A Concordance to the
Plays, Poems, and Translations of
CHRISTOPHER MARLOWE

THE CORNELL CONCORDANCES

S. M. Parrish, *General Editor*

Supervisory Committee

M. H. Abrams
Donald D. Eddy
Ephim Fogel
Alain Seznec

POEMS OF MATTHEW ARNOLD, *edited by S. M. Parrish* (Out of Print)
POEMS OF W. B. YEATS, *edited by S. M. Parrish*
POEMS OF EMILY DICKINSON, *edited by S. P. Rosenbaum*
WRITINGS OF WILLIAM BLAKE, *edited by David V. Erdman*
BYRON'S *DON JUAN, edited by C. W. Hagelman, Jr., and R. J. Barnes*
THÉÂTRE ET POÉSIES DE JEAN RACINE, *edited by Bryant C. Freeman*
BEOWULF, edited by J. B. Bessinger, Jr.
PLAYS OF W. B. YEATS, *edited by Eric Domville*
POEMS OF JONATHAN SWIFT, *edited by Michael Shinagel*
PLAYS OF WILLIAM CONGREVE, *edited by David Mann*
POEMS OF SAMUEL JOHNSON, *edited by Helen Naugle*
FABLES AND TALES OF JEAN DE LA FONTAINE, *edited by J. Allen Tyler*
POEMS OF OSIP MANDELSTAM, *edited by Demetrius J. Koubourlis*
POEMS OF SIR PHILIP SIDNEY, *edited by Herbert S. Donow*
PLAYS AND POEMS OF FEDERICO GARCÍA LORCA, *edited by Alice M. Pollin*
PASCAL'S *PENSÉES, edited by Hugh M. Davidson and Pierre H. Dubé*
COMPLETE WRITINGS OF GEORGE HERBERT, *edited by Mario A. Di Cesare and Rigo Mignani*
THE ANGLO-SAXON POETIC RECORDS, *edited by J. B. Bessinger, Jr.*
POEMS OF BEN JONSON, *edited by Mario A. Di Cesare and Ephim Fogel*
PLAYS, POEMS, AND TRANSLATIONS OF CHRISTOPHER MARLOWE, *edited by Robert J. Fehrenbach, Lea Ann Boone, and Mario A. Di Cesare*

A Concordance to the

Plays, Poems, and Translations of

CHRISTOPHER MARLOWE

Edited by

ROBERT J. FEHRENBACH,

LEA ANN BOONE, *and*

MARIO A. DI CESARE

Cornell University Press

ITHACA AND LONDON

First published 1982 by Cornell University Press.
Published in the United Kingdom by Cornell University Press, Ltd.,
Ely House, 37 Dover Street, London W1X 4HQ.

International Standard Book Number 0-8014-1420-2
Library of Congress Catalog Card Number 81-67175
Printed in the United States of America
Librarians: Library of Congress cataloging information appears on the last page of the book.

For our children

ERRATA

A Concordance to the Plays, Poems, and Translations of Christopher Marlowe

P. xviii, first sentence after the subhead "Variants": *Read* "In the context line, pointed brackets enclose variants from Bowers' copy text or important emendations by other editors."

CONTENTS

PREFACE

You see my Lord, what woorking woordes he hath.
——Theridamas, *Tamburlaine*, Part I

With the exception of *Tamburlaine the Great,* no work of Christopher Marlowe's appeared in print during his lifetime, and nearly all the posthumously printed works are suspected of containing a reviser's or an editor's hand. One was first issued from the press forty years after Marlowe's death, and another exists only in a miserably bad "Bad Quarto," except for a small portion in manuscript which, ironically, may well be the only piece of authentic Marlovian writing extant. Another, as a result of two different but authoritative versions, suffers from what can fairly be called infamous textual and bibliographical problems over which no modern editor has been brave or foolish enough to claim complete victory. Undeterred, or perhaps challenged by such a textual and bibliographical, to say nothing of authorial, state of affairs, modern editors have turned out collections and single editions of Marlowe's works one after another, often agreeing but nearly just as often disagreeing about what is and is not Marlowe's, and about what does and does not constitute an acceptable emendation to his imperfectly transmitted texts.

Such a tricky and unstable textual ground is hardly the ideal footing for compilers of a concordance whose obvious concern is with the authentic words of a writer. The approach taken by Charles Crawford in building his concordance to Marlowe nearly three-quarters of a century ago was to cast his net widely, basing his concordance mainly on Alexander Dyce's 1858 edition but including as well other material generally thought at the time to be Marlowe's.[1] If our task in selecting the works to be concorded has been made easier by the bibliographical scholarship since Crawford, scholarship that has produced agreement about what plays and poems are Marlowe's, the troubling matter of what words to include in a concordance to those accepted works remains, bibliographical and textual scholars being considerably less in accord on that point.

Yet we do not view our task as concordance editors to be the resolution of the numerous textual puzzles surrounding Marlowe's canon, though our concordance may throw light on them for others. What we can and choose to do is base our concordance on a text which not only has been constructed on the soundest textual and bibliographic principles, but which also provides material that allows the

[1]Crawford's concordance was based on all the works now accepted as Marlowe's, as well as *Selimus, Locrine, Edward III,* all the early versions of the *Henry VI* plays including Shakespeare's, George Chapman's additions to *Hero and Leander,* and all the dedications and epigrams associated with these works, as well as several non-Marlovian verse pieces Dyce included in his collection.

flexibility required to concord works so textually controversial. Our choice of Fredson Bowers' Cambridge edition, therefore, has not been arbitrary. For one thing, Bowers' editorial methods and principles produce a text that retains the verbal and orthographical integrity of each individual work. For another, his detailed critical apparatus provides material that enables us to admit other readings while adopting his, the standard scholarly text, as our copy text. Keeping in mind that we are building a concordance and not editing a text, we have taken great care not to engage in reediting Bowers' text, always distinguishing clearly in our concordance between his text and those selected readings chosen from other editors and from early texts that vary from his.

We believe that the user will find this inclusive character of our concordance valuable; we are not, however, unaware that the introduction of numerous variants may, to some degree, impede the casual use of the concordance by the general reader. But then Bowers' very fidelity to the original texts and his elaborate and comprehensive textual notes, all of which have such great value for the student of Marlowe, pose problems for that same general reader. For though Bowers provides typographical uniformity by removing those characteristics that are printer's conventions (normalizing the *v/u* and *i/j* usage, as well as those words with superscribed fonts, w^{th}, y^{e}, y^{t}, etc.), the texts of Marlowe's seven plays, of his translations of two Latin poems, and of his two original poems are presented by Bowers in all the orthographical variety and bibliographical complexity that one would expect to find in any other eleven works by an Elizabethan writer issued by nearly a dozen different printers working without authorial supervision over a period of forty-three years in early printing houses.

The limits of this concordance are thus clear, and users must always keep those limits foremost in mind. When considering an entry in this concordance they must remember that it may very well owe its appearance—its spelling, its context, its use—to *The Massacre at Paris,* say, an appallingly poor memorial reconstruction probably issued within a year of Marlowe's death; or to a text of *Doctor Faustus* published in an expanded form twelve years after the play was first printed in a substantially different text and twenty-four years after the author wrote it; or to the last acts of *The Jew of Malta* issued for the first time forty years after Marlowe's death and in such a manner as to raise the serious possibility of the presence of the revising hand of another playwright whom Marlowe's biographer, John Bakeless, has described as "conscienceless" in such matters.

What we recommend is not despair, but rather judiciousness. A text does exist, and a fine text it is: Bowers' edition, including the critical apparatus and appendix. The primary purpose of this concordance is to direct the reader to the location of a word in that text. Given the nature of our copy text, especially the orthographical variety that derives from the multiple printing houses, frequency counts are questionable as a useful measure of Marlowe's language; they are, however, included in the Appendixes to this volume. Relative frequency counts, generally dangerous as a meaningful tool and virtually useless here, are not. Under the circumstances, the user who desires an accurate and thorough word search must give careful attention to cross-references and must keep an eye peeled for the homograph. The user is also urged to take note of the variant readings provided, thereby quickly becoming aware of instances of major editorial disagreement among modern textual scholars

or of copy-text readings rejected by Bowers. Brief descriptions of our editorial treatment of each play or poem in preparing our copy text for concording follow the description of the general editorial principles we adopted in building this concordance.

THE COPY TEXT AND GENERAL EDITORIAL PRINCIPLES

This concordance is based on the critical old-spelling edition of *The Complete Works of Christopher Marlowe,* Fredson Bowers, editor, published by the Cambridge University Press, second edition, 1981. The concordance does not include the short Latin works, *Illustrissimae Heroinae . . . Mariae Penbrokiae Comitissae* and *In Obitum Honoratissimi Rogeri Manwood,* since a reader interested in the language of these two brief works does not require the assistance of a computer-generated concordance. Also, the two works differ so greatly from the rest of Marlowe's writings—in language (Latin) and nature (formal eulogy and epitaph)—that their inclusion would seriously distort the list of foreign words and the frequency counts. Omitted from the concordance as well are occasional prologues, epilogues, dedications, and captions composed by someone other than Marlowe, lists of *dramatis personae,* Ben Jonson's translation of Ovid's elegy, I.xv, and the additions to *Hero and Leander* by George Chapman, all of which are found in Bowers' edition.

Variants

The variant readings included are of two kinds: (1) those that appear in the copy text as substantive or semisubstantive variants to Bowers' established text (rejected copy text readings), and (2) those emendations made by other editors (a) where there exists considerable disagreement among modern editors, (b) where Bowers indicates in his Textual Notes that despite his necessary editorial choice, a clear, definitive answer to an editorial crux is wanting, and (c) where Bowers stands virtually alone among modern editors. (See also Variants under Notes for Users, below.) Not included in the variant readings are the following: omissions in the copy text, punctuation differences unless part of a variant phrase, word-order differences unless meaning is seriously altered, and those emendations resulting from the application of different editorial principles such as the creation of a modern-spelling text. Variants appearing in both the Historical Collation and the Emendations of Accidentals in Bowers' critical apparatus are included following Bowers' decision to list them as substantive or semisubstantive variants as well as accidentals. Press variants are treated in the same manner. Those orthographical mistakes that appear to Bowers to have been authorial rather than compositorial are included. Variants resulting from line differences alone are omitted. If, however, a variant or emendation is considered peculiarly important despite the principles of selection described here, it is included in the interest of responsible thoroughness. These are very few. On the other hand, on the few occasions when a variant poses extremely difficult problems for concording, we have surrendered to practical realities and omitted it. A good example of this kind of difficulty is represented in our decision to omit

the emendations suggested by the various editors for "snicle hand too fast," in *Jew of Malta,* 4.4.21. The user is advised to consult Bowers' Textual Notes and Historical Collation for information regarding a variant reading in the concordance.

Though our concordance primarily serves as a reference to Bowers' text, by taking note of the variants concorded and by referring to the Historical Collation in Bowers' critical apparatus, readers are able to use our work as a concordance to Bowers' copy texts, and have available to them information that will permit them to consider textual matters about which modern editors have seriously disagreed.

Verse/Prose Designation

Designating lines as either prose or verse has often been a frustrating process. Where we simply could not determine the form of a given line, we sought advice from Professor Bowers, who was himself not infrequently unsure of its status, given the state of his copy texts. This occasional uncertainty about prose/verse designation did not seem to us significant enough, however, to warrant omitting this tool from the concordance.

Speaker Identification

The speaker of each line has been included. Generally, the speakers are identified as they appear in Bowers' text itself, not as they appear in his *dramatis personae* lists. The few exceptions to this practice are noted in the editorial discussion of each play below.

Homographs

Our principle for identifying an index word as homographic is simple: the like or similar words must be different in both etymology and meaning. Beyond distinguishing words by those criteria we have not thought it sound or practical to venture. For several reasons, no attempt is made to separate or define the various homographs. To do so for each homograph, given the complexity and variety of the old-spelling texts, would virtually require building a Marlowe dictionary as well as a Marlowe concordance. For example, if one merely considers the task of sorting out and printing separately the various meanings of WILL, WILLS, WIL, WILS, WILLES, WILL'T, and WILT, to say nothing of all the contracted forms, 'LL, 'L, and LE, the staggering nature of the process becomes apparent. In addition, the end result would doubtless clutter an already varied list of index words. Moreover, a scholar seriously interested in such verbal distinctions could not unreasonably be expected to make decisions different from ours, and would therefore understandably wish to make a thorough contextual study of his own. The least we can do, however, is to inform him and other less wary users where homographs exist. Under the circumstances, it would seem that the least we can do is also, in practical terms, the most we can do.

Cross-references

Old-spelling forms of a word found at a considerable distance from a more recognizable spelling of it, often but not always the modern equivalent, are cross-

referenced. Frequently we have been forced to supply the recognizable form. Our overriding criterion for making cross-references has been usefulness to the reader. Consistency beyond that principle we freely admit has not been adhered to, and odd orthographical forms have not been our only concern. Thus, NURSERIES is cross-referenced to NOURCERY, and NIGH is cross-referenced to NIE, NY, and NYE. Though we expect the user to find on his own an unusual spelling positioned close to the recognizable form, we have cross-referenced some which, despite proximity, may very well not be easily recognized as the word the reader is trying to locate. Thus, both STATURE and STATUTES are cross-referenced from STATUE despite their proximity to it. We have even thought it wise on occasion to insert a modern entry even though it may appear close or even next to the Marlovian word to which it is cross-referenced because of the uncommon ambiguity of the Marlovian spelling. Thus, we added the modern RABBI for cross-referencing to its Marlovian neighbor and plural equivalent RABIES.

Foreign Words

All non-English words are found in the Foreign Words list as well as in their appropriate places in the concordance. We have categorized five non-English languages used by Marlowe (Latin, French, Italian, Spanish, and Greek) and another small group of words which we have designated as Pseudo-Foreign. Proper names (DEL BOSCO, WITTENBERG) are not ordinarily identified as foreign.

Combination Words

In an attempt to retain the old-spelling text in as accurate a detail as possible, we have entered combination words that were spelled in the copy text as multiple words but are today spelled either as a single word or with a hyphen. Our authority for this practice has been the appearance of the combined form in the *OED*. A very few exceptions to this rule exist, notably proper names such as DEL BOSCO, which, despite its absence from the *OED*, appears as a combination word in the concordance.

EDITORIAL NOTES ON INDIVIDUAL WORKS

Dido, Queene of Carthage (Dido): The Latin is taken directly from the *Aeneid* and therefore should not be considered Marlovian. The user is reminded that from 3.1 Cupid is speaking disguised as Ascanius; his speech prefix remains *Cupid*, however.

Tamburlaine the Great, Part I (1Tamb): The two speaking messengers are differentiated in the concordance (*1Msngr* in Act 2 and *2Msngr* in Act 4). Tamburlaine's camp is represented by the speech prefix *All* in Act 2, and the four Damascus virgins speak the lines given to *Omnes* in Act 5.

Tamburlaine the Great, Part II (2Tamb): In the concordance, the three speaking messengers are differentiated (*1Msngr* appears in Act 2, *2Msngr* in Act 3, and *3Msngr* in Act 5). The concordance follows Bowers in distinguishing between the speech prefixes for *Phisitian* (*Phsitn*) and *1. Phisitian* (*1Phstn*) and in not differ-

entiating those lines assigned the speech prefix for *Souldiers* (*Soldrs*). Techelles and Usumcasane speak one line together and in that speech are given the speaker identification *Tec&Us*.

The Jew of Malta (Jew): The stage direction *Within* is left, as in Bowers, without further identification. There is only one Messenger in the play.

The Massacre at Paris (P, printed text; Paris ms, manuscript): Relying solely on the printed text (O^1) for his copy text, Bowers, unlike some modern editors, does not admit the Collier Leaf manuscript version of scene xvii into his text. At the same time, however, he does not doubt its authenticity, and accordingly he includes it as a footnote to the text. Because of its size, we treat it as we do the *Faustus* A-text Appendices (see the description of the *Doctor Faustus* text below) and concord it in addition to the regular text exactly as printed in the Bowers' footnote except to bring it into conformity with the rest of the text by silently altering certain paleographical, not orthographical, characteristics (y^t to *that*, wth to *with*, wch to *which*, *i* to *j*, yor to *your*) and modernizing the *u* and *v* usage. The speech prefix *minion* (*Minion*) in the manuscript compares with that for *Mugeroun* (*Mugern*) in the regular text.

In other matters, *Anjoy* is given the speech prefix *King* from scene xii on and should not be confused with King Charles, who is always given the speech prefix *Charles* (*Charls*). The various numeral speech prefixes in Bowers (*1*., *2*., and *3*.) in scenes ix, xix, and xx are identified in the concordance as *First* and *Second Attendant* in scene ix (*1Atndt* and *2Atndt*) and *First*, *Second*, and *Third Murtherers* in scenes xix and xx (*1Mur*, *2Mur*, and *3Mur*). Bowers' speech prefix *All* in scene xix is identified in the concordance as *All Murtherers* (*AllMur*). His speech prefix *All* in scene xii, a crowd, remains uncharacterized (*All*), and his two instances of *Souldier* in scenes ii and xvii remain undifferentiated in the concordance (*Souldr*).

Edward II (Edw): Departing from our general editorial principle of introducing as variants only those readings from the copy text or from selected modern editions that differ from Bowers' text, we include the two substantive variants found in the manuscript of the first seventy lines in the Dyce copy of Q^2 (1958) because of their special interest if not their authority. Note that the Prince is assigned the speech prefix *King* in the last scene, 5.4, when he becomes King Edward III and should not be confused with King Edward II, who is always assigned the speech prefix *Edward*. Note also that *Bishop*, undifferentiated in its appearance as a speech prefix in the text, is identified in the concordance as the Bishop of Coventry (*BshpCv* in 1.1), the Archbishop of Canterbury (*ArchBp* in 1.2, 1.4, and 5.4), and the Bishop of Winchester (*BshpWn* in 5.1)—all of which are clearly identified in Bowers' stage directions. *Omnes* indicates the three poor men in 1.1, and the two speaking messengers are identified as *1Msngr* (2.2) and *2Msngr* or *Msngr* (5.2) in the concordance.

Doctor Faustus (F, regular text [largely the B-text]; also F, those extended variants found in Bowers' Historical Collation or HC [largely the A-text]; and F App, those rejected scenes Bowers places in an appendix [exclusively the A-text]): The textual difficulties of this play reach bewildering proportions; for this concordance, they posed almost unimaginable problems. Our decision to attempt to concord both the A-text (1604) and the B-text (1616) as treated by Bowers and to identify the major differences between the two as A or B was fraught with difficulties that

we could not entirely overcome; nonetheless, we are persuaded that the concordance provides a tool which will be helpful to Marlowe scholars whatever their editorial choice of text. The text established by Bowers remains at the center of our concordance to *Doctor Faustus*, and is clearly differentiated from the other readings.

Bowers' text is based on B; the variants to his text representing rejected readings, therefore, are generally from A. On occasion he accepts an A reading for his text, and then the variants of rejected readings are from B. Unfortunately, Bowers' text is not subject to as neat analysis as such a description might suggest. The editorial problems are formidable. Therefore the variants are not always identified in the concordance as A or B, especially the briefer variants of a word or two, though a departure from an unidentified line of the regular text can usually be considered a variant from the A-text. The textual source of the larger variants, especially those identified as located in the Historical Collation (HC), are always identified. The rejected A-text scenes placed by Bowers in an appendix are easily identified as A by their location sign: *F App*. The speech prefixes in the appended scenes are regularized to make the appendix material generally conform to the rest of the concorded text, but nothing else has been altered in these A-text readings.

The speech prefix *All* in Act 5 is identified in the concordance as *All Schollers* (*AllSch*); the other appearances of that speech prefix are not differentiated. The two different speech prefixes in Bowers' text, *A Servant* and *Servant*, are identified as *Servnt* alone in the concordance. *Clown*, *Rafe*, and *Frier* in the A-text appendix (*F App*) compare with but are not exact equivalents to *Robin*, *Dick*, and *1Frier* respectively in the regular text.

The First Booke of Lucan (Lucan, First Booke): The only matter that posed a problem in concording this translation was the treatment of **or Luna*, a marginal note to line 585, very possibly made by Marlowe himself. Though not properly a variant, it has nonetheless been so treated as one way to concord it.

Ovid's Elegies (Ovid's Elegies): The introduction of copy-text variants has been complicated by the unusual problem of two copy texts. Bowers has chosen 0^1 as the copy text for ten of the elegies (I.1, 2, 3, 5, 13, 15; II.4, 10; III.6, 13), giving considerable authority at the same time to the 0^3 readings. He has chosen 0^3 as the sole authority for the remaining elegies. The variants we chose for concording reflect his editorial decisions: substantive variants from both 0^1 and 0^3 are concorded for the ten elegies above; only variants from 0^3 are concorded for the rest. The B.J. (Ben Jonson) translation of I.xv is not concorded, nor are the Latin epigrams.

Hero and Leander (Hero and Leander): Only Marlowe's work has been concorded. Chapman's continuation of the poem, as well as his introductions to Marlowe's sestiads as divided by him, have been omitted. So also has the marginal commentary found at I.189–190 (*A periphrasis of night*).

The Passionate Shepherd to His Love (Passionate Shepherd): The most practical way of dealing with the extremely complicated textual issues surrounding this short poem has been to concord the conventional six-stanza version and enter as substantive variants only those differences found in the copy text (*Englands Helicon*) and in the reconstructed conjectural four-stanza version, also printed by Bowers. Thus, the authorially questionable fourth and sixth stanzas of the six-stanza version are included, but the spurious seventh stanza, considered non-Marlovian by Bowers and relegated to his textual notes, is not. The lyric is brief enough for anyone

interested to make his own study of additional variants found in the several contemporary manuscripts (none holograph) without the services of a computer.

NOTES FOR USERS

Order, Format

The book is divided into three parts: the concordance to the texts; the concordance to the stage directions; and a series of appendixes. In the concordances, we have followed the order of Bowers' edition: context lines appearing below the index words are listed sequentially as they occur in each work.

Lines of poetry are identified by short title and line number. *Ovid's Elegies* are identified by book, elegy, and line number; *Hero and Leander*, by sestiad and line number.

Identification of lines from the plays is both richer and occasionally more complex. Each line carries with it not only the conventional act, scene, and line number but also, where appropriate, a P indicating prose text, and a designation (sometimes abbreviated) of the speaker of that line. Where differences among speakers with the same speech prefix are unclear (*Souldier*, mainly), no distinction is made. Where a clear difference could be determined, we have added distinguishing information to Bowers' speech prefixes; thus, *1Msngr* and *2Msngr* appear instead of Bowers' single *Messenger*, and *AllSch* (*All Schollers*) instead of Bowers' *All*. These modifications, as well as instances where we were unable to add clarifying details and instances where a single character receives more than one speaker identification, are noted above, pages xiii–xv. With the exceptions mentioned there, we have identified speakers as they are identified in Bowers' text itself, not as they appear in his normalized lists of *dramatis personae*.

Act, scene, and line designations are straightforward for most of the plays. *The Massacre at Paris* and *Doctor Faustus*, however, presented special problems, both because of divergences among editors regarding scene divisions and because of special additional materials included. See the section Others Editions, below, for a discussion of scene division in modern editions. We have used both scene/line numbers and through-line numbers to designate lines from Bowers' text of *The Massacre at Paris*. The Collier (i.e., Folger) Leaf manuscript is designated as Paris ms, followed by the line number and the page number in Bowers' edition.

Inevitably the text of *Doctor Faustus* presented the greatest complications. We have included the main text of the play, material from Bowers' Historical Collation, and Bowers' Appendix.

1. Lines from the main text of the play are identified both by act, scene, and line number and by through-line number. Lines taken from the A-text are identified by the symbol A. The insertions that Bowers numbered with decimal line numbers (551.0.1ff, 705.0.1ff, and 719.0.1) are, because of space constraints, presented without the medial 0 as 551.1, etc.

2. Readings from Bowers' Historical Collation, which gives significant variant readings of many words and lines, are identified by HC and the page number in Bowers' edition. These variant lines are interleaved with the main text according

to through-line number. The lines are generally identified by textual origin: as A, if taken from the A-text, or, if Bowers has rejected a B-text reading from his main text, as B. A fuller discussion of variants is given below.

3. Readings from Bowers' Appendix, which provides major sections of the A-text, are identified by the page number in Bowers' edition and the line number on that page. Since all of these lines are from the A-text, no specific identification of textual origin is given.

In the stage-directions concordance, short-title abbreviations have been somewhat expanded; otherwise, line identification is similar to that in the main concordance. The first part provides the line in the text at which the stage direction occurs, with the usual double numbering system for *The Massacre at Paris* and *Doctor Faustus*. Line 0 (zero) identifies those stage directions which precede a scene. The final numeral in the line identification indicates the line number of the stage direction itself, since some stage directions run to several lines; for example, *Faustus* 4.1.103.5. The only exceptions are those lines in *Doctor Faustus* to which Bowers has assigned decimal line numbers (551.0.3, 551.0.7, 551.0.13); space did not permit the presentation of the medial zero and the additional decimal indicating the stage direction.

Context

We have sought to preserve the distinction between verse and prose in the treatment of context. The general principle in establishing prose contexts was to read backward and forward on either side of the entry word, with reversals in reading direction signaled by punctuation. Because Marlowe's line has a very strong "forward" direction, the program to generate context read first to the right of the entry word. When punctuation was encountered, the program began reading to the left of the entry word. A "full stop" (period, question mark, exclamation point, beginning or ending of a speech) signaled the end of the context in that direction. If a full stop was not encountered, alternation continued until the context line was filled. This method and these categories of punctuation provided the best contexts for Marlowe's prose most of the time, although variations in the punctuation of the texts and in the characteristics of the lines themselves occasionally caused difficulties.

Since the verse line is very much a unit in Marlowe, it has been used as the context line for verse passages unless circumstances indicated otherwise—enjambment or full stops within the line. In these instances the verse line has been given a context almost as if it were prose, with the qualification that the end of a verse line has been assigned the punctuation value of a half-stop, equivalent to a comma, dash, or semicolon. The end of a verse line is indicated by the slash symbol (or virgule): /. One other punctuation symbol in the text should be noted. The vertical bar (|) in the Collier Leaf manuscript of *The Massacre at Paris* was considered equivalent to a comma in the generation of context.

Whenever a word occurs twice in one line in such a way that the contexts are identical, the line has been printed only once. We have included, however, instances in which a word appearing in adjacent lines generates identical contexts (as in a and b below), since we felt that the inclusion of the second line number might

be of use to some readers. We have also included cases in which a word appearing twice in one line generates two different contexts (b and c below). The following examples illustrate both practices; the text word that generated the context is italicized.

THY
(a) Servants fit for *thy* purpose thou must hire/To teach thy lover, Ovid's Elegies 1.8.87
(b) Servants fit for thy purpose thou must hire/To teach *thy* lover, Ovid's Elegies 1.8.88
(c) thou must hire/To teach thy lover, what *thy* thoughts desire. Ovid's Elegies 1.8.88

Variants

In the context line, pointed brackets enclose variants from early texts other than the copy text or important emendations by other editors. Square brackets enclose Bowers' emendations of the copy text. Punctuation is generally placed outside the brackets. Where possible, variants are placed immediately following the appropriate text word or phrase. As every editor knows, however, the relation between various texts is not always describable in terms of word-for-word substitution. Formatting requirements for machine input and the generation of context created further restrictions. Again, the text of *Doctor Faustus* presented special difficulties. We have not included the variants WERTENBERG or WERTENBERGE in the WITTENBERG and WITTENBERGE contexts, nor MEPHASTOPHILIS in the MEPHISTOPHILIS contexts, because they occur often and would have cluttered the text.

Variant words and phrases were included within the context line if possible. If, however, the variant was an extended phrase or if its inclusion in the context line might impede comprehension, then the variant was presented in a separate line of its own, displayed along with the text line. The identification of these lines is keyed to pages of Bowers' Historical Collation and to the through-line numbers. The through-line number links the variant to the corresponding line in Bowers' text. The HC designation gives the page number from Bowers' Historical Collation and when appropriate indicates that the variant is from the A-text or B-text. A few variants had to be added as "mongrel" lines because of their unusual nature; for example, the following at F480 (HC260):

All ⟨articles prescrib'd⟩ ⟨covenant-articles⟩ betweene us both.

Treatment of extended passages of variant or emended material is as follows: passages of verse are bracketed line by line, while prose passages are bracketed only at the beginning and end. Hence, on occasion, obvious signals of emendation are lacking in some prose passages, such as those in Bowers' emendations from the A-text at 551.1 and following.

Entries

1. *Alphabetization*. Alphabetization follows normal English practice; & and &TC. are alphabetized with ET. Apostrophes and hyphens have been ignored in alphabetization, so that, for example, WAND'RED immediately precedes WANDRED and SOME-TIMES immediately precedes SOMETIMES. A similar practice has been followed

with separate words that we have treated as compounds: WHAT SOEVER, for example, precedes WHATSOEVER.

2. *Compound Words*. Compound words are of two kinds: those containing hyphens and those consisting of words separate in the text but which, on the authority of the *OED*, we have combined. Both kinds are indexed in several ways—under the full form and under each component element. Separate Appendixes contain lists of these words ordered alphabetically, ordered by second component, and ordered by third component.

3. *Apostrophes*. We have given special consideration to two common forms of elision, T' and TH'. Such words are indexed under the entire form and under each of the component parts, with the apostrophe included in the first component. Thus T'ENCOUNTER is indexed also under T', and ENCOUNTER, and TH'ASPIRING is indexed also under TH', and ASPIRING. Separate Appendixes provide complete lists of words containing apostrophes ordered by first element and by second element. The second list should be especially valuable for considering elisions and contractions formed with words such IS, IT, SHALL, and WILL.

4. *Spelling, homographs, and cross-references*. Our text is an old-spelling text. We have not normalized any of Bowers' text or variants, and have made only small changes in the Collier Leaf manuscript, as described in the Editorial Notes, above (p. xiv).

The wide variations in spelling have exacerbated the usual problems in the relation between the form and the meaning of words. One such problem is that of homographs—that is, words which are spelled the same but which have different meanings. We have identified these with the designation (Homograph) following the index word; a list of words containing homographs appears in the Appendixes. Another problem is that of forms which, though spelled differently, apparently have the same meaning or very closely related meanings. Furthermore, some orthographic forms occur in Marlowe which are not easily recognized or which are themselves subject to several variations. For the user's convenience, we have provided cross-references at many points, especially to old-spelling forms, when the old-spelling form in the alphabetical entry list did not occur close to a recognizable form. Note that cross-references are made from the modern form or the recognizable old-spelling form to the less easily recognizable form. When there was not a recognizable form in Marlowe's text, we inserted the modern form that seemed appropriate: e.g., ACHE (See AKE). Cross-references usually direct readers to the base or simple form (for example, singular of noun, infinitive of verb), if that form occurs in Marlowe's text; related forms may be found easily enough in the vicinity. Cross-references for EVER were too extensive to be provided in the concordance, and are given below:

EVER See also AYE, ERE, WHAT ERE, WHAT SO ERE, WHATSOEVER, WHENSOEVER, WHERE ERE, WHERE SO ERE, WHO ERE

5. *Omitted words*. We have omitted six high-frequency words: A (1798 occurrences), AND (5478), IN (1908), OF (3022), THE (5182), and TO (3359). We have, however, indexed the elided forms T' and TH'. (Readers should note that the omitted

words are homographs: A occurs with the meaning "he," as a French word, and as part of compounds such as A DO; IN occurs as a Latin word; OF is a homograph for OFF, as are THE for THEE and TO for TOO.) Tapes or printouts of context lines for the words omitted from the main concordance may be obtained from one of the editors.

Appendixes

The appendixes include lists of frequencies and lists of words containing compound words, apostrophes, foreign words, and homographs. These lists are based upon the entries in the main concordance only; words from the stage directions are not included. The frequency lists are of two kinds: words listed by frequency in alphabetical subgroups (p. 1621) and words listed alphabetically (p. 1657). The alphabetical list contains words occurring four or more times in the text; words occurring one, two, or three times can easily be found in the first frequency list. The frequency lists provide a useful view of Marlowe's vocabulary as well as some indication of linguistic preferences or the predominance of certain conceptual or imagistic themes. We caution all users not to look for exact frequencies in these lists, owing to distortions resulting from the multiple listing of compound words and the inclusion of variants. At the best of times, frequencies can be problematic; given the condition of the texts of Marlowe, no precision can be hoped for.

Other Editions

For most of the texts there is general agreement among modern editors about texts and about scene division. *The Massacre at Paris* and *Doctor Faustus* present some complications. Modern editions of *The Massacre at Paris* include the following:

Bennett	*The Jew of Malta and The Massacre at Paris*, edited by Henry S. Bennett, 1931, repr. 1966.
Greg	*The Massacre at Paris*, edited by W. W. Greg, 1929.
Oliver	*Dido, Queen of Carthage and The Massacre at Paris*, edited by Harold J. Oliver, 1968.
Ribner	*The Complete Plays of Christopher Marlowe*, edited by Irving Ribner, 1963.

Among these editions, scene division diverges after Scene iv. What Bowers marks as Scenes v, vi, and vii, Ribner divides into v, vi, vii, and viii, and Oliver divides into v, vi, vii, viii, and ix. Greg, however, marks the entire passage as Scene v, whereas Bennett divides it into two scenes, v and vi. After this passage the editors agree once again upon scene division, although they disagree upon the inclusion of the Collier Leaf manuscript. The following schema provides a quick guide to scene numbering in the various editions:

Bowers	Greg	Bennett	Ribner	Oliver
i–iv	i–iv	i–iv	i–iv	i–iv
v–vii	v	v–vi	v–viii	v–ix
viii–xxii	vi–xx	vii–xxi	ix–xxiii	x–xxiv

Several modern editions of *Doctor Faustus* besides Bowers' rely mainly on the B-text, including Ribner and the following:

Gill	*Doctor Faustus*, edited by Roma Gill, 1966, 2d corr. impr., 1967.
Greg	*The Tragical History of the Life and Death of Doctor Faustus: A Conjectural Reconstruction*, edited by W. W. Greg, 1950.
Jump	*Doctor Faustus*, edited by John D. Jump, 1962.
Kirschbaum	*The Plays of Christopher Marlowe*, edited by Leo Kirschbaum, 1962.

Differences in scene division among these editions are rather minor. Bowers divides by scene and by act and scene, and provides through-line numbering as well; Jump divides by scene only; all other editors divide by act and scene. Bowers, Gill, Jump, and Kirschbaum include the second chorus (counting the Prologue as a chorus) at the end of Act II (Scene vii in Jump), whereas Greg and Ribner include the same passage in the beginning of Act III. The third chorus is similarly assigned to the end of III by Bowers, Gill, Jump, and Kirschbaum (Scene x), and to the beginning of IV by Greg and Ribner. Act IV is divided into five scenes by Kirschbaum (he leaves Bowers' xii and xiii as one), into seven scenes by Greg, Gill, Ribner, and Jump (Scenes xi–xvii), and into six scenes by Bowers. The variation occurs in Bowers at 1204, which the other editors mark as the beginning of IV.ii, or (Jump) as Scene xii.

ACKNOWLEDGMENTS

The speed with which a computer appears to generate a concordance belies the time and human labor required to prepare material so that the machine can work its wonders. Effort on this concordance has spanned more than a decade, and the labor and assistance given to complete it during that long period were shared by many more than the three of us. We now take the happy opportunity to thank those without whose help this book could never have emerged from SUNY Binghamton's NAS AS/6 Computer.

Had it not been for the assistance and encouragement of Fredson Bowers, this concordance would not have been begun, much less completed. The project started with galleys of his first edition of the Cambridge *Marlowe* and reached completion with the corrected page proofs of his second edition. Throughout the years, his assistance has been both unfailing and generous. We could not have asked for more. The Cambridge University Press was always most cooperative, from granting us permission to use the text to answering queries about the second edition prior to its publication. We are especially grateful also to Stephen M. Parrish, whose idea it was to bring the three of us together to complete a project he had stimulated with his encouragement over the years. His advice, his searching comments, his patience, and his understanding have been invaluable to us. We wish to express our thanks also to those who assisted during the early stages of the project—Marvin Spevack, who pointed out pitfalls; Vinton Dearing, who gave encouragement and

help; and Ted R. Dinterman, who played an important role in the preparation of the text.

We are grateful to the Committee on Faculty Research at the College of William and Mary, which generously supported this project several times over the years, and to the Provost for Graduate Studies and Research at SUNY Binghamton, who provided financial assistance more recently. We are in considerable debt to the staff members of the computer centers at our institutions, especially Betty Greene and Shirley McCallum at William and Mary, and Russell Vaught, Director of the SUNY Binghamton Computer Center, and members of the academic support group and the operations staff. We owe a special debt to the librarians of the tiny West Sussex County Library branch in Arundel; however perplexed they may have been at the unusual and repeated requests made by one of us who lived in a remote English village during a critical period of this project, with remarkable good humor they scoured their county system for necessary books—and found them.

Good humor was also in great store among the wives, Dee Fehrenbach and Carol Lee Di Cesare, and the husband, James Boone, of this editorial trio. Over the years, much understanding and patience was needed, and much was given, along with solid support and help. Through our children, several of whom were born during this long labor, they are remembered in the dedication, which tries to recognize why so much of whatever good we do is done.

As to the errors that remain—and given a work such as this there is no doubt that some do—we claim them as ours alone and ask of the users of this book no more than that asked by an equally human author in the sixteenth century of the readers of his book: that the faults if large and important be "noted with discretion," and if small and insignificant be "concealed with humanity."

ROBERT J. FEHRENBACH
LEA ANN BOONE
MARIO A. DI CESARE

College of William and Mary
State University of New York at Binghamton

ABBREVIATIONS

GENERAL ABBREVIATIONS AND ABBREVIATED TITLES

A	A-text of *Doctor Faustus*; 1604 edition
B	B-text of *Doctor Faustus*; 1616 edition
Dido	*Dido, Queene of Carthage*
Edw *or* Edward II	*Edward II*
F *or* Faustus	*Doctor Faustus*
F App *or* Faustus App	Bowers' A-text Appendix to *Doctor Faustus*
HC	Historical Collation for *Doctor Faustus*
Jew *or* Jew of Malta	*The Jew of Malta*
Lucan, First Booke	*The First Book of Lucan Translated into English*
P (*title col.*) *or* Paris	*The Massacre at Paris*
P (*adj. to speaker*)	Prose
Paris ms	Collier Leaf (Folger) manuscript (*The Massacre at Paris*)
Passionate Shepherd	*The Passionate Shepherd to His Love*
Prolog	Prologue
1Tamb *or* 1Tamburlaine	*Tamburlaine Part I*
2Tamb *or* 2Tamburlaine	*Tamburlaine Part II*

SPEECH PREFIXES BY PLAY

Dido, Queene of Carthage (Dido)

Achat	Achates
Ascan	Ascanius
Cloan	Cloanthus
Ganimd	Ganimed
Jupitr	Jupiter
Illion	Illioneus
Serg	Sergestus

Tamburlaine, Part I (1Tamb)

Attend	Attendant
Bajzth	Bajazeth
Capol	Capolin

Govnr	Governour
Magnet	Magnetes
Meandr	Meander
Menaph	Menaphon
Moroc	Morocus
1Msngr	Messenger (II.iii)
2Msngr	Messenger (IV.1)
Mycet	Mycetes
Ortyg	Ortygius
Philem	Philemus
Prolog	The Prologue
Souldn	Souldan
Souldr	Souldier
Spy	A Spy
Tamb	Tamburlaine
Techel	Techelles
Therid	Theridamas
Usumc	Usumcasane
1Virgn	1. Virgin
2Virgn	2. Virgin
Zenoc	Zenocrate

Tamburlaine, Part II (2Tamb)

Baldwn	Baldwine
Callap	Callapine
Calyph	Calyphas
Capt	Captaine
Celeb	Celebinus
1Citzn	1. Citizen
2Citzn	2. Citizen
Fredrk	Fredericke
Gazell	Gazellus
Govnr	Governour
Jrslem	Jerusalem
Maxim	Maximus
1Msngr	Messenger (II.ii)
2Msngr	Messenger (III.v)
3Msngr	Messenger (V.iii)
Olymp	Olympia
Orcan	Orcanes
Perdic	Perdicas
Phsitn	Phisitian
1Phstn	1. Phisitian
Pionrs	Pioners
Prolog	The Prologue
Sgsmnd	Sigismond
Soldrs	Souldiers
Tamb	Tamburlaine
Tec&Us	Techelles & Usumcasane
Techel	Techelles

Therid	Theridamas
Trebiz	Trebizon
Uribas	Uribassa
Usumc	Usumcasane
Zenoc	Zenocrate

The Jew of Malta (Jew)

Abbass	Abbasse
Abigal	Abigall
Barab	Barabas
Calym	Calymath
Crpntr	Carpenter
Curtzn	Curtezane
1Fryar	1. Fryar
2Fryar	2. Fryar
Govnr	Governor
Ithimr	Ithimore
1Jew	1. Jew
2Jew	2. Jew
3Jew	3. Jew
3Jews	All 3 Jewes
1Knght	1. Knight
2Knght	2. Knight
Lodowk	Lodowicke
Machvl	Machevil (Prologue)
1Merch	1. Merchant
2Merch	2. Merchant
Msngr	Messenger
Mthias	Mathias
1Offcr	1. Officer
2Offcr	2. Officer
Offcrs	Officers
Pilia	Pilia-borza
Servnt	Servant

The Massacre at Paris (P)

Admral	Admirall
1Atndt	1. (ix)
2Atndt	2. (ix)
Capt	Captaine
Cardnl	Cardinall
Charls	Charles
Cutprs	Cutpurse
Duchss	Duchesse
Dumain	Dumaine
Eprnon	Epernoune
Gonzag	Gonzago
Lorein	Loreine
Mntsrl	Mountsorrell

1Msngr	Messenger
1Mur	1. (xix, xx)
2Mur	2. (xix, xx)
3Mur	3. (xix)
Mugern	Mugeroun
Navrre	Navarre
OldQn	Old Queene
Pothec	Pothecarie
Prtsnt	Protestant
QnMarg	Queene Margaret
QnMoth	Queene Mother
Seroun	Seroune
Souldr	Souldier
Srgeon	Surgeon
SrnsWf	Serouns wife
YngGse	Yong Guise

Collier Leaf (Folger) manuscript to *The Massacre at Paris* (Paris ms)

Souldr	Souldier

Edward II (Edw)

ArchBp	Bishop (Archbishop of Canterbury)
Arundl	Arundell
Baldck	Baldock
Bartly	Bartley
Beamnt	Beamont
BshpCv	Bishop (Coventry)
BshpWn	Bishop (Winchester)
Champn	Champion
Gavstn	Gaveston
HrsBoy	Horse boy
Leistr	Leister
Lncstr	Lancaster
1Lord	1. Lord
2Lord	2. Lord
Ltborn	Lightborne
Matrvs	Matrevis
Mortmr	Mortimer
MortSr	Mortimer senior
Msngr *or* 1Msngr *or* 2 Msngr	Messenger
Penbrk	Penbrooke
Poorem	Poore men
1PrMan	1. poore man
2PrMan	2. poore man
3PrMan	3. poore man
Souldr	Souldier
Spencr	Spencer
SpncrP	Spencer pater
SrJohn	Sir John

Trussl	Trussell
Warwck	Warwicke

Doctor Faustus (F)

Archbp	Archbishop
BdAngl	Bad Angel
Belzeb	Belzebub
Benvol	Benvolio
BthCrd	Both Cardinals
1Card	1. Cardinal
1Chor	Chorus (Prologue)
2Chor	Chorus (Act II)
3Chor	Chorus (Act III)
4Chor	Chorus (Act V)
Cornel	Cornelius
Covet	Covetousnesse
Emper	Emperour
Faust	Faustus
Fredrk	Fredericke
1Frier	1. Frier
GdAngl	Good Angel
Glutny	Gluttony
Hostss	Hostesse
HrsCsr	Horse-courser
Ltchry	Letchery
Lucifr	Lucifer
Mephst	Mephostophilis
Mrtino	Martino
Raymnd	Raymond
1Schol	1. Scholler
2Schol	2. Scholler
3Schol	3. Scholler
Servnt	A Servant, Servant
1Soldr	1. Soldier
2Soldr	2. Soldier
Vintnr	Vintner

Faustus Appendix (F App)

Clown	Clo, Clow
Duchss	Dut, Dutch
Duke	Du
Emper	Em, emp
Faust	Fau
Frier	Fri, Frier
HrsCsr	Hors
Knight	Kn, Knight
Lorein	Lor
Mephst	Me, Meph

OldMan	Old
Robin	Ro, Rob, Robin
Vintnr	Vintn, Vintner
Wagner	Wag

Concordance to the
Plays, Poems, and Translations

ABANDON			
Brave men at armes, abandon fruitles feares,	Dido	1.2.32	Iarbus
The king my lord thus to abandon me:	Edw	1.4.177	Queene
(that did remaine/To their afflictions) were t'abandon Roome.	Lucan, First Booke		495
Abandon fruitlesse cold Virginitie,	Hero and Leander		1.317
ABANDON'D			
heapes of stone/Lye in our townes, that houses are abandon'd,	Lucan, First Booke		26
ABANDOND			
Then let her live abandond and forlorne.	Edw	1.4.298	Queene
ABANDONS			
Iarbus dye, seeing she abandons thee.	Dido	3.1.40	Iarbus
ABANUS			
beare wise Bacons, and [Abanus] <Albanus> <Albertus> workes,	F 181	1.1.153	Valdes
ABATE			
Which wil abate the furie of your fit,	2Tamb	5.3.79	Phsitn
Tis warre that must abate these Barons pride.	Edw	2.2.99	Edward
ABATED			
Now waxt she jealous, least his love abated,	Hero and Leander		2.43
ABATES			
Now all feare with my mindes hot love abates,	Ovid's Elegies		1.10.9
ABBASSE			
there must my girle/Intreat the Abbasse to be entertain'd.	Jew	1.2.280	Barab
Grave Abbasse, and you happy Virgins guide,	Jew	1.2.314	Abigal
The Abbasse of the house/Whose zealous admonition I embrace:	Jew	3.3.66	Abigal
The Abbasse sent for me to be confest:	Jew	3.6.3	2Fryar
ABBOTS			
To make his Monkes and Abbots stand like Apes,	F 861	3.1.83	Mephst
ABBYES			
As Monestaries, Priories, Abbyes and halles,	P 138	2.81	Guise
ABETTED			
The gods abetted; Cato likt the other;	Lucan, First Booke		129
ABHOR			
Aye me, such words as these should I abhor,	Hero and Leander		1.339
ABHOR'D			
They seeing it, both Love and him abhor'd,	Hero and Leander		1.463
ABHORRE			
That Earle of Lancaster do I abhorre.	Edw	1.1.76	Gavstn
My Lords, that I abhorre base Gaveston,	Edw	1.4.239	Mortmr
Please her, her hate makes others thee abhorre,	Ovid's Elegies		2.3.11
ABHORS			
Whereas Nobilitie abhors to stay,	Dido	4.3.19	Aeneas
To scourge the pride of such as heaven abhors:	2Tamb	4.1.149	Tamb
ABIDE			
And none but base Aeneas will abide:	Dido	4.3.20	Aeneas
Or els abide the wrath of frowning Jove.	Dido	5.1.54	Hermes
It shall suffice thou darst abide a wound.	2Tamb	3.2.136	Tamb
And there abide till fortune call thee home.	Edw	1.4.126	Edward
Elmes love the Vines, the Vines with Elmes abide,	Ovid's Elegies		2.16.41
ABIDUS			
(Whose tragedie divine Musaeus soong)/Dwelt at Abidus; since	Hero and Leander		1.53
ABIE			
Deare shall you both abie this riotous deede:	Edw	2.2.88	Edward
denies all, with thy bloud must thou/Abie thy conquest past:	Lucan, First Booke		290
ABIGAIL			
Abigail, things past recovery/Are hardly cur'd with	Jew	1.2.236	Barab
ABIGAILE			
Father, for thee lamenteth Abigaile:	Jew	1.2.229	Abigal
ABIGAL			
Peace, Abigal, 'tis I.	Jew	2.1.43	Barab
Oh Abigal, Abigal, that I had thee here too,	Jew	2.1.51	Barab
Tush man, we talk'd of Diamonds, not of Abigal.	Jew	2.3.151	Barab
Then gentle Abigal plight thy faith to me.	Jew	2.3.315	Lodowk
Oh wretched Abigal, what hast [thou] <thee> done?	Jew	2.3.320	Abigal
Then my faire Abigal should frowne on me.	Jew	2.3.332	Lodowk
Lodowicke, it is enough/That I have made thee sure to Abigal.	Jew	2.3.335	Barab
Why Abigal it is not yet long since/That I did labour thy	Jew	3.3.56	1Fryar
Abigal I will, but see thou change no more,	Jew	3.3.70	1Fryar
ABIGALL			
But whither wends my beauteous Abigall?	Jew	1.2.224	Barab
have so manifestly wronged us,/What will not Abigall attempt?	Jew	1.2.276	Abigal
Then Abigall, there must my girle/Intreat the Abbasse to be	Jew	1.2.279	Barab
But here they come; be cunning Abigall.	Jew	1.2.299	Barab
No, Abigall, in this/It is not necessary I be seene.	Jew	1.2.301	Barab
Why how now Abigall, what mak'st thou/Amongst these hateful	Jew	1.2.338	Barab
Nay backe, Abigall,	Jew	1.2.348	Barab
Faire Abigall the rich Jewes daughter/Become a Nun?	Jew	1.2.366	Mthias
and direct the hand/Of Abigall this night; or let the day/Turne	Jew	2.1.15	Barab
Till I have answer of my Abigall.	Jew	2.1.19	Barab
The Loadstarre of my life, if Abigall.	Jew	2.1.42	Barab
That I may have a sight of Abigall;	Jew	2.3.34	Lodowk
Yond walks the Jew, now for faire Abigall.	Jew	2.3.38	Lodowk
I feare me 'tis about faire Abigall.	Jew	2.3.139	Mthias
What, ho, Abigall; open the doore I say.	Jew	2.3.221	Barab
Abigall, bid him welcome for my sake.	Jew	2.3.232	Barab
For now by this has he kist Abigall;	Jew	2.3.246	Barab
Whither but to my faire love Abigall?	Jew	2.3.252	Mthias
the Governors sonne/Will, whether I will or no, have Abigall:	Jew	2.3.258	Barab
And I am sure he is with Abigall.	Jew	2.3.268	Barab
a warning e're he goes/As he shall have small hopes of Abigall.	Jew	2.3.274	Barab
Doe so; loe here I give thee Abigall.	Jew	2.3.345	Barab
My life is not so deare as Abigall.	Jew	2.3.348	Mthias
now Abigall shall see/Whether Mathias holds her deare or no.	Jew	3.2.1	Mthias

ABIGALL (cont.)			
What, Abigall become a Nunne againe?	Jew	3.4.1	Barab
When saw'st thou Abigall?	Jew	3.4.18	Barab
Why, made mine Abigall a Nunne.	Jew	3.4.24	Barab
False, credulous, inconstant Abigall!	Jew	3.4.27	Barab
Now shalt thou see the death of Abigall,	Jew	3.4.62	Barab
What, all dead save onely Abigall?	Jew	3.6.7	2Fryar
Why, Brother, you converted Abigall;	Jew	4.1.106	Barab
your sonne and Mathias were both contracted unto Abigall; [he]	Jew	5.1.29	P Ithimr
ABILITIE			
it is not in my abilitie to present before your eyes, the true	F App	p.237 41	P Faust
ABJECT			
And like base slaves abject our princely mindes/To vile and	2Tamb	5.1.140	Orcan
By heaven, the abject villaine shall not live.	Edw	2.2.106	Mortmr
ABJECTION			
Now throwen to roomes of blacke abjection,	1Tamb	5.1.267	Bajzth
ABJUR'D			
On God, whom Faustus hath abjur'd?	F1849	5.2.53	P Faust
ABJURE			
Full soone wouldst thou abjure this single life.	Dido	3.1.60	Dido
Then sister youle abjure Iarbus love?	Dido	3.1.77	Anna
Abjure the Scriptures, and his Saviour Christ;	F 276	1.3.48	Mephst
conjuring/Is stoutly to abjure [the Trinity] <all godlinesse>,	F 281	1.3.53	Mephst
Abjure this Magicke, turne to God againe.	F 396	2.1.8	Faust
ABLE			
And better able unto other armes.	Dido	3.3.36	Cupid
Be able to withstand and conquer him.	2Tamb	2.2.19	Gazell
Wherein are thirtie thousand able men,	P 139	2.82	Guise
And being able, Ile keep an hoast in pay.	P 840	17.35	Guise
Thou able to maintaine an hoast in pay,	P 841	17.36	Eprnon
He hath a body able to endure,	Edw	5.5.10	Matrvs
'sbloud I am never able to endure these torments.	F1307	4.1.153	P Benvol
forth as by art and power of my spirit I am able to performe.	F App	p.237 39	P Faust
And sweet toucht harpe that to move stones was able?	Ovid's Elegies		3.11.40
ABOARD (See ABOORD, ABOURD)			
ABODE			
grace may sit secure, if none but wee/Doe wot of your abode.	Edw	4.7.27	Monk
Where kingly Neptune and his traine abode.	Hero and Leander		2.166
ABOORD			
Which when I come aboord will hoist up saile,	2Tamb	1.2.24	Callap
But need we not be spied going aboord?	2Tamb	1.2.56	Almeda
My men are all aboord,	Jew	5.5.103	Calym
Lets all aboord, and follow him amaine.	Edw	2.4.47	Mortmr
Come, come aboord, tis but an houres sailing.	Edw	2.4.49	Lncstr
ABORTIVE			
them for the funerall/They have bestowed on my abortive sonne.	2Tamb	4.3.66	Tamb
ABOUND			
And opening dores with creaking noyse abound?	Ovid's Elegies		1.6.50
For wofull haires let piece-torne plumes abound,	Ovid's Elegies		2.6.5
ABOUNDANCE			
The sucking shore with their aboundance swels.	Ovid's Elegies		2.11.14
ABOUNDED			
While thus I speake, the waters more abounded:	Ovid's Elegies		3.5.85
ABOUNDS			
With corne the earth abounds, with vines much more,	Ovid's Elegies		2.16.7
ABOURD			
Come, come abourd, pursue the hatefull Greekes.	Dido	2.1.22	Aeneas
Then got we to our ships, and being abourd,	Dido	2.1.280	Aeneas
Thinking to beare her on my backe abourd,	Dido	2.1.284	Aeneas
Abourd, abourd, since Fates doe bid abourd,	Dido	4.3.21	Aeneas
Troians abourd, and I will follow you,	Dido	4.3.45	Aeneas
They say Aeneas men are going abourd,	Dido	4.4.2	Dido
The sailes were hoysing up, and he abourd.	Dido	4.4.15	Anna
To rid thee of that doubt, abourd againe,	Dido	4.4.21	Dido
Then let Aeneas goe abourd with us.	Dido	4.4.23	Achat
Get you abourd, Aeneas meanes to stay.	Dido	4.4.24	Dido
But when you were abourd twas calme enough,	Dido	4.4.27	Dido
And left me neither saile nor sterne abourd.	Dido	5.1.61	Aeneas
Aeneas, wherefore goe thy men abourd?	Dido	5.1.87	Dido
O Anna, my Aeneas is abourd,	Dido	5.1.194	Dido
Before I came, Aeneas was abourd,	Dido	5.1.226	Anna
ABOUT (See also 'BOUT)			
As made the bloud run downe about mine eares.	Dido	1.1.8	Ganimd
Put thou about thy necke my owne sweet heart,	Dido	1.1.44	Jupitr
Come Ganimed, we must about this geare.	Dido	1.1.121	Jupitr
All which hemd me about, crying, this is he.	Dido	2.1.219	Aeneas
About whose withered necke hung Hecuba,	Dido	2.1.226	Aeneas
Which he disdaining whiskt his sword about,	Dido	2.1.253	Aeneas
Will Dido let me hang about her necke?	Dido	3.1.30	Cupid
As Seaborne Nymphes shall swarme about thy ships,	Dido	3.1.129	Dido
Then Thetis hangs about Apolloes necke,	Dido	3.1.132	Dido
Her silver armes will coll me round about,	Dido	4.3.51	Aeneas
And triple wise intrench her round about:	Dido	5.1.10	Aeneas
Spendst thou thy time about this little boy,	Dido	5.1.51	Hermes
Which is (God knowes) about that Tamburlaine,	1Tamb	1.1.30	Mycet
and about their neckes/Hangs massie chaines of golde downe to	1Tamb	1.2.125	Souldr
And with my hand turne Fortunes wheel about,	1Tamb	1.2.175	Tamb
About them hangs a knot of Amber heire,	1Tamb	2.1.23	Menaph
with winged Steads/All sweating, tilt about the watery heavens,	1Tamb	3.2.79	Agidas
That naked rowe about the Terrene sea.	1Tamb	3.3.50	Tamb
Have fetcht about the Indian continent:	1Tamb	3.3.254	Tamb
About the confines of Bythinia?	1Tamb	4.3.25	Arabia
Millions of men encompasse thee about,	1Tamb	5.1.215	Bajzth

ABOUT (cont.)

Hover about the ugly Ferriman,	1Tamb	5.1.246		Zabina
Quiver about the Axeltree of heaven.	2Tamb	1.1.90		Orcan
And cloath of Arras hung about the walles,	2Tamb	1.2.44		Callap
Their armes to hang about a Ladies necke:	2Tamb	1.3.30		Tamb
stature <statue>/And martch about it with my mourning campe,	2Tamb	2.4.141		Tamb
And with his hoste [martcht] <martch> round about the earth,	2Tamb	3.2.111		Tamb
Yes, my Lord, yes, come lets about it.	2Tamb	3.3.10		Soldrs
A hundred horse shall scout about the plaines/To spie what	2Tamb	3.3.47		Techel
About the Grecian Isles to rob and spoile:	2Tamb	3.5.94		Jrslem
Ile hang a clogge about your necke for running away againe, you	2Tamb	3.5.100	P	Tamb
Run mourning round about the Femals misse,	2Tamb	4.1.188		Tamb
Run tilting round about the firmament,	2Tamb	4.1.203		Tamb
Enrag'd I ran about the fields for thee,	2Tamb	4.2.17		Therid
Wanders about the black circumference,	2Tamb	4.2.90		Therid
Where about lies it?	2Tamb	5.1.120		Tamb
I will about it straight, come Souldiers.	2Tamb	5.1.172		Techel
To some high hill about <above> the citie here.	2Tamb	5.1.216		Therid
Let it be so, about it souldiers:	2Tamb	5.1.217		Tamb
Circled about with Limnasphaltis Lake,	2Tamb	5.2.5		Callap
Marching about the ayer with armed men,	2Tamb	5.2.34		Amasia
Belike they coasted round by Candie shoare/About their Oyles,	Jew	1.1.92		Barab
glide by night/About the place where Treasure hath bin hid:	Jew	2.1.27		Barab
fortune were so good/As but to be about this happy place;	Jew	2.1.32		Abigal
Oh my Lord we will not jarre about the price;	Jew	2.3.65		Barab
I feare me 'tis about faire Abigall.	Jew	2.3.139		Mthias
talke with him was [but]/About the borrowing of a booke or two.	Jew	2.3.156		Mthias
Sometimes I goe about and poyson wells;	Jew	2.3.176		Barab
And like a cunning Jew so cast about,	Jew	2.3.235		Barab
a golden crosse/With Christian posies round about the ring.	Jew	2.3.297		Barab
And now you men of Malta looke about,	Jew	3.5.29		Govnr
he was ready to leape off e're the halter was about his necke;	Jew	4.2.22	P	Ithimr
And winds it twice or thrice about his eare;	Jew	4.3.8		Barab
come, wee'll walke about/The ruin'd Towne, and see the wracke we	Jew	5.2.18		Calym
Goe walke about the City, see thy friends:	Jew	5.2.92		Barab
Then will I, Barabas, about this coyne,	Jew	5.2.107		Govnr
Well, now about effecting this device:	Jew	5.2.117		Barab
And batter all the stones about their eares,	Jew	5.5.30		Barab
And tye white linnen scarfes about their armes.	P 233	4.31		Guise
That swim about and so preserve their lives:	P 419	7.59		Guise
And dayly meet about this time of day,	P 503	9.22		Guise
Now doe I but begin to look about,	P 985	19.55		Guise
As pale as ashes, nay then tis time to look about.	P1001	19.71		Guise
And fire accursed Rome about his eares.	P1200	22.62		King
We will wait heere about the court.	Edw	1.1.49		Omnes
Crownets of pearle about his naked armes,	Edw	1.1.63		Gavstn
He claps his cheekes, and hanges about his neck,	Edw	1.2.51		Queene
Or with those armes that twind about my neck,	Edw	1.4.175		Queene
Ile hang a golden tongue about thy neck,	Edw	1.4.328		Edward
No other jewels hang about my neck/Then these my lord, nor let	Edw	1.4.330		Queene
It is about her lover Gaveston.	Edw	2.1.22		Spencr
About it then, and we will follow you.	Edw	2.2.124		Mortmr
And so I walke with him about the walles,	Edw	2.2.222		Edward
O that mine armes could close this Ile about,	Edw	2.4.17		Queene
And plowes to go about our pallace gates.	Edw	3.1.216		Edward
that one so false/Should come about the person of a prince.	Edw	5.2.105		Mortmr
So,/Now must I about this geare, nere was there any/So finely	Edw	5.5.39		Ltborn
I'le turne all the lice about thee into Familiars, and make	F 362	1.4.20	P	Wagner
First, I will question [with] thee about hell:	F 504	2.1.116		Faust
I, so are all things else; but whereabouts <where about>?	F 507	2.1.119		Faust
next, like a Neckelace I hang about her Necke:	F 667	2.2.116	P	Pride
put off thy cloathes, and I'le conjure thee about presently:	F 747	2.3.26	P	Robin
To beate the beades about the Friers Pates,	F 863	3.1.85		Mephst
Who's that spoke? Friers looke about.	F1040	3.2.60		Pope
yee Lubbers look about/And find the man that doth this villany,	F1055	3.2.75		Pope
Come brethren, let's about our businesse with good devotion.	F1076	3.2.96	P	1Frier
let me have the carrying of him about to shew some trickes.	F1129	3.3.42	P	Robin
since our conference about faire Ladies, which was the	F1681	5.1.8	P	1Schol
or Ile turne al the lice about thee into familiars, and they	F App	p.229 25	P	Wagner
Friers looke about.	F App	p.231 3	P	Pope
Come brethren, lets about our businesse with good devotion.	F App	p.232 29	P	Frier
he keepes such a chafing with my mistris about it, and she has	F App	p.233 8	P	Rafe
Rafe, keepe out, for I am about a roaring peece of worke.	F App	p.233 11	P	Robin
Wel, tone of you hath this goblet about you.	F App	p.235 16	P	Vintnr
about the honour of mine auncestors, how they had wonne by	F App	p.236 19	P	Emper
him now, or Ile breake his glasse-windowes about his eares.	F App	p.240 143	P	HrsCsr
I have none about me, come to my Oastrie, and Ile give them	F App	p.241 161	P	HrsCsr
When all the woods about stand bolt up-right,	Lucan, First Booke	143		
strange and unknown stars were seene/Wandering about the North,	Lucan, First Booke	525		
the suburbe fieldes/Fled, fowle Erinnis stalkt about the wals,	Lucan, First Booke	570		
Then, that the trembling Citizens should walke/About the City;	Lucan, First Booke	592		
About thy neck shall he at pleasure skippe?	Ovid's Elegies	1.4.6		
foote drawes out/Fastning her light web some old beame about.	Ovid's Elegies	1.14.8		
About my head be quivering Mirtle wound,	Ovid's Elegies	1.15.37		
About my temples go triumphant bayes,	Ovid's Elegies	2.12.1		
And the dull snake about thy offrings creepe,	Ovid's Elegies	2.13.13		
Then wreathes about my necke her winding armes,	Ovid's Elegies	2.18.9		
Where round about small birdes most sweetely sing.	Ovid's Elegies	3.1.4		
Alas he runnes too farre about the ring,	Ovid's Elegies	3.2.69		
About her necke hung chaines of peble stone,	Hero and Leander	1.25		
About her naked necke his bare armes threw.	Hero and Leander	1.42		
That hops about the chamber where I lie,	Hero and Leander	1.354		
Having striv'ne in vaine, was now about to crie,	Hero and Leander	1.413		

ABOUT (cont.)			
Then standing at the doore, she turnd about,	Hero and Leander	2.97	
About his armes the purple riband wound,	Hero and Leander	2.106	
Leander striv'd, the waves about him wound,	Hero and Leander	2.159	
He on the suddaine cling'd her so about,	Hero and Leander	2.314	
And round about the chamber this false morne,	Hero and Leander	2.321	
ABOVE			
Which if thou lose shall shine above the waves:	Dido	3.1.121	Dido
by princely deeds/Doth meane to soare above the highest sort.	1Tamb	2.7.33	Therid
wars justice ye repute)/I execute, enjoin'd me from above,	2Tamb	4.1.148	Tamb
Making their fiery gate above the cloudes,	2Tamb	4.3.9	Tamb
Above the threefold Astracisme of heaven,	2Tamb	4.3.62	Tamb
Have made the water swell above the bankes,	2Tamb	5.1.205	Techel
To some high hill about <above> the citie here.	2Tamb	5.1.216	Therid
And live in spight of death above a day.	2Tamb	5.3.101	Tamb
If 'twere above ground I could, and would have it; but hee	Jew	4.2.57	P Ithimr
Thou in those Groves, by Dis above,	Jew	4.2.97	Ithimr
How busie Barrabas is there above/To entertaine us in his	Jew	5.5.52	Calym
But he that sits and rules above the clowdes,	P 42	1.42	Navrre
But what doth move thee above the rest to doe the deed?	P1132	21.26	P Dumain
Thy woorth sweet friend is far above my guifts,	Edw	1.1.161	Edward
And this above the rest, because we heare/That Edmund casts to	Edw	5.2.57	Mortmr
His waxen wings did mount above his reach,	F 21	Prol.21	1Chor
above written being inviolate, full power to fetch or carry the	F 496	2.1.108	P Faust
<Tel me>, are there many Spheares <heavens> above the Moone?	F 586	2.2.35	Faust
Lifting his loftie head above the clouds,	F 912	3.1.134	Pope
this makes me wonder above the rest, that being in the dead	F App	p.242 16	P Duke
And Marius head above cold Tav'ron peering/(His grave broke	Lucan, First Booke	581	
Ah howe thy lot is above my lot blest:	Ovid's Elegies	1.6.46	
But far above the loveliest, Hero shin'd,	Hero and Leander	1.103	
Her vowes above the emptie aire he flings:	Hero and Leander	1.370	
Above our life we love a stedfast friend,	Hero and Leander	2.79	
ABRAHAM			
He is not of the seed of Abraham.	Jew	2.3.230	Barab
ABRAHAMS			
Light Abrahams off-spring; and direct the hand/Of Abigall this	Jew	2.1.14	Barab
ABRAMS			
And herein was old Abrams happinesse:	Jew	1.1.106	Barab
ABREVIATED			
Th'abreviated <breviated> names of holy Saints,	F 238	1.3.10	Faust
ABRIDGE			
Now Bajazeth, abridge thy banefull daies,	1Tamb	5.1.286	Bajzth
Which in a moment will abridge his life:	Edw	5.1.42	Edward
When as my sonne thinkes to abridge my daies.	Edw	5.6.84	Queene
ABROAD			
Whiles I with my Achates roave abroad,	Dido	1.1.175	Aeneas
of my company/Scowting abroad upon these champion plaines,	1Tamb	2.2.40	Spy
I walke abroad a nights/And kill sicke people groaning under	Jew	2.3.174	Barab
begins those deepe ingendred thoughts/To burst abroad, those	P 92	2.35	Guise
And in the day when he shall walke abroad,	Edw	1.1.57	Gavstn
She neither walkes abroad, nor comes in sight:	Edw	2.1.24	Baldck
And dismall Prophesies were spread abroad:	Lucan, First Booke	562	
Now Mars doth rage abroad without all pitty,	Ovid's Elegies	1.8.41	
There harmelesse Swans feed all abroad the river,	Ovid's Elegies	2.6.53	
Horse freed from service range abroad the woods.	Ovid's Elegies	2.9.22	
Her left hand held abroad a regal scepter,	Ovid's Elegies	3.1.13	
And from the channell all abroad surrounded.	Ovid's Elegies	3.5.86	
ABSENCE			
Whose absence make the sun and Moone as darke/As when opposde	2Tamb	2.4.51	Tamb
and hearing your absence in the field, offers to set upon us	2Tamb	5.3.104	P 3Msngr
Hees gone, and for his absence thus I moorne,	Edw	1.4.305	Edward
If in his absence thus he favors him,	Edw	2.2.47	Mortmr
Thy absence made me droope, and pine away,	Edw	2.2.52	Edward
[Where such as beare <bare> his absence but with griefe],	F1141	3.3.54A	3Chor
ABSENT			
Will, being absent, be obdurate still.	Dido	5.1.187	Dido
How have ye spent your absent time from me?	2Tamb	1.3.173	Tamb
What, dar'st thou then be absent from the fight,	2Tamb	4.1.22	Amyras
lie in wait for him/And if we find him absent from his campe,	2Tamb	5.2.57	Callap
While rage is absent, take some friend the paynes.	Ovid's Elegies	1.7.2	
But absent is my fire, lyes ile tell none,	Ovid's Elegies	2.16.11	
ABSOLUTE			
And art a king as absolute as Jove,	2Tamb	4.3.33	Orcan
ABSOLUTELY			
Lastly, he that denies this, shall absolutely lose al he has.	Jew	1.2.76	P Reader
ABSTAINE			
Nor could the youth abstaine, but he must weare/The sacred ring	Hero and Leander	2.108	
ABSTRACTS			
And spurns the Abstracts of thy foolish lawes.	2Tamb	5.1.197	Tamb
ABUNDANCE (See ABOUNDANCE)			
ABUS'D			
Meander come, I am abus'd Meander.	1Tamb	1.1.106	Mycet
Or holy gods with cruell strokes abus'd.	Ovid's Elegies	1.7.6	
ABUS'DE			
Then treasure is abus'de,/When misers keepe it; being put to	Hero and Leander	1.234	
ABUSDE			
Would it not grieve a King to be so abusde,	1Tamb	2.2.5	Mycet
Remember how the Bishop was abusde,	Edw	1.4.59	ArchBp
ABUSE			
How dare you thus abuse my Majesty?	1Tamb	3.3.226	Zabina
Being thy Captive, thus abuse his state,	1Tamb	4.2.60	Zabina
How you abuse the person of the king:	1Tamb	4.2.73	Anippe
Pope Julius did abuse the Churches Rites,	F 928	3.1.150	Pope

ABUSE (cont.)			
How darst thou thus abuse a Gentleman?	F App	p.238 74	Knight
'Tis so: by my witte her abuse is growne.	Ovid's Elegies	3.11.8	
ABUSES			
and she shal looke/That these abuses flow not from her tongue:	1Tamb	4.2.70	Zenoc
I shall now revenge/My fathers vile abuses and mine owne.	2Tamb	3.5.91	Callap
for needfull uses/Ile prove had hands impure with all abuses.	Ovid's Elegies	1.12.16	
At thy deafe dores in verse sing my abuses.	Ovid's Elegies	3.7.24	
ABY (See ABIE)			
ABYDOS (See also ABIDUS)			
The one Abydos, the other Sestos hight.	Hero and Leander	1.4	
ABYDUS			
And thence unto Abydus sooner blowne,	Hero and Leander	2.112	
ACANTHA			
Acantha, Antioch, and Caesaria,	2Tamb	2.1.20	Fredrk
ACCEPT			
I beseech your Worship accept of these forty Dollors.	F1457	4.4.1	P HrsCsr
I beseech you sir accept of this; I am a very poore man, and	F1463	4.4.7	P HrsCsr
Accept him that will serve thee all his youth,	Ovid's Elegies	1.3.5	
Accept him that will love with spotlesse truth:	Ovid's Elegies	1.3.6	
And thou my light accept me how so ever,	Ovid's Elegies	2.17.23	
ACCEPTANCE			
To presse beyond acceptance to your sight.	Dido	3.3.16	Aeneas
ACCESSARY			
Be made an accessary of your deeds;	Jew	2.3.342	Barab
ACCESSE			
grace the Duke of Guise doth crave/Accesse unto your highnes.	P 960	19.30	Eprnon
the President of Paris, that craves accesse unto your grace.	P1157	22.19	P 1Msngr
Desires accesse unto your majestie.	Edw	3.1.149	Spencr
If he have such accesse unto the prince,	Edw	5.2.77	Mortmr
ACCESSORY (See ACCESSARY)			
ACCIDENS			
That was the cause, but yet per accidens:	F 274	1.3.46	Mephst
ACCIDENTALL			
Your vaines are full of accidentall heat,	2Tamb	5.3.84	Phsitn
ACCIDENT'S			
What accident's betided to the Jewes?	Jew	1.1.145	Barab
ACCIDENTS			
To make discourse of some sweet accidents/Have chanc'd thy	1Tamb	5.1.424	Arabia
ACCOMPANIE			
And with the rest accompanie him to his grave?	Edw	5.6.88	Queene
ACCOMPANY			
But wil those Kings accompany your Lord?	1Tamb	3.3.27	Tamb
Let me accompany my gratious mother,	2Tamb	1.3.66	Calyph
ACCOMPLICE (See COMPLICES)			
ACCOMPLISH			
Your Bassoe will accomplish your behest:	1Tamb	3.1.42	Bassoe
And hast thou cast how to accomplish it?	Edw	5.4.24	Mortmr
To accomplish what soever the Doctor please.	F1183	4.1.29	Mrtino
by whome thou canst accomplish what thou list, this therefore	F App	p.236 5	P Emper
I am ready to accomplish your request, so farre forth as by art	F App	p.237 37	P Faust
He readie to accomplish what she wil'd,	Hero and Leander	1.433	
ACCOMPLISHMENTS			
We are not bound to those accomplishments,	2Tamb	2.1.35	Baldwn
ACCOMPLISHT			
To make him famous in accomplisht woorth:	1Tamb	2.1.34	Cosroe
ACCORD			
No, I came now hether of mine owne accord.	F 272	1.3.44	Mephst
ACCORDING			
According to our ancient use, shall beare/The figure of the	2Tamb	3.1.64	Orcan
I have according to instructions in that behalfe,	Edw	4.3.28	P Spencr
Each one according to his gifts respect.	Ovid's Elegies	1.8.38	
Making her joy according to her hire.	Ovid's Elegies	1.10.32	
ACCOSTED			
With chearefull hope thus he accosted her.	Hero and Leander	1.198	
ACCOUNT			
We will account her author of our lives.	Dido	3.1.112	Aeneas
make account of me/As of thy fellow; we are villaines both:	Jew	2.3.213	Barab
But goe you in, I'le thinke upon the account:	Jew	2.3.241	Barab
The account is made, for [Lodovico] <Lodowicke> dyes.	Jew	2.3.242	Barab
ACCOUNTED			
Faire fooles delight to be accounted nice.	Hero and Leander	1.326	
ACCURSED			
At whose accursed feete as overjoyed,	Dido	2.1.177	Aeneas
Why feed ye still on daies accursed beams,	1Tamb	5.1.262	Bajzth
Accursed Bajazeth, whose words of ruth,	1Tamb	5.1.270	Bajzth
Accursed day infected with my griefs,	1Tamb	5.1.291	Bajzth
With that accursed traitor Almeda,	2Tamb	3.2.150	Tamb
Be likewise end to my accursed life.	2Tamb	3.4.82	Olymp
Who stand accursed in the sight of heaven,	Jew	1.2.64	Govnr
Away accursed from thy fathers sight.	Jew	1.2.351	Barab
I'le be reveng'd on this accursed Towne;	Jew	5.1.62	Barab
Accursed Barabas, base Jew, relent?	Jew	5.5.73	Govnr
And fire accursed Rome about his eares.	P1200	22.62	King
Tis done, and now accursed hand fall off.	Edw	1.4.88	Edward
On your accursed traiterous progenie,	Edw	3.1.141	Edward
Accursed wretches, wast in regard of us,	Edw	3.1.233	Edward
Thy hatefull and accursed head shall lie,	Edw	5.6.30	King
accursed head,/Could I have rulde thee then, as I do now,	Edw	5.6.95	King
I, go accursed spirit to ugly hell:	F 627	2.2.76	Faust
Accursed Faustus, [where is mercy now]?	F1739	5.1.66	Faust
Accursed Faustus, <wretch what hast thou done>?	F1739	(HC270)B	Faust
[Accursed Faustus, miserable man],	F1788	5.1.115A	OldMan

ACCURSSED			
Ah wicked king, accurssed Gaveston, ...	Edw	1.2.4	Lncstr
ACCURST			
Accurst be he that first invented war, ...	1Tamb	2.4.1	Mycet
But most accurst, to see the Sun-bright troope/Of heavenly	1Tamb	5.1.324	Zenoc
For my accurst and hatefull perjurie.	2Tamb	2.3.3	Sgsmnd
For this offence be thou accurst of God.	Edw	1.1.199	BshpCv
ACCUSDE			
Because I thinke scorne to be accusde, ...	Edw	5.6.39	Mortmr
Twas his troupe hem'd in Milo being accusde;	Lucan, First Booke		323
Say but thou wert injurously accusde.	Ovid's Elegies		3.13.42
ACCUSE			
have hir'd a slave my man/To accuse me of a thousand villanies:	Jew	5.1.76	Barab
ACCUSING			
Now rash accusing, and thy vaine beliefe, ...	Ovid's Elegies		2.7.13
ACCUSTOME			
As parting friends accustome on the shoare, ...	Dido	4.3.50	Aeneas
ACHATES			
Gentle Achates, reach the Tinder boxe, ...	Dido	1.1.166	Aeneas
Whiles I with my Achates roave abroad, ...	Dido	1.1.175	Aeneas
Achates, tis my mother that is fled, ...	Dido	1.1.240	Aeneas
O my Achates, Theban Niobe, ...	Dido	2.1.3	Aeneas
And in this humor is Achates to, ...	Dido	2.1.10	Achat
Achates though mine eyes say this is stone, ...	Dido	2.1.24	Aeneas
Achates, see King Priam wags his hand, ...	Dido	2.1.29	Aeneas
You are Achates, or I [am] deciv'd.	Dido	2.1.49	Serg
Achates, speake, for I am overjoyed.	Dido	2.1.54	Aeneas
Blest be the time I see Achates face.	Dido	2.1.56	Illion
When thou Achates with thy sword mad'st way, ...	Dido	2.1.268	Aeneas
Achates speake, sorrow hath tired me quite.	Dido	2.1.293	Aeneas
Achates, how doth Carthage please your Lord?	Dido	3.1.97	Dido
And let Achates saile to Italy:	Dido	3.1.115	Dido
Achates, thou shalt be so [manly] <meanly> clad, ...	Dido	3.1.128	Dido
As for Achates, and his followers.	Dido	3.1.176	Dido
Stoute friend Achates, doest thou know this wood? . .	Dido	3.3.50	Aeneas
Achates and Ascanius, well met.	Dido	4.1.28	Dido
Achates come forth, Sergestus, Illioneus, ...	Dido	4.3.13	Aeneas
I would have given Achates store of gold, ...	Dido	4.4.7	Dido
I went to take my farewell of Achates.	Dido	4.4.18	Aeneas
How haps Achates bid me not farewell?	Dido	4.4.19	Dido
Thou and Achates ment to saile away.	Dido	4.4.28	Dido
And thou and I Achates, for revenge, ...	Dido	4.4.88	Aeneas
Achates and the rest shall waite on thee, ...	Dido	5.1.76	Aeneas
Led by Achates to the Troian fleete:	Dido	5.1.84	Dido
Where thou and false Achates first set foote:	Dido	5.1.175	Dido
But see, Achates wils him put to sea, ...	Dido	5.1.258	Dido
ACHE (See AKE)			
ACHELAUS			
I know not what expecting, I ere while/Nam'd Achelaus, Inachus,	Ovid's Elegies		3.5.104
ACHELOUS			
If Achelous, I aske where thy hornes stand, ...	Ovid's Elegies		3.5.35
ACHERON			
Of Stix, of Acheron, and the fiery Lake, ...	F 826	3.1.48	Faust
And night deepe drencht in mystie Acheron, ...	Hero and Leander		1.189
ACHERONTIS			
Sint mihi Dei Acherontis propitii, valeat numen triplex .	F 244	1.3.16	P Faust
ACHIEVE (See ATCHIVE, ATCHIEVE)			
ACHIEVEMENT (See ATCHIVEMENTS)			
ACHILL			
What helpes it me of fierce Achill to sing?	Ovid's Elegies		2.1.29
ACHILLES			
Then speake Aeneas with Achilles tongue, ...	Dido	2.1.121	Aeneas
by which Achilles horse/Drew him in triumph through the .	Dido	2.1.205	Aeneas
Achilles sonne, remember what I was, ...	Dido	2.1.233	Aeneas
And would have grappeld with Achilles sonne, ...	Dido	2.1.251	Aeneas
Wrapped in curles, as fierce Achilles was, ...	1Tamb	2.1.24	Menaph
And set his warlike person to the view/Of fierce Achilles,	2Tamb	3.5.68	Tamb
For if I should as Hector did Achilles, ...	2Tamb	3.5.70	Tamb
Yea, I will wound Achilles in the heele, ...	F1779	5.1.106	Faust
Achilles burnd Briseis being tane away:	Ovid's Elegies		1.9.33
Achilles burnt with face of captive Briseis, ...	Ovid's Elegies		2.8.11
To tragick verse while thou Achilles trainst, ...	Ovid's Elegies		2.18.1
ACHILLIS			
And for Patroclus sterne Achillis droopt:	Edw	1.4.394	MortSr
ACKNOWLEDGE			
Frier, thou dost acknowledge me thy King?	P1164	22.26	King
stand upon; therefore acknowledge your errour, and be attentive.	F 203	1.2.10	P Wagner
A CLOCKE			
Come to my house at one a clocke this night.	Jew	4.1.91	Barab
A COMMING			
My lord of Cornewall is a comming over, ...	Edw	2.1.76	Neece
ACQUAINTANCE			
Whom kindred and acquaintance counites?	Dido	3.2.31	Juno
ACQUAINTED			
loves bowe/His owne flames best acquainted signes may knowe,	Ovid's Elegies		2.1.8
And rule so soone with private hands acquainted. . .	Ovid's Elegies		2.18.16
ACQUAINTS			
And heaven and earth with his unrest acquaints. . . .	Dido	1.1.141	Venus
ACQUITS			
two words, thinke/The cause acquits you not, but I that winke.	Ovid's Elegies		3.13.50
ACRE			
No sirra, in beaten silke and staves acre.	F App	p.229 16	P Wagner
how, how, knaves acre?	F App	p.229 17	P Clown

ACRE (cont.)
Sirra, I say in staves acre. . . . . F App p.229 20 P Wagner
Oho, oho, staves acre, why then belike, if I were your man, F App p.229 21 P Clown
ACT
As lothing Pirrhus for this wicked act: . . . . . Dido 2.1.258 Aeneas
Nor in my act hath fortune mingled chance, ... Ovid's Elegies 2.12.15
ACTAEON
One like Actaeon peeping through the grove, ... Edw 1.1.67 Gavstn
ACTEON
the Emperour, Il'e be Acteon, and turne my selfe to a Stagge. F1255 4.1.101 P Benvol
No sir, but when Acteon died, he left the hornes for you: F App p.237 55 P Faust
Like chast Diana, when Acteon spyde her, ... Hero and Leander 2.261
ACTEONS
In bold Acteons shape to turne a Stagge. . . . . . F1299 4.1.145 Faust
ACTES
The bright shining of whose glorious actes/Lightens the world F App p.237 25 Emper
ACTION
To whom he used action so pitifull, ... Dido 2.1.155 Aeneas
man, ordain'd by heaven/To further every action to the best. 1Tamb 2.1.53 Ortyg
working tooles present/The naked action of my threatned end. 1Tamb 3.2.94 Agidas
An action bloudy and tirannicall: . . . . . . P 208 4.6 Charls
ACTIONS
their Spheares/That guides his steps and actions to the throne, 1Tamb 2.1.17 Menaph
But when you see his actions [top] <stop> his speech, . 1Tamb 2.3.26 Therid
higher meeds/Then erst our states and actions have retain'd, 1Tamb 4.4.132 Therid
ACTOR
Then in this shew let me an Actor be, ... F 854 3.1.76 Faust
ACTORS
They that shalbe actors in this Massacre, ... P 231 4.29 Guise
ACTS
And chiefest Counsailor in all his acts, ... 1Tamb 2.5.11 Cosroe
Domesticke acts, and mine owne warres to sing. . . . . Ovid's Elegies 2.18.12
The subject hides thy wit, mens acts resound, ... Ovid's Elegies 3.1.25
AD (Homograph)
Oro, si quis [adhuc] <ad haec> precibus locus, exue mentem. Dido 5.1.138 Dido
And ad this to them, that all Asia/Lament to see the follie of 1Tamb 1.1.95 Cosroe
And ad more strength to your dominions/Than ever yet confirm'd 1Tamb 5.1.448 Tamb
Which ad much danger to your malladie. . . . . . 2Tamb 5.3.55 Therid
Th'ad best betimes forsake [them] <thee> and their trains, Edw 3.1.202 Lncstr
Ad <And> they were apt to curle an hundred waies, . . Ovid's Elegies 1.14.13
To this ad shame, shame to performe it quaild mee, . . Ovid's Elegies 3.6.37
ADAM
But perish underneath my bitter curse/Like Cain by Adam, for Jew 3.4.33 Barab
me, as Paradise was to Adam the first day of his creation. F 658 2.2.107 P Faust
ADAMANT
Yet he whose [hearts] <heart> of adamant or flint, . . Dido 5.1.234 Anna
Your honor hath an adamant, of power/To drawe a prince. . Edw 2.5.105 Arundl
ADAMANTES
Huge okes, hard Adamantes might she have moved, . . Ovid's Elegies 3.6.57
ADAMANTINE
I mean the Adamantine Destinies, ... Hero and Leander 1.444
ADDE (See also AD)
Shall adde more excellence unto thine Art, ... F1208 4.1.54 Emper
let's devise how we may adde more shame/To the blacke scandall F1377 4.2.53 Fredrk
Adde, Caesar, to these illes Perusian famine; . . . . Lucan, First Booke 41
And while he drinkes, to adde more do not misse, . . . Ovid's Elegies 1.4.52
Adde she was diligent thy locks to braide, . . . Ovid's Elegies 2.7.23
Adde deeds unto thy promises at last. . . . . . Ovid's Elegies 2.16.48
ADDED
Yet as a punishment they added this, ... Hero and Leander 1.469
ADDERS
And walke upon the dreadfull Adders backe, ... F 919 3.1.141 Pope
Adders and serpents, let me breathe a while: . . . . F1980 5.2.184 Faust
Bearing the head with dreadfull [Adders] <Arrowes> clad, . Ovid's Elegies 3.5.14
ADDES
Pleasure addes fuell to my lustfull fire, ... Ovid's Elegies 2.10.25
ADDING
Adding more courage to my conquering mind. . . . . 1Tamb 5.1.515 Tamb
Adding their wealth and treasure to my store. . . . . 2Tamb 4.3.101 Tamb
Adding this golden sentence to our praise; . . . . F 917 3.1.139 Pope
ADDRESSE
Gainst him my Lord must you addresse your power. . . 2Tamb 1.1.19 Gazell
And to her tentes wild me my selfe addresse. . . . Ovid's Elegies 1.9.44
Borne at Peligny, to write more addresse. . . . . Ovid's Elegies 2.1.2
ADDST
Why addst thou starres to heaven, leaves to greene woods . Ovid's Elegies 2.10.13
ADEIW
What will be, shall be: Divinitie adeiw. . . . . . F 75 1.1.47 Faust
ADEW
Adew my Lord, and either change your minde, ... Edw 1.1.130 Lncstr
ADHUC
Oro, si quis [adhuc] <ad haec> precibus locus, exue mentem. Dido 5.1.138 Dido
ADIEU (See ADEIW, ADEW, ADUE)
ADJOINING
Shal now, adjoining al their hands with mine, ... 1Tamb 5.1.493 Tamb
ADJOURNED
This day denyall hath my sport adjourned. . . . . . Ovid's Elegies 1.12.2
ADJOYNING
Adjoyning on Agenors stately towne, ... Dido 1.1.211 Venus
forth will ride/Into these woods, adjoyning to these walles, Dido 3.2.88 Juno
ADJUNCT
Figures of every adjunct to the heavens, ... F 239 1.3.11 Faust
ADJUNCTS
and this curtle-axe/Are adjuncts more beseeming Tamburlaine. 1Tamb 1.2.43 Tamb

ADJUNCTS (cont.)			
Hunger and [thirst] <cold>, right adjuncts of the war.	2Tamb	3.2.58	Tamb
ADMIRABLE			
O this is admirable!	F App	p.233 1	P Robin
ADMIRABLEST			
that Hellen of Greece was the admirablest Lady that ever liv'd:	F1683	5.1.10	P 1Schol
ADMIRAL (See also VIZADMIRALL)			
Prince Condy and my good Lord Admiral,	P 27	1.27	Navrre
What are you hurt my Lord high Admiral?	P 197	3.32	Condy
How fares it with my Lord high Admiral,	P 253	4.51	Charls
ADMIRALL			
Prince Condy, and my good Lord Admirall,	P 2	1.2	Charls
And when thou seest the Admirall ride by,	P 87	2.30	Guise
And it please your grace the Lord high Admirall,	P 243	4.41	Man
What shall we doe now with the Admirall?	P 248	4.46	Charls
Content, I will goe visite the Admirall.	P 251	4.49	Charls
Assure your selfe my good Lord Admirall,	P 262	4.60	Charls
And so be pacient good Lord Admirall,	P 271	4.69	Charls
I let the Admirall be first dispatcht.	P 283	5.10	Retes
The Admirall,/Cheefe standard bearer to the Lutheranes,	P 284	5.11	Guise
Where is the Admirall?	P 300	5.27	Gonzag
Now sirra, what shall we doe with the Admirall?	P 482	9.1	P 1Atndt
Now Madame, how like you our lusty Admirall?	P 494	9.13	Guise
Thou Lancaster, high admirall of our fleete,	Edw	1.4.66	Edward
ADMIRALS			
Away then, break into the Admirals house.	P 282	5.9	Guise
[Cossin] <Cosin> <Cousin>, the Captaine of the Admirals guarde,	P 293	5.20	Anjoy
But look my Lord, ther's some in the Admirals house.	P 297	5.24	Retes
ADMIR'D			
Admir'd I am of those that hate me most:	Jew	Prol.9	Machvl
This day shall make thee be admir'd in Rome.	F 867	3.1.89	Mephst
ADMIRDE			
[As they admirde and wondred at his wit].	F1148	3.3.61A	3Chor
ADMIRE (See also ADMYRE)			
Anna that doth admire thee more then heaven.	Dido	4.2.46	Anna
Let base conceited wits admire vilde things,	Ovid's Elegies		1.15.35
Thou shalt admire no woods or Citties there,	Ovid's Elegies		2.11.11
ADMIRED			
May be admired through the furthest Land.	F 842	3.1.64	Faust
whose admired worth>/<Made Greece with ten yeares warres	F1696	(HC269)B	2Schol
once admired/For wondrous knowledge in our Germane schooles,	F1997	5.3.15	2Schol
ADMIRES			
shall confesse/Theise are the men that all the world admires.	1Tamb	1.2.223	Usumc
whom all the world admires for Majesty, we should thinke	F1686	5.1.13	P 1Schol
Whom all the world admires for majesty.	F1698	5.1.25	2Schol
ADMIRING			
Which some admiring, O thou oft wilt blush/And say he likes me	Ovid's Elegies		1.14.47
And long admiring say by what meanes learnd/Hath this same Poet	Ovid's Elegies		2.1.9
Whence his admiring eyes more pleasure tooke,	Hero and Leander		2.325
ADMISSION (See ADMITION)			
ADMIT			
give Dido leave/To be more modest then her thoughts admit,	Dido	3.1.95	Dido
Therefore at least admit us libertie,	1Tamb	1.2.71	Zenoc
That nobly must admit necessity:	2Tamb	5.3.201	Tamb
Well, daughter, we admit you for a Nun.	Jew	1.2.330	Abbass
But to admit a sale of these thy Turkes/We may not, nay we dare	Jew	2.2.21	Govnr
Admit thou lov'dst not Lodowicke for his [sire] <sinne>,	Jew	3.3.40	Abigal
Admit him neere.	Edw	3.1.150	Edward
earth, the sea, the world it selfe,/Would not admit two Lords:	Lucan, First Booke		111
ADMITION			
Abigal it is not yet long since/That I did labour thy admition,	Jew	3.3.57	1Fryar
ADMITS			
Whose jealousie admits no second Mate,	2Tamb	2.4.12	Tamb
ADMITTED			
the christian King/Is made, for joy of your admitted truce:	2Tamb	2.2.21	Uribas
And is admitted to the Sister-hood.	Jew	1.2.343	1Fryar
To get me be admitted for a Nun.	Jew	3.3.55	Abigal
ADMONISHT			
Jove being admonisht gold had soveraigne power,	Ovid's Elegies		3.7.29
ADMONITION			
The Abbasse of the house/Whose zealous admonition I embrace:	Jew	3.3.67	Abigal
ADMYR'D			
To shew her beautie, which the world admyr'd,	2Tamb	3.2.26	Tamb
ADMYRE			
The Nations far remoov'd admyre me not)/And when my name and	1Tamb	1.2.204	Tamb
ADMYRED			
and dim their eies/That stand and muse at our admyred armes.	1Tamb	2.3.24	Tamb
Their minds, and muses on admyred theames:	1Tamb	5.1.164	Tamb
ADMYRING			
She likewise in admyring spends her time,	Dido	3.2.72	Juno
A DO			
With much a do my hands I scarsely staide.	Ovid's Elegies		1.8.110
ADO			
me but a little straw, and had much ado to escape drowning:	F1487	4.4.31	P HrsCsr
Which so prevail'd, as he with small ado,	Hero and Leander		2.281
ADONIS			
And couch him in Adonis purple downe.	Dido	3.2.100	Venus
I'le be Adonis, thou shalt be Loves Queene.	Jew	4.2.94	Ithimr
Of proud Adonis that before her lies.	Hero and Leander		1.14
Rose-cheekt Adonis) kept a solemne feast.	Hero and Leander		1.93
ADONS			
As when the wilde boare Adons groine had rent.	Ovid's Elegies		3.8.16
ADOPT			
I here adopt thee for mine onely heire,	Jew	3.4.43	Baraba

ADOPT (cont.)			
Spencer, sweet Spencer, I adopt thee heere,	Edw	3.1.144	Edward
ADORE			
Whose [statues] <statutes> we adore in Scythia,	1Tamb	1.2.244	Tamb
Seeke out another Godhead to adore,	2Tamb	5.1.200	Tamb
Ceres and Bacchus Country-men adore,	Ovid's Elegies		3.2.53
ADORN'D			
That late adorn'd the Affrike Potentate,	2Tamb	3.2.124	Tamb
Nor capitall be adorn'd with sacred bayes:	Lucan, First Booke		288
ADORNE			
That fights for honor to adorne your head.	1Tamb	5.1.376	Anippe
These silver haires will more adorne my court,	Edw	1.4.346	Edward
Rich robes, themselves and others do adorne,	Hero and Leander		1.237
Whose carelesse haire, in stead of pearle t'adorne it,	Hero and Leander		1.389
ADORNED			
adorned with my Crowne,/As if thou wert the Empresse of the	1Tamb	3.3.124	Tamb
ADRIAN			
Pope Adrian let me have some right of Law,	F 904	3.1.126	Bruno
ADRIATICK			
but to passe along/Towards Venice by the Adriatick Sea;	Jew	1.1.163	Barab
A DRY			
I, pray do, for Faustus is a dry.	F1052	3.2.72	Faust
ADUE			
Carthage, my friendly host adue,	Dido	4.3.1	Aeneas
ADULTERER			
All being shut out, th'adulterer is within.	Ovid's Elegies		3.4.8
But when in gifts the wise adulterer came,	Ovid's Elegies		3.7.33
ADULTERORS			
Whiles these adulterors surfetted with sinne:	Dido	4.1.20	Iarbus
ADULTEROUS			
But lustfull Jove and his adulterous child,	Dido	3.2.18	Juno
As Prognes to th'adulterous Thracian King,	1Tamb	4.4.24	Zabina
ADVANC'D			
until the bloody flag/Be once advanc'd on my vermilion Tent,	1Tamb	4.2.117	Tamb
My royal chaire of state shall be advanc'd:	2Tamb	1.3.82	Tamb
Quirinus rites and Latian Jove advanc'd/On Alba hill o Vestall	Lucan, First Booke		200
ADVANCE (See also ADVAUNCE)			
From forth her ashes shall advance her head,	Dido	1.1.94	Jupitr
And now my Lords, advance your speares againe,	2Tamb	3.2.43	Tamb
But weele advance them traitors, now tis time/To be avengd on	Edw	3.1.224	Edward
And lives t'advance your standard good my lord.	Edw	4.2.42	Mortmr
Mine enemies will I plague, my friends advance,	Edw	5.4.67	Mortmr
O care-got triumph hetherwards advance.	Ovid's Elegies		2.12.16
ADVANCED			
That was advanced by my Hebes shame,	Dido	3.2.43	Juno
ADVANTAGE			
by expedition/Advantage takes of your unreadinesse.	1Tamb	4.1.39	Capol
Now then my Lord, advantage take hereof,	2Tamb	2.1.22	Fredrk
Taking advantage of your slender power,	2Tamb	2.2.26	1Msngr
And now by that advantage thinkes, belike,	Jew	1.1.184	Barab
And he from whom my most advantage comes,	Jew	5.2.113	Barab
To keepe me here will nought advantage you.	Jew	5.5.117	Calym
And there stay times advantage with your sonne?	Edw	4.2.18	SrJohn
ADVANTAGES			
Let him take all th'advantages he can,	1Tamb	4.1.40	Souldn
then that your Majesty/Take all advantages of time and power,	2Tamb	2.1.12	Fredrk
ADVAUNCE			
May with one word, advaunce us while we live:	Edw	2.1.9	Spencr
Will I advaunce upon this castell walles,	Edw	2.3.24	Mortmr
Advaunce your standard Edward in the field,	Edw	3.1.126	Spencr
And to the seat of Jove it selfe advaunce,	Hero and Leander		1.467
And wanting organs to advaunce a step,	Hero and Leander		2.57
ADVAUNST			
Then shall your meeds and vallours be advaunst/To roomes of	1Tamb	2.3.40	Cosroe
His cole-blacke collours every where advaunst,	1Tamb	5.1.9	Govnr
That must (advaunst in higher pompe than this)/Rifle the	2Tamb	4.3.58	Tamb
Triumphing in his fall whom you advaunst,	2Tamb	5.3.23	Techel
ADVENTURE			
What will we not adventure?	Jew	5.4.9	1Knght
Guise/Dares once adventure without the Kings consent,	P 37	1.37	Admral
Will be the first that shall adventure life.	Edw	2.3.4	Kent
ADVERSE			
Dismount the Cannon of the adverse part,	2Tamb	3.2.81	Tamb
That to the adverse poles of that straight line,	2Tamb	3.4.64	Therid
Nor yet the adverse reking southerne pole,	Lucan, First Booke		54
ADVERTISED			
My Lord, I am advertised from France,	P 900	18.1	Navrre
ADVICE (See also ADVISE)			
Therefore be gon in hast, and with advice,	Edw	3.1.264	Spencr
ADVISDE			
Your grace was ill advisde to take them then,	P 174	3.9	Admral
Anjoy hath well advisde/Your highnes to consider of the thing,	P 219	4.17	Guise
Tis well advisde Dumain, goe see it strait be done.	P 424	7.64	Guise
Be more advisde, walke as a puritane,	Ovid's Elegies		3.13.13
ADVISE			
Drawen with advise of our Ambassadors.	2Tamb	1.1.126	Orcan
Say they, and lovinglie advise your grace,	Edw	3.1.166	Herald
We in meane while madam, must take advise,	Edw	4.6.77	Mortmr
Well use that tricke no more, I would advise you.	F App	p.232 19	Faust
ADVIZE			
But if in so great feare I may advize thee,	Ovid's Elegies		2.13.27
ADVOCATE			
Be thou my advocate unto these peeres.	Edw	1.4.212	Queene

ADVOCATES			
And sue to me to be your Advocates.	1Tamb	3.3.175	Zenoc
AECUS (See EACUS)			
AEGEAN			
Betwixt the Aegean and the Ionian sea,	Lucan, First Booke		101
AEGEUS (See EGEUS)			
AEGIPTIAN			
Whose like Aegiptian Memphis never had/For skill in stars, and	Lucan, First Booke		639
AENEA			
Let it be term'd Aenea by your name.	Dido	5.1.20	Cloan
AENEAS (See also ENEAS)			
Whiles my Aeneas wanders on the Seas,	Dido	1.1.52	Venus
Then dye Aeneas in thine innocence,	Dido	1.1.80	Venus
Since thy Aeneas wandring fate is firme,	Dido	1.1.83	Jupitr
And court Aeneas with your calmie cheere,	Dido	1.1.123	Venus
Whiles my Aeneas spends himselfe in plaints,	Dido	1.1.140	Venus
How neere my sweet Aeneas art thou driven?	Dido	1.1.170	Venus
Of Troy am I, Aeneas is my name,	Dido	1.1.216	Aeneas
Might we but once more see Aeneas face,	Dido	1.2.45	Serg
Why stands my sweete Aeneas thus amazde?	Dido	2.1.2	Achat
O yet this stone doth make Aeneas weepe,	Dido	2.1.15	Aeneas
What meanes Aeneas?	Dido	2.1.23	Achat
Thy mind Aeneas that would have it so/Deludes thy eye sight,	Dido	2.1.31	Achat
Aeneas see, here come the Citizens,	Dido	2.1.37	Achat
I heare Aeneas voyce, but see him not,	Dido	2.1.45	Illion
Aeneas see, Sergestus or his ghost.	Dido	2.1.50	Achat
He [names] <meanes> Aeneas, let us kisse his feete.	Dido	2.1.51	Illion
Live long Aeneas and Ascanius.	Dido	2.1.53	Serg
Why turnes Aeneas from his trustie friends?	Dido	2.1.57	Cloan
Lovely Aeneas, these are Carthage walles,	Dido	2.1.62	Illion
Looke where she comes: Aeneas [view] <viewd> her well.	Dido	2.1.72	Illion
Warlike Aeneas.	Dido	2.1.78	Illion
Warlike Aeneas, and in these base robes?	Dido	2.1.79	Dido
Both happie that Aeneas is our guest:	Dido	2.1.82	Dido
Aeneas is Aeneas, were he clad/In weedes as bad as ever Irus	Dido	2.1.84	Dido
May it please your grace to let Aeneas waite:	Dido	2.1.87	Aeneas
Sit downe Aeneas, sit in Didos place,	Dido	2.1.91	Dido
Ile have it so, Aeneas be content.	Dido	2.1.95	Dido
And who so miserable as Aeneas is?	Dido	2.1.102	Aeneas
And makes Aeneas sinke at Didos feete.	Dido	2.1.117	Aeneas
What, faints Aeneas to remember Troy?	Dido	2.1.118	Dido
Then speake Aeneas with Achilles tongue,	Dido	2.1.121	Aeneas
Burst from the earth, crying, Aeneas flye,	Dido	2.1.207	Aeneas
Ah, how could poore Aeneas scape their hands?	Dido	2.1.220	Dido
O end Aeneas, I can heare no more.	Dido	2.1.243	Dido
Polixena cryed out, Aeneas stay,	Dido	2.1.281	Aeneas
I dye with melting ruth, Aeneas leave.	Dido	2.1.289	Dido
How got Aeneas to the fleete againe?	Dido	2.1.291	Iarbus
As for Aeneas he swomme quickly backe,	Dido	2.1.296	Achat
That she may dote upon Aeneas love:	Dido	2.1.327	Venus
Looke sister how Aeneas little sonne/Playes with your garments	Dido	3.1.20	Anna
Is not Aeneas faire and beautifull?	Dido	3.1.63	Dido
Is not Aeneas worthie Didos love?	Dido	3.1.68	Dido
Aeneas well deserves to be your love,	Dido	3.1.70	Anna
Runne for Aeneas, or Ile flye to him.	Dido	3.1.79	Dido
Dido, that till now/Didst never thinke Aeneas beautifull:	Dido	3.1.83	Dido
And thou Aeneas, Didos treasurie,	Dido	3.1.91	Dido
That will Aeneas shewe your majestie.	Dido	3.1.98	Achat
Aeneas, art thou there?	Dido	3.1.99	Dido
Aeneas, Ile repaire thy Troian ships,	Dido	3.1.113	Dido
Take what ye will, but leave Aeneas here.	Dido	3.1.127	Dido
So that Aeneas may but stay with me.	Dido	3.1.133	Dido
Wherefore would Dido have Aeneas stay?	Dido	3.1.134	Aeneas
Aeneas, thinke not Dido is in love:	Dido	3.1.136	Dido
I had been wedded ere Aeneas came:	Dido	3.1.138	Dido
But speake Aeneas, know you none of these?	Dido	3.1.148	Dido
Aeneas speake,/We two will goe a hunting in the woods,	Dido	3.1.173	Dido
Here lyes my hate, Aeneas cursed brat,	Dido	3.2.1	Juno
Love my Aeneas, and desire is thine,	Dido	3.2.60	Venus
Aeneas, thinke not but I honor thee,	Dido	3.3.1	Dido
Aeneas, be not movde at what he sayes,	Dido	3.3.23	Dido
Aeneas, leave these dumpes and lets away,	Dido	3.3.60	Dido
Revenge me on Aeneas, or on her:	Dido	3.3.70	Iarbus
Aeneas.	Dido	3.4.1	Dido
It is not ought Aeneas may atchieve?	Dido	3.4.11	Aeneas
Aeneas no, although his eyes doe pearce.	Dido	3.4.12	Dido
Aeneas, O Aeneas, quench these flames.	Dido	3.4.23	Dido
Aeneas, thou art he, what did I say?	Dido	3.4.29	Dido
Nay, nothing, but Aeneas loves me not.	Dido	3.4.32	Dido
Aeneas thoughts dare not ascend so high/As Didos heart, which	Dido	3.4.33	Aeneas
Sicheus, not Aeneas be thou calde:	Dido	3.4.59	Dido
Not with Aeneas in the ugly Cave.	Dido	4.1.32	Iarbus
I see Aeneas sticketh in your minde,	Dido	4.1.33	Dido
Graunt she or no, Aeneas must away,	Dido	4.3.7	Aeneas
Cloanthus, haste away, Aeneas calles.	Dido	4.3.14	Aeneas
And none but base Aeneas will abide:	Dido	4.3.20	Aeneas
So she may have Aeneas in her armes.	Dido	4.3.42	Illion
And teares of pearle, crye stay, Aeneas, stay:	Dido	4.3.52	Aeneas
To sea Aeneas, finde out Italy.	Dido	4.3.56	Aeneas
They say Aeneas men are going abourd,	Dido	4.4.2	Dido
Twas time to runne, Aeneas had been gone,	Dido	4.4.14	Anna
Then let Aeneas goe abourd with us.	Dido	4.4.23	Achat
Get you abourd, Aeneas meanes to stay.	Dido	4.4.24	Dido

AENEAS (cont.)			
O false Aeneas, now the sea is rough, ...	Dido	4.4.26	Dido
Aeneas pardon me, for I forgot/That yong Ascanius lay with me	Dido	4.4.31	Dido
And punish me Aeneas for this crime.	Dido	4.4.36	Dido
O how a Crowne becomes Aeneas head!	Dido	4.4.38	Dido
Stay here Aeneas, and commaund as King.	Dido	4.4.39	Dido
A Sword, and not a Scepter fits Aeneas.	Dido	4.4.43	Aeneas
Now lookes Aeneas like immortall Jove, ...	Dido	4.4.45	Dido
And fanne it in Aeneas lovely face, ...	Dido	4.4.49	Dido
This is the harbour that Aeneas seekes, ...	Dido	4.4.59	Aeneas
Aeneas may commaund as many Moores, ...	Dido	4.4.62	Dido
of all these, commaund/Aeneas ride as Carthaginian King. .	Dido	4.4.78	Dido
Aeneas for his parentage deserves/As large a kingdome as is	Dido	4.4.79	Achat
Speakes not Aeneas like a Conqueror?	Dido	4.4.93	Dido
Aeneas will not goe without his sonne:	Dido	4.4.107	Dido
onely Aeneas frowne/Is that which terrifies poore Didos heart:	Dido	4.4.115	Dido
It is Aeneas frowne that ends my daies:	Dido	4.4.120	Dido
And heres Aeneas tackling, oares and sailes.	Dido	4.4.125	Lord
Packt with the windes to beare Aeneas hence?	Dido	4.4.127	Dido
So I may have Aeneas in mine armes.	Dido	4.4.135	Dido
To measure how I prize Aeneas love, ...	Dido	4.4.140	Dido
And told me that Aeneas ment to goe:	Dido	4.4.142	Dido
Why should I blame Aeneas for his flight?	Dido	4.4.148	Dido
Here will Aeneas build a statelier Troy, ...	Dido	5.1.2	Aeneas
Aeneas stay, Joves Herald bids thee stay.	Dido	5.1.24	Hermes
How now Aeneas, sad, what meanes these dumpes? . . .	Dido	5.1.62	Iarbus
I feare I sawe Aeneas little sonne, ...	Dido	5.1.83	Dido
Aeneas, wherefore goe thy men abourd?	Dido	5.1.87	Dido
Aeneas will not faine with his deare love, ...	Dido	5.1.92	Aeneas
But yet Aeneas will not leave his love?	Dido	5.1.98	Dido
These words proceed not from Aeneas heart.	Dido	5.1.102	Dido
Fare well may Dido, so Aeneas stay, ...	Dido	5.1.107	Dido
I dye, if my Aeneas say farewell.	Dido	5.1.108	Dido
O speake like my Aeneas, like my love:	Dido	5.1.112	Dido
O then Aeneas, tis for griefe of thee:	Dido	5.1.116	Dido
Aeneas, say, how canst thou take thy leave?	Dido	5.1.119	Dido
Therefore unkind Aeneas, must thou say, ...	Dido	5.1.123	Dido
Aeneas could not choose but hold thee deare, ...	Dido	5.1.126	Aeneas
That he should take Aeneas from mine armes?	Dido	5.1.130	Dido
It is Aeneas calles Aeneas hence, ...	Dido	5.1.132	Dido
Desires Aeneas to remaine with her:	Dido	5.1.135	Dido
That I might see Aeneas in his face:	Dido	5.1.150	Dido
But wheres Aeneas? ah hees gone hees gone!	Dido	5.1.192	Dido
O Anna, my Aeneas is abourd, ...	Dido	5.1.194	Dido
Wicked Aeneas.	Dido	5.1.199	Anna
Before I came, Aeneas was abourd, ...	Dido	5.1.226	Anna
But I cride out, Aeneas, false Aeneas stay.	Dido	5.1.228	Anna
Which when I viewd, I cride, Aeneas stay, ...	Dido	5.1.232	Anna
Dido, faire Dido wils Aeneas stay:	Dido	5.1.233	Anna
Looke sister, looke lovely Aeneas ships, ...	Dido	5.1.251	Dido
Save, save Aeneas, Didos leefest love!	Dido	5.1.256	Dido
Iarbus, talke not of Aeneas, let him goe, ...	Dido	5.1.283	Dido
And make Aeneas famous through the world, ...	Dido	5.1.293	Dido
Live false Aeneas, truest Dido dyes, ...	Dido	5.1.312	Dido
Dido I come to thee, aye me Aeneas.	Dido	5.1.318	Iarbus
And Venus rules in her Aeneas Citty.	Ovid's Elegies		1.8.42
Aeneas warre, and Titerus shall be read, ...	Ovid's Elegies		1.15.25
So at Aeneas buriall men report, ...	Ovid's Elegies		3.8.13
AEOLIA			
And all Aeolia to be up in armes:	Dido	1.1.63	Venus
AEOLUS			
Where finding Aeolus intrencht with stormes, ...	Dido	1.1.58	Venus
And Aeolus like Agamemnon sounds/The surges, his fierce .	Dido	1.1.68	Venus
Since gloomie Aeolus doth cease to frowne.	Dido	4.1.27	Aeneas
AEQUE			
The motto: Aeque tandem.	Edw	2.2.20	Mortmr
And Aeque tandem shall that canker crie, ...	Edw	2.2.41	Edward
AERII			
Jehovae, Ignei, Aerii, [Aquatici] <Aquatani>, [Terreni], .	F 245	1.3.17	P Faust
AERY			
For earth and al this aery region/Cannot containe the state of	2Tamb	4.1.119	Tamb
AESOPE			
Lives like the Asse that Aesope speaketh of, ...	Jew	5.2.40	Barab
What should I name Aesope, that Thebe lov'd, ...	Ovid's Elegies		3.5.33
AESOPS			
Like Aesops cocke, this jewell he enjoyed, ...	Hero and Leander		2.51
AETNA			
were scortcht/And all the earth like Aetna breathing fire:	2Tamb	5.3.233	Tamb
And cruel field, nere burning Aetna fought:	Lucan, First Booke		43
AETNA'S			
Fierce Mulciber unbarred Aetna's gate, ...	Lucan, First Booke		543
AETNAS			
Epeus horse, to Aetnas hill transformd, ...	Dido	1.1.66	Venus
AETOLIA			
I traveld with him to Aetolia.	Dido	3.1.145	Serg
Not Calydon, nor Aetolia did please:	Ovid's Elegies		3.5.37
A FARRE			
Come backe, come backe, I heare her crye a farre, . . .	Dido	4.3.27	Aeneas
AFFAIRES			
And give you equall place in our affaires.	1Tamb	2.5.14	Cosroe
For he can counsell best in these affaires;	Jew	1.1.142	2Jew
AFFARES			
My wench her dore shut, Joves affares I left, ...	Ovid's Elegies		2.1.17

AFFAYRES			
To too forgetfull of thine owne affayres, ...	Dido	5.1.30	Hermes
AFFECT (See also EFFECT)			
Such honour, stranger, doe I not affect:	Dido	1.1.203	Venus
and Phoebe's waine/Chace Phoebus and inrag'd affect his place,	Lucan, First Booke		78
Wee skorne things lawfull, stolne sweetes we affect, .	Ovid's Elegies		2.19.3
That can effect <affect> a foolish wittalls wife. . .	Ovid's Elegies		2.19.46
And one especiallie doe we affect, ...	Hero and Leander		1.171
AFFECTED			
Hadst thou affected sweet divinitie, ...	F1901	5.2.105	GdAngl
And I beleeve some wench thou hast affected: . . .	Ovid's Elegies		3.5.83
AFFECTER			
The first affecter of your excellence, ...	1Tamb	5.1.379	Philem
AFFECTES			
What so thy minde affectes or fancie likes. . . .	Edw	1.1.170	Edward
AFFECTEST			
I see whom thou affectest:	Ovid's Elegies		3.2.67
AFFECTING			
Affecting thoughts coequall with the cloudes, . . .	1Tamb	1.2.65	Tamb
AFFECTION			
In all affection at thy kingly feet.	2Tamb	1.3.116	Therid
Nor I the affection that I beare to you.	Jew	2.3.291	Barab
Shall slacke my loves affection from his bent. . . .	P 607	12.20	King
Not to be tied to their affection, ...	Edw	3.1.29	Baldck
Affection by the count'nance is descride.	Hero and Leander		2.132
AFFECTIONS			
His deep affections make him passionate.	1Tamb	1.2.164	Techel
and of fire/Doth send such sterne affections to his heart.	2Tamb	4.1.176	Trebiz
With whom I buried al affections, ...	2Tamb	4.2.23	Olymp
First be thou voyd of these affections, ...	Jew	2.3.169	Barab
With all the honors and affections, ...	P1145	22.7	King
And art a bawd to his affections, ...	Edw	1.4.151	Queene
When like desires and affections meet, ...	Hero and Leander		2.30
AFFECTS			
Heaven thou affects, with Romulus, temples brave/Bacchus,	Ovid's Elegies		3.7.51
AFFIDE			
And Crusa unto Zanthus first affide, ...	Ovid's Elegies		3.5.31
AFFIED			
Both to each other quickly were affied.	Hero and Leander		2.26
AFFIRME			
Dares but affirme, that Edwards not true king, . . .	Edw	5.4.76	Champn
AFFLICT			
How can it but afflict my verie soule?	1Tamb	4.4.67	Zenoc
I feare their comming will afflict us all.	Jew	1.1.156	2Jew
worth>/<Made Greece with ten yeares warres afflict poore Troy>?	F1696	(HC269)B	2Schol
But what I may afflict his body with, ...	F1757	5.1.84	Mephst
nor Hanniball/Art cause, no forraine foe could so afflict us,	Lucan, First Booke		31
Parthians y'afflict us more then ye suppose, ...	Lucan, First Booke		107
AFFLICTED			
Nor never with nights sharpe revenge afflicted? . .	Ovid's Elegies		2.19.54
AFFLICTING			
Till surfeiting with our afflicting armes, , ...	P1153	22.15	King
AFFLICTION			
but trust me 'tis a misery/To see a man in such affliction:	Jew	1.2.212	2Jew
AFFLICTIONS			
These taxes and afflictions are befal'ne, ...	Jew	1.2.65	Govnr
And urg'd thereto with my afflictions, ...	Jew	1.2.231	Abigal
Fearing the afflictions which my father feeles, . . .	Jew	1.2.322	Abigal
And wilt not see thine owne afflictions, ...	Jew	1.2.353	1Fryar
(that did remaine/To their afflictions) were t'abandon Roome.	Lucan, First Booke		495
AFFLICTS			
him to his ships/That now afflicts me with his flattering eyes.	Dido	4.2.22	Iarbus
And threaten him whose hand afflicts my soul, ...	2Tamb	5.3.47	Tamb
He, he afflicts Roome that made me Roomes foe. . . .	Lucan, First Booke		205
were we bestead/When comming conqueror, Roome afflicts me thus?	Lucan, First Booke		310
AFFOORD			
Then twentie thousand Indiaes can affoord:	Dido	3.1.93	Dido
issue, at whose byrth/Heaven did affoord a gratious aspect,	2Tamb	3.5.80	Tamb
As all the world cannot affoord the like.	2Tamb	4.2.57	Olymp
with all the pompe/The treasure of my kingdome may affoord.	2Tamb	4.2.98	Therid
the Governors sonne/With all the curtesie you can affoord;	Jew	2.3.226	Barab
AFFOORDED			
thee greater curtesie/Then Barabas would have affoorded thee.	Jew	5.5.62	Govnr
AFFOORDS			
we wish for ought/The world affoords in greatest noveltie,	1Tamb	2.5.73	Tamb
they come to proove/The wounding troubles angry war affoords.	2Tamb	1.3.87	Zenoc
Affoords no hearbs, whose taste may poison thee, . .	2Tamb	4.2.9	Olymp
Affoords this Art no greater miracle?	F 37	1.1.9	Faust
With greatest [torments] <torment> that our hell affoords.	F1755	5.1.82	Faust
AFFORD			
Let us afford him now the bearing hence.	1Tamb	3.2.111	Usumc
I could afford to whip my selfe to death.	Jew	4.1.59	Barab
AFFORDING			
Affording it no shoare, and Phoebe's waine/Chace Phoebus and	Lucan, First Booke		77
AFFRAID			
and for feare I should be affraid, would put it off and come to	2Tamb	4.1.69	P Calyph
AFFRAIDE			
With all his viceroies shall be so affraide, ...	2Tamb	1.3.162	Tamb
AFFRICA			
Create him Prorex of [Assiria] <Affrica>, ...	1Tamb	1.1.89	Cosroe
Duke of [Assiria] <Affrica> and Albania, ...	1Tamb	1.1.164	Ortyg
To safe conduct us thorow Affrica.	1Tamb	1.2.16	Zenoc
(for say not I intreat)/Not once to set his foot in Affrica,	1Tamb	3.1.28	Bajzth

AFFRICA (cont.)			
and my souldiers looke/As if they meant to conquer Affrica.	1Tamb	3.3.10	Tamb
Unpeopling Westerne Affrica and Greece:	1Tamb	3.3.34	Usumc
That damned traine, the scum of Affrica,	1Tamb	3.3.56	Tamb
shall curse the time/That Tamburlaine set foot in Affrica.	1Tamb	3.3.60	Tamb
The greatest Potentate of Affrica.	1Tamb	3.3.63	Bajzth
Shall lead thee Captive thorow Affrica.	1Tamb	3.3.73	Tamb
That we may raigne as kings of Affrica.	1Tamb	3.3.99	Therid
lie weltring in their blood/And Tamburlaine is Lord of Affrica.	1Tamb	3.3.202	Zenoc
And led them Captive into Affrica.	1Tamb	3.3.205	Zabina
And crowne me Emperour of Affrica.	1Tamb	3.3.221	Tamb
Thou shalt not yet be Lord of Affrica.	1Tamb	3.3.223	Zabina
And write my selfe great Lord of Affrica:	1Tamb	3.3.245	Tamb
Whose feet the kings of Affrica have kist.	1Tamb	4.2.65	Zabina
Affrica, and Greece/Follow my Standard and my thundring Drums:	2Tamb	1.1.158	Orcan
These Pioners of Argier in Affrica,	2Tamb	3.3.20	Therid
that all [Assiria] <Affrica>/Which hath bene subject to the	2Tamb	5.1.165	Tamb
Then by the Northerne part of Affrica,	2Tamb	5.3.140	Tamb
That <which> Julius caesar brought from Affrica.	F 824	3.1.46	Mephst
AFFRICK			
And here in Affrick where it seldom raines,	1Tamb	5.1.457	Tamb
And from the boundes of Affrick to the banks/Of Ganges, shall	1Tamb	5.1.520	Tamb
I'le joyne the Hils that bind the Affrick shore,	F 335	1.3.107	Faust
AFFRICKE			
Yet Queene of Affricke, are my ships unrigd,	Dido	3.1.105	Aeneas
Like to a Lyon of scortcht desart Affricke,	Lucan, First Booke		208
To doubtfull Sirtes and drie Affricke, where/A fury leades the	Lucan, First Booke		686
AFFRIGHT			
Affright me not, onely Aeneas frowne/Is that which terrifies	Dido	4.4.115	Dido
traines should reach down to the earth/Could not affright you,	2Tamb	5.1.91	Tamb
Yet, shall the crowing of these cockerels,/Affright a Lion?	Edw	2.2.204	Edward
men/Whom death the greatest of all feares affright not,	Lucan, First Booke		455
Tav'ron peering/(His grave broke open) did affright the Boores.	Lucan, First Booke		582
to scarre/The quivering Romans, but worse things affright them.	Lucan, First Booke		673
spright/Nor hands prepar'd to slaughter, me affright.	Ovid's Elegies		1.6.14
Nor violent South-windes did thee ought affright.	Ovid's Elegies		2.11.52
AFFRIGHTED			
Th'affrighted worlds force bent on publique spoile,	Lucan, First Booke		5
AFFRIGHTS			
Affrights poore fearefull men, and blasts their eyes/With	Lucan, First Booke		155
AFFRIK			
Affrik and Greece have garrisons enough/To make me Soveraigne	1Tamb	3.3.242	Bajzth
AFFRIKE			
Have triumpht over Affrike, and the bounds/Of Europe wher the	1Tamb	1.1.9	Cosroe
Affrike and Europe bordering on your land,	1Tamb	1.1.127	Menaph
That heretofore have fild Persepolis/With Affrike Captaines,	1Tamb	1.1.142	Ceneus
As if the Turke, the Pope, Affrike and Greece,	1Tamb	2.5.85	Tamb
Dread Lord of Affrike, Europe and Asia,	1Tamb	3.1.23	Bajzth
All Affrike is in Armes with Tamburlaine.	2Tamb	1.1.76	Orcan
Not for all Affrike, therefore moove me not.	2Tamb	1.2.12	Almeda
The Westerne part of Affrike, where I view'd/The Ethiopian sea,	2Tamb	1.3.195	Techel
I left the confines and the bounds of Affrike/And made a voyage	2Tamb	1.3.207	Therid
That late adorn'd the Affrike Potentate,	2Tamb	3.2.124	Tamb
AFFRIKS			
And of Argier and Affriks frontier townes/Twise twenty thousand	2Tamb	1.3.119	Therid
A FIRE			
Hoping ere long to set the house a fire;	Jew	2.3.88	Barab
Feare not, I'le so set his heart a fire,	Jew	2.3.375	Ithimr
A FOOTE			
Might I but see that pretie sport a foote,	Dido	1.1.16	Ganimd
AFORE			
That wee might sleepe seven yeeres together afore we wake.	Jew	4.2.131	Ithimr
You lie Drawer, tis afore me:	F App	p.235 17	P Robin
AFRAID (See also AFFRAID, FRAYDE)			
I was afraid the poyson had not wrought;	Jew	4.1.4	Barab
I am not afraid of a devill.	F 375	1.4.33	P Robin
AFRAIDE			
In midst of peace why art of armes afraide?	Ovid's Elegies		1.6.30
AFRAYD			
And would have turn'd againe, but was afrayd,	Hero and Leander		2.8
A FRESH			
Makes walles a fresh with every thing that falles/Into the	2Tamb	5.1.18	Govnr
Why streames it not, that I may write a fresh?	F 455	2.1.67	Faust
AFRICA (See AFFRICA, AFRICK)			
AFRICK			
Our fraught is Grecians, Turks, and Africk Moores.	Jew	2.2.9	Bosco
AFRIGHT (See AFFRIGHT)			
AFRIGHTED			
Herewith afrighted Hero shrunke away,	Hero and Leander		2.253
AFTER			
And after him a thousand Grecians more,	Dido	2.1.185	Aeneas
That after burnt the pride of Asia.	Dido	2.1.187	Aeneas
And after him his band of Mirmidons,	Dido	2.1.216	Aeneas
And after by that Pirrhus sacrifizde.	Dido	2.1.288	Aeneas
Her Lover after Alexander dyed,	Dido	2.1.298	Achat
I, I, Iarbus, after this is done,	Dido	5.1.289	Dido
All running headlong after greedy spoiles:	1Tamb	2.2.45	Meandr
That fiery thirster after Soveraigntie:	1Tamb	2.6.31	Cosroe
Still climing after knowledge infinite,	1Tamb	2.7.24	Tamb
After your rescue to enjoy his choise.	1Tamb	3.2.58	Agidas
Citties and townes/After my name and thine Zenocrate:	1Tamb	4.4.80	Tamb
Then after all these solemne Exequies,	1Tamb	5.1.533	Tamb
And after martch to Turky with our Campe,	2Tamb	1.3.158	Tamb

AFTER (cont.)			
And after this, to scale a castle wal,	2Tamb	3.2.59	Tamb
To triumph after all our victories.	2Tamb	5.1.213	Tamb
And make him after all these overthrowes,	2Tamb	5.2.29	Callap
night; or let the day/Turne to eternall darkenesse after this:	Jew	2.1.16	Barab
And after that I was an Engineere,	Jew	2.3.186	Barab
Then after that was I an Usurer,	Jew	2.3.190	Barab
Hee's with your mother, therefore after him.	Jew	2.3.350	Barab
Thus every villaine ambles after wealth/Although he ne're be	Jew	3.4.52	Barab
yet not appeare/In forty houres after it is tane.	Jew	3.4.72	Barab
And after that, I and my trusty Turke--	Jew	4.1.127	Barab
And now my Lords after these funerals be done,	P 561	11.26	QnMoth
Thus after many threats of wrathfull warre,	Edw	4.3.1	Edward
A gave a long looke after us my lord,	Edw	4.7.30	Spencr
with me, and after meate/We'le canvase every quidditie thereof:	F 190	1.1.162	Faust
That after this life there is any paine?	F 523	2.1.135	Faust
thought you did not sneake up and downe after her for nothing.	F 743	2.3.22	P Dick
To rest his bones after his weary toyle,	F 769	2.3.48	2Chor
to stand gaping after the divels Governor, and can see nothing.	F1244	4.1.90	P Benvol
And hell shall after plague their treacherie.	F1407	4.2.83	Faust
troupe, in tuckt up vestures,/After the Gabine manner:	Lucan, First Booke		596
Watching till after mid-night did not tire thee.	Ovid's Elegies		1.6.44
For after death all men receive their right:	Ovid's Elegies		1.15.40
I loathe, yet after that I loathe, I runne:	Ovid's Elegies		2.4.5
An Altar made after the ancient fashion.	Ovid's Elegies		3.12.10
A worke, that after my death, heere shall dwell	Ovid's Elegies		3.14.20
As after chaunc'd, they did each other spye.	Hero and Leander		1.134
Which after his disceasse, some other gains.	Hero and Leander		1.246
After went Mercurie, who us'd such cunning,	Hero and Leander		1.417
Or thirsting after immortalitie,	Hero and Leander		1.427
But stayd, and after her a letter sent.	Hero and Leander		2.14
AFTERNOONES			
Jove send me more such afternoones as this.	Ovid's Elegies		1.5.26
AFTERWARDS			
But afterwards will Dido graunt me love?	Dido	5.1.288	Iarbus
AGAIN (See also AGAYNE, AGEN)			
And die before I brought you backe again.	2Tamb	1.2.73	Almeda
Thanks king of Morocus, take your crown again.	2Tamb	1.3.137	Tamb
Thanks king of Fesse, take here thy crowne again.	2Tamb	1.3.150	Tamb
Come back again (sweet death) and strike us both:	2Tamb	3.4.12	Olymp
Shal we let goe these kings again my Lord/To gather greater	2Tamb	4.1.82	Amyras
Or that it be rejoin'd again at full,	2Tamb	5.2.58	Callap
Away and bring us word <again> with speed.	F 888	3.1.110	Pope
to lay the fury of this ghost, once again my Lord fall too.	F App	p.232 17	P Pope
AGAINE			
And flourish once againe that erst was dead:	Dido	1.1.95	Jupitr
How got Aeneas to the fleete againe?	Dido	2.1.291	Iarbus
Till I returne and take thee hence againe.	Dido	2.1.339	Venus
Yet must I heare that lothsome name againe?	Dido	3.1.78	Dido
And build the towne againe the Greekes did burne?	Dido	4.3.40	Illion
To rid thee of that doubt, abourd againe,	Dido	4.4.21	Dido
and once againe conspire/Against the life of me poore Carthage	Dido	4.4.131	Dido
And Didos beautie will returne againe:	Dido	5.1.118	Dido
I but heele come againe, he cannot goe,	Dido	5.1.184	Dido
Once didst thou goe, and he came backe againe,	Dido	5.1.196	Dido
But he remembring me shrinkes backe againe:	Dido	5.1.260	Dido
Now must your jewels be restor'd againe:	1Tamb	1.2.114	Tamb
Wel, I meane you shall have it againe.	1Tamb	2.4.36	Tamb
His royall Crowne againe, so highly won.	1Tamb	3.3.219	Zenoc
garrisons enough/To make me Soveraigne of the earth againe.	1Tamb	3.3.243	Bajzth
Put him in againe.	1Tamb	4.2.82	Tamb
Take them away againe and make us slaves.	1Tamb	4.4.133	Therid
and fire, and my blood I bring him againe, teare me in peeces,	1Tamb	5.1.311	P Zabina
If peace, restore it to my hands againe:	2Tamb	1.1.84	Sgsmnd
Wel said Argier, receive thy crowne againe.	2Tamb	1.3.127	Tamb
Come downe from heaven and live with me againe.	2Tamb	2.4.118	Tamb
Forbids the world to build it up againe.	2Tamb	3.2.18	Calyph
And now my Lords, advance your speares againe,	2Tamb	3.2.43	Tamb
This Lady shall have twice so much againe,	2Tamb	3.4.90	Therid
And turne him to his ancient trade againe.	2Tamb	3.5.95	Jrslem
Ile hang a clogge about your necke for running away againe, you	2Tamb	3.5.101	P Tamb
Here Jove, receive his fainting soule againe,	2Tamb	4.1.111	Tamb
And eb againe, as thou departst from me.	2Tamb	4.2.32	Therid
And every line begins with death againe:	2Tamb	4.2.48	Olymp
Come to the tent againe.	2Tamb	4.2.54	Therid
She waines againe, and so shall his I hope,	2Tamb	5.2.47	Callap
Looke where he goes, but see, he comes againe/Because I stay:	2Tamb	5.3.75	Tamb
That Callapine should be my slave againe.	2Tamb	5.3.118	Tamb
Now lanch our Gallies backe againe to Sea,	Jew	1.2.29	Calym
I'le make 'em friends againe.	Jew	2.3.357	Abigal
What, Abigall become a Nunne againe?	Jew	3.4.1	Barab
Art thou againe got to the Nunnery?	Jew	3.4.4	Barab
go set it downe/And come againe so soone as thou hast done,	Jew	3.4.109	Barab
That kisse againe; she runs division of my lips.	Jew	4.2.127	P Ithimr
That I with her may dye and live againe.	P 190	3.25	Navrre
Now Guise shall catholiques flourish once againe,	P 295	5.22	Anjoy
For if these straglers gather head againe,	P 506	9.25	QnMoth
despatch Embassadours/To Poland, to call Henry back againe,	P 556	11.21	QnMoth
O that that damned villaine were alive againe,	P1216	22.78	Eprnon
yett comminge upon you once unawares he frayde you out againe.	Paris	ms13,p390	P Souldr
To see it done, and bring thee safe againe.	Edw	1.1.205	Edward
Madam, returne unto the court againe:	Edw	1.2.56	Mortmr
And is this true to call him home againe?	Edw	1.4.246	Lncstr

AGAINE (cont.)

That hees repeald, and sent for back againe,	Edw	2.1.18		Spencr
I knew the King would have him home againe.	Edw	2.1.78		Spencr
Libels are cast againe thee in the streete,	Edw	2.2.177		Mortmr
Farewell sweete unckle till we meete againe.	Edw	2.4.11		Neece
against your king)/To see his royall soveraigne once againe.	Edw	2.5.7		Gavstn
mine honor undertake/To carrie him, and bring him back againe,	Edw	2.5.80		Penbrk
and I shall never see/My lovely Pierce, my Gaveston againe,	Edw	3.1.8		Edward
Welcome ten thousand times, old man againe.	Edw	3.1.46		Edward
Sib, if this be all/Valoys and I will soone be friends againe.	Edw	3.1.67		Edward
O might I never open these eyes againe,	Edw	4.7.41		Edward
Never againe lift up this drooping head,	Edw	4.7.42		Edward
See monsters see, ile weare my crowne againe,	Edw	5.1.74		Edward
Call them againe my lorde, and speake them faire,	Edw	5.1.91		Leistr
Wet with my teares, and dried againe with sighes,	Edw	5.1.118		Edward
And then from thence to Bartley back againe:	Edw	5.2.61		Mortmr
Now as I speake they fall, and yet with feare/Open againe.	Edw	5.5.96		Edward
Thou wilt returne againe, and therefore stay.	Edw	5.5.99		Edward
And I shall pitie her if she speake againe.	Edw	5.6.86		King
Or being dead, raise them to life againe,	F 53	1.1.25		Faust
in speculation of this Art/Till Mephostophilis returne againe.	F 342	1.3.114		Faust
Here, take your Guilders [againe], I'le none of 'em.	F 371	1.4.29	P	Robin
Abjure this Magicke, turne to God againe.	F 396	2.1.8		Faust
[I and Faustus will turne to God againe].	F 397	2.1.9A		Faust
Then write againe: Faustus gives to thee his soule.	F 458	2.1.70		Faust
So, now the bloud begins to cleere againe:	F 460	2.1.72		Faust
Come Mephostophilis let us dispute againe,	F 584	2.2.33		Faust
be carried thither againe by Gluttony and Letchery <Leachery>],	F 705.2	2.2.156A	P	Sloth
I see hell, and returne againe safe, how happy were I then.	F 714	2.2.166	P	Faust
What Dick, looke to the horses there till I come againe.	F 722	2.3.1	P	Robin
And in eight daies did bring him home againe.	F 767	2.3.46		2Chor
Make haste againe, my good Lord Cardinalls,	F 972	3.1.194		Pope
Come, give it me againe.	F1111	3.3.24	P	Vintnr
to supper, and a Tester in your purse, and go backe againe.	F1122	3.3.35	P	Robin
love with him, I would he would post with him to Rome againe.	F1192	4.1.38	P	Benvol
O may these eye-lids never close againe,	F1332	4.2.8		Benvol
Martino see,/Benvolio's hornes againe.	F1437	4.3.7		Fredrk
'Zons, hornes againe.	F1444	4.3.14		Benvol
late by horse flesh, and this bargaine will set me up againe.	F1465	4.4.9	P	HrsCsr
go rouse him, and make him give me my forty Dollors againe.	F1488	4.4.32	P	HrsCsr
and give me my mony againe, for your horse is turned to a	F1490	4.4.34	P	HrsCsr
Faustus hath his leg againe, and the Horse-courser a bundle of	F1497	4.4.41	P	Faust
But I have it againe now I am awake:	F1657	4.6.100	P	Faust
And with my bloud againe I will confirme/The <My> former vow I	F1749	5.1.76		Faust
Come Hellen, come, give me my soule againe,	F1772	5.1.99		Faust
Faire natures eye, rise, rise againe and make/Perpetuall day:	F1931	5.2.135		Faust
No, no, here take your gridirons againe.	F App	p.230 38	P	Clown
Beare witnesse I give them you againe.	F App	p.230 42	P	Clown
What againe?	F App	p.231 12	P	Pope
and have my fortie dollers againe, or Ile make it the dearest	F App	p.240 136	P	HrsCsr
Faustus has his legge againe, and the Horsecourser I take it,	F App	p.241 164	P	Faust
Againe, this people could not brooke calme peace,	Lucan, First Booke	172		
hils, hence to the mounts/Pirene, and so backe to Rome againe.	Lucan, First Booke	689		
New factions rise; now through the world againe/I goe; o Phoebus	Lucan, First Booke	691		
Strike, so againe hard chaines shall binde thee never,	Ovid's Elegies	1.6.25		
Put in their place thy keembed haires againe.	Ovid's Elegies	1.7.68		
Going out againe passe forth the dore more wisely/And som-what	Ovid's Elegies	1.12.5		
downe againe,/And birds for <from> Memnon yearly shall be	Ovid's Elegies	1.13.3		
Which giving her, she may give thee againe.	Ovid's Elegies	2.2.16		
And purple Love resumes his dartes againe.	Ovid's Elegies	2.9.34		
Thou givest my mistris life, she mine againe.	Ovid's Elegies	2.13.16		
Againe by some in this unpeopled world.	Ovid's Elegies	2.14.12		
By cloyed Charibdis, and againe devoured.	Ovid's Elegies	2.16.26		
And was againe most apt to my desire.	Ovid's Elegies	2.19.16		
But now againe the barriers open lye;	Ovid's Elegies	3.2.77		
What might I crave more if I aske againe?	Ovid's Elegies	3.6.44		
And what I have borne, shame to beare againe.	Ovid's Elegies	3.10.4		
And beat from thence, have lighted there againe.	Hero and Leander	1.24		
Did she uphold to Venus, and againe,	Hero and Leander	1.367		
They granted what he crav'd, and once againe,	Hero and Leander	1.455		
And would have turn'd againe, but was afrayd,	Hero and Leander	2.8		
Jewels being lost are found againe, this never,	Hero and Leander	2.85		
And kist againe, as lovers use to do.	Hero and Leander	2.94		
And up againe, and close beside him swim,	Hero and Leander	2.190		
Againe she knew not how to frame her looke,	Hero and Leander	2.307		

AGAINST (See also GAINST)

To warre against my bordering enemies:	Dido	3.1.135		Dido
Anna, against this Troian doe I pray,	Dido	4.2.30		Iarbus
Were to transgresse against all lawes of love:	Dido	4.3.48		Aeneas
Will leade an hoste against the hatefull Greekes,	Dido	4.4.91		Aeneas
againe conspire/Against the life of me poore Carthage Queene:	Dido	4.4.132		Dido
And openly exclaime against the King.	1Tamb	1.1.149		Ceneus
will flie (my Lords)/To rest secure against my brothers force.	1Tamb	1.1.178		Cosroe
An ods too great, for us to stand against:	1Tamb	1.2.122		Tamb
To cast up hils against the face of heaven:	1Tamb	2.6.3		Cosroe
Be arm'd against the hate of such a foe,	1Tamb	2.6.22		Ortyg
That thus opposeth him against the Gods,	1Tamb	2.6.39		Cosroe
Moov'd me to manage armes against thy state.	1Tamb	2.7.16		Tamb
To lift our swords against the Persean King.	1Tamb	2.7.35		Techel
Against the terrour of the winds and waves.	1Tamb	3.2.84		Agidas
Now strengthen him against the Turkish Bajazeth,	1Tamb	3.3.191		Zenoc
When first he war'd against the Christians.	1Tamb	3.3.200		Zabina
That will maintaine it against a world of Kings.	1Tamb	4.2.81		Tamb

AGAINST (cont.)

Against the Woolfe that angrie Themis sent,	1Tamb	4.3.5	Souldn
And shivered against a craggie rocke.	1Tamb	4.3.34	Souldn
That never nourisht thought against thy rule,	1Tamb	5.1.98	1Virgn
ruthlesly pursewde/Be equally against his life incenst,	1Tamb	5.1.367	Zenoc
Must fight against my life and present love:	1Tamb	5.1.389	Zenoc
And have a greater foe to fight against,	2Tamb	1.1.15	Gazell
Beating in heaps against their Argoses,	2Tamb	1.1.41	Orcan
it out, or manage armes/Against thy selfe or thy confederates:	2Tamb	1.1.129	Sgsmnd
For we will martch against them presently.	2Tamb	1.3.105	Tamb
Larissa plaines/With hostes apeece against this Turkish crue,	2Tamb	1.3.108	Tamb
pitcht against our power/Betwixt Cutheia and Orminius mount:	2Tamb	2.1.17	Fredrk
Against the grace of our profession.	2Tamb	2.1.32	Sgsmnd
All which will joine against this Tamburlain,	2Tamb	3.1.61	Soria
see if coward Calapine/Dare levie armes against our puissance,	2Tamb	3.2.156	Tamb
Ready to levie power against thy throne,	2Tamb	4.1.117	Tamb
And with the flames that beat against the clowdes/Incense the	2Tamb	4.1.194	Tamb
Which beates against this prison to get out,	2Tamb	4.2.35	Olymp
When we are thus defenc'd against our Foe,	2Tamb	5.1.22	Govnr
bank, right opposite/Against the Westerne gate of Babylon.	2Tamb	5.1.122	Govnr
That shakes his sword against thy majesty,	2Tamb	5.1.196	Tamb
To joine with you against this Tamburlaine.	2Tamb	5.2.35	Amasia
Which makes them manage armes against thy state,	2Tamb	5.3.36	Usumc
Come let us march against the powers of heaven,	2Tamb	5.3.48	Tamb
Come carie me to war against the Gods,	2Tamb	5.3.52	Tamb
In vaine I strive and raile against those powers,	2Tamb	5.3.120	Tamb
Graecia, and from thence/To Asia, where I stay against my will,	2Tamb	5.3.142	Tamb
unrelenting eares/Of death and hell be shut against my praiers,	2Tamb	5.3.192	Amyras
Against the inward powers of my heart,	2Tamb	5.3.196	Amyras
Against the wrath and tyranny of death,	2Tamb	5.3.221	Techel
Though some speake openly against my bookes,	Jew	Prol.10	Machvl
And what's our aid against so great a Prince?	Jew	1.2.51	Barab
Perswade our Governor against the Turke;	Jew	2.2.25	1Knght
will follow thee/Against these barbarous mis-beleeving Turkes.	Jew	2.2.46	Govnr
Against my will, and whether I would or no,	Jew	2.3.75	Barab
He has my heart, I smile against my will.	Jew	2.3.287	Abigal
But now against my will I must be chast.	Jew	3.1.4	Curtzn
then goe with me/And helpe me to exclaime against the Jew.	Jew	3.6.46	2Fryar
Feare not, my Lord, for here, against the [sluice] <Truce>,/The	Jew	5.1.86	Barab
they may become/As men that stand and gase against the Sunne.	P 163	2.106	Guise
Excepting against Doctors [axioms],	P 393	7.33	Guise
I meane our warres against the Muscovites:	P 461	8.11	Anjoy
And on the other side against the Turke,	P 462	8.12	Anjoy
these our warres/Against the proud disturbers of the faith,	P 700	14.3	Navrre
To march against the rebellious King Navarre:	P 745	15.3	King
That lift themselves against the perfect truth,	P 799	16.13	Navrre
That the Guise durst stand in armes against the King,	P 877	17.72	Eprnon
That the Guise hath taken armes against the King,	P 901	18.2	Navrre
Offering him aide against his enemies,	P 905	18.6	Bartus
Against the Guisians and their complices.	P 910	18.11	Navrre
For we must aide the King against the Guise.	P 918	18.19	Navrre
How they beare armes against their soveraigne.	P1187	22.49	King
A souldier, that hath serv'd against the Scot.	Edw	1.1.34	3PrMan
What danger tis to stand against your king.	Edw	1.1.97	Edward
My lord, will you take armes against the king?	Edw	1.2.39	Lncstr
But yet lift not your swords against the king.	Edw	1.2.61	ArchBp
Forbeare to levie armes against the king.	Edw	1.2.82	Queene
For tis against my will he should returne.	Edw	1.4.217	Queene
Not I against my nephew.	Edw	1.4.232	MortSr
Tis treason to be up against the king.	Edw	1.4.281	Mortmr
Against our friend the earle of Cornewall comes,	Edw	1.4.375	Edward
Leave now to oppose thy selfe against the king,	Edw	1.4.387	MortSr
Against the stately triumph we decreed?	Edw	2.2.12	Edward
Against the Earle of Cornewall and my brother?	Edw	2.2.35	Edward
That muster rebels thus against your king)/To see his royall	Edw	2.5.6	Gavstn
A bloudie part, flatly against law of armes.	Edw	3.1.121	Spencr
And levie armes against your lawfull king?	Edw	3.1.208	SpncrP
Poore Pierce, and headed him against lawe of armes?	Edw	3.1.238	Edward
Borne armes against thy brother and thy king?	Edw	4.6.6	Kent
Rebell is he that fights against his prince,	Edw	4.6.71	SpncrP
To plaine me to the gods against them both:	Edw	5.1.22	Edward
Conclude against his father what thou wilt,	Edw	5.2.19	Queene
The Wrenne may strive against the Lions strength,	Edw	5.3.34	Edward
Conspir'd against our God with Lucifer,	F 299	1.3.71	Mephst
By desperate thoughts against Joves Deity:	F 317	1.3.89	Faust
I, that is not against our Kingdome:	F 623	2.2.72	P Mephst
In quittance of their late conspiracie/Against our State, and	F 950	3.1.172	Pope
us sway thy thoughts/From this attempt against the Conjurer.	F1326	4.2.2	Mrtino
conquer all the earth, then turne thy force/Against thy selfe:	Lucan, First Booke	23	
While Titan strives against the worlds swift course;	Lucan, First Booke	90	
T'was peace against their wils; betwixt them both/Stept Crassus	Lucan, First Booke	99	
draw the Commons minds/To favour thee, against the Senats will,	Lucan, First Booke	276	
Woods turn'd to ships; both land and sea against us:	Lucan, First Booke	307	
As when against pine bearing Ossa's rocks,	Lucan, First Booke	390	
Against her kind (the barren Mules loth'd issue)/To be cut	Lucan, First Booke	589	
Constrain'd against thy will give it the pezant,	Ovid's Elegies	1.4.65	
For rage against my wench mov'd my rash arme,	Ovid's Elegies	1.7.3	
Against the destinies durst sharpe darts require.	Ovid's Elegies	1.7.10	
A woman against late-built Rome did send/The Sabine Fathers,	Ovid's Elegies	2.12.23	
Thou fightst against me using mine owne verse.	Ovid's Elegies	3.1.38	
I saw a horse against the bitte stiffe-neckt,	Ovid's Elegies	3.4.13	
Who bad thee lie downe here against thy will?	Ovid's Elegies	3.6.78	
Against thy selfe, mans nature, thou wert cunning,	Ovid's Elegies	3.7.45	

AGAINST (cont.)			
That I may love yet, though against my minde.	Ovid's Elegies	3.10.52	
Or is I thinke my wish against the [starres] <starre>?	Ovid's Elegies	3.11.3	
Or shall I plaine some God against me warres?	Ovid's Elegies	3.11.4	
Against my good they were an envious charme.	Ovid's Elegies	3.11.14	
Even sacrilege against her Deitie,	Hero and Leander	1.307	
And would be thought to graunt against her will.	Hero and Leander	1.336	
AGAINSTE			
this is againste the lawe ser:	Paris	ms14,p390	P Souldr
AGAMEMNON			
And Aeolus like Agamemnon sounds/The surges, his fierce	Dido	1.1.68	Venus
Daughter, whom I hold as deare/As Agamemnon did his Iphegen:	Jew	1.1.138	Barab
Great Agamemnon was, men say, amazed,	Ovid's Elegies	1.9.37	
Great Agamemnon lov'd his servant Chriseis.	Ovid's Elegies	2.8.12	
Such was the Greeke pompe, Agamemnon dead,	Ovid's Elegies	3.12.31	
AGAST			
Whereat agast, we were commanded straight/With reverence to	Dido	2.1.167	Aeneas
Surpriz'd with feare of hideous revenge,/I stand agast:	1Tamb	3.2.69	Agidas
Whereat agast, the poore soule gan to crie,	Hero and Leander	2.177	
AGATE (See AGGET)			
AGAVE			
Or fierce Agave mad; or like Megaera/That scar'd Alcides, when	Lucan, First Booke	574	
AGAYNE			
Welcome from Poland Henry once agayne,'	P 589	12.2	QnMoth
AGE			
Youle be a twigger when you come to age.	Dido	4.5.20	Nurse
A grave, and not a lover fits thy age:--	Dido	4.5.30	Nurse
Fourescore is but a girles age, love is sweete:--	Dido	4.5.32	Nurse
that in former age/Hast bene the seat of mightie Conquerors,	1Tamb	1.1.6	Cosroe
Who, when they come unto their fathers age,	1Tamb	3.3.110	Bajzth
Without respect of Sex, degree or age,	1Tamb	4.1.62	2Msngr
Pitie olde age, within whose silver haires/Honor and reverence	1Tamb	5.1.81	1Virgn
soules/From heavens of comfort, yet their age might beare,	1Tamb	5.1.90	1Virgn
In whom the learned Rabies of this age,	2Tamb	4.2.84	Therid
Would in his age be loath to labour so,	Jew	1.1.17	Barab
The comfort of mine age, my childrens hope,	Jew	1.2.150	Barab
A faire young maid scarce fourteene yeares of age,	Jew	1.2.378	Mthias
Is sure to pay for it when his sonne is of age,	Edw	5.4.4	Mortmr
I will requite it when I come to age.	Edw	5.4.100	King
Torment sweet friend, that base and [crooked age] <aged man>,	F1753	5.1.80	Faust
And now least age might waine his state, he casts/For civill	Lucan, First Booke	324	
Beauty not exercisde with age is spent,	Ovid's Elegies	1.8.53	
The gods send thee no house, a poore old age,	Ovid's Elegies	1.8.113	
What age fits Mars, with Venus doth agree,	Ovid's Elegies	1.9.3	
I pray that rotten age you wrackes/And sluttish white-mould	Ovid's Elegies	1.12.29	
Thou leav'st his bed, because hees faint through age,	Ovid's Elegies	1.13.37	
What age of Varroes name shall not be tolde,	Ovid's Elegies	1.15.21	
Which do perchance old age unto them give.	Ovid's Elegies	2.6.28	
What will my age do, age I cannot shunne,	Ovid's Elegies	3.6.17	
Plaies, maskes, and all that stern age counteth evill.	Hero and Leander	1.302	
AGED			
Yet shall the aged Sunne shed forth his [haire] <aire>,	Dido	1.1.159	Achat
Old men with swords thrust through their aged sides,	Dido	2.1.197	Aeneas
To whom the aged King thus trembling spoke:	Dido	2.1.232	Aeneas
O what became of aged Hecuba?	Dido	2.1.290	Anna
Or aged Atlas shoulder out of joynt,	Dido	4.1.12	Achat
Not for my selfe, but aged Barabas:	Jew	1.2.228	Abigal
And rescue aged Edward from his foes,	Edw	5.2.120	Kent
Torment sweet friend, that base and [crooked age] <aged man>,	F1753	5.1.80	Faust
I did not bid thee wed an aged swaine.	Ovid's Elegies	1.13.42	
And aged Saturne in Olympus dwell.	Hero and Leander	1.454	
AGEN			
Agen, sweet youth; did not you, Sir, bring the sweet youth a	Jew	4.2.41	P Ithimr
But new exploits do hale him out agen,	F 770	2.3.49	2Chor
'Zounds the Divel's alive agen.	F1391	4.2.67	P Benvol
AGENORS			
Adjoyning on Agenors stately towne,	Dido	1.1.211	Venus
AGENT			
his man's now at my lodging/That was his Agent, he'll confesse	Jew	5.1.17	Curtzn
Goe call the English Agent hether strait,	P1188	22.50	King
Agent for England, send thy mistres word,	P1194	22.56	King
AGES			
The ages that shall talk of Tamburlain,	1Tamb	4.2.95	Tamb
Whose life nine ages scarce bring out of date.	Ovid's Elegies	2.6.36	
AGGET			
A livelie vine of greene sea agget spread;	Hero and Leander	1.138	
AGGRAVATE (See AGRAVATE)			
AGHAST (See AGAST)			
AGIDAS			
[Agidas], leave to wound me with these words:	1Tamb	3.2.35	Zenoc
See you Agidas how the King salutes you.	1Tamb	3.2.88	Techel
And let Agidas by Agidas die,	1Tamb	3.2.105	Agidas
AGOE			
should be most)/Hath seem'd to be digested long agoe.	1Tamb	3.2.8	Agidas
Although it be digested long agoe,	1Tamb	3.2.9	Zenoc
Not long agoe bestrid a Scythian Steed:	2Tamb	1.3.38	Zenoc
Why so, they barkt a pace a month agoe,	Edw	4.3.12	Edward
Thy speeches long agoe had easde my sorrowes,	Edw	5.1.6	Edward
AGONY			
His anguish and his burning agony.	2Tamb	5.3.209	Amyras
AGOOD			
That I have laugh'd agood to see the cripples/Goe limping home	Jew	2.3.211	Ithimr
AGRAMITHIST			
Forward, and backward, Anagramatis'd <and Agramithist>:	F 233	1.3.9	Faust

AGRAVATE			
To agravate our sodaine miserie.	P 194	3.29	QnMarg
AGREE (See also GREE)			
And scarcely doe agree upon one poynt:	Dido	2.1.109	Dido
For with my nature warre doth best agree.	Edw	1.4.365	MortSr
What age fits Mars, with Venus doth agree,	Ovid's Elegies		1.9.3
Thy hands agree not with the warlike speare.	Ovid's Elegies		2.3.8
How oft, and by what meanes we did agree.	Ovid's Elegies		2.8.28
Never can these by any meanes agree.	Ovid's Elegies		3.4.42
Beauty with lewdnesse doth right ill agree.	Ovid's Elegies		3.10.42
AGREED			
Agreed Casane, we wil honor him.	1Tamb	3.2.113	Techel
Agreed yfaith.	2Tamb	4.1.66	P Perdic
AGREEDE			
Agreede.	P 493	9.12	P 1Atndt
AGREEV'D			
Brother Cosroe, I find my selfe agreev'd,	1Tamb	1.1.1	Mycet
AGRIPPA			
Will be as cunning as Agrippa was,	F 144	1.1.116	Faust
AGROUND			
O happie sand that made him runne aground:	Dido	4.4.95	Dido
AGYDAS (See also AGIDAS)			
So fares Agydas for the late felt frownes/That sent a tempest	1Tamb	3.2.85	Agidas
It saies, Agydas, thou shalt surely die,	1Tamb	3.2.95	Agidas
Then haste Agydas, and prevent the plagues:	1Tamb	3.2.100	Agidas
AH (See also AY, AYE)			
Ah, how could poore Aeneas scape their hands?	Dido	2.1.220	Dido
Ah foolish Dido to forbeare this long!	Dido	5.1.160	Dido
But wheres Aeneas? ah hees gone hees gone!	Dido	5.1.192	Dido
Ah sister, leave these idle fantasies,	Dido	5.1.262	Anna
Ah, Menaphon, why staiest thou thus behind,	1Tamb	1.1.83	Mycet
Ah Menaphon, I passe not for his threates,	1Tamb	1.1.109	Cosroe
Ah Shepheard, pity my distressed plight,	1Tamb	1.2.7	Zenoc
Are <To> <Ah> these resolved noble Scythians?	1Tamb	1.2.225	Therid
They knew not, ah, they knew not simple men,	1Tamb	2.4.2	Mycet
Ah, life and soule still hover in his Breast,	1Tamb	3.2.21	Zenoc
Ah faire Zenocrate,/Let not a man so vile and barbarous,	1Tamb	3.2.25	Agidas
Ah faire Zabina, we have lost the field.	1Tamb	3.3.233	Bajzth
Ah villaines, dare ye touch my sacred armes?	1Tamb	3.3.268	Bajzth
Ah faire Zenocrate, divine Zenocrate,	1Tamb	5.1.135	Tamb
Ah faire Zabina, we may curse his power,	1Tamb	5.1.230	Bajzth
Ah, save that Infant, save him, save him.	1Tamb	5.1.313	P Zabina
Ah Tamburlaine, wert thou the cause of this/That tearm'st	1Tamb	5.1.335	Zenoc
Ah wretched eies, the enemies of my hart,	1Tamb	5.1.340	Zenoc
Ah Madam, this their slavery hath Enforc'd,	1Tamb	5.1.345	Anippe
Ah Tamburlaine, my love, sweet Tamburlaine,	1Tamb	5.1.355	Zenoc
Ah myghty Jove and holy Mahomet,	1Tamb	5.1.363	Zenoc
Ah what may chance to thee Zenocrate?	1Tamb	5.1.371	Zenoc
Ah that the deadly panges I suffer now,	1Tamb	5.1.422	Arabia
Ah were I now but halfe so eloquent/To paint in woords, what	2Tamb	1.2.9	Callap
Ah good my Lord be patient, she is dead,	2Tamb	2.4.119	Therid
Ah sweet Theridamas, say so no more,	2Tamb	2.4.126	Tamb
Ah sacred Mahomet, if this be sin,	2Tamb	3.4.31	Olymp
Ah, pity me my Lord, and draw your sword,	2Tamb	4.2.33	Olymp
Ah cruel Brat, sprung from a tyrants loines,	2Tamb	4.3.54	Jrslem
Ah sacred Mahomet, thou that hast seene/Millions of Turkes	2Tamb	5.2.24	Callap
Ah friends, what shal I doe, I cannot stand,	2Tamb	5.3.51	Tamb
Ah good my Lord, leave these impatient words,	2Tamb	5.3.54	Therid
ah gentle Fryar,/Convert my father that he may be sav'd,	Jew	3.6.38	Abigal
Ah my good Lord, these are the Guisians,	P 260	4.58	Admral
Ah base Shatillian and degenerate,	P 312	5.39	Guise
Ah base Epernoune, were not his highnes heere,	P 831	17.26	Guise
Ah Sextus, be reveng'd upon the King,	P1010	19.80	Guise
Ah this sweet sight is phisick to my soule,	P1020	19.90	King
Ah, had your highnes let him live,	P1183	22.45	Eprnon
Ah curse him not sith he is dead.	P1220	22.82	King
Ah Epernoune, is this thy love to me?	P1235	22.97	King
Trayterouse guise ah thow hast murthered me	Paris	ms17,p390	Minion
Ah words that make me surfet with delight:	Edw	1.1.3	Gavstn
Ah brother, lay not violent hands on him,	Edw	1.1.189	Kent
Ah wicked king, accurssed Gaveston,	Edw	1.2.4	Lncstr
Ah that bewraies their basenes Lancaster,	Edw	1.2.27	Mortmr
Ah none but rude and savage minded men,	Edw	1.4.78	Edward
Ah Mortimer!	Edw	1.4.193	Queene
Ah had some bloudlesse furie rose from hell,	Edw	1.4.316	Edward
Ah furious Mortimer what hast thou done?	Edw	2.2.85	Queene
Ah Spencer, not the riches of my realme/Can ransome him, ah he	Edw	3.1.3	Edward
the riches of my realme/Can ransome him, ah he is markt to die,	Edw	3.1.4	Edward
Ah traitors, have they put my friend to death?	Edw	3.1.91	Edward
Ah sweete sir John, even to the utmost verge/Of Europe, or the	Edw	4.2.29	Queene
Ah nothing greeves me but my little boye,	Edw	4.3.48	Edward
Ah Leister, way how hardly I can brooke/To loose my crowne and	Edw	5.1.51	Edward
Ah pardon me, greefe makes me lunatick.	Edw	5.1.114	Edward
Ah they do dissemble.	Edw	5.2.86	Kent
Faustus gives to thee his soule: [ah] <O> there it staid.	F 456	2.1.68	Faust
[Ah] <O> Christ my Saviour, my Saviour,	F 634	2.2.83	Faust
[Ah] <O> stay good Faustus, stay thy desperate steps.	F1729	5.1.56	OldMan
[Ah] <O> [my sweete] friend,	F1734	5.1.61	Faust
[Ah] <Oh> gentlemen.	F1822	5.2.26	Faust
Ah my sweet chamber-fellow, had I liv'd with thee, then had I	F1824	5.2.28	P Faust
[Ah] <O> gentlemen, heare [me] with patience, and tremble not	F1838	5.2.42	P Faust
Hell, [ah] <O> hell for ever.	F1846	5.2.50	P Faust
[Ah] <O> my God, I would weepe, but the Divell drawes in my	F1850	5.2.54	P Faust

AH (cont.)			
[Ah] <O> gentlemen, I gave them my soule for my cunning.	F1856	5.2.60	Faust
Oh <Ah> Faustus, if thou hadst given eare to me,	F1892	5.2.96	GdAngl
[Ah] <O> Faustus,/Now hast thou but one bare houre to live,	F1926	5.2.130	Faust
One drop [would save my soule, halfe a drop, ah] my Christ.	F1940	5.2.144	Faust
Rend <Ah rend> not my heart, for naming of my Christ,	F1941	5.2.145	Faust
[Ah] <O> halfe the houre is past:	F1957	5.2.161	Faust
[Ah] <Oh> Pythagoras Metemsycosis <metem su cossis>; were that	F1966	5.2.170	Faust
I'le burne my bookes; [ah] <oh> Mephostophilis.	F1982	5.2.186	Faust
Ah Doctor Faustus, that I might prevaile,	F App	p.243 34	OldMan
Ah howe thy lot is above my lot blest:	Ovid's Elegies		1.6.46
Ah often, that her [hale] <haole> head aked, she lying,	Ovid's Elegies		2.19.11
Ah oft how much she might she feignd offence;	Ovid's Elegies		2.19.13
Ah howe oft on hard doores hung I engrav'd,	Ovid's Elegies		3.1.53
Ah Pelops from his coach was almost feld,	Ovid's Elegies		3.2.15
Ah whether is [thy] <they> brests soft nature [fled] <sled>?	Ovid's Elegies		3.7.18
Ah now a name too true thou hast, I finde.	Ovid's Elegies		3.8.4
Ah, she doth more worth then her vices prove.	Ovid's Elegies		3.10.44
Ah simple Hero, learne thy selfe to cherish,	Hero and Leander		1.241
A HUNTING			
We two will goe a hunting in the woods,	Dido	3.1.174	Dido
This day they both a hunting forth will ride/Into these woods,	Dido	3.2.87	Juno
Come sonne, weele ride a hunting in the parke.	Edw	5.4.113	Queene
AID (See also AYD)			
Lifting his prayers to the heavens for aid,	1Tamb	3.2.83	Agidas
Meaning to aid [thee] <them> in this <these> Turkish armes,	2Tamb	1.3.144	Techel
To aid the kings of Soria and Jerusalem.	2Tamb	2.1.21	Fredrk
In partiall aid of that proud Scythian,	2Tamb	2.2.16	Gazell
by the aid of God and his friend Mahomet, Emperour of Natolia,	2Tamb	3.1.3	P Orcan
Aid thy obedient servant Callapine,	2Tamb	5.2.28	Callap
And what's our aid against so great a Prince?	Jew	1.2.51	Barab
Then gentle friends aid me in this attempt,	F 138	1.1.110	Faust
To slay mine enemies, and aid my friends,	F 324	1.3.96	Faust
If you will aid me in this enterprise,	F1334	4.2.10	Benvol
AIDE			
letters to command/Aide and assistance if we stand in need.	1Tamb	1.2.20	Magnet
of Fesse have brought/To aide thee in this Turkish expedition,	2Tamb	1.3.131	Usumc
I march to meet and aide my neigbor kings,	2Tamb	3.1.60	Soria
If God or Mahomet send any aide.	2Tamb	5.2.11	Callap
Offering him aide against his enemies,	P 905	18.6	Bartus
Assure him all the aide we can provide,	P 909	18.10	Navrre
For we must aide the King against the Guise.	P 918	18.19	Navrre
Welcome old man, comst thou in Edwards aide?	Edw	3.1.34	Edward
Is it not, trowe ye, to assemble aide,	Edw	3.1.207	SpncrP
of golde/To Danae, all aide may be denied/To Isabell the Queene,	Edw	3.1.268	Spencr
the ungentle king/Of Fraunce refuseth to give aide of armes,	Edw	4.2.62	SrJohn
not discourage/Your friends that are so forward in your aide.	Edw	4.2.70	Queene
As Isabella <Isabell> gets no aide from thence.	Edw	4.3.16	Edward
To crave the aide and succour of his peeres.	Edw	5.6.21	Queene
My thoughts sole goddes, aide mine enterprise,	Lucan, First Booke		202
Sent aide; so did Alcides port, whose seas/Eate hollow rocks,	Lucan, First Booke		406
AIE			
and with horror aie/Griping our bowels with retorqued	1Tamb	5.1.236	Bajzth
And which (aie me) ever pretendeth ill,	Lucan, First Booke		625
Aie me how high that gale did lift my hope!	Ovid's Elegies		1.6.52
AIER			
Nor yet this aier, beat often with thy sighes,	2Tamb	4.2.10	Olymp
AIERY			
Filling their empty vaines with aiery wine,	2Tamb	3.2.107	Tamb
AILES (See also AYLE)			
What ailes my Queene, is she falne sicke of late?	Dido	3.4.24	Aeneas
What ailes Faustus?	F1823	5.2.27	2Schol
AIM'D			
And as we ever [aim'd] <and> at your behoofe,	1Tamb	2.5.32	Ortyg
His mind was troubled, and he aim'd at war,	Lucan, First Booke		186
AIME (See also AYME)			
This Troians end will be thy envies aime,	Dido	3.3.73	Iarbus
If we should aime at such a dignitie?	1Tamb	2.5.79	Tamb
And resolution honors fairest aime.	P 96	2.39	Guise
For his aspiring thoughts aime at the crowne,	P 923	18.24	Navrre
Villaine thy life, unlesse I misse mine aime.	Edw	2.2.84	Mortmr
I know it lords, it is this life you aime at,	Edw	2.5.48	Gavstn
AIMED			
and fully executes/Matters of importe, aimed at by many,	P 111	2.54	Guise
AIMES			
Edward, this Mortimer aimes at thy life:	Edw	4.6.10	Kent
Who aimes at nothing but externall trash,	F 62	1.1.34	Faust
AIMING			
Stands aiming at me with his murthering dart,	2Tamb	5.3.69	Tamb
AIRE (See also AIER, AYER, AYRE)			
By Saturnes soule, and this earth threatning [haire] <aire>,	Dido	1.1.10	Jupitr
Yet shall the aged Sunne shed forth his [haire] <aire>,	Dido	1.1.159	Achat
Our quivering Lances shaking in the aire,	1Tamb	2.3.18	Tamb
And since we all have suckt one wholsome aire,	1Tamb	2.6.25	Cosroe
Legions of Spirits fleeting in the [aire],	1Tamb	3.3.156	Tamb
make our <your> strokes to wound the sencelesse [aire] <lure>.	1Tamb	3.3.158	Tamb
Now cleare the triple region of the aire,	1Tamb	4.2.30	Tamb
Fill all the aire with fiery meteors.	1Tamb	4.2.52	Tamb
Shaking her silver tresses in the aire,	1Tamb	5.1.141	Tamb
So high within the region of the aire,	1Tamb	5.1.250	Zabina
Which fils the nookes of Hell with standing aire,	1Tamb	5.1.257	Bajzth
Closde in a coffyn mounted up the aire,	2Tamb	1.1.140	Orcan
Whose chearful looks do cleare the clowdy aire/And cloath it in	2Tamb	1.3.3	Tamb

AIRE (cont.)			
Their legs to dance and caper in the aire:	2Tamb	1.3.31	Tamb
Hath suckt the measure of that vitall aire/That feeds the body	2Tamb	2.4.44	Zenoc
If woords might serve, our voice hath rent the aire,	2Tamb	2.4.121	Therid
Whose hornes shall sprinkle through the tainted aire,	2Tamb	3.1.66	Orcan
Flame to the highest region of the aire:	2Tamb	3.2.2	Tamb
And make whole cyties caper in the aire.	2Tamb	3.2.61	Tamb
Hang in the aire as thicke as sunny motes,	2Tamb	3.2.101	Tamb
the Ecchoe and the souldiers crie/Make deafe the aire, and dim	2Tamb	3.3.61	Therid
Over whose Zenith cloth'd in windy aire,	2Tamb	3.4.61	Therid
Whereat thou trembling hid'st thee in the aire,	2Tamb	4.1.130	Tamb
Fill all the aire with troublous bellowing:	2Tamb	4.1.190	Tamb
And breake their burning Lances in the aire,	2Tamb	4.1.204	Tamb
Spangled with Diamonds dancing in the aire,	2Tamb	4.3.117	Tamb
Which makes them fleet aloft and gaspe for aire.	2Tamb	5.1.209	Techel
And shed their feble influence in the aire.	2Tamb	5.3.5	Therid
Birds of the Aire will tell of murders past;	Jew	Prol.16	Machvl
and the fire the aire, and so we shall be poysoned with him.	P 484	9.3	P 1Atndt
And therefore being pursued, it takes the aire:	Edw	2.2.25	Lncstr
And make a bridge, thorough the moving Aire,	F 333	1.3.105	Faust
That with his wings did part the subtle aire,	F 772	2.3.51	2Chor
So high our Dragons soar'd into the aire,	F 849	3.1.71	Faust
The Planets seven, the gloomy aire,	F 999	3.2.19	Mephst
great deserts in erecting that inchanted Castle in the Aire:	F1560	4.6.3	P Duke
O thou art fairer then the evenings <evening> aire,	F1781	5.1.108	Faust
That when you vomite forth into the aire,	F1954	5.2.158	Faust
<O> It strikes, it strikes; now body turne to aire,	F1975	5.2.179	Faust
shall the thickned aire,/Become intemperate?	Lucan, First Booke	645	
now throughout the aire I flie,/To doubtfull Sirtes and drie	Lucan, First Booke	685	
The aire is colde, and sleepe is sweetest now,	Ovid's Elegies	1.13.7	
All you whose pineons in the cleare aire sore,	Ovid's Elegies	2.6.11	
the Puttock hovers/Around the aire, the Cadesse raine	Ovid's Elegies	2.6.34	
To empty aire may go my fearefull speech.	Ovid's Elegies	3.1.62	
The aire with sparkes of living fire was spangled,	Hero and Leander	1.188	
Her vowes above the emptie aire he flings:	Hero and Leander	1.370	
But like exiled aire thrust from his sphere,	Hero and Leander	2.118	
AIRIE			
Shadowing more beauty in their Airie browes,	F 155	1.1.127	Valdes
AIRS			
But come lets walke aside, th'airs not very sweet.	P 497	9.16	QnMoth
AIRY (See also AERY, AIERY, AYRIE)			
Inclroned round with airy mountaine tops,	F 781	3.1.3	Faust
AJAX			
Whom Ajax ravisht in Dianas [Fane] <Fawne>,	Dido	2.1.275	Aeneas
Ajax, maister of the seven-fould shield,/Butcherd the flocks he	Ovid's Elegies	1.7.7	
What good to me wil either Ajax bring?	Ovid's Elegies	2.1.30	
AKE			
The sent whereof doth make my head to ake.	P 171	3.6	OldQn
Deny him oft, feigne now thy head doth ake:	Ovid's Elegies	1.8.73	
Whose bodies with their heavy burthens ake.	Ovid's Elegies	2.13.20	
AKED			
Ah often, that her [hale] <haole> head aked, she lying,	Ovid's Elegies	2.19.11	
AKER			
No slave, in beaten silke, and staves-aker.	F 357	1.4.15	P Wagner
Staves-aker?	F 358	1.4.16	P Robin
AL			
To turne them al upon their proper heades.	1Tamb	4.4.31	Tamb
His Skul al rivin in twain, his braines dasht out?	1Tamb	5.1.306	Zabina
When al their riders chardg'd their quivering speares/Began to	1Tamb	5.1.332	Zenoc
Al sights of power to grace my victory:	1Tamb	5.1.474	Tamb
Shal now, adjoining al their hands with mine,	1Tamb	5.1.493	Tamb
For Tamburlaine takes truce with al the world.	1Tamb	5.1.529	Tamb
And murdrous Fates throwes al his triumphs down.	2Tamb	Prol.5	Prolog
Our Turky blades shal glide through al their throats,	2Tamb	1.1.31	Orcan
Be al a scourge and terror to the world,	2Tamb	1.3.63	Tamb
But neither man nor child in al the land:	2Tamb	1.3.197	Techel
and al the winds shall breath/Through shady leaves of every	2Tamb	2.3.15	Orcan
al the hundred and thirty Kingdomes late contributory to his	2Tamb	3.1.5	P Orcan
From al the crueltie my soule sustaind,	2Tamb	3.1.33	Callap
Nay, when the battaile ends, al we wil meet,	2Tamb	3.5.97	Callap
Let al of us intreat your highnesse pardon.	2Tamb	4.1.98	Tec&Us
For earth and al this aery region/Cannot containe the state of	2Tamb	4.1.119	Tamb
Ile bridle al your tongues/And bind them close with bits of	2Tamb	4.1.181	Tamb
With whom I buried al affections,	2Tamb	4.2.23	Olymp
Shal al be loden with the martiall spoiles/We will convay with	2Tamb	4.3.105	Tamb
And sommon al the shining lamps of heaven/To cast their	2Tamb	5.3.3	Therid
Meet heaven and earth, and here let al things end,	2Tamb	5.3.249	Amyras
Lastly, he that denies this, shall absolutely lose al he has.	Jew	1.2.76	P Reader
you were his father too, Sir, that's al the harm I wish you:	Jew	2.3.41	P Barab
Thanks to you al.	P 599	12.12	King
have a booke wherein I might beholde al spels and incantations,	F 551.1	2.1.164A	P Faust
I might see al characters of <and> planets of the heavens,	F 551.4	2.1.167A	P Faust
wherein I might see al plants, hearbes and trees that grow upon	F 551.9	2.1.172A	P Faust
al> the seven deadly sinnes appeare to thee in their owne	F 655	2.2.104	P Belzeb
I, I thought that was al the land his father left him:	F App	p.229 17	P Clown
or Ile turne al the lice about thee into familiars, and they	F App	p.229 25	P Wagner
al the maidens in our parish dance at my pleasure starke naked	F App	p.233 3	P Robin
I can do al these things easily with it:	F App	p.234 22	P Robin
Drawer, I hope al is payd, God be with you, come Rafe.	F App	p.234 5	P Robin
I have beene al this day seeking one maister Fustian:	F App	p.239 98	P HrsCsr
he wil drinke of al waters, but ride him not into the water,	F App	p.239 111	P Faust
For he hath given to me al his goodes,	F App	p.243 2	Wagner
his owne waight/Keepe him within the ground, his armes al bare,	Lucan, First Booke	140	

AL (cont.)
At al times charging home, and making havock; Lucan, First Booke 148
wittes) was loath'd, and al the world/Ransackt for golde, Lucan, First Booke 167
Then with their feare, and danger al distract, Lucan, First Booke 487
The hirer payeth al, his rent discharg'd/From further duty he Ovid's Elegies 1.10.45
Is dead, al-fowles her exequies frequent. Ovid's Elegies 2.6.2
And fruit from trees, when ther's no wind at al. Ovid's Elegies 3.6.34
ALARME
And with a sodaine and an hot alarme/Drive all their horses 1Tamb 1.2.134 Usumc
And to Leander as a fresh alarme. Hero and Leander 2.284
ALARMES
Choosing a subject fit for feirse alarmes: Ovid's Elegies 1.1.6
Is golden love hid in Mars mid alarmes. Ovid's Elegies 2.18.36
ALARMS
Or cease one day from war and hot alarms, 2Tamb 1.3.183 Usumc
ALARUM (See also LARUMS)
Trumpets and drums, alarum presently, 2Tamb 3.3.62 Techel
Drums strike alarum, raise them from their sport, Edw 2.3.25 Mortmr
Alarum to the fight, Edw 3.1.218 Warwck
ALAS (See also 'LAS)
Alas sweet boy, thou must be still a while, Dido 1.1.164 Aeneas
And I alas, was forst to let her lye. Dido 2.1.279 Aeneas
Alas poore King that labours so in vaine, Dido 4.2.33 Anna
Alas (poore Turke) his fortune is to weake, 1Tamb 3.3.6 Tamb
Alas poore fooles, must you be first shal feele/The sworne 1Tamb 5.1.65 Tamb
Alas my Lord, how should our bleeding harts/Wounded and broken 2Tamb 5.3.161 Amyras
Alas, our number's few,/And Crownes come either by succession Jew 1.1.130 Barab
Alas, my Lord, the summe is overgreat, Jew 1.2.8 Govnr
Alas, my Lord, we are no souldiers: Jew 1.2.50 Barab
Alas, my Lord, the most of us are poore! Jew 1.2.57 1Jew
Alas, Sir, I am a very youth. Jew 2.3.115 P Slave
alas, hath pac'd too long/The fatall Labyrinth of misbeleefe, Jew 3.3.63 Abigal
now out alas,/He is slaine. Jew 4.1.176 Barab
Alas I am a scholler, how should I have golde? P 377 7.17 Ramus
Alas my Lord, the wound is dangerous, P1212 22.74 Srgeon
Alas my Lord, your highnes cannot live. P1223 22.85 Srgeon
Edward, alas my hart relents for thee, Edw 4.6.2 Kent
I rue my lords ill fortune, but alas, Edw 4.6.64 Queene
But we alas are chaste, and you my friends, Edw 4.7.22 Edward
Alas, see where he sits, and hopes unseene, Edw 4.7.51 Leistr
Gone, gone alas, never to make returne. Edw 4.7.104 Spencr
Alas poore soule, would I could ease his greefe. Edw 5.2.26 Queene
Alas poore slave, see how poverty jests in his nakednesse, I F 348 1.4.6 P Wagner
Alas I am undone, what shall I do? F1492 4.4.36 P HrsCsr
Alas poore slave, see how poverty jesteth in his nakednesse, F App p.229 6 P Wagner
Alas sir, I have no more, I pray you speake for me. F App p.239 104 P HrsCsr
Alas, alas, Doctor Fustian quoth a, mas Doctor Lopus was never F App p.240 127 P HrsCsr
Alas, I am undone, what shall I do: F App p.241 154 P HrsCsr
Alas Madame, thats nothing, Mephastophilis, be gone. F App p.242 12 P Faust
[Thy] <They> troubled haires, alas, endur'd great losse. Ovid's Elegies 1.14.24
Alas she almost weepes, and her white cheekes, Ovid's Elegies 1.14.51
Alas a wench is a perpetuall evill. Ovid's Elegies 2.5.4
(Alas my precepts turne my selfe to smart)/We write, or what Ovid's Elegies 2.18.20
Alas he runnes too farre about the ring, Ovid's Elegies 3.2.69
passions to asswage)/Compile sharpe satyrs, but alas too late, Hero and Leander 1.127
So that the truce was broke, and she alas, Hero and Leander 2.285
ALBA
rites and Latian Jove advanc'd/On Alba hill o Vestall flames, Lucan, First Booke 201
The flame in Alba consecrate to Jove, Lucan, First Booke 548
ALBANEES
We have revolted Grecians, Albanees, 2Tamb 1.1.61 Orcan
ALBANIA
Duke of [Assiria] <Affrica> and Albania, 1Tamb 1.1.164 Ortyg
Shall rule the Province of Albania. 1Tamb 2.2.31 Meandr
ALBANUS
beare wise Bacons, and [Abanus] <Albanus> <Albertus> workes, F 181 1.1.153 Valdes
ALBEIT
Albeit the Gods doe know no wanton thought/Had ever residence Dido 3.1.16 Dido
Albeit the world thinke Machevill is dead, Jew Prol.1 Machvl
My Lords, albeit the Queen winne Mortimer, Edw 1.4.230 Lncstr
(Albeit the Moores light Javelin or his speare/Sticks in his Lucan, First Booke 213
This hand (albeit unwilling) should performe it; Lucan, First Booke 379
Albeit the Citty thou wouldst have so ra'st/Be Roome it selfe. Lucan, First Booke 386
And Marriners, albeit the keele be sound, Lucan, First Booke 500
Virginitie, albeit some highly prise it, Hero and Leander 1.262
I, and shee wisht, albeit not from her hart, Hero and Leander 2.37
Albeit Leander rude in love, and raw, Hero and Leander 2.61
Breathlesse albeit he were, he rested not, Hero and Leander 2.229
ALBERTUS
beare wise Bacons, and [Abanus] <Albanus> <Albertus> workes, F 181 1.1.153 Valdes
ALCARON
And by the holy Alcaron I sweare, 1Tamb 3.3.76 Bajzth
Whose holy Alcaron remaines with us, 2Tamb 1.1.138 Orcan
Now Casane, wher's the Turkish Alcaron, 2Tamb 5.1.173 Tamb
To blow thy Alcaron up to thy throne, 2Tamb 5.1.193 Tamb
ALCHEMIST (See ALCUMIST)
ALCIBIADES
Grave Socrates, wilde Alcibiades: Edw 1.4.397 MortSr
ALCIDAMUS
Where her betrothed Lord Alcidamus, 1Tamb 1.2.78 Agidas
ALCIDES
Hang up your weapons on Alcides poste, 1Tamb 5.1.528 Tamb
The headstrong Jades of Thrace, Alcides tam'd, 2Tamb 4.3.12 Tamb

ALCIDES (cont.)
Sent aide; so did Alcides port, whose seas/Eate hollow rocks, — Lucan, First Booke 406
or like Megaera/That scar'd Alcides, when by Junoes taske/He — Lucan, First Booke 575
Thou saiest broke with Alcides angry hand. . . . . — Ovid's Elegies 3.5.36
Romulus, temples brave/Bacchus, Alcides, and now Caesar have. — Ovid's Elegies 3.7.52
Alcides like, by mightie violence, ... — Hero and Leander 2.120

ALCINOUS
[May] <Many> bounteous [lome] <love> Alcinous fruite resigne. — Ovid's Elegies 1.10.56

ALCION
This was Alcion, a Musition, ... — Dido 3.1.159 Dido

ALCORAN (See ALCARON)

ALCUMIST
An ointment which a cunning Alcumist/Distilled from the purest — 2Tamb 4.2.59 Olymp

ALDEBORAN
Raise me to match the faire Aldeboran, ... — 2Tamb 4.3.61 Tamb

ALE
Who payes for the Ale? . . . . — F1666 4.6.109 P Hostss

ALEPO
Here at Alepo with an hoste of men/Lies Tamburlaine, this king — 2Tamb 3.5.3 2Msngr

ALEPPO
Tane from Aleppo, Soldino, Tripoly, ... — 2Tamb 3.1.58 Soria

ALEXANDER
Her Lover after Alexander dyed, ... — Dido 2.1.298 Achat
Where Belus, Ninus and great Alexander/Have rode in triumph, — 2Tamb 5.1.69 Tamb
be it to her as the draught/Of which great Alexander drunke, — Jew 3.4.97 Barab
Great Alexander lovde Ephestion, ... — Edw 1.4.392 MortSr
And as Pope Alexander our Progenitour, ... — F 915 3.1.137 Pope
and warlike semblances/Of Alexander and his beauteous Paramour. — F1171 4.1.17 Mrtino
Great Alexander, and his Paramour, ... — F1232 4.1.78 Emper
Great Alexander and his beauteous Paramour. . . . — F1239 4.1.85 Faust
present the royall shapes/Of Alexander and his Paramour, . — F1250 4.1.96 Faust
and thou bring Alexander and his Paramour before the Emperour, — F1254 4.1.100 P Benvol
this royall Emperour/The mightie Monarch, warlicke Alexander. — F1297 4.1.143 Faust
amongest which kings is Alexander the great, chiefe spectacle — F App p.237 23 P Emper
spirites as can lively resemble Alexander and his Paramour, — F App p.237 46 P Faust
you bring Alexander and his paramour before the emperor? . — F App p.237 51 P Knight

ALEXANDERS
Have not I made blind Homer sing to me/Of Alexanders love, and — F 578 2.2.27 Faust

ALEXANDRIA
To Alexandria, and the frontier townes, ... — 2Tamb 1.1.48 Gazell
By [Cairo] <Cario> runs to Alexandria Bay, ... — 2Tamb 1.2.19 Callap
And here not far from Alexandria, ... — 2Tamb 5.3.131 Tamb
Mine Argosie from Alexandria, ... — Jew 1.1.44 Barab
And saw'st thou not/Mine Argosie at Alexandria? . . . — Jew 1.1.72 Barab
Thou needs must saile by Alexandria. . . . . . . — Jew 1.1.76 Barab
Thine Argosie from Alexandria, ... — Jew 1.1.85 2Merch
At Alexandria, Merchandize unsold: . . . . . . — Jew 4.1.68 Barab

AL-FOWLES
Is dead, al-fowles her exequies frequent. . . . . . — Ovid's Elegies 2.6.2

ALGIERS (See ARGEIRE, ARGIER)

ALIANCE
And all bands of that death presaging aliance. . . . . — Lucan, First Booke 114

ALIED
His name is Spencer, he is well alied, ... — Edw 2.2.249 Gavstn
Armies alied, the kingdoms league uprooted, ... — Lucan, First Booke 4

ALIFE
To steale sands from the shore he loves alife, ... — Ovid's Elegies 2.19.45

ALIGHT
Alight and weare a woful mourning weed. . . . . . — 2Tamb 1.1.44 Orcan
His left hand whereon gold doth ill alight, ... — Ovid's Elegies 3.7.15

A LIKE
Let us both lovers hope, and feare a like, ... — Ovid's Elegies 2.19.5

ALIKE
a match confirmd/Betwixt these two, whose loves are so alike, — Dido 3.2.78 Juno
All fellowes now, disposde alike to sporte, ... — Dido 3.3.5 Dido
Whether you will, all places are alike, ... — Edw 5.1.145 Edward
Eagles alike displaide, darts answering darts. . . . . — Lucan, First Booke 7
Both verses were alike till Love (men say)/Began to smile and — Ovid's Elegies 1.1.7
The sport being such, as both alike sweete try it, . . . — Ovid's Elegies 1.10.33
This kinde of verse is not alike, yet fit, ... — Ovid's Elegies 2.17.21

ALIVE
grim Ceranias seate/Have you oregone, and yet remaine alive? — Dido 1.1.148 Aeneas
He is alive, Troy is not overcome. . . . . . . — Dido 2.1.30 Aeneas
O Illioneus, art thou yet alive? . . . . . . — Dido 2.1.55 Achat
Zenocrate, the loveliest Maide alive, ... — 1Tamb 3.3.117 Tamb
Now all are dead, not one remaines alive. . . . . . — Jew 4.1.7 Barab
Whence none can possibly escape alive: . . . . . . — Jew 5.5.31 Barab
To which thou didst alure me being alive: . . . . . — P1025 19.95 King
When Duke Dumaine his brother is alive, ... — P1055 19.125 King
And make the Guisians stoup that are alive. . . . . — P1071 19.141 King
My brother Cardenall slaine and I alive? . . . . . — P1125 21.19 Dumain
O that that damned villaine were alive againe, ... — P1216 22.78 Eprnon
Lord Edmund and lord Mortimer alive? . . . . . . — Edw 4.2.36 Queene
Not one alive, but shrewdly I suspect, ... — Edw 4.7.28 Spencr
Gone, gone, and doe I remaine alive? . . . . . . — Edw 5.5.91 Edward
Zounds the Divel's alive agen. . . . . — F1391 4.2.67 P Benvol
And Hector dyed his brothers yet alive. . . . . . — Ovid's Elegies 2.6.42

ALL (See also AL, ALL'S)
Why, are not all the Gods at thy commaund, ... — Dido 1.1.30 Jupitr
But as this one Ile teare them all from him, ... — Dido 1.1.40 Jupitr
And charg'd him drowne my sonne with all his traine. . — Dido 1.1.61 Venus
And all Aeolia to be up in armes: . . . . . . — Dido 1.1.63 Venus
Which Pergama did vaunt in all her pride. . . . . . — Dido 1.1.151 Aeneas

ALL (cont.)

men, saw you as you came/Any of all my Sisters wandring here?	Dido	1.1.184	Venus
Live happie in the height of all content,	Dido	1.1.195	Aeneas
But of them all scarce seven doe anchor safe,	Dido	1.1.222	Aeneas
And all of them unburdened of their loade,	Dido	1.1.225	Aeneas
Doe trace these Libian deserts all despisde,	Dido	1.1.228	Aeneas
Forbids all hope to harbour neere our hearts.	Dido	1.2.16	Illion
Disperst them all amongst the wrackfull Rockes:	Dido	1.2.29	Cloan
O were I not at all so thou mightst be.	Dido	2.1.28	Aeneas
Who for Troyes sake hath entertaind us all,	Dido	2.1.64	Illion
In all humilitie I thanke your grace.	Dido	2.1.99	Aeneas
But all in this that Troy is overcome,	Dido	2.1.112	Dido
And so in troopes all marcht to Tenedos:	Dido	2.1.135	Aeneas
All which hemd me about, crying, this is he.	Dido	2.1.219	Aeneas
Not mov'd at all, but smiling at his teares,	Dido	2.1.240	Aeneas
Her cheekes swolne with sighes, her haire all rent,	Dido	2.1.276	Aeneas
For all our ships were launcht into the deepe:	Dido	2.1.285	Aeneas
Or whisking of these leaves, all shall be still,	Dido	2.1.337	Venus
know that thou of all my wooers/(And yet have I had many	Dido	3.1.11	Dido
Is he not eloquent in all his speech?	Dido	3.1.65	Dido
My Sailes all rent in sunder with the winde,	Dido	3.1.106	Aeneas
Yea all my Navie split with Rockes and Shelfes:	Dido	3.1.108	Aeneas
All these and others which I never sawe,	Dido	3.1.150	Dido
Yet none obtaind me, I am free from all.--	Dido	3.1.153	Dido
The rest are such as all the world well knowes,	Dido	3.1.165	Dido
And have no gall at all to grieve my foes:	Dido	3.2.17	Juno
Is this then all the thankes that I shall have,	Dido	3.2.37	Juno
I mustred all the windes unto his wracke,	Dido	3.2.45	Juno
When in the midst of all their gamesome sports,	Dido	3.2.89	Juno
All fellowes now, disposde alike to sporte,	Dido	3.3.5	Dido
What makes Iarbus here of all the rest?	Dido	3.3.13	Dido
How like his father speaketh he in all?	Dido	3.3.41	Anna
Who would not undergoe all kind of toyle,	Dido	3.3.58	Aeneas
Who then of all so cruell may he be,	Dido	3.4.16	Aeneas
As my despised worths, that shun all praise,	Dido	3.4.42	Aeneas
And vow by all the Gods of Hospitalitie,	Dido	3.4.44	Aeneas
In all my life I never knew the like,	Dido	4.1.7	Anna
It haild, it snowde, it lightned all at once.	Dido	4.1.8	Anna
In all this coyle, where have ye left the Queene?	Dido	4.1.14	Iarbus
But where were you Iarbus all this while?	Dido	4.1.31	Dido
Father of gladnesse, and all frollicke thoughts,	Dido	4.2.5	Iarbus
And all the woods Eliza to resound:	Dido	4.2.10	Iarbus
And all the fruites that plentie els sends forth,	Dido	4.2.15	Iarbus
On whom the nimble windes may all day waight,	Dido	4.3.23	Aeneas
And follow your foreseeing starres in all;	Dido	4.3.32	Achat
Were to transgresse against all lawes of love:	Dido	4.3.48	Aeneas
O Dido, patronesse of all our lives,	Dido	4.4.55	Aeneas
Not all the world can take thee from mine armes,	Dido	4.4.61	Dido
All that they have, their lands, their goods, their lives,	Dido	4.4.76	Dido
And I the Goddesse of all these, commaund/Aeneas ride as	Dido	4.4.77	Dido
And sheere ye all asunder with her hands:	Dido	4.4.156	Dido
If that all glorie hath forsaken thee,	Dido	5.1.36	Hermes
If that be all, then cheare thy drooping lookes,	Dido	5.1.71	Iarbus
And all the world calles me a second Helen,	Dido	5.1.144	Dido
And all thy needie followers Noblemen?	Dido	5.1.164	Dido
Which seene to all, though he beheld me not,	Dido	5.1.237	Anna
How can ye goe when he hath all your fleete?	Dido	5.1.242	Anna
And all the Sailers merrie make for joy,	Dido	5.1.259	Dido
And he hath all [my] <thy> fleete, what shall I doe/But dye in	Dido	5.1.268	Dido
That shall consume all that this stranger left,	Dido	5.1.285	Dido
These letters, lines, and perjurd papers all,	Dido	5.1.300	Dido
And order all things at your high dispose,	Dido	5.1.303	Dido
Meaning to mangle all thy Provinces.	1Tamb	1.1.17	Cosroe
Therefore tis best, if so it lik you all,	1Tamb	1.1.51	Mycet
And with thy lookes thou conquerest all thy foes:	1Tamb	1.1.75	Mycet
All loden with the heads of killed men.	1Tamb	1.1.78	Mycet
to them, that all Asia/Lament to see the follie of their King.	1Tamb	1.1.95	Cosroe
And made their spoiles from all our provinces.	1Tamb	1.1.122	Cosroe
Therefore to stay all sodaine mutinies,	1Tamb	1.1.150	Ceneus
Chiefe Lord of all the wide vast Euxine sea,	1Tamb	1.1.167	Ortyg
In spite of all suspected enemies.	1Tamb	1.1.186	Ortyg
I know it wel my Lord, and thanke you all.	1Tamb	1.1.187	Cosroe
Where all my youth I have bene governed,	1Tamb	1.2.13	Zenoc
Not all the Gold in Indias welthy armes,	1Tamb	1.2.85	Tamb
Shall all we offer to Zenocrate,	1Tamb	1.2.104	Tamb
Sent from the King to overcome us all.	1Tamb	1.2.112	Souldr
an hot alarme/Drive all their horses headlong down the hill.	1Tamb	1.2.135	Usumc
Keep all your standings, and not stir a foote,	1Tamb	1.2.150	Tamb
do but joine with me/And we will triumph over all the world.	1Tamb	1.2.173	Tamb
Shall vaile to us, as Lords of all the Lake.	1Tamb	1.2.196	Tamb
And sit with Tamburlaine in all his majestie.	1Tamb	1.2.209	Tamb
And kingdomes at the least we all expect,	1Tamb	1.2.218	Usumc
shall confesse/Theise are the men that all the world admires.	1Tamb	1.2.223	Usumc
Welcome renowmed Persean to us all.	1Tamb	1.2.239	Techel
A pearle more worth, then all the world is plaste:	1Tamb	2.1.12	Menaph
And all conjoin'd to meet the witlesse King,	1Tamb	2.1.64	Cosroe
Beside the spoile of him and all his traine:	1Tamb	2.2.34	Meandr
All running headlong after greedy spoiles:	1Tamb	2.2.45	Meandr
We have our Cammels laden all with gold:	1Tamb	2.2.62	Meandr
In thy approoved Fortunes all my hope,	1Tamb	2.3.2	Cosroe
And makes a passage for all prosperous Armes,	1Tamb	2.3.38	Cosroe
That I with these my friends and all my men,	1Tamb	2.3.43	Tamb
as outwaies the sands/And all the craggie rockes of Caspea.	1Tamb	2.3.48	Tamb

ALL (cont.)

And chiefest Counsailor in all his acts,	1Tamb	2.5.11	Cosroe
And sought your state all honor it deserv'd,	1Tamb	2.5.33	Ortyg
Then will we march to all those Indian Mines,	1Tamb	2.5.41	Cosroe
(Staying to order all the scattered troopes)/Farewell Lord	1Tamb	2.5.45	Cosroe
I, if I could with all my heart my Lord.	1Tamb	2.5.68	Techel
And would not all our souldiers soone consent,	1Tamb	2.5.78	Tamb
And if I prosper, all shall be as sure,	1Tamb	2.5.84	Tamb
And since we all have suckt one wholsome aire,	1Tamb	2.6.25	Cosroe
and all the Starres that make/The loathsome Circle of my dated	1Tamb	2.6.36	Cosroe
Doth teach us all to have aspyring minds:	1Tamb	2.7.20	Tamb
Untill we reach the ripest fruit of all,	1Tamb	2.7.27	Tamb
And sommons all my sences to depart.	1Tamb	2.7.45	Cosroe
Not all the curses which the furies breathe,	1Tamb	2.7.53	Tamb
And all the earthly Potentates conspire,	1Tamb	2.7.59	Tamb
And all pronounst me king of Persea.	1Tamb	2.7.67	Tamb
For all flesh quakes at your magnificence.	1Tamb	3.1.48	Argier
All this is true as holy Mahomet,	1Tamb	3.1.54	Bajzth
And all the trees are blasted with our breathes.	1Tamb	3.1.55	Bajzth
And all the sea my Gallies countermaund.	1Tamb	3.1.63	Bajzth
And all that pierceth Phoebes silver eie,	1Tamb	3.2.19	Agidas
(Auster and Aquilon with winged Steads/All sweating, tilt about	1Tamb	3.2.79	Agidas
strike flames of lightening)/All fearefull foldes his sailes,	1Tamb	3.2.82	Agidas
And rifle all those stately Janisars.	1Tamb	3.3.26	Techel
And all his Captaines that thus stoutly stand,	1Tamb	3.3.79	Bajzth
Why stay we thus prolonging all their lives?	1Tamb	3.3.97	Techel
Fight all couragiously and be you kings.	1Tamb	3.3.101	Tamb
of a bigger size/Than all the brats ysprong from Typhons loins:	1Tamb	3.3.109	Bajzth
And all his Captains bound in captive chaines.	1Tamb	3.3.115	Bajzth
untill thou see/Me martch victoriously with all my men,	1Tamb	3.3.127	Tamb
Which lately made all Europe quake for feare:	1Tamb	3.3.135	Bajzth
Arabians, Moores and Jewes/Enough to cover all Bythinia.	1Tamb	3.3.137	Bajzth
The field is ours, the Turk, his wife and all.	1Tamb	3.3.163	Tamb
Not all the world shall ransom Bajazeth.	1Tamb	3.3.232	Tamb
And all the Ocean by the British shore.	1Tamb	3.3.259	Tamb
Let him take all th'advantages he can,	1Tamb	4.1.40	Souldn
His resolution far exceedeth all:	1Tamb	4.1.48	2Msngr
He raceth all his foes with fire and sword.	1Tamb	4.1.63	2Msngr
For I the chiefest Lamp of all the earth,	1Tamb	4.2.36	Tamb
Fill all the aire with fiery meteors.	1Tamb	4.2.52	Tamb
Not all the Kings and Emperours of the Earth:	1Tamb	4.2.92	Tamb
So shall he have his life, and all the rest.	1Tamb	4.2.115	Tamb
Were in that citie all the world contain'd,	1Tamb	4.2.121	Tamb
And all the friendes of faire Zenocrate,	1Tamb	4.4.88	Tamb
Shead from the heads and hearts of all our Sex,	1Tamb	5.1.26	1Virgn
Before all hope of rescue were denied,	1Tamb	5.1.38	Govnr
Now waxe all pale and withered to the death,	1Tamb	5.1.91	1Virgn
For us, for infants, and for all our bloods,	1Tamb	5.1.97	1Virgn
For all the wealth of Gehons golden waves.	1Tamb	5.1.123	Tamb
Than all my Army to Damascus walles.	1Tamb	5.1.156	Tamb
If all the pens that ever poets held,	1Tamb	5.1.161	Tamb
If all the heavenly Quintessence they still/From their	1Tamb	5.1.165	Tamb
made one Poems period/And all combin'd in Beauties worthinesse,	1Tamb	5.1.170	Tamb
Shal give the world to note, for all my byrth,	1Tamb	5.1.188	Tamb
Or roaring Cannons sever all thy joints,	1Tamb	5.1.223	Bajzth
Let all the swords and Lances in the field,	1Tamb	5.1.225	Zabina
That all the world will see and laugh to scorne,	1Tamb	5.1.252	Zabina
Infecting all the Ghosts with curelesse griefs:	1Tamb	5.1.258	Bajzth
Since other meanes are all forbidden me,	1Tamb	5.1.288	Bajzth
To drive all sorrow from my fainting soule:	1Tamb	5.1.429	Arabia
Since I shall render all into your hands.	1Tamb	5.1.447	Tamb
(Renowmed Tamburlain) to whom all kings/Of force must yeeld	1Tamb	5.1.480	Souldn
And for all blot of foule inchastity,	1Tamb	5.1.486	Tamb
And all the kingdomes and dominions/That late the power of	1Tamb	5.1.508	Tamb
Then after all these solemne Exequies,	1Tamb	5.1.533	Tamb
We all are glutted with the Christians blood,	2Tamb	1.1.14	Gazell
Since Tamburlaine hath mustred all his men,	2Tamb	1.1.46	Gazell
of our Empery/Once lost, All Turkie would be overthrowne:	2Tamb	1.1.56	Orcan
All Asia is in Armes with Tamburlaine.	2Tamb	1.1.72	Orcan
All Affrike is in Armes with Tamburlaine.	2Tamb	1.1.76	Orcan
basely on their knees/In all your names desirde a truce of me?	2Tamb	1.1.97	Orcan
So am I fear'd among all Nations.	2Tamb	1.1.151	Orcan
I thank thee Sigismond, but when I war/All Asia Minor, Affrica,	2Tamb	1.1.158	Orcan
Not for all Affrike, therefore moove me not.	2Tamb	1.2.12	Almeda
kings and more/Upon their knees, all bid me welcome home.	2Tamb	1.2.29	Callap
Choose which thou wilt, all are at thy command.	2Tamb	1.2.31	Callap
shine as bright/As that faire vail that covers all the world:	2Tamb	1.2.50	Callap
And more than this, for all I cannot tell.	2Tamb	1.2.53	Callap
in mine eies/Than all the wealthy kingdomes I subdewed:	2Tamb	1.3.19	Tamb
As all the world shall tremble at their view.	2Tamb	1.3.57	Celeb
They are enough to conquer all the world/And you have won	2Tamb	1.3.67	Calyph
Of all the provinces I have subdued/Thou shalt not have a foot,	2Tamb	1.3.71	Tamb
When we shall meet the Turkish Deputie/And all his Viceroies,	2Tamb	1.3.100	Tamb
My crowne, my selfe, and all the power I have,	2Tamb	1.3.115	Therid
In all affection at thy kingly feet.	2Tamb	1.3.116	Therid
All which have sworne to sacke Natolia:	2Tamb	1.3.121	Therid
And all the men in armour under me,	2Tamb	1.3.135	Usumc
All Barbary is unpeopled for thy sake.	2Tamb	1.3.149	Techel
If all the christall gates of Joves high court/Were opened	2Tamb	1.3.153	Tamb
With all his viceroies shall be so affraide,	2Tamb	1.3.162	Tamb
And all the land unto the coast of Spaine.	2Tamb	1.3.179	Usumc
then that your Majesty/Take all advantages of time and power,	2Tamb	2.1.12	Fredrk
That strikes a terrour to all Turkish hearts,	2Tamb	2.1.15	Fredrk

ALL (cont.)

Natolia hath dismist the greatest part/Of all his armie, pitcht	2Tamb	2.1.17	Fredrk
We may discourage all the pagan troope,	2Tamb	2.1.25	Fredrk
Worthy the worship of all faithfull hearts,	2Tamb	2.2.57	Orcan
Discomfited is all the Christian hoste,	2Tamb	2.3.1	Sgsmnd
End all my penance in my sodaine death,	2Tamb	2.3.7	Sgsmnd
And all with faintnesse and for foule disgrace,	2Tamb	2.4.5	Tamb
her latest breath/All dasled with the hellish mists of death.	2Tamb	2.4.14	Tamb
Use all their voices and their instruments/To entertaine divine	2Tamb	2.4.28	Tamb
And shiver all the starry firmament:	2Tamb	2.4.106	Tamb
And all this raging cannot make her live,	2Tamb	2.4.120	Therid
If teares, our eies have watered all the earth:	2Tamb	2.4.122	Therid
your royall gratitudes/With all the benefits my Empire yeelds:	2Tamb	3.1.9	Callap
As all the world should blot our dignities/Out of the booke of	2Tamb	3.1.18	Callap
All bordring on the Mare-major sea:	2Tamb	3.1.51	Trebiz
The cursed Scythian sets on all their townes,	2Tamb	3.1.55	Trebiz
All which will joine against this Tamburlain,	2Tamb	3.1.61	Soria
Perfourming all your promise to the full:	2Tamb	3.1.76	Jrslem
this table as a Register/Of all her vertues and perfections.	2Tamb	3.2.24	Celeb
Upon the heads of all our enemies.	2Tamb	3.2.42	Tamb
And see him lance his flesh to teach you all.	2Tamb	3.2.114	Tamb
And in my blood wash all your hands at once,	2Tamb	3.2.127	Tamb
And treble all his fathers slaveries.	2Tamb	3.2.158	Tamb
Wherein is all the treasure of the land.	2Tamb	3.3.4	Therid
That with his ruine fils up all the trench.	2Tamb	3.3.26	Therid
Cut off the water, all convoies that can,	2Tamb	3.3.39	Capt
I feele my liver pierc'd and all my vaines,	2Tamb	3.4.6	Capt
and all my entrals bath'd/In blood that straineth from their	2Tamb	3.4.8	Capt
Gods great lieftenant over all the world:	2Tamb	3.5.2	2Msngr
Whet all your swords to mangle Tamburlain,	2Tamb	3.5.15	Callap
hands)/All brandishing their brands of quenchlesse fire,	2Tamb	3.5.27	Orcan
that ever brandisht sword)/Challenge in combat any of you all,	2Tamb	3.5.72	Tamb
And all have jointly sworne thy cruell death,	2Tamb	3.5.112	Soria
while all thy joints/Be rackt and beat asunder with the wheele,	2Tamb	3.5.124	Tamb
Loden with Lawrell wreathes to crowne us all.	2Tamb	3.5.164	Tamb
You shall be princes all immediatly:	2Tamb	3.5.168	Tamb
Were all the lofty mounts of Zona mundi,	2Tamb	4.1.42	Amyras
sonnes have had no shares/In all the honors he proposde for us.	2Tamb	4.1.48	Amyras
which all the good I have/Join'd with my fathers crowne would	2Tamb	4.1.57	Calyph
Fill all the aire with troublous bellowing:	2Tamb	4.1.190	Tamb
Commanding all thy princely eie desires,	2Tamb	4.2.43	Therid
As all the world cannot affoord the like.	2Tamb	4.2.57	Olymp
And simplest extracts of all Minerals,	2Tamb	4.2.61	Olymp
From whence the starres doo borrow all their light,	2Tamb	4.2.89	Therid
Whose body shall be tomb'd with all the pompe/The treasure of	2Tamb	4.2.97	Therid
Survaieng all the glories of the land:	2Tamb	4.3.35	Orcan
Before I conquere all the triple world.	2Tamb	4.3.63	Tamb
And let them equally serve all your turnes.	2Tamb	4.3.73	Tamb
And common souldiers jest with all their Truls.	2Tamb	4.3.91	Tamb
When all the Gods stand gazing at his pomp:	2Tamb	4.3.129	Tamb
Have we not hope, for all our battered walles,	2Tamb	5.1.15	Govnr
That made us all the labour for the towne,	2Tamb	5.1.82	Therid
That with his sword hath quail'd all earthly kings,	2Tamb	5.1.93	Tamb
Do all thy wurst, nor death, nor Tamburlaine,	2Tamb	5.1.112	Govnr
Then for all your valour, you would save your life.	2Tamb	5.1.119	Tamb
Yet shouldst thou die, shoot at him all at once.	2Tamb	5.1.157	Tamb
that all [Assiria] <Affrica>/Which hath bene subject to the	2Tamb	5.1.165	Tamb
Techelles, Drowne them all, man, woman, and child,	2Tamb	5.1.170	Tamb
And all the heapes of supersticious bookes,	2Tamb	5.1.174	Tamb
Slew all his Priests, his kinsmen, and his friends,	2Tamb	5.1.181	Tamb
To triumph after all our victories.	2Tamb	5.1.213	Tamb
Where Tamburlaine with all his armie lies,	2Tamb	5.2.6	Callap
To be reveng'd of all his Villanie.	2Tamb	5.2.23	Callap
And make him after all these overthrowes,	2Tamb	5.2.29	Callap
Yet might your mighty hoste incounter all,	2Tamb	5.2.39	Amasia
Are greatest to discourage all our drifts,	2Tamb	5.2.45	Callap
All Turkie is in armes with Callapine.	2Tamb	5.2.51	Callap
No doubt, but you shal soone recover all.	2Tamb	5.3.99	Phsitn
Then will I comfort all my vital parts,	2Tamb	5.3.100	Tamb
There should not one of all the villaines power/Live to give	2Tamb	5.3.108	Tamb
let me see how much/Is left for me to conquer all the world,	2Tamb	5.3.124	Tamb
That these my boies may finish all my wantes.	2Tamb	5.3.125	Tamb
I conquered all as far as Zansibar.	2Tamb	5.3.139	Tamb
Loe here my sonnes, are all the golden Mines,	2Tamb	5.3.151	Tamb
that shine as bright/As all the Lamps that beautifie the Sky,	2Tamb	5.3.157	Tamb
And live in all your seedes immortally:	2Tamb	5.3.174	Tamb
Nor may our hearts all drown'd in teares of blood,	2Tamb	5.3.214	Usumc
were scortcht/And all the earth like Aetna breathing fire:	2Tamb	5.3.233	Tamb
For earth hath spent the pride of all her fruit,	2Tamb	5.3.250	Amyras
easily in a day/Tell that which may maintaine him all his life.	Jew	1.1.11	Barab
And all his life time hath bin tired,	Jew	1.1.15	Barab
And all the Merchants with other Merchandize/Are safe arriv'd,	Jew	1.1.51	1Merch
For I can see no fruits in all their faith,	Jew	1.1.116	Barab
And all I have is hers. But who comes here?	Jew	1.1.139	Barab
Nay let 'em combat, conquer, and kill all,	Jew	1.1.152	Barab
I feare their comming will afflict us all.	Jew	1.1.156	2Jew
And all the Jewes in Malta must be there.	Jew	1.1.168	2Jew
Umh; All the Jewes in Malta must be there?	Jew	1.1.169	Barab
Which Tribute all in policie, I feare,	Jew	1.1.181	Barab
As all the wealth of Malta cannot pay;	Jew	1.1.183	Barab
Stand all aside, and let the Knights determine,	Jew	1.2.14	Calym
And all good fortune wait on Calymath.	Jew	1.2.33	Govnr
mony of the Turkes shall all be levyed amongst the Jewes,	Jew	1.2.68	P Reader

ALL (cont.)

Either pay that, or we will seize on all.	Jew	1.2.89	Govnr
And make thee poore and scorn'd of all the world, . .	Jew	1.2.108	1Knght
Some Jewes are wicked, as all Christians are:	Jew	1.2.112	Barab
that I descended of/Were all in generall cast away for sinne,	Jew	1.2.114	Barab
which being valued/Amount to more then all the wealth in Malta.	Jew	1.2.134	Offcrs
My ships, my store, and all that I enjoy'd;	Jew	1.2.139	Barab
And having all, you can request no more;	Jew	1.2.140	Barab
flinty hearts/Suppresse all pitty in your stony breasts, .	Jew	1.2.142	Barab
Earths barrennesse, and all mens hatred/Inflict upon them, thou	Jew	1.2.163	Barab
And of me onely have they taken all.	Jew	1.2.179	Barab
And in the Senate reprehend them all, ...	Jew	1.2.233	Abigal
thinke me not all so fond/As negligently to forgoe so much	Jew	1.2.241	Barab
My gold, my gold, and all my wealth is gone. . . .	Jew	1.2.258	Barab
As much I hope as all I hid is worth.	Jew	1.2.336	Barab
Welcome to Malta, and to all of us;	Jew	2.2.20	Govnr
He'de give us present mony for them all.	Jew	2.3.6	1Offcr
Seiz'd all I had, and thrust me out a doores. . . .	Jew	2.3.76	Barab
All that I have shall be at your command.	Jew	2.3.137	Barab
the Governors sonne/With all the curtesie you can affoord;	Jew	2.3.226	Barab
Not for all Malta, therefore sheath your sword; . .	Jew	2.3.270	Barab
But all are Hereticks that are not Jewes;	Jew	2.3.312	Barab
I know not, and that grieves me most of all. . . .	Jew	3.2.21	Govnr
And all unknowne, and unconstrain'd of me, ...	Jew	3.4.3	Barab
All that I have is thine when I am dead, ...	Jew	3.4.44	Barab
And all the poysons of the Stygian poole/Breake from the fiery	Jew	3.4.102	Barab
The wind that bloweth all the world besides, ...	Jew	3.5.3	Basso
Oh brother, brother, all the Nuns are sicke, ...	Jew	3.6.1	1Fryar
What, all dead save onely Abigall?	Jew	3.6.7	2Fryar
And one offence torments me more then all. . . .	Jew	3.6.19	Abigal
Oh brother, all the Nuns are dead, let's bury them. . .	Jew	3.6.44	1Fryar
Now all are dead, not one remaines alive.	Jew	4.1.7	Barab
Good master let me poyson all the Monks.	Jew	4.1.14	Ithimr
What needs all this? I know I am a Jew.	Jew	4.1.33	Barab
for store of wealth may I compare/With all the Jewes in Malta;	Jew	4.1.56	Barab
All this I'le give to some religious house/So I may be baptiz'd	Jew	4.1.75	Barab
You shall convert me, you shall have all my wealth. . .	Jew	4.1.81	Barab
and I am resolv'd/You shall confesse me, and have all my goods.	Jew	4.1.86	Barab
men to suppose/That I will leave my house, my goods, and all,	Jew	4.1.123	Barab
'Tis neatly done, Sir, here's no print at all. . . .	Jew	4.1.151	Ithimr
Otherwise I'le confesse all:--	Jew	4.2.78	P Ithimr
Oh, if that be all, I can picke ope your locks. . .	Jew	4.3.33	Pilia
no childe, and unto whom/Should I leave all but unto Ithimore?	Jew	4.3.45	Barab
Well, I must seeke a meanes to rid 'em all, ...	Jew	4.3.63	Barab
his villany/He will tell all he knowes and I shall dye for't.	Jew	4.3.65	Barab
Nay, I'le have all or none.	Jew	4.4.5	Curtzn
So, now I am reveng'd upon 'em all.	Jew	4.4.42	Barab
Pardona moy, be no in tune yet; so, now, now all be in. .	Jew	4.4.45	P Barab
now at my lodging/That was his Agent, he'll confesse it all.	Jew	5.1.17	Curtzn
One dram of powder more had made all sure.	Jew	5.1.22	Barab
What, all alone? well fare sleepy drinke.	Jew	5.1.61	Barab
May all good fortune follow Calymath.	Jew	5.2.21	Barab
shut/His souldiers, till I have consum'd 'em all with fire?	Jew	5.2.82	Barab
That at one instant all things may be done, ...	Jew	5.2.120	Barab
serve to entertaine/Selim and all his souldiers for a month;	Jew	5.3.31	Msngr
With all thy Bashawes and brave followers.	Jew	5.3.39	Msngr
Are all the Cranes and Pulleyes sure?	Jew	5.5.2	Barab
All fast.	Jew	5.5.2	Servnt
Leave nothing loose, all leveld to my mind.	Jew	5.5.3	Barab
Downe to the Celler, taste of all my wines.	Jew	5.5.7	Barab
For so I live, perish may all the world.	Jew	5.5.10	Barab
He will; and has commanded all his men/To come ashore, and march	Jew	5.5.14	Msngr
Then now are all things as my wish wud have 'em, . . .	Jew	5.5.17	Barab
And batter all the stones about their eares, ...	Jew	5.5.30	Barab
Governour, why stand you all so pittilesse?	Jew	5.5.71	Barab
I would have brought confusion on you all, ...	Jew	5.5.85	Barab
My men are all aboord, ...	Jew	5.5.103	Calym
Blowne up, and all thy souldiers massacred.	Jew	5.5.107	Govnr
Malta prisoner; for come [all] <call> the world/To rescue thee,	Jew	5.5.119	Govnr
That seekes to murder all the Protestants:	P 31	1.31	Navrre
That all the protestants that are in Paris, ...	P 34	1.34	Navrre
Shall fully shew the fury of them all.	P 65	2.8	Guise
Or with seditions weary all the worlde:	P 116	2.59	Guise
All this and more, if more may be comprisde, ...	P 143	2.86	Guise
Since thou hast all the Cardes within thy hands/To shuffle or	P 146	2.89	Guise
Oh fatall was this mariage to us all.	P 202	3.37	Admral
At which they all shall issue out and set the streetes. .	P 237	4.35	Guise
And make a shew as if all were well.	P 250	4.48	QnMoth
see they keep/All trecherous violence from our noble freend,	P 268	4.66	Charls
Repaying all attempts with present death, ...	P 269	4.67	Charls
To kill all that you suspect of heresie.	P 276	5.3	Guise
And therfore meane to murder all I meet.	P 279	5.6	Anjoy
All that I have is but my stipend from the King, . . .	P 378	7.18	Ramus
Marry sir, in having a smack in all, ...	P 385	7.25	Guise
Because my places being but three, contains all his: .	P 405	7.45	Ramus
My Lord, they say/That all the protestants are massacred.	P 432	7.72	Navrre
All this and more your highnes shall commaund, ...	P 479	8.29	Lord
no, to decide all doubts, be rulde by me, lets hang him heere	P 491	9.10	P 2Atndt
For to revenge their deaths upon us all.	P 518	9.37	Cardnl
Ile disinherite him and all the rest:	P 524	9.43	QnMoth
We will with all the speed we can, provide/For Henries .	P 562	11.27	QnMoth
Whose army shall discomfort all your foes, ...	P 579	11.44	Pleshe
In spite of Spaine and all the popish power, ...	P 581	11.46	Pleshe

ALL (cont.)

Truth Pleshe, and God so prosper me in all,	P 584	11.49	Navrre
And all things that a King may wish besides:	P 595	12.8	QnMoth
All this and more hath Henry with his crowne.	P 596	12.9	QnMoth
And long may Henry enjoy all this and more.	P 597	12.10	Cardnl
The guider of all crownes,/Graunt that our deeds may wel	P 599	12.12	King
And all his heaven is to delight himselfe:	P 634	12.47	QnMoth
Tush, all shall dye unles I have my will:	P 653	12.66	QnMoth
What, all alone my love, and writing too:	P 670	13.14	Guise
Is all my love forgot which helde thee deare?	P 684	13.28	Guise
In spite of Spaine and all his heresies.	P 716	14.19	Bartus
Of all my army now in readines,	P 744	15.2	King
And sure if all the proudest Kings/In Christendome, should	P 760	15.18	Guise
And heer by all the Saints in heaven I sweare,	P 765	15.23	Guise
If that be all, the next time that I meet her,	P 781	15.39	Mugern
The Duke is slaine and all his power dispearst,	P 787	16.1	Navrre
Else all France knowes how poor a Duke thou art.	P 844	17.39	Eprnon
I meane to muster all the power I can,	P 849	17.44	Guise
Make a discharge of all my counsell straite,	P 882	17.77	King
And so to quite your grace of all suspect.	P 889	17.84	Eprnon
Assure him all the aide we can provide,	P 909	18.10	Navrre
And all his Minions stoup when I commaund:	P 979	19.49	Guise
And all my former time was spent in vaine:	P 986	19.56	Guise
And heere in presence of you all I sweare,	P1026	19.96	King
(As all the world shall know our Guise is dead)/Rest satisfied	P1042	19.112	King
The Popedome cannot stand, all goes to wrack,	P1087	19.157	QnMoth
And all for thee my Guise: what may I doe?	P1088	19.158	QnMoth
Upon whose heart may all the furies gripe,	P1101	20.11	Cardnl
And all those traitors to the Church of Rome,	P1120	21.14	Dumain
With all the honors and affections,	P1145	22.7	King
For all the wealth and treasure of the world.	P1163	22.25	King
Sweet Eperncune all Rebels under heaven,	P1185	22.47	King
Tell her for all this that I hope to live,	P1196	22.58	King
As Rome and all those popish Prelates there,	P1248	22.110	Navrre
If I speed well, ile entertaine you all.	Edw	1.1.46	Gavstn
All Warwickshire will love him for my sake.	Edw	1.1.128	Warwck
And all the court begins to flatter him.	Edw	1.2.22	Lncstr
All stomack him, but none dare speake a word.	Edw	1.2.26	Lncstr
Were all the Earles and Barons of my minde,	Edw	1.2.28	Mortmr
My lords, to eaze all this, but heare me speake.	Edw	1.2.68	ArchBp
And in the meane time ile intreat you all,	Edw	1.2.77	ArchBp
My lords, now let us all be resolute,	Edw	1.4.45	Mortmr
And share it equally amongst you all,	Edw	1.4.71	Edward
Because he loves me more then all the world:	Edw	1.4.77	Edward
Is all my hope turnd to this hell of greefe.	Edw	1.4.116	Gavstn
To sue unto you all for his repeale:	Edw	1.4.201	Queene
All that he speakes, is nothing, we are resolv'd.	Edw	1.4.251	Warwck
As he will front the mightiest of us all,	Edw	1.4.260	Mortmr
And smelling to a Nosegay all the day,	Edw	2.1.35	Spencr
If all things sort out, as I hope they will,	Edw	2.1.79	Neece
And gets unto the highest bough of all,	Edw	2.2.19	Mortmr
Which all the other fishes deadly hate,	Edw	2.2.24	Lncstr
Sweete husband be content, they all love you.	Edw	2.2.36	Queene
Nay all of them conspire to crosse me thus,	Edw	2.2.95	Edward
Why how now cosin, how fares all our friends?	Edw	2.2.114	Lncstr
Complaines, that thou hast left her all forlorne.	Edw	2.2.173	Lncstr
Heere comes she thats cause of all these jarres.	Edw	2.2.224	Edward
And all in vaine, for when I speake him faire,	Edw	2.4.28	Queene
Lets all aboord, and follow him amaine.	Edw	2.4.47	Mortmr
Breathing, in hope (malgrado all your beards,	Edw	2.5.5	Gavstn
I thanke you all my lords, then I perceive,	Edw	2.5.29	Gavstn
And death is all.	Edw	2.5.31	Gavstn
My lords, king Edward greetes you all by me.	Edw	2.5.33	Arundl
bestow/His teares on that, for that is all he gets/Of Gaveston,	Edw	2.5.53	Mortmr
O must this day be period of my life,/Center of all my blisse!	Edw	2.6.5	Gavstn
For favors done in him, unto us all.	Edw	3.1.42	SpncrP
That powres in lieu of all your goodnes showne,	Edw	3.1.44	Spencr
Souldiers a largis, and thrice welcome all.	Edw	3.1.57	Edward
Sib, if this be all/Valoys and I will soone be friends againe.	Edw	3.1.66	Edward
With all the hast we can dispatch him hence.	Edw	3.1.83	Edward
I did your highnes message to them all,	Edw	3.1.96	Arundl
Yea Spencer, traitors all.	Edw	3.1.102	Edward
By earth, the common mother of us all,	Edw	3.1.128	Edward
By heaven, and all the mooving orbes thereof,	Edw	3.1.129	Edward
And all the honors longing to my crowne,	Edw	3.1.131	Edward
our men with sweat and dust/All chockt well neare, begin to	Edw	3.1.192	SpncrP
I traitors all, rather then thus be bravde,	Edw	3.1.214	Edward
traitors, now tis time/To be avengd on you for all your braves,	Edw	3.1.225	Edward
Do speedie execution on them all,	Edw	3.1.254	Edward
That therewith all enchaunted like the guarde,	Edw	3.1.266	Spencr
of golde/To Danae, all aide may be denied/To Isabell the Queene,	Edw	3.1.268	Spencr
It hath my lord, the warders all a sleepe,	Edw	4.1.15	Mortmr
A boye, our friends do faile us all in Fraunce,	Edw	4.2.1	Queene
and then a Fig/For all my unckles frienship here in Fraunce.	Edw	4.2.5	Prince
And shake off all our fortunes equallie?	Edw	4.2.20	SrJohn
Tould us at our arrivall all the newes,	Edw	4.2.48	Mortmr
Would all were well, and Edward well reclaimd,	Edw	4.2.57	Kent
I thinke king Edward will out-run us all.	Edw	4.2.68	Prince
Binde us in kindenes all at your commaund.	Edw	4.2.73	Kent
that the Queene all discontented and discomforted, is gone,	Edw	4.3.30	P Spencr
this is all the newes of import.	Edw	4.3.36	P Spencr
Your honors in all service, [Levune] <Lewne>.	Edw	4.3.37	P Spencr
England shall welcome you, and all your route.	Edw	4.3.42	Edward

ALL (cont.)

Welcome to England all with prosperous windes,	Edw	4.4.2	Queene
Misgoverned kings are cause of all this wrack,	Edw	4.4.9	Queene
And Edward thou art one among them all,	Edw	4.4.10	Queene
Heere for our countries cause sweare we to him/All homage,	Edw	4.4.20	Mortmr
Vilde wretch, and why hast thou of all unkinde,	Edw	4.6.5	Kent
As to your wisdomes fittest seemes in all.	Edw	4.6.29	Queene
We thanke you all.	Edw	4.6.53	Queene
Some whirle winde fetche them backe, or sincke them all:--	Edw	4.6.59	Mortmr
And all the land I know is up in armes,	Edw	4.7.31	Spencr
the last of all my blisse on earth,/Center of all misfortune.	Edw	4.7.61	Edward
Center of all misfortune. O my starres!	Edw	4.7.62	Edward
Reduce we all our lessons unto this,	Edw	4.7.110	Baldck
To die sweet Spencer, therefore live wee all,	Edw	4.7.111	Baldck
Spencer, all live to die, and rise to fall.	Edw	4.7.112	Baldck
All times and seasons rest you at a stay,	Edw	5.1.67	Edward
He of you all that most desires my bloud,	Edw	5.1.100	Edward
Whether you will, all places are alike,	Edw	5.1.145	Edward
That death ends all, and I can die but once.	Edw	5.1.153	Edward
To erect your sonne with all the speed we may,	Edw	5.2.11	Mortmr
Seeke all the meanes thou canst to make him droope,	Edw	5.2.54	Mortmr
And tell him, that I labour all in vaine,	Edw	5.2.70	Queene
Use Edmund friendly, as if all were well.	Edw	5.2.79	Queene
Whose sight is loathsome to all winged fowles?	Edw	5.3.7	Edward
When all my sences are anoyde with stenche?	Edw	5.3.18	Edward
But all in vaine, so vainely do I strive,	Edw	5.3.35	Edward
O levell all your lookes upon these daring men,	Edw	5.3.39	Edward
And when I frowne, make all the court looke pale,	Edw	5.4.53	Mortmr
Now is all sure, the Queene and Mortimer/Shall rule the realme,	Edw	5.4.65	Mortmr
Thats all?	Edw	5.5.34	Gurney
Foh, heeres a place in deed with all my hart.	Edw	5.5.41	Ltborn
Wherein the filthe of all the castell falles.	Edw	5.5.57	Edward
All tremble at my name, and I feare none,	Edw	5.6.13	Mortmr
Excelling all, [whose sweete delight's] dispute/In th'heavenly	F 18	Prol.18	1Chor
Excelling all, <whose sweete delight disputes>	F 18	(HC256)A	1Chor
Excelling all, <and sweetly can dispute>	F 18	(HC256)B	1Chor
When all is done, Divinitie is best:	F 64	1.1.36	Faust
All things that move betweene the quiet Poles/Shall be at my	F 83	1.1.55	Faust
Then all my labours, plod I ne're so fast.	F 96	1.1.68	Faust
Art/Wherein all natures [treasury] <treasure> is contain'd:	F 102	1.1.74	BdAngl
Resolve me of all ambiguities?	F 107	1.1.79	Faust
And search all corners of the new-found-world/For pleasant	F 111	1.1.83	Faust
And tell the secrets of all forraine Kings:	F 114	1.1.86	Faust
I'le have them wall all Germany with Brasse,	F 115	1.1.87	Faust
And raigne sole King of all [our] Provinces.	F 121	1.1.93	Faust
Whose [shadows] made all Europe honour him.	F 145	1.1.117	Faust
Shall make all Nations to Canonize us:	F 147	1.1.119	Valdes
Hath all the Principles Magick doth require:	F 167	1.1.139	Cornel
And fetch the treasure of all forraine wrackes:	F 172	1.1.144	Cornel
Yea <I> all the wealth that our fore-fathers hid,	F 173	1.1.145	Cornel
And then all other ceremonies learn'd,	F 186	1.1.158	Cornel
conjuring/Is stoutly to abjure [the Trinity] <all godlinesse>,	F 281	1.3.53	Mephst
Arch-regent and Commander of all Spirits.	F 291	1.3.63	Mephst
Letting him live in all voluptuousnesse,	F 320	1.3.92	Faust
I'de give them all for Mephostophilis.	F 331	1.3.103	Faust
I'le turne all the lice about thee into Familiars, and make	F 362	1.4.20	P Wagner
conditionally, that thou performe/All Covenants, and Articles,	F 480	2.1.92	Faust
All <articles prescrib'd> <covenant-articles> betweene us both.	F 480	(HC260)	Faust
To effect all promises betweene us [made] <both>.	F 482	2.1.94	Mephst
at all times, in what shape [or] <and> forme soever he please.	F 491	2.1.103	P Faust
I, so are all things else; but whereabouts <where about>?	F 507	2.1.119	Faust
And to be short <conclude>, when all the world dissolves,	F 513	2.1.125	Mephst
All places shall be hell that is not heaven.	F 515	2.1.127	Mephst
Are all Celestiall bodies but one Globe,	F 587	2.2.36	Faust
And <Faustus all> jointly move upon one Axle-tree,	F 592	2.2.41	Mephst
But <tell me> have they all/One motion, both situ et tempore?	F 595	2.2.44	Faust
All <joyntly> move from East to West, in foure and twenty	F 597	2.2.46	P Mephst
Eclipses, all at one time, but in some years we have more, in	F 615	2.2.64	P Faust
this house, you and all, should turne to Gold, that I might	F 676	2.2.125	P Covet
and all the people in it were turnd> to Gold,	F 676	(HC263)A	P Covet
cannot read, and therefore wish all books burn'd <were burnt>.	F 680	2.2.129	P Envy
O that there would come a famine over <through> all the world,	F 682	2.2.131	P Envy
<through> all the world, that all might die, and I live along,	F 682	2.2.131	P Envy
my parents are all dead, and the devill a peny they have left	F 693	2.2.142	P Glutny
Now Faustus thou hast heard all my progeny, wilt thou bid me to	F 700	2.2.149	P Glutny
<No, Ile see thee hanged, thou wilt eate up all my victualls>.	F 702	(HC264)A	P Faust
[Tut] <But> Faustus, in hell is all manner of delight.	F 713	2.2.165	Lucifr
let me be cloyd/With all things that delight the heart of man.	F 838	3.1.60	Faust
And in despite of all his Holinesse/Restore this Bruno to his	F 898	3.1.120	Faust
And all society of holy men:	F 910	3.1.132	Pope
Is not all power on earth bestowed on us?	F 930	3.1.152	Pope
Then he and thou, and all the world shall stoope,	F 937	3.1.159	Pope
By full consent of all the [reverend] <holy> Synod/Of Priests	F 952	3.1.174	Faust
With all our Colledge of grave Cardinals,	F 968	3.1.190	Pope
That I may walke invisible to all,	F 992	3.2.12	Faust
weare this girdle, then appeare/Invisible to all are here:	F 998	3.2.18	Mephst
So Faustus, now for all their holinesse,	F1004	3.2.24	Mephst
And see that all things be in readinesse,	F1011	3.2.31	Pope
we all are witnesses/That Bruno here was late delivered you,	F1025	3.2.45	Raymnd
Or by our sanctitude you all shall die.	F1057	3.2.77	Pope
The race of all his stout progenitors;	F1168	4.1.14	Mrtino
That all this day the sluggard keepes his bed.	F1176	4.1.22	Mrtino
Thou shalt be famous through all Italy,	F1215	4.1.61	Emper

ALL (cont.)

but for all that, I doe not greatly beleeve him, he lookes as	F1227	4.1.73	P	Benvol
to thinke I have beene such an Asse all this while, to stand	F1243	4.1.89	P	Benvol
in your head for shame, let not all the world wonder at you.	F1292	4.1.138	P	Faust
As all his footmanship shall scarce prevaile,	F1302	4.1.148		Faust
which being all I desire, I am content to remove his hornes.	F1313	4.1.159	P	Faust
And all alone, comes walking in his gowne;	F1358	4.2.34		Fredrk
this blow ends all,/Hell take his soule, his body thus must	F1362	4.2.38		Benvol
That all the world may see my just revenge.	F1382	4.2.58		Benvol
I, [all] <I call> your hearts to recompence this deed.	F1394	4.2.70		Faust
O hellish spite,/Your heads are all set with hornes.	F1442	4.3.12		Benvol
Nay chafe not man, we all are sped.	F1444	4.3.14		Mrtino
And make us laughing stockes to all the world.	F1450	4.3.20		Benvol
why will he not drink of all waters?	F1471	4.4.15	P	HrsCsr
he will drinke of all waters, but ride him not into the water;	F1472	4.4.16	P	Faust
he never left eating, till he had eate up all my loade of hay.	F1531	4.5.27	P	Carter
and whooping in his eares, but all could not wake him:	F1549	4.5.45	P	HrsCsr
This makes me wonder more then all the rest, that at this time	F1578	4.6.21	P	Duke
They all cry out to speake with Doctor Faustus.	F1600	4.6.43		Servnt
I have procur'd your pardons: welcome all.	F1610	4.6.53		Faust
or we'll breake all the barrels in the house, and dash out all	F1618	4.6.61	P	HrsCsr
in the house, and dash out all your braines with your Bottles.	F1619	4.6.62	P	HrsCsr
With all my heart kind Doctor, please thy selfe,	F1623	4.6.66		Duke
we will recompence/With all the love and kindnesse that we may.	F1672	4.6.115		Duke
His Artfull sport, drives all sad thoughts away.	F1673	4.6.116		Duke
which was the beautifullest in all the world, we have	F1682	5.1.9	P	1Schol
whom all the world admires for Majesty, we should thinke	F1686	5.1.13	P	1Schol
Whom all the world admires for majesty.	F1698	5.1.25		2Schol
[Whose heavenly beauty passeth all compare].	F1701	5.1.28A		3Schol
my exhortation/Seemes harsh, and all unpleasant; let it not,	F1718	5.1.45		OldMan
And all is drosse that is not Helena.	F1774	5.1.101		Faust
To over-reach the Divell, but all in vaine;	F1811	5.2.15		Mephst
As in all humble dutie, I do yeeld/My life and lasting service	F1818	5.2.22		Wagner
Is all our pleasure turn'd to melancholy?	F1828	5.2.32		2Schol
I have done, all Germany can witnesse, yea all the world:	F1842	5.2.46	P	Faust
I have done, all Germany can witnesse, yea all the world:	F1843	5.2.47	P	Faust
O what will all thy riches, pleasures, pompes,	F1896	5.2.100		GdAngl
But yet all these are nothing, thou shalt see/Ten thousand	F1919	5.2.123		BdAngl
Nay, thou must feele them, taste the smart of all:	F1922	5.2.126		BdAngl
'twill all be past anone:	F1957	5.2.161		Faust
All beasts are happy, for when they die,	F1969	5.2.173		Faust
All torne asunder by the hand of death.	F1989	5.3.7		2Schol
At which selfe time the house seem'd all on fire,	F1993	5.3.11		3Schol
And all the Students clothed in mourning blacke,	F2000	5.3.18		2Schol
divell, so I should be cald kill divell all the parish over.	F App	p.230 49	P	Clown
all hee divels has hornes, and all shee divels has clifts and	F App	p.230 53	P	Clown
has hornes, and all shee divels has clifts and cloven feete.	F App	p.230 53	P	Clown
Ifaith thats just nothing at all.	F App	p.237 40	P	Knight
which being all I desire, I am content to release him of his	F App	p.238 83	P	Faust
why sir, wil he not drinke of all waters?	F App	p.239 110	P	HrsCsr
As Wagner nere beheld in all his life.	F App	p.243 7		Wagner
First conquer all the earth, then turne thy force/Against	Lucan, First Booke			22
Time ends and to old Chaos all things turne;	Lucan, First Booke			74
All great things crush themselves, such end the gods/Allot the	Lucan, First Booke			81
O Roome thy selfe art cause of all these evils,	Lucan, First Booke			84
And all bands of that death presaging aliance.	Lucan, First Booke			114
Made all shake hands as once the Sabines did;	Lucan, First Booke			118
When all the woods about stand bolt up-right,	Lucan, First Booke			143
even the same that wrack's all great [dominions] <dominion>.	Lucan, First Booke			160
When fortune made us lords of all, wealth flowed,	Lucan, First Booke			161
Force mastered right, the strongest govern'd all.	Lucan, First Booke			177
And armes all naked, who with broken sighes,	Lucan, First Booke			191
This said, he laying aside all lets of war,	Lucan, First Booke			206
Predestinate to ruine; all lands else/Have stable peace, here	Lucan, First Booke			251
Or sea far from the land, so all were whist.	Lucan, First Booke			262
Infringing all excuse of modest shame,	Lucan, First Booke			266
successe/May bring her downe, and with her all the world;	Lucan, First Booke			286
Envy denies all, with thy bloud must thou/Abie thy conquest	Lucan, First Booke			289
share the world thou canst not;/Injoy it all thou maiest:	Lucan, First Booke			292
restrain'd them; but wars love/And Caesars awe dasht all:	Lucan, First Booke			357
This [band] <hand> that all behind us might be quail'd,	Lucan, First Booke			370
by these ten blest ensignes/And all thy several triumphs,	Lucan, First Booke			376
held up, all joyntly cryde/They'ill follow where he please:	Lucan, First Booke			388
And in all quarters musters men for Roome.	Lucan, First Booke			396
men/Whom death the greatest of all feares affright not,	Lucan, First Booke			455
All rise in armes; nor could the bed-rid parents/Keep back	Lucan, First Booke			502
Ranne through the bloud, that turn'd it all to gelly,	Lucan, First Booke			618
Turne all to good, be Augury vaine, and Tages/Th'arts master	Lucan, First Booke			635
Involving all, did Aruns darkly sing.	Lucan, First Booke			637
lawlesse/And casuall; all the starres at randome radge <range>:	Lucan, First Booke			642
Let all Lawes yeeld, sinne beare the name of vertue,	Lucan, First Booke			666
Are all things thine? the Muses Tempe <Temple> thine?	Ovid's Elegies			1.1.19
Thee all shall feare and worship as a King,	Ovid's Elegies			1.2.33
A scorching flame burnes all the standers by.	Ovid's Elegies			1.2.46
Accept him that will serve thee all his youth,	Ovid's Elegies			1.3.5
If thou givest kisses, I shall all disclose,	Ovid's Elegies			1.4.39
Suspitious feare in all my veines will hover,	Ovid's Elegies			1.4.42
When to go homewards we rise all along,	Ovid's Elegies			1.4.55
To leave the rest, all likt me passing well,	Ovid's Elegies			1.5.23
Night, Love, and wine to all extreames perswade:	Ovid's Elegies			1.6.59
All have I spent:	Ovid's Elegies			1.6.61
That I was mad, and barbarous all men cried,	Ovid's Elegies			1.7.19
Now Mars doth rage abroad without all pitty,	Ovid's Elegies			1.8.41

ALL (cont.)			
On all the [bed mens] <beds men> tumbling let him viewe/And thy	Ovid's Elegies	1.8.97	
All Lovers warre, and Cupid hath his tent,	Ovid's Elegies	1.9.1	
Atticke, all lovers are to warre farre sent.	Ovid's Elegies	1.9.2	
Let him surcease: love tries wit best of all.	Ovid's Elegies	1.9.32	
Now all feare with my mindes hot love abates,	Ovid's Elegies	1.10.9	
All for their Mistrisse, what they have, prepare.	Ovid's Elegies	1.10.58	
for needfull uses/Ile prove had hands impure with all abuses.	Ovid's Elegies	1.12.16	
[All] <This> could I beare, but that the wench should rise,/Who	Ovid's Elegies	1.13.25	
Now hast thou left no haires at all to die.	Ovid's Elegies	1.14.2	
painted stands/All naked holding in her wave-moist hands.	Ovid's Elegies	1.14.34	
That all the world [may] <might> ever chaunt my name.	Ovid's Elegies	1.15.8	
While Rome of all the [conquered] <conquering> world is head.	Ovid's Elegies	1.15.26	
For after death all men receive their right:	Ovid's Elegies	1.15.40	
Enjoy the wench, let all else be refusd.	Ovid's Elegies	2.2.30	
To staine all faith in truth, by false crimes use.	Ovid's Elegies	2.2.38	
Trust me all husbands for such faults are sad/Nor make they any	Ovid's Elegies	2.2.51	
Men handle those, all manly hopes resigne,	Ovid's Elegies	2.3.9	
No one face likes me best, all faces moove,	Ovid's Elegies	2.4.9	
To leave my selfe, that am in love [with all] <withall>,	Ovid's Elegies	2.4.31	
And wish hereby them all unknowne to leave.	Ovid's Elegies	2.5.54	
All wasting years have that complaint [out] <not> worne.	Ovid's Elegies	2.6.8	
All you whose pineons in the cleare aire sore,	Ovid's Elegies	2.6.11	
Full concord all your lives was you betwixt,	Ovid's Elegies	2.6.13	
There harmelesse Swans feed all abroad the river,	Ovid's Elegies	2.6.53	
Turnes all the goodly <godly> birdes to what she please.	Ovid's Elegies	2.6.58	
My mouth in speaking did all birds excell.	Ovid's Elegies	2.6.62	
Haples is he that all the night lies quiet/And slumbring,	Ovid's Elegies	2.9.39	
The unjust seas all blewish do appeare.	Ovid's Elegies	2.11.12	
In all thy face will be no crimsen bloud.	Ovid's Elegies	2.11.28	
Ile clip and kisse thee with all contentation,	Ovid's Elegies	2.11.45	
Ile thinke all true, though it be feigned matter.	Ovid's Elegies	2.11.53	
All humaine kinde by their default had perisht.	Ovid's Elegies	2.14.10	
Not though thy face in all things make thee raigne,	Ovid's Elegies	2.17.11	
Nothing I love, that at all times availes me.	Ovid's Elegies	2.19.8	
A laughing stocke thou art to all the citty,	Ovid's Elegies	3.1.21	
Let us all conquer by our mistris favour.	Ovid's Elegies	3.2.18	
Now comes the pompe; themselves let all men cheere:	Ovid's Elegies	3.2.43	
And all things too much in their sole power drenches.	Ovid's Elegies	3.3.26	
All being shut out, th'adulterer is within.	Ovid's Elegies	3.4.8	
Yet by deceit Love did them all surprize.	Ovid's Elegies	3.4.20	
And from the channell all abroad surrounded.	Ovid's Elegies	3.5.86	
And usde all speech that might provoke and stirre.	Ovid's Elegies	3.6.12	
All gaine in darknesse the deepe earth supprest.	Ovid's Elegies	3.7.36	
All, they possesse:	Ovid's Elegies	3.7.57	
Outrageous death profanes all holy things/And on all creatures	Ovid's Elegies	3.8.19	
all holy things/And on all creatures obscure darcknesse brings.	Ovid's Elegies	3.8.20	
Scarse rests of all what a small urne conteines.	Ovid's Elegies	3.8.40	
Thee, goddesse, bountifull all nations judge,	Ovid's Elegies	3.9.5	
Be witnesse Crete (nor Crete doth all things feigne)/Crete	Ovid's Elegies	3.9.19	
our fellow bed, by all/The Gods who by thee to be perjurde fall,	Ovid's Elegies	3.10.45	
What day was that, which all sad haps to bring,	Ovid's Elegies	3.11.1	
There use all tricks, and tread shame under feete.	Ovid's Elegies	3.13.18	
And in the bed hide all the faults you have,	Ovid's Elegies	3.13.20	
Deceive all, let me erre, and thinke I am right,	Ovid's Elegies	3.13.29	
Buskins of shels all silvered, used she,	Hero and Leander	1.31	
For in his lookes were all that men desire,	Hero and Leander	1.84	
Why art thou not in love, and lov'd of all?	Hero and Leander	1.89	
To meet their loves; such as had none at all,	Hero and Leander	1.95	
And all that view'd her, were enamour'd on her.	Hero and Leander	1.118	
So at her presence all surpris'd and tooken,	Hero and Leander	1.122	
And I in dutie will excell all other,	Hero and Leander	1.221	
As heaven preserves all things, so save thou one.	Hero and Leander	1.224	
Like untun'd golden strings all women are,	Hero and Leander	1.229	
All heaven would come to claime this legacie,	Hero and Leander	1.250	
Thinke water farre excels all earthly things:	Hero and Leander	1.260	
Or capable of any forme at all.	Hero and Leander	1.274	
Things that are not at all, are never lost.	Hero and Leander	1.276	
Plaies, maskes, and all that stern age counteth evill.	Hero and Leander	1.302	
Far from the towne (where all is whist and still,	Hero and Leander	1.346	
God knowes I play/With Venus swannes and sparrowes all the day.	Hero and Leander	1.352	
not to love at all, and everie part/Strove to resist the	Hero and Leander	1.363	
Vow'd spotlesse chastitie, but all in vaine.	Hero and Leander	1.368	
All deepe enrag'd, his sinowie bow he bent,	Hero and Leander	1.371	
All women are ambitious naturallie:	Hero and Leander	1.428	
Which taught him all that elder lovers know,	Hero and Leander	2.69	
All headlong throwes her selfe the clouds among/And now Leander	Hero and Leander	2.90	
Through numming cold, all feeble, faint and wan:	Hero and Leander	2.246	
And her all naked to his sight displayd.	Hero and Leander	2.324	
And we will all the pleasures prove,	Passionate Shepherd	2	
Imbroydred all with leaves of Mirtle.	Passionate Shepherd	12	
ALLAY (See LAY)			
ALLAYDE			
The greefes of private men are soone allayde,	Edw	5.1.8	Edward
ALLEAG'D			
Then he alleag'd the Gods would have them stay,	Dido	2.1.141	Aeneas
ALLEDGE			
Yet good my lord, heare what he can alledge.	Edw	1.4.250	Queene
ALLEGE (See ALLEAG'D, ALLEDGE)			
ALLEGEANCE			
O where is dutie and allegeance now?	1Tamb	1.1.101	Mycet
On your allegeance to the sea of Rome,	Edw	1.4.52	ArchBp
Of dutie and allegeance due to thee.	Edw	1.4.62	ArchBp

ALLIANCE (See ALIANCE)

ALLOT

such end the gods/Allot the height of honor, men so strong/By — Lucan, First Booke 82

ALLOTTED

Whose influence hath allotted death and hell; — F1951 5.2.155 Faust

ALLOW

Base boullion for the stampes sake we allow, — Hero and Leander 1.265

ALLOWE

The places lawes this benefit allowe. — Ovid's Elegies 3.2.20

ALLOWES

To hoarse scrich-owles foule shadowes it allowes, — Ovid's Elegies 1.12.19

ALL'S

Besides, if we should let thee goe, all's one, — Jew 5.5.99 Govnr
All's one, for wee'l be bold with his Venison. — F 808 3.1.30 Mephst

ALLUDES

My love alludes to everie historie: — Ovid's Elegies 2.4.44

ALLUR'D

Would have allur'd the vent'rous youth of Greece, — Hero and Leander 1.57

ALLURES (See also ALURE)

Whose sound allures the golden Morpheus, — Hero and Leander 1.349

ALLURING

For I will flye from these alluring eyes, — Dido 4.2.50 Iarbus
And wanton motions of alluring eyes, — Dido 4.3.35 Achat

ALLY (See ALIED)

ALLYED

Were he a stranger, <and> not allyed to me, — F 223 1.2.30 2Schol

ALMAIN

Sclavonians, [Almain Rutters] <Almains, Rutters>, Muffes, and — 2Tamb 1.1.22 Uribas
Slavonians, [Almain Rutters] <Almains, Rutters>, Muffes, and — 2Tamb 1.1.58 Orcan

ALMAINE

Like Almaine Rutters with their horsemens staves, — F 152 1.1.124 Valdes

ALMAINS

Sclavonians, [Almain Rutters] <Almains, Rutters>, Muffes, and — 2Tamb 1.1.22 Uribas
Slavonians, [Almain Rutters] <Almains, Rutters>, Muffes, and — 2Tamb 1.1.58 Orcan

ALMEDA

Sweet Almeda, pity the ruthfull plight/Of Callapine, the sonne — 2Tamb 1.2.1 Callap
Yet heare me speake my gentle Almeda. — 2Tamb 1.2.13 Callap
A litle further, gentle Almeda. — 2Tamb 1.2.17 Callap
Sweet Almeda, scarse halfe a league from hence. — 2Tamb 1.2.55 Callap
Then here I sweare, as I am Almeda, — 2Tamb 1.2.67 Almeda
Thanks gentle Almeda, then let us haste, — 2Tamb 1.2.74 Callap
Then wil I shortly keep my promise Almeda. — 2Tamb 3.1.78 P Callap
With that accursed traitor Almeda, — 2Tamb 3.2.150 Tamb
That curst and damned Traitor Almeda. — 2Tamb 3.2.154 Usumc
See father, how Almeda the Jaylor lookes upon us. — 2Tamb 3.5.116 Celeb
Come Almeda, receive this crowne of me, — 2Tamb 3.5.129 Callap

ALMES

and then I say they use/To send their Almes unto the Nunneries: — Jew 3.4.77 Barab

ALMIGHTY

For if th'almighty take my brother hence, — P 469 8.19 Anjoy

ALMOND

Like to an almond tree ymounted high, — 2Tamb 4.3.119 Tamb

ALMONDS

Ile give thee Sugar-almonds, sweete Conserves, — Dido 2.1.305 Venus
Browne Almonds, Servises, ripe Figs and Dates, — Dido 4.5.5 Nurse

ALMO'S

secret works, and [wash] <washt> their saint/In Almo's floud: — Lucan, First Booke 600

ALMOST

That almost brent the Axeltree of heaven, — 1Tamb 4.2.50 Tamb
of Verna and Bulgaria/And almost to the very walles of Rome, — 2Tamb 2.1.9 Fredrk
Is almost cleane extinguished and spent, — 2Tamb 5.3.89 Phsitn
We now are almost at the new made Nunnery. — Jew 1.2.306 1Fryar
As I am almost desperate for my sinnes: — Jew 3.6.18 Abigal
Is ruth and almost death to call to minde: — P 797 16.11 Navrre
That almost rents the closet of my heart, — Edw 5.3.22 Edward
And I was almost stifeled with the savor. — Edw 5.5.9 Gurney
Saies Faustus come, thine houre is almost come, — F1727 5.1.54 Faust
Alas she almost weepes, and her white cheekes, — Ovid's Elegies 1.14.51
How almost wrackt thy ship in maine seas fell. — Ovid's Elegies 2.11.50
Ah Pelops from his coach was almost feld, — Ovid's Elegies 3.2.15
For under water he was almost dead, — Hero and Leander 2.170

ALOFT

And hoyst aloft on Neptunes hideous hilles, — Dido 3.3.47 Iarbus
my souldiers march/Shal rise aloft and touch the horned Moon, — 2Tamb 1.3.14 Tamb
Which makes them fleet aloft and gaspe for aire. — 2Tamb 5.1.209 Techel
And roof't aloft with curious worke in gold. — F 798 3.1.20 Faust
And mount aloft with them as high as heaven, — F1404 4.2.80 Faust
Or flaming Titan (feeding on the deepe)/Puls them aloft, and — Lucan, First Booke 417
where shall I fall,/Thus borne aloft? — Lucan, First Booke 678
When in this [workes] <worke> first verse I trod aloft, — Ovid's Elegies 1.1.21
Then on the rough Alpes should I tread aloft, — Ovid's Elegies 2.16.19
Will mount aloft, and enter heaven gate, — Hero and Leander 1.466
And then he got him to a rocke aloft. — Hero and Leander 2.148

ALONE

But thou art gone and leav'st me here alone, — Dido 1.1.247 Aeneas
Lords goe before, we two must talke alone. — Dido 3.3.9 Dido
We two will talke alone, what words be these? — Dido 3.3.12 Iarbus
Then haste Cosroe to be king alone, — 1Tamb 2.3.42 Tamb
O let him alone: — 1Tamb 4.4.40 P Tamb
For he is God alone, and none but he. — 2Tamb 5.1.202 Tamb
You know my mind, let me alone with him. — Jew 4.1.100 Barab
Let me alone, doe but you speake him faire: — Jew 4.2.63 Pilia
Let me alone, I'le use him in his kinde. — Jew 4.2.80 Pilia

ALONE (cont.)				
You two alone?	Jew	4.4.22		Curtzn
Let me alone to urge it now I know the meaning.	Jew	4.4.79		Pilia
I'le goe alone, dogs, do not hale me thus.	Jew	5.1.19		Barab
What, all alone? well fare sleepy drinke.	Jew	5.1.61		Barab
For that let me alone, Cousin stay you heer,	P 428	7.68		Anjoy
I, but my Lord let me alone for that,	P 519	9.38		QnMoth
Tush man, let me alone with him,	P 648	12.61		QnMoth
What, all alone my love, and writing too:	P 670	13.14		Guise
Well, let me alone, whose within there?	P 881	17.76		King
Let us alone, I warrant you.	P 939	19.9	P	1Mur
Away, leave me alone to meditate.	P1081	19.151		QnMoth
The Kings alone, it cannot satisfie.	P1109	21.3		Dumain
Tush my Lord, let me alone for that.	P1136	21.30	P	Frier
His highnes is disposde to be alone.	Edw	2.2.135		Guard
Nay, now you are heere alone, ile speake my minde.	Edw	2.2.155		Mortmr
What lord [Arundell] <Matre>, dost thou come alone?	Edw	3.1.89		Edward
And then let me alone to handle him.	Edw	5.2.22		Mortmr
Let me alone, here is the privie seale,	Edw	5.2.37		Mortmr
And all alone, comes walking in his gowne;	F1358	4.2.34		Fredrk
Whose bloud alone must wash away thy guilt.	F App	p.243 45		OldMan
Yet he alone is held in reverence.	Lucan, First Booke			144
shoot) marcht on/And then (when Lucifer did shine alone,	Lucan, First Booke			233
the north-west wind/Nor Zephir rules not, but the north alone,	Lucan, First Booke			408
And their vaild Matron, who alone might view/Minervas statue;	Lucan, First Booke			597
I am alone, were furious Love discarded.	Ovid's Elegies			1.6.34
Let this word, come, alone the tables fill.	Ovid's Elegies			1.11.24
There lives the Phoenix one alone bird ever.	Ovid's Elegies			2.6.54
Yet this is better farre then lie alone,	Ovid's Elegies			2.10.15
Thou doest alone give matter to my wit.	Ovid's Elegies			2.17.34
Why she alone in empty bed oft tarries.	Ovid's Elegies			2.19.42
Where's thy attire? why wand'rest heere alone?	Ovid's Elegies			3.5.55
Verses alone are with continuance crown'd.	Ovid's Elegies			3.8.28
What to have laine alone in empty bed?	Ovid's Elegies			3.8.34
In emptie bed alone my mistris lies.	Ovid's Elegies			3.9.2
Alone Corinna moves my wanton wit.	Ovid's Elegies			3.11.16
Of me Pelignis nation boasts alone,	Ovid's Elegies			3.14.8
But this faire jem, sweet in the losse alone,	Hero and Leander			1.247
By which alone, our reverend fathers say,	Hero and Leander			1.267
As Greece will thinke, if thus you live alone,	Hero and Leander			1.289
Beautie alone is lost, too warily kept.	Hero and Leander			1.328
Leaving Leander in the bed alone.	Hero and Leander			2.312
ALONG				
Sailing along the Orientall sea,	1Tamb	3.3.253		Tamb
And I have martch'd along the river Nile,	2Tamb	1.3.186		Techel
bringing of our ordinance/Along the trench into the battery,	2Tamb	3.3.55		Therid
us haste from hence/Along the cave that leads beyond the foe,	2Tamb	3.4.2		Olymp
Along Armenia and the Caspian sea,	2Tamb	5.3.127		Tamb
And so along the Ethiopian sea,	2Tamb	5.3.137		Tamb
neither, but to passe along/Towards Venice by the Adriatick Sea;	Jew	1.1.162		Barab
the plancke/That runs along the upper chamber floore,	Jew	1.2.297		Barab
See 'em goe pinion'd along by my doore.	Jew	2.3.180		Barab
hence, out of the way/A little, but our men shall go along.	Edw	2.5.101		Penbrk
Madam along, and you my lord, with me,	Edw	4.2.81		SrJohn
and I live along, then thou should'st see how fat I'de <I	F 682	2.2.131	P	Envy
Here, take his triple Crowne along with you,	F 970	3.1.192		Pope
Of these garboiles, whence springs [a long] <along> discourse,	Lucan, First Booke			68
And creepes along the vales, deviding just/The bounds of Italy,	Lucan, First Booke			217
bands were spread/Along Nar floud that into Tiber fals,	Lucan, First Booke			472
When to go homewards we rise all along,	Ovid's Elegies			1.4.55
That runs along his backe, but my rude pen,	Hero and Leander			1.69
ALONGST				
Your Artiers which alongst the vaines convey/The lively spirits	2Tamb	5.3.93		Phsitn
shoots/Alongst the ayre and [nought] <not> resisting it/Falls,	Lucan, First Booke			157
ALOUD				
one, me thought/I heard him shreeke and call aloud for helpe:	F1992	5.3.10		3Schol
ALOUDE				
And ring aloude the knell of Gaveston.	Edw	2.3.26		Mortmr
ALOWD				
And made his capring Triton sound alowd,	Hero and Leander			2.156
ALPES				
Yet was his soule but flowne beyond the Alpes,	Jew	Prol.2		Machvl
Flies ore the Alpes to fruitfull Germany,	F 985	3.2.5		Mephst
Now Caesar overpast the snowy Alpes,	Lucan, First Booke			185
And frozen Alpes thaw'd with resolving winds.	Lucan, First Booke			221
our wintering/Under the Alpes; Roome rageth now in armes/As if	Lucan, First Booke			304
Borne twixt the Alpes and Rhene, which he hath brought/From out	Lucan, First Booke			478
And the Alpes/Shooke the old snow from off their trembling	Lucan, First Booke			551
Then on the rough Alpes should I tread aloft,	Ovid's Elegies			2.16.19
ALPHEUS				
not Alpheus in strange lands to runne,/Th'Arcadian Virgins	Ovid's Elegies			3.5.29
ALREADIE				
Whose armed soule alreadie on the sea,	Dido	3.2.83		Venus
ALREADY				
Your Majesty already hath devisde/A meane, as fit as may be to	2Tamb	4.3.50		Usumc
He knowes it already.	Jew	4.4.60	P	Barab
That they which have already set the street/May know their	P 328	5.55		Guise
Put of that feare, they are already joynde,	P 605	12.18		King
Which are already mustered in the land,	P 726	14.29		1Msngr
Weepst thou already?	Edw	5.5.52		Edward
So Faustus hath <I have> already done, and holds <hold> this	F 283	1.3.55		Faust
Already Faustus hath hazarded that for thee.	F 422	2.1.34		Faust
they are too familiar with me already, swowns they are as bolde	F App	p.230 28	P	Clown

ALSO			
And also furniture for these my men.	Dido	5.1.70	Aeneas
Also much better were they then I tell,	Ovid's Elegies	2.5.55	
Thou also, that wert borne faire, hadst decayed,	Ovid's Elegies	2.14.19	
My Mistris deity also drewe me fro it,	Ovid's Elegies	2.18.17	
Thou also that late tookest mine eyes away,	Ovid's Elegies	2.19.19	
ALTAR (See also ALTERS)			
And at Joves Altar finding Priamus,	Dido	2.1.225	Aeneas
His lips an altar, where Ile offer up/As many kisses as the Sea	Dido	3.1.87	Dido
Upon which Altar I will offer up/My daily sacrifice of sighes	Jew	3.2.31	Govnr
To him, I'le build an Altar and a Church,	F 401	2.1.13	Faust
on the Altar/He laies a ne're-yoakt Bull, and powers downe	Lucan, First Booke		607
An Altar takes mens incense, and oblation,	Ovid's Elegies	3.12.9	
An Altar made after the ancient fashion.	Ovid's Elegies	3.12.10	
And in the midst a silver altar stood,	Hero and Leander	1.157	
From Venus altar to your footsteps bending)/Doth testifie that	Hero and Leander	1.210	
ALTARS			
And this right hand shall make thy Altars crack/With mountaine	Dido	1.1.201	Aeneas
Whose emptie Altars have enlarg'd our illes.	Dido	4.2.3	Iarbus
Staining his Altars with your purple blood:	1Tamb	4.2.4	Bajzth
Upon whose altars thousand soules do lie,	F App	p.235 36	Mephst
In white, with incense Ile thine Altars greete,	Ovid's Elegies	2.13.23	
Who now will care the Altars to perfume?	Ovid's Elegies	3.3.33	
ALTER (Homograph)			
Nothing shall alter us, wee are resolv'd.	Edw	1.4.74	ArchBp
Feare not, the queens words cannot alter him.	Edw	1.4.233	Penbrk
una eademque res legatur duobus, alter rem, alter valorem rei,	F 56	1.1.28	P Faust
eademque res legatur duobus, alter rem, alter valorem rei, &c.	F 56	1.1.28	P Faust
Till time shall alter this our brutish shapes:	F1454	4.3.24	Benvol
why doe the Planets/Alter their course; and vainly dim their	Lucan, First Booke		663
ALTERED			
We see his tents have now bene altered,	1Tamb	5.1.7	Govnr
ALTERS			
And had his alters deckt with duskie lightes:	P 59	2.2	Guise
ALTHOUGH			
Aeneas no, although his eyes doe pearce.	Dido	3.4.12	Dido
Although it be digested long agoe,	1Tamb	3.2.9	Zenoc
Although he sent a thousand armed men/To intercept this haughty	2Tamb	1.2.70	Almeda
Although it shine as brightly as the Sun.	2Tamb	4.1.134	Tamb
Barabas, although thou art in mis-beleefe,	Jew	1.2.352	1Fryar
Although unworthy of that Sister-hood.	Jew	3.3.69	Abigal
ambles after wealth/Although he ne're be richer then in hope:	Jew	3.4.53	Barab
Although my downfall be the deepest hell.	P 104	2.47	Guise
Although my love to thee can hardly [suffer't] <suffer>,	P 747	15.5	King
And although you take out nothing but your owne, yet you put in	P 808	17.3	P Souldr
although I do not doubt but to see you both hang'd the next	F 212	1.2.19	P Wagner
Although the nights be long, I sleepe not tho,	Ovid's Elegies	1.2.3	
Although I would, I cannot him cashiere/Before I be divided	Ovid's Elegies	1.6.35	
Yet although [neither] <either>, mixt of eithers hue,	Ovid's Elegies	1.14.10	
[His Arte excelld, although his witte was weake].	Ovid's Elegies	1.15.14	
and lockes put in the poast/Although of oake, to yeeld to	Ovid's Elegies	2.1.28	
Although the sunne to rive the earth incline,	Ovid's Elegies	2.16.3	
But without thee, although vine-planted ground/Conteines me,	Ovid's Elegies	2.16.33	
Although thou chafe, stolne pleasure is sweet play,	Ovid's Elegies	3.4.31	
Which makes me hope, although I am but base,	Hero and Leander	1.218	
ALURE			
To which thou didst alure me being alive:	P1025	19.95	King
ALWAIES			
And alwaies mooving as the restles Spheares,	1Tamb	2.7.25	Tamb
But God that alwaies doth defend the right,	P 575	11.40	Navrre
But God we know will alwaies put them downe,	P 798	16.12	Navrre
For kinde and loving hast thou alwaies beene:	Edw	5.1.7	Edward
Be alwaies serviceable to us three:	F 150	1.1.122	Valdes
And alwaies be obedient to my will.	F 325	1.3.97	Faust
your right eye be alwaies Diametrally fixt upon my left heele,	F 386	1.4.44	P Wagner
use stirde, and thoughts that alwaies scorn'd/A second place;	Lucan, First Booke		124
Whether the sea roul'd alwaies from that point,	Lucan, First Booke		413
And with my name shall thine be alwaies sung.	Ovid's Elegies	1.3.26	
And alwaies cut him off as he replide.	Hero and Leander	1.196	
That he and Povertie should alwaies kis.	Hero and Leander	1.470	
Love alwaies makes those eloquent that have it.	Hero and Leander	2.72	
ALWAYES			
And alwayes kept the Sexton's armes in ure/With digging graves	Jew	2.3.184	Barab
Goe fetch him straight. I alwayes fear'd that Jew.	Jew	5.1.18	Govnr
Which troopes hath alwayes bin on Cupids side:	Ovid's Elegies	1.2.36	
Doost me of new crimes alwayes guilty frame?	Ovid's Elegies	2.7.1	
Why me that alwayes was thy souldiour found,	Ovid's Elegies	2.9.3	
White birdes to lovers did not alwayes sing.	Ovid's Elegies	3.11.2	
AM			
I am much better for your worthles love,	Dido	1.1.3	Ganimd
Of Troy am I, Aeneas is my name,	Dido	1.1.216	Aeneas
Where am I now? these should be Carthage walles.	Dido	2.1.1	Aeneas
You are Achates, or I [am] deciv'd.	Dido	2.1.49	Serg
Achates, speake, for I am overjoyed.	Dido	2.1.54	Aeneas
But Troy is not, what shall I say I am?	Dido	2.1.76	Aeneas
And now am neither father, Lord, nor King:	Dido	2.1.239	Aeneas
Am I not King of rich Getulia?	Dido	3.1.45	Iarbus
Am not I Queen of Libia? then depart.	Dido	3.1.49	Dido
Yet none obtaind me, I am free from all.--	Dido	3.1.153	Dido
Tut, I am simple, without [minde] <made> to hurt,	Dido	3.2.16	Juno
And yet I am not free, oh would I were.	Dido	3.4.6	Dido
The man that I doe eye where ere I am,	Dido	3.4.18	Dido
How vaine am I to weare this Diadem,	Dido	4.4.40	Aeneas

AM (cont.)

Yet lest he should, for I am full of feare,	Dido	4.4.108	Dido
Nurse I am wearie, will you carrie me?	Dido	4.5.15	Cupid
Say Dido what she will I am not old,	Dido	4.5.21	Nurse
Ile be no more a widowe, I am young,	Dido	4.5.22	Nurse
Iarbus, I am cleane besides my selfe,	Dido	5.1.63	Aeneas
How loth I am to leave these Libian bounds,	Dido	5.1.81	Aeneas
I am commaunded by immortall Jove,	Dido	5.1.99	Aeneas
Am I lesse faire then when thou sawest me first?	Dido	5.1.115	Dido
And I am thus deluded of my boy:	Dido	5.1.219	Dido
I am as true as any one of yours.	Dido	5.1.223	Nurse
Dido I am, unlesse I be deceiv'd,	Dido	5.1.264	Dido
No but I am not, yet I will be straight.	Dido	5.1.271	Dido
I am not wise enough to be a kinge,	1Tamb	1.1.20	Mycet
Meander come, I am abus'd Meander.	1Tamb	1.1.106	Mycet
I am (my Lord), for so you do import.	1Tamb	1.2.33	Zenoc
I am a Lord, for so my deeds shall proove,	1Tamb	1.2.34	Tamb
But this is she with whom I am in love.	1Tamb	1.2.108	Tamb
Whom seekst thou Persean? I am Tamburlain.	1Tamb	1.2.153	Tamb
For you then Maddam, I am out of doubt.	1Tamb	1.2.258	Tamb
Away, I am the King: go, touch me not.	1Tamb	2.4.20	Mycet
I marie am I: have you any suite to me?	1Tamb	2.4.24	Mycet
Me thinks we should not, I am strongly moov'd,	1Tamb	2.5.75	Tamb
Tell him, I am content to take a truce,	1Tamb	3.1.31	Bajzth
I that am tearm'd the Scourge and Wrath of God,	1Tamb	3.3.44	Tamb
thou be plac'd by me/That am the Empresse of the mighty Turke?	1Tamb	3.3.167	Zabina
Cal'st thou me Concubine that am betroath'd/Unto the great and	1Tamb	3.3.169	Zenoc
But I am pleasde you shall not see him there:	1Tamb	5.1.113	Tamb
If I had not bin wounded as I am.	1Tamb	5.1.421	Arabia
And I am pleasde with this my overthrow,	1Tamb	5.1.482	Souldn
forgetst thou I am he/That with the Cannon shooke Vienna	2Tamb	1.1.86	Orcan
So am I fear'd among all Nations.	2Tamb	1.1.151	Orcan
As I am Callapine the Emperour,	2Tamb	1.2.64	Callap
Then here I sweare, as I am Almeda,	2Tamb	1.2.67	Almeda
When you will my Lord, I am ready.	2Tamb	1.2.76	Almeda
When I am old and cannot mannage armes,	2Tamb	1.3.59	Tamb
Your Majesty remembers I am sure/What cruell slaughter of our	2Tamb	2.1.4	Fredrk
Yet I am resolute, and so farewell.	2Tamb	3.3.40	Capt
Madam, I am so far in love with you,	2Tamb	3.4.78	Therid
Why, so he is Casane, I am here,	2Tamb	3.5.62	Tamb
Ye petty kings of Turkye I am come,	2Tamb	3.5.64	Tamb
They say I am a coward, (Perdicas) and I feare as litle their	2Tamb	4.1.67	P Calyph
Nor am I made Arch-monark of the world,	2Tamb	4.1.150	Tamb
Thus am I right the Scourge of highest Jove,	2Tamb	4.3.24	Tamb
Whose Scourge I am, and him will I obey.	2Tamb	5.1.185	Tamb
And let them know that I am Machevill,	Jew	Prol.7	Machvl
Admir'd I am of those that hate me most:	Jew	Prol.9	Machvl
I am asham'd to heare such fooleries.	Jew	Prol.17	Machvl
But whither am I bound, I come not, I,	Jew	Prol.28	Machvl
And now me thinkes that I am one of those:	Jew	2.1.28	Barab
Governor of Malta, hither am I bound;	Jew	2.2.4	Bosco
And so am I, Delbosco is my name;	Jew	2.2.6	Bosco
and Vespasian conquer'd us)/Am I become as wealthy as I was:	Jew	2.3.11	Barab
I am not of the Tribe of Levy, I,	Jew	2.3.18	Barab
Barabas, thou know'st I am the Governors sonne.	Jew	2.3.40	Lodowk
Alas, Sir, I am a very youth.	Jew	2.3.115	P Slave
I am content to lose some of my Crownes;	Jew	2.3.178	Barab
But marke how I am blest for plaguing them,	Jew	2.3.199	Barab
I am a little busie, Sir, pray pardon me.	Jew	2.3.231	Barab
And I am sure he is with Abigall.	Jew	2.3.268	Barab
Oh, is't the custome, then I am resolv'd:	Jew	2.3.329	Lodowk
Oh leave to grieve me, I am griev'd enough.	Jew	3.2.17	Mater
Am I Ithimore?	Jew	3.3.23	P Ithimr
Know, holy Sir, I am bold to sollicite thee.	Jew	3.3.53	Abigal
Ithimore, intreat not for her, I am mov'd,	Jew	3.4.35	Barab
All that I have is thine when I am dead,	Jew	3.4.44	Barab
I am gone.	Jew	3.4.114	Ithimr
And for the Tribute-mony I am sent.	Jew	3.5.10	Basso
As I am almost desperate for my sinnes:	Jew	3.6.18	Abigal
What needs all this? I know I am a Jew.	Jew	4.1.33	Barab
I am a Jew, and therefore am I lost.	Jew	4.1.57	Barab
Then 'tis not for me; and I am resolv'd/You shall confesse me,	Jew	4.1.85	Barab
And I am bound in charitie to requite it,	Jew	4.1.107	Barab
So, now the feare is past, and I am safe:	Jew	4.1.114	Barab
Villaines, I am a sacred person, touch me not.	Jew	4.1.201	1Fryar
base slave as he should be saluted by such a tall man as I am,	Jew	4.2.10	P Pilia
and now would I were gone, I am not worthy to looke upon her.	Jew	4.2.36	P Ithimr
Now am I cleane, or rather fouly out of the way.	Jew	4.2.47	P Ithimr
I am gone.	Jew	4.2.122	P Pilia
I am betraid.--	Jew	4.3.39	Barab
five hundred Crownes that I esteeme,/I am not mov'd at that:	Jew	4.3.41	Barab
Was ever Jew tormented as I am?	Jew	4.3.60	Barab
So, now I am reveng'd upon 'em all.	Jew	4.4.42	Barab
What e're I am, yet Governor heare me speake;	Jew	5.1.9	Curtzn
My name is Barabas; I am a Jew.	Jew	5.1.72	Barab
I now am Governour of Malta; true,	Jew	5.2.29	Barab
And now at length am growne your Governor,	Jew	5.2.70	Barab
returne me word/That thou wilt come, and I am satisfied.	Jew	5.5.12	Barab
I am my Lord, in what your grace commaundes till death.	P 76	2.19	P Pothec
Fye, I am ashamde, how ever that I seeme,	P 124	2.67	Guise
Help sonne Navarre, I am poysoned.	P 176	3.11	OldQn
I vow and sweare as I am King of France,	P 255	4.53	Charls
And that I am not more secure my selfe,	P 264	4.62	Charls

AM (cont.)

Then I am carefull you should be preserved.	P 265	4.63	Charls
I am disguisde and none knows who I am,	P 278	5.5	Anjoy
I am a preacher of the word of God,	P 341	5.68	Lorein
I am as Ramus is, a Christian.	P 374	7.14	Taleus
Alas I am a scholler, how should I have golde?	P 377	7.17	Ramus
And Guise usurpes it, cause I am his wife:	P 661	13.5	Duchss
to speak with him/But cannot, and therfore am enforst to write,	P 663	13.7	Duchss
Am I growne olde, or is thy lust growne yong,	P 681	13.25	Guise
At thy request I am content thou goe,	P 746	15.4	King
Am I thus to be jested at and scornde?	P 758	15.16	Guise
Why I am no traitor to the crowne of France.	P 825	17.20	Guise
I am a Prince of the Valoyses line,/Therfore an enemy to the	P 835	17.30	Guise
I am a juror in the holy league,	P 837	17.32	Guise
Thinke not but I am tragicall within:	P 894	17.89	King
My Lord, I am advertised from France,	P 900	18.1	Navrre
Cousin, assure you I am resolute,	P 973	19.43	King
O my Lord, I am one of them that is set to murder you.	P 992	19.62	P 3Mur
Tut they are pesants, I am Duke of Guise:	P 998	19.68	Guise
Philip and Parma, I am slaine for you:	P1011	19.81	Guise
Murder me not, I am a Cardenall.	P1091	20.1	Cardnl
I am thy brother, and ile revenge thy death,	P1112	21.6	Dumain
I am a Frier of the order of the Jacobyns, that for my	P1130	21.24	P Frier
I vow as I am lawfull King of France,	P1143	22.5	King
That crosse me thus, shall know I am displeasd.	Edw	1.1.79	Edward
Am I a king and must be over rulde?	Edw	1.1.135	Edward
Why shouldst thou kneele, knowest thou not who I am?	Edw	1.1.142	Edward
You know that I am legate to the Pope,	Edw	1.4.51	ArchBp
I see I must, and therefore am content.	Edw	1.4.85	Edward
That I am banishd, and must flie the land.	Edw	1.4.107	Gavstn
Thou from this land, I from my selfe am banisht.	Edw	1.4.118	Edward
And so am I for ever miserable.	Edw	1.4.186	Queene
I am injoynde,/To sue unto you all for his repeale:	Edw	1.4.200	Queene
Plead for him he that will, I am resolvde.	Edw	1.4.214	MortSr
And so am I my lord, diswade the Queene.	Edw	1.4.215	Lncstr
Then so am I, and live to do him service,	Edw	1.4.421	Mortmr
I am none of these common [pedants] <pendants> I,	Edw	2.1.52	Baldck
Come lead the way, I long till I am there.	Edw	2.1.82	Neece
I am that Cedar, shake me not too much,	Edw	2.2.38	Edward
When I thy brother am rejected thus.	Edw	2.2.218	Kent
This way he fled, but I am come too late.	Edw	4.6.1	Kent
Full often am I sowring up to heaven,	Edw	5.1.21	Edward
But when I call to minde I am a king,	Edw	5.1.23	Edward
I weare the crowne, but am contrould by them,	Edw	5.1.29	Edward
Whilst I am lodgd within this cave of care,	Edw	5.1.32	Edward
And thats the cause that I am now remoovde.	Edw	5.1.150	Edward
I know not, but of this am I assured,	Edw	5.1.152	Edward
Let him be king, I am too yong to raigne.	Edw	5.2.93	Prince
Where I am sterv'd for want of sustenance,	Edw	5.3.20	Edward
O Gaveston, it is for thee that I am wrongd,	Edw	5.3.41	Edward
Feard am I more then lov'd, let me be feard,	Edw	5.4.52	Mortmr
And to conclude, I am Protector now,	Edw	5.4.64	Mortmr
I am the Champion that will combate him!	Edw	5.4.78	Champn
Know that I am a king, oh at that name,	Edw	5.5.89	Edward
I am too weake and feeble to resist,	Edw	5.5.108	Edward
Thinke not that I am frighted with thy words,	Edw	5.6.27	King
He hath forgotten me, stay, I am his mother.	Edw	5.6.90	Queene
How am I glutted with conceipt of this?	F 105	1.1.77	Faust
Valdes, as resolute am I in this,	F 161	1.1.133	Faust
But that I am by nature flegmatique, slow to wrath, and prone	F 209	1.2.16	P Wagner
I am a servant to great Lucifer,	F 268	1.3.40	Mephst
Why this is hell: nor am I out of it.	F 304	1.3.76	Mephst
Am not tormented with ten thousand hels,	F 307	1.3.79	Mephst
seene many boyes with [such pickadevaunts] <beards> I am sure.	F 345	1.4.3	P Robin
I am not afraid of a devill.	F 374	1.4.32	P Robin
But <Faustus> I am an instance to prove the contrary:	F 525	2.1.137	Mephst
For I tell thee I am damn'd, and <am> now in hell.	F 526	2.1.138	Mephst
for I am wanton and lascivious, and cannot live without a wife.	F 530	2.1.142	P Faust
Who buzzeth in mine eares I am a spirit?	F 565	2.2.14	Faust
I am resolv'd, Faustus shall not <nere> repent.	F 583	2.2.32	Faust
Well, I am answer'd:	F 618	2.2.67	P Faust
I am Lucifer,	F 639	2.2.88	Lucifr
I am Pride; I disdaine to have any parents:	F 664	2.2.113	P Pride
I am like to Ovids Flea, I can creepe into every corner of a	F 664	2.2.113	P Pride
I am Covetousnesse:	F 674	2.2.123	P Covet
I am Envy, begotten of a Chimney-sweeper, and an Oyster-wife:	F 679	2.2.128	P Envy
I am leane with seeing others eate:	F 681	2.2.130	P Envy
I am Wrath:	F 686	2.2.135	P Wrath
I <who I sir, I> am Gluttony; my parents are all dead, and the	F 693	2.2.142	P Glutny
Hey ho; I am Sloth:	F 705	2.2.154	P Sloth
I am one that loves an inch of raw Mutton, better then an ell	F 708	2.2.160	P Ltchry
brave, prethee let's to it presently, for I am as dry as a dog.	F 751	2.3.30	P Dick
Whilst I am here on earth let me be cloyd/With all things that	F 837	3.1.59	Faust
<Well, I am content, to compasse then some sport>,	F 989	(HC266) A	Faust
Raymond pray fall too, I am beholding/To the Bishop of Millaine,	F1041	3.2.61	Pope
O I am slaine, help me my Lords:	F1068	3.2.88	Pope
I am glad I have found you, you are a couple of fine	F1096	3.3.9	P Vintnr
How am I vexed by these villaines Charmes?	F1117	3.3.30	Mephst
Constantinople have they brought me now <am I hither brought>,	F1118	3.3.31	Mephst
I am content for this once to thrust my head out at a window:	F1199	4.1.45	P Benvol
I, I, and I am content too:	F1254	4.1.100	P Benvol
'sblood I am never able to endure these torments.	F1306	4.1.152	P Benvol
which being all I desire, I am content to remove his hornes.	F1313	4.1.159	P Faust

AM (cont.)			
I am a very poore man, and have lost very much of late by horse	F1463	4.4.7	P HrsCsr
Now am I a made man for ever.	F1476	4.4.20	P HrsCsr
Alas I am undone, what shall I do?	F1492	4.4.36	P HrsCsr
I am eighteene pence on the score, but say nothing, see if she	F1511	4.5.7	P Robin
fell to eating; and as I am a cursen man, he never left eating,	F1530	4.5.26	P Carter
I thanke you, I am fully satisfied.	F1651	4.6.94	P Carter
But I have it againe now I am awake:	F1657	4.6.100	P Faust
Rafe, keepe out, for I am about a roaring peece of worke.	F App	p.233 11	P Robin
How am I vexed with these vilaines charmes?	F App	p.235 37	Mephst
From Constantinople am I hither come,	F App	p.235 38	Mephst
I am content to do whatsoever your majesty shall command me.	F App	p.236 15	P Faust
I am ready to accomplish your request, so farre forth as by art	F App	p.237 37	P Faust
forth as by art and power of my spirit I am able to performe.	F App	p.237 38	P Faust
being all I desire, I am content to release him of his hornes:	F App	p.238 84	P Faust
til I am past this faire and pleasant greene, ile walke on	F App	p.239 96	P Faust
Now am I made man for ever, Ile not leave my horse for fortie:	F App	p.239 114	P HrsCsr
what, doost thinke I am a horse-doctor?	F App	p.240 120	P Faust
Alas, I am undone, what shall I do:	F App	p.241 154	P HrsCsr
My gratious Lord, I am glad it contents you so wel:	F App	p.242 3	P Faust
I am glad they content you so Madam.	F App	p.242 27	P Faust
Pean whither am I halde?	Lucan, First Booke		677
Loe I confesse, I am thy captive I,	Ovid's Elegies		1.2.19
That am descended but of knightly line,	Ovid's Elegies		1.3.8
I am no halfe horse, nor in woods I dwell,	Ovid's Elegies		1.4.9
I have beene wanton, therefore am perplext,	Ovid's Elegies		1.4.45
I am alone, were furious Love discarded.	Ovid's Elegies		1.6.34
Punish I am, if I a Romaine beat,	Ovid's Elegies		1.7.29
That some youth hurt as I am with loves bowe/His owne flames	Ovid's Elegies		2.1.7
love please/[Am] <And> driven like a ship upon rough seas,	Ovid's Elegies		2.4.8
<blushe>, and by that blushfull [glance] <glasse> am tooke:	Ovid's Elegies		2.4.12
To leave my selfe, that am in love [with all] <withall>,	Ovid's Elegies		2.4.31
By thee deceived, by thee surprisde am I,	Ovid's Elegies		2.10.3
Though I am slender, I have store of pith,	Ovid's Elegies		2.10.23
But she conceiv'd of me, or I am sure/I oft have done, what	Ovid's Elegies		2.13.5
He being Judge, I am convinc'd of blame.	Ovid's Elegies		2.17.2
Light am I, and with me, my care, light love,	Ovid's Elegies		3.1.41
Not stronger am I, then the thing I move.	Ovid's Elegies		3.1.42
Couzend, I am the couzeners sacrifice.	Ovid's Elegies		3.3.22
Why being a vestall am I wooed to wed,	Ovid's Elegies		3.5.75
Thou [cousenst] <cousendst> mee, by thee surprizde am I,	Ovid's Elegies		3.6.71
When bad fates take good men, I am forbod,	Ovid's Elegies		3.8.35
Why am I sad, when Proserpine is found,	Ovid's Elegies		3.9.45
I am not as I was before, unwise.	Ovid's Elegies		3.10.32
Deceive all, let me erre, and thinke I am right,	Ovid's Elegies		3.13.29
(Nor am I by such wanton toyes defamde)/Heire of an antient	Ovid's Elegies		3.14.4
Which makes me hope, although I am but base,	Hero and Leander		1.218
You are deceav'd, I am no woman I.	Hero and Leander		2.192
AMAINE			
Returnes amaine: welcome, welcome my love:	Dido	5.1.191	Dido
And spying me, hoyst up the sailes amaine:	Dido	5.1.227	Anna
I, and our lives too, therfore pull amaine.	Jew	4.1.150	Ithimr
And let them march away to France amaine:	P 917	18.18	Navrre
So, pluck amaine,	P1104	20.14	1Mur
Lets all aboord, and follow him amaine.	Edw	2.4.47	Mortmr
Then make for Fraunce amaine, [Levune] <Lewne> away,/Proclaime	Edw	3.1.280	Spencr
So now away, post thither wards amaine.	Edw	5.2.67	Mortmr
I'le wing my selfe and forth-with flie amaine/Unto my Faustus	F1136	3.3.49	Mephst
So wavering Cupid bringes me backe amaine,	Ovid's Elegies		2.9.33
Let souldiour <souldiours> chase his <their> enemies amaine,	Ovid's Elegies		2.10.31
Incenst with savage heat, gallop amaine,	Hero and Leander		1.115
AMASDE			
Amasde, swim up and downe upon the waves,	2Tamb	5.1.207	Techel
AMASIA			
Of Soria, Trebizon and Amasia,	2Tamb	2.3.44	Orcan
Trebizon, Soria, Amasia, Thracia, Illyria, Carmonia and al the	2Tamb	3.1.4	P Orcan
Chio, Famastro, and Amasia,	2Tamb	3.1.50	Trebiz
King of Amasia, now our mighty hoste,	2Tamb	5.2.1	Callap
AMATISTS			
Bags of fiery Opals, Saphires, Amatists,	Jew	1.1.25	Barab
AMAZ'D			
mated and amaz'd/To heare the king thus threaten like himselfe?	1Tamb	1.1.107	Menaph
And hostes of souldiers stand amaz'd at us,	1Tamb	1.2.221	Usumc
These direful signes made Aruns stand amaz'd,	Lucan, First Booke		615
AMAZDE			
Why stands my sweete Aeneas thus amazde?	Dido	2.1.2	Achat
Your sight amazde me, O what destinies/Have brought my sweete	Dido	2.1.59	Aeneas
AMAZE (See also AMASDE)			
That their reflexions may amaze the Perseans.	1Tamb	1.2.140	Tamb
It might amaze your royall majesty.	1Tamb	4.1.16	2Msngr
AMAZED			
So runnes a Matron through th'amazed streetes,	Lucan, First Booke		675
Great Agamemnon was, men say, amazed,	Ovid's Elegies		1.9.37
True love is mute, and oft amazed stands.	Hero and Leander		1.186
AMAZING			
Or songs amazing wilde beasts of the wood?	Ovid's Elegies		3.8.22
AMAZON			
If she be tall, shees like an Amazon,	Ovid's Elegies		2.4.33
AMAZONIA			
To Amazonia under Capricorne,	2Tamb	1.1.74	Orcan
AMAZONIANS			
Wher Amazonians met me in the field:	2Tamb	1.3.192	Techel
AMBASSADORS (See also EMBASSADORS)			
Drawen with advise of our Ambassadors.	2Tamb	1.1.126	Orcan

AMBASSAGE
Now send Ambassage to thy neighbor Kings, ... 1Tamb 2.5.20 Cosroe
AMBER (Homograph)
About them hangs a knot of Amber heire, ... 1Tamb 2.1.23 Menaph
stay with me/Embalm'd with Cassia, Amber Greece and Myrre, 2Tamb 2.4.130 Tamb
[Amber] <Yellow> trest is shee, then on the morne thinke I,/My Ovid's Elegies 2.4.43
With Corall clasps and Amber studs, ... Passionate Shepherd 18
AMBER GREECE
stay with me/Embalm'd with Cassia, Amber Greece and Myrre, 2Tamb 2.4.130 Tamb
AMBIGUITIES
Resolve me of all ambiguities? . . . . F 107 1.1.79 Faust
AMBIGUOUS
Thus in ambiguous tearmes,/Involving all, did Aruns darkly Lucan, First Booke 636
AMBITION
O faintly joyn'd friends with ambition blind, . . . Lucan, First Booke 87
AMBITIOUS
And by profession be ambitious. . . . . 1Tamb 2.6.14 Meandr
Ambitious pride shall make thee fall as low, ... 1Tamb 4.2.76 Bajzth
Which makes me valiant, proud, ambitious, ... 2Tamb 4.1.116 Tamb
Surchargde with surfet of ambitious thoughts: . . . . P 953 19.23 King
Who swolne with venome of ambitious pride, ... Edw 1.2.31 Mortmr
dauntlesse minde/The ambitious Mortimer would seeke to curbe, Edw 5.1.16 Edward
To give ambitious Mortimer my right, ... Edw 5.1.53 Edward
[Ambitious fiends, see how the heavens smiles]/[At your . F1794 5.1.121A OldMan
Ambitious Imp, why seekst thou further charge? . . . Ovid's Elegies 1.1.18
But my ambitious ranging mind approoves? . . . . Ovid's Elegies 2.4.48
All women are ambitious naturallie: . . . . . . Hero and Leander 1.428
AMBLES
Thus every villaine ambles after wealth/Although he ne're be Jew 3.4.52 Barab
AMBROSIA
Giving thee Nectar and Ambrosia, ... 2Tamb 2.4.110 Tamb
AMBUSH
That lie in ambush, waiting for a pray: . . . . . 1Tamb 2.2.17 Meandr
But ere he came, Warwick in ambush laie, ... Edw 3.1.118 Arundl
and our followers/Close in an ambush there behinde the trees, F1342 4.2.18 Benvol
What's here? an ambush to betray my life: . . . . . F1424 4.2.100 Faust
AMEN
[Et omnes sancti. Amen]. F1087 3.2.107A 1Frier
Et omnes sancti Amen. . . . . F App p.233 41 Frier
AMEND
Checking thy body, may amend thy soule. . . . . . F1723 5.1.50 OldMan
AMENDS
Love made me jealous, but to make amends, ... Dido 4.4.33 Dido
The more cause have I now to make amends. . . . . . Edw 5.2.103 Kent
AMERICA
Fraughted with golde of rich America: . . . . . 2Tamb 1.2.35 Callap
To rip the golden bowels of America. . . . . . . P 854 17.49 Guise
And from America the Golden Fleece, ... F 158 1.1.130 Valdes
AMETHYST (See AMATISTS)
AMIABLE
Yet, yet, thou hast an amiable soule, ... F1712 5.1.39 OldMan
AMID
hunters in the chace/Of savage beastes amid the desart woods. 1Tamb 4.3.57 Capol
AMIDST
Shall build his throne amidst those starrie towers, . . . Dido 1.1.98 Jupitr
Thou shalt be drawen amidst the frosen Pooles, ... 1Tamb 1.2.99 Tamb
watch and ward shall keepe his trunke/Amidst these plaines, 2Tamb 2.3.39 Orcan
When he himselfe amidst the thickest troopes/Beats downe our 2Tamb 4.1.25 Amyras
That in a field amidst his enemies, ... Jew 1.2.203 Barab
AMIMONE
Such as Amimone through the drie fields strayed/When on her Ovid's Elegies 1.10.5
AMISSE
Twere not amisse my Lord, if he were searcht. . . . . P1160 22.22 Eprnon
Tis not amisse my liege for eyther part, ... Edw 3.1.190 SpncrP
but this/If feigned, doth well; if true it doth amisse. . Ovid's Elegies 1.8.36
AMITIE
How highly I doe prize this amitie, ... Dido 3.2.67 Juno
And in their smoothnesse, amitie and life: . . . . 1Tamb 2.1.22 Menaph
and strive to be retain'd/In such a great degree of amitie. 1Tamb 2.3.32 Therid
With dutie [and] <not> with amitie we yeeld/Our utmost service 1Tamb 2.3.33 Techel
pitch'd before the gates/And gentle flags of amitie displaid. 1Tamb 4.2.112 Therid
Can you in words make showe of amitie, ... Edw 2.2.32 Edward
AMITY
Thy death broake amity and trainde to war, ... Lucan, First Booke 119
AMONG (See also 'MONG)
So am I fear'd among all Nations. . . . . 2Tamb 1.1.151 Orcan
And harmelesse run among the deadly pikes. . . . . 2Tamb 1.3.46 Tamb
What wilt thou doe among these hatefull fiends? . . . Jew 1.2.345 Barab
Among the rest beare this, and set it there; . . . . Jew 3.4.78 Barab
Yonder is Edward among his flatterers. . . . . . Edw 3.1.196 Mortmr
Among the lords of France with Englands golde, ... Edw 3.1.277 Levune
And Edward thou art one among them all, ... Edw 4.4.10 Queene
Her I suspect among nights spirits to fly, ... Ovid's Elegies 1.8.13
Among day bookes and billes they had laine better/In which the Ovid's Elegies 1.12.25
Behould how quailes among their battailes live, . . . Ovid's Elegies 2.6.27
One among many is to grieve thee tooke. . . . . . Ovid's Elegies 2.7.4
Poore Semele, among so many burn'd; . . . . . . Ovid's Elegies 3.3.37
All headlong throwes her selfe the clouds among/And now Leander Hero and Leander 2.90
AMONGEST
amongest which kings is Alexander the great, chiefe spectacle F App p.237 23 P Emper
AMONGST (See also MONGST)
Disperst them all amongst the wrackfull Rockes: . . . Dido 1.2.29 Cloan
and in this grove/Amongst greene brakes Ile lay Ascanius, Dido 2.1.317 Venus

AMONGST (cont.)			
When ayrie creatures warre amongst themselves:	Dido	4.2.7	Iarbus
Amongst so many crownes of burnisht gold,	2Tamb	1.2.30	Callap
I beleeve there will be some hurt done anon amongst them.	2Tamb	4.1.75	P Calyph
Tush, who amongst 'em knowes not Barrabas?	Jew	1.1.67	Barab
time to make collection/Amongst the Inhabitants of Malta for't.	Jew	1.2.21	Govnr
For to be short, amongst you 'tmust be had.	Jew	1.2.56	Govnr
mony of the Turkes shall all be levyed amongst the Jewes,	Jew	1.2.69	P Reader
long since some of us/Did stray so farre amongst the multitude.	Jew	1.2.309	Abbass
now Abigall, what mak'st thou/Amongst these hateful Christians?	Jew	1.2.339	Barab
But one amongst the rest became our prize:	Jew	2.2.16	Bosco
And I will send amongst the Citizens/And by my letters	Jew	5.2.86	Govnr
There, Carpenters, divide that gold amongst you:	Jew	5.5.5	Barab
which my Lord of Guise/Did make in Paris amongst the Hugonites?	P 515	9.34	QnMoth
And share it equally amongst you all,	Edw	1.4.71	Edward
And read amongst the Statutes Decretall,	F 883	3.1.105	Pope
[Amongst the rest the Emperour is one],	F1150	3.3.63A	3Chor
Amongst the pricking thornes, and sharpest briers,	F1411	4.2.87	Faust
tickle the pretie wenches plackets Ile be amongst them ifaith.	F App	p.231 64	P Clown
carowse, and swill/Amongst the Students, as even now he doth,	F App	p.243 5	Wagner
was)/They call th'Etrurian Augures, amongst whom/The gravest,	Lucan, First Booke		584
AMOROUS (See also AMOUROUS)			
Whose amorous face like Pean sparkles fire,	Dido	3.4.19	Dido
And not stand lingering here for amorous lookes:	Dido	4.3.38	Illion
And when you looke for amorous discourse,	1Tamb	3.2.44	Agidas
Skilful in musicke and in amorous laies:	2Tamb	1.2.37	Callap
But yet me thinks their looks are amorous,	2Tamb	1.3.21	Tamb
For amorous Jove hath snatcht my love from hence,	2Tamb	2.4.107	Tamb
Supposing amorous Jove had sent his sonne,	2Tamb	4.2.18	Therid
Come Amorous wag, first banquet and then sleep.	Jew	4.2.132	Curtzn
Sweete prince I come, these these thy amorous lines,	Edw	1.1.6	Gavstn
Elegian Muse, that warblest amorous laies,	Ovid's Elegies		1.1.33
Take, and receive each secret amorous glaunce.	Ovid's Elegies		1.4.18
Amorous Leander, beautifull and yoong,	Hero and Leander		1.51
Leander, thou art made for amorous play:	Hero and Leander		1.88
Such force and vertue hath an amorous looke.	Hero and Leander		1.166
The mirthfull God of amorous pleasure smil'd,	Hero and Leander		2.39
yet he suspected/Some amorous rites or other were neglected.	Hero and Leander		2.64
Leanders amorous habit soone reveal'd.	Hero and Leander		2.104
AMOUNT			
To what this ten yeares tribute will amount/That we have cast,	Jew	1.2.46	Govnr
which being valued/Amount to more then all the wealth in Malta.	Jew	1.2.134	Offcrs
AMOUROUS			
how may I deserve/Such amourous favours at thy beautious hand?	Dido	3.2.65	Juno
AMPLIFIE			
But amplifie his greefe with bitter words.	Edw	5.2.65	Mortmr
AMYMONE (See AMIMONE)			
AMYRAS			
No, no Amyras, tempt not Fortune so,	2Tamb	4.1.86	Tamb
AN (Homograph; See also ANT)			
And then Ile hugge with you an hundred times.	Dido	1.1.48	Ganimd
An ancient Empire, famoused for armes,	Dido	1.2.21	Cloan
To force an hundred watchfull eyes to sleepe:	Dido	2.1.146	Aeneas
Which sent an eccho to the wounded King:	Dido	2.1.249	Aeneas
His lips an altar, where Ile offer up/As many kisses as the Sea	Dido	3.1.87	Dido
This was an Orator, and thought by words/To compasse me, but	Dido	3.1.155	Dido
Will leade an hoste against the hatefull Greekes,	Dido	4.4.91	Aeneas
The water is an Element, no Nimph,	Dido	4.4.147	Dido
I have an Orchard that hath store of plums,	Dido	4.5.4	Nurse
May have the leading of so great an host,	1Tamb	1.2.48	Tamb
With milke-white Hartes upon an Ivorie sled,	1Tamb	1.2.98	Tamb
An ods too great, for us to stand against:	1Tamb	1.2.122	Tamb
And with a sodaine and an hot alarme/Drive all their horses	1Tamb	1.2.134	Usumc
Deserv'st to have the leading of an hoste?	1Tamb	1.2.171	Tamb
An hundred horsmen of my company/Scowting abroad upon these	1Tamb	2.2.39	Spy
And more than needes to make an Emperour.	1Tamb	2.3.65	Tamb
An uncouth paine torments my grieved soule,	1Tamb	2.7.7	Cosroe
The sweet fruition of an earthly crowne.	1Tamb	2.7.29	Tamb
the Sea-man sees the Hyades/Gather an armye of Cemerian clouds,	1Tamb	3.2.77	Agidas
Dar'st thou that never saw an Emperour,	1Tamb	4.2.58	Zabina
Faire is too foule an Epithite for thee,	1Tamb	5.1.136	Tamb
Would lend an howers license to my tongue:	1Tamb	5.1.423	Arabia
Which kept his father in an yron cage:	2Tamb	1.1.5	Orcan
But (Sigismond) confirme it with an oath,	2Tamb	1.1.131	Orcan
And with an hoste of Moores trainde to the war,	2Tamb	1.3.141	Techel
An hundred kings by scores wil bid him armes,	2Tamb	2.2.11	Gazell
Not dooing Mahomet an injurie,	2Tamb	2.3.34	Orcan
whose taste illuminates/Refined eies with an eternall sight,	2Tamb	2.4.23	Tamb
(An Emperour so honoured for his vertues)/Revives the spirits	2Tamb	3.1.23	Callap
And when I meet an armie in the field,	2Tamb	3.2.38	Tamb
Here at Alepo with an hoste of men/Lies Tamburlaine, this king	2Tamb	3.5.3	2Msngr
Wherein an incorporeall spirit mooves,	2Tamb	4.1.114	Tamb
As when an heard of lusty Cymbrian Buls,	2Tamb	4.1.187	Tamb
I cannot love to be an Emperesse.	2Tamb	4.2.49	Olymp
An ointment which a cunning Alcumist/Distilled from the purest	2Tamb	4.2.59	Olymp
Like to an almond tree ymounted high,	2Tamb	4.3.119	Tamb
And made his state an honor to the heavens,	2Tamb	5.3.12	Therid
And henceforth wish for an eternall night,	Jew	1.2.193	Barab
And time may yeeld us an occasion/Which on the sudden cannot	Jew	1.2.239	Barab
That can so soone forget an injury.	Jew	2.3.19	Barab
Let me see, sirra, are you not an old shaver?	Jew	2.3.114	P Barab
An hundred Crownes, I'le have him; there's the coyne.	Jew	2.3.130	Barab
And after that I was an Engineere,	Jew	2.3.186	Barab

AN (cont.)

Then after that was I an Usurer,	Jew	2.3.190		Barab
One time I was an Hostler in an Inne,	Jew	2.3.205		Ithimr
Be made an accessary of your deeds;	Jew	2.3.342		Barab
a precious powder that I bought/Of an Italian in Ancona once,	Jew	3.4.69		Barab
Open an entrance for the wastfull sea,	Jew	3.5.16		Govnr
An Hebrew borne, and would become a Christian?	Jew	4.1.19		Barab
No, 'tis an order which the Fryars use:	Jew	4.1.134		Barab
Wherein I shall convert an Infidell,	Jew	4.1.162		1Fryar
whom I saluted with an old hempen proverb, Hodie tibi,	Jew	4.2.18	P	Pilia
What an eye she casts on me?	Jew	4.2.128	P	Ithimr
And in an out-house of the City shut/His souldiers, till I have	Jew	5.2.81		Barab
is a monastery/Which standeth as an out-house to the Towne;	Jew	5.3.37		Msngr
An eare, to heare what my detractors say,	P 160	2.103		Guise
An action bloudy and tirannicall:	P 208	4.6		Charls
Why let us burne him for an heretick.	P 483	9.2	P	2Atndt
Ile muster up an army secretly,	P 572	11.37		Navrre
Therfore an enemy to the Burbonites.	P 836	17.31		Guise
And being able, Ile keep an hoast in pay.	P 840	17.35		Guise
Thou able to maintaine an hoast in pay,	P 841	17.36		Eprnon
Why this tis to have an army in the fielde.	P 980	19.50		Guise
That wouldst reward them with an hospitall.	Edw	1.1.38		3PrMan
Shall with their Goate feete daunce an antick hay.	Edw	1.1.60		Gavstn
And in his sportfull hands an Olive tree,	Edw	1.1.64		Gavstn
And running in the likenes of an Hart,	Edw	1.1.69		Gavstn
That villaine Gaveston is made an Earle.	Edw	1.2.11		Lncstr
of Lancaster/That hath more earldomes then an asse can beare,	Edw	1.3.2		Gavstn
he refuse, and then may we/Depose him and elect an other king.	Edw	1.4.55		Mortmr
My heart is as an anvill unto sorrow,	Edw	1.4.312		Edward
Art thou an enemie to my Gaveston?	Edw	2.2.212		Edward
Come, come aboord, tis but an houres sailing.	Edw	2.4.49		Lncstr
Your honor hath an adamant, of power/To drawe a prince.	Edw	2.5.105		Arundl
I long to heare an answer from the Barons/Touching my friend,	Edw	3.1.1		Edward
being strucke/Runnes to an herbe that closeth up the wounds,	Edw	5.1.10		Edward
An other poast, what newes bringes he?	Edw	5.1.128		Leistr
For now we hould an old Wolfe by the eares,	Edw	5.2.7		Mortmr
But read it thus, and thats an other sence:	Edw	5.4.10		Mortmr
I, we must die, an everlasting death.	F 73	1.1.45		Faust
Go and returne an old Franciscan Frier,	F 253	1.3.25		Faust
Was not that Lucifer an Angell once?	F 292	1.3.64		Faust
So, now thou art to bee at an howres warning, whensoever, and	F 369	1.4.27	P	Wagner
To him, I'le build an Altar and a Church,	F 401	2.1.13		Faust
Now will I make an end immediately.	F 461	2.1.73		Faust
But <Faustus> I am an instance to prove the contrary:	F 525	2.1.137		Mephst
So shalt thou shew thy selfe an obedient servant <Do so>,/And	F 652	2.2.101		Lucifr
not speake a word more for a Kings ransome <an other worde>,	F 670	2.2.119	P	Pride
of an old Churle in a <an olde> leather <leatherne> bag;	F 674	2.2.123	P	Covet
I am Envy, begotten of a Chimney-sweeper, and an Oyster-wife:	F 679	2.2.128	P	Envy
out of a Lyons mouth when I was scarce <half> an houre old,	F 687	2.2.136	P	Wrath
O she was an ancient Gentlewoman, her name was <mistress>	F 699	2.2.148	P	Glutny
I'le not speake <an other word for a King's raunsome>.	F 706	(HC264) A	P	Sloth
I'le not speake [an other] word.	F 706	2.2.158	P	Sloth
I am one that loves an inch of raw Mutton, better then an ell	F 708	2.2.160	P	Ltchry
an inch of raw Mutton, better then an ell of fryde Stockfish:	F 709	2.2.161	P	Ltchry
your foolery, for an my Maister come, he'le conjure you 'faith.	F 734	2.3.13	P	Dick
an my Maister come here, I'le clap as faire a paire of hornes	F 736	2.3.15	P	Robin
The way he cut, an English mile in length,	F 792	3.1.14		Faust
Then in this shew let me an Actor be,	F 854	3.1.76		Faust
Fall to, the Divell choke you an you spare.	F1039	3.2.59		Faust
let him come; an he follow us, I'le so conjure him, as he was	F1091	3.3.4	P	Robin
For Apish deeds transformed to an Ape.	F1127	3.3.40		Mephst
O brave, an Ape?	F1128	3.3.41	P	Robin
an your Divels come not away quickly, you shall have me asleepe	F1241	4.1.87	P	Benvol
to thinke I have beene such an Asse all this while, to stand	F1243	4.1.89	P	Benvol
But an I be not reveng'd for this, would I might be turn'd to a	F1318	4.1.164	P	Benvol
Shall I let slip so great an injury,	F1328	4.2.4		Benvol
and our followers/Close in an ambush there behinde the trees,	F1342	4.2.18		Benvol
An excellent policie:	F1389	4.2.65	P	Mrtino
What's here? an ambush to betray my life:	F1424	4.2.100		Faust
Behold an Army comes incontinent.	F1430	4.2.106		Faust
The Duke of Vanholt's an honourable Gentleman, and one to whom	F1503	4.4.47	P	Faust
one of his devils turn'd me into the likenesse of an Apes face.	F1554	4.5.50	P	Dick
Do you remember how you made me weare an Apes--	F1661	4.6.104	P	Dick
Yet, yet, thou hast an amiable soule,	F1712	5.1.39		OldMan
I see an Angell hover <hovers> ore thy head,	F1730	5.1.57		OldMan
Shall be perform'd in twinkling of an eye.	F1767	5.1.94		Mephst
<a threatning Arme, an angry Brow>.	F1944	(HC271) B		Faust
an houres warning whensoever or wheresoever the divell shall	F App	p.230 36	P	Wagner
bleate, and an asse braye, because it is S. Peters holy day.	F App	p.232 27	P	Faust
Vanish vilaines, th'one like an Ape, an other like a Beare, the	F App	p.235 32	P	Mephst
th'one like an Ape, an other like a Beare, the third an Asse,	F App	p.235 32	P	Mephst
like a Beare, the third an Asse, for doing this enterprise.	F App	p.235 33	P	Mephst
presumption, I transforme thee into an Ape, and thee into a Dog,	F App	p.235 44	P	Mephst
How, into an Ape?	F App	p.236 45	P	Robin
him have him, he is an honest felow, and he has a great charge,	F App	p.239 105	P	Mephst
on him; hee has a buttocke as slicke as an Ele; wel god buy sir,	F App	p.240 117	P	HrsCsr
but yet like an asse as I was; I would not be ruled by him, for	F App	p.240 130	P	HrsCsr
an honourable gentleman, to whom I must be no niggard of my	F App	p.241 170	P	Faust
here, here (saith he)/An end of peace; here end polluted lawes;	Lucan, First Booke			227
and with what noise/An armed battaile joines, such and more	Lucan, First Booke			578
Next, an inferiour troupe, in tuckt up vestures,	Lucan, First Booke			595
as being like to prove/An aukward sacrifice, but by the hornes	Lucan, First Booke			611
And dores conjoynd with an hard iron lock.	Ovid's Elegies			1.6.74

AN (cont.)			
He first a Goddesse strooke; an other I.	Ovid's Elegies	1.7.32	
a bawde aright/Give eare, there is an old trot Dipsas hight.	Ovid's Elegies	1.8.2	
Take clustred grapes from an ore-laden vine,	Ovid's Elegies	1.10.55	
I did not bid thee wed an aged swaine.	Ovid's Elegies	1.13.42	
Ad <And> they were apt to curle an hundred waies,	Ovid's Elegies	1.14.13	
And tearmes <termst> [my] <our> works fruits of an idle quill?	Ovid's Elegies	1.15.2	
My hands an unsheath'd shyning weapon have not.	Ovid's Elegies	2.2.64	
Aye me an Eunuch keepes my mistrisse chaste,	Ovid's Elegies	2.3.1	
If she be tall, shees like an Amazon,	Ovid's Elegies	2.4.33	
A yong wench pleaseth, and an old is good,	Ovid's Elegies	2.4.45	
Yea, let my foes sleepe in an emptie bed,	Ovid's Elegies	2.10.17	
Nor can an other say his helpe I tooke.	Ovid's Elegies	2.12.12	
But of my love it will an end procure.	Ovid's Elegies	2.19.52	
An old wood, stands uncut of long yeares space,	Ovid's Elegies	3.1.1	
Pay it not heere, but in an other place.	Ovid's Elegies	3.2.84	
Argus had either way an hundred eyes,	Ovid's Elegies	3.4.19	
Against my good they were an envious charme.	Ovid's Elegies	3.11.14	
There stands an old wood with thick trees darke clouded,	Ovid's Elegies	3.12.7	
An Altar takes mens incense, and oblation,	Ovid's Elegies	3.12.9	
An Altar made after the ancient fashion.	Ovid's Elegies	3.12.10	
But with your robes, put on an honest face,	Ovid's Elegies	3.13.27	
am I by such wanton toyes defamde)/Heire of an antient house,	Ovid's Elegies	3.14.5	
Such force and vertue hath an amorous looke.	Hero and Leander	1.166	
And like an insolent commaunding lover,	Hero and Leander	1.409	
Therefore even as an Index to a booke,	Hero and Leander	2.129	
As from an orient cloud, glymse <glimps'd> here and there.	Hero and Leander	2.320	
ANAGRAMATIS'D			
Forward, and backward, Anagramatis'd <and Agramithist>:	F 237	1.3.9	Faust
ANALITIKES			
Sweet Analitikes <Anulatikes>, tis thou hast ravisht me,	F 34	1.1.6	Faust
ANCESTOR (See AUNCESTERS)			
ANCHISAEON			
Nay, I will have it calde Anchisaeon,	Dido	5.1.22	Aeneas
ANCHISES			
Then would I wish me with Anchises Tombe,	Dido	3.3.44	Aeneas
The King of Carthage, not Anchises sonne:	Dido	3.4.60	Dido
ANCHOR (See also ANCOR)			
But of them all scarce seven doe anchor safe,	Dido	1.1.222	Aeneas
Nor Sterne nor Anchor have our maimed Fleete,	Dido	3.1.109	Aeneas
Shall lie at anchor in the Isle Asant,	1Tamb	3.3.251	Tamb
wherin at anchor lies/A Turkish Gally of my royall fleet,	2Tamb	1.2.20	Callap
Or dieng, be the [author] <anchor> of my death.	2Tamb	2.4.56	Tamb
Was borne I see to be our anchor hold.	Edw	4.2.77	Mortmr
ANCHORS			
Thy Anchors shall be hewed from Christall Rockes,	Dido	3.1.120	Dido
Yet Dido casts her eyes like anchors out,	Dido	4.3.25	Aeneas
Whence is thy ship that anchors in our Rhoad?	Jew	2.2.2	Govnr
Too late you looke back, when with anchors weighd,	Ovid's Elegies	2.11.23	
ANCIENT (See also ANTIENT, AUNTIENT)			
An ancient Empire, famoused for armes,	Dido	1.2.21	Cloan
According to our ancient use, shall beare/The figure of the	2Tamb	3.1.64	Orcan
And turne him to his ancient trade againe.	2Tamb	3.5.95	Jrslem
As ancient Romanes over their Captive Lords,	P 982	19.52	Guise
O she was an ancient Gentlewoman, her name was <mistress>	F 699	2.2.148	P Glutny
And few live that behold their ancient seats;	Lucan, First Booke		27
Had ancient Mothers this vile custome cherisht,	Ovid's Elegies	2.14.9	
An Altar made after the ancient fashion.	Ovid's Elegies	3.12.10	
ANCKLES			
When thy waves brim did scarse my anckles touch.	Ovid's Elegies	3.5.6	
ANCONA			
a precious powder that I bought/Of an Italian in Ancona once,	Jew	3.4.69	Barab
ANCOR			
Yet could I not cast ancor where I meant,	Ovid's Elegies	3.6.6	
ANDROMACHE			
And on Andromache his helmet laces.	Ovid's Elegies	1.9.36	
A NEW			
And in the channell christen him a new.	Edw	1.1.188	Edward
Edward this day hath crownd him king a new.	Edw	3.1.261	Edward
ANEW			
Both whom thou raisest up to toyle anew.	Ovid's Elegies	1.13.22	
ANGELL			
Was not that Lucifer an Angell once?	F 292	1.3.64	Faust
I see an Angell hover <hovers> ore thy head,	F1730	5.1.57	OldMan
And now poore soule must thy good Angell leave thee,	F1907	5.2.111	GdAngl
ANGELO			
Upon the Bridge, call'd Ponte Angelo,	F 817	3.1.39	Mephst
And beare him streight to Ponte Angelo,	F 965	3.1.187	Pope
ANGELS			
(Whose scepter Angels kisse, and Furies dread)/As for their	1Tamb	5.1.94	1Virgn
There Angels in their christal armours fight/A doubtfull	1Tamb	5.1.151	Tamb
Now walk the angels on the walles of heaven,	2Tamb	2.4.15	Tamb
To see the devils mount in Angels throanes,	2Tamb	5.3.32	Usumc
And Angels dive into the pooles of hell.	2Tamb	5.3.33	Usumc
ANGER			
The heavens may frowne, the earth for anger quake,	1Tamb	5.1.231	Bajzth
And jealous anger of his fearefull arme/Be pour'd with rigour	2Tamb	2.1.57	Fredrk
(wanting moisture and remorsefull blood)/Drie up with anger,	2Tamb	4.1.180	Soria
Nor yet thy selfe, the anger of the highest,	2Tamb	5.1.104	Govnr
Bridle thy anger gentle Mortimer.	Edw	1.1.121	Warwck
Anger and wrathfull furie stops my speech.	Edw	1.4.42	Edward
I passe not for their anger, come lets go.	Edw	1.4.142	Edward
Would levie men enough to anger you.	Edw	2.2.152	Mortmr

ANGER (cont.)
My swelling hart for very anger breakes, ... Edw 2.2.200 Edward
Send for him out thence, and I will anger him. . . . . Edw 5.5.13 Gurney
zounds I could eate my selfe for anger, to thinke I have beene F1243 4.1.89 P Benvol
I harm'd: a foe did Diomedes anger move. . . . . . Ovid's Elegies 1.7.34
And as a pray unto blinde anger given, ... Ovid's Elegies 1.7.44
(Anger will helpe thy hands though nere so weake). . . . Ovid's Elegies 1.7.66
Anger delaide doth oft to hate retire. . . . . . Ovid's Elegies 1.8.82
Forbid thine anger to procure my griefe. . . . . . Ovid's Elegies 2.7.14
Yet evilly faining anger, strove she still, ... Hero and Leander 1.335
And here and there her eies through anger rang'd. . . . Hero and Leander 1.360
To slake his anger, if he were displeas'd, ... Hero and Leander 2.49
And red for anger that he stayd so long, ... Hero and Leander 2.89
ANGERS
this angers me,/That he who knowes I love him as my selfe Jew 4.3.41 Barab
ANGLE (Homograph)
For [which] <with> the quinque-angle fourme is meet: . 2Tamb 3.2.64 Tamb
Faire Queene forbeare to angle for the fish, ... Edw 1.4.221 Mortmr
There sat the hang-man for mens neckes to angle. . . Ovid's Elegies 1.12.18
ANGRED
What, hath Iarbus angred her in ought? . . . . . Dido 3.4.13 Aeneas
Not angred me, except in angring thee. . . . . . Dido 3.4.15 Dido
ANGRIE
To sound this angrie message in thine eares. . . . . Dido 5.1.33 Hermes
And dare the force of angrie Jupiter. . . . . . 1Tamb 2.6.4 Cosroe
Though Mars himselfe the angrie God of armes, ... 1Tamb 2.7.58 Tamb
Pursude by hunters, flie his angrie lookes, ... 1Tamb 3.3.193 Zenoc
Against the Woolfe that angrie Themis sent, ... 1Tamb 4.3.5 Souldn
Venus, would she leave/The angrie God of Armes, and lie with me. 1Tamb 5.1.125 Tamb
Shall by the angrie goddesse be transformde, ... Edw 1.1.68 Gavstn
The angrie king hath banished me the court: . . . . Edw 1.4.210 Queene
Likewise the angrie sisters thus deluded, ... Hero and Leander 1.473
Neptune was angrie that hee gave no eare, ... Hero and Leander 2.207
ANGRING
Not angred me, except in angring thee. . . . . . Dido 3.4.15 Dido
ANGRY
or els infernall, mixt/Their angry seeds at his conception: 1Tamb 2.6.10 Meandr
And wrapt in silence of his angry soule. . . . . . 1Tamb 3.2.71 Agidas
Whose lookes might make the angry God of armes, . . . 1Tamb 5.1.326 Zenoc
they come to proove/The wounding troubles angry war affoords. 2Tamb 1.3.87 Zenoc
now let us celebrate/Our happy conquest, and his angry fate. 2Tamb 2.3.47 Orcan
Now by the malice of the angry Skies, ... 2Tamb 2.4.11 Tamb
We must my lord, so will the angry heavens. . . . . Edw 4.7.74 Spencr
[No marvel tho the angry Greekes pursu'd]/[With tenne yeares F1699 5.1.26A 3Schol
<a threatning Arme, an angry Brow>. . . . . . . F1944 (HC271)B Faust
The angry Senate urging Grachus deeds, ... Lucan, First Booke 268
the angry threatning gods/Fill'd both the earth and seas with Lucan, First Booke 522
Angry, I pray that rotten age you wrackes/And sluttish . Ovid's Elegies 1.12.29
But when on thee her angry eyes did rush, ... Ovid's Elegies 2.8.15
The carefull ship-man now feares angry gusts, ... Ovid's Elegies 2.11.25
Angry I was, but feare my wrath exempted. . . . . Ovid's Elegies 2.13.4
Thou saiest broke with Alcides angry hand. . . . . Ovid's Elegies 3.5.36
And knocks his bare brest with selfe-angry hands. . . Ovid's Elegies 3.8.10
ANGUISH
His anguish and his burning agony. . . . . 2Tamb 5.3.209 Amyras
doe not languish/And then report her sicke and full of anguish. Ovid's Elegies 2.2.22
Till she o'recome with anguish, shame, and rage, . . . Hero and Leander 2.333
ANHOLT (See VANHOLT)
A NIGHT
What time a night is't now, sweet Ithimore? . . . . Jew 4.1.157 Barab
A NIGHTS
I walke abroad a nights/And kill sicke people groaning under Jew 2.3.174 Barab
ANIMATE
Would animate grosse clay, and higher set/The drooping thoughts Hero and Leander 2.256
ANIMATED
Being animated by Religious zeale, ... P 848 17.43 Guise
ANIO (See TAV'RON)
ANIPPE
Hearst thou Anippe, how thy drudge doth talk, ... 1Tamb 3.3.182 Zenoc
Chide her Anippe. . . . . 1Tamb 4.2.71 Zenoc
See, se Anippe if they breathe or no. . . . . . 1Tamb 5.1.343 Zenoc
ANJOY
Anjoy hath well advisde/Your highnes to consider of the thing, P 219 4.17 Guise
Anjoy, Dumaine, Gonzago, Retes, sweare by/The argent crosses in P 274 5.1 Guise
Anjoy, Gonzago, Retes, if that you three, ... P 322 5.49 Guise
Anjoy will follow thee. . . . . P 333 5.60 Anjoy
My Lord of Anjoy, there are a hundred Protestants, . . . P 417 7.57 Guise
ANKLE (See ANCKLES)
ANNA
O Anna, didst thou know how sweet love were, ... Dido 3.1.59 Dido
Name not Iarbus, but sweete Anna say, ... Dido 3.1.67 Dido
Anna, good sister Anna goe for him, ... Dido 3.1.75 Dido
Faire Anna, how escapt you from the shower? . . . . Dido 4.1.29 Aeneas
I Anna, is there ought you would with me? . . . . . Dido 4.2.24 Iarbus
Anna, against this Troian doe I pray, ... Dido 4.2.30 Iarbus
Away with Dido, Anna be thy song, ... Dido 4.2.45 Anna
Anna that doth admire thee more then heaven. . . . . Dido 4.2.46 Anna
O Anna, runne unto the water side, ... Dido 4.4.1 Dido
Stay not to answere me, runne Anna runne. . . . . . Dido 4.4.4 Dido
Faire sister Anna leade my lover forth, ... Dido 4.4.65 Dido
O Anna, my Aeneas is abourd, ... Dido 5.1.194 Dido
Request him gently (Anna) to returne, ... Dido 5.1.206 Dido
Run Anna, run, stay not to answere me. . . . . . Dido 5.1.210 Dido

ANNA (cont.)			
O Anna, Anna, I will follow him.	Dido	5.1.241	Dido
O Anna, fetch [Arions] <Orions> Harpe,	Dido	5.1.248	Dido
Anna be glad, now have I found a meane/To rid me from these	Dido	5.1.272	Dido
Goe Anna, bid my servants bring me fire.	Dido	5.1.278	Dido
But Anna now shall honor thee in death,	Dido	5.1.325	Anna
ANNAS			
O sweet Iarbus, Annas sole delight,	Dido	5.1.322	Anna
ANNOY (See also ANOY)			
That by thy vertues freest us from annoy,	Dido	1.1.153	Achat
And urg'd each Element to his annoy:	Dido	3.2.46	Juno
If without battell selfe-wrought wounds annoy them,	Ovid's Elegies	2.14.3	
Nor feared they thy body to annoy?	Ovid's Elegies	3.8.42	
ANNOYES			
Fat love, and too much fulsome me annoyes,	Ovid's Elegies	2.19.25	
ANNOYETH			
Raves in Egyptia, and annoyeth us.	1Tamb	4.3.10	Souldn
ANNUALL			
The annuall pompe goes on the covered ground.	Ovid's Elegies	3.12.12	
ANOINT (See NOINT)			
ANON			
I beleeve there will be some hurt done anon amongst them.	2Tamb	4.1.75	P Calyph
Zoon's what a looking thou keep'st, thou'lt betraye's anon.	Jew	3.1.25	Pilia
Here take my keyes, I'le give 'em thee anon:	Jew	3.4.46	Barab
I hope the poyson'd flowers will worke anon.	Jew	5.1.43	Barab
For anon the Guise will come.	P 941	19.11	Capt
The Cardinals will be plagu'd for this anon.	F 976	3.1.198	Faust
life, Vintner you shall have your cup anon, say nothing Dick:	F1114	3.3.27	P Robin
Il'e make you feele something anon, if my Art faile me not.	F1246	4.1.92	P Faust
zounds hee'l raise up a kennell of Divels I thinke anon:	F1306	4.1.152	P Benvol
And so I leave thee Faustus till anon,	F1924	5.2.128	BdAngl
Anon you shal heare a hogge grunt, a calfe bleate, and an asse	F App	p.232 27	P Faust
ANONE			
For hornes he gave, Il'e have his head anone.	F1361	4.2.37	Benvol
'twill all be past anone:	F1957	5.2.161	Faust
Ile meete with you anone for interrupting me so:	F App	p.238 58	P Faust
AN OTHER			
he refuse, and then may we/Depose him and elect an other king.	Edw	1.4.55	Mortmr
An other poast, what newes bringes he?	Edw	5.1.128	Leistr
not speake a word more for a Kings ransome <an other worde>,	F 670	2.2.119	P Pride
I'le not speake <an other word for a King's raunsome>.	F 706	(HC264)A	P Sloth
I'le not speake [an other] word.	F 706	2.2.158	P Sloth
th'one like an Ape, an other like a Beare, the third an Asse,	F App	p.235 32	P Mephst
He first a Goddesse strooke; an other I.	Ovid's Elegies	1.7.32	
Nor can an other say his helpe I tooke.	Ovid's Elegies	2.12.12	
ANOTHER			
No more my child, now talke another while,	Dido	3.1.26	Dido
And in my thoughts is shrin'd another [love] <Iove>:	Dido	3.1.58	Dido
But I will take another order now,	Dido	3.2.6	Juno
But may be slackt untill another time:	Dido	4.2.26	Anna
Such another word, and I will have thee executed.	1Tamb	2.4.30	Mycet
But see another bloody spectacle.	1Tamb	5.1.339	Zenoc
And me another my Lord.	2Tamb	3.2.133	P Amyras
Seeke out another Godhead to adore,	2Tamb	5.1.200	Tamb
of all the villaines power/Live to give offer of another fight.	2Tamb	5.3.109	Tamb
Well, let it passe, another time shall serve.	Jew	2.3.278	Mthias
Fornication? but that was in another Country:	Jew	4.1.41	Barab
As thou lik'st that, stop me another time.	Jew	4.1.173	1Fryar
when holy Friars turne devils and murder one another.	Jew	4.1.194	P Ithimr
reading of the letter, he look'd like a man of another world.	Jew	4.2.7	P Pilia
to his prayers, as if hee had had another Cure to serve; well,	Jew	4.2.24	P Ithimr
Yet is [their] <there> pacience of another sort,	P 545	11.10	Charls
Thy friend, thy selfe, another Gaveston.	Edw	1.1.143	Edward
Let us assaile his minde another while.	Edw	5.5.12	Matrvs
Then if I gain'd another Monarchie.	F1272	4.1.118	Emper
we'le into another roome and drinke a while, and then we'le go	F1556	4.5.52	P Robin
Another railes at me, and that I write,	Ovid's Elegies	2.4.21	
And one gave place still as another came.	Ovid's Elegies	3.6.64	
As if another Phaeton had got/The guidance of the sunnes rich	Hero and Leander	1.101	
There might you see one sigh, another rage,	Hero and Leander	1.125	
of hers (like that/Which made the world) another world begat,	Hero and Leander	2.292	
ANOY			
Lets see what tempests can anoy me now.	Dido	4.4.60	Aeneas
ANOYDE			
When all my sences are anoyde with stenche?	Edw	5.3.18	Edward
ANSWEARE			
And asking why, this answeare she redoubled,	Ovid's Elegies	2.2.7	
ANSWEARES			
Nemesis answeares, what's my losse to thee?	Ovid's Elegies	3.8.57	
ANSWER			
Till I have answer of my Abigall.	Jew	2.1.19	Barab
Doth she not with her smiling answer you?	Jew	2.3.286	Barab
I pray, mistris, wil you answer me to one question?	Jew	3.3.30	P Ithimr
For by this Answer, broken is the league,	Jew	3.5.34	Govnr
You see I answer him, and yet he stayes;	Jew	4.1.88	Barab
You heare your answer, and you may be gone.	Jew	4.1.92	1Fryar
Yes more then thou canst answer though he live,	Edw	2.2.87	Edward
Madam, I cannot stay to answer you,	Edw	2.4.57	Mortmr
I long to heare an answer from the Barons/Touching my friend,	Edw	3.1.1	Edward
Away, tarrie no answer, but be gon.	Edw	3.1.173	Edward
They stay your answer, will you yeeld your crowne?	Edw	5.1.50	Leistr
This answer weele returne, and so farewell.	Edw	5.1.90	BshpWn
I, stay a while, thou shalt have answer straight.	Edw	5.5.20	Matrvs

ANSWERABLE			
and nothing answerable to the honor of your Imperial majesty,	F App	p.236 14	P Faust
ANSWER'D			
Well, I am answer'd:	F 618	2.2.67	P Faust
This spoke none answer'd, but a murmuring buz/Th'unstable	Lucan, First Booke		353
ANSWERE			
Stay not to answere me, runne Anna runne.	Dido	4.4.4	Dido
Run Anna, run, stay not to answere me.	Dido	5.1.210	Dido
How answere you that?	P 397	7.37	Guise
Ile read them Frier, and then Ile answere thee.	P1171	22.33	King
thats no answere	Paris	ms 7,p390	P Souldr
No more then I would answere were he slaine.	Edw	2.2.86	Mortmr
Welcome grave Fathers, answere presently,	F 946	3.1.168	Pope
that your devill can answere the stealing of this same cup,	F1089	3.3.2	P Dick
Eneas to Elisa answere gives,	Ovid's Elegies		2.18.31
ANSWERED			
[Which Faustus answered with such learned skill],	F1147	3.3.60A	3Chor
To Venus, answered shee, and as shee spake,	Hero and Leander		1.295
They answered Love, nor would vouchsafe so much/As one poore	Hero and Leander		1.383
Which joyfull Hero answered in such sort,	Hero and Leander		2.15
But still the rising billowes answered no.	Hero and Leander		2.152
ANSWERING			
Eagles alike displaide, darts answering darts.	Lucan, First Booke		7
ANT			
And saying, trulie ant may please your honor,	Edw	2.1.40	Spencr
ANTARTICKE			
Leapes from th'Antarticke world unto the skie,	F 231	1.3.3	Faust
ANTARTIQUE			
We meane to traveile to th'Antartique Pole,	1Tamb	4.4.136	Tamb
And from th'Antartique Pole, Eastward behold/As much more land,	2Tamb	5.3.154	Tamb
ANTECHRISTIAN			
Monarck goes/To wrack, and [his] antechristian kingdome falles.	P1198	22.60	King
ANTENOR			
Some say Antenor did betray the towne,	Dido	2.1.110	Dido
ANTICHRISTIAN			
Wherewith thy antichristian churches blaze,	Edw	1.4.99	Edward
ANTICK			
Shall with their Goate feete daunce an antick hay.	Edw	1.1.60	Gavstn
ANTIENT			
Great grand-sires from their antient graves she chides/And with	Ovid's Elegies		1.8.17
Nor let the armes of antient [lines] <lives> beguile thee,	Ovid's Elegies		1.8.65
Behold the signes of antient fight, his skarres,	Ovid's Elegies		3.7.19
am I by such wanton toyes defamde)/Heire of an antient house,	Ovid's Elegies		3.14.5
ANTIOCH			
Acantha, Antioch, and Caesaria,	2Tamb	2.1.20	Fredrk
ANTIPODES (See also ANTYPODES)			
Discendeth downward to th'Antipodes.	2Tamb	1.2.52	Callap
ANTIQUES			
And point like Antiques at his triple Crowne:	F 862	3.1.84	Mephst
ANTS			
Can kinglie Lions fawne on creeping Ants?	Edw	1.4.15	Penbrk
ANTWARPES			
keele at [Antwerpe] <Anwerpe> <Antwarpes> <Antwerpes> bridge,	F 123	1.1.95	Faust
ANTWERPE			
In Florence, Venice, Antwerpe, London, Civill,	Jew	4.1.71	Barab
keele at [Antwerpe] <Anwerpe> <Antwarpes> <Antwerpes> bridge,	F 123	1.1.95	Faust
ANTWERPES			
keele at [Antwerpe] <Anwerpe> <Antwarpes> <Antwerpes> bridge,	F 123	1.1.95	Faust
ANTYPODES			
Begins the day with our Antypodes:	2Tamb	5.3.149	Tamb
ANUBIS			
By fear'd Anubis visage I thee pray,	Ovid's Elegies		2.13.11
ANULATIKES			
Sweet Analitikes <Anulatikes>, tis thou hast ravisht me,	F 34	1.1.6	Faust
ANVILL			
My heart is as an anvill unto sorrow,	Edw	1.4.312	Edward
ANWERPE			
keele at [Antwerpe] <Anwerpe> <Antwarpes> <Antwerpes> bridge,	F 123	1.1.95	Faust
ANY			
men, saw you as you came/Any of all my Sisters wandring here?	Dido	1.1.184	Venus
I neither saw nor heard of any such:	Dido	1.1.187	Aeneas
And have not any coverture but heaven.	Dido	1.1.230	Aeneas
Nor armed to offend in any kind:	Dido	1.2.13	Illion
Who if that any seeke to doe him hurt,	Dido	2.1.321	Venus
For if that any man could conquer me,	Dido	3.1.137	Dido
And meddle not with any that I love:	Dido	3.3.22	Dido
Never to like or love any but her.	Dido	3.4.51	Aeneas
Before my sorrowes tide have any stint.	Dido	4.2.42	Iarbus
If there be any heaven in earth, tis love:	Dido	4.5.27	Nurse
I am as true as any one of yours.	Dido	5.1.223	Nurse
As any prizes out of my precinct.	1Tamb	1.2.28	Tamb
And far from any man that is a foole.	1Tamb	2.4.12	Mycet
I marie am I: have you any suite to me?	1Tamb	2.4.24	Mycet
had the Turkish Emperour/So great a foile by any forraine foe.	1Tamb	3.3.235	Bajzth
Not sparing any that can manage armes.	1Tamb	4.1.57	2Msngr
And now Bajazeth, hast thou any stomacke?	1Tamb	4.4.10	Tamb
If any love remaine in you my Lord,	1Tamb	4.4.68	Zenoc
By any innovation or remorse,	1Tamb	5.1.16	Govnr
As long as any blood or sparke of breath/Can quench or coole	1Tamb	5.1.284	Zabina
if any Christian King/Encroche upon the confines of thy realme,	2Tamb	1.1.146	Orcan
If any heathen potentate or king/Invade Natolia, Sigismond will	2Tamb	1.1.152	Sgsmnd
If any man will hold him, I will strike,	2Tamb	1.3.102	Calyph
We shall not need to nourish any doubt,	2Tamb	3.1.26	Callap

ANY (cont.)

Whose lovely faces never any viewed, ...	2Tamb	3.2.30	Tamb
Quite voide of skars, and cleare from any wound, . .	2Tamb	3.2.112	Tamb
Nor [any] issue foorth, but they shall die:	2Tamb	3.3.33	Techel
Than any Viceroy, King or Emperour.	2Tamb	3.4.43	Olymp
that ever brandisht sword)/Challenge in combat any of you all,	2Tamb	3.5.72	Tamb
not any Element/Shal shrowde thee from the wrath of . .	2Tamb	3.5.126	Tamb
To think our helps will doe him any good.	2Tamb	4.1.21	Calyph
Shrowd any thought may holde my striving hands/From martiall	2Tamb	4.1.95	Tamb
As any thing of price with thy conceit?	2Tamb	5.1.14	Govnr
the towne will never yeeld/As long as any life is in my breast.	2Tamb	5.1.48	Govnr
Now Mahomet, if thou have any power, ...	2Tamb	5.1.187	Tamb
The God that sits in heaven, if any God, ...	2Tamb	5.1.201	Tamb
If God or Mahomet send any aide.	2Tamb	5.2.11	Callap
Pierc'd with the joy of any dignity?	2Tamb	5.3.190	Amyras
Joy any hope of your recovery?	2Tamb	5.3.215	Usumc
I, wealthier farre then any Christian.	Jew	1.1.128	Barab
If any thing shall there concerne our state/Assure your selves	Jew	1.1.172	Barab
And ducke as low as any bare-foot Fryar, ...	Jew	2.3.25	Barab
No; so shall I, if any hurt be done, ...	Jew	2.3.341	Barab
and inquire/For any of the Fryars of Saint [Jaques] <Jaynes>,	Jew	3.3.28	Abigal
into the sea; why I'le doe any thing for your sweet sake.	Jew	3.4.40	P Ithimr
I never heard of any man but he/Malign'd the order of the	Jew	4.1.103	Barab
But not a word to any of your Covent.	Jew	4.1.112	Barab
Why, wantst thou any of thy tale?	Jew	4.3.19	P Barab
Any of 'em will doe it.	Jew	4.4.78	P Ithimr
Thou shalt not live in doubt of any thing.	Jew	5.5.45	Barab
That durst presume for hope of any gaine, ...	P 258	4.56	Charls
And yet didst never sound any thing to the depth. . .	P 386	7.26	Guise
Whatsoever any whisper in mine eares, ...	P 974	19.44	King
I will not yeeld to any such upstart.	Edw	1.4.423	Mortmr
Not Mortimer, nor any of his side, ...	Edw	2.1.4	Spencr
Can get you any favour with great men.	Edw	2.1.41	Spencr
And apt for any kinde of villanie.	Edw	2.1.51	Baldck
Violate any promise to possesse him.	Edw	2.5.64	Warwck
In any case, take heed of childish feare, ...	Edw	5.2.6	Mortmr
Speake curstlie to him, and in any case/Let no man comfort him,	Edw	5.2.63	Mortmr
Thus lives old Edward not reliev'd by any, ...	Edw	5.3.23	Edward
If any Christian, Heathen, Turke, or Jew, ...	Edw	5.4.75	Champn
That were enough to poison any man, ...	Edw	5.5.5	Matrvs
Neede you any thing besides?	Edw	5.5.32	Gurney
geare, nere was there any/So finely handled as this king shalbe.	Edw	5.5.39	Ltborn
<Have you any witnesse on't>?	F 204	(HC258)A	P Wagner
Nor any Potentate of Germany.	F 339	1.3.111	Faust
to a Dog, or a Cat, or a Mouse, or a Rat, or any thing. .	F 383	1.4.41	P Wagner
Why, have you any paine that torture other <tortures others>?	F 432	2.1.44	Faust
That after this life there is any paine?	F 523	2.1.135	Faust
faire/As thou, or any man that [breathes] <breathe> on earth.	F 558	2.2.7	Mephst
Villaine, have I not bound thee to tell me any thing? .	F 622	2.2.71	P Faust
I am Pride; I disdaine to have any parents:	F 664	2.2.113	P Pride
Not to be wonne by any conquering Prince:	F 783	3.1.5	Faust
Or any villany thou canst devise, ...	F 865	3.1.87	Mephst
And doe what ere I please, unseene of any.	F 993	3.2.13	Faust
<to do what I please unseene of any whilst I stay in Rome>.	F 993	(HC266)A	P Faust
in any case, ride him not into the water.	F1468	4.4.12	P Faust
time; but, quoth he, in any case ride him not into the water.	F1541	4.5.37	P HrsCsr
Tel me sirra, hast thou any commings in?	F App	p.229 4	P Wagner
to a dogge, or a catte, or a mouse, or a ratte, or any thing.	F App	p.231 59	P Wagner
if you turne me into any thing, let it be in the likenesse of a	F App	p.231 61	P Clown
for conjuring that ere was invented by any brimstone divel.	F App	p.233 20	P Robin
druncke with ipocrase at any taberne in Europe for nothing,	F App	p.234 23	P Robin
if thou hast any mind to Nan Spit our kitchin maide, then turn	F App	p.234 26	P Robin
before you have him, ride him not into the water at any hand.	F App	p.239 109	P Faust
And they of Nilus mouth (if there live any).	Lucan, First Booke		20
If any one part of vast heaven thou swayest, ...	Lucan, First Booke		56
Wondring if any walked without light.	Ovid's Elegies		1.6.10
No charmed herbes of any harlot skathd thee, ...	Ovid's Elegies		1.14.39
such faults are sad/Nor make they any man that heare them glad.	Ovid's Elegies		2.2.52
I meane not to defend the scapes of any, ...	Ovid's Elegies		2.4.1
If any eie mee with a modest looke, ...	Ovid's Elegies		2.4.11
Nay what is she that any Romane loves, ...	Ovid's Elegies		2.4.47
If I praise any, thy poore haires thou tearest, . . .	Ovid's Elegies		2.7.7
Or any back made rough with stripes imbrace?	Ovid's Elegies		2.7.22
Yet blusht I not, nor usde I any saying, ...	Ovid's Elegies		2.8.7
If any godly care of me thou hast, ...	Ovid's Elegies		2.16.47
To serve a wench if any thinke it shame, ...	Ovid's Elegies		2.17.1
Nor, least she will, can any be restrainde.	Ovid's Elegies		3.4.6
Was not defilde by any gallant wooer.	Ovid's Elegies		3.4.24
She pleaseth best, I feare, if any say.	Ovid's Elegies		3.4.32
Never can these by any meanes agree.	Ovid's Elegies		3.4.42
Least labour so shall winne great grace of any. . . .	Ovid's Elegies		3.4.46
That seeing thy teares can any joy then feele. . . .	Ovid's Elegies		3.5.60
No certaine house thou hast, nor any fountaines. . . .	Ovid's Elegies		3.5.92
Hath any rose so from a fresh yong maide, ...	Ovid's Elegies		3.6.53
Or thinke soft verse in any stead to stand?	Ovid's Elegies		3.7.2
Nor lesse at mans prosperity any grudge.	Ovid's Elegies		3.9.6
Who mine was cald, whom I lov'd more then any, . . .	Ovid's Elegies		3.11.5
Would I my words would any credit beare.	Ovid's Elegies		3.11.20
Died ere he could enjoy the love of any.	Hero and Leander		1.76
No, nor to any one exterior sence, ...	Hero and Leander		1.271
Nor hath it any place of residence, ...	Hero and Leander		1.272
Or capable of any forme at all.	Hero and Leander		1.274

ANY THING

into the sea; why I'le doe any thing for your sweet sake.	Jew	3.4.40	P Ithimr

ANY THING (cont.)			
Thou shalt not live in doubt of any thing. . . .	Jew	5.5.45	Barab
And yet didst never sound any thing to the depth. . .	P 386	7.26	Guise
Neede you any thing besides?	Edw	5.5.32	Gurney
to a Dog, or a Cat, or a Mouse, or a Rat, or any thing. .	F 383	1.4.41	P Wagner
Villaine, have I not bound thee to tell me any thing? .	F 622	2.2.71	P Faust
to a dogge, or a catte, or a mouse, or a ratte, or any thing.	F App	p.231 59	P Wagner
if you turne me into any thing, let it be in the likenesse of a	F App	p.231 61	P Clown
ANYTHING			
I will teach thee to turne thy selfe to anything, to a dogge,	F App	p.231 58	P Wagner
AONIAN			
To waste and spoile the sweet Aonian fieldes. . . .	1Tamb	4.3.6	Souldn
While Mars doth take the Aonian harpe to play? . . .	Ovid's Elegies		1.1.16
Doth say, with her that lov'd the Aonian harpe. . .	Ovid's Elegies		2.18.26
AP			
Take him away, he prates. You Rice ap Howell, . . .	Edw	4.6.73	Mortmr
A PACE			
Why so, they barkt a pace a month agoe, ...	Edw	4.3.12	Edward
Gallop a pace bright Phoebus through the skie, . . .	Edw	4.3.43	Edward
APACE			
Huntsmen, why pitch you not your toyles apace, . . .	Dido	3.3.30	Dido
Came creeping to us with their crownes apace. . . .	1Tamb	2.5.86	Tamb
APAL'D			
With whose outcryes Atrides being apal'd, ...	Dido	2.1.129	Aeneas
APART			
And worshipt by their paine, and lying apart? . . .	Ovid's Elegies		3.9.16
APE			
For Apish deeds transformed to an Ape.	F1127	3.3.40	Mephst
O brave, an Ape?	F1128	3.3.41	P Robin
Vanish vilaines, th'one like an Ape, an other like a Beare, the	F App	p.235 32	P Mephst
presumption, I transforme thee into an Ape, and thee into a Dog,	F App	p.235 44	P Mephst
How, into an Ape?	F App	p.236 45	P Robin
APEECE			
Larissa plaines/With hostes apeece against this Turkish crue,	2Tamb	1.3.108	Tamb
take ye Queens apeece/(I meane such Queens as were kings .	2Tamb	4.3.70	Tamb
APES			
To make his Monkes and Abbots stand like Apes, . . .	F 861	3.1.83	Mephst
one of his devils turn'd me into the likenesse of an Apes face.	F1554	4.5.50	P Dick
Do you remember how you made me weare an Apes-- . .	F1661	4.6.104	P Dick
APHORISMES			
[Is not thy common talke sound Aphorismes]? . . .	F 47	1.1.19A	Faust
APIECE (See APEECE)			
A PIECES (See also APEECE)			
hoary flieces/And riveld cheekes I would have puld a pieces.	Ovid's Elegies		1.8.112
APIS			
And in thy pompe hornd Apis with thee keepe, . . .	Ovid's Elegies		2.13.14
APISH			
For Apish deeds transformed to an Ape.	F1127	3.3.40	Mephst
might be better spent)/In vaine discourse, and apish merriment.	Hero and Leander		1.356
APOLLO (See also PEAN)			
Apollo, Cynthia, and the ceaslesse lamps/That gently look'd	2Tamb	2.4.18	Tamb
Will him to send Apollo hether straight, ...	2Tamb	5.3.62	Tamb
Apollo, Bacchus, and the Muses may, ...	Ovid's Elegies		1.3.11
At me Apollo bends his pliant bowe:	Ovid's Elegies		3.3.29
Whom young Apollo courted for her haire, ...	Hero and Leander		1.6
APOLLOES			
Then Thetis hangs about Apolloes necke, ...	Dido	3.1.132	Dido
I shall not need/To crave Apolloes ayde, or Bacchus helpe;	Lucan, First Booke		65
Apolloes southsayers; and Joves feasting priests; . .	Lucan, First Booke		601
APOLLO'S			
And burned is Apollo's Lawrell bough, ...	F2003	5.3.21	4Chor
APOLLOS			
Doubtles Apollos Axeltree is crackt, ...	Dido	4.1.11	Achat
Nor are Apollos Oracles more true, ...	1Tamb	1.2.212	Tamb
and on his head/A Chaplet brighter than Apollos crowne, .	2Tamb	5.2.33	Amasia
By this Apollos golden harpe began, ...	Hero and Leander		2.327
APOSTOLICALL			
And by authority Apostolicall/Depose him from his Regall .	F 923	3.1.145	Pope
And take our blessing Apostolicall.	F 973	3.1.195	Pope
APOTHECARIE			
Apothecarie.--	P 66	2.9	Guise
APPAL (See also APPAULS, APAL'D)			
Come lady, let not this appal your thoughts. . . .	1Tamb	1.2.1	Tamb
APPARANT			
might ease/The Commons jangling minds, apparant signes arose,	Lucan, First Booke		521
APPARANTLY			
His secret flame apparantly was seene, ...	Hero and Leander		2.135
APPAREAT			
propitiamus vos, ut appareat, et surgat Mephostophilis. .	F 247	1.3.19	P Faust
APPAREL (See 'PARRELL)			
APPAULS			
ugly jointes/Then nature gives, whose sight appauls the mother,	Lucan, First Booke		561
APPEALE			
And now <so> to patient judgements we appeale <our plaude>,	F 9	Prol.9	1Chor
APPEAR'D			
That looking downe the earth appear'd to me, . . .	F 850	3.1.72	Faust
When he appear'd to haplesse Semele:	F1784	5.1.111	Faust
Mourning appear'd, whose hoary hayres were torne, . .	Lucan, First Booke		189
Strange sights appear'd, the angry threatning gods/Fill'd both	Lucan, First Booke		522
At that bunch where the liver is, appear'd/A knob of flesh,	Lucan, First Booke		626
One halfe appear'd, the other halfe was hid. . . .	Hero and Leander		2.316
APPEARD			
Sent from his father Jove, appeard to me, ...	Dido	5.1.95	Aeneas

APPEARDE
As if that Proteus god of shapes appearde. . . . Edw 1.4.411 Mortmr
APPEARE
and the bounds/Of Europe wher the Sun dares scarce appeare, 1Tamb 1.1.10 Cosroe
Were they not summon'd to appeare to day? . . . . . Jew 1.2.35 Govnr
yet not appeare/In forty houres after it is tane. . . Jew 3.4.71 Barab
Did not he charge thee to appeare to me? . . . . . F 271 1.3.43 Faust
that hee shall appeare to the said John Faustus, at all times, F 491 2.1.103 P Faust
And men in harnesse <armour> shall appeare to thee, . . F 548 2.1.160 Mephst
appeare to thee in their owne proper shapes and likenesse. F 656 2.2.105 P Belzeb
First weare this girdle, then appeare/Invisible to all are here: F 997 3.2.17 Mephst
shal appeare before your Grace, in that manner that they best F App p.237 47 P Faust
With stiffe oake propt the gate doth still appeare. . . Ovid's Elegies 1.6.28
That colour rightly did appeare so bloudy. . . . Ovid's Elegies 1.12.12
The unjust seas all blewish do appeare. . . . . Ovid's Elegies 2.11.12
Who on Loves seas more glorious wouldst appeare? . . Hero and Leander 1.228
APPEARES
which here appeares as full/As raies of Cynthia to the clearest 2Tamb 2.3.29 Orcan
It appeares so, pray be bold else-where, ... F1597 4.6.40 Servnt
APPEARING
Not bloudie speares appearing in the ayre, . . . Dido 4.4.117 Dido
APPEAS'D
Soules quiet and appeas'd [sigh'd] <sight> from their graves, Lucan, First Booke 566
O what god would not therewith be appeas'd? . . . Hero and Leander 2.50
APPEASD
The undaunted spirit of Percie was appeasd, . . . Edw 1.1.114 Kent
his grave looke appeasd/The wrastling tumult, and right hand Lucan, First Booke 298
APPEASE
Epeus pine-tree Horse/A sacrifize t'appease Minervas wrath: Dido 2.1.163 Aeneas
And dig for treasure to appease my wrath: . . . . 1Tamb 3.3.265 Tamb
T'appease my wrath, or els Ile torture thee, . . . 2Tamb 3.5.122 Tamb
and let this wound appease/The mortall furie of great . 2Tamb 5.1.153 Govnr
But doubt thou not (revenge doth griefe appease)/With thy Ovid's Elegies 1.7.63
APPEAZE
T'appeaze the wrath of their offended king. . . . Edw 3.1.210 Edward
APPENINES
Ocean to the Traveiler/That restes upon the snowy Appenines: 2Tamb 1.1.111 Sgsmnd
APPETENCE
By nature have a mutuall appetence, ... Hero and Leander 2.56
APPETITE
To make you fierce, and fit my appetite, ... 2Tamb 4.3.17 Tamb
The god thou serv'st is thine owne appetite, . . . F 399 2.1.11 Faust
APPLAUD (See also PLAUDE)
And then applaud his fortunes if you please. . . . 1Tamb Prol.8 Prolog
Thy mother shall from heaven applaud this show, . . Ovid's Elegies 1.2.39
Applaud you Neptune, that dare trust his wave, . . . Ovid's Elegies 3.2.47
Souldiour applaud thy Mars: . . . . Ovid's Elegies 3.2.49
APPLAUDED
Here every band applauded,/And with their hands held up, all Lucan, First Booke 387
APPLAUDING
The people thee applauding thou shalte stand, . . . Ovid's Elegies 1.2.25
APPLAUSE
Save onely that in Beauties just applause, ... 1Tamb 5.1.178 Tamb
And joyed to heare his Theaters applause; . . . . Lucan, First Booke 134
APPLE
I, dearer then the apple of mine eye? . . . . . P 685 13.29 Guise
APPLES
Dewberries, Apples, yellow Orenges, ... Dido 4.5.6 Nurse
With apples like the heads of damned Feends. . . . 2Tamb 2.3.23 Orcan
have fine sport with the boyes, Ile get nuts and apples enow. F App p.236 46 P Robin
With cruell hand why doest greene Apples pull? . . . Ovid's Elegies 2.14.24
Apples, and hony in oakes hollow boughes. . . . . Ovid's Elegies 3.7.40
APPLY
I must apply my selfe to fit those tearmes, . . . 2Tamb 4.1.155 Tamb
Wenches apply your faire lookes to my verse/Which golden love Ovid's Elegies 2.1.37
Faith to the witnesse Joves praise doth apply, . . . Ovid's Elegies 3.9.23
APPOINT
espy'd a time/To search the plancke my father did appoint; Jew 2.1.21 Abigal
Shalt thou appoint/What we shall graunt? . . . . . Edw 2.5.49 Mortmr
Rebels, will they appoint their soveraigne/His sports, his Edw 3.1.174 Edward
But what the heavens appoint, I must obaye, . . . Edw 5.1.56 Edward
Will hatefull Mortimer appoint no rest? . . . . Edw 5.3.5 Edward
APPOINTED
And painefull nights have bin appointed me. . . . Jew 1.2.198 Barab
To see us there appointed for our foes. . . . . Edw 4.2.56 Mortmr
keepe these preachments till you come to the place appointed. Edw 4.7.114 P Rice
APPREHEND
to apprehend/And bring him Captive to your Highnesse throne. 1Tamb 1.1.47 Meandr
To apprehend that paltrie Scythian. . . . . . 1Tamb 1.1.53 Mycet
APPROACH
So, leave me now, let none approach this place. . . Dido 5.1.291 Dido
is by cowards/Left as a pray now Caesar doth approach: . Lucan, First Booke 512
(Their reines let loose) right soone my house approach. . Ovid's Elegies 2.16.50
APPROACHT
That crost them; both which now approacht the camp, . . Lucan, First Booke 270
APPROCH
Or steeds might fal forcd with thick clouds approch. . Ovid's Elegies 1.13.30
APPROCHING
And sigh'd to thinke upon th'approching sunne, . . . Hero and Leander 2.302
APPROCHT
Approcht the swelling streame with drum and ensigne, . Lucan, First Booke 207
APPROOVE
Approove the difference twixt himself and you. . . . 2Tamb 4.1.137 Tamb

APPROOVED				
In thy approoved Fortunes all my hope,	1Tamb	2.3.2		Cosroe
APPROOVES				
But my ambitious ranging mind approoves?	Ovid's Elegies	2.4.48		
This tombe approoves, I pleasde my mistresse well,	Ovid's Elegies	2.6.61		
APPROV'D				
Of horne the bowe was that approv'd their side.	Ovid's Elegies	1.8.48		
APPROVE				
And laboring to approve his quarrell good.	Lucan, First Booke	267		
APPROVES				
Your name approves you made for such like things,	Ovid's Elegies	1.12.27		
APRILL				
Or ever drisling drops of Aprill showers,	1Tamb	4.1.31		Souldn
APT				
For evils are apt to happen every day.	Jew	1.2.223		Barab
And apt for any kinde of villanie.	Edw	2.1.51		Baldck
The Belgians apt to governe Brittish cars;	Lucan, First Booke	427		
How apt her breasts were to be prest by me,	Ovid's Elegies	1.5.20		
<make> slender/And to get out doth like apt members render.	Ovid's Elegies	1.6.6		
Ad <And> they were apt to curle an hundred waies,	Ovid's Elegies	1.14.13		
Good forme there is, yeares apt to play togither,	Ovid's Elegies	2.3.13		
Apt to thy mistrisse, but more apt to me.	Ovid's Elegies	2.8.4		
But though I apt were for such high deseignes,	Ovid's Elegies	2.18.14		
And was againe most apt to my desire.	Ovid's Elegies	2.19.16		
AQUAM				
et consecratam aquam quam nunc spargo; signumque crucis quod	F 248	1.3.20	P	Faust
AQUATANI				
Aerii, [Aquatici] <Aquatani>, [Terreni], spiritus salvete:	F 245	1.3.17	P	Faust
AQUATICI				
Aerii, [Aquatici] <Aquatani>, [Terreni], spiritus salvete:	F 245	1.3.17	P	Faust
AQUILON				
(Auster and Aquilon with winged Steads/All sweating, tilt about	1Tamb	3.2.78		Agidas
ARABIA				
But noble Lord of great Arabia,	1Tamb	4.3.29		Souldn
Great Emperours of Egypt and Arabia,	1Tamb	4.3.51		Capol
For Egypt and Arabia must be mine.	1Tamb	4.4.91		Tamb
of Egypt, the King of Arabia, and the Governour of Damascus.	1Tamb	4.4.114	P	Tamb
Send like defence of faire Arabia.	1Tamb	5.1.402		Zenoc
Lye down Arabia, wounded to the death,	1Tamb	5.1.407		Arabia
With them Arabia too hath left his life,	1Tamb	5.1.473		Tamb
Thy first betrothed Love, Arabia,	1Tamb	5.1.530		Tamb
As dooth the Desart of Arabia/To those that stand on Badgeths	2Tamb	1.1.108		Sgsmnd
So from Arabia desart, and the bounds/Of that sweet land, whose	2Tamb	3.5.35		Orcan
Then martcht I into Egypt and Arabia,	2Tamb	5.3.130		Tamb
In Trace; brought up in Arabia.	Jew	2.3.128	P	Ithimr
ARABIAN				
But let the yong Arabian live in hope,	1Tamb	3.2.57		Agidas
the faire Arabian king/That hath bene disapointed by this	1Tamb	4.1.68		Souldn
And leads with him the great Arabian King,	1Tamb	4.3.64		Souldn
The Souldan and the Arabian king together/Martch on us with	1Tamb	5.1.199		Techel
Madam, your father and th'Arabian king,	1Tamb	5.1.378		Philem
Where in Arabian, Hebrew, Greek, is writ/This towne being burnt	2Tamb	3.2.16		Calyph
ARABIANS				
Arabians, Moores and Jewes/Enough to cover all Bythinia.	1Tamb	3.3.136		Bajzth
Joine your Arabians with the Souldans power:	1Tamb	4.3.16		Souldn
Cicilians, Jewes, Arabians, Turks, and Moors,	2Tamb	1.1.62		Orcan
Well fare the Arabians, who so richly pay/The things they	Jew	1.1.8		Barab
ARABICUS				
And on the south Senus Arabicus,	2Tamb	4.3.104		Tamb
ARACHNE				
Arachne staynes Assyrian ivory.	Ovid's Elegies	2.5.40		
ARARIS				
and brave Theridamas/Have met us by the river Araris:	1Tamb	2.1.63		Cosroe
which by fame is said/To drinke the mightie Parthian Araris,	1Tamb	2.3.16		Tamb
and where swift Rhodanus/Drives Araris to sea; They neere the	Lucan, First Booke	435		
ARATUS				
With sunne and moone Aratus shall remaine.	Ovid's Elegies	1.15.16		
ARAY				
And when they see me march in black aray.	1Tamb	4.2.119		Tamb
Will laugh I feare me at their good aray.	P 673	13.17		Duchss
ARAYED				
The Poets God arayed in robes of gold,	Ovid's Elegies	1.8.59		
A scarlet blush her guilty face arayed.	Ovid's Elegies	2.5.34		
ARBITRAMENT				
submit your selves/To leave your goods to their arbitrament?	Jew	1.2.80		Barab
Are at my Arbitrament; and Barabas/At his discretion may	Jew	5.2.53		Barab
ARC (See ARKE)				
ARCADIAN				
Before whose bow th'Arcadian wild beasts trembled.	Ovid's Elegies	1.7.14		
Th'Arcadian Virgins constant love hath wunne?	Ovid's Elegies	3.5.30		
ARCH				
Arch-Monarke of the world, I offer here,	2Tamb	1.3.114		Therid
Nor am I made Arch-monark of the world,	2Tamb	4.1.150		Tamb
Arch-regent and Commander of all Spirits.	F 291	1.3.63		Mephst
use he's known/To exceed his maister, that arch-traitor Sylla.	Lucan, First Booke	326		
ARCHBISHOP				
Lord Archbishop of Reames, sit downe with us.	F1037	3.2.57		Pope
My good Lord Archbishop, heres a most daintie dish,	F1046	3.2.66		Pope
ARCHES				
Whose arches should be fram'd with bones of Turks,	2Tamb	1.3.94		Amyras
ARCHIPELLAGO				
And thence as far as Archipellago:	2Tamb	1.1.75		Orcan
ARCHITECT				
Thankes be heavens great architect and you.	Edw	4.6.22		Queene

ARCHITECTURE			
can comprehend/The wondrous Architecture of the world:	1Tamb	2.7.22	Tamb
ARCH-MONARK			
Nor am I made Arch-monark of the world,	2Tamb	4.1.150	Tamb
ARCH-MONARKE			
Arch-Monarke of the world, I offer here,	2Tamb	1.3.114	Therid
ARCH-REGENT			
Arch-regent and Commander of all Spirits.	F 291	1.3.63	Mephst
ARCH-TRAITOR			
use he's known/To exceed his maister, that arch-traitor Sylla.	Lucan, First Booke		326
ARCTIC (See ARTICK)			
ARDENTIS			
[Lucifer], Belzebub inferni ardentis monarcha, et Demogorgon,	F 246	1.3.18	P Faust
ARE			
Why, are not all the Gods at thy commaund,	Dido	1.1.30	Jupitr
Are drawne by darknes forth Astraeus tents.	Dido	1.1.73	Venus
On which by tempests furie we are cast.	Dido	1.1.199	Aeneas
Tell us, O tell us that are ignorant,	Dido	1.1.200	Aeneas
But what are you that aske of me these things?	Dido	1.1.214	Venus
Are ballassed with billowes watrie weight.	Dido	1.1.226	Aeneas
But are arived safe not farre from hence:	Dido	1.1.237	Venus
Why, what are you, or wherefore doe you sewe?	Dido	1.2.3	Iarbus
Our hands are not prepar'd to lawles spoyle,	Dido	1.2.12	Illion
The rest we feare are foulded in the flouds.	Dido	1.2.31	Cloan
For we are strangers driven on this shore,	Dido	2.1.43	Aeneas
And scarcely know within what Clime we are.	Dido	2.1.44	Aeneas
You are Achates, or I [am] deciv'd.	Dido	2.1.49	Serg
Lovely Aeneas, these are Carthage walles,	Dido	2.1.62	Illion
Father of fiftie sonnes, but they are slaine,	Dido	2.1.234	Aeneas
Are you Queene Didos sonne?	Dido	2.1.308	Ascan
Yet Queene of Affricke, are my ships unrigd,	Dido	3.1.105	Aeneas
And are not these as faire as faire may be?	Dido	3.1.140	Dido
No Madame, but it seemes that these are Kings.	Dido	3.1.149	Aeneas
The rest are such as all the world well knowes,	Dido	3.1.165	Dido
my Doves are back returnd,/Who warne me of such daunger prest	Dido	3.2.21	Venus
Are not we both sprong of celestiall rase,	Dido	3.2.28	Juno
The day, the night, my Swannes, my sweetes are thine.	Dido	3.2.61	Venus
More then melodious are these words to me,	Dido	3.2.62	Juno
a match confirmd/Betwixt these two, whose loves are so alike,	Dido	3.2.78	Juno
My princely robes thou seest are layd aside,	Dido	3.3.3	Dido
The woods are wide, and we have store of game:	Dido	3.3.6	Dido
How now Getulian, are ye growne so brave,	Dido	3.3.19	Dido
Yea little sonne, are you so forward now?	Dido	3.3.34	Dido
Why, that was in a net, where we are loose,	Dido	3.4.5	Dido
The ayre is cleere, and Southerne windes are whist,	Dido	4.1.25	Aeneas
They say Aeneas men are going abourd,	Dido	4.4.2	Dido
Unworthie are they of a Queenes reward:	Dido	4.4.12	Dido
As in the Sea are little water drops:	Dido	4.4.63	Dido
Are these the sailes that in despight of me,	Dido	4.4.126	Dido
A garden where are Bee hives full of honey,	Dido	4.5.7	Nurse
My vaines are withered, and my sinewes drie,	Dido	4.5.33	Nurse
Triumph, my mates, our travels are at end,	Dido	5.1.1	Aeneas
Why are thy ships new rigd?	Dido	5.1.88	Dido
These words are poyson to poore Didos soule,	Dido	5.1.111	Dido
Leape in mine armes, mine armes are open wide:	Dido	5.1.180	Dido
Sweet sister cease, remember who you are.	Dido	5.1.263	Anna
Go, stout Theridamas, thy words are swords,	1Tamb	1.1.74	Mycet
These are his words, Meander set them downe.	1Tamb	1.1.94	Mycet
there are in readines/Ten thousand horse to carie you from	1Tamb	1.1.184	Ortyg
Are countermanded by a greater man:	1Tamb	1.2.22	Tamb
For they are friends that help to weane my state,	1Tamb	1.2.29	Tamb
and this curtle-axe/Are adjuncts more beseeming Tamburlaine.	1Tamb	1.2.43	Tamb
A thousand Persean horsmen are at hand,	1Tamb	1.2.111	Souldr
But are they rich? And is their armour good?	1Tamb	1.2.123	Tamb
Their plumed helmes are wrought with beaten golde.	1Tamb	1.2.124	Souldr
His fierie eies are fixt upon the earth,	1Tamb	1.2.158	Therid
Nor are Apollos Oracles more true,	1Tamb	1.2.212	Tamb
We are his friends, and if the Persean king/Should offer	1Tamb	1.2.214	Techel
exchange for that/We are assured of by our friends successe.	1Tamb	1.2.217	Techel
shall confesse/Theise are the men that all the world admires.	1Tamb	1.2.223	Usumc
Are <To> <Ah> these resolved noble Scythians?	1Tamb	1.2.225	Therid
These are my friends in whom I more rejoice,	1Tamb	1.2.241	Tamb
Thus farre are we towards Theridamas,	1Tamb	2.1.1	Cosroe
Are fixt his piercing instruments of sight:	1Tamb	2.1.14	Menaph
Then when our powers in points of swords are join'd,	1Tamb	2.1.40	Cosroe
Whose tops are covered with Tartarian thieves,	1Tamb	2.2.16	Meandr
Will quickly win such as are like himselfe.	1Tamb	2.2.28	Meandr
These are the wings shall make it flie as swift,	1Tamb	2.3.57	Tamb
We are enough to scarre the enemy,	1Tamb	2.3.64	Tamb
For Kings are clouts that every man shoots at,	1Tamb	2.4.8	Mycet
from the camp/When Kings themselves are present in the field?	1Tamb	2.4.17	Tamb
Are you the witty King of Persea?	1Tamb	2.4.23	Tamb
same proportion of Elements/Resolve, I hope we are resembled,	1Tamb	2.6.27	Cosroe
And all the trees are blasted with our breathes.	1Tamb	3.1.55	Bajzth
Which dies my lookes so livelesse as they are.	1Tamb	3.2.15	Zenoc
For words are vaine where working tooles present/The naked	1Tamb	3.2.93	Agidas
Turkes are ful of brags/And menace more than they can wel	1Tamb	3.3.3	Tamb
Your men are valiant but their number few,	1Tamb	3.3.11	Bassoe
Then fight couragiously, their crowns are yours.	1Tamb	3.3.30	Tamb
Are punisht with Bastones so grievously,	1Tamb	3.3.52	Tamb
These are the cruell pirates of Argeire,	1Tamb	3.3.55	Tamb
I speake it, and my words are oracles.	1Tamb	3.3.102	Tamb
Whose hands are made to gripe a warlike Lance,	1Tamb	3.3.106	Bajzth

ARE (cont.)

Whose eies are brighter than the Lamps of heaven,	1Tamb	3.3.120		Tamb
Where are your stout contributorie kings?	1Tamb	3.3.214		Tamb
Here Madam, you are Empresse, she is none.	1Tamb	3.3.227		Therid
Are falne in clusters at my conquering feet.	1Tamb	3.3.230		Tamb
Black are his collours, blacke Pavilion,	1Tamb	4.1.59		2Msngr
Pillage and murder are his usuall trades.	1Tamb	4.1.66		Souldn
Are fled from Bajazeth, and remaine with me,	1Tamb	4.2.80		Tamb
are you so daintily brought up, you cannot eat your owne flesh?	1Tamb	4.4.36	P	Tamb
My vaines are pale, my sinowes hard and drie,	1Tamb	4.4.97		Bajzth
Casane, here are the cates you desire to finger, are they not?	1Tamb	4.4.107	P	Tamb
Casane, here are the cates you desire to finger, are they not?	1Tamb	4.4.108	P	Tamb
say you to this (Turke) these are not your contributorie kings.	1Tamb	4.4.118	P	Tamb
And they are worthy she investeth kings.	1Tamb	4.4.129		Tamb
What, are the Turtles fraide out of their neastes?	1Tamb	5.1.64		Tamb
Your fearfull minds are thicke and mistie then,	1Tamb	5.1.110		Tamb
And know my customes are as peremptory/As wrathfull Planets,	1Tamb	5.1.127		Tamb
to their soules I think/As are Thessalian drugs or Mithradate.	1Tamb	5.1.133		Tamb
Pray for us Bajazeth, we are going.	1Tamb	5.1.213		Tamb
the Feends infernall view/As are the blasted banks of Erebus:	1Tamb	5.1.244		Zabina
Since other meanes are all forbidden me,	1Tamb	5.1.288		Bajzth
How are ye glutted with these grievous objects,	1Tamb	5.1.341		Zenoc
Those that are proud of fickle Empery,	1Tamb	5.1.352		Zenoc
When my poore pleasures are devided thus,	1Tamb	5.1.386		Zenoc
And such are objects fit for Tamburlaine.	1Tamb	5.1.475		Tamb
We all are glutted with the Christians blood,	2Tamb	1.1.14		Gazell
Our Tents are pitcht, our men stand in array,	2Tamb	1.1.120		Fredrk
So prest are we, but yet if Sigismond/Speake as a friend, and	2Tamb	1.1.122		Orcan
Choose which thou wilt, all are at thy command.	2Tamb	1.2.31		Callap
But yet me thinks their looks are amorous,	2Tamb	1.3.21		Tamb
Bewraies they are too dainty for the wars.	2Tamb	1.3.28		Tamb
Or els you are not sons of Tamburlaine.	2Tamb	1.3.64		Tamb
They are enough to conquer all the world/And you have won	2Tamb	1.3.67		Calyph
No Madam, these are speeches fit for us,	2Tamb	1.3.88		Celeb
Five hundred Briggandines are under saile,	2Tamb	1.3.122		Therid
In number more than are the drops that fall/When Boreas rents a	2Tamb	1.3.159		Tamb
We are not bound to those accomplishments,	2Tamb	2.1.35		Baldwn
Our faiths are sound, and must be [consumate] <consinuate>,	2Tamb	2.1.47		Sgsmnd
life may be as short to me/As are the daies of sweet Zenocrate:	2Tamb	2.4.37		Tamb
Their Spheares are mounted on the serpents head,	2Tamb	2.4.53		Tamb
Now are those Spheares where Cupid usde to sit,	2Tamb	2.4.81		Tamb
Whose courages are kindled with the flames,	2Tamb	3.1.54		Trebiz
When this is done, then are ye souldiers,	2Tamb	3.2.91		Tamb
Were you that are the friends of Tamburlain,	2Tamb	3.3.35		Capt
How now Madam, what are you doing?	2Tamb	3.4.34		Therid
In number more than are the quyvering leaves/Of Idas forrest,	2Tamb	3.5.5		2Msngr
fighting men/Are come since last we shewed your majesty.	2Tamb	3.5.34		Jrslem
So sirha, now you are a king you must give armes.	2Tamb	3.5.137	P	Tamb
here are Bugges/Wil make the haire stand upright on your heads,	2Tamb	3.5.147		Tamb
when we are fighting, least hee hide his crowne as the foolish	2Tamb	3.5.154	P	Tamb
Thy victories are growne so violent,	2Tamb	4.1.140		Jrslem
Whose cruelties are not so harsh as thine,	2Tamb	4.1.169		Jrslem
like armed men/Are seene to march upon the towers of heaven,	2Tamb	4.1.202		Tamb
For with thy view my joyes are at the full,	2Tamb	4.2.31		Therid
And now the damned soules are free from paine,	2Tamb	4.2.91		Therid
Are not so honoured in their Governour,	2Tamb	4.3.10		Tamb
Where are my common souldiers now that fought/So Lion-like upon	2Tamb	4.3.67		Tamb
Are ye not gone ye villaines with your spoiles?	2Tamb	4.3.84		Tamb
More strong than are the gates of death or hel?	2Tamb	5.1.20		Govnr
When we are thus defenc'd against our Foe,	2Tamb	5.1.22		Govnr
Yet are there Christians of Georgia here,	2Tamb	5.1.31		1Citzn
These Jades are broken winded, and halfe tyr'd,	2Tamb	5.1.129		Tamb
Here they are my Lord.	2Tamb	5.1.177		Usumc
Are greatest to discourage all our drifts,	2Tamb	5.2.45		Callap
But if he die, your glories are disgrac'd,	2Tamb	5.3.15		Therid
Your vaines are full of accidentall heat,	2Tamb	5.3.84		Phsitn
which the heart ingenders/Are partcht and void of spirit,	2Tamb	5.3.95		Phsitn
Thus are the villaines, cowards fled for feare,	2Tamb	5.3.115		Tamb
Loe here my sonnes, are all the golden Mines,	2Tamb	5.3.151		Tamb
Wherein are rockes of Pearle, that shine as bright/As all the	2Tamb	5.3.156		Tamb
Are poyson'd by my climing followers.	Jew	Prol.13		Machvl
Who smiles to see how full his bags are cramb'd,	Jew	Prol.31		Machvl
But he whose steele-bard coffers are cramb'd full,	Jew	1.1.14		Barab
and the bordering Iles/Are gotten up by Nilus winding bankes:	Jew	1.1.43		Barab
Are smoothly gliding downe by Candie shoare/To Malta, through	Jew	1.1.46		Barab
Thy ships are safe, riding in Malta Rhode:	Jew	1.1.50		1Merch
And all the Merchants with other Merchandize/Are safe arriv'd,	Jew	1.1.52		1Merch
The ships are safe thou saist, and richly fraught.	Jew	1.1.54		Barab
They are.	Jew	1.1.55		1Merch
comes to more/Then many Merchants of the Towne are worth,	Jew	1.1.64		1Merch
Tush, they are wise; I know her and her strength:	Jew	1.1.81		Barab
And thus are wee on every side inrich'd:	Jew	1.1.104		Barab
These are the Blessings promis'd to the Jewes,	Jew	1.1.105		Barab
They say we are a scatter'd Nation:	Jew	1.1.121		Barab
Are come from Turkey, and lye in our Rhode:	Jew	1.1.147		1Jew
What need they treat of peace that are in league?	Jew	1.1.158		Barab
The Turkes and those of Malta are in league.	Jew	1.1.159		Barab
Now [Governour], how are you resolv'd?	Jew	1.2.17		Calym
Since your hard conditions are such/That you will needs have	Jew	1.2.18		Govnr
And therefore are we to request your ayd.	Jew	1.2.49		Govnr
Alas, my Lord, we are no souldiers:	Jew	1.2.50		Barab
Alas, my Lord, the most of us are poore!	Jew	1.2.57		1Jew
Are strangers with your tribute to be tax'd?	Jew	1.2.59		Barab

ARE (cont.)

These taxes and afflictions are befal'ne,	Jew	1.2.65		Govnr
And therefore thus we are determined;	Jew	1.2.66		Govnr
Let me be us'd but as my brethren are.	Jew	1.2.91		Barab
Some Jewes are wicked, as all Christians are:	Jew	1.2.112		Barab
Well then my Lord, say, are you satisfied?	Jew	1.2.137		Barab
You that/Were ne're possest of wealth, are pleas'd with want.	Jew	1.2.201		Barab
Great injuries are not so soone forgot.	Jew	1.2.208		Barab
For evils are apt to happen every day.	Jew	1.2.223		Barab
things past recovery/Are hardly cur'd with exclamations.	Jew	1.2.237		Barab
have turn'd my house/Into a Nunnery, and some Nuns are there.	Jew	1.2.278		Barab
We now are almost at the new made Nunnery.	Jew	1.2.306		1Fryar
Claime tribute where thou wilt, we are resolv'd,	Jew	2.2.55		Govnr
bite, yet are our lookes/As innocent and harmelesse as a Lambes.	Jew	2.3.21		Barab
Are wondrous; and indeed doe no man good:	Jew	2.3.82		Barab
And seeing they are not idle, but still doing,	Jew	2.3.83		Barab
Let me see, sirra, are you not an old shaver?	Jew	2.3.114	P	Barab
My Lord farewell: Come Sirra you are mine.	Jew	2.3.134		Barab
make account of me/As of thy fellow; we are villaines both:	Jew	2.3.214		Barab
father, here are letters come/From Ormus, and the Post stayes	Jew	2.3.222		Abigal
But all are Hereticks that are not Jewes;	Jew	2.3.312		Barab
Are there not Jewes enow in Malta,	Jew	2.3.359		Barab
I, part 'em now they are dead: Farewell, farewell.	Jew	3.2.9		Barab
Come, Katherina, our losses equall are,	Jew	3.2.36		Govnr
make her round and plump, and batten more then you are aware.	Jew	3.4.66	P	Ithimr
In Malta are no golden Minerals.	Jew	3.5.6		Govnr
Oh brother, brother, all the Nuns are sicke,	Jew	3.6.1		1Fryar
sent for him, but seeing you are come/Be you my ghostly father;	Jew	3.6.11		Abigal
Oh brother, all the Nuns are dead, let's bury them.	Jew	3.6.44		1Fryar
How sweet the Bels ring now the Nuns are dead/That sound at	Jew	4.1.2		Barab
Now all are dead, not one remaines alive.	Jew	4.1.7		Barab
Thou shalt not need, for now the Nuns are dead,	Jew	4.1.15		Barab
She has confest, and we are both undone,	Jew	4.1.46		Barab
Oh Barabas, their Lawes are strict.	Jew	4.1.82		1Fryar
I know they are, and I will be with you.	Jew	4.1.83		Barab
But are not both these wise men to suppose/That I will leave my	Jew	4.1.122		Barab
Where are my Maids?	Jew	4.2.83		Curtzn
Where painted Carpets o're the meads are hurl'd,	Jew	4.2.91		Ithimr
His hands are hackt, some fingers cut quite off;	Jew	4.3.10		Barab
Sir, here they are.	Jew	4.3.50		Barab
My Lord, the Curtezane and her man are dead;	Jew	5.1.50		1Offcr
Wonder not at it, Sir, the heavens are just:	Jew	5.1.55		Govnr
Since they are dead, let them be buried.	Jew	5.1.57		Govnr
What should I say? we are captives and must yeeld.	Jew	5.2.6		Govnr
Are at my Arbitrament; and Barabas/At his discretion may	Jew	5.2.53		Barab
This, Barabas; since things are in thy power,	Jew	5.2.57		Govnr
This is the life we Jewes are us'd to lead;	Jew	5.2.115		Barab
Are all the Cranes and Pulleyes sure?	Jew	5.5.2		Barab
Then now are all things as my wish wud have 'em,	Jew	5.5.17		Barab
First, for his Army, they are sent before,	Jew	5.5.25		Barab
and underneath/In severall places are field-pieces pitch'd,	Jew	5.5.27		Barab
My men are all aboord,	Jew	5.5.103		Calym
That all the protestants that are in Paris,	P 34	1.34		Navrre
Where are those perfumed gloves which I sent/To be poysoned,	P 70	2.13		Guise
Wherein are thirtie thousand able men,	P 139	2.82		Guise
O gracious God, what times are these?	P 188	3.23		Navrre
What are you hurt my Lord high Admiral?	P 197	3.32		Condy
We are betraide, come my Lords, and let us goe tell the King of	P 199	3.34	P	Navrre
These are the cursed Guisians that doe seeke our death.	P 201	3.36		Admral
Ah my good Lord, these are the Guisians,	P 260	4.58		Admral
Are you a preacher of these heresies?	P 340	5.67		Guise
The Guisians are hard at thy doore,	P 367	7.7		Taleus
My Lord of Anjoy, there are a hundred Protestants,	P 417	7.57		Guise
That are tutors to him and the prince of Condy--	P 427	7.67		Guise
My Lord, they say/That all the protestants are massacred.	P 432	7.72		Navrre
I, so they are, but yet what remedy:	P 433	7.73		Anjoy
Who I? you are deceived, I rose but now.	P 437	7.77		Anjoy
There are a hundred Hugonets and more,	P 501	9.20		Guise
Put of that feare, they are already joynde,	P 605	12.18		King
As now you are, so shall you still persist,	P 608	12.21		King
Which [are] <as> he saith, to kill the Puritans,	P 643	12.56		Cardnl
Are these your secrets that no man must know?	P 678	13.22		Guise
Thou trothles and unjust, what lines are these?	P 680	13.24		Guise
Which are already mustered in the land,	P 726	14.29		1Msngr
For his othes are seldome spent in vaine.	P 773	15.31		Eprnon
And we are grac'd with wreathes of victory:	P 788	16.2		Navrre
What are ye come so soone?	P 815	17.10	P	Souldr
The Pope and King of Spaine are thy good frends,	P 843	17.38		Eprnon
I, those are they that feed him with their golde,	P 845	17.40		King
Then farwell Guise, the King and thou are freends.	P 870	17.65		King
My head shall be my counsell, they are false:	P 884	17.79		King
Come on sirs, what, are you resolutely bent,	P 931	19.1		Capt
Well then, I see you are resolute.	P 938	19.8		Capt
Now Captain of my guarde, are these murtherers ready?	P 947	19.17		King
But are they resolute and armde to kill,	P 949	19.19		King
Tut they are pesants, I am Duke of Guise:	P 998	19.68		Guise
And make the Guisians stoup that are alive.	P1071	19.141		King
Sweete Epernoune, our Friers are holy men,	P1161	22.23		King
For you are stricken with a poysoned knife.	P1213	22.75		Srgeon
yow are wellcome ser have at you	Paris	ms16,p390	P	Souldr
As for the multitude that are but sparkes,	Edw	1.1.20		Gavstn
But how now, what are these?	Edw	1.1.24		Gavstn
Why there are hospitals for such as you,	Edw	1.1.35		Gavstn

ARE (cont.)

these are not men for me,/I must have wanton Poets, pleasant	Edw		1.1.50		Gavstn
And hew these knees that now are growne so stiffe.	Edw		1.1.95		Edward
We and the rest that are his counsellers,	Edw		1.2.69		ArchBp
Are gone towards Lambeth, there let them remaine.	Edw		1.3.5		Gavstn
What? are you mov'd that Gaveston sits heere?	Edw		1.4.8		Edward
We are no traitors, therefore threaten not.	Edw		1.4.25		MortSr
Why are you moov'd, be patient my lord,	Edw		1.4.43		ArchBp
Nothing shall alter us, wee are resolv'd.	Edw		1.4.74		ArchBp
You that are princely borne should shake him off,	Edw		1.4.81		Warwck
Are you content to banish him the realme?	Edw		1.4.84		ArchBp
All that he speakes, is nothing, we are resolv'd.	Edw		1.4.251		Warwck
That now are readie to assaile the Scots.	Edw		1.4.363		Edward
Because the king and he are enemies.	Edw		2.1.5		Spencr
But seeing you are so desirous, thus it is:	Edw		2.2.15		Mortmr
the familie of the Mortimers/Are not so poore, but would they	Edw		2.2.151		Mortmr
Nay, now you are heere alone, ile speake my minde.	Edw		2.2.155		Mortmr
Thy garrisons are beaten out of Fraunce,	Edw		2.2.162		Lncstr
Libels are cast againe thee in the streete,	Edw		2.2.177		Mortmr
My lord, tis thought, the Earles are up in armes.	Edw		2.2.225		Queene
But let them go, and tell me what are these.	Edw		2.2.239		Edward
I feare me you are sent of pollicie,	Edw		2.3.5		Lncstr
These hands are tir'd, with haling of my lord/From Gaveston,	Edw		2.4.26		Queene
Whose eyes are fixt on none but Gaveston:	Edw		2.4.62		Queene
And that the Mortimers are in hand withall,	Edw		3.1.54		Edward
Are to your highnesse vowd and consecrate.	Edw		3.1.171		Herald
with my sword/On those proud rebels that are up in armes,	Edw		3.1.187		Edward
For theile betray thee, traitors as they are.	Edw		3.1.203		Lncstr
The lords are cruell, and the king unkinde,	Edw		4.2.2		Queene
His grace I dare presume will welcome me,/But who are these?	Edw		4.2.34		Queene
But gentle lords, friendles we are in Fraunce.	Edw		4.2.46		Queene
want, and though a many friends/Are made away, as Warwick,	Edw		4.2.52		Mortmr
not discourage/Your friends that are so forward in your aide.	Edw		4.2.70		Queene
our port-maisters/Are not so careles of their kings commaund.	Edw		4.3.23		Edward
with them are gone lord Edmund, and the lord Mortimer, having	Edw		4.3.32	P	Spencr
Misgoverned kings are cause of all this wrack,	Edw		4.4.9		Queene
Lords, sith that we are by sufferance of heaven,	Edw		4.4.17		Mortmr
princely resolution/Fits not the time, away, we are pursu'd.	Edw		4.5.9		Baldck
So are the Spencers, the father and the sonne.	Edw		4.6.44		SrJohn
But we alas are chaste, and you my friends,	Edw		4.7.22		Edward
this drowsines/Betides no good, here even we are betraied.	Edw		4.7.45		Spencr
Our lots are cast, I feare me so is thine.	Edw		4.7.79		Baldck
Hence fained weeds, unfained are my woes,	Edw		4.7.97		Edward
Spencer, I see our soules are fleeted hence,	Edw		4.7.105		Baldck
We are deprivde the sun-shine of our life,	Edw		4.7.106		Baldck
You, and such as you are, have made wise worke in England.	Edw		4.7.114	P	Rice
The greefes of private men are soone allayde,	Edw		5.1.8		Edward
But what are kings, when regiment is gone,	Edw		5.1.26		Edward
Which thoughts are martyred with endles torments.	Edw		5.1.80		Edward
Take it: what are you moovde, pitie you me?	Edw		5.1.102		Edward
Whether you will, all places are alike,	Edw		5.1.145		Edward
Brother Edmund, strive not, we are his friends,	Edw		5.2.114		Queene
My lord, be not pensive, we are your friends.	Edw		5.3.1		Matrvs
Men are ordaind to live in miserie,	Edw		5.3.2		Matrvs
When all my sences are anoyde with stenche?	Edw		5.3.18		Edward
Where lords keepe courts, and kings are lockt in prison!	Edw		5.3.64		Kent
Doe as you are commaunded by my lord.	Edw		5.5.26		Matrvs
And others are but shrubs compard to me,	Edw		5.6.12		Mortmr
Feare not my lord, know that you are a king.	Edw		5.6.24		1Lord
Mother, you are suspected for his death,	Edw		5.6.78		King
Are not thy bils hung up as monuments,	F	48	1.1.20		Faust
And Negromantick bookes are heavenly.	F	77	1.1.49		Faust
I these are those that Faustus most desires.	F	79	1.1.51		Faust
Are but obey'd in their severall Provinces:	F	85	1.1.57		Faust
Both Law and Physicke are for petty wits:	F	134	1.1.106		Faust
You are deceiv'd, for <Yes sir>, I will tell you:	F	206	1.2.13	P	Wagner
damned Art/For which they two are infamous through the world.	F	222	1.2.29		1Schol
By which the spirits are inforc'd to rise:	F	241	1.3.13		Faust
And what are you that live with Lucifer?	F	297	1.3.69		Faust
And are for ever damn'd with Lucifer.	F	300	1.3.72		Mephst
Where are you damn'd?	F	301	1.3.73		Faust
for they are as familiar with me, as if they payd for their	F	364	1.4.22	P	Robin
O they are meanes to bring thee unto heaven.	F	406	2.1.18		GdAngl
My sences are deceiv'd, here's nothing writ:	F	468	2.1.80		Faust
I, so are all things else; but whereabouts <where about>?	F	507	2.1.119		Faust
Where we are tortur'd, and remaine for ever.	F	509	2.1.121		Mephst
but <for> where we are is hell,/And where hell is there must we	F	511	2.1.123		Mephst
[Tush] <No>, these are trifles, and meere old wives Tales.	F	524	2.1.136		Faust
[Here they are in this booke].	F	551.3	2.1.166A	P	Mephst
[Heere they are too].	F	551.7	2.1.170A	P	Mephst
Are laid before me to dispatch my selfe:	F	574	2.2.23		Faust
<Tel me>, are there many Spheares <heavens> above the Moone?	F	586	2.2.35		Faust
Are all Celestiall bodies but one Globe,	F	587	2.2.36		Faust
As are the elements, such are the heavens <spheares>,/Even from	F	589	2.2.38		Mephst
Nor are the names of Saturne, Mars, or Jupiter,	F	594	2.2.43		Mephst
Mars, or Jupiter,/Fain'd, but are [erring] <evening> Starres.	F	595	2.2.44		Mephst
[Tush], these are fresh mens [suppositions] <questions>:	F	606	2.2.55	P	Faust
How many Heavens, or Spheares, are there?	F	609	2.2.58	P	Faust
Why are <have wee> not Conjunctions, Oppositions, Aspects,	F	615	2.2.64	P	Faust
O Faustus they are come to fetch <away> thy soule.	F	641	2.2.90		Faust
We are come to tell thee thou dost injure us.	F	642	2.2.91		Belzeb
we are come from hell in person to shew thee some pastime:	F	654	2.2.103	P	Belzeb
And what are thou the fift?	F	692	2.2.141		Faust

ARE (cont.)

my parents are all dead, and the devill a peny they have left	F 693	2.2.142	P Glutny
Choke thy selfe Glutton: What are thou the sixt?	F 704	2.2.153	Faust
And what are you Mistris Minkes, the seventh and last?	F 707	2.2.159	Faust
Whose bankes are set with Groves of fruitfull Vines.	F 786	3.1.8	Faust
And cause we are no common guests,	F 805	3.1.27	Mephst
<Within whose walles such store of ordnance are>,	F 819	(HC265)A	Mephst
Now tell me Faustus, are we not fitted well?	F 940	3.1.162	Mephst
Behold my Lord, the Cardinals are return'd.	F 945	3.1.167	Raymnd
The sleepy Cardinals are hard at hand,	F 982	3.2.2	Mephst
weare this girdle, then appeare/Invisible to all are here:	F 998	3.2.18	Mephst
we all are witnesses/That Bruno here was late delivered you,	F1025	3.2.45	Raymnd
So, they are safe:	F1035	3.2.55	Faust
O, are you here?	F1096	3.3.9	P Vintnr
am glad I have found you, you are a couple of fine companions:	F1096	3.3.9	P Vintnr
Be it as Faustus please, we are content.	F1253	4.1.99	Emper
These are but shadowes, not substantiall.	F1259	4.1.105	Faust
my thoughts are ravished so/With sight of this renowned	F1260	4.1.106	Emper
If Faustus do it, you are streight resolv'd,	F1298	4.1.144	Faust
O hellish spite,/Your heads are all set with hornes.	F1442	4.3.12	Benvol
Nay chafe not man, we all are sped.	F1444	4.3.14	Mrtino
That spite of spite, our wrongs are doubled?	F1446	4.3.16	Benvol
great bellyed women, do long for things, are rare and dainty.	F1569	4.6.12	P Faust
And trust me, they are the sweetest grapes that e're I tasted.	F1587	4.6.30	P Lady
They are good subject for a merriment.	F1606	4.6.49	Faust
'Faith you are too outragious, but come neere,	F1609	4.6.52	Faust
Nay, hearke you, can you tell me where you are?	F1614	4.6.57	Faust
I marry can I, we are under heaven.	F1615	4.6.58	P Carter
Then I assure thee certainelie they are.	F1650	4.6.93	Faust
We are much beholding to this learned man.	F1670	4.6.113	Lady
So are we Madam, which we will recompence/With all the love and	F1671	4.6.114	Duke
He and his servant Wagner are at hand,	F1813	5.2.17	Mephst
Now worthy Faustus: me thinks your looks are chang'd.	F1821	5.2.25	1Schol
to heaven, and remember [Gods] mercy is <mercies are> infinite.	F1836	5.2.40	P 2Schol
The jawes of hell are open to receive thee.	F1908	5.2.112	GdAngl
There are the Furies tossing damned soules,	F1911	5.2.115	BdAngl
There are live quarters broyling on the coles,	F1913	5.2.117	BdAngl
These, that are fed with soppes of flaming fire,	F1916	5.2.120	BdAngl
But yet all these are nothing, thou shalt see/Ten thousand	F1919	5.2.123	BdAngl
All beasts are happy, for when they die,	F1969	5.2.173	Faust
Their soules are soone dissolv'd in elements,	F1970	5.2.174	Faust
O help us heaven, see, here are Faustus limbs,	F1988	5.3.6	2Schol
they are too familiar with me already, swowns they are as bolde	F App	p.229 27	P Clown
swowns they are as bolde with my flesh, as if they had payd for	F App	p.230 28	P Clown
what, are they gone?	F App	p.230 51	P Clown
What, are you crossing of your selfe?	F App	p.232 18	Faust
keep out, or else you are blowne up, you are dismembred Rafe,	F App	p.233 10	P Robin
or else you are blowne up, you are dismembred Rafe, keepe out,	F App	p.233 11	P Robin
and you are but a &c.	F App	p.234 9	P Robin
two deceased princes which long since are consumed to dust.	F App	p.237 43	P Faust
heere they are my gratious Lord.	F App	p.238 59	P Faust
Sure these are no spirites, but the true substantiall bodies of	F App	p.238 64	P Emper
are you remembred how you crossed me in my conference with the	F App	p.238 76	P Faust
What horse-courser, you are wel met.	F App	p.239 100	P Faust
who are at supper with such belly-cheere,	F App	p.243 6	Wagner
heapes of stone/Lye in our townes, that houses are abandon'd,	Lucan, First Booke	26	
The fates are envious, high seats quickly perish,	Lucan, First Booke	70	
Under great burdens fals are ever greevous;	Lucan, First Booke	71	
Being conquered, we are plaugde with civil war.	Lucan, First Booke	108	
but as the fields/When birds are silent thorough winters rage;	Lucan, First Booke	261	
Where men are ready, lingering ever hurts:	Lucan, First Booke	282	
to warre,/Was so incenst as are Eleius steedes/With clamors:	Lucan, First Booke	294	
Cornets of horse are mustered for the field;	Lucan, First Booke	306	
What, now Scicillian Pirats are suppresst,	Lucan, First Booke	336	
say Pompey, are these worse/Then Pirats of Sycillia?	Lucan, First Booke	346	
the gods are with us,/Neither spoile, nor kingdom seeke we by	Lucan, First Booke	350	
And Trevier; thou being glad that wars are past thee;	Lucan, First Booke	437	
Are blest by such sweet error, this makes them/Run on the	Lucan, First Booke	456	
horsemen fought/Upon Mevanias plaine, where Buls are graz'd;	Lucan, First Booke	470	
When Romans are besieg'd by forraine foes,	Lucan, First Booke	513	
And in the brest of this slaine Bull are crept,	Lucan, First Booke	632	
Or if Fate rule them, Rome thy Cittizens/Are neere some plague:	Lucan, First Booke	644	
We which were Ovids five books, now are three,	Ovid's Elegies	1.1.1	
We are the Muses prophets, none of thine.	Ovid's Elegies	1.1.10	
Great are thy kingdomes, over strong and large,	Ovid's Elegies	1.1.17	
Are all things thine? the Muses Tempe <Temple> thine?	Ovid's Elegies	1.1.19	
My sides are sore with tumbling to and fro.	Ovid's Elegies	1.2.4	
Yong oxen newly yokt are beaten more,	Ovid's Elegies	1.2.13	
And rough jades mouths with stubburn bits are torne,	Ovid's Elegies	1.2.15	
But managde horses heads are lightly borne,	Ovid's Elegies	1.2.16	
Say they are mine, and hands on thee impose.	Ovid's Elegies	1.4.40	
See how the gates with my teares wat'red are.	Ovid's Elegies	1.6.18	
Night shamelesse, wine and Love are fearelesse made.	Ovid's Elegies	1.6.60	
Houses not dwelt in, are with filth forlorne.	Ovid's Elegies	1.8.52	
Nor one or two men are sufficient.	Ovid's Elegies	1.8.54	
Atticke, all lovers are to warre farre sent.	Ovid's Elegies	1.9.2	
Love and Loves sonne are with fierce armes to oddes;	Ovid's Elegies	1.10.19	
Thankes worthely are due for things unbought,	Ovid's Elegies	1.10.43	
For beds ill hyr'd we are indebted nought.	Ovid's Elegies	1.10.44	
are in thy soft brest/But pure simplicity in thee doth rest.	Ovid's Elegies	1.11.9	
Presages are not vaine, when she departed/Nape by stumbling on	Ovid's Elegies	1.12.3	
Slow oxen early in the yoake are pent.	Ovid's Elegies	1.13.16	
By thy meanes women of their rest are bard,	Ovid's Elegies	1.13.23	

ARE (cont.)			
Lost are the goodly lockes, which from their crowne/Phoebus and	Ovid's Elegies	1.14.31	
Wars dustie <rustie> honors are refused being yong,	Ovid's Elegies	1.15.4	
Are both in Fames eternall legend writ.	Ovid's Elegies	1.15.20	
You are unapt my looser lines to heare.	Ovid's Elegies	2.1.4	
Trust me all husbands for such faults are sad/Nor make they any	Ovid's Elegies	2.2.51	
things hidden)/Whence uncleane fowles are said to be forbidden.	Ovid's Elegies	2.6.52	
Both are wel favoured, both rich in array,	Ovid's Elegies	2.10.5	
Why with hid irons are your bowels torne?	Ovid's Elegies	2.14.27	
Sythia, Cilicia, Brittaine are as good,	Ovid's Elegies	2.16.39	
Small doores unfitting for large houses are.	Ovid's Elegies	3.1.40	
Coate-tuckt Dianas legges are painted like them,	Ovid's Elegies	3.2.31	
What, are there Gods?	Ovid's Elegies	3.3.1	
Thy springs are nought but raine and melted snowe:	Ovid's Elegies	3.5.93	
By charmes are running springs and fountaines drie,	Ovid's Elegies	3.6.32	
The gods care we are cald, and men of piety,	Ovid's Elegies	3.8.17	
Verses alone are with continuance crown'd.	Ovid's Elegies	3.8.28	
So Nemesis, so Delia famous are,	Ovid's Elegies	3.8.31	
Why are our pleasures by thy meanes forborne?	Ovid's Elegies	3.9.4	
These gifts are meete to please the powers divine.	Ovid's Elegies	3.9.48	
White Heifers by glad people forth are led,	Ovid's Elegies	3.12.13	
Which with the grasse of Tuscane fields are fed.	Ovid's Elegies	3.12.14	
When you are up and drest, be sage and grave,	Ovid's Elegies	3.13.19	
When two are stript, long ere the course begin,	Hero and Leander	1.169	
faire, mishapen stuffe/Are of behaviour boisterous and ruffe.	Hero and Leander	1.204	
To whom you offer, and whose Nunne you are.	Hero and Leander	1.212	
Like untun'd golden strings all women are,	Hero and Leander	1.229	
for both not us'de,/Are of like worth.	Hero and Leander	1.234	
One is no number, mayds are nothing then,	Hero and Leander	1.255	
Things that are not at all, are never lost.	Hero and Leander	1.276	
But you are faire (aye me) so wondrous faire,	Hero and Leander	1.287	
Are banquets, Dorick musicke, midnight-revell,	Hero and Leander	1.301	
When Venus sweet rites are perform'd and done.	Hero and Leander	1.320	
But Pallas and your mistresse are at strife.	Hero and Leander	1.322	
Women are woon when they begin to jarre.	Hero and Leander	1.332	
Maids are not woon by brutish force and might,	Hero and Leander	1.419	
All women are ambitious naturallie:	Hero and Leander	1.428	
To which the Muses sonnes are only heire:	Hero and Leander	1.476	
And fruitfull wits that in aspiring <inaspiring> are,	Hero and Leander	1.477	
(Sweet are the kisses, the imbracements sweet,	Hero and Leander	2.29	
Jewels being lost are found againe, this never,	Hero and Leander	2.85	
Are reeking water, and dull earthlie fumes.	Hero and Leander	2.116	
You are deceav'd, I am no woman I.	Hero and Leander	2.192	
Such sights as this, to tender maids are rare.	Hero and Leander	2.238	
Rich jewels in the darke are soonest spide.	Hero and Leander	2.240	
ARETHUSA'S			
In wanton Arethusa's [azur'd] <azure> armes,	F1786	5.1.113	Faust
ARGEIRE			
These are the cruell pirates of Argeire,	1Tamb	3.3.55	Tamb
ARGENT			
Gonzago, Retes, sweare by/The argent crosses in your burgonets,	P 275	5.2	Guise
ARGIER			
True (Argier) and tremble at my lookes.	1Tamb	3.1.49	Bajzth
I wil the captive Pioners of Argier,	1Tamb	3.1.58	Bajzth
Kings of Fesse, Moroccus and Argier,	1Tamb	3.3.66	Bajzth
I crowne you here (Theridamas) King of Argier:	1Tamb	4.4.116	P Tamb
Kings of Argier, Morocus, and of Fesse,	1Tamb	4.4.120	Tamb
Welcome Theridamas, king of Argier.	2Tamb	1.3.112	Tamb
And of Argier and Affriks frontier townes/Twise twenty thousand	2Tamb	1.3.119	Therid
That lanching from Argier to Tripoly,	2Tamb	1.3.124	Therid
Wel said Argier, receive thy crowne againe.	2Tamb	1.3.127	Tamb
These Pioners of Argier in Affrica,	2Tamb	3.3.20	Therid
Thou shalt be stately Queene of faire Argier,	2Tamb	4.2.39	Therid
ARGINS			
It must have high Argins and covered waies/To keep the bulwark	2Tamb	3.2.75	Tamb
And over thy Argins and covered waies/Shal play upon the	2Tamb	3.3.23	Therid
ARGIRON			
Ho, Belimoth, Argiron, Asteroth.	F1304	4.1.150	Faust
ARGOLIAN			
Environed with brave Argolian knightes,	1Tamb	4.3.2	Souldn
ARGOS			
And Jasons Argos, and the fleece of golde?	Ovid's Elegies	1.15.22	
The Argos wrackt had deadly waters drunke.	Ovid's Elegies	2.11.6	
ARGOSES			
Beating in heaps against their Argoses,	2Tamb	1.1.41	Orcan
ARGOSIE			
Mine Argosie from Alexandria,	Jew	1.1.44	Barab
And saw'st thou not/Mine Argosie at Alexandria?	Jew	1.1.72	Barab
And yet I wonder at this Argosie.	Jew	1.1.84	Barab
Thine Argosie from Alexandria,	Jew	1.1.85	2Merch
and in mine Argosie/And other ships that came from Egypt last,	Jew	1.2.187	Barab
ARGOSIES			
From <For> Venice shall they drag <dregge> huge Argosies,/And	F 157	1.1.129	Valdes
ARGUE			
Argue their want of courage and of wit:	2Tamb	1.3.24	Tamb
And reason <argue> of divine Astrology.	F 585	2.2.34	Faust
ARGUES			
This argues the entire love of my Lord.	Edw	2.1.63	Neece
Argues thy noble minde and disposition:	Edw	3.1.48	Edward
This argues, that you spilt my fathers bloud,	Edw	5.6.70	King
ARGUEST			
Thou arguest she doth secret markes unfold.	Ovid's Elegies	2.7.6	
ARGUMENT			
And as a sure and grounded argument,	1Tamb	1.2.184	Tamb

ARGUMENT (cont.)			
Zenocrate had bene the argument/Of every Epigram or Eligie.	2Tamb	2.4.94	Tamb
Know ye not yet the argument of Armes?	2Tamb	4.1.100	Tamb
Can not indure by argument of art.	2Tamb	5.3.97	Phsitn
That followes not <necessary> by force of argument, which	F 202	1.2.9	P Wagner
O Poet carelesse of thy argument?	Ovid's Elegies		3.1.16
ARGUMENTS			
These arguments he us'de, and many more,	Hero and Leander		1.329
ARGUMENTUM			
Argumentum [testimonii] <testimonis> est [inartificiale] <in	P 395	7.35	Guise
your nego argumentum/Cannot serve, sirra:	P 397	7.37	Guise
ARGUS			
Argus had either way an hundred eyes,	Ovid's Elegies		3.4.19
The self-same day that he asleepe had layd/Inchaunted Argus,	Hero and Leander		1.388
ARIADAN			
I here invest thee king of Ariadan,	2Tamb	3.5.130	Callap
ARIADNE			
Such Ariadne was, when she bewayles/Her perjur'd Theseus flying	Ovid's Elegies		1.7.15
ARIGHT			
There is, who ere will knowe a bawde aright/Give eare, there is	Ovid's Elegies		1.8.1
ARIMINUM (See ARRIMINUM)			
ARIONS			
O Anna, fetch [Arions] <Orions> Harpe,	Dido	5.1.248	Dido
ARISE			
We meane to take his mornings next arise/For messenger, he will	1Tamb	3.1.38	Bajzth
And fellowes to, what ever stormes arise.	P 615	12.28	King
So shall our sleeping vengeance now arise,	F 879	3.1.101	Pope
These plagues arise from wreake of civill power.	Lucan, First Booke		32
ARISETH			
From whence a dampe continually ariseth,	Edw	5.5.4	Matrvs
ARISTARCHUS			
I view the prince with Aristarchus eyes,	Edw	5.4.54	Mortmr
ARISTOTLE			
And this for Aristotle will I say,	P 408	7.48	Ramus
of artes/Thou suckedst from Plato, and from Aristotle.	Edw	4.7.19	Edward
ARISTOTLES			
And live and die in Aristotles workes.	F 33	1.1.5	Faust
ARIVED			
But are arived safe not farre from hence:	Dido	1.1.237	Venus
ARKE			
And cause the stars fixt in the Southern arke,	2Tamb	3.2.29	Tamb
ARM			
See where my Souldier shot him through the arm.	P 310	5.37	Guise
ARMA			
arma armis: pugnent ipsique nepotes:	Dido	5.1.311	Dido
ARMADOS			
And bring Armados from the coasts of Spaine,	2Tamb	1.2.34	Callap
ARM'D			
And with unwilling souldiers faintly arm'd,	1Tamb	2.1.66	Cosroe
Be arm'd against the hate of such a foe,	1Tamb	2.6.22	Ortyg
tis no matter for thy head, for that's arm'd sufficiently.	F1289	4.1.135	P Emper
And lawes assailde, and arm'd men in the Senate?	Lucan, First Booke		322
sleeping foe tis good/And arm'd to shed unarmed peoples bloud.	Ovid's Elegies		1.9.22
Nor being arm'd fierce troupes to follow farre?	Ovid's Elegies		2.14.2
ARMDE			
But are they resolute and armde to kill,	P 949	19.19	King
ARME (Homograph)			
whet thy winged sword/And lift thy lofty arme into the cloudes,	1Tamb	2.3.52	Cosroe
Shall Tamburlain extend his puisant arme.	1Tamb	3.3.247	Tamb
This arme should send him downe to Erebus,	1Tamb	4.1.45	Souldn
And proove the waight of his victorious arme:	1Tamb	4.3.47	Arabia
To thinke thy puisant never staied arme/Will part their bodies,	1Tamb	5.1.88	1Virgn
As long as life maintaines his mighty arme,	1Tamb	5.1.375	Anippe
Affrick to the banks/Of Ganges, shall his mighty arme extend.	1Tamb	5.1.521	Tamb
And jealous anger of his fearefull arme/Be pour'd with rigour	2Tamb	2.1.57	Fredrk
Then arme my Lords, and issue sodainly,	2Tamb	2.1.60	Sgsmnd
Arme dread Soveraign and my noble Lords.	2Tamb	2.2.24	1Msngr
And hath the power of his outstretched arme,	2Tamb	2.2.42	Orcan
Come sirra, give me your arme.	2Tamb	3.2.134	P Tamb
Cut off this arme that murthered my Love:	2Tamb	4.2.83	Therid
Than you by this unconquered arme of mine.	2Tamb	4.3.16	Tamb
I my good Lord, shot through the arme.	P 198	3.33	Admral
Thus arme in arme, the king and he dooth marche:	Edw	1.2.20	Lncstr
Then Faustus stab thy <thine> Arme couragiously,	F 438	2.1.50	Mephst
for love of thee/Faustus hath <I> cut his <mine> arme, and with	F 443	2.1.55	Faust
Veiw here this <the> bloud that trickles from mine arme,	F 446	2.1.58	Faust
But what is this Inscription on mine Arme?	F 465	2.1.77	Faust
<a threatning Arme, an angry Brow>.	F1944	(HC271)B	Faust
And see [where God]/[Stretcheth out his Arme, and bends his	F1944	5.2.148A	Faust
For rage against my wench mov'd my rash arme,	Ovid's Elegies		1.7.3
Pallas launce strikes me with unconquerd arme.	Ovid's Elegies		3.3.28
And wound them on his arme, and for her mourn'd.	Hero and Leander		1.376
The god put Helles bracelet on his arme,	Hero and Leander		2.179
ARMED			
Nor armed to offend in any kind:	Dido	1.2.13	Illion
Whose armed soule alreadie on the sea,	Dido	3.2.83	Venus
Till I may see thee hem'd with armed men.	1Tamb	2.4.38	Tamb
Sitting in scarlet on their armed speares.	1Tamb	5.1.118	Tamb
Armed with lance into the Egyptian fields,	1Tamb	5.1.381	Philem
Although he sent a thousand armed men/To intercept this haughty	2Tamb	1.2.70	Almeda
place himselfe therin/Must armed wade up to the chin in blood.	2Tamb	1.3.84	Tamb
that like armed men/Are seene to march upon the towers of	2Tamb	4.1.201	Tamb
Marching about the ayer with armed men,	2Tamb	5.2.34	Amasia

ARMED (cont.)			
Arrivde and armed in this princes right, ...	Edw	4.4.18	Mortmr
and with what noise/An armed battaile joines, such and more	Lucan, First Booke		578
With armes or armed men I come not guarded, . . .	Ovid's Elegies		1.6.33
ARMENIA			
Great Lord of Medea and Armenia:	1Tamb	1.1.163	Ortyg
Along Armenia and the Caspian sea, ...	2Tamb	5.3.127	Tamb
Scythia and wilde Armenia had bin yoakt, ...	Lucan, First Booke		19
ARMENIAN			
Then having past Armenian desarts now, ...	1Tamb	2.2.14	Meandr
Armenian Tygers never did so ill, ...	Ovid's Elegies		2.14.35
ARMES (Homograph)			
And I will spend my time in thy bright armes. . . .	Dido	1.1.22	Ganimd
And tricke thy armes and shoulders with my theft. . .	Dido	1.1.45	Jupitr
And all Aeolia to be up in armes:	Dido	1.1.63	Venus
An ancient Empire, famoused for armes, ...	Dido	1.2.21	Cloan
Brave men at armes, abandon fruitles feares, ...	Dido	1.2.32	Iarbus
His armes torne from his shoulders, and his breast/Furrowd with	Dido	2.1.203	Aeneas
This young boy in mine armes, and by the hand/Led faire Creusa	Dido	2.1.266	Aeneas
For Didos sake I take thee in my armes, ...	Dido	2.1.313	Venus
Eate Comfites in mine armes, and I will sing. . . .	Dido	2.1.315	Venus
No Dido will not take me in her armes, ...	Dido	3.1.22	Cupid
Whom I will beare to Ida in mine armes, ...	Dido	3.2.99	Venus
And better able unto other armes.	Dido	3.3.36	Cupid
Then would I wish me in faire Didos armes, ...	Dido	3.3.48	Iarbus
And I must perish in his burning armes.	Dido	3.4.22	Dido
Stoute love in mine armes make thy Italy, ...	Dido	3.4.57	Dido
This is no life for men at armes to live, ...	Dido	4.3.33	Achat
So she may have Aeneas in her armes.	Dido	4.3.42	Illion
Her silver armes will coll me round about, ...	Dido	4.3.51	Aeneas
Not all the world can take thee from mine armes, . . .	Dido	4.4.61	Dido
Or that the Tyrrhen sea were in mine armes, ...	Dido	4.4.101	Dido
So I may have Aeneas in mine armes.	Dido	4.4.135	Dido
That daylie dandlest Cupid in thy armes:	Dido	5.1.45	Aeneas
Who ever since hath luld me in her armes.	Dido	5.1.48	Ascan
That he should take Aeneas from mine armes?	Dido	5.1.130	Dido
Hast thou forgot how many neighbour kings/Were up in armes, for	Dido	5.1.142	Dido
Leape in mine armes, mine armes are open wide: . . .	Dido	5.1.180	Dido
That they may melt and I fall in his armes:	Dido	5.1.245	Dido
prophesies)/To raigne in Asia, and with barbarous Armes, .	1Tamb	1.1.42	Meandr
By whose desires of discipline in Armes, ...	1Tamb	1.1.174	Cosroe
Even in the circle of your Fathers armes:	1Tamb	1.2.5	Tamb
Not all the Gold in Indias welthy armes, ...	1Tamb	1.2.85	Tamb
Weele fight five hundred men at armes to one, ...	1Tamb	1.2.143	Tamb
Draw foorth thy sword, thou mighty man at Armes, . . .	1Tamb	1.2.178	Tamb
Thirsting with soverainty, with love of armes:	1Tamb	2.1.20	Menaph
His armes and fingers long and [sinowy] <snowy>, . . .	1Tamb	2.1.27	Menaph
The world will strive with hostes of men at armes, . .	1Tamb	2.3.13	Tamb
and dim their eies/That stand and muse at our admyred armes.	1Tamb	2.3.24	Tamb
And makes a passage for all prosperous Armes, ...	1Tamb	2.3.38	Cosroe
That ere made passage thorow Persean Armes.	1Tamb	2.3.56	Tamb
Thou breakst the law of Armes unlesse thou kneele, . .	1Tamb	2.4.21	Mycet
So do I thrice renowmed man at armes, ...	1Tamb	2.5.6	Cosroe
Moov'd me to manage armes against thy state.	1Tamb	2.7.16	Tamb
Though Mars himselfe the angrie God of armes, ...	1Tamb	2.7.58	Tamb
Or els to threaten death and deadly armes, ...	1Tamb	3.1.19	Fesse
He be so mad to manage Armes with me, ...	1Tamb	3.1.34	Bajzth
Who when he shall embrace you in his armes, ...	1Tamb	3.2.42	Agidas
Or when the morning holds him in her armes:	1Tamb	3.2.48	Zenoc
Hath now in armes ten thousand Janisaries, ...	1Tamb	3.3.15	Bassoe
And manage words with her as we will armes.	1Tamb	3.3.131	Tamb
Thy souldiers armes could not endure to strike/So many blowes	1Tamb	3.3.143	Bajzth
That dare to manage armes with him, ...	1Tamb	3.3.198	Zabina
Ah villaines, dare ye touch my sacred armes?	1Tamb	3.3.268	Bajzth
Not sparing any that can manage armes.	1Tamb	4.1.57	2Msngr
Of lawfull armes, or martiall discipline:	1Tamb	4.1.65	Souldn
Two hundred thousand foot, brave men at armes, ...	1Tamb	4.3.54	Capol
will make thee slice the brawnes of thy armes into carbonadoes,	1Tamb	4.4.44	P Tamb
And if we should with common rites of Armes, ...	1Tamb	5.1.11	Govnr
Venus, would she leave/The angrie God of Armes, and lie with me.	1Tamb	5.1.125	Tamb
My discipline of armes and Chivalrie, ...	1Tamb	5.1.175	Tamb
I may poure foorth my soule into thine armes, ...	1Tamb	5.1.279	Bajzth
Whose lookes might make the angry God of armes, . . .	1Tamb	5.1.326	Zenoc
eies beholde/That as for her thou bearst these wretched armes,	1Tamb	5.1.409	Arabia
Even so for her thou diest in these armes:	1Tamb	5.1.410	Arabia
Jove viewing me in armes, lookes pale and wan, ...	1Tamb	5.1.452	Tamb
When men presume to manage armes with him.	1Tamb	5.1.478	Tamb
Or as Latonas daughter bent to armes, ...	1Tamb	5.1.514	Tamb
Bringing the strength of Europe to these Armes: . . .	2Tamb	1.1.30	Orcan
All Asia is in Armes with Tamburlaine.	2Tamb	1.1.72	Orcan
All Affrike is in Armes with Tamburlaine.	2Tamb	1.1.76	Orcan
it out, or manage armes/Against thy selfe or thy confederates:	2Tamb	1.1.128	Sgsmnd
when wilt thou leave these armes/And save thy sacred person	2Tamb	1.3.9	Zenoc
Their armes to hang about a Ladies necke:	2Tamb	1.3.30	Tamb
When I am old and cannot mannage armes, ...	2Tamb	1.3.59	Tamb
But while my brothers follow armes my lord, ...	2Tamb	1.3.65	Calyph
Stretching your conquering armes from east to west: . . .	2Tamb	1.3.97	Tamb
frontier townes/Twise twenty thousand valiant men at armes,	2Tamb	1.3.120	Therid
Meaning to aid [thee] <them> in this <these> Turkish armes,	2Tamb	1.3.144	Techel
And stirs your valures to such soddaine armes?	2Tamb	2.1.3	Sgsmnd
to them should not infringe/Our liberty of armes and victory.	2Tamb	2.1.41	Baldwn
An hundred kings by scores wil bid him armes, ...	2Tamb	2.2.11	Gazell
To armes my Lords, on Christ still let us crie, . . .	2Tamb	2.2.63	Orcan

ARMES (cont.)

Hellen, whose beauty sommond Greece to armes, ...	2Tamb	2.4.87		Tamb
Casane and Theridamas to armes:	2Tamb	2.4.102		Tamb
What God so ever holds thee in his armes, ...	2Tamb	2.4.109		Tamb
I have a hundred thousand men in armes, ...	2Tamb	3.1.38		Orcan
shal be plac'd/Wrought with the Persean and Egyptian armes,	2Tamb	3.2.20		Amyras
But keep within the circle of mine armes.	2Tamb	3.2.35		Tamb
Shot through the armes, cut overthwart the hands, . .	2Tamb	3.2.104		Tamb
see if coward Calapine/Dare levie armes against our puissance,	2Tamb	3.2.156		Tamb
And makes the mighty God of armes his slave:	2Tamb	3.4.53		Therid
So sirha, now you are a king you must give armes. . .	2Tamb	3.5.137	P	Tamb
Spirits with desire/Stil to be train'd in armes and chivalry?	2Tamb	4.1.81		Tamb
Know ye not yet the argument of Armes?	2Tamb	4.1.100		Tamb
And I will cast off armes and sit with thee, ...	2Tamb	4.2.44		Therid
All Turkie is in armes with Callapine.	2Tamb	5.2.51		Callap
And never wil we sunder camps and armes, ...	2Tamb	5.2.52		Callap
Which makes them manage armes against thy state, . . .	2Tamb	5.3.36		Usumc
she farre become a bed/Embraced in a friendly lovers armes,	Jew	1.2.372		Mthias
And alwayes kept the Sexton's armes in ure/With digging graves	Jew	2.3.184		Barab
These armes of mine shall be thy Sepulchre.	Jew	3.2.11		Govnr
And as you profitably take up Armes, ...	Jew	3.5.32		Govnr
Knavely spoke, and like a Knight at Armes.	Jew	4.4.9		Pilia
Now, Gentlemen, betake you to your Armes, ...	Jew	5.1.1		Govnr
And tye white linnen scarfes about their armes. . . .	P 233	4.31		Guise
To leavy armes and make these civill broyles:	P 730	14.33		Navrre
In prosecution of these cruell armes, ...	P 796	16.10		Navrre
(aspiring Guise)/Durst be in armes without the Kings consent?	P 829	17.24		Eprnon
That the Guise durst stand in armes against the King, .	P 877	17.72		Eprnon
That the Guise hath taken armes against the King, . . .	P 901	18.2		Navrre
And now will I to armes, come Epernoune:	P1079	19.149		King
Till surfeiting with our afflicting armes, ...	P1153	22.15		King
How they beare armes against their soveraigne.	P1187	22.49		King
So thou wouldst smile and take me in thy <thine> armes. .	Edw	1.1.9		Gavstn
Crownets of pearle about his naked armes, ...	Edw	1.1.63		Gavstn
My lord, will you take armes against the king?	Edw	1.2.39		Lncstr
What neede I, God himselfe is up in armes, ...	Edw	1.2.40		ArchBp
Forbeare to levie armes against the king.	Edw	1.2.82		Queene
Or with those armes that twind about my neck, ...	Edw	1.4.175		Queene
Then may we with some colour rise in armes, ...	Edw	1.4.279		Mortmr
He meanes to make us stoope by force of armes, ...	Edw	2.2.103		Lncstr
My lord, tis thought, the Earles are up in armes. . . .	Edw	2.2.225		Queene
Tell me, where wast thou borne? What is thine armes? .	Edw	2.2.242		Edward
O that mine armes could close this Ile about, ...	Edw	2.4.17		Queene
That like the Greekish strumpet traind to armes/And bloudie	Edw	2.5.15		Lncstr
I see it is your life these armes pursue.	Edw	2.6.2		James
A bloudie part, flatly against law of armes.	Edw	3.1.121		Spencr
The Barons up in armes, by me salute/Your highnes, with long	Edw	3.1.156		Herald
with my sword/On those proud rebels that are up in armes,	Edw	3.1.187		Edward
And levie armes against your lawfull king?	Edw	3.1.208		SpncrP
Poore Pierce, and headed him against lawe of armes? . .	Edw	3.1.238		Edward
the ungentle king/Of Fraunce refuseth to give aide of armes,	Edw	4.2.62		SrJohn
This noble gentleman, forward in armes, ...	Edw	4.2.76		Mortmr
We come in armes to wrecke it with the [sword] <swords>: .	Edw	4.4.23		Mortmr
Borne armes against thy brother and thy king?	Edw	4.6.6		Kent
And all the land I know is up in armes, ...	Edw	4.7.31		Spencr
Armes that pursue our lives with deadly hate.	Edw	4.7.32		Spencr
That in mine armes I would have compast him.	F1262	4.1.108		Emper
In wanton Arethusa's [azur'd] <azure> armes, ...	F1786	5.1.113		Faust
Yet Room is much bound to these civil armes, ...	Lucan, First Booke	44		
And by long rest forgot to manage armes, ...	Lucan, First Booke	131		
his owne waight/Keepe him within the ground, his armes al bare,	Lucan, First Booke	140		
And armes all naked, who with broken sighes, ...	Lucan, First Booke	191		
And snatcht armes neer their houshold gods hung up/Such as	Lucan, First Booke	242		
Roome rageth now in armes/As if the Carthage Hannibal were	Lucan, First Booke	304		
Neither spoile, nor kingdom seeke we by these armes, .	Lucan, First Booke	351		
our lively bodies, and strong armes/Can mainly throw the dart;	Lucan, First Booke	364		
All rise in armes; nor could the bed-rid parents/Keep back	Lucan, First Booke	502		
And they whom fierce Bellonaes fury moves/To wound their armes,	Lucan, First Booke	564		
Clashing of armes was heard, in untrod woods/Shrill voices	Lucan, First Booke	567		
Muse upreard <prepar'd> I [meant] <meane> to sing of armes,	Ovid's Elegies	1.1.5		
With armes to conquer armlesse men is base, ...	Ovid's Elegies	1.2.22		
Let not thy necke by his vile armes be prest, ...	Ovid's Elegies	1.4.35		
What armes and shoulders did I touch and see, ...	Ovid's Elegies	1.5.19		
In midst of peace why art of armes afraide?	Ovid's Elegies	1.6.30		
With armes or armed men I come not guarded, ...	Ovid's Elegies	1.6.33		
Who feares these armes? who wil not go to meete them? .	Ovid's Elegies	1.6.39		
Would of mine armes, my shoulders had beene scanted, .	Ovid's Elegies	1.7.23		
Nor let the armes of antient [lines] <lives> beguile thee,	Ovid's Elegies	1.8.65		
Who slumbring, they rise up in swelling armes. . . .	Ovid's Elegies	1.9.26		
Hector to armes went from his wives embraces, ...	Ovid's Elegies	1.9.35		
Love and Loves sonne are with fierce armes to oddes;	Ovid's Elegies	1.10.19		
Now in her tender armes I sweetly bide, ...	Ovid's Elegies	1.13.5		
But [heldst] <hadst> thou in thine armes some Caephalus, .	Ovid's Elegies	1.13.39		
Thou wert not borne to ride, or armes to beare, . . .	Ovid's Elegies	2.3.7		
Foldes up her armes, and makes low curtesie.	Ovid's Elegies	2.4.30		
Seeing her face, mine upreard armes discended, ...	Ovid's Elegies	2.5.47		
Crowes <crow> [survive] <survives> armes-bearing Pallas hate,	Ovid's Elegies	2.6.35		
We people wholy given thee, feele thine armes, . . .	Ovid's Elegies	2.9.11		
To cruell armes their drunken selves did summon. . . .	Ovid's Elegies	2.12.20		
With thy white armes upon my shoulders seaze, ...	Ovid's Elegies	2.16.29		
And new sworne souldiours maiden armes retainst, . . .	Ovid's Elegies	2.18.2		
Then wreathes about my necke her winding armes, . . .	Ovid's Elegies	2.18.9		
Nor of thee Macer that resoundst forth armes, ...	Ovid's Elegies	2.18.35		

ARMES (cont.)
She on my necke her Ivorie armes did throw, ... Ovid's Elegies 3.6.7
That were as white as is <Her armes farre whiter, then> the Ovid's Elegies 3.6.8
Foole canst thou him in thy white armes embrace? . . Ovid's Elegies 3.7.11
We make Enceladus use a thousand armes, ... Ovid's Elegies 3.11.27
Whom liberty to honest armes compeld, ... Ovid's Elegies 3.14.9
About her naked necke his bare armes threw. . . . . Hero and Leander 1.42
Faire Cinthia wisht, his armes might be her speare, . Hero and Leander 1.59
But from his spreading armes away she cast her, . . Hero and Leander 1.342
Till in his twining armes he lockt her fast, . . . Hero and Leander 1.403
About his armes the purple riband wound, ... Hero and Leander 2.106
He watcht his armes, and as they opend wide, . . . Hero and Leander 2.183
O that these tardie armes of mine were wings, . . . Hero and Leander 2.205
At least vouchsafe these armes some little roome, . . Hero and Leander 2.249
Inclos'd her in his armes and kist her to. . . . Hero and Leander 2.282
Both in each others armes chaind as they layd. . . . Hero and Leander 2.306

ARMES-BEARING
Crowes <crow> [survive] <survives> armes-bearing Pallas hate, Ovid's Elegies 2.6.35

ARMIE
And with the Armie of Theridamas, ... 1Tamb 1.1.176 Cosroe
Have past the armie of the mightie Turke: . . . . 1Tamb 1.2.14 Zenoc
And when their scattered armie is subdu'd, . . . 1Tamb 2.2.68 Meandr
discovered the enemie/Ready to chardge you with a mighty armie. 1Tamb 2.3.50 1Msngr
You know our Armie is invincible: . . . . . . 1Tamb 3.1.7 Bajzth
Europe, and pursue/His scattered armie til they yeeld or die. 1Tamb 3.3.39 Therid
Your threefold armie and my hugie hoste, ... 1Tamb 3.3.94 Bajzth
Natolia hath dismist the greatest part/Of all his armie, pitcht 2Tamb 2.1.17 Fredrk
And when I meet an armie in the field, ... 2Tamb 3.2.38 Tamb
Before we meet the armie of the Turke. . . . . . 2Tamb 3.2.138 Tamb
Where Tamburlaine with all his armie lies, ... 2Tamb 5.2.6 Callap
I and myne armie come to lode thy barke/With soules of thousand 2Tamb 5.3.73 Tamb
hath nowe gathered a fresh Armie, and hearing your absence in 2Tamb 5.3.103 P 3Msngr
That this your armie going severall waies, ... Edw 2.4.42 Queene

ARMIES
Armies of foes resolv'd to winne this towne, ... Dido 4.4.113 Dido
And Generall Lieftenant of my Armies. . . . . . 1Tamb 2.5.9 Cosroe
Now thou art fearfull of thy armies strength, . . . 2Tamb 3.5.75 Orcan
Hovering betwixt our armies, light on me, ... 2Tamb 3.5.163 Tamb
And cuts down armies with his [conquering] <conquerings> wings. 2Tamb 4.1.6 Amyras
And Death with armies of Cymerian spirits/Gives battile gainst 2Tamb 5.3.8 Therid
Your highnes needs not feare mine armies force, . . . P 857 17.52 Guise
Armies alied, the kingdoms league uprooted, ... Lucan, First Booke 4

ARMIS
arma armis: pugnent ipsique nepotes: . . . . . . Dido 5.1.311 Dido

ARMLESSE
With armes to conquer armlesse men is base, ... Ovid's Elegies 1.2.22

ARMOR
This compleat armor, and this curtle-axe/Are adjuncts more 1Tamb 1.2.42 Tamb
Cast off your armor, put on scarlet roabes. . . . . 1Tamb 5.1.524 Tamb
For Mortimer will hang his armor up. . . . . . . Edw 1.1.89 Mortmr
With garish robes, not armor, and thy selfe/Bedaubd with golde, Edw 2.2.184 Mortmr
With her owne armor was my wench defended. . . . . Ovid's Elegies 2.5.48

ARMOUR
Then buckled I mine armour, drew my sword, ... Dido 2.1.200 Aeneas
So in his Armour looketh Tamburlaine: . . . . . 1Tamb 1.2.54 Techel
But are they rich? And is their armour good? . . . . 1Tamb 1.2.123 Tamb
and with our Sun-bright armour as we march, ... 1Tamb 2.3.221 Tamb
Their shoulders broad, for complet armour fit, . . . 1Tamb 3.3.107 Bajzth
Three hundred thousand men in armour clad, ... 1Tamb 4.1.21 2Msngr
His speare, his shield, his horse, his armour, plumes, . 1Tamb 4.1.60 2Msngr
Our warlike hoste in compleat armour rest, ... 2Tamb 1.1.8 Orcan
Armour of proofe, horse, helme, and Curtle-axe, . . . 2Tamb 1.3.44 Tamb
And all the men in armour under me, ... 2Tamb 1.3.135 Usumc
have martcht/Foure hundred miles with armour on their backes, 2Tamb 1.3.175 Usumc
March in your armour thorowe watery Fens, ... 2Tamb 3.2.56 Tamb
Ile ride in golden armour like the Sun, ... 2Tamb 4.3.115 Tamb
And men in harnesse <armour> shall appeare to thee, . . F 548 2.1.160 Mephst
Why letst discordant hands to armour fall? . . . . Ovid's Elegies 3.7.48

ARMOURS
There Angels in their christal armours fight/A doubtfull . 1Tamb 5.1.151 Tamb

ARMS
Now shalt thou feel the force of Turkish arms, ... 1Tamb 3.3.134 Bajzth
When made a victor in these hautie arms, ... 2Tamb 4.1.46 Amyras
Stand up my boyes, and I wil teach ye arms, ... 2Tamb 4.1.103 Tamb

ARMY (See also ARMIE)
Our army will be forty thousand strong, ... 1Tamb 2.1.61 Cosroe
Have view'd the army of the Scythians, ... 1Tamb 2.2.41 Spy
go before and charge/The fainting army of that foolish King. 1Tamb 2.3.62 Cosroe
Than all my Army to Damascus walles. . . . . . . 1Tamb 5.1.156 Tamb
I will dispatch chiefe of my army hence/To faire Natolia, and 2Tamb 1.1.161 Orcan
The treacherous army of the Christians, ... 2Tamb 2.2.25 1Msngr
let us haste and meete/Our Army and our brother of Jerusalem, 2Tamb 2.3.43 Orcan
Ready to charge the army of the Turke. . . . . . 2Tamb 3.4.87 Therid
My royal army is as great as his, ... 2Tamb 3.5.10 Callap
And what our Army royall is esteem'd. . . . . . 2Tamb 3.5.31 Callap
So that the Army royall is esteem'd/Six hundred thousand . 2Tamb 3.5.50 Soria
First, for his Army, they are sent before, ... Jew 5.5.25 Barab
Ile muster up an army secretly, ... P 572 11.37 Navrre
Whose army shall discomfort all your foes, ... P 579 11.44 Pleshe
A mighty army comes from France with speed: . . . . P 725 14.28 1Msngr
Of all my army now in readines, ... P 744 15.2 King
And either never mannage army more, ... P 793 16.7 Bartus
Why this tis to have an army in the fielde. . . . . P 980 19.50 Guise

ARMY (cont.)				
Behold an Army comes incontinent.	F1430	4.2.106		Faust
When Caesar saw his army proane to war,	Lucan, First Booke			393
ARMYE				
the Sea-man sees the Hyades/Gather an armye of Cemerian clouds,	1Tamb	3.2.77		Agidas
the armye I have gathered now shall ayme/more at thie end then	Paris	ms28,p391		Guise
AROSE				
sundry thoughts arose, about the honour of mine auncestors,	F App	p.236 18	P	Emper
might ease/The Commons jangling minds, apparant signes arose,	Lucan, First Booke			521
She stayd not for her robes, but straight arose,	Hero and Leander			2.235
AROUND				
the Puttock hovers/Around the aire, the Cadesse raine	Ovid's Elegies			2.6.34
ARRAS				
And cloath of Arras hung about the walles,	2Tamb	1.2.44		Callap
the ground be <were> perfum'd, and cover'd with cloth of Arras.	F 671	2.2.120	P	Pride
ARRAY (See also ARAY)				
Our Tents are pitcht, our men stand in array,	2Tamb	1.1.120		Fredrk
Both are wel favoured, both rich in array,	Ovid's Elegies			2.10.5
ARREST				
I arrest you of high treason here,	Edw	4.7.57		Leistr
Stand not on titles, but obay th'arrest,	Edw	4.7.58		Leistr
Thou traytor Faustus, I arrest thy soule,	F1743	5.1.70		Mephst
ARRESTS				
And death arrests the organe of my voice,	1Tamb	2.7.8		Cosroe
ARRIMINUM				
And some dim stars) he Arriminum enter'd:	Lucan, First Booke			234
ARRIVALL				
Expects th'arrivall of her highnesse person.	1Tamb	1.2.79		Agidas
whose weeping eies/Since thy arrivall here beheld no Sun,	2Tamb	4.2.2		Olymp
Tould us at our arrivall all the newes,	Edw	4.2.48		Mortmr
ARRIV'D				
Than if you were arriv'd in Siria,	1Tamb	1.2.4		Tamb
And since we have arriv'd in Scythia,	1Tamb	1.2.17		Magnet
Since I arriv'd with my triumphant hoste,	1Tamb	5.1.458		Tamb
And all the Merchants with other Merchandize/Are safe arriv'd,	Jew	1.1.52		1Merch
From the Emperour of Turkey is arriv'd/Great Selim-Calymath,	Jew	1.2.39		Govnr
For Faustus at the Court is late arriv'd,	F1181	4.1.27		Mrtino
ARRIVDE				
How now, what newes, is Gaveston arrivde?	Edw	2.2.6		Edward
That Gaveston is secretlie arrivde,	Edw	2.3.16		Lncstr
Till Edmund be arrivde for Englands good,	Edw	4.1.2		Kent
Arrivde and armed in this princes right,	Edw	4.4.18		Mortmr
ARRIVE (See also ARIVED)				
We quickly may in Turkish seas arrive.	2Tamb	1.2.27		Callap
And send us safely to arrive in France:	P 928	18.29		Navrre
And as I guesse will first arrive at Rome,	F 775	2.3.54		2Chor
ARRIVED				
When he arrived last upon our stage,	2Tamb	Prol.2		Prolog
ARROW				
Then touch her white breast with this arrow head,	Dido	2.1.326		Venus
Thence flew Loves arrow with the golden head,	Hero and Leander			1.161
ARROWE				
Convey this golden arrowe in thy sleeve,	Dido	3.1.3		Cupid
ARROWES				
Cupid shall lay his arrowes in thy lap,	Dido	3.2.56		Venus
Sharpe forked arrowes light upon thy horse:	1Tamb	5.1.217		Bajzth
In spite of thee, forth will thy <thine> arrowes flie,	Ovid's Elegies			1.2.45
Doest joy to have thy hooked Arrowes shaked,	Ovid's Elegies			2.9.13
Bearing the head with dreadfull [Adders] <Arrowes> clad,	Ovid's Elegies			3.5.14
ART (Homograph)				
And my nine Daughters sing when thou art sad,	Dido	1.1.33		Jupitr
Venus, how art thou compast with content,	Dido	1.1.135		Venus
Brave Prince of Troy, thou onely art our God,	Dido	1.1.152		Achat
How neere my sweet Aeneas art thou driven?	Dido	1.1.170		Venus
Thou art a Goddesse that delud'st our eyes,	Dido	1.1.191		Aeneas
But thou art gone and leav'st me here alone,	Dido	1.1.247		Aeneas
O Illioneus, art thou yet alive?	Dido	2.1.55		Achat
What stranger art thou that doest eye me thus?	Dido	2.1.74		Dido
Remember who thou art, speake like thy selfe,	Dido	2.1.100		Dido
Then be assured thou art not miserable.	Dido	2.1.104		Dido
Lest she imagine thou art Venus sonne:	Dido	3.1.4		Cupid
Why staiest thou here? thou art no love of mine.	Dido	3.1.39		Dido
That I should say thou art no love of mine?	Dido	3.1.42		Dido
Aeneas, art thou there?	Dido	3.1.99		Dido
but now thou art here, tell me in sooth/In what might Dido	Dido	3.1.101		Dido
Then never say that thou art miserable,	Dido	3.1.169		Dido
But not so much for thee, thou art but one,	Dido	3.1.175		Dido
Or art thou grievde thy betters presse so nye?	Dido	3.3.18		Iarbus
Aeneas, thou art he, what did I say?	Dido	3.4.29		Dido
And yet I blame thee not, thou art but wood.	Dido	4.4.143		Dido
Which neither art nor reason may atchieve,	Dido	5.1.65		Aeneas
But thou art sprung from Scythian Caucasus,	Dido	5.1.158		Dido
thou art so meane a man)/And seeke not to inrich thy followers,	1Tamb	1.2.8		Zenoc
Art thou but Captaine of a thousand horse,	1Tamb	1.2.168		Tamb
Wherein by curious soveraintie of Art,	1Tamb	2.1.13		Menaph
Wel, wel (Meander) thou art deeply read:	1Tamb	2.2.55		Mycet
Thou art no match for mightie Tamburlaine.	1Tamb	2.4.40		Tamb
Thou art deceiv'd, I heard the Trumpets sound,	1Tamb	3.3.203		Zabina
pray thee tel, why art thou so sad?	1Tamb	4.4.63	P	Tamb
These words assure me boy, thou art my sonne,	2Tamb	1.3.58		Tamb
Thou Christ that art esteem'd omnipotent,	2Tamb	2.2.55		Orcan
Villain, art thou the sonne of Tamburlaine,	2Tamb	3.2.95		Tamb
Nay Captain, thou art weary of thy life,	2Tamb	3.3.18		Techel

ART (cont.)

Death, whether art thou gone that both we live?	2Tamb	3.4.11	Olymp
Tell me sweet boie, art thou content to die?	2Tamb	3.4.18	Olymp
Now thou art fearfull of thy armies strength,	2Tamb	3.5.75	Orcan
And art a king as absolute as Jove,	2Tamb	4.3.33	Orcan
Thou art not woorthy to be worshipped,	2Tamb	5.1.189	Tamb
Can not indure by argument of art.	2Tamb	5.3.97	Phsitn
But art thou master in a ship of mine,	Jew	1.1.61	Barab
Sirra, which of my ships art thou Master of?	Jew	1.1.70	Barab
Tut, Jew, we know thou art no souldier;	Jew	1.2.52	1Knght
Thou art a Merchant, and a monied man,	Jew	1.2.53	1Knght
What art thou, daughter?	Jew	1.2.316	Abbass
Barabas, although thou art in mis-beleefe,	Jew	1.2.352	1Fryar
Now Captaine tell us whither thou art bound?	Jew	2.2.1	Govnr
So much the better, thou art for my turne.	Jew	2.3.129	Barab
Art thou againe got to the Nunnery?	Jew	3.4.4	Barab
Onely know this, that thus thou art to doe:	Jew	3.4.48	Barab
Thou art a--	Jew	4.1.31	2Fryar
I, that thou art a--	Jew	4.1.32	1Fryar
Art thou that Jew whose goods we heard were sold/For	Jew	5.1.73	Calym
Why now I see that you have Art indeed.	Jew	5.5.4	Barab
What art thou?	P 373	7.13	Gonzag
What art thou dead, sweet sonne speak to thy Mother.	P 551	11.16	QnMoth
Else all France knowes how poor a Duke thou art.	P 844	17.39	Eprnon
Art thou King, and hast done this bloudy deed?	P1050	19.120	YngGse
My sonne: thou art a changeling, not my sonne.	P1074	19.144	QnMoth
Now thou art dead, heere is no stay for us:	P1111	21.5	Dumain
But I have no horses. What art thou?	Edw	1.1.28	Gavstn
And what art thou?	Edw	1.1.33	Gavstn
That hardly art a gentleman by birth?	Edw	1.4.29	Mortmr
And art a bawd to his affections,	Edw	1.4.151	Queene
Thou art too familiar with that Mortimer,	Edw	1.4.154	Edward
And witnesse heaven how deere thou art to me.	Edw	1.4.167	Edward
Art thou an enemie to my Gaveston?	Edw	2.2.212	Edward
The fitter art thou Baldock for my turne,	Edw	2.2.245	Edward
But for we know thou art a noble gentleman,	Edw	2.5.68	Mortmr
Then tell thy prince, of whence, and what thou art.	Edw	3.1.35	Edward
thy mother feare/Thou art not markt to many daies on earth.	Edw	3.1.80	Queene
Grone for this greefe, behold how thou art maimed.	Edw	3.1.251	Mortmr
A boye, thou art deceivde at least in this,	Edw	4.2.8	Queene
And Edward thou art one among them all,	Edw	4.4.10	Queene
But haplesse Edward, thou art fondly led,	Edw	5.1.76	Edward
Come forth. Art thou as resolute as thou wast?	Edw	5.4.22	Mortmr
Art thou king, must I die at thy commaund?	Edw	5.4.103	Kent
And therefore tell me, wherefore art thou come?	Edw	5.5.106	Edward
Yet levell at the end of every Art,	F 32	1.1.4	Faust
Affoords this Art no greater miracle?	F 37	1.1.9	Faust
Yet art thou still but Faustus, and a man.	F 51	1.1.23	Faust
Go forward Faustus in that famous Art/Wherein all natures	F 101	1.1.73	BdAngl
Valdes, first let him know the words of Art,	F 185	1.1.157	Cornel
That thou art <he is> falne into that damned Art/For which they	F 221	1.2.28	1Schol
Thou art too ugly to attend on me:	F 252	1.3.24	Faust
Who would not be proficient in this Art?	F 256	1.3.28	Faust
thou art Conjurer laureate]/[That canst commaund great	F 260	1.3.32A	Faust
How comes it then that thou art out of hell?	F 303	1.3.75	Faust
I'le live in speculation of this Art/Till Mephostophilis	F 341	1.3.113	Faust
So, now thou art to bee at an howres warning, whensoever, and	F 369	1.4.27	P Wagner
Not I, thou art Prest, prepare thy selfe, for I will presently	F 372	1.4.30	P Wagner
Go forward Faustus in that famous Art.	F 403	2.1.15	BdAngl
Sweete Faustus leave that execrable Art.	F 404	2.1.16	GdAngl
Faustus thou art safe.	F 414	2.1.26	Faust
[O thou art deceived].	F 551.12	2.1.175A	P Faust
Thou art a spirit, God cannot pity thee.	F 564	2.2.13	BdAngl
[Faustus, thou art damn'd, then swords <guns> and knives],	F 572	2.2.21A	Faust
Thou art damn'd, think thou of hell>.	F 624	2.2.73	P Mephst
<Thinke thou on hell Faustus, for thou art damnd>.	F 624	(HC262)A	Mephst
O what art thou that look'st so [terrible] <terribly>.	F 638	2.2.87	Faust
That shall I soone: What art thou the first?	F 663	2.2.112	Faust
Thou art a proud knave indeed:	F 672	2.2.121	P Faust
What art thou the second?	F 672	2.2.121	P Faust
And what art thou the third?	F 678	2.2.127	P Faust
But what art thou the fourth?	F 685	2.2.134	Faust
By [cunning] <comming> in <of> thine Art to crosse the Pope,/Or	F 859	3.1.81	Mephst
[What there he did in triall of his art],	F1153	3.3.66A	3Chor
The wonder of the world for Magick Art;	F1166	4.1.12	Mrtino
Shall adde more excellence unto thine Art,	F1208	4.1.54	Emper
The Doctor stands prepar'd, by power of Art,	F1222	4.1.68	Faust
Il'e make you feele something anon, if my Art faile me not.	F1246	4.1.92	P Faust
No Art, no cunning, to present these Lords,	F1295	4.1.141	Faust
whose heart <art> conspir'd/Benvolio's shame before the	F1373	4.2.49	Mrtino
What art thou Faustus but a man condemn'd to die?	F1478	4.4.22	Faust
O gentle Faustus leave this damned Art,	F1707	5.1.34	OldMan
Then thou art banisht from the sight of heaven;	F1715	5.1.42	OldMan
Where art thou Faustus? wretch, what hast thou done?	F1724	5.1.51	Faust
[Damned art thou Faustus, damned, despaire and die],	F1725	5.1.52A	Faust
O thou art fairer then the evenings <evening> aire,	F1781	5.1.108	Faust
Brighter art thou then flaming Jupiter,	F1783	5.1.110	Faust
art at an houres warning whensoever or wheresoever the divell	F App	p.230 36	P Wagner
study, shee's borne to beare with me, or else my Art failes.	F App	p.233 17	P Robin
If therefore thou, by cunning of thine Art,	F App	p.237 29	Emper
forth as by art and power of my spirit I am able to performe.	F App	p.237 38	P Faust
what art thou Faustus but a man condemnd to die?	F App	p.240 121	P Faust
neither thou nor Hanniball/Art cause, no forraine foe could so	Lucan, First Booke		31

ART (cont.)
Thou Caesar at this instant art my God, ... Lucan, First Booke 63
O Roome thy selfe art cause of all these evils, . . Lucan, First Booke 84
having lickt/Warme goare from Syllas sword art yet athirst, Lucan, First Booke 331
what ere thou be whom God assignes/This great effect, art hid. Lucan, First Booke 420
Why art thou thus enrag'd? . . . . Lucan, First Booke 659
In midst of peace why art of armes afraide? . . . . Ovid's Elegies 1.6.30
Art carelesse? . . . . Ovid's Elegies 1.6.41
What ere thou art, farewell, be like me paind, ... Ovid's Elegies 1.6.71
As thou art faire, would thou wert fortunate, ... Ovid's Elegies 1.8.27
And whom I like eternize by mine art. . . . . . Ovid's Elegies 1.10.60
Thou art as faire as shee, then kisse and play. . . . Ovid's Elegies 1.13.44
Or if one touch the lute with art and cunning, ... Ovid's Elegies 2.4.27
Light art thou, and more windie then thy winges, . . . Ovid's Elegies 2.9.49
Aye me she cries, to love, why art a shamed? . . . . Ovid's Elegies 2.18.8
What lawfull is, or we professe Loves art, ... Ovid's Elegies 2.18.19
A laughing stocke thou art to all the citty, ... Ovid's Elegies 3.1.21
art thou aye gravely plaied? . . . . Ovid's Elegies 3.1.36
Greater then her, by her leave th'art, Ile say. . . . Ovid's Elegies 3.2.60
In Tiburs field with watry fome art rumbling, ... Ovid's Elegies 3.5.46
Either th'art muddy in mid winter tide: . . . . . Ovid's Elegies 3.5.95
Either th'art witcht with blood <bould> of frogs new dead, Ovid's Elegies 3.6.79
What ere thou art mine art thou: . . . . Ovid's Elegies 3.10.49
Seeing thou art faire, I barre not thy false playing, . Ovid's Elegies 3.13.1
Leander, thou art made for amorous play: . . . . . Hero and Leander 1.88
Why art thou not in love, and lov'd of all? . . . . Hero and Leander 1.89
ARTE (Homograph)
<testimonis> est [inartificiale] <in arte fetiales>. . P 395 7.35 Guise
have heard strange report of thy knowledge in the blacke Arte, F App p.236 2 P Emper
[His Arte excelld, although his witte was weake]. . . Ovid's Elegies 1.15.14
Least Arte should winne her, firmely did inclose. . . Ovid's Elegies 2.12.4
ARTERY (See ARTIER)
ARTES
That in our famous nurseries of artes/Thou suckedst from Plato, Edw 4.7.18 Edward
ARTFULL
His Artfull sport, drives all sad thoughts away. . . . F1673 4.6.116 Duke
ARTICK
Millions of Souldiers cut the Artick line, ... 2Tamb 1.1.29 Orcan
What neede the artick people love star-light, ... Edw 1.1.16 Gavstn
Ocean;/And swept the foming brest of [Artick] <Articks> Rhene. Lucan, First Booke 372
ARTICKS
Ocean;/And swept the foming brest of [Artick] <Articks> Rhene. Lucan, First Booke 372
ARTICLES
Confirm'd by oth and Articles of peace, ... 2Tamb 2.1.29 Sgsmnd
Have I not here the articles of peace, ... 2Tamb 2.2.30 Orcan
Reade there the Articles of our decrees. . . . . . Jew 1.2.67 Govnr
No, Jew, thou hast denied the Articles, ... Jew 1.2.92 Govnr
All <articles prescrib'd> <covenant-articles> betweene us both. F 480 (HC260) Faust
thou performe/All Covenants, and Articles, betweene us both. F 480 2.1.92 Faust
All <articles prescrib'd> <covenant-articles> betweene us both. F 480 (HC260) Faust
and twentie yeares being expired, and these <the> Articles. F 496 2.1.108 P Faust
ARTIER
Sackes every vaine and artier of my heart. . . . . 1Tamb 2.7.10 Cosroe
vaine or Artier feed/The cursed substance of that cruel heart, 2Tamb 4.1.177 Soria
ARTIERS
Your Artiers which alongst the vaines convey/The lively spirits 2Tamb 5.3.93 Phsitn
ARTIFICIALL
Her vaile was artificiall flowers and leaves, ... Hero and Leander 1.19
ARTILERY
Then let us bring our light Artilery, ... 2Tamb 3.3.5 Techel
ARTILLERY
Casemates to place the great Artillery, ... 2Tamb 3.2.78 Tamb
That we may know if our artillery/Will carie full point blancke 2Tamb 3.3.52 Techel
ARTIZAN
Is promised to the Studious Artizan? . . . . . . F 82 1.1.54 Faust
ARTS
See what strange arts necessitie findes out, ... Dido 1.1.169 Venus
Not farre from hence/There is a woman famoused for arts, . Dido 5.1.275 Dido
To practise Magicke and concealed Arts. . . . . . F 129 1.1.101 Faust
all to good, be Augury vaine, and Tages/Th'arts master falce. Lucan, First Booke 636
She magick arts and Thessale charmes doth know, . . . Ovid's Elegies 1.8.5
What man will now take liberall arts in hand, ... Ovid's Elegies 3.7.1
ARUNDELL
How now my lord of Arundell? . . . . Edw 2.5.32 Lncstr
Arundell, say your message. . . . . Edw 2.5.34 Warwck
Arundell, we will gratifie the king/In other matters, he must Edw 2.5.43 Warwck
Arundell no,/We wot, he that the care of realme remits, . Edw 2.5.60 Warwck
Provided this, that you my lord of Arundell/Will joyne with me. Edw 2.5.81 Penbrk
What lord [Arundell] <Matre>, dost thou come alone? . . Edw 3.1.89 Edward
Tell me [Arundell] <Matre>, died he ere thou camst, . . Edw 3.1.92 Edward
Done through the realme, my lord of Arundell/You have the note, Edw 4.3.7 Edward
ARUNS
whom/The gravest, Aruns, dwelt in forsaken Leuca <or Luna>, Lucan, First Booke 585
blasted, Aruns takes/And it inters with murmurs dolorous, Lucan, First Booke 605
These direful signes made Aruns stand amaz'd, ... Lucan, First Booke 615
Involving all, did Aruns darkly sing. . . . . . Lucan, First Booke 637
AS (See also AS'T)
To day when as I fild into your cups, ... Dido 1.1.5 Ganimd
As made the bloud run downe about mine eares. . . . . Dido 1.1.8 Ganimd
As once I did for harming Hercules. . . . . . . Dido 1.1.15 Jupitr
As I exhal'd with thy fire darting beames, ... Dido 1.1.25 Jupitr
When as they would have hal'd thee from my sight: . . . Dido 1.1.27 Jupitr
But as this one Ile teare them all from him, ... Dido 1.1.40 Jupitr

AS (cont.)

And intercepts the day as Dolon erst:	Dido	1.1.71	Venus
When as the waves doe threat our Chrystall world,	Dido	1.1.75	Venus
And Phoebus as in Stygian pooles, refraines/To taint his	Dido	1.1.111	Venus
men, saw you as you came/Any of all my Sisters wandring here?	Dido	1.1.183	Venus
As to instruct us under what good heaven/We breathe as now, and	Dido	1.1.197	Aeneas
As to instruct us under what good heaven/We breathe as now, and	Dido	1.1.198	Aeneas
Whereas Sidonian Dido rules as Queene.	Dido	1.1.213	Venus
As every tide tilts twixt their oken sides:	Dido	1.1.224	Aeneas
As poore distressed miserie may pleade:	Dido	1.2.6	Illion
And every Troian be as welcome here,	Dido	1.2.40	Iarbus
As Jupiter to sillie [Baucis] <Vausis> house:	Dido	1.2.41	Iarbus
As shall surpasse the wonder of our speech.	Dido	1.2.47	Serg
Had not such passions in her head as I.	Dido	2.1.6	Aeneas
And would my prayers (as Pigmalions did)/Could give it life,	Dido	2.1.16	Aeneas
is Aeneas, were he clad/In weedes as bad as ever Irus ware.	Dido	2.1.85	Dido
And if this be thy sonne as I suppose,	Dido	2.1.92	Dido
And who so miserable as Aeneas is?	Dido	2.1.102	Aeneas
And as he spoke, to further his entent/The windes did drive	Dido	2.1.138	Aeneas
and both his eyes/Turnd up to heaven as one resolv'd to dye,	Dido	2.1.152	Aeneas
As therewithall the old man overcome,	Dido	2.1.157	Aeneas
At whose accursed feete as overjoyed,	Dido	2.1.177	Aeneas
As lothing Pirrhus for this wicked act:	Dido	2.1.258	Aeneas
And as we went unto our ships, thou knowest/We sawe Cassandra	Dido	2.1.273	Aeneas
And as I swomme, she standing on the shoare,	Dido	2.1.286	Aeneas
As for Aeneas he swomme quickly backe,	Dido	2.1.296	Achat
As every touch shall wound Queene Didos heart.	Dido	2.1.333	Cupid
altar, where Ile offer up/As many kisses as the Sea hath sands,	Dido	3.1.88	Dido
As without blushing I can aske no more:	Dido	3.1.104	Aeneas
As Seaborne Nymphes shall swarme about thy ships,	Dido	3.1.129	Dido
And are not these as faire as faire may be?	Dido	3.1.140	Dido
The rest are such as all the world well knowes,	Dido	3.1.165	Dido
I was as farre from love, as they from hate.	Dido	3.1.167	Dido
As for Achates, and his followers.	Dido	3.1.176	Dido
Should ere defile so faire a mouth as thine:	Dido	3.2.27	Juno
And banquet as two Sisters with the Gods?	Dido	3.2.29	Juno
That would have kild him sleeping as he lay?	Dido	3.2.39	Juno
As these thy protestations doe paint forth,	Dido	3.2.54	Venus
We two as friends one fortune will devide:	Dido	3.2.55	Venus
Fancie and modestie shall live as mates,	Dido	3.2.58	Venus
Be it as you will have [it] for this once,	Dido	3.2.97	Venus
As I remember, here you shot the Deere,	Dido	3.3.51	Achat
By chance sweete Queene, as Mars and Venus met.	Dido	3.4.4	Aeneas
When as he buts his beames on Floras bed,	Dido	3.4.20	Dido
Aeneas thoughts dare not ascend so high/As Didos heart, which	Dido	3.4.34	Aeneas
As my despised worths, that shun all praise,	Dido	3.4.42	Aeneas
As made disdaine to flye to fancies lap:	Dido	3.4.56	Dido
That can call them forth when as she please,	Dido	4.1.4	Iarbus
When as she meanes to maske the world with clowdes.	Dido	4.1.6	Iarbus
As others did, by running to the wood.	Dido	4.1.30	Anna
And follow them as footemen through the deepe:	Dido	4.3.24	Aeneas
We may as one saile into Italy.	Dido	4.3.30	Aeneas
As parting friends accustome on the shoare,	Dido	4.3.50	Aeneas
Stay here Aeneas, and commaund as King.	Dido	4.4.39	Dido
Aeneas may commaund as many Moores,	Dido	4.4.62	Dido
As in the Sea are little water drops:	Dido	4.4.63	Dido
let him ride/As Didos husband through the Punicke streetes,	Dido	4.4.67	Dido
To waite upon him as their soveraigne Lord.	Dido	4.4.69	Dido
of all these, commaund/Aeneas ride as Carthaginian King.	Dido	4.4.78	Dido
for his parentage deserves/As large a kingdome as is Libia.	Dido	4.4.80	Achat
I shall be planted in as rich a land.	Dido	4.4.82	Aeneas
Doe as I bid thee sister, leade the way,	Dido	4.4.85	Dido
As oft as he attempts to hoyst up saile:	Dido	4.4.103	Dido
Theres not so much as this base tackling too,	Dido	4.4.151	Dido
But what shall it be calde, Troy as before?	Dido	5.1.18	Illion
As how I pray, may I entreate you tell.	Dido	5.1.67	Iarbus
When as I want both rigging for my fleete,	Dido	5.1.69	Aeneas
So thou wouldst prove as true as Paris did,	Dido	5.1.146	Dido
Would, as faire Troy was, Carthage might be sackt,	Dido	5.1.147	Dido
I am as true as any one of yours.	Dido	5.1.223	Nurse
And such conceits as clownage keepes in pay,	1Tamb	Prol.2	Prolog
And as I heare, doth meane to pull my plumes.	1Tamb	1.1.33	Mycet
the verie legges/Whereon our state doth leane, as on a staffe,	1Tamb	1.1.60	Mycet
As did Sir Paris with the Grecian Dame:	1Tamb	1.1.66	Mycet
Embost with silke as best beseemes my state,	1Tamb	1.1.99	Mycet
Passe into Graecia, as did Cyrus once.	1Tamb	1.1.130	Menaph
(If as thou seem'st, thou art so meane a man)/And seeke not to	1Tamb	1.2.8	Zenoc
As easely may you get the Souldans crowne,	1Tamb	1.2.27	Tamb
As any prizes out of my precinct.	1Tamb	1.2.28	Tamb
of his Emperie/By East and west, as Phoebus doth his course:	1Tamb	1.2.40	Tamb
As with their waight shall make the mountains quake,	1Tamb	1.2.49	Tamb
Even as when windy exhalations,	1Tamb	1.2.50	Tamb
As princely Lions when they rouse themselves,	1Tamb	1.2.52	Techel
Even as thou hop'st to be eternized,	1Tamb	1.2.72	Zenoc
As if he now devis'd some Stratageme:	1Tamb	1.2.159	Therid
As if he meant to give my Souldiers pay,	1Tamb	1.2.183	Tamb
And as a sure and grounded argument,	1Tamb	1.2.184	Tamb
Shall vaile to us, as Lords of all the Lake.	1Tamb	1.2.196	Tamb
Both we will raigne as Consuls of the earth,	1Tamb	1.2.197	Tamb
As far as Boreas claps his brazen wings,	1Tamb	1.2.206	Tamb
As long as life maintaines Theridamas.	1Tamb	1.2.231	Therid
Which is as much as if I swore by heaven,	1Tamb	1.2.233	Tamb
You shall have honors, as your merits be:	1Tamb	1.2.255	Tamb

AS (cont.)

Such breadth of shoulders as might mainely beare/Olde Atlas	1Tamb	2.1.10	Menaph
Wrapped in curles, as fierce Achilles was, ...	1Tamb	2.1.24	Menaph
noble Tamburlaine/Shall be my Regent, and remaine as King.	1Tamb	2.1.49	Cosroe
his Diadem/Sought for by such scalde knaves as love him not?	1Tamb	2.2.8	Mycet
Will quickly win such as are like himselfe.	1Tamb	2.2.28	Meandr
But if Cosroe (as our Spials say, ...	1Tamb	2.2.35	Meandr
And as we knew) remaines with Tamburlaine, ...	1Tamb	2.2.36	Meandr
For even as from assured oracle, ...	1Tamb	2.3.4	Cosroe
and with our Sun-bright armour as we march, ...	1Tamb	2.3.221	Tamb
As I shall be commended and excusde/For turning my poore charge	1Tamb	2.3.28	Therid
Which I esteeme as portion of my crown.	1Tamb	2.3.35	Cosroe
as outwaies the sands/And all the craggie rockes of Caspea.	1Tamb	2.3.47	Tamb
These are the wings shall make it flie as swift, . .	1Tamb	2.3.57	Tamb
As dooth the lightening, or the breath of heaven: . .	1Tamb	2.3.58	Tamb
And kill as sure as it swiftly flies.	1Tamb	2.3.59	Tamb
Thinke thee invested now as royally, ...	1Tamb	2.5.2	Tamb
As if as many kinges as could encompasse thee, . . .	1Tamb	2.5.4	Tamb
And as we ever [aim'd] <and> at your behoofe, . . .	1Tamb	2.5.32	Ortyg
A God is not so glorious as a King:	1Tamb	2.5.57	Therid
And if I prosper, all shall be as sure, ...	1Tamb	2.5.84	Tamb
As if the Turke, the Pope, Affrike and Greece, . . .	1Tamb	2.5.85	Tamb
But as he thrust them underneath the hils, . . .	1Tamb	2.6.5	Cosroe
And alwaies mooving as the restles Spheares, . . .	1Tamb	2.7.25	Tamb
For as when Jove did thrust old Saturn down, . . .	1Tamb	2.7.36	Usumc
Shall make me leave so rich a prize as this: . . .	1Tamb	2.7.54	Tamb
As great commander of this Easterne world, . . .	1Tamb	2.7.62	Tamb
As many circumcised Turkes we have, ...	1Tamb	3.1.8	Bajzth
As hath the Ocean or the Terrene sea/Small drops of water, when	1Tamb	3.1.10	Bajzth
As from the mouth of mighty Bajazeth.	1Tamb	3.1.20	Fesse
As fits the Legate of the stately Turk.	1Tamb	3.1.44	Bassoe
All this is true as holy Mahomet, ...	1Tamb	3.1.54	Bajzth
As his exceding favours have deserv'd, ...	1Tamb	3.2.10	Zenoc
And might content the Queene of heaven as well, . .	1Tamb	3.2.11	Zenoc
As it hath chang'd my first conceiv'd disdaine. . .	1Tamb	3.2.12	Zenoc
Which dies my lookes so livelesse as they are. . . .	1Tamb	3.2.15	Zenoc
And leave my body sencelesse as the earth.	1Tamb	3.2.22	Zenoc
And speake of Tamburlaine as he deserves.	1Tamb	3.2.36	Zenoc
As looks the sun through Nilus flowing stream, . . .	1Tamb	3.2.47	Zenoc
That shine as Comets, menacing revenge, ...	1Tamb	3.2.74	Agidas
As when the Sea-man sees the Hyades/Gather an armye of Cemerian	1Tamb	3.2.76	Agidas
and my souldiers looke/As if they meant to conquer Affrica.	1Tamb	3.3.10	Tamb
Withdraw as many more to follow him.	1Tamb	3.3.22	Bassoe
Such as his Highnesse please, but some must stay/To rule the	1Tamb	3.3.28	Bassoe
inlarge/Those Christian Captives, which you keep as slaves,	1Tamb	3.3.47	Tamb
But as I live that towne shall curse the time/That Tamburlaine	1Tamb	3.3.59	Tamb
mighty Turkish Emperor/To talk with one so base as Tamburlaine?	1Tamb	3.3.88	Fesse
That we may raigne as kings of Affrica.	1Tamb	3.3.99	Therid
As if thou wert the Empresse of the world.	1Tamb	3.3.125	Tamb
Which I will bring as Vassals to thy feete.	1Tamb	3.3.129	Tamb
And manage words with her as we will armes.	1Tamb	3.3.131	Tamb
And as the heads of Hydra, so my power/Subdued, shall stand as	1Tamb	3.3.140	Bajzth
of Hydra, so my power/Subdued, shall stand as mighty as before:	1Tamb	3.3.141	Bajzth
not endure to strike/So many blowes as I have heads for thee.	1Tamb	3.3.144	Bajzth
As these my followers willingly would have:	1Tamb	3.3.155	Tamb
As when my Emperour overthrew the Greeks:	1Tamb	3.3.204	Zabina
Straight will I use thee as thy pride deserves: . . .	1Tamb	3.3.206	Zabina
As Crocodiles that unaffrighted rest, ...	1Tamb	4.1.10	Souldn
were that Tamburlaine/As monsterous as Gorgon, prince of Hell,	1Tamb	4.1.18	Souldn
Standard round, that stood/As bristle-pointed as a thorny wood.	1Tamb	4.1.27	2Msngr
As red as scarlet is his furniture, ...	1Tamb	4.1.55	2Msngr
Then as I look downe to the damned Feends, ...	1Tamb	4.2.26	Bajzth
As when a fiery exhalation/Wrapt in the bowels of a freezing	1Tamb	4.2.43	Tamb
As was the fame of [Clymens] <Clymeus> brain-sicke sonne,/That	1Tamb	4.2.49	Tamb
Then when the Sky shal waxe as red as blood, ...	1Tamb	4.2.53	Tamb
Ambitious pride shall make thee fall as low, ...	1Tamb	4.2.76	Bajzth
And every house is as a treasurie.	1Tamb	4.2.109	Tamb
Me thinks we martch as Meliager did, ...	1Tamb	4.3.1	Souldn
As Concubine I feare, to feed his lust.	1Tamb	4.3.42	Souldn
offences feele/Such plagues as heaven and we can poure on him.	1Tamb	4.3.45	Arabia
As frolike as the hunters in the chace/Of savage beastes amid	1Tamb	4.3.56	Capol
And make Damascus spoiles as rich to you, ...	1Tamb	4.4.8	Tamb
As was to Jason Colchos golden fleece.	1Tamb	4.4.9	Tamb
Tamburlane) as I could willingly feed upon thy blood-raw hart.	1Tamb	4.4.11	P Bajzth
And may this banquet proove as omenous, ...	1Tamb	4.4.23	Zabina
As Prognes to th'adulterous Thracian King, ...	1Tamb	4.4.24	Zabina
As far as from the frozen [plage] <place> of heaven, .	1Tamb	4.4.122	Tamb
And be renowm'd, as never Emperours were.	1Tamb	4.4.138	Tamb
Which he observes as parcell of his fame, ...	1Tamb	5.1.14	Govnr
Had never bene erected as they bee, ...	1Tamb	5.1.32	1Virgn
Nor you depend on such weake helps as we.	1Tamb	5.1.33	1Virgn
Endure as we the malice of our stars, ...	1Tamb	5.1.43	Govnr
could they not as well/Have sent ye out, when first my .	1Tamb	5.1.67	Tamb
As now when furie and incensed hate/Flings slaughtering terrour	1Tamb	5.1.71	Tamb
As well for griefe our ruthlesse Governour/Have thus refusde	1Tamb	5.1.92	1Virgn
and Furies dread)/As for their liberties, their loves or lives.	1Tamb	5.1.95	1Virgn
O then for these, and such as we our selves, ...	1Tamb	5.1.96	1Virgn
And wisht as worthy subjects happy meanes, ...	1Tamb	5.1.103	1Virgn
And know my customes are as peremptory/As wrathfull Planets,	1Tamb	5.1.127	Tamb
And know my customes are as peremptory/As wrathfull Planets,	1Tamb	5.1.128	Tamb
A sight as banefull to their soules I think/As are Thessalian	1Tamb	5.1.132	Tamb
to their soules I think/As are Thessalian drugs or Mithradate.	1Tamb	5.1.133	Tamb
So much by much, as dooth Zenocrate.	1Tamb	5.1.159	Tamb

AS (cont.)

Wherein as in a myrrour we perceive/The highest reaches of a	1Tamb	5.1.167	Tamb
As if there were no way but one with us.	1Tamb	5.1.201	Techel
And gore thy body with as many wounds.	1Tamb	5.1.216	Bajzth
Making thee mount as high as Eagles soare.	1Tamb	5.1.224	Bajzth
Stick in his breast, as in their proper roomes.	1Tamb	5.1.226	Zabina
As rules the Skies, and countermands the Gods:	1Tamb	5.1.233	Bajzth
the Feends infernall view/As are the blasted banks of Erebus:	1Tamb	5.1.244	Zabina
As long as any blood or sparke of breath/Can quench or coole	1Tamb	5.1.284	Zabina
As long as life maintaines his mighty arme,	1Tamb	5.1.375	Anippe
Comes now as Turnus gainst Eneas did,	1Tamb	5.1.380	Philem
But as the Gods to end the Troyans toile,	1Tamb	5.1.392	Zenoc
Then as the powers devine have preordainde,	1Tamb	5.1.400	Zenoc
eies beholde/That as for her thou bearst these wretched armes,	1Tamb	5.1.409	Arabia
As much as thy faire body is for me.	1Tamb	5.1.416	Zenoc
As now it bringeth sweetnesse to my wound,	1Tamb	5.1.420	Arabia
If I had not bin wounded as I am.	1Tamb	5.1.421	Arabia
As vast and deep as Euphrates or Nile.	1Tamb	5.1.439	Tamb
The Turk and his great Emperesse as it seems,	1Tamb	5.1.470	Tamb
Wherein as in a mirrour may be seene,	1Tamb	5.1.476	Tamb
If as beseemes a person of thy state,	1Tamb	5.1.483	Souldn
As Juno, when the Giants were supprest,	1Tamb	5.1.510	Tamb
Or as Látonas daughter bent to armes,	1Tamb	5.1.514	Tamb
Shall we with honor (as beseemes) entombe,	1Tamb	5.1.531	Tamb
And means tc fire Turky as he goes:	2Tamb	1.1.18	Gazell
Gyants as big as hugie Polypheme:	2Tamb	1.1.28	Orcan
As martiall presents to our friends at home,	2Tamb	1.1.35	Orcan
And thence as far as Archipellago:	2Tamb	1.1.75	Orcan
Orcanes (as our Legates promist thee)/Wee with our Peeres have	2Tamb	1.1.78	Sgsmnd
for as the Romans usde/I here present thee with a naked sword.	2Tamb	1.1.81	Sgsmnd
As when the massy substance of the earth,	2Tamb	1.1.89	Orcan
That hides these plaines, and seems as vast and wide,	2Tamb	1.1.107	Sgsmnd
As dooth the Desart of Arabia/To those that stand on Badgeths	2Tamb	1.1.108	Sgsmnd
Or as the Ocean to the Traveiler/That restes upon the snowy	2Tamb	1.1.110	Sgsmnd
but yet if Sigismond/Speake as a friend, and stand not upon	2Tamb	1.1.123	Orcan
As memorable witnesse of our league.	2Tamb	1.1.145	Orcan
As faire as was Pigmalions Ivory gyrle,	2Tamb	1.2.38	Callap
And as thou rid'st in triumph through the streets,	2Tamb	1.2.41	Callap
which shine as bright/As that faire vail that covers all the	2Tamb	1.2.49	Callap
shine as bright/As that faire vail that covers all the world:	2Tamb	1.2.50	Callap
my Lord, if I should goe, would you bee as good as your word?	2Tamb	1.2.62	P Almeda
As I am Callapine the Emperour,	2Tamb	1.2.64	Callap
Then here I sweare, as I am Almeda,	2Tamb	1.2.67	Almeda
Not martiall as the sons of Tamburlaine.	2Tamb	1.3.22	Tamb
Their haire as white as milke and soft as Downe,	2Tamb	1.3.25	Tamb
As blacke as Jeat, and hard as Iron or steel,	2Tamb	1.3.27	Tamb
As I cried out for feare he should have falne.	2Tamb	1.3.42	Zenoc
Have under me as many kings as you,	2Tamb	1.3.55	Celeb
As all the world shall tremble at their view.	2Tamb	1.3.57	Celeb
Why may not I my Lord, as wel as he,	2Tamb	1.3.61	Amyras
as if infernall Jove/Meaning to aid [thee] <them> in this	2Tamb	1.3.143	Techel
That though the stones, as at Deucalions flood,	2Tamb	1.3.163	Tamb
But as the faith which they prophanely plight/Is not by	2Tamb	2.1.37	Baldwn
As fell to Saule, to Balaam and the rest,	2Tamb	2.1.54	Fredrk
of the clowdes/And fall as thick as haile upon our heads,	2Tamb	2.2.15	Gazell
Then if there be a Christ, as Christians say,	2Tamb	2.2.39	Orcan
As is our hcly prophet Mahomet,	2Tamb	2.2.44	Orcan
Take here these papers as our sacrifice/And witnesse of thy	2Tamb	2.2.45	Orcan
Yet flourisheth as Flora in her pride,	2Tamb	2.3.22	Orcan
which here appeares as full/As raies of Cynthia to the clearest	2Tamb	2.3.29	Orcan
appeares as full/As raies of Cynthia to the clearest sight?	2Tamb	2.3.30	Orcan
As Centinels to warne th'immortall soules,	2Tamb	2.4.16	Tamb
That this my life may be as short to me/As are the daies of	2Tamb	2.4.36	Tamb
life may be as short to me/As are the daies of sweet Zenocrate:	2Tamb	2.4.37	Tamb
I fare my Lord, as other Emperesses,	2Tamb	2.4.42	Zenoc
Whose absence make the sun and Moone as darke/As when opposde	2Tamb	2.4.51	Tamb
the sun and Moone as darke/As when opposde in one Diamiter,	2Tamb	2.4.52	Tamb
Then in as rich a tombe as Mausolus,	2Tamb	2.4.133	Tamb
rest and have one Epitaph/Writ in as many severall languages,	2Tamb	2.4.135	Tamb
As I have conquered kingdomes with my sword.	2Tamb	2.4.136	Tamb
The houses burnt, wil looke as if they mourn'd,	2Tamb	2.4.139	Tamb
as when Bajazeth/My royall Lord and father fild the throne,	2Tamb	3.1.11	Callap
As all the world should blot our dignities/Out of the booke of	2Tamb	3.1.18	Callap
And raise our honors to as high a pitch/In this our strong and	2Tamb	3.1.30	Callap
And I as many from Jerusalem,	2Tamb	3.1.44	Jrslem
And I as many bring from Trebizon,	2Tamb	3.1.49	Trebiz
and make them seeme as black/As is the Island, where the Furies	2Tamb	3.2.11	Tamb
them seeme as black/As is the Island where the Furies maske,	2Tamb	3.2.12	Tamb
And here this table as a Register/Of all her vertues and	2Tamb	3.2.23	Celeb
As Pilgrimes traveile to our Hemi-spheare,	2Tamb	3.2.32	Tamb
As if Bellona, Goddesse of the war/Threw naked swords and	2Tamb	3.2.40	Tamb
As is that towne, so is my heart consum'd,	2Tamb	3.2.49	Amyras
Whose shattered lims, being tost as high as heaven,	2Tamb	3.2.100	Tamb
Hang in the aire as thicke as sunny motes,	2Tamb	3.2.101	Tamb
a souldier, and this wound/As great a grace and majesty to me,	2Tamb	3.2.118	Tamb
As if a chaire of gold enamiled,	2Tamb	3.2.119	Tamb
Here father, cut it bravely as you did your own.	2Tamb	3.2.135	P Celeb
Killing my selfe, as I have done my sonne,	2Tamb	3.4.35	Olymp
Then scortch a face so beautiful as this,	2Tamb	3.4.74	Techel
My royal army is as great as his,	2Tamb	3.5.10	Callap
Sitting as if they were a telling ridles.	2Tamb	3.5.59	Tamb
Poore soules they looke as if their deaths were neere.	2Tamb	3.5.61	Usumc
As Hector did into the Grecian campe,	2Tamb	3.5.65	Tamb

AS (cont.)

For if I should as Hector did Achilles,	2Tamb	3.5.70		Tamb
And fly my glove as from a Scorpion.	2Tamb	3.5.74		Tamb
So famous as is mighty Tamburlain:	2Tamb	3.5.84		Tamb
As ye shal curse the byrth of Tamburlaine.	2Tamb	3.5.89		Tamb
But as for you (Viceroy) you shal have bits,	2Tamb	3.5.103		Tamb
For as soone as the battaile is done, Ile ride in triumph	2Tamb	3.5.145	P	Tamb
least hee hide his crowne as the foolish king of Persea did.	2Tamb	3.5.154	P	Tamb
Fight as you ever did, like Conquerours,	2Tamb	3.5.160		Tamb
Twill please my mind as wel to heare both you/Have won a heape	2Tamb	4.1.36		Calyph
As if I lay with you for company.	2Tamb	4.1.39		Calyph
I were as soone rewarded with a shot,	2Tamb	4.1.54		Calyph
(Perdicas) and I feare as litle their tara, tantaras, their	2Tamb	4.1.67	P	Calyph
as I doe a naked Lady in a net of golde, and for feare I should	2Tamb	4.1.68	P	Calyph
Although it shine as brightly as the Sun.	2Tamb	4.1.134		Tamb
To scourge the pride of such as heaven abhors:	2Tamb	4.1.149		Tamb
And plague such Pesants as [resist in] <resisting> me/The power	2Tamb	4.1.157		Tamb
And Ile dispose them as it likes me best,	2Tamb	4.1.166		Tamb
Whose cruelties are not so harsh as thine,	2Tamb	4.1.169		Jrslem
As when an heard of lusty Cymbrian Buls,	2Tamb	4.1.187		Tamb
As if they were the teares of Mahomet/For hot consumption of	2Tamb	4.1.196		Tamb
And eb againe, as thou departst from me.	2Tamb	4.2.32		Therid
As all the world cannot affoord the like.	2Tamb	4.2.57		Olymp
Might find as many woondrous myracles,	2Tamb	4.2.85		Therid
As in the Theoria of the world.	2Tamb	4.2.86		Therid
And such a Coachman as great Tamburlaine?	2Tamb	4.3.4		Tamb
As you (ye slaves) in mighty Tamburlain.	2Tamb	4.3.11		Tamb
You shal be fed with flesh as raw as blood,	2Tamb	4.3.18		Tamb
And art a king as absolute as Jove,	2Tamb	4.3.33		Orcan
Come as thou didst in fruitfull Scicilie,	2Tamb	4.3.34		Orcan
And as thou took'st the faire Proserpina,	2Tamb	4.3.36		Orcan
as fit as may be to restraine/These coltish coach-horse tongues	2Tamb	4.3.51		Usumc
(I meane such Queens as were kings Concubines)/Take them,	2Tamb	4.3.71		Tamb
Is not my life and state as deere to me,	2Tamb	5.1.12		Govnr
As any thing of price with thy conceit?	2Tamb	5.1.14		Govnr
the towne will never yeeld/As long as any life is in my breast.	2Tamb	5.1.48		Govnr
As durst resist us till our third daies siege:	2Tamb	5.1.59		Techel
taskes a while/And take such fortune as your fellowes felt.	2Tamb	5.1.137		Tamb
And offer'd me as ransome for thy life,	2Tamb	5.1.156		Tamb
Having as many bullets in his flesh,	2Tamb	5.1.159		Tamb
As there be breaches in her battered wall.	2Tamb	5.1.160		Tamb
As when they swallow Assafitida,	2Tamb	5.1.208		Techel
As your supreame estates instruct our thoughtes,	2Tamb	5.3.20		Techel
But as his birth, life, health and majesty/Were strangely blest	2Tamb	5.3.24		Techel
And that their power is puissant as Joves,	2Tamb	5.3.35		Usumc
Dangerous to those, whose Chrisis is as yours:	2Tamb	5.3.92		Phsitn
As much too high for this disdainfull earth.	2Tamb	5.3.122		Tamb
I conquered all as far as Zansibar.	2Tamb	5.3.139		Tamb
Eastward behold/As much more land, which never was descried,	2Tamb	5.3.155		Tamb
that shine as bright/As all the Lamps that beautifie the Sky,	2Tamb	5.3.156		Tamb
that shine as bright/As all the Lamps that beautifie the Sky,	2Tamb	5.3.157		Tamb
And serve as parcell of my funerall.	2Tamb	5.3.212		Tamb
As precious is the charge thou undertak'st/As that which	2Tamb	5.3.230		Tamb
As that which [Clymens] <Clymeus> brainsicke sonne did guide,	2Tamb	5.3.231		Tamb
learne with awfull eie/To sway a throane as dangerous as his:	2Tamb	5.3.235		Tamb
not full of thoughtes/As pure and fiery as Phyteus beames,	2Tamb	5.3.237		Tamb
But such as love me, gard me from their tongues,	Jew	Prol.6		Machvl
I crave but this, Grace him as he deserves,	Jew	Prol.33		Machvl
As for those [Samnites] <Samintes>, and the men of Uzz,/That	Jew	1.1.4		Barab
As one of them indifferently rated,	Jew	1.1.29		Barab
And as their wealth increaseth, so inclose/Infinite riches in a	Jew	1.1.36		Barab
the Custome-house/Will serve as well as I were present there.	Jew	1.1.58		Barab
Daughter, whom I hold as deare/As Agamemnon did his Iphegen:	Jew	1.1.137		Barab
Daughter, whom I hold as deare/As Agamemnon did his Iphegen:	Jew	1.1.138		Barab
As all the wealth of Malta cannot pay;	Jew	1.1.183		Barab
Let me be us'd but as my brethren are.	Jew	1.2.91		Barab
Some Jewes are wicked, as all Christians are:	Jew	1.2.112		Barab
As if we knew not thy profession?	Jew	1.2.120		Govnr
And not simplicity, as they suggest.	Jew	1.2.161		Barab
as hardly can we brooke/The cruell handling of our selves in	Jew	1.2.174		1Jew
As much as would have bought his beasts and him,	Jew	1.2.189		Barab
As negligently to forgoe so much/Without provision for	Jew	1.2.242		Barab
in distresse/Thinke me so mad as I will hang my selfe,	Jew	1.2.263		Barab
How, as a Nunne?	Jew	1.2.281		Abigal
but be thou so precise/As they may thinke it done of Holinesse.	Jew	1.2.285		Barab
And seeme to them as if thy sinnes were great,	Jew	1.2.287		Barab
As good dissemble that thou never mean'st/As first meane truth,	Jew	1.2.290		Barab
As good dissemble that thou never mean'st/As first meane truth,	Jew	1.2.291		Barab
First let me as a Novice learne to frame/My solitary life to	Jew	1.2.331		Abigal
As much I hope as all I hid is worth.	Jew	1.2.336		Barab
As had you seene her 'twould have mov'd your heart,	Jew	1.2.385		Mthias
And if she be so faire as you report,	Jew	1.2.388		Lodowk
fortune were so good/As but to be about this happy place;	Jew	2.1.32		Abigal
As good goe on, as sit so sadly thus.	Jew	2.1.40		Barab
Singing ore these, as she does ore her young.	Jew	2.1.63		Barab
Delbosco, as thou lovest and honour'st us,	Jew	2.2.24		1Knght
Such as, poore villaines, were ne're thought upon/Till Titus	Jew	2.3.9		Barab
and Vespasian conquer'd us)/Am I become as wealthy as I was:	Jew	2.3.11		Barab
I have bought a house/As great and faire as is the Governors;	Jew	2.3.14		Barab
yet are our lookes/As innocent and harmelesse as a Lambes.	Jew	2.3.22		Barab
And ducke as low as any bare-foot Fryar,	Jew	2.3.25		Barab
And as it were in Catechising sort,	Jew	2.3.73		Barab
As for the Diamond, Sir, I told you of,	Jew	2.3.91		Barab

AS (cont.)

As for the Diamond it shall be yours;	Jew	2.3.135	Barab
Thinke of me as thy father; Sonne farewell.	Jew	2.3.149	Barab
As for the Comment on the Machabees/I have it, Sir, and 'tis at	Jew	2.3.153	Barab
As for my selfe, I walke abroad a nights/And kill sicke people	Jew	2.3.174	Barab
I have as much coyne as will buy the Towne.	Jew	2.3.200	Barab
make account of me/As of thy fellow; we are villaines both:	Jew	2.3.214	Barab
Use him as if he were a--Philistine.	Jew	2.3.228	Barab
As sure as heaven rain'd Manna for the Jewes,	Jew	2.3.248	Barab
Even now as I came home, he slipt me in,	Jew	2.3.267	Barab
a warning e're he goes/As he shall have small hopes of Abigall.	Jew	2.3.274	Barab
Mathias, as thou lov'st me, not a word.	Jew	2.3.277	Barab
but for me, as you went in at dores/You had bin stab'd, but not	Jew	2.3.337	Barab
My life is not so deare as Abigall.	Jew	2.3.348	Mthias
As I behave my selfe in this, imploy me hereafter.	Jew	2.3.379	Ithimr
and as I was taking my choyce, I heard a rumbling in the house;	Jew	3.1.20	P Pilia
As meet they will, and fighting dye; brave sport.	Jew	3.1.30	Ithimr
And then they met, [and] as the story sayes,	Jew	3.3.20	Ithimr
And whilst I live use halfe; spend as my selfe;	Jew	3.4.45	Barab
As fatall be it to her as the draught/Of which great Alexander	Jew	3.4.96	Barab
go set it downe/And come againe so soone as thou hast done,	Jew	3.4.109	Barab
And as you profitably take up Armes,	Jew	3.5.32	Govnr
As I am almost desperate for my sinnes:	Jew	3.6.18	Abigal
As never Jew nor Christian knew the like:	Jew	4.1.118	Barab
Then is it as it should be, take him up.	Jew	4.1.152	Barab
staffe; excellent, he stands as if he were begging of Bacon.	Jew	4.1.154	P Ithimr
As thou lik'st that, stop me another time.	Jew	4.1.173	1Fryar
base slave as he should be saluted by such a tall man as I am,	Jew	4.2.9	P Pilia
base slave as he should be saluted by such a tall man as I am,	Jew	4.2.10	P Pilia
by such a tall man as I am, from such a beautifull dame as you.	Jew	4.2.10	P Pilia
only gave me a nod, as who shold say, Is it even so; and so I	Jew	4.2.12	P Pilia
I never knew a man take his death so patiently as this Fryar;	Jew	4.2.21	P Ithimr
to his prayers, as if hee had had another Cure to serve; well,	Jew	4.2.24	P Ithimr
sort as if he had meant to make cleane my Boots with his lips;	Jew	4.2.30	P Ithimr
this Gentlewoman, who as my selfe, and the rest of the family,	Jew	4.2.43	P Pilia
but hee hides and buries it up as Partridges doe their egges,	Jew	4.2.58	P Ithimr
I, and such as--Goe to, no more, I'le make him send me half he	Jew	4.2.66	P Ithimr
as you love your life send me five hundred crowns, and give the	Jew	4.2.117	P Ithimr
crosbiting, such a Rogue/As is the husband to a hundred whores:	Jew	4.3.14	Barab
Might he not as well come as send; pray bid him come and fetch	Jew	4.3.26	P Barab
That he who knowes I love him as my selfe/Should write in this	Jew	4.3.42	Barab
And unto your good mistris as unknowne.	Jew	4.3.48	Barab
Here take 'em, fellow, with as good a will--	Jew	4.3.52	Barab
As I wud see thee hang'd; oh, love stops my breath:	Jew	4.3.53	Barab
Never lov'd man servant as I doe Ithimore.	Jew	4.3.54	Barab
Was ever Jew tormented as I am?	Jew	4.3.60	Barab
The Governour feeds not as I doe.	Jew	4.4.63	P Barab
As these have spoke so be it to their soules:--	Jew	5.1.42	Barab
Canst thou, as thou reportest, make Malta ours?	Jew	5.1.85	Calym
And Barabas, as erst we promis'd thee,	Jew	5.2.9	Calym
Intreat them well, as we have used thee.	Jew	5.2.17	Calym
And now, as entrance to our safety,	Jew	5.2.22	Barab
When as thy life shall be at their command?	Jew	5.2.33	Barab
And as for Malta's ruine, thinke you not/'Twere slender policy	Jew	5.2.64	Barab
For sith, as once you said, within this Ile/In Malta here, that	Jew	5.2.67	Barab
For as a friend not knowne, but in distresse,	Jew	5.2.72	Barab
Deale truly with us as thou intimatest,	Jew	5.2.85	Govnr
I will be there, and doe as thou desirest;	Jew	5.2.103	Govnr
As be it valued but indifferently,	Jew	5.3.29	Msngr
is a monastery/Which standeth as an out-house to the Towne;	Jew	5.3.37	Msngr
Rather then thus to live as Turkish thrals,	Jew	5.4.8	1Knght
Then now are all things as my wish wud have 'em,	Jew	5.5.17	Barab
Now as for Calymath and his consorts,	Jew	5.5.32	Barab
As sooner shall they drinke the Ocean dry,	Jew	5.5.121	Govnr
And as you know, our difference in Religion/Might be a meanes	P 15	1.15	QnMoth
Him as a childe I dayly winne with words,	P 130	2.73	Guise
As Monestaries, Priories, Abbyes and halles,	P 138	2.81	Guise
within thy hands/To shuffle or cut, take this as surest thing:	P 147	2.90	Guise
As Caesar to his souldiers, so say I:	P 155	2.98	Guise
they may become/As men that stand and gase against the Sunne.	P 163	2.106	Guise
And as we late decreed we may perfourme.	P 206	4.4	QnMoth
And make a shew as if all were well.	P 250	4.48	QnMoth
I vow and sweare as I am King of France,	P 255	4.53	Charls
Will be as resolute as I and Dumaine:	P 323	5.50	Guise
But slay as many as we can come neer.	P 326	5.53	Anjoy
To speek with me from such a man as he?	P 350	6.5	Seroun
I am as Ramus is, a Christian.	P 374	7.14	Taleus
Which as I heare one [Shekius] <Shekins> takes it ill,	P 404	7.44	Ramus
[Sorbonests] <thorbonest>/Attribute as much unto their workes,	P 412	7.52	Ramus
As to the service of the eternall God.	P 413	7.53	Ramus
And sinke them in the river as they swim.	P 423	7.63	Dumain
For Poland is as I have been enformde,	P 454	8.4	Anjoy
As hath sufficient counsaile in himselfe,	P 456	8.6	Anjoy
As I could long ere this have wisht him there.	P 496	9.15	QnMoth
And now Madam as I understand,	P 500	9.19	Guise
I goe as whirl-windes rage before a storme.	P 511	9.30	Guise
As I doe live, so surely shall he dye,	P 521	9.40	QnMoth
And therefore as speedily as I can perfourme,	P 571	11.36	Navrre
As I entend to labour for the truth,	P 585	11.50	Navrre
As now you are, so shall you still persist,	P 608	12.21	King
And like disportes, such as doe fit the Court?	P 629	12.42	King
As not a man may live without our leaves.	P 638	12.51	QnMoth
Madam, as in secrecy I was tolde,	P 641	12.54	Cardnl

AS (cont.)

Which [are] <as> he saith, to kill the Puritans,	P 643	12.56	Cardnl
To such a one my Lord, as when she reads my lines,	P 672	13.16	Duchss
Whom I respect as leaves of boasting greene,	P 720	14.23	Navrre
When I shall vaunt as victor in revenge.	P 722	14.25	Navrre
My Lord, as by our scoutes we understande,	P 724	14.27	1Msngr
But as report doth goe, the Duke of Joyeux/Hath made great sute	P 733	14.36	1Msngr
Which Ile maintaine so long as life doth last:	P 800	16.14	Navrre
possession (as I would I might) yet I meane to keepe you out,	P 814	17.9	P Souldr
Revenge it Henry as thou list or dare,	P 819	17.14	Guise
And as Dictator make or warre or peace,	P 860	17.55	King
But as I live, so sure the Guise shall dye.	P 899	17.94	King
As ancient Romanes over their Captive Lords,	P 982	19.52	Guise
As pale as ashes, nay then tis time to look about.	P1001	19.71	Guise
(As all the world shall know our Guise is dead)/Rest satisfied	P1042	19.112	King
Nere was there King of France so yoakt as I.	P1044	19.114	King
see where she comes, as if she droupt/To heare these newes.	P1062	19.132	Eprnon
I vow as I am lawfull King of France,	P1143	22.5	King
Of such as holde them of the holy church?	P1181	22.43	King
And may it never end in bloud as mine hath done.	P1233	22.95	King
As Rome and all those popish Prelates there,	P1248	22.110	Navrre
And thoughe I come not to keep possessione as I wold I mighte	Paris	ms15 p390	P Souldr
Is as Elizium to a new come soule.	Edw	1.1.11	Gavstn
As for the multitude that are but sparkes,	Edw	1.1.20	Gavstn
Such as desire your worships service.	Edw	1.1.25	Poorem
And as I like your discoursing, ile have you.	Edw	1.1.32	Gavstn
Why there are hospitals for such as you,	Edw	1.1.35	Gavstn
I, I, these wordes of his move me as much,	Edw	1.1.39	Gavstn
As if a Goose should play the Porpintine,	Edw	1.1.40	Gavstn
With haire that gilds the water as it glides,	Edw	1.1.62	Gavstn
Such things as these best please his majestie,	Edw	1.1.71	Gavstn
Embrace me Gaveston as I do thee:	Edw	1.1.141	Edward
Which whiles I have, I thinke my selfe as great,	Edw	1.1.172	Gavstn
As Caesar riding in the Romaine streete,	Edw	1.1.173	Gavstn
As then I did incense the parlement,	Edw	1.1.184	BshpCv
And make him serve thee as thy chaplaine,	Edw	1.1.195	Edward
I give him thee, here use him as thou wilt.	Edw	1.1.196	Edward
And when I come, he frownes, as who should say,	Edw	1.2.53	Queene
Was ever king thus over rulde as I?	Edw	1.4.38	Edward
Subscribe as we have done to his exile.	Edw	1.4.53	ArchBp
As for the peeres that backe the cleargie thus,	Edw	1.4.104	Edward
O might I keepe thee heere, as I doe this,	Edw	1.4.128	Edward
O that we might as well returne as goe.	Edw	1.4.143	Edward
So much as he on cursed Gaveston.	Edw	1.4.181	Queene
And to behold so sweete a sight as that,	Edw	1.4.206	Warwck
And therefore as thou lovest and tendrest me,	Edw	1.4.211	Queene
As thou wilt soone subscribe to his repeale.	Edw	1.4.227	Queene
As he will front the mightiest of us all,	Edw	1.4.260	Mortmr
But were he here, detested as he is,	Edw	1.4.264	Mortmr
And none so much as blame the murtherer,	Edw	1.4.267	Mortmr
Such a one as my Lord of Cornewall is,	Edw	1.4.285	Mortmr
Thinke me as base a groome as Gaveston.	Edw	1.4.291	Mortmr
returnd, this newes will glad him much,/Yet not so much as me.	Edw	1.4.302	Queene
As dooth the want of my sweete Gaveston,	Edw	1.4.307	Edward
My heart is as an anvill unto sorrow,	Edw	1.4.312	Edward
And as grosse vapours perish by the sunne,	Edw	1.4.341	Edward
Live thou with me as my companion.	Edw	1.4.343	Edward
As England shall be quiet, and you safe.	Edw	1.4.358	Mortmr
And as for you, lord Mortimer of Chirke,	Edw	1.4.359	Edward
As fast as Iris, or Joves Mercurie.	Edw	1.4.371	Edward
And promiseth as much as we can wish,	Edw	1.4.399	MortSr
As if that Proteus god of shapes appearde.	Edw	1.4.411	Mortmr
below, the king and he/From out a window, laugh at such as we,	Edw	1.4.417	Mortmr
And as she red, she smild, which makes me thinke,	Edw	2.1.21	Spencr
And now and then, stab as occasion serves.	Edw	2.1.43	Spencr
As is the joy of his returning home.	Edw	2.1.58	Neece
And will be at the court as soone as we.	Edw	2.1.77	Neece
If all things sort out, as I hope they will,	Edw	2.1.79	Neece
What will he do when as he shall be present?	Edw	2.2.48	Mortmr
For as the lovers of faire Danae,	Edw	2.2.53	Edward
As to bestow a looke on such as you.	Edw	2.2.78	Gavstn
As never subject did unto his King.	Edw	2.2.129	Mortmr
I marry, such a garde as this dooth well.	Edw	2.2.131	Mortmr
We never beg, but use such praiers as these.	Edw	2.2.153	Mortmr
If ye be moov'de, revenge it as you can,	Edw	2.2.198	Lncstr
None be so hardie as to touche the King,	Edw	2.3.27	Lncstr
As if he heare I have but talkt with you,	Edw	2.4.54	Queene
But thinke of Mortimer as he deserves.	Edw	2.4.58	Mortmr
As Isabell could live with thee for ever.	Edw	2.4.60	Queene
As by their preachments they will profit much,	Edw	3.1.22	Spencr
As though your highnes were a schoole boy still,	Edw	3.1.30	Baldck
That as the sun-shine shall reflect ore thee:	Edw	3.1.51	Edward
things of more waight/Then fits a prince so yong as I to beare,	Edw	3.1.75	Prince
Neither my lord, for as he was surprizd,	Edw	3.1.94	Arundl
I will have heads, and lives, for him as many,	Edw	3.1.132	Edward
As I have manors, casteis, townes, and towers:	Edw	3.1.133	Edward
And bid me say as plainer to your grace,	Edw	3.1.158	Herald
person you remoove/This Spencer, as a putrifying branche,	Edw	3.1.162	Herald
For theile betray thee, traitors as they are.	Edw	3.1.203	Lncstr
As much as thou in rage out wentst the rest.	Edw	3.1.240	Edward
and though a many friends/Are made away, as Warwick, Lancaster,	Edw	4.2.52	Mortmr
As Isabella <Isabell> gets no aide from thence.	Edw	4.3.16	Edward
Spencer, as true as death,/He is in Englands ground, our	Edw	4.3.21	Edward

AS (cont.)

and as constant report goeth, they intend to give king Edward	Edw	4.3.34	P	Spencr
And windes as equall be to bring them in,	Edw	4.3.51		Edward
As you injurious were to beare them foorth.	Edw	4.3.52		Edward
As to your wisdomes fittest seemes in all.	Edw	4.6.29		Queene
But as the realme and parlement shall please,	Edw	4.6.36		Mortmr
And we must seeke to right it as we may,	Edw	4.6.68		Mortmr
As silent and as carefull will we be,	Edw	4.7.2		Abbot
and fell invasion/Of such as have your majestie in chase,	Edw	4.7.5		Abbot
As daunger of this stormie time requires.	Edw	4.7.7		Abbot
As good be gon, as stay and be benighted.	Edw	4.7.86		Rice
You, and such as you are, have made wise worke in England.	Edw	4.7.114	P	Rice
As with the wings of rancor and disdaine,	Edw	5.1.20		Edward
They passe not for thy frownes as late they did,	Edw	5.1.77		Edward
Such newes as I expect, come Bartley, come,	Edw	5.1.129		Edward
So may his limmes be torne, as is this paper,	Edw	5.1.142		Edward
Favor him my lord, as much as lieth in you.	Edw	5.1.147		Leistr
Even so betide my soule as I use him.	Edw	5.1.148		Bartly
Thinke therefore madam that imports [us] <as> much,	Edw	5.2.10		Mortmr
the greater sway/When as a kings name shall be under writ.	Edw	5.2.14		Mortmr
Whome I esteeme as deare as these mine eyes,	Edw	5.2.18		Queene
As Leicester that had charge of him before.	Edw	5.2.35		BshpWn
But Mortimer, as long as he survives/What safetie rests for us,	Edw	5.2.42		Queene
As thou intendest to rise by Mortimer,	Edw	5.2.52		Mortmr
Who now makes Fortunes wheele turne as he please,	Edw	5.2.53		Mortmr
Feare not my Lord, weele do as you commaund.	Edw	5.2.66		Matrvs
And beare him this, as witnesse of my love.	Edw	5.2.72		Queene
Use Edmund friendly, as if all were well.	Edw	5.2.79		Queene
Heeres channell water, as our charge is given.	Edw	5.3.27		Matrvs
Unpointed as it is, thus shall it goe,	Edw	5.4.13		Mortmr
Come forth. Art thou as resolute as thou wast?	Edw	5.4.22		Mortmr
The proudest lords salute me as I passe,	Edw	5.4.50		Mortmr
Whose lookes were as a breeching to a boye.	Edw	5.4.55		Mortmr
Suscepi that provinciam as they terme it,	Edw	5.4.63		Mortmr
As we were bringing him to Killingworth.	Edw	5.4.85		Souldr
I thought as much.	Edw	5.5.22		Gurney
Doe as you are commaunded by my lord.	Edw	5.5.26		Matrvs
nere was there any/So finely handled as this king shalbe.	Edw	5.5.40		Ltborn
And then thy heart, were it as Gurneys is,	Edw	5.5.53		Edward
Or as Matrevis, hewne from the Caucasus,	Edw	5.5.54		Edward
As doth this water from my tattered robes:	Edw	5.5.67		Edward
But everie jointe shakes as I give it thee:	Edw	5.5.86		Edward
Now as I speake they fall, and yet with feare/Open againe.	Edw	5.5.95		Edward
As for my selfe, I stand as Joves huge tree,	Edw	5.6.11		Mortmr
And had you lov'de him halfe so well as I,	Edw	5.6.35		King
I feard as much, murther cannot be hid.	Edw	5.6.46		Queene
That scornes the world, and as a traveller,	Edw	5.6.65		Mortmr
As thou receivedst thy life from me,	Edw	5.6.68		Queene
When as my sonne thinkes to abridge my daies.	Edw	5.6.84		Queene
Could I have rulde thee then, as I do now,	Edw	5.6.96		King
Nothing so sweet as Magicke is to him,	F 26	Prol.26		1Chor
Are not thy bils hung up as monuments,	F 48	1.1.20		Faust
Stretcheth as farre as doth the mind of man:	F 88	1.1.60		Faust
Be thou on earth as Jove is in the skye,	F 103	1.1.75		BdAngl
as th'infernall spirits/On sweet Musaeus when he came to hell,	F 142	1.1.114		Faust
Will be as cunning as Agrippa was,	F 144	1.1.116		Faust
As Indian Moores, obey their Spanish Lords,	F 148	1.1.120		Valdes
Valdes, as resolute am I in this,	F 161	1.1.133		Faust
As thou to live, therefore object it not.	F 162	1.1.134		Faust
with Valdes and Cornelius, as this wine, if it could speake,	F 216	1.2.23	P	Wagner
Had I as many soules, as there be Starres,	F 330	1.3.102		Faust
for they are as familiar with me, as if they payd for their	F 364	1.4.22	P	Robin
me, as if they payd for their meate and drinke, I can tell you.	F 365	1.4.23	P	Robin
As great as have the humane soules of men.	F 433	2.1.45		Mephst
at some certaine day/Great Lucifer may claime it as his owne,	F 440	2.1.52		Mephst
And then be thou as great as Lucifer.	F 441	2.1.53		Mephst
Speake Faustus, do you deliver this as your Deed?	F 501	2.1.113		Mephst
Were <Be> she as chaste as was Penelope,	F 540	2.1.152		Mephst
As wise as Saba, or as beautifull/As was bright Lucifer before	F 541	2.1.153		Mephst
as Saba, or as beautifull/As was bright Lucifer before his fall.	F 541	2.1.153		Mephst
Saba, or as beautifull/As was bright Lucifer before his fall.	F 542	2.1.154		Mephst
This will I keepe, as chary as my life.	F 551	2.1.163		Faust
I tell thee Faustus it is <tis> not halfe so faire/As thou, or	F 558	2.2.7		Mephst
As is the substance of this centricke earth?	F 588	2.2.37		Faust
As are the elements, such are the heavens <spheares>,/Even from	F 589	2.2.38		Mephst
<as> Saturne in thirty yeares, Jupiter in twelve, Mars in four,	F 604	2.2.53	P	Faust
That sight will be as pleasant to <pleasing unto> me, as	F 657	2.2.106	P	Faust
me, as Paradise was to Adam the first day of his creation.	F 657	2.2.106	P	Faust
[This will I keepe as chary as my life].	F 719.1	2.2.172		Faust
as faire a paire of hornes on's head as e're thou sawest in thy	F 737	2.3.16	P	Robin
a paire of hornes on's head as e're thou sawest in thy life.	F 737	2.3.16	P	Robin
of us here, that have waded as deepe into matters, as other men,	F 740	2.3.19	P	Robin
into matters, as other men, if they were disposed to talke.	F 741	2.3.20	P	Robin
brave, prethee let's to it presently, for I am as dry as a dog.	F 751	2.3.30	P	Dick
And as I guesse will first arrive at Rome,	F 775	2.3.54		2Chor
Hast thou, as earst I did command,	F 801	3.1.23		Faust
As that the double Cannons forg'd of brasse,	F 820	3.1.42		Mephst
<As match the dayes within one compleate yeare>,	F 821	(HC265)A		Mephst
And view their triumphs, as they passe this way.	F 857	3.1.79		Mephst
Thus, as the Gods creepe on with feete of wool,	F 877	3.1.99		Pope
And as they turne their superstitious Bookes,	F 893	3.1.115		Faust
And as Pope Alexander our Progenitour,	F 915	3.1.137		Pope
To light as heavy as the paines of hell.	F 939	3.1.161		Pope

AS (cont.)

two such Cardinals/Ne're serv'd a holy Pope, as we shall do.	F 942	3.1.164		Faust
and the Germane Emperour/Be held as Lollords, and bold	F 955	3.1.177		Faust
And on a proud pac'd Steed, as swift as thought,	F 984	3.2.4		Mephst
As best beseemes this solemne festivall.	F1012	3.2.32		Pope
him, as he was never conjur'd in his life, I warrant him:	F1092	3.3.5	P	Robin
[Where such as beare <bare> his absence but with griefe],	F1141	3.3.54A		3Chor
[As they admirde and wondred at his wit].	F1148	3.3.61A		3Chor
As never yet was seene in Germany.	F1188	4.1.34		Mrtino
shall controule him as well as the Conjurer, I warrant you.	F1203	4.1.49	P	Benvol
he lookes as like [a] conjurer as the Pope to a Coster-monger.	F1228	4.1.74	P	Benvol
Then Faustus as thou late didst promise us,	F1230	4.1.76		Emper
Be it as Faustus please, we are content.	F1253	4.1.99		Emper
As all his footmanship shall scarce prevaile,	F1302	4.1.148		Faust
as to delight your Majesty with some mirth, hath Faustus justly	F1312	4.1.158	P	Faust
Or hew'd this flesh and bones as small as sand,	F1398	4.2.74		Faust
And mount aloft with them as high as heaven,	F1404	4.2.80		Faust
As he intended to dismember me.	F1415	4.2.91		Faust
And stand as Bulwarkes twixt your selves and me,	F1427	4.2.103		Faust
As I was going to Wittenberge t'other day, with a loade of Hay,	F1525	4.5.21	P	Carter
me what he should give me for as much Hay as he could eate;	F1527	4.5.23	P	Carter
bad him take as much as he would for three-farthings; so he	F1528	4.5.24	P	Carter
bad him take as much as he would for three-farthings; so he	F1529	4.5.25	P	Carter
fell to eating; and as I am a cursen man, he never left eating,	F1530	4.5.26	P	Carter
such a horse, as would run over hedge and ditch, and never tyre,	F1538	4.5.34	P	HrsCsr
so delighted me, as nothing in the world could please me more.	F1561	4.6.4	P	Duke
were it now Summer, as it is January, a dead time of the Winter,	F1572	4.6.15	P	Lady
circle it is likewise Summer with them, as in India, Saba,	F1583	4.6.26	P	Faust
spirit that I have, I had these grapes brought as you see.	F1586	4.6.29	P	Faust
us, he were as good commit with his father, as commit with us.	F1603	4.6.46	P	Dick
us, he were as good commit with his father, as commit with us.	F1604	4.6.47	P	Dick
Do as thou wilt Faustus, I give thee leave.	F1607	4.6.50		Duke
such belly-cheere, as Wagner in his life nere saw the like:	F1679	5.1.6	P	Wagner
as to let us see that peerelesse dame of Greece, whom all the	F1685	5.1.12	P	1Schol
[As in this furnace God shal try my faith],	F1792	5.1.119A		OldMan
'Mong which as chiefe, Faustus we come to thee,	F1800	5.2.4		Lucifr
As in all humble dutie, I do yeeld/My life and lasting service	F1818	5.2.22		Wagner
end be such/As every Christian heart laments to thinke on:	F1996	5.3.14		2Schol
you have seene many boyes with such pickadevaunts as I have.	F App	p.229 3	P	Clown
swowns they are as bolde with my flesh, as if they had payd for	F App	p.230 28	P	Clown
with my flesh, as if they had payd for my meate and drinke.	F App	p.230 29	P	Clown
crownes a man were as good have as many english counters,	F App	p.230 33	P	Clown
crownes a man were as good have as many english counters,	F App	p.230 34	P	Clown
hir to thy owne use, as often as thou wilt, and at midnight.	F App	p.234 28	P	Robin
Ile feede thy divel with horse-bread as long as he lives,	F App	p.234 30	P	Rafe
our horses shal eate no hay as long as this lasts.	F App	p.234 3	P	Robin
I shall say, As I was sometime solitary set, within my Closet,	F App	p.236 17	P	Emper
as we that do succeede, or they that shal hereafter possesse	F App	p.236 21	P	Emper
As when I heare but motion made of him,	F App	p.237 27		Emper
forth as by art and power of my spirit I am able to performe.	F App	p.237 38	P	Faust
spirites as can lively resemble Alexander and his Paramour,	F App	p.237 46	P	Faust
Ifaith thats as true as Diana turned me to a stag.	F App	p.237 54	P	Knight
as to delight you with some mirth, hath Faustus worthily	F App	p.238 82	P	Faust
on him; hee has a buttocke as slicke as an Ele; wel god buy sir,	F App	p.239 116	P	HrsCsr
on him; hee has a buttocke as slicke as an Ele; wel god buy sir,	F App	p.240 117	P	HrsCsr
but yet like an asse as I was, I would not be ruled by him, for	F App	p.240 130	P	HrsCsr
nowe summer, as it is January, and the dead time of the winter,	F App	p.242 9	P	Duchss
the contrary circle it is summer with them, as in India, Saba,	F App	p.242 21	P	Faust
had them brought hither, as ye see, how do you like them Madame,	F App	p.242 23	P	Faust
carowse, and swill/Amongst the Students, as even now he doth,	F App	p.243 5		Wagner
As Wagner nere beheld in all his life.	F App	p.243 7		Wagner
As no commiseration may expel,	F App	p.243 43		OldMan
As far as Titan springs where night dims heaven,	Lucan, First Booke			15
as yet thou wants not foes.	Lucan, First Booke			23
Receive with shouts; where thou wilt raigne as King,	Lucan, First Booke			47
even as the slender Isthmos,/Betwixt the Aegean and the Ionian	Lucan, First Booke			100
So when as Crassus wretched death who stayd them,	Lucan, First Booke			104
Made all shake hands as once the Sabines did;	Lucan, First Booke			118
As soone as Caesar got unto the banke/And bounds of Italy;	Lucan, First Booke			225
armes neer their houshold gods hung up/Such as peace yeelds;	Lucan, First Booke			243
As oft as Roome was sackt, here gan the spoile:	Lucan, First Booke			258
but as the fields/When birds are silent thorough winters rage;	Lucan, First Booke			260
to warre,/Was so incenst as are Eleius steedes/With clamors:	Lucan, First Booke			294
rageth now in armes/As if the Carthage Hannibal were neere;	Lucan, First Booke			305
[As] <A> brood of barbarous Tygars having lapt/The bloud of	Lucan, First Booke			327
Must Pompey as his last foe plume on me,	Lucan, First Booke			338
As when against pine bearing Ossa's rocks,	Lucan, First Booke			390
And rustling swing up as the wind fets breath.	Lucan, First Booke			392
And changeth as the Ocean ebbes and flowes:	Lucan, First Booke			412
As if, the only hope (that did remaine/To their afflictions)	Lucan, First Booke			494
As loath to leave Roome whom they held so deere,	Lucan, First Booke			506
is by cowards/Left as a pray now Caesar doth approach:	Lucan, First Booke			512
making men/Dispaire of day; as did Thiestes towne/(Mycenae),	Lucan, First Booke			541
The Ocean swell'd, as high as Spanish Calpe,	Lucan, First Booke			553
To these ostents (as their old custome was)/They call	Lucan, First Booke			583
long struggled, as being like to prove/An aukward sacrifice,	Lucan, First Booke			610
As [Maenas] <Maenus> full of wine on Pindus raves,	Lucan, First Booke			674
Then such as in their bondage feele content.	Ovid's Elegies			1.2.18
Yong men and women, shalt thou lead as thrall,	Ovid's Elegies			1.2.27
shame, and such as seeke loves wrack/Shall follow thee, their	Ovid's Elegies			1.2.31
Thee all shall feare and worship as a King,	Ovid's Elegies			1.2.33
Shall I sit gazing as a bashfull guest,	Ovid's Elegies			1.4.3
Turne round thy gold-ring, as it were to ease thee.	Ovid's Elegies			1.4.26

AS (cont.)

Which gave such light, as twincles in a wood,	Ovid's Elegies	1.5.4
And striving thus as one that would be cast,	Ovid's Elegies	1.5.15
Starke naked as she stood before mine eie,	Ovid's Elegies	1.5.17
Jove send me more such afternoones as this.	Ovid's Elegies	1.5.26
his tender mother/And smiling sayed, be thou as bold as other.	Ovid's Elegies	1.6.12
And as a pray unto blinde anger given,	Ovid's Elegies	1.7.44
Fame saith as I suspect, and in her eyes/Two eye-balles shine,	Ovid's Elegies	1.8.15
As thou art faire, would thou wert fortunate,	Ovid's Elegies	1.8.27
Such is his forme as may with thine compare,	Ovid's Elegies	1.8.33
Let Homer yeeld to such as presents bring,	Ovid's Elegies	1.8.61
Dissemble so, as lov'd he may be thought,	Ovid's Elegies	1.8.71
And as first wrongd the wronged some-times banish,	Ovid's Elegies	1.8.79
When thou hast so much as he gives no more,	Ovid's Elegies	1.8.101
As thus she spake, my shadow me betraide,	Ovid's Elegies	1.8.109
One as a spy doth to his enemies goe,	Ovid's Elegies	1.9.17
The other eyes his rivall as his foe.	Ovid's Elegies	1.9.18
Such as the cause was of two husbands warre,	Ovid's Elegies	1.10.1
Such as was Leda, whom the God deluded/In snowe-white plumes of	Ovid's Elegies	1.10.3
Such as Amimone through the drie fields strayed/When on her	Ovid's Elegies	1.10.5
The sport being such, as both alike sweete try it,	Ovid's Elegies	1.10.33
Yet as if mixt with red leade thou wert ruddy,	Ovid's Elegies	1.12.11
As evill wood throwne in the high-waies lie,	Ovid's Elegies	1.12.13
Thou art as faire as shee, then kisse and play.	Ovid's Elegies	1.13.44
Such as in hilly Idas watry plaines,	Ovid's Elegies	1.14.11
Such were they as [Dione] <Diana> painted stands/All naked	Ovid's Elegies	1.14.33
Ile live, and as he puls me downe, mount higher.	Ovid's Elegies	1.15.42
That some youth hurt as I am with loves bowe/His owne flames	Ovid's Elegies	2.1.7
O would my proofes as vaine might be withstood,	Ovid's Elegies	2.5.7
Even such as by Aurora hath the skie,	Ovid's Elegies	2.5.35
Such as a rose mixt with a lilly breedes,	Ovid's Elegies	2.5.37
Or such, as least long yeares should turne the die,	Ovid's Elegies	2.5.39
Even kembed as they were, her lockes to rend,	Ovid's Elegies	2.5.45
and kissed so sweetely as might make/Wrath-kindled Jove away	Ovid's Elegies	2.5.51
And ever seemed as some new sweete befell.	Ovid's Elegies	2.5.56
[Itis is] <It is as> great, but auntient cause of sorrowe.	Ovid's Elegies	2.6.10
And as a traitour mine owne fault confesse.	Ovid's Elegies	2.8.26
Even as a head-strong courser beares away,	Ovid's Elegies	2.9.29
Or as a sodaine gale thrustes into sea,	Ovid's Elegies	2.9.31
Here of themselves thy shafts come, as if shot,	Ovid's Elegies	2.9.37
Even as a boate, tost by contrarie winde,	Ovid's Elegies	2.10.9
Let such as be mine enemies have none,	Ovid's Elegies	2.10.16
Even as he led his life, so did he die.	Ovid's Elegies	2.10.38
To bring that happy time so soone as may be.	Ovid's Elegies	2.11.56
She whom her husband, guard, and gate as foes,	Ovid's Elegies	2.12.3
me, or I am sure/I oft have done, what might as much procure.	Ovid's Elegies	2.13.6
Fit her so well, as she is fit for me:	Ovid's Elegies	2.15.5
Sythia, Cilicia, Brittaine are as good,	Ovid's Elegies	2.16.39
Which as it seemes, hence winde and sea bereaves.	Ovid's Elegies	2.16.46
Shee in my lap sits still as earst she did.	Ovid's Elegies	2.18.6
As soone as from strange lands Sabinus came,	Ovid's Elegies	2.18.27
Even as sweete meate a glutted stomacke cloyes.	Ovid's Elegies	2.19.26
Each crosse waies corner doth as much expresse.	Ovid's Elegies	3.1.18
She beckt, and prosperous signes gave as she moved.	Ovid's Elegies	3.2.58
The horses seeme, as [thy] <they> desire they knewe.	Ovid's Elegies	3.2.68
The Gods have eyes, and brests as well as men.	Ovid's Elegies	3.3.42
Even as the sicke desire forbidden drinke.	Ovid's Elegies	3.4.18
As his deepe whirle-pooles could not quench the same.	Ovid's Elegies	3.5.42
Idly I lay with her, as if I lovde <her> not,	Ovid's Elegies	3.6.3
That were as white as is <Her armes farre whiter, then> the	Ovid's Elegies	3.6.8
Yet like as if cold hemlocke I had drunke,	Ovid's Elegies	3.6.13
And I grow faint, as with some spirit haunted?	Ovid's Elegies	3.6.36
As she might straight have gone to church and praide:	Ovid's Elegies	3.6.54
Well, I beleeve she kist not as she should,	Ovid's Elegies	3.6.55
And one gave place still as another came.	Ovid's Elegies	3.6.64
Seeing now thou wouldst deceive me as before:	Ovid's Elegies	3.6.70
As when the wilde boare Adons groine had rent.	Ovid's Elegies	3.8.16
She sawe, and as her marrowe tooke the flame,	Ovid's Elegies	3.9.27
As in thy sacrifize we them forbeare?	Ovid's Elegies	3.9.44
I am not as I was before, unwise.	Ovid's Elegies	3.10.32
Nor, as use will not Poets record heare,	Ovid's Elegies	3.11.19
As is the use, the Nunnes in white veyles clad,	Ovid's Elegies	3.12.27
Such as confesse, have lost their good names by it.	Ovid's Elegies	3.13.6
Be more advisde, walke as a puritane,	Ovid's Elegies	3.13.13
And blush, and seeme as you were full of grace.	Ovid's Elegies	3.13.28
And offred as a dower his burning throne,	Hero and Leander	1.7
Many would praise the sweet smell as she past,	Hero and Leander	1.21
Such as the world would woonder to behold:	Hero and Leander	1.34
Which as shee went would cherupe through the bils.	Hero and Leander	1.36
As he imagyn'd Hero was his mother.	Hero and Leander	1.40
As nature wept, thinking she was undone;	Hero and Leander	1.46
His bodie was as straight as Circes wand,	Hero and Leander	1.61
Even as delicious meat is to the tast,	Hero and Leander	1.63
And such as knew he was a man would say,	Hero and Leander	1.87
To meet their loves; such as had none at all,	Hero and Leander	1.95
As if another Phaeton had got/The guidance of the sunnes rich	Hero and Leander	1.101
Even as, when gawdie Nymphs pursue the chace,	Hero and Leander	1.113
And as in furie of a dreadfull fight,	Hero and Leander	1.119
Pyn'd as they went, and thinking on her died.	Hero and Leander	1.130
As after chaunc'd, they did each other spye.	Hero and Leander	1.134
So faire a church as this, had Venus none,	Hero and Leander	1.135
Love kindling fire, to burne such townes as Troy,	Hero and Leander	1.153
And modestly they opened as she rose:	Hero and Leander	1.160

AS (cont.)			
And as shee spake those words, came somewhat nere him.	Hero and Leander	1.180	
He started up, she blusht as one asham'd;	Hero and Leander	1.181	
And alwaies cut him off as he replide.	Hero and Leander	1.196	
To lead thy thoughts, as thy faire lookes doe mine,	Hero and Leander	1.201	
God knowes I cannot force love, as you doe.	Hero and Leander	1.206	
My words shall be as spotlesse as my youth,	Hero and Leander	1.207	
As much as sparkling Diamonds flaring glasse.	Hero and Leander	1.214	
As thou in beautie doest exceed Loves mother/Nor heaven, nor	Hero and Leander	1.222	
As heaven preserves all things, so save thou one.	Hero and Leander	1.224	
In heaping up a masse of drossie pelfe,/Than such as you:	Hero and Leander	1.245	
Differs as much, as wine and water doth.	Hero and Leander	1.264	
As Greece will thinke, if thus you live alone,	Hero and Leander	1.289	
Some one or other keepes you as his owne.	Hero and Leander	1.290	
To Venus, answered shee, and as shee spake,	Hero and Leander	1.295	
Thee as a holy Idiot doth she scorne,	Hero and Leander	1.303	
Such sacrifice as this, Venus demands.	Hero and Leander	1.310	
As put thereby, yet might he hope for mo.	Hero and Leander	1.312	
Aye me, such words as these should I abhor,	Hero and Leander	1.339	
Come thither; As she spake this, her toong tript,	Hero and Leander	1.357	
As might have made heaven stoope to have a touch,	Hero and Leander	1.366	
As made Love sigh, to see his tirannie.	Hero and Leander	1.374	
And as she wept, her teares to pearle he turn'd,	Hero and Leander	1.375	
nor would vouchsafe so much/As one poore word, their hate to	Hero and Leander	1.384	
Glist'red with deaw, as one that seem'd to skorne it:	Hero and Leander	1.390	
Her breath as fragrant as the morning rose,	Hero and Leander	1.391	
As sheap-heards do, her on the ground hee layd,	Hero and Leander	1.405	
As she to heare his tale, left off her running.	Hero and Leander	1.418	
such lovelinesse and beautie had/As could provoke his liking,	Hero and Leander	1.423	
she wanting no excuse/To feed him with delaies, as women use:	Hero and Leander	1.426	
As he ought not performe, nor yet she aske.	Hero and Leander	1.430	
Which being knowne (as what is hid from Jove)?	Hero and Leander	1.436	
As soone as he his wished purpose got,	Hero and Leander	1.460	
Yet as a punishment they added this,	Hero and Leander	1.469	
Wherewith as one displeas'd, away she trips.	Hero and Leander	2.4	
Yet as she went, full often look'd behind,	Hero and Leander	2.5	
As he had hope to scale the beauteous fort,	Hero and Leander	2.16	
As if her name and honour had beene wrong'd,	Hero and Leander	2.35	
And as a brother with his sister toyed,	Hero and Leander	2.52	
As in plaine termes (yet cunningly) he crav'd it,	Hero and Leander	2.71	
And ever as he thought himselfe most nigh it,	Hero and Leander	2.74	
And kist againe, as lovers use to do.	Hero and Leander	2.94	
As loath to see Leander going out.	Hero and Leander	2.98	
As pittying these lovers, downeward creepes.	Hero and Leander	2.100	
Like as the sunne in a Dyameter,	Hero and Leander	2.123	
Therefore even as an Index to a booke,	Hero and Leander	2.129	
For as a hote prowd horse highly disdaines,	Hero and Leander	2.141	
He watcht his armes, and as they opend wide,	Hero and Leander	2.183	
And as he turnd, cast many a lustfull glaunce,	Hero and Leander	2.186	
As for his love, both earth and heaven pyn'd;	Hero and Leander	2.196	
And as he spake, upon the waves he springs.	Hero and Leander	2.206	
He flung at him his mace, but as it went,	Hero and Leander	2.209	
As meaning to be veng'd for darting it.	Hero and Leander	2.212	
went and came, as if he rewd/The greefe which Neptune felt.	Hero and Leander	2.214	
Such sights as this, to tender maids are rare.	Hero and Leander	2.238	
And as her silver body downeward went,	Hero and Leander	2.263	
Yet ever as he greedily assayd/To touch those dainties, she the	Hero and Leander	2.269	
And every lim did as a soldier stout,	Hero and Leander	2.271	
Which so prevail'd, as he with small ado,	Hero and Leander	2.281	
And everie kisse to her was as a charme,	Hero and Leander	2.283	
And to Leander as a fresh alarme.	Hero and Leander	2.284	
Love is not ful of pittie (as men say)/But deaffe and cruell,	Hero and Leander	2.287	
Even as a bird, which in our hands we wring,	Hero and Leander	2.289	
Both in each others armes chaind as they layd.	Hero and Leander	2.306	
But as her naked feet were whipping out,	Hero and Leander	2.313	
As from an orient cloud, glymse <glimps'd> here and there.	Hero and Leander	2.320	
And ran before, as Harbenger of light,	Hero and Leander	2.331	
ASAFOETIDA (See ASSAFITIDA)			
ASANT			
Shall lie at anchor in the Isle Asant,	1Tamb	3.3.251	Tamb
ASCANIA			
Rather Ascania by your little sonne.	Dido	5.1.21	Serg
ASCANIUS			
But bright Ascanius, beauties better worke,	Dido	1.1.96	Jupitr
Ascanius, goe and drie thy drenched lims,	Dido	1.1.174	Aeneas
It is our Captaine, see Ascanius.	Dido	2.1.52	Cloan
Live long Aeneas and Ascanius.	Dido	2.1.53	Serg
Will Dido give to sweete Ascanius:	Dido	2.1.312	Venus
and in this grove/Amongst greene brakes Ile lay Ascanius,	Dido	2.1.317	Venus
Now Cupid turne thee to Ascanius shape,	Dido	2.1.323	Venus
How lovely is Ascanius when he smiles?	Dido	3.1.29	Dido
Take it Ascanius, for thy fathers sake.	Dido	3.1.33	Dido
Come Dido, leave Ascanius, let us walke.	Dido	3.1.34	Iarbus
Goe thou away, Ascanius shall stay.	Dido	3.1.35	Dido
Say vengeance, now shall her Ascanius dye?	Dido	3.2.13	Juno
To harme my sweete Ascanius lovely life.	Dido	3.2.23	Venus
Meane time, Ascanius shall be my charge,	Dido	3.2.98	Venus
Sister, see see Ascanius in his pompe,	Dido	3.3.32	Anna
Achates and Ascanius, well met.	Dido	4.1.28	Dido
me, for I forgot/That yong Ascanius lay with me this night:	Dido	4.4.32	Dido
Goe, bid my Nurse take yong Ascanius,	Dido	4.4.105	Dido
Your Nurse is gone with yong Ascanius,	Dido	4.4.124	Lord
My Lord Ascanius, ye must goe with me.	Dido	4.5.1	Nurse

ASCANIUS (cont.)
Now speake Ascanius, will ye goe or no? . . . . . Dido 4.5.12 Nurse
Yet thinke upon Ascanius prophesie, ... Dido 5.1.38 Hermes
O Dido, your little sonne Ascanius/Is gone! . . . Dido 5.1.212 Nurse
ASCEASD
upon him, next/Himselfe imprisoned, and his goods asceasd, Edw 1.2.37 ArchBp
ASCEND (See also ASSENDS)
Aeneas thoughts dare not ascend so high/As Didos heart, which Dido 3.4.33 Aeneas
Cannot ascend to Fames immortall house, ... Dido 4.3.9 Aeneas
with what a broken hart/And damned spirit I ascend this seat, 2Tamb 5.3.207 Amyras
To ascend our homely stayres? . . . . Jew 5.5.58 Barab
Thus from infernall Dis do we ascend/To view the subjects of F1797 5.2.1 Lucifr
[So that] my soule [may but] ascend to heaven. . . . F1956 5.2.160 Faust
<But let my soule mount and> ascend to heaven. . . . F1956 (HC271)B Faust
should defend/Or great wealth from a judgement seate ascend. Ovid's Elegies 1.10.40
ASCENDS
Whilst on thy backe his hollinesse ascends/Saint Peters Chaire F 869 3.1.91 Raymnd
From Bruno's backe, ascends Saint Peters Chaire. . . F 876 3.1.98 Pope
ASCREUS
Ascreus lives, while grapes with new wine swell, . . Ovid's Elegies 1.15.11
ASCRIB'D
Much lesse can honour bee ascrib'd thereto, . . . Hero and Leander 1.279
ASHAM'D
I am asham'd to heare such fooleries. . . . . . Jew Prol.17 Machvl
Nor of our love to be asham'd we need, ... Ovid's Elegies 2.17.26
He started up, she blusht as one asham'd; . . . . Hero and Leander 1.181
ASHAMDE
Fye, I am ashamde, how ever that I seeme, ... P 124 2.67 Guise
A SHAMED
Aye me she cries, to love, why art a shamed? . . . Ovid's Elegies 2.18.8
ASHAMED
you may be ashamed to burden honest men with a matter of truth. F App p.234 15 P Rafe
Be not ashamed to strippe you being there, ... Ovid's Elegies 3.13.21
ASHES
From forth her ashes shall advance her head, . . . Dido 1.1.94 Jupitr
And from mine ashes let a Conquerour rise, . . . Dido 5.1.306 Dido
As pale as ashes, nay then tis time to look about. . . P1001 19.71 Guise
Nor did thy ashes her last offrings lose. . . . . Ovid's Elegies 3.8.50
And may th'earths weight thy ashes nought molest. . . Ovid's Elegies 3.8.68
ASHIE
came Hectors ghost/With ashie visage, blewish sulphure eyes, Dido 2.1.202 Aeneas
ASHORE
Why then goe bid them come ashore,/And bring with them their Jew 1.1.55 Barab
And bid the Merchants and my men dispatch/And come ashore, and Jew 1.1.101 Barab
And why thou cam'st ashore without our leave? . . . Jew 2.2.3 Govnr
and has commanded all his men/To come ashore, and march through Jew 5.5.15 Msngr
ASIA
Exild forth Europe and wide Asia both, ... Dido 1.1.229 Aeneas
That after burnt the pride of Asia. . . . . . . Dido 2.1.187 Aeneas
Hoping (misled by dreaming prophesies)/To raigne in Asia, and 1Tamb 1.1.42 Meandr
But ere he march in Asia, or display/His vagrant Ensigne in the 1Tamb 1.1.44 Meandr
to them, that all Asia/Lament to see the follie of their King. 1Tamb 1.1.95 Cosroe
To crowne me Emperour of Asia. . . . . 1Tamb 1.1.112 Cosroe
Emperour of Asia, and of Persea, ... 1Tamb 1.1.162 Ortyg
Must grace his bed that conquers Asia: . . . . . . 1Tamb 1.2.37 Tamb
Before I crowne you kings in Asia. . . . . . . 1Tamb 1.2.246 Tamb
Shall make me solely Emperour of Asia: . . . . . . 1Tamb 2.3.39 Cosroe
So do we hope to raign in Asia, ... 1Tamb 2.7.38 Usumc
Long live Tamburlaine, and raigne in Asia. . . . . 1Tamb 2.7.64 All
To charge him to remaine in Asia. . . . . . . 1Tamb 3.1.18 Fesse
Dread Lord of Affrike, Europe and Asia, ... 1Tamb 3.1.23 Bajzth
That made me Emperour of Asia. . . . . 1Tamb 3.3.32 Tamb
Egyptians, Moores and men of Asia, ... 1Tamb 5.1.517 Tamb
Proud Tamburlaine, that now in Asia, ... 2Tamb 1.1.16 Gazell
All Asia is in Armes with Tamburlaine. . . . . . 2Tamb 1.1.72 Orcan
I thank thee Sigismond, but when I war/All Asia Minor, Affrica, 2Tamb 1.1.158 Orcan
From Trebizon in Asia the lesse, ... 2Tamb 3.5.40 Trebiz
And now ye cankred curres of Asia, ... 2Tamb 4.1.132 Tamb
Holla, ye pampered Jades of Asia: . . . . . . 2Tamb 4.3.1 Tamb
Now crowch ye kings of greatest Asia, ... 2Tamb 4.3.98 Tamb
Courted by kings and peeres of Asia, ... 2Tamb 5.1.74 Tamb
Marcheth in Asia major, where the streames, ... 2Tamb 5.2.2 Callap
Graecia, and from thence/To Asia, where I stay against my will, 2Tamb 5.3.142 Tamb
More worth than Asia, and the world beside, ... 2Tamb 5.3.153 Tamb
but for a Queene/Europe, and Asia in firme peace had beene. Ovid's Elegies 2.12.18
ASIAN
Come Asian Viceroies, to your taskes a while/And take such 2Tamb 5.1.136 Tamb
ASIAS
By living Asias mightie Emperour. . . . . 1Tamb 1.2.73 Zenoc
ASIDE
My princely robes thou seest are layd aside, ... Dido 3.3.3 Dido
Stand all aside, and let the Knights determine, . . . Jew 1.2.14 Calym
But stand aside, here comes Don Lodowicke. . . . . Jew 2.3.217 Barab
reading of the letter, he star'd and stamp'd, and turnd aside. Jew 4.2.105 P Pilia
But come lets walke aside, th'airs not very sweet. . . P 497 9.16 QnMoth
the king and the nobles/From the parlament, ile stand aside. Edw 1.1.73 Gavstn
But wherefore walkes yong Mortimer aside? . . . . . Edw 1.4.353 Edward
O Faustus, lay that damned booke aside, ... F 97 1.1.69 GdAngl
stand aside you had best, I charge you in the name of Belzabub: F App p.235 19 P Robin
This said, he laying aside all lets of war, ... Lucan, First Booke 206
There shalt be lov'd: Ilia lay feare aside. . . . Ovid's Elegies 3.5.62
Eryx bright Empresse turnd her lookes aside, ... Ovid's Elegies 3.8.45
And yet at everie word shee turn'd aside, ... Hero and Leander 1.195

ASIDE (cont.)			
And turn'd aside, and to her selfe lamented.	Hero and Leander		2.34
ASKE			
But what are you that aske of me these things?	Dido	1.1.214	Venus
As without blushing I can aske no more:	Dido	3.1.104	Aeneas
The thing that I will dye before I aske,	Dido	3.4.9	Dido
Pardon me though I aske, love makes me aske.	Dido	5.1.90	Dido
Stay Techelles, aske a parlee first.	1Tamb	1.2.137	Tamb
To aske, and have: commaund, and be obeied.	1Tamb	2.5.62	Therid
Doost thou aske him leave?	2Tamb	3.5.134	P Callap
What respit aske you [Governour]?	Jew	1.2.27	Calym
And if he aske why I demand so much, tell him, I scorne to	Jew	4.2.120	P Ithimr
Then pray to God, and aske forgivenes of the King.	P1004	19.74	P 2Mur
Nor will I aske forgivenes of the King.	P1006	19.76	Guise
is gone, whither if you aske, with sir John of Henolt, brother	Edw	4.3.31	P Spencr
Madam, without offence if I may aske,	Edw	4.6.30	Kent
<Aske my fellow if I be a thiefe>.	F 204	(HC258)A	P Wagner
you were not dunces, you would never aske me such a question:	F 207	1.2.14	P Wagner
Then wherefore should you aske me such a question?	F 209	1.2.16	P Wagner
To give me whatsoever I shall aske;	F 322	1.3.94	Faust
And give thee more then thou hast wit to aske.	F 436	2.1.48	Mephst
So, now Faustus aske me what thou wilt.	F 503	2.1.115	Mephst
But wherefore dost thou aske?	F1652	4.6.95	Faust
I aske but right:	Ovid's Elegies		1.3.1
I aske too much, would she but let me love hir,	Ovid's Elegies		1.3.3
Aske thou the boy, what thou enough doest thinke.	Ovid's Elegies		1.4.30
Little I aske, a little entrance make,	Ovid's Elegies		1.6.3
Let them aske some-what, many asking little,	Ovid's Elegies		1.8.89
Yet thinke no scorne to aske a wealthy churle,	Ovid's Elegies		1.10.53
If Achelous, I aske where thy hornes stand,	Ovid's Elegies		3.5.35
What might I crave more if I aske againe?	Ovid's Elegies		3.6.44
Festivall dayes aske Venus, songs, and wine,	Ovid's Elegies		3.9.47
As he ought not performe, nor yet she aske.	Hero and Leander		1.430
ASKED			
asked me what he should give me for as much Hay as he could	F1526	4.5.22	P Carter
ASKES			
The Mare askes not the Horse, the Cowe the Bull,	Ovid's Elegies		1.10.27
If, what I do, she askes, say hope for night,	Ovid's Elegies		1.11.13
Thy labour ever lasts, she askes but little.	Ovid's Elegies		3.1.68
ASKEST			
thou make a Colossus of me, that thou askest me such questions?	F1646	4.6.89	P Faust
ASKING			
Let them aske some-what, many asking little,	Ovid's Elegies		1.8.89
Leave asking, and Ile give what I refraine.	Ovid's Elegies		1.10.64
And asking why, this answeare she redoubled,	Ovid's Elegies		2.2.7
ASK'ST			
Ask'st why I chaunge? because thou crav'st reward:	Ovid's Elegies		1.10.11
ASK'T			
To give I love, but to be ask't disdayne,	Ovid's Elegies		1.10.63
ASKT			
Oft hath she askt us under whom we serv'd,	Dido	2.1.66	Illion
He askt, she gave, and nothing was denied,	Hero and Leander		2.25
A SLEEPE			
It hath my lord, the warders all a sleepe,	Edw	4.1.15	Mortmr
Fast a sleepe I warrant you,	F1173	4.1.19	Mrtino
ASLEEPE			
Now is he fast asleepe, and in this grove/Amongst greene brakes	Dido	2.1.316	Venus
Ithimore, tell me, is the Fryar asleepe?	Jew	4.1.129	Barab
And being asleepe, belike they thought me dead,	Jew	5.1.81	Barab
I, and I fall not asleepe i'th meane time.	F1196	4.1.42	Benvol
come not away quickly, you shall have me asleepe presently:	F1242	4.1.88	P Benvol
What, is he asleepe, or dead?	F1279	4.1.125	Saxony
and there I found him asleepe; I kept a hallowing and whooping	F1548	4.5.44	P HrsCsr
sir, did not I pull off one of your legs when you were asleepe?	F1656	4.6.99	P HrsCsr
Why hee's fast asleepe, come some other time.	F App	p.240 141	P Mephst
See where he is fast asleepe.	F App	p.241 147	P Mephst
The self-same day that he asleepe had layd/Inchaunted Argus,	Hero and Leander		1.387
ASPECT			
And by thy martiall face and stout aspect,	1Tamb	1.2.170	Tamb
First rising in the East with milde aspect,	1Tamb	4.2.37	Tamb
issue, at whose byrth/Heaven did affoord a gratious aspect,	2Tamb	3.5.80	Tamb
My sterne aspect shall make faire Victory,	2Tamb	3.5.162	Tamb
a non-plus at the critical aspect of my terrible countenance.	Jew	4.2.14	P Pilia
Was this that sterne aspect, that awfull frowne,	F1370	4.2.46	Fredrk
ASPECTS			
Conjunctions, Oppositions, Aspects, Eclipses, all at one time,	F 615	2.2.64	P Faust
ASPEN			
Stand staggering like a quivering Aspen leafe,	1Tamb	2.4.4	Mycet
ASPHALTIS			
But from Asphaltis, where I conquer'd you,	2Tamb	4.3.5	Tamb
souldiers now that fought/So Lion-like upon Asphaltis plaines?	2Tamb	4.3.68	Tamb
No, though Asphaltis lake were liquid gold,	2Tamb	5.1.155	Tamb
Thousands of men drown'd in Asphaltis Lake,	2Tamb	5.1.204	Techel
ASPIRE			
And both our soules aspire celestiall thrones.	1Tamb	1.2.237	Tamb
What means this divelish shepheard to aspire/With such a	1Tamb	2.6.1	Cosroe
that in thy wheele/There is a point, to which when men aspire,	Edw	5.6.60	Mortmr
That durst to so great wickednesse aspire.	Ovid's Elegies		3.8.44
ASPIRES			
ragged stonie walles/Immure thy vertue that aspires to heaven?	Edw	3.1.257	Mortmr
ASPIRING			
My Lord I mervaile that th'aspiring Guise/Dares once adventure	P 36	1.36	Admral
Or mount the top with my aspiring winges,	P 103	2.46	Guise

ASPIRING (cont.)
What Peere in France but thou (aspiring Guise)/Durst be in — P 828 17.23 Eprnon
For his aspiring thoughts aime at the crowne, — P 923 18.24 Navrre
Frownst thou thereat, aspiring Lancaster, — Edw 1.1.93 Edward
by aspiring pride and insolence,/For which God threw him from — F 295 1.3.67 Mephst
That threates the starres with her aspiring top, — F 796 3.1.18 Faust
And fruitfull wits that in aspiring <inaspiring> are, — Hero and Leander 1.477

ASPIR'ST
Aspir'st unto the guidance of the sunne. — Edw 1.4.17 Warwck

ASPYRING
Doth teach us all to have aspyring minds: — 1Tamb 2.7.20 Tamb

ASSAFITIDA
As when they swallow Assafitida, — 2Tamb 5.1.208 Techel

ASSAIES
At one selfe instant, she poore soule assaies, — Hero and Leander 1.362

ASSAILDE
Whereas the Fort may fittest be assailde, — 2Tamb 3.2.66 Tamb
And lawes assailde, and arm'd men in the Senate? — Lucan, First Booke 322

ASSAILE
With expedition to assaile the Pagan, — 2Tamb 2.1.62 Sgsmnd
Assaile it and be sure of victorie. — 2Tamb 5.2.59 Callap
These cowards invisiblie assaile hys soule, — 2Tamb 5.3.13 Therid
That now are readie to assaile the Scots. — Edw 1.4.363 Edward
Let us assaile his minde another while. — Edw 5.5.12 Matrvs
And with rough clawes your tender cheekes assaile. — Ovid's Elegies 2.6.4
And envious fates great [goddesses] <goodesses> assaile, — Ovid's Elegies 3.8.2

ASSAULT
And sharpest where th'assault is desperate. — 2Tamb 3.2.67 Tamb
Thou seest us prest to give the last assault, — 2Tamb 5.1.60 Techel
Assault and spare not, we wil never yeeld. — 2Tamb 5.1.62 Govnr
Now whilst you give assault unto the wals, — Jew 5.1.90 Barab
Thou'st doom'd thy selfe, assault it presently. — Jew 5.1.97 Calym
Lay hands upon the earle for this assault. — Edw 5.3.54 Gurney
Here will we stay to bide the first assault, — F1354 4.2.30 Benvol
Shake off these wrinckles that thy front assault, — Ovid's Elegies 1.8.45

ASSAULTS
And save our forces for the hot assaults/Proud Tamburlaine — 2Tamb 1.1.52 Gazell

ASSAY (See also ASSAIES)
Why then Theridamas, Ile first assay, — 1Tamb 2.5.81 Tamb
And with smooth speech, her fancie to assay, — Hero and Leander 1.402

ASSAYD
on the sand/Assayd with honey words to turne them backe: — Dido 2.1.137 Aeneas
Yet ever as he greedily assayd/To touch those dainties, she the — Hero and Leander 2.269

ASSAYED
If such a worke thy mother had assayed. — Ovid's Elegies 2.14.20

ASSE
Lives like the Asse that Aesope speaketh of, — Jew 5.2.40 Barab
of Lancaster/That hath more earldomes then an asse can beare, — Edw 1.3.2 Gavstn
to thinke I have beene such an Asse all this while, to stand — F1243 4.1.89 P Benvol
bleate, and an asse braye, because it is S. Peters holy day. — F App p.232 27 P Faust
like a Beare, the third an Asse, for doing this enterprise. — F App p.235 33 P Mephst
but yet like an asse as I was, I would not be ruled by him, for — F App p.240 130 P HrsCsr
Loe how the miserable great eared Asse, — Ovid's Elegies 2.7.15

ASSEMBLE
Is it not, trowe ye, to assemble aide, — Edw 3.1.207 SpncrP

ASSENDS
More glory by thy vanquisht foes assends. — Ovid's Elegies 2.9.6

ASSENT
And if that Bruno by his owne assent, — F 957 3.1.179 Faust

ASSES
Of labouring Oxen, and five hundred/Shee Asses: — Jew 1.2.185 Barab
He'd joyne long Asses eares to these huge hornes, — F1449 4.3.19 Benvol

ASSIGNES
cause, what ere thou be whom God assignes/This great effect, — Lucan, First Booke 419

ASSIRIA
Create him Prorex of [Assiria] <Affrica>, — 1Tamb 1.1.89 Cosroe
Duke of [Assiria] <Affrica> and Albania, — 1Tamb 1.1.164 Ortyg
that all [Assiria] <Affrica>/Which hath bene subject to the — 2Tamb 5.1.165 Tamb

ASSIRIAN
where brave Assirian Dames/Have rid in pompe like rich — 2Tamb 5.1.76 Tamb
Had fild Assirian Carras wals with bloud, — Lucan, First Booke 105

ASSIRIANS
Whose chariot wheeles have burst th'Assirians bones, — 2Tamb 5.1.71 Tamb

ASSIST
Assist me sweete God, and receive my soule. — Edw 5.5.109 Edward
Our prayers move thee to assist our drift, — Ovid's Elegies 2.3.17
And with thy hand assist [the] <thy> swelling saile. — Ovid's Elegies 2.11.42
Great floods ought to assist young men in love, — Ovid's Elegies 3.5.23

ASSISTANCE
letters to command/Aide and assistance if we stand in need. — 1Tamb 1.2.20 Magnet

ASSOCIATE
With him is Edmund gone associate? — Edw 4.3.39 Edward

ASSOCIATES
Commandes the hearts of his associates, — 1Tamb 4.1.15 2Msngr

ASSUME
That doth assume the Papall government, — F 886 3.1.108 Pope

ASSURANCE
And in assurance of desir'd successe, — 1Tamb 1.1.160 Ortyg
To be esteem'd assurance for our selves, — 2Tamb 2.1.39 Baldwn
the enimie hath made/Gives such assurance of our overthrow, — 2Tamb 5.1.3 Maxim

ASSURE
Thy words assure me of kind successe: — 1Tamb 2.3.60 Cosroe
Yet we assure us of the victorie. — 1Tamb 3.3.35 Usumc

ASSURE (cont.)			
These words assure me boy, thou art my sonne,	2Tamb	1.3.58	Tamb
Assure your Grace tis superstition/To stand so strictly on	2Tamb	2.1.49	Fredrk
shall there concerne our state/Assure your selves I'le looke--	Jew	1.1.173	Barab
Assure thy selfe thou shalt have broth by the eye.	Jew	3.4.92	Barab
Assure your selfe my good Lord Admirall,	P 262	4.60	Charls
Assure him all the aide we can provide,	P 909	18.10	Navrre
Cousin, assure you I am resolute,	P 973	19.43	King
Assure thy selfe thou comst not in my sight.	Edw	1.4.169	Edward
we friends, assure your grace, in England/Would cast up cappes,	Edw	4.2.54	Mortmr
bloud/Assures his <assure my> soule to be great Lucifers,	F 444	2.1.56	Faust
Then I assure thee certainelie they are.	F1650	4.6.93	Faust
ASSURED			
Then be assured thou art not miserable.	Dido	2.1.104	Dido
exchange for that/We are assured of by our friends successe.	1Tamb	1.2.217	Techel
Besides the honor in assured conquestes:	1Tamb	1.2.219	Usumc
For even as from assured oracle,	1Tamb	2.3.4	Cosroe
Whose smiling stars gives him assured hope/Of martiall triumph,	1Tamb	3.3.42	Tamb
I know not, but of this am I assured,	Edw	5.1.152	Edward
Or be assured of our dreadfull curse,	F 938	3.1.160	Pope
ASSURES			
bloud/Assures his <assure my> soule to be great Lucifers,	F 444	2.1.56	Faust
ASSWAGE			
Tis warre that must asswage this tyrantes pride.	P1128	21.22	Dumain
When will the furie of his minde asswage?	Edw	5.3.8	Edward
And some (their violent passions to asswage)/Compile sharpe	Hero and Leander		1.126
ASSYRIAN (See also ASSIRIA, SIRIA)			
Arachne staynes Assyrian ivory.	Ovid's Elegies		2.5.40
AS'T			
conjuring bookes, and now we'le have such knavery, as't passes.	F 724	2.3.3	P Robin
ASTERISM (See ASTRACISME)			
ASTEROTH			
Ho, Belimoth, Argiron, Asteroth.	F1304	4.1.150	Faust
Asteroth, Belimoth, Mephostophilis,	F1402	4.2.78	Faust
ASTONIED			
but most astonied/To see his choller shut in secrete thoughtes,	1Tamb	3.2.69	Agidas
ASTOUNDING			
Threatning the world with high astounding tearms/And scourging	1Tamb	Prol.5	Prolog
ASTRACISME			
Above the threefold Astracisme of heaven,	2Tamb	4.3.62	Tamb
ASTRAEUS			
Are drawne by darknes forth Astraeus tents.	Dido	1.1.73	Venus
ASTRAY			
Chide me sweete Warwick, if I go astray.	Edw	1.4.348	Edward
ASTROLOGIE			
[They put forth questions of Astrologie],	F1146	3.3.59A	3Chor
ASTROLOGY			
He that is grounded in Astrology,	F 165	1.1.137	Cornel
And reason <argue> of divine Astrology.	F 585	2.2.34	Faust
ASTRONOMY			
Learned Faustus/To find <know> the secrets of Astronomy,/Graven	F 755	2.3.34	2Chor
A SUNDER			
Keepe them a sunder, thrust in the king.	Edw	5.3.52	Matrvs
Comes forth her [unkeembd] <unkeembe> locks a sunder tearing.	Ovid's Elegies		3.8.52
ASUNDER (See also SUNDER)			
And sheere ye all asunder with her hands:	Dido	4.4.156	Dido
while all thy joints/Be rackt and beat asunder with the wheele,	2Tamb	3.5.125	Tamb
Doth fall asunder; so that it doth sinke/Into a deepe pit past	Jew	5.5.35	Barab
All torne asunder by the hand of death.	F1989	5.3.7	2Schol
AT			
And bring the Gods to wonder at the game:	Dido	1.1.18	Ganimd
Why, are not all the Gods at thy commaund,	Dido	1.1.30	Jupitr
And Helens rape doth haunt [ye] <thee> at the heeles.	Dido	1.1.144	Aeneas
That crave such favour at your honors feete,	Dido	1.2.5	Illion
Brave men at armes, abandon fruitles feares,	Dido	1.2.32	Iarbus
O were I not at all so thou mightst be.	Dido	2.1.28	Aeneas
Leave to lament lest they laugh at our feares.	Dido	2.1.38	Achat
May I entreate thee to discourse at large,	Dido	2.1.106	Dido
And makes Aeneas sinke at Didos feete.	Dido	2.1.117	Aeneas
His hands bound at his backe, and both his eyes/Turnd up to	Dido	2.1.151	Aeneas
At whose accursed feete as overjoyed,	Dido	2.1.177	Aeneas
Thongs at his heeles, by which Achilles horse/Drew him in	Dido	2.1.205	Aeneas
At last came Pirrhus fell and full of ire,	Dido	2.1.213	Aeneas
And at Joves Altar finding Priamus,	Dido	2.1.225	Aeneas
He with his faulchions poynt raisde up at once,	Dido	2.1.229	Aeneas
Threatning a thousand deaths at every glaunce.	Dido	2.1.231	Aeneas
Not mov'd at all, but smiling at his teares,	Dido	2.1.240	Aeneas
At which the franticke Queene leapt on his face,	Dido	2.1.244	Aeneas
At last the souldiers puld her by the heeles,	Dido	2.1.247	Aeneas
Then from the navell to the throat at once,	Dido	2.1.255	Aeneas
at whose latter gaspe/Joves marble statue gan to bend the brow,	Dido	2.1.256	Aeneas
And he at last depart to Italy,	Dido	2.1.330	Venus
So much have I receiv'd at Didos hands,	Dido	3.1.103	Aeneas
I saw this man at Troy ere Troy was sackt.	Dido	3.1.141	Achat
This man and I were at Olympus games.	Dido	3.1.143	Illion
And have no gall at all to grieve my foes:	Dido	3.2.17	Juno
Who warne me of such daunger prest at hand,	Dido	3.2.22	Venus
how may I deserve/Such amourous favours at thy beautious hand?	Dido	3.2.65	Juno
Aeneas, be not movde at what he sayes,	Dido	3.3.23	Dido
Bearing her bowe and quiver at her backe.	Dido	3.3.55	Achat
Whose Crowne and kingdome rests at thy commande:	Dido	3.4.58	Dido
Hold, take these Jewels at thy Lovers hand,	Dido	3.4.61	Dido
It haild, it snowde, it lightned all at once.	Dido	4.1.8	Anna

AT (cont.)

How now Iarbus, at your prayers so hard?	Dido	4.2.23		Anna
This is no life for men at armes to live,	Dido	4.3.33		Achat
Shall vulgar pesants storme at what I doe?	Dido	4.4.73		Dido
Triumph, my mates, our travels are at end,	Dido	5.1.1		Aeneas
Not past foure thousand paces at the most.	Dido	5.1.17		Aeneas
And hisse at Dido for preserving thee?	Dido	5.1.168		Dido
The Rockes and Sea-gulfes will performe at large,	Dido	5.1.171		Dido
I never vow'd at Aulis gulfe/The desolation of his native Troy,	Dido	5.1.202		Dido
And order all things at your high dispose,	Dido	5.1.303		Dido
At whose byrth-day Cynthia with Saturne joinde,	1Tamb	1.1.13		Cosroe
Now Turkes and Tartars shake their swords at thee,	1Tamb	1.1.16		Cosroe
Or plead for mercie at your highnesse feet.	1Tamb	1.1.73		Therid
were woont to quake/And tremble at the Persean Monarkes name,	1Tamb	1.1.116		Cosroe
With costlie jewels hanging at their eares,	1Tamb	1.1.144		Ceneus
Then did the Macedonians at the spoile/Of great Darius and his	1Tamb	1.1.153		Ceneus
But since I love to live at liberty,	1Tamb	1.2.26		Tamb
Me thinks I see kings kneeling at his feet,	1Tamb	1.2.55		Techel
Therefore at least admit us libertie,	1Tamb	1.2.71		Zenoc
Which graticus starres have promist at my birth.	1Tamb	1.2.92		Tamb
A thousand Persean horsmen are at hand,	1Tamb	1.2.111		Souldr
Come let us meet them at the mountain foot,	1Tamb	1.2.133		Usumc
Weele fight five hundred men at armes to one,	1Tamb	1.2.143		Tamb
Draw foorth thy sword, thou mighty man at Armes,	1Tamb	1.2.178		Tamb
And kingdomes at the least we all expect,	1Tamb	1.2.218		Usumc
And hostes of souldiers stand amaz'd at us,	1Tamb	1.2.221		Usumc
That could perswade at such a sodaine pinch,	1Tamb	2.1.37		Cosroe
The world will strive with hostes of men at armes,	1Tamb	2.3.13		Tamb
and dim their eies/That stand and muse at our admyred armes.	1Tamb	2.3.24		Tamb
The King your Brother is now hard at hand,	1Tamb	2.3.45		Tamb
For Kings are clouts that every man shoots at,	1Tamb	2.4.8		Mycet
So do I thrice renowmed man at armes,	1Tamb	2.5.6		Cosroe
And as we ever [aim'd] <and> at your behoofe,	1Tamb	2.5.32		Ortyg
If we should aime at such a dignitie?	1Tamb	2.5.79		Tamb
or els infernall, mixt/Their angry seeds at his conception:	1Tamb	2.6.10		Meandr
Even at the morning of my happy state,	1Tamb	2.7.4		Cosroe
Who entring at the breach thy sword hath made,	1Tamb	2.7.9		Cosroe
For all flesh quakes at your magnificence.	1Tamb	3.1.48		Argier
True (Argier) and tremble at my lookes.	1Tamb	3.1.49		Bajzth
And strive for life at every stroke they give.	1Tamb	3.3.54		Tamb
Must plead for mercie at his kingly feet,	1Tamb	3.3.174		Zenoc
Are falne in clusters at my conquering feet.	1Tamb	3.3.230		Tamb
Shall lie at anchor in the Isle Asant,	1Tamb	3.3.251		Tamb
And by this meanes Ile win the world at last.	1Tamb	3.3.260		Tamb
And make it swallow both of us at once.	1Tamb	4.2.29		Bajzth
Smile Stars that raign'd at my nativity,	1Tamb	4.2.33		Tamb
Two hundred thousand foot, brave men at armes,	1Tamb	4.3.54		Capol
not the Turke and his wife make a goodly showe at a banquet?	1Tamb	4.4.58	P	Tamb
unto your majesty/May merit favour at your highnesse handes,	1Tamb	4.4.70		Zenoc
Here at Damascus will I make the Point/That shall begin the	1Tamb	4.4.81		Tamb
Behold my sword, what see you at the point?	1Tamb	5.1.108		Tamb
One thought, one grace, one woonder at the least,	1Tamb	5.1.172		Tamb
At every pore let blood comme dropping foorth,	1Tamb	5.1.227		Zabina
Blush heaven, that gave them honor at their birth,	1Tamb	5.1.350		Zenoc
Your love hath fortune so at his command,	1Tamb	5.1.373		Anippe
And therfore grieve not at your overthrow,	1Tamb	5.1.446		Tamb
And make it quake at every drop it drinks:	1Tamb	5.1.462		Tamb
Emperours and kings lie breathlesse at my feet.	1Tamb	5.1.469		Tamb
Left to themselves while we were at the fight,	1Tamb	5.1.471		Tamb
That darted mountaines at her brother Jove:	1Tamb	5.1.511		Tamb
Himselfe in presence shal unfold at large.	2Tamb	Prol.9		Prolog
As martiall presents to our friends at home,	2Tamb	1.1.35		Orcan
Wilt thou have war, then shake this blade at me,	2Tamb	1.1.83		Sgsmnd
But whilst I live will be at truce with thee.	2Tamb	1.1.130		Sgsmnd
wherin at anchor lies/A Turkish Gally of my royall fleet,	2Tamb	1.2.20		Callap
Choose which thou wilt, all are at thy command.	2Tamb	1.2.31		Callap
Trotting the ring, and tilting at a glove:	2Tamb	1.3.39		Zenoc
As all the world shall tremble at their view.	2Tamb	1.3.57		Celeb
In all affection at thy kingly feet.	2Tamb	1.3.116		Therid
frontier townes/Twise twenty thousand valiant men at armes,	2Tamb	1.3.120		Therid
That though the stones, as at Deucalions flood,	2Tamb	1.3.163		Tamb
For since we left you at the Souldans court,	2Tamb	1.3.177		Usumc
And by the coast of Byather at last,	2Tamb	1.3.200		Techel
That would not kill and curse at Gods command,	2Tamb	2.1.55		Fredrk
That is a Gentleman (I know) at least.	2Tamb	3.1.72		Callap
At every towne and castle I besiege,	2Tamb	3.2.36		Tamb
And yet at night carrouse within my tent,	2Tamb	3.2.106		Tamb
And in my blood wash all your hands at once,	2Tamb	3.2.127		Tamb
Til fire and sword have found them at a bay.	2Tamb	3.2.151		Tamb
Stand at the walles, with such a mighty power.	2Tamb	3.3.14		Therid
Who by this time is at Natolia,	2Tamb	3.4.86		Therid
Here at Alepo with an hoste of men/Lies Tamburlaine, this king	2Tamb	3.5.3		2Msngr
issue, at whose byrth/Heaven did affoord a gratious aspect,	2Tamb	3.5.79		Tamb
And cast your crownes in slavery at their feet.	2Tamb	3.5.149		Tamb
The bullets fly at random where they list.	2Tamb	4.1.52		Calyph
Blush, blush faire citie, at thine honors foile,	2Tamb	4.1.107		Tamb
Than he that darted mountaines at thy head,	2Tamb	4.1.128		Tamb
For with thy view my joyes are at the full,	2Tamb	4.2.31		Therid
And have so proud a chariot at your heeles,	2Tamb	4.3.3		Tamb
meet not me/With troopes of harlots at your sloothful heeles.	2Tamb	4.3.82		Tamb
At every little breath that thorow heaven is blowen:	2Tamb	4.3.124		Tamb
When all the Gods stand gazing at his pomp:	2Tamb	4.3.129		Tamb
Then have at him to begin withall.	2Tamb	5.1.152		Therid

AT (cont.)

Yet shouldst thou die, shoot at him all at once.	2Tamb	5.1.157	Tamb
To sue for mercie at your highnesse feete.	2Tamb	5.2.41	Amasia
Yet when the pride of Cynthia is at full,	2Tamb	5.2.46	Callap
chiefe selected men/Of twenty severall kingdomes at the least:	2Tamb	5.2.49	Callap
Nor plowman, Priest, nor Merchant staies at home,	2Tamb	5.2.50	Callap
Or that it be rejoin'd again at full,	2Tamb	5.2.58	Callap
Stands aiming at me with his murthering dart,	2Tamb	5.3.69	Tamb
Who flies away at every glance I give,	2Tamb	5.3.70	Tamb
I came at last to Graecia, and from thence/To Asia, where I	2Tamb	5.3.141	Tamb
And saw'st thou not/Mine Argosie at Alexandria?	Jew	1.1.72	Barab
from Egypt, or by Caire/But at the entry there into the sea,	Jew	1.1.74	Barab
And yet I wonder at this Argosie.	Jew	1.1.84	Barab
Now Bassoes, what demand you at our hands?	Jew	1.2.1	Govnr
What at our hands demand ye?	Jew	1.2.6	Govnr
From nought at first thou camst to little welth,	Jew	1.2.105	1Knght
Had they beene valued at indifferent rate,	Jew	1.2.186	Barab
I had at home, and in mine Argosie/And other ships that came	Jew	1.2.187	Barab
But give him liberty at least to mourne,	Jew	1.2.202	Barab
We now are almost at the new made Nunnery.	Jew	1.2.306	1Fryar
To morrow early I'le be at the doore.	Jew	1.2.361	Barab
No come not at me, if thou wilt be damn'd,	Jew	1.2.362	Barab
Then rise at midnight to a solemne masse.	Jew	1.2.373	Mthias
Or at the least to pitty.	Jew	1.2.387	Mthias
then we [luft] <left>, and [tackt] <tooke>, and fought at ease:	Jew	2.2.14	Bosco
and you were stated here/To be at deadly enmity with Turkes.	Jew	2.2.33	Bosco
But she's at home, and I have bought a house/As great and faire	Jew	2.3.13	Barab
I, I, no doubt but shee's at your command.	Jew	2.3.39	Barab
Your father has deserv'd it at my hands,	Jew	2.3.70	Barab
Good Barabas glance not at our holy Nuns.	Jew	2.3.86	Lodowk
Ratest thou this Moore but at two hundred plats?	Jew	2.3.107	Lodowk
I pray, Sir, be no stranger at my house,	Jew	2.3.136	Barab
All that I have shall be at your command.	Jew	2.3.137	Barab
on the Machabees/I have it, Sir, and 'tis at your command.	Jew	2.3.154	Barab
Be mov'd at nothing, see thou pitty none,	Jew	2.3.171	Barab
Once at Jerusalem, where the pilgrims kneel'd,	Jew	2.3.208	Ithimr
Oh muse not at it, 'tis the Hebrewes guize,	Jew	2.3.325	Barab
but for me, as you went in at dores/You had bin stab'd, but not	Jew	2.3.337	Barab
Till I have set 'em both at enmitie.	Jew	2.3.383	Barab
Though thou deservest hardly at my hands,	Jew	3.3.74	Abigal
The time you tooke for respite, is at hand,	Jew	3.5.8	Basso
which is there/Set downe at large, the Gallants were both	Jew	3.6.29	Abigal
the Nuns are dead/That sound at other times like Tinkers pans?	Jew	4.1.3	Barab
At Alexandria, Merchandize unsold:	Jew	4.1.68	Barab
Come to my house at one a clocke this night.	Jew	4.1.91	Barab
'Tis neatly done, Sir, here's no print at all.	Jew	4.1.151	Ithimr
Why, stricken him that would have stroke at me.	Jew	4.1.175	1Fryar
'Las I could weepe at your calamity.	Jew	4.1.203	Barab
for at the reading of the letter, he look'd like a man of	Jew	4.2.6	P Pilia
a non-plus at the critical aspect of my terrible countenance.	Jew	4.2.13	P Pilia
and the rest of the family, stand or fall at your service.	Jew	4.2.44	P Pilia
Send for a hundred Crownes at least.	Jew	4.2.70	P Pilia
Put in two hundred at least.	Jew	4.2.74	P Pilia
At reading of the letter, he star'd and stamp'd, and turnd	Jew	4.2.104	P Pilia
five hundred Crownes that I esteeme,/I am not mov'd at that:	Jew	4.3.41	Barab
Pray when, Sir, shall I see you at my house?	Jew	4.3.56	Barab
have at it; and doe you heare?	Jew	4.4.2	P Ithimr
Knavely spoke, and like a Knight at Armes.	Jew	4.4.9	Pilia
my Lord, his man's now at my lodging/That was his Agent, he'll	Jew	5.1.16	Curtzn
Wonder not at it, Sir, the heavens are just:	Jew	5.1.55	Govnr
The Jew is here, and rests at your command.	Jew	5.1.83	Barab
thy desert we make thee Governor,/Use them at thy discretion.	Jew	5.2.11	Calym
When as thy life shall be at their command?	Jew	5.2.33	Barab
At least unprofitably lose it not:	Jew	5.2.37	Barab
Are at my Arbitrament; and Barabas/At his discretion may	Jew	5.2.53	Barab
Arbitrament; and Barabas/At his discretion may dispose of both:	Jew	5.2.54	Barab
And now at length am growne your Governor,	Jew	5.2.70	Barab
That at one instant all things may be done,	Jew	5.2.120	Barab
We rent in sunder at our entry:	Jew	5.3.4	Calym
There will he banquet them, but thee at home,	Jew	5.3.38	Msngr
How the slave jeeres at him?	Jew	5.5.56	Govnr
My Lord you need not mervaile at the Guise,	P 39	1.39	Condy
How they did storme at these your nuptiall rites,	P 49	1.49	Admral
And thats the cause that Guise so frowns at us,	P 52	1.52	Navrre
If ever Hymen lowr'd at marriage rites,	P 58	2.1	Guise
Oft have I leveld, and at last have learnd,	P 94	2.37	Guise
and fully executes/Matters of importe, aimed at by many,	P 111	2.54	Guise
At which they all shall issue out and set the streetes.	P 237	4.35	Guise
And at ech corner shall the Kings garde stand.	P 291	5.18	Anjoy
That frightes poore Ramus sitting at his book?	P 362	7.2	Ramus
The Guisians are hard at thy doore,	P 367	7.7	Taleus
Harke, harke they come, Ile leap out at the window.	P 369	7.9	Taleus
With bowes and dartes to shoot at them they see,	P 422	7.62	Dumain
And at the length in Pampelonia crowne,	P 580	11.45	Pleshe
Will laugh I feare me at their good aray.	P 673	13.17	Duchss
At thy request I am content thou goe,	P 746	15.4	King
Am I thus to be jested at and scornde?	P 758	15.16	Guise
How now Mugeroun, metst thou not the Guise at the doore?	P 774	15.32	King
have at ye sir.	P 816	17.11	P Souldr
shewes did entertaine him/And promised to be at his commaund:	P 875	17.70	Eprnon
For his aspiring thoughts aime at the crowne,	P 923	18.24	Navrre
sorte of English priestes/From Doway to the Seminary at Remes,	P1031	19.101	King
Wounded and poysoned, both at once?	P1215	22.77	King

AT (cont.)

yow are wellcome ser have at you	Paris	ms16,p390	P Souldr
gathered now shall ayme/more at thie end then exterpatione	Paris	ms29,p391	Guise
And with the world be still at enmitie:	Edw	1.1.15	Gavstn
That glaunceth at my lips and flieth away:	Edw	1.1.23	Gavstn
thou wouldst do well/To waite at my trencher, and tell me lies	Edw	1.1.31	Gavstn
well/To waite at my trencher, and tell me lies at dinner time,	Edw	1.1.31	Gavstn
Were sworne to your father at his death,	Edw	1.1.83	Mortmr
Shall sleepe within the scabberd at thy neede,	Edw	1.1.87	Mortmr
To floate in bloud, and at thy wanton head,	Edw	1.1.132	Lncstr
With captive kings at his triumphant Carre.	Edw	1.1.174	Gavstn
My lord of Cornewall now, at every worde,	Edw	1.2.17	Lncstr
He nods, and scornes, and smiles at those that passe.	Edw	1.2.24	Warwck
Doth no man take exceptions at the slave?	Edw	1.2.25	MortSr
And at the court gate hang the pessant up,	Edw	1.2.30	Mortmr
And courage to, to be revengde at full.	Edw	1.2.60	Mortmr
At the new temple.	Edw	1.2.75	ArchBp
Their downfall is at hand, their forces downe,	Edw	1.4.18	Mortmr
Now is my heart at ease.	Edw	1.4.91	ArchBp
or at the mariage day/The cup of Hymen had beene full of	Edw	1.4.173	Queene
And Mortimer will rest at your commaund.	Edw	1.4.296	Mortmr
With base outlandish cullions at his heeles,	Edw	1.4.409	Mortmr
below, the king and he/From out a window, laugh at such as we,	Edw	1.4.417	Mortmr
And floute our traine, and jest at our attire:	Edw	1.4.418	Mortmr
Or saying a long grace at a tables end,	Edw	2.1.37	Spencr
That he would take exceptions at my buttons,	Edw	2.1.47	Baldck
And meete me at the parke pale presentlie:	Edw	2.1.73	Neece
And will be at the court as soone as we.	Edw	2.1.77	Neece
Goe sit at home and eate your tenants beefe:	Edw	2.2.75	Gavstn
And come not here to scoffe at Gaveston,	Edw	2.2.76	Gavstn
They rate his ransome at five thousand pound.	Edw	2.2.117	Mortmr
And lame and poore, lie groning at the gates,	Edw	2.2.163	Lncstr
and thy selfe/Bedaubd with golde, rode laughing at the rest,	Edw	2.2.185	Mortmr
For your lemmons you have lost, at Bannocks borne,	Edw	2.2.191	Lncstr
Have at the rebels, and their complices.	Edw	2.2.265	Edward
In vaine I looke for love at Edwards hand,	Edw	2.4.61	Queene
hang him at a bough.	Edw	2.5.24	Warwck
Thou shalt have so much honor at our hands.	Edw	2.5.28	Warwck
I know it lords, it is this life you aime at,	Edw	2.5.48	Gavstn
My lord, weele quicklie be at Cobham.	Edw	2.5.111	HrsBoy
And go in peace, leave us in warres at home.	Edw	3.1.85	Edward
I found them at the first inexorable,	Edw	3.1.103	Arundl
Edward with fire and sword, followes at thy heeles.	Edw	3.1.180	Edward
these Barons and the subtill Queene,/Long [leveld] <levied> at.	Edw	3.1.273	Levune
A boye, thou art deceivde at least in this,	Edw	4.2.8	Queene
And then have at the proudest Spencers head.	Edw	4.2.25	Prince
Tould us at our arrivall all the newes,	Edw	4.2.48	Mortmr
Binde us in kindenes all at your commaund.	Edw	4.2.73	Kent
friends in Belgia have we left,/To cope with friends at home:	Edw	4.4.4	Queene
Edward, this Mortimer aimes at thy life:	Edw	4.6.10	Kent
And hags howle for my death at Charons shore,	Edw	4.7.90	Edward
Where sorrow at my elbow still attends,	Edw	5.1.33	Edward
Two kings in England cannot raigne at once:	Edw	5.1.58	Edward
All times and seasons rest you at a stay,	Edw	5.1.67	Edward
[Till] <And> at the last, he come to Killingworth,	Edw	5.2.60	Mortmr
It is the chiefest marke they levell at.	Edw	5.3.12	Edward
To seeke for mercie at a tyrants hand.	Edw	5.3.36	Edward
But at his lookes Lightborne thou wilt relent.	Edw	5.4.26	Mortmr
At every ten miles end thou hast a horse.	Edw	5.4.42	Mortmr
While at the councell table, grave enough,	Edw	5.4.58	Mortmr
Art thou king, must I die at thy commaund?	Edw	5.4.103	Kent
At our commaund, once more away with him.	Edw	5.4.104	Mortmr
What safetie may I looke for at his hands,	Edw	5.4.109	King
For she relents at this your miserie.	Edw	5.5.49	Ltborn
When for her sake I ran at tilt in Fraunce,	Edw	5.5.69	Edward
Know that I am a king, oh at that name,	Edw	5.5.89	Edward
All tremble at my name, and I feare none,	Edw	5.6.13	Mortmr
Why should I greeve at my declining fall?	Edw	5.6.63	Mortmr
At <of> riper yeares to Wittenberg <Wertenberg> he went,	F 13	Prol.13	1Chor
Yet levell at the end of every Art,	F 32	1.1.4	Faust
Who aimes at nothing but externall trash,	F 62	1.1.34	Faust
that move betweene the quiet Poles/Shall be at my command:	F 84	1.1.56	Faust
keele at [Antwerpe] <Anwerpe> <Antwarpes> <Antwerpes> bridge,	F 123	1.1.95	Faust
Know that your words have won me at the last,	F 128	1.1.100	Faust
my Maister is within at dinner, with Valdes and Cornelius,	F 215	1.2.22	P Wagner
And meet me in my Study, at Midnight,	F 327	1.3.99	Faust
So, now thou art to bee at an howres warning, whensoever, and	F 369	1.4.27	P Wagner
that at some certaine day/Great Lucifer may claime it as his	F 439	2.1.51	Mephst
shall be his servant, and be by him commanded <at his command>.	F 487	2.1.99	P Faust
at all times, in what shape [or] <and> forme soever he please.	F 491	2.1.103	P Faust
Eclipses, all at one time, but in some years we have more, in	F 615	2.2.64	P Faust
Faustus, thou shalt, at midnight I will send for thee;	F 716	2.2.168	Lucifr
And as I guesse will first arrive at Rome,	F 775	2.3.54	2Chor
And point like Antiques at his triple Crowne:	F 862	3.1.84	Mephst
What by the holy Councell held at Trent,	F 884	3.1.106	Pope
The sleepy Cardinals are hard at hand,	F 982	3.2.2	Mephst
I pray my Lords have patience at this troublesome banquet.	F1058	3.2.78	Pope
same cup, for the Vintners boy followes us at the hard heeles.	F1090	3.3.3	P Dick
circle, and stand close at my backe, and stir not for thy life,	F1113	3.3.26	P Robin
[As they admirde and wondred at his wit].	F1148	3.3.61A	3Chor
at whose pallace now]/[Faustus is feasted mongst his noblemen].	F1151	3.3.64A	3Chor
For Faustus at the Court is late arriv'd,	F1181	4.1.27	Mrtino
And at his heeles a thousand furies waite,	F1182	4.1.28	Mrtino

AT (cont.)

The Emperour is at hand, who comes to see/What wonders by	F1197	4.1.43		Mrtino
I am content for this once to thrust my head out at a window:	F1200	4.1.46	P	Benvol
And lay his life at holy Bruno's feet.	F1220	4.1.66		Faust
That we may wonder at their excellence.	F1234	4.1.80		Emper
To satisfie my longing thoughts at full,	F1264	4.1.110		Emper
beast is yon, that thrusts his head out at [the] window.	F1275	4.1.121	P	Faust
in your head for shame, let not all the world wonder at you.	F1292	4.1.138	P	Faust
When every servile groome jeasts at my wrongs,	F1329	4.2.5		Benvol
Close, close, the Conjurer is at hand,	F1357	4.2.33		Fredrk
Tremble and quake at his commanding charmes?	F1372	4.2.48		Fredrk
For loe these Trees remove at my command,	F1426	4.2.102		Faust
me his leg quite off, and now 'tis at home in mine Hostry.	F1551	4.5.47	P	HrsCsr
that at this time of the yeare, when every Tree is barren of	F1578	4.6.21	P	Duke
What rude disturbers have we at the gate?	F1588	4.6.31		Duke
Our servants, and our Courts at thy command.	F1624	4.6.67		Duke
hee's now at supper with the schollers, where ther's such	F1678	5.1.5	P	Wagner
see how the heavens smiles]/[At your repulse, and laughs your	F1795	5.1.122A		OldMan
He and his servant Wagner are at hand,	F1813	5.2.17		Mephst
heare [me] with patience, and tremble not at my speeches.	F1839	5.2.43	P	Faust
And laught to see the poore starve at their gates:	F1918	5.2.122		BdAngl
You Starres that raign'd at my nativity,	F1950	5.2.154		Faust
A hundred thousand, and at last be sav'd.	F1962	5.2.166		Faust
At which selfe time the house seem'd all on fire,	F1993	5.3.11		3Schol
may exhort the wise/Onely to wonder at unlawfull things,	F2007	5.3.25		4Chor
at an houres warning whensoever or wheresoever the divell shall	F App	p.230 36	P	Wagner
in our parish dance at my pleasure starke naked before me,	F App	p.233 4	P	Robin
druncke with ipocrase at any taberne in Europe for nothing,	F App	p.234 23	P	Robin
hir to thy owne use, as often as thou wilt, and at midnight.	F App	p.234 28	P	Robin
Ifaith thats just nothing at all.	F App	p.237 40	P	Knight
at my intreaty release him, he hath done penance sufficient.	F App	p.238 79	P	Emper
before you have him, ride him not into the water at any hand.	F App	p.239 109	P	Faust
my horse be sick, or ill at ease, if I bring his water to you,	F App	p.240 118	P	HrsCsr
rid him into the deepe pond at the townes ende, I was no sooner	F App	p.240 133	P	HrsCsr
who are at supper with such belly-cheere,	F App	p.243 6		Wagner
At Munda let the dreadfull battailes joyne;	Lucan, First Booke			40
The Mutin toyles; the fleet at Leuca suncke;	Lucan, First Booke			42
Thou Caesar at this instant art my God,	Lucan, First Booke			63
A towne with one poore church set them at oddes.	Lucan, First Booke			97
At al times charging home, and making havock;	Lucan, First Booke			148
His mind was troubled, and he aim'd at war,	Lucan, First Booke			186
At night in dreadful vision fearefull Roome,	Lucan, First Booke			188
At last learne wretch to leave thy monarchy;	Lucan, First Booke			335
me,/Because at his commaund I wound not up/My conquering Eagles?	Lucan, First Booke			339
But Roome at thraldoms feet to rid from tyrants.	Lucan, First Booke			352
We grieve at this thy patience and delay:	Lucan, First Booke			362
Sit safe at home and chaunt sweet Poesie.	Lucan, First Booke			445
heady rout/That in chain'd troupes breake forth at every port;	Lucan, First Booke			489
Thou Roome at name of warre runst from thy selfe,	Lucan, First Booke			517
to run their course through empty night/At noone day mustered,	Lucan, First Booke			535
birds/Defil'd the day, and <at night> wilde beastes were seene,	Lucan, First Booke			557
At that bunch where the liver is, appear'd/A knob of flesh,	Lucan, First Booke			626
lawlesse/And casuall; all the starres at randome radge <range>:	Lucan, First Booke			642
Which being not shakt <slackt>, I saw it die at length.	Ovid's Elegies			1.2.12
loves wrack/Shall follow thee, their hands tied at their backe.	Ovid's Elegies			1.2.32
And give woundes infinite at everie turne.	Ovid's Elegies			1.2.44
About thy neck shall he at pleasure skippe?	Ovid's Elegies			1.4.6
When thou doest wish thy husband at the devill.	Ovid's Elegies			1.4.28
At night thy husband clippes thee, I will weepe/And to the	Ovid's Elegies			1.4.61
Like twilight glimps at setting of the sunne,	Ovid's Elegies			1.5.5
Betrayde her selfe, and yeelded at the last.	Ovid's Elegies			1.5.16
By speechlesse lookes we guesse at things succeeding.	Ovid's Elegies			1.11.18
Poore travailers though tierd, rise at thy sight,	Ovid's Elegies			1.13.13
Now hast thou left no haires at all to die.	Ovid's Elegies			1.14.2
Borne at Peligny, to write more addresse.	Ovid's Elegies			2.1.2
And call the sunnes white horses [backe] <blacke> at noone.	Ovid's Elegies			2.1.24
Another railes at me, and that I write,	Ovid's Elegies			2.4.21
I could not be in love with twoo at once,	Ovid's Elegies			2.10.2
That at my funeralles some may weeping crie,	Ovid's Elegies			2.10.37
At Colchis stain'd with childrens bloud men raile,	Ovid's Elegies			2.14.29
And in her bosome strangely fall at last.	Ovid's Elegies			2.15.14
Adde deeds unto thy promises at last.	Ovid's Elegies			2.16.48
Often at length, my wench depart, I bid,	Ovid's Elegies			2.18.5
Love laughed at my cloak, and buskines painted,	Ovid's Elegies			2.18.15
Sappho her vowed harpe laies at Phoebus feete.	Ovid's Elegies			2.18.34
Nothing I love, that at all times availes me.	Ovid's Elegies			2.19.8
Beginne to shut thy house at evening sure.	Ovid's Elegies			2.19.38
Search at the dore who knocks oft in the darke,	Ovid's Elegies			2.19.39
Oft some points at the prophet passing by,	Ovid's Elegies			3.1.19
Some greater worke will urge me on at last.	Ovid's Elegies			3.1.70
But spare my wench thou at her right hand seated,	Ovid's Elegies			3.2.21
At least now conquer, and out-runne the rest:	Ovid's Elegies			3.2.79
At me Apollo bends his pliant bowe:	Ovid's Elegies			3.3.29
At me Joves right-hand lightning hath to throwe.	Ovid's Elegies			3.3.30
And see at home much, that thou nere broughtst thether.	Ovid's Elegies			3.4.48
men point at me for a whore,/Shame, that should make me blush,	Ovid's Elegies			3.5.77
And fruit from trees, when ther's no wind at al.	Ovid's Elegies			3.6.34
And craves his taske, and seekes to be at fight.	Ovid's Elegies			3.6.68
At thy deafe dores in verse sing my abuses.	Ovid's Elegies			3.7.24
So at Aeneas buriall men report,	Ovid's Elegies			3.8.13
Nor lesse at mans prosperity any grudge.	Ovid's Elegies			3.9.6
Who thinkes her to be glad at lovers smart,	Ovid's Elegies			3.9.15
The plough-mans hopes were frustrate at the last.	Ovid's Elegies			3.9.34

AT (cont.)			
Victorious wreathes at length my Temples greete. . .	Ovid's Elegies	3.10.6	
At Sestos, Hero dwelt; Hero the faire, ...	Hero and Leander	1.5	
(Whose tragedie divine Musaeus soong)/Dwelt at Abidus; since	Hero and Leander	1.53	
To meet their loves; such as had none at all, ...	Hero and Leander	1.95	
So at her presence all surpris'd and tooken, ...	Hero and Leander	1.122	
Who ever lov'd, that lov'd not at first sight? . . .	Hero and Leander	1.176	
And yet at everie word shee turn'd aside, ...	Hero and Leander	1.195	
At last, like to a bold sharpe Sophister, ...	Hero and Leander	1.197	
Or capable of any forme at all.	Hero and Leander	1.274	
Things that are not at all, are never lost.	Hero and Leander	1.276	
But Pallas and your mistresse are at strife.	Hero and Leander	1.322	
So having paus'd a while, at last shee said:	Hero and Leander	1.337	
At one selfe instant, she poore soule assaies, ...	Hero and Leander	1.362	
not to love at all, and everie part/Strove to resist the .	Hero and Leander	1.363	
Threatning a thousand deaths at everie glaunce, . . .	Hero and Leander	1.382	
And then he woo'd with kisses, and at last, ...	Hero and Leander	1.404	
At his faire feathered feet, the engins layd, ...	Hero and Leander	1.449	
At last he came, O who can tell the greeting, ...	Hero and Leander	2.23	
These greedie lovers had, at their first meeting. . .	Hero and Leander	2.24	
Then standing at the doore, she turnd about, ...	Hero and Leander	2.97	
At every stroke, betwixt them would he slide, ...	Hero and Leander	2.184	
He flung at him his mace, but as it went, ...	Hero and Leander	2.209	
And knockt and cald, at which celestiall noise, . . .	Hero and Leander	2.231	
At least vouchsafe these armes some little roome, . . .	Hero and Leander	2.249	
(Poore sillie maiden) at his mercie was.	Hero and Leander	2.286	
Seeming not woon, yet woon she was at length, ...	Hero and Leander	2.295	
ATALANTA			
So fayre she was, Atalanta she resembled, ...	Ovid's Elegies	1.7.13	
ATALANTAS			
Swift Atalantas flying legges like these, ...	Ovid's Elegies	3.2.29	
ATAX			
Mild Atax glad it beares not Roman [boats] <bloats>; .	Lucan, First Booke	404	
ATCHIEV'D			
What thinks your greatnes best to be atchiev'd/In pursuit of	1Tamb	3.1.56	Fesse
ATCHIEVE			
It is not ought Aeneas may atchieve?	Dido	3.4.11	Aeneas
Which neither art nor reason may atchieve, ...	Dido	5.1.65	Aeneas
ATCHIVE			
That hanges for every peasant to atchive?	P 98	2.41	Guise
ATCHIVEMENTS			
Whose great atchivements in our forrain warre, ...	Edw	1.4.360	Edward
ATHENS			
And I in Athens with this gentleman, ...	Dido	3.1.146	Cloan
ATHIRST			
having lickt/Warme goare from Syllas sword art yet athirst,	Lucan, First Booke	331	
ATHWART			
then having whiskt/His taile athwart his backe, and crest	Lucan, First Booke	211	
ATLAS			
That earth-borne Atlas groning underprops:	Dido	1.1.99	Jupitr
Or aged Atlas shoulder out of joynt, ...	Dido	4.1.12	Achat
breadth of shoulders as might mainely beare/Olde Atlas burthen.	1Tamb	2.1.11	Menaph
Shaking the burthen mighty Atlas beares:	2Tamb	4.1.129	Tamb
heavens great beames/On Atlas shoulder, shall not lie more	Edw	3.1.77	Prince
Or Atlas head; their saints and houshold gods/Sweate teares to	Lucan, First Booke	554	
ATONEMENT (See ATTONEMENT)			
ATREUS			
The Sunne turnd backe from Atreus cursed table? . . .	Ovid's Elegies	3.11.39	
ATRIDES			
With whose outcryes Atrides being apal'd, ...	Dido	2.1.129	Aeneas
Then that which grim Atrides overthrew:	Dido	5.1.3	Aeneas
With the Atrides many gainde renowne.	Ovid's Elegies	2.12.10	
ATTAIN'D			
Then read no more, thou hast attain'd that <the> end; .	F 38	1.1.10	Faust
Why Faustus, hast thou not attain'd that end?	F 46	1.1.18	Faust
Yet he attain'd by her support to have her, ...	Ovid's Elegies	3.2.17	
ATTAINE			
I could attaine it with a woondrous ease, ...	1Tamb	2.5.77	Tamb
Yet will they reade me, and thereby attaine/To Peters Chayre:	Jew	Prol.11	Machvl
attaine to that degree of high renowne and great authoritie,	F App	p.236 22	P Emper
By which sweete path thou maist attaine the gole/That shall	F App	p.243 36	OldMan
How to attaine, what is denyed, we thinke, ...	Ovid's Elegies	3.4.17	
ATTEMPLESSE			
And rest attemplesse, faint and destitute?	1Tamb	2.5.74	Tamb
ATTEMPT			
But if he dare attempt to stir your siege, ...	1Tamb	3.1.46	Argier
That dare attempt to war with Christians.	2Tamb	2.1.26	Fredrk
have so manifestly wronged us,/What will not Abigall attempt?	Jew	1.2.276	Abigal
To meddle or attempt such dangerous things.	P 38	1.38	Admral
That durst attempt to murder noble Guise.	P1121	21.15	Dumain
But rather praise him for that brave attempt, ...	Edw	1.4.268	Mortmr
A noble attempt, and honourable deed, ...	Edw	3.1.206	SpncrP
Did you attempt his rescue, Edmund speake?	Edw	5.4.86	Mortmr
Then gentle friends aid me in this attempt, ...	F 138	1.1.110	Faust
us sway thy thoughts/From this attempt against the Conjurer.	F1326	4.2.2	Mrtino
Yet to encounter this your weake attempt, ...	F1429	4.2.105	Faust
I will attempt, which is but little worth.	F1758	5.1.85	Mephst
ATTEMPTED			
With whom they have attempted many times, ...	Jew	1.1.164	Barab
She secretly with me such harme attempted, ...	Ovid's Elegies	2.13.3	
Is said to have attempted flight forsooke.	Ovid's Elegies	3.12.20	
ATTEMPTES			
What thinkst thou man, shal come of our attemptes? . .	1Tamb	2.3.3	Cosroe

ATTEMPTES (cont.)			
And make them blest that share in his attemptes. . . .	1Tamb	2.3.9	Tamb
ATTEMPTLESS (See ATTEMPLESSE)			
ATTEMPTS			
Who will eternish Troy in their attempts.	Dido	1.1.108	Jupitr
As oft as he attempts to hoyst up saile:	Dido	4.4.103	Dido
And thou despise the praise of such attempts:	Dido	5.1.37	Hermes
Repaying all attempts with present death, ...	P 269	4.67	Charls
But if that God doe prosper mine attempts, ...	P 927	18.28	Navrre
ATTEND			
A hundreth <hundred> Tartars shall attend on thee, . . .	1Tamb	1.2.93	Tamb
Attend upon the person of your Lord, ...	1Tamb	3.3.62	Bajzth
The Grecian virgins shall attend on thee, ...	2Tamb	1.2.36	Callap
Where wee'll attend the respit you have tane, ...	Jew	1.2.30	Calym
He said he wud attend me in the morne.	Jew	2.1.34	Abigal
I, Barabas, come Bashawes, attend.	Jew	5.5.59	Calym
And doe attend my comming there by this.	Jew	5.5.104	Calym
Thou art too ugly to attend on me:	F 252	1.3.24	Faust
Having thee ever to attend on me, ...	F 321	1.3.93	Faust
Lord Raymond, take your seate, Friers attend, ...	F1010	3.2.30	Pope
What Lollards do attend our Hollinesse, ...	F1049	3.2.69	Pope
Hye to the presence to attend the Emperour.	F1156	4.1.2	Mrtino
Well, go you attend the Emperour:	F1199	4.1.45	P Benvol
of his men to attend you with provision fit for your journey.	F1501	4.4.45	P Wagner
Lest greater dangers <danger> do attend thy drift. . . .	F1752	5.1.79	Mephst
ATTENDANCE			
For this, I waite, that scornes attendance else: . . .	P 106	2.49	Guise
That waite attendance for a gratious looke, ...	Edw	1.4.338	Queene
ATTENDS			
Where sorrow at my elbow still attends, ...	Edw	5.1.33	Edward
What devill attends this damn'd Magician, ...	F1445	4.3.15	Benvol
he doth not chide/Nor to hoist saile attends fit time and tyde.	Ovid's Elegies		1.9.14
ATTENTIVE			
upon; therefore acknowledge your errour, and be attentive.	F 204	1.2.11	P Wagner
ATTENTIVELY			
and see that you walke attentively, and let your right eye be	F 386	1.4.44	P Wagner
ATTICKE			
Atticke, all lovers are to warre farre sent.	Ovid's Elegies		1.9.2
ATTIRE (See also HAIRE-TYERS)			
I know she is a Curtezane by her attire:	Jew	3.1.27	P Ithimr
And floute our traine, and jest at our attire:	Edw	1.4.418	Mortmr
Which made me curate-like in mine attire, ...	Edw	2.1.49	Baldck
and attire/They usde to weare during their time of life, .	F App	p.237 33	Emper
Where's thy attire? why wand'rest heere alone?	Ovid's Elegies		3.5.55
Either she was foule, or her attire was bad, ...	Ovid's Elegies		3.6.1
Some swore he was a maid in mans attire, ...	Hero and Leander		1.83
ATTIRED			
[Is she attired, then shew her graces best]. . . .	Ovid's Elegies		2.4.38
ATTONEMENT			
To make attonement for my labouring soule.	Jew	1.2.326	Abigal
ATTORNEY (See ATTURNEY)			
ATTRACT			
The while thine eyes attract their sought for joyes: .	Dido	1.1.136	Venus
ATTRACTIVE			
Such power attractive shines in princes eies.	1Tamb	2.5.64	Therid
ATTRIBUTE			
[Sorbonests] <thorbonest>/Attribute as much unto their workes,	P 412	7.52	Ramus
ATTURNEY			
bondes contained/From barbarous lips of some Atturney strained.	Ovid's Elegies		1.12.24
AUDACIOUS			
Nor in the pompe of proud audacious deeds, ...	F 5	Prol.5	1Chor
AUGHT (See OUGHT)			
AUGMENT			
But rather will augment then ease my woe?	Dido	5.1.152	Dido
AUGMENTETH			
Where Nile augmenteth the Pelusian sea:	Lucan, First Booke		683
AUGMENTS			
And therefore stil augments his cruelty.	2Tamb	5.3.219	Tamb
AUGURES			
(as their old custome was)/They call th'Etrurian Augures,	Lucan, First Booke		584
Next learned Augures follow;/Apolloes southsayers; and Joves	Lucan, First Booke		600
With Augures Phoebus, Phoebe with hunters standes, . . .	Ovid's Elegies		3.2.51
AUGURY			
all to good, be Augury vaine, and Tages/Th'arts master falce.	Lucan, First Booke		635
AUKWARD			
as being like to prove/An aukward sacrifice, but by the hornes	Lucan, First Booke		611
AULIS			
I never vow'd at Aulis gulfe/The desolation of his native Troy,	Dido	5.1.202	Dido
AUNCESTERS			
This tottered ensigne of my auncesters, ...	Edw	2.3.21	Mortmr
AUNCESTORS			
about the honour of mine auncestors, how they had wonne by	F App	p.236 19	P Emper
AUNTIENT			
[Itis is] <It is as> great, but auntient cause of sorrowe.	Ovid's Elegies		2.6.10
AURORA			
Aurora shall not peepe out of her doores, ...	1Tamb	2.2.10	Mycet
But when Aurora mounts the second time, ...	1Tamb	4.1.54	2Msngr
Aurora whither slidest thou?	Ovid's Elegies		1.13.3
Even such as by Aurora hath the skie, ...	Ovid's Elegies		2.5.35
AUSTER			
(Auster and Aquilon with winged Steads/All sweating, tilt about	1Tamb	3.2.78	Agidas
Looke how when stormy Auster from the breach/Of Libian Syrtes	Lucan, First Booke		496
AUSTRICH			
The king of Boheme, and the Austrich Duke, ...	2Tamb	1.1.95	Orcan

AUT			
Si bene quid de te merui, fuit aut tibi quidquam/Dulce meum,	Dido	5.1.136	Dido
AUTHOR			
We will account her author of our lives.	Dido	3.1.112	Aeneas
Nor Dardanus the author of thy stocke:	Dido	5.1.157	Dido
Or dieng, be the [author] <anchor> of my death.	2Tamb	2.4.56	Tamb
AUTHORITIE			
To plant our selves with such authoritie,	P 637	12.50	QnMoth
attaine to that degree of high renowne and great authoritie,	F App	p.237 23	P Emper
AUTHORITY			
No simple place, no small authority,	Jew	5.2.28	Barab
And since by wrong thou got'st Authority,	Jew	5.2.35	Barab
For he that liveth in Authority,	Jew	5.2.38	Barab
He growes to prowd in his authority,	F 911	3.1.133	Pope
And by authority Apostolicall/Depose him from his Regall	F 923	3.1.145	Pope
AUTUME			
Or withered leaves that Autume shaketh downe:	1Tamb	4.1.32	Souldn
AVAILDE			
But what availde this faith? her rarest hue?	Ovid's Elegies		2.6.17
AVAILE			
'Tis not thy life which can availe me ought,	Jew	5.2.62	Barab
Tis not for his sake, but for our availe:	Edw	1.4.242	Mortmr
O what will all thy riches, pleasures, pompes,/Availe thee now?	F1897	5.2.101	GdAngl
Request milde Zephires helpe for thy availe,	Ovid's Elegies		2.11.41
'Tis doubtfull whether verse availe, or harme,	Ovid's Elegies		3.11.13
AVAILES			
Nothing I love, that at all times availes me.	Ovid's Elegies		2.19.8
AVAILETH			
But what availeth that this traitors dead,	P1054	19.124	King
AVARICE			
Nor staine thy youthfull years with avarice,	Hero and Leander		1.325
AVAUNT			
Avaunt old witch and trouble not my wits.	Dido	3.2.25	Venus
AVENGD			
traitors, now tis time/To be avengd on you for all your braves,	Edw	3.1.225	Edward
AVENGED (See also VENGE)			
And will she be avenged on his life?	Dido	3.4.14	Aeneas
AVENGER (See VENGER)			
AVERNE			
Him the last day in black Averne hath drownd,	Ovid's Elegies		3.8.27
AVERNI			
Th'Averni too, which bouldly faine themselves/The Romanes	Lucan, First Booke		428
AVERNUS			
Or meant to pierce Avernus darksome vaults,	1Tamb	1.2.160	Therid
Dive to the bottome of Avernus poole,	1Tamb	4.4.18	Bajzth
AVOID (See also AVOYD)			
So sir, you have spoke, away, avoid our presence.	Edw	3.1.232	Edward
AVOUCHE			
And will avouche his saying with the sworde,	Edw	5.4.77	Champn
AVOYD			
Then call for mercy, and avoyd despaire.	F1733	5.1.60	OldMan
AW			
Keeping in aw the Bay of Portingale:	1Tamb	3.3.258	Tamb
AWAIT			
Await the sentence of her scornefull eies:	Hero and Leander		1.123
AWAKE			
Hermes awake, and haste to Neptunes realme,	Dido	1.1.114	Jupitr
Awake ye men of Memphis, heare the clange/Of Scythian trumpets,	1Tamb	4.1.1	Souldn
I'le rouse my senses, and awake my selfe.	Jew	1.2.269	Barab
Fryar, awake.	Jew	4.1.143	Barab
you cosoning scab; Maister Doctor awake, and rise, and give me	F1489	4.4.33	P HrsCsr
But I have it againe now I am awake:	F1657	4.6.100	P Faust
And crowing Cocks poore soules to worke awake.	Ovid's Elegies		1.6.66
AWARE			
make her round and plump, and batten more then you are aware.	Jew	3.4.66	P Ithimr
the second time, aware the third, I give you faire warning.	F App	p.232 20	P Faust
A WAY			
No sicknesse harm'd thee, farre be that a way,	Ovid's Elegies		1.14.41
AWAY			
Goe thou away, Ascanius shall stay.	Dido	3.1.35	Dido
Away I say,/Depart from Carthage, come not in my sight.	Dido	3.1.43	Dido
Lest with these sweete thoughts I melt cleane away.	Dido	3.1.76	Dido
And might I live to see thee shipt away,	Dido	3.3.46	Iarbus
Aeneas, leave these dumpes and lets away,	Dido	3.3.60	Dido
Away with Dido, Anna be thy song,	Dido	4.2.45	Anna
Graunt she or no, Aeneas must away,	Dido	4.3.7	Aeneas
Cloanthus, haste away, Aeneas calles.	Dido	4.3.14	Aeneas
It may be he will steale away with them:	Dido	4.4.3	Dido
Thou and Achates ment to saile away.	Dido	4.4.28	Dido
Yet hath she tane away my oares and masts,	Dido	5.1.60	Aeneas
Away with her to prison presently,	Dido	5.1.220	Dido
Away with her, suffer her not to speake.	Dido	5.1.224	Dido
But he clapt under hatches saild away.	Dido	5.1.240	Anna
O sister, sister, take away the Rockes,	Dido	5.1.254	Dido
Must I make ships for him to saile away?	Dido	5.1.266	Dido
Returne with speed, time passeth swift away,	1Tamb	1.1.67	Mycet
And have a thousand horsmen tane away?	1Tamb	2.2.6	Mycet
They cannot take away my crowne from me.	1Tamb	2.4.14	Mycet
Away, I am the King: go, touch me not.	1Tamb	2.4.20	Mycet
I marveile much he stole it not away.	1Tamb	2.4.42	Mycet
The Turkesse let my Loves maid lead away.	1Tamb	3.3.267	Tamb
Take them away againe and make us slaves.	1Tamb	4.4.133	Therid
Away with them I say and shew them death.	1Tamb	5.1.120	Tamb

AWAY (cont.)

Goe to, my child, away, away, away.	1Tamb	5.1.313	P	Zabina
Whose sight with joy would take away my life,	1Tamb	5.1.419		Arabia
Pioners away, and where I stuck the stake,	2Tamb	3.3.41		Therid
Ile hang a clogge about your necke for running away againe, you	2Tamb	3.5.101	P	Tamb
Away, let us to the field, that the villaine may be slaine.	2Tamb	3.5.143	P	Trebiz
Away ye fools, my father needs not me,	2Tamb	4.1.15		Calyph
Come, thou and I wil goe to cardes to drive away the time.	2Tamb	4.1.61	P	Calyph
Away with him hence, let him speake no more:	2Tamb	5.1.125		Tamb
Take them away Theridamas, see them dispatcht.	2Tamb	5.1.134		Tamb
Who flies away at every glance I give,	2Tamb	5.3.70		Tamb
And when I look away, comes stealing on:	2Tamb	5.3.71		Tamb
Villaine away, and hie thee to the field,	2Tamb	5.3.72		Tamb
that I descended of/Were all in generall cast away for sinne,	Jew	1.2.114		Barab
I'de passe away my life in penitence,	Jew	1.2.324		Abigal
Away accursed from thy fathers sight.	Jew	1.2.351		Barab
So will we fight it out; come, let's away:	Jew	2.2.52		Govnr
Thou hast thy Crownes, fellow, come let's away.	Jew	2.3.158		Mater
Lets away.	Jew	2.3.162		1Offcr
Away, for here they come.	Jew	2.3.275		Barab
Away then.	Jew	2.3.380		Barab
Looke not towards him, let's away:	Jew	3.1.24		Pilia
And the horse pestilence to boot; away.	Jew	3.4.113		Barab
Come let's away.	Jew	3.6.52		2Fryar
Rid him away, and goe you home with me.	Jew	4.1.89		Barab
Why goe, get you away.	Jew	4.1.93		2Fryar
Away, I'de wish thee, and let me goe by:	Jew	4.1.170		1Fryar
I must make this villaine away:	Jew	4.3.29	P	Barab
Away with her, she is a Curtezane.	Jew	5.1.8		Govnr
Away with him, his sight is death to me.	Jew	5.1.35		Govnr
Once more away with him; you shall have law.	Jew	5.1.40		Govnr
So, now away and fortifie the Towne.	Jew	5.1.60		Govnr
Away, no more, let him not trouble me.	Jew	5.2.26		Barab
So march away, and let due praise be given/Neither to Fate nor	Jew	5.5.123		Govnr
Away then, break into the Admirals house.	P 282	5.9		Guise
Away with him, cut of his head and handes,	P 316	5.43		Anjoy
Come then, lets away.	P 335	5.62		Guise
Come dragge him away and throw him in a ditch.	P 345	5.72		Guise
Away with them both.	P 442	7.82		Anjoy
Sirs, take him away and throw him in some ditch.	P 499	9.18		Guise
So, dragge them away.	P 535	10.8		Guise
Come Pleshe, lets away whilste time doth serve.	P 587	11.52		Navrre
Sirra, take him away.	P 621	12.34		Guise
But come my Lords, let us away with speed,	P 741	14.44		Navrre
Let us away with triumph to our tents.	P 805	16.19		Navrre
It would be good the Guise were made away,	P 888	17.83		Eprnon
And let them march away to France amaine:	P 917	18.18		Navrre
Mounser of Loraine sinke away to hell,	P1023	19.93		King
Away to prison with him, Ile clippe his winges/Or ere he passe	P1052	19.122		King
Ile clippe his winges/Or ere he passe my handes, away with him.	P1053	19.123		King
Get you away and strangle the Cardinall.	P1059	19.129		King
Away, leave me alone to meditate.	P1081	19.151		QnMoth
Come take him away.	P1106	20.16		1Mur
Come let us away and leavy men,	P1127	21.21		Dumain
That glaunceth at my lips and flieth away:	Edw	1.1.23		Gavstn
But in the meane time Gaveston away,	Edw	1.1.202		Edward
This certifie the Pope, away, take horsse.	Edw	1.2.38		ArchBp
Come then lets away.	Edw	1.2.79		Lncstr
Away I say with hatefull Gaveston.	Edw	1.4.33		Lncstr
Ile see him presently dispatched away.	Edw	1.4.90		Mortmr
Away then, touch me not, come Gaveston.	Edw	1.4.159		Edward
You know my minde, come unckle lets away.	Edw	1.4.424		Mortmr
Thy absence made me droope, and pine away,	Edw	2.2.52		Edward
Come Edmund lets away, and levie men,	Edw	2.2.98		Edward
And unresisted, drave away riche spoiles.	Edw	2.2.167		Lncstr
Away:	Edw	2.2.219		Edward
Why then weele have him privilie made away.	Edw	2.2.236		Gavstn
Come lets away, and when the mariage ends,	Edw	2.2.264		Edward
Take shipping and away to Scarborough,	Edw	2.4.5		Edward
Spencer and I will post away by land.	Edw	2.4.6		Edward
I will not trust them, Gaveston away.	Edw	2.4.8		Edward
From my imbracements thus he breakes away,	Edw	2.4.16		Queene
He turnes away, and smiles upon his minion.	Edw	2.4.29		Queene
Upon him souldiers, take away his weapons.	Edw	2.5.8		Warwck
Souldiers, have him away:	Edw	2.5.26		Warwck
Souldiers away with him.	Edw	2.5.45		Warwck
Souldiers away with him:	Edw	2.5.50		Mortmr
To make away a true man for a theefe.	Edw	2.5.70		Mortmr
Away base groome, robber of kings renowme,	Edw	2.5.72		Mortmr
Returne him on your honor. Sound, away.	Edw	2.5.98		Mortmr
Goe, take the villaine, soldiers come away,	Edw	2.6.11		Warwck
Away.	Edw	2.6.17		Warwck
Away, tarrie no answer, but be gon.	Edw	3.1.173		Edward
Away.	Edw	3.1.184		Edward
Away base upstart, brav'st thou nobles thus?	Edw	3.1.205		Penbrk
A rebels, recreants, you made him away.	Edw	3.1.229		Edward
So sir, you have spoke, away, avoid our presence.	Edw	3.1.232		Edward
Away with them:	Edw	3.1.245		Edward
Away.	Edw	3.1.248		Edward
Then make for Fraunce amaine, [Levune] <Lewne> away,/Proclaime	Edw	3.1.280		Spencr
want, and though a many friends/Are made away, as Warwick,	Edw	4.2.52		Mortmr
What, was I borne to flye and runne away,	Edw	4.5.4		Edward
princely resolution/Fits not the time, away, we are pursu'd.	Edw	4.5.9		Baldck

AWAY (cont.)

Edmund away, Bristow to Longshankes blood/Is false, be not	Edw	4.6.16	Kent
Take him away, he prates. You Rice ap Howell,	Edw	4.6.73	Mortmr
Away with them.	Edw	4.7.68	Rice
Will your Lordships away?	Edw	4.7.116	Rice
My lord, why waste you thus the time away,	Edw	5.1.49	Leistr
But dayes bright beames dooth vanish fast away,	Edw	5.1.69	Edward
Call me not lorde, away, out of my sight:	Edw	5.1.113	Edward
So now away, post thither wards amaine.	Edw	5.2.67	Mortmr
Then I will carrie thee by force away.	Edw	5.2.112	Mortmr
Traitors away, what will you murther me,	Edw	5.3.29	Edward
No, but wash your face, and shave away your beard,	Edw	5.3.31	Gurney
Come, come, away, now put the torches out,	Edw	5.3.47	Matrvs
Take this, away, and never see me more.	Edw	5.4.43	Mortmr
A would have taken the king away perforce,	Edw	5.4.84	Souldr
At our commaund, once more away with him.	Edw	5.4.104	Mortmr
This villain's sent to make away the king.	Edw	5.5.21	Matrvs
I know what I must do, get you away,	Edw	5.5.27	Ltborn
And therefore let us take horse and away.	Edw	5.5.115	Matrvs
Away.	Edw	5.5.120	Gurney
for I will presently raise up two devils to carry thee away:	F 373	1.4.31	P Wagner
I good Wagner, take away the devill then.	F 377	1.4.35	P Robin
Spirits away.	F 378	1.4.36	P Wagner
Away with such vaine fancies, and despaire,	F 392	2.1.4	Faust
O Faustus they are come to fetch <away> thy soule.	F 641	2.2.90	Faust
<talke of the divel, and nothing else: come away>.	F 660	(HC263) A	P Lucifr
Out envious wretch <Away envious rascall>:	F 685	2.2.134	Faust
Away to hell, away: on piper.	F 711	2.2.163	Lucifr
What Robin, you must come away and walk the horses.	F 725	2.3.4	P Dick
Come then let's away.	F 753	2.3.32	P Robin
Come therefore, let's away.	F 830	3.1.52	Faust
Away and bring us word <again> with speed.	F 888	3.1.110	Pope
Away sweet Mephostophilis be gone,	F 975	3.1.197	Faust
That slept both Bruno and his crowne away.	F 988	3.2.8	Faust
be he that stole [away] his holinesse meate from the Table.	F1077	3.2.97	1Frier
Cursed be he that tooke away his holinesse wine.	F1085	3.2.105	1Frier
plague take you, I thought 'twas your knavery to take it away:	F1111	3.3.24	P Vintnr
Away be gone.	F1132	3.3.45	Mephst
Mephostophilis away,	F1236	4.1.82	Faust
an your Divels come not away quickly, you shall have me asleepe	F1241	4.1.87	P Benvol
Away, be gone.	F1273	4.1.119	Faust
Away, you love me not, to urge me thus,	F1327	4.2.3	Benvol
Away.	F1418	4.2.94	Faust
and one to whom I must be no niggard of my cunning; Come, away.	F1504	4.4.48	P Faust
and when I came just in the midst my horse vanisht away, and I	F1544	4.5.40	P HrsCsr
Go Mephostophilis, away.	F1574	4.6.17	P Faust
you thinke to carry it away with your Hey-passe, and Re-passe:	F1664	4.6.107	P Robin
now you have sent away my guesse, I pray who shall pay me for	F1667	4.6.110	P Hostss
His Artfull sport, drives all sad thoughts away.	F1673	4.6.116	Duke
Gentlemen away, least you perish with me.	F1867	5.2.71	P Faust
two divels presently to fetch thee away Baliol and Belcher.	F App	p.230 44	P Wagner
Balioll and Belcher, spirits away.	F App	p.230 50	P Wagner
Cursed be hee that stole away his holinesse meate from/the	F App	p.232 31	Frier
Cursed be he that tooke away his holinesse wine.	F App	p.233 39	Frier
prethee come away, theres a Gentleman tarries to have his	F App	p.233 6	P Rafe
it, and she has sent me to looke thee out, prethee come away.	F App	p.233 9	P Rafe
Away you villaine:	F App	p.240 120	P Faust
pond, but my horse vanisht away, and I sat upon a bottle of hey,	F App	p.240 135	P HrsCsr
niggard of my cunning, come Mephastophilis, let's away to him.	F App	p.241 172	P Faust
Whose bloud alone must wash away thy guilt.	F App	p.243 45	OldMan
each from other, but being worne away/They both burst out,	Lucan, First Booke		102
Two tane away, thy labor will be lesse:	Ovid's Elegies		1.1.4
(men say)/Began to smile and [tooke] <take> one foote away.	Ovid's Elegies		1.1.8
Take these away, where is thy <thine> honor then?	Ovid's Elegies		1.2.38
Nor let the windes away my warnings blowe.	Ovid's Elegies		1.4.12
Night goes away: the dores barre backeward strike.	Ovid's Elegies		1.6.24
Strike backe the barre, night fast away doth goe.	Ovid's Elegies		1.6.32
Night runnes away; with open entrance greete them.	Ovid's Elegies		1.6.40
Night goes away: I pray thee ope the dore.	Ovid's Elegies		1.6.48
nights deawie hoast/March fast away:	Ovid's Elegies		1.6.56
But thou my crowne, from sad haires tane away,	Ovid's Elegies		1.6.67
Take strife away, love doth not well endure.	Ovid's Elegies		1.8.96
Achilles burnd Briseis being tane away:	Ovid's Elegies		1.9.33
Therefore when flint and yron weare away,	Ovid's Elegies		1.15.31
as might make/Wrath-kindled Jove away his thunder shake.	Ovid's Elegies		2.5.52
Pure waters moisture thirst away did keepe.	Ovid's Elegies		2.6.32
Even as a head-strong courser beares away,	Ovid's Elegies		2.9.29
Thou also that late tookest mine eyes away,	Ovid's Elegies		2.19.19
And from my hands the reines will slip away.	Ovid's Elegies		3.2.14
Foule dust, from her faire body, go away.	Ovid's Elegies		3.2.42
By feare depriv'd of strength to runne away.	Ovid's Elegies		3.5.70
Her long haires eare-wrought garland fell away.	Ovid's Elegies		3.9.36
And stole away th'inchaunted gazers mind,	Hero and Leander		1.104
But from his spreading armes away she cast her,	Hero and Leander		1.342
away she ran,/After went Mercurie, who us'd such cunning,	Hero and Leander		1.416
Wherewith as one displeas'd, away she trips.	Hero and Leander		2.4
He would have chac'd away the swelling maine,	Hero and Leander		2.121
Herewith afrighted Hero shrunke away,	Hero and Leander		2.253
And faine by stealth away she would have crept,	Hero and Leander		2.310

AWAYE

Awaye with her, her wordes inforce these teares,	Edw	5.6.85	King

AWDE

And must be awde and governd like a child.	Edw	3.1.31	Baldck

AWE (See also AW)			
restrain'd them; but wars love/And Caesars awe dasht all:	Lucan, First Booke		357
AWFUL			
blacke survey/Great Potentates do kneele with awful feare,	F App	p.235 35	Mephst
AWFULL			
learne with awfull eie/To sway a throane as dangerous as his:	2Tamb	5.3.234	Tamb
Was this that sterne aspect, that awfull frowne,	F1370	4.2.46	Fredrk
A WHILE			
Alas sweet boy, thou must be still a while,	Dido	1.1.164	Aeneas
Iarbus pardon me, and stay a while.	Dido	3.1.46	Dido
And stay a while to heare what I could say,	Dido	5.1.239	Anna
Least if we let them lynger here a while,	1Tamb	2.2.20	Meandr
Here take it for a while, I lend it thee,	1Tamb	2.4.37	Tamb
Come banquet and carouse with us a while,	2Tamb	1.1.165	Orcan
Now will we banquet on these plaines a while,	2Tamb	1.3.157	Tamb
And therefore let them rest a while my Lord.	2Tamb	1.3.184	Usumc
But since my life is lengthened yet a while,	2Tamb	2.4.71	Zenoc
for whose byrth/Olde Rome was proud, but gasde a while on her,	2Tamb	2.4.92	Tamb
But stay a while, summon a parle, Drum,	2Tamb	3.3.11	Therid
to your taskes a while/And take such fortune as your fellowes	2Tamb	5.1.136	Tamb
And could I but a while pursue the field,	2Tamb	5.3.117	Tamb
For though they doe a while increase and multiply,	Jew	2.3.89	Barab
Whither goes Don Mathias? stay a while.	Jew	2.3.251	Barab
That maidens new betroth'd should weepe a while:	Jew	2.3.326	Barab
Then breath a while.	P 241	4.39	Guise
O let me stay and rest me heer a while,	P 536	11.1	Charls
What now remaines, but for a while to feast,	P 627	12.40	King
Then stay a while and Ile goe call the King,	P1017	19.87	Capt
O my Lord, let him live a while.	P1173	22.35	Eprnon
Sweete Mortimer, sit downe by me a while,	Edw	1.4.225	Queene
I for a while, but Baldock marke the end,	Edw	2.1.16	Spencr
To breathe a while, our men with sweat and dust/All chockt well	Edw	3.1.191	SpncrP
But stay a while, let me be king till night,	Edw	5.1.59	Edward
And therefore let me weare it yet a while.	Edw	5.1.83	Edward
I, stay a while, thou shalt have answer straight.	Edw	5.5.20	Matrvs
list a while to me,/And then thy heart, were it as Gurneys is,	Edw	5.5.52	Edward
Lie on this bed, and rest your selfe a while.	Edw	5.5.72	Ltborn
Yet stay a while, forbeare thy bloudie hande,	Edw	5.5.75	Edward
O let me not die yet, stay, O stay a while.	Edw	5.5.101	Edward
A plague upon you, let me sleepe a while.	F1283	4.1.129	Benvol
we'le into another roome and drinke a while, and then we'le go	F1556	4.5.52	P Robin
My Lord, beseech you give me leave a while,	F1621	4.6.64	Faust
Leave me a while, to ponder on my sinnes.	F1736	5.1.63	Faust
Adders and serpents, let me breathe a while:	F1980	5.2.184	Faust
Within a while great heapes grow of a tittle.	Ovid's Elegies		1.8.90
Would Tithon might but talke of thee a while,	Ovid's Elegies		1.13.35
So having paus'd a while, at last shee said:	Hero and Leander		1.337
Harken a while, and I will tell you why:	Hero and Leander		1.385
AWHILE			
Faire Troian, hold my golden bowe awhile,	Dido	3.3.7	Dido
AWKWARD (See also AUKWARD)			
With awkward windes, and sore tempests driven/To fall on	Edw	4.7.34	Baldck
A WOOING			
Well, if he come a wooing he shall speede,	Dido	4.5.36	Nurse
AWRIE			
She hath not trode <tred> awrie that doth denie it,	Ovid's Elegies		3.13.5
AXE			
and this curtle-axe/Are adjuncts more beseeming Tamburlaine.	1Tamb	1.2.42	Tamb
See where it is, the keenest Cutle-axe <curtle-axe>,/That ere	1Tamb	2.3.55	Tamb
and Danes/That with the Holbard, Lance, and murthering Axe,	2Tamb	1.1.23	Uribas
Armour of proofe, horse, helme, and Curtle-axe,	2Tamb	1.3.44	Tamb
or with a Curtle-axe/To hew thy flesh and make a gaping wound?	2Tamb	3.2.96	Tamb
AXELTREE			
Doubtles Apollos Axeltree is crackt,	Dido	4.1.11	Achat
That almost brent the Axeltree of heaven,	1Tamb	4.2.50	Tamb
Quiver about the Axeltree of heaven.	2Tamb	1.1.90	Orcan
AXES			
Who with steele Pol-axes dasht out their braines.	Dido	2.1.199	Aeneas
The burdened axes with thy force will bend;	Lucan, First Booke		57
AXIOMS			
Excepting against Doctors [axioms],	P 393	7.33	Guise
AXIS			
Whose shoulders beare the Axis of the world,	2Tamb	5.3.59	Tamb
AXLE			
And <Faustus all> jointly move upon one Axle-tree,	F 592	2.2.41	Mephst
AXLE-TREE			
And <Faustus all> jointly move upon one Axle-tree,	F 592	2.2.41	Mephst
AXLETREE (See also AXELTREE)			
That drawes the day from heavens cold axletree.	Ovid's Elegies		1.13.2
AXON			
Those of Bituriges and light Axon pikes;	Lucan, First Booke		424
AY (See also AIE, I)			
Ay me!	Dido	1.1.72	Venus
And my pin'd soule resolv'd in liquid [ayre] <ay>,	1Tamb	5.1.300	Bajzth
Ay me, O what a world of land and sea,	Lucan, First Booke		13
AYD			
you to come so farre/Without the ayd or conduct of their ships.	Jew	1.1.94	Barab
And therefore are we to request your ayd.	Jew	1.2.49	Govnr
I'le write unto his Majesty for ayd,	Jew	2.2.40	Bosco
AYDE			
For this so friendly ayde in time of neede.	Dido	1.1.138	Venus
Thankes good Iarbus for thy friendly ayde,	Dido	5.1.75	Aeneas
I shall not need/To crave Apolloes ayde, or Bacchus helpe;	Lucan, First Booke		65

AYDE (cont.)
Must Pompeis followers with strangers ayde, . . . Lucan, First Booke 314
Such rampierd gates beseiged Cittyes ayde, . . . Ovid's Elegies 1.6.29
Pardon me Jove, thy weapons ayde me nought, . . . Ovid's Elegies 2.1.19
We praise: great goddesse ayde my enterprize. . . . Ovid's Elegies 3.2.56
AYE (Homograph; See also AIE, I)
Dido in these flames/Hath burnt her selfe, aye me, unhappie me! Dido 5.1.315 Anna
Dido I come to thee, aye me Aeneas. . . . . . . Dido 5.1.318 Iarbus
Aye me poore soule when these begin to jarre. . . . . Edw 2.2.72 Queene
And sit for aye inthronized in heaven, ... Edw 5.1.109 Edward
Aye me, see where he comes, and they with him, ... Edw 5.6.22 Queene
Aye me I warne what profits some few howers, ... Ovid's Elegies 1.4.59
Aye me, thy body hath no worthy weedes. . . . . . Ovid's Elegies 1.8.26
Aye me rare gifts unworthy such a happe. . . . . . Ovid's Elegies 1.14.54
Aye me an Eunuch keepes my mistrisse chaste, ... Ovid's Elegies 2.3.1
Aye me poore soule, why is my cause so good. . . . . Ovid's Elegies 2.5.8
Aye me why is it knowne to her so well? . . . . . Ovid's Elegies 2.17.8
Aye me she cries, to love, why art a shamed? . . . . Ovid's Elegies 2.18.8
Aye me, let not my warnings cause my paine. . . . . Ovid's Elegies 2.19.34
art thou aye gravely plaied? . . . . Ovid's Elegies 3.1.36
Drye winters aye, and sunnes in heate extreame. . . . Ovid's Elegies 3.5.106
Let me, and them by it be aye be-friended. . . . . Ovid's Elegies 3.12.36
But you are faire (aye me) so wondrous faire, ... Hero and Leander 1.287
Aye me, such words as these should I abhor, ... Hero and Leander 1.339
Aye me, Leander cryde, th'enamoured sunne, ... Hero and Leander 2.202
AYER
Marching about the ayer with armed men, ... 2Tamb 5.2.34 Amasia
AYLE
What a devill ayle you two? . . . . F1179 4.1.25 P Benvol
AYL'ST
Why, what ayl'st thou? . . . . Jew 3.3.6 Abigal
AYM'D
Know, Calymath, I aym'd thy overthrow, ... Jew 5.5.83 Barab
AYME
the armye I have gathered now shall ayme/more at thie end then Paris ms28,p391 Guise
AYRE
The ayre is pleasant, and the soyle most fit/For Cities, and Dido 1.1.178 Achat
To dull the ayre with my discoursive moane. . . . . Dido 1.1.248 Aeneas
Here she was wont to sit, but saving ayre/Is nothing here, and Dido 2.1.13 Achat
And swong her howling in the emptie ayre, ... Dido 2.1.248 Aeneas
The ayre is cleere, and Southerne windes are whist, . . . Dido 4.1.25 Aeneas
Ten thousand Cupids hover in the ayre, ... Dido 4.4.48 Dido
The ayre wherein they breathe, the water, fire, . . . Dido 4.4.75 Dido
Not bloudie speares appearing in the ayre, ... Dido 4.4.117 Dido
And my pin'd soule resolv'd in liquid [ayre] <ay>, . . . 1Tamb 5.1.300 Bajzth
Water and ayre being simbolisde in one, ... 2Tamb 1.3.23 Tamb
That I may vanish ore the earth in ayre, ... Jew 1.2.264 Barab
That I may hover with her in the Ayre, ... Jew 2.1.62 Barab
We turne into the Ayre to purge our selves: . . . . Jew 2.3.46 Barab
Earth melt to ayre, gone is my soveraigne, ... Edw 4.7.103 Spencr
lowly earth/Should drinke his bloud, mounts up into the ayre: Edw 5.1.14 Edward
But can my ayre of life continue long, ... Edw 5.3.17 Edward
[Touching his journey through the world and ayre], . . . F1145 3.3.58A 3Chor
While th'earth the sea, and ayre the earth sustaines; . Lucan, First Booke 89
With cracke of riven ayre and hideous sound, ... Lucan, First Booke 153
shoots/Alongst the ayre and [nought] <not> resisting it/Falls, Lucan, First Booke 157
south were cause/I know not, but the cloudy ayre did frown; Lucan, First Booke 237
and rings of fire/Flie in the ayre, and dreadfull bearded Lucan, First Booke 526
But in the ayre let these words come to nought, . . . Ovid's Elegies 2.14.41
AYRIE
Made Hebe to direct her ayrie wheeles/Into the windie countrie Dido 1.1.56 Venus
When ayrie creatures warre amongst themselves: . . . . Dido 4.2.7 Iarbus
AZAMOR
From Azamor to Tunys neare the sea, ... 2Tamb 1.3.133 Usumc
AZUR'D
In wanton Arethusa's [azur'd] <azure> armes, ... F1786 5.1.113 Faust
AZURE
In wanton Arethusa's [azur'd] <azure> armes, ... F1786 5.1.113 Faust
For here the stately azure pallace stood, ... Hero and Leander 2.165
Which is with azure circling lines empal'd, ... Hero and Leander 2.274
AZURED
Whose azured gates enchased with his name, ... Dido 1.1.101 Jupitr
BABES
And offer luke-warme bloud, of new borne babes. . . . F 402 2.1.14 Faust
And why dire poison give you babes unborne? . . . . Ovid's Elegies 2.14.28
BABILON
Now Babilon, (proud through our spoile) should stoop, . Lucan, First Booke 10
BABLING (See also BRABBLING)
Vaine babling speech, and pleasant peace thou lovedst. . Ovid's Elegies 2.6.26
BABYLON
Till we prepare our martch to Babylon, ... 2Tamb 4.3.93 Tamb
To Babylon my Lords, to Babylon. . . . . . . 2Tamb 4.3.133 Tamb
And this eternisde citie Babylon, ... 2Tamb 5.1.35 Govnr
Thou desperate Governour of Babylon, ... 2Tamb 5.1.49 Therid
The stately buildings of faire Babylon, ... 2Tamb 5.1.63 Tamb
The sturdy Governour of Babylon, ... 2Tamb 5.1.81 Therid
There lies more gold than Babylon is worth, ... 2Tamb 5.1.116 Govnr
bank, right opposite/Against the Westerne gate of Babylon. 2Tamb 5.1.122 Govnr
When this is done, we'll martch from Babylon, ... 2Tamb 5.1.127 Tamb
Shall pay me tribute for, in Babylon. . . . . . 2Tamb 5.1.167 Tamb
And here may we behold great Babylon, ... 2Tamb 5.2.4 Callap
Before his hoste be full from Babylon, ... 2Tamb 5.2.9 Callap

BABYLONIANS			
That he may win the Babylonians hearts,	1Tamb	1.1.90	Cosroe
BACCHINALL			
Yet seemely like a Thracian Bacchinall/That tyr'd doth rashly	Ovid's Elegies	1.14.21	
BACCHUS			
And Bacchus vineyards [over-spread] <ore-spread> the world:	Jew	4.2.92	Ithimr
I shall not need/To crave Apolloes ayde, or Bacchus helpe;	Lucan, First Booke	65	
So having conquerd Inde, was Bacchus hew,	Ovid's Elegies	1.2.47	
Apollo, Bacchus, and the Muses may,	Ovid's Elegies	1.3.11	
from their crowne/Phoebus and Bacchus wisht were hanging downe.	Ovid's Elegies	1.14.32	
Ceres and Bacchus Country-men adore,	Ovid's Elegies	3.2.53	
The fathers thigh should unborne Bacchus lacke.	Ovid's Elegies	3.3.40	
with Romulus, temples brave/Bacchus, Alcides, and now Caesar	Ovid's Elegies	3.7.52	
Horned Bacchus graver furie doth distill,	Ovid's Elegies	3.14.17	
Where by one hand, light headed Bacchus hoong,	Hero and Leander	1.139	
BACHELOR (See BATCHELER)			
BACK			
my Doves are back returnd,/Who warne me of such daunger prest	Dido	3.2.21	Venus
And bid him turne [him] <his> back to war with us,	1Tamb	2.5.100	Tamb
For treading on the back of Bajazeth,	1Tamb	4.2.77	Bajzth
Waiting the back returne of Charons boat,	1Tamb	5.1.464	Tamb
Come back again (sweet death) and strike us both:	2Tamb	3.4.12	Olymp
despatch Embassadours/To Poland, to call Henry back againe,	P 556	11.21	QnMoth
Wee'l beat him back, and drive him to his death,	P 929	18.30	Navrre
So will I now, and thou shalt back to France.	Edw	1.1.185	BshpCv
he comes not back,/Unlesse the sea cast up his shipwrack body.	Edw	1.4.204	Lncstr
And could my crownes revenew bring him back,	Edw	1.4.308	Edward
He weares a lords revenewe on his back,	Edw	1.4.407	Mortmr
That hees repeald, and sent for back againe,	Edw	2.1.18	Spencr
Looke to your owne crowne, if you back him thus.	Edw	2.2.93	Warwck
mine honor undertake/To carrie him, and bring him back againe,	Edw	2.5.80	Penbrk
Upon mine oath I will returne him back.	Edw	2.5.88	Penbrk
to carrie him/Unto your highnes, and to bring him back.	Edw	3.1.100	Arundl
Call thou them back, I have no power to speake.	Edw	5.1.93	Edward
And then from thence to Bartley back againe:	Edw	5.2.61	Mortmr
But bring his head back presently to me.	Edw	5.6.54	King
That on a furies back came post from Rome,	F1161	4.1.7	Fredrk
nor could the bed-rid parents/Keep back their sons, or womens	Lucan, First Booke	503	
My feared hands thrice back she did repell.	Ovid's Elegies	1.7.62	
And makes large streams back to their fountaines flow,	Ovid's Elegies	1.8.6	
And turned streames run back-ward to their fountaines.	Ovid's Elegies	2.1.26	
Her trembling hand writ back she might not doo.	Ovid's Elegies	2.2.6	
Or any back made rough with stripes imbrace?	Ovid's Elegies	2.7.22	
Too late you looke back, when with anchors weighd,	Ovid's Elegies	2.11.23	
I yeeld, and back my wit from battells bring,	Ovid's Elegies	2.18.11	
If I a lover bee by thee held back.	Ovid's Elegies	3.5.22	
Victorious Perseus a wingd steedes back takes.	Ovid's Elegies	3.11.24	
And Rams with hornes their hard heads wreathed back.	Ovid's Elegies	3.12.17	
BACK'D			
And toward Calabria, back'd by Sicily,	Jew	5.3.9	Calym
BACKE			
Have oft driven backe the horses of the night,	Dido	1.1.26	Jupitr
that under his conduct/We might saile backe to Troy, and be	Dido	2.1.18	Aeneas
on the sand/Assayd with honey words to turne them backe:	Dido	2.1.137	Aeneas
His hands bound at his backe, and both his eyes/Turnd up to	Dido	2.1.151	Aeneas
By this I got my father on my backe,	Dido	2.1.265	Aeneas
Thinking to beare her on my backe abourd,	Dido	2.1.284	Aeneas
As for Aeneas he swomme quickly backe,	Dido	2.1.296	Achat
Doth Dido call me backe?	Dido	3.1.53	Iarbus
Bearing her bowe and quiver at her backe.	Dido	3.3.55	Achat
Come backe, come backe, I heare her crye a farre,	Dido	4.3.27	Aeneas
I faine would goe, yet beautie calles me backe:	Dido	4.3.46	Aeneas
And shrunke not backe, knowing my love was there?	Dido	4.4.146	Dido
But he shrinkes backe, and now remembring me,	Dido	5.1.190	Dido
Once didst thou goe, and he came backe againe,	Dido	5.1.196	Dido
Now bring him backe, and thou shalt be a Queene,	Dido	5.1.197	Dido
And ride upon his backe unto my love:	Dido	5.1.250	Dido
But he remembring me shrinkes backe againe:	Dido	5.1.260	Dido
I long to see thee backe returne from thence,	1Tamb	1.1.76	Mycet
Returne our Mules and emptie Camels backe,	1Tamb	1.2.76	Agidas
And die before I brought you backe again.	2Tamb	1.2.73	Almeda
Before whom (mounted on a Lions backe)/Rhamnusia beares a	2Tamb	3.4.56	Therid
Now lanch our Gallies backe againe to Sea,	Jew	1.2.29	Calym
Nay backe, Abigall,	Jew	1.2.348	Barab
Every ones price is written on his backe,	Jew	2.3.3	2Offcr
No, Mathias, no, but sends them backe,/And when he comes, she	Jew	2.3.261	Barab
backe lanes through the Gardens I chanc'd to cast mine eye up	Jew	3.1.17	P Pilia
Though womans modesty should hale me backe,	Jew	4.2.45	Curtzn
As for the peeres that backe the cleargie thus,	Edw	1.4.104	Edward
He will but talke with him and send him backe.	Edw	2.5.59	Arundl
Some whirle winde fetche them backe, or sincke them all:--	Edw	4.6.59	Mortmr
Returne it backe and dip it in my bloud.	Edw	5.1.120	Edward
If thou deny it I must <wil> backe to hell.	F 426	2.1.38	Mephst
And mounted then upon a Dragons backe,	F 771	2.3.50	2Chor
Whilst on thy backe his hollinesse ascends/Saint Peters Chaire	F 869	3.1.91	Raymnd
From Bruno's backe, ascends Saint Peters Chaire.	F 876	3.1.98	Pope
And walke upon the dreadfull Adders backe,	F 919	3.1.141	Pope
circle, and stand close at my backe, and stir not for thy life,	F1113	3.3.26	P Robin
to supper, and a Tester in your purse, and go backe againe.	F1122	3.3.35	P Robin
be thou transformed to/A dog, and carry him upon thy backe;	F1131	3.3.44	Mephst
Go backe, and see the State in readinesse.	F1159	4.1.5	Mrtino
He was upon the devils backe late enough; and if he be so farre	F1190	4.1.36	P Benvol
what, wil you goe on horse backe, or on foote?	F App	p.239 95	P Mephst

BACKE (cont.)			
then having whiskt/His taile athwart his backe, and crest	Lucan, First Booke	211	
hils, hence to the mounts/Pirene, and so backe to Rome againe.	Lucan, First Booke	689	
loves wrack/Shall follow thee, their hands tied at their backe.	Ovid's Elegies	1.2.32	
Strike backe the barre, night fast away doth goe.	Ovid's Elegies	1.6.32	
Or least his love oft beaten backe should waine.	Ovid's Elegies	1.8.76	
Straight being read, will her to write much backe,	Ovid's Elegies	1.11.19	
And call the sunnes white horses [backe] <blacke> at noone.	Ovid's Elegies	2.1.24	
So wavering Cupid bringes me backe amaine,	Ovid's Elegies	2.9.33	
In vaine why flyest backe? force conjoynes us now:	Ovid's Elegies	3.2.19	
For shame presse not her backe with thy hard knee.	Ovid's Elegies	3.2.24	
They call him backe:	Ovid's Elegies	3.2.75	
But when her lover came, had she drawne backe,	Ovid's Elegies	3.3.39	
Flye backe his [streame] <shame> chargd, the streame chargd,	Ovid's Elegies	3.5.44	
The Sunne turnd backe from Atreus cursed table?	Ovid's Elegies	3.11.39	
That runs along his backe, but my rude pen,	Hero and Leander	1.69	
And looking backe, saw Neptune follow him.	Hero and Leander	2.176	
The mace returning backe, his owne hand hit,	Hero and Leander	2.211	
BACKES			
have martcht/Foure hundred miles with armour on their backes,	2Tamb	1.3.175	Usumc
shall sweat/With carrieng pearle and treasure on their backes.	2Tamb	3.5.167	Techel
Go horse these traytors on your fiery backes,	F1403	4.2.79	Faust
BACKEWARD			
Backeward and forwards nere five thousand leagues.	2Tamb	5.3.144	Tamb
Night goes away: the dores barre backeward strike.	Ovid's Elegies	1.6.24	
BACKT			
And backt by stout Lanceres of Germany,	2Tamb	1.1.155	Sgsmnd
BACK-WARD			
And turned streames run back-ward to their fountaines.	Ovid's Elegies	2.1.26	
BACKWARD			
Forward, and backward, Anagramatis'd <and Agramithist>:	F 237	1.3.9	Faust
Now go not backward: no, Faustus, be resolute.	F 394	2.1.6	Faust
Forward and backward, to curse Faustus to hell.	F1075	3.2.95	Faust
Forward and backward, to curse Faustus to hell.	F App	p.232 26	Faust
Or darts which Parthians backward shoot) marcht on/And then	Lucan, First Booke	232	
BACON			
staffe; excellent, he stands as if he were begging of Bacon.	Jew	4.1.155	P Ithimr
my father <grandfather> was a Gammon of Bacon, and my mother	F 696	2.2.145	P Glutny
BACONS			
And beare wise Bacons, and [Abanus] <Albanus> <Albertus>	F 181	1.1.153	Valdes
BAD (Homograph)			
is Aeneas, were he clad/In weedes as bad as ever Irus ware.	Dido	2.1.85	Dido
I have, and sorrow for his bad successe:	1Tamb	4.3.28	Souldn
must now performe/The forme of Faustus fortunes, good or bad,	F 8	Prol.8	1Chor
bad him take as much as he would for three-farthings; so he	F1528	4.5.24	P Carter
Doctor Fauster bad me ride him night and day, and spare him no	F1540	4.5.36	P HrsCsr
Judge you the rest, being tyrde <tride> she bad me kisse.	Ovid's Elegies	1.5.25	
Rhesus fell/And Captive horses bad their Lord fare-well.	Ovid's Elegies	1.9.24	
Or prostitute thy beauty for bad prize.	Ovid's Elegies	1.10.42	
cold hemlocks flower/Wherein bad hony Corsicke Bees did power.	Ovid's Elegies	1.12.10	
Their wedlocks pledges veng'd their husbands bad.	Ovid's Elegies	2.14.32	
Either she was foule, or her attire was bad,	Ovid's Elegies	3.6.1	
Who bad thee lie downe here against thy will?	Ovid's Elegies	3.6.78	
When bad fates take good men, I am forbod,	Ovid's Elegies	3.8.35	
BADE			
by him, for he bade me I should ride him into no water; now,	F App	p.240 130	P HrsCsr
BADGETHS			
Desart of Arabia/To those that stand on Badgeths lofty Tower,	2Tamb	1.1.109	Sgsmnd
BAG			
of an old Churle in a <an olde> leather <leatherne> bag;	F 675	2.2.124	P Covet
BAGDAD (See BADGETHS, BAGDETS)			
BAGDETS			
So now he hangs like Bagdets Governour,	2Tamb	5.1.158	Tamb
BAGGE			
Hide the bagge.	Jew	3.1.23	Curtzn
BAGGS			
The East winds in Ulisses baggs we shut,	Ovid's Elegies	3.11.29	
BAGOUS			
Bagous whose care doth thy Mistrisse bridle,	Ovid's Elegies	2.2.1	
BAGS			
Who smiles to see how full his bags are cramb'd,	Jew	Prol.31	Machvl
Bags of fiery Opals, Saphires, Amatists,	Jew	1.1.25	Barab
up to the Jewes counting-house where I saw some bags of mony,	Jew	3.1.19	P Pilia
And neither gets him friends, nor fils his bags,	Jew	5.2.39	Barab
BAIES			
Pay vowes to Jove, engirt thy hayres with baies,	Ovid's Elegies	1.7.36	
BAILE			
Hands of good fellow, I will be his baile/For this offence:	P 622	12.35	King
BAIRSETH			
Obed in Bairseth, Nones in Portugall,	Jew	1.1.125	Barab
BAITED			
How oft have I beene baited by these peeres?	Edw	2.2.201	Edward
BAJAZETH			
As from the mouth of mighty Bajazeth.	1Tamb	3.1.20	Fesse
I meane t'incounter with that Bajazeth.	1Tamb	3.3.65	Tamb
He cals me Bajazeth, whom you call Lord.	1Tamb	3.3.67	Bajzth
And dar'st thou bluntly call me Bajazeth?	1Tamb	3.3.71	Bajzth
Such good successe happen to Bajazeth.	1Tamb	3.3.116	Zabina
Now strengthen him against the Turkish Bajazeth,	1Tamb	3.3.191	Zenoc
Not all the world shall ransom Bajazeth.	1Tamb	3.3.232	Tamb
For treading on the back of Bajazeth,	1Tamb	4.2.77	Bajzth
Are fled from Bajazeth, and remaine with me,	1Tamb	4.2.80	Tamb
Is this a place for mighty Bajazeth?	1Tamb	4.2.83	Bajzth

Headword / Line	Work	Ref		Speaker
BAJAZETH (cont.)				
There whiles he lives, shal Bajazeth be kept,	1Tamb	4.2.85		Tamb
Shall talke how I have handled Bajazeth.	1Tamb	4.2.97		Tamb
have ye lately heard/The overthrow of mightie Bajazeth,	1Tamb	4.3.24		Arabia
And now Bajazeth, hast thou any stomacke?	1Tamb	4.4.10		Tamb
Eat Bajazeth.	1Tamb	4.4.99	P	Zabina
Hath Bajazeth bene fed to day?	1Tamb	5.1.192		Tamb
Pray for us Bajazeth, we are going.	1Tamb	5.1.213		Tamb
Why live we Bajazeth, and build up neasts,	1Tamb	5.1.249		Zabina
Accursed Bajazeth, whose words of ruth,	1Tamb	5.1.270		Bajzth
Sweet Bajazeth, I will prolong thy life,	1Tamb	5.1.283		Zabina
Now Bajazeth, abridge thy banefull daies,	1Tamb	5.1.286		Bajzth
The braines of Bajazeth, my Lord and Soveraigne?	1Tamb	5.1.307		Zabina
O Bajazeth, my husband and my Lord,	1Tamb	5.1.308		Zabina
O Bajazeth, O Turk, O Emperor.	1Tamb	5.1.309		Zabina
of these Eastern parts/Plac'd by the issue of great Bajazeth,	2Tamb	1.1.2		Orcan
pity the ruthfull plight/Of Callapine, the sonne of Bajazeth,	2Tamb	1.2.2		Callap
son and successive heire to the late mighty Emperour Bajazeth,	2Tamb	3.1.2	P	Orcan
as when Bajazeth/My royall Lord and father fild the throne,	2Tamb	3.1.11		Callap
That since the heire of mighty Bajazeth/(An Emperour so	2Tamb	3.1.22		Callap
BAK'D				
Rude husband-men bak'd not their corne before,	Ovid's Elegies			3.9.7
BALAAM				
As fell to Saule, to Balaam and the rest,	2Tamb	2.1.54		Fredrk
BALANCE (See BALLANCE)				
BALD				
Begin betimes, Occasion's bald behind,	Jew	5.2.44		Barab
<Where thou shalt see a troupe of bald-pate Friers>,	F 833	(HC265) A		Mephst
BALDE				
balde scalpes [thin] <thine> hoary flieces/And riveld cheekes I	Ovid's Elegies			1.8.111
BALDOCK (See also BALDUCK)				
Baldock:	Edw	2.1.6		Spencr
I for a while, but Baldock marke the end,	Edw	2.1.16		Spencr
My name is Baldock, and my gentrie/Is fetcht from Oxford, not	Edw	2.2.243		Baldck
The fitter art thou Baldock for my turne,	Edw	2.2.245		Edward
Baldock is with the king,/A goodly chauncelor, is he not my	Edw	4.6.42		Queene
Is with that smoothe toongd scholler Baldock gone,	Edw	4.6.57		Rice
Baldock, this drowsines/Betides no good, here even we are	Edw	4.7.44		Spencr
BALDOCKE				
How Baldocke, Spencer, and their complices,	Edw	4.6.78		Mortmr
Come Spencer, come Baldocke, come sit downe by me,	Edw	4.7.16		Edward
Spencer and Baldocke, by no other names,	Edw	4.7.56		Leistr
Sweete Spencer, gentle Baldocke, part we must.	Edw	4.7.96		Edward
BALD-PATE				
<Where thou shalt see a troupe of bald-pate Friers>,	F 833	(HC265) A		Mephst
BALDUCK				
Then Balduck, you must cast the scholler off,	Edw	2.1.31		Spencr
Whose there, Balduck?	Edw	2.1.70		Neece
BALEFULL				
To live in greefe and balefull discontent,	Edw	1.2.48		Queene
BALIO				
Let your Balio and your Belcher come here, and Ile knocke them,	F App	p.230 45	P	Clown
BALIOL (See also BANIO)				
two divels presently to fetch thee away Baliol and Belcher.	F App	p.230 44	P	Wagner
BALIOLL				
Balioll and Belcher, spirits away.	F App	p.230 50	P	Wagner
How Balioll and Belcher.	F App	p.231 67	P	Wagner
BALKE				
Sir, must not come so neare and balke their lips.	Edw	2.5.103		Penbrk
Thy mouth to taste of many meates did balke.	Ovid's Elegies			2.6.30
BALL				
Say Paris, now shall Venus have the ball?	Dido	3.2.12		Juno
And Paris judgement of the heavenly ball,	Dido	3.2.44		Juno
charme to keepe the windes/Within the closure of a golden ball,	Dido	4.4.100		Dido
in peeces, give me the sworde with a ball of wildefire upon it.	1Tamb	5.1.312	P	Zabina
BALLACE				
For ballace, emptie Didos treasurie,	Dido	3.1.126		Dido
BALLADS				
Ballads and rimes, made of thy overthrow.	Edw	2.2.178		Mortmr
BALLANCE				
Whose golden Crowne might ballance my content:	Dido	3.4.36		Dido
lives were weigh'd/In equall care and ballance with our owne,	1Tamb	5.1.42		Govnr
Where fancie is in equall ballance pais'd).	Hero and Leander			2.32
BALLASSED (See also BALLACE)				
Are ballassed with billowes watrie weight.	Dido	1.1.226		Aeneas
BALLE				
The golden balle of heavens eternal fire,	2Tamb	2.4.2		Tamb
BALLES				
With balles of wilde fire in their murdering pawes,	Dido	2.1.217		Aeneas
And feast the birds with their bloud-shotten balles,	Dido	3.2.35		Venus
and in her eyes/Two eye-balles shine, and double light thence	Ovid's Elegies			1.8.16
BALS				
of the war/Threw naked swords and sulphur bals of fire,	2Tamb	3.2.41		Tamb
BALSAMUM				
which a cunning Alcumist/Distilled from the purest Balsamum,	2Tamb	4.2.60		Olymp
BALSERA				
And this is Balsera their chiefest hold,	2Tamb	3.3.3		Therid
BAN				
In nights deepe silence why the ban-dogges barke.	Ovid's Elegies			2.19.40
BANCHO				
Great summes of mony lying in the bancho;	Jew	4.1.74		Barab
BANCKES				
Saying, why sadly treadst my banckes upon,	Ovid's Elegies			3.5.53

BAND (Homograph)
And after him his band of Mirmidons, Dido 2.1.216 Aeneas
staid, with wrath and hate/Of our expreslesse band inflictions. 1Tamb 5.1.282 Bajzth
Tis not a black coate and a little band, Edw 2.1.33 Spencr
Loe, with a band of bowmen and of pikes, Edw 3.1.36 SpncrP
To passe the Ocean with a band of men, F 334 1.3.106 Faust
This [band] <hand> that all behind us might be quail'd, Lucan, First Booke 370
Here every band applauded,/And with their hands held up, all Lucan, First Booke 387
Sooth Lovers watch till sleepe the hus-band charmes, Ovid's Elegies 1.9.25
I had in hand/Which for his heaven fell on the Gyants band. Ovid's Elegies 2.1.16
BANDES
Let us unite our royall bandes in one, 1Tamb 4.3.17 Souldn
where/A fury leades the Emathian bandes, from thence/To the Lucan, First Booke 687
Beholde thy kinsmans Caesars prosperous bandes, Ovid's Elegies 1.2.51
BANDIE
Ile bandie with the Barons and the Earles, Edw 1.1.137 Edward
BAN-DOGGES
In nights deepe silence why the ban-dogges barke. Ovid's Elegies 2.19.40
BANDS (Homograph)
Kist him, imbrast him, and unloosde his bands, Dido 2.1.158 Aeneas
Convaid me from their crooked nets and bands: Dido 2.1.222 Aeneas
And warlike bands of Christians renied, 1Tamb 3.1.9 Bajzth
and stout Bythinians/Came to my bands full fifty thousand more, 2Tamb 3.5.42 Trebiz
A dissolution of the slavish Bands/Wherein the Turke hath Jew 5.2.77 Barab
Weaponles must I fall and die in bands, Edw 2.6.3 Gavstn
And all bands of that death presaging aliance. Lucan, First Booke 114
Other that Caesars barbarous bands were spread/Along Nar floud Lucan, First Booke 471
BANE
She humbly did beseech him for our bane, Dido 1.1.60 Venus
In few, the blood of Hydra, Lerna's bane; Jew 3.4.100 Barab
BANEFULL
A sight as banefull to their soules I think/As are Thessalian 1Tamb 5.1.132 Tamb
Enforce thee run upon the banefull pikes. 1Tamb 5.1.220 Bajzth
Now Bajazeth, abridge thy banefull daies, 1Tamb 5.1.286 Bajzth
And feeds upon the banefull tree of hell, 2Tamb 2.3.19 Orcan
BANIO (See also BALIOL)
Banio, Belcher. F 373 1.4.31 P Wagner
O Lord I pray sir, let Banio and Belcher go sleepe. F App p.231 68 P Clown
BANIOS
serve you, would you teach me to raise up Banios and Belcheos? F App p.230 57 P Clown
BANISH
Banish that ticing dame from forth your mouth, Dido 4.3.31 Achat
Yet Barrabas we will not banish thee, Jew 1.2.100 Govnr
with us that be his peeres/To banish or behead that Gaveston? Edw 1.2.43 Mortmr
Either banish him that was the cause thereof, Edw 1.4.60 ArchBp
Are you content to banish him the realme? Edw 1.4.84 ArchBp
How fast they run to banish him I love, Edw 1.4.94 Edward
Can this be true twas good to banish him, Edw 1.4.245 Lncstr
To banish him, and then to call him home, Edw 1.4.275 Mortmr
And therefore brother banish him for ever. Edw 2.2.211 Kent
Then banish that pernicious companie? Edw 3.1.213 Mortmr
Proud Edward, doost thou banish me thy presence? Edw 4.1.5 Kent
And as first wrongd the wronged some-times banish, Ovid's Elegies 1.8.79
BANISHD
That I am banishd, and must flie the land. Edw 1.4.107 Gavstn
BANISHED
The angrie king hath banished me the court: Edw 1.4.210 Queene
BANISHMENT
Confirme his banishment with our handes and seales. Edw 1.2.71 ArchBp
And that his banishment had changd her minde. Edw 2.1.26 Baldck
BANISHT
But I long more to see him banisht hence. Edw 1.4.5 Warwck
Thou from this land, I from my selfe am banisht. Edw 1.4.118 Edward
Or else be banisht from his highnesse presence. Edw 1.4.203 Queene
But he is banisht, theres small hope of him. Edw 2.1.15 Baldck
Then thou art banisht from the sight of heaven; F1715 5.1.42 OldMan
Might presently be banisht into hell, Hero and Leander 1.453
BANK
Under a hollow bank, right opposite/Against the Westerne gate 2Tamb 5.1.121 Govnr
I was begotten on a sunny bank: F 705 2.2.154 P Sloth
BANKE
As soone as Caesar got unto the banke/And bounds of Italy; Lucan, First Booke 225
Girt my shine browe with sea banke mirtle praise <sprays>. Ovid's Elegies 1.1.34
But sundry flouds in one banke never go, Ovid's Elegies 2.17.31
My foote upon the further banke to set. Ovid's Elegies 3.5.12
Rather thou large banke over-flowing river, Ovid's Elegies 3.5.19
BANKES
Who groveling in the mire of Zanthus bankes, Dido 2.1.150 Aeneas
Lie slumbering on the flowrie bankes of Nile, 1Tamb 4.1.9 Souldn
Millions of soules sit on the bankes of Styx, 1Tamb 5.1.463 Tamb
Have made the water swell above the bankes, 2Tamb 5.1.205 Techel
and the bordering Iles/Are gotten up by Nilus winding bankes: Jew 1.1.43 Barab
Whose billowes beating the resistlesse bankes, Jew 3.5.17 Govnr
And bankes raisd higher with their sepulchers: Edw 1.4.103 Edward
Whose bankes are set with Groves of fruitfull Vines. F 786 3.1.8 Faust
With winding bankes that cut it in two parts; F 814 3.1.36 Mephst
They came that dwell/By Nemes fields, and bankes of Satirus, Lucan, First Booke 421
Floud with [reede-growne] <redde-growne> slime bankes, till I Ovid's Elegies 3.5.1
BANKET
where her servitors passe through the hall/Bearing a banket, Dido 2.1.71 Serg
Go presently, and bring a banket forth, F 977 3.1.199 Pope
BANKROUTS (See also BANQUEROUT)
I fill'd the Jailes with Bankrouts in a yeare, Jew 2.3.193 Barab

BANKS			
the Feends infernall view/As are the blasted banks of Erebus:	1Tamb	5.1.244	Zabina
And from the boundes of Affrick to the banks/Of Ganges, shall	1Tamb	5.1.520	Tamb
from faire Natolia/Two hundred leagues, and on Danubius banks,	2Tamb	1.1.7	Orcan
[And] <The> banks ore which gold bearing Tagus flowes.	Ovid's Elegies	1.15.34	
BANNE			
I banne their soules to everlasting paines/And extreme tortures	Jew	1.2.166	Barab
BANNER			
When wert thou in the field with banner spred?	Edw	2.2.182	Mortmr
BANNERS			
And underneath thy banners march who will,	Edw	1.1.88	Mortmr
BANNOCKS			
For your lemmons you have lost, at Bannocks borne,	Edw	2.2.191	Lncstr
BANNOCKS BORNE			
For your lemmons you have lost, at Bannocks borne,	Edw	2.2.191	Lncstr
BANQUEROUT			
better/In which the Merchant wayles his banquerout debter.	Ovid's Elegies	1.12.26	
BANQUET (See also BANKET)			
Your men and you shall banquet in our Court,	Dido	1.2.39	Iarbus
Sit in this chaire and banquet with a Queene,	Dido	2.1.83	Dido
And banquet as two Sisters with the Gods?	Dido	3.2.29	Juno
Or banquet in bright honors burnisht hall,	Dido	4.3.10	Aeneas
Then let us freely banquet and carouse/Full bowles of wine unto	1Tamb	4.4.5	Tamb
And may this banquet proove as omenous,	1Tamb	4.4.23	Zabina
not the Turke and his wife make a goodly showe at a banquet?	1Tamb	4.4.58	P Tamb
Come let us goe and banquet in our tents:	2Tamb	1.1.160	Orcan
Come banquet and carouse with us a while,	2Tamb	1.1.165	Orcan
Now will we banquet on these plaines a while,	2Tamb	1.3.157	Tamb
Then wil we triumph, banquet and carouse,	2Tamb	1.3.218	Tamb
Come let us banquet and carrouse the whiles.	2Tamb	1.3.225	Tamb
provide a running Banquet;/Send to the Merchant, bid him bring	Jew	4.2.83	Curtzn
Come Amorous wag, first banquet and then sleep.	Jew	4.2.132	Curtzn
And banquet with him e're thou leav'st the Ile.	Jew	5.3.19	Msngr
To banquet with him in his Citadell?	Jew	5.3.20	Calym
There will he banquet them, but thee at home,	Jew	5.3.38	Msngr
Was this the banquet he prepar'd for us?	Jew	5.5.95	Calym
I pray my Lords have patience at this troublesome banquet.	F1058	3.2.78	Pope
He would not banquet, and carowse, and swill/Amongst the	F App	p.243 4	Wagner
Thy husband to a banquet goes with me,	Ovid's Elegies	1.4.1	
A brow for Love to banquet roiallye,	Hero and Leander	1.86	
BANQUETS			
Wine-bibbing banquets tell thy naughtinesse,	Ovid's Elegies	3.1.17	
What secret becks in banquets with her youths,	Ovid's Elegies	3.10.23	
Are banquets, Dorick musicke, midnight-revell,	Hero and Leander	1.301	
BANQUETTED			
We banquetted till overcome with wine,	Dido	2.1.178	Aeneas
BAPTIZ'D			
to some religious house/So I may be baptiz'd and live therein.	Jew	4.1.76	Barab
BAR (See also BARRE)			
Nor bar thy mind that magnanimitie,	2Tamb	5.3.200	Tamb
BARABAS (See also BARRABAS)			
Barabas,/Thy ships are safe,	Jew	1.1.49	1Merch
Know Barabas, doth ride in Malta Rhode,	Jew	1.1.86	2Merch
A Fleet of warlike Gallyes, Barabas,	Jew	1.1.146	1Jew
Why, Barabas, they come for peace or warre.	Jew	1.1.161	1Jew
Let's take our leaves; Farewell good Barabas.	Jew	1.1.175	2Jew
And Barabas now search this secret out.	Jew	1.1.177	Barab
Soft Barabas, there's more longs too't than so.	Jew	1.2.45	Govnr
And 'tis thy mony, Barabas, we seeke.	Jew	1.2.54	1Knght
Why Barabas wilt thou be christened?	Jew	1.2.81	Govnr
Out wretched Barabas,	Jew	1.2.118	Govnr
we have seiz'd upon the goods/And wares of Barabas, which being	Jew	1.2.133	Offcrs
Barabas, to staine our hands with blood/Is farre from us and	Jew	1.2.144	Govnr
Content thee, Barabas, thou hast nought but right.	Jew	1.2.152	Govnr
Oh yet be patient, gentle Barabas.	Jew	1.2.169	1Jew
Barabas, as hardly can we brooke/The cruell handling of	Jew	1.2.174	1Jew
Yet brother Barabas remember Job.	Jew	1.2.180	1Jew
Thy fatall birth-day, forlorne Barabas;	Jew	1.2.192	Barab
Good Barabas be patient.	Jew	1.2.199	2Jew
Farewell Barabas.	Jew	1.2.213	2Jew
No, Barabas is borne to better chance,	Jew	1.2.218	Barab
Not for my selfe, but aged Barabas:	Jew	1.2.228	Abigal
The Jew of Malta, wretched Barabas;	Jew	1.2.318	Abigal
Barabas, although thou art in mis-beleefe,	Jew	1.2.352	1Fryar
What, Barabas, whose goods were lately seiz'd?	Jew	1.2.383	Lodowk
Vex'd and tormented runnes poore Barabas/With fatall curses	Jew	2.1.5	Barab
Barabas, thou know'st I am the Governors sonne.	Jew	2.3.40	Lodowk
Whither walk'st thou, Barabas?	Jew	2.3.43	Lodowk
Well, Barabas, canst helpe me to a Diamond?	Jew	2.3.48	Lodowk
No, Barabas, I will deserve it first.	Jew	2.3.68	Lodowk
Good Barabas glance not at our holy Nuns.	Jew	2.3.86	Lodowk
And, Barabas, I'le beare thee company.	Jew	2.3.96	Lodowk
Oh Barabas well met;	Jew	2.3.218	Lodowk
I, Barabas, or else thou wrong'st me much.	Jew	2.3.255	Mthias
Barabas, is not that the widowes sonne?	Jew	2.3.279	Lodowk
Barabas, thou know'st I have lov'd thy daughter long.	Jew	2.3.288	Lodowk
Suffer me, Barabas, but to follow him.	Jew	2.3.340	Mthias
Hard-hearted Father, unkind Barabas,	Jew	3.3.36	Abigal
oh Barabas,/Though thou deservest hardly	Jew	3.3.73	Abigal
Barabas, thou hast--	Jew	4.1.28	2Fryar
I, but Barabas, remember Mathias and Don Lodowick.	Jew	4.1.43	P 2Fryar
Oh good Barabas come to our house.	Jew	4.1.77	1Fryar
Oh no, good Barabas come to our house.	Jew	4.1.78	2Fryar

BARABAS (cont.)			
And Barabas, you know--	Jew	4.1.79	2Fryar
Oh Barabas, their Lawes are strict.	Jew	4.1.82	1Fryar
Good Barabas, come to me.	Jew	4.1.87	2Fryar
But Barabas, who shall be your godfathers,	Jew	4.1.109	1Fryar
I warrant thee, Barabas.	Jew	4.1.113	1Fryar
Good Barabas let me goe.	Jew	4.1.184	1Fryar
Ten hundred thousand crownes,--Master Barabas.	Jew	4.2.71	P Ithimr
Sirra Barabas, send me a hundred crownes.	Jew	4.2.73	P Ithimr
Barabas send me three hundred Crownes.	Jew	4.3.1	Barab
Plaine Barabas: oh that wicked Curtezane!	Jew	4.3.2	Barab
He was not wont to call me Barabas.	Jew	4.3.3	Barab
Dost not know a Jew, one Barabas?	Jew	4.4.56	P Ithimr
So is the Turke, and Barabas the Jew.	Jew	5.1.51	1Offcr
My name is Barabas; I am a Jew.	Jew	5.1.72	Barab
but tell me, Barabas,/Canst thou, as thou reportest, make Malta	Jew	5.1.84	Calym
And Barabas, as erst we promis'd thee,	Jew	5.2.9	Calym
and Barabas we give/To guard thy person, these our Janizaries:	Jew	5.2.15	Calym
Farewell brave Jew, farewell great Barabas.	Jew	5.2.20	Calym
and what boots it thee/Poore Barabas, to be the Governour,	Jew	5.2.32	Barab
No, Barabas, this must be look'd into;	Jew	5.2.34	Barab
But Barabas will be more circumspect.	Jew	5.2.43	Barab
Arbitrament; and Barabas/At his discretion may dispose of both:	Jew	5.2.53	Barab
This, Barabas; since things are in thy power,	Jew	5.2.57	Govnr
'Twere slender policy for Barabas/To dispossesse himselfe of	Jew	5.2.65	Barab
Will Barabas recover Malta's losse?	Jew	5.2.74	Govnr
Will Barabas be good to Christians?	Jew	5.2.75	Govnr
Here is my hand, beleeve me, Barabas,	Jew	5.2.102	Govnr
Then will I, Barabas, about this coyne,	Jew	5.2.107	Govnr
From Barabas, Malta's Governor, I bring/A message unto mighty	Jew	5.3.13	Msngr
Yet would I gladly visit Barabas,	Jew	5.3.24	Calym
For well has Barabas deserv'd of us.	Jew	5.3.25	Calym
here, hold thee, Barabas,/I trust thy word, take what I	Jew	5.5.42	Govnr
Let us salute him. Save thee, Barabas.	Jew	5.5.54	Calym
I, Barabas, come Bashawes, attend.	Jew	5.5.59	Calym
thee greater curtesie/Then Barabas would have affoorded thee.	Jew	5.5.62	Govnr
Accursed Barabas, base Jew, relent?	Jew	5.5.73	Govnr
Then Barabas breath forth thy latest fate,	Jew	5.5.78	Barab
BARBARIAN			
In mannaging those fierce barbarian mindes:	Dido	1.1.92	Jupitr
in crimson silk/Shall ride before the on Barbarian Steeds:	2Tamb	1.2.47	Callap
BARBARIANS			
lust of warre/Hath made Barbarians drunke with Latin bloud?	Lucan, First Booke		9
BARBARISME			
Now poverty great barbarisme we hold.	Ovid's Elegies		3.7.4
BARBAROUS			
I but the barbarous sort doe threat our ships,	Dido	1.2.34	Serg
prophesies)/To raigne in Asia, and with barbarous Armes,	1Tamb	1.1.42	Meandr
Direct my weapon to his barbarous heart,	1Tamb	2.6.38	Cosroe
Barbarous and bloody Tamburlaine,	1Tamb	2.7.1	Cosroe
Let not a man so vile and barbarous,	1Tamb	3.2.26	Agidas
that makest us thus/The slaves to Scythians rude and barbarous.	1Tamb	3.3.271	Zabina
And let them die a death so barbarous.	1Tamb	5.1.351	Zenoc
Now shall his barbarous body be a pray/To beasts and foules,	2Tamb	2.3.14	Orcan
These barbarous Scythians full of cruelty,	2Tamb	3.4.19	Olymp
twixt our selves and thee/In this thy barbarous damned tyranny.	2Tamb	4.1.139	Orcan
Vild Tyrant, barbarous bloody Tamburlain.	2Tamb	5.1.133	Trebiz
will follow thee/Against these barbarous mis-beleeving Turkes.	Jew	2.2.46	Govnr
[As] <A> brood of barbarous Tygars having lapt/The bloud of	Lucan, First Booke		327
And Druides you now in peace renew/Your barbarous customes, and	Lucan, First Booke		447
Other that Caesars barbarous bands were spread/Along Nar floud	Lucan, First Booke		471
And far more barbarous then the French (his vassals)/And that	Lucan, First Booke		476
That I was mad, and barbarous all men cried,	Ovid's Elegies		1.7.19
bondes contained/From barbarous lips of some Atturney strained.	Ovid's Elegies		1.12.24
The barbarous Thratian soldier moov'd with nought,	Hero and Leander		1.81
BARBARS			
Sit downe, for weele be Barbars to your grace.	Edw	5.3.28	Matrvs
BARBARY			
Great Kings of Barbary, and my portly Bassoes,	1Tamb	3.1.1	Bajzth
Ye Moores and valiant men of Barbary,	1Tamb	3.3.89	Moroc
From Barbary unto the Westerne Inde,	1Tamb	5.1.518	Tamb
Is Barbary unpeopled for thy sake,	2Tamb	1.3.134	Usumc
All Barbary is unpeopled for thy sake.	2Tamb	1.3.149	Techel
our men of Barbary have martcht/Foure hundred miles with armour	2Tamb	1.3.174	Usumc
BARCKE			
The [haven] <heaven> touching barcke now nere the lea,	Ovid's Elegies		2.9.32
BARD			
But he whose steele-bard coffers are cramb'd full,	Jew	1.1.14	Barab
Let him within heare bard out lovers prate.	Ovid's Elegies		1.8.78
By thy meanes women of their rest are bard,	Ovid's Elegies		1.13.23
BARDE			
Ile not be barde the court for Gaveston.	Edw	2.2.90	Mortmr
BARDI			
And you French Bardi, whose immortal pens/Renowne the valiant	Lucan, First Booke		443
BARE (Homograph)			
And of my former riches rests no more/But bare remembrance;	Jew	2.1.10	Barab
And ducke as low as any bare-foot Fryar,	Jew	2.3.25	Barab
that but for one bare night/A hundred Duckets have bin freely	Jew	3.1.2	Curtzn
They weare no shirts, and they goe bare-foot too.	Jew	4.1.84	1Fryar
That in the Court I bare so great a traine.	P 968	19.38	Guise
And bare him to his death, and in a trenche/Strake off his	Edw	3.1.119	Arundl
but a [bare] <small> pention, and that buyes me <is> thirty	F 694	2.2.143	P Glutny
[Where such as beare <bare> his absence but with griefe],	F1141	3.3.54A	3Chor

BARE (cont.)			
Now hast thou but one bare houre to live, ...	F1927	5.2.131	Faust
in his nakednesse, the vilaine is bare, and out of service,	F App	p.229 7	P Wagner
Bare downe to hell her sonne, the pledge of peace, . .	Lucan, First Booke	113	
his owne waight/Keepe him within the ground, his armes al bare,	Lucan, First Booke	140	
Strayd bare-foote through sole places on a time. . .	Ovid's Elegies	3.5.50	
And knocks his bare brest with selfe-angry hands. . .	Ovid's Elegies	3.8.10	
About her naked necke his bare armes threw. . . .	Hero and Leander	1.42	
And in his heart revenging malice bare:	Hero and Leander	2.208	
BARE-FOOT			
And ducke as low as any bare-foot Fryar, ...	Jew	2.3.25	Barab
They weare no shirts, and they goe bare-foot too. . .	Jew	4.1.84	1Fryar
BARE-FOOTE			
Strayd bare-foote through sole places on a time. . .	Ovid's Elegies	3.5.50	
BARELY			
The very Custome barely comes to more/Then many Merchants of	Jew	1.1.63	1Merch
So that for proofe, he barely beares the name: . . .	P 131	2.74	Guise
BARGAINE			
late by horse flesh, and this bargaine will set me up againe.	F1465	4.4.9	P HrsCsr
BARK (See also BARCKE, BARQUE)			
Wel, bark ye dogs.	2Tamb	4.1.181	Tamb
BARKE (Homograph)			
I and myne armie come to lode thy barke/With soules of thousand	2Tamb	5.3.73	Tamb
And by the barke a canker creepes me up, ...	Edw	2.2.18	Mortmr
Now on my life, theile neither barke nor bite. . . .	Edw	4.3.13	Edward
The Cedar tall spoyld of his barke retaines. . . .	Ovid's Elegies	1.14.12	
In nights deepe silence why the ban-dogges barke. . .	Ovid's Elegies	2.19.40	
BARKES			
Wound on the barkes of odoriferous trees, ...	Dido	3.1.117	Dido
BARKING			
Both barking Scilla, and the sounding Rocks, ...	Dido	1.1.146	Aeneas
No barking Dogs that Syllaes intrailes beare, . . .	Ovid's Elegies	2.16.23	
BARKT			
Why so, they barkt a pace a month agoe, ...	Edw	4.3.12	Edward
BARNARDINE (See also BERNARDINE)			
Fryar Barnardine goe you with Ithimore.	Jew	4.1.99	Barab
BARONS (See also BARRONS)			
Barons and Earls, your pride hath made me mute, . .	Edw	1.1.107	Kent
Ile bandie with the Barons and the Earles, ...	Edw	1.1.137	Edward
Were all the Earles and Barons of my minde, ...	Edw	1.2.28	Mortmr
Tis warre that must abate these Barons pride. . . .	Edw	2.2.99	Edward
The head-strong Barons shall not limit me. . . .	Edw	2.2.262	Edward
I long to heare an answer from the Barons/Touching my friend,	Edw	3.1.1	Edward
The Barons overbeare me with their pride.	Edw	3.1.9	Edward
suffer uncontrowld/These Barons thus to beard me in my land,	Edw	3.1.14	Spencr
Thou shalt have crownes of us, t'out bid the Barons, .	Edw	3.1.55	Edward
Upon these Barons, harten up your men, ...	Edw	3.1.124	Spencr
My lord, [here] is <heres> a messenger from the Barons,/Desires	Edw	3.1.148	Spencr
The Barons up in armes, by me salute/Your highnes, with long	Edw	3.1.156	Herald
Saint George for England, and the Barons right. . .	Edw	3.1.219	Warwck
Thats it these Barons and the subtill Queene, ...	Edw	3.1.272	Levune
These Barons lay their heads on blocks together, . .	Edw	3.1.274	Baldck
BARQUE			
The crooked Barque hath her swift sailes displayd. . .	Ovid's Elegies	2.11.24	
BARRABAS			
Tush, who amongst 'em knowes not Barrabas?	Jew	1.1.67	Barab
Come therefore let us goe to Barrabas;	Jew	1.1.141	2Jew
Yet Barrabas we will not banish thee, ...	Jew	1.2.100	Govnr
Then shall they ne're be seene of Barrabas:	Jew	1.2.250	Abigal
How busie Barrabas is there above/To entertaine us in his	Jew	5.5.52	Calym
BARRAINE			
Become intemperate? shall the earth be barraine? . .	Lucan, First Booke	646	
BARR'D			
none but their owne sect/Must enter in; men generally barr'd.	Jew	1.2.257	Abigal
BARRE			
by me, for in extremitie/We ought to make barre of no policie.	Jew	1.2.273	Barab
Night goes away: the dores barre backeward strike. . .	Ovid's Elegies	1.6.24	
Strike backe the barre, night fast away doth goe. . .	Ovid's Elegies	1.6.32	
the barre strike from the poast.	Ovid's Elegies	1.6.56	
Seeing thou art faire, I barre not thy false playing, .	Ovid's Elegies	3.13.1	
BARRELS			
Bombards, whole Barrels full of Gunpowder, ...	Jew	5.5.28	Barab
or we'll breake all the barrels in the house, and dash out all	F1618	4.6.61	P HrsCsr
BARREN (See also BARRAINE)			
when every Tree is barren of his fruite, from whence you had	F1579	4.6.22	P Duke
Against her kind (the barren Mules loth'd issue)/To be cut	Lucan, First Booke	589	
BARRENNESSE			
Earths barrennesse, and all mens hatred/Inflict upon them, thou	Jew	1.2.163	Barab
BARRES			
And boult the brazen gates with barres of Iron. . .	Lucan, First Booke	62	
BARRIERS			
And spend some daies in barriers, tourny, tylte, . .	P 628	12.41	King
But now againe the barriers open lye;	Ovid's Elegies	3.2.77	
BARRONS			
Stil wil these Earles and Barrons use me thus? . . .	Edw	2.2.70	Edward
BARTLEY			
Such newes as I expect, come Bartley, come, . . .	Edw	5.1.129	Edward
And save you from your foes, Bartley would die. . .	Edw	5.1.134	Bartly
Your grace must hence with mee to Bartley straight. . .	Edw	5.1.144	Bartly
And thinkes your grace that Bartley will bee cruell? .	Edw	5.1.151	Bartly
Further, or this letter was sealed, Lord Bartley came, .	Edw	5.2.30	BshpWn
The lord of Bartley is so pitifull, ...	Edw	5.2.34	BshpWn
Bartley shall be dischargd, the king remoovde, . . .	Edw	5.2.40	Mortmr

BARTLEY (cont.)			
a letter presently/Unto the Lord of Bartley from our selfe,	Edw	5.2.48	Mortmr
And then from thence to Bartley back againe:	Edw	5.2.61	Mortmr
BARTUS			
Bartus, it shall be so, poast then to Fraunce,	P 907	18.8	Navrre
Bartus be gone, commend me to his grace,	P 911	18.12	Navrre
BASE (Homograph)			
Warlike Aeneas, and in these base robes?	Dido	2.1.79	Dido
O th'inchaunting words of that base slave,	Dido	2.1.161	Aeneas
And none but base Aeneas will abide:	Dido	4.3.20	Aeneas
Theres not so much as this base tackling too,	Dido	4.4.151	Dido
And while the base borne Tartars take it up,	1Tamb	2.2.65	Meandr
Base villaine, darst thou give the lie?	1Tamb	2.4.19	Tamb
mighty Turkish Emperor/To talk with one so base as Tamburlaine?	1Tamb	3.3.88	Fesse
Shall swallow up these base borne Perseans.	1Tamb	3.3.95	Bajzth
Base Concubine, must thou be plac'd by me/That am the Empresse	1Tamb	3.3.166	Zabina
While you faint-hearted base Egyptians,	1Tamb	4.1.8	Souldn
Base villain, vassall, slave to Tamburlaine:	1Tamb	4.2.19	Tamb
A sturdy Felon and a base-bred Thiefe,	1Tamb	4.3.12	Souldn
That such a base usurping vagabond/Should brave a king, or	1Tamb	4.3.21	Souldn
Than this base earth should shroud your majesty:	2Tamb	2.4.60	Zenoc
blot our dignities/Out of the booke of base borne infamies.	2Tamb	3.1.19	Callap
But Shepheards issue, base borne Tamburlaine,	2Tamb	3.5.77	Orcan
Stand up, ye base unworthy souldiers,	2Tamb	4.1.99	Tamb
And like base slaves abject our princely mindes/To vile and	2Tamb	5.1.140	Orcan
never sepulchre/Shall grace that base-borne Tyrant Tamburlaine.	2Tamb	5.2.18	Amasia
See the simplicitie of these base slaves,	Jew	1.2.214	Barab
My death? what, is the base borne peasant mad?	Jew	2.3.281	Lodowk
What, dares the villain write in such base terms?	Jew	3.2.3	Lodowk
base slave as he should be saluted by such a tall man as I am,	Jew	4.2.9	P Pilia
What shall we doe with this base villaine then?	Jew	4.2.62	Curtzn
Accursed Barabas, base Jew, relent?	Jew	5.5.73	Govnr
Then be themselves base subjects to the whip.	P 218	4.16	Anjoy
Ah base Shatillian and degenerate,	P 312	5.39	Guise
Ah base Epernoune, were not his highnes heere,	P 831	17.26	Guise
Farewell base stooping to the lordly peeres,	Edw	1.1.18	Gavstn
But for that base and obscure Gaveston:	Edw	1.1.101	Lncstr
The glozing head of thy base minion throwne.	Edw	1.1.133	Lncstr
Unlesse he be declinde from that base pesant.	Edw	1.4.7	Mortmr
My Lords, that I abhorre base Gaveston,	Edw	1.4.239	Mortmr
How easilie might some base slave be subbornd,	Edw	1.4.265	Mortmr
Thinke me as base a groome as Gaveston.	Edw	1.4.291	Mortmr
With base outlandish cullions at his heeles,	Edw	1.4.409	Mortmr
Base leaden Earles that glorie in your birth,	Edw	2.2.74	Gavstn
Base flatterer, yeeld, and were it not for shame,	Edw	2.5.11	Mortmr
How meanst thou Mortimer? that is over base.	Edw	2.5.71	Gavstn
Away base groome, robber of kings renowme,	Edw	2.5.72	Mortmr
Away base upstart, brav'st thou nobles thus?	Edw	3.1.205	Penbrk
men, and friends/Ere long, to bid the English king a base.	Edw	4.2.66	SrJohn
Base villaines, wherefore doe you gripe mee thus?	Edw	5.3.57	Kent
Strike of my head? base traitor I defie thee.	Edw	5.4.90	Kent
Base fortune, now I see, that in thy wheele/There is a point,	Edw	5.6.59	Mortmr
Now is he borne, of parents base of stocke,	F 11	Prol.11	1Chor
both condemn'd/For lothed Lollords, and base Schismatiques:	F1022	3.2.42	Pope
base pesants stand,/For loe these Trees remove at my command,	F1425	4.2.101	Faust
Torment sweet friend, that base and [crooked age] <aged man>,	F1753	5.1.80	Faust
With armes to conquer armlesse men is base,	Ovid's Elegies		1.2.22
He hath no bosome, where to hide base pelfe.	Ovid's Elegies		1.10.18
Not one in heaven should be more base and vile.	Ovid's Elegies		1.13.36
Let base conceited wits admire vilde things,	Ovid's Elegies		1.15.35
To like a base wench of despisd condition.	Ovid's Elegies		2.7.20
And little Piggs, base Hog-sties sacrifice,	Ovid's Elegies		3.12.16
Which makes me hope, although I am but base,	Hero and Leander		1.218
Base in respect of thee, divine and pure,	Hero and Leander		1.219
Base boullion for the stampes sake we allow,	Hero and Leander		1.265
and higher set/The drooping thoughts of base declining soules,	Hero and Leander		2.257
BASE-BORNE			
never sepulchre/Shall grace that base-borne Tyrant Tamburlaine.	2Tamb	5.2.18	Amasia
BASE BORNE			
And while the base borne Tartars take it up,	1Tamb	2.2.65	Meandr
Shall swallow up these base borne Perseans.	1Tamb	3.3.95	Bajzth
blot our dignities/Out of the booke of base borne infamies.	2Tamb	3.1.19	Callap
But Shepheards issue, base borne Tamburlaine,	2Tamb	3.5.77	Orcan
My death? what, is the base borne peasant mad?	Jew	2.3.281	Lodowk
BASE-BRED			
A sturdy Felon and a base-bred Thiefe,	1Tamb	4.3.12	Souldn
BASELIE			
But this I scorne, that one so baselie borne,	Edw	1.4.403	Mortmr
BASELY			
which basely on their knees/In all your names desirde a truce	2Tamb	1.1.96	Orcan
And will you basely thus submit your selves/To leave your goods	Jew	1.2.79	Barab
And buy it basely too for summes of gold?	Jew	2.2.29	Bosco
That basely seekes the ruine of his Realme.	P 930	18.31	Navrre
That basely seekes to joyne with such a King,	P1115	21.9	Dumain
Why should I die then, or basely despaire?	F 582	2.2.31	Faust
BASENES			
Ah that bewraies their basenes Lancaster,	Edw	1.2.27	Mortmr
BASENESSE			
To dim thy basenesse and obscurity,	1Tamb	4.3.65	Souldn
And let no basenesse in thy haughty breast,	2Tamb	5.3.30	Usumc
BASER			
chariot wil not beare/A guide of baser temper than my selfe,	2Tamb	5.3.243	Tamb
Let mean consaits, and baser men feare death,	P 997	19.67	Guise

BASEST			
Smear'd with blots of basest drudgery:	1Tamb	5.1.268	Bajzth
[Divinitie is basest of the three],	F 135	1.1.107A	Faust
What difference betwixt the richest mine/And basest mold, but	Hero and Leander		1.233
BASHAW			
Welcome, great [Bashaw] <Bashaws>, how fares/Callymath,	Jew	3.5.1	Govnr
Bashaw, in briefe, shalt have no tribute here,	Jew	3.5.11	Govnr
BASHAWES			
And now, brave Bashawes, come, wee'll walke about/The ruin'd	Jew	5.2.18	Calym
With all thy Bashawes and brave followers.	Jew	5.3.39	Msngr
And now, bold Bashawes, let us to our Tents,	Jew	5.3.43	Calym
And with his Bashawes shall be blithely set,	Jew	5.5.38	Barab
my Companion-Bashawes, see I pray/How busie Barrabas is there	Jew	5.5.51	Calym
I, Barabas, come Bashawes, attend.	Jew	5.5.59	Calym
Treason, treason! Bashawes, flye.	Jew	5.5.67	Calym
BASHAWS			
Welcome, great [Bashaw] <Bashaws>, how fares/Callymath,	Jew	3.5.1	Govnr
BASHFULL			
And not unlike a bashfull puretaine,	Edw	5.4.59	Mortmr
Shall I sit gazing as a bashfull guest,	Ovid's Elegies		1.4.3
BASHFULNESSE			
Or, but for bashfulnesse her selfe would crave.	Ovid's Elegies		1.8.44
BASILISKE			
Which with our Bombards shot and Basiliske,	Jew	5.3.3	Calym
And fearelesse spurne the killing Basiliske:	F 921	3.1.143	Pope
BASILISKES			
heare the clange/Of Scythian trumpets, heare the Basiliskes,	1Tamb	4.1.2	Souldn
Close your Port-cullise, charge your Basiliskes,	Jew	3.5.31	Govnr
BASON			
That when the offering-Bason comes to me,	Jew	2.3.28	Barab
BASSOE (See also BASHAW)			
Hie thee my Bassoe fast to Persea,	1Tamb	3.1.21	Bajzth
Your Bassoe will accomplish your behest:	1Tamb	3.1.42	Bassoe
Bassoe, by this thy Lord and maister knowes,	1Tamb	3.3.1	Tamb
When thy great Bassoe-maister and thy selfe,	1Tamb	3.3.173	Zenoc
BASSOE-MAISTER			
When thy great Bassoe-maister and thy selfe,	1Tamb	3.3.173	Zenoc
BASSOES			
Great Kings of Barbary, and my portly Bassoes,	1Tamb	3.1.1	Bajzth
What if you sent the Bassoes of your guard,	1Tamb	3.1.17	Fesse
Bassoes and Janisaries of my Guard,	1Tamb	3.3.61	Bajzth
Come Kings and Bassoes, let us glut our swords/That thirst to	1Tamb	3.3.164	Bajzth
Now king of Bassoes, who is Conqueror?	1Tamb	3.3.212	Tamb
A hundred Bassoes cloath'd in crimson silk/Shall ride before	2Tamb	1.2.46	Callap
Now Bassoes, what demand you at our hands?	Jew	1.2.1	Govnr
BASTARDLY			
Bastardly boy, sprong from some cowards loins,	2Tamb	1.3.69	Tamb
BASTARDS			
Would make me thinke them Bastards, not my sons,	2Tamb	1.3.32	Tamb
BASTONES			
Are punisht with Bastones so grievously,	1Tamb	3.3.52	Tamb
BATAVIANS			
and fierce Batavians,/Whome trumpets clang incites, and those	Lucan, First Booke		432
BATCHELER			
why I has thought thou hadst beene a batcheler, but now I see	F App	p.238 70 P	Emper
BATH'D			
and all my entrals bath'd/In blood that straineth from their	2Tamb	3.4.8	Capt
No faithlesse witch in Thessale waters bath'd thee.	Ovid's Elegies		1.14.40
BATHDE			
Which had ere this bin bathde in streames of blood,	1Tamb	5.1.438	Tamb
BATHE			
Shall bathe him in a spring, and there hard by,	Edw	1.1.66	Gavstn
And rather bathe thy sword in subjects bloud,	Edw	3.1.212	Mortmr
BATHING			
Now lie the Christians bathing in their bloods,	2Tamb	2.3.10	Orcan
BATTAILE			
What should we doe but bid them battaile straight,	1Tamb	2.2.18	Meandr
To bid him battaile ere he passe too farre,	1Tamb	2.5.95	Tamb
Ready for battaile gainst my Lord the King.	1Tamb	5.1.382	Philem
To bid us battaile for our dearest lives.	2Tamb	2.2.28	1Msngr
Our battaile then in martiall maner pitcht,	2Tamb	3.1.63	Orcan
The field wherin this battaile shall be fought,	2Tamb	3.5.18	Callap
Nay, when the battaile ends, al we wil meet,	2Tamb	3.5.97	Callap
For as soone as the battaile is done, Ile ride in triumph	2Tamb	3.5.145 P	Tamb
would let me be put in the front of such a battaile once,	2Tamb	4.1.73 P	Calyph
and with what noise/An armed battaile joines, such and more	Lucan, First Booke		578
BATTAILES			
At Munda let the dreadfull battailes joyne;	Lucan, First Booke		40
Few battailes fought with prosperous successe/May bring her	Lucan, First Booke		285
Behould how quailes among their battailes live,	Ovid's Elegies		2.6.27
Let others tell how winds fierce battailes wage,	Ovid's Elegies		2.11.17
But follow trembling campes, and battailes sterne,	Ovid's Elegies		3.7.26
BATTEL			
From dangerous battel of my conquering Love.	1Tamb	5.1.442	Zenoc
BATTELL			
And bid him battell for his novell Crowne?	1Tamb	2.5.88	Techel
armours fight/A doubtfull battell with my tempted thoughtes,	1Tamb	5.1.152	Tamb
Shall by this battell be the bloody Sea.	2Tamb	1.1.38	Orcan
they intend to give king Edward battell in England, sooner then	Edw	4.3.35 P	Spencr
Who'le set the faire treste [sunne] <sonne> in battell ray,	Ovid's Elegies		1.1.15
If without battell selfe-wrought wounds annoy them,	Ovid's Elegies		2.14.3
BATTELLS			
Succesfull battells gives the God of kings,	Edw	4.6.19	Queene

BATTELLS (cont.)			
I durst the great celestiall battells tell, . . .	Ovid's Elegies		2.1.11
I yeeld, and back my wit from battells bring, . . .	Ovid's Elegies		2.18.11
BATTELS			
footmen that have serv'd/In two set battels fought in Grecia:	1Tamb	3.3.19	Bassoe
BATTEN			
make her round and plump, and batten more then you are aware.	Jew	3.4.66	P Ithimr
BATTER			
with their Cannons mouth'd like Orcus gulfe/Batter the walles,	1Tamb	3.1.66	Bajzth
Will batter Turrets with their manly fists. . . .	1Tamb	3.3.111	Bajzth
Batter our walles, and beat our Turrets downe. . . .	1Tamb	5.1.2	Govnr
And batter downe the castles on the shore. . . .	2Tamb	1.3.126	Therid
Batter the shining pallace of the Sun, ...	2Tamb	2.4.105	Tamb
Raise mounts, batter, intrench, and undermine, ...	2Tamb	3.3.38	Capt
And with brasse-bullets batter downe your Towers, . . .	Jew	3.5.24	Basso
And batter all the stones about their eares, . . .	Jew	5.5.30	Barab
Thy lightning can my life in pieces batter. . . .	Ovid's Elegies		1.6.16
BATTERED			
Have we not hope, for all our battered walles, . . .	2Tamb	5.1.15	Govnr
And make a bridge unto the battered walles. . . .	2Tamb	5.1.68	Tamb
As there be breaches in her battered wall. . . .	2Tamb	5.1.160	Tamb
BATTERING			
Which thousand battering Rams could never pierce, . .	Dido	2.1.175	Aeneas
Shall not defend it from our battering shot. . . .	1Tamb	4.2.107	Tamb
BATTERY			
and covered waies/To keep the bulwark fronts from battery,	2Tamb	3.2.76	Tamb
bringing of our ordinance/Along the trench into the battery,	2Tamb	3.3.55	Therid
BATTILE			
Cymerian spirits/Gives battile gainst the heart of Tamburlaine.	2Tamb	5.3.9	Therid
BATTLE (See also BATTAILE, BATTEL, BATTILE)			
When Troy by ten yeares battle tumbled downe, . . .	Ovid's Elegies		2.12.9
BAUCIS			
As Jupiter to sillie [Baucis] <Vausis> house: . . .	Dido	1.2.41	Iarbus
BAUDE			
Can I but loath a husband growne a baude?	Ovid's Elegies		2.19.57
BAUDS			
Yet greedy Bauds command she curseth still, . . .	Ovid's Elegies		1.10.23
BAWD			
And art a bawd to his affections, ...	Edw	1.4.151	Queene
BAWDE			
There is, who ere will knowe a bawde aright/Give eare, there is	Ovid's Elegies		1.8.1
The bawde I play, lovers to her I guide:	Ovid's Elegies		3.11.11
BAWDS			
While bond-men cheat, fathers [be hard] <hoord>, bawds hoorish,	Ovid's Elegies		1.15.17
BAY (Homograph; See also BAIES)			
To stay my Fleete from loosing forth the Bay: . . .	Dido	4.3.26	Aeneas
Keeping in aw the Bay of Portingale:	1Tamb	3.3.258	Tamb
By [Cairo] <Cario> runs to Alexandria Bay, . . .	2Tamb	1.2.19	Callap
Til fire and sword have found them at a bay. . . .	2Tamb	3.2.151	Tamb
BAYES			
Nor capitall be adorn'd with sacred bayes:	Lucan, First Booke		288
About my temples go triumphant bayes, ...	Ovid's Elegies		2.12.1
Where the French rout engirt themselves with Bayes. . .	Ovid's Elegies		2.13.18
BE (See also BEE, BE'T, BEEST, SHALBE, WILBE)			
And shall have Ganimed, if thou wilt be my love. . .	Dido	1.1.49	Jupitr
And all Aeolia to be up in armes:	Dido	1.1.63	Venus
Poore Troy must now be sackt upon the Sea, . . .	Dido	1.1.64	Venus
And Neptunes waves be envious men of warre, . . .	Dido	1.1.65	Venus
Before he be the Lord of Turnus towne, ...	Dido	1.1.87	Jupitr
Venus farewell, thy sonne shall be our care: . . .	Dido	1.1.120	Jupitr
Great Jupiter, still honourd maist thou be, . . .	Dido	1.1.137	Venus
Though we be now in extreame miserie, ...	Dido	1.1.157	Achat
Alas sweet boy, thou must be still a while, . . .	Dido	1.1.164	Aeneas
But whether thou the Sunnes bright Sister be, . . .	Dido	1.1.193	Aeneas
Fortune hath favord thee what ere thou be, . . .	Dido	1.1.231	Venus
But tell me Troians, Troians if you be, ...	Dido	1.2.17	Iarbus
And every Troian be as welcome here, ...	Dido	1.2.40	Iarbus
Where am I now? these should be Carthage walles. . .	Dido	2.1.1	Aeneas
Me thinkes that towne there should be Troy, yon Idas hill,	Dido	2.1.7	Aeneas
backe to Troy, and be revengde/On these hard harted Grecians,	Dido	2.1.18	Aeneas
O were I not at all so thou mightst be.	Dido	2.1.28	Aeneas
For none of these can be our Generall.	Dido	2.1.46	Illion
Blest be the time I see Achates face.	Dido	2.1.56	Illion
O tell me, for I long to be resolv'd.	Dido	2.1.61	Aeneas
For though my birth be great, my fortunes meane, . .	Dido	2.1.88	Aeneas
Too meane to be companion to a Queene.	Dido	2.1.89	Aeneas
Thy fortune may be greater then thy birth, ...	Dido	2.1.90	Dido
And if this be thy sonne as I suppose, ...	Dido	2.1.92	Dido
Here let him sit, be merrie lovely child.	Dido	2.1.93	Dido
Ile have it so, Aeneas be content.	Dido	2.1.95	Dido
Madame, you shall be my mother.	Dido	2.1.96	Ascan
be merrie man,/Heres to thy better fortune and good starres.	Dido	2.1.97	Dido
Then be assured thou art not miserable.	Dido	2.1.104	Dido
Lest you be mov'd too much with my sad tale. . . .	Dido	2.1.125	Aeneas
And prophecied Troy should be overcome:	Dido	2.1.142	Aeneas
And this yong Prince shall be thy playfellow. . . .	Dido	2.1.307	Venus
These milke white Doves shall be his Centronels: . .	Dido	2.1.320	Venus
Or whisking of these leaves, all shall be still, . .	Dido	2.1.337	Venus
To be inamourd of thy brothers lookes, ...	Dido	3.1.2	Cupid
Feare not Iarbus, Dido may be thine.	Dido	3.1.19	Dido
I shall not be her sonne, she loves me not. . . .	Dido	3.1.23	Cupid
Weepe not sweet boy, thou shalt be Didos sonne, . .	Dido	3.1.24	Dido
Aeneas well deserves to be your love, ...	Dido	3.1.70	Anna

BE (cont.)

His glistering eyes shall be my looking glasse,	Dido	3.1.86	Dido
His lookes shall be my only Librarie,	Dido	3.1.90	Dido
give Dido leave/To be more modest then her thoughts admit,	Dido	3.1.95	Dido
Lest I be made a wonder to the world.	Dido	3.1.96	Dido
Thy Anchors shall be hewed from Christall Rockes,	Dido	3.1.120	Dido
of foulded Lawne, where shall be wrought/The warres of Troy,	Dido	3.1.124	Dido
Achates, thou shalt be so [manly] <meanly> clad,	Dido	3.1.128	Dido
And are not these as faire as faire may be?	Dido	3.1.140	Dido
Unlesse I be deceiv'd disputed once.	Dido	3.1.147	Cloan
O happie shall he be whom Dido loves.	Dido	3.1.168	Aeneas
Because it may be thou shalt be my love:	Dido	3.1.170	Dido
Sister of Jove, if that thy love be such,	Dido	3.2.53	Venus
And Venus, let there be a match confirmd/Betwixt these two,	Dido	3.2.77	Juno
Be it as you will have [it] for this once,	Dido	3.2.97	Venus
Meane time, Ascanius shall be my charge,	Dido	3.2.98	Venus
We two will talke alone, what words be these?	Dido	3.3.12	Iarbus
Aeneas, be not movde at what he sayes,	Dido	3.3.23	Dido
For otherwhile he will be out of joynt.	Dido	3.3.24	Dido
I mother, I shall one day be a man,	Dido	3.3.35	Cupid
To be well stor'd with such a winters tale?	Dido	3.3.59	Aeneas
This Troians end will be thy envies aime,	Dido	3.3.73	Iarbus
Who nere will cease to soare till he be slaine.	Dido	3.3.85	Iarbus
that Dido may desire/And not obtaine, be it in humaine power?	Dido	3.4.8	Aeneas
And will she be avenged on his life?	Dido	3.4.14	Aeneas
Who then of all so cruell may he be,	Dido	3.4.16	Aeneas
Sicheus, not Aeneas be thou calde:	Dido	3.4.59	Dido
And be thou king of Libia, by my guift.	Dido	3.4.64	Dido
But may be slackt untill another time:	Dido	4.2.26	Anna
I would be thankfull for such curtesie.	Dido	4.2.29	Anna
Be rul'd by me, and seeke some other love,	Dido	4.2.35	Anna
Away with Dido, Anna be thy song,	Dido	4.2.45	Anna
And every speech be ended with a kisse:	Dido	4.3.54	Aeneas
It may be he will steale away with them:	Dido	4.4.3	Dido
This kisse shall be faire Didos punishment.	Dido	4.4.37	Aeneas
To be partakers of our honey talke.	Dido	4.4.54	Dido
When I leave thee, death be my punishment,	Dido	4.4.56	Aeneas
I, and unlesse the destinies be false,	Dido	4.4.81	Aeneas
I shall be planted in as rich a land.	Dido	4.4.82	Aeneas
Henceforth you shall be our Carthage Gods:	Dido	4.4.96	Dido
I, but it may be he will leave my love,	Dido	4.4.97	Dido
I cannot see him frowne, it may not be:	Dido	4.4.112	Dido
And would be toyling in the watrie billowes,	Dido	4.4.137	Dido
Youle be a twigger when you come to age.	Dido	4.5.20	Nurse
Ile be no more a widowe, I am young,	Dido	4.5.22	Nurse
If there be any heaven in earth, tis love:	Dido	4.5.27	Nurse
But what shall it be calde, Troy as before?	Dido	5.1.18	Illion
Let it be term'd Aenea by your name.	Dido	5.1.20	Cloan
No marvell Dido though thou be in love,	Dido	5.1.44	Aeneas
If that be all, then cheare thy drooping lookes,	Dido	5.1.71	Iarbus
If it be so, his father meanes to flye:	Dido	5.1.85	Dido
The Gods, what Gods be those that seeke my death?	Dido	5.1.128	Dido
Would, as faire Troy was, Carthage might be sackt,	Dido	5.1.147	Dido
And I be calde a second Helena.	Dido	5.1.148	Dido
And wilt thou not be mov'd with Didos words?	Dido	5.1.155	Dido
Will, being absent, be obdurate still.	Dido	5.1.187	Dido
Now bring him backe, and thou shalt be a Queene,	Dido	5.1.197	Dido
Dido I am, unlesse I be deceiv'd,	Dido	5.1.264	Dido
I, I must be the murderer of my selfe:	Dido	5.1.270	Dido
No but I am not, yet I will be straight.	Dido	5.1.271	Dido
Anna be glad, now have I found a meane/To rid me from these	Dido	5.1.272	Dido
in the darksome Cave/He drew, and swore by to be true to me,	Dido	5.1.296	Dido
They may be still tormented with unrest,	Dido	5.1.305	Dido
Betwixt this land and that be never league,	Dido	5.1.309	Dido
Now to be rulde and governed by a man,	1Tamb	1.1.12	Cosroe
I am not wise enough to be a kinge,	1Tamb	1.1.20	Mycet
That knowe my wit, and can be witnesses:	1Tamb	1.1.22	Mycet
I might command you to be slaine for this,	1Tamb	1.1.23	Mycet
Therefore tis good and meete for to be wise.	1Tamb	1.1.34	Mycet
Thou shalt be leader of this thousand horse,	1Tamb	1.1.62	Mycet
To be reveng'd for these contemptuous words.	1Tamb	1.1.100	Mycet
The [Lords] <Lord> would not be too exasperate,	1Tamb	1.1.182	Ortyg
The jewels and the treasure we have tane/Shall be reserv'd, and	1Tamb	1.2.3	Tamb
And meanes to be a terrour to the world,	1Tamb	1.2.38	Tamb
They shall be kept our forced followers,	1Tamb	1.2.66	Tamb
Even as thou hop'st to be eternized,	1Tamb	1.2.72	Zenoc
Or you my Lordes to be my followers?	1Tamb	1.2.83	Tamb
Thy Garments shall be made of Medean silke,	1Tamb	1.2.95	Tamb
Thou shalt be drawen amidst the frosen Pooles,	1Tamb	1.2.99	Tamb
Which with thy beautie will be soone resolv'd.	1Tamb	1.2.101	Tamb
Techelles, women must be flatered.	1Tamb	1.2.107	Tamb
Now must your jewels be restor'd againe:	1Tamb	1.2.114	Tamb
And I that triumpht so be overcome.	1Tamb	1.2.115	Tamb
You must be forced from me ere you goe:	1Tamb	1.2.120	Tamb
his chaine shall serve/For Manackles, till he be ransom'd home.	1Tamb	1.2.148	Tamb
Noble and milde this Persean seemes to be,	1Tamb	1.2.162	Tamb
Than Tamburlaine be slaine or overcome.	1Tamb	1.2.177	Tamb
That I shall be the Monark of the East,	1Tamb	1.2.185	Tamb
To be my Queen and portly Emperesse.	1Tamb	1.2.187	Tamb
And mightie kings shall be our Senators.	1Tamb	1.2.198	Tamb
admyre me not)/And when my name and honor shall be spread,	1Tamb	1.2.205	Tamb
Then shalt thou be Competitor with me,	1Tamb	1.2.208	Tamb
To be partaker of thy good or ill,	1Tamb	1.2.230	Therid

BE (cont.)

Thus shall my heart be still combinde with thine,	1Tamb	1.2.235		Tamb
Shal want my heart to be with gladnes pierc'd/To do you honor	1Tamb	1.2.250		Therid
You shall have honors, as your merits be:	1Tamb	1.2.255		Tamb
Or els you shall be forc'd with slaverie.	1Tamb	1.2.256		Tamb
I must be pleasde perforce, wretched Zenocrate.	1Tamb	1.2.259		Zenoc
And well his merits show him to be made/His Fortunes maister,	1Tamb	2.1.35		Cosroe
Though straight the passage and the port be made,	1Tamb	2.1.42		Cosroe
In faire Persea noble Tamburlaine/Shall be my Regent, and	1Tamb	2.1.49		Cosroe
Our army will be forty thousand strong,	1Tamb	2.1.61		Cosroe
Would it not grieve a King to be so abusde,	1Tamb	2.2.5		Mycet
And be reclaim'd with princely lenitie.	1Tamb	2.2.38		Meandr
Suppose they be in number infinit,	1Tamb	2.2.43		Meandr
And tis a prety toy to be a Poet.	1Tamb	2.2.54		Mycet
Which you that be but common souldiers,	1Tamb	2.2.63		Meandr
As I shall be commended and excusde/For turning my poore charge	1Tamb	2.3.28		Therid
Would make one thrust and strive to be retain'd/In such a great	1Tamb	2.3.31		Therid
Then shall your meeds and vallours be advaunst/To roomes of	1Tamb	2.3.40		Cosroe
Then haste Cosroe to be king alone,	1Tamb	2.3.42		Tamb
Accurst be he that first invented war,	1Tamb	2.4.1		Mycet
So shall not I be knowen, or if I bee,	1Tamb	2.4.13		Mycet
Is it not brave to be a King, Techelles?	1Tamb	2.5.51		Tamb
Is it not passing brave to be a King,	1Tamb	2.5.53		Tamb
To be a King, is halfe to be a God.	1Tamb	2.5.56		Usumc
To aske, and have: commaund, and be obeied.	1Tamb	2.5.62		Therid
Why say Theridamas, wilt thou be a king?	1Tamb	2.5.65		Tamb
What saies my other friends, wil you be kings?	1Tamb	2.5.67		Tamb
And if I prosper, all shall be as sure,	1Tamb	2.5.84		Tamb
Nay quickly then, before his roome be hot.	1Tamb	2.5.89		Usumc
And by profession be ambitious.	1Tamb	2.6.14		Meandr
Or of what mould or mettel he be made,	1Tamb	2.6.17		Ortyg
Be arm'd against the hate of such a foe,	1Tamb	2.6.22		Ortyg
If Tamburlain be plac'd in Persea.	1Tamb	2.7.39		Usumc
Yet would we not be brav'd with forrain power,	1Tamb	3.1.13		Bajzth
He be so mad to manage Armes with me,	1Tamb	3.1.34		Bajzth
mornings next arise/For messenger, he will not be reclaim'd,	1Tamb	3.1.39		Bajzth
Twere requisite he should be ten times more,	1Tamb	3.1.47		Argier
What thinks your greatnes best to be atchiev'd/In pursuit of	1Tamb	3.1.56		Fesse
And thus the Grecians shall be conquered.	1Tamb	3.1.67		Bajzth
(Which of your whole displeasures should be most)/Hath seem'd	1Tamb	3.2.7		Agidas
should be most)/Hath seem'd to be digested long agoe.	1Tamb	3.2.8		Agidas
Although it be digested long agoe,	1Tamb	3.2.9		Zenoc
Eternall heaven sooner be dissolv'd,	1Tamb	3.2.18		Agidas
Be honored with your love, but for necessity.	1Tamb	3.2.30		Agidas
And might in noble minds be counted princely.	1Tamb	3.2.39		Zenoc
Yet be not so inconstant in your love,	1Tamb	3.2.56		Agidas
He shall be made a chast and lustlesse Eunuke,	1Tamb	3.3.77		Bajzth
Fight all couragiously and be you kings.	1Tamb	3.3.101		Tamb
must thou be plac'd by me/That am the Empresse of the mighty	1Tamb	3.3.166		Zabina
And sue to me to be your Advocates.	1Tamb	3.3.175		Zenoc
Thou shalt be Landresse to my waiting maid.	1Tamb	3.3.177		Zabina
Both for their sausinesse shall be employed,	1Tamb	3.3.184		Zenoc
But that he lives and will be Conquerour.	1Tamb	3.3.211		Zenoc
Thou shalt not yet be Lord of Affrica.	1Tamb	3.3.223		Zabina
Though he be prisoner, he may be ransomed.	1Tamb	3.3.231		Zabina
Now will the Christian miscreants be glad,	1Tamb	3.3.236		Bajzth
For though the glorie of this day be lost,	1Tamb	3.3.241		Bajzth
And be reveng'd for her disparadgement.	1Tamb	4.1.72		Souldn
And be the foot-stoole of great Tamburlain,	1Tamb	4.2.14		Tamb
That may command thee peecemeale to be torne,	1Tamb	4.2.23		Tamb
It shall be said, I made it red my selfe,	1Tamb	4.2.54		Tamb
Let these be warnings for you then my slave,	1Tamb	4.2.72		Anippe
That should be horsed on fower mightie kings.	1Tamb	4.2.78		Bajzth
There whiles he lives, shal Bajazeth be kept,	1Tamb	4.2.85		Tamb
And where I goe be thus in triumph drawne:	1Tamb	4.2.86		Tamb
until the bloody flag/Be once advanc'd on my vermilion Tent,	1Tamb	4.2.117		Tamb
Be so perswaded, that the Souldan is/No more dismaide with	1Tamb	4.3.30		Souldn
But if his highnesse would let them be fed, it would doe them	1Tamb	4.4.34	P	Therid
and then she shall be sure not to be starv'd, and he be	1Tamb	4.4.46	P	Usumc
starv'd, and he be provided for a moneths victuall before hand.	1Tamb	4.4.46	P	Usumc
Content thy selfe, his person shall be safe,	1Tamb	4.4.87		Tamb
If with their lives they will be pleasde to yeeld,	1Tamb	4.4.89		Tamb
Or may be forc'd, to make me Emperour.	1Tamb	4.4.90		Tamb
For Egypt and Arabia must be mine.	1Tamb	4.4.91		Tamb
thou maist thinke thy selfe happie to be fed from my trencher.	1Tamb	4.4.92	P	Tamb
sir, you must be dieted, too much eating will make you surfeit.	1Tamb	4.4.103	P	Tamb
Nor shall they long be thine, I warrant them.	1Tamb	4.4.119		Bajzth
Your byrthes shall be no blemish to your fame,	1Tamb	4.4.127		Tamb
And be renowm'd, as never Emperours were.	1Tamb	4.4.138		Tamb
Until with greater honors I be grac'd.	1Tamb	4.4.140		Tamb
Will never be dispenc'd with til our deaths.	1Tamb	5.1.17		Govnr
Our love of honor loth to be enthral'd/To forraine powers, and	1Tamb	5.1.35		Govnr
Or be the means the overweighing heavens/Have kept to qualifie	1Tamb	5.1.45		Govnr
must you be first shal feele/The sworne destruction of	1Tamb	5.1.65		Tamb
To be investers of thy royall browes,	1Tamb	5.1.104		1Virgn
to prevent/That which mine honor sweares shal be perform'd:	1Tamb	5.1.107		Tamb
Bring him forth, and let us know if the towne be ransackt.	1Tamb	5.1.194	P	Tamb
That may be ministers of my decay.	1Tamb	5.1.289		Bajzth
Let the souldiers be buried.	1Tamb	5.1.316	P	Zabina
On horsmens Lances to be hoisted up,	1Tamb	5.1.328		Zenoc
ruthlesly pursewde/Be equally against his life incenst,	1Tamb	5.1.367		Zenoc
Madam content your self and be resolv'd,	1Tamb	5.1.372		Anippe
And that I might be privy to the state,	1Tamb	5.1.426		Arabia

BE (cont.)

Wherein as in a mirrour may be seene,	1Tamb	5.1.476	Tamb
Shall by this battell be the bloody Sea.	2Tamb	1.1.38	Orcan
of our Empery/Once lost, All Turkie would be overthrowne:	2Tamb	1.1.56	Orcan
let peace be ratified/On these conditions specified before,	2Tamb	1.1.124	Orcan
But whilst I live will be at truce with thee.	2Tamb	1.1.130	Sgsmnd
Born to be Monarch of the Western world:	2Tamb	1.2.3	Callap
Hoping by some means I shall be releast,	2Tamb	1.2.23	Callap
With naked Negros shall thy coach be drawen,	2Tamb	1.2.40	Callap
thy chariot wheels/With Turky Carpets shall be covered:	2Tamb	1.2.43	Callap
But need we not be spied going aboord?	2Tamb	1.2.56	Almeda
Shall I be made a king for my labour?	2Tamb	1.2.62	P Almeda
Thou shalt be crown'd a king and be my mate.	2Tamb	1.2.66	Callap
Least time be past, and lingring let us both.	2Tamb	1.2.75	Callap
Betweene thy sons that shall be Emperours,	2Tamb	1.3.7	Tamb
Which should be like the quilles of Porcupines,	2Tamb	1.3.26	Tamb
Thou shalt be made a King and raigne with me,	2Tamb	1.3.48	Tamb
Thou shalt be king before them, and thy seed/Shall issue	2Tamb	1.3.52	Tamb
Be thou the scourge and terrour of the world.	2Tamb	1.3.60	Tamb
Be tearm'd the scourge and terrour of the world?	2Tamb	1.3.62	Amyras
Be al a scourge and terror to the world,	2Tamb	1.3.63	Tamb
My royal chaire of state shall be advanc'd:	2Tamb	1.3.82	Tamb
Whose arches should be fram'd with bones of Turks,	2Tamb	1.3.94	Amyras
Wel lovely boies, you shal be Emperours both,	2Tamb	1.3.96	Tamb
With all his viceroies shall be so affraide,	2Tamb	1.3.162	Tamb
Were turnde to men, he should be overcome:	2Tamb	1.3.164	Tamb
This should be treacherie and violence,	2Tamb	2.1.31	Sgsmnd
To be esteem'd assurance for our selves,	2Tamb	2.1.39	Baldwn
Our faiths are sound, and must be [consumate] <consinuate>,	2Tamb	2.1.47	Sgsmnd
his fearefull arme/Be pour'd with rigour on our sinfull heads,	2Tamb	2.1.58	Fredrk
Be able to withstand and conquer him.	2Tamb	2.2.19	Gazell
That could not but before be terrified:	2Tamb	2.2.22	Uribas
Can there be such deceit in Christians,	2Tamb	2.2.36	Orcan
Then if there be a Christ, as Christians say,	2Tamb	2.2.39	Orcan
If he be son to everliving Jove,	2Tamb	2.2.41	Orcan
If he be jealous of his name and honor,	2Tamb	2.2.43	Orcan
Be now reveng'd upon this Traitors soule,	2Tamb	2.2.58	Orcan
If there be Christ, we shall have victorie.	2Tamb	2.2.64	Orcan
Now shall his barbarous body be a pray/To beasts and foules,	2Tamb	2.3.14	Orcan
Yet in my thoughts shall Christ be honoured,	2Tamb	2.3.33	Orcan
That this my life may be as short to me/As are the daies of	2Tamb	2.4.36	Tamb
Or dieng, be the [author] <anchor> of my death.	2Tamb	2.4.56	Tamb
Ah good my Lord be patient, she is dead,	2Tamb	2.4.119	Therid
Though she be dead, yet let me think she lives,	2Tamb	2.4.127	Tamb
Where ere her soule be, thou shalt stay with me/Embalm'd with	2Tamb	2.4.129	Tamb
And till I die thou shalt not be interr'd.	2Tamb	2.4.132	Tamb
That may endure till heaven be dissolv'd,	2Tamb	3.2.7	Tamb
And here this mournful streamer shal be plac'd/Wrought with the	2Tamb	3.2.19	Amyras
Thou shalt be set upon my royall tent.	2Tamb	3.2.37	Tamb
Whereas the Fort may fittest be assailde,	2Tamb	3.2.66	Tamb
The ditches must be deepe, the Counterscarps/Narrow and steepe,	2Tamb	3.2.68	Tamb
My Lord, but this is dangerous to be done,	2Tamb	3.2.93	Calyph
We may be slaine or wounded ere we learne.	2Tamb	3.2.94	Calyph
A wound is nothing be it nere so deepe,	2Tamb	3.2.115	Tamb
It may be they will yeeld it quietly,	2Tamb	3.3.12	Therid
of thy hold/Volleies of ordinance til the breach be made,	2Tamb	3.3.25	Therid
Wel, this must be the messenger for thee.	2Tamb	3.4.15	Olymp
Ah sacred Mahomet, if this be sin,	2Tamb	3.4.31	Olymp
Be likewise end to my accursed life.	2Tamb	3.4.82	Olymp
The field wherin this battaile shall be fought,	2Tamb	3.5.18	Callap
And join'd those stars that shall be opposite,	2Tamb	3.5.81	Tamb
By Mahomet he shal be tied in chaines,	2Tamb	3.5.92	Jrslem
And when ye stay, be lasht with whips of wier:	2Tamb	3.5.105	Tamb
while all thy joints/Be rackt and beat asunder with the wheele,	2Tamb	3.5.125	Tamb
Wel, in despight of thee he shall be king:	2Tamb	3.5.128	Callap
Away, let us to the field, that the villaine may be slaine.	2Tamb	3.5.143	P Trebiz
hee shall not be put to that exigent, I warrant thee.	2Tamb	3.5.156	P Soria
You shall be princes all immediatly:	2Tamb	3.5.168	Tamb
but that you wil be thought/More childish valourous than manly	2Tamb	4.1.16	Calyph
What, dar'st thou then be absent from the fight,	2Tamb	4.1.22	Amyras
And oft hath warn'd thee to be stil in field,	2Tamb	4.1.24	Amyras
I take no pleasure to be murtherous,	2Tamb	4.1.29	Calyph
and for feare I should be affraid, would put it off and come to	2Tamb	4.1.69	P Calyph
would let me be put in the front of such a battaile once,	2Tamb	4.1.72	P Calyph
I beleeve there will be some hurt done anon amongst them.	2Tamb	4.1.74	P Calyph
tel me if the warres/Be not a life that may illustrate Gods,	2Tamb	4.1.79	Tamb
Spirits with desire/Stil to be train'd in armes and chivalry?	2Tamb	4.1.81	Tamb
Good my Lord, let him be forgiven for once,	2Tamb	4.1.101	Amyras
Let this invention be the instrument.	2Tamb	4.2.13	Olymp
Thou shalt be stately Queene of faire Argier,	2Tamb	4.2.39	Therid
I cannot love to be an Emperesse.	2Tamb	4.2.49	Olymp
I must and wil be pleasde, and you shall yeeld:	2Tamb	4.2.53	Therid
your weapons point/That wil be blunted if the blow be great.	2Tamb	4.2.80	Olymp
Whose body shall be tomb'd with all the pompe/The treasure of	2Tamb	4.2.97	Therid
You shal be fed with flesh as raw as blood,	2Tamb	4.3.18	Tamb
And thus be drawen with these two idle kings.	2Tamb	4.3.28	Amyras
While these their fellow kings may be refresht.	2Tamb	4.3.31	Tamb
as fit as may be to restraine/These coltish coach-horse tongues	2Tamb	4.3.51	Usumc
Let us not be idle then my Lord,	2Tamb	4.3.95	Techel
But presently be prest to conquer it.	2Tamb	4.3.96	Techel
Shal al be loden with the martiall spoiles/We will convay with	2Tamb	4.3.105	Tamb
Be famous through the furthest continents,	2Tamb	4.3.110	Tamb
For there my Pallace royal shal be plac'd:	2Tamb	4.3.111	Tamb

intollorable wrath/May be suppresst by our submission.	2Tamb	5.1.9	Maxim
Though this be held his last daies dreadfull siege,	2Tamb	5.1.29	1Citzn
Or els be sure thou shalt be forc'd with paines,	2Tamb	5.1.52	Therid
As there be breaches in her battered wall.	2Tamb	5.1.160	Tamb
What shal be done with their wives and children my Lord.	2Tamb	5.1.168	P Techel
Whom I have thought a God? they shal be burnt.	2Tamb	5.1.176	Tamb
Wel said, let there be a fire presently.	2Tamb	5.1.178	Tamb
Thou art not woorthy to be worshipped,	2Tamb	5.1.189	Tamb
And let this Captaine be remoov'd the walles,	2Tamb	5.1.215	Therid
Let it be so, about it souldiers:	2Tamb	5.1.217	Tamb
But foorth ye vassals, what so ere it be,	2Tamb	5.1.221	Tamb
Before his hoste be full from Babylon,	2Tamb	5.2.9	Callap
To be reveng'd of all his Villanie.	2Tamb	5.2.23	Callap
Before himselfe or his be conquered.	2Tamb	5.2.53	Callap
Or that it be rejoin'd again at full,	2Tamb	5.2.58	Callap
Assaile it and be sure of victorie.	2Tamb	5.2.59	Callap
Be not inconstant, carelesse of your fame,	2Tamb	5.3.21	Techel
So honour heaven til heaven dissolved be,	2Tamb	5.3.26	Techel
Shall sicknesse proove me now to be a man,	2Tamb	5.3.44	Tamb
That Callapine should be my slave againe.	2Tamb	5.3.118	Tamb
unrelenting eares/Of death and hell be shut against my praiers,	2Tamb	5.3.192	Amyras
Let it be plac'd by this my fatall chaire,	2Tamb	5.3.211	Tamb
May be upon himselfe reverberate.	2Tamb	5.3.223	Techel
Be warn'd by him then, learne with awfull eie/To sway a throane	2Tamb	5.3.234	Tamb
Let me be envy'd and not pittied!	Jew	Prol.27	Machvl
And let him not be entertain'd the worse/Because he favours me.	Jew	Prol.34	Machvl
Would in his age be loath to labour so,	Jew	1.1.17	Barab
Rather had I a Jew be hated thus,	Jew	1.1.114	Barab
I must confesse we come not to be Kings:	Jew	1.1.129	Barab
Oft have I heard tell, can be permanent.	Jew	1.1.133	Barab
Or let 'em warre, so we be conquerors:	Jew	1.1.151	Barab
And very wisely sayd, it may be so.	Jew	1.1.166	3Jew
And all the Jewes in Malta must be there.	Jew	1.1.168	2Jew
Umh; All the Jewes in Malta must be there?	Jew	1.1.169	Barab
then let every man/Provide him, and be there for fashion-sake.	Jew	1.1.171	Barab
For to be short, amongst you 'tmust be had.	Jew	1.2.56	Govnr
Are strangers with your tribute to be tax'd?	Jew	1.2.59	Barab
mony of the Turkes shall all be levyed amongst the Jewes,	Jew	1.2.68	P Reader
Why Barabas wilt thou be christened?	Jew	1.2.81	Govnr
No, Governour, I will be no convertite.	Jew	1.2.82	Barab
Let me be us'd but as my brethren are.	Jew	1.2.91	Barab
And now it cannot be recall'd.	Jew	1.2.93	Govnr
Shall I be tryed by their transgression?	Jew	1.2.115	Barab
Be patient and thy riches will increase.	Jew	1.2.122	Govnr
I must be forc'd to steale and compasse more.	Jew	1.2.127	Barab
It shall be so: now Officers have you done?	Jew	1.2.131	Govnr
Then be the causers of their misery.	Jew	1.2.148	Barab
'Tis necessary that be look'd unto:	Jew	1.2.157	1Knght
Oh yet be patient, gentle Barabas.	Jew	1.2.169	1Jew
Good Barabas be patient.	Jew	1.2.199	2Jew
Thinke me to be a senselesse lumpe of clay/That will with every	Jew	1.2.216	Barab
Be silent, Daughter, sufferance breeds ease,	Jew	1.2.238	Barab
Then shall they ne're be seene of Barrabas:	Jew	1.2.250	Abigal
Be rul'd by me, for in extremitie/We ought to make barre of no	Jew	1.2.272	Barab
what e're it be to injure them/That have so manifestly wronged	Jew	1.2.274	Abigal
there must my girle/Intreat the Abbasse to be entertain'd.	Jew	1.2.280	Barab
but be thou so precise/As they may thinke it done of Holinesse.	Jew	1.2.284	Barab
Till thou hast gotten to be entertain'd.	Jew	1.2.288	Barab
Well father, say I be entertain'd,	Jew	1.2.294	Abigal
But here they come; be cunning Abigall.	Jew	1.2.299	Barab
No, Abigall, in this/It is not necessary I be seene.	Jew	1.2.302	Barab
Be close, my girle, for this must fetch my gold.	Jew	1.2.304	Barab
The better; for we love not to be seene:	Jew	1.2.307	Abbass
It may be so: but who comes here?	Jew	1.2.313	Abbass
And be a Novice in your Nunnery,	Jew	1.2.325	Abigal
Let us intreat she may be entertain'd.	Jew	1.2.329	2Fryar
Yet let thy daughter be no longer blinde.	Jew	1.2.354	1Fryar
Becomes it Jewes to be so credulous,	Jew	1.2.360	Barab
To morrow early I'le be at the doore.	Jew	1.2.361	Barab
No come not at me, if thou wilt be damn'd,	Jew	1.2.362	Barab
Forget me, see me not, and so be gone.	Jew	1.2.363	Barab
fitter for a tale of love/Then to be tired out with Orizons:	Jew	1.2.370	Mthias
And if she be so faire as you report,	Jew	1.2.388	Lodowk
fortune were so good/As but to be about this happy place;	Jew	2.1.32	Abigal
Will Knights of Malta be in league with Turkes,	Jew	2.2.28	Bosco
and you were stated here/To be at deadly enmity with Turkes.	Jew	2.2.33	Bosco
Therefore be rul'd by me, and keepe the gold:	Jew	2.2.39	Bosco
On this condition shall thy Turkes be sold.	Jew	2.2.42	Govnr
Bosco, thou shalt be Malta's Generall;	Jew	2.2.44	Govnr
Feare not their sale, for they'll be quickly bought.	Jew	2.3.2	1Offcr
And so much must they yeeld or not be sold.	Jew	2.3.4	2Offcr
Or else be gather'd for in our Synagogue;	Jew	2.3.27	Barab
But when he touches it, it will be foild:	Jew	2.3.57	Barab
But now I must be gone to buy a slave.	Jew	2.3.95	Barab
the Towne-seale might be got/To keepe him for his life time	Jew	2.3.103	Barab
Why should this Turke be dearer then that Moore?	Jew	2.3.109	Barab
It may be under colour of shaving, thou'lt cut my throat for my	Jew	2.3.119	P Barab
I must have one that's sickly, and be but for sparing vittles:	Jew	2.3.124	P Barab
As for the Diamond it shall be yours;	Jew	2.3.135	Barab
I pray, Sir, be no stranger at my house,	Jew	2.3.136	Barab
All that I have shall be at your command.	Jew	2.3.137	Barab
And be reveng'd upon the--Governor.	Jew	2.3.143	Barab

BE (cont.)

First be thou voyd of these affections,	Jew	2.3.169		Barab
Be mov'd at nothing, see thou pitty none,	Jew	2.3.171		Barab
Be true and secret, thou shalt want no gold.	Jew	2.3.216		Barab
That ye be both made sure e're you come out.	Jew	2.3.236		Barab
Doe, it is requisite it should be so.	Jew	2.3.239		Barab
That I intend my daughter shall be thine.	Jew	2.3.254		Barab
This gentle Magot, Lodowicke I meane,/Must be deluded:	Jew	2.3.306		Barab
What, shall I be betroth'd to Lodowicke?	Jew	2.3.308		Abigal
Faith is not to be held with Heretickes;	Jew	2.3.311		Barab
I know not, but farewell, I must be gone.	Jew	2.3.322		Abigal
Shee is thy wife, and thou shalt be mine heire.	Jew	2.3.328		Barab
But rather let the brightsome heavens be dim,	Jew	2.3.330		Lodowk
There comes the villaine, now I'le be reveng'd.	Jew	2.3.333		Lodowk
Be quiet Lodowicke, it is enough/That I have made thee sure to	Jew	2.3.334		Barab
Here must no speeches passe, nor swords be drawne.	Jew	2.3.339		Barab
No; so shall I, if any hurt be done,	Jew	2.3.341		Barab
Be made an accessary of your deeds;	Jew	2.3.342		Barab
True; and it shall be cunningly perform'd.	Jew	2.3.367		Barab
No, no, and yet it might be done that way:	Jew	2.3.373		Barab
But now against my will I must be chast.	Jew	3.1.4		Curtzn
So, now they have shew'd themselves to be tall fellowes.	Jew	3.2.7		Barab
These armes of mine shall be thy Sepulchre.	Jew	3.2.11		Govnr
and let them be interr'd/Within one sacred monument of stone;	Jew	3.2.29		Govnr
That by my favour they should both be slaine?	Jew	3.3.39		Abigal
To get me be admitted for a Nun.	Jew	3.3.55		Abigal
Oh therefore, Jacomo, let me be one,	Jew	3.3.68		Abigal
For that will be most heavy to thy soule.	Jew	3.3.71		1Fryar
If so, 'tis time that it be seene into:	Jew	3.4.9		Barab
Be blest of me, nor come within my gates,	Jew	3.4.31		Barab
ambles after wealth/Although he ne're be richer then in hope:	Jew	3.4.53		Barab
Very well, Ithimore, then now be secret;	Jew	3.4.60		Barab
That thou mayst freely live to be my heire.	Jew	3.4.63		Barab
Troth master, I'm loth such a pot of pottage should be spoyld.	Jew	3.4.89	P	Ithimr
As fatall be it to her as the draught/Of which great Alexander	Jew	3.4.96		Barab
That's to be gotten in the Westerne Inde:	Jew	3.5.5		Govnr
And nought is to be look'd for now but warres,	Jew	3.5.35		Govnr
The Abbasse sent for me to be confest:	Jew	3.6.3		2Fryar
Oh what a sad confession will there be?	Jew	3.6.4		2Fryar
but seeing you are come/Be you my ghostly father; and first	Jew	3.6.12		Abigal
Know that Confession must not be reveal'd,	Jew	3.6.33		2Fryar
Shall be condemn'd, and then sent to the fire.	Jew	3.6.36		2Fryar
Convert my father that he may be sav'd,	Jew	3.6.39		Abigal
Thou know'st 'tis death and if it be reveal'd.	Jew	3.6.51		2Fryar
That's brave, master, but think you it wil not be known?	Jew	4.1.8	P	Ithimr
How can it if we two be secret.	Jew	4.1.9		Barab
Thou hast offended, therefore must be damn'd.	Jew	4.1.25		1Fryar
Their voyage will be worth ten thousand Crownes.	Jew	4.1.70		Barab
to some religious house/So I may be baptiz'd and live therein.	Jew	4.1.76		Barab
I know they are, and I will be with you.	Jew	4.1.83		Barab
I'le be with you to night.	Jew	4.1.90		2Fryar
You heare your answer, and you may be gone.	Jew	4.1.92		1Fryar
This is meere frailty, brethren, be content.	Jew	4.1.98		Barab
But Barabas, who shall be your godfathers,	Jew	4.1.109		1Fryar
For presently you shall be shriv'd.	Jew	4.1.110		1Fryar
Marry the Turke shall be one of my godfathers,	Jew	4.1.111		Barab
To fast and be well whipt; I'le none of that.	Jew	4.1.124		Barab
No more but so: it must and shall be done.	Jew	4.1.128		Barab
Blame not us but the proverb, Confes and be hang'd.	Jew	4.1.146	P	Barab
Then is it as it should be, take him up.	Jew	4.1.152		Barab
master, be rul'd by me a little; so, let him leane upon his	Jew	4.1.153	P	Ithimr
Then will not Jacomo be long from hence.	Jew	4.1.159		Barab
I must be forc'd to give in evidence,	Jew	4.1.186		Barab
That being importun'd by this Bernardine/To be a Christian, I	Jew	4.1.188		Barab
Take in the staffe too, for that must be showne:	Jew	4.1.204		Barab
Law wils that each particular be knowne.	Jew	4.1.205		Barab
base slave as he should be saluted by such a tall man as I am,	Jew	4.2.9	P	Pilia
goe whither he will, I'le be none of his followers in haste:	Jew	4.2.25	P	Ithimr
It may be she sees more in me than I can find in my selfe:	Jew	4.2.32	P	Ithimr
he flouts me, what gentry can be in a poore Turke of ten pence?	Jew	4.2.38	P	Ithimr
I'le be gone.	Jew	4.2.39	P	Ithimr
Canst thou be so unkind to leave me thus?	Jew	4.2.52		Curtzn
by this bearer, and this shall be your warrant; if you doe not,	Jew	4.2.76	P	Ithimr
I'le be thy Jason, thou my golden Fleece;	Jew	4.2.90		Ithimr
I'le be Adonis, thou shalt be Loves Queene.	Jew	4.2.94		Ithimr
Shalt live with me and be my love.	Jew	4.2.98		Ithimr
you dine with me, Sir, and you shal be most hartily poyson'd.	Jew	4.3.30	P	Barab
Oh, if that be all, I can picke ope your locks.	Jew	4.3.33		Pilia
Goe to, it shall be so.	Jew	4.4.3		Curtzn
We two, and 'twas never knowne, nor never shall be for me.	Jew	4.4.23	P	Ithimr
Pardona moy, be no in tune yet; so, now, now all be in.	Jew	4.4.45	P	Barab
Very mush, Mounsier, you no be his man?	Jew	4.4.57	P	Barab
Pardona moy, Mounsier, [me] <we> be no well.	Jew	4.4.71		Barab
And see that Malta be well fortifi'd;	Jew	5.1.2		Govnr
And it behoves you to be resolute;	Jew	5.1.3		Govnr
Make fires, heat irons, let the racke be fetch'd.	Jew	5.1.24		Govnr
Nay stay, my Lord, 'tmay be he will confesse.	Jew	5.1.25		1Knght
As these have spoke so be it to their soules:--	Jew	5.1.42		Barab
Be patient, gentle Madam, it was he,	Jew	5.1.46		Govnr
Since they are dead, let them be buried.	Jew	5.1.57		Govnr
To be a prey for Vultures and wild beasts.	Jew	5.1.59		Govnr
I'le be reveng'd on this accursed Towne;	Jew	5.1.62		Barab
If this be true, I'le make thee Governor.	Jew	5.1.95		Calym

BE (cont.)

And if it be not true, then let me dye.	Jew	5.1.96	Barab
much better/To [have] kept thy promise then be thus surpriz'd?	Jew	5.2.5	Calym
Oh villaine, Heaven will be reveng'd on thee.	Jew	5.2.25	Govnr
and what boots it thee/Poore Barabas, to be the Governour,	Jew	5.2.32	Barab
When as thy life shall be at their command?	Jew	5.2.33	Barab
No, Barabas, this must be look'd into;	Jew	5.2.34	Barab
But Barabas will be more circumspect.	Jew	5.2.43	Barab
Governor, good words, be not so furious;	Jew	5.2.61	Barab
Your selves shall see it shall not be forgot:	Jew	5.2.71	Barab
Will Barabas be good to Christians?	Jew	5.2.75	Govnr
Nay, doe thou this, Ferneze, and be free;	Jew	5.2.90	Barab
Where be thou present onely to performe/One stratagem that I'le	Jew	5.2.98	Barab
I will be there, and doe as thou desirest;	Jew	5.2.103	Govnr
Shall be my friend.	Jew	5.2.114	Barab
That at one instant all things may be done,	Jew	5.2.120	Barab
And caus'd the ruines to be new repair'd,	Jew	5.3.2	Calym
I wonder how it could be conquer'd thus?	Jew	5.3.12	Calym
Will be too costly and too troublesome:	Jew	5.3.23	Calym
As be it valued but indifferently,	Jew	5.3.29	Msngr
In this, my Countrimen, be rul'd by me,	Jew	5.4.1	Govnr
For happily I shall be in distresse,	Jew	5.4.6	Govnr
And with his Bashawes shall be blithely set,	Jew	5.5.38	Barab
A warning-peece shall be shot off from the Tower,	Jew	5.5.39	Barab
And fire the house; say, will not this be brave?	Jew	5.5.41	Barab
Let's hence, lest further mischiefe be pretended.	Jew	5.5.96	Calym
for Malta shall be freed,/Or Selim ne're returne to Ottoman.	Jew	5.5.113	Govnr
away, and let due praise be given/Neither to Fate nor Fortune,	Jew	5.5.123	Govnr
May still be feweld in our progenye.	P 8	1.8	Charls
in Religion/Might be a meanes to crosse you in your love.	P 16	1.16	QnMoth
Where are those perfumed gloves which I sent/To be poysoned,	P 71	2.14	Guise
See where they be my good Lord, and he that smelles but to	P 73	2.16	P Pothec
Be gone my freend, present them to her straite.	P 82	2.25	Guise
Which cannot be extinguisht but by bloud.	P 93	2.36	Guise
Although my downfall be the deepest hell.	P 104	2.47	Guise
Of so great matter should be made the ground.	P 126	2.69	Guise
All this and more, if more may be comprisde,	P 143	2.86	Guise
Too late it is my Lord if that be true/To blame her highnes,	P 181	3.16	QnMarg
but I hope it be/Only some naturall passion makes her sicke.	P 182	3.17	QnMarg
Then be themselves base subjects to the whip.	P 218	4.16	Anjoy
Shall dye, be he King or Emperour.	P 235	4.33	Guise
Then I am carefull you should be preserved.	P 265	4.63	Charls
And so be pacient good Lord Admirall,	P 271	4.69	Charls
I sweare by this to be unmercifull.	P 277	5.4	Dumain
I let the Admirall be first dispatcht.	P 283	5.10	Retes
Be murdered in his bed.	P 287	5.14	Guise
It may be it is some other, and he escapte.	P 308	5.35	Anjoy
Shall being dead, be hangd thereon in chaines.	P 321	5.48	Anjoy
Will be as resolute as I and Dumaine:	P 323	5.50	Guise
I sweare by this crosse, wee'l not be partiall,	P 325	5.52	Anjoy
He that will be a flat decotamest,	P 389	7.29	Guise
I knew the Organon to be confusde,	P 406	7.46	Ramus
that despiseth him, can nere/Be good in Logick or Philosophie.	P 410	7.50	Ramus
Tis well advisde Dumain, goe see it strait be done.	P 424	7.64	Guise
the diadem/Of France be cast on me, then with your leaves/I may	P 473	8.23	Anjoy
and the fire the aire, and so we shall be poysoned with him.	P 485	9.4	P 1Atndt
all doubts, be rulde by me, lets hang him heere upon this tree.	P 491	9.10	P 2Atndt
It will be hard for us to worke their deaths.	P 508	9.27	QnMoth
Be gone, delay no time sweet Guise.	P 509	9.28	QnMoth
My Lords, what resteth there now for to be done?	P 554	11.19	QnMoth
Epernoune, goe see it presently be done,	P 558	11.23	QnMoth
And now my Lords after these funerals be done,	P 561	11.26	QnMoth
I tell thee Mugeroun we will be freends,	P 614	12.27	King
Hands of good fellow, I will be his baile/For this offence:	P 622	12.35	King
Till this our Coronation day be past:	P 624	12.37	King
For while she lives Katherine will be Queene.	P 654	12.67	QnMoth
So he be safe he cares not what becomes,	P 739	14.42	Navrre
Am I thus to be jested at and scornde?	P 758	15.16	Guise
I may be stabd, and live till he be dead,	P 778	15.36	Mugern
If that be all, the next time that I meet her,	P 781	15.39	Mugern
you will take upon you to be his, and tyll the ground that he	P 811	17.6	P Souldr
If it be not too free there's the question:	P 812	17.7	P Souldr
(aspiring Guise)/Durst be in armes without the Kings consent?	P 829	17.24	Eprnon
Be patient Guise and threat not Epernoune,	P 833	17.28	King
Least thou perceive the King of France be mov'd.	P 834	17.29	King
Guise, weare our crowne, and be thou King of France,	P 859	17.54	King
Be thou proclaimde a traitor throughout France.	P 864	17.59	King
shewes did entertaine him/And promised to be at his commaund:	P 875	17.70	Eprnon
My head shall be my counsell, they are false:	P 884	17.79	King
And Epernoune I will be rulde by thee.	P 885	17.80	King
It would be good the Guise were made away,	P 888	17.83	Eprnon
Unles he meane to be betraide and dye:	P 898	17.93	King
Which cannot but be thankfully receiv'd.	P 906	18.7	Bartus
Bartus, it shall be so, poast then to Fraunce,	P 907	18.8	Navrre
Bartus be gone, commend me to his grace,	P 911	18.12	Navrre
And tell him ere it be long, Ile visite him.	P 912	18.13	Navrre
Be gone I say, tis time that we were there.	P 919	18.20	Navrre
That wicked Guise I feare me much will be,	P 921	18.22	Navrre
I, I, feare not: stand close, so, be resolute:	P 943	19.13	Capt
They be my good Lord.	P 948	19.18	Capt
Or be suspicious of my deerest freends:	P 972	19.42	King
Nor immortalitie to be reveng'd:	P1008	19.78	Guise
Ah Sextus, be reveng'd upon the King,	P1010	19.80	Guise

BE (cont.)

Tush, to be short, he meant to make me Munke,	P1039	19.109	King
Or else to murder me, and so be King.	P1040	19.110	King
Ile be revengde.	P1051	19.121	YngGse
I slew the Guise, because I would be King.	P1066	19.136	King
Pray God thou be a King now this is done.	P1068	19.138	QnMoth
But now I will be King and rule my selfe,	P1070	19.140	King
Cry out, exclaime, houle till thy throat be hoarce,	P1077	19.147	King
Whose murderous thoughts will be his overthrow.	P1116	21.10	Dumain
It is enough if that Navarre may be/Esteemed faithfull to the	P1147	22.9	Navrre
What irreligeous Pagans partes be these,	P1180	22.42	King
Oh no Navarre, thou must be King of France.	P1225	22.87	King
Long may you live, and still be King of France.	P1226	22.88	Navrre
yf it be not to free theres the questione | now ser where he is	Paris	ms 8,p390 P	Souldr
ser where he is your landlorde you take upon you to be his |	Paris	ms10,p390 P	Souldr
Then live and be the favorit of a king?	Edw	1.1.5	Gavstn
And with the world be still at enmitie:	Edw	1.1.15	Gavstn
I have no warre, and therefore sir be gone.	Edw	1.1.36	Gavstn
Like Sylvian <Sylvan> Nimphes my pages shall be clad,	Edw	1.1.58	Gavstn
Shall by the angrie goddesse be transformde,	Edw	1.1.68	Gavstn
That villaine Mortimer, ile be his death.	Edw	1.1.81	Gavstn
Therefore if he be come, expell him straight.	Edw	1.1.106	Lncstr
Am I a king and must be over rulde?	Edw	1.1.135	Edward
If for these dignities thou be envied,	Edw	1.1.163	Edward
Wouldst thou be lovde and fearde?	Edw	1.1.168	Edward
I priest, and lives to be revengd on thee,	Edw	1.1.178	Edward
And Gaveston unlesse thou be reclaimd,	Edw	1.1.183	BshpCv
Ile be revengd on him for my exile.	Edw	1.1.192	Gavstn
Be thou lord bishop, and receive his rents,	Edw	1.1.194	Edward
For this offence be thou accurst of God.	Edw	1.1.199	BshpCv
Shall be their timeles sepulcher, or mine.	Edw	1.2.6	Lncstr
Unlesse his brest be sword proofe he shall die.	Edw	1.2.8	Mortmr
Will be the ruine of the realme and us.	Edw	1.2.32	Mortmr
Then wil you joine with us that be his peeres/To banish or	Edw	1.2.42	Mortmr
And courage to, to be revengde at full.	Edw	1.2.60	Mortmr
And war must be the meanes, or heele stay stil.	Edw	1.2.63	Warwck
for rather then my lord/Shall be oppress by civill mutinies,	Edw	1.2.65	Queene
Unlesse he be declinde from that base pesant.	Edw	1.4.7	Mortmr
We will not thus be facst and overpeerd.	Edw	1.4.19	Mortmr
Why are you moov'd, be patient my lord,	Edw	1.4.43	ArchBp
My lords, now let us all be resolute,	Edw	1.4.45	Mortmr
The Legate of the Pope will be obayd:	Edw	1.4.64	Edward
You that be noble borne should pitie him.	Edw	1.4.80	Edward
This will be good newes to the common sort.	Edw	1.4.92	Penbrk
Be it or no, he shall not linger here.	Edw	1.4.93	MortSr
Why should a king be subject to a priest?	Edw	1.4.96	Edward
If I be king, not one of them shall live.	Edw	1.4.105	Edward
And thou must hence, or I shall be deposd,	Edw	1.4.110	Edward
But I will raigne to be reveng'd of them,	Edw	1.4.111	Edward
Be governour of Ireland in my stead,	Edw	1.4.125	Edward
Tis something to be pitied of a king.	Edw	1.4.130	Gavstn
I shal be found, and then twil greeve me more.	Edw	1.4.132	Gavstn
Or thou shalt nere be reconcild to me.	Edw	1.4.157	Edward
There weepe, for till my Gaveston be repeald,	Edw	1.4.168	Edward
And be a meanes to call home Gaveston:	Edw	1.4.184	Queene
His wanton humor will be quicklie left.	Edw	1.4.199	Lncstr
Or else be banisht from his highnesse presence.	Edw	1.4.203	Queene
I Mortimer, for till he be restorde,	Edw	1.4.209	Queene
Be thou my advocate unto these peeres.	Edw	1.4.212	Queene
Will you be resolute and hold with me?	Edw	1.4.231	Lncstr
Well of necessitie it must be so.	Edw	1.4.238	Mortmr
Can this be true twas good to banish him,	Edw	1.4.245	Lncstr
In no respect can contraries be true.	Edw	1.4.249	Lncstr
And whereas he shall live and be belovde,	Edw	1.4.261	Mortmr
How easilie might some base slave be subbornd,	Edw	1.4.265	Mortmr
Tis treason to be up against the king.	Edw	1.4.281	Mortmr
My lords, if to performe this I be slack,	Edw	1.4.290	Mortmr
Repeald, the newes is too sweet to be true.	Edw	1.4.323	Edward
If it be so, what will not Edward do?	Edw	1.4.325	Edward
Once more receive my hand, and let this be,	Edw	1.4.334	Edward
Be thou commaunder of our royall fleete,	Edw	1.4.354	Edward
As England shall be quiet, and you safe.	Edw	1.4.358	Mortmr
Be you the generall of the levied troopes,	Edw	1.4.362	Edward
Who in the triumphe will be challenger,	Edw	1.4.382	Edward
What, meane you then to be his follower?	Edw	2.1.12	Baldck
Then hope I by her meanes to be preferd,	Edw	2.1.29	Baldck
You must be proud, bold, pleasant, resolute,	Edw	2.1.42	Spencr
I will not long be from thee though I die:	Edw	2.1.62	Neece
See that my coache be readie, I must hence.	Edw	2.1.71	Neece
It shall be done madam.	Edw	2.1.72	Baldck
And will be at the court as soone as we.	Edw	2.1.77	Neece
Sweete husband be content, they all love you.	Edw	2.2.36	Queene
What will he do when as he shall be present?	Edw	2.2.48	Mortmr
Returne it to their throtes, ile be thy warrant.	Edw	2.2.73	Edward
Ile not be barde the court for Gaveston.	Edw	2.2.90	Mortmr
Moov'd may he be, and perish in his wrath.	Edw	2.2.101	Mortmr
Weel have him ransomd man, be of good cheere.	Edw	2.2.116	Lncstr
Be resolute, and full of secrecie.	Edw	2.2.125	Lncstr
His highnes is disposde to be alone.	Edw	2.2.135	Guard
Shall I still be haunted thus?	Edw	2.2.154	Edward
Looke for rebellion, looke to be deposde,	Edw	2.2.161	Lncstr
If ye be moov'de, revenge it as you can,	Edw	2.2.198	Lncstr
And dare not be revengde, for their power is great:	Edw	2.2.202	Edward

BE (cont.)

If I be cruell, and growe tyrannous,	Edw	2.2.206	Edward
Will be the ruine of the realme and you,	Edw	2.2.209	Kent
Traitor be gone, whine thou with Mortimer.	Edw	2.2.214	Edward
Then to be favoured of your majestie.	Edw	2.2.255	Spencr
He that I list to favour shall be great:	Edw	2.2.263	Edward
Will be the first that shall adventure life.	Edw	2.3.4	Kent
None be so hardie as to touche the King,	Edw	2.3.27	Lncstr
Farre be it from the thought of Lancaster,	Edw	2.4.33	Lncstr
Might be of lesser force, and with the power/That he intendeth	Edw	2.4.43	Queene
Be easilie suppresst: and therefore be gone.	Edw	2.4.45	Queene
Mine honour will be cald in question,	Edw	2.4.55	Queene
And therefore gentle Mortimer be gone.	Edw	2.4.56	Queene
If he be straunge and not regarde my wordes,	Edw	2.4.64	Queene
And Gaveston this blessed day be slaine.	Edw	2.4.69	Queene
He will be mindfull of the curtesie.	Edw	2.5.40	Arundl
My lords, I will be pledge for his returne.	Edw	2.5.66	Arundl
Be thou this night his keeper, in the morning/We will discharge	Edw	2.5.108	Penbrk
in the morning/We will discharge thee of thy charge, be gon.	Edw	2.5.109	Penbrk
My lord, weele quicklie be at Cobham.	Edw	2.5.111	HrsBoy
O must this day be period of my life,	Edw	2.6.4	Gavstn
And yee be men,/Speede to the king.	Edw	2.6.5	Gavstn
not suffer thus your majestie/Be counterbuft of your nobilitie.	Edw	3.1.19	Spencr
Not to be tied to their affection,	Edw	3.1.29	Baldck
And must be awde and governd like a child.	Edw	3.1.31	Baldck
These be the letters, this the messenger.	Edw	3.1.65	Queene
Sib, if this be all/Valoys and I will soone be friends againe.	Edw	3.1.66	Edward
Sib, if this be all/Valoys and I will soone be friends againe.	Edw	3.1.67	Edward
Madam, we will that you with speed be shipt,	Edw	3.1.81	Edward
And promiseth he shall be safe returnd,	Edw	3.1.110	Arundl
If I be Englands king, in lakes of gore/Your headles trunkes,	Edw	3.1.135	Edward
Away, tarrie no answer, but be gon.	Edw	3.1.173	Edward
I traitors all, rather then thus be bravde,	Edw	3.1.214	Edward
traitors, now tis time/To be avengd on you for all your braves,	Edw	3.1.225	Edward
to request/He might be spared to come to speake with us,	Edw	3.1.235	Edward
Be gon.	Edw	3.1.255	Edward
No Edward, Englands scourge, it may not be,	Edw	3.1.258	Mortmr
Therefore be gon in hast, and with advice,	Edw	3.1.264	Spencr
of golde/To Danae, all aide may be denied/To Isabell the Queene,	Edw	3.1.268	Spencr
And Fraunce shall be obdurat with her teares.	Edw	3.1.279	Levune
Till Edmund be arrivde for Englands good,	Edw	4.1.2	Kent
To thinke that we can yet be tun'd together,	Edw	4.2.9	Queene
Till I be strong enough to breake a staffe,	Edw	4.2.24	Prince
But by the sword, my lord, it must be deserv'd.	Edw	4.2.59	Mortmr
Was borne I see to be our anchor hold.	Edw	4.2.77	Mortmr
Sir John of Henolt, be it thy renowne,	Edw	4.2.78	Mortmr
My lord, we have, and if he be in England,	Edw	4.3.19	Spencr
A will be had ere long I doubt it not.	Edw	4.3.20	Spencr
And windes as equall be to bring them in,	Edw	4.3.51	Edward
blood,/Of thine own people patron shouldst thou be/But thou--	Edw	4.4.13	Queene
Nay madam, if you be a warriar,	Edw	4.4.15	Mortmr
to Longshankes blood/Is false, be not found single for suspect:	Edw	4.6.17	Kent
Thankes be heavens great architect and you.	Edw	4.6.22	Queene
So shall your brother be disposed of.	Edw	4.6.37	Mortmr
May in their fall be followed to their end.	Edw	4.6.79	Mortmr
As silent and as carefull will we be,	Edw	4.7.2	Abbot
Upon my life, those be the men ye seeke.	Edw	4.7.46	Mower
my lord I pray be short,/A faire commission warrants what we	Edw	4.7.47	Rice
As good be gon, as stay and be benighted.	Edw	4.7.86	Rice
My lord, be going, care not for these,	Edw	4.7.93	Rice
Be patient good my lord, cease to lament,	Edw	5.1.1	Leistr
So shall not Englands [Vine] <Vines> be perished,	Edw	5.1.47	Edward
But stay a while, let me be king till night,	Edw	5.1.59	Edward
That Edward may be still faire Englands king:	Edw	5.1.68	Edward
Ile not resigne, but whilst I live, [be king].	Edw	5.1.86	Edward
Traitors be gon, and joine you with Mortimer,	Edw	5.1.87	Edward
If he be not, let him choose.	Edw	5.1.95	BshpWn
hands of mine/Shall not be guiltie of so foule a crime.	Edw	5.1.99	Edward
And will be called the murtherer of a king,	Edw	5.1.101	Edward
If with the sight thereof she be not mooved,	Edw	5.1.119	Edward
Unlesse it be with too much clemencie?	Edw	5.1.123	Edward
Will be my death, and welcome shall it be,	Edw	5.1.126	Edward
So may his limmes be torne, as is this paper,	Edw	5.1.142	Edward
Be rulde by me, and we will rule the realme,	Edw	5.2.5	Mortmr
And that I be protector over him,	Edw	5.2.12	Mortmr
the greater sway/When as a kings name shall be under writ.	Edw	5.2.14	Mortmr
Be thou perswaded, that I love thee well,	Edw	5.2.16	Queene
And therefore so the prince my sonne be safe,	Edw	5.2.17	Queene
Thankes gentle Winchester: sirra, be gon.	Edw	5.2.27	Queene
Then let some other be his guardian.	Edw	5.2.36	Queene
Bartley shall be dischargd, the king remoovde,	Edw	5.2.40	Mortmr
Speake, shall he presently be dispatch'd and die?	Edw	5.2.44	Mortmr
It shall be done my lord.	Edw	5.2.51	Matrvs
Our plots and stratagems will soone be dasht.	Edw	5.2.78	Mortmr
Doe looke to be protector over the prince?	Edw	5.2.89	Mortmr
Let him be king, I am too yong to raigne.	Edw	5.2.93	Prince
To be revengde on Mortimer and thee.	Edw	5.2.121	Kent
My lord, be not pensive, we are your friends.	Edw	5.3.1	Matrvs
Must I be vexed like the nightly birde,	Edw	5.3.6	Edward
When will his hart be satisfied with bloud?	Edw	5.3.9	Edward
Sit downe, for weele be Barbars to your grace.	Edw	5.3.28	Matrvs
Least you be knowne, and so be rescued.	Edw	5.3.32	Gurney
Twixt theirs and yours, shall be no enmitie.	Edw	5.3.46	Matrvs

BE (cont.)

Seeing that my brother cannot be releast.	Edw		5.3.67		Kent
That being dead, if it chaunce to be found, . . .	Edw		5.4.14		Mortmr
And we be quit that causde it to be done:	Edw		5.4.16		Mortmr
Shall he be murdered when the deed is done. . . .	Edw		5.4.20		Mortmr
Well, do it bravely, and be secret.	Edw		5.4.28		Mortmr
I care not how it is, so it be not spide:	Edw		5.4.40		Mortmr
Feard am I more then lov'd, let me be feard, . . .	Edw		5.4.52		Mortmr
And that this be the coronation day, ...	Edw		5.4.70		Mortmr
Sonne, be content, I dare not speake a worde. . . .	Edw		5.4.96		Queene
If that my Unckle shall be murthered thus? . . .	Edw		5.4.110		King
See how he must be handled for his labour, . . .	Edw		5.5.23		Matrvs
Yet be not farre off, I shall need your helpe, . . .	Edw		5.5.28		Ltborn
And get me a spit, and let it be red hote. . . .	Edw		5.5.30		Ltborn
My minde may be more stedfast on my God.	Edw		5.5.78		Edward
Nor shall they now be tainted with a kings. . . .	Edw		5.5.82		Ltborn
If you mistrust me, ile be gon my lord.	Edw		5.5.97		Ltborn
if thou now growest penitent/Ile be thy ghostly father, .	Edw		5.6.4		Mortmr
Whether thou wilt be secret in this, ...	Edw		5.6.5		Mortmr
And vowes to be revengd upon us both, ...	Edw		5.6.19		Queene
Because I thinke scorne to be accusde, ...	Edw		5.6.39		Mortmr
Yes, if this be the hand of Mortimer.	Edw		5.6.44		King
I feard as much, murther cannot be hid.	Edw		5.6.46		Queene
And so shalt thou be too: why staies he heere? . . .	Edw		5.6.51		King
Till further triall may be made thereof.	Edw		5.6.80		King
If you be guiltie, though I be your sonne, ...	Edw		5.6.81		King
Be witnesse of my greefe and innocencie.	Edw		5.6.102		King
Having commenc'd, be a Divine in shew, ...	F	31	1.1.3		Faust
Be a Phisitian Faustus, heape up gold, ...	F	42	1.1.14		Faust
And be eterniz'd for some wondrous cure:	F	43	1.1.15		Faust
Then this profession were to be esteem'd.	F	54	1.1.26		Faust
What will be, shall be; Divinitie adeiw.	F	75	1.1.47		Faust
that move betweene the quiet Poles/Shall be at my command:	F	84	1.1.56		Faust
Their conference will be a greater helpe to me, . . .	F	95	1.1.67		Faust
Be thou on earth as Jove is in the skye, ...	F	103	1.1.75		BdAngl
Wherewith the Students shall be bravely clad. . . .	F	118	1.1.90		Faust
Will be as cunning as Agrippa was, ...	F	144	1.1.116		Faust
Be alwaies serviceable to us three:	F	150	1.1.122		Valdes
If learned Faustus will be resolute.	F	160	1.1.132		Valdes
Then doubt not Faustus but to be renowm'd, ...	F	168	1.1.140		Cornel
And then wilt thou be perfecter then I.	F	189	1.1.161		Valdes
upon; therefore acknowledge your errour, and be attentive.	F	204	1.2.11	P	Wagner
<Aske my fellow if I be a thiefe>.	F	204	(HC258)A	P	Wagner
be <and see if hee by> his grave counsell may <can> reclaime	F	226	1.2.33		2Schol
Then feare not Faustus to <but> be resolute/And try the utmost	F	242	1.3.14		Faust
Who would not be proficient in this Art?	F	256	1.3.28		Faust
Be it to make the Moone drop from her Sphere, . . .	F	266	1.3.38		Faust
Whereby he is in danger to be damn'd:	F	279	1.3.51		Mephst
My <His> Ghost be with the old Phylosophers. . . .	F	288	1.3.60		Faust
And alwaies be obedient to my will.	F	325	1.3.97		Faust
Had I as many soules, as there be Starres, ...	F	330	1.3.102		Faust
By him, I'le be great Emperour of the world, ...	F	332	1.3.104		Faust
Sirra, wilt thou be my man and waite on me?	F	354	1.4.12	P	Wagner
then belike if I serve you, I shall be lousy. . . .	F	359	1.4.17	P	Robin
Why so thou shalt be, whether thou dost it or no: . .	F	360	1.4.18	P	Wagner
your right eye be alwaies Diametrally fixt upon my left heele,	F	386	1.4.44	P	Wagner
Now Faustus, must thou needs be damn'd, ...	F	389	2.1.1		Faust
[And] canst <thou> not [now] be sav'd.	F	390	2.1.2		Faust
Now go not backward: no, Faustus, be resolute. . . .	F	394	2.1.6		Faust
Why, the Signory of Embden shall be mine:	F	412	2.1.24		Faust
And I will be thy slave and waite on thee, ...	F	435	2.1.47		Mephst
And then be thou as great as Lucifer.	F	441	2.1.53		Mephst
bloud/Assures his <assure my> soule to be great Lucifers,	F	444	2.1.56		Faust
And let it be propitious for my wish.	F	447	2.1.59		Faust
First, that Faustus may be a spirit in forme and substance.	F	485	2.1.97	P	Faust
that Mephostophilis shall be his servant, and be by him .	F	486	2.1.98	P	Faust
shall be his servant, and be by him commanded <at his command>.	F	486	2.1.98	P	Faust
Fourthly, that he shall be in his chamber or house invisible.	F	490	2.1.102	P	Faust
And where hell is there must we ever be.	F	512	2.1.124		Mephst
And to be short <conclude>, when all the world dissolves,	F	513	2.1.125		Mephst
And every creature shall be purifi'd, ...	F	514	2.1.126		Mephst
All places shall be hell that is not heaven.	F	515	2.1.127		Mephst
Why, dost thou think <think'st thou then> that Faustus shall be	F	518	2.1.130		Faust
Nay, and this be hell, I'le willingly be damn'd <damned here>.	F	527	2.1.139		Faust
Were <Be> she as chaste as was Penelope, ...	F	540	2.1.152		Mephst
[Here they be].	F	551.11	2.1.174A	P	Mephst
Be I a devill yet God may pitty me, ...	F	566	2.2.15		Faust
No Faustus they be but Fables.	F	613	2.2.62	P	Mephst
That sight will be as pleasant to <pleasing unto> me, as .	F	657	2.2.106	P	Faust
unlesse <except> the ground be <were> perfum'd, and cover'd	F	670	2.2.119	P	Pride
live along, then thou should'st see how fat I'de <I would> be.	F	683	2.2.132	P	Envy
in hell, and look to it, for some of you shall be my father.	F	690	2.2.139	P	Wrath
be carried thither againe by Gluttony and Letchery <Leachery>],	F	705.2	2.2.156A	P	Sloth
I, there be of us here, that have waded as deepe into matters,	F	740	2.3.19	P	Robin
Not to be wonne by any conquering Prince:	F	783	3.1.5		Faust
<Faustus I have, and because we wil not be unprovided, .	F	805	(HC265)A	P	Mephst
All's one, for wee'l be bold with his Venison.	F	808	3.1.30		Mephst
<Tut, tis no matter man>, wee'l be bold with his <good cheare>.	F	808	(HC265)A	P	Mephst
Whilst I am here on earth let me be cloyd/With all things that	F	837	3.1.59		Faust
May be admired through the furthest Land.	F	842	3.1.64		Faust
Then in this shew let me an Actor be, ...	F	854	3.1.76		Faust
Let it be so my Faustus, but first stay, ...	F	856	3.1.78		Mephst
This day shall make thee be admir'd in Rome.	F	867	3.1.89		Mephst

BE (cont.)

Or be assured of our dreadfull curse,	F 938	3.1.160		Pope
and the Germane Emperour/Be held as Lollords, and bold	F 955	3.1.177		Faust
He shall be streight condemn'd of heresie,	F 962	3.1.184		Faust
Away sweet Mephostophilis be gone,	F 975	3.1.197		Faust
The Cardinals will be plagu'd for this anon.	F 976	3.1.198		Faust
<Then charme me that I may be invisible>,	F 991	(HC266)A		Faust
Do what thou wilt, thou shalt not be discern'd.	F1005	3.2.25		Mephst
And see that all things be in readinesse,	F1011	3.2.31		Pope
With his rich triple crowne to be reserv'd,	F1027	3.2.47		Raymnd
Curst be your soules to hellish misery.	F1034	3.2.54		Pope
I thinke it be some Ghost crept out of Purgatory, and now is	F1059	3.2.79	P	Archbp
It may be so:	F1062	3.2.82		Pope
Must every bit be spiced with a Crosse?	F1066	3.2.86		Faust
Damb'd be this soule for ever, for this deed.	F1070	3.2.90		Pope
for I can tell you, you'le be curst with Bell, Booke, and	F1072	3.2.92	P	Mephst
be he that stole [away] his holinesse meate from the Table.	F1077	3.2.97		1Frier
Cursed be he that stroke his holinesse a blow [on] the face.	F1079	3.2.99		1Frier
be he that strucke <tooke> fryer Sandelo a blow on the pate.	F1081	3.2.101		1Frier
Cursed be he that disturbeth our holy Dirge.	F1083	3.2.103		1Frier
Cursed be he that tooke away his holinesse wine.	F1085	3.2.105		1Frier
First, be thou turned to this ugly shape,	F1126	3.3.39		Mephst
be thou transformed to/A dog, and carry him upon thy backe;	F1130	3.3.43		Mephst
Away be gone.	F1132	3.3.45		Mephst
Good Fredericke see the roomes be voyded straight,	F1157	4.1.3		Mrtino
and if he be so farre in love with him, I would he would post	F1190	4.1.36	P	Benvol
who comes to see/What wonders by blacke spels may compast be.	F1198	4.1.44		Mrtino
if a man be drunke over night, the Divell cannot hurt him in	F1201	4.1.47	P	Benvol
For ever be belov'd of Carolus.	F1211	4.1.57		Emper
Thou shalt be famous through all Italy,	F1215	4.1.61		Emper
For proofe whereof, if so your Grace be pleas'd,	F1221	4.1.67		Faust
Be it as Faustus please, we are content.	F1253	4.1.99		Emper
the Emperour, Il'e be Acteon, and turne my selfe to a Stagge.	F1255	4.1.101	P	Benvol
How may I prove that saying to be true?	F1268	4.1.114		Emper
Away, be gone.	F1273	4.1.119		Faust
be such Cuckold-makers to clap hornes of honest mens heades	F1316	4.1.162	P	Benvol
But an I be not reveng'd for this, would I might be turn'd to a	F1319	4.1.165	P	Benvol
would I might be turn'd to a gaping Oyster, and drinke nothing	F1319	4.1.165	P	Benvol
Then draw your weapons, and be resolute:	F1335	4.2.11		Benvol
Be ready then, and strike the Peasant downe.	F1359	4.2.35		Fredrk
Mine be that honour then:	F1360	4.2.36		Benvol
Defend me heaven, shall I be haunted still?	F1439	4.3.9		Benvol
and one to whom I must be no niggard of my cunning; Come,	F1504	4.4.48	P	Faust
best beere in Europe, what ho, Hostis; where be these Whores?	F1506	4.5.2	P	Carter
yes, that may be; for I have heard of one, that ha's eate a load	F1533	4.5.29	P	Robin
because I knew him to be such a horse, as would run over hedge	F1538	4.5.34	P	HrsCsr
it may be, that you have taken no pleasure in those sights;	F1565	4.6.8	P	Faust
be it in the world, it shall be yours:	F1567	4.6.10	P	Faust
be it in the world, it shall be yours:	F1568	4.6.11	P	Faust
they should be good, for they come from a farre Country I can	F1576	4.6.19	P	Faust
Why saucy varlets, dare you be so bold.	F1594	4.6.37		Servnt
I hope sir, we have wit enough to be more bold then welcome.	F1595	4.6.38	P	HrsCsr
It appeares so, pray be bold else-where,	F1597	4.6.40		Servnt
we will be wellcome for our mony, and we will pay for what we	F1611	4.6.54	P	Robin
What ho, give's halfe a dosen of Beere here, and be hang'd.	F1613	4.6.56	P	Robin
Be not so furious: come you shall have Beere.	F1620	4.6.63		Faust
that flesh and bloud should be so fraile with your Worship:	F1632	4.6.75	P	Carter
Be both your legs bedfellowes every night together?	F1645	4.6.88	P	Carter
Be silent then, for danger is in words.	F1696	5.1.23		Faust
sight <glorious deed>/Happy and blest be Faustus evermore.	F1705	5.1.32		1Schol
It may be this my exhortation/Seemes harsh, and all unpleasant;	F1717	5.1.44		OldMan
Shall be perform'd in twinkling of an eye.	F1767	5.1.94		Mephst
Here will I dwell, for heaven is <be> in these lippes,	F1773	5.1.100		Faust
I will be Paris <Pacis>, and for love of thee,	F1775	5.1.102		Faust
In stead of Troy shall Wittenberg <Wertenberge> be sack't,/And	F1776	5.1.103		Faust
And none but thou shalt be my Paramour.	F1787	5.1.114		Faust
Here in this roome will wretched Faustus be.	F1804	5.2.8		Mephst
His store of pleasures must be sauc'd with paine.	F1812	5.2.16		Mephst
If it be so, wee'l have Physitians,	F1830	5.2.34		2Schol
But Faustus offence can nere be pardoned, the serpent that	F1837	5.2.41	P	Faust
the serpent that tempted Eve may be saved, but not Faustus.	F1838	5.2.42	P	Faust
For that must be thy mansion, there to dwell.	F1882	5.2.86		Mephst
thou shalt see/Ten thousand tortures that more horrid be.	F1920	5.2.124		BdAngl
And then thou must be damn'd perpetually.	F1928	5.2.132		Faust
or let this houre be but/A yeare, a month, a weeke, a naturall	F1932	5.2.136		Faust
The devill will come, and Faustus must be damn'd.	F1937	5.2.141		Faust
'twill all be past anone:	F1957	5.2.161		Faust
A hundred thousand, and at last be sav'd.	F1962	5.2.166		Faust
flie from me, and I be chang'd/[Unto] <Into> some brutish beast.	F1967	5.2.171		Faust
But mine must live still to be plagu'd in hell.	F1971	5.2.175		Faust
Curst be the parents that ingendred me;	F1972	5.2.176		Faust
O soule be chang'd into <to> [little] <small> water drops,	F1977	5.2.181		Faust
And fall into the Ocean, ne're be found.	F1978	5.2.182		Faust
tho Faustus end be such/As every Christian heart laments to	F1995	5.3.13		2Schol
Doe yee heare, I would be sorie to robbe you of your living.	F App	p.229 18	P	Clown
then belike, if I were your man, I should be ful of vermine.	F App	p.229 22	P	Clown
Gridyrons, what be they?	F App	p.230 31	P	Clown
divell, so I should be cald kill divell all the parish over.	F App	p.230 48	P	Clown
let it be in the likenesse of a little pretie frisking flea,	F App	p.231 61	P	Clown
that I may be here and there and every where, O Ile tickle the	F App	p.231 62	P	Clown
tickle the pretie wenches plackets Ile be amongst them ifaith.	F App	p.231 63	P	Clown
and let thy left eye be diametarily fixt upon my right heele,	F App	p.231 69	P	Wagner
be some ghost newly crept out of Purgatory come to begge a	F App	p.232 14	P	Lorein

BE (cont.)

It may be so, Friers prepare a dirge to lay the fury of this	F App	p.232 16 P	Pope
Cursed be hee that stole away his holinesse meate from/the	F App	p.232 31	Frier
Cursed be hee that strooke his holinesse a blowe on the face.	F App	p.232 33	Frier
Cursed be he that tooke Frier Sandelo a blow on the pate.	F App	p.232 35	Frier
Cursed be he that disturbeth our holy Dirge.	F App	p.232 37	Frier
Cursed be he that tooke away his holinesse wine.	F App	p.233 39	Frier
Drawer, I hope al is payd, God be with you, come Rafe.	F App	p.234 6 P	Robin
you may be ashamed to burden honest men with a matter of truth.	F App	p.234 14 P	Rafe
sixe pence in your purse to pay for your supper, and be gone?	F App	p.235 42 P	Robin
thee into an Ape, and thee into a Dog, and so be gone.	F App	p.235 44 P	Mephst
And I must be a Dogge.	F App	p.236 47 P	Rafe
Ifaith thy head will never be out of the potage pot.	F App	p.236 48 P	Robin
be witnesses to confirme what mine eares have heard reported,	F App	p.236 7 P	Emper
thou doest, thou shalt be no wayes prejudiced or indamaged.	F App	p.236 9 P	Emper
Mephastophilis be gone.	F App	p.237 56 P	Faust
Nay, and you go to conjuring, Ile be gone.	F App	p.237 57 P	Knight
or moale in her necke, how shal I know whether it be so or no?	F App	p.238 61 P	Emper
but hark ye sir, if my horse be sick, or ill at ease, if I bring	F App	p.240 118 P	HrsCsr
I would not be ruled by him, for he bade me I should ride him	F App	p.240 130 P	HrsCsr
Where be they?	F App	p.241 160 P	Mephst
Be gone quickly.	F App	p.241 163 P	Mephst
to whom I must be no niggard of my cunning, come	F App	p.241 171 P	Faust
but it may be Madame, you take no delight in this, I have heard	F App	p.242 4 P	Faust
Alas Madame, thats nothing, Mephastophilis, be gone.	F App	p.242 12 P	Faust
here they be madam, wilt please you taste on them.	F App	p.242 15 P	Faust
hither, as ye see, how do you like them Madame, be they good?	F App	p.242 24 P	Faust
they be the best grapes that ere I tasted in my life before.	F App	p.242 25 P	Duchss
And Carthage soules be glutted with our blouds;	Lucan, First Booke	39	
Undaunted though her former guide be chang'd.	Lucan, First Booke	50	
What God it please thee be, or where to sway:	Lucan, First Booke	52	
Shall never faith be found in fellow kings.	Lucan, First Booke	92	
Who though his root be weake, and his owne waight/Keepe him	Lucan, First Booke	139	
Romans if ye be,/And beare true harts, stay heare:	Lucan, First Booke	193	
wonst thou France; Roome may be won/With farre lesse toile,	Lucan, First Booke	283	
Nor capitall be adorn'd with sacred bayes:	Lucan, First Booke	288	
So be I may be bold to speake a truth,	Lucan, First Booke	361	
This [band] <hand> that all behind us might be quail'd,	Lucan, First Booke	370	
What wals thou wilt be leaveld with the ground,	Lucan, First Booke	384	
Albeit the Citty thou wouldst have so ra'st/Be Roome it selfe.	Lucan, First Booke	387	
cause, what ere thou be whom God assignes/This great effect,	Lucan, First Booke	419	
and that Roome/He looking on by these men should be sackt.	Lucan, First Booke	480	
And Marriners, albeit the keele be sound,	Lucan, First Booke	500	
Mules loth'd issue)/To be cut forth and cast in dismall fiers:	Lucan, First Booke	590	
all to good, be Augury vaine, and Tages/Th'arts master falce.	Lucan, First Booke	635	
Shall townes be swallowed?	Lucan, First Booke	645	
Become intemperate? shall the earth be barraine?	Lucan, First Booke	646	
Shall water be conjeal'd and turn'd to ice?	Lucan, First Booke	647	
And in the fleeting sea the earth be drencht.	Lucan, First Booke	653	
rayes now sing/The fell Nemean beast, th'earth would be fired,	Lucan, First Booke	655	
Two tane away, thy labor will be lesse:	Ovid's Elegies	1.1.4	
Let my first verse be sixe, my last five feete,	Ovid's Elegies	1.1.31	
Although the nights be long, I sleepe not tho,	Ovid's Elegies	1.2.3	
And captive like be manacled and bound.	Ovid's Elegies	1.2.30	
Be thou the happie subject of my Bookes,	Ovid's Elegies	1.3.19	
So likewise we will through the world be rung,	Ovid's Elegies	1.3.25	
And with my name shall thine be alwaies sung.	Ovid's Elegies	1.3.26	
Pray God it may his latest supper be,	Ovid's Elegies	1.4.2	
though I not see/What may be done, yet there before him bee.	Ovid's Elegies	1.4.14	
Thy Rosie cheekes be to thy thombe inclinde.	Ovid's Elegies	1.4.22	
Let thy soft finger to thy eare be brought.	Ovid's Elegies	1.4.24	
Let not thy necke by his vile armes be prest,	Ovid's Elegies	1.4.35	
There will I finde thee, or be found by thee,	Ovid's Elegies	1.4.57	
Forbeare sweet wordes, and be your sport unpleasant.	Ovid's Elegies	1.4.66	
But though this night thy fortune be to trie it,	Ovid's Elegies	1.4.69	
Such light to shamefaste maidens must be showne,	Ovid's Elegies	1.5.7	
Where they may sport, and seeme to be unknowne.	Ovid's Elegies	1.5.8	
Yet strivde she to be covered therewithall,	Ovid's Elegies	1.5.14	
And striving thus as one that would be cast,	Ovid's Elegies	1.5.15	
How apt her breasts were to be prest by me,	Ovid's Elegies	1.5.20	
his tender mother/And smiling sayed, be thou as bold as other.	Ovid's Elegies	1.6.12	
When thou stood'st naked ready to be beate,	Ovid's Elegies	1.6.19	
Gratis thou maiest be free, give like for like,	Ovid's Elegies	1.6.23	
would, I cannot him cashiere/Before I be divided from my geere.	Ovid's Elegies	1.6.36	
Though it be so, shut me not out therefore,	Ovid's Elegies	1.6.47	
What ere thou art, farewell, be like me paind,	Ovid's Elegies	1.6.71	
And to my selfe could I be so injurious?	Ovid's Elegies	1.7.26	
lockes spred/On her white necke but for hurt cheekes be led.	Ovid's Elegies	1.7.40	
wheeles spun/And what with Mares ranck humour may be done.	Ovid's Elegies	1.8.8	
Wert thou rich, poore should not be my state.	Ovid's Elegies	1.8.28	
Brasse shines with use; good garments would be worne,	Ovid's Elegies	1.8.51	
Dissemble so, as lov'd he may be thought,	Ovid's Elegies	1.8.71	
Nor let my words be with the windes hence blowne,	Ovid's Elegies	1.8.106	
Tis shame for eld in warre or love to be.	Ovid's Elegies	1.9.4	
The whore stands to be bought for each mans mony/And seekes	Ovid's Elegies	1.10.21	
Tis shame their wits should be more excelent.	Ovid's Elegies	1.10.26	
To give I love, but to be ask't disdayne,	Ovid's Elegies	1.10.63	
Be sedulous, let no stay cause thee tarry.	Ovid's Elegies	1.11.8	
funerall wood be flying/And thou the waxe stuft full with notes	Ovid's Elegies	1.12.7	
Be broake with wheeles of chariots passing by.	Ovid's Elegies	1.12.14	
And birds for <from> Memnon yearly shall be slaine.	Ovid's Elegies	1.13.4	
Not one in heaven should be more base and vile.	Ovid's Elegies	1.13.36	
Farre off be force, no fire to them may reach,	Ovid's Elegies	1.14.29	

BE (cont.)

No sicknesse harm'd thee, farre be that a way,	Ovid's Elegies	1.14.41
And be heereafter seene with native haire.	Ovid's Elegies	1.14.56
While bond-men cheat, fathers [be hard] <hoord>, bawds hoorish,	Ovid's Elegies	1.15.17
What age of Varroes name shall not be tolde,	Ovid's Elegies	1.15.21
Aeneas warre, and Titerus shall be read,	Ovid's Elegies	1.15.25
Till Cupids bow, and fierie shafts be broken,	Ovid's Elegies	1.15.27
Thy verses sweet Tibullus shall be spoken.	Ovid's Elegies	1.15.28
And Gallus shall be knowne from East to West,	Ovid's Elegies	1.15.29
About my head be quivering Mirtle wound,	Ovid's Elegies	1.15.37
And in sad lovers heads let me be found.	Ovid's Elegies	1.15.38
So Cupid wills, farre hence be the severe,	Ovid's Elegies	2.1.3
While I speake some fewe, yet fit words be idle.	Ovid's Elegies	2.2.2
Keeper if thou be wise cease hate to cherish,	Ovid's Elegies	2.2.9
Feare to be guilty, then thou maiest desemble.	Ovid's Elegies	2.2.18
Enquire not what with Isis may be done/Nor feare least she to	Ovid's Elegies	2.2.25
Let him please, haunt the house, be kindly usd,	Ovid's Elegies	2.2.29
Enjoy the wench, let all else be refusd.	Ovid's Elegies	2.2.30
What can be easier then the thing we pray?	Ovid's Elegies	2.2.66
Thy mistrisse enseignes must be likewise thine.	Ovid's Elegies	2.3.10
Me thinkes she should <would> be nimble when shees downe.	Ovid's Elegies	2.4.14
If she be learned, then for her skill I crave her,	Ovid's Elegies	2.4.17
She would be nimbler, lying with a man.	Ovid's Elegies	2.4.24
If she be tall, shees like an Amazon,	Ovid's Elegies	2.4.33
[I thinke what one undeckt would be, being drest];	Ovid's Elegies	2.4.37
If her white necke be shadowde with blacke haire,	Ovid's Elegies	2.4.41
Cupid flie)/That my chiefe wish should be so oft to die.	Ovid's Elegies	2.5.2
O would my proofes as vaine might be withstood,	Ovid's Elegies	2.5.7
And words that seem'd for certaine markes to be.	Ovid's Elegies	2.5.20
No where can they be taught but in the bed,	Ovid's Elegies	2.5.61
things hidden)/Whence uncleane fowles are said to be forbidden.	Ovid's Elegies	2.6.52
Our pleasant scapes shew thee no clowne to be,	Ovid's Elegies	2.8.3
That might be urg'd to witnesse our false playing.	Ovid's Elegies	2.8.8
Let [me] <her> enjoy [her] <me> oft, oft be debard.	Ovid's Elegies	2.9.46
I could not be in love with twoo at once,	Ovid's Elegies	2.10.2
Let such as be mine enemies have none,	Ovid's Elegies	2.10.16
In all thy face will be no crimsen bloud.	Ovid's Elegies	2.11.28
Whose blast may hether strongly be inclinde,	Ovid's Elegies	2.11.38
Ile thinke all true, though it be feigned matter.	Ovid's Elegies	2.11.53
Let the bright day-starre cause in heaven this day be,	Ovid's Elegies	2.11.55
To bring that happy time so soone as may be.	Ovid's Elegies	2.11.56
What helpes it Woman to be free from warre?	Ovid's Elegies	2.14.1
Deserv'd thereby with death to be tormented.	Ovid's Elegies	2.14.6
[Or] <On> stones, our stockes originall, should be hurld,	Ovid's Elegies	2.14.11
And my presages of no weight be thought.	Ovid's Elegies	2.14.42
Be welcome to her, gladly let her take thee,	Ovid's Elegies	2.15.3
Or [be] a loade thou shouldst refuse to beare.	Ovid's Elegies	2.15.22
In heaven without thee would I not be fixt.	Ovid's Elegies	2.16.14
And falling vallies be the smooth-wayes crowne.	Ovid's Elegies	2.16.52
Let me be slandered, while my fire she hides,	Ovid's Elegies	2.17.3
Small things with greater may be copulate.	Ovid's Elegies	2.17.14
Lay in the mid bed, there be my law giver.	Ovid's Elegies	2.17.24
Nor of our love to be asham'd we need,	Ovid's Elegies	2.17.26
Nor in my bookes shall one but thou be writ,	Ovid's Elegies	2.17.33
Wild me, whose slowe feete sought delay, be flying.	Ovid's Elegies	2.19.12
Thou doest beginne, she shall be mine no longer.	Ovid's Elegies	2.19.48
Shall I poore soule be never interdicted?	Ovid's Elegies	2.19.53
And first [she] <he> sayd, when will thy love be spent,	Ovid's Elegies	3.1.15
This thou wilt say to be a worthy ground.	Ovid's Elegies	3.1.26
Venus without me should be rusticall,	Ovid's Elegies	3.1.43
From no mans reading fearing to be sav'd.	Ovid's Elegies	3.1.54
Yet whom thou favourst, pray may conquerour be.	Ovid's Elegies	3.2.2
Let my new mistris graunt to be beloved:	Ovid's Elegies	3.2.57
For evermore thou shalt my mistris be.	Ovid's Elegies	3.2.62
thou maiest, if that be best,/[A] <Or> while thy tiptoes on the	Ovid's Elegies	3.2.63
Let with strong hand the reine to bend be made.	Ovid's Elegies	3.2.72
So long they be, since she her faith forsooke.	Ovid's Elegies	3.3.4
radiant like starres they be,/By which she perjurd oft hath	Ovid's Elegies	3.3.9
Or if there be a God, he loves fine wenches,	Ovid's Elegies	3.3.25
And I would be none of the Gods severe.	Ovid's Elegies	3.3.46
Nor, least she will, can any be restrainde.	Ovid's Elegies	3.4.6
She must be honest to thy servants credit.	Ovid's Elegies	3.4.36
Kindly thy mistris use, if thou be wise.	Ovid's Elegies	3.4.43
<redde-growne> slime bankes, till I be past/Thy waters stay:	Ovid's Elegies	3.5.1
First to be throwne upon the untill'd ground.	Ovid's Elegies	3.5.16
Nere was, nor shall be, what my verse mentions.	Ovid's Elegies	3.5.18
There shalt be lov'd: Ilia lay feare aside.	Ovid's Elegies	3.5.62
Why might not then my sinews be inchanted,	Ovid's Elegies	3.6.35
I wisht to be received in, <and> in I [get] <got> me,	Ovid's Elegies	3.6.47
And craves his taske, and seekes to be at fight.	Ovid's Elegies	3.6.68
Homer without this shall be nothing worth.	Ovid's Elegies	3.7.28
Souldiours by bloud to be inricht have lucke.	Ovid's Elegies	3.7.54
If of scornd lovers god be venger just,	Ovid's Elegies	3.7.65
And some there be that thinke we have a deity.	Ovid's Elegies	3.8.18
Yet shall thy life be forcibly bereaven.	Ovid's Elegies	3.8.38
Who thinkes her to be glad at lovers smart,	Ovid's Elegies	3.9.15
Be witnesse Crete (nor Crete doth all things feigne)/Crete	Ovid's Elegies	3.9.19
May that shame fall mine enemies chance to be.	Ovid's Elegies	3.10.16
Hearing her to be sicke, I thether ranne,	Ovid's Elegies	3.10.25
fellow bed, by all/The Gods who by thee to be perjurde fall,	Ovid's Elegies	3.10.46
When Thebes, when Troy, when Caesar should be writ,	Ovid's Elegies	3.11.15
Let me, and them by it be aye be-friended.	Ovid's Elegies	3.12.36
Before the roome be cleere, and doore put too.	Ovid's Elegies	3.13.10

BE (cont.)			
And let the world be witnesse of the same?	Ovid's Elegies	3.13.12	
Be more advisde, walke as a puritane,	Ovid's Elegies	3.13.13	
When you are up and drest, be sage and grave,	Ovid's Elegies	3.13.19	
Be not ashamed to strippe you being there,	Ovid's Elegies	3.13.21	
And would be dead, but dying <dead> with thee remaine.	Ovid's Elegies	3.13.40	
Though while the deede be doing you be tooke,	Ovid's Elegies	3.13.43	
Sweare I was blinde, yeeld not <deny>, if you be wise,	Ovid's Elegies	3.13.45	
Where little ground to be inclosd befalles,	Ovid's Elegies	3.14.12	
Faire Cinthia wisht, his armes might be her spheare,	Hero and Leander	1.59	
Though thou be faire, yet be not thine owne thrall.	Hero and Leander	1.90	
Be not unkind and faire, mishapen stuffe/Are of behaviour	Hero and Leander	1.203	
My words shall be as spotlesse as my youth,	Hero and Leander	1.207	
When you fleet hence, can be bequeath'd to none.	Hero and Leander	1.248	
Untill some honourable deed be done.	Hero and Leander	1.282	
Whose name is it, if she be false or not,	Hero and Leander	1.285	
So she be faire, but some vile toongs will blot?	Hero and Leander	1.286	
Love Hero then, and be not tirannous,	Hero and Leander	1.323	
Faire fooles delight to be accounted nice.	Hero and Leander	1.326	
The richest corne dies, if it be not reapt,	Hero and Leander	1.327	
And would be thought to graunt against her will.	Hero and Leander	1.336	
And spends the night (that might be better spent)/In vaine	Hero and Leander	1.355	
Both might enjoy ech other, and be blest.	Hero and Leander	1.380	
To be reveng'd on Jove, did undertake,	Hero and Leander	1.442	
Might presently be banisht into hell,	Hero and Leander	1.453	
But be surpris'd with every garish toy.	Hero and Leander	1.480	
In offring parlie, to be counted light.	Hero and Leander	2.9	
Fearing her owne thoughts made her to be hated.	Hero and Leander	2.44	
O what god would not therewith be appeas'd?	Hero and Leander	2.50	
Supposing nothing else was to be done,	Hero and Leander	2.53	
She, fearing on the rushes to be flung,	Hero and Leander	2.66	
And stay the messenger that would be gon:	Hero and Leander	2.82	
her selfe the clouds among/And now Leander fearing to be mist,	Hero and Leander	2.91	
Saying, let your vowes and promises be kept.	Hero and Leander	2.96	
Home when he came, he seem'd not to be there,	Hero and Leander	2.117	
As meaning to be veng'd for darting it.	Hero and Leander	2.212	
The god seeing him with pittie to be moved,	Hero and Leander	2.219	
Come live with mee, and be my love,	Passionate Shepherd	1	
Come <Then> live with mee, and be my love.	Passionate Shepherd	20	
Then live with mee, and be my love.	Passionate Shepherd	24	
BEADES			
To beate the beades about the Friers Pates,	F 863	3.1.85	Mephst
BEAKE			
Raven that tolls/The sicke mans passeport in her hollow beake,	Jew	2.1.2	Barab
BEAME			
foote drawes out/Fastning her light web some old beame about.	Ovid's Elegies	1.14.8	
BEAMES			
As I exhal'd with thy fire darting beames,	Dido	1.1.25	Jupitr
Lest their grosse eye-beames taint my lovers cheekes:	Dido	3.1.74	Dido
When as he buts his beames on Floras bed,	Dido	3.4.20	Dido
Commaunds me leave these unrenowmed [reames] <beames>,	Dido	4.3.18	Aeneas
Wherewith his burning beames like labouring Bees,	Dido	5.1.12	Aeneas
Nor Sun reflexe his vertuous beames thereon,	1Tamb	3.1.52	Moroc
Whose beames illuminate the lamps of heaven,	2Tamb	1.3.2	Tamb
Now wants the fewell that enflamde his beames:	2Tamb	2.4.4	Tamb
with which I burst/The rusty beames of Janus Temple doores,	2Tamb	2.4.114	Tamb
not full of thoughtes/As pure and fiery as Phyteus beames,	2Tamb	5.3.237	Tamb
not lord and father, heavens great beames/On Atlas shoulder,	Edw	3.1.76	Prince
But dayes bright beames dooth vanish fast away,	Edw	5.1.69	Edward
glorious actes/Lightens the world with his reflecting beames,	F App	p.237 26	Emper
noysome Saturne/Were now exalted, and with blew beames shinde,	Lucan, First Booke	651	
And with his flaring beames mockt ougly night,	Hero and Leander	2.332	
BEAMONT			
Beamont flie,/As fast as Iris, or Joves Mercurie.	Edw	1.4.370	Edward
BEAMS			
flags/Through which sweet mercie threw her gentle beams,	1Tamb	5.1.69	Tamb
Why feed ye still on daies accursed beams,	1Tamb	5.1.262	Bajzth
Whence thou shouldst view thy Roome with squinting beams.	Lucan, First Booke	55	
BEAR			
That in conceit bear Empires on our speares,	1Tamb	1.2.64	Tamb
BEARD			
I tooke him by the [beard] <sterd>, and look'd upon him thus;	Jew	4.2.105	P Pilia
That when he speakes, drawes out his grisly beard,	Jew	4.3.7	Barab
suffer uncontrowld/These Barons thus to beard me in my land,	Edw	3.1.14	Spencr
No, but wash your face, and shave away your beard,	Edw	5.3.31	Gurney
What use shall we put his beard to?	F1383	4.2.59	P Mrtino
BEARDED			
rings of fire/Flie in the ayre, and dreadfull bearded stars,	Lucan, First Booke	526	
BEARDS			
Breathing, in hope (malgrado all your beards,	Edw	2.5.5	Gavstn
seene many boyes with [such pickadevaunts] <beards> I am sure.	F 345	1.4.3	P Robin
BEARE'			
They that deserve paine, beare't with patience.	Ovid's Elegies	2.7.12	
BEARE (Homograph)			
Whom I tooke up to beare unto our ships:	Dido	2.1.277	Aeneas
Thinking to beare her on my backe abourd,	Dido	2.1.284	Aeneas
Whom I will beare to Ida in mine armes,	Dido	3.2.99	Venus
And beare this golden Scepter in my hand?	Dido	4.4.41	Aeneas
And beare him in the countrey to her house,	Dido	4.4.106	Dido
Packt with the windes to beare Aeneas hence?	Dido	4.4.127	Dido
Come beare them in.	Dido	4.4.165	Dido
Sergestus, beare him hence unto our ships,	Dido	5.1.49	Aeneas
That I may learne to beare it patiently,	Dido	5.1.208	Dido

BEARE (cont.)

Nothing can beare me to him but a ship,	Dido	5.1.267	Dido
Such breadth of shoulders as might mainely beare/Olde Atlas	1Tamb	2.1.10	Menaph
Whose fiery cyrcles beare encompassed/A heaven of heavenly	1Tamb	2.1.15	Menaph
soules/From heavens of comfort, yet their age might beare,	1Tamb	5.1.90	1Virgn
a foot, unlesse thou beare/A mind corragious and invincible:	2Tamb	1.3.72	Tamb
ancient use, shall beare/The figure of the semi-circled Moone:	2Tamb	3.1.64	Orcan
Teach you my boyes to beare couragious minds,	2Tamb	3.2.143	Tamb
Beare not the burthen of your enemies joyes,	2Tamb	5.3.22	Techel
Whose shoulders beare the Axis of the world,	2Tamb	5.3.59	Tamb
The nature of thy chariot wil not beare/A guide of baser temper	2Tamb	5.3.242	Tamb
And, Barabas, I'le beare thee company.	Jew	2.3.96	Lodowk
Nor I the affection that I beare to you.	Jew	2.3.291	Barab
Take this and beare it to Mathias streight,	Jew	2.3.370	Barab
Among the rest beare this, and set it there;	Jew	3.4.78	Barab
No, let us beare him to the Magistrates.	Jew	4.1.183	Ithimr
Instead of Sedge and Reed, beare Sugar Canes:	Jew	4.2.96	Ithimr
under Turkish yokes/Shall groning beare the burthen of our ire;	Jew	5.2.8	Calym
Sister, I think your selfe will beare us company.	P 21	1.21	Charls
Come my Lords let us beare her body hence,	P 195	3.30	Admral
proudest Kings/In Christendome, should beare me such derision,	P 761	15.19	Guise
That villain for whom I beare this deep disgrace,	P 766	15.24	Guise
And that the sweet and princely minde you beare,	P1141	22.3	King
How they beare armes against their soveraigne.	P1187	22.49	King
I dye Navarre, come beare me to my Sepulchre.	P1242	22.104	King
Then beare the ship that shall transport thee hence:	Edw	1.1.153	Edward
of Lancaster/That hath more earldomes then an asse can beare,	Edw	1.3.2	Gavstn
Whether will you beare him, stay or ye shall die.	Edw	1.4.24	Edward
But come sweete friend, ile beare thee on thy way.	Edw	1.4.140	Edward
Should beare us downe of the nobilitie,	Edw	1.4.286	Mortmr
Penbrooke shall beare the sword before the king.	Edw	1.4.351	Edward
Spencer, stay you and beare me companie,	Edw	2.1.74	Neece
this fish my lord I beare,/The motto this:	Edw	2.2.27	Lncstr
Is this the love you beare your soveraigne?	Edw	2.2.30	Edward
Do cosin, and ile beare thee companie.	Edw	2.2.121	Lncstr
Content, ile beare my part, holla whose there?	Edw	2.2.130	Lncstr
would I beare/These braves, this rage, and suffer uncontrowld	Edw	3.1.12	Spencr
Boye, see you beare you bravelie to the king,	Edw	3.1.72	Edward
things of more waight/Then fits a prince so yong as I to beare,	Edw	3.1.75	Prince
Choose of our lords to beare you companie,	Edw	3.1.84	Edward
As you injurious were to beare them foorth.	Edw	4.3.52	Edward
A king to beare these words and proud commaunds.	Edw	4.7.71	Abbot
My nobles rule, I beare the name of king,	Edw	5.1.28	Edward
beare this to the queene,/Wet with my teares, and dried againe	Edw	5.1.117	Edward
Not yet my lorde, ile beare you on your waye.	Edw	5.1.155	Leistr
For our behoofe will beare the greater sway/When as a kings	Edw	5.2.13	Mortmr
And beare him this, as witnesse of my love.	Edw	5.2.72	Queene
Matrevis and the rest may beare the blame,	Edw	5.4.15	Mortmr
How often shall I bid you beare him hence?	Edw	5.4.102	Mortmr
And beare the kings to Mortimer our lord,	Edw	5.5.119	Gurney
You could not beare his death thus patiently,	Edw	5.6.36	King
And beare wise Bacons, and [Abanus] <Albanus> <Albertus>	F 181	1.1.153	Valdes
Go beare these <those> tydings to great Lucifer,	F 315	1.3.87	Faust
And beare him to the States of Germany.	F 900	3.1.122	Faust
And beare him streight to Ponte Angelo,	F 965	3.1.187	Pope
O come and help to beare my body hence:	F1069	3.2.89	Pope
[Where such as beare <bare> his absence but with griefe],	F1141	3.3.54A	3Chor
Or Lucifer will beare thee quicke to hell.	F1976	5.2.180	Faust
Beare witnesse I gave them him.	F App	p.230 41	P Wagner
Beare witnesse I give them you againe.	F App	p.230 42	P Clown
study, shee's borne to beare with me, or else my Art failes.	F App	p.233 16	P Robin
th'one like an Ape, an other like a Beare, the third an Asse,	F App	p.235 33	P Mephst
plaine not heavens, but gladly beare these evils/For Neros sake:	Lucan, First Booke		37
Roome was so great it could not beare it selfe:	Lucan, First Booke		72
Romans if ye be,/And beare true harts, stay heare:	Lucan, First Booke		194
Under the frosty beare, or parching East,	Lucan, First Booke		254
Let all Lawes yeeld, sinne beare the name of vertue,	Lucan, First Booke		666
Faire Dames for-beare rewards for nights to crave,	Ovid's Elegies		1.10.47
dore more wisely/And som-what higher beare thy foote precisely.	Ovid's Elegies		1.12.6
[All] <This> could I beare, but that the wench should rise,/Who	Ovid's Elegies		1.13.25
Thou wert not borne to ride, or armes to beare,	Ovid's Elegies		2.3.7
Within my brest no desert empire beare.	Ovid's Elegies		2.9.52
Or [be] a loade thou shouldst refuse to beare.	Ovid's Elegies		2.15.22
No barking Dogs that Syllaes intrailes beare,	Ovid's Elegies		2.16.23
So sweete a burthen I will beare with eaze.	Ovid's Elegies		2.16.30
Knowest not this head a helme was wont to beare,	Ovid's Elegies		3.7.13
She first constraind bulles necks to beare the yoake,	Ovid's Elegies		3.9.13
And what I have borne, shame to beare againe.	Ovid's Elegies		3.10.4
Would I my words would any credit beare.	Ovid's Elegies		3.11.20
Niobe flint, Callist we make a Beare,	Ovid's Elegies		3.11.31
And mingle thighs, yours ever mine to beare.	Ovid's Elegies		3.13.22

BEARER

I charge thee send me three hundred by this bearer, and this	Jew	4.2.75	P Ithimr
send me five hundred crowns, and give the Bearer one hundred.	Jew	4.2.118	P Ithimr
Cheefe standard bearer to the Lutheranes,	P 285	5.12	Guise
Cheef standard bearer to the Lutheranes,	P 313	5.40	Guise
I was both horse-man, foote-man, standard bearer.	Ovid's Elegies		2.12.14

BEARES

Beares figures of renowne and myracle:	1Tamb	2.1.4	Cosroe
Because I heare he beares a valiant mind.	1Tamb	3.1.32	Bajzth
on his silver crest/A snowy Feather spangled white he beares,	1Tamb	4.1.51	2Msngr
That beares the honor of my royall waight.	1Tamb	4.2.21	Tamb
on a Lions backe)/Rhamnusia beares a helmet ful of blood,	2Tamb	3.4.57	Therid

BEARES (cont.)
Shaking the burthen mighty Atlas beares: 2Tamb 4.1.129 Tamb
heare a Culverin discharg'd/By him that beares the Linstocke, Jew 5.4.4 Govnr
So that for proofe, he barely beares the name: P 131 2.74 Guise
But wherfore beares he me such deadly hate? P 779 15.37 Mugern
Because his wife beares thee such kindely love. P 780 15.38 King
Is this the fruite your reconcilement beares? Edw 2.2.31 Edward
And yet she beares a face of love forsooth: Edw 4.6.14 Kent
And by a secret token that he beares, Edw 5.4.19 Mortmr
Mild Atax glad it beares not Roman [boats] <bloats>; Lucan, First Booke 404
If Boreas beares Orithyas rape in minde, Ovid's Elegies 1.6.53
Even as a head-strong courser beares away, Ovid's Elegies 2.9.29
And shaking sobbes his mouth for speeches beares. Ovid's Elegies 3.8.12
A dwarfish beldame beares me companie, Hero and Leander 1.353
BEARE'T
They that deserve paine, beare't with patience. Ovid's Elegies 2.7.12
BEARING
where her servitors passe through the hall/Bearing a banket, Dido 2.1.71 Serg
Bearing his huntspeare bravely in his hand. Dido 3.3.33 Anna
Bearing her bowe and quiver at her backe. Dido 3.3.55 Achat
Bearing his privie signet and his hand: 1Tamb 1.2.15 Zenoc
Let us afford him now the bearing hence. 1Tamb 3.2.111 Usumc
With ugly Furies bearing fiery flags, 2Tamb 1.3.146 Techel
Bearing the vengeance of our fathers wrongs, 2Tamb 3.1.17 Callap
And weary Death with bearing soules to hell. 2Tamb 5.3.77 Tamb
Or mount the sunnes flame bearing <plume bearing> charriot, Lucan, First Booke 48
Bearing old spoiles and conquerors monuments, Lucan, First Booke 138
And on her Turret-bearing head disperst, Lucan, First Booke 190
As when against pine bearing Ossa's rocks, Lucan, First Booke 390
from thence/To the pine bearing hils, hence to the mounts Lucan, First Booke 688
And quiver bearing Dian till the plaine: Ovid's Elegies 1.1.14
[And] <The> banks ore which gold bearing Tagus flowes. Ovid's Elegies 1.15.34
Crowes <crow> [survive] <survives> armes-bearing Pallas hate, Ovid's Elegies 2.6.35
Eurotas cold, and poplar-bearing Po. Ovid's Elegies 2.17.32
Bearing the head with dreadfull [Adders] <Arrowes> clad, Ovid's Elegies 3.5.14
Part of her sorrowe heere thy sister bearing, Ovid's Elegies 3.8.51
From steepe Pine-bearing mountains to the plaine: Hero and Leander 1.116
But he the [days] <day> bright-bearing Car prepar'd. Hero and Leander 2.330
BEARS
The wind that bears him hence, wil fil our sailes, Edw 2.4.48 Lncstr
BEAR'ST
The love thou bear'st unto the house of Guise: P 69 2.12 Guise
BEARST
eies beholde/That as for her thou bearst these wretched armes, 1Tamb 5.1.409 Arabia
BEAST
And every beast the forrest doth send forth, Dido 1.1.161 Achat
Nature, why mad'st me not some poysonous beast, Dido 4.1.21 Iarbus
To tame the pride of this presumptuous Beast, 1Tamb 4.3.15 Souldn
what strange beast is yon, that thrusts his head out at [the] F1274 4.1.120 P Faust
from me, and I be chang'd/[Unto] <Into> some brutish beast. F1968 5.2.172 Faust
The beast long struggled, as being like to prove/An aukward Lucan, First Booke 610
shouldst thou with thy rayes now sing/The fell Nemean beast, Lucan, First Booke 655
Whose workmanship both man and beast deceaves. Hero and Leander 1.20
BEASTES
Stretching their pawes, and threatning heardes of Beastes, 1Tamb 1.2.53 Techel
hunters in the chace/Of savage beastes amid the desart woods. 1Tamb 4.3.57 Capol
birds/Defil'd the day, and <at night> wilde beastes were seene, Lucan, First Booke 557
BEASTS
Or whether men or beasts inhabite it. Dido 1.1.177 Aeneas
The crye of beasts, the ratling of the windes, Dido 2.1.336 Venus
Now shall his barbarous body be a pray/To beasts and foules, 2Tamb 2.3.15 Orcan
then dy like beasts, and fit for nought/But perches for the 2Tamb 4.3.22 Tamb
As much as would have bought his beasts and him, Jew 1.2.189 Barab
To be a prey for Vultures and wild beasts. Jew 5.1.59 Govnr
All beasts are happy, for when they die, F1969 5.2.173 Faust
one that knew/The hearts of beasts, and flight of wandring Lucan, First Booke 587
Before whose bow th'Arcadian wild beasts trembled. Ovid's Elegies 1.7.14
Take from irrationall beasts a president, Ovid's Elegies 1.10.25
Hunters leave taken beasts, pursue the chase, Ovid's Elegies 2.9.9
When strong wilde beasts, she stronger hunts to strike them. Ovid's Elegies 3.2.32
Harmefull to beasts, and to the fields thou proves: Ovid's Elegies 3.5.99
Or songs amazing wilde beasts of the wood? Ovid's Elegies 3.8.22
With strong hand striking wild-beasts brist'led hyde. Ovid's Elegies 3.9.26
With famous pageants, and their home-bred beasts. Ovid's Elegies 3.12.4
BEAT
Batter our walles, and beat our Turrets downe. 1Tamb 5.1.2 Govnr
Whiles only danger beat upon our walles, 1Tamb 5.1.30 1Virgn
Must needs have beauty beat on his conceites. 1Tamb 5.1.182 Tamb
And beat thy braines out of thy conquer'd head: 1Tamb 5.1.287 Bajzth
while all thy joints/Be rackt and beat asunder with the wheele, 2Tamb 3.5.125 Tamb
And with the flames that beat against the clowdes/Incense the 2Tamb 4.1.194 Tamb
Nor yet this aier, beat often with thy sighes, 2Tamb 4.2.10 Olymp
To beat the papall Monarck from our lands, P 802 16.16 Navrre
Wee'l beat him back, and drive him to his death, P 929 18.30 Navrre
Punisht I am, if I a Romaine beat, Ovid's Elegies 1.7.29
And beat from thence, have lighted there againe. Hero and Leander 1.24
Beat downe the bold waves with his triple mace, Hero and Leander 2.172
This head was beat with manie a churlish billow, Hero and Leander 2.251
BEATE
And beate proud Burbon to his native home, P1114 21.8 Dumain
To beate the beades about the Friers Pates, F 863 3.1.85 Mephst
When thou stood'st naked ready to be beate, Ovid's Elegies 1.6.19
Snatching the combe, to beate the wench out drive <drave> her. Ovid's Elegies 1.14.18

BEATE (cont.)			
That Paphos, and the floud-beate Cithera guides.	Ovid's Elegies		2.17.4
I borne much, hoping time would beate thee/To guard her well,	Ovid's Elegies		2.19.49
BEATEN			
Their plumed helmes are wrought with beaten golde.	1Tamb	1.2.124	Souldr
Thy garrisons are beaten out of Fraunce,	Edw	2.2.162	Lncstr
No slave, in beaten silke, and staves-aker.	F 357	1.4.15	P Wagner
No sirra, in beaten silke and staves acre.	F App	p.229 16	P Wagner
Yong oxen newly yokt are beaten more,	Ovid's Elegies		1.2.13
Or least his love oft beaten backe should waine.	Ovid's Elegies		1.8.76
BEATES			
Beates forth my senses from this troubled soule,	Dido	2.1.116	Aeneas
Lantchidol/Beates on the regions with his boysterous blowes,	2Tamb	1.1.70	Orcan
Which beates against this prison to get out,	2Tamb	4.2.35	Olymp
And beates his braines to catch us in his trap,	P 53	1.53	Navrre
Which beates upon it like the Cyclops hammers,	Edw	1.4.313	Edward
Beates Thracian Boreas; or when trees [bowe] <bowde> down,	Lucan, First Booke		391
BEATING			
joyntly both/Beating their breasts and falling on the ground,	Dido	2.1.228	Aeneas
Beating in heaps against their Argoses,	2Tamb	1.1.41	Orcan
Whose billowes beating the resistlesse bankes,	Jew	3.5.17	Govnr
Duld with much beating slowly forth doth passe.	Ovid's Elegies		2.7.16
BEATS			
troopes/Beats downe our foes to flesh our taintlesse swords?	2Tamb	4.1.26	Amyras
Sits wringing of her hands, and beats her brest.	Edw	1.4.188	Lncstr
Cupid beats downe her praiers with his wings,	Hero and Leander		1.369
BEAUMONT (See BEAMONT)			
BEAUTEOUS (See also BEAUTIOUS)			
Beauteous Rubyes, sparkling Diamonds,	Jew	1.1.27	Barab
But whither wends my beauteous Abigall?	Jew	1.2.224	Barab
and warlike semblances/Of Alexander and his beauteous Paramour.	F1171	4.1.17	Mrtino
Great Alexander and his beauteous Paramour.	F1239	4.1.85	Faust
And bring with him his beauteous Paramour,	F App	p.237 32	Emper
The rites/In which Loves beauteous Empresse most delites,/Are	Hero and Leander		1.300
As he had hope to scale the beauteous fort,	Hero and Leander		2.16
BEAUTIE			
Grace my immortall beautie with this boone,	Dido	1.1.21	Ganimd
And shrowdes thy beautie in this borrowd shape:	Dido	1.1.192	Aeneas
Yeelds up her beautie to a strangers bed,	Dido	4.2.17	Iarbus
I faine would goe, yet beautie calles me backe:	Dido	4.3.46	Aeneas
been/When Didos beautie [chaind] <chaungd> thine eyes to her:	Dido	5.1.114	Dido
And Didos beautie will returne againe:	Dido	5.1.118	Dido
Which with thy beautie will be soone resolv'd.	1Tamb	1.2.101	Tamb
Gazing upon the beautie of their lookes:	1Tamb	5.1.334	Zenoc
To shew her beautie, which the world admyr'd,	2Tamb	3.2.26	Tamb
The pride and beautie of her princely seat,	2Tamb	4.3.109	Tamb
With beautie of thy wings, thy faire haire guilded,	Ovid's Elegies		1.2.41
And of such wondrous beautie her bereft:	Hero and Leander		1.48
Enamoured of his beautie had he beene,	Hero and Leander		1.78
So was her beautie to the standers by.	Hero and Leander		1.106
As thou in beautie doest exceed Loves mother/Nor heaven, nor	Hero and Leander		1.222
Beautie alone is lost, too warily kept.	Hero and Leander		1.328
That she such lovelinesse and beautie had/As could provoke his	Hero and Leander		1.422
So beautie, sweetly quickens when t'is ny,	Hero and Leander		2.126
BEAUTIES			
But bright Ascanius, beauties better worke,	Dido	1.1.96	Jupitr
That with their beauties grac'd the Memphion fields:	1Tamb	4.2.104	Tamb
made one Poems period/And all combin'd in Beauties worthinesse,	1Tamb	5.1.170	Tamb
Save onely that in Beauties just applause,	1Tamb	5.1.178	Tamb
Muffle your beauties with eternall clowdes,	2Tamb	5.3.6	Therid
I flie her lust, but follow beauties creature;	Ovid's Elegies		3.10.37
BEAUTIFIE			
Thou shalt not beautifie Larissa plaines,	2Tamb	3.2.34	Tamb
that shine as bright/As all the Lamps that beautifie the Sky,	2Tamb	5.3.157	Tamb
BEAUTIFIED			
Whose heavenly presence beautified with health,	2Tamb	2.4.49	Tamb
BEAUTIFUL			
Then scortch a face so beautiful as this,	2Tamb	3.4.74	Techel
BEAUTIFULL			
Is not Aeneas faire and beautifull?	Dido	3.1.63	Dido
Dido, that till now/Didst never thinke Aeneas beautifull:	Dido	3.1.83	Dido
And matchlesse beautifull;/As had you seene her 'twould have	Jew	1.2.384	Mthias
by such a tall man as I am, from such a beautifull dame as you.	Jew	4.2.10	P Pilia
as Saba, or as beautifull/As was bright Lucifer before his fall.	F 541	2.1.153	Mephst
Amorous Leander, beautifull and yoong,	Hero and Leander		1.51
BEAUTIFULLEST			
which was the beautifullest in all the world, we have	F1682	5.1.9	P 1Schol
BEAUTIFYING			
And beautifying the Empire of this Queene,	Dido	5.1.28	Hermes
BEAUTIOUS			
Whose beautious burden well might make you proude,	Dido	1.1.124	Venus
how may I deserve/Such amourous favours at thy beautious hand?	Dido	3.2.65	Juno
Would first my beautious wenches moist lips touch,	Ovid's Elegies		2.15.17
For her ill-beautious Mother judgd to slaughter?	Ovid's Elegies		3.3.18
BEAUTY			
Wher Beauty, mother to the Muses sits,	1Tamb	5.1.144	Tamb
What is beauty, saith my sufferings then?	1Tamb	5.1.160	Tamb
Must needs have beauty beat on his conceites.	1Tamb	5.1.182	Tamb
Blacke is the beauty of the brightest day,	2Tamb	2.4.1	Tamb
Her sacred beauty hath enchaunted heaven,	2Tamb	2.4.85	Tamb
Hellen, whose beauty sommond Greece to armes,	2Tamb	2.4.87	Tamb
Which with thy beauty thou wast woont to light,	2Tamb	4.2.16	Therid
Oh girle, oh gold, oh beauty, oh my blisse!	Jew	2.1.54	Barab

BEAUTY (cont.)			
And Natures beauty choake with stifeling clouds,	Jew	2.3.331	Lodowk
And yet I know my beauty doth not faile.	Jew	3.1.5	Curtzn
Shadowing more beauty in their Airie browes,	F 155	1.1.127	Valdes
[Whose heavenly beauty passeth all compare].	F1701	5.1.28A	3Schol
Clad in the beauty of a thousand starres:	F1782	5.1.109	Faust
Wrinckles in beauty is a grievous fault.	Ovid's Elegies		1.8.46
Beauty not exercisde with age is spent,	Ovid's Elegies		1.8.53
No more this beauty mine eyes captivates.	Ovid's Elegies		1.10.10
Or prostitute thy beauty for bad prize.	Ovid's Elegies		1.10.42
Unmeete is beauty without use to wither.	Ovid's Elegies		2.3.14
By chaunce her beauty never shined fuller.	Ovid's Elegies		2.5.42
Beauty gives heart, Corinnas lookes excell,	Ovid's Elegies		2.17.7
maides society/Falsely to sweare, their beauty hath some deity.	Ovid's Elegies		3.3.12
Beauty with lewdnesse doth right ill agree.	Ovid's Elegies		3.10.42
BEAVERS			
and that buyes me <is> thirty meales a day, and ten Beavers:	F 695	2.2.144	P Glutny
BECAME			
O what became of aged Hecuba?	Dido	2.1.290	Anna
But what became of faire Zenocrate,	2Tamb	Prol.6	Prolog
But one amongst the rest became our prize:	Jew	2.2.16	Bosco
BECAUSE (See also 'CAUSE)			
There Zanthus streame, because here's Priamus,	Dido	2.1.8	Aeneas
Because his lothsome sight offends mine eye,	Dido	3.1.57	Dido
Because it may be thou shalt be my love:	Dido	3.1.170	Dido
It was because I sawe no King like thee,	Dido	3.4.35	Dido
Because I feard your grace would keepe me here.	Dido	4.4.20	Achat
It cannot choose, because it comes from you.	1Tamb	1.1.56	Cosroe
(I cal it meane, because being yet obscure,	1Tamb	1.2.203	Tamb
Because I heare he beares a valiant mind.	1Tamb	3.1.32	Bajzth
Because it is my countries, and my Fathers.	1Tamb	4.2.124	Zenoc
Because this place bereft me of my Love:	2Tamb	2.4.138	Tamb
Because my deare Zenocrate is dead.	2Tamb	3.2.14	Tamb
Because the corners there may fall more flat,	2Tamb	3.2.65	Tamb
Looke where he goes, but see, he comes againe/Because I stay:	2Tamb	5.3.76	Tamb
And let him not be entertain'd the worse/Because he favours me.	Jew	Prol.35	Machvl
Because we vail'd not to the [Turkish] <Spanish> Fleet,/Their	Jew	2.2.11	Bosco
Because he is young and has more qualities.	Jew	2.3.110	1Offcr
Because the Pryor <Governor> <Sire> dispossest thee once,/And	Jew	3.3.43	Abigal
No, but I grieve because she liv'd so long.	Jew	4.1.18	Barab
early; with intent to goe/Unto your Friery, because you staid.	Jew	4.1.192	Barab
Because the house of Burbon now comes in,	P 50	1.50	Admral
Because my places being but three, contains all his:	P 405	7.45	Ramus
And thats because the blockish [Sorbonests] <thorbonest>	P 411	7.51	Ramus
Because his wife beares thee such kindely love.	P 780	15.38	King
I slew the Guise, because I would be King.	P1066	19.136	King
Because he loves me more then all the world:	Edw	1.4.77	Edward
Because my lords, it was not thought upon:	Edw	1.4.273	Mortmr
Because the king and he are enemies.	Edw	2.1.5	Spencr
Because his majestie so earnestlie/Desires to see the man	Edw	2.5.77	Penbrk
Because we heare Lord Bruse dooth sell his land,	Edw	3.1.53	Edward
Because your highnesse hath beene slack in homage,	Edw	3.1.63	Queene
My lords, because our soveraigne sends for him,	Edw	3.1.109	Arundl
rest, because we heare/That Edmund casts to worke his libertie,	Edw	5.2.57	Mortmr
Because I thinke scorne to be accusde,	Edw	5.6.39	Mortmr
Because thou hast depriv'd me of those Joyes.	F 554	2.2.3	Faust
<Faustus I have, and because we wil not be unprovided,	F 805	(HC265)A	P Mephst
more, take him, because I see thou hast a good minde to him.	F1461	4.4.5	P Faust
because I knew him to be such a horse, as would run over hedge	F1537	4.5.33	P HrsCsr
bleate, and an asse braye, because it is S. Peters holy day.	F App	p.232 28	P Faust
me,/Because at his commaund I wound not up/My conquering Eagles?	Lucan, First Booke		339
Ask'st why I chaunge? because thou crav'st reward:	Ovid's Elegies		1.10.11
Thou leav'st his bed, because hees faint through age,	Ovid's Elegies		1.13.37
[Doest] punish <ye >me, because yeares make him waine?	Ovid's Elegies		1.13.41
Because [thy] <they> care too much thy Mistresse troubled.	Ovid's Elegies		2.2.8
If not, because shees simple I would have her.	Ovid's Elegies		2.4.18
Because thy belly should rough wrinckles lacke,	Ovid's Elegies		2.14.7
Because on him thy care doth hap to rest.	Ovid's Elegies		3.2.8
Who, because meanes want, doeth not, she doth.	Ovid's Elegies		3.4.4
Because the keeper may come say, I did it,	Ovid's Elegies		3.4.35
Because she tooke more from her than she left,	Hero and Leander		1.47
Greefe makes her pale, because she mooves not there.	Hero and Leander		1.60
And fell in drops like teares, because they mist him.	Hero and Leander		2.174
BECKS			
View me, my becks, and speaking countenance:	Ovid's Elegies		1.4.17
What secret becks in banquets with her youths,	Ovid's Elegies		3.10.23
BECKT			
She beckt, and prosperous signes gave as she moved.	Ovid's Elegies		3.2.58
BECOME			
May we become immortall like the Gods.	1Tamb	1.2.201	Tamb
A friendly parle might become ye both.	2Tamb	1.1.117	Gazell
let me see how well/Thou wilt become thy fathers majestie.	2Tamb	5.3.184	Tamb
hee that denies to pay, shal straight become a Christian.	Jew	1.2.73	P Reader
Faire Abigall the rich Jewes daughter/Become a Nun?	Jew	1.2.367	Mthias
And better would she farre become a bed/Embraced in a friendly	Jew	1.2.371	Mthias
and Vespasian conquer'd us)/Am I become as wealthy as I was:	Jew	2.3.11	Barab
What, Abigall become a Nunne againe?	Jew	3.4.1	Barab
And for his sake did I become a Nunne.	Jew	3.6.25	Abigal
An Hebrew borne, and would become a Christian?	Jew	4.1.19	Barab
What thinkst thou shall become of it and thee?	Jew	5.2.56	Barab
they may become/As men that stand and gase against the Sunne.	P 162	2.105	Guise
It may become thee yet,/To let us take our farewell of his	Edw	4.7.68	Spencr
And Leister say, what shall become of us?	Edw	4.7.81	Edward

BECOME (cont.)			
I wonder what's become of Faustus that/Was wont to make our	F 194	1.2.1	1Schol
friends, what shall become of Faustus being in hell for ever?	F1846	5.2.50	P Faust
Become intemperate? shall the earth be barraine?	Lucan, First Booke	646	
They well become thee, then to spare them turne.	Ovid's Elegies	1.14.28	
BECOMES			
O how a Crowne becomes Aeneas head!	Dido	4.4.38	Dido
Becomes it Jewes to be so credulous,	Jew	1.2.360	Barab
Beleeve me Guise he becomes the place so well,	P 495	9.14	QnMoth
So he be safe he cares not what becomes,	P 739	14.42	Navrre
This haught resolve becomes your majestie,	Edw	3.1.28	Baldck
That holy shape becomes a devill best.	F 254	1.3.26	Faust
red shame becomes white cheekes, but this/If feigned, doth	Ovid's Elegies	1.8.35	
The unjust Judge for bribes becomes a stale.	Ovid's Elegies	1.10.38	
BED			
To sweeten out the slumbers of thy bed:	Dido	1.1.37	Jupitr
When as he buts his beames on Floras bed,	Dido	3.4.20	Dido
Yeelds up her beautie to a strangers bed,	Dido	4.2.17	Iarbus
The dreames (brave mates) that did beset my bed,	Dido	4.3.16	Aeneas
Must grace his bed that conquers Asia:	1Tamb	1.2.37	Tamb
Pitie the mariage bed, where many a Lord/In prime and glorie of	1Tamb	5.1.83	1Virgn
I should be affraid, would put it off and come to bed with me.	2Tamb	4.1.70	P Calyph
And better would she farre become a bed/Embraced in a friendly	Jew	1.2.371	Mthias
Nor goe to bed, but sleepes in his owne clothes;	Jew	4.1.132	Ithimr
<humble> intreates your Majestie/To visite him sick in his bed.	P 246	4.44	Man
Be murdered in his bed.	P 287	5.14	Guise
And so convey him closely to his bed.	P 450	7.90	Guise
And in this bed of [honor] <honors> die with fame.	Edw	4.5.7	Edward
Who spots my nuptiall bed with infamie,	Edw	5.1.31	Edward
Lie on this bed, and rest your selfe a while.	Edw	5.5.72	Ltborn
And bring them every morning to thy bed:	F 538	2.1.150	Mephst
That all this day the sluggard keepes his bed.	F1176	4.1.22	Mrtino
in armes; nor could the bed-rid parents/Keep back their sons,	Lucan, First Booke	502	
What makes my bed seem hard seeing it is soft?	Ovid's Elegies	1.2.1	
When his limbes he spread/Upon the bed, but on my foote first	Ovid's Elegies	1.4.16	
Resembling faire Semiramis going to bed,	Ovid's Elegies	1.5.11	
On all the [bed mens] <beds men> tumbling let him viewe/And thy	Ovid's Elegies	1.8.97	
Tis shame to grow rich by bed merchandize,	Ovid's Elegies	1.10.41	
Thou leav'st his bed, because hees faint through age,	Ovid's Elegies	1.13.37	
Halfe sleeping on a purple bed she rested,	Ovid's Elegies	1.14.20	
And therefore filles the bed she lies uppon:	Ovid's Elegies	2.4.34	
No where can they be taught but in the bed,	Ovid's Elegies	2.5.61	
Is charg'd to violate her mistresse bed.	Ovid's Elegies	2.7.18	
Yea, let my foes sleepe in an emptie bed,	Ovid's Elegies	2.10.17	
Loe country Gods, and [known] <know> bed to forsake,	Ovid's Elegies	2.11.7	
Lay in the mid bed, there be my law giver.	Ovid's Elegies	2.17.24	
Why she alone in empty bed oft tarries.	Ovid's Elegies	2.19.42	
And slipt from bed cloth'd in a loose night-gowne,	Ovid's Elegies	3.1.51	
Deflowr'd and stained in unlawfull bed?	Ovid's Elegies	3.5.76	
And like a burthen greevde the bed that mooved not.	Ovid's Elegies	3.6.4	
Or jaded camst thou from some others bed.	Ovid's Elegies	3.6.80	
What to have laine alone in empty bed?	Ovid's Elegies	3.8.34	
In emptie bed alone my mistris lies.	Ovid's Elegies	3.9.2	
This was [their] <there> meate, the soft grasse was their bed.	Ovid's Elegies	3.9.10	
O by our fellow bed, by all/The Gods who by thee to be perjurde	Ovid's Elegies	3.10.45	
The bed is for lascivious toyings meete,	Ovid's Elegies	3.13.17	
And in the bed hide all the faults you have,	Ovid's Elegies	3.13.20	
This bed, and that by tumbling made uneven,	Ovid's Elegies	3.13.32	
Jove, slylie stealing from his sisters bed,	Hero and Leander	1.147	
And seeking refuge, slipt into her bed.	Hero and Leander	2.244	
Me in thy bed and maiden bosome take,	Hero and Leander	2.248	
With both her hands she made the bed a tent,	Hero and Leander	2.264	
Leaving Leander in the bed alone.	Hero and Leander	2.312	
Thus neere the bed she blushing stood upright,	Hero and Leander	2.317	
BEDAUBD			
and thy selfe/Bedaubd with golde, rode laughing at the rest,	Edw	2.2.185	Mortmr
BEDDE			
To rest my limbes, uppon a bedde I lay,	Ovid's Elegies	1.5.2	
BEDFELLOW			
Tis Taleus, Ramus bedfellow.	P 372	7.12	Retes
me thinkes you should have a wooden bedfellow of one of 'em.	F1654	4.6.97	P Carter
BEDFELLOWES			
Be both your legs bedfellowes every night together?	F1645	4.6.88	P Carter
BEDRED			
Whereat he lifted up his bedred lims,	Dido	2.1.250	Aeneas
BED-RID			
in armes; nor could the bed-rid parents/Keep back their sons,	Lucan, First Booke	502	
BEDS			
The people started; young men left their beds,	Lucan, First Booke	241	
On all the [bed mens] <beds men> tumbling let him viewe/And thy	Ovid's Elegies	1.8.97	
For beds ill hyr'd we are indebted nought.	Ovid's Elegies	1.10.44	
And in the forme of beds weele strowe soft sand,	Ovid's Elegies	2.11.47	
And I will make thee beds of Roses,	Passionate Shepherd	9	
BEDSTED			
And with your pastime let the bedsted creake,	Ovid's Elegies	3.13.26	
BEE (Homograph)			
A garden where are Bee hives full of honey,	Dido	4.5.7	Nurse
So shall not I be knowen, or if I bee,	1Tamb	2.4.13	Mycet
Then must his kindled wrath bee quencht with blood:	1Tamb	4.1.56	2Msngr
with freatting, and then she will not bee woorth the eating.	1Tamb	4.4.50	P Tamb
Had never bene erected as they bee,	1Tamb	5.1.32	1Virgn
my Lord, if I should goe, would you bee as good as your word?	2Tamb	1.2.62	P Almeda
But say my lord, where shall this meeting bee?	Edw	1.2.74	Warwck

BEE (cont.)			
And there let him bee,	Edw	3.1.197	Lncstr
And thinkes your grace that Bartley will bee cruell?	Edw	5.1.151	Bartly
But bee content, seeing it his highnesse pleasure.	Edw	5.2.94	Queene
So, now thou art to bee at an howres warning, whensoever, and	F 369	1.4.27	P Wagner
if that bee true, I have a charme in my head, shall controule	F1202	4.1.48	P Benvol
And Faustus shall bee cur'd.	F1831	5.2.35	2Schol
though I not see/What may be done, yet there before him bee.	Ovid's Elegies		1.4.14
No pritty wenches keeper maist thou bee:	Ovid's Elegies		1.6.63
Bee not to see with wonted eyes inclinde,	Ovid's Elegies		1.14.37
And of just compasse for her knuckles bee.	Ovid's Elegies		2.15.6
If I a lover bee by thee held back.	Ovid's Elegies		3.5.22
Who sayd with gratefull voyce perpetuall bee?	Ovid's Elegies		3.5.98
Or lesse faire, or lesse lewd would thou mightst bee,	Ovid's Elegies		3.10.41
Under whose shade the Wood-gods love to bee.	Hero and Leander		1.156
Then shouldst thou bee his prisoner who is thine.	Hero and Leander		1.202
one shalt thou bee,/Though never-singling Hymen couple thee.	Hero and Leander		1.257
Much lesse can honour bee ascrib'd thereto,	Hero and Leander		1.279
Which made his love through Sestos to bee knowne,	Hero and Leander		2.111
BEEF			
not a stone of beef a day will maintaine you in these chops;	Jew	2.3.124	P Barab
BEEFE			
Goe sit at home and eate your tenants beefe:	Edw	2.2.75	Gavstn
Pickeld-herring <Pickle-herring>, and Martin Martlemasse-beefe:	F 698	2.2.147	P Glutny
BEE HIVES			
A garden where are Bee hives full of honey,	Dido	4.5.7	Nurse
BEELZEBUB (See also BELZABUB, BELZEBUB)			
There is no chiefe but onely Beelzebub:	F 284	1.3.56	Faust
BEEN (See also BENE, BIN)			
O had that ticing strumpet nere been borne:	Dido	2.1.300	Dido
I feare me Dido hath been counted light,	Dido	3.1.14	Dido
I had been wedded ere Aeneas came:	Dido	3.1.138	Dido
Have been most urgent suiters for my love,	Dido	3.1.151	Dido
Twas time to runne, Aeneas had been gone,	Dido	4.4.14	Anna
Welcome sweet child, where hast thou been this long?	Dido	5.1.46	Aeneas
the time hath been/When Didos beautie [chaind] <chaungd> thine	Dido	5.1.113	Dido
I had not thought he had been so brave a man.	Jew	4.4.16	Curtzn
Should have been murdered the other night?	P 35	1.35	Navrre
Hath he been hurt with villaines in the street?	P 254	4.52	Charls
Wherein hath Ramus been so offencious?	P 384	7.24	Ramus
For Poland is as I have been enformde,	P 454	8.4	Anjoy
Had late been pluckt from out faire Cupids wing:	P 668	13.12	Duchss
Or hath my love been so obscurde in thee,	P 682	13.26	Guise
BEENE			
Had they beene valued at indifferent rate,	Jew	1.2.186	Barab
I must needs say that I have beene a great usurer.	Jew	4.1.39	Barab
I have beene zealous in the Jewish faith,	Jew	4.1.51	Barab
Musician, hast beene in Malta long?	Jew	4.4.54	Curtzn
had it not beene much better/To [have] kept thy promise then be	Jew	5.2.4	Calym
That I with speed should have beene put to death.	P1118	21.12	Dumain
I have beene a great sinner in my dayes, and the deed is	P1133	21.27	P Frier
Then thou hast beene of me since thy exile.	Edw	1.1.145	Edward
at the mariage day/The cup of Hymen had beene full of poyson,	Edw	1.4.174	Queene
I had beene stifled, and not lived to see,	Edw	1.4.176	Queene
But I had thought the match had beene broke off,	Edw	2.1.25	Baldck
How oft have I beene baited by these peeres?	Edw	2.2.201	Edward
Yea gentle Spencer, we have beene too milde,	Edw	3.1.24	Edward
Because your highnesse hath beene slack in homage,	Edw	3.1.63	Queene
Have beene by thee restored and comforted.	Edw	4.2.80	Mortmr
O hadst thou ever beene a king, thy hart/Pierced deeply with	Edw	4.7.9	Edward
For kinde and loving hast thou alwaies beene:	Edw	5.1.7	Edward
And Isabell, whose eyes [being] <beene> turnd to steele,	Edw	5.1.104	Edward
And thousand desperate maladies beene cur'd <eas'd>?	F 50	1.1.22	Faust
to thinke I have beene such an Asse all this while, to stand	F1243	4.1.89	P Benvol
thinking some hidden mystery had beene in the horse, I had	F1485	4.4.29	P HrsCsr
remember that I have beene a student here these thirty yeares,	F1840	5.2.44	P Faust
why I has thought thou hadst beene a batcheler, but now I see	F App	p.238 70	P Emper
I have beene al this day seeking one maister Fustian:	F App	p.239 98	P HrsCsr
I have beene wanton, therefore am perplext,	Ovid's Elegies		1.4.45
Would of mine armes, my shoulders had beene scanted,	Ovid's Elegies		1.7.23
But what had beene more faire had they beene kept?	Ovid's Elegies		1.14.3
And in the morne beene lively nerethelesse.	Ovid's Elegies		2.10.28
but for a Queene/Europe, and Asia in firme peace had beene.	Ovid's Elegies		2.12.18
He had not beene that conquering Rome did build.	Ovid's Elegies		2.14.16
The earth of Caesars had beene destitute.	Ovid's Elegies		2.14.18
Would I had beene my mistresse gentle prey,	Ovid's Elegies		2.17.5
Troy had not yet beene ten yeares siege out-stander,	Ovid's Elegies		3.5.27
My bones had beene, while yet I was a maide.	Ovid's Elegies		3.5.74
Since Heroes time, hath halfe the world beene blacke.	Hero and Leander		1.50
Had they beene cut, and unto Colchos borne,	Hero and Leander		1.56
Enamoured of his beautie had he beene,	Hero and Leander		1.78
As if her name and honour had beene wrong'd,	Hero and Leander		2.35
Leanders Father knew where hee had beene,	Hero and Leander		2.136
BEERE			
Gentlewoman, her name was <mistress> Margery March-beere:	F 700	2.2.149	P Glutny
Maisters, I'le bring you to the best beere in Europe, what ho,	F1505	4.5.1	P Carter
Why Hostesse, I say, fetch us some Beere.	F1518	4.5.14	P Dick
What ho, give's halfe a dosen of Beere here, and be hang'd.	F1612	4.6.55	P Robin
Zons fill us some Beere, or we'll breake all the barrels in the	F1618	4.6.61	P HrsCsr
Be not so furious: come you shall have Beere.	F1620	4.6.63	Faust
I humbly thanke your grace: then fetch some Beere.	F1625	4.6.68	Faust
BEES			
Wherewith his burning beames like labouring Bees,	Dido	5.1.12	Aeneas

BEES (cont.)
cold hemlocks flower/Wherein bad hony Corsicke Bees did power. . Ovid's Elegies 1.12.10
And there for honie, bees have sought in vaine, . . Hero and Leander 1.23

BEEST
Now if thou beest a pitying God of power, ... Dido 4.2.19 Iarbus
So thou shalt, whether thou beest with me, or no: . . F App p.229 22 P Wagner

BEFALL
This goddesse company doth to me befall. . . . . . Ovid's Elegies 3.1.44

BEFALLES
Where little ground to be inclosd befalles, ... Ovid's Elegies 3.14.12

BEFAL'NE
These taxes and afflictions are befal'ne, ... Jew 1.2.65 Govnr

BEFELL
[And in their conference of what befell], ... F1144 3.3.57A 3Chor
And ever seemed as some new sweete befell. . . . . Ovid's Elegies 2.5.56

BEFORE (See also AFORE, ERE)
Before he be the Lord of Turnus towne, ... Dido 1.1.87 Jupitr
Before that Boreas buckled with your sailes? . . . . Dido 1.2.19 Iarbus
Lords goe before, we two must talke alone. . . . . Dido 3.3.9 Dido
Ile dye before a stranger have that grace: . . . . Dido 3.3.11 Iarbus
Preferd before a man of majestie: . . . . . . Dido 3.3.65 Iarbus
The thing that I will dye before I aske, ... Dido 3.4.9 Dido
And yet desire to have before I dye. . . . . . . Dido 3.4.10 Dido
Before my sorrowes tide have any stint. . . . . . Dido 4.2.42 Iarbus
But what shall it be calde, Troy as before? . . . . Dido 5.1.18 Illion
Before I came, Aeneas was abourd, ... Dido 5.1.226 Anna
Before the Moone renew her borrowed light, ... 1Tamb 1.1.69 Therid
We knew my Lord, before we brought the crowne, ... 1Tamb 1.1.179 Ortyg
Before we part with our possession. . . . . . . 1Tamb 1.2.144 Tamb
Before I crowne you kings in Asia. . . . . 1Tamb 1.2.246 Tamb
go before and charge/The fainting army of that foolish King. 1Tamb 2.3.61 Cosroe
Nay quickly then, before his roome be hot. . . . . 1Tamb 2.5.89 Usumc
Nor raise our siege before the Gretians yeeld, ... 1Tamb 3.1.14 Bajzth
Or breathles lie before the citie walles. . . . . . 1Tamb 3.1.15 Bajzth
And if before the Sun have measured heaven/With triple circuit 1Tamb 3.1.36 Bajzth
Before such hap fall to Zenocrate. . . . . 1Tamb 3.2.20 Agidas
I prophecied before and now I proove, ... 1Tamb 3.2.90 Agidas
of Hydra, so my power/Subdued, shall stand as mighty as before: 1Tamb 3.3.141 Bajzth
Before I yeeld to such a slavery. . . . . 1Tamb 4.2.18 Bajzth
Before thou met my husband in the field, ... 1Tamb 4.2.59 Zabina
If they would lay their crownes before my feet, . . . 1Tamb 4.2.93 Tamb
Your tentes of white now pitch'd before the gates/And gentle 1Tamb 4.2.111 Therid
Halfe dead for feare before they feele my wrath: . . 1Tamb 4.4.4 Tamb
starv'd, and he be provided for a moneths victuall before hand. 1Tamb 4.4.47 P Usumc
Before all hope of rescue were denied, ... 1Tamb 5.1.38 Govnr
Then here before the majesty of heaven, ... 1Tamb 5.1.48 2Virgn
Wagons of gold were set before my tent: . . . . . 2Tamb 1.1.99 Orcan
let peace be ratified/On these conditions specified before, . 2Tamb 1.1.125 Orcan
in crimson silk/Shall ride before the on Barbarian Steeds: 2Tamb 1.2.47 Callap
And die before I brought you backe again. . . . . 2Tamb 1.2.73 Almeda
And not before, my sweet Zenocrate: . . . . . . 2Tamb 1.3.15 Tamb
Thou shalt be king before them, and thy seed/Shall issue . 2Tamb 1.3.52 Tamb
Dismaies their mindes before they come to proove/The wounding 2Tamb 1.3.86 Zenoc
Will quickly ride before Natolia: . . . . 2Tamb 1.3.125 Therid
lead him bound in chaines/Unto Damasco, where I staid before. 2Tamb 1.3.205 Techel
make no period/Untill Natolia kneele before your feet. . 2Tamb 1.3.217 Therid
That could not but before be terrified: . . . . . 2Tamb 2.2.22 Uribas
and holy Seraphins/That sing and play before the king of kings, 2Tamb 2.4.27 Tamb
Yet let me kisse my Lord before I die, ... 2Tamb 2.4.69 Zenoc
And had she liv'd before the siege of Troy, ... 2Tamb 2.4.86 Tamb
Before we meet the armie of the Turke. . . . . . 2Tamb 3.2.138 Tamb
That we have sent before to fire the townes, ... 2Tamb 3.2.147 Tamb
And lie in trench before thy castle walles, ... 2Tamb 3.3.31 Techel
And purge my soule before it come to thee. . . . . 2Tamb 3.4.33 Olymp
Before whom (mounted on a Lions backe)/Rhamnusia beares a 2Tamb 3.4.56 Therid
I goe into the field before I need? . . . . . . 2Tamb 4.1.51 Calyph
Before I conquere all the triple world. . . . . . 2Tamb 4.3.63 Tamb
Lost long before you knew what honour meant. . . . 2Tamb 4.3.87 Tamb
Before I bide the wrath of Tamburlaine. 2Tamb 5.1.42 2Citzn
Before his hoste be full from Babylon, ... 2Tamb 5.2.9 Callap
Before himselfe or his be conquered. . . . . . . 2Tamb 5.2.53 Callap
That I may see thee crown'd before I die. . . . . . 2Tamb 5.3.179 Tamb
And send my soule before my father die, ... 2Tamb 5.3.208 Amyras
Fearing the worst of this before it fell, ... Jew 1.2.246 Barab
Seeme not to know me here before your mother/Lest she mistrust Jew 2.3.146 Barab
Will winne the Towne, or dye before the wals. . . . Jew 5.1.5 Govnr
First, for his Army, they are sent before, ... Jew 5.5.25 Barab
My Mother poysoned heere before my face: . . . . . P 187 3.22 Navrre
O let me pray before I dye. . . . . P 301 5.28 Admral
O let me pray before I take my death. . . . . . P 352 6.7 Seroun
I goe as whirl-windes rage before a storme. . . . . P 511 9.30 Guise
Poland diadem, before/You were invested in the crowne of France. P 612 12.25 Mugern
King, why so thou wert before. . . . . P1067 19.137 QnMoth
Then heere wee'l lye before [Lutetia] <Lucrecia> walles, . P1151 22.13 King
I, but how chance this was not done before? . . . . Edw 1.4.272 Lncstr
Penbrooke shall beare the sword before the king. . . . Edw 1.4.351 Edward
A Velvet cap'de cloake, fac'st before with Serge, . . . Edw 2.1.34 Spencr
by me, yet but he may/See him before he dies, for why he saies, Edw 2.5.37 Arundl
majestie so earnestlie/Desires to see the man before his death, Edw 2.5.78 Penbrk
His life, my lord, before your princely feete. . . . Edw 3.1.45 Spencr
As Leicester that had charge of him before. . . . . Edw 5.2.35 BshpWn
And let me see the stroke before it comes, ... Edw 5.5.76 Edward
Which he preferres before his chiefest blisse; . . . . F 27 Prol.27 1Chor

BEFORE (cont.)			
Saba, or as beautifull/As was bright Lucifer before his fall.	F 542	2.1.154	Mephst
Are laid before me to dispatch my selfe:	F 574	2.2.23	Faust
And crouch before the Papall dignity:	F 874	3.1.96	Pope
So, so, was never Divell thus blest before.	F 974	3.1.196	Mephst
Before the Pope and royall Emperour,	F1187	4.1.33	Mrtino
Present before this royall Emperour,	F1238	4.1.84	Faust
and thou bring Alexander and his Paramour before the Emperour,	F1255	4.1.101	P Benvol
Or bring before this royall Emperour/The mightie Monarch,	F1296	4.1.142	Faust
heart <art> conspir'd/Benvolio's shame before the Emperour?	F1374	4.2.50	Mrtino
why did not Faustus tell us of this before, that Divines might	F1862	5.2.66	P 1Schol
in our parish dance at my pleasure starke naked before me,	F App	p.233 4	P Robin
it is not in my abilitie to present before your eyes, the true	F App	p.237 42	P Faust
shal appeare before your Grace, in that manner that they best	F App	p.237 47	P Faust
you bring Alexander and his paramour before the emperor?	F App	p.237 52	P Knight
but I must tel you one thing before you have him, ride him not	F App	p.239 108	P Faust
they be the best grapes that ere I tasted in my life before.	F App	p.242 26	P Duchss
And shal he triumph long before his time,	Lucan, First Booke		316
peoples minds, and laide before their eies/Slaughter to come,	Lucan, First Booke		466
when by Junoes taske/He had before lookt Pluto in the face.	Lucan, First Booke		576
For these before the rest preferreth he:	Ovid's Elegies		1.1.2
Then oxen which have drawne the plow before.	Ovid's Elegies		1.2.14
Before thy husband come, though I not see/What may be done, yet	Ovid's Elegies		1.4.13
though I not see/What may be done, yet there before him bee.	Ovid's Elegies		1.4.14
Starke naked as she stood before mine eie,	Ovid's Elegies		1.5.17
would, I cannot him cashiere/Before I be divided from my geere.	Ovid's Elegies		1.6.36
Before whose bow th'Arcadian wild beasts trembled.	Ovid's Elegies		1.7.14
Before her feete thrice prostrate downe I fell,	Ovid's Elegies		1.7.61
He Citties greate, this thresholds lies before:	Ovid's Elegies		1.9.19
Oft was she drest before mine eyes, yet never,	Ovid's Elegies		1.14.17
Before Callimachus one preferres me farre,	Ovid's Elegies		2.4.19
My selfe will bring vowed gifts before thy feete,	Ovid's Elegies		2.13.24
Jove liked her better then he did before.	Ovid's Elegies		2.19.30
And yet remaines the face she had before.	Ovid's Elegies		3.3.2
Faire white with rose red was before commixt:	Ovid's Elegies		3.3.5
And nine sweete bouts had we before day light.	Ovid's Elegies		3.6.26
Seeing now thou wouldst deceive me as before:	Ovid's Elegies		3.6.70
For bloudshed knighted, before me preferr'd.	Ovid's Elegies		3.7.10
Rude husband-men bak'd not their corne before,	Ovid's Elegies		3.9.7
I am not as I was before, unwise.	Ovid's Elegies		3.10.32
Before the roome be cleere, and doore put too.	Ovid's Elegies		3.13.10
And before folke immodest speeches shunne,	Ovid's Elegies		3.13.16
Of proud Adonis that before her lies.	Hero and Leander		1.14
Wherewith she yeelded, that was woon before.	Hero and Leander		1.330
And she her selfe before the pointed time,	Hero and Leander		2.20
Brought foorth the day before the day was borne.	Hero and Leander		2.322
And ran before, as Harbenger of light,	Hero and Leander		2.331
BEFORE HAND			
starv'd, and he be provided for a moneths victuall before hand.	1Tamb	4.4.47	P Usumc
BE-FRIENDED			
Let me, and them by it be aye be-friended.	Ovid's Elegies		3.12.36
BEG			
We never beg, but use such praiers as these.	Edw	2.2.153	Mortmr
BEGAN (See also GAN)			
Began to crye, let us unto our ships,	Dido	2.1.127	Aeneas
chardg'd their quivering speares/Began to checke the ground,	1Tamb	5.1.333	Zenoc
Here I began to martch towards Persea,	2Tamb	5.3.126	Tamb
Which is from Scythia, where I first began,	2Tamb	5.3.143	Tamb
But suddenly the wind began to rise,	Jew	2.2.13	Bosco
studied Physicke, and began/To practise first upon the Italian;	Jew	2.3.181	Barab
(men say)/Began to smile and [tooke] <take> one foote away.	Ovid's Elegies		1.1.8
And sweetly on his pipe began to play,	Hero and Leander		1.401
he stayd his furie, and began/To give her leave to rise:	Hero and Leander		1.415
Saturne and Ops, began their golden raigne.	Hero and Leander		1.456
Leander being up, began to swim,	Hero and Leander		2.175
Whereon Leander sitting, thus began,	Hero and Leander		2.245
By this Apollos golden harpe began,	Hero and Leander		2.327
BEGAT			
of hers (like that/Which made the world) another world begat,	Hero and Leander		2.292
BEGET			
Will not these delaies beget my hopes?	Edw	2.5.47	Gavstn
BEGETS			
Begets the quiet of king Edwards land,	Edw	3.1.263	Spencr
Begets a world of idle fantasies,	F1810	5.2.14	Mephst
BEGGARS			
Why should we live, O wretches, beggars, slaves,	1Tamb	5.1.248	Zabina
BEGGE			
out of Purgatory come to begge a pardon of your holinesse.	F App	p.232 15	P Lorein
BEGGERS			
To beggers shut, to bringers ope thy gate,	Ovid's Elegies		1.8.77
BEGGERY			
And for his conscience lives in beggery.	Jew	1.1.120	Barab
BEGGING			
staffe; excellent, he stands as if he were begging of Bacon.	Jew	4.1.154	P Ithimr
BEGIN			
Begin in troopes to threaten civill warre,	1Tamb	1.1.148	Ceneus
will I make the Point/That shall begin the Perpendicular.	1Tamb	4.4.82	Tamb
That there begin and nourish every part,	2Tamb	3.4.7	Capt
Then have at him to begin withall.	2Tamb	5.1.152	Therid
And 'bout this time the Nuns begin to wake;	Jew	2.1.56	Abigal
Begin betimes, Occasion's bald behind,	Jew	5.2.44	Barab
Which when they heare, they shall begin to kill:	P 239	4.37	Guise
Stay my Lord, let me begin the psalme.	P 344	5.71	Anjoy

BEGIN (cont.)			
Now doe I but begin to look about,	P 985	19.55	Guise
Aye me poore soule when these begin to jarre.	Edw	2.2.72	Queene
sweat and dust/All chockt well neare, begin to faint for heate,	Edw	3.1.192	SpncrP
The commons now begin to pitie him,	Edw	5.4.2	Mortmr
and begin/To sound the depth of that thou wilt professe,	F 29	1.1.1	Faust
set my countenance like a Precisian, and begin to speake thus:	F 214	1.2.21	P Wagner
Faustus, begin thine Incantations,	F 233	1.3.5	Faust
Since first the worlds creation did begin.	F1985	5.3.3	1Schol
When two are stript, long ere the course begin,	Hero and Leander		1.169
Women are woon when they begin to jarre.	Hero and Leander		1.332
BEGINNE			
Beginne to shut thy house at evening sure.	Ovid's Elegies		2.19.38
Thou doest beginne, she shall be mine no longer.	Ovid's Elegies		2.19.48
BEGINNER			
Welcome the first beginner of my blisse:	Jew	2.1.50	Barab
BEGINNES			
Now frosty night her flight beginnes to take,	Ovid's Elegies		1.6.65
BEGINNING			
No Madam, but the beginning of your joy,	2Tamb	3.4.83	Techel
BEGINS			
My soule begins to take her flight to hell:	1Tamb	2.7.44	Cosroe
when the Moon begins/To joine in one her semi-circled hornes:	1Tamb	3.1.11	Bajzth
Then Victorie begins to take her flight,	1Tamb	3.3.160	Tamb
And every line begins with death againe:	2Tamb	4.2.48	Olymp
How like his cursed father he begins,	2Tamb	4.3.55	Jrslem
Begins the day with our Antypodes:	2Tamb	5.3.149	Tamb
But now begins the extremity of heat/To pinch me with	Jew	5.5.87	Barab
Guise, begins those deepe ingendred thoughts/To burst abroad,	P 91	2.34	Guise
How Charles our sonne begins for to lament/For the late nights	P 513	9.32	QnMoth
O holde me up, my sight begins to faile,	P 548	11.13	Charls
And all the court begins to flatter him.	Edw	1.2.22	Lncstr
Now Mortimer begins our tragedie.	Edw	5.6.23	Queene
So, now the bloud begins to cleere againe:	F 460	2.1.72	Faust
the first letter of my name begins with Letchery <leachery>.	F 710	2.2.162	P Ltchry
[Sathan begins to sift me with his pride]:	F1791	5.1.118A	OldMan
all lands else/Have stable peace, here wars rage first begins,	Lucan, First Booke		252
Shall Dian fanne when love begins to glowe?	Ovid's Elegies		1.1.12
And now begins Leander to display/Loves holy fire, with words,	Hero and Leander		1.192
BEGIRT			
What care I though the Earles begirt us round?	Edw	2.2.223	Edward
Begirt with weapons, and with enemies round,	Edw	3.1.95	Arundl
BE GON			
in the morning/We will discharge thee of thy charge, be gon.	Edw	2.5.109	Penbrk
Away, tarrie no answer, but be gon.	Edw	3.1.173	Edward
Be gon.	Edw	3.1.255	Edward
Therefore be gon in hast, and with advice,	Edw	3.1.264	Spencr
As good be gon, as stay and be benighted.	Edw	4.7.86	Rice
Traitors be gon, and joine you with Mortimer,	Edw	5.1.87	Edward
Thankes gentle Winchester: sirra, be gon.	Edw	5.2.27	Queene
If you mistrust me, ile be gon my lord.	Edw	5.5.97	Ltborn
BEGON			
Welcome grave Fryar; Ithamore begon,	Jew	3.3.52	Abigal
BE GONE			
Forget me, see me not, and so be gone.	Jew	1.2.363	Barab
But now I must be gone to buy a slave.	Jew	2.3.95	Barab
Be gone I say, tis time that we were there.	P 919	18.20	Navrre
Traitor be gone, whine thou with Mortimer.	Edw	2.2.214	Edward
Be easilie supprest: and therefore be gone.	Edw	2.4.45	Queene
Away be gone.	F1132	3.3.45	Mephst
thee into an Ape, and thee into a Dog, and so be gone.	F App	p.235 44	P Mephst
Mephastophilis be gone.	F App	p.237 56	P Faust
Be gone quickly.	F App	p.241 163	P Mephst
Alas Madame, thats nothing, Mephastophilis, be gone.	F App	p.242 12	P Faust
BEGONE			
God-a-mercy nose; come let's begone.	Jew	4.1.23	Ithimr
Why does he goe to thy house? let him begone.	Jew	4.1.101	1Fryar
On then, begone.	Jew	5.4.10	Govnr
BEGONNE			
Thinking to quench the sparckles new begonne.	Hero and Leander		2.138
BEGOTTEN			
begotten of an old Churle in a <an olde> leather <leatherne>	F 674	2.2.123	P Covet
I am Envy, begotten of a Chimney-sweeper, and an Oyster-wife:	F 679	2.2.128	P Envy
I was begotten on a sunny bank:	F 705	2.2.154	P Sloth
BEGUIL'D			
Both held in hand, and flatly both beguil'd.	Jew	3.3.3	Ithimr
To see how he this captive Nymph beguil'd.	Hero and Leander		2.40
BEGUILD			
This was my mother that beguild the Queene,	Dido	5.1.42	Aeneas
BEGUILE			
Nor let the armes of antient [lines] <lives> beguile thee,	Ovid's Elegies		1.8.65
BEGUILED			
I thinke some Fairies have beguiled me.	Dido	5.1.215	Nurse
BEGUN			
And Phoebus had forsooke my worke begun.	Ovid's Elegies		3.11.18
BEGUNNE			
Or night being past, and yet not day begunne.	Ovid's Elegies		1.5.6
BEHALFE			
I have according to instructions in that behalfe,	Edw	4.3.29	P Spencr
BEHAV'D			
But wish thou hadst behav'd thee otherwise.	Jew	5.5.75	Govnr
BEHAVE			
As I behave my selfe in this, imploy me hereafter.	Jew	2.3.379	Ithimr

BEHAVE (cont.)			
But how thou shouldst behave thy selfe now know;	Ovid's Elegies		1.4.11
BEHAVIOUR			
Heere I display my lewd and loose behaviour.	Ovid's Elegies		2.4.4
doth favour/That seekes the conquest by her loose behaviour.	Ovid's Elegies		2.5.12
faire, mishapen stuffe/Are of behaviour boisterous and ruffe.	Hero and Leander		1.204
BEHEAD			
with us that be his peeres/To banish or behead that Gaveston?	Edw	1.2.43	Mortmr
BEHELD			
Which seene to all, though he beheld me not,	Dido	5.1.237	Anna
Having beheld devine Zenocrate,	1Tamb	5.1.418	Arabia
Hast thou beheld a peale of ordinance strike/A ring of pikes,	2Tamb	3.2.98	Tamb
whose weeping eies/Since thy arrivall here beheld no Sun,	2Tamb	4.2.2	Olymp
The strangest sight, in my opinion,/That ever I beheld.	Jew	1.2.377	Mthias
O the sweetest face that ever I beheld!	Jew	3.1.26	P Ithimr
And what might please mine eye, I there beheld.	F 853	3.1.75	Faust
As Wagner nere beheld in all his life.	F App	p.243 7	Wagner
Hippodameias lookes while he beheld.	Ovid's Elegies		3.2.16
BEHEST (See also HEST)			
Yet must he not gainsay the Gods behest.	Dido	5.1.127	Aeneas
Your Bassoe will accomplish your behest:	1Tamb	3.1.42	Bassoe
BEHIGHT			
She smilde, and with quicke eyes behight some grace:	Ovid's Elegies		3.2.83
BEHIND			
Now if thou goest, what canst thou leave behind,	Dido	5.1.151	Dido
Ah, Menaphon, why staiest thou thus behind,	1Tamb	1.1.83	Mycet
And make the power I have left behind/(Too litle to defend our	2Tamb	2.2.59	Orcan
And left your slender carkasses behind,	2Tamb	4.1.38	Calyph
Begin betimes, Occasion's bald behind,	Jew	5.2.44	Barab
And leave the Mortimers conquerers behind?	Edw	4.5.5	Edward
This [band] <hand> that all behind us might be quail'd,	Lucan, First Booke		370
(his vassals)/And that he lags behind with them of purpose,	Lucan, First Booke		477
And sit thou rounder, that behind us see,	Ovid's Elegies		3.2.23
Yet as she went, full often look'd behind,	Hero and Leander		2.5
BEHINDE			
and our followers/Close in an ambush there behinde the trees,	F1342	4.2.18	Benvol
BEHOLD (See also BEHOULD)			
might behold/Young infants swimming in their parents bloud,	Dido	2.1.192	Aeneas
Behold where both of them come forth the Cave.	Dido	4.1.16	Anna
And from a turret Ile behold my love.	Dido	4.4.86	Dido
Behold, my Lord, Ortigius and the rest,	1Tamb	1.1.134	Menaph
Behold my sword, what see you at the point?	1Tamb	5.1.108	Tamb
What do mine eies behold, my husband dead?	1Tamb	5.1.305	Zabina
Behold the Turke and his great Emperesse.	1Tamb	5.1.354	Zenoc
Behold the Turk and his great Emperesse.	1Tamb	5.1.357	Zenoc
Behold the Turke and his great Emperesse.	1Tamb	5.1.362	Zenoc
Behold Zenocrate, the cursed object/Whose Fortunes never	1Tamb	5.1.413	Zenoc
Behold her wounded in conceit for thee,	1Tamb	5.1.415	Zenoc
power and puritie/Behold and venge this Traitors perjury.	2Tamb	2.2.54	Orcan
Behold me here divine Zenocrate,	2Tamb	2.4.111	Tamb
While I sit smiling to behold the sight.	2Tamb	3.2.128	Tamb
And him faire Lady shall thy eies behold.	2Tamb	3.4.67	Therid
And here may we behold great Babylon,	2Tamb	5.2.4	Callap
And from th'Antartique Pole, Eastward behold/As much more land,	2Tamb	5.3.154	Tamb
Cannot behold the teares ye shed for me,	2Tamb	5.3.218	Tamb
And here behold (unseene) where I have found/The gold, the	Jew	2.1.22	Abigal
And to behold so sweete a sight as that,	Edw	1.4.206	Warwck
Then I doe to behold your Majestie.	Edw	2.2.63	Gavstn
shall I never see,/Never behold thee now?	Edw	3.1.69	Edward
Grone for this greefe, behold how thou art maimed.	Edw	3.1.251	Mortmr
When I behold the heavens then I repent/And curse thee wicked	F 552	2.2.1	Faust
behold <see al> the seven deadly sinnes appeare to thee in	F 655	2.2.104	P Belzeb
Behold this Silver Belt whereto is fixt/Seven golden [keys]	F 932	3.1.154	Pope
Behold my Lord, the Cardinals are return'd.	F 945	3.1.167	Raymnd
We would behold that famous Conquerour,	F1231	4.1.77	Emper
Behold an Army comes incontinent.	F1430	4.2.106	Faust
You shall behold that peerelesse dame of Greece,	F1692	5.1.19	Faust
Hadst thou kept on that way, Faustus behold,	F1903	5.2.107	GdAngl
And few live that behold their ancient seats;	Lucan, First Booke		27
Behold what gives the Poet but new verses?	Ovid's Elegies		1.8.57
If some faire wench me secretly behold,	Ovid's Elegies		2.7.5
Behold Cypassis wont to dresse thy head,	Ovid's Elegies		2.7.17
Behold the signes of antient fight, his skarres,	Ovid's Elegies		3.7.19
Such as the world would woonder to behold:	Hero and Leander		1.34
What we behold is censur'd by our eies.	Hero and Leander		1.174
in being bold/To eie those parts, which no eie should behold.	Hero and Leander		1.408
And from her countenance behold ye might,	Hero and Leander		2.318
BEHOLDE			
And let the majestie of heaven beholde/Their Scourge and	1Tamb	4.2.31	Tamb
And let Zenocrates faire eies beholde/That as for her thou	1Tamb	5.1.408	Arabia
That those which doe beholde, they may become/As men that stand	P 162	2.105	Guise
Then in this bloudy brunt they may beholde,	P 713	14.16	Bartus
Goe fetch his sonne for to beholde his death:	P1021	19.91	King
have a booke wherein I might beholde al spels and incantations,	F 551.1	2.1.164A	P Faust
Beholde thy kinsmans Caesars prosperous bandes,	Ovid's Elegies		1.2.51
BEHOLDING			
Raymond pray fall too, I am beholding/To the Bishop of Millaine,	F1041	3.2.61	Pope
We are much beholding to this learned man.	F1670	4.6.113	Lady
Majesty, we should thinke our selves much beholding unto you.	F1687	5.1.14	P 1Schol
my Lord, and whilst I live, Rest beholding for this curtesie.	F App	p.243 31	P Duchss
BEHOLDS			
That when my mistresse there beholds thee cast,	Ovid's Elegies		1.6.69
BEHOOFE			
And as we ever [aim'd] <and> at your behoofe,	1Tamb	2.5.32	Ortyg

BEHOOFE (cont.)			
Nay, for the realms behoofe and for the kings.	Edw	1.4.243	Mortmr
And in your quarrell and the realmes behoofe,	Edw	2.3.3	Kent
For our behoofe will beare the greater sway/When as a kings	Edw	5.2.13	Mortmr
BEHOULD			
Behould how quailes among their battailes live,	Ovid's Elegies		2.6.27
BEHOVES			
And it behoves you to be resolute;	Jew	5.1.3	Govnr
BEING			
And had my being from thy bubling froth:	Dido	1.1.129	Venus
With whose outcryes Atrides being apal'd,	Dido	2.1.129	Aeneas
Then got we to our ships, and being abourd,	Dido	2.1.280	Aeneas
In being too familiar with Iarbus:	Dido	3.1.15	Dido
For being intangled by a strangers lookes:	Dido	5.1.145	Dido
Will, being absent, be obdurate still.	Dido	5.1.187	Dido
(I cal it meane, because being yet obscure,	1Tamb	1.2.203	Tamb
Yet being void of Martiall discipline,	1Tamb	2.2.44	Meandr
Scarce being seated in my royall throne,	1Tamb	2.7.5	Cosroe
Being supposde his worthlesse Concubine,	1Tamb	3.2.29	Agidas
the King of Persea/(Being a Shepheard) seem'd to love you much,	1Tamb	3.2.60	Agidas
Being thy Captive, thus abuse his state,	1Tamb	4.2.60	Zabina
Water and ayre being simbolisde in one,	2Tamb	1.3.23	Tamb
Which being wroth, sends lightning from his eies,	2Tamb	1.3.76	Tamb
With whom (being women) I vouchsaft a league,	2Tamb	1.3.193	Techel
transfourme my love/In whose sweet being I repose my life,	2Tamb	2.4.48	Tamb
Being a handfull to a mighty hoste,	2Tamb	3.1.40	Orcan
matter sir, for being a king, for Tamburlain came up of nothing.	2Tamb	3.1.73	P Almeda
That being fiery meteors, may presage,	2Tamb	3.2.4	Tamb
Greek, is writ/This towne being burnt by Tamburlaine the great,	2Tamb	3.2.17	Calyph
Being burnt to cynders for your mothers death.	2Tamb	3.2.46	Tamb
Whose shattered lims, being tost as high as heaven,	2Tamb	3.2.100	Tamb
That being concocted, turnes to crimson blood,	2Tamb	3.2.108	Tamb
Cloth'd with a pitchy cloud for being seene.	2Tamb	4.1.131	Tamb
Being caried thither by the cannons force,	2Tamb	5.1.66	Tamb
Which being faint and weary with the siege,	2Tamb	5.2.7	Callap
Which being the cause of life, imports your death.	2Tamb	5.3.90	Phsitn
Being distant lesse than ful a hundred leagues,	2Tamb	5.3.133	Tamb
which being valued/Amount to more then all the wealth in Malta.	Jew	1.2.133	Offcrs
being bought, the Towne-seale might be got/To keepe him for his	Jew	2.3.103	Barab
And few or none scape but by being purg'd.	Jew	2.3.106	Barab
Being young I studied Physicke, and began/To practise first	Jew	2.3.181	Barab
it, and the Priest/That makes it knowne, being degraded first,	Jew	3.6.35	2Fryar
That being importun'd by this Bernardine/To be a Christian, I	Jew	4.1.187	Barab
being driven to a non-plus at the critical aspect of my	Jew	4.2.13	P Pilia
but the Exercise being done, see where he comes.	Jew	4.2.20	P Pilia
And being asleepe, belike they thought me dead,	Jew	5.1.81	Barab
The floore whereof, this Cable being cut,	Jew	5.5.34	Barab
And then the watchword being given, a bell shall ring,	P 238	4.36	Guise
The head being of, the members cannot stand.	P 296	5.23	Anjoy
Shall being dead, be hangd thereon in chaines.	P 321	5.48	Anjoy
Because my places being but three, contains all his:	P 405	7.45	Ramus
And being able, Ile keep an hoast in pay.	P 840	17.35	Guise
Being animated by Religious zeale,	P 848	17.43	Guise
To which thou didst alure me being alive:	P1025	19.95	King
Lord Percie of the North being highly mov'd,	Edw	1.1.110	Kent
Were he a peasant, being my minion,	Edw	1.4.30	Edward
Which being caught, strikes him that takes it dead,	Edw	1.4.222	Mortmr
And being like pins heads, blame me for the bignesse,	Edw	2.1.48	Baldck
And therefore being pursued, it takes the aire:	Edw	2.2.25	Lncstr
Thy court is naked, being bereft of those,	Edw	2.2.174	Mortmr
For being delivered unto Penbrookes men,	Edw	3.1.116	Arundl
Being of countenance in your countrey here,	Edw	4.6.75	Mortmr
the forrest Deare being strucke/Runnes to an herbe that closeth	Edw	5.1.9	Edward
And Isabell, whose eyes [being] <beene> turnd to steele,	Edw	5.1.104	Edward
And gripe the sorer being gript himselfe.	Edw	5.2.9	Mortmr
Thou being his unckle, and the next of bloud,	Edw	5.2.88	Mortmr
That being dead, if it chaunce to be found,	Edw	5.4.14	Mortmr
Till being interrupted by my friends,	Edw	5.4.62	Mortmr
Being in a vault up to the knees in water,	Edw	5.5.2	Matrvs
They give me bread and water being a king,	Edw	5.5.62	Edward
Or being dead, raise them to life againe,	F 53	1.1.25	Faust
<that> you, being Licentiats <licentiate>, should stand upon;	F 203	1.2.10	P Wagner
In being depriv'd of everlasting blisse?	F 308	1.3.80	Mephst
so passionate/For being deprived of the Joyes of heaven?	F 312	1.3.84	Faust
grant unto them that foure and twentie yeares being expired,	F 496	2.1.108	P Faust
above written being inviolate, full power to fetch or carry the	F 497	2.1.109	P Faust
Where sitting <Being seated> in a Chariot burning bright,	F 758	2.3.37	2Chor
which being all I desire, I am content to remove his hornes.	F1313	4.1.159	P Faust
He is not well with being over solitarie.	F1829	5.2.33	3Schol
<Belike he is growne into some sicknesse, by> being over	F1829	(HC270)A	P 3Schol
friends, what shall become of Faustus being in hell for ever?	F1847	5.2.51	P Faust
which being all I desire, I am content to release him of his	F App	p.238 83	P Faust
that being in the dead time of winter, and in the month of	F App	p.242 17	P Duke
thee (seeing thou being old/Must shine a star) shal heaven	Lucan, First Booke		45
each from other, but being worne away/They both burst out,	Lucan, First Booke		102
Being conquered, we are plaugde with civil war.	Lucan, First Booke		108
And being popular sought by liberal gifts,	Lucan, First Booke		132
Being three daies old inforst the floud to swell,	Lucan, First Booke		220
Which being broke the foot had easie passage.	Lucan, First Booke		224
But law being put to silence by the wars,	Lucan, First Booke		278
Twas his troupe hem'd in Milo being accusde;	Lucan, First Booke		323
And Trevier; thou being glad that wars are past thee;	Lucan, First Booke		437
And shame to spare life which being lost is wonne.	Lucan, First Booke		458

BEING (cont.)
These being come, their huge power made him bould/To mannage   Lucan, First Booke   462
long struggled, as being like to prove/An aukward sacrifice,   Lucan, First Booke   610
This said, being tir'd with fury she sunke downe.   Lucan, First Booke   694
Being fittest matter for a wanton wit,   Ovid's Elegies   1.1.24
Which being not shakt <slackt>, I saw it die at length.   Ovid's Elegies   1.2.12
Or night being past, and yet not day begunne.   Ovid's Elegies   1.5.6
being thin, the harme was small,/Yet strivde she to be covered   Ovid's Elegies   1.5.13
Judge you the rest, being tyrde <tride> she bad me kisse.   Ovid's Elegies   1.5.25
she being wise,/Sees not the morne on rosie horses rise.   Ovid's Elegies   1.8.3
Who seekes, for being faire, a night to have,   Ovid's Elegies   1.8.67
Least they should fly, being tane, the tirant play.   Ovid's Elegies   1.8.70
Achilles burnd Briseis being tane away: Ovid's Elegies   1.9.33
The sport being such, as both alike sweete try it,   Ovid's Elegies   1.10.33
Straight being read, will her to write much backe,   Ovid's Elegies   1.11.19
to her I consecrate/My faithfull tables being vile maple late.   Ovid's Elegies   1.11.28
being fine and thinne/Like to the silke the curious Seres   Ovid's Elegies   1.14.5
Why in thy glasse doest looke being discontent?   Ovid's Elegies   1.14.36
Wars dustie <rustie> honors are refused being yong,   Ovid's Elegies   1.15.4
to thee being cast do happe/Sharpe stripes, she sitteth in the   Ovid's Elegies   2.2.61
Or justifie my vices being many,   Ovid's Elegies   2.4.2
And she thats coy I like for being no clowne,   Ovid's Elegies   2.4.13
[I thinke what one undeckt would be, being drest];   Ovid's Elegies   2.4.37
Now many guests were gone, the feast being done,   Ovid's Elegies   2.5.21
But being present, might that worke the best,   Ovid's Elegies   2.8.17
Being requirde, with speedy helpe relieve?   Ovid's Elegies   2.9.8
Being wrackt, carowse the sea tir'd by their ships: Ovid's Elegies   2.10.34
There wine being fild, thou many things shalt tell,   Ovid's Elegies   2.11.49
Nor being arm'd fierce troupes to follow farre?   Ovid's Elegies   2.14.2
He being Judge, I am convinc'd of blame.   Ovid's Elegies   2.17.2
Oft couzen me, oft being wooed say nay.   Ovid's Elegies   2.19.20
All being shut out, th'adulterer is within.   Ovid's Elegies   3.4.8
Like lightning go, his strugling mouth being checkt.   Ovid's Elegies   3.4.14
Why being a vestall am I wooed to wed,   Ovid's Elegies   3.5.75
I blush, [that] <and> being youthfull, hot, and lustie,   Ovid's Elegies   3.6.19
Why mockst thou me she cried, or being ill,   Ovid's Elegies   3.6.77
Jove being admonisht gold had soveraigne power,   Ovid's Elegies   3.7.29
And Venus grieves, Tibullus life being spent,   Ovid's Elegies   3.8.15
Being fit broken with the crooked share,   Ovid's Elegies   3.9.32
Be not ashamed to strippe you being there,   Ovid's Elegies   3.13.21
And being justified by two words, thinke/The cause acquits you   Ovid's Elegies   3.13.49
Their fellowes being slaine or put to flight,   Hero and Leander   1.120
When misers keepe it; being put to lone,   Hero and Leander   1.235
Of that which hath no being, doe not boast,   Hero and Leander   1.275
Beyond the bounds of shame, in being bold/To eie those parts,   Hero and Leander   1.407
Which being knowne (as what is hid from Jove)?   Hero and Leander   1.436
He being a novice, knew not what she meant,   Hero and Leander   2.13
By being possest of him for whom she long'd: Hero and Leander   2.36
Jewels being lost are found againe, this never,   Hero and Leander   2.85
But being separated and remooved,   Hero and Leander   2.127
Leander being up, began to swim,   Hero and Leander   2.175
By this Leander being nere the land,   Hero and Leander   2.227
Being sodainly betraide, dyv'd downe to hide her.   Hero and Leander   2.262

BEL
And now stay/That bel that to the devils mattins rings.   P 448   7.88   Guise

BELCH
and Belcher come here, I'le belch him: F 374   1.4.32   P Robin

BELCHEOS
serve you, would you teach me to raise up Banios and Belcheos?   F App   p.230 57   P Clown

BELCHER
Banio, Belcher.   F 373   1.4.31   P Wagner
Belcher?   F 374   1.4.32   P Robin
and Belcher come here, I'le belch him: F 374   1.4.32   P Robin
O per se o, demogorgon, Belcher and Mephostophilis.   F1115   3.3.28   P Robin
two divels presently to fetch thee away Baliol and Belcher.   F App   p.230 44   P Wagner
Let your Balio and your Belcher come here, and Ile knocke them,   F App   p.230 45   P Clown
Balioll and Belcher, spirits away.   F App   p.230 50   P Wagner
How Balioll and Belcher.   F App   p.231 67   P Wagner
O Lord I pray sir, let Banio and Belcher go sleepe.   F App   p.231 68   P Clown

BELDAME
A dwarfish beldame beares me companie,   Hero and Leander   1.353

BELEEFE
Barabas, although thou art in mis-beleefe,   Jew   1.2.352   1Fryar
For she that varies from me in beleefe/Gives great presumption   Jew   3.4.10   Barab

BELEEVE
I beleeve there will be some hurt done anon amongst them.   2Tamb   4.1.74   P Calyph
Beleeve me, Noble Lodowicke, I have seene/The strangest sight,   Jew   1.2.375   Mthias
But doe you thinke that I beleeve his words?   Jew   4.1.105   Barab
Here is my hand, beleeve me, Barabas,   Jew   5.2.102   Govnr
Beleeve me Guise he becomes the place so well,   P 495   9.14   QnMoth
Beleeve me this jest bites sore.   P 771   15.29   King
I doe not greatly beleeve him, he lookes as like [a] conjurer   F1228   4.1.74   P Benvol
Beleeve me maister Doctor, this merriment hath much pleased me.   F App   p.242 1   P Duke
Beleeve me master Doctor, this makes me wonder above the rest,   F App   p.242 16   P Duke
Beleeve me Maister doctor, they be the best grapes that ere I   F App   p.242 25   P Duchss
Beleeve me, whom we feare, we wish to perish.   Ovid's Elegies   2.2.10
There good birds rest (if we beleeve things hidden)/Whence   Ovid's Elegies   2.6.51
and what each one speakes/Beleeve, no tempest the beleever   Ovid's Elegies   2.11.22
And I beleeve some wench thou hast affected: Ovid's Elegies   3.5.83
Well, I beleeve she kist not as she should,   Ovid's Elegies   3.6.55
Beleeve me Hero, honour is not wone,   Hero and Leander   1.281

BELEEVER
what each one speakes/Beleeve, no tempest the beleever wreakes.   Ovid's Elegies   2.11.22

BELEEVES				
And this townes well knowne customes not beleeves, . .	Ovid's Elegies	3.4.38		
BELEEVING				
will follow thee/Against these barbarous mis-beleeving Turkes.	Jew	2.2.46		Govnr
BELGASAR				
And sent them marching up to Belgasar, ...	2Tamb	2.1.19		Fredrk
BELGIA				
Our kindest friends in Belgia have we left, . . .	Edw	4.4.3		Queene
BELGIANS				
The Belgians apt to governe Brittish cars; . . .	Lucan, First Booke	427		
BELIAL (See BALIOL, BANIO)				
BELIEFE (See also BELEEFE)				
Now rash accusing, and thy vaine beliefe, ...	Ovid's Elegies	2.7.13		
And doth the world in fond beliefe deteine. . . .	Ovid's Elegies	3.3.24		
BELIEVE (See BELEEVE)				
BELIKE				
belike he hath not bene watered to day, give him some drinke.	1Tamb	4.4.54	P	Tamb
Belike they coasted round by Candie shoare/About their Oyles,	Jew	1.1.91		Barab
And now by that advantage thinkes, belike, . . .	Jew	1.1.184		Barab
Belike he has some new tricke for a purse; . . .	Jew	2.3.101		Barab
Belike there is some Ceremony in't.	Jew	3.4.83		Barab
And being asleepe, belike they thought me dead, . .	Jew	5.1.81		Barab
Why then belike/We must sinne, and so consequently die, .	F 71	1.1.43		Faust
then belike if I serve you, I shall be lousy. . . .	F 358	1.4.16	P	Robin
and see where they come, belike the feast is done. . .	F1680	5.1.7	P	Wagner
<Belike he is growne into some sicknesse, by> being over	F1829	(HC270)A	P	3Schol
staves acre, why then belike, if I were your man, I should be	F App	p.229 21	P	Clown
See where they come: belike the feast is ended. . .	F App	p.243 8		Wagner
BELIMOTH				
Ho, Belimoth, Argiron, Asteroth.	F1304	4.1.150		Faust
Asteroth, Belimoth, Mephostophilis, ...	F1402	4.2.78		Faust
BELIMOTHE				
Go Belimothe, and take this caitife hence, . . .	F1408	4.2.84		Faust
BELL (See also BEL)				
And then the watchword being given, a bell shall ring, .	P 238	4.36		Guise
And never cease untill that bell shall cease, ...	P 240	4.38		Guise
set the street/May know their watchword, then tole the bell,	P 329	5.56		Guise
for I can tell you, you'le be curst with Bell, Booke, and	F1072	3.2.92	P	Mephst
Bell, Booke, and Candle; Candle, Booke, and Bell, . .	F1074	3.2.94		Faust
Nay I know not, we shalbe curst with bell, booke, and candle.	F App	p.232 23	P	Mephst
bell, booke, and candle, candle, booke, and bell,/Forward and	F App	p.232 25		Faust
BELLAMIRA				
and he gave me a letter from one Madam Bellamira, saluting me	Jew	4.2.30	P	Ithimr
me; Sweet Bellamira, would I had my Masters wealth for thy sake.	Jew	4.2.55	P	Ithimr
Thus Bellamira esteemes of gold;	Jew	4.2.125		Curtzn
BELLES				
Ringing with joy their superstitious belles: . . .	1Tamb	3.3.237		Bajzth
BELLIE				
How smoothe a bellie, under her waste sawe I, . . .	Ovid's Elegies	1.5.21		
How smooth his brest was, and how white his bellie, . .	Hero and Leander	1.66		
BELLIED				
that great bellied women do long for some dainties or other,	F App	p.242 5	P	Faust
BELLIES				
Had Venus spoilde her bellies Troyane fruite, . . .	Ovid's Elegies	2.14.17		
BELLONA				
As if Bellona, Goddesse of the war/Threw naked swords and	2Tamb	3.2.40		Tamb
BELLONAES				
And they whom fierce Bellonaes fury moves/To wound their armes,	Lucan, First Booke	563		
BELLOWED				
H'had never bellowed in a brasen Bull/Of great ones envy; o'th	Jew	Prol.25		Machvl
BELLOWING				
Fill all the aire with troublous bellowing:	2Tamb	4.1.190		Tamb
And for his love Europa, bellowing loud, ...	Hero and Leander	1.149		
BELLY				
Nor me neither, I cannot out-run you Constable, oh my belly.	Jew	5.1.21	P	Ithimr
hold belly hold, and wee'le not pay one peny for it. .	F 749	2.3.28	P	Robin
<Whose summum bonum is in belly-cheare>.	F 834	(HC265)A		Mephst
where ther's such belly-cheere, as Wagner in his life nere saw	F1679	5.1.6	P	Wagner
who are at supper with such belly-cheere, ...	F App	p.243 6		Wagner
Because thy belly should rough wrinckles lacke, . .	Ovid's Elegies	2.14.7		
BELLY-CHEARE				
<Whose summum bonum is in belly-cheare>.	F 834	(HC265)A		Mephst
BELLY-CHEERE				
where ther's such belly-cheere, as Wagner in his life nere saw	F1679	5.1.6	P	Wagner
who are at supper with such belly-cheere, ...	F App	p.243 6		Wagner
BELLYED				
I have heard that great bellyed women, do long for things, are	F1568	4.6.11	P	Faust
BELONG				
For unto us the Promise doth belong.	Jew	2.3.47		Barab
BELONGING				
And tricks belonging unto Brokery, ...	Jew	2.3.192		Barab
BELONGS (See also LONGS)				
or whatsoever stile/Belongs unto your name, vouchsafe of ruth	Dido	2.1.40		Aeneas
Humilitie belongs to common groomes.	Dido	2.1.101		Dido
to whom in justice it belongs/To punish this unnaturall revolt:	Edw	4.6.8		Kent
Proud Lucifer, that State belongs to me:	F 871	3.1.93		Bruno
BELOV'D				
For ever be belov'd of Carolus.	F1211	4.1.57		Emper
And live belov'd of mightie Carolus.	F1324	4.1.170		Emper
A heavenly Nimph, belov'd of humane swaines, . . .	Hero and Leander	1.216		
BELOVDE				
And whereas he shall live and be belovde, ...	Edw	1.4.261		Mortmr
BELOVED				
mine armes, and by the hand/Led faire Creusa my beloved wife,	Dido	2.1.267		Aeneas

BELOVED (cont.)
Dearely beloved brother, thus tis written. . . . . P 343 5.70 Guise
Shall I not moorne for my beloved lord, ... Edw 5.6.87 Queene
Let my new mistris graunt to be beloved: . . . . . Ovid's Elegies 3.2.57
Thereon concluded that he was beloved. . . . . . Hero and Leander 2.220

BELOW
And from their knees, even to their hoofes below, . . . 1Tamb 1.1.79 Mycet
Whiles other walke below, the king and he/From out a window, Edw 1.4.416 Mortmr
Canst raise this man from hollow vaults below, ... F App p.237 30 Emper

BELOWE
A gloomie fellow in a meade belowe, ... Edw 4.7.29 Spencr

BELS
How sweet the Bels ring now the Nuns are dead/That sound at Jew 4.1.2 Barab
Let Plutos bels ring out my fatall knell, ... Edw 4.7.89 Edward

BELSEBORAMS
Belseborams framanto pacostiphos tostu Mephastophilis, . F App p.235 24 P Robin

BELT
Behold this Silver Belt whereto is fixt/Seven golden [keys] F 932 3.1.154 Pope
A belt of straw, and Ivie buds, ... Passionate Shepherd 17

BELUS
Where Belus, Ninus and great Alexander/Have rode in triumph, 2Tamb 5.1.69 Tamb

BELZABUB
stand aside you had best, I charge you in the name of Belzabub: F App p.235 19 P Robin

BELZEBUB
[Lucifer], Belzebub inferni ardentis monarcha, et Demogorgon, F 246 1.3.18 P Faust
Despair in GOD, and trust in Belzebub: . . . . . F 393 2.1.5 Faust
Wherein is fixt the love of Belzebub, ... F 400 2.1.12 Faust

BEND
at whose latter gaspe/Joves marble statue gan to bend the brow, Dido 2.1.257 Aeneas
Give me a look, that when I bend the browes, ... P 157 2.100 Guise
Whether, O whether doost thou bend thy steps? . . . . Edw 4.2.12 Queene
The burdened axes with thy force will bend; . . . . Lucan, First Booke 57
Let Nereus bend the waves unto this shore, ... Ovid's Elegies 2.11.39
Let with strong hand the reine to bend be made. . . . Ovid's Elegies 3.2.72

BENDING
hollow hanging of a hill/And crooked bending of a craggy rock, 2Tamb 1.2.58 Callap
high; but headlong pitcht/Her burning head on bending Hespery. Lucan, First Booke 545
From Venus altar to your footsteps bending)/Doth testifie that Hero and Leander 1.210

BENDS
God]/[Stretcheth out his Arme, and bends his irefull Browes]: F1944 5.2.148A Faust
When most her husband bends the browes and frownes, . . . Ovid's Elegies 2.2.33
At me Apollo bends his pliant bowe: . . . . . . Ovid's Elegies 3.3.29

BENE (Homograph)
Si bene quid de te merui, fuit aut tibi quidquam/Dulce meum, Dido 5.1.136 Dido
that in former age/Hast bene the seat of mightie Conquerors, 1Tamb 1.1.7 Cosroe
Where all my youth I have bene governed, ... 1Tamb 1.2.13 Zenoc
faire Arabian king/That hath bene disapointed by this slave, 1Tamb 4.1.69 Souldn
For Fame I feare hath bene too prodigall, ... 1Tamb 4.3.48 Arabia
belike he hath not bene watered to day, give him some drinke. 1Tamb 4.4.55 P Tamb
We see his tents have now bene altered, ... 1Tamb 5.1.7 Govnr
Had never bene erected as they bee, ... 1Tamb 5.1.32 1Virgn
Hath Bajazeth bene fed to day? . . . . 1Tamb 5.1.192 Tamb
Bene oft resolv'd in bloody purple showers, ... 1Tamb 5.1.460 Tamb
And have bene crown'd for prooved worthynesse: . . . . 1Tamb 5.1.491 Tamb
And Christ or Mahomet hath bene my friend. . . . . 2Tamb 2.3.11 Orcan
Had not bene nam'd in Homers Iliads: . . . . . . 2Tamb 2.4.89 Tamb
Her name had bene in every line he wrote: . . . . . 2Tamb 2.4.90 Tamb
Nor Lesbia, nor Corrinna had bene nam'd, ... 2Tamb 2.4.93 Tamb
Zenocrate had bene the argument/Of every Epigram or Eligie. 2Tamb 2.4.94 Tamb
<Affrica>/Which hath bene subject to the Persean king, . 2Tamb 5.1.166 Tamb
That have bene tearm'd the terrour of the world? . . . 2Tamb 5.3.45 Tamb
Bene disserere est finis logices. . . . . F 35 1.1.7 Faust

BENEATH
And treading him beneath thy loathsome feet, ... 1Tamb 4.2.64 Zabina
From whence her vaile reacht to the ground beneath. . . Hero and Leander 1.18

BENEFIT
The places lawes this benefit allowe. . . . . . Ovid's Elegies 3.2.20

BENEFITE
Now eies, injoy your latest benefite, ... 2Tamb 5.3.224 Tamb
Nay for the Popes sake, and thine owne benefite. . . . P 827 17.22 Eprnon
the great Gods greeved they had bestowde/This <The> benefite, Ovid's Elegies 3.6.46

BENEFITS
your royall gratitudes/With all the benefits my Empire yeelds: 2Tamb 3.1.9 Callap

BENIGHTED
As good be gon, as stay and be benighted. . . . . . Edw 4.7.86 Rice

BENT
Or as Latonas daughter bent to armes, ... 1Tamb 5.1.514 Tamb
Shall slacke my loves affection from his bent. . . . P 607 12.20 King
Come on sirs, what, are you resolutely bent, ... P 931 19.1 Capt
Th'affrighted worlds force bent on publique spoile, . . . Lucan, First Booke 5
And fates so bent, least sloth and long delay/Might crosse him, Lucan, First Booke 394
And bent his sinewy bow upon his knee, ... Ovid's Elegies 1.1.27
The gate halfe ope my bent side in will take. . . . Ovid's Elegies 1.6.4
My nayles to scratch her lovely cheekes I bent. . . . Ovid's Elegies 1.7.50
With wheeles bent inward now the ring-turne ride. . . . Ovid's Elegies 3.2.12
All deepe enrag'd, his sinowie bow he bent, ... Hero and Leander 1.371

BENUMB'D
My jointes benumb'd, unlesse I eat, I die. . . . . 1Tamb 4.4.98 Bajzth

BENUMM'D
They shooke for feare, and cold benumm'd their lims, . . Lucan, First Booke 248

BENUMMED
Yet words in thy benummed palate rung, ... Ovid's Elegies 2.6.47

BENVOLIO
Where is Benvolio? . . . . F1168 4.1.18 Fredrk

BENVOLIO (cont.)			
What hoe, Benvolio.	F1178	4.1.24	Mrtino
hornes most strangely fastened/Upon the head of yong Benvolio.	F1278	4.1.124	Emper
What ho, Benvolio.	F1282	4.1.128	Emper
Looke up Benvolio, tis the Emperour calls.	F1286	4.1.132	Saxony
Nay sweet Benvolio, let us sway thy thoughts/From this attempt	F1325	4.2.1	Mrtino
here will Benvolio die,/But Faustus death shall quit my	F1336	4.2.12	Benvol
Where shall we place our selves Benvolio?	F1353	4.2.29	Mrtino
What ho, Benvolio.	F1431	4.3.1	Mrtino
How now Benvolio?	F1438	4.3.8	Mrtino
What shall we then do deere Benvolio?	F1451	4.3.21	Mrtino
BENVOLIO'S			
Benvolio's head was grac't with hornes to day?	F1331	4.2.7	Benvol
heart <art> conspir'd/Benvolio's shame before the Emperour?	F1374	4.2.50	Mrtino
Martino see,/Benvolio's hornes againe.	F1437	4.3.7	Fredrk
BEQUEATH			
Bequeath her young ones to our scanted foode.	Dido	1.1.162	Achat
To whom poore Dido doth bequeath revenge.	Dido	5.1.173	Dido
But now <Faustus> thou must bequeath it solemnly,	F 423	2.1.35	Mephst
BEQUEATH'D			
And Faustus hath bequeath'd his soule to Lucifer.	F 464	2.1.76	Faust
When you fleet hence, can be bequeath'd to none.	Hero and Leander		1.248
BEREAVE			
And now shall move you to bereave my life.	Jew	1.2.143	Barab
And quite bereave thee of salvation.	F1709	5.1.36	OldMan
BEREAVEN			
Yet shall thy life be forcibly bereaven.	Ovid's Elegies		3.8.38
BEREAVES			
Which as it seemes, hence winde and sea bereaves.	Ovid's Elegies		2.16.46
BEREFT			
Because this place bereft me of my Love:	2Tamb	2.4.138	Tamb
Thy court is naked, being bereft of those,	Edw	2.2.174	Mortmr
And of such wondrous beautie her bereft:	Hero and Leander		1.48
BERKELEY (See BARTLEY)			
BERNARDINE (See also BARNARDINE)			
Now Fryar Bernardine I come to you,	Jew	4.1.125	Barab
But soft, is not this Bernardine?	Jew	4.1.164	1Fryar
Bernardine--/Wilt thou not speake?	Jew	4.1.168	1Fryar
Who is it? Bernardine?	Jew	4.1.176	Barab
That being importun'd by this Bernardine/To be a Christian, I	Jew	4.1.187	Barab
lov'd Rice, that Fryar Bernardine slept in his owne clothes.	Jew	4.4.76	P Ithimr
Marry, even he that strangled Bernardine, poyson'd the Nuns, and	Jew	5.1.33	P Ithimr
BESCRATCH			
Bescratch mine eyes, spare not my lockes to breake,	Ovid's Elegies		1.7.65
BESEECH			
She humbly did beseech him for our bane,	Dido	1.1.60	Venus
Maddame, I beseech your grace to except this simple gift.	P 166	3.1	P Pothec
I beseech your Worship accept of these forty Dollors.	F1457	4.4.1	P HrsCsr
I beseech you sir accept of this; I am a very poore man, and	F1463	4.4.7	P HrsCsr
I do beseech your grace let them come in,	F1605	4.6.48	Faust
My Lord, beseech you give me leave a while,	F1621	4.6.64	Faust
She left; I say'd, you both I must beseech,	Ovid's Elegies		3.1.61
And her in humble manner thus beseech.	Hero and Leander		1.314
BESEEM'D			
She viewed the earth: the earth to viewe, beseem'd her.	Ovid's Elegies		2.5.43
BESEEME			
A prison may beseeme his holinesse.	Edw	1.1.207	Gavstn
Warwicke, these words do ill beseeme thy years.	Edw	2.2.94	Kent
BESEEMES			
This place beseemes me not, O pardon me.	Dido	2.1.94	Aeneas
Embost with silke as best beseemes my state,	1Tamb	1.1.99	Mycet
If as beseemes a person of thy state,	1Tamb	5.1.483	Souldn
Shall we with honor (as beseemes) entombe,	1Tamb	5.1.531	Tamb
Beseemes it thee to contradict thy king?	Edw	1.1.92	Edward
As best beseemes this solemne festivall.	F1012	3.2.32	Pope
To serve for pay beseemes not wanton gods.	Ovid's Elegies		1.10.20
BESEEMING			
and this curtle-axe/Are adjuncts more beseeming Tamburlaine.	1Tamb	1.2.43	Tamb
Saying, Poet heers a worke beseeming thee.	Ovid's Elegies		1.1.28
BESEIGED			
Such rampierd gates beseiged Cittyes ayde,	Ovid's Elegies		1.6.29
BESET			
When yet both sea and sands beset their ships,	Dido	1.1.110	Venus
The dreames (brave mates) that did beset my bed,	Dido	4.3.16	Aeneas
them thither, and then/Beset his house that not a man may live.	P 289	5.16	Guise
BESIDE			
Beside the spoile of him and all his traine:	1Tamb	2.2.34	Meandr
More worth than Asia, and the world beside,	2Tamb	5.3.153	Tamb
Nuns, strangled a Fryar, and I know not what mischiefe beside.	Jew	5.1.14	P Pilia
Beside, the more to manifest our love,	Edw	3.1.52	Edward
Beside <Besides> the gates, and high Pyramydes,	F 823	3.1.45	Mephst
And up againe, and close beside him swim,	Hero and Leander		2.190
BESIDES			
Iarbus, I am cleane besides my selfe,	Dido	5.1.63	Aeneas
Besides rich presents from the puisant Cham,	1Tamb	1.2.18	Magnet
Besides thy share of this Egyptian prise,	1Tamb	1.2.190	Tamb
Besides the honor in assured conquestes:	1Tamb	1.2.219	Usumc
Besides fifteene contributorie kings,	1Tamb	3.3.14	Bassoe
Besides, king Sigismond hath brought from Christendome,	2Tamb	1.1.20	Uribas
Besides my Lord, this day is Criticall,	2Tamb	5.3.91	Phsitn
Besides, my girle, thinke me not all so fond/As negligently to	Jew	1.2.241	Barab
Ten thousand Portagues besides great Perles,	Jew	1.2.244	Barab
The wind that bloweth all the world besides,	Jew	3.5.3	Basso

BESIDES (cont.)				
And besides, the Wench is dead.	Jew	4.1.42		Barab
Besides I know not how much weight in Pearle/Orient and round,	Jew	4.1.66		Barab
besides the slaughter of these Gentlemen, poyson'd his owne	Jew	5.1.12	P	Pilia
Besides, if we should let thee goe, all's one,	Jew	5.5.99		Govnr
Besides a thousand sturdy student Catholicks,	P 140	2.83		Guise
Besides my heart relentes that noble men,	P 211	4.9		Charls
And all things that a King may wish besides:	P 595	12.8		QnMoth
But you will saye you leave him rome enoughe besides:	Paris	ms 7,p390	P	Souldr
Foure Earldomes have I besides Lancaster,	Edw	1.1.102		Lncstr
I, and besides, lord Chamberlaine of the realme,	Edw	1.2.13		Warwck
Neede you any thing besides?	Edw	5.5.32		Gurney
Beside <Besides> the gates, and high Pyramydes,	F 823	3.1.45		Mephst
of golden plate; besides two thousand duckets ready coin'd:	F1676	5.1.3	P	Wagner
BESIEG'D				
My lord, to see my fathers towne besieg'd,	1Tamb	4.4.65		Zenoc
Vienna was besieg'd, and I was there,	2Tamb	1.1.103		Sgsmnd
Which when the citie was besieg'd I hid,	2Tamb	5.1.117		Govnr
Since this Towne was besieg'd, my gaine growes cold:	Jew	3.1.1		Curtzn
When Romans are besieg'd by forraine foes,	Lucan, First Booke			513
BESIEGE				
Besiege the ofspring of our kingly loynes,	Dido	1.1.116		Jupitr
At every towne and castle I besiege,	2Tamb	3.2.36		Tamb
Besiege a fort, to undermine a towne,	2Tamb	3.2.60		Tamb
BESMER'D				
Besmer'd with blood, that makes a dainty show.	1Tamb	1.1.80		Mycet
BESPAKE				
The earle of Penbrooke mildlie thus bespake.	Edw	3.1.108		Arundl
his spreading armes away she cast her,/And thus bespake him:	Hero and Leander			1.343
BESPEAKE				
My gentle lord, bespeake these nobles faire,	Edw	1.4.337		Queene
BESPOKE				
And staring, thus bespoke: what mean'st thou Caesar?	Lucan, First Booke			192
BEST				
Therefore tis best, if so it lik you all,	1Tamb	1.1.51		Mycet
Embost with silke as best beseemes my state,	1Tamb	1.1.99		Mycet
man, ordain'd by heaven/To further every action to the best.	1Tamb	2.1.53		Ortyg
What thinks your greatnes best to be atchiev'd/In pursuit of	1Tamb	3.1.56		Fesse
For Wil and Shall best fitteth Tamburlain,	1Tamb	3.3.41		Tamb
No Tamburlain, though now thou gat the best,	1Tamb	3.3.222		Zabina
Give her the Crowne Turkesse, you wer best.	1Tamb	3.3.224		Therid
In champion grounds, what figure serves you best,	2Tamb	3.2.63		Tamb
And Ile dispose them as it likes me best,	2Tamb	4.1.166		Tamb
So, now their best is done to honour me,	2Tamb	5.1.131		Tamb
For he can counsell best in these affaires;	Jew	1.1.142		2Jew
I, marke him, you were best, for this is he	Jew	2.3.132		Barab
told him he were best to send it; then he hug'd and imbrac'd	Jew	4.2.106	P	Pilia
words, Sir, and send it you, were best see; there's his letter.	Jew	4.3.24	P	Pilia
Ha, to the Jew, and send me mony you were best.	Jew	4.4.12	P	Ithimr
And meditate how we may grace us best/To solemnize our	Jew	5.3.44		Calym
That like I best that flyes beyond my reach.	P 99	2.42		Guise
Your Majesty were best goe visite him,	P 249	4.47		QnMoth
Such things as these best please his majestie,	Edw	1.1.71		Gavstn
For with my nature warre doth best agree.	Edw	1.4.365		MortSr
Th'ad best betimes forsake [them] <thee> and their trains,	Edw	3.1.202		Lncstr
When all is done, Divinitie is best:	F 64	1.1.36		Faust
That holy shape becomes a devill best.	F 254	1.3.26		Faust
you had best leave your foolery, for an my Maister come, he'le	F 734	2.3.13	P	Dick
And then devise what best contents thy minde,	F 858	3.1.80		Mephst
As best beseemes this solemne festivall.	F1012	3.2.32		Pope
best looke that your devill can answere the stealing of this	F1088	3.3.1	P	Dick
Maisters, I'le bring you to the best beere in Europe, what ho,	F1505	4.5.1	P	Carter
stand aside you had best, I charge you in the name of Belzabub:	F App	p.235 19	P	Robin
in that manner that they best liv'd in, in their most	F App	p.237 48	P	Faust
they be the best grapes that ere I tasted in my life before.	F App	p.242 25	P	Duchss
The midst is best; that place is pure, and bright,	Lucan, First Booke			58
While others touch the damsell I love best?	Ovid's Elegies			1.4.4
Let him surcease: love tries wit best of all.	Ovid's Elegies			1.9.32
So shall Licoris whom he loved best:	Ovid's Elegies			1.15.30
loves bowe/His owne flames best acquainted signes may knowe,	Ovid's Elegies			2.1.8
Who first depriv'd yong boyes of their best part,	Ovid's Elegies			2.3.3
No one face likes me best, all faces moove,	Ovid's Elegies			2.4.9
[Is she attired, then shew her graces best].	Ovid's Elegies			2.4.38
The Parrat given me, the farre [worlds] <words> best choice.	Ovid's Elegies			2.6.38
The greedy spirits take the best things first,	Ovid's Elegies			2.6.39
But being present, might that worke the best,	Ovid's Elegies			2.8.17
What horse-driver thou favourst most is best,	Ovid's Elegies			3.2.7
thou maiest, if that be best,/[A] <Or> while thy tiptoes on the	Ovid's Elegies			3.2.63
She pleaseth best, I feare, if any say.	Ovid's Elegies			3.4.32
And kindly gave her, what she liked best.	Ovid's Elegies			3.5.82
BESTEAD				
Pursu'd us hither, how were we bestead/When comming conqueror,	Lucan, First Booke			309
BESTOW				
As to bestow a looke on such as you.	Edw	2.2.78		Gavstn
Weele send his head by thee, let him bestow/His teares on that,	Edw	2.5.52		Mortmr
Not so my Lord, least he bestow more cost,	Edw	2.5.55		Lncstr
BESTOWD				
Which I bestowd upon his followers:	Dido	4.4.162		Dido
BESTOWDE				
I thinke the great Gods greeved they had bestowde/This <The>	Ovid's Elegies			3.6.45
BESTOWE				
Bestowe that treasure on the lords of Fraunce,	Edw	3.1.265		Spencr
While thou hast time yet to bestowe that gift.	Ovid's Elegies			2.3.18

BESTOWE (cont.)			
Yet in the meane time wilt small windes bestowe,	Ovid's Elegies	3.2.37	
Which wealth, cold winter doth on thee bestowe.	Ovid's Elegies	3.5.94	
BESTOWED			
them for the funerall/They have bestowed on my abortive sonne.	2Tamb	4.3.66	Tamb
lascivious showes/And prodigall gifts bestowed on Gaveston,	Edw	2.2.158	Mortmr
There see him safe bestowed, and for the rest,	Edw	3.1.253	Edward
Is not all pcwer on earth bestowed on us?	F 930	3.1.152	Pope
BESTRID			
Not long agoe bestrid a Scythian Steed:	2Tamb	1.3.38	Zenoc
BE'T			
And so they triumph, be't with whom ye wil.	Lucan, First Booke	342	
BETAKE			
Now, Gentlemen, betake you to your Armes,	Jew	5.1.1	Govnr
BETIDE			
Wherein no danger shall betide thy life,	Jew	5.2.100	Barab
Even so betide my soule as I use him.	Edw	5.1.148	Bartly
Nay, we will stay with thee, betide what may,	F1338	4.2.14	Fredrk
BETIDED			
What accident's betided to the Jewes?	Jew	1.1.145	Barab
BETIDES			
this drowsines/Betides no good, here even we are betraied.	Edw	4.7.45	Spencr
BETIMES			
Begin betimes, Occasion's bald behind,	Jew	5.2.44	Barab
Th'ad best betimes forsake [them] <thee> and their trains,	Edw	3.1.202	Lncstr
Madam, tis good to looke to him betimes.	Edw	4.6.39	Mortmr
BETOKENING			
Betokening valour and excesse of strength:	1Tamb	2.1.28	Menaph
BETRAID			
I am betraid.--	Jew	4.3.39	Barab
BETRAIDE			
Betraide by fortune and suspitious love,	1Tamb	3.2.66	Agidas
We are betraide, come my Lords, and let us goe tell the King of	P 199	3.34	P Navrre
Unles he meane to be betraide and dye:	P 898	17.93	King
False Gurney hath betraide me and himselfe.	Edw	5.6.45	Mortmr
As thus she spake, my shadow me betraide,	Ovid's Elegies	1.8.109	
Being sodainly betraide, dyv'd downe to hide her.	Hero and Leander	2.262	
BETRAIED			
And Helena betraied Deiphobus,	Dido	2.1.297	Achat
That hath betraied my gracious Soveraigne,	2Tamb	3.2.153	Usumc
this drowsines/Betides no good, here even we are betraied.	Edw	4.7.45	Spencr
My lord, he hath betraied the king his brother,	Edw	5.2.106	Mortmr
BETRAIES			
And love that is conceal'd, betraies poore lovers.	Hero and Leander	2.134	
BETRAY			
Some say Antenor did betray the towne,	Dido	2.1.110	Dido
O if I speake/I shall betray my selfe:--	Dido	3.1.173	Dido
Why wilt thou so betray thy sonnes good hap?	Dido	5.1.31	Hermes
Plac'd by my brother, will betray his Lord:	P 294	5.21	Anjoy
For theile betray thee, traitors as they are.	Edw	3.1.203	Lncstr
Do you betray us and our companie.	Edw	4.7.25	Edward
Betray us both, therefore let me flie.	Edw	5.6.8	Matrvs
What's here? an ambush to betray my life:	F1424	4.2.100	Faust
Thou coosnest boyes of sleepe, and dost betray them/To Pedants,	Ovid's Elegies	1.13.17	
BETRAYD			
So Heroes ruddie cheeke, Hero betrayd,	Hero and Leander	2.323	
BETRAYDE			
Betrayde her selfe, and yeelded at the last.	Ovid's Elegies	1.5.16	
BETRAYED			
Whose loosnes hath betrayed thy land to spoyle,	Edw	4.4.11	Queene
BETRAYE'S			
Zoon's what a looking thou keep'st, thou'lt betraye's anon.	Jew	3.1.25	Pilia
BETROATH'D			
Cal'st thou me Concubine that am betroath'd/Unto the great and	1Tamb	3.3.169	Zenoc
BETROTH'D			
But tell me Maddam, is your grace betroth'd?	1Tamb	1.2.32	Tamb
What, shall I be betroth'd to Lodowicke?	Jew	2.3.308	Abigal
That maidens new betroth'd should weepe a while:	Jew	2.3.326	Barab
BETROTHED			
Where her betrothed Lord Alcidamus,	1Tamb	1.2.78	Agidas
My father and my first betrothed love,	1Tamb	5.1.388	Zenoc
Thy first betrothed Love, Arabia,	1Tamb	5.1.530	Tamb
Or maides that their betrothed husbands spie.	Ovid's Elegies	2.5.36	
BETTER			
I am much better for your worthles love,	Dido	1.1.3	Ganimd
But bright Ascanius, beauties better worke,	Dido	1.1.96	Jupitr
Heres to thy better fortune and good starres.	Dido	2.1.98	Dido
And better able unto other armes.	Dido	3.3.36	Cupid
Better he frowne, then I should dye for griefe:	Dido	4.4.111	Dido
I know you have a better wit than I.	1Tamb	1.1.5	Mycet
we have tane/Shall be reserv'd, and you in better state,	1Tamb	1.2.3	Tamb
thee (sweet Ortigius)/Better replies shall proove my purposes.	1Tamb	2.5.37	Cosroe
What better president than mightie Jove?	1Tamb	2.7.17	Tamb
Zenocrate, looke better to your slave.	1Tamb	4.2.68	Tamb
twere better he kild his wife, and then she shall be sure not	1Tamb	4.4.45	P Usumc
Me thinks, tis a great deale better than a consort of musicke.	1Tamb	4.4.60	P Therid
And better one want for a common good,	Jew	1.2.98	Govnr
No, Barabas is borne to better chance,	Jew	1.2.218	Barab
it,/A counterfet profession is better/Then unseene hypocrisie.	Jew	1.2.292	Barab
The better; for we love not to be seene:	Jew	1.2.307	Abbass
And better would she farre become a bed/Embraced in a friendly	Jew	1.2.371	Mthias
I like it much the better.	Jew	2.3.61	Lodowk
You'le like it better farre a nights than dayes.	Jew	2.3.63	Barab

BETTER (cont.)			
So much the better, thou art for my turne.	Jew	2.3.129	Barab
No, this is the better, mother, view this well.	Jew	2.3.145	Mthias
Peace, Ithimore, 'tis better so then spar'd.	Jew	3.4.91	Barab
had it not beene much better/To [have] kept thy promise then be	Jew	5.2.4	Calym
And I reduc'd it into better forme.	P 407	7.47	Ramus
Or else employ them in some better cause.	P 794	16.8	Bartus
Learne then to rule us better and the realme.	Edw	1.4.39	Lncstr
The worst is death, and better die to live,	Edw	3.1.243	Lncstr
A loves me better than a thousand Spencers.	Edw	4.2.7	Prince
But Mortimer reservde for better hap,	Edw	4.2.40	Mortmr
and bid him rule/Better then I, yet how have I transgrest,	Edw	5.1.122	Edward
an inch of raw Mutton, better then an ell of fryde Stockfish:	F 709	2.2.161	P Ltchry
And in this sight thou better pleasest me,	F1271	4.1.117	Emper
I would request no better meate, then a dish of ripe grapes.	F1573	4.6.16	P Lady
I would desire no better meate then a dish of ripe grapes.	F App	p.242 10	P Duchss
Better I could part of my selfe have wanted.	Ovid's Elegies		1.7.24
Slaughter and mischiefs instruments, no better,	Ovid's Elegies		1.7.27
blotted letter/On the last edge to stay mine eyes the better.	Ovid's Elegies		1.11.22
Among day bookes and billes they had laine better/In which the	Ovid's Elegies		1.12.25
Also much better were they then I tell,	Ovid's Elegies		2.5.55
Better then I their quiver knowes them not.	Ovid's Elegies		2.9.38
Yet this is better farre then lie alone,	Ovid's Elegies		2.10.15
My selfe that better dye with loving may/Had seene, my mother	Ovid's Elegies		2.14.21
Jove liked her better then he did before.	Ovid's Elegies		2.19.30
But better things it gave, corne without ploughes,	Ovid's Elegies		3.7.39
Yet better ist, then if Corcyras Ile/Had thee unknowne interr'd	Ovid's Elegies		3.8.47
And spends the night (that might be better spent)/In vaine	Hero and Leander		1.355
Then muse not, Cupids sute no better sped,	Hero and Leander		1.483
BETTERS			
Or art thou grievde thy betters presse so nye?	Dido	3.3.18	Iarbus
BETWEEN			
In civill broiles between Navarre and me?	P1038	19.108	King
BETWEENE			
Betweene thy sons that shall be Emperours,	2Tamb	1.3.7	Tamb
Betweene you both, shorten the time I pray,	Edw	4.3.45	Edward
All things that move betweene the quiet Poles/Shall be at my	F 83	1.1.55	Faust
thou performe/All Covenants, and Articles, betweene us both.	F 480	2.1.92	Faust
All <articles prescrib'd> <covenant-articles> betweene us both.	F 480	(HC260)	Faust
To effect all promises betweene us [made] <both>.	F 482	2.1.94	Mephst
me for the matter, for sure the cup is betweene you two.	F1108	3.3.21	P Vintnr
BETWIXT (See also 'TWIXT, TWIXT)			
let there be a match confirmd/Betwixt these two, whose loves	Dido	3.2.78	Juno
Which I will breake betwixt a Lyons jawes.	Dido	3.3.38	Cupid
Betwixt this land and that be never league,	Dido	5.1.309	Dido
Betwixt the hollow hanging of a hill/And crooked bending of a	2Tamb	1.2.57	Callap
Betwixt the citie Zula and Danubius,	2Tamb	2.1.7	Fredrk
pitcht against our power/Betwixt Cutheia and Orminius mount:	2Tamb	2.1.18	Fredrk
Betwixt which, shall our ordinance thunder foorth,	2Tamb	3.3.58	Therid
Hovering betwixt our armies, light on me,	2Tamb	3.5.163	Tamb
and those other Iles/That lye betwixt the Mediterranean seas.	Jew	1.2.4	Basso
Why joine you force to share the world betwixt you?	Lucan, First Booke		88
peace against their wils; betwixt them both/Stept Crassus in:	Lucan, First Booke		99
Betwixt the Aegean and the Ionian sea,	Lucan, First Booke		101
words she sayd/While closely hid betwixt two dores I layed.	Ovid's Elegies		1.8.22
Full concord all your lives was you betwixt,	Ovid's Elegies		2.6.13
Pollux and Castor, might I stand betwixt,	Ovid's Elegies		2.16.13
Now shine her lookes pure white and red betwixt.	Ovid's Elegies		3.3.6
What difference betwixt the richest mine/And basest mold, but	Hero and Leander		1.232
At every stroke, betwixt them would he slide,	Hero and Leander		2.184
BEWAILD			
Heav'n starre Electra that bewaild her sisters?	Ovid's Elegies		3.11.37
BEWAILE			
Bewaile my chaunce, the sad booke is returned,	Ovid's Elegies		1.12.1
Bewaile I onely, though I them lament.	Ovid's Elegies		2.5.60
Go goodly <godly> birdes, striking your breasts bewaile,	Ovid's Elegies		2.6.3
And mother-murtherd Itis [they] <thee> bewaile,	Ovid's Elegies		2.14.30
BEWARE (See also AWARE)			
Might well have moved your highnes to beware/How you did meddle	P 179	3.14	Navrre
Beware least he unrival'd loves secure,	Ovid's Elegies		1.8.95
BEWAYLES			
when she bewayles/Her perjur'd Theseus flying vowes and sayles,	Ovid's Elegies		1.7.15
BEWITCHING			
O thou bewitching fiend, 'twas thy temptation,	F1883	5.2.87	Faust
BEWITCHT (See also WITCHT)			
Is it not straunge, that he is thus bewitcht?	Edw	1.2.55	MortSr
BEWRAIES			
Nor speech bewraies ought humaine in thy birth,	Dido	1.1.190	Aeneas
Bewraies they are too dainty for the wars.	2Tamb	1.3.28	Tamb
Ah that bewraies their basenes Lancaster,	Edw	1.2.27	Mortmr
His countenance bewraies he is displeasd.	Edw	1.2.34	Lncstr
BEWRAY			
Yet never shall these lips bewray thy life.	Jew	3.3.75	Abigal
To whom shall I bewray my secrets now,	P1083	19.153	QnMoth
No gifts given secretly thy crime bewray.	Ovid's Elegies		2.5.6
[And] <Or> hidden secrets openlie to bewray?	Ovid's Elegies		3.13.8
BEWRAYD			
And smiling wantonly, his love bewrayd.	Hero and Leander		2.182
BEWRAYDE			
Who that our bodies were comprest bewrayde?	Ovid's Elegies		2.8.5
BEYOND			
To presse beyond acceptance to your sight.	Dido	3.3.16	Aeneas
of Natolia/Confirm[illegible] this league beyond Danubius streame,	2Tamb	1.1.149	Orcan

BEYOND (cont.)			
us haste frcm hence/Along the cave that leads beyond the foe,	2Tamb	3.4.2	Olymp
Yet was his soule but flowne beyond the Alpes, . . .	Jew	Prol.2	Machvl
That like I best that flyes beyond my reach. . . .	P 99	2.42	Guise
of your Prince Electors, farre/Beyond the reach of my desertes:	P 453	8.3	Anjoy
Thou shouldst not plod one foote beyond this place. . .	Edw	1.1.181	Gavstn
Nay there you lie, 'tis beyond us both.	F1109	3.3.22	P Robin
Beyond thy robes thy dangling [lockes] <lackes> had sweept.	Ovid's Elegies		1.14.4
he often strayd/Beyond the bounds of shame, in being bold/To	Hero and Leander		1.407
BIBBING			
Wine-bibbing banquets tell thy naughtinesse, ...	Ovid's Elegies		3.1.17
BIBLE			
Jeromes Bible Faustus, view it well:	F 65	1.1.37	Faust
BICKERING			
Presume a bickering with your Emperour:	1Tamb	3.1.4	Bajzth
BID			
Wherefore doth Dido bid Iarbus goe?	Dido	3.1.56	Anna
Abourd, abourd, since Fates doe bid abourd, ...	Dido	4.3.21	Aeneas
How haps Achates bid me not farewell?	Dido	4.4.19	Dido
Doe as I bid thee sister, leade the way, ...	Dido	4.4.85	Dido
Goe, bid my Nurse take yong Ascanius, ...	Dido	4.4.105	Dido
Goe Anna, bid my servants bring me fire.	Dido	5.1.278	Dido
What should we doe but bid them battaile straight, . . .	1Tamb	2.2.18	Meandr
And bid him battell for his novell Crowne?	1Tamb	2.5.88	Techel
To bid him battaile ere he passe too farre, ...	1Tamb	2.5.95	Tamb
And bid him turne [him] <his> back to war with us, . . .	1Tamb	2.5.100	Tamb
Then stay thou with him, say I bid thee so. . . .	1Tamb	3.1.35	Bajzth
kings and more/Upon their knees, all bid me welcome home.	2Tamb	1.2.29	Callap
Jove shall send his winged Messenger/To bid me sheath my sword,	2Tamb	1.3.167	Tamb
An hundred kings by scores wil bid him armes, ...	2Tamb	2.2.11	Gazell
To bid us battaile for our dearest lives.	2Tamb	2.2.28	1Msngr
Harkening when he shall bid them plague the world. . . .	2Tamb	3.4.60	Therid
Why then goe bid them come ashore,/And bring with them their	Jew	1.1.55	Barab
And bid my Factor bring his loading in.	Jew	1.1.83	Barab
goe/And bid the Merchants and my men dispatch/And come ashore,	Jew	1.1.100	Barab
Abigall, bid him welcome for my sake.	Jew	2.3.232	Barab
Send to the Merchant, bid him bring me silkes, ...	Jew	4.2.84	Curtzn
And bid the Jeweller come hither too.	Jew	4.2.86	Ithimr
he not as well come as send; pray bid him come and fetch it:	Jew	4.3.26	P Barab
Pilia-borza, bid the Fidler give me the posey in his hat there.	Jew	4.4.35	P Curtzn
now; Bid him deliver thee a thousand Crownes, by the same token,	Jew	4.4.75	P Ithimr
And bid him come without delay to us.	P 559	11.24	QnMoth
Thou shalt have crownes of us, t'out bid the Barons, .	Edw	3.1.55	Edward
And bid me say as plainer to your grace, ...	Edw	3.1.158	Herald
men, and friends/Ere long, to bid the English king a base.	Edw	4.2.66	SrJohn
Commend me to my sonne, and bid him rule/Better then I, yet how	Edw	5.1.121	Edward
How often shall I bid you beare him hence?	Edw	5.4.102	Mortmr
Bid [on kai me on] <Oncaymaeon> farewell, <and> Galen come:	F 40	1.1.12	Faust
thou hast heard all my progeny, wilt thou bid me to supper?	F 701	2.2.150	P Glutny
I hope his Holinesse will bid us welcome.	F 807	3.1.29	Faust
Go bid the Hostler deliver him unto you, and remember what I	F1474	4.4.18	P Faust
you remember you bid he should not ride [him] into the water?	F1636	4.6.79	P Carter
shouldst thou bid me/Intombe my sword within my brothers .	Lucan, First Booke		376
I did not bid thee wed an aged swaine.	Ovid's Elegies		1.13.42
Often at length, my wench depart, I bid, ...	Ovid's Elegies		2.18.5
To pleasure me, for-bid me to corive with thee. . . .	Ovid's Elegies		2.19.60
BIDE			
My selfe will bide the danger of the brunt.	1Tamb	1.2.151	Tamb
I would not bide the furie of my father:	2Tamb	4.1.45	Amyras
Before I bide the wrath of Tamburlaine.	2Tamb	5.1.42	2Citzn
And that shal bide no more regard of parlie.	2Tamb	5.1.61	Techel
The earle of Warwick would not bide the hearing, . . .	Edw	3.1.104	Arundl
Here will we stay to bide the first assault, ...	F1354	4.2.30	Benvol
Then men from war shal bide in league, and ease, . . .	Lucan, First Booke		60
alwaies scorn'd/A second place; Pompey could bide no equall,	Lucan, First Booke		125
We bide the first brunt, safer might we dwel, ...	Lucan, First Booke		253
Now in her tender armes I sweetly bide, ...	Ovid's Elegies		1.13.5
And bide sore losse, with endlesse infamie.	Ovid's Elegies		3.6.72
BIDENTALL			
it inters with murmurs dolorous,/And cals the place Bidentall:	Lucan, First Booke		607
BIDS			
A wofull tale bids Dido to unfould, ...	Dido	2.1.114	Aeneas
Aeneas stay, Joves Herald bids thee stay.	Dido	5.1.24	Hermes
With speede he bids me saile to Italy, ...	Dido	5.1.68	Aeneas
He bids you prophesie what it imports.	1Tamb	3.2.89	Techel
Stoop villaine, stoope, stoope for so he bids, ...	1Tamb	4.2.22	Tamb
I cannot chuse, seeing my father bids:--	Jew	2.3.316	Abigal
And bids thee whet thy sword on Sextus bones, ...	P1237	22.99	King
Containes his death, yet bids them save his life. . . .	Edw	5.4.7	Mortmr
But bids his darts from perjurd girles retire. . . .	Ovid's Elegies		3.3.36
BIEN			
Bien para todos mi ganado no es:	Jew	2.1.39	Barab
BIG			
Gyants as big as hugie Polypheme:	2Tamb	1.1.28	Orcan
That he hath in store a Pearle so big, ...	Jew	5.3.27	Msngr
And that he's much chang'd, looking wild and big, . . .	Lucan, First Booke		475
BIGGER			
Their lims more large and of a bigger size/Than all the brats	1Tamb	3.3.108	Bajzth
No bigger then my hand in quantity.	F 851	3.1.73	Faust
BIGNESSE			
And being like pins heads, blame me for the bignesse, .	Edw	2.1.48	Baldck
BILEDULL			
From strong Tesella unto Biledull, ...	2Tamb	1.3.148	Techel

BILL (Homograph; See also BYLL)				
Into what corner peeres my Halcions bill?	Jew	1.1.39		Barab
I writ them a bill with mine owne bloud, the date is expired:	F1860	5.2.64	P	Faust
BILLES (Homograph)				
What traitor have wee there with blades and billes?	Edw	5.4.82		Mortmr
Among day bookes and billes they had laine better/In which the	Ovid's Elegies			1.12.25
BILLOW				
This head was beat with manie a churlish billow,	Hero and Leander			2.251
BILLOWES				
And rests a pray to every billowes pride.	Dido	1.1.53		Venus
Are ballassed with billowes watrie weight.	Dido	1.1.226		Aeneas
his entent/The windes did drive huge billowes to the shoare,	Dido	2.1.139		Aeneas
And would be toyling in the watrie billowes,	Dido	4.4.137		Dido
Flote up and downe where ere the billowes drive?	Dido	5.1.58		Aeneas
And thou shalt perish in the billowes waies,	Dido	5.1.172		Dido
See see, the billowes heave him up to heaven,	Dido	5.1.252		Dido
Whose billowes beating the resistlesse bankes,	Jew	3.5.17		Govnr
But still the rising billowes answered no.	Hero and Leander			2.152
BILS (Homograph)				
Shaking their swords, their speares and yron bils,	1Tamb	4.1.25		2Msngr
And bring with them their bils of entry:	Jew	1.1.56		Barab
Browne bils, and targetiers, foure hundred strong,	Edw	3.1.37		SpncrP
Are not thy bils hung up as monuments,	F 48	1.1.20		Faust
Which as shee went would cherupe through the bils.	Hero and Leander			1.36
BIN				
whose moaning entercourse/Hath hetherto bin staid, with wrath	1Tamb	5.1.281		Bajzth
If I had not bin wounded as I am.	1Tamb	5.1.421		Arabia
Which had ere this bin bathde in streames of blood,	1Tamb	5.1.438		Tamb
And all his life time hath bin tired,	Jew	1.1.15		Barab
And painefull nights have bin appointed me.	Jew	1.2.198		Barab
glide by night/About the place where Treasure hath bin hid:	Jew	2.1.27		Barab
Here comes the Jew, had not his goods bin seiz'd,	Jew	2.3.5		1Offcr
They hop'd my daughter would ha bin a Nun;	Jew	2.3.12		Barab
as you went in at dores/You had bin stab'd, but not a word on't	Jew	2.3.338		Barab
The time has bin, that but for one bare night/A hundred Duckets	Jew	3.1.2		Curtzn
but for one bare night/A hundred Duckets have bin freely given:	Jew	3.1.3		Curtzn
for your sake, and said what a faithfull servant you had bin.	Jew	4.2.110	P	Pilia
Whose face has bin a grind-stone for mens swords,	Jew	4.3.9		Barab
If greater falshood ever has bin done.	Jew	5.5.50		Barab
I would he never had bin flattered more.	Edw	4.4.30		Kent
Scythia and wilde Armenia had bin yoakt,	Lucan, First Booke			19
You would have thought their houses had bin fierd/Or	Lucan, First Booke			490
Which troopes hath alwayes bin on Cupids side:	Ovid's Elegies			1.2.36
BIND				
And bind her hand and foote with golden cordes,	Dido	1.1.14		Jupitr
Come bind them both and one lead in the Turke.	1Tamb	3.3.266		Tamb
victorie we yeeld/May bind the temples of his conquering head,	1Tamb	5.1.56		2Virgn
Or bind thee in eternall torments wrath.	2Tamb	3.5.113		Soria
your tongues/And bind them close with bits of burnisht steele,	2Tamb	4.1.182		Tamb
Go bind the villaine, he shall hang in chaines,	2Tamb	5.1.84		Tamb
Goe now and bind the Burghers hand and foot,	2Tamb	5.1.161		Tamb
I'le joyne the Hils that bind the Affrick shore,	F 335	1.3.107		Faust
thou dost not presently bind thy selfe to me for seven yeares,	F 361	1.4.19	P	Wagner
And bind thy soule, that at some certaine day/Great Lucifer may	F 439	2.1.51		Mephst
BINDE				
Whose operation is to binde, infect,	Jew	3.4.70		Barab
Shall binde me ever to your highnes will,	P 11	1.11		Navrre
And binde it wholy to the Sea of Rome:	P 926	18.27		Navrre
Binde us in kindenes all at your commaund.	Edw	4.2.73		Kent
Binde him, and so convey him to the court.	Edw	5.3.58		Gurney
To binde or loose, lock fast, condemne, or judge,	F 935	3.1.157		Pope
and binde your selfe presently unto me for seaven yeeres, or	F App	p.229 24	P	Wagner
Strike, so againe hard chaines shall binde thee never,	Ovid's Elegies			1.6.25
Binde fast my hands, they have deserved chaines,	Ovid's Elegies			1.7.1
Thou ring that shalt my faire girles finger binde,	Ovid's Elegies			2.15.1
BINDES				
He bindes his temples with a frowning cloude,	2Tamb	2.4.6		Tamb
yet for that love and duety bindes me thereunto, I am content	F App	p.236 15	P	Faust
BINDING				
Chaining of Eunuches, binding gally-slaves.	Jew	2.3.204		Ithimr
BIRCHIN				
it will weare out ten birchin broomes I warrant you.	F1385	4.2.61	P	Benvol
BIRD (See also BYRDS)				
From Junos bird Ile pluck her spotted pride,	Dido	1.1.34		Jupitr
The golden stature of their feathered bird/That spreads her	1Tamb	4.2.105		Tamb
No such voice-feigning bird was on the ground,	Ovid's Elegies			2.6.23
There lives the Phoenix one alone bird ever.	Ovid's Elegies			2.6.54
There Junoes bird displayes his gorgious feather,	Ovid's Elegies			2.6.55
Bird-changed Progne doth her Itys teare.	Ovid's Elegies			3.11.32
Even as a bird, which in our hands we wring,	Hero and Leander			2.289
BIRD-CHANGED				
Bird-changed Progne doth her Itys teare.	Ovid's Elegies			3.11.32
BIRDE				
Must I be vexed like the nightly birde,	Edw	5.3.6		Edward
BIRDES				
And her old body in birdes plumes to lie.	Ovid's Elegies			1.8.14
And birdes send forth shrill notes from everie bow.	Ovid's Elegies			1.13.8
Go goodly <godly> birdes, striking your breasts bewaile,	Ovid's Elegies			2.6.3
Thy tunes let this rare birdes sad funerall borrowe,	Ovid's Elegies			2.6.9
Birdes haples glory, death thy life doth quench.	Ovid's Elegies			2.6.20
Turnes all the goodly <godly> birdes to what she please.	Ovid's Elegies			2.6.58
Where round about small birdes most sweetely sing.	Ovid's Elegies			3.1.4
White birdes to lovers did not alwayes sing.	Ovid's Elegies			3.11.2

BIRDS			
And feast the birds with their bloud-shotten balles,	Dido	3.2.35	Venus
Birds of the Aire will tell of murders past;	Jew	Prol.16	Machvl
but as the fields/When birds are silent thorough winters rage;	Lucan, First Booke		261
Crownes fell from holy statues, ominous birds/Defil'd the day,	Lucan, First Booke		556
Thee Pompous birds and him two tygres drew.	Ovid's Elegies		1.2.48
And birds for <from> Memnon yearly shall be slaine.	Ovid's Elegies		1.13.4
There good birds rest (if we beleeve things hidden)/Whence	Ovid's Elegies		2.6.51
My mouth in speaking did all birds excell.	Ovid's Elegies		2.6.62
BIRTH (See also BYRTH)			
Shall yeeld to dignitie a dubble birth,	Dido	1.1.107	Jupitr
Nor speech bewraies ought humaine in thy birth,	Dido	1.1.190	Aeneas
For though my birth be great, my fortunes meane,	Dido	2.1.88	Aeneas
Thy fortune may be greater then thy birth,	Dido	2.1.90	Dido
Which graticus starres have promist at my birth.	1Tamb	1.2.92	Tamb
Blush heaven, that gave them honor at their birth,	1Tamb	5.1.350	Zenoc
But as his birth, life, health and majesty/Were strangely blest	2Tamb	5.3.24	Techel
Thy fatall birth-day, forlorne Barabas;	Jew	1.2.192	Barab
Now let me know thy name, and therewithall/Thy birth, condition,	Jew	2.3.164	Barab
Faith, Sir, my birth is but meane, my name's Ithimor,	Jew	2.3.165	Ithimr
these may well suffice/For one of greater birth then Gaveston.	Edw	1.1.159	Kent
What man of noble birth can brooke this sight?	Edw	1.4.12	MortSr
That hardly art a gentleman by birth?	Edw	1.4.29	Mortmr
Base leaden Earles that glorie in your birth,	Edw	2.2.74	Gavstn
not a thought so villanous/Can harbor in a man of noble birth.	Edw	5.1.132	Bartly
By keeping of thy birth make but a shift.	Ovid's Elegies		1.8.94
Nor do I like the country of my birth.	Ovid's Elegies		2.16.38
What gift with me was on her birth day sent,	Ovid's Elegies		3.1.57
BIRTH-DAY			
Thy fatall birth-day, forlorne Barabas;	Jew	1.2.192	Barab
BIRTH DAY			
What gift with me was on her birth day sent,	Ovid's Elegies		3.1.57
BIRTHES			
Prodigious birthes with more and ugly jointes/Then nature	Lucan, First Booke		560
BISHOP			
Be thou lord bishop, and receive his rents,	Edw	1.1.194	Edward
Tis true, the Bishop is in the tower,	Edw	1.2.1	Warwck
Remember how the Bishop was abusde,	Edw	1.4.59	ArchBp
I am beholding/To the Bishop of Millaine, for this so rare a	F1042	3.2.62	Pope
here is a daintie dish was sent me from the Bishop of Millaine.	F App	p.231 6 P	Pope
BISHOPRICK			
The Bishoprick of Coventrie is his.	Edw	1.2.45	ArchBp
BIT (Homograph; See also BYTS)			
what, not a bit?	1Tamb	4.4.54 P	Tamb
Must every bit be spiced with a Crosse?	F1066	3.2.86	Faust
Spits foorth the ringled bit, and with his hoves,	Hero and Leander		2.143
BITE			
And when we grin we bite, yet are our lookes/As innocent and	Jew	2.3.21	Barab
Now on my life, theile neither barke nor bite.	Edw	4.3.13	Edward
The living, not the dead can envie bite,	Ovid's Elegies		1.15.39
Let this care some-times bite thee to the quick,	Ovid's Elegies		2.19.43
BITES			
Sharp hunger bites upon and gripes the root,	1Tamb	5.1.273	Bajzth
Beleeve me this jest bites sore.	P 771	15.29	King
BITHYNIA (See also BYTHINIA)			
I meane to meet him in Bithynia:	1Tamb	3.3.2	Tamb
In mid Bithynia 'tis said Inachus,	Ovid's Elegies		3.5.25
BITING			
The sheepeherd nipt with biting winters rage,	Edw	2.2.61	Gavstn
BITS			
But as for you (Viceroy) you shal have bits,	2Tamb	3.5.103	Tamb
your tongues/And bind them close with bits of burnisht steele,	2Tamb	4.1.182	Tamb
And rough jades mouths with stubburn bits are torne,	Ovid's Elegies		1.2.15
BITTE			
I saw a horse against the bitte stiffe-neckt,	Ovid's Elegies		3.4.13
BITTER			
Nor yet imposd, with such a bitter hate.	2Tamb	4.1.170	Jrslem
To practize tauntes and bitter tyrannies?	2Tamb	4.3.56	Jrslem
But perish underneath my bitter curse/Like Cain by Adam, for	Jew	3.4.32	Barab
was thy parting hence/Bitter and irkesome to my sobbing heart.	Edw	2.2.58	Edward
But amplifie his greefe with bitter words.	Edw	5.2.65	Mortmr
Oft bitter juice brings to the sicke reliefe.	Ovid's Elegies		3.10.8
BITTERLY			
And in his name rebukt me bitterly,	Dido	5.1.96	Aeneas
BITTERNESS (See BYTTERNESSE)			
BITURIGES			
Those of Bituriges and light Axon pikes;	Lucan, First Booke		424
BLABBE			
he will lament/And say this blabbe shall suffer punnishment.	Ovid's Elegies		2.2.60
BLABBING			
And blabbing Tantalus in mid-waters put.	Ovid's Elegies		3.11.30
BLACK			
Black are his collours, blacke Pavilion,	1Tamb	4.1.59	2Msngr
And when they see me march in black aray.	1Tamb	4.2.119	Tamb
and make them seeme as black/As is the Island where the Furies	2Tamb	3.2.11	Tamb
Wanders about the black circumference,	2Tamb	4.2.90	Therid
and fit for nought/But perches for the black and fatall Ravens.	2Tamb	4.3.23	Tamb
And with their pawes drench his black soule in hell.	P1102	20.12	Cardnl
Tis not a black coate and a little band,	Edw	2.1.33	Spencr
But we must part, when heav'n with black night lowers.	Ovid's Elegies		1.4.60
Mars in the deed the black-smithes net did stable,	Ovid's Elegies		1.9.39
Not black, nor golden were they to our viewe,	Ovid's Elegies		1.14.9
Elisium hath a wood of holme trees black,	Ovid's Elegies		2.6.49

BLACK (cont.)			
Him the last day in black Averne hath drownd,	Ovid's Elegies	3.8.27	
BLACKE			
And dive into blacke tempests treasurie,	Dido	4.1.5	Iarbus
O Queene of Carthage, wert thou ugly blacke,	Dido	5.1.125	Aeneas
The Ocean, Terrene, and the cole-blacke sea,	1Tamb	3.1.25	Bajzth
Black are his collours, blacke Pavilion,	1Tamb	4.1.59	2Msngr
His cole-blacke collours every where advaunst,	1Tamb	5.1.9	Govnr
Furies from the blacke Cocitus lake,	1Tamb	5.1.218	Bajzth
Now throwen to roomes of blacke abjection,	1Tamb	5.1.267	Bajzth
Streamers white, Red, Blacke.	1Tamb	5.1.315	P Zabina
Natolians, Sorians, blacke Egyptians,	2Tamb	1.1.63	Orcan
As blacke as Jeat, and hard as Iron or steel,	2Tamb	1.3.27	Tamb
Should pierce the blacke circumference of hell,	2Tamb	1.3.145	Techel
Blacke is the beauty of the brightest day,	2Tamb	2.4.1	Tamb
And wake blacke Jove to crouch and kneele to me,	2Tamb	5.1.98	Tamb
And set blacke streamers in the firmament,	2Tamb	5.3.49	Tamb
Such reasons make white blacke, and darke night day.	Edw	1.4.247	Lncstr
who comes to see/What wonders by blacke spels may compast be.	F1198	4.1.44	Mrtino
may adde more shame/To the blacke scandall of his hated name.	F1378	4.2.54	Fredrk
Sith blacke disgrace hath thus eclipst our fame,	F1455	4.3.25	Benvol
Those soules which sinne seales the blacke sonnes of hell,	F1799	5.2.3	Lucifr
And all the Students clothed in mourning blacke,	F2000	5.3.18	2Schol
under whose blacke survey/Great Potentates do kneele with awful	F App	p.235 34	Mephst
have heard strange report of thy knowledge in the blacke Arte,	F App	p.236 2	P Emper
olde swords/With ugly teeth of blacke rust fouly scarr'd:	Lucan, First Booke	245	
Cole-blacke Charibdis whirl'd a sea of bloud;	Lucan, First Booke	546	
such and more strange/Blacke night brought forth in secret:	Lucan, First Booke	579	
Memnon the elfe/Received his cole-blacke colour from thy selfe.	Ovid's Elegies	1.13.32	
And call the sunnes white horses [backe] <blacke> at noone.	Ovid's Elegies	2.1.24	
I sawe ones legges with fetters blacke and blewe,	Ovid's Elegies	2.2.47	
If her white necke be shadowde with blacke haire,	Ovid's Elegies	2.4.41	
While thus I speake, blacke dust her white robes ray:	Ovid's Elegies	3.2.41	
Since Heroes time, hath halfe the world beene blacke.	Hero and Leander	1.50	
BLACKNESSE			
cullor scard him; a dead blacknesse/Ranne through the bloud,	Lucan, First Booke	617	
BLACK-SMITHES			
Mars in the deed the black-smithes net did stable,	Ovid's Elegies	1.9.39	
BLADE			
Wilt thou have war, then shake this blade at me,	2Tamb	1.1.83	Sgsmnd
BLADES			
Our Turky blades shal glide through al their throats,	2Tamb	1.1.31	Orcan
My horsmen brandish their unruly blades.	2Tamb	5.1.79	Tamb
What traitor have wee there with blades and billes?	Edw	5.4.82	Mortmr
BLAME			
And yet I blame thee not, thou art but wood.	Dido	4.4.143	Dido
Why should I blame Aeneas for his flight?	Dido	4.4.148	Dido
O Dido, blame not him, but breake his oares,	Dido	4.4.149	Dido
Blame not us but the proverb, Confes and be hang'd.	Jew	4.1.146	P Barab
I execute, and he sustaines the blame.	P 132	2.75	Guise
Too late it is my Lord if that be true/To blame her highnes,	P 182	3.17	QnMarg
They were to blame that said I was displeasde,	P 969	19.39	King
And none so much as blame the murtherer,	Edw	1.4.267	Mortmr
And being like pins heads, blame me for the bignesse,	Edw	2.1.48	Baldck
Matrevis and the rest may beare the blame,	Edw	5.4.15	Mortmr
I blame thee not to sleepe much, having such a head of thine	F1284	4.1.130	P Emper
If blame, dissembling of my fault thou fearest.	Ovid's Elegies	2.7.8	
The losse of such a wench much blame will gather,	Ovid's Elegies	2.11.35	
He being Judge, I am convinc'd of blame.	Ovid's Elegies	2.17.2	
BLANCKE			
if our artillery/Will carie full point blancke unto their wals.	2Tamb	3.3.53	Techel
BLASPHEM'D			
on God, whom Faustus hath blasphem'd?	F1850	5.2.54	P Faust
BLASPHEMDE			
That hath blasphemde the holy Church of Rome,	P 531	10.4	Guise
BLASPHEMOUS			
Christians death/And scourge their foule blasphemous Paganisme?	2Tamb	2.1.53	Fredrk
BLASPHEMY			
to restraine/These coltish coach-horse tongues from blasphemy.	2Tamb	4.3.52	Usumc
Reade, reade the Scriptures: that is blasphemy.	F 100	1.1.72	GdAngl
BLAST			
Though every blast it nod, and seeme to fal,	Lucan, First Booke	142	
We erre: a strong blast seem'd the gates to ope:	Ovid's Elegies	1.6.51	
Thou Goddesse doest command a warme South-blast,	Ovid's Elegies	2.8.19	
Whose blast may hether strongly be inclinde,	Ovid's Elegies	2.11.38	
BLASTED			
And all the trees are blasted with our breathes.	1Tamb	3.1.55	Bajzth
the Feends infernall view/As are the blasted banks of Erebus:	1Tamb	5.1.244	Zabina
Whose pining heart, her inward sighes have blasted,	Edw	2.4.24	Queene
from the northren climat snatching fier/Blasted the Capitoll:	Lucan, First Booke	533	
Looke what the lightning blasted, Aruns takes/And it inters	Lucan, First Booke	605	
BLASTING			
To follow swiftly blasting infamie.	Hero and Leander	1.292	
BLASTS			
Fearing the force of Boreas boistrous blasts.	1Tamb	2.4.5	Mycet
the winds/To drive their substance with successefull blasts?	Jew	1.1.111	Barab
fearefull men, and blasts their eyes/With overthwarting flames,	Lucan, First Booke	155	
BLAZ'D			
And sundry fiery meteors blaz'd in heaven;	Lucan, First Booke	529	
BLAZE			
Wherewith thy antichristian churches blaze,	Edw	1.4.99	Edward
Heavens turne it to a blaze of quenchelesse fier,	Edw	5.1.44	Edward
BLAZED			
Till with the fire that from his count'nance blazed,	Hero and Leander	1.164	

BLAZING			
Nor blazing Commets threatens Didos death,	Dido	4.4.119	Dido
Over my Zenith hang a blazing star,	2Tamb	3.2.6	Tamb
Were full of Commets and of blazing stars,	2Tamb	5.1.89	Tamb
Where crown'd with blazing light and majestie,	Hero and Leander	1.110	
BLAZON			
Can hardly blazon foorth the loves of men,	Hero and Leander	1.70	
BLEARE			
But her bleare eyes, balde scalpes [thin] <thine> hoary flieces	Ovid's Elegies	1.8.111	
BLEATE			
you shal heare a hogge grunt, a calfe bleate, and an asse braye,	F App	p.232 27	P Faust
BLEED			
Lest Faustus make your shaven crownes to bleed.	F1007	3.2.27	Faust
BLEEDES			
That bleedes within me for this strange exchange.	Edw	5.1.35	Edward
BLEEDING			
dooth gastly death/With greedy tallents gripe my bleeding hart,	1Tamb	2.7.49	Cosroe
And tell my soule mor tales of bleeding ruth?	1Tamb	5.1.342	Zenoc
how should our bleeding harts/Wounded and broken with your	2Tamb	5.3.161	Amyras
When this fresh bleeding wound Leander viewd,	Hero and Leander	2.213	
BLEMISH			
It is a blemish to the Majestie/And high estate of mightie	1Tamb	4.3.19	Souldn
Your byrthes shall be no blemish to your fame,	1Tamb	4.4.127	Tamb
For she is that huge blemish in our eye,	P 80	2.23	Guise
Wily Corinna sawe this blemish in me,	Ovid's Elegies	2.19.9	
By her footes blemish greater grace she tooke.	Ovid's Elegies	3.1.10	
Receives no blemish, but oft-times more grace,	Hero and Leander	1.217	
BLESSE			
Heaven blesse me; what, a Fryar a murderer?	Jew	4.1.196	Barab
and so the Lord blesse you, preserve you, and keepe you, my	F 217	1.2.24	P Wagner
BLESSED			
O blessed tempests that did drive him in,	Dido	4.4.94	Dido
And Gaveston this blessed day be slaine.	Edw	2.4.69	Queene
and for this blessed sight <glorious deed>/Happy and blest be	F1704	5.1.31	1Schol
<Wee'l take our leaves>, and for this blessed sight	F1704	(HC269)B	1Schol
seate of God, the Throne of the Blessed, the Kingdome of Joy,	F1845	5.2.49	P Faust
lies quiet/And slumbring, thinkes himselfe much blessed by it.	Ovid's Elegies	2.9.40	
But long this blessed time continued not;	Hero and Leander	1.459	
Should know the pleasure of this blessed night,	Hero and Leander	2.304	
BLESSEDNES			
in whose gratious lookes/The blessednes of Gaveston remaines,	Edw	1.4.121	Gavstn
BLESSING			
I charge thee on my blessing that thou leave/These divels, and	Jew	1.2.346	Barab
What a blessing has he given't?	Jew	3.4.106	P Ithimr
And take our blessing Apostolicall.	F 973	3.1.195	Pope
BLESSINGS			
These are the Blessings promis'd to the Jewes,	Jew	1.1.105	Barab
BLEST			
Blest be the time I see Achates face.	Dido	2.1.56	Illion
Lyes it in Didos hands to make thee blest,	Dido	2.1.103	Dido
And make them blest that share in his attemptes.	1Tamb	2.3.9	Tamb
health and majesty/Were strangely blest and governed by heaven,	2Tamb	5.3.25	Techel
But marke how I am blest for plaguing them,	Jew	2.3.199	Barab
Be blest of me, nor come within my gates,	Jew	3.4.31	Barab
Whom God hath blest for hating Papestry.	P1208	22.70	King
would he lov'd me/But halfe so much, then were I treble blest.	Edw	1.4.304	Queene
And make me blest with your sage conference.	F 126	1.1.98	Faust
So, so, was never Divell thus blest before.	F 974	3.1.196	Mephst
sight <glorious deed>/Happy and blest be Faustus evermore.	F1705	5.1.32	1Schol
by these ten blest ensignes/And all thy several triumphs,	Lucan, First Booke	375	
Are blest by such sweet error, this makes them/Run on the	Lucan, First Booke	456	
Ah howe thy lot is above my lot blest:	Ovid's Elegies	1.6.46	
Mistris thou knowest, thou hast a blest youth pleas'd,	Ovid's Elegies	1.8.23	
Blest ring thou in my mistris hand shalt lye,	Ovid's Elegies	2.15.7	
Why was I blest?	Ovid's Elegies	3.6.49	
Both might enjoy ech other, and be blest.	Hero and Leander	1.380	
BLEW			
Pluto's blew fire, and Hecat's tree,	F1001	3.2.21	Mephst
noysome Saturne/Were now exalted, and with blew beames shinde,	Lucan, First Booke	651	
let him viewe/And thy neck with lascivious markes made blew.	Ovid's Elegies	1.8.98	
Her kirtle blew, whereon was many a staine,	Hero and Leander	1.15	
BLEWE			
Meeter it were her lips were blewe with kissing/And on her	Ovid's Elegies	1.7.41	
I sawe ones legges with fetters blacke and blewe,	Ovid's Elegies	2.2.47	
BLEWISH			
came Hectors ghost/With ashie visage, blewish sulphure eyes,	Dido	2.1.202	Aeneas
The unjust seas all blewish do appeare.	Ovid's Elegies	2.11.12	
BLIND			
I will confute those blind Geographers/That make a triple	1Tamb	4.4.75	Tamb
Blind, Fryer, I wrecke not thy perswasions.	Jew	1.2.355	Barab
Have not I made blind Homer sing to me/Of Alexanders love, and	F 577	2.2.26	Faust
O faintly joyn'd friends with ambition blind,	Lucan, First Booke	87	
And looking in her face, was strooken blind.	Hero and Leander	1.38	
BLINDE			
Yet let thy daughter be no longer blinde.	Jew	1.2.354	1Fryar
And as a pray unto blinde anger given,	Ovid's Elegies	1.7.44	
Had then swum over, but the way was blinde.	Ovid's Elegies	2.16.32	
Sweare I was blinde, yeeld not <deny>, if you be wise,	Ovid's Elegies	3.13.45	
BLINDES			
Blindes Europs eyes and troubleth our estate:	P 152	2.95	Guise
BLINK			
fethered steele/So thick upon the blink-ei'd Burghers heads,	2Tamb	1.1.93	Orcan
BLINK-EI'D			
fethered steele/So thick upon the blink-ei'd Burghers heads,	2Tamb	1.1.93	Orcan

BLIS			
By which love sailes to regions full of blis),	Hero and Leander		2.276
BLISSE			
That perfect blisse and sole felicitie,	1Tamb	2.7.28	Tamb
Welcome the first beginner of my blisse:	Jew	2.1.50	Barab
Oh girle, oh gold, oh beauty, oh my blisse!	Jew	2.1.54	Barab
What greater blisse can hap to Gaveston,	Edw	1.1.4	Gavstn
O must this day be period of my life,/Center of all my blisse!	Edw	2.6.5	Gavstn
the last of all my blisse on earth,/Center of all misfortune.	Edw	4.7.61	Edward
That like a mountaine overwhelmes my blisse,	Edw	5.1.54	Edward
Which he preferres before his chiefest blisse;	F 27	Prol.27	1Chor
In being depriv'd of everlasting blisse?	F 308	1.3.80	Mephst
Pleasures unspeakeable, blisse without end.	F1900	5.2.104	GdAngl
not onely kisse/But force thee give him my stolne honey blisse.	Ovid's Elegies		1.4.64
Such blisse is onely common to us two,	Ovid's Elegies		2.5.31
We humane creatures should enjoy that blisse.	Hero and Leander		1.254
BLITHELY			
And with his Bashawes shall be blithely set,	Jew	5.5.38	Barab
BLOATS			
Mild Atax glad it beares not Roman [boats] <bloats>;	Lucan, First Booke		404
BLOCK			
Weele haile him by the eares unto the block.	Edw	2.2.91	Lncstr
And farewell cruell posts, rough thresholds block,	Ovid's Elegies		1.6.73
BLOCKE			
But I will soone put by that stumbling blocke,	Dido	4.1.34	Dido
Meane while, have hence this rebell to the blocke,	Edw	4.6.69	Mortmr
Like a dull Cipher, or rude blocke I lay,	Ovid's Elegies		3.6.15
BLOCKISH			
And thats because the blockish [Sorbonests] <thorbonest>	P 411	7.51	Ramus
BLOCKS			
These Barons lay their heads on blocks together,	Edw	3.1.274	Baldck
BLOIS (See BLOYSE)			
BLOOD (See also 'SBLOUD, BLOUD)			
Besmer'd with blood, that makes a dainty show.	1Tamb	1.1.80	Mycet
That none can quence but blood and Emperie.	1Tamb	2.6.33	Cosroe
And with my blood my life slides through my wound,	1Tamb	2.7.43	Cosroe
Will rattle foorth his facts of war and blood.	1Tamb	3.2.45	Agidas
That make quick havock of the Christian blood.	1Tamb	3.3.58	Tamb
glut our swords/That thirst to drinke the feble Perseans blood.	1Tamb	3.3.165	Bajzth
By this the Turks lie weltring in their blood/And Tamburlaine	1Tamb	3.3.201	Zenoc
That satiate with spoile refuseth blood.	1Tamb	4.1.53	2Msngr
Then must his kindled wrath bee quencht with blood:	1Tamb	4.1.56	2Msngr
Staining his Altars with your purple blood:	1Tamb	4.2.4	Bajzth
Then when the Sky shal waxe as red as blood,	1Tamb	4.2.53	Tamb
To make me think of nought but blood and war.	1Tamb	4.2.55	Tamb
Reflexing hewes of blood upon their heads,	1Tamb	4.4.2	Tamb
Tamburlane) as I could willingly feed upon thy blood-raw hart.	1Tamb	4.4.12	P Bajzth
(Uttered with teares of wretchednesse and blood,	1Tamb	5.1.25	1Virgn
Embraceth now with teares of ruth and blood,	1Tamb	5.1.85	1Virgn
At every pore let blood comme dropping foorth,	1Tamb	5.1.227	Zabina
As long as any blood or sparke of breath/Can quench or coole	1Tamb	5.1.284	Zabina
and fire, and my blood I bring him againe, teare me in peeces,	1Tamb	5.1.310	P Zabina
Damascus walles di'd with Egyptian blood:	1Tamb	5.1.320	Zenoc
Leaving thy blood for witnesse of thy love.	1Tamb	5.1.411	Arabia
Which had ere this bin bathde in streames of blood,	1Tamb	5.1.438	Tamb
His honor, that consists in sheading blood,	1Tamb	5.1.477	Tamb
We all are glutted with the Christians blood,	2Tamb	1.1.14	Gazell
place himselfe therin/Must armed wade up to the chin in blood.	2Tamb	1.3.84	Tamb
For if his chaire were in a sea of blood,	2Tamb	1.3.89	Celeb
And I would strive to swim through pooles of blood,	2Tamb	1.3.92	Amyras
Such lavish will I make of Turkish blood,	2Tamb	1.3.165	Tamb
If griefe, our murthered harts have straind forth blood.	2Tamb	2.4.123	Therid
Dieng their lances with their streaming blood,	2Tamb	3.2.105	Tamb
That being concocted, turnes to crimson blood,	2Tamb	3.2.108	Tamb
That by the warres lost not a dram of blood,	2Tamb	3.2.113	Tamb
Blood is the God of Wars rich livery.	2Tamb	3.2.116	Tamb
And in my blood wash all your hands at once,	2Tamb	3.2.127	Tamb
My boy, Thou shalt not loose a drop of blood,	2Tamb	3.2.137	Tamb
my entrals bath'd/In blood that straineth from their orifex.	2Tamb	3.4.9	Capt
on a Lions backe)/Rhamnusia beares a helmet ful of blood,	2Tamb	3.4.57	Therid
Nor care for blood when wine wil quench my thirst.	2Tamb	4.1.30	Calyph
with the meteors/Of blood and fire thy tyrannies have made,	2Tamb	4.1.142	Jrslem
Will poure down blood and fire on thy head:	2Tamb	4.1.143	Jrslem
In war, in blood, in death, in crueltie,	2Tamb	4.1.156	Tamb
But (wanting moisture and remorsefull blood)/Drie up with	2Tamb	4.1.179	Soria
You shal be fed with flesh as raw as blood,	2Tamb	4.3.18	Tamb
The Monster that hath drunke a sea of blood,	2Tamb	5.2.13	Amasia
Whereby the moisture of your blood is dried,	2Tamb	5.3.85	Phsitn
Nor may our hearts all drown'd in teares of blood,	2Tamb	5.3.214	Usumc
sure/When like the [Dracos] <Drancus> they were writ in blood.	Jew	Prol.21	Machvl
to staine our hands with blood/Is farre from us and our	Jew	1.2.144	Govnr
And these my teares to blood, that he might live.	Jew	3.2.19	Govnr
That we may venge their blood upon their heads.	Jew	3.2.28	Mater
In few, the blood of Hydra, Lerna's bane;	Jew	3.4.100	Barab
Shall buy that strumpets favour with his blood,	P 768	15.26	Guise
And made the channels overflow with blood,	Edw	4.4.12	Queene
Edmund away, Bristow to Longshankes blood/Is false, be not found	Edw	4.6.16	Kent
the Divel for a shoulder of mutton, though it were blood rawe.	F App	p.229 9	P Wagner
to the Divel for a shoulder of mutton though twere blood rawe?	F App	p.229 11	P Clown
Either th'art witcht with blood <bould> of frogs new dead,	Ovid's Elegies		3.6.79
On Hellespont guiltie of True-loves blood,	Hero and Leander		1.1
Made with the blood of wretched Lovers slaine.	Hero and Leander		1.16
Blood-quaffing Mars, heaving the yron net,	Hero and Leander		1.151

BLOOD (cont.)			
There Hero sacrificing turtles blood, ...	Hero and Leander		1.158
BLOODLES			
soules passe not to silent Erebus/Or Plutoes bloodles kingdom,	Lucan, First Booke		452
BLOODLESSE			
My bloodlesse body waxeth chill and colde, . . .	1Tamb	2.7.42	Cosroe
her bloodlesse white lookes shewed/Like marble from the Parian	Ovid's Elegies		1.7.51
BLOOD-QUAFFING			
Blood-quaffing Mars, heaving the yron net, . . .	Hero and Leander		1.151
BLOOD-RAW			
Tamburlane) as I could willingly feed upon thy blood-raw hart.	1Tamb	4.4.12	P Bajzth
BLOODS			
For us, for infants, and for all our bloods, . . .	1Tamb	5.1.97	1Virgn
I am sure/What cruell slaughter of our Christian bloods, .	2Tamb	2.1.5	Fredrk
Now lie the Christians bathing in their bloods, . .	2Tamb	2.3.10	Orcan
And with our bloods, revenge our bloods on thee. . .	2Tamb	4.1.145	Jrslem
BLOODY			
Barbarous and bloody Tamburlaine, ...	1Tamb	2.7.1	Cosroe
Bloody and insatiate Tamburlain.	1Tamb	2.7.11	Cosroe
And when she sees our bloody Collours spread, . . .	1Tamb	3.3.159	Tamb
But if he stay until the bloody flag/Be once advanc'd on my	1Tamb	4.2.116	Tamb
My Lord it is the bloody Tamburlaine, ...	1Tamb	4.3.11	Souldn
Now hang our bloody collours by Damascus, ...	1Tamb	4.4.1	Tamb
Drawes bloody humours from my feeble partes, . . .	1Tamb	4.4.95	Bajzth
But see another bloody spectacle.	1Tamb	5.1.339	Zenoc
Bene oft resolv'd in bloody purple showers, . . .	1Tamb	5.1.460	Tamb
And make this champion mead a bloody Fen.	2Tamb	1.1.32	Orcan
Shall by this battell be the bloody Sea.	2Tamb	1.1.38	Orcan
Bloody and breathlesse for his villany.	2Tamb	2.3.13	Gazell
To martch with me under this bloody flag:	2Tamb	2.4.116	Tamb
Dreadlesse of blowes, of bloody wounds and death: . .	2Tamb	3.2.140	Tamb
Tis not thy bloody tents can make me yeeld, . . .	2Tamb	5.1.103	Govnr
Vild Tyrant, barbarous bloody Tamburlain.	2Tamb	5.1.133	Trebiz
BLOOMES			
queintly dect/With bloomes more white than Hericinas browes,	2Tamb	4.3.122	Tamb
BLOSSOMS			
Whose tender blossoms tremble every one, ...	2Tamb	4.3.123	Tamb
BLOT			
And for all blot of foule inchastity, ...	1Tamb	5.1.486	Tamb
As all the world should blot our dignities/Out of the booke of	2Tamb	3.1.18	Callap
So she be faire, but some vile toongs will blot? . .	Hero and Leander		1.286
BLOTS			
Smear'd with blots of basest drudgery:	1Tamb	5.1.268	Bajzth
BLOTTED			
and some blotted letter/On the last edge to stay mine eyes the	Ovid's Elegies		1.11.21
BLOUD			
As made the bloud run downe about mine eares. . . .	Dido	1.1.8	Ganimd
But first in bloud must his good fortune bud, . . .	Dido	1.1.86	Jupitr
might behold/Young infants swimming in their parents bloud,	Dido	2.1.193	Aeneas
His harnesse dropping bloud, and on his speare/The mangled head	Dido	2.1.214	Aeneas
And dipt it in the old Kings chill cold bloud, . . .	Dido	2.1.260	Aeneas
And feast the birds with their bloud-shotten balles, .	Dido	3.2.35	Venus
I would have either drunke his dying bloud, . . .	Dido	3.3.28	Iarbus
Whose bloud will reconcile thee to content, . . .	Dido	3.3.74	Iarbus
And mixe her bloud with thine, this shall I doe, . .	Dido	5.1.326	Anna
Honor is bought with bloud and not with gold. . . .	Jew	2.2.56	Govnr
Which Ile desolve with bloud and crueltie. . . .	P 26	1.26	QnMoth
And will revenge the bloud of innocents, ...	P 44	1.44	Navrre
Which cannot be extinguisht but by bloud.	P 93	2.36	Guise
Shall buy her love even with his dearest bloud. . .	P 697	13.41	Guise
What, will you fyle your handes with Churchmens bloud? .	P1093	20.3	Cardnl
Shed your bloud?	P1094	20.4	2Mur
And may it never end in bloud as mine hath done. . .	P1233	22.95	King
But he that makes most lavish of his bloud. . . .	P1240	22.102	King
To floate in bloud, and at thy wanton head, . . .	Edw	1.1.132	Lncstr
What we have done, our hart bloud shall maintaine. . .	Edw	1.4.40	Mortmr
Ile have his bloud, or die in seeking it.	Edw	2.2.107	Warwck
And let their lives bloud slake thy furies hunger: . .	Edw	2.2.205	Edward
That you may drinke your fill, and quaffe in bloud, . .	Edw	3.1.137	Edward
That if without effusion of bloud, ...	Edw	3.1.159	Herald
And rather bathe thy sword in subjects bloud, . . .	Edw	3.1.212	Mortmr
that the lowly earth/Should drinke his bloud, mounts up into	Edw	5.1.14	Edward
Their bloud and yours shall seale these treacheries. .	Edw	5.1.89	Edward
He of you all that most desires my bloud, ...	Edw	5.1.100	Edward
Returne it backe and dip it in my bloud.	Edw	5.1.120	Edward
Thou being his unckle, and the next of bloud, . . .	Edw	5.2.88	Mortmr
When will his hart be satisfied with bloud? . . .	Edw	5.3.9	Edward
And none of both [them] <then> thirst for Edmunds bloud. .	Edw	5.4.107	Kent
O would my bloud dropt out from every vaine, . . .	Edw	5.5.66	Edward
These handes were never stainde with innocent bloud, .	Edw	5.5.81	Ltborn
Spill not the bloud of gentle Mortimer.	Edw	5.6.69	Queene
This argues, that you spilt my fathers bloud, . . .	Edw	5.6.70	King
I spill his bloud? no.	Edw	5.6.72	Queene
to the devill, for a shoulder of Mutton, tho it were bloud raw.	F 351	1.4.9	P Wagner
And offer luke-warme bloud, of new borne babes. . .	F 402	2.1.14	Faust
And wright a Deed of Gift with thine owne bloud; . .	F 424	2.1.36	Mephst
and with his <my> proper bloud/Assures his <assure my> soule to	F 443	2.1.55	Faust
Veiw here this <the> bloud that trickles from mine arme, .	F 446	2.1.58	Faust
My bloud congeales, and I can write no more. . . .	F 451	2.1.63	Faust
What might the staying of my bloud portend? . . .	F 453	2.1.65	Faust
So, now the bloud begins to cleere againe: . . .	F 460	2.1.72	Faust
flesh [and] bloud, <or goods> into their habitation . .	F 498	2.1.110	P Faust
Bloud, he speakes terribly:	F1227	4.1.73	P Benvol

BLOUD (cont.)			
that flesh and bloud should be so fraile with your Worship:	F1632	4.6.75	P Carter
And with my bloud againe I will confirme/The <My> former vow I	F1749	5.1.76	Faust
Fond worldling, now his heart bloud dries with griefe; .	F1808	5.2.12	Mephst
Gush forth bloud in stead of teares, yea life and soule: .	F1851	5.2.55	P Faust
I writ them a bill with mine owne bloud, the date is expired:	F1860	5.2.64	P Faust
[See see where Christs bloud streames in the firmament], .	F1939	5.2.143A	Faust
One drop <of bloud will save me; oh> my Christ. . . .	F1940	(HC271)B	Faust
[Yet for Christs sake, whose bloud hath ransom'd me], .	F1959	5.2.163A	Faust
Breake heart, drop bloud, and mingle it with teares, .	F App	p.243 38	OldMan
Whose bloud alone must wash away thy guilt.	F App	p.243 45	OldMan
lust of warre/Hath made Barbarians drunke with Latin bloud?	Lucan, First Booke		9
Roomes infant walles were steept in brothers bloud; . .	Lucan, First Booke		95
Had fild Assirian Carras wals with bloud, ...	Lucan, First Booke		105
And glad when bloud, and ruine made him way: . . .	Lucan, First Booke		151
stil poore/Did vild deeds, then t'was worth the price of bloud,	Lucan, First Booke		175
denies all, with thy bloud must thou/Abie thy conquest past:	Lucan, First Booke		289
See how they quit our [bloud shed] <bloudshed> in the North;	Lucan, First Booke		302
of barbarous Tygars having lapt/The bloud of many a heard,	Lucan, First Booke		328
Jawes flesht with bloud continue murderous. . . .	Lucan, First Booke		332
even nowe when youthfull bloud/Pricks forth our lively bodies,	Lucan, First Booke		363
The stubborne Nervians staind with Cottas bloud; . .	Lucan, First Booke		430
Cole-blacke Charibdis whirl'd a sea of bloud; . . .	Lucan, First Booke		546
In steed of red bloud wallowed venemous gore. . . .	Lucan, First Booke		614
a dead blacknesse/Ranne through the bloud, that turn'd it all	Lucan, First Booke		618
My bloud, the teares were that from her descended. . .	Ovid's Elegies		1.7.60
(If I have faith) I sawe the starres drop bloud, . .	Ovid's Elegies		1.8.11
sleeping foe tis good/And arm'd to shed unarmed peoples bloud.	Ovid's Elegies		1.9.22
And with his <their> bloud eternall honour gaine, . .	Ovid's Elegies		2.10.32
In all thy face will be no crimsen bloud.	Ovid's Elegies		2.11.28
Which without bloud-shed doth the pray inherit. . .	Ovid's Elegies		2.12.6
At Colchis stain'd with childrens bloud men raile, . .	Ovid's Elegies		2.14.29
And rockes dyed crimson with Prometheus bloud. . . .	Ovid's Elegies		2.16.40
A target bore: bloud sprinckled was his right. . . .	Ovid's Elegies		3.7.16
Souldiours by bloud to be inricht have lucke. . . .	Ovid's Elegies		3.7.54
Gallus that [car'dst] <carst> not bloud, and life to spend.	Ovid's Elegies		3.8.64
And thorough everie vaine doth cold bloud runne, . .	Ovid's Elegies		3.13.38
BLOUDIE			
Not bloudie speares appearing in the ayre, . . .	Dido	4.4.117	Dido
like the Greekish strumpet traind to armes/And bloudie warres,	Edw	2.5.16	Lncstr
A bloudie part, flatly against law of armes. . . .	Edw	3.1.121	Spencr
That so my bloudie colours may suggest/Remembrance of revenge	Edw	3.1.139	Edward
Yet stay a while, forbeare thy bloudie hande, . . .	Edw	5.5.75	Edward
BLOUDLES			
Whether now shal these olde bloudles soules repaire? .	Lucan, First Booke		343
BLOUDLESSE			
Ah had some bloudlesse furie rose from hell, . . .	Edw	1.4.316	Edward
BLOUDS			
And Carthage soules be glutted with our blouds; . .	Lucan, First Booke		39
BLOUD-SHED			
Which without bloud-shed doth the pray inherit. . .	Ovid's Elegies		2.12.6
BLOUDSHED			
Cause yet more bloudshed:	Edw	2.5.83	Warwck
See how they quit our [bloud shed] <bloudshed> in the North;	Lucan, First Booke		302
For bloudshed knighted, before me preferr'd. . . .	Ovid's Elegies		3.7.10
BLOUD-SHOTTEN			
And feast the birds with their bloud-shotten balles, .	Dido	3.2.35	Venus
BLOUDY			
If ever sunne stainde heaven with bloudy clowdes, . .	P 60	2.3	Guise
An action bloudy and tirannicall:	P 208	4.6	Charls
Thou traitor Guise, lay of thy bloudy hands. . . .	P 439	7.79	Navrre
Then in this bloudy brunt they may beholde, . . .	P 713	14.16	Bartus
And in remembrance of those bloudy broyles, . . .	P1024	19.94	King
Art thou King, and hast done this bloudy deed? . . .	P1050	19.120	YngGse
These bloudy hands shall teare his triple Crowne, . .	P1199	22.61	King
That hatcheth up such bloudy practises.	P1205	22.67	King
Who wounds me with the name of Mortimer/That bloudy man? .	Edw	4.7.39	Edward
To keepe his Carkasse from their bloudy phangs. . .	F1303	4.1.149	Faust
and where [Jove] <it> seemes/Bloudy like Dian, whom the .	Lucan, First Booke		442
Curling their bloudy lockes, howle dreadfull things, .	Lucan, First Booke		565
That colour rightly did appeare so bloudy. . . .	Ovid's Elegies		1.12.12
Verses [deduce] <reduce> the horned bloudy moone/And call the	Ovid's Elegies		2.1.23
they manadge peace, and rawe warres bloudy jawes, . .	Ovid's Elegies		3.7.58
BLOW (Homograph)			
The sea is rough, the windes blow to the shoare. . .	Dido	4.4.25	Aeneas
Blow windes, threaten ye Rockes and sandie shelfes, . .	Dido	4.4.58	Aeneas
To ward the blow, and shield me safe from harme. . .	1Tamb	1.2.181	Tamb
And you shall se't rebated with the blow.	2Tamb	4.2.70	Olymp
your weapons point/That wil be blunted if the blow be great.	2Tamb	4.2.80	Olymp
And blow the morning from their nosterils, ...	2Tamb	4.3.8	Tamb
To blow thy Alcaron up to thy throne, ...	2Tamb	5.1.193	Tamb
Cursed be he that stroke his holinesse a blow [on] the face.	F1079	3.2.99	1Frier
be he that strucke <tooke> fryer Sandelo a blow on the pate.	F1081	3.2.101	1Frier
this blow ends all,/Hell take his soule, his body thus must	F1362	4.2.38	Benvol
Cursed be he that tooke Frier Sandelo a blow on the pate.	F App	p.232 35	Frier
That from thy fanne, mov'd by my hand may blow? . .	Ovid's Elegies		3.2.38
BLOWE (Homograph)			
Faire blowes the winde for Fraunce, blowe gentle gale, .	Edw	4.1.1	Kent
sleepe, to take a quill/And blowe a little powder in his eares,	Edw	5.4.35	Ltborn
Cursed be hee that strooke his holinesse a blowe on the face.	F App	p.232 33	Frier
Nor let the windes away my warnings blowe. . . .	Ovid's Elegies		1.4.12
Which stormie South-windes into sea did blowe? . . .	Ovid's Elegies		2.6.44
Hether the windes blowe, here the spring-tide rore. . .	Ovid's Elegies		2.11.40

BLOWEN			
At every little breath that thorow heaven is blowen:	2Tamb	4.3.124	Tamb
BLOWES (Homograph)			
That will nct shield me from her shrewish blowes:	Dido	1.1.4	Ganimd
not endure to strike/So many blowes as I have heads for thee.	1Tamb	3.3.144	Bajzth
Lantchidol/Beates on the regions with his boysterous blowes,	2Tamb	1.1.70	Orcan
Dreadlesse of blowes, of bloody wounds and death:	2Tamb	3.2.140	Tamb
Faire blowes the winde for Fraunce, blowe gentle gale,	Edw	4.1.1	Kent
Whence the wind blowes stil forced to and fro;	Lucan, First Booke		414
BLOWETH			
The wind that bloweth all the world besides,	Jew	3.5.3	Basso
BLOWNE			
Blowne up, and all thy souldiers massacred.	Jew	5.5.107	Govnr
keep out, or else you are blowne up, you are dismembred Rafe,	F App	p.233 10 P	Robin
Like Popler leaves blcwne with a stormy flawe,	Ovid's Elegies		1.7.54
Nor let my words be with the windes hence blowne,	Ovid's Elegies		1.8.106
And thence unto Abydus sooner blowne,	Hero and Leander		2.112
BLOYSE			
Ile secretly convay me unto Bloyse,	P 895	17.90	King
BLUBBERED			
Their blubbered cheekes and hartie humble mones/Will melt his	1Tamb	5.1.21	Govnr
BLUBBRED			
And wofull Dido by these blubbred cheekes,	Dido	5.1.133	Dido
BLUE (See BLEW)			
BLUNTED			
your weapons point/That wil be blunted if the blow be great.	2Tamb	4.2.80	Olymp
BLUNTER			
Fare well sterne warre, for blunter Poets meete.	Ovid's Elegies		1.1.32
BLUNTLY			
And dar'st thou bluntly call me Bajazeth?	1Tamb	3.3.71	Bajzth
And dar'st thou bluntly call me Tamburlaine?	1Tamb	3.3.74	Tamb
BLUSH			
Blush blush for shame, why shouldst thou thinke of love?	Dido	4.5.29	Nurse
Blush heaven, that gave them honor at their birth,	1Tamb	5.1.350	Zenoc
Blush, blush faire citie, at thine honors foile,	2Tamb	4.1.107	Tamb
Blush heaven to loose the honor of thy name,	2Tamb	5.3.28	Usumc
O thou oft wilt blush/And say he likes me for my borrowed bush,	Ovid's Elegies		1.14.47
A scarlet blush her guilty face arayed.	Ovid's Elegies		2.5.34
In both [thy] <my> cheekes she did perceive thee blush,	Ovid's Elegies		2.8.16
Shame, that should make me blush, I have no more.	Ovid's Elegies		3.5.78
I blush, [that] <and> being youthfull, hot, and lustie,	Ovid's Elegies		3.6.19
And blush, and seeme as you were full of grace.	Ovid's Elegies		3.13.28
BLUSHE			
I [burne] <blushe>, and by that blushfull [glance] <glasse> am	Ovid's Elegies		2.4.12
BLUSHFULL			
<blushe>, and by that blushfull [glance] <glasse> am tooke:	Ovid's Elegies		2.4.12
BLUSHING			
Blushing Roses, purple Hyacinthe:	Dido	2.1.319	Venus
As without blushing I can aske no more:	Dido	3.1.104	Aeneas
And brancht with blushing corall to the knee;	Hero and Leander		1.32
Thus neere the bed she blushing stood upright,	Hero and Leander		2.317
BLUSHT			
She blusht:	Ovid's Elegies		1.8.35
I chid no mcre, she blusht, and therefore heard me,	Ovid's Elegies		1.13.47
Yet blusht I not, nor usde I any saying,	Ovid's Elegies		2.8.7
He started up, she blusht as one asham'd;	Hero and Leander		1.181
BLUSTRING			
Whether the gods, or blustring south were cause/I know not, but	Lucan, First Booke		236
BOARD (See BOORD, BOURD)			
BOARE (See also BORE)			
To chace the savage [Calidonian] <Caldonian> Boare:	1Tamb	4.3.3	Souldn
As when the wilde boare Adons groine had rent.	Ovid's Elegies		3.8.16
Which by the wild boare in the woods was shorne.	Ovid's Elegies		3.9.40
BOAST			
Yet boast nct of it, for I love thee not,	Dido	3.1.171	Dido
put in the poast/Although of oake, to yeeld to verses boast.	Ovid's Elegies		2.1.28
Of that which hath no being, doe not boast,	Hero and Leander		1.275
BOASTING			
Whom I respect as leaves of boasting greene,	P 720	14.23	Navrre
He liv'd secure boasting his former deeds,	Lucan, First Booke		135
Boasting his parentage, would needs discover/The way to new	Hero and Leander		1.410
BOASTS			
Of me Pelignis nation boasts alone,	Ovid's Elegies		3.14.8
BOAT			
Waiting the back returne of Charons boat,	1Tamb	5.1.464	Tamb
BOATE			
Even as a boate, tost by contrarie winde,	Ovid's Elegies		2.10.9
Thou hast nc bridge, nor boate with ropes to throw,	Ovid's Elegies		3.5.3
BOATS			
Mild Atax glad it beares not Roman [boats] <bloats>;	Lucan, First Booke		404
BODIE			
And let me linke [thy] <my> bodie to my <thy> lips,	Dido	4.3.28	Aeneas
The jealous bodie of his fearfull wife,	1Tamb	5.1.86	1Virgn
And on their points his fleshlesse bodie feedes.	1Tamb	5.1.115	Tamb
And cast her bodie in the burning flame,	2Tamb	3.4.71	Olymp
Then, gentle sleepe, where e're his bodie rests,	Jew	2.1.35	Abigal
And cleare my bodie from foule excrements.	Edw	5.3.26	Edward
Not one wen in her bodie could I spie,	Ovid's Elegies		1.5.18
I clinged her naked bodie, downe she fell,	Ovid's Elegies		1.5.24
His bodie was as straight as Circes wand,	Hero and Leander		1.61
Therefore unto his bodie, hirs he clung,	Hero and Leander		2.65
BODIES			
Untill our bodies turne to Elements:	1Tamb	1.2.236	Tamb

BODIES (cont.)				
A heaven of heavenly bodies in their Spheares/That guides his	1Tamb	2.1.16		Menaph
Burdening their bodies with your heavie chaines,	1Tamb	3.3.48		Tamb
We have their crownes, their bodies strowe the fielde.	1Tamb	3.3.215		Techel
To thinke thy puisant never staied arme/Will part their bodies,	1Tamb	5.1.89		1Virgn
And wounded bodies gasping yet for life.	1Tamb	5.1.323		Zenoc
The slaughtered bodies of these Christians.	2Tamb	1.1.36		Orcan
minute end our daies, and one sepulcher/Containe our bodies:	2Tamb	3.4.14		Olymp
pride/And leads your glories <bodies> sheep-like to the sword.	2Tamb	4.1.77		Tamb
My bodies mortified lineaments/Should exercise the motions of	2Tamb	5.3.188		Amyras
For this, this earth sustaines my bodies [waight],	P 114	2.57		Guise
lakes of gore/Your headles trunkes, your bodies will I traile,	Edw	3.1.136		Edward
My mindes distempered, and my bodies numde,	Edw	5.5.64		Edward
The end of Physicke is our bodies health:	F 45	1.1.17		Faust
Are all Celestiall bodies but one Globe,	F 587	2.2.36		Faust
On burning forkes: their bodies [boyle] <broyle> in lead.	F1912	5.2.116		BdAngl
bodies of those two deceased princes which long since are	F App	p.237 42	P	Faust
but the true substantiall bodies of those two deceased princes.	F App	p.238 64	P	Emper
even nowe when youthfull bloud/Pricks forth our lively bodies,	Lucan, First Booke			364
Who that our bodies were comprest bewrayde?	Ovid's Elegies			2.8.5
And in the midst their bodies largely spread:	Ovid's Elegies			2.10.18
Whose bodies with their heavy burthens ake.	Ovid's Elegies			2.13.20
To plague your bodies with such harmefull strokes?	Ovid's Elegies			2.14.34
I loath her manners, love her bodies feature.	Ovid's Elegies			3.10.38
BODKIN				
Thy very haires will the hot bodkin teach.	Ovid's Elegies			1.14.30
BODY				
My bloodlesse body waxeth chill and colde,	1Tamb	2.7.42		Cosroe
And leave my body sencelesse as the earth.	1Tamb	3.2.22		Zenoc
Keeping his kingly body in a Cage,	1Tamb	4.2.61		Zabina
And gore thy body with as many wounds.	1Tamb	5.1.216		Bajzth
As much as thy faire body is for me.	1Tamb	5.1.416		Zenoc
Whose glorious body when he left the world,	2Tamb	1.1.139		Orcan
Now shall his barbarous body be a pray/To beasts and foules,	2Tamb	2.3.14		Orcan
of that vitall aire/That feeds the body with his dated health,	2Tamb	2.4.45		Zenoc
That dares torment the body of my Love,	2Tamb	2.4.79		Tamb
Whose body with his fathers I have burnt,	2Tamb	3.4.36		Olymp
That most may vex his body and his soule.	2Tamb	3.5.99		Callap
Whose body shall be tomb'd with all the pompe/The treasure of	2Tamb	4.2.97		Therid
Nor if my body could have stopt the breach,	2Tamb	5.1.101		Govnr
Up with him then, his body shalbe scard.	2Tamb	5.1.114		Tamb
What daring God torments my body thus,	2Tamb	5.3.42		Tamb
For if thy body thrive not full of thoughtes/As pure and fiery	2Tamb	5.3.236		Tamb
My body feeles, my soule dooth weepe to see/Your sweet desires	2Tamb	5.3.246		Tamb
I have don't, but no body knowes it but you two, I may escape.	Jew	4.1.180	P	1Fryar
Dead, my Lord, and here they bring his body.	Jew	5.1.53		1Offcr
For the Jewes body, throw that o're the wals,	Jew	5.1.58		Govnr
Weakneth his body, and will waste his Realme,	P 128	2.71		Guise
Come my Lords let us beare her body hence,	P 195	3.30		Admral
Come let us take his body hence.	P 564	11.29		QnMoth
Come Lords, take up the body of the King,	P1245	22.107		Navrre
And goods and body given to Gaveston.	Edw	1.2.2		Warwck
Unlesse the sea cast up his shipwrack body.	Edw	1.4.205		Lncstr
And body with continuall moorning wasted:	Edw	2.4.25		Queene
He hath a body able to endure,	Edw	5.5.10		Matrvs
But not too hard, least that you bruse his body.	Edw	5.5.113		Ltborn
Come let us cast the body in the mote,	Edw	5.5.118		Gurney
His kingly body was too soone interrde.	Edw	5.6.32		King
And universall body of the law <Church>.	F 60	1.1.32		Faust
A Deed of Gift, of body and of soule:	F 478	2.1.90		Faust
by these presents doe give both body and soule to Lucifer,	F 494	2.1.106	P	Faust
carry the said John Faustus, body and soule, flesh [and] bloud,	F 498	2.1.110	P	Faust
I, and body too, but what of that:	F 521	2.1.133		Faust
my selfe when I could get none <had no body> to fight withall:	F 689	2.2.138	P	Wrath
That no eye may thy body see.	F1003	3.2.23		Mephst
O come and help to beare my body hence:	F1069	3.2.89		Pope
Hell take his soule, his body thus must fall.	F1363	4.2.39		Benvol
I, that's the head, and here the body lies,	F1375	4.2.51		Benvol
and now sirs, having divided him, what shall the body doe?	F1390	4.2.66	P	Mrtino
And had you cut my body with your swords,	F1397	4.2.73		Faust
Checking thy body, may amend thy soule.	F1723	5.1.50		OldMan
But what I may afflict his body with,	F1757	5.1.84		Mephst
A surfet of deadly sin, that hath damn'd both body and soule.	F1833	5.2.37	P	Faust
to fetch me <both> body and soule, if I once gave eare to	F1865	5.2.69	P	Faust
<O> It strikes, it strikes; now body turne to aire,	F1975	5.2.179		Faust
Heere's no body, if it like your Holynesse.	F App	p.231 4	P	Frier
His body (not his boughs) send forth a shade;	Lucan, First Booke			141
Or Plutoes bloodles kingdom, but else where/Resume a body:	Lucan, First Booke			453
Long Love my body to such use [makes] <make> slender/And to get	Ovid's Elegies			1.6.5
And her old body in birdes plumes to lie.	Ovid's Elegies			1.8.14
Aye me, thy body hath no worthy weedes.	Ovid's Elegies			1.8.26
Foule dust, from her faire body, go away.	Ovid's Elegies			3.2.42
Though thou her body guard, her minde is staind:	Ovid's Elegies			3.4.5
Thy feare is, then her body, valued more.	Ovid's Elegies			3.4.30
Or shade, or body was [I] <Io>, who can say?	Ovid's Elegies			3.6.16
What ere he hath his body gaind in warres.	Ovid's Elegies			3.7.20
Burnes his dead body in the funerall flame.	Ovid's Elegies			3.8.6
Nor feared they thy body to annoy?	Ovid's Elegies			3.8.42
To lay my body on the hard moist floore.	Ovid's Elegies			3.10.10
And like light Salmacis, her body throes/Upon his bosome, where	Hero and Leander			2.46
And as her silver body downeward went,	Hero and Leander			2.263
BODYE				
O no, his bodye will infect the fire, and the fire the aire, and	P 484	9.3	P	1Atndt

BOETES			
And leave his steeds to faire Boetes charge:	2Tamb	1.3.170	Tamb
BOHEME			
The king of Boheme, and the Austrich Duke,	2Tamb	1.1.95	Orcan
BOHEMIA			
Now say my Lords of Buda and Bohemia,	2Tamb	2.1.1	Sgsmnd
BOIE			
Tell me sweet boie, art thou content to die?	2Tamb	3.4.18	Olymp
BOIES			
Zabina, mother of three braver boies,	1Tamb	3.3.103	Bajzth
Wel lovely boies, you shal be Emperours both,	2Tamb	1.3.96	Tamb
But now my boies, leave off, and list to me,	2Tamb	3.2.53	Tamb
That these my boies may finish all my wantes.	2Tamb	5.3.125	Tamb
Looke here my boies, see what a world of ground,	2Tamb	5.3.145	Tamb
Here lovely boies, what death forbids my life,	2Tamb	5.3.159	Tamb
Farewel my boies, my dearest friends, farewel,	2Tamb	5.3.245	Tamb
BOIL (See BOYLE)			
BOISTEROUS (See also BOYSTEROUS)			
faire, mishapen stuffe/Are of behaviour boisterous and ruffe.	Hero and Leander		1.204
BOISTROUS			
Fearing the force of Boreas boistrous blasts.	1Tamb	2.4.5	Mycet
Nor [leane] <leave> thy soft head on his boistrous brest.	Ovid's Elegies		1.4.36
And raging Seas in boistrous South-winds plough.	Ovid's Elegies		2.16.22
BOLD (See also BOULD)			
Know, holy Sir, I am bold to sollicite thee.	Jew	3.3.53	Abigal
And now, bold Bashawes, let us to our Tents,	Jew	5.3.43	Calym
You must be proud, bold, pleasant, resolute,	Edw	2.1.42	Spencr
All's one, for wee'l be bold with his Venison.	F 808	3.1.30	Mephst
<Tut, tis no matter man>, wee'l be bold with his <good cheare>.	F 808	(HC265)A P	Mephst
Germane Emperour/Be held as Lollords, and bold Schismatiques,	F 955	3.1.177	Faust
In bold Acteons shape to turne a Stagge.	F1299	4.1.145	Faust
Why saucy varlets, dare you be so bold.	F1594	4.6.37	Servnt
I hope sir, we have wit enough to be more bold then welcome.	F1595	4.6.38 P	HrsCsr
It appeares so, pray be bold else-where,	F1597	4.6.40	Servnt
So be I may be bold to speake a truth,	Lucan, First Booke		361
his tender mother/And smiling sayed, be thou as bold as other.	Ovid's Elegies		1.6.12
Her, from his swift waves, the bold floud perceav'd,	Ovid's Elegies		3.5.51
At last, like to a bold sharpe Sophister,	Hero and Leander		1.197
Beyond the bounds of shame, in being bold/To eie those parts,	Hero and Leander		1.407
Beat downe the bold waves with his triple mace,	Hero and Leander		2.172
BOLDE			
swowns they are as bolde with my flesh, as if they had payd for	F App	p.230 28 P	Clown
BOLDLY			
Your Majesty may boldly goe and see.	F1269	4.1.115	Faust
Then Souldiers boldly fight; if Faustus die,	F1346	4.2.22	Benvol
Your highnes may boldly go and see.	F App	p.238 63 P	Faust
He's happy, that his love dares boldly credit,	Ovid's Elegies		2.5.9
BOLSTERED			
The pillers that have bolstered up those tearmes,	1Tamb	3.3.229	Tamb
BOLT (See also BOULT)			
When all the woods about stand bolt up-right,	Lucan, First Booke		143
BOMBARDS			
Which with our Bombards shot and Basiliske,	Jew	5.3.3	Calym
Bombards, whole Barrels full of Gunpowder,	Jew	5.5.28	Barab
BOND			
While bond-men cheat, fathers [be hard] <hoord>, bawds hoorish,	Ovid's Elegies		1.15.17
What if a man with bond-women offend,	Ovid's Elegies		2.8.9
BONDAGE			
accidents/Have chanc'd thy merits in this worthles bondage.	1Tamb	5.1.425	Arabia
That freed me from the bondage of my foe:	2Tamb	3.1.69	Callap
My Viceroies bondage under Tamburlaine,	2Tamb	5.2.21	Callap
Then such as in their bondage feele content.	Ovid's Elegies		1.2.18
BONDES			
More fitly had [they] <thy> wrangling bondes contained/From	Ovid's Elegies		1.12.23
BONDMAN			
And he my bondman, let me have law,	Jew	5.1.38	Barab
BOND-MEN			
While bond-men cheat, fathers [be hard] <hoord>, bawds hoorish,	Ovid's Elegies		1.15.17
BOND-WOMEN			
What if a man with bond-women offend,	Ovid's Elegies		2.8.9
BONES			
foule Idolaters/Shall make me bonfires with their filthy bones,	1Tamb	3.3.240	Bajzth
Whose arches should be fram'd with bones of Turks,	2Tamb	1.3.94	Amyras
Whose chariot wheeles have burst th'Assirians bones,	2Tamb	5.1.71	Tamb
And bids thee whet thy sword on Sextus bones,	P1237	22.99	King
To rest his bones after his weary toyle,	F 769	2.3.48	2Chor
Or hew'd this flesh and bones as small as sand,	F1398	4.2.74	Faust
That rowling downe, may breake the villaines bones,	F1414	4.2.90	Faust
what Colonies/To rest their bones?	Lucan, First Booke		346
That my dead bones may in their grave lie soft.	Ovid's Elegies		1.8.108
Then though death rackes <rakes> my bones in funerall fier,	Ovid's Elegies		1.15.41
A grave her bones hides, on her corps great <small> grave,	Ovid's Elegies		2.6.59
In naked bones? love hath my bones left naked.	Ovid's Elegies		2.9.14
My bones had beene, while yet I was a maide.	Ovid's Elegies		3.5.74
Thy bones I pray may in the urne safe rest,	Ovid's Elegies		3.8.67
BONET			
With Cupids myrtle was his bonet crownd,	Hero and Leander		2.105
BONFIRES			
And making bonfires for my overthrow.	1Tamb	3.3.238	Bajzth
foule Idolaters/Shall make me bonfires with their filthy bones,	1Tamb	3.3.240	Bajzth
BONNET			
whom he vouchsafes/For vailing of his bonnet one good looke.	Edw	1.2.19	Lncstr
BONUM			
Edwardum occidere nolite timere bonum est.	Edw	5.4.8	Mortmr

BONUM (cont.)				
Edwardum occidere nolite timere bonum est.	Edw	5.4.11		Mortmr
Summum bonum medicinae sanitas, ...	F 44	1.1.16		Faust
<Whose summum bonum is in belly-cheare>.	F 834	(HC265)A		Mephst
BOOK				
That frightes poore Ramus sitting at his book?	P 362	7.2		Ramus
'Snayles, what hast thou got there, a book?	F 730	2.3.9	P	Dick
I had never seene Wittenberg <Wertenberge>, never read book:	F1842	5.2.46	P	Faust
BOOKE				
blot our dignities/Out of the booke of base borne infamies.	2Tamb	3.1.19		Callap
talke with him was [but]/About the borrowing of a booke or two.	Jew	2.3.156		Mthias
Sirra, Jew, remember the booke.	Jew	2.3.159		Mthias
O Faustus, lay that damned booke aside, ...	F 97	1.1.69		GdAngl
<Here>, take this booke, <and> peruse it [thoroughly] <well>:	F 543	2.1.155		Mephst
Thankes Mephostophilis for this sweete booke.	F 550	2.1.162		Faust
have a booke wherein I might beholde al spels and incantations,	F 551.1	2.1.164A	P	Faust
[Here they are in this booke].	F 551.3	2.1.166A	P	Mephst
booke where I might see al characters of <and> planets of the	F 551.4	2.1.167A	P	Faust
[Nay let me have one booke more, and then I have done, wherein	F 551.8	2.1.171A	P	Faust
Meane while peruse this booke, and view it throughly, .	F 717	2.2.169		Lucifr
<in mean time take this booke, peruse it throwly>, . .	F 717	(HC264)A		Lucifr
tell me, in good sadnesse Robin, is that a conjuring booke?	F 744	2.3.23	P	Dick
Graven in the booke of Joves high firmament, ...	F 756	2.3.35		2Chor
Then wherefore would you have me view that booke? . .	F1023	3.2.43		Pope
I can tell you, you'le be curst with Bell, Booke, and Candle.	F1072	3.2.92	P	Mephst
Bell, Booke, and Candle; Candle, Booke, and Bell, . .	F1074	3.2.94		Faust
Damb'd up thy passage; when thou took'st the booke, . .	F1887	5.2.91		Mephst
Nay I know not, we shalbe curst with bell, booke, and candle.	F App	p.232 23	P	Mephst
bell, booke, and candle, candle, booke, and bell,/Forward and	F App	p.232 25		Faust
what doest thou with that same booke thou canst not reade?	F App	p.233 13	P	Rafe
Why Robin what booke is that?	F App	p.233 18	P	Rafe
What booke?	F App	p.233 19	P	Robin
booke for conjuring that ere was invented by any brimstone	F App	p.233 19	P	Robin
tell thee, we were for ever made by this doctor Faustus booke?	F App	p.234 2	P	Robin
Bewaile my chaunce, the sad booke is returned, ...	Ovid's Elegies			1.12.1
It is more safe to sleepe, to read a booke, ...	Ovid's Elegies			2.11.31
And I see when you ope the two leavde booke:	Ovid's Elegies			3.13.44
Therefore even as an Index to a booke, ...	Hero and Leander			2.129
BOOKES				
And all the heapes of superstitious bookes, ...	2Tamb	5.1.174		Tamb
Though some speake openly against my bookes, ...	Jew	Prol.10		Machvl
And Negromantick bookes are heavenly.	F 77	1.1.49		Faust
Faustus, these bookes, thy wit, and our experience, . .	F 146	1.1.118		Valdes
I have gotten one of Doctor Faustus conjuring bookes, and now	F 723	2.3.2	P	Robin
And as they turne their superstitious Bookes, ...	F 893	3.1.115		Faust
I'le burne my bookes; [ah] <oh> Mephostophilis. . . .	F1982	5.2.186		Faust
Be thou the happie subject of my Bookes, ...	Ovid's Elegies			1.3.19
Among day bookes and billes they had laine better/In which the	Ovid's Elegies			1.12.25
Seeing she likes my bookes, why should we jarre? . .	Ovid's Elegies			2.4.20
Nor in my bookes shall one but thou be writ, . . .	Ovid's Elegies			2.17.33
When our bookes did my mistris faire content, ...	Ovid's Elegies			3.7.5
Erre I? or by my [bookes] <lookes> is she so knowne? .	Ovid's Elegies			3.11.7
BOOKS				
cannot read, and therefore wish all books burn'd <were burnt>.	F 680	2.2.129	P	Envy
here I ha stolne one of doctor Faustus conjuring books, and	F App	p.233 2	P	Robin
We which were Ovids five books, now are three, ...	Ovid's Elegies			1.1.1
BOONE				
Grace my immortall beautie with this boone, ...	Dido	1.1.21		Ganimd
And lighten our extreames with this one boone, ...	Dido	1.1.196		Aeneas
BOORD				
with the scraps/My servitures shall bring the from my boord.	1Tamb	4.2.88		Tamb
The boord is marked thus that covers it.	Jew	1.2.350		Barab
The boord is marked thus that covers it, ...	Jew	1.2.356		Barab
Strike on the boord like them that pray for evill, . . .	Ovid's Elegies			1.4.27
Not silent were thine eyes, the boord with wine/Was scribled,	Ovid's Elegies			2.5.17
Had spread the boord, with roses strowed the roome, . .	Hero and Leander			2.21
BOORDED				
Yet boorded I the golden Chie twise, ...	Ovid's Elegies			3.6.23
BOORE				
Grosse gold, from them runs headlong to the boore. . .	Hero and Leander			1.472
BOORES				
Tav'ron peering/(His grave broke open) did affright the Boores.	Lucan, First Booke			582
BOOT				
And the horse pestilence to boot; away.	Jew	3.4.113		Barab
BOOTED				
Come fellowes, it booted not for us to strive, ...	Edw	2.6.18		James
BOOTES (Homograph; See also BOETES)				
I must conceale/The torment, that it bootes me not reveale,/And	Dido	3.4.26		Dido
Or faire Bootes sends his cheerefull light, ...	1Tamb	1.2.207		Tamb
It bootes me not to threat, I must speake faire, . . .	Edw	1.4.63		Edward
That bootes not, therefore gentle madam goe.	Edw	5.6.91		2Lord
What bootes it then to thinke on <of> God or Heaven? .	F 391	2.1.3		Faust
goe and make cleane our bootes which lie foule upon our handes,	F App	p.234 33	P	Robin
BOOTLES				
Bootles I sawe it was to warre with fate, ...	Dido	3.2.49		Juno
BOOTLESSE				
lamps of heaven/To cast their bootlesse fires to the earth,	2Tamb	5.3.4		Therid
BOOTS (Homograph)				
sort as if he had meant to make cleane my Boots with his lips;	Jew	4.2.31	P	Ithimr
me/My life's in danger, and what boots it thee/Poore Barabas,	Jew	5.2.31		Barab
BORDER				
Nape free-borne, whose cunning hath no border, ...	Ovid's Elegies			1.11.2
BORDERED				
Her wide sleeves greene, and bordered with a grove, . .	Hero and Leander			1.11

BORDERERS
The Northren borderers seeing [their] <the> houses burnt,/Their — Edw 2.2.179 Lncstr

BORDERING
To warre against my bordering enemies: . . . . — Dido 3.1.135 Dido
Affrike and Europe bordering on your land, ... — 1Tamb 1.1.127 Menaph
Riso, Sancina, and the bordering townes, ... — 2Tamb 3.1.52 Trebiz
Bordering on Mare Roso neere to Meca. . . . . . — 2Tamb 3.5.131 Callap
I sent for Egypt and the bordering Iles/Are gotten up by Nilus — Jew 1.1.42 Barab
To mannage greater deeds; the bordering townes/He garrison'd; — Lucan, First Booke 463

BORDERS
Where straying in our borders up and downe, . . . — Dido 4.2.12 Iarbus

BORDRING
All bordring on the Mare-major sea: . . . . . — 2Tamb 3.1.51 Trebiz

BORE (Homograph)
And overtake the tusked Bore in chase. . . . . — Dido 1.1.208 Venus
And bore yong Cupid unto Cypresse Ile. . . . . — Dido 5.1.41 Hermes
With earthes revenge and how Olimpus toppe/High Ossa bore, — Ovid's Elegies 2.1.14
And some few pastures Pallas Olives bore. . . . . — Ovid's Elegies 2.16.8
A target bore: bloud sprinckled was his right. . . . — Ovid's Elegies 3.7.16

BOREAS
Drawne through the heavens by Steedes of Boreas brood, . — Dido 1.1.55 Venus
Before that Boreas buckled with your sailes? . . . — Dido 1.2.19 Iarbus
As far as Boreas claps his brazen wings, ... — 1Tamb 1.2.206 Tamb
Fearing the force of Boreas boistrous blasts. . . . — 1Tamb 2.4.5 Mycet
drops that fall/When Boreas rents a thousand swelling cloudes, — 2Tamb 1.3.160 Tamb
Beates Thracian Boreas; or when trees [bowe] <bowde> down, — Lucan, First Booke 391
If Boreas beares Orithyas rape in minde, ... — Ovid's Elegies 1.6.53
With Icy Boreas, and the Southerne gale: . . . . — Ovid's Elegies 2.11.10

BORGIAS
And with her let it worke like Borgias wine, . . . — Jew 3.4.98 Barab

BORN
Born to be Monarch of the western world: . . . . — 2Tamb 1.2.3 Callap
Oh earth-mettall'd villaines, and no Hebrews born! . . — Jew 1.2.78 Barab

BORNE (Homograph)
That earth-borne Atlas groning underprops: . . . — Dido 1.1.99 Jupitr
Had not the heavens conceav'd with hel-borne clowdes, . — Dido 1.1.125 Venus
O had that ticing strumpet nere been borne: . . . — Dido 2.1.300 Dido
I know this face, he is a Persian borne, ... — Dido 3.1.144 Serg
And while the base borne Tartars take it up, . . . — 1Tamb 2.2.65 Meandr
Shall swallow up these base borne Perseans. . . . — 1Tamb 3.3.95 Bajzth
The countrie wasted where my selfe was borne, . . . — 1Tamb 4.4.66 Zenoc
blot our dignities/Out of the booke of base borne infamies. — 2Tamb 3.1.19 Callap
To signifie she was a princesse borne, ... — 2Tamb 3.2.21 Amyras
But Shepheards issue, base borne Tamburlaine, . . . — 2Tamb 3.5.77 Orcan
Vile monster, borne of some infernal hag, ... — 2Tamb 5.1.110 Govnr
never sepulchre/Shall grace that base-borne Tyrant Tamburlaine. — 2Tamb 5.2.18 Amasia
Oh silly brethren, borne to see this day! . . . . — Jew 1.2.170 Barab
No, Barabas is borne to better chance, ... — Jew 1.2.218 Barab
Where was thou borne? . . . . — Jew 2.3.127 P Barab
My death? what, is the base borne peasant mad? . . . — Jew 2.3.281 Lodowk
An Hebrew borne, and would become a Christian? . . . — Jew 4.1.19 Barab
I cannot speak for greefe: when thou wast borne, . . . — P1072 19.142 QnMoth
You that be noble borne should pitie him. . . . . — Edw 1.4.80 Edward
You that are princely borne should shake him off, . . . — Edw 1.4.81 Warwck
For howsoever we have borne it out, ... — Edw 1.4.280 Mortmr
But this I scorne, that one so baselie borne, . . . — Edw 1.4.403 Mortmr
For your lemmons you have lost, at Bannocks borne, . . — Edw 2.2.191 Lncstr
Tell me, where wast thou borne? What is thine armes? . . — Edw 2.2.242 Edward
Was borne I see to be our anchor hold. . . . . — Edw 4.2.77 Mortmr
What, was I borne to flye and runne away, ... — Edw 4.5.4 Edward
Borne armes against thy brother and thy king? . . . — Edw 4.6.6 Kent
Now is he borne, of parents base of stocke, ... — F 11 Prol.11 1Chor
And offer luke-warme bloud, of new borne babes. . . . — F 402 2.1.14 Faust
I was borne in hell, and look to it, for some of you shall be — F 690 2.2.139 P Wrath
study, shee's borne to beare with me, or else my Art failes. — F App p.233 16 P Robin
you that with me have borne/A thousand brunts, and tride me ful — Lucan, First Booke 300
Borne twixt the Alpes and Rhene, which he hath brought/From out — Lucan, First Booke 478
where shall I fall,/Thus borne aloft? . . . . . — Lucan, First Booke 678
Lets yeeld, a burden easly borne is light. . . . . — Ovid's Elegies 1.2.10
But managde horses heads are lightly borne, ... — Ovid's Elegies 1.2.16
Nape free-borne, whose cunning hath no border, . . . — Ovid's Elegies 1.11.2
Borne at Peligny, to write more addresse. . . . . — Ovid's Elegies 2.1.2
Thou wert not borne to ride, or armes to beare, . . . — Ovid's Elegies 2.3.7
Thou also, that wert borne faire, hadst decayed, . . . — Ovid's Elegies 2.14.19
Long have I borne much, hoping time would beate thee/To guard — Ovid's Elegies 2.19.49
By suffring much not borne by thy severity. . . . — Ovid's Elegies 3.1.48
A free-borne wench, no right 'tis up to locke: . . . — Ovid's Elegies 3.4.33
Remus and Romulus, Ilias twinne-borne seed. . . . — Ovid's Elegies 3.4.40
Long have I borne much, mad thy faults me make: . . . — Ovid's Elegies 3.10.1
And what I have borne, shame to beare againe. . . . — Ovid's Elegies 3.10.4
Had they beene cut, and unto Colchos borne, ... — Hero and Leander 1.56
What vertue is it that is borne with us? . . . . — Hero and Leander 1.278
Heavens winged herrald, Jove-borne Mercury, ... — Hero and Leander 1.386
Brought foorth the day before the day was borne. . . . — Hero and Leander 2.322

BORNO
There having sackt Borno the Kingly seat, ... — 2Tamb 1.3.203 Techel
From thence to Nubia neere Borno Lake, ... — 2Tamb 5.3.136 Tamb

BORROW
Disdaine to borrow light of Cynthia, ... — 1Tamb 4.2.35 Tamb
From whence the starres doo borrow all their light, . . — 2Tamb 4.2.89 Therid

BORROWD
And shrowdes thy beautie in this borrowd shape: . . . — Dido 1.1.192 Aeneas

BORROWE
And cause the Sun to borrowe light of you. . . . — 1Tamb 4.2.40 Tamb

BORROWE (cont.)			
Thy tunes let this rare birdes sad funerall borrowe,	Ovid's Elegies	2.6.9	
BORROWED			
Before the Moone renew her borrowed light,	1Tamb	1.1.69	Therid
O thou oft wilt blush/And say he likes me for my borrowed bush,	Ovid's Elegies	1.14.48	
BORROWING			
talke with him was [but]/About the borrowing of a booke or two.	Jew	2.3.156	Mthias
BOSCO			
Martin del Bosco, I have heard of thee;	Jew	2.2.19	Govnr
Bosco, thou shalt be Malta's Generall;	Jew	2.2.44	Govnr
BOSOME			
In whose faire bosome I will locke more wealth,	Dido	3.1.92	Dido
And I for pitie harbord in my bosome,	Dido	5.1.166	Dido
With what a flinty bosome should I joy,	2Tamb	5.3.185	Amyras
My bosome [inmate] <inmates> <intimates>, but I must dissemble.	Jew	4.1.47	Barab
The king, upon whose bosome let me die,	Edw	1.1.14	Gavstn
Weele hale him from the bosome of the king,	Edw	1.2.29	Mortmr
I burne, love in my idle bosome sits.	Ovid's Elegies	1.1.30	
Wilt lying under him his bosome clippe?	Ovid's Elegies	1.4.5	
He hath no bosome, where to hide base pelfe.	Ovid's Elegies	1.10.18	
And from my mistris bosome let me rise:	Ovid's Elegies	2.10.20	
Conquer'd Corinna in my bosome layes.	Ovid's Elegies	2.12.2	
And in her bosome strangely fall at last.	Ovid's Elegies	2.15.14	
The maide to hide me in her bosome let not.	Ovid's Elegies	3.1.56	
To hide thee in my bosome straight repaire.	Ovid's Elegies	3.2.76	
Her wofull bosome a warme shower did drowne.	Ovid's Elegies	3.5.68	
And oftentimes into her bosome flew,	Hero and Leander	1.41	
her body throes/Upon his bosome, where with yeelding eyes,	Hero and Leander	2.47	
Me in thy bed and maiden bosome take,	Hero and Leander	2.248	
BOSOMES			
spirits may vex/Your slavish bosomes with continuall paines,	2Tamb	5.1.46	Govnr
Thy bosomes Roseat buds let him not finger,	Ovid's Elegies	1.4.37	
BOSSE			
Disdainful Turkesse and unreverend Bosse,	1Tamb	3.3.168	Zenoc
BOTH			
When yet both sea and sands beset their ships,	Dido	1.1.110	Venus
And call both Thetis and [Cimothoe] <Cimodoae> <Cymodoce>,/To	Dido	1.1.132	Venus
Both barking Scilla, and the sounding Rocks,	Dido	1.1.146	Aeneas
Exild forth Europe and wide Asia both,	Dido	1.1.229	Aeneas
Both happie that Aeneas is our guest:	Dido	2.1.82	Dido
and both his eyes/Turnd up to heaven as one resolv'd to dye,	Dido	2.1.151	Aeneas
and joyntly both/Beating their breasts and falling on the	Dido	2.1.227	Aeneas
Forgetting both his want of strength and hands,	Dido	2.1.252	Aeneas
Then pull out both mine eyes, or let me dye.	Dido	3.1.55	Iarbus
Are not we both sprong of celestiall rase,	Dido	3.2.28	Juno
And both our Deities conjoynd in one,	Dido	3.2.79	Juno
This day they both a hunting forth will ride/Into these woods,	Dido	3.2.87	Juno
Behold where both of them come forth the Cave.	Dido	4.1.16	Anna
I might have stakte them both unto the earth,	Dido	4.1.23	Iarbus
With whom we did devide both lawes and land,	Dido	4.2.14	Iarbus
Or drop out both mine eyes in drisling teares,	Dido	4.2.41	Iarbus
When as I want both rigging for my fleete,	Dido	5.1.69	Aeneas
That hath dishonord her and Carthage both?	Dido	5.1.280	Iarbus
Wanting both pay and martiall discipline,	1Tamb	1.1.147	Ceneus
Both may invest you Empresse of the East:	1Tamb	1.2.46	Tamb
Both we wil walke upon the lofty clifts,	1Tamb	1.2.193	Tamb
Both we will raigne as Consuls of the earth,	1Tamb	1.2.197	Tamb
And both our soules aspire celestiall thrones.	1Tamb	1.2.237	Tamb
Usumcasane and Techelles both,	1Tamb	2.3.36	Cosroe
For want of nourishment to feed them both,	1Tamb	2.7.47	Cosroe
And feareful vengeance light upon you both.	1Tamb	2.7.52	Cosroe
Both for their sausinesse shall be employed,	1Tamb	3.3.184	Zenoc
Come bind them both and one lead in the Turke.	1Tamb	3.3.266	Tamb
And make it swallow both of us at once.	1Tamb	4.2.29	Bajzth
I thus conceiving and subduing both:	1Tamb	5.1.183	Tamb
No breath nor sence, nor motion in them both.	1Tamb	5.1.344	Anippe
not but faire Zenocrate/Will soone consent to satisfy us both.	1Tamb	5.1.499	Tamb
A friendly parle might become ye both.	2Tamb	1.1.117	Gazell
Least time be past, and lingring let us both.	2Tamb	1.2.75	Callap
When heaven shal cease to moove on both the poles/And when the	2Tamb	1.3.12	Tamb
Wel lovely boies, you shal be Emperours both,	2Tamb	1.3.96	Tamb
And solemne covenants we have both confirm'd,	2Tamb	2.2.31	Orcan
And died a traitor both to heaven and earth,	2Tamb	2.3.37	Orcan
We wil both watch and ward shall keepe his trunke/Amidst these	2Tamb	2.3.38	Orcan
We both will rest and have one Epitaph/Writ in as many severall	2Tamb	2.4.134	Tamb
Both we (Theridamas) wil intrench our men,	2Tamb	3.3.49	Techel
Death, whether art thou gone that both we live?	2Tamb	3.4.11	Olymp
Come back again (sweet death) and strike us both:	2Tamb	3.4.12	Olymp
And carie both our soules, where his remaines.	2Tamb	3.4.17	Olymp
And quickly rid thee both of paine and life.	2Tamb	3.4.25	Olymp
Madam, sooner shall fire consume us both,	2Tamb	3.4.73	Techel
Welcome Theridamas and Techelles both,	2Tamb	3.5.150	Tamb
Goe, goe tall stripling, fight you for us both,	2Tamb	4.1.33	Calyph
Twill please my mind as wel to heare both you/Have won a heape	2Tamb	4.1.36	Calyph
Take them, and hang them both up presently.	2Tamb	5.1.132	Tamb
First let thy Scythyan horse teare both our limmes/Rather then	2Tamb	5.1.138	Orcan
I meant to cut a channell to them both,	2Tamb	5.3.134	Tamb
By equall portions into both your breasts:	2Tamb	5.3.171	Tamb
For both their woorths wil equall him no more.	2Tamb	5.3.253	Amyras
But I have sworne to frustrate both their hopes,	Jew	2.3.142	Barab
make account of me/As of thy fellow; we are villaines both:	Jew	2.3.214	Barab
Both circumcized, we hate Christians both:	Jew	2.3.215	Barab
That ye be both made sure e're you come out.	Jew	2.3.236	Barab

BOTH (cont.)

Father, why have you thus incenst them both?	Jew	2.3.356	Abigal
I thinke by this/You purchase both their lives; is it not so?	Jew	2.3.366	Ithimr
Till I have set 'em both at enmitie.	Jew	2.3.383	Barab
Both held in hand, and flatly both beguil'd.	Jew	3.3.3	Ithimr
In dolefull wise they ended both their dayes.	Jew	3.3.21	Ithimr
That by my favour they should both be slaine?	Jew	3.3.39	Abigal
My father did contract me to 'em both:	Jew	3.6.22	Abigal
Both jealous of my love, envied each other:	Jew	3.6.27	Abigal
is there/Set downe at large, the Gallants were both slaine.	Jew	3.6.29	Abigal
She has confest, and we are both undone,	Jew	4.1.46	Barab
Now I have such a plot for both their lives,	Jew	4.1.117	Barab
But are not both these wise men to suppose/That I will leave my	Jew	4.1.122	Barab
son; he and I kild 'em both, and yet never touch'd 'em.	Jew	4.4.18	P Ithimr
your sonne and Mathias were both contracted unto Abigall; [he]	Jew	5.1.29	P Ithimr
Arbitrament; and Barabas/At his discretion may dispose of both:	Jew	5.2.54	Barab
Thus loving neither, will I live with both,	Jew	5.2.111	Barab
Away with them both.	P 442	7.82	Anjoy
Rich Princes both, and mighty Emperours:	P 463	8.13	Anjoy
they Henries heart/Will not both harbour love and Majestie?	P 604	12.17	King
Of King or Country, no not for them both.	P 740	14.43	Navrre
of Guise you and your wife/Doe both salute our lovely Minions.	P 753	15.11	King
Wounded and poysoned, both at once?	P1215	22.77	King
To whom the sunne shines both by day and night.	Edw	1.1.17	Gavstn
And both the Mortimers, two goodly men,	Edw	1.3.3	Gavstn
Deare shall you both abie this riotous deede:	Edw	2.2.88	Edward
Would Lancaster and he had both carroust,	Edw	2.2.237	Edward
I charge you roundly off with both their heads,	Edw	3.1.247	Edward
Betweene you both, shorten the time I pray,	Edw	4.3.45	Edward
To plaine me to the gods against them both:	Edw	5.1.22	Edward
And joyntly both yeeld up their wished right.	Edw	5.1.63	Edward
That if he slip will seaze upon us both,	Edw	5.2.8	Mortmr
For me, both thou, and both the Spencers died,	Edw	5.3.42	Edward
And none of both [them] <then> thirst for Edmunds bloud.	Edw	5.4.107	Kent
Betray us both, therefore let me flie.	Edw	5.6.8	Matrvs
And vowes to be revengd upon us both,	Edw	5.6.19	Queene
Both Law and Physicke are for petty wits:	F 134	1.1.106	Faust
I do not doubt but to see you both hang'd the next Sessions.	F 212	1.2.19	P Wagner
And both contributary to my Crowne.	F 337	1.3.109	Faust
thou performe/All Covenants, and Articles, betweene us both.	F 480	2.1.92	Faust
All <articles prescrib'd> <covenant-articles> betweene us both.	F 480	(HC260)	Faust
To effect all promises betweene us [made] <both>.	F 482	2.1.94	Mephst
by these presents doe give both body and soule to Lucifer,	F 494	2.1.106	P Faust
But <tell me> have they all/One motion, both situ et tempore?	F 596	2.2.45	Faust
Both he and thou shalt stand excommunicate,	F 908	3.1.130	Pope
That slept both Bruno and his crowne away.	F 988	3.2.8	Faust
Were by the holy Councell both condemn'd/For lothed Lollords,	F1021	3.2.41	Pope
Nay there you lie, 'tis beyond us both.	F1109	3.3.22	P Robin
Both love and serve the Germane Emperour,	F1219	4.1.65	Faust
Be both your legs bedfellowes every night together?	F1645	4.6.88	P Carter
Both come from drawing Faustus latest will.	F1814	5.2.18	Mephst
A surfet of deadly sin, that hath damn'd both body and soule.	F1833	5.2.37	P Faust
for which Faustus hath lost both Germany and the world, yea	F1843	5.2.47	P Faust
to fetch me <both> body and soule, if I once gave eare to	F1865	5.2.69	P Faust
Both in their right shapes, gesture, and attire/They usde to	F App	p.237 33	Emper
Thou shalt both satisfie my just desire,	F App	p.237 35	Emper
peace against their wils; betwixt them both/Stept Crassus in:	Lucan, First Booke	99	
but being worne away/They both burst out, and each incounter	Lucan, First Booke	103	
superior, which of both/Had justest cause unlawful tis to judge:	Lucan, First Booke	126	
Both differ'd much, Pompey was strooke in yeares,	Lucan, First Booke	130	
That crost them; both which now approacht the camp,	Lucan, First Booke	270	
Woods turn'd to ships; both land and sea against us:	Lucan, First Booke	307	
Which is nor sea, nor land, but oft times both,	Lucan, First Booke	411	
and flying/Left hateful warre decreed to both the Consuls.	Lucan, First Booke	486	
threatning gods/Fill'd both the earth and seas with prodegies;	Lucan, First Booke	523	
Both verses were alike till Love (men say)/Began to smile and	Ovid's Elegies	1.1.7	
Both of them watch: each on the hard earth sleepes:	Ovid's Elegies	1.9.7	
And lets what both delight, what both desire,	Ovid's Elegies	1.10.31	
The sport being such, as both alike sweete try it,	Ovid's Elegies	1.10.33	
The lawier and the client <both do> hate thy view,	Ovid's Elegies	1.13.21	
Both whom thou raisest up to toyle anew.	Ovid's Elegies	1.13.22	
Are both in Fames eternall legend writ.	Ovid's Elegies	1.15.20	
And what she likes, let both hold ratifide.	Ovid's Elegies	2.2.32	
More he deserv'd, to both great harme he fram'd,	Ovid's Elegies	2.2.49	
Both short and long please me, for I love both:	Ovid's Elegies	2.4.36	
In both [thy] <my> cheekes she did perceive thee blush,	Ovid's Elegies	2.8.16	
So of both people shalt thou homage gaine.	Ovid's Elegies	2.9.54	
Both are wel favoured, both rich in array,	Ovid's Elegies	2.10.5	
Both to the Sea-nimphes, and the Sea-nimphes father.	Ovid's Elegies	2.11.36	
I was both horse-man, foote-man, standard bearer.	Ovid's Elegies	2.12.14	
Both unkinde parents, but for causes sad,	Ovid's Elegies	2.14.31	
Let us both lovers hope, and feare a like,	Ovid's Elegies	2.19.5	
She left; I say'd, you both I must beseech,	Ovid's Elegies	3.1.61	
Though both of us performd our true intent,	Ovid's Elegies	3.6.5	
Worthy she was to move both Gods and men,	Ovid's Elegies	3.6.59	
If I should give, both would the house forbeare.	Ovid's Elegies	3.7.64	
Both loves to whom my heart long time did yeeld,	Ovid's Elegies	3.14.15	
Whose workmanship both man and beast deceaves.	Hero and Leander	1.20	
Where both deliberat, the love is slight,	Hero and Leander	1.175	
for both not us'de,/Are of like worth.	Hero and Leander	1.233	
Compar'd with marriage, had you tried them both,	Hero and Leander	1.263	
Both might enjoy ech other, and be blest.	Hero and Leander	1.380	
They seeing it, both Love and him abhor'd,	Hero and Leander	1.463	

BOTH (cont.)			
Both to each other quickly were affied.	Hero and Leander		2.26
As for his love, both earth and heaven pyn'd;	Hero and Leander		2.196
With both her hands she made the bed a tent,	Hero and Leander		2.264
Both in each others armes chaind as they layd.	Hero and Leander		2.306
BOTTLE (Homograph)			
bottle-nos'd knave to my Master, that ever Gentleman had.	Jew	3.3.10	P Ithimr
for your horse is turned to a bottle of Hay,--Maister Doctor.	F1490	4.4.34	P HrsCsr
horse vanisht away, and I sate straddling upon a bottle of Hay.	F1545	4.5.41	P HrsCsr
and I sat upon a bottle of hey, never so neare drowning in my	F App	p.240 135	P HrsCsr
Fustian, fortie dollers, fortie dollers for a bottle of hey.	F App	p.241 149	P HrsCsr
the Horsecourser I take it, a bottle of hey for his labour; wel,	F App	p.241 165	P Faust
BOTTLE-NOS'D			
bottle-nos'd knave to my Master, that ever Gentleman had.	Jew	3.3.10	P Ithimr
BOTTLES			
in the house, and dash out all your braines with your Bottles.	F1619	4.6.62	P HrsCsr
BOTTOME			
Dive to the bottome of Avernus poole,	1Tamb	4.4.18	Bajzth
And puld him to the bottome, where the ground/Was strewd with	Hero and Leander		2.160
BOUGH (See also BOW, BOWES)			
And gets unto the highest bough of all,	Edw	2.2.19	Mortmr
hang him at a bough.	Edw	2.5.24	Warwck
And burned is Apollo's Lawrell bough,	F2003	5.3.21	4Chor
BOUGHES			
Vultures and furies nestled in the boughes.	Ovid's Elegies		1.12.20
Apples, and hony in oakes hollow boughes.	Ovid's Elegies		3.7.40
BOUGHS			
His body (not his boughs) send forth a shade;	Lucan, First Booke		141
BOUGHT			
Share equally the gold that bought their lives,	1Tamb	2.2.70	Meandr
That bought my Spanish Oyles, and Wines of Greece,	Jew	1.1.5	Barab
As much as would have bought his beasts and him,	Jew	1.2.189	Barab
Honor is bought with bloud and not with gold.	Jew	2.2.56	Govnr
Feare not their sale, for they'll be quickly bought.	Jew	2.3.2	1Offcr
and I have bought a house/As great and faire as is the	Jew	2.3.13	Barab
being bought, the Towne-seale might be got/To keepe him for his	Jew	2.3.103	Barab
It is a precious powder that I bought/Of an Italian in Ancona	Jew	3.4.68	Barab
And thinke I gaind, having bought so deare a friend.	Edw	1.4.310	Edward
and peoples voices/Bought by themselves and solde, and every	Lucan, First Booke		181
The whore stands to be bought for each mans mony/And seekes	Ovid's Elegies		1.10.21
BOULD			
When yre, or hope provokt, heady, and bould,	Lucan, First Booke		147
come, their huge power made him bould/To mannage greater deeds;	Lucan, First Booke		462
Who but a souldiour or a lover is bould/To suffer storme mixt	Ovid's Elegies		1.9.15
Either th'art witcht with blood <bould> of frogs new dead,	Ovid's Elegies		3.6.79
BOULDLY			
Ile bouldly quarter out the fields of Rome;	Lucan, First Booke		383
too, which bouldly faine themselves/The Romanes brethren,	Lucan, First Booke		428
BOULES			
wines/Shall common Souldiers drink in quaffing boules,	2Tamb	1.3.222	Tamb
Then drerie Mars, carowsing Nectar boules.	Hero and Leander		2.258
BOULLION			
Base boullion for the stampes sake we allow,	Hero and Leander		1.265
BOULT			
And boult the brazen gates with barres of Iron.	Lucan, First Booke		62
BOULTS			
He shall to prison, and there die in boults.	Edw	1.1.197	Gavstn
Now when he should not jette, he boults upright,	Ovid's Elegies		3.6.67
BOUND (Homograph)			
No bounds but heaven shall bound his Emperie,	Dido	1.1.100	Jupitr
Unto what fruitfull quarters were ye bound,	Dido	1.2.18	Iarbus
His hands bound at his backe, and both his eyes/Turnd up to	Dido	2.1.151	Aeneas
I hold the Fates bound fast in yron chaines,	1Tamb	1.2.174	Tamb
And all his Captains bound in captive chaines.	1Tamb	3.3.115	Bajzth
I took the king, and lead him bound in chaines/Unto Damasco,	2Tamb	1.3.204	Techel
We are not bound to those accomplishments,	2Tamb	2.1.35	Baldwn
Whom I brought bound unto Damascus walles.	2Tamb	3.2.125	Tamb
our mighty hoste/Shal bring thee bound unto the Generals tent.	2Tamb	3.5.111	Trebiz
But whither am I bound, I come not, I,	Jew	Prol.28	Machvl
Now Captaine tell us whither thou art bound?	Jew	2.2.1	Govnr
Governor of Malta, hither am I bound;	Jew	2.2.4	Bosco
And I am bound in charitie to requite it,	Jew	4.1.107	Barab
Hearing his Soveraigne was bound for Sea,	Jew	5.3.15	Msngr
I did no more then I was bound to do,	Edw	1.1.182	BshpCv
Bound to your highnes everlastinglie,	Edw	3.1.41	SpncrP
Villaine, have I not bound thee to tell me any thing?	F 622	2.2.71	P Faust
Yet Room is much bound to these civil armes,	Lucan, First Booke		44
And captive like be manacled and bound.	Ovid's Elegies		1.2.30
Unworthy porter, bound in chaines full sore,	Ovid's Elegies		1.6.1
BOUNDES			
And from the boundes of Affrick to the banks/Of Ganges, shall	1Tamb	5.1.520	Tamb
And passe their fixed boundes exceedingly.	2Tamb	4.3.47	Therid
BOUNDLESSE			
Poets large power is boundlesse, and immense,	Ovid's Elegies		3.11.41
BOUNDS (Homograph)			
And heaven and earth the bounds of thy delight?	Dido	1.1.31	Jupitr
No bounds but heaven shall bound his Emperie,	Dido	1.1.100	Jupitr
How loth I am to leave these Libian bounds,	Dido	5.1.81	Aeneas
and the bounds/Of Europe wher the Sun dares scarce appeare,	1Tamb	1.1.9	Cosroe
I left the confines and the bounds of Affrike/And made a voyage	2Tamb	1.3.207	Therid
Judaea, Gaza, and Scalonians bounds,	2Tamb	3.1.45	Jrslem
That from the bounds of Phrigia to the sea/Which washeth Cyprus	2Tamb	3.5.11	Callap
So from Arabia desart, and the bounds/Of that sweet land, whose	2Tamb	3.5.35	Orcan

BOUNDS (cont.)
The greatest warres within our Christian bounds, P 460 8.10 Anjoy
<Unhappies> <Unhappy is> Edward, chaste from Englands bounds. Edw 4.6.62 Kent
vales, deviding just/The bounds of Italy, from Cisalpin Fraunce; Lucan, First Booke 218
As soone as Caesar got unto the banke/And bounds of Italy; Lucan, First Booke 226
Slide in thy bounds, so shalt thou runne for ever. Ovid's Elegies 3.5.20
he often strayd/Beyond the bounds of shame, in being bold/To Hero and Leander 1.407
BOUNTEOUS
Doctor, yet ere you goe, expect from me a bounteous reward. F App p.239 89 P Emper
[May] <Many> bounteous [lome] <love> Alcinous fruite resigne. Ovid's Elegies 1.10.56
BOUNTIFULL
Thee, goddesse, bountifull all nations judge, Ovid's Elegies 3.9.5
BOUNTY
For deeds of bounty or nobility: 2Tamb 4.1.152 Tamb
BOURBON (See also BURBON)
Now let the house of Bourbon weare the crowne, P1232 22.94 King
BOURD
Our Masts the furious windes strooke over bourd: Dido 3.1.110 Aeneas
'BOUT
And 'bout this time the Nuns begin to wake; Jew 2.1.56 Abigal
BOUTS
And nine sweete bouts had we before day light. Ovid's Elegies 3.6.26
BOW (Homograph)
I, and my mother gave me this fine bow. Dido 2.1.309 Cupid
Shall I have such a quiver and a bow? Dido 2.1.310 Ascan
Such bow, such quiver, and such golden shafts, Dido 2.1.311 Venus
And bent his sinewy bow upon his knee, Ovid's Elegies 1.1.27
Before whose bow th'Arcadian wild beasts trembled. Ovid's Elegies 1.7.14
And birdes send forth shrill notes from everie bow. Ovid's Elegies 1.13.8
Till Cupids bow, and fierie shafts be broken, Ovid's Elegies 1.15.27
Why burnes thy brand, why strikes thy bow thy friends? Ovid's Elegies 2.9.5
All deepe enrag'd, his sinowie bow he bent, Hero and Leander 1.371
BOWDE
Beates Thracian Boreas; or when trees [bowe] <bowde> down,/And Lucan, First Booke 391
BOWE (Homograph)
maides to weare/Their bowe and quiver in this modest sort, Dido 1.1.205 Venus
Faire Troian, hold my golden bowe awhile, Dido 3.3.7 Dido
Bearing her bowe and quiver at her backe. Dido 3.3.55 Achat
By heaven and earth, and my faire brothers bowe, Dido 3.4.45 Aeneas
My knee shall bowe to none but to the king. Edw 1.1.19 Gavstn
Beates Thracian Boreas; or when trees [bowe] <bowde> down,/And Lucan, First Booke 391
[What] <That> if thy Mother take Dianas bowe, Ovid's Elegies 1.1.11
Of horne the bowe was that approv'd their side. Ovid's Elegies 1.8.48
And tis suppos'd Loves bowe hath wounded thee, Ovid's Elegies 1.11.11
That some youth hurt as I am with loves bowe/His owne flames Ovid's Elegies 2.1.7
I sweare by Venus, and the wingd boyes bowe, Ovid's Elegies 2.7.27
At me Apollo bends his pliant bowe: Ovid's Elegies 3.3.29
His broken bowe, his fire-brand without light. Ovid's Elegies 3.8.8
BOWELS
Which glided through the bowels of the Greekes. 1Tamb 3.3.92 Argier
Trampling their bowels with our horses hooffes: 1Tamb 3.3.150 Tamb
First shalt thou rip my bowels with thy sword, 1Tamb 4.2.16 Bajzth
a fiery exhalation/Wrapt in the bowels of a freezing cloude, 1Tamb 4.2.44 Tamb
with horror aie/Griping our bowels with retorqued thoughtes, 1Tamb 5.1.237 Bajzth
Should breake out off the bowels of the clowdes/And fall as 2Tamb 2.2.14 Gazell
I long to pierce his bowels with my sword, 2Tamb 3.2.152 Usumc
Or rip thy bowels, and rend out thy heart, 2Tamb 3.5.121 Tamb
Ripping the bowels of the earth for them, Jew 1.1.109 Barab
Rifling the bowels of her treasurie, P 135 2.78 Guise
To rip the golden bowels of America. P 854 17.49 Guise
Within the bowels of these Elements, F 508 2.1.120 Mephst
thou bid me/Intombe my sword within my brothers bowels; Lucan, First Booke 377
And stain'd the bowels with darke lothsome spots: Lucan, First Booke 619
Why with hid irons are your bowels torne? Ovid's Elegies 2.14.27
BOWER
Unto the watry mornings ruddy [bower] <hower>, 1Tamb 4.4.123 Tamb
Unto the shining bower where Cynthia sits, 2Tamb 3.4.50 Therid
That now should shine on Thetis glassie bower, Hero and Leander 2.203
BOWERS
Whose eies shot fire from their Ivory bowers, 2Tamb 2.4.9 Tamb
BOWES (Homograph)
You shall have leaves and windfall bowes enow/Neere to these Dido 1.1.172 Aeneas
With bowes and dartes to shoot at them they see, P 422 7.62 Dumain
Penelope in bowes her youths strength tride, Ovid's Elegies 1.8.47
BOWLE
A bowle of poison to each others health: Edw 2.2.238 Edward
BOWLES
banquet and carouse/Full bowles of wine unto the God of war, 1Tamb 4.4.6 Tamb
And happily with full Natolian bowles/Of Greekish wine now let 2Tamb 2.3.45 Orcan
Goe swill in bowles of Sacke and Muscadine: Jew 5.5.6 Barab
BOWMEN
Loe, with a band of bowmen and of pikes, Edw 3.1.36 SpncrP
BOWRE
That Nature shall dissolve this earthly bowre. Ovid's Elegies 1.15.24
BOX
I but sir sauce box, know you in what place? F1616 4.6.59 Servnt
BOXE
Gentle Achates, reach the Tinder boxe, Dido 1.1.166 Aeneas
BOY (See also BOIE)
And playing with that female wanton boy, Dido 1.1.51 Venus
What shall I doe to save thee my sweet boy? Dido 1.1.74 Venus
Alas sweet boy, thou must be still a while, Dido 1.1.164 Aeneas
This young boy in mine armes, and by the hand/Led faire Creusa Dido 2.1.266 Aeneas

BOY (cont.)			
Weepe not sweet boy, thou shalt be Didos sonne,	Dido	3.1.24	Dido
The boy wherein false destinie delights,	Dido	3.2.2	Juno
If thou but lay thy fingers on my boy.	Dido	3.2.36	Venus
That I might live to see this boy a man,	Dido	4.5.18	Nurse
Spendst thou thy time about this little boy,	Dido	5.1.51	Hermes
And I am thus deluded of my boy:	Dido	5.1.219	Dido
This lovely boy the yongest of the three,	2Tamb	1.3.37	Zenoc
Wel done my boy, thou shalt have shield and lance,	2Tamb	1.3.43	Tamb
These words assure me boy, thou art my sonne,	2Tamb	1.3.58	Tamb
Bastardly boy, sprong from some cowards loins,	2Tamb	1.3.69	Tamb
My boy, Thou shalt not loose a drop of blood,	2Tamb	3.2.137	Tamb
O cowardly boy, fie for shame, come foorth.	2Tamb	4.1.31	Celeb
Souldier shall defile/His manly fingers with so faint a boy.	2Tamb	4.1.164	Tamb
Thy youth forbids such ease my kingly boy,	2Tamb	4.3.29	Tamb
I Turke, I tel thee, this same Boy is he,	2Tamb	4.3.57	Tamb
Tis brave indeed my boy, wel done,	2Tamb	5.1.150	Tamb
Sit up my boy, and with those silken raines,	2Tamb	5.3.202	Tamb
Boy, look where your father lyes.	P1046	19.116	King
As though your highnes were a schoole boy still,	Edw	3.1.30	Baldck
That shall we presently know, <for see> here comes his boy.	F 196	1.2.3	2Schol
Come hither sirra boy.	F 343	1.4.1	P Wagner
Boy?	F 344	1.4.2	P Robin
boy in your face, you have seene many boyes with [such	F 344	1.4.2	P Robin
same cup, for the Vintners boy followes us at the hard heeles.	F1089	3.3.2	P Dick
Sirra boy, come hither.	F App	p.229 1	P Wagner
How, boy?	F App	p.229 2	P Clown
swowns boy, I hope you have seene many boyes with such	F App	p.229 2	P Clown
Boy quotha?	F App	p.229 3	P Clown
Wel, come give me your money, my boy wil deliver him to you:	F App	p.239 107	P Faust
slicke as an Ele; wel god buy sir, your boy wil deliver him me:	F App	p.240 117	P HrsCsr
Rash boy, who gave thee power to change a line?	Ovid's Elegies	1.1.9	
Aske thou the boy, what thou enough doest thinke.	Ovid's Elegies	1.4.30	
Love is a naked boy, his yeares saunce staine,	Ovid's Elegies	1.10.15	
O boy that lyest so slothfull in my heart.	Ovid's Elegies	2.9.2	
Strike boy, I offer thee my naked brest,	Ovid's Elegies	2.9.35	
Thee gentle Venus, and the boy that flies,	Ovid's Elegies	3.2.55	
A little boy druncke teate-distilling showers.	Ovid's Elegies	3.9.22	
Sylvanus weeping for the lovely boy/That now is turn'd into a	Hero and Leander	1.154	
Playd with a boy so faire and [so] kind,	Hero and Leander	2.195	
BOYE			
Sometime a lovelie boye in Dians shape,	Edw	1.1.61	Gavstn
Boye, see you beare you bravelie to the king,	Edw	3.1.72	Edward
A boye, this towardnes makes thy mother feare/Thou art not	Edw	3.1.79	Queene
A boye, our friends do faile us all in Fraunce,	Edw	4.2.1	Queene
A boye, thou art deceivde at least in this,	Edw	4.2.8	Queene
Ah nothing greeves me but my little boye,	Edw	4.3.48	Edward
Whose lookes were as a breeching to a boye.	Edw	5.4.55	Mortmr
Feare not sweete boye, ile garde thee from thy foes,	Edw	5.4.111	Queene
Then sue for life unto a paltrie boye.	Edw	5.6.57	Mortmr
BOYES			
Boyes leave to mourne, this towne shall ever mourne,	2Tamb	3.2.45	Tamb
Come boyes and with your fingers search my wound,	2Tamb	3.2.126	Tamb
Now my boyes, what think you of a wound?	2Tamb	3.2.129	Tamb
Teach you my boyes to beare couragious minds,	2Tamb	3.2.143	Tamb
Bring them my boyes, and tel me if the warres/Be not a life	2Tamb	4.1.78	Tamb
Stand up my boyes, and I wil teach ye arms,	2Tamb	4.1.103	Tamb
seene many boyes with [such pickadevaunts] <beards> I am sure.	F 345	1.4.3	P Robin
you have seene many boyes with such pickadevaunts as I have.	F App	p.229 2	P Clown
Ile have fine sport with the boyes, Ile get nuts and apples	F App	p.236 46	P Robin
Thou coosnest boyes of sleepe, and dost betray them/To Pedants,	Ovid's Elegies	1.13.17	
And rude boyes toucht with unknowne love me reade,	Ovid's Elegies	2.1.6	
Who first depriv'd yong boyes of their best part,	Ovid's Elegies	2.3.3	
I sweare by Venus, and the wingd boyes bowe,	Ovid's Elegies	2.7.27	
Now is the goat brought through the boyes with darts,	Ovid's Elegies	3.12.21	
BOYLE			
On burning forkes: their bodies [boyle] <broyle> in lead.	F1912	5.2.116	BdAngl
BOYSTEROUS			
Lantchidol/Beates on the regions with his boysterous blowes,	2Tamb	1.1.70	Orcan
Come breake these deafe dores with thy boysterous wind.	Ovid's Elegies	1.6.54	
BRABBLING			
Brabbling Marcellus; Cato whom fooles reverence;	Lucan, First Booke	313	
BRACELET			
The god put Helles bracelet on his arme,	Hero and Leander	2.179	
BRACELETS			
Ile make me bracelets of his golden haire,	Dido	3.1.85	Dido
These golden bracelets, and this wedding ring,	Dido	3.4.62	Dido
He sends her letters, bracelets, jewels, rings.	Jew	2.3.259	Barab
BRACKISH			
Whereas the Southerne winde with brackish breath,	Dido	1.2.28	Cloan
BRAG			
scambled up/More wealth by farre then those that brag of faith.	Jew	1.1.123	Barab
BRAGS			
Turkes are ful of brags/And menace more than they can wel	1Tamb	3.3.3	Tamb
BRAIDE			
Adde she was diligent thy locks to braide,	Ovid's Elegies	2.7.23	
BRAIN			
As was the fame of [Clymens] <Clymeus> brain-sicke sonne,/That	1Tamb	4.2.49	Tamb
the fatall poyson/Workes within my head, my brain pan breakes,	P 185	3.20	OldQn
BRAINDE			
The proud corrupters of the light-brainde king,	Edw	5.2.2	Mortmr
BRAINE			
denied/To shed [their] <his> influence in his fickle braine,	1Tamb	1.1.15	Cosroe

BRAINE (cont.)			
And with the noise turnes up my giddie braine, . . .	Edw	1.4.314	Edward
His conscience kils it, and his labouring braine, . .	F1809	5.2.13	Mephst
See Love with me, wine moderate in my braine, . . .	Ovid's Elegies	1.6.37	
BRAINES			
Who with steele Pol-axes dasht out their braines. . .	Dido	2.1.199	Aeneas
down murthering shot from heaven/To dash the Scythians braines,	1Tamb	3.3.197	Zabina
And beat thy braines out of thy conquer'd head: . .	1Tamb	5.1.287	Bajzth
His Skul al rivin in twain, his braines dasht out? . .	1Tamb	5.1.306	Zabina
The braines of Bajazeth, my Lord and Soveraigne? . .	1Tamb	5.1.307	Zabina
And sprinkled with the braines of slaughtered men, . .	2Tamb	1.3.81	Tamb
The poisoned braines of this proud Scythian. . . .	2Tamb	3.1.67	Orcan
And strowes the way with braines of slaughtered men: .	2Tamb	3.4.58	Therid
I may knocke out his braines with them, and lock you in the	2Tamb	3.5.141	P Tamb
whose scalding drops wil pierce thy seething braines, .	2Tamb	4.1.144	Jrslem
And beates his braines to catch us in his trap, . .	P 53	1.53	Navrre
My sinnewes shrinke, my braines turne upside downe, . .	P 549	11.14	Charls
god>,/Here <Faustus> tire my <trie thy> braines to get a Deity.	F 90	1.1.62	Faust
in the house, and dash out all your braines with your Bottles.	F1619	4.6.62	P HrsCsr
BRAINS			
I, master, he's slain; Look how his brains drop out on's nose.	Jew	4.1.178	P Ithimr
BRAINSICK			
Come unckle, let us leave the brainsick king, . . .	Edw	1.1.125	Mortmr
BRAIN-SICKE			
As was the fame of [Clymens] <Clymeus> brain-sicke sonne,/That	1Tamb	4.2.49	Tamb
BRAINSICKE			
As that which [Clymens] <Clymeus> brainsicke sonne did guide,	2Tamb	5.3.231	Tamb
BRAKE			
Foorth from those two tralucent cesternes brake, . .	Hero and Leander	1.296	
BRAKES			
and in this grove/Amongst greene brakes Ile lay Ascanius,	Dido	2.1.317	Venus
BRANCH			
The wicked branch of curst Valois his line. . . .	P1013	19.83	Guise
Cut is the branch that might have growne full straight, .	F2002	5.3.20	4Chor
BRANCHE			
person you remoove/This Spencer, as a putrifying branche,	Edw	3.1.162	Herald
BRANCHES			
On whose top-branches Kinglie Eagles pearch, . . .	Edw	2.2.17	Mortmr
BRANCHT			
And brancht with blushing corall to the knee; . . .	Hero and Leander	1.32	
BRAND			
And with my brand these gorgeous houses burne. . . .	Ovid's Elegies	1.6.58	
Why burnes thy brand, why strikes thy bow thy friends? .	Ovid's Elegies	2.9.5	
His broken bowe, his fire-brand without light. . . .	Ovid's Elegies	3.8.8	
BRANDISH			
My horsmen brandish their unruly blades.	2Tamb	5.1.79	Tamb
BRANDISHING			
hands)/All brandishing their brands of quenchlesse fire, .	2Tamb	3.5.27	Orcan
BRANDISHT			
(The worthiest knight that ever brandisht sword)/Challenge in	2Tamb	3.5.71	Tamb
I saw a brandisht fire increase in strength, . . .	Ovid's Elegies	1.2.11	
BRANDS			
hands)/All brandishing their brands of quenchlesse fire, .	2Tamb	3.5.27	Orcan
BRASEN			
H'had never bellowed in a brasen Bull/Of great ones envy; o'th	Jew	Prol.25	Machvl
When she was lockt up in a brasen tower, ...	Edw	2.2.54	Edward
BRASSE			
And fetter them in Vulcans sturdie brasse, . . .	Dido	1.1.118	Jupitr
Tho countermin'd <countermur'd> with walls of brasse, to love,	Jew	1.2.386	Mthias
And with brasse-bullets batter downe your Towers, . .	Jew	3.5.24	Basso
I'le have them wall all Germany with Brasse, . . .	F 115	1.1.87	Faust
<And double Canons, fram'd of carved brasse>, . . .	F 820	(HC265)A	Mephst
As that the double Cannons forg'd of brasse, . . .	F 820	3.1.42	Mephst
Brasse shines with use; good garments would be worne, .	Ovid's Elegies	1.8.51	
The posts of brasse, the walles of iron were. . . .	Ovid's Elegies	3.7.32	
Gold, silver, irons heavy weight, and brasse, . . .	Ovid's Elegies	3.7.37	
Vessels of Brasse oft handled, brightly shine, . . .	Hero and Leander	1.231	
BRASSE-BULLETS			
And with brasse-bullets batter downe your Towers, . .	Jew	3.5.24	Basso
BRAT			
Here lyes my hate, Aeneas cursed brat, ...	Dido	3.2.1	Juno
Making them burie this effeminate brat, ...	2Tamb	4.1.162	Tamb
Ah cruel Brat, sprung from a tyrants loines, . . .	2Tamb	4.3.54	Jrslem
BRATS			
of a bigger size/Than all the brats ysprong from Typhons loins:	1Tamb	3.3.109	Bajzth
BRAV'D			
Yet would we not be brav'd with forrain power, . . .	1Tamb	3.1.13	Bajzth
Brav'd Mowberie in presence of the king, ...	Edw	1.1.111	Kent
BRAVDE			
I traitors all, rather then thus be bravde, . . .	Edw	3.1.214	Edward
BRAVE			
Brave Prince of Troy, thou onely art our God, . . .	Dido	1.1.152	Achat
Follow ye Troians, follow this brave Lord, . . .	Dido	1.2.1	Illion
Brave men at armes, abandon fruitles feares, . . .	Dido	1.2.32	Iarbus
Brave Prince, welcome to Carthage and to me, . . .	Dido	2.1.81	Dido
How now Getulian, are ye growne so brave, ...	Dido	3.3.19	Dido
The dreames (brave mates) that did beset my bed, . .	Dido	4.3.16	Aeneas
What length or bredth shal this brave towne containe? .	Dido	5.1.16	Achat
In every part exceeding brave and rich.	1Tamb	1.2.127	Souldr
He sends this Souldans daughter rich and brave, . .	1Tamb	1.2.186	Tamb
When Tamburlain and brave Theridamas/Have met us by the river	1Tamb	2.1.62	Cosroe
Is it not brave to be a King, Techelles?	1Tamb	2.5.51	Tamb
Is it not passing brave to be a King, ...	1Tamb	2.5.53	Tamb

BRAVE (cont.)				
Brave horses, bred on the white Tartarian hils: . .	1Tamb	3.3.151		Tamb
Environed with brave Argolian knightes, ...	1Tamb	4.3.2		Souldn
That such a base usurping vagabond/Should brave a king, or	1Tamb	4.3.22		Souldn
Two hundred thousand foot, brave men at armes, . . .	1Tamb	4.3.54		Capol
land, whose brave Metropolis/Reedified the faire Semyramis,	2Tamb	3.5.36		Orcan
where brave Assirian Dames/Have rid in pompe like rich .	2Tamb	5.1.76		Tamb
See now my Lord how brave the Captaine hangs. . . .	2Tamb	5.1.149		Amyras
Tis brave indeed my boy, wel done, ...	2Tamb	5.1.150		Tamb
Kingdomes made waste, brave cities sackt and burnt, . .	2Tamb	5.2.26		Callap
Farewell great [Governor], and brave Knights of Malta. .	Jew	1.2.32		Calym
Oh brave, master, I worship your nose for this. . .	Jew	2.3.173		Ithimr
As meet they will, and fighting dye; brave sport. . .	Jew	3.1.30		Ithimr
That's brave, master, but think you it wil not be known? .	Jew	4.1.8	P	Ithimr
I had not thought he had been so brave a man. . . .	Jew	4.4.16		Curtzn
And now, brave Bashawes, come, wee'll walke about/The ruin'd	Jew	5.2.18		Calym
Farewell brave Jew, farewell great Barabas. . . .	Jew	5.2.20		Calym
With all thy Bashawes and brave followers. . . .	Jew	5.3.39		Msngr
And fire the house; say, will not this be brave? . .	Jew	5.5.41		Barab
Yet dare you brave the king unto his face. . . .	Edw	1.1.116		Kent
But rather praise him for that brave attempt, . . .	Edw	1.4.268		Mortmr
The yonger Mortimer is growne so brave, ...	Edw	2.2.232		Edward
Unnatural wars, where subjects brave their king, . .	Edw	3.1.86		Queene
O brave Wagner.	F 384	1.4.42	P	Robin
O brave, prethee let's to it presently, for I am as dry as a	F 751	2.3.30	P	Dick
O brave, an Ape?	F1128	3.3.41	P	Robin
O brave Doctor.	F1546	4.5.42	P	All
O brave Robin, shal I have Nan Spit, and to mine owne use?	F App	p.234 29	P	Rafe
thats brave, Ile have fine sport with the boyes, Ile get nuts	F App	p.236 45	P	Robin
Ide make a brave living on him; hee has a buttocke as slicke as	F App	p.239 116	P	HrsCsr
thou affects, with Romulus, temples brave/Bacchus, Alcides,	Ovid's Elegies			3.7.51
BRAVELIE				
Boye, see you beare you bravelie to the king, . . .	Edw	3.1.72		Edward
Tell me sirs, was it not bravelie done?	Edw	5.5.116		Ltborn
BRAVELY				
Bearing his huntspeare bravely in his hand. . . .	Dido	3.3.33		Anna
Here father, cut it bravely as you did your own. . .	2Tamb	3.2.135	P	Celeb
Twas bravely done, and like a souldiers wife. . . .	2Tamb	3.4.38		Techel
Oh bravely fought, and yet they thrust not home. . .	Jew	3.2.5		Barab
Oh bravely done.	Jew	4.4.19		Pilia
'Twas bravely done:	Jew	5.1.84		Calym
Maintaine it bravely by firme policy, ...	Jew	5.2.36		Barab
Well, do it bravely, and be secret.	Edw	5.4.28		Mortmr
Wherewith the Students shall be bravely clad. . . .	F 118	1.1.90		Faust
But you shall heare how bravely I serv'd him for it; I went me	F1547	4.5.43	P	HrsCsr
I would bravely runne,/On swift steedes mounted till the race	Ovid's Elegies			3.2.9
BRAVER				
Zabina, mother of three braver boies, ...	1Tamb	3.3.103		Bajzth
But yet I have a braver way then these.	Edw	5.4.37		Ltborn
BRAVES				
would I beare/These braves, this rage, and suffer uncontrowld	Edw	3.1.13		Spencr
traitors, now tis time/To be avengd on you for all your braves,	Edw	3.1.225		Edward
BRAVEST				
I have the bravest, gravest, secret, subtil, bottle-nos'd knave	Jew	3.3.9	P	Ithimr
Oh, my master has the bravest policy.	Jew	3.3.12	P	Ithimr
I'le tell you the bravest tale how a Conjurer serv'd me; you	F1521	4.5.17	P	Carter
BRAV'ST				
Away base upstart, brav'st thou nobles thus? . . .	Edw	3.1.205		Penbrk
BRAWLE				
Brawle not (I warne you) for your lechery, . . .	2Tamb	4.3.75		Tamb
BRAWLING				
Nor that I studie not the brawling lawes, ...	Ovid's Elegies			1.15.5
BRAWNES				
will make thee slice the brawnes of thy armes into carbonadoes,	1Tamb	4.4.44	P	Tamb
BRAYE				
bleate, and an asse braye, because it is S. Peters holy day.	F App	p.232 27	P	Faust
BRAZEN (See also BRASEN)				
Then gan the windes breake ope their brazen doores, . .	Dido	1.1.62		Venus
As far as Boreas claps his brazen wings, ...	1Tamb	1.2.206		Tamb
And boult the brazen gates with barres of Iron. . .	Lucan, First Booke			62
In brazen tower had not Danae dwelt, ...	Ovid's Elegies			2.19.27
Was Danaes statue in a brazen tower, ...	Hero and Leander			1.146
BREACH				
Inforst a wide breach in that rampierd wall, . . .	Dido	2.1.174		Aeneas
And through the breach did march into the streetes, . .	Dido	2.1.189		Aeneas
Who entring at the breach thy sword hath made, . . .	1Tamb	2.7.9		Cosroe
Murther the Foe and save [the] <their> walles from breach.	2Tamb	3.2.82		Tamb
Filling the ditches with the walles wide breach, . .	2Tamb	3.3.7		Techel
of thy hold/Volleies of ordinance til the breach be made,	2Tamb	3.3.25		Therid
the breach the enimie hath made/Gives such assurance of our	2Tamb	5.1.2		Maxim
Yet could not enter till the breach was made. . . .	2Tamb	5.1.100		Tamb
Nor if my body could have stopt the breach, . . .	2Tamb	5.1.101		Govnr
Faiths breach, and hence came war to most men welcom. .	Lucan, First Booke			184
Looke how when stormy Auster from the breach/Of Libian Syrtes	Lucan, First Booke			496
BREACHES				
And with the breaches fall, smoake, fire, and dust, . .	2Tamb	3.3.59		Therid
As there be breaches in her battered wall. . . .	2Tamb	5.1.160		Tamb
BREAD				
That labours with a load of bread and wine, . . .	Jew	5.2.41		Barab
They give me bread and water being a king, . . .	Edw	5.5.62		Edward
Ile feede thy divel with horse-bread as long as he lives,	F App	p.234 30	P	Rafe
BREADTH				
Such breadth of shoulders as might mainely beare/Olde Atlas	1Tamb	2.1.10		Menaph

BREAK (See also BROAKE)			
Turn'd to dispaire, would break my wretched breast,	2Tamb	2.4.64	Zenoc
we wil break the hedges of their mouths/And pul their kicking	2Tamb	4.3.48	Techel
Away then, break into the Admirals house.	P 282	5.9	Guise
My heart doth break, I faint and dye.	P 550	11.15	Charls
BREAKE			
Then gan the windes breake ope their brazen doores,	Dido	1.1.62	Venus
Which I will breake betwixt a Lyons jawes.	Dido	3.3.38	Cupid
O Dido, blame not him, but breake his oares,	Dido	4.4.149	Dido
Theile breake his ships, O Proteus, Neptune, Jove,	Dido	5.1.255	Dido
I long to breake my speare upon his crest,	1Tamb	4.3.46	Arabia
Breake up the earth, and with their firebrands,	1Tamb	5.1.219	Bajzth
From whence the issues of my thoughts doe breake:	1Tamb	5.1.274	Bajzth
To breake his sword, and mildly treat of love,	1Tamb	5.1.327	Zenoc
Should breake out off the bowels of the clowdes/And fall as	2Tamb	2.2.14	Gazell
And with the cannon breake the frame of heaven,	2Tamb	2.4.104	Tamb
And breake their burning Lances in the aire,	2Tamb	4.1.204	Tamb
Breake through the hedges of their hateful mouthes,	2Tamb	4.3.46	Therid
For if we breake our day, we breake the league,	Jew	1.2.158	1Knght
and thou hast, breake my head with it, I'le forgive thee.	Jew	2.3.112	P Barab
poysons of the Stygian poole/Breake from the fiery kingdome;	Jew	3.4.103	Barab
Didst breake prison?	Jew	5.1.78	Calym
And know my lord, ere I will breake my oath,	Edw	1.1.85	Mortmr
Till I be strong enough to breake a staffe,	Edw	4.2.24	Prince
Breake may his heart with grones: deere Frederik see,	F1366	4.2.42	Benvol
That rowling downe, may breake the villaines bones,	F1414	4.2.90	Faust
or we'll breake all the barrels in the house, and dash out all	F1618	4.6.61	P HrsCsr
him now, or Ile breake his glasse-windowes about his eares.	F App	p.240 142	P HrsCsr
Breake heart, drop bloud, and mingle it with teares,	F App	p.243 38	OldMan
heady rout/That in chain'd troupes breake forth at every port;	Lucan, First Booke		489
Come breake these deafe dores with thy boysterous wind.	Ovid's Elegies		1.6.54
Bescratch mine eyes, spare not my lockes to breake,	Ovid's Elegies		1.7.65
How oft, that either wind would breake thy coche,	Ovid's Elegies		1.13.29
Even from your cheekes parte of a voice did breake.	Ovid's Elegies		2.5.16
With her I durst the Lybian Syrtes breake through,	Ovid's Elegies		2.16.21
A kind of twilight breake, which through the heare,	Hero and Leander		2.319
BREAKERS			
Upon the cursed breakers of our peace.	P 270	4.68	Charls
BREAKES			
the fatall poyson/Workes within my head, my brain pan breakes,	P 185	3.20	OldQn
Witnesse this hart, that sighing for thee breakes,	Edw	1.4.165	Queene
My swelling hart for very anger breakes,	Edw	2.2.200	Edward
From my imbracements thus he breakes away,	Edw	2.4.16	Queene
O speake no more my lorde, this breakes my heart.	Edw	5.5.71	Ltborn
So when this worlds compounded union breakes,	Lucan, First Booke		73
This breakes Towne gates, but he his Mistris dore.	Ovid's Elegies		1.9.20
To have his head control'd, but breakes the raines,	Hero and Leander		2.142
BREAKING			
for that one Laocoon/Breaking a speare upon his hollow breast,	Dido	2.1.165	Aeneas
Breaking my steeled lance, with which I burst/The rusty beames	2Tamb	2.4.113	Tamb
My daily diet, is heart breaking sobs,	Edw	5.3.21	Edward
BREAKS			
From whom the thunder and the lightning breaks,	2Tamb	5.1.184	Tamb
now breaks the kings hate forth,/And he confesseth that he	Edw	1.4.193	Queene
BREAKST			
Thou breakst the law of Armes unlesse thou kneele,	1Tamb	2.4.21	Mycet
BREAST (See also BREST)			
for that one Laocoon/Breaking a speare upon his hollow breast,	Dido	2.1.165	Aeneas
torne from his shoulders, and his breast/Furrowd with wounds,	Dido	2.1.203	Aeneas
Treading upon his breast, strooke off his hands.	Dido	2.1.242	Aeneas
Then touch her white breast with this arrow head,	Dido	2.1.326	Venus
Then shall I touch her breast and conquer her.	Dido	3.1.6	Cupid
doe know no wanton thought/Had ever residence in Didos breast.	Dido	3.1.17	Dido
That he might suffer shipwracke on my breast,	Dido	4.4.102	Dido
Why did it suffer thee to touch her breast,	Dido	4.4.145	Dido
Ah, life and soule still hover in his Breast,	1Tamb	3.2.21	Zenoc
Stick in his breast, as in their proper roomes.	1Tamb	5.1.226	Zabina
Fetch me some water for my burning breast,	1Tamb	5.1.276	Bajzth
Whose head hath deepest scarres, whose breast most woundes,	2Tamb	1.3.75	Tamb
Turn'd to dispaire, would break my wretched breast,	2Tamb	2.4.64	Zenoc
And Eagles wings join'd to her feathered breast,	2Tamb	3.4.62	Therid
Wrath kindled in the furnace of his breast,	2Tamb	4.1.9	Celeb
the towne will never yeeld/As long as any life is in my breast.	2Tamb	5.1.48	Govnr
That I may sheath it in this breast of mine,	2Tamb	5.1.143	Jrslem
And let no basenesse in thy haughty breast,	2Tamb	5.3.30	Usumc
Come let us chardge our speares and pierce his breast,	2Tamb	5.3.58	Tamb
Pinning upon his breast a long great Scrowle/How I with	Jew	2.3.197	Barab
O no, his soule is fled from out his breast,	P 552	11.17	QnMoth
Hell strives with grace for conquest in my breast:	F1741	5.1.68	Faust
BREASTS			
joyntly both/Beating their breasts and falling on the ground,	Dido	2.1.228	Aeneas
Warring within our breasts for regiment,	1Tamb	2.7.19	Tamb
some your children)/Might have intreated your obdurate breasts,	1Tamb	5.1.28	1Virgn
By equall portions into both your breasts:	2Tamb	5.3.171	Tamb
flinty hearts/Suppresse all pitty in your stony breasts,	Jew	1.2.142	Barab
Then has <in> the white breasts of the Queene of love.	F 156	1.1.128	Valdes
We sing, whose conquering swords their own breasts launcht,	Lucan, First Booke		3
How apt her breasts were to be prest by me,	Ovid's Elegies		1.5.20
The filthy prison faithlesse breasts restraines.	Ovid's Elegies		2.2.42
Go goodly <godly> birdes, striking your breasts bewaile,	Ovid's Elegies		2.6.3
BREATH			
Whereas the Southerne winde with brackish breath,	Dido	1.2.28	Cloan
Who for her sonnes death wept out life and breath,	Dido	2.1.4	Aeneas

Line	Work	Reference	Speaker
BREATH (cont.)			
In vaine my love thou spendst thy fainting breath,	Dido	5.1.153	Aeneas
And rue our ends senceles of life or breath:	Dido	5.1.328	Anna
On which the breath of heaven delights to play,	1Tamb	2.1.25	Menaph
As dooth the lightening, or the breath of heaven:	1Tamb	2.3.58	Tamb
And when they chance to breath and rest a space,	1Tamb	3.3.51	Tamb
As long as any blood or sparke of breath/Can quench or coole	1Tamb	5.1.284	Zabina
No breath ncr sence, nor motion in them both.	1Tamb	5.1.344	Anippe
and al the winds shall breath/Through shady leaves of every	2Tamb	2.3.15	Orcan
Drawes in the comfort of her latest breath/All dasled with the	2Tamb	2.4.13	Tamb
At every little breath that thorow heaven is blowen:	2Tamb	4.3.124	Tamb
The breath of life, and burthen of my soule,	2Tamb	5.3.186	Amyras
Oh that my sighs could turne to lively breath;	Jew	3.2.18	Govnr
The jouyce of Hebon, and Cocitus breath,	Jew	3.4.101	Barab
As I wud see thee hang'd; oh, love stops my breath:	Jew	4.3.53	Barab
Like thy breath, sweet-hart, no violet like 'em.	Jew	4.4.40	Ithimr
Then Barabas breath forth thy latest fate,	Jew	5.5.78	Barab
Then breath a while.	P 241	4.39	Guise
There shall not a Hugonet breath in France.	P 324	5.51	Guise
Breath out that life wherein my death was hid,	P 954	19.24	King
Shape we our course to Ireland there to breath.	Edw	4.5.3	Spencr
And rustling swing up as the wind fets breath.	Lucan, First Booke		392
Long shalt thou rest when Fates expire thy breath.	Ovid's Elegies		2.9.42
In sleeping shall I fearelesse drawe my breath?	Ovid's Elegies		2.19.55
When t'was the odour which her breath foorth cast.	Hero and Leander		1.22
Her breath as fragrant as the morning rose,	Hero and Leander		1.391
BREATH'D			
And I had breath'd a man made free from harme.	F1400	4.2.76	Faust
Breath'd darkenesse forth (darke night is Cupids day).	Hero and Leander		1.191
He kist her, and breath'd life into her lips,	Hero and Leander		2.3
BREATHE			
As to instruct us under what good heaven/We breathe as now, and	Dido	1.1.198	Aeneas
The ayre wherein they breathe, the water, fire,	Dido	4.4.75	Dido
Not all the curses which the furies breathe,	1Tamb	2.7.53	Tamb
And let her horses from their nostrels breathe/Rebellious winds	1Tamb	5.1.297	Bajzth
See, se Anippe if they breathe or no.	1Tamb	5.1.343	Zenoc
To breathe a while, our men with sweat and dust/All chockt well	Edw	3.1.191	SpncrP
And dyms the Welkin, with her pitchy breathe:	F 232	1.3.4	Faust
faire/As thou, or any man that [breathes] <breathe> on earth.	F 558	2.2.7	Mephst
was limitted/For foure and twenty yeares, to breathe on earth?	F1396	4.2.72	Faust
Adders and serpents, let me breathe a while:	F1980	5.2.184	Faust
BREATHED			
O Samarcanda, where I breathed first,	2Tamb	4.1.105	Tamb
BREATHES			
And all the trees are blasted with our breathes.	1Tamb	3.1.55	Bajzth
faire/As thou, or any man that [breathes] <breathe> on earth.	F 558	2.2.7	Mephst
BREATHING			
were scortcht/And all the earth like Aetna breathing fire:	2Tamb	5.3.233	Tamb
Breathing, in hope (malgrado all your beards,	Edw	2.5.5	Gavstn
street like to a Firmament/Glistered with breathing stars,	Hero and Leander		1.98
BREATHLES			
Or breathles lie before the citie walles.	1Tamb	3.1.15	Bajzth
BREATHLESSE			
Emperours and kings lie breathlesse at my feet.	1Tamb	5.1.469	Tamb
Bloody and breathlesse for his villany.	2Tamb	2.3.13	Gazell
and sacrifice/Mountaines of breathlesse men to Mahomet,	2Tamb	3.5.55	Callap
Breathlesse albeit he were, he rested not,	Hero and Leander		2.229
Breathlesse spoke some thing, and sigh'd out the rest;	Hero and Leander		2.280
BRED			
Brave horses, bred on the white Tartarian hils:	1Tamb	3.3.151	Tamb
A sturdy Felon and a base-bred Thiefe,	1Tamb	4.3.12	Souldn
Bred in the concave of some monstrous rocke:	F App	p.238 73	Knight
Suffring much cold by hoary nights frost bred.	Ovid's Elegies		2.19.22
What profit to us hath our pure life bred?	Ovid's Elegies		3.8.33
With famous pageants, and their home-bred beasts.	Ovid's Elegies		3.12.4
BREDTH			
What length or bredth shal this brave towne containe?	Dido	5.1.16	Achat
BREECHING			
Whose lookes were as a breeching to a boye.	Edw	5.4.55	Mortmr
BREED			
When looks breed love, with lookes to gaine the prize.	1Tamb	2.5.63	Therid
Breed litle strength to our securitie,	2Tamb	2.1.43	Sgsmnd
Will every savour breed a pangue of death?	P 72	2.15	Guise
Nor then was land, or sea, to breed such hate,	Lucan, First Booke		96
Where Mars his sonnes not without fault did breed,	Ovid's Elegies		3.4.39
BREEDE			
My stay no crime, my flight no joy shall breede,	Ovid's Elegies		2.17.25
Keepe her for me, my more desire to breede.	Ovid's Elegies		2.19.2
Oxen in whose mouthes burning flames did breede?	Ovid's Elegies		3.11.36
BREEDES			
Or if he loves, thy tale breedes his misfortune.	Ovid's Elegies		2.2.54
Such as a rose mixt with a lilly breedes,	Ovid's Elegies		2.5.37
BREEDS			
Be silent, Daughter, sufferance breeds ease,	Jew	1.2.238	Barab
al the world/Ransackt for golde, which breeds the world decay;	Lucan, First Booke		168
Some hidden influence breeds like effect.	Hero and Leander		2.60
BRENT			
That almost brent the Axeltree of heaven,	1Tamb	4.2.50	Tamb
BREST			
is massacred)/Infect thy gracious brest with fresh supply,	P 193	3.28	QnMarg
Upon the hauty mountains of my brest:	P 718	14.21	Navrre
Then come proud Guise and heere disgordge thy brest,	P 952	19.22	King
O the fatall poyson workes within my brest,	P1221	22.83	King

BREST (cont.)			
And dart her plumes, thinking to pierce my brest,	Edw	1.1.41	Gavstn
Unlesse his brest be sword proofe he shall die.	Edw	1.2.8	Mortmr
Sits wringing of her hands, and beats her brest.	Edw	1.4.188	Lncstr
Here man, rip up this panting brest of mine,	Edw	4.7.66	Edward
And tell thy message to my naked brest.	Edw	5.1.130	Edward
If mine will serve, unbowell straight this brest,	Edw	5.3.10	Edward
Ocean;/And swept the foming brest of [Artick] <Articks> Rhene.	Lucan, First Booke	372	
And in the brest of this slaine Bull are crept,	Lucan, First Booke	632	
Nor [leane] <leave> thy soft head on his boistrous brest.	Ovid's Elegies	1.4.36	
are in thy soft brest/But pure simplicity in thee doth rest.	Ovid's Elegies	1.11.9	
Strike boy, I offer thee my naked brest,	Ovid's Elegies	2.9.35	
Within my brest no desert empire beare.	Ovid's Elegies	2.9.52	
Ist womens love my captive brest doth frie?	Ovid's Elegies	3.2.40	
And fiercely knockst thy brest that open lyes?	Ovid's Elegies	3.5.58	
Tis said the slippery streame held up her brest,	Ovid's Elegies	3.5.81	
And knocks his bare brest with selfe-angry hands.	Ovid's Elegies	3.8.10	
A clowne, nor no love from her warme brest yeelds.	Ovid's Elegies	3.9.18	
Dishonest love my wearied brest forsake,	Ovid's Elegies	3.10.2	
Now love, and hate my light brest each way move;	Ovid's Elegies	3.10.33	
And laid his childish head upon her brest,	Hero and Leander	1.43	
How smooth his brest was, and how white his bellie,	Hero and Leander	1.66	
dive into the water, and there prie/Upon his brest, his thighs,	Hero and Leander	2.189	
Wherein Leander on her quivering brest,	Hero and Leander	2.279	
BRESTED			
Flint-brested Pallas joies in single life,	Hero and Leander	1.321	
BRESTS			
The Gods have eyes, and brests as well as men.	Ovid's Elegies	3.3.42	
Ah whether is [thy] <they> brests soft nature [fled] <sled>?	Ovid's Elegies	3.7.18	
In gentle brests,/Relenting thoughts, remorse and pittie rests.	Hero and Leander	2.215	
BRETHREN			
Was there such brethren, sweet Meander, say,	1Tamb	2.2.51	Mycet
I know you will; well brethren let us goe.	Jew	1.1.174	1Jew
Let me be us'd but as my brethren are.	Jew	1.2.91	Barab
Oh silly brethren, borne to see this day!	Jew	1.2.170	Barab
This is meere frailty, brethren, be content.	Jew	4.1.98	Barab
Truely my deere brethren, my Maister is within at dinner, with	F 215	1.2.22	P Wagner
you, and keepe you, my deere brethren <my deare brethren>.	F 218	1.2.25	P Wagner
Come brethren, let's about our businesse with good devotion.	F1076	3.2.96	P 1Frier
Come brethren, lets about our businesse with good devotion.	F App	p.232 29	P Frier
which bouldly faine themselves/The Romanes brethren, sprung of	Lucan, First Booke	429	
BREVIATED			
Th'abreviated <breviated> names of holy Saints,	F 238	1.3.10	Faust
BRIAR (See BRIERS)			
BRIBDE			
(Whom from his youth he bribde) needs make him king?	Lucan, First Booke	315	
BRIBES			
The unjust Judge for bribes becomes a stale.	Ovid's Elegies	1.10.38	
BRICKE			
<The> streetes straight forth, and paved with finest bricke,	F 789	3.1.11	Faust
BRIDE			
Marveile not though the faire Bride did incite/The drunken	Ovid's Elegies	1.4.7	
BRIDGE			
Or make a bridge of murthered Carcases,	2Tamb	1.3.93	Amyras
And make a bridge unto the battered walles.	2Tamb	5.1.68	Tamb
I feare the Guisians have past the bridge,	P 363	7.3	Ramus
Goe place some men upon the bridge,	P 421	7.61	Dumain
keele at [Antwerpe] <Anwerpe> <Antwarpes> <Antwerpes> bridge,	F 123	1.1.95	Faust
And make a bridge, thorough the moving Aire,	F 333	1.3.105	Faust
Upon the bridge, call'd Ponte Angelo,	F 817	3.1.39	Mephst
Thou hast no bridge, nor boate with ropes to throw,	Ovid's Elegies	3.5.3	
BRIDGES			
Over the which [foure] <two> stately Bridges leane,	F 815	3.1.37	Mephst
BRIDLE			
Ile bridle al your tongues/And bind them close with bits of	2Tamb	4.1.181	Tamb
To bridle their contemptuous cursing tongues,	2Tamb	4.3.44	Therid
They will talk still my Lord, if you doe not bridle them.	2Tamb	5.1.146	P Amyras
Bridle them, and let me to my coach.	2Tamb	5.1.148	Tamb
Bridle the steeled stomackes of those Jades.	2Tamb	5.3.203	Tamb
Bridle thy anger gentle Mortimer.	Edw	1.1.121	Warwck
Bagous whose care doth thy Mistrisse bridle,	Ovid's Elegies	2.2.1	
And on his loose mane the loose bridle laide.	Ovid's Elegies	3.4.16	
BRIEFE			
Bashaw, in briefe, shalt have no tribute here,	Jew	3.5.11	Govnr
BRIERS			
Amongst the pricking thornes, and sharpest briers,	F1411	4.2.87	Faust
BRIGANDINE			
Rowing with Christians in a Brigandine,	2Tamb	3.5.93	Jrslem
BRIGGANDINES			
The Galles and those pilling Briggandines,	1Tamb	3.3.248	Tamb
Five hundred Briggandines are under saile,	2Tamb	1.3.122	Therid
BRIGHT			
And I will spend my time in thy bright armes.	Dido	1.1.22	Ganimd
But bright Ascanius, beauties better worke,	Dido	1.1.96	Jupitr
But whether thou the Sunnes bright Sister be,	Dido	1.1.193	Aeneas
Or banquet in bright honors burnisht hall,	Dido	4.3.10	Aeneas
and with our Sun-bright armour as we march,	1Tamb	2.3.221	Tamb
That rooffes of golde, and sun-bright Pallaces,	1Tamb	4.2.62	Zabina
to see the Sun-bright troope/Of heavenly vyrgins and unspotted	1Tamb	5.1.324	Zenoc
which shine as bright/As that faire vail that covers all the	2Tamb	1.2.49	Callap
Now bright Zenocrate, the worlds faire eie,	2Tamb	1.3.1	Tamb
A greater Lamp than that bright eie of heaven,	2Tamb	4.2.88	Therid
Pav'd with bright Christall, and enchac'd with starres,	2Tamb	4.3.128	Tamb

BRIGHT (cont.)				
that shine as bright/As all the Lamps that beautifie the Sky,	2Tamb	5.3.156		Tamb
Lord Lodowicke, it sparkles bright and faire.	Jew	2.3.58		Barab
Gallop a pace bright Phoebus through the skie,	Edw	4.3.43		Edward
But dayes bright beames dooth vanish fast away,	Edw	5.1.69		Edward
Saba, or as beautifull/As was bright Lucifer before his fall.	F 542	2.1.154		Mephst
Where sitting <Being seated> in a Chariot burning bright,	F 758	2.3.37		2Chor
From the bright circle of the horned Moone,	F 762	2.3.41		2Chor
to see the Monuments/And situation of bright splendent Rome,	F 829	3.1.51		Faust
That Faustus name, whilst this bright frame doth stand,	F 841	3.1.63		Faust
hadst set/In yonder throne, like those bright shining Saints,	F1905	5.2.109		GdAngl
The bright shining of whose glorious actes/Lightens the world	F App	p.237 25		Emper
And with bright restles fire compasse the earth,	Lucan, First Booke			49
The midst is best; that place is pure, and bright,	Lucan, First Booke			58
Sword-girt Orions side glisters too bright.	Lucan, First Booke			664
Let the bright day-starre cause in heaven this day be,	Ovid's Elegies			2.11.55
So through the world shold bright renown expresse me.	Ovid's Elegies			3.1.64
Eryx bright Empresse turnd her lookes aside,	Ovid's Elegies			3.8.45
For much it greev'd her that the bright day-light,	Hero and Leander			2.303
But he the [days] <day> bright-bearing Car prepar'd.	Hero and Leander			2.330
BRIGHT-BEARING				
But he the [days] <day> bright-bearing Car prepar'd.	Hero and Leander			2.330
BRIGHTER				
Brighter than is the silver [Rhodope] <Rhodolfe>,	1Tamb	1.2.88		Tamb
Whose eies are brighter than the Lamps of heaven,	1Tamb	3.3.120		Tamb
and on his head/A Chaplet brighter than Apollos crowne,	2Tamb	5.2.33		Amasia
Brighter art thou then flaming Jupiter,	F1783	5.1.110		Faust
BRIGHTEST				
Blacke is the beauty of the brightest day,	2Tamb	2.4.1		Tamb
BRIGHTLY				
Although it shine as brightly as the Sun.	2Tamb	4.1.134		Tamb
Vessels of Brasse oft handled, brightly shine,	Hero and Leander			1.231
BRIGHTNES				
Whose brightnes such pernitious upstarts dim,	Edw	3.1.165		Herald
BRIGHTNESSE				
And dim the brightnesse of their neighbor Lamps:	1Tamb	4.2.34		Tamb
BRIGHTSOME				
But rather let the brightsome heavens be dim,	Jew	2.3.330		Lodowk
BRIM				
When thy waves brim did scarse my anckles touch.	Ovid's Elegies			3.5.6
BRIMSTONE				
for conjuring that ere was invented by any brimstone divel.	F App	p.233 20	P	Robin
BRINCKE				
And faintnes numm'd his steps there on the brincke:	Lucan, First Booke			196
BRING				
And bring the Gods to wonder at the game:	Dido	1.1.18		Ganimd
Come in with me, Ile bring you to my Queene,	Dido	1.2.42		Iarbus
And bring forth mightie Kings to Carthage towne,	Dido	3.2.75		Juno
Come servants, come bring forth the Sacrifize,	Dido	4.2.1		Iarbus
Bring me his oares, his tackling, and his sailes:	Dido	4.4.109		Dido
The Sunne from Egypt shall rich odors bring,	Dido	5.1.11		Aeneas
And givest not eare unto the charge I bring?	Dido	5.1.52		Hermes
Now bring him backe, and thou shalt be a Queene,	Dido	5.1.197		Dido
Goe Anna, bid my servants bring me fire.	Dido	5.1.278		Dido
to apprehend/And bring him Captive to your Highnesse throne.	1Tamb	1.1.48		Meandr
Let him bring millions infinite of men,	1Tamb	3.3.33		Usumc
Untill I bring this sturdy Tamburlain,	1Tamb	3.3.114		Bajzth
Which I will bring as Vassals to thy feete.	1Tamb	3.3.129		Tamb
Come bring them in, and for this happy conquest/Triumph, and	1Tamb	3.3.272		Tamb
Bring out my foot-stocle.	1Tamb	4.2.1		Tamb
with the scraps/My servitures shall bring the from my boord.	1Tamb	4.2.88		Tamb
Come bring in the Turke.	1Tamb	4.2.126		Tamb
And in your hands bring hellish poison up,	1Tamb	4.4.19		Bajzth
Were but to bring our wilfull overthrow,	1Tamb	5.1.5		Govnr
And bring us pardon in your chearfull lookes.	1Tamb	5.1.47		Govnr
Bring him forth, and let us know if the towne be ransackt.	1Tamb	5.1.194	P	Tamb
Not I, bring milk and fire, and my blood I bring him againe,	1Tamb	5.1.310	P	Zabina
and fire, and my blood I bring him againe, teare me in peeces,	1Tamb	5.1.311	P	Zabina
And bring Armados from the coasts of Spaine,	2Tamb	1.2.34		Callap
And I as many bring from Trebizon,	2Tamb	3.1.49		Trebiz
And bring him captive to your highnesse feet.	2Tamb	3.1.62		Soria
Then let us bring our light Artilery,	2Tamb	3.3.5		Techel
That bring fresh water to thy men and thee:	2Tamb	3.3.30		Techel
our mighty hoste/Shal bring thee bound unto the Generals tent.	2Tamb	3.5.111		Trebiz
Sirha, prepare whips, and bring my chariot to my Tent:	2Tamb	3.5.144	P	Tamb
Bring them my boyes, and tel me if the warres/Be not a life	2Tamb	4.1.78		Tamb
Then bring those Turkish harlots to my tent,	2Tamb	4.1.165		Tamb
Come bring them in to our Pavilion.	2Tamb	4.1.206		Tamb
And bring with them their bils of entry:	Jew	1.1.56		Barab
And twenty Waggons to bring up the ware.	Jew	1.1.60		Barab
And bid my Factor bring his loading in.	Jew	1.1.83		Barab
What? bring you Scripture to confirm your wrongs?	Jew	1.2.110		Barab
not a man surviv'd/To bring the haplesse newes to Christendome.	Jew	2.2.51		Bosco
To bring me to religious purity,	Jew	2.3.72		Barab
And bring his gold into our treasury.	Jew	4.1.163		1Fryar
sweet youth; did not you, Sir, bring the sweet youth a letter?	Jew	4.2.41	P	Ithimr
Send to the Merchant, bid him bring me silkes,	Jew	4.2.84		Curtzn
Oh bring us to the Governor.	Jew	5.1.7		Curtzn
I bring thee newes by whom thy sonne was slaine:	Jew	5.1.10		Curtzn
Dead, my Lord, and here they bring his body.	Jew	5.1.53		1Offcr
Doe but bring this to passe which thou pretendest,	Jew	5.2.84		Govnr
And bring it with me to thee in the evening.	Jew	5.2.108		Govnr
Malta's Governor, I bring/A message unto mighty Calymath;	Jew	5.3.13		Msngr

BRING (cont.)			
To bring the will of our desires to end.	P 144	2.87	Guise
To work the way to bring this thing to passe:	P 649	12.62	QnMoth
I come to bring you newes, that your brother the Cardinall of	P1122	21.16	P Frier
To see it done, and bring thee safe againe.	Edw	1.1.205	Edward
And could my crownes revenew bring him back,	Edw	1.4.308	Edward
My gratious lord, I come to bring you newes.	Edw	1.4.320	Queene
Nay, stay my lord, I come to bring you newes,	Edw	2.2.141	Mortmr
mine honor undertake/To carrie him, and bring him back againe,	Edw	2.5.80	Penbrk
to carrie him/Unto your highnes, and to bring him back.	Edw	3.1.100	Arundl
Reward for them can bring in Mortimer?	Edw	4.3.18	Edward
And windes as equall be to bring them in,	Edw	4.3.51	Edward
Farewell, I know the next newes that they bring,	Edw	5.1.125	Edward
Unlesse thou bring me newes of Edwards death.	Edw	5.4.46	Mortmr
I, I, so: when I call you, bring it in.	Edw	5.5.35	Ltborn
To comfort you, and bring you joyfull newes.	Edw	5.5.43	Ltborn
What murtherer? bring foorth the man I sent.	Edw	5.6.49	Mortmr
Bring him unto a hurdle, drag him foorth,	Edw	5.6.52	King
But bring his head back presently to me.	Edw	5.6.54	King
hearse, where it shall lie,/And bring my funerall robes:	Edw	5.6.95	King
I'le leavy souldiers with the coyne they bring,	F 119	1.1.91	Faust
O they are meanes to bring thee unto heaven.	F 406	2.1.18	GdAngl
Mephostophilis come/And bring glad tydings from great Lucifer.	F 416	2.1.28	Faust
Mephostophilis shall doe for him, and bring him whatsoever.	F 488	2.1.100	P Faust
And bring them every morning to thy bed:	F 538	2.1.150	Mephst
and you have done me great injury to bring me from thence, let	F 705.2	2.2.156A	P Sloth
And in eight daies did bring him home againe.	F 767	2.3.46	2Chor
Away and bring us word <again> with speed.	F 888	3.1.110	Pope
Go presently, and bring a banket forth,	F 977	3.1.199	Pope
Unlesse you bring them forth immediatly:	F1031	3.2.51	Pope
And bring in presence of his Majesty,	F1169	4.1.15	Mrtino
and thou bring Alexander and his Paramour before the Emperour,	F1254	4.1.100	P Benvol
Or bring before this royall Emperour/The mightie Monarch,	F1296	4.1.142	Faust
Maisters, I'le bring you to the best beere in Europe, what ho,	F1505	4.5.1	P Carter
And bring with him his beauteous Paramour,	F App	p.237 32	Emper
you bring Alexander and his paramour before the emperor?	F App	p.237 51	P Knight
at ease, if I bring his water to you, youle tel me what it is?	F App	p.240 118	P HrsCsr
let thy sword bring us home.	Lucan, First Booke		280
battailes fought with prosperous successe/May bring her downe,	Lucan, First Booke		286
To him I pray it no delight may bring,	Ovid's Elegies		1.4.67
Let Homer yeeld to such as presents bring,	Ovid's Elegies		1.8.61
What good to me wil either Ajax bring?	Ovid's Elegies		2.1.30
Whose life nine ages scarce bring out of date.	Ovid's Elegies		2.6.36
To bring that happy time so soone as may be.	Ovid's Elegies		2.11.56
My selfe will bring vowed gifts before thy feete,	Ovid's Elegies		2.13.24
Though Hindes in brookes the running waters bring,	Ovid's Elegies		2.16.35
I yeeld, and back my wit from battells bring,	Ovid's Elegies		2.18.11
What doest? thy wagon in lesse compasse bring.	Ovid's Elegies		3.2.70
What day was that, which all sad haps to bring,	Ovid's Elegies		3.11.1
How such a Poet could you bring forth, sayes,	Ovid's Elegies		3.14.13
BRINGERS			
To beggers shut, to bringers ope thy gate,	Ovid's Elegies		1.8.77
BRINGES			
An other poast, what newes bringes he?	Edw	5.1.128	Leistr
The number two no good divining bringes.	Ovid's Elegies		1.12.28
So wavering Cupid bringes me backe amaine,	Ovid's Elegies		2.9.33
Whether the subtile maide lines bringes and carries,	Ovid's Elegies		2.19.41
BRINGETH			
As now it bringeth sweetnesse to my wound,	1Tamb	5.1.420	Arabia
BRINGING			
Bringing the Crowne to make you Emperour.	1Tamb	1.1.135	Menaph
Bringing the strength of Europe to these Armes:	2Tamb	1.1.30	Orcan
Then see the bringing of our ordinance/Along the trench into	2Tamb	3.3.54	Therid
As we were bringing him to Killingworth.	Edw	5.4.85	Souldr
Bringing with us lasting damnation,	F1801	5.2.5	Lucifr
Slaughter to come, and swiftly bringing newes/Of present war,	Lucan, First Booke		467
BRINGS			
Who brings that Traitors head Theridamas,	1Tamb	2.2.32	Meandr
The more he brings, the greater is the spoile,	1Tamb	3.3.23	Techel
What other heavie news now brings Philemus?	1Tamb	5.1.377	Zenoc
He brings a world of people to the field,	2Tamb	1.1.67	Orcan
And see he brings it: Now, Governor, the summe?	Jew	5.5.19	Barab
The iterating of these lines brings gold;	F 544	2.1.156	Mephst
The framing of this circle on the ground/Brings Thunder,	F 546	2.1.158	Mephst
so (if truth you sing)/Death brings long life.	Lucan, First Booke		454
And brings good fortune, a rich lover plants/His love on thee,	Ovid's Elegies		1.8.31
Joyes with uncertaine faith thou takest and brings.	Ovid's Elegies		2.9.50
And say it brings her that preserveth me;	Ovid's Elegies		2.11.44
Loe Cupid brings his quiver spoyled quite,	Ovid's Elegies		3.8.7
all holy things/And on all creatures obscure darcknesse brings.	Ovid's Elegies		3.8.20
Oft bitter juice brings to the sicke reliefe.	Ovid's Elegies		3.10.8
BRINGST			
Then come thou neer, and tell what newes thou bringst.	P1166	22.28	King
BRINISH			
Phrigia to the sea/Which washeth Cyprus with his brinish waves,	2Tamb	3.5.12	Callap
And since this earth, dew'd with thy brinish teares,	2Tamb	4.2.8	Olymp
BRINKE (See also BRINCKE)			
Least water-nymphs should pull him from the brinke.	Hero and Leander		2.198
BRISEIS			
Achilles burnd Briseis being tane away:	Ovid's Elegies		1.9.33
Achilles burnt with face of captive Briseis,	Ovid's Elegies		2.8.11
BRISKE			
I have not seene a dapper jack so briske,	Edw	1.4.412	Mortmr

BRISTLE			
Standard round, that stood/As bristle-pointed as a thorny wood.	1Tamb	4.1.27	2Msngr
BRIST'LED			
With strong hand striking wild-beasts brist'led hyde.	Ovid's Elegies		3.9.26
BRISTLE-POINTED			
Standard round, that stood/As bristle-pointed as a thorny wood.	1Tamb	4.1.27	2Msngr
BRISTOW			
Come friends to Bristow, there to make us strong,	Edw	4.3.50	Edward
Edmund away, Bristow to Longshankes blood/Is false, be not found	Edw	4.6.16	Kent
My lord, the Maior of Bristow knows our mind.	Edw	4.6.40	Queene
Madam, the Maior and Citizens of Bristow,	Edw	4.6.47	Rice
BRITAINE			
To reade a lecture here in [Britanie] <Britaine>,	Jew	Prol.29	Machvl
BRITANIE			
To reade a lecture here in [Britanie] <Britaine>,	Jew	Prol.29	Machvl
Unto the proudest peere of Britanie:	Edw	2.2.42	Edward
BRITISH			
And all the Ocean by the British shore.	1Tamb	3.3.259	Tamb
BRITTAINE			
Sythia, Cilicia, Brittaine are as good,	Ovid's Elegies		2.16.39
BRITTISH			
The Belgians apt to governe Brittish cars;	Lucan, First Booke		427
BROACH (See BROUCH)			
BROAD			
Their shoulders broad, for complet armour fit,	1Tamb	3.3.107	Bajzth
Counterscarps/Narrow and steepe, the wals made high and broad,	2Tamb	3.2.69	Tamb
Where we will have [Gabions] <Galions> of sixe foot broad,/To	2Tamb	3.3.56	Therid
Quiet your self, you shall have the broad seale,	Edw	2.2.147	Edward
BROAKE			
Thy death broake amity and trainde to war,	Lucan, First Booke		119
That lawes were broake, Tribunes with Consuls strove,	Lucan, First Booke		179
Be broake with wheeles of chariots passing by.	Ovid's Elegies		1.12.14
And untild ground with crooked plough-shares broake.	Ovid's Elegies		3.9.14
BROILE (See also BROYLE)			
I have done what I could to stay this broile.	P 434	7.74	Anjoy
BROILES			
And now Navarre whilste that these broiles doe last,	P 565	11.30	Navrre
In making forraine warres and civile broiles.	P1029	19.99	King
In civill broiles between Navarre and me?	P1038	19.108	King
Corrupter of thy king, cause of these broiles,	Edw	2.5.10	Mortmr
In civill broiles makes kin and country men/Slaughter	Edw	4.4.6	Queene
Might they have won whom civil broiles have slaine,	Lucan, First Booke		14
Many a yeare these [furious] <firious> broiles let last,	Lucan, First Booke		667
out the date/Of slaughter; onely civill broiles make peace.	Lucan, First Booke		671
And with intestine broiles the world destroy,	Hero and Leander		1.251
BROKE			
since thou hast broke the league/By flat denyall of the	Jew	3.5.19	Basso
But I had thought the match had beene broke off,	Edw	2.1.25	Baldck
Which being broke the foot had easie passage.	Lucan, First Booke		224
Tav'ron peering/(His grave broke open) did affright the Boores.	Lucan, First Booke		582
Thou saiest broke with Alcides angry hand.	Ovid's Elegies		3.5.36
So that the truce was broke, and she alas,	Hero and Leander		2.285
BROKEN			
And by that meanes repaire his broken ships,	Dido	2.1.328	Venus
My Oares broken, and my Tackling lost,	Dido	3.1.107	Aeneas
That like unruly never broken Jades,	2Tamb	4.3.45	Therid
These Jades are broken winded, and halfe tyr'd,	2Tamb	5.1.129	Tamb
bleeding harts/Wounded and broken with your Highnesse griefe,	2Tamb	5.3.162	Amyras
with what a broken hart/And damned spirit I ascend this seat,	2Tamb	5.3.206	Amyras
For by this Answer, broken is the league,	Jew	3.5.34	Govnr
day, and ful of strife/Disolve the engins of the broken world.	Lucan, First Booke		80
And armes all naked, who with broken sighes,	Lucan, First Booke		191
Till Cupids bow, and fierie shafts be broken,	Ovid's Elegies		1.15.27
Snakes leape by verse from caves of broken mountaines/And	Ovid's Elegies		2.1.25
His broken bowe, his fire-brand without light.	Ovid's Elegies		3.8.8
Being fit broken with the crooked share,	Ovid's Elegies		3.9.32
BROKEN WINDED			
These Jades are broken winded, and halfe tyr'd,	2Tamb	5.1.129	Tamb
BROKERY			
And tricks belonging unto Brokery,	Jew	2.3.192	Barab
BROOD			
Drawne through the heavens by Steedes of Boreas brood,	Dido	1.1.55	Venus
[As] <A> brood of barbarous Tygars having lapt/The bloud of	Lucan, First Booke		327
have concluded/That Midas brood shall sit in Honors chaire,	Hero and Leander		1.475
BROOK			
I cannot brook thy hauty insolence,	P 862	17.57	King
BROOKE			
as hardly can we brooke/The cruell handling of our selves in	Jew	1.2.174	1Jew
I cannot brooke these hautie menaces:	Edw	1.1.134	Edward
Cease brother, for I cannot brooke these words:	Edw	1.1.160	Edward
What man of noble birth can brooke this sight?	Edw	1.4.12	MortSr
Think you that we can brooke this upstart pride?	Edw	1.4.41	Warwck
But cannot brooke a night growne mushrump,	Edw	1.4.284	Mortmr
My Lord I cannot brooke these injuries.	Edw	2.2.71	Gavstn
way how hardly I can brooke/To loose my crowne and kingdome,	Edw	5.1.51	Edward
Againe, this people could not brooke calme peace,	Lucan, First Booke		172
But I no partner of my glory brooke,	Ovid's Elegies		2.12.11
BROOKES			
Though Hindes in brookes the running waters bring,	Ovid's Elegies		2.16.35
BROOMES			
it will weare out ten birchin broomes I warrant you.	F1385	4.2.61	P Benvol
BROTH			
Assure thy selfe thou shalt have broth by the eye.	Jew	3.4.92	Barab

BROTH (cont.)			
I feare they know we sent the poyson'd broth.	Jew	4.1.26	Barab
I carried the broth that poyson'd the Nuns, and he and I,	Jew	4.4.20	P Ithimr
BROTHER			
O how would I with Helens brother laugh,	Dido	1.1.17	Ganimd
And made me take my brother for my sonne:	Dido	5.1.43	Aeneas
Brother Cosroe, I find my selfe agreev'd,	1Tamb	1.1.1	Mycet
Good brother tell the cause unto my Lords,	1Tamb	1.1.4	Mycet
Brother, I see your meaning well enough.	1Tamb	1.1.18	Mycet
What, shall I call thee brother?	1Tamb	1.1.103	Mycet
your investion so neere/The residence of your dispised brother,	1Tamb	1.1.181	Ortyg
And of that false Cosroe, my traiterous brother.	1Tamb	2.2.4	Mycet
The King your Brother is now hard at hand,	1Tamb	2.3.45	Tamb
My witlesse brother to the Christians lost:	1Tamb	2.5.42	Cosroe
That darted mountaines at her brother Jove:	1Tamb	5.1.511	Tamb
let us haste and meete/Our Army and our brother of Jerusalem,	2Tamb	2.3.43	Orcan
Now brother, follow we our fathers sword,	2Tamb	4.1.4	Amyras
Call foorth our laisie brother from the tent,	2Tamb	4.1.7	Celeb
Brother, ho, what, given so much to sleep/You cannot leave it,	2Tamb	4.1.11	Amyras
And take my other toward brother here,	2Tamb	4.1.34	Calyph
Yet brother Barabas remember Job.	Jew	1.2.180	1Jew
No doubt, brother, but this proceedeth of the spirit.	Jew	1.2.327	1Fryar
I, and of a moving spirit too, brother; but come,	Jew	1.2.328	2Fryar
Oh brother, brother, all the Nuns are sicke,	Jew	3.6.1	1Fryar
Oh brother, all the Nuns are dead, let's bury them.	Jew	3.6.44	1Fryar
Why, Brother, you converted Abigall;	Jew	4.1.106	Barab
Prince of Navarre my honourable brother,	P 1	1.1	Charls
but did you mark the Cardinall/The Guises brother, and the Duke	P 48	1.48	Admral
Plac'd by my brother, will betray his Lord:	P 294	5.21	Anjoy
Dearely beloved brother, thus tis written.	P 343	5.70	Guise
Yet by my brother Charles our King of France,	P 464	8.14	Anjoy
For if th'almighty take my brother hence,	P 469	8.19	Anjoy
O no, my loving brother of Navarre.	P 543	11.8	Charls
Thy brother Guise and we may now provide,	P 636	12.49	QnMoth
My brother Guise hath gathered a power of men,	P 642	12.55	Cardnl
Ile dispatch him with his brother presently,	P 651	12.64	QnMoth
when Duke Dumaine his brother is alive,	P1055	19.125	King
Yet lives/My brother Duke Dumaine, and many moe:	P1099	20.9	Cardnl
My noble brother murthered by the King,	P1107	21.1	Dumain
I am thy brother, and ile revenge thy death,	P1112	21.6	Dumain
brother the Cardinall of Loraine by the Kings consent is lately	P1122	21.16	P Frier
My brother Cardenall slaine and I alive?	P1125	21.19	Dumain
Brother of Navarre, I sorrow much,	P1139	22.1	King
Thankes to my Kingly Brother of Navarre.	P1150	22.12	King
Brother revenge it, and let these their heads,	Edw	1.1.117	Kent
Brother displaie my ensignes in the field,	Edw	1.1.136	Edward
I know it, brother welcome home my friend.	Edw	1.1.148	Edward
Brother, the least of these may well suffice/For one of greater	Edw	1.1.158	Kent
Cease brother, for I cannot brooke these words:	Edw	1.1.160	Edward
Ah brother, lay not violent hands on him,	Edw	1.1.189	Kent
Against the Earle of Cornewall and my brother?	Edw	2.2.35	Edward
Brother, doe you heare them?	Edw	2.2.69	Kent
And therefore brother banish him for ever.	Edw	2.2.211	Kent
When I thy brother am rejected thus.	Edw	2.2.218	Kent
He is your brother, therefore have we cause/To cast the worst,	Edw	2.3.7	Warwck
And to the king my brother there complaine,	Edw	2.4.66	Queene
That lord Valoyes our brother, king of Fraunce,	Edw	3.1.62	Queene
Brother, in regard of thee and of thy land,	Edw	3.1.230	Kent
A brother, no, a butcher of thy friends,	Edw	4.1.4	Kent
Yea gentle brother, and the God of heaven,	Edw	4.2.74	Queene
sir John of Henolt, brother to the Marquesse, into Flaunders:	Edw	4.3.31	P Spencr
Borne armes against thy brother and thy king?	Edw	4.6.6	Kent
So shall your brother be disposed of.	Edw	4.6.37	Mortmr
To set his brother free, no more but so.	Edw	5.2.33	BshpWn
Well, if my Lorde your brother were enlargde.	Edw	5.2.82	Queene
Brother, you know it is impossible.	Edw	5.2.97	Queene
My lord, he hath betraied the king his brother,	Edw	5.2.106	Mortmr
Brother Edmund, strive not, we are his friends,	Edw	5.2.114	Queene
O gentle brother, helpe to rescue me.	Edw	5.3.51	Edward
Seeing that my brother cannot be releast.	Edw	5.3.67	Kent
Either my brother or his sonne is king,	Edw	5.4.106	Kent
None such the sister gives her brother grave,	Ovid's Elegies		2.5.25
Or one that with her tender brother lies,	Ovid's Elegies		3.6.22
And as a brother with his sister toyed,	Hero and Leander		2.52
BROTHER'S			
my bitter curse/Like Cain by Adam, for his brother's death.	Jew	3.4.33	Barab
BROTHERS			
To be inamourd of thy brothers lookes,	Dido	3.1.2	Cupid
By heaven and earth, and my faire brothers bowe,	Dido	3.4.45	Aeneas
And languish in my brothers government:	1Tamb	1.1.156	Cosroe
will flie (my Lords)/To rest secure against my brothers force.	1Tamb	1.1.178	Cosroe
That leads to Pallace of my brothers life,	1Tamb	2.1.43	Cosroe
Like to the cruell brothers of the earth,	1Tamb	2.2.47	Meandr
Meander, you that were our brothers Guide,	1Tamb	2.5.10	Cosroe
The Lords and Captaines of my brothers campe,	1Tamb	2.5.26	Cosroe
And now Lord Tamburlaine, my brothers Campe/I leave to thee, and	1Tamb	2.5.38	Cosroe
I long to sit upon my brothers throne.	1Tamb	2.5.47	Cosroe
If thou exceed thy elder Brothers worth,	2Tamb	1.3.50	Tamb
But while my brothers follow armes my lord,	2Tamb	1.3.65	Calyph
Brothers to holy Mahomet himselfe,	2Tamb	3.3.36	Capt
To weare his brothers crowne and dignity.	P 557	11.22	QnMoth
Roomes infant walles were steept in brothers bloud;	Lucan, First Booke		95
thou bid me/Intombe my sword within my brothers bowels;	Lucan, First Booke		377

BROTHERS (cont.)
having fild/Her meeting hornes to match her brothers light, — Lucan, First Booke 536
a double point/Rose like the Theban brothers funerall fire; — Lucan, First Booke 550
And Hector dyed his brothers yet alive. — Ovid's Elegies 2.6.42

BROUCH
And a fine brouch to put in my hat, — Dido 1.1.47 Ganimd

BROUGHT
destinies/Have brought my sweete companions in such plight? — Dido 2.1.60 Aeneas
And brought unto the Court of Priamus: — Dido 2.1.154 Aeneas
And dead to honour that hath brought me up. — Dido 3.3.45 Aeneas
Whom I have brought from Ida where he slept, — Dido 5.1.40 Hermes
We knew my Lord, before we brought the crowne, — 1Tamb 1.1.179 Ortyg
Brought to the war by men of Tripoly: — 1Tamb 3.3.17 Bassoe
Whom I have brought to see their overthrow. — 1Tamb 3.3.81 Bajzth
are you so daintily brought up, you cannot eat your owne flesh? — 1Tamb 4.4.37 P Tamb
Brought up and propped by the hand of fame, — 1Tamb 5.1.265 Bajzth
Besides, king Sigismond hath brought from Christendome, — 2Tamb 1.1.20 Uribas
And die before I brought you backe again. — 2Tamb 1.2.73 Almeda
I and my neighbor King of Fesse have brought/To aide thee in — 2Tamb 1.3.130 Usumc
Whom I brought bound unto Damascus walles. — 2Tamb 3.2.125 Tamb
sudden fall/Has humbled her and brought her downe to this: — Jew 1.2.368 Mthias
In Trace; brought up in Arabia. — Jew 2.3.128 P Ithimr
When you have brought her home, come to my house; — Jew 2.3.148 Barab
What, hast thou brought the Ladle with thee too? — Jew 3.4.57 Barab
I have brought you a Ladle. — Jew 3.4.59 P Ithimr
I would have brought confusion on you all, — Jew 5.5.85 Barab
And brought by murder to their timeles ends. — P 46 1.46 Navrre
Having brought the Earle of Cornewall on his way, — Edw 1.4.300 Queene
Much more a king brought up so tenderlie. — Edw 5.5.6 Matrvs
Whereas his kinsmen chiefly brought him up; — F 14 Prol.14 1Chor
That <which> Julius caesar brought from Affrica. — F 824 3.1.46 Mephst
You brought us word even now, it was decreed, — F1019 3.2.39 Pope
Constantinople have they brought me now <am I hither brought>, — F1118 3.3.31 Mephst
spirit that I have, I had these grapes brought as you see. — F1586 4.6.29 P Faust
And brought the spoyles to rich Dardania: — F1695 5.1.22 Faust
I have brought you forty dollers for your horse. — F App p.239 101 P HrsCsr
swift spirit that I have, I had them brought hither, as ye see, — F App p.242 23 P Faust
The soldiours pray, and rapine brought in ryot, — Lucan, First Booke 163
and Rhene, which he hath brought/From out their Northren parts, — Lucan, First Booke 478
such and more strange/Blacke night brought forth in secret: — Lucan, First Booke 579
Let thy soft finger to thy eare be brought. — Ovid's Elegies 1.4.24
Her shut gates greater lightning then thyne brought. — Ovid's Elegies 2.1.20
But Venus often to her Mars such brought. — Ovid's Elegies 2.5.28
First Victory is brought with large spred wing, — Ovid's Elegies 3.2.45
Now is the goat brought through the boyes with darts, — Ovid's Elegies 3.12.21
Brought foorth the day before the day was borne. — Hero and Leander 2.322

BROUGHTST
And see at home much, that thou nere broughtst thether. — Ovid's Elegies 3.4.48

BROW
at whose latter gaspe/Joves marble statue gan to bend the brow, — Dido 2.1.257 Aeneas
Sometimes, like a Perriwig, I sit upon her Brow: — F 666 2.2.115 P Pride
<a threatning Arme, an angry Brow>. — F1944 (HC271)B Faust
A brow for Love to banquet roiallye, — Hero and Leander 1.86

BROWE
Girt my shine browe with sea banke mirtle praise <sprays>. — Ovid's Elegies 1.1.34
Though her sowre looks a Sabines browe resemble, — Ovid's Elegies 2.4.15

BROWES
Whose night and day descendeth from thy browes: — Dido 1.1.156 Achat
And he with frowning browes and fiery lookes, — 1Tamb 1.2.56 Techel
That by Characters graven in thy browes, — 1Tamb 1.2.169 Tamb
His lofty browes in foldes, do figure death, — 1Tamb 2.1.21 Menaph
Upon his browes was pourtraid ugly death, — 1Tamb 3.2.72 Agidas
To hide the folded furrowes of his browes, — 1Tamb 5.1.57 2Virgn
To be investers of thy royall browes, — 1Tamb 5.1.104 1Virgn
Sleep'st every night with conquest on thy browes, — 1Tamb 5.1.359 Zenoc
shadowing in her browes/Triumphes and Trophees for my — 1Tamb 5.1.512 Tamb
And in the furrowes of his frowning browes, — 2Tamb 1.3.77 Tamb
Can never wash from thy distained browes. — 2Tamb 4.1.110 Tamb
queintly dect/With bloomes more white than Hericinas browes, — 2Tamb 4.3.122 Tamb
Give me a look, that when I bend the browes, — P 157 2.100 Guise
The sworde shall plane the furrowes of thy browes, — Edw 1.1.94 Edward
I see my tragedie written in thy browes, — Edw 5.5.74 Edward
Shadowing more beauty in their Airie browes, — F 155 1.1.127 Valdes
God]/[Stretcheth out his Arme, and bends his irefull Browes]: — F1944 5.2.148A Faust
Words without voyce shall on my eye browes sit, — Ovid's Elegies 1.4.19
When most her husband bends the browes and frownes, — Ovid's Elegies 2.2.33
I sawe your nodding eye-browes much to speake, — Ovid's Elegies 2.5.15
Their <Your> youthfull browes with Ivie girt to meete him,/With — Ovid's Elegies 3.8.61

BROWNE
Browne Almonds, Servises, ripe Figs and Dates, — Dido 4.5.5 Nurse
Browne bils, and targetiers, foure hundred strong, — Edw 3.1.37 SpncrP
[And nut-browne girles in doing have no fellowe]. — Ovid's Elegies 2.4.40
Let me lie with thee browne Cypasse to day. — Ovid's Elegies 2.8.22

BROYLE
On burning forkes: their bodies [boyle] <broyle> in lead. — F1912 5.2.116 BdAngl

BROYLES
Daily inur'd to broyles and Massacres, — Dido 2.1.124 Aeneas
To leavy armes and make these civill broyles: — P 730 14.33 Navrre
And in remembrance of those bloudy broyles, — P1024 19.94 King

BROYLING
There are live quarters broyling on the coles, — F1913 5.2.117 BdAngl

BRUCE (See BRUSE)
BRUISE (See BRUSE)

BRUNO			
Saxon Bruno stoope,/Whilst on thy backe his hollinesse ascends	F 868	3.1.90	Raymnd
despite of all his Holinesse/Restore this Bruno to his liberty,	F 899	3.1.121	Faust
Concerning Bruno and the Emperour,	F 948	3.1.170	Pope
That Bruno, and the Germane Emperour/Be held as Lollords, and	F 954	3.1.176	Faust
And if that Bruno by his owne assent,	F 957	3.1.179	Faust
To censure Bruno, that is posted hence,	F 983	3.2.3	Mephst
That slept both Bruno and his crowne away.	F 988	3.2.8	Faust
Concerning Bruno and the Emperour.	F1015	3.2.35	1Card
That Bruno and the cursed Emperour/Were by the holy Councell	F1020	3.2.40	Pope
we all are witnesses/That Bruno here was late delivered you,	F1026	3.2.46	Raymnd
But where is Bruno our elected Pope,	F1160	4.1.6	Fredrk
thine, in setting Bruno free/From his and our professed enemy,	F1206	4.1.52	Emper
And if this Bruno thou hast late redeem'd,	F1212	4.1.58	Emper
BRUNO'S			
From Bruno's backe, ascends Saint Peters Chaire.	F 876	3.1.98	Pope
So kindly yesternight to Bruno's health,	F1175	4.1.21	Mrtino
And lay his life at holy Bruno's feet.	F1220	4.1.66	Faust
BRUNT			
My selfe will bide the danger of the brunt.	1Tamb	1.2.151	Tamb
Then in this bloudy brunt they may beholde,	P 713	14.16	Bartus
Yea stranger engines for the brunt of warre,	F 122	1.1.94	Faust
We bide the first brunt, safer might we dwel,	Lucan, First Booke		253
BRUNTS			
you that with me have borne/A thousand brunts, and tride me ful	Lucan, First Booke		301
BRUSE (Homograph)			
Because we heare Lord Bruse dooth sell his land,	Edw	3.1.53	Edward
But not too hard, least that you bruse his body.	Edw	5.5.113	Ltborn
BRUTISH			
Till time shall alter this our brutish shapes:	F1454	4.3.24	Benvol
from me, and I be chang'd/[Unto] <Into> some brutish beast.	F1968	5.2.172	Faust
Maids are not woon by brutish force and might,	Hero and Leander		1.419
BUBLING			
And had my being from thy bubling froth:	Dido	1.1.129	Venus
BUCKLED			
Before that Boreas buckled with your sailes?	Dido	1.2.19	Iarbus
Then buckled I mine armour, drew my sword,	Dido	2.1.200	Aeneas
BUCKLER			
Tis not the king can buckler Gaveston,	Edw	1.4.288	Mortmr
[King] <Kind> Edward is not heere to buckler thee.	Edw	2.5.18	Lncstr
BUCKLES			
With buckles of the purest gold.	Passionate Shepherd		16
BUD			
But first in bloud must his good fortune bud,	Dido	1.1.86	Jupitr
BUDA			
Now say my Lords of Buda and Bohemia,	2Tamb	2.1.1	Sgsmnd
BUDS			
Thy bosomes Roseat buds let him not finger,	Ovid's Elegies		1.4.37
A belt of straw, and Ivie buds,	Passionate Shepherd		17
BUGGES			
here are Bugges/Wil make the haire stand upright on your heads,	2Tamb	3.5.147	Tamb
BUILD			
Shall build his throne amidst those starrie towers,	Dido	1.1.98	Jupitr
She crav'd a hide of ground to build a towne,	Dido	4.2.13	Iarbus
Why, let us build a Citie of our owne,	Dido	4.3.37	Illion
And build the towne againe the Greekes did burne?	Dido	4.3.40	Illion
Here will Aeneas build a statelier Troy,	Dido	5.1.2	Aeneas
Why live we Bajazeth, and build up neasts,	1Tamb	5.1.249	Zabina
Forbids the world to build it up againe.	2Tamb	3.2.18	Calyph
And to command the citie, I will build/A Cytadell, that all	2Tamb	5.1.164	Tamb
To him, I'le build an Altar and a Church,	F 401	2.1.13	Faust
With strawie cabins now her courts should build.	Ovid's Elegies		2.9.18
He had not beene that conquering Rome did build.	Ovid's Elegies		2.14.16
BUILDE			
For this, my quenchles thirst whereon I builde,	P 107	2.50	Guise
Or who will helpe to builde Religion?	P1084	19.154	QnMoth
BUILDED			
Ride golden Love in Chariots richly builded.	Ovid's Elegies		1.2.42
A stately builded ship, well rig'd and tall,	Hero and Leander		1.225
BUILDING			
Why cosin, stand you building Cities here,	Dido	5.1.27	Hermes
BUILDINGS			
That shaken thrise, makes Natures buildings quake,	Dido	1.1.11	Jupitr
The stately buildings of faire Babylon,	2Tamb	5.1.63	Tamb
Ile fire his crased buildings and [inforse] <incense>/The	P1201	22.63	King
Ile fire thy crased buildings, and enforce/The papall towers,	Edw	1.4.100	Edward
[The] <Whose> buildings faire, and gorgeous to the eye,	F 788	3.1.10	Faust
BUILDS			
Who builds a pallace and rams up the gate,	Hero and Leander		1.239
BUILT			
that a strong built Citadell/Commands much more then letters	Jew	Prol.22	Machvl
And on that hope my happinesse is built:	Jew	3.4.17	Barab
And hath not he that built the walles of Thebes/With ravishing	F 579	2.2.28	Faust
that guardst/Roomes mighty walles built on Tarpeian rocke,	Lucan, First Booke		198
A woman against late-built Rome did send/The Sabine Fathers,	Ovid's Elegies		2.12.23
Built walles high towred with a prosperous hand.	Ovid's Elegies		3.12.34
BULGARIA			
How through the midst of Verna and Bulgaria/And almost to the	2Tamb	2.1.8	Fredrk
BULKE			
The Duke of Guise stampes on thy liveles bulke.	P 315	5.42	Guise
BULL			
And make faire Europe mounted on her bull,	2Tamb	1.1.42	Orcan
H'had never bellowed in a brasen Bull/Of great ones envy; o'th	Jew	Prol.25	Machvl

BULL (cont.)			
on the Altar/He laies a ne're-yoakt Bull, and powers downe	Lucan, First Booke		608
And in the brest of this slaine Bull are crept,	Lucan, First Booke		632
And she to whom in shape of [Swanne] <Bull> Jove came.	Ovid's Elegies		1.3.22
And she that on a faind Bull swamme to land,	Ovid's Elegies		1.3.23
and I fear'd the Bull and Eagle/And what ere love made Jove	Ovid's Elegies		1.10.7
The Mare askes not the Horse, the Cowe the Bull,	Ovid's Elegies		1.10.27
BULLES			
She first constraind bulles necks to beare the yoake,	Ovid's Elegies		3.9.13
Bulles hate the yoake, yet what they hate have still.	Ovid's Elegies		3.10.36
Or his Bulles hornes Europas hand doth hold.	Ovid's Elegies		3.11.34
BULLET			
And closde in compasse of the killing bullet,	1Tamb	2.1.41	Cosroe
And every bullet dipt in poisoned drugs.	1Tamb	5.1.222	Bajzth
A deadly bullet gliding through my side,	2Tamb	3.4.4	Capt
BULLETS			
And bullets like Joves dreadfull Thunderbolts,	1Tamb	2.3.19	Tamb
Direct our Bullets and our weapons pointes/And make our <your>	1Tamb	3.3.157	Tamb
The bullets fly at random where they list.	2Tamb	4.1.52	Calyph
Having as many bullets in his flesh,	2Tamb	5.1.159	Tamb
Wee'll send [thee] <the> bullets wrapt in smoake and fire:	Jew	2.2.54	Govnr
And with brasse-bullets batter downe your Towers,	Jew	3.5.24	Basso
the darke/(Swifter then bullets throwne from Spanish slinges,	Lucan, First Booke		231
BULLION			
Whole Chests of Gold, in Bullion, and in Coyne,	Jew	4.1.65	Barab
BULLS			
I saw how Bulls for a white Heifer strive,	Ovid's Elegies		2.12.25
BULS			
As when an heard of lusty Cymbrian Buls,	2Tamb	4.1.187	Tamb
horsemen fought/Upon Mevanias plaine, where Buls are graz'd;	Lucan, First Booke		470
BULWARK			
and covered waies/To keep the bulwark fronts from battery,	2Tamb	3.2.76	Tamb
BULWARKES			
Carkasses/Shall serve for walles and bulwarkes to the rest:	1Tamb	3.3.139	Bajzth
And stand as Bulwarkes twixt your selves and me,	F1427	4.2.103	Faust
BULWARKS			
The Bulwarks and the rampiers large and strong,	2Tamb	3.2.70	Tamb
Shal play upon the bulwarks of thy hold/Volleies of ordinance	2Tamb	3.3.24	Therid
BUNCH			
let him hang a bunch of keies on his standerd, to put him in	2Tamb	3.5.139 P	Tamb
At that bunch where the liver is, appear'd/A knob of flesh,	Lucan, First Booke		626
BUNDLE			
and the Horse-courser a bundle of hay for his forty Dollors.	F1497	4.4.41 P	Faust
BURBON			
Because the house of Burbon now comes in,	P 50	1.50	Admral
But tis the house of Burbon that he meanes.	P 644	12.57	Cardnl
And beate proud Burbon to his native home,	P1114	21.8	Dumain
BURBONITES			
Therfore an enemy to the Burbonites.	P 836	17.31	Guise
BURDEN (See also BURTHEN)			
Whose beautious burden well might make you proude,	Dido	1.1.124	Venus
you may be ashamed to burden honest men with a matter of truth.	F App	p.234 15 P	Rafe
Lets yeeld, a burden easly borne is light.	Ovid's Elegies		1.2.10
BURDENED			
The burdened axes with thy force will bend;	Lucan, First Booke		57
BURDENING			
Burdening their bodies with your heavie chaines,	1Tamb	3.3.48	Tamb
BURDENS			
Under great burdens fals are ever greevous;	Lucan, First Booke		71
BURGHERS			
fethered steele/So thick upon the blink-ei'd Burghers heads,	2Tamb	1.1.93	Orcan
Goe now and bind the Burghers hand and foot,	2Tamb	5.1.161	Tamb
BURGONET			
A Burgonet of steele, and not a Crowne,	Dido	4.4.42	Aeneas
Now every man put of his burgonet,	P 449	7.89	Guise
BURGONETS			
Shall weare white crosses on their Burgonets,	P 232	4.30	Guise
Gonzago, Retes, sweare by/The argent crosses in your burgonets,	P 275	5.2	Guise
BURIALL (See also BURYALL)			
Which if it chaunce, Ile give ye buriall,	Dido	5.1.176	Dido
And crave his triple worthy buriall.	1Tamb	3.2.112	Usumc
And every earth is fit for buriall.	Edw	5.1.146	Edward
So at Aeneas buriall men report,	Ovid's Elegies		3.8.13
BURIALS			
There I enrich'd the Priests with burials,	Jew	2.3.183	Barab
BURIE			
Making them burie this effeminate brat,	2Tamb	4.1.162	Tamb
BURIED			
Let the souldiers be buried.	1Tamb	5.1.316 P	Zabina
With whom I buried al affections,	2Tamb	4.2.23	Olymp
Since they are dead, let them be buried.	Jew	5.1.57	Govnr
BURIES			
but hee hides and buries it up as Partridges doe their egges,	Jew	4.2.58	P Ithimr
BURLADIE			
burladie I had neede have it wel roasted, and good sawce to it,	F App	p.229 11 P	Clown
BURLY			
There was such hurly burly in the heavens:	Dido	4.1.10	Achat
BURN'D			
cannot read, and therefore wish all books burn'd <were burnt>.	F 680	2.2.129 P	Envy
Poore Semele, among so many burn'd;	Ovid's Elegies		3.3.37
BURND			
Achilles burnd Briseis being tane away:	Ovid's Elegies		1.9.33
Love conquer'd shame, the furrowes dry were burnd,	Ovid's Elegies		3.9.29

BURNE (See also BRENT)			
And build the towne againe the Greekes did burne?	Dido	4.3.40	Illion
Now Dido, with these reliques burne thy selfe,	Dido	5.1.292	Dido
Thou shalt burne first, thy crime is worse then his:	Dido	5.1.297	Dido
Shall burne to cinders in this pretious flame.	Dido	5.1.301	Dido
And burne him in the fury of that flame,	1Tamb	2.6.32	Cosroe
Will sooner burne the glorious frame of Heaven,	1Tamb	4.2.10	Tamb
And vow to burne the villaines cruell heart.	2Tamb	3.1.56	Trebiz
So, burne the turrets of this cursed towne,	2Tamb	3.2.1	Tamb
That suffers flames of fire to burne the writ/Wherein the sum	2Tamb	5.1.190	Tamb
Why let us burne him for an heretick.	P 483	9.2	P 2Atndt
[To burne his Scriptures, slay his Ministers],	F 650	2.2.99A	Faust
I'le burne my bookes; [ah] <oh> Mephostophilis.	F1982	5.2.186	Faust
I burne, love in my idle bosome sits.	Ovid's Elegies		1.1.30
Unlesse I erre, full many shalt thou burne,	Ovid's Elegies		1.2.43
And with my brand these gorgeous houses burne.	Ovid's Elegies		1.6.58
I cryed, tis sinne, tis sinne, these haires to burne,	Ovid's Elegies		1.14.27
I [burne] <blushe>, and by that blushfull [glance] <glasse> am	Ovid's Elegies		2.4.12
for neither sunne nor wind/Would burne or parch her hands,	Hero and Leander		1.28
Eternall heaven to burne, for so it seem'd,	Hero and Leander		1.100
Love kindling fire, to burne such townes as Troy,	Hero and Leander		1.153
BURNED			
And burned is Apollo's Lawrell bough,	F2003	5.3.21	4Chor
BURNES			
I to the Torrid Zone where midday burnes,	Lucan, First Booke		16
A scorching flame burnes all the standers by.	Ovid's Elegies		1.2.46
Why burnes thy brand, why strikes thy bow thy friends?	Ovid's Elegies		2.9.5
And this is he whom fierce love burnes, they cry.	Ovid's Elegies		3.1.20
Burnes his dead body in the funerall flame.	Ovid's Elegies		3.8.6
And by thine eyes whose radiance burnes out mine.	Ovid's Elegies		3.10.48
Burnes where it cherisht, murders where it loved.	Hero and Leander		2.128
BURNING			
And I must perish in his burning armes.	Dido	3.4.22	Dido
Wherewith his burning beames like labouring Bees,	Dido	5.1.12	Aeneas
And prest out fire from their burning jawes:	1Tamb	2.6.6	Cosroe
Fetch me some water for my burning breast,	1Tamb	5.1.276	Bajzth
Shall lead his soule through Orcus burning gulfe:	2Tamb	2.3.25	Orcan
And let the burning of Larissa wals,	2Tamb	3.2.141	Tamb
And cast her bodie in the burning flame,	2Tamb	3.4.71	Olymp
Searing thy hatefull flesh with burning yrons,	2Tamb	3.5.123	Tamb
And breake their burning Lances in the aire,	2Tamb	4.1.204	Tamb
His anguish and his burning agony.	2Tamb	5.3.209	Amyras
No, but I doe it through a burning zeale,	Jew	2.3.87	Barab
This which I urge, is of a burning zeale,	Edw	1.4.256	Mortmr
Where sitting <Being seated> in a Chariot burning bright,	F 758	2.3.37	2Chor
Of ever-burning Phlegeton, I sweare,	F 827	3.1.49	Faust
Now with the flames of ever-burning fire,	F1135	3.3.48	Mephst
that shall pierce through/The Ebon gates of ever-burning hell,	F1224	4.1.70	Faust
On burning forkes: their bodies [boyle] <broyle> in lead.	F1912	5.2.116	BdAngl
this ever-burning chaire,/Is for ore-tortur'd soules to rest	F1914	5.2.118	BdAngl
And cruel field, nere burning Aetna fought:	Lucan, First Booke		43
His burning chariot plung'd in sable cloudes,	Lucan, First Booke		539
high; but headlong pitcht/Her burning head on bending Hespery.	Lucan, First Booke		545
The threatning Scorpion with the burning taile/And fier'st his	Lucan, First Booke		658
Oxen in whose mouthes burning flames did breede?	Ovid's Elegies		3.11.36
And offred as a dower his burning throne,	Hero and Leander		1.7
And shot a shaft that burning from him went,	Hero and Leander		1.372
BURNISHT			
Or banquet in bright honors burnisht hall,	Dido	4.3.10	Aeneas
Amongst so many crownes of burnisht gold,	2Tamb	1.2.30	Callap
your tongues/And bind them close with bits of burnisht steele,	2Tamb	4.1.182	Tamb
BURNT			
That after burnt the pride of Asia.	Dido	2.1.187	Aeneas
Which made the funerall flame that burnt faire Troy:	Dido	2.1.218	Aeneas
Viewing the fire wherewith rich Ilion burnt.	Dido	2.1.264	Aeneas
helpe Iarbus, Dido in these flames/Hath burnt her selfe, aye me,	Dido	5.1.315	Anna
The houses burnt, wil looke as if they mourn'd,	2Tamb	2.4.139	Tamb
Greek, is writ/This towne being burnt by Tamburlaine the great,	2Tamb	3.2.17	Calyph
Being burnt to cynders for your mothers death.	2Tamb	3.2.46	Tamb
Whose body with his fathers I have burnt,	2Tamb	3.4.36	Olymp
Whom I have thought a God? they shal be burnt.	2Tamb	5.1.176	Tamb
Kingdomes made waste, brave cities sackt and burnt,	2Tamb	5.2.26	Callap
The Northren borderers seeing [their] <the> houses burnt,/Their	Edw	2.2.179	Lncstr
cannot read, and therefore wish all books burn'd <were burnt>.	F 680	2.2.129	P Envy
And on a pile of Fagots burnt to death.	F 963	3.1.185	Faust
And burnt the toplesse Towers of Ilium?	F1769	5.1.96	Faust
Achilles burnt with face of captive Briseis,	Ovid's Elegies		2.8.11
Ere these were seene, I burnt: what will these do?	Ovid's Elegies		3.2.33
BURST			
Burst from the earth, crying, Aeneas flye,	Dido	2.1.207	Aeneas
Why burst you not, and they fell in the seas?	Dido	4.4.154	Dido
with which I burst/The rusty beames of Janus Temple doores,	2Tamb	2.4.113	Tamb
Whose chariot wheeles have burst th'Assirians bones,	2Tamb	5.1.71	Tamb
begins those deepe ingendred thoughts/To burst abroad, those	P 92	2.35	Guise
but being worne away/They both burst out, and each incounter	Lucan, First Booke		103
BURTHEN			
breadth of shoulders as might mainely beare/Olde Atlas burthen.	1Tamb	2.1.11	Menaph
and rid your royall shoulders/Of such a burthen, as outwaies	1Tamb	2.3.47	Tamb
Shaking the burthen mighty Atlas beares:	2Tamb	4.1.129	Tamb
Beare not the burthen of your enemies joyes,	2Tamb	5.3.22	Techel
The breath of life, and burthen of my soule,	2Tamb	5.3.186	Amyras
Oh holy Fryars, the burthen of my sinnes/Lye heavy on my soule;	Jew	4.1.48	Barab
under Turkish yokes/Shall groning beare the burthen of our ire;	Jew	5.2.8	Calym

BURTHEN (cont.)			
Oh how the burthen irkes, that we should shun.	Ovid's Elegies	2.4.6	
While rashly her wombes burthen she casts out,	Ovid's Elegies	2.13.1	
So sweete a burthen I will beare with eaze.	Ovid's Elegies	2.16.30	
And like a burthen greevde the bed that mooved not.	Ovid's Elegies	3.6.4	
BURTHENS			
Whose bodies with their heavy burthens ake.	Ovid's Elegies	2.13.20	
BURY (See also BURIE)			
Oh brother, all the Nuns are dead, let's bury them.	Jew	3.6.44	1Fryar
First helpe to bury this, then goe with me/And helpe me to	Jew	3.6.45	2Fryar
BURYALL			
We'll give his mangled limbs due buryall:	F1999	5.3.17	2Schol
BURYING			
In burying him, then he hath ever earned.	Edw	2.5.56	Lncstr
BUSH			
Here in this bush disguised will I stand,	Dido	1.1.139	Venus
O thou oft wilt blush/And say he likes me for my borrowed bush,	Ovid's Elegies	1.14.48	
BUSHY			
That I may conjure in some bushy <lustie> Grove,	F 178	1.1.150	Faust
BUSIE			
I am a little busie, Sir, pray pardon me.	Jew	2.3.231	Barab
How busie Barrabas is there above/To entertaine us in his	Jew	5.5.52	Calym
BUSINES			
Nay, no such waightie busines of import,	Dido	4.2.25	Anna
And now my Lords let us closely to our busines.	P 332	5.59	Guise
I have some busines, leave me to my selfe.	Edw	1.1.48	Gavstn
BUSINESSE			
For I have other businesse for thee.	Jew	3.4.110	Barab
And thus farre roundly goes the businesse:	Jew	5.2.110	Barab
Come brethren, let's about our businesse with good devotion.	F1076	3.2.96	P 1Frier
Come brethren, lets about our businesse with good devotion.	F App	p.232 29	P Frier
BUSINESSES			
round by Candie shoare/About their Oyles, or other businesses.	Jew	1.1.92	Barab
BUSKIN			
The Lydian buskin [in] fit [paces] <places> kept her.	Ovid's Elegies	3.1.14	
BUSKIND			
And Love triumpheth ore his buskind Poet.	Ovid's Elegies	2.18.18	
BUSKINES			
Love laughed at my cloak, and buskines painted,	Ovid's Elegies	2.18.15	
BUSKINS			
This saied, she mov'd her buskins gaily varnisht,	Ovid's Elegies	3.1.31	
With scepters, and high buskins th'one would dresse me,	Ovid's Elegies	3.1.63	
Buskins of shels all silvered, used she,	Hero and Leander	1.31	
BUSSETH			
Something still busseth in mine eares,	Edw	5.5.103	Edward
BUSY (See BUSIE)			
BUT			
I vow, if she but once frowne on thee more,	Dido	1.1.12	Jupitr
Might I but see that pretie sport a foote,	Dido	1.1.16	Ganimd
But as this one Ile teare them all from him,	Dido	1.1.40	Jupitr
Doe thou but say their colour pleaseth me.	Dido	1.1.41	Jupitr
But first in bloud must his good fortune bud,	Dido	1.1.86	Jupitr
But bright Ascanius, beauties better worke,	Dido	1.1.96	Jupitr
No bounds but heaven shall bound his Emperie,	Dido	1.1.100	Jupitr
Doe thou but smile, and clowdie heaven will cleare,	Dido	1.1.155	Achat
But what may I faire Virgin call your name?	Dido	1.1.188	Aeneas
But whether thou the Sunnes bright Sister be,	Dido	1.1.193	Aeneas
But for the land whereof thou doest enquire,	Dido	1.1.209	Venus
But what are you that aske of me these things?	Dido	1.1.214	Venus
But of them all scarce seven doe anchor safe,	Dido	1.1.222	Aeneas
But haples I, God wot, poore and unknowne,	Dido	1.1.227	Aeneas
And have not any coverture but heaven.	Dido	1.1.230	Aeneas
But are arived safe not farre from hence:	Dido	1.1.237	Venus
But thou art gone and leav'st me here alone,	Dido	1.1.247	Aeneas
But tell me Troians, Troians if you be,	Dido	1.2.17	Iarbus
I but the barbarous sort doe threat our ships,	Dido	1.2.34	Serg
Might we but once more see Aeneas face,	Dido	1.2.45	Serg
I cannot choose but fall upon my knees,	Dido	2.1.11	Achat
Here she was wont to sit, but saving ayre/Is nothing here, and	Dido	2.1.13	Achat
but saving ayre/Is nothing here, and what is this but stone?	Dido	2.1.14	Achat
I heare Aeneas voyce, but see him not,	Dido	2.1.45	Illion
But Illioneus goes not in such robes.	Dido	2.1.48	Achat
Well may I view her, but she sees not me.	Dido	2.1.73	Aeneas
But Troy is not, what shall I say I am?	Dido	2.1.76	Aeneas
But all in this that Troy is overcome,	Dido	2.1.112	Dido
Peeres/Heare me, but yet with Mirmidons harsh eares,	Dido	2.1.123	Aeneas
But Priamus impatient of delay,	Dido	2.1.173	Aeneas
Father of fiftie sonnes, but they are slaine,	Dido	2.1.234	Aeneas
Lord of my fortune, but my fortunes turnd,	Dido	2.1.235	Aeneas
King of this Citie, but my Troy is fired,	Dido	2.1.236	Aeneas
Yet who so wretched but desires to live?	Dido	2.1.238	Aeneas
Not mov'd at all, but smiling at his teares,	Dido	2.1.240	Aeneas
But suddenly the Grecians followed us,	Dido	2.1.278	Aeneas
But how scapt Helen, she that causde this warre?	Dido	2.1.292	Dido
But that I may enjoy what I desire:	Dido	3.1.9	Iarbus
But Dido is the favour I request.	Dido	3.1.18	Iarbus
No, but I charge thee never looke on me.	Dido	3.1.54	Dido
O that Iarbus could but fancie me.	Dido	3.1.62	Anna
Name not Iarbus, but sweete Anna say,	Dido	3.1.67	Dido
But tell them none shall gaze on him but I,	Dido	3.1.73	Dido
But now for quittance of this oversight,	Dido	3.1.84	Dido
but now thou art here, tell me in sooth/In what might Dido	Dido	3.1.101	Dido
shall be wrought/The warres of Troy, but not Troyes overthrow:	Dido	3.1.125	Dido

BUT (cont.)

Take what ye will, but leave Aeneas here.	Dido	3.1.127	Dido
So that Aeneas may but stay with me.	Dido	3.1.133	Dido
But speake Aeneas, know you none of these?	Dido	3.1.148	Dido
No Madame, but it seemes that these are Kings.	Dido	3.1.149	Aeneas
and thought by words/To compasse me, but yet he was deceiv'd:	Dido	3.1.156	Dido
But his fantastick humours pleasde not me:	Dido	3.1.158	Dido
But playd he nere so sweet, I let him goe:	Dido	3.1.160	Dido
But I had gold enough and cast him off:	Dido	3.1.162	Dido
But weapons gree not with my tender yeares:	Dido	3.1.164	Dido
But not so much for thee, thou art but one,	Dido	3.1.175	Dido
But I will take another order now,	Dido	3.2.6	Juno
But lustfull Jove and his adulterous child,	Dido	3.2.18	Juno
But I will teare thy eyes fro forth thy head,	Dido	3.2.34	Venus
If thou but lay thy fingers on my boy.	Dido	3.2.36	Venus
But that thou maist more easilie perceive,	Dido	3.2.66	Juno
And cannot talke nor thinke of ought but him:	Dido	3.2.73	Juno
But much I feare my sonne will nere consent,	Dido	3.2.82	Venus
Aeneas, thinke not but I honor thee,	Dido	3.3.1	Dido
But love and duetie led him on perhaps,	Dido	3.3.15	Aeneas
But should that man of men (Dido except)/Have taunted me in	Dido	3.3.26	Iarbus
But Dido that now holdeth him so deare,	Dido	3.3.76	Iarbus
But time will discontinue her content,	Dido	3.3.78	Iarbus
And then, what then? Iarbus shall but love:	Dido	3.3.82	Iarbus
Not sicke my love, but sicke:--	Dido	3.4.25	Dido
Nay, nothing, but Aeneas loves me not.	Dido	3.4.32	Dido
But now that I have found what to effect,	Dido	3.4.37	Dido
Never to like or love any but her.	Dido	3.4.51	Aeneas
But where were you Iarbus all this while?	Dido	4.1.31	Dido
But I will soone put by that stumbling blocke,	Dido	4.1.34	Dido
But may be slackt untill another time:	Dido	4.2.26	Anna
When sleepe but newly had imbrast the night,	Dido	4.3.17	Aeneas
And none but base Aeneas will abide:	Dido	4.3.20	Aeneas
But if I use such ceremonious thankes,	Dido	4.3.49	Aeneas
But when you were abourd twas calme enough,	Dido	4.4.27	Dido
Love made me jealous, but to make amends,	Dido	4.4.33	Dido
I, but it may be he will leave my love,	Dido	4.4.97	Dido
But though he goe, he stayes in Carthage still,	Dido	4.4.133	Dido
O cursed tree, hadst thou but wit or sense,	Dido	4.4.139	Dido
And yet I blame thee not, thou art but wood.	Dido	4.4.143	Dido
O Dido, blame not him, but breake his oares,	Dido	4.4.149	Dido
But dares to heape up sorrowe to my heart:	Dido	4.4.152	Dido
But hereby child, we shall get thither straight.	Dido	4.5.14	Nurse
Fourescore is but a girles age, love is sweete:--	Dido	4.5.32	Nurse
But what shall it be calde, Troy as before?	Dido	5.1.18	Illion
But that eternall Jupiter commands.	Dido	5.1.82	Aeneas
But here he is, now Dido trie thy wit.	Dido	5.1.86	Dido
But yet Aeneas will not leave his love?	Dido	5.1.98	Dido
Aeneas could not choose but hold thee deare,	Dido	5.1.126	Aeneas
But rather will augment then ease my woe?	Dido	5.1.152	Dido
But thou art sprung from Scythian Caucasus,	Dido	5.1.158	Dido
I but heele come againe, he cannot goe,	Dido	5.1.184	Dido
But he shrinkes backe, and now remembring me,	Dido	5.1.190	Dido
But wheres Aeneas? ah hees gone hees gone!	Dido	5.1.192	Dido
I crave but this, he stay a tide or two,	Dido	5.1.207	Dido
But I cride out, Aeneas, false Aeneas stay.	Dido	5.1.228	Anna
But he clapt under hatches saild away.	Dido	5.1.240	Anna
But see, Achates wils him put to sea,	Dido	5.1.258	Dido
But he remembring me shrinkes backe againe:	Dido	5.1.260	Dido
Nothing can beare me to him but a ship,	Dido	5.1.267	Dido
fleete, what shall I doe/But dye in furie of this oversight?	Dido	5.1.269	Dido
No but I am not, yet I will be straight.	Dido	5.1.271	Dido
But afterwards will Dido graunt me love?	Dido	5.1.288	Iarbus
None in the world shall have my love but thou:	Dido	5.1.290	Dido
But Anna now shall honor thee in death,	Dido	5.1.325	Anna
View but his picture in this tragicke glasse,	1Tamb	Prol.7	Prolog
But I refer me to my noble men,	1Tamb	1.1.21	Mycet
I meane it not, but yet I know I might,	1Tamb	1.1.26	Mycet
But ere he march in Asia, or display/His vagrant Ensigne in the	1Tamb	1.1.44	Meandr
Go frowning foorth, but come thou smyling home,	1Tamb	1.1.65	Mycet
But Tamburlaine, and that Tartarian rout,	1Tamb	1.1.71	Therid
But this it is that doth excruciate/The verie substance of my	1Tamb	1.1.113	Cosroe
But Menaphon, what means this trumpets sound?	1Tamb	1.1.133	Cosroe
I doubt not shortly but to raigne sole king,	1Tamb	1.1.175	Cosroe
But now you see these letters and commandes,	1Tamb	1.2.21	Tamb
But since I love to live at liberty,	1Tamb	1.2.26	Tamb
But tell me Maddam, is your grace betroth'd?	1Tamb	1.2.32	Tamb
But Lady, this faire face and heavenly hew,	1Tamb	1.2.36	Tamb
And these that seeme but silly country Swaines,	1Tamb	1.2.47	Tamb
But since they measure our deserts so meane,	1Tamb	1.2.63	Tamb
We will report but well of Tamburlaine.	1Tamb	1.2.81	Magnet
But this is she with whom I am in love.	1Tamb	1.2.108	Tamb
But are they rich? And is their armour good?	1Tamb	1.2.123	Tamb
But if they offer word or violence,	1Tamb	1.2.142	Tamb
Art thou but Captaine of a thousand horse,	1Tamb	1.2.168	Tamb
Forsake thy king and do but joine with me/And we will triumph	1Tamb	1.2.172	Tamb
Intending but to rase my charmed skin:	1Tamb	1.2.179	Tamb
But shall I proove a Traitor to my King?	1Tamb	1.2.226	Therid
No, but the trustie friend of Tamburlaine.	1Tamb	1.2.227	Tamb
But tell me, that hast seene him, Menaphon,	1Tamb	2.1.5	Cosroe
But I will have Cosroe by the head,	1Tamb	2.2.11	Mycet
What should we doe but bid them battaile straight,	1Tamb	2.2.18	Meandr
But if Cosroe (as our Spials say,	1Tamb	2.2.35	Meandr

BUT (cont.)

Which you that be but common souldiers,	1Tamb	2.2.63	Meandr
And doubt you not, but if you favour me,	1Tamb	2.3.10	Tamb
Was but a handful to that we will have.	1Tamb	2.3.17	Tamb
But when you see his actions [top] <stop> his speech,	1Tamb	2.3.26	Therid
I would intreat you to speak but three wise wordes.	1Tamb	2.4.25	Tamb
And none shall keepe the crowne but Tamburlaine:	1Tamb	2.5.7	Cosroe
Make but a jest to win the Persean crowne.	1Tamb	2.5.98	Tamb
But give him warning and more warriours.	1Tamb	2.5.103	Tamb
But as he thrust them underneath the hils,	1Tamb	2.6.5	Cosroe
That none can quence but blood and Emperie.	1Tamb	2.6.33	Cosroe
If you but say that Tamburlaine shall raigne.	1Tamb	2.7.63	Tamb
But if presuming on his silly power,	1Tamb	3.1.33	Bajzth
But if he dare attempt to stir your siege,	1Tamb	3.1.46	Argier
Be honored with your love, but for necessity.	1Tamb	3.2.30	Agidas
Your Highnesse needs not doubt but in short time,	1Tamb	3.2.32	Agidas
But let the yong Arabian live in hope,	1Tamb	3.2.57	Agidas
but most astonied/To see his choller shut in secrete thoughtes,	1Tamb	3.2.69	Agidas
Your men are valiant but their number few,	1Tamb	3.3.11	Bassoe
But wil those Kings accompany your Lord?	1Tamb	3.3.27	Tamb
but some must stay/To rule the provinces he late subdude.	1Tamb	3.3.28	Bassoe
But as I live that towne shall curse the time/That Tamburlaine	1Tamb	3.3.59	Tamb
But every common souldier of my Camp/Shall smile to see thy	1Tamb	3.3.85	Tamb
That never fought but had the victorie:	1Tamb	3.3.153	Tamb
But come my Lords, to weapons let us fall.	1Tamb	3.3.162	Tamb
But I shall turne her into other weedes,	1Tamb	3.3.180	Ebea
But that he lives and will be Conquerour.	1Tamb	3.3.211	Zenoc
But ere I die those foule Idolaters/Shall make me bonfires with	1Tamb	3.3.239	Bajzth
But speake, what power hath he?	1Tamb	4.1.20	Souldn
But Tamburlaine, by expedition/Advantage takes of your	1Tamb	4.1.38	Capol
But when Aurora mounts the second time,	1Tamb	4.1.54	2Msngr
But if these threats moove not submission,	1Tamb	4.1.58	2Msngr
But Villaine, thou that wishest this to me,	1Tamb	4.2.12	Tamb
But fixed now in the Meridian line,	1Tamb	4.2.38	Tamb
But ere I martch to wealthy Persea,	1Tamb	4.2.47	Tamb
To make me think of nought but blood and war.	1Tamb	4.2.55	Tamb
I doubt not but the Governour will yeeld,	1Tamb	4.2.113	Therid
But if he stay until the bloody flag/Be once advanc'd on my	1Tamb	4.2.116	Tamb
Not one should scape: but perish by our swords.	1Tamb	4.2.122	Tamb
But noble Lord of great Arabia,	1Tamb	4.3.29	Souldn
Famous for nothing but for theft and spoile,	1Tamb	4.3.66	Souldn
But if his highnesse would let them be fed, it would doe them	1Tamb	4.4.34	P Therid
for if she live but a while longer, shee will fall into a	1Tamb	4.4.49	P Tamb
but why is it?	1Tamb	4.4.64	P Tamb
How can it but afflict my verie soule?	1Tamb	4.4.67	Zenoc
I (my Lord) but none save kinges must feede with these.	1Tamb	4.4.109	P Therid
Were but to bring our wilfull overthrow,	1Tamb	5.1.5	Govnr
Nothing but feare and fatall steele my Lord.	1Tamb	5.1.109	1Virgn
But I am pleasde you shall not see him there:	1Tamb	5.1.113	Tamb
But goe my Lords, put the rest to the sword.	1Tamb	5.1.134	Tamb
But how unseemly is it for my Sex,	1Tamb	5.1.174	Tamb
As if there were no way but one with us.	1Tamb	5.1.201	Techel
But let us save the reverend Souldans life,	1Tamb	5.1.204	Therid
But such a Star hath influence in his sword,	1Tamb	5.1.232	Bajzth
But most accurst, to see the Sun-bright troope/Of heavenly	1Tamb	5.1.324	Zenoc
But see another bloody spectacle.	1Tamb	5.1.339	Zenoc
But as the Gods to end the Troyans toile,	1Tamb	5.1.392	Zenoc
But making now a vertue of thy sight,	1Tamb	5.1.428	Arabia
But here these kings that on my fortunes wait,	1Tamb	5.1.490	Tamb
Then doubt I not but faire Zenocrate/Will soone consent to	1Tamb	5.1.498	Tamb
But what became of faire Zenocrate,	2Tamb	Prol.6	Prolog
and Danes/[Feares] <feare> not Orcanes, but great Tamburlaine:	2Tamb	1.1.59	Orcan
Nor he but Fortune that hath made him great.	2Tamb	1.1.60	Orcan
Then County-Pallatine, but now a king:	2Tamb	1.1.104	Sgsmnd
But now Orcanes, view my royall hoste,	2Tamb	1.1.106	Sgsmnd
So prest are we, but yet if Sigismond/Speake as a friend, and	2Tamb	1.1.122	Orcan
But whilst I live will be at truce with thee.	2Tamb	1.1.130	Sgsmnd
But (Sigismond) confirme it with an oath,	2Tamb	1.1.131	Orcan
I thank thee Sigismond, but when I war/All Asia Minor, Affrica,	2Tamb	1.1.157	Orcan
with my heart/Wish your release, but he whose wrath is death,	2Tamb	1.2.6	Almeda
Ah were I now but halfe so eloquent/To paint in woords, what	2Tamb	1.2.9	Callap
But need we not be spied going aboord?	2Tamb	1.2.56	Almeda
but tel me my Lord, if I should goe, would you bee as good as	2Tamb	1.2.61	P Almeda
But yet me thinks their looks are amorous,	2Tamb	1.3.21	Tamb
But that I know they issued from thy wombe,	2Tamb	1.3.33	Tamb
That never look'd on man but Tamburlaine.	2Tamb	1.3.34	Tamb
But when they list, their conquering fathers hart:	2Tamb	1.3.36	Zenoc
But while my brothers follow armes my lord,	2Tamb	1.3.65	Calyph
But now my friends, let me examine ye,	2Tamb	1.3.172	Tamb
But neither man nor child in al the land:	2Tamb	1.3.197	Techel
But cals not then your Grace to memorie/The league we lately	2Tamb	2.1.27	Sgsmnd
But as the faith which they prophanely plight/Is not by	2Tamb	2.1.37	Baldwn
That could not but before be terrified:	2Tamb	2.2.22	Uribas
But in their deeds deny him for their Christ:	2Tamb	2.2.40	Orcan
But every where fils every Continent,	2Tamb	2.2.51	Orcan
Tis but the fortune of the wars my Lord,	2Tamb	2.3.31	Gazell
no more, but deck the heavens/To entertaine divine Zenocrate.	2Tamb	2.4.20	Tamb
For should I but suspect your death by mine,	2Tamb	2.4.61	Zenoc
But let me die my Love, yet let me die,	2Tamb	2.4.66	Zenoc
But since my life is lengthened yet a while,	2Tamb	2.4.71	Zenoc
for whose byrth/Olde Rome was proud, but gasde a while on her,	2Tamb	2.4.92	Tamb
Not lapt in lead but in a sheet of gold,	2Tamb	2.4.131	Tamb
And now I doubt not but your royall cares/Hath so provided for	2Tamb	3.1.20	Callap

BUT (cont.)

But that proud Fortune, who hath followed long/The martiall	2Tamb	3.1.27	Callap
But keep within the circle of mine armes.	2Tamb	3.2.35	Tamb
But now my boies, leave off, and list to me,	2Tamb	3.2.53	Tamb
My Lord, but this is dangerous to be done,	2Tamb	3.2.93	Calyph
But then run desperate through the thickest throngs,	2Tamb	3.2.139	Tamb
But stay a while, summon a parle, Drum,	2Tamb	3.3.11	Therid
Nor [any] issue foorth, but they shall die:	2Tamb	3.3.33	Techel
But Lady goe with us to Tamburlaine,	2Tamb	3.4.45	Therid
No Madam, but the beginning of your joy,	2Tamb	3.4.83	Techel
Nor ere returne but with the victory,	2Tamb	3.5.44	Trebiz
But yet Ile save their lives and make them slaves.	2Tamb	3.5.63	Tamb
But Shepheards issue, base borne Tamburlaine,	2Tamb	3.5.77	Orcan
But as for you (Viceroy) you shal have bits,	2Tamb	3.5.103	Tamb
But Tamburlaine, first thou shalt kneele to us/And humbly crave	2Tamb	3.5.108	Orcan
But now my followers and my loving friends,	2Tamb	3.5.159	Tamb
but that you wil be thought/More childish valourous than manly	2Tamb	4.1.16	Calyph
Content my Lord, but what shal we play for?	2Tamb	4.1.63	P Perdic
But matchlesse strength and magnanimity?	2Tamb	4.1.85	Amyras
But wher's this coward, villaine, not my sonne,	2Tamb	4.1.89	Tamb
But traitor to my name and majesty.	2Tamb	4.1.90	Tamb
But follie, sloth, and damned idlenesse:	2Tamb	4.1.126	Tamb
But since I exercise a greater name,	2Tamb	4.1.153	Tamb
But (wanting moisture and remorsefull blood)/Drie up with	2Tamb	4.1.179	Soria
But closde within the compasse of a tent,	2Tamb	4.2.3	Olymp
But when I saw the place obscure and darke,	2Tamb	4.2.15	Therid
But now I finde thee, and that feare is past.	2Tamb	4.2.20	Therid
entertaine a thought/That tends to love, but meditate on death,	2Tamb	4.2.26	Olymp
Nothing, but stil thy husband and thy sonne?	2Tamb	4.2.37	Therid
But that where every period ends with death,	2Tamb	4.2.47	Olymp
With which if you but noint your tender Skin,	2Tamb	4.2.65	Olymp
But was prevented by his sodaine end.	2Tamb	4.2.74	Olymp
What, can ye draw but twenty miles a day,	2Tamb	4.3.2	Tamb
But from Asphaltis, where I conquer'd you,	2Tamb	4.3.5	Tamb
and fit for nought/But perches for the black and fatall Ravens.	2Tamb	4.3.23	Tamb
twere but time indeed,/Lost long before you knew what honour	2Tamb	4.3.86	Tamb
But presently be prest to conquer it.	2Tamb	4.3.96	Techel
And have no terrour but his threatning lookes?	2Tamb	5.1.23	Govnr
not perswade you to submission,/But stil the ports were shut:	2Tamb	5.1.95	Tamb
Should I but touch the rusty gates of hell,	2Tamb	5.1.96	Tamb
But I have sent volleies of shot to you,	2Tamb	5.1.99	Tamb
But Tamburlain, in Lymnasphaltis lake,	2Tamb	5.1.115	Govnr
Save but my life and I wil give it thee.	2Tamb	5.1.118	Govnr
For he is God alone, and none but he.	2Tamb	5.1.202	Tamb
But that we leave sufficient garrison/And presently depart to	2Tamb	5.1.211	Tamb
But stay, I feele my selfe distempered sudainly.	2Tamb	5.1.218	Tamb
Something Techelles, but I know not what,	2Tamb	5.1.220	Tamb
But foorth ye vassals, what so ere it be,	2Tamb	5.1.221	Tamb
Doubt not my lord, but we shal conquer him.	2Tamb	5.2.12	Amasia
And but one hoste is left to honor thee:	2Tamb	5.2.27	Callap
But if he die, your glories are disgrac'd,	2Tamb	5.3.15	Therid
But as his birth, life, health and majesty/Were strangely blest	2Tamb	5.3.24	Techel
Looke where he goes, but see, he comes againe/Because I stay:	2Tamb	5.3.75	Tamb
But of a substance more divine and pure,	2Tamb	5.3.88	Phsitn
No doubt, but you shal soone recover all.	2Tamb	5.3.99	Phsitn
And could I but a while pursue the field,	2Tamb	5.3.117	Tamb
But I perceive my martial strength is spent,	2Tamb	5.3.119	Tamb
But sons, this subject not of force enough,	2Tamb	5.3.168	Tamb
Yet was his soule but flowne beyond the Alpes,	Jew	Prol.2	Machvl
But such as love me, gard me from their tongues,	Jew	Prol.6	Machvl
I count Religion but a childish Toy,	Jew	Prol.14	Machvl
And hold there is no sinne but Ignorance.	Jew	Prol.15	Machvl
But whither am I bound, I come not, I,	Jew	Prol.28	Machvl
But to present the Tragedy of a Jew,	Jew	Prol.30	Machvl
I crave but this, Grace him as he deserves,	Jew	Prol.33	Machvl
But he whose steele-bard coffers are cramb'd full,	Jew	1.1.14	Barab
But now how stands the wind?	Jew	1.1.38	Barab
But who comes heare? How now.	Jew	1.1.48	Barab
But art thou master in a ship of mine,	Jew	1.1.61	Barab
from Egypt, or by Caire/But at the entry there into the sea,	Jew	1.1.74	Barab
But this we heard some of our sea-men say,	Jew	1.1.78	1Merch
[But] <by> goe, goe thou thy wayes, discharge thy Ship,	Jew	1.1.82	Barab
But 'twas ill done of you to come so farre/Without the ayd or	Jew	1.1.93	Barab
Who hateth me but for my happinesse?	Jew	1.1.112	Barab
Or who is honour'd now but for his wealth?	Jew	1.1.113	Barab
But malice, falshood, and excessive pride,	Jew	1.1.117	Barab
but we have scambled up/More wealth by farre then those that	Jew	1.1.122	Barab
But one sole Daughter, whom I hold as deare/As Agamemnon did	Jew	1.1.137	Barab
And all I have is hers. But who comes here?	Jew	1.1.139	Barab
neither, but to passe along/Towards Venice by the Adriatick Sea;	Jew	1.1.162	Barab
But never could effect their Stratagem.	Jew	1.1.165	Barab
But there's a meeting in the Senate-house,	Jew	1.1.167	2Jew
'twere in my power/To favour you, but 'tis my fathers cause,	Jew	1.2.11	Calym
But a month.	Jew	1.2.27	Govnr
We grant a month, but see you keep your promise.	Jew	1.2.28	Calym
we have cast, but cannot compasse it/By reason of the warres,	Jew	1.2.47	Govnr
Let me be us'd but as my brethren are.	Jew	1.2.91	Barab
But here in Malta, where thou gotst thy wealth,	Jew	1.2.101	Govnr
'Tis not our fault, but thy inherent sinne.	Jew	1.2.109	1Knght
But say the Tribe that I descended of/Were all in generall cast	Jew	1.2.113	Barab
I, but theft is worse:	Jew	1.2.125	Barab
Content thee, Barabas, thou hast nought but right.	Jew	1.2.152	Govnr
But take it to you i'th devils name.	Jew	1.2.154	Barab

BUT (cont.)

And that will prove but simple policie.	Jew	1.2.159	1Knght
You were a multitude, and I but one,	Jew	1.2.178	Barab
but for every one of those,/Had they beene valued at	Jew	1.2.185	Barab
So that not he, but I may curse the day,	Jew	1.2.191	Barab
But give him liberty at least to mourne,	Jew	1.2.202	Barab
Our words will but increase his extasie.	Jew	1.2.210	1Jew
but trust me 'tis a misery/To see a man in such affliction:	Jew	1.2.211	2Jew
That measure nought but by the present time.	Jew	1.2.220	Barab
But whither wends my beauteous Abigall?	Jew	1.2.224	Barab
Not for my selfe, but aged Barabas:	Jew	1.2.228	Abigal
But I will learne to leave these fruitlesse teares,	Jew	1.2.230	Abigal
But they will give me leave once more, I trow,	Jew	1.2.252	Barab
To make a Nunnery, where none but their owne sect/Must enter in;	Jew	1.2.256	Abigal
I, but father they will suspect me there.	Jew	1.2.283	Abigal
but be thou so precise/As they may thinke it done of Holinesse.	Jew	1.2.284	Barab
But here they come; be cunning Abigall.	Jew	1.2.299	Barab
But, Madam, this house/And waters of this new made Nunnery	Jew	1.2.310	1Fryar
It may be so: but who comes here?	Jew	1.2.313	Abbass
No doubt, brother, but this proceedeth of the spirit.	Jew	1.2.327	1Fryar
I, and of a moving spirit too, brother; but come,	Jew	1.2.328	2Fryar
divine precepts/And mine owne industry, but to profit much.	Jew	1.2.335	Abigal
But say, What was she?	Jew	1.2.382	Lodowk
And of my former riches rests no more/But bare remembrance;	Jew	2.1.10	Barab
fortune were so good/As but to be about this happy place;	Jew	2.1.32	Abigal
But stay, what starre shines yonder in the East?	Jew	2.1.41	Barab
But I will practise thy enlargement thence:	Jew	2.1.53	Barab
But suddenly the wind began to rise,	Jew	2.2.13	Bosco
But one amongst the rest became our prize:	Jew	2.2.16	Bosco
But to admit a sale of these thy Turkes/We may not, nay we dare	Jew	2.2.21	Govnr
This truce we have is but in hope of gold,	Jew	2.2.26	1Knght
Captaine we know it, but our force is small.	Jew	2.2.34	Govnr
But she's at home, and I have bought a house/As great and faire	Jew	2.3.13	Barab
I, I, no doubt but shee's at your command.	Jew	2.3.39	Barab
but e're he shall have her	Jew	2.3.51	Barab
But when he touches it, it will be foild:	Jew	2.3.57	Barab
Pointed it is, good Sir,--but not for you.	Jew	2.3.60	Barab
I, but my Lord, the harvest is farre off:	Jew	2.3.79	Barab
And seeing they are not idle, but still doing,	Jew	2.3.83	Barab
No, but I doe it through a burning zeale,	Jew	2.3.87	Barab
It shall goe hard but I will see your death.	Jew	2.3.94	Barab
But now I must be gone to buy a slave.	Jew	2.3.95	Barab
And few or none scape but by being purg'd.	Jew	2.3.106	Barab
Ratest thou this Moore but at two hundred plats?	Jew	2.3.107	Lodowk
I must have one that's sickly, and be but for sparing vittles:	Jew	2.3.124	P Barab
But I have sworne to frustrate both their hopes,	Jew	2.3.142	Barab
But wherefore talk'd Don Lodowick with you?	Jew	2.3.150	Mthias
and my talke with him was [but]/About the borrowing of a booke	Jew	2.3.155	Mthias
Faith, Sir, my birth is but meane, my name's Ithimor,	Jew	2.3.165	Ithimr
But to thy selfe smile when the Christians moane.	Jew	2.3.172	Barab
But marke how I am blest for plaguing them,	Jew	2.3.199	Barab
But tell me now, How hast thou spent thy time?	Jew	2.3.201	Barab
But stand aside, here comes Don Lodowicke.	Jew	2.3.217	Barab
But goe you in, I'le thinke upon the account:	Jew	2.3.241	Barab
Whither but to my faire love Abigall?	Jew	2.3.252	Mthias
No, Mathias, no, but sends them backe,/And when he comes, she	Jew	2.3.261	Barab
But steale you in, and seeme to see him not;	Jew	2.3.272	Barab
no, but happily he stands in feare/Of that which you, I thinke,	Jew	2.3.282	Barab
Oh but I know your Lordship wud disdaine/To marry with the	Jew	2.3.294	Barab
'Tis not thy wealth, but her that I esteeme,	Jew	2.3.298	Lodowk
But keepe thy heart till Don Mathias comes.	Jew	2.3.307	Barab
But all are Hereticks that are not Jewes;	Jew	2.3.312	Barab
Nothing but death shall part my love and me.	Jew	2.3.317	Abigal
So have not I, but yet I hope I shall.	Jew	2.3.319	Barab
I know not, but farewell, I must be gone.	Jew	2.3.322	Abigal
Stay her,--but let her not speake one word more.	Jew	2.3.323	Barab
But rather let the brightsome heavens be dim,	Jew	2.3.330	Lodowk
Well, but for me, as you went in at dores/You had bin stab'd,	Jew	2.3.337	Barab
went in at dores/You had bin stab'd, but not a word on't now;	Jew	2.3.338	Barab
Suffer me, Barabas, but to follow him.	Jew	2.3.340	Mthias
But thou must dote upon a Christian?	Jew	2.3.360	Barab
I cannot choose but like thy readinesse:	Jew	2.3.377	Barab
that but for one bare night/A hundred Duckets have bin freely	Jew	3.1.2	Curtzn
But now against my will I must be chast.	Jew	3.1.4	Curtzn
I, but the Jew has gold,	Jew	3.1.14	Pilia
but here's the Jews man.	Jew	3.1.21	P Pilia
But thou wert set upon extreme revenge,	Jew	3.3.42	Abigal
And couldst not venge it, but upon his sonne,	Jew	3.3.44	Abigal
Nor on his sonne, but by Mathias meanes;	Jew	3.3.45	Abigal
Nor on Mathias, but by murdering me.	Jew	3.3.46	Abigal
But I perceive there is no love on earth,	Jew	3.3.47	Abigal
But here comes cursed Ithimore with the Fryar.	Jew	3.3.49	Abigal
But now experience, purchased with griefe,	Jew	3.3.61	Abigal
Abigal I will, but see thou change no more,	Jew	3.3.70	1Fryar
But who comes here?	Jew	3.4.13	Barab
For I have now no hope but even in thee;	Jew	3.4.16	Barab
But let 'em goe:	Jew	3.4.28	Barab
But perish underneath my bitter curse/Like Cain by Adam, for	Jew	3.4.32	Barab
I cannot thinke but that thou hat'st my life.	Jew	3.4.38	Barab
Oh trusty Ithimore; no servant, but my friend;	Jew	3.4.42	Barab
Goe buy thee garments: but thou shalt not want:	Jew	3.4.47	Barab
But first goe fetch me in the pot of Rice/That for our supper	Jew	3.4.49	Barab
But hush't.	Jew	3.4.54	Barab

BUT (cont.)

I but Ithimore seest thou this?	Jew	3.4.67	Barab
And nought is to be look'd for now but warres,	Jew	3.5.35	Govnr
sent for him, but seeing you are come/Be you my ghostly father;	Jew	3.6.11	Abigal
But e're I came--	Jew	3.6.15	Abigal
But I must to the Jew and exclaime on him,	Jew	3.6.42	2Fryar
No, but a worse thing:	Jew	3.6.50	2Fryar
That's brave, master, but think you it wil not be known?	Jew	4.1.8	P Ithimr
But here's a royall Monastry hard by,	Jew	4.1.13	Ithimr
No, but I grieve because she liv'd so long.	Jew	4.1.18	Barab
Fornication? but that was in another Country:	Jew	4.1.41	Barab
I, but Barabas, remember Mathias and Don Lodowick.	Jew	4.1.43	P 2Fryar
My bosome [inmate] <inmates> <intimates>, but I must dissemble.	Jew	4.1.47	Barab
may I compare/With all the Jewes in Malta; but what is wealth?	Jew	4.1.56	Barab
And so could I; but pennance will not serve.	Jew	4.1.60	Ithimr
But yesterday two ships went from this Towne,	Jew	4.1.69	Barab
I never heard of any man but he/Malign'd the order of the	Jew	4.1.103	Barab
But doe you thinke that I beleeve his words?	Jew	4.1.105	Barab
And so I will, oh Jacomo, faile not but come.	Jew	4.1.108	Barab
But Barabas, who shall be your godfathers,	Jew	4.1.109	1Fryar
But not a word to any of your Covent.	Jew	4.1.112	Barab
But are not both these wise men to suppose/That I will leave my	Jew	4.1.122	Barab
No more but so: it must and shall be done.	Jew	4.1.128	Barab
Nor goe to bed, but sleepes in his owne clothes;	Jew	4.1.132	Ithimr
Blame not us but the proverb, Confes and be hang'd.	Jew	4.1.146	P Barab
Who would not thinke but that this Fryar liv'd?	Jew	4.1.156	Barab
But soft, is not this Bernardine?	Jew	4.1.164	1Fryar
I have don't, but no body knowes it but you two, I may escape.	Jew	4.1.180	P 1Fryar
The Law shall touch you, we'll but lead you, we:	Jew	4.1.202	Barab
but the Exercise being done, see where he comes.	Jew	4.2.20	P Pilia
And ye did but know how she loves you, Sir.	Jew	4.2.53	Pilia
but hee hides and buries it up as Partridges doe their egges,	Jew	4.2.57	P Ithimr
Let me alone, doe but you speake him faire:	Jew	4.2.63	Pilia
But you know some secrets of the Jew,	Jew	4.2.64	Pilia
Write not so submissively, but threatning him.	Jew	4.2.72	P Pilia
and this shall be your warrant; if you doe not, no more but so.	Jew	4.2.76	P Ithimr
Content, but we will leave this paltry land,	Jew	4.2.88	Ithimr
But came it freely, did the Cow give down her milk freely?	Jew	4.2.102	P Ithimr
But ten?	Jew	4.2.114	P Ithimr
'Tis not thy mony, but thy selfe I weigh:	Jew	4.2.124	Curtzn
But thus of thee.--	Jew	4.2.126	Curtzn
But if I get him, Coupe de Gorge for that.	Jew	4.3.5	Barab
And when he comes: Oh that he were but here!	Jew	4.3.17	Barab
No; but three hundred will not serve his turne.	Jew	4.3.20	P Pilia
no childe, and unto whom/Should I leave all but unto Ithimore?	Jew	4.3.45	Barab
Here's many words but no crownes; the crownes.	Jew	4.3.46	P Pilia
nothing; but I know what I know.	Jew	4.4.14	P Ithimr
And fit it should: but first let's ha more gold.	Jew	4.4.26	Curtzn
Had we but proofe of this--	Jew	5.1.15	Govnr
I carried it, I confesse, but who writ it?	Jew	5.1.32	P Ithimr
I was imprison'd, but escap'd their hands.	Jew	5.1.77	Barab
but tell me, Barabas,/Canst thou, as thou reportest, make Malta	Jew	5.1.84	Calym
But Malta hates me, and in hating me/My life's in danger, and	Jew	5.2.30	Barab
But Barabas will be more circumspect.	Jew	5.2.43	Barab
too late/Thou seek'st for much, but canst not compasse it.	Jew	5.2.46	Barab
I see no reason but of Malta's wracke,	Jew	5.2.58	Govnr
Nor hope of thee but extreme cruelty,	Jew	5.2.59	Govnr
For as a friend not knowne, but in distresse,	Jew	5.2.72	Barab
Doe but bring this to passe which thou pretendest,	Jew	5.2.84	Govnr
Doe so, but faile not; now farewell Ferneze:	Jew	5.2.109	Barab
As be it valued but indifferently,	Jew	5.3.29	Msngr
There will he banquet them, but thee at home,	Jew	5.3.38	Msngr
There wanteth nothing but the Governors pelfe,	Jew	5.5.18	Barab
But wish thou hadst behav'd thee otherwise.	Jew	5.5.75	Govnr
And had I but escap'd this stratagem,	Jew	5.5.84	Barab
But now begins the extremity of heat/To pinch me with	Jew	5.5.87	Barab
But I have rather chose to save thy life.	Jew	5.5.94	Govnr
due praise be given/Neither to Fate nor Fortune, but to Heaven.	Jew	5.5.124	Govnr
From time to time, but specially in this,	P 10	1.10	Navrre
Now Guise may storme but doe us little hurt:	P 28	1.28	Navrre
But he that sits and rules above the clowdes,	P 42	1.42	Navrre
My Lord, but did you mark the Cardinall/The Guises brother, and	P 47	1.47	Admral
they be my good Lord, and he that smelles but to them, dyes.	P 74	2.17	P Pothec
Which cannot be extinguisht but by bloud.	P 93	2.36	Guise
I but, Navarre, Navarre.	P 149	2.92	Guise
Tis but a nook of France,/Sufficient yet for such a pettie	P 149	2.92	Guise
Him will we--but first lets follow those in France,	P 153	2.96	Guise
Not wel, but do remember such a man.	P 173	3.8	OldQn
but I hope it be/Only some naturall passion makes her sicke.	P 182	3.17	QnMarg
But look my Lord, ther's some in the Admirals house.	P 297	5.24	Retes
He mist him neer, but we have strook him now.	P 311	5.38	Guise
But slay as many as we can come neer.	P 326	5.53	Anjoy
All that I have is but my stipend from the King,	P 378	7.18	Ramus
Which is no sooner receiv'd but it is spent.	P 379	7.19	Ramus
And seen in nothing but Epitomies:	P 390	7.30	Guise
O good my Lord, let me but speak a word.	P 399	7.39	Ramus
But in my latter houre to purge my selfe,	P 402	7.42	Ramus
Because my places being but three, contains all his:	P 405	7.45	Ramus
I, so they are, but yet what remedy:	P 433	7.73	Anjoy
But yet my Lord the report doth run,	P 435	7.75	Navrre
Who I? you are deceived, I rose but now.	P 437	7.77	Anjoy
But come lets walke aside, th'airs not very sweet.	P 497	9.16	QnMoth
I, but my Lord let me alone for that,	P 519	9.38	QnMoth

BUT (cont.)

For Ile rule France, but they shall weare the crowne:	P 525	9.44	QnMoth
O Mounser de Guise, heare me but speake.	P 529	10.2	Prtsnt
But God will sure restore you to your health.	P 542	11.7	Navrre
But that we presently despatch Embassadours/To Poland, to call	P 555	11.20	QnMoth
But God that alwaies doth defend the right,	P 575	11.40	Navrre
Cannot but march with many graces more:	P 578	11.43	Pleshe
What now remaines, but for a while to feast,	P 627	12.40	King
But tis the house of Burbon that he meanes.	P 644	12.57	Cardnl
Faine would I finde some means to speak with him/But cannot,	P 663	13.7	Duchss
But Madam I must see.	P 677	13.21	Guise
Is Guises glory but a clowdy mist,	P 686	13.30	Guise
But villaine he to whom these lines should goe,	P 696	13.40	Guise
But for you know our quarrell is no more,	P 704	14.7	Navrre
But to defend their strange inventions,	P 705	14.8	Navrre
But canst thou tell who is their generall?	P 731	14.34	Navrre
But as report doth goe, the Duke of Joyeux/Hath made great sute	P 733	14.36	1Msngr
But he doth lurke within his drousie couch,	P 737	14.40	Navrre
But come my Lords, let us away with speed,	P 741	14.44	Navrre
I know none els but holdes them in disgrace:	P 764	15.22	Guise
But wherfore beares he me such deadly hate?	P 779	15.37	Mugern
But which way is he gone?	P 783	15.41	Mugern
But God we know will alwaies put them downe,	P 798	16.12	Navrre
And although you take out nothing but your owne, yet you put in	P 808	17.3	P Souldr
But we presume it is not for our good.	P 824	17.19	King
What Peere in France but thou (aspiring Guise)/Durst be in	P 828	17.23	Eprnon
What should I doe but stand upon my guarde?	P 839	17.34	Guise
But trust him not my Lord,	P 871	17.66	Eprnon
Thinke not but I am tragicall within:	P 894	17.89	King
But as I live, so sure the Guise shall dye.	P 899	17.94	King
Which cannot but be thankfully receiv'd.	P 906	18.7	Bartus
But if that God doe prosper mine attempts,	P 927	18.28	Navrre
But when will he come that we may murther him?	P 937	19.7	P 3Mur
But are they resolute and armde to kill,	P 949	19.19	King
Now doe I but begin to look about,	P 985	19.55	Guise
But see where he comes.	P1018	19.88	Capt
But what availeth that this traitors dead,	P1054	19.124	King
But now I will be King and rule my selfe,	P1070	19.140	King
But sorrow seaze upon my toyling soule,	P1089	19.159	QnMoth
Then there is no remedye but I must dye?	P1096	20.6	Cardnl
But thats prevented, for to end his life,	P1119	21.13	Dumain
My Lord, here me but speak.	P1129	21.23	P Frier
But what doth move thee above the rest to doe the deed?	P1132	21.26	P Dumain
But how wilt thou get opportunitye?	P1135	21.29	Dumain
Yes Navarre, but not to death I hope.	P1177	22.39	King
Weep not sweet Navarre, but revenge my death.	P1234	22.96	King
But he that makes most lavish of his bloud.	P1240	22.102	King
thoughe you take out none but your owne treasure	Paris	ms 3,p390	P Souldr
But you will saye you leave him rome enoughe besides:	Paris	ms 6,p390	P Souldr
But that it harbors him I hold so deare,	Edw	1.1.13	Gavstn
My knee shall bowe to none but to the king.	Edw	1.1.19	Gavstn
As for the multitude that are but sparkes,	Edw	1.1.20	Gavstn
But how now, what are these?	Edw	1.1.24	Gavstn
But I have no horses. What art thou?	Edw	1.1.28	Gavstn
But yet it is no paine to speake men faire,	Edw	1.1.42	Gavstn
But for that base and obscure Gaveston:	Edw	1.1.101	Lncstr
But now ile speake, and to the proofe I hope:	Edw	1.1.108	Kent
He should have lost his head, but with his looke,	Edw	1.1.113	Kent
Ile give thee more, for but to honour thee,	Edw	1.1.164	Edward
But is that wicked Gaveston returnd?	Edw	1.1.177	BshpCv
Tis true, and but for reverence of these robes,	Edw	1.1.180	Gavstn
No, spare his life, but seaze upon his goods,	Edw	1.1.193	Edward
But in the meane time Gaveston away,	Edw	1.1.202	Edward
All stomack him, but none dare speake a word.	Edw	1.2.26	Lncstr
But dotes upon the love of Gaveston.	Edw	1.2.50	Queene
But yet lift not your swords against the king.	Edw	1.2.61	ArchBp
No, but weele lift Gaveston from hence.	Edw	1.2.62	Lncstr
My lords, to eaze all this, but heare me speake.	Edw	1.2.68	ArchBp
But say my lord, where shall this meeting bee?	Edw	1.2.74	Warwck
But I long more to see him banisht hence.	Edw	1.4.5	Warwck
No, threaten not my lord, but pay them home.	Edw	1.4.26	Gavstn
I there it goes, but yet I will not yeeld,	Edw	1.4.56	Edward
Then linger not my lord but do it straight.	Edw	1.4.58	Lncstr
Ah none but rude and savage minded men,	Edw	1.4.78	Edward
But I will raigne to be reveng'd of them,	Edw	1.4.111	Edward
But to forsake you, in whose gratious lookes/The blessednes of	Edw	1.4.120	Gavstn
Happie were I, but now most miserable.	Edw	1.4.129	Edward
But come sweete friend, ile beare thee on thy way.	Edw	1.4.140	Edward
On whom but on my husband should I fawne?	Edw	1.4.146	Queene
But thou must call mine honor thus in question?	Edw	1.4.152	Queene
But I would wish thee reconcile the lords,	Edw	1.4.156	Edward
But that will more exasperate his wrath,	Edw	1.4.182	Queene
Theres none here, but would run his horse to death.	Edw	1.4.207	Warwck
But madam, would you have us cal him home?	Edw	1.4.208	Mortmr
It is impossible, but speake your minde.	Edw	1.4.228	Mortmr
Then thus, but none shal heare it but our selves.	Edw	1.4.229	Queene
No? doe but marke how earnestly she pleads.	Edw	1.4.234	Warwck
Tis not for his sake, but for our availe:	Edw	1.4.242	Mortmr
Why then my lord, give me but leave to speak.	Edw	1.4.254	Mortmr
But nephew, do not play the sophister.	Edw	1.4.255	MortSr
Marke you but that my lord of Lancaster.	Edw	1.4.263	Warwck
But were he here, detested as he is,	Edw	1.4.264	Mortmr
But rather praise him for that brave attempt,	Edw	1.4.268	Mortmr

BUT (cont.)

I, but how chance this was not done before?	Edw	1.4.272	Lncstr
But how if he do not Nephew?	Edw	1.4.278	MortSr
But cannot brooke a night growne mushrump,	Edw	1.4.284	Mortmr
But see in happie time, my lord the king,	Edw	1.4.299	Queene
would he lov'd me/But halfe so much, then were I treble blest.	Edw	1.4.304	Queene
But will you love me, if you finde it so?	Edw	1.4.324	Queene
For Gaveston, but not for Isabell.	Edw	1.4.326	Queene
But wherefore walkes yong Mortimer aside?	Edw	1.4.353	Edward
And not kings onelie, but the wisest men,	Edw	1.4.395	MortSr
But this I scorne, that one so baselie borne,	Edw	1.4.403	Mortmr
But nephew, now you see the king is changd.	Edw	1.4.420	MortSr
But whiles I have a sword, a hand, a hart,	Edw	1.4.422	Mortmr
But he that hath the favour of a king,	Edw	2.1.8	Spencr
But he is banisht, theres small hope of him.	Edw	2.1.15	Baldck
I for a while, but Baldock marke the end,	Edw	2.1.16	Spencr
But I had thought the match had beene broke off,	Edw	2.1.25	Baldck
And use them but of meere hypocrisie.	Edw	2.1.45	Baldck
But one of those that saith quandoquidem,	Edw	2.1.54	Spencr
But rest thee here where Gaveston shall sleepe.	Edw	2.1.65	Neece
Nothing but Gaveston, what means your grace?	Edw	2.2.7	Mortmr
But tell me Mortimer, whats thy devise,	Edw	2.2.11	Edward
But seeing you are so desirous, thus it is:	Edw	2.2.15	Mortmr
No sooner is it up, but thers a foule,	Edw	2.2.26	Lncstr
What call you this but private libelling,	Edw	2.2.34	Edward
But if I live, ile tread upon their heads,	Edw	2.2.96	Edward
Who should defray the money, but the King,	Edw	2.2.118	Mortmr
Whither else but to the King.	Edw	2.2.134	Mortmr
Why, so he may, but we will speake to him.	Edw	2.2.136	Lncstr
the Mortimers/Are not so poore, but would they sell their land,	Edw	2.2.151	Mortmr
We never beg, but use such praiers as these.	Edw	2.2.153	Mortmr
Who loves thee? but a sort of flatterers.	Edw	2.2.171	Mortmr
But once, and then thy souldiers marcht like players,	Edw	2.2.183	Mortmr
Poore Gaveston, that hast no friend but me,	Edw	2.2.220	Edward
But let them go, and tell me what are these.	Edw	2.2.239	Edward
But I respect neither their love nor hate.	Edw	2.2.261	Gavstn
But whats the reason you should leave him now?	Edw	2.3.13	Penbrk
But neither spare you Gaveston, nor his friends.	Edw	2.3.28	Lncstr
Heavens can witnesse, I love none but you.	Edw	2.4.15	Queene
No madam, but that cursed Gaveston.	Edw	2.4.32	Lncstr
We would but rid the realme of Gaveston,	Edw	2.4.35	Lncstr
Come, come aboord, tis but an houres sailing.	Edw	2.4.49	Lncstr
As if he heare I have but talkt with you,	Edw	2.4.54	Queene
But thinke of Mortimer as he deserves.	Edw	2.4.58	Mortmr
Whose eyes are fixt on none but Gaveston:	Edw	2.4.62	Queene
But yet I hope my sorrowes will have end,	Edw	2.4.68	Queene
But for thou wert the favorit of a King,	Edw	2.5.27	Warwck
Intreateth you by me, yet but he may/See him before he dies, for	Edw	2.5.36	Arundl
He will but talke with him and send him backe.	Edw	2.5.59	Arundl
But for we know thou art a noble gentleman,	Edw	2.5.68	Mortmr
That we have taken him, but must we now/Leave him on had-I-wist,	Edw	2.5.84	Warwck
But if you dare trust Penbrooke with the prisoner,	Edw	2.5.87	Penbrk
hence, out of the way/A little, but our men shall go along.	Edw	2.5.101	Penbrk
Too kinde to them, but now have drawne our sword,	Edw	3.1.25	Edward
And Spencer, spare them not, but lay it on.	Edw	3.1.56	Edward
But to my Gaveston:	Edw	3.1.68	Edward
But ere he came, Warwick in ambush laie,	Edw	3.1.118	Arundl
Away, tarrie no answer, but be gon.	Edw	3.1.173	Edward
But justice of the quarrell and the cause,	Edw	3.1.222	Edward
But weele advance them traitors, now tis time/To be avengd on	Edw	3.1.224	Edward
Tis but temporall that thou canst inflict.	Edw	3.1.242	Warwck
Yea, but [Levune] <Lewne> thou seest,/These Barons lay their	Edw	3.1.273	Baldck
But ile to Fraunce, and cheere the wronged Queene,	Edw	4.1.6	Kent
But hath thy potion wrought so happilie?	Edw	4.1.14	Kent
But hath your grace got shipping unto Fraunce?	Edw	4.1.17	Mortmr
But droope not madam, noble mindes contemne/Despaire:	Edw	4.2.16	SrJohn
His grace I dare presume will welcome me,/But who are these?	Edw	4.2.34	Queene
But Mortimer reservde for better hap,	Edw	4.2.40	Mortmr
But gentle lords, friendles we are in Fraunce.	Edw	4.2.46	Queene
but madam, right makes roome,/Where weapons want, and though a	Edw	4.2.50	Mortmr
But by the sword, my lord, it must be deserv'd.	Edw	4.2.59	Mortmr
Ah nothing greeves me but my little boye,	Edw	4.3.48	Edward
their sides/With their owne weapons gorde, but whats the helpe?	Edw	4.4.8	Queene
Of thine own people patron shouldst thou be/But thou--	Edw	4.4.14	Queene
This way he fled, but I am come too late.	Edw	4.6.1	Kent
O fly him then, but Edmund calme this rage,	Edw	4.6.11	Kent
But as the realme and parlement shall please,	Edw	4.6.36	Mortmr
But wheres the king and the other Spencer fled?	Edw	4.6.55	Mortmr
And shipt but late for Ireland with the king.	Edw	4.6.58	Rice
I rue my lords ill fortune, but alas,	Edw	4.6.64	Queene
Could not but take compassion of my state.	Edw	4.7.11	Edward
But what is he, whome rule and emperie/Have not in life or	Edw	4.7.14	Edward
But we alas are chaste, and you my friends,	Edw	4.7.22	Edward
grace may sit secure, if none but wee/Doe wot of your abode.	Edw	4.7.26	Monk
Not one alive, but shrewdly I suspect,	Edw	4.7.28	Spencr
But Leister leave to growe so passionate,	Edw	4.7.55	Leistr
Stand not on titles, but obay th'arrest,	Edw	4.7.58	Leistr
For friends hath Edward none, but these, and these,	Edw	4.7.91	Edward
The greefes of private men are soone allayde,/But not of kings:	Edw	5.1.9	Edward
But when the imperiall Lions flesh is gorde,	Edw	5.1.11	Edward
But when I call to minde I am a king,	Edw	5.1.23	Edward
But what are kings, when regiment is gone,	Edw	5.1.26	Edward
But perfect shadowes in a sun-shine day?	Edw	5.1.27	Edward

BUT (cont.)

I weare the crowne, but am contrould by them,	Edw		5.1.29	Edward
But tell me, must I now resigne my crowne,	Edw		5.1.36	Edward
But if proud Mortimer do weare this crowne,	Edw		5.1.43	Edward
But Edwards name survives, though Edward dies.	Edw		5.1.48	Edward
But what the heavens appoint, I must obaye,	Edw		5.1.56	Edward
But stay a while, let me be king till night,	Edw		5.1.59	Edward
But dayes bright beames dooth vanish fast away,	Edw		5.1.69	Edward
But haplesse Edward, thou art fondly led,	Edw		5.1.76	Edward
But seekes to make a new elected king,	Edw		5.1.78	Edward
But that I feele the crowne upon my head,	Edw		5.1.82	Edward
Ile not resigne, but whilst I live, [be king].	Edw		5.1.86	Edward
I might, but heavens and earth conspire/To make me miserable:	Edw		5.1.96	Edward
I know not, but of this am I assured,	Edw		5.1.152	Edward
That death ends all, and I can die but once.	Edw		5.1.153	Edward
In health madam, but full of pensivenes.	Edw		5.2.25	Msngr
To set his brother free, no more but so.	Edw		5.2.33	BshpWn
And none but we shall know where he lieth.	Edw		5.2.41	Mortmr
But Mortimer, as long as he survives/What safetie rests for us,	Edw		5.2.42	Queene
But amplifie his greefe with bitter words.	Edw		5.2.65	Mortmr
But she that gave him life, I meane the Queene?	Edw		5.2.91	Kent
But bee content, seeing it his highnesse pleasure.	Edw		5.2.94	Queene
Let me but see him first, and then I will.	Edw		5.2.95	Prince
But hee repents, and sorrowes for it now.	Edw		5.2.108	Prince
With you I will, but not with Mortimer.	Edw		5.2.110	Prince
But can my ayre of life continue long,	Edw		5.3.17	Edward
No, but wash your face, and shave away your beard,	Edw		5.3.31	Gurney
But all in vaine, so vainely do I strive,	Edw		5.3.35	Edward
Souldiers, let me but talke to him one worde.	Edw		5.3.53	Kent
Where is the court but heere, heere is the king,	Edw		5.3.59	Kent
But read it thus, and thats an other sence:	Edw		5.4.10	Mortmr
But at his lookes Lightborne thou wilt relent.	Edw		5.4.26	Mortmr
But yet I have a braver way then these.	Edw		5.4.37	Ltborn
Dares but affirme, that Edwards not true king,	Edw		5.4.76	Champn
But seeing I cannot, ile entreate for him:	Edw		5.4.98	King
Let me but stay and speake, I will not go,	Edw		5.4.105	Kent
yesternight/I opened but the doore to throw him meate,/And I	Edw		5.5.8	Gurney
But stay, whose this?	Edw		5.5.14	Matrvs
These lookes of thine can harbor nought but death.	Edw		5.5.73	Edward
But everie jointe shakes as I give it thee:	Edw		5.5.86	Edward
But that greefe keepes me waking, I shoulde sleepe,	Edw		5.5.93	Edward
But not too hard, least that you bruse his body.	Edw		5.5.113	Ltborn
And others are but shrubs compard to me,	Edw		5.6.12	Mortmr
I, I, but he teares his haire, and wrings his handes,	Edw		5.6.18	Queene
But you I feare, conspirde with Mortimer.	Edw		5.6.37	King
But hath your grace no other proofe then this?	Edw		5.6.43	Mortmr
But bring his head back presently to me.	Edw		5.6.54	King
Yet art thou still but Faustus, and a man.	F	51	1.1.23	Faust
Who aimes at nothing but externall trash,	F	62	1.1.34	Faust
Are but obey'd in their severall Provinces:	F	85	1.1.57	Faust
But his dominion that exceeds <excells> in this,	F	87	1.1.59	Faust
[Yet not your words onely, but mine owne fantasie],	F	130	1.1.102A	Faust
no object, for my head]/[But ruminates on Negromantique skill].	F	132	1.1.104A	Faust
Then doubt not Faustus but to be renowm'd,	F	168	1.1.140	Cornel
Yes, I know, but that followes not.	F	200	1.2.7	P Wagner
But that I am by nature flegmatique, slow to wrath, and prone	F	209	1.2.16	P Wagner
I do not doubt but to see you both hang'd the next Sessions.	F	212	1.2.19	P Wagner
But come, let us go, and informe the Rector:	F	225	1.2.32	2Schol
<O but> I feare me, nothing will <can> reclaime him now.	F	227	1.2.34	1Schol
Then feare not Faustus to <but> be resolute/And try the utmost	F	242	1.3.14	Faust
That was the cause, but yet per accidens:	F	274	1.3.46	Mephst
There is no chiefe but onely Beelzebub:	F	284	1.3.56	Faust
But leaving these vaine trifles of mens soules,	F	289	1.3.61	Faust
The Emperour shall not live, but by my leave,	F	338	1.3.110	Faust
but hearke you Maister, will you teach me this conjuring	F	380	1.4.38	P Robin
But now <Faustus> thou must bequeath it solemnly,	F	423	2.1.35	Mephst
But tell me Faustus, shall I have thy soule?	F	434	2.1.46	Mephst
But Faustus/<thou must> Write it in manner of a Deed of Gift.	F	448	2.1.60	Mephst
I so I do <will>; but Mephostophilis,	F	450	2.1.62	Faust
But what is this Inscription on mine Arme?	F	465	2.1.77	Faust
Nothing Faustus but to delight thy mind <withall>,/And let thee	F	473	2.1.85	Mephst
But may I raise such <up> spirits when I please?	F	475	2.1.87	Faust
But yet conditionally, that thou performe/All Covenants, and	F	479	2.1.91	Faust
I, so are all things else; but whereabouts <where about>?	F	507	2.1.119	Faust
but <for> where we are is hell,/And where hell is there must we	F	511	2.1.123	Mephst
I, and body too, but what of that:	F	521	2.1.133	Faust
But <Faustus> I am an instance to prove the contrary:	F	525	2.1.137	Mephst
But leaving <off> this, let me have a wife, the fairest Maid in	F	529	2.1.141	P Faust
<Tut Faustus>, Marriage is but a ceremoniall toy,	F	535	2.1.147	Mephst
But <why Faustus> think'st thou heaven is such a glorious	F	556	2.2.5	Mephst
I, but Faustus never shall repent.	F	568	2.2.17	BdAngl
[But feareful ecchoes thunder <thunders> in mine eares],	F	571	2.2.20A	Faust
Are all Celestiall bodies but one Globe,	F	587	2.2.36	Faust
Mars, or Jupiter,/Fain'd, but are [erring] <evening> Starres.	F	595	2.2.44	Mephst
But <tell me> have they all/One motion, both situ et tempore?	F	595	2.2.44	Faust
but differ in their motions <motion> upon the poles of the	F	598	2.2.47	P Mephst
But tell me, hath every Spheare a Dominion, or Intelligentia	F	607	2.2.56	P Faust
But is there not Coelum igneum, [and] <&> <et> Christalinum?	F	612	2.2.61	P Faust
No Faustus they be but Fables.	F	613	2.2.62	P Mephst
all at one time, but in some years we have more, in some lesse?	F	616	2.2.65	P Faust
I, that is not against our kingdome: <but> this is.	F	623	2.2.72	P Mephst
There's none but I have interest in the same.	F	637	2.2.86	Lucifr
not of Paradice or <nor> Creation, but marke the <this> shew.	F	659	2.2.108	P Lucifr

BUT (cont.)

But fye, what a smell <scent> is heere?	F 668	2.2.117	P	Pride
but must thou sit, and I stand?	F 683	2.2.132	P	Envy
But what art thou the fourth?	F 685	2.2.134		Faust
but a [bare] <small> pention, and that buyes me <is> thirty	F 694	2.2.143	P	Glutny
<O> But my godmother, O she was an ancient Gentlewoman, her	F 699	2.2.148	P	Glutny
[Tut] <But> Faustus, in hell is all manner of delight.	F 713	2.2.165		Lucifr
But I prethee tell me, in good sadnesse Robin, is that a	F 743	2.3.22	P	Dick
Do but speake what thou't have me to do, and I'le do't:	F 745	2.3.24	P	Robin
Or if thou't go but to the Taverne with me, I'le give thee	F 747	2.3.26	P	Robin
But new exploits do hale him out agen,	F 770	2.3.49		2Chor
But tell me now, what resting place is this?	F 800	3.1.22		Faust
But <And> now my Faustus, that thou maist perceive,	F 809	3.1.31		Mephst
Let it be so my Faustus, but first stay,	F 856	3.1.78		Mephst
But thus I fall to Peter, not to thee.	F 872	3.1.94		Bruno
But wee'le pul downe his haughty insolence:	F 914	3.1.136		Pope
But whilst they sleepe within the Consistory,	F 943	3.1.165		Faust
But now, that Faustus may delight his minde,	F 989	3.2.9		Faust
you heartily sir; for wee cal'd you but in jeast I promise you.	F1123	3.3.36	P	Dick
[Where such as beare <bare> his absence but with griefe],	F1141	3.3.54A		3Chor
But where is Bruno our elected Pope,	F1160	4.1.6		Fredrk
but for all that, I doe not greatly beleeve him, he lookes as	F1227	4.1.73	P	Benvol
But in dumbe silence let them come and goe.	F1252	4.1.98		Faust
These are but shadowes, not substantiall.	F1259	4.1.105		Faust
But Faustus, since I may not speake to them,	F1263	4.1.109		Emper
He sleeps my Lord, but dreames not of his hornes.	F1280	4.1.126		Faust
But an I be not reveng'd for this, would I might be turn'd to a	F1318	4.1.164	P	Benvol
turn'd to a gaping Oyster, and drinke nothing but salt water.	F1320	4.1.166	P	Benvol
But Faustus death shall quit my infamie.	F1337	4.2.13		Benvol
But yet my [heart's] <heart> more ponderous then my head,	F1351	4.2.27		Benvol
O were that damned Hell-hound but in place,	F1355	4.2.31		Benvol
But wherefore doe I dally my revenge?	F1401	4.2.77		Faust
sell him, but if thou likest him for ten Dollors more, take him,	F1460	4.4.4	P	Faust
him o're hedge and ditch, and spare him not; but do you heare?	F1468	4.4.12	P	Faust
waters, but ride him not into the water; o're hedge and ditch,	F1472	4.4.16	P	Faust
hedge and ditch, or where thou wilt, but not into the water:	F1473	4.4.17	P	Faust
What art thou Faustus but a man condemn'd to die?	F1478	4.4.22		Faust
I had nothing under me but a little straw, and had much ado to	F1486	4.4.30	P	HrsCsr
Murder or not murder, now he has but one leg, I'le out-run him,	F1494	4.4.38	P	HrsCsr
on the score, but say nothing, see if she have forgotten me.	F1511	4.5.7	P	Robin
and spare him no time; but, quoth he, in any case ride him not	F1541	4.5.37	P	HrsCsr
what did I but rid him into a great river, and when I came just	F1543	4.5.39	P	HrsCsr
But you shall heare how bravely I serv'd him for it; I went me	F1547	4.5.43	P	HrsCsr
and whooping in his eares, but all could not wake him:	F1549	4.5.45	P	HrsCsr
And has the Doctor but one leg then?	F1553	4.5.49	P	Dick
grace to thinke but well of that which Faustus hath performed.	F1564	4.6.7	P	Faust
But gratious Lady, it may be, that you have taken no pleasure	F1565	4.6.8	P	Faust
This is but a small matter:	F1574	4.6.17	P	Faust
'Faith you are too outragious, but come neere,	F1609	4.6.52		Faust
I but sir sauce box, know you in what place?	F1616	4.6.59		Servnt
sir, I would make nothing of you, but I would faine know that.	F1648	4.6.91	P	Carter
But wherefore dost thou aske?	F1652	4.6.95		Faust
but me thinkes you should have a wooden bedfellow of one of	F1653	4.6.96	P	Carter
But I have it againe now I am awake:	F1657	4.6.100	P	Faust
Or envy of thee, but in tender love,	F1720	5.1.47		OldMan
Faustus I leave thee, but with griefe of heart,	F1737	5.1.64		OldMan
<I goe sweete Faustus, but with heavy cheare>,	F1737	(HC269)A		OldMan
But what I may afflict his body with,	F1757	5.1.84		Mephst
I will attempt, which is but little worth.	F1758	5.1.85		Mephst
And none but thou shalt be my Paramour.	F1787	5.1.114		Faust
How should he, but in <with> desperate lunacie.	F1807	5.2.11		Mephst
To over-reach the Divell, but all in vaine;	F1811	5.2.15		Mephst
thee, then had I lived still, but now must <I> dye eternally.	F1825	5.2.29	P	Faust
<to cure him, tis but a surffet, never feare man>.	F1831	(HC270)A	P	2Schol
Tis but a surfet sir, feare nothing.	F1832	5.2.36		3Schol
But Faustus offence can nere be pardoned, the serpent that	F1837	5.2.41	P	Faust
the serpent that tempted Eve may be saved, but not Faustus.	F1838	5.2.42	P	Faust
<O> my God, I would weepe, but the Divell drawes in my teares.	F1850	5.2.54	P	Faust
up my hands, but see they hold 'em <them>, they hold 'em <them>.	F1853	5.2.57	P	Faust
God forbade it indeed, but Faustus hath done it:	F1858	5.2.62	P	Faust
but the Divel threatned to teare me in peeces if I nam'd God:	F1864	5.2.68	P	Faust
Talke not of me, but save your selves and depart.	F1869	5.2.73	P	Faust
but let us into the next roome, and [there] pray for him.	F1871	5.2.75	P	1Schol
But thou didst love the world.	F1894	5.2.98		GdAngl
Nothing but vexe thee more,/To want in hell, that had on earth	F1897	5.2.101		BdAngl
But yet all these are nothing, thou shalt see/Ten thousand	F1919	5.2.123		BdAngl
Now hast thou but one bare houre to live,	F1927	5.2.131		Faust
or let this houre be but/A yeare, a month, a weeke, a naturall	F1932	5.2.136		Faust
<But let my soule mount and> ascend to heaven.	F1956	(HC271)B		Faust
[So that] my soule [may but] ascend to heaven.	F1956	5.2.160		Faust
But mine must live still to be plagu'd in hell.	F1971	5.2.175		Faust
but sirra, leave your jesting, and binde your selfe presently	F App	p.229 22	P	Wagner
but for the name of french crownes a man were as good have as	F App	p.230 33	P	Clown
Truly but you shall.	F App	p.230 40	P	Clown
But do you hear?	F App	p.230 56	P	Clown
But doe you heare Wagner?	F App	p.231 66	P	Clown
But Robin, here comes the vintner.	F App	p.234 4	P	Rafe
and you are but a &c.	F App	p.234 10	P	Robin
As when I heare but motion made of him,	F App	p.237 27		Emper
But if it like your Grace, it is not in my abilitie to present	F App	p.237 41	P	Faust
But such spirites as can lively resemble Alexander and his	F App	p.237 46	P	Faust
No sir, but when Acteon died, he left the hornes for you:	F App	p.237 55	P	Faust
but the true substantiall bodies of those two deceased princes.	F App	p.238 64	P	Emper

BUT (cont.)

but now I see thou hast a wife, that not only gives thee	F App	p.238 70 P Emper
gives thee hornes, but makes thee weare them, feele on thy head.	F App	p.238 71 P Emper
theres no haste but good, are you remembred how you crossed me	F App	p.238 76 P Faust
but I must tel you one thing before you have him, ride him not	F App	p.239 108 P Faust
but ride him not into the water, ride him over hedge or ditch,	F App	p.239 111 P Faust
hedge or ditch, or where thou wilt, but not into the water.	F App	p.239 112 P Faust
if he had but the qualitie of hey ding, ding, hey, ding, ding,	F App	p.239 115 P HrsCsr
but hark ye sir, if my horse be sick, or ill at ease, if I	F App	p.240 117 P HrsCsr
what art thou Faustus but a man condemnd to die?	F App	p.240 121 P Faust
but yet like an asse as I was, I would not be ruled by him, for	F App	p.240 129 P HrsCsr
pond, but my horse vanisht away, and I sat upon a bottle of hey,	F App	p.240 134 P HrsCsr
but Ile seeke out my Doctor, and have my fortie dollers againe,	F App	p.240 136 P HrsCsr
But I wil speake with him.	F App	p.240 140 P HrsCsr
but it may be Madame, you take no delight in this, I have heard	F App	p.242 4 P Faust
But mercie Faustus of thy Saviour sweete,	F App	p.243 44 OldMan
But if for Nero (then unborne) the fates/Would find no other	Lucan, First Booke	33
plaine not heavens, but gladly beare these evils/For Neros sake:	Lucan, First Booke	37
But neither chuse the north t'erect thy seat;	Lucan, First Booke	53
each from other, but being worne away/They both burst out,	Lucan, First Booke	102
Shaming to strive but where he did subdue,	Lucan, First Booke	146
Such humors stirde them up; but this warrs seed,	Lucan, First Booke	159
Which issues from a small spring, is but shallow,	Lucan, First Booke	216
But now the winters wrath and wat'ry moone,	Lucan, First Booke	219
south were cause/I know not, but the cloudy ayre did frown;	Lucan, First Booke	237
But seeing white Eagles, and Roomes flags wel known,	Lucan, First Booke	246
but as the fields/When birds are silent thorough winters rage;	Lucan, First Booke	260
But gods and fortune prickt him to this war,	Lucan, First Booke	265
But law being put to silence by the wars,	Lucan, First Booke	278
But Roome at thraldoms feet to rid from tyrants.	Lucan, First Booke	352
none answer'd, but a murmuring buz/Th'unstable people made:	Lucan, First Booke	353
prone) restrain'd them; but wars love/And Caesars awe dasht all:	Lucan, First Booke	356
the north-west wind/Nor Zephir rules not, but the north alone,	Lucan, First Booke	408
Which is nor sea, nor land, but oft times both,	Lucan, First Booke	411
Or Plutoes bloodles kingdom, but else where/Resume a body:	Lucan, First Booke	452
to heart/With this vaine terror; but the Court, the Senate;	Lucan, First Booke	484
easie grant men great estates,/But hardly grace to keepe them:	Lucan, First Booke	509
high; but headlong pitcht/Her burning head on bending Hespery.	Lucan, First Booke	544
but by the hornes/The quick priest pull'd him on his knees and	Lucan, First Booke	611
No vaine sprung out but from the yawning gash,	Lucan, First Booke	613
But Figulus more seene in heavenly mysteries,	Lucan, First Booke	638
But thy fiers hurt not; Mars, 'tis thou enflam'st/The	Lucan, First Booke	657
to scarre/The quivering Romans, but worse things affright them.	Lucan, First Booke	673
Thus I complaind, but Love unlockt his quiver,	Ovid's Elegies	1.1.25
Oh woe is me, he never shootes but hits,	Ovid's Elegies	1.1.29
But managde horses heads are lightly borne,	Ovid's Elegies	1.2.16
I aske but right:	Ovid's Elegies	1.3.1
I aske too much, would she but let me love hir,	Ovid's Elegies	1.3.3
That am descended but of knightly line,	Ovid's Elegies	1.3.8
My spotlesse life, which but to Gods [gives] <give> place,	Ovid's Elegies	1.3.13
I love but one, and hir I love change never,	Ovid's Elegies	1.3.15
But how thou shouldst behave thy selfe now know;	Ovid's Elegies	1.4.11
his limbes he spread/Upon the bed, but on my foote first tread.	Ovid's Elegies	1.4.16
Yet this Ile see, but if thy gowne ought cover,	Ovid's Elegies	1.4.41
Do not thou so, but throw thy mantle hence,	Ovid's Elegies	1.4.49
Entreat thy husband drinke, but do not kisse,	Ovid's Elegies	1.4.51
But we must part, when heav'n with black night lowers.	Ovid's Elegies	1.4.60
not onely kisse/But force thee give him my stolne honey blisse.	Ovid's Elegies	1.4.64
But though this night thy fortune be to trie it,	Ovid's Elegies	1.4.69
But in times past I fear'd vaine shades, and night,	Ovid's Elegies	1.6.9
But what entreates for thee some-times tooke place,	Ovid's Elegies	1.6.21
But now perchaunce thy wench with thee doth rest,	Ovid's Elegies	1.6.45
But thou my crowne, from sad haires tane away,	Ovid's Elegies	1.6.67
But secretlie her lockes with checks did trounce mee,	Ovid's Elegies	1.7.21
lockes spred/On her white necke but for hurt cheekes be led.	Ovid's Elegies	1.7.40
But though I like a swelling floud was driven,	Ovid's Elegies	1.7.43
But cruelly her tresses having rent,	Ovid's Elegies	1.7.49
But doubt thou not (revenge doth griefe appease)/With thy	Ovid's Elegies	1.7.63
red shame becomes white cheekes, but this/If feigned, doth well;	Ovid's Elegies	1.8.35
Or, but for bashfulnesse her selfe would crave.	Ovid's Elegies	1.8.44
Behold what gives the Poet but new verses?	Ovid's Elegies	1.8.57
But never give a spatious time to ire,	Ovid's Elegies	1.8.81
By keeping of thy birth make but a shift.	Ovid's Elegies	1.8.94
But her bleare eyes, balde scalpes [thin] <thine> hoary flieces	Ovid's Elegies	1.8.111
Who but a souldiour or a lover is bould/To suffer storme mixt	Ovid's Elegies	1.9.15
This breakes Towne gates, but he his Mistris dore.	Ovid's Elegies	1.9.20
And hath no cloathes, but open doth remaine.	Ovid's Elegies	1.10.16
To give I love, but to be ask't disdayne,	Ovid's Elegies	1.10.63
are in thy soft brest/But pure simplicity in thee doth rest.	Ovid's Elegies	1.11.10
give her my writ/But see that forth-with shee peruseth it.	Ovid's Elegies	1.11.16
But when thou comest they of their courses faile.	Ovid's Elegies	1.13.12
[All] <This> could I beare, but that the wench should rise,/Who	Ovid's Elegies	1.13.25
Would Tithon might but talke of thee a while,	Ovid's Elegies	1.13.35
But [heldst] <hadst> thou in thine armes some Caephalus,	Ovid's Elegies	1.13.39
Jove that thou shouldst not hast but wait his leasure,	Ovid's Elegies	1.13.45
Yet lingered not the day, but morning scard me.	Ovid's Elegies	1.13.48
But what had beene more faire had they beene kept?	Ovid's Elegies	1.14.3
But I remember when it was my fame.	Ovid's Elegies	1.14.50
But when I praise a pretty wenches face/Shee in requitall doth	Ovid's Elegies	2.1.33
But furiously he follow his loves fire/And [thinke] <thinkes>	Ovid's Elegies	2.2.13
But yet sometimes to chide thee let her fall/Counterfet teares:	Ovid's Elegies	2.2.35
but where love please/[Am] <And> driven like a ship upon rough	Ovid's Elegies	2.4.7
I thinke sheele doe, but deepely can dissemble.	Ovid's Elegies	2.4.16

BUT (cont.)

But my ambitious ranging mind approoves?	Ovid's Elegies	2.4.48
But such kinde wenches let their lovers have.	Ovid's Elegies	2.5.26
But Venus often to her Mars such brought.	Ovid's Elegies	2.5.28
No where can they be taught but in the bed,	Ovid's Elegies	2.5.61
[Itis is] <It is as> great, but auntient cause of sorrowe.	Ovid's Elegies	2.6.10
But most thou friendly turtle-dove, deplore.	Ovid's Elegies	2.6.12
But what availde this faith? her rarest hue?	Ovid's Elegies	2.6.17
Worthy to keembe none but a Goddesse faire,	Ovid's Elegies	2.8.2
Apt to thy mistrisse, but more apt to me.	Ovid's Elegies	2.8.4
But when on thee her angry eyes did rush,	Ovid's Elegies	2.8.15
But being present, might that worke the best,	Ovid's Elegies	2.8.17
Yet should I curse a God, if he but said,	Ovid's Elegies	2.9.25
Foole, what is sleepe but image of cold death,	Ovid's Elegies	2.9.41
But me let crafty damsells words deceive,	Ovid's Elegies	2.9.43
But may soft love rowse up my drowsie eies,	Ovid's Elegies	2.10.19
Nor want I strength, but weight to presse her with:	Ovid's Elegies	2.10.24
But when I die, would I might droope with doing,	Ovid's Elegies	2.10.35
So farre 'tis safe, but to go farther dread.	Ovid's Elegies	2.11.16
But if that Triton tosse the troubled floud,	Ovid's Elegies	2.11.27
But if my words with winged stormes hence slip,	Ovid's Elegies	2.11.33
But to my share a captive damsell falles.	Ovid's Elegies	2.12.8
But I no partner of my glory brooke,	Ovid's Elegies	2.12.11
Nor is my warres cause new, but for a Queene/Europe, and Asia in	Ovid's Elegies	2.12.17
And me with many, but yet me without murther,	Ovid's Elegies	2.12.27
Angry I was, but feare my wrath exempted.	Ovid's Elegies	2.13.4
But she conceiv'd of me, or I am sure/I oft have done, what	Ovid's Elegies	2.13.5
Do but deserve gifts with this title grav'd.	Ovid's Elegies	2.13.26
But if in so great feare I may advize thee,	Ovid's Elegies	2.13.27
Both unkinde parents, but for causes sad,	Ovid's Elegies	2.14.31
But tender Damsels do it, though with paine,	Ovid's Elegies	2.14.37
But in the ayre let these words come to nought,	Ovid's Elegies	2.14.41
But in lesse compasse her small fingers knit.	Ovid's Elegies	2.15.20
But seeing thee, I thinke my thing will swell,	Ovid's Elegies	2.15.25
A small, but wholesome soyle with watrie veynes.	Ovid's Elegies	2.16.2
But absent is my fire, lyes ile tell none,	Ovid's Elegies	2.16.11
But if sterne Neptunes windie powre prevaile,	Ovid's Elegies	2.16.27
Had then swum over, but the way was blinde.	Ovid's Elegies	2.16.32
But without thee, although vine-planted ground/Conteines me,	Ovid's Elegies	2.16.33
But when she comes, [you] <your> swelling mounts sinck downe,	Ovid's Elegies	2.16.51
But by her glasse disdainefull pride she learnes,	Ovid's Elegies	2.17.9
Nor she her selfe but first trim'd up discernes.	Ovid's Elegies	2.17.10
But sundry flouds in one banke never go,	Ovid's Elegies	2.17.31
Nor in my bookes shall one but thou be writ,	Ovid's Elegies	2.17.33
But though I apt were for such high deseignes,	Ovid's Elegies	2.18.14
But thou of thy faire damsell too secure,	Ovid's Elegies	2.19.37
But of my love it will an end procure.	Ovid's Elegies	2.19.52
Can I but loath a husband growne a baude?	Ovid's Elegies	2.19.57
But till the [keeper] <keepes> went forth, I forget not,	Ovid's Elegies	3.1.55
But cruelly by her was drown'd and rent.	Ovid's Elegies	3.1.58
Thy labour ever lasts, she askes but little.	Ovid's Elegies	3.1.68
But spare my wench thou at her right hand seated,	Ovid's Elegies	3.2.21
But on the ground thy cloathes too loosely lie,	Ovid's Elegies	3.2.25
But now againe the barriers open lye;	Ovid's Elegies	3.2.77
Pay it not heere, but in an other place.	Ovid's Elegies	3.2.84
But did you not so envy Cepheus Daughter,	Ovid's Elegies	3.3.17
But by my paine to purge her perjuries,	Ovid's Elegies	3.3.21
But bids his darts from perjurd girles retire.	Ovid's Elegies	3.3.36
But when her lover came, had she drawne backe,	Ovid's Elegies	3.3.39
But yet their gift more moderately use,	Ovid's Elegies	3.3.47
Nor doth her face please, but her husbands love;	Ovid's Elegies	3.4.27
She is not chaste, that's kept, but a deare whore:	Ovid's Elegies	3.4.29
But woods and groves keepe your faults undetected.	Ovid's Elegies	3.5.84
Thou hast no name, but com'st from snowy mountaines;	Ovid's Elegies	3.5.91
Thy springs are nought but raine and melted snowe:	Ovid's Elegies	3.5.93
But for thy merits I wish thee, white streame,	Ovid's Elegies	3.5.105
I prove neither youth nor man, but old and rustie.	Ovid's Elegies	3.6.20
But neither was I man, nor lived then.	Ovid's Elegies	3.6.60
What sweete thought is there but I had the same?	Ovid's Elegies	3.6.63
But when she saw it would by no meanes stand,	Ovid's Elegies	3.6.75
But still droupt downe, regarding not her hand,	Ovid's Elegies	3.6.76
But follow trembling campes, and battailes sterne,	Ovid's Elegies	3.7.26
But when in gifts the wise adulterer came,	Ovid's Elegies	3.7.33
But better things it gave, corne without ploughes,	Ovid's Elegies	3.7.39
If ought remaines of us but name, and spirit,	Ovid's Elegies	3.8.59
But with my rivall sicke she was not than.	Ovid's Elegies	3.10.26
But victory, I thinke, will hap to love.	Ovid's Elegies	3.10.34
I flie her lust, but follow beauties creature;	Ovid's Elegies	3.10.37
But let not mee poore soule know of thy straying.	Ovid's Elegies	3.13.2
But that thou wouldst dissemble when tis paste.	Ovid's Elegies	3.13.4
But with your robes, put on an honest face,	Ovid's Elegies	3.13.27
And would be dead, but dying <dead> with thee remaine.	Ovid's Elegies	3.13.40
Ile not sift much, but hold thee soone excusde,	Ovid's Elegies	3.13.41
Say but thou wert injuriously accusde.	Ovid's Elegies	3.13.42
Teach but your tongue to say, I did it not,	Ovid's Elegies	3.13.48
two words, thinke/The cause acquits you not, but I that winke.	Ovid's Elegies	3.13.50
sunne nor wind/Would burne or parch her hands, but to her mind,	Hero and Leander	1.28
But this is true, so like was one the other,	Hero and Leander	1.39
That runs along his backe, but my rude pen,	Hero and Leander	1.69
But far above the loveliest, Hero shin'd,	Hero and Leander	1.103
passions to asswage)/Compile sharpe satyrs, but alas too late,	Hero and Leander	1.127
He kneel'd, but unto her devoutly praid;	Hero and Leander	1.177
O shun me not, but heare me ere you goe,	Hero and Leander	1.205

BUT (cont.)
Receives no blemish, but oft-times more grace, — Hero and Leander 1.217
Which makes me hope, although I am but base, — Hero and Leander 1.218
difference betwixt the richest mine/And basest mold, but use? — Hero and Leander 1.233
But this faire jem, sweet in the losse alone, — Hero and Leander 1.247
But they that dayly tast neat wine, despise it. — Hero and Leander 1.261
So she be faire, but some vile toongs will blot? — Hero and Leander 1.286
But you are faire (aye me) so wondrous faire, — Hero and Leander 1.287
But Pallas and your mistresse are at strife. — Hero and Leander 1.322
But heale the heart, that thou hast wounded thus, — Hero and Leander 1.324
Heroes lookes yeelded, but her words made warre, — Hero and Leander 1.331
But from his spreading armes away she cast her, — Hero and Leander 1.342
Vow'd spotlesse chastitie, but all in vaine. — Hero and Leander 1.368
But with a ghastly dreadfull countenaunce, — Hero and Leander 1.381
but she,/Whose only dower was her chastitie, — Hero and Leander 1.411
But speeches full of pleasure and delight. — Hero and Leander 1.420
These he regarded not, but did intreat, — Hero and Leander 1.451
But long this blessed time continued not; — Hero and Leander 1.459
And but that Learning, in despight of Fate, — Hero and Leander 1.465
But be surpris'd with every garish toy. — Hero and Leander 1.480
And would have turn'd againe, but was afrayd, — Hero and Leander 2.8
But stayd, and after her a letter sent. — Hero and Leander 2.14
For hitherto hee did but fan the fire, — Hero and Leander 2.41
But know you not that creatures wanting sence, — Hero and Leander 2.55
T'is lost but once, and once lost, lost for ever. — Hero and Leander 2.86
But what the secret trustie night conceal'd, — Hero and Leander 2.103
but he must weare/The sacred ring wherewith she was endow'd, — Hero and Leander 2.108
Whose waight consists in nothing but her name, — Hero and Leander 2.114
But like exiled aire thrust from his sphere, — Hero and Leander 2.118
But being separated and remooved, — Hero and Leander 2.127
O none but gods have power their love to hide, — Hero and Leander 2.131
But love resisted once, growes passionate, — Hero and Leander 2.139
To have his head control'd, but breakes the raines, — Hero and Leander 2.142
What is it now, but mad Leander dares? — Hero and Leander 2.146
But still the rising billowes answered no. — Hero and Leander 2.152
But when he knew it was not Ganimed, — Hero and Leander 2.169
He flung at him his mace, but as it went, — Hero and Leander 2.209
But vicious, harebraind, and illit'rat hinds? — Hero and Leander 2.218
She stayd not for her robes, but straight arose, — Hero and Leander 2.235
Love is not ful of pittie (as men say)/But deaffe and cruell, — Hero and Leander 2.288
In such warres women use but halfe their strength. — Hero and Leander 2.296
describe, but hee/That puls or shakes it from the golden tree: — Hero and Leander 2.299
But as her naked feet were whipping out, — Hero and Leander 2.313
But he the [days] <day> bright-bearing Car prepar'd. — Hero and Leander 2.330

BUTCHER
This butcher whil'st his hands were yet held up, — Dido 2.1.241 Aeneas
A brother, no, a butcher of thy friends, — Edw 4.1.4 Kent

BUTCHERD
Butcherd the flocks he found in spatious field, — Ovid's Elegies 1.7.8

BUTS
When as he buts his beames on Floras bed, — Dido 3.4.20 Dido

BUTTING
And then large limits had their butting lands, — Lucan, First Booke 169

BUTTOCKE
on him; hee has a buttocke as slicke as an Ele; wel god buy sir, — F App p.239 116 P HrsCsr

BUTTONS
Come sir, give me my buttons and heers your eare. — P 620 12.33 Mugern
That he would take exceptions at my buttons, — Edw 2.1.47 Baldck
and they shall serve for buttons to his lips, to keepe his — F1387 4.2.63 P Benvol

BUY (Homograph)
Shall buy the meanest souldier in my traine. — 1Tamb 1.2.86 Tamb
And wouldst thou have me buy thy Fathers love/With such a — 1Tamb 4.4.83 Tamb
And buy it basely too for summes of gold? — Jew 2.2.29 Bosco
But now I must be gone to buy a slave. — Jew 2.3.95 Barab
I'le buy you, and marry you to Lady vanity, if you doe well. — Jew 2.3.116 P Barab
I have as much coyne as will buy the Towne. — Jew 2.3.200 Barab
Goe buy thee garments: but thou shalt not want: — Jew 3.4.47 Barab
Shall buy her love even with his dearest bloud. — P 697 13.41 Guise
Shall buy that strumpets favour with his blood, — P 768 15.26 Guise
So he will buy my service with his soule. — F 421 2.1.33 Mephst
thou canst not buy so good a horse, for so small a price: — F1459 4.4.3 P Faust
I went to him yesterday to buy a horse of him, and he would by — F1536 4.5.32 P HrsCsr
slicke as an Ele; wel god buy sir, your boy wil deliver him me: — F App p.240 117 P HrsCsr
Would he not buy thee thou for him shouldst care. — Ovid's Elegies 1.8.34
Why should one sell it, and the other buy it? — Ovid's Elegies 1.10.34

BUYES
and that buyes me <is> thirty meales a day, and ten Beavers: — F 694 2.2.143 P Glutny

BUZ
none answer'd, but a murmuring buz/Th'unstable people made: — Lucan, First Booke 353

BUZZETH (See also BUSSETH)
Who buzzeth in mine eares I am a spirit? — F 565 2.2.14 Faust

BY (See also BURLADIE, BUY)
By Saturnes soule, and this earth threatning [haire] <aire>, — Dido 1.1.10 Jupitr
Drawne through the heavens by Steedes of Boreas brood, — Dido 1.1.55 Venus
Are drawne by darknes forth Astraeus tents. — Dido 1.1.73 Venus
Till that a Princesse priest conceav'd by Mars, — Dido 1.1.106 Jupitr
Priams misfortune followes us by sea, — Dido 1.1.143 Aeneas
That by thy vertues freest us from annoy, — Dido 1.1.153 Achat
On which by tempests furie we are cast. — Dido 1.1.199 Aeneas
Who driven by warre from forth my native world, — Dido 1.1.217 Aeneas
And they so wrackt and weltred by the waves, — Dido 1.1.223 Aeneas
I know her by the movings of her feete: — Dido 1.1.241 Aeneas
There is a place Hesperia term'd by us, — Dido 1.2.20 Cloan

BY (cont.)

By this the Campe was come unto the walles,	Dido	2.1.188	Aeneas
Virgins halfe dead dragged by their golden haire,	Dido	2.1.195	Aeneas
by which Achilles horse/Drew him in triumph through the	Dido	2.1.205	Aeneas
And in his eyelids hanging by the nayles,	Dido	2.1.245	Aeneas
At last the souldiers puld her by the heeles,	Dido	2.1.247	Aeneas
By this I got my father on my backe,	Dido	2.1.265	Aeneas
in mine armes, and by the hand/Led faire Creusa my beloved wife,	Dido	2.1.266	Aeneas
Was by the cruell Mirmidons surprizd,	Dido	2.1.287	Aeneas
And after by that Pirrhus sacrifizde.	Dido	2.1.288	Aeneas
And by that meanes repaire his broken ships,	Dido	2.1.328	Venus
This was an Orator, and thought by words/To compasse me, but yet	Dido	3.1.155	Dido
Yet how <here> <now> I sweare by heaven and him I love,	Dido	3.1.166	Dido
That was advanced by my Hebes shame,	Dido	3.2.43	Juno
And thy faire peacockes by my pigeons pearch:	Dido	3.2.59	Venus
Women may wrong by priviledge of love:	Dido	3.3.25	Iarbus
By chance sweete Queene, as Mars and Venus met.	Dido	3.4.4	Aeneas
What meanes faire Dido by this doubtfull speech?	Dido	3.4.31	Aeneas
And vow by all the Gods of Hospitalitie,	Dido	3.4.44	Aeneas
By heaven and earth, and my faire brothers bowe,	Dido	3.4.45	Aeneas
By Paphos, Capys, and the purple Sea,	Dido	3.4.46	Aeneas
And by this Sword that saved me from the Greekes,	Dido	3.4.48	Aeneas
And be thou king of Libia, by my guift.	Dido	3.4.64	Dido
As others did, by running to the wood.	Dido	4.1.30	Anna
But I will soone put by that stumbling blocke,	Dido	4.1.34	Dido
And dive into her heart by coloured lookes.	Dido	4.2.32	Iarbus
Be rul'd by me, and seeke some other love,	Dido	4.2.35	Anna
That tyed together by the striving tongues,	Dido	4.3.29	Aeneas
Let it be term'd Aenea by your name.	Dido	5.1.20	Cloan
Rather Ascania by your little sonne.	Dido	5.1.21	Serg
Nor I devise by what meanes to contrive.	Dido	5.1.66	Aeneas
Led by Achates to the Troian fleete:	Dido	5.1.84	Dido
I am commaunded by immortall Jove,	Dido	5.1.99	Aeneas
And wofull Dido by these blubbred cheekes,	Dido	5.1.133	Dido
By this right hand, and by our spousall rites,	Dido	5.1.134	Dido
For being intangled by a strangers lookes:	Dido	5.1.145	Dido
Had I a sonne by thee, the griefe were lesse,	Dido	5.1.149	Dido
By this is he got to the water side,	Dido	5.1.188	Dido
And, see the Sailers take him by the hand,	Dido	5.1.189	Dido
I know not what you meane by treason, I,	Dido	5.1.222	Nurse
in the darksome Cave/He drew, and swore by to be true to me,	Dido	5.1.296	Dido
By plowing up his Countries with the Sword:	Dido	5.1.308	Dido
Now to be rulde and governed by a man,	1Tamb	1.1.12	Cosroe
[Trading] <Treading> by land unto the Westerne Isles,	1Tamb	1.1.38	Meandr
Hoping (misled by dreaming prophesies)/To raigne in Asia, and	1Tamb	1.1.41	Meandr
Your Grace hath taken order by Theridamas,	1Tamb	1.1.46	Meandr
Shall either perish by our warlike hands,	1Tamb	1.1.72	Therid
And foot by foot follow Theridamas.	1Tamb	1.1.86	Mycet
Well here I sweare by this my royal seat--	1Tamb	1.1.97	Mycet
The plot is laid by Persean Noble men,	1Tamb	1.1.110	Cosroe
By curing of this maimed Emperie.	1Tamb	1.1.126	Menaph
By whose desires of discipline in Armes,	1Tamb	1.1.174	Cosroe
By lawlesse rapine from a silly maide.	1Tamb	1.2.10	Zenoc
Are countermanded by a greater man:	1Tamb	1.2.22	Tamb
And yet a shepheard by my Parentage:	1Tamb	1.2.35	Tamb
Measuring the limits of his Emperie/By East and west, as	1Tamb	1.2.40	Tamb
By living Asias mightie Emperour.	1Tamb	1.2.73	Zenoc
That by Characters graven in thy browes,	1Tamb	1.2.169	Tamb
And by thy martiall face and stout aspect,	1Tamb	1.2.170	Tamb
And by those steps that he hath scal'd the heavens,	1Tamb	1.2.200	Tamb
exchange for that/We are assured of by our friends successe.	1Tamb	1.2.217	Techel
Which is as much as if I swore by heaven,	1Tamb	1.2.233	Tamb
And by the love of Pyllades and Orestes,	1Tamb	1.2.243	Tamb
Wherein by curious soveraintie of Art,	1Tamb	2.1.13	Menaph
the man, ordain'd by heaven/To further every action to the best.	1Tamb	2.1.52	Ortyg
What will he doe supported by a king?	1Tamb	2.1.57	Ceneus
and brave Theridamas/Have met us by the river Araris:	1Tamb	2.1.63	Cosroe
his Diadem/Sought for by such scalde knaves as love him not?	1Tamb	2.2.8	Mycet
wel then, by heavens I sweare,/Aurora shall not peepe out of	1Tamb	2.2.9	Mycet
But I will have Cosroe by the head,	1Tamb	2.2.11	Mycet
They gather strength by power of fresh supplies.	1Tamb	2.2.21	Meandr
That live by rapine and by lawlesse spoile,	1Tamb	2.2.23	Meandr
which by fame is said/To drinke the mightie Parthian Araris,	1Tamb	2.3.15	Tamb
How those were hit by pelting Cannon shot,	1Tamb	2.4.3	Mycet
Even by the mighty hand of Tamburlaine,	1Tamb	2.5.3	Tamb
Judge by thy selfe Theridamas, not me,	1Tamb	2.5.93	Tamb
And by profession be ambitious.	1Tamb	2.6.14	Meandr
nor by princely deeds/Doth meane to soare above the highest	1Tamb	2.7.32	Therid
The spring is hindred by your smoothering host,	1Tamb	3.1.50	Moroc
that by leaden pipes/Runs to the citie from the mountain	1Tamb	3.1.59	Bajzth
That no reliefe or succour come by Land.	1Tamb	3.1.62	Bajzth
a heavenly face/Should by hearts sorrow wax so wan and pale,	1Tamb	3.2.5	Agidas
When your offensive rape by Tamburlaine,	1Tamb	3.2.6	Agidas
Betraide by fortune and suspitious love,	1Tamb	3.2.66	Agidas
To dy by this resolved hand of thine,	1Tamb	3.2.98	Agidas
And let Agidas by Agidas die,	1Tamb	3.2.105	Agidas
Bassoe, by this thy Lord and maister knowes,	1Tamb	3.3.1	Tamb
Brought to the war by men of Tripoly:	1Tamb	3.3.17	Bassoe
For when they perish by our warlike hands,	1Tamb	3.3.24	Techel
By Mahomet, my Kinsmans sepulcher,	1Tamb	3.3.75	Bajzth
And by the holy Alcaron I sweare,	1Tamb	3.3.76	Bajzth
By this my sword that conquer'd Persea,	1Tamb	3.3.82	Tamb
I long to see those crownes won by our swords,	1Tamb	3.3.98	Therid

BY (cont.)

Sit downe by her:	1Tamb	3.3.124		Tamb
must thou be plac'd by me/That am the Empresse of the mighty	1Tamb	3.3.166		Zabina
Pursude by hunters, flie his angrie lookes,	1Tamb	3.3.193		Zenoc
By this the Turks lie weltring in their blood/And Tamburlaine	1Tamb	3.3.201		Zenoc
Thou, by the fortune of this damned [foile] <soile>.	1Tamb	3.3.213		Bajzth
had the Turkish Emperour/So great a foile by any forraine foe.	1Tamb	3.3.235		Bajzth
And all the Ocean by the British shore.	1Tamb	3.3.259		Tamb
And by this meanes Ile win the world at last.	1Tamb	3.3.260		Tamb
Yet would the Souldane by his conquering power,	1Tamb	4.1.33		Souldn
Tamburlaine, by expedition/Advantage takes of your unreadinesse.	1Tamb	4.1.38		Capol
faire Arabian king/That hath bene disapointed by this slave,	1Tamb	4.1.69		Souldn
Unworthy king, that by thy crueltie,	1Tamb	4.2.56		Zabina
Shall sit by him and starve to death himselfe.	1Tamb	4.2.90		Tamb
Not one should scape: but perish by our swords.	1Tamb	4.2.122		Tamb
By murder raised to the Persean Crowne,	1Tamb	4.3.13		Souldn
Now hang our bloody collours by Damascus,	1Tamb	4.4.1		Tamb
Nay, thine owne is easier to come by, plucke out that, and twil	1Tamb	4.4.13	P	Tamb
you suffer these outragious curses by these slaves of yours?	1Tamb	4.4.27	P	Zenoc
Preserving life, by hasting cruell death.	1Tamb	4.4.96		Bajzth
And thence by land unto the Torrid Zone,	1Tamb	4.4.124		Tamb
By [valure] <value and by magnanimity.	1Tamb	4.4.126		Tamb
By any innovation or remorse,	1Tamb	5.1.16		Govnr
Keeping his circuit by the slicing edge.	1Tamb	5.1.112		Tamb
So much by much, as dooth Zenocrate.	1Tamb	5.1.159		Tamb
By living long in this oppression,	1Tamb	5.1.251		Zabina
Brought up and propped by the hand of fame,	1Tamb	5.1.265		Bajzth
And rackt by dutie from my cursed heart:	1Tamb	5.1.387		Zenoc
Must Tamburlaine by their resistlesse powers,	1Tamb	5.1.397		Zenoc
And griesly death, by running to and fro,	1Tamb	5.1.455		Tamb
Even by this hand that shall establish them,	1Tamb	5.1.492		Tamb
That purchac'd kingdomes by your martiall deeds,	1Tamb	5.1.523		Tamb
of these Eastern parts/Plac'd by the issue of great Bajazeth,	2Tamb	1.1.2		Orcan
Shall by this battell be the bloody Sea.	2Tamb	1.1.38		Orcan
And sweare in sight of heaven and by thy Christ.	2Tamb	1.1.132		Orcan
By him that made the world and sav'd my soule,	2Tamb	1.1.133		Sgsmnd
By sacred Mahomet, the friend of God,	2Tamb	1.1.137		Orcan
And backt by stout Lanceres of Germany,	2Tamb	1.1.155		Sgsmnd
Yet here detain'd by cruell Tamburlaine.	2Tamb	1.2.4		Callap
No speach to that end, by your favour sir.	2Tamb	1.2.14		Almeda
By [Cairo] <Cario> runs--	2Tamb	1.2.15		Callap
By [Cairo] <Cario> runs to Alexandria Bay,	2Tamb	1.2.19		Callap
Hoping by some means I shall be releast,	2Tamb	1.2.23		Callap
And by the hand of Mahomet I sweare,	2Tamb	1.2.65		Callap
Plac'd by her side, looke on their mothers face.	2Tamb	1.3.20		Tamb
For I have sworne by sacred Mahomet,	2Tamb	1.3.109		Tamb
Whose triple Myter I did take by force,	2Tamb	1.3.189		Techel
And by the coast of Byather at last,	2Tamb	1.3.200		Techel
Where by the river Tyros I subdew'd/Stoka, Padalia, and	2Tamb	1.3.209		Therid
From thence I crost the Gulfe, call'd by the name/Mare magiore,	2Tamb	1.3.214		Therid
Confirm'd by oth and Articles of peace,	2Tamb	2.1.29		Sgsmnd
faith which they prophanely plight/Is not by necessary pollycy,	2Tamb	2.1.38		Baldwn
An hundred kings by scores wil bid him armes,	2Tamb	2.2.11		Gazell
He by his Christ, and I by Mahomet?	2Tamb	2.2.32		Orcan
Now by the malice of the angry Skies,	2Tamb	2.4.11		Tamb
For should I but suspect your death by mine,	2Tamb	2.4.61		Zenoc
To haile the fatall Sisters by the haire,	2Tamb	2.4.99		Tamb
by the aid of God and his friend Mahomet, Emperour of Natolia,	2Tamb	3.1.2	P	Orcan
By this my friendly keepers happy meanes,	2Tamb	3.1.34		Callap
Greek, is writ/This towne being burnt by Tamburlaine the great,	2Tamb	3.2.17		Calyph
By plaine and easie demonstration,	2Tamb	3.2.84		Tamb
Invincible by nature of the place.	2Tamb	3.2.90		Tamb
That by the warres lost not a dram of blood,	2Tamb	3.2.113		Tamb
And few or none shall perish by their shot.	2Tamb	3.3.45		Therid
Therefore die by thy loving mothers hand,	2Tamb	3.4.23		Olymp
By whose proud side the ugly furies run,	2Tamb	3.4.59		Therid
Who by this time is at Natolia,	2Tamb	3.4.86		Therid
By Mahomet not one of them shal live.	2Tamb	3.5.17		Callap
by your highnesse hands)/All brandishing their brands of	2Tamb	3.5.26		Orcan
By Mahomet he shal be tied in chaines,	2Tamb	3.5.92		Jrslem
By Mahomet, thy mighty friend I sweare,	2Tamb	4.1.121		Tamb
And by the state of his supremacie,	2Tamb	4.1.136		Tamb
Crown'd and invested by the hand of Jove,	2Tamb	4.1.151		Tamb
And til by vision, or by speach I heare/Immortall Jove say,	2Tamb	4.1.198		Tamb
Tempered by science metaphisicall,	2Tamb	4.2.63		Olymp
But was prevented by his sodaine end.	2Tamb	4.2.74		Olymp
Than you by this unconquered arme of mine.	2Tamb	4.3.16		Tamb
By which I hold my name and majesty.	2Tamb	4.3.26		Tamb
intollorable wrath/May be suppresst by our submission.	2Tamb	5.1.9		Maxim
Being caried thither by the cannons force,	2Tamb	5.1.66		Tamb
Courted by kings and peeres of Asia,	2Tamb	5.1.74		Tamb
And yet I live untoucht by Mahomet:	2Tamb	5.1.182		Tamb
Where men report, thou sitt'st by God himselfe,	2Tamb	5.1.194		Tamb
And fishes [fed] <feed> by humaine carkasses,	2Tamb	5.1.206		Techel
And that vile Carkasse drawne by warlike kings,	2Tamb	5.2.16		Amasia
thou that hast seene/Millions of Turkes perish by Tamburlaine,	2Tamb	5.2.25		Callap
health and majesty/Were strangely blest and governed by heaven,	2Tamb	5.3.25		Techel
that the soule/Wanting those Organnons by which it mooves,	2Tamb	5.3.96		Phsitn
Can not indure by argument of art.	2Tamb	5.3.97		Phsitn
Like Summers vapours, vanisht by the Sun.	2Tamb	5.3.116		Tamb
Then by the Northerne part of Affrica,	2Tamb	5.3.140		Tamb
For by your life we entertaine our lives.	2Tamb	5.3.167		Celeb
By equall portions into both your breasts:	2Tamb	5.3.171		Tamb

BY (cont.)

Let it be plac'd by this my fatall chaire,	2Tamb	5.3.211	Tamb
Be warn'd by him then, learne with awfull eie/To sway a throane	2Tamb	5.3.234	Tamb
rebelling Jades/Wil take occasion by the slenderest haire,	2Tamb	5.3.239	Tamb
Are poyson'd by my climing followers.	Jew	Prol.13	Machvl
Receive them free, and sell them by the weight;	Jew	1.1.24	Barab
East and by-South:	Jew	1.1.41	Barab
and the bordering Iles/Are gotten up by Nilus winding bankes:	Jew	1.1.43	Barab
Are smoothly gliding downe by Candie shoare/To Malta, through	Jew	1.1.46	Barab
from Egypt, or by Caire/But at the entry there into the sea,	Jew	1.1.73	Barab
Thou needs must saile by Alexandria.	Jew	1.1.76	Barab
[But] <by> goe, goe thou thy wayes, discharge thy Ship,	Jew	1.1.82	Barab
you came not with those other ships/That sail'd by Egypt?	Jew	1.1.90	Barab
Belike they coasted round by Candie shoare/About their Oyles,	Jew	1.1.91	Barab
we were wafted by a Spanish Fleet/That never left us till	Jew	1.1.95	2Merch
Thus trowles our fortune in by land and Sea,	Jew	1.1.103	Barab
scambled up/More wealth by farre then those that brag of faith.	Jew	1.1.123	Barab
And Crownes come either by succession/Or urg'd by force; and	Jew	1.1.131	Barab
And Crownes come either by succession/Or urg'd by force; and	Jew	1.1.132	Barab
but to passe along/Towards Venice by the Adriatick Sea;	Jew	1.1.163	Barab
And now by that advantage thinkes, belike,	Jew	1.1.184	Barab
And 'tis more Kingly to obtaine by peace/Then to enforce	Jew	1.2.25	Calym
to obtaine by peace/Then to enforce conditions by constraint.	Jew	1.2.26	Calym
but cannot compasse it/By reason of the warres, that robb'd our	Jew	1.2.48	Govnr
Why know you what you did by this device?	Jew	1.2.84	Barab
Shall I be tryed by their transgression?	Jew	1.2.115	Barab
That measure nought but by the present time.	Jew	1.2.220	Barab
Be rul'd by me, for in extremitie/We ought to make barre of no	Jew	1.2.272	Barab
I doe not doubt by your divine precepts/And mine owne industry,	Jew	1.2.334	Abigal
And speake of spirits and ghosts that glide by night/About the	Jew	2.1.26	Barab
and by my fingers take/A kisse from him that sends it from his	Jew	2.1.58	Barab
nay we dare not give consent/By reason of a Tributary league.	Jew	2.2.23	Govnr
Therefore be rul'd by me, and keepe the gold:	Jew	2.2.39	Bosco
How showes it by night?	Jew	2.3.62	Lodowk
And few or none scape but by being purg'd.	Jew	2.3.106	Barab
That by my helpe shall doe much villanie.	Jew	2.3.133	Barab
And I will teach [thee] that shall sticke by thee:	Jew	2.3.168	Barab
See 'em goe pinion'd along by my doore.	Jew	2.3.180	Barab
For now by this has he kist Abigall;	Jew	2.3.246	Barab
Faith Master, I thinke by this/You purchase both their lives; is	Jew	2.3.365	Ithimr
Tell me, how cam'st thou by this?	Jew	3.1.16	Curtzn
I know she is a Curtezane by her attire:	Jew	3.1.27	P Ithimr
hadst thou perish'd by the Turke,/Wretched Ferneze might have	Jew	3.2.13	Govnr
That by my favour they should both be slaine?	Jew	3.3.39	Abigal
Nor on his sonne, but by Mathias meanes;	Jew	3.3.45	Abigal
Nor on Mathias, but by murdering me.	Jew	3.3.46	Abigal
But perish underneath my bitter curse/Like Cain by Adam, for	Jew	3.4.33	Barab
Assure thy selfe thou shalt have broth by the eye.	Jew	3.4.92	Barab
hast broke the league/By flat denyall of the promis'd Tribute,	Jew	3.5.20	Basso
For by this Answer, broken is the league,	Jew	3.5.34	Govnr
And by my father's practice, which is there/Set downe at large,	Jew	3.6.28	Abigal
But here's a royall Monastry hard by,	Jew	4.1.13	Ithimr
I will not say that by a forged challenge they met.	Jew	4.1.45	P 2Fryar
master, be rul'd by me a little; so, let him leane upon his	Jew	4.1.153	P Ithimr
Away, I'de wish thee, and let me goe by:	Jew	4.1.170	1Fryar
That being importun'd by this Bernardine/To be a Christian, I	Jew	4.1.187	Barab
base slave as he should be saluted by such a tall man as I am,	Jew	4.2.9	P Pilia
By no meanes possible.	Jew	4.2.61	P Ithimr
I charge thee send me three hundred by this bearer, and this	Jew	4.2.75	P Ithimr
Thou in those Groves, by Dis above,	Jew	4.2.97	Ithimr
I tooke him by the [beard] <sterd>, and look'd upon him thus;	Jew	4.2.105	P Pilia
And I by him must send three hundred crownes.	Jew	4.3.15	Barab
I'le send by word of mouth now; Bid him deliver thee a thousand	Jew	4.4.74	P Ithimr
a thousand Crownes, by the same token, that the Nuns lov'd Rice,	Jew	4.4.75	P Ithimr
I bring thee newes by whom thy sonne was slaine:	Jew	5.1.10	Curtzn
Was my Mathias murder'd by the Jew?	Jew	5.1.44	Mater
For by my meanes Calymath shall enter in.	Jew	5.1.63	Barab
And by this meanes the City is your owne.	Jew	5.1.94	Barab
Thus hast thou gotten, by thy policie,	Jew	5.2.27	Barab
And since by wrong thou got'st Authority,	Jew	5.2.35	Barab
Maintaine it bravely by firme policy,	Jew	5.2.36	Barab
Now Governor--stand by there, wait within.--	Jew	5.2.50	Barab
And by my letters privately procure/Great summes of mony for	Jew	5.2.87	Govnr
And toward Calabria, back'd by Sicily,	Jew	5.3.9	Calym
In this, my Countrimen, be rul'd by me,	Jew	5.4.1	Govnr
heare a Culverin discharg'd/By him that beares the Linstocke,	Jew	5.4.4	Govnr
A kingly kinde of trade to purchase Townes/By treachery, and	Jew	5.5.48	Barab
trade to purchase Townes/By treachery, and sell 'em by deceit?	Jew	5.5.48	Barab
And doe attend my comming there by this.	Jew	5.5.104	Calym
For he that did by treason worke our fall,	Jew	5.5.109	Govnr
By treason hath delivered thee to us:	Jew	5.5.110	Govnr
That Guise hath slaine by treason of his heart,	P 45	1.45	Navrre
And brought by murder to their timeles ends.	P 46	1.46	Navrre
And when thou seest the Admirall ride by,	P 87	2.30	Guise
Which cannot be extinguisht but by bloud.	P 93	2.36	Guise
and fully executes/Matters of importe, aimed at by many,	P 111	2.54	Guise
Yet understoode by none.	P 112	2.55	Guise
And by that priviledge to worke upon,	P 121	2.64	Guise
Gonzago, Retes, sweare by/The argent crosses in your burgonets,	P 274	5.1	Guise
I sweare by this to be unmercifull.	P 277	5.4	Dumain
Plac'd by my brother, will betray his Lord:	P 294	5.21	Anjoy
Cosin tis he, I know him by his look.	P 309	5.36	Guise
I sweare by this crosse, wee'l not be partiall,	P 325	5.52	Anjoy

BY (cont.)

Yet by my brother Charles our King of France,	P 464	8.14	Anjoy
And by his graces councell it is thought,	P 465	8.15	Anjoy
By due discent the Regall seat is mine.	P 470	8.20	Anjoy
That if by death of Charles, the diadem/Of France be cast on	P 472	8.22	Anjoy
water the fish, and by the fish our selves when we eate them.	P 488	9.7	P 2Atndt
all doubts, be rulde by me, lets hang him heere upon this tree.	P 491	9.10	P 2Atndt
No by my faith Madam.	P 498	9.17	Guise
It is my due by just succession:	P 570	11.35	Navrre
My Lord, as by our scoutes we understande,	P 724	14.27	1Msngr
And heer by all the Saints in heaven I sweare,	P 765	15.23	Guise
That livest by forraine exhibition?	P 842	17.37	Eprnon
Being animated by Religious zeale,	P 848	17.43	Guise
Dismisse thy campe or else by our Edict,	P 863	17.58	King
And Epernoune I will be rulde by thee.	P 885	17.80	King
Now by the holy sacrament I sweare,	P 981	19.51	Guise
Stand close, he is comming, I know him by his voice.	P1000	19.70	P 1Mur
To dye by Pesantes, what a greefe is this?	P1009	19.79	Guise
My noble brother murthered by the King,	P1107	21.1	Dumain
of Loraine by the Kings consent is lately strangled unto death.	P1123	21.17	P Frier
And sends <send> his dutie by these speedye lines,	P1169	22.31	Frier
Shall take example by [his] <their> punishment,	P1186	22.48	King
And rulde in France by Henries fatall death.	P1250	22.112	Navrre
and will needs enter by defaulte | whatt thoughe you were once	Paris	ms11,p390	P Souldr
To whom the sunne shines both by day and night.	Edw	1.1.17	Gavstn
Farewell, and perish by a souldiers hand,	Edw	1.1.37	3PrMan
Therefore ile have Italian maskes by night,	Edw	1.1.55	Gavstn
Shall bathe him in a spring, and there hard by,	Edw	1.1.66	Gavstn
Shall by the angrie goddesse be transformde,	Edw	1.1.68	Gavstn
By yelping hounds puld downe, and seeme to die.	Edw	1.1.70	Gavstn
for rather then my lord/Shall be opprest by civill mutinies,	Edw	1.2.65	Queene
Your grace doth wel to place him by your side,	Edw	1.4.10	Lncstr
That hardly art a gentleman by birth?	Edw	1.4.29	Mortmr
And by thy meanes is Gaveston exilde.	Edw	1.4.155	Edward
Sweete Mortimer, sit downe by me a while,	Edw	1.4.225	Queene
And as grosse vapours perish by the sunne,	Edw	1.4.341	Edward
Thou seest by nature he is milde and calme,	Edw	1.4.388	MortSr
Should by his soveraignes favour grow so pert,	Edw	1.4.404	Mortmr
Then hope I by her meanes to be preferd,	Edw	2.1.29	Baldck
And by the barke a canker creepes me up,	Edw	2.2.18	Mortmr
Weele haile him by the eares unto the block.	Edw	2.2.91	Lncstr
He meanes to make us stoope by force of armes,	Edw	2.2.103	Lncstr
By heaven, the abject villaine shall not live.	Edw	2.2.106	Mortmr
My unckles taken prisoner by the Scots.	Edw	2.2.115	Mortmr
Mine unckles taken prisoner by the Scots.	Edw	2.2.142	Mortmr
How oft have I beene baited by these peeres?	Edw	2.2.201	Edward
Spencer and I will post away by land.	Edw	2.4.6	Edward
Hees gone by water unto Scarborough,	Edw	2.4.37	Queene
Go souldiers take him hence, for by my sword,	Edw	2.5.20	Warwck
My lords, king Edward greetes you all by me.	Edw	2.5.33	Arundl
Intreateth you by me, yet but he may/See him before he dies,	Edw	2.5.36	Arundl
Weele send his head by thee, let him bestow/His teares on that,	Edw	2.5.52	Mortmr
As by their preachments they will profit much,	Edw	3.1.22	Spencr
Informeth us, by letters and by words,	Edw	3.1.61	Queene
By earth, the common mother of us all,	Edw	3.1.128	Edward
By heaven, and all the mooving orbes thereof,	Edw	3.1.129	Edward
By this right hand, and by my fathers sword,	Edw	3.1.130	Edward
The Barons up in armes, by me salute/Your highnes, with long	Edw	3.1.156	Herald
Now lustie lords, now not by chance of warre,	Edw	3.1.221	Edward
But by the sword, my lord, it must be deserv'd.	Edw	4.2.59	Mortmr
Have beene by thee restored and comforted.	Edw	4.2.80	Mortmr
Lords, sith that we are by sufferance of heaven,	Edw	4.4.17	Mortmr
Present by me this traitor to the state,	Edw	4.6.49	Rice
Come Spencer, come Baldocke, come sit downe by me,	Edw	4.7.16	Edward
The Queenes commission, urgd by Mortimer,	Edw	4.7.49	Leistr
Spencer and Baldocke, by no other names,	Edw	4.7.56	Leistr
For we shall see them shorter by the heads.	Edw	4.7.94	Rice
I weare the crowne, but am contrould by them,	Edw	5.1.29	Edward
By Mortimer, and my unconstant Queene,	Edw	5.1.30	Edward
For hees a lambe, encompassed by Woolves,	Edw	5.1.41	Edward
By Mortimer, whose name is written here,	Edw	5.1.139	Edward
Be rulde by me, and we will rule the realme,	Edw	5.2.5	Mortmr
For now we hould an old Wolfe by the eares,	Edw	5.2.7	Mortmr
I would hee were, so it were not by my meanes.	Edw	5.2.45	Queene
As thou intendest to rise by Mortimer,	Edw	5.2.52	Mortmr
Remoove him still from place to place by night,	Edw	5.2.59	Mortmr
And by the way to make him fret the more,	Edw	5.2.62	Mortmr
Then I will carrie thee by force away.	Edw	5.2.112	Mortmr
Thus lives old Edward not reliev'd by any,	Edw	5.3.23	Edward
And so must die, though pitied by many.	Edw	5.3.24	Edward
Weele enter in by darkenes to Killingworth.	Edw	5.3.48	Matrvs
This letter written by a friend of ours,	Edw	5.4.6	Mortmr
And by a secret token that he beares,	Edw	5.4.19	Mortmr
Till being interrupted by my friends,	Edw	5.4.62	Mortmr
Long live king Edward, by the grace of God/King of England, and	Edw	5.4.73	ArchBp
Doe as you are commaunded by my lord.	Edw	5.5.26	Matrvs
Or else die by the hand of Mortimer.	Edw	5.6.6	Mortmr
To witnesse to the world, that by thy meanes,	Edw	5.6.31	King
Tis my hand, what gather you by this.	Edw	5.6.47	Mortmr
Or Lapland Giants trotting by our sides:	F 153	1.1.125	Valdes
Faustus may try his cunning by himselfe.	F 187	1.1.159	Cornel
That followes not <necessary> by force of argument, which	F 202	1.2.9	P Wagner
But that I am by nature flegmatique, slow to wrath, and prone	F 209	1.2.16	P Wagner

BY (cont.)

<and see if hee by> his grave counsell may <can> reclaime him.	F 226	1.2.33		2Schol
By which the spirits are inforc'd to rise:	F 241	1.3.13		Faust
by aspiring pride and insolence,/For which God threw him from	F 295	1.3.67		Mephst
By desperate thoughts against Joves Deity:	F 317	1.3.89		Faust
By him, I'le be great Emperour of the world,	F 332	1.3.104		Faust
The Emperour shall not live, but by my leave,	F 338	1.3.110		Faust
When Mephostophilis shall stand by me,	F 413	2.1.25		Faust
Faustus, I sweare by Hell and Lucifer,	F 481	2.1.93		Mephst
shall be his servant, and be by him commanded <at his command>.	F 486	2.1.98	P	Faust
by these presents doe give both body and soule to Lucifer,	F 493	2.1.105	P	Faust
By me John Faustus.	F 500	2.1.112	P	Faust
be carried thither againe by Gluttony and Letchery <Leachery>],	F 705.2	2.2.156A	P	Sloth
Drawne by the strength of yoked <yoky> Dragons neckes;	F 759	2.3.38		2Chor
Not to be wonne by any conquering Prince:	F 783	3.1.5		Faust
Now by the Kingdomes of Infernall Rule,	F 825	3.1.47		Faust
come then stand by me/And thou shalt see them come immediately.	F 843	3.1.65		Mephst
By [cunning] <comming> in <of> thine Art to crosse the Pope,/Or	F 859	3.1.81		Mephst
What by the holy Councell held at Trent,	F 884	3.1.106		Pope
I was elected by the Emperour.	F 905	3.1.127		Bruno
And by authority Apostolicall/Depose him from his Regall	F 923	3.1.145		Pope
By full consent of all the [reverend] <holy> Synod/Of Priests	F 952	3.1.174		Faust
And if that Bruno by his owne assent,	F 957	3.1.179		Faust
And by your death to clime Saint Peters Chaire,	F 960	3.1.182		Faust
And by their folly make some <us> merriment,	F 990	3.2.10		Faust
Were by the holy Councell both condemn'd/For lothed Lollords,	F1021	3.2.41		Pope
By holy Paul we saw them not.	F1029	3.2.49		BthCrd
By Peter you shall dye,	F1030	3.2.50		Pope
Or by our sanctitude you all shall die.	F1057	3.2.77		Pope
How am I vexed by these villaines Charmes?	F1117	3.3.30		Mephst
By Lady sir, you have had a shroud journey of it, will it	F1120	3.3.33	P	Robin
who comes to see/What wonders by blacke spels may compast be.	F1198	4.1.44		Mrtino
Then if by powerfull Necromantick spels,	F1209	4.1.55		Emper
The Doctor stands prepar'd, by power of Art,	F1222	4.1.68		Faust
Why how now sir Knight, what, hang'd by the hornes?	F1290	4.1.136	P	Faust
By this (I know) the Conjurer is neere,	F1343	4.2.19		Benvol
My head is lighter then it was by th'hornes,	F1350	4.2.26		Benvol
Through which the Furies drag'd me by the heeles.	F1435	4.3.5		Mrtino
and have lost very much of late by horse flesh, and this	F1464	4.4.8	P	HrsCsr
Who's this, that stands so solemnly by himselfe:	F1513	4.5.9	P	Hostss
and he would by no meanes sell him under forty Dollors; so sir,	F1537	4.5.33	P	HrsCsr
I seeing that, tooke him by the leg, and never rested pulling,	F1550	4.5.46	P	HrsCsr
by meanes of a swift spirit that I have, I had these grapes	F1585	4.6.28	P	Faust
My woodden leg? what dost thou meane by that?	F1628	4.6.71		Faust
If sin by custome grow not into nature:	F1713	5.1.40		OldMan
<Belike he is growne into some sicknesse, by> being over	F1829	(HC270)A	P	3Schol
All torne asunder by the hand of death.	F1989	5.3.7		2Schol
and so by that meanes I shal see more then ere I felt, or saw	F App	p.233 4	P	Robin
for conjuring that ere was invented by any brimstone divel.	F App	p.233 20	P	Robin
tell thee, we were for ever made by this doctor Faustus booke?	F App	p.234 1	P	Robin
stand by, Ile scowre you for a goblet, stand aside you had	F App	p.235 18	P	Robin
by whome thou canst accomplish what thou list, this therefore	F App	p.236 4	P	Emper
by the honor of mine Imperial crowne, that what ever thou	F App	p.236 8	P	Emper
how they had wonne by prowesse such exploits, gote such riches,	F App	p.236 19	P	Emper
If therefore thou, by cunning of thine Art,	F App	p.237 29		Emper
forth as by art and power of my spirit I am able to performe.	F App	p.237 38	P	Faust
I would not be ruled by him, for he bade me I should ride him	F App	p.240 130	P	HrsCsr
in the month of January, how you shuld come by these grapes.	F App	p.242 18	P	Duke
and by means of a swift spirit that I have, I had them brought	F App	p.242 22	P	Faust
By which sweete path thou maist attaine the gole/That shall	F App	p.243 36		OldMan
And strive to shine by day, and ful of strife/Disolve the	Lucan, First Booke	79		
Allot the height of honor, men so strong/By land, and sea, no	Lucan, First Booke	83		
for Julia/Snatcht hence by cruel fates with ominous howles,	Lucan, First Booke	112		
And by long rest forgot to manage armes,	Lucan, First Booke	131		
And being popular sought by liberal gifts,	Lucan, First Booke	132		
and peoples voices/Bought by themselves and solde, and every	Lucan, First Booke	181		
But law being put to silence by the wars,	Lucan, First Booke	278		
What should I talke of mens corne reapt by force,	Lucan, First Booke	318		
And by him kept of purpose for a dearth?	Lucan, First Booke	319		
Who sees not warre sit by the quivering Judge;	Lucan, First Booke	320		
Neither spoile, nor kingdom seeke we by these armes,	Lucan, First Booke	351		
Is conquest got by civill war so hainous?	Lucan, First Booke	367		
by these ten blest ensignes/And all thy several triumphs,	Lucan, First Booke	375		
They by Lemannus nooke forsooke their tents;	Lucan, First Booke	397		
Under the rockes by crooked Vogesus;	Lucan, First Booke	399		
They came that dwell/By Nemes fields, and bankes of Satirus,	Lucan, First Booke	421		
and those that dwel/By Cyngas streame, and where swift Rhodanus	Lucan, First Booke	434		
Are blest by such sweet error, this makes them/Run on the	Lucan, First Booke	456		
and that Roome/He looking on by these men should be sackt.	Lucan, First Booke	480		
The world (were it together) is by cowards/Left as a pray now	Lucan, First Booke	511		
When Romans are besieg'd by forraine foes,	Lucan, First Booke	513		
when by Junces taske/He had before lookt Pluto in the face.	Lucan, First Booke	575		
but by the hornes/The quick priest pull'd him on his knees and	Lucan, First Booke	611		
By these he seeing what myschiefes must ensue,	Lucan, First Booke	629		
Smooth speeches, feare and rage shall by thee ride,	Ovid's Elegies	1.2.35		
A scorching flame burnes all the standers by.	Ovid's Elegies	1.2.46		
By verses horned Io got hir name,	Ovid's Elegies	1.3.21		
Lines thou shalt read in wine by my hand writ.	Ovid's Elegies	1.4.20		
Let not thy necke by his vile armes be prest,	Ovid's Elegies	1.4.35		
There will I finde thee, or be found by thee,	Ovid's Elegies	1.4.57		
How apt her breasts were to be prest by me,	Ovid's Elegies	1.5.20		
By chaunce I heard her talke, these words she sayd/While	Ovid's Elegies	1.8.21		
By many hands great wealth is quickly got.	Ovid's Elegies	1.8.92		

BY (cont.)

By keeping of thy birth make but a shift.	Ovid's Elegies	1.8.94
If this thou doest, to me by long use knowne,	Ovid's Elegies	1.8.105
each mans mony/And seekes vild wealth by selling of her Cony,	Ovid's Elegies	1.10.22
and thou gaine by the pleasure/Which man and woman reape in	Ovid's Elegies	1.10.35
Tis shame to grow rich by bed merchandize,	Ovid's Elegies	1.10.41
And whom I like eternize by mine art.	Ovid's Elegies	1.10.60
Corinna clips me oft by thy perswasion,	Ovid's Elegies	1.11.5
By speechlesse lookes we guesse at things succeeding.	Ovid's Elegies	1.11.18
when she departed/Nape by stumbling on the thre-shold started.	Ovid's Elegies	1.12.4
Be broake with wheeles of chariots passing by.	Ovid's Elegies	1.12.14
If ever, now well lies she by my side.	Ovid's Elegies	1.13.6
The painfull Hinde by thee to field is sent,	Ovid's Elegies	1.13.15
By thy meanes women of their rest are bard,	Ovid's Elegies	1.13.23
By thine owne hand and fault thy hurt doth growe,	Ovid's Elegies	1.14.43
And long admiring say by what meanes learnd/Hath this same Poet	Ovid's Elegies	2.1.9
Snakes leape by verse from caves of broken mountaines/And	Ovid's Elegies	2.1.25
Stolne liberty she may by thee obtaine,	Ovid's Elegies	2.2.15
To staine all faith in truth, by false crimes use.	Ovid's Elegies	2.2.38
By whom the husband his wives incest knewe.	Ovid's Elegies	2.2.48
She safe by favour of her judge doth rest.	Ovid's Elegies	2.2.56
<blushe>, and by that blushfull [glance] <glasse> am tooke:	Ovid's Elegies	2.4.12
doth favour/That seekes the conquest by her loose behaviour.	Ovid's Elegies	2.5.12
Even such as by Aurora hath the skie,	Ovid's Elegies	2.5.35
By chaunce her beauty never shined fuller.	Ovid's Elegies	2.5.42
I sweare by Venus, and the wingd boyes bowe,	Ovid's Elegies	2.7.27
By Venus Deity how did I protest.	Ovid's Elegies	2.8.18
How oft, and by what meanes we did agree.	Ovid's Elegies	2.8.28
More glory by thy vanquisht foes assends.	Ovid's Elegies	2.9.6
His sword layed by, safe, though rude places yeelds.	Ovid's Elegies	2.9.20
lies quiet/And slumbring, thinkes himselfe much blessed by it.	Ovid's Elegies	2.9.40
Great joyes by hope I inly shall conceive.	Ovid's Elegies	2.9.44
Cupid by thee, Mars in great doubt doth trample,	Ovid's Elegies	2.9.47
And thy step-father fights by thy example.	Ovid's Elegies	2.9.48
By thee deceived, by thee surprisde am I,	Ovid's Elegies	2.10.3
Even as a boate, tost by contrarie winde,	Ovid's Elegies	2.10.9
Being wrackt, carowse the sea tir'd by their ships:	Ovid's Elegies	2.10.34
taught/Ill waies by rough seas wondring waves first taught,	Ovid's Elegies	2.11.2
When Troy by ten yeares battle tumbled downe,	Ovid's Elegies	2.12.9
By seaven huge mouthes into the sea is [skipping] <slipping>,	Ovid's Elegies	2.13.10
By fear'd Anubis visage I thee pray,	Ovid's Elegies	2.13.11
All humaine kinde by their default had perisht.	Ovid's Elegies	2.14.10
Againe by some in this unpeopled world.	Ovid's Elegies	2.14.12
I could my selfe by secret Magicke shift.	Ovid's Elegies	2.15.10
And by the rising herbes, where cleare springs slide,	Ovid's Elegies	2.16.9
By cloyed Charibdis, and againe devoured.	Ovid's Elegies	2.16.26
By me, and by my starres, thy radiant eyes.	Ovid's Elegies	2.16.44
But by her glasse disdainefull pride she learnes,	Ovid's Elegies	2.17.9
Venus with Vulcan, though smiths tooles laide by,	Ovid's Elegies	2.17.19
And many by me to get glory crave.	Ovid's Elegies	2.17.28
And craftily knowes by what meanes to winne me.	Ovid's Elegies	2.19.10
Suffring much cold by hoary nights frost bred.	Ovid's Elegies	2.19.22
A mothers joy by Jove she had not felt.	Ovid's Elegies	2.19.28
What ever haps, by suffrance harme is done,	Ovid's Elegies	2.19.35
By thy default thou doest our joyes defraude.	Ovid's Elegies	2.19.58
By her footes blemish greater grace she tooke.	Ovid's Elegies	3.1.10
Oft some points at the prophet passing by,	Ovid's Elegies	3.1.19
And by those numbers is thy first youth spent.	Ovid's Elegies	3.1.28
By suffring much not borne by thy severity.	Ovid's Elegies	3.1.48
By me Corinna learnes, cousening her guard,	Ovid's Elegies	3.1.49
But cruelly by her was drown'd and rent.	Ovid's Elegies	3.1.58
Yet he attain'd by her support to have her,	Ovid's Elegies	3.2.17
Let us all conquer by our mistris favour.	Ovid's Elegies	3.2.18
By thy sides touching ill she is entreated.	Ovid's Elegies	3.2.22
By these I judge, delight me may the rest,	Ovid's Elegies	3.2.35
That from thy fanne, mov'd by my hand may blow?	Ovid's Elegies	3.2.38
Greater then her, by her leave th'art, Ile say.	Ovid's Elegies	3.2.60
And each give signes by casting up his cloake.	Ovid's Elegies	3.2.74
By which she perjurd oft hath lyed [to] <by> me.	Ovid's Elegies	3.3.10
By her eyes I remember late she swore,	Ovid's Elegies	3.3.13
And by mine eyes, and mine were pained sore.	Ovid's Elegies	3.3.14
But by my paine to purge her perjuries,	Ovid's Elegies	3.3.21
Nor canst by watching keepe her minde from sinne.	Ovid's Elegies	3.4.7
Forbeare to kindle vice by prohibition,	Ovid's Elegies	3.4.11
Yet by deceit Love did them all surprize.	Ovid's Elegies	3.4.20
Was not defilde by any gallant wooer.	Ovid's Elegies	3.4.24
Never can these by any meanes agree.	Ovid's Elegies	3.4.42
If standing here I can by no meanes get,	Ovid's Elegies	3.5.11
If I a lover bee by thee held back.	Ovid's Elegies	3.5.22
Rich Nile by seaven mouthes to the vast sea flowing,	Ovid's Elegies	3.5.39
Is by Evadne thought to take such flame,	Ovid's Elegies	3.5.41
By feare depriv'd of strength to runne away.	Ovid's Elegies	3.5.70
By charmes are running springs and fountaines drie,	Ovid's Elegies	3.6.32
By charmes maste drops from okes, from vines grapes fall,	Ovid's Elegies	3.6.33
Thou [cousenst] <cousendst> mee, by thee surprizde am I,	Ovid's Elegies	3.6.71
But when she saw it would by no meanes stand,	Ovid's Elegies	3.6.75
Souldiours by bloud to be inricht have lucke.	Ovid's Elegies	3.7.54
Where Linus by his father Phoebus layed/To sing with his	Ovid's Elegies	3.8.23
By secreat thoughts to thinke there is a god.	Ovid's Elegies	3.8.36
Why are our pleasures by thy meanes forborne?	Ovid's Elegies	3.9.4
And worshipt by their paine, and lying apart?	Ovid's Elegies	3.9.16
Which by the wild boare in the woods was shorne.	Ovid's Elegies	3.9.40
good growes by this griefe,/Oft bitter juice brings to the	Ovid's Elegies	3.10.7

BY (cont.)			
The people by my company she pleasd,	Ovid's Elegies	3.10.19	
O by our fellow bed, by all/The Gods who by thee to be perjurde	Ovid's Elegies	3.10.45	
our fellow bed, by all/The Gods who by thee to be perjurde fall,	Ovid's Elegies	3.10.45	
fellow bed, by all/The Gods who by thee to be perjurde fall,	Ovid's Elegies	3.10.46	
And by thy face to me a powre divine,	Ovid's Elegies	3.10.47	
And by thine eyes whose radiance burnes out mine.	Ovid's Elegies	3.10.48	
Wilt have me willing, or to love by force?	Ovid's Elegies	3.10.50	
Erre I? or by my [bookes] <lookes> is she so knowne?	Ovid's Elegies	3.11.7	
'Tis so: by my witte her abuse is growne.	Ovid's Elegies	3.11.8	
The wench by my fault is set forth to sell.	Ovid's Elegies	3.11.10	
Her gate by my hands is set open wide.	Ovid's Elegies	3.11.12	
Scylla by us her fathers rich haire steales,	Ovid's Elegies	3.11.21	
And men inthralld by Mermaids singing charmes.	Ovid's Elegies	3.11.28	
We toucht the walles, Camillus wonne by thee.	Ovid's Elegies	3.12.2	
White Heifers by glad people forth are led,	Ovid's Elegies	3.12.13	
By whom disclosd, she in the high woods tooke,	Ovid's Elegies	3.12.19	
Let me, and them by it be aye be-friended.	Ovid's Elegies	3.12.36	
Such as confesse, have lost their good names by it.	Ovid's Elegies	3.13.6	
What madnesse ist to tell night <nights> prankes by day,	Ovid's Elegies	3.13.7	
This bed, and that by tumbling made uneven,	Ovid's Elegies	3.13.32	
And being justified by two words, thinke/The cause acquits you	Ovid's Elegies	3.13.49	
(Nor am I by such wanton toyes defamde)/Heire of an antient	Ovid's Elegies	3.14.4	
Not onely by warres rage made Gentleman.	Ovid's Elegies	3.14.6	
[Seaborderers] <Seaborders>, disjoin'd by Neptunes might:	Hero and Leander	1.3	
Which lightned by her necke, like Diamonds shone.	Hero and Leander	1.26	
So was her beautie to the standers by.	Hero and Leander	1.106	
Where by one hand, light headed Bacchus hoong,	Hero and Leander	1.139	
For will in us is over-rul'd by fate.	Hero and Leander	1.168	
What we behold is censur'd by our eies.	Hero and Leander	1.174	
These lovers parled by the touch of hands,	Hero and Leander	1.185	
Well therefore by the gods decreed it is,	Hero and Leander	1.253	
By which alone, our reverend fathers say,	Hero and Leander	1.267	
Honour is purchac'd by the deedes wee do.	Hero and Leander	1.280	
Maids are not woon by brutish force and might,	Hero and Leander	1.419	
Than for the fire filcht by Prometheus;	Hero and Leander	1.438	
By this, sad Hero, with love unacquainted,	Hero and Leander	2.1	
To linger by the way, and once she stayd,	Hero and Leander	2.7	
And therefore to her tower he got by stealth.	Hero and Leander	2.18	
By being possest of him for whom she long'd:	Hero and Leander	2.36	
By nature have a mutuall appetence,	Hero and Leander	2.56	
Mov'd by Loves force, unto ech other lep?	Hero and Leander	2.58	
Shee, with a kind of graunting, put him by it,	Hero and Leander	2.73	
Sad Hero wroong him by the hand, and wept,	Hero and Leander	2.95	
Alcides like, by mightie violence,	Hero and Leander	2.120	
Affection by the count'nance is descride.	Hero and Leander	2.132	
By this Leander being nere the land,	Hero and Leander	2.227	
By those white limmes, which sparckled through the lawne.	Hero and Leander	2.242	
By which love sailes to regions full of blis),	Hero and Leander	2.276	
And faine by stealth away she would have crept,	Hero and Leander	2.310	
By this Apollos golden harpe began,	Hero and Leander	2.327	
By shallow Rivers, to whose falls,	Passionate Shepherd	7	
BYATHER			
And by the coast of Byather at last,	2Tamb	1.3.200	Techel
BYLL			
Is it unwilling I should write this byll?	F 454	2.1.66	Faust
this byll is ended,/And Faustus hath bequeath'd his soule to	F 463	2.1.75	Faust
BYRDS			
Melodious byrds [sing] <sings> Madrigalls.	Passionate Shepherd	8	
BYRON			
Viceroy of Byron, wisely hast thou said:	2Tamb	1.1.54	Orcan
To Byron here where thus I honor you?	2Tamb	4.3.6	Tamb
BYRTH			
At whose byrth-day Cynthia with Saturne joinde,	1Tamb	1.1.13	Cosroe
Shal give the world to note, for all my byrth,	1Tamb	5.1.188	Tamb
Or had those wanton Poets, for whose byrth/Olde Rome was proud,	2Tamb	2.4.91	Tamb
issue, at whose byrth/Heaven did affoord a gratious aspect,	2Tamb	3.5.79	Tamb
As ye shal curse the byrth of Tamburlaine.	2Tamb	3.5.89	Tamb
His byrth, his life, his health and majesty.	2Tamb	5.3.27	Techel
BYRTH-DAY			
At whose byrth-day Cynthia with Saturne joinde,	1Tamb	1.1.13	Cosroe
BYRTHES			
Your byrthes shall be no blemish to your fame,	1Tamb	4.4.127	Tamb
BY-SOUTH			
East and by-South:	Jew	1.1.41	Barab
BYTHINIA			
Arabians, Moores and Jewes/Enough to cover all Bythinia.	1Tamb	3.3.137	Bajzth
Even in Bythinia, when I took this Turke:	1Tamb	4.2.42	Tamb
These Mores that drew him from Bythinia,	1Tamb	4.2.98	Tamb
About the confines of Bythinia?	1Tamb	4.3.25	Arabia
And thence unto Bythinia, where I tooke/The Turke and his great	2Tamb	5.3.128	Tamb
BYTHINIANS			
[Illirians] <Illicians>, Thracians, and Bythinians,	2Tamb	1.1.64	Orcan
Naturalized Turks and stout Bythinians/Came to my bands full	2Tamb	3.5.41	Trebiz
BYTS			
Your Majesty must get some byts for these,	2Tamb	4.3.43	Therid
BYTTERNESSE			
That Zoacum, that fruit of bytternesse,	2Tamb	2.3.20	Orcan
CABINET (See CABONET)			
CABINS			
With strawie cabins now her courts should build.	Ovid's Elegies	2.9.18	
CABLE			
The floore whereof, this Cable being cut,	Jew	5.5.34	Barab

CABONET			
Mounted his royall Cabonet.	P 957	19.27	Eprnon
CADESSE			
Puttock hovers/Around the aire, the Cadesse raine discovers,	Ovid's Elegies		2.6.34
CAEPHALUS			
Say that thy love with Caephalus were not knowne,	Ovid's Elegies		1.13.33
But [heldst] <hadst> thou in thine armes some Caephalus,	Ovid's Elegies		1.13.39
CAESAR			
What right had Caesar to the [Empery] <Empire>?	Jew	Prol.19	Machvl
As Caesar tc his souldiers, so say I:	P 155	2.98	Guise
Yet Caesar shall goe forth.	P 996	19.66	Guise
Thus Caesar did goe foorth, and thus he dyed.	P1015	19.85	Guise
As Caesar riding in the Romaine streete,	Edw	1.1.173	Gavstn
That <which> Julius caesar brought from Affrica.	F 824	3.1.46	Mephst
Adde, Caesar, to these illes Perusian famine;	Lucan, First Booke		41
[There] <Their> Caesar may'st thou shine and no cloud dim thee;	Lucan, First Booke		59
Thou Caesar at this instant art my God,	Lucan, First Booke		63
Nor Caesar no superior, which of both/Had justest cause	Lucan, First Booke		126
Now Caesar cverpast the snowy Alpes,	Lucan, First Booke		185
And staring, thus bespoke: what mean'st thou Caesar?	Lucan, First Booke		192
Caesar is thine, so please it thee, thy soldier;	Lucan, First Booke		204
As soone as Caesar got unto the banke/And bounds of Italy;	Lucan, First Booke		225
And lofty Caesar in the thickest throng,	Lucan, First Booke		247
One that was feed for Caesar, and whose tongue/Could tune the	Lucan, First Booke		272
Caesar (said he) while eloquence prevail'd,	Lucan, First Booke		274
And therewith Caesar prone ennough to warre,	Lucan, First Booke		293
Caesar; he whom I heare thy trumpets charge/I hould no Romaine;	Lucan, First Booke		374
When Caesar saw his army proane to war,	Lucan, First Booke		393
is by cowards/Left as a pray now Caesar doth approach:	Lucan, First Booke		512
and every vaine/Did threaten horror from the host of Caesar;	Lucan, First Booke		621
Romulus, temples brave/Bacchus, Alcides, and now Caesar have.	Ovid's Elegies		3.7.52
When Thebes, when Troy, when Caesar should be writ,	Ovid's Elegies		3.11.15
CAESARIA			
Acantha, Antioch, and Caesaria,	2Tamb	2.1.20	Fredrk
CAESARS			
My Campe is like to Julius Caesars Hoste,	1Tamb	3.3.152	Tamb
Caesars, and Pompeys jarring love soone ended,	Lucan, First Booke		98
would dim/Olde triumphs, and that Caesars conquering France,	Lucan, First Booke		122
Each side had great partakers; Caesars cause,	Lucan, First Booke		128
Caesars renowne for war was lesse, he restles,	Lucan, First Booke		145
this spectacle/Stroake Caesars hart with feare, his hayre	Lucan, First Booke		195
And Caesars mind unsetled musing stood;	Lucan, First Booke		264
restrain'd them; but wars love/And Caesars awe dasht all:	Lucan, First Booke		357
The Santons that rejoyce in Caesars love,	Lucan, First Booke		423
Other that Caesars barbarous bands were spread/Along Nar floud	Lucan, First Booke		471
Beholde thy kinsmans Caesars prosperous bandes,	Ovid's Elegies		1.2.51
The earth of Caesars had beene destitute.	Ovid's Elegies		2.14.18
CAGE			
Keeping his kingly body in a Cage,	1Tamb	4.2.61	Zabina
Shall ransome him, or take him from his cage.	1Tamb	4.2.94	Tamb
Which kept his father in an yron cage:	2Tamb	1.1.5	Orcan
CAGES			
Keeping in yron cages Emperours.	2Tamb	1.3.49	Tamb
CAICKE			
You likewise that repulst the Caicke foe,	Lucan, First Booke		459
CAIN			
yet let me talke to her;/This off-spring of Cain, this Jebusite	Jew	2.3.301	Barab
But perish underneath my bitter curse/Like Cain by Adam, for	Jew	3.4.33	Barab
CAIRE			
from Egypt, or by Caire/But at the entry there into the sea,	Jew	1.1.73	Barab
CAIRO			
By [Cairo] <Cario> runs--	2Tamb	1.2.15	Callap
By [Cairo] <Cario> runs to Alexandria Bay,	2Tamb	1.2.19	Callap
CAIRON			
Marching from Cairon northward with his camp,	2Tamb	1.1.47	Gazell
CAITIFE			
Go Belimothe, and take this caitife hence,	F1408	4.2.84	Faust
CAL (Homograph)			
(I cal it meane, because being yet obscure,	1Tamb	1.2.203	Tamb
And made Canarea cal us kings and Lords,	2Tamb	1.3.181	Usumc
But madam, would you have us cal him home?	Edw	1.4.208	Mortmr
liver/Squis'd matter; through the cal, the intralls pearde,	Lucan, First Booke		624
CALABRIA			
And toward Calabria, back'd by Sicily,	Jew	5.3.9	Calym
CALABRIAN			
Lachrima Christi and Calabrian wines/Shall common Souldiers	2Tamb	1.3.221	Tamb
CALAMITY			
May serve in perill of calamity/To ransome great Kings from	Jew	1.1.31	Barab
'Las I could weepe at your calamity.	Jew	4.1.203	Barab
CALAPINE			
And sacred Lord, the mighty Calapine:	2Tamb	1.1.3	Orcan
Then let us see if coward Calapine/Dare levie armes against our	2Tamb	3.2.155	Tamb
CALAPINES			
I, my Lord, he was Calapines keeper.	2Tamb	3.5.152	P Therid
CAL'D			
where the mighty Christian Priest/Cal'd John the great, sits in	2Tamb	1.3.188	Techel
And now that Henry is cal'd from Polland,	P 569	11.34	Navrre
In Germany, within a Towne cal'd [Rhode] <Rhodes>:	F 12	Prol.12	1Chor
you heartily sir; for wee cal'd you but in jeast I promise you.	F1123	3.3.36	P Dick
The towne of Sestos cal'd it Venus glasse.	Hero and Leander		1.142
CALD			
Mine honour will be cald in question,	Edw	2.4.55	Queene
Care of my countrie cald me to this warre.	Edw	4.6.65	Queene

CALD (cont.)
divell, so I should be cald kill divell all the parish over. — F App p.230 48 P Clown
The gods care we are cald, and men of piety, — Ovid's Elegies 3.8.17
Who mine was cald, whom I lov'd more then any, — Ovid's Elegies 3.11.5
The lustie god imbrast him, cald him love, — Hero and Leander 2.167
He cald it in, for love made him repent. — Hero and Leander 2.210
And knockt and cald, at which celestiall noise, — Hero and Leander 2.231

CALDE
good heaven/We breathe as now, and what this world is calde, — Dido 1.1.198 Aeneas
And therewithall he calde false Sinon forth, — Dido 2.1.143 Aeneas
Sicheus, not Aeneas be thou calde: — Dido 3.4.59 Dido
And seeke a forraine land calde Italy: — Dido 4.4.98 Dido
But what shall it be calde, Troy as before? — Dido 5.1.18 Illion
Nay, I will have it calde Anchisaeon, — Dido 5.1.22 Aeneas
And I be calde a second Helena. — Dido 5.1.148 Dido
Yea, and she soothde me up, and calde me sir <sire>, — Ovid's Elegies 3.6.11

CALDONIAN
To chace the savage [Calidonian] <Caldonian> Boare: — 1Tamb 4.3.3 Souldn

CALEPINUS
Calepinus Cyricelibes, otherwise Cybelius, son and successive — 2Tamb 3.1.1 P Orcan

CALFE
you shal heare a hogge grunt, a calfe bleate, and an asse braye, — F App p.232 27 P Faust

CALIDONIAN
To chace the savage [Calidonian] <Caldonian> Boare: — 1Tamb 4.3.3 Souldn

CALL (See also CAL, CALS)
Sit on my knee, and call for thy content, — Dido 1.1.28 Jupitr
And call both Thetis and [Cimothoe] <Cimodoae> <Cymodoce>,/To — Dido 1.1.132 Venus
But what may I faire Virgin call your name? — Dido 1.1.188 Aeneas
Which now we call Italia of his name, — Dido 1.2.23 Cloan
Doth Dido call me backe? — Dido 3.1.53 Iarbus
Troy shall no more call him her second hope, — Dido 3.2.8 Juno
That can call them forth when as she please, — Dido 4.1.4 Iarbus
Since destinie doth call me from [thy] <the> shoare: — Dido 4.3.2 Aeneas
What willes our Lord, or wherefore did he call? — Dido 4.3.15 Achat
Dido is thine, henceforth Ile call thee Lord: — Dido 4.4.84 Dido
I, so youle dwell with me and call me mother. — Dido 4.5.16 Nurse
Call him not wicked, sister, speake him faire, — Dido 5.1.200 Dido
What, shall I call thee brother? — 1Tamb 1.1.103 Mycet
He cals me Bajazeth, whom you call Lord. — 1Tamb 3.3.67 Bajzth
And dar'st thou bluntly call me Bajazeth? — 1Tamb 3.3.71 Bajzth
And dar'st thou bluntly call me Tamburlaine? — 1Tamb 3.3.74 Tamb
Call foorth our laisie brother from the tent, — 2Tamb 4.1.7 Celeb
Call up the souldiers to defend these wals. — 2Tamb 5.1.56 Govnr
Summon thy sences, call thy wits together: — Jew 1.1.178 Barab
Goe one and call those Jewes of Malta hither: — Jew 1.2.34 Govnr
Heave up my shoulders when they call me dogge, — Jew 2.3.24 Barab
How, dost call me rogue? — Jew 4.1.96 1Fryar
He was not wont to call me Barabas. — Jew 4.3.3 Barab
Malta prisoner; for come [all] <call> the world/To rescue thee, — Jew 5.5.119 Govnr
Why, darst thou presume to call on Christ, — P 356 6.11 Mntsrl
despatch Embassadours/To Poland, to call Henry back againe, — P 556 11.21 QnMoth
Is ruth and almost death to call to minde: — P 797 16.11 Navrre
Then stay a while and Ile goe call the King, — P1017 19.87 Capt
Goe call a surgeon hether strait. — P1179 22.41 Navrre
Goe call the English Agent hether strait, — P1188 22.50 King
And there abide till fortune call thee home. — Edw 1.4.126 Edward
But thou must call mine honor thus in question? — Edw 1.4.152 Queene
And be a meanes to call home Gaveston: — Edw 1.4.184 Queene
And is this true to call him home againe? — Edw 1.4.246 Lncstr
To banish him, and then to call him home, — Edw 1.4.275 Mortmr
Diablo, what passions call you these? — Edw 1.4.319 Lncstr
What call you this but private libelling, — Edw 2.2.34 Edward
Nephew, your father, I dare not call him king. — Edw 4.6.33 Kent
But when I call to minde I am a king, — Edw 5.1.23 Edward
Call them againe my lorde, and speake them faire, — Edw 5.1.91 Leistr
Call thou them back, I have no power to speake. — Edw 5.1.93 Edward
Call me not lorde, away, out of my sight: — Edw 5.1.113 Edward
Whose there? call hither Gurney and Matrevis. — Edw 5.2.38 Mortmr
I, I, so: when I call you, bring it in. — Edw 5.5.35 Ltborn
What doctrine call you this? Che sera, sera: — F 74 1.1.46 Faust
call me Maister Wagner, and see that you walke attentively, — F 385 1.4.43 P Wagner
Tell me, where is the place that men call Hell? — F 505 2.1.117 Faust
See, see his window's ope, we'l call to him. — F1177 4.1.23 Fredrk
This sport is excellent: wee'l call and wake him. — F1281 4.1.127 Emper
I, [all] <I call> your hearts to recompence this deed. — F1394 4.2.70 Faust
Tush, Christ did call the Theefe upon the Crosse, — F1482 4.4.26 Faust
Then call for mercy, and avoyd despaire. — F1733 5.1.60 OldMan
Yet Faustus call on God. — F1848 5.2.52 P 2Schol
Yet will I call on him: O spare me Lucifer. — F1942 5.2.146 Faust
one, me thought/I heard him shreeke and call aloud for helpe: — F1992 5.3.10 3Schol
call me Maister Wagner, and let thy left eye be diametarily — F App p.231 69 P Wagner
One of you call him foorth. — F App p.238 68 P Emper
Tush, Christ did call the thiefe upon the Crosse, — F App p.240 125 Faust
helpe Mephastophilis, call the Officers, my legge, my legge. — F App p.241 155 P Faust
(as their old custome was)/They call th'Etrurian Augures, — Lucan, First Booke 584
Therefore who ere love sloathfulnesse doth call, — Ovid's Elegies 1.9.31
And call the sunnes white horses [backe] <blacke> at noone. — Ovid's Elegies 2.1.24
and thee lewd hangman call. — Ovid's Elegies 2.2.36
They call him backe: — Ovid's Elegies 3.2.75
Men foolishly doe call it vertuous, — Hero and Leander 1.277

CALLAPINE (See also CALAPINE, CALLEPINE)
pity the ruthfull plight/Of Callapine, the sonne of Bajazeth, — 2Tamb 1.2.2 Callap
As I am Callapine the Emperour, — 2Tamb 1.2.64 Callap

CALLAPINE (ccnt.)				
Shall so torment thee and that Callapine, ...	2Tamb	3.5.85		Tamb
Callapine, Ile hang a clogge about your necke for running away	2Tamb	3.5.100	P	Tamb
Aid thy obedient servant Callapine, ...	2Tamb	5.2.28		Callap
Renowmed Generall mighty Callapine, ...	2Tamb	5.2.36		Amasia
All Turkie is in armes with Callapine.	2Tamb	5.2.51		Callap
yong Callapine that lately fled from your majesty, hath nowe	2Tamb	5.3.102	P	3Msngr
That Callapine should be my slave againe.	2Tamb	5.3.118		Tamb
What Callapine, a little curtesie.	Jew	1.2.23		Calym
CALL'D				
And call'd the Gods to witnesse of my vow, ...	1Tamb	1.2.234		Tamb
From thence I crost the Gulfe, call'd by the name/Mare magiore,	2Tamb	1.3.214		Therid
This Even they use in Malta here ('tis call'd/Saint Jaques	Jew	3.4.75		Barab
Upon the Bridge, call'd Ponte Angelo, ...	F 817	3.1.39		Mephst
CALLED				
And will be called the murtherer of a king, ...	Edw	5.1.101		Edward
CALLEPINE				
Renowmed Emperour, mighty Callepine, ...	2Tamb	3.5.1		2Msngr
CALLEPINUS				
Long live Callepinus, Emperour of Turky.	2Tamb	3.1.6	P	Orcan
CALLES				
That calles my soule from forth his living seate, . .	Dido	3.4.53		Dido
Cloanthus, haste away, Aeneas calles.	Dido	4.3.14		Aeneas
I faine would goe, yet beautie calles me backe: . .	Dido	4.3.46		Aeneas
And Mercury to flye for what he calles?	Dido	4.4.47		Dido
It is Aeneas calles Aeneas hence, ...	Dido	5.1.132		Dido
And all the world calles me a second Helen, ...	Dido	5.1.144		Dido
CALLIMACHUS				
[The world shall of Callimachus ever speake], . . .	Ovid's Elegies	1.15.13		
Before Callimachus one preferres me farre, . . .	Ovid's Elegies	2.4.19		
CALLING				
And grace your calling with a greater sway.	1Tamb	2.5.31		Cosroe
Calling the Provinces, Citties and townes/After my name and	1Tamb	4.4.79		Tamb
And calling Christ for record of our trueths? . . .	2Tamb	2.1.30		Sgsmnd
CALLIST				
Niobe flint, Callist we make a Beare, ...	Ovid's Elegies	3.11.31		
CALLS				
Looke up Benvolio, tis the Emperour calls.	F1286	4.1.132		Saxony
Hell claimes his <calls for> right, and with a roaring voyce,	F1726	5.1.53		Faust
Calls for the payment of my latest yeares, ...	F App	p.239 93		Faust
CALLYMATH				
how fares Callymath, What wind drives you thus into Malta	Jew	3.5.2	P	Govnr
For Callymath, when he hath view'd the Towne, ...	Jew	5.2.105		Barab
CALMDE				
She that hath calmde the furie of my sword, ...	1Tamb	5.1.437		Tamb
CALME				
But when you were abourd twas calme enough, ...	Dido	4.4.27		Dido
And calme the rage of thundring Jupiter:	1Tamb	3.3.123		Tamb
And Epernoune though I seeme milde and calme, ...	P 893	17.88		King
Thou seest by nature he is milde and calme, ...	Edw	1.4.388		MortSr
O fly him then, but Edmund calme this rage, ...	Edw	4.6.11		Kent
course that time doth runne with calme and silent foote, .	F App	p.239 91	P	Faust
Againe, this people could not brooke calme peace, . .	Lucan, First Booke	172		
CALMIE				
And court Aeneas with your calmie cheere, ...	Dido	1.1.123		Venus
CALOR				
The Humidum and Calor, which some holde/Is not a parcell of the	2Tamb	5.3.86		Phsitn
CALPE				
The Ocean swell'd, as high as Spanish Calpe, ...	Lucan, First Booke	553		
CALS				
He cals me Bajazeth, whom you call Lord.	1Tamb	3.3.67		Bajzth
But cals not then your Grace to memorie/The league we lately	2Tamb	2.1.27		Sgsmnd
Now, he that cals himself the scourge of Jove, ...	2Tamb	3.5.21		Orcan
it inters with murmurs dolorous,/And cals the place Bidentall:	Lucan, First Booke	607		
CAL'ST				
Cal'st thou me Concubine that am betroath'd/Unto the great and	1Tamb	3.3.169		Zenoc
CALST				
Thou calst on <talkst of> Christ contrary to thy promise.	F 643	2.2.92		Lucifr
CALVES				
And calves from whose feard front no threatning flyes, .	Ovid's Elegies	3.12.15		
CALVUS				
With Calvus learnd Catullus comes <come> and greete him. .	Ovid's Elegies	3.8.62		
CALYDON				
Not Calydon, nor Aetolia did please:	Ovid's Elegies	3.5.37		
CALYMATH (See also CALLYMATH)				
Then give us leave, great Selim-Calymath.	Jew	1.2.13		Govnr
And all good fortune wait on Calymath.	Jew	1.2.33		Govnr
From the Emperour of Turkey is arriv'd/Great Selim-Calymath,	Jew	1.2.40		Govnr
What is the summe that Calymath requires?	Jew	2.2.35		Bosco
Proud-daring Calymath, instead of gold, ...	Jew	2.2.53		Govnr
To you of Malta thus saith Calymath:	Jew	3.5.7		Basso
For Selim-Calymath shall come himselfe, ...	Jew	3.5.23		Basso
And let's provide to welcome Calymath:	Jew	3.5.30		Govnr
For Calymath having hover'd here so long, ...	Jew	5.1.4		Govnr
For by my meanes Calymath shall enter in.	Jew	5.1.63		Barab
May all good fortune follow Calymath.	Jew	5.2.21		Barab
What will you give me if I render you/The life of Calymath,	Jew	5.2.80		Barab
To a solemne feast/I will invite young Selim-Calymath,/Where be	Jew	5.2.97		Barab
Malta's Governor, I bring/A message unto mighty Calymath;	Jew	5.3.14		Msngr
Now Selim-Calymath, returne me word/That thou wilt come, and I	Jew	5.5.11		Barab
Now as for Calymath and his consorts, ...	Jew	5.5.32		Barab
Welcome great Calymath.	Jew	5.5.55		Barab
Will't please thee, mighty Selim-Calymath, ...	Jew	5.5.57		Barab

CALYMATH (cont.)			
Stay, Calymath;	Jew	5.5.60	Govnr
See Calymath, this was devis'd for thee.	Jew	5.5.66	Govnr
Know, Calymath, I aym'd thy overthrow,	Jew	5.5.83	Barab
Content thee, Calymath, here thou must stay,	Jew	5.5.118	Govnr
CALYPSO			
Love-snarde Calypso is supposde to pray,	Ovid's Elegies		2.17.15
CAME			
men, saw you as you came/Any of all my Sisters wandring here?	Dido	1.1.183	Venus
Where when they came, Ulysses on the sand/Assayd with honey	Dido	2.1.136	Aeneas
And so came in this fatall instrument:	Dido	2.1.176	Aeneas
And thinking to goe downe, came Hectors ghost/With ashie visage,	Dido	2.1.201	Aeneas
At last came Pirrhus fell and full of ire,	Dido	2.1.213	Aeneas
I had been wedded ere Aeneas came:	Dido	3.1.138	Dido
Some came in person, others sent their Legats:	Dido	3.1.152	Dido
O Serpent that came creeping from the shoare,	Dido	5.1.165	Dido
Once didst thou goe, and he came backe againe,	Dido	5.1.196	Dido
Before I came, Aeneas was abourd,	Dido	5.1.226	Anna
When first he came on shoare, perish thou to:	Dido	5.1.299	Dido
Came creeping to us with their crownes apace.	1Tamb	2.5.86	Tamb
We came from Turky to confirme a league,	2Tamb	1.1.115	Gazell
I came to Cubar, where the Negros dwell,	2Tamb	1.3.201	Techel
Then crost the sea and came to Oblia,	2Tamb	1.3.211	Therid
sir, for being a king, for Tamburlain came up of nothing.	2Tamb	3.1.74	P Almeda
Came forty thousand warlike foot and horse,	2Tamb	3.5.38	Orcan
and stout Bythinians/Came to my bands full fifty thousand more,	2Tamb	3.5.42	Trebiz
I came at last to Graecia, and from thence/To Asia, where I	2Tamb	5.3.141	Tamb
How chance you came not with those other ships/That sail'd by	Jew	1.1.89	Barab
Know Knights of Malta, that we came from Rhodes,	Jew	1.2.2	Basso
and in mine Argosie/And other ships that came from Egypt last,	Jew	1.2.188	Barab
The Christian Ile of Rhodes, from whence you came,	Jew	2.2.31	Bosco
Even now as I came home, he slipt me in,	Jew	2.3.267	Barab
But e're I came--	Jew	3.6.15	Abigal
I smelt 'em e're they came.	Jew	4.1.22	Barab
But came it freely, did the Cow give down her milk freely?	Jew	4.2.102	P Ithimr
You know that I came lately out of France,	Edw	1.1.44	Gavstn
And even now, a poast came from the court,	Edw	2.1.19	Spencr
This letter came from my sweete Gaveston,	Edw	2.1.59	Neece
And thereof came it, that the fleering Scots,	Edw	2.2.188	Lncstr
Well, and how fortunes that he came not?	Edw	3.1.113	Edward
But ere he came, Warwick in ambush laie,	Edw	3.1.118	Arundl
Further, or this letter was sealed, Lord Bartley came,	Edw	5.2.30	BshpWn
as th'infernall spirits/On sweet Musaeus when he came to hell,	F 143	1.1.115	Faust
No, I came now hether of mine owne accord.	F 272	1.3.44	Mephst
The Pope shall curse that Faustus came to Rome.	F 903	3.1.125	Faust
That on a furies back came post from Rome,	F1161	4.1.7	Fredrk
and when I came just in the midst my horse vanisht away, and I	F1544	4.5.40	P HrsCsr
Hence came it that th'edicts were overrul'd,	Lucan, First Booke		178
Faiths breach, and hence came war to most men welcom.	Lucan, First Booke		184
And many came from shallow Isara,	Lucan, First Booke		400
And others came from that uncertaine shore,	Lucan, First Booke		410
They came that dwell/By Nemes fields, and bankes of Satirus,	Lucan, First Booke		420
And she to whom in shape of [Swanne] <Bull> Jove came.	Ovid's Elegies		1.3.22
Then came Corinna in a long loose gowne,	Ovid's Elegies		1.5.9
Forth-with Love came, no darke night-flying spright/Nor hands	Ovid's Elegies		1.6.13
The seventh day came, none following mightst thou see,	Ovid's Elegies		2.6.45
As soone as from strange lands Sabinus came,	Ovid's Elegies		2.18.27
Elegia came with haires perfumed sweete,	Ovid's Elegies		3.1.7
Then with huge steps came violent Tragedie,	Ovid's Elegies		3.1.11
To sit, and talke with thee I hether came,	Ovid's Elegies		3.2.3
But when her lover came, had she drawne backe,	Ovid's Elegies		3.3.39
Came forth a mother, though a maide there put.	Ovid's Elegies		3.4.22
And one gave place still as another came.	Ovid's Elegies		3.6.64
To winne the maide came in a golden shewer.	Ovid's Elegies		3.7.30
But when in gifts the wise adulterer came,	Ovid's Elegies		3.7.33
Came lovers home, from this great festivall.	Hero and Leander		1.96
And as shee spake those words, came somewhat nere him.	Hero and Leander		1.180
At last he came, O who can tell the greeting,	Hero and Leander		2.23
Home when he came, he seem'd not to be there,	Hero and Leander		2.117
His colour went and came, as if he rewd/The greefe which	Hero and Leander		2.214
The neerer that he came, the more she fled,	Hero and Leander		2.243
CAMELS			
Returne our Mules and emptie Camels backe,	1Tamb	1.2.76	Agidas
Goe send 'um threescore Camels, thirty Mules,	Jew	1.1.59	Barab
Three thousand Camels, and two hundred yoake/Of labouring Oxen,	Jew	1.2.183	Barab
CAMILLUS			
The ground which Curius and Camillus till'd,	Lucan, First Booke		170
We toucht the walles, Camillus wonne by thee.	Ovid's Elegies		3.12.2
CAMMELS			
We have our Cammels laden all with gold:	1Tamb	2.2.62	Meandr
CAMP			
stragling from the camp/When Kings themselves are present in	1Tamb	2.4.16	Tamb
View well my Camp, and speake indifferently,	1Tamb	3.3.8	Tamb
But every common souldier of my Camp/Shall smile to see thy	1Tamb	3.3.85	Tamb
More then his Camp of stout Hungarians,	2Tamb	1.1.21	Uribas
Marching from Cairon northward with his camp,	2Tamb	1.1.47	Gazell
They have not long since massacred our Camp.	2Tamb	2.1.10	Fredrk
as the battaile is done, Ile ride in triumph through the Camp.	2Tamb	3.5.146	P Tamb
That crost them; both which now approacht the camp,	Lucan, First Booke		270
CAMPANIA			
Then up to Naples rich Campania,	F 787	3.1.9	Faust
CAMPE			
Gave up their voyces to dislodge the Campe,	Dido	2.1.134	Aeneas

CAMPE (cont.)			
the Greekish spyes/To hast to Tenedos and tell the Campe:	Dido	2.1.181	Aeneas
By this the Campe was come unto the walles, ...	Dido	2.1.188	Aeneas
Achilles horse/Drew him in triumph through the Greekish Campe,	Dido	2.1.206	Aeneas
The Lords and Captaines of my brothers campe, ...	1Tamb	2.5.26	Cosroe
And now Lord Tamburlaine, my brothers Campe/I leave to thee, and	1Tamb	2.5.38	Cosroe
My Campe is like to Julius Caesars Hoste, ...	1Tamb	3.3.152	Tamb
And after martch to Turky with our Campe, ...	2Tamb	1.3.158	Tamb
Where unresisted I remoov'd my campe.	2Tamb	1.3.199	Techel
stature <statue>/And martch about it with my mourning campe,	2Tamb	2.4.141	Tamb
[Those] <Whose> looks will shed such influence in my campe,/As	2Tamb	3.2.39	Tamb
As Hector did into the Grecian campe, ...	2Tamb	3.5.65	Tamb
If halfe our campe should sit and sleepe with me, . . .	2Tamb	4.1.18	Calyph
lie in wait for him/And if we find him absent from his campe,	2Tamb	5.2.57	Callap
Dismisse thy campe or else by our Edict, ...	P 863	17.58	King
Intending to dislodge my campe with speed.	P 869	17.64	Guise
in a trenche/Strake off his head, and marcht unto the campe.	Edw	3.1.120	Arundl
And frontier Varus that the campe is farre, ...	Lucan, First Booke		405
CAMPES			
But follow trembling campes, and battailes sterne, . .	Ovid's Elegies		3.7.26
CAMPS			
And never wil we sunder camps and armes, ...	2Tamb	5.2.52	Callap
CAM'ST			
And cam'st to Dido like a Fisher swaine?	Dido	5.1.162	Dido
And why thou cam'st ashore without our leave?	Jew	2.2.3	Govnr
Tell me, how cam'st thou by this?	Jew	3.1.16	Curtzn
CAMST			
From nought at first thou camst to little welth, . . .	Jew	1.2.105	1Knght
Tell me [Arundell] <Matre>, died he ere thou camst, . .	Edw	3.1.92	Edward
Or jaded camst thou from some others bed.	Ovid's Elegies		3.6.80
CAN			
I, this is it, you can sit toying there, ...	Dido	1.1.50	Venus
For none of these can be our Generall.	Dido	2.1.46	Illion
O end Aeneas, I can heare no more.	Dido	2.1.243	Dido
Then twentie thousand Indiaes can affoord:	Dido	3.1.93	Dido
As without blushing I can aske no more:	Dido	3.1.104	Aeneas
Ungentle, can she wrong Iarbus so?	Dido	3.3.10	Iarbus
I, and outface him to, doe what he can.	Dido	3.3.40	Cupid
If that your majestie can looke so lowe, ...	Dido	3.4.41	Aeneas
That can call them forth when as she please, ...	Dido	4.1.4	Iarbus
Nay, where is my warlike father, can you tell?	Dido	4.1.15	Cupid
Come forth the Cave: can heaven endure this sight? . . .	Dido	4.1.17	Iarbus
Lets see what tempests can anoy me now.	Dido	4.4.60	Aeneas
Not all the world can take thee from mine armes, . . .	Dido	4.4.61	Dido
Drive if you can my house to Italy:	Dido	4.4.129	Dido
Not from my heart, for I can hardly goe, ...	Dido	5.1.103	Aeneas
How can ye goe when he hath all your fleete?	Dido	5.1.242	Anna
Nothing can beare me to him but a ship, ...	Dido	5.1.267	Dido
What can my teares or cryes prevaile me now?	Dido	5.1.319	Anna
That knowe my wit, and can be witnesses:	1Tamb	1.1.22	Mycet
He that can take or slaughter Tamburlaine, ...	1Tamb	2.2.30	Meandr
So I can when I see my time.	1Tamb	2.4.26	Mycet
To one that can commaund what longs thereto:	1Tamb	2.5.23	Cosroe
enjoy in heaven/Can not compare with kingly joyes in earth.	1Tamb	2.5.59	Therid
Nay, though I praise it, I can live without it. . . .	1Tamb	2.5.66	Therid
That none can quence but blood and Emperie.	1Tamb	2.6.33	Cosroe
whose faculties can comprehend/The wondrous Architecture of the	1Tamb	2.7.21	Tamb
For neither rain can fall upon the earth, ...	1Tamb	3.1.51	Moroc
How can you fancie one that lookes so fierce, ...	1Tamb	3.2.40	Agidas
are ful of brags/And menace more than they can wel performe:	1Tamb	3.3.4	Tamb
If he think good, can from his garrisons, ...	1Tamb	3.3.21	Bassoe
How can ye suffer these indignities?	1Tamb	3.3.90	Moroc
Let him take all th'advantages he can, ...	1Tamb	4.1.40	Souldn
Not sparing any that can manage armes.	1Tamb	4.1.57	2Msngr
offences feele/Such plagues as heaven and we can poure on him.	1Tamb	4.3.45	Arabia
Ye Furies that can maske invisible, ...	1Tamb	4.4.17	Bajzth
can you suffer these outragious curses by these slaves of	1Tamb	4.4.26	P Zenoc
How can it but afflict my verie soule?	1Tamb	4.4.67	Zenoc
Which into words no vertue can digest:	1Tamb	5.1.173	Tamb
sparke of breath/Can quench or coole the torments of my griefe.	1Tamb	5.1.285	Zabina
She lies so close that none can find her out. . . .	2Tamb	1.2.60	Callap
Can there be such deceit in Christians, ...	2Tamb	2.2.36	Orcan
Cut off the water, all convoies that can, ...	2Tamb	3.3.39	Capt
For think ye I can live, and see him dead?	2Tamb	3.4.27	Sonne
Can never wash from thy distained browes.	2Tamb	4.1.110	Tamb
Nor Pistol, Sword, nor Lance can pierce your flesh. . . .	2Tamb	4.2.66	Olymp
What, can ye draw but twenty miles a day, ...	2Tamb	4.3.2	Tamb
If you can live with it, then live, and draw/My chariot swifter	2Tamb	4.3.20	Tamb
Tis not thy bloody tents can make me yeeld, ...	2Tamb	5.1.103	Govnr
Torture or paine can daunt my dreadlesse minde. . . .	2Tamb	5.1.113	Govnr
Sicknes or death can never conquer me.	2Tamb	5.1.222	Tamb
Is greater far, than they can thus subdue.	2Tamb	5.3.39	Usumc
Can not indure by argument of art.	2Tamb	5.3.97	Phsitn
That can endure so well your royall presence, ...	2Tamb	5.3.111	Usumc
built Citadell/Commands much more then letters can import:	Jew	Prol.23	Machvl
the Easterne rockes/Without controule can picke his riches up,	Jew	1.1.22	Barab
For I can see no fruits in all their faith, ...	Jew	1.1.116	Barab
Oft have I heard tell, can be permanent.	Jew	1.1.133	Barab
For he can counsell best in these affaires;	Jew	1.1.142	2Jew
Christians; what, or how can I multiply?	Jew	1.2.103	Barab
And which of you can charge me otherwise?	Jew	1.2.117	Barab
And having all, you can request no more;	Jew	1.2.140	Barab
as hardly can we brooke/The cruell handling of our selves in	Jew	1.2.174	1Jew

CAN (cont.)

No sleepe can fasten on my watchfull eyes,	Jew	2.1.17		Barab
That can so soone forget an injury.	Jew	2.3.19		Barab
We Jewes can fawne like Spaniels when we please;	Jew	2.3.20		Barab
What, can he steale that you demand so much?	Jew	2.3.100		Barab
No Sir, I can cut and shave.	Jew	2.3.113	P	Slave
the Governors sonne/With all the curtesie you can affoord;	Jew	2.3.226		Barab
Thou know'st, and heaven can witnesse it is true,	Jew	2.3.253		Barab
And now I can no longer hold my minde.	Jew	2.3.290		Lodowk
What greater gift can poore Mathias have?	Jew	2.3.346		Mthias
How can it if we two be secret.	Jew	4.1.9		Barab
Doe what I can he will not strip himselfe,	Jew	4.1.131		Ithimr
No, none can heare him, cry he ne're so loud.	Jew	4.1.136		Ithimr
It may be she sees more in me than I can find in my selfe:	Jew	4.2.33	P	Ithimr
he flouts me, what gentry can be in a poore Turke of ten pence?	Jew	4.2.38	P	Ithimr
I can with-hold no longer; welcome sweet love.	Jew	4.2.46		Curtzn
And you can have it, Sir, and if you please.	Jew	4.2.56		Pilia
Oh, if that be all, I can picke ope your locks.	Jew	4.3.33		Pilia
For none of this can prejudice my life.	Jew	5.1.39		Barab
my good Lord, one that can spy a place/Where you may enter, and	Jew	5.1.70		Barab
'Tis not thy life which can availe me ought,	Jew	5.2.62		Barab
Whence none can possibly escape alive:	Jew	5.5.31		Barab
But slay as many as we can come neer.	P 326	5.53		Anjoy
that despiseth him, can nere/Be good in Logick or Philosophie.	P 409	7.49		Ramus
We will with all the speed we can, provide/For Henries	P 562	11.27		QnMoth
And therefore as speedily as I can perfourme,	P 571	11.36		Navrre
Although my love to thee can hardly [suffer't] <suffer>,	P 747	15.5		King
I meane to muster all the power I can,	P 849	17.44		Guise
Assure him all the aide we can provide,	P 909	18.10		Navrre
What greater blisse can hap to Gaveston,	Edw	1.1.4		Gavstn
I can ride.	Edw	1.1.27		1PrMan
I can no longer keepe me from my lord.	Edw	1.1.139		Gavstn
of Lancaster/That hath more earldomes then an asse can beare,	Edw	1.3.2		Gavstn
What man of noble birth can brooke this sight?	Edw	1.4.12		MortSr
Can kinglie Lions fawne on creeping Ants?	Edw	1.4.15		Penbrk
Think you that we can brooke this upstart pride?	Edw	1.4.41		Warwck
Curse me, depose me, doe the worst you can.	Edw	1.4.57		Edward
Can this be true twas good to banish him,	Edw	1.4.245		Lncstr
In no respect can contraries be true.	Edw	1.4.249		Lncstr
Yet good my lord, heare what he can alledge.	Edw	1.4.250		Queene
Tis not the king can buckler Gaveston,	Edw	1.4.288		Mortmr
I love him more/Then he can Gaveston, would he lov'd me/But	Edw	1.4.303		Queene
And promiseth as much as we can wish,	Edw	1.4.399		MortSr
Can get you any favour with great men.	Edw	2.1.41		Spencr
Can you in words make showe of amitie,	Edw	2.2.32		Edward
If ye be moov'de, revenge it as you can,	Edw	2.2.198		Lncstr
Do what they can, weele live in Tinmoth here,	Edw	2.2.221		Edward
Heavens can witnesse, I love none but you.	Edw	2.4.15		Queene
When, can you tell?	Edw	2.5.60		Warwck
not the riches of my realme/Can ransome him, ah he is markt to	Edw	3.1.4		Edward
With all the hast we can dispatch him hence.	Edw	3.1.83		Edward
can ragged stonie walles/Immure thy vertue that aspires to	Edw	3.1.256		Mortmr
To thinke that we can yet be tun'd together,	Edw	4.2.9		Queene
Reward for them can bring in Mortimer?	Edw	4.3.18		Edward
Edward battell in England, sooner then he can looke for them:	Edw	4.3.35	P	Spencr
way how hardly I can brooke/To loose my crowne and kingdome,	Edw	5.1.51		Edward
not a thought so villanous/Can harbor in a man of noble birth.	Edw	5.1.132		Bartly
That death ends all, and I can die but once.	Edw	5.1.153		Edward
But can my ayre of life continue long,	Edw	5.3.17		Edward
More then we can enflict, and therefore now,	Edw	5.5.11		Matrvs
And what eyes can refraine from shedding teares,	Edw	5.5.50		Ltborn
These lookes of thine can harbor nought but death.	Edw	5.5.73		Edward
Excelling all, <and sweetly can dispute>	F 18	(HC256)B		1Chor
[Nor can they raise the winde, or rend the cloudes]:	F 86	1.1.58A		Faust
The spirits tell me they can dry the sea,	F 171	1.1.143		Cornel
For e're I sleep, I'le try what I can do:	F 192	1.1.164		Faust
<and see if hee by> his grave counsell may <can> reclaime him.	F 226	1.2.33		2Schol
<O but> I feare me, nothing will <can> reclaime him now.	F 227	1.2.34		1Schol
Yet let us see <trie> what we can do.	F 228	1.2.35		2Schol
resolute/And try the utmost <uttermost> Magicke can performe.	F 243	1.3.15		Faust
and good sauce to it, if I pay so deere, I can tell you.	F 353	1.4.11	P	Robin
me, as if they payd for their meate and drinke, I can tell you.	F 366	1.4.24	P	Robin
shall stand by me,/What [god] <power> can hurt me <thee>?	F 414	2.1.26		Faust
My bloud congeales, and I can write no more.	F 451	2.1.63		Faust
And let thee see <shewe thee> what Magicke can performe.	F 474	2.1.86		Mephst
Scarce can I name salvation, faith, or heaven,	F 570	2.2.19		Faust
<Tush>, These slender questions <trifles> Wagner can decide:	F 600	2.2.49		Faust
Never too late, if Faustus will <can> repent.	F 631	2.2.80		GdAngl
like to Ovids Flea, I can creepe into every corner of a Wench:	F 665	2.2.114	P	Pride
And therefore none of his Decrees can stand.	F 929	3.1.151		Pope
for I can tell you, you'le be curst with Bell, Booke, and	F1072	3.2.92	P	Mephst
that your devill can answere the stealing of this same cup,	F1088	3.3.1	P	Dick
what you say, we looke not like cup-stealers I can tell you.	F1100	3.3.13	P	Robin
your searching; we scorne to steale your cups I can tell you.	F1106	3.3.19	P	Dick
when, can you tell?	F1112	3.3.25	P	Robin
to stand gaping after the divels Governor, and can see nothing.	F1244	4.1.90	P	Benvol
be good, for they come from a farre Country I can tell you.	F1577	4.6.20	P	Faust
Nay, hearke you, can you tell me where you are?	F1614	4.6.57		Faust
I marry can I, we are under heaven.	F1615	4.6.58	P	Carter
No mortall can expresse the paines of hell.	F1716	5.1.43		OldMan
But Faustus offence can nere be pardoned, the serpent that	F1837	5.2.41	P	Faust
I have done, all Germany can witnesse, yea all the world:	F1842	5.2.46	P	Faust
you <yee> heare, come not unto me, for nothing can rescue me.	F1874	5.2.78	P	Faust

CAN (cont.)

are live quarters broyling on the coles,/That ner'e can die: F1914 5.2.118 BdAngl
my maister and mistris shal finde that I can reade, he for his F App p.233 15 P Robin
I can do al these things easily with it: . . . . F App p.234 22 P Robin
can make thee druncke with ipocrase at any taberne in Europe F App p.234 22 P Robin
nor in the whole world can compare with thee, for the rare F App p.236 3 P Emper
spirites as can lively resemble Alexander and his Paramour, F App p.237 46 P Faust
and strong armes/Can mainly throw the dart; wilt thou indure Lucan, First Booke 365
Yet more will happen then I can unfold; . . . . Lucan, First Booke 634
Then scarse can Phoebus say, this harpe is mine. . . Ovid's Elegies 1.1.20
Or lies he close, and shoots where none can spie him? . Ovid's Elegies 1.2.6
Thy lightning can my life in pieces batter. . . . Ovid's Elegies 1.6.16
a rich lover plants/His love on thee, and can supply thy wants. Ovid's Elegies 1.8.32
Farmes out her-self on nights for what she can. . . Ovid's Elegies 1.10.30
Who can indure, save him with whom none lies? . . Ovid's Elegies 1.13.26
The living, not the dead can envie bite, ... Ovid's Elegies 1.15.39
What can be easier then the thing we pray? . . . Ovid's Elegies 2.2.66
I thinke sheele doe, but deepely can dissemble. . . Ovid's Elegies 2.4.16
To whom his wench can say, I never did it. . . . Ovid's Elegies 2.5.10
No where can they be taught but in the bed, . . . Ovid's Elegies 2.5.61
If one can doote, if not, two everie night, . . . Ovid's Elegies 2.10.22
Nor can an other say his helpe I tooke. . . . Ovid's Elegies 2.12.12
That can effect <affect> a foolish wittalls wife. . . Ovid's Elegies 2.19.46
Thou suffrest what no husband can endure, ... Ovid's Elegies 2.19.51
Can I but loath a husband growne a baude? . . . . Ovid's Elegies 2.19.57
Nor, least she will, can any be restrainde. . . . Ovid's Elegies 3.4.6
Never can these by any meanes agree. . . . . Ovid's Elegies 3.4.42
If standing here I can by no meanes get, ... Ovid's Elegies 3.5.11
That seeing thy teares can any joy then feele. . . . Ovid's Elegies 3.5.60
Or shade, or body was [I] <Io>, who can say? . . . . Ovid's Elegies 3.6.16
Can deafe [eares] <yeares> take delight when Phemius sings,/Or Ovid's Elegies 3.6.61
One [her] <she> commands, who many things can give. . . Ovid's Elegies 3.7.62
Ile hate, if I can; if not, love gainst my will: . . Ovid's Elegies 3.10.35
Nor with thee, nor without thee can I live, . . . Ovid's Elegies 3.10.39
And I shall thinke you chaste, do what you can. . . Ovid's Elegies 3.13.14
toyes defamde)/Heire of an antient house, if helpe that can, Ovid's Elegies 3.14.5
Can hardly blazon foorth the loves of men, ... Hero and Leander 1.70
When you fleet hence, can be bequeath'd to none. . . Hero and Leander 1.248
Much lesse can honour bee ascrib'd thereto, . . . Hero and Leander 1.279
At last he came, O who can tell the greeting, . . . Hero and Leander 2.23
Whose fruit none rightly can describe, but hee/That puls or Hero and Leander 2.299

CANAAN

Nor e're shall see the land of Canaan, ... Jew 2.3.303 Barab

CANAPIE

when thou goest, a golden Canapie/Enchac'd with pretious stones, 2Tamb 1.2.48 Callap
pearle of welthie India/Were mounted here under a Canapie: 2Tamb 3.2.122 Tamb

CANAREA

And made Canarea cal us kings and Lords, ... 2Tamb 1.3.181 Usumc

CANCELL

I seale, I cancell, I do what I will, ... Edw 5.4.51 Mortmr

CANCERS

Even from the midst of fiery Cancers Tropick, ... 2Tamb 1.1.73 Orcan
Lies westward from the midst of Cancers line, ... 2Tamb 5.3.146 Tamb

CANDIE

Are smoothly gliding downe by Candie shoare/To Malta, through Jew 1.1.46 Barab
Belike they coasted round by Candie shoare/About their Oyles, Jew 1.1.91 Barab

CANDLE

Hold, take this candle and goe light a fire, ... Dido 1.1.171 Aeneas
I can tell you, you'le be curst with Bell, Booke, and Candle. F1073 3.2.93 P Mephst
Bell, Booke, and Candle; Candle, Booke, and Bell, . . . F1074 3.2.94 Faust
Nay I know not, we shalbe curst with bell, booke, and candle. F App p.232 24 P Mephst
bell, booke, and candle, candle, booke, and bell,/Forward and F App p.232 25 Faust

CANDY (See also CANDIE, CREETE)

Candy, and those other Iles/That lye betwixt the Mediterranean Jew 1.2.3 Basso
What's Cyprus, Candy, and those other Iles/To us, or Malta? Jew 1.2.5 Govnr

CANDYAN

The goddesse sawe Iasion on Candyan Ide, ... Ovid's Elegies 3.9.25

CANES

Instead of Sedge and Reed, beare Sugar Canes: . . . . Jew 4.2.96 Ithimr

CANKER

And by the barke a canker creepes me up, ... Edw 2.2.18 Mortmr
And Aeque tandem shall that canker crie, ... Edw 2.2.41 Edward

CANKRED

And now ye cankred curres of Asia, ... 2Tamb 4.1.132 Tamb

CANNON (See also CANONS)

How those were hit by pelting Cannon shot, ... 1Tamb 2.4.3 Mycet
thou I am he/That with the Cannon shooke Vienna walles, . 2Tamb 1.1.87 Orcan
And with the cannon breake the frame of heaven, . . 2Tamb 2.4.104 Tamb
Dismount the Cannon of the adverse part, ... 2Tamb 3.2.81 Tamb
For though thy cannon shooke the citie walles, . . . 2Tamb 5.1.105 Govnr

CANNONIERS

To save our Cannoniers from musket shot, ... 2Tamb 3.3.57 Therid

CANNONS

And with their Cannons mouth'd like Orcus gulfe/Batter the 1Tamb 3.1.65 Bajzth
While thundring Cannons rattle on their Skins. . . . 1Tamb 4.1.11 Souldn
Or roaring Cannons sever all thy joints, ... 1Tamb 5.1.223 Bajzth
Even in the cannons face shall raise a hill/Of earth and fagots 2Tamb 3.3.21 Therid
And ratling cannons thunder in our eares/Our proper ruine, 2Tamb 4.1.13 Amyras
their swordes or their cannons, as I doe a naked Lady in a net 2Tamb 4.1.68 P Calyph
Being caried thither by the cannons force, ... 2Tamb 5.1.66 Tamb
As that the double Cannons forg'd of brasse, ... F 820 3.1.42 Mephst

CAN NOT

enjoy in heaven/Can not compare with kingly joyes in earth. 1Tamb 2.5.59 Therid

CAN NOT (cont.)

Can not indure by argument of art.	2Tamb	5.3.97		Phsitn

CANNOT

Yet much I marvell that I cannot finde, ...	Dido	1.1.180		Achat
I cannot choose but fall upon my knees, ...	Dido	2.1.11		Achat
What happened to the Queene we cannot shewe, . . .	Dido	2.1.294		Achat
O no God wot, I cannot watch my time, ...	Dido	3.2.14		Juno
And cannot talke nor thinke of ought but him: . . .	Dido	3.2.73		Juno
Mine eye is fixt where fancie cannot start, . . .	Dido	4.2.37		Iarbus
Cannot ascend to Fames immortall house, ...	Dido	4.3.9		Aeneas
I cannot see him frowne, it may not be:	Dido	4.4.112		Dido
I but heele come againe, he cannot goe, ...	Dido	5.1.184		Dido
It cannot choose, because it comes from you. . . .	1Tamb	1.1.56		Cosroe
They cannot take away my crowne from me.	1Tamb	2.4.14		Mycet
And cannot terrefie his mightie hoste.	1Tamb	3.3.12		Bassoe
are you so daintily brought up, you cannot eat your owne flesh?	1Tamb	4.4.37	P	Tamb
Tis like he wil, when he cannot let it.	1Tamb	4.4.53	P	Techel
And more than this, for all I cannot tell.	2Tamb	1.2.53		Callap
When I am old and cannot mannage armes, ...	2Tamb	1.3.59		Tamb
And all this raging cannot make her live, ...	2Tamb	2.4.120		Therid
Lies heavy on my heart, I cannot live.	2Tamb	3.4.5		Capt
given so much to sleep/You cannot leave it, when our enemies	2Tamb	4.1.12		Amyras
al this aery region/Cannot containe the state of Tamburlaine.	2Tamb	4.1.120		Tamb
I cannot love to be an Emperesse.	2Tamb	4.2.49		Olymp
As all the world cannot affoord the like.	2Tamb	4.2.57		Olymp
He cannot heare the voice of Tamburlain, ...	2Tamb	5.1.199		Tamb
Ah friends, what shal I doe, I cannot stand, ...	2Tamb	5.3.51		Tamb
And cannot last, it is so violent.	2Tamb	5.3.65		Techel
Cannot behold the teares ye shed for me, ...	2Tamb	5.3.218		Tamb
I cannot tell, but we have scambled up/More wealth by farre	Jew	1.1.122		Barab
As all the wealth of Malta cannot pay;	Jew	1.1.183		Barab
we have cast, but cannot compasse it/By reason of the warres,	Jew	1.2.47		Govnr
And now it cannot be recall'd.	Jew	1.2.93		Govnr
us an occasion/Which on the sudden cannot serve the turne.	Jew	1.2.240		Barab
What, hand in hand, I cannot suffer this.	Jew	2.3.276		Mthias
I cannot chuse, seeing my father bids:--	Jew	2.3.316		Abigal
I cannot stay; for if my mother come, ...	Jew	2.3.353		Mthias
I cannot take my leave of him for teares:	Jew	2.3.355		Abigal
I cannot choose but like thy readinesse:	Jew	2.3.377		Barab
I cannot thinke but that thou hat'st my life. . . .	Jew	3.4.38		Barab
so, and yet I cannot tell, for at the reading of the letter,	Jew	4.2.6	P	Pilia
I cannot doe it, I have lost my keyes.	Jew	4.3.32		Barab
Nor me neither, I cannot out-run you Constable, oh my belly.	Jew	5.1.20	P	Ithimr
I cannot feast my men in Malta wals, ...	Jew	5.3.34		Calym
And villaines, know you cannot helpe me now. . . .	Jew	5.5.77		Barab
Which cannot be extinguisht but by bloud.	P 93	2.36		Guise
The head being of, the members cannot stand. . . .	P 296	5.23		Anjoy
your nego argumentum/Cannot serve, sirra:	P 398	7.38		Guise
Cannot but march with many graces more:	P 578	11.43		Pleshe
Faine would I finde some means to speak with him/But cannot,	P 663	13.7		Duchss
what your intent is yet we cannot learn, ...	P 823	17.18		King
I cannot brook thy hauty insolence, ...	P 862	17.57		King
Which cannot but be thankfully receiv'd.	P 906	18.7		Bartus
I cannot speak for greefe: when thou wast borne, . . .	P1072	19.142		QnMoth
The Popedome cannot stand, all goes to wrack, . . .	P1087	19.157		QnMoth
The Kings alone, it cannot satisfie.	P1109	21.3		Dumain
Alas my Lord, your highnes cannot live.	P1223	22.85		Srgeon
I cannot, nor I will not, I must speake.	Edw	1.1.122		Mortmr
I cannot brooke these hautie menaces:	Edw	1.1.134		Edward
Cease brother, for I cannot brooke these words: . . .	Edw	1.1.160		Edward
Stay Gaveston, I cannot leave thee thus.	Edw	1.4.135		Edward
Feare not, the queens words cannot alter him. . . .	Edw	1.4.233		Penbrk
But cannot brooke a night growne mushrump, ...	Edw	1.4.284		Mortmr
That cannot speake without propterea quod.	Edw	2.1.53		Baldck
My Lord I cannot brooke these injuries.	Edw	2.2.71		Gavstn
Pursue him quicklie, and he cannot scape, ...	Edw	2.4.38		Queene
Madam, I cannot stay to answer you, ...	Edw	2.4.57		Mortmr
Your lordship cannot priviledge your head.	Edw	4.6.70		Mortmr
What cannot gallant Mortimer with the Queene? . . .	Edw	4.7.50		Leistr
Two kings in England cannot raigne at once:	Edw	5.1.58		Edward
Seeing that my brother cannot be releast.	Edw	5.3.67		Kent
Sweete mother, if I cannot pardon him, ...	Edw	5.4.94		King
But seeing I cannot, ile entreate for him:	Edw	5.4.98		King
I feard as much, murther cannot be hid.	Edw	5.6.46		Queene
for I am wanton and lascivious, and cannot live without a wife.	F 530	2.1.142	P	Faust
Thou art a spirit, God cannot pity thee.	F 564	2.2.13		BdAngl
My heart is <hearts so> hardned, I cannot repent: . .	F 569	2.2.18		Faust
Christ cannot save thy soule, for he is just, . . .	F 636	2.2.85		Lucifr
I cannot read, and therefore wish all books burn'd <were .	F 680	2.2.129	P	Envy
And therefore tho we would we cannot erre.	F 931	3.1.153		Pope
drunke over night, the Divell cannot hurt him in the morning:	F1201	4.1.47	P	Benvol
His faith is great, I cannot touch his soule;	F1756	5.1.83		Mephst
I cannot sel him so:	F App	p.239 103	P	Faust
you cannot speake with him.	F App	p.240 139	P	Mephst
Dominion cannot suffer partnership;	Lucan, First Booke	93		
If loftie titles cannot make me thine, ...	Ovid's Elegies	1.3.7		
would, I cannot him cashiere/Before I be divided from my geere.	Ovid's Elegies	1.6.35		
That cannot Venus mutuall pleasure taste.	Ovid's Elegies	2.3.2		
I cannot rule my selfe, but where love please/[Am] <And> driven	Ovid's Elegies	2.4.7		
What gate thy stately words cannot unlocke, ...	Ovid's Elegies	3.1.45		
Cannot a faire one, if not chast, please thee? . . .	Ovid's Elegies	3.4.41		
What will my age do, age I cannot shunne, ...	Ovid's Elegies	3.6.17		
And lookes uppon the fruits he cannot touch. . . .	Ovid's Elegies	3.6.52		

CANNOT (cont.)			
God knowes I cannot force love, as you doe.	Hero and Leander		1.206
CANON			
The Canon Law forbids it, and the Priest/That makes it knowne,	Jew	3.6.34	2Fryar
CANONIZE			
Shall make all Nations to Canonize us:	F 147	1.1.119	Valdes
CANONS			
<And double Canons, fram'd of carved brasse>,	F 820	(HC265)A	Mephst
CANOPUS			
Thou that frequents Canopus pleasant fields,	Ovid's Elegies		2.13.7
CANOPY (See CANAPIE)			
CANST			
Aeneas, say, how canst thou take thy leave?	Dido	5.1.119	Dido
canst thou take her hand?	Dido	5.1.121	Dido
Now if thou goest, what canst thou leave behind,	Dido	5.1.151	Dido
That with thy lookes canst cleare the darkened Sky:	1Tamb	3.3.122	Tamb
How canst thou think of this and offer war?	2Tamb	1.1.102	Orcan
And canst thou Coward stand in feare of death?	2Tamb	3.2.102	Tamb
Live still; and if thou canst, get more.	Jew	1.2.102	Govnr
Well, Barabas, canst helpe me to a Diamond?	Jew	2.3.48	Lodowk
Canst thou be so unkind to leave me thus?	Jew	4.2.52	Curtzn
Canst thou, as thou reportest, make Malta ours?	Jew	5.1.85	Calym
too late/Thou seek'st for much, but canst not compasse it.	Jew	5.2.46	Barab
And let me see what mony thou canst make;	Jew	5.2.94	Barab
See his end first, and flye then if thou canst.	Jew	5.5.69	Govnr
The ruines done to Malta and to us,/Thou canst not part:	Jew	5.5.113	Govnr
But canst thou tell who is their generall?	P 731	14.34	Navrre
What canst thou doe?	Edw	1.1.26	Gavstn
Yes more then thou canst answer though he live,	Edw	2.2.87	Edward
Tis but temporall that thou canst inflict.	Edw	3.1.242	Warwck
Seeke all the meanes thou canst to make him droope,	Edw	5.2.54	Mortmr
Conjurer laureate]/[That canst commaund great Mephostophilis],	F 261	1.3.33A	Faust
[And] canst <thou> not [now] be sav'd.	F 390	2.1.2	Faust
why thou canst not tell ne're a word on't.	F 731	2.3.10 P	Dick
Or any villany thou canst devise,	F 865	3.1.87	Mephst
thou canst not buy so good a horse, for so small a price:	F1459	4.4.3 P	Faust
what doest thou with that same booke thou canst not reade?	F App	p.233 14 P	Rafe
Canst thou conjure with it?	F App	p.233 21 P	Rafe
by whome thou canst accomplish what thou list, this therefore	F App	p.236 5 P	Emper
Canst raise this man from hollow vaults below,	F App	p.237 30	Emper
decrees/To expel the father; share the world thou canst not;	Lucan, First Booke		291
There touch what ever thou canst touch of mee.	Ovid's Elegies		1.4.58
And I deserve more then thou canst in verity,	Ovid's Elegies		3.1.47
Nor canst by watching keepe her minde from sinne.	Ovid's Elegies		3.4.7
Foole canst thou him in thy white armes embrace?	Ovid's Elegies		3.7.11
Foole canst thou lie in his enfolding space?	Ovid's Elegies		3.7.12
Canst touch that hand wherewith some one lie dead?	Ovid's Elegies		3.7.17
CANTERBURIES			
Here comes my lord of Canterburies grace.	Edw	1.2.33	Warwck
CANVASE			
with me, and after meate/We'le canvase every quidditie thereof:	F 191	1.1.163	Faust
CAP (See also CAPPES)			
and in his tuskan cap/A jewell of more value then the crowne.	Edw	1.4.414	Mortmr
A cap of flowers, and a kirtle,	Passionate Shepherd		11
CAPABLE			
Or capable of any forme at all.	Hero and Leander		1.274
CAP'DE			
A Velvet cap'de cloake, fac'st before with Serge,	Edw	2.1.34	Spencr
CAPER (See also CAPRING)			
Their legs to dance and caper in the aire:	2Tamb	1.3.31	Tamb
And make whole cyties caper in the aire.	2Tamb	3.2.61	Tamb
CAPITALL			
Nor capitall be adorn'd with sacred bayes:	Lucan, First Booke		288
CAPITOLL			
from the northren climat snatching fier/Blasted the Capitoll:	Lucan, First Booke		533
CAPOLIN			
See Capolin, the faire Arabian king/That hath bene disapointed	1Tamb	4.1.68	Souldn
Capolin, hast thou survaid our powers?	1Tamb	4.3.50	Souldn
CAPPES			
in England/would cast up cappes, and clap their hands for joy,	Edw	4.2.55	Mortmr
CAPRICORNE			
To Amazonia under Capricorne,	2Tamb	1.1.74	Orcan
Cutting the Tropicke line of Capricorne,	2Tamb	5.3.138	Tamb
CAPRING			
And made his capring Triton sound alowd,	Hero and Leander		2.156
CAPTAIN			
Nay Captain, thou art weary of thy life,	2Tamb	3.3.18	Techel
Now Captain of my guarde, are these murtherers ready?	P 947	19.17	King
CAPTAINE			
It is our Captaine, see Ascanius.	Dido	2.1.52	Cloan
The chiefest Captaine of Mycetes hoste,	1Tamb	1.1.58	Mycet
Art thou but Captaine of a thousand horse,	1Tamb	1.2.168	Tamb
Captaine, that thou yeeld up thy hold to us.	2Tamb	3.3.16	Therid
Captaine, these Moores shall cut the leaden pipes,	2Tamb	3.3.29	Techel
And therefore Captaine, yeeld it quietly.	2Tamb	3.3.34	Techel
See now my Lord how brave the Captaine hangs.	2Tamb	5.1.149	Amyras
And let this Captaine be remoov'd the walles,	2Tamb	5.1.215	Therid
Captaine, the force of Tamburlaine is great,	2Tamb	5.2.42	Callap
Now Captaine tell us whither thou art bound?	Jew	2.2.1	Govnr
Captaine we know it, but our force is small.	Jew	2.2.34	Govnr
[Cossin] <Cosin> <Cousin>, the Captaine of the Admirals guarde,	P 293	5.20	Anjoy
CAPTAINES			
Summoned the Captaines to his princely tent,	Dido	2.1.130	Aeneas

CAPTAINES (cont.)				
And Captaines of the Medean garrisons, ...	1Tamb	1.1.111		Cosroe
That heretofore have fild Persepolis/With Affrike Captaines,	1Tamb	1.1.142		Ceneus
The Lords and Captaines of my brothers campe, ...	1Tamb	2.5.26		Cosroe
Dco not my captaines and my souldiers looke/As if they meant to	1Tamb	3.3.9		Tamb
And all his Captaines that thus stoutly stand, . . .	1Tamb	3.3.79		Bajzth
His sonnes, his Captaines and his followers, . . .	2Tamb	3.5.16		Callap
To prison with the Governour and these/Captaines, his consorts	Jew	5.2.24		Barab
These Captaines emulous of each others glory. . . .	Lucan, First Booke	120		
Roome that flowes/With Citizens and [Captives] <Captaines>, and	Lucan, First Booke	510		
What yeares in souldiours Captaines do require, . .	Ovid's Elegies	1.9.5		
His Mistris dores this; that his Captaines keepes. . .	Ovid's Elegies	1.9.8		
CAPTAIN'S				
The Captain's slaine, the rest remaine our slaves, . . .	Jew	2.2.17		Bosco
CAPTAINS				
And all his Captains bound in captive chaines. . . .	1Tamb	3.3.115		Bajzth
CAPTIVATES				
No more this beauty mine eyes captivates.	Ovid's Elegies	1.10.10		
CAPTIVE				
We heare they led her captive into Greece.	Dido	2.1.295		Achat
to apprehend/And bring him Captive to your Highnesse throne.	1Tamb	1.1.48		Meandr
Spurning their crownes from off their captive heads. .	1Tamb	1.2.57		Techel
I wil the captive Pioners of Argier, ...	1Tamb	3.1.58		Bajzth
Shall lead thee Captive thorow Affrica.	1Tamb	3.3.73		Tamb
And all his Captains bound in captive chaines. . . .	1Tamb	3.3.115		Bajzth
And led them Captive into Affrica.	1Tamb	3.3.205		Zabina
Being thy Captive, thus abuse his state, ...	1Tamb	4.2.60		Zabina
And bring him captive to your highnesse feet. . . .	2Tamb	3.1.62		Soria
That we may tread upon his captive necke, ...	2Tamb	3.2.157		Tamb
Now vaile your pride you captive Christians, . . .	Jew	5.2.1		Calym
As ancient Romanes over their Captive Lords, . . .	P 982	19.52		Guise
With captive kings at his triumphant Carre. . . .	Edw	1.1.174		Gavstn
Tis cruell love turmoyles my captive hart. . . .	Ovid's Elegies	1.2.8		
Loe I confesse, I am thy captive I, ...	Ovid's Elegies	1.2.19		
And captive like be manacled and bound.	Ovid's Elegies	1.2.30		
Let the sad captive formost with lockes spred/On her white	Ovid's Elegies	1.7.39		
Rhesus fell/And Captive horses bad their Lord fare-well. .	Ovid's Elegies	1.9.24		
Now Germany shall captive haire-tyers send thee, . .	Ovid's Elegies	1.14.45		
Achilles burnt with face of captive Briseis, . . .	Ovid's Elegies	2.8.11		
But to my share a captive damsell falles. . . .	Ovid's Elegies	2.12.8		
Ist womens love my captive brest doth frie? . . .	Ovid's Elegies	3.2.40		
To see how he this captive Nymph beguil'd. . . .	Hero and Leander	2.40		
CAPTIVES				
and then inlarge/Those Christian Captives, which you keep as	1Tamb	3.3.47		Tamb
To make these captives reine their lavish tongues. . .	1Tamb	4.2.67		Techel
What should I say? we are captives and must yeeld. . .	Jew	5.2.6		Govnr
Roome that flowes/With Citizens and [Captives] <Captaines>, and	Lucan, First Booke	510		
CAPTIVITIE				
And he himselfe lies in captivitie.	Edw	5.2.4		Mortmr
CAPTIVITY				
Their cruel death, mine owne captivity, ...	2Tamb	5.2.20		Callap
in perill of calamity/To ransome great Kings from captivity.	Jew	1.1.32		Barab
CAPYS				
By Paphos, Capys, and the purple Sea, ...	Dido	3.4.46		Aeneas
CAR (See also CARRE)				
But he the [days] <day> bright-bearing Car prepar'd. .	Hero and Leander	2.330		
CARBONADOES				
will make thee slice the brawnes of thy armes into carbonadoes,	1Tamb	4.4.44	P	Tamb
CARCASES (See also CARKASSE)				
And weepe upon your liveles carcases, ...	Dido	5.1.177		Dido
on Damascus wals/Have hoisted up their slaughtered carcases.	1Tamb	5.1.131		Techel
Or make a bridge of murthered Carcases, ...	2Tamb	1.3.93		Amyras
CARD				
Thou setst their labouring hands to spin and card. . .	Ovid's Elegies	1.13.24		
CARDENALL				
Murder me not, I am a Cardenall.	P1091	20.1		Cardnl
My brother Cardenall slaine and I alive?	P1125	21.19		Dumain
CARDES				
Ile to cardes: Perdicas.	2Tamb	4.1.59		Calyph
Come, thou and I wil goe to cardes to drive away the time.	2Tamb	4.1.61	P	Calyph
Since thou hast all the Cardes within thy hands/To shuffle or	P 146	2.89		Guise
CARDINALL (See also CARDENALL)				
My Lord, but did you mark the Cardinall/The Guises brother, and	P 47	1.47		Admral
My Lord Cardinall of Loraine, tell me, ...	P 631	12.44		QnMoth
And that young Cardinall that is growne so proud? . .	P1056	19.126		King
Get you away and strangle the Cardinall.	P1059	19.129		King
Yours my Lord Cardinall, you should have saide. . .	P1103	20.13		1Mur
Cardinall of Loraine by the Kings consent is lately strangled	P1123	21.17	P	Frier
Was sent me from a Cardinall in France.	F1047	3.2.67		Pope
My Lord, this dish was sent me from the Cardinall of Florence.	F App	p.231 9	P	Pope
CARDINALLS				
Make haste againe, my good Lord Cardinalls, ...	F 972	3.1.194		Pope
CARDINALS				
Or clap huge hornes, upon the Cardinals heads: . . .	F 864	3.1.86		Mephst
Lord Cardinals of France and Padua, ...	F 881	3.1.103		Pope
Follow the Cardinals to the Consistory;	F 892	3.1.114		Faust
Mephostophilis, and two such Cardinals/Ne're serv'd a holy Pope,	F 941	3.1.163		Faust
Behold my Lord, the Cardinals are return'd. . . .	F 945	3.1.167		Raymnd
With all our Colledge of grave Cardinals, ...	F 968	3.1.190		Pope
The Cardinals will be plagu'd for this anon. . . .	F 976	3.1.198		Faust
The sleepy Cardinals are hard at hand, ...	F 982	3.2.2		Mephst
Faustus no more: see where the Cardinals come. . . .	F1008	3.2.28		Mephst
Welcome Lord Cardinals: come sit downe.	F1009	3.2.29		Pope

CAR'DST			
Gallus that [car'dst] <carst> not bloud, and life to spend.	Ovid's Elegies	3.8.64	
CARE			
Content thee Cytherea in thy care,	Dido	1.1.82	Jupitr
Venus farewell, thy sonne shall be our care:	Dido	1.1.120	Jupitr
You sonnes of care, companions of my course,	Dido	1.1.142	Aeneas
So youle love me, I care not if I doe.	Dido	4.5.17	Cupid
To entertaine some care of our securities,	1Tamb	5.1.29	1Virgn
Wel, lovely Virgins, think our countries care,	1Tamb	5.1.34	Govnr
lives were weigh'd/In equall care and ballance with our owne,	1Tamb	5.1.42	Govnr
Depriv'd of care, my heart with comfort dies,	1Tamb	5.1.431	Arabia
Then carie me I care not where you will,	2Tamb	3.4.80	Olymp
Nor care for blood when wine wil quench my thirst.	2Tamb	4.1.30	Calyph
I care not, nor the towne will never yeeld/As long as any life	2Tamb	5.1.47	Govnr
Nay, I care not how much she loves me; Sweet Bellamira, would I	Jew	4.2.54	P Ithimr
Have speciall care that no man sally forth/Till you shall heare	Jew	5.4.2	Govnr
Tush, Governor, take thou no care for that,	Jew	5.5.102	Calym
To have some care for feare of enemies.	P 224	4.22	QnMoth
The sole endevour of your princely care,	P 714	14.17	Bartus
What care I though the Earles begirt us round?	Edw	2.2.223	Edward
We wot, he that the care of realme remits,	Edw	2.5.61	Warwck
Of love and care unto his royall person,	Edw	4.6.25	Queene
Your loving care in this,/Deserveth princelie favors and	Edw	4.6.53	Mortmr
Care of my countrie cald me to this warre.	Edw	4.6.65	Queene
Madam, have done with care and sad complaint,	Edw	4.6.66	Mortmr
good father on thy lap/Lay I this head, laden with mickle care,	Edw	4.7.40	Edward
My lord, be going, care not for these,	Edw	4.7.93	Rice
Whilst I am lodgd within this cave of care,	Edw	5.1.32	Edward
I care not how it is, so it be not spide:	Edw	5.4.40	Mortmr
Have care to walke in middle of the throng.	Ovid's Elegies	1.4.56	
Would he not buy thee thou for him shouldst care.	Ovid's Elegies	1.8.34	
A faire maides care expeld this sluggishnesse,	Ovid's Elegies	1.9.43	
Let poore men show their service, faith, and care;	Ovid's Elegies	1.10.57	
Bagous whose care doth thy Mistrisse bridle,	Ovid's Elegies	2.2.1	
Because [thy] <they> care too much thy Mistresse troubled.	Ovid's Elegies	2.2.8	
O care-got triumph hetherwards advance.	Ovid's Elegies	2.12.16	
If any godly care of me thou hast,	Ovid's Elegies	2.16.47	
Phedra, and Hipolite may read, my care is,	Ovid's Elegies	2.18.24	
Let this care some-times bite thee to the quick,	Ovid's Elegies	2.19.43	
Light am I, and with me, my care, light love,	Ovid's Elegies	3.1.41	
Because on him thy care doth hap to rest.	Ovid's Elegies	3.2.8	
Who now will care the Altars to perfume?	Ovid's Elegies	3.3.33	
What's kept, we covet more: the care makes theft:	Ovid's Elegies	3.4.25	
The gods care we are cald, and men of piety,	Ovid's Elegies	3.8.17	
The one his first love, th'other his new care.	Ovid's Elegies	3.8.32	
CAREFULL			
Then I am carefull you should be preserved.	P 265	4.63	Charls
As silent and as carefull will we be,	Edw	4.7.2	Abbot
The carefull prison is more meete for thee.	Ovid's Elegies	1.6.64	
The carefull ship-man now feares angry gusts,	Ovid's Elegies	2.11.25	
When carefull Rome in doubt their prowesse held.	Ovid's Elegies	3.14.10	
CAREFULLY			
and carefully maintaine/The wealth and safety of your kingdomes	P 477	8.27	Anjoy
CARE-GOT			
O care-got triumph hetherwards advance.	Ovid's Elegies	2.12.16	
CARELES			
our port-maisters/Are not so careles of their kings commaund.	Edw	4.3.23	Edward
CARELESLY			
Then carelesly I rent my haire for griefe,	Dido	5.1.236	Anna
CARELESSE			
Their carelesse swords shal lanch their fellowes throats/And	1Tamb	2.2.49	Meandr
Be not inconstant, carelesse of your fame,	2Tamb	5.3.21	Techel
Art carelesse?	Ovid's Elegies	1.6.41	
Carelesse, farewell, with my falt not distaind.	Ovid's Elegies	1.6.72	
O Poet carelesse of thy argument?	Ovid's Elegies	3.1.16	
To please the carelesse and disdainfull eies,	Hero and Leander	1.13	
Whose carelesse haire, in stead of pearle t'adorne it,	Hero and Leander	1.389	
To spurne in carelesse sort, the shipwracke treasure.	Hero and Leander	2.164	
CARES			
And quell those hopes that thus employ your [cares] <eares>.	Dido	4.1.35	Dido
No no, she cares not how we sinke or swimme,	Dido	4.3.41	Illion
And cares so litle for their prophet Christ.	2Tamb	2.2.35	Gazell
And now I doubt not but your royall cares/Hath so provided for	2Tamb	3.1.20	Callap
So he be safe he cares not what becomes,	P 739	14.42	Navrre
Immortall powers, that knowes the painfull cares,	Edw	5.3.37	Edward
CARIBDIS			
How Scyllaes and Caribdis waters rage.	Ovid's Elegies	2.11.18	
CARIE			
are in readines/Ten thousand horse to carie you from hence,	1Tamb	1.1.185	Ortyg
Whose vertues carie with it life and death,	1Tamb	2.5.61	Therid
Shall carie wrapt within his scarlet waves,	2Tamb	1.1.34	Orcan
if our artillery/Will carie full point blancke unto their wals.	2Tamb	3.3.53	Techel
And carie both our soules, where his remaines.	2Tamb	3.4.17	Olymp
Then carie me I care not where you will,	2Tamb	3.4.80	Olymp
Come carie me to war against the Gods,	2Tamb	5.3.52	Tamb
CARIED			
Being caried thither by the cannons force,	2Tamb	5.1.66	Tamb
Caried the famous golden-fleeced sheepe.	Ovid's Elegies	2.11.4	
CARIES			
that in her wings/Caries the fearfull thunderbolts of Jove.	2Tamb	1.1.101	Orcan
CARIO			
By [Cairo] <Cario> runs--	2Tamb	1.2.15	Callap
By [Cairo] <Cario> runs to Alexandria Bay,	2Tamb	1.2.19	Callap

CARKASSE
And that vile Carkasse drawne by warlike kings, 2Tamb 5.2.16 Amasia
To keepe his Carkasse from their bloudy phangs. F1303 4.1.149 Faust
CARKASSES
Headles carkasses piled up in heapes, Dido 2.1.194 Aeneas
And you march on their slaughtered carkasses: 1Tamb 2.2.69 Meandr
their slaughtered Carkasses/Shall serve for walles and 1Tamb 3.3.138 Bajzth
And left your slender carkasses behind, 2Tamb 4.1.38 Calyph
Drawen with these kings on heaps of carkasses. 2Tamb 5.1.72 Tamb
And fishes [fed] <feed> by humaine carkasses, 2Tamb 5.1.206 Techel
to lode thy barke/With soules of thousand mangled carkasses. 2Tamb 5.3.74 Tamb
CARMONIA
Carmonia and al the hundred and thirty Kingdomes late 2Tamb 3.1.4 P Orcan
CARNON
by leaden pipes/Runs to the citie from the mountain Carnon. 1Tamb 3.1.60 Bajzth
CAROLUS
[Carolus the fift, at whose pallace now]/[Faustus is feasted F1151 3.3.64A 3Chor
And he intends to shew great Carolus, F1167 4.1.13 Mrtino
For ever be belov'd of Carolus. F1211 4.1.57 Emper
These gracious words, most royall Carolus, F1217 4.1.63 Faust
And live belov'd of mightie Carolus. F1324 4.1.170 Emper
CAROUSE (See also CARROUSE)
Then let us freely banquet and carouse/Full bowles of wine unto 1Tamb 4.4.5 Tamb
Come banquet and carouse with us a while, 2Tamb 1.1.165 Orcan
Then wil we triumph, banquet and carouse, 2Tamb 1.3.218 Tamb
CAROWSE
would not banquet, and carowse, and swill/Amongst the Students, F App p.243 4 Wagner
Being wrackt, carowse the sea tir'd by their ships: Ovid's Elegies 2.10.34
CAROWSING
Then drerie Mars, carowsing Nectar boules. Hero and Leander 2.258
CARPATHIAN
My [false] <selfe> othes in Carpathian seas to cast. Ovid's Elegies 2.8.20
CARPENTERS
There, Carpenters, divide that gold amongst you: Jew 5.5.5 Barab
CARPEST
Envie, why carpest thou my time is spent so ill, Ovid's Elegies 1.15.1
CARPETS
thy chariot wheels/With Turky Carpets shall be covered: 2Tamb 1.2.43 Callap
Where painted Carpets o're the meads are hurl'd, Jew 4.2.91 Ithimr
CARRAS
Had fild Assirian Carras wals with bloud, Lucan, First Booke 105
CARRE
With captive kings at his triumphant Carre. Edw 1.1.174 Gavstn
And duskie night, in rustie iron carre: Edw 4.3.44 Edward
(When yawning dragons draw her thirling carre, Hero and Leander 1.108
CARRECT
And of a Carrect of this quantity, Jew 1.1.30 Barab
CARRIAGE
And early mountest thy hatefull carriage: Ovid's Elegies 1.13.38
Dang'd downe to hell her loathsome carriage. Hero and Leander 2.334
CARRIE
Nurse I am wearie, will you carrie me? Dido 4.5.15 Cupid
I will upon mine honor undertake/To carrie him, and bring him Edw 2.5.80 Penbrk
That I would undertake to carrie him/Unto your highnes, and to Edw 3.1.99 Arundl
Then I will carrie thee by force away. Edw 5.2.112 Mortmr
CARRIED
my master writ it, and I carried it, first to Lodowicke, and Jew 3.3.19 P Ithimr
I carried the broth that poyson'd the Nuns, and he and I, Jew 4.4.20 P Ithimr
Who carried that challenge? Jew 5.1.31 Barab
I carried it, I confesse, but who writ it? Jew 5.1.32 P Ithimr
be carried thither againe by Gluttony and Letchery <Leachery>], F 705.2 2.2.156A P Sloth
CARRIENG
shall sweat/With carrieng pearle and treasure on their backes. 2Tamb 3.5.167 Techel
CARRIES
Their sway of fleight carries the heady rout/That in chain'd Lucan, First Booke 488
Whether the subtile maide lines bringes and carries, Ovid's Elegies 2.19.41
CARROUSE
Come let us banquet and carrouse the whiles. 2Tamb 1.3.225 Tamb
And yet at night carrouse within my tent, 2Tamb 3.2.106 Tamb
CARROUST
Would Lancaster and he had both carroust, Edw 2.2.237 Edward
CARRY (See also CARIE, CARRIE)
for I will presently raise up two devils to carry thee away: F 373 1.4.31 P Wagner
full power to fetch or carry the said John Faustus, body and F 497 2.1.109 P Faust
be thou transformed to/A dog, and carry him upon thy backe; F1131 3.3.44 Mephst
you thinke to carry it away with your Hey-passe, and Re-passe: F1664 4.6.107 P Robin
Receive these lines, them to my Mistrisse carry, Ovid's Elegies 1.11.7
CARRYING
let me have the carrying of him about to shew some trickes. F1128 3.3.41 P Robin
CARRY'T
I'le carry't to the Nuns with a powder. Jew 3.4.112 P Ithimr
CARS
The Belgians apt to governe Brittish cars; Lucan, First Booke 427
CARST
Gallus that [car'dst] <carst> not bloud, and life to spend. Ovid's Elegies 3.8.64
CARTHAGE
Since Carthage knowes to entertaine distresse. Dido 1.2.33 Iarbus
Where am I now? these should be Carthage walles. Dido 2.1.1 Aeneas
Lovely Aeneas, these are Carthage walles, Dido 2.1.62 Illion
Brave Prince, welcome to Carthage and to me, Dido 2.1.81 Dido
Or els in Carthage make his kingly throne. Dido 2.1.331 Venus
Depart from Carthage, come not in my sight. Dido 3.1.44 Dido
Yet not from Carthage for a thousand worlds. Dido 3.1.51 Iarbus

Line	Work	Ref.		Speaker
CARTHAGE (cont.)				
Achates, how doth Carthage please your Lord?	Dido	3.1.97		Dido
And bring forth mightie Kings to Carthage towne,	Dido	3.2.75		Juno
Then to the Carthage Queene that dyes for him.	Dido	3.4.40		Dido
The King of Carthage, not Anchises sonne:	Dido	3.4.60		Dido
Carthage, my friendly host adue,	Dido	4.3.1		Aeneas
Hath not the Carthage Queene mine onely sonne?	Dido	4.4.29		Aeneas
Henceforth you shall be our Carthage Gods:	Dido	4.4.96		Dido
againe conspire/Against the life of me poore Carthage Queene:	Dido	4.4.132		Dido
But though he goe, he stayes in Carthage still,	Dido	4.4.133		Dido
And let rich Carthage fleete upon the seas,	Dido	4.4.134		Dido
Is this the wood that grew in Carthage plaines,	Dido	4.4.136		Dido
Ye shall no more offend the Carthage Queene.	Dido	4.4.158		Dido
Carthage shall vaunt her pettie walles no more,	Dido	5.1.4		Aeneas
Welcome to Carthage new erected towne.	Dido	5.1.26		Aeneas
Say thou wilt stay in Carthage with [thy] <my> Queene,	Dido	5.1.117		Dido
O Queene of Carthage, wert thou ugly blacke,	Dido	5.1.125		Aeneas
How Carthage did rebell, Iarbus storme,	Dido	5.1.143		Dido
Would, as faire Troy was, Carthage might be sackt,	Dido	5.1.147		Dido
That hath dishonord her and Carthage both?	Dido	5.1.280		Iarbus
And Carthage soules be glutted with our blouds;	Lucan, First Booke			39
And furious Cymbrians and of Carthage Moores,	Lucan, First Booke			257
rageth now in armes/As if the Carthage Hannibal were neere;	Lucan, First Booke			305
CARTHAGENS				
Where Mars did mate the warlicke Carthagens <Carthaginians>,	F 2	Prol.2		1Chor
CARTHAGINIAN				
And Dido and you Carthaginian Peeres/Heare me, but yet with	Dido	2.1.122		Aeneas
Now Cupid cause the Carthaginian Queene,	Dido	3.1.1		Cupid
of all these, commaund/Aeneas ride as Carthaginian King.	Dido	4.4.78		Dido
CARTHAGINIANS				
Where Mars did mate the warlicke Carthagens <Carthaginians>,	F 2	Prol.2		1Chor
CARVED				
<And double Canons, fram'd of carved brasse>,	F 820	(HC265)A		Mephst
Wherein was Proteus carved, and o'rehead,	Hero and Leander			1.137
CARY				
So sure did your father write, and I cary the chalenge.	Jew	3.3.25	P	Ithimr
CASANE				
Techelles, and Casane, welcome him.	1Tamb	1.2.238		Tamb
Why then Casane, shall we wish for ought/The world affoords in	1Tamb	2.5.72		Tamb
Agreed Casane, we wil honor him.	1Tamb	3.2.113		Techel
Techelles and Casane, here are the cates you desire to finger,	1Tamb	4.4.107	P	Tamb
Techelles, and Casane/Promist to meet me on Larissa plaines	2Tamb	1.3.106		Tamb
They shal Casane, and tis time yfaith.	2Tamb	1.3.185		Tamb
Casane and Theridamas to armes:	2Tamb	2.4.102		Tamb
Sorrow no more my sweet Casane now:	2Tamb	3.2.44		Tamb
How now Casane?	2Tamb	3.5.58		Tamb
Why, so he is Casane, I am here,	2Tamb	3.5.62		Tamb
Theridamas, Techelles, and Casane,	2Tamb	4.1.159		Tamb
Now Casane, wher's the Turkish Alcaron,	2Tamb	5.1.173		Tamb
So Casane, fling them in the fire.	2Tamb	5.1.186		Tamb
I know it wil Casane:	2Tamb	5.3.113		Tamb
Casane no, the Monarke of the earth,	2Tamb	5.3.216		Tamb
CASE (Homograph)				
In what a lamentable case were I,	1Tamb	2.4.6		Mycet
a heavie case,/When force to force is knit, and sword and	Edw	4.4.4		Queene
In any case, take heed of childish feare,	Edw	5.2.6		Mortmr
Speake curstlie to him, and in any case/Let no man comfort him,	Edw	5.2.63		Mortmr
A petty <pretty> case of paltry Legacies:	F 57	1.1.29		Faust
run up and downe the world with these <this> case of Rapiers,	F 688	2.2.137	P	Wrath
in any case, ride him not into the water.	F1468	4.4.12	P	Faust
time; but, quoth he, in any case ride him not into the water.	F1541	4.5.37	P	HrsCsr
CASEMATES				
Casemates to place the great Artillery,	2Tamb	3.2.78		Tamb
CASEMENT				
Ile set the casement open that the windes/May enter in, and	Dido	4.4.130		Dido
CASHIERE				
would, I cannot him cashiere/Before I be divided from my geere.	Ovid's Elegies			1.6.35
CASPEA				
as outwaies the sands/And all the craggie rockes of Caspea.	1Tamb	2.3.48		Tamb
CASPEAN				
Fled to the Caspean or the Ocean maine?	1Tamb	1.1.102		Mycet
CASPIAN				
And of the ever raging Caspian Lake:	1Tamb	1.1.168		Ortyg
with Russian stems/Plow up huge furrowes in the Caspian sea,	1Tamb	1.2.195		Tamb
The Terrene west, the Caspian north north-east,	2Tamb	4.3.103		Tamb
Along Armenia and the Caspian sea,	2Tamb	5.3.127		Tamb
Through rocks more steepe and sharp than Caspian cliftes.	2Tamb	5.3.241		Tamb
CASSANDRA				
thou knowest/We sawe Cassandra sprauling in the streetes,	Dido	2.1.274		Aeneas
So chast Minerva did Cassandra fall,	Ovid's Elegies			1.7.17
CASSIA				
thou shalt stay with me/Embalm'd with Cassia, Amber Greece and	2Tamb	2.4.130		Tamb
CAST				
On which by tempests furie we are cast.	Dido	1.1.199		Aeneas
But I had gold enough and cast him off:	Dido	3.1.162		Dido
I traytor, and the waves shall cast thee up,	Dido	5.1.174		Dido
To cast up hils against the face of heaven:	1Tamb	2.6.3		Cosroe
Or winged snakes of Lerna cast your stings,	1Tamb	4.4.21		Bajzth
Earth cast up fountaines from thy entralles,	1Tamb	5.1.347		Zenoc
Cast off your armor, put on scarlet roabes.	1Tamb	5.1.524		Tamb
Cast up the earth towards the castle wall,	2Tamb	3.3.43		Therid
And cast her bodie in the burning flame,	2Tamb	3.4.71		Olymp
Goe villaine, cast thee headlong from a rock,	2Tamb	3.5.120		Tamb

CAST (cont.)

And cast your crownes in slavery at their feet.	2Tamb	3.5.149	Tamb
And I will cast off armes and sit with thee,	2Tamb	4.2.44	Therid
And cast the fame of Ilions Tower to hell.	2Tamb	4.3.113	Tamb
For I wil cast my selfe from off these walles,	2Tamb	5.1.40	2Citzn
And cast them headlong in the cities lake:	2Tamb	5.1.162	Tamb
lamps of heaven/To cast their bootlesse fires to the earth,	2Tamb	5.3.4	Therid
And when they cast me off,/Are poyson'd by my climing	Jew	Prol.12	Machvl
To what this ten yeares tribute will amount/That we have cast,	Jew	1.2.47	Govnr
that I descended of/Were all in generall cast away for sinne,	Jew	1.2.114	Barab
And cast with cunning for the time to come:	Jew	1.2.222	Barab
Converse not with him, he is cast off from heaven.	Jew	2.3.157	Mater
And like a cunning Jew so cast about,	Jew	2.3.235	Barab
cast mine eye up to the Jewes counting-house where I saw some	Jew	3.1.18	P Pilia
And thus we cast it:	Jew	5.2.96	Barab
the diadem/Of France be cast on me, then with your leaves/I may	P 473	8.23	Anjoy
She cast her hatefull stomack to the earth.	P1154	22.16	King
Unlesse the sea cast up his shipwrack body.	Edw	1.4.205	Lncstr
Then Balduck, you must cast the scholler off,	Edw	2.1.31	Spencr
Libels are cast againe thee in the streete,	Edw	2.2.177	Mortmr
therefore have we cause/To cast the worst, and doubt of your	Edw	2.3.8	Warwck
in England/Would cast up cappes, and clap their hands for joy,	Edw	4.2.55	Mortmr
Our lots are cast, I feare me so is thine.	Edw	4.7.79	Baldck
And hast thou cast how to accomplish it?	Edw	5.4.24	Mortmr
Come let us cast the body in the mote,	Edw	5.5.118	Gurney
Cast no more doubts; Mephostophilis come/And bring glad tydings	F 415	2.1.27	Faust
Cast downe our Foot-stoole.	F 868	3.1.90	Pope
To cast his Magicke charmes, that shall pierce through/The Ebon	F1223	4.1.69	Faust
I'le out-run him, and cast this leg into some ditch or other.	F1495	4.4.39	P HrsCsr
Mules loth'd issue)/To be cut forth and cast in dismall fiers:	Lucan, First Booke		590
Even in his face his offered [Gobbets] <Goblets> cast.	Ovid's Elegies		1.4.34
And striving thus as one that would be cast,	Ovid's Elegies		1.5.15
That when my mistresse there beholds thee cast,	Ovid's Elegies		1.6.69
to thee being cast do happe/Sharpe stripes, she sitteth in the	Ovid's Elegies		2.2.61
My [false] <selfe> oathes in Carpathian seas to cast.	Ovid's Elegies		2.8.20
Yet could I not cast ancor where I meant,	Ovid's Elegies		3.6.6
With that her loose gowne on, from me she cast her,	Ovid's Elegies		3.6.81
And seedes were equally in large fields cast,	Ovid's Elegies		3.9.33
When t'was the odour which her breath foorth cast.	Hero and Leander		1.22
But from his spreading armes away she cast her,	Hero and Leander		1.342
And as he turnd, cast many a lustfull glaunce,	Hero and Leander		2.186
Cast downe his wearie feet, and felt the sand.	Hero and Leander		2.228
His hands he cast upon her like a snare,	Hero and Leander		2.259

CASTELL

Will I advaunce upon this castell walles,	Edw	2.3.24	Mortmr
Madam, stay you within this castell here.	Edw	2.4.50	Mortmr
Imagine Killingworth castell were your court,	Edw	5.1.2	Leistr
To which the channels of the castell runne,	Edw	5.5.3	Matrvs
Wherein the filthe of all the castell falles.	Edw	5.5.57	Edward

CASTELS

Lets to our castels, for the king is moovde.	Edw	2.2.100	Warwck
As I have manors, castels, townes, and towers:	Edw	3.1.133	Edward

CASTILIANO

Hey Rivo Castiliano, a man's a man.	Jew	4.4.10	P Ithimr

CASTING

And each give signes by casting up his cloake.	Ovid's Elegies		3.2.74

CASTLE

At every towne and castle I besiege,	2Tamb	3.2.36	Tamb
And after this, to scale a castle wal,	2Tamb	3.2.59	Tamb
And lie in trench before thy castle walles,	2Tamb	3.3.31	Techel
Cast up the earth towards the castle wall,	2Tamb	3.3.43	Therid
measure the height/And distance of the castle from the trench,	2Tamb	3.3.51	Techel
Hence will I haste to Killingworth castle,	Edw	5.2.119	Kent
Erected is a Castle passing strong,	F 818	3.1.40	Mephst
I have a Castle joyning neere these woods,	F1452	4.3.22	Benvol
great deserts in erecting that inchanted Castle in the Aire:	F1560	4.6.3	P Duke

CASTLES

And batter downe the castles on the shore.	2Tamb	1.3.126	Therid
Jove throwes downe woods, and Castles with his fire:	Ovid's Elegies		3.3.35

CASTOR

Pollux and Castor, might I stand betwixt,	Ovid's Elegies		2.16.13
pleace <please> Pollux, Castor [love] <loves> horsemen more.	Ovid's Elegies		3.2.54

CASTS

Yet Dido casts her eyes like anchors out,	Dido	4.3.25	Aeneas
And casts a pale complexion on his cheeks.	1Tamb	3.2.75	Agidas
And casts a flash of lightning to the earth.	1Tamb	4.2.46	Tamb
What an eye she casts on me?	Jew	4.2.128	P Ithimr
See what a scornfull looke the pesant casts.	Edw	1.4.14	MortSr
rest, because we heare/That Edmund casts to worke his libertie,	Edw	5.2.58	Mortmr
now least age might waine his state, he casts/For civill warre,	Lucan, First Booke		324
While rashly her wombes burthen she casts out,	Ovid's Elegies		2.13.1

CASUALL

The worlds swift course is lawlesse/And casuall; all the	Lucan, First Booke		642

CASUALTIE

Whom casualtie of sea hath made such friends?	Dido	3.2.76	Juno

CAT (See also CATTE)

teach thee to turne thy selfe to a Dog, or a Cat, or a Mouse,	F 383	1.4.41	P Wagner
A Dog, or a Cat, or a Mouse, or a Rat?	F 384	1.4.42	P Robin

CATCH

And beates his braines to catch us in his trap,	P 53	1.53	Navrre
And guides my feete least stumbling falles they catch.	Ovid's Elegies		1.6.8

CATCHING

buttons to his lips, to keepe his tongue from catching cold.	F1388	4.2.64	P Benvol

CATECHISING			
And as it were in Catechising sort, ...	Jew	2.3.73	Barab
CATERPILLERS			
Look, look, master, here come two religious Caterpillers.	Jew	4.1.21	P Ithimr
CATES			
Casane, here are the cates you desire to finger, are they not?	1Tamb	4.4.108	P Tamb
Cookes shall have pensions to provide us cates, . .	2Tamb	1.3.219	Tamb
CATHOLICK			
O let him goe, he is a catholick.	P 375	7.15	Retes
Then shall the Catholick faith of Rome, ...	P 639	12.52	QnMoth
I, and the catholick Philip King of Spaine, ...	P 852	17.47	Guise
CATHOLICKES			
from Spaine the stately Catholickes/Sends Indian golde to coyne	P 117	2.60	Guise
CATHOLICKS			
Besides a thousand sturdy student Catholicks, ...	P 140	2.83	Guise
That it may keenly slice the Catholicks.	P1238	22.100	King
CATHOLIKE			
Vizadmirall unto the Catholike King.	Jew	2.2.7	Bosco
CATHOLIQUES			
Now Guise shall catholiques flourish once againe, . .	P 295	5.22	Anjoy
CATILINE			
That like the lawles Catiline of Rome, ...	Edw	4.6.51	Rice
CATO			
The gods abetted; Cato likt the other;	Lucan, First Booke		129
Brabbling Marcellus; Cato whom fooles reverence; . .	Lucan, First Booke		313
CATS			
Play, Fidler, or I'le cut your cats guts into chitterlins.	Jew	4.4.44	P Ithimr
CATTE			
to anything, to a dogge, or a catte, or a mouse, or a ratte,	F App	p.231 59	P Wagner
a Christian fellow to a dogge or a catte, a mouse or a ratte?	F App	p.231 60	P Clown
CATTELL			
Cattell were seene that muttered humane speech: . .	Lucan, First Booke		559
CATUL			
in Catul Verone,/Of me Pelignis nation boasts alone, .	Ovid's Elegies		3.14.7
CATULLUS			
With Calvus learnd Catullus comes <come> and greete him. .	Ovid's Elegies		3.8.62
CATZERIE			
and looks/Like one that is imploy'd in Catzerie/And crosbiting,	Jew	4.3.12	Barab
CAUCASUS			
But thou art sprung from Scythian Caucasus, ...	Dido	5.1.158	Dido
Or as Matrevis, hewne from the Caucasus, ...	Edw	5.5.54	Edward
CAUGHT			
Which being caught, strikes him that takes it dead, . .	Edw	1.4.222	Mortmr
CAUL (See CAL)			
CAUS'D			
And caus'd the ruines to be new repair'd, ...	Jew	5.3.2	Calym
And a rich neck-lace caus'd that punnishment. . . .	Ovid's Elegies		1.10.52
CAUSDE			
causde the Greekish spyes/To hast to Tenedos and tell the	Dido	2.1.180	Aeneas
But how scapt Helen, she that causde this warre? . .	Dido	2.1.292	Dido
That causde the eldest sonne of heavenly Ops, ...	1Tamb	2.7.13	Tamb
And we be quit that causde it to be done:	Edw	5.4.16	Mortmr
Nuts were thy food, and Poppie causde thee sleepe, . .	Ovid's Elegies		2.6.31
'CAUSE			
Yes, 'cause you use to confesse.	Jew	4.1.145	Ithimr
CAUSE			
Now Cupid cause the Carthaginian Queene, ...	Dido	3.1.1	Cupid
Yet if you would partake with me the cause/Of this devotion	Dido	4.2.27	Anna
Good brother tell the cause unto my Lords, ...	1Tamb	1.1.4	Mycet
Declare the cause of my conceived griefe, ...	1Tamb	1.1.29	Mycet
And cause them to withdraw their forces home, ...	1Tamb	1.1.131	Menaph
And cause the souldiers that thus honour me, ...	1Tamb	1.1.172	Cosroe
may I presume/To know the cause of these unquiet fits: .	1Tamb	3.2.2	Agidas
And cause the Sun to borrowe light of you.	1Tamb	4.2.40	Tamb
wert thou the cause of this/That tearm'st Zenocrate thy dearest	1Tamb	5.1.335	Zenoc
Since Death denies me further cause of joy, ...	1Tamb	5.1.430	Arabia
And for that cause the Christians shall have peace. . .	2Tamb	1.1.57	Orcan
And cause the stars fixt in the Southern arke, ...	2Tamb	3.2.29	Tamb
And cause some milder spirits governe you.	2Tamb	5.3.80	Phsitn
Which being the cause of life, imports your death. . .	2Tamb	5.3.90	Phsitn
'twere in my power/To favour you, but 'tis my fathers cause,	Jew	1.2.11	Calym
Excesse of wealth is cause of covetousnesse:	Jew	1.2.123	Govnr
And thats the cause that Guise so frowns at us, . . .	P 52	1.52	Navrre
And Guise usurpes it, cause I am his wife:	P 661	13.5	Duchss
Or else employ them in some better cause.	P 794	16.8	Bartus
I challenge thee for treason in the cause.	P 830	17.25	Eprnon
Ere I shall want, will cause his Indians, ...	P 853	17.48	Guise
Did he not cause the King of Spaines huge fleete, . . .	P1033	19.103	King
That wert the onely cause of his exile.	Edw	1.1.179	Edward
Either banish him that was the cause thereof, ...	Edw	1.4.60	ArchBp
Heere comes she thats cause of all these jarres. . . .	Edw	2.2.224	Edward
Thus do you still suspect me without cause.	Edw	2.2.227	Queene
He is your brother, therefore have we cause/To cast the worst,	Edw	2.3.7	Warwck
Corrupter of thy king, cause of these broiles, ...	Edw	2.5.10	Mortmr
it is our countries cause,/That here severelie we will execute	Edw	2.5.22	Warwck
Cause yet more bloudshed:	Edw	2.5.83	Warwck
No James, it is my countries cause I follow.	Edw	2.6.10	Warwck
Some treason, or some villanie was cause.	Edw	3.1.114	Spencr
But justice of the quarrell and the cause, ...	Edw	3.1.222	Edward
Nature, yeeld to my countries cause in this.	Edw	4.1.3	Kent
Misgoverned kings are cause of all this wrack, ...	Edw	4.4.9	Queene
Heere for our countries cause sweare we to him/All homage,	Edw	4.4.19	Mortmr
I can brooke/To loose my crowne and kingdome, without cause,	Edw	5.1.52	Edward

CAUSE (cont.)			
And thats the cause that I am now remoovde.	Edw	5.1.150	Edward
That wast a cause of his imprisonment?	Edw	5.2.102	Mortmr
The more cause have I now to make amends.	Edw	5.2.103	Kent
Yet he that is the cause of Edwards death,	Edw	5.4.3	Mortmr
Still feare I, and I know not whats the cause,	Edw	5.5.85	Edward
That was the cause, but yet per accidens:	F 274	1.3.46	Mephst
And cause we are no common guests,	F 805	3.1.27	Mephst
heere's some on's have cause to know him; did he conjure thee	F1523	4.5.19	P HrsCsr
cause two divels presently to fetch thee away Baliol and	F App	p.230 43	P Wagner
And give me cause to praise thee whilst I live.	F App	p.237 36	Emper
neither thou nor Hanniball/Art cause, no forraine foe could so	Lucan, First Booke		31
O Roome thy selfe art cause of all these evils,	Lucan, First Booke		84
which of both/Had justest cause unlawful tis to judge:	Lucan, First Booke		127
Each side had great partakers; Caesars cause,	Lucan, First Booke		128
Warre and the destinies shall trie my cause.	Lucan, First Booke		229
Whether the gods, or blustring south were cause/I know not, but	Lucan, First Booke		236
for unto me/Thou cause, what ere thou be whom God assignes/This	Lucan, First Booke		419
Were Love the cause, it's like I shoulde descry him,	Ovid's Elegies		1.2.5
Either love, or cause that I may never hate:	Ovid's Elegies		1.3.2
Such as the cause was of two husbands warre,	Ovid's Elegies		1.10.1
This cause hath thee from pleasing me debard.	Ovid's Elegies		1.10.12
Be sedulous, let no stay cause thee tarry.	Ovid's Elegies		1.11.8
And did to thee no cause of dolour raise.	Ovid's Elegies		1.14.14
Nor set my voyce to sale in everie cause?	Ovid's Elegies		1.15.6
Aye me poore soule, why is my cause so good.	Ovid's Elegies		2.5.8
[Itis is] <It is as> great, but auntient cause of sorrowe.	Ovid's Elegies		2.6.10
To take repulse, and cause her shew my lust?	Ovid's Elegies		2.7.26
Let the bright day-starre cause in heaven this day be,	Ovid's Elegies		2.11.55
Nor is my warres cause new, but for a Queene/Europe, and Asia	Ovid's Elegies		2.12.17
Aye me, let not my warnings cause my paine.	Ovid's Elegies		2.19.34
And was the second cause why vigor failde mee:	Ovid's Elegies		3.6.38
And with sweete words cause deafe rockes to have loved <moned>,	Ovid's Elegies		3.6.58
My love was cause that more mens love she seazd.	Ovid's Elegies		3.10.20
Wee cause feete flie, wee mingle haires with snakes,	Ovid's Elegies		3.11.23
two words, thinke/The cause acquits you not, but I that winke.	Ovid's Elegies		3.13.50
CAUSELES			
Fie Venus, that such causeles words of wrath,	Dido	3.2.26	Juno
CAUSERS			
Then be the causers of their misery.	Jew	1.2.148	Barab
Hold, let's inquire the causers of their deaths,	Jew	3.2.27	Mater
Till they [reveal] the causers of our smarts,	Jew	3.2.34	Govnr
CAUSES			
The causes first I purpose to unfould/Of these garboiles,	Lucan, First Booke		67
When causes fale thee to require a gift,	Ovid's Elegies		1.8.93
Vaine causes faine of him the true to hide,	Ovid's Elegies		2.2.31
Both unkinde parents, but for causes sad,	Ovid's Elegies		2.14.31
CAVALIEROS			
Raise Cavalieros higher than the cloudes,	2Tamb	2.4.103	Tamb
With Cavalieros and thicke counterforts,	2Tamb	3.2.71	Tamb
CAVE			
Then in one Cave the Queene and he shall meete,	Dido	3.2.92	Juno
Tell me deare love, how found you out this Cave?	Dido	3.4.3	Dido
Behold where both of them come forth the Cave.	Dido	4.1.16	Anna
Come forth the Cave: can heaven endure this sight?	Dido	4.1.17	Iarbus
Whil'st they were sporting in this darksome Cave?	Dido	4.1.24	Iarbus
Not with Aeneas in the ugly Cave.	Dido	4.1.32	Iarbus
Here lye the Sword that in the darksome Cave/He drew, and swore	Dido	5.1.295	Dido
us haste from hence/Along the cave that leads beyond the foe,	2Tamb	3.4.2	Olymp
Nor thy close Cave a sword to murther thee,	2Tamb	4.2.12	Olymp
Whilst I am lodgd within this cave of care,	Edw	5.1.32	Edward
CAVES			
And hale the stubborne Furies from their caves,	F1225	4.1.71	Faust
Snakes leape by verse from caves of broken mountaines/And	Ovid's Elegies		2.1.25
CAY (See KAI)			
CAYC (See CAICKE)			
CAZATES			
From thence unto Cazates did I martch,	2Tamb	1.3.191	Techel
CAZZO			
Cazzo, diabolo.	Jew	4.1.20	Barab
CEASDE			
A griping paine hath ceasde upon my heart:	P 537	11.2	Charls
CEASE			
Who nere will cease to soare till he be slaine.	Dido	3.3.85	Iarbus
Since gloomie Aeolus doth cease to frowne.	Dido	4.1.27	Aeneas
Sweet sister cease, remember who you are.	Dido	5.1.263	Anna
When heaven shal cease to moove on both the poles/And when the	2Tamb	1.3.12	Tamb
Or cease one day from war and hot alarms,	2Tamb	1.3.183	Usumc
Some musicke, and my fit wil cease my Lord.	2Tamb	2.4.77	Zenoc
or by speach I heare/Immortall Jove say, Cease my Tamburlaine,	2Tamb	4.1.199	Tamb
Sit stil my gratious Lord, this griefe wil cease,	2Tamb	5.3.64	Techel
And never cease untill that bell shall cease,	P 240	4.38	Guise
Cease brother, for I cannot brooke these words:	Edw	1.1.160	Edward
No speaking will prevaile, and therefore cease.	Edw	1.4.220	Penbrk
Cease to lament, and tell us wheres the king?	Edw	2.4.30	Mortmr
Be patient good my lord, cease to lament,	Edw	5.1.1	Leistr
We will informe thee e're our conference cease.	F 184	1.1.156	Valdes
That time may cease, and midnight never come.	F1930	5.2.134	Faust
Keeper if thou be wise cease hate to cherish,	Ovid's Elegies		2.2.9
O Cupid that doest never cease my smart,	Ovid's Elegies		2.9.1
CEASELESSE			
With ceaselesse and disconsolate conceits,	1Tamb	3.2.14	Zenoc
CEASLES			
And make our soules resolve in ceasles teares:	1Tamb	5.1.272	Bajaze

CEASLESSE			
and the ceaslesse lamps/That gently look'd upon this loathsome	2Tamb	2.4.18	Tamb
CEASSLES			
To doo their ceassles homag to my sword:	1Tamb	5.1.456	Tamb
CEDAR			
Or scattered like the lofty Cedar trees, ...	1Tamb	4.2.24	Tamb
A loftie Cedar tree faire flourishing, ...	Edw	2.2.16	Mortmr
I am that Cedar, shake me not too much, ...	Edw	2.2.38	Edward
The Cedar tall spoyld of his barke retaines.	Ovid's Elegies		1.14.12
CELEBRATE			
Of Greekish wine now let us celebrate/Our happy conquest,	2Tamb	2.3.46	Orcan
To celebrate your fathers exequies, ...	Edw	1.1.176	BshpCv
CELEBRATED			
We wil our celebrated rites of mariage solemnize. . . .	1Tamb	5.1.534	Tamb
manie cities sacrifice/He celebrated her [sad] <said> funerall,	2Tamb	Prol.8	Prolog
CELESTIAL			
attaine the gole/That shall conduct thee to celestial rest.	F App	p.243 37	OldMan
CELESTIALL			
Are not we both sprong of celestiall rase, ...	Dido	3.2.28	Juno
And both our soules aspire celestiall thrones.	1Tamb	1.2.237	Tamb
Upon the lofty and celestiall mount, ...	2Tamb	4.3.120	Tamb
Continue ever thou celestiall sunne, ...	Edw	5.1.64	Edward
Are all Celestiall bodies but one Globe, ...	F 587	2.2.36	Faust
O thou hast lost celestiall happinesse, ...	F1899	5.2.103	GdAngl
Confused stars shal meete, celestiall fire/Fleete on the flouds,	Lucan, First Booke		75
I durst the great celestiall battells tell, ...	Ovid's Elegies		2.1.11
Nor is't of earth or mold celestiall, ...	Hero and Leander		1.273
And knockt and cald, at which celestiall noise, . . .	Hero and Leander		2.231
CELLER			
Downe to the Celler, taste of all my wines.	Jew	5.5.7	Barab
CELLERS			
Cellers of Wine, and Sollers full of Wheat, ...	Jew	4.1.63	Barab
CELS			
that dwels/In tow'red courts, is oft in sheapheards cels).	Hero and Leander		1.394
CEMERIAN			
the Sea-man sees the Hyades/Gather an armye of Cemerian clouds,	1Tamb	3.2.77	Agidas
CENSTE			
fondlie hast thow in censte the guises sowle	Paris	ms25,p391	Guise
CENSUR'D			
What we behold is censur'd by our eies.	Hero and Leander		1.174
CENSURE			
To censure Bruno, that is posted hence, ...	F 983	3.2.3	Mephst
CENTAURES			
Bride did incite/The drunken Centaures to a sodaine fight.	Ovid's Elegies		1.4.8
The Laphithes, and the Centaures for a woman, ...	Ovid's Elegies		2.12.19
CENTER			
Pierce through the center of my withered heart, . . .	1Tamb	5.1.303	Bajzth
My realme, the Center of our Empery/Once lost, All Turkie would	2Tamb	1.1.55	Orcan
Whose darts do pierce the Center of my soule:	2Tamb	2.4.84	Tamb
O must this day be period of my life,/Center of all my blisse!	Edw	2.6.5	Gavstn
Center of all misfortune. O my starres!	Edw	4.7.62	Edward
new to enter/Warres, just Latinus, in thy kingdomes center:	Ovid's Elegies		2.12.22
CENTERS			
That have not past the Centers latitude, ...	2Tamb	3.2.31	Tamb
CENTINELS			
As Centinels to warne th'immortall soules, ...	2Tamb	2.4.16	Tamb
CENTRICKE			
As is the substance of this centricke earth?	F 588	2.2.37	Faust
CENTRONELS			
These milke white Doves shall be his Centronels: . . .	Dido	2.1.320	Venus
CENTURION			
then Laelius/The chiefe Centurion crown'd with Oaken leaves,	Lucan, First Booke		358
CEPHALUS (See also CAEPHALUS)			
Or Cephalus with lustie Thebane youths, ...	1Tamb	4.3.4	Souldn
CEPHEUS			
But did you not so envy Cepheus Daughter, ...	Ovid's Elegies		3.3.17
CERANIAS			
The Cyclops shelves, and grim Ceranias seate/Have you oregone,	Dido	1.1.147	Aeneas
CERANNIA			
what [rockes] <rocke> the feard Cerannia <Ceraunia> threat,	Ovid's Elegies		2.11.19
CERAUNIA			
what [rockes] <rocke> the feard Cerannia <Ceraunia> threat,	Ovid's Elegies		2.11.19
CERBERUS			
The triple headed Cerberus would howle, ...	2Tamb	5.1.97	Tamb
CEREMONIALL			
<Tut Faustus>, Marriage is but a ceremoniall toy, . . .	F 535	2.1.147	Mephst
CEREMONIES			
And then all other ceremonies learn'd, ...	F 186	1.1.158	Cornel
CEREMONIOUS			
But if I use such ceremonious thankes, ...	Dido	4.3.49	Aeneas
CEREMONY			
Belike there is some Ceremony in't.	Jew	3.4.83	Barab
CERES			
And fertile in faire Ceres furrowed wealth, ...	Dido	1.2.22	Cloan
Joying the fruit of Ceres garden plot, ...	2Tamb	4.3.37	Orcan
In woodie groves ist meete that Ceres Raigne, ...	Ovid's Elegies		1.1.13
Ceres and Bacchus Country-men adore, ...	Ovid's Elegies		3.2.53
Come were the times of Ceres sacrifize, ...	Ovid's Elegies		3.9.1
Golden-hair'd Ceres crownd with eares of corne, . . .	Ovid's Elegies		3.9.3
First Ceres taught the seede in fields to swell, . . .	Ovid's Elegies		3.9.11
Ceres, I thinke, no knowne fault will deny.	Ovid's Elegies		3.9.24
Where Ceres went each place was harvest there. . . .	Ovid's Elegies		3.9.38
Ceres what sports to thee so grievous were, ...	Ovid's Elegies		3.9.43

CERTAINE			
that at some certaine day/Great Lucifer may claime it as his	F 439	2.1.51	Mephst
And words that seem'd for certaine markes to be.	Ovid's Elegies		2.5.20
Shee oft hath serv'd thee upon certaine dayes,	Ovid's Elegies		2.13.17
No certaine house thou hast, nor any fountaines.	Ovid's Elegies		3.5.92
CERTAINELIE			
Then I assure thee certainelie they are.	F1650	4.6.93	Faust
CERTIFIE			
This certifie the Pope, away, take horsse.	Edw	1.2.38	ArchBp
We will in hast go certifie our Lord.	Edw	2.6.19	James
And certifie what Edwards loosenes is.	Edw	4.1.7	Kent
CESTERNES			
Foorth from those two tralucent cesternes brake,	Hero and Leander		1.296
CHAC'D			
He would have chac'd away the swelling maine,	Hero and Leander		2.121
CHACE			
To chace the savage [Calidonian] <Caldonian> Boare:	1Tamb	4.3.3	Souldn
As frolike as the hunters in the chace/Of savage beastes amid	1Tamb	4.3.56	Capol
and Phoebe's waine/Chace Phoebus and inrag'd affect his place,	Lucan, First Booke		78
Even as, when gawdie Nymphs pursue the chace,	Hero and Leander		1.113
CHAFE			
Nay chafe not man, we all are sped.	F1444	4.3.14	Mrtino
Although thou chafe, stolne pleasure is sweet play,	Ovid's Elegies		3.4.31
CHAFING			
he keepes such a chafing with my mistris about it, and she has	F App	p.233 8	P Rafe
And heaven tormented with thy chafing heate,	Lucan, First Booke		656
CHAIN'D			
And I was chain'd to follies of the world:	Jew	3.3.60	Abigal
heady rout/That in chain'd troupes breake forth at every port;	Lucan, First Booke		489
CHAIND			
been/When Didos beautie [chaind] <chaungd> thine eyes to her:	Dido	5.1.114	Dido
who though lockt and chaind in stalls,/Souse downe the wals,	Lucan, First Booke		295
Both in each others armes chaind as they layd.	Hero and Leander		2.306
CHAINE			
Shall chaine felicitie unto their throne.	Dido	3.2.80	Juno
Or take him prisoner, and his chaine shall serve/For Manackles,	1Tamb	1.2.147	Tamb
Now have I freed my selfe, and fled the chaine,	Ovid's Elegies		3.10.3
CHAINES			
For tackling, let him take the chaines of gold,	Dido	4.4.161	Dido
their neckes/Hangs massie chaines of golde downe to the waste,	1Tamb	1.2.126	Souldr
I hold the Fates bound fast in yron chaines,	1Tamb	1.2.174	Tamb
Burdening their bodies with your heavie chaines,	1Tamb	3.3.48	Tamb
And all his Captains bound in captive chaines.	1Tamb	3.3.115	Bajzth
I took the king, and lead him bound in chaines/Unto Damasco,	2Tamb	1.3.204	Techel
The Dyvils there in chaines of quencelesse flame,	2Tamb	2.3.24	Orcan
By Mahomet he shal be tied in chaines,	2Tamb	3.5.92	Jrslem
Go bind the villaine, he shall hang in chaines,	2Tamb	5.1.84	Tamb
Hang him up in chaines upon the citie walles,	2Tamb	5.1.108	Tamb
Shall being dead, be hangd thereon in chaines.	P 321	5.48	Anjoy
Fetters the Euxin sea, with chaines of yce:	Lucan, First Booke		18
Unworthy porter, bound in chaines full sore,	Ovid's Elegies		1.6.1
Strike, so againe hard chaines shall binde thee never,	Ovid's Elegies		1.6.25
Binde fast my hands, they have deserved chaines,	Ovid's Elegies		1.7.1
Deserved chaines these cursed hands shall fetter,	Ovid's Elegies		1.7.28
On tell-tales neckes thou seest the linke-knitt chaines,	Ovid's Elegies		2.2.41
About her necke hung chaines of peble stone,	Hero and Leander		1.25
CHAINING			
Chaining of Eunuches, binding gally-slaves.	Jew	2.3.204	Ithimr
CHAIRE (See also CHAYRE)			
Sit in this chaire and banquet with a Queene,	Dido	2.1.83	Dido
To thrust his doting father from his chaire,	1Tamb	2.7.14	Tamb
Sit here upon this royal chaire of state,	1Tamb	3.3.112	Bajzth
Make ready my Coch, my chaire, my jewels, I come, I come, I	1Tamb	5.1.317	P Zabina
My royal chaire of state shall be advanc'd:	2Tamb	1.3.82	Tamb
For if his chaire were in a sea of blood,	2Tamb	1.3.89	Celeb
As if a chaire of gold enamiled,	2Tamb	3.2.119	Tamb
turrets of my Court/Sit like to Venus in her chaire of state,	2Tamb	4.2.42	Therid
Let it be plac'd by this my fatall chaire,	2Tamb	5.3.211	Tamb
hollinesse ascends/Saint Peters Chaire and State Pontificall.	F 870	3.1.92	Raymnd
From Bruno's backe, ascends Saint Peters Chaire.	F 876	3.1.98	Pope
And by your death to clime Saint Peters Chaire,	F 960	3.1.182	Faust
And sit in Peters Chaire, despite of chance,	F1214	4.1.60	Emper
this ever-burning chaire,/Is for ore-tortur'd soules to rest	F1914	5.2.118	BdAngl
have concluded/That Midas brood shall sit in Honors chaire,	Hero and Leander		1.475
CHALENGE			
So sure did your father write, and I cary the chalenge.	Jew	3.3.25	P Ithimr
CHALLENGE			
To challenge us with your comparisons?	Dido	3.3.20	Dido
that ever brandisht sword)/Challenge in combat any of you all,	2Tamb	3.5.72	Tamb
It is a challenge feign'd from Lodowicke.	Jew	2.3.374	Barab
Well, I have deliver'd the challenge in such sort,	Jew	3.1.29	Ithimr
Why the devil invented a challenge, my master writ it, and I	Jew	3.3.18	P Ithimr
I will not say that by a forged challenge they met.	Jew	4.1.45	P 2Fryar
contracted unto Abigall; [he] forg'd a counterfeit challenge.	Jew	5.1.30	P Ithimr
Who carried that challenge?	Jew	5.1.31	Barab
He forged the daring challenge made them fight.	Jew	5.1.47	Govnr
I fram'd the challenge that did make them meet:	Jew	5.5.82	Barab
They justly challenge their protection:	P 210	4.8	Charls
I challenge thee for treason in the cause.	P 830	17.25	Eprnon
CHALLENGER			
Who in the triumphe will be challenger,	Edw	1.4.382	Edward
CHAM			
Besides rich presents from the puisant Cham,	1Tamb	1.2.18	Magnet

CHAM (cont.)			
'Twas sent me for a present from the great Cham.	Jew	4.4.68	Barab
CHAMBER			
Ile hang ye in the chamber where I lye,	Dido	4.4.128	Dido
send for them/To do the work my chamber maid disdaines.	1Tamb	3.3.188	Anippe
the plancke/That runs along the upper chamber floore,	Jew	1.2.297	Barab
Spaine is the counsell chamber of the pope,	P 709	14.12	Navrre
and use a counterfeite key to his privie Chamber doore:	P 807	17.2	P Souldr
Then sirs take your standings within this Chamber,	P 940	19.10	Capt
duke a cuckolde and use a counterfeyt key to his privy chamber	Paris	ms 2,p390	P Souldr
Into the councell chamber he is gone,	Edw	5.6.20	Queene
Fourthly, that he shall be in his chamber or house invisible.	F 490	2.1.102	P Faust
I chuse his privy chamber for our use.	F 806	3.1.28	Mephst
I have taken up his holinesse privy chamber for our use>.	F 806	(HC265)A	P Mephst
Come leave thy chamber first, and thou shalt see/This Conjurer	F1185	4.1.31	Mrtino
Ah my sweet chamber-fellow, had I liv'd with thee, then had I	F1824	5.2.28	P Faust
That hops about the chamber where I lie,	Hero and Leander		1.354
And round about the chamber this false morne,	Hero and Leander		2.321
CHAMBER-FELLOW			
Ah my sweet chamber-fellow, had I liv'd with thee, then had I	F1824	5.2.28	P Faust
CHAMBERLAINE			
I heere create thee Lord high Chamberlaine,	Edw	1.1.154	Edward
I, and besides, lord Chamberlaine of the realme,	Edw	1.2.13	Warwck
Salute him? yes: welcome Lord Chamberlaine.	Edw	2.2.65	Lncstr
love we do create thee/Earle of Gloster, and lord Chamberlaine,	Edw	3.1.146	Edward
CHAMBER MAID			
send for them/To do the work my chamber maid disdaines.	1Tamb	3.3.188	Anippe
CHAMBERS			
the night time secretly would I steale/To travellers Chambers,	Jew	2.3.207	Ithimr
The other Chambers open towards the street.	Jew	4.1.138	Barab
CHAMPION			
of my company/Scowting abroad upon these champion plaines,	1Tamb	2.2.40	Spy
And make this champion mead a bloody Fen.	2Tamb	1.1.32	Orcan
In champion grounds, what figure serves you best,	2Tamb	3.2.63	Tamb
I am the Champion that will combate him!	Edw	5.4.78	Champn
Champion, heeres to thee.	Edw	5.4.80	King
CHAMPIONS			
Champions pleace <please> Pollux, Castor [love] <loves>	Ovid's Elegies		3.2.54
CHANC'D			
accidents/Have chanc'd thy merits in this worthles bondage.	1Tamb	5.1.425	Arabia
chanc'd to cast mine eye up to the Jewes counting-house where I	Jew	3.1.18	P Pilia
CHANCE (See also CHAUNCE)			
By chance sweete Queene, as Mars and Venus met.	Dido	3.4.4	Aeneas
And when they chance to breath and rest a space,	1Tamb	3.3.51	Tamb
Ah what may chance to thee Zenocrate?	1Tamb	5.1.371	Zenoc
That they may say, it is not chance doth this,	2Tamb	4.1.84	Amyras
How chance you came not with those other ships/That sail'd by	Jew	1.1.89	Barab
I, let me sorrow for this sudden chance,	Jew	1.2.206	Barab
No, Barabas is borne to better chance,	Jew	1.2.218	Barab
I, but how chance this was not done before?	Edw	1.4.272	Lncstr
Now lustie lords, now not by chance of warre,	Edw	3.1.221	Edward
And sit in Peters Chaire, despite of chance,	F1214	4.1.60	Emper
Nor in my act hath fortune mingled chance,	Ovid's Elegies		2.12.15
May that shame fall mine enemies chance to be.	Ovid's Elegies		3.10.16
CHANCES			
And dangerous chances of the wrathfull war?	2Tamb	1.3.11	Zenoc
CHANG'D			
And let them know the Persean King is chang'd:	1Tamb	2.5.21	Cosroe
As it hath chang'd my first conceiv'd disdaine.	1Tamb	3.2.12	Zenoc
Why on the sudden is your colour chang'd?	Jew	2.3.321	Lodowk
Now worthy Faustus: me thinks your looks are chang'd.	F1821	5.2.25	1Schol
flie from me, and I be chang'd/[Unto] <Into> some brutish beast.	F1967	5.2.171	Faust
O soule be chang'd into <to> [little] <small> water drops,	F1977	5.2.181	Faust
Undaunted though her former guide be chang'd.	Lucan, First Booke		50
And that he's much chang'd, looking wild and big,	Lucan, First Booke		475
And sodainly her former colour chang'd,	Hero and Leander		1.359
CHANGD			
She smiles, now for my life his mind is changd.	Edw	1.4.236	Warwck
But nephew, now you see the king is changd.	Edw	1.4.420	MortSr
And that his banishment had changd her minde.	Edw	2.1.26	Baldck
CHANGE (See also CHAUNGE)			
Nor change my Martiall observations,	1Tamb	5.1.122	Tamb
Wherin the change I use condemns my faith,	1Tamb	5.1.390	Zenoc
From paine to paine, whose change shal never end:	2Tamb	2.3.26	Orcan
Wanes with enforst and necessary change.	2Tamb	2.4.46	Zenoc
May never such a change transfourme my love/In whose sweet	2Tamb	2.4.47	Tamb
A woful change my Lord, that daunts our thoughts,	2Tamb	5.3.181	Therid
Mute a the sudden; here's a sudden change.	Jew	2.3.324	Lodowk
Abigal I will, but see thou change no more,	Jew	3.3.70	1Fryar
Oh raskall! I change my selfe twice a day.	Jew	4.4.65	Barab
We know that noble mindes change not their thoughts/For wearing	P 610	12.23	Mugern
That change their coulour when the winter comes,	P 721	14.24	Navrre
Adew my Lord, and either change your minde,	Edw	1.1.130	Lncstr
Let this gift change thy minde, and save thy soule,	Edw	5.5.88	Edward
I charge thee to returne, and change thy shape,	F 251	1.3.23	Faust
I, thinke so still, till experience change thy mind.	F 517	2.1.129	Mephst
Rash boy, who gave thee power to change a line?	Ovid's Elegies		1.1.9
I love but one, and hir I love change never,	Ovid's Elegies		1.3.15
Or voice that howe to change the wilde notes knew?	Ovid's Elegies		2.6.18
Charmes change corne to grasse, and makes it dye,	Ovid's Elegies		3.6.31
O let him change goods so ill got to dust.	Ovid's Elegies		3.7.66
CHANGED			
Bird-changed Progne doth her Itys teare.	Ovid's Elegies		3.11.32

CHANGELING			
My sonne: thou art a changeling, not my sonne.	P1074	19.144	QnMoth
CHANGETH			
And changeth as the Ocean ebbes and flowes:	Lucan, First Booke		412
CHANNELL			
And cleave him to the channell with my sword.	2Tamb	1.3.103	Calyph
I meant to cut a channell to them both,	2Tamb	5.3.134	Tamb
And in the channell christen him a new.	Edw	1.1.188	Edward
With slaughtered priests [make] <may> Tibers channell swell,	Edw	1.4.102	Edward
Heeres channell water, as our charge is given.	Edw	5.3.27	Matrvs
And where swift Nile in his large channell slipping <skipping>,	Ovid's Elegies		2.13.9
And from the channell all abroad surrounded.	Ovid's Elegies		3.5.86
CHANNELS			
Downe to the channels of your hatefull throats,	2Tamb	4.1.183	Tamb
for the running streames/And common channels of the City.	Jew	5.1.89	Barab
And made the channels overflow with blood,	Edw	4.4.12	Queene
To which the channels of the castell runne,	Edw	5.5.3	Matrvs
CHANT (See CHAUNT)			
CHAOS			
Than when she gave eternall Chaos forme,	2Tamb	3.4.76	Techel
Time ends and to old Chaos all things turne;	Lucan, First Booke		74
Which th'earth from ougly Chaos den up-wayd:	Hero and Leander		1.450
CHAPLAINE			
And make him serve thee as thy chaplaine,	Edw	1.1.195	Edward
CHAPLET			
and on his head/A Chaplet brighter than Apollos crowne,	2Tamb	5.2.33	Amasia
CHARACTERS			
That by Characters graven in thy browes,	1Tamb	1.2.169	Tamb
Lines, Circles, [Signes], Letters, [and] Characters,	F 78	1.1.50	Faust
And Characters of Signes, and [erring] <evening> Starres,	F 240	1.3.12	Faust
I might see al characters of <and> planets of the heavens,	F 551.4	2.1.167A P	Faust
CHARDG'D			
Chardg'd with a thousand horse, to apprehend/And bring him	1Tamb	1.1.47	Meandr
When al their riders chardg'd their quivering speares/Began to	1Tamb	5.1.332	Zenoc
CHARDGE			
discovered the enemie/Ready to chardge you with a mighty armie.	1Tamb	2.3.50	1Msngr
A jest to chardge on twenty thousand men?	1Tamb	2.5.91	Therid
straight goe charge a few of them/To chardge these Dames,	1Tamb	5.1.117	Tamb
Come let us chardge our speares and pierce his breast,	2Tamb	5.3.58	Tamb
CHARG'D			
And charg'd him drowne my sonne with all his traine.	Dido	1.1.61	Venus
Is charg'd to violate her mistresse bed.	Ovid's Elegies		2.7.18
CHARGD			
Flye backe his [streame] <shame> chargd, the streame chargd,	Ovid's Elegies		3.5.44
his [streame] <shame> chargd, the streame chargd, gave place.	Ovid's Elegies		3.5.44
CHARGE			
Charge him from me to turne his stormie powers,	Dido	1.1.117	Jupitr
No, but I charge thee never looke on me.	Dido	3.1.54	Dido
Meane time, Ascanius shall be my charge,	Dido	3.2.98	Venus
I charge thee put to sea and stay not here.	Dido	4.4.22	Dido
Those that dislike what Dido gives in charge,	Dido	4.4.71	Dido
And givest not eare unto the charge I bring?	Dido	5.1.52	Hermes
Jove hath heapt on me such a desperate charge,	Dido	5.1.64	Aeneas
Then heare thy charge, valiant Theridamas,	1Tamb	1.1.57	Mycet
Go on my Lord, and give your charge I say,	1Tamb	2.2.57	Mycet
and excusde/For turning my poore charge to his direction.	1Tamb	2.3.29	Therid
go before and charge/The fainting army of that foolish King.	1Tamb	2.3.61	Cosroe
To charge him to remaine in Asia.	1Tamb	3.1.18	Fesse
straight goe charge a few of them/To chardge these Dames,	1Tamb	5.1.116	Tamb
Ready to charge you ere you stir your feet.	2Tamb	1.1.121	Fredrk
And I will teach thee how to charge thy foe,	2Tamb	1.3.45	Tamb
And leave his steeds to faire Boetes charge:	2Tamb	1.3.170	Tamb
Go Uribassa, give it straight in charge.	2Tamb	2.3.40	Orcan
Hast thou not seene my horsmen charge the foe,	2Tamb	3.2.103	Tamb
Ready to charge the army of the Turke.	2Tamb	3.4.87	Therid
As precious is the charge thou undertak'st/As that which	2Tamb	5.3.230	Tamb
I have no charge, nor many children,	Jew	1.1.136	Barab
And which of you can charge me otherwise?	Jew	1.2.117	Barab
I charge thee on my blessing that thou leave/These divels, and	Jew	1.2.346	Barab
Give charge to Morpheus that he may dreame/A golden dreame, and	Jew	2.1.36	Abigal
Close your Port-cullise, charge your Basiliskes,	Jew	3.5.31	Govnr
I charge thee send me three hundred by this bearer, and this	Jew	4.2.75	P Ithimr
Sound a charge there.	Jew	5.5.63	1Knght
Why, hardst thou not the trumpet sound a charge?	Jew	5.5.105	Govnr
That charge is mine.	P 290	5.17	Anjoy
I thankfully shall undertake the charge/Of you and yours, and	P 476	8.26	Anjoy
Lord Mortimer, we leave you to your charge:	Edw	1.4.373	Edward
in the morning/We will discharge thee of thy charge, be gon.	Edw	2.5.109	Penbrk
Then shall your charge committed to my trust.	Edw	3.1.78	Prince
I charge you roundly off with both their heads,	Edw	3.1.247	Edward
That I resigne my charge.	Edw	5.1.136	Leistr
As Leicester that had charge of him before.	Edw	5.2.35	BshpWn
Sister, Edward is my charge, redeeme him.	Edw	5.2.116	Kent
Not so my liege, the Queene hath given this charge,	Edw	5.3.13	Gurney
Heeres channell water, as our charge is given.	Edw	5.3.27	Matrvs
Lord Mortimer, now take him to your charge.	Edw	5.4.81	Queene
I charge thee to returne, and change thy shape,	F 251	1.3.23	Faust
I charge thee waite upon me whilst I live/To do what ever	F 264	1.3.36	Faust
Did not he charge thee to appeare to me?	F 271	1.3.43	Faust
here, take him to your charge,/And beare him streight to Ponte	F 964	3.1.186	Pope
Your Grace mistakes, you gave us no such charge.	F1024	3.2.44	1Card
Fly hence, dispatch my charge immediatly.	F1416	4.2.92	Faust
stand aside you had best, I charge you in the name of Belzabub:	F App	p.235 19 P	Robin

CHARGE (cont.)			
felow, and he has a great charge, neither wife nor childe.	F App	p.239 106	P Mephst
Caesar; he whom I heare thy trumpets charge/I hould no Romaine;	Lucan, First Booke	374	
Ambitious Imp, why seekst thou further charge? . . .	Ovid's Elegies	1.1.18	
I charge thee marke her eyes and front in reading, . .	Ovid's Elegies	1.11.17	
CHARGED			
And thou, if falsely charged to wrong thy friend, . .	Ovid's Elegies	3.8.63	
CHARGING			
At al times charging home, and making havock; . . .	Lucan, First Booke	148	
CHARIBDIS			
Cole-blacke Charibdis whirl'd a sea of bloud; . . .	Lucan, First Booke	546	
By cloyed Charibdis, and againe devoured.	Ovid's Elegies	2.16.26	
CHARILY			
That which so long so charily she kept, ...	Hero and Leander	2.309	
CHARIOT (See also CHARRIOT)			
Shall draw the chariot of my Emperesse, ...	1Tamb	3.3.80	Bajzth
The pavement underneath thy chariot wheels/With Turky Carpets	2Tamb	1.2.42	Callap
in the stable, when you shall come sweating from my chariot.	2Tamb	3.5.142	P Tamb
Sirha, prepare whips, and bring my chariot to my Tent: .	2Tamb	3.5.144	P Tamb
And have so proud a chariot at your heeles, ...	2Tamb	4.3.3	Tamb
live, and draw/My chariot swifter than the racking cloudes:	2Tamb	4.3.21	Tamb
They shall to morrow draw my chariot, ...	2Tamb	4.3.30	Tamb
Mounted his shining [chariot] <chariots>, gilt with fire,	2Tamb	4.3.126	Tamb
Whose chariot wheeles have burst th'Assirians bones, .	2Tamb	5.1.71	Tamb
teare both our limmes/Rather then we should draw thy chariot,	2Tamb	5.1.139	Orcan
And mount my royall chariot of estate, ...	2Tamb	5.3.178	Tamb
Guiding thy chariot with thy Fathers hand.	2Tamb	5.3.229	Tamb
The nature of thy chariot wil not beare/A guide of baser temper	2Tamb	5.3.242	Tamb
Where sitting <Being seated> in a Chariot burning bright,	F 758	2.3.37	2Chor
His burning chariot plung'd in sable cloudes, . . .	Lucan, First Booke	539	
And let the troupes which shall thy Chariot follow, . .	Ovid's Elegies	1.7.37	
Fower chariot-horses from the lists even ends. . . .	Ovid's Elegies	3.2.66	
Now wish the chariot, whence corne [seedes] <fields> were	Ovid's Elegies	3.5.15	
Phaeton had got/The guidance of the sunnes rich chariot. .	Hero and Leander	1.102	
CHARIOT-HORSES			
Fower chariot-horses from the lists even ends. . . .	Ovid's Elegies	3.2.66	
CHARIOTS			
Juno, false Juno in her Chariots pompe, ...	Dido	1.1.54	Venus
Mounted his shining [chariot] <chariots>, gilt with fire,	2Tamb	4.3.126	Tamb
And he shall follow my proud Chariots wheeles. . . .	P 984	19.54	Guise
Vulcan will give thee Chariots rich and faire. . . .	Ovid's Elegies	1.2.24	
Ride golden Love in Chariots richly builded. . . .	Ovid's Elegies	1.2.42	
Be broake with wheeles of chariots passing by. . . .	Ovid's Elegies	1.12.14	
CHARITIE			
And I am bound in charitie to requite it, ...	Jew	4.1.107	Barab
CHARITY			
Even for charity I may spit intoo't.	Jew	2.3.29	Barab
Who of meere charity and Christian ruth, ...	Jew	2.3.71	Barab
To undoe a Jew is charity, and not sinne.	Jew	4.4.81	Ithimr
CHARLES (See also CAROLUS)			
Under pretence of helping Charles the fifth, ...	Jew	2.3.188	Barab
Yet by my brother Charles our King of France, ...	P 464	8.14	Anjoy
That if by death of Charles, the diadem/Of France be cast on	P 472	8.22	Anjoy
How Charles our sonne begins for to lament/For the late nights	P 513	9.32	QnMoth
CHARME			
O that I had a charme to keepe the windes/Within the closure of	Dido	4.4.99	Dido
<Then charme me that I may be invisible>, ...	F 991	(HC266)A	Faust
Sweet Mephostophilis so charme me here, ...	F 991	3.2.11	Faust
And charme thee with this Magicke wand, ...	F 996	3.2.16	Mephst
I have a charme in my head, shall controule him as well as the	F1202	4.1.48	P Benvol
This Magicke, that will charme thy soule to hell, . .	F1708	5.1.35	OldMan
Against my good they were an envious charme. . . .	Ovid's Elegies	3.11.14	
Did charme her nimble feet, and made her stay, . . .	Hero and Leander	1.399	
And everie kisse to her was as a charme, ...	Hero and Leander	2.283	
CHARMED			
Intending but to rase my charmed skin:	1Tamb	1.2.179	Tamb
Volleyes of shot pierce through thy charmed Skin, . .	1Tamb	5.1.221	Bajzth
No charmed herbes of any harlot skathd thee, . . .	Ovid's Elegies	1.14.39	
Or when the Moone travailes with charmed steedes. . .	Ovid's Elegies	2.5.38	
CHARMES			
How am I vexed by these villaines Charmes?	F1117	3.3.30	Mephst
To cast his Magicke charmes, that shall pierce through/The Ebon	F1223	4.1.69	Faust
Tremble and quake at his commanding charmes? . . .	F1372	4.2.48	Fredrk
How am I vexed with these vilaines charmes? . . .	F App	p.235 37	Mephst
She magick arts and Thessale charmes doth know, . . .	Ovid's Elegies	1.8.5	
she chides/And with long charmes the solide earth divides.	Ovid's Elegies	1.8.18	
Sooth Lovers watch till sleepe the hus-band charmes, .	Ovid's Elegies	1.9.25	
Charmes change corne to grasse, and makes it dye, . .	Ovid's Elegies	3.6.31	
By charmes are running springs and fountaines drie, . .	Ovid's Elegies	3.6.32	
By charmes maste drops from okes, from vines grapes fall,	Ovid's Elegies	3.6.33	
And men inthralld by Mermaids singing charmes. . . .	Ovid's Elegies	3.11.28	
CHARMING			
That charming Circes walking on the waves, ...	Edw	1.4.172	Queene
CHARMS			
What, wast my limbs through some Thesalian charms, . .	Ovid's Elegies	3.6.27	
CHARONS			
Waiting the back returne of Charons boat, ...	1Tamb	5.1.464	Tamb
And hags howle for my death at Charons shore, ...	Edw	4.7.90	Edward
CHARRIOT			
Or mount the sunnes flame bearing <plume bearing> charriot,	Lucan, First Booke	48	
CHARY			
This will I keepe, as chary as my life.	F 551	2.1.163	Faust
[This will I keepe as chary as my life].	F 719.1	2.2.172	Faust

CHARYBDIS (See CARIBDIS, CHARIBDIS)
CHASE (See also CHACE)
And overtake the tusked Bore in chase. Dido 1.1.208 Venus
Weel chase the Stars from heaven, and dim their eies/That stand 1Tamb 2.3.23 Tamb
That had the Gallies of the Turke in chase. Jew 1.1.97 2Merch
Their creeping Gallyes had us in the chase: Jew 2.2.12 Bosco
Proud traytor Mortimer why doost thou chase/Thy lawfull king Edw 4.6.3 Kent
and fell invasion/Of such as have your majestie in chase, Edw 4.7.5 Abbot
And chase the Prince of Parma from our Land, F 120 1.1.92 Faust
Hunters leave taken beasts, pursue the chase, Ovid's Elegies 2.9.9
Let souldiour <souldiours> chase his <their> enemies amaine, Ovid's Elegies 2.10.31
CHAST
Or one of chast Dianas fellow Nimphs, Dido 1.1.194 Aeneas
He shall be made a chast and lustlesse Eunuke, 1Tamb 3.3.77 Bajzth
And made my house a place for Nuns most chast. Jew 2.3.77 Barab
But now against my will I must be chast. Jew 3.1.4 Curtzn
Chast, and devout, much sorrowing for my sinnes, Jew 3.6.14 Abigal
So chast Minerva did Cassandra fall, Ovid's Elegies 1.7.17
She drawes chast women to incontinence, Ovid's Elegies 1.8.19
Faire women play, shee's chast whom none will have, Ovid's Elegies 1.8.43
fire/And [thinke] <thinkes> her chast whom many doe desire. Ovid's Elegies 2.2.14
Who, without feare, is chaste, is chast in sooth: Ovid's Elegies 3.4.3
Cannot a faire one, if not chast, please thee? Ovid's Elegies 3.4.41
Now, Sabine-like, though chast she seemes to live, Ovid's Elegies 3.7.61
Chast Hero to her selfe thus softly said: Hero and Leander 1.178
Like chast Diana, when Acteon spyde her, Hero and Leander 2.261
CHASTE (Homograph)
Which we have chaste into the river [Sene] <Rene>, P 418 7.58 Guise
<Unhappies> <Unhappy is> Edward, chaste from Englands bounds. Edw 4.6.62 Kent
But we alas are chaste, and you my friends, Edw 4.7.22 Edward
Were <Be> she as chaste as was Penelope, F 540 2.1.152 Mephst
Aye me an Eunuch keepes my mistrisse chaste, Ovid's Elegies 2.3.1
Who, without feare, is chaste, is chast in sooth: Ovid's Elegies 3.4.3
She is not chaste, that's kept, but a deare whore: Ovid's Elegies 3.4.29
The Priests to Juno did prepare chaste feasts, Ovid's Elegies 3.12.3
Nor do I give thee counsaile to live chaste, Ovid's Elegies 3.13.3
And I shall thinke you chaste, do what you can. Ovid's Elegies 3.13.14
CHASTEST
Some one of these might make the chastest fall. Ovid's Elegies 2.4.32
CHASTISE
And tell them I will come to chastise them, Edw 3.1.178 Edward
CHASTITIE
To entertaine this Queene of chastitie, 2Tamb 4.2.96 Therid
Seeke you for chastitie, immortall fame, Hero and Leander 1.283
For thou in vowing chastitie, hast sworne/To rob her name and Hero and Leander 1.304
Vow'd spotlesse chastitie, but all in vaine. Hero and Leander 1.368
Whose only dower was her chastitie, Hero and Leander 1.412
When first religious chastitie she vow'd: Hero and Leander 2.110
CHASTIZE
Now serve to chastize shipboyes for their faults, Dido 4.4.157 Dido
CHATILLON (See SHATILLIAN)
CHAUNC'D
As after chaunc'd, they did each other spye. Hero and Leander 1.134
CHAUNCE
Which if it chaunce, Ile give ye buriall, Dido 5.1.176 Dido
Let not this heavy chaunce my dearest Lord, P 191 3.26 QnMarg
and in any case/Let no man comfort him, if he chaunce to weepe, Edw 5.2.64 Mortmr
That being dead, if it chaunce to be found, Edw 5.4.14 Mortmr
By chaunce I heard her talke, these words she sayd/While Ovid's Elegies 1.8.21
Bewaile my chaunce, the sad booke is returned, Ovid's Elegies 1.12.1
what meanes learnd/Hath this same Poet my sad chaunce discernd? Ovid's Elegies 2.1.10
By chaunce her beauty never shined fuller. Ovid's Elegies 2.5.42
Such chaunce let me have: Ovid's Elegies 3.2.9
CHAUNCELLOR
My lord, you shalbe Chauncellor of the realme, Edw 1.4.65 Edward
CHAUNCELOR
A goodly chauncelor, is he not my lord? Edw 4.6.43 Queene
CHAUNGD
Wherefore I [chaungd] <chaunge> my counsell with the time, Dido 3.2.51 Juno
been/When Didos beautie [chaind] <chaungd> thine eyes to her: Dido 5.1.114 Dido
Had chaungd my shape, or at the mariage day/The cup of Hymen Edw 1.4.173 Queene
CHAUNGE
Wherefore I [chaungd] <chaunge> my counsell with the time, Dido 3.2.51 Juno
And to a Scepter chaunge his golden shafts, Dido 3.2.57 Venus
That imitate the Moone in every chaunge, Dido 3.3.67 Iarbus
I may nor will list to such loathsome chaunge, Dido 4.2.47 Iarbus
Ask'st why I chaunge? because thou crav'st reward: Ovid's Elegies 1.10.11
CHAUNGING
And chaunging heavens may those good daies returne, Dido 1.1.150 Aeneas
CHAUNT
Sit safe at home and chaunt sweet Poesie. Lucan, First Booke 445
That all the world [may] <might> ever chaunt my name. Ovid's Elegies 1.15.8
CHAYRE
Yet will they reade me, and thereby attaine/To Peters Chayre: Jew Prol.12 Machvl
CHE
What doctrine call you this? Che sera, sera: F 74 1.1.46 Faust
CHEAR
That would with pity chear Zabinas heart, 1Tamb 5.1.271 Bajzth
CHEARE
If that be all, then cheare thy drooping lookes, Dido 5.1.71 Iarbus
Yet musicke woulde doe well to cheare up Zenocrate: 1Tamb 4.4.62 P Tamb
<Tut, tis no matter man>, wee'l be bold with his <good cheare>. F 808 (HC265)A P Mephst
<Whose summum bonum is in belly-cheare>. F 834 (HC265)A Mephst

CHEARE (cont.)			
<I goe sweete Faustus, but with heavy cheare>,	F1737	(HC269)A	OldMan
tearmes, with sad and heavie cheare/Complaind to Cupid;	Hero and Leander	1.440	
CHEAREFULL			
With chearefull hope thus he accosted her.	Hero and Leander	1.198	
CHEARES			
This doth delight me, this my courage cheares.	Ovid's Elegies	2.19.24	
CHEARFUL			
Whose chearful looks do cleare the clowdy aire/And cloath it in	2Tamb	1.3.3	Tamb
CHEARFULL			
And bring us pardon in your chearfull lookes.	1Tamb	5.1.47	Govnr
CHEAT			
While bond-men cheat, fathers [be hard] <hoord>, bawds hoorish,	Ovid's Elegies	1.15.17	
CHECK			
To countermaund our will and check our freends.	P 846	17.41	King
CHECKE			
chardg'd their quivering speares/Began to checke the ground,	1Tamb	5.1.333	Zenoc
CHECKES			
ringled bit, and with his hoves,/Checkes the submissive ground:	Hero and Leander	2.144	
CHECKING			
Checking thy body, may amend thy soule.	F1723	5.1.50	OldMan
CHECKS			
But secretlie her lookes with checks did trounce mee,	Ovid's Elegies	1.7.21	
CHECKT			
Like lightning go, his strugling mouth being checkt.	Ovid's Elegies	3.4.14	
CHEEF			
Cheef standard bearer to the Lutheranes,	P 313	5.40	Guise
CHEEFE			
Cheefe standard bearer to the Lutheranes,	P 285	5.12	Guise
Cheefe Secretarie to the state and me,	Edw	1.1.155	Edward
CHEEFELY			
Cheefely since under safetie of our word,	P 209	4.7	Charls
CHEEFEST			
That perill is the cheefest way to happines,	P 95	2.38	Guise
CHEEK			
the slave looks like a hogs cheek new sindg'd.	Jew	2.3.42	P Barab
CHEEK'DE			
And Libas, and the white cheek'de Pitho thrise,	Ovid's Elegies	3.6.24	
CHEEKE			
A pleasant smiling cheeke, a speaking eye,	Hero and Leander	1.85	
So Heroes ruddie cheeke, Hero betrayd,	Hero and Leander	2.323	
CHEEKES			
Her cheekes swolne with sighes, her haire all rent,	Dido	2.1.276	Aeneas
Lest their grosse eye-beames taint my lovers cheekes:	Dido	3.1.74	Dido
And wofull Dido by these blubbred cheekes,	Dido	5.1.133	Dido
Their blubbered cheekes and hartie humble mones/Will melt his	1Tamb	5.1.21	Govnr
Whose cheekes and hearts so punisht with conceit,	1Tamb	5.1.87	1Virgn
Hath stain'd thy cheekes, and made thee look like death,	2Tamb	4.2.4	Olymp
He claps his cheekes, and hanges about his neck,	Edw	1.2.51	Queene
Thy Rosie cheekes be to thy thombe inclinde.	Ovid's Elegies	1.4.22	
lockes spred/On her white necke but for hurt cheekes be led.	Ovid's Elegies	1.7.40	
My nayles to scratch her lovely cheekes I bent.	Ovid's Elegies	1.7.50	
And downe her cheekes, the trickling teares did flow,	Ovid's Elegies	1.7.57	
red shame becomes white cheekes, but this/If feigned, doth	Ovid's Elegies	1.8.35	
That this, or that man may thy cheekes moist keepe.	Ovid's Elegies	1.8.84	
hoary flieces/And riveld cheekes I would have puld a pieces.	Ovid's Elegies	1.8.112	
Alas she almost weepes, and her white cheekes,	Ovid's Elegies	1.14.51	
Even from your cheekes parte of a voice did breake.	Ovid's Elegies	2.5.16	
And scratch her faire soft cheekes I did intend.	Ovid's Elegies	2.5.46	
And with rough clawes your tender cheekes assaile.	Ovid's Elegies	2.6.4	
In both [thy] <my> cheekes she did perceive thee blush,	Ovid's Elegies	2.8.16	
Her cheekes were scratcht, her goodly haires discheveld.	Ovid's Elegies	3.5.48	
Those orient cheekes and lippes, exceeding his/That leapt into	Hero and Leander	1.73	
And silver tincture of her cheekes, that drew/The love of	Hero and Leander	1.396	
He clapt his plumpe cheekes, with his tresses playd,	Hero and Leander	2.181	
CHEEKS			
Thence rise the tears that so distain my cheeks,	1Tamb	3.2.64	Zenoc
And casts a pale complexion on his cheeks.	1Tamb	3.2.75	Agidas
With haire discheweld wip'st thy watery cheeks:	1Tamb	5.1.139	Tamb
And wet thy cheeks for their untimely deathes:	1Tamb	5.1.348	Zenoc
When wandring Phoebes Ivory cheeks were scortcht/And all the	2Tamb	5.3.232	Tamb
CHEEKT			
White-cheekt Penelope knewe Ulisses signe,	Ovid's Elegies	2.18.29	
Rose-cheekt Adonis) kept a solemne feast.	Hero and Leander	1.93	
CHEERE (See also CHEAR, CHEARE)			
And court Aeneas with your calmie cheere,	Dido	1.1.123	Venus
Therefore cheere up your mindes, prepare to fight,	1Tamb	2.2.29	Meandr
Let's cheere our souldiers to incounter him,	1Tamb	2.6.29	Cosroe
Weel have him ransomd man, be of good cheere.	Edw	2.2.116	Lncstr
But ile to Fraunce, and cheere the wronged Queene,	Edw	4.1.6	Kent
Madam, what cheere?	Edw	4.2.13	SrJohn
where ther's such belly-cheere, as Wagner in his life nere saw	F1679	5.1.6	P Wagner
who are at supper with such belly-cheere,	F App	p.243 6	Wagner
Cheere up thy selfe, thy losse thou maiest repaire,	Ovid's Elegies	1.14.55	
Now comes the pompe; themselves let all men cheere:	Ovid's Elegies	3.2.43	
CHEEREFULL			
Or faire Bootes sends his cheerefull light,	1Tamb	1.2.207	Tamb
Pay natures debt with cheerefull countenance,	Edw	4.7.109	Baldck
CHEERELES			
Never so cheereles, nor so farre distrest.	Edw	4.2.14	Queene
CHEERES			
Nothing Cornelius; O this cheeres my soule:	F 176	1.1.148	Faust
CHERELY			
Who hoping to imbrace thee, cherely swome.	Hero and Leander	2.250	

CHERISH			
Cherish thy valour stil with fresh supplies:	2Tamb	4.1.87	Tamb
And now and then, to cherish Christian theeves, . .	Jew	2.3.177	Barab
To cherish vertue and nobilitie, ...	Edw	3.1.167	Herald
Unnaturall king, to slaughter noble men/And cherish flatterers:	Edw	4.1.9	Kent
Keeper if thou be wise cease hate to cherish, ...	Ovid's Elegies		2.2.9
Ah simple Hero, learne thy selfe to cherish, ...	Hero and Leander		1.241
CHERISHT			
Had ancient Mothers this vile custome cherisht, . .	Ovid's Elegies		2.14.9
Burnes where it cherisht, murders where it loved. . .	Hero and Leander		2.128
CHERUBINS			
The Cherubins and holy Seraphins/That sing and play before the	2Tamb	2.4.26	Tamb
CHERUPE			
Which as shee went would cherupe through the bils. . .	Hero and Leander		1.36
CHEST			
that I might locke you safe into <uppe in> my <goode> Chest:	F 677	2.2.126	P Covet
CHESTS			
Whole Chests of Gold, in Bullion, and in Coyne, . .	Jew	4.1.65	Barab
CHID			
I chid no more, she blusht, and therefore heard me, . .	Ovid's Elegies		1.13.47
CHIDE			
See where they come, how might I doe to chide? . . .	Dido	4.4.13	Dido
Chide her Anippe.	1Tamb	4.2.71	Zenoc
Chide me sweete Warwick, if I go astray.	Edw	1.4.348	Edward
Wa'st not enough the fearefull Wench to chide? . . .	Ovid's Elegies		1.7.45
East windes he doth not chide/Nor to hoist saile attends fit	Ovid's Elegies		1.9.13
But yet sometimes to chide thee let her fall/Counterfet teares:	Ovid's Elegies		2.2.35
Now let her flatter me, now chide me hard, ...	Ovid's Elegies		2.9.45
CHIDES			
Great grand-sires from their antient graves she chides/And with	Ovid's Elegies		1.8.17
CHIE			
Yet boorded I the golden Chie twise, ...	Ovid's Elegies		3.6.23
CHIEFE (See also CHEEF)			
Chiefe Lord of all the wide vast Euxine sea, ...	1Tamb	1.1.167	Ortyg
I will dispatch chiefe of my army hence/To faire Natolia, and	2Tamb	1.1.161	Orcan
For we have here the chiefe selected men/Of twenty severall	2Tamb	5.2.48	Callap
There is no chiefe but onely Beelzebub:	F 284	1.3.56	Faust
Chiefe Lord and Regent of perpetuall night.	F 445	2.1.57	Faust
'Mong which as chiefe, Faustus we come to thee, . . .	F1800	5.2.4	Lucifr
chiefe spectacle of the worldes preheminence, The bright .	F App	p.237 24	P Emper
then Laelius/The chiefe Centurion crown'd with Oaken leaves,	Lucan, First Booke		358
chiefe leader of Rooms force,/So be I may be bold to speake a	Lucan, First Booke		360
Cupid flie)/That my chiefe wish should be so oft to die. .	Ovid's Elegies		2.5.2
When the chiefe pompe comes, lowd the people hollow, .	Ovid's Elegies		3.12.29
CHIEFELY			
Chiefely on thy lips let not his lips linger.	Ovid's Elegies		1.4.38
Chiefely shew him the gifts, which others send: . .	Ovid's Elegies		1.8.99
That victory doth chiefely triumph merit, ...	Ovid's Elegies		2.12.5
CHIEFEST			
The chiefest Captaine of Mycetes hoste, ...	1Tamb	1.1.58	Mycet
And chiefest Counsailor in all his acts, ...	1Tamb	2.5.11	Cosroe
The chiefest God, first moover of that Spheare/Enchac'd with	1Tamb	4.2.8	Tamb
For I the chiefest Lamp of all the earth, ...	1Tamb	4.2.36	Tamb
And place their chiefest good in earthly pompe: . .	1Tamb	5.1.353	Zenoc
And this is Balsera their chiefest hold, ...	2Tamb	3.3.3	Therid
His father was my chiefest enemie.	Jew	2.3.250	Barab
Warwick shalbe my chiefest counseller:	Edw	1.4.345	Edward
It is the chiefest marke they levell at.	Edw	5.3.12	Edward
Which he preferres before his chiefest blisse;	F 27	Prol.27	1Chor
Is to dispute well Logickes chiefest end?	F 36	1.1.8	Faust
CHIEFLY			
That will we chiefly see unto, Theridamas, ...	1Tamb	5.1.206	Tamb
Whereas his kinsmen chiefly brought him up; . . .	F 14	Prol.14	1Chor
CHILD			
Here let him sit, be merrie lovely child.	Dido	2.1.93	Dido
And so I will sweete child:	Dido	2.1.97	Dido
Faire child stay thou with Didos waiting maide, . . .	Dido	2.1.304	Venus
No more my child, now talke another while, ...	Dido	3.1.26	Dido
But lustfull Jove and his adulterous child, ...	Dido	3.2.18	Juno
But hereby child, we shall get thither straight. . . .	Dido	4.5.14	Nurse
Welcome sweet child, where hast thou been this long? .	Dido	5.1.46	Aeneas
That fed upon the substance of his child.	1Tamb	4.4.25	Zabina
Goe to, my child, away, away, away.	1Tamb	5.1.313	P Zabina
But neither man nor child in al the land:	2Tamb	1.3.197	Techel
Wherein he spareth neither man nor child, ...	2Tamb	5.1.30	1Citzn
Techelles, Drowne them all, man, woman, and child, . .	2Tamb	5.1.170	Tamb
Child of perdition, and thy fathers shame, ...	Jew	1.2.344	Barab
And so has she done you, even from a child. . . .	Jew	2.3.289	Barab
What, has he crucified a child?	Jew	3.6.49	1Fryar
And must be awde and governd like a child. . . .	Edw	3.1.31	Baldck
Oft dyes she that her paunch-wrapt child hath slaine. .	Ovid's Elegies		2.14.38
Which I Pelignis foster-child have framde, ...	Ovid's Elegies		3.14.3
CHILDE			
You know I have no childe, and unto whom/Should I leave all but	Jew	4.3.44	Barab
Him as a childe I dayly winne with words, ...	P 130	2.73	Guise
Having read unto her since she was a childe. . . .	Edw	2.1.30	Baldck
What if he have? the king is yet a childe.	Edw	5.6.17	Mortmr
felow, and he has a great charge, neither wife nor childe.	F App	p.239 106	P Mephst
If watry Thetis had her childe fordone?	Ovid's Elegies		2.14.14
CHILDISH			
That love is childish which consists in words. . . .	Dido	3.1.10	Iarbus
you wil be thought/More childish valourous than manly wise:	2Tamb	4.1.17	Calyph
I count Religion but a childish Toy, ...	Jew	Prol.14	Machvl

CHILDISH (cont.)
Henry thy King wipes of these childish teares, ... P1236 22.98 King
In any case, take heed of childish feare, ... Edw 5.2.6 Mortmr
Some thing he whispers in his childish eares. . . . . Edw 5.2.76 Queene
And laid his childish head upon her brest, ... Hero and Leander 1.43
CHILDREN
and some your children)/Might have intreated your obdurate 1Tamb 5.1.27 1Virgn
my children stoops your pride/And leads your glories <bodies> 2Tamb 4.1.76 Tamb
Yeeld up the towne, save our wives and children: . . 2Tamb 5.1.39 2Citzn
What shal be done with their wives and children my Lord. . 2Tamb 5.1.168 P Techel
I have no charge, nor many children, ... Jew 1.1.136 Barab
I'le helpe to slay their children and their wives, . . Jew 5.1.64 Barab
Their wives and children slaine, run up and downe, . . Edw 2.2.180 Lncstr
CHILDRENS
The comfort of mine age, my childrens hope, ... Jew 1.2.150 Barab
At Colchis stain'd with childrens bloud men raile, . . Ovid's Elegies 2.14.29
CHILL
And dipt it in the old Kings chill cold bloud, ... Dido 2.1.260 Aeneas
My bloodlesse body waxeth chill and colde, ... 1Tamb 2.7.42 Cosroe
CHIMNEY
I am Envy, begotten of a Chimney-sweeper, and an Oyster-wife: F 679 2.2.128 P Envy
CHIMNEY-SWEEPER
I am Envy, begotten of a Chimney-sweeper, and an Oyster-wife: F 679 2.2.128 P Envy
CHIMNY
Wee'l sell it to a Chimny-sweeper: . . . . . . F1384 4.2.60 P Benvol
CHIMNY-SWEEPER
Wee'l sell it to a Chimny-sweeper: . . . . . . F1384 4.2.60 P Benvol
CHIN
place himselfe therin/Must armed wade up to the chin in blood. 2Tamb 1.3.84 Tamb
CHINESE (See SERES)
CHIO
Chio, Famastro, and Amasia, ... 2Tamb 3.1.50 Trebiz
CHIRKE
And as for you, lord Mortimer of Chirke, ... Edw 1.4.359 Edward
CHIRRUP (See CHERUPE)
CHITTERLINS
Play, Fidler, or I'le cut your cats guts into chitterlins. Jew 4.4.44 P Ithimr
CHIVALRIE
My discipline of armes and Chivalrie, ... 1Tamb 5.1.175 Tamb
CHIVALRY
Spirits with desire/Stil to be train'd in armes and chivalry? 2Tamb 4.1.81 Tamb
CHOAKE
And Natures beauty choake with stifeling clouds, . . Jew 2.3.331 Lodowk
Or choake your soveraigne with puddle water? . . . Edw 5.3.30 Edward
Fall too, and the divel choake you and you spare. . . F App p.231 2 P Faust
CHOAKT
And choakt with thorns, that greedy earth wants hinds, . Lucan, First Booke 29
CHOCKT
our men with sweat and dust/All chockt well neare, begin to Edw 3.1.192 SpncrP
CHOICE (See also CHOYSE)
The Parrat given me, the farre [worlds] <words> best choice. Ovid's Elegies 2.6.38
CHOISE
After your rescue to enjoy his choise. . . . . . 1Tamb 3.2.58 Agidas
CHOISEST
And heaven consum'd his choisest living fire. . . . 2Tamb 5.3.251 Amyras
CHOKE (See also CHOAKE, CHOCKT)
Then the devill choke thee. . . . . F 703 2.2.152 P Glutny
Choke thy selfe Glutton: What are thou the sixt? . . F 704 2.2.153 Faust
Fall to, the Divell choke you an you spare. . . . F1039 3.2.59 Faust
CHOLLER
but most astonied/To see his choller shut in secrete thoughtes, 1Tamb 3.2.70 Agidas
CHOOSE (See also CHUSE)
I cannot choose but fall upon my knees, ... Dido 2.1.11 Achat
Aeneas could not choose but hold thee deare, ... Dido 5.1.126 Aeneas
It cannot choose, because it comes from you. . . . 1Tamb 1.1.56 Cosroe
Choose which thou wilt, all are at thy command. . . 2Tamb 1.2.31 Callap
Your Majesty may choose some pointed time, ... 2Tamb 3.1.75 Jrslem
I cannot choose but like thy readinesse: . . . . . Jew 2.3.377 Barab
Choose of our lords to beare you companie, ... Edw 3.1.84 Edward
If he be not, let him choose. . . . . Edw 5.1.95 BshpWn
growest penitent/Ile be thy ghostly father, therefore choose, Edw 5.6.4 Mortmr
choose this course,/Wilt have me willing, or to love by force? Ovid's Elegies 3.10.49
CHOOSING
Choosing a subject fit for feirse alarmes: . . . . Ovid's Elegies 1.1.6
CHOPS
not a stone of beef a day will maintaine you in these chops; Jew 2.3.125 P Barab
CHOSE
But I have rather chose to save thy life. . . . . . Jew 5.5.94 Govnr
CHOSEN
And her chosen freend? . . . . P 756 15.14 King
Your selfe, and those your chosen companie, ... Edw 4.7.6 Abbot
CHOYCE
and as I was taking my choyce, I heard a rumbling in the house; Jew 3.1.20 P Pilia
hes to have the choyce of his owne freeland | yf it be not to Paris ms 8,p390 P Souldr
CHOYSE
The choyse is hard, I must dissemble. . . . . . P 865 17.60 Guise
CHRISEIS
Great Agamemnon lov'd his servant Chriseis. . . . Ovid's Elegies 2.8.12
CHRISIS
Dangerous to those, whose Chrisis is as yours: . . . . 2Tamb 5.3.92 Phsitn
CHRIST (See also 'SBLOUD, 'SNAYLES, SWOWNS, ZOUNDS)
And sweare in sight of heaven and by thy Christ. . . 2Tamb 1.1.132 Orcan
Sweet Jesus Christ, I sollemnly protest, ... 2Tamb 1.1.135 Sgsmnd

CHRIST (cont.)			
And calling Christ for record of our trueths?	2Tamb	2.1.30	Sgsmnd
He by his Christ, and I by Mahomet?	2Tamb	2.2.32	Orcan
And cares so litle for their prophet Christ.	2Tamb	2.2.35	Gazell
Then if there be a Christ, as Christians say,	2Tamb	2.2.39	Orcan
But in their deeds deny him for their Christ:	2Tamb	2.2.40	Orcan
Thou Christ that art esteem'd omnipotent,	2Tamb	2.2.55	Orcan
To armes my Lords, on Christ still let us crie,	2Tamb	2.2.63	Orcan
If there be Christ, we shall have victorie.	2Tamb	2.2.64	Orcan
And Christ or Mahomet hath bene my friend.	2Tamb	2.3.11	Orcan
Which we referd to justice of his Christ,	2Tamb	2.3.28	Orcan
Yet in my thoughts shall Christ be honoured,	2Tamb	2.3.33	Orcan
O Christ my Saviour--	P 354	6.9	Seroun
Christ, villaine?	P 355	6.10	Mntsrl
Why, darst thou presume to call on Christ,	P 356	6.11	Mntsrl
Abjure the Scriptures, and his Saviour Christ;	F 276	1.3.48	Mephst
[Ah] <O> Christ my Saviour, my Saviour,	F 634	2.2.83	Faust
Christ cannot save thy soule, for he is just,	F 636	2.2.85	Lucifr
Thou calst on <talkst of> Christ contrary to thy promise.	F 643	2.2.92	Lucifr
Tush, Christ did call the Theete upon the Crosse,	F1482	4.4.26	Faust
One drop <of bloud will save me; oh> my Christ.	F1940	(HC271)B	Faust
One drop [would save my soule, halfe a drop, ah] my Christ.	F1940	5.2.144	Faust
Rend <Ah rend> not my heart, for naming of my Christ,	F1941	5.2.145	Faust
Tush, Christ did call the thiefe upon the Crosse,	F App	p.240 125	Faust
CHRISTAL			
There Angels in their christal armours fight/A doubtfull	1Tamb	5.1.151	Tamb
CHRISTALINUM			
But is there not Coelum igneum, [and] <&> <et> Christalinum?	F 612	2.2.61	P Faust
CHRISTALL			
Thy Anchors shall be hewed from Christall Rockes,	Dido	3.1.120	Dido
do cleare the clowdy aire/And cloath it in a christall liverie,	2Tamb	1.3.4	Tamb
If all the christall gates of Joves high court/Were opened	2Tamb	1.3.153	Tamb
The christall springs whose taste illuminates/Refined eies with	2Tamb	2.4.22	Tamb
souldiers crie/Make deafe the aire, and dim the Christall Sky.	2Tamb	3.3.61	Therid
Like lovely Thetis in a Christall robe:	2Tamb	3.4.51	Therid
city Samarcanda/And christall waves of fresh Jaertis streame,	2Tamb	4.3.108	Tamb
Pav'd with bright Christall, and enchac'd with starres,	2Tamb	4.3.128	Tamb
Of Christall shining faire, the pavement was,	Hero and Leander		1.141
CHRISTEN			
And in the channell christen him a new.	Edw	1.1.188	Edward
CHRISTENDOME			
Least you subdue the pride of Christendome?	1Tamb	1.1.132	Menaph
Besides, king Sigismond hath brought from Christendome,	2Tamb	1.1.20	Uribas
The holy lawes of Christendome injoine:	2Tamb	2.1.36	Baldwn
not a man surviv'd/To bring the haplesse newes to Christendome.	Jew	2.2.51	Bosco
to see the cripples/Goe limping home to Christendome on stilts.	Jew	2.3.212	Ithimr
And sure if all the proudest Kings/In Christendome, should	P 761	15.19	Guise
CHRISTENED			
Why Barabas wilt thou be christened?	Jew	1.2.81	Govnr
CHRISTI			
Lachrima Christi and Calabrian wines/Shall common Souldiers	2Tamb	1.3.221	Tamb
CHRISTIAN			
And Christian Merchants that with Russian stems/Plow up huge	1Tamb	1.2.194	Tamb
and then inlarge/Those Christian Captives, which you keep as	1Tamb	3.3.47	Tamb
That make quick havock of the Christian blood.	1Tamb	3.3.58	Tamb
Now will the Christian miscreants be glad,	1Tamb	3.3.236	Bajzth
Shall we parle with the Christian,/Or crosse the streame, and	2Tamb	1.1.11	Orcan
if any Christian King/Encroche upon the confines of thy realme,	2Tamb	1.1.146	Orcan
A thousand Gallies mann'd with Christian slaves/I freely give	2Tamb	1.2.32	Callap
Machda, where the mighty Christian Priest/Cal'd John the great,	2Tamb	1.3.187	Techel
I am sure/What cruell slaughter of our Christian bloods,	2Tamb	2.1.5	Fredrk
Me thinks I see how glad the christian King/Is made, for joy of	2Tamb	2.2.20	Uribas
Discomfited is all the Christian hoste,	2Tamb	2.3.1	Sgsmnd
Some, that in conquest of the perjur'd Christian,	2Tamb	3.1.39	Orcan
Then pittied in a Christian poverty:	Jew	1.1.115	Barab
I, wealthier farre then any Christian.	Jew	1.1.128	Barab
hee that denies to pay, shal straight become a Christian.	Jew	1.2.74	P Reader
How, a Christian? Hum, what's here to doe?	Jew	1.2.75	Barab
The Christian Ile of Rhodes, from whence you came,	Jew	2.2.31	Bosco
Who of meere charity and Christian ruth,	Jew	2.3.71	Barab
And now and then, to cherish Christian theeves,	Jew	2.3.177	Barab
In setting Christian villages on fire,	Jew	2.3.203	Ithimr
a golden crosse/With Christian posies round about the ring.	Jew	2.3.297	Barab
It's no sinne to deceive a Christian;	Jew	2.3.309	Barab
But thou must dote upon a Christian?	Jew	2.3.360	Barab
And witnesse that I dye a Christian.	Jew	3.6.40	Abigal
An Hebrew borne, and would become a Christian?	Jew	4.1.19	Barab
Is't not too late now to turne Christian?	Jew	4.1.50	Barab
As never Jew nor Christian knew the like:	Jew	4.1.118	Barab
That being importun'd by this Bernardine/To be a Christian, I	Jew	4.1.188	Barab
will you turne Christian, when holy Friars turne devils and	Jew	4.1.193	P Ithimr
I am as Ramus is, a Christian.	P 374	7.14	Taleus
The greatest warres within our Christian bounds,	P 460	8.10	Anjoy
Let Christian princes that shall heare of this,	P1041	19.111	King
If any Christian, Heathen, Turke, or Jew,	Edw	5.4.75	Champn
end be such/As every Christian heart laments to thinke on:	F1996	5.3.14	2Schol
a Christian fellow to a dogge or a catte, a mouse or a ratte?	F App	p.231 60	P Clown
CHRISTIANS			
My witlesse brother to the Christians lost:	1Tamb	2.5.42	Cosroe
And warlike bands of Christians renied,	1Tamb	3.1.9	Bajzth
When first he war'd against the Christians.	1Tamb	3.3.200	Zabina
And hover in the straightes for Christians wracke,	1Tamb	3.3.250	Tamb
We all are glutted with the Christians blood,	2Tamb	1.1.14	Gazell

CHRISTIANS (cont.)			
The slaughtered bodies of these Christians.	2Tamb	1.1.36	Orcan
Shall meet those Christians fleeting with the tyde,	2Tamb	1.1.40	Orcan
And for that cause the Christians shall have peace.	2Tamb	1.1.57	Orcan
Therefore Viceroies the Christians must have peace.	2Tamb	1.1.77	Orcan
That dare attempt to war with Christians.	2Tamb	2.1.26	Fredrk
That God hath given to venge our Christians death/And scourge	2Tamb	2.1.52	Fredrk
The treacherous army of the Christians,	2Tamb	2.2.25	1Msngr
Traitors, villaines, damned Christians.	2Tamb	2.2.29	Orcan
Can there be such deceit in Christians,	2Tamb	2.2.36	Orcan
Then if there be a Christ, as Christians say,	2Tamb	2.2.39	Orcan
and confound/The trustlesse force of those false Christians.	2Tamb	2.2.62	Orcan
Now lie the Christians bathing in their bloods,	2Tamb	2.3.10	Orcan
Rowing with Christians in a Brigandine,	2Tamb	3.5.93	Jrslem
Yet are there Christians of Georgia here,	2Tamb	5.1.31	1Citzn
Give us a peacefull rule, make Christians Kings,	Jew	1.1.134	Barab
Christians; what, or how can I multiply?	Jew	1.2.103	Barab
Some Jewes are wicked, as all Christians are:	Jew	1.2.112	Barab
the plight/Wherein these Christians have oppressed me:	Jew	1.2.271	Barab
now Abigall, what mak'st thou/Amongst these hateful Christians?	Jew	1.2.339	Barab
poore Barabas/With fatall curses towards these Christians.	Jew	2.1.6	Barab
in spite of these swine-eating Christians,	Jew	2.3.7	Barab
But to thy selfe smile when the Christians moane.	Jew	2.3.172	Barab
Both circumcized, we hate Christians both:	Jew	2.3.215	Barab
There is no musicke to a Christians knell:	Jew	4.1.1	Barab
Now vaile your pride you captive Christians,	Jew	5.2.1	Calym
Will Barabas be good to Christians?	Jew	5.2.75	Govnr
And reason too, for Christians doe the like:	Jew	5.2.116	Barab
Helpe, helpe me, Christians, helpe.	Jew	5.5.65	Barab
Oh helpe me, Selim, helpe me, Christians.	Jew	5.5.70	Barab
Damn'd Christians, dogges, and Turkish Infidels;	Jew	5.5.86	Barab
Tell me, you Christians, what doth this portend?	Jew	5.5.90	Calym
Nay rather, Christians, let me goe to Turkey,	Jew	5.5.115	Calym
CHRISTS			
[See see where Christs bloud streames in the firmament],	F1939	5.2.143A	Faust
[Yet for Christs sake, whose bloud hath ransom'd me],	F1959	5.2.163A	Faust
CHRONICLE			
And in the Chronicle, enrowle his name,	Edw	1.4.269	Mortmr
CHRYSTALL (See also CHRISTAL)			
When as the waves doe threat our Chrystall world,	Dido	1.1.75	Venus
And clad her in a Chrystall liverie,	Dido	5.1.6	Aeneas
CHUF			
Chuf-like had I not gold, and could not use it?	Ovid's Elegies		3.6.50
CHUFFE			
See a rich chuffe whose wounds great wealth inferr'd,	Ovid's Elegies		3.7.9
CHUF-LIKE			
Chuf-like had I not gold, and could not use it?	Ovid's Elegies		3.6.50
CHURCH			
Come my Lords lets go to the Church and pray,	P 55	1.55	Navrre
That hath blasphemde the holy Church of Rome,	P 531	10.4	Guise
And all those traitors to the Church of Rome,	P1120	21.14	Dumain
Of such as holde them of the holy church?	P1181	22.43	King
To ruinate that wicked Church of Rome,	P1204	22.66	King
What? will they tyrannize upon the Church?	Edw	1.2.3	Lncstr
When violence is offered to the church.	Edw	1.2.41	ArchBp
And universall body of the law <Church>.	F 60	1.1.32	Faust
<Consissylogismes>/Gravel'd the Pastors of the Germane Church,	F 140	1.1.112	Faust
To him, I'le build an Altar and a Church,	F 401	2.1.13	Faust
And like a Steeple over-peeres the Church.	F 913	3.1.135	Pope
Most sacred Patron of the Church of Rome,	F 951	3.1.173	Faust
A towne with one poore church set them at oddes.	Lucan, First Booke		97
These troupes should soone pull down the church of Jove.	Lucan, First Booke		381
As she might straight have gone to church and praide:	Ovid's Elegies		3.6.54
So faire a church as this, had Venus none,	Hero and Leander		1.135
CHURCHES			
To fire the Churches, pull their houses downe,	Jew	5.1.65	Barab
Wherewith thy antichristian churches blaze,	Edw	1.4.99	Edward
[And make my spirites pull his churches downe].	F 651	2.2.100A	Faust
And interdict from Churches priviledge,	F 909	3.1.131	Pope
Pope Julius did abuse the Churches Rites,	F 928	3.1.150	Pope
And proud disturbers of the Churches peace.	F 956	3.1.178	Faust
And leave it in the Churches treasury.	F 971	3.1.193	Pope
And put into the Churches treasury.	F1028	3.2.48	Raymnd
CHURCHMENS			
What, will you fyle your handes with Churchmens bloud?	P1093	20.3	Cardnl
CHURLE			
of an old Churle in a <an olde> leather <leatherne> bag;	F 674	2.2.123	P Covet
Yet thinke no scorne to aske a wealthy churle,	Ovid's Elegies		1.10.53
CHURLES			
Onely our loves let not such rich churles gaine,	Ovid's Elegies		3.7.59
CHURLISH			
On mooved hookes set ope the churlish dore.	Ovid's Elegies		1.6.2
This head was beat with manie a churlish billow,	Hero and Leander		2.251
CHUSE			
I cannot chuse, seeing my father bids:--	Jew	2.3.316	Abigal
And rather chuse to seek your countries good,	P 221	4.19	Guise
I chuse his privy chamber for our use.	F 806	3.1.28	Mephst
But neither chuse the north t'erect thy seat;	Lucan, First Booke		53
CICILIANS			
Cicilians, Jewes, Arabians, Turks, and Moors,	2Tamb	1.1.62	Orcan
CILICIA			
Sythia, Cilicia, Brittaine are as good,	Ovid's Elegies		2.16.39

CIMBRIAN (See CYMBRIAN)				
CIMMERIAN (See CEMERIAN, CYMERIAN)				
CIMODOAE				
And call both Thetis and [Cimotnoe] <Cimodoae> <Cymodoce>,/To	Dido	1.1.132		Venus
CIMOTHOE				
And call both Thetis and [Cimothoe] <Cimodoae> <Cymodoce>,/To	Dido	1.1.132		Venus
CINCA (See CYNGAS)				
CINDERS (See also CYNDERS)				
Shall burne to cinders in this pretious flame.	Dido	5.1.301		Dido
CINTHIA				
Faire Cinthia wisht, his armes might be her spheare, .	Hero and Leander	1.59		
CINTHIA'S				
Outshines Cinthia's rayes:	Jew	2.3.62		Barab
CIPHER (See also CYPHER)				
Like a dull Cipher, or rude blocke I lay, ...	Ovid's Elegies	3.6.15		
CIRCES				
Which Circes sent Sicheus when he lived:	Dido	4.4.11		Dido
That charming Circes walking on the waves, . . .	Edw	1.4.172		Queene
His bodie was as straight as Circes wand, ...	Hero and Leander	1.61		
CIRCLE (See also CYRCLES)				
Even in the circle of your Fathers armes:	1Tamb	1.2.5		Tamb
the Starres that make/The loathsome Circle of my dated life,	1Tamb	2.6.37		Cosroe
But keep within the circle of mine armes.	2Tamb	3.2.35		Tamb
And make swift Rhine, circle faire Wittenberge <Wertenberge>:	F 116	1.1.88		Faust
Within this circle is Jehova's Name, ...	F 236	1.3.8		Faust
The framing of this circle on the ground/Brings Thunder, .	F 545	2.1.157		Mephst
keep out of the circle, I say, least I send you into the Ostry	F 732	2.3.11	P	Robin
From the bright circle of the horned Moone, ...	F 762	2.3.41		2Chor
Dick, make me a circle, and stand close at my backe, and stir	F1112	3.3.25	P	Robin
in the contrary circle it is likewise Summer with them, as in	F1583	4.6.26	P	Faust
us, in the contrary circle it is summer with them, as in India,	F App	p.242 21	P	Faust
CIRCLED				
when the Moon begins/To joine in one her semi-circled hornes:	1Tamb	3.1.12		Bajzth
ancient use, shall beare/The figure of the semi-circled Moone:	2Tamb	3.1.65		Orcan
Circled about with Limnasphaltis Lake, ...	2Tamb	5.2.5		Callap
While these thus in and out had circled Roome, . . .	Lucan, First Booke	604		
CIRCLES				
Lines, Circles, [Signes], Letters, [and] Characters, .	F 78	1.1.50		Faust
the yeare is divided into two circles over the whole world, so	F1581	4.6.24	P	Faust
and ifaith I meane to search some circles for my owne use:	F App	p.233 2	P	Robin
the yeere is divided into twoo circles over the whole worlde,	F App	p.242 19	P	Faust
CIRCLING				
Which is with azure circling lines empal'd, ...	Hero and Leander	2.274		
CIRCUIT				
have measured heaven/With triple circuit thou regreet us not,	1Tamb	3.1.37		Bajzth
Keeping his circuit by the slicing edge.	1Tamb	5.1.112		Tamb
CIRCUMCIS'D				
He never put on cleane shirt since he was circumcis'd. .	Jew	4.4.64	P	Ithimr
CIRCUMCISED				
As many circumcised Turkes we have, ...	1Tamb	3.1.8		Bajzth
CIRCUMCIZ'D				
(Unchosen Nation, never circumciz'd;	Jew	2.3.8		Barab
CIRCUMCIZED				
Both circumcized, we hate Christians both:	Jew	2.3.215		Barab
CIRCUMFERENCE				
Should pierce the blacke circumference of hell, . .	2Tamb	1.3.145		Techel
Wanders about the black circumference, ...	2Tamb	4.2.90		Therid
And whirling round with this circumference, ...	F 764	2.3.43		2Chor
CIRCUMSCRIB'D				
Hell hath no limits, nor is circumscrib'd, ...	F 510	2.1.122		Mephst
CIRCUMSCRIPTIBLE				
Nor in one place is circumscriptible, ...	2Tamb	2.2.50		Orcan
CIRCUMSPECT				
But Barabas will be more circumspect.	Jew	5.2.43		Barab
CIRCUMSTANCE				
No person, place, or time, or circumstance, ...	P 606	12.19		King
CISALPIN				
deviding just/The bounds of Italy, from Cisalpin Fraunce;	Lucan, First Booke	218		
CISTERN (See CESTERNES)				
CITADELL (See also CYTADELL)				
that a strong built Citadell/Commands much more then letters	Jew	Prol.22		Machvl
would intreat your Majesty/To come and see his homely Citadell,	Jew	5.3.18		Msngr
To banquet with him in his Citadell?	Jew	5.3.20		Calym
That thou maist feast them in thy Citadell. . . .	Jew	5.5.16		Msngr
CITHEIDAS				
Will quickly flye to [Cithereas] <Citheidas> fist. . .	Dido	2.1.322		Venus
CITHERA				
That Paphos, and the floud-beate Cithera guides. . .	Ovid's Elegies	2.17.4		
CITHEREA'S				
The sweetest flower in Citherea's field, ...	Jew	1.2.379		Mthias
CITHEREAS				
Will quickly flye to [Cithereas] <Citheidas> fist. . .	Dido	2.1.322		Venus
CITIE				
King of this Citie, but my Troy is fired, ...	Dido	2.1.236		Aeneas
Why, let us build a Citie of our owne, ...	Dido	4.3.37		Illion
Or breathles lie before the citie walles.	1Tamb	3.1.15		Bajzth
by leaden pipes/Runs to the citie from the mountain Carnon.	1Tamb	3.1.60		Bajzth
feathered bird/That spreads her wings upon the citie wals,	1Tamb	4.2.106		Tamb
Were in that citie all the world contain'd, . . .	1Tamb	4.2.121		Tamb
While they walke quivering on their citie walles, . .	1Tamb	4.4.3		Tamb
Threaten our citie with a generall spoile: . . .	1Tamb	5.1.10		Govnr
(sweet Virgins) on whose safe return/Depends our citie, .	1Tamb	5.1.63		Govnr

CITIE (cont.)			
Betwixt the citie Zula and Danubius,	2Tamb	2.1.7	Fredrk
And so unto my citie of Damasco,	2Tamb	3.1.59	Soria
Blush, blush faire citie, at thine honors foile,	2Tamb	4.1.107	Tamb
Or hold our citie from the Conquerours hands.	2Tamb	5.1.5	Maxim
The citie and my native countries weale,	2Tamb	5.1.13	Govnr
And this eternisde citie Babylon,	2Tamb	5.1.35	Govnr
Yeeld speedily the citie to our hands,	2Tamb	5.1.51	Therid
For though thy cannon shooke the citie walles,	2Tamb	5.1.105	Govnr
Hang him up in chaines upon the citie walles,	2Tamb	5.1.108	Tamb
Which when the citie was besieg'd I hid,	2Tamb	5.1.117	Govnr
And to command the citie, I will build/A Cytadell, that all	2Tamb	5.1.164	Tamb
To some high hill about <above> the citie here.	2Tamb	5.1.216	Therid
Not that I love the citie or the men,	Edw	1.1.12	Gavstn
in every good towne and Citie>,	F 699	(HC264) A	P Glutny
CITIES			
and the soyle most fit/For Cities, and societies supports:	Dido	1.1.179	Achat
For many tales goe of that Cities fall,	Dido	2.1.108	Dido
Why cosin, stand you building Cities here,	Dido	5.1.27	Hermes
martiall spoile/Of conquered kingdomes, and of Cities sackt.	1Tamb	1.2.192	Tamb
best to be atchiev'd/In pursuit of the Cities overthrow?	1Tamb	3.1.57	Fesse
And with how manie cities sacrifice/He celebrated her [sad]	2Tamb	Prol.7	Prolog
The towers and cities of these hatefull Turks,	2Tamb	3.2.148	Tamb
Halla is repair'd/And neighbor cities of your highnesse land,	2Tamb	3.5.47	Soria
and utterly consume/Your cities and your golden pallaces,	2Tamb	4.1.193	Tamb
That whips downe cities, and controwleth crownes,	2Tamb	4.3.100	Tamb
And cast them headlong in the cities lake:	2Tamb	5.1.162	Tamb
Kingdomes made waste, brave cities sackt and burnt,	2Tamb	5.2.26	Callap
Halfe of my substance is a Cities wealth.	Jew	1.2.85	Barab
Wherby whole Cities have escap't the plague,	F 49	1.1.21	Faust
CITIZEN			
For saving of a Romaine Citizen,	Lucan, First Booke		359
CITIZENS			
Aeneas see, here come the Citizens,	Dido	2.1.37	Achat
What if the Citizens repine thereat?	Dido	4.4.70	Anna
And I will send amongst the Citizens/And by my letters	Jew	5.2.86	Govnr
and how the Citizens/With gifts and shewes did entertaine him	P 873	17.68	Eprnon
Madam, the Maior and Citizens of Bristow,	Edw	4.6.47	Rice
Roome that flowes/With Citizens and [Captives] <Captaines>, and	Lucan, First Booke		510
Then, that the trembling Citizens should walke/About the City;	Lucan, First Booke		591
CITTIE			
Girting this strumpet Cittie with our siege,	P1152	22.14	King
Silent the Cittie is:	Ovid's Elegies		1.6.55
CITTIES			
Provinces, Citties and townes/After my name and thine Zenocrate:	1Tamb	4.4.79	Tamb
He Citties greate, this thresholds lies before:	Ovid's Elegies		1.9.19
Thou shalt admire no woods or Citties there,	Ovid's Elegies		2.11.11
Why girt'st thy citties with a towred wall?	Ovid's Elegies		3.7.47
In view and opposit two citties stood,	Hero and Leander		1.2
CITTIZENS			
Or if Fate rule them, Rome thy Cittizens/Are neere some plague:	Lucan, First Booke		643
CITTY			
Albeit the Citty thou wouldst have so ra'st/Be Roome it selfe.	Lucan, First Booke		386
inconsiderate multitude/Thorough the Citty hurried headlong on,	Lucan, First Booke		493
even so the Citty left,/All rise in armes; nor could the	Lucan, First Booke		501
And wilt not trust thy Citty walls one night:	Lucan, First Booke		518
gods/Sweate teares to shew the travailes of their citty.	Lucan, First Booke		555
And Venus rules in her Aeneas Citty.	Ovid's Elegies		1.8.42
A laughing stocke thou art to all the citty,	Ovid's Elegies		3.1.21
CITTYES			
Such rampierd gates beseiged Cittyes ayde,	Ovid's Elegies		1.6.29
CITY (See also CITIE, CITTIE, CYTIES)			
Then shal my native city Samarcanda/And christall waves of	2Tamb	4.3.107	Tamb
I ha the poyson of the City for him,	Jew	2.3.53	Barab
First will we race the City wals our selves,	Jew	3.5.13	Govnr
Talke not of racing downe your City wals,	Jew	3.5.21	Basso
for the running streames/And common channels of the City.	Jew	5.1.89	Barab
And by this meanes the City is your owne.	Jew	5.1.94	Barab
And in this City still have had successe,	Jew	5.2.69	Barab
And in an out-house of the City shut/His souldiers, till I have	Jew	5.2.81	Barab
Goe walke about the City, see thy friends:	Jew	5.2.92	Barab
Thus have we view'd the City, seene the sacke,	Jew	5.3.1	Calym
Know that this City stands upon seven hils,	F 811	3.1.33	Mephst
Then, that the trembling Citizens should walke/About the City;	Lucan, First Booke		592
CIVIL			
Might they have won whom civil broiles have slaine,	Lucan, First Booke		14
Yet Room is much bound to these civil armes,	Lucan, First Booke		44
Being conquered, we are plaugde with civil war.	Lucan, First Booke		108
CIVILE			
In making forraine warres and civile broiles.	P1029	19.99	King
CIVILL			
Begin in troopes to threaten civill warre,	1Tamb	1.1.148	Ceneus
In Florence, Venice, Antwerpe, London, Civill,	Jew	4.1.71	Barab
To leavy armes and make these civill broyles:	P 730	14.33	Navrre
In civill broiles between Navarre and me?	P1038	19.108	King
for rather then my lord/Shall be opprest by civill mutinies,	Edw	1.2.65	Queene
That to my face he threatens civill warres.	Edw	2.2.233	Edward
Make Englands civill townes huge heapes of stones,	Edw	3.1.215	Edward
In civill broiles makes kin and country men/Slaughter	Edw	4.4.6	Queene
Wars worse then civill on Thessalian playnes,	Lucan, First Booke		1
These plagues arise from wreake of civill power.	Lucan, First Booke		32
he casts/For civill warre, wherein through use he's known/To	Lucan, First Booke		325
Is conquest got by civill war so hainous?	Lucan, First Booke		367

CIVILL (cont.)			
out the date/Of slaughter; onely civill broiles make peace.	Lucan, First Booke		671
CLAD			
And clad us in these wealthie robes we weare.	Dido	2.1.65	Illion
is Aeneas, were he clad/In weedes as bad as ever Irus ware.	Dido	2.1.84	Dido
Achates, thou shalt be so [manly] <meanly> clad,	Dido	3.1.128	Dido
And clad her in a Chrystall liverie,	Dido	5.1.6	Aeneas
Three hundred thousand men in armour clad,	1Tamb	4.1.21	2Msngr
Like Sylvian <Sylvan> Nimphes my pages shall be clad,	Edw	1.1.58	Gavstn
Wherewith the Students shall be bravely clad.	F 118	1.1.90	Faust
Clad in the beauty of a thousand starres:	F1782	5.1.109	Faust
Bearing the head with dreadfull [Adders] <Arrowes> clad,	Ovid's Elegies		3.5.14
As is the use, the Nunnes in white veyles clad,	Ovid's Elegies		3.12.27
CLAIME			
Claime tribute where thou wilt, we are resolv'd,	Jew	2.2.55	Govnr
at some certaine day/Great Lucifer may claime it as his owne,	F 440	2.1.52	Mephst
All heaven would come to claime this legacie,	Hero and Leander		1.250
CLAIMES			
Hell claimes his <calls for> right, and with a roaring voyce,	F1726	5.1.53	Faust
CLAMBER'D			
and in the night I clamber'd up with my hooks, and as I was	Jew	3.1.19	P Pilia
CLAMORS			
Was so incenst as are Eleius steedes/With clamors:	Lucan, First Booke		295
CLANG			
Whome trumpets clang incites, and those that dwel/By Cyngas	Lucan, First Booke		433
CLANGE			
Awake ye men of Memphis, heare the clange/Of Scythian trumpets,	1Tamb	4.1.1	Souldn
colours, with confused noise/Of trumpets clange, shril cornets,	Lucan, First Booke		240
CLAP			
Have you no doubts my lords, ile [clap so] <claps> close,/Among	Edw	3.1.276	Levune
in England/Would cast up cappes, and clap their hands for joy,	Edw	4.2.55	Mortmr
clap as faire a paire of hornes on's head as e're thou sawest	F 737	2.3.16	P Robin
Or clap huge hornes, upon the Cardinals heads:	F 864	3.1.86	Mephst
to clap hornes of honest mens heades o'this order,	F1317	4.1.163	P Benvol
CLAPS			
As far as Boreas claps his brazen wings,	1Tamb	1.2.206	Tamb
He claps his cheekes, and hanges about his neck,	Edw	1.2.51	Queene
Have you no doubts my lords, ile [clap so] <claps> close,/Among	Edw	3.1.276	Levune
CLAPT			
But he clapt under hatches saild away.	Dido	5.1.240	Anna
He clapt his plumpe cheekes, with his tresses playd,	Hero and Leander		2.181
CLAREMONT (See CLEREMONT)			
CLARET			
and my mother <grandmother> was a Hogshead of Claret Wine.	F 697	2.2.146	P Glutny
give thee white wine, red wine, claret wine, Sacke, Muskadine,	F 748	2.3.27	P Robin
CLARKE			
Clarke of the crowne, direct our warrant forth,	Edw	1.4.369	Edward
CLASHING			
Clashing of armes was heard, in untrod woods/Shrill voices	Lucan, First Booke		567
CLASPS			
With Corall clasps and Amber studs,	Passionate Shepherd		18
CLAWES (See also CLEYES)			
And with rough clawes your tender cheekes assaile.	Ovid's Elegies		2.6.4
CLAY			
Thinke me to be a senselesse lumpe of clay/That will with every	Jew	1.2.216	Barab
Would animate grosse clay, and higher set/The drooping thoughts	Hero and Leander		2.256
CLEANE			
Lest with these sweete thoughts I melt cleane away.	Dido	3.1.76	Dido
While Italy is cleane out of thy minde?	Dido	5.1.29	Hermes
Iarbus, I am cleane besides my selfe,	Dido	5.1.63	Aeneas
Here Turk, wilt thou have a cleane trencher?	1Tamb	4.4.101	P Tamb
Is almost cleane extinguished and spent,	2Tamb	5.3.89	Phsitn
These silly men mistake the matter cleane.	Jew	1.1.179	Barab
sort as if he had meant to make cleane my Boots with his lips;	Jew	4.2.31	P Ithimr
Now am I cleane, or rather fouly out of the way.	Jew	4.2.47	P Ithimr
He never put on cleane shirt since he was circumcis'd.	Jew	4.4.64	P Ithimr
What they intend, the hangman frustrates cleane.	Edw	3.1.275	Baldck
sweet embraces <imbracings> may extinguish cleare <cleane>,	F1763	5.1.90	Faust
his horse, and he would have his things rubd and made cleane:	F App	p.233 7	P Rafe
goe and make cleane our bootes which lie foule upon our handes,	F App	p.234 32	P Robin
CLEARE (See also CLEERE)			
Doe thou but smile, and clowdie heaven will cleare,	Dido	1.1.155	Achat
That with thy lookes canst cleare the darkened Sky:	1Tamb	3.3.122	Tamb
Now cleare the triple region of the aire,	1Tamb	4.2.30	Tamb
I record heaven, her heavenly selfe is cleare:	1Tamb	5.1.487	Tamb
Whose chearful looks do cleare the clowdy aire/And cloath it in	2Tamb	1.3.3	Tamb
Quite voide of skars, and cleare from any wound,	2Tamb	3.2.112	Tamb
And cleare my bodie from foule excrements.	Edw	5.3.26	Edward
sweet embraces <imbracings> may extinguish cleare <cleane>,	F1763	5.1.90	Faust
All you whose pineons in the cleare aire sore,	Ovid's Elegies		2.6.11
And by the rising herbes, where cleare springs slide,	Ovid's Elegies		2.16.9
CLEAREST			
appeares as full/As raies of Cynthia to the clearest sight?	2Tamb	2.3.30	Orcan
CLEARGIE			
As for the peeres that backe the cleargie thus,	Edw	1.4.104	Edward
CLEAVE (Homograph)			
Our Crowne the pin that thousands seeke to cleave.	1Tamb	2.4.9	Mycet
And cleave his Pericranion with thy sword.	2Tamb	1.3.101	Tamb
And cleave him to the channell with my sword.	2Tamb	1.3.103	Calyph
Hold him, and cleave him too, or Ile cleave thee,	2Tamb	1.3.104	Tamb
And wound the earth, that it may cleave in twaine,	2Tamb	2.4.97	Tamb
With strong plough shares no man the earth did cleave,	Ovid's Elegies		3.7.41
CLEAVES			
Least to the waxe the hold-fast drye gemme cleaves,	Ovid's Elegies		2.5.16

CLEERE				
Or day so cleere so suddenly orecast?	Dido	4.1.2		Achat
The ayre is cleere, and Southerne windes are whist,	Dido	4.1.25		Aeneas
So, now the bloud begins to cleere againe:	F 460	2.1.72		Faust
Before the roome be cleere, and doore put too.	Ovid's Elegies			3.13.10
CLEFT (See CLIFTS)				
CLEMENCIE				
Offer our safeties to his clemencie,	1Tamb	5.1.12		Govnr
Unlesse it be with too much clemencie?	Edw	5.1.123		Edward
CLEREMONT				
And there unhorste the duke of Cleremont.	Edw	5.5.70		Edward
CLERGY (See CLEARGIE)				
CLERK (See CLARKE)				
CLEYES				
Scorpion with the burning taile/And fier'st his cleyes.	Lucan, First Booke			659
CLIENT				
The lawier and the client <both do> hate thy view,	Ovid's Elegies			1.13.21
CLIFTES				
Through rocks more steepe and sharp than Caspian cliftes.	2Tamb	5.3.241		Tamb
CLIFTS (Homograph)				
Both we wil walke upon the lofty clifts,	1Tamb	1.2.193		Tamb
has hornes, and all shee divels has clifts and cloven feete.	F App	p.230 54	P	Clown
CLIMAT				
And from the northren climat snatching fier/Blasted the	Lucan, First Booke			532
CLIMBE				
Or climbe up to my Counting-house window:	Jew	4.3.34	P	Barab
CLIME (Homograph)				
And scarcely know within what Clime we are.	Dido	2.1.44		Aeneas
Let never silent night possesse this clime,	Edw	5.1.65		Edward
And by your death to clime Saint Peters Chaire,	F 960	3.1.182		Faust
Wide open stood the doore, hee need not clime,	Hero and Leander			2.19
CLIMING				
Still climing after knowledge infinite,	1Tamb	2.7.24		Tamb
Are poyson'd by my climing followers.	Jew	Prol.13		Machvl
CLING'D				
He on the suddaine cling'd her so about,	Hero and Leander			2.314
CLINGED				
I clinged her naked bodie, downe she fell,	Ovid's Elegies			1.5.24
CLIP				
Ile clip and kisse thee with all contentation,	Ovid's Elegies			2.11.45
CLIPPE (Homograph)				
With him, Ile clippe his winges/Or ere he passe my handes,	P1052	19.122		King
Wilt lying under him his bosome clippe?	Ovid's Elegies			1.4.5
CLIPPES				
At night thy husband clippes thee, I will weepe/And to the	Ovid's Elegies			1.4.61
CLIPS				
Corinna clips me oft by thy perswasion,	Ovid's Elegies			1.11.5
CLOAK				
Love laughed at my cloak, and buskines painted,	Ovid's Elegies			2.18.15
CLOAKE				
He weares a short Italian hooded cloake,	Edw	1.4.413		Mortmr
A Velvet cap'de cloake, fac'st before with Serge,	Edw	2.1.34		Spencr
Sterne was her front, her [cloake] <looke> on ground did lie.	Ovid's Elegies			3.1.12
And each give signes by casting up his cloake.	Ovid's Elegies			3.2.74
CLOAKES				
Navarre that cloakes them underneath his wings,	P 855	17.50		Guise
CLOANTHUS				
Cloanthus, haste away, Aeneas calles.	Dido	4.3.14		Aeneas
CLOATH				
And held the cloath of pleasance whiles you dranke,	Dido	1.1.6		Ganimd
The townes-men maske in silke and cloath of gold,	1Tamb	4.2.108		Tamb
And cloath of Arras hung about the walles,	2Tamb	1.2.44		Callap
do cleare the clowdy aire/And cloath it in a christall liverie,	2Tamb	1.3.4		Tamb
And cloth'd in costly cloath of massy gold,	2Tamb	4.2.40		Therid
CLOATH'D				
Here lye the garment which I cloath'd him in,	Dido	5.1.298		Dido
A hundred Bassoes cloath'd in crimson silk/Shall ride before	2Tamb	1.2.46		Callap
CLOATHED				
And cloathed in a spotted Leopards skin.	Dido	1.1.186		Venus
CLOATHES				
put off thy cloathes, and I'le conjure thee about presently:	F 746	2.3.25	P	Robin
And hath no cloathes, but open doth remaine.	Ovid's Elegies			1.10.16
But on the ground thy cloathes too loosely lie,	Ovid's Elegies			3.2.25
CLOCKE				
Come to my house at one a clocke this night.	Jew	4.1.91		Barab
The Stars move still, Time runs, the Clocke will strike,	F1936	5.2.140		Faust
CLOGD				
Whose golden fortunes clogd with courtly ease,	Dido	4.3.8		Aeneas
CLOGGE				
Ile hang a clogge about your necke for running away againe, you	2Tamb	3.5.100	P	Tamb
CLOISTER (See CLOYSTER)				
CLOS'D				
Were with Jove clos'd in Stigian Emperie.	Hero and Leander			1.458
CLOSD				
For not these ten daies have these eyes lids closd.	Edw	5.5.94		Edward
CLOSDE				
And closde in compasse of the killing bullet,	1Tamb	2.1.41		Cosroe
Closde in a coffyn mounted up the aire,	2Tamb	1.1.140		Orcan
But closde within the compasse of a tent,	2Tamb	4.2.3		Olymp
CLOSE				
Therefore in pollicie I thinke it good/To hide it close:	1Tamb	2.4.11		Mycet
Since thy desired hand shall close mine eies.	1Tamb	5.1.432		Arabia
She lies so close that none can find her out.	2Tamb	1.2.60		Callap

CLOSE (cont.)				
your tongues/And bind them close with bits of burnisht steele,	2Tamb	4.1.182		Tamb
Nor thy close Cave a sword to murther thee,	2Tamb	4.2.12		Olymp
There have I hid close underneath the plancke/That runs along	Jew	1.2.296		Barab
Be close, my girle, for this must fetch my gold.	Jew	1.2.304		Barab
Close your Port-cullise, charge your Basiliskes,	Jew	3.5.31		Govnr
So I have heard; pray therefore keepe it close.	Jew	3.6.37		Abigal
Stand close, for here they come:	Jew	5.5.46		Barab
I, I, feare not: stand close, so, be resolute:	P 943	19.13		Capt
Stand close, he is comming, I know him by his voice.	P1000	19.70	P	1Mur
Or looking downeward, with your eye lids close,	Edw	2.1.39		Spencr
O that mine armes could close this Ile about,	Edw	2.4.17		Queene
Have you no doubts my lords, ile [clap so] <claps> close,/Among	Edw	3.1.276		Levune
Come death, and with thy fingers close my eyes,	Edw	5.1.110		Edward
circle, and stand close at my backe, and stir not for thy life,	F1113	3.3.26	P	Robin
O may these eye-lids never close againe,	F1332	4.2.8		Benvol
and our followers/Close in an ambush there behinde the trees,	F1342	4.2.18		Benvol
Close, close, the Conjurer is at hand,	F1357	4.2.33		Fredrk
Or lies he close, and shoots where none can spie him?	Ovid's Elegies			1.2.6
Heere while I walke hid close in shadie grove,	Ovid's Elegies			3.1.5
Thy dying eyes here did thy mother close,	Ovid's Elegies			3.8.49
When have not I fixt to thy side close layed?	Ovid's Elegies			3.10.17
Vaild to the ground, vailing her eie-lids close,	Hero and Leander			1.159
And up againe, and close beside him swim,	Hero and Leander			2.190
CLOSELY				
I closely hid.	Jew	1.2.247		Barab
And now my Lords let us closely to our busines.	P 332	5.59		Guise
And so convey him closely to his bed.	P 450	7.90		Guise
words she sayd/While closely hid betwixt two dores I layed.	Ovid's Elegies			1.8.22
Time flying slides hence closely, and deceaves us,	Ovid's Elegies			1.8.49
CLOSET				
That almost rents the closet of my heart,	Edw	5.3.22		Edward
sometime solitary set, within my Closet, sundry thoughts arose,	F App	p.236 18	P	Emper
CLOSETH				
being strucke/Runnes to an herbe that closeth up the wounds,	Edw	5.1.10		Edward
CLOSURE				
charme to keepe the windes/Within the closure of a golden ball,	Dido	4.4.100		Dido
CLOTH (See also CLOATH)				
the ground be <were> perfum'd, and cover'd with cloth of Arras.	F 671	2.2.120	P	Pride
CLOTH'D				
And I sat downe, cloth'd with the massie robe,	2Tamb	3.2.123		Tamb
Over whose Zenith cloth'd in windy aire,	2Tamb	3.4.61		Therid
Cloth'd with a pitchy cloud for being seene.	2Tamb	4.1.131		Tamb
And cloth'd in costly cloath of massy gold,	2Tamb	4.2.40		Therid
And slipt from bed cloth'd in a loose night-gowne,	Ovid's Elegies			3.1.51
CLOTHE (See CLOATH)				
CLOTHED				
I see great Mahomet/Clothed in purple clowdes, and on his head	2Tamb	5.2.32		Amasia
And all the Students clothed in mourning blacke,	F2000	5.3.18		2Schol
CLOTHES				
Nor goe to bed, but sleepes in his owne clothes;	Jew	4.1.132		Ithimr
lov'd Rice, that Fryar Bernardine slept in his owne clothes.	Jew	4.4.77	P	Ithimr
I and my wench oft under clothes did lurke,	Ovid's Elegies			1.4.47
CLOUD (See also CLOWDES)				
Cloth'd with a pitchy cloud for being seene.	2Tamb	4.1.131		Tamb
Into the entrals of yon labouring cloud,	F1953	5.2.157		Faust
[There] <Their> Caesar may'st thou shine and no cloud dim thee;	Lucan, First Booke			59
And tumbling with the Rainbow in a cloud:	Hero and Leander			1.150
As from an orient cloud, glymse <glimps'd> here and there.	Hero and Leander			2.320
CLOUDE				
a fiery exhalation/Wrapt in the bowels of a freezing cloude,	1Tamb	4.2.44		Tamb
He bindes his temples with a frowning cloude,	2Tamb	2.4.6		Tamb
CLOUDED				
There stands an old wood with thick trees darke clouded,	Ovid's Elegies			3.12.7
CLOUDES				
Affecting thoughts coequall with the cloudes,	1Tamb	1.2.65		Tamb
whet thy winged sword/And lift thy lofty arme into the cloudes,	1Tamb	2.3.52		Cosroe
Have swelling cloudes drawen from wide gasping woundes,	1Tamb	5.1.459		Tamb
drops that fall/When Boreas rents a thousand swelling cloudes,	2Tamb	1.3.160		Tamb
Raise Cavalieros higher than the cloudes,	2Tamb	2.4.103		Tamb
Looke like the parti-coloured cloudes of heaven,	2Tamb	3.1.47		Jrslem
Making their fiery gate above the cloudes,	2Tamb	4.3.9		Tamb
live, and draw/My chariot swifter than the racking cloudes:	2Tamb	4.3.21		Tamb
Whose lofty Pillers, higher than the cloudes,	2Tamb	5.1.64		Tamb
[Nor can they raise the winde, or rend the cloudes]:	F 86	1.1.58A		Faust
He viewes the cloudes, the Planets, and the Starres,	F 760	2.3.39		2Chor
So thunder which the wind teares from the cloudes,	Lucan, First Booke			152
His burning chariot plung'd in sable cloudes,	Lucan, First Booke			539
When she will, cloudes the darckned heav'n obscure,	Ovid's Elegies			1.8.9
CLOUDIE				
So that in silence of the cloudie night,	Hero and Leander			2.101
CLOUDS				
the Sea-man sees the Hyades/Gather an armye of Cemerian clouds,	1Tamb	3.2.77		Agidas
her rusty coach/Engyrt with tempests wrapt in pitchy clouds,	1Tamb	5.1.295		Bajzth
That clouds of darkenesse may inclose my flesh,	Jew	1.2.194		Barab
And Natures beauty choake with stifeling clouds,	Jew	2.3.331		Lodowk
Lifting his loftie head above the clouds,	F 912	3.1.134		Pope
Lightning in silence, stole forth without clouds,	Lucan, First Booke			531
Or steeds might fal forcd with thick clouds approch.	Ovid's Elegies			1.13.30
All headlong throwes her selfe the clouds among/And now Leander	Hero and Leander			2.90
CLOUDY				
south were cause/I know not, but the cloudy ayre did frown;	Lucan, First Booke			237
CLOUTS				
For Kings are clouts that every man shoots at,	1Tamb	2.4.8		Mycete

CLOVEN
has hornes, and all shee divels has clifts and cloven feete. F App p.230 54 P Clown
CLOWDES
her ayrie wheeles/Into the windie countrie of the clowdes, Dido 1.1.57 Venus
Had not the heavens conceav'd with hel-borne clowdes, . Dido 1.1.125 Venus
And heaven was darkned with tempestuous clowdes: . . Dido 2.1.140 Aeneas
Ile make the Clowdes dissolve their watrie workes, . . Dido 3.2.90 Juno
Kind clowdes that sent forth such a curteous storme, . Dido 3.4.55 Dido
When as she meanes to maske the world with clowdes. . . Dido 4.1.6 Iarbus
Eternall Jove, great master of the Clowdes, . . . Dido 4.2.4 Iarbus
O that the Clowdes were here wherein thou [fledst] <fleest>, Dido 4.4.50 Dido
Should breake out off the bowels of the clowdes/And fall as 2Tamb 2.2.14 Gazell
And with the flames that beat against the clowdes/Incense the 2Tamb 4.1.194 Tamb
I see great Mahomet/Clothed in purple clowdes, and on his head 2Tamb 5.2.32 Amasia
Muffle your beauties with eternall clowdes, . . . 2Tamb 5.3.6 Therid
But he that sits and rules above the clowdes, . . . P 42 1.42 Navrre
If ever sunne stainde heaven with bloudy clowdes, . . P 60 2.3 Guise
CLOWDIE
Doe thou but smile, and clowdie heaven will cleare, . . Dido 1.1.155 Achat
CLOWDY
Whose chearful looks do cleare the clowdy aire/And cloath it in 2Tamb 1.3.3 Tamb
Is Guises glory but a clowdy mist, ... P 686 13.30 Guise
CLOWNAGE
And such conceits as clownage keepes in pay, . . . 1Tamb Prol.2 Prolog
CLOWNE
And she thats coy I like for being no clowne, . . . Ovid's Elegies 2.4.13
Our pleasant scapes shew thee no clowne to be, . . . Ovid's Elegies 2.8.3
Clowne, from my journey why doest me deterre? . . . Ovid's Elegies 3.5.88
A clowne, ncr no love from her warme brest yeelds. . . Ovid's Elegies 3.9.18
And still inrich the loftie servile clowne, . . . Hero and Leander 1.481
CLOWNISH
He is too clownish, whom a lewd wife grieves, . . . Ovid's Elegies 3.4.37
CLOY
Let one wench cloy me with sweete loves delight, . . Ovid's Elegies 2.10.21
CLOYD
Whilst I am here on earth let me be cloyd/With all things that F 837 3.1.59 Faust
CLOYE
For such outragious passions cloye my soule, . . . Edw 5.1.19 Edward
CLOYED
By cloyed Charibdis, and againe devoured. . . . . Ovid's Elegies 2.16.26
CLOYES
Even as sweete meate a glutted stomacke cloyes. . . Ovid's Elegies 2.19.26
CLOYSTER
of my knowledge in one cloyster keeps,/Five hundred fatte P 141 2.84 Guise
CLUNG
Therefore unto his bodie, hirs he clung, ... Hero and Leander 2.65
CLUSTERS
Are falne in clusters at my conquering feet. . . . 1Tamb 3.3.230 Tamb
CLUSTRED
Take clustred grapes from an ore-laden vine, . . . Ovid's Elegies 1.10.55
CLYMENS
As was the fame of [Clymens] <Clymeus> brain-sicke sonne,/That 1Tamb 4.2.49 Tamb
As that which [Clymens] <Clymeus> brainsicke sonne did guide, 2Tamb 5.3.231 Tamb
CLYMEUS
As was the fame of [Clymens] <Clymeus> brain-sicke sonne,/That 1Tamb 4.2.49 Tamb
As that which [Clymens] <Clymeus> brainsicke sonne did guide, 2Tamb 5.3.231 Tamb
COACH (See also COCH, COCHE)
Let ugly darknesse with her rusty coach/Engyrt with tempests 1Tamb 5.1.294 Bajzth
With naked Negros shall thy coach be drawen, . . . 2Tamb 1.2.40 Callap
Let me have coach my Lord, that I may ride, . . . 2Tamb 4.3.27 Amyras
to restraine/These coltish coach-horse tongues from blasphemy. 2Tamb 4.3.52 Usumc
Then in my coach like Saturnes royal son, . . . 2Tamb 4.3.125 Tamb
Bridle them, and let me to my coach. . . . . 2Tamb 5.1.148 Tamb
More then heavens coach, the pride of Phaeton. . . 2Tamb 5.3.244 Tamb
And with swift Naggs drawing thy little Coach, . . . Ovid's Elegies 2.16.49
Ah Pelops from his coach was almost feld, ... Ovid's Elegies 3.2.15
COACHE
See that my coache be readie, I must hence. . . . Edw 2.1.71 Neece
COACH-HORSE
to restraine/These coltish coach-horse tongues from blasphemy. 2Tamb 4.3.52 Usumc
COACHMAN
And such a Coachman as great Tamburlaine? . . . . 2Tamb 4.3.4 Tamb
COAL (See COLE)
COARSE
Unto mount Faucon will we dragge his coarse: . . . P 319 5.46 Anjoy
COAST
To know what coast the winde hath driven us on, . . Dido 1.1.176 Aeneas
In sending thee unto this curteous Coast: . . . . Dido 1.1.232 Venus
And all the land unto the coast of Spaine. . . . 2Tamb 1.3.179 Usumc
And by the coast of Byather at last, ... 2Tamb 1.3.200 Techel
For late upon the coast of Corsica, ... Jew 2.2.10 Bosco
Turmoiles the coast, and enterance forbids; . . . Lucan, First Booke 409
COASTED
Belike they coasted round by Candie shoare/About their Oyles, Jew 1.1.91 Barab
COASTES
And keep those relicks from our countries coastes. . . P 803 16.17 Navrre
COASTS
And bring Armados from the coasts of Spaine, . . . 2Tamb 1.2.34 Callap
COAT
My sword stroke fire from his coat of steele, . . . 1Tamb 4.2.41 Tamb
COATE
Tis not a black coate and a little band, ... Edw 2.1.33 Spencr
Nor shamefully her coate pull ore her crowne, . . . Ovid's Elegies 1.7.47

COATE (cont.)			
Coate-tuckt Dianas legges are painted like them,	Ovid's Elegies	3.2.31	
her coate hood-winckt her fearefull eyes,/And into water	Ovid's Elegies	3.5.79	
COATES			
The common souldiers rich imbrodered coates,	Dido	4.4.9	Dido
Whose ransome made them martch in coates of gold,	1Tamb	1.1.143	Ceneus
COATE-TUCKT			
Coate-tuckt Dianas legges are painted like them,	Ovid's Elegies	3.2.31	
COBHAM			
My lord, weele quicklie be at Cobham.	Edw	2.5.111	HrsBoy
COCH			
Make ready my Coch, my chaire, my jewels, I come, I come, I	1Tamb	5.1.317	P Zabina
And harnest like my horses, draw my coch,	2Tamb	3.5.104	Tamb
COCHE			
How oft, that either wind would breake thy coche,	Ovid's Elegies	1.13.29	
COCITUS			
Furies from the blacke Cocitus lake,	1Tamb	5.1.218	Bajzth
The jouyce of Hebon, and Cocitus breath,	Jew	3.4.101	Barab
COCKE			
Like Aesops cocke, this jewell he enjoyed,	Hero and Leander	2.51	
COCKERELS			
Yet, shall the crowing of these cockerels,	Edw	2.2.203	Edward
COCKS			
And crowing Cocks poore soules to worke awake.	Ovid's Elegies	1.6.66	
COCYTUS (See COCITUS)			
CODEMIA			
by the river Tyros I subdew'd/Stoka, Padalia, and Codemia.	2Tamb	1.3.210	Therid
COELUM			
But is there not Coelum igneum, [and] <&> <et> Christalinum?	F 612	2.2.61	P Faust
COEQUALL			
Affecting thoughts coequall with the cloudes,	1Tamb	1.2.65	Tamb
COFFER			
My purse, my Coffer, and my selfe is thine.	Jew	3.4.93	Barab
COFFERS			
Out of the coffers of our treasurie.	2Tamb	3.4.91	Therid
But he whose steele-bard coffers are cramb'd full,	Jew	1.1.14	Barab
COFFIN			
Pierce through the coffin and the sheet of gold,	2Tamb	5.3.226	Tamb
COFFYN			
Closde in a coffyn mounted up the aire,	2Tamb	1.1.140	Orcan
COIL (See COYLE)			
COIN'D (See also COYNE)			
of golden plate; besides two thousand duckets ready coin'd:	F1676	5.1.3	P Wagner
COLCHIS			
At Colchis stain'd with childrens bloud men raile,	Ovid's Elegies	2.14.29	
COLCHOS			
As was to Jason Colchos golden fleece.	1Tamb	4.4.9	Tamb
Had they beene cut, and unto Colchos borne,	Hero and Leander	1.56	
COLD (Homograph)			
And dipt it in the old Kings chill cold bloud,	Dido	2.1.260	Aeneas
Is drie and cold, and now dooth gastly death/With greedy	1Tamb	2.7.48	Cosroe
Sustaine the scortching heat and freezing cold,	2Tamb	3.2.57	Tamb
Hunger and [thirst] <cold>, right adjuncts of the war.	2Tamb	3.2.58	Tamb
Since this Towne was besieg'd, my gaine growes cold:	Jew	3.1.1	Curtzn
I dranke of Poppy and cold mandrake juyce;	Jew	5.1.80	Barab
exhalatione/which our great sonn of fraunce cold not effecte	Paris	ms20,p390	Guise
buttons to his lips, to keepe his tongue from catching cold.	F1388	4.2.64	P Benvol
They shooke for feare, and cold benumm'd their lims,	Lucan, First Booke	248	
And Marius head above cold Tav'ron peering/(His grave broke	Lucan, First Booke	581	
If cold noysome Saturne/Were now exalted, and with blew beames	Lucan, First Booke	650	
is bould/To suffer storme mixt snowes with nights sharpe cold?	Ovid's Elegies	1.9.16	
Which I thinke gather'd from cold hemlocks flower/Wherein bad	Ovid's Elegies	1.12.9	
That drawes the day from heavens cold axletree.	Ovid's Elegies	1.13.2	
Foole, what is sleepe but image of cold death,	Ovid's Elegies	2.9.41	
Upon the cold earth pensive let them lay,	Ovid's Elegies	2.16.15	
Eurotas cold, and poplar-bearing Po.	Ovid's Elegies	2.17.32	
Suffring much cold by hoary nights frost bred.	Ovid's Elegies	2.19.22	
Grew pale, and in cold foords hot lecherous.	Ovid's Elegies	3.5.26	
Which wealth, cold winter doth on thee bestowe.	Ovid's Elegies	3.5.94	
Yet like as if cold hemlocke I had drunke,	Ovid's Elegies	3.6.13	
And thorough everie vaine doth cold bloud runne,	Ovid's Elegies	3.13.38	
Abandon fruitlesse cold Virginitie,	Hero and Leander	1.317	
Through numming cold, all feeble, faint and wan:	Hero and Leander	2.246	
Fayre lined slippers for the cold:	Passionate Shepherd	15	
COLDE			
For freezing meteors and conjealed colde:	1Tamb	1.1.11	Cosroe
My bloodlesse body waxeth chill and colde,	1Tamb	2.7.42	Cosroe
Then let the stony dart of sencelesse colde,	1Tamb	5.1.302	Bajzth
The aire is colde, and sleepe is sweetest now,	Ovid's Elegies	1.13.7	
COLDLY			
And see how coldly his lookes make deniall.	Edw	1.4.235	Lncstr
COLE			
The Ocean, Terrene, and the cole-blacke sea,	1Tamb	3.1.25	Bajzth
His cole-blacke collours every where advaunst,	1Tamb	5.1.9	Govnr
Cole-blacke Charibdis whirl'd a sea of bloud;	Lucan, First Booke	546	
Memnon the elfe/Received his cole-blacke colour from thy selfe.	Ovid's Elegies	1.13.32	
COLEBLACK			
hate/Flings slaughtering terrour from my coleblack tents.	1Tamb	5.1.72	Tamb
COLE-BLACKE			
The Ocean, Terrene, and the cole-blacke sea,	1Tamb	3.1.25	Bajzth
His cole-blacke collours every where advaunst,	1Tamb	5.1.9	Govnr
Cole-blacke Charibdis whirl'd a sea of bloud;	Lucan, First Booke	546	
Memnon the elfe/Received his cole-blacke colour from thy selfe.	Ovid's Elegies	1.13.32	

COLEBLACKE			
Whose coleblacke faces make their foes retire, . . .	2Tamb	1.3.142	Techel
COLES			
There are live quarters broyling on the coles, . . .	F1913	5.2.117	BdAngl
COLL			
Her silver armes will coll me round about, . . .	Dido	4.3.51	Aeneas
COLLECTION			
We may have time to make collection/Amongst the Inhabitants of	Jew	1.2.20	Govnr
COLLEDGE			
With all our Colledge of grave Cardinals, ...	F 968	3.1.190	Pope
COLLEDGES			
Paris hath full five hundred Colledges, ...	P 137	2.80	Guise
COLLIARS			
Nere was there Colliars sonne so full of pride. . .	P 416	7.56	Anjoy
COLLORS			
Under my collors march ten thousand Greeks, ...	2Tamb	1.3.118	Therid
COLLOURS			
Or spread his collours in Grecia, ...	1Tamb	3.1.29	Bajzth
And when she sees our bloody Collours spread, . . .	1Tamb	3.3.159	Tamb
Hath spread his collours to our high disgrace: . . .	1Tamb	4.1.7	Souldn
Black are his collours, blacke Pavilion, ...	1Tamb	4.1.59	2Msngr
Now hang our bloody collours by Damascus, ...	1Tamb	4.4.1	Tamb
His cole-blacke collours every where advaunst, . . .	1Tamb	5.1.9	Govnr
COLONIES			
what Colonies/To rest their bones?	Lucan, First Booke		345
COLOSSUS			
Wouldst thou make a Colossus of me, that thou askest me such	F1646	4.6.89	P Faust
COLOUR (See also COLLORS, COJLOUR, CULLOR)			
Doe thou but say their colour pleaseth me.	Dido	1.1.41	Jupitr
It may be under colour of shaving, thou'lt cut my throat for my	Jew	2.3.119	P Barab
Why on the sudden is your colour chang'd?	Jew	2.3.321	Lodowk
Then may we with some colour rise in armes, . . .	Edw	1.4.279	Mortmr
That colour rightly did appeare so bloudy.	Ovid's Elegies		1.12.12
Memnon the elfe/Received his cole-blacke colour from thy selfe.	Ovid's Elegies		1.13.32
To these, or some of these like was her colour, . .	Ovid's Elegies		2.5.41
And sodainly her former colour chang'd, ...	Hero and Leander		1.359
His colour went and came, as if he rewd/The greefe which .	Hero and Leander		2.214
COLOURED			
And dive into her heart by coloured lookes.	Dido	4.2.32	Iarbus
And slice the Sea with sable coloured ships, ...	Dido	4.3.22	Aeneas
Looke like the parti-coloured cloudes of heaven, . .	2Tamb	3.1.47	Jrslem
Whose frame is paved with sundry coloured stones, . .	F 797	3.1.19	Faust
COLOURING			
Leave colouring thy tresses I did cry, ...	Ovid's Elegies		1.14.1
COLOURS			
That so my bloudie colours may suggest/Remembrance of revenge	Edw	3.1.139	Edward
And weare thy colours on my plumed crest.	F1778	5.1.105	Faust
There spred the colours, with confused noise/Of trumpets .	Lucan, First Booke		239
COLTISH			
to restraine/These coltish coach-horse tongues from blasphemy.	2Tamb	4.3.52	Usumc
COLTS			
their mouths/And pul their kicking colts out of their pastures.	2Tamb	4.3.49	Techel
COMBAT			
that ever brandisht sword)/Challenge in combat any of you all,	2Tamb	3.5.72	Tamb
Nay let 'em combat, conquer, and kill all, ...	Jew	1.1.152	Barab
And I will combat with weake Menelaus, ...	F1777	5.1.104	Faust
COMBATE			
I am the Champion that will combate him!	Edw	5.4.78	Champn
COMBE (See also KEEMBE, KEMBD)			
Snatching the combe, to beate the wench out drive <drave> her.	Ovid's Elegies		1.14.18
COMBES			
Nor hath the needle, or the combes teeth reft them, . .	Ovid's Elegies		1.14.15
COMBIN'D			
made one Poems period/And all combin'd in Beauties worthinesse,	1Tamb	5.1.170	Tamb
COMBINDE			
Thus shall my heart be still combinde with thine, . .	1Tamb	1.2.235	Tamb
COMBINE			
Nor thy soft foote with his hard foote combine. . .	Ovid's Elegies		1.4.44
COME (See also COMM'ST, COMME, COMST)			
Come gentle Ganimed and play with me, ...	Dido	1.1.1	Jupitr
Come Ganimed, we must about this geare.	Dido	1.1.121	Jupitr
What? doe I see my sonne now come on shoare: . . .	Dido	1.1.134	Venus
Whence may you come, or whither will you goe? . . .	Dido	1.1.215	Venus
We come not we to wrong your Libian Gods, ...	Dido	1.2.10	Illion
Come in with me, Ile bring you to my Queene, . . .	Dido	1.2.42	Iarbus
Come, come abourd, pursue the hatefull Greekes. . .	Dido	2.1.22	Aeneas
Aeneas see, here come the Citizens, ...	Dido	2.1.37	Achat
By this the Campe was come unto the walles, . . .	Dido	2.1.188	Aeneas
Come let us thinke upon some pleasing sport, . . .	Dido	2.1.302	Dido
Come Dido, leave Ascanius, let us walke.	Dido	3.1.34	Iarbus
Depart from Carthage, come not in my sight. . . .	Dido	3.1.44	Dido
Behold where both of them come forth the Cave. . . .	Dido	4.1.16	Anna
Come forth the Cave: can heaven endure this sight? . .	Dido	4.1.17	Iarbus
Come Dido, let us hasten to the towne, ...	Dido	4.1.26	Aeneas
Come servants, come bring forth the Sacrifize, . . .	Dido	4.2.1	Iarbus
Servants, come fetch these emptie vessels here, . . .	Dido	4.2.49	Iarbus
Achates come forth, Sergestus, Illioneus, ...	Dido	4.3.13	Aeneas
Come backe, come backe, I heare her crye a farre, . .	Dido	4.3.27	Aeneas
See where they come, how might I doe to chide? . . .	Dido	4.4.13	Dido
Come beare them in.	Dido	4.4.165	Dido
Come come, Ile goe, how farre hence is your house? . .	Dido	4.5.13	Cupid
Youle be a twigger when you come to age.	Dido	4.5.20	Nurse
Come Nurse.	Dido	4.5.35	Cupid

COME (cont.)

Well, if he come a wooing he shall speede,	Dido	4.5.36		Nurse
I but heele come againe, he cannot goe,	Dido	5.1.184		Dido
Now is he come on shoare safe without hurt:	Dido	5.1.257		Dido
Dido I come to thee, aye me Aeneas.	Dido	5.1.318		Iarbus
Now sweet Iarbus stay, I come to thee.	Dido	5.1.329		Anna
Go frowning foorth, but come thou smyling home,	1Tamb	1.1.65		Mycet
Meander come, I am abus'd Meander.	1Tamb	1.1.106		Mycet
Come lady, let not this appal your thoughts.	1Tamb	1.2.1		Tamb
Come let us meet them at the mountain foot,	1Tamb	1.2.133		Usumc
Come let us martch.	1Tamb	1.2.136		Techel
And looke we friendly on them when they come:	1Tamb	1.2.141		Tamb
I heare them come, shal we encounter them?	1Tamb	1.2.149		Techel
Come my Meander, let us to this geere,	1Tamb	2.2.1		Mycet
What thinkst thou man, shal come of our attemptes?	1Tamb	2.3.3		Cosroe
Come, Tamburlain, now whet thy winged sword/And lift thy lofty	1Tamb	2.3.51		Cosroe
Usumcasane and Techelles come,	1Tamb	2.3.63		Tamb
Come give it me.	1Tamb	2.4.31		Mycet
That no reliefe or succour come by Land.	1Tamb	3.1.62		Bajzth
Who, when they come unto their fathers age,	1Tamb	3.3.110		Bajzth
But come my Lords, to weapons let us fall.	1Tamb	3.3.162		Tamb
Come Kings and Bassoes, let us glut our swords/That thirst to	1Tamb	3.3.164		Bajzth
For we will scorne they should come nere our selves.	1Tamb	3.3.186		Zenoc
If Mahomet should come from heaven and sweare,	1Tamb	3.3.208		Zenoc
Come bind them both and one lead in the Turke.	1Tamb	3.3.266		Tamb
Come bring them in, and for this happy conquest/Triumph, and	1Tamb	3.3.272		Tamb
Come bring in the Turke.	1Tamb	4.2.126		Tamb
Nay, thine owne is easier to come by, plucke out that, and twil	1Tamb	4.4.13	P	Tamb
Make ready my Coch, my chaire, my jewels, I come, I come, I come	1Tamb	5.1.318	P	Zabina
ready my Coch, my chaire, my jewels, I come, I come, I come.	1Tamb	5.1.318	P	Zabina
Come happy Father of Zenocrate,	1Tamb	5.1.433		Tamb
Where ere I come the fatall sisters sweat,	1Tamb	5.1.454		Tamb
Come let us goe and banquet in our tents:	2Tamb	1.1.160		Orcan
Come banquet and carouse with us a while,	2Tamb	1.1.165		Orcan
Which when I come aboord will hoist up saile,	2Tamb	1.2.24		Callap
Dismaies their mindes before they come to proove/The wounding	2Tamb	1.3.86		Zenoc
The trumpets sound, Zenocrate, they come.	2Tamb	1.3.111		Tamb
Come let us banquet and carrouse the whiles.	2Tamb	1.3.225		Tamb
And now come we to make his sinowes shake,	2Tamb	2.2.9		Gazell
Come downe from heaven and live with me againe.	2Tamb	2.4.118		Tamb
Come boyes and with your fingers search my wound,	2Tamb	3.2.126		Tamb
Come sirra, give me your arme.	2Tamb	3.2.134	P	Tamb
Usumcasane now come let us martch/Towards Techelles and	2Tamb	3.2.145		Tamb
Yes, my Lord, yes, come lets about it.	2Tamb	3.3.10		Soldrs
That no supply of victuall shall come in,	2Tamb	3.3.32		Techel
Come good my Lord, and let us haste from hence/Along the cave	2Tamb	3.4.1		Olymp
Come back again (sweet death) and strike us both:	2Tamb	3.4.12		Olymp
And purge my soule before it come to thee.	2Tamb	3.4.33		Olymp
Come.	2Tamb	3.4.68		Therid
Come willinglie, therfore.	2Tamb	3.4.84		Techel
fighting men/Are come since last we shewed your majesty.	2Tamb	3.5.34		Jrslem
Come puissant Viceroies, let us to the field,	2Tamb	3.5.53		Callap
Ye petty kings of Turkye I am come,	2Tamb	3.5.64		Tamb
againe, you shall not trouble me thus to come and fetch you.	2Tamb	3.5.101	P	Tamb
Come Almeda, receive this crowne of me,	2Tamb	3.5.129		Callap
in the stable, when you shall come sweating from my chariot.	2Tamb	3.5.142	P	Tamb
Come fight ye Turks, or yeeld us victory.	2Tamb	3.5.169		Tamb
O cowardly boy, fie for shame, come foorth.	2Tamb	4.1.31		Celeb
Come, thou and I wil goe to cardes to drive away the time.	2Tamb	4.1.61	P	Calyph
I should be affraid, would put it off and come to bed with me.	2Tamb	4.1.70	P	Calyph
Come bring them in to our Pavilion.	2Tamb	4.1.206		Tamb
Come to the tent againe.	2Tamb	4.2.54		Therid
Come as thou didst in fruitfull Scicilie,	2Tamb	4.3.34		Orcan
Come once in furie and survay his pride,	2Tamb	4.3.41		Orcan
And tremble when ye heare this Scourge wil come,	2Tamb	4.3.99		Tamb
Come Asian Viceroies, to your taskes a while/And take such	2Tamb	5.1.136		Tamb
I will about it straight, come Souldiers.	2Tamb	5.1.172		Techel
Come downe thy selfe and worke a myracle,	2Tamb	5.1.188		Tamb
Should come in person to resist your power,	2Tamb	5.2.38		Amasia
Come Souldiers, let us lie in wait for him/And if we find him	2Tamb	5.2.56		Callap
Techelles and the rest, come take your swords,	2Tamb	5.3.46		Tamb
Come let us march against the powers of heaven,	2Tamb	5.3.48		Tamb
Come carie me to war against the Gods,	2Tamb	5.3.52		Tamb
Come let us chardge our speares and pierce his breast,	2Tamb	5.3.58		Tamb
I and myne armie come to lode thy barke/With soules of thousand	2Tamb	5.3.73		Tamb
now the Guize is dead, is come from France/To view this Land,	Jew	Prol.3		Machvl
But whither am I bound, I come not, I,	Jew	Prol.28		Machvl
sent me to know/Whether your selfe will come and custome them.	Jew	1.1.53		1Merch
Why then goe bid them come ashore,/And bring with them their	Jew	1.1.55		Barab
So then, there's somewhat come.	Jew	1.1.69		Barab
Thou couldst not come from Egypt, or by Caire/But at the entry	Jew	1.1.73		Barab
But 'twas ill done of you to come so farre/Without the ayd or	Jew	1.1.93		Barab
And bid the Merchants and my men dispatch/And come ashore, and	Jew	1.1.101		Barab
I must confesse we come not to be Kings:	Jew	1.1.129		Barab
And Crownes come either by succession/Or urg'd by force; and	Jew	1.1.131		Barab
Come therefore let us goe to Barrabas;	Jew	1.1.141		2Jew
Are come from Turkey, and lye in our Rhode:	Jew	1.1.147		1Jew
Why let 'em come, so they come not to warre;	Jew	1.1.150		Barab
They would not come in warlike manner thus.	Jew	1.1.155		1Jew
Why, Barabas, they come for peace or warre.	Jew	1.1.161		1Jew
They were, my Lord, and here they come.	Jew	1.2.36		Offcrs
Yes, give me leave, and Hebrews now come neare.	Jew	1.2.38		Govnr
Come, let us in, and gather of these goods/The mony for this	Jew	1.2.155		Govnr

COME (cont.)

Come, let us leave him in his irefull mood,	Jew	1.2.209	1Jew
And cast with cunning for the time to come:	Jew	1.2.222	Barab
But here they come; be cunning Abigall.	Jew	1.2.299	Barab
I, and of a moving spirit too, brother; but come,	Jew	1.2.328	2Fryar
Come daughter, follow us.	Jew	1.2.337	Abbass
No come not at me, if thou wilt be damn'd,	Jew	1.2.362	Barab
Come and receive the Treasure I have found.	Jew	2.1.38	Abigal
So will we fight it out; come, let's away:	Jew	2.2.52	Govnr
Come to my house and I will giv't your honour--	Jew	2.3.66	Barab
Come home and there's no price shall make us part,	Jew	2.3.92	Barab
Come then, here's the marketplace; whats the price of this	Jew	2.3.97	P Barab
My Lord farewell: Come Sirra you are mine.	Jew	2.3.134	Barab
When you have brought her home, come to my house;	Jew	2.3.148	Barab
Thou hast thy Crownes, fellow, come let's away.	Jew	2.3.158	Mater
Come, I have made a reasonable market,	Jew	2.3.161	1Offcr
father, here are letters come/From Ormus, and the Post stayes	Jew	2.3.222	Abigal
That ye be both made sure e're you come out.	Jew	2.3.236	Barab
looking out/When you should come and hale him from the doore.	Jew	2.3.265	Barab
Away, for here they come.	Jew	2.3.275	Barab
Nor our Messias that is yet to come,	Jew	2.3.304	Barab
I cannot stay; for if my mother come,	Jew	2.3.353	Mthias
and from Padua/Were wont to come rare witted Gentlemen,	Jew	3.1.7	Curtzn
Come, Katherina, our losses equall are,	Jew	3.2.36	Govnr
And say, I pray them come and speake with me.	Jew	3.3.29	Abigal
Come, shall we goe?	Jew	3.3.76	1Fryar
Oh Ithimore come neere;/Come neere, my love, come neere, thy	Jew	3.4.13	Barab
Come neere, my love, come neere, thy masters life,	Jew	3.4.14	Barab
Be blest of me, nor come within my gates,	Jew	3.4.31	Barab
go set it downe/And come againe so soone as thou hast done,	Jew	3.4.109	Barab
For Selim-Calymath shall come himselfe,	Jew	3.5.23	Basso
sent for him, but seeing you are come/Be you my ghostly father;	Jew	3.6.11	Abigal
Come let's away.	Jew	3.6.52	2Fryar
Look, look, master, here come two religious Caterpillers.	Jew	4.1.21	P Ithimr
God-a-mercy nose; come let's begone.	Jew	4.1.23	Ithimr
Oh good Barabas come to our house.	Jew	4.1.77	1Fryar
Oh no, good Barabas come to our house.	Jew	4.1.78	2Fryar
Good Barabas, come to me.	Jew	4.1.87	2Fryar
Come to my house at one a clocke this night.	Jew	4.1.91	Barab
And so I will, oh Jacomo, faile not but come.	Jew	4.1.108	Barab
Now Fryar Bernardine I come to you,	Jew	4.1.125	Barab
Come on, sirra,/Off with your girdle,	Jew	4.1.141	Barab
And understanding I should come this way,	Jew	4.1.165	1Fryar
Come Ithimore, let's helpe to take him hence.	Jew	4.1.200	Barab
And what think'st thou, will he come?	Jew	4.2.5	P Curtzn
with his lips; the effect was, that I should come to her house.	Jew	4.2.32	P Ithimr
And bid the Jeweller come hither too.	Jew	4.2.86	Ithimr
Come my deare love, let's in and sleepe together.	Jew	4.2.129	Curtzn
Come Amorous wag, first banquet and then sleep.	Jew	4.2.132	Curtzn
Might he not as well come as send; pray bid him come and fetch	Jew	4.3.26	P Barab
he not as well come as send; pray bid him come and fetch it:	Jew	4.3.26	P Barab
To have a shag-rag knave to come [demand]/Three hundred	Jew	4.3.61	Barab
Come gentle Ithimore, lye in my lap.	Jew	4.4.27	Curtzn
A French Musician, come let's heare your skill?	Jew	4.4.30	Curtzn
The meaning has a meaning; come let's in:	Jew	4.4.80	Ithimr
brave Bashawes, come, wee'll walke about/The ruin'd Towne, and	Jew	5.2.18	Calym
would intreat your Majesty/To come and see his homely Citadell,	Jew	5.3.18	Msngr
Then issue out and come to rescue me,	Jew	5.4.5	Govnr
returne me word/That thou wilt come, and I am satisfied.	Jew	5.5.12	Barab
Now sirra, what, will he come?	Jew	5.5.13	Barab
and has commanded all his men/To come ashore, and march through	Jew	5.5.15	Msngr
Stand close, for here they come:	Jew	5.5.46	Barab
Come, my Companion-Bashawes, see I pray/How busie Barrabas is	Jew	5.5.51	Calym
I, Barabas, come Bashawes, attend.	Jew	5.5.59	Calym
Malta prisoner; for come [all] <call> the world/To rescue thee,	Jew	5.5.119	Govnr
Come Mother,/Let us goe to honor this solemnitie.	P 24	1.24	Charls
Come my Lords lets go to the Church and pray,	P 55	1.55	Navrre
Now come thou forth and play thy tragick part,	P 85	2.28	Guise
The plot is laide, and things shall come to passe,	P 164	2.107	Guise
Come my Lords let us beare her body hence,	P 195	3.30	Admral
betraide, come my Lords, and let us goe tell the King of this.	P 199	3.34	P Navrre
Come sirs follow me.	P 292	5.19	Gonzag
In lucky time, come let us keep this lane,	P 298	5.25	Anjoy
But slay as many as we can come neer.	P 326	5.53	Anjoy
Come then, lets away.	P 335	5.62	Guise
Come dragge him away and throw him in a ditch.	P 345	5.72	Guise
Husband come down, heer's one would speak with you from the	P 348	6.3	P SrnsWf
Harke, harke they come, Ile leap out at the window.	P 369	7.9	Taleus
Come Ramus, more golde, or thou shalt have the stabbe.	P 376	7.16	Gonzag
Come let us goe tell the King.	P 440	7.80	Condy
Come sirs, Ile whip you to death with my punniards point.	P 441	7.81	Guise
Then come my Lords, lets goe.	P 481	8.31	Anjoy
But come lets walke aside, th'airs not very sweet.	P 497	9.16	QnMoth
Come my Lord [let] <lets> us goe.	P 527	9.46	QnMoth
And bid him come without delay to us.	P 559	11.24	QnMoth
Come let us take his body hence.	P 564	11.29	QnMoth
Come Pleshe, lets away whilste time doth serve.	P 587	11.52	Navrre
Come sir, give me my buttons and heers your eare.	P 620	12.33	Mugern
Come my [Lord] <Lords>, let us goe seek the Guise,	P 655	12.68	QnMoth
That he may come and meet me in some place,	P 664	13.8	Duchss
In Gods name, let them come.	P 728	14.31	Navrre
I would the Guise in his steed might have come,	P 736	14.39	Navrre
But come my Lords, let us away with speed,	P 741	14.44	Navrre

COME (cont.)

come Epernoune/Lets goe seek the Duke and make them freends.	P 785	15.43	King
Come my Lords, now that this storme is overpast,	P 804	16.18	Navrre
come not to take possession (as I would I might) yet I meane to	P 813	17.8	P Souldr
what are ye come so soone?	P 815	17.10	P Souldr
Come on sirs, what, are you resolutely bent,	P 931	19.1	Capt
What, will you not feare when you see him come?	P 933	19.3	Capt
But when will he come that we may murther him?	P 937	19.7	P 3Mur
For anon the Guise will come.	P 941	19.11	Capt
Then come proud Guise and heere disgordge thy brest,	P 952	19.22	King
Let him come in.	P 961	19.31	King
Come Guise and see thy traiterous guile outreacht,	P 962	19.32	King
And now will I to armes, come Epernoune:	P1079	19.149	King
Come take him away.	P1106	20.16	1Mur
I come to bring you newes, that your brother the Cardinall of	P1122	21.16	P Frier
Come let us away and leavy men,	P1127	21.21	Dumain
Frier come with me,	P1137	21.31	Dumain
Let him come in.	P1158	22.20	King
Then come thou neer, and tell what newes thou bringst.	P1166	22.28	King
I dye Navarre, come beare me to my Sepulchre.	P1242	22.104	King
Come Lords, take up the body of the King,	P1245	22.107	Navrre
And thoughe I come not to keep possessione as I wold I mighte	Paris	ms14,p390	P Souldr
yet I come to keepe you out ser.	Paris	ms15,p390	P Souldr
My father is deceast, come Gaveston,	Edw	1.1.1	Gavstn
Sweete prince I come, these these thy amorous lines,	Edw	1.1.6	Gavstn
Is as Elizium to a new come soule.	Edw	1.1.11	Gavstn
Therefore if he be come, expell him straight.	Edw	1.1.106	Lncstr
Come unckle, let us leave the brainsick king,	Edw	1.1.125	Mortmr
Come follow me, and thou shalt have my guarde,	Edw	1.1.204	Edward
And when I come, he frownes, as who should say,	Edw	1.2.53	Queene
and yet ere that day come,/The king shall lose his crowne, for	Edw	1.2.58	Mortmr
Come then lets away.	Edw	1.2.79	Lncstr
Come, come, subscribe.	Edw	1.4.75	Lncstr
Ile come to thee, my love shall neare decline.	Edw	1.4.115	Edward
But come sweete friend, ile beare thee on thy way.	Edw	1.4.140	Edward
I passe not for their anger, come lets go.	Edw	1.4.142	Edward
Away then, touch me not, come Gaveston.	Edw	1.4.159	Edward
My gratious lord, I come to bring you newes.	Edw	1.4.320	Queene
Thankes gentle Warwick, come lets in and revell.	Edw	1.4.385	Edward
You know my minde, come unckle lets away.	Edw	1.4.424	Mortmr
I know thou couldst not come and visit me.	Edw	2.1.61	Neece
Come lead the way, I long till I am there.	Edw	2.1.82	Neece
And come not here to scoffe at Gaveston,	Edw	2.2.76	Gavstn
Out of my presence, come not neere the court.	Edw	2.2.89	Edward
Come Edmund lets away, and levie men,	Edw	2.2.98	Edward
Nay, stay my lord, I come to bring you newes,	Edw	2.2.141	Mortmr
Come lets away, and when the mariage ends,	Edw	2.2.264	Edward
I come to joine with you, and leave the king,	Edw	2.3.2	Kent
Come, come aboord, tis but an houres sailing.	Edw	2.4.49	Lncstr
Sweete soveraigne, yet I come/To see thee ere I die.	Edw	2.5.94	Gavstn
Sir, must not come so neare and balke their lips.	Edw	2.5.103	Penbrk
Come hether James,/I do commit this Gaveston to thee,	Edw	2.5.106	Penbrk
Goe, take the villaine, soldiers come away,	Edw	2.6.11	Warwck
Come, let thy shadow parley with king Edward.	Edw	2.6.14	Warwck
Come fellowes, it booted not for us to strive,	Edw	2.6.18	James
I come in person to your majestie,	Edw	3.1.39	SpncrP
What lord [Arundell] <Matre>, dost thou come alone?	Edw	3.1.89	Edward
And tell them I will come to chastise them,	Edw	3.1.178	Edward
Heere come the rebels.	Edw	3.1.194	Spencr
to request/He might be spared to come to speake with us,	Edw	3.1.235	Edward
How now, what newes with thee, from whence come these?	Edw	4.3.24	Edward
Come friends to Bristow, there to make us strong,	Edw	4.3.50	Edward
We come in armes to wrecke it with the [sword] <swords>:	Edw	4.4.23	Mortmr
Edward will thinke we come to flatter him.	Edw	4.4.29	SrJohn
This way he fled, but I am come too late.	Edw	4.6.1	Kent
Come Spencer, come Baldocke, come sit downe by me,	Edw	4.7.16	Edward
Come, come, keepe these preachments till you come to the place	Edw	4.7.113	P Rice
come, keepe these preachments till you come to the place	Edw	4.7.113	P Rice
keepe these preachments till you come to the place appointed.	Edw	4.7.113	P Rice
Come death, and with thy fingers close my eyes,	Edw	5.1.110	Edward
Such newes as I expect, come Bartley, come,	Edw	5.1.129	Edward
[Till] <And> at the last, he come to Killingworth,	Edw	5.2.60	Mortmr
Sweete sonne come hither, I must talke with thee.	Edw	5.2.87	Queene
that one so false/Should come about the person of a prince.	Edw	5.2.105	Mortmr
Come sonne, and go with this gentle Lorde and me.	Edw	5.2.109	Queene
Therefore come, dalliance dangereth our lives.	Edw	5.3.3	Matrvs
Come, come, away, now put the torches out,	Edw	5.3.47	Matrvs
Come forth. Art thou as resolute as thou wast?	Edw	5.4.22	Mortmr
I will requite it when I come to age.	Edw	5.4.100	King
Come sonne, weele ride a hunting in the parke.	Edw	5.4.113	Queene
He is a traitor, thinke not on him, come.	Edw	5.4.115	Queene
And therefore tell me, wherefore art thou come?	Edw	5.5.106	Edward
To rid thee of thy life. Matrevis come.	Edw	5.5.107	Ltborn
Come let us cast the body in the mote,	Edw	5.5.118	Gurney
Then come sweete death, and rid me of this greefe.	Edw	5.6.92	Queene
Bid [on kai me on] <Oncaymaeon> farewell, <and> Galen come:	F 40	1.1.12	Faust
Come Germane Valdes and Cornelius,	F 125	1.1.97	Faust
Come, shew me some demonstrations Magicall,	F 177	1.1.149	Faust
Then come and dine with me, and after meate/We'le canvase every	F 190	1.1.162	Faust
for you to come within fortie foot of the place of execution,	F 211	1.2.18	P Wagner
But come, let us go, and informe the Rector:	F 225	1.2.32	2Schol
Nor will we come unlesse he use such meanes,	F 278	1.3.50	Mephst
Come hither sirra boy.	F 343	1.4.1	P Wagner

COME (cont.)

and Belcher come here, I'le belch him:	F 374	1.4.32	P	Robin
Mephostophilis come/And bring glad tydings from great Lucifer.	F 415	2.1.27		Faust
Ist not midnight? come Mephostophilis <Mephastophilis>.	F 417	2.1.29		Faust
See <come> Faustus, here is <heres> fire, set it on.	F 459	2.1.71		Mephst
<Come>, I thinke Hel's a fable.	F 516	2.1.128		Faust
<Well thou wilt have one, sit there till I come,	F 531	(HC261)A	P	Mephst
Come Mephostophilis let us dispute againe,	F 584	2.2.33		Faust
O Faustus they are come to fetch <away> thy soule.	F 641	2.2.90		Faust
We are come to tell thee thou dost injure us.	F 642	2.2.91		Belzeb
we are come from hell in person to shew thee some pastime:	F 654	2.2.103	P	Belzeb
<talke of the divel, and nothing else: come away>.	F 660	(HC263)A	P	Lucifr
O that there would come a famine over <through> all the world,	F 681	2.2.130	P	Envy
come downe with a vengeance.	F 684	2.2.133	P	Envy
I <O I> come of a Royall Pedigree <parentage>, my father	F 696	2.2.145	P	Glutny
Farewell great Lucifer: come Mephostophilis.	F 721	2.2.173		Faust
What Dick, looke to the horses there till I come againe.	F 722	2.3.1	P	Robin
What Robin, you must come away and walk the horses.	F 725	2.3.4	P	Dick
your foolery, for an my Maister come, he'le conjure you 'faith.	F 735	2.3.14	P	Dick
an my Maister come here, I'le clap as faire a paire of hornes	F 737	2.3.16	P	Robin
Come then let's away.	F 753	2.3.32	P	Robin
Come therefore, let's away.	F 830	3.1.52		Faust
come then stand by me/And thou shalt see them come immediately.	F 843	3.1.65		Mephst
come then stand by me/And thou shalt see them come immediately.	F 844	3.1.66		Mephst
And I'le performe it Faustus: heark they come:	F 866	3.1.88		Mephst
Now Faustus, come prepare thy selfe for mirth,	F 981	3.2.1		Mephst
Faustus no more: see where the Cardinals come.	F1008	3.2.28		Mephst
Welcome Lord Cardinals: come sit downe.	F1009	3.2.29		Pope
Purgatory, and now is come unto your holinesse for his pardon.	F1060	3.2.80	P	Archbp
O come and help to beare my body hence:	F1069	3.2.89		Pope
Come brethren, let's about our businesse with good devotion.	F1076	3.2.96	P	1Frier
'Tis no matter, let him come; an he follow us, I'le so conjure	F1091	3.3.4	P	Robin
hold the cup Dick, come, come, search me, search me.	F1102	3.3.15	P	Robin
hold the cup Dick, come, come, search me, search me.	F1103	3.3.16	P	Robin
Come on sirra, let me search you now.	F1104	3.3.17	P	Vintnr
Come, give it me againe.	F1111	3.3.24	P	Vintnr
come Dick, come.	F1134	3.3.47	P	Robin
Come leave thy chamber first, and thou shalt see/This Conjurer	F1185	4.1.31		Mrtino
Speake, wilt thou come and see this sport?	F1193	4.1.39		Fredrk
an your Divels come not away quickly, you shall have me asleepe	F1241	4.1.87	P	Benvol
But in dumbe silence let them come and goe.	F1252	4.1.98		Faust
Come Faustus while the Emperour lives.	F1321	4.1.167		Emper
And kill that Doctor if he come this way.	F1339	4.2.15		Fredrk
Come souldiers, follow me unto the grove,	F1348	4.2.24		Fredrk
Come, let's devise how we may adde more shame/To the blacke	F1377	4.2.53		Fredrk
Come sirs, prepare your selves in readinesse,	F1420	4.2.96		1Soldr
and one to whom I must be no niggard of my cunning; Come, away.	F1504	4.4.48	P	Faust
Come my Maisters, I'le bring you to the best beere in Europe,	F1505	4.5.1	P	Carter
Come sirs, what shall we do now till mine Hostesse comes?	F1520	4.5.16	P	Dick
be good, for they come from a farre Country I can tell you.	F1576	4.6.19	P	Faust
I do beseech your grace let them come in,	F1605	4.6.48		Faust
'Faith you are too outragious, but come neere,	F1609	4.6.52		Faust
Be not so furious: come you shall have Beere.	F1620	4.6.63		Faust
and see where they come, belike the feast is done.	F1680	5.1.7	P	Wagner
Then Faustus, will repentance come too late,	F1714	5.1.41		OldMan
Saies Faustus come, thine houre is almost come,	F1727	5.1.54		Faust
And Faustus now will come to do thee right.	F1728	5.1.55		Faust
Come Hellen, come, give me my soule againe,	F1772	5.1.99		Faust
'Mong which as chiefe, Faustus we come to thee,	F1800	5.2.4		Lucifr
To wait upon thy soule; the time is come/Which makes it forfeit.	F1802	5.2.6		Lucifr
Both come from drawing Faustus latest will.	F1814	5.2.18		Mephst
See where they come.	F1815	5.2.19		Mephst
this is the time <the time wil come>, and he will fetch mee.	F1861	5.2.65	P	Faust
you <yee> heare, come not unto me, for nothing can rescue me.	F1874	5.2.78	P	Faust
That time may cease, and midnight never come.	F1930	5.2.134		Faust
The devill will come, and Faustus must be damn'd.	F1937	5.2.141		Faust
Mountaines and Hils, come, come, and fall on me,	F1945	5.2.149		Faust
Ugly hell gape not; come not Lucifer,	F1981	5.2.185		Faust
Come Gentlemen, let us go visit Faustus,	F1983	5.3.1		1Schol
Sirra boy, come hither.	F App	p.229 1	P	Wagner
Let your Balio and your Belcher come here, and Ile knocke them,	F App	p.230 45	P	Clown
Wel sirra, come.	F App	p.231 65	P	Wagner
out of Purgatory come to begge a pardon of your holinesse.	F App	p.232 15	P	Lorein
Come on Mephastophilis, what shall we do?	F App	p.232 22	P	Faust
Come brethren, lets about our businesse with good devotion.	F App	p.232 29	P	Frier
prethee come away, theres a Gentleman tarries to have his	F App	p.233 6	P	Rafe
it, and she has sent me to looke thee out, prethee come away.	F App	p.233 9	P	Rafe
Come, what doest thou with that same booke thou canst not	F App	p.233 13	P	Rafe
Come Rafe, did not I tell thee, we were for ever made by this	F App	p.234 1	P	Robin
Drawer, I hope al is payd, God be with you, come Rafe.	F App	p.234 6	P	Robin
From Constantinople am I hither come,	F App	p.235 38		Mephst
Wel, come give me your money, my boy wil deliver him to you:	F App	p.239 107	P	Faust
Why hee's fast asleepe, come some other time.	F App	p.240 141	P	Mephst
Come villaine to the Constable.	F App	p.241 157	P	Mephst
I have none about me, come to my Oastrie, and Ile give them you.	F App	p.241 161	P	HrsCsr
niggard of my cunning, come Mephastophilis, let's away to him.	F App	p.241 171	P	Faust
in the month of January, how you shuld come by these grapes.	F App	p.242 18	P	Duke
Come, Madame, let us in, where you must wel reward this learned	F App	p.243 28	P	Duke
Come, maister Doctor follow us, and receive your reward.	F App	p.243 33	P	Duke
See where they come: belike the feast is ended.	F App	p.243 8		Wagner
Let come their [leader] <leaders whom long peace hath quail'd;	Lucan, First Booke			311
These being come, their huge power made him bould/To mannage	Lucan, First Booke			462
and laide before their eies/Slaughter to come, and swiftly	Lucan, First Booke			467

COME (cont.)			
Before thy husband come, though I not see/What may be done, yet	Ovid's Elegies	1.4.13	
When our lascivious toyes come in thy minde,	Ovid's Elegies	1.4.21	
With armes or armed men I come not guarded,	Ovid's Elegies	1.6.33	
Come breake these deafe dores with thy boysterous wind.	Ovid's Elegies	1.6.54	
From dog-kept flocks come preys to woolves most gratefull.	Ovid's Elegies	1.8.56	
Let this word, come, alone the tables fill.	Ovid's Elegies	1.11.24	
Or that unlike the line from whence I [sprong] <come>,	Ovid's Elegies	1.15.3	
To over-come, so oft to fight I shame.	Ovid's Elegies	2.7.2	
Here of themselves thy shafts come, as if shot,	Ovid's Elegies	2.9.37	
But in the ayre let these words come to nought,	Ovid's Elegies	2.14.41	
Then warres, and from thy tents wilt come to mine.	Ovid's Elegies	2.18.40	
Come therefore, and to long verse shorter frame.	Ovid's Elegies	3.1.66	
Goddesse come here, make my love conquering.	Ovid's Elegies	3.2.46	
Because the keeper may come say, I did it,	Ovid's Elegies	3.4.35	
With Calvus learnd Catullus comes <come> and greete him.	Ovid's Elegies	3.8.62	
Come were the times of Ceres sacrifize,	Ovid's Elegies	3.9.1	
Practise a thousand sports when there you come,	Ovid's Elegies	3.13.24	
All heaven would come to claime this legacie,	Hero and Leander	1.250	
Come thither; As she spake this, her toong tript,	Hero and Leander	1.357	
For unawares (Come thither) from her slipt,	Hero and Leander	1.358	
And oft look't out, and mus'd he did not come.	Hero and Leander	2.22	
To part in twaine, that hee might come and go,	Hero and Leander	2.151	
And crying, Love I come, leapt lively in.	Hero and Leander	2.154	
Come live with mee, and be my love,	Passionate Shepherd	1	
Come <Then> live with mee, and be my love.	Passionate Shepherd	20	
COMEDIES			
Sweete speeches, comedies, and pleasing showes,	Edw	1.1.56	Gavstn
COMELIEST			
This Moore is comeliest, is he not? speake son.	Jew	2.3.144	Mater
COMELY			
Could I therefore her comely tresses teare?	Ovid's Elegies	1.7.11	
She looked sad: sad, comely I esteem'd her.	Ovid's Elegies	2.5.44	
Comely tall was she, comely tall shee's yet.	Ovid's Elegies	3.3.8	
COMES			
See how the night Ulysses-like comes forth,	Dido	1.1.70	Venus
Looke where she comes: Aeneas [view] <viewd> her well.	Dido	2.1.72	Illion
You shall not hurt my father when he comes.	Dido	3.1.80	Cupid
O here he comes, love, love, give Dido leave/To be more modest	Dido	3.1.94	Dido
My sister comes, I like not her sad lookes.	Dido	5.1.225	Dido
See where he comes, welcome, welcome my love.	Dido	5.1.261	Dido
It cannot choose, because it comes from you.	1Tamb	1.1.56	Cosroe
See how he comes?	1Tamb	3.3.3	Tamb
Now Tamburlaine, the mightie Souldane comes,	1Tamb	4.3.63	Souldn
And tels for trueth, submissions comes too late.	1Tamb	5.1.73	Tamb
Comes now as Turnus gainst Eneas did,	1Tamb	5.1.380	Philem
Comes marching on us, and determines straight,	2Tamb	2.2.27	1Msngr
the plaines/To spie what force comes to relieve the holde.	2Tamb	3.3.48	Techel
He comes and findes his sonnes have had no shares/In all the	2Tamb	4.1.47	Amyras
And when I look away, comes stealing on:	2Tamb	5.3.71	Tamb
Looke where he goes, but see, he comes againe/Because I stay:	2Tamb	5.3.75	Tamb
Hence comes it, that a strong built Citadell/Commands much more	Jew	Prol.22	Machvl
But who comes heare? How now.	Jew	1.1.48	Barab
The very Custome barely comes to more/Then many Merchants of	Jew	1.1.63	1Merch
And all I have is hers. But who comes here?	Jew	1.1.139	Barab
For he can counsell best in these affaires;/And here he comes.	Jew	1.1.143	2Jew
It may be so: but who comes here?	Jew	1.2.313	Abbass
Here comes the Jew, had not his goods bin seiz'd,	Jew	2.3.5	1Offcr
That when the offering-Bason comes to me,	Jew	2.3.28	Barab
Here comes Don Lodowicke the Governor's sonne,	Jew	2.3.30	Barab
Yonder comes Don Mathias, let us stay;	Jew	2.3.140	Barab
But stand aside, here comes Don Lodowicke.	Jew	2.3.217	Barab
And when he comes, she lockes her selfe up fast;	Jew	2.3.262	Barab
But keepe thy heart till Don Mathias comes.	Jew	2.3.307	Barab
There comes the villaine, now I'le be reveng'd.	Jew	2.3.333	Lodowk
Nay, if you will, stay till she comes her selfe.	Jew	2.3.352	Barab
And tell him that it comes from Lodowicke.	Jew	2.3.371	Barab
That he shall verily thinke it comes from him.	Jew	2.3.376	Ithimr
And now, save Pilia-borza, comes there none.	Jew	3.1.9	Curtzn
And here he comes.	Jew	3.1.11	Curtzn
But here comes cursed Ithimore with the Fryar.	Jew	3.3.49	Abigal
But who comes here?	Jew	3.4.13	Barab
What if I murder'd him e're Jacomo comes?	Jew	4.1.116	Barab
but the Exercise being done, see where he comes.	Jew	4.2.20	P Pilia
here's her house, and here she comes, and now would I were gone,	Jew	4.2.35	P Ithimr
And when he comes: Oh that he were but here!	Jew	4.3.17	Barab
And he from whom my most advantage comes,	Jew	5.2.113	Barab
Here, hold that knife, and when thou seest he comes,	Jew	5.5.37	Barab
Because the house of Burbon now comes in,	P 50	1.50	Admral
What fearfull cries comes from the river [Sene] <Rene>,/That	P 361	7.1	Ramus
That change their coulour when the winter comes,	P 721	14.24	Navrre
A mighty army comes from France with speed:	P 725	14.28	1Msngr
But see where he comes.	P1018	19.88	Capt
see where she comes, as if she droupt/To heare these newes.	P1062	19.132	Eprnon
Heere comes the king and the nobles/From the parlament, ile	Edw	1.1.72	Gavstn
Here comes my lord of Canterburies grace.	Edw	1.2.33	Warwck
he comes not back,/Unlesse the sea cast up his shipwrack body.	Edw	1.4.204	Lncstr
Against our friend the earle of Cornewall comes,	Edw	1.4.375	Edward
She neither walkes abroad, nor comes in sight:	Edw	2.1.24	Baldck
Leave of this jesting, here my lady comes.	Edw	2.1.56	Baldck
That shall wee see, looke where his lordship comes.	Edw	2.2.49	Lncstr
Heere comes she thats cause of all these jarres.	Edw	2.2.224	Edward
No, here he comes, now let them spoile and kill:	Edw	2.4.3	Edward

COMES (cont.)				
How comes it, that the king and he is parted?	Edw	2.4.41		Mortmr
My lord, here comes the Queene.	Edw	3.1.58		Spencr
Comes Leister then in Isabellas name,	Edw	4.7.64		Edward
Heere comes the yong prince, with the Earle of Kent.	Edw	5.2.75		Mortmr
How now, who comes there?	Edw	5.3.49		Gurney
None comes, sound trumpets.	Edw	5.4.79		Mortmr
Whose there, what light is that, wherefore comes thou?	Edw	5.5.42		Edward
And let me see the stroke before it comes,	Edw	5.5.76		Edward
Aye me, see where he comes, and they with him,	Edw	5.6.22		Queene
Heere comes the hearse, helpe me to moorne, my lords:	Edw	5.6.98		King
That shall we presently know, <for see> here comes his boy.	F 196	1.2.3		2Schol
How comes it then that he is Prince of Devils?	F 294	1.3.66		Faust
How comes it then that thou art out of hell?	F 303	1.3.75		Faust
Yonder he comes:	F1094	3.3.7	P	Dick
And with him comes the Germane Conjurer,	F1164	4.1.10		Mrtino
who comes to see/What wonders by blacke spels may compast be.	F1197	4.1.43		Mrtino
And all alone, comes walking in his gowne;	F1358	4.2.34		Fredrk
See, see, he comes.	F1362	4.2.38		Mrtino
See where he comes, dispatch, and kill the slave.	F1423	4.2.99		2Soldr
Behold an Army comes incontinent.	F1430	4.2.106		Faust
Come sirs, what shall we do now till mine Hostesse comes?	F1520	4.5.16	P	Dick
Looke sirs, comes he not, comes he not?	F1826	5.2.30	P	Faust
But Robin, here comes the vintner.	F App	p.234 4	P	Rafe
Her name comes from the thing:	Ovid's Elegies	1.8.3		
Now on <ore> the sea from her old love comes shee,	Ovid's Elegies	1.13.1		
But when she comes, [you] <your> swelling mounts sinck downe,	Ovid's Elegies	2.16.51		
Now comes the pompe; themselves let all men cheere:	Ovid's Elegies	3.2.43		
The shout is nigh; the golden pompe comes heere.	Ovid's Elegies	3.2.44		
Comes forth her [unkeembd] <unkeembe> locks a sunder tearing.	Ovid's Elegies	3.8.52		
With Calvus learnd Catullus comes <come> and greete him.	Ovid's Elegies	3.8.62		
Where Juno comes, each youth, and pretty maide,	Ovid's Elegies	3.12.23		
When the chiefe pompe comes, lowd the people hollow,	Ovid's Elegies	3.12.29		
COMEST				
But when thou comest they of their courses faile.	Ovid's Elegies	1.13.12		
COMETS (See also COMMETS)				
That shine as Comets, menacing revenge,	1Tamb	3.2.74		Agidas
COMFITES				
Eate Comfites in mine armes, and I will sing.	Dido	2.1.315		Venus
Eating sweet Comfites with Queene Didos maide,	Dido	5.1.47		Ascan
COMFORT				
and prevent their soules/From heavens of comfort, yet their age	1Tamb	5.1.90		1Virgn
To coole and comfort me with longer date,	1Tamb	5.1.277		Bajzth
Depriv'd of care, my heart with comfort dies,	1Tamb	5.1.431		Arabia
Drawes in the comfort of her latest breath/All dasled with the	2Tamb	2.4.13		Tamb
The comfort of my future happinesse/And hope to meet your	2Tamb	2.4.62		Zenoc
Then will I comfort all my vital parts,	2Tamb	5.3.100		Tamb
The comfort of mine age, my childrens hope,	Jew	1.2.150		Barab
That has no further comfort for his maime.	Jew	2.1.11		Barab
Comfort your selfe my Lord and have no doubt,	P 541	11.6		Navrre
We will finde comfort, money, men, and friends/Ere long, to bid	Edw	4.2.65		SrJohn
Leister, if gentle words might comfort me,	Edw	5.1.5		Edward
And in this torment, comfort finde I none,	Edw	5.1.81		Edward
and in any case/Let no man comfort him, if he chaunce to weepe,	Edw	5.2.64		Mortmr
To comfort you, and bring you joyfull newes.	Edw	5.5.43		Ltborn
Small comfort findes poore Edward in thy lookes,	Edw	5.5.44		Edward
I feele thy words to comfort my distressed soule,	F1735	5.1.62		Faust
COMFORTED				
Have beene by thee restored and comforted.	Edw	4.2.80		Mortmr
COMFORTINGS				
Those words of favour, and those comfortings,	1Tamb	3.2.62		Agidas
COMFORTLES				
This is no seate for one thats comfortles,	Dido	2.1.86		Aeneas
COMFORTS				
These words revive my thoughts and comforts me,	P1209	22.71		Navrre
These comforts that you give our wofull queene,	Edw	4.2.72		Kent
COMING (See also COMMING)				
And makes our hopes survive to [coming] <cunning> joyes:	Dido	1.1.154		Achat
COMMAND				
I might command you to be slaine for this,	1Tamb	1.1.23		Mycet
We have his highnesse letters to command/Aide and assistance if	1Tamb	1.2.19		Magnet
That may command thee peecemeale to be torne,	1Tamb	4.2.23		Tamb
Your love hath fortune so at his command,	1Tamb	5.1.373		Anippe
Choose which thou wilt, all are at thy command.	2Tamb	1.2.31		Callap
That would not kill and curse at Gods command,	2Tamb	2.1.55		Fredrk
And to command the citie, I will build/A Cytadell, that all	2Tamb	5.1.164		Tamb
I, I, no doubt but shee's at your command.	Jew	2.3.39		Barab
All that I have shall be at your command.	Jew	2.3.137		Barab
on the Machabees/I have it, Sir, and 'tis at your command.	Jew	2.3.154		Barab
The Jew is here, and rests at your command.	Jew	5.1.83		Barab
'Tis our command:	Jew	5.2.15		Calym
When as thy life shall be at their command?	Jew	5.2.33		Barab
Two lofty Turrets that command the Towne.	Jew	5.3.11		Calym
that move betweene the quiet Poles/Shall be at my command:	F 84	1.1.56		Faust
upon me whilst I live/To do what ever Faustus shall command:	F 265	1.3.37		Faust
shall be his servant, and be by him commanded <at his command>.	F 487	2.1.99	P	Faust
Hast thou, as earst I did command,	F 801	3.1.23		Faust
Go then command our Priests to sing a Dirge,	F1063	3.2.83		Pope
Thou couldst command the worlds obedience:	F1210	4.1.56		Emper
Thou shalt command the state of Germany,	F1323	4.1.169		Emper
For loe these Trees remove at my command,	F1426	4.2.102		Faust
Our servants, and our Courts at thy command.	F1624	4.6.67		Duke
I am content to do whatsoever your majesty shall command me.	F App	p.236 16	P	Faust

COMMAND (cont.)
Yet greedy Bauds command she curseth still, . . . Ovid's Elegies 1.10.23
Thou Goddesse doest command a warme South-blast, . . Ovid's Elegies 2.8.19
COMMANDE
Whose Crowne and kingdome rests at thy commande: . . Dido 3.4.58 Dido
COMMANDED
we were commanded straight/With reverence to draw it into Troy. Dido 2.1.167 Aeneas
He will; and has commanded all his men/To come ashore, and march Jew 5.5.14 Msngr
shall be his servant, and be by him commanded <at his command>. F 487 2.1.99 P Faust
COMMANDEMENT
Giving commandement to our generall hoste, ... 2Tamb 2.1.61 Sgsmnd
COMMANDEMENTE
A voustre commandemente Madam. . . . . Jew 4.4.38 Barab
COMMANDER
As great commander of this Easterne world, ... 1Tamb 2.7.62 Tamb
My Lord, the great Commander of the worlde, ... 1Tamb 3.3.13 Bassoe
And every one Commander of a world. . . . . . . 2Tamb 1.3.8 Tamb
Lord and Commander of these elements. . . . . . F 104 1.1.76 BdAngl
Arch-regent and Commander of all Spirits. . . . . . F 291 1.3.63 Mephst
COMMANDES
But now you see these letters and commandes, ... 1Tamb 1.2.21 Tamb
Commandes the hearts of his associates, ... 1Tamb 4.1.15 2Msngr
COMMANDING
Commanding all thy princely eie desires, ... 2Tamb 4.2.43 Therid
Tremble and quake at his commanding charmes? . . . . F1372 4.2.48 Fredrk
COMMANDS
But that eternall Jupiter commands. . . . . Dido 5.1.82 Aeneas
Wils and commands (for say not I intreat)/Not once to set his 1Tamb 3.1.27 Bajzth
Since Fate commands, and proud necessity. . . . . . 2Tamb 5.3.205 Therid
built Citadell/Commands much more then letters can import: Jew Prol.23 Machvl
In what Queen Mother or your grace commands. . . . . P 12 1.12 Navrre
The hautie Dane commands the narrow seas, ... Edw 2.2.168 Mortmr
No more then he commands, must we performe. . . . . F 270 1.3.42 Mephst
To compasse whatsoere your grace commands. . . . . F1226 4.1.72 Faust
First he commands such monsters Nature hatcht/Against her kind Lucan, First Booke 588
Cupid commands to move his ensignes further. . . . . Ovid's Elegies 2.12.28
One [her] <she> commands, who many things can give. . . Ovid's Elegies 3.7.62
COMMANDST
Ready to execute what thou commandst <desirst>. . . F 549 2.1.161 Mephst
COMMAUND
Why, are not all the Gods at thy commaund, ... Dido 1.1.30 Jupitr
Stay here Aeneas, and commaund as King. . . . . . Dido 4.4.39 Dido
Aeneas may commaund as many Moores, ... Dido 4.4.62 Dido
Commaund my guard to slay for their offence: . . . . Dido 4.4.72 Dido
of all these, commaund/Aeneas ride as Carthaginian King. . Dido 4.4.77 Dido
To one that can commaund what longs thereto: . . . . 1Tamb 2.5.23 Cosroe
To aske, and have: commaund, and be obeied. . . . . 1Tamb 2.5.62 Therid
That let your lives commaund in spight of death. . . . 2Tamb 5.3.160 Tamb
All this and more your highnes shall commaund, ... P 479 8.29 Lord
shewes did entertaine him/And promised to be at his commaund: P 875 17.70 Eprnon
And all his Minions stoup when I commaund: . . . . P 979 19.49 Guise
Whose service he may still commaund till death. . . . P1149 22.11 Navrre
Save or condemne, and in our name commaund, ... Edw 1.1.169 Edward
And Mortimer will rest at your commaund. . . . . . Edw 1.4.296 Mortmr
In this, or ought, your highnes shall commaund us. . . . Edw 1.4.384 Warwck
Binde us in kindenes all at your commaund. . . . . Edw 4.2.73 Kent
our port-maisters/Are not so careles of their kings commaund. Edw 4.3.23 Edward
Feare not my Lord, weele do as you commaund. . . . . Edw 5.2.66 Matrvs
The prince I rule, the queene do I commaund, ... Edw 5.4.48 Mortmr
And what I list commaund, who dare controwle? . . . . Edw 5.4.68 Mortmr
Nor I, and yet me thinkes I should commaund, ... Edw 5.4.97 King
Art thou king, must I die at thy commaund? . . . . Edw 5.4.103 Kent
At our commaund, once more away with him. . . . . . Edw 5.4.104 Mortmr
Conjurer laureate]/[That canst commaund great Mephostophilis], F 261 1.3.33A Faust
Five yeeres I lengthned thy commaund in France: . . . Lucan, First Booke 277
me,/Because at his commaund I wound not up/My conquering Eagles? Lucan, First Booke 339
COMMAUNDED
I am commaunded by immortall Jove, ... Dido 5.1.99 Aeneas
Doe as you are commaunded by my lord. . . . . . Edw 5.5.26 Matrvs
COMMAUNDER
Be thou commaunder of our royall fleete, ... Edw 1.4.354 Edward
COMMAUNDES
I am my Lord, in what your grace commaundes till death. . P 76 2.19 P Pothec
COMMAUNDING
And like an insolent commaunding lover, ... Hero and Leander 1.409
COMMAUNDS
Commaunds me leave these unrenowmed [reames] <beames>, . Dido 4.3.18 Aeneas
A king to beare these words and proud commaunds. . . . Edw 4.7.71 Abbot
My lorde, the counsell of the Queene commaunds, . . . Edw 5.1.135 Leistr
COMME
At every pore let blood comme dropping foorth, ... 1Tamb 5.1.227 Zabina
COMMENC'D
Having commenc'd, be a Divine in shew, ... F 31 1.1.3 Faust
COMMEND
Commend me to him, Sir, most humbly, ... Jew 4.3.47 Barab
Bartus be gone, commend me to his grace, ... P 911 18.12 Navrre
Weel make quick worke, commend me to your maister/My friend, and Edw 2.6.12 Warwck
Commend me to my sonne, and bid him rule/Better then I, yet how Edw 5.1.121 Edward
Commend me humblie to his Majestie, ... Edw 5.2.69 Queene
Wagner, commend me to me deerest friends, ... F 91 1.1.63 Faust
Rude man, 'tis vaine, thy damsell to commend/To keepers trust: Ovid's Elegies 3.4.1
COMMENDED
As I shall be commended and excusde/For turning my poore charge 1Tamb 2.3.28 Therid

COMMENDED (cont.)
He to th'Hetrurians Junoes feast commended, Ovid's Elegies 3.12.35
COMMENT
As for the Comment on the Machabees/I have it, Sir, and 'tis at Jew 2.3.153 Barab
That others needs to comment on my text? P 683 13.27 Guise
COMMENTS
And comments vollumes with her Yvory pen, 1Tamb 5.1.145 Tamb
COMMETS
Nor blazing Commets threatens Didos death, Dido 4.4.119 Dido
Were full of Commets and of blazing stars, 2Tamb 5.1.89 Tamb
And Commets that presage the fal of kingdoms. Lucan, First Booke 527
COMMING
To stay my comming gainst proud Tamburlaine. 2Tamb 1.1.163 Orcan
Waiting my comming to the river side, 2Tamb 1.2.22 Callap
I feare their comming will afflict us all. Jew 1.1.156 2Jew
And I shall dye too, for I feele death comming. Jew 3.6.8 Abigal
And doe attend my comming there by this. Jew 5.5.104 Calym
Stand close, he is comming, I know him by his voice. P1000 19.70 P 1Mur
My lord of Cornewall is a comming over, Edw 2.1.76 Neece
be,/That this proud Pope may Faustus [cunning] <comming> see. F 855 3.1.77 Faust
By [cunning] <comming> in <of> thine Art to crosse the Pope,/Or F 859 3.1.81 Mephst
His Majesty is comming to the Hall; F1158 4.1.4 Mrtino
And comming to the foord of Rubicon, Lucan, First Booke 187
how were we bestead/When comming conqueror, Roome afflicts me Lucan, First Booke 310
COMMINGE
yett comminge upon you once unawares he frayde you out againe. Paris ms12,p390 P Souldr
COMMINGS
Sirra, hast thou no commings in? F 346 1.4.4 P Wagner
Tel me sirra, hast thou any commings in? F App p.229 4 P Wagner
COMMINGS IN
Tel me sirra, hast thou any commings in? F App p.229 4 P Wagner
COMMISERATION
As no commiseration may expel, F App p.243 43 OldMan
COMMISSION
That's more then is in our Commission. Jew 1.2.22 Basso
If your commission serve to warrant this, P 475 8.25 Anjoy
A faire commission warrants what we do. Edw 4.7.48 Rice
The Queenes commission, urgd by Mortimer, Edw 4.7.49 Leistr
COMMIT
When shall you see a Jew commit the like? Jew 4.1.197 Barab
Why do you not commit him to the tower? Edw 2.2.234 Gavstn
I do commit this Gaveston to thee, Edw 2.5.107 Penbrk
Commit not to my youth things of more waight/Then fits a prince Edw 3.1.74 Prince
And therefore we commit you to the Tower, Edw 5.6.79 King
Will you sir? Commit the Rascals. F1602 4.6.45 Duke
Commit with us, he were as good commit with his father, as F1603 4.6.46 P Dick
us, he were as good commit with his father, as commit with us. F1603 4.6.46 P Dick
us, he were as good commit with his father, as commit with us. F1604 4.6.47 P Dick
COMMITS
Daily commits incivill outrages, 1Tamb 1.1.40 Meandr
COMMIT'ST
honour, and thereby/Commit'st a sinne far worse than perjurie. Hero and Leander 1.306
COMMITTED
Thou hast committed-- Jew 4.1.40 2Fryar
Then shall your charge committed to my trust. Edw 3.1.78 Prince
To these my love I foolishly committed/And then with sweete Ovid's Elegies 1.12.21
COMMITTING
Committing headdie ryots, incest, rapes: Hero and Leander 1.144
COMMIXT
Faire white with rose red was before commixt: Ovid's Elegies 3.3.5
COMMODIOUS
Thy service for nights scapes is knowne commodious/And to give Ovid's Elegies 1.11.3
COMMON
Humilitie belongs to common groomes. Dido 2.1.101 Dido
The common souldiers rich imbrodered coates, Dido 4.4.9 Dido
Which you that be but common souldiers, 1Tamb 2.2.63 Meandr
And gives no more than common courtesies. 1Tamb 3.2.63 Agidas
But every common souldier of my Camp/Shall smile to see thy 1Tamb 3.3.85 Tamb
To dresse the common souldiers meat and drink. 1Tamb 3.3.185 Zenoc
And if we should with common rites of Armes, 1Tamb 5.1.11 Govnr
wines/Shall common Souldiers drink in quaffing boules, 2Tamb 1.3.222 Tamb
The common souldiers of our mighty hoste/Shal bring thee bound 2Tamb 3.5.110 Trebiz
For not a common Souldier shall defile/His manly fingers with 2Tamb 4.1.163 Tamb
Where are my common souldiers now that fought/So Lion-like upon 2Tamb 4.3.67 Tamb
The violence of thy common Souldiours lust? 2Tamb 4.3.80 Orcan
And common souldiers jest with all their Truls. 2Tamb 4.3.91 Tamb
And better one want for a common good, Jew 1.2.98 Govnr
And fram'd of finer mold then common men, Jew 1.2.219 Barab
for the running streames/And common channels of the City. Jew 5.1.89 Barab
What glory is there in a common good, P 97 2.40 Guise
And common profit of Religion. P 647 12.60 Cardnl
This will be good newes to the common sort. Edw 1.4.92 Penbrk
Deserves no common place, nor meane reward: Edw 1.4.361 Edward
I am none of these common [pedants] <pendants> I, Edw 2.1.52 Baldck
By earth, the common mother of us all, Edw 3.1.128 Edward
[Is not thy common talke sound Aphorismes]? F 47 1.1.19A Faust
And cause we are no common guests, F 805 3.1.27 Mephst
Such blisse is onely common to us two, Ovid's Elegies 2.5.31
I feare with me is common now to many. Ovid's Elegies 3.11.6
COMMONS
And commons of this mightie Monarchie, 1Tamb 1.1.138 Ortyg
And when the commons and the nobles joyne, Edw 1.4.287 Mortmr
The murmuring commons overstretched hath. Edw 2.2.160 Mortmr

COMMONS (cont.)
The commons now begin to pitie him, Edw 5.4.2 Mortmr
To gaine the light unstable commons love, Lucan, First Booke 133
And I might pleade, and draw the Commons minds/To favour thee, Lucan, First Booke 275
Nor were the Commons only strooke to heart/With this vaine Lucan, First Booke 483
least some one hope might ease/The Commons jangling minds, Lucan, First Booke 521

COMMONWEALE
O miserable is that commonweale, Edw 5.3.63 Kent

COMM'ST
death, why comm'st thou not? 2Tamb 3.4.14 Olymp

COMPACT
A man compact of craft and perjurie, Dido 2.1.144 Aeneas
Compact of Rapine, Pyracie, and spoile, 1Tamb 4.3.8 Souldn

COMPANIE
We could have gone without your companie. Dido 3.3.14 Dido
Spencer, stay you and beare me companie, Edw 2.1.74 Neece
Do cosin, and ile beare thee companie. Edw 2.2.121 Lncstr
Choose of our lords to beare you companie, Edw 3.1.84 Edward
their soveraigne/His sports, his pleasures, and his companie: Edw 3.1.175 Edward
Till hee pay deerely for their companie. Edw 3.1.198 Lncstr
Then banish that pernicious companie? Edw 3.1.213 Mortmr
Your selfe, and those your chosen companie, Edw 4.7.6 Abbot
Do you betray us and our companie. Edw 4.7.25 Edward
To take my life, my companie from me? Edw 4.7.65 Edward
To companie my hart with sad laments, Edw 5.1.34 Edward
A dwarfish beldame beares me companie, Hero and Leander 1.353

COMPANIES
Straight summon'd he his severall companies/Unto the standard: Lucan, First Booke 297

COMPANION
Too meane to be companion to a Queene. Dido 2.1.89 Aeneas
my Companion-Bashawes, see I pray/How busie Barrabas is there Jew 5.5.51 Calym
Live thou with me as my companion. Edw 1.4.343 Edward
No, his companion, for he loves me well, Edw 2.1.13 Spencr
And this is my companion Prince in hell. F 640 2.2.89 Lucifr

COMPANION-BASHAWES
my Companion-Bashawes, see I pray/How busie Barrabas is there Jew 5.5.51 Calym

COMPANIONS
You sonnes of care, companions of my course, Dido 1.1.142 Aeneas
destinies/Have brought my sweete companions in such plight? Dido 2.1.60 Aeneas
Pesant, goe seeke companions like thy selfe, Dido 3.3.21 Dido
Question with thy companions and thy mates. Edw 2.5.73 Mortmr
am glad I have found you, you are a couple of fine companions: F1097 3.3.10 P Vintnr
[I meane his friends and nearest companions], F1142 3.3.55A 3Chor

COMPANY
An hundred horsmen of my company/Scowting abroad upon these 1Tamb 2.2.39 Spy
As if I lay with you for company. 2Tamb 4.1.39 Calyph
dooth weepe to see/Your sweet desires depriv'd my company, 2Tamb 5.3.247 Tamb
And, Barabas, I'le beare thee company. Jew 2.3.96 Lodowk
So might my man and I hang with you for company. Jew 4.1.182 Barab
Sister, I think your selfe will beare us company. P 21 1.21 Charls
having in their company divers of your nation, and others, Edw 4.3.33 P Spencr
the Duke of Vanholt doth earnestly entreate your company, and F1501 4.4.45 P Wagner
Sir, the Duke of Vanholt doth earnestly entreate your company. F App p.241 169 P Wagner
This goddesse company doth to me befall. Ovid's Elegies 3.1.44
The people by my company she pleasd, Ovid's Elegies 3.10.19

COMPAR'D
Compar'd with marriage, had you tried them both, Hero and Leander 1.263

COMPARD
And others are but shrubs compard to me, Edw 5.6.12 Mortmr

COMPARE
enjoy in heaven/Can not compare with kingly joyes in earth. 1Tamb 2.5.59 Therid
And now for store of wealth may I compare/With all the Jewes in Jew 4.1.55 Barab
[Whose heavenly beauty passeth all compare]. F1701 5.1.28A 3Schol
nor in the whole world can compare with thee, for the rare F App p.236 3 P Emper
Such is his forme as may with thine compare, Ovid's Elegies 1.8.33
Thy lofty stile with mine I not compare, Ovid's Elegies 3.1.39

COMPARISONS
To challenge us with your comparisons? Dido 3.3.20 Dido

COMPARST
Though thou comparst him to a flying Fish, Edw 2.2.43 Edward

COMPASSE
and thought by words/To compasse me, but yet he was deceiv'd: Dido 3.1.156 Dido
And closde in compasse of the killing bullet, 1Tamb 2.1.41 Cosroe
But closde within the compasse of a tent, 2Tamb 4.2.3 Olymp
we have cast, but cannot compasse it/By reason of the warres, Jew 1.2.47 Govnr
I must be forc'd to steale and compasse more. Jew 1.2.127 Barab
too late/Thou seek'st for much, but canst not compasse it. Jew 5.2.46 Barab
Within the compasse of a deadly toyle, P 205 4.3 QnMoth
Within the concave compasse of the Pole, F 765 2.3.44 2Chor
Within the compasse of one compleat yeare: F 822 3.1.44 Mephst
Thou know'st within the compasse of eight daies, F 847 3.1.69 Faust
<Well, I am content, to compasse then some sport>, F 989 (HC266)A Faust
With Magicke spels so compasse thee, F1002 3.2.22 Mephst
To compasse whatsoere your grace commands. F1226 4.1.72 Faust
And with bright restles fire compasse the earth, Lucan, First Booke 49
And of just compasse for her knuckles bee. Ovid's Elegies 2.15.6
But in lesse compasse her small fingers knit. Ovid's Elegies 2.15.20
What doest? thy wagon in lesse compasse bring. Ovid's Elegies 3.2.70

COMPASSION
On whom ruth and compassion ever waites, Dido 4.2.20 Iarbus
Yet in compassion of his wretched state, 1Tamb 4.3.35 Souldn
Compassion, love, vaine hope, and hartlesse feare, Jew 2.3.170 Barab
Could not but take compassion of my state. Edw 4.7.11 Edward

COMPAST			
Venus, how art thou compast with content,	Dido	1.1.135	Venus
Vast Gruntland compast with the frozen sea,	2Tamb	1.1.26	Orcan
Compast with Lethe, Styx, and Phlegeton,	2Tamb	3.2.13	Tamb
who comes to see/What wonders by blacke spels may compast be.	F1198	4.1.44	Mrtino
That in mine armes I would have compast him.	F1262	4.1.108	Emper
COMPELD			
Whom liberty to honest armes compeld,	Ovid's Elegies		3.14.9
COMPELST			
And thou compelst this prince to weare the crowne.	Edw	5.4.88	Kent
COMPETITOR			
Then shalt thou be Competitor with me,	1Tamb	1.2.208	Tamb
COMPILE			
Long hast thou loyterd, greater workes compile.	Ovid's Elegies		3.1.24
some (their violent passions to asswage)/Compile sharpe satyrs,	Hero and Leander		1.127
COMPLAIN (See also PLAINE)			
Oft have I heard your Majestie complain,	1Tamb	1.1.35	Meandr
COMPLAIN'D			
And muttering much, thus to themselves complain'd:	Lucan, First Booke		249
COMPLAIND			
Thus I complaind, but Love unlockt his quiver,	Ovid's Elegies		1.1.25
with sad and heavie cheare/Complaind to Cupid; Cupid for his	Hero and Leander		1.441
COMPLAINE			
That doe complaine the wounds of thousand waves,	Dido	1.2.8	Illion
I must say so, paine forceth me complaine.	P 540	11.5	Charls
For heele complaine unto the sea of Rome.	Edw	1.1.190	Kent
Let him complaine unto the sea of hell,	Edw	1.1.191	Gavstn
And to the king my brother there complaine,	Edw	2.4.66	Queene
First I complaine of imbecilitie,	Edw	5.4.60	Mortmr
COMPLAINES			
Complaines, that thou hast left her all forlorne.	Edw	2.2.173	Lncstr
COMPLAINT			
Madam, have done with care and sad complaint,	Edw	4.6.66	Mortmr
All wasting years have that complaint [out] <not> worne.	Ovid's Elegies		2.6.8
COMPLEAT			
This compleat armor, and this curtle-axe/Are adjuncts more	1Tamb	1.2.42	Tamb
Our warlike hoste in compleat armour rest,	2Tamb	1.1.8	Orcan
And shine in compleat vertue more than they,	2Tamb	1.3.51	Tamb
Within the compasse of one compleat yeare:	F 822	3.1.44	Mephst
COMPLEATE			
<As match the dayes within one compleate yeare>,	F 821	(HC265)A	Mephst
COMPLET			
Their shoulders broad, for complet armour fit,	1Tamb	3.3.107	Bajzth
COMPLEXION			
Pale of complexion:	1Tamb	2.1.19	Menaph
And casts a pale complexion on his cheeks.	1Tamb	3.2.75	Agidas
COMPLICES			
Against the Guisians and their complices.	P 910	18.11	Navrre
Have at the rebels, and their complices.	Edw	2.2.265	Edward
Thou comst from Mortimer and his complices,	Edw	3.1.153	Edward
How Baldocke, Spencer, and their complices,	Edw	4.6.78	Mortmr
COMPOSDE			
Whose sight composde of furie and of fire/Doth send such sterne	2Tamb	4.1.175	Trebiz
COMPOUND			
Thou mad'st thy head with compound poyson flow.	Ovid's Elegies		1.14.44
COMPOUNDED			
So when this worlds compounded union breakes,	Lucan, First Booke		73
COMPREHEND			
whose faculties can comprehend/The wondrous Architecture of the	1Tamb	2.7.21	Tamb
COMPREST			
Who that our bodies were comprest bewrayde?	Ovid's Elegies		2.8.5
COMPRISDE			
All this and more, if more may be comprisde,	P 143	2.86	Guise
COMPRIZ'D			
In whose sweete person is compriz'd the Sum/Of natures Skill	1Tamb	5.1.78	1Virgn
COMPULSION			
Not of compulsion or necessitie.	Edw	5.1.4	Leistr
COM'ST			
Nay [to] thine owne cost, villaine, if thou com'st.	Jew	4.3.59	Barab
Thou hast no name, but com'st from snowy mountaines;	Ovid's Elegies		3.5.91
COMST			
Assure thy selfe thou comst not in my sight.	Edw	1.4.169	Edward
Welcome old man, comst thou in Edwards aide?	Edw	3.1.34	Edward
Thou comst from Mortimer and his complices,	Edw	3.1.153	Edward
Villaine, I know thou comst to murther me.	Edw	5.5.45	Edward
Nor shalt thou triumph when thou comst to Roome;	Lucan, First Booke		287
CONCAVE			
Fenc'd with the concave of a monstrous rocke,	2Tamb	3.2.89	Tamb
lookes is much more majesty/Than from the Concave superficies,	2Tamb	3.4.48	Therid
Within the concave compasse of the Pole,	F 765	2.3.44	2Chor
Bred in the concave of some monstrous rocke:	F App	p.238 73	Knight
CONCEAL'D			
But what the secret trustie night conceal'd,	Hero and Leander		2.103
And love that is conceal'd, betraies poore lovers.	Hero and Leander		2.134
CONCEALE			
I must conceale/The torment, that it bootes me not reveale,	Dido	3.4.25	Dido
CONCEALED			
To practise Magicke and concealed Arts.	F 129	1.1.101	Faust
CONCEALES			
And Scyllaes wombe mad raging dogs conceales.	Ovid's Elegies		3.11.22
CONCEAV'D			
Till that a Princesse priest conceav'd by Mars,	Dido	1.1.106	Jupitr
Had not the heavens conceav'd with hel-borne clowdes,	Dido	1.1.125	Venus

CONCEIPT				
How am I glutted with conceipt of this?	F 105	1.1.77		Faust
CONCEIPTED				
O dull conceipted Dido, that till now/Didst never thinke Aeneas	Dido	3.1.82		Dido
CONCEIT (See also CONSAITS)				
That in conceit bear Empires on our speares,	1Tamb	1.2.64		Tamb
Whose cheekes and hearts so punisht with conceit,	1Tamb	5.1.87		1Virgn
nor the Turk/Troubled my sences with conceit of foile,	1Tamb	5.1.158		Tamb
Behold her wounded in conceit for thee,	1Tamb	5.1.415		Zenoc
As any thing of price with thy conceit?	2Tamb	5.1.14		Govnr
Till swolne with cunning of a selfe conceit,	F 20	Prol.20		1Chor
Then rest thee Faustus quiet in conceit.	F1483	4.4.27		Faust
Then rest thee Faustus quiet in conceit.	F App	p.240 126		Faust
CONCEITED				
Let base conceited wits admire vilde things,	Ovid's Elegies			1.15.35
CONCEITES				
Must needs have beauty beat on his conceites.	1Tamb	5.1.182		Tamb
CONCEITS				
And such conceits as clownage keepes in pay,	1Tamb	Prol.2		Prolog
With ceaselesse and disconsolate conceits,	1Tamb	3.2.14		Zenoc
CONCEIV'D				
As it hath chang'd my first conceiv'd disdaine.	1Tamb	3.2.12		Zenoc
But she conceiv'd of me, or I am sure/I oft have done, what	Ovid's Elegies			2.13.5
CONCEIVE (See also CONCEAV'D)				
Whereat the Souldiers will conceive more joy,	1Tamb	1.1.152		Ceneus
Conceive a second life in endlesse mercie.	2Tamb	2.3.9		Sgsmnd
Great joyes by hope I inly shall conceive.	Ovid's Elegies			2.9.44
CONCEIVED				
Declare the cause of my conceived griefe,	1Tamb	1.1.29		Mycet
CONCEIVING				
I thus conceiving and subduing both:	1Tamb	5.1.183		Tamb
friends and fellow kings)/Makes me to surfet in conceiving joy.	2Tamb	1.3.152		Tamb
CONCEPTION				
or els infernall, mixt/Their angry seeds at his conception:	1Tamb	2.6.10		Meandr
CONCERNE				
If any thing shall there concerne our state/Assure your selves	Jew	1.1.172		Barab
CONCERNES				
What els my lords, for it concernes me neere,	Edw	1.2.44		ArchBp
CONCERNETH				
Now then here know that it concerneth us--	Jew	1.2.42		Govnr
CONCERNING				
Concerning Bruno and the Emperour,	F 948	3.1.170		Pope
Concerning Bruno and the Emperour.	F1015	3.2.35		1Card
CONCISE				
have with [concise] <subtle> Sillogismes <Consissylogismes>	F 139	1.1.111		Faust
CONCLUDE				
Conclude a league of honor to my hope.	1Tamb	5.1.399		Zenoc
the king of Hungary/Should meet our person to conclude a truce.	2Tamb	1.1.10		Orcan
To conclude, he gave me ten crownes.	Jew	4.2.113	P	Pilia
Conclude against his father what thou wilt,	Edw	5.2.19		Queene
And to conclude, I am Protector now,	Edw	5.4.64		Mortmr
And to be short <conclude>, when all the world dissolves,	F 513	2.1.125		Mephst
CONCLUDED				
have concluded/That Midas brood shall sit in Honors chaire,	Hero and Leander			1.474
Thereon concluded that he was beloved.	Hero and Leander			2.220
CONCLUSION				
Whose short conclusion will seale up their hearts,	Dido	3.2.94		Juno
CONCOCTED				
That being concocted, turnes to crimson blood,	2Tamb	3.2.108		Tamb
CONCORD				
Full concord all your lives was you betwixt,	Ovid's Elegies			2.6.13
CONCUBINE				
Being supposde his worthlesse Concubine,	1Tamb	3.2.29		Agidas
Base Concubine, must thou be plac'd by me/That am the Empresse	1Tamb	3.3.166		Zabina
Cal'st thou me Concubine that am betroath'd/Unto the great and	1Tamb	3.3.169		Zenoc
The Souldans daughter for his Concubine,	1Tamb	4.1.5		Souldn
As Concubine I feare, to feed his lust.	1Tamb	4.3.42		Souldn
a hundred of the Jewes Crownes that I had such a Concubine.	Jew	3.1.28	P	Ithimr
CONCUBINES				
And in my Sarell tend my Concubines:	1Tamb	3.3.78		Bajzth
Who shal kisse the fairest of the Turkes Concubines first, when	2Tamb	4.1.64	P	Calyph
the pavilions/Of these proud Turks, and take their Concubines,	2Tamb	4.1.161		Tamb
Now fetch me out the Turkish Concubines,	2Tamb	4.3.64		Tamb
(I meane such Queens as were kings Concubines)/Take them,	2Tamb	4.3.71		Tamb
CONDEMN'D				
Shall be condemn'd, and then sent to the fire.	Jew	3.6.36		2Fryar
He shall be streight condemn'd of heresie,	F 962	3.1.184		Faust
Were by the holy Councell both condemn'd/For lothed Lollords,	F1021	3.2.41		Pope
What art thou Faustus but a man condemn'd to die?	F1478	4.4.22		Faust
CONDEMND				
what art thou Faustus but a man condemnd to die?	F App	p.240 121	P	Faust
CONDEMNE				
Save or condemne, and in our name commaund,	Edw	1.1.169		Edward
To binde or loose, lock fast, condemne, or judge,	F 935	3.1.157		Pope
Condemne his eyes, and say there is no tryall.	Ovid's Elegies			2.2.58
CONDEMNS				
Wherin the change I use condemns my faith,	1Tamb	5.1.390		Zenoc
CONDITION				
On this condition shall thy Turkes be sold.	Jew	2.2.42		Govnr
name, and therewithall/Thy birth, condition, and profession.	Jew	2.3.164		Barab
Of that condition I wil drink it up; here's to thee.	Jew	4.4.4	P	Ithimr
On that condition Lancaster will graunt.	Edw	1.4.292		Lncstr
condition Ile feede thy divel with horse-bread as long as he	F App	p.234 30	P	Rafe

CONDITION (cont.)				
To like a base wench of despisd condition.	Ovid's Elegies			2.7.20
CONDITIONALLY				
Conditionally that thou wilt stay with me,	Dido	3.1.114		Dido
But yet conditionally, that thou performe/All Covenants, and	F 479	2.1.91		Faust
CONDITIONS				
let peace be ratified/On these conditions specified before,	2Tamb	1.1.125		Orcan
Of whose conditions, and our solemne othes/Sign'd with our	2Tamb	1.1.143		Orcan
Since your hard conditions are such/That you will needs have	Jew	1.2.18		Govnr
to obtaine by peace/Then to enforce conditions by constraint.	Jew	1.2.26		Calym
On these conditions following:	F 484	2.1.96	P	Faust
CONDUCT				
it life, that under his conduct/We might saile backe to Troy,	Dido	2.1.17		Aeneas
To safe conduct us thorow Affrica.	1Tamb	1.2.16		Zenoc
you must expect/Letters of conduct from my mightinesse,	1Tamb	1.2.24		Tamb
And lead thy thousand horse with my conduct,	1Tamb	1.2.189		Tamb
and the Easterne theeves/Under the conduct of one Tamburlaine,	1Tamb	3.1.3		Bajzth
Thou that in conduct of thy happy stars,	1Tamb	5.1.358		Zenoc
Yet would I venture to conduct your Grace,	2Tamb	1.2.72		Almeda
you to come so farre/Without the ayd or conduct of their ships.	Jew	1.1.94		Barab
Gonzago conduct them thither, and then/Beset his house that not	P 288	5.15		Guise
attaine the gole/That shall conduct thee to celestial rest.	F App	p.243 37		OldMan
CONDUCTED				
Conducted me within the walles of Rome?	F 802	3.1.24		Faust
CONDY				
Prince Condy, and my good Lord Admirall,	P 2	1.2		Charls
Prince Condy and my good Lord Admiral,	P 27	1.27		Navrre
That are tutors to him and the prince of Condy--	P 427	7.67		Guise
CONFEDERATES				
it out, or manage armes/Against thy selfe or thy confederates:	2Tamb	1.1.129		Sgsmnd
Governour and these/Captaines, his consorts and confederates.	Jew	5.2.24		Barab
and here to pine in feare/Of Mortimer and his confederates.	Edw	4.7.36		Baldck
CONFERENCE				
Their conference will be a greater helpe to me,	F 95	1.1.67		Faust
And make me blest with your sage conference.	F 126	1.1.98		Faust
We will informe thee e're our conference cease.	F 184	1.1.156		Valdes
[And in their conference of what befell],	F1144	3.3.57A		3Chor
since our conference about faire Ladies, which was the	F1681	5.1.8	P	1Schol
how you crossed me in my conference with the emperour?	F App	p.238 77	P	Faust
CONFES				
Blame not us but the proverb, Confes and be hang'd.	Jew	4.1.146	P	Barab
CONFESSE				
When with their fearfull tongues they shall confesse/Theise are	1Tamb	1.2.222		Usumc
Though I confesse the othes they undertake,	2Tamb	2.1.42		Sgsmnd
I must confesse we come not to be Kings:	Jew	1.1.129		Barab
To worke my peace, this I confesse to thee;	Jew	3.6.31		Abigal
and I am resolv'd/You shall confesse me, and have all my goods.	Jew	4.1.86		Barab
Yes, 'cause you use to confesse.	Jew	4.1.145		Ithimr
Tell him you will confesse.	Jew	4.2.77	P	Pilia
Otherwise I'le confesse all:--	Jew	4.2.78	P	Ithimr
Or else I will confesse: I, there it goes:	Jew	4.3.4		Barab
now at my lodging/That was his Agent, he'll confesse it all.	Jew	5.1.17		Curtzn
Nay stay, my Lord, 'tmay be he will confesse.	Jew	5.1.25		1Knght
Confesse; what meane you, Lords, who should confesse?	Jew	5.1.26		Barab
I confesse; your sonne and Mathias were both contracted unto	Jew	5.1.28	P	Ithimr
I carried it, I confesse, but who writ it?	Jew	5.1.32	P	Ithimr
My Lords of Poland I must needs confesse,	P 451	8.1		Anjoy
I have deserv'd a scourge I must confesse,	P 544	11.9		Charls
I doe confesse it Faustus, and rejoyce;	F1885	5.2.89		Mephst
confesse my selfe farre inferior to the report men have	F App	p.236 12	P	Faust
a signe of grace in you, when you will confesse the trueth.	F App	p.237 45	P	Knight
Loe I confesse, I am thy captive I,	Ovid's Elegies			1.2.19
For I confesse, if that might merite favour,	Ovid's Elegies			2.4.3
And as a traitour mine owne fault confesse.	Ovid's Elegies			2.8.26
Such as confesse, have lost their good names by it.	Ovid's Elegies			3.13.6
CONFESSETH				
And he confesseth that he loves me not.	Edw	1.4.194		Queene
CONFESSING				
Confessing this, why doest thou touch him than?	Ovid's Elegies			3.7.22
CONFESSION				
Oh what a sad confession will there be?	Jew	3.6.4		2Fryar
Know that Confession must not be reveal'd,	Jew	3.6.33		2Fryar
CONFEST				
The Abbasse sent for me to be confest:	Jew	3.6.3		2Fryar
She has confest, and we are both undone,	Jew	4.1.46		Barab
CONFINES				
And in your confines with his lawlesse traine,	1Tamb	1.1.39		Meandr
About the confines of Bythinia?	1Tamb	4.3.25		Arabia
if any Christian King/Encroche upon the confines of thy realme,	2Tamb	1.1.147		Orcan
I left the confines and the bounds of Affrike/And made a voyage	2Tamb	1.3.207		Therid
CONFIRM				
What? bring you Scripture to confirm your wrongs?	Jew	1.2.110		Barab
CONFIRMATION				
Were it for confirmation of a League,	Jew	1.1.154		1Jew
CONFIRM'D				
to your dominions/Than ever yet confirm'd th'Egyptian Crown.	1Tamb	5.1.449		Tamb
of Natolia/Confirm'd this league beyond Danubius streame,	2Tamb	1.1.149		Orcan
Confirm'd by oth and Articles of peace,	2Tamb	2.1.29		Sgsmnd
And solemne covenants we have both confirm'd,	2Tamb	2.2.31		Orcan
CONFIRMD				
And Venus, let there be a match confirmd/Betwixt these two,	Dido	3.2.77		Juno
CONFIRME				
Who shall confirme my words with further deedes.	Dido	1.2.43		Iarbus

CONFIRME (cont.)				
He needed nct with wcrds confirme my feare,	1Tamb	3.2.92		Agidas
And I wil sheath it to confirme the same.	2Tamb	1.1.85		Sgsmnd
We came from Turky to confirme a league,	2Tamb	1.1.115		Gazell
But (Sigismcnd) confirme it with an oath,	2Tamb	1.1.131		Orcan
Confirme his banishment with our handes and seales.	Edw	1.2.71		ArchBp
What we confirme the king will frustrate.	Edw	1.2.72		Lncstr
And with my bloud againe I will confirme/The <My> former vow I	F1749	5.1.76		Faust
be witnesses to confirme what mine eares have heard reported,	F App	p.236 7	P	Emper
My mistris wish confirme with my request.	Ovid's Elegies	3.2.80		
CONFIRMING				
Confirming it with Ibis holy name,	1Tamb	4.3.37		Souldn
CONFOUND				
Sufficient to discomfort and confound/The trustlesse force of	2Tamb	2.2.61		Orcan
And furie wculd confound my present rest.	2Tamb	2.4.65		Zenoc
For I confound <He confounds> hell in Elizium:	F 287	1.3.59		Faust
Confound these passicns with a quiet sleepe:	F1481	4.4.25		Faust
Confound these passions with a quiet sleepe:	F App	p.240 124		Faust
And quite confound natures sweet harmony.	Hero and Leander	1.252		
CONFOUNDED				
That live confounded in disordered troopes,	1Tamb	2.2.60		Meandr
CONFOUNDS				
For I confound <He confounds> hell in Elizium:	F 287	1.3.59		Faust
CONFRONT				
And do confront and countermaund their king.	Edw	3.1.188		Edward
CONFRONTER				
This proud confronter of the Emperour,	F 897	3.1.119		Faust
CONFUSDE				
I knew the Organon to be confusde,	P 406	7.46		Ramus
CONFUSED				
Frighted with this confused noyse, I rose,	Dido	2.1.191		Aeneas
Confused stars shal meete, celestiall fire/Fleete on the	Lucan, First Booke	75		
There spred the colours, with confused noise/Of trumpets clange,	Lucan, First Booke	239		
CONFUSION				
Confusion light on him that helps thee thus.	1Tamb	4.2.84		Bajzth
Hel and confusion light upon their heads,	2Tamb	2.2.33		Gazell
I would have brought confusion on you all,	Jew	5.5.85		Barab
Then wilt thou tumble in confusion.	F1925	5.2.129		BdAngl
CONFUSIONS				
Shall finde it written on confusions front,	Dido	3.2.19		Juno
CONFUTE				
I will confute those blind Geographers/That make a triple	1Tamb	4.4.75		Tamb
CONGE				
And with a lowly conge to the ground,	Edw	5.4.49		Mortmr
CONGEALES				
My bloud congeales, and I can write no more.	F 451	2.1.63		Faust
CONGRATULATE (See GRATULATE)				
CONJEAL'D				
Shall water be conjeal'd and turn'd to ice?	Lucan, First Booke	647		
CONJEALED				
For freezing meteors and conjealed colde:	1Tamb	1.1.11		Cosroe
CONJOIN'D				
And all conjoin'd to meet the witlesse King,	1Tamb	2.1.64		Cosroe
CONJOYND				
And both our Deities conjoynd in one,	Dido	3.2.79		Juno
And dores ccnjoynd with an hard iron lock.	Ovid's Elegies	1.6.74		
CONJOYNES				
In vaine why flyest backe? force conjoynes us now:	Ovid's Elegies	3.2.19		
CONJUNCTIONS				
Why are <have wee> not Conjunctions, Oppositions, Aspects,	F 615	2.2.64	P	Faust
CONJUR'D				
him, as he was never conjur'd in his life, I warrant him:	F1092	3.3.5	P	Robin
CONJURE				
That I may conjure in some bushy <lustie> Grove,	F 178	1.1.150		Faust
This night I'le conjure tho I die therefore.	F 193	1.1.165		Faust
your foolery, for an my Maister come, he'le conjure you 'faith.	F 735	2.3.14	P	Dick
My Maister conjure me?	F 736	2.3.15	P	Robin
put off thy cloathes, and I'le conjure thee about presently:	F 746	2.3.25	P	Robin
us, I'le so conjure him, as he was never conjur'd in his life,	F1092	3.3.5	P	Robin
some on's have cause to know him; did he conjure thee too?	F1524	4.5.20	P	HrsCsr
Canst thou conjure with it?	F App	p.233 21	P	Rafe
CONJURER				
thou art Conjurer laureate]/[That canst commaund great	F 260	1.3.32A		Faust
And with him comes the Germane Conjurer,	F1164	4.1.10		Mrtino
and thou shalt see/This Conjurer performe such rare exploits,	F1186	4.1.32		Mrtino
shall controule him as well as the Conjurer, I warrant you.	F1203	4.1.49	P	Benvol
he lookes as like [a] conjurer as the Pope to a Coster-monger.	F1228	4.1.74	P	Benvol
us sway thy thoughts/From this attempt against the Conjurer.	F1326	4.2.2		Mrtino
Till with my sword I have that Conjurer slaine.	F1333	4.2.9		Benvol
By this (I know) the Conjurer is neere,	F1343	4.2.19		Benvol
And pants untill I see that Conjurer dead.	F1352	4.2.28		Benvol
Close, close, the Conjurer is at hand,	F1357	4.2.33		Fredrk
I heard them parly with the Conjurer.	F1422	4.2.98		1Soldr
I'le tell ycu the bravest tale how a Conjurer serv'd me; you	F1521	4.5.17	P	Carter
Ifaith he lookes much like a conjurer.	F App	p.236 11	P	Knight
CONJURING				
Did not my conjuring [speeches] raise thee? speake.	F 273	1.3.45		Faust
Therefore the shortest cut for conjuring/Is stoutly to abjure	F 280	1.3.52		Mephst
you Maister, will you teach me this conjuring Occupation?	F 381	1.4.39	P	Robin
I have gotten one of Doctor Faustus conjuring bookes, and now	F 723	2.3.2	P	Robin
tell me, in good sadnesse Robin, is that a conjuring booke?	F 744	2.3.23	P	Dick
Has not the Pope enough of conjuring yet?	F1189	4.1.35	P	Benvol
You whoreson conjuring scab, do you remember how you cosened me	F1662	4.6.105	P	HrsCsr

CONJURING (cont.)
here I ha stolne one of doctor Faustus conjuring books, and F App p.233 2 P Robin
for conjuring that ere was invented by any brimstone divel. F App p.233 20 P Robin
in Europe for nothing, thats one of my conjuring workes. . F App p.234 24 P Robin
upon our handes, and then to our conjuring in the divels name. F App p.234 33 P Robin
Nay, and you go to conjuring, Ile be gone. . . . F App p.237 57 P Knight

CONNING
conning his neck-verse I take it, looking of a Fryars . Jew 4.2.17 P Pilia

CONQUER
Then shall I touch her breast and conquer her. . . . Dido 3.1.6 Cupid
For if that any man could conquer me, ... Dido 3.1.137 Dido
and my souldiers looke/As if they meant to conquer Affrica. 1Tamb 3.3.10 Tamb
They are enough to conquer all the world/And you have won 2Tamb 1.3.67 Calyph
Be able to withstand and conquer him. . . . . 2Tamb 2.2.19 Gazell
Conquer, sacke, and utterly consume/Your cities and your golden 2Tamb 4.1.192 Tamb
It seemes they meant to conquer us my Lord, . . . 2Tamb 4.3.88 Therid
But presently be prest to conquer it. . . . . 2Tamb 4.3.96 Techel
Sicknes or death can never conquer me. . . . . 2Tamb 5.1.222 Tamb
Doubt not my lord, but we shal conquer him. . . . 2Tamb 5.2.12 Amasia
And seeks to conquer mighty Tamburlaine, ... 2Tamb 5.3.43 Tamb
let me see how much/Is left for me to conquer all the world, 2Tamb 5.3.124 Tamb
Nay let 'em combat, conquer, and kill all, . . . Jew 1.1.152 Barab
Then conquer Malta, or endanger us. . . . . . Jew 5.5.122 Govnr
First conquer all the earth, then turne thy force/Against Lucan, First Booke 22
With armes to conquer armlesse men is base, . . . Ovid's Elegies 1.2.22
Let us all conquer by our mistris favour. . . . . Ovid's Elegies 3.2.18
At least now conquer, and out-runne the rest: . . . Ovid's Elegies 3.2.79

CONQUER'D
By this my sword that conquer'd Persea, ... 1Tamb 3.3.82 Tamb
And beat thy braines out of thy conquer'd head: . . 1Tamb 5.1.287 Bajzth
I, liquid golde when we have conquer'd him, . . . 2Tamb 1.3.223 Tamb
But from Asphaltis, where I conquer'd you, . . . 2Tamb 4.3.5 Tamb
Till Titus and Vespasian conquer'd us)/Am I become as wealthy Jew 2.3.10 Barab
And how secure this conquer'd Iland stands/Inviron'd with the Jew 5.3.6 Calym
I wonder how it could be conquer'd thus? . . . . Jew 5.3.12 Calym
Had not sweete pleasure conquer'd deepe despaire. . . F 576 2.2.25 Faust
spread these flags that ten years space have conquer'd, . Lucan, First Booke 348
Conquer'd Corinna in my bosome layes. . . . . Ovid's Elegies 2.12.2
Love conquer'd shame, the furrowes dry were burnd, . . Ovid's Elegies 3.9.29

CONQUERD
So having conquerd Inde, was Bacchus hew, ... Ovid's Elegies 1.2.47
Io, a strong man conquerd this Wench, hollow. . . . Ovid's Elegies 1.7.38
The weary souldiour hath the conquerd fields, . . . Ovid's Elegies 2.9.19

CONQUERE
Before I conquere all the triple world. . . . . 2Tamb 4.3.63 Tamb

CONQUERED
horse shall sweat with martiall spoile/Of conquered kingdomes, 1Tamb 1.2.192 Tamb
Won with thy words, and conquered with thy looks, . . 1Tamb 1.2.228 Therid
And thus the Grecians shall be conquered. . . . . 1Tamb 3.1.67 Bajzth
My royall Lord is slaine or conquered, ... 1Tamb 3.3.209 Zenoc
As I have conquered kingdomes with my sword. . . . 2Tamb 2.4.136 Tamb
View me thy father that hath conquered kings, . . . 2Tamb 3.2.110 Tamb
No hope is left to save this conquered hold. . . . 2Tamb 3.4.3 Olymp
Turkes Concubines first, when my father hath conquered them. 2Tamb 4.1.65 P Calyph
Thorow the streets with troops of conquered kings, . . 2Tamb 4.3.114 Tamb
Upon the ruines of this conquered towne. . . . . 2Tamb 5.1.85 Tamb
Before himselfe or his be conquered. . . . . . 2Tamb 5.2.53 Callap
I conquered all as far as Zansibar. . . . . . 2Tamb 5.3.139 Tamb
Being conquered, we are plaugde with civil war. . . . Lucan, First Booke 108
And hold my conquered hands for thee to tie. . . . Ovid's Elegies 1.2.20
Who gardes [the] <thee> conquered with his conquering hands. Ovid's Elegies 1.2.52
While Rome of all the [conquered] <conquering> world is head. Ovid's Elegies 1.15.26

CONQUERERS
And leave the Mortimers conquerers behind? . . . Edw 4.5.5 Edward

CONQUEREST
And with thy lookes thou conquerest all thy foes: . . 1Tamb 1.1.75 Mycet
Thou with these souldiers conquerest gods and men, . . Ovid's Elegies 1.2.37

CONQUERING
tearms/And scourging kingdoms with his conquering sword. . 1Tamb Prol.6 Prolog
Where kings shall crouch unto our conquering swords, . 1Tamb 1.2.220 Usumc
This hand shal set them on your conquering heads: . . 1Tamb 3.3.31 Tamb
Our conquering swords shall marshal us the way/We use to march 1Tamb 3.3.148 Tamb
Are falne in clusters at my conquering feet. . . . 1Tamb 3.3.230 Tamb
Yet would the Souldane by his conquering power, . . 1Tamb 4.1.33 Souldn
Conquering the people underneath our feet, . . . 1Tamb 4.4.137 Tamb
victorie we yeeld/May bind the temples of his conquering head, 1Tamb 5.1.56 2Virgn
From dangerous battel of my conquering Love. . . . 1Tamb 5.1.442 Zenoc
Adding more courage to my conquering mind. . . . 1Tamb 5.1.515 Tamb
Neere Guyrons head doth set his conquering feet, . . 2Tamb 1.1.17 Gazell
But when they list, their conquering fathers hart: . . 2Tamb 1.3.36 Zenoc
Stretching your conquering armes from east to west: . . 2Tamb 1.3.97 Tamb
And conquering that, made haste to Nubia, ... 2Tamb 1.3.202 Techel
And cuts down armies with his [conquering] <conquerings> wings. 2Tamb 4.1.6 Amyras
For conquering the Tyrant of the world. . . . . 2Tamb 5.2.55 Callap
And kneele for mercy to your conquering foe: . . . Jew 5.2.2 Calym
The conquering [Hercules] <Hector> for Hilas wept, . . Edw 1.4.393 Mort.Sr
Not to be wonne by any conquering Prince: . . . . F 783 3.1.5 Faust
We sing, whose conquering swords their own breasts launcht, Lucan, First Booke 3
would dim/Olde triumphs, and that Caesars conquering France, Lucan, First Booke 122
Because at his commaund I wound not up/My conquering Eagles? Lucan, First Booke 340
Who gardes [the] <thee> conquered with his conquering hands. Ovid's Elegies 1.2.52
While Rome of all the [conquered] <conquering> world is head. Ovid's Elegies 1.15.26
He had not beene that conquering Rome did build. . . Ovid's Elegies 2.14.16

CONQUERING (cont.)			
The other gives my love a conquering name,	Ovid's Elegies	3.1.65	
Goddesse come here, make my love conquering.	Ovid's Elegies	3.2.46	
CONQUERINGS			
And cuts down armies with his [conquering] <conquerings> wings.	2Tamb	4.1.6	Amyras
CONQUEROR			
Speakes not Aeneas like a Conqueror?	Dido	4.4.93	Dido
Now king of Bassoes, who is Conqueror?	1Tamb	3.3.212	Tamb
how were we bestead/When comming conqueror, Roome afflicts me	Lucan, First Booke		310
Go now thou Conqueror, glorious triumphs raise,	Ovid's Elegies		1.7.35
CONQUERORS			
that in former age/Hast bene the seat of mightie Conquerors,	1Tamb	1.1.7	Cosroe
Thy wit will make us Conquerors to day.	1Tamb	2.2.58	Mycet
Or let 'em warre, so we be conquerors:	Jew	1.1.151	Barab
Bearing old spoiles and conquerors monuments,	Lucan, First Booke		138
CONQUEROUR			
And from mine ashes let a Conquerour rise,	Dido	5.1.306	Dido
To gaine the tytle of a Conquerour,	1Tamb	1.1.125	Menaph
Great King and conquerour of Grecia,	1Tamb	3.1.24	Bajzth
That I may see him issue Conquerour.	1Tamb	3.3.194	Zenoc
But that he lives and will be Conquerour.	1Tamb	3.3.211	Zenoc
And use us like a loving Conquerour.	1Tamb	5.1.23	Govnr
And never meant to make a Conquerour,	2Tamb	3.5.83	Tamb
And use us like a loving Conquerour.	2Tamb	5.1.28	1Citzn
We would behold that famous Conquerour,	F1231	4.1.77	Emper
where lies intombde this famous Conquerour,	F App	p.237 31	Emper
Yet whom thou favourst, pray may conquerour be.	Ovid's Elegies		3.2.2
CONQUEROURS			
Fight as you ever did, like Conquerours,	2Tamb	3.5.160	Tamb
Or hold our citie from the Conquerours hands.	2Tamb	5.1.5	Maxim
CONQUERS			
Must grace his bed that conquers Asia:	1Tamb	1.2.37	Tamb
CONQUEST			
Come bring them in, and for this happy conquest/Triumph, and	1Tamb	3.3.272	Tamb
Lord, and fresh supply/Of conquest, and of spoile is offered us.	1Tamb	5.1.197	Techel
whose worthinesse/Deserves a conquest over every hart:	1Tamb	5.1.208	Tamb
Sleep'st every night with conquest on thy browes,	1Tamb	5.1.359	Zenoc
And let not conquest ruthlesly pursewde/Be equally against his	1Tamb	5.1.366	Zenoc
Meaning to make a conquest of our land:	2Tamb	1.1.49	Gazell
Of Greekish wine now let us celebrate/Our happy conquest, and	2Tamb	2.3.47	Orcan
Some, that in conquest of the perjur'd Christian,	2Tamb	3.1.39	Orcan
And threaten conquest on our Soveraigne:	2Tamb	5.3.14	Therid
Hell strives with grace for conquest in my breast:	F1741	5.1.68	Faust
denies all, with thy bloud must thou/Abie thy conquest past:	Lucan, First Booke		290
Is conquest got by civill war so hainous?	Lucan, First Booke		367
doth favour/That seekes the conquest by her loose behaviour.	Ovid's Elegies		2.5.12
CONQUESTES			
Besides the honor in assured conquestes:	1Tamb	1.2.219	Usumc
CONQUESTS			
I hate thee not, to thee my conquests stoope,	Lucan, First Booke		203
CONSAITS			
Let mean consaits, and baser men feare death,	P 997	19.67	Guise
CONSCIENCE			
It works remorse of conscience in me,	2Tamb	4.1.28	Calyph
Happily some haplesse man hath conscience,	Jew	1.1.119	Barab
And for his conscience lives in beggery.	Jew	1.1.120	Barab
Should for their conscience taste such rutheles ends.	P 214	4.12	Charls
the Jacobyns, that for my conscience sake will kill the King.	P1130	21.24	P Frier
His conscience kils it, and his labouring braine,	F1809	5.2.13	Mephst
CONSECRATAM			
et consecratam aquam quam nunc spargo; signumque crucis quod	F 248	1.3.20	P Faust
CONSECRATE			
Are to your highnesse vowd and consecrate.	Edw	3.1.171	Herald
The flame in Alba consecrate to Jove,	Lucan, First Booke		548
Subscribing that to her I consecrate/My faithfull tables being	Ovid's Elegies		1.11.27
CONSENT			
But much I feare my sonne will nere consent,	Dido	3.2.82	Venus
And would not all our souldiers soone consent,	1Tamb	2.5.78	Tamb
not but faire Zenocrate/Will soone consent to satisfy us both.	1Tamb	5.1.499	Tamb
nay we dare not give consent/By reason of a Tributary league.	Jew	2.2.22	Govnr
Yet crave I thy consent.	Jew	2.3.299	Lodowk
With free consent a hundred thousand pounds.	Jew	5.5.20	Govnr
If that the King had given consent thereto,	P 33	1.33	Navrre
Guise/Dares once adventure without the Kings consent,	P 37	1.37	Admral
(aspiring Guise)/Durst be in armes without the Kings consent?	P 829	17.24	Eprnon
of Loraine by the Kings consent is lately strangled unto death.	P1123	21.17	P Frier
Will meete, and with a generall consent,	Edw	1.2.70	ArchBp
Without election, and a true consent:	F 887	3.1.109	Pope
By full consent of all the [reverend] <holy> Synod/Of Priests	F 952	3.1.174	Faust
CONSEQUENTLY			
Why then belike/We must sinne, and so consequently die,/I, we	F 72	1.1.44	Faust
CONSERVE			
Live still my Love and so conserve my life,	2Tamb	2.4.55	Tamb
CONSERVES			
Ile give thee Sugar-almonds, sweete Conserves,	Dido	2.1.305	Venus
CONSIDER			
I hope your Highnesse will consider us.	Jew	1.2.9	Govnr
Anjoy hath well advisde/Your highnes to consider of the thing,	P 220	4.18	Guise
CONSIDERING			
Considering of these dangerous times.	P 175	3.10	Admral
CONSINUATE			
Our faiths are sound, and must be [consumate] <consinuate>,	2Tamb	2.1.47	Sgsmnd
CONSISSYLOGISMES			
have with [concise] <subtle> Sillogismes <Consissylogismes>	F 135	1.1.111	Faust

CONSISTORY			
Go forth-with to our holy Consistory,	F 882	3.1.104	Pope
Follow the Cardinals to the Consistory;	F 892	3.1.114	Faust
But whilst they sleepe within the Consistory,	F 943	3.1.165	Faust
To morrow, sitting in our Consistory,	F 967	3.1.189	Pope
To morrow we would sit i'th Consistory,	F1017	3.2.37	Pope
CONSISTS			
That love is childish which consists in words.	Dido	3.1.10	Iarbus
His honor, that consists in sheading blood,	1Tamb	5.1.477	Tamb
Made of the mould whereof thy selfe consists,	2Tamb	4.1.115	Tamb
of judgement frame/This is the ware wherein consists my wealth:	Jew	1.1.33	Barab
His heart consists of flint, and hardest steele,	Ovid's Elegies		3.5.59
Whose waight consists in nothing but her name,	Hero and Leander		2.114
CONSORT			
Me thinks, tis a great deale better than a consort of musicke.	1Tamb	4.4.60	P Therid
Will not his grace consort the Emperour?	F1162	4.1.8	Fredrk
Who doubts, with Pelius, Thetis did consort,	Ovid's Elegies		2.17.17
CONSORTS			
Governour and these/Captaines, his consorts and confederates.	Jew	5.2.24	Barab
Now as for Calymath and his consorts,	Jew	5.5.32	Barab
CONSPIRACIE			
In quittance of their late conspiracie/Against our State, and	F 949	3.1.171	Pope
CONSPIR'D			
And melting, heavens conspir'd his over-throw:	F 22	Prol.22	1Chor
Conspir'd against our God with Lucifer,	F 299	1.3.71	Mephst
whose heart <art> conspir'd/Benvolio's shame before the	F1373	4.2.49	Mrtino
CONSPIRDE			
But you I feare, conspirde with Mortimer.	Edw	5.6.37	King
CONSPIRE			
and once againe conspire/Against the life of me poore Carthage	Dido	4.4.131	Dido
And all the earthly Potentates conspire,	1Tamb	2.7.59	Tamb
Then it should so conspire my overthrow.	1Tamb	4.2.11	Tamb
Now let the treacherous Mortimers conspire,	Edw	1.1.149	Edward
Nay all of them conspire to crosse me thus,	Edw	2.2.95	Edward
diest, for Mortimer/And Isabell doe kisse while they conspire,	Edw	4.6.13	Kent
Elect, conspire, install, do what you will,	Edw	5.1.88	Edward
I might, but heavens and earth conspire/To make me miserable:	Edw	5.1.96	Edward
CONSTABLE			
Nor me neither, I cannot out-run you Constable, oh my belly.	Jew	5.1.20	P Ithimr
Come villaine to the Constable.	F App	p.241 157	P Mephst
CONSTANT			
and as constant report goeth, they intend to give king Edward	Edw	4.3.34	P Spencr
And to the end your constant faith stood fixt.	Ovid's Elegies		2.6.14
Th'Arcadian Virgins constant love hath wunne?	Ovid's Elegies		3.5.30
CONSTANTINOPLE			
from our dreadful siege/Of the famous Grecian Constantinople.	1Tamb	3.1.6	Bajzth
Constantinople have they brought me now <am I hither brought>,	F1118	3.3.31	Mephst
From Constantinople am I hither come,	F App	p.235 38	Mephst
How, from Constantinople?	F App	p.235 40	P Robin
CONSTANTLY			
To me to morrow constantly deny it.	Ovid's Elegies		1.4.70
CONSTER			
Whats heere? I know not how to conster it.	Edw	5.5.15	Gurney
CONSTRAIN'D			
Constrain'd against thy will give it the pezant,	Ovid's Elegies		1.4.65
CONSTRAIND			
And doth constraind, what you do of good will.	Ovid's Elegies		1.10.24
She first constraind bulles necks to beare the yoake,	Ovid's Elegies		3.9.13
CONSTRAINED			
And let thine eyes constrained learne to weepe,	Ovid's Elegies		1.8.83
CONSTRAINT			
to obtaine by peace/Then to enforce conditions by constraint.	Jew	1.2.26	Calym
CONSTRUE (See CONSTER)			
CONSULS			
Both we will raigne as Consuls of the earth,	1Tamb	1.2.197	Tamb
That lawes were broake, Tribunes with Consuls strove,	Lucan, First Booke		179
and flying/Left hateful warre decreed to both the Consuls.	Lucan, First Booke		486
CONSUMATE			
Our faiths are sound, and must be [consumate] <consinuate>,	2Tamb	2.1.47	Sgsmnd
We think it good to goe and consumate/The rest, with hearing of	P 19	1.19	Charls
CONSUM'D			
As is that towne, so is my heart consum'd,	2Tamb	3.2.49	Amyras
And heaven consum'd his choisest living fire.	2Tamb	5.3.251	Amyras
shut/His souldiers, till I have consum'd 'em all with fire?	Jew	5.2.82	Barab
CONSUME			
Where daliance doth consume a Souldiers strength,	Dido	4.3.34	Achat
How long shall I with griefe consume my daies,	Dido	5.1.281	Iarbus
That shall consume all that this stranger left,	Dido	5.1.285	Dido
So scatter and consume them in his rage,	1Tamb	4.1.34	Souldn
This cursed towne will I consume with fire,	2Tamb	2.4.137	Tamb
Madam, sooner shall fire consume us both,	2Tamb	3.4.73	Techel
remorsefull blood)/Drie up with anger, and consume with heat.	2Tamb	4.1.180	Soria
sacke, and utterly consume/Your cities and your golden pallaces,	2Tamb	4.1.192	Tamb
Tut, men should not their courage so consume.	Ovid's Elegies		3.3.34
CONSUMED			
two deceased princes which long since are consumed to dust.	F App	p.237 43	P Faust
CONSUMES			
His life that so consumes Zenocrate,	1Tamb	5.1.154	Tamb
CONSUMING			
Like water gushing from consuming snowe.	Ovid's Elegies		1.7.58
CONSUMMATUM			
Consummatum est:	F 463	2.1.75	Faust
CONSUMPTION			
shee will fall into a consumption with freatting, and then she	1Tamb	4.4.49	P Tamb

CONSUMPTION (cont.)			
teares of Mahomet/For hot consumption of his countries pride:	2Tamb	4.1.197	Tamb
CONTAGION			
of the silent night/Doth shake contagion from her sable wings;	Jew	2.1.4	Barab
CONTAGIOUS			
Contagious smels, and vapors to infect thee, . . .	2Tamb	4.2.11	Olymp
CONTAIN'D			
Were in that citie all the world contain'd, ...	1Tamb	4.2.121	Tamb
Art/Wherein all natures [treasury] <treasure> is contain'd:	F 102	1.1.74	BdAngl
Do [match] <watch> the number of the daies contain'd, .	F 821	3.1.43	Mephst
A small thin skinne contain'd the vital parts, . . .	Lucan, First Booke		622
CONTAINE			
Each word she sayes will then containe a Crowne, . .	Dido	4.3.53	Aeneas
What length or bredth shal this brave towne containe? .	Dido	5.1.16	Achat
minute end our daies, and one sepulcher/Containe our bodies:	2Tamb	3.4.14	Olymp
al this aery region/Cannot containe the state of Tamburlaine.	2Tamb	4.1.120	Tamb
Yet scarse my hands from thee containe I well. . . .	Ovid's Elegies		1.4.10
CONTAINED			
More fitly had [they] <thy> wrangling bondes contained/From	Ovid's Elegies		1.12.23
CONTAINES			
To hold the fiery spirit it containes, ...	2Tamb	5.3.169	Tamb
Containes his death, yet bids them save his life. . .	Edw	5.4.7	Mortmr
containes <containeth> for to delight thine eyes <thee with>,	F 810	3.1.32	Mephst
Sulmo, Pelignies third part me containes, ...	Ovid's Elegies		2.16.1
CONTAINETH			
containes <containeth> for to delight thine eyes <thee with>,	F 810	3.1.32	Mephst
CONTAINS			
Because my places being but three, contains all his: .	P 405	7.45	Ramus
CONTEINE			
For five score Nimphes, or more our flouds conteine. .	Ovid's Elegies		3.5.64
CONTEINES			
although vine-planted ground/Conteines me, though the streames	Ovid's Elegies		2.16.34
Scarse rests of all what a small urne conteines. . .	Ovid's Elegies		3.8.40
CONTEMNE			
But droope not madam, noble mindes contemne/Despaire: .	Edw	4.2.16	SrJohn
CONTEMNER			
and to subdew/This proud contemner of thy dreadfull power,	2Tamb	4.3.40	Orcan
CONTEMPLATIVE			
Father, this life contemplative is heaven, ...	Edw	4.7.20	Edward
CONTEMPT			
Pardon my Love, oh pardon his contempt, ...	1Tamb	5.1.364	Zenoc
CONTEMPTIBLE			
[Unpleasant, harsh, contemptible and vilde]:	F 136	1.1.108A	Faust
CONTEMPTUOUS			
To be reveng'd for these contemptuous words. . . .	1Tamb	1.1.100	Mycet
To bridle their contemptuous cursing tongues, . . .	2Tamb	4.3.44	Therid
CONTEND			
To prove him foolish did I ere contend?	Ovid's Elegies		2.8.10
CONTENT (Homograph)			
Sit on my knee, and call for thy content, ...	Dido	1.1.28	Jupitr
Content thee Cytherea in thy care, ...	Dido	1.1.82	Jupitr
Venus, how art thou compast with content, ...	Dido	1.1.135	Venus
Live happie in the height of all content, ...	Dido	1.1.195	Aeneas
Ile have it so, Aeneas be content.	Dido	2.1.95	Dido
That overcloy my soule with their content:	Dido	3.2.63	Juno
Whose bloud will reconcile thee to content, ...	Dido	3.3.74	Iarbus
But time will discontinue her content, ...	Dido	3.3.78	Iarbus
Whose golden Crowne might ballance my content: . . .	Dido	3.4.36	Dido
Tell him, I am content to take a truce, ...	1Tamb	3.1.31	Bajzth
And might content the Queene of heaven as well, . . .	1Tamb	3.2.11	Zenoc
Content thy selfe, his person shall be safe, ...	1Tamb	4.4.87	Tamb
Madam content your self and be resolv'd, ...	1Tamb	5.1.372	Anippe
Tell me sweet boie, art thou content to die? . . .	2Tamb	3.4.18	Olymp
Content my Lord, but what shal we play for?	2Tamb	4.1.63	P Perdic
Live [continent] <content> then (ye slaves) and meet not me	2Tamb	4.3.81	Tamb
Content thee, Barabas, thou hast nought but right. . .	Jew	1.2.152	Govnr
I am content to lose some of my Crownes;	Jew	2.3.178	Barab
This is meere frailty, brethren, be content.	Jew	4.1.98	Barab
Content, but we will leave this paltry land, ...	Jew	4.2.88	Ithimr
Content thee, Calymath, here thou must stay, ...	Jew	5.5.118	Govnr
Content, I will goe visite the Admirall.	P 251	4.49	Charls
At thy request I am content thou goe, ...	P 746	15.4	King
Content.	Edw	1.2.76	Mortmr
if this content you not,/Make severall kingdomes of this .	Edw	1.4.69	Edward
Are you content to banish him the realme?	Edw	1.4.84	ArchBp
I see I must, and therefore am content.	Edw	1.4.85	Edward
Sweete husband be content, they all love you. . . .	Edw	2.2.36	Queene
Content, ile beare my part, holla whose there? . . .	Edw	2.2.130	Lncstr
So shall my eyes receive their last content, ...	Edw	5.1.61	Edward
But bee content, seeing it his highnesse pleasure. . .	Edw	5.2.94	Queene
Sonne, be content, I dare not speake a worde. . . .	Edw	5.4.96	Queene
<Well, I am content, to compasse then some sport>, . .	F 989	(HC266)A	Faust
I am content for this once to thrust my head out at a window:	F1199	4.1.45	P Benvol
Be it as Faustus please, we are content.	F1253	4.1.99	Emper
I, I, and I am content too:	F1254	4.1.100	P Benvol
which being all I desire, I am content to remove his hornes.	F1314	4.1.160	P Faust
Madam, I will do more then this for your content. . .	F1575	4.6.18	P Faust
I'le gage my credit, 'twill content your grace. . . .	F1622	4.6.65	Faust
I am content to do whatsoever your majesty shall command me.	F App	p.236 15	P Faust
I doubt not shal sufficiently content your Imperiall majesty.	F App	p.237 49	P Faust
being all I desire, I am content to release him of his hornes:	F App	p.238 84	P Faust
thing then this, so it would content you, you should have it	F App	p.242 14	P Faust
I am glad they content you so Madam.	F App	p.242 27	P Faust

CONTENT (cont.)				
Then such as in their bondage feele content.	Ovid's Elegies	1.2.18		
Thy muse hath played what may milde girles content,	Ovid's Elegies	3.1.27		
When our bookes did my mistris faire content,	Ovid's Elegies	3.7.5		
with th'earth thou wert content,/Why seek'st not heav'n the	Ovid's Elegies	3.7.49		
CONTENTATION				
Ile clip and kisse thee with all contentation,	Ovid's Elegies	2.11.45		
CONTENTED				
Then shal I die with full contented heart,	1Tamb	5.1.417		Arabia
CONTENTMENT				
Of thy deserv'd contentment and thy love:	1Tamb	5.1.427		Arabia
CONTENTS				
And then devise what best contents thy minde,	F 858	3.1.80		Mephst
My gratious Lord, I am glad it contents you so wel:	F App	p.242 3	P	Faust
CONTERMIN'D				
Strong contermin'd <countermur'd> with other petty Iles;	Jew	5.3.8		Calym
CONTINENT				
And continent to your Dominions:	1Tamb	1.1.128		Menaph
Have fetcht about the Indian continent:	1Tamb	3.3.254		Tamb
And made it dance upon the Continent:	2Tamb	1.1.88		Orcan
But every where fils every Continent,	2Tamb	2.2.51		Orcan
Live [continent] <content> then (ye slaves) and meet not me	2Tamb	4.3.81		Tamb
And make that Country <land>, continent to Spaine,	F 336	1.3.108		Faust
CONTINENTS				
Be famous through the furthest continents,	2Tamb	4.3.110		Tamb
CONTINUALL				
spirits may vex/Your slavish bosomes with continuall paines,	2Tamb	5.1.46		Govnr
And body with continuall moorning wasted:	Edw	2.4.25		Queene
CONTINUALLY				
From whence a dampe continually ariseth,	Edw	5.5.4		Matrvs
One plaies continually upon a Drum,	Edw	5.5.61		Edward
CONTINUANCE				
Verses alone are with continuance crown'd.	Ovid's Elegies	3.8.28		
CONTINUE				
Continue ever thou celestiall sunne,	Edw	5.1.64		Edward
But can my ayre of life continue long,	Edw	5.3.17		Edward
Jawes flesht with bloud continue murderous.	Lucan, First Booke	332		
onely gives us peace, o Rome continue/The course of mischiefe,	Lucan, First Booke	669		
So shall my love continue many yeares,	Ovid's Elegies	2.19.23		
CONTINUED				
But long this blessed time continued not;	Hero and Leander	1.459		
CONTRACT				
My father did contract me to 'em both:	Jew	3.6.22		Abigal
CONTRACTED				
your sonne and Mathias were both contracted unto Abigall; [he]	Jew	5.1.29	P	Ithimr
CONTRADICT				
To contradict which, I say Ramus shall dye:	P 396	7.36		Guise
Beseemes it thee to contradict thy king?	Edw	1.1.92		Edward
CONTRARIA				
league,/Littora littoribus contraria, fluctibus undas/Imprecor:	Dido	5.1.310		Dido
CONTRARIE				
Even as a boate, tost by contrarie winde,	Ovid's Elegies	2.10.9		
CONTRARIES				
In no respect can contraries be true.	Edw	1.4.249		Lncstr
CONTRARY				
But <Faustus> I am an instance to prove the contrary:	F 525	2.1.137		Mephst
Thou calst on <talkst of> Christ contrary to thy promise.	F 643	2.2.92		Lucifr
in the contrary circle it is likewise Summer with them, as in	F1583	4.6.26	P	Faust
us, in the contrary circle it is summer with them, as in India,	F App	p.242 21	P	Faust
CONTRIBUTARY				
And both contributary to my Crowne.	F 337	1.3.109		Faust
CONTRIBUTE				
Long to the Turke did Malta contribute;	Jew	1.1.180		Barab
Then let them with us contribute.	Jew	1.2.61		2Knght
CONTRIBUTORIE				
Besides fifteene contributorie kings,	1Tamb	3.3.14		Bassoe
Where are your stout contributorie kings?	1Tamb	3.3.214		Tamb
these three crownes, and pledge me, my contributorie Kings.	1Tamb	4.4.115	P	Tamb
say you to this (Turke) these are not your contributorie kings.	1Tamb	4.4.118	P	Tamb
CONTRIBUTORY				
Wel said my stout contributory kings,	1Tamb	3.3.93		Bajzth
Queen of fifteene contributory Queens,	1Tamb	5.1.266		Bajzth
and thirty Kingdomes late contributory to his mighty father.	2Tamb	3.1.5	P	Orcan
CONTRITION				
Contrition, Prayer, Repentance?	F 405	2.1.17		Faust
CONTRIVE				
Nor I devise by what meanes to contrive.	Dido	5.1.66		Aeneas
CONTRIVES				
Contrives, imagines and fully executes/Matters of importe,	P 110	2.53		Guise
CONTROL'D				
To have his head control'd, but breakes the raines,	Hero and Leander	2.142		
CONTROLL				
That dares controll us in our Territories.	1Tamb	4.3.14		Souldn
CONTROLLE				
So, raigne my sonne, scourge and controlle those slaves,	2Tamb	5.3.228		Tamb
CONTROULD				
I weare the crowne, but am contrould by them,	Edw	5.1.29		Edward
CONTROULE				
Controule proud Fate, and cut the thred of time.	Dido	1.1.29		Jupitr
And silver whistles to controule the windes,	Dido	4.4.10		Dido
the Easterne rockes/Without controule can picke his riches up,	Jew	1.1.22		Barab
shall controule him as well as the Conjurer, I warrant you.	F1203	4.1.49	P	Benvol
CONTROULEMENT				
Let him without controulement have his will	Edw	1.4.390		Mortmr

CONTROULMENT				
Tis not in her controulment, nor in ours,	Edw	4.6.35		Mortmr
CONTROWLE				
And what I list commaund, who dare controwle?	Edw	5.4.68		Mortmr
CONTROWLETH				
That whips downe cities, and controwleth crownes,	2Tamb	4.3.100		Tamb
CONVAID				
Convaid me from their crooked nets and bands:	Dido	2.1.222		Aeneas
CONVAY				
Then let some holy trance convay my thoughts,	2Tamb	2.4.34		Tamb
The winged Hermes, to convay thee hence:	2Tamb	4.2.19		Therid
with the martiall spoiles/We will convay with us to Persea.	2Tamb	4.3.106		Tamb
Ile secretly convay me unto Bloyse,	P 895	17.90		King
And to the gates of hell convay me hence,	Edw	4.7.88		Edward
CONVEIE				
Whose there? conveie this priest to the tower.	Edw	1.1.200		Edward
That shall conveie it, and performe the rest,	Edw	5.4.18		Mortmr
CONVENIUNT				
Quam male conveniunt:	Edw	1.4.13		MortSr
CONVENT (See COVENT)				
CONVERSE				
Converse not with him, he is cast off from heaven.	Jew	2.3.157		Mater
CONVERST				
Where is the Fryar that converst with me?	Jew	3.6.9		Abigal
CONVERT				
Convert his mansion to a Nunnery,	Jew	1.2.129		1Knght
Convert my father that he may be sav'd,	Jew	3.6.39		Abigal
You shall convert me, you shall have all my wealth.	Jew	4.1.81		Barab
Wherein I shall convert an Infidell,	Jew	4.1.162		1Fryar
CONVERTED				
Why, Brother, you converted Abigall;	Jew	4.1.106		Barab
CONVERTITE				
No, Governour, I will be no convertite.	Jew	1.2.82		Barab
CONVEY (See also CONVAID, CONVAY, CONVEIE)				
Convey this golden arrowe in thy sleeve,	Dido	3.1.3		Cupid
Convey events of mercie to his heart:	1Tamb	5.1.54		2Virgn
Your Artiers which alongst the vaines convey/The lively spirits	2Tamb	5.3.93		Phsitn
And so convey him closely to his bed.	P 450	7.90		Guise
So, convey this to the counsell presently.	P 892	17.87		King
Convey hence Gaveston, thaile murder him.	Edw	2.2.82		Edward
Binde him, and so convey him to the court.	Edw	5.3.58		Gurney
CONVINC'D				
He being Judge, I am convinc'd of blame.	Ovid's Elegies		2.17.2	
CONVOIES				
Cut off the water, all convoies that can,	2Tamb	3.3.39		Capt
CONY				
each mans mony/And seekes vild wealth by selling of her Cony,	Ovid's Elegies		1.10.22	
COOKES				
Cookes shall have pensions to provide us cates,	2Tamb	1.3.219		Tamb
COOLE				
To make thee fannes wherewith to coole thy face,	Dido	1.1.35		Jupitr
To coole and comfort me with longer date,	1Tamb	5.1.277		Bajzth
sparke of breath/Can quench or coole the torments of my griefe.	1Tamb	5.1.285		Zabina
O water gentle friends to coole my thirst,	Edw	5.3.25		Edward
And coole gales shake the tall trees leavy spring,	Ovid's Elegies		2.16.36	
or parch her hands, but to her mind,/Or warme or coole them:	Hero and Leander		1.29	
COOLING				
Sleepe my sweete nephew in these cooling shades,	Dido	2.1.334		Venus
That of the cooling river durst not drinke,	Hero and Leander		2.197	
COOSNEST				
Thou coosnest boyes of sleepe, and dost betray them/To Pedants,	Ovid's Elegies		1.13.17	
COPE				
friends in Belgia have we left,/To cope with friends at home:	Edw	4.4.4		Queene
COPULATE				
Small things with greater may be copulate.	Ovid's Elegies		2.17.14	
CORALL				
And brancht with blushing corall to the knee;	Hero and Leander		1.32	
With Corall clasps and Amber studs,	Passionate Shepherd		18	
CORCYRAS				
then if Corcyras Ile/Had thee unknowne interr'd in ground most	Ovid's Elegies		3.8.47	
CORD				
To give thee knowledge when to cut the cord,	Jew	5.5.40		Barab
CORDES				
And bind her hand and foote with golden cordes,	Dido	1.1.14		Jupitr
CORDS				
How stand the cords? How hang these hinges, fast?	Jew	5.5.1		Barab
CORINNA (See also CORRINNA)				
Then came Corinna in a long loose gowne,	Ovid's Elegies		1.5.9	
Corinna clips me oft by thy perswasion,	Ovid's Elegies		1.11.5	
Farewell Corinna cryed thy dying tongue.	Ovid's Elegies		2.6.48	
Whence knowes Corinna that with thee I playde?	Ovid's Elegies		2.8.6	
Corinna meanes, and dangerous wayes to take.	Ovid's Elegies		2.11.8	
Conquer'd Corinna in my bosome layes.	Ovid's Elegies		2.12.2	
Wearie Corinna hath her life in doubt.	Ovid's Elegies		2.13.2	
Subscribing, Naso with Corinna sav'd:	Ovid's Elegies		2.13.25	
Wily Corinna sawe this blemish in me,	Ovid's Elegies		2.19.9	
By me Corinna learnes, cousening her guard,	Ovid's Elegies		3.1.49	
Corinna cravde it in a summers night,	Ovid's Elegies		3.6.25	
Alone Corinna moves my wanton wit.	Ovid's Elegies		3.11.16	
CORINNAS				
Beauty gives heart, Corinnas lookes excell,	Ovid's Elegies		2.17.7	
CORINNE				
I know a wench reports her selfe Corinne,	Ovid's Elegies		2.17.29	

CORIVE
To pleasure me, for-bid me to corive with thee. . . Ovid's Elegies 2.19.60
CORNE
What should I talke of mens corne reapt by force, . . Lucan, First Booke 318
Or men with crooked sickles corne downe fell. . . . Ovid's Elegies 1.15.12
With corne the earth abounds, with vines much more, . . Ovid's Elegies 2.16.7
wish the chariot, whence corne [seedes] <fields> were found, Ovid's Elegies 3.5.15
Charmes change corne to grasse, and makes it dye, . . Ovid's Elegies 3.6.31
But better things it gave, corne without ploughes, . . Ovid's Elegies 3.7.39
Golden-hair'd Ceres crownd with eares of corne, . . Ovid's Elegies 3.9.3
Rude husband-men bak'd not their corne before, . . . Ovid's Elegies 3.9.7
And ripe-earde corne with sharpe-edg'd sithes to fell. . Ovid's Elegies 3.9.12
And corne with least part of it selfe returnd. . . . Ovid's Elegies 3.9.30
Ida the seate of groves did sing with corne, . . . Ovid's Elegies 3.9.39
The richest corne dies, if it be not reapt, . . . Hero and Leander 1.327
CORNELIUS
The Germane Valdes and Cornelius, ... F 92 1.1.64 Faust
Come Germane Valdes and Cornelius, ... F 125 1.1.97 Faust
Valdes, sweete Valdes, and Cornelius, ... F 127 1.1.99 Faust
Nothing Cornelius; O this cheeres my soule: . . . . F 176 1.1.148 Faust
is within at dinner, with Valdes and Cornelius, as this wine, F 215 1.2.22 P Wagner
CORNER
Shall fling in every corner of the field: . . . . . 1Tamb 2.2.64 Meandr
Into what corner peeres my Halcions bill? . . . . . Jew 1.1.39 Barab
And at ech corner shall the Kings garde stand. . . . . P 291 5.18 Anjoy
So I may have some nooke or corner left, ... Edw 1.4.72 Edward
like to Ovids Flea, I can creepe into every corner of a Wench: F 665 2.2.114 P Pride
Each crosse waies corner doth as much expresse. . . Ovid's Elegies 3.1.18
And to some corner secretly have gone, ... Hero and Leander 2.311
CORNERS
Because the corners there may fall more flat, ... 2Tamb 3.2.65 Tamb
And search all corners of the new-found-world/For pleasant F 111 1.1.83 Faust
CORNETS
noise/Of trumpets clange, shril cornets, whistling fifes; Lucan, First Booke 240
Cornets of horse are mustered for the field; . . . . Lucan, First Booke 306
CORNEWALL
Earle of Cornewall, king and lord of Man. . . . . . Edw 1.1.156 Edward
My lord of Cornewall now, at every worde, ... Edw 1.2.17 Lncstr
Such a one as my Lord of Cornewall is, ... Edw 1.4.285 Mortmr
Having brought the Earle of Cornewall on his way, . . Edw 1.4.300 Queene
Against our friend the earle of Cornewall comes, . . Edw 1.4.375 Edward
The liberall earle of Cornewall is the man, ... Edw 2.1.10 Spencr
My lord of Cornewall is a comming over, ... Edw 2.1.76 Neece
Against the Earle of Cornewall and my brother? . . . Edw 2.2.35 Edward
Welcome is the good Earle of Cornewall. . . . . . Edw 2.2.66 Mortmr
CORONATION
the speed we can, provide/For Henries coronation from Polonie: P 563 11.28 QnMoth
Till this our Coronation day be past: . . . . . P 624 12.37 King
Our solemne rites of Coronation done, ... P 626 12.39 King
And that this be the coronation day, ... Edw 5.4.70 Mortmr
CORPO
Corpo di dic stay, you shall have halfe, ... Jew 1.2.90 Barab
CORPS (Homograph; See also COARSE)
The keepers hands and corps-dugard to passe/The souldiours, and Ovid's Elegies 1.9.27
A grave her bones hides, on her corps great <small> grave, Ovid's Elegies 2.6.59
CORPS-DUGARD
The keepers hands and corps-dugard to passe/The souldiours, and Ovid's Elegies 1.9.27
CORPUS
For is he not Corpus naturale? . . . . F 208 1.2.15 P Wagner
CORRAGE
Wherein was neither corrage, strength or wit, ... 2Tamb 4.1.125 Tamb
My heart did never quake, or corrage faint. . . . . 2Tamb 5.1.106 Govnr
CORRAGIOUS
a foot, unlesse thou beare/A mind corragious and invincible: 2Tamb 1.3.73 Tamb
CORRAGIOUSLY
Strike up the Drum and martch corragiously, ... 1Tamb 2.2.72 Meandr
CORRALL
Mingled with corrall and with [orient] <orientall> pearle: 2Tamb 1.3.224 Tamb
the ground/Was strewd with pearle, and in low corrall groves, Hero and Leander 2.161
CORRECTS
That with thy gloomie hand corrects the heaven, . . Dido 4.2.6 Iarbus
CORRINNA
Nor Lesbia, nor Corrinna had bene nam'd, ... 2Tamb 2.4.93 Tamb
CORRIVE (See CORIVE)
CORRUPT
Oh twill corrupt the water, and the water the fish, and by the P 488 9.7 P 2Atndt
CORRUPTED
Onely corrupted in religion, ... P 212 4.10 Charls
This ground which is corrupted with their steps, . . Edw 1.2.5 Lncstr
CORRUPTER
Corrupter of thy king, cause of these broiles, ... Edw 2.5.10 Mortmr
CORRUPTERS
The proud corrupters of the light-brainde king, . . Edw 5.2.2 Mortmr
CORRUPTION
and every yeare/Frauds and corruption in the field of Mars; Lucan, First Booke 182
CORRUPTS
Ist not enough, that thou corrupts my lord, ... Edw 1.4.150 Queene
The stench whereof corrupts the inward soule/With such . F App p.243 41 OldMan
CORSE (See COARSE)
CORSICA
For late upon the coast of Corsica, ... Jew 2.2.10 Bosco
CORSICKE
cold hemlocks flower/Wherein bad hony Corsicke Bees did power. Ovid's Elegies 1.12.10

COSENED
Do you remember sir, how you cosened me and eat up my load of-- F1659 4.6.102 P Carter
scab, do you remember how you cosened me with <of> a ho-- F1663 4.6.106 P HrsCsr
COSENING
O what a cosening Doctor was this? . . . . . F1484 4.4.28 P HrsCsr
COSIN (Homograph)
My cosin Helen taught it me in Troy. . . . . . . Dido 3.1.28 Cupid
Why cosin, stand you building Cities here, ... Dido 5.1.27 Hermes
[Cossin] <Ccsin> <Cousin>, take twenty of our strongest guarde, P 266 4.64 Charls
[Cossin] <Ccsin> <Cousin>, the Captaine of the Admirals guarde, P 293 5.20 Anjoy
Now cosin view him well, ... P 307 5.34 Anjoy
Cosin tis he, I know him by his look. . . . . . P 309 5.36 Guise
So kindely Cosin of Guise you and your wife/Doe both salute our P 752 15.10 King
And you good Cosin to imagine it. . . . . . . P 970 19.40 King
Cosin, our hands I hope shall fence our heads, ... Edw 1.1.123 Mortmr
Unto our cosin, the earle of Glosters heire. . . . . Edw 1.4.379 Edward
Cosin it is no dealing with him now, ... Edw 2.2.102 Lncstr
Why how now cosin, how fares all our friends? . . . . Edw 2.2.114 Lncstr
Do cosin, and ile beare thee companie. . . . . . Edw 2.2.121 Lncstr
Cosin, and if he will not ransome him, ... Edw 2.2.127 Mortmr
Cosin, this day shalbe your mariage feast, ... Edw 2.2.256 Edward
COSMOGRAPHY
He now is gone to prove Cosmography, ... F 773 2.3.52 2Chor
COSONING
Ho sirra Doctor, you cosoning scab; Maister Doctor awake, and F1489 4.4.33 P HrsCsr
COSROE
Brother Cosroe, I find my selfe agreev'd, ... 1Tamb 1.1.1 Mycet
Magnificent and mightie Prince Cosroe, ... 1Tamb 1.1.136 Ortyg
Long live Cosroe mighty Emperour. . . . . . . 1Tamb 1.1.169 Ortyg
And of that false Cosroe, my traiterous brother. . . 1Tamb 2.2.4 Mycet
But I will have Cosroe by the head, ... 1Tamb 2.2.11 Mycet
But if Cosrce (as our Spials say, ... 1Tamb 2.2.35 Meandr
with amitie we yeeld/Our utmost service to the faire Cosroe. 1Tamb 2.3.34 Techel
Then haste Cosroe to be king alone, ... 1Tamb 2.3.42 Tamb
Holde thee Cosroe, weare two imperiall Crownes. . . 1Tamb 2.5.1 Tamb
then Cosroe raign/And governe Persea in her former pomp: . 1Tamb 2.5.18 Cosroe
COSSIN
[Cossin] <Ccsin> <Cousin>, take twenty of our strongest guarde, P 266 4.64 Charls
[Cossin] <Ccsin> <Cousin>, the Captaine of the Admirals guarde, P 293 5.20 Anjoy
COST
Soone enough to your cost, Sir: . . . . Jew 4.3.57 Pilia
Nay [to] thine owne cost, villaine, if thou com'st. . . Jew 4.3.59 Barab
Spare for no cost, we will requite your love. . . . Edw 1.4.383 Edward
Not so my Lord, least he bestow more cost, ... Edw 2.5.55 Lncstr
thy divel with horse-bread as long as he lives, of free cost. F App p.234 31 P Rafe
his labour; wel, this tricke shal cost him fortie dollers more. F App p.241 166 P Faust
COSTER
he lookes as like [a] conjurer as the Pope to a Coster-monger. F1229 4.1.75 P Benvol
COSTER-MONGER
he lookes as like [a] conjurer as the Pope to a Coster-monger. F1229 4.1.75 P Benvol
COSTING
From Paris next, costing the Realme of France, ... F 784 3.1.6 Faust
COSTLIE
With costlie jewels hanging at their eares, ... 1Tamb 1.1.144 Ceneus
COSTLY
And cloth'd in costly cloath of massy gold, ... 2Tamb 4.2.40 Therid
And seildsene costly stones of so great price, ... Jew 1.1.28 Barab
Rich costly Jewels, and Stones infinite, ... Jew 1.2.245 Barab
Will be too costly and too troublesome: . . . . . Jew 5.3.23 Calym
COSTS
That measures costs, and kingdomes of the earth: . . . F 774 2.3.53 2Chor
COTTAGES
And martch in cottages of strowed weeds: . . . . . 1Tamb 5.1.187 Tamb
COTTAS
The stubborne Nervians staind with Cottas bloud; . . . Lucan, First Booke 430
COUCH
And couch him in Adonis purple downe. . . . . . Dido 3.2.100 Venus
But he doth lurke within his drousie couch, ... P 737 14.40 Navrre
COUGHT
I lately cought, will have a new made wound, ... Ovid's Elegies 1.2.29
let hir <he> that cought me late,/Either love, or cause that I Ovid's Elegies 1.3.1
COULD (See also COLD)
And would my prayers (as Pigmalions did)/Could give it life, Dido 2.1.17 Aeneas
Through which it could not enter twas so huge. . . . Dido 2.1.171 Aeneas
Which thousand battering Rams could never pierce, . . . Dido 2.1.175 Aeneas
Ah, how could poore Aeneas scape their hands? . . . . Dido 2.1.220 Dido
Through which he could not passe for slaughtred men: . Dido 2.1.262 Aeneas
mightier Kings)/Hast had the greatest favours I could give: Dido 3.1.13 Dido
O that Iarbus could but fancie me. . . . . . . Dido 3.1.62 Anna
For if that any man could conquer me, ... Dido 3.1.137 Dido
Well could I like this reconcilements meanes, ... Dido 3.2.81 Venus
We could have gone without your companie. . . . . Dido 3.3.14 Dido
Aeneas could not choose but hold thee deare, ... Dido 5.1.126 Aeneas
My teares nor plaints could mollifie a whit: . . . . Dido 5.1.235 Anna
And stay a while to heare what I could say, ... Dido 5.1.239 Anna
Could use perswasions more patheticall. . . . . . 1Tamb 1.2.211 Therid
That could perswade at such a sodaine pinch, ... 1Tamb 2.1.37 Cosroe
And he that could with giftes and promises/Inveigle him that 1Tamb 2.2.25 Meandr
As if as many kinges as could encompasse thee, ... 1Tamb 2.5.4 Tamb
I, if I could with all my heart my Lord. . . . . 1Tamb 2.5.68 Techel
I could attaine it with a woondrous ease, ... 1Tamb 2.5.77 Tamb
Thy souldiers armes could not endure to strike/So many blowes 1Tamb 3.3.143 Bajzth
Nay could their numbers countervail the stars, ... 1Tamb 4.1.30 Souldn

COULD (cont.)

Tamburlane) as I could willingly feed upon thy blood-raw hart. | 1Tamb 4.4.11 | P Bajzth
could they not as well/Have sent ye out, when first my . | 1Tamb 5.1.67 | Tamb
It could not more delight me than your sight. . . . . | 2Tamb 1.3.156 | Tamb
That could not but before be terrified: . . . . . | 2Tamb 2.2.22 | Uribas
traines should reach down to the earth/Could not affright you, | 2Tamb 5.1.91 | Tamb
Could not perswade you to submission, ... | 2Tamb 5.1.94 | Tamb
Yet could not enter till the breach was made. . . . . | 2Tamb 5.1.100 | Tamb
Nor if my body could have stopt the breach, ... | 2Tamb 5.1.101 | Govnr
A thousand deathes could not torment our hearts/More than the | 2Tamb 5.1.144 | Jrslem
Me thinks I could sustaine a thousand deaths, ... | 2Tamb 5.2.22 | Callap
And could I but a while pursue the field, ... | 2Tamb 5.3.117 | Tamb
But never could effect their Stratagem. . . . . . | Jew 1.1.165 | Barab
Oh that my sighs could turne to lively breath; . . . . | Jew 3.2.18 | Govnr
I could afford to whip my selfe to death. . . . . . | Jew 4.1.59 | Barab
And so could I; but pennance will not serve. . . . . | Jew 4.1.60 | Ithimr
Yet if he knew our meanings, could he scape? . . . . | Jew 4.1.135 | Barab
Why, a Turke could ha done no more. . . . . . . | Jew 4.1.198 | P Ithimr
'Las I could weepe at your calamity. . . . . . . | Jew 4.1.203 | Barab
If 'twere above ground I could, and would have it; but hee | Jew 4.2.57 | P Ithimr
What greater misery could heaven inflict? . . . . . | Jew 5.2.14 | Govnr
I wonder how it could be conquer'd thus? . . . . . | Jew 5.3.12 | Calym
And in the mean time my Lord, could we devise, ... | P 425 7.65 | Guise
I have done what I could to stay this broile. . . . . | P 434 7.74 | Anjoy
As I could long ere this have wisht him there. . . . . | P 496 9.15 | QnMoth
And could my crownes revenew bring him back, ... | Edw 1.4.308 | Edward
O that mine armes could close this Ile about, ... | Edw 2.4.17 | Queene
As Isabell could live with thee for ever. . . . . . | Edw 2.4.60 | Queene
Could not but take compassion of my state. . . . . | Edw 4.7.11 | Edward
Alas poore soule, would I could ease his greefe. . . . | Edw 5.2.26 | Queene
You could not beare his death thus patiently, ... | Edw 5.6.36 | King
Could I have rulde thee then, as I do now, ... | Edw 5.6.96 | King
this wine, if it could speake, <it> would informe your Worships: | F 216 1.2.23 | P Wagner
my selfe when I could get none <had no body> to fight withall: | F 689 2.2.138 | P Wrath
zounds I could eate my selfe for anger, to thinke I have beene | F1242 4.1.88 | P Benvol
me what he should give me for as much Hay as he could eate; | F1527 4.5.23 | P Carter
and whooping in his eares, but all could not wake him: . | F1549 4.5.45 | P HrsCsr
so delighted me, as nothing in the world could please me more. | F1561 4.6.4 | P Duke
nor Hanniball/Art cause, no forraine foe could so afflict us, | Lucan, First Booke | 31
Roome was so great it could not beare it selfe: . . | Lucan, First Booke | 72
men so strong/By land, and sea, no forreine force could ruine: | Lucan, First Booke | 83
alwaies scorn'd/A second place; Pompey could bide no equall, | Lucan, First Booke | 125
Againe, this people could not brooke calme peace, . . | Lucan, First Booke | 172
and whose tongue/Could tune the people to the Nobles mind: | Lucan, First Booke | 273
And Sequana that well could manage steeds; . . . | Lucan, First Booke | 426
in armes; nor could the bed-rid parents/Keep back their sons, | Lucan, First Booke | 502
Not one wen in her bodie could I spie, ... | Ovid's Elegies | 1.5.18
Could I therefore her comely tresses teare? . . . | Ovid's Elegies | 1.7.11
Better I could part of my selfe have wanted. . . . | Ovid's Elegies | 1.7.24
And to my selfe could I be so injurious? . . . . . | Ovid's Elegies | 1.7.26
[All] <This> could I beare, but that the wench should rise,/Who | Ovid's Elegies | 1.13.25
I could not be in love with twoo at once, ... | Ovid's Elegies | 2.10.2
I could my selfe by secret Magicke shift. . . . . | Ovid's Elegies | 2.15.10
As his deepe whirle-pooles could not quench the same. . | Ovid's Elegies | 3.5.42
Yet could I not cast ancor where I meant, ... | Ovid's Elegies | 3.6.6
Chuf-like had I not gold, and could not use it? . . | Ovid's Elegies | 3.6.50
Nor usde the slight nor <and> cunning which she could, . | Ovid's Elegies | 3.6.56
Thee sacred Poet could sad flames destroy? . . . . | Ovid's Elegies | 3.8.41
How such a Poet could you bring forth, sayes, . . . | Ovid's Elegies | 3.14.13
I could tell ye,/How smooth his brest was, and how white his | Hero and Leander | 1.65
Died ere he could enjoy the love of any. . . . . . | Hero and Leander | 1.76
Or if it could, downe from th'enameld skie, ... | Hero and Leander | 1.249
such lovelinesse and beautie had/As could provoke his liking, | Hero and Leander | 1.423
Nor could the youth abstaine, but he must weare/The sacred ring | Hero and Leander | 2.108
Than he could saile, for incorporeal Fame, ... | Hero and Leander | 2.113

COULDST

Thou couldst not come from Egypt, or by Caire/But at the entry | Jew 1.1.73 | Barab
And couldst not venge it, but upon his sonne, . . . | Jew 3.3.44 | Abigal
For with thy Gallyes couldst thou not get hence, . . | Jew 5.5.100 | Govnr
I know thou couldst not come and visit me. . . . | Edw 2.1.61 | Neece
Couldst <wouldst> thou make men <man> to live eternally, . | F 52 1.1.24 | Faust
Thou couldst command the worlds obedience: . . . | F1210 4.1.56 | Emper

COULOUR

That change their coulour when the winter comes, . . | P 721 14.24 | Navrre

COULOURS

Plaies with her goary coulours of revenge, . . . | P 719 14.22 | Navrre

COUNCELL

And sit in councell to invent some paine, ... | 2Tamb 3.5.98 | Callap
And by his graces councell it is thought, ... | P 465 8.15 | Anjoy
While at the councell table, grave enough, ... | Edw 5.4.58 | Mortmr
Into the councell chamber he is gone, ... | Edw 5.6.20 | Queene
What by the holy Councell held at Trent, ... | F 884 3.1.106 | Pope
What have our holy Councell there decreed, ... | F 947 3.1.169 | Pope
Were by the holy Councell both condemn'd/For lothed Lollords, | F1021 3.2.41 | Pope

COUNCELLERS

And see what we your councellers have done. . . . | Edw 1.4.44 | ArchBp

COUNITES

Whom kindred and acquaintance counites? . . . . | Dido 3.2.31 | Juno

COUNSAILE

As hath sufficient counsaile in himselfe, ... | P 456 8.6 | Anjoy
Nor do I give thee counsaile to live chaste, . . . | Ovid's Elegies | 3.13.3
And nothing more than counsaile, lovers hate. . . . | Hero and Leander | 2.140

COUNSAILOR

And chiefest Counsailor in all his acts, ... | 1Tamb 2.5.11 | Cosroe

COUNSELL			
Wherefore I [chaungd] <chaunge> my counsell with the time,	Dido	3.2.51	Juno
For he can counsell best in these affaires;	Jew	1.1.142	2Jew
And they this day sit in the Counsell-house/To entertaine them	Jew	1.1.148	1Jew
Spaine is the counsell chamber of the pope, ...	P 709	14.12	Navrre
Make a discharge of all my counsell straite, . . .	P 882	17.77	King
My head shall be my counsell, they are false: . . .	P 884	17.79	King
So, convey this to the counsell presently. . . .	P 892	17.87	King
My lorde, the counsell of the Queene commaunds, . .	Edw	5.1.135	Leistr
<and see if hee by> his grave counsell may <can> reclaime him.	F 226	1.2.33	2Schol
The thing and place shall counsell us the rest. . .	Ovid's Elegies		1.4.54
COUNSELLER			
Warwick shalbe my chiefest counseller:	Edw	1.4.345	Edward
COUNSELLERS			
We and the rest that are his counsellers, ...	Edw	1.2.69	ArchBp
COUNSELL-HOUSE			
And they this day sit in the Counsell-house/To entertaine them	Jew	1.1.148	1Jew
COUNSELLOR (See also COUNCELLERS)			
Meander, thou my faithfull Counsellor, ...	1Tamb	1.1.28	Mycet
COUNT (See also COUNTY)			
I count Religion but a childish Toy, ...	Jew	Prol.14	Machvl
Fye; what a trouble tis to count this trash.	Jew	1.1.7	Barab
In this I count me highly gratified, ...	Edw	1.4.295	Mortmr
COUNTED			
I feare me Dido hath been counted light, ...	Dido	3.1.14	Dido
And might in noble minds be counted princely. . . .	1Tamb	3.2.39	Zenoc
In offring parlie, to be counted light.	Hero and Leander		2.9
COUNTENANCE (See also COUNT'NANCE)			
And shadow his displeased countenance, ...	1Tamb	5.1.58	2Virgn
a non-plus at the critical aspect of my terrible countenance.	Jew	4.2.14	P Pilia
His countenance bewraies he is displeasd.	Edw	1.2.34	Lncstr
Is thus misled to countenance their ils.	Edw	4.3.49	Edward
Being of countenance in your countrey here, ...	Edw	4.6.75	Mortmr
Pay natures debt with cheerefull countenance, ...	Edw	4.7.109	Baldck
I will set my countenance like a Precisian, and begin to speake	F 213	1.2.20	P Wagner
View me, my becks, and speaking countenance:	Ovid's Elegies		1.4.17
And from her countenance behold ye might, ...	Hero and Leander		2.318
COUNTENAUNCE			
But with a ghastly dreadfull countenaunce, ...	Hero and Leander		1.381
COUNTERBUFT			
not suffer thus your majestie/Be counterbuft of your nobilitie.	Edw	3.1.19	Spencr
COUNTERFEIT			
Make me the gastly counterfeit of death.	1Tamb	3.2.17	Zenoc
contracted unto Abigall; [he] forg'd a counterfeit challenge.	Jew	5.1.29	P Ithimr
COUNTERFEITE			
and use a counterfeite key to his privie Chamber doore: .	P 807	17.2	P Souldr
COUNTERFET			
it,/A counterfet profession is better/Then unseene hypocrisie.	Jew	1.2.292	Barab
But yet sometimes to chide thee let her fall/Counterfet teares:	Ovid's Elegies		2.2.36
COUNTERFEYT			
duke a cuckolde and use a counterfeyt key to his privy chamber	Paris	ms 2,p390	P Souldr
COUNTERFORTS			
With Cavalieros and thicke counterforts, ...	2Tamb	3.2.71	Tamb
COUNTERMANDED			
Are countermanded by a greater man:	1Tamb	1.2.22	Tamb
Nay he was King and countermanded me, ...	P1069	19.139	King
COUNTERMANDS			
As rules the Skies, and countermands the Gods: . . .	1Tamb	5.1.233	Bajzth
COUNTERMAUND			
And all the sea my Gallies countermaund.	1Tamb	3.1.63	Bajzth
To countermaund our will and check our freends. . .	P 846	17.41	King
And do confront and countermaund their king. . . .	Edw	3.1.188	Edward
COUNTERMIN'D			
Tho countermin'd <countermur'd> with walls of brasse, to love,	Jew	1.2.386	Mthias
COUNTERMINES			
It must have privy ditches, countermines, ...	2Tamb	3.2.73	Tamb
COUNTERMUR'D			
Tho countermin'd <countermur'd> with walls of brasse, to love,	Jew	1.2.386	Mthias
Strong contermin'd <countermur'd> with other petty Iles; .	Jew	5.3.8	Calym
COUNTERPOISE			
And with this wait Ile counterpoise a Crowne, . . .	P 115	2.58	Guise
COUNTERS			
crownes a man were as good have as many english counters,	F App	p.230 34	P Clown
COUNTERSCARPS			
The ditches must be deepe, the Counterscarps/Narrow and steepe,	2Tamb	3.2.68	Tamb
COUNTERVAIL			
Nay could their numbers countervail the stars, . . .	1Tamb	4.1.30	Souldn
COUNTERVAILE			
It will not countervaile his paines I hope, ...	P 735	14.38	Navrre
COUNTETH			
Plaies, maskes, and all that stern age counteth evill. .	Hero and Leander		1.302
COUNTING			
up to the Jewes counting-house where I saw some bags of mony,	Jew	3.1.18	P Pilia
Or climbe up to my Counting-house window:	Jew	4.3.34	P Barab
enough, and therfore talke not to me of your Counting-house:	Jew	4.3.37	P Pilia
COUNTING-HOUSE			
up to the Jewes counting-house where I saw some bags of mony,	Jew	3.1.18	P Pilia
Or climbe up to my Counting-house window:	Jew	4.3.34	P Barab
enough, and therfore talke not to me of your Counting-house:	Jew	4.3.37	P Pilia
COUNT'NANCE			
Till with the fire that from his count'nance blazed, .	Hero and Leander		1.164
Affection by the count'nance is descride.	Hero and Leander		2.132
COUNTREY			
And beare him in the countrey to her house, ...	Dido	4.4.106	Dido

COUNTREY (cont.)			
Being of countenance in your countrey here,	Edw	4.6.75	Mortmr
fierce men of Rhene/Leaving your countrey open to the spoile.	Lucan, First Booke		461
COUNTRIE			
her ayrie wheeles/Into the windie countrie of the clowdes,	Dido	1.1.57	Venus
This countrie swarmes with vile outragious men,	1Tamb	2.2.22	Meandr
The countrie wasted where my selfe was borne,	1Tamb	4.4.66	Zenoc
To pacifie my countrie and my love,	1Tamb	5.1.396	Zenoc
Than honor of thy countrie or thy name?	2Tamb	5.1.11	Govnr
To mend the king, and do our countrie good:	Edw	1.4.257	Mortmr
Care of my countrie cald me to this warre.	Edw	4.6.65	Queene
Your king hath wrongd your countrie and himselfe,	Edw	4.6.67	Mortmr
That in the vast uplandish countrie dwelt,	Hero and Leander		1.80
he asleepe had layd/Inchaunted Argus, spied a countrie mayd,	Hero and Leander		1.388
COUNTRIES			
By plowing up his Countries with the Sword:	Dido	5.1.308	Dido
And vow to weare it for my countries good:	1Tamb	1.1.158	Cosroe
Because it is my countries, and my Fathers.	1Tamb	4.2.124	Zenoc
Wel, lovely Virgins, think our countries care,	1Tamb	5.1.34	Govnr
That in thy passion for thy countries love,	1Tamb	5.1.137	Tamb
teares of Mahomet/For hot consumption of his countries pride:	2Tamb	4.1.197	Tamb
The citie and my native countries weale,	2Tamb	5.1.13	Govnr
And rather chuse to seek your countries good,	P 221	4.19	Guise
And tell him that tis for his Countries good,	P 646	12.59	Cardnl
In honor of our God and countries good.	P 708	14.11	Navrre
And keep those relicks from our countries coastes.	P 803	16.17	Navrre
Thou proud disturber of thy countries peace,	Edw	2.5.9	Mortmr
it is our countries cause,/That here severelie we will execute	Edw	2.5.22	Warwck
No James, it is my countries cause I follow.	Edw	2.6.10	Warwck
Nature, yeeld to my countries cause in this.	Edw	4.1.3	Kent
Heere for our countries cause sweare we to him/All homage,	Edw	4.4.19	Mortmr
Goes to discover countries yet unknowne.	Edw	5.6.66	Mortmr
and such Countries that lye farre East, where they have fruit	F1584	4.6.27	P Faust
and farther countries in the East, and by means of a swift	F App	p.242 22	P Faust
COUNTRIMEN			
Leave us my Lord, and loving countrimen,	1Tamb	5.1.60	2Virgn
Thy Fathers subjects and thy countrimen.	1Tamb	5.1.321	Zenoc
In this, my Countrimen, be rul'd by me,	Jew	5.4.1	Govnr
Now lords, our loving friends and countrimen,	Edw	4.4.1	Queene
COUNTRY (See also COUNTREY)			
these Medean Lords/To Memphis, from my uncles country of Medea,	1Tamb	1.2.12	Zenoc
And these that seeme but silly country Swaines,	1Tamb	1.2.47	Tamb
To save your King and country from decay:	1Tamb	2.6.35	Cosroe
Fornication? but that was in another Country:	Jew	4.1.41	Barab
Heere hast thou a country voide of feares,	P 591	12.4	QnMoth
Of King or Country, no not for them both.	P 740	14.43	Navrre
In civill broiles makes kin and country men/Slaughter	Edw	4.4.6	Queene
And make that Country <land>, continent to Spaine,	F 336	1.3.108	Faust
be good, for they come from a farre Country I can tell you.	F1577	4.6.20	P Faust
Loe country Gods, and [known] <know> bed to forsake,	Ovid's Elegies		2.11.7
Nor do I like the country of my birth.	Ovid's Elegies		2.16.38
Ceres and Bacchus Country-men adore,	Ovid's Elegies		3.2.53
Which fact, and country wealth Halesus fled.	Ovid's Elegies		3.12.32
COUNTRY-MEN			
Ceres and Bacchus Country-men adore,	Ovid's Elegies		3.2.53
COUNTRYMEN (See also COUNTRIMEN)			
Why, how now Countrymen?	Jew	1.1.143	Barab
COUNTY			
That thou thy self, then County-Pallatine,	2Tamb	1.1.94	Orcan
Then County-Pallatine, but now a king:	2Tamb	1.1.104	Sgsmnd
COUNTY-PALLATINE			
That thou thy self, then County-Pallatine,	2Tamb	1.1.94	Orcan
Then County-Pallatine, but now a king:	2Tamb	1.1.104	Sgsmnd
COUPE			
But if I get him, Coupe de Gorge for that.	Jew	4.3.5	Barab
COUPLE			
am glad I have found you, you are a couple of fine companions:	F1097	3.3.10	P Vintnr
Though never-singling Hymen couple thee.	Hero and Leander		1.258
COURAGE (See also CORRAGE)			
Adding more courage to my conquering mind.	1Tamb	5.1.515	Tamb
Argue their want of courage and of wit:	2Tamb	1.3.24	Tamb
I think I make your courage something quaile.	2Tamb	5.1.126	Tamb
And courage to, to be revengde at full.	Edw	1.2.60	Mortmr
Shee looking on them did more courage give.	Ovid's Elegies		2.12.26
This doth delight me, this my courage cheares.	Ovid's Elegies		2.19.24
Tut, men should not their courage so consume.	Ovid's Elegies		3.3.34
His side past service, and his courage spent.	Ovid's Elegies		3.10.14
COURAGES			
Yet should our courages and steeled crestes,	2Tamb	2.2.17	Gazell
Whose courages are kindled with the flames,	2Tamb	3.1.54	Trebiz
What faintnesse should dismay our courages,	2Tamb	5.1.21	Govnr
COURAGIOUS			
Couragious and full of hardinesse:	1Tamb	4.3.55	Capol
Teach you my boyes to beare couragious minds,	2Tamb	3.2.143	Tamb
Couragious Lancaster, imbrace thy king,	Edw	1.4.340	Edward
COURAGIOUSLY			
Then shall we fight couragiously with them.	1Tamb	1.2.128	Tamb
Then fight couragiously, their crowns are yours.	1Tamb	3.3.30	Tamb
Fight all couragiously and be you kings.	1Tamb	3.3.101	Tamb
So now couragiously encounter them;	Jew	3.5.33	Govnr
Then Faustus stab thy <thine> Arme couragiously,	F 438	2.1.50	Mephst
COURSE			
You sonnes of care, companions of my course,	Dido	1.1.142	Aeneas

COURSE (cont.)			
That intercepts the course of my desire:	Dido	4.2.48	Iarbus
of his Emperie/By East and west, as Phoebus doth his course:	1Tamb	1.2.40	Tamb
With litle slaughter take Meanders course,	1Tamb	2.5.27	Cosroe
And measure every wandring plannets course:	1Tamb	2.7.23	Tamb
Therfore I tooke my course to Manico:	2Tamb	1.3.198	Techel
No, pardon me, the Law must have his course.	Jew	4.1.185	Barab
Shape we our course to Ireland there to breath.	Edw	4.5.3	Spencr
[Hee stayde his course, and so returned home],	F1140	3.3.53A	3Chor
course that time doth runne with calme and silent foote,	F App	p.239 90 P	Faust
While Titan strives against the worlds swift course;	Lucan, First Booke		90
Which wont to run their course through empty night/At noone day	Lucan, First Booke		534
The worlds swift course is lawlesse/And casuall; all the	Lucan, First Booke		641
why doe the Planets/Alter their course; and vainly dim their	Lucan, First Booke		663
o Rome continue/The course of mischiefe, and stretch out the	Lucan, First Booke		670
Thou viewst the course, I thee:	Ovid's Elegies		3.2.5
choose this course,/Wilt have me willing, or to love by force?	Ovid's Elegies		3.10.49
When two are stript, long ere the course begin,	Hero and Leander		1.169
COURSER			
and the Horse-courser a bundle of hay for his forty Dollors.	F1497	4.4.41 P	Faust
do not you remember a Horse-courser you sold a horse to?	F1633	4.6.76 P	Carter
What horse-courser, you are wel met.	F App	p.239 100 P	Faust
Even as a head-strong courser beares away,	Ovid's Elegies		2.9.29
COURSES			
But when thou comest they of their courses faile.	Ovid's Elegies		1.13.12
COURT			
And court Aeneas with your calmie cheere,	Dido	1.1.123	Venus
A Gods name on and hast thee to the Court,	Dido	1.1.233	Venus
Your men and you shall banquet in our Court,	Dido	1.2.39	Iarbus
And brought unto the Court of Priamus:	Dido	2.1.154	Aeneas
And wanton Mermaides court thee with sweete songs,	Dido	3.1.130	Dido
And feedes his eyes with favours of her Court,	Dido	3.2.71	Juno
If all the christall gates of Joves high court/Were opened	2Tamb	1.3.153	Tamb
For since we left you at the Souldans court,	2Tamb	1.3.177	Usumc
Upon the marble turrets of my Court/Sit like to Venus in her	2Tamb	4.2.41	Therid
Theridamas, haste to the court of Jove,	2Tamb	5.3.61	Tamb
And like disportes, such as doe fit the Court?	P 629	12.42	King
<make> a walk/On purpose from the Court to meet with him.	P 784	15.42	Mugern
That in the Court I bare so great a traine.	P 968	19.38	Guise
We will wait heere about the court.	Edw	1.1.49	Omnes
And all the court begins to flatter him.	Edw	1.2.22	Lncstr
And at the court gate hang the pessant up,	Edw	1.2.30	Mortmr
Madam, returne unto the court againe:	Edw	1.2.56	Mortmr
The angrie king hath banished me the court:	Edw	1.4.210	Queene
These silver haires will more adorne my court,	Edw	1.4.346	Edward
And Midas like he jets it in the court,	Edw	1.4.408	Mortmr
And even now, a poast came from the court,	Edw	2.1.19	Spencr
And learne to court it like a Gentleman,	Edw	2.1.32	Spencr
He wils me to repaire unto the court,	Edw	2.1.67	Neece
And will be at the court as soone as we.	Edw	2.1.77	Neece
Out of my presence, come not neere the court.	Edw	2.2.89	Edward
Ile not be barde the court for Gaveston.	Edw	2.2.90	Mortmr
Thy court is naked, being bereft of those,	Edw	2.2.174	Mortmr
The king of England, nor the court of Fraunce,	Edw	4.2.22	Prince
Imagine Killingworth castell were your court,	Edw	5.1.2	Leistr
Binde him, and so convey him to the court.	Edw	5.3.58	Gurney
Where is the court but heere, heere is the king,	Edw	5.3.59	Kent
The court is where lord Mortimer remaines,	Edw	5.3.61	Matrvs
Wherefore stay we? on sirs to the court.	Edw	5.3.65	Souldr
And when I frowne, make all the court looke pale,	Edw	5.4.53	Mortmr
To see the Pope and manner of his Court,	F 776	2.3.55	2Chor
flie amaine/Unto my Faustus to the great Turkes Court.	F1137	3.3.50	Mephst
For Faustus at the Court is late arriv'd,	F1181	4.1.27	Mrtino
Thrice learned Faustus, welcome to our Court.	F1205	4.1.51	Emper
to heart/With this vaine terror; but the Court, the Senate;	Lucan, First Booke		484
to thee our Court stands open wide,/There shalt be lov'd:	Ovid's Elegies		3.5.61
Faire-fac'd Iulus, he went forth thy court.	Ovid's Elegies		3.8.14
paths, wheron the gods might trace/To Joves high court.	Hero and Leander		1.299
COURTED			
Courted by kings and peeres of Asia,	2Tamb	5.1.74	Tamb
Whom young Apollo courted for her haire,	Hero and Leander		1.6
And knowing Hermes courted her, was glad/That she such	Hero and Leander		1.421
COURTEOUS (See CURTEOUS)			
COURTESAN (See CURTEZANE)			
COURTESIES (See also CURTESIE)			
And gives no more than common courtesies.	1Tamb	3.2.63	Agidas
COURTIER			
And this a Spartan Courtier vaine and wilde,	Dido	3.1.157	Dido
COURTING			
Infernall Dis is courting of my Love,	2Tamb	4.2.93	Therid
COURTLY			
Whose golden fortunes clogd with courtly ease,	Dido	4.3.8	Aeneas
COURTS			
Where lords keepe courts, and kings are lockt in prison!	Edw	5.3.64	Kent
Nor sporting in the dalliance of love/In Courts of Kings, where	F 4	Prol.4	1Chor
tane the view]/[Of rarest things, and royal courts of kings],	F1139	3.3.52A	3Chor
Our servants, and our Courts at thy command.	F1624	4.6.67	Duke
With strawie cabins now her courts should build.	Ovid's Elegies		2.9.18
Courts shut the poore out; wealth gives estimation,	Ovid's Elegies		3.7.55
(for loftie pride that dwels/In tow'red courts, is oft in	Hero and Leander		1.394
COUSENDST			
Thou [cousenst] <cousendst> mee, by thee surprizde am I,	Ovid's Elegies		3.6.71
COUSENING			
By me Corinna learnes, cousening her guard,	Ovid's Elegies		3.1.49

COUSENST			
Thou [cousenst] <cousendst> mee, by thee surprizde am I,	Ovid's Elegies		3.6.71
COUSIN (See also CUZ)			
[Cossin] <Ccsin> <Cousin>, take twenty of our strongest guarde,	P 266	4.64	Charls
[Cossin] <Ccsin> <Cousin>, the Captaine of the Admirals guarde,	P 293	5.20	Anjoy
For that let me alone, Cousin stay you heer,	P 428	7.68	Anjoy
Good morrow to my loving Cousin of Guise.	P 965	19.35	King
Cousin, assure you I am resolute,	P 973	19.43	King
COUZEN			
Oft couzen me, oft being wooed say nay.	Ovid's Elegies		2.19.20
COUZEND			
Couzend, I am the couzeners sacrifice.	Ovid's Elegies		3.3.22
COUZENERS			
Couzend, I am the couzeners sacrifice.	Ovid's Elegies		3.3.22
COUZENST			
Nor, if thou couzenst one, dread to for-sweare,	Ovid's Elegies		1.8.85
COVENANT			
With Poland therfore must I covenant thus,	P 471	8.21	Anjoy
All <articles prescrib'd> <covenant-articles> betweene us both.	F 480	(HC260)	Faust
COVENANT-ARTICLES			
All <articles prescrib'd> <covenant-articles> betweene us both.	F 480	(HC260)	Faust
COVENANTS			
And solemne covenants we have both confirm'd,	2Tamb	2.2.31	Orcan
conditionally, that thou performe/All Covenants, and Articles,	F 480	2.1.92	Faust
Hence leagues, and covenants; Fortune thee I follow,	Lucan, First Booke		228
COVENT			
But not a word to any of your Covent.	Jew	4.1.112	Barab
COVENTRIE			
Whether goes my Lord of Coventrie so fast?	Edw	1.1.175	Edward
The Bishoprick of Coventrie is his.	Edw	1.2.45	ArchBp
COVER			
Arabians, Moores and Jewes/Enough to cover all Bythinia.	1Tamb	3.3.137	Bajzth
Yet this Ile see, but if thy gowne ought cover,	Ovid's Elegies		1.4.41
And treades the deserts snowy heapes [do] <to> cover.	Ovid's Elegies		1.9.12
To cover it, spilt water in <on> the place.	Ovid's Elegies		3.6.84
COVER'D			
the ground be <were> perfum'd, and cover'd with cloth of Arras.	F 670	2.2.119	P Pride
COVERED			
Whose tops are covered with Tartarian thieves,	1Tamb	2.2.16	Meandr
thy chariot wheels/With Turky Carpets shall be covered:	2Tamb	1.2.43	Callap
<superfluities>/Is covered with a liquid purple veile,	2Tamb	1.3.80	Tamb
It must have high Argins and covered waies/To keep the bulwark	2Tamb	3.2.75	Tamb
And over thy Argins and covered waies/Shal play upon the	2Tamb	3.3.23	Therid
Yet strivde she to be covered therewithall,	Ovid's Elegies		1.5.14
The annuall pompe goes on the covered ground.	Ovid's Elegies		3.12.12
COVERLET			
Or why slips downe the Coverlet so oft?	Ovid's Elegies		1.2.2
COVERS			
shine as bright/As that faire vail that covers all the world:	2Tamb	1.2.50	Callap
Covers the hils, the valleies and the plaines.	2Tamb	3.5.13	Callap
The boord is marked thus that covers it.	Jew	1.2.350	Barab
COVERTURE			
And have not any coverture but heaven.	Dido	1.1.230	Aeneas
O'recast with dim and darksome coverture.	Hero and Leander		2.266
COVET			
What's kept, we covet more: the care makes theft:	Ovid's Elegies		3.4.25
COVETOUS			
Hard harted to the poore, a covetous wretch,	Jew	4.1.52	Barab
COVETOUSNESSE			
Excesse of wealth is cause of covetousnesse:	Jew	1.2.123	Govnr
And covetousnesse, oh 'tis a monstrous sinne.	Jew	1.2.124	Govnr
I am Covetousnesse:	F 674	2.2.123	P Covet
COVETS			
Who covets lawfull things takes leaves from woods,	Ovid's Elegies		2.19.31
COW			
But came it freely, did the Cow give down her milk freely?	Jew	4.2.102	P Ithimr
COWARD			
fearful coward, stragling from the camp/When Kings themselves	1Tamb	2.4.16	Tamb
What Coward wold not fight for such a prize?	1Tamb	3.3.100	Usumc
And canst thou Coward stand in feare of death?	2Tamb	3.2.102	Tamb
And hunt that Coward, faintheart runaway,	2Tamb	3.2.149	Tamb
Then let us see if coward Calapine/Dare levie armes against our	2Tamb	3.2.155	Tamb
They say I am a coward, (Perdicas) and I feare as litle their	2Tamb	4.1.67	P Calyph
But wher's this coward, villaine, not my sonne,	2Tamb	4.1.89	Tamb
COWARDISE			
Knowing my father hates thy cowardise,	2Tamb	4.1.23	Amyras
My wisedome shall excuse my cowardise:	2Tamb	4.1.50	Calyph
COWARDIZE			
Would not with too much cowardize or feare,	1Tamb	5.1.37	Govnr
COWARDLY			
We will not steale upon him cowardly,	1Tamb	2.5.102	Tamb
O cowardly boy, fie for shame, come foorth.	2Tamb	4.1.31	Celeb
COWARDS			
cowards and fainthearted runawaies,/Looke for orations when the	1Tamb	1.2.130	Techel
Bastardly boy, sprong from some cowards loins,	2Tamb	1.3.69	Tamb
Villaines, cowards, Traitors to our state,	2Tamb	5.1.43	Govnr
These cowards invisiblie assaile hys soule,	2Tamb	5.3.13	Therid
Thus are the villaines, cowards fled for feare,	2Tamb	5.3.115	Tamb
The world (were it together) is by cowards/Left as a pray now	Lucan, First Booke		511
COWE			
The Mare askes not the Horse, the Cowe the Bull,	Ovid's Elegies		1.10.27
COY			
And she thats coy I like for being no clowne,	Ovid's Elegies		2.4.13

COYLE			
In all this coyle, where have ye left the Queene?	Dido	4.1.14	Iarbus
What a coyle they keepe, I beleeve there will be some hurt done	2Tamb	4.1.74	P Calyph
Why how now Maisters, what a coyle is there?	F1591	4.6.34	Servnt
COYNE			
Would make a miracle of thus much coyne:	Jew	1.1.13	Barab
An hundred Crownes, I'le have him; there's the coyne.	Jew	2.3.130	Barab
I have as much coyne as will buy the Towne.	Jew	2.3.200	Barab
whole Chests of Gold, in Bullion, and in Coyne,	Jew	4.1.65	Barab
Then will I, Barabas, about this coyne,	Jew	5.2.107	Govnr
Catholickes/Sends Indian golde to coyne me French ecues:	P 118	2.61	Guise
I'le leavy souldiers with the coyne they bring,	F 119	1.1.91	Faust
COZENING (See also COOSNEST, COSENED, COSONING, COUSEN)			
And with extorting, cozening, forfeiting,	Jew	2.3.191	Barab
CRACK			
And this right hand shall make thy Altars crack/With mountaine	Dido	1.1.201	Aeneas
CRACKE			
Fighting for passage, [makes] <make> the Welkin cracke,	1Tamb	4.2.45	Tamb
The cracke, the Ecchoe and the souldiers crie/Make deafe the	2Tamb	3.3.60	Therid
With cracke of riven ayre and hideous sound,	Lucan, First Booke		153
CRACKT			
Doubtles Apollos Axeltree is crackt,	Dido	4.1.11	Achat
CRAFT			
A man compact of craft and perjurie,	Dido	2.1.144	Aeneas
CRAFTES			
To thee Minerva turne the craftes-mens hands.	Ovid's Elegies		3.2.52
CRAFTES-MENS			
To thee Minerva turne the craftes-mens hands.	Ovid's Elegies		3.2.52
CRAFTILY			
And craftily knowes by what meanes to winne me.	Ovid's Elegies		2.19.10
CRAFTY			
But me let crafty damsells words deceive,	Ovid's Elegies		2.9.43
CRAGGIE			
as outwaies the sands/And all the craggie rockes of Caspea.	1Tamb	2.3.48	Tamb
And shivered against a craggie rocke.	1Tamb	4.3.34	Souldn
CRAGGY			
hollow hanging of a hill/And crooked bending of a craggy rock,	2Tamb	1.2.58	Callap
CRAMB'D			
Who smiles to see how full his bags are cramb'd,	Jew	Prol.31	Machvl
But he whose steele-bard coffers are cramb'd full,	Jew	1.1.14	Barab
CRAMS			
Then crams salt levin on his crooked knife;	Lucan, First Booke		609
CRANES			
Are all the Cranes and Pulleyes sure?	Jew	5.5.2	Barab
CRAS			
tibi, cras mihi, and so I left him to the mercy of the Hangman:	Jew	4.2.19	P Pilia
CRASED			
Ile fire his crased buildings and [inforse] <incense>/The	P1201	22.63	King
Ile fire thy crased buildings, and enforce/The papall towers,	Edw	1.4.100	Edward
CRASSUS			
While slaughtred Crassus ghost walks unreveng'd,	Lucan, First Booke		11
peace against their wils; betwixt them both/Stept Crassus in:	Lucan, First Booke		100
So when as Crassus wretched death who stayd them,	Lucan, First Booke		104
CRAV'D			
She crav'd a hide of ground to build a towne,	Dido	4.2.13	Iarbus
They granted what he crav'd, and once againe,	Hero and Leander		1.455
As in plaine termes (yet cunningly) he crav'd it,	Hero and Leander		2.71
CRAVDE			
Corinna cravde it in a summers night,	Ovid's Elegies		3.6.25
CRAVE			
That crave such favour at your honors feete,	Dido	1.2.5	Illion
I crave but this, he stay a tide or two,	Dido	5.1.207	Dido
And crave his triple worthy buriall.	1Tamb	3.2.112	Usumc
thou shalt kneele to us/And humbly crave a pardon for thy life.	2Tamb	3.5.109	Orcan
I crave but this, Grace him as he deserves,	Jew	Prol.33	Machvl
Yet crave I thy consent.	Jew	2.3.299	Lodowk
And please your grace the Duke of Guise doth crave/Accesse unto	P 959	19.29	Eprnon
And princely Edwards right we crave the crowne.	Edw	5.1.39	BshpWn
To crave the aide and succour of his peeres.	Edw	5.6.21	Queene
One thing good servant let me crave of thee,	F1759	5.1.86	Faust
I shall not need/To crave Apolloes ayde, or Bacchus helpe;	Lucan, First Booke		65
Or, but for bashfulnesse her selfe would crave.	Ovid's Elegies		1.8.44
What he will give, with greater instance crave.	Ovid's Elegies		1.8.68
Faire Dames for-beare rewards for nights to crave,	Ovid's Elegies		1.10.47
To meete for poyson or vilde facts we crave not,	Ovid's Elegies		2.2.63
If she be learned, then for her skill I crave her,	Ovid's Elegies		2.4.17
And many by me to get glory crave.	Ovid's Elegies		2.17.28
Nor Romane stocke scorne me so much (I crave)/Gifts then my	Ovid's Elegies		3.5.65
What might I crave more if I aske againe?	Ovid's Elegies		3.6.44
And crave the helpe of sheap-heards that were nie.	Hero and Leander		1.414
CRAVES			
That humbly craves upon her knees to stay,	2Tamb	3.4.70	Olymp
And with that summe he craves might we wage warre.	Jew	2.2.27	1Knght
the President of Paris, that craves accesse unto your grace.	P1157	22.19	P 1Msngr
For that security craves <great> Lucifer.	F 425	2.1.37	Mephst
And craves his taske, and seekes to be at fight.	Ovid's Elegies		3.6.68
CRAVING			
Humblye craving your gracious reply.	P1170	22.32	Frier
CRAV'ST			
Ask'st why I chaunge? because thou crav'st reward:	Ovid's Elegies		1.10.11
CRAZED (See also CRASED)			
how you durst with so much wealth/Trust such a crazed Vessell,	Jew	1.1.80	1Merch
CREAKE			
And with your pastime let the bedsted creake,	Ovid's Elegies		3.13.26

CREAKING
And opening dores with creaking noyse abound? Ovid's Elegies 1.6.50
CREATE
Create him Prorex of [Assiria] <Affrica>, 1Tamb 1.1.89 Cosroe
I heere create thee Lord high Chamberlaine, Edw 1.1.154 Edward
Spencer, I heere create thee earle of Wilshire, Edw 3.1.49 Edward
And meerely of our love we do create thee/Earle of Gloster, and Edw 3.1.145 Edward
We heere create our welbeloved sonne, Edw 4.6.24 Queene
CREATED
Created of the massy dregges of earth, 2Tamb 4.1.123 Tamb
Spencer the sonne, created earle of Gloster, Edw 4.6.56 Rice
CREATION
me, as Paradise was to Adam the first day of his creation. F 658 2.2.107 P Faust
Talke not of Paradice or <nor> Creation, but marke the <this> F 659 2.2.108 P Lucifr
Since first the worlds creation did begin. F1985 5.3.3 1Schol
CREATURE
And every creature shall be purifi'd, F 514 2.1.126 Mephst
Why wert thou not a creature wanting soule? F1964 5.2.168 Faust
I flie her lust, but follow beauties creature; Ovid's Elegies 3.10.37
Faire creature, let me speake without offence, Hero and Leander 1.199
CREATURES
When ayrie creatures warre amongst themselves: Dido 4.2.7 Iarbus
Inhumaine creatures, nurst with Tigers milke, Edw 5.1.71 Edward
all holy things/And on all creatures obscure darcknesse brings. Ovid's Elegies 3.8.20
We humane creatures should enjoy that blisse. Hero and Leander 1.254
But know you not that creatures wanting sence, Hero and Leander 2.55
CREDIBLE
Tis credible some [god-head] <good head> haunts the place. Ovid's Elegies 3.1.2
CREDIT
I hope our credit in the Custome-house/Will serve as well as I Jew 1.1.57 Barab
And is thy credit not enough for that? Jew 1.1.62 Barab
And therefore farre exceeds my credit, Sir. Jew 1.1.65 1Merch
I'le gage my credit, 'twill content your grace. F1622 4.6.65 Faust
Though himselfe see; heele credit her denyall, Ovid's Elegies 2.2.57
He's happy, that his love dares boldly credit, Ovid's Elegies 2.5.9
She must be honest to thy servants credit. Ovid's Elegies 3.4.36
Would I my words would any credit beare. Ovid's Elegies 3.11.20
CREDITE
How may I credite these thy flattering termes, Dido 1.1.109 Venus
CREDULITY
Now your credulity harme to me hath raisd. Ovid's Elegies 3.11.44
CREDULOUS
Becomes it Jewes to be so credulous, Jew 1.2.360 Barab
False, credulous, inconstant Abigall! Jew 3.4.27 Barab
(Love is too full of faith, too credulous, Hero and Leander 2.221
CREEKES
Deep rivers, havens, creekes, and litle seas, 2Tamb 3.2.87 Tamb
CREEPE
And on my knees creepe to Jerusalem. Jew 4.1.62 Barab
Whose mounting thoughts did never creepe so low, Edw 2.2.77 Gavstn
like to Ovids Flea, I can creepe into every corner of a Wench: F 665 2.2.114 P Pride
Thus, as the Gods creepe on with feete of wool, F 877 3.1.99 Pope
And the dull snake about thy offrings creepe, Ovid's Elegies 2.13.13
CREEPES
And by the barke a canker creepes me up, Edw 2.2.18 Mortmr
And creepes along the vales, deviding just/The bounds of Italy, Lucan, First Booke 217
As pittying these lovers, downeward creepes. Hero and Leander 2.100
CREEPING
O Serpent that came creeping from the shoare, Dido 5.1.165 Dido
Came creeping to us with their crownes apace. 1Tamb 2.5.86 Tamb
Their creeping Gallyes had us in the chase: Jew 2.2.12 Bosco
Can kinglie Lions fawne on creeping Ants? Edw 1.4.15 Penbrk
CREETE
Where twixt the Isles of Cyprus and of Creete, 2Tamb 1.2.26 Callap
CREPT
I thinke it be some Ghost crept out of Purgatory, and now is F1060 3.2.80 P Archbp
crept out of Purgatory come to begge a pardon of your F App p.232 14 P Lorein
And in the brest of this slaine Bull are crept, Lucan, First Booke 632
And faine by stealth away she would have crept, Hero and Leander 2.310
CREST
and on his silver crest/A snowy Feather spangled white he 1Tamb 4.1.50 2Msngr
I long to breake my speare upon his crest, 1Tamb 4.3.46 Arabia
Nodding and shaking of thy spangled crest, Edw 2.2.186 Mortmr
Weele steele it on their crest, and powle their tops. Edw 3.1.27 Edward
And weare thy colours on my plumed crest. F1778 5.1.105 Faust
having whiskt/His taile athwart his backe, and crest heav'd up, Lucan, First Booke 211
CRESTES
And shining stones upon their loftie Crestes: 1Tamb 1.1.145 Ceneus
Yet should our courages and steeled crestes, 2Tamb 2.2.17 Gazell
CRESTS
Fortune her selfe dooth sit upon our Crests. 1Tamb 2.2.73 Meandr
CRETE (See also CREETE)
Be witnesse Crete (nor Crete doth all things feigne)/Crete Ovid's Elegies 3.9.19
things feigne)/Crete proud that Jove her nourcery maintaine. Ovid's Elegies 3.9.20
Onely was Crete fruitfull that plenteous yeare, Ovid's Elegies 3.9.37
CREUSA
mine armes, and by the hand/Led faire Creusa my beloved wife, Dido 2.1.267 Aeneas
CREW (See CRUE)
CRIDE
But I cride out, Aeneas, false Aeneas stay. Dido 5.1.228 Anna
Which when I viewd, I cride, Aeneas stay, Dido 5.1.232 Anna
He thus cride out: Lucan, First Booke 197
these he seeing what myschiefes must ensue,/Cride out, O gods! Lucan, First Booke 630

CRIE			
To armes my Lords, on Christ still let us crie,	2Tamb	2.2.63	Orcan
cracke, the Ecchoe and the souldiers crie/Make deafe the aire,	2Tamb	3.3.60	Therid
With open crie pursues the wounded Stag:	2Tamb	3.5.7	2Msngr
Crie quittance Madam then, and love not him.	Edw	1.4.195	Mortmr
And Aeque tandem shall that canker crie,	Edw	2.2.41	Edward
I feare mee that this crie will raise the towne,	Edw	5.5.114	Matrvs
That at my funeralles some may weeping crie,	Ovid's Elegies		2.10.37
Having striv'ne in vaine, was now about to crie,	Hero and Leander		1.413
Whereat agast, the poore soule gan to crie,	Hero and Leander		2.177
CRIED			
As I cried out for feare he should have falne.	2Tamb	1.3.42	Zenoc
That I was mad, and barbarous all men cried,	Ovid's Elegies		1.7.19
Why mockst thou me she cried, or being ill,	Ovid's Elegies		3.6.77
CRIES			
What fearfull cries comes from the river [Sene] <Rene>,/That	P 361	7.1	Ramus
With gastlie murmure of my sighes and cries,	Edw	1.4.179	Queene
Such fearefull shrikes, and cries, were never heard,	F1986	5.3.4	1Schol
Aye me she cries, to love, why art a shamed?	Ovid's Elegies		2.18.8
CRIME (See also CRYME)			
And punish me Aeneas for this crime.	Dido	4.4.36	Dido
Thou shalt burne first, thy crime is worse then his:	Dido	5.1.297	Dido
hands of mine/Shall not be guiltie of so foule a crime.	Edw	5.1.99	Edward
And least the sad signes of my crime remaine,	Ovid's Elegies		1.7.67
No gifts given secretly thy crime bewray.	Ovid's Elegies		2.5.6
My selfe unguilty of this crime I know.	Ovid's Elegies		2.7.28
My stay no crime, my flight no joy shall breede,	Ovid's Elegies		2.17.25
She wailing Mars sinne, and her uncles crime,	Ovid's Elegies		3.5.49
CRIMES			
the inward soule/With such flagitious crimes of hainous sinnes,	F App	p.243 42	OldMan
To staine all faith in truth, by false crimes use.	Ovid's Elegies		2.2.38
Doost me of new crimes alwayes guilty frame?	Ovid's Elegies		2.7.1
CRIMSEN			
In all thy face will be no crimsen bloud.	Ovid's Elegies		2.11.28
CRIMSON			
A hundred Bassoes cloath'd in crimson silk/Shall ride before	2Tamb	1.2.46	Callap
That being concocted, turnes to crimson blood,	2Tamb	3.2.108	Tamb
And rockes dyed crimson with Prometheus bloud.	Ovid's Elegies		2.16.40
CRIPPLES			
That I have laugh'd agood to see the cripples/Goe limping home	Jew	2.3.211	Ithimr
CRISPY			
take/In crocked [tramells] <trannels> crispy curles to make.	Ovid's Elegies		1.14.26
CRITICAL			
a non-plus at the critical aspect of my terrible countenance.	Jew	4.2.14	P Pilia
CRITICALL			
Besides my Lord, this day is Criticall,	2Tamb	5.3.91	Phsitn
The Sessions day is criticall to theeves,	Jew	2.3.105	Barab
CROCODILES			
As Crocodiles that unaffrighted rest,	1Tamb	4.1.10	Souldn
CROOKED			
Convaid me from their crooked nets and bands:	Dido	2.1.222	Aeneas
hollow hanging of a hill/And crooked bending of a craggy rock,	2Tamb	1.2.58	Callap
Torment sweet friend, that base and [crooked age] <aged man>,	F1753	5.1.80	Faust
The thunder hov'd horse in a crooked line,	Lucan, First Booke		222
Under the rockes by crooked Vogesus;	Lucan, First Booke		399
Shaking her snakie haire and crooked pine/With flaming toppe,	Lucan, First Booke		571
Then crams salt levin on his crooked knife;	Lucan, First Booke		609
take/In crocked [tramells] <trannels> crispy curles to make.	Ovid's Elegies		1.14.26
Or men with crooked sickles corne downe fell.	Ovid's Elegies		1.15.12
The crooked Barque hath her swift sailes displayd.	Ovid's Elegies		2.11.24
Nor thy gulfes crooked Malea, would I feare.	Ovid's Elegies		2.16.24
And untild ground with crooked plough-shares broake.	Ovid's Elegies		3.9.14
Being fit broken with the crooked share,	Ovid's Elegies		3.9.32
Or crooked Dolphin when the sailer sings;	Hero and Leander		2.234
CROPT			
Cropt from the pleasures of the fruitfull earth,	Jew	1.2.380	Mthias
CROSBITING			
Like one that is imploy'd in Catzerie/And crosbiting, such a	Jew	4.3.13	Barab
CROSSE			
Or crosse the streame, and meet him in the field?	2Tamb	1.1.12	Orcan
And yet I'le give her many a golden crosse/With Christian	Jew	2.3.296	Barab
My heart misgives me, that to crosse your love,	Jew	2.3.349	Barab
in Religion/Might be a meanes to crosse you in your love.	P 16	1.16	QnMoth
Then pray unto our Ladye, kisse this crosse.	P 302	5.29	Gonzag
And he that living hated so the crosse,	P 320	5.47	Anjoy
I sweare by this crosse, wee'l not be partiall,	P 325	5.52	Anjoy
And if he grudge or crosse his Mothers will,	P 523	9.42	QnMoth
Might seeme <seek> to crosse me in mine enterprise.	P 574	11.39	Navrre
That crosse me thus, shall know I am displeasd.	Edw	1.1.79	Edward
To crosse to Lambeth, and there stay with me.	Edw	1.2.78	ArchBp
Nay all of them conspire to crosse me thus,	Edw	2.2.95	Edward
France/Makes friends, to crosse the seas with her yong sonne,	Edw	3.1.270	Spencr
By [cunning] <comming> in <of> thine Art to crosse the Pope,/Or	F 859	3.1.81	Mephst
Must every bit be spiced with a Crosse?	F1066	3.2.86	Faust
Tush, Christ did call the Theefe upon the Crosse,	F1482	4.4.26	Faust
Tush, Christ did call the thiefe upon the Crosse,	F App	p.240 125	Faust
least sloth and long delay/Might crosse him, he withdrew his	Lucan, First Booke		395
Each crosse waies corner doth as much expresse.	Ovid's Elegies		3.1.18
CROSSED			
how you crossed me in my conference with the emperour?	F App	p.238 77	P Faust
CROSSES			
Shall weare white crosses on their Burgonets,	P 232	4.30	Guise
Gonzago, Retes, sweare by/The argent crosses in your burgonets,	P 275	5.2	Guise

CROSSING
What, are you crossing of your selfe? F App p.232 18 Faust
CROST
Wee with our Peeres have crost Danubius stream/To treat of 2Tamb 1.1.79 Sgsmnd
Then crost the sea and came to Oblia, 2Tamb 1.3.211 Therid
From thence I crost the Gulfe, call'd by the name/Mare magiore, 2Tamb 1.3.214 Therid
Then when sir Paris crost the seas with <for> her, F1694 5.1.21 Faust
That crost them; both which now approacht the camp, Lucan, First Booke 270
CROUCH
Where kings shall crouch unto our conquering swords, 1Tamb 1.2.220 Usumc
And wake blacke Jove to crouch and kneele to me, 2Tamb 5.1.98 Tamb
And crouch before the Papall dignity: F 874 3.1.96 Pope
CROW
Crowes <crow> [survive] <survives> armes-bearing Pallas hate, Ovid's Elegies 2.6.35
CROWCH
Now crowch ye kings of greatest Asia, 2Tamb 4.3.98 Tamb
CROWES
Crowes <crow> [survive] <survives> armes-bearing Pallas hate, Ovid's Elegies 2.6.35
CROWING
Yet, shall the crowing of these cockerels, Edw 2.2.203 Edward
And crowing Cocks poore soules to worke awake. Ovid's Elegies 1.6.66
CROWN
Which I esteeme as portion of my crown. 1Tamb 2.3.35 Cosroe
The thirst of raigne and sweetnes of a crown, 1Tamb 2.7.12 Tamb
Each man a crown? why kingly fought ifaith. 1Tamb 3.3.216 Tamb
Nay take the Turkish Crown from her, Zenocrate, 1Tamb 3.3.220 Tamb
Though with the losse of Egypt and my Crown. 1Tamb 5.1.444 Souldn
to your dominions/Than ever yet confirm'd th'Egyptian Crown. 1Tamb 5.1.449 Tamb
And here's the crown my Lord, help set it on. 1Tamb 5.1.505 Usumc
Thanks king of Morocus, take your crown again. 2Tamb 1.3.137 Tamb
Go too sirha, take your crown, and make up the halfe dozen. 2Tamb 3.5.135 P Tamb
CROWN'D
With greatest pompe had crown'd thee Emperour. 1Tamb 2.5.5 Tamb
And have bene crown'd for prooved worthynesse: 1Tamb 5.1.491 Tamb
Thou shalt be crown'd a king and be my mate. 2Tamb 1.2.66 Callap
Crown'd and invested by the hand of Jove, 2Tamb 4.1.151 Tamb
That I may see thee crown'd before I die. 2Tamb 5.3.179 Tamb
then Laelius/The chiefe Centurion crown'd with Oaken leaves, Lucan, First Booke 358
Verses alone are with continuance crown'd. Ovid's Elegies 3.8.28
Where crown'd with blazing light and majestie, Hero and Leander 1.110
CROWND
Edward this day hath crownd him king a new. Edw 3.1.261 Edward
Golden-hair'd Ceres crownd with eares of corne, Ovid's Elegies 3.9.3
Now my ship in the wished haven crownd, Ovid's Elegies 3.10.29
With Cupids myrtle was his bonet crownd, Hero and Leander 2.105
CROWNE
And here Queene Dido weares th'imperiall Crowne, Dido 2.1.63 Illion
Whose golden Crowne might ballance my content: Dido 3.4.36 Dido
Whose Crowne and kingdome rests at thy commande: Dido 3.4.58 Dido
Each word she sayes will then containe a Crowne, Dido 4.3.53 Aeneas
Weare the emperiall Crowne of Libia, Dido 4.4.34 Dido
O how a Crowne becomes Aeneas head! Dido 4.4.38 Dido
A Burgonet of steele, and not a Crowne, Dido 4.4.42 Aeneas
To crowne me Emperour of Asia. 1Tamb 1.1.112 Cosroe
Bringing the Crowne to make you Emperour. 1Tamb 1.1.135 Menaph
I willingly receive th'emperiall crowne, 1Tamb 1.1.157 Cosroe
We here doo crowne thee Monarch of the East, 1Tamb 1.1.161 Ortyg
We knew my Lord, before we brought the crowne, 1Tamb 1.1.179 Ortyg
As easely may you get the Souldans crowne, 1Tamb 1.2.27 Tamb
Than the possession of the Persean Crowne, 1Tamb 1.2.91 Tamb
Than dooth the King of Persea in his Crowne: 1Tamb 1.2.242 Tamb
Before I crowne you kings in Asia. 1Tamb 1.2.246 Tamb
In happy hower we have set the Crowne/Upon your kingly head, 1Tamb 2.1.50 Ortyg
That it may reach the King of Perseas crowne, 1Tamb 2.3.53 Cosroe
Our Crowne the pin that thousands seeke to cleave. 1Tamb 2.4.9 Mycet
They cannot take away my crowne from me. 1Tamb 2.4.14 Mycet
Is this your Crowne? 1Tamb 2.4.27 Tamb
And none shall keepe the crowne but Tamburlaine: 1Tamb 2.5.7 Cosroe
To weare a Crowne enchac'd with pearle and golde, 1Tamb 2.5.60 Therid
That if I should desire the Persean Crowne, 1Tamb 2.5.76 Tamb
And bid him battell for his novell Crowne? 1Tamb 2.5.88 Techel
Make but a jest to win the Persean crowne. 1Tamb 2.5.98 Tamb
Thus to deprive me of my crowne and life. 1Tamb 2.7.2 Cosroe
The sweet fruition of an earthly crowne. 1Tamb 2.7.29 Tamb
Neptune and Dis gain'd each of them a Crowne, 1Tamb 2.7.37 Usumc
And on thy head weare my Emperiall crowne, 1Tamb 3.3.113 Bajzth
adorned with my Crowne,/As if thou wert the Empresse of the 1Tamb 3.3.124 Tamb
Til then take thou my crowne, vaunt of my worth, 1Tamb 3.3.130 Tamb
His royall Crowne againe, so highly won. 1Tamb 3.3.219 Zenoc
And crowne me Emperour of Affrica. 1Tamb 3.3.221 Tamb
Give her the Crowne Turkesse, you wer best. 1Tamb 3.3.224 Therid
By murder raised to the Persean Crowne, 1Tamb 4.3.13 Souldn
vagabond/Should brave a king, or weare a princely crowne. 1Tamb 4.3.22 Souldn
I crowne you here (Theridamas) King of Argier: 1Tamb 4.4.116 P Tamb
Zenocrate, I will not crowne thee yet, 1Tamb 4.4.139 Tamb
That sees my crowne, my honor and my name, 1Tamb 5.1.260 Bajzth
time to grace/Her princely Temples with the Persean crowne: 1Tamb 5.1.489 Tamb
Then let us set the crowne upon her head, 1Tamb 5.1.501 Therid
And here we crowne thee Queene of Persea, 1Tamb 5.1.507 Tamb
For he shall weare the crowne of Persea, 2Tamb 1.3.74 Tamb
And sirha, if you meane to weare a crowne, 2Tamb 1.3.98 Tamb
My crowne, my selfe, and all the power I have, 2Tamb 1.3.115 Therid
Wel said Argier, receive thy crowne againe. 2Tamb 1.3.127 Tamb

CROWNE (cont.)				
Which with my crowne I gladly offer thee.	2Tamb	1.3.136		Usumc
I here present thee with the crowne of Fesse,	2Tamb	1.3.140		Techel
Thanks king of Fesse, take here thy crowne again.	2Tamb	1.3.150		Tamb
And made him sweare obedience to my crowne.	2Tamb	1.3.190		Techel
Come Almeda, receive this crowne of me,	2Tamb	3.5.129		Callap
least hee hide his crowne as the foolish king of Persea did.	2Tamb	3.5.154	P	Tamb
Loden with Lawrell wreathes to crowne us all.	2Tamb	3.5.164		Tamb
the good I have/Join'd with my fathers crowne would never cure.	2Tamb	4.1.58		Calyph
and on his head/A Chaplet brighter than Apollos crowne,	2Tamb	5.2.33		Amasia
First take my Scourge and my imperiall Crowne,	2Tamb	5.3.177		Tamb
Many will talke of Title to a Crowne:	Jew	Prol.18		Machvl
Give him a crowne, and fill me out more wine.	Jew	4.4.46		Ithimr
And joynes your linnage to the crowne of France?	P 51	1.51		Admral
And with this wait Ile counterpoise a Crowne,	P 115	2.58		Guise
That hinder our possession to the crowne:	P 154	2.97		Guise
A royall seate, a scepter and a crowne:	P 161	2.104		Guise
That if I undertake to weare the crowne/Of Poland, it may	P 466	8.16		Anjoy
prejudice their hope/Of my inheritance to the crowne of France:	P 468	8.18		Anjoy
For Polands crowne and kingly diadem.	P 480	8.30		Lord
For Ile rule France, but they shall weare the crowne:	P 525	9.44		QnMoth
To weare his brothers crowne and dignity.	P 557	11.22		QnMoth
And at the length in Pampelonia crowne,	P 580	11.45		Pleshe
All this and more hath Henry with his crowne.	P 596	12.9		QnMoth
noble mindes change not their thoughts/For wearing of a crowne:	P 611	12.24		Mugern
diadem, before/You were invested in the crowne of France.	P 613	12.26		Mugern
Why I am no traitor to the crowne of France.	P 825	17.20		Guise
And know my Lord, the Pope will sell his triple crowne,	P 851	17.46		Guise
Guise, weare our crowne, and be thou King of France,	P 859	17.54		King
For his aspiring thoughts aime at the crowne,	P 923	18.24		Navrre
Wicked Navarre will get the crowne of France,	P1086	19.156		QnMoth
These bloudy hands shall teare his triple Crowne,	P1199	22.61		King
Now let the house of Bourbon weare the crowne,	P1232	22.94		King
The king shall lose his crowne, for we have power,	Edw	1.2.59		Mortmr
Warwicke and Lancaster, weare you my crowne,	Edw	1.4.37		Edward
Clarke of the crowne, direct our warrant forth,	Edw	1.4.369		Edward
and in his tuskan cap/A jewell of more value then the crowne.	Edw	1.4.415		Mortmr
Looke to your owne crowne, if you back him thus.	Edw	2.2.93		Warwck
And all the honors longing to my crowne,	Edw	3.1.131		Edward
I weare the crowne, but am contrould by them,	Edw	5.1.29		Edward
But tell me, must I now resigne my crowne,	Edw	5.1.36		Edward
And princely Edwards right we crave the crowne.	Edw	5.1.39		BshpWn
But if proud Mortimer do weare this crowne,	Edw	5.1.43		Edward
They stay your answer, will you yeeld your crowne?	Edw	5.1.50		Leistr
way how hardly I can brooke/To loose my crowne and kingdome,	Edw	5.1.52		Edward
Here, take my crowne, the life of Edward too,	Edw	5.1.57		Edward
That I may gaze upon this glittering crowne,	Edw	5.1.60		Edward
And needes I must resigne my wished crowne.	Edw	5.1.70		Edward
See monsters see, ile weare my crowne againe,	Edw	5.1.74		Edward
But that I feele the crowne upon my head,	Edw	5.1.82		Edward
heere receive my crowne.	Edw	5.1.97		Edward
The king hath willingly resignde his crowne.	Edw	5.2.28		BshpWn
Mother, perswade me not to weare the crowne,	Edw	5.2.92		Prince
And thou compelst this prince to weare the crowne.	Edw	5.4.88		Kent
I feele a hell of greefe: where is my crowne?	Edw	5.5.90		Edward
And both contributary to my Crowne.	F 337	1.3.109		Faust
And point like Antiques at his triple Crowne:	F 862	3.1.84		Mephst
Here, take his triple Crowne along with you,	F 970	3.1.192		Pope
That slept both Bruno and his crowne away.	F 988	3.2.8		Faust
With his rich triple crowne to be reserv'd,	F1027	3.2.47		Raymnd
by the honor of mine Imperial crowne, that what ever thou	F App	p.236 8	P	Emper
And on my haires a crowne of flowers remaine.	Ovid's Elegies	1.6.38		
But thou my crowne, from sad haires tane away,	Ovid's Elegies	1.6.67		
Nor shamefully her coate pull ore her crowne,	Ovid's Elegies	1.7.47		
which from their crowne/Phoebus and Bacchus wisht were hanging	Ovid's Elegies	1.14.31		
And falling vallies be the smooth-wayes crowne.	Ovid's Elegies	2.16.52		
Jewels, and gold their Virgin tresses crowne,	Ovid's Elegies	3.12.25		
CROWNED				
and thy seed/Shall issue crowned from their mothers wombe.	2Tamb	1.3.53		Tamb
CROWNES				
Spurning their crownes from off their captive heads.	1Tamb	1.2.57		Techel
Holde thee Cosroe, weare two imperiall Crownes.	1Tamb	2.5.1		Tamb
Came creeping to us with their crownes apace.	1Tamb	2.5.86		Tamb
I long to see those crownes won by our swords,	1Tamb	3.3.98		Therid
We have their crownes, their bodies strowe the fielde.	1Tamb	3.3.215		Techel
If they would lay their crownes before my feet,	1Tamb	4.2.93		Tamb
Now take these three crownes, and pledge me, my contributorie	1Tamb	4.4.115	P	Tamb
That fights for Scepters and for slippery crownes,	1Tamb	5.1.356		Zenoc
whom all kings/Of force must yeeld their crownes and Emperies:	1Tamb	5.1.481		Souldn
Amongst so many crownes of burnisht gold,	2Tamb	1.2.30		Callap
And cast your crownes in slavery at their feet.	2Tamb	3.5.149		Tamb
Now in their glories shine the golden crownes/Of these proud	2Tamb	4.1.1		Amyras
That whips downe cities, and controwleth crownes,	2Tamb	4.3.100		Tamb
And Crownes come either by succession/Or urg'd by force; and	Jew	1.1.131		Barab
A hundred thousand Crownes.	Jew	2.2.36		Govnr
An hundred Crownes, I'le have him; there's the coyne.	Jew	2.3.130		Barab
Thou hast thy Crownes, fellow, come let's away.	Jew	2.3.158		Mater
I am content to lose some of my Crownes;	Jew	2.3.178		Barab
a hundred of the Jewes Crownes that I had such a Concubine.	Jew	3.1.28	P	Ithimr
Their voyage will be worth ten thousand Crownes.	Jew	4.1.70		Barab
Send for a hundred Crownes at least.	Jew	4.2.70	P	Pilia
Ten hundred thousand crownes,--Master Barabas.	Jew	4.2.71	P	Ithimr
Sirra Barabas, send me a hundred crownes.	Jew	4.2.73	P	Ithimr

CROWNES (cont.)

To conclude, he gave me ten crownes.	Jew	4.2.113	P Pilia
Write for five hundred Crownes.	Jew	4.2.116	P Pilia
tell him, I scorne to write a line under a hundred crownes.	Jew	4.2.121	P Ithimr
Barabas send me three hundred Crownes.	Jew	4.3.1	Barab
And I by him must send three hundred crownes.	Jew	4.3.15	Barab
No god-a-mercy, shall I have these crownes?	Jew	4.3.31	Pilia
'Tis not five hundred Crownes that I esteeme,	Jew	4.3.40	Barab
Here's many words but no crownes; the crownes.	Jew	4.3.46	P Pilia
have a shag-rag knave to come [demand]/Three hundred Crownes,	Jew	4.3.62	Barab
[demand]/Three hundred Crownes, and then five hundred Crownes?	Jew	4.3.62	Barab
There's two crownes for thee, play.	Jew	4.4.47	Pilia
now; Bid him deliver thee a thousand Crownes, by the same token,	Jew	4.4.75	P Ithimr
And then Ile guerdon thee with store of crownes.	P 89	2.32	Guise
The guider of all crownes,/Graunt that our deeds may wel	P 599	12.12	King
And could my crownes revenew bring him back,	Edw	1.4.308	Edward
Thou shalt have crownes of us, t'out bid the Barons,	Edw	3.1.55	Edward
Lest Faustus make your shaven crownes to bleed.	F1007	3.2.27	Faust
Why french crownes.	F App	p.230 32	P Wagner
crownes a man were as good have as many english counters,	F App	p.230 33	P Clown
Crownes fell from holy statues, ominous birds/Defil'd the day,	Lucan, First Booke		556
His fauning wench with her desire he crownes.	Ovid's Elegies		2.2.34

CROWNETS

Crownets of pearle about his naked armes,	Edw	1.1.63	Gavstn

CROWNS

Then fight couragiously, their crowns are yours.	1Tamb	3.3.30	Tamb
marketplace; whats the price of this slave, two hundred Crowns?	Jew	2.3.98	P Barab
as you love your life send me five hundred crowns, and give the	Jew	4.2.118	P Ithimr

CRUCIFIED

What, has he crucified a child?	Jew	3.6.49	1Fryar

CRUCIS

signumque crucis quod nunc facio; et per vota nostra ipse nunc	F 249	1.3.21	P Faust

CRUE

To race and scatter thy inglorious crue,	1Tamb	4.3.67	Souldn
Larissa plaines/With hostes apeece against this Turkish crue,	2Tamb	1.3.108	Tamb

CRUEL

(cruel Tamburlane) as I could willingly feed upon thy blood-raw	1Tamb	4.4.11	P Bajzth
vaine or Artier feed/The cursed substance of that cruel heart,	2Tamb	4.1.178	Soria
Ah cruel Brat, sprung from a tyrants loines,	2Tamb	4.3.54	Jrslem
Shouldst thou have entred, cruel Tamburlaine:	2Tamb	5.1.102	Govnr
Their cruel death, mine owne captivity,	2Tamb	5.2.20	Callap
Untill the cruel Giants war was done)/We plaine not heavens,	Lucan, First Booke		36
And cruel field, nere burning Aetna fought:	Lucan, First Booke		43
for Julia/Snatcht hence by cruel fates with ominous howles,	Lucan, First Booke		112

CRUELL

Too cruell, why wilt thou forsake me thus?	Dido	1.1.243	Aeneas
Save, save, O save our ships from cruell fire,	Dido	1.2.7	Illion
Was by the cruell Mirmidons surprizd,	Dido	2.1.287	Aeneas
O love, O hate, O cruell womens hearts,	Dido	3.3.66	Iarbus
Who then of all so cruell may he be,	Dido	3.4.16	Aeneas
Like to the cruell brothers of the earth,	1Tamb	2.2.47	Meandr
These are the cruell pirates of Argeire,	1Tamb	3.3.55	Tamb
Preserving life, by hasting cruell death.	1Tamb	4.4.96	Bajzth
And guiltlesly endure a cruell death.	1Tamb	5.1.329	Zenoc
Yet here detain'd by cruell Tamburlaine.	2Tamb	1.2.4	Callap
I am sure/What cruell slaughter of our Christian bloods,	2Tamb	2.1.5	Fredrk
T'incounter with the cruell Tamburlain,	2Tamb	2.2.5	Orcan
And vow to burne the villaines cruell heart.	2Tamb	3.1.56	Trebiz
Least cruell Scythians should dismember him.	2Tamb	3.4.37	Olymp
And all have jointly sworne thy cruell death,	2Tamb	3.5.112	Soria
hardly can we brooke/The cruell handling of our selves in this:	Jew	1.2.175	1Jew
In prosecution of these cruell armes,	P 796	16.10	Navrre
If I be cruell, and growe tyrannous,	Edw	2.2.206	Edward
The lords are cruell, and the king unkinde,	Edw	4.2.2	Queene
Nay so will hell, and cruell Mortimer,	Edw	4.7.75	Edward
And thinkes your grace that Bartley will bee cruell?	Edw	5.1.151	Bartly
Tis cruell love turmoyles my captive hart.	Ovid's Elegies		1.2.8
And farewell cruell posts, rough thresholds block,	Ovid's Elegies		1.6.73
Or holy gods with cruell strokes abus'd.	Ovid's Elegies		1.7.6
dost betray them/To Pedants, that with cruell lashes pay them.	Ovid's Elegies		1.13.18
He's cruell, and too much his griefe doth favour/That seekes	Ovid's Elegies		2.5.11
To cruell armes their drunken selves did summon.	Ovid's Elegies		2.12.20
With cruell hand why doest greene Apples pull?	Ovid's Elegies		2.14.24
Cruell is he, that loves whom none protect.	Ovid's Elegies		2.19.4
Love is not ful of pittie (as men say)/But deaffe and cruell,	Hero and Leander		2.288

CRUELLY

But cruelly her tresses having rent,	Ovid's Elegies		1.7.49
But cruelly by her was drown'd and rent.	Ovid's Elegies		3.1.58

CRUELST

With terrours to the last and cruelst hew:	1Tamb	5.1.8	Govnr

CRUELTIE

Unworthy king, that by thy crueltie,	1Tamb	4.2.56	Zabina
From al the crueltie my soule sustaind,	2Tamb	3.1.33	Callap
In war, in blood, in death, in crueltie,	2Tamb	4.1.156	Tamb
Which Ile desolve with bloud and crueltie.	P 26	1.26	QnMoth

CRUELTIES

Whose cruelties are not so harsh as thine,	2Tamb	4.1.169	Jrslem

CRUELTY

And ruthlesse cruelty of Tamburlaine.	1Tamb	5.1.346	Anippe
Harbors revenge, war, death and cruelty:	2Tamb	1.3.78	Tamb
These barbarous Scythians full of cruelty,	2Tamb	3.4.19	Olymp
O mercilesse infernall cruelty.	2Tamb	4.3.85	Jrslem
And therefore stil augments his cruelty.	2Tamb	5.3.219	Tamb

CRUELTY (cont.)			
Nor hope of thee but extreme cruelty,	Jew	5.2.59	Govnr
CRUSA			
And Crusa unto Zanthus first affide,	Ovid's Elegies	3.5.31	
CRUSH			
All great things crush themselves, such end the gods/Allot the	Lucan, First Booke	81	
CRY (See also CRIE)			
And cry me mercie, noble King.	1Tamb	2.4.22	Mycet
No, none can heare him, cry he ne're so loud.	Jew	4.1.136	Ithimr
Whilste I cry placet like a Senator.	P 861	17.56	King
Cry out, exclaime, houle till thy throat be hoarce,	P1077	19.147	King
They all cry out to speake with Doctor Faustus.	F1600	4.6.43	Servnt
Then wouldst thou cry, stay night and runne not thus.	Ovid's Elegies	1.13.40	
Leave colouring thy tresses I did cry,	Ovid's Elegies	1.14.1	
And this is he whom fierce love burnes, they cry.	Ovid's Elegies	3.1.20	
CRY'DE			
O Hero, Hero, thus he cry'de full oft,	Hero and Leander	2.147	
CRYDE			
For saving of a Romaine Citizen,/Stept forth, and cryde:	Lucan, First Booke	360	
held up, all joyntly cryde/They'ill follow where he please:	Lucan, First Booke	388	
Aye me, Leander cryde, th'enamoured sunne,	Hero and Leander	2.202	
CRYE			
Began to crye, let us unto our ships,	Dido	2.1.127	Aeneas
The crye of beasts, the ratling of the windes,	Dido	2.1.336	Venus
Come backe, come backe, I heare her crye a farre,	Dido	4.3.27	Aeneas
And teares of pearle, crye stay, Aeneas, stay:	Dido	4.3.52	Aeneas
What meanes my sister thus to rave and crye?	Dido	5.1.193	Anna
CRYED			
Where meeting with the rest, kill kill they cryed.	Dido	2.1.190	Aeneas
Polixena cryed out, Aeneas stay,	Dido	2.1.281	Aeneas
I cryed, tis sinne, tis sinne, these haires to burne,	Ovid's Elegies	1.14.27	
What doest, I cryed, transportst thou my delight?	Ovid's Elegies	2.5.29	
Farewell Corinna cryed thy dying tongue.	Ovid's Elegies	2.6.48	
CRYES			
What can my teares or cryes prevaile me now?	Dido	5.1.319	Anna
CRYING			
Burst from the earth, crying, Aeneas flye,	Dido	2.1.207	Aeneas
All which hemd me about, crying, this is he.	Dido	2.1.219	Aeneas
And crying, Love I come, leapt lively in.	Hero and Leander	2.154	
CRYMES			
There Paris is, and Helens crymes record,	Ovid's Elegies	2.18.37	
CRYSTAL (See CHRISTAL, CHRISTALL, CHRYSTALL)			
CUBAR			
I came to Cubar, where the Negros dwell,	2Tamb	1.3.201	Techel
CUCKOLD			
Cuckold-makers to clap hornes of honest mens heades o'this	F1317	4.1.163	P Benvol
CUCKOLDE			
that dares make the Duke a cuckolde, and use a counterfeite key	P 806	17.1	P Souldr
duke a cuckolde and use a counterfeyt key to his privy chamber	Paris	ms 1,p390	P Souldr
CUCKOLD-MAKERS			
Cuckold-makers to clap hornes of honest mens heades o'this	F1317	4.1.163	P Benvol
CUI			
Major sum quam cui possit fortuna nocere.	Edw	5.4.69	Mortmr
CULL			
I'le cull thee out the fairest Curtezans,	F 537	2.1.149	Mephst
CULLIONS			
With base outlandish cullions at his heeles,	Edw	1.4.409	Mortmr
CULLISE			
Close your Port-cullise, charge your Basiliskes,	Jew	3.5.31	Govnr
CULLOR			
The very cullor scard him; a dead blacknesse/Ranne through the	Lucan, First Booke	617	
CULPABLE			
Would I were culpable of some offence,	Ovid's Elegies	2.7.11	
CULVERIN			
Till you shall heare a Culverin discharg'd/By him that beares	Jew	5.4.3	Govnr
CUNNING			
And makes our hopes survive to [coming] <cunning> joyes:	Dido	1.1.154	Achat
An ointment which a cunning Alcumist/Distilled from the purest	2Tamb	4.2.59	Olymp
And cast with cunning for the time to come:	Jew	1.2.222	Barab
But here they come; be cunning Abigall.	Jew	1.2.299	Barab
And like a cunning Jew so cast about,	Jew	2.3.235	Barab
And like a cunning spirit feigne some lye,	Jew	2.3.382	Barab
Till swolne with cunning of a selfe conceit,	F 20	Prol.20	1Chor
Will be as cunning as Agrippa was,	F 144	1.1.116	Faust
Faustus may try his cunning by himselfe.	F 187	1.1.159	Cornel
be,/That this proud Pope may Faustus [cunning] <comming> see.	F 855	3.1.77	Faust
By [cunning] <comming> in <of> thine Art to crosse the Pope,/Or	F 859	3.1.81	Mephst
Now Robin, now or never shew thy cunning.	F1095	3.3.8	P Dick
No Art, no cunning, to present these Lords,	F1295	4.1.141	Faust
and one to whom I must be no niggard of my cunning; Come,	F1504	4.4.48	P Faust
[Ah] <O> gentlemen, I gave them my soule for my cunning.	F1856	5.2.60	Faust
If therefore thou, by cunning of thine Art,	F App	p.237 29	Emper
to whom I must be no niggard of my cunning, come	F App	p.241 171	P Faust
And they of Rhene and Leuca, cunning darters,	Lucan, First Booke	425	
Nape free-borne, whose cunning hath no border,	Ovid's Elegies	1.11.2	
Or if one touch the lute with art and cunning,	Ovid's Elegies	2.4.27	
The Thracian Harpe with cunning to have strooke,	Ovid's Elegies	2.11.32	
(O face most cunning mine eyes to detaine)/Thou oughtst	Ovid's Elegies	2.17.12	
Nor usde the slight nor <and> cunning which she could,	Ovid's Elegies	3.6.56	
Against thy selfe, mans nature, thou wert cunning,	Ovid's Elegies	3.7.45	
After went Mercurie, who us'd such cunning,	Hero and Leander	1.417	
CUNNINGLIE			
And therefore will I do it cunninglie.	Edw	5.4.5	Mortmr

CUNNINGLY				
True; and it shall be cunningly perform'd.	Jew	2.3.367		Barab
As in plaine termes (yet cunningly) he crav'd it,	Hero and Leander	2.71		
And cunningly to yeeld her selfe she sought.	Hero and Leander	2.294		
CUP				
O where is Ganimed to hold his cup,	Dido	4.4.46		Dido
And squease it in the cup of Tamburlain.	1Tamb	4.4.20		Bajzth
at the mariage day/The cup of Hymen had beene full of poyson,	Edw	1.4.174		Queene
that your devill can answere the stealing of this same cup,	F1089	3.3.2	P	Dick
let me see the cup.	F1093	3.3.6	P	Robin
pray where's the cup you stole from the Taverne?	F1097	3.3.10	P	Vintnr
we steale a cup?	F1099	3.3.12	P	Robin
what you say, we looke not like cup-stealers I can tell you.	F1100	3.3.13	P	Robin
hold the cup Dick, come, come, search me, search me.	F1102	3.3.15	P	Robin
do, hold the cup Robin, I feare not your searching; we scorne to	F1105	3.3.18	P	Dick
me for the matter, for sure the cup is betweene you two.	F1107	3.3.20	P	Vintnr
life, Vintner you shall have your cup anon, say nothing Dick:	F1114	3.3.27	P	Robin
When thou hast tasted, I will take the cup,	Ovid's Elegies	1.4.31		
Stole some from Hebe (Hebe, Joves cup fil'd),	Hero and Leander	1.434		
CUPID				
Now Cupid turne thee to Ascanius shape,	Dido	2.1.323		Venus
Now Cupid cause the Carthaginian Queene,	Dido	3.1.1		Cupid
Cupid shall lay his arrowes in thy lap,	Dido	3.2.56		Venus
And bore yong Cupid unto Cypresse Ile.	Dido	5.1.41		Hermes
That daylie dandlest Cupid in thy armes:	Dido	5.1.45		Aeneas
Now are those Spheares where Cupid usde to sit,	2Tamb	2.4.81		Tamb
All Lovers warre, and Cupid hath his tent,	Ovid's Elegies	1.9.1		
Will you for gaine have Cupid sell himselfe?	Ovid's Elegies	1.10.17		
So Cupid wills, farre hence be the severe,	Ovid's Elegies	2.1.3		
No love is so dere (quiverd Cupid flie)/That my chiefe wish	Ovid's Elegies	2.5.1		
O Cupid that doest never cease my smart,	Ovid's Elegies	2.9.1		
So wavering Cupid bringes me backe amaine,	Ovid's Elegies	2.9.33		
Cupid by thee, Mars in great doubt doth trample,	Ovid's Elegies	2.9.47		
Cupid commands to move his ensignes further.	Ovid's Elegies	2.12.28		
Loe Cupid brings his quiver spoyled quite,	Ovid's Elegies	3.8.7		
Some say, for her the fairest Cupid pyn'd,	Hero and Leander	1.37		
Cupid beats downe her praiers with his wings,	Hero and Leander	1.369		
with sad and heavie cheare/Complaind to Cupid; Cupid for his	Hero and Leander	1.441		
sad and heavie cheare/Complaind to Cupid; Cupid for his sake,	Hero and Leander	1.441		
For from the earth to heaven, is Cupid rais'd,	Hero and Leander	2.31		
CUPIDE				
And Cupide who hath markt me for thy pray,	Ovid's Elegies	1.3.12		
CUPIDS				
Prometheus hath put on Cupids shape,	Dido	3.4.21		Dido
Ten thousand Cupids hover in the ayre,	Dido	4.4.48		Dido
Had late been pluckt from out faire Cupids wing:	P 668	13.12		Duchss
Which troopes hath alwayes bin on Cupids side:	Ovid's Elegies	1.2.36		
Till Cupids bow, and fierie shafts be broken,	Ovid's Elegies	1.15.27		
Breath'd darkenesse forth (darke night is Cupids day).	Hero and Leander	1.191		
Thus having swallow'd Cupids golden hooke,	Hero and Leander	1.333		
Then muse not, Cupids sute no better sped,	Hero and Leander	1.483		
With Cupids myrtle was his bonet crownd,	Hero and Leander	2.105		
CUPS				
To day when as I fild into your cups,	Dido	1.1.5		Ganimd
your searching; we scorne to steale your cups I can tell you.	F1106	3.3.19	P	Dick
CUP-STEALERS				
what you say, we looke not like cup-stealers I can tell you.	F1100	3.3.13	P	Robin
CURATE				
Which made me curate-like in mine attire,	Edw	2.1.49		Baldck
CURATE-LIKE				
Which made me curate-like in mine attire,	Edw	2.1.49		Baldck
CURBE				
dauntlesse minde/The ambitious Mortimer would seeke to curbe,	Edw	5.1.16		Edward
CUR'D				
things past recovery/Are hardly cur'd with exclamations.	Jew	1.2.237		Barab
And thousand desperate maladies beene cur'd <eas'd>?	F 50	1.1.22		Faust
And Faustus shall bee cur'd.	F1831	5.2.35		2Schol
CURE				
To cure my minde that melts for unkind love.	Dido	5.1.287		Dido
the good I have/Join'd with my fathers crowne would never cure.	2Tamb	4.1.58		Calyph
To cure me, or Ile fetch him downe my selfe.	2Tamb	5.3.63		Tamb
to his prayers, as if hee had had another Cure to serve; well,	Jew	4.2.25	P	Ithimr
And be eterniz'd for some wondrous cure:	F 43	1.1.15		Faust
<to cure him, tis but a surffet, never feare man>.	F1831	(HC270)A	P	2Schol
CURELESSE				
Infecting all the Ghosts with curelesse griefs:	1Tamb	5.1.258		Bajzth
CURING				
By curing of this maimed Emperie.	1Tamb	1.1.126		Menaph
CURIO				
And with them Curio, sometime Tribune too,	Lucan, First Booke	271		
thus Curio spake,/And therewith Caesar prone ennough to warre,	Lucan, First Booke	292		
CURIOUS (See also CURRIOUS)				
Wherein by curious soveraintie of Art,	1Tamb	2.1.13		Menaph
And roof't aloft with curious worke in gold.	F 798	3.1.20		Faust
fine and thinne/Like to the silke the curious Seres spinne,	Ovid's Elegies	1.14.6		
And vanquisht people curious dressings lend thee,	Ovid's Elegies	1.14.46		
Or Thamiras in curious painted things?	Ovid's Elegies	3.6.62		
That heavenly path, with many a curious dint,	Hero and Leander	1.68		
CURIUS				
The ground which Curius and Camillus till'd,	Lucan, First Booke	170		
CURLE				
Ad <And> they were apt to curle an hundred waies,	Ovid's Elegies	1.14.13		
CURLED				
And gives the viper curled Dogge three heads.	Ovid's Elegies	3.11.26		

CURLED (cont.)
Her painted fanne of curled plumes let fall, — Hero and Leander 2.11

CURLES
Wrapped in curles, as fierce Achilles was, — 1Tamb 2.1.24 Menaph
take/In crooked [tramelis] <trannels> crispy curles to make. — Ovid's Elegies 1.14.26

CURLING
Curling their bloudy lockes, howle dreadfull things, — Lucan, First Booke 565

CURRES
And now ye cankred curres of Asia, — 2Tamb 4.1.132 Tamb

CURRIOUS
And in this sweet and currious harmony, — 2Tamb 2.4.30 Tamb

CURRITE
O lente lente currite noctis equi: — F1935 5.2.139 Faust

CURSE
Iarbus, curse that unrevenging Jove, — Dido 4.1.18 Iarbus
But as I live that towne shall curse the time/That Tamburlaine — 1Tamb 3.3.59 Tamb
Ah faire Zabina, we may curse his power, — 1Tamb 5.1.230 Bajzth
That would not kill and curse at Gods command, — 2Tamb 2.1.55 Fredrk
As ye shal curse the byrth of Tamburlaine. — 2Tamb 3.5.89 Tamb
If your first curse fall heavy on thy head, — Jew 1.2.107 1Knght
The plagues of Egypt, and the curse of heaven, — Jew 1.2.162 Barab
So that not he, but I may curse the day, — Jew 1.2.191 Barab
But perish underneath my bitter curse/Like Cain by Adam, for — Jew 3.4.32 Barab
Dye life, flye soule, tongue curse thy fill and dye. — Jew 5.5.89 Barab
I curse thee and exclaime thee miscreant, — P1075 19.145 QnMoth
Ah curse him not sith he is dead. — P1220 22.82 King
Shall curse the time that ere Navarre was King, — P1249 22.111 Navrre
Curse him, if he refuse, and then may we/Depose him and elect — Edw 1.4.54 Mortmr
Curse me, depose me, doe the worst you can. — Edw 1.4.57 Edward
the heavens then I repent/And curse thee wicked Mephostophilis, — F 553 2.2.2 Faust
The Pope shall curse that Faustus came to Rome. — F 903 3.1.125 Faust
And curse the people that submit to him; — F 907 3.1.129 Pope
Or be assured of our dreadfull curse, — F 938 3.1.160 Pope
The Pope will curse them for their sloth to day, — F 987 3.2.7 Faust
Forward and backward, to curse Faustus to hell. — F1075 3.2.95 Faust
No Faustus, curse thy selfe, curse Lucifer, — F1973 5.2.177 Faust
Forward and backward, to curse Faustus to hell. — F App p.232 26 Faust
Yet should I curse a God, if he but said, — Ovid's Elegies 2.9.25

CURSED
Here lyes my hate, Aeneas cursed brat, — Dido 3.2.1 Juno
O cursed tree, hadst thou but wit or sense, — Dido 4.4.139 Dido
O cursed hagge and false dissembling wretch! — Dido 5.1.216 Dido
Traytoresse too [keene] <keend> <kind> and cursed Sorceresse. — Dido 5.1.221 Dido
Cursed Iarbus, dye to expiate/The griefe that tires upon thine — Dido 5.1.316 Iarbus
O cursed Mahomet that makest us thus/The slaves to Scythians — 1Tamb 3.3.270 Zabina
And rackt by dutie from my cursed heart: — 1Tamb 5.1.387 Zenoc
What cursed power guides the murthering hands, — 1Tamb 5.1.403 Arabia
the cursed object/Whose Fortunes never mastered her griefs: — 1Tamb 5.1.413 Zenoc
Even straight: and farewell cursed Tamburlaine. — 2Tamb 1.2.77 Callap
This cursed towne will I consume with fire, — 2Tamb 2.4.137 Tamb
Whose cursed fate hath so dismembred it, — 2Tamb 3.1.13 Callap
not but your royall cares/Hath so provided for this cursed foe, — 2Tamb 3.1.21 Callap
Scourging the pride of cursed Tamburlain. — 2Tamb 3.1.37 Callap
The cursed Scythian sets on all their townes, — 2Tamb 3.1.55 Trebiz
So, burne the turrets of this cursed towne, — 2Tamb 3.2.1 Tamb
vaine or Artier feed/The cursed substance of that cruel heart, — 2Tamb 4.1.178 Soria
How like his cursed father he begins, — 2Tamb 4.3.55 Jrslem
To triumph over cursed Tamburlaine. — 2Tamb 5.2.30 Callap
But here comes cursed Ithimore with the Fryar. — Jew 3.3.49 Abigal
These are the cursed Guisians that doe seeke our death. — P 201 3.36 Admral
Upon the cursed breakers of our peace. — P 270 4.68 Charls
To revenge our deaths upon that cursed King, — P1100 20.10 Cardnl
So much as he on cursed Gaveston. — Edw 1.4.181 Queene
No madam, but that cursed Gaveston. — Edw 2.4.32 Lncstr
Raigne showers of vengeance on my cursed head/Thou God, to whom — Edw 4.6.7 Kent
He surfets upon cursed Necromancie: — F 25 Prol.25 1Chor
That Bruno and the cursed Emperour/Were by the holy Councell — F1020 3.2.40 Pope
Cursed be he that stole [away] his holinesse meate from the — F1077 3.2.97 1Frier
Cursed be he that stroke his holinesse a blow [on] the face. — F1079 3.2.99 1Frier
Cursed be he that strucke <tooke> fryer Sandelo a blow on the — F1081 3.2.101 1Frier
Cursed be he that disturbeth our holy Dirge. — F1083 3.2.103 1Frier
Cursed be he that tooke away his holinesse wine. — F1085 3.2.105 1Frier
To purge the rashnesse of this cursed deed, — F1125 3.3.38 Mephst
Cursed be hee that stole away his holinesse meate from/the — F App p.232 31 Frier
Cursed be hee that strooke his holinesse a blowe on the face. — F App p.232 33 Frier
Cursed be he that tooke Frier Sandelo a blow on the pate. — F App p.232 35 Frier
Cursed be he that disturbeth our holy Dirge. — F App p.232 37 Frier
Cursed be he that tooke away his holinesse wine. — F App p.233 39 Frier
Deserved chaines these cursed hands shall fetter, — Ovid's Elegies 1.7.28
The Sunne turnd backe from Atreus cursed table? — Ovid's Elegies 3.11.39
On this feast day, O cursed day and hower, — Hero and Leander 1.131

CURSEN
fell to eating; and as I am a cursen man, he never left eating, — F1530 4.5.26 P Carter

CURSES
Not all the curses which the furies breathe, — 1Tamb 2.7.53 Tamb
you suffer these outragious curses by these slaves of yours? — 1Tamb 4.4.26 P Zenoc
them see (divine Zenocrate)/I glorie in the curses of my foes, — 1Tamb 4.4.29 Tamb
poore Barabas/With fatall curses towards these Christians. — Jew 2.1.6 Barab

CURSETH
Yet greedy Bauds command she curseth still, — Ovid's Elegies 1.10.23

CURSING
To bridle their contemptuous cursing tongues, — 2Tamb 4.3.44 Therid
Cursing the name of thee and Gaveston. — Edw 2.2.181 Lncstr

CURST
That curst and damned Traitor Almeda. 2Tamb 3.2.154 Usumc
The wicked branch of curst Valois his line. P1013 19.83 Guise
Curst be your soules to hellish misery. F1034 3.2.54 Pope
for I can tell you, you'le be curst with Bell, Booke, and F1072 3.2.92 P Mephst
Curst be the parents that ingendred me; F1972 5.2.176 Faust
Nay I know not, we shalbe curst with bell, booke, and candle. F App p.232 23 P Mephst
CURSTLIE
Speake curstlie to him, and in any case/Let no man comfort him, Edw 5.2.63 Mortmr
CURTAINES
from every flanke/May scoure the outward curtaines of the Fort, 2Tamb 3.2.80 Tamb
CURTEOUS
In sending thee unto this curteous Coast: Dido 1.1.232 Venus
Kind clowdes that sent forth such a curteous storme, Dido 3.4.55 Dido
And for I see your curteous intent to pleasure me, I wil not F App p.242 8 P Duchss
CURTESIE
I would be thankfull for such curtesie. Dido 4.2.29 Anna
Whil'st I rest thankfull for this curtesie. Dido 5.1.77 Aeneas
What Callapine, a little curtesie. Jew 1.2.23 Calym
the Governors sonne/With all the curtesie you can affoord; Jew 2.3.226 Barab
For I will shew thee greater curtesie/Then Barabas would have Jew 5.5.61 Govnr
A Jewes curtesie: Jew 5.5.108 Govnr
He will be mindfull of the curtesie. Edw 2.5.40 Arundl
Then I pray remember your curtesie. F1641 4.6.84 P Carter
my Lord, and whilst I live, Rest beholding for this curtesie. F App p.243 31 P Duchss
Foldes up her armes, and makes low curtesie. Ovid's Elegies 2.4.30
CURTEZANE
I know she is a Curtezane by her attire: Jew 3.1.27 P Ithimr
Plaine Barabas: oh that wicked Curtezane! Jew 4.3.2 Barab
Away with her, she is a Curtezane. Jew 5.1.8 Govnr
Shee is a Curtezane and he a theefe, Jew 5.1.37 Barab
My Lord, the Curtezane and her man are dead; Jew 5.1.50 1Offcr
CURTEZANS
I'le cull thee out the fairest Curtezans, F 537 2.1.149 Mephst
CURTLE
and this curtle-axe/Are adjuncts more beseeming Tamburlaine. 1Tamb 1.2.42 Tamb
See where it is, the keenest Cutle-axe <curtle-axe>,/That ere 1Tamb 2.3.55 Tamb
Armour of proofe, horse, helme, and Curtle-axe, 2Tamb 1.3.44 Tamb
or with a Curtle-axe/To hew thy flesh and make a gaping wound? 2Tamb 3.2.96 Tamb
CURTLE-AXE
and this curtle-axe/Are adjuncts more beseeming Tamburlaine. 1Tamb 1.2.42 Tamb
See where it is, the keenest Cutle-axe <curtle-axe>,/That ere 1Tamb 2.3.55 Tamb
Armour of proofe, horse, helme, and Curtle-axe, 2Tamb 1.3.44 Tamb
or with a Curtle-axe/To hew thy flesh and make a gaping wound? 2Tamb 3.2.96 Tamb
CURVET
He raign'd him straight and made him so curvet, 2Tamb 1.3.41 Zenoc
CUSTOME
I feare the custome proper to his sword, 1Tamb 5.1.13 Govnr
They know my custome: 1Tamb 5.1.67 Tamb
sent me to know/Whether your selfe will come and custome them. Jew 1.1.53 1Merch
I hope our credit in the Custome-house/Will serve as well as I Jew 1.1.57 Barab
The very Custome barely comes to more/Then many Merchants of Jew 1.1.63 1Merch
'tis a custome held with us,/That when we speake with Gentiles Jew 2.3.44 Barab
Oh, is't the custome, then I am resolv'd: Jew 2.3.329 Lodowk
[And] Faustus custome is not to deny/The just [requests] F1690 5.1.17 Faust
<It is not Faustus custome> to deny F1690 (HC269) B Faust
If sin by custome grow not into nature: F1713 5.1.40 OldMan
To these ostents (as their old custome was)/They call Lucan, First Booke 583
Had ancient Mothers this vile custome cherisht, Ovid's Elegies 2.14.9
CUSTOME-HOUSE
I hope our credit in the Custome-house/Will serve as well as I Jew 1.1.57 Barab
CUSTOMES
And know my customes are as peremptory/As wrathfull Planets, 1Tamb 5.1.127 Tamb
And Druides you now in peace renew/Your barbarous customes, and Lucan, First Booke 447
And this townes well knowne customes not beleeves, Ovid's Elegies 3.4.38
CUT
Controule proud Fate, and cut the thred of time. Dido 1.1.29 Jupitr
And cut a passage through his toples hilles: Dido 4.3.12 Aeneas
Cut of the water, that by leaden pipes/Runs to the citie from 1Tamb 3.1.59 Bajzth
That sacrificing slice and cut your flesh, 1Tamb 4.2.3 Bajzth
Millions of Souldiers cut the Artick line, 2Tamb 1.1.29 Orcan
slaves/I freely give thee, which shall cut the straights, 2Tamb 1.2.33 Callap
Shot through the armes, cut overthwart the hands, 2Tamb 3.2.104 Tamb
Here father, cut it bravely as you did your own. 2Tamb 3.2.135 P Celeb
Captaine, these Moores shall cut the leaden pipes, 2Tamb 3.3.29 Techel
Cut off the water, all convoies that can, 2Tamb 3.3.39 Capt
Cut off this arme that murthered my Love: 2Tamb 4.2.83 Therid
I meant to cut a channell to them both, 2Tamb 5.3.134 Tamb
No Sir, I can cut and shave. Jew 2.3.113 P Slave
be under colour of shaving, thou'lt cut my throat for my goods. Jew 2.3.120 P Barab
I steale/To travellers Chambers, and there cut their throats: Jew 2.3.207 Ithimr
I'de cut thy throat if I did. Jew 4.1.11 Barab
His hands are hackt, some fingers cut quite off; Jew 4.3.10 Barab
Play, Fidler, or I'le cut your cats guts into chitterlins. Jew 4.4.44 P Ithimr
The floore whereof, this Cable being cut, Jew 5.5.34 Barab
To give thee knowledge when to cut the cord, Jew 5.5.40 Barab
thou hast all the Cardes within thy hands/To shuffle or cut, P 147 2.90 Guise
Away with him, cut of his head and handes, P 316 5.43 Anjoy
Therefore the shortest cut for conjuring/Is stoutly to abjure F 280 1.3.52 Mephst
for love of thee/Faustus hath <I> cut his <mine> arme, and with F 443 2.1.55 Faust
The way he cut, an English mile in length, F 792 3.1.14 Faust
With winding bankes that cut it in two parts; F 814 3.1.36 Mephst
And had you cut my body with your swords, F1397 4.2.73 Faust

CUT (cont.)
Cut is the branch that might have growne full straight, . F2002 5.3.20 4Chor
Mules loth'd issue)/To be cut forth and cast in dismall fiers: Lucan, First Booke 590
Had they beene cut, and unto Colchos borne, ... Hero and Leander 1.56
And alwaies cut him off as he replide. . . . . . Hero and Leander 1.196

CUTHEIA
pitcht against our power/Betwixt Cutheia and Orminius mount: 2Tamb 2.1.18 Fredrk

CUTLASS (See CURTLE-AXE)

CUTLE
See where it is, the keenest Cutle-axe <curtle-axe>,/That ere 1Tamb 2.3.55 Tamb

CUTLE-AXE
See where it is, the keenest Cutle-axe <curtle-axe>,/That ere 1Tamb 2.3.55 Tamb

CUTS
When death cuts off the progres of his pomp, ... 2Tamb Prol.4 Prolog
And cuts down armies with his [conquering] <conquerings> wings. 2Tamb 4.1.6 Amyras

CUTTING
Cutting the Tropicke line of Capricorne, ... 2Tamb 5.3.138 Tamb

CUZ
And so sweet Cuz farwell. . . . . P 976 19.46 King

CYBELIUS
otherwise Cybelius, son and successive heire to the late mighty 2Tamb 3.1.1 P Orcan

CYCLOPIAN
Shall threat the Gods more than Cyclopian warres, . . 1Tamb 2.3.21 Tamb

CYCLOPS
The Cyclops shelves, and grim Ceranias seate/Have you oregone, Dido 1.1.147 Aeneas
Which beates upon it like the Cyclops hammers, . . . Edw 1.4.313 Edward
Which limping Vulcan and his Cyclops set: . . . . . Hero and Leander 1.152

CYMBRIAN
As when an heard of lusty Cymbrian Buls, ... 2Tamb 4.1.187 Tamb

CYMBRIANS
And furious Cymbrians and of Carthage Moores, . . . Lucan, First Booke 257

CYMERIAN
More than Cymerian Stix or Distinie. . . . . . . 1Tamb 5.1.234 Bajzth
And Death with armies of Cymerian spirits/Gives battile gainst 2Tamb 5.3.8 Therid

CYMODOCE
And call both Thetis and [Cimothoe] <Cimodoae> <Cymodoce>,/To Dido 1.1.132 Venus

CYNDERS
Being burnt to cynders for your mothers death. . . . 2Tamb 3.2.46 Tamb

CYNGAS
and those that dwel/By Cyngas streame, and where swift Rhodanus Lucan, First Booke 434

CYNTHIA (See also CINTHIA)
At whose byrth-day Cynthia with Saturne joinde, . . 1Tamb 1.1.13 Cosroe
Disdaine to borrow light of Cynthia, ... 1Tamb 4.2.35 Tamb
Open thou shining vaile of Cynthia/And make a passage from the 2Tamb 2.2.47 Orcan
appeares as full/As raies of Cynthia to the clearest sight? 2Tamb 2.3.30 Orcan
Cynthia, and the ceaslesse lamps/That gently look'd upon this 2Tamb 2.4.18 Tamb
Unto the shining bower where Cynthia sits, ... 2Tamb 3.4.50 Therid
Yet when the pride of Cynthia is at full, ... 2Tamb 5.2.46 Callap
Or Cynthia nights Queene waights upon the day; . . . . Lucan, First Booke 91

CYNTHIAS
operation and more force/Than Cynthias in the watery wildernes, 2Tamb 4.2.30 Therid

CYPASSE
Let me lie with thee browne Cypasse to day. . . . . Ovid's Elegies 2.8.22

CYPASSIS
Behold Cypassis wont to dresse thy head, ... Ovid's Elegies 2.7.17
Cypassis that a thousand wayes trimst haire, ... Ovid's Elegies 2.8.1

CYPRES
for the lovely boy/That now is turn'd into a Cypres tree, Hero and Leander 1.155

CYPRESSE
And bore yong Cupid unto Cypresse Ile. . . . . . Dido 5.1.41 Hermes

CYPRUS
Where twixt the Isles of Cyprus and of Creete, ... 2Tamb 1.2.26 Callap
Phrigia to the sea/Which washeth Cyprus with his brinish waves, 2Tamb 3.5.12 Callap
From Cyprus, Candy, and those other Iles/That lye betwixt the Jew 1.2.3 Basso
What's Cyprus, Candy, and those other Iles/To us, or Malta? Jew 1.2.5 Govnr

CYRCLES
Whose fiery cyrcles beare encompassed/A heaven of heavenly 1Tamb 2.1.15 Menaph

CYRICELIBES
Calepinus Cyricelibes, otherwise Cybelius, son and successive 2Tamb 3.1.1 P Orcan

CYRUS
Passe into Graecia, as did Cyrus once. . . . . . 1Tamb 1.1.130 Menaph

CYTADELL
I will build/A Cytadell, that all [Assiria] <Affrica>/Which 2Tamb 5.1.165 Tamb

CYTHARA (See CITHARA)

CYTHARIA (See CITHERIA)

CYTHEREA
Content thee Cytherea in thy care, ... Dido 1.1.82 Jupitr

CYTIES
And make whole cyties caper in the aire. . . . . 2Tamb 3.2.61 Tamb

DAGGER
Here is my dagger, dispatch her while she is fat, for if she 1Tamb 4.4.48 P Tamb
and a Dagger with a hilt like a warming-pan, and he gave me a Jew 4.2.28 P Ithimr

DAIES
And chaunging heavens may those good daies returne, . . . Dido 1.1.150 Aeneas
It is Aeneas frowne that ends my daies: . . . . Dido 4.4.120 Dido
How long shall I with griefe consume my daies, . . . Dido 5.1.281 Iarbus
Why feed ye still on daies accursed beams, ... 1Tamb 5.1.262 Bajzth
Now Bajazeth, abridge thy banefull daies, ... 1Tamb 5.1.286 Bajzth
life may be as short to me/As are the daies of sweet Zenocrate: 2Tamb 2.4.37 Tamb
One minute end our daies, and one sepulcher/Containe our . 2Tamb 3.4.13 Olymp
And for his sake here will I end my daies. . . . . 2Tamb 3.4.44 Olymp
Though this be held his last daies dreadfull siege, . . 2Tamb 5.1.29 1Citzn
As durst resist us till our third daies siege: . . . 2Tamb 5.1.59 Techel

DAIES (cont.)				
O graunt sweet God my daies may end with hers, ...	P 189	3.24		Navrre
And spend some daies in barriers, tourny, tylte, . .	P 628	12.41		King
thy mother feare/Thou art not markt to many daies on earth.	Edw	3.1.80		Queene
For not these ten daies have these eyes lids closd. . .	Edw	5.5.94		Edward
When as my sonne thinkes to abridge my daies. . . .	Edw	5.6.84		Queene
Venus, and Mercury in a yeare; the Moone in twenty eight daies.	F 606	2.2.55	P	Faust
And in eight daies did bring him home againe. . . .	F 767	2.3.46		2Chor
Do [match] <watch> the number of the daies contain'd, .	F 821	3.1.43		Mephst
Thou know'st within the compasse of eight daies, . .	F 847	3.1.69		Faust
Being three daies old inforst the floud to swell, . .	Lucan, First Booke			220
DAILY				
Daily inur'd to broyles and Massacres, ...	Dido	2.1.124		Aeneas
Daily commits incivill outrages, ...	1Tamb	1.1.40		Meandr
Altar I will offer up/My daily sacrifice of sighes and teares,	Jew	3.2.32		Govnr
And daily will enrich thee with our favour, ...	Edw	3.1.50		Edward
My daily diet, is heart breaking sobs, ...	Edw	5.3.21		Edward
DAINTIE				
And make her daintie fingers fall to woorke. . . .	1Tamb	3.3.181		Ebea
My good Lord Archbishop, heres a most daintie dish, . .	F1046	3.2.66		Pope
here is a daintie dish was sent me from the Bishop of Millaine.	F App	p.231 5	P	Pope
DAINTIES				
And glut us with the dainties of the world, ...	2Tamb	1.3.220		Tamb
that great bellied women do long for some dainties or other,	F App	p.242 5	P	Faust
Yet ever as he greedily assayd/To touch those dainties, she the	Hero and Leander			2.270
DAINTILY				
are you so daintily brought up, you cannot eat your owne flesh?	1Tamb	4.4.36	P	Tamb
DAINTY				
Besmer'd with blood, that makes a dainty show. . . .	1Tamb	1.1.80		Mycet
Too harsh a subject for your dainty eares. . . .	1Tamb	3.2.46		Agidas
Bewraies they are too dainty for the wars. . . .	2Tamb	1.3.28		Tamb
Here have I made a dainty Gallery, ...	Jew	5.5.33		Barab
great bellyed women, do long for things, are rare and dainty.	F1569	4.6.12	P	Faust
DALIANCE				
Where daliance doth consume a Souldiers strength, . .	Dido	4.3.34		Achat
yeares of liberty/I'le spend in pleasure and in daliance,	F 840	3.1.62		Faust
DALLIANCE				
Therefore come, dalliance dangereth our lives. . . .	Edw	5.3.3		Matrvs
Nor sporting in the dalliance of love/In Courts of Kings, where	F 3	Prol.3		1Chor
DALLIE				
To dallie with Idalian Ganimed:	Hero and Leander			1.148
DALLY				
Wherein I may not, nay I dare not dally.	Jew	1.2.12		Calym
But wherefore doe I dally my revenge?	F1401	4.2.77		Faust
DALLYING				
Long dallying with Hero, nothing saw/That might delight him	Hero and Leander			2.62
DAM (See also DAMB'D)				
And <of> his dam <dame> to.	F 646	2.2.95		Belzeb
DAMASCO				
and lead him bound in chaines/Unto Damasco, where I staid	2Tamb	1.3.205		Techel
And so unto my citie of Damasco, ...	2Tamb	3.1.59		Soria
DAMASCUS				
That roaring, shake Damascus turrets downe. . . .	1Tamb	4.1.3		Souldn
Or leave Damascus and th'Egyptian fields, ...	1Tamb	4.2.48		Tamb
To faire Damascus, where we now remaine, ...	1Tamb	4.2.99		Tamb
Now may we see Damascus lofty towers, ...	1Tamb	4.2.102		Tamb
Offering Damascus to your Majesty.	1Tamb	4.2.114		Therid
And hasten to remoove Damascus siege.	1Tamb	4.3.18		Souldn
your sounding Drummes/Direct our Souldiers to Damascus walles.	1Tamb	4.3.62		Souldn
Now hang our bloody collours by Damascus, ...	1Tamb	4.4.1		Tamb
And make Damascus spoiles as rich to you, ...	1Tamb	4.4.8		Tamb
Then raise your seige from faire Damascus walles, . .	1Tamb	4.4.71		Zenoc
Here at Damascus will I make the Point/That shall begin the	1Tamb	4.4.81		Tamb
of Egypt, the King of Arabia, and the Governour of Damascus.	1Tamb	4.4.114	P	Tamb
you be first shal feele/The sworne destruction of Damascus.	1Tamb	5.1.66		Tamb
Pittie our plightes, O pitie poore Damascus: . . .	1Tamb	5.1.80		1Virgn
and on Damascus wals/Have hoisted up their slaughtered .	1Tamb	5.1.130		Techel
Than all my Army to Damascus walles.	1Tamb	5.1.156		Tamb
Damascus walles di'd with Egyptian blood:	1Tamb	5.1.320		Zenoc
Whom I brought bound unto Damascus walles. . . .	2Tamb	3.2.125		Tamb
DAMB'D (Homograph)				
Damb'd be this soule for ever, for this deed.	F1070	3.2.90		Pope
Damb'd up thy passage; when thou took'st the booke, . .	F1887	5.2.91		Mephst
DAME				
Banish that ticing dame from forth your mouth, . . .	Dido	4.3.31		Achat
As did Sir Paris with the Grecian Dame:	1Tamb	1.1.66		Mycet
by such a tall man as I am, from such a beautifull dame as you.	Jew	4.2.10	P	Pilia
And <of> his dam <dame> to.	F 646	2.2.95		Belzeb
as to let us see that peerelesse dame of Greece, whom all the	F1685	5.1.12	P	1Schol
You shall behold that peerelesse dame of Greece, . .	F1692	5.1.19		Faust
Praysing for me some unknowne Guelder dame, . . .	Ovid's Elegies			1.14.49
DAMES				
straight goe charge a few of them/To chardge these Dames,	1Tamb	5.1.117		Tamb
To exercise upon such guiltlesse Dames, ...	2Tamb	4.3.79		Orcan
where brave Assirian Dames/Have rid in pompe like rich .	2Tamb	5.1.76		Tamb
Faire Dames for-beare rewards for nights to crave, . .	Ovid's Elegies			1.10.47
DAMNATION				
This word Damnation, terrifies not me <him>, ...	F 286	1.3.58		Faust
Bringing with us lasting damnation, ...	F1801	5.2.5		Lucifr
DAMN'D				
No come not at me, if thou wilt be damn'd,	Jew	1.2.362		Barab
Thou hast offended, therefore must be damn'd.	Jew	4.1.25		1Fryar
What a damn'd slave was I?	Jew	5.1.23		Barab

DAMN'D (cont.)
Damn'd Christians, dogges, and Turkish Infidels; Jew 5.5.86 Barab
Whereby he is in danger to be damn'd: F 279 1.3.51 Mephst
And are for ever damn'd with Lucifer. F 300 1.3.72 Mephst
Where are you damn'd? F 301 1.3.73 Faust
Now Faustus, must thou needs be damn'd, F 389 2.1.1 Faust
Why, dost thou think <think'st thou then> that Faustus shall be F 518 2.1.130 Faust
For I tell thee I am damn'd, and <am> now in hell. F 526 2.1.138 Mephst
Nay, and this be hell, I'le willingly be damn'd <damned here>. F 527 2.1.139 Faust
[Faustus, thou art damn'd, then swords <guns> and knives], F 572 2.2.21A Faust
Thou art damn'd, think thou of hell>. F 624 2.2.73 P Mephst
'Tis thou hast damn'd distressed Faustus soule. F 628 2.2.77 Faust
What devill attends this damn'd Magician, F1445 4.3.15 Benvol
A surfet of deadly sin, that hath damn'd both body and soule. F1833 5.2.37 P Faust
And then thou must be damn'd perpetually. F1928 5.2.132 Faust
The devill will come, and Faustus must be damn'd. F1937 5.2.141 Faust

DAMND
<Thinke thou on hell Faustus, for thou art damnd>. F 624 (HC262)A Mephst

DAMNED (See also DAMB'D)
That damned traine, the scum of Affrica, 1Tamb 3.3.56 Tamb
Thou, by the fortune of this damned [foile] <soile>. 1Tamb 3.3.213 Bajzth
Then as I looke downe to the damned Feends, 1Tamb 4.2.26 Bajzth
And madnesse send his damned soule to hell. 1Tamb 5.1.229 Zabina
Traitors, villaines, damned Christians. 2Tamb 2.2.29 Orcan
With apples like the heads of damned Feends. 2Tamb 2.3.23 Orcan
That curst and damned Traitor Almeda. 2Tamb 3.2.154 Usumc
Villaine, traitor, damned fugitive, 2Tamb 3.5.117 Tamb
But follie, sloth, and damned idlenesse: 2Tamb 4.1.126 Tamb
twixt our selves and thee/In this thy barbarous damned tyranny. 2Tamb 4.1.139 Orcan
O damned monster, nay a Feend of Hell, 2Tamb 4.1.168 Jrslem
And now the damned soules are free from paine, 2Tamb 4.2.91 Therid
with what a broken hart/And damned spirit I ascend this seat, 2Tamb 5.3.207 Amyras
that thou leave/These divels, and their damned heresie. Jew 1.2.347 Barab
Take hence that damned villaine from my sight. P1182 22.44 King
O that that damned villaine were alive againe, P1216 22.78 Eprnon
O Faustus, lay that damned booke aside, F 97 1.1.69 GdAngl
That thou art <he is> falne into that damned Art/For which they F 221 1.2.28 1Schol
Nay, and this be hell, I'le willingly be damn'd <damned here>. F 527 2.1.139 Faust
Onely for pleasure of these damned slaves. F1119 3.3.32 Mephst
O were that damned Hell-hound but in place, F1355 4.2.31 Benvol
Was this that damned head, whose heart <art> conspir'd F1373 4.2.49 Mrtino
O gentle Faustus leave this damned Art, F1707 5.1.34 OldMan
[Damned art thou Faustus, damned, despaire and die], F1725 5.1.52A Faust
There are the Furies tossing damned soules, F1911 5.2.115 BdAngl
<O> No end is limited to damned soules. F1963 5.2.167 Faust
With dreadfull horror of these damned fiends. F1994 5.3.12 3Schol
Onely for pleasure of these damned slaves. F App p.235 39 Mephst
Thou damned wretch, and execrable dogge, F App p.238 72 Knight

DAMON
Whom I may tearme a Damon for thy love. 1Tamb 1.1.50 Mycet

DAMPE
From whence a dampe continually ariseth, Edw 5.5.4 Matrvs

DAMS
many a heard, whilst with their dams/They kennel'd in Hircania, Lucan, First Booke 328

DAMSELL
While others touch the damsell I love best? Ovid's Elegies 1.4.4
I sawe the damsell walking yesterday/There where the porch doth Ovid's Elegies 2.2.3
But to my share a captive damsell falles. Ovid's Elegies 2.12.8
But thou of thy faire damsell too secure, Ovid's Elegies 2.19.37
Rude man, 'tis vaine, thy damsell to commend/To keepers trust: Ovid's Elegies 3.4.1

DAMSELLS
But me let crafty damsells words deceive, Ovid's Elegies 2.9.43

DAMSELS
But tender Damsels do it, though with paine, Ovid's Elegies 2.14.37

DANAE
For as the lovers of faire Danae, Edw 2.2.53 Edward
That suffered Jove to passe in showers of golde/To Danae, all Edw 3.1.268 Spencr
In brazen tower had not Danae dwelt, Ovid's Elegies 2.19.27
In stone, and Yron walles Danae shut, Ovid's Elegies 3.4.21

DANAES
Was Danaes statue in a brazen tower, Hero and Leander 1.146

DANAUS
yesterday/There where the porch doth Danaus fact display. Ovid's Elegies 2.2.4

DANC'D
That danc'd with glorie on the silver waves, 2Tamb 2.4.3 Tamb

DANCE (See also DAUNCE)
And made it dance upon the Continent: 2Tamb 1.1.88 Orcan
Their legs to dance and caper in the aire: 2Tamb 1.3.31 Tamb
And Nigra Silva, where the Devils dance, 2Tamb 1.3.212 Therid
If thou't dance naked, put off thy cloathes, and I'le conjure F 746 2.3.25 P Robin
in our parish dance at my pleasure starke naked before me, F App p.233 3 P Robin

DANCING
Spangled with Diamonds dancing in the aire, 2Tamb 4.3.117 Tamb

DANDLEST
That daylie dandlest Cupid in thy armes: Dido 5.1.45 Aeneas

DANE
The hautie Dane commands the narrow seas, Edw 2.2.168 Mortmr

DANES
Rutters>, Muffes, and Danes/That with the Holbard, Lance, and 2Tamb 1.1.22 Uribas
Muffes, and Danes/[Feares] <feare> not Orcanes, but great 2Tamb 1.1.58 Orcan

DANG'D
Dang'd downe to hell her loathsome carriage. Hero and Leander 2.334

DANGER (See also DAUNGER)
My selfe will bide the danger of the brunt. 1Tamb 1.2.151 Tamb

DANGER (cont.)			
Whiles only danger beat upon our walles,	1Tamb	5.1.30	1Virgn
Which ad much danger to your malladie.	2Tamb	5.3.55	Therid
<Hipostates>/Thick and obscure doth make your danger great,	2Tamb	5.3.83	Phsitn
and in hating me/My life's in danger, and what boots it thee	Jew	5.2.31	Barab
Wherein no danger shall betide thy life,	Jew	5.2.100	Barab
Regarding still the danger of thy life.	P 748	15.6	King
What danger tis to stand against your king.	Edw	1.1.97	Edward
The danger of his soule would make me mourne:	F 224	1.2.31	2Schol
Whereby he is in danger to be damn'd:	F 279	1.3.51	Mephst
Be silent then, for danger is in words.	F1696	5.1.23	Faust
Lest greater dangers <danger> do attend thy drift.	F1752	5.1.79	Mephst
Pray heaven the Doctor have escapt the danger.	F1987	5.3.5	1Schol
Then with their feare, and danger al distract,	Lucan, First Booke		487
DANGERETH			
Therefore come, dalliance dangereth our lives.	Edw	5.3.3	Matrvs
DANGEROUS			
These more than dangerous warrants of our death,	1Tamb	5.1.31	1Virgn
From dangerous battel of my conquering Love.	1Tamb	5.1.442	Zenoc
And dangerous chances of the wrathfull war?	2Tamb	1.3.11	Zenoc
My Lord, but this is dangerous to be done,	2Tamb	3.2.93	Calyph
Dangerous to those, whose Chrisis is as yours:	2Tamb	5.3.92	Phsitn
learne with awfull eie/To sway a throane as dangerous as his:	2Tamb	5.3.235	Tamb
To meddle or attempt such dangerous things.	P 38	1.38	Admral
Considering of these dangerous times.	P 175	3.10	Admral
to beware/How you did meddle with such dangerous giftes.	P 180	3.15	Navrre
Alas my Lord, the wound is dangerous,	P1212	22.74	Srgeon
Corinna meanes, and dangerous wayes to take.	Ovid's Elegies		2.11.8
DANGERS			
How many dangers have we over past?	Dido	1.1.145	Aeneas
Lest greater dangers <danger> do attend thy drift.	F1752	5.1.79	Mephst
DANGLING			
Beyond thy robes thy dangling [lockes] <lackes> had sweept.	Ovid's Elegies		1.14.4
His dangling tresses that were never shorne,	Hero and Leander		1.55
DANUBIUS			
from faire Natolia/Two hundred leagues, and on Danubius banks,	2Tamb	1.1.7	Orcan
Danubius stream that runs to Trebizon,	2Tamb	1.1.33	Orcan
The Terrene main wherin Danubius fals,	2Tamb	1.1.37	Orcan
Wee with our Peeres have crost Danubius stream/To treat of	2Tamb	1.1.79	Sgsmnd
of Natolia/Confirm'd this league beyond Danubius streame,	2Tamb	1.1.149	Orcan
Betwixt the citie Zula and Danubius,	2Tamb	2.1.7	Fredrk
DAPPER			
I have not seene a dapper jack so briske,	Edw	1.4.412	Mortmr
DARBIE			
Darbie, Salsburie, Lincolne, Leicester,	Edw	1.1.103	Lncstr
DARCKNED			
When she will, cloudes the darckned heav'n obscure,	Ovid's Elegies		1.8.9
DARCKNESSE			
all holy things/And on all creatures obscure darcknesse brings.	Ovid's Elegies		3.8.20
DARDANIA			
And brought the spoyles to rich Dardania:	F1695	5.1.22	Faust
DARDANUS			
Nor Dardanus the author of thy stocke:	Dido	5.1.157	Dido
DARE			
Aeneas thoughts dare not ascend so high/As Didos heart, which	Dido	3.4.33	Aeneas
His looks do menace heaven and dare the Gods,	1Tamb	1.2.157	Therid
And dare the force of angrie Jupiter.	1Tamb	2.6.4	Cosroe
But if he dare attempt to stir your siege,	1Tamb	3.1.46	Argier
That dare to manage armes with him,	1Tamb	3.3.198	Zabina
How dare you thus abuse my Majesty?	1Tamb	3.3.226	Zabina
Ah villaines, dare ye touch my sacred armes?	1Tamb	3.3.268	Bajzth
And not to dare ech other to the field:	2Tamb	1.1.116	Gazell
That dare attempt to war with Christians.	2Tamb	2.1.26	Fredrk
see if coward Calapine/Dare levie armes against our puissance,	2Tamb	3.2.156	Tamb
Wherein I may not, nay I dare not dally.	Jew	1.2.12	Calym
nay we dare not give consent/By reason of a Tributary league.	Jew	2.2.22	Govnr
Revenge it Henry as thou list or dare,	P 819	17.14	Guise
Yet dare you brave the king unto his face.	Edw	1.1.116	Kent
All stomack him, but none dare speake a word.	Edw	1.2.26	Lncstr
And dare not be revengde, for their power is great:	Edw	2.2.202	Edward
I dare not, for the people love him well.	Edw	2.2.235	Edward
But if you dare trust Penbrooke with the prisoner,	Edw	2.5.87	Penbrk
His grace I dare presume will welcome me,	Edw	4.2.33	Queene
Nephew, your father, I dare not call him king.	Edw	4.6.33	Kent
And what I list commaund, who dare controwle?	Edw	5.4.68	Mortmr
Sonne, be content, I dare not speake a worde.	Edw	5.4.96	Queene
Lets see who dare impeache me for his death?	Edw	5.6.14	Mortmr
Who is the man dare say I murdered him?	Edw	5.6.40	Mortmr
Why saucy varlets, dare you be so bold.	F1594	4.6.37	Servnt
Applaud you Neptune, that dare trust his wave,	Ovid's Elegies		3.2.47
DARES			
What? dares she strike the darling of my thoughts?	Dido	1.1.9	Jupitr
But dares to heape up sorrowe to my heart:	Dido	4.4.152	Dido
and the bounds/Of Europe wher the Sun dares scarce appeare,	1Tamb	1.1.10	Cosroe
He dares so doubtlesly resolve of rule,	1Tamb	2.6.13	Meandr
That dares controll us in our Territories.	1Tamb	4.3.14	Souldn
That dares torment the body of my Love,	2Tamb	2.4.79	Tamb
What is it dares distemper Tamburlain?	2Tamb	5.1.219	Techel
What, dares the villain write in such base terms?	Jew	3.2.3	Lodowk
Guise/Dares once adventure without the Kings consent,	P 37	1.37	Admral
that dares make the Duke a cuckolde, and use a counterfeite key	P 806	17.1	P Souldr
dares make a duke a cuckolde and use a counterfeyt key to his	Paris	ms 1,p390	P Souldr
Dares but affirme, that Edwards not true king,	Edw	5.4.76	Champn

DARES (cont.)			
He's happy, that his love dares boldly credit, . . .	Ovid's Elegies	2.5.9	
Nor dares the Lyonesse her young whelpes kill. . . .	Ovid's Elegies	2.14.36	
What is it now, but mad Leander dares?	Hero and Leander	2.146	
DAREST			
What, darest thou looke a Lyon in the face? . . .	Dido	3.3.39	Dido
DARING			
What daring God torments my body thus, ...	2Tamb	5.3.42	Tamb
Proud-daring Calymath, instead of gold, ...	Jew	2.2.53	Govnr
He forged the daring challenge made them fight. . .	Jew	5.1.47	Govnr
O levell all your lookes upon these daring men, . .	Edw	5.3.39	Edward
One sweares his troupes of daring horsemen fought/Upon Mevanias	Lucan, First Booke	469	
DARIUS			
at the spoile/Of great Darius and his wealthy hoast. .	1Tamb	1.1.154	Ceneus
DARKE			
Whose absence make the sun and Moone as darke/As when opposde	2Tamb	2.4.51	Tamb
But when I saw the place obscure and darke, . . .	2Tamb	4.2.15	Therid
There's a darke entry where they take it in, . . .	Jew	3.4.79	Barab
Such reasons make white blacke, and darke night day. .	Edw	1.4.247	Lncstr
the restles generall through the darke/(Swifter then bullets	Lucan, First Booke	230	
And stain'd the bowels with darke lothsome spots: . .	Lucan, First Booke	619	
no darke night-flying spright/Nor hands prepar'd to slaughter,	Ovid's Elegies	1.6.13	
Thou with thy quilles mightst make greene Emeralds darke,	Ovid's Elegies	2.6.21	
Search at the dore who knocks oft in the darke, . .	Ovid's Elegies	2.19.39	
There stands an old wood with thick trees darke clouded, .	Ovid's Elegies	3.12.7	
Breath'd darkenesse forth (darke night is Cupids day). .	Hero and Leander	1.191	
And ran into the darke her selfe to hide, ...	Hero and Leander	2.239	
Rich jewels in the darke are soonest spide. . . .	Hero and Leander	2.240	
DARKEN (See also DARCKNED)			
Ready to darken earth with endlesse night: . . .	2Tamb	2.4.7	Tamb
DARKENED			
That with thy lookes canst cleare the darkened Sky: . .	1Tamb	3.3.122	Tamb
DARKENES			
Weele enter in by darkenes to Killingworth. . . .	Edw	5.3.48	Matrvs
DARKENESSE			
That clouds of darkenesse may inclose my flesh, . .	Jew	1.2.194	Barab
night; or let the day/Turne to eternall darkenesse after this:	Jew	2.1.16	Barab
Breath'd darkenesse forth (darke night is Cupids day). .	Hero and Leander	1.191	
DARKESOME			
And hasting to me, neither darkesome night, . . .	Ovid's Elegies	2.11.51	
DARKLY			
Involving all, did Aruns darkly sing.	Lucan, First Booke	637	
DARKNED			
And heaven was darkned with tempestuous clowdes: . .	Dido	2.1.140	Aeneas
DARKNES			
Are drawne by darknes forth Astraeus tents. . . .	Dido	1.1.73	Venus
To shroud his shame in darknes of the night. . . .	1Tamb	4.1.46	Souldn
DARKNESSE (See also DARCKNESSE)			
Let ugly darknesse with her rusty coach/Engyrt with tempests	1Tamb	5.1.294	Bajzth
For hell and darknesse pitch their pitchy tentes, . .	2Tamb	5.3.7	Therid
And whelm'd the world in darknesse, making men/Dispaire of day;	Lucan, First Booke	540	
All gaine in darknesse the deepe earth suppreșt. . .	Ovid's Elegies	3.7.36	
DARKSOME			
Whil'st they were sporting in this darksome Cave? . .	Dido	4.1.24	Iarbus
Here lye the Sword that in the darksome Cave/He drew, and swore	Dido	5.1.295	Dido
Or meant to pierce Avernus darksome vaults, . . .	1Tamb	1.2.160	Therid
O'recast with dim and darksome coverture.	Hero and Leander	2.266	
DARLING			
What? dares she strike the darling of my thoughts? . .	Dido	1.1.9	Jupitr
DAROTES			
Darotes streames, wherin at anchor lies/A Turkish Gally of my	2Tamb	1.2.20	Callap
DAR'ST			
That dar'st presume thy Soveraigne for to mocke. . .	1Tamb	1.1.105	Mycet
And dar'st thou bluntly call me Bajazeth?	1Tamb	3.3.71	Bajzth
And dar'st thou bluntly call me Tamburlaine? . . .	1Tamb	3.3.74	Tamb
Dar'st thou that never saw an Emperour, ...	1Tamb	4.2.58	Zabina
What, dar'st thou then be absent from the fight, . .	2Tamb	4.1.22	Amyras
I did it, and revenge it if thou dar'st. . . .	Jew	3.2.4	Mthias
DARST			
Base villaine, darst thou give the lie?	1Tamb	2.4.19	Tamb
It shall suffice thou darst abide a wound. . . .	2Tamb	3.2.136	Tamb
Why, darst thou presume to call on Christ, . . .	P 356	6.11	Mntsrl
revenge it henry yf thow liste or darst	Paris	ms23,p391	Guise
How darst thou thus abuse a Gentleman?	F App	p.238 74	Knight
DART			
Then let the stony dart of sencelesse colde, . . .	1Tamb	5.1.302	Bajzth
Stands aiming at me with his murthering dart, . . .	2Tamb	5.3.69	Tamb
And dart her plumes, thinking to pierce my brest, . .	Edw	1.1.41	Gavstn
and strong armes/Can mainly throw the dart; wilt thou indure	Lucan, First Booke	365	
T'was so, he stroke me with a slender dart, . . .	Ovid's Elegies	1.2.7	
And for a good verse drawe the first dart forth, . .	Ovid's Elegies	3.7.27	
DARTED			
That darted mountaines at her brother Jove: . . .	1Tamb	5.1.511	Tamb
Than he that darted mountaines at thy head, . . .	2Tamb	4.1.128	Tamb
DARTERS			
And they of Rhene and Leuca, cunning darters, . . .	Lucan, First Booke	425	
DARTES			
Forgetst thou that I sent a shower of dartes/Mingled with	2Tamb	1.1.91	Orcan
With bowes and dartes to shoot at them they see, . .	P 422	7.62	Dumain
And purple Love resumes his dartes againe. . . .	Ovid's Elegies	2.9.34	
DARTING			
As I exhal'd with thy fire darting beames, . . .	Dido	1.1.25	Jupitr
As meaning to be veng'd for darting it.	Hero and Leander	2.212	

DARTS			
Darts forth her light to Lavinias shoare.	Dido	3.2.84	Venus
And with one shaft provoke ten thousand darts:	Dido	3.3.72	Iarbus
Whose flintie darts slept in Tipheus den,	Dido	4.1.19	Iarbus
And will my guard with Mauritanian darts,	Dido	4.4.68	Dido
Whose darts do pierce the Center of my soule:	2Tamb	2.4.84	Tamb
Eagles alike displaide, darts answering darts.	Lucan, First Booke		7
Or darts which Parthians backward shoot) marcht on/And then	Lucan, First Booke		232
headles darts, olde swords/With ugly teeth of blacke rust fouly	Lucan, First Booke		244
Against the destinies durst sharpe darts require.	Ovid's Elegies		1.7.10
Toyes, and light Elegies my darts I tooke,	Ovid's Elegies		2.1.21
But bids his darts from perjurd girles retire.	Ovid's Elegies		3.3.36
Now is the goat brought through the boyes with darts,	Ovid's Elegies		3.12.21
DASH			
down murthering shot from heaven/To dash the Scythians braines,	1Tamb	3.3.197	Zabina
To dash the heavie headed Edmunds drift,	Edw	5.2.39	Mortmr
Or dash the pride of this solemnity;	F 860	3.1.82	Mephst
in the house, and dash out all your braines with your Bottles.	F1619	4.6.62	P HrsCsr
Would dash the wreath thou wearst for Pirats wracke.	Lucan, First Booke		123
DASHT			
Who with steele Pol-axes dasht out their braines.	Dido	2.1.199	Aeneas
His Skul al rivin in twain, his braines dasht out?	1Tamb	5.1.306	Zabina
Our plots and stratagems will soone be dasht.	Edw	5.2.78	Mortmr
restrain'd them; but wars love/And Caesars awe dasht all:	Lucan, First Booke		357
DASLED			
her latest breath/All dasled with the hellish mists of death.	2Tamb	2.4.14	Tamb
DATE (Homograph)			
To coole and comfort me with longer date,	1Tamb	5.1.277	Bajzth
And though they think their painfull date is out,	2Tamb	5.3.34	Usumc
I writ them a bill with mine owne bloud, the date is expired:	F1861	5.2.65	P Faust
The course of mischiefe, and stretch out the date/Of slaughter;	Lucan, First Booke		670
Whose life nine ages scarce bring out of date.	Ovid's Elegies		2.6.36
Memphis, and Pharos that sweete date trees yeelds,	Ovid's Elegies		2.13.8
DATED			
the Starres that make/The loathsome Circle of my dated life,	1Tamb	2.6.37	Cosroe
of that vitall aire/That feeds the body with his dated health,	2Tamb	2.4.45	Zenoc
DATES			
Browne Almonds, Servises, ripe Figs and Dates,	Dido	4.5.5	Nurse
DAUB (See BEDAUBD)			
DAUGHTER			
Daughter unto the Nimphs Hesperides,	Dido	5.1.276	Dido
He sends this Souldans daughter rich and brave,	1Tamb	1.2.186	Tamb
The Souldans daughter for his Concubine,	1Tamb	4.1.5	Souldn
Of my faire daughter, and his princely Love:	1Tamb	4.1.70	Souldn
Thy princely daughter here shall set thee free.	1Tamb	5.1.436	Tamb
Or as Latonas daughter bent to armes,	1Tamb	5.1.514	Tamb
But one sole Daughter, whom I hold as deare/As Agamemnon did	Jew	1.1.137	Barab
So they spare me, my daughter, and my wealth.	Jew	1.1.153	Barab
Oh what has made my lovely daughter sad?	Jew	1.2.225	Barab
Be silent, Daughter, sufferance breeds ease,	Jew	1.2.238	Barab
Daughter, I have it:	Jew	1.2.270	Barab
I, Daughter, for Religion/Hides many mischiefes from suspition.	Jew	1.2.281	Barab
What art thou, daughter?	Jew	1.2.316	Abbass
The hopelesse daughter of a haplesse Jew,	Jew	1.2.317	Abigal
Well, daughter, say, what is thy suit with us?	Jew	1.2.321	Abbass
Well, daughter, we admit you for a Nun.	Jew	1.2.330	Abbass
Come daughter, follow us.	Jew	1.2.337	Abbass
Yet let thy daughter be no longer blinde.	Jew	1.2.354	1Fryar
Seduced Daughter, Goe, forget not.	Jew	1.2.359	Barab
Faire Abigall the rich Jewes daughter/Become a Nun?	Jew	1.2.366	Mthias
Why, the rich Jewes daughter.	Jew	1.2.382	Mthias
They hop'd my daughter would ha bin a Nun;	Jew	2.3.12	Barab
I meane my daughter:--	Jew	2.3.51	Barab
He loves my daughter, and she holds him deare:	Jew	2.3.141	Barab
Give me the letters, daughter, doe you heare?	Jew	2.3.224	Barab
Daughter, a word more; kisse him, speake him faire,	Jew	2.3.234	Barab
That I intend my daughter shall be thine.	Jew	2.3.254	Barab
My daughter here, a paltry silly girle.	Jew	2.3.284	Barab
Barabas, thou know'st I have lov'd thy daughter long.	Jew	2.3.288	Lodowk
your Lordship wud disdaine/To marry with the daughter of a Jew:	Jew	2.3.295	Barab
This follows well, and therefore daughter feare not.	Jew	2.3.313	Barab
Thy daughter--	Jew	4.1.34	2Fryar
I, thy daughter--	Jew	4.1.35	1Fryar
One turn'd my daugnter, therefore he shall dye;	Jew	4.1.119	Barab
poyson'd his owne daughter and the Nuns, strangled a Fryar,	Jew	5.1.13	P Pilia
strangled Bernardine, poyson'd the Nuns, and his owne daughter.	Jew	5.1.34	P Ithimr
That linke you in mariage with our daughter heer:	P 14	1.14	QnMoth
On Priams loose-trest daughter when he gazed.	Ovid's Elegies		1.9.38
But did you not so envy Cepheus Daughter,	Ovid's Elegies		3.3.17
DAUGHTERS			
And my nine Daughters sing when thou art sad,	Dido	1.1.33	Jupitr
Doe you not sorrow for your daughters death?	Jew	4.1.17	Ithimr
Thebe who Mother of five Daughters prov'd?	Ovid's Elegies		3.5.34
DAUNCE			
Vulcan shall daunce to make thee laughing sport,	Dido	1.1.32	Jupitr
Making it daunce with wanton majestie:	1Tamb	2.1.26	Menaph
Shall with their Goate feete daunce an antick hay.	Edw	1.1.60	Gavstn
And steale a kisse, and then run out and daunce,	Hero and Leander		2.185
The Sheepheards Swaines shall daunce and sing,	Passionate Shepherd		21
DAUNGER			
Who warne me of such daunger prest at hand,	Dido	3.2.22	Venus
As daunger of this stormie time requires.	Edw	4.7.7	Abbot
DAUNT			
Torture or paine can daunt my dreadlesse minde.	2Tamb	5.1.113	Govnr

DAUNT (cont.)				
Intends our Muse to vaunt <daunt> his heavenly verse; .	F 6	Prol.6		1Chor
DAUNTED				
late felt frownes/That sent a tempest to my daunted thoughtes,	1Tamb	3.2.86		Agidas
And glut it not with stale and daunted foes. . . .	2Tamb	4.1.88		Tamb
DAUNTLESSE				
whose dauntlesse minde/The ambitious Mortimer would seeke to	Edw	5.1.15		Edward
DAUNTS				
A woful change my Lord, that daunts our thoughts, . .	2Tamb	5.3.181		Therid
DAY (See also DAIES)				
To day when as I fild into your cups, ...	Dido	1.1.5		Ganimd
My Juno ware upon her marriage day, ...	Dido	1.1.43		Jupitr
And intercepts the day as Dolon erst:	Dido	1.1.71		Venus
Whose night and day descendeth from thy browes: . . .	Dido	1.1.156		Achat
The day, the night, my Swannes, my sweetes are thine. .	Dido	3.2.61		Venus
This day they both a hunting forth will ride/Into these woods,	Dido	3.2.87		Juno
I mother, I shall one day be a man, ...	Dido	3.3.35		Cupid
turne the hand of fate/Unto that happie day of my delight,	Dido	3.3.81		Iarbus
Or day so cleere so suddenly orecast?	Dido	4.1.2		Achat
On whom the nimble windes may all day waight, . . .	Dido	4.3.23		Aeneas
Wherein the day may evermore delight:	Dido	5.1.7		Aeneas
this day swift Mercury/When I was laying a platforme for these	Dido	5.1.93		Aeneas
At whose byrth-day Cynthia with Saturne joinde, . . .	1Tamb	1.1.13		Cosroe
Our life is fraile, and we may die to day.	1Tamb	1.1.68		Mycet
Thy wit will make us Conquerors to day.	1Tamb	2.2.58		Mycet
For though the glorie of this day be lost, ...	1Tamb	3.3.241		Bajzth
The first day when he pitcheth downe his tentes, . . .	1Tamb	4.1.49		2Msngr
Even from this day to Platoes wondrous yeare, ...	1Tamb	4.2.96		Tamb
That Tamburlaine shall rue the day, the hower, . . .	1Tamb	4.3.38		Souldn
belike he hath not bene watered to day, give him some drinke.	1Tamb	4.4.55	P	Tamb
Hath Bajazeth bene fed to day?	1Tamb	5.1.192		Tamb
Accursed day infected with my griefs, ...	1Tamb	5.1.291		Bajzth
Or cease one day from war and hot alarms, ...	2Tamb	1.3.183		Usumc
Blacke is the beauty of the brightest day, ...	2Tamb	2.4.1		Tamb
The glorie of this happy day is yours:	2Tamb	3.5.161		Tamb
May never day give vertue to his eies, ...	2Tamb	4.1.174		Trebiz
What, can ye draw but twenty miles a day, ...	2Tamb	4.3.2		Tamb
Besides my Lord, this day is Criticall, ...	2Tamb	5.3.91		Phsitn
Yet if your majesty may escape this day, ...	2Tamb	5.3.98		Phsitn
And live in spight of death above a day.	2Tamb	5.3.101		Tamb
Begins the day with our Antypodes:	2Tamb	5.3.149		Tamb
Whereof a man may easily in a day/Tell that which may maintaine	Jew	1.1.10		Barab
And they this day sit in the Counsell-house/To entertaine them	Jew	1.1.148		1Jew
Were they not summon'd to appeare to day?	Jew	1.2.35		Govnr
For if we breake our day, we breake the league, . . .	Jew	1.2.158		1Knght
Oh silly brethren, borne to see this day!	Jew	1.2.170		Barab
So that not he, but I may curse the day, ...	Jew	1.2.191		Barab
Thy fatall birth-day, forlorne Barabas;	Jew	1.2.192		Barab
For evils are apt to happen every day.	Jew	1.2.223		Barab
night; or let the day/Turne to eternall darkenesse after this:	Jew	2.1.15		Barab
Now Phoebus ope the eye-lids of the day, ...	Jew	2.1.60		Barab
The Sessions day is criticall to theeves, ...	Jew	2.3.105		Barab
not a stone of beef a day will maintaine you in these chops;	Jew	2.3.124	P	Barab
To day.	Jew	3.4.19	P	Ithimr
Oh unhappy day, ...	Jew	3.4.26		Barab
Oh raskall! I change my selfe twice a day.	Jew	4.4.65		Barab
Oh fatall day, to fall into the hands/Of such a Traitor and	Jew	5.2.12		Govnr
If ever day were turnde to ugly night, ...	P 62	2.5		Guise
This day, this houre, this fatall night, ...	P 64	2.7		Guise
And dayly meet about this time of day, ...	P 503	9.22		Guise
Till this our Coronation day be past:	P 624	12.37		King
To whom the sunne shines both by day and night. . . .	Edw	1.1.17		Gavstn
And in the day when he shall walke abroad, ...	Edw	1.1.57		Gavstn
and yet ere that day come,/The king shall lose his crowne, for	Edw	1.2.58		Mortmr
or at the mariage day/The cup of Hymen had beene full of .	Edw	1.4.173		Queene
Such reasons make white blacke, and darke night day. .	Edw	1.4.247		Lncstr
That day, if not for him, yet for my sake, ...	Edw	1.4.381		Edward
And smelling to a Nosegay all the day, ...	Edw	2.1.35		Spencr
Seeing that he talkes thus of my mariage day?	Edw	2.1.69		Neece
Cosin, this day shalbe your mariage feast, ...	Edw	2.2.256		Edward
And Gaveston this blessed day be slaine.	Edw	2.4.69		Queene
O must this day be period of my life, ...	Edw	2.6.4		Gavstn
This day I shall powre vengeance with my sword/On those proud	Edw	3.1.186		Edward
Edward this day hath crownd him king a new.	Edw	3.1.261		Edward
That I may see that most desired day, ...	Edw	4.3.46		Edward
O day!	Edw	4.7.61		Edward
That waites your pleasure, and the day growes old. . .	Edw	4.7.85		Leistr
But perfect shadowes in a sun-shine day?	Edw	5.1.27		Edward
And that this be the coronation day, ...	Edw	5.4.70		Mortmr
that at some certaine day/Great Lucifer may claime it as his	F 439	2.1.51		Mephst
That the first is finisht in a naturall day?	F 603	2.2.52		Faust
me, as Paradise was to Adam the first day of his creation.	F 658	2.2.107	P	Faust
and that buyes me <is> thirty meales a day, and ten Beavers:	F 695	2.2.144	P	Glutny
The which <That to> this day is highly solemnized. . . .	F 778	2.3.57		2Chor
The which this day with high solemnity, ...	F 833	3.1.55		Mephst
This day is held through Rome and Italy, ...	F 834	3.1.56		Mephst
This day shall make thee be admir'd in Rome.	F 867	3.1.89		Mephst
The Pope will curse them for their sloth to day, . . .	F 987	3.2.7		Faust
That all this day the sluggard keepes his bed. . . .	F1176	4.1.22		Mrtino
Benvolio's head was grac't with hornes to day?	F1331	4.2.7		Benvol
I warrant you sir; O joyfull day:	F1476	4.4.20	P	HrsCsr
As I was going to Wittenberge t'other day, with a loade of Hay,	F1526	4.5.22	P	Carter
Doctor Fauster bad me ride him night and day, and spare him no	F1540	4.5.36	P	HrsCsr

DAY (cont.)			
Faire natures eye, rise, rise againe and make/Perpetuall day:	F1932	5.2.136	Faust
this houre be but/A yeare, a month, a weeke, a naturall day,	F1933	5.2.137	Faust
bleate, and an asse braye, because it is S. Peters holy day.	F App	p.232 28 P	Faust
I have beene al this day seeking one maister Fustian:	F App	p.239 98 P	HrsCsr
And strive to shine by day, and ful of strife/Disolve the	Lucan, First Booke		79
Or Cynthia nights Queene waights upon the day;	Lucan, First Booke		91
Day rose and viewde these tumultes of the war;	Lucan, First Booke		235
to run their course through empty night/At noone day mustered,	Lucan, First Booke		535
making men/Dispaire of day; as did Thiestes towne/(Mycenae),	Lucan, First Booke		541
ominous birds/Defil'd the day, and <at night> wilde beastes	Lucan, First Booke		557
In summers heate, and midtime of the day,	Ovid's Elegies		1.5.1
Or night being past, and yet not day begunne.	Ovid's Elegies		1.5.6
When she will, day shines every where most pure.	Ovid's Elegies		1.8.10
This day denyall hath my sport adjourned.	Ovid's Elegies		1.12.2
Among day bookes and billes they had laine better/In which the	Ovid's Elegies		1.12.25
That drawes the day from heavens cold axletree.	Ovid's Elegies		1.13.2
The Moone sleepes with Endemion everie day,	Ovid's Elegies		1.13.43
Yet lingered not the day, but morning scard me.	Ovid's Elegies		1.13.48
The seventh day came, none following mightst thou see,	Ovid's Elegies		2.6.45
Let me lie with thee browne Cypasse to day.	Ovid's Elegies		2.8.22
Let the bright day-starre cause in heaven this day be,	Ovid's Elegies		2.11.55
with loving may/Had seene, my mother killing me, [no] <to> day.	Ovid's Elegies		2.14.22
What gift with me was on her birth day sent,	Ovid's Elegies		3.1.57
What day and night to travaile in her quest?	Ovid's Elegies		3.5.10
And nine sweete bouts had we before day light.	Ovid's Elegies		3.6.26
Him the last day in black Averne hath drownd,	Ovid's Elegies		3.8.27
What day was that, which all sad haps to bring,	Ovid's Elegies		3.11.1
What madnesse ist to tell night <nights> prankes by day,	Ovid's Elegies		3.13.7
On this feast day, O cursed day and hower,	Hero and Leander		1.131
Breath'd darkenesse forth (darke night is Cupids day).	Hero and Leander		1.191
God knowes I play/With Venus swannes and sparrowes all the day.	Hero and Leander		1.352
The self-same day that he asleepe had layd/Inchaunted Argus,	Hero and Leander		1.387
And to this day is everie scholler poore,	Hero and Leander		1.471
For much it greev'd her that the bright day-light,	Hero and Leander		2.303
Brought foorth the day before the day was borne.	Hero and Leander		2.322
But he the [days] <day> bright-bearing Car prepar'd.	Hero and Leander		2.330
DAYES			
You'le like it better farre a nights than dayes.	Jew	2.3.63	Barab
In dolefull wise they ended both their dayes.	Jew	3.3.21	Ithimr
I have beene a great sinner in my dayes, and the deed is	P1133	21.27 P	Frier
I do remember in my fathers dayes,	Edw	1.1.109	Kent
But dayes bright beames dooth vanish fast away,	Edw	5.1.69	Edward
This ten dayes space, and least that I should sleepe,	Edw	5.5.60	Edward
<As match the dayes within one compleate yeare>,	F 821	(HC265)A	Mephst
Shortning my dayes and thred of vitall life,	F App	p.239 92	Faust
Shee oft hath serv'd thee upon certaine dayes,	Ovid's Elegies		2.13.17
Festivall dayes aske Venus, songs, and wine,	Ovid's Elegies		3.9.47
DAYLIE			
That daylie dandlest Cupid in thy armes:	Dido	5.1.45	Aeneas
DAY-LIGHT			
For much it greev'd her that the bright day-light,	Hero and Leander		2.303
DAY LIGHT			
And nine sweete bouts had we before day light.	Ovid's Elegies		3.6.26
DAYLY			
Him as a childe I dayly winne with words,	P 130	2.73	Guise
And dayly meet about this time of day,	P 503	9.22	Guise
Love <Jove> knowes with such like praiers, I dayly move hir:	Ovid's Elegies		1.3.4
But they that dayly tast neat wine, despise it.	Hero and Leander		1.261
DAYS			
But he the [days] <day> bright-bearing Car prepar'd.	Hero and Leander		2.330
DAY-STARRE			
Let the bright day-starre cause in heaven this day be,	Ovid's Elegies		2.11.55
DAZZLE (See DASLED)			
DE (Homograph)			
Si bene quid de te merui, fuit aut tibi quidquam/Dulce meum,	Dido	5.1.136	Dido
Hermoso Placer de los Dineros.	Jew	2.1.64	Barab
But if I get him, Coupe de Gorge for that.	Jew	4.3.5	Barab
O Mounser de Guise, heare me but speake.	P 529	10.2	Prtsnt
DEAD			
And flourish once againe that erst was dead:	Dido	1.1.95	Jupitr
that would have it so/Deludes thy eye sight, Priamus is dead.	Dido	2.1.32	Achat
And Priam dead, yet how we heare no newes.	Dido	2.1.113	Dido
Virgins halfe dead dragged by their golden haire,	Dido	2.1.195	Aeneas
And dead to honour that hath brought me up.	Dido	3.3.45	Aeneas
And dead to scorne that hath pursued me so.	Dido	3.3.49	Iarbus
Dido is dead,	Dido	5.1.320	Anna
heaven/To dash the Scythians braines, and strike them dead,	1Tamb	3.3.197	Zabina
Halfe dead for feare before they feele my wrath:	1Tamb	4.4.4	Tamb
What do mine eies behold, my husband dead?	1Tamb	5.1.305	Zabina
What, is she dead?	2Tamb	2.4.96	Tamb
Ah good my Lord be patient, she is dead,	2Tamb	2.4.119	Therid
Nothing prevailes, for she is dead my Lord.	2Tamb	2.4.124	Therid
For she is dead? thy words doo pierce my soule.	2Tamb	2.4.125	Tamb
Though she be dead, yet let me think she lives,	2Tamb	2.4.127	Tamb
Because my deare Zenocrate is dead.	2Tamb	3.2.14	Tamb
For think ye I can live, and see him dead?	2Tamb	3.4.27	Sonne
Albeit the world thinke Machevill is dead,	Jew	Prol.1	Machvl
And now the Guize is dead, is come from France/To view this	Jew	Prol.3	Machvl
armes in ure/With digging graves and ringing dead mens knels:	Jew	2.3.185	Barab
I, part 'em now they are dead: Farewell, farewell.	Jew	3.2.9	Barab
All that I have is thine when I am dead,	Jew	3.4.44	Barab
What, all dead save onely Abigall?	Jew	3.6.7	2Fryar

Line	Work	Ref	Speaker
DEAD (cont.)			
Oh brother, all the Nuns are dead, let's bury them.	Jew	3.6.44	1Fryar
How sweet the Bels ring now the Nuns are dead/That sound at	Jew	4.1.2	Barab
Now all are dead, not one remaines alive.	Jew	4.1.7	Barab
Thou shalt not need, for now the Nuns are dead,	Jew	4.1.15	Barab
And besides, the Wench is dead.	Jew	4.1.42	Barab
My Lord, the Curtezane and her man are dead;	Jew	5.1.50	1Offcr
Dead?	Jew	5.1.52	Govnr
Dead, my Lord, and here they bring his body.	Jew	5.1.53	1Offcr
Since they are dead, let them be buried.	Jew	5.1.57	Govnr
And being asleepe, belike they thought me dead,	Jew	5.1.81	Barab
Gonzago, what, is he dead?	P 304	5.31	Guise
Shall being dead, be hangd thereon in chaines.	P 321	5.48	Anjoy
What art thou dead, sweet sonne speak to thy Mother.	P 551	11.16	QnMoth
I may be stabd, and live till he be dead,	P 778	15.36	Mugern
(As all the world shall know our Guise is dead)/Rest satisfied	P1042	19.112	King
But what availeth that this traitors dead,	P1054	19.124	King
For since the Guise is dead, I will not live.	P1090	19.160	QnMoth
Now thou art dead, heere is no stay for us:	P1111	21.5	Dumain
Ah curse him not sith he is dead.	P1220	22.82	King
Which being caught, strikes him that takes it dead,	Edw	1.4.222	Mortmr
Do you not wish that Gaveston were dead?	Edw	1.4.252	Mortmr
And with my kinglie scepter stroke me dead,	Edw	1.4.317	Edward
Seeing that our Lord th'earle of Glosters dead,	Edw	2.1.2	Baldck
Which swept the desart shore of that dead sea,	Edw	2.3.22	Mortmr
Yea my good lord, for Gaveston is dead.	Edw	3.1.90	Arundl
That you were dead, or very neare your death.	Edw	4.2.38	Queene
Why, is he dead?	Edw	5.2.98	Prince
That being dead, if it chaunce to be found,	Edw	5.4.14	Mortmr
Ist done, Matrevis, and the murtherer dead?	Edw	5.6.1	Mortmr
His fathers dead, and we have murdered him.	Edw	5.6.16	Queene
Or being dead, raise them to life againe,	F 53	1.1.25	Faust
my parents are all dead, and the devill a peny they have left	F 693	2.2.142	P Glutny
What, is he asleepe, or dead?	F1279	4.1.125	Saxony
And pants untill I see that Conjurer dead.	F1352	4.2.28	Benvol
The Divel's dead, the Furies now may laugh.	F1369	4.2.45	Benvol
a dead time of the winter, I would request no better meate,	F1572	4.6.15	P Lady
and the dead time of the winter, I would desire no better meate	F App	p.242 10	P Duchss
that being in the dead time of winter, and in the month of	F App	p.242 17	P Duke
cullor scard him; a dead blacknesse/Ranne through the bloud,	Lucan, First Booke	617	
of flesh, whereof one halfe did looke/Dead, and discoulour'd;	Lucan, First Booke	628	
Her halfe dead joynts, and trembling limmes I sawe,	Ovid's Elegies	1.7.53	
That my dead bones may in their grave lie soft.	Ovid's Elegies	1.8.108	
The living, not the dead can envie bite,	Ovid's Elegies	1.15.39	
Is dead, al-fowles her exequies frequent.	Ovid's Elegies	2.6.2	
Dead is that speaking image of mans voice,	Ovid's Elegies	2.6.37	
With Laodameia mate to her dead Lord.	Ovid's Elegies	2.18.38	
Yet notwithstanding, like one dead it lay,	Ovid's Elegies	3.6.65	
Either th'art witcht with blood <bould> of frogs new dead,	Ovid's Elegies	3.6.79	
Canst touch that hand wherewith some one lie dead?	Ovid's Elegies	3.7.17	
Burnes his dead body in the funerall flame.	Ovid's Elegies	3.8.6	
Such was the Greeke pompe, Agamemnon dead,	Ovid's Elegies	3.12.31	
And would be dead, but dying <dead> with thee remaine.	Ovid's Elegies	3.13.40	
Poore soldiers stand with fear of death dead strooken,	Hero and Leander	1.121	
For under water he was almost dead,	Hero and Leander	2.170	
DEADLY			
Or els to threaten death and deadly armes,	1Tamb	3.1.19	Fesse
destruction/Redeeme you from this deadly servitude.	1Tamb	3.2.34	Agidas
Ah that the deadly panges I suffer now,	1Tamb	5.1.422	Arabia
crost Danubius stream/To treat of friendly peace or deadly war:	2Tamb	1.1.80	Sgsmnd
And harmelesse run among the deadly pikes.	2Tamb	1.3.46	Tamb
A deadly bullet gliding through my side,	2Tamb	3.4.4	Capt
Wil send a deadly lightening to his heart.	2Tamb	4.1.10	Celeb
and you were stated here/To be at deadly enmity with Turkes.	Jew	2.2.33	Bosco
Which he hath pitcht within his deadly toyle.	P 54	1.54	Navrre
within the compasse of a deadly toyle,	P 205	4.3	QnMoth
But wherfore beares he me such deadly hate?	P 779	15.37	Mugern
Whose light was deadly to the Protestants:	P 945	19.15	Capt
Which all the other fishes deadly hate,	Edw	2.2.24	Lncstr
Armes that pursue our lives with deadly hate.	Edw	4.7.32	Spencr
deadly sinnes appeare to thee in their owne proper shapes and	F 655	2.2.104	P Belzeb
A surfet of deadly sin, that hath damn'd both body and soule.	F1833	5.2.37	P Faust
Trumpets and drums, like deadly threatning other,	Lucan, First Booke	6	
Under sweete hony deadly poison lurkes.	Ovid's Elegies	1.8.104	
The Argos wrackt had deadly waters drunke.	Ovid's Elegies	2.11.6	
Mars girts his deadly sword on for my harme:	Ovid's Elegies	3.3.27	
They offred him the deadly fatall knife,	Hero and Leander	1.447	
DEADS			
That deads the royall vine, whose golden leaves/Empale your	Edw	3.1.163	Herald
DEAFE			
the Ecchoe and the souldiers crie/Make deafe the aire, and dim	2Tamb	3.3.61	Therid
Come breake these deafe dores with thy boysterous wind.	Ovid's Elegies	1.6.54	
If he loves not, deafe eares thou doest importune,	Ovid's Elegies	2.2.53	
And with sweete words cause deafe rockes to have loved <moned>,	Ovid's Elegies	3.6.58	
Can deafe [eares] <yeares> take delight when Phemius sings,/Or	Ovid's Elegies	3.6.61	
At thy deafe dores in verse sing my abuses.	Ovid's Elegies	3.7.24	
DEAFFE			
Love is not ful of pittie (as men say)/But deaffe and cruell,	Hero and Leander	2.288	
DEALE			
Me thinks, tis a great deale better than a consort of musicke.	1Tamb	4.4.60	P Therid
Deale truly with us as thou intimatest,	Jew	5.2.85	Govnr
That right or wrong, thou deale thy selfe a King.	P 148	2.91	Guise
Deale you my lords in this, my loving lords,	Edw	4.6.28	Queene

DEALE (cont.)			
How will you deale with Edward in his fall?	Edw	4.6.31	Kent
DEALETH			
The man that dealeth righteously shall live:	Jew	1.2.116	Barab
DEALING			
Cosin it is no dealing with him now,	Edw	2.2.102	Lncstr
DEALT			
That thus have dealt with me in my distresse.	Jew	1.2.168	Barab
behalfe, dealt with the king of Fraunce his lords, and effected,	Edw	4.3.29	P Spencr
DEARE (Homograph; See also DEERE, DERE)			
But Dido that now holdeth him so deare,	Dido	3.3.76	Iarbus
Tell me deare love, how found you out this Cave?	Dido	3.4.3	Dido
Aeneas will not faine with his deare love,	Dido	5.1.92	Aeneas
Aeneas could not choose but hold thee deare,	Dido	5.1.126	Aeneas
Iarbus slaine, Iarbus my deare love,	Dido	5.1.321	Anna
Too deare a witnesse for such love my Lord.	1Tamb	5.1.412	Zenoc
Wel met my only deare Zenocrate,	1Tamb	5.1.443	Souldn
Because my deare Zenocrate is dead.	2Tamb	3.2.14	Tamb
Daughter, whom I hold as deare/As Agamemnon did his Iphegen:	Jew	1.1.137	Barab
He loves my daughter, and she holds him deare:	Jew	2.3.141	Barab
My life is not so deare as Abigall.	Jew	2.3.348	Mthias
now Abigall shall see/Whether Mathias holds her deare or no.	Jew	3.2.2	Mthias
Mathias was the man that I held deare,	Jew	3.6.24	Abigal
Come my deare love, let's in and sleepe together.	Jew	4.2.129	Curtzn
Is all my love forgot which helde thee deare?	P 684	13.28	Guise
Which your wife writ to my deare Minion,	P 755	15.13	King
But that it harbors him I hold so deare,	Edw	1.1.13	Gavstn
How deare my lord is to poore Isabell.	Edw	1.4.166	Queene
And thinke I gaind, having bought so deare a friend.	Edw	1.4.310	Edward
Deare shall you both abie this riotous deede:	Edw	2.2.88	Edward
the forrest Deare being strucke/Runnes to an herbe that closeth	Edw	5.1.9	Edward
Whome I esteeme as deare as these mine eyes,	Edw	5.2.18	Queene
you, and keepe you, my deere brethren <my deare brethren>.	F 218	1.2.25	P Wagner
I might have then my parents deare misus'd,	Ovid's Elegies		1.7.5
She is not chaste, that's kept, but a deare whore:	Ovid's Elegies		3.4.29
(For his sake whom their goddesse held so deare,	Hero and Leander		1.92
DEARELY			
And for thy sake, whom I so dearely love,	Jew	3.4.61	Barab
Dearely beloved brother, thus tis written.	P 343	5.70	Guise
The Sabine gauntlets were too dearely wunne/That unto death did	Ovid's Elegies		1.10.49
DEARER			
Whose lives were dearer to Zenocrate/Than her owne life, or	1Tamb	5.1.337	Zenoc
My Lord deceast, was dearer unto me,	2Tamb	3.4.42	Olymp
Why should this Turke be dearer then that Moore?	Jew	2.3.109	Barab
I, dearer then the apple of mine eye?	P 685	13.29	Guise
DEAREST			
the cause of this/That tearm'st Zenocrate thy dearest love?	1Tamb	5.1.336	Zenoc
To bid us battaile for our dearest lives.	2Tamb	2.2.28	1Msngr
Farewel my boies, my dearest friends, farewel,	2Tamb	5.3.245	Tamb
Let not this heavy chaunce my dearest Lord,	P 191	3.26	QnMarg
That I may write unto my dearest Lord.	P 659	13.3	Duchss
Shall buy her love even with his dearest bloud.	P 697	13.41	Guise
That ever I vouchsafte my dearest freends.	P1146	22.8	King
my fortie dollers againe, or Ile make it the dearest horse:	F App	p.240 137	P HrsCsr
DEARLY			
I meane the peeres, whom thou shouldst dearly love:	Edw	2.2.176	Mortmr
DEARTH			
Threatning a death <dearth> and famine to this land,	2Tamb	3.2.9	Tamb
And by him kept of purpose for a dearth?	Lucan, First Booke		319
DEATH			
Who for her sonnes death wept out life and breath,	Dido	2.1.4	Aeneas
Was with two winged Serpents stung to death.	Dido	2.1.166	Aeneas
That sav'd your famisht souldiers lives from death,	Dido	3.3.52	Achat
I, this it is which wounds me to the death,	Dido	3.3.63	Iarbus
Will dye with very tidings of his death:	Dido	3.3.77	Iarbus
When I leave thee, death be my punishment,	Dido	4.4.56	Aeneas
Nor blazing Commets threatens Didos death,	Dido	4.4.119	Dido
The Gods, what Gods be those that seeke my death?	Dido	5.1.128	Dido
But Anna now shall honor thee in death,	Dido	5.1.325	Anna
That Gods and men may pitie this my death,	Dido	5.1.327	Anna
Have sworne the death of wicked Tamburlaine.	1Tamb	1.1.64	Mycet
That even to death will follow Tamburlaine.	1Tamb	1.2.59	Usumc
And they will never leave thee till the death.	1Tamb	1.2.248	Tamb
His lofty browes in foldes, do figure death,	1Tamb	2.1.21	Menaph
And fall like mellowed fruit, with shakes of death,	1Tamb	2.1.47	Cosroe
Whose vertues carie with it life and death,	1Tamb	2.5.61	Therid
Vowing our loves to equall death and life.	1Tamb	2.6.28	Cosroe
And death arrests the organe of my voice,	1Tamb	2.7.8	Cosroe
and now dooth gastly death/With greedy tallents gripe my	1Tamb	2.7.48	Cosroe
Or els to threaten death and deadly armes,	1Tamb	3.1.19	Fesse
Make me the gastly counterfeit of death.	1Tamb	3.2.17	Zenoc
Upon his browes was pourtraid ugly death,	1Tamb	3.2.72	Agidas
And Jetty Feathers menace death and hell.	1Tamb	4.1.61	2Msngr
And sacrifice my heart to death and hell,	1Tamb	4.2.17	Bajzth
Shall sit by him and starve to death himselfe.	1Tamb	4.2.90	Tamb
Preserving life, by hasting cruell death.	1Tamb	4.4.96	Bajzth
These more than dangerous warrants of our death,	1Tamb	5.1.31	1Virgn
Now waxe all pale and withered to the death,	1Tamb	5.1.91	1Virgn
For there sits Death, there sits imperious Death,	1Tamb	5.1.111	Tamb
few of them/To chardge these Dames, and shew my servant death,	1Tamb	5.1.117	Tamb
Away with them I say and shew them death.	1Tamb	5.1.120	Tamb
are as peremptory/As wrathfull Planets, death, or destinie.	1Tamb	5.1.128	Tamb
What, have your horsmen shewen the virgins Death?	1Tamb	5.1.129	Tamb

DEATH (cont.)

Hel, death, Tamburlain, Hell.	1Tamb	5.1.316	P Zabina
And guiltlesly endure a cruell death.	1Tamb	5.1.329	Zenoc
And let them die a death so barbarous.	1Tamb	5.1.351	Zenoc
Lye down Arabia, wounded to the death,	1Tamb	5.1.407	Arabia
Since Death denies me further cause of joy,	1Tamb	5.1.430	Arabia
And griesly death, by running to and fro,	1Tamb	5.1.455	Tamb
Wher death cuts off the progres of his pomp,	2Tamb	Prol.4	Prolog
with my heart/Wish your release, but he whose wrath is death,	2Tamb	1.2.6	Almeda
Now goe I to revenge my fathers death.	2Tamb	1.2.78	Callap
Harbors revenge, war, death and cruelty:	2Tamb	1.3.78	Tamb
That God hath given to venge our Christians death/And scourge	2Tamb	2.1.52	Fredrk
End all my penance in my sodaine death,	2Tamb	2.3.7	Sgsmnd
And let this death wherein to sinne I die,	2Tamb	2.3.8	Sgsmnd
her latest breath/All dasled with the hellish mists of death.	2Tamb	2.4.14	Tamb
Or dieng, be the [author] <anchor> of my death.	2Tamb	2.4.56	Tamb
For should I but suspect your death by mine,	2Tamb	2.4.61	Zenoc
Sweet sons farewell, in death resemble me,	2Tamb	2.4.75	Zenoc
Sadly supplied with pale and ghastly death,	2Tamb	2.4.83	Tamb
Letting out death and tyrannising war,	2Tamb	2.4.115	Tamb
Death and destruction to th'inhabitants.	2Tamb	3.2.5	Tamb
Threatning a death <dearth> and famine to this land,	2Tamb	3.2.9	Tamb
Being burnt to cynders for your mothers death.	2Tamb	3.2.46	Tamb
With griefe and sorrow for my mothers death.	2Tamb	3.2.50	Amyras
My mothers death hath mortified my mind,	2Tamb	3.2.51	Celeb
And canst thou Coward stand in feare of death?	2Tamb	3.2.102	Tamb
Dreadlesse of blowes, of bloody wounds and death:	2Tamb	3.2.140	Tamb
Death, whether art thou gone that both we live?	2Tamb	3.4.11	Olymp
Come back again (sweet death) and strike us both:	2Tamb	3.4.12	Olymp
death, why comm'st thou not?	2Tamb	3.4.14	Olymp
Now ugly death stretch out thy Sable wings,	2Tamb	3.4.16	Olymp
On whom death and the fatall sisters waite,	2Tamb	3.4.54	Therid
Then welcome Tamburlaine unto thy death.	2Tamb	3.5.52	Callap
And all have jointly sworne thy cruell death,	2Tamb	3.5.112	Soria
Seest thou not death within my wrathfull looks?	2Tamb	3.5.119	Tamb
In war, in blood, in death, in crueltie,	2Tamb	4.1.156	Tamb
Hath stain'd thy cheekes, and made thee look like death,	2Tamb	4.2.4	Olymp
My Lord and husbandes death, with my sweete sons,	2Tamb	4.2.22	Olymp
entertaine a thought/That tends to love, but meditate on death,	2Tamb	4.2.26	Olymp
But that where every period ends with death,	2Tamb	4.2.47	Olymp
And every line begins with death againe:	2Tamb	4.2.48	Olymp
More strong than are the gates of death or hel?	2Tamb	5.1.20	Govnr
Or die some death of quickest violence,	2Tamb	5.1.41	2Citzn
And let my souldiers shoot the slave to death.	2Tamb	5.1.109	Tamb
Do all thy wurst, nor death, nor Tamburlaine,	2Tamb	5.1.112	Govnr
Sicknes or death can never conquer me.	2Tamb	5.1.222	Tamb
Their cruel death, mine owne captivity,	2Tamb	5.2.20	Callap
And Death with armies of Cymerian spirits/Gives battile gainst	2Tamb	5.3.8	Therid
where my slave, the uglie monster death/Shaking and quivering,	2Tamb	5.3.67	Tamb
And weary Death with bearing soules to hell.	2Tamb	5.3.77	Tamb
Which being the cause of life, imports your death.	2Tamb	5.3.90	Phsitn
And live in spight of death above a day.	2Tamb	5.3.101	Tamb
In spight of death I will goe show my face.	2Tamb	5.3.114	Tamb
Here lovely boies, what death forbids my life,	2Tamb	5.3.159	Tamb
That let your lives commaund in spight of death.	2Tamb	5.3.160	Tamb
unrelenting eares/Of death and hell be shut against my praiers,	2Tamb	5.3.192	Amyras
Against the wrath and tyranny of death,	2Tamb	5.3.221	Techel
Let earth and heaven his timelesse death deplore,	2Tamb	5.3.252	Amyras
And for a pound to sweat himselfe to death:	Jew	1.1.18	Barab
Strength to my soule, death to mine enemy;	Jew	2.1.49	Barab
It shall goe hard but I will see your death.	Jew	2.3.94	Barab
I, and take heed, for he hath sworne your death.	Jew	2.3.280	Barab
My death? what, is the base borne peasant mad?	Jew	2.3.281	Lodowk
Nothing but death shall part my love and me.	Jew	2.3.317	Abigal
Wretched Ferneze might have veng'd thy death.	Jew	3.2.14	Govnr
Thy sonne slew mine, and I'le revenge his death.	Jew	3.2.15	Mater
my bitter curse/Like Cain by Adam, for his brother's death.	Jew	3.4.33	Barab
Now shalt thou see the death of Abigall,	Jew	3.4.62	Barab
And I shall dye too, for I feele death comming.	Jew	3.6.8	Abigal
Death seizeth on my heart:	Jew	3.6.38	Abigal
Thou know'st 'tis death and if it be reveal'd.	Jew	3.6.51	2Fryar
Doe you not sorrow for your daughters death?	Jew	4.1.17	Ithimr
I could afford to whip my selfe to death.	Jew	4.1.59	Barab
I never knew a man take his death so patiently as this Fryar;	Jew	4.2.21	P Ithimr
The scent thereof was death, I poyson'd it.	Jew	4.4.43	Barab
Away with him, his sight is death to me.	Jew	5.1.35	Govnr
This sudden death of his is very strange.	Jew	5.1.54	Bosco
And, rowing in a Gally, whipt to death.	Jew	5.1.68	Barab
Nor feare I death, nor will I flatter thee.	Jew	5.2.60	Govnr
May not desolve, till death desolve our lives,	P 5	1.5	Charls
Will every savour breed a pangue of death?	P 72	2.15	Guise
I am my Lord, in what your grace commaundes till death.	P 77	2.20	P Pothec
Discharge thy musket and perfourme his death:	P 88	2.31	Guise
Pale death may walke in furrowes of my face:	P 158	2.101	Guise
These are the cursed Guisians that doe seeke our death.	P 201	3.36	Admral
And I will goe take order for his death.	P 252	4.50	Guise
To finde and to repay the man with death:	P 256	4.54	Charls
With death delay'd and torments never usde,	P 257	4.55	Charls
Repaying all attempts with present death,	P 269	4.67	Charls
O let me pray before I take my death.	P 352	6.7	Seroun
Come sirs, Ile whip you to death with my punniards point.	P 441	7.81	Guise
That if by death of Charles, the diadem/Of France be cast on	P 472	8.22	Anjoy
A sodaine pang, the messenger of death.	P 538	11.3	Charls

DEATH (cont.)

For he hath solemnely sworne thy death.	P 777	15.35	King
Is ruth and almost death to call to minde:	P 797	16.11	Navrre
Wee'l beat him back, and drive him to his death,	P 929	18.30	Navrre
Breath out that life wherein my death was hid,	P 954	19.24	King
And end thy endles treasons with thy death.	P 955	19.25	King
Let mean consaits, and baser men feare death,	P 997	19.67	Guise
Goe fetch his sonne for to beholde his death:	P1021	19.91	King
Oh what may I doe, for to revenge thy death?	P1108	21.2	Dumain
I am thy brother, and ile revenge thy death,	P1112	21.6	Dumain
That I with speed should have beene put to death.	P1118	21.12	Dumain
of Loraine by the Kings consent is lately strangled unto death.	P1124	21.18	P Frier
Whose service he may still commaund till death.	P1149	22.11	Navrre
Yes Navarre, but not to death I hope.	P1177	22.39	King
God shield your grace from such a sodaine death:	P1178	22.40	Navrre
That we might torture him with some new found death.	P1217	22.79	Eprnon
He died a death too good, the devill of hell/Torture his wicked	P1218	22.80	Bartus
Weep not sweet Navarre, but revenge my death.	P1234	22.96	King
And then I vow for to revenge his death,	P1247	22.109	Navrre
And rulde in France by Henries fatall death.	P1250	22.112	Navrre
That villaine Mortimer, ile be his death.	Edw	1.1.81	Gavstn
Were sworne to your father at his death,	Edw	1.1.83	Mortmr
Theres none here, but would run his horse to death.	Edw	1.4.207	Warwck
When I forsake thee, death seaze on my heart,	Edw	2.1.64	Neece
And threatenest death whether he rise or fall,	Edw	2.2.44	Edward
To prosecute that Gaveston to the death.	Edw	2.2.105	Lncstr
Looke for no other fortune wretch then death,	Edw	2.5.17	Lncstr
And death is all.	Edw	2.5.31	Gavstn
majestie so earnestlie/Desires to see the man before his death,	Edw	2.5.78	Penbrk
Ah traitors, have they put my friend to death?	Edw	3.1.91	Edward
Or didst thou see my friend to take his death?	Edw	3.1.93	Edward
And bare him to his death, and in a trenche/Strake off his	Edw	3.1.119	Arundl
The worst is death, and better die to live,	Edw	3.1.243	Lncstr
That you were dead, or very neare your death.	Edw	4.2.38	Queene
Spencer, as true as death,/He is in Englands ground, our	Edw	4.3.21	Edward
Fie on that love that hatcheth death and hate.	Edw	4.6.15	Kent
rule and emperie/Have not in life or death made miserable?	Edw	4.7.15	Edward
And hags howle for my death at Charons shore,	Edw	4.7.90	Edward
Come death, and with thy fingers close my eyes,	Edw	5.1.110	Edward
Will be my death, and welcome shall it be,	Edw	5.1.126	Edward
To wretched men death is felicitie.	Edw	5.1.127	Edward
That death ends all, and I can die but once.	Edw	5.1.153	Edward
I, lead me whether you will, even to my death,	Edw	5.3.66	Kent
Yet he that is the cause of Edwards death,	Edw	5.4.3	Mortmr
Containes his death, yet bids them save his life.	Edw	5.4.7	Mortmr
Unlesse thou bring me newes of Edwards death.	Edw	5.4.46	Mortmr
Had Edmund liv'de, he would have sought thy death.	Edw	5.4.112	Queene
These lookes of thine can harbor nought but death.	Edw	5.5.73	Edward
Lets see who dare impeache me for his death?	Edw	5.6.14	Mortmr
You could not beare his death thus patiently,	Edw	5.6.36	King
Mother, you are suspected for his death,	Edw	5.6.78	King
Nay, to my death, for too long have I lived,	Edw	5.6.83	Queene
Then come sweete death, and rid me of this greefe.	Edw	5.6.92	Queene
The reward of sin is death? that's hard:	F 67	1.1.39	Faust
I, we must die, an everlasting death.	F 73	1.1.45	Faust
Seeing Faustus hath incur'd eternall death,	F 316	1.3.88	Faust
blind Homer sing to me/Of Alexanders love, and Oenons death?	F 578	2.2.27	Faust
And smite with death thy hated enterprise.	F 880	3.1.102	Pope
And by your death to clime Saint Peters Chaire,	F 960	3.1.182	Faust
And on a pile of Fagots burnt to death.	F 963	3.1.185	Faust
We will determine of his life or death.	F 969	3.1.191	Pope
But Faustus death shall quit my infamie.	F1337	4.2.13	Benvol
what he meanes, if death were nie, he would not frolick thus:	F1677	5.1.4	P Wagner
What shall I doe to shun the snares of death?	F1742	5.1.69	Faust
Whose influence hath allotted death and hell;	F1951	5.2.155	Faust
All torne asunder by the hand of death.	F1989	5.3.7	2Schol
And yet me thinkes, if that death were neere,	F App	p.243 3	Wagner
So when as Crassus wretched death who stayd them,	Lucan, First Booke	104	
And all bands of that death presaging aliance.	Lucan, First Booke	114	
Thy death broake amity and trainde to war,	Lucan, First Booke	119	
Our friends death; and our wounds; our wintering/Under the	Lucan, First Booke	303	
so (if truth you sing)/Death brings long life.	Lucan, First Booke	454	
men/Whom death the greatest of all feares affright not,	Lucan, First Booke	455	
O Gods what death prepare ye?	Lucan, First Booke	648	
the death of many men/Meetes in one period.	Lucan, First Booke	649	
too dearely wunne/That unto death did presse the holy Nunne.	Ovid's Elegies	1.10.50	
For after death all men receive their right:	Ovid's Elegies	1.15.40	
Then though death rackes <rakes> my bones in funerall fier,	Ovid's Elegies	1.15.41	
Him timelesse death tooke, she was deifide.	Ovid's Elegies	2.2.46	
Minding thy fault, with death I wish to revill,	Ovid's Elegies	2.5.3	
Birdes haples glory, death thy life doth quench.	Ovid's Elegies	2.6.20	
Foole, what is sleepe but image of cold death,	Ovid's Elegies	2.9.41	
And to the Gods for that death Ovid prayes.	Ovid's Elegies	2.10.30	
And with the waters sees death neere him thrusts,	Ovid's Elegies	2.11.26	
Deserv'd thereby with death to be tormented.	Ovid's Elegies	2.14.6	
Wilt nothing do, why I should wish thy death?	Ovid's Elegies	2.19.56	
Outrageous death profanes all holy things/And on all creatures	Ovid's Elegies	3.8.19	
His fainting hand in death engrasped mee.	Ovid's Elegies	3.8.58	
With these thy soule walkes, soules if death release,	Ovid's Elegies	3.8.65	
A worke, that after my death, heere shall dwell	Ovid's Elegies	3.14.20	
Poore soldiers stand with fear of death dead strooken,	Hero and Leander	1.121	

DEATHES

And wet thy cheeks for their untimely deathes:	1Tamb	5.1.348	Zenoc

DEATHES (cont.)
A thousand deathes could not torment our hearts/More than the — 2Tamb 5.1.144 Jrslem

DEATHS
Whose memorie like pale deaths stony mace, ... — Dido 2.1.115 Aeneas
Threatning a thousand deaths at every glaunce. . . . — Dido 2.1.231 Aeneas
Will never be dispenc'd with til our deaths. . . . — 1Tamb 5.1.17 Govnr
Poore soules they looke as if their deaths were neere. . — 2Tamb 3.5.61 Usumc
Me thinks I could sustaine a thousand deaths, . . . — 2Tamb 5.2.22 Callap
Hold, let's inquire the causers of their deaths, . . — Jew 3.2.27 Mater
And was my father furtherer of their deaths? . . . — Jew 3.3.22 Abigal
('tis so) of my device/In Don Mathias and Lodovicoes deaths: — Jew 3.4.8 Barab
Their deaths were like their lives, then think not of 'em; — Jew 5.1.56 Govnr
It will be hard for us to worke their deaths. . . . — P 508 9.27 QnMoth
For to revenge their deaths upon us all. . . . . — P 518 9.37 Cardnl
Oh I have my deaths wound, give me leave to speak. . . — P1003 19.73 Guise
To revenge our deaths upon that cursed King, . . . — P1100 20.10 Cardnl
No, rather will I die a thousand deaths, ... — Edw 1.4.196 Queene
Trust in good verse, Tibullus feeles deaths paines, . . — Ovid's Elegies 3.8.39
Threatning a thousand deaths at everie glaunce, . . — Hero and Leander 1.382

DEAW
Glist'red with deaw, as one that seem'd to skorne it: . — Hero and Leander 1.390

DEAWE
Pierian deawe to Poets is distild. . . . . . . — Ovid's Elegies 3.8.26

DEAWIE
nights deawie hoast/March fast away: . . . . . . — Ovid's Elegies 1.6.55

DEBARD
This cause hath thee from pleasing me debard. . . . — Ovid's Elegies 1.10.12
Let [me] <her> enjoy [her] <me> oft, oft be debard. . . — Ovid's Elegies 2.9.46

DEBONAIRE
So yoong, so gentle, and so debonaire, ... — Hero and Leander 1.288

DEBT
Pay natures debt with cheerefull countenance, . . . — Edw 4.7.109 Baldck

DEBTER
better/In which the Merchant wayles his banquerout debter. — Ovid's Elegies 1.12.26

DEBTS
Have I debts owing; and in most of these, ... — Jew 4.1.73 Barab

DECAY
To save your King and country from decay: . . . . — 1Tamb 2.6.35 Cosroe
That may be ministers of my decay. . . . . . . — 1Tamb 5.1.289 Bajzth
al the world/Ransackt for golde, which breeds the world decay; — Lucan, First Booke 168
No envious tongue wrought thy thicke lockes decay. . . — Ovid's Elegies 1.14.42
Verse is immortall, and shall nere decay. . . . . — Ovid's Elegies 1.15.32

DECAYED
Thou also, that wert borne faire, hadst decayed, . . . — Ovid's Elegies 2.14.19

DECEASE (See DISCEASSE)

DECEASED
neece, the onely heire/Unto the Earle of Gloster late deceased. — Edw 2.2.259 Edward
two deceased princes which long since are consumed to dust. — F App p.237 42 P Faust
but the true substantiall bodies of those two deceased princes. — F App p.238 65 P Emper

DECEAST
My Lord deceast, was dearer unto me, ... — 2Tamb 3.4.42 Olymp
Did he not injure Mounser thats deceast? . . . . . — P1035 19.105 King
My father is deceast, come Gaveston, ... — Edw 1.1.1 Gavstn

DECEAV'D
You are deceav'd, I am no woman I. . . . . . . — Hero and Leander 2.192

DECEAVE
With lying lips my God-head to deceave, ... — Ovid's Elegies 3.3.44

DECEAVES
Time flying slides hence closely, and deceaves us, . . . — Ovid's Elegies 1.8.49
Whose workmanship both man and beast deceaves. . . . — Hero and Leander 1.20

DECEIT
Can there be such deceit in Christians, ... — 2Tamb 2.2.36 Orcan
trade to purchase Townes/By treachery, and sell 'em by deceit? — Jew 5.5.48 Barab
Father, thy face should harbor no deceit, ... — Edw 4.7.8 Edward
Yet by deceit Love did them all surprize. . . . . . — Ovid's Elegies 3.4.20

DECEITFULL
To dote upon deceitfull Mercurie. . . . . . . — Hero and Leander 1.446

DECEITS
That to deceits it may me forward pricke. . . . . . — Ovid's Elegies 2.19.44

DECEIV'D
Unlesse I be deceiv'd disputed once. . . . . . . — Dido 3.1.147 Cloan
and thought by words/To compasse me, but yet he was deceiv'd: — Dido 3.1.156 Dido
Dido I am, unlesse I be deceiv'd, ... — Dido 5.1.264 Dido
Thou art deceiv'd, I heard the Trumpets sound, ... — 1Tamb 3.3.203 Zabina
You are deceiv'd, for <Yes sir>, I will tell you: . . . — F 206 1.2.13 P Wagner
My sences are deceiv'd, here's nothing writ: . . . . — F 468 2.1.80 Faust

DECEIVDE
A boye, thou art deceivde at least in this, ... — Edw 4.2.8 Queene

DECEIVE (See also DECEAV'D, DECIV'D)
It's no sinne to deceive a Christian; . . . . . — Jew 2.3.309 Barab
If we say that we have no sinne we deceive our selves, and — F 69 1.1.41 P Faust
Shee may deceive thee, though thou her protect, . . . — Ovid's Elegies 2.3.15
But me let crafty damsells words deceive, ... — Ovid's Elegies 2.9.43
if she unpunisht you deceive,/For others faults, why do I losse — Ovid's Elegies 3.3.15
Seeing now thou wouldst deceive me as before: . . . . — Ovid's Elegies 3.6.70
Deceive all, let me erre, and thinke I am right, . . . — Ovid's Elegies 3.13.29
Who taught thee Rhethoricke to deceive a maid? . . . . — Hero and Leander 1.338

DECEIVED
Who I? you are deceived, I rose but now. . . . . . — P 437 7.77 Anjoy
[O thou art deceived]. . . . . — F 551.12 2.1.175A P Faust
By thee deceived, by thee surprisde am I, ... — Ovid's Elegies 2.10.3

DECEIV'ST
Or in these shades deceiv'st mine eye so oft? . . . . — Dido 1.1.244 Aeneas

DECENT			
A decent forme, thinne robe, a lovers looke,	Ovid's Elegies		3.1.9
DECIDE			
no, to decide all doubts, be rulde by me, lets hang him heere	P 491	9.10	P 2Atndt
<Tush>, These slender questions <trifles> Wagner can decide:	F 600	2.2.49	Faust
DECIV'D			
You are Achates, or I [am] deciv'd.	Dido	2.1.49	Serg
DECK (See also DECT)			
no more, but deck the heavens/To entertaine divine Zenocrate.	2Tamb	2.4.20	Tamb
DECKT			
And had his alters deckt with duskie lightes:	P 59	2.2	Guise
DECLAIME			
Why suffer you that peasant to declaime?	P 414	7.54	Guise
DECLARE			
Declare the cause of my conceived griefe,	1Tamb	1.1.29	Mycet
DECLIN'D			
Kind Jupiter hath low declin'd himselfe;	Lucan, First Booke		660
DECLINDE			
Unlesse he be declinde from that base pesant.	Edw	1.4.7	Mortmr
DECLINE			
Ile come to thee, my love shall neare decline.	Edw	1.4.115	Edward
DECLINING			
Whereas the Sun declining from our sight,	2Tamb	5.3.148	Tamb
Why should I greeve at my declining fall?	Edw	5.6.63	Mortmr
and higher set/The drooping thoughts of base declining soules,	Hero and Leander		2.257
DECOTAMEST			
He that will be a flat decotamest,	P 389	7.29	Guise
DECREAST			
Seeing the number of their men decreast,	Dido	2.1.132	Aeneas
DECREE			
Sir, halfe is the penalty of our decree,	Jew	1.2.88	Govnr
DECREED			
Have you not heard of late how he decreed,	P 32	1.32	Navrre
And as we late decreed we may perfourme.	P 206	4.4	QnMoth
Against the stately triumph we decreed?	Edw	2.2.12	Edward
I, my most gratious lord, so tis decreed.	Edw	5.1.138	Bartly
The sacred Sinod hath decreed for him,	F 885	3.1.107	Pope
What have our holy Councell there decreed,	F 947	3.1.169	Pope
<holy> Synod/Of Priests and Prelates, it is thus decreed:	F 953	3.1.175	Faust
The Statutes Decretall have thus decreed,	F 961	3.1.183	Faust
You brought us word even now, it was decreed,	F1019	3.2.39	Pope
and flying/Left hateful warre decreed to both the Consuls.	Lucan, First Booke		486
Well therefore by the gods decreed it is,	Hero and Leander		1.253
DECREES			
Reade there the Articles of our decrees.	Jew	1.2.67	Govnr
And therefore none of his Decrees can stand.	F 929	3.1.151	Pope
the sonne decrees/To expel the father; share the world thou	Lucan, First Booke		290
DECRETALL			
And read amongst the Statutes Decretall,	F 883	3.1.105	Pope
The Statutes Decretall have thus decreed,	F 961	3.1.183	Faust
DECT			
Of [ever] <every> greene Selinus queintly dect/With bloomes	2Tamb	4.3.121	Tamb
DEDICATE			
To whom Faustus doth dedicate himselfe.	F 285	1.3.57	Faust
DEDUCE			
Verses [deduce] <reduce> the horned bloudy moone/And call the	Ovid's Elegies		2.1.23
DEED			
My hand is ready to performe the deed,	1Tamb	5.1.503	Techel
My Lord, if ever you did deed of ruth,	2Tamb	5.1.24	1Citzn
I, so thou shalt, 'tis thou must doe the deed:	Jew	2.3.369	Barab
A Fryar? false villaine, he hath done the deed.	Jew	3.4.22	Barab
My father slaine, who hath done this deed?	P1047	19.117	YngGse
Art thou King, and hast done this bloudy deed?	P1050	19.120	YngGse
But what doth move thee above the rest to doe the deed?	P1132	21.26	P Dumain
beene a great sinner in my dayes, and the deed is meritorious.	P1134	21.28	P Frier
A noble attempt, and honourable deed,	Edw	3.1.206	SpncrP
Shall he be murdered when the deed is done.	Edw	5.4.20	Mortmr
Foh, heeres a place in deed with all my hart.	Edw	5.5.41	Ltborn
And wright a Deed of Gift with thine owne bloud;	F 424	2.1.36	Mephst
But Faustus/<thou must> Write it in manner of a Deed of Gift.	F 449	2.1.61	Mephst
A Deed of Gift, of body and of soule:	F 478	2.1.90	Faust
Speake Faustus, do you deliver this as your Deed?	F 501	2.1.113	Mephst
long e're this, I should have done the deed <slaine my selfe>,	F 575	2.2.24	Faust
We will depose the Emperour for that deed,	F 906	3.1.128	Pope
Damb'd be this soule for ever, for this deed.	F1070	3.2.90	Pope
To purge the rashnesse of this cursed deed,	F1125	3.3.38	Mephst
This deed of thine, in setting Bruno free/From his and our	F1206	4.1.52	Emper
I, [all] <I call> your hearts to recompence this deed.	F1394	4.2.70	Faust
and for this blessed sight <glorious deed>/Happy and blest be	F1704	5.1.31	1Schol
Mars in the deed the black-smithes net did stable,	Ovid's Elegies		1.9.39
Untill some honourable deed be done.	Hero and Leander		1.282
DEEDE			
Deare shall you both abie this riotous deede:	Edw	2.2.88	Edward
Though while the deede be doing you be tooke,	Ovid's Elegies		3.13.43
DEEDES			
Who shall confirme my words with further deedes.	Dido	1.2.43	Iarbus
To roialise the deedes of Tamburlaine:	1Tamb	2.3.8	Tamb
No intercepted lines thy deedes display,	Ovid's Elegies		2.5.5
Honour is purchac'd by the deedes wee do.	Hero and Leander		1.280
DEEDS			
I am a Lord, for so my deeds shall proove,	1Tamb	1.2.34	Tamb
To some direction in your martiall deeds,	1Tamb	2.3.12	Tamb
nor by princely deeds/Doth meane to soare above the highest	1Tamb	2.7.32	Therid

DEEDS (cont.)			
And makes my deeds infamous through the world.	1Tamb	5.1.391	Zenoc
That purchac'd kingdomes by your martiall deeds,	1Tamb	5.1.523	Tamb
so eloquent/To paint in woords, what Ile perfourme in deeds,	2Tamb	1.2.10	Callap
But in their deeds deny him for their Christ:	2Tamb	2.2.40	Orcan
For deeds of bounty or nobility:	2Tamb	4.1.152	Tamb
Be made an accessary of your deeds;	Jew	2.3.342	Barab
Now Selim note the unhallowed deeds of Jewes:	Jew	5.5.92	Govnr
Graunt that our deeds may wel deserve your loves:	P 600	12.13	King
Nor in the pompe of proud audacious deeds,	F 5	Prol.5	1Chor
For Apish deeds transformed to an Ape.	F1127	3.3.40	Mephst
Thou feard'st (great Pompey) that late deeds would dim/Olde	Lucan, First Booke	121	
He liv'd secure boasting his former deeds,	Lucan, First Booke	135	
greedy desire stil poore/Did vild deeds, then t'was worth the	Lucan, First Booke	175	
The angry Senate urging Grachus deeds,	Lucan, First Booke	268	
their huge power made him bould/To mannage greater deeds; the	Lucan, First Booke	463	
If thou deniest foole, Ile our deeds expresse,	Ovid's Elegies	2.8.25	
Adde deeds unto thy promises at last.	Ovid's Elegies	2.16.48	
Her deeds gaine hate, her face entreateth love:	Ovid's Elegies	3.10.43	
And few great lords in vertuous deeds shall joy,	Hero and Leander	1.479	
DEEM'D			
And deem'd renowne to spoile their native towne,	Lucan, First Booke	176	
Frighted the melancholie earth, which deem'd,	Hero and Leander	1.99	
DEEME			
What graced Kings, in me no shame I deeme.	Ovid's Elegies	2.8.14	
DEEP			
His deep affections make him passionate.	1Tamb	1.2.164	Techel
As vast and deep as Euphrates or Nile.	1Tamb	5.1.439	Tamb
Deep rivers, havens, creekes, and litle seas,	2Tamb	3.2.87	Tamb
Gonzago poste you to Orleance, Retes to Deep,	P 445	7.85	Guise
That villain for whom I beare this deep disgrace,	P 766	15.24	Guise
And to the vast deep sea fresh water flouds?	Ovid's Elegies	2.10.14	
DEEPE			
With twise twelve Phrigian ships I plowed the deepe,	Dido	1.1.220	Aeneas
For all our ships were launcht into the deepe:	Dido	2.1.285	Aeneas
And follow them as footemen through the deepe:	Dido	4.3.24	Aeneas
How should I put into the raging deepe,	Dido	5.1.55	Aeneas
And now downe falles the keeles into the deepe:	Dido	5.1.253	Dido
The ditches must be deepe, the Counterscarps/Narrow and steepe,	2Tamb	3.2.68	Tamb
A wound is nothing be it nere so deepe,	2Tamb	3.2.115	Tamb
Were woont to guide the seaman in the deepe,	2Tamb	5.1.65	Tamb
to everlasting paines/And extreme tortures of the fiery deepe,	Jew	1.2.167	Barab
asunder; so that it doth sinke/Into a deepe pit past recovery.	Jew	5.5.36	Barab
Guise, begins those deepe ingendred thoughts/To burst abroad,	P 91	2.34	Guise
The wound I warrant ye is deepe my Lord,	P1192	22.54	King
Had not sweete pleasure conquer'd deepe despaire.	F 576	2.2.25	Faust
of us here, that have waded as deepe into matters, as other men,	F 740	2.3.19	P Robin
With wals of Flint, and deepe intrenched Lakes,	F 782	3.1.4	Faust
rid him into the deepe pond at the townes ende, I was no sooner	F App	p.240 133	P HrsCsr
Or flaming Titan (feeding on the deepe)/Puls them aloft, and	Lucan, First Booke	416	
Which rashly twixt the sharpe rocks in the deepe,	Ovid's Elegies	2.11.3	
In nights deepe silence why the ban-dogges barke.	Ovid's Elegies	2.19.40	
And in thy foule deepe waters thicke thou [gushest] <rushest>.	Ovid's Elegies	3.5.8	
As his deepe whirle-pooles could not quench the same.	Ovid's Elegies	3.5.42	
O would in my fore-fathers tombe deepe layde,	Ovid's Elegies	3.5.73	
All gaine in darknesse the deepe earth supprest.	Ovid's Elegies	3.7.36	
Men kept the shoare, and sailde not into deepe.	Ovid's Elegies	3.7.44	
And night deepe drencht in mystie Acheron,	Hero and Leander	1.189	
All deepe enrag'd, his sinowie bow he bent,	Hero and Leander	1.371	
When deepe perswading Oratorie failes.	Hero and Leander	2.226	
DEEPELY			
I deepely sorrow for your trecherous wrong:	P 263	4.61	Charls
I thinke sheele doe, but deepely can dissemble.	Ovid's Elegies	2.4.16	
Love deepely grounded, hardly is dissembled.	Hero and Leander	1.184	
DEEPER			
The more she striv'd, the deeper was she strooke.	Hero and Leander	1.334	
DEEPEST			
Whose head hath deepest scarres, whose breast most woundes,	2Tamb	1.3.75	Tamb
Embracing thee with deepest of his love,	2Tamb	4.1.109	Tamb
A reaching thought will search his deepest wits,	Jew	1.2.221	Barab
Although my downfall be the deepest hell.	P 104	2.47	Guise
DEEPLY			
Wel, wel (Meander) thou art deeply read:	1Tamb	2.2.55	Mycet
Whose operation is to binde, infect,/And poyson deeply:	Jew	3.4.71	Barab
a king, thy hart/Pierced deeply with sence of my distresse,	Edw	4.7.10	Edward
DEEPNESSE			
Whose deepnesse doth intice such forward wits,	F2008	5.3.26	4Chor
DEERE (Homograph; See also DEARE)			
And rowse the light foote Deere from forth their laire?	Dido	3.3.31	Dido
As I remember, here you shot the Deere,	Dido	3.3.51	Achat
Is not my life and state as deere to me,	2Tamb	5.1.12	Govnr
Now have we got the fatall stragling deere,	P 204	4.2	QnMoth
And witnesse heaven how deere thou art to me.	Edw	1.4.167	Edward
Truely my deere brethren, my Maister is within at dinner, with	F 214	1.2.21	P Wagner
you, and keepe you, my deere brethren <my deare brethren>.	F 217	1.2.24	P Wagner
rosted, and good sauce to it, if I pay so deere, I can tell you.	F 353	1.4.11	P Robin
Breake may his heart with grones: deere Frederik see,	F1366	4.2.42	Benvol
Deere Frederick here,	F1433	4.3.3	Mrtino
What shall we then do deere Benvolio?	F1451	4.3.21	Mrtino
O my deere Faustus what imports this feare?	F1827	5.2.31	1Schol
have it wel roasted, and good sawce to it, if I pay so deere.	F App	p.229 12	P Clown
As loath to leave Roome whom they held so deere,	Lucan, First Booke	506	
DEERELY			
Till hee pay deerely for their companie.	Edw	3.1.198	Lncstr

DEERELY (cont.)
Yes Faustus, and most deerely lov'd of God. — F 293 1.3.65 Mephst
would not yeeld/So soone to part from that she deerely held. — Hero and Leander 2.84

DEEREST
Or be suspicious of my deerest freends: — P 972 19.42 King
And share the kingdom with thy deerest friend. — Edw 1.1.2 Gavstn
To frolike with my deerest Gaveston. — Edw 1.4.73 Edward
answer from the Barons/Touching my friend, my deerest Gaveston. — Edw 3.1.2 Edward
And for the murther of my deerest friend, — Edw 3.1.226 Edward
Wagner, commend me to me deerest friends, — F 91 1.1.63 Faust

DEFAM'D
The man did grieve, the woman was defam'd. — Ovid's Elegies 2.2.50

DEFAMDE
(Nor am I by such wanton toyes defamde)/Heire of an antient — Ovid's Elegies 3.14.4

DEFAME
Yet those infirmities that thus defame/Their faiths, their — 2Tamb 2.1.44 Sgsmnd
wilt thou so defame/The hatefull fortunes of thy victory, — 2Tamb 4.3.77 Orcan

DEFAULT
All humaine kinde by their default had perisht. — Ovid's Elegies 2.14.10
By thy default thou doest our joyes defraude. — Ovid's Elegies 2.19.58

DEFAULTE
and will needs enter by defaulte | whatt thoughe you were once — Paris ms11,p390 P Souldr

DEFECTS
That should detaine thy eye in his defects? — Dido 3.4.17 Aeneas

DEFENC'D
When we are thus defenc'd against our Foe, — 2Tamb 5.1.22 Govnr

DEFENCE
In whose defence he fought so valiantly: — Dido 2.1.119 Dido
In love of honor and defence of right, — 1Tamb 2.6.21 Ortyg
Send like defence of faire Arabia. — 1Tamb 5.1.402 Zenoc
Hath he not made me in the Popes defence, — P1036 19.106 King
what needes defence/When [un-protected] <un-protested> ther is — Ovid's Elegies 2.2.11

DEFEND
Defend his freedome gainst a Monarchie: — 1Tamb 2.1.56 Ceneus
Shall not defend it from our battering shot. — 1Tamb 4.2.107 Tamb
(Too litle to defend our guiltlesse lives)/Sufficient to — 2Tamb 2.2.60 Orcan
And secret issuings to defend the ditch. — 2Tamb 3.2.74 Tamb
Which til it may defend you, labour low: — 2Tamb 3.3.44 Therid
And wil defend it in despight of thee. — 2Tamb 5.1.55 Govnr
Call up the souldiers to defend these wals. — 2Tamb 5.1.56 Govnr
That God may still defend the right of France: — P 56 1.56 Navrre
But God that alwaies doth defend the right, — P 575 11.40 Navrre
But to defend their strange inventions, — P 705 14.8 Navrre
Sworne to defend king Edwards royall right, — Edw 3.1.38 SpncrP
Souldiers, good harts, defend your soveraignes right, — Edw 3.1.182 Edward
Defend me heaven, shall I be haunted still? — F1439 4.3.9 Benvol
Tis shame sould tongues the guilty should defend/Or great — Ovid's Elegies 1.10.39
Defend the ensignes of thy warre in mee. — Ovid's Elegies 1.11.12
I meane not to defend the scapes of any, — Ovid's Elegies 2.4.1
their wits should them defend. — Ovid's Elegies 3.4.2
Defend the fort, and keep the foe-man out. — Hero and Leander 2.272

DEFENDED
With her owne armor was my wench defended. — Ovid's Elegies 2.5.48

DEFENDERS
The Gods, defenders of the innocent, — 1Tamb 1.2.68 Zenoc

DEFENSE (See DEFENCE)

DEFERRE
Mad streame, why doest our mutuall joyes deferre? — Ovid's Elegies 3.5.87

DEFIANCE
Now in defiance of that woonted love, — 2Tamb 5.3.10 Therid

DEFIE
Now send our Heralds to defie the King, — Edw 2.2.110 Lncstr
Strike of my head? base traitor I defie thee. — Edw 5.4.90 Kent

DEFIL'D
ominous birds/Defil'd the day, and <at night> wilde beastes — Lucan, First Booke 557

DEFILDE
Was not defilde by any gallant wooer. — Ovid's Elegies 3.4.24

DEFILE (See also FYLE)
Should ere defile so faire a mouth as thine: — Dido 3.2.27 Juno
For not a common Souldier shall defile/His manly fingers with — 2Tamb 4.1.163 Tamb

DEFILES
Se impious warre defiles the Senat house, — Lucan, First Booke 690

DEFLOWR'D
Deflowr'd except, within thy Temple wall. — Ovid's Elegies 1.7.18
Deflowr'd and stained in unlawfull bed? — Ovid's Elegies 3.5.76

DEFRAUDE
By thy default thou doest our joyes defraude. — Ovid's Elegies 2.19.58

DEFRAY
Who should defray the money, but the King, — Edw 2.2.118 Mortmr

DEFY (See DEFIE)

DEGENERATE
Ah base Shatillian and degenerate, — P 312 5.39 Guise

DEGESTIONE
enoughe to worke/thy Just degestione with extreamest shame — Paris ms27,p391 Guise

DEGRADED
it, and the Priest/That makes it knowne, being degraded first, — Jew 3.6.35 2Fryar

DEGREE
and strive to be retain'd/In such a great degree of amitie. — 1Tamb 2.3.32 Therid
Without respect of Sex, degree or age, — 1Tamb 4.1.62 2Msngr
attaine to that degree of high renowne and great authoritie, — F App p.236 22 P Emper

DEI
Sint mihi Dei Acherontis propitii, valeat numen triplex — F 244 1.3.16 P Faust

DEIANIRA
One Deianira was more worth then these. — Ovid's Elegies 3.5.38

DEIFIDE			
Him timelesse death tooke, she was deifide.	Ovid's Elegies	2.2.46	
DEIGNE			
Hard hearted, wilt not deigne to heare me speake?	Dido	4.2.54	Anna
DEIGNST			
Thou deignst unequall lines should thee rehearse,	Ovid's Elegies	3.1.37	
DEIPHOBUS			
And Helena betraied Deiphobus,	Dido	2.1.297	Achat
DEITIE			
And wrong my deitie with high disgrace:	Dido	3.2.5	Juno
Even sacrilege against her Deitie,	Hero and Leander	1.307	
DEITIES			
And both our Deities conjoynd in one,	Dido	3.2.79	Juno
DEITY			
god>,/Here <Faustus> tire my <trie thy> braines to get a Deity.	F 90	1.1.62	Faust
By desperate thoughts against Joves Deity:	F 317	1.3.89	Faust
By Venus Deity how did I protest.	Ovid's Elegies	2.8.18	
My Mistris deity also drewe me fro it,	Ovid's Elegies	2.18.17	
maides society/Falsely to sweare, their beauty hath some deity.	Ovid's Elegies	3.3.12	
And some there be that thinke we have a deity.	Ovid's Elegies	3.8.18	
Who sees it, graunts some deity there is shrowded.	Ovid's Elegies	3.12.8	
DEJECT			
When on thy lappe thine eyes thou dost deject,	Ovid's Elegies	1.8.37	
DELAIDE			
Anger delaide doth oft to hate retire.	Ovid's Elegies	1.8.82	
DELAIES			
Will not these delaies beget my hopes?	Edw	2.5.47	Gavstn
she wanting no excuse/To feed him with delaies, as women use:	Hero and Leander	1.426	
DELAY			
But Priamus impatient of delay,	Dido	2.1.173	Aeneas
Doe so sweet Guise, let us delay no time,	P 505	9.24	QnMoth
Be gone, delay no time sweet Guise.	P 509	9.28	QnMoth
And bid him come without delay to us.	P 559	11.24	QnMoth
What, suffer you the traitor to delay?	Edw	5.6.67	King
We grieve at this thy patience and delay:	Lucan, First Booke	362	
And fates so bent, least sloth and long delay/Might crosse him,	Lucan, First Booke	394	
Wild me, whose slowe feete sought delay, be flying.	Ovid's Elegies	2.19.12	
DELAY'D			
With death delay'd and torments never usde,	P 257	4.55	Charls
DEL BOSCO			
Martin del Bosco, I have heard of thee;	Jew	2.2.19	Govnr
DELBOSCO			
And so am I, Delbosco is my name;	Jew	2.2.6	Bosco
Delbosco, as thou lovest and honour'st us,	Jew	2.2.24	1Knght
DELIA			
So Nemesis, so Delia famous are,	Ovid's Elegies	3.8.31	
Delia departing, happier lov'd, she saith,	Ovid's Elegies	3.8.55	
DELIAN			
What more then Delian musicke doe I heare,	Dido	3.4.52	Dido
DELIBERAT			
Where both deliberat, the love is slight,	Hero and Leander	1.175	
DELICATES			
new-found-world/For pleasant fruites, and Princely delicates.	F 112	1.1.84	Faust
Were gluttons, and lov'd only delicates,	F1917	5.2.121	BdAngl
DELICIOUS			
Even as delicious meat is to the tast,	Hero and Leander	1.63	
DELICT			
Forgive her gratious Gods this one delict,	Ovid's Elegies	2.14.43	
DELIGHT (See also DELYGHT)			
And heaven and earth the bounds of thy delight?	Dido	1.1.31	Jupitr
Through which the water shall delight to play:	Dido	3.1.119	Dido
O how these irksome labours now delight,	Dido	3.3.56	Aeneas
turne the hand of fate/Unto that happie day of my delight,	Dido	3.3.81	Iarbus
To move unto the measures of delight:	Dido	3.4.54	Dido
In this delight of dying pensivenes:	Dido	4.2.44	Anna
Wherein the day may evermore delight:	Dido	5.1.7	Aeneas
O sweet Iarbus, Annas sole delight,	Dido	5.1.322	Anna
It could not more delight me than your sight.	2Tamb	1.3.156	Tamb
And waters of this new made Nunnery/Will much delight you.	Jew	1.2.312	1Fryar
And all his heaven is to delight himselfe:	P 634	12.47	QnMoth
Lye there the Kings delight, and Guises scorne.	P 818	17.13	Guise
Ah words that make me surfet with delight:	Edw	1.1.3	Gavstn
Musicke and poetrie is his delight,	Edw	1.1.54	Gavstn
To hide those parts which men delight to see,	Edw	1.1.65	Gavstn
Excelling all, <whose sweete delight disputes>	F 18	(HC256) A	1Chor
O what a world of profite and delight,	F 80	1.1.52	Faust
I'le fetch him somewhat to delight his minde.	F 471	2.1.83	Mephst
Nothing Faustus but to delight thy mind <withall>,/And let thee	F 473	2.1.85	Mephst
O how this sight doth delight <this feedes> my soule.	F 712	2.2.164	Faust
[Tut] <But> Faustus, in hell is all manner of delight.	F 713	2.2.165	Lucifr
Past with delight the stately Towne of Trier:	F 780	3.1.2	Faust
containes <containeth> for to delight thine eyes <thee with>,	F 810	3.1.32	Mephst
let me be cloyd/With all things that delight the heart of man.	F 838	3.1.60	Faust
But now, that Faustus may delight his minde,	F 989	3.2.9	Faust
as to delight your Majesty with some mirth, hath Faustus justly	F1312	4.1.158	P Faust
as to delight you with some mirth, hath Faustus worthily	F App	p.238 82	P Faust
you take no delight in this, I have heard that great bellied	F App	p.242 4	P Faust
Roome, if thou take delight in impious warre,	Lucan, First Booke	21	
Men tooke delight in Jewels, houses, plate,	Lucan, First Booke	164	
To him I pray it no delight may bring,	Ovid's Elegies	1.4.67	
And lets what both delight, what both desire,	Ovid's Elegies	1.10.31	
What doest, I cryed, transportst thou my delight?	Ovid's Elegies	2.5.29	
Let one wench cloy me with sweete loves delight,	Ovid's Elegies	2.10.21	

DELIGHT (cont.)
This doth delight me, this my courage cheares. . . . . Ovid's Elegies 2.19.24
By these I judge, delight me may the rest, ... Ovid's Elegies 3.2.35
Can deafe [eares] <yeares> take delight when Phemius sings,/Or Ovid's Elegies 3.6.61
Faire fooles delight to be accounted nice. . . . . Hero and Leander 1.326
But speeches full of pleasure and delight. . . . Hero and Leander 1.420
nothing saw/That might delight him more, yet he suspected/Some Hero and Leander 2.63
For thy delight each May-morning. . . . . . . Passionate Shepherd 22
DELIGHTED
the sight whereof so delighted me, as nothing in the world F1561 4.6.4 P Duke
My idle thoughts delighted her no more, ... Ovid's Elegies 3.6.39
DELIGHTETH
For her that so delighteth in thy paine: . . . . . Dido 4.2.34 Anna
DELIGHTFULL
Weake Elegies, delightfull Muse farewell; . . . . . Ovid's Elegies 3.14.19
DELIGHT'S
[whose sweete delight's] dispute/In th'heavenly matters of F 18 Prol.18 1Chor
DELIGHTS
The boy wherein false destinie delights, ... Dido 3.2.2 Juno
On which the breath of heaven delights to play, . . . 1Tamb 2.1.25 Menaph
If these delights thy minde may move; . . . . Passionate Shepherd 23
DELITE
for they tooke delite/To play upon those hands, they were so Hero and Leander 1.29
DELITES
The rites/In which Loves beauteous Empresse most delites,/Are Hero and Leander 1.300
DELIVER
Deliver them into my treasurie. . . . . 1Tamb 3.3.217 Tamb
And didst thou deliver my letter? . . . . . . Jew 4.2.3 P Curtzn
now; Bid him deliver thee a thousand Crownes, by the same token, Jew 4.4.75 P Ithimr
My lord of Penbrooke, we deliver him you, ... Edw 2.5.97 Mortmr
Deliver this to Gurney and Matrevis, ... Edw 5.4.41 Mortmr
Speake Faustus, do you deliver this as your Deed? . . . F 501 2.1.113 Mephst
Go bid the Hostler deliver him unto you, and remember what I F1474 4.4.18 P Faust
Wel, come give me your money, my boy wil deliver him to you: F App p.239 107 P Faust
slicke as an Ele; wel god buy sir, your boy wil deliver him me: F App p.240 117 P HrsCsr
DELIVER'D
Well, I have deliver'd the challenge in such sort, . . . Jew 3.1.29 Ithimr
DELIVERED
By treason hath delivered thee to us: . . . . . Jew 5.5.110 Govnr
For being delivered unto Penbrookes men, ... Edw 3.1.116 Arundl
we all are witnesses/That Bruno here was late delivered you, F1026 3.2.46 Raymnd
DELPHIAN
Then heeretofore the Delphian <Dolphian> Oracle. . . . F 170 1.1.142 Cornel
DELUDED
And I am thus deluded of my boy: . . . . . . Dido 5.1.219 Dido
This gentle Magot, Lodowicke I meane,/Must be deluded: . Jew 2.3.306 Barab
whom the God deluded/In snowe-white plumes of a false swanne Ovid's Elegies 1.10.3
Likewise the angrie sisters thus deluded, ... Hero and Leander 1.473
DELUDES
Thy mind Aeneas that would have it so/Deludes thy eye sight, Dido 2.1.32 Achat
DELUDING
With follie and false hope deluding us). . . . . . Hero and Leander 2.222
DELUD'ST
Thou art a Goddesse that delud'st our eyes, ... Dido 1.1.191 Aeneas
DELYGHT
lye there the kinges delyght and guises scorne . . . Paris ms22,p390 Guise
DEMAND
Now Bassoes, what demand you at our hands? . . . . Jew 1.2.1 Govnr
What at our hands demand ye? . . . . Jew 1.2.6 Govnr
What, can he steale that you demand so much? . . . . Jew 2.3.100 Barab
And if he aske why I demand so much, tell him, I scorne to Jew 4.2.120 P Ithimr
To have a shag-rag knave to come [demand]/Three hundred . Jew 4.3.61 Barab
To tell me whatsoever I demand: . . . . F 323 1.3.95 Faust
Your grace demand no questions of the King, ... F1251 4.1.97 Faust
And then demand of them, what they would have. . . . F1590 4.6.33 Duke
DEMANDES
O Faustus leave these frivolous demandes, ... F 309 1.3.81 Mephst
DEMANDING
Demanding him of them, entreating rather, ... Edw 3.1.97 Arundl
DEMANDS
Such sacrifice as this, Venus demands. . . . . Hero and Leander 1.310
DEMEANE
To marke him how he doth demeane himselfe. F1806 5.2.10 Belzeb
DEMI (See also DEMY)
A sound Magitian is a Demi-god <mighty god>, ... F 89 1.1.61 Faust
DEMI-GOD
A sound Magitian is a Demi-god <mighty god>, ... F 89 1.1.61 Faust
DEMOGORGON (See also DEMY, GORGON, ORGON)
inferni ardentis monarcha, et Demogorgon, propitiamus vos, F 246 1.3.18 P Faust
O per se o, demogorgon, Belcher and Mephostophilis. . . F1114 3.3.27 P Robin
DEMONSTRATION
By plaine and easie demonstration, ... 2Tamb 3.2.84 Tamb
DEMONSTRATIONS
Come, shew me some demonstrations Magicall, ... F 177 1.1.149 Faust
DEMOPHOON
Or Phillis teares that her [Demophoon] <Domoophon> misses,/What Ovid's Elegies 2.18.22
DEMY
o per se, o, [demy] <deny> orgon, gorgon: . . . . . F 728 2.3.7 P Robin
DEN (See also DENNE)
Whose flintie darts slept in Tipheus den, ... Dido 4.1.19 Iarbus
Which th'earth from ougly Chaos den up-wayd: . . . . Hero and Leander 1.450
DENDE
Why enviest me, this hostile [denne] <dende> unbarre, . Ovid's Elegies 1.6.17

DENIALL (See also DENYALL)
And see how coldly his lookes make deniall. — Edw 1.4.235 Lncstr

DENI'D
And some, that she refrain'd teares, have deni'd. — Ovid's Elegies 3.8.46

DENIE
Denie my soule fruition of her joy, — 2Tamb 5.3.194 Amyras
And tell me, would the rebels denie me that? — Edw 3.1.101 Edward
She hath not trode <tred> awrie that doth denie it, — Ovid's Elegies 3.13.5
Slippe still, onely denie it when tis done, — Ovid's Elegies 3.13.15
Thereat she smild, and did denie him so, — Hero and Leander 1.311
And neither would denie, nor graunt his sute. — Hero and Leander 1.424

DENIED
the Sun and Mercurie denied/To shed [their] <his> influence in — 1Tamb 1.1.14 Cosroe
Before all hope of rescue were denied, — 1Tamb 5.1.38 Govnr
No, Jew, thou hast denied the Articles, — Jew 1.2.92 Govnr
of golde/To Danae, all aide may be denied/To Isabell the Queene, — Edw 3.1.268 Spencr
And many seeing great princes were denied, — Hero and Leander 1.129
He askt, she gave, and nothing was denied, — Hero and Leander 2.25

DENIES
Since Death denies me further cause of joy, — 1Tamb 5.1.430 Arabia
hee that denies to pay, shal straight become a Christian. — Jew 1.2.73 P Reader
Lastly, he that denies this, shall absolutely lose al he has. — Jew 1.2.76 P Reader
Envy denies all, with thy bloud must thou/Abie thy conquest — Lucan, First Booke 289

DENIEST
If thou deniest foole, Ile our deeds expresse, — Ovid's Elegies 2.8.25

DENNE
Why enviest me, this hostile [denne] <dende> unbarre, — Ovid's Elegies 1.6.17

DENY
What ist sweet wagge I should deny thy youth? — Dido 1.1.23 Jupitr
But in their deeds deny him for their Christ: — 2Tamb 2.2.40 Orcan
Flourish in France, and none deny the same. — P 640 12.53 QnMoth
And if he doe deny what I doe say, — P 650 12.63 QnMoth
If thou deny it I must <wil> backe to hell. — F 426 2.1.38 Mephst
o per se, o, [demy] <deny> orgon, gorgon: — F 728 2.3.7 P Robin
Deny it not, we all are witnesses/That Bruno here was late — F1025 3.2.45 Raymnd
[And] Faustus custome is not to deny/The just [requests] — F1690 5.1.17 Faust
<It is not Faustus custome> to deny — F1690 (HC269)B Faust
To me to morrow constantly deny it. — Ovid's Elegies 1.4.70
Deny him oft, feigne now thy head doth ake: — Ovid's Elegies 1.8.73
Ceres, I thinke, no knowne fault will deny. — Ovid's Elegies 3.9.24
Sweare I was blinde, yeeld not <deny>, if you be wise, — Ovid's Elegies 3.13.45

DENYALL
hast broke the league/By flat denyall of the promis'd Tribute, — Jew 3.5.20 Basso
This day denyall hath my sport adjourned. — Ovid's Elegies 1.12.2
Though himselfe see; heele credit her denyall, — Ovid's Elegies 2.2.57

DENYED
and when they flatly had denyed,/Refusing to receive me pledge — Edw 3.1.106 Arundl
How to attaine, what is denyed, we thinke, — Ovid's Elegies 3.4.17

DENYING
wood be flying/And thou the waxe stuft full with notes denying, — Ovid's Elegies 1.12.8

DENY'T
Never deny't, for I know you have it, and I'le search you. — F1101 3.3.14 P Vintnr

DEPART
And he at last depart to Italy, — Dido 2.1.330 Venus
Depart from Carthage, come not in my sight. — Dido 3.1.44 Dido
Am not I Queen of Libia? then depart. — Dido 3.1.49 Dido
If he depart thus suddenly, I dye: — Dido 5.1.209 Dido
And sommons all my sences to depart. — 1Tamb 2.7.45 Cosroe
And then depart we to our territories. — 2Tamb 1.1.166 Orcan
I know thou wouldst depart from hence with me. — 2Tamb 1.2.11 Callap
we leave sufficient garrison/And presently depart to Persea, — 2Tamb 5.1.212 Tamb
And not depart untill I see you free. — Jew 2.2.41 Bosco
Trouble her not, sweet Lodowicke depart: — Jew 2.3.327 Barab
intreat your Highnesse/Not to depart till he has feasted you. — Jew 5.3.33 Msngr
For shame subscribe, and let the lowne depart. — Edw 1.4.82 Warwck
That whether I will or no thou must depart: — Edw 1.4.124 Edward
If not, depart: — F1336 4.2.12 Benvol
[Let us depart], and for this blessed sight <glorious deed> — F1704 5.1.31 1Schol
Talke not of me, but save your selves and depart. — F1869 5.2.73 P Faust
Often at length, my wench depart, I bid, — Ovid's Elegies 2.18.5
That he would leave her turret and depart. — Hero and Leander 2.38

DEPARTED
when she departed/Nape by stumbling on the thre-shold started. — Ovid's Elegies 1.12.3

DEPARTING
Delia departing, happier lov'd, she saith, — Ovid's Elegies 3.8.55

DEPARTST
And eb againe, as thou departst from me. — 2Tamb 4.2.32 Therid

DEPEND
Nor you depend on such weake helps as we. — 1Tamb 5.1.33 1Virgn

DEPENDS
(sweet Virgins) on whose safe return/Depends our citie, — 1Tamb 5.1.63 Govnr
On whose good fortune Spencers hope depends. — Edw 2.1.11 Spencr

DEPLORE
Let earth and heaven his timelesse death deplore, — 2Tamb 5.3.252 Amyras
But most thou friendly turtle-dove, deplore. — Ovid's Elegies 2.6.12

DEPOSD
And thou must hence, or I shall be deposd, — Edw 1.4.110 Edward

DEPOSDE
Looke for rebellion, looke to be deposde, — Edw 2.2.161 Lncstr
First would I heare newes that hee were deposde, — Edw 5.2.21 Mortmr
I heare of late he hath deposde himselfe. — Edw 5.2.83 Kent

DEPOSE
Pope excommunicate, Philip depose, — P1012 19.82 Guise

DEPOSE (cont.)
he refuse, and then may we/Depose him and elect an other king. | Edw 1.4.55 | Mortmr
Curse me, depose me, doe the worst you can. | Edw 1.4.57 | Edward
We will depose the Emperour for that deed, | F 906 3.1.128 | Pope
authority Apostolicall/Depose him from his Regall Government. | F 924 3.1.146 | Pope

DEPRIV'D
Depriv'd of care, my heart with comfort dies, | 1Tamb 5.1.431 | Arabia
dooth weepe to see/Your sweet desires depriv'd my company, | 2Tamb 5.3.247 | Tamb
In being depriv'd of everlasting blisse? | F 308 1.3.80 | Mephst
Because thou hast depriv'd me of those Joyes. | F 554 2.2.3 | Faust
That hath depriv'd thee of the joies of heaven. | F1974 5.2.178 | Faust
Who first depriv'd yong boyes of their best part, | Ovid's Elegies | 2.3.3
By feare depriv'd of strength to runne away. | Ovid's Elegies | 3.5.70

DEPRIVDE
We are deprivde the sun-shine of our life, | Edw 4.7.106 | Baldck

DEPRIVE
Thus to deprive me of my crowne and life. | 1Tamb 2.7.2 | Cosroe

DEPRIVED
so passionate/For being deprived of the Joyes of heaven? | F 312 1.3.84 | Faust

DEPRIVES
For when my loathing it of heate deprives me, | Ovid's Elegies | 2.9.27

DEPTH
And yet didst never sound any thing to the depth. | P 386 7.26 | Guise
and begin/To sound the depth of that thou wilt professe, | F 30 1.1.2 | Faust

DEPUTIE
When we shall meet the Turkish Deputie/And all his Viceroies, | 2Tamb 1.3.99 | Tamb

DERBY (See DARBIE)

DERE
No love is so dere (quiverd Cupid flie)/That my chiefe wish | Ovid's Elegies | 2.5.1

DERISION
proudest Kings/In Christendome, should beare me such derision, | P 761 15.19 | Guise

DESART
hunters in the chace/Of savage beastes amid the desart woods. | 1Tamb 4.3.57 | Capol
As dooth the Desart of Arabia/To those that stand on Badgeths | 2Tamb 1.1.108 | Sgsmnd
So from Arabia desart, and the bounds/Of that sweet land, whose | 2Tamb 3.5.35 | Orcan
Scarce shall you finde a man of more desart. | Edw 2.2.251 | Gavstn
Which swept the desart shore of that dead sea, | Edw 2.3.22 | Mortmr
Like to a Lyon of scortcht desart Affricke, | Lucan, First Booke | 208
Well, leade us then to Syrtes desart shoare; | Lucan, First Booke | 368

DESARTS
Then having past Armenian desarts now, | 1Tamb 2.2.14 | Meandr

DESCEND (See also DISCEND)
From whence my radiant mother did descend, | Dido 3.4.47 | Aeneas

DESCENDED
But say the Tribe that I descended of/Were all in generall cast | Jew 1.2.113 | Barab
That am descended but of knightly line, | Ovid's Elegies | 1.3.8
My bloud, the teares were that from her descended. | Ovid's Elegies | 1.7.60

DESCENDETH
Whose night and day descendeth from thy browes: | Dido 1.1.156 | Achat

DESCENDING
Hermes this night descending in a dreame, | Dido 4.3.3 | Aeneas
This sacrifice (whose sweet perfume descending, | Hero and Leander | 1.209

DESCENDS
Descends upon my radiant Heroes tower. | Hero and Leander | 2.204

DESCENT (See also DISCENT)
And my divine descent from sceptred Jove: | Dido 1.1.219 | Aeneas

DESCRIBE
Whose fruit none rightly can describe, but hee/That puls or | Hero and Leander | 2.299

DESCRIDE
Affection by the count'nance is descride. | Hero and Leander | 2.132

DESCRIED
Eastward behold/As much more land, which never was descried, | 2Tamb 5.3.155 | Tamb

DESCRY
Were Love the cause, it's like I shoulde descry him, | Ovid's Elegies | 1.2.5

DESEIGNES
But though I apt were for such high deseignes, | Ovid's Elegies | 2.18.14

DESEMBLE
Feare to be guilty, then thou maiest desemble. | Ovid's Elegies | 2.2.18

DESERT (Homograph; See also DESART)
If you retaine desert of holinesse, | 2Tamb 5.3.19 | Techel
For thy desert we make thee Governor, | Jew 5.2.10 | Calym
In recompence of this thy high desert, | F1322 4.1.168 | Emper
Within my brest no desert empire beare. | Ovid's Elegies | 2.9.52

DESERTES
of your Prince Electors, farre/Beyond the reach of my desertes: | P 453 8.3 | Anjoy
And yeeld your thoughts to height of my desertes. | P 602 12.15 | King

DESERTS (Homograph)
Doe trace these Libian deserts all despisde, | Dido 1.1.228 | Aeneas
But since they measure our deserts so meane, | 1Tamb 1.2.63 | Tamb
We might have punisht him to his deserts. | P1184 22.46 | Eprnon
great deserts in erecting that inchanted Castle in the Aire: | F1559 4.6.2 P | Duke
What seates for their deserts? | Lucan, First Booke | 344
And treades the deserts snowy heapes [do] <to> cover. | Ovid's Elegies | 1.9.12

DESERV'D
No, live Iarbus, what hast thou deserv'd, | Dido 3.1.41 | Dido
Something thou hast deserv'd.-- | Dido 3.1.43 | Dido
And sought your state all honor it deserv'd, | 1Tamb 2.5.33 | Ortyg
As his exceding favours have deserv'd, | 1Tamb 3.2.10 | Zenoc
Of thy deserv'd contentment and thy love: | 1Tamb 5.1.427 | Arabia
You partiall heavens, have I deserv'd this plague? | Jew 1.2.259 | Barab
Your father has deserv'd it at my hands, | Jew 2.3.70 | Barab
For well has Barabas deserv'd of us. | Jew 5.3.25 | Calym
I have deserv'd a scourge I must confesse, | P 544 11.9 | Charls

DESERV'D (cont.)			
But by the sword, my lord, it must be deserv'd.	Edw	4.2.59	Mortmr
More he deserv'd, to both great harme he fram'd,	Ovid's Elegies		2.2.49
Deserv'd thereby with death to be tormented.	Ovid's Elegies		2.14.6
DESERVD			
Wherein my lord, have I deservd these words?	Edw	1.4.163	Queene
DESERV'DE			
So well hast thou deserv'de sweete Mortimer.	Edw	2.4.59	Queene
DESERVE			
how may I deserve/Such amourous favours at thy beautious hand?	Dido	3.2.64	Juno
Deserve these tytles I endow you with,	1Tamb	4.4.125	Tamb
If we deserve them not with higher meeds/Then erst our states	1Tamb	4.4.131	Therid
No, Barabas, I will deserve it first.	Jew	2.3.68	Lodowk
Graunt that our deeds may wel deserve your loves:	P 600	12.13	King
They that deserve paine, beare't with patience.	Ovid's Elegies		2.7.12
Do but deserve gifts with this title grav'd.	Ovid's Elegies		2.13.26
And I deserve more then thou canst in verity,	Ovid's Elegies		3.1.47
Though neither gods nor men may thee deserve,	Hero and Leander		1.315
DESERVED			
In this my mortall well deserved wound,	2Tamb	2.3.6	Sgsmnd
Binde fast my hands, they have deserved chaines,	Ovid's Elegies		1.7.1
Deserved chaines these cursed hands shall fetter,	Ovid's Elegies		1.7.28
DESERVES			
Aeneas well deserves to be your love,	Dido	3.1.70	Anna
Aeneas for his parentage deserves/As large a kingdome as is	Dido	4.4.79	Achat
And speake of Tamburlaine as he deserves.	1Tamb	3.2.36	Zenoc
Straight will I use thee as thy pride deserves:	1Tamb	3.3.206	Zabina
whose worthinesse/Deserves a conquest over every hart:	1Tamb	5.1.208	Tamb
I crave but this, Grace him as he deserves,	Jew	Prol.33	Machvl
Deserves no common place, nor meane reward:	Edw	1.4.361	Edward
But thinke of Mortimer as he deserves.	Edw	2.4.58	Mortmr
DESERVEST			
Though thou deservest hardly at my hands,	Jew	3.3.74	Abigal
DESERVETH			
Deserveth princelie favors and rewardes,	Edw	4.6.54	Mortmr
DESERV'ST			
Deserv'st to have the leading of an hoste?	1Tamb	1.2.171	Tamb
DESIGN (See DESEIGNES)			
DESINE			
Desine meque tuis incendere teque querelis,	Dido	5.1.139	Aeneas
DESINIT			
[Seeing ubi desinit philosophus, ibi incipit medicus].	F 41	1.1.13A	Faust
DESIR'D			
And in assurance of desir'd successe,	1Tamb	1.1.160	Ortyg
Now that I have obtain'd what I desir'd <desire>/I'le live in	F 340	1.3.112	Faust
DESIRDE			
basely on their knees/In all your names desirde a truce of me?	2Tamb	1.1.97	Orcan
Desirde her more, and waxt outragious,	Edw	2.2.55	Edward
DESIRE			
But that I may enjoy what I desire:	Dido	3.1.9	Iarbus
Love my Aeneas, and desire is thine,	Dido	3.2.60	Venus
And make love drunken with thy sweete desire:	Dido	3.3.75	Iarbus
Why, what is it that Dido may desire/And not obtaine, be it in	Dido	3.4.7	Aeneas
And yet desire to have before I dye.	Dido	3.4.10	Dido
That intercepts the course of my desire:	Dido	4.2.48	Iarbus
Like his desire, lift upwards and divine,	1Tamb	2.1.8	Menaph
That if I should desire the Persean Crowne,	1Tamb	2.5.76	Tamb
Casane, here are the cates you desire to finger, are they not?	1Tamb	4.4.108 P	Tamb
And tickle not your Spirits with desire/Stil to be train'd in	2Tamb	4.1.80	Tamb
The wind that bloweth all the world besides,/Desire of gold.	Jew	3.5.4	Basso
Desire of gold, great Sir?	Jew	3.5.4	Govnr
Not for my life doe I desire this pause,	P 401	7.41	Ramus
Such as desire your worships service.	Edw	1.1.25	Poorem
Faire Isabell, now have we our desire,	Edw	5.2.1	Mortmr
And sue to me for that that I desire,	Edw	5.4.57	Mortmr
Now that I have obtain'd what I desir'd <desire>/I'le live in	F 340	1.3.112	Faust
<I would desire, that this house,	F 675	(HC263)A P	Covet
which being all I desire, I am content to remove his hornes.	F1313	4.1.159 P	Faust
I pray you tell me, what is the thing you most desire to have?	F1567	4.6.10 P	Faust
To glut the longing of my hearts desire,	F1760	5.1.87	Faust
This, or what else my Faustus shall <thou shalt> desire,	F1766	5.1.93	Mephst
Thou shalt both satisfie my just desire,	F App	p.237 35	Emper
which being all I desire, I am content to release him of his	F App	p.238 84 P	Faust
I would desire no better meate then a dish of ripe grapes.	F App	p.242 10 P	Duchss
Quarrels were rife, greedy desire stil poore/Did vild deeds,	Lucan, First Booke		174
this makes them/Run on the swords point and desire to die,	Lucan, First Booke		457
thou must hire/To teach thy lover, what thy thoughts desire.	Ovid's Elegies		1.8.88
Those in their lovers, pretty maydes desire.	Ovid's Elegies		1.9.6
And lets what both delight, what both desire,	Ovid's Elegies		1.10.31
Let Maydes whom hot desire to husbands leade,	Ovid's Elegies		2.1.5
fire/And [thinke] <thinkes> her chast whom many doe desire.	Ovid's Elegies		2.2.14
His fauning wench with her desire he crownes.	Ovid's Elegies		2.2.34
I pay them home with that they most desire:	Ovid's Elegies		2.10.26
Keepe her for me, my more desire to breede.	Ovid's Elegies		2.19.2
And was againe most apt to my desire.	Ovid's Elegies		2.19.16
The horses seeme, as [thy] <they> desire they knewe.	Ovid's Elegies		3.2.68
Even as the sicke desire forbidden drinke.	Ovid's Elegies		3.4.18
Law-giving Minos did such yeares desire;	Ovid's Elegies		3.9.41
And doubt to which desire the palme to give.	Ovid's Elegies		3.10.40
For in his lookes were all that men desire,	Hero and Leander		1.84
DESIRED			
Since thy desired hand shall close mine eies.	1Tamb	5.1.432	Arabia
That I may see that most desired day,	Edw	4.3.46	Edward

DESIRES			
Yet who so wretched but desires to live?	Dido	2.1.238	Aeneas
Desires Aeneas to remaine with her:	Dido	5.1.135	Dido
By whose desires of discipline in Armes,	1Tamb	1.1.174	Cosroe
Commanding all thy princely eie desires,	2Tamb	4.2.43	Therid
dooth weepe to see/Your sweet desires depriv'd my company,	2Tamb	5.3.247	Tamb
Then my desires were fully satisfied,	Jew	2.1.52	Barab
To bring the will of our desires to end.	P 144	2.87	Guise
majestie so earnestlie/Desires to see the man before his death,	Edw	2.5.78	Penbrk
Desires accesse unto your majestie.	Edw	3.1.149	Spencr
He of you all that most desires my bloud,	Edw	5.1.100	Edward
I these are those that Faustus most desires.	F 79	1.1.51	Faust
kind I will make knowne unto you what my heart desires to have,	F1571	4.6.14	P Lady
I wil not hide from you the thing my heart desires, and were it	F App	p.242 9	P Duchss
Destroying what withstood his proud desires,	Lucan, First Booke		150
Mine owne desires why should my selfe not flatter?	Ovid's Elegies		2.11.54
When like desires and affections meet,	Hero and Leander		2.30
DESIREST			
I will be there, and doe as thou desirest;	Jew	5.2.103	Govnr
DESIROUS			
But seeing you are so desirous, thus it is:	Edw	2.2.15	Mortmr
DESIRST			
Ready to execute what thou commandst <desirst>.	F 549	2.1.161	Mephst
DESOLATE			
Shall see it ruinous and desolate.	Hero and Leander		1.240
DESOLATION			
I never vow'd at Aulis gulfe/The desolation of his native Troy,	Dido	5.1.203	Dido
DESOLVE			
May not desolve, till death desolve our lives,	P 5	1.5	Charls
Which Ile desolve with bloud and crueltie.	P 26	1.26	QnMoth
DESPAIR (See also DISPAIRE)			
Despair in GOD, and trust in Belzebub:	F 393	2.1.5	Faust
DESPAIRE			
time/Have tane their flight, and left me in despaire;	Jew	2.1.8	Barab
But droope not madam, noble mindes contemne/Despaire:	Edw	4.2.17	SrJohn
Away with such vaine fancies, and despaire,	F 392	2.1.4	Faust
Had not sweete pleasure conquer'd deepe despaire.	F 576	2.2.25	Faust
Why should I die then, or basely despaire?	F 582	2.2.31	Faust
Despaire doth drive distrust into my thoughts.	F1480	4.4.24	Faust
[Damned art thou Faustus, damned, despaire and die],	F1725	5.1.52A	Faust
Then call for mercy, and avoyd despaire.	F1733	5.1.60	OldMan
I do repent, and yet I doe despaire,	F1740	5.1.67	Faust
Therefore despaire, thinke onely upon hell;	F1881	5.2.85	Mephst
'tis too late, despaire, farewell,/Fooles that will laugh on	F1890	5.2.94	Mephst
DESPAIRING			
Which fils my mind with strange despairing thoughts,	Edw	5.1.79	Edward
DESPATCH			
Despatch then quickly.	P 353	6.8	Mntsrl
But that we presently despatch Embassadours/To Poland, to call	P 555	11.20	QnMoth
DESPERATE			
Yet flung I forth, and desperate of my life,	Dido	2.1.210	Aeneas
Jove hath heapt on me such a desperate charge,	Dido	5.1.64	Aeneas
And make us desperate of our threatned lives:	1Tamb	5.1.6	Govnr
Raving, impatient, desperate and mad,	2Tamb	2.4.112	Tamb
And sharpest where th'assault is desperate.	2Tamb	3.2.67	Tamb
But then run desperate through the thickest throngs,	2Tamb	3.2.139	Tamb
Thou desperate Governour of Babylon,	2Tamb	5.1.49	Therid
To make me desperate in my poverty?	Jew	1.2.261	Barab
As I am almost desperate for my sinnes:	Jew	3.6.18	Abigal
A desperate and unnaturall resolution,	Edw	3.1.217	Warwck
And thousand desperate maladies beene cur'd <eas'd>?	F 50	1.1.22	Faust
Performe what desperate enterprise I will?	F 108	1.1.80	Faust
By desperate thoughts against Joves Deity:	F 317	1.3.89	Faust
[Ah] <O> stay good Faustus, stay thy desperate steps.	F1729	5.1.56	OldMan
How should he, but in <with> desperate lunacie.	F1807	5.2.11	Mephst
DESPERATELY			
And into water desperately she flies.	Ovid's Elegies		3.5.80
DESPERATLY			
Have desperatly dispatcht their slavish lives:	1Tamb	5.1.472	Tamb
DESPIGHT			
Are these the sailes that in despight of me,	Dido	4.4.126	Dido
Yet will I weare it in despight of them,	1Tamb	2.7.61	Tamb
And meane to fetch thee in despight of him.	1Tamb	3.1.40	Bajzth
That holds you from your father in despight,	1Tamb	3.2.27	Agidas
Whom he detaineth in despight of us,	1Tamb	4.1.44	Souldn
Which in despight of them I set on fire:	2Tamb	1.3.213	Therid
Wel, in despight of thee he shall be king:	2Tamb	3.5.128	Callap
And wil defend it in despight of thee.	2Tamb	5.1.55	Govnr
And but that Learning, in despight of Fate,	Hero and Leander		1.465
DESPISD			
To like a base wench of despisd condition.	Ovid's Elegies		2.7.20
DESPISDE			
Doe trace these Libian deserts all despisde,	Dido	1.1.228	Aeneas
DESPISE (See also DISPISED, DESPIZE)			
And thou despise the praise of such attempts:	Dido	5.1.37	Hermes
Make me despise this transitorie pompe,	Edw	5.1.108	Edward
Looke gently, and rough husbands lawes despise.	Ovid's Elegies		3.4.44
But they that dayly tast neat wine, despise it.	Hero and Leander		1.261
his promise, did despise/The love of th'everlasting Destinies.	Hero and Leander		1.461
DESPISED			
As my despised worths, that shun all praise,	Dido	3.4.42	Aeneas
DESPISETH			
That he that despiseth him, can nere/Be good in Logick or	P 409	7.49	Ramus

DESPISING
the water fcr a kis/Of his owne shadow, and despising many, — Hero and Leander 1.75
DESPITE (See also DESPIGHT, DISPIGHT)
Thus in despite of thy Religion, — P 314 5.41 Guise
I did it only in despite of thee. — P 820 17.15 Guise
Despite of times, despite of enemies. — Edw 3.1.147 Edward
And in despite of all his Holinesse/Restore this Bruno to his — F 898 3.1.120 Faust
And sit in Peters Chaire, despite of chance, — F1214 4.1.60 Emper
DESPIZE
The vaine name of inferiour slaves despize. — Ovid's Elegies 1.8.64
DESTENIE
The yeares that fatall destenie shall give, — Ovid's Elegies 1.3.17
DESTINIE (See also DISTINIE)
The boy wherein false destinie delights, — Dido 3.2.2 Juno
Since destinie doth call me from [thy] <the> shoare: — Dido 4.3.2 Aeneas
What fatall destinie envies me thus, — Dido 5.1.323 Anna
are as peremptory/As wrathfull Planets, death, or destinie. — 1Tamb 5.1.128 Tamb
DESTINIES
O what destinies/Have brought my sweete companions in such — Dido 2.1.59 Aeneas
Swell raging seas, frowne wayward destinies, — Dido 4.4.57 Aeneas
I, and unlesse the destinies be false, — Dido 4.4.81 Aeneas
Warre and the destinies shall trie my cause. — Lucan, First Booke 229
Against the destinies durst sharpe darts require. — Ovid's Elegies 1.7.10
Then towards the pallace of the Destinies, — Hero and Leander 1.377
I mean the Adamantine Destinies, — Hero and Leander 1.444
his promise, did despise/The love of th'everlasting Destinies. — Hero and Leander 1.462
DESTITUTE
And rest attemplesse, faint and destitute? — 1Tamb 2.5.74 Tamb
The earth of Caesars had beene destitute. — Ovid's Elegies 2.14.18
DESTROY
Troianes destroy the Greeke wealth, while you may. — Ovid's Elegies 1.9.34
And their owne privie weapon'd hands destroy them. — Ovid's Elegies 2.14.4
Thee sacred Poet could sad flames destroy? — Ovid's Elegies 3.8.41
And with intestine broiles the world destroy, — Hero and Leander 1.251
DESTROYING
Destroying what withstood his proud desires, — Lucan, First Booke 150
DESTRUCTION
He will with Tamburlaines destruction/Redeeme you from this — 1Tamb 3.2.33 Agidas
you be first shal feele/The sworne destruction of Damascus. — 1Tamb 5.1.66 Tamb
Death and destruction to th'inhabitants. — 2Tamb 3.2.5 Tamb
DETAIN'D
Yet here detain'd by cruell Tamburlaine. — 2Tamb 1.2.4 Callap
DETAINE
That should detaine thy eye in his defects? — Dido 3.4.17 Aeneas
(O face most cunning mine eyes to detaine)/Thou oughtst — Ovid's Elegies 2.17.12
That him frcm her unjustly did detaine. — Hero and Leander 2.122
DETAINETH
partake with me the cause/Of this devotion that detaineth you, — Dido 4.2.28 Anna
Whom he detaineth in despight of us, — 1Tamb 4.1.44 Souldn
DETEINE
And doth the world in fond beliefe deteine. — Ovid's Elegies 3.3.24
DETERMIN'D
Have you determin'd what to say to them? — Jew 1.2.37 1Knght
Thus he determin'd to have handled thee, — Jew 5.5.93 Govnr
we have determin'd with our selves, that Hellen of Greece was — F1683 5.1.10 P 1Schol
DETERMINDE
That have I not determinde with my selfe. — Dido 5.1.19 Aeneas
DETERMINE
Stand all aside, and let the Knights determine, — Jew 1.2.14 Calym
What you determine, I will ratifie. — P 227 4.25 Charls
And then determine of this enterprise. — P 656 12.69 QnMoth
We will determine of his life or death. — F 969 3.1.191 Pope
And there determine of his punishment? — F1018 3.2.38 Pope
What two determine never wants effect. — Ovid's Elegies 2.3.16
yong-mens mates, to go/If they determine to persever so. — Ovid's Elegies 2.16.18
DETERMINED
And therefore thus we are determined; — Jew 1.2.66 Govnr
DETERMINES
Comes marching on us, and determines straight, — 2Tamb 2.2.27 1Msngr
DETERRE
Clowne, from my journey why doest me deterre? — Ovid's Elegies 3.5.88
DETESTED
And rid the world of those detested troopes? — 1Tamb 2.2.19 Meandr
And then shall we in this detested guyse, — 1Tamb 5.1.235 Bajzth
Rather than yeeld to his detested suit, — 2Tamb 4.2.6 Olymp
What this detested Jacobin hath done. — P1195 22.57 King
But were he here, detested as he is, — Edw 1.4.264 Mortmr
DETESTING
And in detesting such a divelish Thiefe, — 1Tamb 2.6.20 Ortyg
DETESTS
My policie detests prevention: — Jew 5.2.121 Barab
DETRACTORS
An eare, to heare what my detractors say, — P 160 2.103 Guise
DEUCALION
What, would the Gods have me, Deucalion like, — Dido 5.1.57 Aeneas
DEUCALIONS
That though the stones, as at Deucalions flood, — 2Tamb 1.3.163 Tamb
Then Gaynimede would renew Deucalions flood, — Lucan, First Booke 652
DEVICE
Why know you what you did by this device? — Jew 1.2.84 Barab
I feare she knowes ('tis so) of my device/In Don Mathias and — Jew 3.4.7 Barab
Well, now about effecting this device: — Jew 5.2.117 Barab
Mother, how like you this device of mine? — P1065 19.135 King

DEVICE (cont.)
Stand graticus gloomie night to his device. Edw 4.1.11 Kent
DEVIDE
We two as friends one fortune will devide: Dido 3.2.55 Venus
With whom we did devide both lawes and land, Dido 4.2.14 Iarbus
Rifling this Fort, devide in equall shares: 2Tamb 3.4.89 Therid
kings Concubines)/Take them, devide them and their jewels too, 2Tamb 4.3.72 Tamb
Why doth my mistresse from me oft devide? Ovid's Elegies 2.16.42
DEVIDED
When my poore pleasures are devided thus, 1Tamb 5.1.386 Zenoc
My flesh devided in your precious shapes, 2Tamb 5.3.172 Tamb
DEVIDES
Who with the Sunne devides one radiant shape, Dido 1.1.97 Jupitr
DEVIDING
And creepes along the vales, deviding just/The bounds of Italy, Lucan, First Booke 217
DEVIL (See also DIVEL, DIVELLS, DYVILS)
Why the devil invented a challenge, my master writ it, and I Jew 3.3.18 P Ithimr
saies, he that eats with the devil had need of a long spoone. Jew 3.4.58 P Ithimr
Speak softly sir, least the devil heare you: F1180 4.1.26 Mrtino
DEVILISH (See DIVELISH, DIVELLISH)
DEVILL
a death too good, the devill of hell/Torture his wicked soule. P1218 22.80 Bartus
Too servile <The devill> and illiberall for mee. F 63 1.1.35 Faust
That holy shape becomes a devill best. F 254 1.3.26 Faust
that <I know> he would give his soule to the devill, for a F 350 1.4.8 P Wagner
whensoever, and wheresoever the devill shall fetch thee. F 370 1.4.28 P Wagner
I am not afraid of a devill. F 375 1.4.33 P Robin
I good Wagner, take away the devill then. F 377 1.4.35 P Robin
I, take it, and the devill give thee good of it <on't>. F 502 2.1.114 Faust
Be I a devill yet God may pitty me, F 566 2.2.15 Faust
Thinke [of] <on> the devill. F 645 2.2.94 Lucifr
and the devill a peny they have left me, but a [bare] <small> F 693 2.2.142 P Glutny
Then the devill choke thee. F 703 2.2.152 P Glutny
that your devill can answere the stealing of this same cup, F1088 3.3.1 P Dick
What a devill ayle you two? F1179 4.1.25 P Benvol
What devill attends this damn'd Magician, F1445 4.3.15 Benvol
The devill will come, and Faustus must be damn'd. F1937 5.2.141 Faust
When thou doest wish thy husband at the devill. Ovid's Elegies 1.4.28
DEVILS
First legions of devils shall teare thee in peeces. 1Tamb 4.4.38 P Bajzth
And Nigra Silva, where the Devils dance, 2Tamb 1.3.212 Therid
Where legions of devils (knowing he must die/Here in Natolia, 2Tamb 3.5.25 Orcan
To see the devils mount in Angels throanes, 2Tamb 5.3.32 Usumc
But take it to you i'th devils name. Jew 1.2.154 Barab
when holy Friars turne devils and murder one another. Jew 4.1.194 P Ithimr
Devils doe your worst, [I'le] <I> live in spite of you. Jew 5.1.41 Barab
And now stay/That bel that to the devils mattins rings. P 448 7.88 Guise
And try if devils will obey thy Hest, F 234 1.3.6 Faust
How comes it then that he is Prince of Devils? F 294 1.3.66 Faust
for I will presently raise up two devils to carry thee away: F 373 1.4.31 P Wagner
If thou repent, devils will <shall> teare thee in peeces. F 632 2.2.81 BdAngl
He was upon the devils backe late enough; and if he be so farre F1190 4.1.36 P Benvol
one of his devils turn'd me into the likenesse of an Apes face. F1554 4.5.50 P Dick
The devils whom Faustus serv'd have torne him thus: F1990 5.3.8 3Schol
DEVINE
And makes my soule devine her overthrow. 1Tamb 3.2.87 Agidas
Then as the powers devine have preordainde, 1Tamb 5.1.400 Zenoc
Having beheld devine Zenocrate, 1Tamb 5.1.418 Arabia
To entertaine devine Zenocrate. 2Tamb 2.4.17 Tamb
DEVIS'D
As if he now devis'd some Stratageme: 1Tamb 1.2.159 Therid
See Calymath, this was devis'd for thee. Jew 5.5.66 Govnr
DEVISDE
Your Majesty already hath devisde/A meane, as fit as may be to 2Tamb 4.3.50 Usumc
DEVISE
Nor I devise by what meanes to contrive. Dido 5.1.66 Aeneas
You must devise some torment worsse, my Lord, 1Tamb 4.2.66 Techel
That this devise may proove propitious, 1Tamb 5.1.52 2Virgn
Devise some meanes to rid thee of thy life, 2Tamb 4.2.5 Olymp
And in the mean time my Lord, could we devise, P 425 7.65 Guise
But tell me Mortimer, whats thy devise, Edw 2.2.11 Edward
And then devise what best contents thy minde, F 858 3.1.80 Mephst
Or any villany thou canst devise, F 865 3.1.87 Mephst
let's devise how we may adde more shame/To the blacke scandall F1377 4.2.53 Fredrk
DEVISION
Thou swearest, devision should not twixt us rise, Ovid's Elegies 2.16.43
DEVOIRE
To do your highnes service and devoire, Edw 5.1.133 Bartly
DEVORCE
Faire Queene of love, I will devorce these doubts, Dido 3.2.85 Juno
Yet ere thou go, see how I do devorce Edw 3.1.176 Edward
DEVORSED
And though devorsed from king Edwards eyes, Edw 2.5.3 Gavstn
DEVOTION
partake with me the cause/Of this devotion that detaineth you, Dido 4.2.28 Anna
Come brethren, let's about our businesse with good devotion. F1076 3.2.96 P 1Frier
Come brethren, lets about our businesse with good devotion. F App p.232 30 P Frier
DEVOURED
By cloyed Charibdis, and againe devoured. Ovid's Elegies 2.16.26
DEVOURING
Hence interest and devouring usury sprang, Lucan, First Booke 183
DEVOUT
Chast, and devout, much sorrowing for my sinnes, Jew 3.6.14 Abigal

DEVOUTELY			
And pray devoutely to the Prince of hell.	F 282	1.3.54	Mephst
DEVOUTLY			
Pronounce this thrice devoutly to thy selfe,	F 547	2.1.159	Mephst
He kneel'd, but unto her devoutly praid;	Hero and Leander		1.177
DEW (See also DEAW)			
My head, the latest honor dew to it,	Edw	5.1.62	Edward
DEWBERRIES			
Dewberries, Apples, yellow Orenges,	Dido	4.5.6	Nurse
DEW'D			
And since this earth, dew'd with thy brinish teares,	2Tamb	4.2.8	Olymp
DI			
Corpo di dio stay, you shall have halfe,	Jew	1.2.90	Barab
DIABLO			
Diablo, what passions call you these?	Edw	1.4.319	Lncstr
DIABOLE			
Religion: O Diabole.	P 123	2.66	Guise
DIABOLO			
Cazzo, diabolo.	Jew	4.1.20	Barab
DIADEM (See also DYADEM)			
How vaine am I to weare this Diadem,	Dido	4.4.40	Aeneas
Present thee with th'Emperiall Diadem.	1Tamb	1.1.139	Ortyg
And when the princely Persean Diadem,	1Tamb	2.1.45	Cosroe
And which is worst to have his Diadem/Sought for by such scalde	1Tamb	2.2.7	Mycet
To dispossesse me of this Diadem:	1Tamb	2.7.60	Tamb
Even with the true Egyptian Diadem.	1Tamb	5.1.105	1Virgn
And thereon set the Diadem of Fraunce,	P 101	2.44	Guise
That if by death of Charles, the diadem/Of France be cast on me,	P 472	8.22	Anjoy
For Polands crowne and kingly diadem.	P 480	8.30	Lord
And Henry then shall weare the diadem.	P 522	9.41	QnMoth
Hath worne the Poland diadem, before/You were invested in the	P 612	12.25	Mugern
And then shall Mounser weare the diadem.	P 652	12.65	QnMoth
whose golden leaves/Empale your princelie head, your diadem,	Edw	3.1.164	Herald
My diadem I meane, and guiltlesse life.	Edw	5.1.73	Edward
In peace possesse the triple Diadem,	F1213	4.1.59	Emper
DIADEME			
Ne're king more sought to keepe his diademe,	Hero and Leander		2.77
DIAMETARILY			
and let thy left eye be diametarily fixt upon my right heele,	F App	p.231 70	P Wagner
DIAMETRALLY			
your right eye be alwaies Diametrally fixt upon my left heele,	F 386	1.4.44	P Wagner
DIAMITER (See also DYAMETER)			
the sun and Moone as darke/As when opposde in one Diamiter,	2Tamb	2.4.52	Tamb
DIAMOND			
Well, Barabas, canst helpe me to a Diamond?	Jew	2.3.48	Lodowk
The Diamond that I talke of, ne'r was foild:	Jew	2.3.56	Barab
As for the Diamond, Sir, I told you of,	Jew	2.3.91	Barab
As for the Diamond it shall be yours;	Jew	2.3.135	Barab
Where is the Diamond you told me of?	Jew	2.3.219	Lodowk
This is thy Diamond, tell me, shall I have it?	Jew	2.3.292	Lodowk
A Diamond set in lead his worth retaines,	Hero and Leander		1.215
DIAMONDES			
Enchac'd with Diamondes, Saphyres, Rubies/And fairest pearle of	2Tamb	3.2.120	Tamb
DIAMONDS			
Spangled with Diamonds dancing in the aire,	2Tamb	4.3.117	Tamb
Beauteous Rubyes, sparkling Diamonds,	Jew	1.1.27	Barab
Oh, Sir, your father had my Diamonds.	Jew	2.3.49	Barab
Tush man, we talk'd of Diamonds, not of Abigal.	Jew	2.3.151	Barab
Which lightned by her necke, like Diamonds shone.	Hero and Leander		1.26
As much as sparkling Diamonds flaring glasse.	Hero and Leander		1.214
DIAN			
and where [Jove] <it> seemes/Bloudy like Dian, whom the	Lucan, First Booke		442
Shall Dian fanne when love begins to glowe?	Ovid's Elegies		1.1.12
And quiver bearing Dian till the plaine:	Ovid's Elegies		1.1.14
DIANA			
And Il'e play Diana, and send you the hornes presently.	F1257	4.1.103	P Faust
Ifaith thats as true as Diana turned me to a stag.	F App	p.237 54	P Knight
Such were they as [Dione] <Diana> painted stands/All naked	Ovid's Elegies		1.14.33
Phoebus gave not Diana such tis thought,	Ovid's Elegies		2.5.27
Like chast Diana, when Acteon spyde her,	Hero and Leander		2.261
DIANAS			
Or one of chast Dianas fellow Nimphs,	Dido	1.1.194	Aeneas
Whom Ajax ravisht in Dianas [Fane] <Fawne>,	Dido	2.1.275	Aeneas
Whose glittering pompe Dianas shrowdes supplies,	Dido	3.3.4	Dido
[What] <That> if thy Mother take Dianas bowe,	Ovid's Elegies		1.1.11
Coate-tuckt Dianas legges are painted like them,	Ovid's Elegies		3.2.31
And know that some have wrong'd Dianas name?	Hero and Leander		1.284
DIANS			
Sometime a lovelie boye in Dians shape,	Edw	1.1.61	Gavstn
DICATUS			
per vota nostra ipse nunc surgat nobis dicatus Mephostophilis.	F 250	1.3.22	P Faust
DICHOTOMIST (See DECOTAMEST)			
DICK			
What Dick, looke to the horses there till I come againe.	F 722	2.3.1	P Robin
hold the cup Dick, come, come, search me, search me.	F1102	3.3.15	P Robin
Dick, make me a circle, and stand close at my backe, and stir	F1112	3.3.25	P Robin
life, Vintner you shall have your cup anon, say nothing Dick:	F1114	3.3.27	P Robin
come Dick, come.	F1134	3.3.47	P Robin
Sirra Dick, dost thou know why I stand so mute?	F1509	4.5.5	P Robin
Ha, ha, ha, dost heare him Dick, he has forgot his legge.	F1629	4.6.72	P Carter
DICTATOR			
And as Dictator make or warre or peace,	P 860	17.55	King

DID

As once I did for harming Hercules.	Dido	1.1.15	Jupitr
She humbly did beseech him for our bane,	Dido	1.1.60	Venus
Which Pergama did vaunt in all her pride.	Dido	1.1.151	Aeneas
That in such peace long time did rule the same:	Dido	1.2.24	Cloan
And would my prayers (as Pigmalions did)/Could give it life,	Dido	2.1.16	Aeneas
Some say Antenor did betray the towne,	Dido	2.1.110	Dido
his entent/The windes did drive huge billowes to the shoare,	Dido	2.1.139	Aeneas
These hands did helpe to hale it to the gates,	Dido	2.1.170	Aeneas
And through the breach did march into the streetes,	Dido	2.1.189	Aeneas
Aeneas, thou art he, what did I say?	Dido	3.4.29	Dido
From whence my radiant mother did descend,	Dido	3.4.47	Aeneas
Did ever men see such a sudden storme?	Dido	4.1.1	Achat
As others did, by running to the wood.	Dido	4.1.30	Anna
With whom we did devide both lawes and land,	Dido	4.2.14	Iarbus
What willes our Lord, or wherefore did he call?	Dido	4.3.15	Achat
The dreames (brave mates) that did beset my bed,	Dido	4.3.16	Aeneas
And build the towne againe the Greekes did burne?	Dido	4.3.40	Illion
O blessed tempests that did drive him in,	Dido	4.4.94	Dido
Why did it suffer thee to touch her breast,	Dido	4.4.145	Dido
How Carthage did rebell, Iarbus storme,	Dido	5.1.143	Dido
So thou wouldst prove as true as Paris did,	Dido	5.1.146	Dido
As did Sir Paris with the Grecian Dame:	1Tamb	1.1.66	Mycet
Passe into Graecia, as did Cyrus once.	1Tamb	1.1.130	Menaph
Then did the Macedonians at the spoile/Of great Darius and his	1Tamb	1.1.153	Ceneus
For as when Jove did thrust old Saturn down,	1Tamb	2.7.36	Usumc
The heat and moisture which did feed each other,	1Tamb	2.7.46	Cosroe
Or when Minerva did with Neptune strive.	1Tamb	3.2.52	Zenoc
that in his infancie/Did pash the jawes of Serpents venomous:	1Tamb	3.3.105	Bajzth
Nay (mightie Souldan) did your greatnes see/The frowning lookes	1Tamb	4.1.12	2Msngr
Me thinks we martch as Meliager did,	1Tamb	4.3.1	Souldn
Comes now as Turnus gainst Eneas did,	1Tamb	5.1.380	Philem
And what we did, was in extremity:	2Tamb	1.1.105	Sgsmnd
Yet never did they recreate themselves,	2Tamb	1.3.182	Usumc
Whose triple Myter I did take by force,	2Tamb	1.3.189	Techel
From thence unto Cazates did I martch,	2Tamb	1.3.191	Techel
And with my power did march to Zansibar,	2Tamb	1.3.194	Techel
Here father, cut it bravely as you did your own.	2Tamb	3.2.135	P Celeb
As Hector did into the Grecian campe,	2Tamb	3.5.65	Tamb
For if I should as Hector did Achilles,	2Tamb	3.5.70	Tamb
issue, at whose byrth/Heaven did affoord a gratious aspect,	2Tamb	3.5.80	Tamb
least hee hide his crowne as the foolish king of Persea did.	2Tamb	3.5.155	P Tamb
Fight as you ever did, like Conquerours,	2Tamb	3.5.160	Tamb
My Lord, if ever you did deed of ruth,	2Tamb	5.1.24	1Citzn
we offer more/Than ever yet we did to such proud slaves,	2Tamb	5.1.58	Techel
My heart did never quake, or corrage faint.	2Tamb	5.1.106	Govnr
As that which [Clymens] <Clymeus> brainsicke sonne did guide,	2Tamb	5.3.231	Tamb
Daughter, whom I hold as deare/As Agamemnon did his Iphegen:	Jew	1.1.138	Barab
Long to the Turke did Malta contribute;	Jew	1.1.180	Barab
Why know you what you did by this device?	Jew	1.2.84	Barab
Why did you yeeld to their extortion?	Jew	1.2.177	Barab
I did.	Jew	1.2.279	Abigal
long since some of us/Did stray so farre amongst the multitude.	Jew	1.2.309	Abbass
espy'd a time/To search the plancke my father did appoint;	Jew	2.1.21	Abigal
I did it, and revenge it if thou dar'st.	Jew	3.2.4	Mthias
And so did Lodowicke him.	Jew	3.2.22	Govnr
Lend me that weapon that did kill my sonne,	Jew	3.2.23	Mater
So sure did your father write, and I cary the chalenge.	Jew	3.3.25	P Ithimr
Abigal it is not yet long since/That I did labour thy admition,	Jew	3.3.57	1Fryar
And so did faire Maria send for me:	Jew	3.6.5	1Fryar
I did offend high heaven so grievously,	Jew	3.6.17	Abigal
My father did contract me to 'em both:	Jew	3.6.22	Abigal
And for his sake did I become a Nunne.	Jew	3.6.25	Abigal
I'de cut thy throat if I did.	Jew	4.1.11	Barab
Why true, therefore did I place him there:	Jew	4.1.137	Barab
I did.	Jew	4.2.2	P Pilia
I did.	Jew	4.2.4	P Pilia
sweet youth; did not you, Sir, bring the sweet youth a letter?	Jew	4.2.41	P Ithimr
I did Sir, and from this Gentlewoman, who as my selfe, and the	Jew	4.2.43	P Pilia
And ye did but know how she loves you, Sir.	Jew	4.2.53	Pilia
But came it freely, did the Cow give down her milk freely?	Jew	4.2.102	P Ithimr
So did you when you stole my gold.	Jew	4.4.50	Barab
Mathias did it not, it was the Jew.	Jew	5.1.11	Curtzn
I fram'd the challenge that did make them meet:	Jew	5.5.82	Barab
For he that did by treason worke our fall,	Jew	5.5.109	Govnr
My Lord, but did you mark the Cardinall/The Guises brother, and	P 47	1.47	Admral
How they did storme at these your nuptiall rites,	P 49	1.49	Admral
to beware/How you did meddle with such dangerous giftes.	P 180	3.15	Navrre
which my Lord of Guise/Did make in Paris amongst the Hugonites?	P 515	9.34	QnMoth
I did it only in despite of thee.	P 820	17.15	Guise
with gifts and shewes did entertaine him/And promised to be at	P 874	17.69	Eprnon
Did they of Paris entertaine him so?	P 879	17.74	King
Thus Caesar did goe foorth, and thus he dyed.	P1015	19.85	Guise
Did he not draw a sorte of English priestes/From Doway to the	P1030	19.100	King
Did he not cause the King of Spaines huge fleete,	P1033	19.103	King
Did he not injure Mounser thats deceast?	P1035	19.105	King
I did it onely in dispight of thee	Paris	ms24,p391	Guise
I did no more then I was bound to do,	Edw	1.1.182	BshpCv
As then I did incense the parlement,	Edw	1.1.184	BshpCv
Did never sorrow go so neere my heart,	Edw	1.4.306	Edward
Desirde her more, and waxt outragious,/So did it sure with me:	Edw	2.2.56	Edward
Whose mounting thoughts did never creepe so low,	Edw	2.2.77	Gavstn
As never subject did unto his King.	Edw	2.2.129	Mortmr

DID (cont.)

Did you retaine your fathers magnanimitie,	Edw	3.1.16	Spencr
I did your highnes message to them all,	Edw	3.1.96	Arundl
Did they remoove that flatterer from thy throne.	Edw	3.1.231	Kent
They passe not for thy frownes as late they did,	Edw	5.1.77	Edward
Did you attempt his rescue, Edmund speake?	Edw	5.4.86	Mortmr
Mortimer, I did, he is our king,	Edw	5.4.87	Kent
Where Mars did mate the warlicke Carthagens <Carthaginians>,	F 2	Prol.2	1Chor
His waxen wings did mount above his reach,	F 21	Prol.21	1Chor
Did not he charge thee to appeare to me?	F 271	1.3.43	Faust
Did not my conjuring [speeches] raise thee? speake.	F 273	1.3.45	Faust
thought you did not sneake up and downe after her for nothing.	F 742	2.3.21	P Dick
Did mount him up <himselfe> to scale Olimpus top.	F 757	2.3.36	2Chor
And in eight daies did bring him home againe.	F 767	2.3.46	2Chor
That with his wings did part the subtle aire,	F 772	2.3.51	2Chor
Hast thou, as earst I did command,	F 801	3.1.23	Faust
There did we view the Kingdomes of the world,	F 852	3.1.74	Faust
Pope Julius did abuse the Churches Rites,	F 928	3.1.150	Pope
Did seeke to weare the triple Dyadem,	F 959	3.1.181	Faust
Did I not tell you,/To morrow we would sit i'th Consistory,	F1016	3.2.36	Pope
[Did gratulate his safetie with kinde words],	F1143	3.3.56A	3Chor
[What there he did in triall of his art],	F1153	3.3.66A	3Chor
Tush, Christ did call the Theefe upon the Crosse,	F1482	4.4.26	Faust
some on's have cause to know him; did he conjure thee too?	F1524	4.5.20	P HrsCsr
what did I but rid him into a great river, and when I came just	F1543	4.5.39	P HrsCsr
sir, did not I pull off one of your legs when you were asleepe?	F1655	4.6.98	P HrsCsr
Why did not Faustus tell us of this before, that Divines might	F1862	5.2.66	P 1Schol
Since first the worlds creation did begin.	F1985	5.3.3	1Schol
did not I tell thee, we were for ever made by this doctor	F App	p.234 1	P Robin
Tush, Christ did call the thiefe upon the Crosse,	F App	p.240 125	Faust
Made all shake hands as once the Sabines did;	Lucan, First Booke	118	
Shaming to strive but where he did subdue,	Lucan, First Booke	146	
greedy desire stil poore/Did vild deeds, then t'was worth the	Lucan, First Booke	175	
shoot) marcht on/And then (when Lucifer did shine alone,	Lucan, First Booke	233	
south were cause/I know not, but the cloudy ayre did frown;	Lucan, First Booke	237	
Sent aide; so did Alcides port, whose seas/Eate hollow rocks,	Lucan, First Booke	406	
fame increast true feare, and did invade/The peoples minds,	Lucan, First Booke	465	
Thus in his fright did each man strengthen Fame,	Lucan, First Booke	481	
the only hope (that did remaine/To their afflictions) were	Lucan, First Booke	494	
making men/Dispaire of day; as did Thiestes towne/(Mycenae),	Lucan, First Booke	541	
Tav'ron peering/(His grave broke open) did affright the Boores.	Lucan, First Booke	582	
and every vaine/Did threaten horror from the host of Caesar;	Lucan, First Booke	621	
appear'd/A knob of flesh, whereof one halfe did looke/Dead, and	Lucan, First Booke	627	
Involving all, did Aruns darkly sing.	Lucan, First Booke	637	
Marveile not though the faire Bride did incite/The drunken	Ovid's Elegies	1.4.7	
If hee gives thee what first himselfe did tast,	Ovid's Elegies	1.4.33	
I and my wench oft under clothes did lurke,	Ovid's Elegies	1.4.47	
What armes and shoulders did I touch and see,	Ovid's Elegies	1.5.19	
For thee I did thy mistris faire entreate.	Ovid's Elegies	1.6.20	
Well I remember when I first did hire thee,	Ovid's Elegies	1.6.43	
Watching till after mid-night did not tire thee.	Ovid's Elegies	1.6.44	
Aie me how high that gale did lift my hope!	Ovid's Elegies	1.6.52	
She may perceive how we the time did wast:	Ovid's Elegies	1.6.70	
My Mistresse weepes whom my mad hand did harme.	Ovid's Elegies	1.7.4	
So chast Minerva did Cassandra fall,	Ovid's Elegies	1.7.17	
But secretlie her lookes with checks did trounce mee,	Ovid's Elegies	1.7.21	
Her teares, she silent, guilty did pronounce me.	Ovid's Elegies	1.7.22	
I harm'd: a foe did Diomedes anger move.	Ovid's Elegies	1.7.34	
And downe her cheekes, the trickling teares did flow,	Ovid's Elegies	1.7.57	
Then first I did perceive I had offended,	Ovid's Elegies	1.7.59	
My feared hands thrice back she did repell.	Ovid's Elegies	1.7.62	
Mars in the deed the black-smithes net did stable,	Ovid's Elegies	1.9.39	
too dearely wunne/That unto death did presse the holy Nunne.	Ovid's Elegies	1.10.50	
cold hemlocks flower/Wherein bad hony Corsicke Bees did power.	Ovid's Elegies	1.12.10	
That colour rightly did appeare so bloudy.	Ovid's Elegies	1.12.12	
Poore wretches on the tree themselves did strangle,	Ovid's Elegies	1.12.17	
I did not bid thee wed an aged swaine.	Ovid's Elegies	1.13.42	
Leave colouring thy tresses I did cry,	Ovid's Elegies	1.14.1	
And did to thee no cause of dolour raise.	Ovid's Elegies	1.14.14	
How patiently hot irons they did take/In crooked [tramells]	Ovid's Elegies	1.14.25	
Or wofull Hector whom wilde jades did teare?	Ovid's Elegies	2.1.32	
Shee pleas'd me, soone I sent, and did her woo,	Ovid's Elegies	2.2.5	
Let him goe forth knowne, that unknowne did enter,	Ovid's Elegies	2.2.20	
The man did grieve, the woman was defam'd.	Ovid's Elegies	2.2.50	
To whom his wench can say, I never did it.	Ovid's Elegies	2.5.10	
Even from your cheekes parte of a voice did breake.	Ovid's Elegies	2.5.16	
And scratch her faire soft cheekes I did intend.	Ovid's Elegies	2.5.46	
What Pylades did to Orestes prove,	Ovid's Elegies	2.6.15	
Thy mouth to taste of many meates did balke.	Ovid's Elegies	2.6.30	
Pure waters moisture thirst away did keepe.	Ovid's Elegies	2.6.32	
Thersites did Protesilaus survive,	Ovid's Elegies	2.6.41	
Which stormie South-windes into sea did blowe?	Ovid's Elegies	2.6.44	
My mouth in speaking did all birds excell.	Ovid's Elegies	2.6.62	
To prove him foolish did I ere contend?	Ovid's Elegies	2.8.10	
But when on thee her angry eyes did rush,	Ovid's Elegies	2.8.15	
In both [thy] <my> cheekes she did perceive thee blush,	Ovid's Elegies	2.8.16	
By Venus Deity how did I protest.	Ovid's Elegies	2.8.18	
How oft, and by what meanes we did agree.	Ovid's Elegies	2.8.28	
Did not Pelides whom his Speare did grieve,	Ovid's Elegies	2.9.7	
Even as he led his life, so did he die.	Ovid's Elegies	2.10.38	
Nor violent South-windes did thee ought affright.	Ovid's Elegies	2.11.52	
Least Arte should winne her, firmely did inclose.	Ovid's Elegies	2.12.4	
To cruell armes their drunken selves did summon.	Ovid's Elegies	2.12.20	

DID (cont.)

A woman against late-built Rome did send/The Sabine Fathers,	Ovid's Elegies	2.12.23
Shee looking on them did more courage give	Ovid's Elegies	2.12.26
He had not beene that conquering Rome did build.	Ovid's Elegies	2.14.16
Armenian Tygers never did so ill,	Ovid's Elegies	2.14.35
Who doubts, with Pelius, Thetis did consort,	Ovid's Elegies	2.17.17
Shee in my lap sits still as earst she did.	Ovid's Elegies	2.18.6
And writings did from diverse places frame,	Ovid's Elegies	2.18.28
Jove liked her better then he did before.	Ovid's Elegies	2.19.30
Sterne was her front, her [cloake] <looke> on ground did lie.	Ovid's Elegies	3.1.12
Wish in his hands graspt did Hippomenes.	Ovid's Elegies	3.2.30
But did you not so envy Cepheus Daughter,	Ovid's Elegies	3.3.17
My selfe would sweare, the wenches true did sweare,	Ovid's Elegies	3.3.45
Yet by deceit Love did them all surprize.	Ovid's Elegies	3.4.20
Because the keeper may come say, I did it,	Ovid's Elegies	3.4.35
Where Mars his sonnes not without fault did breed,	Ovid's Elegies	3.4.39
When thy waves brim did scarse my anckles touch.	Ovid's Elegies	3.5.6
They say Peneus neere Phthias towne did hide.	Ovid's Elegies	3.5.32
Not Calydon, nor Aetolia did please:	Ovid's Elegies	3.5.37
Her wofull bosome a warme shower did drowne.	Ovid's Elegies	3.5.68
Thrice she prepar'd to flie, thrice she did stay,	Ovid's Elegies	3.5.69
She on my necke her Ivorie armes did throw,	Ovid's Elegies	3.6.7
Then did the robe or garment which she wore <more>,	Ovid's Elegies	3.6.40
Nay more, the wench did not disdaine a whit,	Ovid's Elegies	3.6.73
When our bookes did my mistris faire content,	Ovid's Elegies	3.7.5
This side that serves thee, a sharpe sword did weare.	Ovid's Elegies	3.7.14
With strong plough shares no man the earth did cleave,	Ovid's Elegies	3.7.41
The ditcher no markes on the ground did leave.	Ovid's Elegies	3.7.42
Nor hanging oares the troubled seas did sweepe,	Ovid's Elegies	3.7.43
If Thetis, and the morne their sonnes did waile,	Ovid's Elegies	3.8.1
To Thracian Orpheus what did parents good?	Ovid's Elegies	3.8.21
And that slowe webbe nights fals-hood did unframe.	Ovid's Elegies	3.8.30
Thy dying eyes here did thy mother close,	Ovid's Elegies	3.8.49
Nor did thy ashes her last offrings lose.	Ovid's Elegies	3.8.50
When well-toss'd mattocks did the ground prepare,	Ovid's Elegies	3.9.31
The graine-rich goddesse in high woods did stray,	Ovid's Elegies	3.9.35
Ida the seate of groves did sing with corne,	Ovid's Elegies	3.9.39
Law-giving Minos did such yeares desire;	Ovid's Elegies	3.9.41
White birdes to lovers did not alwayes sing.	Ovid's Elegies	3.11.2
And justly: for her praise why did I tell?	Ovid's Elegies	3.11.9
Oxen in whose mouthes burning flames did breede?	Ovid's Elegies	3.11.36
The Priests to Juno did prepare chaste feasts,	Ovid's Elegies	3.12.3
Onely the Goddesse hated Goate did lack,	Ovid's Elegies	3.12.18
Teach but your tongue to say, I did it not,	Ovid's Elegies	3.13.48
Both loves to whom my heart long time did yeeld,	Ovid's Elegies	3.14.15
And whose immortall fingars did imprint,	Hero and Leander	1.67
As after chaunc'd, they did each other spye.	Hero and Leander	1.134
Thereat she smild, and did denie him so,	Hero and Leander	1.311
Did she uphold to Venus, and againe,	Hero and Leander	1.367
Did charme her nimble feet, and made her stay,	Hero and Leander	1.399
To be reveng'd on Jove, did undertake,	Hero and Leander	1.442
These he regarded not, but did intreat,	Hero and Leander	1.451
his promise, did despise/The love of th'everlasting Destinies.	Hero and Leander	1.461
And many poore excuses did she find,	Hero and Leander	2.6
And oft look't out, and mus'd he did not come.	Hero and Leander	2.22
And what he did, she willingly requited.	Hero and Leander	2.28
For hitherto hee did but fan the fire,	Hero and Leander	2.41
Though it was morning, did he take his flight.	Hero and Leander	2.102
That him from her unjustly did detaine.	Hero and Leander	2.122
And every lim did as a soldier stout,	Hero and Leander	2.271
Till gentle parlie did the truce obtaine.	Hero and Leander	2.278

DIDO

Whereas Sidonian Dido rules as Queene.	Dido	1.1.213	Venus
Where Dido will receive ye with her smiles:	Dido	1.1.234	Venus
And here Queene Dido weares th'imperiall Crowne,	Dido	2.1.63	Illion
passe through the hall/Bearing a banket, Dido is not farre.	Dido	2.1.71	Serg
Renowmed Dido, tis our Generall:	Dido	2.1.77	Illion
A wofull tale bids Dido to unfould,	Dido	2.1.114	Aeneas
And Dido and you Carthaginian Peeres/Heare me, but yet with	Dido	2.1.122	Aeneas
And then--O Dido, pardon me.	Dido	2.1.159	Aeneas
Will Dido give to sweete Ascanius:	Dido	2.1.312	Venus
And goe to Dido, who in stead of him/Will set thee on her lap	Dido	2.1.324	Venus
How long faire Dido shall I pine for thee?	Dido	3.1.7	Iarbus
I feare me Dido hath been counted light,	Dido	3.1.14	Dido
But Dido is the favour I request.	Dido	3.1.18	Iarbus
Feare not Iarbus, Dido may be thine.	Dido	3.1.19	Dido
No Dido will not take me in her armes,	Dido	3.1.22	Cupid
Will Dido let me hang about her necke?	Dido	3.1.30	Cupid
Come Dido, leave Ascanius, let us walke.	Dido	3.1.34	Iarbus
Doth Dido call me backe?	Dido	3.1.53	Iarbus
Wherefore doth Dido bid Iarbus goe?	Dido	3.1.56	Anna
O dull conceipted Dido, that till now/Didst never thinke Aeneas	Dido	3.1.82	Dido
love, give Dido leave/To be more modest then her thoughts admit,	Dido	3.1.94	Dido
here, tell me in sooth/In what might Dido highly pleasure thee.	Dido	3.1.102	Dido
Which piteous wants if Dido will supplie,	Dido	3.1.111	Aeneas
Wherefore would Dido have Aeneas stay?	Dido	3.1.134	Aeneas
Aeneas, thinke not Dido is in love:	Dido	3.1.136	Dido
O happie shall he be whom Dido loves.	Dido	3.1.168	Aeneas
Thy sonne thou knowest with Dido now remaines,	Dido	3.2.70	Juno
But should that man of men (Dido except)/Have taunted me in	Dido	3.3.26	Iarbus
But Dido that now holdeth him so deare,	Dido	3.3.76	Iarbus
Dido.	Dido	3.4.2	Aeneas
Why, what is it that Dido may desire/And not obtaine, be it in	Dido	3.4.7	Aeneas

DIDO (cont.)

what meanes faire Dido by this doubtfull speech?	Dido	3.4.31	Aeneas
whiles Dido lives and rules in Junos towne,	Dido	3.4.50	Aeneas
Come Dido, let us hasten to the towne,	Dido	4.1.26	Aeneas
Away with Dido, Anna be thy song,	Dido	4.2.45	Anna
Yet Dido casts her eyes like anchors out,	Dido	4.3.25	Aeneas
Will Dido raise old Priam forth his grave,	Dido	4.3.39	Illion
And not let Dido understand their drift:	Dido	4.4.6	Dido
O princely Dido, give me leave to speake,	Dido	4.4.17	Aeneas
Thinkes Dido I will goe and leave him here?	Dido	4.4.30	Aeneas
O Dido, patronesse of all our lives,	Dido	4.4.55	Aeneas
Those that dislike what Dido gives in charge,	Dido	4.4.71	Dido
Dido is thine, henceforth Ile call thee Lord:	Dido	4.4.84	Dido
O Dido, blame not him, but breake his oares,	Dido	4.4.149	Dido
For this will Dido tye ye full of knots,	Dido	4.4.155	Dido
Say Dido what she will I am not old,	Dido	4.5.21	Nurse
No marvell Dido though thou be in love,	Dido	5.1.44	Aeneas
Lest Dido spying him keepe him for a pledge.	Dido	5.1.50	Aeneas
But here he is, now Dido trie thy wit.	Dido	5.1.86	Dido
And yet I may not stay, Dido farewell.	Dido	5.1.104	Aeneas
Fare well may Dido, so Aeneas stay,	Dido	5.1.107	Dido
Wilt thou kisse Dido?	Dido	5.1.120	Dido
O thy lips have sworne/To stay with Dido:	Dido	5.1.121	Dido
And wofull Dido by these blubbred cheekes,	Dido	5.1.133	Dido
Ah foolish Dido to forbeare this long!	Dido	5.1.160	Dido
And cam'st to Dido like a Fisher swaine?	Dido	5.1.162	Dido
And hisse at Dido for preserving thee?	Dido	5.1.168	Dido
To whom poore Dido doth bequeath revenge.	Dido	5.1.173	Dido
O Dido, your little sonne Ascanius/Is gone!	Dido	5.1.212	Nurse
Dido, faire Dido wils Aeneas stay:	Dido	5.1.233	Anna
Dido I am, unlesse I be deceiv'd,	Dido	5.1.264	Dido
How long will Dido mourne a strangers flight,	Dido	5.1.279	Iarbus
But afterwards will Dido graunt me love?	Dido	5.1.288	Iarbus
Now Dido, with these reliques burne thy selfe,	Dido	5.1.292	Dido
Live false Aeneas, truest Dido dyes,	Dido	5.1.312	Dido
O helpe Iarbus, Dido in these flames/Hath burnt her selfe, aye	Dido	5.1.314	Anna
Dido I come to thee, aye me Aeneas.	Dido	5.1.318	Iarbus
Dido is dead,	Dido	5.1.320	Anna
And what poore Dido with her drawne sword sharpe,	Ovid's Elegies	2.18.25	

DIDOS

Sit downe Aeneas, sit in Didos place,	Dido	2.1.91	Dido
Lyes it in Didos hands to make thee blest,	Dido	2.1.103	Dido
And makes Aeneas sinke at Didos feete.	Dido	2.1.117	Aeneas
Faire child stay thou with Didos waiting maide,	Dido	2.1.304	Venus
Are you Queene Didos sonne?	Dido	2.1.308	Ascan
For Didos sake I take thee in my armes,	Dido	2.1.313	Venus
As every touch shall wound Queene Didos heart.	Dido	2.1.333	Cupid
doe know no wanton thought/Had ever residence in Didos breast.	Dido	3.1.17	Dido
Weepe not sweet boy, thou shalt be Didos sonne,	Dido	3.1.24	Dido
Is not Aeneas worthie Didos love?	Dido	3.1.68	Dido
And thou Aeneas, Didos treasurie,	Dido	3.1.91	Dido
So much have I receiv'd at Didos hands,	Dido	3.1.103	Aeneas
For ballace, emptie Didos treasurie,	Dido	3.1.126	Dido
Then would I wish me in faire Didos armes,	Dido	3.3.48	Iarbus
Aeneas thoughts dare not ascend so high/As Didos heart, which	Dido	3.4.34	Aeneas
This kisse shall be faire Didos punishment.	Dido	4.4.37	Aeneas
let him ride/As Didos husband through the Punicke streetes,	Dido	4.4.67	Dido
onely Aeneas frowne/Is that which terrifies poore Didos heart:	Dido	4.4.116	Dido
Nor blazing Commets threatens Didos death,	Dido	4.4.119	Dido
Eating sweet Comfites with Queene Didos maide,	Dido	5.1.47	Ascan
Farewell: is this the mends for Didos love?	Dido	5.1.105	Dido
These words are poyson to poore Didos soule,	Dido	5.1.111	Dido
been/When Didos beautie [chaind] <chaungd> thine eyes to her:	Dido	5.1.114	Dido
And Didos beautie will returne againe:	Dido	5.1.118	Dido
And wilt thou not be mov'd with Didos words?	Dido	5.1.155	Dido
Save, save Aeneas, Didos leefest love!	Dido	5.1.256	Dido

DIDST

O Anna, didst thou know how sweet love were,	Dido	3.1.59	Dido
Dido, that till now/Didst never thinke Aeneas beautifull:	Dido	3.1.83	Dido
Once didst thou goe, and he came backe againe,	Dido	5.1.196	Dido
I, Didst thou ever see a fairer?	1Tamb	2.4.28	Mycet
Come as thou didst in fruitfull Scicilie,	2Tamb	4.3.34	Orcan
And then thou didst not like that holy life.	Jew	3.3.58	1Fryar
Pilia-borza, didst thou meet with Ithimore?	Jew	4.2.1	P Curtzn
And didst thou deliver my letter?	Jew	4.2.3	P Curtzn
And where didst meet him?	Jew	4.2.15	P Curtzn
Didst breake prison?	Jew	5.1.78	Calym
And yet didst never sound any thing to the depth.	P 386	7.26	Guise
To which thou didst alure me being alive:	P1025	19.95	King
Or didst thou see my friend to take his death?	Edw	3.1.93	Edward
That thither thou didst send a murtherer.	Edw	5.6.48	King
<Why, didst thou not say thou knewst>?	F 204	(HC258)A	P 2Schol
Then Faustus as thou late didst promise us,	F1230	4.1.76	Emper
But thou didst love the world.	F1894	5.2.98	GdAngl
[wretch] <wench> I sawe when thou didst thinke I slumbred,	Ovid's Elegies	2.5.13	
I know not whom thou lewdly didst imbrace,	Ovid's Elegies	3.10.11	

DIE (Homograph; See also DY, DYE)

Our life is fraile, and we may die to day.	1Tamb	1.1.68	Mycet
Theridamas and Tamburlaine, I die,	1Tamb	2.7.51	Cosroe
That I may live and die with Tamburlaine.	1Tamb	3.2.24	Zenoc
It saies, Agydas, thou shalt surely die,	1Tamb	3.2.95	Agidas
And let Agidas by Agidas die,	1Tamb	3.2.105	Agidas
Europe, and pursue/His scattered armie til they yeeld or die.	1Tamb	3.3.39	Therid

DIE (cont.)

Let thousands die, their slaughtered Carkasses/Shall serve for	1Tamb	3.3.138		Bajzth
Prepare thy selfe to live and die my slave.	1Tamb	3.3.207		Zabina
But ere I die those foule Idolaters/Shall make me bonfires with	1Tamb	3.3.239		Bajzth
Ile make the kings of India ere I die,	1Tamb	3.3.263		Tamb
My jointes benumb'd, unlesse I eat, I die.	1Tamb	4.4.98		Bajzth
And let them die a death so barbarous.	1Tamb	5.1.351		Zenoc
Then shal I die with full contented heart,	1Tamb	5.1.417		Arabia
And die before I brought you backe again.	2Tamb	1.2.73		Almeda
And let this death wherein to sinne I die,	2Tamb	2.3.8		Sgsmnd
But let me die my Love, yet let me die,	2Tamb	2.4.66		Zenoc
With love and patience let your true love die,	2Tamb	2.4.67		Zenoc
Yet let me kisse my Lord before I die,	2Tamb	2.4.69		Zenoc
And let me die with kissing of my Lord.	2Tamb	2.4.70		Zenoc
And till I die thou shalt not be interr'd.	2Tamb	2.4.132		Tamb
And fear'st to die, or with a Curtle-axe/To hew thy flesh and	2Tamb	3.2.96		Tamb
Nor [any] issue foorth, but they shall die:	2Tamb	3.3.33		Techel
Farewell sweet wife, sweet son farewell, I die.	2Tamb	3.4.10		Capt
Tell me sweet boie, art thou content to die?	2Tamb	3.4.18		Olymp
Therefore die by thy loving mothers hand,	2Tamb	3.4.23		Olymp
Where legions of devils (knowing he must die/Here in Natolia,	2Tamb	3.5.25		Orcan
For every man that so offends shall die.	2Tamb	4.3.76		Tamb
Or die some death of quickest violence,	2Tamb	5.1.41		2Citzn
Yet shouldst thou die, shoot at him all at once.	2Tamb	5.1.157		Tamb
But if he die, your glories are disgrac'd,	2Tamb	5.3.15		Therid
For if he die, thy glorie is disgrac'd,	2Tamb	5.3.40		Usumc
Not last Techelles, no, for I shall die.	2Tamb	5.3.66		Tamb
And shall I die, and this unconquered?	2Tamb	5.3.150		Tamb
And shal I die, and this unconquered?	2Tamb	5.3.158		Tamb
Shal still retaine my spirit, though I die,	2Tamb	5.3.173		Tamb
That I may see thee crown'd before I die.	2Tamb	5.3.179		Tamb
Leading a life that onely strives to die,	2Tamb	5.3.197		Amyras
And send my soule before my father die,	2Tamb	5.3.208		Amyras
For Tamburlaine, the Scourge of God must die.	2Tamb	5.3.248		Tamb
The king, upon whose bosome let me die,	Edw	1.1.14		Gavstn
By yelping hounds puld downe, and seeme to die.	Edw	1.1.70		Gavstn
And eyther die, or live with Gaveston.	Edw	1.1.138		Edward
He shall to prison, and there die in boults.	Edw	1.1.197		Gavstn
Unlesse his brest be sword proofe he shall die.	Edw	1.2.8		Mortmr
Whether will you beare him, stay or ye shall die.	Edw	1.4.24		Edward
No, rather will I die a thousand deaths,	Edw	1.4.196		Queene
I will not long be from thee though I die:	Edw	2.1.62		Neece
Ile have his bloud, or die in seeking it.	Edw	2.2.107		Warwck
Tell us where he remaines, and he shall die.	Edw	2.4.36		Lncstr
And sends you word, he knowes that die he shall,	Edw	2.5.38		Arundl
Sweete soveraigne, yet I come/To see thee ere I die.	Edw	2.5.95		Gavstn
Weaponles must I fall and die in bands,	Edw	2.6.3		Gavstn
the riches of my realme/Can ransome him, ah he is markt to die,	Edw	3.1.4		Edward
O shall I speake, or shall I sigh and die!	Edw	3.1.122		Edward
The worst is death, and better die to live,	Edw	3.1.243		Lncstr
And in this bed of [honor] <honors> die with fame.	Edw	4.5.7		Edward
And these must die under a tyrants sword.	Edw	4.7.92		Edward
To die sweet Spencer, therefore live wee all,	Edw	4.7.111		Baldck
Spencer, all live to die, and rise to fall.	Edw	4.7.112		Baldck
And save you from your foes, Bartley would die.	Edw	5.1.134		Bartly
That death ends all, and I can die but once.	Edw	5.1.153		Edward
Speake, shall he presently be dispatch'd and die?	Edw	5.2.44		Mortmr
And so must die, though pitied by many.	Edw	5.3.24		Edward
Wish well to mine, then tush, for them ile die.	Edw	5.3.45		Edward
Edmund, yeeld thou thy self, or thou shalt die.	Edw	5.3.56		Matrvs
The king must die, or Mortimer goes downe,	Edw	5.4.1		Mortmr
Feare not to kill the king tis good he die.	Edw	5.4.9		Mortmr
My lord, he is your enemie, and shall die.	Edw	5.4.92		Mortmr
Art thou king, must I die at thy commaund?	Edw	5.4.103		Kent
O let me not die yet, stay, O stay a while.	Edw	5.5.101		Edward
Or else die by the hand of Mortimer.	Edw	5.6.6		Mortmr
And thou shalt die, and on his mournefull hearse,	Edw	5.6.29		King
Madam, intreat not, I will rather die,	Edw	5.6.56		Mortmr
And live and die in Aristotles workes.	F 33	1.1.5		Faust
Why then belike/We must sinne, and so consequently die,/I, we	F 72	1.1.44		Faust
I, we must die, an everlasting death.	F 73	1.1.45		Faust
This night I'le conjure tho I die therefore.	F 193	1.1.165		Faust
Why should I die then, or basely despaire?	F 582	2.2.31		Faust
<through> all the world, that all might die, and I live along,	F 682	2.2.131	P	Envy
Or by our sanctitude you all shall die.	F1057	3.2.77		Pope
here will Benvolio die,/But Faustus death shall quit my	F1336	4.2.12		Benvol
Then Souldiers boldly fight; if Faustus die,	F1346	4.2.22		Benvol
We'le rather die with griefe, then live with shame.	F1456	4.3.26		Benvol
What art thou Faustus but a man condemn'd to die?	F1478	4.4.22		Faust
I think my Maister means to die shortly, he has made his will,	F1674	5.1.1	P	Wagner
[Damned art thou Faustus, damned, despaire and die],	F1725	5.1.52A		Faust
are live quarters broyling on the coles,/That ner'e can die:	F1914	5.2.118		BdAngl
All beasts are happy, for when they die,	F1969	5.2.173		Faust
what art thou Faustus but a man condemnd to die?	F App	p.240 121	P	Faust
I thinke my maister meanes to die shortly,	F App	p.243 1		Wagner
this makes them/Run on the swords point and desire to die,	Lucan, First Booke			457
Which being not shakt <slackt>, I saw it die at length.	Ovid's Elegies			1.2.12
Ile live with thee, and die, or <ere> thou shalt <shall> grieve.	Ovid's Elegies			1.3.18
Now hast thou left no haires at all to die.	Ovid's Elegies			1.14.2
Cupid flie)/That my chiefe wish should be so oft to die.	Ovid's Elegies			2.5.2
Or such, as least long yeares should turne the die,	Ovid's Elegies			2.5.39
If ill, thou saiest I die for others love.	Ovid's Elegies			2.7.10
But when I die, would I might droope with doing,	Ovid's Elegies			2.10.35

DIE (cont.)			
Even as he led his life, so did he die.	Ovid's Elegies	2.10.38	
Live godly, thou shalt die, though honour heaven,	Ovid's Elegies	3.8.37	
O let mee viste Hero ere I die.	Hero and Leander	2.178	
DIED (Homograph)			
And died a traitor both to heaven and earth,	2Tamb	2.3.37	Orcan
Sweet Guise, would he had died so thou wert heere:	P1082	19.152	QnMoth
He died a death too good, the devill of hell/Torture his wicked	P1218	22.80	Bartus
Tell me [Arundell] <Matre>, died he ere thou camst,	Edw	3.1.92	Edward
For me, both thou, and both the Spencers died,	Edw	5.3.42	Edward
I, I, and none shall know which way he died.	Edw	5.4.25	Ltborn
No sir, but when Acteon died, he left the hornes for you:	F App	p.237 55 P	Faust
Died red with shame, to hide from shame she seekes.	Ovid's Elegies	1.14.52	
Died ere he could enjoy the love of any.	Hero and Leander	1.76	
Pyn'd as they went, and thinking on her died.	Hero and Leander	1.130	
DIENG (Homograph)			
Or dieng, be the [author] <anchor> of my death.	2Tamb	2.4.56	Tamb
Dieng their lances with their streaming blood,	2Tamb	3.2.105	Tamb
DIES (Homograph)			
Which dies my lookes so livelesse as they are.	1Tamb	3.2.15	Zenoc
He dies, and those that kept us out so long.	1Tamb	4.2.118	Tamb
Depriv'd of care, my heart with comfort dies,	1Tamb	5.1.431	Arabia
And feed my mind that dies for want of her:	2Tamb	2.4.128	Tamb
by me, yet but he may/See him before he dies, for why he saies,	Edw	2.5.37	Arundl
Too true it is, quem dies vidit veniens superbum,	Edw	4.7.53	Leistr
Hunc dies vidit fugiens jacentem.	Edw	4.7.54	Leistr
But Edwards name survives, though Edward dies.	Edw	5.1.48	Edward
Gurney, I wonder the king dies not,	Edw	5.5.1	Matrvs
He whom she favours lives, the other dies.	Hero and Leander	1.124	
The richest corne dies, if it be not reapt,	Hero and Leander	1.327	
DIEST			
Even so for her thou diest in these armes:	1Tamb	5.1.410	Arabia
Dissemble or thou diest, for Mortimer/And Isabell doe kisse	Edw	4.6.12	Kent
DIET (See also DYET)			
diet your selves, you knowe I shall have occasion shortly to	2Tamb	3.5.114 P	Tamb
My daily diet, is heart breaking sobs,	Edw	5.3.21	Edward
And scorn'd old sparing diet, and ware robes/Too light for	Lucan, First Booke	165	
DIETED			
sir, you must be dieted, too much eating will make you surfeit.	1Tamb	4.4.103 P	Tamb
DIEU			
Mort dieu.	Edw	1.1.90	Gavstn
DIFFER			
differ in their motions <motion> upon the poles of the	F 598	2.2.47 P	Mephst
DIFFER'D			
Both differ'd much, Pompey was strooke in yeares,	Lucan, First Booke	130	
DIFFERENCE			
Approove the difference twixt himself and you.	2Tamb	4.1.137	Tamb
Thou shewest the difference twixt our selves and thee/In this	2Tamb	4.1.138	Orcan
Has made me see the difference of things.	Jew	3.3.62	Abigal
our difference in Religion/Might be a meanes to crosse you in	P 15	1.15	QnMoth
What difference betwixt the richest mine/And basest mold, but	Hero and Leander	1.232	
DIFFERS			
Differs as much, as wine and water doth.	Hero and Leander	1.264	
DIG			
And dig for treasure to appease my wrath:	1Tamb	3.3.265	Tamb
DIGEST			
Fall to, and never may your meat digest.	1Tamb	4.4.16	Bajzth
Which into words no vertue can digest:	1Tamb	5.1.173	Tamb
DIGESTED			
should be most)/Hath seem'd to be digested long agoe.	1Tamb	3.2.8	Agidas
Although it be digested long agoe,	1Tamb	3.2.9	Zenoc
Oft in the morne her haires not yet digested,	Ovid's Elegies	1.14.19	
DIGESTION (See DEGESTIONE)			
DIGG'D			
The rocke is hollow, and of purpose digg'd,	Jew	5.1.87	Barab
DIGGING			
armes in ure/With digging graves and ringing dead mens knels:	Jew	2.3.185	Barab
DIGNITIE			
Shall yeeld to dignitie a dubble birth,	Dido	1.1.107	Jupitr
If we should aime at such a dignitie?	1Tamb	2.5.79	Tamb
And see the figure of my dignitie,	2Tamb	4.3.25	Tamb
their late conspiracie/Against our State, and Papall dignitie?	F 950	3.1.172	Pope
DIGNITIES			
Thy names and tytles, and thy dignities,	1Tamb	4.2.79	Tamb
As all the world should blot our dignities/Out of the booke of	2Tamb	3.1.18	Callap
If for these dignities thou be envied,	Edw	1.1.163	Edward
queene in peace may reposesse/Her dignities and honors,	Edw	4.4.25	Mortmr
DIGNITY			
those that lead my horse/Have to their names tytles of dignity,	1Tamb	3.3.70	Bajzth
Pierc'd with the joy of any dignity?	2Tamb	5.3.190	Amyras
To weare his brothers crowne and dignity.	P 557	11.22	QnMoth
And crouch before the Papall dignity:	F 874	3.1.96	Pope
DILIGENT			
Adde she was diligent thy locks to braide,	Ovid's Elegies	2.7.23	
DIM			
and dim their eies/That stand and muse at our admyred armes.	1Tamb	2.3.23	Tamb
And dim the brightnesse of their neighbor Lamps:	1Tamb	4.2.34	Tamb
To dim thy basenesse and obscurity,	1Tamb	4.3.65	Souldn
souldiers crie/Make deafe the aire, and dim the Christall Sky.	2Tamb	3.3.61	Therid
But rather let the brightsome heavens be dim,	Jew	2.3.330	Lodowk
Whose brightnes such pernitious upstarts dim,	Edw	3.1.165	Herald
[There] <Their> Caesar may'st thou shine and no cloud dim thee;	Lucan, First Booke	59	
Thou feard'st (great Pompey) that late deeds would dim/Olde	Lucan, First Booke	121	

Context	Work	Reference	Speaker
DIM (cont.)			
And some dim stars) he Arriminum enter'd:	Lucan, First Booke		234
the Planets/Alter their course; and vainly dim their vertue?	Lucan, First Booke		663
O'recast with dim and darksome coverture.	Hero and Leander		2.266
DIMENSIONS			
Intrench with those dimensions I prescribed: . . .	2Tamb	3.3.42	Therid
DIMS (See also DYMS)			
As far as Titan springs where night dims heaven, . .	Lucan, First Booke		15
DINE			
please you dine with me, Sir, and you shal be most hartily	Jew	4.3.29	P Barab
Then come and dine with me, and after meate/We'le canvase every	F 190	1.1.162	Faust
DINEROS			
Hermoso Placer de los Dineros.	Jew	2.1.64	Barab
DING			
if he had but the qualitie of hey ding, ding, hey, ding, ding,	F App	p.239 115	P HrsCsr
ding, hey, ding, ding, Ide make a brave living on him; hee has	F App	p.239 116	P HrsCsr
ding, ding, Ide make a brave living on him; hee has a buttocke	F App	p.239 116	P HrsCsr
DINNER			
Lets goe my Lords, our dinner staies for us.	P 630	12.43	King
well/To waite at my trencher, and tell me lies at dinner time,	Edw	1.1.31	Gavstn
my Maister is within at dinner, with Valdes and Cornelius,	F 215	1.2.22	P Wagner
DINT			
That heavenly path, with many a curious dint, ...	Hero and Leander		1.68
DIO			
Corpo di dio stay, you shall have halfe, ...	Jew	1.2.90	Barab
DIOMEDES			
I harm'd: a foe did Diomedes anger move.	Ovid's Elegies		1.7.34
DIONE			
Such were they as [Dione] <Diana> painted stands/All naked	Ovid's Elegies		1.14.33
DIONISIUS			
[Where] <When> Siracusian Dionisius reign'd, ...	Jew	5.3.10	Calym
DIP			
Returne it backe and dip it in my bloud.	Edw	5.1.120	Edward
DIPS			
Lay her whole tongue hid, mine in hers she dips. . .	Ovid's Elegies		2.5.58
DIPSAS			
a bawde aright/Give eare, there is an old trot Dipsas hight.	Ovid's Elegies		1.8.2
DIPT			
And dipt it in the old Kings chill cold bloud, ...	Dido	2.1.260	Aeneas
And every bullet dipt in poisoned drugs.	1Tamb	5.1.222	Bajzth
DIRE			
Dire league of partners in a kingdome last not. . .	Lucan, First Booke		86
And why dire poison give you babes unborne?	Ovid's Elegies		2.14.28
DIRECT			
Made Hebe to direct her ayrie wheeles/Into the windie countrie	Dido	1.1.56	Venus
To whom sweet Menaphon, direct me straight.	1Tamb	2.1.68	Cosroe
Direct my weapon to his barbarous heart, ...	1Tamb	2.6.38	Cosroe
Direct our Bullets and our weapons pointes/And make our <your>	1Tamb	3.3.157	Tamb
your sounding Drummes/Direct our Souldiers to Damascus walles.	1Tamb	4.3.62	Souldn
Abrahams off-spring; and direct the hand/Of Abigall this night;	Jew	2.1.14	Barab
Clarke of the crowne, direct our warrant forth, . . .	Edw	1.4.369	Edward
DIRECTION			
To some direction in your martiall deeds, ...	1Tamb	2.3.12	Tamb
and excusde/For turning my poore charge to his direction.	1Tamb	2.3.29	Therid
And under your direction see they keep/All trecherous violence	P 267	4.65	Charls
DIREFUL			
These direful signes made Aruns stand amaz'd, ...	Lucan, First Booke		615
DIRGE			
Go then command our Priests to sing a Dirge, ...	F1063	3.2.83	Pope
Cursed be he that disturbeth our holy Dirge.	F1083	3.2.103	1Frier
Friers prepare a dirge to lay the fury of this ghost, once	F App	p.232 16	P Pope
Cursed be he that disturbeth our holy Dirge.	F App	p.232 37	Frier
DIRT (See also DURT)			
lumpe of clay/That will with every water wash to dirt: .	Jew	1.2.217	Barab
DIS			
Neptune and Dis gain'd each of them a Crowne, ...	1Tamb	2.7.37	Usumc
Infernall Dis is courting of my Love, ...	2Tamb	4.2.93	Therid
Thou in those Groves, by Dis above, ...	Jew	4.2.97	Ithimr
Thus from infernall Dis do we ascend/To view the subjects of	F1797	5.2.1	Lucifr
And Juno like with Dis raignes under ground?	Ovid's Elegies		3.9.46
Than Dis, on heapes of gold fixing his looke. . . .	Hero and Leander		2.326
DISAPOINTED			
faire Arabian king/That hath bene disapointed by this slave,	1Tamb	4.1.69	Souldn
DISARM'D			
Doth see his souldiers slaine, himselfe disarm'd, . .	Jew	1.2.204	Barab
DISASTER			
Know you not of Mathias and Don Lodowickes disaster? .	Jew	3.3.16	P Ithimr
DISCARDED			
I am alone, were furious Love discarded.	Ovid's Elegies		1.6.34
DISCARDES			
If she discardes thee, what use servest thou for? . .	Ovid's Elegies		2.3.12
DISCEASSE			
Which after his disceasse, some other gains.	Hero and Leander		1.246
DISCEND			
And we discend into th'infernall vaults, ...	2Tamb	2.4.98	Tamb
DISCENDED			
Or els discended to his winding traine:	2Tamb	2.4.54	Tamb
Seeing her face, mine upreard armes discended, . . .	Ovid's Elegies		2.5.47
DISCENDETH			
Discendeth downward to th'Antipodes.	2Tamb	1.2.52	Callap
DISCENT			
By due discent the Regall seat is mine.	P 470	8.20	Anjoy
DISCERN'D			
Do what thou wilt, thou shalt not be discern'd. . .	F1001	3.2.25	Mephst

DISCERND
what meanes learnd/Hath this same Poet my sad chaunce discernd? Ovid's Elegies 2.1.10
DISCERNES
Nor she her selfe but first trim'd up discernes. . . Ovid's Elegies 2.17.10
DISCHARG'D
men dispatch/And come ashore, and see the fraught discharg'd. Jew 1.1.101 Barab
Pray pardon me, I must goe see a ship discharg'd. . . Jew 4.2.51 P Ithimr
Till you shall heare a Culverin discharg'd/By him that beares Jew 5.4.3 Govnr
his rent discharg'd/From further duty he rests then inlarg'd. Ovid's Elegies 1.10.45
DISCHARGD
Bartley shall be dischargd, the king remoovde, ... Edw 5.2.40 Mortmr
DISCHARGE
[But] <by> goe, goe thou thy wayes, discharge thy Ship, . Jew 1.1.82 Barab
Discharge thy musket and perfourme his death: . . . . P 88 2.31 Guise
Make a discharge of all my counsell straite, ... P 882 17.77 King
Or I will presentlie discharge these lords, ... Edw 1.4.61 ArchBp
in the morning/We will discharge thee of thy charge, be gon. Edw 2.5.109 Penbrk
DISCHEVELD
And strewe thy walkes with my discheveld haire. . . Dido 4.2.56 Anna
Her cheekes were scratcht, her goodly haires discheveld. . Ovid's Elegies 3.5.48
DISCHEWELD
With haire discheweld wip'st thy watery cheeks: . . 1Tamb 5.1.139 Tamb
DISCIPLINE
Wanting both pay and martiall discipline, ... 1Tamb 1.1.147 Ceneus
By whose desires of discipline in Armes, ... 1Tamb 1.1.174 Cosroe
Yet being void of Martiall discipline, ... 1Tamb 2.2.44 Meandr
Of lawfull armes, or martiall discipline: . . . . . 1Tamb 4.1.65 Souldn
My discipline of armes and Chivalrie, ... 1Tamb 5.1.175 Tamb
DISCIPULUS
and I will make thee go, like Qui mihi discipulus. . . F 355 1.4.13 P Wagner
thou serve me, and Ile make thee go like Qui mihi discipulus? F App p.229 14 P Wagner
DISCLOSD
By whom disclosd, she in the high woods tooke, . . . Ovid's Elegies 3.12.19
DISCLOSE
Doe shame her worst, I will disclose my griefe:-- . . Dido 3.4.28 Dido
If thou givest kisses, I shall all disclose, . . . Ovid's Elegies 1.4.39
DISCLOSING
Disclosing Phoebus furie in this sort: . . . . . Lucan, First Booke 676
DISCOLOURED (See also DISCOULOUR'D)
The wals were of discoloured Jasper stone, . . . Hero and Leander 1.136
DISCOMFITED
Discomfited is all the Christian hoste, ... 2Tamb 2.3.1 Sgsmnd
DISCOMFORT
Sufficient to discomfort and confound/The trustlesse force of 2Tamb 2.2.61 Orcan
Whose army shall discomfort all your foes, ... P 579 11.44 Pleshe
DISCOMFORTED
that the Queene all discontented and discomforted, is gone, Edw 4.3.30 P Spencr
DISCONSOLATE
With ceaselesse and disconsolate conceits, . . . 1Tamb 3.2.14 Zenoc
DISCONTENT
Wounded with shame, and kill'd with discontent, . . 2Tamb 4.1.94 Tamb
Wherfore is Guy of Warwicke discontent? . . . . . Edw 1.2.10 Mortmr
To live in greefe and balefull discontent, ... Edw 1.2.48 Queene
Newes of dishonor lord, and discontent, ... Edw 3.1.59 Queene
Why in thy glasse doest looke being discontent? . . Ovid's Elegies 1.14.36
Shall discontent run into regions farre; . . . . . Hero and Leander 1.478
DISCONTENTED
that the Queene all discontented and discomforted, is gone, Edw 4.3.30 P Spencr
DISCONTINUE
But time will discontinue her content, ... Dido 3.3.78 Iarbus
DISCORDANT
Why letst discordant hands to armour fall? . . . Ovid's Elegies 3.7.48
DISCOULOUR'D
did looke/Dead, and discoulour'd; th'other leane and thinne. Lucan, First Booke 628
DISCOURAGE
We may discourage all the pagan troope, ... 2Tamb 2.1.25 Fredrk
Are greatest to discourage all our drifts, ... 2Tamb 5.2.45 Callap
and you must not discourage/Your friends that are so forward in Edw 4.2.69 Queene
DISCOURSE
May I entreate thee to discourse at large, . . . Dido 2.1.106 Dido
And interchangeably discourse their thoughts, . . . Dido 3.2.93 Juno
And when you looke for amorous discourse, ... 1Tamb 3.2.44 Agidas
To make discourse of some sweet accidents/Have chanc'd thy 1Tamb 5.1.424 Arabia
Spending my life in sweet discourse of love. . . . 2Tamb 4.2.45 Therid
No such discourse is pleasant in mine eares, . . . 2Tamb 4.2.46 Olymp
Of these garboiles, whence springs [a long] <along> discourse, Lucan, First Booke 68
the night (that might be better spent)/In vaine discourse, Hero and Leander 1.356
DISCOURSING
And as I like your discoursing, ile have you. . . . Edw 1.1.32 Gavstn
DISCOURSIVE
To dull the ayre with my discoursive moane. . . . Dido 1.1.248 Aeneas
DISCOVER
Goes to discover countries yet unknowne. . . . . Edw 5.6.66 Mortmr
his parentage, would needs discover/The way to new Elisium: Hero and Leander 1.410
DISCOVERED
East India and the late discovered Isles, ... 1Tamb 1.1.166 Ortyg
we have discovered the enemie/Ready to chardge you with a 1Tamb 2.3.49 1Msngr
That never sea-man yet discovered: . . . . . 2Tamb 1.1.71 Orcan
DISCOVERS
Puttock hovers/Around the aire, the Cadesse raine discovers, Ovid's Elegies 2.6.34
The light of hidden fire it selfe discovers, . . . Hero and Leander 2.133
DISCOV'RD
Had not my Doves discov'rd thy entent: . . . . Dido 3.2.33 Venus

DISCRETION			
thy desert we make thee Governor,/Use them at thy discretion.	Jew	5.2.11	Calym
Arbitrament; and Barabas/At his discretion may dispose of both:	Jew	5.2.54	Barab
DISDAINDE			
To yeeld their love to more then one disdainde. . .	Ovid's Elegies		1.8.40
DISDAINE (See also DISTAIN, S'DAINST)			
What shall I doe thus wronged with disdaine?	Dido	3.3.69	Iarbus
As made disdaine to flye to fancies lap:	Dido	3.4.56	Dido
Whose foming galle with rage and high disdaine, . .	1Tamb	1.1.63	Mycet
Lie here ye weedes that I disdaine to weare, . . .	1Tamb	1.2.41	Tamb
Durst in disdaine of wrong and tyrannie, ...	1Tamb	2.1.55	Ceneus
As it hath chang'd my first conceiv'd disdaine. . .	1Tamb	3.2.12	Zenoc
Disdaine to borrow light of Cynthia, ...	1Tamb	4.2.35	Tamb
And Villanesse to shame, disdaine, and misery: . . .	1Tamb	5.1.269	Bajzth
Oh but I know your Lordship wud disdaine/To marry with the	Jew	2.3.294	Barab
'Tis silver, I disdaine it.	Jew	3.1.13	Curtzn
Yet I disdaine not to doe this for you.	Edw	2.2.79	Lncstr
As with the wings of rancor and disdaine, ...	Edw	5.1.20	Edward
I am Pride; I disdaine to have any parents:	F 664	2.2.113	P Pride
Nay more, the wench did not disdaine a whit, . . .	Ovid's Elegies		3.6.73
DISDAINEFULL			
Fall prostrate on the lowe disdainefull earth. . . .	1Tamb	4.2.13	Tamb
But by her glasse disdainefull pride she learnes, . .	Ovid's Elegies		2.17.9
DISDAINES			
Disdaines Zenocrate to live with me?	1Tamb	1.2.82	Tamb
send for them/To do the work my chamber maid disdaines. .	1Tamb	3.3.188	Anippe
For as a hote prowd horse highly disdaines, ...	Hero and Leander		2.141
DISDAINFUL			
Disdainful Turkesse and unreverend Bosse, ...	1Tamb	3.3.168	Zenoc
DISDAINFULL			
Reflexing them on your disdainfull eies:	1Tamb	5.1.70	Tamb
As much too high for this disdainfull earth. . . .	2Tamb	5.3.122	Tamb
To please the carelesse and disdainfull eies, . . .	Hero and Leander		1.13
DISDAINFULLY			
Steeds, disdainfully/With wanton paces trampling on the ground.	1Tamb	4.1.22	2Msngr
DISDAINING			
Which he disdaining whiskt his sword about, ...	Dido	2.1.253	Aeneas
DISDAYNE			
To give I love, but to be ask't disdayne, ...	Ovid's Elegies		1.10.63
DISGORDGE			
Then come proud Guise and heere disgordge thy brest, .	P 952	19.22	King
DISGRAC'D			
And since this miscreant hath disgrac'd his faith, . .	2Tamb	2.3.36	Orcan
But if he die, your glories are disgrac'd, ...	2Tamb	5.3.15	Therid
For if he die, thy glorie is disgrac'd, ...	2Tamb	5.3.40	Usumc
DISGRACE			
And wrong my deitie with high disgrace:	Dido	3.2.5	Juno
Hath spread his colours to our high disgrace:	1Tamb	4.1.7	Souldn
And all with faintnesse and for foule disgrace, . . .	2Tamb	2.4.5	Tamb
from hence/Ne're shall she grieve me more with her disgrace;	Jew	3.4.29	Barab
I know none els but holdes them in disgrace:	P 764	15.22	Guise
That villain for whom I beare this deep disgrace, . .	P 766	15.24	Guise
The life of thee shall salve this foule disgrace. . .	Edw	2.2.83	Gavstn
To Englands high disgrace, have made this Jig, . . .	Edw	2.2.189	Lncstr
O disgrace to my person:	F 344	1.4.2	P Robin
Thou soone shouldst see me quit my foule disgrace. . .	F1356	4.2.32	Benvol
Sith blacke disgrace hath thus eclipst our fame, . .	F1455	4.3.25	Benvol
Now inward faults thy outward forme disgrace. . . .	Ovid's Elegies		1.10.14
And least her maide should know of this disgrace, . .	Ovid's Elegies		3.6.83
DISGUISDE			
I am disguisde and none knows who I am, ...	P 278	5.5	Anjoy
DISGUISED			
Here in this bush disguised will I stand, ...	Dido	1.1.139	Venus
DISGUIZE			
I will in some disguize goe see the slave, ...	Jew	4.3.67	Barab
DISH			
And leave your venoms in this Tyrants dish.	1Tamb	4.4.22	Bajzth
My good Lord Archbishop, heres a most daintie dish, . .	F1046	3.2.66	Pope
I would request no better meate, then a dish of ripe grapes.	F1573	4.6.16	P Lady
here is a daintie dish was sent me from the Bishop of Millaine.	F App	p.231 5	P Pope
My Lord, this dish was sent me from the Cardinall of Florence.	F App	p.231 9	P Pope
I would desire no better meate then a dish of ripe grapes.	F App	p.242 11	P Duchss
DISHONEST			
Dishonest love my wearied brest forsake, ...	Ovid's Elegies		3.10.2
DISHONOR			
Let the dishonor of the paines I feele, ...	2Tamb	2.3.5	Sgsmnd
You doo dishonor to his majesty, ...	2Tamb	4.1.20	Calyph
Thou doost dishonor manhood, and thy house.	2Tamb	4.1.32	Celeb
Whose drift is onely to dishonor thee.	2Tamb	4.2.7	Olymp
Fie Mortimer, dishonor not thy selfe, ...	Edw	1.4.244	Lncstr
Your lordship doth dishonor to your selfe, ...	Edw	2.6.8	James
Newes of dishonor lord, and discontent, ...	Edw	3.1.59	Queene
Your lives and my dishonor they pursue, ...	Edw	4.7.23	Edward
DISHONORD			
That hath dishonord her and Carthage both?	Dido	5.1.280	Iarbus
DISHONOUR			
Shame and dishonour to a souldiers name, ...	Edw	2.5.12	Mortmr
I heere and there go witty with dishonour.	Ovid's Elegies		3.7.8
DISHONOURED			
Whether he have dishonoured me or no.	P 769	15.27	Guise
DISINHERITE			
Ile disinherite him and all the rest:	P 524	9.43	QnMoth
DISJOIN'D			
[Seaborderers] <Seaborders>, disjoin'd by Neptunes might:	Hero and Leander		1.3

DISJOYNE
Why is it then displeasure should disjoyne, Dido 3.2.30 Juno
DISLIKE
Those that dislike what Dido gives in charge, Dido 4.4.71 Dido
Or loving, doth dislike of something done. Jew 3.4.12 Barab
DISLODGE
Gave up their voyces to dislodge the Campe, Dido 2.1.134 Aeneas
Intending to dislodge my campe with speed. P 869 17.64 Guise
DISLOYALTYE
Not to suspect disloyaltye in thee, P 975 19.45 King
DISMAIDE
that the Souldan is/No more dismaide with tidings of his fall, 1Tamb 4.3.31 Souldn
and the victories/Wherewith he hath so sore dismaide the world, 2Tamb 5.2.44 Callap
DISMAIES
Dismaies their mindes before they come to proove/The wounding 2Tamb 1.3.86 Zenoc
DISMALL
piller led'st/The sonnes of Israel through the dismall shades, Jew 2.1.13 Barab
And dismall Prophesies were spread abroad: Lucan, First Booke 562
Mules loth'd issue)/To be cut forth and cast in dismall fiers: Lucan, First Booke 590
DISMAY
much like so many suns/That halfe dismay the majesty of heaven: 2Tamb 4.1.3 Amyras
Whose shyning Turrets shal dismay the heavens, 2Tamb 4.3.112 Tamb
What faintnesse should dismay our courages, 2Tamb 5.1.21 Govnr
Which onely will dismay the enemy. 2Tamb 5.3.112 Usumc
DISMEMBER
Least cruell Scythians should dismember him. 2Tamb 3.4.37 Olymp
As he intended to dismember me. F1415 4.2.91 Faust
DISMEMBRED
Whose cursed fate hath so dismembred it, 2Tamb 3.1.13 Callap
or else you are blowne up, you are dismembred Rafe, keepe out, F App p.233 11 P Robin
DISMISSE
Dismisse thy campe or else by our Edict, P 863 17.58 King
DISMIST
Natolia hath dismist the greatest part/Of all his armie, pitcht 2Tamb 2.1.16 Fredrk
DISMOUNT
Dismount the Cannon of the adverse part, 2Tamb 3.2.81 Tamb
DISOBEDIENCE
For disobedience to my soveraigne Lord, F1744 5.1.71 Mephst
DISOLVE
day, and ful of strife/Disolve the engins of the broken world. Lucan, First Booke 80
DISORDERED
That live confounded in disordered troopes, 1Tamb 2.2.60 Meandr
DISPAIRE
Turn'd to dispaire, would break my wretched breast, 2Tamb 2.4.64 Zenoc
Dispaire doth drive distrust unto my thoughts, F App p.240 123 Faust
making men/Dispaire of day; as did Thiestes towne/(Mycenae), Lucan, First Booke 541
DISPARADGEMENT
And be reveng'd for her disparadgement. 1Tamb 4.1.72 Souldn
DISPARAGE
My lord, you may not thus disparage us, Edw 1.4.32 Lncstr
DISPATCH (See also DESPATCH)
dispatch her while she is fat, for if she live but a while 1Tamb 4.4.48 P Tamb
I will dispatch chiefe of my army hence/To faire Natolia, and 2Tamb 1.1.161 Orcan
Mother dispatch me, or Ile kil my selfe, 2Tamb 3.4.26 Sonne
goe/And bid the Merchants and my men dispatch/And come ashore, Jew 1.1.100 Barab
Ile dispatch him with his brother presently, P 651 12.64 QnMoth
With all the hast we can dispatch him hence. Edw 3.1.83 Edward
Are laid before me to dispatch my selfe: F 574 2.2.23 Faust
Dispatch it soone, F 902 3.1.124 Faust
Fly hence, dispatch my charge immediatly. F1416 4.2.92 Faust
See where he comes, dispatch, and kill the slave. F1423 4.2.99 2Soldr
DISPATCH'D
Speake, shall he presently be dispatch'd and die? Edw 5.2.44 Mortmr
DISPATCHE
O spare me, or dispatche me in a trice. Edw 5.5.111 Edward
DISPATCHED
Ile see him presently dispatched away. Edw 1.4.90 Mortmr
DISPATCHT
Have desperatly dispatcht their slavish lives: 1Tamb 5.1.472 Tamb
Take them away Theridamas, see them dispatcht. 2Tamb 5.1.134 Tamb
I let the Admirall be first dispatcht. P 283 5.10 Retes
DISPEARST
The Duke is slaine and all his power dispearst, P 787 16.1 Navrre
DISPENC'D
Will never be dispenc'd with til our deaths. 1Tamb 5.1.17 Govnr
DISPENSATION
A pension and a dispensation too: P 120 2.63 Guise
DISPENSIVE
tis superstition/To stand so strictly on dispensive faith: 2Tamb 2.1.50 Fredrk
DISPERSE (See also DISPEARST)
And disperse themselves throughout the Realme of France, P 507 9.26 QnMoth
DISPERST
Disperst them all amongst the wrackfull Rockes: Dido 1.2.29 Cloan
And on her Turret-bearing head disperst, Lucan, First Booke 190
DISPIGHT
I did it onely in dispight of thee Paris ms24,p391 Guise
DISPISED
your investion so neere/The residence of your dispised brother, 1Tamb 1.1.181 Ortyg
DISPLACING
Displacing me; and of thy house they meane/To make a Nunnery, Jew 1.2.255 Abigal
DISPLAID
pitch'd before the gates/And gentle flags of amitie displaid. 1Tamb 4.2.112 Therid
DISPLAIDE
Eagles alike displaide, darts answering darts. Lucan, First Booke 7

DISPLAIE			
Brother displaie my ensignes in the field,	Edw	1.1.136	Edward
DISPLAST			
Like one start up your haire tost and displast,	Ovid's Elegies		3.13.33
DISPLAY			
in Asia, or display/His vagrant Ensigne in the Persean fields,	1Tamb	1.1.44	Meandr
And in your shields display your rancorous minds?	Edw	2.2.33	Edward
A traitors, will they still display their pride?	Edw	3.1.172	Spencr
yesterday/There where the porch doth Danaus fact display.	Ovid's Elegies		2.2.4
Heere I display my lewd and loose behaviour.	Ovid's Elegies		2.4.4
No intercepted lines thy deedes display,	Ovid's Elegies		2.5.5
And now begins Leander to display/Loves holy fire, with words,	Hero and Leander		1.192
DISPLAYD			
The crooked Barque hath her swift sailes displayd.	Ovid's Elegies		2.11.24
And [them] <then> like Mars and Ericine displayd,	Hero and Leander		2.305
And her all naked to his sight displayd.	Hero and Leander		2.324
DISPLAYED			
Shew large wayes with their garments there displayed.	Ovid's Elegies		3.12.24
DISPLAYES			
There Junoes bird displayes his gorgious feather,	Ovid's Elegies		2.6.55
DISPLEAS'D			
to unfould/What you intend, great Jove is now displeas'd,	Lucan, First Booke		631
Wherewith as one displeas'd, away she trips.	Hero and Leander		2.4
To slake his anger, if he were displeas'd,	Hero and Leander		2.49
Imagining, that Ganimed displeas'd,	Hero and Leander		2.157
DISPLEASD			
That crosse me thus, shall know I am displeasd.	Edw	1.1.79	Edward
His countenance bewraies he is displeasd.	Edw	1.2.34	Lncstr
DISPLEASDE			
They were to blame that said I was displeasde,	P 969	19.39	King
DISPLEASED			
And shadow his displeased countenance,	1Tamb	5.1.58	2Virgn
DISPLEASES			
yett you putt in that displeases him | And fill up his rome	Paris	ms 4,p390	P Souldr
DISPLEASETH			
yet you put in that which displeaseth him, and so forestall his	P 809	17.4	P Souldr
DISPLEASURE			
Why is it then displeasure should disjoyne,	Dido	3.2.30	Juno
And searching farther for the gods displeasure,	Lucan, First Booke		616
DISPLEASURES			
(Which of your whole displeasures should be most)/Hath seem'd	1Tamb	3.2.7	Agidas
DISPORTES			
And like disportes, such as doe fit the Court?	P 629	12.42	King
DISPOSDE			
All fellowes now, disposde alike to sporte,	Dido	3.3.5	Dido
His highnes is disposde to be alone.	Edw	2.2.135	Guard
DISPOSE			
And order all things at your high dispose,	Dido	5.1.303	Dido
And Ile dispose them as it likes me best,	2Tamb	4.1.166	Tamb
Arbitrament; and Barabas/At his discretion may dispose of both:	Jew	5.2.54	Barab
DISPOSED			
Onelie disposed to martiall Stratagems?	1Tamb	3.2.41	Agidas
So shall your brother be disposed of.	Edw	4.6.37	Mortmr
into matters, as other men, if they were disposed to talke.	F 741	2.3.20	P Robin
DISPOSITION			
Argues thy noble minde and disposition:	Edw	3.1.48	Edward
DISPOSITIONS			
heavens, that I might knowe their motions and dispositions].	F 551.6	2.1.169A	P Faust
<examine> them of their <several> names and dispositions.	F 662	2.2.111	P Belzeb
DISPOSSESSE			
To dispossesse me of this Diadem:	1Tamb	2.7.60	Tamb
policy for Barabas/To dispossesse himselfe of such a place?	Jew	5.2.66	Barab
DISPOSSEST			
Because the Pryor <Governor> <Sire> dispossest thee once,/And	Jew	3.3.43	Abigal
DISPRED			
And on thy thre-shold let me lie dispred,	Ovid's Elegies		2.19.21
DISPUTE			
[whose sweete delight's] dispute/In th'heavenly matters of	F 18	Prol.18	1Chor
Excelling all, <and sweetly can dispute>	F 18	(HC256)B	1Chor
Is to dispute well Logickes chiefest end?	F 36	1.1.8	Faust
Come Mephostophilis let us dispute againe,	F 584	2.2.33	Faust
DISPUTED			
Unlesse I be deceiv'd disputed once.	Dido	3.1.147	Cloan
DISPUTES			
Excelling all, <whose sweete delight disputes>	F 18	(HC256)A	1Chor
DISPUTING			
What, sleeping, eating, walking and disputing?	F 528	2.1.140	Faust
DISQUIET			
Disquiet Seas lay downe your swelling lookes,	Dido	1.1.122	Venus
DISSEMBLE (See also DESEMBLE)			
That I dissemble not, trie it on me.	2Tamb	4.2.76	Olymp
Thus father shall I much dissemble.	Jew	1.2.289	Abigal
As good dissemble that thou never mean'st/As first meane truth,	Jew	1.2.290	Barab
thou never mean'st/As first meane truth, and then dissemble it,	Jew	1.2.291	Barab
Dissemble, sweare, protest, vow to love him,	Jew	2.3.229	Barab
My bosome [inmate] <inmates> <intimates>, but I must dissemble.	Jew	4.1.47	Barab
The choyse is hard, I must dissemble.	P 865	17.60	Guise
My lord, dissemble with her, speake her faire.	Edw	2.2.229	Gavstn
Dissemble or thou diest, for Mortimer/And Isabell doe kisse	Edw	4.6.12	Kent
Ah they do dissemble.	Edw	5.2.86	Kent
What meanes thou to dissemble with me thus?	Edw	5.5.80	Edward
Dissemble so, as lov'd he may be thought,	Ovid's Elegies		1.8.71
I thinke sheele doe, but deepely can dissemble.	Ovid's Elegies		2.4.16

DISSEMBLE (cont.)			
But that thou wouldst dissemble when tis paste. . .	Ovid's Elegies	3.13.4	
DISSEMBLED			
Finely dissembled, do so still sweet Queene. . . .	Edw	5.2.74	Mortmr
Love deepely grounded, hardly is dissembled. . . .	Hero and Leander	1.184	
DISSEMBLING			
O cursed hagge and false dissembling wretch! . . .	Dido	5.1.216	Dido
And shake off smooth dissembling flatterers: . . .	Edw	3.1.169	Herald
If blame, dissembling of my fault thou fearest. . .	Ovid's Elegies	2.7.8	
With privy signes, and talke dissembling truths? . .	Ovid's Elegies	3.10.24	
DISSERERE			
Bene disserere est finis logices.	F 35	1.1.7	Faust
DISSEVER			
That on the sudden shall dissever it, ...	Jew	5.5.29	Barab
DISSEVERED			
Thy streetes strowed with dissevered jointes of men, .	1Tamb	5.1.322	Zenoc
Until my soule dissevered from this flesh, . . .	2Tamb	4.3.131	Tamb
DISSOLUTION			
Even till the dissolution of the world, ...	2Tamb	3.5.82	Tamb
A dissolution of the slavish Bands/Wherein the Turke hath	Jew	5.2.77	Barab
DISSOLV'D			
Eternall heaven sooner be dissolv'd, ...	1Tamb	3.2.18	Agidas
That may endure till heaven be dissolv'd, ...	2Tamb	3.2.7	Tamb
Their soules are soone dissolv'd in elements, . . .	F1970	5.2.174	Faust
Now light had quite dissolv'd the mysty [night] <might>, .	Lucan, First Booke	263	
DISSOLVE (See also DESOLVE, DISOLVE)			
Ile make the Clowdes dissolve their watrie workes, . .	Dido	3.2.90	Juno
And sooner let the fiery Element/Dissolve, and make your .	2Tamb	2.4.59	Zenoc
I'le fetch thee fire to dissolve it streight. . . .	F 452	2.1.64	Mephst
That Nature shall dissolve this earthly bowre. . . .	Ovid's Elegies	1.15.24	
DISSOLVED			
So honour heaven til heaven dissolved be, ...	2Tamb	5.3.26	Techel
DISSOLVES			
And to be short <conclude>, when all the world dissolves,	F 513	2.1.125	Mephst
DISSWADE			
That durst disswade me from thy Lucifer, ...	F1754	5.1.81	Faust
Those <These> thoughts that do disswade me from my vow, .	F1764	5.1.91	Faust
DISTAFFE			
And the fates distaffe emptie stood to thee, . . .	Ovid's Elegies	2.6.46	
DISTAIN			
Thence rise the tears that so distain my cheeks, . .	1Tamb	3.2.64	Zenoc
DISTAIND			
Carelesse, farewell, with my falt not distaind. . .	Ovid's Elegies	1.6.72	
DISTAINED			
Can never wash from thy distained browes.	2Tamb	4.1.110	Tamb
DISTANCE			
measure the height/And distance of the castle from the trench,	2Tamb	3.3.51	Techel
DISTANT			
Being distant lesse than ful a hundred leagues, . .	2Tamb	5.3.133	Tamb
DISTEMPER			
What is it dares distemper Tamburlain?	2Tamb	5.1.219	Techel
DISTEMPER'D			
Nor quiet enter my distemper'd thoughts, ...	Jew	2.1.18	Barab
DISTEMPERED			
And thinke we prattle with distempered spirits: . .	1Tamb	1.2.62	Tamb
But stay, I feele my selfe distempered sudainly. . .	2Tamb	5.1.218	Tamb
My mindes distempered, and my bodies numde, . . .	Edw	5.5.64	Edward
DISTILD			
Pierian deawe to Poets is distild.	Ovid's Elegies	3.8.26	
DISTILL			
Horned Bacchus graver furie doth distill, ...	Ovid's Elegies	3.14.17	
DISTILLED			
which a cunning Alcumist/Distilled from the purest Balsamum,	2Tamb	4.2.60	Olymp
DISTILLING			
And let these teares distilling from mine eyes, . .	Edw	5.6.101	King
A little boy druncke teate-distilling showers. . . .	Ovid's Elegies	3.9.22	
DISTINGUISH			
And therefore ne're distinguish of the wrong. . . .	Jew	1.2.151	Barab
DISTINIE			
More than Cymerian Stix or Distinie.	1Tamb	5.1.234	Bajzth
DISTRACT			
Then with their feare, and danger al distract, . . .	Lucan, First Booke	487	
Was divers waies distract with love, and shame. . .	Ovid's Elegies	3.9.28	
DISTRESSE			
And plaine to him the summe of your distresse. . . .	Dido	1.2.2	Illion
Since Carthage knowes to entertaine distresse. . . .	Dido	1.2.33	Iarbus
In feare and feeling of the like distresse, ...	1Tamb	5.1.361	Zenoc
That Tamburlaine may pitie our distresse, ...	2Tamb	5.1.27	1Citzn
That thus have dealt with me in my distresse. . . .	Jew	1.2.168	Barab
Why pine not I, and dye in this distresse?	Jew	1.2.173	Barab
And knowing me impatient in distresse/Thinke me so mad as I	Jew	1.2.262	Barab
Wilt thou forsake mee too in my distresse, ...	Jew	1.2.358	Barab
For as a friend not knowne, but in distresse, . . .	Jew	5.2.72	Barab
For happily I shall be in distresse, ...	Jew	5.4.6	Govnr
That Englands Queene, and nobles in distresse, . . .	Edw	4.2.79	Mortmr
a king, thy hart/Pierced deeply with sence of my distresse,	Edw	4.7.10	Edward
DISTRESSED			
As poore distressed miserie may pleade:	Dido	1.2.6	Illion
Ah Shepheard, pity my distressed plight, ...	1Tamb	1.2.7	Zenoc
Pitty the state of a distressed Maid.	Jew	1.2.315	Abigal
O miserable and distressed Queene!	Edw	1.4.170	Queene
To this distressed Queene his sister heere, ...	Edw	4.2.63	SrJohn
That waites upon my poore distressed soule, . . .	Edw	5.3.38	Edward

DISTRESSED (cont.)
'Tis thou hast damn'd distressed Faustus soule. . . F 628 2.2.77 Faust
Helpe <seeke> to save distressed Faustus soule. . . F 635 2.2.84 Faust
I feele thy words to comfort my distressed soule, . . F1735 5.1.62 Faust
DISTREST
Distrest Olympia, whose weeping eies/Since thy arrivall here 2Tamb 4.2.1 Olymp
Never so cheereles, nor so farre distrest. . . . . Edw 4.2.14 Queene
DISTRUST
Despaire doth drive distrust into my thoughts. . . . F1480 4.4.24 Faust
Dispaire doth drive distrust unto my thoughts, . . . F App p.240 123 Faust
DISTURBE
What is the reason you disturbe the Duke? . . . . . F1592 4.6.35 Servnt
DISTURBER
Thou proud disturber of thy countries peace, ... Edw 2.5.9 Mortmr
DISTURBERS
these our warres/Against the proud disturbers of the faith, P 700 14.3 Navrre
And proud disturbers of the Churches peace. . . . . F 956 3.1.178 Faust
What rude disturbers have we at the gate? . . . . . F1588 4.6.31 Duke
DISTURBETH
Cursed be he that disturbeth our holy Dirge. F1083 3.2.103 1Frier
Cursed be he that disturbeth our holy Dirge. . . . . F App p.232 37 Frier
DISWADE (See also DISSWADE)
And so am I my lord, diswade the Queene. . . . . . Edw 1.4.215 Lncstr
O Lancaster, let him diswade the king, ... Edw 1.4.216 Queene
DITCH
And secret issuings to defend the ditch. . . . . . 2Tamb 3.2.74 Tamb
Come dragge him away and throw him in a ditch. . . . P 345 5.72 Guise
Then throw him into the ditch. . . . . P 490 9.9 P 1Atndt
Sirs, take him away and throw him in some ditch. . . . P 499 9.18 Guise
that you may ride him o're hedge and ditch, and spare him not; F1468 4.4.12 P Faust
not into the water; o're hedge and ditch, or where thou wilt, F1473 4.4.17 P Faust
I'le out-run him, and cast this leg into some ditch or other. F1495 4.4.39 P HrsCsr
such a horse, as would run over hedge and ditch, and never tyre, F1538 4.5.34 P HrsCsr
the water, ride him over hedge or ditch, or where thou wilt, F App p.239 112 P Faust
DITCHED
No little ditched townes, no lowlie walles, ... Ovid's Elegies 2.12.7
DITCHER
The ditcher no markes on the ground did leave. . . . . Ovid's Elegies 3.7.42
DITCHES
The ditches must be deepe, the Counterscarps/Narrow and steepe, 2Tamb 3.2.68 Tamb
It must have privy ditches, countermines, ... 2Tamb 3.2.73 Tamb
Filling the ditches with the walles wide breach, . . . 2Tamb 3.3.7 Techel
DITTY
While without shame thou singst thy lewdnesse ditty. . Ovid's Elegies 3.1.22
DIVE (See also DYV'D)
And dive into blacke tempests treasurie, ... Dido 4.1.5 Iarbus
And dive into her heart by coloured lookes. . . . . Dido 4.2.32 Iarbus
Dive to the bottome of Avernus poole, ... 1Tamb 4.4.18 Bajzth
And Angels dive into the pooles of hell. . . . . . 2Tamb 5.3.33 Usumc
And dive into the water, and there prie/Upon his brest, his Hero and Leander 2.188
DIVEL
<talke of the divel, and nothing else: come away>. . . F 660 (HC263)A P Lucifr
<Farewel Faustus, and thinke on the divel>. . . . . F 720 (HC264)A Lucifr
but the Divel threatned to teare me in peeces if I nam'd God: F1864 5.2.68 P Faust
he would give his soule to the Divel for a shoulder of mutton, F App p.229 8 P Wagner
to the Divel for a shoulder of mutton though twere blood rawe? F App p.229 10 P Clown
Fall too, and the divel choake you and you spare. . . F App p.231 2 P Faust
for conjuring that ere was invented by any brimstone divel. F App p.233 20 P Robin
Ile feede thy divel with horse-bread as long as he lives, F App p.234 30 P Rafe
good divel forgive me now, and Ile never rob thy Library more. F App p.235 30 P Robin
DIVELISH
What means this divelish shepheard to aspire/With such a . 1Tamb 2.6.1 Cosroe
And in detesting such a divelish Thiefe, ... 1Tamb 2.6.20 Ortyg
DIVELL
So, so, was never Divell thus blest before. . . . . F 974 3.1.196 Mephst
Fall to, the Divell choke you an you spare. . . . . F1039 3.2.59 Faust
drunke over night, the Divell cannot hurt him in the morning: F1201 4.1.47 P Benvol
He must needs goe that the Divell drives. . . . . . F1419 4.2.95 Fredrk
Doe not persever in it like a Divell; . . . . . F1711 5.1.38 OldMan
To over-reach the Divell, but all in vaine; . . . . F1811 5.2.15 Mephst
<O> my God, I would weepe, but the Divell drawes in my teares. F1851 5.2.55 P Faust
Hell, or the Divell, had had no power on thee. . . . F1902 5.2.106 GdAngl
warning whensoever or wheresoever the divell shall fetch thee. F App p.230 37 P Wagner
hee has kild the divell, so I should be cald kill divell all F App p.230 48 P Clown
divell, so I should be cald kill divell all the parish over. F App p.230 48 P Clown
there was a hee divell and a shee divell, Ile tell you how you F App p.230 52 P Clown
DIVELLISH
For falling to a divellish exercise, ... F 23 Prol.23 1Chor
DIVEL'S
The Divel's dead, the Furies now may laugh. . . . . F1369 4.2.45 Benvol
Zounds the Divel's alive agen. . . . . F1391 4.2.67 P Benvol
DIVELS
I thinke it was the divels revelling night, ... Dido 4.1.9 Achat
I charge thee on my blessing that thou leave/These divels, and Jew 1.2.347 Barab
Ile fetch thee a wife in the divels name>. . . . . F 531 (HC261)A P Mephst
an your Divels come not away quickly, you shall have me asleepe F1241 4.1.87 P Benvol
to stand gaping after the divels Governor, and can see nothing. F1244 4.1.90 P Benvol
zounds hee'l raise up a kennell of Divels I thinke anon: . F1305 4.1.151 P Benvol
two divels presently to fetch thee away Baliol and Belcher. F App p.230 43 P Wagner
they were never so knocht since they were divels, say I should F App p.230 46 P Clown
all hee divels has hornes, and all shee divels has clifts and F App p.230 53 P Clown
has hornes, and all shee divels has clifts and cloven feete. F App p.230 54 P Clown
upon our handes, and then to our conjuring in the divels name. F App p.234 34 P Robin

DIVERS			
having in their company divers of your nation, and others,	Edw	4.3.33	P Spencr
The youthfull sort to divers pastimes runne. . . .	Ovid's Elegies	2.5.22	
Was divers waies distract with love, and shame. . .	Ovid's Elegies	3.9.28	
DIVERSE			
And writings did from diverse places frame, . . .	Ovid's Elegies	2.18.28	
DIVIDE (See also DEVIDE)			
Which forc'd their hands divide united hearts: . . .	Jew	3.2.35	Govnr
There, Carpenters, divide that gold amongst you: . .	Jew	5.5.5	Barab
DIVIDED			
and now sirs, having divided him, what shall the body doe?	F1389	4.2.65	P Mrtino
the yeare is divided into two circles over the whole world, so	F1581	4.6.24	P Faust
the yeere is divided into twoo circles over the whole worlde,	F App	p.242 19	P Faust
would, I cannot him cashiere/Before I be divided from my geere.	Ovid's Elegies	1.6.36	
DIVIDES			
she chides/And with long charmes the solide earth divides.	Ovid's Elegies	1.8.18	
DIVINE (See also DEVINE)			
And my divine descent from sceptred Jove:	Dido	1.1.219	Aeneas
Like his desire, lift upwards and divine, ...	1Tamb	2.1.8	Menaph
Some powers divine, or els infernall, mixt/Their angry seeds at	1Tamb	2.6.9	Meandr
To let them see (divine Zenocrate)/I glorie in the curses of my	1Tamb	4.4.28	Tamb
For whome the Powers divine have made the world, . .	1Tamb	5.1.76	1Virgn
Ah faire Zenocrate, divine Zenocrate, ...	1Tamb	5.1.135	Tamb
Then sit thou downe divine Zenocrate, ...	1Tamb	5.1.506	Tamb
no more, but deck the heavens/To entertaine divine Zenocrate.	2Tamb	2.4.21	Tamb
silver runs through Paradice/To entertaine divine Zenocrate.	2Tamb	2.4.25	Tamb
voices and their instruments/To entertaine divine Zenocrate.	2Tamb	2.4.29	Tamb
out his hand in highest majesty/To entertaine divine Zenocrate.	2Tamb	2.4.33	Tamb
Behold me here divine Zenocrate, ...	2Tamb	2.4.111	Tamb
Sweet picture of divine Zenocrate, ...	2Tamb	3.2.27	Tamb
Were not subdew'd with valour more divine, ...	2Tamb	4.3.15	Tamb
But of a substance more divine and pure, ...	2Tamb	5.3.88	Phsitn
I doe not doubt by your divine precepts/And mine owne industry,	Jew	1.2.334	Abigal
Having commenc'd, be a Divine in shew, ...	F 31	1.1.3	Faust
And reason <argue> of divine Astrology.	F 585	2.2.34	Faust
the sacred priests/That with divine lustration purg'd the wals,	Lucan, First Booke	593	
These gifts are meete to please the powers divine. . .	Ovid's Elegies	3.9.48	
And by thy face to me a powre divine, ...	Ovid's Elegies	3.10.47	
(Whose tragedie divine Musaeus soong)/Dwelt at Abidus; since	Hero and Leander	1.52	
Base in respect of thee, divine and pure, ...	Hero and Leander	1.219	
DIVINES			
tell us of this before, that Divines might have prayd for thee?	F1863	5.2.67	P 1Schol
DIVINING			
The number two no good divining bringes.	Ovid's Elegies	1.12.28	
DIVINITIE			
So much <soone> he profits in Divinitie, ...	F 15	Prol.15	1Chor
When all is done, Divinitie is best:	F 64	1.1.36	Faust
What will be, shall be; Divinitie adeiw.	F 75	1.1.47	Faust
[Divinitie is basest of the three], ...	F 135	1.1.107A	Faust
me <both> body and soule, if I once gave eare to Divinitie:	F1866	5.2.70	P Faust
Hadst thou affected sweet divinitie, ...	F1901	5.2.105	GdAngl
DIVISION (See also DEVISION)			
That kisse againe; she runs division of my lips. . .	Jew	4.2.127	P Ithimr
DIVORCE (See DEVORCE)			
DIXI			
And ipse dixi with this quidditie, ...	P 394	7.34	Guise
DO (See also DO'T, DOE, DOO, DOOST, DOOTE, DOST)			
I am (my Lord), for so you do import.	1Tamb	1.2.33	Zenoc
These Lords (perhaps) do scorne our estimates, . . .	1Tamb	1.2.61	Tamb
His looks do menace heaven and dare the Gods, . . .	1Tamb	1.2.157	Therid
Forsake thy king and do but joine with me/And we will triumph	1Tamb	1.2.172	Tamb
heart to be with gladnes pierc'd/To do you honor and securitie.	1Tamb	1.2.251	Therid
His lofty browes in foldes, do figure death, . . .	1Tamb	2.1.21	Menaph
So do I thrice renowmed man at armes, ...	1Tamb	2.5.6	Cosroe
From one that knew not what a King should do, . . .	1Tamb	2.5.22	Cosroe
So do we hope to raign in Asia, ...	1Tamb	2.7.38	Usumc
send for them/To do the work my chamber maid disdaines. .	1Tamb	3.3.188	Anippe
What do mine eies behold, my husband dead?	1Tamb	5.1.305	Zabina
Whose chearful looks do cleare the clowdy aire/And cloath it in	2Tamb	1.3.3	Tamb
Phisitions, wil no phisicke do her good?	2Tamb	2.4.38	Tamb
Whose darts do pierce the Center of my soule: . . .	2Tamb	2.4.84	Tamb
Do us such honor and supremacie, ...	2Tamb	3.1.16	Callap
To you? Why, do you thinke me weary of it? . . .	2Tamb	3.3.17	Capt
And should I goe and do nor harme nor good, . . .	2Tamb	4.1.56	Calyph
Hath trode the Meisures, do my souldiers martch, . .	2Tamb	5.1.75	Tamb
Do all thy wurst, nor death, nor Tamburlaine, . . .	2Tamb	5.1.112	Govnr
Your paines do pierce our soules, no hope survives, . .	2Tamb	5.3.166	Celeb
Do the [Turkes] <Turke> weigh so much?	Jew	2.3.98	P Barab
I'le goe alone, dogs, do not hale me thus. . . .	Jew	5.1.19	Barab
Not wel, but do remember such a man.	P 173	3.8	OldQn
Navarre, give me thy hand, I heere do sweare, . . .	P1203	22.65	King
Let me see, thou wouldst do well/To waite at my trencher, and	Edw	1.1.30	Gavstn
Do: these are not men for me, ...	Edw	1.1.50	Gavstn
That Earle of Lancaster do I abhorre.	Edw	1.1.76	Gavstn
My lord, why do you thus incense your peeres, . . .	Edw	1.1.99	Lncstr
I do remember in my fathers dayes, ...	Edw	1.1.109	Kent
Embrace me Gaveston as I do thee:	Edw	1.1.141	Edward
I did no more then I was bound to do, ...	Edw	1.1.182	BshpCv
What should a priest do with so faire a house? . . .	Edw	1.1.206	Gavstn
Then linger not my lord but do it straight. . . .	Edw	1.4.58	Lncstr
They would not stir, were it to do me good: . . .	Edw	1.4.95	Edward
Seeing I must go, do not renew my sorrow.	Edw	1.4.137	Gavstn
Do you not wish that Gaveston were dead?	Edw	1.4.252	Mortmr

DO (cont.)

But nephew, do not play the sophister.	Edw	1.4.255	MortSr
To mend the king, and do our countrie good:	Edw	1.4.257	Mortmr
But how if he do not Nephew?	Edw	1.4.278	MortSr
If it be so, what will not Edward do?	Edw	1.4.325	Edward
Then so am I, and live to do him service,	Edw	1.4.421	Mortmr
a factious lord/Shall hardly do himselfe good, much lesse us,	Edw	2.1.7	Spencr
why do I stay,/Seeing that he talkes thus of my mariage day?	Edw	2.1.68	Neece
What will he do when as he shall be present?	Edw	2.2.48	Mortmr
Warwicke, these words do ill beseeme thy years.	Edw	2.2.94	Kent
Do cosin, and ile beare thee companie.	Edw	2.2.121	Lncstr
Do what they can, weele live in Tinmoth here,	Edw	2.2.221	Edward
Thus do you still suspect me without cause.	Edw	2.2.227	Queene
Why do you not commit him to the tower?	Edw	2.2.234	Gavstn
Penbrooke, what wilt thou do?	Edw	2.5.82	Warwck
Nay, do your pleasures, I know how twill proove.	Edw	2.5.93	Warwck
I do commit this Gaveston to thee,	Edw	2.5.107	Penbrk
And do your message with a majestie.	Edw	3.1.73	Edward
And meerely of our love we do create thee/Earle of Gloster, and	Edw	3.1.145	Edward
Yet ere thou go, see how I do devorce	Edw	3.1.176	Edward
Why do we sound retreat?	Edw	3.1.185	Edward
And do confront and countermaund their king.	Edw	3.1.188	Edward
What rebels, do you shrinke, and sound retreat?	Edw	3.1.200	Edward
Do speedie execution on them all,	Edw	3.1.254	Edward
A boye, our friends do faile us all in Fraunce,	Edw	4.2.1	Queene
Oh my sweet hart, how do I mone thy wrongs,	Edw	4.2.27	Queene
Much happier then your friends in England do.	Edw	4.2.35	Kent
My lord of Gloster, do you heare the newes?	Edw	4.3.4	Edward
Shall do good service to her Majestie,	Edw	4.6.74	Mortmr
Do you betray us and our companie.	Edw	4.7.25	Edward
A faire commission warrants what we do.	Edw	4.7.48	Rice
Why do you lowre unkindly on a king?	Edw	4.7.63	Edward
The gentle heavens have not to do in this.	Edw	4.7.76	Edward
But if proud Mortimer do weare this crowne,	Edw	5.1.43	Edward
Elect, conspire, install, do what you will,	Edw	5.1.88	Edward
And thus, most humbly do we take our leave.	Edw	5.1.124	Trussl
To do your highnes service and devoire,	Edw	5.1.133	Bartly
Feare not my Lord, weele do as you commaund.	Edw	5.2.66	Matrvs
Finely dissembled, do so still sweet Queene.	Edw	5.2.74	Mortmr
Ah they do dissemble.	Edw	5.2.86	Kent
I, do sweete Nephew.	Edw	5.2.96	Kent
But all in vaine, so vainely do I strive,	Edw	5.3.35	Edward
And therefore will I do it cunninglie.	Edw	5.4.5	Mortmr
Well, do it bravely, and be secret.	Edw	5.4.28	Mortmr
That will I quicklie do, farewell my lord.	Edw	5.4.47	Ltborn
The prince I rule, the queene do I commaund,	Edw	5.4.48	Mortmr
I seale, I cancell, I do what I will,	Edw	5.4.51	Mortmr
And so do I, Matrevis:	Edw	5.5.7	Gurney
I know what I must do, get you away,	Edw	5.5.27	Ltborn
Farre is it from my hart to do you harme,	Edw	5.5.47	Ltborn
Could I have rulde thee then, as I do now,	Edw	5.6.96	King
For e're I sleep, I'le try what I can do:	F 192	1.1.164	Faust
I do not doubt but to see you both hang'd the next Sessions.	F 212	1.2.19	P Wagner
Yet let us see <trie> what we can do.	F 228	1.2.35	2Schol
Now Faustus what wouldst thou have me do?	F 263	1.3.35	Mephst
upon me whilst I live/To do what ever Faustus shall command:	F 265	1.3.37	Faust
[makes men] <make them> foolish that do use <trust> them most.	F 408	2.1.20	BdAngl
And tell me, what good will my soule do thy Lord?	F 428	2.1.40	Faust
I so I do <will>; but Mephostophilis,	F 450	2.1.62	Faust
What will not I do to obtaine his soule?	F 462	2.1.74	Mephst
I Faustus, and do greater things then these.	F 476	2.1.88	Mephst
Speake Faustus, do you deliver this as your Deed?	F 501	2.1.113	Mephst
So shalt thou shew thy selfe an obedient servant <Do so>,/And	F 652	2.2.101	Lucifr
And then turning my selfe to a wrought Smocke do what I list.	F 668	2.2.117	P Pride
Thou needst not do that, for my Mistresse hath done it.	F 739	2.3.18	P Dick
Do but speake what thou't have me to do, and I'le do't:	F 745	2.3.24	P Robin
But new exploits do hale him out agen,	F 770	2.3.49	2Chor
Do [match] <watch> the number of the daies contain'd,	F 821	3.1.43	Mephst
That I do long to see the Monuments/And situation of bright	F 828	3.1.50	Faust
two such Cardinals/Ne're serv'd a holy Pope, as we shall do.	F 942	3.1.164	Faust
<to do what I please unseene of any whilst I stay in Rome>.	F 993	(HC266)A	P Faust
Do what thou wilt, thou shalt not be discern'd.	F1005	3.2.25	Mephst
What Lollards do attend our Hollinesse,	F1049	3.2.69	Pope
I, pray do, for Faustus is a dry.	F1052	3.2.72	Faust
Now Faustus, what will you do now?	F1071	3.2.91	P Mephst
I, I, do, do, hold the cup Robin, I feare not your searching;	F1105	3.3.18	P Dick
I, do, do, hold the cup Robin, I feare not your searching; we	F1105	3.3.18	P Dick
If Faustus do it, you are streight resolv'd,	F1298	4.1.144	Faust
What may we do, that we may hide our shames?	F1447	4.3.17	Fredrk
What shall we then do deere Benvolio?	F1451	4.3.21	Mrtino
him o're hedge and ditch, and spare him not; but do you heare?	F1468	4.4.12	P Faust
Alas I am undone, what shall I do?	F1492	4.4.36	P HrsCsr
O Hostisse how do you?	F1515	4.5.11	P Robin
Come sirs, what shall we do now till mine Hostesse comes?	F1520	4.5.16	P Dick
I do thinke my selfe my good Lord, highly recompenced, in that	F1563	4.6.6	P Faust
great bellyed women, do long for things, are rare and dainty.	F1568	4.6.11	P Faust
Madam, I will do more then this for your content.	F1575	4.6.18	P Faust
I do beseech your grace let them come in,	F1605	4.6.48	Faust
Do as thou wilt Faustus, I give thee leave.	F1607	4.6.50	Duke
do not you remember a Horse-courser you sold a horse to?	F1633	4.6.76	P Carter
do you remember you bid he should not ride [him] into the	F1636	4.6.79	P Carter
Yes, I do verie well remember that.	F1638	4.6.81	P Faust
And do you remember nothing of your leg?	F1639	4.6.82	P Carter

DC (cont.)
do you heare sir, did not I pull off one of your legs when you F1655 4.6.98 P HrsCsr
Do you remember sir, how you cosened me and eat up my load of-- F1659 4.6.102 P Carter
Do you remember how you made me weare an Apes-- F1661 4.6.104 P Dick
scab, do you remember how you cosened me with <of> a ho-- F1662 4.6.105 P HrsCsr
do you remember the dogs fa-- F1665 4.6.108 P Robin
And Faustus now will come to do thee right. F1728 5.1.55 Faust
I do repent, and yet I doe despaire, F1740 5.1.67 Faust
I do repent I ere offended him, F1746 5.1.73 Faust
Do it then Faustus <quickly>, with unfained heart, F1751 5.1.78 Mephst
Lest greater dangers <danger> do attend thy drift. F1752 5.1.79 Mephst
Those <These> thoughts that do disswade me from my vow, F1764 5.1.91 Faust
Thus from infernall Dis do we ascend/To view the subjects of F1797 5.2.1 Lucifr
dutie, I do yeeld/My life and lasting service for your love. F1818 5.2.22 Wagner
O what may <shal> we do to save Faustus? F1868 5.2.72 P 2Schol
wel, do you heare sirra? F App p.230 30 P Wagner
have as many english counters, and what should I do with these? F App p.230 34 P Clown
do ye see yonder tall fellow in the round slop, hee has kild F App p.230 47 P Clown
But do you hear? F App p.230 56 P Clown
Come on Mephastophilis, what shall we do? F App p.232 22 P Faust
I can do al these things easily with it: F App p.234 22 P Robin
blacke survey/Great Potentates do kneele with awful feare, F App p.235 35 Mephst
Upon whose altars thousand soules do lie, F App p.235 36 Mephst
I am content to do whatsoever your majesty shall command me. F App p.236 15 P Faust
as we that do succeede, or they that shal hereafter possesse F App p.236 21 P Emper
Do you heare maister Doctor? F App p.237 51 P Knight
Do you heare sir? F App p.239 101 P HrsCsr
O yonder is his snipper snapper, do you heare? F App p.240 138 P HrsCsr
Alas, I am undone, what shall I do: F App p.241 154 P HrsCsr
that great bellied women do long for some dainties or other, F App p.242 5 P Faust
hither, as ye see, how do you like them Madame, be they good? F App p.242 23 P Faust
When I (my light) do or say ought that please thee, Ovid's Elegies 1.4.25
Do not thou so, but throw thy mantle hence, Ovid's Elegies 1.4.49
Entreat thy husband drinke, but do not kisse, Ovid's Elegies 1.4.51
And while he drinkes, to adde more do not misse, Ovid's Elegies 1.4.52
Or if it do, to thee no joy thence spring: Ovid's Elegies 1.4.68
or do the turned hinges sound,/And opening dores with creaking Ovid's Elegies 1.6.49
With much a do my hands I scarsely staide. Ovid's Elegies 1.8.110
What yeares in souldiours Captaines do require, Ovid's Elegies 1.9.5
And treades the deserts snowy heapes [do] <to> cover. Ovid's Elegies 1.9.12
And doth constraind, what you do of good will. Ovid's Elegies 1.10.24
Garments do weare, jewells and gold do wast, Ovid's Elegies 1.10.61
If, what I do, she askes, say hope for night, Ovid's Elegies 1.11.13
The lawier and the client <both do> hate thy view, Ovid's Elegies 1.13.21
Do this and soone thou shalt thy freedome reape. Ovid's Elegies 2.2.40
to thee being cast do happe/Sharpe stripes, she sitteth in the Ovid's Elegies 2.2.61
I knew your speech (what do not lovers see)? Ovid's Elegies 2.5.19
In this sweete good, why hath a third to do? Ovid's Elegies 2.5.32
Which do perchance old age unto them give. Ovid's Elegies 2.6.28
And then things round do ever further pace. Ovid's Elegies 2.9.10
The unjust seas all blewish do appeare. Ovid's Elegies 2.11.12
Do but deserve gifts with this title grav'd. Ovid's Elegies 2.13.26
But tender Damsels do it, though with paine, Ovid's Elegies 2.14.37
Nor do I like the country of my birth. Ovid's Elegies 2.16.38
What should I do with fortune that nere failes me? Ovid's Elegies 2.19.7
Wilt nothing do, why I should wish thy death? Ovid's Elegies 2.19.56
Ere these were seene, I burnt: what will these do? Ovid's Elegies 3.2.33
For others faults, why do I losse receive? Ovid's Elegies 3.3.16
Who may offend, sinnes least; power to do ill, Ovid's Elegies 3.4.9
Great floods the force of it do often prove. Ovid's Elegies 3.5.24
What will my age do, age I cannot shunne, Ovid's Elegies 3.6.17
May spelles and droughs <drugges> do sillie soules such harmes? Ovid's Elegies 3.6.28
Nor do I give thee counsaile to live chaste, Ovid's Elegies 3.13.3
The strumpet with the stranger will not do, Ovid's Elegies 3.13.9
And I shall thinke you chaste, do what you can. Ovid's Elegies 3.13.14
Graunt this, that what you do I may not see, Ovid's Elegies 3.13.35
Rich robes, themselves and others do adorne, Hero and Leander 1.237
Even so for mens impression do we you. Hero and Leander 1.266
Honour is purchac'd by the deedes wee do. Hero and Leander 1.280
As sheap-heards do, her on the ground hee layd, Hero and Leander 1.405
And kist againe, as lovers use to do. Hero and Leander 2.94

DOCKE
The Docke in harbours ships drawne from the flouds, Ovid's Elegies 2.9.21

DOCTOR
Doctor, by these presents doe give both body and soule to F 493 2.1.105 P Faust
I have gotten one of Doctor Faustus conjuring bookes, and now F 723 2.3.2 P Robin
To accomplish what soever the Doctor please. F1183 4.1.29 Mrtino
The Doctor stands prepar'd, by power of Art, F1222 4.1.68 Faust
Well Master Doctor, an your Divels come not away quickly, you F1241 4.1.87 P Benvol
Zounds Doctor, is this your villany? F1293 4.1.139 P Benvol
the Doctor has no skill,/No Art, no cunning, to present these F1294 4.1.140 Faust
Then good Master Doctor, F1308 4.1.154 Emper
And kill that Doctor if he come this way. F1339 4.2.15 Fredrk
Grone you Master Doctor? F1365 4.2.41 Fredrk
O what a cosening Doctor was this? F1484 4.4.28 P HrsCsr
Ho sirra Doctor, you cosoning scab; Maister Doctor awake, and F1488 4.4.32 P HrsCsr
you cosoning scab; Maister Doctor awake, and rise, and give me F1489 4.4.33 P HrsCsr
for your horse is turned to a bottle of Hay,--Maister Doctor. F1491 4.4.35 P HrsCsr
bravest tale how a Conjurer serv'd me; you know Doctor Fauster? F1522 4.5.18 P Carter
Doctor Fauster bad me ride him night and day, and spare him no F1540 4.5.36 P HrsCsr
O brave Doctor. F1546 4.5.42 P All
And has the Doctor but one leg then? F1553 4.5.49 P Dick
and drinke a while, and then we'le go seeke out the Doctor. F1557 4.5.53 P Robin

DOCTOR (cont.)				
Thankes Maister Doctor, for these pleasant sights, nor know I	F1558	4.6.1	P	Duke
True Maister Doctor, and since I finde you so kind I will make	F1570	4.6.13	P	Lady
They all cry out to speake with Doctor Faustus.	F1600	4.6.43		Servnt
With all my heart kind Doctor, please thy selfe,	F1623	4.6.66		Duke
there spake a Doctor indeed, and 'faith Ile drinke a health to	F1626	4.6.69	P	HrsCsr
O horrible, had the Doctor three legs?	F1658	4.6.101	P	All
heare you Maister Doctor, now you have sent away my guesse, I	F1666	4.6.109	P	Hostss
Master Doctor Faustus, since our conference about faire Ladies,	F1681	5.1.8	P	1Schol
therefore Master Doctor, if you will doe us so much <that>	F1684	5.1.11	P	1Schol
Pray heaven the Doctor have escapt the danger.	F1987	5.3.5		1Schol
here I ha stolne one of doctor Faustus conjuring books, and	F App	p.233 1	P	Robin
tell thee, we were for ever made by this doctor Faustus booke?	F App	p.234 2	P	Robin
Maister doctor Faustus, I have heard strange report of thy	F App	p.236 1	P	Emper
Then doctor Faustus, marke what I shall say, As I was sometime	F App	p.236 17	P	Emper
I mary master doctor, now theres a signe of grace in you, when	F App	p.237 44	P	Knight
Go to maister Doctor, let me see them presently.	F App	p.237 50	P	Emper
Do you heare maister Doctor?	F App	p.237 51	P	Knight
Maister Doctor, I heard this Lady while she liv'd had a wart or	F App	p.238 60	P	Emper
Good Maister Doctor, at my intreaty release him, he hath done	F App	p.238 79	P	Emper
Farewel maister Doctor, yet ere you goe, expect from me a	F App	p.239 88	P	Emper
masse see where he is, God save you maister doctor.	F App	p.239 99	P	HrsCsr
what, doost thinke I am a horse-doctor?	F App	p.240 120	P	Faust
Doctor Fustian quoth a, mas Doctor Lopus was never such a	F App	p.240 127	P	HrsCsr
mas Doctor Lopus was never such a Doctor, has given me a	F App	p.240 127	P	HrsCsr
mas Doctor Lopus was never such a Doctor, has given me a	F App	p.240 128	P	HrsCsr
but Ile seeke out my Doctor, and have my fortie dollers againe,	F App	p.240 136	P	HrsCsr
this is he, God save ye maister doctor, maister doctor, maister	F App	p.241 148	P	HrsCsr
save ye maister doctor, maister doctor, maister doctor Fustian,	F App	p.241 148	P	HrsCsr
maister doctor, maister doctor Fustian, fortie dollers, fortie	F App	p.241 149	P	HrsCsr
Beleeve me maister Doctor, this merriment hath much pleased me.	F App	p.242 1	P	Duke
Thankes, good maister doctor.	F App	p.242 7	P	Duchss
Beleeve me master Doctor, this makes me wonder above the rest,	F App	p.242 16	P	Duke
Beleeve me Maister doctor, they be the best grapes that ere I	F App	p.242 25	P	Duchss
Come, maister Doctor follow us, and receive your reward.	F App	p.243 33	P	Duke
Ah Doctor Faustus, that I might prevaile,	F App	p.243 34		OldMan
DOCTORS				
Excepting against Doctors [axioms],	P 393	7.33		Guise
That shortly he was grac'd with Doctors name,	F 17	Prol.17		1Chor
DOCTRINE				
What doctrine call you this? Che sera, sera:	F 74	1.1.46		Faust
DOE				
Doe thou but say their colour pleaseth me.	Dido	1.1.41		Jupitr
What shall I doe to save thee my sweet boy?	Dido	1.1.74		Venus
When as the waves doe threat our Chrystall world,	Dido	1.1.75		Venus
What? doe I see my sonne now come on shoare:	Dido	1.1.134		Venus
Doe thou but smile, and clowdie heaven will cleare,	Dido	1.1.155		Achat
Such honour, stranger, doe I not affect:	Dido	1.1.203		Venus
But of them all scarce seven doe anchor safe,	Dido	1.1.222		Aeneas
Doe trace these Libian deserts all despisde,	Dido	1.1.228		Aeneas
Why, what are you, or wherefore doe you sewe?	Dido	1.2.3		Iarbus
That doe complaine the wounds of thousand waves,	Dido	1.2.8		Illion
I but the barbarous sort doe threat our ships,	Dido	1.2.34		Serg
And scarcely doe agree upon one poynt:	Dido	2.1.109		Dido
Who if that any seeke to doe him hurt,	Dido	2.1.321		Venus
Albeit the Gods doe know no wanton thought/Had ever residence	Dido	3.1.16		Dido
Yet now I doe repent me of his ruth,	Dido	3.2.47		Juno
As these thy protestations doe paint forth,	Dido	3.2.54		Venus
How highly I doe prize this amitie,	Dido	3.2.67		Juno
Why, man of Troy, doe I offend thine eyes?	Dido	3.3.17		Iarbus
I, and outface him to, doe what he can.	Dido	3.3.40		Cupid
What shall I doe thus wronged with disdaine?	Dido	3.3.69		Iarbus
Aeneas no, although his eyes doe pearce.	Dido	3.4.12		Dido
The man that I doe eye where ere I am,	Dido	3.4.18		Dido
Doe shame her worst, I will disclose my griefe:--	Dido	3.4.28		Dido
What more then Delian musicke doe I heare,	Dido	3.4.52		Dido
Anna, against this Troian doe I pray,	Dido	4.2.30		Iarbus
That doe pursue my peace where ere it goes.	Dido	4.2.51		Iarbus
Abourd, abourd, since Fates doe bid abourd,	Dido	4.3.21		Aeneas
See where they come, how might I doe to chide?	Dido	4.4.13		Dido
Shall vulgar pesants storme at what I doe?	Dido	4.4.73		Dido
Doe as I bid thee sister, leade the way,	Dido	4.4.85		Dido
So youle love me, I care not if I doe.	Dido	4.5.17		Cupid
Why doe I thinke of love now I should dye?	Dido	4.5.34		Nurse
Whom doe I see, Joves winged messenger?	Dido	5.1.25		Aeneas
Doe Troians use to quit their Lovers thus?	Dido	5.1.106		Dido
O no, the Gods wey not what Lovers doe,	Dido	5.1.131		Dido
I hope that that which love forbids me doe,	Dido	5.1.170		Dido
fleete, what shall I doe/But dye in furie of this oversight?	Dido	5.1.268		Dido
And mixe her bloud with thine, this shall I doe,	Dido	5.1.326		Anna
You may doe well to kisse it then.	1Tamb	1.1.98		Cosroe
What will he doe supported by a king?	1Tamb	2.1.57		Ceneus
What should we doe but bid them battaile straight,	1Tamb	2.2.18		Meandr
highnesse would let them be fed, it would doe them more good.	1Tamb	4.4.35	P	Therid
Yet musicke woulde doe well to cheare up Zenocrate:	1Tamb	4.4.62	P	Tamb
From whence the issues of my thoughts doe breake:	1Tamb	5.1.274		Bajzth
I doe you honor in the simile,	2Tamb	3.5.69		Tamb
To think our helps will doe him any good.	2Tamb	4.1.21		Calyph
as I doe a naked Lady in a net of golde, and for feare I should	2Tamb	4.1.68	P	Calyph
And what the jealousie of warres must doe.	2Tamb	4.1.104		Tamb
They will talk still my Lord, if you doe not bridle them.	2Tamb	5.1.146	P	Amyras
Ah friends, what shal I doe, I cannot stand,	2Tamb	5.3.51		Tamb
What more may Heaven doe for earthly man/Then thus to powre out	Jew	1.1.107		Barab

DOE (cont.)

Doe so; Farewell Zaareth, farewell Temainte.	Jew	1.1.176	Barab
Your Lordship shall doe well to let them have it.	Jew	1.2.44	Barab
How, a Christian? Hum, what's here to doe?	Jew	1.2.75	Barab
I doe not doubt by your divine precepts/And mine owne industry,	Jew	1.2.334	Abigal
What wilt thou doe among these hatefull fiends?	Jew	1.2.345	Barab
So doe I too.	Jew	2.3.61	Barab
Are wondrous; and indeed doe no man good:	Jew	2.3.82	Barab
No, but I doe it through a burning zeale,	Jew	2.3.87	Barab
For though they doe a while increase and multiply,	Jew	2.3.89	Barab
I'le buy you, and marry you to Lady vanity, if you doe well.	Jew	2.3.117	P Barab
That by my helpe shall doe much villanie.	Jew	2.3.133	Barab
Give me the letters, daughter, doe you heare?	Jew	2.3.224	Barab
Doe, it is requisite it should be so.	Jew	2.3.239	Barab
Doe so; loe here I give thee Abigall.	Jew	2.3.345	Barab
I, so thou shalt, 'tis thou must doe the deed:	Jew	2.3.369	Barab
into the sea; why I'le doe any thing for your sweet sake.	Jew	3.4.40	P Ithimr
Onely know this, that thus thou art to doe:	Jew	3.4.48	Barab
Pray doe, and let me help you, master.	Jew	3.4.86	P Ithimr
Prethe doe: what saist thou now?	Jew	3.4.88	Barab
What shall I doe with it?	Jew	3.4.107	P Ithimr
Doe you not sorrow for your daughters death?	Jew	4.1.17	Ithimr
And so doe I, master, therfore speake 'em faire.	Jew	4.1.27	Ithimr
But doe you thinke that I beleeve his words?	Jew	4.1.105	Barab
Doe what I can he will not strip himselfe,	Jew	4.1.131	Ithimr
What, doe you meane to strangle me?	Jew	4.1.144	2Fryar
but hee hides and buries it up as Partridges doe their egges,	Jew	4.2.58	P Ithimr
What shall we doe with this base villaine then?	Jew	4.2.62	Curtzn
Let me alone, doe but you speake him faire:	Jew	4.2.63	Pilia
Which if they were reveal'd, would doe him harme.	Jew	4.2.65	Pilia
and this shall be your warrant; if you doe not, no more but so.	Jew	4.2.76	P Ithimr
I cannot doe it, I have lost my keyes.	Jew	4.3.32	Barab
Never lov'd man servant as I doe Ithimore.	Jew	4.3.54	Barab
have at it; and doe you heare?	Jew	4.4.2	P Ithimr
There, if thou lov'st me doe not leave a drop.	Jew	4.4.6	P Ithimr
What wudst thou doe if he should send thee none?	Jew	4.4.13	Pilia
Doe? nothing; but I know what I know.	Jew	4.4.14	P Ithimr
Whilst I in thy incony lap doe tumble.	Jew	4.4.29	Ithimr
The Governour feeds not as I doe.	Jew	4.4.63	P Barab
Any of 'em will doe it.	Jew	4.4.78	P Ithimr
Devils doe your worst, [I'le] <I> live in spite of you.	Jew	5.1.41	Barab
Yet you doe live, and live for me you shall:	Jew	5.2.63	Barab
Doe but bring this to passe which thou pretendest,	Jew	5.2.84	Govnr
Nay more, doe this, and live thou Governor still.	Jew	5.2.89	Govnr
Nay, doe thou this, Ferneze, and be free;	Jew	5.2.90	Barab
I will be there, and doe as thou desirest;	Jew	5.2.103	Govnr
Doe so, but faile not; now farewell Ferneze:	Jew	5.2.109	Barab
And reason too, for Christians doe the like:	Jew	5.2.116	Barab
No, Selim, doe not flye;	Jew	5.5.68	Govnr
And doe attend my comming there by this.	Jew	5.5.104	Calym
Now Guise may storme but doe us little hurt:	P 28	1.28	Navrre
That those which doe beholde, they may become/As men that stand	P 162	2.105	Guise
These are the cursed Guisians that doe seeke our death.	P 201	3.36	Admral
What shall we doe now with the Admirall?	P 248	4.46	Charls
Not for my life doe I desire this pause,	P 401	7.41	Ramus
How may we doe? I feare me they will live.	P 420	7.60	Guise
Now sirra, what shall we doe with the Admirall?	P 482	9.1	P 1Atndt
What shall we doe then?	P 486	9.5	P 2Atndt
Which in the woods doe holde their synagogue:	P 502	9.21	Guise
Doe so sweet Guise, let us delay no time,	P 505	9.24	QnMoth
As I doe live, so surely shall he dye,	P 521	9.40	QnMoth
And he nor heares, nor sees us what we doe:	P 553	11.18	QnMoth
And now Navarre whilste that these broiles doe last,	P 565	11.30	Navrre
To punish those that doe prophane this holy feast.	P 617	12.30	Mugern
And like disportes, such as doe fit the Court?	P 629	12.42	King
And if he doe deny what I doe say,	P 650	12.63	QnMoth
Now doe I see that from the very first,	P 694	13.38	Guise
Not yet my Lord, for thereon doe they stay:	P 732	14.35	1Msngr
of Guise you and your wife/Doe both salute our lovely Minions.	P 753	15.11	King
What should I doe but stand upon my guarde?	P 839	17.34	Guise
And then Ile tell thee what I meane to doe.	P 891	17.86	King
But if that God doe prosper mine attempts,	P 927	18.28	Navrre
Now doe I but begin to look about,	P 985	19.55	Guise
And all for thee my Guise: what may I doe?	P1088	19.158	QnMoth
Oh what may I doe, for to revenge thy death?	P1108	21.2	Dumain
But what doth move thee above the rest to doe the deed?	P1132	21.26	P Dumain
Which if I doe, the Papall Monarck goes/To wrack, and [his]	P1197	22.59	King
What canst thou doe?	Edw	1.1.26	Gavstn
Curse me, depose me, doe the worst you can.	Edw	1.4.57	Edward
O might I keepe thee heere, as I doe this,	Edw	1.4.128	Edward
No? doe but marke how earnestly she pleads.	Edw	1.4.234	Warwck
Then I doe to behold your Majestie.	Edw	2.2.63	Gavstn
Brother, doe you heare them?	Edw	2.2.69	Kent
Yet I disdaine not to doe this for you.	Edw	2.2.79	Lncstr
The lords are cruell, and the king unkinde,/What shall we doe?	Edw	4.2.3	Queene
Her friends doe multiply and yours doe fayle,	Edw	4.5.2	Spencr
diest, for Mortimer/And Isabell doe kisse while they conspire,	Edw	4.6.13	Kent
Tell me good unckle, what Edward doe you meane?	Edw	4.6.32	Prince
grace may sit secure, if none but wee/Doe wot of your abode.	Edw	4.7.27	Monk
Doe looke to be protector over the prince?	Edw	5.2.89	Mortmr
Base villaines, wherefore doe you gripe mee thus?	Edw	5.3.57	Kent
Doe as you are commaunded by my lord.	Edw	5.5.26	Matrvs
Gone, gone, and doe I remaine alive?	Edw	5.5.91	Edward

DOE (cont.)

I doe not thinke her so unnaturall.	Edw	5.6.76		King
that Mephostophilis shall doe for him, and bring him	F 488	2.1.100	P	Faust
by these presents doe give both body and soule to Lucifer,	F 493	2.1.105	P	Faust
<indeede I doe, what doe I not>?	F 668	(HC263)A	P	Pride
And doe what ere I please, unseene of any.	F 993	3.2.13		Faust
I doe not greatly beleeve him, he lookes as like [a] conjurer	F1227	4.1.73	P	Benvol
My gracious Lord, you doe forget your selfe,	F1258	4.1.104		Faust
What shall [his] eyes doe?	F1386	4.2.62	P	Fredrk
and now sirs, having divided him, what shall the body doe?	F1390	4.2.66	P	Mrtino
But wherefore doe I dally my revenge?	F1401	4.2.77		Faust
if you will doe us so much <that> favour, as to let us see that	F1685	5.1.12	P	1Schol
Doe not persever in it like a Divell;	F1711	5.1.38		OldMan
I do repent, and yet I doe despaire,	F1740	5.1.67		Faust
What shall I doe to shun the snares of death?	F1742	5.1.69		Faust
I doe confesse it Faustus, and rejoyce;	F1885	5.2.89		Mephst
Doe yee heare, I would be sorie to robbe you of your living.	F App	p.229 18	P	Clown
Doe you heare sir?	F App	p.229 27	P	Clown
But doe you heare Wagner?	F App	p.231 66	P	Clown
Misericordia pro nobis, what shal I doe?	F App	p.235 30	P	Robin
why doe the Planets/Alter their course; and vainly dim their	Lucan, First Booke	662		
Yeelding or striving <strugling> doe we give him might,	Ovid's Elegies	1.2.9		
fire/And [thinke] <thinkes> her chast whom many doe desire.	Ovid's Elegies	2.2.14		
Let him goe see her though she doe not languish/And then report	Ovid's Elegies	2.2.21		
I thinke sheele doe, but deepely can dissemble.	Ovid's Elegies	2.4.16		
And one especiallie doe we affect,	Hero and Leander	1.171		
To lead thy thoughts, as thy faire lookes doe mine,	Hero and Leander	1.201		
God knowes I cannot force love, as you doe.	Hero and Leander	1.206		
Of that which hath no being, doe not boast,	Hero and Leander	1.275		
Men foolishly doe call it vertuous,	Hero and Leander	1.277		
And swore the sea should never doe him harme.	Hero and Leander	2.180		
DOES				
He tells you true, my maisters, so he does.	1Tamb	2.2.74		Mycet
Your extreme right does me exceeding wrong:	Jew	1.2.153		Barab
Singing ore these, as she does ore her young.	Jew	2.1.63		Barab
What sparkle does it give without a foile?	Jew	2.3.55		Lodowk
Does she receive them?	Jew	2.3.260		Mthias
Why does he goe to thy house? let him begone.	Jew	4.1.101		1Fryar
I, I, he does not stand much upon that.	F1630	4.6.73	P	HrsCsr
DOEST				
But for the land whereof thou doest enquire,	Dido	1.1.209		Venus
What stranger art thou that doest eye me thus?	Dido	2.1.74		Dido
Tis not enough that thou doest graunt me love,	Dido	3.1.8		Iarbus
Stoute friend Achates, doest thou know this wood?	Dido	3.3.50		Aeneas
what doest thou with that same booke thou canst not reade?	F App	p.233 13	P	Rafe
that what ever thou doest, thou shalt be no wayes prejudiced or	F App	p.236 9	P	Emper
When thou doest wish thy husband at the devill.	Ovid's Elegies	1.4.28		
Aske thou the boy, what thou enough doest thinke.	Ovid's Elegies	1.4.30		
Hard-hearted Porter doest and wilt not heare?	Ovid's Elegies	1.6.27		
Make a small price, while thou thy nets doest lay,	Ovid's Elegies	1.8.69		
If this thou doest, to me by long use knowne,	Ovid's Elegies	1.8.105		
[Doest] punish <ye >me, because yeares make him waine?	Ovid's Elegies	1.13.41		
Why doest thy ill kembd tresses losse lament?	Ovid's Elegies	1.14.35		
Why in thy glasse doest looke being discontent?	Ovid's Elegies	1.14.36		
If he loves not, deafe eares thou doest importune,	Ovid's Elegies	2.2.53		
What doest, I cryed, transportst thou my delight?	Ovid's Elegies	2.5.29		
Why Philomele doest Tereus leudnesse mourne?	Ovid's Elegies	2.6.7		
If I looke well, thou thinkest thou doest not move,	Ovid's Elegies	2.7.9		
Thou Goddesse doest command a warme South-blast,	Ovid's Elegies	2.8.19		
and doest refuse;/Well maiest thou one thing for thy Mistresse	Ovid's Elegies	2.8.23		
O Cupid that doest never cease my smart,	Ovid's Elegies	2.9.1		
Doest harme, and in thy tents why doest me wound?	Ovid's Elegies	2.9.4		
Doest joy to have thy hooked Arrowes shaked,	Ovid's Elegies	2.9.13		
On labouring women thou doest pitty take,	Ovid's Elegies	2.13.19		
With cruell hand why doest greene Apples pull?	Ovid's Elegies	2.14.24		
Thou doest alone give matter to my wit.	Ovid's Elegies	2.17.34		
Thou doest beginne, she shall be mine no longer.	Ovid's Elegies	2.19.48		
By thy default thou doest our joyes defraude.	Ovid's Elegies	2.19.58		
What doest? thy wagon in lesse compasse bring.	Ovid's Elegies	3.2.70		
What doest, unhappy?	Ovid's Elegies	3.2.71		
Mad streame, why doest our mutuall joyes deferre?	Ovid's Elegies	3.5.87		
Clowne, from my journey why doest me deterre?	Ovid's Elegies	3.5.88		
Or full of dust doest on the drye earth slide.	Ovid's Elegies	3.5.96		
Confessing this, why doest thou touch him than?	Ovid's Elegies	3.7.22		
What doest with seas?	Ovid's Elegies	3.7.49		
As thou in beautie doest exceed Loves mother/Nor heaven, nor	Hero and Leander	1.222		
DOETH				
Who, because meanes want, doeth not, she doth.	Ovid's Elegies	3.4.4		
DOG				
[and] <To> pull the triple headed dog from hell.	1Tamb	1.2.161		Therid
suborn'd/That villaine there, that slave, that Turkish dog,	2Tamb	3.5.87		Tamb
I sirra, I'le teach thee to turne thy selfe to a Dog, or a Cat,	F 382	1.4.40	P	Wagner
A Dog, or a Cat, or a Mouse, or a Rat?	F 384	1.4.42	P	Robin
brave, prethee let's to it presently, for I am as dry as a dog.	F 752	2.3.31	P	Dick
be thou transformed to/A dog, and carry him upon thy backe;	F1131	3.3.44		Mephst
A dog?	F1133	3.3.46	P	Robin
thee into an Ape, and thee into a Dog, and so be gone.	F App	p.235 44	P	Mephst
From dog-kept flocks come preys to woolves most gratefull.	Ovid's Elegies	1.8.56		
And the Icarian froward Dog-starre shine,	Ovid's Elegies	2.16.4		
DOGGE				
Heave up my shoulders when they call me dogge,	Jew	2.3.24		Barab
thee to turne thy selfe to anything, to a dogge, or a catte,	F App	p.231 58	P	Wagner
a Christian fellow to a dogge or a catte, a mouse or a ratte?	F App	p.231 60	P	Clown

DOGGE (cont.)				
And I must be a Dogge.	F App	p.236 47	P	Rafe
Thou damned wretch, and execrable dogge,	F App	p.238 72		Knight
And gives the viper curled Dogge three heads.	Ovid's Elegies	3.11.26		
DOGGES				
Damn'd Christians, dogges, and Turkish Infidels;	Jew	5.5.86		Barab
In nights deepe silence why the ban-dogges barke.	Ovid's Elegies	2.19.40		
DOG-KEPT				
From dog-kept flocks come preys to woolves most gratefull.	Ovid's Elegies	1.8.56		
DOGS				
Wel, bark ye dogs.	2Tamb	4.1.181		Tamb
I'le goe alone, dogs, do not hale me thus.	Jew	5.1.19		Barab
do you remember the dogs fa--	F1665	4.6.108	P	Robin
No barking Dogs that Syllaes intrailes beare,	Ovid's Elegies	2.16.23		
And Scyllaes wombe mad raging dogs conceales.	Ovid's Elegies	3.11.22		
DOG-STARRE				
And the Icarian froward Dog-starre shine,	Ovid's Elegies	2.16.4		
DOING				
How now Madam, what are you doing?	2Tamb	3.4.34		Therid
And seeing they are not idle, but still doing,	Jew	2.3.83		Barab
like a Beare, the third an Asse, for doing this enterprise.	F App	p.235 33	P	Mephst
[And nut-browne girles in doing have no fellowe].	Ovid's Elegies	2.4.40		
But when I die, would I might droope with doing,	Ovid's Elegies	2.10.35		
And doing wrong made shew of innocence.	Ovid's Elegies	2.19.14		
Though while the deede be doing you be tooke,	Ovid's Elegies	3.13.43		
DOLEFULL				
In dolefull wise they ended both their dayes.	Jew	3.3.21		Ithimr
DOLEFULLY				
Wherewith she strooken, look'd so dolefully,	Hero and Leander	1.373		
DOLLERS				
I have brought you forty dollers for your horse.	F App	p.239 101	P	HrsCsr
has purg'd me of fortie Dollers, I shall never see them more:	F App	p.240 129	P	HrsCsr
and have my fortie dollers againe, or Ile make it the dearest	F App	p.240 136	P	HrsCsr
Fustian, fortie dollers, fortie dollers for a bottle of hey.	F App	p.241 149	P	HrsCsr
O Lord sir, let me goe, and Ile give you fortie dollers more.	F App	p.241 158	P	HrsCsr
his labour; wel, this tricke shal cost him fortie dollers more.	F App	p.241 166	P	Faust
DOLLORS				
I beseech your Worship accept of these forty Dollors.	F1458	4.4.2	P	HrsCsr
sell him, but if thou likest him for ten Dollors more, take him,	F1461	4.4.5	P	Faust
go rouse him, and make him give me my forty Dollors againe.	F1488	4.4.32	P	HrsCsr
and the Horse-courser a bundle of hay for his forty Dollors.	F1498	4.4.42	P	Faust
and he would by no meanes sell him under forty Dollors; so sir,	F1537	4.5.33	P	HrsCsr
DOLON				
And intercepts the day as Dolon erst:	Dido	1.1.71		Venus
DOLORIS				
Solamen miseris socios habuisse doloris.	F 431	2.1.43		Mephst
DOLOROUS				
blasted, Aruns takes/And it inters with murmurs dolorous,	Lucan, First Booke	606		
DOLOUR				
And did to thee no cause of dolour raise.	Ovid's Elegies	1.14.14		
DOLOURS				
Your passions make your dolours to increase.	Edw	5.3.15		Gurney
DOLPHIAN				
Then heeretofore the Delphian <Dolphian> Oracle.	F 170	1.1.142		Cornel
DOLPHIN				
That I may tice a Dolphin to the shoare,	Dido	5.1.249		Dido
Or crooked Dolphin when the sailer sings;	Hero and Leander	2.234		
DOMESTICKE				
Domesticke acts, and mine owne warres to sing.	Ovid's Elegies	2.18.12		
DOMINE				
O nomine Domine, what meanst thou Robin?	F App	p.235 26	P	Vintnr
DOMINION				
But his dominion that exceeds <excells> in this,	F 87	1.1.59		Faust
hath every Spheare a Dominion, or Intelligentia <Inteligentij>?	F 607	2.2.56	P	Faust
Dominion cannot suffer partnership;	Lucan, First Booke	93		
even the same that wrack's all great [dominions] <dominion>.	Lucan, First Booke	160		
DOMINIONS				
And continent to your Dominions:	1Tamb	1.1.128		Menaph
And ad more strength to your dominions/Than ever yet confirm'd	1Tamb	5.1.448		Tamb
And all the kingdomes and dominions/That late the power of	1Tamb	5.1.508		Tamb
even the same that wrack's all great [dominions] <dominion>.	Lucan, First Booke	160		
DOMINUS				
Maledicat Dominus.	F1078	3.2.98		1Frier
Maledicat Dominus.	F1080	3.2.100		1Frier
Maledicat Dominus.	F1082	3.2.102		1Frier
Maledicat Dominus.	F1084	3.2.104		1Frier
Maledicat Dominus.	F1086	3.2.106		1Frier
maledicat dominus.	F App	p.232 32		Frier
maledicat dominus.	F App	p.232 34		Frier
maledicat dominus.	F App	p.233 40		Frier
DOMOOPHON				
Or Phillis teares that her [Demophoon] <Domoophon> misses,/What	Ovid's Elegies	2.18.22		
DOMUS				
fuit aut tibi quidquam/Dulce meum, miserere domus labentis:	Dido	5.1.137		Dido
DON				
Why how now Don Mathias, in a dump?	Jew	1.2.374		Lodowk
Here comes Don Lodowicke the Governor's sonne,	Jew	2.3.30		Barab
For Don Mathias tels me she is faire.	Jew	2.3.35		Lodowk
Yonder comes Don Mathias, let us stay;	Jew	2.3.140		Barab
But wherefore talk'd Don Lodowick with you?	Jew	2.3.150		Mthias
But stand aside, here comes Don Lodowicke.	Jew	2.3.217		Barab
O father, Don Mathias is my love.	Jew	2.3.237		Abigal
So sure shall he and Don Mathias dye:	Jew	2.3.249		Barab

DON (cont.)

Whither goes Don Mathias? stay a while.	Jew	2.3.251		Barab
Why, loves she Don Mathias?	Jew	2.3.285		Lodowk
But keepe thy heart till Don Mathias comes.	Jew	2.3.307		Barab
I will have Don Mathias, he is my love.	Jew	2.3.361		Abigal
Know you not of Mathias and Don Lodowickes disaster?	Jew	3.3.16	P	Ithimr
Yet Don Mathias ne're offended thee:	Jew	3.3.41		Abigal
('tis so) of my device/In Don Mathias and Lodovicoes deaths:	Jew	3.4.8		Barab
You knew Mathias and Don Lodowicke?	Jew	3.6.20		Abigal
First to Don Lodowicke, him I never lov'd;	Jew	3.6.23		Abigal
I, but Barabas, remember Mathias and Don Lodowick.	Jew	4.1.43	P	2Fryar

DONE (See also DOONE)

I, I, Iarbus, after this is done,	Dido	5.1.289		Dido
Faith, and Techelles, it was manly done:	1Tamb	3.2.109		Usumc
Wel done my boy, thou shalt have shield and lance,	2Tamb	1.3.43		Tamb
Well done Techelles: what saith Theridamas?	2Tamb	1.3.206		Tamb
When this is done, then are ye souldiers,	2Tamb	3.2.91		Tamb
My Lord, but this is dangerous to be done,	2Tamb	3.2.93		Calyph
Killing my selfe, as I have done my sonne,	2Tamb	3.4.35		Olymp
Twas bravely done, and like a souldiers wife.	2Tamb	3.4.38		Techel
For as soone as the battaile is done, Ile ride in triumph	2Tamb	3.5.145	P	Tamb
I beleeve there will be some hurt done anon amongst them.	2Tamb	4.1.74	P	Calyph
When this is done, we'll martch from Babylon,	2Tamb	5.1.127		Tamb
So, now their best is done to honour me,	2Tamb	5.1.131		Tamb
Tis brave indeed my boy, wel done,	2Tamb	5.1.150		Tamb
What shal be done with their wives and children my Lord.	2Tamb	5.1.168	P	Techel
But 'twas ill done of you to come so farre/Without the ayd or	Jew	1.1.93		Barab
Tush, tell not me 'twas done of policie.	Jew	1.1.140		1Jew
It shall be so: now Officers have you done?	Jew	1.2.131		Govnr
Till they reduce the wrongs done to my father.	Jew	1.2.235		Abigal
but be thou so precise/As they may thinke it done of Holinesse.	Jew	1.2.285		Barab
And so has she done you, even from a child.	Jew	2.3.289		Barab
Oh wretched Abigal, what hast [thou] <thee> done?	Jew	2.3.320		Abigal
No; so shall I, if any hurt be done,	Jew	2.3.341		Barab
No, no, and yet it might be done that way:	Jew	2.3.373		Barab
Or loving, doth dislike of something done.	Jew	3.4.12		Barab
A Fryar? false villaine, he hath done the deed.	Jew	3.4.22		Barab
go set it downe/And come againe so soone as thou hast done,	Jew	3.4.109		Barab
Pay me my wages for my worke is done.	Jew	3.4.115		Ithimr
Why? what has he done?	Jew	3.6.47		1Fryar
Or though it wrought, it would have done no good,	Jew	4.1.5		Barab
No more but so: it must and shall be done.	Jew	4.1.128		Barab
'Tis neatly done, Sir, here's no print at all.	Jew	4.1.151		Ithimr
Why, how now Jacomo, what hast thou done?	Jew	4.1.174		Barab
Why, a Turke could ha done no more.	Jew	4.1.198	P	Ithimr
but the Exercise being done, see where he comes.	Jew	4.2.20	P	Pilia
Oh bravely done.	Jew	4.4.19		Pilia
'Twas bravely done:	Jew	5.1.84		Calym
That at one instant all things may be done,	Jew	5.2.120		Barab
If greater falshood ever has bin done.	Jew	5.5.50		Barab
thy father hath made good/The ruines done to Malta and to us,	Jew	5.5.112		Govnr
gloves which I sent/To be poysoned, hast thou done them?	P 71	2.14		Guise
Tis well advisde Dumain, goe see it strait be done.	P 424	7.64		Guise
I have done what I could to stay this broile.	P 434	7.74		Anjoy
My Lords, what resteth there now for to be done?	P 554	11.19		QnMoth
Epernoune, goe see it presently be done,	P 558	11.23		QnMoth
And now my Lords after these funerals be done,	P 561	11.26		QnMoth
Our solemne rites of Coronation done,	P 626	12.39		King
What I have done tis for the Gospell sake.	P 826	17.21		Guise
Pardon thee, why what hast thou done?	P 991	19.61		Guise
What, have you done?	P1016	19.86		Capt
My father slaine, who hath done this deed?	P1047	19.117		YngGse
Art thou King, and hast done this bloudy deed?	P1050	19.120		YngGse
Pray God thou be a King now this is done.	P1068	19.138		QnMoth
What this detested Jacobin hath done.	P1195	22.57		King
And may it never end in bloud as mine hath done.	P1233	22.95		King
To see it done, and bring thee safe againe.	Edw	1.1.205		Edward
What we have done, our hart bloud shall maintaine.	Edw	1.4.40		Mortmr
And see what we your councellers have done.	Edw	1.4.44		ArchBp
Subscribe as we have done to his exile.	Edw	1.4.53		ArchBp
Tis done, and now accursed hand fall off.	Edw	1.4.88		Edward
I, but how chance this was not done before?	Edw	1.4.272		Lncstr
It shalbe done my gratious Lord.	Edw	1.4.372		Beamnt
It shall be done madam.	Edw	2.1.72		Baldck
Ah furious Mortimer what hast thou done?	Edw	2.2.85		Queene
For favors done in him, unto us all.	Edw	3.1.42		SpncrP
they say there is great execution/Done through the realme, my	Edw	4.3.7		Edward
And for the open wronges and injuries/Edward hath done to us,	Edw	4.4.22		Mortmr
Madam, have done with care and sad complaint,	Edw	4.6.66		Mortmr
That Mortimer and Isabell have done.	Edw	5.1.25		Edward
Have done their homage to the loftie gallowes,	Edw	5.2.3		Mortmr
And when tis done, we will subscribe our name.	Edw	5.2.50		Mortmr
It shall be done my lord.	Edw	5.2.51		Matrvs
And we be quit that causde it to be done:	Edw	5.4.16		Mortmr
Shall he be murdered when the deed is done.	Edw	5.4.20		Mortmr
What hath he done?	Edw	5.4.83		King
And when the murders done,/See how he must be handled for his	Edw	5.5.22		Matrvs
Yet will it melt, ere I have done my tale.	Edw	5.5.55		Edward
Tell me sirs, was it not bravelie done?	Edw	5.5.116		Ltborn
Ist done, Matrevis, and the murtherer dead?	Edw	5.6.1		Mortmr
When all is done, Divinitie is best:	F 64	1.1.36		Faust
So Faustus hath <I have> already done, and holds <hold> this	F 283	1.3.55		Faust
booke more, and then I have done, wherein I might see al plants,	F 551.8	2.1.171A	P	Faust

DONE (cont.)
long e're this, I should have done the deed <slaine my selfe>, F 575 2.2.24 Faust
and you have done me great injury to bring me from thence, let F 705.1 2.2.155A P Sloth
Thou needst not do that, for my Mistresse hath done it. F 739 2.3.18 P Dick
He has done penance now sufficently. F1310 4.1.156 Emper
not so much for injury done to me, as to delight your Majesty F1311 4.1.157 P Faust
and see where they come, belike the feast is done. F1680 5.1.7 P Wagner
Where art thou Faustus? wretch, what hast thou done? F1724 5.1.51 Faust
Accursed Faustus, <wretch what hast thou done>? F1739 (HC270)B Faust
and what wonders I have done, all Germany can witnesse, yea all F1842 5.2.46 P Faust
God forbade it indeed, but Faustus hath done it: F1858 5.2.62 P Faust
Oft have I thought to have done so: F1864 5.2.68 P Faust
Vilaine I say, undo what thou hast done. F App p.238 75 Knight
at my intreaty release him, he hath done penance sufficient. F App p.238 80 P Emper
Now my good Lord having done my duety, I humbly take my leave. F App p.238 86 P Faust
Untill the cruel Giants war was done)/We plaine not heavens, Lucan, First Booke 36
Yet for long service done, reward these men, Lucan, First Booke 341
though I not see/What may be done, yet there before him bee. Ovid's Elegies 1.4.14
wheeles spun/And what with Mares ranck humour may be done. Ovid's Elegies 1.8.8
Th'opposed starre of Mars hath done thee harme, Ovid's Elegies 1.8.29
Hundred-hand Gyges, and had done it well, Ovid's Elegies 2.1.12
Enquire not what with Isis may be done/Nor feare least she to Ovid's Elegies 2.2.25
Now many guests were gone, the feast being done, Ovid's Elegies 2.5.21
of me, or I am sure/I oft have done, what might as much procure. Ovid's Elegies 2.13.6
What ever haps, by suffrance harme is done, Ovid's Elegies 2.19.35
On swift steedes mounted till the race were done. Ovid's Elegies 3.2.10
Seeing <When> in my prime my force is spent and done? Ovid's Elegies 3.6.18
With Muse oppos'd would I my lines had done, Ovid's Elegies 3.11.17
Slippe still, onely denie it when tis done, Ovid's Elegies 3.13.15
My soule fleetes when I thinke what you have done, Ovid's Elegies 3.13.37
Untill some honourable deed be done. Hero and Leander 1.282
When Venus sweet rites are perform'd and done. Hero and Leander 1.320
Supposing nothing else was to be done, Hero and Leander 2.53
Ere halfe this tale was done,/Aye me, Leander cryde, Hero and Leander 2.201
And now she wisht this night were never done, Hero and Leander 2.301

DON'T
Good sirs I have don't, but no body knowes it but you two, I Jew 4.1.180 P 1Fryar

DOO
We here doo crowne thee Monarch of the East, 1Tamb 1.1.161 Ortyg
Thee doo I make my Regent of Persea, 1Tamb 2.5.8 Cosroe
Doo not my captaines and my souldiers looke/As if they meant to 1Tamb 3.3.9 Tamb
To doo their ceassles homag to my sword: 1Tamb 5.1.456 Tamb
For she is dead? thy words doo pierce my soule. 2Tamb 2.4.125 Tamb
I would not yeeld it: therefore doo your worst. 2Tamb 3.3.37 Capt
You doo dishonor to his majesty, 2Tamb 4.1.20 Calyph
From whence the starres doo borrow all their light, 2Tamb 4.2.89 Therid
Her trembling hand writ back she might not doo. Ovid's Elegies 2.2.6

DOOING
Not dooing Mahomet an injurie, 2Tamb 2.3.34 Orcan

DOOM'D
Thou'st doom'd thy selfe, assault it presently. Jew 5.1.97 Calym

DOOME
I take thy doome for satisfaction. 1Tamb 2.3.5 Cosroe

DOONE
Well doone, Ned. Edw 1.1.98 Gavstn

DOORE (See also DORE)
To morrow early I'le be at the doore. Jew 1.2.361 Barab
See 'em goe pinion'd along by my doore. Jew 2.3.180 Barab
What, ho, Abigall; open the doore I say. Jew 2.3.221 Barab
looking out/When you should come and hale him from the doore. Jew 2.3.265 Barab
The Guisians are hard at thy doore, P 367 7.7 Taleus
How now Mugeroun, metst thou not the Guise at the doore? P 774 15.32 King
and use a counterfeite key to his privie Chamber doore: P 807 17.2 P Souldr
yesternight/I opened but the doore to throw him meate,/And I Edw 5.5.8 Gurney
Before the roome be cleere, and doore put too. Ovid's Elegies 3.13.10
Wide open stood the doore, hee need not clime, Hero and Leander 2.19
Then standing at the doore, she turnd about, Hero and Leander 2.97

DOORES
Then gan the windes breake ope their brazen doores, Dido 1.1.62 Venus
Aurora shall not peepe out of her doores, 1Tamb 2.2.10 Mycet
with which I burst/The rusty beames of Janus Temple doores, 2Tamb 2.4.114 Tamb
Opening the doores of his rich treasurie, 2Tamb 4.2.95 Therid
Seiz'd all I had, and thrust me out a doores, Jew 2.3.76 Barab
Small doores unfitting for large houses are. Ovid's Elegies 3.1.40
Ah howe oft on hard doores hung I engrav'd, Ovid's Elegies 3.1.53

DOOST
Doost thou think that Mahomet wil suffer this? 1Tamb 4.4.52 P Therid
Doost thou aske him leave? 2Tamb 3.5.134 P Callap
Thou doost dishonor manhood, and thy house. 2Tamb 4.1.32 Celeb
And long thou shalt not stay, or if thou doost, Edw 1.4.114 Edward
Proud Edward, doost thou banish me thy presence? Edw 4.1.5 Kent
Whether, O whether doost thou bend thy steps? Edw 4.2.12 Queene
If, doost thou say? Edw 4.3.21 Edward
Proud traytor Mortimer why doost thou chase/Thy lawfull king Edw 4.6.3 Kent
Inconstant Edmund, doost thou favor him, Edw 5.2.101 Mortmr
what, doost thinke I am a horse-doctor? F App p.240 120 P Faust
Doost me of new crimes alwayes guilty frame? Ovid's Elegies 2.7.1

DOOTE
If one can doote, if not, two everie night, Ovid's Elegies 2.10.22

DOOTH
Dooth pray uppon my flockes of Passengers, 1Tamb 1.1.32 Mycet
Than dooth the King of Persea in his Crowne: 1Tamb 1.2.242 Tamb
Fortune her selfe dooth sit upon our Crests. 1Tamb 2.2.73 Meandr

DOOTH (cont.)
As dooth the lightening, or the breath of heaven: 1Tamb 2.3.58 Tamb
and now dooth gastly death/With greedy tallents gripe my 1Tamb 2.7.48 Cosroe
dooth not the Turke and his wife make a goodly showe at a 1Tamb 4.4.57 P Tamb
Stil dooth this man or rather God of war, 1Tamb 5.1.1 Govnr
So much by much, as dooth Zenocrate. 1Tamb 5.1.159 Tamb
As dooth the Desart of Arabia/To those that stand on Badgeths 2Tamb 1.1.108 Sgsmnd
our hearts/More than the thought of this dooth vexe our soules. 2Tamb 5.1.145 Jrslem
my soule dooth weepe to see/Your sweet desires depriv'd my 2Tamb 5.3.246 Tamb
Thus arme in arme, the king and he dooth marche: Edw 1.2.20 Lncstr
As dooth the want of my sweete Gaveston, Edw 1.4.307 Edward
I marry, such a garde as this dooth well. Edw 2.2.131 Mortmr
Because we heare Lord Bruse dooth sell his land, Edw 3.1.53 Edward
But dayes bright beames dooth vanish fast away, Edw 5.1.69 Edward
DORE
On mooved hookes set ope the churlish dore. Ovid's Elegies 1.6.2
Night goes away: I pray thee ope the dore. Ovid's Elegies 1.6.48
This breakes Towne gates, but he his Mistris dore. Ovid's Elegies 1.9.20
Going out againe passe forth the dore more wisely/And som-what Ovid's Elegies 1.12.5
My wench her dore shut, Joves affares I left, Ovid's Elegies 2.1.17
Search at the dore who knocks oft in the darke, Ovid's Elegies 2.19.39
To get the dore with little noise unbard. Ovid's Elegies 3.1.50
I have sustainde so oft thrust from the dore, Ovid's Elegies 3.10.9
And drunke with gladnesse, to the dore she goes. Hero and Leander 2.236
DORES
but for me, as you went in at dores/You had bin stab'd, but not Jew 2.3.337 Barab
I will weepe/And to the dores sight of thy selfe [will] keepe: Ovid's Elegies 1.4.62
Night goes away: the dores barre backeward strike. Ovid's Elegies 1.6.24
And opening dores with creaking noyse abound? Ovid's Elegies 1.6.50
Come breake these deafe dores with thy boysterous wind. Ovid's Elegies 1.6.54
O harder then the dores thou gardest I prove thee. Ovid's Elegies 1.6.62
And dores conjoynd with an hard iron lock. Ovid's Elegies 1.6.74
words she sayd/While closely hid betwixt two dores I layed. Ovid's Elegies 1.8.22
His Mistris dores this; that his Captaines keepes. Ovid's Elegies 1.9.8
Quickly soft words hard dores wide open strooke. Ovid's Elegies 2.1.22
Verses ope dores, and lockes put in the poast/Although of oake, Ovid's Elegies 2.1.27
At thy deafe dores in verse sing my abuses. Ovid's Elegies 3.7.24
DORICK
Are banquets, Dorick musicke, midnight-revell, Hero and Leander 1.301
DOSEN
What ho, give's halfe a dosen of Beere here, and be hang'd. F1612 4.6.55 P Robin
DOST
How, dost call me rogue? Jew 4.1.96 1Fryar
Dost not know a Jew, one Barabas? Jew 4.4.56 P Ithimr
Villaine, why dost thou look so gastly? speake. P 989 19.59 Guise
Frier, thou dost acknowledge me thy King? P1164 22.26 King
Which of the nobles dost thou meane to serve? Edw 2.1.3 Baldck
What lord [Arundell] <Matre>, dost thou come alone? Edw 3.1.89 Edward
Why, dost not thou know then? F 199 1.2.6 P 2Schol
Why so thou shalt be, whether thou dost it or no: F 360 1.4.18 P Wagner
thou dost not presently bind thy selfe to me for seven yeares, F 361 1.4.19 P Wagner
Why, dost thou think <think'st thou then> that Faustus shall be F 518 2.1.130 Faust
<Tel Faustus, how dost thou like thy wife>? F 533 (HC261)A P Mephst
We are come to tell thee thou dost injure us. F 642 2.2.91 Belzeb
<Now Faustus, how dost thou like this>? F 711 (HC264)A Lucifr
Sirra Dick, dost thou know why I stand so mute? F1509 4.5.5 P Robin
My woodden leg? what dost thou meane by that? F1628 4.6.71 Faust
Ha, ha, ha, dost heare him Dick, he has forgot his legge. F1629 4.6.72 P Carter
But wherefore dost thou aske? F1652 4.6.95 Faust
Say Wagner, thou hast perus'd my will,/How dost thou like it? F1817 5.2.21 Faust
When on thy lappe thine eyes thou dost deject, Ovid's Elegies 1.8.37
Thou coosnest boyes of sleepe, and dost betray them/To Pedants, Ovid's Elegies 1.13.17
DO'T
Do but speake what thou't have me to do, and I'le do't: F 745 2.3.24 P Robin
DOTE
That she may dote upon Aeneas love: Dido 2.1.327 Venus
But thou must dote upon a Christian? Jew 2.3.360 Barab
dote on them your selfe,/I know none els but holdes them in P 763 15.21 Guise
And yet heele ever dote on Gaveston, Edw 1.4.185 Queene
To dote upon deceitfull Mercurie. Hero and Leander 1.446
DOTED
For never doted Jove on Ganimed, Edw 1.4.180 Queene
DOTES
But dotes upon the love of Gaveston. Edw 1.2.50 Queene
And seeing his minde so dotes on Gaveston, Edw 1.4.389 MortSr
DOTH (See also DOETH, DOOTH)
And Helens rape doth haunt [ye] <thee> at the heeles. Dido 1.1.144 Aeneas
And every beast the forrest doth send forth, Dido 1.1.161 Achat
O yet this stone doth make Aeneas weepe, Dido 2.1.15 Aeneas
Doth Dido call me backe? Dido 3.1.53 Iarbus
Wherefore doth Dido bid Iarbus goe? Dido 3.1.56 Anna
Achates, how doth Carthage please your Lord? Dido 3.1.97 Dido
So doth he now, though not with equall gaine, Dido 3.3.83 Iarbus
Since gloomie Aeolus doth cease to frowne. Dido 4.1.27 Aeneas
Anna that doth admire thee more then heaven. Dido 4.2.46 Anna
Since destinie doth call me from [thy] <the> shoare: Dido 4.3.2 Aeneas
Where daliance doth consume a Souldiers strength, Dido 4.3.34 Achat
And in the midst doth run a silver streame, Dido 4.5.9 Nurse
To whom poore Dido doth bequeath revenge. Dido 5.1.173 Dido
And as I heare, doth meane to pull my plumes. 1Tamb 1.1.33 Mycet
and the verie legges/Whereon our state doth leane, as on a 1Tamb 1.1.60 Mycet
But this it is that doth excruciate/The verie substance of my 1Tamb 1.1.113 Cosroe
of his Emperie/By East and west, as Phoebus doth his course: 1Tamb 1.2.40 Tamb

DCTH (cont.)

Nature doth strive with Fortune and his stars,	1Tamb	2.1.33	Cosroe
Doth teach us all to have aspyring minds:	1Tamb	2.7.20	Tamb
by princely deeds/Doth meane to soare above the highest sort.	1Tamb	2.7.33	Therid
Hearst thou Anippe, how thy drudge doth talk,	1Tamb	3.3.182	Zenoc
my spirit doth foresee/The utter ruine of thy men and thee.	1Tamb	4.3.59	Arabia
Neere Guyrons head doth set his conquering feet,	2Tamb	1.1.17	Gazell
That fighting, knowes not what retreat doth meane,	2Tamb	3.5.43	Trebiz
That they may say, it is not chance doth this,	2Tamb	4.1.84	Amyras
and of fire/Doth send such sterne affections to his heart.	2Tamb	4.1.176	Trebiz
<Hipostates>/Thick and obscure doth make your danger great,	2Tamb	5.3.83	Phsitn
Know Barabas, doth ride in Malta Rhode,	Jew	1.1.86	2Merch
Doth see his souldiers slaine, himselfe disarm'd,	Jew	1.2.204	Barab
of the silent night/Doth shake contagion from her sable wings;	Jew	2.1.4	Barab
For unto us the Promise doth belong.	Jew	2.3.47	Barab
Doth she not with her smiling answer you?	Jew	2.3.286	Barab
And yet I know my beauty doth not faile.	Jew	3.1.5	Curtzn
Or loving, doth dislike of something done.	Jew	3.4.12	Barab
Doth fall asunder; so that it doth sinke/Into a deepe pit past	Jew	5.5.35	Barab
asunder; so that it doth sinke/Into a deepe pit past recovery.	Jew	5.5.35	Barab
Tell me, you Christians, what doth this portend?	Jew	5.5.90	Calym
For what he doth the Pope will ratifie:	P 40	1.40	Condy
Doth heare and see the praiers of the just:	P 43	1.43	Navrre
The sent whereof doth make my head to ake.	P 171	3.6	OldQn
Doth not your grace know the man that gave them you?	P 172	3.7	Navrre
My heart doth faint, I dye.	P 186	3.21	OldQn
But yet my Lord the report doth run,	P 435	7.75	Navrre
My heart doth break, I faint and dye.	P 550	11.15	Charls
But God that alwaies doth defend the right,	P 575	11.40	Navrre
Come Pleshe, lets away whilste time doth serve.	P 587	11.52	Navrre
O would to God this quill that heere doth write,	P 667	13.11	Duchss
But as report doth goe, the Duke of Joyeux/Hath made great sute	P 733	14.36	1Msngr
But he doth lurke within his drousie couch,	P 737	14.40	Navrre
Thus God we see doth ever guide the right,	P 789	16.3	Navrre
Which Ile maintaine so long as life doth last:	P 800	16.14	Navrre
And please your grace the Duke of Guise doth crave/Accesse unto	P 959	19.29	Eprnon
But what doth move thee above the rest to doe the deed?	P1132	21.26	P Dumain
Doth no man take exceptions at the slave?	Edw	1.2.25	MortSr
Your grace doth wel to place him by your side,	Edw	1.4.10	Lncstr
For with my nature warre doth best agree.	Edw	1.4.365	MortSr
And so doth Lancaster:	Edw	2.2.109	Lncstr
Your lordship doth dishonor to your selfe,	Edw	2.6.8	James
As doth this water from my tattered robes:	Edw	5.5.67	Edward
Stretcheth as farre as doth the mind of man:	F 88	1.1.60	Faust
Hath all the Principles Magick doth require:	F 167	1.1.139	Cornel
To whom Faustus doth dedicate himselfe.	F 285	1.3.57	Faust
O how this sight doth delight <this feedes> my soule.	F 712	2.2.164	Faust
That Faustus name, whilst this bright frame doth stand,	F 841	3.1.63	Faust
That doth assume the Papall government,	F 886	3.1.108	Pope
yee Lubbers look about/And find the man that doth this villany,	F1056	3.2.76	Pope
Despaire doth drive distrust into my thoughts.	F1480	4.4.24	Faust
the Duke of Vanholt doth earnestly entreate your company, and	F1500	4.4.44	P Wagner
To marke him how he doth demeane himselfe.	F1806	5.2.10	Belzeb
Whose deepnesse doth intice such forward wits,	F2008	5.3.26	4Chor
course that time doth runne with calme and silent foote,	F App	p.239 91	P Faust
Thy fatall time doth drawe to finall ende,	F App	p.240 122	Faust
Dispaire doth drive distrust unto my thoughts,	F App	p.240 123	Faust
Sir, the Duke of Vanholt doth earnestly entreate your company.	F App	p.241 168	P Wagner
carowse, and swill/Amongst the Students, as even now he doth,	F App	p.243 5	Wagner
is by cowards/Left as a pray now Caesar doth approach:	Lucan, First Booke		512
While Mars doth take the Aonian harpe to play?	Ovid's Elegies		1.1.16
Unwilling Lovers, love doth more torment,	Ovid's Elegies		1.2.17
<make> slender/And to get out doth like apt members render.	Ovid's Elegies		1.6.6
With stiffe oake propt the gate doth still appeare.	Ovid's Elegies		1.6.28
Strike backe the barre, night fast away doth goe.	Ovid's Elegies		1.6.32
But now perchaunce thy wench with thee doth rest,	Ovid's Elegies		1.6.45
But doubt thou not (revenge doth griefe appease)/With thy	Ovid's Elegies		1.7.63
She magick arts and Thessale charmes doth know,	Ovid's Elegies		1.8.5
Nor doth her tongue want harmefull eloquence.	Ovid's Elegies		1.8.20
Venus thy side doth warme,/And brings good fortune, a rich	Ovid's Elegies		1.8.30
cheekes, but this/If feigned, doth well; if true it doth amisse.	Ovid's Elegies		1.8.36
but this/If feigned, doth well; if true it doth amisse.	Ovid's Elegies		1.8.36
Now Mars doth rage abroad without all pitty,	Ovid's Elegies		1.8.41
Of his gilt Harpe the well tun'd strings doth hold.	Ovid's Elegies		1.8.60
Deny him oft, feigne now thy head doth ake:	Ovid's Elegies		1.8.73
Anger delaide doth oft to hate retire.	Ovid's Elegies		1.8.82
Take strife away, love doth not well endure.	Ovid's Elegies		1.8.96
What age fits Mars, with Venus doth agree,	Ovid's Elegies		1.9.3
East windes he doth not chide/Nor to hoist saile attends fit	Ovid's Elegies		1.9.13
One as a spy doth to his enemies goe,	Ovid's Elegies		1.9.17
Therefore who ere love sloathfulnesse doth call,	Ovid's Elegies		1.9.31
And hath no cloathes, but open doth remaine.	Ovid's Elegies		1.10.16
And doth constraind, what you do of good will.	Ovid's Elegies		1.10.24
Nor the milde Ewe gifts from the Ramme doth pull.	Ovid's Elegies		1.10.28
The fame that verse gives doth for ever last.	Ovid's Elegies		1.10.62
are in thy soft brest/But pure simplicity in thee doth rest.	Ovid's Elegies		1.11.10
The rest my hand doth in my letters write.	Ovid's Elegies		1.11.14
Bacchinall/That tyr'd doth rashly on the greene grasse fall.	Ovid's Elegies		1.14.22
By thine owne hand and fault thy hurt doth growe,	Ovid's Elegies		1.14.43
Or [into] <to the> sea swift Symois [doth] <shall> slide.	Ovid's Elegies		1.15.10
a pretty wenches face/Shee in requitall doth me oft imbrace.	Ovid's Elegies		2.1.34
lookes to my verse/Which golden love doth unto me rehearse.	Ovid's Elegies		2.1.38
Bagous whose care doth thy Mistrisse bridle,	Ovid's Elegies		2.2.1

DOTH (cont.)

Line	Work	Reference	Speaker
yesterday/There where the porch doth Danaus fact display.	Ovid's Elegies	2.2.4	
She safe by favour of her judge doth rest.	Ovid's Elegies	2.2.56	
[A white wench thralles me, so doth golden yellowe],	Ovid's Elegies	2.4.39	
and too much his griefe doth favour/That seekes the conquest by	Ovid's Elegies	2.5.11	
Birdes haples glory, death thy life doth quench.	Ovid's Elegies	2.6.20	
Whose earth doth not perpetuall greene-grasse lacke,	Ovid's Elegies	2.6.50	
Thou arguest she doth secret markes unfold.	Ovid's Elegies	2.7.6	
Duld with much beating slowly forth doth passe.	Ovid's Elegies	2.7.16	
Heere thou hast strength, here thy right hand doth rest.	Ovid's Elegies	2.9.36	
Cupid by thee, Mars in great doubt doth trample,	Ovid's Elegies	2.9.47	
This seemes the fairest, so doth that to mee,	Ovid's Elegies	2.10.7	
[And] this doth please me most, and so doth she.	Ovid's Elegies	2.10.8	
That victory doth chiefely triumph merit,	Ovid's Elegies	2.12.5	
Which without bloud-shed doth the pray inherit.	Ovid's Elegies	2.12.6	
A grassie turffe the moistened earth doth hide.	Ovid's Elegies	2.16.10	
Why doth my mistresse from me oft devide?	Ovid's Elegies	2.16.42	
Doth say, with her that lov'd the Aonian harpe.	Ovid's Elegies	2.18.26	
Jasons sad letter doth Hipsipile greete,	Ovid's Elegies	2.18.33	
This doth delight me, this my courage cheares.	Ovid's Elegies	2.19.24	
Each crosse waies corner doth as much expresse.	Ovid's Elegies	3.1.18	
This goddesse company doth to me befall.	Ovid's Elegies	3.1.44	
Because on him thy care doth hap to rest.	Ovid's Elegies	3.2.8	
Ist womens love my captive brest doth frie?	Ovid's Elegies	3.2.40	
And unrevengd mockt Gods with me doth scoffe.	Ovid's Elegies	3.3.20	
And doth the world in fond beliefe deteine.	Ovid's Elegies	3.3.24	
Who, because meanes want, doeth not, she doth.	Ovid's Elegies	3.4.4	
The fainting seedes of naughtinesse doth kill.	Ovid's Elegies	3.4.10	
Nor doth her face please, but her husbands love;	Ovid's Elegies	3.4.27	
Which wealth, cold winter doth on thee bestowe.	Ovid's Elegies	3.5.94	
His left hand whereon gold doth ill alight,	Ovid's Elegies	3.7.15	
For me, she doth keeper, and husband feare,	Ovid's Elegies	3.7.63	
Tibullus doth Elysiums joy inherit.	Ovid's Elegies	3.8.60	
The godly, sweete Tibullus doth increase.	Ovid's Elegies	3.8.66	
Be witnesse Crete (nor Crete doth all things feigne)/Crete	Ovid's Elegies	3.9.19	
Faith to the witnesse Joves praise doth apply,	Ovid's Elegies	3.9.23	
Beauty with lewdnesse doth right ill agree.	Ovid's Elegies	3.10.42	
Ah, she doth more worth then her vices prove.	Ovid's Elegies	3.10.44	
Bird-changed Progne doth her Itys teare.	Ovid's Elegies	3.11.32	
Or his Bulles hornes Europas hand doth hold.	Ovid's Elegies	3.11.34	
Here when the Pipe with solemne tunes doth sound,	Ovid's Elegies	3.12.11	
And she her vestall virgin Priests doth follow.	Ovid's Elegies	3.12.30	
She hath not trode <tred> awrie that doth denie it,	Ovid's Elegies	3.13.5	
And thorough everie vaine doth cold bloud runne,	Ovid's Elegies	3.13.38	
Horned Bacchus graver furie doth distill,	Ovid's Elegies	3.14.17	
footsteps bending)/Doth testifie that you exceed her farre,	Hero and Leander	1.211	
Differs as much, as wine and water doth.	Hero and Leander	1.264	
Thee as a holy Idiot doth she scorne,	Hero and Leander	1.303	

DOTING

Line	Work	Reference	Speaker
To thrust his doting father from his chaire,	1Tamb	2.7.14	Tamb

DOUAI (See DOWAY)

DOUBLE (See also DUBBLE)

Line	Work	Reference	Speaker
Nor quit good turnes with double fee downe told:	Dido	3.2.15	Juno
Who knowes not the double motion of the Planets?	F 602	2.2.51	Faust
<And double Canons, fram'd of carved brasse>,	F 820	(HC265) A	Mephst
As that the double Cannons forg'd of brasse,	F 820	3.1.42	Mephst
and with a double point/Rose like the Theban brothers funerall	Lucan, First Booke	549	
her eyes/Two eye-balles shine, and double light thence flies.	Ovid's Elegies	1.8.16	

DOUBLED

Line	Work	Reference	Speaker
That spite of spite, our wrongs are doubled?	F1446	4.3.16	Benvol
Mounts, and raine-doubled floods he passeth over,	Ovid's Elegies	1.9.11	

DOUBLEST

Line	Work	Reference	Speaker
Venus, why doublest thou my endlesse smart?	Ovid's Elegies	2.10.11	

DOUBT

Line	Work	Reference	Speaker
To rid thee of that doubt, abourd againe,	Dido	4.4.21	Dido
Doubt not my Lord and gratious Soveraigne,	1Tamb	1.1.70	Therid
I doubt not shortly but to raigne sole king,	1Tamb	1.1.175	Cosroe
For you then Maddam, I am out of doubt.	1Tamb	1.2.258	Tamb
And doubt you not, but if you favour me,	1Tamb	2.3.10	Tamb
Your Highnesse needs not doubt but in short time,	1Tamb	3.2.32	Agidas
I doubt not but the Governour will yeeld,	1Tamb	4.2.113	Therid
Then doubt I not but faire Zenocrate/Will soone consent to	1Tamb	5.1.498	Tamb
And now I doubt not but your royall cares/Hath so provided for	2Tamb	3.1.20	Callap
We shall not need to nourish any doubt,	2Tamb	3.1.26	Callap
Doubt not my lord, but we shal conquer him.	2Tamb	5.2.12	Amasia
No doubt, but you shal soone recover all.	2Tamb	5.3.99	Phsitn
No doubt, brother, but this proceedeth of the spirit.	Jew	1.2.327	1Fryar
I doe not doubt by your divine precepts/And mine owne industry,	Jew	1.2.334	Abigal
I, I, no doubt but shee's at your command.	Jew	2.3.39	Barab
No doubt your soule shall reape the fruit of it.	Jew	2.3.78	Lodowk
Thou shalt not live in doubt of any thing.	Jew	5.5.45	Barab
Comfort your selfe my Lord and have no doubt,	P 541	11.6	Navrre
Twere hard with me if I should doubt my kinne,	P 971	19.41	King
have we cause/To cast the worst, and doubt of your revolt.	Edw	2.3.8	Warwck
No doubt, such lessons they will teach the rest,	Edw	3.1.21	Spencr
I doubt it not my lord, right will prevaile.	Edw	3.1.189	Spencr
doubt yee not,/We will finde comfort, money, men, and friends	Edw	4.2.64	SrJohn
A will be had ere long I doubt it not.	Edw	4.3.20	Spencr
They shalbe started thence I doubt it not.	Edw	4.6.60	Mortmr
Have you no doubt my Lorde, have you no feare,	Edw	4.7.1	Abbot
Then doubt not Faustus but to be renowm'd,	F 168	1.1.140	Cornel
I do not doubt but to see you both hang'd the next Sessions.	F 212	1.2.19	P Wagner
I there's no doubt of that, for me thinkes you make no hast to	F1516	4.5.12	P Hostss

DOUBT (cont.)			
I doubt not shal sufficiently content your Imperiall majesty.	F App	p.237 48	P Faust
But doubt thou not (revenge doth griefe appease)/With thy	Ovid's Elegies	1.7.63	
Cupid by thee, Mars in great doubt doth trample,	Ovid's Elegies	2.9.47	
Wearie Corinna hath her life in doubt.	Ovid's Elegies	2.13.2	
And doubt to which desire the palme to give.	Ovid's Elegies	3.10.40	
When carefull Rome in doubt their prowesse held.	Ovid's Elegies	3.14.10	
DOUBTFULL			
What meanes faire Dido by this doubtfull speech?	Dido	3.4.31	Aeneas
armours fight/A doubtfull battell with my tempted thoughtes,	1Tamb	5.1.152	Tamb
From doubtfull Roome wrongly expel'd the Tribunes,	Lucan, First Booke	269	
To doubtfull Sirtes and drie Affricke, where/A fury leades the	Lucan, First Booke	686	
Doubtfull is warre and love, the vanquisht rise/And who thou	Ovid's Elegies	1.9.29	
'Tis doubtfull whether verse availe, or harme,	Ovid's Elegies	3.11.13	
DOUBTLES			
Doubtles Apollos Axeltree is crackt,	Dido	4.1.11	Achat
Doubtles these northren men/Whom death the greatest of all	Lucan, First Booke	454	
DOUBTLESLY			
He dares so doubtlesly resolve of rule,	1Tamb	2.6.13	Meandr
DOUBTS			
Faire Queene of love, I will devorce these doubts,	Dido	3.2.85	Juno
To lighten doubts and frustrate subtile foes.	P 457	8.7	Anjoy
no, to decide all doubts, be rulde by me, lets hang him heere	P 491	9.10	P 2Atndt
Have you no doubts my lords, ile [clap so] <claps> close,/Among	Edw	3.1.276	Levune
Cast no more doubts; Mephostophilis come/And bring glad tydings	F 415	2.1.27	Faust
Who doubts, with Pelius, Thetis did consort,	Ovid's Elegies	2.17.17	
DOUBTST			
What doubtst thou us?	Lucan, First Booke	363	
DOVE			
will I shew my selfe to have more of the Serpent then the Dove;	Jew	2.3.37	P Barab
But most thou friendly turtle-dove, deplore.	Ovid's Elegies	2.6.12	
Such to the parrat was the turtle dove.	Ovid's Elegies	2.6.16	
DOVES			
These milke white Doves shall be his Centronels:	Dido	2.1.320	Venus
my Doves are back returnd,/Who warne me of such daunger prest	Dido	3.2.21	Venus
Had not my Doves discov'rd thy entent:	Dido	3.2.33	Venus
Yoke Venus Doves, put Mirtle on thy haire,	Ovid's Elegies	1.2.23	
And loving Doves kisse eagerly together.	Ovid's Elegies	2.6.56	
DOWAY			
sorte of English priestes/From Doway to the Seminary at Remes,	P1031	19.101	King
DOWER			
And offred as a dower his burning throne,	Hero and Leander	1.7	
Whose only dower was her chastitie,	Hero and Leander	1.412	
DOWN			
an hot alarme/Drive all their horses headlong down the hill.	1Tamb	1.2.135	Usumc
See how he raines down heaps of gold in showers,	1Tamb	1.2.182	Tamb
For as when Jove did thrust old Saturn down,	1Tamb	2.7.36	Usumc
And make him raine down murthering shot from heaven/To dash the	1Tamb	3.3.196	Zabina
With mournfull streamers hanging down their heads,	1Tamb	4.2.120	Tamb
Lye down Arabia, wounded to the death,	1Tamb	5.1.407	Arabia
And murdrous Fates throwes al his triumphs down.	2Tamb	Prol.5	Prolog
And cuts down armies with his [conquering] <conquerings> wings.	2Tamb	4.1.6	Amyras
Will poure down blood and fire on thy head:	2Tamb	4.1.143	Jrslem
Whose flaming traines should reach down to the earth/Could not	2Tamb	5.1.90	Tamb
But came it freely, did the Cow give down her milk freely?	Jew	4.2.102	P Ithimr
Then throw him down.	P 306	5.33	Guise
Husband come down, heer's one would speak with you from the	P 348	6.3	P SrnsWf
So, set it down and leave me to my selfe.	P 666	13.10	Duchss
That thinke with high lookes thus to tread me down.	Edw	2.2.97	Edward
That rampiers fallen down, huge heapes of stone/Lye in our	Lucan, First Booke	25	
Yea and thy father to, and swords thrown down,	Lucan, First Booke	117	
These troupes should soone pull down the church of Jove.	Lucan, First Booke	381	
Beates Thracian Boreas; or when trees [bowe] <bowde> down,/And	Lucan, First Booke	391	
It mocked me, hung down the head and suncke,	Ovid's Elegies	3.6.14	
fire filcht by Prometheus;/And thrusts him down from heaven:	Hero and Leander	1.439	
DOWNE (Homograph)			
As made the bloud run downe about mine eares.	Dido	1.1.8	Ganimd
And Venus Swannes shall shed their silver downe,	Dido	1.1.36	Jupitr
Disquiet Seas lay downe your swelling lookes,	Dido	1.1.122	Venus
Sit downe Aeneas, sit in Didos place,	Dido	2.1.91	Dido
And thinking to goe downe, came Hectors ghost/With ashie	Dido	2.1.201	Aeneas
And with the [wind] <wound> thereof the King fell downe:	Dido	2.1.254	Aeneas
Nor quit good turnes with double fee downe told:	Dido	3.2.15	Juno
And couch him in Adonis purple downe.	Dido	3.2.100	Venus
Where straying in our borders up and downe,	Dido	4.2.12	Iarbus
And when we whisper, then the starres fall downe,	Dido	4.4.53	Dido
Flote up and downe where ere the billowes drive?	Dido	5.1.58	Aeneas
And now downe falles the keeles into the deepe:	Dido	5.1.253	Dido
These are his words, Meander set them downe.	1Tamb	1.1.94	Mycet
their neckes/Hangs massie chaines of golde downe to the waste,	1Tamb	1.2.126	Souldr
Two thousand horse shall forrage up and downe,	1Tamb	3.1.61	Bajzth
Sit downe by her:	1Tamb	3.3.124	Tamb
That roaring, shake Damascus turrets downe.	1Tamb	4.1.3	Souldn
Or withered leaves that Autume shaketh downe:	1Tamb	4.1.32	Souldn
This arme should send him downe to Erebus,	1Tamb	4.1.45	Souldn
The first day when he pitcheth downe his tentes,	1Tamb	4.1.49	2Msngr
Then as I look downe to the damned Feends,	1Tamb	4.2.26	Bajzth
Batter our walles, and beat our Turrets downe.	1Tamb	5.1.2	Govnr
Downe with him, downe with him.	1Tamb	5.1.312	P Zabina
The Sun was downe.	1Tamb	5.1.314	P Zabina
Then sit thou downe divine Zenocrate,	1Tamb	5.1.506	Tamb
The sailes wrapt up, the mast and tacklings downe,	2Tamb	1.2.59	Callap
Their haire as white as milke and soft as Downe,	2Tamb	1.3.25	Tamb

DOWNE (cont.)

And batter downe the castles on the shore.	2Tamb	1.3.126	Therid
Come downe from heaven and live with me againe.	2Tamb	2.4.118	Tamb
Will poure it downe in showers on our heads:	2Tamb	3.1.36	Callap
And I sat downe, cloth'd with the massie robe,	2Tamb	3.2.123	Tamb
troopes/Beats downe our foes to flesh our taintlesse swords?	2Tamb	4.1.26	Amyras
Downe to the channels of your hatefull throats,	2Tamb	4.1.183	Tamb
That whips downe cities, and controwleth crownes,	2Tamb	4.3.100	Tamb
Come downe thy selfe and worke a myracle,	2Tamb	5.1.188	Tamb
Why send'st thou not a furious whyrlwind downe,	2Tamb	5.1.192	Tamb
Amasde, swim up and downe upon the waves,	2Tamb	5.1.207	Techel
To cure me, or Ile fetch him downe my selfe.	2Tamb	5.3.63	Tamb
Are smoothly gliding downe by Candie shoare/To Malta, through	Jew	1.1.46	Barab
sudden fall/Has humbled her and brought her downe to this:	Jew	1.2.368	Mthias
Oh my sweet Ithimore go set it downe/And come againe so soone	Jew	3.4.108	Barab
Lay waste the Iland, hew the Temples downe,	Jew	3.5.14	Govnr
Talke not of racing downe your City wals,	Jew	3.5.21	Basso
And with brasse-bullets batter downe your Towers,	Jew	3.5.24	Basso
which is there/Set downe at large, the Gallants were both	Jew	3.6.29	Abigal
To fire the Churches, pull their houses downe,	Jew	5.1.65	Barab
Downe to the Celler, taste of all my wines.	Jew	5.5.7	Barab
What order wil you set downe for the Massacre?	P 229	4.27	QnMoth
And if they storme, I then may pull them downe.	P 526	9.45	QnMoth
Downe with the Hugonites, murder them.	P 528	10.1	Guise
My sinnewes shrinke, my braines turne upside downe,	P 549	11.14	Charls
But God we know will alwaies put them downe,	P 798	16.12	Navrre
Downe with him, downe with him.	P1002	19.72	P AllMur
By yelping hounds puld downe, and seeme to die.	Edw	1.1.70	Gavstn
Their downfall is at hand, their forces downe,	Edw	1.4.18	Mortmr
For every looke, my lord, drops downe a teare,	Edw	1.4.136	Gavstn
Sweete Mortimer, sit downe by me a while,	Edw	1.4.225	Queene
Should beare us downe of the nobilitie,	Edw	1.4.286	Mortmr
I have the [gesses] <gresses> that will pull you downe,	Edw	2.2.40	Edward
And make the people sweare to put him downe.	Edw	2.2.111	Lncstr
Their wives and children slaine, run up and downe,	Edw	2.2.180	Lncstr
Where womens favors hung like labels downe.	Edw	2.2.187	Mortmr
Come Spencer, come Baldocke, come sit downe by me,	Edw	4.7.16	Edward
Sit downe, for weele be Barbars to your grace.	Edw	5.3.28	Matrvs
Lay downe your weapons, traitors, yeeld the king.	Edw	5.3.55	Kent
The king must die, or Mortimer goes downe,	Edw	5.4.1	Mortmr
Or open his mouth, and powre quick silver downe,	Edw	5.4.36	Ltborn
Your overwatchde my lord, lie downe and rest.	Edw	5.5.92	Ltborn
So, lay the table downe, and stampe on it,	Edw	5.5.112	Ltborn
a point, to which when men aspire,/They tumble hedlong downe:	Edw	5.6.61	Mortmr
If unto [God] <heaven>, hee'le throw me <thee> downe to hell.	F 467	2.1.79	Faust
[And make my spirites pull his churches downe].	F 651	2.2.100A	Faust
downe and thou shalt behold <see al> the seven deadly sinnes	F 655	2.2.104	P Belzeb
come downe with a vengeance.	F 684	2.2.133	P Envy
run up and downe the world with these <this> case of Rapiers,	F 688	2.2.137	P Wrath
thought you did not sneake up and downe after her for nothing.	F 743	2.3.22	P Dick
That looking downe the earth appear'd to me,	F 850	3.1.72	Faust
Cast downe our Foot-stoole.	F 868	3.1.90	Pope
But wee'le pul downe his haughty insolence:	F 914	3.1.136	Pope
Treading the Lyon, and the Dragon downe,	F 920	3.1.142	Pope
Faustus thou shalt, then kneele downe presently,	F 994	3.2.14	Mephst
Welcome Lord Cardinals: come sit downe.	F1009	3.2.29	Pope
Lord Archbishop of Reames, sit downe with us.	F1037	3.2.57	Pope
Be ready then, and strike the Peasant downe.	F1359	4.2.35	Fredrk
That rowling downe, may breake the villaines bones,	F1414	4.2.90	Faust
O I'le leape up to [my God] <heaven>: who puls me downe?	F1938	5.2.142	Faust
Bare downe to hell her sonne, the pledge of peace,	Lucan, First Booke	113	
battailes fought with prosperous successe/May bring her downe,	Lucan, First Booke	286	
Souse downe the wals, and make a passage forth:	Lucan, First Booke	296	
the Altar/He laies a ne're-yoakt Bull, and powers downe wine,	Lucan, First Booke	608	
This said, being tir'd with fury she sunke downe.	Lucan, First Booke	694	
Or why slips downe the Coverlet so oft?	Ovid's Elegies	1.2.2	
If hee lyes downe with Wine and sleepe opprest,	Ovid's Elegies	1.4.53	
Her white necke hid with tresses hanging downe,	Ovid's Elegies	1.5.10	
I clinged her naked bodie, downe she fell,	Ovid's Elegies	1.5.24	
Which to her wast her girdle still kept downe.	Ovid's Elegies	1.7.48	
And downe her cheekes, the trickling teares did flow,	Ovid's Elegies	1.7.57	
Before her feete thrice prostrate downe I fell,	Ovid's Elegies	1.7.61	
rise/And who thou never think'st should fall downe lies.	Ovid's Elegies	1.9.30	
downe againe,/And birds for <from> Memnon yearly shall be	Ovid's Elegies	1.13.3	
from their crowne/Phoebus and Bacchus wisht were hanging downe.	Ovid's Elegies	1.14.32	
Or men with crooked sickles corne downe fell.	Ovid's Elegies	1.15.12	
Ile live, and as he puls me downe, mount higher.	Ovid's Elegies	1.15.42	
the time more short/Lay downe thy forehead in thy lap to snort.	Ovid's Elegies	2.2.24	
Me thinkes she should <would> be nimble when shees downe.	Ovid's Elegies	2.4.14	
When Troy by ten yeares battle tumbled downe,	Ovid's Elegies	2.12.9	
But when she comes, [you] <your> swelling mounts sinck downe,	Ovid's Elegies	2.16.51	
lofty wordes stout Tragedie (she sayd)/Why treadst me downe?	Ovid's Elegies	3.1.36	
To move her feete unheard in [setting] <sitting> downe.	Ovid's Elegies	3.1.52	
Thy legges hang-downe:	Ovid's Elegies	3.2.63	
Jove throwes downe woods, and Castles with his fire:	Ovid's Elegies	3.3.35	
Nor passe I thee, who hollow rocks downe tumbling,	Ovid's Elegies	3.5.45	
shee her modest eyes held downe,/Her wofull bosome a warme	Ovid's Elegies	3.5.67	
Lie downe with shame, and see thou stirre no more,	Ovid's Elegies	3.6.69	
But still droupt downe, regarding not her hand,	Ovid's Elegies	3.6.76	
Who bad thee lie downe here against thy will?	Ovid's Elegies	3.6.78	
And stately robes to their gilt feete hang downe.	Ovid's Elegies	3.12.26	
Or if it could, downe from th'enameld skie,	Hero and Leander	1.249	
of liquid pearle, which downe her face/Made milk-white paths,	Hero and Leander	1.297	

DOWNE (cont.)			
Cupid beats downe her praiers with his wings,	Hero and Leander	1.369	
The while upon a hillocke downe he lay,	Hero and Leander	1.400	
Who with incroching guile, keepes learning downe.	Hero and Leander	1.482	
Viewing Leanders face, fell downe and fainted.	Hero and Leander	2.2	
And kept it downe that it might mount the hier.	Hero and Leander	2.42	
Beat downe the bold waves with his triple mace,	Hero and Leander	2.172	
Cast downe his wearie feet, and felt the sand.	Hero and Leander	2.228	
Being sodainly betraide, dyv'd downe to hide her.	Hero and Leander	2.262	
Dang'd downe to hell her loathsome carriage.	Hero and Leander	2.334	
DOWNEWARD			
Or looking downeward, with your eye lids close,	Edw	2.1.39	Spencr
As pittying these lovers, downeward creepes.	Hero and Leander	2.100	
And as her silver body downeward went,	Hero and Leander	2.263	
DOWNFALL			
Presage the downfall of my Emperie,	Dido	4.4.118	Dido
To worke my downfall and untimely end.	1Tamb	2.7.6	Cosroe
Although my downfall be the deepest hell.	P 104	2.47	Guise
Their downfall is at hand, their forces downe,	Edw	1.4.18	Mortmr
DOWNWARD			
Discendeth downward to th'Antipodes.	2Tamb	1.2.52	Callap
DOWNWARDS			
Shine downwards now no more, but deck the heavens/To entertaine	2Tamb	2.4.20	Tamb
DOWNY			
When they were slender, and like downy mosse,	Ovid's Elegies	1.14.23	
DOZEN (See also DOSEN)			
Go too sirha, take your crown, and make up the halfe dozen.	2Tamb	3.5.136	P Tamb
Three and fifty dozen, I'le pledge thee.	Jew	4.4.8	P Ithimr
DRACOS			
sure/When like the [Dracos] <Drancus> they were writ in blood.	Jew	Prol.21	Machvl
DRAG			
Bring him unto a hurdle, drag him foorth,	Edw	5.6.52	King
From <For> Venice shall they drag <dregge> huge Argosies,/And	F 157	1.1.129	Valdes
DRAG'D			
Through which the Furies drag'd me by the heeles.	F1435	4.3.5	Mrtino
DRAGGE			
Unto mount Faucon will we dragge his coarse:	P 319	5.46	Anjoy
Come dragge him away and throw him in a ditch.	P 345	5.72	Guise
So, dragge them away.	P 535	10.8	Guise
Take thou this other, dragge him through the woods,	F1410	4.2.86	Faust
DRAGGED			
Virgins halfe dead dragged by their golden haire,	Dido	2.1.195	Aeneas
DRAGON			
My Ship, the flying Dragon, is of Spaine,	Jew	2.2.5	Bosco
Treading the Lyon, and the Dragon downe,	F 920	3.1.142	Pope
DRAGONS			
Sprong of the teeth of Dragons venomous,	1Tamb	2.2.48	Meandr
That sprong of teeth of Dragons venomous?	1Tamb	2.2.52	Mycet
Flieng Dragons, lightning, fearfull thunderclaps,	2Tamb	3.2.10	Tamb
Drawne by the strength of yoked <yoky> Dragons neckes;	F 759	2.3.38	2Chor
From East to West his Dragons swiftly glide,	F 766	2.3.45	2Chor
And mounted then upon a Dragons backe,	F 771	2.3.50	2Chor
So high our Dragons soar'd into the aire,	F 849	3.1.71	Faust
(When yawning dragons draw her thirling carre,	Hero and Leander	1.108	
DRAM			
That by the warres lost not a dram of blood,	2Tamb	3.2.113	Tamb
One dram of powder more had made all sure.	Jew	5.1.22	Barab
DRANCUS			
sure/When like the [Dracos] <Drancus> they were writ in blood.	Jew	Prol.21	Machvl
DRANKE			
And held the cloath of pleasance whiles you dranke,	Dido	1.1.6	Ganimd
I dranke of Poppy and cold mandrake juyce;	Jew	5.1.80	Barab
DRAUGHT (See also DROUGHS)			
As fatall be it to her as the draught/Of which great Alexander	Jew	3.4.96	Barab
A draught of flowing Nectar, she requested,	Hero and Leander	1.431	
DRAVE			
And unresisted, drave away riche spoiles.	Edw	2.2.167	Lncstr
Snatching the combe, to beate the wench out drive <drave> her.	Ovid's Elegies	1.14.18	
DRAW			
we were commanded straight/With reverence to draw it into Troy.	Dido	2.1.168	Aeneas
Draw foorth thy sword, thou mighty man at Armes,	1Tamb	1.2.178	Tamb
Which thy prolonged Fates may draw on thee:	1Tamb	3.2.101	Agidas
Shall draw the chariot of my Emperesse,	1Tamb	3.3.80	Bajzth
Never to draw it out, or manage armes/Against thy selfe or thy	2Tamb	1.1.128	Sgsmnd
Techelles, draw thy sword,/And wound the earth, that it may	2Tamb	2.4.96	Tamb
That hanging here, wil draw the Gods from heaven:	2Tamb	3.2.28	Tamb
And harnest like my horses, draw my coch,	2Tamb	3.5.104	Tamb
Ah, pity me my Lord, and draw your sword,	2Tamb	4.2.33	Olymp
What, can ye draw but twenty miles a day,	2Tamb	4.3.2	Tamb
then live, and draw/My chariot swifter than the racking cloudes:	2Tamb	4.3.20	Tamb
They shall to morrow draw my chariot,	2Tamb	4.3.30	Tamb
Wel, now Ile make it quake, go draw him up,	2Tamb	5.1.107	Tamb
teare both our limmes/Rather then we should draw thy chariot,	2Tamb	5.1.139	Orcan
draw you slaves,/In spight of death I will goe show my face.	2Tamb	5.3.113	Tamb
And draw thee peecemeale like Hyppolitus,	2Tamb	5.3.240	Tamb
Did he not draw a sorte of English priestes/From Doway to the	P1030	19.100	King
of a string/May draw the pliant king which way I please:	Edw	1.1.53	Gavstn
Then draw your weapons, and be resolute:	F1335	4.2.11	Benvol
Now draw up Faustus like a foggy mist,	F1952	5.2.156	Faust
My Lord of Lorraine, wilt please you draw neare.	F App	p.231 1	P Pope
And I might pleade, and draw the Commons minds/To favour thee,	Lucan, First Booke	275	
(When yawning dragons draw her thirling carre,	Hero and Leander	1.108	
DRAWE			
Your honor hath an adamant, of power/To drawe a prince.	Edw	2.5.105	Arundl

DRAWE (cont.)			
Thy fatall time doth drawe to finall ende,	F App	p.240 122	Faust
In sleeping shall I fearelesse drawe my breath?	Ovid's Elegies		2.19.55
And for a good verse drawe the first dart forth,	Ovid's Elegies		3.7.27
DRAWEN			
Thou shalt be drawen amidst the frosen Pooles,	1Tamb	1.2.99	Tamb
Have swelling cloudes drawen from wide gasping woundes,	1Tamb	5.1.459	Tamb
Drawen with advise of our Ambassadors.	2Tamb	1.1.126	Orcan
With naked Negros shall thy coach be drawen,	2Tamb	1.2.40	Callap
And thus be drawen with these two idle kings.	2Tamb	4.3.28	Amyras
And drawen with princely Eagles through the path,	2Tamb	4.3.127	Tamb
Drawen with these kings on heaps of carkasses.	2Tamb	5.1.72	Tamb
DRAWER			
Drawer, I hope al is payd, God be with you, come Rafe.	F App	p.234 5	P Robin
You lie Drawer, tis afore me:	F App	p.235 17	P Robin
DRAWES			
Drawes bloody humours from my feeble partes,	1Tamb	4.4.95	Bajzth
Drawes in the comfort of her latest breath/All dasled with the	2Tamb	2.4.13	Tamb
That when he speakes, drawes out his grisly beard,	Jew	4.3.7	Barab
Thy fatall time drawes to a finall end;	F1479	4.4.23	Faust
<O> my God, I would weepe, but the Divell drawes in my teares.	F1851	5.2.55	P Faust
She drawes chast women to incontinence,	Ovid's Elegies		1.8.19
That drawes the day from heavens cold axletree.	Ovid's Elegies		1.13.2
Or thrids which spiders slender foote drawes out/Fastning her	Ovid's Elegies		1.14.7
DRAWETH			
Father, it draweth towards midnight now,	Jew	2.1.55	Abigal
DRAWING			
Drawing from it the shining Lamps of heaven.	2Tamb	3.4.77	Techel
Both come from drawing Faustus latest will.	F1814	5.2.18	Mephst
And with swift Naggs drawing thy little Coach,	Ovid's Elegies		2.16.49
DRAWNE			
Drawne through the heavens by Steedes of Boreas brood,	Dido	1.1.55	Venus
Are drawne by darknes forth Astraeus tents.	Dido	1.1.73	Venus
And where I goe be thus in triumph drawne:	1Tamb	4.2.86	Tamb
And that vile Carkasse drawne by warlike kings,	2Tamb	5.2.16	Amasia
Here must no speeches passe, nor swords be drawne.	Jew	2.3.339	Barab
Have drawne thy treasure drie, and made thee weake,	Edw	2.2.159	Mortmr
Too kinde to them, but now have drawne our sword,	Edw	3.1.25	Edward
Drawne by the strength of yoked <yoky> Dragons neckes;	F 759	2.3.38	2Chor
Then oxen which have drawne the plow before.	Ovid's Elegies		1.2.14
The Docke in harbours ships drawne from the flouds,	Ovid's Elegies		2.9.21
And what poore Dido with her drawne sword sharpe,	Ovid's Elegies		2.18.25
But when her lover came, had she drawne backe,	Ovid's Elegies		3.3.39
The lining, purple silke, with guilt starres drawne,	Hero and Leander		1.10
Unto her was he led, or rather drawne,	Hero and Leander		2.241
DRAWS			
Wars radge draws neare; and to the swords strong hand,	Lucan, First Booke		665
DREAD			
Dread Lord of Affrike, Europe and Asia,	1Tamb	3.1.23	Bajzth
Feends looke on me, and thou dread God of hell,	1Tamb	4.2.27	Bajzth
scepter Angels kisse, and Furies dread)/As for their liberties,	1Tamb	5.1.94	1Virgn
Arme dread Soveraign and my noble Lords.	2Tamb	2.2.24	1Msngr
Nor, if thou couzenst one, dread to for-sweare,	Ovid's Elegies		1.8.85
So farre 'tis safe, but to go farther dread.	Ovid's Elegies		2.11.16
The wronged Gods dread faire ones to offend,	Ovid's Elegies		3.3.31
DREADFUL			
And thinks to rouse us from our dreadful siege/Of the famous	1Tamb	3.1.5	Bajzth
At night in dreadful vision fearefull Roome,	Lucan, First Booke		188
DREADFULL			
And bullets like Joves dreadfull Thunderbolts,	1Tamb	2.3.19	Tamb
nostrels breathe/Rebellious winds and dreadfull thunderclaps:	1Tamb	5.1.298	Bajzth
O just and dreadfull punisher of sinne,	2Tamb	2.3.4	Sgsmnd
and to subdew/This proud contemner of thy dreadfull power,	2Tamb	4.3.40	Orcan
Though this be held his last daies dreadfull siege,	2Tamb	5.1.29	1Citzn
And walke upon the dreadfull Adders backe,	F 919	3.1.141	Pope
Or be assured of our dreadfull curse,	F 938	3.1.160	Pope
For such a dreadfull night, was never seene,	F1984	5.3.2	1Schol
With dreadfull horror of these damned fiends.	F1994	5.3.12	3Schol
At Munda let the dreadfull battailes joyne;	Lucan, First Booke		40
rings of fire/Flie in the ayre, and dreadfull bearded stars,	Lucan, First Booke		526
Curling their bloudy lockes, howle dreadfull things,	Lucan, First Booke		565
Bearing the head with dreadfull [Adders] <Arrowes> clad,	Ovid's Elegies		3.5.14
And as in furie of a dreadfull fight,	Hero and Leander		1.119
But with a ghastly dreadfull countenaunce,	Hero and Leander		1.381
DREADLESSE			
Dreadlesse of blowes, of bloody wounds and death:	2Tamb	3.2.140	Tamb
Torture or paine can daunt my dreadlesse minde.	2Tamb	5.1.113	Govnr
DREAME			
Hermes this night descending in a dreame,	Dido	4.3.3	Aeneas
Fond men, what dreame you of their multitudes?	Jew	1.1.157	Barab
Give charge to Morpheus that he may dreame/A golden dreame, and	Jew	2.1.36	Abigal
Give charge to Morpheus that he may dreame/A golden dreame, and	Jew	2.1.37	Abigal
stands in feare/Of that which you, I thinke, ne're dreame upon,	Jew	2.3.283	Barab
then will I wake thee from this folishe dreame/and lett thee	Paris	ms32,p391	Guise
DREAMES			
The dreames (brave mates) that did beset my bed,	Dido	4.3.16	Aeneas
He sleeps my Lord, but dreames not of his hornes.	F1280	4.1.126	Faust
DREAMING			
Hoping (misled by dreaming prophesies)/To raigne in Asia, and	1Tamb	1.1.41	Meandr
DREARY (See also DRERIE)			
O dreary Engines of my loathed sight,	1Tamb	5.1.259	Bajzth
DREGGE			
From <For> Venice shall they drag <dregge> huge Argosies,/And	F 157	1.1.129	Valdes

DREGGES			
Created of the massy dregges of earth,	2Tamb	4.1.123	Tamb
DREGS			
Fed with the fresh supply of earthly dregs,	2Tamb	3.2.8	Tamb
DRENCH			
And drench Silvanus dwellings with their shewers,	Dido	3.2.91	Juno
Here's a drench to poyson a whole stable of Flanders mares:	Jew	3.4.111	P Ithimr
And with their pawes drench his black soule in hell.	P1102	20.12	Cardnl
DRENCHED			
Ascanius, goe and drie thy drenched lims,	Dido	1.1.174	Aeneas
DRENCHES			
And all things too much in their sole power drenches.	Ovid's Elegies		3.3.26
DRENCHT			
And in the fleeting sea the earth be drencht.	Lucan, First Booke		653
And night deepe drencht in mystie Acheron,	Hero and Leander		1.189
DRERIE			
Then drerie Mars, carowsing Nectar boules.	Hero and Leander		2.258
DRESSE			
Till we have fire to dresse the meate we kild:	Dido	1.1.165	Aeneas
To dresse the common souldiers meat and drink.	1Tamb	3.3.185	Zenoc
Feardst thou to dresse them?	Ovid's Elegies		1.14.5
Behold Cypassis wont to dresse thy head,	Ovid's Elegies		2.7.17
With scepters, and high buskins th'one would dresse me,	Ovid's Elegies		3.1.63
DRESSINGS			
And vanquisht people curious dressings lend thee,	Ovid's Elegies		1.14.46
DREST			
Oft was she drest before mine eyes, yet never,	Ovid's Elegies		1.14.17
[I thinke what one undeckt would be, being drest];	Ovid's Elegies		2.4.37
When you are up and drest, be sage and grave,	Ovid's Elegies		3.13.19
DREW			
Then buckled I mine armour, drew my sword,	Dido	2.1.200	Aeneas
Achilles horse/Drew him in triumph through the Greekish Campe,	Dido	2.1.206	Aeneas
Here lye the Sword that in the darksome Cave/He drew, and swore	Dido	5.1.296	Dido
These Mores that drew him from Bythinia,	1Tamb	4.2.98	Tamb
And drew a thousand ships to Tenedos,	2Tamb	2.4.88	Tamb
Thee Pompous birds and him two tygres drew.	Ovid's Elegies		1.2.48
tincture of her cheekes, that drew/The love of everie swaine:	Hero and Leander		1.396
DREWE			
My Mistris deity also drewe me fro it,	Ovid's Elegies		2.18.17
DRIE			
Ascanius, goe and drie thy drenched lims,	Dido	1.1.174	Aeneas
And drie with griefe was turnd into a stone,	Dido	2.1.5	Aeneas
My vaines are withered, and my sinewes drie,	Dido	4.5.33	Nurse
Is drie and cold, and now dooth gastly death/With greedy	1Tamb	2.7.48	Cosroe
My vaines are pale, my sinowes hard and drie,	1Tamb	4.4.97	Bajzth
(wanting moisture and remorsefull blood)/Drie up with anger,	2Tamb	4.1.180	Soria
Have drawne thy treasure drie, and made thee weake,	Edw	2.2.159	Mortmr
To doubtfull Sirtes and drie Affricke, where/A fury leades the	Lucan, First Booke		686
Such as Amimone through the drie fields strayed/When on her	Ovid's Elegies		1.10.5
By charmes are running springs and fountaines drie,	Ovid's Elegies		3.6.32
DRIED			
Whereby the moisture of your blood is dried,	2Tamb	5.3.85	Phsitn
Wet with my teares, and dried againe with sighes,	Edw	5.1.118	Edward
DRIES			
Fond worldling, now his heart bloud dries with griefe;	F1808	5.2.12	Mephst
DRIFT			
And not let Dido understand their drift:	Dido	4.4.6	Dido
Whose drift is onely to dishonor thee.	2Tamb	4.2.7	Olymp
To dash the heavie headed Edmunds drift,	Edw	5.2.39	Mortmr
Lest greater dangers <danger> do attend thy drift.	F1752	5.1.79	Mephst
Our prayers move thee to assist our drift,	Ovid's Elegies		2.3.17
DRIFTES			
Will never prosper your intended driftes,	1Tamb	1.2.69	Zenoc
DRIFTS			
Are greatest to discourage all our drifts,	2Tamb	5.2.45	Callap
DRINK			
To dresse the common souldiers meat and drink.	1Tamb	3.3.185	Zenoc
wines/Shall common Souldiers drink in quaffing boules,	2Tamb	1.3.222	Tamb
Pleaseth your Majesty to drink this potion,	2Tamb	5.3.78	Phsitn
Of that condition I wil drink it up; here's to thee.	Jew	4.4.4	P Ithimr
Lord Raymond, I drink unto your grace.	F1053	3.2.73	Pope
Why will he not drink of all waters?	F1470	4.4.14	P HrsCsr
I, I, the house is good enough to drink in:	F1617	4.6.60	P HrsCsr
DRINKE			
which by fame is said/To drinke the mightie Parthian Araris,	1Tamb	2.3.16	Tamb
glut our swords/That thirst to drinke the feble Perseans blood.	1Tamb	3.3.165	Bajzth
belike he hath not bene watered to day, give him some drinke.	1Tamb	4.4.55	P Tamb
To drinke the river Nile or Euphrates,	2Tamb	3.1.42	Orcan
And drinke in pailes the strongest Muscadell:	2Tamb	4.3.19	Tamb
I'le pledge thee, love, and therefore drinke it off.	Jew	4.4.1	Curtzn
Wilt drinke French-man, here's to thee with a--pox on this	Jew	4.4.32	P Ithimr
What, all alone? well fare sleepy drinke.	Jew	5.1.61	Barab
And if you like them, drinke your fill and dye:	Jew	5.5.9	Barab
As sooner shall they drinke the Ocean dry,	Jew	5.5.121	Govnr
That you may drinke your fill, and quaffe in bloud,	Edw	3.1.137	Edward
that the lowly earth/Should drinke his bloud, mounts up into	Edw	5.1.14	Edward
me, as if they payd for their meate and drinke, I can tell you.	F 365	1.4.23	P Robin
Drinke to our late and happy victory.	F 980	3.1.202	Pope
turn'd to a gaping Oyster, and drinke nothing but salt water.	F1320	4.1.166	P Benvol
he will drinke of all waters, but ride him not into the water;	F1472	4.4.16	P Faust
Some more drinke Hostesse.	F1555	4.5.51	P Carter
we'le into another roome and drinke a while, and then we'le go	F1556	4.5.52	P Robin
'faith Ile drinke a health to thy wooden leg for that word.	F1627	4.6.70	P HrsCsr

DRINKE (cont.)			
with my flesh, as if they had payd for my meate and drinke.	F App	p.230 29	P Clown
my Lord Ile drinke to your grace	F App	p.231 12	P Pope
why sir, wil he not drinke of all waters?	F App	p.239 110	P HrsCsr
he wil drinke of al waters, but ride him not into the water,	F App	p.239 111	P Faust
What wine he fills thee, wisely will him drinke,	Ovid's Elegies		1.4.29
Entreat thy husband drinke, but do not kisse,	Ovid's Elegies		1.4.51
Nor servile water shalt thou drinke for ever.	Ovid's Elegies		1.6.26
Even as the sicke desire forbidden drinke.	Ovid's Elegies		3.4.18
Wild savages, that drinke of running springs,	Hero and Leander		1.259
That of the cooling river durst not drinke,	Hero and Leander		2.197
DRINKES			
And while he drinkes, to adde more do not misse,	Ovid's Elegies		1.4.52
And drinkes stolne waters in surrownding floudes.	Ovid's Elegies		2.19.32
DRINKS			
And make it quake at every drop it drinks:	1Tamb	5.1.462	Tamb
DRINKST			
And where thou drinkst, on that part I will sup.	Ovid's Elegies		1.4.32
DRISLING			
Or drop out both mine eyes in drisling teares,	Dido	4.2.41	Iarbus
Or ever drisling drops of Aprill showers,	1Tamb	4.1.31	Souldn
Longing to view Orions drisling looke <looks>,	F 230	1.3.2	Faust
DRISSELL			
Or that these teares that drissell from mine eyes,	Edw	2.4.19	Queene
DRIVE (See also DRAVE)			
his entent/The windes did drive huge billowes to the shoare,	Dido	2.1.139	Aeneas
O blessed tempests that did drive him in,	Dido	4.4.94	Dido
Drive if you can my house to Italy:	Dido	4.4.129	Dido
Flote up and downe where ere the billowes drive?	Dido	5.1.58	Aeneas
Then gan they drive into the Ocean,	Dido	5.1.231	Anna
an hot alarme/Drive all their horses headlong down the hill.	1Tamb	1.2.135	Usumc
To drive all sorrow from my fainting soule:	1Tamb	5.1.429	Arabia
Come, thou and I wil goe to cardes to drive away the time.	2Tamb	4.1.61	P Calyph
the winds/To drive their substance with successefull blasts?	Jew	1.1.111	Barab
Shall drive no plaintes into the Guises eares,	P 532	10.5	Guise
Wee'l beat him back, and drive him to his death,	P 929	18.30	Navrre
Despaire doth drive distrust into my thoughts.	F1480	4.4.24	Faust
Dispaire doth drive distrust unto my thoughts,	F App	p.240 123	Faust
Snatching the combe, to beate the wench out drive <drave> her.	Ovid's Elegies		1.14.18
DRIVEN			
Have oft driven backe the horses of the night,	Dido	1.1.26	Jupitr
How neere my sweet Aeneas art thou driven?	Dido	1.1.170	Venus
To know what coast the winde hath driven us on,	Dido	1.1.176	Aeneas
Who driven by warre from forth my native world,	Dido	1.1.217	Aeneas
For we are strangers driven on this shore,	Dido	2.1.43	Aeneas
driven to a non-plus at the critical aspect of my terrible	Jew	4.2.13	P Pilia
With awkward windes, and sore tempests driven/To fall on shoare,	Edw	4.7.34	Baldck
wars,/We from our houses driven, most willingly/Suffered exile:	Lucan, First Booke		279
But though I like a swelling floud was driven,	Ovid's Elegies		1.7.43
love please/[Am] <And> driven like a ship upon rough seas,	Ovid's Elegies		2.4.8
DRIVER			
What horse-driver thou favourst most is best,	Ovid's Elegies		3.2.7
DRIVES			
fares Callymath, What wind drives you thus into Malta rhode?	Jew	3.5.2	P Govnr
To what event my secret purpose drives,	Jew	5.2.122	Barab
And drives his nobles to these exigents/For Gaveston, will if	Edw	2.5.62	Warwck
He must needs goe that the Divell drives.	F1419	4.2.95	Fredrk
His Artfull sport, drives all sad thoughts away.	F1673	4.6.116	Duke
and where swift Rhodanus/Drives Araris to sea; They neere the	Lucan, First Booke		435
I know not whether my mindes whirle-wind drives me.	Ovid's Elegies		2.9.28
DRIZZLE (See DRISSELL)			
DROOPE (See also DROUP)			
Wel, since I see the state of Persea droope,	1Tamb	1.1.155	Cosroe
Speake not unto her, let her droope and pine.	Edw	1.4.162	Edward
Thy absence made me droope, and pine away,	Edw	2.2.52	Edward
But droope not madam, noble mindes contemne/Despaire:	Edw	4.2.16	SrJohn
My lord, why droope you thus?	Edw	4.7.60	Leistr
Seeke all the meanes thou canst to make him droope,	Edw	5.2.54	Mortmr
But when I die, would I might droope with doing,	Ovid's Elegies		2.10.35
DROOPES			
Earth droopes and saies, that hell in heaven is plac'd.	2Tamb	5.3.16	Therid
Earth droopes and saies that hel in heaven is plac'd.	2Tamb	5.3.41	Usumc
DROOPING			
If that be all, then cheare thy drooping lookes,	Dido	5.1.71	Iarbus
Drooping and pining for Zenocrate.	2Tamb	2.4.142	Tamb
Never againe lift up this drooping head,	Edw	4.7.42	Edward
and higher set/The drooping thoughts of base declining soules,	Hero and Leander		2.257
DROOPS			
How now, why droops the earle of Lancaster?	Edw	1.2.9	MortSr
DROOPT			
And for Patroclus sterne Achillis droopt:	Edw	1.4.394	MortSr
DROP			
Or drop out both mine eyes in drisling teares,	Dido	4.2.41	Iarbus
And make it quake at every drop it drinks:	1Tamb	5.1.462	Tamb
My boy, Thou shalt not loose a drop of blood,	2Tamb	3.2.137	Tamb
I, master, he's slain; look how his brains drop out on's nose.	Jew	4.1.178	P Ithimr
There, if thou lov'st me doe not leave a drop.	Jew	4.4.6	P Ithimr
Be it to make the Moone drop from her Sphere,	F 266	1.3.38	Faust
One drop [would save my soule, halfe a drop, ah] my Christ.	F1940	5.2.144	Faust
One drop <of bloud will save me; oh> my Christ.	F1940	(HC271)B	Faust
One drop [would save my soule, halfe a drop, ah] my Christ.	F1940	5.2.144	Faust
Breake heart, drop bloud, and mingle it with teares,	F App	p.243 38	OldMan
(If I have faith) I sawe the starres drop bloud,	Ovid's Elegies		1.8.11

DROPPING
His harnesse dropping bloud, and on his speare/The mangled head — Dido 2.1.214 Aeneas
At every pore let blood comme dropping foorth, — 1Tamb 5.1.227 Zabina
would have thought their houses had bin fierd/Or dropping-ripe, — Lucan, First Booke 491

DROPPING-RIPE
would have thought their houses had bin fierd/Or dropping-ripe, — Lucan, First Booke 491

DROPS
As in the Sea are little water drops: — Dido 4.4.63 Dido
As hath the Ocean or the Terrene sea/Small drops of water, when — 1Tamb 3.1.11 Bajzth
Or ever drisling drops of Aprill showers, — 1Tamb 4.1.31 Souldn
In number more than are the drops that fall/When Boreas rents a — 2Tamb 1.3.159 Tamb
And drops of scalding lead, while all thy joints/Be rackt and — 2Tamb 3.5.124 Tamb
Whose scalding drops wil pierce thy seething braines, — 2Tamb 4.1.144 Jrslem
For every looke, my lord, drops downe a teare, — Edw 1.4.136 Gavstn
O soule be chang'd into <to> [little] <small> water drops, — F1977 5.2.181 Faust
By charmes maste drops from okes, from vines grapes fall, — Ovid's Elegies 3.6.33
And fell in drops like teares, because they mist him. — Hero and Leander 2.174

DROPT
O would my bloud dropt out from every vaine, — Edw 5.5.66 Edward

DROSSE
And all is drosse that is not Helena. — F1774 5.1.101 Faust

DROSSIE
In heaping up a masse of drossie pelfe, — Hero and Leander 1.244

DROUGHS
May spelles and droughs <drugges> do sillie soules such harmes? — Ovid's Elegies 3.6.28

DROUP
And let her droup, my heart is light enough. — P1064 19.134 King

DROUPING
Drouping more then a Rose puld yesterday: — Ovid's Elegies 3.6.66
How piteously with drouping wings he stands, — Ovid's Elegies 3.8.9

DROUPT
see where she comes, as if she droupt/To heare these newes. — P1062 19.132 Eprnon
But still droupt downe, regarding not her hand, — Ovid's Elegies 3.6.76

DROUSIE
But he doth lurke within his drousie couch, — P 737 14.40 Navrre

DROWN'D
Thousands of men drown'd in Asphaltis Lake, — 2Tamb 5.1.204 Techel
Nor may our hearts all drown'd in teares of blood, — 2Tamb 5.3.214 Usumc
But cruelly by her was drown'd and rent. — Ovid's Elegies 3.1.58

DROWND
Him the last day in black Averne hath drownd, — Ovid's Elegies 3.8.27

DROWNE
And charg'd him drowne my sonne with all his traine. — Dido 1.1.61 Venus
Techelles, Drowne them all, man, woman, and child, — 2Tamb 5.1.170 Tamb
Her wofull bosome a warme shower did drowne. — Ovid's Elegies 3.5.68

DROWNED
No flowing waves with drowned ships forth poured, — Ovid's Elegies 2.16.25

DROWNING
me but a little straw, and had much ado to escape drowning: — F1487 4.4.31 P HrsCsr
I sat upon a bottle of hey, never so neare drowning in my life: — F App p.240 135 P HrsCsr

DROWSIE
But may soft love rowse up my drowsie eies, — Ovid's Elegies 2.10.19

DROWSINES
Baldock, this drowsines/Betides no good, here even we are — Edw 4.7.44 Spencr

DROWSY (See also DROUSIE)
Strike them with sloth, and drowsy idlenesse; — F 894 3.1.116 Faust

DRUDGE
Hearst thou Anippe, how thy drudge doth talk, — 1Tamb 3.3.182 Zenoc
This <His> study fits a Mercenarie drudge, — F 61 1.1.33 Faust

DRUDGERIE
I may not dure this female drudgerie, — Dido 4.3.55 Aeneas

DRUDGERY
Smear'd with blots of basest drudgery: — 1Tamb 5.1.268 Bajzth

DRUGGES
May spelles and droughs <drugges> do sillie soules such harmes? — Ovid's Elegies 3.6.28

DRUGS
to their soules I think/As are Thessalian drugs or Mithradate. — 1Tamb 5.1.133 Tamb
And every bullet dipt in poisoned drugs. — 1Tamb 5.1.222 Bajzth
Inestimable drugs and precious stones, — 2Tamb 5.3.152 Tamb
Ware-houses stuft with spices and with drugs, — Jew 4.1.64 Barab

DRUIDES
And Druides you now in peace renew/Your barbarous customes, and — Lucan, First Booke 446

DRUM
Strike up the Drum and martch corragiously, — 1Tamb 2.2.72 Meandr
Then strike up Drum, and all the Starres that make/The — 1Tamb 2.6.36 Cosroe
But stay a while, summon a parle, Drum, — 2Tamb 3.3.11 Therid
One plaies continually upon a Drum, — Edw 5.5.61 Edward
Approcht the swelling streame with drum and ensigne, — Lucan, First Booke 207

DRUMMES
let your sounding Drummes/Direct our Souldiers to Damascus — 1Tamb 4.3.61 Souldn

DRUMS
Drums, why sound ye not when Meander speaks. — 1Tamb 2.2.75 Mycet
Affrica, and Greece/Follow my Standard and my thundring Drums: — 2Tamb 1.1.159 Orcan
Trumpets and drums, alarum presently, — 2Tamb 3.3.62 Techel
when our enemies drums/And ratling cannons thunder in our eares — 2Tamb 4.1.12 Amyras
No, strike the drums, and in revenge of this, — 2Tamb 5.3.57 Tamb
Drums strike alarum, raise them from their sport, — Edw 2.3.25 Mortmr
Sound drums and trumpets, marche with me my friends, — Edw 3.1.260 Edward
Trumpets and drums, like deadly threatning other, — Lucan, First Booke 6

DRUNCKE
druncke with ipocrase at any taberne in Europe for nothing, — F App p.234 23 P Robin
A little boy druncke teate-distilling showers. — Ovid's Elegies 3.9.22

DRUNKE
I would have either drunke his dying bloud, — Dido 3.3.28 Iarbus

DRUNKE (cont.)			
The Monster that hath drunke a sea of blood,	2Tamb	5.2.13	Amasia
be it to her as the draught/Of which great Alexander drunke,	Jew	3.4.97	Barab
if a man be drunke over night, the Divell cannot hurt him in	F1201	4.1.47	P Benvol
lust of warre/Hath made Barbarians drunke with Latin bloud?	Lucan, First Booke		9
Not drunke, your faults [in] <on> the spilt wine I numbred.	Ovid's Elegies		2.5.14
The Argos wrackt had deadly waters drunke.	Ovid's Elegies		2.11.6
What thirstie traveller ever drunke of thee?	Ovid's Elegies		3.5.97
Yet like as if cold hemlocke I had drunke,	Ovid's Elegies		3.6.13
And drunke with gladnesse, to the dore she goes.	Hero and Leander		2.236
DRUNKEN			
And make love drunken with thy sweete desire:	Dido	3.3.75	Iarbus
here's to thee with a--pox on this drunken hick-up.	Jew	4.4.33	P Ithimr
Bride did incite/The drunken Centaures to a sodaine fight.	Ovid's Elegies		1.4.8
To cruell armes their drunken selves did summon.	Ovid's Elegies		2.12.20
DRY			
As sooner shall they drinke the Ocean dry,	Jew	5.5.121	Govnr
The spirits tell me they can dry the sea,	F 171	1.1.143	Cornel
brave, prethee let's to it presently, for I am as dry as a dog.	F 751	2.3.30	P Dick
I, pray do, for Faustus is a dry.	F1052	3.2.72	Faust
Love conquer'd shame, the furrowes dry were burnd,	Ovid's Elegies		3.9.29
DRYE			
Least to the waxe the hold-fast drye gemme cleaves,	Ovid's Elegies		2.15.16
Drye Enipeus, Tyro to embrace,	Ovid's Elegies		3.5.43
Or full of dust doest on the drye earth slide.	Ovid's Elegies		3.5.96
Drye winters aye, and sunnes in heate extreame.	Ovid's Elegies		3.5.106
DRYFOOT			
That you may dryfoot martch through lakes and pooles,	2Tamb	3.2.86	Tamb
DU (See also DIEU, DUGARD)			
Mor du, wert <were> not the fruit within thy wombe,	P 688	13.32	Guise
Par [le] <la> mor du, Il mora.	P 770	15.28	Guise
DUBBLE			
Shall yeeld to dignitie a dubble birth,	Dido	1.1.107	Jupitr
DUCAT (See DUCKETS)			
DUCKE			
And ducke as low as any bare-foot Fryar,	Jew	2.3.25	Barab
When, ducke you?	Jew	3.3.51	P Ithimr
DUCKETS			
but for one bare night/A hundred Duckets have bin freely given:	Jew	3.1.3	Curtzn
of golden plate; besides two thousand duckets ready coin'd:	F1676	5.1.3	P Wagner
DUE (See also DEW)			
away, and let due praise be given/Neither to Fate nor Fortune,	Jew	5.5.123	Govnr
By due discent the Regall seat is mine.	P 470	8.20	Anjoy
It is my due by just succession:	P 570	11.35	Navrre
Of dutie and allegeance due to thee.	Edw	1.4.62	ArchBp
We'll give his mangled limbs due buryall:	F1999	5.3.17	2Schol
Thankes worthely are due for things unbought,	Ovid's Elegies		1.10.43
DUETIE			
But love and duetie led him on perhaps,	Dido	3.3.15	Aeneas
DUETY			
yet for that love and duety bindes me thereunto, I am content	F App	p.236 15	P Faust
Now my good Lord having done my duety, I humbly take my leave.	F App	p.238 86	P Faust
DUGARD			
The keepers hands and corps-dugard to passe/The souldiours, and	Ovid's Elegies		1.9.27
DUKE			
Duke of [Assiria] <Affrica> and Albania,	1Tamb	1.1.164	Ortyg
The king of Boheme, and the Austrich Duke,	2Tamb	1.1.95	Orcan
you mark the Cardinall/The Guises brother, and the Duke Dumain:	P 48	1.48	Admral
The late suspition of the Duke of Guise,	P 178	3.13	Navrre
My noble sonne, and princely Duke of Guise,	P 203	4.1	QnMoth
And to my Nephew heere the Duke of Guise:	P 226	4.24	Charls
The Duke of Guise stampes on thy liveles bulke.	P 315	5.42	Guise
Mountsorrell from the Duke of Guise.	P 347	6.2	Mntsrl
down, heer's one would speak with you from the Duke of Guise.	P 349	6.4	P SrnsWf
the Duke of Joyeux/Hath made great sute unto the King therfore.	P 733	14.36	1Msngr
come Epernoune/Lets goe seek the Duke and make them freends.	P 786	15.44	King
The Duke is slaine and all his power dispearst,	P 787	16.1	Navrre
that dares make the Duke a cuckolde, and use a counterfeite key	P 806	17.1	P Souldr
Thou shouldst perceive the Duke of Guise is mov'd.	P 832	17.27	Guise
Else all France knowes how poor a Duke thou art.	P 844	17.39	Eprnon
And please your grace the Duke of Guise doth crave/Accesse unto	P 959	19.29	Eprnon
For in thee is the Duke of Guises hope.	P 988	19.58	Guise
Tut they are pesants, I am Duke of Guise:	P 998	19.68	Guise
When Duke Dumaine his brother is alive,	P1055	19.125	King
And will him in my name to kill the Duke.	P1058	19.128	King
These two will make one entire Duke of Guise,	P1060	19.130	King
Yet lives/My brother Duke Dumaine, and many moe:	P1099	20.9	Cardnl
Sweet Duke of Guise our prop to leane upon,	P1110	21.4	Dumain
duke a cuckolde and use a counterfeyt key to his privy chamber	Paris	ms 1,p390	P Souldr
And there unhorste the duke of Cleremont.	Edw	5.5.70	Edward
see Duke of Saxony,/Two spreading hornes most strangely	F1276	4.1.122	Emper
the Duke of Vanholt doth earnestly entreate your company, and	F1500	4.4.44	P Wagner
The Duke of Vanholt's an honourable Gentleman, and one to whom	F1503	4.4.47	P Faust
What is the reason you disturbe the Duke?	F1592	4.6.35	Servnt
And trouble not the Duke.	F1598	4.6.41	Servnt
Sir, the Duke of Vanholt doth earnestly entreate your company.	F App	p.241 168	P Wagner
The Duke of Vanholt!	F App	p.241 170	P Faust
DUKEDOMES			
the Persean king/Should offer present Dukedomes to our state,	1Tamb	1.2.215	Techel
DULCE			
fuit aut tibi quidquam/Dulce meum, miserere domus labentis:	Dido	5.1.137	Dido
DULD			
Duld with much beating slowly forth doth passe.	Ovid's Elegies		2.7.16

DULL			
To dull the ayre with my discoursive moane.	Dido	1.1.248	Aeneas
O dull conceipted Dido, that till now/Didst never thinke Aeneas	Dido	3.1.82	Dido
My selfe was dull, and faint, to sloth inclinde,	Ovid's Elegies		1.9.41
commodious/And to give signes dull wit to thee is odious.	Ovid's Elegies		1.11.4
Thy dull hand stayes thy striving enemies harmes.	Ovid's Elegies		2.9.12
And the dull snake about thy offrings creepe,	Ovid's Elegies		2.13.13
Like a dull Cipher, or rude blocke I lay,	Ovid's Elegies		3.6.15
Are reeking water, and dull earthlie fumes.	Hero and Leander		2.116
DUM			
Therefore with dum imbracement let us part.	Edw	1.4.134	Edward
Thus while dum signs their yeelding harts entangled,	Hero and Leander		1.187
DUMAIN			
you mark the Cardinall/The Guises brother, and the Duke Dumain:	P 48	1.48	Admral
Tis well advisde Dumain, goe see it strait be done.	P 424	7.64	Guise
DUMAINE			
Anjoy, Dumaine, Gonzago, Retes, sweare by/The argent crosses in	P 274	5.1	Guise
Will be as resolute as I and Dumaine:	P 323	5.50	Guise
And so will Dumaine.	P 334	5.61	Dumain
When Duke Dumaine his brother is alive,	P1055	19.125	King
Yet lives/My brother Duke Dumaine, and many moe:	P1099	20.9	Cardnl
DUMBE (See also DUM)			
But in dumbe silence let them come and goe.	F1252	4.1.98	Faust
DUMP			
Why how now Don Mathias, in a dump?	Jew	1.2.374	Lodowk
DUMPES			
Aeneas, leave these dumpes and lets away,	Dido	3.3.60	Dido
How now Aeneas, sad, what meanes these dumpes?	Dido	5.1.62	Iarbus
DUNCES			
yet if you were not dunces, you would never aske me such a	F 207	1.2.14	P Wagner
DUNGEON			
Within a dungeon Englands king is kept,	Edw	5.3.19	Edward
Heeres a light to go into the dungeon.	Edw	5.5.37	Gurney
This dungeon where they keepe me, is the sincke,	Edw	5.5.56	Edward
DUOBUS			
Si una eademque res legatur duobus, alter rem, alter valorem	F 56	1.1.28	P Faust
DURE			
I may not dure this female drudgerie,	Dido	4.3.55	Aeneas
DURING			
and attire/They usde to weare during their time of life,	F App	p.237 34	Emper
DURST			
That durst thus proudly wrong our kinsmans peace.	Dido	1.1.119	Jupitr
Durst in disdaine of wrong and tyrannie,	1Tamb	2.1.55	Ceneus
As durst resist us till our third daies siege:	2Tamb	5.1.59	Techel
They wondred how you durst with so much wealth/Trust such a	Jew	1.1.79	1Merch
That durst presume for hope of any gaine,	P 258	4.56	Charls
(aspiring Guise)/Durst be in armes without the Kings consent?	P 829	17.24	Eprnon
That the Guise durst stand in armes against the King,	P 877	17.72	Eprnon
That durst attempt to murder noble Guise.	P1121	21.15	Dumain
That durst disswade me from thy Lucifer,	F1754	5.1.81	Faust
whispered they, and none durst speake/And shew their feare,	Lucan, First Booke		259
Against the destinies durst sharpe darts require.	Ovid's Elegies		1.7.10
I durst the great celestiall battells tell,	Ovid's Elegies		2.1.11
With her I durst the Lybian Syrtes breake through,	Ovid's Elegies		2.16.21
That durst to so great wickednesse aspire.	Ovid's Elegies		3.8.44
That of the cooling river durst not drinke,	Hero and Leander		2.197
DURT			
And hurle him in some lake of mud and durt:	F1409	4.2.85	Faust
Halfe smother'd in a Lake of mud and durt,	F1434	4.3.4	Mrtino
DUSKIE			
And had his alters deckt with duskie lightes:	P 59	2.2	Guise
And duskie night, in rustie iron carre:	Edw	4.3.44	Edward
DUST			
And with the breaches fall, smoake, fire, and dust,	2Tamb	3.3.59	Therid
a while, our men with sweat and dust/All chockt well neare,	Edw	3.1.191	SpncrP
two deceased princes which long since are consumed to dust.	F App	p.237 43	P Faust
While thus I speake, blacke dust her white robes ray:	Ovid's Elegies		3.2.41
Foule dust, from her faire body, go away.	Ovid's Elegies		3.2.42
Or full of dust doest on the drye earth slide.	Ovid's Elegies		3.5.96
O let him change goods so ill got to dust.	Ovid's Elegies		3.7.66
DUSTIE			
Wars dustie <rustie> honors are refused being yong,	Ovid's Elegies		1.15.4
DUTCH			
God forgive me, he speakes Dutch fustian:	F App	p.231 72	P Clown
DUTIE			
O where is dutie and allegeance now?	1Tamb	1.1.101	Mycet
With dutie [and] <not> with amitie we yeeld/Our utmost service	1Tamb	2.3.33	Techel
With utmost vertue of my faith and dutie.	1Tamb	2.5.17	Meandr
And rackt by dutie from my cursed heart:	1Tamb	5.1.387	Zenoc
And sends <send> his dutie by these speedye lines,	P1169	22.31	Frier
Is this the dutie that you owe your king?	Edw	1.4.22	Kent
Of dutie and allegeance due to thee.	Edw	1.4.62	ArchBp
My dutie to your honor [premised] <promised>, &c. I have	Edw	4.3.28	P Spencr
In signe of love and dutie to this presence,	Edw	4.6.48	Rice
As in all humble dutie, I do yeeld/My life and lasting service	F1818	5.2.22	Wagner
And I in dutie will excell all other,	Hero and Leander		1.221
DUTIES			
We know our duties, let him know his peeres.	Edw	1.4.23	Warwck
DUTIFULL			
Dutifull service may thy love procure,	Hero and Leander		1.220
DUTY (See also DUETIE)			
Now shame and duty, love and feare presents/A thousand sorrowes	1Tamb	5.1.383	Zenoc
My duty waits on you.	Jew	3.3.76	Abigal

DUTY (cont.)
his rent discharg'd/From further duty he rests then inlarg'd. Ovid's Elegies 1.10.46
DWARFISH
A dwarfish beldame beares me companie, ... Hero and Leander 1.353
DWEL
We bide the first brunt, safer might we dwel, . . . Lucan, First Booke 253
trumpets clang incites, and those that dwel/By Cyngas streame, Lucan, First Booke 433
DWELL
If that thy fancie in his feathers dwell, ... Dido 1.1.39 Jupitr
I, so youle dwell with me and call me mother. . . . Dido 4.5.16 Nurse
I came to Cubar, where the Negros dwell, ... 2Tamb 1.3.201 Techel
And there in spite of Malta will I dwell: . . . . . Jew 2.3.15 Barab
Here will I dwell, for heaven is <be> in these lippes, . F1773 5.1.100 Faust
For that must be thy mansion, there to dwell. . . . F1882 5.2.86 Mephst
They came that dwell/By Nemes fields, and bankes of Satirus, Lucan, First Booke 420
In unfeld woods, and sacred groves you dwell, . . . Lucan, First Booke 448
I am no halfe horse, nor in woods I dwell, . . . Ovid's Elegies 1.4.9
A worke, that after my death, heere shall dwell . . Ovid's Elegies 3.14.20
And aged Saturne in Olympus dwell. . . . . . . Hero and Leander 1.454
DWELLETH
I thinke some fell Inchantresse dwelleth here, . . . Dido 4.1.3 Iarbus
DWELLINGS
And drench Silvanus dwellings with their shewers, . . Dido 3.2.91 Juno
DWELS
prowd she was, (for loftie pride that dwels/In tow'red courts, Hero and Leander 1.393
DWELT
whom/The gravest, Aruns, dwelt in forsaken Leuca <or Luna>, Lucan, First Booke 585
Houses not dwelt in, are with filth forlorne. . . . Ovid's Elegies 1.8.52
In brazen tower had not Danae dwelt, ... Ovid's Elegies 2.19.27
At Sestos, Hero dwelt; Hero the faire, ... Hero and Leander 1.5
(Whose tragedie divine Musaeus soong)/Dwelt at Abidus; since Hero and Leander 1.53
Musaeus soong)/Dwelt at Abidus; since him, dwelt there none, Hero and Leander 1.53
That in the vast uplandish countrie dwelt, ... Hero and Leander 1.80
DY
To dy by this resolved hand of thine, ... 1Tamb 3.2.98 Agidas
then dy like beasts, and fit for nought/But perches for the 2Tamb 4.3.22 Tamb
DYADEM
Did seeke to weare the triple Dyadem, ... F 959 3.1.181 Faust
DYAMETER
Like as the sunne in a Dyameter, ... Hero and Leander 2.123
DYE
Then dye Aeneas in thine innocence, ... Dido 1.1.80 Venus
And when I know it is not, then I dye. . . . . . Dido 2.1.9 Aeneas
and both his eyes/Turnd up to heaven as one resolv'd to dye, Dido 2.1.152 Aeneas
I dye with melting ruth, Aeneas leave. . . . . . Dido 2.1.289 Dido
Iarbus dye, seeing she abandons thee. . . . . . Dido 3.1.40 Iarbus
Then pull out both mine eyes, or let me dye. . . . Dido 3.1.55 Iarbus
Say vengeance, now shall her Ascanius dye? . . . . Dido 3.2.13 Juno
Ile dye before a stranger have that grace: . . . . Dido 3.3.11 Iarbus
Will dye with very tidings of his death: . . . . . Dido 3.3.77 Iarbus
The thing that I will dye before I aske, ... Dido 3.4.9 Dido
And yet desire to have before I dye. . . . . . . Dido 3.4.10 Dido
Better he frowne, then I should dye for griefe: . . . Dido 4.4.111 Dido
If he forsake me not, I never dye, ... Dido 4.4.121 Dido
Why doe I thinke of love now I should dye? . . . . Dido 4.5.34 Nurse
I dye, if my Aeneas say farewell. . . . . . . Dido 5.1.108 Dido
If he depart thus suddenly, I dye: . . . . . . Dido 5.1.209 Dido
fleete, what shall I doe/But dye in furie of this oversight? Dido 5.1.269 Dido
dye to expiate/The griefe that tires upon thine inward soule. Dido 5.1.316 Iarbus
Why pine not I, and dye in this distresse? . . . . Jew 1.2.173 Barab
For I had rather dye, then see her thus. . . . . Jew 1.2.357 Barab
And when I dye, here shall my spirit walke. . . . . Jew 2.1.30 Barab
So sure shall he and Don Mathias dye: . . . . . Jew 2.3.249 Barab
Shee'll dye with griefe. . . . . Jew 2.3.354 Mthias
As meet they will, and fighting dye; brave sport. . . . Jew 3.1.30 Ithimr
And on that rather should Ferneze dye. . . . . . Jew 3.2.26 Govnr
And Physicke will not helpe them; they must dye. . . . Jew 3.6.2 1Fryar
And I shall dye too, for I feele death comming. . . . Jew 3.6.8 Abigal
And witnesse that I dye a Christian. . . . . . . Jew 3.6.40 Abigal
They'll dye with griefe. . . . . Jew 4.1.16 Barab
Oh speake not of her, then I dye with griefe. . . . Jew 4.1.36 Barab
One turn'd my daughter, therefore he shall dye; . . . Jew 4.1.119 Barab
his villany/He will tell all he knowes and I shall dye for't. Jew 4.3.65 Barab
Will winne the Towne, or dye before the wals. . . . Jew 5.1.5 Govnr
And dye he shall, for we will never yeeld. . . . . Jew 5.1.6 1Knght
And if it be not true, then let me dye. . . . . . Jew 5.1.96 Barab
And if you like them, drinke your fill and dye: . . . Jew 5.5.9 Barab
Dye life, flye soule, tongue curse thy fill and dye. . Jew 5.5.89 Barab
My heart doth faint, I dye. . . . . P 186 3.21 OldQn
That I with her may dye and live againe. . . . . . P 190 3.25 Navrre
Shall dye, be he King or Emperour. . . . . . . P 235 4.33 Guise
O let me pray before I dye. . . . . P 301 5.28 Admral
To contradict which, I say Ramus shall dye: . . . . P 396 7.36 Guise
As I doe live, so surely shall he dye, ... P 521 9.40 QnMoth
My heart doth break, I faint and dye. . . . . . P 550 11.15 Charls
Tush, all shall dye unles I have my will: . . . . . P 653 12.66 QnMoth
Unles he meane to be betraide and dye: . . . . . P 898 17.93 King
But as I live, so sure the Guise shall dye. . . . . P 899 17.94 King
To dye by Pesantes, what a greefe is this? . . . . P1009 19.79 Guise
Then there is no remedye but I must dye? . . . . . P1096 20.6 Cardnl
I my good Lord, and will dye therein. . . . . . P1165 22.27 Frier
No, let the villaine dye, and feele in hell, ... P1174 22.36 King
What, shall the French king dye,/Wounded and poysoned, both at P1214 22.76 King

DYE (cont.)
Or else dye Epernoune. P1227 22.89 Eprnon
Sweet Epernoune thy King must dye. P1228 22.90 King
I dye Navarre, come beare me to my Sepulchre. P1242 22.104 King
By Peter you shall dye, F1030 3.2.50 Pope
thee, then had I lived still, but now must <I> dye eternally. F1825 5.2.29 P Faust
My selfe that better dye with loving may/Had seene, my mother Ovid's Elegies 2.14.21
Charmes change corne to grasse, and makes it dye, Ovid's Elegies 3.6.31

DYED (Homograph)
Her Lover after Alexander dyed, Dido 2.1.298 Achat
her as the draught/Of which great Alexander drunke, and dyed: Jew 3.4.97 Barab
Thus Caesar did goe foorth, and thus he dyed. P1015 19.85 Guise
And Hector dyed his brothers yet alive. Ovid's Elegies 2.6.42
And rockes dyed crimson with Prometheus bloud. Ovid's Elegies 2.16.40

DYES
Then to the Carthage Queene that dyes for him. Dido 3.4.40 Dido
Live false Aeneas, truest Dido dyes, Dido 5.1.312 Dido
The account is made, for [Lodovico] <Lodowicke> dyes. Jew 2.3.242 Barab
Reveale it not, for then my father dyes. Jew 3.6.32 Abigal
they be my good Lord, and he that smelles but to them, dyes. P 74 2.17 P Pothec
And tell her Henry dyes her faithfull freend. P1244 22.106 King
Oft dyes she that her paunch-wrapt child hath slaine. Ovid's Elegies 2.14.38
Shee dyes, and with loose haires to grave is sent, Ovid's Elegies 2.14.39

DYET
That have so oft serv'd pretty wenches dyet. Ovid's Elegies 2.9.24

DYING
I would have either drunke his dying bloud, Dido 3.3.28 Iarbus
In this delight of dying pensivenes: Dido 4.2.44 Anna
ingendred thoughts/To burst abroad, those never dying flames, P 92 2.35 Guise
O never more lift up this dying hart! Edw 4.7.43 Edward
Farewell Corinna cryed thy dying tongue. Ovid's Elegies 2.6.48
Thy dying eyes here did thy mother close, Ovid's Elegies 3.8.49
And would be dead, but dying <dead> with thee remaine. Ovid's Elegies 3.13.40

DYMS
And dyms the Welkin, with her pitchy breathe: F 232 1.3.4 Faust

DYV'D
Being sodainly betraide, dyv'd downe to hide her. Hero and Leander 2.262

DYVILS
The Dyvils there in chaines of quencelesse flame, 2Tamb 2.3.24 Orcan

E.
A per se, a, t. h. e. the: F 728 2.3.7 P Robin

EACH (See also ECH)
And urg'd each Element to his annoy: Dido 3.2.46 Juno
Each word she sayes will then containe a Crowne, Dido 4.3.53 Aeneas
Neptune and Dis gain'd each of them a Crowne, 1Tamb 2.7.37 Usumc
The heat and moisture which did feed each other, 1Tamb 2.7.46 Cosroe
Each man a crown? why kingly fought ifaith. 1Tamb 3.3.216 Tamb
othes/Sign'd with our handes, each shal retaine a scrowle: 2Tamb 1.1.144 Orcan
And hundred thousands subjects to each score: 2Tamb 2.2.12 Gazell
the Jewes, and each of them to pay one halfe of his estate. Jew 1.2.69 P Reader
Both jealous of my love, envied each other: Jew 3.6.27 Abigal
Law wils that each particular be knowne. Jew 4.1.205 Barab
A bowle of poison to each others health: Edw 2.2.238 Edward
My lord Mortimer, and you my lords each one, Edw 2.5.74 Penbrk
Mutually folded in each others Spheares <orbe>, F 591 2.2.40 Mephst
That make <makes> safe passage, to each part of Rome. F 816 3.1.38 Mephst
Keepes each from other, but being worne away/They both burst Lucan, First Booke 102
being worne away/They both burst out, and each incounter other: Lucan, First Booke 103
These Captaines emulous of each others glory. Lucan, First Booke 120
Each side had great partakers; Caesars cause, Lucan, First Booke 128
Thus in his fright did each man strengthen Fame, Lucan, First Booke 481
Take, and receive each secret amorous glaunce. Ovid's Elegies 1.4.18
Each one according to his gifts respect. Ovid's Elegies 1.8.38
Both of them watch: each on the hard earth sleepes: Ovid's Elegies 1.9.7
The whore stands to be bought for each mans mony/And seekes Ovid's Elegies 1.10.21
Let others tell this, and what each one speakes/Beleeve, no Ovid's Elegies 2.11.21
Each little hill shall for a table stand: Ovid's Elegies 2.11.48
Each crosse waies corner doth as much expresse. Ovid's Elegies 3.1.18
And each give signes by casting up his cloake. Ovid's Elegies 3.2.74
Where Ceres went each place was harvest there. Ovid's Elegies 3.9.38
Now love, and hate my light brest each way move; Ovid's Elegies 3.10.33
Where Juno comes, each youth, and pretty maide, Ovid's Elegies 3.12.23
As after chaunc'd, they did each other spye. Hero and Leander 1.134
Of two gold Ingots like in each respect. Hero and Leander 1.172
Both to each other quickly were affied. Hero and Leander 2.26
Both in each others armes chaind as they layd. Hero and Leander 2.306
For thy delight each May-morning. Passionate Shepherd 22

EACUS
Revenge it Radamanth and Eacus, 2Tamb 4.1.171 Orcan

EADEMQUE
Si una eademque res legatur duobus, alter rem, alter valorem F 56 1.1.28 P Faust

EAGER
Arabian king together/Martch on us with such eager violence, 1Tamb 5.1.200 Techel

EAGERLIE
And eagerlie she kist me with her tongue, Ovid's Elegies 3.6.9

EAGERLY
And loving Doves kisse eagerly together. Ovid's Elegies 2.6.56

EAGLE (See also EGLES)
and I fear'd the Bull and Eagle/And what ere love made Jove Ovid's Elegies 1.10.7

EAGLES
Making thee mount as high as Eagles soare. 1Tamb 5.1.224 Bajzth
And Eagles wings join'd to her feathered breast, 2Tamb 3.4.62 Therid
And drawen with princely Eagles through the path, 2Tamb 4.3.127 Tamb

EAGLES (cont.)

On whose top-branches Kinglie Eagles pearch, . . . Edw 2.2.17 Mortmr
And you the Eagles, sore ye nere so high, . . . Edw 2.2.39 Edward
Eagles alike displaide, darts answering darts. . . . Lucan, First Booke 7
But seeing white Eagles, and Roomes flags wel known, . Lucan, First Booke 246
Because at his commaund I wound not up/My conquering Eagles? Lucan, First Booke 340

EARDE

And ripe-earde corne with sharpe-edg'd sithes to fell. . Ovid's Elegies 3.9.12

EARE

I would have a jewell for mine eare, ... Dido 1.1.46 Ganimd
And givest not eare unto the charge I bring? . . . Dido 5.1.52 Hermes
And winds it twice or thrice about his eare; . . . Jew 4.3.8 Barab
An eare, to heare what my detractors say, ... P 160 2.103 Guise
O Lord, mine eare. . . . . P 619 12.32 Cutprs
Come sir, give me my buttons and heers your eare. . . P 620 12.33 Mugern
O something soundeth in mine [eares] <eare>,/Abjure this . F 395 2.1.7 Faust
me <both> body and soule, if I once gave eare to Divinitie: F1866 5.2.70 P Faust
Oh <Ah> Faustus, if thou hadst given eare to me, . . F1892 5.2.96 GdAngl
Gave eare to me,/And now must taste hels paines perpetually. F1894 5.2.98 BdAngl
Let thy soft finger to thy eare be brought. . . . Ovid's Elegies 1.4.24
Giving the windes my words running in thine eare? . . Ovid's Elegies 1.6.42
who ere will knowe a bawde aright/Give eare, there is an old Ovid's Elegies 1.8.2
Venus to mockt men lendes a sencelesse eare. . . . Ovid's Elegies 1.8.86
Her long haires eare-wrought garland fell away. . . Ovid's Elegies 3.9.36
Neptune was angrie that hee gave no eare, ... Hero and Leander 2.207
And now she lets him whisper in her eare, ... Hero and Leander 2.267

EARED

Loe how the miserable great eared Asse, ... Ovid's Elegies 2.7.15

EARES (Homograph)

As made the bloud run downe about mine eares. . . . Dido 1.1.8 Ganimd
Peeres/Heare me, but yet with Mirmidons harsh eares, . Dido 2.1.123 Aeneas
And quell those hopes that thus employ your [cares] <eares>. Dido 4.1.35 Dido
To sound this angrie message in thine eares. . . . Dido 5.1.33 Hermes
With costlie jewels hanging at their eares, . . . 1Tamb 1.1.144 Ceneus
Too harsh a subject for your dainty eares. . . . 1Tamb 3.2.46 Agidas
And through the eies and eares of Tamburlaine, . . . 1Tamb 5.1.53 2Virgn
And ratling cannons thunder in our eares/Our proper ruine, 2Tamb 4.1.13 Amyras
No such discourse is pleasant in mine eares, . . . 2Tamb 4.2.46 Olymp
if the unrelenting eares/Of death and hell be shut against my 2Tamb 5.3.191 Amyras
And batter all the stones about their eares, . . . Jew 5.5.30 Barab
Shall drive no plaintes into the Guises eares, . . . P 532 10.5 Guise
Whatsoever any whisper in mine eares, ... P 974 19.44 King
And fire accursed Rome about his eares. . . . . P1200 22.62 King
Smiles in his face, and whispers in his eares, . . . Edw 1.2.52 Queene
Weele haile him by the eares unto the block. . . . Edw 2.2.91 Lncstr
Ile thunder such a peale into his eares, ... Edw 2.2.128 Mortmr
For now we hould an old Wolfe by the eares, . . . Edw 5.2.7 Mortmr
Some thing he whispers in his childish eares. . . . Edw 5.2.76 Queene
sleepe, to take a quill/And blowe a little powder in his eares, Edw 5.4.35 Ltborn
Something still busseth in mine eares, ... Edw 5.5.103 Edward
O something soundeth in mine [eares] <eare>,/Abjure this . F 395 2.1.7 Faust
Who buzzeth in mine eares I am a spirit? . . . . F 565 2.2.14 Faust
[But feareful ecchoes thunder <thunders> in mine eares], . F 571 2.2.20A Faust
He'd joyne long Asses eares to these huge hornes, . . F1449 4.3.19 Benvol
I kept a hallowing and whooping in his eares, but all could not F1549 4.5.45 P HrsCsr
be witnesses to confirme what mine eares have heard reported, F App p.236 7 P Emper
him now, or Ile breake his glasse-windowes about his eares. F App p.240 143 P HrsCsr
Or slender eares, with gentle Zephire shaken, . . . Ovid's Elegies 1.7.55
If he loves not, deafe eares thou doest importune, . . Ovid's Elegies 2.2.53
Can deafe [eares] <yeares> take delight when Phemius sings,/Or Ovid's Elegies 3.6.61
Golden-hair'd Ceres crownd with eares of corne, . . Ovid's Elegies 3.9.3
Which like sweet musicke entred Heroes eares, . . . Hero and Leander 1.194

EARE-WROUGHT

Her long haires eare-wrought garland fell away. . . Ovid's Elegies 3.9.36

EARLDOMES

Foure Earldomes have I besides Lancaster, ... Edw 1.1.102 Lncstr
of Lancaster/That hath more earldomes then an asse can beare, Edw 1.3.2 Gavstn

EARLE

That Earle of Lancaster do I abhorre. . . . . Edw 1.1.76 Gavstn
Mine unckle heere, this Earle, and I my selfe, . . . Edw 1.1.82 Mortmr
And that high minded earle of Lancaster, ... Edw 1.1.150 Edward
Earle of Cornewall, king and lord of Man. . . . . Edw 1.1.156 Edward
How now, why droops the earle of Lancaster? . . . Edw 1.2.9 MortSr
That villaine Gaveston is made an Earle. . . . . Edw 1.2.11 Lncstr
For no where else the new earle is so safe. . . . Edw 1.4.11 Lncstr
And with the earle of Kent that favors him. . . . Edw 1.4.34 MortSr
Having brought the Earle of Cornewall on his way, . . Edw 1.4.300 Queene
Against our friend the earle of Cornewall comes, . . Edw 1.4.375 Edward
Unto our cosin, the earle of Glosters heire. . . . Edw 1.4.379 Edward
Freely enjoy that vaine light-headed earle, . . . Edw 1.4.400 MortSr
Seeing that our Lord th'earle of Glosters dead, . . . Edw 2.1.2 Baldck
The liberall earle of Cornewall is the man, . . . Edw 2.1.10 Spencr
Against the Earle of Cornewall and my brother? . . . Edw 2.2.35 Edward
Welcome is the good Earle of Cornewall. . . . . Edw 2.2.66 Mortmr
neece, the onely heire/Unto the Earle of Gloster late deceased. Edw 2.2.259 Edward
I have enformd the Earle of Lancaster. . . . . Edw 2.3.14 Kent
Treacherous earle, shall I not see the king? . . . Edw 2.6.15 Gavstn
Spencer, I heere create thee earle of Wilshire, . . . Edw 3.1.49 Edward
The earle of Warwick would not bide the hearing, . . Edw 3.1.104 Arundl
The earle of Penbrooke mildlie thus bespake. . . . Edw 3.1.108 Arundl
The earle of Warwick seazde him on his way, . . . Edw 3.1.115 Arundl
And meerely of our love we do create thee/Earle of Gloster, and Edw 3.1.146 Edward
Spencer the sonne, created earle of Gloster, . . . Edw 4.6.56 Rice

EARLE (cont.)			
Heere comes the yong prince, with the Earle of Kent.	Edw	5.2.75	Mortmr
Isabell is neerer then the earle of Kent.	Edw	5.2.115	Queene
Guarde the king sure, it is the earle of Kent.	Edw	5.3.50	Matrvs
Lay hands upon the earle for this assault.	Edw	5.3.54	Gurney
Edmund the Earle of Kent.	Edw	5.4.83	Souldr
EARLES			
Ile bandie with the Barons and the Earles,	Edw	1.1.137	Edward
Were all the Earles and Barons of my minde,	Edw	1.2.28	Mortmr
Yong Mortimer and his unckle shalbe earles,	Edw	1.4.67	Edward
Stil wil these Earles and Barrons use me thus?	Edw	2.2.70	Edward
Base leaden Earles that glorie in your birth,	Edw	2.2.74	Gavstn
What care I though the Earles begirt us round?	Edw	2.2.223	Edward
My lord, tis thought, the Earles are up in armes.	Edw	2.2.225	Queene
Flie, flie, my lords, the earles have got the holde,	Edw	2.4.4	Edward
EARLS			
Barons and Earls, your pride hath made me mute,	Edw	1.1.107	Kent
EARLY			
To morrow early I'le be at the doore.	Jew	1.2.361	Barab
Was up thus early; with intent to goe/Unto your Friery, because	Jew	4.1.191	Barab
Slow oxen early in the yoake are pent.	Ovid's Elegies	1.13.16	
And early mountest thy hatefull carriage:	Ovid's Elegies	1.13.38	
EARNED			
In burying him, then he hath ever earned.	Edw	2.5.56	Lncstr
EARNES			
My heart with pittie earnes to see this sight,	Edw	4.7.70	Abbot
EARNESTLIE			
Because his majestie so earnestlie/Desires to see the man	Edw	2.5.77	Penbrk
EARNESTLY			
No? doe but marke how earnestly she pleads.	Edw	1.4.234	Warwck
Request them earnestly to visit me.	F 93	1.1.65	Faust
the Duke of Vanholt doth earnestly entreate your company, and	F1500	4.4.44	P Wagner
Sir, the Duke of Vanholt doth earnestly entreate your company.	F App	p.241 168	P Wagner
EARST			
Hast thou, as earst I did command,	F 801	3.1.23	Faust
Shee in my lap sits still as earst she did.	Ovid's Elegies	2.18.6	
EARTH			
By Saturnes soule, and this earth threatning [haire] <aire>,	Dido	1.1.10	Jupitr
To hang her meteor like twixt heaven and earth,	Dido	1.1.13	Jupitr
And heaven and earth the bounds of thy delight?	Dido	1.1.31	Jupitr
That earth-borne Atlas groning underprops:	Dido	1.1.99	Jupitr
And heaven and earth with his unrest acquaints.	Dido	1.1.141	Venus
No steps of men imprinted in the earth.	Dido	1.1.181	Achat
And from the first earth interdict our feete.	Dido	1.2.37	Serg
Burst from the earth, crying, Aeneas flye,	Dido	2.1.207	Aeneas
By heaven and earth, and my faire brothers bowe,	Dido	3.4.45	Aeneas
I might have stakte them both unto the earth,	Dido	4.1.23	Iarbus
If there be any heaven in earth, tis love:	Dido	4.5.27	Nurse
Witnes the Gods, and witnes heaven and earth,	Dido	5.1.80	Aeneas
Fighting for passage, tilt within the earth.	1Tamb	1.2.51	Tamb
His fierie eies are fixt upon the earth,	1Tamb	1.2.158	Therid
Both we will raigne as Consuls of the earth,	1Tamb	1.2.197	Tamb
Like to the cruell brothers of the earth,	1Tamb	2.2.47	Meandr
enjoy in heaven/Can not compare with kingly joyes in earth.	1Tamb	2.5.59	Therid
What God or Feend, or spirit of the earth,	1Tamb	2.6.15	Ortyg
Whether from earth, or hell, or heaven he grow.	1Tamb	2.6.23	Ortyg
For he is grosse and like the massie earth,	1Tamb	2.7.31	Therid
Most great and puisant Monarke of the earth,	1Tamb	3.1.41	Bassoe
For neither rain can fall upon the earth,	1Tamb	3.1.51	Moroc
And leave my body sencelesse as the earth.	1Tamb	3.2.22	Zenoc
garrisons enough/To make me Soveraigne of the earth againe.	1Tamb	3.3.243	Bajzth
Fall prostrate on the lowe disdainefull earth.	1Tamb	4.2.13	Tamb
With Eban Scepter strike this hatefull earth,	1Tamb	4.2.28	Bajzth
For I the chiefest Lamp of all the earth,	1Tamb	4.2.36	Tamb
And casts a flash of lightning to the earth.	1Tamb	4.2.46	Tamb
Not all the Kings and Emperours of the Earth:	1Tamb	4.2.92	Tamb
Most happy King and Emperour of the earth,	1Tamb	5.1.74	1Virgn
Rain'st on the earth resolved pearle in showers,	1Tamb	5.1.142	Tamb
Breake up the earth, and with their firebrands,	1Tamb	5.1.219	Bajzth
The heavens may frowne, the earth for anger quake,	1Tamb	5.1.231	Bajzth
Gape earth, and let the Feends infernall view/As are the	1Tamb	5.1.242	Zabina
Smother the earth with never fading mistes:	1Tamb	5.1.296	Bajzth
Earth cast up fountaines from thy entralles,	1Tamb	5.1.347	Zenoc
A meteor that might terrify the earth,	1Tamb	5.1.461	Tamb
As when the massy substance of the earth,	2Tamb	1.1.89	Orcan
And died a traitor both to heaven and earth,	2Tamb	2.3.37	Orcan
Ready to darken earth with endlesse night:	2Tamb	2.4.7	Tamb
ceaslesse lamps/That gently look'd upon this loathsome earth,	2Tamb	2.4.19	Tamb
Than this base earth should shroud your majesty:	2Tamb	2.4.60	Zenoc
And wound the earth, that it may cleave in twaine,	2Tamb	2.4.97	Tamb
If teares, our eies have watered all the earth:	2Tamb	2.4.122	Therid
And with his hoste [marcht] <martch> round about the earth,	2Tamb	3.2.111	Tamb
shall raise a hill/Of earth and fagots higher than thy Fort,	2Tamb	3.3.22	Therid
Cast up the earth towards the castle wall,	2Tamb	3.3.43	Therid
Ile make thee wish the earth had swallowed thee:	2Tamb	3.5.118	Tamb
For earth and al this aery region/Cannot containe the state of	2Tamb	4.1.119	Tamb
Created of the massy dregges of earth,	2Tamb	4.1.123	Tamb
that earth may eccho foorth/The far resounding torments ye	2Tamb	4.1.185	Tamb
And since this earth, dew'd with thy brinish teares,	2Tamb	4.2.8	Olymp
O thou that swaiest the region under earth,	2Tamb	4.3.32	Orcan
If Jove esteeming me too good for earth,	2Tamb	4.3.60	Tamb
Fall to the earth, and pierce the pit of Hel,	2Tamb	5.1.44	Govnr
Whose flaming traines should reach down to the earth/Could not	2Tamb	5.1.90	Tamb

EARTH (cont.)

And sent from hell to tyrannise on earth,	2Tamb	5.1.111	Govnr
lamps of heaven/To cast their bootlesse fires to the earth,	2Tamb	5.3.4	Therid
Earth droopes and saies, that hell in heaven is plac'd.	2Tamb	5.3.16	Therid
Earth droopes and saies that hel in heaven is plac'd.	2Tamb	5.3.41	Usumc
That if I perish, heaven and earth may fade.	2Tamb	5.3.60	Tamb
As much too high for this disdainfull earth.	2Tamb	5.3.122	Tamb
Casane no, the Monarke of the earth,	2Tamb	5.3.216	Tamb
were scortcht/And all the earth like Aetna breathing fire:	2Tamb	5.3.233	Tamb
Meet heaven and earth, and here let al things end,	2Tamb	5.3.249	Amyras
For earth hath spent the pride of all her fruit,	2Tamb	5.3.250	Amyras
Let earth and heaven his timelesse death deplore,	2Tamb	5.3.252	Amyras
Ripping the bowels of the earth for them,	Jew	1.1.109	Barab
Oh earth-mettall'd villaines, and no Hebrews born!	Jew	1.2.78	Barab
And here upon my knees, striking the earth,	Jew	1.2.165	Barab
That I may vanish ore the earth in ayre,	Jew	1.2.264	Barab
Cropt from the pleasures of the fruitfull earth,	Jew	1.2.380	Mthias
But I perceive there is no love on earth,	Jew	3.3.47	Abigal
buries it up as Partridges doe their egges, under the earth.	Jew	4.2.59	P Ithimr
For this, hath heaven engendred me of earth,	P 113	2.56	Guise
For this, this earth sustaines my bodies [waight],	P 114	2.57	Guise
To make his glory great upon the earth.	P 790	16.4	Navrre
She cast her hatefull stomack to the earth.	P1154	22.16	King
<incense>/The papall towers to kisse the [lowly] <holy> earth.	P1202	22.64	King
Like frantick Juno will I fill the earth,	Edw	1.4.178	Queene
thy mother feare/Thou art not markt to many daies on earth.	Edw	3.1.80	Queene
By earth, the common mother of us all,	Edw	3.1.128	Edward
the last of all my blisse on earth,/Center of all misfortune.	Edw	4.7.61	Edward
In heaven wee may, in earth never shall wee meete,	Edw	4.7.80	Edward
Earth melt to ayre, gone is my soveraigne,	Edw	4.7.103	Spencr
highly scorning, that the lowly earth/Should drinke his bloud,	Edw	5.1.13	Edward
I might, but heavens and earth conspire/To make me miserable:	Edw	5.1.96	Edward
And every earth is fit for buriall.	Edw	5.1.146	Edward
Be thou on earth as Jove is in the skye,	F 103	1.1.75	BdAngl
Within the massy entrailes of the earth:	F 174	1.1.146	Cornel
Now that the gloomy shadow of the night <earth>,	F 229	1.3.1	Faust
see al plants, hearbes and trees that grow upon the earth].	F 551.10	2.1.173A	P Faust
faire/As thou, or any man that [breathes] <breathe> on earth.	F 558	2.2.7	Mephst
As is the substance of this centricke earth?	F 588	2.2.37	Faust
That measures costs, and kingdomes of the earth:	F 774	2.3.53	2Chor
Whilst I am here on earth let me be cloyd/With all things that	F 837	3.1.59	Faust
We veiw'd the face of heaven, of earth and hell.	F 848	3.1.70	Faust
That looking downe the earth appear'd to me,	F 850	3.1.72	Faust
Is not all power on earth bestowed on us?	F 930	3.1.152	Pope
That this faire Lady, whilest she liv'd on earth,	F1266	4.1.112	Emper
was limitted/For foure and twenty yeares, to breathe on earth?	F1396	4.2.72	Faust
Fooles that will laugh on earth, [must] <most> weepe in hell.	F1891	5.2.95	Mephst
To want in hell, that had on earth such store.	F1898	5.2.102	BdAngl
Then will I headlong run into the earth:	F1948	5.2.152	Faust
Gape earth; O no, it will not harbour me.	F1949	5.2.153	Faust
First conquer all the earth, then turne thy force/Against	Lucan, First Booke		22
And choakt with thorns, that greedy earth wants hinds,	Lucan, First Booke		29
And with bright restles fire compasse the earth,	Lucan, First Booke		49
fire/Fleete on the flouds, the earth shoulder the sea,	Lucan, First Booke		76
While th'earth the sea, and ayre the earth sustaines;	Lucan, First Booke		89
our Empire, fortune that made Roome/Governe the earth, the sea,	Lucan, First Booke		110
threatning gods/Fill'd both the earth and seas with prodegies;	Lucan, First Booke		523
The earth went off hir hinges; And the Alpes/Shooke the old	Lucan, First Booke		551
Become intemperate? shall the earth be barraine?	Lucan, First Booke		646
And in the fleeting sea the earth be drencht.	Lucan, First Booke		653
rayes now sing/The fell Nemean beast, th'earth would be fired,	Lucan, First Booke		655
she chides/And with long charmes the solide earth divides.	Ovid's Elegies		1.8.18
Both of them watch: each on the hard earth sleepes:	Ovid's Elegies		1.9.7
She viewed the earth: the earth to viewe, beseem'd her.	Ovid's Elegies		2.5.43
Whose earth doth not perpetuall greene-grasse lacke,	Ovid's Elegies		2.6.50
And he is happy whom the earth holds, say.	Ovid's Elegies		2.11.30
The earth of Caesars had beene destitute.	Ovid's Elegies		2.14.18
Although the sunne to rive the earth incline,	Ovid's Elegies		2.16.3
With corne the earth abounds, with vines much more,	Ovid's Elegies		2.16.7
A grassie turffe the moistened earth doth hide.	Ovid's Elegies		2.16.10
Upon the cold earth pensive let them lay,	Ovid's Elegies		2.16.15
The sea I use not: me my earth must have.	Ovid's Elegies		3.2.48
Or full of dust doest on the drye earth slide.	Ovid's Elegies		3.5.96
All gaine in darknesse the deepe earth supprest.	Ovid's Elegies		3.7.36
With strong plough shares no man the earth did cleave,	Ovid's Elegies		3.7.41
with th'earth thou wert content,/Why seek'st not heav'n the	Ovid's Elegies		3.7.49
Gold from the earth in steade of fruits we pluck,	Ovid's Elegies		3.7.53
Nor on the earth was knowne the name of floore.	Ovid's Elegies		3.9.8
Frighted the melancholie earth, which deem'd,	Hero and Leander		1.99
his golden earth remains,/Which after his disceasse, some other	Hero and Leander		1.245
Nor is't of earth or mold celestiall,	Hero and Leander		1.273
And those on whom heaven, earth, and hell relies,	Hero and Leander		1.443
Which th'earth from ougly Chaos den up-wayd:	Hero and Leander		1.450
For from the earth to heaven, is Cupid rais'd,	Hero and Leander		2.31
As for his love, both earth and heaven pyn'd;	Hero and Leander		2.196

EARTH-BORNE

That earth-borne Atlas groning underprops:	Dido	1.1.99	Jupitr

EARTHE

And guide this massy substance of the earthe,	2Tamb	5.3.18	Techel

EARTHES

With earthes revenge and how Olimpus toppe/High Ossa bore,	Ovid's Elegies		2.1.13

EARTHLIE

Are reeking water, and dull earthlie fumes.	Hero and Leander		2.116

EARTHLY			
The sweet fruition of an earthly crowne.	1Tamb	2.7.29	Tamb
And all the earthly Potentates conspire,	1Tamb	2.7.59	Tamb
And place their chiefest good in earthly pompe:	1Tamb	5.1.353	Zenoc
Of earthly fortune, and respect of pitie,	1Tamb	5.1.365	Zenoc
And mighty Tamburlaine, our earthly God,	2Tamb	1.3.138	Techel
Fed with the fresh supply of earthly dregs,	2Tamb	3.2.8	Tamb
The Emperour of the world, and earthly God,	2Tamb	3.5.22	Orcan
That with his sword hath quail'd all earthly kings,	2Tamb	5.1.93	Tamb
Unto the rising of this earthly globe,	2Tamb	5.3.147	Tamb
What more may heaven doe for earthly man/Then thus to powre out	Jew	1.1.107	Barab
That Nature shall dissolve this earthly bowre.	Ovid's Elegies		1.15.24
Thinke water farre excels all earthly things:	Hero and Leander		1.260
EARTH-METTALL'D			
Oh earth-mettall'd villaines, and no Hebrews born!	Jew	1.2.78	Barab
EARTHQUAKES			
tooles/Makes Earthquakes in the hearts of men and heaven.	2Tamb	2.2.8	Orcan
EARTHS			
Earths barrennesse, and all mens hatred/Inflict upon them, thou	Jew	1.2.163	Barab
Strooke with th'earths suddaine shadow waxed pale,	Lucan, First Booke		537
And may th'earths weight thy ashes nought molest.	Ovid's Elegies		3.8.68
EAS'D			
And thousand desperate maladies beene cur'd <eas'd>?	F 50	1.1.22	Faust
EASD			
This poore revenge hath something easd my minde,	Edw	5.1.141	Edward
EASDE			
Thy speeches long agoe had easde my sorrowes,	Edw	5.1.6	Edward
EASE (See also EAZE)			
Whose golden fortunes clogd with courtly ease,	Dido	4.3.8	Aeneas
But rather will augment then ease my woe?	Dido	5.1.152	Dido
I could attaine it with a woondrous ease,	1Tamb	2.5.77	Tamb
It would not ease the sorrow I sustaine.	2Tamb	3.2.48	Calyph
Take you the honor, I will take my ease,	2Tamb	4.1.49	Calyph
Thy youth forbids such ease my kingly boy,	2Tamb	4.3.29	Tamb
Then feeles your majesty no sovereraigne ease,	2Tamb	5.3.213	Usumc
Be silent, Daughter, sufferance breeds ease,	Jew	1.2.238	Barab
then we [luft] <left>, and [tackt] <tooke>, and fought at ease:	Jew	2.2.14	Bosco
And whilste he sleepes securely thus in ease,	P 635	12.48	QnMoth
Now is my heart at ease.	Edw	1.4.91	ArchBp
You will this greefe have ease and remedie,	Edw	3.1.160	Herald
Alas poore soule, would I could ease his greefe.	Edw	5.2.26	Queene
To ease his greefe, and worke his libertie:	Edw	5.2.71	Queene
my horse be sick, or ill at ease, if I bring his water to you,	F App	p.240 118 P	HrsCsr
Then men from war shal bide in league, and ease,	Lucan, First Booke		60
Now evermore least some one hope might ease/The Commons	Lucan, First Booke		520
Turne round thy gold-ring, as it were to ease thee.	Ovid's Elegies		1.4.26
Pleasure, and ease had mollifide my minde.	Ovid's Elegies		1.9.42
EASELY			
How easely may you with a mightie hoste,	1Tamb	1.1.129	Menaph
As easely may you get the Souldans crowne,	1Tamb	1.2.27	Tamb
EASIE			
By plaine and easie demonstration,	2Tamb	3.2.84	Tamb
And for a present easie proofe hereof,	2Tamb	4.2.75	Olymp
Which being broke the foot had easie passage.	Lucan, First Booke		224
O gods that easie grant men great estates,	Lucan, First Booke		508
EASIER			
Nay, thine owne is easier to come by, plucke out that, and twil	1Tamb	4.4.13 P	Tamb
What can be easier then the thing we pray?	Ovid's Elegies		2.2.66
EASILIE			
But that thou maist more easilie perceive,	Dido	3.2.66	Juno
How easilie might some base slave be subbornd,	Edw	1.4.265	Mortmr
Be easilie supprest: and therefore be gone.	Edw	2.4.45	Queene
Yea madam, and they scape not easilie,	Edw	4.6.41	Mortmr
EASILY			
Whereof a man may easily in a day/Tell that which may maintaine	Jew	1.1.10	Barab
Governour, it was not got so easily;	Jew	1.2.86	Barab
I can do al these things easily with it:	F App	p.234 22 P	Robin
Nor is it easily prov'd though manifest,	Ovid's Elegies		2.2.55
EASLY			
Lets yeeld, a burden easly borne is light.	Ovid's Elegies		1.2.10
EAST			
To make himselfe the Monarch of the East:	1Tamb	1.1.43	Meandr
We here doo crowne thee Monarch of the East,	1Tamb	1.1.161	Ortyg
East India and the late discovered Isles,	1Tamb	1.1.166	Ortyg
Measuring the limits of his Emperie/By East and west, as	1Tamb	1.2.40	Tamb
Both may invest you Empresse of the East:	1Tamb	1.2.46	Tamb
That I shall be the Monark of the East,	1Tamb	1.2.185	Tamb
So from the East unto the furthest West,	1Tamb	3.3.246	Tamb
First rising in the East with milde aspect,	1Tamb	4.2.37	Tamb
Stretching your conquering armes from east to west:	2Tamb	1.3.97	Tamb
And wife unto the Monarke of the East.	2Tamb	3.2.22	Amyras
The Terrene west, the Caspian north north-east,	2Tamb	4.3.103	Tamb
Ha, to the East? yes: See how stands the Vanes?	Jew	1.1.40	Barab
East and by-South:	Jew	1.1.41	Barab
But stay, what starre shines yonder in the East?	Jew	2.1.41	Barab
to Lucifer, Prince of the East, and his Minister Mephostophilis,	F 494	2.1.106 P	Faust
All <joyntly> move from East to West, in foure and twenty	F 597	2.2.46 P	Mephst
From East to West his Dragons swiftly glide,	F 766	2.3.45	2Chor
From thence to Venice, Padua, and the [rest] <East>,	F 794	3.1.16	Faust
and such Countries that lye farre East, where they have fruit	F1584	4.6.27 P	Faust
and farther countries in the East, and by means of a swift	F App	p.242 22 P	Faust
Under the frosty beare, or parching East,	Lucan, First Booke		254
did Thiestes towne/(Mycenae), Phoebus flying through the East:	Lucan, First Booke		542

EAST (cont.)
thou lead'st me toward th'east,/Where Nile augmenteth the Lucan, First Booke 682
East windes he doth not chide/Nor to hoist saile attends fit Ovid's Elegies 1.9.13
And Gallus shall be knowne from East to West, ... Ovid's Elegies 1.15.29
The parrat from east India to me sent, ... Ovid's Elegies 2.6.1
For thee the East and West winds make me pale, ... Ovid's Elegies 2.11.9
The East winds in Ulisses baggs we shut, ... Ovid's Elegies 3.11.29
EASTERN
Egregious Viceroyes of these Eastern parts/Plac'd by the issue 2Tamb 1.1.1 Orcan
EASTERNE
Have swarm'd in troopes into the Easterne India: . . 1Tamb 1.1.120 Cosroe
As great commander of this Easterne world, ... 1Tamb 2.7.62 Tamb
the Tartars and the Easterne theeves/Under the conduct of one 1Tamb 3.1.2 Bajzth
will keep it for/The richest present of this Easterne world. 2Tamb 4.2.78 Therid
that in the Easterne rockes/Without controule can picke his Jew 1.1.21 Barab
EASTWARD
And from th'Antartique Pole, Eastward behold/As much more land, 2Tamb 5.3.154 Tamb
EAST WINDS
The East winds in Ulisses baggs we shut, ... Ovid's Elegies 3.11.29
EAT
are you so daintily brought up, you cannot eat your owne flesh? 1Tamb 4.4.37 P Tamb
here, eat sir, take it from my swords point, or Ile thrust it to 1Tamb 4.4.40 P Tamb
and eat it, or I will make thee slice the brawnes of thy armes 1Tamb 4.4.43 P Tamb
slice the brawnes of thy armes into carbonadoes, and eat them. 1Tamb 4.4.44 P Tamb
Faste and welcome sir, while hunger make you eat. . . 1Tamb 4.4.56 P Tamb
My jointes benumb'd, unlesse I eat, I die. . . . . 1Tamb 4.4.98 Bajzth
Eat Bajazeth. . . . . 1Tamb 4.4.99 P Zabina
Do you remember sir, how you cosened me and eat up my load of-- F1659 4.6.102 P Carter
EATE
Eate Comfites in mine armes, and I will sing. . . . Dido 2.1.315 Venus
The Foules shall eate, for never sepulchre/Shall grace that 2Tamb 5.2.17 Amasia
water the fish, and by the fish our selves when we eate them. P 489 9.8 P 2Atndt
Goe sit at home and eate your tenants beefe: . . . . Edw 2.2.75 Gavstn
I am leane with seeing others eate: . . . . . . F 681 2.2.130 P Envy
<No, Ile see thee hanged, thou wilt eate up all my victualls>. F 702 (HC264)A P Faust
zounds I could eate my selfe for anger, to thinke I have beene F1242 4.1.88 P Benvol
me what he should give me for as much Hay as he could eate; F1527 4.5.23 P Carter
he never left eating, till he had eate up all my loade of hay. F1531 4.5.27 P Carter
O monstrous, eate a whole load of Hay! . . . . . F1532 4.5.28 P All
be; for I have heard of one, that ha's eate a load of logges. F1534 4.5.30 P Robin
our horses shal eate no hay as long as this lasts. . . F App p.234 3 P Robin
whose seas/Eate hollow rocks, and where the north-west wind/Nor Lucan, First Booke 407
EATING
Eating sweet Comfites with Queene Didos maide, ... Dido 5.1.47 Ascan
with freatting, and then she will not bee woorth the eating. 1Tamb 4.4.51 P Tamb
sir, you must be dieted, too much eating will make you surfeit. 1Tamb 4.4.103 P Tamb
In spite of these swine-eating Christians, ... Jew 2.3.7 Barab
What, sleeping, eating, walking and disputing? . . . F 528 2.1.140 Faust
gave me my mony, and fell to eating; and as I am a cursen man, F1530 4.5.26 P Carter
he never left eating, till he had eate up all my loade of hay. F1531 4.5.27 P Carter
EATS
saies, he that eats with the devil had need of a long spoone. Jew 3.4.58 P Ithimr
EAZE
My lords, to eaze all this, but heare me speake. . . Edw 1.2.68 ArchBp
So sweete a burthen I will beare with eaze. . . . Ovid's Elegies 2.16.30
EB
And eb againe, as thou departst from me. . . . . 2Tamb 4.2.32 Therid
EBAN
With Eban Scepter strike this hatefull earth, ... 1Tamb 4.2.28 Bajzth
EBBES
And changeth as the Ocean ebbes and flowes: . . . . Lucan, First Booke 412
EBEA
How lik'st thou her Ebea, will she serve? . . . . . 1Tamb 3.3.178 Zabina
EBENA
Eies when that Ebena steps to heaven, ... 1Tamb 5.1.147 Tamb
EBON
that shall pierce through/The Ebon gates of ever-burning hell, F1224 4.1.70 Faust
ECCE
ecce signum, heeres a simple purchase for horse-keepers, our F App p.234 2 P Robin
ECCHO
Which sent an eccho to the wounded King: . . . . . Dido 2.1.249 Aeneas
that earth may eccho foorth/The far resounding torments ye 2Tamb 4.1.185 Tamb
ECCHOE
cracke, the Ecchoe and the souldiers crie/Make deafe the aire, 2Tamb 3.3.60 Therid
ECCHOES
Whose hideous ecchoes make the welkin howle, ... Dido 4.2.9 Iarbus
[But feareful ecchoes thunder <thunders> in mine eares], . F 571 2.2.20A Faust
ECH
Whereto ech man of rule hath given his hand, ... 1Tamb 5.1.102 1Virgn
And not to dare ech other to the field: . . . . 2Tamb 1.1.116 Gazell
And at ech corner shall the Kings garde stand. . . . P 291 5.18 Anjoy
Both might enjoy ech other, and be blest. . . . . Hero and Leander 1.380
Mov'd by Loves force, unto ech other lep? . . . . . Hero and Leander 2.58
ECLIPSES
Aspects, Eclipses, all at one time, but in some years we have F 615 2.2.64 P Faust
ECLIPST
Sith blacke disgrace hath thus eclipst our fame, . . . F1455 4.3.25 Benvol
ECSTASY (See EXTASIE)
ECUES
Catholickes/Sends Indian golde to coyne me French ecues: . P 118 2.61 Guise
EDG'D
And ripe-earde corne with sharpe-edg'd sithes to fell. . Ovid's Elegies 3.9.12
EDGE
Keeping his circuit by the slicing edge. . . . . . 1Tamb 5.1.112 Tamb

EDGE (cont.)			
blotted letter/On the last edge to stay mine eyes the better.	Ovid's Elegies	1.11.22	
EDGED			
That with the sharpnes of my edged sting,	Dido	4.1.22	Iarbus
EDICT			
Dismisse thy campe or else by our Edict,	P 863	17.58	King
EDICTS			
Hence came it that th'edicts were overrul'd,	Lucan, First Booke		178
EDMUND			
Edmund, the mightie prince of Lancaster/That hath more	Edw	1.3.1	Gavstn
Come Edmund lets away, and levie men,	Edw	2.2.98	Edward
Stay Edmund, never was Plantagenet/False of his word, and	Edw	2.3.11	Mortmr
Till Edmund be arrivde for Englands good,	Edw	4.1.2	Kent
Lord Edmund and lord Mortimer alive?	Edw	4.2.36	Queene
with them are gone lord Edmund, and the lord Mortimer, having	Edw	4.3.32	P Spencr
With him is Edmund gone associate?	Edw	4.3.39	Edward
O fly him then, but Edmund calme this rage,	Edw	4.6.11	Kent
Edmund away, Bristow to Longshankes blood/Is false, be not	Edw	4.6.16	Kent
I like not this relenting moode in Edmund,	Edw	4.6.38	Mortmr
And we have heard that Edmund laid a plot,	Edw	5.2.32	BshpWn
rest, because we heare/That Edmund casts to worke his libertie,	Edw	5.2.58	Mortmr
Use Edmund friendly, as if all were well.	Edw	5.2.79	Queene
Inconstant Edmund, doost thou favor him,	Edw	5.2.101	Mortmr
Brother Edmund, strive not, we are his friends,	Edw	5.2.114	Queene
Edmund, yeeld thou thy self, or thou shalt die.	Edw	5.3.56	Matrvs
Edmund the Earle of Kent.	Edw	5.4.83	Souldr
Did you attempt his rescue, Edmund speake?	Edw	5.4.86	Mortmr
Had Edmund liv'de, he would have sought thy death.	Edw	5.4.112	Queene
And shall my Uncle Edmund ride with us?	Edw	5.4.114	King
EDMUNDS			
To dash the heavie headed Edmunds drift,	Edw	5.2.39	Mortmr
And none of both [them] <then> thirst for Edmunds bloud.	Edw	5.4.107	Kent
EDWARD			
Is Edward pleazd with kinglie regiment.	Edw	1.1.165	Edward
If it be so, what will not Edward do?	Edw	1.4.325	Edward
Edward, unfolde thy pawes,/And let their lives bloud slake thy	Edw	2.2.204	Edward
[King] <Kind> Edward is not heere to buckler thee.	Edw	2.5.18	Lncstr
My lords, king Edward greetes you all by me.	Edw	2.5.33	Arundl
Renowmed Edward, how thy name/Revives poore Gaveston.	Edw	2.5.41	Gavstn
it is this life you aime at,/Yet graunt king Edward this.	Edw	2.5.49	Gavstn
Come, let thy shadow parley with king Edward.	Edw	2.6.14	Warwck
Were I king Edward, Englands soveraigne,	Edw	3.1.10	Spencr
the lovelie Elenor of Spaine,/Great Edward Longshankes issue:	Edw	3.1.12	Spencr
Long live my soveraigne the noble Edward,	Edw	3.1.32	SpncrP
Advaunce your standard Edward in the field,	Edw	3.1.126	Spencr
Long live king Edward, Englands lawful lord.	Edw	3.1.151	Herald
Edward with fire and sword, followes at thy heeles.	Edw	3.1.180	Edward
Yonder is Edward among his flatterers.	Edw	3.1.196	Mortmr
No Edward, no, thy flatterers faint and flie.	Edw	3.1.201	Mortmr
Then Edward, thou wilt fight it to the last,	Edw	3.1.211	Mortmr
No Edward, Englands scourge, it may not be,	Edw	3.1.258	Mortmr
Edward this day hath crownd him king a new.	Edw	3.1.261	Edward
Proud Edward, doost thou banish me thy presence?	Edw	4.1.5	Kent
Would all were well, and Edward well reclaimd,	Edw	4.2.57	Kent
I thinke king Edward will out-run us all.	Edw	4.2.68	Prince
Triumpheth Englands Edward with his friends,	Edw	4.3.2	Edward
And triumph Edward with his friends uncontrould.	Edw	4.3.3	Edward
they intend to give king Edward battell in England, sooner then	Edw	4.3.35	P Spencr
And Edward thou art one among them all,	Edw	4.4.10	Queene
And for the open wronges and injuries/Edward hath done to us,	Edw	4.4.22	Mortmr
Edward will thinke we come to flatter him.	Edw	4.4.29	SrJohn
Edward, alas my hart relents for thee,	Edw	4.6.2	Kent
Edward, this Mortimer aimes at thy life:	Edw	4.6.10	Kent
How will you deale with Edward in his fall?	Edw	4.6.31	Kent
Tell me good unckle, what Edward doe you meane?	Edw	4.6.32	Prince
This, Edward, is the ruine of the realme.	Edw	4.6.45	Kent
[Unhappie] <Unhappies> <Unhappy is> Edward, chaste from	Edw	4.6.62	Kent
For friends hath Edward none, but these, and these,	Edw	4.7.91	Edward
is noble Edward gone,/Parted from hence, never to see us more!	Edw	4.7.100	Spencr
But Edwards name survives, though Edward dies.	Edw	5.1.48	Edward
Here, take my crowne, the life of Edward too,	Edw	5.1.57	Edward
That Edward may be still faire Englands king:	Edw	5.1.68	Edward
But haplesse Edward, thou art fondly led,	Edw	5.1.76	Edward
Sister, Edward is my charge, redeeme him.	Edw	5.2.116	Kent
Edward is my sonne, and I will keepe him.	Edw	5.2.117	Queene
And rescue aged Edward from his foes,	Edw	5.2.120	Kent
Friends, whither must unhappie Edward go,	Edw	5.3.4	Edward
Thus lives old Edward not reliev'd by any,	Edw	5.3.23	Edward
Long live king Edward, by the grace of God/King of England, and	Edw	5.4.73	ArchBp
Small comfort findes poore Edward in thy lookes,	Edw	5.5.44	Edward
EDWARDS			
Here Mortimer, sit thou in Edwards throne,	Edw	1.4.36	Edward
In vaine I looke for love at Edwards hand,	Edw	2.4.61	Queene
And though devorsed from king Edwards eyes,	Edw	2.5.3	Gavstn
Welcome old man, comst thou in Edwards aide?	Edw	3.1.34	Edward
Sworne to defend king Edwards royall right,	Edw	3.1.38	SpncrP
Saint George for England, and king Edwards right.	Edw	3.1.220	Edward
Begets the quiet of king Edwards land,	Edw	3.1.263	Spencr
Proclaime king Edwards warres and victories.	Edw	3.1.281	Spencr
And certifie what Edwards loosenes is.	Edw	4.1.7	Kent
So fought not they that fought in Edwards right.	Edw	4.6.72	SpncrP
And princely Edwards right we crave the crowne.	Edw	5.1.39	BshpWn
No, tis for Mortimer, not Edwards head,	Edw	5.1.40	Edward

EDWARDS (cont.)			
But Edwards name survives, though Edward dies.	Edw	5.1.48	Edward
Yet he that is the cause of Edwards death,	Edw	5.4.3	Mortmr
Unlesse thou bring me newes of Edwards death.	Edw	5.4.46	Mortmr
Dares but affirme, that Edwards not true king,	Edw	5.4.76	Champn
EDWARDUM			
Edwardum occidere nolite timere bonum est.	Edw	5.4.8	Mortmr
Edwardum occidere nolite timere bonum est.	Edw	5.4.11	Mortmr
Edwardum occidere nolite timere,	Edw	5.5.17	Matrvs
EEL (See ELE)			
EFFECT (Homograph)			
But now that I have found what to effect,	Dido	3.4.37	Dido
But never could effect their Stratagem.	Jew	1.1.165	Barab
with his lips; the effect was, that I should come to her house.	Jew	4.2.31	P Ithimr
To effect all promises betweene us [made] <both>.	F 482	2.1.94	Mephst
what ere thou be whom God assignes/This great effect, art hid.	Lucan, First Booke		420
What two determine never wants effect.	Ovid's Elegies		2.3.16
That can effect <affect> a foolish wittalls wife.	Ovid's Elegies		2.19.46
Some hidden influence breeds like effect.	Hero and Leander		2.60
EFFECTE			
exhalatione/which our great sonn of fraunce cold not effecte	Paris	ms20,p390	Guise
EFFECTED			
and effected, that the Queene all discontented and	Edw	4.3.30	P Spencr
EFFECTING			
Well, now about effecting this device:	Jew	5.2.117	Barab
For not effecting of his holines will.	P 878	17.73	Eprnon
EFFECTS			
(For whose effects my soule is massacred)/Infect thy gracious	P 192	3.27	QnMarg
world can compare with thee, for the rare effects of Magicke:	F App	p.236 3	P Emper
EFFEMINATE			
Effeminate our mindes inur'd to warre.	Dido	4.3.36	Achat
To harbour thoughts effeminate and faint?	1Tamb	5.1.177	Tamb
Making them burie this effeminate brat,	2Tamb	4.1.162	Tamb
EFFUSION			
That if without effusion of bloud,	Edw	3.1.159	Herald
EGERIA			
Egeria with just Numa had good sport,	Ovid's Elegies		2.17.18
EGEUS			
That King Egeus fed with humaine flesh,	2Tamb	4.3.13	Tamb
EGGES			
but hee hides and buries it up as Partridges doe their egges,	Jew	4.2.58	P Ithimr
EGLES			
Or seemed faire walde in with Egles wings,	Dido	1.1.20	Ganimd
EGO			
Ego mihimet sum semper proximus.	Jew	1.1.189	Barab
EGREGIOUS			
Egregious Viceroyes of these Eastern parts/Plac'd by the issue	2Tamb	1.1.1	Orcan
EGYPT			
The Sunne from Egypt shall rich odors bring,	Dido	5.1.11	Aeneas
How now my Lords of Egypt and Zenocrate?	1Tamb	1.2.113	Tamb
Great Emperours of Egypt and Arabia,	1Tamb	4.3.51	Capol
Zenocrate, were Egypt Joves owne land,	1Tamb	4.4.73	Tamb
For Egypt and Arabia must be mine.	1Tamb	4.4.91	Tamb
Wel, here is now to the Souldane of Egypt, the King of Arabia,	1Tamb	4.4.113	P Tamb
Though with the losse of Egypt and my Crown.	1Tamb	5.1.444	Souldn
Who lives in Egypt, prisoner to that slave,	2Tamb	1.1.4	Orcan
Where Egypt and the Turkish Empire parts,	2Tamb	1.3.6	Tamb
Then martcht I into Egypt and Arabia,	2Tamb	5.3.130	Tamb
I sent for Egypt and the bordering Iles/Are gotten up by Nilus	Jew	1.1.42	Barab
Thou couldst not come from Egypt, or by Caire/But at the entry	Jew	1.1.73	Barab
you came not with those other ships/That sail'd by Egypt?	Jew	1.1.90	Barab
The plagues of Egypt, and the curse of heaven,	Jew	1.2.162	Barab
and in mine Argosie/And other ships that came from Egypt last,	Jew	1.2.188	Barab
EGYPTIA			
The mightie Souldan of Egyptia.	1Tamb	1.2.6	Tamb
Raves in Egyptia, and annoyeth us.	1Tamb	4.3.10	Souldn
when holy Fates/Shall stablish me in strong Egyptia,	1Tamb	4.4.135	Tamb
And holy Patrones <Patrons> of Egyptia,	1Tamb	5.1.49	2Virgn
EGYPTIAN (See also AEGIPTIAN)			
Besides thy share of this Egyptian prise,	1Tamb	1.2.190	Tamb
Or leave Damascus and th'Egyptian fields,	1Tamb	4.2.48	Tamb
Even with the true Egyptian Diadem.	1Tamb	5.1.105	1Virgn
Damascus walles di'd with Egyptian blood:	1Tamb	5.1.320	Zenoc
Armed with lance into the Egyptian fields,	1Tamb	5.1.381	Philem
to your dominions/Than ever yet confirm'd th'Egyptian Crown.	1Tamb	5.1.449	Tamb
shal be plac'd/Wrought with the Persean and Egyptian armes,	2Tamb	3.2.20	Amyras
EGYPTIANS			
While you faint-hearted base Egyptians,	1Tamb	4.1.8	Souldn
I will not spare these proud Egyptians,	1Tamb	5.1.121	Tamb
Egyptians, Moores and men of Asia,	1Tamb	5.1.517	Tamb
Natolians, Sorians, blacke Egyptians,	2Tamb	1.1.63	Orcan
EGYPTS			
For Egypts freedom and the Souldans life:	1Tamb	5.1.153	Tamb
EI'D			
fethered steele/So thick upon the blink-ei'd Burghers heads,	2Tamb	1.1.93	Orcan
EIE			
And all that pierceth Phoebes silver eie,	1Tamb	3.2.19	Agidas
Fit objects for thy princely eie to pierce.	2Tamb	1.2.45	Callap
Now bright Zenocrate, the worlds faire eie,	2Tamb	1.3.1	Tamb
Commanding all thy princely eie desires,	2Tamb	4.2.43	Therid
A greater Lamp than that bright eie of heaven,	2Tamb	4.2.88	Therid
The horse that guide the golden eie of heaven,	2Tamb	4.3.7	Tamb
learne with awfull eie/To sway a throane as dangerous as his:	2Tamb	5.3.234	Tamb

EIE (cont.)
Starke naked as she stood before mine eie, — Ovid's Elegies 1.5.17
If any eie mee with a modest looke, — Ovid's Elegies 2.4.11
Vaild to the ground, vailing her eie-lids close, — Hero and Leander 1.159
Is neither essence subject to the eie, — Hero and Leander 1.270
in being bold/To eie those parts, which no eie should behold. — Hero and Leander 1.408
And [throw] <threw> him gawdie toies to please his eie, — Hero and Leander 2.187

EIELESSE
And eielesse Monster that torments my soule, — 2Tamb 5.3.217 Tamb

EIE-LIDS
Vaild to the ground, vailing her eie-lids close, — Hero and Leander 1.159

EIES
Till with their eies [they] <thee> view us Emperours. — 1Tamb 1.2.67 Tamb
His fierie eies are fixt upon the earth, — 1Tamb 1.2.158 Therid
and dim their eies/That stand and muse at our admyred armes. — 1Tamb 2.3.23 Tamb
Such power attractive shines in princes eies. — 1Tamb 2.5.64 Therid
And in his eies the furie of his hart, — 1Tamb 3.2.73 Agidas
whose eies are brighter than the Lamps of heaven, — 1Tamb 3.3.120 Tamb
That with his terrour and imperious eies, — 1Tamb 4.1.14 2Msngr
And through the eies and eares of Tamburlaine, — 1Tamb 5.1.53 2Virgn
Reflexing them on your disdainfull eies: — 1Tamb 5.1.70 Tamb
Taking instructions from thy flowing eies: — 1Tamb 5.1.146 Tamb
Eies when that Ebena steps to heaven, — 1Tamb 5.1.147 Tamb
What do mine eies behold, my husband dead? — 1Tamb 5.1.305 Zabina
Ah wretched eies, the enemies of my hart, — 1Tamb 5.1.340 Zenoc
And let Zenocrates faire eies beholde/That as for her thou — 1Tamb 5.1.408 Arabia
Since thy desired hand shall close mine eies. — 1Tamb 5.1.432 Arabia
more precious in mine eies/Than all the wealthy kingdomes I — 2Tamb 1.3.18 Tamb
Which being wroth, sends lightning from his eies, — 2Tamb 1.3.76 Tamb
Whose eies shot fire from their Ivory bowers, — 2Tamb 2.4.9 Tamb
whose taste illuminates/Refined eies with an eternall sight, — 2Tamb 2.4.23 Tamb
If teares, our eies have watered all the earth: — 2Tamb 2.4.122 Therid
And him faire Lady shall thy eies behold. — 2Tamb 3.4.67 Therid
How may my hart, thus fired with mine eies, — 2Tamb 4.1.93 Tamb
May never day give vertue to his eies, — 2Tamb 4.1.174 Trebiz
whose weeping eies/Since thy arrivall here beheld no Sun, — 2Tamb 4.2.1 Olymp
Now eies, injoy your latest benefite, — 2Tamb 5.3.224 Tamb
eies may be witnesses to confirme what mine eares have heard — F App p.236 6 P Emper
peoples minds, and laide before their eies/Slaughter to come, — Lucan, First Booke 466
But may soft love rowse up my drowsie eies, — Ovid's Elegies 2.10.19
And I will trust your words more then mine eies. — Ovid's Elegies 3.13.46
To please the carelesse and disdainfull eies, — Hero and Leander 1.13
That my slacke muse, sings of Leanders eies, — Hero and Leander 1.72
Await the sentence of her scornefull eies: — Hero and Leander 1.123
What we behold is censur'd by our eies. — Hero and Leander 1.174
And here and there her eies through anger rang'd. — Hero and Leander 1.360

EIGHT
Venus, and Mercury in a yeare; the Moone in twenty eight daies. — F 606 2.2.55 P Faust
And in eight daies did bring him home againe. — F 767 2.3.46 2Chor
Thou know'st within the compasse of eight daies, — F 847 3.1.69 Faust
I tell thee he has not slept this eight nights. — F App p.240 144 P Mephst
And he have not slept this eight weekes Ile speake with him. — F App p.240 145 P HrsCsr

EIGHTEENE
I am eighteene pence on the score, but say nothing, see if she — F1511 4.5.7 P Robin

EITHER (See also EYTHER)
I would have either drunke his dying bloud, — Dido 3.3.28 Iarbus
And I will either move the thoughtles flint, — Dido 4.2.40 Iarbus
Shall either perish by our warlike hands, — 1Tamb 1.1.72 Therid
And either lanch his greedy thirsting throat, — 1Tamb 1.2.146 Tamb
And Crownes come either by succession/Or urg'd by force; and — Jew 1.1.131 Barab
Either pay that, or we will seize on all. — Jew 1.2.89 Govnr
Ile either rend it with my nayles to naught, — P 102 2.45 Guise
And either never mannage army more, — P 793 16.7 Bartus
Adew my Lord, and either change your minde, — Edw 1.1.130 Lncstr
And either have our wils, or lose our lives. — Edw 1.4.46 Mortmr
Either banish him that was the cause thereof, — Edw 1.4.60 ArchBp
Either my brother or his sonne is king, — Edw 5.4.106 Kent
They stai'd not either to pray or sacrifice, — Lucan, First Booke 504
Either love, or cause that I may never hate: — Ovid's Elegies 1.3.2
How oft, that either wind would breake thy coche, — Ovid's Elegies 1.13.29
Yet although [neither] <either>, mixt of eithers hue, — Ovid's Elegies 1.14.10
What good to me wil either Ajax bring? — Ovid's Elegies 2.1.30
In what gulfe either Syrtes have their seate. — Ovid's Elegies 2.11.20
let either heed/What please them, and their eyes let either — Ovid's Elegies 3.2.5
either heed/What please them, and their eyes let either feede. — Ovid's Elegies 3.2.6
Argus had either way an hundred eyes, — Ovid's Elegies 3.4.19
Either th'art muddy in mid winter tide: — Ovid's Elegies 3.5.95
Either she was foule, or her attire was bad, — Ovid's Elegies 3.6.1
Either th'art witcht with blood <bould> of frogs new dead, — Ovid's Elegies 3.6.79

EITHERS
Yet although [neither] <either>, mixt of eithers hue, — Ovid's Elegies 1.14.10

ELBOW
Where sorrow at my elbow still attends, — Edw 5.1.33 Edward

ELD
Tis shame for eld in warre or love to be. — Ovid's Elegies 1.9.4

ELDER (Homograph)
If thou exceed thy elder Brothers worth, — 2Tamb 1.3.50 Tamb
he weares, Judas left under the Elder when he hang'd himselfe. — Jew 4.4.66 P Ithimr
Which taught him all that elder lovers know, — Hero and Leander 2.69

ELDEST
That causde the eldest sonne of heavenly Ops, — 1Tamb 2.7.13 Tamb

ELE
on him; hee has a buttocke as slicke as an Ele; wel god buy sir, — F App p.240 117 P HrsCsr

ELEANOR (See ELENOR)			
ELECT			
And of extremities elect the least.	1Tamb	3.2.96	Agidas
he refuse, and then may we/Depose him and elect an other king.	Edw	1.4.55	Mortmr
Elect, conspire, install, do what you will,	Edw	5.1.88	Edward
ELECTED			
But seekes to make a new elected king,	Edw	5.1.78	Edward
I was elected by the Emperour.	F 905	3.1.127	Bruno
But where is Bruno our elected Pope,	F1160	4.1.6	Fredrk
ELECTION			
Without election, and a true consent:	F 887	3.1.109	Pope
ELECTORS			
The offer of your Prince Electors, farre/Beyond the reach of my	P 452	8.2	Anjoy
ELECTRA			
Heav'n starre Electra that bewaild her sisters?	Ovid's Elegies		3.11.37
ELEGIA			
Elegia came with haires perfumed sweete,	Ovid's Elegies		3.1.7
Sad Elegia thy wofull haires unbinde:	Ovid's Elegies		3.8.3
ELEGIAN			
Elegian Muse, that warblest amorous laies,	Ovid's Elegies		1.1.33
ELEGIES			
Toyes, and light Elegies my darts I tooke,	Ovid's Elegies		2.1.21
This last end to my Elegies is set,	Ovid's Elegies		3.14.2
Weake Elegies, delightfull Muse farewell;	Ovid's Elegies		3.14.19
ELEGY (See ELIGIE)			
ELEIUS			
to warre,/Was so incenst as are Eleius steedes/With clamors:	Lucan, First Booke		294
ELEMENT			
And urg'd each Element to his annoy:	Dido	3.2.46	Juno
The water is an Element, no Nimph,	Dido	4.4.147	Dido
And sooner let the fiery Element/Dissolve, and make your	2Tamb	2.4.58	Zenoc
not any Element/Shal shrowde thee from the wrath of	2Tamb	3.5.126	Tamb
more than if the region/Next underneath the Element of fire,	2Tamb	5.1.88	Tamb
Stand still you watches of the element,	Edw	5.1.66	Edward
So shall the spirits <subjects> of every element,	F 149	1.1.121	Valdes
ELEMENTS			
Untill our bodies turne to Elements:	1Tamb	1.2.236	Tamb
And with the same proportion of Elements/Resolve, I hope we are	1Tamb	2.6.26	Cosroe
Nature that fram'd us of foure Elements,	1Tamb	2.7.18	Tamb
The scum and tartar of the Elements,	2Tamb	4.1.124	Tamb
and Calor, which some holde/Is not a parcell of the Elements,	2Tamb	5.3.87	Phsitn
Lord and Commander of these elements.	F 104	1.1.76	BdAngl
Within the bowels of these Elements,	F 508	2.1.120	Mephst
As are the elements, such are the heavens <spheares>,/Even from	F 589	2.2.38	Mephst
Their soules are soone dissolv'd in elements,	F1970	5.2.174	Faust
ELENOR			
Sonne to the lovelie Elenor of Spaine,	Edw	3.1.11	Spencr
ELFE			
Memnon the elfe/Received his cole-blacke colour from thy selfe.	Ovid's Elegies		1.13.31
ELIGIE			
Zenocrate had bene the argument/Of every Epigram or Eligie.	2Tamb	2.4.95	Tamb
ELISA			
Eneas to Elisa answere gives,	Ovid's Elegies		2.18.31
ELISIAN			
To get a passage to Elisian.	1Tamb	5.1.247	Zabina
Hell and Elisian swarme with ghosts of men,	1Tamb	5.1.465	Tamb
Now Hell is fairer than Elisian,	2Tamb	4.2.87	Therid
ELISIUM			
Elisium hath a wood of holme trees black,	Ovid's Elegies		2.6.49
his parentage, would needs discover/The way to new Elisium:	Hero and Leander		1.411
ELIZA			
And all the woods Eliza to resound:	Dido	4.2.10	Iarbus
ELIZIUM			
Is as Elizium to a new come soule.	Edw	1.1.11	Gavstn
For I confound <He confounds> hell in Elizium:	F 287	1.3.59	Faust
ELL			
an inch of raw Mutton, better then an ell of fryde Stockfish:	F 709	2.2.161	P Ltchry
ELMES			
Elmes love the Vines, the Vines with Elmes abide,	Ovid's Elegies		2.16.41
ELOQUENCE			
Caesar (said he) while eloquence prevail'd,	Lucan, First Booke		274
Nor doth her tongue want harmefull eloquence.	Ovid's Elegies		1.8.20
ELOQUENT			
Is he not eloquent in all his speech?	Dido	3.1.65	Dido
Ah were I now but halfe so eloquent/To paint in woords, what	2Tamb	1.2.9	Callap
Love alwaies makes those eloquent that have it.	Hero and Leander		2.72
ELS			
Or els in Carthage make his kingly throne.	Dido	2.1.331	Venus
Or els I would have given my life in gage.	Dido	3.3.29	Iarbus
And all the fruites that plentie els sends forth,	Dido	4.2.15	Iarbus
Ile have a husband, or els a lover.	Dido	4.5.23	Nurse
Or els abide the wrath of frowning Jove.	Dido	5.1.54	Hermes
Or els Ile make a prayer unto the waves,	Dido	5.1.246	Dido
Or els you shall be forc'd with slaverie.	1Tamb	1.2.256	Tamb
or els infernall, mixt/Their angry seeds at his conception:	1Tamb	2.6.9	Meandr
Or els to threaten death and deadly armes,	1Tamb	3.1.19	Fesse
Or els unite you to his life and soule,	1Tamb	3.2.23	Zenoc
Or els I sweare to have you whipt stark nak'd.	1Tamb	4.2.74	Anippe
Els should I much forget my self, my Lord.	1Tamb	5.1.500	Zenoc
Or els you are not sons of Tamburlaine.	2Tamb	1.3.64	Tamb
Or els discended to his winding traine:	2Tamb	2.4.54	Tamb
Or els invent some torture worse than that.	2Tamb	3.4.22	Olymp
T'appease my wrath, or els Ile torture thee,	2Tamb	3.5.122	Tamb

ELS (cont.)
Or els be sure thou shalt be forc'd with paines, 2Tamb 5.1.52 Therid
I know none els but holdes them in disgrace: P 764 15.22 Guise
What els my lords, for it concernes me neere, Edw 1.2.44 ArchBp
Els would you nct intreate for Mortimer. Edw 5.6.71 King
Or els will maidens, yong-mens mates, to go/If they determine Ovid's Elegies 2.16.17
ELSE
Or else be gather'd for in our Synagogue; Jew 2.3.27 Barab
I, Barabas, or else thou wrong'st me much. Jew 2.3.255 Mthias
Or else I will confesse: I, there it goes: Jew 4.3.4 Barab
I, and the rest too, or else-- Jew 4.3.28 P Pilia
so, or how else,/The Jew is here, and rests at your command. Jew 5.1.82 Barab
For this, I waite, that scornes attendance else: P 106 2.49 Guise
Or else employ them in some better cause. P 794 16.8 Bartus
Else all France knowes how poor a Duke thou art. P 844 17.39 Eprnon
Dismisse thy campe or else by our Edict, P 863 17.58 King
Or else to murder me, and so be King. P1040 19.110 King
Or else dye Epernoune. P1227 22.89 Eprnon
For no where else the new earle is so safe. Edw 1.4.11 Lncstr
For no where else seekes he felicitie. Edw 1.4.122 Gavstn
Or else be banisht from his highnesse presence. Edw 1.4.203 Queene
Whither else but to the King. Edw 2.2.134 Mortmr
And you shall ransome him, or else-- Edw 2.2.145 Mortmr
that is all he gets/Of Gaveston, or else his sencelesse trunck. Edw 2.5.54 Mortmr
Remember thee fellow? what else? Edw 4.7.118 Rice
What else my lord? and farre more resolute. Edw 5.4.23 Ltborn
let him have the king,/What else? Edw 5.5.25 Matrvs
What else, a table and a fetherbed. Edw 5.5.33 Ltborn
Or else die by the hand of Mortimer. Edw 5.6.6 Mortmr
Will make thee vow to study nothing else. F 164 1.1.136 Cornel
And whatsoever else is requisite, F 183 1.1.155 Valdes
I, so are all things else; but whereabouts <where about>? F 507 2.1.119 Faust
<talke of the divel, and nothing else: come away>. F 660 (HC263)A P Lucifr
It appeares so, pray be bold else-where, F1597 4.6.40 Servnt
This, or what else my Faustus shall <thou shalt> desire, F1766 5.1.93 Mephst
I, and goings out too, you may see else. F App p.229 5 P Clown
keep out, or else you are blowne up, you are dismembred Rafe, F App p.233 10 P Robin
study, shee's borne to beare with me, or else my Art failes. F App p.233 17 P Robin
Predestinate to ruine; all lands else/Have stable peace, here Lucan, First Booke 251
Or Plutoes bloodles kingdom, but else where/Resume a body: Lucan, First Booke 452
Enjoy the wench, let all else be refusd. Ovid's Elegies 2.2.30
Supposing nothing else was to be done, Hero and Leander 2.53
ELSE-WHERE
It appeares so, pray be bold else-where, F1597 4.6.40 Servnt
ELSE WHERE
Or Plutoes bloodles kingdom, but else where/Resume a body: Lucan, First Booke 452
ELYSIUMS (See also ELIZIUM)
Tibullus doth Elysiums joy inherit. Ovid's Elegies 3.8.60
'EM (Homograph)
Goe tell 'em the Jew of Malta sent thee, man: Jew 1.1.66 Barab
Tush, who amongst 'em knowes not Barrabas? Jew 1.1.67 Barab
Sir we saw 'em not. Jew 1.1.90 2Merch
Why let 'em come, so they come not to warre; Jew 1.1.150 Barab
Or let 'em warre, so we be conquerors: Jew 1.1.151 Barab
Nay let 'em combat, conquer, and kill all, Jew 1.1.152 Barab
Why let 'em enter, let 'em take the Towne. Jew 1.1.190 Barab
Let 'em suspect, but be thou so precise/As they may thinke it Jew 1.2.284 Barab
Intreat 'em faire, and give them friendly speech, Jew 1.2.286 Barab
This is the Market-place, here let 'em stand: Jew 2.3.1 1Offcr
See 'em goe pinion'd along by my doore. Jew 2.3.180 Barab
I'le make 'em friends againe. Jew 2.3.357 Abigal
You'll make 'em friends? Jew 2.3.358 Barab
Till I have set 'em both at enmitie. Jew 2.3.383 Barab
Part 'em, part 'em. Jew 3.2.8 Within
I, part 'em now they are dead: Farewell, farewell. Jew 3.2.9 Barab
But let 'em goe: Jew 3.4.28 Barab
Here take my keyes, I'le give 'em thee anon: Jew 3.4.46 Barab
My father did contract me to 'em both: Jew 3.6.22 Abigal
I smelt 'em e're they came. Jew 4.1.22 Barab
And so doe I, master, therfore speake 'em faire. Jew 4.1.27 Ithimr
Part 'em, master, part 'em. Jew 4.1.97 P Ithimr
Fie upon 'em, master, will you turne Christian, when holy Jew 4.1.193 P Ithimr
Here take 'em, fellow, with as good a will-- Jew 4.3.52 Barab
Well, I must seeke a meanes to rid 'em all, Jew 4.3.63 Barab
son; he and I kild 'em both, and yet never touch'd 'em. Jew 4.4.18 P Ithimr
Like thy breath, sweet-hart, no violet like 'em. Jew 4.4.40 Ithimr
So, now I am reveng'd upon 'em all. Jew 4.4.42 Barab
Any of 'em will doe it. Jew 4.4.78 P Ithimr
Their deaths were like their lives, then think not of 'em; Jew 5.1.56 Govnr
shut/His souldiers, till I have consum'd 'em all with fire? Jew 5.2.82 Barab
Tush, send not letters to 'em, goe thy selfe, Jew 5.2.93 Barab
Then now are all things as my wish wud have 'em, Jew 5.5.17 Barab
trade to purchase Townes/By treachery, and sell 'em by deceit? Jew 5.5.48 Barab
I, and tis likewise thought you favour him <them> <'em> <hem>. Edw 2.2.226 Edward
Here, take your Guilders [againe], I'le none of 'em. F 371 1.4.29 P Robin
me thinkes you should have a wooden bedfellow of one of 'em. F1654 4.6.97 P Carter
up my hands, but see they hold 'em <them>, they hold 'em <them>. F1853 5.2.57 P Faust
my hands, but see they hold 'em <them>, they hold 'em <them>. F1853 5.2.57 P Faust
EMATHIAN
where/A fury leades the Emathian bandes, from thence/To the Lucan, First Booke 687
EMBALM'D
thou shalt stay with me/Embalm'd with Cassia, Amber Greece and 2Tamb 2.4.130 Tamb
EMBARK (See IMBARKT)

EMBASE (See IMBAST)			
EMBASSADORS			
What forraine prince sends thee embassadors? . . .	Edw	2.2.170	Lncstr
EMBASSADOURS			
But that we presently despatch Embassadours/To Poland, to call	P 555	11.20	QnMoth
EMBASSAGE (See AMBASSAGE)			
EMBASSIE			
in the Counsell-house/To entertaine them and their Embassie.	Jew	1.1.149	1Jew
EMBDEN			
Why, the Signory of Embden shall be mine:	F 412	2.1.24	Faust
EMBERS			
Rakt up in embers of their povertie, ...	Edw	1.1.21	Gavstn
EMBOST			
Embost with silke as best beseemes my state, ...	1Tamb	1.1.99	Mycet
EMBRACE (See also EMBRAC'D)			
Who when he shall embrace you in his armes, ...	1Tamb	3.2.42	Agidas
The Abbasse of the house/Whose zealous admonition I embrace:	Jew	3.3.67	Abigal
Embrace me Gaveston as I do thee:	Edw	1.1.141	Edward
Drye Enipeus, Tyro to embrace, ...	Ovid's Elegies		3.5.43
Foole canst thou him in thy white armes embrace? . .	Ovid's Elegies		3.7.11
EMBRACED			
she farre become a bed/Embraced in a friendly lovers armes,	Jew	1.2.372	Mthias
EMBRACES			
sweet embraces <imbracings> may extinguish cleare <cleane>,	F1763	5.1.90	Faust
Hector to armes went from his wives embraces, . . .	Ovid's Elegies		1.9.35
EMBRACETH			
Embraceth now with teares of ruth and blood, ...	1Tamb	5.1.85	1Virgn
EMBRACING			
Embracing thee with deepest of his love, ...	2Tamb	4.1.109	Tamb
EMBROIDER (See IMBRODERED)			
EMDEN (See EMBDEN)			
EMERALDS			
Thou with thy quilles mightst make greene Emeralds darke,	Ovid's Elegies		2.6.21
EMERAULDS			
Jacints, hard Topas, grasse-greene Emeraulds, ...	Jew	1.1.26	Barab
EMPAL'D			
Which is with azure circling lines empal'd, ...	Hero and Leander		2.274
EMPALE			
whose golden leaves/Empale your princelie head, your diadem,	Edw	3.1.164	Herald
EMPERESSE			
To be my Queen and portly Emperesse.	1Tamb	1.2.187	Tamb
Shall draw the chariot of my Emperesse, ...	1Tamb	3.3.80	Bajzth
he persecutes/The noble Turke and his great Emperesse? .	1Tamb	4.3.27	Arabia
You see my wife, my Queene and Emperesse, ...	1Tamb	5.1.264	Bajzth
Behold the Turke and his great Emperesse.	1Tamb	5.1.354	Zenoc
Behold the Turk and his great Emperesse.	1Tamb	5.1.357	Zenoc
Behold the Turke and his great Emperesse.	1Tamb	5.1.362	Zenoc
In this great Turk and haplesse Emperesse.	1Tamb	5.1.368	Zenoc
The Turk and his great Emperesse as it seems, ...	1Tamb	5.1.470	Tamb
With this great Turke and his faire Emperesse: . . .	1Tamb	5.1.532	Tamb
I cannot love to be an Emperesse.	2Tamb	4.2.49	Olymp
EMPERESSES			
I fare my Lord, as other Emperesses, ...	2Tamb	2.4.42	Zenoc
EMPERIALL			
Weare the emperiall Crowne of Libia, ...	Dido	4.4.34	Dido
Present thee with th'Emperiall Diadem.	1Tamb	1.1.139	Ortyg
I willingly receive th'emperiall crowne, ...	1Tamb	1.1.157	Cosroe
And place himselfe in the Emperiall heaven, ...	1Tamb	2.7.15	Tamb
And on thy head weare my Emperiall crowne, ...	1Tamb	3.3.113	Bajzth
Having the power from the Emperiall heaven, ...	1Tamb	4.4.30	Tamb
Even from the Moone unto the Emperiall Orbe, ...	F 590	2.2.39	Mephst
the seven Planets, the Firmament, and the Emperiall heaven.	F 611	2.2.60	P Mephst
EMPERIE			
No bounds but heaven shall bound his Emperie, ...	Dido	1.1.100	Jupitr
Presage the downfall of my Emperie, ...	Dido	4.4.118	Dido
By curing of this maimed Emperie.	1Tamb	1.1.126	Menaph
Measuring the limits of his Emperie/By East and west, as .	1Tamb	1.2.39	Tamb
That none can quence but blood and Emperie.	1Tamb	2.6.33	Cosroe
whome rule and emperie/Have not in life or death made .	Edw	4.7.14	Edward
Were with Jove clos'd in Stigian Emperie.	Hero and Leander		1.458
EMPERIES			
whom all kings/Of force must yeeld their crownes and Emperies:	1Tamb	5.1.481	Souldn
EMPERIOUS			
Tis more then kingly or Emperious.	P 759	15.17	Guise
EMPEROR			
What meanes the mighty Turkish Emperor/To talk with one so base	1Tamb	3.3.87	Fesse
O Bajazeth, O Turk, O Emperor.	1Tamb	5.1.309	Zabina
you bring Alexander and his paramour before the emperor? .	F App	p.237 52	P Knight
Which made thee Emperor; thee (seeing thou being old/Must shine	Lucan, First Booke		45
EMPERORS			
Emperors and Kings,/Are but obey'd in their severall Provinces:	F 84	1.1.56	Faust
EMPEROUR			
To crowne me Emperour of Asia.	1Tamb	1.1.112	Cosroe
Bringing the Crowne to make you Emperour.	1Tamb	1.1.135	Menaph
We will invest your Highnesse Emperour:	1Tamb	1.1.151	Ceneus
Emperour of Asia, and of Persea, ...	1Tamb	1.1.162	Ortyg
Long live Cosroe mighty Emperour.	1Tamb	1.1.169	Ortyg
By living Asias mightie Emperour.	1Tamb	1.2.73	Zenoc
I see the folly of thy Emperour:	1Tamb	1.2.167	Tamb
Shall make me solely Emperour of Asia:	1Tamb	2.3.39	Cosroe
And more than needes to make an Emperour.	1Tamb	2.3.65	Tamb
With greatest pompe had crown'd thee Emperour.	1Tamb	2.5.5	Tamb
Most happy Emperour in humblest tearms/I vow my service to your	1Tamb	2.5.15	Meandr

EMPEROUR (cont.)			
Presume a bickering with your Emperour:	1Tamb	3.1.4	Bajzth
Renowmed Emperour, and mighty Generall,	1Tamb	3.1.16	Fesse
Tell him thy Lord the Turkish Emperour,	1Tamb	3.1.22	Bajzth
That made me Emperour of Asia.	1Tamb	3.3.32	Tamb
More mighty than the Turkish Emperour:	1Tamb	3.3.37	Therid
As when my Emperour overthrew the Greeks:	1Tamb	3.3.204	Zabina
And crowne me Emperour of Affrica.	1Tamb	3.3.221	Tamb
And never had the Turkish Emperour/So great a foile by any	1Tamb	3.3.234	Bajzth
Dar'st thou that never saw an Emperour,	1Tamb	4.2.58	Zabina
Or may be forc'd, to make me Emperour.	1Tamb	4.4.90	Tamb
Most happy King and Emperour of the earth,	1Tamb	5.1.74	1Virgn
(sacred Emperour)/The prostrate service of this wretched towne.	1Tamb	5.1.99	1Virgn
As I am Callapine the Emperour,	2Tamb	1.2.64	Callap
son and successive heire to the late mighty Emperour Bajazeth,	2Tamb	3.1.2	P Orcan
of God and his friend Mahomet, Emperour of Natolia, Jerusalem,	2Tamb	3.1.3	P Orcan
Long live Callepinus, Emperour of Turky.	2Tamb	3.1.6	P Orcan
(An Emperour so honoured for his vertues)/Revives the spirits	2Tamb	3.1.23	Callap
Than any Viceroy, King or Emperour.	2Tamb	3.4.43	Olymp
Renowmed Emperour, mighty Callepine,	2Tamb	3.5.1	2Msngr
The Emperour of the world, and earthly God,	2Tamb	3.5.22	Orcan
To note me Emperour of the three fold world:	2Tamb	4.3.118	Tamb
From the Emperour of Turkey is arriv'd/Great Selim-Calymath,	Jew	1.2.39	Govnr
Shall dye, be he King or Emperour.	P 235	4.33	Guise
By him, I'le be great Emperour of the world,	F 332	1.3.104	Faust
The Emperour shall not live, but by my leave,	F 338	1.3.110	Faust
This proud confronter of the Emperour,	F 897	3.1.119	Faust
I was elected by the Emperour.	F 905	3.1.127	Bruno
We will depose the Emperour for that deed,	F 906	3.1.128	Pope
Concerning Bruno and the Emperour,	F 948	3.1.170	Pope
That Bruno, and the Germane Emperour/Be held as Lollords, and	F 954	3.1.176	Faust
There to salute the wofull Emperour.	F 986	3.2.6	Mephst
Concerning Bruno and the Emperour.	F1015	3.2.35	1Card
That Bruno and the cursed Emperour/Were by the holy Councell	F1020	3.2.40	Pope
[Amongst the rest the Emperour is one],	F1150	3.3.63A	3Chor
Hye to the presence to attend the Emperour.	F1156	4.1.2	Mrtino
Will not his grace consort the Emperour?	F1162	4.1.8	Fredrk
Before the Pope and royall Emperour,	F1187	4.1.33	Mrtino
The Emperour is at hand, who comes to see/What wonders by	F1197	4.1.43	Mrtino
Well, go you attend the Emperour:	F1199	4.1.45	P Benvol
And honour'd of the Germane Emperour.	F1216	4.1.62	Emper
Both love and serve the Germane Emperour,	F1219	4.1.65	Faust
Present before this royall Emperour,	F1238	4.1.84	Faust
and thou bring Alexander and his Paramour before the Emperour,	F1255	4.1.101	P Benvol
thoughts are ravished so/With sight of this renowned Emperour,	F1261	4.1.107	Emper
Looke up Benvolio, tis the Emperour calls.	F1286	4.1.132	Saxony
The Emperour? where? O zounds my head.	F1287	4.1.133	Benvol
Or bring before this royall Emperour/The mightie Monarch,	F1296	4.1.142	Faust
Come Faustus while the Emperour lives.	F1321	4.1.167	Emper
heart <art> conspir'd/Benvolio's shame before the Emperour?	F1374	4.2.50	Mrtino
how you crossed me in my conference with the emperour?	F App	p.238 77	P Faust
EMPEROURS			
Till with their eies [they] <thee> view us Emperours.	1Tamb	1.2.67	Tamb
heaven beholde/Their Scourge and Terrour treade on Emperours.	1Tamb	4.2.32	Tamb
Not all the Kings and Emperours of the Earth:	1Tamb	4.2.92	Tamb
a blemish to the Majestie/And high estate of mightie Emperours,	1Tamb	4.3.20	Souldn
Great Emperours of Egypt and Arabia,	1Tamb	4.3.51	Capol
And be renowm'd, as never Emperours were.	1Tamb	4.4.138	Tamb
Emperours and kings lie breathlesse at my feet.	1Tamb	5.1.469	Tamb
Betweene thy sons that shall be Emperours,	2Tamb	1.3.7	Tamb
Keeping in yron cages Emperours.	2Tamb	1.3.49	Tamb
Wel lovely boies, you shal be Emperours both,	2Tamb	1.3.96	Tamb
Rich Princes both, and mighty Emperours:	P 463	8.13	Anjoy
That Peters heires should tread on Emperours,	F 918	3.1.140	Pope
To hold the Emperours their lawfull Lords.	F 927	3.1.149	Bruno
I saw him kneele, and kisse the Emperours hand,	F1344	4.2.20	Benvol
EMPERY (See also EMPERIE)			
Those that are proud of fickle Empery,	1Tamb	5.1.352	Zenoc
My realme, the Center of our Empery/Once lost, All Turkie would	2Tamb	1.1.55	Orcan
To make it parcel of my Empery.	2Tamb	1.3.110	Tamb
What right had Caesar to the [Empery] <Empire>?	Jew	Prol.19	Machvl
EMPIRE			
An ancient Empire, famoused for armes,	Dido	1.2.21	Cloan
And beautifying the Empire of this Queene,	Dido	5.1.28	Hermes
Where Egypt and the Turkish Empire parts,	2Tamb	1.3.6	Tamb
your royall gratitudes/With all the benefits my Empire yeelds:	2Tamb	3.1.9	Callap
What right had Caesar to the [Empery] <Empire>?	Jew	Prol.19	Machvl
how that none in my Empire, nor in the whole world can compare	F App	p.236 2	P Emper
Swords share our Empire, fortune that made Roome/Governe the	Lucan, First Booke		109
Within my brest no desert empire beare.	Ovid's Elegies		2.9.52
EMPIRES			
That in conceit bear Empires on our speares,	1Tamb	1.2.64	Tamb
EMPLOY (See also IMPLOY)			
And quell those hopes that thus employ your [cares] <eares>.	Dido	4.1.35	Dido
Or else employ them in some better cause.	P 794	16.8	Bartus
Madam in this matter/We will employ you and your little sonne,	Edw	3.1.70	Edward
EMPLOYD			
In which unhappie worke was I employd,	Dido	2.1.169	Aeneas
EMPLOYED			
Both for their sausinesse shall be employed,	1Tamb	3.3.184	Zenoc
EMPRESSE (See also EMPERESSE)			
O sister, were you Empresse of the world,	Dido	3.1.69	Anna
Both may invest you Empresse of the East:	1Tamb	1.2.46	Tamb

EMPRESSE (cont.)			
As if thou wert the Empresse of the world.	1Tamb	3.3.125	Tamb
thou be plac'd by me/That am the Empresse of the mighty Turke?	1Tamb	3.3.167	Zabina
Here Madam, you are Empresse, she is none. . . .	1Tamb	3.3.227	Therid
where I tooke/The Turke and his great Empresse prisoners,	2Tamb	5.3.129	Tamb
Eryx bright Empresse turnd her lookes aside, . . .	Ovid's Elegies		3.8.45
The rites/In which Loves beauteous Empresse most delites,/Are	Hero and Leander		1.300
EMPTIE			
And swong her howling in the emptie ayre, ...	Dido	2.1.248	Aeneas
For ballace, emptie Didos treasurie, ...	Dido	3.1.126	Dido
Whose emptie Altars have enlarg'd our illes. . . .	Dido	4.2.3	Iarbus
Servants, come fetch these emptie vessels here, . .	Dido	4.2.49	Iarbus
Returne our Mules and emptie Camels backe, . . .	1Tamb	1.2.76	Agidas
And the fates distaffe emptie stood to thee, . . .	Ovid's Elegies		2.6.46
Yea, let my foes sleepe in an emptie bed, ...	Ovid's Elegies		2.10.17
In emptie bed alone my mistris lies.	Ovid's Elegies		3.9.2
Lone women like to emptie houses perish.	Hero and Leander		1.242
Her vowes above the emptie aire he flings: . . .	Hero and Leander		1.370
EMPTY			
My empty stomacke ful of idle heat, ...	1Tamb	4.4.94	Bajzth
Filling their empty vaines with aiery wine, . . .	2Tamb	3.2.107	Tamb
Which wont to run their course through empty night/At noone day	Lucan, First Booke		534
Why she alone in empty bed oft tarries.	Ovid's Elegies		2.19.42
To empty aire may go my fearefull speech.	Ovid's Elegies		3.1.62
What to have laine alone in empty bed?	Ovid's Elegies		3.8.34
EMULOUS			
These Captaines emulous of each others glory. . . .	Lucan, First Booke		120
ENAMELD			
Their swords enameld, and about their neckes/Hangs massie	1Tamb	1.2.125	Souldr
Or if it could, downe from th'enameld skie, . . .	Hero and Leander		1.249
ENAMILED			
As if a chaire of gold enamiled, ...	2Tamb	3.2.119	Tamb
ENAMOUR'D			
And all that view'd her, were enamour'd on her. . .	Hero and Leander		1.118
ENAMOURED (See also INAMOURED)			
Enamoured of his beautie had he beene, ...	Hero and Leander		1.78
And thus Leander was enamoured.	Hero and Leander		1.162
On her, this god/Enamoured was, and with his snakie rod,/Did	Hero and Leander		1.398
Aye me, Leander cryde, th'enamoured sunne, . . .	Hero and Leander		2.202
ENCAMP (See INCAMPE)			
ENCELADUS			
We make Enceladus use a thousand armes, ...	Ovid's Elegies		3.11.27
ENCHAC'D			
To weare a Crowne enchac'd with pearle and golde, . .	1Tamb	2.5.60	Therid
of that Spheare/Enchac'd with thousands ever shining lamps,	1Tamb	4.2.9	Tamb
a golden Canapie/Enchac'd with pretious stones, which shine as	2Tamb	1.2.49	Callap
Enchac'd with Diamondes, Saphyres, Rubies/And fairest pearle of	2Tamb	3.2.120	Tamb
Pav'd with bright Christall, and enchac'd with starres, .	2Tamb	4.3.128	Tamb
ENCHANT (See ENCHAUNTED, INCHANTED, INCHAUNTED)			
ENCHANTMENTS			
What stronge enchantments tice my yeelding soule? . .	1Tamb	1.2.224	Therid
ENCHANTRESS (See INCHANTRESSE)			
ENCHASED			
Whose azured gates enchased with his name, ...	Dido	1.1.101	Jupitr
ENCHAST			
Enchast with precious juelles of mine owne: . . .	1Tamb	1.2.96	Tamb
ENCHAUNTED			
Her sacred beauty hath enchaunted heaven, ...	2Tamb	2.4.85	Tamb
That therewith all enchaunted like the guarde, . . .	Edw	3.1.266	Spencr
ENCLOSE (See INCLOSE)			
ENCOMPASSE			
As if as many kinges as could encompasse thee, . . .	1Tamb	2.5.4	Tamb
Millions of men encompasse thee about, ...	1Tamb	5.1.215	Bajzth
ENCOMPASSED			
Whose fiery cyrcles beare encompassed/A heaven of heavenly	1Tamb	2.1.15	Menaph
For hees a lambe, encompassed by Woolves, ...	Edw	5.1.41	Edward
ENCOUNTER (See also INCOUNTER)			
I heare them come, shal we encounter them? . . .	1Tamb	1.2.149	Techel
Yet scarse enough t'encounter Tamburlaine. . . .	2Tamb	1.1.66	Orcan
to as high a pitch/In this our strong and fortunate encounter.	2Tamb	3.1.31	Callap
Wee may lie ready to encounter him, ...	2Tamb	5.2.8	Callap
So now couragiously encounter them;	Jew	3.5.33	Govnr
Yet to encounter this your weake attempt, ...	F1429	4.2.105	Faust
ENCREASE			
Of whose encrease I set some longing hope, ...	P 689	13.33	Guise
Knowing her scapes thine honour shall encrease, . .	Ovid's Elegies		2.2.27
ENCROCHE (See also INCROCHING)			
if any Christian King/Encroche upon the confines of thy realme,	2Tamb	1.1.147	Orcan
END			
And in the end subdue them with his sword, ...	Dido	1.1.90	Jupitr
O end Aeneas, I can heare no more.	Dido	2.1.243	Dido
This Troians end will be thy envies aime, ...	Dido	3.3.73	Iarbus
Triumph, my mates, our travels are at end, ...	Dido	5.1.1	Aeneas
or to what end/Launcht from the haven, lye they in the Rhode?	Dido	5.1.88	Dido
To worke my downfall and untimely end.	1Tamb	2.7.6	Cosroe
working tooles present/The naked action of my threatned end.	1Tamb	3.2.94	Agidas
And have no hope to end our extasies.	1Tamb	5.1.238	Bajzth
Fortune, nor no hope of end/To our infamous monstrous slaveries?	1Tamb	5.1.240	Zabina
But as the Gods to end the Troyans toile, ...	1Tamb	5.1.392	Zenoc
No speach to that end, by your favour sir. . . .	2Tamb	1.2.14	Almeda
End all my penance in my sodaine death, ...	2Tamb	2.3.7	Sgsmnd
From paine to paine, whose change shal never end: . .	2Tamb	2.3.26	Orcan
That touch the end of famous Euphrates.	2Tamb	3.1.53	Trebiz

END (cont.)			
One minute end our daies, and one sepulcher/Containe our	2Tamb	3.4.13	Olymp
And for his sake here will I end my daies.	2Tamb	3.4.44	Olymp
And let the end of this my fatall journey,	2Tamb	3.4.81	Olymp
Be likewise end to my accursed life.	2Tamb	3.4.82	Olymp
Shal end the warlike progresse he intends,	2Tamb	3.5.23	Orcan
Thinke of thy end, this sword shall lance thy throat.	2Tamb	3.5.78	Orcan
But was prevented by his sodaine end.	2Tamb	4.2.74	Olymp
Meet heaven and earth, and here let al things end,	2Tamb	5.3.249	Amyras
So, say how was their end?	Jew	3.6.26	2Fryar
See his end first, and flye then if thou canst.	Jew	5.5.69	Govnr
fury of thy torments, strive/To end thy life with resolution:	Jew	5.5.80	Barab
To bring the will of our desires to end.	P 144	2.87	Guise
O graunt sweet God my daies may end with hers,	P 189	3.24	Navrre
Yet will we not that the Massacre shall end:	P 444	7.84	Guise
And end thy endles treasons with thy death.	P 955	19.25	King
But thats prevented, for to end his life,	P1119	21.13	Dumain
And may it never end in bloud as mine hath done.	P1233	22.95	King
gathered now shall ayme/more at thie end then exterpatione	Paris	ms29,p391	Guise
I for a while, but Baldock marke the end,	Edw	2.1.16	Spencr
Or saying a long grace at a tables end,	Edw	2.1.37	Spencr
But yet I hope my sorrowes will have end,	Edw	2.4.68	Queene
God end them once, my lord I take my leave,	Edw	3.1.87	Queene
May in their fall be followed to their end.	Edw	4.6.79	Mortmr
At every ten miles end thou hast a horse.	Edw	5.4.42	Mortmr
Yet levell at the end of every Art,	F 32	1.1.4	Faust
Is to dispute well Logickes chiefest end?	F 36	1.1.8	Faust
Then read no more, thou hast attain'd that <the> end;	F 38	1.1.10	Faust
The end of Physicke is our bodies health:	F 45	1.1.17	Faust
Why Faustus, hast thou not attain'd that end?	F 46	1.1.18	Faust
Now will I make an end immediately.	F 461	2.1.73	Faust
Thus will I end his griefes immediatly.	F1367	4.2.43	Benvol
Thy fatall time drawes to a finall end;	F1479	4.4.23	Faust
Pleasures unspeakeable, blisse without end.	F1900	5.2.104	GdAngl
Impose some end to my incessant paine:	F1960	5.2.164	Faust
<O> No end is limited to damned soules.	F1963	5.2.167	Faust
tho Faustus end be such/As every Christian heart laments to	F1995	5.3.13	2Schol
crush themselves, such end the gods/Allot the height of honor,	Lucan, First Booke	81	
here, here (saith he)/An end of peace; here end polluted lawes;	Lucan, First Booke	227	
Speake, when shall this thy long usurpt power end?	Lucan, First Booke	333	
What end of mischiefe?	Lucan, First Booke	334	
Why should we wish the gods should ever end them?	Lucan, First Booke	668	
Her valiant lover followes without end.	Ovid's Elegies	1.9.10	
Ill gotten goods good end will never have.	Ovid's Elegies	1.10.48	
And to the end your constant faith stood fixt.	Ovid's Elegies	2.6.14	
But of my love it will an end procure.	Ovid's Elegies	2.19.52	
This last end to my Elegies is set,	Ovid's Elegies	3.14.2	
ENDAMAGE (See INDAMAGED)			
ENDANGER			
Then conquer Malta, or endanger us.	Jew	5.5.122	Govnr
ENDE			
Thy fatall time doth drawe to finall ende,	F App	p.240 122	Faust
rid him into the deepe pond at the townes ende, I was no sooner	F App	p.240 133 P	HrsCsr
ENDEAVOR (See ENDEVOUR, INDEVOR)			
ENDED			
And every speech be ended with a kisse:	Dido	4.3.54	Aeneas
In dolefull wise they ended both their dayes.	Jew	3.3.21	Ithimr
this byll is ended,/And Faustus hath bequeath'd his soule to	F 463	2.1.75	Faust
See where they come: belike the feast is ended.	F App	p.243 8	Wagner
Caesars, and Pompeys jarring love soone ended,	Lucan, First Booke	98	
ENDEMION			
The Moone sleepes with Endemion everie day,	Ovid's Elegies	1.13.43	
ENDEVOUR			
The sole endevour of your princely care,	P 714	14.17	Bartus
ENDLES			
Hide now thy stained face in endles night,	1Tamb	5.1.292	Bajzth
And end thy endles treasons with thy death.	P 955	19.25	King
Which thoughts are martyred with endles torments.	Edw	5.1.80	Edward
ENDLESSE			
and protestations/Of endlesse honor to thee for her love.	1Tamb	5.1.497	Souldn
May in his endlesse power and puritie/Behold and venge this	2Tamb	2.2.53	Orcan
Conceive a second life in endlesse mercie.	2Tamb	2.3.9	Sgsmnd
Ready to darken earth with endlesse night:	2Tamb	2.4.7	Tamb
Who kils him shall have gold, and endlesse love.	F1349	4.2.25	Fredrk
Venus, why doublest thou my endlesse smart?	Ovid's Elegies	2.10.11	
And bide sore losse, with endlesse infamie.	Ovid's Elegies	3.6.72	
ENDOW			
Deserve these tytles I endow you with,	1Tamb	4.4.125	Tamb
ENDOW'D			
but he must weare/The sacred ring wherewith she was endow'd,	Hero and Leander	2.109	
ENDS			
It is Aeneas frowne that ends my daies:	Dido	4.4.120	Dido
And rue our ends senceles of life or breath:	Dido	5.1.328	Anna
Nay, when the battaile ends, al we wil meet,	2Tamb	3.5.97	Callap
But that where every period ends with death,	2Tamb	4.2.47	Olymp
Wearying his fingers ends with telling it,	Jew	1.1.16	Barab
And brought by murder to their timeles ends.	P 46	1.46	Navrre
Should for their conscience taste such rutheles ends.	P 214	4.12	Charls
Valoyses lyne ends in my tragedie.	P1231	22.93	King
Come lets away, and when the mariage ends,	Edw	2.2.264	Edward
That death ends all, and I can die but once.	Edw	5.1.153	Edward
this blow ends all,/Hell take his soule, his body thus must	F1362	4.2.38	Benvol
Time ends and to old Chaos all things turne;	Lucan, First Booke	74	

ENDS (cont.)			
Fower chariot-horses from the lists even ends.	Ovid's Elegies	3.2.66	
ENDUE (See INDUE)			
ENDUR'D			
[Thy] <They> troubled haires, alas, endur'd great losse.	Ovid's Elegies	1.14.24	
ENDURE (See also DURE, INDURE)			
Come forth the Cave: can heaven endure this sight?	Dido	4.1.17	Iarbus
Thy souldiers armes could not endure to strike/So many blowes	1Tamb	3.3.143	Bajzth
Endure as we the malice of our stars,	1Tamb	5.1.43	Govnr
And guiltlesly endure a cruell death.	1Tamb	5.1.329	Zenoc
That may endure till heaven be dissolv'd,	2Tamb	3.2.7	Tamb
That can endure so well your royall presence,	2Tamb	5.3.111	Usumc
I wil endure a melancholie life,	Edw	1.2.66	Queene
He hath a bcdy able tc endure,	Edw	5.5.10	Matrvs
'sbloud I am never able to endure these torments.	F1307	4.1.153	P Benvol
Take strife away, love doth not well endure.	Ovid's Elegies	1.8.96	
Thou suffrest what no husband can endure,	Ovid's Elegies	2.19.51	
Some other seeke, whc will these things endure.	Ovid's Elegies	3.10.28	
ENDYMION (See ENDEMION)			
ENEAS			
Comes now as Turnus gainst Eneas did,	1Tamb	5.1.380	Philem
And fatally enricht Eneas love.	1Tamb	5.1.394	Zenoc
Eneas to Elisa answere gives,	Ovid's Elegies	2.18.31	
ENEMIE			
we have discovered the enemie/Ready to chardge you with a	1Tamb	2.3.49	1Msngr
Thou hast procur'd a greater enemie,	2Tamb	4.1.127	Tamb
His father was my chiefest enemie.	Jew	2.3.250	Barab
Art thou an enemie to my Gaveston?	Edw	2.2.212	Edward
Mine enemie hath pitied my estate,	Edw	5.1.149	Edward
My lord, he is your enemie, and shall die.	Edw	5.4.92	Mortmr
The gentle queene of Loves sole enemie.	Hero and Leander	1.318	
ENEMIES			
To warre against my bordering enemies:	Dido	3.1.135	Dido
In spite of all suspected enemies.	1Tamb	1.1.186	Ortyg
Ah wretched eies, the enemies of my hart,	1Tamb	5.1.340	Zenoc
That no escape may save their enemies:	1Tamb	5.1.405	Arabia
Upon the heads of all our enemies.	2Tamb	3.2.42	Tamb
To see the slaughter of our enemies.	2Tamb	3.5.57	Callap
when our enemies drums/And ratling cannons thunder in our eares	2Tamb	4.1.12	Amyras
Beare not the burthen of your enemies joyes,	2Tamb	5.3.22	Techel
That in a field amidst his enemies,	Jew	1.2.203	Barab
Who made them enemies?	Jew	3.2.20	Mater
And rather seeke to scourge their enemies,	P 217	4.15	Anjoy
To have some care for feare of enemies.	P 224	4.22	QnMoth
Tis for your safetie and your enemies wrack.	P 858	17.53	Guise
Offering him aide against his enemies,	P 905	18.6	Bartus
I would freelie give it to his enemies,	Edw	1.4.309	Edward
My lord, ile marshall so your enemies,	Edw	1.4.357	Mortmr
Because the king and he are enemies.	Edw	2.1.5	Spencr
Begirt with weapons, and with enemies round,	Edw	3.1.95	Arundl
Despite of times, despite of enemies.	Edw	3.1.147	Edward
Mine enemies will I plague, my friends advance,	Edw	5.4.67	Mortmr
To slay mine enemies, and aid my friends,	F 324	1.3.96	Faust
One as a spy doth to his enemies goe,	Ovid's Elegies	1.9.17	
Thy dull hand stayes thy striving enemies harmes.	Ovid's Elegies	2.9.12	
Let such as be mine enemies have none,	Ovid's Elegies	2.10.16	
Let souldiour <souldiours> chase his <their> enemies amaine,	Ovid's Elegies	2.10.31	
May that shame fall mine enemies chance to be.	Ovid's Elegies	3.10.16	
ENEMY (See also ENIMIE)			
We are enough to scarre the enemy,	1Tamb	2.3.64	Tamb
Which onely will dismay the enemy.	2Tamb	5.3.112	Usumc
Strength to my soule, death to mine enemy;	Jew	2.1.49	Barab
Slew friend and enemy with my stratagems.	Jew	2.3.189	Barab
Therfore an enemy tc the Burbonites.	P 836	17.31	Guise
That ever I was prov'd your enemy,	P1140	22.2	King
thine, in setting Bruno free/From his and our professed enemy,	F1207	4.1.53	Emper
Fearing the enemy <ruine> of thy haplesse <hopelesse> soule.	F1738	5.1.65	OldMan
ENFLAMDE			
Now wants the fewell that enflamde his beames:	2Tamb	2.4.4	Tamb
ENFLAM'ST			
'tis thou enflam'st/The threatning Scorpion with the burning	Lucan, First Booke	657	
ENFLICT			
More then we can enflict, and therefore now,	Edw	5.5.11	Matrvs
ENFOLDING			
Foole canst thou lie in his enfolding space?	Ovid's Elegies	3.7.12	
ENFORC'D			
Ah Madam, this their slavery hath Enforc'd,	1Tamb	5.1.345	Anippe
ENFORCE (See also INFORCE, INFORSE)			
Enforce thee run upon the banefull pikes.	1Tamb	5.1.220	Bajzth
to obtaine by peace/Then to enforce conditions by constraint.	Jew	1.2.26	Calym
Ile fire thy crased buildings, and enforce/The papall towers, to	Edw	1.4.100	Edward
Which makes him quickly re-enforce his speech,	Hero and Leander	1.313	
ENFORCING			
With shivering speares enforcing thunderclaps,	1Tamb	3.2.80	Agidas
ENFORMD			
I have enformd the Earle of Lancaster.	Edw	2.3.14	Kent
ENFORMDE			
For Poland is as I have been enformde,	P 454	8.4	Anjoy
ENFORST			
Wanes with enforst and necessary change.	2Tamb	2.4.46	Zenoc
to speak with him/But cannot, and therfore am enforst to write,	P 663	13.7	Duchss
Might have enforst me to have swum from France,	Edw	1.1.7	Gavstn
ENGENDRED (See also INGENDER)			
For this, hath heaven engendred me of earth,	P 113	2.56	Guise

ENGINEERE			
And after that I was an Engineere,	Jew	2.3.186	Barab
ENGINES			
O dreary Engines of my loathed sight,	1Tamb	5.1.259	Bajzth
I will with Engines, never exercisde,	2Tamb	4.1.191	Tamb
Yea stranger engines for the brunt of warre,	F 122	1.1.94	Faust
ENGINS			
Their warlike Engins and munition/Exceed the forces of their	1Tamb	4.1.28	2Msngr
day, and ful of strife/Disolve the engins of the broken world.	Lucan, First Booke		80
At his faire feathered feet, the engins layd,	Hero and Leander		1.449
ENGIRT			
Engirt the temples of his hatefull head,	Edw	5.1.46	Edward
Pay vowes to Jove, engirt thy hayres with baies,	Ovid's Elegies		1.7.36
Where the French rout engirt themselves with Bayes.	Ovid's Elegies		2.13.18
ENGLAND			
And with the Queene of England joyne my force,	P 801	16.15	Navrre
To threaten England and to menace me?	P1034	19.104	King
Ile send my sister England newes of this,	P1189	22.51	King
Agent for England, send thy mistres word,	P1194	22.56	King
And to the Queene of England specially,	P1207	22.69	King
Salute the Queene of England in my name,	P1243	22.105	King
As England shall be quiet, and you safe.	Edw	1.4.358	Mortmr
Now is the king of England riche and strong,	Edw	1.4.366	Queene
Maids of England, sore may you moorne,	Edw	2.2.190	Lncstr
What weeneth the king of England,	Edw	2.2.193	Lncstr
Saint George for England, and the Barons right.	Edw	3.1.219	Warwck
Saint George for England, and king Edwards right.	Edw	3.1.220	Edward
England, unkinde to thy nobilitie,	Edw	3.1.250	Mortmr
Madam, returne to England,/And please my father well, and then	Edw	4.2.3	Prince
The king of England, nor the court of Fraunce,	Edw	4.2.22	Prince
Much happier then your friends in England do.	Edw	4.2.35	Kent
assure your grace, in England/would cast up cappes, and clap	Edw	4.2.54	Mortmr
My Lords of England, sith the ungentle king/Of Fraunce refuseth	Edw	4.2.61	SrJohn
My lord, we have, and if he be in England,	Edw	4.3.19	Spencr
they intend to give king Edward battell in England, sooner then	Edw	4.3.35	P Spencr
England shall welcome you, and all your route.	Edw	4.3.42	Edward
Welcome to England all with prosperous windes,	Edw	4.4.2	Queene
You, and such as you are, have made wise worke in England.	Edw	4.7.115	P Rice
Two kings in England cannot raigne at once:	Edw	5.1.58	Edward
by the grace of God/King of England, and lorde of Ireland.	Edw	5.4.74	ArchBp
ENGLANDS			
To Englands high disgrace, have made this Jig,	Edw	2.2.189	Lncstr
Were I king Edward, Englands soveraigne,	Edw	3.1.10	Spencr
If I be Englands king, in lakes of gore/Your headles trunkes,	Edw	3.1.135	Edward
Long live king Edward, Englands lawful lord.	Edw	3.1.151	Herald
Make Englands civill townes huge heapes of stones,	Edw	3.1.215	Edward
No Edward, Englands scourge, it may not be,	Edw	3.1.258	Mortmr
Among the lords of France with Englands golde,	Edw	3.1.277	Levune
Till Edmund be arrivde for Englands good,	Edw	4.1.2	Kent
For Englands honor, peace, and quietnes.	Edw	4.2.58	Kent
That Englands Queene, and nobles in distresse,	Edw	4.2.79	Mortmr
That Englands peeres may Henolts welcome see.	Edw	4.2.82	SrJohn
Triumpheth Englands Edward with his friends,	Edw	4.3.2	Edward
I trowe/The lords of Fraunce love Englands gold so well,	Edw	4.3.15	Edward
He is in Englands ground, our port-maisters/Are not so careles	Edw	4.3.22	Edward
That Englands queene in peace may reposesse/Her dignities and	Edw	4.4.24	Mortmr
That havocks Englands wealth and treasurie.	Edw	4.4.27	Mortmr
Reveld in Englands wealth and treasurie.	Edw	4.6.52	Rice
<Unhappies> <Unhappy is> Edward, chaste from Englands bounds.	Edw	4.6.62	Kent
Your grace mistakes, it is for Englands good,	Edw	5.1.38	BshpWn
So shall not Englands [Vine] <Vines> be perished,	Edw	5.1.47	Edward
That Edward may be still faire Englands king:	Edw	5.1.68	Edward
Within a dungeon Englands king is kept,	Edw	5.3.19	Edward
That wronges their liege and soveraigne, Englands king.	Edw	5.3.40	Edward
ENGLISH			
Did he not draw a sorte of English priestes/From Doway to the	P1030	19.100	King
Goe call the English Agent hether strait,	P1188	22.50	King
Lives uncontroulde within the English pale,	Edw	2.2.165	Lncstr
men, and friends/Ere long, to bid the English king a base.	Edw	4.2.66	SrJohn
The way he cut, an English mile in length,	F 792	3.1.14	Faust
crownes a man were as good have as many english counters,	F App	p.230 34	P Clown
ENGRAFT (See INGRAFT)			
ENGRASPED			
His fainting hand in death engrasped mee.	Ovid's Elegies		3.8.58
ENGRAV'D (See also GRAV'D)			
Ah howe oft on hard doores hung I engrav'd,	Ovid's Elegies		3.1.53
ENGRAVEN			
To feede her eyes with his engraven fame.	Dido	1.1.103	Jupitr
ENGYRT			
her rusty coach/Engyrt with tempests wrapt in pitchy clouds,	1Tamb	5.1.295	Bajzth
ENIMIE			
the breach the enimie hath made/Gives such assurance of our	2Tamb	5.1.2	Maxim
ENIPEUS			
Drye Enipeus, Tyro to embrace,	Ovid's Elegies		3.5.43
ENJOIN'D (See also INJOINE, INJOYNDE)			
wars justice ye repute)/I execute, enjoin'd me from above,	2Tamb	4.1.148	Tamb
ENJOY (See also INJOY)			
But that I may enjoy what I desire:	Dido	3.1.9	Iarbus
I thinke the pleasure they enjoy in heaven/Can not compare with	1Tamb	2.5.58	Therid
After your rescue to enjoy his choise.	1Tamb	3.2.58	Agidas
for us to see them, and for Tamburlaine onely to enjoy them.	1Tamb	4.4.112	P Techel
And long may Henry enjoy all this and more.	P 597	12.10	Cardnl
It shall suffice me to enjoy your love,	Edw	1.1.171	Gavstn

ENJOY (cont.)
Freely enjoy that vaine light-headed earle, . . . Edw 1.4.400 MortSr
Enjoy the wench, let all else be refusd. . . . . Ovid's Elegies 2.2.30
Let [me] <her> enjoy [her] <me> oft, oft be debard. . . Ovid's Elegies 2.9.46
Died ere he could enjoy the love of any. . . . . Hero and Leander 1.76
We humane creatures should enjoy that blisse. . . . Hero and Leander 1.254
Both might enjoy ech other, and be blest. . . . . Hero and Leander 1.380

ENJOY'D
My ships, my store, and all that I enjoy'd; . . . Jew 1.2.139 Barab

ENJOYED
Like Aesops cocke, this jewell he enjoyed, . . . Hero and Leander 2.51

ENLARG'D
Whose emptie Altars have enlarg'd our illes. . . . Dido 4.2.3 Iarbus

ENLARGDE
Well, if my Lorde your brother were enlargde. . . . Edw 5.2.82 Queene

ENLARGE (See also INLARGE)
Governor, I enlarge thee, live with me, ... Jew 5.2.91 Barab
Enlarge his Kingdome. . . . . F 429 2.1.41 Mephst

ENLARGEMENT
But I will practise thy enlargement thence: . . . Jew 2.1.53 Barab

ENMITIE
Till I have set 'em both at enmitie. . . . . . Jew 2.3.383 Barab
And with the world be still at enmitie: . . . . . Edw 1.1.15 Gavstn
Twixt theirs and yours, shall be no enmitie. . . . Edw 5.3.46 Matrvs

ENMITY
and you were stated here/To be at deadly enmity with Turkes. Jew 2.2.33 Bosco

ENNIUS
Rude Ennius, and Plautus full of wit, ... Ovid's Elegies 1.15.19

ENNOUGH
And therewith Caesar prone ennough to warre, . . . Lucan, First Booke 293

ENOUGH (See also ENOW, INOUGH, YNOW)
Tis not enough that thou doest graunt me love, . . . Dido 3.1.8 Iarbus
But I had gold enough and cast him off: . . . . Dido 3.1.162 Dido
But when you were abourd twas calme enough, ... Dido 4.4.27 Dido
Brother, I see your meaning well enough. . . . . 1Tamb 1.1.18 Mycet
I am not wise enough to be a kinge, ... 1Tamb 1.1.20 Mycet
We are enough to scarre the enemy, ... 1Tamb 2.3.64 Tamb
Arabians, Moores and Jewes/Enough to cover all Bythinia. 1Tamb 3.3.137 Bajzth
Affrik and Greece have garrisons enough/To make me Soveraigne 1Tamb 3.3.242 Bajzth
Tis enough for us to see them, and for Tamburlaine onely to 1Tamb 4.4.111 P Techel
Enough to swallow forcelesse Sigismond, ... 2Tamb 1.1.65 Orcan
Yet scarse enough t'encounter Tamburlaine. . . . . 2Tamb 1.1.66 Orcan
They are enough to conquer all the world/And you have won 2Tamb 1.3.67 Calyph
conquer all the world/And you have won enough for me to keep. 2Tamb 1.3.68 Calyph
My father were enough to scar the foe: . . . . . 2Tamb 4.1.19 Calyph
But sons, this subject not of force enough, ... 2Tamb 5.3.168 Tamb
And is thy credit not enough for that? . . . . . Jew 1.1.62 Barab
I, like enough, why then let every man/Provide him, and be there Jew 1.1.170 Barab
And yet have kept enough to live upon; . . . . . Jew 1.2.190 Barab
Thy father has enough in store for thee. . . . . Jew 1.2.227 Barab
I weigh it thus much; I have wealth enough. . . . . Jew 2.3.245 Barab
Lodowicke, it is enough/That I have made thee sure to Abigal. Jew 2.3.334 Barab
Oh leave to grieve me, I am griev'd enough. . . . . Jew 3.2.17 Mater
The other knowes enough to have my life, ... Jew 4.1.120 Barab
I know enough, and therfore talke not to me of your . . Jew 4.3.36 P Pilia
Soone enough to your cost, Sir: . . . . Jew 4.3.57 Pilia
And let her droup, my heart is light enough. . . . P1064 19.134 King
It is enough if that Navarre may be/Esteemed faithfull to the P1147 22.9 Navrre
Wilshire hath men enough to save our heads. . . . Edw 1.1.127 MortSr
Live where thou wilt, ile send thee gould enough, . . . Edw 1.4.113 Edward
Ist not enough, that thou corrupts my lord, ... Edw 1.4.150 Queene
Tis like enough, for since he was exild, ... Edw 2.1.23 Baldck
Though inwardly licentious enough, ... Edw 2.1.50 Baldck
Looke to your owne heads, his is sure enough. . . . . Edw 2.2.92 Edward
Would levie men enough to anger you. . . . . . Edw 2.2.152 Mortmr
is it not enough/That we have taken him, but must we now . Edw 2.5.83 Warwck
Till I be strong enough to breake a staffe, ... Edw 4.2.24 Prince
Fellow enough: . . . . Edw 4.7.47 Rice
While at the councell table, grave enough, ... Edw 5.4.58 Mortmr
That were enough to poison any man, ... Edw 5.5.5 Matrvs
It is enough: . . . . F 964 3.1.186 Pope
Has not the Pope enough of conjuring yet? . . . . . F1189 4.1.35 P Benvol
He was upon the devils backe late enough; and if he be so farre F1190 4.1.36 P Benvol
I hope sir, we have wit enough to be more bold then welcome. F1595 4.6.38 P HrsCsr
I, I, the house is good enough to drink in: . . . . F1617 4.6.60 P HrsCsr
O, I have seene enough to torture me. . . . . . F1921 5.2.125 Faust
These sad presages were enough to scarre/The quivering Romans, Lucan, First Booke 672
Aske thou the boy, what thou enough doest thinke. . . Ovid's Elegies 1.4.30
Wa'st not enough the fearefull Wench to chide? . . . Ovid's Elegies 1.7.45
Tis not enough, she shakes your record off, ... Ovid's Elegies 3.3.19

ENOUGHE
But you will saye you leave him rome enoughe besides: . Paris ms 7,p390 P Souldr
that of it self was hote enoughe to worke/thy Just degestione Paris ms26,p391 Guise

ENOW (See also YNOW)
You shall have leaves and windfall bowes enow/Neere to these Dido 1.1.172 Aeneas
Are there not Jewes enow in Malta, ... Jew 2.3.359 Barab
have fine sport with the boyes, Ile get nuts and apples enow. F App p.236 46 P Robin

ENQUIRE (See also INQUIRE)
But for the land whereof thou doest enquire, ... Dido 1.1.209 Venus
Enquire not what with Isis may be done/Nor feare least she to Ovid's Elegies 2.2.25

ENQUIRY
Nor make enquiry who hath sent it them. . . . . . Jew 3.4.81 Barab

ENRAG'D
Enrag'd I ran about the fields for thee, ... 2Tamb 4.2.17 Therid

ENRAG'D (cont.)
Why art thou thus enrag'd? Lucan, First Booke 659
All deepe enrag'd, his sinowie bow he bent, Hero and Leander 1.371
ENRAGED (See also INRAG'D)
Yet rending with enraged thumbe her tresses, Ovid's Elegies 3.5.71
ENRICH (See also INRICH)
And daily will enrich thee with our favour, Edw 3.1.50 Edward
ENRICH'D
There I enrich'd the Priests with burials, Jew 2.3.183 Barab
ENRICHT
And fatally enricht Eneas love. 1Tamb 5.1.394 Zenoc
ENROLDE
Enrolde in flames and fiery smoldering mistes, 1Tamb 2.3.20 Tamb
ENROWLE
And in the Chronicle, enrowle his name, Edw 1.4.269 Mortmr
ENSEIGNES
Thy mistrisse enseignes must be likewise thine. Ovid's Elegies 2.3.10
ENSIGNE
in Asia, or display/His vagrant Ensigne in the Persean fields, 1Tamb 1.1.45 Meandr
To swarme unto the Ensigne I support. 1Tamb 2.3.14 Tamb
This tottered ensigne of my auncesters, Edw 2.3.21 Mortmr
Approcht the swelling streame with drum and ensigne, Lucan, First Booke 207
ENSIGNES
That on mount Sinay with their ensignes spread, 2Tamb 3.1.46 Jrslem
Brother displaie my ensignes in the field, Edw 1.1.136 Edward
Looke next to see us with our ensignes spred. Edw 2.2.199 Lncstr
by these ten blest ensignes/And all thy several triumphs, Lucan, First Booke 375
And that his owne ten ensignes, and the rest/Marcht not Lucan, First Booke 473
Defend the ensignes of thy warre in mee. Ovid's Elegies 1.11.12
Cupid commands to move his ensignes further. Ovid's Elegies 2.12.28
Your golden ensignes [plucke] <pluckt> out of my field, Ovid's Elegies 3.14.16
ENSUE (See also INSUE)
By these he seeing what myschiefes must ensue, Lucan, First Booke 629
ENTANGLED
Thus while dum signs their yeelding harts entangled, Hero and Leander 1.187
ENTEND
For I entend a private Sacrifize, Dido 5.1.286 Dido
As I entend to labour for the truth, P 585 11.50 Navrre
O Lord no: for we entend to strangle you. P1095 20.5 2Mur
ENTENDS
Entends ere long to sport him in the skie. Dido 1.1.77 Venus
ENTENT
to further his entent/The windes did drive huge billowes to the Dido 2.1.138 Aeneas
Had not my Doves discov'rd thy entent: Dido 3.2.33 Venus
ENTER
Through which it could not enter twas so huge. Dido 2.1.171 Aeneas
Ile set the casement open that the windes/May enter in, and Dido 4.4.131 Dido
like Orcus gulfe/Batter the walles, and we will enter in: 1Tamb 3.1.66 Bajzth
and I might enter in/To see the state and majesty of heaven, 2Tamb 1.3.154 Tamb
And enter in, to seaze upon the gold: 2Tamb 3.3.8 Techel
And when we enter in, not heaven it selfe/Shall ransome thee, 2Tamb 3.3.27 Therid
Yet could not enter till the breach was made. 2Tamb 5.1.100 Tamb
Why let 'em enter, let 'em take the Towne. Jew 1.1.190 Barab
where none but their owne sect/Must enter in; men generally Jew 1.2.257 Abigal
Nor quiet enter my distemper'd thoughts, Jew 2.1.18 Barab
For by my meanes Calymath shall enter in. Jew 5.1.63 Barab
one that can spy a place/Where you may enter, and surprize the Jew 5.1.71 Barab
Open the gates for you to enter in, Jew 5.1.93 Barab
and will needs enter by defaulte | whatt thoughe you were once Paris ms11,p390 P Souldr
Weele enter in by darkenes to Killingworth. Edw 5.3.48 Matrvs
Let him goe forth knowne, that unknowne did enter, Ovid's Elegies 2.2.20
A woman forc'd the Troyanes new to enter/Warres, just Latinus, Ovid's Elegies 2.12.21
Will mount aloft, and enter heaven gate, Hero and Leander 1.466
ENTERANCE
Turmoiles the coast, and enterance forbids; Lucan, First Booke 409
ENTERCOURSE
whose moaning entercourse/Hath hetherto bin staid, with wrath 1Tamb 5.1.280 Bajzth
ENTER'D
Enter'd the Monastery, and underneath/In severall places are Jew 5.5.26 Barab
And some dim stars) he Arriminum enter'd: Lucan, First Booke 234
ENTERPRISE
Might seeme <seek> to crosse me in mine enterprise. P 574 11.39 Navrre
And then determine of this enterprise. P 656 12.69 QnMoth
Performê what desperate enterprise I will? F 108 1.1.80 Faust
And smite with death thy hated enterprise. F 880 3.1.102 Pope
If you will aid me in this enterprise, F1334 4.2.10 Benvol
like a Beare, the third an Asse, for doing this enterprise. F App p.235 33 P Mephst
My thoughts sole goddes, aide mine enterprise, Lucan, First Booke 202
ENTERPRIZE
sent a thousand armed men/To intercept this haughty enterprize, 2Tamb 1.2.71 Almeda
We praise: great goddesse ayde my enterprize. Ovid's Elegies 3.2.56
ENTERTAIN'D
And let him not be entertain'd the worse/Because he favours me. Jew Prol.34 Machvl
there must my girle/Intreat the Abbasse to be entertain'd. Jew 1.2.280 Barab
Till thou hast gotten to be entertain'd. Jew 1.2.288 Barab
Well father, say I be entertain'd, Jew 1.2.294 Abigal
Let us intreat she may be entertain'd. Jew 1.2.329 2Fryar
ENTERTAIND
Who for Troyes sake hath entertaind us all, Dido 2.1.64 Illion
ENTERTAINE
Since Carthage knowes to entertaine distresse. Dido 1.2.33 Iarbus
The woman that thou wild us entertaine, Dido 4.2.11 Iarbus
Should have prepar'd to entertaine his Grace? 1Tamb 4.2.63 Zabina

ENTERTAINE (ccnt.)			
To entertaine scme care ot our securities,	1Tamb	5.1.29	1Virgn
To entertaine devine Zenocrate.	2Tamb	2.4.17	Tamb
nc more, but deck the heavens/To entertaine divine Zenocrate.	2Tamb	2.4.21	Tamb
silver runs through Paradice/To entertaine divine Zenocrate.	2Tamb	2.4.25	Tamb
voices and their instruments/To entertaine divine Zenocrate.	2Tamb	2.4.29	Tamb
out his hand in highest majesty/To entertaine divine Zenocrate.	2Tamb	2.4.33	Tamb
And guard the gates to entertaine his soule.	2Tamb	3.5.29	Orcan
Forbids my mind to entertaine a thought/That tends to love, but	2Tamb	4.2.25	Olymp
To entertaine this Queene of chastitie,	2Tamb	4.2.96	Therid
For by your life we entertaine our lives.	2Tamb	5.3.167	Celeb
in the Counsell-hcuse/To entertaine them and their Embassie.	Jew	1.1.149	1Jew
Entertaine Lodowicke the Governors sonne/With all the curtesie	Jew	2.3.225	Barab
The price thereof will serve to entertaine/Selim and all his	Jew	5.3.30	Msngr
busie Barrabas is there above/To entertaine us in his Gallery;	Jew	5.5.53	Calym
With gifts and shewes did entertaine him/And promised to be at	P 874	17.69	Eprnon
Did they of Paris entertaine him so?	P 879	17.74	King
If I speed well, ile entertaine you all.	Edw	1.1.46	Gavstn
Mait please your grace to entertaine them now.	Edw	2.2.241	Neece
ENTERTAINMENT			
The entertainment we have had of him,	1Tamb	3.2.37	Zenoc
ENTHRAL'D			
Our love of honcr loth to be enthral'd/To forraine powers, and	1Tamb	5.1.35	Govnr
ENTHRALLED			
Though my right hand have thus enthralled thee,	1Tamb	5.1.435	Tamb
ENTHRONE (See INTHRONIZED)			
ENTICE (See INTICE, TICE)			
ENTIRE (See also INTIRELY)			
These two will make cne entire Duke of Guise,	P1060	19.130	King
This argues the entire love of my Lord.	Edw	2.1.63	Neece
ENTOMBE (See also INTOMBE, TOMB'D)			
Shall we with honcr (as beseemes) entombe,	1Tamb	5.1.531	Tamb
ENTOMBES			
And in my lcve entombes the hope of Fraunce:	P 134	2.77	Guise
ENTRAILES (See also INTRAILES, INTRALLS)			
and suddenly/Frcm out his entrailes, Neoptolemus/Setting his	Dido	2.1.183	Aeneas
Within the massy entrailes cf the earth:	F 174	1.1.146	Cornel
ENTRALLED (See INTHRALLD)			
ENTRALLES			
Earth cast up fountaines from thy entralles,	1Tamb	5.1.347	Zenoc
ENTRALS			
and all my entrals bath'd/In blood that straineth from their	2Tamb	3.4.8	Capt
Into the entrals cf ycn labouring cloud,	F1953	5.2.157	Faust
ENTRANCE (See also ENTERANCE)			
Open an entrance for the wastfull sea,	Jew	3.5.16	Govnr
And now, as entrance to our safety,	Jew	5.2.22	Barab
Shall in the entrance of this Massacre,	P 286	5.13	Guise
Little I aske, a little entrance make,	Ovid's Elegies		1.6.3
Night runnes away; with open entrance greete them.	Ovid's Elegies		1.6.40
ENTRAP (See INTRAP)			
ENTREAT (See also INTREAT)			
I must entreat him, I must speake him faire,	Edw	1.4.183	Queene
Entreat thy husband drinke, but do not kisse,	Ovid's Elegies		1.4.51
ENTREATE			
May I entreate thee tc discourse at large,	Dido	2.1.106	Dido
As how I pray, may I entreate you tell.	Dido	5.1.67	Iarbus
But seeing I cannct, ile entreate for him:	Edw	5.4.98	King
the Duke of Vanholt dcth earnestly entreate your company, and	F1501	4.4.45	P Wagner
Sir, the Duke of Vanholt doth earnestly entreate your company.	F App	p.241 168	P Wagner
For thee I did thy mistris faire entreate.	Ovid's Elegies		1.6.20
beate thee/To guard her well, that well I might entreate thee.	Ovid's Elegies		2.19.50
ENTREATED			
By thy sides touching ill she is entreated.	Ovid's Elegies		3.2.22
ENTREATES			
But what entreates for thee some-times tooke place,	Ovid's Elegies		1.6.21
ENTREATETH			
Her deeds gaine hate, her face entreateth love:	Ovid's Elegies		3.10.43
ENTREATING			
Demanding him of them, entreating rather,	Edw	3.1.97	Arundl
ENTREATY (See INTREATY)			
ENTRED			
O had it never entred, Troy had stood.	Dido	2.1.172	Aeneas
Shouldst thcu have entred, cruel Tamburlaine:	2Tamb	5.1.102	Govnr
For had your highnesse seene with what a pompe/He entred Paris,	P 873	17.68	Eprnon
Which like sweet musicke entred Heroes eares,	Hero and Leander		1.194
Entred the crchard of Th'esperides,	Hero and Leander		2.298
ENTRENCH (See INTRENCH)			
ENTRING			
Who entring at the breach thy sword hath made,	1Tamb	2.7.9	Cosroe
ENTRY			
And bring with them their bils of entry:	Jew	1.1.56	Barab
from Egypt, cr by Caire/But at the entry there into the sea,	Jew	1.1.74	Barab
There's a darke entry where they take it in,	Jew	3.4.79	Barab
We rent in sunder at our entry:	Jew	5.3.4	Calym
ENTRYE			
therefore your entrye is mere Intrusione	Paris	ms13,p390	P Souldr
ENVENOM (See INVENOMBD, INVENOME)			
ENVIDE			
The more thcu look'st, the more the gowne envide.	Ovid's Elegies		3.2.28
ENVIE			
And planted love where envie erst had sprong.	Dido	3.2.52	Juno
Envie, why carpest thou my time is spent so ill,	Ovid's Elegies		1.15.1
The living, not the dead can envie bite,	Ovid's Elegies		1.15.39

ENVIE (cont.)			
My selfe poore wretch mine owne gifts now envie.	Ovid's Elegies	2.15.8	
(Trust me) land-streame thou shalt no envie lack,	Ovid's Elegies	3.5.21	
ENVIED			
Wretches of Troy, envied of the windes,	Dido	1.2.4	Illion
Both jealous of my love, envied each other:	Jew	3.6.27	Abigal
If for these dignities thou be envied,	Edw	1.1.163	Edward
ENVIES			
This Troians end will be thy envies aime,	Dido	3.3.73	Iarbus
What fatall destinie envies me thus,	Dido	5.1.323	Anna
ENVIEST			
Why enviest me, this hostile [denne] <dende> unbarre,	Ovid's Elegies	1.6.17	
ENVIOUS			
And Neptunes waves be envious men of warre,	Dido	1.1.65	Venus
Heavens envious of our joyes is waxen pale,	Dido	4.4.52	Dido
To stop the mallice of his envious heart,	P 30	1.30	Navrre
Out envious wretch <Away envious rascall>:	F 685	2.2.134	Faust
The fates are envious, high seats quickly perish,	Lucan, First Booke		70
No envious tongue wrought thy thicke lockes decay.	Ovid's Elegies		1.14.42
Envious garments so good legges to hide,	Ovid's Elegies		3.2.27
And envious fates great [goddesses] <goodesses> assaile,	Ovid's Elegies		3.8.2
Against my good they were an envious charme.	Ovid's Elegies		3.11.14
ENVIRONED (See also INVIRONED)			
Environed with brave Argolian knightes,	1Tamb	4.3.2	Souldn
Environed with troopes of noble men,	1Tamb	5.1.526	Tamb
How is my soule environed,	2Tamb	5.1.34	Govnr
ENVIRONING			
Environing their Standard round, that stood/As bristle-pointed	1Tamb	4.1.26	2Msngr
ENVY (See also INVIE)			
H'had never bellowed in a brasen Bull/Of great ones envy; o'th	Jew	Prol.26	Machvl
I am Envy, begotten of a Chimney-sweeper, and an Oyster-wife:	F 679	2.2.128 P	Envy
Or envy of thee, but in tender love,	F1720	5.1.47	OldMan
Envy denies all, with thy bloud must thou/Abie thy conquest	Lucan, First Booke		289
Envy hath rapt thee, no fierce warres thou movedst,	Ovid's Elegies		2.6.25
But did you not so envy Cepheus Daughter,	Ovid's Elegies		3.3.17
ENVY'D			
Let me be envy'd and not pittied!	Jew	Prol.27	Machvl
EPERNOUNE			
Epernoune, goe see it presently be done,	P 558	11.23	QnMoth
Farwell to my Lord of Guise and Epernoune.	P 750	15.8	Joyeux
come Epernoune/Lets goe seek the Duke and make them freends.	P 785	15.43	King
Ah base Epernoune, were not his highnes heere,	P 831	17.26	Guise
Be patient Guise and threat not Epernoune,	P 833	17.28	King
And Epernoune I will be rulde by thee.	P 885	17.80	King
And Epernoune though I seeme milde and calme,	P 893	17.88	King
Holla verlete, hey: Epernoune, where is the King?	P 956	19.26	Guise
And now will I to armes, come Epernoune:	P1079	19.149	King
Sweete Epernoune, our Friers are holy men,	P1161	22.23	King
Sweet Epernoune all Rebels under heaven,	P1185	22.47	King
Or else dye Epernoune.	P1227	22.89	Eprnon
Sweet Epernoune thy King must dye.	P1228	22.90	King
Ah Epernoune, is this thy love to me?	P1235	22.97	King
EPEUS			
Epeus horse, to Aetnas hill transformd,	Dido	1.1.66	Venus
And him, Epeus having made the horse,	Dido	2.1.147	Aeneas
Made him to thinke Epeus pine-tree Horse/A sacrifize t'appease	Dido	2.1.162	Aeneas
EPHESTION			
Great Alexander lovde Ephestion,	Edw	1.4.392	MortSr
EPIGRAM			
Zenocrate had bene the argument/Of every Epigram or Eligie.	2Tamb	2.4.95	Tamb
EPITAPH			
We both will rest and have one Epitaph/Writ in as many severall	2Tamb	2.4.134	Tamb
EPITHITE			
Faire is too foule an Epithite for thee,	1Tamb	5.1.136	Tamb
EPITOMIES			
And seen in nothing but Epitomies:	P 390	7.30	Guise
EQUALL			
So doth he now, though not with equall gaine,	Dido	3.3.83	Iarbus
And give you equall place in our affaires.	1Tamb	2.5.14	Cosroe
Vowing our loves to equall death and life.	1Tamb	2.6.28	Cosroe
lives were weigh'd/In equall care and ballance with our owne,	1Tamb	5.1.42	Govnr
Rifling this Fort, devide in equall shares:	2Tamb	3.4.89	Therid
By equall portions into both your breasts:	2Tamb	5.3.171	Tamb
For both their woorths wil equall him no more.	2Tamb	5.3.253	Amyras
Come, Katherina, our losses equall are,	Jew	3.2.36	Govnr
Then of true griefe let us take equall share.	Jew	3.2.37	Govnr
Therefore to equall it receive my hart.	Edw	1.1.162	Edward
And windes as equall be to bring them in,	Edw	4.3.51	Edward
alwaies scorn'd/A second place; Pompey could bide no equall,	Lucan, First Booke		125
by the pleasure/Which man and woman reape in equall measure?	Ovid's Elegies		1.10.36
Where fancie is in equall ballance pais'd).	Hero and Leander		2.32
EQUALLIE			
And shake off all our fortunes equallie?	Edw	4.2.20	SrJohn
For now I love two women equallie:	Ovid's Elegies		2.10.4
He wounds with love, and forst them equallie,	Hero and Leander		1.445
EQUALLY			
Share equally the gold that bought their lives,	1Tamb	2.2.70	Meandr
ruthlesly pursewde/Be equally against his life incenst,	1Tamb	5.1.367	Zenoc
And let them equally serve all your turnes.	2Tamb	4.3.73	Tamb
How, equally?	Jew	1.2.62	Barab
And share it equally amongst you all,	Edw	1.4.71	Edward
And seedes were equally in large fields cast,	Ovid's Elegies		3.9.33
EQUI			
O lente lente currite noctis equi:	F1931	5.2.139	Faust

EQUINOCTIALL			
Men from the farthest Equinoctiall line,	1Tamb	1.1.119	Cosroe
EQUIVOLENCE			
[Quarter <Quarters> the towne in foure equivolence].	F 790	3.1.12A	Faust
E'RE (See also ERE)			
And leave no memory that e're I was.	Jew	1.2.265	Barab
what e're it be to injure them/That have so manifestly wronged	Jew	1.2.274	Abigal
Then, gentle sleepe, where e're his bodie rests,	Jew	2.1.35	Abigal
but e're he shall have her	Jew	2.3.51	Barab
That ye be both made sure e're you come out.	Jew	2.3.236	Barab
I'le give him such a warning e're he goes/As he shall have	Jew	2.3.273	Barab
Nor e're shall see the land of Canaan,	Jew	2.3.303	Barab
But e're I came--	Jew	3.6.15	Abigal
I smelt 'em e're they came.	Jew	4.1.22	Barab
What if I murder'd him e're Jacomo comes?	Jew	4.1.116	Barab
he was ready to leape off e're the halter was about his necke;	Jew	4.2.22	P Ithimr
What e're I am, yet Governor heare me speake;	Jew	5.1.9	Curtzn
And banquet with him e're thou leav'st the Ile.	Jew	5.3.19	Msngr
We will informe thee e're our conference cease.	F 184	1.1.156	Valdes
For e're I sleep, I'le try what I can do:	F 192	1.1.164	Faust
And long e're this, I should have done the deed <slaine	F 575	2.2.24	Faust
a paire of hornes on's head as e're thou sawest in thy life.	F 737	2.3.16	P Robin
And trust me, they are the sweetest grapes that e're I tasted.	F1587	4.6.30	P Lady
ERE (Homograph; See also WHAT ERE, WHATSOERE)			
Sweet Jupiter, if ere I pleasde thine eye,	Dido	1.1.19	Ganimd
Entends ere long to sport him in the skie.	Dido	1.1.77	Venus
Fortune hath favord thee what ere thou be,	Dido	1.1.231	Venus
So lovely is he that where ere he goes,	Dido	3.1.71	Anna
I had been wedded ere Aeneas came:	Dido	3.1.138	Dido
I saw this man at Troy ere Troy was sackt.	Dido	3.1.141	Achat
Should ere defile so faire a mouth as thine:	Dido	3.2.27	Juno
The man that I doe eye where ere I am,	Dido	3.4.18	Dido
That doe pursue my peace where ere it goes.	Dido	4.2.51	Iarbus
Flote up and downe where ere the billowes drive?	Dido	5.1.58	Aeneas
And they shall have what thing so ere thou needst.	Dido	5.1.74	Iarbus
But ere he march in Asia, or display/His vagrant Ensigne in the	1Tamb	1.1.44	Meandr
You must be forced from me ere you goe:	1Tamb	1.2.120	Tamb
That ere made passage thorow Persean Armes.	1Tamb	2.3.56	Tamb
To bid him battaile ere he passe too farre,	1Tamb	2.5.95	Tamb
him assured hope/Of martiall triumph, ere he meete his foes:	1Tamb	3.3.43	Tamb
But ere I die those foule Idolaters/Shall make me bonfires with	1Tamb	3.3.239	Bajzth
Ile make the kings of India ere I die,	1Tamb	3.3.263	Tamb
But ere I martch to wealthy Persea,	1Tamb	4.2.47	Tamb
Which had ere this bin bathde in streames of blood,	1Tamb	5.1.438	Tamb
Where ere I come the fatall sisters sweat,	1Tamb	5.1.454	Tamb
Ready to charge you ere you stir your feet.	2Tamb	1.1.121	Fredrk
Ere I would loose the tytle of a king.	2Tamb	1.3.91	Celeb
Ere I would loose the tytle of a king.	2Tamb	1.3.95	Amyras
Where ere her soule be, thou shalt stay with me/Embalm'd with	2Tamb	2.4.129	Tamb
We may be slaine or wounded ere we learne.	2Tamb	3.2.94	Calyph
Nor ere returne but with the victory,	2Tamb	3.5.44	Trebiz
But foorth ye vassals, what so ere it be,	2Tamb	5.1.221	Tamb
How ere the world goe, I'le make sure for one,	Jew	1.1.186	Barab
Hoping ere long to set the house a fire;	Jew	2.3.88	Barab
As I could long ere this have wisht him there.	P 496	9.15	QnMoth
Ere I shall want, will cause his Indians,	P 853	17.48	Guise
And tell him ere it be long, Ile visite him.	P 912	18.13	Navrre
Ile clippe his winges/Or ere he passe my handes, away with him.	P1053	19.123	King
Shall curse the time that ere Navarre was King,	P1249	22.111	Navrre
And know my lord, ere I will breake my oath,	Edw	1.1.85	Mortmr
Ere Gaveston shall stay within the realme.	Edw	1.1.105	Lncstr
and yet ere that day come,/The king shall lose his crowne, for	Edw	1.2.58	Mortmr
Ere my sweete Gaveston shall part from me,	Edw	1.4.48	Edward
me, for his sake/Ile grace thee with a higher stile ere long.	Edw	2.2.253	Edward
Sweete soveraigne, yet I come/To see thee ere I die.	Edw	2.5.95	Gavstn
Tell me [Arundell] <Matre>, died he ere thou camst,	Edw	3.1.92	Edward
But ere he came, Warwick in ambush laie,	Edw	3.1.118	Arundl
Yet ere thou go, see how I do devorce	Edw	3.1.176	Edward
For which ere long, their heads shall satisfie,	Edw	3.1.209	Edward
men, and friends/Ere long, to bid the English king a base.	Edw	4.2.66	SrJohn
A will be had ere long I doubt it not.	Edw	4.3.20	Spencr
Ere farther we proceede my noble lordes,	Edw	4.6.23	Queene
Yet will it melt, ere I have done my tale.	Edw	5.5.55	Edward
Long ere with Iron hands they punish men,	F 878	3.1.100	Pope
And doe what ere I please, unseene of any.	F 993	3.2.13	Faust
I do repent I ere offended him,	F1746	5.1.73	Faust
and so by that meanes I shal see more then ere I felt, or saw	F App	p.233 5	P Robin
for conjuring that ere was invented by any brimstone divel.	F App	p.233 20	P Robin
with you, I must yet have a goblet payde from you ere you goe.	F App	p.234 8	P Vintnr
Doctor, yet ere you goe, expect from me a bounteous reward.	F App	p.239 88	P Emper
Ile make you wake ere I goe.	F App	p.241 153	P HrsCsr
they be the best grapes that ere I tasted in my life before.	F App	p.242 26	P Duchss
And ere he sees the sea looseth his name;	Lucan, First Booke	402	
cause, what ere thou be whom God assignes/This great effect,	Lucan, First Booke	419	
live with thee, and die, or <ere> thou shalt <shall> grieve.	Ovid's Elegies	1.3.18	
What ere thou art, farewell, be like me paind,	Ovid's Elegies	1.6.71	
There is, who ere will knowe a bawde aright/Give eare, there is	Ovid's Elegies	1.8.1	
to passe/The souldiours, and poore lovers worke ere was.	Ovid's Elegies	1.9.28	
Therefore who ere love sloathfulnesse doth call,	Ovid's Elegies	1.9.31	
Bull and Eagle/And what ere love made Jove should thee invegle.	Ovid's Elegies	1.10.8	
Ere thou rise starres teach seamen where to saile,	Ovid's Elegies	1.13.11	
I that ere-while was fierce, now humbly sue,	Ovid's Elegies	2.5.49	
To prove him foolish did I ere contend?	Ovid's Elegies	2.8.10	

ERE (cont.)
And who ere see her, worthily lament. Ovid's Elegies 2.14.40
Ere these were seene, I burnt: what will these do? Ovid's Elegies 3.2.33
How long her lockes were, ere her oath she tooke: Ovid's Elegies 3.3.3
I know not what expecting, I ere while/Nam'd Achelaus, Inachus, Ovid's Elegies 3.5.103
What ere he hath his body gaind in warres. Ovid's Elegies 3.7.20
What ere thou art mine art thou: Ovid's Elegies 3.10.49
How small so ere, Ile you for greatest praise. Ovid's Elegies 3.14.14
Died ere he could enjoy the love of any. Hero and Leander 1.76
When two are stript, long ere the course begin, Hero and Leander 1.169
O shun me not, but heare me ere you goe, Hero and Leander 1.205
O let mee viste Hero ere I die. Hero and Leander 2.178
Ere halfe this tale was done,/Aye me, Leander cryde, Hero and Leander 2.201

EREBUS
This arme should send him downe to Erebus, 1Tamb 4.1.45 Souldn
the Feends infernall view/As are the blasted banks of Erebus: 1Tamb 5.1.244 Zabina
That soules passe not to silent Erebus/Or Plutoes bloodles Lucan, First Booke 451

ERECT
To erect your sonne with all the speed we may, Edw 5.2.11 Mortmr
But neither chuse the north t'erect thy seat; Lucan, First Booke 53

ERECTED
Welcome to Carthage new erected towne. Dido 5.1.26 Aeneas
Had never bene erected as they bee, 1Tamb 5.1.32 1Virgn
Erected is a Castle passing strong, F 818 3.1.40 Mephst

ERECTING
great deserts in erecting that inchanted Castle in the Aire: F1560 4.6.3 P Duke

ERE-WHILE
I that ere-while was fierce, now humbly sue, Ovid's Elegies 2.5.49

ERICINE
And [them] <then> like Mars and Ericine displayd, Hero and Leander 2.305

ERINNIS
the suburbe fieldes/Fled, fowle Erinnis stalkt about the wals, Lucan, First Booke 570

ERRE
And therefore tho we would we cannot erre. F 931 3.1.153 Pope
Unlesse I erre, full many shalt thou burne, Ovid's Elegies 1.2.43
Erre we? or do the turned hinges sound, Ovid's Elegies 1.6.49
We erre: a strong blast seem'd the gates to ope: Ovid's Elegies 1.6.51
Unlesse I erre to these thou more incline, Ovid's Elegies 2.18.39
Erre I? or mirtle in her right hand lies. Ovid's Elegies 3.1.34
Erre I? or by my [bookes] <lookes> is she so knowne? Ovid's Elegies 3.11.7
Deceive all, let me erre, and thinke I am right, Ovid's Elegies 3.13.29

ERRING
And Characters of Signes, and [erring] <evening> Starres,/By F 240 1.3.12 Faust
Mars, or Jupiter,/Fain'd, but are [erring] <evening> Starres. F 595 2.2.44 Mephst

ERROR
Are blest by such sweet error, this makes them/Run on the Lucan, First Booke 456

ERROUR
stand upon; therefore acknowledge your errour, and be attentive. F 204 1.2.11 P Wagner

ERST (See also EARST)
And intercepts the day as Dolon erst: Dido 1.1.71 Venus
And flourish once againe that erst was dead: Dido 1.1.95 Jupitr
That erst-while issued from thy watrie loynes, Dido 1.1.128 Venus
And planted love where envie erst had sprong. Dido 3.2.52 Juno
higher meeds/Then erst our states and actions have retain'd, 1Tamb 4.4.132 Therid
With greater power than erst his pride hath felt, 2Tamb 2.2.10 Gazell
And Barabas, as erst we promis'd thee, Jew 5.2.9 Calym

ERST-WHILE (See also ERE-WHILE)
That erst-while issued from thy watrie loynes, Dido 1.1.128 Venus

ERYCINE (See ERICINE, HERICINAS)

ERYX
Eryx bright Empresse turnd her lookes aside, Ovid's Elegies 3.8.45

ES
Bien para todos mi ganado no es: Jew 2.1.39 Barab

ESCAP'D
I was imprison'd, but escap'd their hands. Jew 5.1.77 Barab
And had I but escap'd this stratagem, Jew 5.5.84 Barab

ESCAPE (See also SCAPE, SCAPT)
And overjoy my thoughts with their escape: Dido 3.3.57 Aeneas
That no escape may save their enemies: 1Tamb 5.1.405 Arabia
For so hath heaven provided my escape, 2Tamb 3.1.32 Callap
Yet if your majesty may escape this day, 2Tamb 5.3.98 Phsitn
I have don't, but no body knowes it but you two, I may escape. Jew 4.1.181 P 1Fryar
Whence none can possibly escape alive: Jew 5.5.31 Barab
Let none escape, murder the Hugonets. P 337 5.64 Guise
Tue, tue, tue, let none escape: P 534 10.7 Guise
Mortimer I stay thy sweet escape, Edw 4.1.10 Kent
T'escape their hands that seeke to reave his life: Edw 4.7.52 Leistr
me but a little straw, and had much ado to escape drowning: F1487 4.4.31 P HrsCsr
With slender trench they escape night stratagems, Lucan, First Booke 514

ESCAP'T
Wherby whole Cities have escap't the plague, F 49 1.1.21 Faust

ESCAPT
From thence a fewe of us escapt to land, Dido 1.2.30 Cloan
So I escapt the furious Pirrhus wrath: Dido 2.1.223 Aeneas
Faire Anna, how escapt you from the shower? Dido 4.1.29 Aeneas
Yet lustie lords I have escapt your handes, Edw 2.5.1 Gavstn
A villaines, hath that Mortimer escapt? Edw 4.3.38 Edward
Pray heaven the Doctor have escapt the danger. F1987 5.3.5 1Schol

ESCAPTE
It may be it is some other, and he escapte. P 308 5.35 Anjoy

ESPECIALLIE
And one especiallie doe we affect, Hero and Leander 1.171

ESPECIALLY
Especially in women of [our] <your> yeares.-- Dido 4.5.28 Nurse

ESPECIALLY (cont.)
Especially with our olde mothers helpe. P1061 19.131 King
ESPERIDES
Entred the orchard of Th'esperides, Hero and Leander 2.298
ESPY'D
Now have I happily espy'd a time/To search the plancke my Jew 2.1.20 Abigal
ESPY'DE
Now had the morne espy'de her lovers steeds, Hero and Leander 2.87
ESSENCE
A Forme not meet to give that subject essence, 2Tamb 4.1.112 Tamb
Your soul gives essence to our wretched subjects, 2Tamb 5.3.164 Amyras
Is neither essence subject to the eie, Hero and Leander 1.270
ESSENTIALL
In which the essentiall fourme of Marble stone, 2Tamb 4.2.62 Olymp
EST
<testimonis> est [inartificiale] <in arte fetiales>. P 395 7.35 Guise
The motto this: Undique mors est. Edw 2.2.28 Lncstr
Edwardum occidere nolite timere bonum est. Edw 5.4.8 Mortmr
Edwardum occidere nolite timere bonum est. Edw 5.4.11 Mortmr
Bene disserere est finis logices. F 35 1.1.7 Faust
Stipendium peccati mors est: F 66 1.1.38 P Faust
Si peccasse negamus, fallimur, et nulla est in nobis veritas: F 68 1.1.40 P Faust
Consummatum est: F 463 2.1.75 Faust
ESTABLISH (See also STABLISH)
Even by this hand that shall establish them, 1Tamb 5.1.492 Tamb
ESTATE
In spight of them shall malice my estate. 1Tamb 1.1.159 Cosroe
Joine with me now in this my meane estate, 1Tamb 1.2.202 Tamb
a blemish to the Majestie/And high estate of mightie Emperours, 1Tamb 4.3.20 Souldn
Mount up your royall places of estate, 1Tamb 5.1.525 Tamb
And mount my royall chariot of estate, 2Tamb 5.3.178 Tamb
the Jewes, and each of them to pay one halfe of his estate. Jew 1.2.70 P Reader
Blindes Europs eyes and troubleth our estate: P 152 2.95 Guise
Mine enemie hath pitied my estate, Edw 5.1.149 Edward
in their most florishing estate, which I doubt not shal F App p.237 48 P Faust
ESTATES
As your supreame estates instruct our thoughtes, 2Tamb 5.3.20 Techel
O gods that easie grant men great estates, Lucan, First Booke 508
ESTEEM'D
To be esteem'd assurance for our selves, 2Tamb 2.1.39 Baldwn
Thou Christ that art esteem'd omnipotent, 2Tamb 2.2.55 Orcan
And what our Army royall is esteem'd. 2Tamb 3.5.31 Callap
So that the Army royall is esteem'd/Six hundred thousand 2Tamb 3.5.50 Soria
Then this profession were to be esteem'd. F 54 1.1.26 Faust
She looked sad: sad, comely I esteem'd her. Ovid's Elegies 2.5.44
ESTEEMDST
Was I: thou liv'dst, while thou esteemdst my faith. Ovid's Elegies 3.8.56
ESTEEME
And Maddam, whatsoever you esteeme/Of this successe, and losse 1Tamb 1.2.44 Tamb
Which I esteeme as portion of my crown. 1Tamb 2.3.35 Cosroe
Why I esteeme the injury farre lesse, Jew 1.2.146 Barab
'Tis not thy wealth, but her that I esteeme, Jew 2.3.298 Lodowk
'Tis not five hundred Crownes that I esteeme, Jew 4.3.40 Barab
And have old servitors in high esteeme, Edw 3.1.168 Herald
Whome I esteeme as deare as these mine eyes, Edw 5.2.18 Queene
Greater then these my selfe I not esteeme, Ovid's Elegies 2.8.13
Healthfull Peligny I esteeme nought worth, Ovid's Elegies 2.16.37
ESTEEMED
that Navarre may be/Esteemed faithfull to the King of France: P1148 22.10 Navrre
ESTEEMES
Thus Bellamira esteemes of gold; Jew 4.2.125 Curtzn
ESTEEMING
If Jove esteeming me too good for earth, 2Tamb 4.3.60 Tamb
ESTEEMS
What, thinkst thou Tamburlain esteems thy gold? 1Tamb 3.3.262 Tamb
ESTIMATE
And higher would I reare my estimate, 1Tamb 3.2.53 Zenoc
ESTIMATES
These Lords (perhaps) do scorne our estimates, 1Tamb 1.2.61 Tamb
ESTIMATION
Courts shut the poore out; wealth gives estimation, Ovid's Elegies 3.7.55
ESUS (See HESUS)
ET
et istam/Oro, si quis [adhuc] <ad haec> precibus locus, Dido 5.1.137 Dido
Si peccasse negamus, fallimur, et nulla est in nobis veritas: F 68 1.1.40 P Faust
inferni ardentis monarcha, et Demogorgon, propitiamus vos, F 246 1.3.18 P Faust
propitiamus vos, ut appareat, et surgat Mephostophilis. F 247 1.3.19 P Faust
et consecratam aquam quam nunc spargo; signumque crucis quod F 248 1.3.20 P Faust
nunc facio; et per vota nostra ipse nunc surgat nobis dicatus F 249 1.3.21 P Faust
But <tell me> have they all/One motion, both situ et tempore? F 596 2.2.45 Faust
But is there not Coelum igneum, [and] <&> <et> Christalinum? F 612 2.2.61 P Faust
[Et omnes sancti. Amen]. F1087 3.2.107A 1Frier
Et omnes sancti Amen. F App p.233 41 Frier
& (ET)
But is there not Coelum igneum, [and] <&> <et> Christalinum? F 612 2.2.61 P Faust
&C.
&c. I have according to instructions in that behalfe, dealt Edw 4.3.28 P Spencr
eademque res legatur duobus, alter rem, alter valorem rei, &c. F 56 1.1.28 P Faust
ha, Stipendium, &c. F 66 1.1.38 P Faust
male, &c. F App p.232 36 Frier
male, &c. F App p.232 38 Frier
and you are but a &c. F App p.234 10 P Robin
Belseborams framanto pacostiphos tostu Mephastophilis, &c. F App p.235 25 P Robin

ETERNAL			
The golden balle of heavens eternal fire,	2Tamb	2.4.2	Tamb
O then ye Powers that sway eternal seates,	2Tamb	5.3.17	Techel
ETERNALL			
And race th'eternall Register of time:	Dido	3.2.7	Juno
Harke to a motion of eternall league,	Dido	3.2.68	Juno
Eternall Jove, great master of the Clowdes,	Dido	4.2.4	Iarbus
But that eternall Jupiter commands.	Dido	5.1.82	Aeneas
Eternall heaven sooner be dissolv'd,	1Tamb	3.2.18	Agidas
whose taste illuminates/Refined eies with an eternall sight,	2Tamb	2.4.23	Tamb
Than when she gave eternall Chaos forme,	2Tamb	3.4.76	Techel
Or bind thee in eternall torments wrath.	2Tamb	3.5.113	Soria
in] <resisting> me/The power of heavens eternall majesty.	2Tamb	4.1.158	Tamb
Muffle your beauties with eternall clowdes,	2Tamb	5.3.6	Therid
And henceforth wish for an eternall night,	Jew	1.2.193	Barab
night; or let the day/Turne to eternall darkenesse after this:	Jew	2.1.16	Barab
Farre from the Sonne that gives eternall life.	Jew	3.3.65	Abigal
As to the service of the eternall God.	P 413	7.53	Ramus
And heere protest eternall love to thee,	P1206	22.68	King
And tasted the eternall Joyes of heaven,	F 306	1.3.78	Mephst
Seeing Faustus hath incur'd eternall death,	F 316	1.3.88	Faust
and twenty yeares hath Faustus lost eternall joy and felicitie.	F1860	5.2.64	P Faust
Hath rob'd me of eternall happinesse.	F1884	5.2.88	Faust
Thy scope is mortall, mine eternall fame,	Ovid's Elegies	1.15.7	
Are both in Fames eternall legend writ.	Ovid's Elegies	1.15.20	
And with his <their> bloud eternall honour gaine,	Ovid's Elegies	2.10.32	
Insooth th'eternall powers graunt maides society/Falsely to	Ovid's Elegies	3.3.11	
Eternall heaven to burne, for so it seem'd,	Hero and Leander	1.100	
ETERNALLY			
And with this stab slumber eternally.	1Tamb	3.2.106	Agidas
Couldst <Wouldst> thou make men <man> to live eternally,	F 52	1.1.24	Faust
thee, then had I lived still, but now must <I> dye eternally.	F1825	5.2.29	P Faust
ETERNISDE			
And this eternisde citie Babylon,	2Tamb	5.1.35	Govnr
ETERNISH			
Who will eternish Troy in their attempts.	Dido	1.1.108	Jupitr
ETERNITIE			
For in his lookes I see eternitie,	Dido	4.4.122	Dido
ETERNIZ'D			
And be eterniz'd for some wondrous cure:	F 43	1.1.15	Faust
ETERNIZE			
This is the time that must eternize me,	2Tamb	5.2.54	Callap
And whom I like eternize by mine art.	Ovid's Elegies	1.10.60	
ETERNIZED			
Even as thou hop'st to be eternized,	1Tamb	1.2.72	Zenoc
ETHIOPIAN			
of Affrike, where I view'd/The Ethiopian sea, rivers and lakes:	2Tamb	1.3.196	Techel
And so along the Ethiopian sea,	2Tamb	5.3.137	Tamb
ETRURIAN			
(as their old custome was)/They call th'Etrurian Augures,	Lucan, First Booke	584	
EUNUCH			
Aye me an Eunuch keepes my mistrisse chaste,	Ovid's Elegies	2.3.1	
EUNUCHES			
Chaining of Eunuches, binding gally-slaves.	Jew	2.3.204	Ithimr
EUNUKE			
He shall be made a chast and lustlesse Eunuke,	1Tamb	3.3.77	Bajzth
EUPHRATES			
As vast and deep as Euphrates or Nile.	1Tamb	5.1.439	Tamb
To drinke the river Nile or Euphrates,	2Tamb	3.1.42	Orcan
That touch the end of famous Euphrates.	2Tamb	3.1.53	Trebiz
Of Euphrates and Tigris swiftly runs,	2Tamb	5.2.3	Callap
EUROPA			
Whom Troiane ships fecht from Europa farre.	Ovid's Elegies	1.10.2	
And for his love Europa, bellowing loud,	Hero and Leander	1.149	
EUROPAS			
Or his Bulles hornes Europas hand doth hold.	Ovid's Elegies	3.11.34	
EUROPE			
Exild forth Europe and wide Asia both,	Dido	1.1.229	Aeneas
and the bounds/Of Europe wher the Sun dares scarce appeare,	1Tamb	1.1.10	Cosroe
Affrike and Europe bordering on your land,	1Tamb	1.1.127	Menaph
Dread Lord of Affrike, Europe and Asia,	1Tamb	3.1.23	Bajzth
Shall rouse him out of Europe, and pursue/His scattered armie	1Tamb	3.3.38	Therid
Which lately made all Europe quake for feare:	1Tamb	3.3.135	Bajzth
Bringing the strength of Europe to these Armes:	2Tamb	1.1.30	Orcan
And make faire Europe mounted on her bull,	2Tamb	1.1.42	Orcan
And we from Europe to the same intent,	2Tamb	1.1.118	Fredrk
and the bounds of Affrike/And made a voyage into Europe,	2Tamb	1.3.208	Therid
even to the utmost verge/Of Europe, or the shore of Tanaise,	Edw	4.2.30	Queene
Whose [shadows] made all Europe honour him.	F 145	1.1.117	Faust
Maisters, I'le bring you to the best beere in Europe, what ho,	F1506	4.5.2	P Carter
druncke with ipocrase at any taberne in Europe for nothing,	F App	p.234 23	P Robin
new, but for a Queene/Europe, and Asia in firme peace had beene.	Ovid's Elegies	2.12.18	
EUROP'S			
My Lord, Remember that to Europ's shame,	Jew	2.2.30	Bosco
EUROPS			
Blindes Europs eyes and troubleth our estate:	P 152	2.95	Guise
EUROTAS			
Eurotas cold, and poplar-bearing Po.	Ovid's Elegies	2.17.32	
EUXIN			
Fetters the Euxin sea, with chaines of yce:	Lucan, First Booke	18	
EUXINE			
Chiefe Lord of all the wide vast Euxine sea,	1Tamb	1.1.167	Ortyg
The Euxine sea North to Natolia,	2Tamb	4.3.102	Tamb

EVADNE
Is by Evadne thought to take such flame, ... Ovid's Elegies 3.5.41
EVASION
Never to harme me made thy faith evasion. . . . . . Ovid's Elegies 1.11.6
EVE
the serpent that tempted Eve may be saved, but not Faustus. F1838 5.2.42 P Faust
EVEN (Homograph)
And from their knees, even to their hoofes below, . . 1Tamb 1.1.79 Mycet
Even in the circle of your Fathers armes: . . . . . 1Tamb 1.2.5 Tamb
Even as when windy exhalations, ... 1Tamb 1.2.50 Tamb
That even to death will follow Tamburlaine. . . . . 1Tamb 1.2.59 Usumc
Even as thou hop'st to be eternized, ... 1Tamb 1.2.72 Zenoc
For even as from assured oracle, ... 1Tamb 2.3.4 Cosroe
Even by the mighty hand of Tamburlaine, ... 1Tamb 2.5.3 Tamb
Even at the morning of my happy state, ... 1Tamb 2.7.4 Cosroe
Even he that in a trice vanquisht two kings, ... 1Tamb 3.3.36 Therid
Even from Persepolis to Mexico, ... 1Tamb 3.3.255 Tamb
Even in Bythinia, when I took this Turke: . . . . . 1Tamb 4.2.42 Tamb
Even from this day to Platoes wondrous yeare, ... 1Tamb 4.2.96 Tamb
Even with the true Egyptian Diadem. 1Tamb 5.1.105 1Virgn
Even from the fiery spangled vaile of heaven, ... 1Tamb 5.1.185 Tamb
I, even I speake to her. . . . . 1Tamb 5.1.314 P Zabina
Even so for her thou diest in these armes: . . . . 1Tamb 5.1.410 Arabia
Even by this hand that shall establish them, ... 1Tamb 5.1.492 Tamb
Even from the midst of fiery Cancers Tropick, ... 2Tamb 1.1.73 Orcan
Even straight: and farewell cursed Tamburlaine. . . . 2Tamb 1.2.77 Callap
Even in the cannons face shall raise a hill/Of earth and fagots 2Tamb 3.3.21 Therid
Even till the dissolution of the world, ... 2Tamb 3.5.82 Tamb
Even for charity I may spit intoo't. . . . . . . Jew 2.3.29 Barab
Even for your Honourable fathers sake. . . . . . Jew 2.3.93 Barab
Even now as I came home, he slipt me in, ... Jew 2.3.267 Barab
And so has she done you, even from a child. . . . . Jew 2.3.289 Barab
For I have now no hope but even in thee; . . . . . Jew 3.4.16 Barab
This Even they use in Malta here ('tis call'd/Saint Jaques Jew 3.4.75 Barab
Saint Jaques Even) and then I say they use/To send their Almes Jew 3.4.76 Barab
as who shold say, Is it even so; and so I left him, being driven Jew 4.2.13 P Pilia
Marry, even he that strangled Bernardine, poyson'd the Nuns, and Jew 5.1.33 P Ithimr
Shall buy her love even with his dearest bloud. . . . P 697 13.41 Guise
Even for your words that have incenst me so, ... P 767 15.25 Guise
Even so let hatred with thy [soveraignes] <soveraigne> smile. Edw 1.4.342 Edward
And even now, a poast came from the court, ... Edw 2.1.19 Spencr
For now, even now, we marche to make them stoope, . . . Edw 3.1.183 Edward
Ah sweete sir John, even to the utmost verge/Of Europe, or the Edw 4.2.29 Queene
this drowsines/Betides no good, here even we are betraied. Edw 4.7.45 Spencr
Even so betide my soule as I use him. . . . . . Edw 5.1.148 Bartly
I, lead me whether you will, even to my death, . . . Edw 5.3.66 Kent
That <and> even then when I shall lose my life, . . . Edw 5.5.77 Edward
I see it plaine, even heere <in this place> is writ/Homo fuge: F 469 2.1.81 Faust
Even from the Moone unto the Emperiall Orbe, ... F 590 2.2.39 Mephst
Even to the height of Primum Mobile: . . . . . . F 763 2.3.42 2Chor
You brought us word even now, it was decreed, ... F1019 3.2.39 Pope
carowse, and swill/Amongst the Students, as even now he doth, F App p.243 5 Wagner
even as the slender Isthmos,/Betwixt the Aegean and the Ionian Lucan, First Booke 100
even the same that wrack's all great [dominions] <dominion>. Lucan, First Booke 160
even nowe when youthfull bloud/Pricks forth our lively bodies, Lucan, First Booke 363
even so the City left,/All rise in armes; nor could the . Lucan, First Booke 501
Even in his face his offered [Gobbets] <Goblets> cast. . Ovid's Elegies 1.4.34
Even Jove himselfe out off my wit was reft. . . . . Ovid's Elegies 2.1.18
To quaver on her lippes even in her song, ... Ovid's Elegies 2.4.26
Even from your cheekes parte of a voice did breake. . . Ovid's Elegies 2.5.16
Even such as by Aurora hath the skie, ... Ovid's Elegies 2.5.35
Even kembed as they were, her lockes to rend, ... Ovid's Elegies 2.5.45
Even as a head-strong courser beares away, ... Ovid's Elegies 2.9.29
Even as a boate, tost by contrarie winde, ... Ovid's Elegies 2.10.9
Even as he led his life, so did he die. . . . . . Ovid's Elegies 2.10.38
And even the ring performe a mans part well. . . . . Ovid's Elegies 2.15.26
Even as sweete meate a glutted stomacke cloyes. . . . Ovid's Elegies 2.19.26
Fower chariot-horses from the lists even ends. . . . Ovid's Elegies 3.2.66
Even as the sicke desire forbidden drinke. . . . . Ovid's Elegies 3.4.18
Even her I had, and she had me in vaine, ... Ovid's Elegies 3.6.43
Even as delicious meat is to the tast, ... Hero and Leander 1.63
Even as, when gawdie Nymphs pursue the chace, ... Hero and Leander 1.113
Even so for mens impression do we you. . . . . . Hero and Leander 1.266
Even sacrilege against her Deitie, ... Hero and Leander 1.307
Therefore even as an Index to a booke, ... Hero and Leander 2.129
Even as a bird, which in our hands we wring, ... Hero and Leander 2.289
EVENING
And bring it with me to thee in the evening. . . . . Jew 5.2.108 Govnr
Wee'll in this Summer Evening feast with him. . . . . Jew 5.3.41 Calym
And Characters of Signes, and [erring] <evening> Starres,/By F 240 1.3.12 Faust
Mars, or Jupiter,/Fain'd, but are [erring] <evening> Starres. F 595 2.2.44 Mephst
O thou art fairer then the evenings <evening> aire, . . . F1781 5.1.108 Faust
Beginne to shut thy house at evening sure. . . . . Ovid's Elegies 2.19.38
EVENINGS
In silence of thy solemn Evenings walk, ... 1Tamb 5.1.148 Tamb
O thou art fairer then the evenings <evening> aire, . . . F1781 5.1.108 Faust
EVENT
To what event my secret purpose drives, ... Jew 5.2.122 Barab
EVENTS
And might, if my extreams had full events, ... 1Tamb 3.2.16 Zenoc
Convey events of mercie to his heart: 1Tamb 5.1.54 2Virgn
EVER (See Preface for cross-references)
is Aeneas, were he clad/In weedes as bad as ever Irus ware. Dido 2.1.85 Dido

EVER (cont.)

doe know no wanton thought/Had ever residence in Didos breast.	Dido	3.1.17	Dido
And like the Planets ever love to raunge:	Dido	3.3.68	Iarbus
Did ever men see such a sudden storme?	Dido	4.1.1	Achat
On whom ruth and compassion ever waites,	Dido	4.2.20	Iarbus
Who ever since hath luld me in her armes.	Dido	5.1.48	Ascan
Nor ever viclated faith to him:	Dido	5.1.205	Dido
And of the ever raging Caspian Lake:	1Tamb	1.1.168	Ortyg
I, Didst thou ever see a fairer?	1Tamb	2.4.28	Mycet
And as we ever [aim'd] <and> at your behoofe,	1Tamb	2.5.32	Ortyg
Where flames shall ever feed upon his soule.	1Tamb	2.6.8	Cosroe
The strangest men that ever nature made,	1Tamb	2.7.40	Cosroe
Or ever drisling drops of Aprill showers,	1Tamb	4.1.31	Souldn
of that Spheare/Enchac'd with thousands ever shining lamps,	1Tamb	4.2.9	Tamb
If all the pens that ever poets held,	1Tamb	5.1.161	Tamb
Where shaking ghosts with ever howling grones,	1Tamb	5.1.245	Zabina
to your dominions/Than ever yet confirm'd th'Egyptian Crown.	1Tamb	5.1.449	Tamb
What God so ever holds thee in his armes,	2Tamb	2.4.109	Tamb
Boyes leave to mourne, this towne shall ever mourne,	2Tamb	3.2.45	Tamb
For ever terme, the Perseans sepulchre,	2Tamb	3.5.19	Callap
(The worthiest knight that ever brandisht sword)/Challenge in	2Tamb	3.5.71	Tamb
Fight as you ever did, like Conquerours,	2Tamb	3.5.160	Tamb
Of [ever] <every> greene Selinus queintly dect/With bloomes	2Tamb	4.3.121	Tamb
My Lord, if ever you did deed of ruth,	2Tamb	5.1.24	1Citzn
Whose state he ever pitied and reliev'd,	2Tamb	5.1.32	1Citzn
My Lord, if ever you wil win our hearts,	2Tamb	5.1.38	2Citzn
More exquisite than ever Traitor felt.	2Tamb	5.1.53	Therid
we offer more/Than ever yet we did to such proud slaves,	2Tamb	5.1.58	Techel
The strangest sight, in my opinion,/That ever I beheld.	Jew	1.2.377	Mthias
O the sweetest face that ever I beheld!	Jew	3.1.26	P Ithimr
Why, was there ever seene such villany,	Jew	3.3.1	Ithimr
bottle-nos'd knave to my Master, that ever Gentleman had.	Jew	3.3.10	P Ithimr
was ever pot of rice porredge so sauc't?	Jew	3.4.106	P Ithimr
that she loves me ever since she saw me, and who would not	Jew	4.2.34	P Ithimr
Was ever Jew tormented as I am?	Jew	4.3.60	Barab
And I will warrant Malta free for ever.	Jew	5.2.101	Barab
If greater falshood ever has bin done.	Jew	5.5.50	Barab
Shall binde me ever to your highnes will,	P 11	1.11	Navrre
If ever Hymen lowr'd at marriage rites,	P 58	2.1	Guise
If ever sunne stainde heaven with bloudy clowdes,	P 60	2.3	Guise
If ever day were turnde to ugly night,	P 62	2.5	Guise
Fye, I am ashamde, how ever that I seeme,	P 124	2.67	Guise
And fellowes to, what ever stormes arise.	P 615	12.28	King
Thus God we see doth ever guide the right,	P 789	16.3	Navrre
That ever I was prov'd your enemy,	P1140	22.2	King
Was ever troubled with injurious warres:	P1142	22.4	King
That ever I vouchsafte my dearest freends.	P1146	22.8	King
Was ever king thus over rulde as I?	Edw	1.4.38	Edward
And yet heele ever dote on Gaveston,	Edw	1.4.185	Queene
And so am I for ever miserable.	Edw	1.4.186	Queene
And therefore brother banish him for ever.	Edw	2.2.211	Kent
As Isabell could live with thee for ever.	Edw	2.4.60	Queene
In burying him, then he hath ever earned.	Edw	2.5.56	Lncstr
O hadst thou ever beene a king, thy hart/Pierced deeply with	Edw	4.7.9	Edward
Continue ever thou celestiall sunne,	Edw	5.1.64	Edward
The Spencers ghostes, where ever they remaine,	Edw	5.3.44	Edward
upon me whilst I live/To do what ever Faustus shall command:	F 265	1.3.37	Faust
And are for ever damn'd with Lucifer.	F 300	1.3.72	Mephst
Having thee ever to attend on me,	F 321	1.3.93	Faust
Where we are tortur'd, and remaine for ever.	F 509	2.1.121	Mephst
And where hell is there must we ever be.	F 512	2.1.124	Mephst
ever since <I> have run up and downe the world with these	F 687	2.2.136	P Wrath
[where I have laine ever since, and you have done me great	F 705.1	2.2.155A	P Sloth
Of ever-burning Phlegeton, I sweare,	F 827	3.1.49	Faust
Damb'd be this soule for ever, for this deed.	F1070	3.2.90	Pope
Now with the flames of ever-burning fire,	F1135	3.3.48	Mephst
For ever be belov'd of Carolus.	F1211	4.1.57	Emper
that shall pierce through/The Ebon gates of ever-burning hell,	F1224	4.1.70	Faust
Now am I a made man for ever.	F1477	4.4.21	P HrsCsr
that Hellen of Greece was the admirablest Lady that ever liv'd:	F1684	5.1.11	P 1Schol
the Kingdome of Joy, and must remaine in hell for ever.	F1846	5.2.50	P Faust
Hell, [ah] <O> hell for ever.	F1846	5.2.50	P Faust
friends, what shall become of Faustus being in hell for ever?	F1847	5.2.51	P Faust
this ever-burning chaire,/Is for ore-tortur'd soules to rest	F1914	5.2.118	BdAngl
Stand still you ever moving Spheares of heaven,	F1929	5.2.133	Faust
tell thee, we were for ever made by this doctor Faustus booke?	F App	p.234 1	P Robin
that what ever thou doest, thou shalt be no wayes prejudiced or	F App	p.236 9	P Emper
Now am I made man for ever, Ile not leave my horse for fortie:	F App	p.239 114	P HrsCsr
Under great burdens fals are ever greevous;	Lucan, First Booke		71
Where men are ready, lingering ever hurts:	Lucan, First Booke		282
And which (aie me) ever pretendeth ill,	Lucan, First Booke		625
Why should we wish the gods should ever end them?	Lucan, First Booke		668
If men have Faith, Ile live with thee for ever.	Ovid's Elegies		1.3.16
There touch what ever thou canst touch of mee.	Ovid's Elegies		1.4.58
Nor servile water shalt thou drinke for ever.	Ovid's Elegies		1.6.26
The fame that verse gives doth for ever last.	Ovid's Elegies		1.10.62
If ever, now well lies she by my side.	Ovid's Elegies		1.13.6
The maide that kembd them ever safely left them.	Ovid's Elegies		1.14.16
That all the world [may] <might> ever chaunt my name.	Ovid's Elegies		1.15.8
[The world shall of Callimachus ever speake],	Ovid's Elegies		1.15.13
For ever lasts high Sophocles proud vaine,	Ovid's Elegies		1.15.15
If ever wench had made luke-warme thy love:	Ovid's Elegies		2.3.6
A hundred reasons makes <make> me ever love.	Ovid's Elegies		2.4.10

EVER (cont.)			
And ever seemed as some new sweete befell.	Ovid's Elegies	2.5.56	
There lives the Phoenix one alone bird ever.	Ovid's Elegies	2.6.54	
And then things found do ever further pace.	Ovid's Elegies	2.9.10	
And thou my light accept me how so ever,	Ovid's Elegies	2.17.23	
What ever haps, by suffrance harme is done,	Ovid's Elegies	2.19.35	
Thy labour ever lasts, she askes but little.	Ovid's Elegies	3.1.68	
Slide in thy bounds, so shalt thou runne for ever.	Ovid's Elegies	3.5.20	
What thirstie traveller ever drunke of thee?	Ovid's Elegies	3.5.97	
See Homer from whose fountaine ever fild,	Ovid's Elegies	3.8.25	
And mingle thighs, yours ever mine to beare.	Ovid's Elegies	3.13.22	
Who ever lov'd, that lov'd not at first sight?	Hero and Leander	1.176	
And ever as he thought himselfe most nigh it,	Hero and Leander	2.74	
T'is lost but once, and once lost, lost for ever.	Hero and Leander	2.86	
Yet ever as he greedily assayd/To touch those dainties, she the	Hero and Leander	2.269	
EVER-BURNING			
Of ever-burning Phlegeton, I sweare,	F 827	3.1.49	Faust
Now with the flames of ever-burning fire,	F1135	3.3.48	Mephst
that shall pierce through/The Ebon gates of ever-burning hell,	F1224	4.1.70	Faust
this ever-burning chaire,/Is for ore-tortur'd soules to rest	F1914	5.2.118	BdAngl
EVERIE			
But everie jointe shakes as I give it thee:	Edw	5.5.86	Edward
And give woundes infinite at everie turne.	Ovid's Elegies	1.2.44	
And birdes send forth shrill notes from everie bow.	Ovid's Elegies	1.13.8	
The Moone sleepes with Endemion everie day,	Ovid's Elegies	1.13.43	
Nor set my voyce to sale in everie cause?	Ovid's Elegies	1.15.6	
My love alludes to everie historie:	Ovid's Elegies	2.4.44	
If one can doote, if not, two everie night,	Ovid's Elegies	2.10.22	
And thorough everie vaine doth cold bloud runne,	Ovid's Elegies	3.13.38	
The men of wealthie Sestos, everie yeare,	Hero and Leander	1.91	
For everie street like to a Firmament/Glistered with breathing	Hero and Leander	1.97	
And yet at everie word shee turn'd aside,	Hero and Leander	1.195	
Women receave perfection everie way.	Hero and Leander	1.268	
all, and everie part/Strove to resist the motions of her hart.	Hero and Leander	1.363	
Threatning a thousand deaths at everie glaunce,	Hero and Leander	1.382	
tincture of her cheekes, that drew/The love of everie swaine:	Hero and Leander	1.397	
And to this day is everie scholler poore,	Hero and Leander	1.471	
and there prie/Upon his brest, his thighs, and everie lim,	Hero and Leander	2.189	
And everie kisse to her was as a charme,	Hero and Leander	2.283	
EVERIE DAY			
The Moone sleepes with Endemion everie day,	Ovid's Elegies	1.13.43	
EVERLASTING			
I banne their soules to everlasting paines/And extreme tortures	Jew	1.2.166	Barab
I, we must die, an everlasting death.	F 73	1.1.45	Faust
In being depriv'd of everlasting blisse?	F 308	1.3.80	Mephst
his promise, did despise/The love of th'everlasting Destinies.	Hero and Leander	1.462	
EVERLASTINGLIE			
Bound to your highnes everlastinglie,	Edw	3.1.41	SpncrP
EVERLIVING			
O highest Lamp of everliving Jove,	1Tamb	5.1.290	Bajzth
If he be son to everliving Jove,	2Tamb	2.2.41	Orcan
EVERMORE			
Wherein the day may evermore delight:	Dido	5.1.7	Aeneas
whose silver haires/Honor and reverence evermore have raign'd,	1Tamb	5.1.82	1Virgn
sight <glorious deed>/Happy and blest be Faustus evermore.	F1705	5.1.32	1Schol
dams/They kennel'd in Hircania, evermore/Wil rage and pray:	Lucan, First Booke	329	
Now evermore least some one hope might ease/The Commons	Lucan, First Booke	520	
For evermore thou shalt my mistris be.	Ovid's Elegies	3.2.62	
Stone still he stood, and evermore he gazed,	Hero and Leander	1.163	
EVERY			
And rests a pray to every billowes pride.	Dido	1.1.53	Venus
And every beast the forrest doth send forth,	Dido	1.1.161	Achat
As every tide tilts twixt their oken sides:	Dido	1.1.224	Aeneas
And spare our lives whom every spite pursues.	Dido	1.2.9	Illion
And every Troian be as welcome here,	Dido	1.2.40	Iarbus
Threatning a thousand deaths at every glaunce.	Dido	2.1.231	Aeneas
As every touch shall wound Queene Didos heart.	Dido	2.1.333	Cupid
That imitate the Moone in every chaunge,	Dido	3.3.67	Iarbus
And every speech be ended with a kisse:	Dido	4.3.54	Aeneas
In every part exceeding brave and rich.	1Tamb	1.2.127	Souldr
In every part proportioned like the man,	1Tamb	2.1.29	Menaph
man, ordain'd by heaven/To further every action to the best.	1Tamb	2.1.53	Ortyg
Shall fling in every corner of the field:	1Tamb	2.2.64	Meandr
For Kings are clouts that every man shoots at,	1Tamb	2.4.8	Mycet
Sackes every vaine and artier of my heart.	1Tamb	2.7.10	Cosroe
And measure every wandring plannets course:	1Tamb	2.7.23	Tamb
And strive for life at every stroke they give.	1Tamb	3.3.54	Tamb
But every common souldier of my Camp/Shall smile to see thy	1Tamb	3.3.85	Tamb
Make heaven to frowne and every fixed starre/To sucke up poison	1Tamb	4.2.5	Bajzth
And every house is as a treasurie.	1Tamb	4.2.109	Tamb
His cole-blacke collours every where advaunst,	1Tamb	5.1.9	Govnr
And every sweetnes that inspir'd their harts,	1Tamb	5.1.163	Tamb
And every warriour that is rapt with love/Of fame, of valour,	1Tamb	5.1.180	Tamb
whose worthinesse/Deserves a conquest over every hart:	1Tamb	5.1.208	Tamb
And every bullet dipt in poisoned drugs.	1Tamb	5.1.222	Bajzth
At every pore let blood comme dropping foorth,	1Tamb	5.1.227	Zabina
For every fell and stout Tartarian Stead/That stampt on others	1Tamb	5.1.330	Zenoc
Sleep'st every night with conquest on thy browes,	1Tamb	5.1.359	Zenoc
And make it quake at every drop it drinks:	1Tamb	5.1.462	Tamb
And every one Commander of a world.	2Tamb	1.3.8	Tamb
But every where fils every Continent,	2Tamb	2.2.51	Orcan
shall breath/Through shady leaves of every sencelesse tree,	2Tamb	2.3.16	Orcan
And tempered every soule with lively heat,	2Tamb	2.4.10	Tamb

EVERY (cont.)			
Her name had bene in every line he wrote:	2Tamb	2.4.90	Tamb
Zenocrate had bene the argument/Of every Epigram or Eligie.	2Tamb	2.4.95	Tamb
At every towne and castle I besiege,	2Tamb	3.2.36	Tamb
And store of ordinance that from every flanke/May scoure the	2Tamb	3.2.79	Tamb
That there begin and nourish every part,	2Tamb	3.4.7	Capt
But that where every period ends with death,	2Tamb	4.2.47	Olymp
And every line begins with death againe:	2Tamb	4.2.48	Olymp
For every Fury gazeth on her lookes:	2Tamb	4.2.92	Therid
For every man that so offends shall die.	2Tamb	4.3.76	Tamb
Of [ever] <every> greene Selinus queintly dect/With bloomes	2Tamb	4.3.121	Tamb
Whose tender blossoms tremble every one,	2Tamb	4.3.123	Tamb
At every little breath that thorow heaven is blowen:	2Tamb	4.3.124	Tamb
Makes walles a fresh with every thing that falles/Into the	2Tamb	5.1.18	Govnr
Who flies away at every glance I give,	2Tamb	5.3.70	Tamb
And thus are wee on every side inrich'd:	Jew	1.1.104	Barab
Many in France, and wealthy every one:	Jew	1.1.127	Barab
like enough, why then let every man/Provide him, and be there	Jew	1.1.170	Barab
but for every one of those,/Had they beene valued at	Jew	1.2.185	Barab
lumpe of clay/That will with every water wash to dirt:	Jew	1.2.217	Barab
For evils are apt to happen every day.	Jew	1.2.223	Barab
Every ones price is written on his backe,	Jew	2.3.3	2Offcr
And every Moone made some or other mad,	Jew	2.3.195	Barab
Thus every villaine ambles after wealth/Although he ne're be	Jew	3.4.52	Barab
For every yeare they swell, and yet they live;	Jew	4.1.6	Barab
Will every savour breed a pangue of death?	P 72	2.15	Guise
That hanges for every peasant to atchive?	P 98	2.41	Guise
And every hower I will visite you.	P 272	4.70	Charls
Now every man put of his burgonet,	P 449	7.89	Guise
My lord of Cornewall now, at every worde,	Edw	1.2.17	Lncstr
My lord I heare it whispered every where,	Edw	1.4.106	Gavstn
For every looke, my lord, drops downe a teare,	Edw	1.4.136	Gavstn
And every earth is fit for buriall.	Edw	5.1.146	Edward
At every ten miles end thou hast a horse.	Edw	5.4.42	Mortmr
O would my bloud dropt out from every vaine,	Edw	5.5.66	Edward
Yet levell at the end of every Art,	F 32	1.1.4	Faust
So shall the spirits <subjects> of every element,	F 149	1.1.121	Valdes
with me, and after meate/We'le canvase every quidditie thereof:	F 191	1.1.163	Faust
Figures of every adjunct to the heavens,	F 239	1.3.11	Faust
And every creature shall be purifi'd,	F 514	2.1.126	Mephst
And bring them every morning to thy bed:	F 538	2.1.150	Mephst
hath every Spheare a Dominion, or Intelligentia <Inteligentij>?	F 607	2.2.56	P Faust
like to Ovids Flea, I can creepe into every corner of a Wench:	F 665	2.2.114	P Pride
in every good towne and Citie>,	F 699	(HC264) A	P Glutny
Must every bit be spiced with a Crosse?	F1066	3.2.86	Faust
[Now is his fame spread forth in every land],	F1149	3.3.62A	3Chor
When every servile groome jeasts at my wrongs,	F1329	4.2.5	Benvol
when every Tree is barren of his fruite, from whence you had	F1579	4.6.22	P Duke
Be both your legs bedfellowes every night together?	F1645	4.6.88	P Carter
end be such/As every Christian heart laments to thinke on:	F1996	5.3.14	2Schol
that I may be here and there and every where, O Ile tickle the	F App	p.231 63	P Clown
Nature, and every power shal give thee place,	Lucan, First Booke		51
Though every blast it nod, and seeme to fal,	Lucan, First Booke		142
and every yeare/Frauds and corruption in the field of Mars;	Lucan, First Booke		181
Here every band applauded,/And with their hands held up, all	Lucan, First Booke		387
heady rout/That in chain'd troupes breake forth at every port;	Lucan, First Booke		489
and every vaine/Did threaten horror from the host of Caesar;	Lucan, First Booke		620
When she will, day shines every where most pure.	Ovid's Elegies		1.8.10
If thy great fame in every region stood?	Ovid's Elegies		3.5.90
But be surpris'd with every garish toy.	Hero and Leander		1.480
At every stroke, betwixt them would he slide,	Hero and Leander		2.184
And every lim did as a soldier stout,	Hero and Leander		2.271
EVERY DAY			
For evils are apt to happen every day.	Jew	1.2.223	Barab
EVERY ONES			
Every ones price is written on his backe,	Jew	2.3.3	2Offcr
EVERY THING			
Makes walles a fresh with every thing that falles/Into the	2Tamb	5.1.18	Govnr
EVERY WHERE			
His cole-blacke collours every where advaunst,	1Tamb	5.1.9	Govnr
But every where fils every Continent,	2Tamb	2.2.51	Orcan
My lord I heare it whispered every where,	Edw	1.4.106	Gavstn
that I may be here and there and every where, O Ile tickle the	F App	p.231 63	P Clown
When she will, day shines every where most pure.	Ovid's Elegies		1.8.10
EVIDENCE			
I must be forc'd to give in evidence,	Jew	4.1.186	Barab
EVILL			
Strike on the boord like them that pray for evill,	Ovid's Elegies		1.4.27
As evill wood throwne in the high-waies lie,	Ovid's Elegies		1.12.13
Alas a wench is a perpetuall evill.	Ovid's Elegies		2.5.4
Plaies, maskes, and all that stern age counteth evill.	Hero and Leander		1.302
EVILLY			
Yet evilly faining anger, strove she still,	Hero and Leander		1.335
EVILS			
For evils are apt to happen every day.	Jew	1.2.223	Barab
plaine not heavens, but gladly beare these evils/For Neros sake:	Lucan, First Booke		37
O Roome thy selfe art cause of all these evils,	Lucan, First Booke		84
EWE			
Nor the milde Ewe gifts from the Ramme doth pull.	Ovid's Elegies		1.10.28
EXALTED			
If cold noysome Saturne/Were now exalted, and with blew beames	Lucan, First Booke		651
EXAMINE			
But now my friends, let me examine ye,	2Tamb	1.3.172	Tamb

EXAMINE (cont.)			
<examine> them of their <several> names and dispositions.	F 661	2.2.110	P Belzeb
EXAMPLE			
No, for this example I'le remaine a Jew:	Jew	4.1.195	Barab
Shall take example by [his] <their> punishment,	P1186	22.48	King
And thy step-father fights by thy example.	Ovid's Elegies		2.9.48
EXASPERATE			
The [Lords] <Lord> would not be too exasperate,	1Tamb	1.1.182	Ortyg
But that will more exasperate his wrath,	Edw	1.4.182	Queene
EXCEDING			
As his exceding favours have deserv'd,	1Tamb	3.2.10	Zenoc
EXCEED			
Engins and munition/Exceed the forces of their martial men.	1Tamb	4.1.29	2Msngr
If thou exceed thy elder Brothers worth,	2Tamb	1.3.50	Tamb
Let not thy love exceed thyne honor sonne,	2Tamb	5.3.199	Tamb
My lord, these titles far exceed my worth.	Edw	1.1.157	Gavstn
wherein through use he's known/To exceed his maister, that	Lucan, First Booke		326
were wont/In large spread heire to exceed the rest of France;	Lucan, First Booke		439
footsteps bending)/Doth testifie that you exceed her farre,	Hero and Leander		1.211
As thou in beautie doest exceed Loves mother/Nor heaven, nor	Hero and Leander		1.222
EXCEEDES			
none thy face exceedes,/Aye me, thy body hath no worthy weedes.	Ovid's Elegies		1.8.25
EXCEEDETH			
His resolution far exceedeth all:	1Tamb	4.1.48	2Msngr
EXCEEDING			
In every part exceeding brave and rich.	1Tamb	1.2.127	Souldr
Laden with riches, and exceeding store/Of Persian silkes, of	Jew	1.1.87	2Merch
Your extreme right does me exceeding wrong:	Jew	1.2.153	Barab
and lippes, exceeding his/That leapt into the water for a kis	Hero and Leander		1.73
EXCEEDINGLY			
And passe their fixed boundes exceedingly.	2Tamb	4.3.47	Therid
EXCEEDS			
Which make reports it far exceeds the Kings.	1Tamb	2.2.42	Spy
And therefore farre exceeds my credit, Sir.	Jew	1.1.65	1Merch
But his dominion that exceeds <excells> in this,	F 87	1.1.59	Faust
EXCELENT			
Tis shame their wits should be more excelent.	Ovid's Elegies		1.10.26
EXCELL			
My mouth in speaking did all birds excell.	Ovid's Elegies		2.6.62
Beauty gives heart, Corinnas lookes excell,	Ovid's Elegies		2.17.7
And I in dutie will excell all other,	Hero and Leander		1.221
EXCELLD			
[His Arte excelld, although his witte was weake].	Ovid's Elegies		1.15.14
EXCELLENCE (See also INEXCELLENCE)			
The first affecter of your excellence,	1Tamb	5.1.379	Philem
How fares it this morning with your excellence?	P 966	19.36	King
Shall adde more excellence unto thine Art,	F1208	4.1.54	Emper
That we may wonder at their excellence.	F1234	4.1.80	Emper
[And only Paragon of excellence],	F1703	5.1.30A	1Schol
EXCELLENCY			
And in your lives your fathers excellency.	2Tamb	2.4.76	Zenoc
EXCELLENT			
staffe; excellent, he stands as if he were begging of Bacon.	Jew	4.1.154	P Ithimr
Oh excellent!	Jew	5.5.42	Govnr
Excellent well, take this for thy rewarde.	Edw	5.5.117	Gurney
was> made for man; then he's <therefore is man> more excellent.	F 560	2.2.9	Mephst
that's excellent:	F1133	3.3.46	P Robin
This sport is excellent: wee'l call and wake him.	F1281	4.1.127	Emper
An excellent policie:	F1389	4.2.65	P Mrtino
that's excellent, for one of his devils turn'd me into the	F1553	4.5.49	P Dick
EXCELLING			
Excelling all, [whose sweete delight's] dispute/In th'heavenly	F 18	Prol.18	1Chor
Excelling all, <whose sweete delight disputes>	F 18	(HC256)A	1Chor
Excelling all, <and sweetly can dispute>	F 18	(HC256)B	1Chor
EXCELLS			
But his dominion that exceeds <excells> in this,	F 87	1.1.59	Faust
EXCELS			
Thinke water farre excels all earthly things:	Hero and Leander		1.260
EXCEPT			
But should that man of men (Dido except)/Have taunted me in	Dido	3.3.26	Iarbus
Not angred me, except in angring thee.	Dido	3.4.15	Dido
Except he place his Tables in the streets.	Jew	5.3.35	Calym
Maddame, I beseech your grace to except this simple gift.	P 166	3.1	P Pothec
unlesse <except> the ground be <were> perfum'd, and cover'd	F 670	2.2.119	P Pride
Deflowr'd except, within thy Temple wall.	Ovid's Elegies		1.7.18
EXCEPTING			
Excepting against Doctors [axioms],	P 393	7.33	Guise
EXCEPTIONS			
Doth no man take exceptions at the slave?	Edw	1.2.25	MortSr
That he would take exceptions at my buttons,	Edw	2.1.47	Baldck
EXCESSE			
Betokening valour and excesse of strength:	1Tamb	2.1.28	Menaph
Excesse of wealth is cause of covetousnesse:	Jew	1.2.123	Govnr
EXCESSIVE			
But malice, falshood, and excessive pride,	Jew	1.1.117	Barab
EXCHANGE			
We thinke it losse to make exchange for that/We are assured of	1Tamb	1.2.216	Techel
That bleedes within me for this strange exchange.	Edw	5.1.35	Edward
EXCLAIME			
And openly exclaime against the King.	1Tamb	1.1.149	Ceneus
But I must to the Jew and exclaime on him,	Jew	3.6.42	2Fryar
then goe with me/And helpe me to exclaime against the Jew.	Jew	3.6.46	2Fryar
I curse thee and exclaime thee miscreant,	P1075	19.145	QnMoth

EXCLAIME (cont.)			
Cry out, exclaime, houle till thy throat be hoarce,	P1077	19.147	King
EXCLAIMES			
With fierce exclaimes run to the Senate-house,	Jew	1.2.232	Abigal
EXCLAMATIONS			
things past recovery/Are hardly cur'd with exclamations.	Jew	1.2.237	Barab
EXCLAMES			
Grave [Governor], list not to his exclames:	Jew	1.2.128	1Knght
EXCLUDING			
Excluding Regions which I meane to trace,	1Tamb	4.4.77	Tamb
EXCLUD'ST			
[That from thy soule exclud'st the grace of heaven],	F1789	5.1.116A	OldMan
EXCLUDST			
Excludst a lover, how wouldst use a foe?	Ovid's Elegies		1.6.31
EXCOMMUNICATE			
Pope excommunicate, Philip depose,	P1012	19.82	Guise
Both he and thou shalt stand excommunicate,	F 908	3.1.130	Pope
EXCREMENTS			
And cleare my bodie from foule excrements.	Edw	5.3.26	Edward
EXCRUCIAT			
May styl excruciat his tormented thoughts.	1Tamb	5.1.301	Bajzth
EXCRUCIATE			
But this it is that doth excruciate/The verie substance of my	1Tamb	1.1.113	Cosroe
Wherewith he may excruciate thy soule.	1Tamb	3.2.104	Agidas
EXCUSDE			
As I shall be commended and excusde/For turning my poore charge	1Tamb	2.3.28	Therid
Ile not sift much, but hold thee soone excusde,	Ovid's Elegies		3.13.41
EXCUSE (See also SCUSE)			
On your submission we with thanks excuse,	1Tamb	2.5.13	Cosroe
My wisedome shall excuse my cowardise:	2Tamb	4.1.50	Calyph
What needst thou, love, thus to excuse thy selfe?	Edw	2.1.60	Neece
Infringing all excuse of modest shame,	Lucan, First Booke		266
Object thou then what she may well excuse,	Ovid's Elegies		2.2.37
vowd he love, she wanting no excuse/To feed him with delaies,	Hero and Leander		1.425
EXCUSES			
And many poore excuses did she find,	Hero and Leander		2.6
EXECRABLE			
Sweete Faustus leave that execrable Art.	F 404	2.1.16	GdAngl
Thou damned wretch, and execrable dogge,	F App	p.238 72	Knight
EXECUTE			
(If tyrannies wars justice ye repute)/I execute, enjoin'd me	2Tamb	4.1.148	Tamb
I execute, and he sustaines the blame.	P 132	2.75	Guise
cause,/That here severelie we will execute/Upon thy person:	Edw	2.5.23	Warwck
Ready to execute what thou commandst <desirst>.	F 549	2.1.161	Mephst
EXECUTED			
Such another word, and I will have thee executed.	1Tamb	2.4.30	Mycet
EXECUTES			
Contrives, imagines and fully executes/Matters of importe, aimed	P 110	2.53	Guise
EXECUTION			
The rest forward with execution,	2Tamb	5.1.124	Tamb
looking of a Fryars Execution, whom I saluted with an old	Jew	4.2.18	P Pilia
going to the execution, a fellow met me with a muschatoes like	Jew	4.2.27	P Ithimr
Do speedie execution on them all,	Edw	3.1.254	Edward
man, they say there is great execution/Done through the realme,	Edw	4.3.6	Edward
for you to come within fortie foot of the place of execution,	F 211	1.2.18	P Wagner
EXEMPT			
What? is not pietie exempt from woe?	Dido	1.1.79	Venus
And must maintaine my life exempt from servitude.	1Tamb	1.2.31	Tamb
EXEMPTED			
Angry I was, but feare my wrath exempted.	Ovid's Elegies		2.13.4
EXEQUIES			
Then after all these solemne Exequies,	1Tamb	5.1.533	Tamb
To celebrate your fathers exequies,	Edw	1.1.176	BshpCv
Is dead, al-fowles her exequies frequent.	Ovid's Elegies		2.6.2
EXERCISDE			
I will with Engines, never exercisde,	2Tamb	4.1.191	Tamb
Beauty not exercisde with age is spent,	Ovid's Elegies		1.8.53
EXERCISE			
lord, specially having so smal a walke, and so litle exercise.	1Tamb	4.4.106	P Therid
But since I exercise a greater name,	2Tamb	4.1.153	Tamb
To exercise upon such guiltlesse Dames,	2Tamb	4.3.79	Orcan
mortified lineaments/Should exercise the motions of my heart,	2Tamb	5.3.189	Amyras
but the Exercise being done, see where he comes.	Jew	4.2.20	P Pilia
For falling to a divellish exercise,	F 23	Prol.23	1Chor
EXHALATION			
As when a fiery exhalation/Wrapt in the bowels of a freezing	1Tamb	4.2.43	Tamb
EXHALATIONE			
thus fall Imperfett exhalatione/which our great sonn of fraunce	Paris	ms19,p390	Guise
EXHALATIONS			
Even as when windy exhalations,	1Tamb	1.2.50	Tamb
And kindle heaps of exhalations,	2Tamb	3.2.3	Tamb
EXHAL'D			
As I exhal'd with thy fire darting beames,	Dido	1.1.25	Jupitr
EXHALED			
Shall here unburden their exhaled sweetes,	Dido	5.1.14	Aeneas
EXHEREDITARE			
Exhereditare filium non potest pater, nisi--Such is the	F 58	1.1.30	P Faust
EXHIBITION			
That livest by forraine exhibition?	P 842	17.37	Eprnon
EXHORT			
Whose fiendfull fortune may exhort the wise/Onely to wonder at	F2006	5.3.24	4Chor
EXHORTATION			
It may be this my exhortation/Seemes harsh, and all unpleasant;	F1717	5.1.44	OldMan

EXIGENT				
hee shall nct be put to that exigent, I warrant thee.	2Tamb	3.5.156	P	Soria
EXIGENTS				
And drives his nobles to these exigents/For Gaveston, will if	Edw	2.5.62		Warwck
EXILD				
Exild forth Europe and wide Asia both,	Dido	1.1.229		Aeneas
Tis like encugh, for since he was exild,	Edw	2.1.23		Baldck
EXILDE				
And by thy meanes is Gaveston exilde.	Edw	1.4.155		Edward
EXILE				
Then thou hast beene of me since thy exile.	Edw	1.1.145		Edward
That wert the onely cause of his exile.	Edw	1.1.179		Edward
Ile be revengd on him for my exile.	Edw	1.1.192		Gavstn
That slie inveigling Frenchman weele exile,	Edw	1.2.57		Mortmr
Here is the forme of Gavestons exile:	Edw	1.4.1		Lncstr
Subscribe as we have done to his exile.	Edw	1.4.53		ArchBp
The greefe for his exile was not so much,	Edw	2.1.57		Neece
We from our houses driven, most willingly/Suffered exile:	Lucan, First Booke			280
Poore lover with thy gransires I exile thee.	Ovid's Elegies			1.8.66
EXILED				
The sight of London tc my exiled eyes,	Edw	1.1.10		Gavstn
But like exiled aire thrust from his sphere,	Hero and Leander			2.118
EXPECT				
And through my prcvinces you must expect/Letters of conduct	1Tamb	1.2.23		Tamb
And kingdomes at the least we all expect,	1Tamb	1.2.218		Usumc
our neighbour kings/Expect our power and our royall presence,	2Tamb	2.2.4		Orcan
Such newes as I expect, come Bartley, come,	Edw	5.1.129		Edward
Doctor, yet ere you goe, expect from me a bounteous reward.	F App	p.239 88	P	Emper
EXPECTED				
May triumph in our long expected Fate.	1Tamb	2.3.44		Tamb
EXPECTING				
I know not what expecting, I ere while/Nam'd Achelaus, Inachus,	Ovid's Elegies			3.5.103
EXPECTS				
Expects th'arrivall of her highnesse person.	1Tamb	1.2.79		Agidas
EXPECTST				
Vaine man, what Monarky expectst thou here?	Dido	5.1.34		Hermes
EXPEDITION				
And for the expeditien of this war,	1Tamb	3.3.20		Bassoe
Tamburlaine, by expedition/Advantage takes of your unreadinesse.	1Tamb	4.1.38		Capol
of Fesse have brought/To aide thee in this Turkish expedition,	2Tamb	1.3.131		Usumc
With expedition to assaile the Pagan,	2Tamb	2.1.62		Sgsmnd
Whether we next make expedition.	2Tamb	4.3.94		Tamb
EXPEL				
As no commiseration may expel,	F App	p.243 43		OldMan
the sonne decrees/To expel the father; share the world thou	Lucan, First Booke			291
EXPEL'D				
From doubtfull Roome wrongly expel'd the Tribunes,	Lucan, First Booke			269
EXPELD				
A faire maides care expeld this sluggishnesse,	Ovid's Elegies			1.9.43
EXPELL				
Expell the hate wherewith he paines our soules.	2Tamb	4.1.173		Orcan
And he meanes quickly to expell you hence;	Jew	2.2.38		Bosco
Therefore if he be ccme, expell him straight.	Edw	1.1.106		Lncstr
A trifle, weele expell him when we please:	Edw	2.2.10		Edward
EXPENCE				
defence/When [un-protected] <un-protested> ther is no expence?	Ovid's Elegies			2.2.12
EXPERIENCE				
And now to make experience of my love,	Dido	4.4.64		Dido
But now experience, purchased with griefe,	Jew	3.3.61		Abigal
Faustus, these bookes, thy wit, and our experience,	F 146	1.1.118		Valdes
I, thinke sc still, till experience change thy mind.	F 517	2.1.129		Mephst
EXPERT				
With twenty thousand expert souldiers.	1Tamb	2.5.25		Cosroe
A hundred thousand expert souldiers:	2Tamb	1.3.132		Usumc
EXPIAT				
To expiat which sinne, kisse and shake hands,	Hero and Leander			1.309
EXPIATE				
dye to expiate/The griefe that tires upon thine inward soule.	Dido	5.1.316		Iarbus
EXPIRE				
Long shalt thou rest when Fates expire thy breath.	Ovid's Elegies			2.9.42
EXPIRED				
grant unto them that foure and twentie yeares being expired,	F 496	2.1.108	P	Faust
I writ them a bill with mine owne bloud, the date is expired:	F1861	5.2.65	P	Faust
EXPLOITS				
But new exploits do hale him out agen,	F 770	2.3.49		2Chor
and thou shalt see/This Conjurer performe such rare exploits,	F1186	4.1.32		Mrtino
how they had wonne by prowesse such exploits, gote such riches,	F App	p.236 20	P	Emper
EXPRESLESSE				
staid, with wrath and hate/Of our expreslesse band inflictions.	1Tamb	5.1.282		Bajzth
EXPRESSE				
Yet insufficient to expresse the same:	1Tamb	1.1.2		Mycet
Yet have I words left to expresse my joy:	Edw	2.2.60		Gavstn
No mortall can expresse the paines of hell.	F1716	5.1.43		OldMan
If thou deniest foole, Ile our deeds expresse,	Ovid's Elegies			2.8.25
Each crosse waies ccrner doth as much expresse.	Ovid's Elegies			3.1.18
So through the world shold bright renown expresse me.	Ovid's Elegies			3.1.64
EXPRESSES				
Her trembling mouth these unmeete sounds expresses.	Ovid's Elegies			3.5.72
EXQUISITE				
More exquisite than ever Traitor felt.	2Tamb	5.1.53		Therid
EXTASIE				
Our words will but increase his extasie.	Jew	1.2.210		1Jew

EXTASIES			
And have no hope to end our extasies.	1Tamb	5.1.238	Bajzth
EXTEND			
Shall Tamburlain extend his puisant arme.	1Tamb	3.3.247	Tamb
Affrick to the banks/Of Ganges, shall his mighty arme extend.	1Tamb	5.1.521	Tamb
EXTENDED			
And let your hates extended in his paines,	2Tamb	4.1.172	Orcan
EXTERIOR			
No, nor to any one exterior sence,	Hero and Leander		1.271
EXTERNALL			
who aimes at nothing but externall trash,	F 62	1.1.34	Faust
EXTERPATIONE			
gathered now shall ayme/more at thie end then exterpatione	Paris	ms29,p391	Guise
EXTINGUISH			
sweet embraces <imbracings> may extinguish cleare <cleane>,	F1763	5.1.90	Faust
EXTINGUISHED			
Is almost cleane extinguished and spent,	2Tamb	5.3.89	Phsitn
EXTINGUISHT			
which cannot be extinguisht but by bloud.	P 93	2.36	Guise
EXTIRPATION (See EXTERPATIONE)			
EXTOL			
Your speech will stay, or so extol his worth,	1Tamb	2.3.27	Therid
EXTORTING			
And with extorting, cozening, forfeiting,	Jew	2.3.191	Barab
EXTORTION			
Why did you yeeld to their extortion?	Jew	1.2.177	Barab
EXTRACTS			
And simplest extracts of all Minerals,	2Tamb	4.2.61	Olymp
EXTREAME			
Though we be now in extreame miserie,	Dido	1.1.157	Achat
In which extreame my minde here murthered is:	Edw	5.1.55	Edward
Drye winters aye, and sunnes in heate extreame.	Ovid's Elegies		3.5.106
EXTREAMES			
And lighten our extreames with this one boone,	Dido	1.1.196	Aeneas
overweighing heavens/Have kept to qualifie these hot extreames,	1Tamb	5.1.46	Govnr
Night, Love, and wine to all extreames perswade:	Ovid's Elegies		1.6.59
EXTREAMEST			
enoughe to worke/thy Just degestione with extreamest shame	Paris	ms27,p391	Guise
EXTREAMS			
And might, if my extreams had full events,	1Tamb	3.2.16	Zenoc
EXTREME			
Your extreme right does me exceeding wrong:	Jew	1.2.153	Barab
to everlasting paines/And extreme tortures of the fiery deepe,	Jew	1.2.167	Barab
And hide these extreme sorrowes from mine eyes:	Jew	1.2.195	Barab
But thou wert set upon extreme revenge,	Jew	3.3.42	Abigal
Nor hope of thee but extreme cruelty,	Jew	5.2.59	Govnr
EXTREMITIE			
To succour him in this extremitie.	Dido	1.1.133	Venus
by me, for in extremitie/We ought to make barre of no policie.	Jew	1.2.272	Barab
EXTREMITIES			
And of extremities elect the least.	1Tamb	3.2.96	Agidas
EXTREMITY			
And what we did, was in extremity:	2Tamb	1.1.105	Sgsmnd
But now begins the extremity of heat/To pinch me with	Jew	5.5.87	Barab
EXUE			
Oro, si quis [adhuc] <ad haec> precibus locus, exue mentem.	Dido	5.1.138	Dido
EYDE			
While Junos watch-man Io too much eyde,	Ovid's Elegies		2.2.45
EYE (See also EIE)			
Sweet Jupiter, if ere I pleasde thine eye,	Dido	1.1.19	Ganimd
Or in these shades deceiv'st mine eye so oft?	Dido	1.1.244	Aeneas
Thy mind Aeneas that would have it so/Deludes thy eye sight,	Dido	2.1.32	Achat
What stranger art thou that doest eye me thus?	Dido	2.1.74	Dido
Because his lothsome sight offends mine eye,	Dido	3.1.57	Dido
Lest their grosse eye-beames taint my lovers cheekes:	Dido	3.1.74	Dido
That should detaine thy eye in his defects?	Dido	3.4.17	Aeneas
The man that I doe eye where ere I am,	Dido	3.4.18	Dido
Mine eye is fixt where fancie cannot start,	Dido	4.2.37	Iarbus
And looke upon him with a Mermaides eye,	Dido	5.1.201	Dido
Now Phoebus ope the eye-lids of the day,	Jew	2.1.60	Barab
eye up to the Jewes counting-house where I saw some bags of	Jew	3.1.18	P Pilia
Assure thy selfe thou shalt have broth by the eye.	Jew	3.4.92	Barab
What an eye she casts on me?	Jew	4.2.128	P Ithimr
For she is that huge blemish in our eye,	P 80	2.23	Guise
I, dearer then the apple of mine eye?	P 685	13.29	Guise
In sight and judgement of thy lustfull eye?	P 687	13.31	Guise
Or looking downeward, with your eye lids close,	Edw	2.1.39	Spencr
your right eye be alwaies Diametrally fixt upon my left heele,	F 386	1.4.44	P Wagner
She whom thine eye shall like, thy heart shall have,	F 539	2.1.151	Mephst
[The] <Whose> buildings faire, and gorgeous to the eye,	F 788	3.1.10	Faust
And what might please mine eye, I there beheld.	F 853	3.1.75	Faust
That no eye may thy body see.	F1003	3.2.23	Mephst
O may these eye-lids never close againe,	F1332	4.2.8	Benvol
Shall be perform'd in twinkling of an eye.	F1767	5.1.94	Mephst
the Scriptures, then I turn'd the leaves/And led thine eye.	F1889	5.2.93	Mephst
Faire natures eye, rise, rise againe and make/Perpetuall day:	F1931	5.2.135	Faust
and let thy left eye be diametarily fixt upon my right heele,	F App	p.231 69	P Wagner
Words without voyce shall on my eye browes sit,	Ovid's Elegies		1.4.19
and in her eyes/Two eye-balles shine, and double light thence	Ovid's Elegies		1.8.16
I sawe your nodding eye-browes much to speake,	Ovid's Elegies		2.5.15
A pleasant smiling cheeke, a speaking eye,	Hero and Leander		1.85
EYE-BALLES			
and in her eyes/Two eye-balles shine, and double light thence	Ovid's Elegies		1.8.16

EYE-BEAMES			
Lest their grosse eye-beames taint my lovers cheekes:	Dido	3.1.74	Dido
EYE-BROWES			
I sawe your nodding eye-browes much to speake,	Ovid's Elegies		2.5.15
EYE BROWES			
Words without voyce shall on my eye browes sit,	Ovid's Elegies		1.4.19
EYE-LIDS			
Now Phoebus ope the eye-lids of the day,	Jew	2.1.60	Barab
O may these eye-lids never close againe,	F1332	4.2.8	Benvol
EYE LIDS			
Or looking downeward, with your eye lids close,	Edw	2.1.39	Spencr
EYELIDS			
And in his eyelids hanging by the nayles,	Dido	2.1.245	Aeneas
EYES			
Whose face reflects such pleasure to mine eyes,	Dido	1.1.24	Jupitr
To feede her eyes with his engraven fame.	Dido	1.1.103	Jupitr
The while thine eyes attract their sought for joyes:	Dido	1.1.136	Venus
Thou art a Goddesse that delud'st our eyes,	Dido	1.1.191	Aeneas
Achates though mine eyes say this is stone,	Dido	2.1.24	Aeneas
To force an hundred watchfull eyes to sleepe:	Dido	2.1.146	Aeneas
and both his eyes/Turnd up to heaven as one resolv'd to dye,	Dido	2.1.151	Aeneas
came Hectors ghost/With ashie visage, blewish sulphure eyes,	Dido	2.1.202	Aeneas
And with Megeras eyes stared in their face,	Dido	2.1.230	Aeneas
Then pull out both mine eyes, or let me dye.	Dido	3.1.55	Iarbus
His glistering eyes shall be my looking glasse,	Dido	3.1.86	Dido
But I will teare thy eyes fro forth thy head,	Dido	3.2.34	Venus
And feedes his eyes with favours of her Court,	Dido	3.2.71	Juno
Why, man of Troy, doe I offend thine eyes?	Dido	3.3.17	Iarbus
Aeneas no, although his eyes doe pearce.	Dido	3.4.12	Dido
And rather had seeme faire [to] Sirens eyes,	Dido	3.4.39	Dido
him to his ships/That now afflicts me with his flattering eyes.	Dido	4.2.22	Iarbus
Or drop out both mine eyes in drisling teares,	Dido	4.2.41	Iarbus
For I will flye from these alluring eyes,	Dido	4.2.50	Iarbus
Yet Dido casts her eyes like anchors out,	Dido	4.3.25	Aeneas
And wanton motions of alluring eyes,	Dido	4.3.35	Achat
been/When Didos beautie [chaind] <chaungd> thine eyes to her:	Dido	5.1.114	Dido
And hide these extreme sorrowes from mine eyes:	Jew	1.2.195	Barab
No sleepe can fasten on my watchfull eyes,	Jew	2.1.17	Barab
Blindes Europs eyes and troubleth our estate:	P 152	2.95	Guise
Her eyes and lookes sow'd seeds of perjury,	P 695	13.39	Guise
The sight of London to my exiled eyes,	Edw	1.1.10	Gavstn
Or that these teares that drissell from mine eyes,	Edw	2.4.19	Queene
Whose eyes are fixt on none but Gaveston:	Edw	2.4.62	Queene
And though devorsed from king Edwards eyes,	Edw	2.5.3	Gavstn
O might I never open these eyes againe,	Edw	4.7.41	Edward
Make for a new life man, throw up thy eyes,	Edw	4.7.107	Baldck
So shall my eyes receive their last content,	Edw	5.1.61	Edward
And Isabell, whose eyes [being] <beene> turnd to steele,	Edw	5.1.104	Edward
Come death, and with thy fingers close my eyes,	Edw	5.1.110	Edward
Whome I esteeme as deare as these mine eyes,	Edw	5.2.18	Queene
I view the prince with Aristarchus eyes,	Edw	5.4.54	Mortmr
And what eyes can refraine from shedding teares,	Edw	5.5.50	Ltborn
For not these ten daies have these eyes lids closd.	Edw	5.5.94	Edward
And let these teares distilling from mine eyes,	Edw	5.6.101	King
containes <containeth> for to delight thine eyes <thee with>,	F 810	3.1.32	Mephst
[I leave untold, your eyes shall see performd].	F1154	3.3.67A	3Chor
What shall [his] eyes doe?	F1386	4.2.62	P Fredrk
wee'l put out his eyes, and they shall serve for buttons to his	F1387	4.2.63	P Benvol
Now Faustus let thine eyes with horror stare/Into that vaste	F1909	5.2.113	BdAngl
it is not in my abilitie to present before your eyes, the true	F App	p.237 42	P Faust
fearefull men, and blasts their eyes/With overthwarting flames,	Lucan, First Booke		155
Bescratch mine eyes, spare not my lockes to breake,	Ovid's Elegies		1.7.65
Fame saith as I suspect, and in her eyes/Two eye-balles shine,	Ovid's Elegies		1.8.15
When on thy lappe thine eyes thou dost deject,	Ovid's Elegies		1.8.37
And let thine eyes constrained learne to weepe,	Ovid's Elegies		1.8.83
But her bleare eyes, balde scalpes [thin] <thine> hoary flieces	Ovid's Elegies		1.8.111
The other eyes his rivall as his foe.	Ovid's Elegies		1.9.18
No more this beauty mine eyes captivates.	Ovid's Elegies		1.10.10
I charge thee marke her eyes and front in reading,	Ovid's Elegies		1.11.17
blotted letter/On the last edge to stay mine eyes the better.	Ovid's Elegies		1.11.22
Oft was she drest before mine eyes, yet never,	Ovid's Elegies		1.14.17
Bee not to see with wonted eyes inclinde,	Ovid's Elegies		1.14.37
Condemne his eyes, and say there is no tryall.	Ovid's Elegies		2.2.58
Not silent were thine eyes, the boord with wine/Was scribled,	Ovid's Elegies		2.5.17
But when on thee her angry eyes did rush,	Ovid's Elegies		2.8.15
By me, and by my starres, thy radiant eyes.	Ovid's Elegies		2.16.44
(O face most cunning mine eyes to detaine)/Thou oughtst	Ovid's Elegies		2.17.12
Thou also that late tookest mine eyes away,	Ovid's Elegies		2.19.19
The other smilde, (I wot) with wanton eyes,	Ovid's Elegies		3.1.33
either heed/What please them, and their eyes let either feede.	Ovid's Elegies		3.2.6
She smilde, and with quicke eyes behight some grace:	Ovid's Elegies		3.2.83
Sharpe eyes she had:	Ovid's Elegies		3.3.9
By her eyes I remember late she swore,	Ovid's Elegies		3.3.13
And by mine eyes, and mine were pained sore.	Ovid's Elegies		3.3.14
The Gods have eyes, and brests as well as men.	Ovid's Elegies		3.3.42
Or in mine eyes good wench no paine transfuse.	Ovid's Elegies		3.3.48
Argus had either way an hundred eyes,	Ovid's Elegies		3.4.19
Why weepst? and spoilst with teares thy watry eyes?	Ovid's Elegies		3.5.57
shee her modest eyes held downe,/Her wofull bosome a warme	Ovid's Elegies		3.5.67
her coate hood-winckt her fearefull eyes,/And into water	Ovid's Elegies		3.5.79
Thy dying eyes here did thy mother close,	Ovid's Elegies		3.8.49
And by thine eyes whose radiance burnes out mine.	Ovid's Elegies		3.10.48
her body throes/Upon his bosome, where with yeelding eyes,	Hero and Leander		2.47

EYES (cont.)			
Whence his admiring eyes more pleasure tooke,	Hero and Leander	2.325	
EYE SIGHT			
Thy mind Aeneas that would have it so/Deludes thy eye sight,	Dido	2.1.32	Achat
EYTHER			
And eyther die, or live with Gaveston.	Edw	1.1.138	Edward
Tis not amisse my liege for eyther part,	Edw	3.1.190	SpncrP
FA			
do you remember the dogs fa--	F1665	4.6.108	P Robin
FABLE			
<Come>, I thinke Hel's a fable.	F 516	2.1.128	Faust
In heaven was never more notorious fable.	Ovid's Elegies	1.9.40	
FABLES			
No Faustus they be but Fables.	F 613	2.2.62	P Mephst
FAC'D (See also FACST)			
Is't not a sweet fac'd youth, Pilia?	Jew	4.2.40	P Curtzn
Faire-fac'd Iulus, he went forth thy court.	Ovid's Elegies	3.8.14	
FACE (See also FA)			
Whose face reflects such pleasure to mine eyes,	Dido	1.1.24	Jupitr
To make thee fannes wherewith to coole thy face,	Dido	1.1.35	Jupitr
Might we but once more see Aeneas face,	Dido	1.2.45	Serg
Blest be the time I see Achates face.	Dido	2.1.56	Illion
And with Megeras eyes stared in their face,	Dido	2.1.230	Aeneas
At which the franticke Queene leapt on his face,	Dido	2.1.244	Aeneas
The people swarme to gaze him in the face.	Dido	3.1.72	Anna
I know this face, he is a Persian borne,	Dido	3.1.144	Serg
heire of [fame] <furie>, the favorite of the [fates] <face>,	Dido	3.2.3	Juno
What, darest thou looke a Lyon in the face?	Dido	3.3.39	Dido
Whose amorous face like Pean sparkles fire,	Dido	3.4.19	Dido
And fanne it in Aeneas lovely face,	Dido	4.4.49	Dido
That I might see Aeneas in his face:	Dido	5.1.150	Dido
Why star'st thou in my face?	Dido	5.1.179	Dido
But Lady, this faire face and heavenly hew,	1Tamb	1.2.36	Tamb
And by thy martiall face and stout aspect,	1Tamb	1.2.170	Tamb
The face and personage of a woondrous man:	1Tamb	2.1.32	Cosroe
To cast up hils against the face of heaven:	1Tamb	2.6.3	Cosroe
Tis more then pitty such a heavenly face/Should by hearts	1Tamb	3.2.4	Agidas
And sprinklest Saphyrs on thy shining face,	1Tamb	5.1.143	Tamb
Hide now thy stained face in endles night,	1Tamb	5.1.292	Bajzth
Fling the meat in his face.	1Tamb	5.1.315	P Zabina
Plac'd by her side, looke on their mothers face.	2Tamb	1.3.20	Tamb
Even in the cannons face shall raise a hill/Of earth and fagots	2Tamb	3.3.21	Therid
Then scortch a face so beautiful as this,	2Tamb	3.4.74	Techel
In spight of death I will goe show my face.	2Tamb	5.3.114	Tamb
O the sweetest face that ever I beheld!	Jew	3.1.26	P Ithimr
Whose face has bin a grind-stone for mens swords,	Jew	4.3.9	Barab
Pale death may walke in furrowes of my face:	P 158	2.101	Guise
My Mother poysoned heere before my face:	P 187	3.22	Navrre
Yet dare you brave the king unto his face.	Edw	1.1.116	Kent
Smiles in his face, and whispers in his eares,	Edw	1.2.52	Queene
That to my face he threatens civill warres.	Edw	2.2.233	Edward
Traitor on thy face, rebellious Lancaster.	Edw	3.1.204	Spencr
And yet she beares a face of love forsooth:	Edw	4.6.14	Kent
Father, thy face should harbor no deceit,	Edw	4.7.8	Edward
No, but wash your face, and shave away your beard,	Edw	5.3.31	Gurney
For which God threw him from the face of heaven.	F 296	1.3.68	Mephst
Think'st thou that I [who] saw the face of God,	F 305	1.3.77	Mephst
boy in your face, you have seene many boyes with [such	F 344	1.4.2	P Robin
We veiw'd the face of heaven, of earth and hell.	F 848	3.1.70	Faust
Cursed be he that stroke his holinesse a blow [on] the face.	F1079	3.2.99	1Frier
Never out face me for the matter, for sure the cup is betweene	F1107	3.3.20	P Vintnr
one of his devils turn'd me into the likenesse of an Apes face.	F1554	4.5.50	P Dick
Was this the face that Launcht a thousand ships,	F1768	5.1.95	Faust
Cursed be hee that strooke his holinesse a blowe on the face.	F App	p.232 33	Frier
when by Junoes taske/He had before lookt Pluto in the face.	Lucan, First Booke	576	
Even in his face his offered [Gobbets] <Goblets> cast.	Ovid's Elegies	1.4.34	
griefe appease)/With thy sharpe nayles upon my face to seaze.	Ovid's Elegies	1.7.64	
none thy face exceedes,/Aye me, thy body hath no worthy weedes.	Ovid's Elegies	1.8.25	
While thou wert plaine, I lov'd thy minde and face:	Ovid's Elegies	1.10.13	
Nor morning starres shunne thy uprising face.	Ovid's Elegies	1.13.28	
But when I praise a pretty wenches face/Shee in requitall doth	Ovid's Elegies	2.1.33	
No one face likes me best, all faces moove,	Ovid's Elegies	2.4.9	
A scarlet blush her guilty face arayed.	Ovid's Elegies	2.5.34	
Seeing her face, mine upreard armes discended,	Ovid's Elegies	2.5.47	
Achilles burnt with face of captive Briseis,	Ovid's Elegies	2.8.11	
In all thy face will be no crimsen bloud.	Ovid's Elegies	2.11.28	
Not though thy face in all things make thee raigne,	Ovid's Elegies	2.17.11	
(O face most cunning mine eyes to detaine)/Thou oughtst	Ovid's Elegies	2.17.12	
And yet remaines the face she had before.	Ovid's Elegies	3.3.2	
Nor doth her face please, but her husbands love;	Ovid's Elegies	3.4.27	
Her deeds gaine hate, her face entreateth love:	Ovid's Elegies	3.10.43	
And by thy face to me a powre divine,	Ovid's Elegies	3.10.47	
But with your robes, put on an honest face,	Ovid's Elegies	3.13.27	
And looking in her face, was strooken blind.	Hero and Leander	1.38	
of liquid pearle, which downe her face/Made milk-white paths,	Hero and Leander	1.297	
Viewing Leanders face, fell downe and fainted.	Hero and Leander	2.2	
He heav'd him up, and looking on his face,	Hero and Leander	2.171	
FACES			
In whose sterne faces shin'd the quenchles fire,	Dido	2.1.186	Aeneas
Whose coleblacke faces make their foes retire,	2Tamb	1.3.142	Techel
Whose lovely faces never any viewed,	2Tamb	3.2.30	Tamb
order, Il'e nere trust smooth faces, and small ruffes more.	F1318	4.1.164	P Benvol

FACES (cont.)
And on their faces heapes of Roses strow. . . . . . Ovid's Elegies 1.2.40
No one face likes me best, all faces moove, . . . Ovid's Elegies 2.4.9

FACIO
signumque crucis quod nunc facio; et per vota nostra ipse nunc F 249 1.3.21 P Faust

FAC'ST
A Velvet cap'de cloake, fac'st before with Serge, . . Edw 2.1.34 Spencr

FACST
We will not thus be facst and overpeerd. . . . . . Edw 1.4.19 Mortmr

FACT
yesterday/There where the porch doth Danaus fact display. Ovid's Elegies 2.2.4
Which fact, and country wealth Halesus fled. . . . Ovid's Elegies 3.12.32

FACTION
And others of our partie and faction, ... Edw 4.2.53 Mortmr

FACTIONS
New factions rise; now through the world againe/I goe; o . Lucan, First Booke 691

FACTIOUS
To overthrow those [sectious] <sexious> <factious> Puritans: P 850 17.45 Guise
this of me, a factious lord/Shall hardly do himselfe good, Edw 2.1.6 Spencr

FACTOR
And bid my Factor bring his loading in. . . . . . Jew 1.1.83 Barab
My Factor sends me word a Merchant's fled/That owes me for a Jew 2.3.243 Barab

FACTORS
Nay on my life it is my Factors hand, ... Jew 2.3.240 Barab

FACTS
Will rattle foorth his facts of war and blood. . . . . 1Tamb 3.2.45 Agidas
To meete for poyson or vilde facts we crave not, . . Ovid's Elegies 2.2.63

FACULTIES
whose faculties can comprehend/The wondrous Architecture of the 1Tamb 2.7.21 Tamb

FADE
That if I perish, heaven and earth may fade. . . . 2Tamb 5.3.60 Tamb
her good wishes fade,/Let with strong hand the reine to bend be Ovid's Elegies 3.2.71

FADING
Whose fading weale of victorie forsooke, ... Dido 1.2.15 Illion
Smother the earth with never fading mistes: . . . . 1Tamb 5.1.296 Bajzth

FAGOTS
shall raise a hill/Of earth and fagots higher than thy Fort, 2Tamb 3.3.22 Therid
And on a pile of Fagots burnt to death. . . . . . F 963 3.1.185 Faust

FAIL (See FAIE)

FAILDE
And was the second cause why vigor failde mee: . . . . Ovid's Elegies 3.6.38

FAILE (See also FAYLE)
And yet I know my beauty doth not faile. . . . . . Jew 3.1.5 Curtzn
And so I will, oh Jaccmo, faile not but come. . . . Jew 4.1.108 Barab
Doe so, but faile nct; now farewell Ferneze: . . . . Jew 5.2.109 Barab
O holde me up, my sight begins to faile, ... P 548 11.13 Charls
A boye, our friends do faile us all in Fraunce, . . . Edw 4.2.1 Queene
Il'e make you feele something anon, if my Art faile me not. F1246 4.1.92 P Faust
But when thou comest they of their courses faile. . . Ovid's Elegies 1.13.12
And waters force, force helping Gods to faile, . . . Ovid's Elegies 2.16.28

FAILES
study, shee's borne to beare with me, or else my Art failes. F App p.233 17 P Robin
What should I do with fortune that nere failes me? . . Ovid's Elegies 2.19.7
When deepe perswading Oratorie failes. . . . . . Hero and Leander 2.226

FAIN'D
Mars, or Jupiter,/Fain'd, but are [erring] <evening> Starres. F 595 2.2.44 Mephst

FAIND
And without ground, fear'd, what themselves had faind: . Lucan, First Booke 482
And she that on a faind Bull swamme to land, ... Ovid's Elegies 1.3.23

FAINE (Homograph)
I faine would goe, yet beautie calles me backe: . . . Dido 4.3.46 Aeneas
Aeneas will not faine with his deare love, ... Dido 5.1.92 Aeneas
Faine would I finde some means to speak with him/But cannot, P 662 13.6 Duchss
faine would I have a booke wherein I might beholde al spels and F 551.1 2.1.164A P Faust
I know you'd <faine> see the Pope/And take some part of holy F 831 3.1.53 Mephst
sir, I would make nothing of you, but I would faine know that. F1649 4.6.92 P Carter
too, which bouldly faine themselves/The Romanes brethren, Lucan, First Booke 428
Vaine causes faine of him the true to hide, ... Ovid's Elegies 2.2.31
And faine by stealth away she would have crept, . . . Hero and Leander 2.310

FAINED
Hence fained weeds, unfained are my woes, ... Edw 4.7.97 Edward

FAINING
Yet evilly faining anger, strove she still, ... Hero and Leander 1.335

FAINT
Father I faint, good father give me meate. . . . . Dido 1.1.163 Ascan
And rest attemplesse, faint and destitute? . . . . 1Tamb 2.5.74 Tamb
while you faint-hearted base Egyptians, ... 1Tamb 4.1.8 Souldn
To harbour thoughts effeminate and faint? . . . . . 1Tamb 5.1.177 Tamb
Souldier shall defile/His manly fingers with so faint a boy. 2Tamb 4.1.164 Tamb
My heart did never quake, or corrage faint. . . . . 2Tamb 5.1.106 Govnr
Which being faint and weary with the siege, ... 2Tamb 5.2.7 Callap
My heart doth faint, I dye. . . . . P 186 3.21 OldQn
My heart doth break, I faint and dye. . . . . . . P 550 11.15 Charls
sweat and dust/All chockt well neare, begin to faint for heate, Edw 3.1.192 SpncrP
No Edward, no, thy flatterers faint and flie. . . . Edw 3.1.201 Mortmr
Venus is faint; swift Hermes retrograde; . . . . . Lucan, First Booke 661
My selfe was dull, and faint, to sloth inclinde, . . . Ovid's Elegies 1.9.41
Thou leav'st his bed, because hees faint through age, . Ovid's Elegies 1.13.37
And I grow faint, as with some spirit haunted? . . . Ovid's Elegies 3.6.36
Through numming cold, all feeble, faint and wan: . . . Hero and Leander 2.246

FAINTED
Viewing Leanders face, fell downe and fainted. . . . Hero and Leander 2.2

FAINTHEART
And hunt that coward, faintheart runaway, ... 2Tamb 3.2.149 Tamb

FAINTHEART (cont.)			
Fill'd with a packe of faintheart Fugitives,	2Tamb	5.1.36	Govnr
FAINT-HEARTED			
While you faint-hearted base Egyptians,	1Tamb	4.1.8	Souldn
FAINTHEARTED			
cowards and fainthearted runawaies,/Looke for orations when the	1Tamb	1.2.130	Techel
FAINTING			
In vaine my love thou spendst thy fainting breath,	Dido	5.1.153	Aeneas
go before and charge/The fainting army of that foolish King.	1Tamb	2.3.62	Cosroe
To drive all sorrow from my fainting soule:	1Tamb	5.1.429	Arabia
Here Jove, receive his fainting soule againe,	2Tamb	4.1.111	Tamb
Which [strike] <strikes> a terror to my fainting soule.	F 310	1.3.82	Mephst
The fainting seedes of naughtinesse doth kill.	Ovid's Elegies		3.4.10
His fainting hand in death engrasped mee.	Ovid's Elegies		3.8.58
FAINTLY			
And with unwilling souldiers faintly arm'd,	1Tamb	2.1.66	Cosroe
O faintly joyn'd friends with ambition blind,	Lucan, First Booke		87
FAINTNES			
And faintnes numm'd his steps there on the brincke:	Lucan, First Booke		196
FAINTNESSE			
And all with faintnesse and for foule disgrace,	2Tamb	2.4.5	Tamb
What faintnesse should dismay our courages,	2Tamb	5.1.21	Govnr
FAINTS			
What, faints Aeneas to remember Troy?	Dido	2.1.118	Dido
FAIR (See also FAYRE)			
Sindge these fair plaines, and make them seeme as black/As is	2Tamb	3.2.11	Tamb
FAIRE			
Or seemed faire walde in with Egles wings,	Dido	1.1.20	Ganimd
In those faire walles I promist him of yore:	Dido	1.1.85	Jupitr
But what may I faire Virgin call your name?	Dido	1.1.188	Aeneas
And fertile in faire Ceres furrowed wealth,	Dido	1.2.22	Cloan
vouchsafe of ruth/To tell us who inhabits this faire towne,	Dido	2.1.41	Aeneas
Which made the funerall flame that burnt faire Troy:	Dido	2.1.218	Aeneas
mine armes, and by the hand/Led faire Creusa my beloved wife,	Dido	2.1.267	Aeneas
Faire child stay thou with Didos waiting maide,	Dido	2.1.304	Venus
I will faire mother, and so play my part,	Dido	2.1.332	Cupid
How long faire Dido shall I pine for thee?	Dido	3.1.7	Iarbus
Is not Aeneas faire and beautifull?	Dido	3.1.63	Dido
In whose faire bosome I will locke more wealth,	Dido	3.1.92	Dido
And are not these as faire as faire may be?	Dido	3.1.140	Dido
I this in Greece when Paris stole faire Helen.	Dido	3.1.142	Aeneas
Should ere defile so faire a mouth as thine:	Dido	3.2.27	Juno
And thy faire peacockes by my pigeons pearch:	Dido	3.2.59	Venus
Faire Queene of love, I will devorce these doubts,	Dido	3.2.85	Juno
Faire Troian, hold my golden bowe awhile,	Dido	3.3.7	Dido
Then would I wish me in faire Didos armes,	Dido	3.3.48	Iarbus
And here we met faire Venus virgine like,	Dido	3.3.54	Achat
What meanes faire Dido by this doubtfull speech?	Dido	3.4.31	Aeneas
And rather had seeme faire [to] Sirens eyes,	Dido	3.4.39	Dido
By heaven and earth, and my faire brothers bowe,	Dido	3.4.45	Aeneas
Faire Anna, how escapt you from the shower?	Dido	4.1.29	Aeneas
This kisse shall be faire Didos punishment.	Dido	4.4.37	Aeneas
Faire sister Anna leade my lover forth,	Dido	4.4.65	Dido
Am I lesse faire then when thou sawest me first?	Dido	5.1.115	Dido
Would, as faire Troy was, Carthage might be sackt,	Dido	5.1.147	Dido
Call him not wicked, sister, speake him faire,	Dido	5.1.200	Dido
I goe faire sister, heavens graunt good successe.	Dido	5.1.211	Anna
Dido, faire Dido wils Aeneas stay:	Dido	5.1.233	Anna
But Lady, this faire face and heavenly hew,	1Tamb	1.2.36	Tamb
And then my selfe to faire Zenocrate.	1Tamb	1.2.105	Tamb
Or faire Bootes sends his cheerefull light,	1Tamb	1.2.207	Tamb
And now faire Madam, and my noble Lords,	1Tamb	1.2.253	Tamb
In faire Persea noble Tamburlaine/Shall be my Regent, and	1Tamb	2.1.48	Cosroe
with amitie we yeeld/Our utmost service to the faire Cosroe.	1Tamb	2.3.34	Techel
And now we will to faire Persepolis,	1Tamb	2.5.24	Cosroe
To follow me to faire Persepolis.	1Tamb	2.5.40	Cosroe
Ah faire Zenocrate,/Let not a man so vile and barbarous,	1Tamb	3.2.25	Agidas
So lookes my Lordly love, faire Tamburlaine.	1Tamb	3.2.49	Zenoc
Ah faire Zabina, we have lost the field.	1Tamb	3.3.233	Bajzth
Yet in revenge of faire Zenocrate,	1Tamb	4.1.43	Souldn
the faire Arabian king/That hath bene disapointed by this	1Tamb	4.1.68	Souldn
Of my faire daughter, and his princely Love:	1Tamb	4.1.70	Souldn
To faire Damascus, where we now remaine,	1Tamb	4.2.99	Tamb
Or kept the faire Zenocrate so long,	1Tamb	4.3.41	Souldn
Then raise your seige from faire Damascus walles,	1Tamb	4.4.71	Zenoc
And all the friendes of faire Zenocrate,	1Tamb	4.4.88	Tamb
Ah faire Zenocrate, divine Zenocrate,	1Tamb	5.1.135	Tamb
Faire is too foule an Epithite for thee,	1Tamb	5.1.136	Tamb
For faire Zenocrate, that so laments his state.	1Tamb	5.1.205	Therid
Ah faire Zabina, we may curse his power,	1Tamb	5.1.230	Bajzth
Send like defence of faire Arabia.	1Tamb	5.1.402	Zenoc
And let Zenocrates faire eies beholde/That as for her thou	1Tamb	5.1.408	Arabia
As much as thy faire body is for me.	1Tamb	5.1.416	Zenoc
Then doubt I not but faire Zenocrate/Will soone consent to	1Tamb	5.1.498	Tamb
With this great Turke and his faire Emperesse:	1Tamb	5.1.532	Tamb
But what became of faire Zenocrate,	2Tamb	Prol.6	Prolog
Now have we martcht from faire Natolia/Two hundred leagues, and	2Tamb	1.1.6	Orcan
And make faire Europe mounted on her bull,	2Tamb	1.1.42	Orcan
I will dispatch chiefe of my army hence/To faire Natolia, and	2Tamb	1.1.162	Orcan
As faire as was Pigmalions Ivory gyrle,	2Tamb	1.2.38	Callap
shine as bright/As that faire vail that covers all the world:	2Tamb	1.2.50	Callap
Now bright Zenocrate, the worlds faire eie,	2Tamb	1.3.1	Tamb
Now rest thee here on faire Larissa Plaines,	2Tamb	1.3.5	Tamb

FAIRE (cont.)

And leave his steeds to faire Boetes charge:	2Tamb	1.3.170	Tamb
Now will we march frcm proud Orminius mount/To faire Natolia,	2Tamb	2.2.3	Orcan
Tell me, how fares my faire Zenocrate?	2Tamb	2.4.41	Tamb
For taking hence my faire Zenocrate.	2Tamb	2.4.101	Tamb
That shew faire weather to the neighbor morne.	2Tamb	3.1.48	Jrslem
And him faire Lady shall thy eies behold.	2Tamb	3.4.67	Therid
land, whose brave Metropolis/Reedified the faire Semyramis,	2Tamb	3.5.37	Orcan
My sterne aspect shall make faire Victory,	2Tamb	3.5.162	Tamb
Blush, blush faire citie, at thine honors foile,	2Tamb	4.1.107	Tamb
Thou shalt be stately Queene of faire Argier,	2Tamb	4.2.39	Therid
And as thou took'st the faire Proserpina,	2Tamb	4.3.36	Orcan
Raise me to match the faire Aldeboran,	2Tamb	4.3.61	Tamb
The stately buildings of faire Babylon,	2Tamb	5.1.63	Tamb
Now in the place where faire Semiramis,	2Tamb	5.1.73	Tamb
Now fetch the hearse of faire Zenocrate,	2Tamb	5.3.210	Tamb
Intreat 'em faire, and give them friendly speech,	Jew	1.2.286	Barab
Faire Abigall the rich Jewes daughter/Become a Nun?	Jew	1.2.366	Mthias
A faire young maid scarce fourteene yeares of age,	Jew	1.2.378	Mthias
Is she so faire?	Jew	1.2.384	Lodowk
And if she be so faire as you report,	Jew	1.2.388	Lodowk
I have bought a house/As great and faire as is the Governors;	Jew	2.3.14	Barab
For Don Mathias tels me she is faire.	Jew	2.3.35	Lodowk
Yond walks the Jew, now for faire Abigall.	Jew	2.3.38	Lodowk
Lord Lodowicke, it sparkles bright and faire.	Jew	2.3.58	Barab
I feare me 'tis about faire Abigall.	Jew	2.3.139	Mthias
Daughter, a word more; kisse him, speake him faire,	Jew	2.3.234	Barab
Whither but to my faire love Abigall?	Jew	2.3.252	Mthias
Then my faire Abigal should frowne on me.	Jew	2.3.332	Lodowk
Shall Lodowicke rob me of so faire a love?	Jew	2.3.347	Mthias
And so did faire Maria send for me:	Jew	3.6.5	1Fryar
And so doe I, master, therfore speake 'em faire.	Jew	4.1.27	Ithimr
I'le feast you, lodge you, give you faire words,	Jew	4.1.126	Barab
Let me alone, doe but you speake him faire:	Jew	4.2.63	Pilia
Had late been pluckt from out faire Cupids wing:	P 668	13.12	Duchss
But yet it is no paine to speake men faire,	Edw	1.1.42	Gavstn
What should a priest do with so faire a house?	Edw	1.1.206	Gavstn
It bootes me not to threat, I must speake faire,	Edw	1.4.63	Edward
I must entreat him, I must speake him faire,	Edw	1.4.183	Queene
Faire Queene forbeare to angle for the fish,	Edw	1.4.221	Mortmr
For thee faire Queene, if thou lovest Gaveston,	Edw	1.4.327	Edward
My gentle lord, bespeake these nobles faire,	Edw	1.4.337	Queene
A loftie Cedar tree faire flourishing,	Edw	2.2.16	Mortmr
For as the lovers of faire Danae,	Edw	2.2.53	Edward
My lord, dissemble with her, speake her faire.	Edw	2.2.229	Gavstn
And all in vaine, for when I speake him faire,	Edw	2.4.28	Queene
Faire blowes the winde for Fraunce, blowe gentle gale,	Edw	4.1.1	Kent
A faire commission warrants what we do.	Edw	4.7.48	Rice
That Edward may be still faire Englands king:	Edw	5.1.68	Edward
Call them againe my lorde, and speake them faire,	Edw	5.1.91	Leistr
Faire Isabell, now have we our desire,	Edw	5.2.1	Mortmr
Farewell faire Queene, weepe not for Mortimer,	Edw	5.6.64	Mortmr
And make swift Rhine, circle faire Wittenberge <Wertenberge>:	F 116	1.1.88	Faust
I tell thee Faustus it is <tis> not halfe so faire/As thou, or	F 557	2.2.6	Mephst
faire a paire of hornes on's head as e're thou sawest in thy	F 737	2.3.16	P Robin
[The] <Whose> buildings faire, and gorgeous to the eye,	F 788	3.1.10	Faust
That this faire Lady, whilest she liv'd on earth,	F1266	4.1.112	Emper
since our conference about faire Ladies, which was the	F1682	5.1.9	P 1Schol
<Was this faire Hellen, whose admired worth>/<Made Greece with	F1696	(HC269)B	2Schol
Faire natures eye, rise, rise againe and make/Perpetuall day:	F1931	5.2.135	Faust
the second time, aware the third, I give you faire warning.	F App	p.232 21	P Faust
til I am past this faire and pleasant greene, ile walke on	F App	p.239 96	P Faust
Who'le set the faire treste [sunne] <sonne> in battell ray,	Ovid's Elegies		1.1.15
Vulcan will give thee Chariots rich and faire.	Ovid's Elegies		1.2.24
With beautie of thy wings, thy faire haire guilded,	Ovid's Elegies		1.2.41
That I may write things worthy thy faire lookes:	Ovid's Elegies		1.3.20
Marveile not though the faire Bride did incite/The drunken	Ovid's Elegies		1.4.7
Resembling faire Semiramis going to bed,	Ovid's Elegies		1.5.11
For thee I did thy mistris faire entreate.	Ovid's Elegies		1.6.20
As thou art faire, would thou wert fortunate,	Ovid's Elegies		1.8.27
Faire women play, shee's chast whom none will have,	Ovid's Elegies		1.8.43
Who seekes, for being faire, a night to have,	Ovid's Elegies		1.8.67
A faire maides care expeld this sluggishnesse,	Ovid's Elegies		1.9.43
Faire Dames for-beare rewards for nights to crave,	Ovid's Elegies		1.10.47
I hate faire Paper should writte matter lacke.	Ovid's Elegies		1.11.20
Thou art as faire as shee, then kisse and play.	Ovid's Elegies		1.13.44
But what had beene more faire had they beene kept?	Ovid's Elegies		1.14.3
Faire Phoebus leade me to the Muses springs.	Ovid's Elegies		1.15.36
Wenches apply your faire lookes to my verse/Which golden love	Ovid's Elegies		2.1.37
Why so was Ledas, yet was Leda faire.	Ovid's Elegies		2.4.42
And scratch her faire soft cheekes I did intend.	Ovid's Elegies		2.5.46
If some faire wench me secretly behold,	Ovid's Elegies		2.7.5
Worthy to keembe none but a Goddesse faire,	Ovid's Elegies		2.8.2
Yet Love, if thou with thy faire mother heare,	Ovid's Elegies		2.9.51
Thou also, that wert borne faire, hadst decayed,	Ovid's Elegies		2.14.19
Thou ring that shalt my faire girles finger binde,	Ovid's Elegies		2.15.1
Since some faire one I should of force obey.	Ovid's Elegies		2.17.6
What would not she give that faire name to winne?	Ovid's Elegies		2.17.30
To please me, what faire termes and sweet words ha's shee,	Ovid's Elegies		2.19.17
But thou of thy faire damsell too secure,	Ovid's Elegies		2.19.37
Foule dust, from her faire body, go away.	Ovid's Elegies		3.2.42
Faire white with rose red was before commixt:	Ovid's Elegies		3.3.5
The wronged Gods dread faire ones to offend,	Ovid's Elegies		3.3.31

FAIRE (cont.)

Cannot a faire one, if not chast, please thee?	Ovid's Elegies	3.4.41	
When our bockes did my mistris faire content, . . .	Ovid's Elegies	3.7.5	
Faire-fac'd Iulus, he went forth thy court.	Ovid's Elegies	3.8.14	
Or lesse faire, or lesse lewd would thou mightst bee, .	Ovid's Elegies	3.10.41	
Seeing thou art faire, I barre not thy false playing, .	Ovid's Elegies	3.13.1	
At Sestos, Hero dwelt; Hero the faire, ...	Hero and Leander	1.5	
So lovely faire was Hero, Venus Nun, ...	Hero and Leander	1.45	
Faire Cinthia wisht, his armes might be her spheare, .	Hero and Leander	1.59	
Though thou be faire, yet be not thine owne thrall. . .	Hero and Leander	1.90	
So faire a church as this, had Venus none, . . .	Hero and Leander	1.135	
Of Christall shining faire, the pavement was, . . .	Hero and Leander	1.141	
Faire creature, let me speake without offence, . . .	Hero and Leander	1.199	
To lead thy thoughts, as thy faire lookes doe mine, . .	Hero and Leander	1.201	
Be not unkind and faire, mishapen stuffe/Are of behaviour	Hero and Leander	1.203	
But this faire jem, sweet in the losse alone, . . .	Hero and Leander	1.247	
So she be faire, but some vile toongs will blot? . .	Hero and Leander	1.286	
But you are faire (aye me) so wondrous faire, . . .	Hero and Leander	1.287	
Faire fooles delight to be accounted nice. . . .	Hero and Leander	1.326	
And too too well the faire vermilion knew, . . .	Hero and Leander	1.395	
At his faire feathered feet, the engins layd, . . .	Hero and Leander	1.449	
Playd with a boy so faire and [so] kind, ...	Hero and Leander	2.195	

FAIRE-FAC'D

Faire-fac'd Iulus, he went forth thy court.	Ovid's Elegies	3.8.14	

FAIRER

For I will grace them with a fairer frame, ...	Dido	5.1.5	Aeneas
Fairer than whitest snow on Scythian hils, ...	1Tamb	1.2.89	Tamb
I, Didst thou ever see a fairer?	1Tamb	2.4.28	Mycet
Fairer than rockes of pearle and pretious stone, . .	1Tamb	3.3.118	Tamb
Now Hell is fairer than Elisian, ...	2Tamb	4.2.87	Therid
O thou art fairer then the evenings <evening> aire, . .	F1781	5.1.108	Faust

FAIREST

And fairest pearle of welthie India/Were mounted here under a	2Tamb	3.2.121	Tamb
Who shal kisse the fairest of the Turkes Concubines first, when	2Tamb	4.1.64	P Calyph
And resolution honors fairest aime.	P 96	2.39	Guise
the fairest Maid in Germany, for I am wanton and lascivious,	F 529	2.1.141	P Faust
I'le cull thee out the fairest Curtezans, ...	F 537	2.1.149	Mephst
This seemes the fairest, so doth that to mee, . . .	Ovid's Elegies	2.10.7	
Some say, for her the fairest Cupid pyn'd, . . .	Hero and Leander	1.37	

FAIRIES

I thinke some Fairies have beguiled me.	Dido	5.1.215	Nurse

'FAITH (See also YFAITH)

the horses, I scorn't 'faith, I have other matters in hand,	F 726	2.3.5	P Robin
That's like, 'faith:	F 734	2.3.13	P Dick
your foolery, for an my Maister come, he'le conjure you 'faith.	F 735	2.3.14	P Dick
'Faith you are too outragious, but come neere, . . .	F1609	4.6.52	Faust
'faith Ile drinke a health to thy wooden leg for that word.	F1626	4.6.69	P HrsCsr

FAITH (See also FAYTHE, IFAITH, YFAITH)

Thy hand and mine have plighted mutuall faith, . . .	Dido	5.1.122	Dido
Nor ever violated faith to him:	Dido	5.1.205	Dido
And make him false his faith unto his King, . . .	1Tamb	2.2.27	Meandr
With utmost vertue of my faith and dutie. . . .	1Tamb	2.5.17	Meandr
Twil proove a pretie jest (in faith) my friends. . .	1Tamb	2.5.90	Tamb
Faith, and Techelles, it was manly done:	1Tamb	3.2.109	Usumc
Wherin the change I use condemns my faith, . . .	1Tamb	5.1.390	Zenoc
In whom no faith nor true religion rests, ...	2Tamb	2.1.34	Baldwn
But as the faith which they prophanely plight/Is not by .	2Tamb	2.1.37	Baldwn
tis superstition/To stand so strictly on dispensive faith:	2Tamb	2.1.50	Fredrk
And since this miscreant hath disgrac'd his faith, . .	2Tamb	2.3.36	Orcan
Nor you in faith, but that you wil be thought/More childish	2Tamb.	4.1.16	Calyph
For I can see no fruits in all their faith, ...	Jew	1.1.116	Barab
scambled up/More wealth by farre then those that brag of faith.	Jew	1.1.123	Barab
Proceed from sinne, or want of faith in us, . . .	Jew	1.2.323	Abigal
Hinder her not, thou man of little faith, ...	Jew	1.2.340	1Fryar
Faith, Sir, my birth is but meane, my name's Ithimor, .	Jew	2.3.165	Ithimr
Faith, Master,/In setting Christian villages on fire, . .	Jew	2.3.202	Ithimr
Faith is not to be held with Heretickes;	Jew	2.3.311	Barab
Then gentle Abigal plight thy faith to me.	Jew	2.3.315	Lodowk
Faith Master, I thinke by this/You purchase both their lives;	Jew	2.3.365	Ithimr
Faith, walking the backe lanes through the Gardens I chanc'd to	Jew	3.1.17	P Pilia
I have beene zealous in the Jewish faith, ...	Jew	4.1.51	Barab
No by my faith Madam.	P 498	9.17	Guise
Then shall the Catholick faith of Rome, ...	P 639	12.52	QnMoth
these our warres/Against the proud disturbers of the faith,	P 700	14.3	Navrre
To plant the true succession of the faith, ...	P 715	14.18	Bartus
How now my Lord, faith this is more then need, . . .	P 757	15.15	Guise
Scarce can I name salvation, faith, or heaven, . . .	F 570	2.2.19	Faust
No faith, not much upon a wooden leg.	F1631	4.6.74	Faust
His faith is great, I cannot touch his soule; . . .	F1756	5.1.83	Mephst
[As in this furnace God shal try my faith], . . .	F1792	5.1.119A	OldMan
[My faith, vile hel, shall triumph over thee], . . .	F1793	5.1.120A	OldMan
Shall never faith be found in fellow kings. . . .	Lucan, First Booke	92	
If men have Faith, Ile live with thee for ever. . . .	Ovid's Elegies	1.3.16	
(If I have faith) I sawe the starres drop bloud, . . .	Ovid's Elegies	1.8.11	
Let poore men show their service, faith, and care; . .	Ovid's Elegies	1.10.57	
Never to harme me made thy faith evasion.	Ovid's Elegies	1.11.6	
To staine all faith in truth, by false crimes use. . .	Ovid's Elegies	2.2.38	
And to the end your constant faith stood fixt. . . .	Ovid's Elegies	2.6.14	
But what availde this faith? her rarest hue? . . .	Ovid's Elegies	2.6.17	
Joyes with uncertaine faith thou takest and brings. . .	Ovid's Elegies	2.9.50	
Let her my faith with thee given understand. . . .	Ovid's Elegies	2.15.28	
So long they be, since she her faith forsooke. . . .	Ovid's Elegies	3.3.4	
Was I: thou liv'dst, while thou esteemdst my faith. . .	Ovid's Elegies	3.8.56	

FAITH (cont.)

Faith to the witnesse Joves praise doth apply, . . .	Ovid's Elegies	3.9.23		
(Love is too full of faith, too credulous, . . .	Hero and Leander	2.221		

FAITHFULL

Meander, thou my faithfull Counsellor, ...	1Tamb	1.1.28		Mycet
Worthy the worship of all faithfull hearts, ...	2Tamb	2.2.57		Orcan
for your sake, and said what a faithfull servant you had bin.	Jew	4.2.109	P	Pilia
that Navarre may be/Esteemed faithfull to the King of France:	P1148	22.10		Navrre
And tell her Henry dyes her faithfull freend. . . .	P1244	22.106		King
Our friend [Levune] <Lewne>, faithfull and full of trust,	Edw	3.1.60		Queene
to her I consecrate/My faithfull tables being vile maple late.	Ovid's Elegies	1.11.28		
For faithfull love will never turne to hate. . . .	Hero and Leander	1.128		

FAITHLESSE

No faithlesse witch in Thessale waters bath'd thee. . .	Ovid's Elegies	1.14.40		
The filthy prison faithlesse breasts restraines. . .	Ovid's Elegies	2.2.42		

FAITHS

Yet those infirmities that thus defame/Their faiths, their	2Tamb	2.1.45		Sgsmnd
Our faiths are sound, and must be [consumate] <consinuate>,	2Tamb	2.1.47		Sgsmnd
Faiths breach, and hence came war to most men welcom. .	Lucan, First Booke	184		

FAL

Go to, fal to your meat:	1Tamb	4.4.54	P	Tamb
Fal starres that governe his nativity, ...	2Tamb	5.3.2		Therid
Though every blast it nod, and seeme to fal, ...	Lucan, First Booke	142		
Which makes the maine saile fal with hideous sound; . .	Lucan, First Booke	498		
And Commets that presage the fal of kingdoms. . . .	Lucan, First Booke	527		
Or steeds might fal forcd with thick clouds approch. .	Ovid's Elegies	1.13.30		

FALCE

all to good, be Augury vaine, and Tages/Th'arts master falce.	Lucan, First Booke	636		

FALCHION (See FAULCHIONS)

FALCONET (See FAUKNETS)

FALE

When causes fale thee to require a gift, ...	Ovid's Elegies	1.8.93		

FALL

I cannot choose but fall upon my knees, ...	Dido	2.1.11		Achat
For many tales goe of that Cities fall, ...	Dido	2.1.108		Dido
And when we whisper, then the starres fall downe, . . .	Dido	4.4.53		Dido
That they may melt and I fall in his armes:	Dido	5.1.245		Dido
And sooner shall the Sun fall from his Spheare, . . .	1Tamb	1.2.176		Tamb
And fall like mellowed fruit, with shakes of death, . . .	1Tamb	2.1.47		Cosroe
For neither rain can fall upon the earth, ...	1Tamb	3.1.51		Moroc
Before such hap fall to Zenocrate.	1Tamb	3.2.20		Agidas
Thy fall shall make me famous through the world: . . .	1Tamb	3.3.83		Tamb
But come my Lords, to weapons let us fall.	1Tamb	3.3.162		Tamb
And make her daintie fingers fall to woorke.	1Tamb	3.3.181		Ebea
That not a man should live to rue their fall.	1Tamb	4.1.35		Souldn
Fall prostrate on the lowe disdainefull earth.	1Tamb	4.2.13		Tamb
Ambitious pride shall make thee fall as low, ...	1Tamb	4.2.76		Bajzth
that the Souldan is/No more dismaide with tidings of his fall,	1Tamb	4.3.31		Souldn
Wel Zenocrate, Techelles, and the rest, fall to your victuals.	1Tamb	4.4.15	P	Tamb
Fall to, and never may your meat digest.	1Tamb	4.4.16		Bajzth
Sirra, why fall you not too, are you so daintily brought up, you	1Tamb	4.4.36	P	Tamb
shee will fall into a consumption with freatting, and then she	1Tamb	4.4.49	P	Tamb
In number more than are the drops that fall/When Boreas rents a	2Tamb	1.3.159		Tamb
of the clowdes/And fall as thick as haile upon our heads,	2Tamb	2.2.15		Gazell
Because the corners there may fall more flat, ...	2Tamb	3.2.65		Tamb
And with the breaches fall, smoake, fire, and dust, . . .	2Tamb	3.3.59		Therid
Fall to the earth, and pierce the pit of Hel, ...	2Tamb	5.1.44		Govnr
Triumphing in his fall whom you advaunst, ...	2Tamb	5.3.23		Techel
If your first curse fall heavy on thy head, ...	Jew	1.2.107		1Knght
her fathers sudden fall/Has humbled her and brought her downe	Jew	1.2.367		Mthias
and the rest of the family, stand or fall at your service.	Jew	4.2.44	P	Pilia
to fall into the hands/Of such a Traitor and unhallowed Jew!	Jew	5.2.12		Govnr
Doth fall asunder; so that it doth sinke/Into a deepe pit past	Jew	5.5.35		Barab
For he that did by treason worke our fall, ...	Jew	5.5.109		Govnr
Now must he fall and perish in his height.	P 946	19.16		Capt
thus fall Imperfett exhalatione/which our great sonn of fraunce	Paris	ms19,p390		Guise
Tis done, and now accursed hand fall off.	Edw	1.4.88		Edward
And threatenest death whether he rise or fall, ...	Edw	2.2.44		Edward
Upon my weapons point here shouldst thou fall, ...	Edw	2.5.13		Mortmr
Weaponles must I fall and die in bands, ...	Edw	2.6.3		Gavstn
How will you deale with Edward in his fall?	Edw	4.6.31		Kent
May in their fall be followed to their end.	Edw	4.6.79		Mortmr
and sore tempests driven/To fall on shoare, and here to pine in	Edw	4.7.35		Baldck
Spencer, all live to die, and rise to fall.	Edw	4.7.112		Baldck
Now as I speake they fall, and yet with feare/Open againe.	Edw	5.5.95		Edward
Why should I greeve at my declining fall?	Edw	5.6.63		Mortmr
Saba, or as beautifull/As was bright Lucifer before his fall.	F 542	2.1.154		Mephst
We saw the River Maine, fall into Rhine <Rhines>, . . .	F 785	3.1.7		Faust
But thus I fall to Peter, not to thee.	F 872	3.1.94		Bruno
Fall to, the Divell choke you an you spare.	F1039	3.2.59		Faust
Lord Raymond pray fall too, I am beholding/To the Bishop of	F1041	3.2.61		Pope
I, and I fall not asleepe i'th meane time.	F1196	4.1.42		Benvol
Hell take his soule, his body thus must fall.	F1363	4.2.39		Benvol
He that loves pleasure, must for pleasure fall. . . .	F1923	5.2.127		BdAngl
Mountaines and Hils, come, come, and fall on me, . . .	F1945	5.2.149		Faust
And fall into the Ocean, ne're be found.	F1978	5.2.182		Faust
Faustus is gone, regard his hellish fall, ...	F2005	5.3.23		4Chor
Fall too, and the divel choake you and you spare. . . .	F App	p.231 2	P	Faust
to lay the fury of this ghost, once again my Lord fall too.	F App	p.232 17	P	Pope
had bin fierd/Or dropping-ripe, ready to fall with Ruine,	Lucan, First Booke	491		
where shall I fall,/Thus borne aloft?	Lucan, First Booke	677		
So chast Minerva did Cassandra fall, ...	Ovid's Elegies	1.7.17		
rise/And who thou never think'st should fall downe lies. .	Ovid's Elegies	1.9.30		

Context	Work	Reference	Speaker
FALL (cont.)			
Bacchinall/That tyr'd doth rashly on the greene grasse fall.	Ovid's Elegies	1.14.22	
But yet sometimes to chide thee let her fall/Counterfet teares:	Ovid's Elegies	2.2.35	
Some one of these might make the chastest fall.	Ovid's Elegies	2.4.32	
For thy returne shall fall the vowd oblation,	Ovid's Elegies	2.11.46	
Fruites ripe will fall, let springing things increase,	Ovid's Elegies	2.14.25	
And in her bosome strangely fall at last.	Ovid's Elegies	2.15.14	
By charmes maste drops from okes, from vines grapes fall,	Ovid's Elegies	3.6.33	
Why letst discordant hands to armour fall?	Ovid's Elegies	3.7.48	
May that shame fall mine enemies chance to be.	Ovid's Elegies	3.10.16	
fellow bed, by all/The Gods who by thee to be perjurde fall,	Ovid's Elegies	3.10.46	
Her painted fanne of curled plumes let fall,	Hero and Leander	2.11	
FALLEN			
That rampiers fallen down, huge heapes of stone/Lye in our	Lucan, First Booke	25	
FALLES			
And now downe falles the keeles into the deepe:	Dido	5.1.253	Dido
Makes walles a fresh with every thing that falles/Into the	2Tamb	5.1.18	Govnr
Monarck goes/To wrack, and [his] antechristian kingdome falles.	P1198	22.60	King
Wherein the filthe of all the castell falles.	Edw	5.5.57	Edward
And guides my feete least stumbling falles they catch.	Ovid's Elegies	1.6.8	
But to my share a captive damsell falles.	Ovid's Elegies	2.12.8	
FALLIMUR			
Si peccasse negamus, fallimur, et nulla est in nobis veritas:	F 68	1.1.40	P Faust
FALLING			
joyntly both/Beating their breasts and falling on the ground,	Dido	2.1.228	Aeneas
For falling to a divellish exercise,	F 23	Prol.23	1Chor
Teares falling from repentant heavinesse/Of thy most vilde and	F App	p.243 39	OldMan
Maides words more vaine and light then falling leaves,	Ovid's Elegies	2.16.45	
And falling vallies be the smooth-wayes crowne.	Ovid's Elegies	2.16.52	
FALLS			
Alongst the ayre and [nought] <not> resisting it/Falls, and	Lucan, First Booke	158	
By shallow Rivers, to whose falls,	Passionate Shepherd	7	
FALNE			
What ailes my Queene, is she falne sicke of late?	Dido	3.4.24	Aeneas
Are falne in clusters at my conquering feet.	1Tamb	3.3.230	Tamb
As I cried out for feare he should have falne.	2Tamb	1.3.42	Zenoc
That thou art <he is> falne into that damned Art/For which they	F 221	1.2.28	1Schol
FALS (Homograph)			
The Terrene main wherin Danubius fals,	2Tamb	1.1.37	Orcan
Now fals the star whose influence governes France,	P 944	19.14	Capt
Under great burdens fals are ever greevous;	Lucan, First Booke	71	
Who running long, fals in a greater floud,	Lucan, First Booke	401	
bands were spread/Along Nar floud that into Tiber fals,	Lucan, First Booke	472	
And that slowe webbe nights fals-hood did unframe.	Ovid's Elegies	3.8.30	
FALSE (See also FALCE)			
Juno, false Juno in her Chariots pompe,	Dido	1.1.54	Venus
False Jupiter, rewardst thou vertue so?	Dido	1.1.78	Venus
And therewithall he calde false Sinon forth,	Dido	2.1.143	Aeneas
The boy wherein false destinie delights,	Dido	3.2.2	Juno
O false Aeneas, now the sea is rough,	Dido	4.4.26	Dido
I, and unlesse the destinies be false,	Dido	4.4.81	Aeneas
Where thou and false Achates first set foote:	Dido	5.1.175	Dido
O cursed hagge and false dissembling wretch!	Dido	5.1.216	Dido
But I cride out, Aeneas, false Aeneas stay.	Dido	5.1.228	Anna
Live false Aeneas, truest Dido dyes,	Dido	5.1.312	Dido
And of that false Cosroe, my traiterous brother.	1Tamb	2.2.4	Mycet
And make him false his faith unto his King,	1Tamb	2.2.27	Meandr
Treacherous and false Theridamas,	1Tamb	2.7.3	Cosroe
and confound/The trustlesse force of those false Christians.	2Tamb	2.2.62	Orcan
To false his service to his Soveraigne,	2Tamb	3.5.88	Tamb
False, and unkinde; what, hast thou lost thy father?	Jew	3.4.2	Barab
A Fryar? false villaine, he hath done the deed.	Jew	3.4.22	Barab
False, credulous, inconstant Abigall!	Jew	3.4.27	Barab
My head shall be my counsell, they are false:	P 884	17.79	King
Tis true sweete Gaveston, oh were it false.	Edw	1.4.108	Edward
never was Plantagenet/False of his word, and therefore trust we	Edw	2.3.12	Mortmr
Bristow to Longshankes blood/Is false, be not found single for	Edw	4.6.17	Kent
And that unnaturall Queene false Isabell,	Edw	5.1.17	Edward
that one so false/Should come about the person of a prince.	Edw	5.2.104	Mortmr
False Gurney hath betraide me and himselfe.	Edw	5.6.45	Mortmr
False Prelates, for this hatefull treachery,	F1033	3.2.53	Pope
Griping his false hornes with hir virgin hand:	Ovid's Elegies	1.3.24	
God deluded/In snowe-white plumes of a false swanne included.	Ovid's Elegies	1.10.4	
To staine all faith in truth, by false crimes use.	Ovid's Elegies	2.2.38	
That might be urg'd to witnesse our false playing.	Ovid's Elegies	2.8.8	
My [false] <selfe> oathes in Carpathian seas to cast.	Ovid's Elegies	2.8.20	
Seeing thou art faire, I barre not thy false playing,	Ovid's Elegies	3.13.1	
Whose name is it, if she be false or not,	Hero and Leander	1.285	
With follie and false hope deluding us).	Hero and Leander	2.222	
And round about the chamber this false morne,	Hero and Leander	2.321	
FALSELY			
th'eternall powers graunt maides society/Falsely to sweare,	Ovid's Elegies	3.3.12	
And thou, if falsely charged to wrong thy friend,	Ovid's Elegies	3.8.63	
And my wench ought to have seem'd falsely praisd,	Ovid's Elegies	3.11.43	
FALS-HOOD			
And that slowe webbe nights fals-hood did unframe.	Ovid's Elegies	3.8.30	
FALSHOOD			
But malice, falshood, and excessive pride,	Jew	1.1.117	Barab
If greater falshood ever has bin done.	Jew	5.5.50	Barab
FALT			
Carelesse, farewell, with my falt not distaind.	Ovid's Elegies	1.6.72	
FAMASTRO			
Chio, Famastro, and Amasia,	2Tamb	3.1.50	Trebiz

FAME				
To feede her eyes with his engraven fame.	Dido	1.1.103		Jupitr
The heire of [fame] <furie>, the favorite of the [fates]	Dido	3.2.3		Juno
I followe one that loveth fame for me,	Dido	3.4.38		Dido
And valiant Tamburlaine, the man of fame,	1Tamb	2.1.2		Cosroe
which by fame is said/To drinke the mightie Parthian Araris,	1Tamb	2.3.15		Tamb
And ransome them with fame and usurie.	1Tamb	2.5.43		Cosroe
As was the fame of [Clymens] <Clymeus> brain-sicke sonne,/That	1Tamb	4.2.49		Tamb
For Fame I feare hath bene too prodigall,	1Tamb	4.3.48		Arabia
Your byrthes shall be no blemish to your fame,	1Tamb	4.4.127		Tamb
Which he observes as parcell of his fame,	1Tamb	5.1.14		Govnr
And every warriour that is rapt with love/Of fame, of valour,	1Tamb	5.1.181		Tamb
Brought up and propped by the hand of fame,	1Tamb	5.1.265		Bajzth
To spread my fame through hell and up to heaven:	1Tamb	5.1.467		Tamb
Fame hovereth, sounding of her golden Trumpe:	2Tamb	3.4.63		Therid
person to the view/Of fierce Achilles, rivall of his fame.	2Tamb	3.5.68		Tamb
And cast the fame of Ilions Tower to hell.	2Tamb	4.3.113		Tamb
Be not inconstant, carelesse of your fame,	2Tamb	5.3.21		Techel
And in this bed of [honor] <honors> die with fame.	Edw	4.5.7		Edward
[Now is his fame spread forth in every land],	F1149	3.3.62A		3Chor
The learned Faustus, fame of Wittenberge,	F1165	4.1.11		Mrtino
Sith blacke disgrace hath thus eclipst our fame,	F1455	4.3.25		Benvol
Vaine fame increast true feare, and did invade/The peoples	Lucan, First Booke	465		
Thus in his fright did each man strengthen Fame,	Lucan, First Booke	481		
Fame saith as I suspect, and in her eyes/Two eye-balles shine,	Ovid's Elegies	1.8.15		
The fame that verse gives doth for ever last.	Ovid's Elegies	1.10.62		
But I remember when it was my fame.	Ovid's Elegies	1.14.50		
Thy scope is mortall, mine eternall fame,	Ovid's Elegies	1.15.7		
If thy great fame in every region stood?	Ovid's Elegies	3.5.90		
Tibullus, thy workes Poet, and thy fame,	Ovid's Elegies	3.8.5		
The worke of Poets lasts Troyes labours fame,	Ovid's Elegies	3.8.29		
Seeke you for chastitie, immortall fame,	Hero and Leander	1.283		
Than he could saile, for incorporeal Fame,	Hero and Leander	2.113		
FAMES				
Cannot ascend to Fames immortall house,	Dido	4.3.9		Aeneas
Are both in Fames eternall legend writ.	Ovid's Elegies	1.15.20		
FAMILIAR				
And tell our griefes in more familiar termes:	Dido	1.1.246		Aeneas
In being too familiar with Iarbus:	Dido	3.1.15		Dido
Thou art too familiar with that Mortimer,	Edw	1.4.154		Edward
for they are as familiar with me, as if they payd for their	F 365	1.4.23	P	Robin
they are too familiar with me already, swowns they are as bolde	F App	p.230 28	P	Clown
they say thou hast a familiar spirit, by whome thou canst	F App	p.236 4	P	Emper
FAMILIARS				
I'le turne all the lice about thee into Familiars, and make	F 362	1.4.20	P	Wagner
or Ile turne al the lice about thee into familiars, and they	F App	p.229 25	P	Wagner
FAMILIE				
My lord, the familie of the Mortimers/Are not so poore, but	Edw	2.2.150		Mortmr
FAMILY				
not heaven it selfe/Shall ransome thee, thy wife and family.	2Tamb	3.3.28		Therid
and the rest of the family, stand or fall at your service.	Jew	4.2.44	P	Pilia
FAMINE				
Threatning a death <dearth> and famine to this land,	2Tamb	3.2.9		Tamb
O that there would come a famine over <through> all the world,	F 682	2.2.131	P	Envy
Adde, Caesar, to these illes Perusian famine;	Lucan, First Booke	41		
FAMISHT				
That sav'd your famisht souldiers lives from death,	Dido	3.3.52		Achat
FAMOUS				
And make Aeneas famous through the world,	Dido	5.1.293		Dido
To make him famous in accomplisht woorth:	1Tamb	2.1.34		Cosroe
from our dreadful siege/Of the famous Grecian Constantinople.	1Tamb	3.1.6		Bajzth
Thy fall shall make me famous through the world:	1Tamb	3.3.83		Tamb
Famous for nothing but for theft and spoile,	1Tamb	4.3.66		Souldn
That touch the end of famous Euphrates.	2Tamb	3.1.53		Trebiz
So famous as is mighty Tamburlain:	2Tamb	3.5.84		Tamb
Be famous through the furthest continents,	2Tamb	4.3.110		Tamb
When this our famous lake of Limnasphaltis/Makes walles a fresh	2Tamb	5.1.17		Govnr
The ruine of that famous Realme of France:	P 922	18.23		Navrre
That in our famous nurseries of artes/Thou suckedst from Plato,	Edw	4.7.18		Edward
Go forward Faustus in that famous Art/Wherein all natures	F 101	1.1.73		BdAngl
Go forward Faustus in that famous Art.	F 403	2.1.15		BdAngl
Thou shalt be famous through all Italy,	F1215	4.1.61		Emper
We would behold that famous Conquerour,	F1231	4.1.77		Emper
where lies intombde this famous Conquerour,	F App	p.237 31		Emper
Heroes, O <of> famous names/Farewel, your favour nought my minde	Ovid's Elegies	2.1.35		
Caried the famous golden-fleeced sheepe.	Ovid's Elegies	2.11.4		
So Nemesis, so Delia famous are,	Ovid's Elegies	3.8.31		
With famous pageants, and their home-bred beasts.	Ovid's Elegies	3.12.4		
FAMOUSED				
An ancient Empire, famoused for armes,	Dido	1.2.21		Cloan
Not farre from hence/There is a woman famoused for arts,	Dido	5.1.275		Dido
FAN (See also FANNE)				
Then <or>, like a Fan of Feathers, I kisse her [lippes]; And	F 667	2.2.116	P	Pride
For hitherto hee did but fan the fire,	Hero and Leander	2.41		
FANCIE				
If that thy fancie in his feathers dwell,	Dido	1.1.39		Jupitr
O that Iarbus could but fancie me.	Dido	3.1.62		Anna
Fancie and modestie shall live as mates,	Dido	3.2.58		Venus
Mine eye is fixt where fancie cannot start,	Dido	4.2.37		Iarbus
How can you fancie one that lookes so fierce,	1Tamb	3.2.40		Agidas
What so thy minde affectes or fancie likes.	Edw	1.1.170		Edward
And with smooth speech, her fancie to assay,	Hero and Leander	1.402		
Where fancie is in equall ballance pais'd).	Hero and Leander	2.32		

FANCIE (cont.)			
Wherefore Leanders fancie to surprize,	Hero and Leander	2.223	
FANCIES			
And mould her minde unto newe fancies shapes:	Dido	3.3.79	Iarbus
As made disdaine to flye to fancies lap:	Dido	3.4.56	Dido
Away with such vaine fancies, and despaire,	F 392	2.1.4	Faust
FANE (See also PHANE)			
Whom Ajax ravisht in Dianas [Fane] <Fawne>,	Dido	2.1.275	Aeneas
FANG (See PHANGS)			
FANNE			
What will you give me now? Ile have this Fanne.	Dido	3.1.32	Cupid
And fanne it in Aeneas lovely face,	Dido	4.4.49	Dido
Ile [fawne] <fanne> first on the winde,/That glaunceth at my	Edw	1.1.22	Gavstn
Shall Dian fanne when love begins to glowe?	Ovid's Elegies	1.1.12	
That from thy fanne, mov'd by my hand may blow?	Ovid's Elegies	3.2.38	
Her painted fanne of curled plumes let fall,	Hero and Leander	2.11	
FANNES			
To make thee fannes wherewith to coole thy face,	Dido	1.1.35	Jupitr
FANTASIE			
[Yet not your words onely, but mine owne fantasie],	F 130	1.1.102A	Faust
FANTASIES			
Ah sister, leave these idle fantasies,	Dido	5.1.262	Anna
Begets a world of idle fantasies,	F1810	5.2.14	Mephst
FANTASTICK			
But his fantastick humours pleasde not me:	Dido	3.1.158	Dido
Whose proud fantastick liveries make such show,	Edw	1.4.410	Mortmr
FAR			
To see a Phrigian far fet [on] <o'er> <forfeit to> the sea,	Dido	3.3.64	Iarbus
The Nations far remoov'd admyre me not)/And when my name and	1Tamb	1.2.204	Tamb
As far as Boreas claps his brazen wings,	1Tamb	1.2.206	Tamb
Which make reports it far exceeds the Kings.	1Tamb	2.2.42	Spy
And far from any man that is a foole.	1Tamb	2.4.12	Mycet
I judge the purchase more important far.	1Tamb	2.5.92	Therid
Is far from villanie or servitude.	1Tamb	3.2.38	Zenoc
His resolution far exceedeth all:	1Tamb	4.1.48	2Msngr
As far as from the frozen [plage] <place> of heaven,	1Tamb	4.4.122	Tamb
And thence as far as Archipellago:	2Tamb	1.1.75	Orcan
How far hence lies the Galley, say you?	2Tamb	1.2.54	Almeda
Madam, I am so far in love with you,	2Tamb	3.4.78	Therid
And sooner far than he that never fights.	2Tamb	4.1.55	Calyph
earth may eccho foorth/The far resounding torments ye sustaine,	2Tamb	4.1.186	Tamb
Is greater far, than they can thus subdue.	2Tamb	5.3.39	Usumc
And here not far from Alexandria,	2Tamb	5.3.131	Tamb
I conquered all as far as Zansibar.	2Tamb	5.3.139	Tamb
My lord, these titles far exceed my worth.	Edw	1.1.157	Gavstn
Thy woorth sweet friend is far above my guifts,	Edw	1.1.161	Edward
As far as Titan springs where night dims heaven,	Lucan, First Booke	15	
This need no forraine proofe, nor far fet story:	Lucan, First Booke	94	
Or sea far from the land, so all were whist.	Lucan, First Booke	262	
And far more barbarous then the French (his vassals)/And that	Lucan, First Booke	476	
But far above the loveliest, Hero shin'd,	Hero and Leander	1.103	
honour, and thereby/Commit'st a sinne far worse than perjurie.	Hero and Leander	1.306	
Far from the towne (where all is whist and still,	Hero and Leander	1.346	
FARE			
Fare well may Dido, so Aeneas stay,	Dido	5.1.107	Dido
And feeding them with thin and slender fare,	1Tamb	3.3.49	Tamb
I fare my Lord, as other Emperesses,	2Tamb	2.4.42	Zenoc
Well fare the Arabians, who so richly pay/The things they	Jew	1.1.8	Barab
I, fare you well.	Jew	1.2.213	Barab
Fare you well.	Jew	4.3.58	Pilia
What, all alone? well fare sleepy drinke.	Jew	5.1.61	Barab
How now my Lords, how fare you?	P 430	7.70	Anjoy
Fare well sterne warre, for blunter Poets meete.	Ovid's Elegies	1.1.32	
Rhesus fell/And Captive horses bad their Lord fare-well.	Ovid's Elegies	1.9.24	
FARES			
So fares Agydas for the late felt frownes/That sent a tempest	1Tamb	3.2.85	Agidas
Tell me, how fares my faire Zenocrate?	2Tamb	2.4.41	Tamb
Welcome, great [Bashaw] <Bashaws>, how fares/Callymath,	Jew	3.5.1	Govnr
How fares it with my Lord high Admiral,	P 253	4.51	Charls
How fares it this morning with your excellence?	P 966	19.36	King
Madam, how fares your grace?	Edw	1.4.192	Mortmr
Why how now cosin, how fares all our friends?	Edw	2.2.114	Lncstr
And so it fares with me, whose dauntlesse minde/The ambitious	Edw	5.1.15	Edward
How fares my lord the king?	Edw	5.2.24	Queene
How fares my honorable lord of Kent?	Edw	5.2.80	Mortmr
In health sweete Mortimer, how fares your grace?	Edw	5.2.81	Kent
The more he is restrain'd, the woorse he fares,	Hero and Leander	2.145	
FAREWEL			
Theridamas, farewel ten thousand times.	1Tamb	1.1.82	Mycet
Farewel my boies, my dearest friends, farewel,	2Tamb	5.3.245	Tamb
<Farewel Faustus, and thinke on the divel>.	F 720	(HC264)A	Lucifr
Farewel maister Doctor, yet ere you goe, expect from me a	F App	p.239 88 P	Emper
O <of> famous names/Farewel, your favour nought my minde	Ovid's Elegies	2.1.36	
FARE-WELL			
Rhesus fell/And Captive horses bad their Lord fare-well.	Ovid's Elegies	1.9.24	
FARE WELL			
Fare well sterne warre, for blunter Poets meete.	Ovid's Elegies	1.1.32	
FAREWELL (See also FARWEL, FARWELL)			
Venus farewell, thy sonne shall be our care:	Dido	1.1.120	Jupitr
To leave her so and not once say farewell,	Dido	4.3.47	Aeneas
I went to take my farewell of Achates.	Dido	4.4.18	Aeneas
How haps Achates bid me not farewell?	Dido	4.4.19	Dido
And yet I may not stay, Dido farewell.	Dido	5.1.104	Aeneas

FAREWELL (cont.)

Farewell: is this the mends for Didos love?	Dido	5.1.105	Dido
I dye, if my Aeneas say farewell.	Dido	5.1.108	Dido
Then let me goe and never say farewell?	Dido	5.1.109	Aeneas
Let me goe, farewell, I must from hence,	Dido	5.1.110	Dido
Then let me goe, and never say farewell?	Dido	5.1.124	Dido
For though thou hast the heart to say farewell,	Dido	5.1.182	Dido
to order all the scattered troopes)/Farewell Lord Regent,	1Tamb	2.5.46	Cosroe
Farewell (sweet Virgins) on whose safe return/Depends our	1Tamb	5.1.62	Govnr
Even straight: and farewell cursed Tamburlaine.	2Tamb	1.2.77	Callap
Sweet sons farewell, in death resemble me,	2Tamb	2.4.75	Zenoc
Yet I am resolute, and so farewell.	2Tamb	3.3.40	Capt
Farewell sweet wife, sweet son farewell, I die.	2Tamb	3.4.10	Capt
Let's take our leaves; Farewell good Barabas.	Jew	1.1.175	2Jew
Doe so; Farewell Zaareth, farewell Temainte.	Jew	1.1.176	Barab
Farewell great [Governor], and brave Knights of Malta.	Jew	1.2.32	Calym
Farewell Barabas.	Jew	1.2.213	2Jew
Farewell, Remember to morrow morning.	Jew	1.2.364	Barab
Farewell Mathias.	Jew	1.2.393	Lodowk
Farewell Lodowicke.	Jew	1.2.393	Mthias
Farewell my joy, and by my fingers take/A kisse from him that	Jew	2.1.58	Barab
My Lord farewell: Come Sirra you are mine.	Jew	2.3.134	Barab
Thinke of me as thy father; Sonne farewell.	Jew	2.3.149	Barab
I know not, but farewell, I must be gone.	Jew	2.3.322	Abigal
I, part 'em now they are dead: Farewell, farewell.	Jew	3.2.9	Barab
And so farewell.	Jew	3.5.27	Basso
Farewell:/And now you men of Malta looke about,	Jew	3.5.28	Govnr
Farewell Fidler: One letter more to the Jew.	Jew	4.4.72	Pilia
Farewell brave Jew, farewell great Barabas.	Jew	5.2.20	Calym
Doe so, but faile not; now farewell Ferneze:	Jew	5.2.109	Barab
Farewell grave Governor.	Jew	5.4.10	1Knght
Farewell base stooping to the lordly peeres,	Edw	1.1.18	Gavstn
Farewell, and perish by a souldiers hand,	Edw	1.1.37	3PrMan
Madam farewell.	Edw	1.2.80	Mortmr
Farewell sweet Mortimer, and for my sake,	Edw	1.2.81	Queene
And so will I, and then my lord farewell.	Edw	2.2.156	Lncstr
Farewell my Lord.	Edw	2.4.9	Gavstn
Ladie, farewell.	Edw	2.4.10	Edward
Farewell sweete unckle till we meete againe.	Edw	2.4.11	Neece
Farewell sweete Gaveston, and farewell Neece.	Edw	2.4.12	Edward
No farewell, to poore Isabell, thy Queene?	Edw	2.4.13	Queene
Farewell vaine worlde.	Edw	3.1.249	Warwck
Sweete Mortimer farewell.	Edw	3.1.249	Lncstr
To let us take our farewell of his grace.	Edw	4.7.69	Spencr
Hence fained weeds, unfained are my woes,/Father, farewell:	Edw	4.7.98	Edward
And go I must, life farewell with my friends.	Edw	4.7.99	Edward
This answer weele returne, and so farewell.	Edw	5.1.90	BshpWn
Farewell, I know the next newes that they bring,	Edw	5.1.125	Edward
Leicester, farewell.	Edw	5.1.154	Edward
Thither shall your honour go, and so farewell.	Edw	5.3.62	Matrvs
That will I quicklie do, farewell my lord.	Edw	5.4.47	Ltborn
Farewell faire Queene, weepe not for Mortimer,	Edw	5.6.64	Mortmr
Bid [on kai me on] <Oncaymaeon> farewell, <and> Galen come:	F 40	1.1.12	Faust
Physicke farewell: where is Justinian?	F 55	1.1.27	Faust
Now Faustus farewell.	F 720	2.2.172	Lucifr
Farewell great Lucifer: come Mephostophilis.	F 721	2.2.173	Faust
Gentlemen farewell: the same wish I to you.	F1706	5.1.33	Faust
Gentlemen farewell:/if I live till morning,	F1877	5.2.81	P Faust
Faustus, farewell.	F1879	5.2.83	AllSch
'tis too late, despaire, farewell,/Fooles that will laugh on	F1890	5.2.94	Mephst
What ere thou art, farewell, be like me paind,	Ovid's Elegies		1.6.71
Carelesse, farewell, with my falt not distaind.	Ovid's Elegies		1.6.72
And farewell cruell posts, rough thresholds block,	Ovid's Elegies		1.6.73
Farewell Corinna cryed thy dying tongue.	Ovid's Elegies		2.6.48
Weake Elegies, delightfull Muse farewell;	Ovid's Elegies		3.14.19
FAR FET			
This need no forraine proofe, nor far fet story:	Lucan, First Booke		94
FARMES			
Farmes out her-self on nights for what she can.	Ovid's Elegies		1.10.30
FARRE			
But are arived safe not farre from hence:	Dido	1.1.237	Venus
Such force is farre from our unweaponed thoughts,	Dido	1.2.14	Illion
passe through the hall/Bearing a banket, Dido is not farre.	Dido	2.1.71	Serg
I was as farre from love, as they from hate.	Dido	3.1.167	Dido
Come backe, come backe, I heare her crye a farre,	Dido	4.3.27	Aeneas
Come come, Ile goe, how farre hence is your house?	Dido	4.5.13	Cupid
Not farre from hence/There is a woman famoused for arts,	Dido	5.1.274	Dido
Thus farre are we towards Theridamas,	1Tamb	2.1.1	Cosroe
To bid him battaile ere he passe too farre,	1Tamb	2.5.95	Tamb
And therefore farre exceeds my credit, Sir.	Jew	1.1.65	1Merch
with so much wealth/Trust such a crazed Vessell, and so farre.	Jew	1.1.80	1Merch
But 'twas ill done of you to come so farre/Without the ayd or	Jew	1.1.93	Barab
scambled up/More wealth by farre then those that brag of faith.	Jew	1.1.123	Barab
I, wealthier farre then any Christian.	Jew	1.1.128	Barab
our hands with blood/Is farre from us and our profession.	Jew	1.2.145	Govnr
Why I esteeme the injury farre lesse,	Jew	1.2.146	Barab
long since some of us/Did stray so farre amongst the multitude.	Jew	1.2.309	Abbass
And better would she farre become a bed/Embraced in a friendly	Jew	1.2.371	Mthias
You'le like it better farre a nights than dayes.	Jew	2.3.63	Barab
I, but my Lord, the harvest is farre off:	Jew	2.3.79	Barab
Farre from the Sonne that gives eternall life.	Jew	3.3.65	Abigal
You shall not need trouble your selves so farre,	Jew	3.5.22	Basso
And thus farre roundly goes the businesse:	Jew	5.2.110	Barab

Line	Work	Ref	Speaker
FARRE (cont.)			
of your Prince Electors, farre/Beyond the reach of my desertes:	P 452	8.2	Anjoy
and now thy sight/Is sweeter farre, then was thy parting hence	Edw	2.2.57	Edward
Farre be it from the thought of Lancaster,	Edw	2.4.33	Lncstr
And if you gratifie his grace so farre,	Edw	2.5.39	Arundl
My house is not farre hence, out of the way/A little, but our	Edw	2.5.100	Penbrk
Mortimers hope surmounts his fortune farre.	Edw	3.1.259	Mortmr
that we can yet be tun'd together,/No, no, we jarre too farre.	Edw	4.2.10	Queene
Never so cheereles, nor so farre distrest.	Edw	4.2.14	Queene
What else my lord? and farre more resolute.	Edw	5.4.23	Ltborn
Yet be not farre off, I shall need your helpe,	Edw	5.5.28	Ltborn
Farre is it from my hart to do you harme,	Edw	5.5.47	Ltborn
Stretcheth as farre as doth the mind of man:	F 88	1.1.60	Faust
and if he be so farre in love with him, I would he would post	F1190	4.1.36	P Benvol
be good, for they come from a farre Country I can tell you.	F1577	4.6.20	P Faust
and such Countries that lye farre East, where they have fruit	F1584	4.6.27	P Faust
my selfe farre inferior to the report men have published,	F App	p.236 13	P Faust
farre forth as by art and power of my spirit I am able to	F App	p.237 38	P Faust
Roome may be won/With farre lesse toile, and yet the honors	Lucan, First Booke	284	
And frontier Varus that the campe is farre,	Lucan, First Booke	405	
Atticke, all lovers are to warre farre sent.	Ovid's Elegies	1.9.2	
Souldiers must travaile farre:	Ovid's Elegies	1.9.9	
Whom Troiane ships fecht from Europa farre.	Ovid's Elegies	1.10.2	
Farre off be force, no fire to them may reach,	Ovid's Elegies	1.14.29	
No sicknesse harm'd thee, farre be that a way,	Ovid's Elegies	1.14.41	
So Cupid wills, farre hence be the severe,	Ovid's Elegies	2.1.3	
Before Callimachus one preferres me farre,	Ovid's Elegies	2.4.19	
The Parrat given me, the farre [worlds] <words> best choice.	Ovid's Elegies	2.6.38	
Yet this is better farre then lie alone,	Ovid's Elegies	2.10.15	
So farre 'tis safe, but to go farther dread.	Ovid's Elegies	2.11.16	
Nor being arm'd fierce troupes to follow farre?	Ovid's Elegies	2.14.2	
Alas he runnes too farre about the ring,	Ovid's Elegies	3.2.69	
That were as white as is <Her armes farre whiter, then> the	Ovid's Elegies	3.6.8	
footsteps bending)/Doth testifie that you exceed her farre,	Hero and Leander	1.211	
Thinke water farre excels all earthly things:	Hero and Leander	1.260	
Shall discontent run into regions farre;	Hero and Leander	1.478	
Fires and inflames objects remooved farre,	Hero and Leander	2.124	
FARTHER			
Yet since a farther passion feeds my thoughts,	1Tamb	3.2.13	Zenoc
Ere farther we proceede my noble lordes,	Edw	4.6.23	Queene
and farther countries in the East, and by means of a swift	F App	p.242 21	P Faust
And searching farther for the gods displeasure,	Lucan, First Booke	616	
So farre 'tis safe, but to go farther dread.	Ovid's Elegies	2.11.16	
FARTHEST			
Men from the farthest Equinoctiall line,	1Tamb	1.1.119	Cosroe
That fill the midst of farthest Tartary,	2Tamb	4.1.43	Amyras
FARTHINGS			
bad him take as much as he would for three-farthings; so he	F1529	4.5.25	P Carter
FARWEL			
farwel he, Faustus has his legge againe, and the Horsecourser I	F App	p.241 164	P Faust
FARWELL			
Farwell to my Lord of Guise and Epernoune.	P 750	15.8	Joyeux
Health and harty farwell to my Lord Joyeux.	P 751	15.9	Guise
Then farwell Guise, the King and thou are freends.	P 870	17.65	King
And so sweet Cuz farwell.	P 976	19.46	King
If that will not suffice, farwell my lords.	Edw	2.3.10	Kent
FASHION			
then let every man/Provide him, and be there for fashion-sake.	Jew	1.1.171	Barab
An Altar made after the ancient fashion.	Ovid's Elegies	3.12.10	
FASHIONED			
Of stature tall, and straightly fashioned,	1Tamb	2.1.7	Menaph
FASHIONS			
And fashions men with true nobility.	1Tamb	5.1.190	Tamb
FASHION-SAKE			
then let every man/Provide him, and be there for fashion-sake.	Jew	1.1.171	Barab
FAST (Homograph)			
Now is he fast asleepe, and in this grove/Amongst greene brakes	Dido	2.1.316	Venus
I hold the Fates bound fast in yron chaines,	1Tamb	1.2.174	Tamb
Hie thee my Bassoe fast to Persea,	1Tamb	3.1.21	Bajzth
And when he comes, she lockes her selfe up fast;	Jew	2.3.262	Barab
To fast, to pray, and weare a shirt of haire,	Jew	4.1.61	Barab
To fast and be well whipt; I'le none of that.	Jew	4.1.124	Barab
the Nuns, and he and I, snicle hand too fast, strangled a Fryar.	Jew	4.4.21	P Ithimr
How stand the cords? How hang these hinges, fast?	Jew	5.5.1	Barab
All fast.	Jew	5.5.2	Servnt
Whether goes my Lord of Coventrie so fast?	Edw	1.1.175	Edward
Madam, whether walks your majestie so fast?	Edw	1.2.46	Mortmr
How fast they run to banish him I love,	Edw	1.4.94	Edward
As fast as Iris, or Joves Mercurie.	Edw	1.4.371	Edward
But dayes bright beames dooth vanish fast away,	Edw	5.1.69	Edward
Then all my labours, plod I ne're so fast.	F 96	1.1.68	Faust
Seven golden [keys] <seales> fast sealed with seven seales,	F 933	3.1.155	Pope
To binde or loose, lock fast, condemne, or judge,	F 935	3.1.157	Pope
And in the strongest Tower inclose him fast.	F 966	3.1.188	Pope
Fast a sleepe I warrant you,	F1173	4.1.19	Mrtino
O not so fast sir, theres no haste but good, are you remembred	F App	p.238 76	P Faust
Why hee's fast asleepe, come some other time.	F App	p.240 141	P Mephst
See where he is fast asleepe.	F App	p.241 147	P Mephst
Strike backe the barre, night fast away doth goe.	Ovid's Elegies	1.6.32	
nights deawie hoast/March fast away:	Ovid's Elegies	1.6.56	
Binde fast my hands, they have deserved chaines,	Ovid's Elegies	1.7.1	
I would get off though straight, and sticking fast,	Ovid's Elegies	2.15.13	
Least to the waxe the hold-fast drye gemme cleaves,	Ovid's Elegies	2.15.16	

FAST (cont.)				
She prais'd me, yet the gate shutt fast upon her,	Ovid's Elegies	3.7.7		
Till in his twining armes he lockt her fast,	Hero and Leander	1.403		
FASTE				
Faste and welcome sir, while hunger make you eat.	1Tamb	4.4.56	P	Tamb
FASTEN				
No sleepe can fasten on my watchfull eyes,	Jew	2.1.17		Barab
FASTENED				
Two spreading hornes most strangely fastened/Upon the head of	F1277	4.1.123		Emper
FASTNING				
foote drawes out/Fastning her light web some old beame about.	Ovid's Elegies	1.14.8		
FAT (See also FATTE)				
dispatch her while she is fat, for if she live but a while	1Tamb	4.4.48	P	Tamb
live along, then thou should'st see how fat I'de <I would> be.	F 683	2.2.132	P	Envy
Fat love, and too much fulsome me annoyes,	Ovid's Elegies	2.19.25		
FATALL				
And so came in this fatall instrument:	Dido	2.1.176		Aeneas
What fatall destinie envies me thus,	Dido	5.1.323		Anna
Nothing but feare and fatall steele my Lord.	1Tamb	5.1.109		1Virgn
Whom should I wish the fatall victory,	1Tamb	5.1.385		Zenoc
Where ere I come the fatall sisters sweat,	1Tamb	5.1.454		Tamb
To haile the fatall Sisters by the haire,	2Tamb	2.4.99		Tamb
On whom death and the fatall sisters waite,	2Tamb	3.4.54		Therid
And let the end of this my fatall journey,	2Tamb	3.4.81		Olymp
and fit for nought/But perches for the black and fatall Ravens.	2Tamb	4.3.23		Tamb
Let it be plac'd by this my fatall chaire,	2Tamb	5.3.211		Tamb
Thy fatall birth-day, forlorne Barabas;	Jew	1.2.192		Barab
poore Barabas/With fatall curses towards these Christians.	Jew	2.1.6		Barab
alas, hath pac'd too long/The fatall Labyrinth of misbeleefe,	Jew	3.3.64		Abigal
As fatall be it to her as the draught/Of which great Alexander	Jew	3.4.96		Barab
Oh fatall day, to fall into the hands/Of such a Traitor and	Jew	5.2.12		Govnr
This day, this houre, this fatall night,	P 64	2.7		Guise
sweet Margaret, the fatall poyson/Workes within my head, my	P 184	3.19		OldQn
Oh fatall was this mariage to us all.	P 202	3.37		Admral
Now have we got the fatall stragling deere,	P 204	4.2		QnMoth
O the fatall poyson workes within my brest,	P1221	22.83		King
And rulde in France by Henries fatall death.	P1250	22.112		Navrre
Let Plutos bels ring out my fatall knell,	Edw	4.7.89		Edward
Thy fatall time drawes to a finall end;	F1479	4.4.23		Faust
Thy fatall time doth drawe to finall ende,	F App	p.240 122		Faust
The yeares that fatall destenie shall give,	Ovid's Elegies	1.3.17		
They offred him the deadly fatall knife,	Hero and Leander	1.447		
FATALLY				
And fatally enricht Eneas love.	1Tamb	5.1.394		Zenoc
FATE				
Controule proud Fate, and cut the thred of time.	Dido	1.1.29		Jupitr
Since thy Aeneas wandring fate is firme,	Dido	1.1.83		Jupitr
Whereas the Wind-god warring now with Fate,	Dido	1.1.115		Jupitr
Pluck up your hearts, since fate still rests our friend,	Dido	1.1.149		Aeneas
Bootles I sawe it was to warre with fate,	Dido	3.2.49		Juno
turne the hand of fate/Unto that happie day of my delight,	Dido	3.3.80		Iarbus
May triumph in our long expected Fate.	1Tamb	2.3.44		Tamb
now let us celebrate/Our happy conquest, and his angry fate.	2Tamb	2.3.47		Orcan
Whose cursed fate hath so dismembred it,	2Tamb	3.1.13		Callap
Since Fate commands, and proud necessity.	2Tamb	5.3.205		Therid
Then Barabas breath forth thy latest fate,	Jew	5.5.78		Barab
and let due praise be given/Neither to Fate nor Fortune, but to	Jew	5.5.124		Govnr
Or if Fate rule them, Rome thy Cittizens/Are neere some plague:	Lucan, First Booke	643		
For will in us is over-rul'd by fate.	Hero and Leander	1.168		
And but that Learning, in despight of Fate,	Hero and Leander	1.465		
FATES				
heire of [fame] <furie>, the favorite of the [fates] <face>,	Dido	3.2.3		Juno
Abourd, abourd, since Fates doe bid abourd,	Dido	4.3.21		Aeneas
I hold the Fates bound fast in yron chaines,	1Tamb	1.2.174		Tamb
For Fates and Oracles [of] heaven have sworne,	1Tamb	2.3.7		Tamb
Which thy prolonged Fates may draw on thee:	1Tamb	3.2.101		Agidas
Theridamas, when holy Fates/Shall stablish me in strong Egyptia,	1Tamb	4.4.134		Tamb
And murdrous Fates throwes al his triumphs down.	2Tamb	Prol.5		Prolog
realme, and sith the fates/Have made his father so infortunate,	Edw	4.6.26		Queene
But if for Nero (then unborne) the fates/Would find no other	Lucan, First Booke	33		
The fates are envious, high seats quickly perish,	Lucan, First Booke	70		
for Julia/Snatcht hence by cruel fates with ominous howles,	Lucan, First Booke	112		
And fates so bent, least sloth and long delay/Might crosse him,	Lucan, First Booke	394		
And the fates distaffe emptie stood to thee,	Ovid's Elegies	2.6.46		
Long shalt thou rest when Fates expire thy breath.	Ovid's Elegies	2.9.42		
And envious fates great [goddesses] <goodesses> assaile,	Ovid's Elegies	3.8.2		
When bad fates take good men, I am forbod,	Ovid's Elegies	3.8.35		
Seeing in their loves, the Fates were injured.	Hero and Leander	1.484		
FATHER				
Father I faint, good father give me meate.	Dido	1.1.163		Ascan
Sweete father leave to weepe, this is not he:	Dido	2.1.35		Ascan
Father of fiftie sonnes, but they are slaine,	Dido	2.1.234		Aeneas
And now am neither father, Lord, nor King:	Dido	2.1.239		Aeneas
By this I got my father on my backe,	Dido	2.1.265		Aeneas
You shall not hurt my father when he comes.	Dido	3.1.80		Cupid
No, for thy sake Ile love thy father well.	Dido	3.1.81		Dido
How like his father speaketh he in all?	Dido	3.3.41		Anna
Nay, where is my warlike father, can you tell?	Dido	4.1.15		Cupid
Father of gladnesse, and all frollicke thoughts,	Dido	4.2.5		Iarbus
If it be so, his father meanes to flye:	Dido	5.1.85		Dido
Sent from his father Jove, appeard to me,	Dido	5.1.95		Aeneas
To thrust his doting father from his chaire,	1Tamb	2.7.14		Tamb
That holds you from your father in despight,	1Tamb	3.2.27		Agidas

FATHER (cont.)

And with my father take a frindly truce.	1Tamb	4.4.72		Zenoc
Madam, your father and th'Arabian king,	1Tamb	5.1.378		Philem
My father and my first betrothed love,	1Tamb	5.1.388		Zenoc
Come happy Father of Zenocrate,	1Tamb	5.1.433		Tamb
To see the king my Father issue safe,	1Tamb	5.1.441		Zenoc
Which kept his father in an yron cage:	2Tamb	1.1.5		Orcan
Yes father, you shal see me if I live,	2Tamb	1.3.54		Celeb
and thirty Kingdomes late contributory to his mighty father.	2Tamb	3.1.6	P	Orcan
as when Bajazeth/My royall Lord and father fild the throne,	2Tamb	3.1.12		Callap
View me thy father that hath conquered kings,	2Tamb	3.2.110		Tamb
give me a wound father.	2Tamb	3.2.132	P	Celeb
Here father, cut it bravely as you did your own.	2Tamb	3.2.135	P	Celeb
Sweet mother strike, that I may meet my father.	2Tamb	3.4.30		Sonne
See father, how Almeda the Jaylor lookes upon us.	2Tamb	3.5.116		Celeb
For if my father misse him in the field,	2Tamb	4.1.8		Celeb
Away ye fools, my father needs not me,	2Tamb	4.1.15		Calyph
My father were enough to scar the foe:	2Tamb	4.1.19		Calyph
Knowing my father hates thy cowardise,	2Tamb	4.1.23		Amyras
I would not bide the furie of my father:	2Tamb	4.1.45		Amyras
Turkes Concubines first, when my father hath conquered them.	2Tamb	4.1.65	P	Calyph
father would let me be put in the front of such a battaile	2Tamb	4.1.72	P	Calyph
How like his cursed father he begins,	2Tamb	4.3.55		Jrslem
O father, if the unrelenting eares/Of death and hell be shut	2Tamb	5.3.191		Amyras
And send my soule before my father die,	2Tamb	5.3.208		Amyras
Thy father has enough in store for thee.	Jew	1.2.227		Barab
Father, for thee lamenteth Abigaile:	Jew	1.2.229		Abigal
Till they reduce the wrongs done to my father.	Jew	1.2.235		Abigal
Where father?	Jew	1.2.248		Abigal
Father, what e're it be to injure them/That have so manifestly	Jew	1.2.274		Abigal
I, but father they will suspect me there.	Jew	1.2.283		Abigal
Thus father shall I much dissemble.	Jew	1.2.289		Abigal
Well father, say I be entertain'd,	Jew	1.2.294		Abigal
Then father, goe with me.	Jew	1.2.300		Abigal
Fearing the afflictions which my father feeles,	Jew	1.2.322		Abigal
Father, give me--	Jew	1.2.348		Abigal
espy'd a time/To search the plancke my father did appoint;	Jew	2.1.21		Abigal
Then father here receive thy happinesse.	Jew	2.1.44		Abigal
Father, it draweth towards midnight now,	Jew	2.1.55		Abigal
I wud you were his father too, Sir, that's al the harm I wish	Jew	2.3.41	P	Barab
Oh, Sir, your father had my Diamonds.	Jew	2.3.49		Barab
Your father has deserv'd it at my hands,	Jew	2.3.70		Barab
Thinke of me as thy father; Sonne farewell.	Jew	2.3.149		Barab
In good time, father, here are letters come/From Ormus, and the	Jew	2.3.222		Abigal
O father, Don Mathias is my love.	Jew	2.3.237		Abigal
His father was my chiefest enemie.	Jew	2.3.250		Barab
I cannot chuse, seeing my father bids:--	Jew	2.3.316		Abigal
Father, why have you thus incenst them both?	Jew	2.3.356		Abigal
Say, knave, why rail'st upon my father thus?	Jew	3.3.11		Abigal
And was my father furtherer of their deaths?	Jew	3.3.22		Abigal
So sure did your father write, and I cary the chalenge.	Jew	3.3.25	P	Ithimr
Hard-hearted Father, unkind Barabas,	Jew	3.3.36		Abigal
False, and unkinde; what, hast thou lost thy father?	Jew	3.4.2		Barab
and invenome her/That like a fiend hath left her father thus.	Jew	3.4.105		Barab
but seeing you are come/Be you my ghostly father; and first	Jew	3.6.12		Abigal
My father did contract me to 'em both:	Jew	3.6.22		Abigal
Reveale it not, for then my father dyes.	Jew	3.6.32		Abigal
Convert my father that he may be sav'd,	Jew	3.6.39		Abigal
till thy father hath made good/The ruines done to Malta and to	Jew	5.5.111		Govnr
Boy, look where your father lyes.	P1046	19.116		King
My father slaine, who hath done this deed?	P1047	19.117		YngGse
My father is deceast, come Gaveston,	Edw	1.1.1		Gavstn
Were sworne to your father at his death,	Edw	1.1.83		Mortmr
Spencer, the father of Hugh Spencer there,	Edw	3.1.40		SpncrP
Thy father Spencer?	Edw	3.1.43		Edward
And feare not lord and father, heavens great beames/On Atlas	Edw	3.1.76		Prince
And please my father well, and then a Fig/For all my unckles	Edw	4.2.4		Prince
How meane you, and the king my father lives?	Edw	4.2.43		Prince
realme, and sith the fates/Have made his father so infortunate,	Edw	4.6.27		Queene
Nephew, your father, I dare not call him king.	Edw	4.6.33		Kent
So are the Spencers, the father and the sonne.	Edw	4.6.44		SrJohn
Spencer, the father to that wanton Spencer,	Edw	4.6.50		Rice
Shall I not see the king my father yet?	Edw	4.6.61		Prince
Father, thy face should harbor no deceit,	Edw	4.7.8		Edward
Father, this life contemplative is heaven,	Edw	4.7.20		Edward
good father on thy lap/Lay I this head, laden with mickle care,	Edw	4.7.39		Edward
Hence fained weeds, unfained are my woes,/Father, farewell:	Edw	4.7.98		Edward
Conclude against his father what thou wilt,	Edw	5.2.19		Queene
if thou now growest penitent/Ile be thy ghostly father,	Edw	5.6.4		Mortmr
Forbid not me to weepe, he was my father,	Edw	5.6.34		King
Traitor, in me my loving father speakes,	Edw	5.6.41		King
Sweete father heere, unto thy murdered ghost,	Edw	5.6.99		King
I had neither father nor mother, I leapt out of a Lyons mouth	F 686	2.2.135	P	Wrath
in hell, and look to it, for some of you shall be my father.	F 691	2.2.140	P	Wrath
my father <grandfather> was a Gammon of Bacon, and my mother	F 696	2.2.145	P	Glutny
Let us salute his reverend Father-hood.	F 944	3.1.166		Faust
us, he were as good commit with his father, as commit with us.	F1603	4.6.46	P	Dick
I, I thought that was al the land his father left him:	F App	p.229 18	P	Clown
Yea and thy father to, and swords thrown down,	Lucan, First Booke			117
the sonne decrees/To expel the father; share the world thou	Lucan, First Booke			291
And thy step-father fights by thy example.	Ovid's Elegies			2.9.48
Both to the Sea-nimphes, and the Sea-nimphes father.	Ovid's Elegies			2.11.36
Till then, rough was her father, she severe,	Ovid's Elegies			3.7.31

FATHER (cont.)			
Where Linus by his father Phoebus layed/To sing with his .	Ovid's Elegies	3.8.23	
Leanders Father knew where hee had beene, ...	Hero and Leander	2.136	
FATHER-HOOD			
Let us salute his reverend Father-hood.	F 944	3.1.166	Faust
FATHER'S			
That was my father's fault.	Jew	3.3.72	Abigal
Thy father's, how?	Jew	3.3.72	1Fryar
And by my father's practice, which is there/Set downe at large,	Jew	3.6.28	Abigal
My father's murdered through thy treacherie, ...	Edw	5.6.28	King
FATHERS			
Yet he undaunted tooke his fathers flagge, ...	Dido	2.1.259	Aeneas
Take it Ascanius, for thy fathers sake.	Dido	3.1.33	Dido
Of my old fathers name.	Dido	5.1.23	Aeneas
Even in the circle of your Fathers armes:	1Tamb	1.2.5	Tamb
Who, when they come unto their fathers age, ...	1Tamb	3.3.110	Bajzth
Because it is my countries, and my Fathers.	1Tamb	4.2.124	Zenoc
My lord, to see my fathers towne besieg'd, ...	1Tamb	4.4.65	Zenoc
And wouldst thou have me buy thy Fathers love/With such a	1Tamb	4.4.83	Tamb
And feare to see thy kingly Fathers harme, ...	1Tamb	5.1.138	Tamb
Thy Fathers subjects and thy countrimen.	1Tamb	5.1.321	Zenoc
With happy safty of my fathers life, ...	1Tamb	5.1.401	Zenoc
Now goe I to revenge my fathers death.	2Tamb	1.2.78	Callap
But when they list, their conquering fathers hart: . .	2Tamb	1.3.36	Zenoc
And in your lives your fathers excellency.	2Tamb	2.4.76	Zenoc
Bearing the vengeance of our fathers wrongs, ...	2Tamb	3.1.17	Callap
In grievous memorie of his fathers shame, ...	2Tamb	3.1.25	Callap
And treble all his fathers slaveries.	2Tamb	3.2.158	Tamb
Whose body with his fathers I have burnt, ...	2Tamb	3.4.36	Olymp
I shall now revenge/My fathers vile abuses and mine owne.	2Tamb	3.5.91	Callap
Now brother, follow we our fathers sword, ...	2Tamb	4.1.4	Amyras
thunder in our eares/Our proper ruine, and our fathers foile?	2Tamb	4.1.14	Amyras
the good I have/Join'd with my fathers crowne would never cure.	2Tamb	4.1.58	Calyph
let me see how well/Thou wilt become thy fathers majestie.	2Tamb	5.3.184	Tamb
Guiding thy chariot with thy Fathers hand.	2Tamb	5.3.229	Tamb
'twere in my power/To favour you, but 'tis my fathers cause,	Jew	1.2.11	Calym
Child of perdition, and thy fathers shame, ...	Jew	1.2.344	Barab
Away accursed from thy fathers sight.	Jew	1.2.351	Barab
her fathers sudden fall/Has humbled her and brought her downe	Jew	1.2.367	Mthias
Now that my fathers fortune were so good/As but to be about	Jew	2.1.31	Abigal
One that I love for his good fathers sake.	Jew	2.3.31	Barab
Even for your Honourable fathers sake.	Jew	2.3.93	Barab
Welcome to France thy fathers royall seate, ...	P 590	12.3	QnMoth
I do remember in my fathers dayes, ...	Edw	1.1.109	Kent
To celebrate your fathers exequies, ...	Edw	1.1.176	BshpCv
Which for his fathers sake leane to the king, ...	Edw	1.4.283	Mortmr
Two of my fathers servants whilst he liv'de, ...	Edw	2.2.240	Neece
Did you retaine your fathers magnanimitie, ...	Edw	3.1.16	Spencr
By this right hand, and by my fathers sword, ...	Edw	3.1.130	Edward
And step into his fathers regiment.	Edw	3.1.271	Spencr
His fathers dead, and we have murdered him.	Edw	5.6.16	Queene
This argues, that you spilt my fathers bloud, ...	Edw	5.6.70	King
Goe fetche my fathers hearse, where it shall lie, . . .	Edw	5.6.94	King
Yea <I> all the wealth that our fore-fathers hid, . .	F 173	1.1.145	Cornel
Welcome grave Fathers, answere presently, ...	F 946	3.1.168	Pope
Or fathers throate; or womens groning wombe;	Lucan, First Booke	378	
The fathers selves leapt from their seats; and flying/Left	Lucan, First Booke	485	
While bond-men cheat, fathers [be hard] <hoord>, bawds hoorish,	Ovid's Elegies	1.15.17	
A woman against late-built Rome did send/The Sabine Fathers,	Ovid's Elegies	2.12.24	
The fathers thigh should unborne Bacchus lacke. . . .	Ovid's Elegies	3.3.40	
O would in my fore-fathers tombe deepe layde, ...	Ovid's Elegies	3.5.73	
Scylla by us her fathers rich haire steales, ...	Ovid's Elegies	3.11.21	
By which alone, our reverend fathers say, ...	Hero and Leander	1.267	
That Jove, usurper of his fathers seat, ...	Hero and Leander	1.452	
FATTE			
Five hundred fatte Franciscan Fryers and priestes. . . .	P 142	2.85	Guise
FAUCON			
Unto mount Faucon will we dragge his coarse:	P 319	5.46	Anjoy
FAUKNETS			
Minions, Fauknets, and Sakars to the trench, ...	2Tamb	3.3.6	Techel
FAULCHIONS			
He with his faulchions poynt raisde up at once, . . .	Dido	2.1.229	Aeneas
FAULT (See also FALT)			
Not for so small a fault my soveraigne Lord.	1Tamb	1.1.25	Meandr
That's not our fault:	Jew	1.1.130	Barab
'Tis not our fault, but thy inherent sinne.	Jew	1.2.109	1Knght
That was my father's fault.	Jew	3.3.72	Abigal
Wrinckles in beauty is a grievous fault.	Ovid's Elegies	1.8.46	
Thy fault with his fault so repuls'd will vanish. . . .	Ovid's Elegies	1.8.80	
By thine owne hand and fault thy hurt doth growe, . . .	Ovid's Elegies	1.14.43	
Wilt thou her fault learne, she may make thee tremble, .	Ovid's Elegies	2.2.17	
Minding thy fault, with death I wish to revill, . . .	Ovid's Elegies	2.5.3	
If blame, dissembling of my fault thou fearest. . . .	Ovid's Elegies	2.7.8	
And as a traitour mine owne fault confesse.	Ovid's Elegies	2.8.26	
And on the next fault punishment inflict.	Ovid's Elegies	2.14.44	
Where Mars his sonnes not without fault did breed, . . .	Ovid's Elegies	3.4.39	
Ceres, I thinke, no knowne fault will deny.	Ovid's Elegies	3.9.24	
The wench by my fault is set forth to sell.	Ovid's Elegies	3.11.10	
FAULTS			
Now serve to chastize shipboyes for their faults, . . .	Dido	4.4.157	Dido
Now inward faults thy outward forme disgrace.	Ovid's Elegies	1.10.14	
Trust me all husbands for such faults are sad/Nor make they any	Ovid's Elegies	2.2.51	
Not drunke, your faults [in] <on> the spilt wine I numbred.	Ovid's Elegies	2.5.14	

FAULTS (cont.)			
For others faults, why do I losse receive?	Ovid's Elegies	3.3.16	
But woods and groves keepe your faults undetected.	Ovid's Elegies	3.5.84	
Long have I borne much, mad thy faults me make:	Ovid's Elegies	3.10.1	
And in the bed hide all the faults you have,	Ovid's Elegies	3.13.20	
FAUNING			
His fauning wench with her desire he crownes.	Ovid's Elegies	2.2.34	
FAUSTER			
bravest tale how a Conjurer serv'd me; you know Doctor Fauster?	F1522	4.5.18	P Carter
Doctor Fauster bad me ride him night and day, and spare him no	F1540	4.5.36	P HrsCsr
FAUSTUS			
we must now performe/The forme of Faustus fortunes, good or	F 8	Prol.8	1Chor
And speake for Faustus in his infancie.	F 10	Prol.10	1Chor
Settle thy studies Faustus, and begin/To sound the depth of	F 29	1.1.1	Faust
A greater subject fitteth Faustus wit:	F 39	1.1.11	Faust
Be a Phisitian Faustus, heape up gold,	F 42	1.1.14	Faust
Why Faustus, hast thou not attain'd that end?	F 46	1.1.18	Faust
Yet art thou still but Faustus, and a man.	F 51	1.1.23	Faust
Jeromes Bible Faustus, view it well:	F 65	1.1.37	Faust
I these are those that Faustus most desires.	F 79	1.1.51	Faust
god>,/Here <Faustus> tire my <trie thy> braines to get a Deity.	F 90	1.1.62	Faust
O Faustus, lay that damned booke aside,	F 97	1.1.69	GdAngl
Go forward Faustus in that famous Art/Wherein all natures	F 101	1.1.73	BdAngl
Faustus, these bookes, thy wit, and our experience,	F 146	1.1.118	Valdes
If learned Faustus will be resolute.	F 160	1.1.132	Valdes
Then doubt not Faustus but to be renowm'd,	F 168	1.1.140	Cornel
Then tell me Faustus what shall we three want?	F 175	1.1.147	Cornel
Faustus may try his cunning by himselfe.	F 187	1.1.159	Cornel
I wonder what's become of Faustus that/Was wont to make our	F 194	1.2.1	1Schol
O Faustus <Nay>,/Then I feare that which I have long	F 219	1.2.26	1Schol
Faustus, begin thine Incantations,	F 233	1.3.5	Faust
Then feare not Faustus to <but> be resolute/And try the utmost	F 242	1.3.14	Faust
[Now <No> Faustus, thou art Conjurer laureate]/[That canst	F 260	1.3.32A	Faust
Now Faustus what wouldst thou have me do?	F 263	1.3.35	Mephst
upon me whilst I live/To do what ever Faustus shall command:	F 265	1.3.37	Faust
So Faustus hath <I have> already done, and holds <hold> this	F 283	1.3.55	Faust
To whom Faustus doth dedicate himselfe.	F 285	1.3.57	Faust
Yes Faustus, and most deerely lov'd of God.	F 293	1.3.65	Mephst
O Faustus leave these frivolous demandes,	F 309	1.3.81	Mephst
Learne thou of Faustus manly fortitude,	F 313	1.3.85	Faust
Seeing Faustus hath incur'd eternall death,	F 316	1.3.88	Faust
I will Faustus.	F 329	1.3.101	Mephst
Now Faustus, must thou needs be damn'd,	F 389	2.1.1	Faust
Now go not backward: no, Faustus, be resolute.	F 394	2.1.6	Faust
[I and Faustus will turne to God againe].	F 397	2.1.9A	Faust
Go forward Faustus in that famous Art.	F 403	2.1.15	BdAngl
Sweete Faustus leave that execrable Art.	F 404	2.1.16	GdAngl
Sweet Faustus think of heaven, and heavenly things.	F 409	2.1.21	GdAngl
No Faustus, thinke of honour and of wealth.	F 410	2.1.22	BdAngl
Faustus thou art safe.	F 414	2.1.26	Faust
That I shall waite on Faustus whilst he lives,	F 420	2.1.32	Mephst
Already Faustus hath hazarded that for thee.	F 422	2.1.34	Faust
But now <Faustus> thou must bequeath it solemnly,	F 423	2.1.35	Mephst
But tell me Faustus, shall I have thy soule?	F 434	2.1.46	Mephst
Then Faustus stab thy <thine> Arme couragiously,	F 438	2.1.50	Mephst
for love of thee/Faustus hath <I> cut his <mine> arme, and with	F 443	2.1.55	Faust
But Faustus/<thou must> Write it in manner of a Deed of Gift.	F 448	2.1.60	Mephst
Faustus gives to thee his soule: [ah] <O> there it staid.	F 456	2.1.68	Faust
Then write againe: Faustus gives to thee his soule.	F 458	2.1.70	Faust
See <come> Faustus, here is <heres> fire, set it on.	F 459	2.1.71	Mephst
And Faustus hath bequeath'd his soule to Lucifer.	F 464	2.1.76	Faust
yet shall not Faustus flye.	F 470	2.1.82	Faust
Nothing Faustus but to delight thy mind <withall>,/And let thee	F 473	2.1.85	Mephst
I Faustus, and do greater things then these.	F 476	2.1.88	Mephst
Faustus, I sweare by Hell and Lucifer,	F 481	2.1.93	Mephst
First, that Faustus may be a spirit in forme and substance.	F 485	2.1.97	P Faust
that hee shall appeare to the said John Faustus, at all times,	F 491	2.1.103	P Faust
I John Faustus of Wittenberg <Wertenberge>, Doctor, by these	F 493	2.1.105	P Faust
full power to fetch or carry the said John Faustus, body and	F 498	2.1.110	P Faust
By me John Faustus.	F 500	2.1.112	P Faust
Speake Faustus, do you deliver this as your Deed?	F 501	2.1.113	Mephst
So, now Faustus aske me what thou wilt.	F 503	2.1.115	Mephst
Why, dost thou think <think'st thou then> that Faustus shall be	F 518	2.1.130	Faust
Think'st thou that Faustus, is so fond to imagine,	F 522	2.1.134	Faust
But <Faustus> I am an instance to prove the contrary:	F 525	2.1.137	Mephst
<How, a wife? I prithee Faustus talke not of a wife>.	F 530	(HC261)A	P Mephst
Well Faustus, thou shalt have a wife.	F 531	2.1.143	Mephst
Now Faustus wilt thou have a wife?	F 533	2.1.145	Mephst
<Tel Faustus, how dost thou like thy wife>?	F 533	(HC261)A	P Mephst
<Tut Faustus>, Marriage is but a ceremoniall toy,	F 535	2.1.147	Mephst
'Twas thine own seeking Faustus, thanke thy selfe.	F 555	2.2.4	Mephst
<why Faustus> think'st thou heaven is such a glorious thing?	F 556	2.2.5	Mephst
I tell thee Faustus it is <tis> not halfe so faire/As thou, or	F 557	2.2.6	Mephst
Faustus repent, yet God will pitty thee.	F 563	2.2.12	GdAngl
I, but Faustus never shall repent.	F 568	2.2.17	BdAngl
[Faustus, thou art damn'd, then swords <guns> and knives],	F 572	2.2.21A	Faust
I am resolv'd, Faustus shall not <nere> repent.	F 583	2.2.32	Faust
And <Faustus all> jointly move upon one Axle-tree,	F 592	2.2.41	Mephst
No Faustus they be but Fables.	F 613	2.2.62	P Mephst
Move me not Faustus <for I will not tell thee>.	F 621	2.2.70	P Mephst
<Thinke thou on hell Faustus, for thou art damnd>.	F 624	(HC262)A	Mephst
Thinke Faustus upon God, that made the world.	F 625	2.2.74	P Faust
'Tis thou hast damn'd distressed Faustus soule.	F 628	2.2.77	Faust

FAUSTUS (cont.)

Never too late, if Faustus will <can> repent.	F 631	2.2.80	GdAngl
Helpe <seeke> to save distressed Faustus soule.	F 635	2.2.84	Faust
O Faustus they are come to fetch <away> thy soule.	F 641	2.2.90	Faust
Nor will [I] <Faustus> henceforth:	F 647	2.2.96	Faust
And Faustus vowes never to looke to heaven,	F 648	2.2.97	Faust
Faustus we are come from hell in person to shew thee some	F 654	2.2.103	P Belzeb
Now Faustus, question <examine> them of their <several> names	F 661	2.2.110	P Belzeb
Now Faustus thou hast heard all my progeny, wilt thou bid me to	F 700	2.2.149	P Glutny
<Now Faustus, how dost thou like this>?	F 711	(HC264) A	Lucifr
[Tut] <But> Faustus, in hell is all manner of delight.	F 713	2.2.165	Lucifr
Faustus, thou shalt, at midnight I will send for thee;	F 716	2.2.168	Lucifr
Now Faustus farewell.	F 720	2.2.172	Lucifr
<Farewel Faustus, and thinke on the divel>.	F 720	(HC264) A	Lucifr
I have gotten one of Doctor Faustus conjuring bookes, and now	F 723	2.3.2	P Robin
Learned Faustus/To find <know> the secrets of Astronomy,	F 754	2.3.33	2Chor
Thus hitherto hath Faustus spent his time.	F 799	3.1.21	Faust
I have my Faustus, and for proofe thereof,	F 803	3.1.25	Mephst
<Faustus I have, and because we wil not be unprovided,	F 805	(HC265) A	P Mephst
But <And> now my Faustus, that thou maist perceive,	F 809	3.1.31	Mephst
Nay stay my Faustus:	F 831	3.1.53	Mephst
That Faustus name, whilst this bright frame doth stand,	F 841	3.1.63	Faust
'Tis well said Faustus, come then stand by me/And thou shalt	F 843	3.1.65	Mephst
be,/That this proud Pope may Faustus [cunning] <comming> see.	F 855	3.1.77	Faust
Let it be so my Faustus, but first stay,	F 856	3.1.78	Mephst
And I'le performe it Faustus: heark they come:	F 866	3.1.88	Mephst
Faustus, I goe.	F 901	3.1.123	Mephst
The Pope shall curse that Faustus came to Rome.	F 903	3.1.125	Faust
Now tell me Faustus, are we not fitted well?	F 940	3.1.162	Mephst
Now Faustus, come prepare thy selfe for mirth,	F 981	3.2.1	Mephst
But now, that Faustus may delight his minde,	F 989	3.2.9	Faust
Faustus thou shalt, then kneele downe presently,	F 994	3.2.14	Mephst
So Faustus, now for all their holinesse,	F1004	3.2.24	Mephst
Lest Faustus make your shaven crownes to bleed.	F1007	3.2.27	Faust
Faustus no more: see where the Cardinals come.	F1008	3.2.28	Mephst
now Faustus to the feast,/The Pope had never such a frolicke	F1035	3.2.55	Faust
I, pray do, for Faustus is a dry.	F1052	3.2.72	Faust
Now Faustus, what will you do now?	F1071	3.2.91	P Mephst
Forward and backward, to curse Faustus to hell.	F1075	3.2.95	Faust
flie amaine/Unto my Faustus to the great Turkes Court.	F1137	3.3.50	Mephst
[When Faustus had with pleasure tane the view]/[Of rarest	F1138	3.3.51A	3Chor
[Which Faustus answered with such learned skill],	F1147	3.3.60A	3Chor
at whose pallace now]/[Faustus is feasted mongst his noblemen].	F1152	3.3.65A	3Chor
The learned Faustus, fame of Wittenberge,	F1165	4.1.11	Mrtino
For Faustus at the Court is late arriv'd,	F1181	4.1.27	Mrtino
Thrice learned Faustus, welcome to our Court.	F1205	4.1.51	Emper
Shall make poore Faustus to his utmost power,	F1218	4.1.64	Faust
Then Faustus as thou late didst promise us,	F1230	4.1.76	Emper
Faustus I will.	F1240	4.1.86	Mephst
Be it as Faustus please, we are content.	F1253	4.1.99	Emper
But Faustus, since I may not speake to them,	F1263	4.1.109	Emper
Faustus I see it plaine,	F1270	4.1.116	Emper
If Faustus do it, you are streight resolv'd,	F1298	4.1.144	Faust
hath Faustus justly requited this injurious knight, which being	F1312	4.1.158	P Faust
Come Faustus while the Emperour lives.	F1321	4.1.167	Emper
But Faustus death shall quit my infamie.	F1337	4.2.13	Benvol
Then Souldiers boldly fight; if Faustus die,	F1346	4.2.22	Benvol
Faustus will have heads and hands,/I, [all] <I call> your	F1393	4.2.69	Faust
Pitie us gentle Faustus, save our lives.	F1417	4.2.93	Fredrk
Then Faustus try thy skill:	F1425	4.2.101	Faust
What art thou Faustus but a man condemn'd to die?	F1478	4.4.22	Faust
Then rest thee Faustus quiet in conceit.	F1483	4.4.27	Faust
Faustus hath his leg againe, and the Horse-courser a bundle of	F1496	4.4.40	P Faust
grace to thinke but well of that which Faustus hath performed.	F1565	4.6.8	P Faust
They all cry out to speake with Doctor Faustus.	F1600	4.6.43	Servnt
Do as thou wilt Faustus, I give thee leave.	F1607	4.6.50	Duke
Master Doctor Faustus, since our conference about faire Ladies,	F1681	5.1.8	P 1Schol
[And] Faustus custome is not to deny/The just [requests]	F1690	5.1.17	Faust
<It is not Faustus custome> to deny	F1690	(HC269) B	Faust
sight <glorious deed>/Happy and blest be Faustus evermore.	F1705	5.1.32	1Schol
O gentle Faustus leave this damned Art,	F1707	5.1.34	OldMan
Then Faustus, will repentance come too late,	F1714	5.1.41	OldMan
Where art thou Faustus? wretch, what hast thou done?	F1724	5.1.51	Faust
[Damned art thou Faustus, damned, despaire and die],	F1725	5.1.52A	Faust
Saies Faustus come, thine houre is almost come,	F1727	5.1.54	Faust
And Faustus now will come to do thee right.	F1728	5.1.55	Faust
[Ah] <O> stay good Faustus, stay thy desperate steps.	F1729	5.1.56	OldMan
Faustus I leave thee, but with griefe of heart,	F1737	5.1.64	OldMan
<I goe sweete Faustus, but with heavy cheare>,	F1737	(HC269) A	OldMan
Accursed Faustus, [where is mercy now]?	F1739	5.1.66	Faust
Accursed Faustus, <wretch what hast thou done>?	F1739	(HC270) B	Faust
Thou traytor Faustus, I arrest thy soule,	F1743	5.1.70	Mephst
Do it then Faustus <quickly>, with unfained heart,	F1751	5.1.78	Mephst
<Faustus> This, or what else my Faustus shall <thou shalt>	F1766	5.1.93	Mephst
This, or what else my Faustus shall <thou shalt> desire,	F1766	5.1.93	Mephst
[Accursed Faustus, miserable man],	F1788	5.1.115A	OldMan
'Mong which as chiefe, Faustus we come to thee,	F1800	5.2.4	Lucifr
Here in this roome will wretched Faustus be.	F1804	5.2.8	Mephst
Both come from drawing Faustus latest will.	F1814	5.2.18	Mephst
Now worthy Faustus: me thinks your looks are chang'd.	F1821	5.2.25	1Schol
What ailes Faustus?	F1823	5.2.27	2Schol
<What meanes Faustus>?	F1827	(HC270) A	P 2Schol
O my deere Faustus what imports this feare?	F1827	5.2.31	1Schol

FAUSTUS (cont.)				
And Faustus shall bee cur'd.	F1831	5.2.35		2Schol
Yet Faustus looke up to heaven, and remember [Gods] mercy is	F1835	5.2.39	P	2Schol
But Faustus offence can nere be pardoned, the serpent that	F1837	5.2.41	P	Faust
the serpent that tempted Eve may be saved, but not Faustus.	F1838	5.2.42	P	Faust
for which Faustus hath lost both Germany and the world, yea	F1843	5.2.47	P	Faust
friends, what shall become of Faustus being in hell for ever?	F1847	5.2.51	P	Faust
Yet Faustus call on God.	F1848	5.2.52	P	2Schol
On God, whom Faustus hath abjur'd?	F1849	5.2.53	P	Faust
on God, whom Faustus hath blasphem'd?	F1850	5.2.54	P	Faust
Who, Faustus?	F1854	5.2.58	P	AllSch
God forbade it indeed, but Faustus hath done it:	F1858	5.2.62	P	Faust
and twenty yeares hath Faustus lost eternall joy and felicitie.	F1859	5.2.63	P	Faust
Why did not Faustus tell us of this before, that Divines might	F1862	5.2.66	P	1Schol
O what may <shal> we do to save Faustus?	F1868	5.2.72	P	2Schol
God will strengthen me, I will stay with Faustus.	F1870	5.2.74	P	3Schol
if not, Faustus is gone to hell.	F1878	5.2.82	P	Faust
Faustus, farewell.	F1879	5.2.83		AllSch
I, Faustus, now thou hast no hope of heaven,	F1880	5.2.84		Mephst
I doe confesse it Faustus, and rejoyce;	F1885	5.2.89		Mephst
Oh <Ah> Faustus, if thou hadst given eare to me,	F1892	5.2.96		GdAngl
Hadst thou kept on that way, Faustus behold,	F1903	5.2.107		GdAngl
Now Faustus let thine eyes with horror stare/Into that vaste	F1909	5.2.113		BdAngl
And so I leave thee Faustus till anon,	F1924	5.2.128		BdAngl
[Ah] <O> Faustus,/Now hast thou but one bare houre to live,	F1926	5.2.130		Faust
That Faustus may repent, and save his soule.	F1934	5.2.138		Faust
The devill will come, and Faustus must be damn'd.	F1937	5.2.141		Faust
Now draw up Faustus like a foggy mist,	F1952	5.2.156		Faust
Let Faustus live in hell a thousand yeares,	F1961	5.2.165		Faust
No Faustus, curse thy selfe, curse Lucifer,	F1973	5.2.177		Faust
Come Gentlemen, let us go visit Faustus,	F1983	5.3.1		1Schol
O help us heaven, see, here are Faustus limbs,	F1988	5.3.6		2Schol
The devils whom Faustus serv'd have torne him thus:	F1990	5.3.8		3Schol
tho Faustus end be such/As every Christian heart laments to	F1995	5.3.13		2Schol
Faustus is gone, regard his hellish fall,	F2005	5.3.23		4Chor
Forward and backward, to curse Faustus to hell.	F App	p.232 26		Faust
here I ha stolne one of doctor Faustus conjuring books, and	F App	p.233 2	P	Robin
tell thee, we were for ever made by this doctor Faustus booke?	F App	p.234 2	P	Robin
Maister doctor Faustus, I have heard strange report of thy	F App	p.236 1	P	Emper
Then doctor Faustus, marke what I shall say, As I was sometime	F App	p.236 17	P	Emper
hath Faustus worthily requited this injurious knight, which	F App	p.238 83	P	Faust
what art thou Faustus but a man condemnd to die?	F App	p.240 121	P	Faust
Then rest thee Faustus quiet in conceit.	F App	p.240 126		Faust
Faustus has his legge againe, and the Horsecourser I take it,	F App	p.241 164	P	Faust
Ah Doctor Faustus, that I might prevaile,	F App	p.243 34		OldMan
But mercie Faustus of thy Saviour sweete,	F App	p.243 44		OldMan
FAVOR				
Favor him my lord, as much as lieth in you.	Edw	5.1.147		Leistr
Inconstant Edmund, doost thou favor him,	Edw	5.2.101		Mortmr
I meane so sir with your favor.	F App	p.234 11	P	Vintnr
FAVORD				
Fortune hath favord thee what ere thou be,	Dido	1.1.231		Venus
FAVORET				
Good Pierce of Gaveston my sweet favoret,	Edw	3.1.228		Edward
FAVORIT				
Then live and be the favorit of a king?	Edw	1.1.5		Gavstn
But for thou wert the favorit of a King,	Edw	2.5.27		Warwck
I have no mistris, nor no favorit,	Ovid's Elegies			1.1.23
FAVORITE				
heire of [fame] <furie>, the favorite of the [fates] <face>,	Dido	3.2.3		Juno
FAVORS				
And with the earle of Kent that favors him.	Edw	1.4.34		MortSr
If in his absence thus he favors him,	Edw	2.2.47		Mortmr
Where womens favors hung like labels downe.	Edw	2.2.187		Mortmr
For favors done in him, unto us all.	Edw	3.1.42		SpncrP
Deserveth princelie favors and rewardes,	Edw	4.6.54		Mortmr
FAVOUR				
That crave such favour at your honors feete,	Dido	1.2.5		Illion
But Dido is the favour I request.	Dido	3.1.18		Iarbus
And doubt you not, but if you favour me,	1Tamb	2.3.10		Tamb
Those words of favour, and those comfortings,	1Tamb	3.2.62		Agidas
unto your majesty/May merit favour at your highnesse handes,	1Tamb	4.4.70		Zenoc
No speach to that end, by your favour sir.	2Tamb	1.2.14		Almeda
'twere in my power/To favour you, but 'tis my fathers cause,	Jew	1.2.11		Calym
To make me shew them favour severally,	Jew	3.3.38		Abigal
That by my favour they should both be slaine?	Jew	3.3.39		Abigal
Shall buy that strumpets favour with his blood,	P 768	15.26		Guise
Now sues the King for favour to the Guise,	P 978	19.48		Guise
And when this favour Isabell forgets,	Edw	1.4.297		Queene
Should by his soveraignes favour grow so pert,	Edw	1.4.404		Mortmr
But he that hath the favour of a king,	Edw	2.1.8		Spencr
Can get you any favour with great men.	Edw	2.1.41		Spencr
I, and tis likewise thought you favour him <them> <'em> <hem>.	Edw	2.2.226		Edward
He that I list to favour shall be great:	Edw	2.2.263		Edward
And daily will enrich thee with our favour,	Edw	3.1.50		Edward
if you will doe us so much <that> favour, as to let us see that	F1685	5.1.12	P	1Schol
and draw the Commons minds/To favour thee, against the Senats	Lucan, First Booke			276
famous names/Farewel, your favour nought my minde inflames.	Ovid's Elegies			2.1.36
She safe by favour of her judge doth rest.	Ovid's Elegies			2.2.56
For I confesse, if that might merite favour,	Ovid's Elegies			2.4.3
and too much his griefe doth favour/That seekes the conquest by	Ovid's Elegies			2.5.11
Yet Galatea favour thou her ship.	Ovid's Elegies			2.11.34
My wench, Lucina, I intreat thee favour,	Ovid's Elegies			2.13.21

FAVOUR (cont.)			
Let us all conquer by our mistris favour.	Ovid's Elegies	3.2.18	
One slowe we favour, Romans him revoke:	Ovid's Elegies	3.2.73	
Was moov'd with him, and for his favour sought.	Hero and Leander	1.82	
Now he her favour and good will had wone.	Hero and Leander	2.54	
FAVOURED			
I, and it greeves me that I favoured him.	Edw	2.2.213	Kent
Then to be favoured of your majestie.	Edw	2.2.255	Spencr
Both are wel favoured, both rich in array,	Ovid's Elegies	2.10.5	
FAVOUREDLY			
With his stumpe-foote he halts ill-favouredly.	Ovid's Elegies	2.17.20	
FAVOURLES			
Yes, and Iarbus foule and favourles.	Dido	3.1.64	Anna
FAVOURS			
mightier Kings)/Hast had the greatest favours I could give:	Dido	3.1.13	Dido
Flinging in favours of more soveraigne worth,	Dido	3.1.131	Dido
how may I deserve/Such amourous favours at thy beautious hand?	Dido	3.2.65	Juno
And feedes his eyes with favours of her Court,	Dido	3.2.71	Juno
Now let him hang my favours on his masts,	Dido	4.4.159	Dido
As his exceding favours have deserv'd,	1Tamb	3.2.10	Zenoc
And let him not be entertain'd the worse/Because he favours me.	Jew	Prol.35	Machvl
The many favours which your grace hath showne,	P 9	1.9	Navrre
Remooveles from the favours of your King.	P 609	12.22	King
He whom she favours lives, the other dies.	Hero and Leander	1.124	
FAVOURST			
Yet whom thou favourst, pray may conquerour be.	Ovid's Elegies	3.2.2	
What horse-driver thou favourst most is best,	Ovid's Elegies	3.2.7	
FAWNE (Homograph; See also FAUNING)			
Whom Ajax ravisht in Dianas [Fane] <Fawne>,	Dido	2.1.275	Aeneas
We Jewes can fawne like Spaniels when we please;	Jew	2.3.20	Barab
Ile [fawne] <fanne> first on the winde,/That glaunceth at my	Edw	1.1.22	Gavstn
Can kinglie Lions fawne on creeping Ants?	Edw	1.4.15	Penbrk
Fawne not on me French strumpet, get thee gone.	Edw	1.4.145	Edward
On whom but on my husband should I fawne?	Edw	1.4.146	Queene
FAWNES			
Gote-footed Satyrs, and up-staring <upstarting> Fawnes,	Hero and Leander	2.200	
FAYLE			
Her friends doe multiply and yours doe fayle,	Edw	4.5.2	Spencr
FAYRE			
So fayre she was, Atalanta she resembled,	Ovid's Elegies	1.7.13	
Fayre lined slippers for the cold:	Passionate Shepherd	15	
FAYTHE			
and that thow most reposest one my faythe	Paris	ms31,p391	Guise
FEALTIE			
cause sweare we to him/All homage, fealtie and forwardnes,	Edw	4.4.20	Mortmr
FEAR			
Poore soldiers stand with fear of death dead strooken,	Hero and Leander	1.121	
FEAR'D			
So am I fear'd among all Nations.	2Tamb	1.1.151	Orcan
Goe fetch him straight. I alwayes fear'd that Jew.	Jew	5.1.18	Govnr
Nay, they fear'd not to speak in the streetes,	P 876	17.71	Eprnon
And without ground, fear'd, what themselves had faind:	Lucan, First Booke	482	
Wel might these feare, when Pompey fear'd and fled.	Lucan, First Booke	519	
But in times past I fear'd vaine shades, and night,	Ovid's Elegies	1.6.9	
and I fear'd the Bull and Eagle/And what ere love made Jove	Ovid's Elegies	1.10.7	
By fear'd Anubis visage I thee pray,	Ovid's Elegies	2.13.11	
FEARD			
Because I feard your grace would keepe me here.	Dido	4.4.20	Achat
Feard am I more then lov'd, let me be feard,	Edw	5.4.52	Mortmr
I feard as much, murther cannot be hid.	Edw	5.6.46	Queene
what [rockes] <rocke> the feard Cerannia <Ceraunia> threat,	Ovid's Elegies	2.11.19	
God is a name, no substance, feard in vaine,	Ovid's Elegies	3.3.23	
And calves from whose feard front no threatning flyes,	Ovid's Elegies	3.12.15	
FEARDE			
Wouldst thou be lovde and fearde?	Edw	1.1.168	Edward
FEARD'ST			
Thou feard'st (great Pompey) that late deeds would dim/Olde	Lucan, First Booke	121	
FEARDST			
Feardst thou to dresse them?	Ovid's Elegies	1.14.5	
FEARE			
The rest we feare are foulded in the flouds.	Dido	1.2.31	Cloan
I feare me Dido hath been counted light,	Dido	3.1.14	Dido
Feare not Iarbus, Dido may be thine.	Dido	3.1.19	Dido
But much I feare my sonne will nere consent,	Dido	3.2.82	Venus
Yet lest he should, for I am full of feare,	Dido	4.4.108	Dido
I feare I sawe Aeneas little sonne,	Dido	5.1.83	Dido
Surpriz'd with feare of hideous revenge,	1Tamb	3.2.68	Agidas
He needed not with words confirme my feare,	1Tamb	3.2.92	Agidas
Go wander free from feare of Tyrants rage,	1Tamb	3.2.102	Agidas
The onely feare and terrour of the world,	1Tamb	3.3.45	Tamb
Which lately made all Europe quake for feare:	1Tamb	3.3.135	Bajzth
As Concubine I feare, to feed his lust.	1Tamb	4.3.42	Souldn
For Fame I feare hath bene too prodigall,	1Tamb	4.3.48	Arabia
Halfe dead for feare before they feele my wrath:	1Tamb	4.4.4	Tamb
I feare the custome proper to his sword,	1Tamb	5.1.13	Govnr
Would not with too much cowardize or feare,	1Tamb	5.1.37	Govnr
Nothing but feare and fatall steele my Lord.	1Tamb	5.1.109	1Virgn
And feare to see thy kingly Fathers harme,	1Tamb	5.1.138	Tamb
Shake with their waight in signe of feare and griefe:	1Tamb	5.1.349	Zenoc
In feare and feeling of the like distresse,	1Tamb	5.1.361	Zenoc
love and feare presents/A thousand sorrowes to my martyred	1Tamb	5.1.383	Zenoc
and Danes/[Feares] <feare> not Orcanes, but great Tamburlaine:	2Tamb	1.1.59	Orcan
As I cried out for feare he should have falne.	2Tamb	1.3.42	Zenoc

FEARE (cont.)

And quake for feare, as if infernall Jove/Meaning to aid [thee]	2Tamb	1.3.143	Techel
And canst thou Coward stand in feare of death?	2Tamb	3.2.102	Tamb
And wilt thou shun the field for feare of woundes?	2Tamb	3.2.109	Tamb
(Perdicas) and I feare as litle their tara, tantaras, their	2Tamb	4.1.67	P Calyph
and for feare I should be affraid, would put it off and come to	2Tamb	4.1.69	P Calyph
Such a feare (my Lord) would never make yee retire.	2Tamb	4.1.71	P Perdic
But now I finde thee, and that feare is past.	2Tamb	4.2.20	Therid
Feare not my Lord, I see great Mahomet/Clothed in purple	2Tamb	5.2.31	Amasia
monster death/Shaking and quivering, pale and wan for feare,	2Tamb	5.3.68	Tamb
Thus are the villaines, cowards fled for feare,	2Tamb	5.3.115	Tamb
I feare their comming will afflict us all.	Jew	1.1.156	2Jew
Which Tribute all in policie, I feare,	Jew	1.1.181	Barab
Feare not their sale, for they'll be quickly bought.	Jew	2.3.2	1Offcr
I feare me 'tis about faire Abigall.	Jew	2.3.139	Mthias
Compassion, love, vaine hope, and hartlesse feare,	Jew	2.3.170	Barab
no, but happily he stands in feare/Of that which you, I thinke,	Jew	2.3.282	Barab
This followes well, and therefore daughter feare not.	Jew	2.3.313	Barab
Feare not, I'le so set his heart a fire,	Jew	2.3.375	Ithimr
I feare she knowes ('tis so) of my device/In Don Mathias and	Jew	3.4.7	Barab
And make him stand in feare of me.	Jew	3.6.43	2Fryar
For my part feare you not.	Jew	4.1.10	Ithimr
I feare they know we sent the poyson'd broth.	Jew	4.1.26	Barab
So, now the feare is past, and I am safe:	Jew	4.1.114	Barab
I feare me he mistrusts what we intend.	Jew	4.1.133	Ithimr
Rather for feare then love.	Jew	4.2.107	P Ithimr
Feare not, my Lord, for here, against the [sluice] <Truce>,/The	Jew	5.1.86	Barab
not thine opportunity, for feare too late/Thou seek'st for much,	Jew	5.2.45	Barab
Nor feare I death, nor will I flatter thee.	Jew	5.2.60	Govnr
I feare me, Messenger, to feast my traine/Within a Towne of	Jew	5.3.21	Calym
To have some care for feare of enemies.	P 224	4.22	QnMoth
I feare the Guisians have past the bridge,	P 363	7.3	Ramus
How may we doe? I feare me they will live.	P 420	7.60	Guise
For feare that Guise joyn'd with the King of Spaine,	P 573	11.38	Navrre
Put of that feare, they are already joynde,	P 605	12.18	King
Will laugh I feare me at their good aray.	P 673	13.17	Duchss
Your highnes needs not feare mine armies force,	P 857	17.52	Guise
That wicked Guise I feare me much will be,	P 921	18.22	Navrre
What, will you not feare when you see him come?	P 933	19.3	Capt
Feare him said you?	P 934	19.4	P 1Mur
I, I, feare not: stand close, so, be resolute:	P 943	19.13	Capt
Let mean consaits, and baser men feare death,	P 997	19.67	Guise
And princes with their lookes ingender feare.	P 999	19.69	Guise
The king I feare hath ill intreated her.	Edw	1.4.189	Warwck
Feare ye not Madam, now his minions gone,	Edw	1.4.198	Lncstr
Feare not, the queens words cannot alter him.	Edw	1.4.233	Penbrk
And feare to offend the meanest noble man.	Edw	1.4.277	Mortmr
I feare me he is wrackt upon the sea.	Edw	2.2.2	Edward
I feare me you are sent of pollicie,	Edw	2.3.5	Lncstr
I feare me he is slaine my gratious lord.	Edw	2.4.2	Spencr
And feare not lord and father, heavens great beames/On Atlas	Edw	3.1.76	Prince
this towardnes makes thy mother feare/Thou art not markt to	Edw	3.1.79	Queene
Feare it not.	Edw	4.1.18	Kent
To them that fight in right and feare his wrath:	Edw	4.6.20	Queene
Have you no doubt my Lorde, have you no feare,	Edw	4.7.1	Abbot
and here to pine in feare/Of Mortimer and his confederates.	Edw	4.7.35	Baldck
Our lots are cast, I feare me so is thine.	Edw	4.7.79	Baldck
What, feare you not the furie of your king?	Edw	5.1.75	Edward
In any case, take heed of childish feare,	Edw	5.2.6	Mortmr
Feare not my Lord, weele do as you commaund.	Edw	5.2.66	Matrvs
Feare not to kill the king tis good he die.	Edw	5.4.9	Mortmr
Kill not the king tis good to feare the worst.	Edw	5.4.12	Mortmr
Feare not sweete boye, ile garde thee from thy foes,	Edw	5.4.111	Queene
Feare not you that.	Edw	5.5.36	Matrvs
Still feare I, and I know not whats the cause,	Edw	5.5.85	Edward
Now as I speake they fall, and yet with feare/Open againe.	Edw	5.5.95	Edward
This feare is that which makes me tremble thus,	Edw	5.5.105	Edward
I feare mee that this crie will raise the towne,	Edw	5.5.114	Matrvs
Gurney, my lord, is fled, and will I feare,	Edw	5.6.7	Matrvs
All tremble at my name, and I feare none,	Edw	5.6.13	Mortmr
Feare not my lord, know that you are a king.	Edw	5.6.24	1Lord
But you I feare, conspirde with Mortimer.	Edw	5.6.37	King
My lord, I feare me it will proove too true.	Edw	5.6.77	2Lord
Then I feare that which I have long suspected:	F 220	1.2.27	1Schol
<O but> I feare me, nothing will <can> reclaime him now.	F 227	1.2.34	1Schol
Then feare not Faustus to <but> be resolute/And try the utmost	F 242	1.3.14	Faust
I feare not your searching; we scorne to steale your cups I can	F1105	3.3.18	P Dick
Nay feare not man, we have no power to kill.	F1440	4.3.10	Mrtino
O my deere Faustus what imports this feare?	F1827	5.2.31	1Schol
<to cure him, tis but a surffet, never feare man>.	F1831	(HC270)A	P 2Schol
Tis but a surfet sir, feare nothing.	F1832	5.2.36	3Schol
blacke survey/Great Potentates do kneele with awful feare,	F App	p.235 35	Mephst
feare me) never attaine to that degree of high renowne and	F App	p.236 22	P Emper
this spectacle/Stroake Caesars hart with feare, his hayre	Lucan, First Booke		195
They shooke for feare, and cold benumm'd their lims,	Lucan, First Booke		248
they, and none durst speake/And shew their feare, or griefe:	Lucan, First Booke		260
Vaine fame increast true feare, and did invade/The peoples	Lucan, First Booke		465
Then with their feare, and danger al distract,	Lucan, First Booke		487
Wel might these feare, when Pompey fear'd and fled.	Lucan, First Booke		519
My feare transcends my words,/Yet more will happen then I can	Lucan, First Booke		633
Thee all shall feare and worship as a King,	Ovid's Elegies		1.2.33
Smooth speeches, feare and rage shall by thee ride,	Ovid's Elegies		1.2.35
Suspitious feare in all my veines will hover,	Ovid's Elegies		1.4.42

FEARE (cont.)			
Thee feare I too much:	Ovid's Elegies	1.6.15	
She nothing said, pale feare her tongue had tyed.	Ovid's Elegies	1.7.20	
Now all feare with my mindes hot love abates,	Ovid's Elegies	1.10.9	
Beleeve me, whom we feare, we wish to perish.	Ovid's Elegies	2.2.10	
Feare to be guilty, then thou maiest desemble.	Ovid's Elegies	2.2.18	
Isis may be done/Nor feare least she to th'theater's runne.	Ovid's Elegies	2.2.26	
Angry I was, but feare my wrath exempted.	Ovid's Elegies	2.13.4	
But if in so great feare I may advize thee,	Ovid's Elegies	2.13.27	
My life, that I will shame thee never feare,	Ovid's Elegies	2.15.21	
Nor thy gulfes crooked Malea, would I feare.	Ovid's Elegies	2.16.24	
Let us both lovers hope, and feare a like,	Ovid's Elegies	2.19.5	
And feare those, that to feare them least intend.	Ovid's Elegies	3.3.32	
Who, without feare, is chaste, is chast in sooth:	Ovid's Elegies	3.4.3	
Thy feare is, then her body, valued more.	Ovid's Elegies	3.4.30	
She pleaseth best, I feare, if any say.	Ovid's Elegies	3.4.32	
Feare not: to thee our Court stands open wide,	Ovid's Elegies	3.5.61	
There shalt be lov'd: Ilia lay feare aside.	Ovid's Elegies	3.5.62	
By feare depriv'd of strength to runne away.	Ovid's Elegies	3.5.70	
For me, she doth keeper, and husband feare,	Ovid's Elegies	3.7.63	
I feare with me is common now to many.	Ovid's Elegies	3.11.6	
Where seeing a naked man, she scriecht for feare,	Hero and Leander	2.237	
She overcome with shame and sallow feare,	Hero and Leander	2.260	
FEARED			
My feared hands thrice back she did repell.	Ovid's Elegies	1.7.62	
Nor feared they thy body to annoy?	Ovid's Elegies	3.8.42	
FEAREFUL			
[But feareful ecchoes thunder <thunders> in mine eares],	F 571	2.2.20A	Faust
FEAREFULL			
Since with the spirit of his fearefull pride,	1Tamb	2.6.12	Meandr
And fearefull vengeance light upon you both.	1Tamb	2.7.52	Cosroe
strike flames of lightening)/All fearefull foldes his sailes,	1Tamb	3.2.82	Agidas
And jealous anger of his fearefull arme/Be pour'd with rigour	2Tamb	2.1.57	Fredrk
Such fearefull shrikes, and cries, were never heard,	F1986	5.3.4	1Schol
Affrights poore fearefull men, and blasts their eyes/With	Lucan, First Booke	155	
At night in dreadful vision fearefull Roome,	Lucan, First Booke	188	
Wa'st not enough the fearefull Wench to chide?	Ovid's Elegies	1.7.45	
To empty aire may go my fearefull speech.	Ovid's Elegies	3.1.62	
her coate hood-winckt her fearefull eyes,/And into water	Ovid's Elegies	3.5.79	
FEARELESSE			
And fearelesse spurne the killing Basiliske:	F 921	3.1.143	Pope
Night shamelesse, wine and Love are fearelesse made.	Ovid's Elegies	1.6.60	
In sleeping shall I fearelesse drawe my breath?	Ovid's Elegies	2.19.55	
FEARES			
Brave men at armes, abandon fruitles feares,	Dido	1.2.32	Iarbus
Leave to lament lest they laugh at our feares.	Dido	2.1.38	Achat
and Danes/[Feares] <feare> not Orcanes, but great Tamburlaine:	2Tamb	1.1.59	Orcan
Heere hast thou a country voide of feares,	P 591	12.4	QnMoth
Now while their part is weake, and feares, march hence,	Lucan, First Booke	281	
men/Whom death the greatest of all feares affright not,	Lucan, First Booke	455	
Who feares these armes? who wil not go to meete them?	Ovid's Elegies	1.6.39	
Ungrate why feignest new feares?	Ovid's Elegies	2.8.23	
The carefull ship-man now feares angry gusts,	Ovid's Elegies	2.11.25	
FEAREST			
If blame, dissembling of my fault thou fearest.	Ovid's Elegies	2.7.8	
FEARFUL			
fearful coward, stragling from the camp/When Kings themselves	1Tamb	2.4.16	Tamb
FEARFULL			
When with their fearfull tongues they shall confesse/Theise are	1Tamb	1.2.222	Usumc
And let his foes like flockes of fearfull Roes,	1Tamb	3.3.192	Zenoc
The jealous bodie of his fearfull wife,	1Tamb	5.1.86	1Virgn
Your fearfull minds are thicke and mistie then,	1Tamb	5.1.110	Tamb
that in her wings/Caries the fearfull thunderbolts of Jove.	2Tamb	1.1.101	Orcan
Flieng Dragons, lightning, fearfull thunderclaps,	2Tamb	3.2.10	Tamb
Now thou art fearfull of thy armies strength,	2Tamb	3.5.75	Orcan
What fearfull cries comes from the river [Sene] <Rene>,/That	P 361	7.1	Ramus
FEARFULLY			
I see how fearfully ye would refuse,	2Tamb	3.5.73	Tamb
FEARING			
Fearing the force of Boreas boistrous blasts.	1Tamb	2.4.5	Mycet
Fearing his love through my unworthynesse.	1Tamb	3.2.65	Zenoc
Fearing my power should pull him from his throne.	1Tamb	5.1.453	Tamb
Fearing the worst of this before it fell,	Jew	1.2.246	Barab
Fearing the afflictions which my father feeles,	Jew	1.2.322	Abigal
Fearing the enemy <ruine> of thy haplesse <hopelesse> soule.	F1738	5.1.65	OldMan
From no mans reading fearing to be sav'd.	Ovid's Elegies	3.1.54	
Fearing her owne thoughts made her to be hated.	Hero and Leander	2.44	
She, fearing on the rushes to be flung,	Hero and Leander	2.66	
her selfe the clouds among/And now Leander fearing to be mist,	Hero and Leander	2.91	
FEAR'ST			
And fear'st to die, or with a Curtle-axe/To hew thy flesh and	2Tamb	3.2.96	Tamb
FEARST			
Fearst thou thy person? thou shalt have a guard:	Edw	1.1.166	Edward
FEAST			
And feast the birds with their bloud-shotten balles,	Dido	3.2.35	Venus
this happy conquest/Triumph, and solemnize a martiall feast.	1Tamb	3.3.273	Tamb
I'le feast you, lodge you, give you faire words,	Jew	4.1.126	Barab
To a solemne feast/I will invite young Selim-Calymath,	Jew	5.2.96	Barab
And then to make provision for the feast,	Jew	5.2.119	Barab
to feast my traine/Within a Towne of warre so lately pillag'd,	Jew	5.3.21	Calym
I cannot feast my men in Malta wals,	Jew	5.3.34	Calym
Wee'll in this Summer Evening feast with him.	Jew	5.3.41	Calym
we may grace us best/To solemnize our Governors great feast.	Jew	5.3.45	Calym

Line	Work	Ref	Speaker
FEAST (cont.)			
That thou maist feast them in thy Citadell.	Jew	5.5.16	Msngr
To punish those that doe prophane this holy feast.	P 617	12.30	Mugern
What now remaines, but for a while to feast,	P 627	12.40	King
Now let us in, and feast it roiallie:	Edw	1.4.374	Edward
Cosin, this day shalbe your mariage feast,	Edw	2.2.256	Edward
And take some part of holy Peters feast,	F 777	2.3.56	2Chor
<faine> see the Pope/And take some part of holy Peters feast,	F 832	3.1.54	Mephst
That we may solemnize Saint Peters feast,	F 978	3.1.200	Pope
now Faustus to the feast,/The Pope had never such a frolicke	F1035	3.2.55	Faust
and see where they come, belike the feast is done.	F1680	5.1.7	P Wagner
See where they come: belike the feast is ended.	F App	p.243 8	Wagner
Now many guests were gone, the feast being done,	Ovid's Elegies	2.5.21	
He to th'Hetrurians Junoes feast commended,	Ovid's Elegies	3.12.35	
Rose-cheekt Adonis) kept a solemne feast.	Hero and Leander	1.93	
On this feast day, O cursed day and hower,	Hero and Leander	1.131	
FEASTED			
intreat your Highnesse/Not to depart till he has feasted you.	Jew	5.3.33	Msngr
at whose pallace now]/[Faustus is feasted mongst his noblemen].	F1152	3.3.65A	3Chor
Wherewith the king of Gods and men is feasted.	Hero and Leander	1.432	
FEASTING			
Apolloes southsayers; and Joves feasting priests;	Lucan, First Booke	601	
FEASTS			
So shalt thou go with youths to feasts together,	Ovid's Elegies	3.4.47	
The Priests to Juno did prepare chaste feasts,	Ovid's Elegies	3.12.3	
FEATHER (See also FETHERED)			
on his silver crest/A snowy Feather spangled white he beares,	1Tamb	4.1.51	2Msngr
There Junoes bird displayes his gorgious feather,	Ovid's Elegies	2.6.55	
FEATHERBED (See FETHERBED)			
FEATHERED			
The golden stature of their feathered bird/That spreads her	1Tamb	4.2.105	Tamb
And Eagles wings join'd to her feathered breast,	2Tamb	3.4.62	Therid
At his faire feathered feet, the engins layd,	Hero and Leander	1.449	
FEATHERS			
If that thy fancie in his feathers dwell,	Dido	1.1.39	Jupitr
And sticke these spangled feathers in thy hat,	Dido	2.1.314	Venus
And Jetty Feathers menace death and hell.	1Tamb	4.1.61	2Msngr
Then <or>, like a Fan of Feathers, I kisse her [lippes]; And	F 667	2.2.116	P Pride
FEATURE			
I loath her manners, love her bodies feature.	Ovid's Elegies	3.10.38	
FEBLE			
glut our swords/That thirst to drinke the feble Perseans blood.	1Tamb	3.3.165	Bajzth
And shed their feble influence in the aire.	2Tamb	5.3.5	Therid
FECHT			
Whom Troiane ships fecht from Europa farre.	Ovid's Elegies	1.10.2	
FED			
That fed upon the substance of his child.	1Tamb	4.4.25	Zabina
But if his highnesse would let them be fed, it would doe them	1Tamb	4.4.34	P Therid
thou maist thinke thy selfe happie to be fed from my trencher.	1Tamb	4.4.92	P Tamb
Had fed the feeling of their maisters thoughts,	1Tamb	5.1.162	Tamb
Hath Bajazeth bene fed to day?	1Tamb	5.1.192	Tamb
Fed with the fresh supply of earthly dregs,	2Tamb	3.2.8	Tamb
That King Egeus fed with humaine flesh,	2Tamb	4.3.13	Tamb
You shal be fed with flesh as raw as blood,	2Tamb	4.3.18	Tamb
And fishes [fed] <feed> by humaine carkasses,	2Tamb	5.1.206	Techel
These, that are fed with soppes of flaming fire,	F1916	5.2.120	BdAngl
On mast of oakes, first oracles, men fed,	Ovid's Elegies	3.9.9	
Which with the grasse of Tuscane fields are fed.	Ovid's Elegies	3.12.14	
FEE			
Nor quit good turnes with double fee downe told:	Dido	3.2.15	Juno
Yet gentle monkes, for treasure, golde nor fee,	Edw	4.7.24	Edward
FEEBLE (See also FEBLE)			
Drawes bloody humours from my feeble partes,	1Tamb	4.4.95	Bajzth
I am too weake and feeble to resist,	Edw	5.5.108	Edward
Through numming cold, all feeble, faint and wan:	Hero and Leander	2.246	
FEED			
I goe to feed the humour of my Love,	Dido	3.1.50	Iarbus
Where flames shall ever feed upon his soule.	1Tamb	2.6.8	Cosroe
The heat and moisture which did feed each other,	1Tamb	2.7.46	Cosroe
For want of nourishment to feed them both,	1Tamb	2.7.47	Cosroe
And thou his wife shalt feed him with the scraps/My servitures	1Tamb	4.2.87	Tamb
As Concubine I feare, to feed his lust.	1Tamb	4.3.42	Souldn
Tamburlane) as I could willingly feed upon thy blood-raw hart.	1Tamb	4.4.12	P Bajzth
Why feed ye still on daies accursed beams,	1Tamb	5.1.262	Bajzth
And feed my mind that dies for want of her:	2Tamb	2.4.128	Tamb
Ile have you learne to feed on provander,	2Tamb	3.5.106	Tamb
vaine or Artier feed/The cursed substance of that cruel heart,	2Tamb	4.1.177	Soria
And fishes [fed] <feed> by humaine carkasses,	2Tamb	5.1.206	Techel
I, those are they that feed him with their golde,	P 845	17.40	King
One that was feed for Caesar, and whose tongue/Could tune the	Lucan, First Booke	272	
There harmelesse Swans feed all abroad the river,	Ovid's Elegies	2.6.53	
she wanting no excuse/To feed him with delaies, as women use:	Hero and Leander	1.426	
FEEDE			
To feede her eyes with his engraven fame.	Dido	1.1.103	Jupitr
And feede infection with his [let] <left> out life:	Dido	3.2.11	Juno
Feede you slave, thou maist thinke thy selfe happie to be fed	1Tamb	4.4.92	P Tamb
I (my Lord) but none save kinges must feede with these.	1Tamb	4.4.109	P Therid
Ile feede thy divel with horse-bread as long as he lives,	F App	p.234 30	P Rafe
either heed/What please them, and their eyes let either feede.	Ovid's Elegies	3.2.6	
Seeing the Sheepheards feede theyr flocks,	Passionate Shepherd	6	
FEEDES			
And feedes his eyes with favours of her Court,	Dido	3.2.71	Juno
And on their points his fleshlesse bodie feedes.	1Tamb	5.1.115	Tamb

FEEDES (cont.)			
O how this sight doth delight <this feedes> my soule.	F 712	2.2.164	Faust
FEEDING			
And feeding them with thin and slender fare,	1Tamb	3.3.49	Tamb
Or flaming Titan (feeding on the deepe)/Puls them aloft, and	Lucan, First Booke		416
FEEDS			
Yet since a farther passion feeds my thoughts,	1Tamb	3.2.13	Zenoc
And feeds upon the banefull tree of hell,	2Tamb	2.3.19	Orcan
of that vitall aire/That feeds the body with his dated health,	2Tamb	2.4.45	Zenoc
That feeds upon her sonnes and husbands flesh.	2Tamb	3.4.72	Olymp
The Governour feeds not as I doe.	Jew	4.4.63	P Barab
FEEL			
Now shalt thou feel the force of Turkish arms,	1Tamb	3.3.134	Bajzth
FEELD			
Yea madam, and they scape not easilie,/That fled the feeld.	Edw	4.6.42	Mortmr
FEELE			
Leave words and let them feele your lances pointes,	1Tamb	3.3.91	Argier
Let Tamburlaine for his offences feele/Such plagues as heaven	1Tamb	4.3.44	Arabia
Halfe dead for feare before they feele my wrath:	1Tamb	4.4.4	Tamb
must you be first shal feele/The sworne destruction of	1Tamb	5.1.65	Tamb
To feele the lovely warmth of shepheards flames,	1Tamb	5.1.186	Tamb
Let the dishonor of the paines I feele,	2Tamb	2.3.5	Sgsmnd
I feele my liver pierc'd and all my vaines,	2Tamb	3.4.6	Capt
Now you shal feele the strength of Tamburlain,	2Tamb	4.1.135	Tamb
But stay, I feele my selfe distempered sudainly.	2Tamb	5.1.218	Tamb
Yet make them feele the strength of Tamburlain,	2Tamb	5.3.37	Usumc
And I shall dye too, for I feele death comming.	Jew	3.6.8	Abigal
Shall feele the house of Lorayne is his foe:	P 856	17.51	Guise
No, let the villaine dye, and feele in hell,	P1174	22.36	King
But that I feele the crowne upon my head,	Edw	5.1.82	Edward
I feele a hell of greefe: where is my crowne?	Edw	5.5.90	Edward
Il'e make you feele something anon, if my Art faile me not.	F1246	4.1.92	P Faust
It is your owne you meane, feele on your head.	F1443	4.3.13	Fredrk
I feele thy words to comfort my distressed soule,	F1735	5.1.62	Faust
Nay, thou must feele them, taste the smart of all:	F1922	5.2.126	BdAngl
thee hornes, but makes thee weare them, feele on thy head.	F App	p.238 71	P Emper
Then such as in their bondage feele content.	Ovid's Elegies		1.2.18
We people wholy given thee, feele thine armes,	Ovid's Elegies		2.9.11
That seeing thy teares can any joy then feele.	Ovid's Elegies		3.5.60
And wisht the goddesse long might feele loves fire.	Ovid's Elegies		3.9.42
FEELES			
Then feeles your majesty no sovereaigne ease,	2Tamb	5.3.213	Usumc
My body feeles, my soule dooth weepe to see/Your sweet desires	2Tamb	5.3.246	Tamb
Fearing the afflictions which my father feeles,	Jew	1.2.322	Abigal
Trust in good verse, Tibullus feeles deaths paines,	Ovid's Elegies		3.8.39
FEELING			
Had fed the feeling of their maisters thoughts,	1Tamb	5.1.162	Tamb
In feare and feeling of the like distresse,	1Tamb	5.1.361	Zenoc
A very feeling one; have not the Nuns fine sport with the	Jew	3.3.32	P Ithimr
FEEND			
What God or Feend, or spirit of the earth,	1Tamb	2.6.15	Ortyg
No Feend, no Fortune, nor no hope of end/To our infamous	1Tamb	5.1.240	Zabina
O damned monster, nay a Feend of Hell,	2Tamb	4.1.168	Jrslem
FEENDS			
Then as I looke downe to the damned Feends,	1Tamb	4.2.26	Bajzth
Feends looke on me, and thou dread God of hell,	1Tamb	4.2.27	Bajzth
and let the Feends infernall view/As are the blasted banks of	1Tamb	5.1.242	Zabina
With apples like the heads of damned Feends.	2Tamb	2.3.23	Orcan
FEET			
Or plead for mercie at your highnesse feet.	1Tamb	1.1.73	Therid
Me thinks I see kings kneeling at his feet,	1Tamb	1.2.55	Techel
Must plead for mercie at his kingly feet,	1Tamb	3.3.174	Zenoc
Are falne in clusters at my conquering feet.	1Tamb	3.3.230	Tamb
And treading him beneath thy loathsome feet,	1Tamb	4.2.64	Zabina
Whose feet the kings of Affrica have kist.	1Tamb	4.2.65	Zabina
If they would lay their crownes before my feet,	1Tamb	4.2.93	Tamb
He stamps it under his feet my Lord.	1Tamb	4.4.42	P Therid
Conquering the people underneath our feet,	1Tamb	4.4.137	Tamb
Emperours and kings lie breathlesse at my feet.	1Tamb	5.1.469	Tamb
Neere Guyrons head doth set his conquering feet,	2Tamb	1.1.17	Gazell
Ready to charge you ere you stir your feet.	2Tamb	1.1.121	Fredrk
In all affection at thy kingly feet.	2Tamb	1.3.116	Therid
make no period/Untill Natolia kneele before your feet.	2Tamb	1.3.217	Therid
And bring him captive to your highnesse feet.	2Tamb	3.1.62	Soria
And cast your crownes in slavery at their feet.	2Tamb	3.5.149	Tamb
And lay his life at holy Bruno's feet.	F1220	4.1.66	Faust
But Roome at thraldoms feet to rid from tyrants.	Lucan, First Booke		352
Did charme her nimble feet, and made her stay,	Hero and Leander		1.399
At his faire feathered feet, the engins layd,	Hero and Leander		1.449
Cast downe his wearie feet, and felt the sand.	Hero and Leander		2.228
But as her naked feet were whipping out,	Hero and Leander		2.313
FEETE			
I know her by the movings of her feete:	Dido	1.1.241	Aeneas
That crave such favour at your honors feete,	Dido	1.2.5	Illion
And from the first earth interdict our feete.	Dido	1.2.37	Serg
He [names] <meanes> Aeneas, let us kisse his feete.	Dido	2.1.51	Illion
And makes Aeneas sinke at Didos feete.	Dido	2.1.117	Aeneas
At whose accursed feete as overjoyed,	Dido	2.1.177	Aeneas
Which I will bring as Vassals to thy feete.	1Tamb	3.3.129	Tamb
That treadeth Fortune underneath his feete,	2Tamb	3.4.52	Therid
To sue for mercie at your highnesse feete.	2Tamb	5.2.41	Amasia
How should I step or stir my hatefull feete,	2Tamb	5.3.195	Amyras
Shall with their Goate feete daunce an antick hay.	Edw	1.1.60	Gavstn

FEETE (cont.)			
His life, my lord, before your princely feete.	Edw	3.1.45	Spencr
Thus, as the Gods creepe on with feete of wool,	F 877	3.1.99	Pope
has hornes, and all shee divels has clifts and cloven feete.	F App	p.230 54 P	Clown
Let my first verse be sixe, my last five feete,	Ovid's Elegies		1.1.31
And guides my feete least stumbling falles they catch.	Ovid's Elegies		1.6.8
Before her feete thrice prostrate downe I fell,	Ovid's Elegies		1.7.61
Maides on the shore, with marble white feete tread,	Ovid's Elegies		2.11.15
My selfe will bring vowed gifts before thy feete,	Ovid's Elegies		2.13.24
Sappho her vowed harpe laies at Phoebus feete.	Ovid's Elegies		2.18.34
wild me, whose slowe feete sought delay, be flying.	Ovid's Elegies		2.19.12
And one, I thinke, was longer, of her feete.	Ovid's Elegies		3.1.8
To move her feete unheard in [setting] <sitting> downe.	Ovid's Elegies		3.1.52
In skipping out her naked feete much grac'd her.	Ovid's Elegies		3.6.82
We vanquish, and tread tam'd love under feete,	Ovid's Elegies		3.10.5
Wee cause feete flie, wee mingle haires with snakes,	Ovid's Elegies		3.11.23
And stately robes to their gilt feete hang downe.	Ovid's Elegies		3.12.26
There use all tricks, and tread shame under feete.	Ovid's Elegies		3.13.18
FEIGN'D			
It is a challenge feign'd from Lodowicke.	Jew	2.3.374	Barab
FEIGND			
Ah oft how much she might she feignd offence;	Ovid's Elegies		2.19.13
FEIGNE (See also FAINE)			
And like a cunning spirit feigne some lye,	Jew	2.3.382	Barab
Deny him oft, feigne now thy head doth ake:	Ovid's Elegies		1.8.73
Be witnesse Crete (nor Crete doth all things feigne)/Crete	Ovid's Elegies		3.9.19
FEIGNED			
red shame becomes white cheekes, but this/If feigned, doth well;	Ovid's Elegies		1.8.36
Ile thinke all true, though it be feigned matter.	Ovid's Elegies		2.11.53
FEIGNEST			
Ungrate why feignest new feares?	Ovid's Elegies		2.8.23
FEIGNING			
No such voice-feigning bird was on the ground,	Ovid's Elegies		2.6.23
FEIRSE			
Choosing a subject fit for feirse alarmes:	Ovid's Elegies		1.1.6
FELD			
Ah Pelops from his coach was almost feld,	Ovid's Elegies		3.2.15
FELICITIE			
Shall chaine felicitie unto their throne.	Dido	3.2.80	Juno
That perfect blisse and sole felicitie,	1Tamb	2.7.28	Tamb
For no where else seekes he felicitie.	Edw	1.4.122	Gavstn
To wretched men death is felicitie.	Edw	5.1.127	Edward
and twenty yeares hath Faustus lost eternall joy and felicitie.	F1860	5.2.64 P	Faust
FELICITY			
My gold, my fortune, my felicity;	Jew	2.1.48	Barab
FELL (Homograph; See also FELD)			
At last came Pirrhus fell and full of ire,	Dido	2.1.213	Aeneas
And with the [wind] <wound> thereof the King fell downe:	Dido	2.1.254	Aeneas
I thinke some fell Inchantresse dwelleth here,	Dido	4.1.3	Iarbus
Why burst you not, and they fell in the seas?	Dido	4.4.154	Dido
For every fell and stout Tartarian Stead/That stampt on others	1Tamb	5.1.330	Zenoc
As fell to Saule, to Balaam and the rest,	2Tamb	2.1.54	Fredrk
Fearing the worst of this before it fell,	Jew	1.2.246	Barab
and fell invasion/Of such as have your majestie in chase,	Edw	4.7.4	Abbot
Unhappy spirits that [fell] <live> with Lucifer,	F 298	1.3.70	Mephst
gave me my mony, and fell to eating; and as I am a cursen man,	F1530	4.5.26 P	Carter
Who seeing hunters pauseth till fell wrath/And kingly rage	Lucan, First Booke		209
to Hesus, and fell Mercury <(Jove)>/They offer humane flesh,	Lucan, First Booke		440
Crownes fell from holy statues, ominous birds/Defil'd the day,	Lucan, First Booke		556
shouldst thou with thy rayes now sing/The fell Nemean beast,	Lucan, First Booke		655
I clinged her naked bodie, downe she fell,	Ovid's Elegies		1.5.24
Before her feete thrice prostrate downe I fell,	Ovid's Elegies		1.7.61
So the fierce troupes of Thracian Rhesus fell/And Captive	Ovid's Elegies		1.9.23
Or men with crooked sickles corne downe fell.	Ovid's Elegies		1.15.12
I had in hand/Which for his heaven fell on the Gyants band.	Ovid's Elegies		2.1.16
How almost wrackt thy ship in maine seas fell.	Ovid's Elegies		2.11.50
And ripe-earde corne with sharpe-edg'd sithes to fell.	Ovid's Elegies		3.9.12
Her long haires eare-wrought garland fell away.	Ovid's Elegies		3.9.36
Viewing Leanders face, fell downe and fainted.	Hero and Leander		2.2
And fell in drops like teares, because they mist him.	Hero and Leander		2.174
FELLOW (See also FELOW)			
Or one of chast Dianas fellow Nimphs,	Dido	1.1.194	Aeneas
Your presence (loving friends and fellow kings)/Makes me to	2Tamb	1.3.151	Tamb
While these their fellow kings may be refresht.	2Tamb	4.3.31	Tamb
Thou hast thy Crownes, fellow, come let's away.	Jew	2.3.158	Mater
make account of me/As of thy fellow; we are villaines both:	Jew	2.3.214	Barab
a fellow met me with a muschatoes like a Ravens wing, and a	Jew	4.2.27 P	Ithimr
Here take 'em, fellow, with as good a will--	Jew	4.3.52	Barab
How now fellow, what newes?	P 242	4.40	Charls
Hands of good fellow, I will be his baile/For this offence:	P 622	12.35	King
A gloomie fellow in a meade belowe,	Edw	4.7.29	Spencr
Fellow enough:	Edw	4.7.47	Rice
Remember thee fellow? what else?	Edw	4.7.118	Rice
<Aske my fellow if I be a thiefe>.	F 204	(HC258)A P	Wagner
Ah my sweet chamber-fellow, had I liv'd with thee, then had I	F1824	5.2.28 P	Faust
do ye see yonder tall fellow in the round slop, hee has kild	F App	p.230 47 P	Clown
a Christian fellow to a dogge or a catte, a mouse or a ratte?	F App	p.231 60 P	Clown
Shall never faith be found in fellow kings.	Lucan, First Booke		92
I have thy husband, guard, and fellow plaied.	Ovid's Elegies		3.10.18
O by our fellow bed, by all/The Gods who by thee to be perjurde	Ovid's Elegies		3.10.45
FELLOWE			
[And nut-browne girles in doing have no fellowe].	Ovid's Elegies		2.4.40
FELLOWES			
All fellowes now, disposde alike to sporte,	Dido	3.3.5	Dido

FELLOWES (cont.)			
Their carelesse swords shal lanch their fellowes throats/And	1Tamb	2.2.49	Meandr
taskes a while/And take such fortune as your fellowes felt.	2Tamb	5.1.137	Tamb
So, now they have shew'd themselves to be tall fellowes.	Jew	3.2.7	Barab
And fellowes to, what ever stormes arise.	P 615	12.28	King
Come fellowes, it booted not for us to strive,	Edw	2.6.18	James
Their fellowes being slaine or put to flight,	Hero and Leander		1.120
FELON			
A sturdy Felon and a base-bred Thiefe,	1Tamb	4.3.12	Souldn
FELOW			
I must say somewhat to your felow, you sir.	F App	p.234 13	P Vintnr
him have him, he is an honest felow, and he has a great charge,	F App	p.239 105	P Mephst
FELT			
Sc fares Agydas for the late felt frownes/That sent a tempest	1Tamb	3.2.85	Agidas
With greater power than erst his pride hath felt,	2Tamb	2.2.10	Gazell
More exquisite than ever Traitor felt.	2Tamb	5.1.53	Therid
taskes a while/And take such fortune as your fellowes felt.	2Tamb	5.1.137	Tamb
no soule in hell/Hath felt more torment then poore Gaveston.	Edw	1.1.147	Gavstn
and so by that meanes I shal see more then ere I felt, or saw	F App	p.233 5	P Robin
A mothers jcy by Jove she had not felt.	Ovid's Elegies		2.19.28
went and came, as if he rewd/The greefe which Neptune felt.	Hero and Leander		2.215
Cast downe his wearie feet, and felt the sand.	Hero and Leander		2.228
FEMALE			
And playing with that female wanton boy,	Dido	1.1.51	Venus
I may not dure this female drudgerie,	Dido	4.3.55	Aeneas
FEMALS			
Run mourning round about the Femals misse,	2Tamb	4.1.188	Tamb
FEN			
And make this champion mead a bloody Fen.	2Tamb	1.1.32	Orcan
FENC'D			
Fenc'd with the concave of a monstrous rocke,	2Tamb	3.2.89	Tamb
FENCE			
Cosin, our hands I hope shall fence our heads,	Edw	1.1.123	Mortmr
FENS			
every fixed starre/To sucke up poison from the moorish Fens,	1Tamb	4.2.6	Bajzth
March in your armour thorowe watery Fens,	2Tamb	3.2.56	Tamb
FERMAMENT			
a fyery meteor in the fermament	Paris	ms21,p390	Guise
FERNEZE			
Wretched Ferneze might have veng'd thy death.	Jew	3.2.14	Govnr
And on that rather should Ferneze dye.	Jew	3.2.26	Govnr
Ferneze, 'twas thy sonne that murder'd him.	Jew	5.1.45	Mater
Ferneze, speake, had it not beene much better/To [have] kept	Jew	5.2.4	Calym
Nay, doe thou this, Ferneze, and be free;	Jew	5.2.90	Barab
Doe so, but faile not; now farewell Ferneze:	Jew	5.2.109	Barab
FERNEZES			
Having Fernezes hand, whose heart I'le have;	Jew	2.3.16	Barab
FERRIMAN			
Hover about the ugly Ferriman,	1Tamb	5.1.246	Zabina
FERTILE			
And fertile in faire Ceres furrowed wealth,	Dido	1.2.22	Cloan
And on the soft ground fertile greene grasse growe.	Ovid's Elegies		2.16.6
Nor is she, though she loves the fertile fields,	Ovid's Elegies		3.9.17
FESSE			
Kings of Fesse, Moroccus and Argier,	1Tamb	3.3.66	Bajzth
Techelles King of Fesse, and Usumcasane King of Morocus.	1Tamb	4.4.117	P Tamb
Kings of Argier, Moroccus, and of Fesse,	1Tamb	4.4.120	Tamb
Kings of Morocus and of Fesse, welcome.	2Tamb	1.3.128	Tamb
I and my neighbor King of Fesse have brought/To aide thee in	2Tamb	1.3.130	Usumc
I here present thee with the crowne of Fesse,	2Tamb	1.3.140	Techel
Thanks king of Fesse, take here thy crowne again.	2Tamb	1.3.150	Tamb
FESTIVALL			
As best beseemes this solemne festivall.	F1012	3.2.32	Pope
Festivall dayes aske Venus, songs, and wine,	Ovid's Elegies		3.9.47
Came lovers home, from this great festivall.	Hero and Leander		1.96
FET			
To see a Phrigian far fet [on] <o'er> <forfeit to> the sea,	Dido	3.3.64	Iarbus
This need no forraine proofe, nor far fet story:	Lucan, First Booke		94
Whose lively heat like fire from heaven fet,	Hero and Leander		2.255
FETCH (See also FECHT, FETS)			
Goe fetch the garment which Sicheus ware:	Dido	2.1.80	Dido
Servants, come fetch these emptie vessels here,	Dido	4.2.49	Iarbus
From golden India Ganges will I fetch,	Dido	5.1.8	Aeneas
O Anna, fetch [Arions] <Orions> Harpe,	Dido	5.1.248	Dido
And meane to fetch thee in despight of him.	1Tamb	3.1.40	Bajzth
He meet me in the field and fetch thee hence?	1Tamb	3.3.5	Tamb
Fetch me some water for my burning breast,	1Tamb	5.1.276	Bajzth
againe, you shall not trouble me thus to come and fetch you.	2Tamb	3.5.102	P Tamb
Now fetch me out the Turkish Concubines,	2Tamb	4.3.64	Tamb
To cure me, or Ile fetch him downe my selfe.	2Tamb	5.3.63	Tamb
Now fetch the hearse of faire Zenocrate,	2Tamb	5.3.210	Tamb
Be close, my girle, for this must fetch my gold.	Jew	1.2.304	Barab
But first goe fetch me in the pot of Rice/That for our supper	Jew	3.4.49	Barab
he not as well come as send; pray bid him come and fetch it:	Jew	4.3.27	P Barab
Goe fetch him straight. I alwayes fear'd that Jew.	Jew	5.1.18	Govnr
Goe fetch me pen and inke.	P 657	13.1	Duchss
Goe fetch his sonne for to beholde his death:	P1021	19.91	King
Then I may fetch from this ritch treasurie:	Edw	1.4.332	Queene
Shall I make spirits fetch me what I please?	F 106	1.1.78	Faust
And fetch the treasure of all forraine wrackes:	F 172	1.1.144	Cornel
Whensoever, and wheresoever the devill shall fetch thee.	F 370	1.4.28	P Wagner
I'le fetch thee fire to dissolve it streight.	F 452	2.1.64	Mephst
I'le fetch him somewhat to delight his minde.	F 471	2.1.83	Mephst

FETCH (cont.)				
full power to fetch or carry the said John Faustus, body and	F 497	2.1.109	P	Faust
<Nay sweete Mephastophilis fetch me one, for I will have one>.	F 530	(HC261)A	P	Faust
Ile fetch thee a wife in the divels name>.	F 531	(HC261)A	P	Mephst
O Faustus they are come to fetch <away> thy soule.	F 641	2.2.90		Faust
Go Mephostophilis, fetch them in.	F 660	2.2.109	P	Lucifr
Fetch me some wine.	F1051	3.2.71		Pope
Why Hostesse, I say, fetch us some Beere.	F1518	4.5.14	P	Dick
I humbly thanke your grace: then fetch some Beere.	F1625	4.6.68		Faust
this is the time <the time wil come>, and he will fetch mee.	F1861	5.2.65	P	Faust
to fetch me <both> body and soule, if I once gave eare to	F1865	5.2.69	P	Faust
warning whensoever or wheresoever the divell shall fetch thee.	F App	p.230 37	P	Wagner
two divels presently to fetch thee away Baliol and Belcher.	F App	p.230 43	P	Wagner
FETCH'D				
Make fires, heat irons, let the racke be fetch'd.	Jew	5.1.24		Govnr
FETCHE				
Some whirle winde fetche them backe, or sincke them all:--	Edw	4.6.59		Mortmr
Goe fetche my fathers hearse, where it shall lie,	Edw	5.6.94		King
FETCHT				
Have fetcht about the Indian continent:	1Tamb	3.3.254		Tamb
and my gentrie/Is fetcht from Oxford, not from Heraldrie.	Edw	2.2.244		Baldck
FETHERBED				
What else, a table and a fetherbed.	Edw	5.5.33		Ltborn
FETHERED				
Mingled with powdered shot and fethered steele/So thick upon	2Tamb	1.1.92		Orcan
FETIALES				
<testimonis> est [inartificiale] <in arte fetiales>.	P 395	7.35		Guise
FETS				
And rustling swing up as the wind fets breath.	Lucan, First Booke			392
FETTER				
And fetter them in Vulcans sturdie brasse,	Dido	1.1.118		Jupitr
Deserved chaines these cursed hands shall fetter,	Ovid's Elegies			1.7.28
FETTERS				
Fetters the Euxin sea, with chaines of yce:	Lucan, First Booke			18
I sawe ones legges with fetters blacke and blewe,	Ovid's Elegies			2.2.47
FEW				
Your men are valiant but their number few,	1Tamb	3.3.11		Bassoe
straight goe charge a few of them/To chardge these Dames,	1Tamb	5.1.116		Tamb
And few or none shall perish by their shot.	2Tamb	3.3.45		Therid
Alas, our number's few,/And Crownes come either by succession	Jew	1.1.130		Barab
And few or none scape but by being purg'd.	Jew	2.3.106		Barab
In few, the blood of Hydra, Lerna's bane;	Jew	3.4.100		Barab
And few live that behold their ancient seats;	Lucan, First Booke			27
Few battailes fought with prosperous successe/May bring her	Lucan, First Booke			285
Aye me I warne what profits some few howers,	Ovid's Elegies			1.4.59
And some few pastures Pallas Olives bore.	Ovid's Elegies			2.16.8
Few love, what others have unguarded left.	Ovid's Elegies			3.4.26
And few great lords in vertuous deeds shall joy,	Hero and Leander			1.479
FEWE				
From thence a fewe of us escapt to land,	Dido	1.2.30		Cloan
While I speake some fewe, yet fit words be idle.	Ovid's Elegies			2.2.2
FEWELD				
May still be feweld in our progenye.	P 8	1.8		Charls
FEWELL				
Now wants the fewell that enflamde his beames:	2Tamb	2.4.4		Tamb
FEZ (See FESSE)				
FICKLE				
denied/To shed [their] <his> influence in his fickle braine,	1Tamb	1.1.15		Cosroe
Those that are proud of fickle Empery,	1Tamb	5.1.352		Zenoc
FIDLER				
Pilia-borza, bid the Fidler give me the posey in his hat there.	Jew	4.4.35	P	Curtzn
Play, Fidler, or I'le cut your cats guts into chitterlins.	Jew	4.4.44	P	Ithimr
Whether now, Fidler?	Jew	4.4.70		Pilia
Farewell Fidler: One letter more to the Jew.	Jew	4.4.72		Pilia
FIE (See also FYE)				
Fie Venus, that such causeles words of wrath,	Dido	3.2.26		Juno
O cowardly boy, fie for shame, come foorth.	2Tamb	4.1.31		Celeb
Fie upon 'em, master, will you turne Christian, when holy	Jew	4.1.193	P	Ithimr
Fie Mortimer, dishonor not thy selfe,	Edw	1.4.244		Lncstr
Fie on that love that hatcheth death and hate.	Edw	4.6.15		Kent
fie, fie, pull in your head for shame, let not all the world	F1291	4.1.137	P	Faust
FIELD (See also FEELD)				
fild Persepolis/With Affrike Captaines, taken in the field:	1Tamb	1.1.142		Ceneus
Shall fling in every corner of the field:	1Tamb	2.2.64		Meandr
from the camp/When Kings themselves are present in the field?	1Tamb	2.4.17		Tamb
He meet me in the field and fetch thee hence?	1Tamb	3.3.5		Tamb
hardy Tamburlaine)/What tis to meet me in the open field,	1Tamb	3.3.146		Bajzth
The field is ours, the Turk, his wife and all.	1Tamb	3.3.163		Tamb
Ah faire Zabina, we have lost the field.	1Tamb	3.3.233		Bajzth
Before thou met my husband in the field,	1Tamb	4.2.59		Zabina
And now my footstoole, if I loose the field,	1Tamb	5.1.209		Tamb
Till we have made us ready for the field.	1Tamb	5.1.212		Tamb
Let all the swords and Lances in the field,	1Tamb	5.1.225		Zabina
Or crosse the streame, and meet him in the field?	2Tamb	1.1.12		Orcan
He brings a world of people to the field,	2Tamb	1.1.67		Orcan
And not to dare ech other to the field:	2Tamb	1.1.116		Gazell
For in a field whose [superficies] <superfluities>/Is covered	2Tamb	1.3.79		Tamb
Messenger/To bid me sheath my sword, and leave the field:	2Tamb	1.3.167		Tamb
Wher Amazonians met me in the field:	2Tamb	1.3.192		Techel
And when I meet an armie in the field,	2Tamb	3.2.38		Tamb
And wilt thou shun the field for feare of woundes?	2Tamb	3.2.109		Tamb
The field wherin this battaile shall be fought,	2Tamb	3.5.18		Callap
Come puissant Viceroies, let us to the field,	2Tamb	3.5.53		Callap

FIELD (cont.)			
Away, let us to the field, that the villaine may be slaine.	2Tamb	3.5.143	P Trebiz
I smile to think, how when this field is fought,	2Tamb	3.5.165	Techel
For if my father misse him in the field,	2Tamb	4.1.8	Celeb
And oft hath warn'd thee to be stil in field,	2Tamb	4.1.24	Amyras
wel to heare both you/Have won a heape of honor in the field,	2Tamb	4.1.37	Calyph
I goe into the field before I need?	2Tamb	4.1.51	Calyph
And we wil force him to the field hereafter.	2Tamb	4.1.102	Amyras
Villaine away, and hie thee to the field,	2Tamb	5.3.72	Tamb
and hearing your absence in the field, offers to set upon us	2Tamb	5.3.104	P 3Msngr
And could I but a while pursue the field,	2Tamb	5.3.117	Tamb
That in a field amidst his enemies,	Jew	1.2.203	Barab
The sweetest flower in Citherea's field,	Jew	1.2.379	Mthias
and underneath/In severall places are field-pieces pitch'd,	Jew	5.5.27	Barab
To send his power to meet us in the field.	P 712	14.15	Navrre
And meanes to meet your highnes in the field.	P 727	14.30	1Msngr
Brother displaie my ensignes in the field,	Edw	1.1.136	Edward
When wert thou in the field with banner spred?	Edw	2.2.182	Mortmr
Advaunce your standard Edward in the field,	Edw	3.1.126	Spencr
When we may meet these traitors in the field.	Edw	4.3.47	Edward
And cruel field, nere burning Aetna fought:	Lucan, First Booke		43
Like to a tall oake in a fruitfull field,	Lucan, First Booke		137
and every yeare/Frauds and corruption in the field of Mars;	Lucan, First Booke		182
Cornets of horse are mustered for the field;	Lucan, First Booke		306
Butcherd the flocks he found in spatious field,	Ovid's Elegies		1.7.8
The painfull Hinde by thee to field is sent,	Ovid's Elegies		1.13.15
I guide and souldiour wunne the field and weare her,	Ovid's Elegies		2.12.13
In Tiburs field with watry fome art rumbling,	Ovid's Elegies		3.5.46
Your golden ensignes [plucke] <pluckt> out of my field,	Ovid's Elegies		3.14.16
FIELDE			
We have their crownes, their bodies strowe the fielde.	1Tamb	3.3.215	Techel
Why this tis to have an army in the fielde.	P 980	19.50	Guise
FIELDES			
Till he hath furrowed Neptunes glassie fieldes,	Dido	4.3.11	Aeneas
To waste and spoile the sweet Aonian fieldes.	1Tamb	4.3.6	Souldn
Those that inhabited the suburbe fieldes/Fled, fowle Erinnis	Lucan, First Booke		569
they governe fieldes, and lawes,/they manadge peace, and rawe	Ovid's Elegies		3.7.57
That Vallies, groves, hills and fieldes,	Passionate Shepherd		3
FIELD-PIECES			
and underneath/In severall places are field-pieces pitch'd,	Jew	5.5.27	Barab
FIELDS			
in Asia, or display/His vagrant Ensigne in the Persean fields,	1Tamb	1.1.45	Meandr
Or leave Damascus and th'Egyptian fields,	1Tamb	4.2.48	Tamb
That with their beauties grac'd the Memphion fields:	1Tamb	4.2.104	Tamb
Armed with lance into the Egyptian fields,	1Tamb	5.1.381	Philem
That I have sent from sundry foughten fields,	1Tamb	5.1.466	Tamb
Enrag'd I ran about the fields for thee,	2Tamb	4.2.17	Therid
Not marching <now> in the fields of Thrasimen,	F 1	Prol.1	1Chor
Was stretcht unto the fields of hinds unknowne;	Lucan, First Booke		171
but as the fields/When birds are silent thorough winters rage;	Lucan, First Booke		260
Ile bouldly quarter out the fields of Rome;	Lucan, First Booke		383
They came that dwell/By Nemes fields, and bankes of Satirus,	Lucan, First Booke		421
Such as Amimone through the drie fields strayed/When on her	Ovid's Elegies		1.10.5
The weary souldiour hath the conquerd fields,	Ovid's Elegies		2.9.19
Thou that frequents Canopus pleasant fields,	Ovid's Elegies		2.13.7
Pelignian fields [with] <which> liqued rivers flowe,	Ovid's Elegies		2.16.5
ground/Conteines me, though the streames in fields surround,	Ovid's Elegies		2.16.34
wish the chariot, whence corne [seedes] <fields> were found,	Ovid's Elegies		3.5.15
Harmefull to beasts, and to the fields thou proves:	Ovid's Elegies		3.5.99
First Ceres taught the seede in fields to swell,	Ovid's Elegies		3.9.11
Nor is she, though she loves the fertile fields,	Ovid's Elegies		3.9.17
And seedes were equally in large fields cast,	Ovid's Elegies		3.9.33
Which with the grasse of Tuscane fields are fed.	Ovid's Elegies		3.12.14
FIEND (See also FEEND)			
and invenome her/That like a fiend hath left her father thus.	Jew	3.4.105	Barab
O thou bewitching fiend, 'twas thy temptation,	F1883	5.2.87	Faust
much like that hellish fiend/Which made the sterne Lycurgus	Lucan, First Booke		572
FIENDFULL			
Whose fiendfull fortune may exhort the wise/Onely to wonder at	F2006	5.3.24	4Chor
FIENDS			
What wilt thou doe among these hatefull fiends?	Jew	1.2.345	Barab
[Ambitious fiends, see how the heavens smiles]/[At your	F1794	5.1.121A	OldMan
With dreadfull horror of these damned fiends.	F1994	5.3.12	3Schol
FIER			
Rent sphere of heaven, and fier forsake thy orbe,	Edw	4.7.102	Spencr
Heavens turne it to a blaze of quenchelesse fier,	Edw	5.1.44	Edward
See that in the next roome I have a fier,	Edw	5.5.29	Ltborn
And from the northren climat snatching fier/Blasted the	Lucan, First Booke		532
Then though death rackes <rakes> my bones in funerall fier,	Ovid's Elegies		1.15.41
FIERCE (See also FEIRSE)			
sounds/The surges, his fierce souldiers, to the spoyle:	Dido	1.1.69	Venus
In mannaging those fierce barbarian mindes:	Dido	1.1.92	Jupitr
Wrapped in curles, as fierce Achilles was,	1Tamb	2.1.24	Menaph
How can you fancie one that lookes so fierce,	1Tamb	3.2.40	Agidas
And set his warlike person to the view/Of fierce Achilles,	2Tamb	3.5.68	Tamb
To make you fierce, and fit my appetite,	2Tamb	4.3.17	Tamb
With fierce exclaimes run to the Senate-house,	Jew	1.2.232	Abigal
[My God, my God] <O mercy heaven>, looke not so fierce on me;	F1979	5.2.183	Faust
Fierce Pirhus, neither thou nor Hanniball/Art cause, no	Lucan, First Booke		30
and fierce Batavians,/Whome trumpets clang incites, and those	Lucan, First Booke		432
and you fierce men of Rhene/Leaving your countrey open to the	Lucan, First Booke		460
Fierce Mulciber unbarred Aetna's gate,	Lucan, First Booke		543
Fierce Mastives hould; the vestall fires went out,	Lucan, First Booke		547

FIERCE (cont.)			
And they whom fierce Bellonaes fury moves/To wound their armes,	Lucan, First Booke	563	
Or fierce Agave mad; or like Megaera/That scar'd Alcides, when	Lucan, First Booke	574	
So the fierce troupes of Thracian Rhesus fell/And Captive	Ovid's Elegies	1.9.23	
Love and Loves sonne are with fierce armes to oddes; .	Ovid's Elegies	1.10.19	
What helpes it me of fierce Achill to sing? . . .	Ovid's Elegies	2.1.29	
I that ere-while was fierce, now humbly sue, . . .	Ovid's Elegies	2.5.49	
Envy hath rapt thee, no fierce warres thou movedst, . .	Ovid's Elegies	2.6.25	
Let others tell how winds fierce battailes wage, . .	Ovid's Elegies	2.11.17	
Nor being arm'd fierce troupes to follow farre? . .	Ovid's Elegies	2.14.2	
And this is he whom fierce love burnes, they cry. . .	Ovid's Elegies	3.1.20	
FIERCELY			
And fiercely knockst thy brest that open lyes? . . .	Ovid's Elegies	3.5.58	
FIERD			
You would have thought their houses had bin fierd/Or .	Lucan, First Booke	490	
FIERIE			
His fierie eies are fixt upon the earth, ...	1Tamb	1.2.158	Therid
Till Cupids bow, and fierie shafts be broken, . . .	Ovid's Elegies	1.15.27	
FIERS			
Mules loth'd issue)/To be cut forth and cast in dismall fiers:	Lucan, First Booke	590	
But thy fiers hurt not; Mars, 'tis thou enflam'st/The .	Lucan, First Booke	657	
FIER'ST			
Scorpion with the burning taile/And fier'st his cleyes. .	Lucan, First Booke	659	
FIERY (See also FYERY)			
And he with frowning browes and fiery lookes, . . .	1Tamb	1.2.56	Techel
Whose fiery cyrcles beare encompassed/A heaven of heavenly	1Tamb	2.1.15	Menaph
Enrolde in flames and fiery smoldering mistes, . . .	1Tamb	2.3.20	Tamb
That fiery thirster after Soveraigntie:	1Tamb	2.6.31	Cosroe
did your greatnes see/The frowning lookes of fiery Tamburlaine,	1Tamb	4.1.13	2Msngr
As when a fiery exhalation/Wrapt in the bowels of a freezing	1Tamb	4.2.43	Tamb
Fill all the aire with fiery meteors.	1Tamb	4.2.52	Tamb
Even from the fiery spangled vaile of heaven, . . .	1Tamb	5.1.185	Tamb
Even from the midst of fiery Cancers Tropick, . . .	2Tamb	1.1.73	Orcan
With ugly Furies bearing fiery flags, ...	2Tamb	1.3.146	Techel
And sooner let the fiery Element/Dissolve, and make your .	2Tamb	2.4.58	Zenoc
That being fiery meteors, may presage, ...	2Tamb	3.2.4	Tamb
Making their fiery gate above the cloudes, . . .	2Tamb	4.3.9	Tamb
To hold the fiery spirit it containes, ...	2Tamb	5.3.169	Tamb
not full of thoughtes/As pure and fiery as Phyteus beames,	2Tamb	5.3.237	Tamb
Bags of fiery Opals, Saphires, Amatists, ...	Jew	1.1.25	Barab
to everlasting paines/And extreme tortures of the fiery deepe,	Jew	1.2.167	Barab
Oh thou that with a fiery piller led'st/The sonnes of Israel	Jew	2.1.12	Barab
poysons of the Stygian poole/Breake from the fiery kingdome;	Jew	3.4.103	Barab
fiery keele at [Antwerpe] <Anwerpe> <Antwarpes> <Antwerpes>	F 123	1.1.95	Faust
Of Stix, of Acheron, and the fiery Lake, ...	F 826	3.1.48	Faust
Go horse these traytors on your fiery backes, . . .	F1403	4.2.79	Faust
And sundry fiery meteors blaz'd in heaven; . . .	Lucan, First Booke	529	
FIFES			
noise/Of trumpets clange, shril cornets, whistling fifes;	Lucan, First Booke	240	
FIFT			
And what are thou the fift?	F 692	2.2.141	Faust
[Carolus the fift, at whose pallace now]/[Faustus is feasted	F1151	3.3.64A	3Chor
FIFTEENE			
Besides fifteene contributorie kings, ...	1Tamb	3.3.14	Bassoe
Queen of fifteene contributory Queens, ...	1Tamb	5.1.266	Bajzth
And laine in leagre fifteene moneths and more, . . .	2Tamb	1.3.176	Usumc
FIFTH (See also FIFT)			
Under pretence of helping Charles the fifth, . . .	Jew	2.3.188	Barab
FIFTIE			
Father of fiftie sonnes, but they are slaine, . . .	Dido	2.1.234	Aeneas
For Troy, for Priam, for his fiftie sonnes, . . .	Dido	4.4.89	Aeneas
Wun on the fiftie headed Vuolgas waves, ...	1Tamb	1.2.103	Tamb
FIFTY			
A hundred and fifty thousand horse, ...	1Tamb	4.3.53	Capol
and stout Bythinians/Came to my bands full fifty thousand more,	2Tamb	3.5.42	Trebiz
Three and fifty dozen, I'le pledge thee.	Jew	4.4.8	P Ithimr
if thou likst him for fifty, take him.	F App	p.239 103	P Faust
FIG			
and then a Fig/For all my unckles frienship here in Fraunce.	Edw	4.2.4	Prince
We have no reason for it, therefore a fig for him. . .	F1593	4.6.36	P Dick
FIGHT			
Then shall we fight couragiously with them. . . .	1Tamb	1.2.128	Tamb
Weele fight five hundred men at armes to one, . . .	1Tamb	1.2.143	Tamb
Therefore cheere up your mindes, prepare to fight, . .	1Tamb	2.2.29	Meandr
Then fight couragiously, their crowns are yours. . .	1Tamb	3.3.30	Tamb
What Coward wold not fight for such a prize? . . .	1Tamb	3.3.100	Usumc
Fight all couragiously and be you kings. . . .	1Tamb	3.3.101	Tamb
There Angels in their christal armours fight/A doubtfull .	1Tamb	5.1.151	Tamb
Must fight against my life and present love: . . .	1Tamb	5.1.389	Zenoc
Left to themselves while we were at the fight, . . .	1Tamb	5.1.471	Tamb
And have a greater foe to fight against, ...	2Tamb	1.1.15	Gazell
For halfe the world shall perish in this fight: . .	2Tamb	1.3.171	Tamb
Thou wouldst with overmatch of person fight, . . .	2Tamb	3.5.76	Orcan
Fight as you ever did, like Conquerours, ...	2Tamb	3.5.160	Tamb
Come fight ye Turks, or yeeld us victory. . . .	2Tamb	3.5.169	Tamb
What, dar'st thou then be absent from the fight, . .	2Tamb	4.1.22	Amyras
Goe, goe tall stripling, fight you for us both, . .	2Tamb	4.1.33	Calyph
of all the villaines power/Live to give offer of another fight.	2Tamb	5.3.109	Tamb
So will we fight it out; come, let's away: . . .	Jew	2.2.52	Govnr
He forged the daring challenge made them fight. . .	Jew	5.1.47	Govnr
We must with resolute mindes resolve to fight, . . .	P 707	14.10	Navrre
And place our selves in order for the fight. . . .	P 742	14.45	Navrre
Fight in the quarrell of this valiant Prince, . . .	P1229	22.91	King

FIGHT (cont.)

And with this sword, Penbrooke wil fight for you.	Edw	1.4.352	Penbrk
Then Edward, thou wilt fight it to the last,	Edw	3.1.211	Mortmr
Alarum to the fight,	Edw	3.1.218	Warwck
To them that fight in right and feare his wrath:	Edw	4.6.20	Queene
my selfe when I could get none <had no body> to fight withall:	F 689	2.2.138	P Wrath
Then Souldiers boldly fight; if Faustus die,	F1346	4.2.22	Benvol
Bride did incite/The drunken Centaures to a sodaine fight.	Ovid's Elegies		1.4.8
And souldiours make them ready to the fight,	Ovid's Elegies		1.13.14
To over-come, so oft to fight I shame.	Ovid's Elegies		2.7.2
And craves his taske, and seekes to be at fight.	Ovid's Elegies		3.6.68
Behold the signes of antient fight, his skarres,	Ovid's Elegies		3.7.19
And as in furie of a dreadfull fight,	Hero and Leander		1.119

FIGHTING

Fighting for passage, tilt within the earth.	1Tamb	1.2.51	Tamb
You fighting more for honor than for gold,	1Tamb	2.2.66	Meandr
had you time to sort/Your fighting men, and raise your royall	1Tamb	4.1.37	Capol
Fighting for passage, [makes] <make> the Welkin cracke,	1Tamb	4.2.45	Tamb
three score thousand fighting men/Are come since last we shewed	2Tamb	3.5.33	Jrslem
That fighting, knowes not what retreat doth meane,	2Tamb	3.5.43	Trebiz
royall is esteem'd/Six hundred thousand valiant fighting men.	2Tamb	3.5.51	Soria
when we are fighting, least hee hide his crowne as the foolish	2Tamb	3.5.154	P Tamb
As meet they will, and fighting dye; brave sport.	Jew	3.1.30	Ithimr

FIGHTS

That fights for Scepters and for slippery crownes,	1Tamb	5.1.356	Zenoc
That fights for honor to adorne your head.	1Tamb	5.1.376	Anippe
And sooner far than he that never fights.	2Tamb	4.1.55	Calyph
Rebell is he that fights against his prince,	Edw	4.6.71	SpncrP
And thy step-father fights by thy example.	Ovid's Elegies		2.9.48

FIGHTST

Why fightst gainst oddes?	Ovid's Elegies		2.2.61
Thou fightst against me using mine owne verse.	Ovid's Elegies		3.1.38

FIGS

Browne Almonds, Servises, ripe Figs and Dates,	Dido	4.5.5	Nurse

FIGULUS

But Figulus more seene in heavenly mysteries,	Lucan, First Booke		638

FIGURE

His lofty browes in foldes, do figure death,	1Tamb	2.1.21	Menaph
Whose shape is figure of the highest God?	2Tamb	2.2.38	Orcan
ancient use, shall beare/The figure of the semi-circled Moone:	2Tamb	3.1.65	Orcan
In champion grounds, what figure serves you best,	2Tamb	3.2.63	Tamb
And see the figure of my dignitie,	2Tamb	4.3.25	Tamb

FIGURES

Beares figures of renowne and myracle:	1Tamb	2.1.4	Cosroe
Figures of every adjunct to the heavens,	F 239	1.3.11	Faust

FIL

Now fil the mouth of Limnasphaltes lake,	2Tamb	5.1.67	Tamb
The wind that bears him hence, wil fil our sailes,	Edw	2.4.48	Lncstr

FILCHT

Than for the fire filcht by Prometheus;	Hero and Leander		1.438

FIL'D

Stole some from Hebe (Hebe, Joves cup fil'd),	Hero and Leander		1.434

FILD

To day when as I fild into your cups,	Dido	1.1.5	Ganimd
Triton I know hath fild his trumpe with Troy,	Dido	1.1.130	Venus
That heretofore have fild Persepolis/With Affrike Captaines,	1Tamb	1.1.141	Ceneus
as when Bajazeth/My royall Lord and father fild the throne,	2Tamb	3.1.12	Callap
fild with the meteors/Of blood and fire thy tyrannies have	2Tamb	4.1.141	Jrslem
Had fild Assirian Carras wals with bloud,	Lucan, First Booke		105
townes/He garrison'd; and Italy he fild with soldiours.	Lucan, First Booke		464
Phoebe having fild/Her meeting hornes to match her brothers	Lucan, First Booke		535
A little fild thee, and for love of talke,	Ovid's Elegies		2.6.29
Rome if her strength the huge world had not fild,	Ovid's Elegies		2.9.17
There wine being fild, thou many things shalt tell,	Ovid's Elegies		2.11.49
Yet tragedies, and scepters fild my lines,	Ovid's Elegies		2.18.13
See Homer from whose fountaine ever fild,	Ovid's Elegies		3.8.25
When fruite fild Tuscia should a wife give me,	Ovid's Elegies		3.12.1

FILIUM

Exhereditare filium non potest pater, nisi--Such is the	F 58	1.1.30	P Faust

FILL

O keepe them still, and let me gaze my fill:	Dido	4.4.44	Dido
Fill all the aire with fiery meteors.	1Tamb	4.2.52	Tamb
That meanes to fill your helmets full of golde:	1Tamb	4.4.7	Tamb
That fill the midst of farthest Tartary,	2Tamb	4.1.43	Amyras
Fill all the aire with troublous bellowing:	2Tamb	4.1.190	Tamb
Love thee, fill me three glasses.	Jew	4.4.7	Curtzn
Give him a crowne, and fill me out more wine.	Jew	4.4.46	Ithimr
And if you like them, drinke your fill and dye:	Jew	5.5.9	Barab
Dye life, flye soule, tongue curse thy fill and dye.	Jew	5.5.89	Barab
displeases him | And fill up his rome that he shold occupie.	Paris	ms 4,p390	P Souldr
And therefore give me leave to looke my fill,	Edw	1.4.139	Edward
Like frantick Juno will I fill the earth,	Edw	1.4.178	Queene
That you may drinke your fill, and quaffe in bloud,	Edw	3.1.137	Edward
I'le have them fill the publique Schooles with [silke] <skill>,	F 117	1.1.89	Faust
Zons fill us some Beere, or we'll breake all the barrels in the	F1618	4.6.61	P HrsCsr
me sir, me sir, search your fill:	F App	p.234 14	P Rafe
Let this word, come, alone the tables fill.	Ovid's Elegies		1.11.24
To fill my lawes thy wanton spirit frame.	Ovid's Elegies		3.1.30

FILL'D

Fill'd with a packe of faintheart Fugitives,	2Tamb	5.1.36	Govnr
I fill'd the Jailes with Bankrouts in a yeare,	Jew	2.3.193	Barab
threatning gods/Fill'd both the earth and seas with prodegies;	Lucan, First Booke		523

FILLES

And therefore filles the bed she lies uppon:	Ovid's Elegies		2.4.34

FILLING
Filling their empty vaines with aiery wine, | 2Tamb 3.2.107 | Tamb
Filling the ditches with the walles wide breach, | 2Tamb 3.3.7 | Techel
Filling the world, leapes out and throwes forth fire, | Lucan, First Booke 154
FILLS
What wine he fills thee, wisely will him drinke, | Ovid's Elegies 1.4.29
FILS
Which fils the nookes of Hell with standing aire, | 1Tamb 5.1.257 | Bajzth
But every where fils every Continent, | 2Tamb 2.2.51 | Orcan
That with his ruine fils up all the trench. | 2Tamb 3.3.26 | Therid
And neither gets him friends, nor fils his bags, | Jew 5.2.39 | Barab
Which fils my mind with strange despairing thoughts, | Edw 5.1.79 | Edward
Those with sweet water oft her handmaid fils, | Hero and Leander 1.35
FILTH
The liver swell'd with filth, and every vaine/Did threaten | Lucan, First Booke 620
Houses not dwelt in, are with filth forlorne. | Ovid's Elegies 1.8.52
FILTHE
Wherein the filthe of all the castell falles. | Edw 5.5.57 | Edward
FILTHINESSE
heavinesse/Of thy most vilde and loathsome filthinesse, | F App p.243 40 | OldMan
FILTHY
foule Idolaters/Shall make me bonfires with their filthy bones, | 1Tamb 3.3.240 | Bajzth
The filthy prison faithlesse breasts restraines. | Ovid's Elegies 2.2.42
What should I tell her vaine tongues filthy lyes, | Ovid's Elegies 3.10.21
FINALL
So for a finall Issue to my griefes, | 1Tamb 5.1.395 | Zenoc
Thy fatall time drawes to a finall end; | F1479 4.4.23 | Faust
Thy fatall time doth drawe to finall ende, | F App p.240 122 | Faust
FIND
Brother Cosroe, I find my selfe agreev'd, | 1Tamb 1.1.1 | Mycet
Then thou shalt find my vaunts substantiall. | 1Tamb 1.2.213 | Tamb
Then let me find no further time to grace/Her princely Temples | 1Tamb 5.1.488 | Tamb
She lies so close that none can find her out. | 2Tamb 1.2.60 | Callap
Might find as many woondrous myracles, | 2Tamb 4.2.85 | Therid
lie in wait for him/And if we find him absent from his campe, | 2Tamb 5.2.57 | Callap
It may be she sees more in me than I can find in my selfe: | Jew 4.2.33 | P Ithimr
And is't not possible to find it out? | Jew 4.2.60 | Pilia
Learned Faustus/To find <know> the secrets of Astronomy,/Graven | F 755 2.3.34 | 2Chor
yee Lubbers look about/And find the man that doth this villany, | F1056 3.2.76 | Pope
for Nero (then unborne) the fates/Would find no other meanes, | Lucan, First Booke 34
And many poore excuses did she find, | Hero and Leander 2.6
FINDE
Yet much I marvell that I cannot finde, | Dido 1.1.180 | Achat
Shall finde it written on confusions front, | Dido 3.2.19 | Juno
And finde the way to wearie such fond thoughts: | Dido 3.2.86 | Juno
To sea Aeneas, finde out Italy. | Dido 4.3.56 | Aeneas
But now I finde thee, and that feare is past. | 2Tamb 4.2.20 | Therid
To finde and to repay the man with death: | P 256 4.54 | Charls
Faine would I finde some means to speak with him/But cannot, | P 662 13.6 | Duchss
But will you love me, if you finde it so? | Edw 1.4.324 | Queene
Scarce shall you finde a man of more desart. | Edw 2.2.251 | Gavstn
We will finde comfort, money, men, and friends/Ere long, to bid | Edw 4.2.65 | SrJohn
And in this torment, comfort finde I none, | Edw 5.1.81 | Edward
Thinke not to finde me slack or pitifull. | Edw 5.6.82 | King
finde you so kind I will make knowne unto you what my heart | F1570 4.6.13 | P Lady
my maister and mistris shal finde that I can reade, he for his | F App p.233 15 | P Robin
There will I finde thee, or be found by thee, | Ovid's Elegies 1.4.57
To finde, what worke my muse might move, I strove. | Ovid's Elegies 3.1.6
Ah now a name too true thou hast, I finde. | Ovid's Elegies 3.8.4
FINDES
See what strange arts necessitie findes out, | Dido 1.1.169 | Venus
He comes and findes his sonnes have had no shares/In all the | 2Tamb 4.1.47 | Amyras
Small comfort findes poore Edward in thy lookes, | Edw 5.5.44 | Edward
FINDING
Where finding Aeolus intrencht with stormes, | Dido 1.1.58 | Venus
And at Joves Altar finding Priamus, | Dido 2.1.225 | Aeneas
FINE
And a fine brouch to put in my hat, | Dido 1.1.47 | Ganimd
I, and my mother gave me this fine bow. | Dido 2.1.309 | Cupid
Madame, she thinks perhaps she is too fine. | 1Tamb 3.3.179 | Ebea
one; have not the Nuns fine sport with the Fryars now and then? | Jew 3.3.32 | P Ithimr
am glad I have found you, you are a couple of fine companions: | F1097 3.3.10 | P Vintnr
Ile have fine sport with the boyes, Ile get nuts and apples | F App p.236 45 | P Robin
being fine and thinne/Like to the silke the curious Seres | Ovid's Elegies 1.14.5
Or if there be a God, he loves fine wenches, | Ovid's Elegies 3.3.25
FINELY
Finely dissembled, do so still sweet Queene. | Edw 5.2.74 | Mortmr
nere was there any/So finely handled as this king shalbe. | Edw 5.5.40 | Ltborn
FINER
And fram'd of finer mold then common men, | Jew 1.2.219 | Barab
FINEST
<The> streetes straight forth, and paved with finest bricke, | F 789 3.1.11 | Faust
A gowne made of the finest wooll, | Passionate Shepherd 13
FINGARS
And whose immortall fingars did imprint, | Hero and Leander 1.67
FINGER
Casane, here are the cates you desire to finger, are they not? | 1Tamb 4.4.108 | P Tamb
Let thy soft finger to thy eare be brought. | Ovid's Elegies 1.4.24
Thy bosomes Roseat buds let him not finger, | Ovid's Elegies 1.4.37
Thou ring that shalt my faire girles finger binde, | Ovid's Elegies 2.15.1
FINGERS
If thou but lay thy fingers on my boy. | Dido 3.2.36 | Venus
His armes and fingers long and [sinowy] <snowy>, | 1Tamb 2.1.27 | Menaph

FINGERS (cont.)
And make her daintie fingers fall to woorke. 1Tamb 3.3.181 Ebea
Their fingers made to quaver on a Lute, 2Tamb 1.3.29 Tamb
Come boyes and with your fingers search my wound, 2Tamb 3.2.126 Tamb
Souldier shall defile/His manly fingers with so faint a boy. 2Tamb 4.1.164 Tamb
Wearying his fingers ends with telling it, Jew 1.1.16 Barab
and by my fingers take/A kisse from him that sends it from his Jew 2.1.58 Barab
His hands are hackt, some fingers cut quite off; Jew 4.3.10 Barab
Me thinkes he fingers very well. Jew 4.4.49 Pilia
Come death, and with thy fingers close my eyes, Edw 5.1.110 Edward
the boord with wine/Was scribled, and thy fingers writ a line. Ovid's Elegies 2.5.18
But in lesse compasse her small fingers knit. Ovid's Elegies 2.15.20

FINGRED
The needy groome that never fingred groat, Jew 1.1.12 Barab

FINIS
Bene disserere est finis logices. F 35 1.1.7 Faust

FINISH
That these my boies may finish all my wantes. 2Tamb 5.3.125 Tamb
Made two nights one to finish up his pleasure. Ovid's Elegies 1.13.46

FINISHED
And when this just revenge is finished, P 318 5.45 Anjoy

FINISHT
That the first is finisht in a naturall day? F 603 2.2.52 Faust

FIR'D
Some have we fir'd, and many have we sunke; Jew 2.2.15 Bosco
Why, then the house was fir'd,/Blowne up, and all thy souldiers Jew 5.5.106 Govnr

FIRE (See also FIER)
As I exhal'd with thy fire darting beames, Dido 1.1.25 Jupitr
Till we have fire to dresse the meate we kild: Dido 1.1.165 Aeneas
That we may make a fire to warme us with, Dido 1.1.167 Aeneas
Hold, take this candle and goe light a fire, Dido 1.1.171 Aeneas
Save, save, O save our ships from cruell fire, Dido 1.2.7 Illion
In whose sterne faces shin'd the quenchles fire, Dido 2.1.186 Aeneas
Troy is a fire, the Grecians have the towne. Dido 2.1.208 Aeneas
With balles of wilde fire in their murdering pawes, Dido 2.1.217 Aeneas
Viewing the fire wherewith rich Ilion burnt. Dido 2.1.264 Aeneas
Whose amorous face like Pean sparkles fire, Dido 3.4.19 Dido
The ayre wherein they breathe, the water, fire, Dido 4.4.75 Dido
And fire proude Lacedemon ore their heads. Dido 4.4.92 Aeneas
Goe Anna, bid my servants bring me fire. Dido 5.1.278 Dido
Lay to thy hands and helpe me make a fire, Dido 5.1.284 Dido
And prest out fire from their burning jawes: 1Tamb 2.6.6 Cosroe
He raceth all his foes with fire and sword. 1Tamb 4.1.63 2Msngr
Will send up fire to your turning Spheares, 1Tamb 4.2.39 Tamb
My sword stroke fire from his coat of steele, 1Tamb 4.2.41 Tamb
Not I, bring milk and fire, and my blood I bring him againe, 1Tamb 5.1.310 P Zabina
And means to fire Turky as he goes: 2Tamb 1.1.18 Gazell
Which in despight of them I set on fire: 2Tamb 1.3.213 Therid
That in the midst of fire is ingraft, 2Tamb 2.3.21 Orcan
The golden balle of heavens eternal fire, 2Tamb 2.4.2 Tamb
Whose eies shot fire from their Ivory bowers, 2Tamb 2.4.9 Tamb
This cursed towne will I consume with fire, 2Tamb 2.4.137 Tamb
of the war/Threw naked swords and sulphur bals of fire, 2Tamb 3.2.41 Tamb
That we have sent before to fire the townes, 2Tamb 3.2.147 Tamb
Til fire and sword have found them at a bay. 2Tamb 3.2.151 Tamb
And with the breaches fall, smoake, fire, and dust, 2Tamb 3.3.59 Therid
Madam, sooner shall fire consume us both, 2Tamb 3.4.73 Techel
Fire the towne and overrun the land. 2Tamb 3.5.9 2Msngr
hands)/All brandishing their brands of quenchlesse fire, 2Tamb 3.5.27 Orcan
And joy'd the fire of this martiall flesh, 2Tamb 4.1.106 Tamb
with the meteors/Of blood and fire thy tyrannies have made, 2Tamb 4.1.142 Jrslem
Will poure down blood and fire on thy head: 2Tamb 4.1.143 Jrslem
Whose sight composde of furie and of fire/Doth send such sterne 2Tamb 4.1.175 Trebiz
Mounted his shining [chariot] <chariots>, gilt with fire, 2Tamb 4.3.126 Tamb
more than if the region/Next underneath the Element of fire, 2Tamb 5.1.88 Tamb
Wel said, let there be a fire presently. 2Tamb 5.1.178 Tamb
So Casane, fling them in the fire. 2Tamb 5.1.186 Tamb
That suffers flames of fire to burne the writ/Wherein the sum 2Tamb 5.1.190 Tamb
were scortcht/And all the earth like Aetna breathing fire: 2Tamb 5.3.233 Tamb
And heaven consum'd his choisest living fire. 2Tamb 5.3.251 Amyras
Wee'll send [thee] <the> bullets wrapt in smoake and fire: Jew 2.2.54 Govnr
Hoping ere long to set the house a fire; Jew 2.3.88 Barab
In setting Christian villages on fire, Jew 2.3.203 Ithimr
Feare not, I'le so set his heart a fire, Jew 2.3.375 Ithimr
me in the pot of Rice/That for our supper stands upon the fire. Jew 3.4.50 Barab
Shall be condemn'd, and then sent to the fire. Jew 3.6.36 2Fryar
To fire the Churches, pull their houses downe, Jew 5.1.65 Barab
shut/His souldiers, till I have consum'd 'em all with fire? Jew 5.2.82 Barab
And fire the house; say, will not this be brave? Jew 5.5.41 Barab
O no, his bodye will infect the fire, and the fire the aire, and P 484 9.3 P 1Atndt
and the fire the aire, and so we shall be poysoned with him. P 484 9.3 P 1Atndt
Which they will put us to with sword and fire: P 706 14.9 Navrre
And fire accursed Rome about his eares. P1200 22.62 King
Ile fire his crased buildings and [inforse] <incense>/The P1201 22.63 King
Fire Paris where these trecherous rebels lurke. P1241 22.103 King
Ile fire thy crased buildings, and enforce/The papall towers, Edw 1.4.100 Edward
And marche to fire them from their starting holes. Edw 3.1.127 Spencr
Edward with fire and sword, followes at thy heeles. Edw 3.1.180 Edward
Will sooner sparkle fire then shed a teare: Edw 5.1.105 Edward
I'le fetch thee fire to dissolve it straight. F 452 2.1.64 Mephst
See <come> Faustus, here is <heres> fire, set it on. F 459 2.1.71 Mephst
Pluto's blew fire, and Hecat's tree, F1001 3.2.21 Mephst
Now with the flames of ever-burning fire, F1135 3.3.48 Mephst

FIRE (cont.)			
These, that are fed with soppes of flaming fire,	F1916	5.2.120	BdAngl
At which selfe time the house seem'd all on fire,	F1993	5.3.11	3Schol
And with bright restles fire compasse the earth,	Lucan, First Booke		49
Confused stars shal meete, celestiall fire/Fleete on the flouds,	Lucan, First Booke		75
Filling the world, leapes out and throwes forth fire,	Lucan, First Booke		154
Or rob the gods; or sacred temples fire;	Lucan, First Booke		380
Wandering about the North, and rings of fire/Flie in the ayre,	Lucan, First Booke		525
a double point/Rose like the Theban brothers funerall fire;	Lucan, First Booke		550
I saw a brandisht fire increase in strength,	Ovid's Elegies		1.2.11
Or I more sterne then fire or sword will turne,	Ovid's Elegies		1.6.57
Farre off be force, no fire to them may reach,	Ovid's Elegies		1.14.29
But furiously he follow his loves fire/And [thinke] <thinkes>	Ovid's Elegies		2.2.13
Pleasure addes fuell to my lustfull fire,	Ovid's Elegies		2.10.25
But absent is my fire, lyes ile tell none,	Ovid's Elegies		2.16.11
Let me be slandered, while my fire she hides,	Ovid's Elegies		2.17.3
So having vext she nourisht my warme fire,	Ovid's Elegies		2.19.15
Jove throwes downe woods, and Castles with his fire:	Ovid's Elegies		3.3.35
Yet might her touch make youthfull Pilius fire,	Ovid's Elegies		3.6.41
His broken bowe, his fire-brand without light.	Ovid's Elegies		3.8.8
The holy gods gilt temples they might fire,	Ovid's Elegies		3.8.43
With thine, nor this last fire their presence misses.	Ovid's Elegies		3.8.54
And wisht the goddesse long might feele loves fire.	Ovid's Elegies		3.9.42
Love kindling fire, to burne such townes as Troy,	Hero and Leander		1.153
Till with the fire that from his count'nance blazed,	Hero and Leander		1.164
The aire with sparkes of living fire was spangled,	Hero and Leander		1.188
And now begins Leander to display/Loves holy fire, with words,	Hero and Leander		1.193
Than for the fire filcht by Prometheus;	Hero and Leander		1.438
For hitherto hee did but fan the fire,	Hero and Leander		2.41
The light of hidden fire it selfe discovers,	Hero and Leander		2.133
Whose lively heat like fire from heaven fet,	Hero and Leander		2.255
FIRE-BRAND			
His broken bowe, his fire-brand without light.	Ovid's Elegies		3.8.8
FIREBRANDS			
Breake up the earth, and with their firebrands,	1Tamb	5.1.219	Bajzth
FIRED			
King of this Citie, but my Troy is fired,	Dido	2.1.236	Aeneas
How may my hart, thus fired with mine eies,	2Tamb	4.1.93	Tamb
rayes now sing/The fell Nemean beast, th'earth would be fired,	Lucan, First Booke		655
FIRES			
lamps of heaven/To cast their bootlesse fires to the earth,	2Tamb	5.3.4	Therid
Make fires, heat irons, let the racke be fetch'd.	Jew	5.1.24	Govnr
Fierce Mastives hould; the vestall fires went out,	Lucan, First Booke		547
Fires and inflames objects remooved farre,	Hero and Leander		2.124
FIRIOUS			
Many a yeare these [furious] <firious> broiles let last,	Lucan, First Booke		667
FIRMAMENT (See also FERMAMENT)			
And shiver all the starry firmament:	2Tamb	2.4.106	Tamb
Who now with Jove opens the firmament,	2Tamb	3.5.56	Callap
Run tilting round about the firmament,	2Tamb	4.1.203	Tamb
And set blacke streamers in the firmament,	2Tamb	5.3.49	Tamb
the seven Planets, the Firmament, and the Emperiall heaven.	F 610	2.2.59	P Mephst
Graven in the booke of Joves high firmament,	F 756	2.3.35	2Chor
[See see where Christs bloud streames in the firmament],	F1939	5.2.143A	Faust
For everie street like to a Firmament/Glistered with breathing	Hero and Leander		1.97
FIRME			
Since thy Aeneas wandring fate is firme,	Dido	1.1.83	Jupitr
Maintaine it bravely by firme policy,	Jew	5.2.36	Barab
but for a Queene/Europe, and Asia in firme peace had beene.	Ovid's Elegies		2.12.18
FIRMELY			
Least Arte should winne her, firmely did inclose.	Ovid's Elegies		2.12.4
FIRST			
But first in bloud must his good fortune bud,	Dido	1.1.86	Jupitr
And from the first earth interdict our feete.	Dido	1.2.37	Serg
When first you set your foote upon the shoare,	Dido	3.3.53	Achat
Am I lesse faire then when thou sawest me first?	Dido	5.1.115	Dido
Where thou and false Achates first set foote:	Dido	5.1.175	Dido
Thou shalt burne first, thy crime is worse then his:	Dido	5.1.297	Dido
When first he came on shoare, perish thou to:	Dido	5.1.299	Dido
Stay Techelles, aske a parlee first.	1Tamb	1.2.137	Tamb
Accurst be he that first invented war,	1Tamb	2.4.1	Mycet
Why then Theridamas, Ile first assay,	1Tamb	2.5.81	Tamb
As it hath chang'd my first conceiv'd disdaine.	1Tamb	3.2.12	Zenoc
You see though first the King of Persea/(Being a Shepheard)	1Tamb	3.2.59	Agidas
Wil first subdue the Turke, and then inlarge/Those Christian	1Tamb	3.3.46	Tamb
When first he war'd against the Christians.	1Tamb	3.3.200	Zabina
The first day when he pitcheth downe his tentes,	1Tamb	4.1.49	2Msngr
first moover of that Spheare/Enchac'd with thousands ever	1Tamb	4.2.8	Tamb
First shalt thou rip my bowels with thy sword,	1Tamb	4.2.16	Bajzth
First rising in the East with milde aspect,	1Tamb	4.2.37	Tamb
First legions of devils shall teare thee in peeces.	1Tamb	4.4.38	P Bajzth
must you be first shal feele/The sworne destruction of	1Tamb	5.1.65	Tamb
when first my milkwhite flags/Through which sweet mercie threw	1Tamb	5.1.68	Tamb
The first affecter of your excellence,	1Tamb	5.1.379	Philem
My father and my first betrothed love,	1Tamb	5.1.388	Zenoc
Thy first betrothed Love, Arabia,	1Tamb	5.1.530	Tamb
first thou shalt kneele to us/And humbly crave a pardon for thy	2Tamb	3.5.108	Orcan
Who shal kisse the fairest of the Turkes Concubines first, when	2Tamb	4.1.65	P Calyph
O Samarcanda, where I breathed first,	2Tamb	4.1.105	Tamb
First let thy Scythyan horse teare both our limmes/Rather then	2Tamb	5.1.138	Orcan
Shoot first my Lord, and then the rest shall follow.	2Tamb	5.1.151	Tamb
Which is from Scythia, where I first began,	2Tamb	5.3.143	Tamb
First take my Scourge and my imperiall Crowne,	2Tamb	5.3.177	Tamb

FIRST (cont.)

Might first made Kings, and Lawes were then most sure/When like	Jew	Prol.20	Machvl
First, the tribute mony of the Turkes shall all be levyed	Jew	1.2.68	P Reader
From nought at first thou camst to little welth,	Jew	1.2.105	1Knght
If your first curse fall heavy on thy head,	Jew	1.2.107	1Knght
As good dissemble that thou never mean'st/As first meane truth,	Jew	1.2.291	Barab
First let me as a Novice learne to frame/My solitary life to	Jew	1.2.331	Abigal
Welcome the first beginner of my blisse:	Jew	2.1.50	Barab
No, Barabas, I will deserve it first.	Jew	2.3.68	Lodowk
First be thou voyd of these affections,	Jew	2.3.169	Barab
studied Physicke, and began/To practise first upon the Italian;	Jew	2.3.182	Barab
and I carried it, first to Lodowicke, and imprimis to Mathias.	Jew	3.3.19	P Ithimr
But first goe fetch me in the pot of Rice/That for our supper	Jew	3.4.49	Barab
Stay, let me spice it first.	Jew	3.4.85	Barab
Pray let me taste first.	Jew	3.4.87	P Ithimr
Stay, first let me stirre it Ithimore.	Jew	3.4.95	Barab
First will we race the City wals our selves,	Jew	3.5.13	Govnr
seeing you are come/Be you my ghostly father; and first know,	Jew	3.6.12	Abigal
First to Don Lodowicke, him I never lov'd;	Jew	3.6.23	Abigal
it, and the Priest/That makes it knowne, being degraded first,	Jew	3.6.35	2Fryar
First helpe to bury this, then goe with me/And helpe me to	Jew	3.6.45	2Fryar
Come Amorous wag, first banquet and then sleep.	Jew	4.2.132	Curtzn
And fit it should: but first let's ha more gold.	Jew	4.4.26	Curtzn
Must tuna my Lute for sound, twang twang first.	Jew	4.4.31	Barab
First to surprize great Selims souldiers,	Jew	5.2.118	Barab
First, for his Army, they are sent before,	Jew	5.5.25	Barab
No, Governor, I'le satisfie thee first,	Jew	5.5.44	Barab
See his end first, and flye then if thou canst.	Jew	5.5.69	Govnr
That kindled first this motion in our hearts,	P 7	1.7	Charls
Him will we--but first lets follow those in France,	P 153	2.96	Guise
I let the Admirall be first dispatcht.	P 283	5.10	Retes
Now doe I see that from the very first,	P 694	13.38	Guise
First let us set our hand and seale to this,	P 890	17.85	King
Ile [fawne] <fanne> first on the winde,/That glaunceth at my	Edw	1.1.22	Gavstn
First were his sacred garments rent and torne,	Edw	1.2.35	ArchBp
And may it proove more happie then the first.	Edw	1.4.336	Queene
Our Ladies first love is not wavering,	Edw	2.1.27	Spencr
Will be the first that shall adventure life.	Edw	2.3.4	Kent
I found them at the first inexorable,	Edw	3.1.103	Arundl
First would I heare newes that hee were deposde,	Edw	5.2.21	Mortmr
Let me but see him first, and then I will.	Edw	5.2.95	Prince
Tis not the first time I have killed a man.	Edw	5.4.30	Ltborn
First I complaine of imbecilitie,	Edw	5.4.60	Mortmr
Valdes, first let him know the words of Art,	F 185	1.1.157	Cornel
First I'le instruct thee in the rudiments,	F 188	1.1.160	Valdes
First, that Faustus may be a spirit in forme and substance.	F 485	2.1.97	P Faust
First, I will question [with] thee about hell:	F 504	2.1.116	Faust
That the first is finisht in a naturall day?	F 603	2.2.52	Faust
me, as Paradise was to Adam the first day of his creation.	F 658	2.2.107	P Faust
That shall I soone: What art thou the first?	F 663	2.2.112	Faust
the first letter of my name begins with Letchery <leachery>.	F 709	2.2.161	P Ltchry
And as I guesse will first arrive at Rome,	F 775	2.3.54	2Chor
Let it be so my Faustus, but first stay,	F 856	3.1.78	Mephst
First weare this girdle, then appeare/Invisible to all are	F 997	3.2.17	Mephst
First, may it please your sacred Holinesse,	F1013	3.2.33	1Card
First, be thou turned to this ugly shape,	F1126	3.3.39	Mephst
Come leave thy chamber first, and thou shalt see/This Conjurer	F1185	4.1.31	Mrtino
Here will we stay to bide the first assault,	F1354	4.2.30	Benvol
First, on his head, in quittance of my wrongs,	F1379	4.2.55	Benvol
and let them hang/Within the window where he yoak'd me first,	F1381	4.2.57	Benvol
Since first the worlds creation did begin.	F1985	5.3.3	1Schol
first, I can make thee druncke with ipocrase at any taberne in	F App	p.234 22	P Robin
First conquer all the earth, then turne thy force/Against	Lucan, First Booke		22
The causes first I purpose to unfould/Of these garboiles,	Lucan, First Booke		67
To scape the violence of the streame first waded,	Lucan, First Booke		223
all lands else/Have stable peace, here wars rage first begins,	Lucan, First Booke		252
We bide the first brunt, safer might we dwel,	Lucan, First Booke		253
We first sustain'd the uproares of the Gaules,	Lucan, First Booke		256
First he commands such monsters Nature hatcht/Against her kind	Lucan, First Booke		588
When in this [workes] <worke> first verse I trod aloft,	Ovid's Elegies		1.1.21
Let my first verse be sixe, my last five feete,	Ovid's Elegies		1.1.31
his limbes he spread/Upon the bed, but on my foote first tread.	Ovid's Elegies		1.4.16
If hee gives thee what first himselfe did tast,	Ovid's Elegies		1.4.33
Well I remember when I first did hire thee,	Ovid's Elegies		1.6.43
He first a Goddesse strooke; an other I.	Ovid's Elegies		1.7.32
Then first I did perceive I had offended,	Ovid's Elegies		1.7.59
And as first wrongd the wronged some-times banish,	Ovid's Elegies		1.8.79
Who first depriv'd yong boyes of their best part,	Ovid's Elegies		2.3.3
The greedy spirits take the best things first,	Ovid's Elegies		2.6.39
taught/Ill waies by rough seas wondring waves first taught,	Ovid's Elegies		2.11.2
I from the shore thy knowne ship first will see,	Ovid's Elegies		2.11.43
Who unborne infants first to slay invented,	Ovid's Elegies		2.14.5
Would first my beautious wenches moist lips touch,	Ovid's Elegies		2.15.17
Nor she her selfe but first trim'd up discernes.	Ovid's Elegies		2.17.10
And first [she] <he> sayd, when will thy love be spent,	Ovid's Elegies		3.1.15
And by those numbers is thy first youth spent.	Ovid's Elegies		3.1.28
First of thy minde the happy seedes I knewe,	Ovid's Elegies		3.1.59
First Victory is brought with large spred wing,	Ovid's Elegies		3.2.45
First to be throwne upon the untill'd ground.	Ovid's Elegies		3.5.16
And Crusa unto Zanthus first affide,	Ovid's Elegies		3.5.31
And for a good verse drawe the first dart forth,	Ovid's Elegies		3.7.27
The one his first love, th'other his new care.	Ovid's Elegies		3.8.32
Nemesis and thy first wench joyne their kisses,	Ovid's Elegies		3.8.53

FIRST (cont.)			
On mast of cakes, first oracles, men fed,	Ovid's Elegies	3.9.9	
First Ceres taught the seede in fields to swell,	Ovid's Elegies	3.9.11	
She first constraind bulles necks to beare the yoake,	Ovid's Elegies	3.9.13	
Proteus what should I name? teeth, Thebes first seed?	Ovid's Elegies	3.11.35	
And give to him that the first wound imparts.	Ovid's Elegies	3.12.22	
Who ever lov'd, that lov'd not at first sight?	Hero and Leander	1.176	
These greedie lovers had, at their first meeting.	Hero and Leander	2.24	
When first religious chastitie she vow'd:	Hero and Leander	2.110	
FISH			
and the water the fish, and by the fish our selves when we eate	P 488	9.7	P 2Atndt
water the fish, and by the fish our selves when we eate them.	P 489	9.8	P 2Atndt
Faire Queene forbeare to angle for the fish,	Edw	1.4.221	Mortmr
Plinie reports, there is a flying Fish,	Edw	2.2.23	Lncstr
this fish my lord I beare,/The motto this:	Edw	2.2.27	Lncstr
Though thou comparst him to a flying Fish,	Edw	2.2.43	Edward
FISHER			
And cam'st to Dido like a Fisher swaine?	Dido	5.1.162	Dido
FISHES			
Where thou shalt see the red gild fishes leape,	Dido	4.5.10	Nurse
And fishes [fed] <feed> by humaine carkasses,	2Tamb	5.1.206	Techel
Which all the other fishes deadly hate,	Edw	2.2.24	Lncstr
FIST			
Will quickly flye to [Cithereas] <Citheidas> fist.	Dido	2.1.322	Venus
FISTS			
Will batter Turrets with their manly fists.	1Tamb	3.3.111	Bajzth
FIT (Homograph)			
The ayre is pleasant, and the soyle most fit/For Cities, and	Dido	1.1.178	Achat
Fit Souldiers for the wicked Tamburlaine.	1Tamb	2.2.24	Meandr
Their shoulders broad, for complet armour fit,	1Tamb	3.3.107	Bajzth
And such are objects fit for Tamburlaine.	1Tamb	5.1.475	Tamb
Fit objects for thy princely eie to pierce.	2Tamb	1.2.45	Callap
No Madam, these are speeches fit for us,	2Tamb	1.3.88	Celeb
And if she passe this fit, the worst is past.	2Tamb	2.4.40	1Phstn
Some musicke, and my fit wil cease my Lord.	2Tamb	2.4.77	Zenoc
Proud furie and intollorable fit,	2Tamb	2.4.78	Tamb
Fit for the followers of great Tamburlaine.	2Tamb	3.2.144	Tamb
I must apply my selfe to fit those tearmes,	2Tamb	4.1.155	Tamb
To make you fierce, and fit my appetite,	2Tamb	4.3.17	Tamb
and fit for nought/But perches for the black and fatall Ravens.	2Tamb	4.3.22	Tamb
as fit as may be to restraine/These coltish coach-horse tongues	2Tamb	4.3.51	Usumc
Which wil abate the furie of your fit,	2Tamb	5.3.79	Phsitn
And fit it should: but first let's ha more gold.	Jew	4.4.26	Curtzn
My opportunity may serve me fit,	P 566	11.31	Navrre
And like disportes, such as doe fit the Court?	P 629	12.42	King
Then hath your grace fit oportunitie,	P 903	18.4	Bartus
And every earth is fit for buriall.	Edw	5.1.146	Edward
of his men to attend you with provision fit for your journey.	F1502	4.4.46	P Wagner
Choosing a subject fit for feirse alarmes:	Ovid's Elegies	1.1.6	
Servants fit for thy purpose thou must hire/To teach thy lover,	Ovid's Elegies	1.8.87	
he doth not chide/Nor to hoist saile attends fit time and tyde.	Ovid's Elegies	1.9.14	
While I speake some fewe, yet fit words be idle.	Ovid's Elegies	2.2.2	
Fit her so well, as she is fit for me:	Ovid's Elegies	2.15.5	
This kinde of verse is not alike, yet fit,	Ovid's Elegies	2.17.21	
The Lydian buskin [in] fit [paces] <places> kept her.	Ovid's Elegies	3.1.14	
Her foote was small: her footes forme is most fit:	Ovid's Elegies	3.3.7	
Being fit broken with the crooked share,	Ovid's Elegies	3.9.32	
FITLY			
More fitly had [they] <thy> wrangling bondes contained/From	Ovid's Elegies	1.12.23	
FITS (Homograph)			
A Sword, and not a Scepter fits Aeneas.	Dido	4.4.43	Aeneas
A grave, and not a lover fits thy age:--	Dido	4.5.30	Nurse
a greater [task]/Fits Menaphon, than warring with a Thiefe:	1Tamb	1.1.88	Cosroe
As fits the Legate of the stately Turk.	1Tamb	3.1.44	Bassoe
may I presume/To know the cause of these unquiet fits:	1Tamb	3.2.2	Agidas
Which me thinkes fits not their profession.	Jew	1.1.118	Barab
things of more waight/Then fits a prince so yong as I to beare,	Edw	3.1.75	Prince
O no my lord, this princely resolution/Fits not the time, away,	Edw	4.5.9	Baldck
This <His> study fits a Mercenarie drudge,	F 61	1.1.33	Faust
What age fits Mars, with Venus doth agree,	Ovid's Elegies	1.9.3	
FITTED			
Now tell me Faustus, are we not fitted well?	F 940	3.1.162	Mephst
committed/And then with sweete words to my Mistrisse fitted.	Ovid's Elegies	1.12.22	
FITTER			
A fitter subject for a pensive soule.	2Tamb	4.2.27	Olymp
she were fitter for a tale of love/Then to be tired out with	Jew	1.2.369	Mthias
The fitter art thou Baldock for my turne,	Edw	2.2.245	Edward
FITTEST			
Whereas the Fort may fittest be assailde,	2Tamb	3.2.66	Tamb
As to your wisdomes fittest seemes in all.	Edw	4.6.29	Queene
Being fittest matter for a wanton wit,	Ovid's Elegies	1.1.24	
FITTETH			
For Wil and Shall best fitteth Tamburlain,	1Tamb	3.3.41	Tamb
A greater subject fitteth Faustus wit:	F 39	1.1.11	Faust
FIVE			
My martiall prises with five hundred men,	1Tamb	1.2.102	Tamb
A thousand horsmen? We five hundred foote?	1Tamb	1.2.121	Tamb
Weele fight five hundred men at armes to one,	1Tamb	1.2.143	Tamb
Five hundred thousand footmen threatning shot,	1Tamb	4.1.24	2Msngr
A monster of five hundred thousand heades,	1Tamb	4.3.7	Souldn
Five hundred Briggandines are under saile,	2Tamb	1.3.122	Therid
Backeward and forwards nere five thousand leagues.	2Tamb	5.3.144	Tamb
hundred yoake/Of labouring Oxen, and five hundred/Shee Asses:	Jew	1.2.184	Barab

FIVE (cont.)			
Write for five hundred Crownes.	Jew	4.2.116	P Pilia
as you love your life send me five hundred crowns, and give the	Jew	4.2.117	P Ithimr
No Sir; and therefore I must have five hundred more. .	Jew	4.3.22	P Pilia
'Tis not five hundred Crownes that I esteeme, ...	Jew	4.3.40	Barab
[demand]/Three hundred Crownes, and then five hundred Crownes?	Jew	4.3.62	Barab
I'le lead five hundred souldiers through the Vault, . .	Jew	5.1.91	Barab
Paris hath full five hundred Colledges, ...	P 137	2.80	Guise
Five hundred fatte Franciscan Fryers and priestes. . .	P 142	2.85	Guise
They rate his ransome at five thousand pound. . . .	Edw	2.2.117	Mortmr
Five yeeres I lengthned thy commaund in France: . .	Lucan, First Booke		277
We which were Ovids five books, now are three, . . .	Ovid's Elegies		1.1.1
If reading five thou plainst of tediousnesse, . . .	Ovid's Elegies		1.1.3
Let my first verse be sixe, my last five feete, . .	Ovid's Elegies		1.1.31
Thebe who Mother of five Daughters prov'd? . . .	Ovid's Elegies		3.5.34
For five score Nimphes, or more our flouds conteine. .	Ovid's Elegies		3.5.64
FIXED			
Make heaven to frowne and every fixed starre/To sucke up poison	1Tamb	4.2.5	Bajzth
But fixed now in the Meridian line, ...	1Tamb	4.2.38	Tamb
Gives light to Phoebus and the fixed stars, ...	2Tamb	2.4.50	Tamb
And passe their fixed boundes exceedingly.	2Tamb	4.3.47	Therid
FIXING			
Than Dis, on heapes of gold fixing his looke. . . .	Hero and Leander		2.326
FIXT			
Mine eye is fixt where fancie cannot start, ...	Dido	4.2.37	Iarbus
His fierie eies are fixt upon the earth, ...	1Tamb	1.2.158	Therid
Are fixt his piercing instruments of sight:	1Tamb	2.1.14	Menaph
And cause the stars fixt in the Southern arke, . . .	2Tamb	3.2.29	Tamb
Whose eyes are fixt on none but Gaveston:	Edw	2.4.62	Queene
your right eye be alwaies Diametrally fixt upon my left heele,	F 386	1.4.44	P Wagner
Wherein is fixt the love of Belzebub, ...	F 400	2.1.12	Faust
Behold this Silver Belt whereto is fixt/Seven golden [keys]	F 932	3.1.154	Pope
and let thy left eye be diametarily fixt upon my right heele,	F App	p.231 70	P Wagner
And to the end your constant faith stood fixt. . . .	Ovid's Elegies		2.6.14
In heaven without thee would I not be fixt. . . .	Ovid's Elegies		2.16.14
When have not I fixt to thy side close layed? . . .	Ovid's Elegies		3.10.17
FLAG			
But if he stay until the bloody flag/Be once advanc'd on my	1Tamb	4.2.116	Tamb
To martch with me under this bloody flag:	2Tamb	2.4.116	Tamb
FLAGGE			
Yet he undaunted tooke his fathers flagge, ...	Dido	2.1.259	Aeneas
FLAGGES			
Then hang out flagges (my Lord) of humble truce, . .	2Tamb	5.1.6	Maxim
FLAGITIOUS			
the inward soule/With such flagitious crimes of hainous sinnes,	F App	p.243 42	OldMan
FLAGS			
pitch'd before the gates/And gentle flags of amitie displaid.	1Tamb	4.2.112	Therid
when first my milkwhite flags/Through which sweet mercie threw	1Tamb	5.1.68	Tamb
With ugly Furies bearing fiery flags, ...	2Tamb	1.3.146	Techel
Offer submission, hang up flags of truce, ...	2Tamb	5.1.26	1Citzn
But seeing white Eagles, and Roomes flags wel known, .	Lucan, First Booke		246
spread these flags that ten years space have conquer'd, .	Lucan, First Booke		348
FLAME			
Which made the funerall flame that burnt faire Troy: .	Dido	2.1.218	Aeneas
Shall burne to cinders in this pretious flame. . . .	Dido	5.1.301	Dido
And burne him in the fury of that flame, ...	1Tamb	2.6.32	Cosroe
The Dyvils there in chaines of quencelesse flame, . .	2Tamb	2.3.24	Orcan
Flame to the highest region of the aire:	2Tamb	3.2.2	Tamb
And cast her bodie in the burning flame, ...	2Tamb	3.4.71	Olymp
Or mount the sunnes flame bearing <plume bearing> charriot,	Lucan, First Booke		48
The flame in Alba consecrate to Jove, ...	Lucan, First Booke		548
A scorching flame burnes all the standers by. . . .	Ovid's Elegies		1.2.46
That thou maiest know with love thou mak'st me flame. .	Ovid's Elegies		3.2.4
Flames into flame, flouds thou powrest seas into. . .	Ovid's Elegies		3.2.34
Is by Evadne thought to take such flame, ...	Ovid's Elegies		3.5.41
Burnes his dead body in the funerall flame. . . .	Ovid's Elegies		3.8.6
She sawe, and as her marrowe tooke the flame, . . .	Ovid's Elegies		3.9.27
His secret flame apparantly was seene, ...	Hero and Leander		2.135
FLAME BEARING			
Or mount the sunnes flame bearing <plume bearing> charriot,	Lucan, First Booke		48
FLAMED			
Which flamed not on high; but headlong pitcht/Her burning head	Lucan, First Booke		544
FLAMEN (See FLAMINS)			
FLAMES			
Aeneas, O Aeneas, quench these flames.	Dido	3.4.23	Dido
O helpe Iarbus, Dido in these flames/Hath burnt her selfe, aye	Dido	5.1.314	Anna
Enrolde in flames and fiery smoldering mistes, . . .	1Tamb	2.3.20	Tamb
Where flames shall ever feed upon his soule. . . .	1Tamb	2.6.8	Cosroe
And from their shieldes strike flames of lightening)/All .	1Tamb	3.2.81	Agidas
To feele the lovely warmth of shepheards flames, . .	1Tamb	5.1.186	Tamb
Whose courages are kindled with the flames, ...	2Tamb	3.1.54	Trebiz
And with the flames that beat against the clowdes/Incense the	2Tamb	4.1.194	Tamb
That suffers flames of fire to burne the writ/Wherein the sum	2Tamb	5.1.190	Tamb
ingendred thoughts/To burst abroad, those never dying flames,	P 92	2.35	Guise
Now with the flames of ever-burning fire, ...	F1135	3.3.48	Mephst
and blasts their eyes/With overthwarting flames, and raging	Lucan, First Booke		156
rites and Latian Jove advanc'd/On Alba hill o Vestall flames,	Lucan, First Booke		201
The flattering skie gliter'd in often flames, ...	Lucan, First Booke		528
loves bowe/His owne flames best acquainted signes may knowe,	Ovid's Elegies		2.1.8
Flames into flame, flouds thou powrest seas into. . .	Ovid's Elegies		3.2.34
Thee sacred Poet could sad flames destroy? . . .	Ovid's Elegies		3.8.41
Oxen in whose mouthes burning flames did breede? . .	Ovid's Elegies		3.11.36
FLAMING			
Whose flaming traines should reach down to the earth/Could not	2Tamb	5.1.90	Tamb

FLAMING (cont.)			
Brighter art thou then flaming Jupiter,	F1783	5.1.110	Faust
These, that are fed with soppes of flaming fire,	F1916	5.2.120	BdAngl
Or flaming Titan (feeding on the deepe)/Puls them aloft, and	Lucan, First Booke	416	
Shaking her snakie haire and crooked pine/With flaming toppe,	Lucan, First Booke	572	
FLAMINS			
And Flamins last, with networke wollen vailes.	Lucan, First Booke	603	
FLANDERS (See also FLAUNDERS)			
Here's a drench to poyson a whole stable of Flanders mares:	Jew	3.4.111	P Ithimr
FLANKE			
And store of ordinance that from every flanke/May scoure the	2Tamb	3.2.79	Tamb
FLARING			
As much as sparkling Diamonds flaring glasse.	Hero and Leander	1.214	
And with his flaring beames mockt ougly night,	Hero and Leander	2.332	
FLASH			
And casts a flash of lightning to the earth.	1Tamb	4.2.46	Tamb
FLAT			
Because the corners there may fall more flat,	2Tamb	3.2.65	Tamb
hast broke the league/By flat denyall of the promis'd Tribute,	Jew	3.5.20	Basso
He that will be a flat decotamest,	P 389	7.29	Guise
well, Ile folow him, Ile serve him, thats flat.	F App	p.231 73	P Clown
FLATERED			
Techelles, women must be flatered.	1Tamb	1.2.107	Tamb
FLATLY			
Both held in hand, and flatly both beguil'd.	Jew	3.3.3	Ithimr
and when they flatly had denyed,/Refusing to receive me pledge	Edw	3.1.106	Arundl
A bloudie part, flatly against law of armes.	Edw	3.1.121	Spencr
FLATTER			
Nor feare I death, nor will I flatter thee.	Jew	5.2.60	Govnr
Tell me Surgeon and flatter not, may I live?	P1222	22.84	King
Ile flatter these, and make them live in hope:	Edw	1.1.43	Gavstn
And all the court begins to flatter him.	Edw	1.2.22	Lncstr
Edward will thinke we come to flatter him.	Edw	4.4.29	SrJohn
only thee I flatter,/Thy lightning can my life in pieces	Ovid's Elegies	1.6.15	
Let thy tongue flatter, while thy minde harme-workes:	Ovid's Elegies	1.8.103	
And strumpets flatter, shall Menander flourish.	Ovid's Elegies	1.15.18	
Now let her flatter me, now chide me hard,	Ovid's Elegies	2.9.45	
Mine owne desires why should my selfe not flatter?	Ovid's Elegies	2.11.54	
Flatter, intreat, promise, protest and sweare,	Hero and Leander	2.268	
FLATTERED			
I would he never had bin flattered more.	Edw	4.4.30	Kent
FLATTERER			
Base flatterer, yeeld, and were it not for shame,	Edw	2.5.11	Mortmr
Did they remoove that flatterer from thy throne.	Edw	3.1.231	Kent
FLATTERERS			
Who loves thee? but a sort of flatterers.	Edw	2.2.171	Mortmr
And shake off smooth dissembling flatterers:	Edw	3.1.169	Herald
Yonder is Edward among his flatterers.	Edw	3.1.196	Mortmr
No Edward, no, thy flatterers faint and flie.	Edw	3.1.201	Mortmr
Unnaturall king, to slaughter noble men/And cherish flatterers:	Edw	4.1.9	Kent
The king will nere forsake his flatterers.	Edw	4.2.60	Mortmr
and withall/We may remoove these flatterers from the king,	Edw	4.4.26	Mortmr
FLATTERIES			
Leave thy once powerfull words, and flatteries,	Ovid's Elegies	3.10.31	
FLATTERING			
How may I credite these thy flattering termes,	Dido	1.1.109	Venus
him to his ships/That now afflicts me with his flattering eyes.	Dido	4.2.22	Iarbus
The flattering skie gliter'd in often flames,	Lucan, First Booke	528	
FLATT'RING			
My flatt'ring speeches soone wide open knocke.	Ovid's Elegies	3.1.46	
FLAUNDERS			
sir John of Henolt, brother to the Marquesse, into Flaunders:	Edw	4.3.32	P Spencr
FLAWE			
Like Popler leaves blowne with a stormy flawe,	Ovid's Elegies	1.7.54	
FLEA			
I am like to Ovids Flea, I can creepe into every corner of a	F 665	2.2.114	P Pride
let it be in the likenesse of a little pretie frisking flea,	F App	p.231 62	P Clown
FLED			
Achates, tis my mother that is fled,	Dido	1.1.240	Aeneas
Yet manhood would not serve, of force we fled,	Dido	2.1.272	Aeneas
Who having wrought her shame, is straight way fled:	Dido	4.2.18	Iarbus
Fled to the Caspean or the Ocean maine?	1Tamb	1.1.102	Mycet
Are fled from Bajazeth, and remaine with me,	1Tamb	4.2.80	Tamb
yong Callapine that lately fled from your majesty, hath nowe	2Tamb	5.3.102	P 3Msngr
Thus are the villaines, cowards fled for feare,	2Tamb	5.3.115	Tamb
My Factor sends me word a Merchant's fled/That owes me for a	Jew	2.3.243	Barab
O no, his soule is fled from out his breast,	P 552	11.17	QnMoth
This way he fled, but I am come too late.	Edw	4.6.1	Kent
Yea madam, and they scape not easilie,/That fled the feeld.	Edw	4.6.42	Mortmr
But wheres the king and the other Spencer fled?	Edw	4.6.55	Mortmr
Gurney, my lord, is fled, and will I feare,	Edw	5.6.7	Matrvs
Wel might these feare, when Pompey fear'd and fled.	Lucan, First Booke	519	
Those that inhabited the suburbe fieldes/Fled, fowle Erinnis	Lucan, First Booke	570	
Ah whether is [thy] <they> brests soft nature [fled] <sled>?	Ovid's Elegies	3.7.18	
Now have I freed my selfe, and fled the chaine,	Ovid's Elegies	3.10.3	
Which fact, and country wealth Halesus fled.	Ovid's Elegies	3.12.32	
Like to the tree of Tantalus she fled,	Hero and Leander	2.75	
The neerer that he came, the more she fled,	Hero and Leander	2.243	
FLEDST			
O that the Clowdes were here wherein thou [fledst] <fleest>,	Dido	4.4.50	Dido
FLEE (See FLIE, FLY)			
FLEECE (See also FLIECES)			
As was to Jason Colchos golden fleece.	1Tamb	4.4.9	Tamb

FLEECE (cont.)			
I'le be thy Jason, thou my golden Fleece:	Jew	4.2.90	Ithimr
And from America the Golden Fleece,	F 158	1.1.130	Valdes
And Jasons Argos, and the fleece of golde?	Ovid's Elegies	1.15.22	
To hazard more, than for the golden Fleece.	Hero and Leander	1.58	
FLEECED			
Caried the famous golden-fleeced sheepe.	Ovid's Elegies	2.11.4	
FLEERING			
And thereof came it, that the fleering Scots,	Edw	2.2.188	Lncstr
FLEEST			
O that the Clowdes were here wherein thou [fledst] <fleest>,	Dido	4.4.50	Dido
FLEET (Homograph)			
wherin at anchor lies/A Turkish Gally of my royall fleet,	2Tamb	1.2.21	Callap
Which makes them fleet aloft and gaspe for aire.	2Tamb	5.1.209	Techel
we were wafted by a Spanish Fleet/That never left us till	Jew	1.1.95	2Merch
A Fleet of warlike Gallyes, Barabas,	Jew	1.1.146	1Jew
Because we vail'd not to the [Turkish] <Spanish> Fleet,/Their	Jew	2.2.11	Bosco
The Mutin toyles; the fleet at Leuca suncke;	Lucan, First Booke	42	
When you fleet hence, can be bequeath'd to none.	Hero and Leander	1.248	
FLEETE (Homograph)			
How got Aeneas to the fleete againe?	Dido	2.1.291	Iarbus
Nor Sterne nor Anchor have our maimed Fleete,	Dido	3.1.109	Aeneas
To stay my Fleete from loosing forth the Bay:	Dido	4.3.26	Aeneas
And let rich Carthage fleete upon the seas,	Dido	4.4.134	Dido
Though she repairde my fleete and gave me ships,	Dido	5.1.59	Aeneas
When as I want both rigging for my fleete,	Dido	5.1.69	Aeneas
Led by Achates to the Troian fleete:	Dido	5.1.84	Dido
How can ye goe when he hath all your fleete?	Dido	5.1.242	Anna
And he hath all [my] <thy> fleete, what shall I doe/But dye in	Dido	5.1.268	Dido
Untill the Persean Fleete and men of war,	1Tamb	3.3.252	Tamb
Did he not cause the King of Spaines huge fleete,	P1033	19.103	King
I, to the tower, the fleete, or where thou wilt.	Edw	1.1.198	Edward
This Ile shall fleete upon the Ocean,	Edw	1.4.49	Edward
Thou Lancaster, high admirall of our fleete,	Edw	1.4.66	Edward
Be thou commaunder of our royall fleete,	Edw	1.4.354	Edward
celestiall fire/Fleete on the flouds, the earth shoulder the	Lucan, First Booke	76	
FLEETED			
Spencer, I see our soules are fleeted hence,	Edw	4.7.105	Baldck
FLEETES			
My soule fleetes when I thinke what you have done,	Ovid's Elegies	3.13.37	
FLEETING			
Legions of Spirits fleeting in the [aire],	1Tamb	3.3.156	Tamb
Shall meet those Christians fleeting with the tyde,	2Tamb	1.1.40	Orcan
And in the fleeting sea the earth be drencht.	Lucan, First Booke	653	
FLEGMATIQUE			
But that I am by nature flegmatique, slow to wrath, and prone	F 209	1.2.16	P Wagner
FLEIGHT			
Their sway of fleight carries the heady rout/That in chain'd	Lucan, First Booke	488	
FLEMISH			
Heere in the river rides a Flemish hoie,	Edw	2.4.46	Mortmr
FLESH			
For all flesh quakes at your magnificence.	1Tamb	3.1.48	Argier
That sacrificing slice and cut your flesh,	1Tamb	4.2.3	Bajzth
are you so daintily brought up, you cannot eat your owne flesh?	1Tamb	4.4.37	P Tamb
That when this fraile and transitory flesh/Hath suckt the	2Tamb	2.4.43	Zenoc
or with a Curtle-axe/To hew thy flesh and make a gaping wound?	2Tamb	3.2.97	Tamb
And see him lance his flesh to teach you all.	2Tamb	3.2.114	Tamb
That feeds upon her sonnes and husbands flesh.	2Tamb	3.4.72	Olymp
Searing thy hatefull flesh with burning yrons,	2Tamb	3.5.123	Tamb
troopes/Beats downe our foes to flesh our taintlesse swords?	2Tamb	4.1.26	Amyras
And joy'd the fire of this martiall flesh,	2Tamb	4.1.106	Tamb
Whose matter is the flesh of Tamburlain,	2Tamb	4.1.113	Tamb
Nor Pistol, Sword, nor Lance can pierce your flesh.	2Tamb	4.2.66	Olymp
That King Egeus fed with humaine flesh,	2Tamb	4.3.13	Tamb
You shal be fed with flesh as raw as blood,	2Tamb	4.3.18	Tamb
Until my soule dissevered from this flesh,	2Tamb	4.3.131	Tamb
Having as many bullets in his flesh,	2Tamb	5.1.159	Tamb
Whose matter is incorporat in your flesh.	2Tamb	5.3.165	Amyras
My flesh devided in your precious shapes,	2Tamb	5.3.172	Tamb
That clouds of darkenesse may inclose my flesh,	Jew	1.2.194	Barab
But when the imperiall Lions flesh is gorde,	Edw	5.1.11	Edward
flesh [and] bloud, <or goods> into their habitation	F 498	2.1.110	P Faust
Or hew'd this flesh and bones as small as sand,	F1398	4.2.74	Faust
and have lost very much of late by horse flesh, and this	F1464	4.4.8	P HrsCsr
that flesh and bloud should be so fraile with your Worship:	F1632	4.6.75	P Carter
Revolt, or I'le in peece-meale teare thy flesh.	F1745	5.1.72	Mephst
swowns they are as bolde with my flesh, as if they had payd for	F App	p.230 28	P Clown
and fell Mercury <(Jove)>/They offer humane flesh, and where	Lucan, First Booke	441	
is, appear'd/A knob of flesh, whereof one halfe did looke/Dead,	Lucan, First Booke	627	
FLESHLESSE			
And on their points his fleshlesse bodie feedes.	1Tamb	5.1.115	Tamb
FLESHLY			
Or treason in the fleshly heart of man,	2Tamb	2.2.37	Orcan
FLESHT			
Jawes flesht with bloud continue murderous.	Lucan, First Booke	332	
FLEW			
And oftentimes into her bosome flew,	Hero and Leander	1.41	
Thence flew Loves arrow with the golden head,	Hero and Leander	1.161	
FLEXIBLE			
Then let his grace, whose youth is flexible,	Edw	1.4.398	MortSr
FLIE (Homograph)			
Whether we presently will flie (my Lords)/To rest secure	1Tamb	1.1.177	Cosroe
These are the wings shall make it flie as swift,	1Tamb	2.3.57	Tamb

FLIE (cont.)

Pursude by hunters, flie his angrie lookes,	1Tamb	3.3.193	Zenoc
My looks shall make them flie, and might I follow,	2Tamb	5.3.107	Tamb
That I am banishd, and must flie the land.	Edw	1.4.107	Gavstn
Beamont flie,/As fast as Iris, or Joves Mercurie.	Edw	1.4.370	Edward
Wigmore shall flie, to set my unckle free.	Edw	2.2.196	Mortmr
Flie, flie, my lords, the earles have got the holde,	Edw	2.4.4	Edward
No Edward, no, thy flatterers faint and flie.	Edw	3.1.201	Mortmr
Betray us both, therefore let me flie.	Edw	5.6.8	Matrvs
Flie to the Savages.	Edw	5.6.9	Mortmr
I'le have them flie to [India] <Indian> for gold;	F 109	1.1.81	Faust
I'le wing my selfe and forth-with flie amaine/Unto my Faustus	F1136	3.3.49	Mephst
[Hence hel, for hence I flie unto my God].	F1796	5.1.123A	OldMan
This soule should flie from me, and I be chang'd/[Unto] <Into>	F1967	5.2.171	Faust
Peace through the world from Janus Phane shal flie,	Lucan, First Booke		61
These hands shall thrust the ram, and make them flie,	Lucan, First Booke		385
Th'irrevocable people flie in troupes.	Lucan, First Booke		507
and rings of fire/Flie in the ayre, and dreadfull bearded	Lucan, First Booke		526
now throughout the aire I flie,/To doubtfull Sirtes and drie	Lucan, First Booke		685
In spite of thee, forth will thy <thine> arrowes flie,	Ovid's Elegies		1.2.45
No love is so dere (quiverd Cupid flie)/That my chiefe wish	Ovid's Elegies		2.5.1
And forth the gay troupes on swift horses flie.	Ovid's Elegies		3.2.78
Thrice she prepar'd to flie, thrice she did stay,	Ovid's Elegies		3.5.69
I flie her lust, but follow beauties creature;	Ovid's Elegies		3.10.37
Wee cause feete flie, wee mingle haires with snakes,	Ovid's Elegies		3.11.23
Then Hero hate me not, nor from me flie,	Hero and Leander		1.291
FLIECES			
balde scalpes [thin] <thine> hoary flieces/And riveld cheekes I	Ovid's Elegies		1.8.111
FLIENG			
Flieng Dragons, lightning, fearfull thunderclaps,	2Tamb	3.2.10	Tamb
FLIES (Homograph)			
And kill as sure as it swiftly flies.	1Tamb	2.3.59	Tamb
That flies with fury swifter than our thoughts,	2Tamb	4.1.5	Amyras
Who flies away at every glance I give,	2Tamb	5.3.70	Tamb
Flies ore the Alpes to fruitfull Germany,	F 985	3.2.5	Mephst
This Traytor flies unto some steepie rocke,	F1413	4.2.89	Faust
Her lips sucke <suckes> forth my soule, see where it flies.	F1771	5.1.98	Faust
her eyes/Two eye-balles shine, and double light thence flies.	Ovid's Elegies		1.8.16
What flies, I followe, what followes me I shunne.	Ovid's Elegies		2.19.36
Thee gentle Venus, and the boy that flies,	Ovid's Elegies		3.2.55
And into water desperately she flies.	Ovid's Elegies		3.5.80
Laden with languishment and griefe he flies.	Hero and Leander		1.378
To the rich Ocean for gifts he flies.	Hero and Leander		2.224
FLIEST			
[And fliest the throne of his tribunall seate],	F1790	5.1.117A	OldMan
FLIETH			
That glaunceth at my lips and flieth away:	Edw	1.1.23	Gavstn
FLIGHT (Homograph; See also FLEIGHT)			
Why should I blame Aeneas for his flight?	Dido	4.4.148	Dido
How long will Dido mourne a strangers flight,	Dido	5.1.279	Iarbus
My soule begins to take her flight to hell:	1Tamb	2.7.44	Cosroe
Then Victorie begins to take her flight,	1Tamb	3.3.160	Tamb
pleasures of swift-footed time/Have tane their flight,	Jew	2.1.8	Barab
that knew/The hearts of beasts, and flight of wandring foules;	Lucan, First Booke		587
Now frosty night her flight beginnes to take,	Ovid's Elegies		1.6.65
My stay no crime, my flight no joy shall breede,	Ovid's Elegies		2.17.25
Is said to have attempted flight forsooke.	Ovid's Elegies		3.12.20
Their fellowes being slaine or put to flight,	Hero and Leander		1.120
So on she goes, and in her idle flight,	Hero and Leander		2.10
Though it was morning, did he take his flight.	Hero and Leander		2.102
FLING (See also FLONG)			
Shall fling in every corner of the field:	1Tamb	2.2.64	Meandr
Fling the meat in his face.	1Tamb	5.1.315	P Zabina
So Casane, fling them in the fire.	2Tamb	5.1.186	Tamb
FLINGING			
Flinging in favours of more soveraigne worth,	Dido	3.1.131	Dido
FLINGS			
hate/Flings slaughtering terrour from my coleblack tents.	1Tamb	5.1.72	Tamb
Her vowes above the emptie aire he flings:	Hero and Leander		1.370
FLINT			
And I will either move the thoughtles flint,	Dido	4.2.40	Iarbus
Yet he whose [hearts] <heart> of adamant or flint,	Dido	5.1.234	Anna
With wals of Flint, and deepe intrenched Lakes,	F 782	3.1.4	Faust
Nor flint, nor iron, are in thy soft brest/But pure simplicity	Ovid's Elegies		1.11.9
Therefore when flint and yron weare away,	Ovid's Elegies		1.15.31
His heart consists of flint, and hardest steele,	Ovid's Elegies		3.5.59
Niobe flint, Callist we make a Beare,	Ovid's Elegies		3.11.31
Flint-brested Pallas joies in single life,	Hero and Leander		1.321
FLINT-BRESTED			
Flint-brested Pallas joies in single life,	Hero and Leander		1.321
FLINTIE			
Whose flintie darts slept in Tipheus den,	Dido	4.1.19	Iarbus
FLINTY			
With what a flinty bosome should I joy,	2Tamb	5.3.185	Amyras
Unlesse your unrelenting flinty hearts/Suppresse all pitty in	Jew	1.2.141	Barab
FLOATE (See also FLEET, FLOTE)			
To floate in bloud, and at thy wanton head,	Edw	1.1.132	Lncstr
FLOCKE			
Why flocke you thus to me in multitudes?	Jew	1.1.144	Barab
FLOCKES			
Dooth pray uppon my flockes of Passengers,	1Tamb	1.1.32	Mycet
And let his foes like flockes of fearfull Roes,	1Tamb	3.3.192	Zenoc
FLOCKS			
Butcherd the flocks he found in spatious field,	Ovid's Elegies		1.7.8

FLOCKS (cont.)
From dog-kept flocks come preys to woolves most gratefull. Ovid's Elegies 1.8.56
Seeing the Sheepheards feede theyr flocks, . . . Passionate Shepherd 6
FLONG
And under mine her wanton thigh she flong, . . . Ovid's Elegies 3.6.10
FLOOD (See also FLOUD)
That though the stones, as at Deucalions flood, . . 2Tamb 1.3.163 Tamb
Then Gaynimede would renew Deucalions flood, . . . Lucan, First Booke 652
She proudly sits) more over-rules the flood, . . . Hero and Leander 1.111
FLOORE
the plancke/That runs along the upper chamber floore, . Jew 1.2.297 Barab
The floore whereof, this Cable being cut, ... Jew 5.5.34 Barab
Nor on the earth was knowne the name of floore. . . Ovid's Elegies 3.9.8
To lay my body on the hard moist floore. . . . . Ovid's Elegies 3.10.10
That Meremaid-like unto the floore she slid, . . . Hero and Leander 2.315
FLORA
And like to Flora in her mornings pride, ... 1Tamb 5.1.140 Tamb
Yet flourisheth as Flora in her pride, ... 2Tamb 2.3.22 Orcan
FLORAS
When as he buts his beames on Floras bed, ... Dido 3.4.20 Dido
FLORENCE
I learn'd in Florence how to kisse my hand, ... Jew 2.3.23 Barab
In Florence, Venice, Antwerpe, London, Civill, . . . Jew 4.1.71 Barab
My Lord, this dish was sent me from the Cardinall of Florence. F App p.231 10 P Pope
FLORISHING
in their most florishing estate, which I doubt not shal . F App p.237 48 P Faust
FLOTE
Flote up and downe where ere the billowes drive? . . Dido 5.1.58 Aeneas
FLOTES
That now I hope flotes on the Irish seas. . . . . . Edw 1.4.224 Mortmr
FLOUD
Being three daies old inforst the floud to swell, . . Lucan, First Booke 220
Who running long, fals in a greater floud, ... Lucan, First Booke 401
bands were spread/Along Nar floud that into Tiber fals, . Lucan, First Booke 472
secret works, and [wash] <washt> their saint/In Almo's floud: Lucan, First Booke 600
But though I like a swelling floud was driven, . . . Ovid's Elegies 1.7.43
But if that Triton tosse the troubled floud, . . . Ovid's Elegies 2.11.27
That Paphos, and the floud-beate Cithera guides. . . Ovid's Elegies 2.17.4
Floud with [reede-growne] <redde-growne> slime bankes, till I Ovid's Elegies 3.5.1
Her, from his swift waves, the bold floud perceav'd, . Ovid's Elegies 3.5.51
How wouldst thou flowe wert thou a noble floud, . . Ovid's Elegies 3.5.89
FLOUD-BEATE
That Paphos, and the floud-beate Cithera guides. . . Ovid's Elegies 2.17.4
FLOUDES
And drinkes stolne waters in surrownding floudes. . . Ovid's Elegies 2.19.32
FLOUDS
And Proteus raising hils of flouds on high, ... Dido 1.1.76 Venus
The rest we feare are foulded in the flouds. . . . . Dido 1.2.31 Cloan
celestiall fire/Fleete on the flouds, the earth shoulder the Lucan, First Booke 76
Mounts, and raine-doubled flouds he passeth over, . . Ovid's Elegies 1.9.11
The Docke in harbours ships drawne from the flouds, . . Ovid's Elegies 2.9.21
And to the vast deep sea fresh water flouds? . . . Ovid's Elegies 2.10.14
But sundry flouds in one banke never go, ... Ovid's Elegies 2.17.31
Flames into flame, flouds thou powrest seas into. . . Ovid's Elegies 3.2.34
Great flouds ought to assist young men in love, . . Ovid's Elegies 3.5.23
Great flouds the force of it do often prove. . . . Ovid's Elegies 3.5.24
For five score Nimphes, or more our flouds conteine. . Ovid's Elegies 3.5.64
To this I fondly loves of flouds told plainly: . . . Ovid's Elegies 3.5.101
FLOURE
For know, that underneath this radiant floure, . . . Hero and Leander 1.145
FLOURISH
And flourish once againe that erst was dead: . . . Dido 1.1.95 Jupitr
Then here in me shall flourish Priams race, ... Dido 4.4.87 Aeneas
And make his Gospel flourish in this land. . . . . P 57 1.57 Navrre
Now Guise shall catholiques flourish once againe, . . P 295 5.22 Anjoy
Flourish in France, and none deny the same. . . . . P 640 12.53 QnMoth
And strumpets flatter, shall Menander flourish. . . Ovid's Elegies 1.15.18
FLOURISHETH
Yet flourisheth as Flora in her pride, ... 2Tamb 2.3.22 Orcan
FLOURISHING
A loftie Cedar tree faire flourishing, ... Edw 2.2.16 Mortmr
FLOUTE
And floute our traine, and jest at our attire: . . . Edw 1.4.418 Mortmr
FLOUTS
he flouts me, what gentry can be in a poore Turke of ten pence? Jew 4.2.38 P Ithimr
FLOW
and she shal looke/That these abuses flow not from her tongue: 1Tamb 4.2.70 Zenoc
And downe her cheekes, the trickling teares did flow, . Ovid's Elegies 1.7.57
And makes large streams back to their fountaines flow, . Ovid's Elegies 1.8.6
Thou mad'st thy head with compound poyson flow. . . Ovid's Elegies 1.14.44
FLOWE
Pelignian fields [with] <which> liqued rivers flowe, . Ovid's Elegies 2.16.5
How wouldst thou flowe wert thou a noble floud, . . Ovid's Elegies 3.5.89
FLOWED
When fortune made us lords of all, wealth flowed, . . Lucan, First Booke 161
FLOWER (See also FLOURE)
The sweetest flower in Citherea's field, ... Jew 1.2.379 Mthias
Which I thinke gather'd from cold hemlocks flower/Wherein bad Ovid's Elegies 1.12.9
FLOWERS
Musk-roses, and a thousand sort of flowers, ... Dido 4.5.8 Nurse
Quintessence they still/From their immortall flowers of Poesy, 1Tamb 5.1.166 Tamb
How sweet, my Ithimore, the flowers smell. . . . Jew 4.4.39 Curtzn
I hope the poyson'd flowers will worke anon. . . . Jew 5.1.43 Barab

FLOWERS (cont.)			
I learnde in Naples how to poison flowers,	Edw	5.4.31	Ltborn
And on my haires a crowne of flowers remaine.	Ovid's Elegies		1.6.38
Her vaile was artificiall flowers and leaves,	Hero and Leander		1.19
A cap of flowers, and a kirtle,	Passionate Shepherd		11
FLOWES			
And changeth as the Ocean ebbes and flowes:	Lucan, First Booke		412
Roome that flowes/With Citizens and [Captives] <Captaines>, and	Lucan, First Booke		509
[And] <The> banks ore which gold bearing Tagus flowes.	Ovid's Elegies		1.15.34
FLOWING			
As looks the sun through Nilus flowing stream,	1Tamb	3.2.47	Zenoc
Taking instructions from thy flowing eies:	1Tamb	5.1.146	Tamb
Just through the midst runnes flowing Tybers streame,	F 813	3.1.35	Mephst
No flowing waves with drowned ships forth poured,	Ovid's Elegies		2.16.25
Rather thou large banke over-flowing river,	Ovid's Elegies		3.5.19
Rich Nile by seaven mouthes to the vast sea flowing,	Ovid's Elegies		3.5.39
A draught of flowing Nectar, she requested,	Hero and Leander		1.431
FLOWNE			
Yet was his soule but flowne beyond the Alpes,	Jew	Prol.2	Machvl
FLOWRIE			
Lie slumbering on the flowrie bankes of Nile,	1Tamb	4.1.9	Souldn
FLOWRING			
And made the flowring pride of Wittenberg <Wertenberge>	F 141	1.1.113	Faust
FLUCTIBUS			
league,/Littora littoribus contraria, fluctibus undas/Imprecor:	Dido	5.1.310	Dido
FLUNG			
And with maine force flung on a ring of pikes,	Dido	2.1.196	Aeneas
Yet flung I forth, and desperate of my life,	Dido	2.1.210	Aeneas
She, fearing on the rushes to be flung,	Hero and Leander		2.66
He flung at him his mace, but as it went,	Hero and Leander		2.209
FLUTTERS			
Foorth plungeth, and oft flutters with her wing,	Hero and Leander		2.290
FLY (Homograph; See also FLIE)			
And fly my glove as from a Scorpion.	2Tamb	3.5.74	Tamb
The bullets fly at random where they list.	2Tamb	4.1.52	Calyph
And fly my presence if thou looke to live.	P 692	13.36	Guise
Fly, fly, my Lord, the Queene is over strong,	Edw	4.5.1	Spencr
O fly him then, but Edmund calme this rage,	Edw	4.6.11	Kent
Fly hence, dispatch my charge immediatly.	F1416	4.2.92	Faust
Her I suspect among nights spirits to fly,	Ovid's Elegies		1.8.13
Least they should fly, being tane, the tirant play.	Ovid's Elegies		1.8.70
FLYE (Homograph)			
Stay gentle Venus, flye not from thy sonne,	Dido	1.1.242	Aeneas
Burst from the earth, crying, Aeneas flye,	Dido	2.1.207	Aeneas
Will quickly flye to [Cithereas] <Citheidas> fist.	Dido	2.1.322	Venus
Runne for Aeneas, or Ile flye to him.	Dido	3.1.79	Dido
As made disdaine to flye to fancies lap:	Dido	3.4.56	Dido
For I will flye from these alluring eyes,	Dido	4.2.50	Iarbus
And Mercury to flye for what he calles?	Dido	4.4.47	Dido
If it be so, his father meanes to flye:	Dido	5.1.85	Dido
Treason, treason! Bashawes, flye.	Jew	5.5.67	Calym
No, Selim, doe not flye;	Jew	5.5.68	Govnr
See his end first, and flye then if thou canst.	Jew	5.5.69	Govnr
Dye life, flye soule, tongue curse thy fill and dye.	Jew	5.5.89	Barab
Flye Ramus flye, if thou wilt save thy life.	P 365	7.5	Taleus
Tell me Taleus, wherfore should I flye?	P 366	7.6	Ramus
Holde thee tall Souldier, take thee this and flye.	P 817	17.12	Guise
Hold thee tale soldier take the this and flye	Paris	ms18,p390	Guise
What, was I borne to flye and runne away,	Edw	4.5.4	Edward
We flye in hope to get his glorious soule:	F 277	1.3.49	Mephst
Homo fuge: whether should I flye?	F 466	2.1.78	Faust
yet shall not Faustus flye.	F 470	2.1.82	Faust
Flye backe his [streame] <shame> chargd, the streame chargd,	Ovid's Elegies		3.5.44
FLYES (Homograph)			
That like I best that flyes beyond my reach.	P 99	2.42	Guise
And calves from whose feard front no threatning flyes,	Ovid's Elegies		3.12.15
FLYEST			
In vaine why flyest backe? force conjoynes us now:	Ovid's Elegies		3.2.19
FLYING (Homograph)			
My Ship, the flying Dragon, is of Spaine,	Jew	2.2.5	Bosco
Plinie reports, there is a flying Fish,	Edw	2.2.23	Lncstr
Though thou comparst him to a flying Fish,	Edw	2.2.43	Edward
and flying/Left hateful warre decreed to both the Consuls.	Lucan, First Booke		485
did Thiestes towne/(Mycenae), Phoebus flying through the East:	Lucan, First Booke		542
no darke night-flying spright/Nor hands prepar'd to slaughter,	Ovid's Elegies		1.6.13
when she bewayles/Her perjur'd Theseus flying vowes and sayles,	Ovid's Elegies		1.7.16
Time flying slides hence closely, and deceaves us,	Ovid's Elegies		1.8.49
funerall wood be flying/And thou the waxe stuft full with notes	Ovid's Elegies		1.12.7
Water in waters, and fruite flying touch/Tantalus seekes, his	Ovid's Elegies		2.2.43
Wild me, whose slowe feete sought delay, be flying.	Ovid's Elegies		2.19.12
Swift Atalantas flying legges like these,	Ovid's Elegies		3.2.29
FOAM (See FOME)			
FOE			
Juno, my mortall foe, what make you here?	Dido	3.2.24	Venus
No, a foe,/Monster of Nature, shame unto thy stocke,	1Tamb	1.1.103	Mycet
Looke for orations when the foe is neere.	1Tamb	1.2.131	Techel
Be arm'd against the hate of such a foe,	1Tamb	2.6.22	Ortyg
marshal us the way/We use to march upon the slaughtered foe:	1Tamb	3.3.149	Tamb
had the Turkish Emperour/So great a foile by any forraine foe.	1Tamb	3.3.235	Bajzth
And have a greater foe to fight against,	2Tamb	1.1.15	Gazell
And I will teach thee how to charge thy foe,	2Tamb	1.3.45	Tamb
not but your royall cares/Hath so provided for this cursed foe,	2Tamb	3.1.21	Callap
That freed me from the bondage of my foe:	2Tamb	3.1.69	Callap

FOE (cont.)			
Murther the Foe and save [the] <their> walles from breach.	2Tamb	3.2.82	Tamb
Hast thou not seene my horsmen charge the foe,	2Tamb	3.2.103	Tamb
us haste from hence/Along the cave that leads beyond the foe,	2Tamb	3.4.2	Olymp
My father were enough to scar the foe:	2Tamb	4.1.19	Calyph
When we are thus defenc'd against our Foe,	2Tamb	5.1.22	Govnr
And kneele for mercy to your conquering foe:	Jew	5.2.2	Calym
Shall feele the house of Lorayne is his foe:	P 856	17.51	Guise
nor Hanniball/Art cause, no forraine foe could so afflict us,	Lucan, First Booke		31
He, he afflicts Roome that made me Roomes foe.	Lucan, First Booke		205
Must Pompey as his last foe plume on me,	Lucan, First Booke		338
You likewise that repulst the Caicke foe,	Lucan, First Booke		459
Excludst a lover, how wouldst use a foe?	Ovid's Elegies		1.6.31
I harm'd: a foe did Diomedes anger move.	Ovid's Elegies		1.7.34
The other eyes his rivall as his foe.	Ovid's Elegies		1.9.18
Oft to invade the sleeping foe tis good/And arm'd to shed	Ovid's Elegies		1.9.21
Defend the fort, and keep the foe-man out.	Hero and Leander		2.272
FOE-MAN			
Defend the fort, and keep the foe-man out.	Hero and Leander		2.272
FOES			
And have no gall at all to grieve my foes:	Dido	3.2.17	Juno
Armies of foes resolv'd to winne this towne,	Dido	4.4.113	Dido
That holds us up, and foiles our neighbour foes.	1Tamb	1.1.61	Mycet
And with thy lookes thou conquerest all thy foes:	1Tamb	1.1.75	Mycet
A thousand sworne and overmatching foes:	1Tamb	2.1.39	Cosroe
him assured hope/Of martiall triumph, ere he meete his foes:	1Tamb	3.3.43	Tamb
And let his foes like flockes of fearfull Roes,	1Tamb	3.3.192	Zenoc
He raceth all his foes with fire and sword.	1Tamb	4.1.63	2Msngr
them see (divine Zenocrate)/I glorie in the curses of my foes,	1Tamb	4.4.29	Tamb
Whose coleblacke faces make their foes retire,	2Tamb	1.3.142	Techel
troopes/Beats downe our foes to flesh our taintlesse swords?	2Tamb	4.1.26	Amyras
And glut it not with stale and daunted foes.	2Tamb	4.1.88	Tamb
To lighten doubts and frustrate subtile foes.	P 457	8.7	Anjoy
Whose army shall discomfort all your foes,	P 579	11.44	Pleshe
And give her warning of her trecherous foes.	P1190	22.52	King
This sword of mine that should offend your foes,	Edw	1.1.86	Mortmr
To see us there appointed for our foes.	Edw	4.2.56	Mortmr
And save you from your foes, Bartley would die.	Edw	5.1.134	Bartly
And rescue aged Edward from his foes,	Edw	5.2.120	Kent
Feare not sweete boye, ile garde thee from thy foes,	Edw	5.4.111	Queene
as yet thou wants not foes.	Lucan, First Booke		23
When Romans are besieg'd by forraine foes,	Lucan, First Booke		513
Why grapples Rome, and makes war, having no foes?	Lucan, First Booke		681
More glory by thy vanquisht foes assends.	Ovid's Elegies		2.9.6
Yea, let my foes sleepe in an emptie bed,	Ovid's Elegies		2.10.17
She whom her husband, guard, and gate as foes,	Ovid's Elegies		2.12.3
FOGGY			
Now draw up Faustus like a foggy mist,	F1952	5.2.156	Faust
FOH			
Foh, me thinkes they stinke like a Holly-Hoke.	Jew	4.4.41	Pilia
Foh, heeres a place in deed with all my hart.	Edw	5.5.41	Ltborn
FOILD (Homograph)			
The Diamond that I talke of, ne'r was foild:	Jew	2.3.56	Barab
But when he touches it, it will be foild:	Jew	2.3.57	Barab
They whom the Lingones foild with painted speares,	Lucan, First Booke		398
FOILE (Homograph)			
Thou, by the fortune of this damned [foile] <soile>.	1Tamb	3.3.213	Bajzth
had the Turkish Emperour/So great a foile by any forraine foe.	1Tamb	3.3.235	Bajzth
nor the Turk/Troubled my sences with conceit of foile,	1Tamb	5.1.158	Tamb
What saiest thou yet Gazellus to his foile:	2Tamb	2.3.27	Orcan
thunder in our eares/Our proper ruine, and our fathers foile?	2Tamb	4.1.14	Amyras
Blush, blush faire citie, at thine honors foile,	2Tamb	4.1.107	Tamb
What sparkle does it give without a foile?	Jew	2.3.55	Lodowk
FOILES			
That holds us up, and foiles our neighbour foes.	1Tamb	1.1.61	Mycet
FOLD (See also FOULD)			
To note me Emperour of the three fold world:	2Tamb	4.3.118	Tamb
In token of our seven-fold power from heaven,	F 934	3.1.156	Pope
FOLDED			
To hide the folded furrowes of his browes,	1Tamb	5.1.57	2Virgn
Mutually folded in each others Spheares <orbe>,	F 591	2.2.40	Mephst
FOLDES			
His lofty browes in foldes, do figure death,	1Tamb	2.1.21	Menaph
strike flames of lightening)/All fearefull foldes his sailes,	1Tamb	3.2.82	Agidas
Foldes up her armes, and makes low curtesie.	Ovid's Elegies		2.4.30
FOLISHE			
then will I wake thee from thie folishe dreame/and lett thee	Paris	ms32,p391	Guise
FOLKE			
And before folke immodest speeches shunne,	Ovid's Elegies		3.13.16
FOLKES			
divels, say I should kill one of them, what would folkes say?	F App	p.230 47 P	Clown
FOLLIE			
to them, that all Asia/Lament to see the follie of their King.	1Tamb	1.1.96	Cosroe
But follie, sloth, and damned idlenesse:	2Tamb	4.1.126	Tamb
With follie and false hope deluding us).	Hero and Leander		2.222
FOLLIES			
And I was chain'd to follies of the world:	Jew	3.3.60	Abigal
FOLLOW (See also FOLOW)			
Follow ye Troians, follow this brave Lord,	Dido	1.2.1	Illion
And if my mother goe, Ile follow her.	Dido	3.1.38	Cupid
Ile follow thee with outcryes nere the lesse,	Dido	4.2.55	Anna
And follow them as footemen through the deepe:	Dido	4.3.24	Aeneas
And follow your foreseeing starres in all;	Dido	4.3.32	Achat

Line	Work	Reference	Speaker
FOLLOW (cont.)			
Troians abourd, and I will follow you,	Dido	4.3.45	Aeneas
O Anna, Anna, I will follow him.	Dido	5.1.241	Dido
And foot by foot follow Theridamas.	1Tamb	1.1.86	Mycet
That even to death will follow Tamburlaine.	1Tamb	1.2.59	Usumc
To follow me to faire Persepolis.	1Tamb	2.5.40	Cosroe
Haste thee Techelles, we will follow thee.	1Tamb	2.5.104	Tamb
Withdraw as many more to follow him.	1Tamb	3.3.22	Bassoe
Affrica, and Greece/Follow my Standard and my thundring Drums:	2Tamb	1.1.159	Orcan
If thou wilt love the warres and follow me,	2Tamb	1.3.47	Tamb
But while my brothers follow armes my lord,	2Tamb	1.3.65	Calyph
Now brother, follow we our fathers sword,	2Tamb	4.1.4	Amyras
Shoot first my Lord, and then the rest shall follow.	2Tamb	5.1.151	Tamb
My looks shall make them flie, and might I follow,	2Tamb	5.3.107	Tamb
Well father, say I be entertain'd,/What then shall follow?	Jew	1.2.295	Abigal
This shall follow then;/There have I hid close underneath the	Jew	1.2.295	Barab
Come daughter, follow us.	Jew	1.2.337	Abbass
We and our warlike Knights will follow thee/Against these	Jew	2.2.45	Govnr
Suffer me, Barabas, but to follow him.	Jew	2.3.340	Mthias
May all good fortune follow Calymath.	Jew	5.2.21	Barab
Him will we--but first lets follow those in France,	P 153	2.96	Guise
Come sirs follow me.	P 292	5.19	Gonzag
Anjoy will follow thee.	P 333	5.60	Anjoy
Loreine, Loreine, follow Loreine.	P 339	5.66	Guise
And when you see me in, then follow hard.	P 429	7.69	Anjoy
And he shall follow my proud Chariots wheeles.	P 984	19.54	Guise
Come follow me, and thou shalt have my guarde,	Edw	1.1.204	Edward
About it then, and we will follow you.	Edw	2.2.124	Mortmr
And ile follow thee.	Edw	2.3.20	Warwck
Lets all abcord, and follow him amaine.	Edw	2.4.47	Mortmr
No James, it is my countries cause I follow.	Edw	2.6.10	Warwck
And this our sonne, [Levune] <Lewne> shall follow you,	Edw	3.1.82	Edward
To follow these rebellious runnagates.	Edw	4.6.76	Mortmr
Follow me to the towne.	Edw	4.7.119	Rice
And may not follow thee without his leave;	F 269	1.3.41	Mephst
Now sirra follow me.	F 379	1.4.37	P Wagner
Follow the Cardinals to the Consistory;	F 892	3.1.114	Faust
let him come; an he follow us, I'le so conjure him, as he was	F1091	3.3.4	P Robin
Come souldiers, follow me unto the grove,	F1348	4.2.24	Fredrk
If we should follow him to worke revenge,	F1448	4.3.18	Benvol
Well sirra follow me.	F App	p.230 55	P Wagner
Come, maister Doctor follow us, and receive your reward.	F App	p.243 33	P Duke
Hence leagues, and covenants; Fortune thee I follow,	Lucan, First Booke	228	
held up, all joyntly cryde/They'ill follow where he please:	Lucan, First Booke	389	
Or that the wandring maine follow the moone;	Lucan, First Booke	415	
Next learned Augures follow;/Apolloes southsayers; and Joves	Lucan, First Booke	600	
and such as seeke loves wrack/Shall follow thee, their hands	Ovid's Elegies	1.2.32	
And let the troupes which shall thy Chariot follow,	Ovid's Elegies	1.7.37	
But furiously he follow his loves fire/And [thinke] <thinkes>	Ovid's Elegies	2.2.13	
Nor being arm'd fierce troupes to follow farre?	Ovid's Elegies	2.14.2	
But follow trembling campes, and battailes sterne,	Ovid's Elegies	3.7.26	
I flie her lust, but follow beauties creature;	Ovid's Elegies	3.10.37	
And she her vestall virgin Priests doth follow.	Ovid's Elegies	3.12.30	
To follow swiftly blasting infamie.	Hero and Leander	1.292	
And looking backe, saw Neptune follow him.	Hero and Leander	2.176	
FOLLOWE			
I followe one that loveth fame for me,	Dido	3.4.38	Dido
What flies, I followe, what followes me I shunne.	Ovid's Elegies	2.19.36	
FOLLOWED			
But suddenly the Grecians followed us,	Dido	2.1.278	Aeneas
who hath followed long/The martiall sword of mighty	2Tamb	3.1.27	Callap
May in their fall be followed to their end.	Edw	4.6.79	Mortmr
Innumerable joyes had followed thee.	F1893	5.2.97	GdAngl
FOLLOWER			
What, meane you then to be his follower?	Edw	2.1.12	Baldck
FOLLOWERS			
As for Achates, and his followers.	Dido	3.1.176	Dido
Which I bestowd upon his followers:	Dido	4.4.162	Dido
Let some of those thy followers goe with me,	Dido	5.1.73	Iarbus
And all thy needie followers Noblemen?	Dido	5.1.164	Dido
thou art so meane a man)/And seeke not to inrich thy followers,	1Tamb	1.2.9	Zenoc
Nobly resolv'd, sweet friends and followers.	1Tamb	1.2.60	Tamb
They shall be kept our forced followers,	1Tamb	1.2.66	Tamb
Or you my Lordes to be my followers?	1Tamb	1.2.83	Tamb
As these my followers willingly would have:	1Tamb	3.3.155	Tamb
Techelles, and my loving followers,	1Tamb	4.2.101	Tamb
And now my Lords and loving followers,	1Tamb	5.1.522	Tamb
Fit for the followers of great Tamburlaine.	2Tamb	3.2.144	Tamb
His sonnes, his Captaines and his followers,	2Tamb	3.5.16	Callap
But now my followers and my loving friends,	2Tamb	3.5.159	Tamb
Are poyson'd by my climing followers.	Jew	Prol.13	Machvl
goe whither he will, I'le be none of his followers in haste:	Jew	4.2.26	P Ithimr
With all thy Bashawes and brave followers.	Jew	5.3.39	Msngr
Let us with these our followers scale the walles,	Edw	2.3.18	Lncstr
and our followers/Close in an ambush there behinde the trees,	F1341	4.2.17	Benvol
Must Pompeis followers with strangers ayde,	Lucan, First Booke	314	
FOLLOWES			
Priams misfortune followes us by sea,	Dido	1.1.143	Aeneas
This followes well, and therefore daughter feare not.	Jew	2.3.313	Barab
Edward with fire and sword, followes at thy heeles.	Edw	3.1.180	Edward
Yes, I know, but that followes not.	F 200	1.2.7	P Wagner
That followes not <necessary> by force of argument, which	F 202	1.2.9	P Wagner
same cup, for the Vintners boy followes us at the hard heeles.	F1089	3.3.2	P Dick

FOLLOWES (cont.)
Her valiant lover followes without end. . . . . . Ovid's Elegies 1.9.10
What flies, I followe, what followes me I shunne. . . Ovid's Elegies 2.19.36
FOLLOWING
And stung with furie of their following, ... 2Tamb 4.1.189 Tamb
On these conditions following: . . . . F 484 2.1.96 P Faust
Then seeing I grace thy show in following thee, . . Ovid's Elegies 1.2.49
The seventh day came, none following mightst thou see, . Ovid's Elegies 2.6.45
FOLLY (See also FOLLIE)
I see the folly of thy Emperour: . . . . . . 1Tamb 1.2.167 Tamb
And by their folly make some <us> merriment, . . . F 990 3.2.10 Faust
FOLOW
well, Ile folow him, Ile serve him, thats flat. . . F App p.231 72 P Clown
FOME
In Tiburs field with watry fome art rumbling, . . . Ovid's Elegies 3.5.46
FOMING
Whose foming galle with rage and high disdaine, . . 1Tamb 1.1.63 Mycet
Ocean;/And swept the foming brest of [Artick] <Articks> Rhene. Lucan, First Booke 372
FOND
And finde the way to wearie such fond thoughts: . . Dido 3.2.86 Juno
fond man, that were to warre gainst heaven,/And with one shaft Dido 3.3.71 Iarbus
Fond men, what dreame you of their multitudes? . . . Jew 1.1.157 Barab
thinke me not all so fond/As negligently to forgoe so much Jew 1.2.241 Barab
Think'st thou that Faustus, is so fond to imagine, . . F 522 2.1.134 Faust
Fond worldling, now his heart bloud dries with griefe; . F1808 5.2.12 Mephst
And doth the world in fond beliefe deteine. . . . Ovid's Elegies 3.3.24
FONDLIE
fondlie hast thow in censte the guises sowle . . . Paris ms25,p391 Guise
FONDLY
But haplesse Edward, thou art fondly led, ... Edw 5.1.76 Edward
To this I fondly loves of floods told plainly: . . . Ovid's Elegies 3.5.101
FOOD
For he that gives him other food than this: . . . 1Tamb 4.2.89 Tamb
Nuts were thy food, and Poppie causde thee sleepe, . . Ovid's Elegies 2.6.31
FOODE
Bequeath her young ones to our scanted foode. . . . Dido 1.1.162 Achat
FOOLE
Meete with the foole, and rid your royall shoulders/Of such a 1Tamb 2.3.46 Tamb
And far from any man that is a foole. . . . . . 1Tamb 2.4.12 Mycet
of the Serpent then the Dove; that is, more knave than foole. Jew 2.3.37 P Barab
If thou deniest foole, Ile our deeds expresse, . . . Ovid's Elegies 2.8.25
Foole, what is sleepe but image of cold death, . . . Ovid's Elegies 2.9.41
Foole if to keepe thy wife thou hast no neede, . . . Ovid's Elegies 2.19.1
Foole canst thou him in thy white armes embrace? . . Ovid's Elegies 3.7.11
Foole canst thou lie in his enfolding space? . . . Ovid's Elegies 3.7.12
FOOLERIES
I am asham'd to heare such fooleries. . . . . . Jew Prol.17 Machvl
FOOLERY
you had best leave your foolery, for an my Maister come, he'le F 734 2.3.13 P Dick
FOOLES
Alas poore fooles, must you be first shal feele/The sworne 1Tamb 5.1.65 Tamb
Fooles that will laugh on earth, [must] <most> weepe in hell. F1891 5.2.95 Mephst
Brabbling Marcellus; Cato whom fooles reverence; . . Lucan, First Booke 313
Faire fooles delight to be accounted nice. . . . . Hero and Leander 1.326
FOOLISH (See also FOLISHE)
O foolish Troians that would steale from hence, . . Dido 4.4.5 Dido
O what meane I to have such foolish thoughts! . . . Dido 4.5.25 Nurse
Foolish is love, a toy.-- . . . . Dido 4.5.26 Nurse
Ah foolish Dido to forbeare this long! . . . . . Dido 5.1.160 Dido
go before and charge/The fainting army of that foolish King. 1Tamb 2.3.62 Cosroe
Thou knowest not (foolish hardy Tamburlaine)/What tis to meet 1Tamb 3.3.145 Bajzth
least hee hide his crowne as the foolish king of Persea did. 2Tamb 3.5.155 P Tamb
Yeeld foolish Governour, we offer more/Than ever yet we did to 2Tamb 5.1.57 Techel
And spurns the Abstracts of thy foolish lawes. . . . 2Tamb 5.1.197 Tamb
[makes men] <make them> foolish that do use <trust> them most. F 408 2.1.20 BdAngl
To prove him foolish did I ere contend? . . . . . Ovid's Elegies 2.8.10
That can effect <affect> a foolish wittalls wife. . . Ovid's Elegies 2.19.46
FOOLISHLY
To these my love I foolishly committed/And then with sweete Ovid's Elegies 1.12.21
Men foolishly doe call it vertuous, ... Hero and Leander 1.277
FOOLS
Away ye fools, my father needs not me, ... 2Tamb 4.1.15 Calyph
FOORD
And comming to the foord of Rubicon, ... Lucan, First Booke 187
And from the mid foord his hoarse voice upheav'd, . . Ovid's Elegies 3.5.52
FOORDS
Grew pale, and in cold foords hot lecherous. . . . Ovid's Elegies 3.5.26
FOORTH
Go frowning foorth, but come thou smyling home, . . 1Tamb 1.1.65 Mycet
Draw foorth thy sword, thou mighty man at Armes, . . 1Tamb 1.2.178 Tamb
Will rattle foorth his facts of war and blood. . . . 1Tamb 3.2.45 Agidas
At every pore let blood comme dropping foorth, . . . 1Tamb 5.1.227 Zabina
I may poure foorth my soule into thine armes, . . . 1Tamb 5.1.279 Bajzth
And soon put foorth into the Terrene sea: . . . . 2Tamb 1.2.25 Callap
Nor [any] issue foorth, but they shall die: . . . . 2Tamb 3.3.33 Techel
Betwixt which, shall our ordinance thunder foorth, . . 2Tamb 3.3.58 Therid
Call foorth our laisie brother from the tent, . . . 2Tamb 4.1.7 Celeb
O cowardly boy, fie for shame, come foorth. . . . 2Tamb 4.1.31 Celeb
that earth may eccho foorth/The far resounding torments ye 2Tamb 4.1.185 Tamb
But foorth ye vassals, what so ere it be, ... 2Tamb 5.1.221 Tamb
in the next roome, therefore good my Lord goe not foorth. P 995 19.65 P 3Mur
Thus Caesar did goe foorth, and thus he dyed. . . . P1015 19.85 Guise
Letters my lord, and tidings foorth of Fraunce, . . Edw 4.3.25 Post

FOORTH (cont.)
As you injurious were to beare them foorth. Edw 4.3.52 Edward
What murtherer? bring foorth the man I sent. Edw 5.6.49 Mortmr
Bring him unto a hurdle, drag him foorth, Edw 5.6.52 King
One of you call him foorth. F App p.238 68 P Emper
When t'was the odour which her breath foorth cast. Hero and Leander 1.22
Can hardly blazon foorth the loves of men, Hero and Leander 1.70
So ran the people foorth to gaze upon her, Hero and Leander 1.117
Foorth from those two tralucent cesternes brake, Hero and Leander 1.296
Sends foorth a ratling murmure to the land, Hero and Leander 1.348
Spits foorth the ringled bit, and with his hoves, Hero and Leander 2.143
Foorth plungeth, and oft flutters with her wing, Hero and Leander 2.290
Brought foorth the day before the day was borne. Hero and Leander 2.322
To sound foorth musicke to the Ocean, Hero and Leander 2.328

FOOT
And foot by foot follow Theridamas. 1Tamb 1.1.86 Mycet
Come let us meet them at the mountain foot, 1Tamb 1.2.133 Usumc
(for say not I intreat)/Not once to set his foot in Affrica, 1Tamb 3.1.28 Bajzth
shall curse the time/That Tamburlaine set foot in Affrica. 1Tamb 3.3.60 Tamb
The Souldane would not start a foot from him. 1Tamb 4.1.19 Souldn
Bring out my foot-stoole. 1Tamb 4.2.1 Tamb
And be the foot-stoole of great Tamburlain, 1Tamb 4.2.14 Tamb
Two hundred thousand foot, brave men at armes, 1Tamb 4.3.54 Capol
Of all the provinces I have subdued/Thou shalt not have a foot, 2Tamb 1.3.72 Tamb
Where we will have [Gabions] <Galions> of sixe foot broad,/To 2Tamb 3.3.56 Therid
Came forty thousand warlike foot and horse, 2Tamb 3.5.38 Orcan
Ten thousand horse, and thirty thousand foot, 2Tamb 3.5.48 Soria
Goe now and bind the Burghers hand and foot, 2Tamb 5.1.161 Tamb
To see thy foot-stoole set upon thy head, 2Tamb 5.3.29 Usumc
And ducke as low as any bare-foot Fryar, Jew 2.3.25 Barab
They weare no shirts, and they goe bare-foot too. Jew 4.1.84 1Fryar
Upon mine owne free-hold within fortie foot of the gallowes, Jew 4.2.16 P Pilia
Who set themselves to tread us under foot, P 702 14.5 Navrre
for you to come within fortie foot of the place of execution, F 211 1.2.18 P Wagner
Cast downe our Foot-stoole. F 868 3.1.90 Pope
Which being broke the foot had easie passage. Lucan, First Booke 224

FOOTE
And bind her hand and foote with golden cordes, Dido 1.1.14 Jupitr
Might I but see that pretie sport a foote, Dido 1.1.16 Ganimd
And rowse the light foote Deere from forth their laire? Dido 3.3.31 Dido
When first you set your foote upon the shoare, Dido 3.3.53 Achat
Where thou and false Achates first set foote: Dido 5.1.175 Dido
A thousand horsmen? We five hundred foote? 1Tamb 1.2.121 Tamb
Keep all your standings, and not stir a foote, 1Tamb 1.2.150 Tamb
Thou shouldst not plod one foote beyond this place. Edw 1.1.181 Gavstn
The King of Fraunce sets foote in Normandie. Edw 2.2.9 Mortmr
course that time doth runne with calme and silent foote, F App p.239 91 P Faust
what, wil you goe on horse backe, or on foote? F App p.239 95 P Mephst
I am past this faire and pleasant greene, ile walke on foote. F App p.239 97 P Faust
(men say)/Began to smile and [tooke] <take> one foote away. Ovid's Elegies 1.1.8
his limbes he spread/Upon the bed, but on my foote first tread. Ovid's Elegies 1.4.16
Nor thy soft foote with his hard foote combine. Ovid's Elegies 1.4.44
dore more wisely/And som-what higher beare thy foote precisely. Ovid's Elegies 1.12.6
Or thrids which spiders slender foote drawes out/Fastning her Ovid's Elegies 1.14.7
I was both horse-man, foote-man, standard bearer. Ovid's Elegies 2.12.14
With his stumpe-foote he halts ill-favouredly. Ovid's Elegies 2.17.20
[A] <Or> while thy tiptoes on the foote-stoole rest. Ovid's Elegies 3.2.64
Her foote was small: her footes forme is most fit: Ovid's Elegies 3.3.7
My foote upon the further banke to set. Ovid's Elegies 3.5.12
Strayd bare-foote through sole places on a time. Ovid's Elegies 3.5.50

FOOTED
The incertaine pleasures of swift-footed time/Have tane their Jew 2.1.7 Barab
Wretched Ixions shaggie footed race, Hero and Leander 1.114
Gote-footed Satyrs, and up-staring <upstarting> Fawnes, Hero and Leander 2.200

FOOTE-MAN
I was both horse-man, foote-man, standard bearer. Ovid's Elegies 2.12.14

FOOTEMEN
And follow them as footemen through the deepe: Dido 4.3.24 Aeneas

FOOTES
By her footes blemish greater grace she tooke. Ovid's Elegies 3.1.10
Her foote was small: her footes forme is most fit: Ovid's Elegies 3.3.7

FOOTE-STOOLE
[A] <Or> while thy tiptoes on the foote-stoole rest. Ovid's Elegies 3.2.64

FOOTMANSHIP
As all his footmanship shall scarce prevaile, F1302 4.1.148 Faust

FOOTMEN
Then shall our footmen lie within the trench, 1Tamb 3.1.64 Bajzth
Two hundred thousand footmen that have serv'd/In two set 1Tamb 3.3.18 Bassoe
We meane to seate our footmen on their Steeds, 1Tamb 3.3.25 Techel
Five hundred thousand footmen threatning shot, 1Tamb 4.1.24 2Msngr

FOOTSTEPS
From Venus altar to your footsteps bending)/Doth testifie that Hero and Leander 1.210

FOOT-STOOLE
Bring out my foot-stoole. 1Tamb 4.2.1 Tamb
And be the foot-stoole of great Tamburlain, 1Tamb 4.2.14 Tamb
To see thy foot-stoole set upon thy head, 2Tamb 5.3.29 Usumc
Cast downe our Foot-stoole. F 868 3.1.90 Pope

FOOTSTOOLE
And now my footstoole, if I loose the field, 1Tamb 5.1.209 Tamb
And makes his footstoole on securitie: P 738 14.41 Navrre

FOR
I am much better for your worthles love, Dido 1.1.3 Ganimd
She reacht me such a rap for that I spilde, Dido 1.1.7 Ganimd

FOR (cont.)

As once I did for harming Hercules.	Dido	1.1.15	Jupitr
Sit on my knee, and call for thy content,	Dido	1.1.28	Jupitr
I would have a jewell for mine eare,	Dido	1.1.46	Ganimd
She humbly did beseech him for our bane,	Dido	1.1.60	Venus
I will take order for that presently:	Dido	1.1.113	Jupitr
For my sake pitie him Oceanus,	Dido	1.1.127	Venus
The while thine eyes attract their sought for joyes:	Dido	1.1.136	Venus
For this so friendly ayde in time of neede.	Dido	1.1.138	Venus
and the soyle most fit/For Cities, and societies supports:	Dido	1.1.179	Achat
Now is the time for me to play my part:	Dido	1.1.182	Venus
It is the use for [Tirien] <Turen> maides to weare/Their bowe	Dido	1.1.204	Venus
And suite themselves in purple for the nonce,	Dido	1.1.206	Venus
But for the land whereof thou doest enquire,	Dido	1.1.209	Venus
And for thy ships which thou supposest lost,	Dido	1.1.235	Venus
An ancient Empire, famoused for armes,	Dido	1.2.21	Cloan
Thankes gentle Lord for such unlookt for grace.	Dido	1.2.44	Serg
Who for her sonnes death wept out life and breath,	Dido	2.1.4	Aeneas
For were it Priam he would smile on me.	Dido	2.1.36	Ascan
For we are strangers driven on this shore,	Dido	2.1.43	Aeneas
For none of these can be our Generall.	Dido	2.1.46	Illion
Achates, speake, for I am overjoyed.	Dido	2.1.54	Aeneas
O tell me, for I long to be resolv'd.	Dido	2.1.61	Aeneas
Who for Troyes sake hath entertaind us all,	Dido	2.1.64	Illion
And when we told her she would weepe for griefe,	Dido	2.1.67	Illion
This is no seate for one thats comfortles,	Dido	2.1.86	Aeneas
For though my birth be great, my fortunes meane,	Dido	2.1.88	Aeneas
For many tales goe of that Cities fall,	Dido	2.1.108	Dido
The rather for that one Laocoon/Breaking a speare upon his	Dido	2.1.164	Aeneas
Kneeling for mercie to a Greekish lad,	Dido	2.1.198	Aeneas
As lothing Pirrhus for this wicked act:	Dido	2.1.258	Aeneas
Through which he could not passe for slaughtred men:	Dido	2.1.262	Aeneas
For all our ships were launcht into the deepe:	Dido	2.1.285	Aeneas
As for Aeneas he swomme quickly backe,	Dido	2.1.296	Achat
For Didos sake I take thee in my armes,	Dido	2.1.313	Venus
How long faire Dido shall I pine for thee?	Dido	3.1.7	Iarbus
Take it Ascanius, for thy fathers sake.	Dido	3.1.33	Dido
Yet not from Carthage for a thousand worlds.	Dido	3.1.51	Iarbus
Anna, good sister Anna goe for him,	Dido	3.1.75	Dido
Runne for Aeneas, or Ile flye to him.	Dido	3.1.79	Dido
No, for thy sake Ile love thy father well.	Dido	3.1.81	Dido
But now for quittance of this oversight,	Dido	3.1.84	Dido
I understand your highnesse sent for me.	Dido	3.1.100	Aeneas
For ballace, emptie Didos treasurie,	Dido	3.1.126	Dido
For if that any man could conquer me,	Dido	3.1.137	Dido
Have been most urgent suiters for my love,	Dido	3.1.151	Dido
Yet boast not of it, for I love thee not,	Dido	3.1.171	Dido
But not so much for thee, thou art but one,	Dido	3.1.175	Dido
As for Achates, and his followers.	Dido	3.1.176	Dido
For here in spight of heaven Ile murder him,	Dido	3.2.10	Juno
For saving him from Snakes and Serpents stings,	Dido	3.2.38	Juno
When for the hate of Troian Ganimed,	Dido	3.2.42	Juno
Be it as you will have [it] for this once,	Dido	3.2.97	Venus
For otherwhile he will be out of joynt.	Dido	3.3.24	Dido
I followe one that loveth fame for me,	Dido	3.4.38	Dido
Then to the Carthage Queene that dyes for him.	Dido	3.4.40	Dido
I would be thankfull for such curtesie.	Dido	4.2.29	Anna
For her that so delighteth in thy paine:	Dido	4.2.34	Anna
For I will flye from these alluring eyes,	Dido	4.2.50	Iarbus
For I have honey to present thee with:	Dido	4.2.53	Anna
This is no life for men at armes to live,	Dido	4.3.33	Achat
And not stand lingering here for amorous lookes:	Dido	4.3.38	Illion
me, for I forgot/That yong Ascanius lay with me this night:	Dido	4.4.31	Dido
And punish me Aeneas for this crime.	Dido	4.4.36	Dido
And Mercury to flye for what he calles?	Dido	4.4.47	Dido
Commaund my guard to slay for their offence:	Dido	4.4.72	Dido
Aeneas for his parentage deserves/As large a kingdome as is	Dido	4.4.79	Achat
And thou and I Achates, for revenge,	Dido	4.4.88	Aeneas
For Troy, for Priam, for his fiftie sonnes,	Dido	4.4.89	Aeneas
Yet lest he should, for I am full of feare,	Dido	4.4.108	Dido
Better he frowne, then I should dye for griefe:	Dido	4.4.111	Dido
For in his lookes I see eternitie,	Dido	4.4.122	Dido
Why should I blame Aeneas for his flight?	Dido	4.4.148	Dido
For this will Dido tye ye full of knots,	Dido	4.4.155	Dido
Now serve to chastize shipboyes for their faults,	Dido	4.4.157	Dido
For tackling, let him take the chaines of gold,	Dido	4.4.161	Dido
Blush blush for shame, why shouldst thou thinke of love?	Dido	4.5.29	Nurse
For I will grace them with a fairer frame,	Dido	5.1.5	Aeneas
And made me take my brother for my sonne:	Dido	5.1.43	Aeneas
Lest Dido spying him keepe him for a pledge.	Dido	5.1.50	Aeneas
Who have no sailes nor tackling for my ships?	Dido	5.1.56	Aeneas
When as I want both rigging for my fleete,	Dido	5.1.69	Aeneas
And also furniture for these my men.	Dido	5.1.70	Aeneas
For I will furnish thee with such supplies:	Dido	5.1.72	Iarbus
Thankes good Iarbus for thy friendly ayde,	Dido	5.1.75	Aeneas
Whil'st I rest thankfull for this curtesie.	Dido	5.1.77	Aeneas
swift Mercury/When I was laying a platforme for these walles,	Dido	5.1.94	Aeneas
For lingering here, neglecting Italy.	Dido	5.1.97	Aeneas
Not from my heart, for I can hardly goe,	Dido	5.1.103	Aeneas
Farewell: is this the mends for Didos love?	Dido	5.1.105	Dido
O then Aeneas, tis for griefe of thee:	Dido	5.1.116	Dido
many neighbour kings/Were up in armes, for making thee my love?	Dido	5.1.142	Dido
For being intangled by a strangers lookes:	Dido	5.1.145	Dido

FOR (cont.)

And I for pitie harbord in my bosome,	Dido	5.1.166	Dido
And hisse at Dido for preserving thee?	Dido	5.1.168	Dido
For though thou hast the heart to say farewell,	Dido	5.1.182	Dido
Thou for some pettie guift hast let him goe,	Dido	5.1.218	Dido
Then carelesly I rent my haire for griefe,	Dido	5.1.236	Anna
And all the Sailers merrie make for joy,	Dido	5.1.259	Dido
And must I rave thus for a runnagate?	Dido	5.1.265	Dido
Must I make ships for him to saile away?	Dido	5.1.266	Dido
Not farre from hence/There is a woman famoused for arts,	Dido	5.1.275	Dido
And reape no guerdon for my truest love?	Dido	5.1.282	Iarbus
For I entend a private Sacrifize,	Dido	5.1.286	Dido
To cure my minde that melts for unkind love.	Dido	5.1.287	Dido
For perjurie and slaughter of a Queene:	Dido	5.1.294	Dido
For it requires a great and thundring speech:	1Tamb	1.1.3	Mycet
For freezing meteors and conjealed colde:	1Tamb	1.1.11	Cosroe
I might command you to be slaine for this,	1Tamb	1.1.23	Mycet
Not for so small a fault my soveraigne Lord.	1Tamb	1.1.25	Meandr
Therefore tis good and meete for to be wise.	1Tamb	1.1.34	Mycet
Whom I may tearme a Damon for thy love.	1Tamb	1.1.50	Mycet
Or plead for mercie at your highnesse feet.	1Tamb	1.1.73	Therid
When other men prease forward for renowne:	1Tamb	1.1.84	Mycet
To be reveng'd for these contemptuous words.	1Tamb	1.1.100	Mycet
That dar'st presume thy Soveraigne for to mocke.	1Tamb	1.1.105	Mycet
Ah Menaphon, I passe not for his threates,	1Tamb	1.1.109	Cosroe
And vow to weare it for my countries good:	1Tamb	1.1.158	Cosroe
For they are friends that help to weane my state,	1Tamb	1.2.29	Tamb
I am (my Lord), for so you do import.	1Tamb	1.2.33	Zenoc
I am a Lord, for so my deeds shall proove,	1Tamb	1.2.34	Tamb
Fighting for passage, tilt within the earth.	1Tamb	1.2.51	Tamb
May serve for ransome to our liberties:	1Tamb	1.2.75	Agidas
An ods too great, for us to stand against:	1Tamb	1.2.122	Tamb
Looke for orations when the foe is neere.	1Tamb	1.2.131	Techel
Our swordes shall play the Orators for us.	1Tamb	1.2.132	Techel
and his chaine shall serve/For Manackles, till he be ransom'd	1Tamb	1.2.148	Tamb
We thinke it losse to make exchange for that/We are assured of	1Tamb	1.2.216	Techel
For you then Maddam, I am out of doubt.	1Tamb	1.2.258	Tamb
And stuft with treasure for his highest thoughts?	1Tamb	2.1.59	Ceneus
his Diadem/Sought for by such scalde knaves as love him not?	1Tamb	2.2.8	Mycet
That lie in ambush, waiting for a pray:	1Tamb	2.2.17	Meandr
Fit Souldiers for the wicked Tamburlaine.	1Tamb	2.2.24	Meandr
You fighting more for honor than for gold,	1Tamb	2.2.66	Meandr
For even as from assured oracle,	1Tamb	2.3.4	Cosroe
I take thy doome for satisfaction.	1Tamb	2.3.5	Cosroe
For Fates and Oracles [of] heaven have sworne,	1Tamb	2.3.7	Tamb
and excusde/For turning my poore charge to his direction.	1Tamb	2.3.29	Therid
And makes a passage for all prosperous Armes,	1Tamb	2.3.38	Cosroe
For Kings are clouts that every man shoots at,	1Tamb	2.4.8	Mycet
Here take it for a while, I lend it thee,	1Tamb	2.4.37	Tamb
Thou art no match for mightie Tamburlaine.	1Tamb	2.4.40	Tamb
shall we wish for ought/The world affoords in greatest	1Tamb	2.5.72	Tamb
Then thou for Parthia, they for Scythia and Medea.	1Tamb	2.5.83	Tamb
And bid him battell for his novell Crowne?	1Tamb	2.5.88	Techel
For presently Techelles here shal haste,	1Tamb	2.5.94	Tamb
Goe on for me.	1Tamb	2.5.106	Therid
For he was never sprong of humaine race,	1Tamb	2.6.11	Meandr
Warring within our breasts for regiment,	1Tamb	2.7.19	Tamb
For he is grosse and like the massie earth,	1Tamb	2.7.31	Therid
For as when Jove did thrust old Saturn down,	1Tamb	2.7.36	Usumc
For want of nourishment to feed them both,	1Tamb	2.7.47	Cosroe
Wils and commands (for say not I intreat)/Not once to set his	1Tamb	3.1.27	Bajzth
We meane to take his mornings next arise/For messenger, he will	1Tamb	3.1.39	Bajzth
For all flesh quakes at your magnificence.	1Tamb	3.1.48	Argier
For neither rain can fall upon the earth,	1Tamb	3.1.51	Moroc
Be honored with your love, but for necessity.	1Tamb	3.2.30	Agidas
And when you looke for amorous discourse,	1Tamb	3.2.44	Agidas
Too harsh a subject for your dainty eares.	1Tamb	3.2.46	Agidas
They sung for honor gainst Pierides,	1Tamb	3.2.51	Zenoc
Lifting his prayers to the heavens for aid,	1Tamb	3.2.83	Agidas
So fares Agydas for the late felt frownes/That sent a tempest	1Tamb	3.2.85	Agidas
For words are vaine where working tooles present/The naked	1Tamb	3.2.93	Agidas
And for the expedition of this war,	1Tamb	3.3.20	Bassoe
For when they perish by our warlike hands,	1Tamb	3.3.24	Techel
For Wil and Shall best fitteth Tamburlain,	1Tamb	3.3.41	Tamb
And strive for life at every stroke they give.	1Tamb	3.3.54	Tamb
What Coward wold not fight for such a prize?	1Tamb	3.3.100	Usumc
Their shoulders broad, for complet armour fit,	1Tamb	3.3.107	Bajzth
Which lately made all Europe quake for feare:	1Tamb	3.3.135	Bajzth
Carkasses/Shall serve for walles and bulwarkes to the rest:	1Tamb	3.3.139	Bajzth
not endure to strike/So many blowes as I have heads for thee.	1Tamb	3.3.144	Bajzth
That leave no ground for thee to martch upon.	1Tamb	3.3.147	Bajzth
Must plead for mercie at his kingly feet,	1Tamb	3.3.174	Zenoc
Both for their sausinesse shall be employed,	1Tamb	3.3.184	Zenoc
For we will scorne they should come nere our selves.	1Tamb	3.3.186	Zenoc
Yet somtimes let your highnesse send for them/To do the work my	1Tamb	3.3.187	Anippe
And making bonfires for my overthrow.	1Tamb	3.3.238	Bajzth
For though the glorie of this day be lost,	1Tamb	3.3.241	Bajzth
And hover in the straightes for Christians wracke,	1Tamb	3.3.250	Tamb
Offer their mines (to sew for peace) to me,	1Tamb	3.3.264	Tamb
And dig for treasure to appease my wrath:	1Tamb	3.3.265	Tamb
Come bring them in, and for this happy conquest/Triumph, and	1Tamb	3.3.272	Tamb
The Souldans daughter for his Concubine,	1Tamb	4.1.5	Souldn
And be reveng'd for her disparadgement.	1Tamb	4.1.72	Souldn

Stoop villaine, stoope, stoope for so he bids,	1Tamb	4.2.22	Tamb
For I the chiefest Lamp of all the earth,	1Tamb	4.2.36	Tamb
Fighting for passage, [makes] <make> the Welkin cracke,	1Tamb	4.2.45	Tamb
Let these be warnings for you then my slave,	1Tamb	4.2.72	Anippe
For treading on the back of Bajazeth,	1Tamb	4.2.77	Bajzth
Is this a place for mighty Bajazeth?	1Tamb	4.2.83	Bajzth
For he that gives him other food than this:	1Tamb	4.2.89	Tamb
Yet would you have some pitie for my sake,	1Tamb	4.2.123	Zenoc
Not for the world Zenocrate, if I have sworn:	1Tamb	4.2.125	Tamb
I have, and sorrow for his bad successe:	1Tamb	4.3.28	Souldn
Let Tamburlaine for his offences feele/Such plagues as heaven	1Tamb	4.3.44	Arabia
For Fame I feare hath bene too prodigall,	1Tamb	4.3.48	Arabia
Famous for nothing but for theft and spoile,	1Tamb	4.3.66	Souldn
Halfe dead for feare before they feele my wrath:	1Tamb	4.4.4	Tamb
starv'd, and he be provided for a moneths victuall before hand.	1Tamb	4.4.46	P Usumc
for if she live but a while longer, shee will fall into a	1Tamb	4.4.49	P Tamb
Yet give me leave to plead for him my Lord.	1Tamb	4.4.86	Zenoc
For Egypt and Arabia must be mine.	1Tamb	4.4.91	Tamb
Tis enough for us to see them, and for Tamburlaine onely to	1Tamb	4.4.111	P Techel
for us to see them, and for Tamburlaine onely to enjoy them.	1Tamb	4.4.111	P Techel
For vertue is the fount whence honor springs.	1Tamb	4.4.128	Tamb
Therefore, for these our harmlesse virgines sakes,	1Tamb	5.1.18	Govnr
And tels for trueth, submissions comes too late.	1Tamb	5.1.73	Tamb
For whome the Powers divine have made the world,	1Tamb	5.1.76	1Virgn
As well for griefe our ruthlesse Governour/Have thus refusde	1Tamb	5.1.92	1Virgn
and Furies dread)/As for their liberties, their loves or lives.	1Tamb	5.1.95	1Virgn
O then for these, and such as we our selves,	1Tamb	5.1.96	1Virgn
For us, for infants, and for all our bloods,	1Tamb	5.1.97	1Virgn
For there sits Death, there sits imperious Death,	1Tamb	5.1.111	Tamb
For all the wealth of Gehons golden waves.	1Tamb	5.1.123	Tamb
Or for the love of Venus, would she leave/The angrie God of	1Tamb	5.1.124	Tamb
Faire is too foule an Epithite for thee,	1Tamb	5.1.136	Tamb
That in thy passion for thy countries love,	1Tamb	5.1.137	Tamb
For Egypts freedom and the Souldans life:	1Tamb	5.1.153	Tamb
But how unseemly is it for my Sex,	1Tamb	5.1.174	Tamb
Shal give the world to note, for all my byrth,	1Tamb	5.1.188	Tamb
For faire Zenocrate, that so laments his state.	1Tamb	5.1.205	Therid
For sweet Zenocrate, whose worthinesse/Deserves a conquest over	1Tamb	5.1.207	Tamb
Till we have made us ready for the field.	1Tamb	5.1.212	Tamb
Pray for us Bajazeth, we are going.	1Tamb	5.1.213	Tamb
The heavens may frowne, the earth for anger quake,	1Tamb	5.1.231	Bajzth
Fetch me some water for my burning breast,	1Tamb	5.1.276	Bajzth
And make a passage for my loathed life.	1Tamb	5.1.304	Bajzth
And wounded bodies gasping yet for life.	1Tamb	5.1.323	Zenoc
For every fell and stout Tartarian Stead/That stampt on others	1Tamb	5.1.330	Zenoc
And wet thy cheeks for their untimely deathes:	1Tamb	5.1.348	Zenoc
That fights for Scepters and for slippery crownes,	1Tamb	5.1.356	Zenoc
That fights for honor to adorne your head.	1Tamb	5.1.376	Anippe
Ready for battaile gainst my Lord the King.	1Tamb	5.1.382	Philem
So for a finall Issue to my griefes,	1Tamb	5.1.395	Zenoc
eies beholde/That as for her thou bearst these wretched armes,	1Tamb	5.1.409	Arabia
Even so for her thou diest in these armes:	1Tamb	5.1.410	Arabia
Leaving thy blood for witnesse of thy love.	1Tamb	5.1.411	Arabia
Too deare a witnesse for such love my Lord.	1Tamb	5.1.412	Zenoc
Behold her wounded in conceit for thee,	1Tamb	5.1.415	Zenoc
As much as thy faire body is for me.	1Tamb	5.1.416	Zenoc
And such are objects fit for Tamburlaine.	1Tamb	5.1.475	Tamb
And for all blot of foule inchastity,	1Tamb	5.1.486	Tamb
And have bene crown'd for prooved worthynesse:	1Tamb	5.1.491	Tamb
and protestations/Of endlesse honor to thee for her love.	1Tamb	5.1.497	Souldn
That long hath lingred for so high a seat.	1Tamb	5.1.502	Therid
For now her mariage time shall worke us rest.	1Tamb	5.1.504	Techel
in her browes/Triumphes and Trophees for my victories:	1Tamb	5.1.513	Tamb
For Tamburlaine takes truce with al the world.	1Tamb	5.1.529	Tamb
Tis requisit to parle for a peace/With Sigismond the king of	2Tamb	1.1.50	Gazell
And save our forces for the hot assaults/Proud Tamburlaine	2Tamb	1.1.52	Gazell
And for that cause the Christians shall have peace.	2Tamb	1.1.57	Orcan
for as the Romans usde/I here present thee with a naked sword.	2Tamb	1.1.81	Sgsmnd
Not for all Affrike, therefore moove me not.	2Tamb	1.2.12	Almeda
Fit objects for thy princely eie to pierce.	2Tamb	1.2.45	Callap
And more than this, for all I cannot tell.	2Tamb	1.2.53	Callap
Shall I be made a king for my labour?	2Tamb	1.2.63	P Almeda
(For that's the style and tytle I have yet)/Although he sent a	2Tamb	1.2.69	Almeda
Bewraies they are too dainty for the wars.	2Tamb	1.3.28	Tamb
As I cried out for feare he should have falne.	2Tamb	1.3.42	Zenoc
conquer all the world/And you have won enough for me to keep.	2Tamb	1.3.68	Calyph
For he shall weare the crowne of Persea,	2Tamb	1.3.74	Tamb
For in a field whose [superficies] <superfluities>/Is covered	2Tamb	1.3.79	Tamb
No Madam, these are speeches fit for us,	2Tamb	1.3.88	Celeb
For if his chaire were in a sea of blood,	2Tamb	1.3.89	Celeb
For we will martch against them presently.	2Tamb	1.3.105	Tamb
For I have sworne by sacred Mahomet,	2Tamb	1.3.109	Tamb
Meet for your service on the sea, my Lord,	2Tamb	1.3.123	Therid
Is Barbary unpeopled for thy sake,	2Tamb	1.3.134	Usumc
And quake for feare, as if infernall Jove/Meaning to aid [thee]	2Tamb	1.3.143	Techel
All Barbary is unpeopled for thy sake.	2Tamb	1.3.149	Techel
For halfe the world shall perish in this fight:	2Tamb	1.3.171	Tamb
For since we left you at the Souldans court,	2Tamb	1.3.177	Usumc
Your Highnesse knowes for Tamburlaines repaire,	2Tamb	2.1.14	Fredrk
And calling Christ for record of our trueths?	2Tamb	2.1.30	Sgsmnd
for with such Infidels,/In whom no faith nor true religion	2Tamb	2.1.33	Baldwn
To be esteem'd assurance for our selves,	2Tamb	2.1.39	Baldwn

FOR (cont.)

the christian King/Is made, for joy of your admitted truce:	2Tamb	2.2.21		Uribas
To bid us battaile for our dearest lives.	2Tamb	2.2.28		1Msngr
And cares so litle for their prophet Christ.	2Tamb	2.2.35		Gazell
But in their deeds deny him for their Christ:	2Tamb	2.2.40		Orcan
For my accurst and hatefull perjurie.	2Tamb	2.3.3		Sgsmnd
Bloody and breathlesse for his villany.	2Tamb	2.3.13		Gazell
Murmures and hisses for his hainous sin.	2Tamb	2.3.17		Orcan
keepe his trunke/Amidst these plaines, for Foules to pray upon.	2Tamb	2.3.39		Orcan
And all with faintnesse and for foule disgrace,	2Tamb	2.4.5		Tamb
For should I but suspect your death by mine,	2Tamb	2.4.61		Zenoc
Or had those wanton Poets, for whose byrth/Olde Rome was proud,	2Tamb	2.4.91		Tamb
For taking hence my faire Zenocrate.	2Tamb	2.4.101		Tamb
For amorous Jove hath snatcht my love from hence,	2Tamb	2.4.107		Tamb
Nothing prevailes, for she is dead my Lord.	2Tamb	2.4.124		Therid
For she is dead? thy words doo pierce my soule.	2Tamb	2.4.125		Tamb
And feed my mind that dies for want of her:	2Tamb	2.4.128		Tamb
Drooping and pining for Zenocrate.	2Tamb	2.4.142		Tamb
not but your royall cares/Hath so provided for this cursed foe,	2Tamb	3.1.21		Callap
(An Emperour so honoured for his vertues)/Revives the spirits	2Tamb	3.1.23		Callap
For so hath heaven provided my escape,	2Tamb	3.1.32		Callap
And for their power, ynow to win the world.	2Tamb	3.1.43		Orcan
Wel then my noble Lords, for this my friend,	2Tamb	3.1.68		Callap
matter sir, for being a king, for Tamburlain came up of nothing.	2Tamb	3.1.73	P	Almeda
sir, for being a king, for Tamburlain came up of nothing.	2Tamb	3.1.73	P	Almeda
Tis nought for your majesty to give a kingdome.	2Tamb	3.1.77		Jrslem
Being burnt to cynders for your mothers death.	2Tamb	3.2.46		Tamb
If I had wept a sea of teares for her,	2Tamb	3.2.47		Calyph
With griefe and sorrow for my mothers death.	2Tamb	3.2.50		Amyras
For [which] <with> the quinque-angle fourme is meet:	2Tamb	3.2.64		Tamb
When this is learn'd for service on the land,	2Tamb	3.2.83		Tamb
And wilt thou shun the field for feare of woundes?	2Tamb	3.2.109		Tamb
Fit for the followers of great Tamburlaine.	2Tamb	3.2.144		Tamb
Wel, this must be the messenger for thee.	2Tamb	3.4.15		Olymp
For think ye I can live, and see him dead?	2Tamb	3.4.27		Sonne
And for his sake here will I end my daies.	2Tamb	3.4.44		Olymp
For ever terme, the Perseans sepulchre,	2Tamb	3.5.19		Callap
For if I should as Hector did Achilles,	2Tamb	3.5.70		Tamb
Ile hang a clogge about your necke for running away againe, you	2Tamb	3.5.101	P	Tamb
But as for you (Viceroy) you shal have bits,	2Tamb	3.5.103		Tamb
thou shalt kneele to us/And humbly crave a pardon for thy life.	2Tamb	3.5.109		Orcan
For if thou livest, not any Element/Shal shrowde thee from the	2Tamb	3.5.126		Tamb
For as soone as the battaile is done, Ile ride in triumph	2Tamb	3.5.145	P	Tamb
For if my father misse him in the field,	2Tamb	4.1.8		Celeb
Nor care for blood when wine wil quench my thirst.	2Tamb	4.1.30		Calyph
O cowardly boy, fie for shame, come foorth.	2Tamb	4.1.31		Celeb
Goe, goe tall stripling, fight you for us both,	2Tamb	4.1.33		Calyph
For person like to proove a second Mars.	2Tamb	4.1.35		Calyph
As if I lay with you for company.	2Tamb	4.1.39		Calyph
Turn'd into pearle and proffered for my stay,	2Tamb	4.1.44		Amyras
sonnes have had no shares/In all the honors he proposde for us.	2Tamb	4.1.48		Amyras
Content my Lord, but what shal we play for?	2Tamb	4.1.63	P	Perdic
and for feare I should be affraid, would put it off and come to	2Tamb	4.1.69	P	Calyph
Good my Lord, let him be forgiven for once,	2Tamb	4.1.101		Amyras
For earth and al this aery region/Cannot containe the state of	2Tamb	4.1.119		Tamb
Cloth'd with a pitchy cloud for being seene.	2Tamb	4.1.131		Tamb
For deeds of bounty or nobility:	2Tamb	4.1.152		Tamb
For not a common Souldier shall defile/His manly fingers with	2Tamb	4.1.163		Tamb
teares of Mahomet/For hot consumption of his countries pride:	2Tamb	4.1.197		Tamb
For honor of my woondrous victories.	2Tamb	4.1.205		Tamb
Enrag'd I ran about the fields for thee,	2Tamb	4.2.17		Therid
A fitter subject for a pensive soule.	2Tamb	4.2.27		Olymp
For with thy view my joyes are at the full,	2Tamb	4.2.31		Therid
Making a passage for my troubled soule,	2Tamb	4.2.34		Olymp
And for a present easie proofe hereof,	2Tamb	4.2.75		Olymp
and will keep it for/The richest present of this Easterne	2Tamb	4.2.77		Therid
For every Fury gazeth on her lookes:	2Tamb	4.2.92		Therid
Inventing maskes and stately showes for her,	2Tamb	4.2.94		Therid
and fit for nought/But perches for the black and fatall Ravens.	2Tamb	4.3.22		Tamb
and fit for nought/But perches for the black and fatall Ravens.	2Tamb	4.3.23		Tamb
For love, for honor, and to make her Queene,	2Tamb	4.3.38		Orcan
So for just hate, for shame, and to subdew/This proud contemner	2Tamb	4.3.39		Orcan
for shame, and to subdew/This proud contemner of thy dreadfull	2Tamb	4.3.39		Orcan
Your Majesty must get some byts for these,	2Tamb	4.3.43		Therid
If Jove esteeming me too good for earth,	2Tamb	4.3.60		Tamb
I will prefer them for the funerall/They have bestowed on my	2Tamb	4.3.65		Tamb
Brawle not (I warne you) for your lechery,	2Tamb	4.3.75		Tamb
For every man that so offends shall die.	2Tamb	4.3.76		Tamb
And make us jeasting Pageants for their Trulles.	2Tamb	4.3.89		Therid
For there my Pallace royal shal be plac'd:	2Tamb	4.3.111		Tamb
Have we not hope, for all our battered walles,	2Tamb	5.1.15		Govnr
For I wil cast my selfe from off these walles,	2Tamb	5.1.40		2Citzn
That made us all the labour for the towne,	2Tamb	5.1.82		Therid
For though thy cannon shooke the citie walles,	2Tamb	5.1.105		Govnr
Then for all your valour, you would save your life.	2Tamb	5.1.119		Tamb
And offer'd me as ransome for thy life,	2Tamb	5.1.156		Tamb
Shall pay me tribute for, in Babylon.	2Tamb	5.1.167		Tamb
For he is God alone, and none but he.	2Tamb	5.1.202		Tamb
Which makes them fleet aloft and gaspe for aire.	2Tamb	5.1.209		Techel
And yet gapes stil for more to quench his thirst,	2Tamb	5.2.14		Amasia
for never sepulchre/Shall grace that base-borne Tyrant	2Tamb	5.2.17		Amasia
To sue for mercie at your highnesse feete.	2Tamb	5.2.41		Amasia
For we have here the chiefe selected men/Of twenty severall	2Tamb	5.2.48		Callap

FOR (cont.)

For conquering the Tyrant of the world.	2Tamb	5.2.55	Callap
let us lie in wait for him/And if we find him absent from his	2Tamb	5.2.56	Callap
For hell and darknesse pitch their pitchy tentes,	2Tamb	5.3.7	Therid
For if he die, thy glorie is disgrac'd,	2Tamb	5.3.40	Usumc
Not last Techelles, no, for I shall die.	2Tamb	5.3.66	Tamb
monster death/Shaking and quivering, pale and wan for feare,	2Tamb	5.3.68	Tamb
Thus are the villaines, cowards fled for feare,	2Tamb	5.3.115	Tamb
As much too high for this disdainfull earth.	2Tamb	5.3.122	Tamb
let me see how much/Is left for me to conquer all the world,	2Tamb	5.3.124	Tamb
For by your life we entertaine our lives.	2Tamb	5.3.167	Celeb
Cannot behold the teares ye shed for me,	2Tamb	5.3.218	Tamb
For if thy body thrive not full of thoughtes/As pure and fiery	2Tamb	5.3.236	Tamb
For Tamburlaine, the Scourge of God must die.	2Tamb	5.3.248	Tamb
For earth hath spent the pride of all her fruit,	2Tamb	5.3.250	Amyras
For both their woorths wil equall him no more.	2Tamb	5.3.253	Amyras
As for those [Samnites] <Samintes>, and the men of Uzz,/That	Jew	1.1.4	Barab
so richly pay/The things they traffique for with wedge of gold,	Jew	1.1.9	Barab
And for a pound to sweat himselfe to death:	Jew	1.1.18	Barab
I sent for Egypt and the bordering Iles/Are gotten up by Nilus	Jew	1.1.42	Barab
And is thy credit not enough for that?	Jew	1.1.62	Barab
What more may Heaven doe for earthly man/Then thus to powre out	Jew	1.1.107	Barab
Ripping the bowels of the earth for them,	Jew	1.1.109	Barab
Who hateth me but for my happinesse?	Jew	1.1.112	Barab
Or who is honour'd now but for his wealth?	Jew	1.1.113	Barab
For I can see no fruits in all their faith,	Jew	1.1.116	Barab
And for his conscience lives in beggery.	Jew	1.1.120	Barab
That thirst so much for Principality.	Jew	1.1.135	Barab
For he can counsell best in these affaires;	Jew	1.1.142	2Jew
Were it for confirmation of a League,	Jew	1.1.154	1Jew
Why, Barabas, they come for peace or warre.	Jew	1.1.161	1Jew
Happily for neither, but to passe along/Towards Venice by the	Jew	1.1.162	Barab
then let every man/Provide him, and be there for fashion-sake.	Jew	1.1.171	Barab
How ere the world goe, I'le make sure for one,	Jew	1.1.186	Barab
For happily we shall not tarry here:	Jew	1.2.16	Calym
And for the mony send our messenger.	Jew	1.2.31	Calym
For to be short, amongst you 'tmust be had.	Jew	1.2.56	Govnr
For through our sufferance of your hatefull lives,	Jew	1.2.63	Govnr
And better one want for a common good,	Jew	1.2.98	Govnr
Then many perish for a private man:	Jew	1.2.99	Govnr
that I descended of/Were all in generall cast away for sinne,	Jew	1.2.114	Barab
For that is theft; and if you rob me thus,	Jew	1.2.126	Barab
Then wee'll take order for the residue.	Jew	1.2.136	Govnr
gather of these goods/The mony for this tribute of the Turke.	Jew	1.2.156	Govnr
For if we breake our day, we breake the league,	Jew	1.2.158	1Knght
but for every one of those,/Had they beene valued at	Jew	1.2.185	Barab
And henceforth wish for an eternall night,	Jew	1.2.193	Barab
For onely I have toyl'd to inherit here/The months of vanity	Jew	1.2.196	Barab
I, let me sorrow for this sudden chance,	Jew	1.2.206	Barab
Who for the villaines have no wit themselves,	Jew	1.2.215	Barab
And cast with cunning for the time to come:	Jew	1.2.222	Barab
For evils are apt to happen every day.	Jew	1.2.223	Barab
What, woman, moane not for a little losse:	Jew	1.2.226	Barab
Thy father has enough in store for thee.	Jew	1.2.227	Barab
Not for my selfe, but aged Barabas:	Jew	1.2.228	Abigal
Father, for thee lamenteth Abigaile:	Jew	1.2.229	Abigal
to forgoe so much/Without provision for thy selfe and me.	Jew	1.2.243	Barab
For they have seiz'd upon thy house and wares.	Jew	1.2.251	Abigal
For there I left the Governour placing Nunnes,	Jew	1.2.254	Abigal
by me, for in extremitie/We ought to make barre of no policie.	Jew	1.2.272	Barab
I, Daughter, for Religion/Hides many mischiefes from suspition.	Jew	1.2.281	Barab
The gold and Jewels which I kept for thee.	Jew	1.2.298	Barab
For I will seeme offended with thee for't.	Jew	1.2.303	Barab
Be close, my girle, for this must fetch my gold.	Jew	1.2.304	Barab
The better; for we love not to be seene:	Jew	1.2.307	Abbass
To make attonement for my labouring soule.	Jew	1.2.326	Abigal
Well, daughter, we admit you for a Nun.	Jew	1.2.330	Abbass
For she has mortified her selfe.	Jew	1.2.341	1Fryar
For I had rather dye, then see her thus.	Jew	1.2.357	Barab
she were fitter for a tale of love/Then to be tired out with	Jew	1.2.369	Mthias
That has no further comfort for his maime.	Jew	2.1.11	Barab
For whilst I live, here lives my soules sole hope,	Jew	2.1.29	Barab
And for the Raven wake the morning Larke,	Jew	2.1.61	Barab
For late upon the coast of Corsica,	Jew	2.2.10	Bosco
And buy it basely too for summes of gold?	Jew	2.2.29	Bosco
I'le write unto his Majesty for ayd,	Jew	2.2.40	Bosco
For when their hideous force inviron'd Rhodes,	Jew	2.2.48	Bosco
Feare not their sale, for they'll be quickly bought.	Jew	2.3.2	1Offcr
He'de give us present mony for them all.	Jew	2.3.6	1Offcr
Or else be gather'd for in our Synagogue;	Jew	2.3.27	Barab
Even for charity I may spit intoo't.	Jew	2.3.29	Barab
One that I love for his good fathers sake.	Jew	2.3.31	Barab
For Don Mathias tels me she is faire.	Jew	2.3.35	Lodowk
Yond walks the Jew, now for faire Abigall.	Jew	2.3.38	Lodowk
For unto us the Promise doth belong.	Jew	2.3.47	Barab
I ha the poyson of the City for him,	Jew	2.3.53	Barab
Pointed it is, good Sir,--but not for you.	Jew	2.3.60	Barab
And made my house a place for Nuns most chast.	Jew	2.3.77	Barab
of those Nuns/And holy Fryers, having mony for their paines,	Jew	2.3.81	Barab
For though they doe a while increase and multiply,	Jew	2.3.89	Barab
As for the Diamond, Sir, I told you of,	Jew	2.3.91	Barab
Even for your Honourable fathers sake.	Jew	2.3.93	Barab
Belike he has some new tricke for a purse;	Jew	2.3.101	Barab

FOR (cont.)

might be got/To keepe him for his life time from the gallowes.	Jew	2.3.104		Barab
be under colour of shaving, thou'lt cut my throat for my goods.	Jew	2.3.120	P	Barab
I must have one that's sickly, and be but for sparing vittles:	Jew	2.3.124	P	Barab
So much the better, thou art for my turne.	Jew	2.3.129		Barab
I, marke him, you were best, for this is he	Jew	2.3.132		Barab
As for the Diamond it shall be yours;	Jew	2.3.135		Barab
As for the Comment on the Machabees/I have it, Sir, and 'tis at	Jew	2.3.153		Barab
Oh brave, master, I worship your nose for this.	Jew	2.3.173		Ithimr
As for my selfe, I walke abroad a nights/And kill sicke people	Jew	2.3.174		Barab
And now and then one hang himselfe for griefe,	Jew	2.3.196		Barab
But marke how I am blest for plaguing them,	Jew	2.3.199		Barab
I have it for you, Sir; please you walke in with me:	Jew	2.3.220		Barab
Abigall, bid him welcome for my sake.	Jew	2.3.232		Barab
For your sake and his own he's welcome hither.	Jew	2.3.233		Abigal
The account is made, for [Lodovico] <Lodowicke> dyes.	Jew	2.3.242		Barab
word a Merchant's fled/That owes me for a hundred Tun of Wine:	Jew	2.3.244		Barab
For now by this has he kist Abigall;	Jew	2.3.246		Barab
As sure as heaven rain'd Manna for the Jewes,	Jew	2.3.248		Barab
Not for all Malta, therefore sheath your sword;	Jew	2.3.270		Barab
Away, for here they come.	Jew	2.3.275		Barab
I, and take heed, for he hath sworne your death.	Jew	2.3.280		Barab
For they themselves hold it a principle,	Jew	2.3.310		Barab
Now have I that for which my soule hath long'd.	Jew	2.3.318		Lodowk
Well, but for me, as you went in at dores/You had bin stab'd,	Jew	2.3.337		Barab
For this I'le have his heart.	Jew	2.3.344		Mthias
I cannot stay; for if my mother come,	Jew	2.3.353		Mthias
I cannot take my leave of him for teares:	Jew	2.3.355		Abigal
that but for one bare night/A hundred Duckets have bin freely	Jew	3.1.2		Curtzn
Hold thee, wench, there's something for thee to spend.	Jew	3.1.12		Pilia
and inquire/For any of the Fryars of Saint [Jaques] <Jaynes>,	Jew	3.3.28		Abigal
Admit thou lov'dst not Lodowicke for his [sire] <sinne>,	Jew	3.3.40		Abigal
To get me be admitted for a Nun.	Jew	3.3.55		Abigal
For that will be most heavy to thy soule.	Jew	3.3.71		1Fryar
For she that varies from me in beleefe/Gives great presumption	Jew	3.4.10		Barab
For I have now no hope but even in thee;	Jew	3.4.16		Barab
That's no lye, for she sent me for him.	Jew	3.4.25	P	Ithimr
my bitter curse/Like Cain by Adam, for his brother's death.	Jew	3.4.33		Barab
Ithimore, intreat not for her, I am mov'd,	Jew	3.4.35		Barab
into the sea; why I'le doe any thing for your sweet sake.	Jew	3.4.40	P	Ithimr
I here adopt thee for mine onely heire,	Jew	3.4.43		Barab
me in the pot of Rice/That for our supper stands upon the fire.	Jew	3.4.50		Barab
And for thy sake, whom I so dearely love,	Jew	3.4.61		Barab
For I have other businesse for thee.	Jew	3.4.110		Barab
Pay me my wages for my worke is done.	Jew	3.4.115		Ithimr
The time you tooke for respite, is at hand,	Jew	3.5.8		Basso
For the performance of your promise past;	Jew	3.5.9		Basso
And for the Tribute-mony I am sent.	Jew	3.5.10		Basso
Open an entrance for the wastfull sea,	Jew	3.5.16		Govnr
For Selim-Calymath shall come himselfe,	Jew	3.5.23		Basso
Malta to a wildernesse/For these intolerable wrongs of yours;	Jew	3.5.26		Basso
For by this Answer, broken is the league,	Jew	3.5.34		Govnr
And nought is to be look'd for now but warres,	Jew	3.5.35		Govnr
The Abbasse sent for me to be confest:	Jew	3.6.3		2Fryar
And so did faire Maria send for me:	Jew	3.6.5		1Fryar
And I shall dye too, for I feele death comming.	Jew	3.6.8		Abigal
I sent for him, but seeing you are come/Be you my ghostly	Jew	3.6.11		Abigal
Chast, and devout, much sorrowing for my sinnes,	Jew	3.6.14		Abigal
As I am almost desperate for my sinnes:	Jew	3.6.18		Abigal
And for his sake did I become a Nunne.	Jew	3.6.25		Abigal
Reveale it not, for then my father dyes.	Jew	3.6.32		Abigal
For every yeare they swell, and yet they live;	Jew	4.1.6		Barab
For my part feare you not.	Jew	4.1.10		Ithimr
Thou shalt not need, for now the Nuns are dead,	Jew	4.1.15		Barab
Doe you not sorrow for your daughters death?	Jew	4.1.17		Ithimr
That would for Lucars sake have sold my soule.	Jew	4.1.53		Barab
A hundred for a hundred I have tane;	Jew	4.1.54		Barab
And now for store of wealth may I compare/With all the Jewes in	Jew	4.1.55		Barab
Would pennance serve for this my sinne,	Jew	4.1.58		Barab
Then 'tis not for me; and I am resolv'd/You shall confesse me,	Jew	4.1.85		Barab
I will not goe for thee.	Jew	4.1.94		1Fryar
For presently you shall be shriv'd.	Jew	4.1.110		1Fryar
For he that shriv'd her is within my house.	Jew	4.1.115		Barab
Now I have such a plot for both their lives,	Jew	4.1.117		Barab
And see, a staffe stands ready for the purpose:	Jew	4.1.172		1Fryar
So might my man and I hang with you for company.	Jew	4.1.182		Barab
No, for this example I'le remaine a Jew:	Jew	4.1.195		Barab
Take in the staffe too, for that must be showne:	Jew	4.1.204		Barab
for at the reading of the letter, he look'd like a man of	Jew	4.2.6	P	Pilia
for she writes further, that she loves me ever since she saw	Jew	4.2.33	P	Ithimr
Sweet Bellamira, would I had my Masters wealth for thy sake.	Jew	4.2.55	P	Ithimr
Send for a hundred Crownes at least.	Jew	4.2.70	P	Pilia
Rather for feare then love.	Jew	4.2.107	P	Ithimr
and told me he lov'd me for your sake, and said what a	Jew	4.2.109	P	Pilia
Write for five hundred Crownes.	Jew	4.2.116	P	Pilia
Take thou the mony, spend it for my sake.	Jew	4.2.123		Ithimr
But if I get him, Coupe de Gorge for that.	Jew	4.3.5		Barab
Whose face has bin a grind-stone for mens swords,	Jew	4.3.9		Barab
what hee writes for you, ye shall have streight.	Jew	4.3.27	P	Barab
for in his villany/He will tell all he knowes and I shall dye	Jew	4.3.64		Barab
We two, and 'twas never knowne, nor never shall be for me.	Jew	4.4.24	P	Ithimr
Must tuna my Lute for sound, twang twang first.	Jew	4.4.31		Barab
There's two crownes for thee, play.	Jew	4.4.47		Pilia

FOR (cont.)

'Twas sent me for a present from the great Cham.	Jew	4.4.68	Barab
For Calymath having hover'd here so long,	Jew	5.1.4	Govnr
And dye he shall, for we will never yeeld.	Jew	5.1.6	1Knght
For what?	Jew	5.1.36	Barab
For none of this can prejudice my life.	Jew	5.1.39	Barab
For the Jewes body, throw that o're the wals,	Jew	5.1.58	Govnr
To be a prey for Vultures and wild beasts.	Jew	5.1.59	Govnr
For by my meanes Calymath shall enter in.	Jew	5.1.63	Barab
thou that Jew whose goods we heard were sold/For Tribute-mony?	Jew	5.1.74	Calym
Feare not, my Lord, for here, against the [sluice] <Truce>,/The	Jew	5.1.86	Barab
To make a passage for the running streames/And common channels	Jew	5.1.88	Barab
Open the gates for you to enter in,	Jew	5.1.93	Barab
And kneele for mercy to your conquering foe:	Jew	5.2.2	Calym
For thy desert we make thee Governor,	Jew	5.2.10	Calym
For he that liveth in Authority,	Jew	5.2.38	Barab
not thine opportunity, for feare too late/Thou seek'st for much,	Jew	5.2.45	Barab
for feare too late/Thou seek'st for much, but canst not	Jew	5.2.46	Barab
This is the reason that I sent for thee;	Jew	5.2.51	Barab
Yet you doe live, and live for me you shall:	Jew	5.2.63	Barab
And as for Malta's ruine, thinke you not/'Twere slender policy	Jew	5.2.64	Barab
'Twere slender policy for Barabas/To dispossesse himselfe of	Jew	5.2.65	Barab
For sith, as once you said, within this Ile/In Malta here, that	Jew	5.2.67	Barab
For as a friend not knowne, but in distresse,	Jew	5.2.72	Barab
privately procure/Great summes of mony for thy recompence:	Jew	5.2.88	Govnr
And I will warrant Malta free for ever.	Jew	5.2.101	Barab
For Callymath, when he hath view'd the Towne,	Jew	5.2.105	Barab
And reason too, for Christians doe the like:	Jew	5.2.116	Barab
And then to make provision for the feast,	Jew	5.2.119	Barab
Hearing his Soveraigne was bound for Sea,	Jew	5.3.15	Msngr
For well has Barabas deserv'd of us.	Jew	5.3.25	Calym
Selim, for that, thus saith the Governor,	Jew	5.3.26	Msngr
serve to entertaine/Selim and all his souldiers for a month;	Jew	5.3.31	Msngr
For happily I shall be in distresse,	Jew	5.4.6	Govnr
For so I live, perish may all the world.	Jew	5.5.10	Barab
For if I keepe not promise, trust not me.	Jew	5.5.23	Barab
First, for his Army, they are sent before,	Jew	5.5.25	Barab
Now as for Calymath and his consorts,	Jew	5.5.32	Barab
Stand close, for here they come:	Jew	5.5.46	Barab
For I will shew thee greater curtesie/Then Barabas would have	Jew	5.5.61	Govnr
See Calymath, this was devis'd for thee.	Jew	5.5.66	Govnr
Was this the banquet he prepar'd for us?	Jew	5.5.95	Calym
Nay, Selim, stay, for since we have thee here,	Jew	5.5.97	Govnr
For with thy Gallyes couldst thou not get hence,	Jew	5.5.100	Govnr
Tush, Governor, take thou no care for that,	Jew	5.5.102	Calym
For he that did by treason worke our fall,	Jew	5.5.109	Govnr
for Malta shall be freed,/Or Selim ne're returne to Ottoman.	Jew	5.5.113	Govnr
Malta prisoner; for come [all] <call> the world/To rescue thee,	Jew	5.5.119	Govnr
For what he doth the Pope will ratifie:	P 40	1.40	Condy
For she is that huge blemish in our eye,	P 80	2.23	Guise
That hanges for every peasant to atchive?	P 98	2.41	Guise
For this, I wake, when others think I sleepe,	P 105	2.48	Guise
For this, I waite, that scornes attendance else:	P 106	2.49	Guise
For this, my quenchles thirst whereon I builde,	P 107	2.50	Guise
For this, this head, this heart, this hand and sworde,	P 109	2.52	Guise
For this, hath heaven engendred me of earth,	P 113	2.56	Guise
For this, this earth sustaines my bodies [waight],	P 114	2.57	Guise
For this, from Spaine the stately Catholickes/Sends Indian	P 117	2.60	Guise
For this have I a largesse from the Pope,	P 119	2.62	Guise
So that for proofe, he barely beares the name:	P 131	2.74	Guise
The Mother Queene workes wonders for my sake,	P 133	2.76	Guise
Sufficient yet for such a pettie King:	P 150	2.93	Guise
Where resolution strives for victory.	P 165	2.108	Guise
(For whose effects my soule is massacred)/Infect thy gracious	P 192	3.27	QnMarg
Should for their conscience taste such rutheles ends.	P 214	4.12	Charls
To have some care for feare of enemies.	P 224	4.22	QnMoth
What order wil you set downe for the Massacre?	P 229	4.27	QnMoth
And I will goe take order for his death.	P 252	4.50	Guise
That durst presume for hope of any gaine,	P 258	4.56	Charls
I deepely sorrow for your trecherous wrong:	P 263	4.61	Charls
And send them for a present to the Pope:	P 317	5.44	Anjoy
I, I, for this Seroune, and thou shalt [ha't] <hate>.	P 351	6.6	Mntsrl
Not for my life doe I desire this pause,	P 401	7.41	Ramus
And this for Aristotle will I say,	P 408	7.48	Ramus
For that let me alone, Cousin stay you heer,	P 428	7.68	Anjoy
And now sirs for this night let our fury stay.	P 443	7.83	Guise
For Poland is as I have been enformde,	P 454	8.4	Anjoy
For if th'almighty take my brother hence,	P 469	8.19	Anjoy
For Polands crowne and kingly diadem.	P 480	8.30	Lord
Why let us burne him for an heretick.	P 483	9.2	P 2Atndt
For if these straglers gather head againe,	P 506	9.25	QnMoth
It will be hard for us to worke their deaths.	P 508	9.27	QnMoth
How Charles our sonne begins for to lament/For the late nights	P 513	9.32	QnMoth
For the late nights worke which my Lord of Guise/Did make in	P 514	9.33	QnMoth
For to revenge their deaths upon us all.	P 518	9.37	Cardnl
I, but my Lord let me alone for that,	P 519	9.38	QnMoth
For Katherine must have her will in France:	P 520	9.39	QnMoth
For Ile rule France, but they shall weare the crowne:	P 525	9.44	QnMoth
My Lords, what resteth there now for to be done?	P 554	11.19	QnMoth
the speed we can, provide/For Henries coronation from Polonie:	P 563	11.28	QnMoth
For heers no saftie in the Realme for me,	P 568	11.33	Navrre
For feare that Guise joyn'd with the King of Spaine,	P 573	11.38	Navrre
As I entend to labour for the truth,	P 585	11.50	Navrre

FOR (cont.)

A watchfull Senate for ordaining lawes,	P 593	12.6	QnMoth
noble mindes change not their thoughts/For wearing of a crowne:	P 611	12.24	Mugern
Hands of good fellow, I will be his baile/For this offence:	P 623	12.36	King
What now remaines, but for a while to feast,	P 627	12.40	King
Lets goe my Lords, our dinner staies for us.	P 630	12.43	King
And tell him that tis for his Countries good,	P 646	12.59	Cardnl
For while she lives Katherine will be Queene.	P 654	12.67	QnMoth
Hence strumpet, hide thy head for shame,	P 691	13.35	Guise
But for you know our quarrell is no more,	P 704	14.7	Navrre
And Guise for Spaine hath now incenst the King,	P 711	14.14	Navrre
Not yet my Lord, for thereon doe they stay:	P 732	14.35	1Msngr
Of King or Country, no not for them both.	P 740	14.43	Navrre
And place our selves in order for the fight.	P 742	14.45	Navrre
That villain for whom I beare this deep disgrace,	P 766	15.24	Guise
Even for your words that have incenst me so,	P 767	15.25	Guise
For his othes are seldome spent in vaine.	P 773	15.31	Eprnon
For he hath solemnely sworne thy death.	P 777	15.35	King
But we presume it is not for our good.	P 824	17.19	King
What I have done tis for the Gospell sake.	P 826	17.21	Guise
Nay for the Popes sake, and thine owne benefite.	P 827	17.22	Eprnon
I challenge thee for treason in the cause.	P 830	17.25	Eprnon
Tis for your safetie and your enemies wrack.	P 858	17.53	Guise
For had your highnesse seene with what a pompe/He entred Paris,	P 872	17.67	Eprnon
For not effecting of his holines will.	P 878	17.73	Eprnon
I think for safety of your royall person,	P 887	17.82	Eprnon
For now that Paris takes the Guises parte,	P 896	17.91	King
Heere is no staying for the King of France,	P 897	17.92	King
For we must aide the King against the Guise.	P 918	18.19	Navrre
For his aspiring thoughts aime at the crowne,	P 923	18.24	Navrre
For anon the Guise will come.	P 941	19.11	Capt
And perish in the pit thou mad'st for me.	P 963	19.33	King
Now sues the King for favour to the Guise,	P 978	19.48	Guise
For in thee is the Duke of Guises hope.	P 988	19.58	Guise
Philip and Parma, I am slaine for you:	P1011	19.81	Guise
Goe fetch his sonne for to beholde his death:	P1021	19.91	King
I cannot speak for greefe: when thou wast borne,	P1072	19.142	QnMoth
And all for thee my Guise: what may I doe?	P1088	19.158	QnMoth
For since the Guise is dead, I will not live.	P1090	19.160	QnMoth
O Lord no: for we entend to strangle you.	P1095	20.5	2Mur
Oh what may I doe, for to revenge thy death?	P1108	21.2	Dumain
Now thou art dead, heere is no stay for us:	P1111	21.5	Dumain
But thats prevented, for to end his life,	P1119	21.13	Dumain
the Jacobyns, that for my conscience sake will kill the King.	P1130	21.24	P Frier
Tush my Lord, let me alone for that.	P1136	21.30	P Frier
For all the wealth and treasure of the world.	P1163	22.25	King
Just torments for his trechery.	P1175	22.37	King
Agent for England, send thy mistres word,	P1194	22.56	King
Tell her for all this that I hope to live,	P1196	22.58	King
whom God hath blest for hating Papestry.	P1208	22.70	King
For you are stricken with a poysoned knife.	P1213	22.75	Srgeon
For he is your lawfull King and my next heire:	P1230	22.92	King
And then I vow for to revenge his death,	P1247	22.109	Navrre
As for the multitude that are but sparkes,	Edw	1.1.20	Gavstn
Why there are hospitals for such as you,	Edw	1.1.35	Gavstn
these are not men for me,/I must have wanton Poets, pleasant	Edw	1.1.50	Gavstn
For Mortimer will hang his armor up.	Edw	1.1.89	Mortmr
But for that base and obscure Gaveston:	Edw	1.1.101	Lncstr
For which, had not his highnes lov'd him well,	Edw	1.1.112	Kent
Preach upon poles for trespasse of their tongues.	Edw	1.1.118	Kent
All Warwickshire will love him for my sake.	Edw	1.1.128	Warwck
these may well suffice/For one of greater birth then Gaveston.	Edw	1.1.159	Kent
Cease brother, for I cannot brooke these words:	Edw	1.1.160	Edward
If for these dignities thou be envied,	Edw	1.1.163	Edward
Ile give thee more, for but to honour thee,	Edw	1.1.164	Edward
Tis true, and but for reverence of these robes,	Edw	1.1.180	Gavstn
For heele complaine unto the sea of Rome.	Edw	1.1.190	Kent
Ile be revengd on him for my exile.	Edw	1.1.192	Gavstn
For this offence be thou accurst of God.	Edw	1.1.199	BshpCv
whom he vouchsafes/For vailing of his bonnet one good looke.	Edw	1.2.19	Lncstr
what els my lords, for it concernes me neere,	Edw	1.2.44	ArchBp
For now my lord the king regardes me not,	Edw	1.2.49	Queene
The king shall lose his crowne, for we have power,	Edw	1.2.59	Mortmr
for rather then my lord/Shall be opprest by civill mutinies,	Edw	1.2.64	Queene
Farewell sweet Mortimer, and for my sake,	Edw	1.2.81	Queene
For no where else the new earle is so safe.	Edw	1.4.11	Lncstr
Meete you for this, proud overdaring peeres?	Edw	1.4.47	Edward
For shame subscribe, and let the lowne depart.	Edw	1.4.82	Warwck
The king is love-sick for his minion.	Edw	1.4.87	Mortmr
For these thy superstitious taperlights,	Edw	1.4.98	Edward
As for the peeres that backe the cleargie thus,	Edw	1.4.104	Edward
For no where else seekes he felicitie.	Edw	1.4.122	Gavstn
For every looke, my lord, drops downe a teare,	Edw	1.4.136	Gavstn
I passe not for their anger, come lets go.	Edw	1.4.142	Edward
Witnesse this hart, that sighing for thee breakes,	Edw	1.4.165	Queene
There weepe, for till my Gaveston be repeald,	Edw	1.4.168	Edward
For never doted Jove on Ganimed,	Edw	1.4.180	Queene
And so am I for ever miserable.	Edw	1.4.186	Queene
To sue unto you all for his repeale:	Edw	1.4.201	Queene
For his repeale, Madam!	Edw	1.4.204	Lncstr
I Mortimer, for till he be restorde,	Edw	1.4.209	Queene
What, would ye have me plead for Gaveston?	Edw	1.4.213	Mortmr
Plead for him he that will, I am resolvde.	Edw	1.4.214	MortSr

FOR (cont.)

For tis against my will he should returne.	Edw	1.4.217	Queene
Then speake not for him, let the pesant go.	Edw	1.4.218	Warwck
Tis for my selfe I speake, and not for him.	Edw	1.4.219	Queene
Faire Queene forbeare to angle for the fish,	Edw	1.4.221	Mortmr
She smiles, now for my life his mind is changd.	Edw	1.4.236	Warwck
And therefore though I pleade for his repeall,	Edw	1.4.241	Mortmr
Tis not for his sake, but for our availe:	Edw	1.4.242	Mortmr
Nay, for the realms behoofe and for the kings.	Edw	1.4.243	Mortmr
Tis hard for us to worke his overthrow.	Edw	1.4.262	Mortmr
But rather praise him for that brave attempt,	Edw	1.4.268	Mortmr
For purging of the realme of such a plague.	Edw	1.4.270	Mortmr
For howsoever we have borne it out,	Edw	1.4.280	Mortmr
Which for his fathers sake leane to the king,	Edw	1.4.283	Mortmr
Hees gone, and for his absence thus I moorne,	Edw	1.4.305	Edward
And makes me frantick for my Gaveston:	Edw	1.4.315	Edward
For Gaveston, but not for Isabell.	Edw	1.4.326	Queene
For thee faire Queene, if thou lovest Gaveston,	Edw	1.4.327	Edward
That waite attendance for a gratious looke,	Edw	1.4.338	Queene
And with this sword, Penbrooke wil fight for you.	Edw	1.4.352	Penbrk
And as for you, lord Mortimer of Chirke,	Edw	1.4.359	Edward
For with my nature warre doth best agree.	Edw	1.4.365	MortSr
the crowne, direct our warrant forth,/For Gaveston to Ireland:	Edw	1.4.370	Edward
For wot you not that I have made him sure,	Edw	1.4.378	Edward
That day, if not for him, yet for my sake,	Edw	1.4.381	Edward
Spare for no cost, we will requite your love.	Edw	1.4.383	Edward
The conquering [Hercules] <Hector> for Hilas wept,	Edw	1.4.393	MortSr
And for Patroclus sterne Achillis droopt:	Edw	1.4.394	MortSr
For riper yeares will weane him from such toyes.	Edw	1.4.401	MortSr
While souldiers mutinie for want of paie.	Edw	1.4.406	Mortmr
No, his companion, for he loves me well,	Edw	2.1.13	Spencr
I for a while, but Baldock marke the end,	Edw	2.1.16	Spencr
That hees repeald, and sent for back againe,	Edw	2.1.18	Spencr
Tis like enough, for since he was exild,	Edw	2.1.23	Baldck
My life for thine she will have Gaveston.	Edw	2.1.28	Spencr
And being like pins heads, blame me for the bignesse,	Edw	2.1.48	Baldck
And apt for any kinde of villanie.	Edw	2.1.51	Baldck
The greefe for his exile was not so much,	Edw	2.1.57	Neece
For I have joyfull newes to tell thee of,	Edw	2.1.75	Neece
For as the lovers of faire Danae,	Edw	2.2.53	Edward
Yet I disdaine not to doe this for you.	Edw	2.2.79	Lncstr
Ile not be barde the court for Gaveston.	Edw	2.2.90	Mortmr
Lets to our castels, for the king is moovde.	Edw	2.2.100	Warwck
To gather for him thoroughout the realme.	Edw	2.2.148	Edward
Looke for rebellion, looke to be deposde,	Edw	2.2.161	Lncstr
For your lemmons you have lost, at Bannocks borne,	Edw	2.2.191	Lncstr
My swelling hart for very anger breakes,	Edw	2.2.200	Edward
And dare not be revengde, for their power is great:	Edw	2.2.202	Edward
For now the wrathfull nobles threaten warres,	Edw	2.2.210	Kent
And therefore brother banish him for ever.	Edw	2.2.211	Kent
I dare not, for the people love him well.	Edw	2.2.235	Edward
The fitter art thou Baldock for my turne,	Edw	2.2.245	Edward
For my sake let him waite upon your grace,	Edw	2.2.250	Gavstn
me, for his sake/Ile grace thee with a higher stile ere long.	Edw	2.2.252	Edward
Yes, yes, for Mortimer your lovers sake.	Edw	2.4.14	Edward
And all in vaine, for when I speake him faire,	Edw	2.4.28	Queene
As Isabell could live with thee for ever.	Edw	2.4.60	Queene
In vaine I looke for love at Edwards hand,	Edw	2.4.61	Queene
Base flatterer, yeeld, and were it not for shame,	Edw	2.5.11	Mortmr
Looke for no other fortune wretch then death,	Edw	2.5.17	Lncstr
Go souldiers take him hence, for by my sword,	Edw	2.5.20	Warwck
But for thou wert the favorit of a King,	Edw	2.5.27	Warwck
by me, yet but he may/See him before he dies, for why he saies,	Edw	2.5.37	Arundl
bestow/His teares on that, for that is all he gets/Of Gaveston,	Edw	2.5.53	Mortmr
And drives his nobles to these exigents/For Gaveston, will if	Edw	2.5.63	Warwck
My lords, I will be pledge for his returne.	Edw	2.5.66	Arundl
But for we know thou art a noble gentleman,	Edw	2.5.68	Mortmr
To make away a true man for a theefe.	Edw	2.5.70	Mortmr
Come fellowes, it booted not for us to strive,	Edw	2.6.18	James
For favors done in him, unto us all.	Edw	3.1.42	SpncrP
To make my preparation for Fraunce.	Edw	3.1.88	Queene
Yea my good lord, for Gaveston is dead.	Edw	3.1.90	Arundl
Neither my lord, for as he was surprizd,	Edw	3.1.94	Arundl
Refusing to receive me pledge for him,	Edw	3.1.107	Arundl
My lords, because our soveraigne sends for him,	Edw	3.1.109	Arundl
For being delivered unto Penbrookes men,	Edw	3.1.116	Arundl
I will have heads, and lives, for him as many,	Edw	3.1.132	Edward
them I will come to chastise them,/For murthering Gaveston:	Edw	3.1.179	Edward
For now, even now, we marche to make them stoope,	Edw	3.1.183	Edward
Tis not amisse my liege for eyther part,	Edw	3.1.190	SpncrP
sweat and dust/All chockt well neare, begin to faint for heate,	Edw	3.1.192	SpncrP
Till hee pay deerely for their companie.	Edw	3.1.198	Lncstr
For theile betray thee, traitors as they are.	Edw	3.1.203	Lncstr
For which ere long, their heads shall satisfie,	Edw	3.1.209	Edward
Saint George for England, and the Barons right.	Edw	3.1.219	Warwck
Saint George for England, and king Edwards right.	Edw	3.1.220	Edward
traitors, now tis time/To be avengd on you for all your braves,	Edw	3.1.225	Edward
And for the murther of my deerest friend,	Edw	3.1.226	Edward
And Penbrooke undertooke for his returne,	Edw	3.1.236	Edward
For which thy head shall over looke the rest,	Edw	3.1.239	Edward
Grone for this greefe, behold how thou art maimed.	Edw	3.1.251	Mortmr
There see him safe bestowed, and for the rest,	Edw	3.1.253	Edward
Then make for Fraunce amaine, [Levune] <Lewne> away,/Proclaime	Edw	3.1.280	Spencr

FOR (cont.)

Faire blowes the winde for Fraunce, blowe gentle gale,	Edw	4.1.1	Kent
Till Edmund be arrivde for Englands good,	Edw	4.1.2	Kent
and then a Fig/For all my unckles frienship here in Fraunce.	Edw	4.2.5	Prince
But Mortimer reservde for better hap,	Edw	4.2.40	Mortmr
in England/Would cast up cappes, and clap their hands for joy,	Edw	4.2.55	Mortmr
To see us there appointed for our foes.	Edw	4.2.56	Mortmr
For Englands honor, peace, and quietnes.	Edw	4.2.58	Kent
Reward for them can bring in Mortimer?	Edw	4.3.18	Edward
Edward battell in England, sooner then he can looke for them:	Edw	4.3.35	P Spencr
Heere for our countries cause sweare we to him/All homage,	Edw	4.4.19	Mortmr
And for the open wronges and injuries/Edward hath done to us,	Edw	4.4.21	Mortmr
Edward, alas my hart relents for thee,	Edw	4.6.2	Kent
diest, for Mortimer/And Isabell doe kisse while they conspire,	Edw	4.6.12	Kent
to Longshankes blood/Is faise, be not found single for suspect:	Edw	4.6.17	Kent
And shipt but late for Ireland with the king.	Edw	4.6.58	Rice
Yet gentle monkes, for treasure, golde nor fee,	Edw	4.7.24	Edward
We were imbarkt for Ireland, wretched we,	Edw	4.7.33	Baldck
Here is a Litter readie for your grace,	Edw	4.7.84	Leistr
And hags howle for my death at Charons shore,	Edw	4.7.90	Edward
For friends hath Edward none, but these, and these,	Edw	4.7.91	Edward
My lord, be going, care not for these,	Edw	4.7.93	Rice
For we shall see them shorter by the heads.	Edw	4.7.94	Rice
Leister, thou staist for me,/And go I must, life farewell with	Edw	4.7.98	Edward
Make for a new life man, throw up thy eyes,	Edw	4.7.107	Baldck
And that you lay for pleasure here a space,	Edw	5.1.3	Leistr
For kinde and loving hast thou alwaies beene:	Edw	5.1.7	Edward
For such outragious passions cloye my soule,	Edw	5.1.19	Edward
That bleedes within me for this strange exchange.	Edw	5.1.35	Edward
Your grace mistakes, it is for Englands good,	Edw	5.1.38	BshpWn
No, tis for Mortimer, not Edwards head,	Edw	5.1.40	Edward
For hees a lambe, encompassed by Woolves,	Edw	5.1.41	Edward
Why gape you for your soveraignes overthrow?	Edw	5.1.72	Edward
They passe not for thy frownes as late they did,	Edw	5.1.77	Edward
For if they goe, the prince shall lose his right.	Edw	5.1.92	Leistr
Then send for unrelenting Mortimer/And Isabell, whose eyes	Edw	5.1.103	Edward
Yet stay, for rather then I will looke on them,	Edw	5.1.106	Edward
And sit for aye inthronized in heaven,	Edw	5.1.109	Edward
And every earth is fit for buriall.	Edw	5.1.146	Edward
For now we hould an old Wolfe by the eares,	Edw	5.2.7	Mortmr
For our behoofe will beare the greater sway/When as a kings	Edw	5.2.13	Mortmr
O happie newes, send for the prince my sonne.	Edw	5.2.29	Queene
as long as he survives/What safetie rests for us, or for my	Edw	5.2.43	Queene
long as he survives/What safetie rests for us, or for my sonne?	Edw	5.2.43	Queene
But hee repents, and sorrowes for it now.	Edw	5.2.108	Prince
Where I am sterv'd for want of sustenance,	Edw	5.3.20	Edward
Sit downe, for weele be Barbars to your grace.	Edw	5.3.28	Matrvs
To seeke for mercie at a tyrants hand.	Edw	5.3.36	Edward
O Gaveston, it is for thee that I am wrongd,	Edw	5.3.41	Edward
For me, both thou, and both the Spencers died,	Edw	5.3.42	Edward
And for your sakes, a thousand wronges ile take,	Edw	5.3.43	Edward
Wish well to mine, then tush, for them ile die.	Edw	5.3.45	Edward
Lay hands upon the earle for this assault.	Edw	5.3.54	Gurney
Is sure to pay for it when his sonne is of age,	Edw	5.4.4	Mortmr
And sue to me for that that I desire,	Edw	5.4.57	Mortmr
Intreate my lord Protector for his life.	Edw	5.4.95	King
But seeing I cannot, ile entreate for him:	Edw	5.4.98	King
Tis for your highnesse good, and for the realmes.	Edw	5.4.101	Mortmr
And none of both [them] <then> thirst for Edmunds bloud.	Edw	5.4.107	Kent
What safetie may I looke for at his hands,	Edw	5.4.109	King
Send for him out thence, and I will anger him.	Edw	5.5.13	Gurney
Gurney, it was left unpointed for the nonce,	Edw	5.5.16	Matrvs
See how he must be handled for his labour,	Edw	5.5.23	Matrvs
For she relents at this your miserie.	Edw	5.5.49	Ltborn
So that for want of sleepe and sustenance,	Edw	5.5.63	Edward
When for her sake I ran at tilt in Fraunce,	Edw	5.5.69	Edward
Forgive my thought, for having such a thought,	Edw	5.5.83	Edward
For not these ten daies have these eyes lids closd.	Edw	5.5.94	Edward
No, no, for if thou meanst to murther me,	Edw	5.5.98	Edward
Runne for the table.	Edw	5.5.110	Ltborn
Excellent well, take this for thy rewarde.	Edw	5.5.117	Gurney
As for my selfe, I stand as Joves huge tree,	Edw	5.6.11	Mortmr
Lets see who dare impeache me for his death?	Edw	5.6.14	Mortmr
For my sake sweete sonne pittie Mortimer.	Edw	5.6.55	Queene
Then sue for life unto a paltrie boye.	Edw	5.6.57	Mortmr
Farewell faire Queene, weepe not for Mortimer,	Edw	5.6.64	Mortmr
Els would you not intreate for Mortimer.	Edw	5.6.71	King
I, madam, you, for so the rumor runnes.	Edw	5.6.73	King
That rumor is untrue, for loving thee,	Edw	5.6.74	Queene
Mother, you are suspected for his death,	Edw	5.6.78	King
Nay, to my death, for too long have I lived,	Edw	5.6.83	Queene
Shall I not moorne for my beloved lord,	Edw	5.6.87	Queene
And speake for Faustus in his infancie.	F 10	Prol.10	1Chor
For falling to a divellish exercise,	F 23	Prol.23	1Chor
And be eterniz'd for some wondrous cure:	F 43	1.1.15	Faust
Too servile <The devill> and illiberall for mee.	F 63	1.1.35	Faust
I'le have them flie to [India] <Indian> for gold;	F 109	1.1.81	Faust
Ransacke the Ocean for Orient Pearle,	F 110	1.1.82	Faust
search all corners of the new-found-world/For pleasant fruites,	F 112	1.1.84	Faust
Yea stranger engines for the brunt of warre,	F 122	1.1.94	Faust
no object, for my head]/[But ruminates on Negromantique skill].	F 131	1.1.103A	Faust
Both Law and Physicke are for petty wits:	F 134	1.1.106	Faust
From <For> Venice shall they drag <dregge> huge Argosies,/And	F 157	1.1.129	Valdes

FOR (cont.)

And more frequented for this mysterie,	F 169	1.1.141	Cornel
For e're I sleep, I'le try what I can do:	F 192	1.1.164	Faust
That shall we presently know, <for see> here comes his boy.	F 196	1.2.3	2Schol
You are deceiv'd, for <Yes sir>, I will tell you:	F 206	1.2.13	P Wagner
For is he not Corpus naturale?	F 207	1.2.14	P Wagner
for you to come within fortie foot of the place of execution,	F 211	1.2.18	P Wagner
damned Art/For which they two are infamous through the world.	F 222	1.2.29	1Schol
<yet should I grieve for him>:	F 224	(HC258) A	2Schol
For when we heare one racke the name of God,	F 275	1.3.47	Mephst
Therefore the shortest cut for conjuring/Is stoutly to abjure	F 280	1.3.52	Mephst
For I confound <He confounds> hell in Elizium:	F 287	1.3.59	Faust
For which God threw him from the face of heaven.	F 296	1.3.68	Mephst
And are for ever damn'd with Lucifer.	F 300	1.3.72	Mephst
so passionate/For being deprived of the Joyes of heaven?	F 312	1.3.84	Faust
I'de give them all for Mephostophilis.	F 331	1.3.103	Faust
to the devill, for a shoulder of Mutton, tho it were bloud raw.	F 350	1.4.8	P Wagner
for sirra, if thou dost not presently bind thy selfe to me for	F 360	1.4.18	P Wagner
thou dost not presently bind thy selfe to me for seven yeares,	F 361	1.4.19	P Wagner
for they are as familiar with me, as if they payd for their	F 364	1.4.22	P Robin
me, as if they payd for their meate and drinke, I can tell you.	F 365	1.4.23	P Robin
for I will presently raise up two devils to carry thee away:	F 372	1.4.30	P Wagner
Already Faustus hath hazarded that for thee.	F 422	2.1.34	Faust
For that security craves <great> Lucifer.	F 425	2.1.37	Mephst
for love of thee/Faustus hath <I> cut his <mine> arme,	F 442	2.1.54	Faust
And let it be propitious for my wish.	F 447	2.1.59	Faust
<Then theres inough for a thousand soules>,	F 477	(HC260) A	Faust
that Mephostophilis shall doe for him, and bring him	F 488	2.1.100	P Faust
Where we are tortur'd, and remaine for ever.	F 509	2.1.121	Mephst
but <for> where we are is hell,/And where hell is there must we	F 511	2.1.123	Mephst
for here's the scrowle/In which <Wherein> thou hast given thy	F 519	2.1.131	Mephst
For I tell thee I am damn'd, and <am> now in hell.	F 526	2.1.138	Mephst
for I am wanton and lascivious, and cannot live without a wife.	F 530	2.1.142	P Faust
<Nay sweete Mephastophilis fetch me one, for I will have one>.	F 530	(HC261) A	P Faust
<A plague on her for a hote whore>.	F 534	(HC261) A	P Faust
Thankes Mephostophilis for this sweete booke.	F 550	2.1.162	Faust
'Twas <It was> made for man; then he's <therefore is man> more	F 560	2.2.9	Mephst
If Heaven was <it were> made for man, 'twas made for me:	F 561	2.2.10	Faust
Move me not Faustus <for I will not tell thee>.	F 621	2.2.70	P Mephst
<Thinke thou on hell Faustus, for thou art damnd>.	F 624	(HC262) A	Mephst
Christ cannot save thy soule, for he is just,	F 636	2.2.85	Lucifr
pardon [me] <him> for <in> this,/And Faustus vowes never to	F 647	2.2.96	Faust
And we will highly gratify thee for it.	F 653	2.2.102	Lucifr
not speake a word more for a Kings ransome <an other worde>,	F 669	2.2.118	P Pride
in hell, and look to it, for some of you shall be my father.	F 690	2.2.139	P Wrath
I'le not speake <an other word for a King's raunsome>.	F 706	(HC264) A	P Sloth
I'le not speake <a word more for a kings ransome>.	F 706	(HC264) B	P Sloth
Faustus, thou shalt, at midnight I will send for thee;	F 716	2.2.168	Lucifr
your foolery, for an my Maister come, he'le conjure you 'faith.	F 734	2.3.13	P Dick
Thou needst not do that, for my Mistresse hath done it.	F 739	2.3.18	P Dick
thought you did not sneake up and downe after her for nothing.	F 743	2.3.22	P Dick
hold belly hold, and wee'le not pay one peny for it.	F 750	2.3.29	P Robin
brave, prethee let's to it presently, for I am as dry as a dog.	F 751	2.3.30	P Dick
I have my Faustus, and for proofe thereof,	F 803	3.1.25	Mephst
I chuse his privy chamber for our use.	F 806	3.1.28	Mephst
I have taken up his holinesse privy chamber for our use>.	F 806	(HC265) A	P Mephst
All's one, for wee'l be bold with his Venison.	F 808	3.1.30	Mephst
containes <containeth> for to delight thine eyes <thee with>,	F 810	3.1.32	Mephst
Sound Trumpets then, for thus Saint Peters Heire,	F 875	3.1.97	Pope
The sacred Sinod hath decreed for him,	F 885	3.1.107	Pope
We will depose the Emperour for that deed,	F 906	3.1.128	Pope
For him, and the succeeding Popes of Rome,	F 926	3.1.148	Bruno
The Cardinals will be plagu'd for this anon.	F 976	3.1.198	Faust
Now Faustus, come prepare thy selfe for mirth,	F 981	3.2.1	Mephst
The Pope will curse them for their sloth to day,	F 987	3.2.7	Faust
So Faustus, now for all their holinesse,	F1004	3.2.24	Mephst
Were by the holy Councell both condemn'd/For lothed Lollords,	F1022	3.2.42	Pope
False Prelates, for this hatefull treachery,	F1033	3.2.53	Pope
To the Bishop of Millaine, for this so rare a present.	F1042	3.2.62	Pope
I, pray do, for Faustus is a dry.	F1052	3.2.72	Faust
Purgatory, and now is come unto your holinesse for his pardon.	F1060	3.2.80	P Archbp
Damb'd be this soule for ever, for this deed.	F1070	3.2.90	Pope
for I can tell you, you'le be curst with Bell, Booke, and	F1072	3.2.92	P Mephst
same cup, for the Vintners boy followes us at the hard heeles.	F1089	3.3.2	P Dick
Never deny't, for I know you have it, and I'le search you.	F1101	3.3.14	P Vintnr
Never out face me for the matter, for sure the cup is betweene	F1107	3.3.20	P Vintnr
me for the matter, for sure the cup is betweene you two.	F1107	3.3.20	P Vintnr
and stir not for thy life, Vintner you shall have your cup	F1113	3.3.26	P Robin
Onely for pleasure of these damned slaves.	F1119	3.3.32	Mephst
you heartily sir; for wee cal'd you but in jeast I promise you.	F1123	3.3.36	P Dick
For Apish deeds transformed to an Ape.	F1127	3.3.40	Mephst
to their porridge-pots, for I'le into the Kitchin presently:	F1134	3.3.47	P Robin
The wonder of the world for Magick Art;	F1166	4.1.12	Mrtino
For Faustus at the Court is late arriv'd,	F1181	4.1.27	Mrtino
I am content for this once to thrust my head out at a window:	F1199	4.1.45	P Benvol
for they say, if a man be drunke over night, the Divell cannot	F1200	4.1.46	P Benvol
For ever be belov'd of Carolus.	F1211	4.1.57	Emper
For proofe whereof, if so your Grace be pleas'd,	F1221	4.1.67	Faust
but for all that, I doe not greatly beleeve him, he lookes as	F1227	4.1.73	P Benvol
zounds I could eate my selfe for anger, to thinke I have beene	F1243	4.1.89	P Benvol
hold, tis no matter for thy head, for that's arm'd sufficiently.	F1288	4.1.134	P Emper
tis no matter for thy head, for that's arm'd sufficiently.	F1289	4.1.135	P Emper
pull in your head for shame, let not all the world wonder at	F1291	4.1.137	P Faust

FOR (cont.)

good my Lord intreate for me:	F1306	4.1.152	P	Benvol
not so much for injury done to me, as to delight your Majesty	F1311	4.1.157	P	Faust
But an I be not reveng'd for this, would I might be turn'd to a	F1319	4.1.165	P	Benvol
For hornes he gave, Il'e have his head anone.	F1361	4.2.37		Benvol
Justly rewarded for his villanies.	F1376	4.2.52		Benvol
and they shall serve for buttons to his lips, to keepe his	F1387	4.2.63	P	Benvol
Give him his head for Gods sake.	F1392	4.2.68	P	Fredrk
I was limitted/For foure and twenty yeares, to breathe on	F1396	4.2.72		Faust
For loe these Trees remove at my command,	F1426	4.2.102		Faust
thou canst not buy so good a horse, for so small a price:	F1459	4.4.3	P	Faust
sell him, but if thou likest him for ten Dollors more, take him,	F1460	4.4.4	P	Faust
Now am I a made man for ever.	F1477	4.4.21	P	HrsCsr
for your horse is turned to a bottle of Hay,--Maister Doctor.	F1490	4.4.34	P	HrsCsr
and the Horse-courser a bundle of hay for his forty Dollors.	F1497	4.4.41	P	Faust
of his men to attend you with provision fit for your journey.	F1502	4.4.46	P	Wagner
doubt of that, for me thinkes you make no hast to wipe it out.	F1516	4.5.12	P	Hostss
me what he should give me for as much Hay as he could eate;	F1527	4.5.23	P	Carter
bad him take as much as he would for three-farthings; so he	F1529	4.5.25	P	Carter
be; for I have heard of one, that ha's eate a load of logges.	F1533	4.5.29	P	Robin
But you shall heare how bravely I serv'd him for it; I went me	F1547	4.5.43	P	HrsCsr
for one of his devils turn'd me into the likenesse of an Apes	F1553	4.5.49	P	Dick
for these pleasant sights, nor know I how sufficiently to	F1558	4.6.1	P	Duke
great bellyed women, do long for things, are rare and dainty.	F1569	4.6.12	P	Faust
Madam, I will do more then this for your content.	F1575	4.6.18	P	Faust
be good, for they come from a farre Country I can tell you.	F1576	4.6.19	P	Faust
We have no reason for it, therefore a fig for him.	F1593	4.6.36	P	Dick
They are good subject for a merriment.	F1606	4.6.49		Faust
we will be wellcome for our mony, and we will pay for what we	F1611	4.6.54	P	Robin
be wellcome for our mony, and we will pay for what we take:	F1612	4.6.55	P	Robin
'faith Ile drinke a health to thy woodden leg for that word.	F1627	4.6.70	P	HrsCsr
For nothing sir:	F1653	4.6.96	P	Carter
Who payes for the Ale?	F1666	4.6.109	P	Hostss
have sent away my guesse, I pray who shall pay me for my A--	F1667	4.6.110	P	Hostss
whom all the world admires for Majesty, we should thinke	F1686	5.1.13	P	1Schol
For that I know your friendship is unfain'd,	F1689	5.1.16		Faust
No [otherwaies] <otherwise> for pompe or <and> Majesty,	F1693	5.1.20		Faust
Then when sir Paris crost the seas with <for> her,	F1694	5.1.21		Faust
Be silent then, for danger is in words.	F1696	5.1.23		Faust
Whom all the world admires for majesty.	F1698	5.1.25		2Schol
and for this blessed sight <glorious deed>/Happy and blest be	F1704	5.1.31		1Schol
<Wee'l take our leaves>, and for this blessed sight	F1704	(HC269)B		1Schol
For gentle sonne, I speake it not in wrath,	F1719	5.1.46		OldMan
Hell claimes his <calls for> right, and with a roaring voyce,	F1726	5.1.53		Faust
Then call for mercy, and avoyd despaire.	F1733	5.1.60		OldMan
Hell strives with grace for conquest in my breast:	F1741	5.1.68		Faust
For disobedience to my soveraigne Lord,	F1744	5.1.71		Mephst
Here will I dwell, for heaven is <be> in these lippes,	F1773	5.1.100		Faust
I will be Paris <Pacis>, and for love of thee,	F1775	5.1.102		Faust
And then returne to Hellen for a kisse.	F1780	5.1.107		Faust
[Hence hel, for hence I flie unto my God].	F1796	5.1.123A		OldMan
dutie, I do yeeld/My life and lasting service for your love.	F1819	5.2.23		Wagner
for which Faustus hath lost both Germany and the world, yea	F1843	5.2.47	P	Faust
the Kingdome of Joy, and must remaine in hell for ever.	F1846	5.2.50	P	Faust
Hell, [ah] <O> hell for ever.	F1846	5.2.50	P	Faust
friends, what shall become of Faustus being in hell for ever?	F1847	5.2.51	P	Faust
[Ah] <O> gentlemen, I gave them my soule for my cunning.	F1856	5.2.60		Faust
for the vaine pleasure of foure and twenty yeares hath Faustus	F1858	5.2.62	P	Faust
tell us of this before, that Divines might have prayd for thee?	F1863	5.2.67	P	1Schol
but let us into the next roome, and [there] pray for him.	F1872	5.2.76	P	1Schol
I, pray for me, pray for me:	F1873	5.2.77	P	Faust
you <yee> heare, come not unto me, for nothing can rescue me.	F1874	5.2.78	P	Faust
For that must be thy mansion, there to dwell.	F1882	5.2.86		Mephst
Is for ore-tortur'd soules to rest them in.	F1915	5.2.119		BdAngl
He that loves pleasure, must for pleasure fall.	F1923	5.2.127		BdAngl
Rend <Ah rend> not my heart, for naming of my Christ,	F1941	5.2.145		Faust
<O, if my soule must suffer for my sinne>,	F1958	(HC271)B		Faust
[Yet for Christs sake, whose bloud hath ransom'd me],	F1959	5.2.163A		Faust
All beasts are happy, for when they die,	F1969	5.2.173		Faust
For such a dreadfull night, was never seene,	F1984	5.3.2		1Schol
For twixt the houres of twelve and one, me thought/I heard him	F1991	5.3.9		3Schol
one, me thought/I heard him shreeke and call aloud for helpe:	F1992	5.3.10		3Schol
Yet for he was a Scholler, once admired/For wondrous knowledge	F1997	5.3.15		2Schol
once admired/For wondrous knowledge in our Germane schooles,	F1998	5.3.16		2Schol
he would give his soule to the Divel for a shoulder of mutton,	F App	p.229 8	P	Wagner
to the Divel for a shoulder of mutton though twere blood rawe?	F App	p.229 10	P	Clown
and binde your selfe presently unto me for seaven yeeres, or	F App	p.229 24	P	Wagner
with my flesh, as if they had payd for my meate and drinke.	F App	p.230 29	P	Clown
for the name of french crownes a man were as good have as many	F App	p.230 33	P	Clown
and ifaith I meane to search some circles for my owne use:	F App	p.233 3	P	Robin
Rafe, keepe out, for I am about a roaring peece of worke.	F App	p.233 11	P	Robin
I can reade, he for his forehead, she for her private study,	F App	p.233 16	P	Robin
she for her private study, shee's borne to beare with me,	F App	p.233 16	P	Robin
for conjuring that ere was invented by any brimstone divel.	F App	p.233 19	P	Robin
druncke with ipocrase at any taberne in Europe for nothing,	F App	p.234 23	P	Robin
tell thee, we were for ever made by this doctor Faustus booke?	F App	p.234 1	P	Robin
heeres a simple purchase for horse-keepers, our horses shal	F App	p.234 3	P	Robin
stand by, Ile scowre you for a goblet, stand aside you had best,	F App	p.235 18	P	Robin
like a Beare, the third an Asse, for doing this enterprise.	F App	p.235 33	P	Mephst
Onely for pleasure of these damned slaves.	F App	p.235 39		Mephst
wil you take sixe pence in your purse to pay for your supper,	F App	p.235 41	P	Robin
villaines, for your presumption, I transforme thee into an Ape,	F App	p.235 43	P	Mephst
world can compare with thee, for the rare effects of Magicke:	F App	p.236 3	P	Emper

FOR (cont.)

yet for that love and duety bindes me thereunto, I am content	F App	p.236 14 P Faust
No sir, but when Acteon died, he left the hornes for you:	F App	p.237 55 P Faust
Ile meete with you anone for interrupting me so:	F App	p.238 58 P Faust
send for the knight that was so pleasent with me here of late?	F App	p.238 66 P Faust
I thinke I have met with you for it.	F App	p.238 78 P Faust
so much for the injury hee offred me heere in your presence,	F App	p.238 81 P Faust
Calls for the payment of my latest yeares,	F App	p.239 93 Faust
I have brought you forty dollers for your horse.	F App	p.239 101 P HrsCsr
if thou likst him for fifty, take him.	F App	p.239 103 P Faust
Alas sir, I have no more, I pray you speake for me.	F App	p.239 104 P HrsCsr
Now am I made man for ever, Ile not leave my horse for fortie:	F App	p.239 114 P HrsCsr
Now am I made man for ever, Ile not leave my horse for fortie:	F App	p.239 115 P HrsCsr
by him, for he bade me I should ride him into no water; now,	F App	p.240 130 P HrsCsr
Fustian, fortie dollers, fortie dollers for a bottle of hey.	F App	p.241 149 P HrsCsr
the Horsecourser I take it, a bottle of hey for his labour; wel,	F App	p.241 165 P Faust
that great bellied women do long for some dainties or other,	F App	p.242 5 P Faust
And for I see your curteous intent to pleasure me, I wil not	F App	p.242 8 P Duchss
this learned man for the great kindnes he hath shewd to you.	F App	p.243 29 P Duke
my Lord, and whilst I live, Rest beholding for this curtesie.	F App	p.243 31 P Duchss
For he hath given to me al his goodes,	F App	p.243 2 Wagner
Will ye wadge war, for which you shall not triumph?	Lucan, First Booke	12
But if for Nero (then unborne) the fates/Would find no other	Lucan, First Booke	33
not heavens, but gladly beare these evils/For Neros sake:	Lucan, First Booke	38
His losse made way for Roman outrages.	Lucan, First Booke	106
for Julia/Snatcht hence by cruel fates with ominous howles,	Lucan, First Booke	111
Would dash the wreath thou wearst for Pirats wracke.	Lucan, First Booke	123
Caesars renowne for war was lesse, he restles,	Lucan, First Booke	145
and ware robes/Too light for women; Poverty (who hatcht/Roomes	Lucan, First Booke	166
and al the world/Ransackt for golde, which breeds the world	Lucan, First Booke	168
They shooke for feare, and cold benumm'd their lims,	Lucan, First Booke	248
One that was feed for Caesar, and whose tongue/Could tune the	Lucan, First Booke	272
Cornets of horse are mustered for the field;	Lucan, First Booke	306
And by him kept of purpose for a dearth?	Lucan, First Booke	319
he casts/For civill warre, wherein through use he's known/To	Lucan, First Booke	325
Yet for long service done, reward these men,	Lucan, First Booke	341
What seates for their deserts?	Lucan, First Booke	344
what store of ground/For servitors to till?	Lucan, First Booke	345
For saving of a Romaine Citizen,	Lucan, First Booke	359
And in all quarters musters men for Roome.	Lucan, First Booke	396
Philosophers looke you, for unto me/Thou cause, what ere thou be	Lucan, First Booke	418
For you hold/That soules passe not to silent Erebus	Lucan, First Booke	450
And searching farther for the gods displeasure,	Lucan, First Booke	616
Whose like Aegiptian Memphis never had/For skill in stars, and	Lucan, First Booke	640
For these before the rest preferreth he:	Ovid's Elegies	1.1.2
Choosing a subject fit for feirse alarmes:	Ovid's Elegies	1.1.6
Being fittest matter for a wanton wit,	Ovid's Elegies	1.1.24
Fare well sterne warre, for blunter Poets meete.	Ovid's Elegies	1.1.32
And hold my conquered hands for thee to tie.	Ovid's Elegies	1.2.20
What needes thou warre, I sue to thee for grace,	Ovid's Elegies	1.2.21
And Cupide who hath markt me for thy pray,	Ovid's Elegies	1.3.12
If men have Faith, Ile live with thee for ever.	Ovid's Elegies	1.3.16
Strike on the boord like them that pray for evill,	Ovid's Elegies	1.4.27
For thee I did thy mistris faire entreate.	Ovid's Elegies	1.6.20
But what entreates for thee some-times tooke place,	Ovid's Elegies	1.6.21
(O mischiefe) now for me obtaine small grace.	Ovid's Elegies	1.6.22
Gratis thou maiest be free, give like for like,	Ovid's Elegies	1.6.23
Nor servile water shalt thou drinke for ever.	Ovid's Elegies	1.6.26
The carefull prison is more meete for thee.	Ovid's Elegies	1.6.64
For rage against my wench mov'd my rash arme,	Ovid's Elegies	1.7.3
lockes spred/On her white necke but for hurt cheekes be led.	Ovid's Elegies	1.7.40
Would he not buy thee thou for him shouldst care.	Ovid's Elegies	1.8.34
Or, but for bashfulnesse her selfe would crave.	Ovid's Elegies	1.8.44
Who seekes, for being faire, a night to have,	Ovid's Elegies	1.8.67
And take heed least he gets that love for nought.	Ovid's Elegies	1.8.72
Nor, if thou couzenst one, dread to for-sweare,	Ovid's Elegies	1.8.85
Servants fit for thy purpose thou must hire/To teach thy lover,	Ovid's Elegies	1.8.87
Tis shame for eld in warre or love to be.	Ovid's Elegies	1.9.4
Will you for gaine have Cupid sell himselfe?	Ovid's Elegies	1.10.17
To serve for pay beseemes not wanton gods.	Ovid's Elegies	1.10.20
The whore stands to be bought for each mans mony/And seekes	Ovid's Elegies	1.10.21
Farmes out her-self on nights for what she can.	Ovid's Elegies	1.10.30
The unjust Judge for bribes becomes a stale.	Ovid's Elegies	1.10.38
Or prostitute thy beauty for bad prize.	Ovid's Elegies	1.10.42
Thankes worthely are due for things unbought,	Ovid's Elegies	1.10.43
For beds ill hyr'd we are indebted nought.	Ovid's Elegies	1.10.44
Faire Dames for-beare rewards for nights to crave,	Ovid's Elegies	1.10.47
All for their Mistrisse, what they have, prepare.	Ovid's Elegies	1.10.58
The fame that verse gives doth for ever last.	Ovid's Elegies	1.10.62
Thy service for nights scapes is knowne commodious/And to give	Ovid's Elegies	1.11.3
If, what I do, she askes, say hope for night,	Ovid's Elegies	1.11.13
And him that hew'd you out for needfull uses/Ile prove had	Ovid's Elegies	1.12.15
There sat the hang-man for mens neckes to angle.	Ovid's Elegies	1.12.18
Your name approves you made for such like things,	Ovid's Elegies	1.12.27
And birds for <from> Memnon yearly shall be slaine.	Ovid's Elegies	1.13.4
O thou oft wilt blush/And say he likes me for my borrowed bush,	Ovid's Elegies	1.14.48
Praysing for me some unknowne Guelder dame,	Ovid's Elegies	1.14.49
For ever lasts high Sophocles proud vaine,	Ovid's Elegies	1.15.15
For after death all men receive their right:	Ovid's Elegies	1.15.40
I had in hand/Which for his heaven fell on the Gyants band.	Ovid's Elegies	2.1.16
Trust me all husbands for such faults are sad/Nor make they any	Ovid's Elegies	2.2.51
To meete for poyson or vilde facts we crave not,	Ovid's Elegies	2.2.63
If she discardes thee, what use servest thou for?	Ovid's Elegies	2.3.12

FOR (cont.)

For I confesse, if that might merite favour,	Ovid's Elegies	2.4.3
And she thats coy I like for being no clowne,	Ovid's Elegies	2.4.13
If she be learned, then for her skill I crave her,	Ovid's Elegies	2.4.17
Who would not love those hands for their swift running?	Ovid's Elegies	2.4.28
Both short and long please me, for I love both:	Ovid's Elegies	2.4.36
This for her looks, that for her woman-hood:	Ovid's Elegies	2.4.46
And words that seem'd for certaine markes to be.	Ovid's Elegies	2.5.20
Tis ill they pleas'd so much, for in my lips,	Ovid's Elegies	2.5.57
For wofull haires let piece-torne plumes abound,	Ovid's Elegies	2.6.5
For long shrild trumpets let your notes resound.	Ovid's Elegies	2.6.6
A little fild thee, and for love of talke,	Ovid's Elegies	2.6.29
My wenches vowes for thee what should I show,	Ovid's Elegies	2.6.43
If ill, thou saiest I die for others love.	Ovid's Elegies	2.7.10
And for her skill to thee a gratefull maide.	Ovid's Elegies	2.7.24
For which good turne my sweete reward repay,	Ovid's Elegies	2.8.21
Well maiest thou one thing for thy Mistresse use.	Ovid's Elegies	2.8.24
And time it was for me to live in quiet,	Ovid's Elegies	2.9.23
For when my loathing it of heate deprives me,	Ovid's Elegies	2.9.27
For now I love two women equallie:	Ovid's Elegies	2.10.4
And to the Gods for that death Ovid prayes.	Ovid's Elegies	2.10.30
For thee the East and West winds make me pale,	Ovid's Elegies	2.11.9
Request milde Zephires helpe for thy availe,	Ovid's Elegies	2.11.41
For thy returne shall fall the vowd oblation,	Ovid's Elegies	2.11.46
Each little hill shall for a table stand:	Ovid's Elegies	2.11.48
Nor is my warres cause new, but for a Queene/Europe, and Asia in	Ovid's Elegies	2.12.17
The Laphithes, and the Centaures for a woman,	Ovid's Elegies	2.12.19
I saw how Bulls for a white Heifer strive,	Ovid's Elegies	2.12.25
Both unkinde parents, but for causes sad,	Ovid's Elegies	2.14.31
Fit her so well, as she is fit for me:	Ovid's Elegies	2.15.5
And of just compasse for her knuckles bee.	Ovid's Elegies	2.15.6
to detaine)/Thou oughtst therefore to scorne me for thy mate,	Ovid's Elegies	2.17.13
For great revenews I good verses have,	Ovid's Elegies	2.17.27
But though I apt were for such high deseignes,	Ovid's Elegies	2.18.14
Keepe her for me, my more desire to breede.	Ovid's Elegies	2.19.2
And may repulse place for our wishes strike.	Ovid's Elegies	2.19.6
To pleasure me, for-bid me to corive with thee.	Ovid's Elegies	2.19.60
Small doores unfitting for large houses are.	Ovid's Elegies	3.1.40
For shame presse not her backe with thy hard knee.	Ovid's Elegies	3.2.24
For evermore thou shalt my mistris be.	Ovid's Elegies	3.2.62
For others faults, why do I losse receive?	Ovid's Elegies	3.3.16
For her ill-beautious Mother judgd to slaughter?	Ovid's Elegies	3.3.18
Mars girts his deadly sword on for my harme:	Ovid's Elegies	3.3.27
Slide in thy bounds, so shalt thou runne for ever.	Ovid's Elegies	3.5.20
For five score Nimphes, or more our flouds conteine.	Ovid's Elegies	3.5.64
men point at me for a whore,/Shame, that should make me blush,	Ovid's Elegies	3.5.77
But for thy merits I wish thee, white streame,	Ovid's Elegies	3.5.105
For bloudshed knighted, before me preferr'd.	Ovid's Elegies	3.7.10
And for a good verse drawe the first dart forth,	Ovid's Elegies	3.7.27
Tis well, if some wench for the poore remaine.	Ovid's Elegies	3.7.60
For me, she doth keeper, and husband feare,	Ovid's Elegies	3.7.63
And shaking sobbes his mouth for speeches beares.	Ovid's Elegies	3.8.12
And justly: for her praise why did I tell?	Ovid's Elegies	3.11.9
The bed is for lascivious toyings meete,	Ovid's Elegies	3.13.17
How small so ere, Ile you for greatest praise.	Ovid's Elegies	3.14.14
Whom young Apollo courted for her haire,	Hero and Leander	1.6
Where she should sit for men to gaze upon.	Hero and Leander	1.8
And there for honie, bees have sought in vaine,	Hero and Leander	1.23
She ware no gloves for neither sunne nor wind/Would burne or	Hero and Leander	1.27
for they tooke delite/To play upon those hands, they were so	Hero and Leander	1.29
Some say, for her the fairest Cupid pyn'd,	Hero and Leander	1.37
For whom succeeding times make greater mone.	Hero and Leander	1.54
To hazard more, than for the golden Fleece.	Hero and Leander	1.58
his/That leapt into the water for a kis/Of his owne shadow,	Hero and Leander	1.74
Was moov'd with him, and for his favour sought.	Hero and Leander	1.82
For in his lookes were all that men desire,	Hero and Leander	1.84
A brow for Love to banquet roiallye,	Hero and Leander	1.86
Leander, thou art made for amorous play:	Hero and Leander	1.88
(For his sake whom their goddesse held so deare,	Hero and Leander	1.92
For everie street like to a Firmament/Glistered with breathing	Hero and Leander	1.97
Eternall heaven to burne, for so it seem'd,	Hero and Leander	1.100
For like Sea-nimphs inveigling harmony,	Hero and Leander	1.105
For faithfull love will never turne to hate.	Hero and Leander	1.128
For know, that underneath this radiant floure,	Hero and Leander	1.145
And for his love Europa, bellowing loud,	Hero and Leander	1.149
Sylvanus weeping for the lovely boy/That now is turn'd into a	Hero and Leander	1.154
For will in us is over-rul'd by fate.	Hero and Leander	1.168
for both not us'de,/Are of like worth.	Hero and Leander	1.233
In time it will returne us two for one.	Hero and Leander	1.236
Base boullion for the stampes sake we allow,	Hero and Leander	1.265
Even so for mens impression do we you.	Hero and Leander	1.266
Seeke you for chastitie, immortall fame,	Hero and Leander	1.283
For thou in vowing chastitie, hast sworne/To rob her name and	Hero and Leander	1.304
As put thereby, yet might he hope for mo.	Hero and Leander	1.312
Yet for her sake whom you have vow'd to serve,	Hero and Leander	1.316
And yet I like them for the Orator.	Hero and Leander	1.340
For unawares (Come thither) from her slipt,	Hero and Leander	1.358
And wound them on his arme, and for her mourn'd.	Hero and Leander	1.376
prowd she was, (for loftie pride that dwels/In tow'red courts,	Hero and Leander	1.393
Than for the fire filcht by Prometheus;	Hero and Leander	1.438
sad and heavie cheare/Complaind to Cupid; Cupid for his sake,	Hero and Leander	1.441
For from the earth to heaven, is Cupid rais'd,	Hero and Leander	2.31
By being possest of him for whom she long'd:	Hero and Leander	2.36

FOR (cont.)
For hitherto hee did but fan the fire, ... Hero and Leander 2.41
T'is lost but once, and once lost, lost for ever. . . Hero and Leander 2.86
And red for anger that he stayd so long, ... Hero and Leander 2.89
Than he could saile, for incorporeal Fame, ... Hero and Leander 2.113
And for the same mildly rebuk't his sonne, ... Hero and Leander 2.137
For as a hote prowd horse highly disdaines, ... Hero and Leander 2.141
For here the stately azure pallace stood, ... Hero and Leander 2.165
For under water he was almost dead, ... Hero and Leander 2.170
As for his love, both earth and heaven pyn'd; . . . . Hero and Leander 2.196
He cald it in, for love made him repent. . . . . . Hero and Leander 2.210
As meaning to be veng'd for darting it. . . . . . Hero and Leander 2.212
To the rich Ocean for gifts he flies. . . . . . . Hero and Leander 2.224
She stayd not for her robes, but straight arose, . . . Hero and Leander 2.235
Where seeing a naked man, she scriecht for feare, . . . Hero and Leander 2.237
If not for love, yet love for pittie sake, ... Hero and Leander 2.247
For though the rising yv'rie mount he scal'd, ... Hero and Leander 2.273
For much it greev'd her that the bright day-light, . . . Hero and Leander 2.303
Fayre lined slippers for the cold: . . . . Passionate Shepherd 15
For thy delight each May-morning. . . . . Passionate Shepherd 22

FORAGE (See FORRAGE)

FORBADE
God forbade it indeed, but Faustus hath done it: . . . F1858 5.2.62 P Faust

FORBARE
Forbare no wanton words you there would speake, . . . Ovid's Elegies 3.13.25

FOR-BEARE
Faire Dames for-beare rewards for nights to crave, . . . Ovid's Elegies 1.10.47

FORBEARE
Ah foolish Dido to forbeare this long! . . . . . . Dido 5.1.160 Dido
Forbeare to levie armes against the king. . . . . . Edw 1.2.82 Queene
Faire Queene forbeare to angle for the fish, ... Edw 1.4.221 Mortmr
Yet stay a while, forbeare thy bloudie hande, ... Edw 5.5.75 Edward
Forbeare to hurt thy selfe in spoyling mee. . . . . Ovid's Elegies 1.2.50
Forbeare sweet wordes, and be your sport unpleasant. . . Ovid's Elegies 1.4.66
Forbeare to kindle vice by prohibition, ... Ovid's Elegies 3.4.11
If I should give, both would the house forbeare. . . . Ovid's Elegies 3.7.64
As in thy sacrifize we them forbeare? . . . . . . Ovid's Elegies 3.9.44
Gentle youth forbeare/To touch the sacred garments which I Hero and Leander 1.343

FOR-BID
To pleasure me, for-bid me to corive with thee. . . . Ovid's Elegies 2.19.60

FORBID (See also FORBOD)
Oh heaven forbid I should have such a thought. . . . . Jew 2.3.256 Barab
The heavens forbid your highnes such mishap. . . . . P 177 3.12 QnMarg
No, God forbid. . . . . Edw 5.2.99 Queene
Forbid not me to weepe, he was my father, ... Edw 5.6.34 King
O God forbid. . . . . F1857 5.2.61 AllSch
Forbid thine anger to procure my griefe. . . . . . Ovid's Elegies 2.7.14

FORBIDDEN
Since other meanes are all forbidden me, ... 1Tamb 5.1.288 Bajzth
things hidden)/Whence uncleane fowles are said to be forbidden. Ovid's Elegies 2.6.52
Even as the sicke desire forbidden drinke. . . . . . Ovid's Elegies 3.4.18

FORBIDS
Forbids all hope to harbour neere our hearts. . . . . Dido 1.2.16 Illion
I hope that that which love forbids me doe, ... Dido 5.1.170 Dido
Forbids you further liberty than this. . . . . . . 2Tamb 1.2.8 Almeda
Forbids the world to build it up againe. . . . . . . 2Tamb 3.2.18 Calyph
Forbids my mind to entertaine a thought/That tends to love, but 2Tamb 4.2.25 Olymp
Thy youth forbids such ease my kingly boy, ... 2Tamb 4.3.29 Tamb
Here lovely boies, what death forbids my life, ... 2Tamb 5.3.159 Tamb
The Canon Law forbids it, and the Priest/That makes it knowne, Jew 3.6.34 2Fryar
Turmoiles the coast, and enterance forbids; . . . . . Lucan, First Booke 409
or ist sleepe forbids thee heare,/Giving the windes my words Ovid's Elegies 1.6.41

FORBOD
When bad fates take good men, I am forbod, ... Ovid's Elegies 3.8.35

FORBORNE
Why are our pleasures by thy meanes forborne? . . . . Ovid's Elegies 3.9.4

FORC'D
Or els you shall be forc'd with slaverie. . . . . . . 1Tamb 1.2.256 Tamb
Or may be forc'd, to make me Emperour. . . . . . . 1Tamb 4.4.90 Tamb
Or els be sure thou shalt be forc'd with paines, ... 2Tamb 5.1.52 Therid
I must be forc'd to steale and compasse more. . . . . Jew 1.2.127 Barab
Which forc'd their hands divide united hearts: . . . . Jew 3.2.35 Govnr
I must be forc'd to give in evidence, ... Jew 4.1.186 Barab
A woman forc'd the Troyanes new to enter/Warres, just Latinus, Ovid's Elegies 2.12.21

FORCD
Or steeds might fal forcd with thick clouds approch. . . Ovid's Elegies 1.13.30

FORCE (See also FORST)
Or force her smile that hetherto hath frownd: . . . . Dido 1.1.88 Jupitr
Such force is farre from our unweaponed thoughts, . . . Dido 1.2.14 Illion
To force an hundred watchfull eyes to sleepe: . . . . Dido 2.1.146 Aeneas
And with maine force flung on a ring of pikes, ... Dido 2.1.196 Aeneas
Yet manhood would not serve, of force we fled, ... Dido 2.1.272 Aeneas
And therefore must of force. . . . . Dido 5.1.101 Aeneas
will flie (my Lords)/To rest secure against my brothers force. 1Tamb 1.1.178 Cosroe
Fearing the force of Boreas boistrous blasts. . . . . 1Tamb 2.4.5 Mycet
And dare the force of angrie Jupiter. . . . . 1Tamb 2.6.4 Cosroe
Now shalt thou feel the force of Turkish arms, ... 1Tamb 3.3.134 Bajzth
Where they shall meete, and joine their force in one, . . 1Tamb 3.3.257 Tamb
whom all kings/Of force must yeeld their crownes and Emperies: 1Tamb 5.1.481 Souldn
Whose triple Myter I did take by force, ... 2Tamb 1.3.189 Techel
and confound/The trustlesse force of those false Christians. 2Tamb 2.2.62 Orcan
the plaines/To spie what force comes to relieve the holde. 2Tamb 3.3.48 Techel
And we wil force him to the field hereafter. . . . . 2Tamb 4.1.102 Amyras

FORCE (cont.)			
Have greater operation and more force/Than Cynthias in the	2Tamb	4.2.29	Therid
Being caried thither by the cannons force,	2Tamb	5.1.66	Tamb
Captaine, the force of Tamburlaine is great,	2Tamb	5.2.42	Callap
But sons, this subject not of force enough,	2Tamb	5.3.168	Tamb
And Crownes come either by succession/Or urg'd by force; and	Jew	1.1.132	Barab
Captaine we know it, but our force is small.	Jew	2.2.34	Govnr
For when their hideous force inviron'd Rhodes,	Jew	2.2.48	Bosco
nay then I'le force my way;/And see, a staffe stands ready for	Jew	4.1.171	1Fryar
And with the Queene of England joyne my force,	P 801	16.15	Navrre
Your highnes needs not feare mine armies force,	P 857	17.52	Guise
He meanes to make us stoope by force of armes,	Edw	2.2.103	Lncstr
Might be of lesser force, and with the power/That he intendeth	Edw	2.4.43	Queene
When force to force is knit, and sword and gleave/In civill	Edw	4.4.5	Queene
Then I will carrie thee by force away.	Edw	5.2.112	Mortmr
That followes not <necessary> by force of argument, which	F 202	1.2.9	P Wagner
Such is the force of Magicke, and my spels.	F 259	1.3.31	Faust
Th'affrighted worlds force bent on publique spoile,	Lucan, First Booke		5
conquer all the earth, then turne thy force/Against thy selfe:	Lucan, First Booke		22
The burdened axes with thy force will bend;	Lucan, First Booke		57
men so strong/By land, and sea, no forreine force could ruine:	Lucan, First Booke		83
Why joine you force to share the world betwixt you?	Lucan, First Booke		88
Force mastered right, the strongest govern'd all.	Lucan, First Booke		177
What should I talke of mens corne reapt by force,	Lucan, First Booke		318
Lets use our tried force, they that now thwart right/In wars	Lucan, First Booke		349
chiefe leader of Rooms force,/So be I may be bold to speake a	Lucan, First Booke		360
not onely kisse/But force thee give him my stolne honey blisse.	Ovid's Elegies		1.4.64
Farre off be force, no fire to them may reach,	Ovid's Elegies		1.14.29
And waters force, force helping Gods to faile,	Ovid's Elegies		2.16.28
Since some faire one I should of force obey.	Ovid's Elegies		2.17.6
In vaine why flyest backe? force conjoynes us now:	Ovid's Elegies		3.2.19
Great flouds the force of it do often prove.	Ovid's Elegies		3.5.24
Seeing <When> in my prime my force is spent and done?	Ovid's Elegies		3.6.18
Wilt have me willing, or to love by force?	Ovid's Elegies		3.10.50
Such force and vertue hath an amorous looke.	Hero and Leander		1.166
God knowes I cannot force love, as you doe.	Hero and Leander		1.206
Maids are not woon by brutish force and might,	Hero and Leander		1.419
Mov'd by Loves force, unto ech other lep?	Hero and Leander		2.58
FORCED			
They shall be kept our forced followers,	1Tamb	1.2.66	Tamb
You must be forced from me ere you goe:	1Tamb	1.2.120	Tamb
Whence the wind blowes stil forced to and fro;	Lucan, First Booke		414
FORCELESSE			
Enough to swallow forcelesse Sigismond,	2Tamb	1.1.65	Orcan
FORCES			
And cause them to withdraw their forces home,	1Tamb	1.1.131	Menaph
Engins and munition/Exceed the forces of their martial men.	1Tamb	4.1.29	2Msngr
And save our forces for the hot assaults/Proud Tamburlaine	2Tamb	1.1.52	Gazell
To live secure, and keep his forces out,	2Tamb	5.1.16	Govnr
Their downfall is at hand, their forces downe,	Edw	1.4.18	Mortmr
FORCETH			
I must say so, paine forceth me complaine.	P 540	11.5	Charls
FORCIBLE			
Lookes so remorcefull, vowes so forcible,	Dido	2.1.156	Aeneas
FORCIBLY			
Yet shall thy life be forcibly bereaven.	Ovid's Elegies		3.8.38
FORD (See FOORD)			
FORDONE			
If watry Thetis had her childe fordone?	Ovid's Elegies		2.14.14
FORE			
Yea <I> all the wealth that our fore-fathers hid,	F 173	1.1.145	Cornel
O would in my fore-fathers tombe deepe layde,	Ovid's Elegies		3.5.73
FORE-FATHERS			
Yea <I> all the wealth that our fore-fathers hid,	F 173	1.1.145	Cornel
O would in my fore-fathers tombe deepe layde,	Ovid's Elegies		3.5.73
FOREGOTTEN			
and when thow thinkst I have foregotten this	Paris	ms20,p391	Guise
FOREHEAD (See also FORHEAD)			
I can reade, he for his forehead, she for her private study,	F App	p.233 16	P Robin
the time more short/Lay downe thy forehead in thy lap to snort.	Ovid's Elegies		2.2.24
FOREIGN (See FORRAIN, FORREINE, FORREN)			
FOREMOST (See FORMOST)			
FORESEE			
my spirit doth foresee/The utter ruine of thy men and thee.	1Tamb	4.3.59	Arabia
FORESEEING			
And follow your foreseeing starres in all;	Dido	4.3.32	Achat
FOREST (See FORREST)			
FORESTALL			
and so forestall his market, and set up your standing where you	P 809	17.4	P Souldr
FORESTALLE			
forestalle the markett and sett upe your standinge where you	Paris	ms 5,p390	P Souldr
FOR EVER			
For ever terme, the Perseans sepulchre,	2Tamb	3.5.19	Callap
And I will warrant Malta free for ever.	Jew	5.2.101	Barab
And so am I for ever miserable.	Edw	1.4.186	Queene
And therefore brother banish him for ever.	Edw	2.2.211	Kent
As Isabell could live with thee for ever.	Edw	2.4.60	Queene
And are for ever damn'd with Lucifer.	F 300	1.3.72	Mephst
Where we are tortur'd, and remaine for ever.	F 509	2.1.121	Mephst
Damb'd be this soule for ever, for this deed.	F1070	3.2.90	Pope
For ever be belov'd of Carolus.	F1211	4.1.57	Emper
Now am I a made man for ever.	F1477	4.4.21	P HrsCsr
the Kingdome of Joy, and must remaine in hell for ever.	F1846	5.2.50	P Faust

FOR EVER (cont.)			
Hell, [ah] <O> hell for ever.	F1846	5.2.50	P Faust
friends, what shall become of Faustus being in hell for ever?	F1847	5.2.51	P Faust
tell thee, we were for ever made by this doctor Faustus booke?	F App	p.234 1	P Robin
Now am I made man for ever, Ile not leave my horse for fortie:	F App	p.239 114	P HrsCsr
If men have Faith, Ile live with thee for ever.	Ovid's Elegies		1.3.16
Nor servile water shalt thou drinke for ever.	Ovid's Elegies		1.6.26
The fame that verse gives doth for ever last.	Ovid's Elegies		1.10.62
Slide in thy bounds, so shalt thou runne for ever.	Ovid's Elegies		3.5.20
T'is lost but once, and once lost, lost for ever.	Hero and Leander		2.86
FOREWARNE			
My Lord, I must forewarne your Majesty,	F1248	4.1.94	Faust
Now I forewarne, unlesse to keepe her stronger,	Ovid's Elegies		2.19.47
FORFEIT			
To see a Phrigian far fet [on] <o'er> <forfeit to> the sea,	Dido	3.3.64	Iarbus
wait upon thy soule; the time is come/Which makes it forfeit.	F1803	5.2.7	Lucifr
FORFEITING			
And with extorting, cozening, forfeiting,	Jew	2.3.191	Barab
FORG'D			
contracted unto Abigall; [he] forg'd a counterfeit challenge.	Jew	5.1.29	P Ithimr
As that the double Cannons forg'd of brasse,	F 820	3.1.42	Mephst
FORGED			
I will not say that by a forged challenge they met.	Jew	4.1.45	P 2Fryar
He forged the daring challenge made them fight.	Jew	5.1.47	Govnr
FORGET (See also FOREGOTTEN)			
Els should I much forget my self, my Lord.	1Tamb	5.1.500	Zenoc
Seduced Daughter, Goe, forget not.	Jew	1.2.359	Barab
Forget me, see me not, and so be gone.	Jew	1.2.363	Barab
That can so soone forget an injury.	Jew	2.3.19	Barab
Or if I live, let me forget my selfe.	Edw	5.1.111	Edward
My gracious Lord, you doe forget your selfe,	F1258	4.1.104	Faust
But till the [keeper] <keepes> went forth, I forget not,	Ovid's Elegies		3.1.55
FORGETFULL			
To too forgetfull of thine owne affayres,	Dido	5.1.30	Hermes
FORGETS			
And when this favour Isabell forgets,	Edw	1.4.297	Queene
FORGETST			
forgetst thou I am he/That with the Cannon shooke Vienna	2Tamb	1.1.86	Orcan
Forgetst thou that I sent a shower of dartes/Mingled with	2Tamb	1.1.91	Orcan
Forgetst thou, that to have me raise my siege,	2Tamb	1.1.98	Orcan
FORGETTING			
Forgetting both his want of strength and hands,	Dido	2.1.252	Aeneas
FORGIVE			
and thou hast, breake my head with it, I'le forgive thee.	Jew	2.3.112	P Barab
O God forgive my sins.	P 303	5.30	Admral
Forgive my thought, for having such a thought,	Edw	5.5.83	Edward
God forgive me, he speakes Dutch fustian:	F App	p.231 72	P Clown
good divel forgive me now, and Ile never rob thy Library more.	F App	p.235 31	P Robin
Forgive her gratious Gods this one delict,	Ovid's Elegies		2.14.43
FORGIVEN			
Good my Lord, let him be forgiven for once,	2Tamb	4.1.101	Amyras
FORGIVENES			
Then pray to God, and aske forgivenes of the King.	P1004	19.74	P 2Mur
Nor will I aske forgivenes of the King.	P1006	19.76	Guise
FORGOE			
As negligently to forgoe so much/Without provision for	Jew	1.2.242	Barab
FORGOT			
Something it was that now I have forgot.	Dido	3.4.30	Dido
me, for I forgot/That yong Ascanius lay with me this night:	Dido	4.4.31	Dido
Hast thou forgot how many neighbour kings/Were up in armes, for	Dido	5.1.141	Dido
Great injuries are not so soone forgot.	Jew	1.2.208	Barab
Your selves shall see it shall not be forgot:	Jew	5.2.71	Barab
Is all my love forgot which helde thee deare?	P 684	13.28	Guise
Pardon me sweet, I forgot my selfe.	Edw	2.2.230	Edward
Ha, ha, ha, dost heare him Dick, he has forgot his legge.	F1629	4.6.72	P Carter
And by long rest forgot to manage armes,	Lucan, First Booke		131
FORGOTTEN			
He hath forgotten me, stay, I am his mother.	Edw	5.6.90	Queene
on the score, but say nothing, see if she have forgotten me.	F1512	4.5.8	P Robin
Ha' you forgotten me?	F1664	4.6.107	P Robin
FORHEAD			
The man that in the forhead of his fortune,	1Tamb	2.1.3	Cosroe
FORKED			
Sharpe forked arrowes light upon thy horse:	1Tamb	5.1.217	Bajzth
Hell and the Furies forked haire,	F1000	3.2.20	Mephst
Il'e naile huge forked hornes, and let them hang/Within the	F1380	4.2.56	Benvol
FORKES			
On burning forkes: their bodies [boyle] <broyle> in lead.	F1912	5.2.116	BdAngl
FORLORNE			
Thy fatall birth-day, forlorne Barabas;	Jew	1.2.192	Barab
Then let her live abandond and forlorne.	Edw	1.4.298	Queene
Complaines, that thou hast left her all forlorne.	Edw	2.2.173	Lncstr
Houses not dwelt in, are with filth forlorne.	Ovid's Elegies		1.8.52
FORMALL			
Spencer, thou knowest I hate such formall toies,	Edw	2.1.44	Baldck
Through regular and formall puritie.	Hero and Leander		1.308
FORME (See also FOURME)			
Whose lookes set forth no mortall forme to view,	Dido	1.1.189	Aeneas
Than when she gave eternall Chaos forme,	2Tamb	3.4.76	Techel
A Forme not meet to give that subject essence,	2Tamb	4.1.112	Tamb
And I reduc'd it into better forme.	P 407	7.47	Ramus
Here is the forme of Gavestons exile:	Edw	1.4.1	Lncstr
And hath a speciall gift to forme a verbe.	Edw	2.1.55	Spencr

FORME (cont.)			
we must now performe/The forme of Faustus fortunes, good or	F 8	Prol.8	1Chor
First, that Faustus may be a spirit in forme and substance.	F 485	2.1.97	P Faust
at all times, in what shape [or] <and> forme soever he please.	F 492	2.1.104	P Faust
Such is his forme as may with thine compare,	Ovid's Elegies		1.8.33
Now inward faults thy outward forme disgrace.	Ovid's Elegies		1.10.14
Good forme there is, yeares apt to play togither,	Ovid's Elegies		2.3.13
And in the forme of beds weele strowe soft sand,	Ovid's Elegies		2.11.47
A decent forme, thinne robe, a lovers looke,	Ovid's Elegies		3.1.9
Her foote was small: her footes forme is most fit:	Ovid's Elegies		3.3.7
Or capable of any forme at all.	Hero and Leander		1.274
FORMER			
To make us live unto our former heate,	Dido	1.1.160	Achat
that in former age/Hast bene the seat of mightie Conquerors,	1Tamb	1.1.6	Cosroe
then Cosroe raign/And governe Persea in her former pomp:	1Tamb	2.5.19	Cosroe
Now will i gratify your former good,	1Tamb	2.5.30	Cosroe
The former triumphes of our mightines,	1Tamb	5.1.253	Zabina
And of my former riches rests no more/But bare remembrance;	Jew	2.1.9	Barab
And all my former time was spent in vaine:	P 986	19.56	Guise
againe I will confirme/The <My> former vow I made to Lucifer.	F1750	5.1.77	Faust
Undaunted though her former guide be chang'd.	Lucan, First Booke		50
He liv'd secure boasting his former deeds,	Lucan, First Booke		135
And sodainly her former colour chang'd,	Hero and Leander		1.359
FORMOST			
Let the sad captive formost with lockes spred/On her white	Ovid's Elegies		1.7.39
FORNICATION			
Fornication? but that was in another Country:	Jew	4.1.41	Barab
FORRAGE			
Two thousand horse shall forrage up and downe,	1Tamb	3.1.61	Bajzth
FORRAIN			
Yet would we not be brav'd with forrain power,	1Tamb	3.1.13	Bajzth
Whose great atchivements in our forrain warre,	Edw	1.4.360	Edward
FORRAINE			
And seeke a forraine land calde Italy:	Dido	4.4.98	Dido
had the Turkish Emperour/So great a foile by any forraine foe.	1Tamb	3.3.235	Bajzth
Our love of honor loth to be enthral'd/To forraine powers, and	1Tamb	5.1.36	Govnr
That livest by forraine exhibition?	P 842	17.37	Eprnon
In making forraine warres and civile broiles.	P1029	19.99	King
What forraine prince sends thee embassadors?	Edw	2.2.170	Lncstr
And tell the secrets of all forraine Kings:	F 114	1.1.86	Faust
And fetch the treasure of all forraine wrackes:	F 172	1.1.144	Cornel
nor Hanniball/Art cause, no forraine foe could so afflict us,	Lucan, First Booke		31
This need no forraine proofe, nor far fet story:	Lucan, First Booke		94
Had forraine wars ill thriv'd; or wrathful France/Pursu'd us	Lucan, First Booke		308
When Romans are besieg'd by forraine foes,	Lucan, First Booke		513
FORREINE			
men so strong/By land, and sea, no forreine force could ruine:	Lucan, First Booke		83
FORREN			
Set in a forren place, and straight from thence,	Hero and Leander		2.119
FORREST			
And every beast the forrest doth send forth,	Dido	1.1.161	Achat
In number more than are the quyvering leaves/Of Idas forrest,	2Tamb	3.5.6	2Msngr
Unto the forrest gentle Mortimer,	Edw	1.2.47	Queene
the forrest Deare being strucke/Runnes to an herbe that closeth	Edw	5.1.9	Edward
FORRESTS			
Where Woods and Forrests goe in goodly greene,	Jew	4.2.93	Ithimr
FORSAKE			
Too cruell, why wilt thou forsake me thus?	Dido	1.1.243	Aeneas
If he forsake me not, I never dye,	Dido	4.4.121	Dido
Forsake thy king and do but joine with me/And we will triumph	1Tamb	1.2.172	Tamb
Wilt thou forsake mee too in my distresse,	Jew	1.2.358	Barab
But to forsake you, in whose gratious lookes/The blessednes of	Edw	1.4.120	Gavstn
When I forsake thee, death seaze on my heart,	Edw	2.1.64	Neece
Th'ad best betimes forsake [them] <thee> and their trains,	Edw	3.1.202	Lncstr
The king will nere forsake his flatterers.	Edw	4.2.60	Mortmr
Rent sphere of heaven, and fier forsake thy orbe,	Edw	4.7.102	Spencr
Loe country Gods, and [known] <know> bed to forsake,	Ovid's Elegies		2.11.7
Dishonest love my wearied brest forsake,	Ovid's Elegies		3.10.2
FORSAKEN			
If that all glorie hath forsaken thee,	Dido	5.1.36	Hermes
whom/The gravest, Aruns, dwelt in forsaken Leuca <or Luna>,	Lucan, First Booke		585
FORSLOWD			
they had bestowde/This <The> benefite, which lewdly I forslowd:	Ovid's Elegies		3.6.46
FORSLOWE			
Forslowe no time, sweet Lancaster lets march.	Edw	2.4.40	Warwck
FORSOOKE			
Whose fading weale of victorie forsooke,	Dido	1.2.15	Illion
They by Lemannus nooke forsooke their tents;	Lucan, First Booke		397
So long they be, since she her faith forsooke.	Ovid's Elegies		3.3.4
And Phoebus had forsooke my worke begun.	Ovid's Elegies		3.11.18
Is said to have attempted flight forsooke.	Ovid's Elegies		3.12.20
FORSOOTH			
I will forsooth, Mistris.	Jew	3.3.35	P Ithimr
And he forsooth must goe and preach in Germany:	P 392	7.32	Guise
And yet she beares a face of love forsooth:	Edw	4.6.14	Kent
FORST			
And I alas, was forst to let her lye.	Dido	2.1.279	Aeneas
When I was forst to leave my Gaveston.	Edw	1.4.318	Edward
He wounds with love, and forst them equallie,	Hero and Leander		1.445
FOR-SWEARE			
Nor, if thou couzenst one, dread to for-sweare,	Ovid's Elegies		1.8.85
FORSWORE			
her selfe she hath forswore,/And yet remaines the face she had	Ovid's Elegies		3.3.1

FOR'T			
time to make collection/Amongst the Inhabitants of Malta for't.	Jew	1.2.21	Govnr
For I will seeme offended with thee for't.	Jew	1.2.303	Barab
Give me a Reame of paper, we'll have a kingdome of gold for't.	Jew	4.2.115	P Ithimr
his villany/He will tell all he knowes and I shall dye for't.	Jew	4.3.65	Barab
FORT			
Besiege a fort, to undermine a towne,	2Tamb	3.2.60	Tamb
Whereas the Fort may fittest be assailde,	2Tamb	3.2.66	Tamb
from every flanke/May scoure the outward curtaines of the Fort,	2Tamb	3.2.80	Tamb
shall raise a hill/Of earth and fagots higher than thy Fort,	2Tamb	3.3.22	Therid
Rifling this Fort, devide in equall shares:	2Tamb	3.4.89	Therid
As he had hope to scale the beauteous fort,	Hero and Leander		2.16
Defend the fort, and keep the foe-man out.	Hero and Leander		2.272
FORTH (See also FOORTH)			
See how the night Ulysses-like comes forth,	Dido	1.1.70	Venus
Are drawne by darknes forth Astraeus tents.	Dido	1.1.73	Venus
From forth her ashes shall advance her head,	Dido	1.1.94	Jupitr
Yet shall the aged Sunne shed forth his [haire] <aire>,	Dido	1.1.159	Achat
And every beast the forrest doth send forth,	Dido	1.1.161	Achat
Whose lookes set forth no mortall forme to view,	Dido	1.1.189	Aeneas
Who driven by warre from forth my native world,	Dido	1.1.217	Aeneas
Exild forth Europe and wide Asia both,	Dido	1.1.229	Aeneas
Beates forth my senses from this troubled soule,	Dido	2.1.116	Aeneas
And therewithall he calde false Sinon forth,	Dido	2.1.143	Aeneas
Neoptolemus/Setting his speare upon the ground, leapt forth,	Dido	2.1.184	Aeneas
Yet flung I forth, and desperate of my life,	Dido	2.1.210	Aeneas
But I will teare thy eyes fro forth thy head,	Dido	3.2.34	Venus
As these thy protestations doe paint forth,	Dido	3.2.54	Venus
And bring forth mightie Kings to Carthage towne,	Dido	3.2.75	Juno
Darts forth her light to Lavinias shoare.	Dido	3.2.84	Venus
This day they both a hunting forth will ride/Into these woods,	Dido	3.2.87	Juno
And rowse the light foote Deere from forth their laire?	Dido	3.3.31	Dido
That calles my soule from forth his living seate,	Dido	3.4.53	Dido
Kind clowdes that sent forth such a curteous storme,	Dido	3.4.55	Dido
That can call them forth when as she please,	Dido	4.1.4	Iarbus
Behold where both of them come forth the Cave.	Dido	4.1.16	Anna
Come forth the Cave: can heaven endure this sight?	Dido	4.1.17	Iarbus
Come servants, come bring forth the Sacrifize,	Dido	4.2.1	Iarbus
And all the fruites that plentie els sends forth,	Dido	4.2.15	Iarbus
Achates come forth, Sergestus, Illioneus,	Dido	4.3.13	Aeneas
To stay my Fleete from loosing forth the Bay:	Dido	4.3.26	Aeneas
Banish that ticing dame from forth your mouth,	Dido	4.3.31	Achat
Will Dido raise old Priam forth his grave,	Dido	4.3.39	Illion
Faire sister Anna leade my lover forth,	Dido	4.4.65	Dido
These were the instruments that launcht him forth,	Dido	4.4.150	Dido
Bring him forth, and let us know if the towne be ransackt.	1Tamb	5.1.194	P Tamb
If griefe, our murthered harts have straind forth blood.	2Tamb	2.4.123	Therid
Have speciall care that no man sally forth/Till you shall heare	Jew	5.4.2	Govnr
Then Barabas breath forth thy latest fate,	Jew	5.5.78	Barab
Now come thou forth and play thy tragick part,	P 85	2.28	Guise
Yet Caesar shall goe forth.	P 996	19.66	Guise
To hatch forth treason gainst their naturall Queene?	P1032	19.102	King
And roote Valoys his line from forth of France,	P1113	21.7	Dumain
now breaks the kings hate forth,/And he confesseth that he	Edw	1.4.193	Queene
Clarke of the crowne, direct our warrant forth,	Edw	1.4.369	Edward
Come forth. Art thou as resolute as thou wast?	Edw	5.4.22	Mortmr
[Whose] <The> streetes straight forth, and paved with finest	F 789	3.1.11	Faust
Go forth-with to our holy Consistory,	F 882	3.1.104	Pope
Go presently, and bring a banket forth,	F 977	3.1.199	Pope
Unlesse you bring them forth immediatly:	F1031	3.2.51	Pope
I'le wing my selfe and forth-with flie amaine/Unto my Faustus	F1136	3.3.49	Mephst
[They put forth questions of Astrologie],	F1146	3.3.59A	3Chor
[Now is his fame spread forth in every land],	F1149	3.3.62A	3Chor
Her lips sucke <suckes> forth my soule, see where it flies.	F1771	5.1.98	Faust
Gush forth bloud in stead of teares, yea life and soule:	F1851	5.2.55	P Faust
That when you vomite forth into the aire,	F1954	5.2.158	Faust
forth as by art and power of my spirit I am able to performe.	F App	p.237 38	P Faust
His body (not his boughs) send forth a shade;	Lucan, First Booke		141
Filling the world, leapes out and throwes forth fire,	Lucan, First Booke		154
Souse downe the wals, and make a passage forth:	Lucan, First Booke		296
For saving of a Romaine Citizen,/Stept forth, and cryde:	Lucan, First Booke		360
even nowe when youthfull bloud/Pricks forth our lively bodies,	Lucan, First Booke		364
heady rout/That in chain'd troupes breake forth at every port;	Lucan, First Booke		489
Lightning in silence, stole forth without clouds,	Lucan, First Booke		531
such and more strange/Blacke night brought forth in secret:	Lucan, First Booke		579
Mules loth'd issue)/To be cut forth and cast in dismall fiers:	Lucan, First Booke		590
In spite of thee, forth will thy <thine> arrowes flie,	Ovid's Elegies		1.2.45
Forth-with Love came, no darke night-flying spright/Nor hands	Ovid's Elegies		1.6.13
the wench forth send,/Her valiant lover followes without end.	Ovid's Elegies		1.9.9
The sonne slew her, that forth to meete him went,	Ovid's Elegies		1.10.51
give her my writ/But see that forth-with shee peruseth it.	Ovid's Elegies		1.11.16
Going out againe passe forth the dore more wisely/And som-what	Ovid's Elegies		1.12.5
And birdes send forth shrill notes from everie bow.	Ovid's Elegies		1.13.8
Let him goe forth knowne, that unknowne did enter,	Ovid's Elegies		2.2.20
Duld with much beating slowly forth doth passe.	Ovid's Elegies		2.7.16
No flowing waves with drowned ships forth poured,	Ovid's Elegies		2.16.25
Nor of thee Macer that resoundst forth armes,	Ovid's Elegies		2.18.35
But till the [keeper] <keepes> went forth, I forget not,	Ovid's Elegies		3.1.55
And forth the gay troupes on swift horses flie.	Ovid's Elegies		3.2.78
Came forth a mother, though a maide there put.	Ovid's Elegies		3.4.22
And for a good verse drawe the first dart forth,	Ovid's Elegies		3.7.27
Faire-fac'd Iulus, he went forth thy court.	Ovid's Elegies		3.8.14
Comes forth her [unkeembd] <unkeembe> locks a sunder tearing.	Ovid's Elegies		3.8.52

FORTH (cont.)
I saw when forth a tyred lover went, ... Ovid's Elegies 3.10.13
The wench by my fault is set forth to sell. . . . Ovid's Elegies 3.11.10
White Heifers by glad people forth are led, . . . Ovid's Elegies 3.12.13
How such a Poet could you bring forth, sayes, . . . Ovid's Elegies 3.14.13
Breath'd darkenesse forth (darke night is Cupids day). . Hero and Leander 1.191

FORTH-WITH
Go forth-with to our holy Consistory, ... F 882 3.1.104 Pope
I'le wing my selfe and forth-with flie amaine/Unto my Faustus F1136 3.3.49 Mephst
Forth-with Love came, no darke night-flying spright/Nor hands Ovid's Elegies 1.6.13
give her my writ/But see that forth-with shee peruseth it. Ovid's Elegies 1.11.16

FORTIE
Upon mine owne free-hold within fortie foot of the gallowes, Jew 4.2.16 P Pilia
for you to come within fortie foot of the place of execution, F 211 1.2.18 P Wagner
Now am I made man for ever, Ile not leave my horse for fortie: F App p.239 115 P HrsCsr
has purg'd me of fortie Dollers, I shall never see them more: F App p.240 129 P HrsCsr
and have my fortie dollers againe, or Ile make it the dearest F App p.240 136 P HrsCsr
Fustian, fortie dollers, fortie dollers for a bottle of hey. F App p.241 149 P HrsCsr
O Lord sir, let me goe, and Ile give you fortie dollers more. F App p.241 158 P HrsCsr
his labour; wel, this tricke shal cost him fortie dollers more. F App p.241 166 P Faust

FORTIFI'D
And see that Malta be well fortifi'd; . . . . . Jew 5.1.2 Govnr

FORTIFIE
Then next, the way to fortifie your men, ... 2Tamb 3.2.62 Tamb
So, now away and fortifie the Towne. . . . . . Jew 5.1.60 Govnr

FORTITUDE
Learne thou of Faustus manly fortitude, ... F 313 1.3.85 Faust

FORTRESSE
And make a Fortresse in the raging waves, ... 2Tamb 3.2.88 Tamb

FORTUNA
Major sum quam cui possit fortuna nocere. . . . . Edw 5.4.69 Mortmr

FORTUNATE
My mind presageth fortunate successe, ... 1Tamb 4.3.58 Arabia
to as high a pitch/In this our strong and fortunate encounter. 2Tamb 3.1.31 Callap
In peace triumphant, fortunate in warres. . . . . Edw 3.1.33 SpncrP
As thou art faire, would thou wert fortunate, . . . Ovid's Elegies 1.8.27

FORTUNE
But first in bloud must his good fortune bud, ... Dido 1.1.86 Jupitr
Fortune hath favord thee what ere thou be, ... Dido 1.1.231 Venus
Thy fortune may be greater then thy birth, ... Dido 2.1.90 Dido
Heres to thy better fortune and good starres. . . . Dido 2.1.98 Dido
Lord of my fortune, but my fortunes turnd, ... Dido 2.1.235 Aeneas
We two as friends one fortune will devide: . . . . Dido 3.2.55 Venus
Since Fortune gives you opportunity, ... 1Tamb 1.1.124 Menaph
Such hope, such fortune have the thousand horse. . . . 1Tamb 1.2.118 Tamb
The man that in the forhead of his fortune, ... 1Tamb 2.1.3 Cosroe
Nature doth strive with Fortune and his stars, . . . 1Tamb 2.1.33 Cosroe
Proud is his fortune if we pierce it not. . . . . 1Tamb 2.1.44 Cosroe
Fortune her selfe dooth sit upon our Crests. . . . 1Tamb 2.2.73 Meandr
Betraide by fortune and suspitious love, ... 1Tamb 3.2.66 Agidas
Alas (poore Turke) his fortune is to weake, ... 1Tamb 3.3.6 Tamb
Thou, by the fortune of this damned [foile] <soile>. . 1Tamb 3.3.213 Bajzth
no Fortune, nor no hope of end/To our infamous monstrous 1Tamb 5.1.240 Zabina
Of earthly fortune, and respect of pitie, ... 1Tamb 5.1.365 Zenoc
Your love hath fortune so at his command, ... 1Tamb 5.1.373 Anippe
Nor fortune keep them selves from victory. . . . . 1Tamb 5.1.406 Arabia
Nor he but Fortune that hath made him great. . . . 2Tamb 1.1.60 Orcan
That in the fortune of their overthrow, ... 2Tamb 2.1.24 Fredrk
Tis but the fortune of the wars my Lord, ... 2Tamb 2.3.31 Gazell
But that proud Fortune, who hath followed long/The martiall 2Tamb 3.1.27 Callap
That treadeth Fortune underneath his feete, ... 2Tamb 3.4.52 Therid
No, no Amyras, tempt not Fortune so, ... 2Tamb 4.1.86 Tamb
taskes a while/And take such fortune as your fellowes felt. 2Tamb 5.1.137 Tamb
His fortune greater, and the victories/Wherewith he hath so 2Tamb 5.2.43 Callap
Thus trowles our fortune in by land and Sea, ... Jew 1.1.103 Barab
And all good fortune wait on Calymath. . . . . . Jew 1.2.33 Govnr
Now that my fathers fortune were so good/As but to be about Jew 2.1.31 Abigal
My gold, my fortune, my felicity; . . . . . . Jew 2.1.48 Barab
May all good fortune follow Calymath. . . . . . Jew 5.2.21 Barab
and let due praise be given/Neither to Fate nor Fortune, but to Jew 5.5.124 Govnr
And so they shall, if fortune speed my will, ... P 601 12.14 King
And there abide till fortune call thee home. . . . . Edw 1.4.126 Edward
On whose good fortune Spencers hope depends. . . . Edw 2.1.11 Spencr
Looke for no other fortune wretch then death, . . . Edw 2.5.17 Lncstr
Mortimers hope surmounts his fortune farre. . . . . Edw 3.1.259 Mortmr
I rue my lords ill fortune, but alas, ... Edw 4.6.64 Queene
Base fortune, now I see, that in thy wheele/There is a point, Edw 5.6.59 Mortmr
Whose fiendfull fortune may exhort the wise/Onely to wonder at F2006 5.3.24 4Chor
share our Empire, fortune that made Roome/Governe the earth, Lucan, First Booke 109
Urging his fortune, trusting in the gods, ... Lucan, First Booke 149
When fortune made us lords of all, wealth flowed, . . . Lucan, First Booke 161
Hence leagues, and covenants; Fortune thee I follow, . . Lucan, First Booke 228
But gods and fortune prickt him to this war, ... Lucan, First Booke 265
But though this night thy fortune be to trie it, . . . Ovid's Elegies 1.4.69
And brings good fortune, a rich lover plants/His love on thee, Ovid's Elegies 1.8.31
Nor in my act hath fortune mingled chance, ... Ovid's Elegies 2.12.15
What should I do with fortune that nere failes me? . . . Ovid's Elegies 2.19.7

FORTUNES
And so I leave thee to thy fortunes lot, ... Dido 1.1.238 Venus
For though my birth be great, my fortunes meane, . . . Dido 2.1.88 Aeneas
Lord of my fortune, but my fortunes turnd, ... Dido 2.1.235 Aeneas
Whose golden fortunes clogd with courtly ease, . . . Dido 4.3.8 Aeneas
And then applaud his fortunes if you please. . . . . 1Tamb Prol.8 Prolog

FORTUNES (cont.)			
And with my hand turne Fortunes wheel about,	1Tamb	1.2.175	Tamb
And well his merits show him to be made/His Fortunes maister,	1Tamb	2.1.36	Cosroe
In thy approoved Fortunes all my hope,	1Tamb	2.3.2	Cosroe
And let my Fortunes and my valour sway,	1Tamb	2.3.11	Tamb
the cursed object/Whose Fortunes never mastered her griefs:	1Tamb	5.1.414	Zenoc
But here these kings that on my fortunes wait,	1Tamb	5.1.490	Tamb
wilt thou so defame/The hatefull fortunes of thy victory,	2Tamb	4.3.78	Orcan
Well, and how fortunes that he came not?	Edw	3.1.113	Edward
And shake off all our fortunes equallie?	Edw	4.2.20	SrJohn
Who now makes Fortunes wheele turne as he please,	Edw	5.2.53	Mortmr
we must now performe/The forme of Faustus fortunes, good or	F 8	Prol.8	1Chor
FORTY (See also FORTIE)			
Our army will be forty thousand strong,	1Tamb	2.1.61	Cosroe
Came forty thousand warlike foot and horse,	2Tamb	3.5.38	Orcan
yet not appeare/In forty houres after it is tane.	Jew	3.4.72	Barab
I beseech your Worship accept of these forty Dollors.	F1457	4.4.1	P HrsCsr
go rouse him, and make him give me my forty Dollors againe.	F1488	4.4.32	P HrsCsr
and the Horse-courser a bundle of hay for his forty Dollors.	F1497	4.4.41	P Faust
and he would by no meanes sell him under forty Dollors; so sir,	F1537	4.5.33	P HrsCsr
I have brought you forty dollers for your horse.	F App	p.239 101	P HrsCsr
FORWARD			
Yea little sonne, are you so forward now?	Dido	3.3.34	Dido
When other men prease forward for renowne:	1Tamb	1.1.84	Mycet
We wil Techelles, forward then ye Jades:	2Tamb	4.3.97	Tamb
The rest forward with execution,	2Tamb	5.1.124	Tamb
And so lets forward to the Massacre.	P 330	5.57	Guise
not discourage/Your friends that are so forward in your aide.	Edw	4.2.70	Queene
This noble gentleman, forward in armes,	Edw	4.2.76	Mortmr
Sound trumpets my lord and forward let us martch,	Edw	4.4.28	SrJohn
Go forward Faustus in that famous Art/Wherein all natures	F 101	1.1.73	BdAngl
Forward, and backward, Anagramatis'd <and Agramithist>:	F 237	1.3.9	Faust
Go forward Faustus in that famous Art.	F 403	2.1.15	BdAngl
Forward and backward, to curse Faustus to hell.	F1075	3.2.95	Faust
Whose deepnesse doth intice such forward wits,	F2008	5.3.26	4Chor
Forward and backward, to curse Faustus to hell.	F App	p.232 26	Faust
That to deceits it may me forward pricke.	Ovid's Elegies		2.19.44
FORWARDNES			
cause sweare we to him/All homage, fealtie and forwardnes,	Edw	4.4.20	Mortmr
FORWARDS			
Backeward and forwards nere five thousand leagues.	2Tamb	5.3.144	Tamb
FOSTER			
Which I Pelignis foster-child have framde,	Ovid's Elegies		3.14.3
FOSTER-CHILD			
Which I Pelignis foster-child have framde,	Ovid's Elegies		3.14.3
FOUGHT			
In whose defence he fought so valiantly:	Dido	2.1.119	Dido
and had not we/Fought manfully, I had not told this tale:	Dido	2.1.271	Aeneas
footmen that have serv'd/In two set battels fought in Grecia:	1Tamb	3.3.19	Bassoe
That never fought but had the victorie:	1Tamb	3.3.153	Tamb
Each man a crown? why kingly fought ifaith.	1Tamb	3.3.216	Tamb
The field wherin this battaile shall be fought,	2Tamb	3.5.18	Callap
I smile to think, how when this field is fought,	2Tamb	3.5.165	Techel
Where are my common souldiers now that fought/So Lion-like upon	2Tamb	4.3.67	Tamb
then we [luft] <left>, and [tackt] <tooke>, and fought at ease:	Jew	2.2.14	Bosco
They fought it out, and not a man surviv'd/To bring the	Jew	2.2.50	Bosco
Oh bravely fought, and yet they thrust not home.	Jew	3.2.5	Barab
So fought not they that fought in Edwards right.	Edw	4.6.72	SpncrP
And cruel field, nere burning Aetna fought:	Lucan, First Booke		43
Few battailes fought with prosperous successe/May bring her	Lucan, First Booke		285
One sweares his troupes of daring horsemen fought/Upon Mevanias	Lucan, First Booke		469
To have this skirmish fought, let it suffice thee.	Ovid's Elegies		2.13.28
FOUGHTEN			
That I have sent from sundry foughten fields,	1Tamb	5.1.466	Tamb
FOULD			
Ajax, maister of the seven-fould shield,/Butcherd the flocks he	Ovid's Elegies		1.7.7
FOULDED			
The rest we feare are foulded in the flouds.	Dido	1.2.31	Cloan
The sailes of foulded Lawne, where shall be wrought/The warres	Dido	3.1.124	Dido
FOULDING			
Foulding his hand in hers, and joyntly both/Beating their	Dido	2.1.227	Aeneas
FOULE (Homograph; See also FOWLE)			
Yes, and Iarbus foule and favourles.	Dido	3.1.64	Anna
But ere I die those foule Idolaters/Shall make me bonfires with	1Tamb	3.3.239	Bajzth
Faire is too foule an Epithite for thee,	1Tamb	5.1.136	Tamb
And for all blot of foule inchastity,	1Tamb	5.1.486	Tamb
Stampt with the princely Foule that in her wings/Caries the	2Tamb	1.1.100	Orcan
Christians death/And scourge their foule blasphemous Paganisme?	2Tamb	2.1.53	Fredrk
And all with faintnesse and for foule disgrace,	2Tamb	2.4.5	Tamb
No sooner is it up, but thers a foule,	Edw	2.2.26	Lncstr
The life of thee shall salve this foule disgrace.	Edw	2.2.83	Gavstn
hands of mine/Shall not be guiltie of so foule a crime.	Edw	5.1.99	Edward
And cleare my bodie from foule excrements.	Edw	5.3.26	Edward
Thou soone shouldst see me quit my foule disgrace.	F1356	4.2.32	Benvol
goe and make cleane our bootes which lie foule upon our handes,	F App	p.234 33	P Robin
To hoarse scrich-owles foule shadowes it allowes,	Ovid's Elegies		1.12.19
Foule dust, from her faire body, go away.	Ovid's Elegies		3.2.42
And in thy foule deepe waters thicke thou [gushest] <rushest>.	Ovid's Elegies		3.5.8
Either she was foule, or her attire was bad,	Ovid's Elegies		3.6.1
FOULES			
Now shall his barbarous body be a pray/To beasts and foules,	2Tamb	2.3.15	Orcan
keepe his trunke/Amidst these plaines, for Foules to pray upon.	2Tamb	2.3.39	Orcan
The Foules shall eate, for never sepulchre/Shall grace that	2Tamb	5.2.17	Amasia

FOULES (cont.)			
that knew/The hearts of beasts, and flight of wandring foules;	Lucan, First Booke	587	
FOULY			
Now am I cleane, or rather fouly out of the way.	Jew	4.2.47	P Ithimr
olde swords/With ugly teeth of blacke rust fouly scarr'd:	Lucan, First Booke	245	
FOUND			
And rost our new found victuals on this shoare.	Dido	1.1.168	Aeneas
Tell me deare love, how found you out this Cave?	Dido	3.4.3	Dido
But now that I have found what to effect,	Dido	3.4.37	Dido
now have I found a meane/To rid me from these thoughts of	Dido	5.1.272	Dido
Til fire and sword have found them at a bay.	2Tamb	3.2.151	Tamb
And Moores, in whom was never pitie found,	2Tamb	3.4.20	Olymp
Found in the Temples of that Mahomet,	2Tamb	5.1.175	Tamb
And here behold (unseene) where I have found/The gold, the	Jew	2.1.22	Abigal
Come and receive the Treasure I have found.	Jew	2.1.38	Abigal
That we might torture him with some new found death.	P1217	22.79	Eprnon
I shal be found, and then twil greeve me more.	Edw	1.4.132	Gavstn
I found them at the first inexorable,	Edw	3.1.103	Arundl
to Longshankes blood/Is false, be not found single for suspect:	Edw	4.6.17	Kent
That being dead, if it chaunce to be found,	Edw	5.4.14	Mortmr
And search all corners of the new-found-world/For pleasant	F 111	1.1.83	Faust
I am glad I have found you, you are a couple of fine	F1096	3.3.9	P Vintnr
and there I found him asleepe; I kept a hallowing and whooping	F1548	4.5.44	P HrsCsr
And fall into the Ocean, ne're be found.	F1978	5.2.182	Faust
Shall never faith be found in fellow kings.	Lucan, First Booke	92	
There will I finde thee, or be found by thee,	Ovid's Elegies	1.4.57	
Butcherd the flocks he found in spatious field,	Ovid's Elegies	1.7.8	
And in sad lovers heads let me be found.	Ovid's Elegies	1.15.38	
Why me that alwayes was thy souldiour found,	Ovid's Elegies	2.9.3	
And then things found do ever further pace.	Ovid's Elegies	2.9.10	
wish the chariot, whence corne [seedes] <fields> were found,	Ovid's Elegies	3.5.15	
In hell were harbourd, here was found no masse.	Ovid's Elegies	3.7.38	
Why am I sad, when Proserpine is found,	Ovid's Elegies	3.9.45	
Jewels being lost are found againe, this never,	Hero and Leander	2.85	
FOUNDATION			
And raise a new foundation to old Troy,	Dido	5.1.79	Aeneas
FOUNT			
For vertue is the fount whence honor springs.	1Tamb	4.4.128	Tamb
FOUNTAINE			
See Homer from whose fountaine ever fild,	Ovid's Elegies	3.8.25	
FOUNTAINES			
Earth cast up fountaines from thy entralles,	1Tamb	5.1.347	Zenoc
And makes large streams back to their fountaines flow,	Ovid's Elegies	1.8.6	
And turned streames run back-ward to their fountaines.	Ovid's Elegies	2.1.26	
No certaine house thou hast, nor any fountaines.	Ovid's Elegies	3.5.92	
By charmes are running springs and fountaines drie,	Ovid's Elegies	3.6.32	
FOUR (See also FOWER)			
thirty yeares, Jupiter in twelve, Mars in four, the Sun, Venus,	F 605	2.2.54	P Faust
FOURE			
Not past foure thousand paces at the most.	Dido	5.1.17	Aeneas
Nature that fram'd us of foure Elements,	1Tamb	2.7.18	Tamb
have martcht/Foure hundred miles with armour on their backes,	2Tamb	1.3.175	Usumc
Two, three, foure month Madam.	Jew	4.4.55	P Barab
Foure Earldomes have I besides Lancaster,	Edw	1.1.102	Lncstr
Browne bils, and targetiers, foure hundred strong,	Edw	3.1.37	SpncrP
So he will spare him foure and twenty yeares,	F 319	1.3.91	Faust
grant unto them that foure and twentie yeares being expired,	F 496	2.1.108	P Faust
West, in foure and twenty houres, upon the poles of the world,	F 597	2.2.46	P Mephst
[Quarter <Quarters> the towne in foure equivolence].	F 790	3.1.12A	Faust
Over the which [foure] <two> stately Bridges leane,	F 815	3.1.37	Mephst
My foure and twenty yeares of liberty/I'le spend in pleasure	F 839	3.1.61	Faust
I was limitted/For foure and twenty yeares, to breathe on	F1396	4.2.72	Faust
foure and twenty yeares hath Faustus lost eternall joy and	F1859	5.2.63	P Faust
FOURESCORE			
Fourescore is but a girles age, love is sweete:--	Dido	4.5.32	Nurse
FOURME			
For [which] <with> the quinque-angle fourme is meet:	2Tamb	3.2.64	Tamb
In which the essentiall fourme of Marble stone,	2Tamb	4.2.62	Olymp
FOURTEENE			
A faire young maid scarce fourteene yeares of age,	Jew	1.2.378	Mthias
FOURTH			
But what art thou the fourth?	F 685	2.2.134	Faust
FOURTHLY			
Fourthly, that he shall be in his chamber or house invisible.	F 490	2.1.102	P Faust
FOWER			
That should be horsed on fower mightie kings.	1Tamb	4.2.78	Bajzth
Fower chariot-horses from the lists even ends.	Ovid's Elegies	3.2.66	
FOWLE			
the suburbe fieldes/Fled, fowle Erinnis stalkt about the wals,	Lucan, First Booke	570	
FOWLES (See also FOULE)			
White Swannes, and many lovely water fowles:	Dido	4.5.11	Nurse
Whose sight is loathsome to all winged fowles?	Edw	5.3.7	Edward
Is dead, al-fowles her exequies frequent.	Ovid's Elegies	2.6.2	
things hidden)/Whence uncleane fowles are said to be forbidden.	Ovid's Elegies	2.6.52	
FOWLEST			
Nor fowlest Harpie that shall swallow him.	Edw	2.2.46	Edward
FOXE			
That like a Foxe in midst of harvest time,	1Tamb	1.1.31	Mycet
FRAGRANT			
Her breath as fragrant as the morning rose,	Hero and Leander	1.391	
And when hee sported in the fragrant lawnes,	Hero and Leander	2.199	
And a thousand fragrant [posies] <poesies>,	Passionate Shepherd	10	
FRAIDE			
What, are the Turtles fraide out of their neastes?	1Tamb	5.1.64	Tamb

FRAILE			
Our life is fraile, and we may die to day.	1Tamb	1.1.68	Mycet
That when this fraile and transitory flesh/Hath suckt the	2Tamb	2.4.43	Zenoc
Then were my thoughts so fraile and unconfirm'd,	Jew	3.3.59	Abigal
that flesh and bloud should be so fraile with your Worship:	F1632	4.6.75	P Carter
FRAILTY			
This is meere frailty, brethren, be content.	Jew	4.1.98	Barab
FRAMANTO			
Belseborams framanto pacostiphos tostu Mephastophilis,	F App	p.235 24	P Robin
FRAM'D			
Nature that fram'd us of foure Elements,	1Tamb	2.7.18	Tamb
Whose arches should be fram'd with bones of Turks,	2Tamb	1.3.94	Amyras
And fram'd of finer mold then common men,	Jew	1.2.219	Barab
I fram'd the challenge that did make them meet:	Jew	5.5.82	Barab
<And double Canons, fram'd of carved brasse>,	F 820	(HC265) A	Mephst
More he deserv'd, to both great harme he fram'd,	Ovid's Elegies		2.2.49
FRAMDE			
My policye hath framde religion.	P 122	2.65	Guise
Which I Pelignis foster-child have framde,	Ovid's Elegies		3.14.3
FRAME			
For I will grace them with a fairer frame,	Dido	5.1.5	Aeneas
Ile frame me wings of waxe like Icarus,	Dido	5.1.243	Dido
And now ye gods that guide the starrie frame,	Dido	5.1.302	Dido
Will sooner burne the glorious frame of Heaven,	1Tamb	4.2.10	Tamb
And with the cannon breake the frame of heaven,	2Tamb	2.4.104	Tamb
Which measureth the glorious frame of heaven,	2Tamb	3.4.65	Therid
In frame of which, Nature hath shewed more skill,	2Tamb	3.4.75	Techel
And thus me thinkes should men of judgement frame/This is the	Jew	1.1.34	Barab
First let me as a Novice learne to frame/My solitary life to	Jew	1.2.331	Abigal
Whose frame is paved with sundry coloured stones,	F 797	3.1.19	Faust
That Faustus name, whilst this bright frame doth stand,	F 841	3.1.63	Faust
Doost me of new crimes alwayes guilty frame?	Ovid's Elegies		2.7.1
And writings did from diverse places frame,	Ovid's Elegies		2.18.28
To fill my lawes thy wanton spirit frame.	Ovid's Elegies		3.1.30
Come therefore, and to long verse shorter frame.	Ovid's Elegies		3.1.66
Againe she knew not how to frame her looke,	Hero and Leander		2.307
FRAMED			
halfe to weping framed,/Aye me she cries, to love, why art	Ovid's Elegies		2.18.7
FRAMING			
The framing of this circle on the ground/Brings Thunder,	F 545	2.1.157	Mephst
FRANCE (See also FRAUNCE)			
now the Guize is dead, is come from France/To view this Land,	Jew	Prol.3	Machvl
Many in France, and wealthy every one:	Jew	1.1.127	Barab
And in the warres 'twixt France and Germanie,	Jew	2.3.187	Barab
And joynes your linnage to the crowne of France?	P 51	1.51	Admral
That God may still defend the right of France:	P 56	1.56	Navrre
Tis but a nook of France,/Sufficient yet for such a pettie	P 149	2.92	Guise
Him will we--but first lets follow those in France,	P 153	2.96	Guise
I vow and sweare as I am King of France,	P 255	4.53	Charls
There shall not a Hugonet breath in France.	P 324	5.51	Guise
Yet by my brother Charles our King of France,	P 464	8.14	Anjoy
prejudice their hope/Of my inheritance to the crowne of France:	P 468	8.18	Anjoy
the diadem/Of France be cast on me, then with your leaves/I may	P 473	8.23	Anjoy
And disperse themselves throughout the Realme of France,	P 507	9.26	QnMoth
For Katherine must have her will in France:	P 520	9.39	QnMoth
For Ile rule France, but they shall weare the crowne:	P 525	9.44	QnMoth
To steale from France, and hye me to my home.	P 567	11.32	Navrre
Welcome to France thy fathers royall seate,	P 590	12.3	QnMoth
diadem, before/You were invested in the crowne of France.	P 613	12.26	Mugern
Flourish in France, and none deny the same.	P 640	12.53	QnMoth
A mighty army comes from France with speed:	P 725	14.28	1Msngr
Why I am no traitor to the crowne of France.	P 825	17.20	Guise
What Peere in France but thou (aspiring Guise)/Durst be in	P 828	17.23	Eprnon
Least thou perceive the King of France be mov'd.	P 834	17.29	King
Else all France knowes how poor a Duke thou art.	P 844	17.39	Eprnon
Guise, weare our crowne, and be thou King of France,	P 859	17.54	King
Be thou proclaimde a traitor throughout France.	P 864	17.59	King
Heere is no staying for the King of France,	P 897	17.92	King
My Lord, I am advertised from France,	P 900	18.1	Navrre
To shew your love unto the King of France:	P 904	18.5	Bartus
And let them march away to France amaine:	P 917	18.18	Navrre
The ruine of that famous Realme of France:	P 922	18.23	Navrre
And send us safely to arrive in France:	P 928	18.29	Navrre
Now fals the star whose influence governes France,	P 944	19.14	Capt
I nere was King of France untill this houre:	P1027	19.97	King
Nere was there King of France so yoakt as I.	P1044	19.114	King
Traitor to God, and to the realme of France.	P1076	19.146	QnMoth
Wicked Navarre will get the crowne of France,	P1086	19.156	QnMoth
And roote Valoys his line from forth of France,	P1113	21.7	Dumain
I vow as I am lawfull King of France,	P1143	22.5	King
that Navarre may be/Esteemed faithfull to the King of France:	P1148	22.10	Navrre
Oh no Navarre, thou must be King of France.	P1225	22.87	King
Long may you live, and still be King of France.	P1226	22.88	Navrre
And rulde in France by Henries fatall death.	P1250	22.112	Navrre
Might have enforst me to have swum from France,	Edw	1.1.7	Gavstn
You know that I came lately out of France,	Edw	1.1.44	Gavstn
So will I now, and thou shalt back to France.	Edw	1.1.185	BshpCv
Would when I left sweet France and was imbarkt,	Edw	1.4.171	Queene
My sonne and I will over into France,	Edw	2.4.65	Queene
denied/To Isabell the Queene, that now in France/Makes friends,	Edw	3.1.269	Spencr
Among the lords of France with Englands golde,	Edw	3.1.277	Levune
From Paris next, costing the Realme of France,	F 784	3.1.6	Faust
Lord Cardinals of France and Padua,	F 881	3.1.103	Pope

FRANCE (cont.)			
Was sent me from a Cardinall in France.	F1047	3.2.67	Pope
would dim/Olde triumphs, and that Caesars conquering France,	Lucan, First Booke		122
O wals unfortunate too neere to France, ...	Lucan, First Booke		250
Five yeeres I lengthned thy commaund in France: . .	Lucan, First Booke		277
In ten yeares wonst thou France; Roome may be won/With farre	Lucan, First Booke		283
forraine wars ill thriv'd; or wrathful France/Pursu'd us hither,	Lucan, First Booke		308
delay/Might crosse him, he withdrew his troupes from France,	Lucan, First Booke		395
were wont/In large spread heire to exceed the rest of France;	Lucan, First Booke		439
FRANCISCAN			
Five hundred fatte Franciscan Fryers and priestes. . .	P 142	2.85	Guise
Go and returne an old Franciscan Frier, ...	F 253	1.3.25	Faust
FRANKEFORD			
Frankeford, Lubecke, Mosco, and where not, ...	Jew	4.1.72	Barab
FRANTICK			
Like frantick Juno will I fill the earth, ...	Edw	1.4.178	Queene
And makes me frantick for my Gaveston:	Edw	1.4.315	Edward
FRANTICKE			
At which the franticke Queene leapt on his face, . .	Dido	2.1.244	Aeneas
FRATRIS			
[Quin redis <regis> Mephostophilis fratris imagine]. .	F 262	1.3.34A	Faust
FRAUDS			
and every yeare/Frauds and corruption in the field of Mars;	Lucan, First Booke		182
FRAUGHT			
The ships are safe thou saist, and richly fraught. . .	Jew	1.1.54	Barab
men dispatch/And come ashore, and see the fraught discharg'd.	Jew	1.1.101	Barab
Our fraught is Grecians, Turks, and Africk Moores. . .	Jew	2.2.9	Bosco
FRAUGHTED			
Fraughted with golde of rich America:	2Tamb	1.2.35	Callap
FRAUNCE			
That makes these upstart heresies in Fraunce:	P 81	2.24	Guise
And thereon set the Diadem of Fraunce, ...	P 101	2.44	Guise
And in my love entombes the hope of Fraunce:	P 134	2.77	Guise
Bartus, it shall be so, poast then to Fraunce, . . .	P 907	18.8	Navrre
exhalatione/which our great sonn of fraunce cold not effecte	Paris	ms20,p390	Guise
Looke where the sister of the king of Fraunce, . . .	Edw	1.4.187	Lncstr
The King of Fraunce sets foote in Normandie. . . .	Edw	2.2.9	Mortmr
Thy garrisons are beaten out of Fraunce, ...	Edw	2.2.162	Lncstr
That lord Valoyes our brother, king of Fraunce, . .	Edw	3.1.62	Queene
You shall go parley with the king of Fraunce. . . .	Edw	3.1.71	Edward
To make my preparation for Fraunce.	Edw	3.1.88	Queene
Bestowe that treasure on the lords of Fraunce, . . .	Edw	3.1.265	Spencr
And Fraunce shall be obdurat with her teares. . . .	Edw	3.1.279	Levune
Then make for Fraunce amaine, [Levune] <Lewne> away,/Proclaime	Edw	3.1.280	Spencr
Faire blowes the winde for Fraunce, blowe gentle gale, .	Edw	4.1.1	Kent
But ile to Fraunce, and cheere the wronged Queene, . .	Edw	4.1.6	Kent
But hath your grace got shipping unto Fraunce? . . .	Edw	4.1.17	Mortmr
A boye, our friends do faile us all in Fraunce, . . .	Edw	4.2.1	Queene
and then a Fig/For all my unckles frienship here in Fraunce.	Edw	4.2.5	Prince
Unhappie Isabell, when Fraunce rejects, ...	Edw	4.2.11	Queene
The king of England, nor the court of Fraunce, . . .	Edw	4.2.22	Prince
Welcome to Fraunce:	Edw	4.2.37	Queene
But gentle lords, friendles we are in Fraunce. . . .	Edw	4.2.46	Queene
the ungentle king/Of Fraunce refuseth to give aide of armes,	Edw	4.2.62	SrJohn
Now sirs, the newes from Fraunce.	Edw	4.3.14	Edward
I trowe/The lords of Fraunce love Englands gold so well, .	Edw	4.3.15	Edward
Letters my lord, and tidings foorth of Fraunce, . . .	Edw	4.3.25	Post
behalfe, dealt with the king of Fraunce his lords, and effected,	Edw	4.3.29	P Spencr
When for her sake I ran at tilt in Fraunce, ...	Edw	5.5.69	Edward
deviding just/The bounds of Italy, from Cisalpin Fraunce;	Lucan, First Booke		218
FRAYDE			
yett comminge upon you once unawares he frayde you out againe.	Paris	ms12,p390	P Souldr
FREATTING			
shee will fall into a consumption with freatting, and then she	1Tamb	4.4.50	P Tamb
FREDERICK			
Here, what Frederick, ho.	F1431	4.3.1	Benvol
Deere Frederick here, ...	F1433	4.3.3	Mrtino
FREDERICKE			
Trode on the neck of Germane Fredericke, ...	F 916	3.1.138	Pope
Good Fredericke see the roomes be voyded straight, . .	F1157	4.1.3	Mrtino
Then gentle Fredericke hie thee to the grove, . . .	F1340	4.2.16	Benvol
FREDERIK			
Breake may his heart with grones: deere Frederik see, .	F1366	4.2.42	Benvol
FREE			
Free from the murmure of these running streames, . . .	Dido	2.1.335	Venus
Yet none obtaind me, I am free from all.--	Dido	3.1.153	Dido
And yet I am not free, oh would I were.	Dido	3.4.6	Dido
Go wander free from feare of Tyrants rage, ...	1Tamb	3.2.102	Agidas
Returne with victorie, and free from wound.	1Tamb	3.3.133	Zenoc
Thy princely daughter here shall set thee free. . . .	1Tamb	5.1.436	Tamb
leave these armes/And save thy sacred person free from scathe:	2Tamb	1.3.10	Zenoc
And now the damned soules are free from paine, . . .	2Tamb	4.2.91	Therid
Receive them free, and sell them by the weight; . . .	Jew	1.1.24	Barab
And not depart untill I see you free.	Jew	2.2.41	Bosco
Upon mine owne free-hold within fortie foot of the gallowes,	Jew	4.2.16	P Pilia
Nay, doe thou this, Ferneze, and be free;	Jew	5.2.90	Barab
Here is my hand that I'le set Malta free:	Jew	5.2.95	Barab
And I will warrant Malta free for ever.	Jew	5.2.101	Barab
With free consent a hundred thousand pounds.	Jew	5.5.20	Govnr
that he himself should occupy, which is his own free land.	P 812	17.7	P Souldr
If it be not too free there's the question:	P 813	17.8	P Souldr
yf it be not to free theres the questione | now ser where he is	Paris	ms 9,p390	P Souldr
Wigmore shall flie, to set my unckle free.	Edw	2.2.196	Mortmr

FREE (cont.)
Free from suspect, and fell invasion/Of such as have your Edw 4.7.4 Abbot
To set his brother free, no more but so. . . . . . Edw 5.2.33 BshpWn
thine, in setting Bruno free/From his and our professed enemy, F1206 4.1.52 Emper
And I had breath'd a man made free from harme. . . . . F1400 4.2.76 Faust
thy divel with horse-bread as long as he lives, of free cost. F App p.234 31 P Rafe
Gratis thou maiest be free, give like for like, . . Ovid's Elegies 1.6.23
Nape free-borne, whose cunning hath no border, . . Ovid's Elegies 1.11.2
What helpes it Woman to be free from warre? . . . Ovid's Elegies 2.14.1
A free-borne wench, no right 'tis up to locke: . . . Ovid's Elegies 3.4.33

FREE-BORNE
Nape free-borne, whose cunning hath no border, . . . Ovid's Elegies 1.11.2
A free-borne wench, no right 'tis up to locke: . . . Ovid's Elegies 3.4.33

FREED
That freed me from the bondage of my foe: . . . . . 2Tamb 3.1.69 Callap
for Malta shall be freed,/Or Selim ne're returne to Ottoman. Jew 5.5.113 Govnr
Horse freed from service range abroad the woods. . . Ovid's Elegies 2.9.22
Now have I freed my selfe, and fled the chaine, . . Ovid's Elegies 3.10.3

FREEDOM
For Egypts freedom and the Souldans life: . . . . . 1Tamb 5.1.153 Tamb

FREEDOME
Defend his freedome gainst a Monarchie: . . . . 1Tamb 2.1.56 Ceneus
Them freedome without war might not suffice, . . . Lucan, First Booke 173
Do this and soone thou shalt thy freedome reape. . . Ovid's Elegies 2.2.40

FREE-HOLD
Upon mine owne free-hold within fortie foot of the gallowes, Jew 4.2.16 P Pilia

FREELAND
hes to have the choyce of his owne freeland | yf it be not to Paris ms 8,p390 P Souldr

FREELIE
I would freelie give it to his enemies, ... Edw 1.4.309 Edward

FREELY
Then let us freely banquet and carouse/Full bowles of wine unto 1Tamb 4.4.5 Tamb
Gallies mann'd with Christian slaves/I freely give thee, . 2Tamb 1.2.33 Callap
but for one bare night/A hundred Duckets have bin freely given: Jew 3.1.3 Curtzn
That thou mayst freely live to be my heire. . . . . Jew 3.4.63 Barab
But came it freely, did the Cow give down her milk freely? Jew 4.2.102 P Ithimr
But came it freely, did the Cow give down her milk freely? Jew 4.2.103 P Ithimr
Freely enjoy that vaine light-headed earle, ... Edw 1.4.400 MortSr

FREEND
Freend Sigismond, and peeres of Hungary, ... 2Tamb 1.1.164 Orcan
Thankes my good freend, I will requite thy love. . . P 78 2.21 Guise
Be gone my freend, present them to her straite. . . P 82 2.25 Guise
Thanks my good freend, holde, take thou this reward. . P 168 3.3 OldQn
see they keep/All trecherous violence from our noble freend, P 268 4.66 Charls
And her chosen freend? . . . . P 756 15.14 King
And tell her Henry dyes her faithfull freend. . . . . P1244 22.106 King

FREENDS
Stab him I say and send him to his freends in hell. . . P 415 7.55 Guise
God graunt my neerest freends may prove no worse. . . P 547 11.12 Charls
I tell thee Mugeroun we will be freends, ... P 614 12.27 King
come Epernoune/Lets goe seek the Duke and make them freends. P 786 15.44 King
To countermaund our will and check our freends. . . . P 846 17.41 King
Then farwell Guise, the King and thou are freends. . . P 870 17.65 King
Or be suspicious of my deerest freends: . . . . . P 972 19.42 King
That ever I vouchsafte my dearest freends. . . . . P1146 22.8 King

FREEST
That by thy vertues freest us from annoy, ... Dido 1.1.153 Achat

FREEZING
For freezing meteors and conjealed colde: . . . . . 1Tamb 1.1.11 Cosroe
a fiery exhalation/Wrapt in the bowels of a freezing cloude, 1Tamb 4.2.44 Tamb
Sustaine the scortching heat and freezing cold, . . . 2Tamb 3.2.57 Tamb

FRENCH
A French Musician, come let's heare your skill? . . . Jew 4.4.30 Curtzn
Wilt drinke French-man, here's to thee with a--pox on this Jew 4.4.32 P Ithimr
Catholickes/Sends Indian golde to coyne me French ecues: . P 118 2.61 Guise
what, shall the French king dye,/Wounded and poysoned, both at P1214 22.76 King
Fawne not on me French strumpet, get thee gone. . . . Edw 1.4.145 Edward
Why french crownes. . . . . F App p.230 32 P Wagner
french crownes a man were as good have as many english . F App p.230 33 P Clown
And you French Bardi, whose immortal pens/Renowne the valiant Lucan, First Booke 443
And far more barbarous then the French (his vassals)/And that Lucan, First Booke 476
Where the French rout engirt themselves with Bayes. . . Ovid's Elegies 2.13.18

FRENCH-MAN
Wilt drinke French-man, here's to thee with a--pox on this Jew 4.4.32 P Ithimr

FRENCHMAN
Wel, let that peevish Frenchman guard him sure, . . . Edw 1.2.7 Mortmr
That slie inveigling Frenchman weele exile, ... Edw 1.2.57 Mortmr

FRENDS
My Lord, twere good to make them frends, ... P 772 15.30 Eprnon
The Pope and King of Spaine are thy good frends, . . . P 843 17.38 Eprnon

FREQUENT
Is dead, al-fowles her exequies frequent. . . . . . Ovid's Elegies 2.6.2
Why seek'st not heav'n the third realme to frequent? . Ovid's Elegies 3.7.50

FREQUENTED
And more frequented for this mysterie, ... F 169 1.1.141 Cornel

FREQUENTS
Thou that frequents Canopus pleasant fields, ... Ovid's Elegies 2.13.7

FRESH
They gather strength by power of fresh supplies. . . . 1Tamb 2.2.21 Meandr
May have fresh warning to go war with us, ... 1Tamb 4.1.71 Souldn
The town is ours my Lord, and fresh supply/Of conquest, and of 1Tamb 5.1.196 Techel
Fed with the fresh supply of earthly dregs, ... 2Tamb 3.2.8 Tamb
That bring fresh water to thy men and thee: . . . . 2Tamb 3.3.30 Techel

FRESH (cont.)
Cherish thy valour stil with fresh supplies: 2Tamb 4.1.87 Tamb
city Samarcanda/And christall waves of fresh Jaertis streame, 2Tamb 4.3.108 Tamb
Makes walles a fresh with every thing that falles/Into the 2Tamb 5.1.18 Govnr
Unharnesse them, and let me have fresh horse: 2Tamb 5.1.130 Tamb
hath nowe gathered a fresh Armie, and hearing your absence in 2Tamb 5.3.103 P 3Msngr
without fresh men to rigge and furnish them. Jew 5.5.101 Govnr
is massacred)/Infect thy gracious brest with fresh supply, P 193 3.28 QnMarg
Why streames it not, that I may write a fresh? F 455 2.1.67 Faust
[Tush], these are fresh mens [suppositions] <questions>: F 606 2.2.55 P Faust
And to the vast deep sea fresh water flouds? Ovid's Elegies 2.10.14
Hath any rose so from a fresh yong maide, Ovid's Elegies 3.6.53
When this fresh bleeding wound Leander viewd, Hero and Leander 2.213
And to Leander as a fresh alarme. Hero and Leander 2.284

FRESH MENS
[Tush], these are fresh mens [suppositions] <questions>: F 606 2.2.55 P Faust

FRET (See also FREATTING)
And by the way to make him fret the more, Edw 5.2.62 Mortmr

FRIARS (See also FRIER, FRYAR, FRYER)
when holy Friars turne devils and murder one another. Jew 4.1.194 P Ithimr

FRIARY (See FRIERY)

FRIE
Ist womens love my captive brest doth frie? Ovid's Elegies 3.2.40

FRIEND (See also FREEND, FRENDS, FRINDLY)
Pluck up your hearts, since fate still rests our friend, Dido 1.1.149 Aeneas
Stoute friend Achates, doest thou know this wood? Dido 3.3.50 Aeneas
No, but the trustie friend of Tamburlaine. 1Tamb 1.2.227 Tamb
Theridamas my friend, take here my hand, 1Tamb 1.2.232 Tamb
but yet if Sigismond/Speake as a friend, and stand not upon 2Tamb 1.1.123 Orcan
By sacred Mahomet, the friend of God, 2Tamb 1.1.137 Orcan
And Christ or Mahomet hath bene my friend. 2Tamb 2.3.11 Orcan
by the aid of God and his friend Mahomet, Emperour of Natolia, 2Tamb 3.1.3 P Orcan
Wel then my noble Lords, for this my friend, 2Tamb 3.1.68 Callap
Knowing two kings, the [friends] <friend> to Tamburlain, 2Tamb 3.3.13 Therid
By Mahomet, thy mighty friend I sweare, 2Tamb 4.1.121 Tamb
Slew friend and enemy with my stratagems. Jew 2.3.189 Barab
Oh trusty Ithimore; no servant, but my friend; Jew 3.4.42 Barab
For as a friend not knowne, but in distresse, Jew 5.2.72 Barab
Shall be my friend. Jew 5.2.114 Barab
And share the kingdom with thy deerest friend. Edw 1.1.2 Gavstn
Thy friend, thy selfe, another Gaveston. Edw 1.1.143 Edward
I know it, brother welcome home my friend. Edw 1.1.148 Edward
Thy woorth sweet friend is far above my guifts, Edw 1.1.161 Edward
And therefore sweete friend, take it patiently, Edw 1.4.112 Edward
But come sweete friend, ile beare thee on thy way. Edw 1.4.140 Edward
And thinke I gaind, having bought so deare a friend. Edw 1.4.310 Edward
Against our friend the earle of Cornewall comes, Edw 1.4.375 Edward
A friend of mine told me in secrecie, Edw 2.1.17 Spencr
Welcome to Tinmouth, welcome to thy friend, Edw 2.2.51 Edward
Poore Gaveston, that hast no friend but me, Edw 2.2.220 Edward
O treacherous Warwicke thus to wrong thy friend! Edw 2.6.1 Gavstn
And wrong our lord, your honorable friend. Edw 2.6.9 James
commend me to your maister/My friend, and tell him that I Edw 2.6.13 Warwck
I long to heare an answer from the Barons/Touching my friend, Edw 3.1.2 Edward
Our friend [Levune] <Lewne>, faithfull and full of trust, Edw 3.1.60 Queene
Ah traitors, have they put my friend to death? Edw 3.1.91 Edward
Or didst thou see my friend to take his death? Edw 3.1.93 Edward
And for the murther of my deerest friend, Edw 3.1.226 Edward
Mounsier le Grand, a noble friend of yours, Edw 4.2.47 Mortmr
This letter written by a friend of ours, Edw 5.4.6 Mortmr
O help me gentle friend; where is Martino? F1432 4.3.2 Fredrk
Friend, thou canst not buy so good a horse, for so small a F1459 4.4.3 P Faust
[Ah] <O> [my sweete] friend, F1734 5.1.61 Faust
Torment sweet friend, that base and [crooked age] <aged man>, F1753 5.1.80 Faust
Tempt not God sweet friend, but let us into the next roome, and F1871 5.2.75 P 1Schol
not so good friend, burladie I had neede have it wel roasted, F App p.229 11 P Clown
While rage is absent, take some friend the paynes. Ovid's Elegies 1.7.2
And thou, if falsely charged to wrong thy friend, Ovid's Elegies 3.8.63
Above our life we love a stedfast friend, Hero and Leander 2.79

FRIENDED
Let me, and them by it be aye be-friended. Ovid's Elegies 3.12.36

FRIENDES
Ortigius and Menaphon, my trustie friendes, 1Tamb 2.5.29 Cosroe
And all the friendes of faire Zenocrate, 1Tamb 4.4.88 Tamb

FRIENDLES
That thus oppresse poore friendles passengers. 1Tamb 1.2.70 Zenoc
But gentle lords, friendles we are in Fraunce. Edw 4.2.46 Queene

FRIENDLY
For this so friendly ayde in time of neede. Dido 1.1.138 Venus
Then would we hope to quite such friendly turnes, Dido 1.2.46 Serg
Carthage, my friendly host adue, Dido 4.3.1 Aeneas
Thankes good Iarbus for thy friendly ayde, Dido 5.1.75 Aeneas
And looke we friendly on them when they come: 1Tamb 1.2.141 Tamb
crost Danubius stream/To treat of friendly peace or deadly war: 2Tamb 1.1.80 Sgsmnd
A friendly parle might become ye both. 2Tamb 1.1.117 Gazell
By this my friendly keepers happy meanes, 2Tamb 3.1.34 Callap
Wel then my friendly Lordes, what now remaines/But that we 2Tamb 5.1.210 Tamb
Intreat 'em faire, and give them friendly speech, Jew 1.2.286 Barab
she farre become a bed/Embraced in a friendly lovers armes, Jew 1.2.372 Mthias
Use Edmund friendly, as if all were well. Edw 5.2.79 Queene
But most thou friendly turtle-dove, deplore. Ovid's Elegies 2.6.12

FRIENDS
Why turnes Aeneas from his trustie friends? Dido 2.1.57 Cloan

FRIENDS (cont.)				
That hath sc many unresisted friends:	Dido	3.2.50		Juno
We two as friends one fortune will devide:	Dido	3.2.55		Venus
Whom casualtie of sea hath made such friends?	Dido	3.2.76		Juno
To Italy, sweete friends to Italy,	Dido	4.3.43		Cloan
As parting friends accustome on the shoare,	Dido	4.3.50		Aeneas
For they are friends that help to weane my state,	1Tamb	1.2.29		Tamb
Nobly resolv'd, sweet friends and followers.	1Tamb	1.2.60		Tamb
We are his friends, and if the Persean king/Should offer	1Tamb	1.2.214		Techel
exchange for that/We are assured of by our friends successe.	1Tamb	1.2.217		Techel
These are my friends in whom I more rejoice,	1Tamb	1.2.241		Tamb
And these his two renowmed friends my Lord,	1Tamb	2.3.30		Therid
That I with these my friends and all my men,	1Tamb	2.3.43		Tamb
troopes)/Farewell Lord Regent, and his happie friends,	1Tamb	2.5.46		Cosroe
What saies my other friends, wil you be kings?	1Tamb	2.5.67		Tamb
Twil proove a pretie jest (in faith) my friends.	1Tamb	2.5.90		Tamb
And that made us, the friends of Tamburlaine,	1Tamb	2.7.34		Techel
As martiall presents to our friends at home,	2Tamb	1.1.35		Orcan
Your presence (loving friends and fellow kings)/Makes me to	2Tamb	1.3.151		Tamb
But now my friends, let me examine ye,	2Tamb	1.3.172		Tamb
Knowing two kings, the [friends] <friend> to Tamburlain,	2Tamb	3.3.13		Therid
If thou withstand the friends of Tamburlain.	2Tamb	3.3.19		Techel
Were you that are the friends of Tamburlain,	2Tamb	3.3.35		Capt
But now my followers and my loving friends,	2Tamb	3.5.159		Tamb
Slew all his Priests, his kinsmen, and his friends,	2Tamb	5.1.181		Tamb
Ah friends, what shal I doe, I cannot stand,	2Tamb	5.3.51		Tamb
Farewel my boies, my dearest friends, farewel,	2Tamb	5.3.245		Tamb
from France/To view this Land, and frolicke with his friends.	Jew	Prol.4		Machvl
I'le make 'em friends againe.	Jew	2.3.357		Abigal
You'll make 'em friends?	Jew	2.3.358		Barab
And neither gets him friends, nor fils his bags,	Jew	5.2.39		Barab
Goe walke about the City, see thy friends:	Jew	5.2.92		Barab
And Northward Gaveston hath many friends.	Edw	1.1.129		Lncstr
Which may in Ireland purchase him such friends,	Edw	1.4.259		Mortmr
Why how now cosin, how fares all our friends?	Edw	2.2.114		Lncstr
But neither spare you Gaveston, nor his friends.	Edw	2.3.28		Lncstr
Sib, if this be all/Valoys and I will soone be friends againe.	Edw	3.1.67		Edward
Let them not unrevengd murther your friends,	Edw	3.1.125		Spencr
Sound drums and trumpets, marche with me my friends,	Edw	3.1.260		Edward
that now in France/Makes friends, to crosse the seas with her	Edw	3.1.270		Spencr
A brother, nc, a butcher of thy friends,	Edw	4.1.4		Kent
A boye, our friends do faile us all in Fraunce,	Edw	4.2.1		Queene
How say you my Lord, will you go with your friends,	Edw	4.2.19		SrJohn
Much happier then your friends in England do.	Edw	4.2.35		Kent
Where weapons want, and though a many friends/Are made away, as	Edw	4.2.51		Mortmr
Yet have we friends, assure your grace, in England/Would cast	Edw	4.2.54		Mortmr
men, and friends/Ere long, to bid the English king a base.	Edw	4.2.65		SrJohn
not discourage/Your friends that are so forward in your aide.	Edw	4.2.70		Queene
Triumpheth Englands Edward with his friends,	Edw	4.3.2		Edward
And triumph Edward with his friends uncontrould.	Edw	4.3.3		Edward
Come friends to Bristow, there to make us strong,	Edw	4.3.50		Edward
Now lords, our loving friends and countrimen,	Edw	4.4.1		Queene
Our kindest friends in Belgia have we left,	Edw	4.4.3		Queene
friends in Belgia have we left,/To cope with friends at home:	Edw	4.4.4		Queene
Her friends doe multiply and yours doe fayle,	Edw	4.5.2		Spencr
But we alas are chaste, and you my friends,	Edw	4.7.22		Edward
And take my heart, in reskew of my friends.	Edw	4.7.67		Edward
For friends hath Edward none, but these, and these,	Edw	4.7.91		Edward
And go I must, life farewell with my friends.	Edw	4.7.99		Edward
Brother Edmund, strive not, we are his friends,	Edw	5.2.114		Queene
My lord, be not pensive, we are your friends.	Edw	5.3.1		Matrvs
Friends, whither must unhappie Edward go,	Edw	5.3.4		Edward
O water gentle friends to coole my thirst,	Edw	5.3.25		Edward
Till being interrupted by my friends,	Edw	5.4.62		Mortmr
Mine enemies will I plague, my friends advance,	Edw	5.4.67		Mortmr
Wagner, commend me to me deerest friends,	F 91	1.1.63		Faust
Then gentle friends aid me in this attempt,	F 138	1.1.110		Faust
To slay mine enemies, and aid my friends,	F 324	1.3.96		Faust
[I meane his friends and nearest companions],	F1142	3.3.55A		3Chor
My friends transformed thus:	F1441	4.3.11		Benvol
Why, how now my [good] <goods> friends?	F1608	4.6.51		Faust
Sweet friends, what shall become of Faustus being in hell	F1846	5.2.50	P	Faust
O faintly joyn'd friends with ambition blind,	Lucan, First Booke			87
Our friends death; and our wounds; our wintering/Under the	Lucan, First Booke			303
Why burnes thy brand, why strikes thy bow thy friends?	Ovid's Elegies			2.9.5
Honour what friends thy wife gives, sheele give many:	Ovid's Elegies			3.4.45
FRIENDSHIP				
Ile rather loose his friendship I, then graunt.	Edw	1.4.237		Lncstr
For that I know your friendship is unfain'd,	F1689	5.1.16		Faust
FRIENSHIP				
and then a Fig/For all my unckles frienship here in Fraunce.	Edw	4.2.5		Prince
FRIER				
I am a Frier of the order of the Jacobyns, that for my	P1130	21.24	P	Frier
Frier come with me,	P1137	21.31		Dumain
your Majestie heere is a Frier of the order of the Jacobins,	P1155	22.17	P	1Msngr
Frier, thou dost acknowledge me thy King?	P1164	22.26		King
Ile read them Frier, and then Ile answere thee.	P1171	22.33		King
Go and returne an old Franciscan Frier,	F 253	1.3.25		Faust
Cursed be he that tooke Frier Sandelo a blow on the pate.	F App	p.232 35		Frier
FRIERS				
I like not this Friers look.	P1159	22.21		Eprnon
Sweete Epernoune, our Friers are holy men,	P1161	22.23		King
<Where thou shalt see a troupe of bald-pate Friers>,	F 833	(HC265)A		Mephst

FRIERS (cont.)			
To beate the beades about the Friers Pates,	F 863	3.1.85	Mephst
now Friers take heed,/Lest Faustus make your shaven crownes to	F1006	3.2.26	Faust
Lord Raymond, take your seate, Friers attend,	F1010	3.2.30	Pope
Who's that spoke? Friers looke about.	F1040	3.2.60	Pope
Friers looke about.	F App	p.231 3 P	Pope
Friers prepare a dirge to lay the fury of this ghost, once	F App	p.232 16 P	Pope
FRIERY			
early; with intent to goe/Unto your Friery, because you staid.	Jew	4.1.192	Barab
FRIGHT			
The name of Mortimer shall fright the king,	Edw	1.4.6	Mortmr
Thus in his fright did each man strengthen Fame,	Lucan, First Booke	481	
FRIGHTED (See also FRAYDE)			
Frighted with this confused noyse, I rose,	Dido	2.1.191	Aeneas
Thinke not that I am frighted with thy words,	Edw	5.6.27	King
Frighted the melancholie earth, which deem'd,	Hero and Leander	1.99	
FRIGHTES			
That frightes poore Ramus sitting at his book?	P 362	7.2	Ramus
FRINDLY			
And with my father take a frindly truce.	1Tamb	4.4.72	Zenoc
FRISKING			
let it be in the likenesse of a little pretie frisking flea,	F App	p.231 62 P	Clown
FRIVOLOUS			
O Faustus leave these frivolous demandes,	F 309	1.3.81	Mephst
FRO			
But I will teare thy eyes fro forth thy head,	Dido	3.2.34	Venus
And griesly death, by running to and fro,	1Tamb	5.1.455	Tamb
Whence the wind blowes stil forced to and fro;	Lucan, First Booke	414	
My sides are sore with tumbling to and fro.	Ovid's Elegies	1.2.4	
My Mistris deity also drewe me fro it,	Ovid's Elegies	2.18.17	
FROGS			
Either th'art witcht with blood <bould> of frogs new dead,	Ovid's Elegies	3.6.79	
FROLICK			
what he meanes, if death were nie, he would not frolick thus:	F1677	5.1.4 P	Wagner
FROLICKE			
from France/To view this Land, and frolicke with his friends.	Jew	Prol.4	Machvl
The Pope had never such a frolicke guest.	F1036	3.2.56	Faust
FROLICKS			
Frolicks not more to see the paynted springe,	Edw	2.2.62	Gavstn
FROLIKE			
As frolike as the hunters in the chace/Of savage beastes amid	1Tamb	4.3.56	Capol
To frolike with my deerest Gaveston.	Edw	1.4.73	Edward
FROLLICK			
And let him frollick with his minion.	Edw	1.2.67	Queene
FROLLICKE			
Father of gladnesse, and all frollicke thoughts,	Dido	4.2.5	Iarbus
FROLLICKS			
And here in Tinmoth frollicks with the king.	Edw	2.3.17	Lncstr
FROM (See also FRO)			
That will not shield me from her shrewish blowes:	Dido	1.1.4	Ganimd
When as they would have hal'd thee from my sight:	Dido	1.1.27	Jupitr
From Junos bird Ile pluck her spotted pride,	Dido	1.1.34	Jupitr
But as this one Ile teare them all from him,	Dido	1.1.40	Jupitr
What? is not pietie exempt from woe?	Dido	1.1.79	Venus
From forth her ashes shall advance her head,	Dido	1.1.94	Jupitr
Charge him from me to turne his stormie powers,	Dido	1.1.117	Jupitr
Vaild his resplendant glorie from your view.	Dido	1.1.126	Venus
That erst-while issued from thy watrie loynes,	Dido	1.1.128	Venus
And had my being from thy bubling froth:	Dido	1.1.129	Venus
That by thy vertues freest us from annoy,	Dido	1.1.153	Achat
Whose night and day descendeth from thy browes:	Dido	1.1.156	Achat
Who driven by warre from forth my native world,	Dido	1.1.217	Aeneas
And my divine descent from sceptred Jove:	Dido	1.1.219	Aeneas
But are arived safe not farre from hence:	Dido	1.1.237	Venus
Stay gentle Venus, flye not from thy sonne,	Dido	1.1.242	Aeneas
Save, save, O save our ships from cruell fire,	Dido	1.2.7	Illion
Or steale your houshold lares from their shrines:	Dido	1.2.11	Illion
Such force is farre from our unweaponed thoughts,	Dido	1.2.14	Illion
From thence a fewe of us escapt to land,	Dido	1.2.30	Cloan
And from the first earth interdict our feete.	Dido	1.2.37	Serg
Why turnes Aeneas from his trustie friends?	Dido	2.1.57	Cloan
Beates forth my senses from this troubled soule,	Dido	2.1.116	Aeneas
and suddenly/From out his entrailes, Neoptolemus/Setting his	Dido	2.1.183	Aeneas
And looking from a turret, might behold/Young infants swimming	Dido	2.1.192	Aeneas
His armes torne from his shoulders, and his breast/Furrowd with	Dido	2.1.203	Aeneas
Burst from the earth, crying, Aeneas flye,	Dido	2.1.207	Aeneas
Convaid me from their crooked nets and bands:	Dido	2.1.222	Aeneas
Then from the navell to the throat at once,	Dido	2.1.255	Aeneas
To rid me from these melancholly thoughts.	Dido	2.1.303	Dido
Free from the murmure of these running streames,	Dido	2.1.335	Venus
Depart from Carthage, come not in my sight.	Dido	3.1.44	Dido
Yet not from Carthage for a thousand worlds.	Dido	3.1.51	Iarbus
Thy Anchors shall be hewed from Christall Rockes,	Dido	3.1.120	Dido
Yet none obtaind me, I am free from all.--	Dido	3.1.153	Dido
I was as farre from love, as they from hate.	Dido	3.1.167	Dido
For saving him from Snakes and Serpents stings,	Dido	3.2.38	Juno
And rowse the light foote Deere from forth their laire?	Dido	3.3.31	Dido
That sav'd your famisht souldiers lives from death,	Dido	3.3.52	Achat
From whence my radiant mother did descend,	Dido	3.4.47	Aeneas
And by this Sword that saved me from the Greekes,	Dido	3.4.48	Aeneas
That calles my soule from forth his living seate,	Dido	3.4.53	Dido
Faire Anna, how escapt you from the shower?	Dido	4.1.29	Aeneas
For I will flye from these alluring eyes,	Dido	4.2.50	Iarbus

FROM (cont.)

Since destinie doth call me from [thy] <the> shoare:	Dido	4.3.2		Aeneas
To stay my Fleete frcm loosing forth the Bay:	Dido	4.3.26		Aeneas
Banish that ticing dame from forth your mouth,	Dido	4.3.31		Achat
O foolish Troians that would steale from hence,	Dido	4.4.5		Dido
Not all the world can take thee from mine armes,	Dido	4.4.61		Dido
And from a turret Ile behold my love.	Dido	4.4.86		Dido
Thou wouldst have leapt from out the Sailers hands,	Dido	4.4.141		Dido
From golden India Ganges will I fetch,	Dido	5.1.8		Aeneas
The Sunne from Egypt shall rich odors bring,	Dido	5.1.11		Aeneas
The king of Gods sent me from highest heaven,	Dido	5.1.32		Hermes
Whom I have brought from Ida where he slept,	Dido	5.1.40		Hermes
or to what end/Launcht from the haven, lye they in the Rhode?	Dido	5.1.89		Dido
Aeneas will not faine with his deare love,/I must from hence:	Dido	5.1.93		Aeneas
Sent from his father Jove, appeard to me,	Dido	5.1.95		Aeneas
These words proceed not from Aeneas heart.	Dido	5.1.102		Dido
Not from my heart, for I can hardly goe,	Dido	5.1.103		Aeneas
Let me goe, farewell, I must from hence,	Dido	5.1.110		Dido
That he should take Aeneas from mine armes?	Dido	5.1.130		Dido
But thou art sprung from Scythian Caucasus,	Dido	5.1.158		Dido
O Serpent that came creeping from the shoare,	Dido	5.1.165		Dido
If not, turne from me, and Ile turne from thee:	Dido	5.1.181		Dido
And in the morning he was stolne from me,	Dido	5.1.214		Nurse
have I found a meane/To rid me from these thoughts of Lunacie:	Dido	5.1.273		Dido
Not farre from hence/There is a woman famoused for arts,	Dido	5.1.274		Dido
And from mine ashes let a Conquerour rise,	Dido	5.1.306		Dido
From jygging vaines of riming mother wits,	1Tamb	Prol.1		Prolog
It cannot choose, because it comes from you.	1Tamb	1.1.56		Cosroe
I long to see thee backe returne from thence,	1Tamb	1.1.76		Mycet
And from their knees, even to their hoofes below,	1Tamb	1.1.79		Mycet
Which will revolt from Persean government,	1Tamb	1.1.91		Cosroe
Men from the farthest Equinoctiall line,	1Tamb	1.1.119		Cosroe
And made their spoiles from all our provinces.	1Tamb	1.1.122		Cosroe
are in readines/Ten thousand horse to carie you from hence,	1Tamb	1.1.185		Ortyg
By lawlesse rapine from a silly maide.	1Tamb	1.2.10		Zenoc
these Medean Lords/To Memphis, from my uncles country of Medea,	1Tamb	1.2.12		Zenoc
Besides rich presents from the puisant Cham,	1Tamb	1.2.18		Magnet
you must expect/Letters of conduct from my mightinesse,	1Tamb	1.2.24		Tamb
And must maintaine my life exempt from servitude.	1Tamb	1.2.31		Tamb
Spurning their crownes from off their captive heads.	1Tamb	1.2.57		Techel
Sent from the King to overcome us all.	1Tamb	1.2.112		Souldr
You must be forced from me ere you goe:	1Tamb	1.2.120		Tamb
[and] <To> pull the triple headed dog from hell.	1Tamb	1.2.161		Therid
And sooner shall the Sun fall from his Spheare,	1Tamb	1.2.176		Tamb
And Jove himselfe will stretch his hand from heaven,	1Tamb	1.2.180		Tamb
To ward the blow, and shield me safe from harme.	1Tamb	1.2.181		Tamb
Thy selfe and them shall never part from me,	1Tamb	1.2.245		Tamb
For even as from assured oracle,	1Tamb	2.3.4		Cosroe
Weel chase the Stars from heaven, and dim their eies/That stand	1Tamb	2.3.23		Tamb
And far from any man that is a foole.	1Tamb	2.4.12		Mycet
They cannot take away my crowne from me.	1Tamb	2.4.14		Mycet
stragling from the camp/When Kings themselves are present in	1Tamb	2.4.16		Tamb
Then shalt thou see me pull it from thy head:	1Tamb	2.4.39		Tamb
From one that knew not what a King should do,	1Tamb	2.5.22		Cosroe
And prest out fire from their burning jawes:	1Tamb	2.6.6		Cosroe
Whether from earth, or hell, or heaven he grow.	1Tamb	2.6.23		Ortyg
To save your King and country from decay:	1Tamb	2.6.35		Cosroe
To thrust his doting father from his chaire,	1Tamb	2.7.14		Tamb
And thinks to rouse us from our dreadful siege/Of the famous	1Tamb	3.1.5		Bajzth
As from the mouth of mighty Bajazeth.	1Tamb	3.1.20		Fesse
by leaden pipes/Runs to the citie from the mountain Carnon.	1Tamb	3.1.60		Bajzth
That holds you from your father in despight,	1Tamb	3.2.27		Agidas
And keeps you from the honors of a Queene,	1Tamb	3.2.28		Agidas
destruction/Redeeme ycu from this deadly servitude.	1Tamb	3.2.34		Agidas
Is far from villanie or servitude.	1Tamb	3.2.38		Zenoc
And from their shieldes strike flames of lightening)/All	1Tamb	3.2.81		Agidas
Go wander free from feare of Tyrants rage,	1Tamb	3.2.102		Agidas
Remooved from the Torments and the hell:	1Tamb	3.2.103		Agidas
If he think good, can from his garrisons,	1Tamb	3.3.21		Bassoe
of a bigger size/Than all the brats ysprong from Typhons loins:	1Tamb	3.3.109		Bajzth
Returne with victorie, and free from wound.	1Tamb	3.3.133		Zenoc
And make him raine down murthering shot from heaven/To dash the	1Tamb	3.3.196		Zabina
If Mahomet should come from heaven and sweare,	1Tamb	3.3.208		Zenoc
Nay take the Turkish Crown from her, Zenocrate,	1Tamb	3.3.220		Tamb
So from the East unto the furthest West,	1Tamb	3.3.246		Tamb
Even from Persepolis to Mexico,	1Tamb	3.3.255		Tamb
The Souldane would not start a foot from him.	1Tamb	4.1.19		Souldn
every fixed starre/To sucke up poison from the moorish Fens,	1Tamb	4.2.6		Bajzth
My sword stroke fire from his coat of steele,	1Tamb	4.2.41		Tamb
and she shal looke/That these abuses flow not from her tongue:	1Tamb	4.2.70		Zenoc
Are fled from Bajazeth, and remaine with me,	1Tamb	4.2.80		Tamb
with the scraps/My servitures shall bring the from my boord.	1Tamb	4.2.88		Tamb
Shall ransome him, or take him from his cage.	1Tamb	4.2.94		Tamb
Even from this day to Platoes wondrous yeare,	1Tamb	4.2.96		Tamb
These Mores that drew him from Bythinia,	1Tamb	4.2.98		Tamb
Shall not defend it from our battering shot.	1Tamb	4.2.107		Tamb
Having the power from the Emperiall heaven,	1Tamb	4.4.30		Tamb
take it from my swords point, or Ile thrust it to thy heart.	1Tamb	4.4.40	P	Tamb
Then raise your seige from faire Damascus walles,	1Tamb	4.4.71		Zenoc
thou maist thinke thy selfe happie to be fed from my trencher.	1Tamb	4.4.92	P	Tamb
Drawes bloody humours from my feeble partes,	1Tamb	4.4.95		Bajzth
As far as from the frozen [plage] <place> of heaven,	1Tamb	4.4.122		Tamb
Or hope of rescue from the Souldans power,	1Tamb	5.1.4		Govnr

FROM (cont.)

Shead from the heads and hearts of all our Sex,	1Tamb	5.1.26	1Virgn
hate/Flings slaughtering terrour from my coleblack tents.	1Tamb	5.1.72	Tamb
and prevent their soules/From heavens of comfort, yet their age	1Tamb	5.1.90	1Virgn
Taking instructions from thy flowing eies:	1Tamb	5.1.146	Tamb
Quintessence they still/From their immortall flowers of Poesy,	1Tamb	5.1.166	Tamb
Even from the fiery spangled vaile of heaven,	1Tamb	5.1.185	Tamb
Here let him stay my maysters from the tents,	1Tamb	5.1.211	Tamb
Furies from the blacke Cocitus lake,	1Tamb	5.1.218	Bajzth
From whence the issues of my thoughts doe breake:	1Tamb	5.1.274	Bajzth
And let her horses from their nostrels breathe/Rebellious winds	1Tamb	5.1.297	Bajzth
Earth cast up fountaines from thy entralles,	1Tamb	5.1.347	Zenoc
And rackt by dutie from my cursed heart:	1Tamb	5.1.387	Zenoc
Nor fortune keep them selves from victory.	1Tamb	5.1.406	Arabia
To drive all sorrow from my fainting soule:	1Tamb	5.1.429	Arabia
From dangerous battel of my conquering Love.	1Tamb	5.1.442	Zenoc
Fearing my power should pull him from his throne.	1Tamb	5.1.453	Tamb
Have swelling cloudes drawen from wide gasping woundes,	1Tamb	5.1.459	Tamb
That I have sent from sundry foughten fields,	1Tamb	5.1.466	Tamb
From Barbary unto the Westerne Inde,	1Tamb	5.1.518	Tamb
And from the boundes of Affrick to the banks/Of Ganges, shall	1Tamb	5.1.520	Tamb
Now have we martcht from faire Natolia/Two hundred leagues, and	2Tamb	1.1.6	Orcan
Besides, king Sigismond hath brought from Christendome,	2Tamb	1.1.20	Uribas
Though from the shortest Northren Paralell,	2Tamb	1.1.25	Orcan
Marching from Cairon northward with his camp,	2Tamb	1.1.47	Gazell
From Scythia to the Orientall Plage/Of India, wher raging	2Tamb	1.1.68	Orcan
Even from the midst of fiery Cancers Tropick,	2Tamb	1.1.73	Orcan
We came from Turky to confirme a league,	2Tamb	1.1.115	Gazell
And we from Europe to the same intent,	2Tamb	1.1.118	Fredrk
I know thou wouldst depart from hence with me.	2Tamb	1.2.11	Callap
And bring Armados from the coasts of Spaine,	2Tamb	1.2.34	Callap
When Phoebus leaping from his Hemi-Spheare,	2Tamb	1.2.51	Callap
Sweet Almeda, scarse halfe a league from hence.	2Tamb	1.2.55	Callap
leave these armes/And save thy sacred person free from scathe:	2Tamb	1.3.10	Zenoc
But that I know they issued from thy wombe,	2Tamb	1.3.33	Tamb
and thy seed/Shall issue crowned from their mothers wombe.	2Tamb	1.3.53	Tamb
Bastardly boy, sprong from some cowards loins,	2Tamb	1.3.69	Tamb
Which being wroth, sends lightning from his eies,	2Tamb	1.3.76	Tamb
Stretching your conquering armes from east to west:	2Tamb	1.3.97	Tamb
Turkish Deputie/And all his Viceroies, snatch it from his head,	2Tamb	1.3.100	Tamb
That lanching from Argier to Tripoly,	2Tamb	1.3.124	Therid
From Azamor to Tunys neare the sea,	2Tamb	1.3.133	Usumc
From strong Tesella unto Biledull,	2Tamb	1.3.148	Techel
How have ye spent your absent time from me?	2Tamb	1.3.173	Tamb
Or cease one day from war and hot alarms,	2Tamb	1.3.183	Usumc
From thence unto Cazates did I martch,	2Tamb	1.3.191	Techel
From thence I crost the Gulfe, call'd by the name/Mare magiore,	2Tamb	1.3.214	Therid
Now will we march from proud Orminius mount/To faire Natolia,	2Tamb	2.2.2	Orcan
And make a passage from the imperiall heaven/That he that sits	2Tamb	2.2.48	Orcan
And God hath thundered vengeance from on high,	2Tamb	2.3.2	Sgsmnd
From paine to paine, whose change shal never end:	2Tamb	2.3.26	Orcan
Whose eies shot fire from their Ivory bowers,	2Tamb	2.4.9	Tamb
For amorous Jove hath snatcht my love from hence,	2Tamb	2.4.107	Tamb
Come downe from heaven and live with me againe.	2Tamb	2.4.118	Tamb
From al the crueltie my soule sustaind,	2Tamb	3.1.33	Callap
And I as many from Jerusalem,	2Tamb	3.1.44	Jrslem
And I as many bring from Trebizon,	2Tamb	3.1.49	Trebiz
From Soria with seventy thousand strong,	2Tamb	3.1.57	Soria
Tane from Aleppo, Soldino, Tripoly,	2Tamb	3.1.58	Soria
That freed me from the bondage of my foe:	2Tamb	3.1.69	Callap
That hanging here, wil draw the Gods from heaven:	2Tamb	3.2.28	Tamb
and covered waies/To keep the bulwark fronts from battery,	2Tamb	3.2.76	Tamb
And store of ordinance that from every flanke/May scoure the	2Tamb	3.2.79	Tamb
Murther the Foe and save [the] <their> walles from breach.	2Tamb	3.2.82	Tamb
Quite voide of skars, and cleare from any wound,	2Tamb	3.2.112	Tamb
Thus have wee martcht Northwarde from Tamburlaine,	2Tamb	3.3.1	Therid
measure the height/And distance of the castle from the trench,	2Tamb	3.3.51	Techel
To save our Cannoniers from musket shot,	2Tamb	3.3.57	Therid
and let us haste from hence/Along the cave that leads beyond	2Tamb	3.4.1	Olymp
my entrals bath'd/In blood that straineth from their orifex.	2Tamb	3.4.9	Capt
lookes is much more majesty/Than from the Concave superficies,	2Tamb	3.4.48	Therid
Drawing from it the shining Lamps of heaven.	2Tamb	3.4.77	Techel
That from the bounds of Phrigia to the sea/Which washeth Cyprus	2Tamb	3.5.11	Callap
From Palestina and Jerusalem,	2Tamb	3.5.32	Jrslem
So from Arabia desart, and the bounds/Of that sweet land, whose	2Tamb	3.5.35	Orcan
From Trebizon in Asia the lesse,	2Tamb	3.5.40	Trebiz
Of Sorians from Halla is repair'd/And neighbor cities of your	2Tamb	3.5.46	Soria
And fly my glove as from a Scorpion.	2Tamb	3.5.74	Tamb
Goe villaine, cast thee headlong from a rock,	2Tamb	3.5.120	Tamb
any Element/Shal shrowde thee from the wrath of Tamburlaine.	2Tamb	3.5.127	Tamb
in the stable, when you shall come sweating from my chariot.	2Tamb	3.5.142	P Tamb
Call foorth our laisie brother from the tent,	2Tamb	4.1.7	Celeb
What, dar'st thou then be absent from the fight,	2Tamb	4.1.22	Amyras
my striving hands/From martiall justice on thy wretched soule.	2Tamb	4.1.96	Tamb
Can never wash from thy distained browes.	2Tamb	4.1.110	Tamb
wars justice ye repute)/I execute, enjoin'd me from above,	2Tamb	4.1.148	Tamb
And eb againe, as thou departst from me.	2Tamb	4.2.32	Therid
which a cunning Alcumist/Distilled from the purest Balsamum,	2Tamb	4.2.60	Olymp
And Spels of magicke from the mouthes of spirits,	2Tamb	4.2.64	Olymp
From whence the starres doo borrow all their light,	2Tamb	4.2.89	Therid
And now the damned soules are free from paine,	2Tamb	4.2.91	Therid
But from Asphaltis, where I conquer'd you,	2Tamb	4.3.5	Tamb
And blow the morning from their nosterils,	2Tamb	4.3.8	Tamb

FROM (cont.)

to restraine/These coltish coach-horse tongues from blasphemy.	2Tamb	4.3.52	Usumc
Ah cruel Brat, sprung from a tyrants loines,	2Tamb	4.3.54	Jrslem
Until my soule dissevered from this flesh,	2Tamb	4.3.131	Tamb
Or hold our citie from the Conquerours hands.	2Tamb	5.1.5	Maxim
For I wil cast my selfe from off these walles,	2Tamb	5.1.40	2Citzn
And sent from hell to tyrannise on earth,	2Tamb	5.1.111	Govnr
When this is done, we'll martch from Babylon,	2Tamb	5.1.127	Tamb
From whom the thunder and the lightning breaks,	2Tamb	5.1.184	Tamb
Before his hoste be full from Babylon,	2Tamb	5.2.9	Callap
lie in wait for him/And if we find him absent from his campe,	2Tamb	5.2.57	Callap
yong Callapine that lately fled from your majesty, hath nowe	2Tamb	5.3.102	P 3Msngr
And here not far from Alexandria,	2Tamb	5.3.131	Tamb
From thence to Nubia neere Borno Lake,	2Tamb	5.3.136	Tamb
I came at last to Graecia, and from thence/To Asia, where I stay	2Tamb	5.3.141	Tamb
Which is from Scythia, where I first began,	2Tamb	5.3.143	Tamb
Lies westward from the midst of Cancers line,	2Tamb	5.3.146	Tamb
Whereas the Sun declining from our sight,	2Tamb	5.3.148	Tamb
And from th'Antartique Pole, Eastward behold/As much more land,	2Tamb	5.3.154	Tamb
now the Guize is dead, is come from France/To view this Land,	Jew	Prol.3	Machvl
But such as love me, gard me from their tongues,	Jew	Prol.6	Machvl
in perill of calamity/To ransome great Kings from captivity.	Jew	1.1.32	Barab
Their meanes of traffique from the vulgar trade,	Jew	1.1.35	Barab
Mine Argosie from Alexandria,	Jew	1.1.44	Barab
Thou couldst not come from Egypt, or by Caire/But at the entry	Jew	1.1.73	Barab
Thine Argosie from Alexandria,	Jew	1.1.85	2Merch
Are come from Turkey, and lye in our Rhode:	Jew	1.1.147	1Jew
Know Knights of Malta, that we came from Rhodes,	Jew	1.2.2	Basso
From Cyprus, Candy, and those other Iles/That lye betwixt the	Jew	1.2.3	Basso
From the Emperour of Turkey is arriv'd/Great Selim-Calymath,	Jew	1.2.39	Govnr
From nought at first thou camst to little welth,	Jew	1.2.105	1Knght
From little unto more, from more to most:	Jew	1.2.106	1Knght
tush, take not from me then,/For that is theft; and if you rob	Jew	1.2.125	Barab
our hands with blood/Is farre from us and our profession.	Jew	1.2.145	Govnr
and in mine Argosie/And other ships that came from Egypt last,	Jew	1.2.188	Barab
And hide these extreme sorrowes from mine eyes:	Jew	1.2.195	Barab
I, Daughter, for Religion/Hides many mischiefes from suspition.	Jew	1.2.282	Barab
Proceed from sinne, or want of faith in us,	Jew	1.2.323	Abigal
Away accursed from thy fathers sight.	Jew	1.2.351	Barab
Cropt from the pleasures of the fruitfull earth,	Jew	1.2.380	Mthias
of the silent night/Doth shake contagion from her sable wings;	Jew	2.1.4	Barab
my fingers take/A kisse from him that sends it from his soule.	Jew	2.1.59	Barab
The Christian Ile of Rhodes, from whence you came,	Jew	2.2.31	Bosco
might be got/To keepe him for his life time from the gallowes.	Jew	2.3.104	Barab
Converse not with him, he is cast off from heaven.	Jew	2.3.157	Mater
here are letters come/From Ormus, and the Post stayes here	Jew	2.3.223	Abigal
looking out/When you should come and hale him from the doore.	Jew	2.3.265	Barab
And so has she done you, even from a child.	Jew	2.3.289	Barab
And tell him that it comes from Lodowicke.	Jew	2.3.371	Barab
It is a challenge feign'd from Lodowicke.	Jew	2.3.374	Barab
That he shall verily thinke it comes from him.	Jew	2.3.376	Ithimr
From Venice Merchants, and from Padua/Were wont to come	Jew	3.1.6	Curtzn
and from Padua/Were wont to come rare witted Gentlemen,	Jew	3.1.6	Curtzn
And he is very seldome from my house;	Jew	3.1.10	Curtzn
Farre from the Sonne that gives eternall life.	Jew	3.3.65	Abigal
For she that varies from me in beleefe/Gives great presumption	Jew	3.4.10	Barab
from hence/Ne're shall she grieve me more with her disgrace;	Jew	3.4.28	Barab
poysons of the Stygian poole/Breake from the fiery kingdome;	Jew	3.4.103	Barab
But yesterday two ships went from this Towne,	Jew	4.1.69	Barab
Then will not Jacomo be long from hence.	Jew	4.1.159	Barab
by such a tall man as I am, from such a beautifull dame as you.	Jew	4.2.10	P Pilia
and he gave me a letter from one Madam Bellamira, saluting me	Jew	4.2.29	P Ithimr
I did Sir, and from this Gentlewoman, who as my selfe, and the	Jew	4.2.43	P Pilia
I'le goe steale some mony from my Master to make me hansome:	Jew	4.2.49	P Ithimr
And saile from hence to Greece, to lovely Greece,	Jew	4.2.89	Ithimr
'Twas sent me for a present from the great Cham.	Jew	4.4.68	Barab
And he from whom my most advantage comes,	Jew	5.2.113	Barab
From Barabas, Malta's Governor, I bring/A message unto mighty	Jew	5.3.13	Msngr
A warning-peece shall be shot off from the Tower,	Jew	5.5.39	Barab
From time to time, but specially in this,	P 10	1.10	Navrre
from Spaine the stately Catholickes/Sends Indian golde to coyne	P 117	2.60	Guise
For this have I a largesse from the Pope,	P 119	2.62	Guise
Then Ile have a peale of ordinance shot from the tower,	P 236	4.34	Guise
see they keep/All trecherous violence from our noble freend,	P 268	4.66	Charls
Mountsorrell from the Duke of Guise.	P 347	6.2	Mntsrl
down, heer's one would speak with you from the Duke of Guise.	P 349	6.4	P SrnsWf
To speek with me from such a man as he?	P 350	6.5	Seroun
What fearfull cries comes from the river [Sene] <Rene>,/That	P 361	7.1	Ramus
All that I have is but my stipend from the King,	P 378	7.18	Ramus
To get those pedantes from the King Navarre,	P 426	7.66	Guise
O no, his soule is fled from out his breast,	P 552	11.17	QnMoth
the speed we can, provide/For Henries coronation from Polonie:	P 563	11.28	QnMoth
To steale from France, and hye me to my home.	P 567	11.32	Navrre
And now that Henry is cal'd from Polland,	P 569	11.34	Navrre
That holdes it from your highnesse wrongfully:	P 582	11.47	Pleshe
Welcome from Poland Henry once agayne,	P 589	12.2	QnMoth
Shall slacke my loves affection from his bent.	P 607	12.20	King
Remooveles from the favours of your King.	P 609	12.22	King
Had late been pluckt from out faire Cupids wing:	P 668	13.12	Duchss
Now doe I see that from the very first,	P 694	13.38	Guise
And rent our true religion from this land:	P 703	14.6	Navrre
A mighty army comes from France with speed:	P 725	14.28	1Msngr
<make> a walk/On purpose from the Court to meet with him.	P 784	15.42	Mugern

FROM (cont.)

To beat the papall Monarck from our lands,	P 802	16.16	Navrre
And keep those relicks from our countries coastes.	P 803	16.17	Navrre
My Lord, I am advertised from France,	P 900	18.1	Navrre
And that Paris is revolted from his grace.	P 902	18.3	Navrre
sorte of English priestes/From Doway to the Seminary at Remes,	P1031	19.101	King
Wert thou the Pope thou mightst not scape from us.	P1092	20.2	1Mur
And roote Valoys his line from forth of France,	P1113	21.7	Dumain
sent from the President of Paris, that craves accesse unto your	P1156	22.18	P 1Msngr
God shield your grace from such a sodaine death:	P1178	22.40	Navrre
Take hence that damned villaine from my sight.	P1182	22.44	King
then will I wake thee from this folishe dreame/and lett thee	Paris	ms32,p391	Guise
Might have enforst me to have swum from France,	Edw	1.1.7	Gavstn
Heere comes the king and the nobles/From the parlament, ile	Edw	1.1.73	Gavstn
I can no longer keepe me from my lord.	Edw	1.1.139	Gavstn
And since I went from hence, no soule in hell/Hath felt more	Edw	1.1.146	Gavstn
Why post we not from hence to levie men?	Edw	1.2.16	Mortmr
Weele hale him from the bosome of the king,	Edw	1.2.29	Mortmr
No, but weele lift Gaveston from hence.	Edw	1.2.62	Lncstr
Then may we lawfully revolt from him.	Edw	1.2.73	Mortmr
Unlesse he be declinde from that base pesant.	Edw	1.4.7	Mortmr
Ere my sweete Gaveston shall part from me,	Edw	1.4.48	Edward
Thou from this land, I from my selfe am banisht.	Edw	1.4.118	Edward
To go from hence, greeves not poore Gaveston,	Edw	1.4.119	Gavstn
Or else be banisht from his highnesse presence.	Edw	1.4.203	Queene
Weele pull him from the strongest hould he hath.	Edw	1.4.289	Mortmr
Ah had some bloudlesse furie rose from hell,	Edw	1.4.316	Edward
Then I may fetch from this ritch treasurie:	Edw	1.4.332	Queene
For riper yeares will weane him from such toyes.	Edw	1.4.401	MortSr
below, the king and he/From out a window, laugh at such as we,	Edw	1.4.417	Mortmr
And even now, a poast came from the court,	Edw	2.1.19	Spencr
With letters to our ladie from the King,	Edw	2.1.20	Spencr
This letter came from my sweete Gaveston,	Edw	2.1.59	Neece
I will not long be from thee though I die:	Edw	2.1.62	Neece
Letters, from whence?	Edw	2.2.112	Mortmr
From Scotland my lord.	Edw	2.2.113	1Msngr
and my gentrie/Is fetcht from Oxford, not from Heraldrie.	Edw	2.2.244	Baldck
Drums strike alarum, raise them from their sport,	Edw	2.3.25	Mortmr
From my imbracements thus he breakes away,	Edw	2.4.16	Queene
Or that these teares that drissell from mine eyes,	Edw	2.4.19	Queene
with haling of my lord/From Gaveston, from wicked Gaveston,	Edw	2.4.27	Queene
Farre be it from the thought of Lancaster,	Edw	2.4.33	Lncstr
And though devorsed from king Edwards eyes,	Edw	2.5.3	Gavstn
I long to heare an answer from the Barons/Touching my friend,	Edw	3.1.1	Edward
And marche to fire them from their starting holes.	Edw	3.1.127	Spencr
My lord, [here] is <heres> a messenger from the Barons,/Desires	Edw	3.1.148	Spencr
Thou comst from Mortimer and his complices,	Edw	3.1.153	Edward
That from your princely person you remoove/This Spencer, as a	Edw	3.1.161	Herald
see how I do devorce/Spencer from me:	Edw	3.1.177	Edward
Did they remoove that flatterer from thy throne.	Edw	3.1.231	Kent
Shall have me from my gratious mothers side,	Edw	4.2.23	Prince
From the lieutenant of the tower my lord.	Edw	4.3.9	Arundl
Now sirs, the newes from Fraunce.	Edw	4.3.14	Edward
As Isabella <Isabell> gets no aide from thence.	Edw	4.3.16	Edward
How now, what newes with thee, from whence come these?	Edw	4.3.24	Edward
To you my lord of Gloster from [Levune] <Lewne>.	Edw	4.3.26	Post
and withall/We may remoove these flatterers from the king,	Edw	4.4.26	Mortmr
<Unhappies> <Unhappy is> Edward, chaste from Englands bounds.	Edw	4.6.62	Kent
Free from suspect, and fell invasion/Of such as have your	Edw	4.7.4	Abbot
That in our famous nurseries of artes/Thou suckedst from Plato,	Edw	4.7.19	Edward
of artes/Thou suckedst from Plato, and from Aristotle.	Edw	4.7.19	Edward
To take my life, my companie from me?	Edw	4.7.65	Edward
Parted from hence, never to see us more!	Edw	4.7.101	Spencr
And save you from your foes, Bartley would die.	Edw	5.1.134	Bartly
Letters, from whence?	Edw	5.2.23	Mortmr
From Killingworth my lorde.	Edw	5.2.23	2Msngr
So that he now is gone from Killingworth,	Edw	5.2.31	BshpWn
a letter presently/Unto the Lord of Bartley from our selfe,	Edw	5.2.48	Mortmr
Remoove him still from place to place by night,	Edw	5.2.59	Mortmr
And then from thence to Bartley back againe:	Edw	5.2.61	Mortmr
I would those wordes proceeded from your heart.	Edw	5.2.100	Kent
And rescue aged Edward from his foes,	Edw	5.2.120	Kent
And cleare my bodie from foule excrements.	Edw	5.3.26	Edward
Feare not sweete boye, ile garde thee from thy foes,	Edw	5.4.111	Queene
From whence a dampe continually ariseth,	Edw	5.5.4	Matrvs
Farre is it from my hart to do you harme,	Edw	5.5.47	Ltborn
And what eyes can refraine from shedding teares,	Edw	5.5.50	Ltborn
Or as Matrevis, hewne from the Caucasus,	Edw	5.5.54	Edward
O would my bloud dropt out from every vaine,	Edw	5.5.66	Edward
As doth this water from my tattered robes:	Edw	5.5.67	Edward
As thou receivedst thy life from me,	Edw	5.6.68	Queene
And let these teares distilling from mine eyes,	Edw	5.6.101	King
And chase the Prince of Parma from our Land,	F 120	1.1.92	Faust
From <For> Venice shall they drag <dregge> huge Argosies,/And	F 157	1.1.129	Valdes
And from America the Golden Fleece,	F 158	1.1.130	Valdes
Leapes from th'Antarticke world unto the skie,	F 231	1.3.3	Faust
Be it to make the Moone drop from her Sphere,	F 266	1.3.38	Faust
For which God threw him from the face of heaven.	F 296	1.3.68	Mephst
Mephostophilis come/And bring glad tydings from great Lucifer.	F 416	2.1.28	Faust
Veiw here this <the> bloud that trickles from mine arme,	F 446	2.1.58	Faust
Even from the Moone unto the Emperiall Orbe,	F 590	2.2.39	Mephst
All <joyntly> move from East to West, in foure and twenty	F 597	2.2.46	P Mephst
we are come from hell in person to shew thee some pastime:	F 654	2.2.103	P Belzeb

FROM (cont.)

and you have done me great injury to bring me from thence, let	F 705.2	2.2.156A	P Sloth
keepe further from me O thou illiterate, and unlearned Hostler.	F 728	2.3.7	P Robin
From the bright circle of the horned Moone, . . .	F 762	2.3.41	2Chor
From East to West his Dragons swiftly glide, . . .	F 766	2.3.45	2Chor
From Paris next, costing the Realme of France, . . .	F 784	3.1.6	Faust
From thence to Venice, Padua, and the [rest] <East>, .	F 794	3.1.16	Faust
That <which> Julius caesar brought from Affrica. . .	F 824	3.1.46	Mephst
From Bruno's backe, ascends Saint Peters Chaire. . .	F 876	3.1.98	Pope
And interdict from Churches priviledge, ...	F 909	3.1.131	Pope
authority Apostolicall/Depose him from his Regall Government.	F 924	3.1.146	Pope
In token of our seven-fold power from heaven, . . .	F 934	3.1.156	Pope
How now? who snatch't the meat from me!	F1044	3.2.64	Pope
Was sent me from a Cardinall in France.	F1047	3.2.67	Pope
be he that stole [away] his holinesse meate from the Table.	F1077	3.2.97	1Frier
pray where's the cup you stole from the Taverne? . .	F1097	3.3.10	P Vintnr
From Constantinople have they brought me now <am I hither	F1118	3.3.31	Mephst
That on a furies back came post from Rome, . . .	F1161	4.1.7	Fredrk
thine, in setting Bruno free/From his and our professed enemy,	F1207	4.1.53	Emper
And hale the stubborne Furies from their caves, . .	F1225	4.1.71	Faust
To keepe his Carkasse from their bloudy phangs. . .	F1303	4.1.149	Faust
us sway thy thoughts/From this attempt against the Conjurer.	F1326	4.2.2	Mrtino
buttons to his lips, to keepe his tongue from catching cold.	F1388	4.2.64	P Benvol
And I had breath'd a man made free from harme. . . .	F1400	4.2.76	Faust
To sheild me from your hated treachery:	F1428	4.2.104	Faust
be good, for they come from a farre Country I can tell you.	F1577	4.6.20	P Faust
is barren of his fruite, from whence you had these ripe grapes.	F1579	4.6.22	P Duke
From whence, by meanes of a swift spirit that I have, I had	F1585	4.6.28	P Faust
Then thou art banisht from the sight of heaven; . .	F1715	5.1.42	OldMan
That durst disswade me from thy Lucifer, ...	F1754	5.1.81	Faust
Those <These> thoughts that do disswade me from my vow, .	F1764	5.1.91	Faust
[That from thy soule exclud'st the grace of heaven], .	F1789	5.1.116A	OldMan
Thus from infernall Dis do we ascend/To view the subjects of	F1797	5.2.1	Lucifr
Both come from drawing Faustus latest will. . . .	F1814	5.2.18	Mephst
And hide me from the heavy wrath of [God] <heaven>. . .	F1946	5.2.150	Faust
My limbes may issue from your smoky mouthes, . . .	F1955	5.2.159	Faust
This soule should flie from me, and I be chang'd/[Unto] <Into>	F1967	5.2.171	Faust
here is a daintie dish was sent me from the Bishop of Millaine.	F App	p.231 5	P Pope
How now, whose that which snatcht the meate from me? .	F App	p.231 8	P Pope
My Lord, this dish was sent me from the Cardinall of Florence.	F App	p.231 9	P Pope
Cursed be hee that stole away his holinesse meate from/the	F App	p.232 31	Frier
with you, I must yet have a goblet payde from you ere you goe.	F App	p.234 8	P Vintnr
From Constantinople am I hither come, ...	F App	p.235 38	Mephst
How, from Constantinople?	F App	p.235 40	P Robin
Canst raise this man from hollow vaults below, . . .	F App	p.237 30	Emper
Doctor, yet ere you goe, expect from me a bounteous reward.	F App	p.239 88	P Emper
I wil not hide from you the thing my heart desires, and were it	F App	p.242 9	P Duchss
Teares falling from repentant heavinesse/Of thy most vilde and	F App	p.243 39	OldMan
These plagues arise from wreake of civill power. . .	Lucan, First Booke		32
Then men from war shal bide in league, and ease, . .	Lucan, First Booke		60
Peace through the world from Janus Phane shal flie, . .	Lucan, First Booke		61
Keepes each from other, but being worne away/They both burst	Lucan, First Booke		102
So thunder which the wind teares from the cloudes, . .	Lucan, First Booke		152
Which issues from a small spring, is but shallow, . .	Lucan, First Booke		216
deviding just/The bounds of Italy, from Cisalpin Fraunce;	Lucan, First Booke		218
the darke/(Swifter then bullets throwne from Spanish slinges,	Lucan, First Booke		231
Or sea far from the land, so all were whist. . . .	Lucan, First Booke		262
From doubtfull Roome wrongly expel'd the Tribunes, . .	Lucan, First Booke		269
wars,/We from our houses driven, most willingly/Suffered exile:	Lucan, First Booke		279
(Whom from his youth he bribde) needs make him king? .	Lucan, First Booke		315
having lickt/Warme goare from Syllas sword art yet athirst,	Lucan, First Booke		331
But Roome at thraldoms feet to rid from tyrants. . .	Lucan, First Booke		352
delay/Might crosse him, he withdrew his troupes from France,	Lucan, First Booke		395
And many came from shallow Isara, ...	Lucan, First Booke		400
And others came from that uncertaine shore, . . .	Lucan, First Booke		410
Whether the sea roul'd alwaies from that point, . .	Lucan, First Booke		413
which he hath brought/From out their Northren parts, and that	Lucan, First Booke		479
The fathers selves leapt from their seats; and flying/Left	Lucan, First Booke		485
Looke how when stormy Auster from the breach/Of Libian Syrtes	Lucan, First Booke		496
The Pilot from the helme leapes in the sea; . . .	Lucan, First Booke		499
Thou Roome at name of warre runst from thy selfe, . .	Lucan, First Booke		517
And from the northren climat snatching fier/Blasted the .	Lucan, First Booke		532
the Alpes/Shooke the old snow from off their trembling laps.	Lucan, First Booke		552
Crownes fell from holy statues, ominous birds/Defil'd the day,	Lucan, First Booke		556
Soules quiet and appeas'd [sigh'd] <sight> from their graves,	Lucan, First Booke		566
No vaine sprung out but from the yawning gash, . . .	Lucan, First Booke		613
and every vaine/Did threaten horror from the host of Caesar;	Lucan, First Booke		621
The heart stird not, and from the gaping liver/Squis'd matter;	Lucan, First Booke		623
the Emathian bandes, from thence/To the pine bearing hils,	Lucan, First Booke		687
Thy mother shall from heaven applaud this show, . .	Ovid's Elegies		1.2.39
Yet scarse my hands from thee containe I well. . . .	Ovid's Elegies		1.4.10
would, I cannot him cashiere/Before I be divided from my geere.	Ovid's Elegies		1.6.36
the barre strike from the poast.	Ovid's Elegies		1.6.56
But thou my crowne, from sad haires tane away, . . .	Ovid's Elegies		1.6.67
lookes shewed/Like marble from the Parian Mountaines hewed.	Ovid's Elegies		1.7.52
Like water gushing from consuming snowe.	Ovid's Elegies		1.7.58
My bloud, the teares were that from her descended. . .	Ovid's Elegies		1.7.60
Her name comes from the thing:	Ovid's Elegies		1.8.3
Great grand-sires from their antient graves she chides/And with	Ovid's Elegies		1.8.17
From dog-kept flocks come preys to woolves most gratefull.	Ovid's Elegies		1.8.56
If he gives nothing, let him from thee wend. . . .	Ovid's Elegies		1.8.100
Hector to armes went from his wives embraces, . . .	Ovid's Elegies		1.9.35
Whom Troiane ships fecht from Europa farre. . . .	Ovid's Elegies		1.10.2

FROM (cont.)

This cause hath thee from pleasing me debard.	Ovid's Elegies	1.10.12
Take from irrationall beasts a president,	Ovid's Elegies	1.10.25
Nor the milde Ewe gifts from the Ramme doth pull.	Ovid's Elegies	1.10.28
Only a Woman gets spoiles from a Man,	Ovid's Elegies	1.10.29
should defend/Or great wealth from a judgement seate ascend.	Ovid's Elegies	1.10.40
his rent discharg'd/From further duty he rests then inlarg'd.	Ovid's Elegies	1.10.46
Take clustred grapes from an ore-laden vine,	Ovid's Elegies	1.10.55
Which I thinke gather'd from cold hemlocks flower/Wherein bad	Ovid's Elegies	1.12.9
bondes contained/From barbarous lips of some Atturney strained.	Ovid's Elegies	1.12.24
Now on <ore> the sea from her old love comes shee,	Ovid's Elegies	1.13.1
That drawes the day from heavens cold axletree.	Ovid's Elegies	1.13.2
And birds for <from> Memnon yearly shall be slaine.	Ovid's Elegies	1.13.4
And birdes send forth shrill notes from everie bow.	Ovid's Elegies	1.13.8
Memnon the elfe/Received his cole-blacke colour from thy selfe.	Ovid's Elegies	1.13.32
which from their crowne/Phoebus and Bacchus wisht were hanging	Ovid's Elegies	1.14.31
Died red with shame, to hide from shame she seekes.	Ovid's Elegies	1.14.52
Or that unlike the line from whence I [sprong] <come>,	Ovid's Elegies	1.15.3
And Gallus shall be knowne from East to West,	Ovid's Elegies	1.15.29
Snakes leape by verse from caves of broken mountaines/And	Ovid's Elegies	2.1.25
Even from your cheekes parte of a voice did breake.	Ovid's Elegies	2.5.16
The parrat from east India to me sent,	Ovid's Elegies	2.6.1
The Gods from this sinne rid me of suspition,	Ovid's Elegies	2.7.19
The Docke in harbours ships drawne from the flouds,	Ovid's Elegies	2.9.21
Horse freed from service range abroad the woods.	Ovid's Elegies	2.9.22
And from my mistris bosome let me rise:	Ovid's Elegies	2.10.20
The lofty Pine from high mount Pelion raught/Ill waies by rough	Ovid's Elegies	2.11.1
I from the shore thy knowne ship first will see,	Ovid's Elegies	2.11.43
What helpes it Woman to be free from warre?	Ovid's Elegies	2.14.1
Why takest increasing grapes from Vine-trees full?	Ovid's Elegies	2.14.23
go small gift from hand,/Let her my faith with thee given	Ovid's Elegies	2.15.27
Why doth my mistresse from me oft devide?	Ovid's Elegies	2.16.42
I yeeld, and back my wit from battells bring,	Ovid's Elegies	2.18.11
As soone as from strange lands Sabinus came,	Ovid's Elegies	2.18.27
And writings did from diverse places frame,	Ovid's Elegies	2.18.28
Then warres, and from thy tents wilt come to mine.	Ovid's Elegies	2.18.40
Who covets lawfull things takes leaves from woods,	Ovid's Elegies	2.19.31
To steale sands from the shore he loves alife,	Ovid's Elegies	2.19.45
And slipt from bed cloth'd in a loose night-gowne,	Ovid's Elegies	3.1.51
From no mans reading fearing to be sav'd.	Ovid's Elegies	3.1.54
Thou hast my gift, which she would from thee sue.	Ovid's Elegies	3.1.60
And from my hands the reines will slip away.	Ovid's Elegies	3.2.14
Ah Pelops from his coach was almost feld,	Ovid's Elegies	3.2.15
That from thy fanne, mov'd by my hand may blow?	Ovid's Elegies	3.2.38
Foule dust, from her faire body, go away.	Ovid's Elegies	3.2.42
Fower chariot-horses from the lists even ends.	Ovid's Elegies	3.2.66
But bids his darts from perjurd girles retire.	Ovid's Elegies	3.3.36
Nor canst by watching keepe her minde from sinne.	Ovid's Elegies	3.4.7
With snow thaw'd from the next hill now thou rushest,	Ovid's Elegies	3.5.7
Who so well keepes his waters head from knowing,	Ovid's Elegies	3.5.40
Her, from his swift waves, the bold floud perceav'd,	Ovid's Elegies	3.5.51
And from the mid foord his hoarse voice upheav'd,	Ovid's Elegies	3.5.52
Ilia, sprung from Idaean Laomedon?	Ovid's Elegies	3.5.54
And from the channell all abroad surrounded.	Ovid's Elegies	3.5.86
Clowne, from my journey why doest me deterre?	Ovid's Elegies	3.5.88
Thou hast no name, but com'st from snowy mountaines;	Ovid's Elegies	3.5.91
By charmes maste drops from okes, from vines grapes fall,	Ovid's Elegies	3.6.33
And fruit from trees, when ther's no wind at al.	Ovid's Elegies	3.6.34
Hath any rose so from a fresh yong maide,	Ovid's Elegies	3.6.53
Or jaded camst thou from some others bed.	Ovid's Elegies	3.6.80
With that her loose gowne on, from me she cast her,	Ovid's Elegies	3.6.81
Gold from the earth in steade of fruits we pluck,	Ovid's Elegies	3.7.53
See Homer from whose fountaine ever fild,	Ovid's Elegies	3.8.25
A clowne, nor no love from her warme brest yeelds.	Ovid's Elegies	3.9.18
I have sustainde so oft thrust from the dore,	Ovid's Elegies	3.10.9
The Sunne turnd backe from Atreus cursed table?	Ovid's Elegies	3.11.39
And calves from whose feard front no threatning flyes,	Ovid's Elegies	3.12.15
From him that yeelds the garland <palme> is quickly got,	Ovid's Elegies	3.13.47
From whence her vaile reacht to the ground beneath.	Hero and Leander	1.18
And beat from thence, have lighted there againe.	Hero and Leander	1.24
Because she tooke more from her than she left,	Hero and Leander	1.47
Jove might have sipt out Nectar from his hand.	Hero and Leander	1.62
Came lovers home, from this great festivall.	Hero and Leander	1.96
From Latmus mount up to the glomie skie,	Hero and Leander	1.109
From steepe Pine-bearing mountains to the plaine:	Hero and Leander	1.116
Went Hero thorow Sestos, from her tower/To Venus temple, [where]	Hero and Leander	1.132
And with the other, wine from grapes out wroong.	Hero and Leander	1.140
Jove, slylie stealing from his sisters bed,	Hero and Leander	1.147
Till with the fire that from his count'nance blazed,	Hero and Leander	1.164
From Venus altar to your footsteps bending)/Doth testifie that	Hero and Leander	1.210
Or if it could, downe from th'enameld skie,	Hero and Leander	1.249
Then Hero hate me not, nor from me flie,	Hero and Leander	1.291
Foorth from those two tralucent cesternes brake,	Hero and Leander	1.296
But from his spreading armes away she cast her,	Hero and Leander	1.342
Far from the towne (where all is whist and still,	Hero and Leander	1.346
For unawares (Come thither) from her slipt,	Hero and Leander	1.358
And shot a shaft that burning from him went,	Hero and Leander	1.372
Stole some from Hebe (Hebe, Joves cup fil'd),	Hero and Leander	1.434
Which being knowne (as what is hid from Jove)?	Hero and Leander	1.436
fire filcht by Prometheus;/And thrusts him down from heaven:	Hero and Leander	1.439
Which th'earth from ougly Chaos den up-wayd:	Hero and Leander	1.450
Grosse gold, from them runs headlong to the boore.	Hero and Leander	1.472
For from the earth to heaven, is Cupid rais'd,	Hero and Leander	2.31

FROM (cont.)
I, and shee wisht, albeit not from her hart, — Hero and Leander 2.37
would not yeeld/So soone to part from that she deerely held. — Hero and Leander 2.84
But like exiled aire thrust from his sphere, — Hero and Leander 2.118
Set in a forren place, and straight from thence, — Hero and Leander 2.119
That him from her unjustly did detaine. — Hero and Leander 2.122
Least water-nymphs should pull him from the brinke. — Hero and Leander 2.198
Whose lively heat like fire from heaven fet, — Hero and Leander 2.255
describe, but hee/That puls or shakes it from the golden tree: — Hero and Leander 2.300
And from her countenance behold ye might, — Hero and Leander 2.318
As from an orient cloud, glymse <glimps'd> here and there. — Hero and Leander 2.320
Which from our pretty Lambes we pull, — Passionate Shepherd 14

FRONT
Shall finde it written on confusions front, — Dido 3.2.19 Juno
would let me be put in the front of such a battaile once, — 2Tamb 4.1.72 P Calyph
As he will front the mightiest of us all, — Edw 1.4.260 Mortmr
Shake off these wrinckles that thy front assault, — Ovid's Elegies 1.8.45
I charge thee marke her eyes and front in reading, — Ovid's Elegies 1.11.17
Sterne was her front, her [cloake] <looke> on ground did lie. — Ovid's Elegies 3.1.12
And calves from whose feard front no threatning flyes, — Ovid's Elegies 3.12.15

FRONTIER
To Alexandria, and the frontier townes, — 2Tamb 1.1.48 Gazell
And of Argier and Affriks frontier townes/Twise twenty thousand — 2Tamb 1.3.119 Therid
Unto the frontier point of Soria: — 2Tamb 3.3.2 Therid
And frontier Varus that the campe is farre, — Lucan, First Booke 405

FRONTIRE
Wagons or tents, then in this frontire towne. — Lucan, First Booke 255

FRONTS
and covered waies/To keep the bulwark fronts from battery, — 2Tamb 3.2.76 Tamb

FROSEN
Thou shalt be drawen amidst the frosen Pooles, — 1Tamb 1.2.99 Tamb

FROST
Suffring much cold by hoary nights frost bred. — Ovid's Elegies 2.19.22

FROSTY
Under the frosty beare, or parching East, — Lucan, First Booke 254
Now frosty night her flight beginnes to take, — Ovid's Elegies 1.6.65

FROTH
And had my being from thy bubling froth: — Dido 1.1.129 Venus

FROWARD
And the Icarian froward Dog-starre shine, — Ovid's Elegies 2.16.4

FROWN
south were cause/I know not, but the cloudy ayre did frown; — Lucan, First Booke 237

FROWND
Or force her smile that hetherto hath frownd: — Dido 1.1.88 Jupitr

FROWNE
I vow, if she but once frowne on thee more, — Dido 1.1.12 Jupitr
Since gloomie Aeolus doth cease to frowne. — Dido 4.1.27 Aeneas
Swell raging seas, frowne wayward destinies, — Dido 4.4.57 Aeneas
What if I sinke his ships? O heele frowne: — Dido 4.4.110 Dido
Better he frowne, then I should dye for griefe: — Dido 4.4.111 Dido
I cannot see him frowne, it may not be: — Dido 4.4.112 Dido
onely Aeneas frowne/Is that which terrifies poore Didos heart: — Dido 4.4.115 Dido
It is Aeneas frowne that ends my daies: — Dido 4.4.120 Dido
Make heaven to frowne and every fixed starre/To sucke up poison — 1Tamb 4.2.5 Bajzth
The heavens may frowne, the earth for anger quake, — 1Tamb 5.1.231 Bajzth
Then my faire Abigal should frowne on me. — Jew 2.3.332 Lodowk
The peeres will frowne. — Edw 1.4.141 Gavstn
And when I frowne, make all the court looke pale, — Edw 5.4.53 Mortmr
Was this that sterne aspect, that awfull frowne, — F1370 4.2.46 Fredrk

FROWNES
So fares Agydas for the late felt frownes/That sent a tempest — 1Tamb 3.2.85 Agidas
The killing frownes of jealousie and love. — 1Tamb 3.2.91 Agidas
And when I come, he frownes, as who should say, — Edw 1.2.53 Queene
They passe not for thy frownes as late they did, — Edw 5.1.77 Edward
When most her husband bends the browes and frownes, — Ovid's Elegies 2.2.33

FROWNING
Or els abide the wrath of frowning Jove. — Dido 5.1.54 Hermes
Go frowning foorth, but come thou smyling home, — 1Tamb 1.1.65 Mycet
And he with frowning browes and fiery lookes, — 1Tamb 1.2.56 Techel
Threatned with frowning wrath and jealousie, — 1Tamb 3.2.67 Agidas
did your greatnes see/The frowning lookes of fiery Tamburlaine, — 1Tamb 4.1.13 2Msngr
And in the furrowes of his frowning browes, — 2Tamb 1.3.77 Tamb
He bindes his temples with a frowning cloude, — 2Tamb 2.4.6 Tamb
With furious words and frowning visages, — 2Tamb 5.1.78 Tamb

FROWNS
And thats the cause that Guise so frowns at us, — P 52 1.52 Navrre

FROWNST
Frownst thou thereat, aspiring Lancaster, — Edw 1.1.93 Edward

FROZEN (See also FROSEN)
As far as from the frozen [plage] <place> of heaven, — 1Tamb 4.4.122 Tamb
Vast Gruntland compast with the frozen sea, — 2Tamb 1.1.26 Orcan
And frozen Alpes thaw'd with resolving winds. — Lucan, First Booke 221

FRUIT
And fall like mellowed fruit, with shakes of death, — 1Tamb 2.1.47 Cosroe
Untill we reach the ripest fruit of all, — 1Tamb 2.7.27 Tamb
That Zoacum, that fruit of bytternesse, — 2Tamb 2.3.20 Orcan
Joying the fruit of Ceres garden plot, — 2Tamb 4.3.37 Orcan
For earth hath spent the pride of all her fruit, — 2Tamb 5.3.250 Amyras
No doubt your soule shall reape the fruit of it. — Jew 2.3.78 Lodowk
'Tis likely they in time may reape some fruit, — Jew 2.3.84 Barab
Mor du, wert <were> not the fruit within thy wombe, — P 688 13.32 Guise
that lye farre East, where they have fruit twice a yeare. — F1584 4.6.27 P Faust
And fruit from trees, when ther's no wind at al. — Ovid's Elegies 3.6.34

FRUIT (cont.)			
Whose fruit none rightly can describe, but hee/That puls or	Hero and Leander		2.299
FRUITE			
Is this the fruite your reconcilement beares? . . .	Edw	2.2.31	Edward
when every Tree is barren of his fruite, from whence you had	F1579	4.6.22	P Duke
[May] <Many> bounteous [lome] <love> Alcinous fruite resigne.	Ovid's Elegies		1.10.56
Water in waters, and fruite flying touch/Tantalus seekes, his	Ovid's Elegies		2.2.43
Had Venus spoilde her bellies Troyane fruite, . . .	Ovid's Elegies		2.14.17
When fruite fild Tuscia should a wife give me, . . .	Ovid's Elegies		3.12.1
FRUITES			
And all the fruites that plentie els sends forth, . .	Dido	4.2.15	Iarbus
search all corners of the new-found-world/For pleasant fruites,	F 112	1.1.84	Faust
Fruites ripe will fall, let springing things increase, .	Ovid's Elegies		2.14.25
FRUITFULL			
Unto what fruitfull quarters were ye bound, . . .	Dido	1.2.18	Iarbus
Hath summond me to fruitfull Italy:	Dido	4.3.4	Aeneas
Come as thou didst in fruitfull Scicilie, ...	2Tamb	4.3.34	Orcan
Cropt from the pleasures of the fruitfull earth, . .	Jew	1.2.380	Mthias
[The fruitfull plot of Scholerisme grac'd], . . .	F 16	Prol.16	1Chor
Whose bankes are set with Groves of fruitfull Vines. .	F 786	3.1.8	Faust
Flies ore the Alpes to fruitfull Germany, ...	F 985	3.2.5	Mephst
Like to a tall oake in a fruitfull field, ...	Lucan, First Booke		137
Onely was Crete fruitfull that plenteous yeare, . .	Ovid's Elegies		3.9.37
And fruitfull wits that in aspiring <inaspiring> are, .	Hero and Leander		1.477
FRUITION			
The sweet fruition of an earthly crowne.	1Tamb	2.7.29	Tamb
Denie my soule fruition of her joy, ...	2Tamb	5.3.194	Amyras
Sooner shall kindnesse gaine thy wills fruition. . .	Ovid's Elegies		3.4.12
FRUITLES			
Brave men at armes, abandon fruitles feares, . . .	Dido	1.2.32	Iarbus
FRUITLESSE			
But I will learne to leave these fruitlesse teares, . .	Jew	1.2.230	Abigal
Abandon fruitlesse cold Virginitie, ...	Hero and Leander		1.317
FRUITS			
For I can see no fruits in all their faith, . . .	Jew	1.1.116	Barab
Rather illusions, fruits of lunacy, ...	F 407	2.1.19	BdAngl
And tearmes <termst> [my] <our> works fruits of an idle quill?	Ovid's Elegies		1.15.2
And lookes uppon the fruits he cannot touch. . . .	Ovid's Elegies		3.6.52
Gold from the earth in steade of fruits we pluck, . .	Ovid's Elegies		3.7.53
FRUSTRATE			
But I have sworne to frustrate both their hopes, . .	Jew	2.3.142	Barab
To lighten doubts and frustrate subtile foes. . . .	P 457	8.7	Anjoy
What we confirme the king will frustrate.	Edw	1.2.72	Lncstr
The plough-mans hopes were frustrate at the last. . .	Ovid's Elegies		3.9.34
FRUSTRATES			
What they intend, the hangman frustrates cleane. . .	Edw	3.1.275	Baldck
FRY (See FRIE)			
FRYAR			
And ducke as low as any bare-foot Fryar, ...	Jew	2.3.25	Barab
But here comes cursed Ithimore with the Fryar. . . .	Jew	3.3.49	Abigal
Welcome grave Fryar; Ithamore begon, ...	Jew	3.3.52	Abigal
A Fryar.	Jew	3.4.21	P Ithimr
A Fryar? false villaine, he hath done the deed. . .	Jew	3.4.22	Barab
Where is the Fryar that converst with me?	Jew	3.6.9	Abigal
ah gentle Fryar,/Convert my father that he may be sav'd, .	Jew	3.6.38	Abigal
Fryar Barnardine goe you with Ithimore.	Jew	4.1.99	Barab
Now Fryar Bernardine I come to you, ...	Jew	4.1.125	Barab
Ithimore, tell me, is the Fryar asleepe?	Jew	4.1.129	Barab
Fryar, awake.	Jew	4.1.143	Barab
Who would not thinke but that this Fryar liv'd? . .	Jew	4.1.156	Barab
Heaven blesse me; what, a Fryar a murderer? . . .	Jew	4.1.196	Barab
I never knew a man take his death so patiently as this Fryar;	Jew	4.2.22	P Ithimr
Nuns, and he and I, snicle hand too fast, strangled a Fryar.	Jew	4.4.21	P Ithimr
lov'd Rice, that Fryar Bernardine slept in his owne clothes.	Jew	4.4.76	P Ithimr
Nuns, strangled a Fryar, and I know not what mischiefe beside.	Jew	5.1.13	P Pilia
FRYARS			
and inquire/For any of the Fryars of Saint [Jaques] <Jaynes>,	Jew	3.3.28	Abigal
one; have not the Nuns fine sport with the Fryars now and then?	Jew	3.3.33	P Ithimr
Oh holy Fryars, the burthen of my sinnes/Lye heavy on my soule;	Jew	4.1.48	Barab
No, 'tis an order which the Fryars use:	Jew	4.1.134	Barab
looking of a Fryars Execution, whom I saluted with an old	Jew	4.2.17	P Pilia
FRYDE			
an inch of raw Mutton, better then an ell of fryde Stockfish:	F 709	2.2.161	P Ltchry
FRYER			
Blind, Fryer, I wrecke not thy perswasions. . . .	Jew	1.2.355	Barab
be he that strucke <tooke> fryer Sandelo a blow on the pate.	F1081	3.2.101	1Frier
FRYERS			
And yet I know the prayers of those Nuns/And holy Fryers,	Jew	2.3.81	Barab
Five hundred fatte Franciscan Fryers and priestes. . .	P 142	2.85	Guise
FUELL (See also FEWELL)			
Pleasure addes fuell to my lustfull fire, ...	Ovid's Elegies		2.10.25
FUGE			
Homo fuge: whether should I flye?	F 466	2.1.78	Faust
I see it plaine, even heere <in this place> is writ/Homo fuge:	F 470	2.1.82	Faust
FUGIENS			
Hunc dies vidit fugiens jacentem.	Edw	4.7.54	Leistr
FUGITIVE			
Villaine, traitor, damned fugitive, ...	2Tamb	3.5.117	Tamb
FUGITIVES			
Fill'd with a packe of faintheart Fugitives, ...	2Tamb	5.1.36	Govnr
FUIT			
Si bene quid de te merui, fuit aut tibi quidquam/Dulce meum,	Dido	5.1.136	Dido
FUL			
Ful true thou speakst, and like thy selfe my lord, . .	1Tamb	1.1.49	Mycete

FUL (cont.)

Turkes are ful of brags/And menace more than they can wel	1Tamb	3.3.3	Tamb
My empty stomacke ful of idle heat,	1Tamb	4.4.94	Bajzth
on a Lions backe)/Rhamnusia beares a helmet ful of blood,	2Tamb	3.4.57	Therid
Being distant lesse than ful a hundred leagues,	2Tamb	5.3.133	Tamb
Now shall I prove and guerdon to the ful,	P 68	2.11	Guise
then belike, if I were your man, I should be ful of vermine.	F App	p.229 22 P	Clown
day, and ful of strife/Disolve the engins of the broken world.	Lucan, First Booke		79
me have borne/A thousand brunts, and tride me ful ten yeeres,	Lucan, First Booke		301
Love is not ful of pittie (as men say)/But deaffe and cruell,	Hero and Leander		2.287

FULFIL'D

I have fulfil'd your highnes wil, my Lord,	2Tamb	5.1.203	Techel

FULL

And full three Sommers likewise shall he waste,	Dido	1.1.91	Jupitr
At last came Pirrhus fell and full of ire,	Dido	2.1.213	Aeneas
Full soone wouldst thou abjure this single life.	Dido	3.1.60	Dido
Oares of massie Ivorie full of holes,	Dido	3.1.118	Dido
Yet lest he should, for I am full of feare,	Dido	4.4.108	Dido
For this will Dido tye ye full of knots,	Dido	4.4.155	Dido
A garden where are Bee hives full of honey,	Dido	4.5.7	Nurse
O my Lord, tis sweet and full of pompe.	1Tamb	2.5.55	Techel
And might, if my extreams had full events,	1Tamb	3.2.16	Zenoc
Couragious and full of hardinesse:	1Tamb	4.3.55	Capol
banquet and carouse/Full bowles of wine unto the God of war,	1Tamb	4.4.6	Tamb
That meanes to fill your helmets full of golde:	1Tamb	4.4.7	Tamb
Then shal I die with full contented heart,	1Tamb	5.1.417	Arabia
which here appeares as full/As raies of Cynthia to the clearest	2Tamb	2.3.29	Orcan
And happily with full Natolian bowles/Of Greekish wine now let	2Tamb	2.3.45	Orcan
Perfourming all your promise to the full:	2Tamb	3.1.76	Jrslem
if our artillery/Will carie full point blancke unto their wals.	2Tamb	3.3.53	Techel
These barbarous Scythians full of cruelty,	2Tamb	3.4.19	Olymp
and stout Bythinians/Came to my bands full fifty thousand more,	2Tamb	3.5.42	Trebiz
For with thy view my joyes are at the full,	2Tamb	4.2.31	Therid
Were full of Commets and of blazing stars,	2Tamb	5.1.89	Tamb
There is a God full of revenging wrath,	2Tamb	5.1.183	Tamb
Before his hoste be full from Babylon,	2Tamb	5.2.9	Callap
Yet when the pride of Cynthia is at full,	2Tamb	5.2.46	Callap
Or that it be rejoin'd again at full,	2Tamb	5.2.58	Callap
Your vaines are full of accidentall heat,	2Tamb	5.3.84	Phsitn
For if thy body thrive not full of thoughtes/As pure and fiery	2Tamb	5.3.236	Tamb
Who smiles to see how full his bags are cramb'd,	Jew	Prol.31	Machvl
But he whose steele-bard coffers are cramb'd full,	Jew	1.1.14	Barab
Cellers of Wine, and Sollers full of Wheat,	Jew	4.1.63	Barab
Bombards, whole Barrels full of Gunpowder,	Jew	5.5.28	Barab
Paris hath full five hundred Colledges,	P 137	2.80	Guise
Nere was there Colliars sonne so full of pride.	P 416	7.56	Anjoy
And courage to, to be revengde at full.	Edw	1.2.60	Mortmr
at the mariage day/The cup of Hymen had beene full of poyson,	Edw	1.4.174	Queene
Be resolute, and full of secrecie.	Edw	2.2.125	Lncstr
Our friend [Levune] <Lewne>, faithfull and full of trust,	Edw	3.1.60	Queene
Whilom I was, powerfull and full of pompe,	Edw	4.7.13	Edward
Full often am I sowring up to heaven,	Edw	5.1.21	Edward
In health madam, but full of pensivenes.	Edw	5.2.25	Msngr
And have these joies in full possession.	F 179	1.1.151	Faust
Full of obedience and humility,	F 258	1.3.30	Faust
full power to fetch or carry the said John Faustus, body and	F 497	2.1.109 P	Faust
By full consent of all the [reverend] <holy> Synod/Of Priests	F 952	3.1.174	Faust
To satisfie my longing thoughts at full,	F1264	4.1.110	Emper
And with a vyoll full of pretious grace,	F1731	5.1.58	OldMan
Cut is the branch that might have growne full straight,	F2002	5.3.20	4Chor
Memphis never had/For skill in stars, and tune-full planeting,	Lucan, First Booke		640
As [Maenas] <Maenus> full of wine on Pindus raves,	Lucan, First Booke		674
Unlesse I erre, full many shalt thou burne,	Ovid's Elegies		1.2.43
Unworthy porter, bound in chaines full sore,	Ovid's Elegies		1.6.1
wood be flying/And thou the waxe stuft full with notes denying,	Ovid's Elegies		1.12.8
Rude Ennius, and Plautus full of wit,	Ovid's Elegies		1.15.19
doe not languish/And then report her sicke and full of anguish.	Ovid's Elegies		2.2.22
Full concord all your lives was you betwixt,	Ovid's Elegies		2.6.13
Why takest increasing grapes from Vine-trees full?	Ovid's Elegies		2.14.23
Or full of dust doest on the drye earth slide.	Ovid's Elegies		3.5.96
And blush, and seeme as you were full of grace.	Ovid's Elegies		3.13.28
Full of simplicitie and naked truth.	Hero and Leander		1.208
But speeches full of pleasure and delight.	Hero and Leander		1.420
Yet as she went, full often look'd behind,	Hero and Leander		2.5
O Hero, Hero, thus he cry'de full oft,	Hero and Leander		2.147
(Love is too full of faith, too credulous,	Hero and Leander		2.221
By which love sailes to regions full of blis),	Hero and Leander		2.276

FULLER

By chaunce her beauty never shined fuller.	Ovid's Elegies		2.5.42

FULLY

Then my desires were fully satisfied,	Jew	2.1.52	Barab
Shall fully shew the fury of them all.	P 65	2.8	Guise
Contrives, imagines and fully executes/Matters of importe, aimed	P 110	2.53	Guise
I thanke you, I am fully satisfied.	F1651	4.6.94	P Carter

FULNESSE

I meane in fulnesse of perfection.	Jew	2.3.85	Barab

FULSOME

Fat love, and too much fulsome me annoyes,	Ovid's Elegies		2.19.25

FUMES

And plant our pleasant suburbes with her fumes.	Dido	5.1.15	Aeneas
Are reeking water, and dull earthlie fumes.	Hero and Leander		2.116

FUNERALL

Which made the funerall flame that burnt faire Troy:	Dido	2.1.218	Aeneas

FUNERALL (cont.)

manie cities sacrifice/He celebrated her [sad] <said> funerall,	2Tamb	Prol.8	Prolog
I will prefer them for the funerall/They have bestowed on my	2Tamb	4.3.65	Tamb
And serve as parcell of my funerall.	2Tamb	5.3.212	Tamb
hearse, where it shall lie,/And bring my funerall robes: .	Edw	5.6.95	King
Shall waite upon his heavy funerall.	F2001	5.3.19	2Schol
a double point/Rose like the Theban brothers funerall fire;	Lucan, First Booke		550
funerall wood be flying/And thou the waxe stuft full with notes	Ovid's Elegies		1.12.7
Then though death rackes <rakes> my bones in funerall fier,	Ovid's Elegies		1.15.41
Thy tunes let this rare birdes sad funerall borrowe, .	Ovid's Elegies		2.6.9
Burnes his dead body in the funerall flame. . . .	Ovid's Elegies		3.8.6

FUNERALLES

That at my funeralles some may weeping crie, . . .	Ovid's Elegies		2.10.37

FUNERALS

And now my Lords after these funerals be done, . . .	P 561	11.26	QnMoth

FURIE

On which by tempests furie we are cast.	Dido	1.1.199	Aeneas
The heire of [fame] <furie>, the favorite of the [fates] .	Dido	3.2.3	Juno
fleete, what shall I doe/But dye in furie of this oversight?	Dido	5.1.269	Dido
Least he incurre the furie of my wrath.	1Tamb	3.1.30	Bajzth
And in his eies the furie of his hart, ...	1Tamb	3.2.73	Agidas
Let griefe and furie hasten on revenge, ...	1Tamb	4.3.43	Arabia
and hartie humble mones/Will melt his furie into some remorse:	1Tamb	5.1.22	Govnr
As now when furie and incensed hate/Flings slaughtering terrour	1Tamb	5.1.71	Tamb
She that hath calmde the furie of my sword, ...	1Tamb	5.1.437	Tamb
And furie would confound my present rest.	2Tamb	2.4.65	Zenoc
Your griefe and furie hurtes my second life: . . .	2Tamb	2.4.68	Zenoc
Proud furie and intollorable fit, ...	2Tamb	2.4.78	Tamb
I would not bide the furie of my father:	2Tamb	4.1.45	Amyras
Whose sight composde of furie and of fire/Doth send such sterne	2Tamb	4.1.175	Trebiz
And stung with furie of their following, ...	2Tamb	4.1.189	Tamb
Come once in furie and survay his pride, ...	2Tamb	4.3.41	Orcan
let this wound appease/The mortall furie of great Tamburlain.	2Tamb	5.1.154	Govnr
Which wil abate the furie of your fit, ...	2Tamb	5.3.79	Phsitn
Anger and wrathfull furie stops my speech.	Edw	1.4.42	Edward
Ah had some bloudlesse furie rose from hell, . . .	Edw	1.4.316	Edward
What, feare you not the furie of your king? . . .	Edw	5.1.75	Edward
When will the furie of his minde asswage?	Edw	5.3.8	Edward
Disclosing Phoebus furie in this sort:	Lucan, First Booke		676
Horned Bacchus graver furie doth distill, ...	Ovid's Elegies		3.14.17
And as in furie of a dreadfull fight, ...	Hero and Leander		1.119
Herewith he stayd his furie, and began/To give her leave to	Hero and Leander		1.415

FURIES

Not all the curses which the furies breathe, ...	1Tamb	2.7.53	Tamb
Ye Furies that can maske invisible, ...	1Tamb	4.4.17	Bajzth
scepter Angels kisse, and Furies dread)/As for their liberties,	1Tamb	5.1.94	1Virgn
Furies from the blacke Cocitus lake, ...	1Tamb	5.1.218	Bajzth
With ugly Furies bearing fiery flags, ...	2Tamb	1.3.146	Techel
them seeme as black/As is the Island where the Furies maske,	2Tamb	3.2.12	Tamb
By whose proud side the ugly furies run, ...	2Tamb	3.4.59	Therid
Upon whose heart may all the furies gripe, ...	P1101	20.11	Cardnl
And let their lives bloud slake thy furies hunger: . .	Edw	2.2.205	Edward
Hell and the Furies forked haire, ...	F1000	3.2.20	Mephst
That on a furies back came post from Rome, ...	F1161	4.1.7	Fredrk
And at his heeles a thousand furies waite, ...	F1182	4.1.28	Mrtino
And hale the stubborne Furies from their caves, . . .	F1225	4.1.71	Faust
The Divel's dead, the Furies now may laugh. . . .	F1369	4.2.45	Benvol
Through which the Furies drag'd me by the heeles. . .	F1435	4.3.5	Mrtino
There are the Furies tossing damned soules, ...	F1911	5.2.115	BdAngl
Vultures and furies nestled in the boughes. . . .	Ovid's Elegies		1.12.20

FURIOUS

So I escapt the furious Pirrhus wrath:	Dido	2.1.223	Aeneas
Our Masts the furious windes strooke over bourd: . . .	Dido	3.1.110	Aeneas
With furious words and frowning visages, ...	2Tamb	5.1.78	Tamb
Why send'st thou not a furious whyrlwind downe, . . .	2Tamb	5.1.192	Tamb
Governor, good words, be not so furious;	Jew	5.2.61	Barab
Ah furious Mortimer what hast thou done?	Edw	2.2.85	Queene
Be not so furious: come you shall have Beere. . . .	F1620	4.6.63	Faust
And furious Cymbrians and of Carthage Moores, . . .	Lucan, First Booke		257
Many a yeare these [furious] <firious> broiles let last,	Lucan, First Booke		667
I am alone, were furious Love discarded.	Ovid's Elegies		1.6.34
To mine owne selfe have I had strength so furious? . .	Ovid's Elegies		1.7.25
He inly storm'd, and waxt more furious, ...	Hero and Leander		1.437

FURIOUSLY

But furiously he follow his loves fire/And [thinke] <thinkes>	Ovid's Elegies		2.2.13

FURNACE

Wrath kindled in the furnace of his breast, ...	2Tamb	4.1.9	Celeb
[As in this furnace God shal try my faith], ...	F1792	5.1.119A	OldMan

FURNISH

For I will furnish thee with such supplies:	Dido	5.1.72	Iarbus
Without fresh men to rigge and furnish them. . . .	Jew	5.5.101	Govnr

FURNITURE

And also furniture for these my men.	Dido	5.1.70	Aeneas
so imbellished/With Natures pride, and richest furniture?	1Tamb	1.2.156	Therid
As red as scarlet is his furniture, ...	1Tamb	4.1.55	2Msngr

FURROWD

and his breast/Furrowd with wounds, and that which made me	Dido	2.1.204	Aeneas

FURROWED

And fertile in faire Ceres furrowed wealth, ...	Dido	1.2.22	Cloan
Till he hath furrowed Neptunes glassie fieldes, . . .	Dido	4.3.11	Aeneas

FURROWES

with Russian stems/Plow up huge furrowes in the Caspian sea,	1Tamb	1.2.195	Tamb
To hide the folded furrowes of his browes, ...	1Tamb	5.1.57	2Virgn

FURROWES (cont.)
And in the furrowes of his frowning browes, . . . 2Tamb 1.3.77 Tamb
Pale death may walke in furrowes of my face: . . . P 158 2.101 Guise
The sworde shall plane the furrowes of thy browes, . . Edw 1.1.94 Edward
Love conquer'd shame, the furrowes dry were burnd, . . Ovid's Elegies 3.9.29

FURTHER
Who shall confirme my words with further deedes. . . Dido 1.2.43 Iarbus
to further his entent/The windes did drive huge billowes to the Dido 2.1.138 Aeneas
man, ordain'd by heaven/To further every action to the best. 1Tamb 2.1.53 Ortyg
Since Death denies me further cause of joy, ... 1Tamb 5.1.430 Arabia
Then let me find no further time to grace/Her princely Temples 1Tamb 5.1.488 Tamb
Forbids you further liberty than this. . . . . . 2Tamb 1.2.8 Almeda
A litle further, gentle Almeda. . . . . 2Tamb 1.2.17 Callap
That has no further comfort for his maime. . . . . Jew 2.1.11 Barab
No further: . . . . Jew 2.3.44 Barab
for she writes further, that she loves me ever since she saw Jew 4.2.33 P Ithimr
Let's hence, lest further mischiefe be pretended. . . Jew 5.5.96 Calym
Further, or this letter was sealed, Lord Bartley came, . Edw 5.2.30 BshpWn
Till further triall may be made thereof. . . . . Edw 5.6.80 King
keepe further from me O thou illiterate, and unlearned Hostler. F 728 2.3.7 P Robin
Ambitious Imp, why seekst thou further charge? . . . . Ovid's Elegies 1.1.18
his rent discharg'd/From further duty he rests then inlarg'd. Ovid's Elegies 1.10.46
And then things found do ever further pace. . . . . Ovid's Elegies 2.9.10
Cupid commands to move his ensignes further. . . . Ovid's Elegies 2.12.28
My foote upon the further banke to set. . . . . . Ovid's Elegies 3.5.12

FURTHERER
And was my father furtherer of their deaths? . . . . Jew 3.3.22 Abigal

FURTHERMORE
furthermore grant unto them that foure and twentie yeares being F 495 2.1.107 P Faust

FURTHEST
So from the East unto the furthest West, ... 1Tamb 3.3.246 Tamb
Be famous through the furthest continents, ... 2Tamb 4.3.110 Tamb
May be admired through the furthest Land. . . . . . F 842 3.1.64 Faust

FURY (See also FURIE)
And burne him in the fury of that flame, ... 1Tamb 2.6.32 Cosroe
That flies with fury swifter than our thoughts, . . . 2Tamb 4.1.5 Amyras
Such is the sodaine fury of my love, ... 2Tamb 4.2.52 Therid
For every Fury gazeth on her lookes: . . . . . . 2Tamb 4.2.92 Therid
And in the fury of thy torments, strive/To end thy life with Jew 5.5.79 Barab
Shall fully shew the fury of them all. . . . . . P 65 2.8 Guise
And now sirs for this night let our fury stay. . . . P 443 7.83 Guise
To lay the fury of this same troublesome ghost. . . . F1064 3.2.84 Pope
Go pacifie their fury, set it ope, ... F1589 4.6.32 Duke
Friers prepare a dirge to lay the fury of this ghost, once F App p.232 16 P Pope
And they whom fierce Bellonaes fury moves/To wound their armes, Lucan, First Booke 563
where/A fury leades the Emathian bandes, from thence/To the Lucan, First Booke 687
This said, being tir'd with fury she sunke downe. . . Lucan, First Booke 694

FUSTIAN
God forgive me, he speakes Dutch fustian: . . . . . . F App p.231 72 P Clown
I have beene al this day seeking one maister Fustian: . F App p.239 98 P HrsCsr
Doctor Fustian quoth a, mas Doctor Lopus was never such a F App p.240 127 P HrsCsr
maister doctor, maister doctor Fustian, fortie dollers, fortie F App p.241 149 P HrsCsr

FUTURE
The comfort of my future happinesse/And hope to meet your 2Tamb 2.4.62 Zenoc
And pitty of thy future miserie. . . . . F1721 5.1.48 OldMan

FYE
Fye; what a trouble tis to count this trash. . . . . Jew 1.1.7 Barab
Fye, I am ashamde, how ever that I seeme, ... P 124 2.67 Guise
But fye, what a smell <scent> is heere? . . . . . F 669 2.2.118 P Pride

FYERY
a fyery meteor in the fermament . . . . Paris ms21,p390 Guise

FYLE
What, will you fyle your handes with Churchmens bloud? . P1093 20.3 Cardnl

GABINE
troupe, in tuckt up vestures,/After the Gabine manner: . Lucan, First Booke 596

GABIONS
Where we will have [Gabions] <Galions> of sixe foot broad,/To 2Tamb 3.3.56 Therid

GAETULIA (See GETULIA)

GAGE
Or els I would have given my life in gage. . . . . Dido 3.3.29 Iarbus
I'le gage my credit, 'twill content your grace. . . . F1622 4.6.65 Faust

GAILY
This saied, she mov'd her buskins gaily varnisht, . . Ovid's Elegies 3.1.31

GAIN'D
Neptune and Dis gain'd each of them a Crowne, ... 1Tamb 2.7.37 Usumc
Then if I gain'd another Monarchie. . . . . . . F1272 4.1.118 Emper

GAIND
And thinke I gaind, having bought so deare a friend. . Edw 1.4.310 Edward
What ere he hath his body gaind in warres. . . . . Ovid's Elegies 3.7.20

GAINDE
With the Atrides many gainde renowne. . . . . . . Ovid's Elegies 2.12.10

GAINE
So doth he now, though not with equall gaine, ... Dido 3.3.83 Iarbus
To gaine the tytle of a Conquerour, ... 1Tamb 1.1.125 Menaph
And more regarding gaine than victory: . . . . . . 1Tamb 2.2.46 Meandr
When looks breed love, with lookes to gaine the prize. . 1Tamb 2.5.63 Therid
And lose more labor than the gaine will quight. . . . 1Tamb 2.5.96 Tamb
Since this Towne was besieg'd, my gaine growes cold: . Jew 3.1.1 Curtzn
That durst presume for hope of any gaine, ... P 258 4.56 Charls
To gaine the light unstable commons love, ... Lucan, First Booke 133
Receive him soone, least patient use he gaine, ... Ovid's Elegies 1.8.75
Will you for gaine have Cupid sell himselfe? . . . . . Ovid's Elegies 1.10.17
and thou gaine by the pleasure/Which man and woman reape in Ovid's Elegies 1.10.35

GAINE (cont.)			
flying touch/Tantalus seekes, his long tongues gaine is such.	Ovid's Elegies		2.2.44
So of both people shalt thou homage gaine.	Ovid's Elegies		2.9.54
And with his <their> bloud eternall honour gaine,	Ovid's Elegies		2.10.32
He holdes the palme: my palme is yet to gaine.	Ovid's Elegies		3.2.82
Sooner shall kindnesse gaine thy wills fruition.	Ovid's Elegies		3.4.12
All gaine in darknesse the deepe earth supprest.	Ovid's Elegies		3.7.36
Onely our loves let not such rich churles gaine,	Ovid's Elegies		3.7.59
Her deeds gaine hate, her face entreateth love:	Ovid's Elegies		3.10.43
GAINS			
Which after his discease, some other gains.	Hero and Leander		1.246
GAINSAY			
Yet must he not gainsay the Gods behest.	Dido	5.1.127	Aeneas
GAINST			
fond man, that were to warre gainst heaven,/And with one shaft	Dido	3.3.71	Iarbus
And gainst the Generall we will lift our swords,	1Tamb	1.2.145	Tamb
Defend his freedome gainst a Monarchie:	1Tamb	2.1.56	Ceneus
They sung for honor gainst Pierides,	1Tamb	3.2.51	Zenoc
Comes now as Turnus gainst Eneas did,	1Tamb	5.1.380	Philem
Ready for battaile gainst my Lord the King.	1Tamb	5.1.382	Philem
Gainst him my Lord must you addresse your power.	2Tamb	1.1.19	Gazell
To stay my comming gainst proud Tamburlaine.	2Tamb	1.1.163	Orcan
kings again my Lord/To gather greater numbers gainst our power,	2Tamb	4.1.83	Amyras
Cymerian spirits/Gives battile gainst the heart of Tamburlaine.	2Tamb	5.3.9	Therid
To hatch forth treason gainst their naturall Queene?	P1032	19.102	King
Why fightst gainst oddes?	Ovid's Elegies		2.2.61
Ile hate, if I can; if not, love gainst my will:	Ovid's Elegies		3.10.35
GAIT (See GATE)			
GALATEA			
Yet Galatea favour thou her ship.	Ovid's Elegies		2.11.34
GALE			
Faire blowes the winde for Fraunce, blowe gentle gale,	Edw	4.1.1	Kent
Aie me how high that gale did lift my hope!	Ovid's Elegies		1.6.52
Or as a sodaine gale thrustes into sea,	Ovid's Elegies		2.9.31
With Icy Boreas, and the Southerne gale:	Ovid's Elegies		2.11.10
GALEN			
Bid [on kai me on] <Oncaymaeon> farewell, <and> Galen come:	F 40	1.1.12	Faust
GALES			
And coole gales shake the tall trees leavy spring,	Ovid's Elegies		2.16.36
GALIONS			
Where we will have [Gabions] <Galions> of sixe foot broad,/To	2Tamb	3.3.56	Therid
GALL			
And have no gall at all to grieve my foes:	Dido	3.2.17	Juno
GALLANT			
What cannot gallant Mortimer with the Queene?	Edw	4.7.50	Leistr
Was not defilde by any gallant wooer.	Ovid's Elegies		3.4.24
GALLANTS			
is there/Set downe at large, the Gallants were both slaine.	Jew	3.6.29	Abigal
GALLE			
Whose foming galle with rage and high disdaine,	1Tamb	1.1.63	Mycet
GALLEON (See GALIONS)			
GALLERY			
That I may, walking in my Gallery,	Jew	2.3.179	Barab
Here have I made a dainty Gallery,	Jew	5.5.33	Barab
busie Barrabas is there above/To entertaine us in his Gallery;	Jew	5.5.53	Calym
GALLES			
The Galles and those pilling Briggandines,	1Tamb	3.3.248	Tamb
GALLEY			
How far hence lies the Galley, say you?	2Tamb	1.2.54	Almeda
GALLIES			
And all the sea my Gallies countermaund.	1Tamb	3.1.63	Bajzth
That they lie panting on the Gallies side,	1Tamb	3.3.53	Tamb
A thousand Gallies mann'd with Christian slaves/I freely give	2Tamb	1.2.32	Callap
That had the Gallies of the Turke in chase.	Jew	1.1.97	2Merch
And send to keepe our Gallies under-saile,	Jew	1.2.15	Calym
Now lanch our Gallies backe againe to Sea,	Jew	1.2.29	Calym
GALLOP			
Gallop a pace bright Phoebus through the skie,	Edw	4.3.43	Edward
Incenst with savage heat, gallop amaine,	Hero and Leander		1.115
GALLOWES			
might be got/To keepe him for his life time from the gallowes.	Jew	2.3.104	Barab
Upon mine owne free-hold within fortie foot of the gallowes,	Jew	4.2.17	P Pilia
Have done their homage to the loftie gallowes,	Edw	5.2.3	Mortmr
GALLUS			
And Gallus shall be knowne from East to West,	Ovid's Elegies		1.15.29
Gallus that [car'dst] <carst> not bloud, and life to spend.	Ovid's Elegies		3.8.64
GALLY			
wherin at anchor lies/A Turkish Gally of my royall fleet,	2Tamb	1.2.21	Callap
Chaining of Eunuches, binding gally-slaves.	Jew	2.3.204	Ithimr
And, rowing in a Gally, whipt to death.	Jew	5.1.68	Barab
GALLYES			
A Fleet of warlike Gallyes, Barabas,	Jew	1.1.146	1Jew
Their creeping Gallyes had us in the chase:	Jew	2.2.12	Bosco
For with thy Gallyes couldst thou not get hence,	Jew	5.5.100	Govnr
GALLY-SLAVES			
Chaining of Eunuches, binding gally-slaves.	Jew	2.3.204	Ithimr
GAMBALS			
And in their rusticke gambals proudly say,	F1330	4.2.6	Benvol
GAME			
And bring the Gods to wonder at the game:	Dido	1.1.18	Ganimd
The woods are wide, and we have store of game:	Dido	3.3.6	Dido
With Venus game who will a servant grace?	Ovid's Elegies		2.7.21
GAMES			
This man and I were at Olympus games.	Dido	3.1.143	Illion

GAMESOME
When in the midst of all their gamesome sports, Dido 3.2.89 Juno
GAMMON
my father <grandfather> was a Gammon of Bacon, and my mother F 696 2.2.145 P Glutny
GAN
Then gan the windes breake ope their brazen doores, Dido 1.1.62 Venus
at whose latter gaspe/Joves marble statue gan to bend the brow, Dido 2.1.257 Aeneas
Then gan he wagge his hand, which yet held up, Dido 5.1.229 Anna
Then gan they drive into the Ocean, Dido 5.1.231 Anna
They gan to move him to redresse my ruth, Dido 5.1.238 Anna
As oft as Roome was sackt, here gan the spoile: Lucan, First Booke 258
And now the same gan so to scorch and glow, Hero and Leander 2.70
Whereat agast, the poore soule gan to crie, Hero and Leander 2.177
GANADO
Bien para todos mi ganado no es: Jew 2.1.39 Barab
GANGES
From golden India Ganges will I fetch, Dido 5.1.8 Aeneas
And from the boundes of Affrick to the banks/Of Ganges, shall 1Tamb 5.1.521 Tamb
GANIMED (See also GAYNIMEDE)
Come gentle Ganimed and play with me, Dido 1.1.1 Jupitr
And shall have Ganimed, if thou wilt be my love. Dido 1.1.49 Jupitr
Come Ganimed, we must about this geare. Dido 1.1.121 Jupitr
When for the hate of Troian Ganimed, Dido 3.2.42 Juno
O where is Ganimed to hold his cup, Dido 4.4.46 Dido
For never doted Jove on Ganimed, Edw 1.4.180 Queene
To dallie with Idalian Ganimed: Hero and Leander 1.148
Imagining, that Ganimed displeas'd, Hero and Leander 2.157
But when he knew it was not Ganimed, Hero and Leander 2.169
GANIMEDE (See GAYNIMEDE)
GAPE
Gape earth, and let the Feends infernall view/As are the 1Tamb 5.1.242 Zabina
Why gape you for your soveraignes overthrow? Edw 5.1.72 Edward
Gape earth; O no, it will not harbour me. F1949 5.2.153 Faust
Ugly hell gape not; come not Lucifer, F1981 5.2.185 Faust
GAPES
And yet gapes stil for more to quench his thirst, 2Tamb 5.2.14 Amasia
GAPING
or with a Curtle-axe/To hew thy flesh and make a gaping wound? 2Tamb 3.2.97 Tamb
to stand gaping after the divels Governor, and can see nothing. F1244 4.1.90 P Benvol
would I might be turn'd to a gaping Oyster, and drinke nothing F1319 4.1.165 P Benvol
The heart stird not, and from the gaping liver/Squis'd matter; Lucan, First Booke 623
GARBOILES
The causes first I purpose to unfould/Of these garboiles, Lucan, First Booke 68
GARD (See also DUGARD)
But such as love me, gard me from their tongues, Jew Prol.6 Machvl
GARDE
And at ech corner shall the Kings garde stand. P 291 5.18 Anjoy
I marry, such a garde as this dooth well. Edw 2.2.131 Mortmr
Feare not sweete boye, ile garde thee from thy foes, Edw 5.4.111 Queene
GARDEN
A garden where are Bee hives full of honey, Dido 4.5.7 Nurse
Joying the fruit of Ceres garden plot, 2Tamb 4.3.37 Orcan
GARDENS
Gardens I chanc'd to cast mine eye up to the Jewes Jew 3.1.17 P Pilia
GARDES
Who gardes [the] <thee> conquered with his conquering hands. Ovid's Elegies 1.2.52
GARDEST
O harder then the dores thou gardest I prove thee. Ovid's Elegies 1.6.62
GARDING
Warily garding that which I ha got. Jew 1.1.188 Barab
GARISH
With garish robes, not armor, and thy selfe/Bedaubd with golde, Edw 2.2.184 Mortmr
But be surpris'd with every garish toy. Hero and Leander 1.480
GARLAND
Her long haires eare-wrought garland fell away. Ovid's Elegies 3.9.36
From him that yeelds the garland <palme> is quickly got, Ovid's Elegies 3.13.47
GARMENT
Goe fetch the garment which Sicheus ware: Dido 2.1.80 Dido
Here lye the garment which I cloath'd him in, Dido 5.1.298 Dido
Then did the robe or garment which she wore <more>, Ovid's Elegies 3.6.40
GARMENTS
little sonne/Playes with your garments and imbraceth you. Dido 3.1.21 Anna
Thy Garments shall be made of Medean silke, 1Tamb 1.2.95 Tamb
Goe buy thee garments: but thou shalt not want: Jew 3.4.47 Barab
First were his sacred garments rent and torne, Edw 1.2.35 ArchBp
Brasse shines with use; good garments would be worne, Ovid's Elegies 1.8.51
Garments do weare, jewells and gold do wast, Ovid's Elegies 1.10.61
Envious garments so good legges to hide, Ovid's Elegies 3.2.27
Shew large wayes with their garments there displayed. Ovid's Elegies 3.12.24
The outside of her garments were of lawne, Hero and Leander 1.9
youth forbeare/To touch the sacred garments which I weare. Hero and Leander 1.344
GARNISHT
shooke her head with thicke locks garnisht. Ovid's Elegies 3.1.32
GARRISON
But that we leave sufficient garrison/And presently depart to 2Tamb 5.1.211 Tamb
GARRISON'D
the bordering townes/He garrison'd; and Italy he fild with Lucan, First Booke 464
GARRISONS
And Captaines of the Medean garrisons, 1Tamb 1.1.111 Cosroe
If he think good, can from his garrisons, 1Tamb 3.3.21 Bassoe
Affrik and Greece have garrisons enough/To make me Soveraigne 1Tamb 3.3.242 Bajzth
Those walled garrisons wil I subdue, 1Tamb 3.3.244 Tamb
Thy garrisons are beaten out of Fraunce, Edw 2.2.162 Lncstr

GARRISONS (cont.)			
The yellow Ruthens left their garrisons;	Lucan, First Booke		403
GASDE			
for whose byrth/Olde Rome was proud, but gasde a while on her,	2Tamb	2.4.92	Tamb
GASE			
they may become/As men that stand and gase against the Sunne.	P 163	2.106	Guise
GASH			
No vaine sprung out but from the yawning gash,	Lucan, First Booke		613
GASPE			
at whose latter gaspe/Joves marble statue gan to bend the brow,	Dido	2.1.256	Aeneas
which makes them fleet aloft and gaspe for aire.	2Tamb	5.1.209	Techel
GASPING			
And wounded bodies gasping yet for life.	1Tamb	5.1.323	Zenoc
Have swelling cloudes drawen from wide gasping woundes,	1Tamb	5.1.459	Tamb
GASPT			
And like Leander gaspt upon the sande,	Edw	1.1.8	Gavstn
GASTLIE			
With gastlie murmure of my sighes and cries,	Edw	1.4.179	Queene
GASTLY			
and now dooth gastly death/With greedy tallents gripe my	1Tamb	2.7.48	Cosroe
Make me the gastly counterfeit of death.	1Tamb	3.2.17	Zenoc
Villaine, why dost thou look so gastly? speake.	P 989	19.59	Guise
GAT			
No Tamburlain, though now thou gat the best,	1Tamb	3.3.222	Zabina
Twas I my lord that gat the victory,	1Tamb	5.1.445	Tamb
GATE (Homograph)			
Making their fiery gate above the cloudes,	2Tamb	4.3.9	Tamb
bank, right opposite/Against the Westerne gate of Babylon.	2Tamb	5.1.122	Govnr
And at the court gate hang the pessant up,	Edw	1.2.30	Mortmr
What rude disturbers have we at the gate?	F1588	4.6.31	Duke
Fierce Mulciber unbarred Aetna's gate,	Lucan, First Booke		543
The gate halfe ope my bent side in will take.	Ovid's Elegies		1.6.4
With stiffe oake propt the gate doth still appeare.	Ovid's Elegies		1.6.28
To beggers shut, to bringers ope thy gate,	Ovid's Elegies		1.8.77
She whom her husband, guard, and gate as foes,	Ovid's Elegies		2.12.3
What gate thy stately words cannot unlocke,	Ovid's Elegies		3.1.45
She prais'd me, yet the gate shutt fast upon her,	Ovid's Elegies		3.7.7
Her gate by my hands is set open wide.	Ovid's Elegies		3.11.12
Who builds a pallace and rams up the gate,	Hero and Leander		1.239
Will mount aloft, and enter heaven gate,	Hero and Leander		1.466
GATES			
Whose azured gates enchased with his name,	Dido	1.1.101	Jupitr
Our Phrigian [shepherds] <shepherd> haled within the gates,/And	Dido	2.1.153	Aeneas
These hands did helpe to hale it to the gates,	Dido	2.1.170	Aeneas
When she that rules in Rhamnis golden gates,	1Tamb	2.3.37	Cosroe
Your tentes of white now pitch'd before the gates/And gentle	1Tamb	4.2.111	Therid
If all the christall gates of Joves high court/Were opened	2Tamb	1.3.153	Tamb
And guard the gates to entertaine his soule.	2Tamb	3.5.29	Orcan
More strong than are the gates of death or hel?	2Tamb	5.1.20	Govnr
Should I but touch the rusty gates of hell,	2Tamb	5.1.96	Tamb
Be blest of me, nor come within my gates,	Jew	3.4.31	Barab
Open the gates for you to enter in,	Jew	5.1.93	Barab
And lame and poore, lie groning at the gates,	Edw	2.2.163	Lncstr
And plowes to go about our pallace gates.	Edw	3.1.216	Edward
And to the gates of hell convay me hence,	Edw	4.7.88	Edward
Beside <Besides> the gates, and high Pyramydes,	F 823	3.1.45	Mephst
that shall pierce through/The Ebon gates of ever-burning hell,	F1224	4.1.70	Faust
And laught to see the poore starve at their gates:	F1918	5.2.122	BdAngl
And boult the brazen gates with barres of Iron.	Lucan, First Booke		62
See how the gates with my teares wat'red are.	Ovid's Elegies		1.6.18
Such rampierd gates beseiged Cittyes ayde,	Ovid's Elegies		1.6.29
We erre: a strong blast seem'd the gates to ope:	Ovid's Elegies		1.6.51
This breakes Towne gates, but he his Mistris dore.	Ovid's Elegies		1.9.20
Her shut gates greater lightning then thyne brought.	Ovid's Elegies		2.1.20
GATHER			
They gather strength by power of fresh supplies.	1Tamb	2.2.21	Meandr
the Sea-man sees the Hyades/Gather an armye of Cemerian clouds,	1Tamb	3.2.77	Agidas
kings again my Lord/To gather greater numbers gainst our power,	2Tamb	4.1.83	Amyras
and gather of these goods/The mony for this tribute of the	Jew	1.2.155	Govnr
For if these straglers gather head againe,	P 506	9.25	QnMoth
Will to Newcastell heere, and gather head.	Edw	2.2.123	Warwck
To gather for him thoroughout the realme.	Edw	2.2.148	Edward
Tis my hand, what gather you by this.	Edw	5.6.47	Mortmr
The losse of such a wench much blame will gather,	Ovid's Elegies		2.11.35
Gather them up, or lift them loe will I.	Ovid's Elegies		3.2.26
GATHER'D			
Or else be gather'd for in our Synagogue;	Jew	2.3.27	Barab
Which I thinke gather'd from cold hemlocks flower/Wherein bad	Ovid's Elegies		1.12.9
GATHERED			
hath nowe gathered a fresh Armie, and hearing your absence in	2Tamb	5.3.103	P 3Msngr
My brother Guise hath gathered a power of men,	P 642	12.55	Cardnl
of Guise, we understand that you/Have gathered a power of men.	P 822	17.17	King
the armye I have gathered now shall ayme/more at thie end then	Paris	ms28,p391	Guise
GATHERING			
In [skilfull] <skilfuld> gathering ruffled haires in order,	Ovid's Elegies		1.11.1
GAUDIE (See also GAWDIE)			
Then gaudie silkes, or rich imbrotherie.	Edw	1.4.347	Edward
GAULES			
We first sustain'd the uproares of the Gaules,	Lucan, First Booke		256
GAUNTLETS			
The Sabine gauntlets were too dearely wunne/That unto death did	Ovid's Elegies		1.10.49
GAVE			
Who looking on the scarres we Troians gave,	Dido	2.1.131	Aeneas

GAVE (cont.)

Gave up their voyces to dislodge the Campe,	Dido	2.1.134	Aeneas
I, and my mother gave me this fine bow.	Dido	2.1.309	Cupid
Though she repairde my fleete and gave me ships,	Dido	5.1.59	Aeneas
And Tygers of Hircania gave thee sucke:	Dido	5.1.159	Dido
You lie, I gave it you.	1Tamb	2.4.33	Mycet
Blush heaven, that gave them honor at their birth,	1Tamb	5.1.350	Zenoc
Zenocrate that gave him light and life,	2Tamb	2.4.8	Tamb
Than when she gave eternall Chaos forme,	2Tamb	3.4.76	Techel
Why gave you not your husband some of it,	2Tamb	4.2.71	Therid
Looke, Katherin, looke, thy sonne gave mine these wounds.	Jew	3.2.16	Govnr
Not a wise word, only gave me a nod, as who shold say, Is it	Jew	4.2.12	P Pilia
and he gave me a letter from one Madam Bellamira, saluting me	Jew	4.2.29	P Ithimr
To conclude, he gave me ten crownes.	Jew	4.2.113	P Pilia
Doth not your grace know the man that gave them you?	P 172	3.7	Navrre
I thanke them, gave me leave to passe in peace:	Edw	4.1.16	Mortmr
A gave a long looke after us my lord,	Edw	4.7.30	Spencr
But she that gave him life, I meane the Queene?	Edw	5.2.91	Kent
Your Grace mistakes, you gave us no such charge.	F1024	3.2.44	1Card
For hornes he gave, Il'e have his head anone.	F1361	4.2.37	Benvol
so he presently gave me my mony, and fell to eating;	F1529	4.5.25	P Carter
and never tyre, I gave him his money; so when I had my horse,	F1539	4.5.35	P HrsCsr
[Ah] <O> gentlemen, I gave them my soule for my cunning.	F1856	5.2.60	Faust
me <both> body and soule, if I once gave eare to Divinitie:	F1866	5.2.70	P Faust
Gave eare to me,/And now must taste hels paines perpetually.	F1894	5.2.98	BdAngl
Beare witnesse I gave them him.	F App	p.230 41	P Wagner
Rash boy, who gave thee power to change a line?	Ovid's Elegies		1.1.9
Which gave such light, as twincles in a wood,	Ovid's Elegies		1.5.4
With selfe same woundes he gave, he ought to smart.	Ovid's Elegies		2.3.4
Phoebus gave not Diana such tis thought,	Ovid's Elegies		2.5.27
Great gods what kisses, and how many gave she?	Ovid's Elegies		2.19.18
She gave me leave, soft loves in time make hast,	Ovid's Elegies		3.1.69
She beckt, and prosperous signes gave as she moved.	Ovid's Elegies		3.2.58
his [streame] <shame> chargd, the streame chargd, gave place.	Ovid's Elegies		3.5.44
And kindly gave her, what she liked best.	Ovid's Elegies		3.5.82
And one gave place still as another came.	Ovid's Elegies		3.6.64
But better things it gave, corne without ploughes,	Ovid's Elegies		3.7.39
And gave it to his simple rustike love,	Hero and Leander		1.435
He askt, she gave, and nothing was denied,	Hero and Leander		2.25
Neptune was angrie that hee gave no eare,	Hero and Leander		2.207

GAVESTON

My father is deceast, come Gaveston,	Edw	1.1.1	Gavstn
What greater blisse can hap to Gaveston,	Edw	1.1.4	Gavstn
If you love us my lord, hate Gaveston.	Edw	1.1.80	MortSr
I will have Gaveston, and you shall know,	Edw	1.1.96	Edward
But for that base and obscure Gaveston:	Edw	1.1.101	Lncstr
Ere Gaveston shall stay within the realme.	Edw	1.1.105	Lncstr
And Northward Gaveston hath many friends.	Edw	1.1.129	Lncstr
And eyther die, or live with Gaveston.	Edw	1.1.138	Edward
What Gaveston, welcome:	Edw	1.1.140	Edward
Embrace me Gaveston as I do thee:	Edw	1.1.141	Edward
Thy friend, thy selfe, another Gaveston.	Edw	1.1.143	Edward
no soule in hell/Hath felt more torment then poore Gaveston.	Edw	1.1.147	Gavstn
these may well suffice/For one of greater birth then Gaveston.	Edw	1.1.159	Kent
But is that wicked Gaveston returnd?	Edw	1.1.177	BshpCv
And Gaveston unlesse thou be reclaimd,	Edw	1.1.183	BshpCv
But in the meane time Gaveston away,	Edw	1.1.202	Edward
And goods and body given to Gaveston.	Edw	1.2.2	Warwck
Ah wicked king, accurssed Gaveston,	Edw	1.2.4	Lncstr
That villaine Gaveston is made an Earle.	Edw	1.2.11	Lncstr
with us that be his peeres/To banish or behead that Gaveston?	Edw	1.2.43	Mortmr
But dotes upon the love of Gaveston.	Edw	1.2.50	Queene
Go whether thou wilt seeing I have Gaveston.	Edw	1.2.54	Queene
No, but weele lift Gaveston from hence.	Edw	1.2.62	Lncstr
What? are you mov'd that Gaveston sits heere?	Edw	1.4.8	Edward
Lay hands on that traitor Gaveston.	Edw	1.4.21	MortSr
Away I say with hatefull Gaveston.	Edw	1.4.33	Lncstr
Ere my sweete Gaveston shall part from me,	Edw	1.4.48	Edward
To frolike with my deerest Gaveston.	Edw	1.4.73	Edward
Would seeke the ruine of my Gaveston,	Edw	1.4.79	Edward
Tis true sweete Gaveston, oh were it false.	Edw	1.4.108	Edward
To go from hence, greeves not poore Gaveston,	Edw	1.4.119	Gavstn
in whose gratious lookes/The blessednes of Gaveston remaines,	Edw	1.4.121	Gavstn
Thou shalt not hence, ile hide thee Gaveston.	Edw	1.4.131	Edward
Stay Gaveston, I cannot leave thee thus.	Edw	1.4.135	Edward
In saying this, thou wrongst me Gaveston,	Edw	1.4.149	Queene
And by thy meanes is Gaveston exilde.	Edw	1.4.155	Edward
Away then, touch me not, come Gaveston.	Edw	1.4.159	Edward
There weepe, for till my Gaveston be repeald,	Edw	1.4.168	Edward
So much as he on cursed Gaveston.	Edw	1.4.181	Queene
And be a meanes to call home Gaveston:	Edw	1.4.184	Queene
And yet heele ever dote on Gaveston,	Edw	1.4.185	Queene
I know tis long of Gaveston she weepes.	Edw	1.4.191	Mortmr
What, would ye have me plead for Gaveston?	Edw	1.4.213	Mortmr
I meane that vile Torpedo, Gaveston,	Edw	1.4.223	Mortmr
My Lords, that I abhorre base Gaveston,	Edw	1.4.239	Mortmr
Do you not wish that Gaveston were dead?	Edw	1.4.252	Mortmr
Know you not Gaveston hath store of golde,	Edw	1.4.258	Mortmr
Tis not the king can buckler Gaveston,	Edw	1.4.288	Mortmr
Thinke me as base a groome as Gaveston.	Edw	1.4.291	Mortmr
I love him more/Then he can Gaveston, would he lov'd me/But	Edw	1.4.303	Queene
As dooth the want of my sweete Gaveston,	Edw	1.4.307	Edward
And makes me frantick for my Gaveston:	Edw	1.4.315	Edward

GAVESTON (cont.)
When I was forst to leave my Gaveston. Edw 1.4.318 Edward
That Gaveston, my Lord, shalbe repeald. Edw 1.4.322 Queene
For Gaveston, but not for Isabell. Edw 1.4.326 Queene
For thee faire Queene, if thou lovest Gaveston, Edw 1.4.327 Edward
the crowne, direct our warrant forth,/For Gaveston to Ireland: Edw 1.4.370 Edward
And seeing his minde so dotes on Gaveston, Edw 1.4.389 MortSr
It is about her lover Gaveston. Edw 2.1.22 Spencr
My life for thine she will have Gaveston. Edw 2.1.28 Spencr
This letter came from my sweete Gaveston, Edw 2.1.59 Neece
But rest thee here where Gaveston shall sleepe. Edw 2.1.65 Neece
He wils me to repaire unto the court,/And meete my Gaveston: Edw 2.1.68 Neece
How now, what newes, is Gaveston arrivde? Edw 2.2.6 Edward
Nothing but Gaveston, what means your grace? Edw 2.2.7 Mortmr
They love me not that hate my Gaveston. Edw 2.2.37 Edward
My Gaveston,/Welcome to Tinmouth, Edw 2.2.50 Edward
Will none of you salute my Gaveston? Edw 2.2.64 Edward
And come not here to scoffe at Gaveston, Edw 2.2.76 Gavstn
Convey hence Gaveston, thaile murder him. Edw 2.2.82 Edward
Ile not be barde the court for Gaveston. Edw 2.2.90 Mortmr
To prosecute that Gaveston to the death. Edw 2.2.105 Lncstr
Your minion Gaveston hath taught you this. Edw 2.2.149 Lncstr
lascivious showes/And prodigall gifts bestowed on Gaveston, Edw 2.2.158 Mortmr
Cursing the name of thee and Gaveston. Edw 2.2.181 Lncstr
My lord, I see your love to Gaveston, Edw 2.2.208 Kent
Art thou an enemie to my Gaveston? Edw 2.2.212 Edward
So will I, rather then with Gaveston. Edw 2.2.215 Kent
Poore Gaveston, that hast no friend but me, Edw 2.2.220 Edward
Knowest thou him Gaveston? Edw 2.2.248 Edward
And Gaveston, thinke that I love thee well, Edw 2.2.257 Edward
That Gaveston is secretlie arrivde, Edw 2.3.16 Lncstr
And ring aloude the knell of Gaveston. Edw 2.3.26 Mortmr
But neither spare you Gaveston, nor his friends. Edw 2.3.28 Lncstr
O tell me Spencer, where is Gaveston? Edw 2.4.1 Edward
I will not trust them, Gaveston away. Edw 2.4.8 Edward
Farewell sweete Gaveston, and farewell Neece. Edw 2.4.12 Edward
with haling of my lord/From Gaveston, from wicked Gaveston, Edw 2.4.27 Queene
No madam, but that cursed Gaveston. Edw 2.4.32 Lncstr
We would but rid the realme of Gaveston, Edw 2.4.35 Lncstr
Whose eyes are fixt on none but Gaveston: Edw 2.4.62 Queene
How Gaveston hath robd me of his love: Edw 2.4.67 Queene
And Gaveston this blessed day be slaine. Edw 2.4.69 Queene
Yet liveth Pierce of Gaveston unsurprizd, Edw 2.5.4 Gavstn
Gaveston, short warning/Shall serve thy turne: Edw 2.5.21 Warwck
Hearing that you had taken Gaveston, Edw 2.5.35 Arundl
Renowmed Edward, how thy name/Revives poore Gaveston. Edw 2.5.42 Gavstn
for that is all he gets/Of Gaveston, or else his senceless Edw 2.5.54 Mortmr
And drives his nobles to these exigents/For Gaveston, will if Edw 2.5.63 Warwck
Touching the sending of this Gaveston, Edw 2.5.76 Penbrk
I do commit this Gaveston to thee, Edw 2.5.107 Penbrk
Unhappie Gaveston, whether goest thou now. Edw 2.5.110 Gavstn
Strive you no longer, I will have that Gaveston. Edw 2.6.7 Warwck
answer from the Barons/Touching my friend, my deerest Gaveston. Edw 3.1.2 Edward
and I shall never see/My lovely Pierce, my Gaveston againe, Edw 3.1.8 Edward
And if they send me not my Gaveston, Edw 3.1.26 Edward
But to my Gaveston: Edw 3.1.68 Edward
Yea my good lord, for Gaveston is dead. Edw 3.1.90 Arundl
You villaines that have slaine my Gaveston: Edw 3.1.142 Edward
them I will come to chastise them,/For murthering Gaveston: Edw 3.1.179 Edward
Good Pierce of Gaveston my sweet favoret, Edw 3.1.228 Edward
O Gaveston, it is for thee that I am wrongd, Edw 5.3.41 Edward

GAVESTONS
Here is the forme of Gavestons exile: Edw 1.4.1 Lncstr

GAWDIE
Even as, when gawdie Nymphs pursue the chace, Hero and Leander 1.113
And [throw] <threw> him gawdie toies to please his eie, Hero and Leander 2.187

GAY
And forth the gay troupes on swift horses flie. Ovid's Elegies 3.2.78

GAYNIMEDE
Then Gaynimede would renew Deucalions flood, Lucan, First Booke 652

GAZA
Judaea, Gaza, and Scalonians bounds, 2Tamb 3.1.45 Jrslem

GAZE (See also GASDE, GASE)
The people swarme to gaze him in the face. Dido 3.1.72 Anna
But tell them none shall gaze on him but I, Dido 3.1.73 Dido
O keepe them still, and let me gaze my fill: Dido 4.4.44 Dido
Onely to gaze upon Zenocrate. 2Tamb 3.2.33 Tamb
That I may gaze upon this glittering crowne, Edw 5.1.60 Edward
And gaze not on it least it tempt thy soule, F 98 1.1.70 GdAngl
Where she should sit for men to gaze upon. Hero and Leander 1.8
So ran the people foorth to gaze upon her, Hero and Leander 1.117
Loves mother/Nor heaven, nor thou, were made to gaze upon, Hero and Leander 1.223

GAZED
On Priams loose-trest daughter when he gazed. Ovid's Elegies 1.9.38
Stone still he stood, and evermore he gazed, Hero and Leander 1.163

GAZELLUS
Gazellus, Uribassa, and the rest, 2Tamb 2.2.1 Orcan
What saiest thou yet Gazellus to his foile: 2Tamb 2.3.27 Orcan
And now Gazellus, let us haste and meete/Our Army and our 2Tamb 2.3.42 Orcan

GAZERS
And stole away th'inchaunted gazers mind, Hero and Leander 1.104

GAZES
He staide, and on thy lookes his gazes seaz'd. Ovid's Elegies 1.8.24

GAZETH			
For every Fury gazeth on her lookes:	2Tamb	4.2.92	Therid
GAZING			
Gazing upon the beautie of their lookes:	1Tamb	5.1.334	Zenoc
When all the Gods stand gazing at his pomp:	2Tamb	4.3.129	Tamb
Shall I sit gazing as a bashfull guest,	Ovid's Elegies		1.4.3
GEARE			
Come Ganimed, we must about this geare.	Dido	1.1.121	Jupitr
yet I meane to keepe you out, which I will if this geare holde:	P 815	17.10	P Souldr
So,/Now must I about this geare, nere was there any/So finely	Edw	5.5.39	Ltborn
GEBENNA			
Under whose hoary rocks Gebenna hangs;	Lucan, First Booke		436
GEERE			
Come my Meander, let us to this geere,	1Tamb	2.2.1	Mycet
would, I cannot him cashiere/Before I be divided from my geere.	Ovid's Elegies		1.6.36
GEHENNAM			
per Jehovam, Gehennam, et consecratam aquam quam nunc spargo;	F 248	1.3.20	P Faust
GEHONS			
For all the wealth of Gehons golden waves.	1Tamb	5.1.123	Tamb
GELLY			
Ranne through the bloud, that turn'd it all to gelly,	Lucan, First Booke		618
GEMME (See also JEM)			
Least to the waxe the hold-fast drye gemme cleaves,	Ovid's Elegies		2.15.16
And through the gemme let thy lost waters pash.	Ovid's Elegies		2.15.24
Than Hero this inestimable gemme.	Hero and Leander		2.78
GEMS			
these linked gems,/My Juno ware	Dido	1.1.42	Jupitr
GENERAL			
Which if your General refuse or scorne,	2Tamb	1.1.119	Fredrk
GENERALL			
For none of these can be our Generall.	Dido	2.1.46	Illion
Renowmed Dido, tis our Generall:	Dido	2.1.77	Illion
And gainst the Generall we will lift our swords,	1Tamb	1.2.145	Tamb
And Generall Lieftenant of my Armies.	1Tamb	2.5.9	Cosroe
Renowmed Emperour, and mighty Generall,	1Tamb	3.1.16	Fesse
Threaten our citie with a generall spoile:	1Tamb	5.1.10	Govnr
Meaning to make me Generall of the world,	1Tamb	5.1.451	Tamb
The generall welcomes Tamburlain receiv'd,	2Tamb	Prol.1	Prolog
Giving commandement to our generall hoste,	2Tamb	2.1.61	Sgsmnd
Souldiers now let us meet the Generall,	2Tamb	3.4.85	Therid
And satisfie the peoples generall praiers,	2Tamb	5.1.7	Maxim
Renowmed Generall mighty Callapine,	2Tamb	5.2.36	Amasia
that I descended of/Were all in generall cast away for sinne,	Jew	1.2.114	Barab
Bosco, thou shalt be Malta's Generall;	Jew	2.2.44	Govnr
But canst thou tell who is their generall?	P 731	14.34	Navrre
My sweet Joyeux, I make thee Generall,	P 743	15.1	King
Will meete, and with a generall consent,	Edw	1.2.70	ArchBp
Be you the generall of the levied troopes,	Edw	1.4.362	Edward
Weele have a generall tilt and turnament,	Edw	1.4.376	Edward
the restles generall through the darke/(Swifter then bullets	Lucan, First Booke		230
GENERALLY			
none but their owne sect/Must enter in; men generally barr'd.	Jew	1.2.257	Abigal
GENERALS			
our mighty hoste/Shal bring thee bound unto the Generals tent.	2Tamb	3.5.111	Trebiz
GENNET			
And seated on my Gennet, let him ride/As Didos husband through	Dido	4.4.66	Dido
GENTILES			
That when we speake with Gentiles like to you,	Jew	2.3.45	Barab
GENTLE			
Come gentle Ganimed and play with me,	Dido	1.1.1	Jupitr
Gentle Achates, reach the Tinder boxe,	Dido	1.1.166	Aeneas
Stay gentle Venus, flye not from thy sonne,	Dido	1.1.242	Aeneas
Thankes gentle Lord for such unlookt for grace.	Dido	1.2.44	Serg
Make much of them gentle Theridamas,	1Tamb	1.2.247	Tamb
pitch'd before the gates/And gentle flags of amitie displaid.	1Tamb	4.2.112	Therid
flags/Through which sweet mercie threw her gentle beams,	1Tamb	5.1.69	Tamb
With vertue of a gentle victorie,	1Tamb	5.1.398	Zenoc
Yet heare me speake my gentle Almeda.	2Tamb	1.2.13	Callap
A litle further, gentle Almeda.	2Tamb	1.2.17	Callap
Thanks gentle Almeda, then let us haste,	2Tamb	1.2.74	Callap
Oh yet be patient, gentle Barabas.	Jew	1.2.169	1Jew
Then, gentle sleepe, where e're his bodie rests,	Jew	2.1.35	Abigal
This gentle Magot, Lodowicke I meane,	Jew	2.3.305	Barab
Then gentle Abigal plight thy faith to me.	Jew	2.3.315	Lodowk
ah gentle Fryar,/Convert my father that he may be sav'd,	Jew	3.6.38	Abigal
Now, gentle Ithimore, lye in my lap.	Jew	4.2.82	Curtzn
Whither will I not goe with gentle Ithimore?	Jew	4.2.99	Curtzn
Come gentle Ithimore, lye in my lap.	Jew	4.4.27	Curtzn
Be patient, gentle Madam, it was he,	Jew	5.1.46	Govnr
The gentle King whose pleasure uncontrolde,	P 127	2.70	Guise
Though gentle mindes should pittie others paines,	P 215	4.13	Anjoy
Remember you the letter gentle sir,	P 754	15.12	King
Bridle thy anger gentle Mortimer.	Edw	1.1.121	Warwck
Unto the forrest gentle Mortimer,	Edw	1.2.47	Queene
My gentle lord, bespeake these nobles faire,	Edw	1.4.337	Queene
Thankes gentle Warwick, come lets in and revell.	Edw	1.4.385	Edward
Thy gentle Queene, sole sister to Valoys,	Edw	2.2.172	Lncstr
And therefore gentle Mortimer be gone.	Edw	2.4.56	Queene
Yea gentle Spencer, we have beene too milde,	Edw	3.1.24	Edward
Faire blowes the winde for Fraunce, blowe gentle gale,	Edw	4.1.1	Kent
But gentle lords, friendles we are in Fraunce.	Edw	4.2.46	Queene
Yea gentle brother, and the God of heaven,	Edw	4.2.74	Queene
Yet gentle monkes, for treasure, golde nor fee,	Edw	4.7.24	Edward

GENTLE (cont.)			
The gentle heavens have not to do in this.	Edw	4.7.76	Edward
Sweete Spencer, gentle Baldocke, part we must.	Edw	4.7.96	Edward
Leister, if gentle words might comfort me,	Edw	5.1.5	Edward
Thankes gentle Winchester: sirra, be gon.	Edw	5.2.27	Queene
Come sonne, and go with this gentle Lorde and me.	Edw	5.2.109	Queene
O water gentle friends to coole my thirst,	Edw	5.3.25	Edward
O gentle brother, helpe to rescue me.	Edw	5.3.51	Edward
Spill not the bloud of gentle Mortimer.	Edw	5.6.69	Queene
That bootes not, therefore gentle madam goe.	Edw	5.6.91	2Lord
Then gentle friends aid me in this attempt,	F 138	1.1.110	Faust
Nay stay my gentle Mephostophilis,	F 845	3.1.67	Faust
Go hast thee gentle Mephostophilis,	F 891	3.1.113	Faust
Then gentle Fredericke hie thee to the grove,	F1340	4.2.16	Benvol
Whilst with my gentle Mephostophilis,	F1412	4.2.88	Faust
Pitie us gentle Faustus, save our lives.	F1417	4.2.93	Fredrk
O help me gentle friend; where is Martino?	F1432	4.3.2	Fredrk
O gentle Faustus leave this damned Art,	F1707	5.1.34	OldMan
For gentle sonne, I speake it not in wrath,	F1719	5.1.46	OldMan
Or slender eares, with gentle Zephire shaken,	Ovid's Elegies		1.7.55
To kinde requests thou wouldst more gentle prove,	Ovid's Elegies		2.3.5
Would I had beene my mistresse gentle prey,	Ovid's Elegies		2.17.5
Thee gentle Venus, and the boy that flies,	Ovid's Elegies		3.2.55
Relenting Heroes gentle heart was strooke,	Hero and Leander		1.165
So yoong, so gentle, and so debonaire,	Hero and Leander		1.288
The gentle queene of Loves sole enemie.	Hero and Leander		1.318
Gentle youth forbeare/To touch the sacred garments which I	Hero and Leander		1.343
The more a gentle pleasing heat revived,	Hero and Leander		2.68
In gentle brests,/Relenting thoughts, remorse and pittie rests.	Hero and Leander		2.215
Till gentle parlie did the truce obtaine.	Hero and Leander		2.278
GENTLEMAN			
And I in Athens with this gentleman,	Dido	3.1.146	Cloan
That is a Gentleman (I know) at least.	2Tamb	3.1.72	Callap
bottle-nos'd knave to my Master, that ever Gentleman had.	Jew	3.3.10	P Ithimr
This is the Gentleman you writ to.	Jew	4.2.37	P Pilia
Gentleman, he flouts me, what gentry can be in a poore Turke of	Jew	4.2.38	P Ithimr
That hardly art a gentleman by birth?	Edw	1.4.29	Mortmr
And learne to court it like a Gentleman,	Edw	2.1.32	Spencr
But for we know thou art a noble gentleman,	Edw	2.5.68	Mortmr
The Marques is a noble Gentleman,	Edw	4.2.32	Queene
This noble gentleman, forward in armes,	Edw	4.2.76	Mortmr
The Duke of Vanholt's an honourable Gentleman, and one to whom	F1503	4.4.47	P Faust
theres a Gentleman tarries to have his horse, and he would have	F App	p.233 6	P Rafe
How darst thou thus abuse a Gentleman?	F App	p.238 74	Knight
an honourable gentleman, to whom I must be no niggard of my	F App	p.241 170	P Faust
Not onely by warres rage made Gentleman.	Ovid's Elegies		3.14.6
GENTLEMEN			
The warlike Souldiers, and the Gentlemen,	1Tamb	1.1.140	Ceneus
Leading a troope of Gentlemen and Lords,	1Tamb	2.1.58	Ceneus
And live like Gentlemen in Persea.	1Tamb	2.2.71	Meandr
and from Padua/Were wont to come rare witted Gentlemen,	Jew	3.1.7	Curtzn
Now, Gentlemen, betake you to your Armes,	Jew	5.1.1	Govnr
besides the slaughter of these Gentlemen, poyson'd his owne	Jew	5.1.12	P Pilia
Ladies of honor, Knightes and Gentlemen,	P 213	4.11	Charls
<daunt> his heavenly verse;/Onely this, Gentles <Gentlemen>:	F 7	Prol.7	1Chor
What ho, Officers, Gentlemen,	F1155	4.1.1	Mrtino
Make hast to help these noble Gentlemen,	F1421	4.2.97	1Soldr
Gentlemen,/For that I know your friendship is unfain'd,	F1688	5.1.15	Faust
Gentlemen farewell: the same wish I to you.	F1706	5.1.33	Faust
Gramercies Wagner. Welcome gentlemen.	F1820	5.2.24	Faust
[Ah] <Oh> gentlemen.	F1822	5.2.26	Faust
[Ah] <O> gentlemen, heare [me] with patience, and tremble not	F1838	5.2.42	P Faust
[Ah] <O> gentlemen, I gave them my soule for my cunning.	F1856	5.2.60	Faust
Gentlemen away, least you perish with me.	F1867	5.2.71	P Faust
Gentlemen farewell:/if I live till morning,	F1877	5.2.81	P Faust
Come Gentlemen, let us go visit Faustus,	F1983	5.3.1	1Schol
Well Gentlemen, tho Faustus end be such/As every Christian	F1995	5.3.13	2Schol
GENTLES			
<daunt> his heavenly verse;/Onely this, Gentles <Gentlemen>:	F 7	Prol.7	1Chor
GENTLEWOMAN			
I did Sir, and from this Gentlewoman, who as my selfe, and the	Jew	4.2.43	P Pilia
<a jolly gentlewoman, and welbeloved	F 699	(HC264)A	P Glutny
O she was an ancient Gentlewoman, her name was <mistress>	F 699	2.2.148	P Glutny
GENTLY			
Request him gently (Anna) to returne,	Dido	5.1.206	Dido
ceaslesse lamps/That gently look'd upon this loathsome earth,	2Tamb	2.4.19	Tamb
Who gently now wil lance thy Ivory throat,	2Tamb	3.4.24	Olymp
Lie with him gently, when his limbes he spread/Upon the bed,	Ovid's Elegies		1.4.15
Looke gently, and rough husbands lawes despise.	Ovid's Elegies		3.4.44
GENTRIE			
My name is Baldock, and my gentrie/Is fetcht from Oxford, not	Edw	2.2.243	Baldck
GENTRY			
he flouts me, what gentry can be in a poore Turke of ten pence?	Jew	4.2.38	P Ithimr
GEOGRAPHERS			
I will confute those blind Geographers/That make a triple	1Tamb	4.4.75	Tamb
GEORGE			
Saint George for England, and the Barons right.	Edw	3.1.219	Warwck
Saint George for England, and king Edwards right.	Edw	3.1.220	Edward
GEORGEAN			
And [pitcht] <pitch> our tents under the Georgean hilles,	1Tamb	2.2.15	Meandr
GEORGIA			
Yet are there Christians of Georgia here,	2Tamb	5.1.31	1Citzn
GERMAN (See also ALMAINE, ALMAINS, ALMANS)			
Without inforcement of the German Peeres,	F 954	3.1.180	Faust

GERMANE			
The Germane Valdes and Cornelius,	F 92	1.1.64	Faust
Come Germane Valdes and Cornelius,	F 125	1.1.97	Faust
<Consissylogismes>/Gravel'd the Pastors of the Germane Church,	F 140	1.1.112	Faust
Trode on the neck of Germane Fredericke,	F 916	3.1.138	Pope
That Bruno, and the Germane Emperour/Be held as Lollords, and	F 954	3.1.176	Faust
And with him comes the Germane Conjurer,	F1164	4.1.10	Mrtino
And honour'd of the Germane Emperour.	F1216	4.1.62	Emper
Both love and serve the Germane Emperour,	F1219	4.1.65	Faust
once admired/For wondrous knowledge in our Germane schooles,	F1998	5.3.16	2Schol
GERMANIE			
And in the warres 'twixt France and Germanie,	Jew	2.3.187	Barab
GERMANY			
And backt by stout Lanceres of Germany,	2Tamb	1.1.155	Sgsmnd
And he forsooth must goe and preach in Germany:	P 392	7.32	Guise
In Germany, within a Towne cal'd [Rhode] <Rhodes>:	F 12	Prol.12	1Chor
I'le have them wall all Germany with Brasse,	F 115	1.1.87	Faust
Nor any Potentate of Germany.	F 339	1.3.111	Faust
the fairest Maid in Germany, for I am wanton and lascivious,	F 529	2.1.141	P Faust
And beare him to the States of Germany.	F 900	3.1.122	Faust
Flies ore the Alpes to fruitfull Germany,	F 985	3.2.5	Mephst
As never yet was seene in Germany.	F1188	4.1.34	Mrtino
Thou shalt command the state of Germany,	F1323	4.1.169	Emper
I have done, all Germany can witnesse, yea all the world:	F1842	5.2.46	P Faust
for which Faustus hath lost both Germany and the world, yea	F1843	5.2.47	P Faust
Now Germany shall captive haire-tyers send thee,	Ovid's Elegies		1.14.45
GESSES			
I have the [gesses] <gresses> that will pull you downe,	Edw	2.2.40	Edward
GESTURE			
gesture, and attire/They usde to weare during their time of	F App	p.237 33	Emper
GET (See also GAT)			
Get you abourd, Aeneas meanes to stay.	Dido	4.4.24	Dido
But hereby child, we shall get thither straight.	Dido	4.5.14	Nurse
As easely may you get the Souldans crowne,	1Tamb	1.2.27	Tamb
To get the Persean Kingdome to my selfe:	1Tamb	2.5.82	Tamb
To get a passage to Elisian.	1Tamb	5.1.247	Zabina
Which beates against this prison to get out,	2Tamb	4.2.35	Olymp
Your Majesty must get some byts for these,	2Tamb	4.3.43	Therid
Wil get his pardon if your grace would send.	2Tamb	5.1.33	1Citzn
Have strangers leave with us to get their wealth?	Jew	1.2.60	2Knght
Live still; and if thou canst, get more.	Jew	1.2.102	Govnr
get ye gon.	Jew	3.3.34	P Abigal
To get me be admitted for a Nun.	Jew	3.3.55	Abigal
Why goe, get you away.	Jew	4.1.93	2Fryar
But if I get him, Coupe de Gorge for that.	Jew	4.3.5	Barab
For with thy Gallyes couldst thou not get hence,	Jew	5.5.100	Govnr
To get those pedantes from the King Navarre,	P 426	7.66	Guise
Get you away and strangle the Cardinall.	P1059	19.129	King
Wicked Navarre will get the crowne of France,	P1086	19.156	QnMoth
But how wilt thou get opportunitye?	P1135	21.29	Dumain
Fawne not on me French strumpet, get thee gone.	Edw	1.4.145	Edward
Can get you any favour with great men.	Edw	2.1.41	Spencr
now get thee to thy lords,/And tell them I will come to	Edw	3.1.177	Edward
hie thee, get thee gone,/Edward with fire and sword, followes	Edw	3.1.179	Edward
I know what I must do, get you away,	Edw	5.5.27	Ltborn
And get me a spit, and let it be red hote.	Edw	5.5.30	Ltborn
god>,/Here <Faustus> tire my <trie thy> braines to get a Deity.	F 90	1.1.62	Faust
We flye in hope to get his glorious soule:	F 277	1.3.49	Mephst
my selfe when I could get none <had no body> to fight withall:	F 689	2.2.138	P Wrath
have fine sport with the boyes, Ile get nuts and apples enow.	F App	p.236 46	P Robin
<make> slender/And to get out doth like apt members render.	Ovid's Elegies		1.6.6
I would get off though straight, and sticking fast,	Ovid's Elegies		2.15.13
And many by me to get glory crave.	Ovid's Elegies		2.17.28
To get the dore with little noise unbard.	Ovid's Elegies		3.1.50
If standing here I can by no meanes get,	Ovid's Elegies		3.5.11
I wisht to be received in, <and> in I [get] <got> me,	Ovid's Elegies		3.6.47
Tender loves Mother a new Poet get,	Ovid's Elegies		3.14.1
GETS			
And neither gets him friends, nor fils his bags,	Jew	5.2.39	Barab
And gets unto the highest bough of all,	Edw	2.2.19	Mortmr
bestow/His teares on that, for that is all he gets/Of Gaveston,	Edw	2.5.53	Mortmr
As Isabella <Isabell> gets no aide from thence.	Edw	4.3.16	Edward
And take heed least he gets that love for nought.	Ovid's Elegies		1.8.72
Only a Woman gets spoiles from a Man,	Ovid's Elegies		1.10.29
GETULIA			
Am I not King of rich Getulia?	Dido	3.1.45	Iarbus
What telst thou me of rich Getulia?	Dido	3.1.48	Dido
GETULIAN			
How now Getulian, are ye growne so brave,	Dido	3.3.19	Dido
GHASTLY (See also GASTLY)			
Sadly supplied with pale and ghastly death,	2Tamb	2.4.83	Tamb
With jawes wide open ghastly roaring out;	Lucan, First Booke		212
But with a ghastly dreadfull countenaunce,	Hero and Leander		1.381
GHOASTS			
untrod woods/Shrill voices schright, and ghoasts incounter men.	Lucan, First Booke		568
GHOST			
Aeneas see, Sergestus or his ghost.	Dido	2.1.50	Achat
And thinking to goe downe, came Hectors ghost/With ashie visage,	Dido	2.1.201	Aeneas
Sweete father heere, unto thy murdered ghost,	Edw	5.6.99	King
My <His> Ghost be with the old Phylosophers.	F 288	1.3.60	Faust
I thinke it be some Ghost crept out of Purgatory, and now is	F1059	3.2.79	P Archbp
To lay the fury of this same troublesome ghost.	F1064	3.2.84	Pope
ghost newly crept out of Purgatory come to begge a pardon of	F App	p.232 14	P Lorein

GHOST (cont.)			
Friers prepare a dirge to lay the fury of this ghost, once	F App	p.232 17 P	Pope
While slaughtred Crassus ghost walks unreveng'd,	Lucan, First Booke		11
Sylla's ghost/Was seene to walke, singing sad Oracles,	Lucan, First Booke		579
GHOSTES			
The Spencers ghostes, where ever they remaine,	Edw	5.3.44	Edward
GHOSTLY			
but seeing you are come/Be you my ghostly father; and first	Jew	3.6.12	Abigal
if thou now growest penitent/Ile be thy ghostly father,	Edw	5.6.4	Mortmr
GHOSTS			
And guarded with a thousand grislie ghosts,	Dido	1.1.59	Venus
and with this sword/Sent many of their savadge ghosts to hell.	Dido	2.1.212	Aeneas
where shaking ghosts with ever howling grones,	1Tamb	5.1.245	Zabina
Infecting all the Ghosts with curelesse griefs:	1Tamb	5.1.258	Bajzth
Hell and Elisian swarme with ghosts of men,	1Tamb	5.1.465	Tamb
And speake of spirits and ghosts that glide by night/About the	Jew	2.1.26	Barab
GIANTLY			
divelish shepheard to aspire/With such a Giantly presumption,	1Tamb	2.6.2	Cosroe
GIANTS (See also GYANTS)			
As Juno, when the Giants were suppresst,	1Tamb	5.1.510	Tamb
Or Lapland Giants trotting by our sides:	F 153	1.1.125	Valdes
Untill the cruel Giants war was done)/We plaine not heavens,	Lucan, First Booke		36
GIBRALTER (See also JUBALTER)			
We kept the narrow straight of Gibralter,	2Tamb	1.3.180	Usumc
GIDDIE			
And with the noise turnes up my giddie braine,	Edw	1.4.314	Edward
GIFT (See also GUIFT)			
What greater gift can poore Mathias have?	Jew	2.3.346	Mthias
Maddame, I beseech your grace to except this simple gift.	P 167	3.2	P Pothec
And hath a speciall gift to forme a verbe.	Edw	2.1.55	Spencr
Let this gift change thy minde, and save thy soule,	Edw	5.5.88	Edward
And wright a Deed of Gift with thine owne bloud;	F 424	2.1.36	Mephst
But Faustus/<thou must> Write it in manner of a Deed of Gift.	F 449	2.1.61	Mephst
A Deed of Gift, of body and of soule:	F 478	2.1.90	Faust
When causes fale thee to require a gift,	Ovid's Elegies		1.8.93
While thou hast time yet to bestowe that gift.	Ovid's Elegies		2.3.18
O would that sodainly into my gift,	Ovid's Elegies		2.15.9
go small gift from hand,/Let her my faith with thee given	Ovid's Elegies		2.15.27
What gift with me was on her birth day sent,	Ovid's Elegies		3.1.57
Thou hast my gift, which she would from thee sue.	Ovid's Elegies		3.1.60
But yet their gift more moderately use,	Ovid's Elegies		3.3.47
'Tis wisedome to give much, a gift prevailes,	Hero and Leander		2.225
GIFTES			
And he that could with giftes and promises/Inveigle him that	1Tamb	2.2.25	Meandr
to beware/How you did meddle with such dangerous giftes.	P 180	3.15	Navrre
GIFTS			
Victuall his Souldiers, give him wealthie gifts,	Dido	2.1.329	Venus
With gifts and shewes did entertaine him/And promised to be at	P 874	17.69	Eprnon
lascivious showes/And prodigall gifts bestowed on Gaveston,	Edw	2.2.158	Mortmr
And glutted now <more> with learnings golden gifts,	F 24	Prol.24	1Chor
And being popular sought by liberal gifts,	Lucan, First Booke		132
Each one according to his gifts respect.	Ovid's Elegies		1.8.38
Chiefely shew him the gifts, which others send:	Ovid's Elegies		1.8.99
Nor the milde Ewe gifts from the Ramme doth pull.	Ovid's Elegies		1.10.28
He wants no gifts into thy lap to hurle.	Ovid's Elegies		1.10.54
Aye me rare gifts unworthy such a happe.	Ovid's Elegies		1.14.54
No gifts given secretly thy crime bewray.	Ovid's Elegies		2.5.6
My selfe will bring vowed gifts before thy feete,	Ovid's Elegies		2.13.24
Do but deserve gifts with this title grav'd.	Ovid's Elegies		2.13.26
My selfe poore wretch mine owne gifts now envie.	Ovid's Elegies		2.15.8
much (I crave)/Gifts then my promise greater thou shalt have.	Ovid's Elegies		3.5.66
But when in gifts the wise adulterer came,	Ovid's Elegies		3.7.33
These gifts are meete to please the powers divine.	Ovid's Elegies		3.9.48
To the rich Ocean for gifts he flies.	Hero and Leander		2.224
GIHON (See GEHONS)			
GILD (See also GUILDED)			
Where thou shalt see the red gild fishes leape,	Dido	4.5.10	Nurse
GILDED			
And take in signe thereof this gilded wreath,	1Tamb	5.1.101	1Virgn
GILDERS			
holde, take these gilders.	F App	p.230 30	P Wagner
GILDS			
With haire that gilds the water as it glides,	Edw	1.1.62	Gavstn
GILT (See also GUILT)			
Mounted his shining [chariot] <chariots>, gilt with fire,	2Tamb	4.3.126	Tamb
Of his gilt Harpe the well tun'd strings doth hold.	Ovid's Elegies		1.8.60
The holy gods gilt temples they might fire,	Ovid's Elegies		3.8.43
And stately robes to their gilt feete hang downe.	Ovid's Elegies		3.12.26
GILTY			
Gilty, my Lord, I confesse; your sonne and Mathias were both	Jew	5.1.28	P Ithimr
GIRD			
Untill I gird my quiver to my side:	Dido	3.3.8	Dido
GIRDED			
Having a quiver girded to her side,	Dido	1.1.185	Venus
GIRDLE			
A silver girdle, and a golden purse,	Dido	2.1.306	Venus
Off with your girdle, make a hansom noose;	Jew	4.1.142	Barab
First weare this girdle, then appeare/Invisible to all are	F 997	3.2.17	Mephst
Which to her wast her girdle still kept downe.	Ovid's Elegies		1.7.48
GIRD'ST			
Why gird'st thy citties with a towred wall?	Ovid's Elegies		3.7.47
GIRLE (See also GYRLE)			
I tell thee shamelesse girle,/Thou shalt be Landresse to my	1Tamb	3.3.176	Zabina

GIRLE (cont.)			
my girle, thinke me not all so fond/As negligently to forgoe so	Jew	1.2.241	Barab
In my house, my girle.	Jew	1.2.249	Barab
there must my girle/Intreat the Abbasse to be entertain'd.	Jew	1.2.279	Barab
Be close, my girle, for this must fetch my gold.	Jew	1.2.304	Barab
Oh my girle,/My gold, my fortune, my felicity;	Jew	2.1.47	Barab
Oh girle, oh gold, oh beauty, oh my blisse!	Jew	2.1.54	Barab
My daughter here, a paltry silly girle.	Jew	2.3.284	Barab
GIRLES			
Fourescore is but a girles age, love is sweete:--	Dido	4.5.32	Nurse
[And nut-browne girles in doing have no fellowe].	Ovid's Elegies		2.4.40
Thou ring that shalt my faire girles finger binde,	Ovid's Elegies		2.15.1
Thy muse hath played what may milde girles content,	Ovid's Elegies		3.1.27
But bids his darts from perjurd girles retire.	Ovid's Elegies		3.3.36
GIRT (See also GYRT)			
Sword-girt Orions side glisters too bright.	Lucan, First Booke		664
Girt my shine browe with sea banke mirtle praise <sprays>.	Ovid's Elegies		1.1.34
Their <Your> youthfull browes with Ivie girt to meete him,/With	Ovid's Elegies		3.8.61
GIRTING			
Girting this strumpet Cittie with our siege,	P1152	22.14	King
GIRTS			
Mars girts his deadly sword on for my harme:	Ovid's Elegies		3.3.27
GIVE			
Father I faint, good father give me meate.	Dido	1.1.163	Ascan
And would my prayers (as Pigmalions did)/Could give it life,	Dido	2.1.17	Aeneas
Then would it leape out to give Priam life:	Dido	2.1.27	Aeneas
Ile give thee Sugar-almonds, sweete Conserves,	Dido	2.1.305	Venus
Will Dido give to sweete Ascanius:	Dido	2.1.312	Venus
Victuall his Souldiers, give him wealthie gifts,	Dido	2.1.329	Venus
mightier Kings)/Hast had the greatest favours I could give:	Dido	3.1.13	Dido
I wagge, and give thee leave to kisse her to.	Dido	3.1.31	Dido
What will you give me now? Ile have this Fanne.	Dido	3.1.32	Cupid
love, give Dido leave/To be more modest then her thoughts admit,	Dido	3.1.94	Dido
Ile give thee tackling made of riveld gold,	Dido	3.1.116	Dido
With this my hand I give to you my heart,	Dido	3.4.43	Aeneas
O princely Dido, give me leave to speake,	Dido	4.4.17	Aeneas
Which if it chaunce, Ile give ye buriall,	Dido	5.1.176	Dido
As if he meant to give my Souldiers pay,	1Tamb	1.2.183	Tamb
Go on my Lord, and give your charge I say,	1Tamb	2.2.57	Mycet
Base villaine, darst thou give the lie?	1Tamb	2.4.19	Tamb
Come give it me.	1Tamb	2.4.31	Mycet
And give you equall place in our affaires.	1Tamb	2.5.14	Cosroe
But give him warning and more warriours.	1Tamb	2.5.103	Tamb
And strive for life at every stroke they give.	1Tamb	3.3.54	Tamb
Give her the Crowne Turkesse, you wer best.	1Tamb	3.3.224	Therid
I pray you give them leave Madam, this speech is a goodly	1Tamb	4.4.32	P Techel
belike he hath not bene watered to day, give him some drinke.	1Tamb	4.4.55	P Tamb
Yet give me leave to plead for him my Lord.	1Tamb	4.4.86	Zenoc
Shal give the world to note, for all my byrth,	1Tamb	5.1.188	Tamb
Give him his liquor?	1Tamb	5.1.310	P Zabina
in peeces, give me the sworde with a ball of wildefire upon it.	1Tamb	5.1.311	P Zabina
Then here I sheath it, and give thee my hand,	2Tamb	1.1.127	Sgsmnd
Gallies mann'd with Christian slaves/I freely give thee,	2Tamb	1.2.33	Callap
Should not give us presumption to the like.	2Tamb	2.1.46	Sgsmnd
Go Uribassa, give it straight in charge.	2Tamb	2.3.40	Orcan
Tis nought for your majesty to give a kingdome.	2Tamb	3.1.77	Jrslem
give me a wound father.	2Tamb	3.2.132	P Celeb
Come sirra, give me your arme.	2Tamb	3.2.134	P Tamb
Give me your knife (good mother) or strike home:	2Tamb	3.4.28	Sonne
So sirha, now you are a king you must give armes.	2Tamb	3.5.137	P Tamb
A Forme not meet to give that subject essence,	2Tamb	4.1.112	Tamb
May never day give vertue to his eies,	2Tamb	4.1.174	Trebiz
Ile give your Grace a present of such price,	2Tamb	4.2.56	Olymp
Thou seest us prest to give the last assault,	2Tamb	5.1.60	Techel
Save but my life and I wil give it thee.	2Tamb	5.1.118	Govnr
Who flies away at every glance I give,	2Tamb	5.3.70	Tamb
of all the villaines power/Live to give offer of another fight.	2Tamb	5.3.109	Tamb
Give me a Map, then let me see how much/Is left for me to	2Tamb	5.3.123	Tamb
Give me the Merchants of the Indian Mynes,	Jew	1.1.19	Barab
Give us a peacefull rule, make Christians Kings,	Jew	1.1.134	Barab
Then give us leave, great Selim-Calymath.	Jew	1.2.13	Govnr
Yes, give me leave, and Hebrews now come neare.	Jew	1.2.38	Govnr
Oh my Lord we will give halfe.	Jew	1.2.77	3Jews
But give him liberty at least to mourne,	Jew	1.2.202	Barab
But they will give me leave once more, I trow,	Jew	1.2.252	Barab
Intreat 'em faire, and give them friendly speech,	Jew	1.2.286	Barab
Father, give me--	Jew	1.2.348	Abigal
Give charge to Morpheus that he may dreame/A golden dreame, and	Jew	2.1.36	Abigal
nay we dare not give consent/By reason of a Tributary league.	Jew	2.2.22	Govnr
He'de give us present mony for them all.	Jew	2.3.6	1Offcr
What sparkle does it give without a foile?	Jew	2.3.55	Lodowk
Give me the letters, daughter, doe you heare?	Jew	2.3.224	Barab
I'le give him such a warning e're he goes/As he shall have	Jew	2.3.273	Barab
And yet I'le give her many a golden crosse/With Christian	Jew	2.3.296	Barab
Doe so; loe here I give thee Abigall.	Jew	2.3.345	Barab
give a hundred of the Jewes Crownes that I had such a	Jew	3.1.27	P Ithimr
Here take my keyes, I'le give 'em thee anon:	Jew	3.4.46	Barab
All this I'le give to some religious house/So I may be baptiz'd	Jew	4.1.75	Barab
I'le give him something and so stop his mouth.	Jew	4.1.102	Barab
I'le feast you, lodge you, give you faire words,	Jew	4.1.126	Barab
I must be forc'd to give in evidence,	Jew	4.1.186	Barab
And give my goods and substance to your house,	Jew	4.1.190	Barab
But came it freely, did the Cow give down her milk freely?	Jew	4.2.102	P Ithimr

GIVE (cont.)

Give me a Reame of paper, we'll have a kingdome of gold for't.	Jew	4.2.114	P Ithimr
send me five hundred crowns, and give the Bearer one hundred.	Jew	4.2.118	P Ithimr
Pilia-borza, bid the Fidler give me the posey in his hat there.	Jew	4.4.35	P Curtzn
Sirra, you must give my mistris your posey. . . .	Jew	4.4.37	Pilia
Give him a crowne, and fill me out more wine. . . .	Jew	4.4.46	Ithimr
Now whilst you give assault unto the wals, . . .	Jew	5.1.90	Barab
and Barabas we give/To guard thy person, these our Janizaries:	Jew	5.2.15	Calym
What wilt thou give me, Governor, to procure/A dissolution of	Jew	5.2.76	Barab
What will you give me if I render you/The life of Calymath,	Jew	5.2.79	Barab
What will you give him that procureth this? . . .	Jew	5.2.83	Barab
To give thee knowledge when to cut the cord, . . .	Jew	5.5.40	Barab
Give me a look, that when I bend the browes, . . .	P 157	2.100	Guise
Then may it please your Majestie to give me leave, . .	P 616	12.29	Mugern
Come sir, give me my buttons and heers your eare. . .	P 620	12.33	Mugern
You will give us our money?	P 942	19.12	P AllMur
Oh I have my deaths wound, give me leave to speak. . .	P1003	19.73	Guise
And give her warning of her trecherous foes. . . .	P1190	22.52	King
Navarre, give me thy hand, I heere do sweare, . . .	P1203	22.65	King
These will I sell to give my souldiers paye, . . .	Edw	1.1.104	Lncstr
Ile give thee more, for but to honour thee, . . .	Edw	1.1.164	Edward
I give him thee, here use him as thou wilt. . . .	Edw	1.1.196	Edward
Give me the paper.	Edw	1.4.3	ArchBp
Give it me, ile have it published in the streetes. . .	Edw	1.4.89	Lncstr
And therefore give me leave to looke my fill, . . .	Edw	1.4.139	Edward
Why then my lord, give me but leave to speak. . . .	Edw	1.4.254	Mortmr
I would freelie give it to his enemies, ...	Edw	1.4.309	Edward
Ile give the onset.	Edw	2.3.20	Mortmr
Then give him me.	Edw	2.5.94	Penbrk
the ungentle king/Of Fraunce refuseth to give aide of armes,	Edw	4.2.62	SrJohn
These comforts that you give our wofull queene, . .	Edw	4.2.72	Kent
they intend to give king Edward battell in England, sooner then	Edw	4.3.34	P Spencr
Give me my horse and lets r'enforce our troupes: . .	Edw	4.5.6	Edward
To give ambitious Mortimer my right, ...	Edw	5.1.53	Edward
And neither give him kinde word, nor good looke. . .	Edw	5.2.55	Mortmr
And give my heart to Isabell and him, ...	Edw	5.3.11	Edward
You shall not need to give instructions, ...	Edw	5.4.29	Ltborn
They give me bread and water being a king, . . .	Edw	5.5.62	Edward
But everie jointe shakes as I give it thee: . . .	Edw	5.5.86	Edward
To give me whatsoever I shall aske;	F 322	1.3.94	Faust
I'de give them all for Mephostophilis.	F 331	1.3.103	Faust
that <I know> he would give his soule to the devill, for a	F 350	1.4.8	P Wagner
And give thee more then thou hast wit to aske. . . .	F 436	2.1.48	Mephst
I Mephostophilis, I'le <I> give it him <thee>. . . .	F 437	2.1.49	Faust
by these presents doe give both body and soule to Lucifer,	F 494	2.1.106	P Faust
I, take it, and the devill give thee good of it <on't>. .	F 502	2.1.114	Faust
but to the Taverne with me, I'le give thee white wine, red wine,	F 748	2.3.27	P Robin
Come, give it me againe.	F1111	3.3.24	P Vintnr
Give him his head for Gods sake.	F1392	4.2.68	P Fredrk
Well, I will not stand with thee, give me the money: .	F1466	4.4.10	P Faust
go rouse him, and make him give me my forty Dollors againe.	F1488	4.4.32	P HrsCsr
and give me my mony againe, for your horse is turned to a	F1489	4.4.33	P HrsCsr
me what he should give me for as much Hay as he could eate;	F1527	4.5.23	P Carter
Do as thou wilt Faustus, I give thee leave. . . .	F1607	4.6.50	Duke
My Lord, beseech you give me leave a while, . . .	F1621	4.6.64	Faust
Come Hellen, come, give me my soule againe, . . .	F1772	5.1.99	Faust
We'll give his mangled limbs due buryall:	F1999	5.3.17	2Schol
he would give his soule to the Divel for a shoulder of mutton,	F App	p.229 8	P Wagner
Beare witnesse I give them you againe.	F App	p.230 42	P Clown
the second time, aware the third, I give you faire warning.	F App	p.232 20	P Faust
And give me cause to praise thee whilst I live. . .	F App	p.237 36	Emper
Wel, come give me your money, my boy wil deliver him to you:	F App	p.239 107	P Faust
O Lord sir, let me goe, and Ile give you fortie dollers more.	F App	p.241 158	P HrsCsr
have none about me, come to my Oastrie, and Ile give them you.	F App	p.241 162	P HrsCsr
Nature, and every power shal give thee place, . . .	Lucan, First Booke	51	
Yeelding or striving <strugling> doe we give him might, .	Ovid's Elegies	1.2.9	
Vulcan will give thee Chariots rich and faire. . . .	Ovid's Elegies	1.2.24	
And give woundes infinite at everie turne. . . .	Ovid's Elegies	1.2.44	
My spotlesse life, which but to Gods [gives] <give> place,	Ovid's Elegies	1.3.13	
The yeares that fatall destenie shall give, . . .	Ovid's Elegies	1.3.17	
not onely kisse/But force thee give him my stolne honey blisse.	Ovid's Elegies	1.4.64	
Constrain'd against thy will give it the pezant, . .	Ovid's Elegies	1.4.65	
Gratis thou maiest be free, give like for like, . .	Ovid's Elegies	1.6.23	
who ere will knowe a bawde aright/Give eare, there is an old	Ovid's Elegies	1.8.2	
(Trust me) to give, it is a witty thing.	Ovid's Elegies	1.8.62	
What he will give, with greater instance crave. . .	Ovid's Elegies	1.8.68	
But never give a spatious time to ire, ...	Ovid's Elegies	1.8.81	
To give I love, but to be ask't disdayne, ...	Ovid's Elegies	1.10.63	
Leave asking, and Ile give what I refraine. . . .	Ovid's Elegies	1.10.64	
commodious/And to give signes dull wit to thee is odious.	Ovid's Elegies	1.11.4	
give her my writ/But see that forth-with shee peruseth it.	Ovid's Elegies	1.11.15	
How oft wisht I night would not give thee place, . .	Ovid's Elegies	1.13.27	
Let Kings give place to verse, and kingly showes, . .	Ovid's Elegies	1.15.33	
Which giving her, she may give thee againe. . . .	Ovid's Elegies	2.2.16	
Which do perchance old age unto them give. . . .	Ovid's Elegies	2.6.28	
Shee looking on them did more courage give. . . .	Ovid's Elegies	2.12.26	
And why dire poison give you babes unborne? . . .	Ovid's Elegies	2.14.28	
What would not she give that faire name to winne? . .	Ovid's Elegies	2.17.30	
Thou doest alone give matter to my wit.	Ovid's Elegies	2.17.34	
Now give the Roman Tragedie a name, ...	Ovid's Elegies	3.1.29	
And each give signes by casting up his cloake. . . .	Ovid's Elegies	3.2.74	
Were I a God, I should give women leave, ...	Ovid's Elegies	3.3.43	
Honour what friends thy wife gives, sheele give many: .	Ovid's Elegies	3.4.45	

GIVE (cont.)

One [her] <she> commands, who many things can give.	Ovid's Elegies	3.7.62	
If I should give, both would the house forbeare.	Ovid's Elegies	3.7.64	
And doubt to which desire the palme to give.	Ovid's Elegies	3.10.40	
When fruite fild Tuscia should a wife give me,	Ovid's Elegies	3.12.1	
And give to him that the first wound imparts.	Ovid's Elegies	3.12.22	
Nor do I give thee counsaile to live chaste,	Ovid's Elegies	3.13.3	
he stayd his furie, and began/To give her leave to rise:	Hero and Leander	1.416	
'Tis wisedome to give much, a gift prevailes,	Hero and Leander	2.225	
GIVEN			
Or els I would have given my life in gage.	Dido	3.3.29	Iarbus
I would have given Achates store of gold,	Dido	4.4.7	Dido
If Nature had not given me wisedomes lore?	1Tamb	2.4.7	Mycet
Whereto ech man of rule hath given his hand,	1Tamb	5.1.102	1Virgn
That God hath given to venge our Christians death/And scourge	2Tamb	2.1.52	Fredrk
And take the victorie our God hath given.	2Tamb	2.1.63	Sgsmnd
what, given so much to sleep/You cannot leave it, when our	2Tamb	4.1.11	Amyras
but for one bare night/A hundred Duckets have bin freely given:	Jew	3.1.3	Curtzn
away, and let due praise be given/Neither to Fate nor Fortune,	Jew	5.5.123	Govnr
If that the King had given consent thereto,	P 33	1.33	Navrre
And then the watchword being given, a bell shall ring,	P 238	4.36	Guise
And goods and body given to Gaveston.	Edw	1.2.2	Warwck
Not so my liege, the Queene hath given this charge,	Edw	5.3.13	Gurney
Heeres channell water, as our charge is given.	Edw	5.3.27	Matrvs
In which <Wherein> thou hast given thy soule to Lucifer.	F 520	2.1.132	Mephst
he has made his will, and given me his wealth, his house, his	F1675	5.1.2	P Wagner
Oh <Ah> Faustus, if thou hadst given eare to me,	F1892	5.2.96	GdAngl
has given me a purgation, has purg'd me of fortie Dollers,	F App	p.240 128	P HrsCsr
For he hath given to me al his goodes,	F App	p.243 2	Wagner
had heaven given thee longer life/Thou hadst restrainde thy	Lucan, First Booke	115	
And sentence given in rings of naked swords,	Lucan, First Booke	321	
I gladly graunt my parents given to save,	Ovid's Elegies	1.3.10	
And as a pray unto blinde anger given,	Ovid's Elegies	1.7.44	
No gifts given secretly thy crime bewray.	Ovid's Elegies	2.5.6	
What helpes it thou wert given to please my wench,	Ovid's Elegies	2.6.19	
The Parrat given me, the farre [worlds] <words> best choice.	Ovid's Elegies	2.6.38	
We people wholy given thee, feele thine armes,	Ovid's Elegies	2.9.11	
Let her my faith with thee given understand.	Ovid's Elegies	2.15.28	
Why see I lines so oft receivde and given,	Ovid's Elegies	3.13.31	
GIVEN'T			
What a blessing has he given't?	Jew	3.4.106	P Ithimr
GIVER			
Lay in the mid bed, there be my law giver.	Ovid's Elegies	2.17.24	
GIVERS			
Wherein is seene the givers loving minde:	Ovid's Elegies	2.15.2	
GIVE'S			
What ho, give's halfe a dosen of Beere here, and be hang'd.	F1612	4.6.55	P Robin
GIVES			
Those that dislike what Dido gives in charge,	Dido	4.4.71	Dido
The ground is mine that gives them sustenance,	Dido	4.4.74	Dido
Since Fortune gives you opportunity,	1Tamb	1.1.124	Menaph
And gives no more than common courtesies.	1Tamb	3.2.63	Agidas
Whose smiling stars gives him assured hope/Of martiall triumph,	1Tamb	3.3.42	Tamb
For he that gives him other food than this:	1Tamb	4.2.89	Tamb
Gives light to Phoebus and the fixed stars,	2Tamb	2.4.50	Tamb
the enimie hath made/Gives such assurance of our overthrow,	2Tamb	5.1.3	Maxim
Cymerian spirits/Gives battile gainst the heart of Tamburlaine.	2Tamb	5.3.9	Therid
Your soul gives essence to our wretched subjects,	2Tamb	5.3.164	Amyras
Farre from the Sonne that gives eternall life.	Jew	3.3.65	Abigal
me in beleefe/Gives great presumption that she loves me not;	Jew	3.4.11	Barab
How liberally the villain gives me mine own gold.	Jew	4.4.48	P Barab
Succesfull battells gives the God of kings,	Edw	4.6.19	Queene
Faustus gives to thee his soule: [ah] <O> there it staid.	F 456	2.1.68	Faust
Then write againe: Faustus gives to thee his soule.	F 458	2.1.70	Faust
that not only gives thee hornes, but makes thee weare them,	F App	p.238 70	P Emper
birthes with more and ugly jointes/Then nature gives,	Lucan, First Booke	561	
War onely gives us peace, o Rome continue/The course of	Lucan, First Booke	669	
My spotlesse life, which but to Gods [gives] <give> place,	Ovid's Elegies	1.3.13	
If hee gives thee what first himselfe did tast,	Ovid's Elegies	1.4.33	
Behold what gives the Poet but new verses?	Ovid's Elegies	1.8.57	
If he gives nothing, let him from thee wend.	Ovid's Elegies	1.8.100	
When thou hast so much as he gives no more,	Ovid's Elegies	1.8.101	
The fame that verse gives doth for ever last.	Ovid's Elegies	1.10.62	
None such the sister gives her brother grave,	Ovid's Elegies	2.5.25	
Beauty gives heart, Corinnas lookes excell,	Ovid's Elegies	2.17.7	
And thousand kisses gives, that worke my harmes:	Ovid's Elegies	2.18.10	
Eneas to Elisa answere gives,	Ovid's Elegies	2.18.31	
The other gives my love a conquering name,	Ovid's Elegies	3.1.65	
Honour what friends thy wife gives, sheele give many:	Ovid's Elegies	3.4.45	
Courts shut the poore out; wealth gives estimation,	Ovid's Elegies	3.7.55	
And gives the viper curled Dogge three heads.	Ovid's Elegies	3.11.26	
GIVEST			
And givest not eare unto the charge I bring?	Dido	5.1.52	Hermes
If thou givest kisses, I shall all disclose,	Ovid's Elegies	1.4.39	
Thou givest my mistris life, she mine againe.	Ovid's Elegies	2.13.16	
GIVING			
Giving commandement to our generall hoste,	2Tamb	2.1.61	Sgsmnd
Giving thee Nectar and Ambrosia,	2Tamb	2.4.110	Tamb
Giving the windes my words running in thine eare?	Ovid's Elegies	1.6.42	
Which giving her, she may give thee againe.	Ovid's Elegies	2.2.16	
Law-giving Minos did such yeares desire;	Ovid's Elegies	3.9.41	
GIV'T			
Come to my house and I will giv't your honour--	Jew	2.3.66	Barab

GLAD			
Anna be glad, now have I found a meane/To rid me from these	Dido	5.1.272	Dido
Now will the Christian miscreants be glad,	1Tamb	3.3.236	Bajzth
Me thinks I see how glad the christian King/Is made, for joy of	2Tamb	2.2.20	Uribas
I'le make him send me half he has, and glad he scapes so too.	Jew	4.2.67	P Ithimr
Is new returnd, this newes will glad him much,	Edw	1.4.301	Queene
Mephostophilis come/And bring glad tydings from great Lucifer.	F 416	2.1.28	Faust
I am glad I have found you, you are a couple of fine	F1096	3.3.9	P Vintnr
My gratious Lord, I am glad it contents you so wel:	F App	p.242 3	P Faust
I am glad they content you so Madam.	F App	p.242 27	P Faust
And glad when bloud, and ruine made him way:	Lucan, First Booke		151
Mild Atax glad it beares not Roman [boats] <bloats>;	Lucan, First Booke		404
And Trevier; thou being glad that wars are past thee;	Lucan, First Booke		437
such faults are sad/Nor make they any man that heare them glad.	Ovid's Elegies		2.2.52
Who thinkes her to be glad at lovers smart,	Ovid's Elegies		3.9.15
White Heifers by glad people forth are led,	Ovid's Elegies		3.12.13
courted her, was glad/That she such lovelinesse and beautie had	Hero and Leander		1.421
GLADLY			
And gladly yeeld them to my gracious rule:	1Tamb	2.5.28	Cosroe
Which with my crowne I gladly offer thee.	2Tamb	1.3.136	Usumc
Yet would I gladly visit Barabas,	Jew	5.3.24	Calym
plaine not heavens, but gladly beare these evils/For Neros sake:	Lucan, First Booke		37
I gladly graunt my parents given to save,	Ovid's Elegies		1.3.10
Be welcome to her, gladly let her take thee,	Ovid's Elegies		2.15.3
GLADNES			
Shal want my heart to be with gladnes pierc'd/To do you honor	1Tamb	1.2.250	Therid
GLADNESSE			
Father of gladnesse, and all frollicke thoughts,	Dido	4.2.5	Iarbus
And drunke with gladnesse, to the dore she goes.	Hero and Leander		2.236
GLAIVE (See GLEAVE)			
GLANCE (See also GLAUNCE)			
Who flies away at every glance I give,	2Tamb	5.3.70	Tamb
Good Barabas glance not at our holy Nuns.	Jew	2.3.86	Lodowk
<blushe>, and by that blushfull [glance] <glasse> am tooke:	Ovid's Elegies		2.4.12
GLASSE			
His glistering eyes shall be my looking glasse,	Dido	3.1.86	Dido
View but his picture in this tragicke glasse,	1Tamb	Prol.7	Prolog
him now, or Ile breake his glasse-windowes about his eares.	F App	p.240 142	P HrsCsr
Why in thy glasse doest looke being discontent?	Ovid's Elegies		1.14.36
<blushe>, and by that blushfull [glance] <glasse> am tooke:	Ovid's Elegies		2.4.12
But by her glasse disdaineful pride she learnes,	Ovid's Elegies		2.17.9
The towne of Sestos cal'd it Venus glasse.	Hero and Leander		1.142
As much as sparkling Diamonds flaring glasse.	Hero and Leander		1.214
GLASSES			
Love thee, fill me three glasses.	Jew	4.4.7	Curtzn
GLASSE-WINDOWES			
him now, or Ile breake his glasse-windowes about his eares.	F App	p.240 142	P HrsCsr
GLASSIE			
Till he hath furrowed Neptunes glassie fieldes,	Dido	4.3.11	Aeneas
That now should shine on Thetis glassie bower,	Hero and Leander		2.203
GLAUNCE			
Threatning a thousand deaths at every glaunce.	Dido	2.1.231	Aeneas
Take, and receive each secret amorous glaunce.	Ovid's Elegies		1.4.18
Threatning a thousand deaths at everie glaunce,	Hero and Leander		1.382
And as he turnd, cast many a lustfull glaunce,	Hero and Leander		2.186
GLAUNCETH			
That glaunceth at my lips and flieth away:	Edw	1.1.23	Gavstn
GLEAVE			
and sword and gleave/In civill broiles makes kin and country	Edw	4.4.5	Queene
GLIDE			
Our Turky blades shal glide through al their throats,	2Tamb	1.1.31	Orcan
And speake of spirits and ghosts that glide by night/About the	Jew	2.1.26	Barab
From East to West his Dragons swiftly glide,	F 766	2.3.45	2Chor
GLIDED			
Which glided through the bowels of the Greekes.	1Tamb	3.3.92	Argier
GLIDES			
With haire that gilds the water as it glides,	Edw	1.1.62	Gavstn
GLIDING			
A deadly bullet gliding through my side,	2Tamb	3.4.4	Capt
Are smoothly gliding downe by Candie shoare/To Malta, through	Jew	1.1.46	Barab
GLIMPS			
Like twilight glimps at setting of the sunne,	Ovid's Elegies		1.5.5
GLIMPS'D			
As from an orient cloud, glymse <glimps'd> here and there.	Hero and Leander		2.320
GLISTERED			
street like to a Firmament/Glistered with breathing stars,	Hero and Leander		1.98
GLISTERING			
His glistering eyes shall be my looking glasse,	Dido	3.1.86	Dido
GLISTERS			
Sword-girt Orions side glisters too bright.	Lucan, First Booke		664
The ships, whose God-head in the sea now glisters?	Ovid's Elegies		3.11.38
GLIST'RED			
Glist'red with deaw, as one that seem'd to skorne it:	Hero and Leander		1.390
GLITER'D			
The flattering skie gliter'd in often flames,	Lucan, First Booke		528
GLITTERING			
Whose glittering pompe Dianas shrowdes supplies,	Dido	3.3.4	Dido
That I may gaze upon this glittering crowne,	Edw	5.1.60	Edward
GLOBE			
Unto the rising of this earthly globe,	2Tamb	5.3.147	Tamb
Are all Celestiall bodies but one Globe,	F 587	2.2.36	Faust
Much like a globe, (a globe may I tearme this,	Hero and Leander		2.275
GLOMIE			
From Latmus mount up to the glomie skie,	Hero and Leander		1.109

GLOOMIE			
When suddenly gloomie Orion rose,	Dido	1.2.26	Cloan
Since gloomie Aeolus doth cease to frowne.	Dido	4.1.27	Aeneas
That I may pacifie that gloomie Jove,	Dido	4.2.2	Iarbus
That with thy gloomie hand corrects the heaven,	Dido	4.2.6	Iarbus
Stand graticus gloomie night to his device.	Edw	4.1.11	Kent
A gloomie fellow in a meade belowe,	Edw	4.7.29	Spencr
GLOOMY			
Now that the gloomy shadow of the night <earth>,	F 229	1.3.1	Faust
The Planets seven, the gloomy aire,	F 999	3.2.19	Mephst
And this gloomy night,/Here in this roome will wretched Faustus	F1803	5.2.7	Mephst
GLORIE			
Vaild his resplendant glorie from your view.	Dido	1.1.126	Venus
If that all glorie hath forsaken thee,	Dido	5.1.36	Hermes
For though the glorie of this day be lost,	1Tamb	3.3.241	Bajzth
them see (divine Zenocrate)/I glorie in the curses of my foes,	1Tamb	4.4.29	Tamb
bed, where many a Lord/In prime and glorie of his loving joy,	1Tamb	5.1.84	1Virgn
That Vertue solely is the sum of glorie,	1Tamb	5.1.189	Tamb
That danc'd with glorie on the silver waves,	2Tamb	2.4.3	Tamb
The glorie of this happy day is yours:	2Tamb	3.5.161	Tamb
For if he die, thy glorie is disgrac'd,	2Tamb	5.3.40	Usumc
Base leaden Earles that glorie in your birth,	Edw	2.2.74	Gavstn
GLORIES			
Now in their glories shine the golden crownes/Of these proud	2Tamb	4.1.1	Amyras
pride/And leads your glories <bodies> sheep-like to the sword.	2Tamb	4.1.77	Tamb
Survaieng all the glories of the land:	2Tamb	4.3.35	Orcan
But if he die, your glories are disgrac'd,	2Tamb	5.3.15	Therid
GLORIOUS			
A God is not so glorious as a King:	1Tamb	2.5.57	Therid
The slave usurps the glorious name of war.	1Tamb	4.1.67	Souldn
And poure it in this glorious Tyrants throat.	1Tamb	4.2.7	Bajzth
Will sooner burne the glorious frame of Heaven,	1Tamb	4.2.10	Tamb
Whose glorious body when he left the world,	2Tamb	1.1.139	Orcan
Which measureth the glorious frame of heaven,	2Tamb	3.4.65	Therid
That makes a king seeme glorious to the world,	Edw	2.2.175	Mortmr
We flye in hope to get his glorious soule:	F 277	1.3.49	Mephst
<why Faustus> think'st thou heaven is such a glorious thing?	F 556	2.2.5	Mephst
and for this blessed sight <glorious deed>/Happy and blest be	F1704	5.1.31	1Schol
The bright shining of whose glorious actes/Lightens the world	F App	p.237 25	Emper
Go now thou Conqueror, glorious triumphs raise,	Ovid's Elegies		1.7.35
Who on Loves seas more glorious wouldst appeare?	Hero and Leander		1.228
GLORY			
What glory is there in a common good,	P 97	2.40	Guise
Is Guises glory but a clowdy mist,	P 686	13.30	Guise
To make his glory great upon the earth.	P 790	16.4	Navrre
The Protestants will glory and insulte,	P1085	19.155	QnMoth
In what resplendant glory thou hadst set/In yonder throne, like	F1904	5.2.108	GdAngl
These Captaines emulous of each others glory.	Lucan, First Booke		120
Birdes haples glory, death thy life doth quench.	Ovid's Elegies		2.6.20
More glory by thy vanquisht foes assends.	Ovid's Elegies		2.9.6
But I no partner of my glory brooke,	Ovid's Elegies		2.12.11
And many by me to get glory crave.	Ovid's Elegies		2.17.28
Where Venus in her naked glory strove,	Hero and Leander		1.12
GLOSE (See also GLOZING)			
Her mind pure, and her toong untaught to glose.	Hero and Leander		1.392
GLOSTER			
neece, the onely heire/Unto the Earle of Gloster late deceased.	Edw	2.2.259	Edward
And meerely of our love we do create thee/Earle of Gloster, and	Edw	3.1.146	Edward
My lord of Gloster, do you heare the newes?	Edw	4.3.4	Edward
Gloster, I trowe/The lords of Fraunce love Englands gold so	Edw	4.3.14	Edward
To you my lord of Gloster from [Levune] <Lewne>.	Edw	4.3.26	Post
Spencer the sonne, created earle of Gloster,	Edw	4.6.56	Rice
GLOSTERS			
Unto our cosin, the earle of Glosters heire.	Edw	1.4.379	Edward
Seeing that our Lord th'earle of Glosters dead,	Edw	2.1.2	Baldck
GLOVE			
Trotting the ring, and tilting at a glove:	2Tamb	1.3.39	Zenoc
And fly my glove as from a Scorpion.	2Tamb	3.5.74	Tamb
GLOVES			
Where are those perfumed gloves which I sent/To be poysoned,	P 70	2.13	Guise
Me thinkes the gloves have a very strong perfume,	P 170	3.5	OldQn
She ware no gloves for neither sunne nor wind/Would burne or	Hero and Leander		1.27
GLOW			
And now the same gan so to scorch and glow,	Hero and Leander		2.70
GLOWE			
Shall Dian fanne when love begins to glowe?	Ovid's Elegies		1.1.12
GLOZING (See also GLOSE)			
The glozing head of thy base minion throwne.	Edw	1.1.133	Lncstr
GLUT			
let us glut our swords/That thirst to drinke the feble Perseans	1Tamb	3.3.164	Bajzth
And glut us with the dainties of the world,	2Tamb	1.3.220	Tamb
And glut it not with stale and daunted foes.	2Tamb	4.1.88	Tamb
And glut your longings with a heaven of joy.	2Tamb	5.3.227	Tamb
To glut the longing of my hearts desire,	F1760	5.1.87	Faust
GLUTTED			
How are ye glutted with these grievous objects,	1Tamb	5.1.341	Zenoc
We all are glutted with the Christians blood,	2Tamb	1.1.14	Gazell
And glutted now <more> with learnings golden gifts,	F 24	Prol.24	1Chor
How am I glutted with conceipt of this?	F 105	1.1.77	Faust
And Carthage soules be glutted with our blouds;	Lucan, First Booke		39
Even as sweete meate a glutted stomacke cloyes.	Ovid's Elegies		2.19.26
GLUTTON			
Choke thy selfe Glutton: What are thou the sixt?	F 704	2.2.153	Faust

GLUTTONS			
Were gluttons, and lov'd only delicates,	F1917	5.2.121	BdAngl
GLUTTONY			
I <who I sir, I> am Gluttony; my parents are all dead, and the	F 693	2.2.142	P Glutny
be carried thither againe by Gluttony and Letchery <Leachery>],	F 705.3	2.2.157A	P Sloth
GLYMSE			
As from an orient cloud, glymse <glimps'd> here and there.	Hero and Leander		2.320
GO (See also GOE, GOST)			
Go frowning foorth, but come thou smyling home,	1Tamb	1.1.65	Mycet
Go, stout Theridamas, thy words are swords,	1Tamb	1.1.74	Mycet
Go Menaphon, go into Scythia,	1Tamb	1.1.85	Mycet
Go on my Lord, and give your charge I say,	1Tamb	2.2.57	Mycet
Go valiant Souldier, go before and charge/The fainting army of	1Tamb	2.3.61	Cosroe
go before and charge/The fainting army of that foolish King.	1Tamb	2.3.61	Cosroe
Away, I am the King: go, touch me not.	1Tamb	2.4.20	Mycet
Go wander free from feare of Tyrants rage,	1Tamb	3.2.102	Agidas
May have fresh warning to go war with us,	1Tamb	4.1.71	Souldn
Go to, fal to your meat:	1Tamb	4.4.54	P Tamb
Go, never to returne with victorie:	1Tamb	5.1.214	Bajzth
Go Uribassa, give it straight in charge.	2Tamb	2.3.40	Orcan
Go too sirha, take your crown, and make up the halfe dozen.	2Tamb	3.5.135	P Tamb
Go bind the villaine, he shall hang in chaines,	2Tamb	5.1.84	Tamb
Wel, now Ile make it quake, go draw him up,	2Tamb	5.1.107	Tamb
Go thither some of you and take his gold,	2Tamb	5.1.123	Tamb
Go to, sirra sauce, is this your question?	Jew	3.3.34	P Abigal
Oh my sweet Ithimore go set it downe/And come againe so soone	Jew	3.4.108	Barab
Come my Lords lets go to the Church and pray,	P 55	1.55	Navrre
Wants thou gold? go to my treasurie:	Edw	1.1.167	Edward
Go whether thou wilt seeing I have Gaveston.	Edw	1.2.54	Queene
To go from hence, greeves not poore Gaveston,	Edw	1.4.119	Gavstn
Seeing I must go, do not renew my sorrow.	Edw	1.4.137	Gavstn
I passe not for their anger, come lets go.	Edw	1.4.142	Edward
Then speake not for him, let the pesant go.	Edw	1.4.218	Warwck
Did never sorrow go so neere my heart,	Edw	1.4.306	Edward
Chide me sweete Warwick, if I go astray.	Edw	1.4.348	Edward
But let them go, and tell me what are these.	Edw	2.2.239	Edward
Go souldiers take him hence, for by my sword,	Edw	2.5.20	Warwck
him, but must we now/Leave him on had-I-wist, and let him go?	Edw	2.5.85	Warwck
Why I say, let him go on Penbrookes word.	Edw	2.5.90	Lncstr
My Lord, you shall go with me,	Edw	2.5.99	Penbrk
hence, out of the way/A little, but our men shall go along.	Edw	2.5.101	Penbrk
We will in hast go certifie our Lord.	Edw	2.6.19	James
You shall go parley with the king of Fraunce.	Edw	3.1.71	Edward
And go in peace, leave us in warres at home.	Edw	3.1.85	Edward
Yet ere thou go, see how I do devorce	Edw	3.1.176	Edward
And plowes to go about our pallace gates.	Edw	3.1.216	Edward
Go take that haughtie Mortimer to the tower,	Edw	3.1.252	Edward
How say you my Lord, will you go with your friends,	Edw	4.2.19	SrJohn
distressed Queene his sister heere,/Go you with her to Henolt:	Edw	4.2.64	SrJohn
Your majestie must go to Killingworth.	Edw	4.7.82	Leistr
Must! tis somwhat hard, when kings must go.	Edw	4.7.83	Edward
And go I must, life farewell with my friends.	Edw	4.7.99	Edward
Come sonne, and go with this gentle Lorde and me.	Edw	5.2.109	Queene
Friends, whither must unhappie Edward go,	Edw	5.3.4	Edward
Thither shall your honour go, and so farewell.	Edw	5.3.62	Matrvs
The trumpets sound, I must go take my place.	Edw	5.4.72	Mortmr
Let me but stay and speake, I will not go,	Edw	5.4.105	Kent
Heeres a light to go into the dungeon.	Edw	5.5.37	Gurney
Go forward Faustus in that famous Art/Wherein all natures	F 101	1.1.73	BdAngl
Go to sirra, leave your jesting, and tell us where he is.	F 201	1.2.8	P 1Schol
But come, let us go, and informe the Rector:	F 225	1.2.32	2Schol
Go and returne an old Franciscan Frier,	F 253	1.3.25	Faust
Go beare these <those> tydings to great Lucifer,	F 315	1.3.87	Faust
Go, and returne to mighty Lucifer,	F 326	1.3.98	Faust
and I will make thee go, like Qui mihi discipulus.	F 355	1.4.13	P Wagner
Now go not backward: no, Faustus, be resolute.	F 394	2.1.6	Faust
Go forward Faustus in that famous Art.	F 403	2.1.15	BdAngl
I, go accursed spirit to ugly hell:	F 627	2.2.76	Faust
Go Mephostophilis, fetch them in.	F 660	2.2.109	P Lucifr
Or if thou't go but to the Taverne with me, I'le give thee	F 747	2.3.26	P Robin
And grant me my request, and then I go.	F 846	3.1.68	Faust
Go forth-with to our holy Consistory,	F 882	3.1.104	Pope
We go my Lord.	F 889	3.1.111	1Card
Go hast thee gentle Mephostophilis,	F 891	3.1.113	Faust
Go presently, and bring a banket forth,	F 977	3.1.199	Pope
Go then command our Priests to sing a Dirge,	F1063	3.2.83	Pope
to supper, and a Tester in your purse, and go backe againe.	F1122	3.3.35	P Robin
Go backe, and see the State in readinesse.	F1159	4.1.5	Mrtino
Well, go you attend the Emperour:	F1199	4.1.45	P Benvol
Go horse these traytors on your fiery backes,	F1403	4.2.79	Faust
Go Belimothe, and take this caitife hence,	F1408	4.2.84	Faust
Go bid the Hostler deliver him unto you, and remember what I	F1474	4.4.18	P Faust
Well I'le go rouse him, and make him give me my forty Dollors	F1487	4.4.31	P HrsCsr
and drinke a while, and then we'le go seeke out the Doctor.	F1557	4.5.53	P Robin
Go Mephostophilis, away.	F1574	4.6.17	P Faust
Go pacifie their fury, set it ope,	F1589	4.6.32	Duke
Come Gentlemen, let us go visit Faustus,	F1983	5.3.1	1Schol
thou serve me, and Ile make thee go like Qui mihi discipulus?	F App	p.229 13	P Wagner
O Lord I pray sir, let Banio and Belcher go sleepe.	F App	p.231 68	P Clown
Go to maister Doctor, let me see them presently.	F App	p.237 50	P Emper
Nay, and you go to conjuring, Ile be gone.	F App	p.237 57	P Knight
Your highnes may boldly go and see.	F App	p.238 63	P Faust
When to go homewards we rise all along,	Ovid's Elegies		1.4.55

GO (cont.)

Who feares these armes? who wil not go to meete them?	Ovid's Elegies	1.6.39	
Go now thou Conqueror, glorious triumphs raise,	Ovid's Elegies	1.7.35	
Go goodly <godly> birdes, striking your breasts bewaile,	Ovid's Elegies	2.6.3	
So farre 'tis safe, but to go farther dread.	Ovid's Elegies	2.11.16	
Go, minding to returne with prosperous winde,	Ovid's Elegies	2.11.37	
About my temples go triumphant bayes,	Ovid's Elegies	2.12.1	
go small gift from hand,/Let her my faith with thee given	Ovid's Elegies	2.15.27	
yong-mens mates, to go/If they determine to persever so.	Ovid's Elegies	2.16.17	
But sundry flouds in one banke never go,	Ovid's Elegies	2.17.31	
To empty aire may go my fearefull speech.	Ovid's Elegies	3.1.62	
Foule dust, from her faire body, go away.	Ovid's Elegies	3.2.42	
Like lightning go, his strugling mouth being checkt.	Ovid's Elegies	3.4.14	
So shalt thou go with youths to feasts together,	Ovid's Elegies	3.4.47	
I might not go, whether my papers went.	Ovid's Elegies	3.7.6	
I heere and there go witty with dishonour.	Ovid's Elegies	3.7.8	
Long was he taking leave, and loath to go,	Hero and Leander	2.93	
To part in twaine, that hee might come and go,	Hero and Leander	2.151	
GOAL (See GOLE)			
GOARE			
weapons point here shouldst thou fall,/And welter in thy goare.	Edw	2.5.14	Mortmr
having lickt/Warme goare from Syllas sword art yet athirst,	Lucan, First Booke	331	
GOARY			
Plaies with her goary coulours of revenge,	P 719	14.22	Navrre
GOAT (See also GOTE)			
Now is the goat brought through the boyes with darts,	Ovid's Elegies	3.12.21	
GOATE			
Shall with their Goate feete daunce an antick hay.	Edw	1.1.60	Gavstn
Onely the Goddesse hated Goate did lack,	Ovid's Elegies	3.12.18	
GOBBETS			
Even in his face his offered [Gobbets] <Goblets> cast.	Ovid's Elegies	1.4.34	
GOBLET			
with you, I must yet have a goblet payde from you ere you goe.	F App	p.234 7	P Vintnr
I a goblet Rafe, I a goblet?	F App	p.234 9	P Robin
I a goblet?	F App	p.234 10	P Robin
Wel, tone of you hath this goblet about you.	F App	p.235 16	P Vintnr
stand by, Ile scowre you for a goblet, stand aside you had best,	F App	p.235 18	P Robin
looke to the goblet Rafe.	F App	p.235 20	P Robin
looke to the goblet Rafe, Polypragmos Belseborams framanto	F App	p.235 24	P Robin
thou hast no goblet.	F App	p.235 27	P Vintnr
Peccatum peccatorum, heeres thy goblet, good Vintner.	F App	p.235 28	P Rafe
GOBLETS			
Even in his face his offered [Gobbets] <Goblets> cast.	Ovid's Elegies	1.4.34	
GOD			
Whereas the Wind-god warring now with Fate,	Dido	1.1.115	Jupitr
Brave Prince of Troy, thou onely art our God,	Dido	1.1.152	Achat
But haples I, God wot, poore and unknowne,	Dido	1.1.227	Aeneas
And yet God knowes intangled unto one.--	Dido	3.1.154	Dido
O no God wot, I cannot watch my time,	Dido	3.2.14	Juno
O God of heaven, turne the hand of fate/Unto that happie day of	Dido	3.3.80	Iarbus
Now if thou beest a pitying God of power,	Dido	4.2.19	Iarbus
Which is (God knowes) about that Tamburlaine,	1Tamb	1.1.30	Mycet
Sound up the trumpets then, God save the King.	1Tamb	1.1.188	Ortyg
To be a King, is halfe to be a God.	1Tamb	2.5.56	Usumc
A God is not so glorious as a King:	1Tamb	2.5.57	Therid
What God or Feend, or spirit of the earth,	1Tamb	2.6.15	Ortyg
Though Mars himselfe the angrie God of armes,	1Tamb	2.7.58	Tamb
Than Juno sister to the highest God,	1Tamb	3.2.54	Zenoc
I that am tearm'd the Scourge and Wrath of God,	1Tamb	3.3.44	Tamb
Now Mahomet, solicit God himselfe,	1Tamb	3.3.195	Zabina
The chiefest God, first moover of that Spheare/Enchac'd with	1Tamb	4.2.8	Tamb
Feends looke on me, and thou dread God of hell,	1Tamb	4.2.27	Bajzth
The Scum of men, the hate and Scourge of God,	1Tamb	4.3.9	Souldn
banquet and carouse/Full bowles of wine unto the God of war,	1Tamb	4.4.6	Tamb
Stil dooth this man or rather God of war,	1Tamb	5.1.1	Govnr
Venus, would she leave/The angrie God of Armes, and lie with me.	1Tamb	5.1.125	Tamb
Then is there left no Mahomet, no God,	1Tamb	5.1.239	Zabina
Whose lookes might make the angry God of armes,	1Tamb	5.1.326	Zenoc
The God of war resignes his roume to me,	1Tamb	5.1.450	Tamb
Mighty hath God and Mahomet made thy hand/(Renowmed Tamburlain)	1Tamb	5.1.479	Souldn
The sonne of God and issue of a Mayd,	2Tamb	1.1.134	Sgsmnd
By sacred Mahomet, the friend of God,	2Tamb	1.1.137	Orcan
And mighty Tamburlaine, our earthly God,	2Tamb	1.3.138	Techel
That God hath given to venge our Christians death/And scourge	2Tamb	2.1.52	Fredrk
And take the victorie our God hath given.	2Tamb	2.1.63	Sgsmnd
Whose shape is figure of the highest God?	2Tamb	2.2.38	Orcan
If thou wilt proove thy selfe a perfect God,	2Tamb	2.2.56	Orcan
And God hath thundered vengeance from on high,	2Tamb	2.3.2	Sgsmnd
The God that tunes this musicke to our soules,	2Tamb	2.4.31	Tamb
And scourge the Scourge of the immortall God:	2Tamb	2.4.80	Tamb
What God so ever holds thee in his armes,	2Tamb	2.4.109	Tamb
by the aid of God and his friend Mahomet, Emperour of Natolia,	2Tamb	3.1.3	P Orcan
Blood is the God of Wars rich livery.	2Tamb	3.2.116	Tamb
Intreat a pardon of the God of heaven,	2Tamb	3.4.32	Olymp
And makes the mighty God of armes his slave:	2Tamb	3.4.53	Therid
The Emperour of the world, and earthly God,	2Tamb	3.5.22	Orcan
The Scourge of God and terrour of the world,	2Tamb	4.1.154	Tamb
Whom I have thought a God? they shal be burnt.	2Tamb	5.1.176	Tamb
There is a God full of revenging wrath,	2Tamb	5.1.183	Tamb
Where men report, thou sitt'st by God himselfe,	2Tamb	5.1.194	Tamb
The God that sits in heaven, if any God,	2Tamb	5.1.201	Tamb
For he is God alone, and none but he.	2Tamb	5.1.202	Tamb
If God or Mahomet send any aide.	2Tamb	5.2.11	Callap

GOD (cont.)

Though God himselfe and holy Mahomet,	2Tamb	5.2.37	Amasia
What daring God torments my body thus,	2Tamb	5.3.42	Tamb
Then let some God oppose his holy power,	2Tamb	5.3.220	Techel
For Tamburlaine, the Scourge of God must die.	2Tamb	5.3.248	Tamb
God-a-mercy nose; come let's begone.	Jew	4.1.23	Ithimr
No god-a-mercy, shall I have these crownes?	Jew	4.3.31	Pilia
That God may still defend the right of France:	P 56	1.56	Navrre
O gracious God, what times are these?	P 188	3.23	Navrre
O graunt sweet God my daies may end with hers,	P 189	3.24	Navrre
O God forgive my sins.	P 303	5.30	Admral
I am a preacher of the word of God,	P 341	5.68	Lorein
O let me pray unto my God.	P 359	6.14	Seroun
As to the service of the eternall God.	P 413	7.53	Ramus
But God will sure restore you to your health.	P 542	11.7	Navrre
God graunt my neerest freends may prove no worse.	P 547	11.12	Charls
But God that alwaies doth defend the right,	P 575	11.40	Navrre
Truth Pleshe, and God so prosper me in all,	P 584	11.49	Navrre
O would to God this quill that heere doth write,	P 667	13.11	Duchss
In honor of our God and countries good.	P 708	14.11	Navrre
Thus God we see doth ever guide the right,	P 789	16.3	Navrre
But God we know will alwaies put them downe,	P 798	16.12	Navrre
But if that God doe prosper mine attempts,	P 927	18.28	Navrre
Then pray to God, and aske forgivenes of the King.	P1004	19.74	P 2Mur
Pray God thou be a King now this is done.	P1068	19.138	QnMoth
Traitor to God, and to the realme of France.	P1076	19.146	QnMoth
God shield your grace from such a sodaine death:	P1178	22.40	Navrre
Whom God hath blest for hating Papestry.	P1208	22.70	King
For this offence be thou accurst of God.	Edw	1.1.199	BshpCv
What neede I, God himselfe is up in armes,	Edw	1.2.40	ArchBp
As if that Proteus god of shapes appearde.	Edw	1.4.411	Mortmr
God end them once, my lord I take my leave,	Edw	3.1.87	Queene
Yea gentle brother, and the God of heaven,	Edw	4.2.74	Queene
Raigne showers of vengeance on my cursed head/Thou God, to whom	Edw	4.6.8	Kent
Succesfull battells gives the God of kings,	Edw	4.6.19	Queene
God save Queene Isabell, and her princely sonne.	Edw	4.6.46	Rice
now sweete God of heaven,/Make me despise this transitorie	Edw	5.1.107	Edward
No, God forbid.	Edw	5.2.99	Queene
Long live king Edward, by the grace of God/King of England, and	Edw	5.4.73	ArchBp
My minde may be more stedfast on my God.	Edw	5.5.78	Edward
Assist me sweete God, and receive my soule.	Edw	5.5.109	Edward
A sound Magitian is a Demi-god <mighty god>,	F 89	1.1.61	Faust
God in heaven knowes.	F 198	1.2.5	P Wagner
For when we heare one racke the name of God,	F 275	1.3.47	Mephst
Yes Faustus, and most deerely lov'd of God.	F 293	1.3.65	Mephst
For which God threw him from the face of heaven.	F 296	1.3.68	Mephst
Conspir'd against our God with Lucifer,	F 299	1.3.71	Mephst
Think'st thou that I [who] saw the face of God,	F 305	1.3.77	Mephst
What bootes it then to thinke on <of> God or Heaven?	F 391	2.1.3	Faust
Despair in GOD, and trust in Belzebub:	F 393	2.1.5	Faust
Abjure this Magicke, turne to God againe.	F 396	2.1.8	Faust
[I and Faustus will turne to God againe].	F 397	2.1.9A	Faust
[To God]? <Why> he loves thee not:	F 398	2.1.10	Faust
The god thou serv'st is thine owne appetite,	F 399	2.1.11	Faust
shall stand by me,/What [god] <power> can hurt me <thee>?	F 414	2.1.26	Faust
If unto [God] <heaven>, hee'le throw me <thee> downe to hell.	F 467	2.1.79	Faust
Faustus repent, yet God will pitty thee.	F 563	2.2.12	GdAngl
Thou art a spirit, God cannot pity thee.	F 564	2.2.13	BdAngl
Be I a devill yet God may pitty me,	F 566	2.2.15	Faust
Yea <I>, God will pitty me if I repent.	F 567	2.2.16	Faust
Thinke Faustus upon God, that made the world.	F 625	2.2.74	P Faust
Thou should'st not thinke on <of> God.	F 644	2.2.93	Belzeb
[Never to name God, or to pray to him],	F 649	2.2.98A	Faust
[As in this furnace God shal try my faith],	F1792	5.1.119A	OldMan
[Hence hel, for hence I flie unto my God].	F1796	5.1.123A	OldMan
heaven the seate of God, the Throne of the Blessed, the	F1844	5.2.48	P Faust
Yet Faustus call on God.	F1848	5.2.52	P 2Schol
On God, whom Faustus hath abjur'd?	F1849	5.2.53	P Faust
on God, whom Faustus hath blasphem'd?	F1849	5.2.53	P Faust
[Ah] <O> my God, I would weepe, but the Divell drawes in my	F1850	5.2.54	P Faust
O God forbid.	F1857	5.2.61	AllSch
God forbade it indeed, but Faustus hath done it:	F1858	5.2.62	P Faust
but the Divel threatned to teare me in peeces if I nam'd God:	F1865	5.2.69	P Faust
God will strengthen me, I will stay with Faustus.	F1870	5.2.74	P 3Schol
Tempt not God sweet friend, but let us into the next roome, and	F1871	5.2.75	P 1Schol
thou, and we will pray, that God may have mercie upon thee.	F1875	5.2.79	P 2Schol
O I'le leape up to [my God] <heaven>: who puls me downe?	F1938	5.2.142	Faust
And see [where God]/[Stretcheth out his Arme, and bends his	F1943	5.2.147	Faust
And hide me from the heavy wrath of [God] <heaven>.	F1946	5.2.150	Faust
[O God, if thou wilt not have mercy on my soule],	F1958	5.2.162A	Faust
[My God, my God] <O mercy heaven>, looke not so fierce on me;	F1979	5.2.183	Faust
God forgive me, he speakes Dutch fustian:	F App	p.231 72	P Clown
Drawer, I hope al is payd, God be with you, come Rafe.	F App	p.234 6	P Robin
masse see where he is, God save you maister doctor.	F App	p.239 99	P HrsCsr
slicke as an Ele; wel god buy sir, your boy wil deliver him me:	F App	p.240 117	P HrsCsr
this is he, God save ye maister doctor, maister doctor, maister	F App	p.241 148	P HrsCsr
What God it please thee be, or where to sway:	Lucan, First Booke		52
Thou Caesar at this instant art my God,	Lucan, First Booke		63
cause, what ere thou be whom God assignes/This great effect,	Lucan, First Booke		419
Pray God it may his latest supper be,	Ovid's Elegies		1.4.2
The Poets God arayed in robes of gold,	Ovid's Elegies		1.8.59
whom the God deluded/In snowe-white plumes of a false swanne	Ovid's Elegies		1.10.3
Yet should I curse a God, if he but said,	Ovid's Elegies		2.9.25

GOD (cont.)			
Tis credible some [god-head] <good head> haunts the place.	Ovid's Elegies	3.1.2	
God is a name, no substance, feard in vaine,	Ovid's Elegies	3.3.23	
Or if there be a God, he loves fine wenches,	Ovid's Elegies	3.3.25	
Were I a God, I should give women leave,	Ovid's Elegies	3.3.43	
With lying lips my God-head to deceave,	Ovid's Elegies	3.3.44	
If of scornd lovers god be venger just,	Ovid's Elegies	3.7.65	
By secreat thoughts to thinke there is a god.	Ovid's Elegies	3.8.36	
And to my losse God-wronging perjuries?	Ovid's Elegies	3.10.22	
Or shall I plaine some God against me warres?	Ovid's Elegies	3.11.4	
The ships, whose God-head in the sea now glisters?	Ovid's Elegies	3.11.38	
God knowes I cannot force love, as you doe.	Hero and Leander	1.206	
and there God knowes I play/With Venus swannes and sparrowes	Hero and Leander	1.351	
On her, this god/Enamoured was, and with his snakie rod,	Hero and Leander	1.397	
The mirthfull God of amorous pleasure smil'd,	Hero and Leander	2.39	
O what god would not therewith be appeas'd?	Hero and Leander	2.50	
Whereat the saphir visag'd god grew prowd,	Hero and Leander	2.155	
The lustie god imbrast him, cald him love,	Hero and Leander	2.167	
The god put Helles bracelet on his arme,	Hero and Leander	2.179	
The god seeing him with pittie to be moved,	Hero and Leander	2.219	
GOD-A-MERCY			
God-a-mercy nose; come let's begone.	Jew	4.1.23	Ithimr
No god-a-mercy, shall I have these crownes?	Jew	4.3.31	Pilia
GOD BUY			
slicke as an Ele; wel god buy sir, your boy wil deliver him me:	F App	p.240 117	P HrsCsr
GODDES			
My thoughts sole goddes, aide mine enterprise,	Lucan, First Booke	202	
GODDESSE			
Thou art a Goddesse that delud'st our eyes,	Dido	1.1.191	Aeneas
And I the Goddesse of all these, commaund/Aeneas ride as	Dido	4.4.77	Dido
Thy mother was no Goddesse perjurd man,	Dido	5.1.156	Dido
Goddesse of the war/Threw naked swords and sulphur bals of	2Tamb	3.2.40	Tamb
Shall by the angrie goddesse be transformde,	Edw	1.1.68	Gavstn
He first a Goddesse strooke; an other I.	Ovid's Elegies	1.7.32	
Worthy to keembe none but a Goddesse faire,	Ovid's Elegies	2.8.2	
Thou Goddesse doest command a warme South-blast,	Ovid's Elegies	2.8.19	
This goddesse company doth to me befall.	Ovid's Elegies	3.1.44	
Goddesse come here, make my love conquering.	Ovid's Elegies	3.2.46	
We praise: great goddesse ayde my enterprize.	Ovid's Elegies	3.2.56	
Thee, goddesse, bountifull all nations judge,	Ovid's Elegies	3.9.5	
The goddesse sawe Iasion on Candyan Ide,	Ovid's Elegies	3.9.25	
The graine-rich goddesse in high woods did stray,	Ovid's Elegies	3.9.35	
And wisht the goddesse long might feele loves fire.	Ovid's Elegies	3.9.42	
Onely the Goddesse hated Goate did lack,	Ovid's Elegies	3.12.18	
(For his sake whom their goddesse held so deare,	Hero and Leander	1.92	
GODDESSES			
And envious fates great [goddesses] <goodesses> assaile,	Ovid's Elegies	3.8.2	
GODFATHERS			
But Barabas, who shall be your godfathers,	Jew	4.1.109	1Fryar
Marry the Turke shall be one of my godfathers,	Jew	4.1.111	Barab
My godfathers were these:	F 697	2.2.146	P Glutny
GOD-HEAD			
Tis credible some [god-head] <good head> haunts the place.	Ovid's Elegies	3.1.2	
With lying lips my God-head to deceave,	Ovid's Elegies	3.3.44	
The ships, whose God-head in the sea now glisters?	Ovid's Elegies	3.11.38	
GODHEAD			
Seeke out another Godhead to adore,	2Tamb	5.1.200	Tamb
GODLINESSE			
conjuring/Is stoutly to abjure [the Trinity] <all godlinesse>,	F 281	1.3.53	Mephst
GODLY			
Go goodly <godly> birdes, striking your breasts bewaile,	Ovid's Elegies	2.6.3	
Turnes all the goodly <godly> birdes to what she please.	Ovid's Elegies	2.6.58	
If any godly care of me thou hast,	Ovid's Elegies	2.16.47	
Live godly, thou shalt die, though honour heaven,	Ovid's Elegies	3.8.37	
The godly, sweete Tibullus doth increase.	Ovid's Elegies	3.8.66	
GODMOTHER			
<O> But my godmother, O she was an ancient Gentlewoman, her	F 699	2.2.148	P Glutny
GODS (See also SWOWNS, ZOUNDS)			
And bring the Gods to wonder at the game:	Dido	1.1.18	Ganimd
Why, are not all the Gods at thy commaund,	Dido	1.1.30	Jupitr
A Gods name on and hast thee to the Court,	Dido	1.1.233	Venus
We come not we to wrong your Libian Gods,	Dido	1.2.10	Illion
Then he alleag'd the Gods would have them stay,	Dido	2.1.141	Aeneas
Albeit the Gods doe know no wanton thought/Had ever residence	Dido	3.1.16	Dido
And banquet as two Sisters with the Gods?	Dido	3.2.29	Juno
And vow by all the Gods of Hospitalitie,	Dido	3.4.44	Aeneas
Henceforth you shall be our Carthage Gods:	Dido	4.4.96	Dido
The king of Gods sent me from highest heaven,	Dido	5.1.32	Hermes
What, would the Gods have me, Deucalion like,	Dido	5.1.57	Aeneas
Witnes the Gods, and witnes heaven and earth,	Dido	5.1.80	Aeneas
Yet must he not gainsay the Gods behest.	Dido	5.1.127	Aeneas
The Gods, what Gods be those that seeke my death?	Dido	5.1.128	Dido
O no, the Gods wey not what Lovers doe,	Dido	5.1.131	Dido
And now ye gods that guide the starrie frame,	Dido	5.1.302	Dido
That Gods and men may pitie this my death,	Dido	5.1.327	Anna
The Gods, defenders of the innocent,	1Tamb	1.2.68	Zenoc
His looks do menace heaven and dare the Gods,	1Tamb	1.2.157	Therid
May we become immortall like the Gods.	1Tamb	1.2.201	Tamb
Not Hermes Prolocutor to the Gods,	1Tamb	1.2.210	Therid
And call'd the Gods to witnesse of my vow,	1Tamb	1.2.234	Tamb
Shall threat the Gods more than Cyclopian warres,	1Tamb	2.3.21	Tamb
O Gods, is this Tamburlaine the thiefe,	1Tamb	2.4.41	Mycet
That thus opposeth him against the Gods,	1Tamb	2.6.39	Cosroe

GODS (cont.)			
Than if the Gods had held a Parliament:	1Tamb	2.7.66	Tamb
Ye Gods and powers that governe Persea,	1Tamb	3.3.189	Zenoc
That which hath [stoopt] <stopt> the tempest of the Gods,	1Tamb	5.1.184	Tamb
As rules the Skies, and countermands the Gods:	1Tamb	5.1.233	Bajzth
But as the Gods to end the Troyans toile,	1Tamb	5.1.392	Zenoc
That would not kill and curse at Gods command,	2Tamb	2.1.55	Fredrk
That hanging here, wil draw the Gods from heaven:	2Tamb	3.2.28	Tamb
Gods great lieftenant over all the world:	2Tamb	3.5.2	2Msngr
tel me if the warres/Be not a life that may illustrate Gods,	2Tamb	4.1.79	Tamb
When all the Gods stand gazing at his pomp:	2Tamb	4.3.129	Tamb
To signifie the slaughter of the Gods.	2Tamb	5.3.50	Tamb
Come carie me to war against the Gods,	2Tamb	5.3.52	Tamb
In Gods name, let them come.	P 728	14.31	Navrre
Welcome a Gods name Madam and your sonne,	Edw	4.3.41	Edward
To plaine me to the gods against them both:	Edw	5.1.22	Edward
And heape Gods heavy wrath upon thy head.	F 99	1.1.71	GdAngl
Thus, as the Gods creepe on with feete of wool,	F 877	3.1.99	Pope
Give him his head for Gods sake.	F1392	4.2.68	P Fredrk
to heaven, and remember [Gods] mercy is <mercies are> infinite.	F1835	5.2.39	P 2Schol
other meanes, (and gods not sleightly/Purchase immortal thrones;	Lucan, First Booke		34
crush themselves, such end the gods/Allot the height of honor,	Lucan, First Booke		81
The gods abetted; Cato likt the other;	Lucan, First Booke		129
Urging his fortune, trusting in the gods,	Lucan, First Booke		149
Ye gods of Phrigia and Iulus line,	Lucan, First Booke		199
Whether the gods, or blustring south were cause/I know not, but	Lucan, First Booke		236
And snatcht armes neer their houshold gods hung up/Such as	Lucan, First Booke		242
But gods and fortune prickt him to this war,	Lucan, First Booke		265
the gods are with us,/Neither spoile, nor kingdom seeke we by	Lucan, First Booke		350
their houshold gods/And love to Room (thogh slaughter steeld	Lucan, First Booke		354
Or rob the gods; or sacred temples fire;	Lucan, First Booke		380
And only gods and heavenly powers you know,	Lucan, First Booke		449
Their houshould gods restrain them not, none lingered,	Lucan, First Booke		505
O gods that easie grant men great estates,	Lucan, First Booke		508
the angry threatning gods/Fill'd both the earth and seas with	Lucan, First Booke		522
their saints and houshold gods/Sweate teares to shew the	Lucan, First Booke		554
And searching farther for the gods displeasure,	Lucan, First Booke		616
these he seeing what myschiefes must ensue,/Cride out, O gods!	Lucan, First Booke		630
O Gods what death prepare ye?	Lucan, First Booke		648
Why should we wish the gods should ever end them?	Lucan, First Booke		668
Thou with these souldiers conquerest gods and men,	Ovid's Elegies		1.2.37
My spotlesse life, which but to Gods [gives] <give> place,	Ovid's Elegies		1.3.13
Or holy gods with cruell strokes abus'd.	Ovid's Elegies		1.7.6
The gods send thee no house, a poore old age,	Ovid's Elegies		1.8.113
To serve for pay beseemes not wanton gods.	Ovid's Elegies		1.10.20
The Gods from this sinne rid me of suspition,	Ovid's Elegies		2.7.19
And to the Gods for that death Ovid prayes.	Ovid's Elegies		2.10.30
Loe country Gods, and [known] <know> bed to forsake,	Ovid's Elegies		2.11.7
Forgive her gratious Gods this one delict,	Ovid's Elegies		2.14.43
And waters force, force helping Gods to faile,	Ovid's Elegies		2.16.28
Great gods what kisses, and how many gave she?	Ovid's Elegies		2.19.18
The Gods, and their rich pompe witnesse with me,	Ovid's Elegies		3.2.61
What, are there Gods?	Ovid's Elegies		3.3.1
Say gods: if she unpunisht you deceive,	Ovid's Elegies		3.3.15
And unrevengd mockt Gods with me doth scoffe.	Ovid's Elegies		3.3.20
The wronged Gods dread faire ones to offend,	Ovid's Elegies		3.3.31
The Gods have eyes, and brests as well as men.	Ovid's Elegies		3.3.42
And I would be none of the Gods severe.	Ovid's Elegies		3.3.46
I thinke the great Gods greeved they had bestowde/This <The>	Ovid's Elegies		3.6.45
Worthy she was to move both Gods and men,	Ovid's Elegies		3.6.59
The gods care we are cald, and men of piety,	Ovid's Elegies		3.8.17
The holy gods gilt temples they might fire,	Ovid's Elegies		3.8.43
fellow bed, by all/The Gods who by thee to be perjurde fall,	Ovid's Elegies		3.10.46
blazon foorth the loves of men,/Much lesse of powerfull gods.	Hero and Leander		1.71
There might you see the gods in sundrie shapes,	Hero and Leander		1.143
Under whose shade the Wood-gods love to bee.	Hero and Leander		1.156
Well therefore by the gods decreed it is,	Hero and Leander		1.253
paths, wheron the gods might trace/To Joves high court.	Hero and Leander		1.298
Though neither gods nor men may thee deserve,	Hero and Leander		1.315
Wherewith the king of Gods and men is feasted.	Hero and Leander		1.432
O none but gods have power their love to hide,	Hero and Leander		2.131
GOD-WRONGING			
And to my losse God-wronging perjuries?	Ovid's Elegies		3.10.22
GOE			
Hold, take this candle and goe light a fire,	Dido	1.1.171	Aeneas
Ascanius, goe and drie thy drenched lims,	Dido	1.1.174	Aeneas
Whence may you come, or whither will you goe?	Dido	1.1.215	Venus
Goe fetch the garment which Sicheus ware:	Dido	2.1.80	Dido
For many tales goe of that Cities fall,	Dido	2.1.108	Dido
And thinking to goe downe, came Hectors ghost/With ashie	Dido	2.1.201	Aeneas
And goe to Dido, who in stead of him/Will set thee on her lap	Dido	2.1.324	Venus
Goe thou away, Ascanius shall stay.	Dido	3.1.35	Dido
O stay Iarbus, and Ile goe with thee.	Dido	3.1.37	Dido
And if my mother goe, Ile follow her.	Dido	3.1.38	Cupid
I goe to feed the humour of my Love,	Dido	3.1.50	Iarbus
Wherefore doth Dido bid Iarbus goe?	Dido	3.1.56	Anna
Anna, good sister Anna goe for him,	Dido	3.1.75	Dido
But playd he nere so sweet, I let him goe:	Dido	3.1.160	Dido
We two will goe a hunting in the woods,	Dido	3.1.174	Dido
That thus in person goe with thee to hunt:	Dido	3.3.2	Dido
Lords goe before, we two must talke alone.	Dido	3.3.9	Dido
Pesant, goe seeke companions like thy selfe,	Dido	3.3.21	Dido
Let my Phenissa graunt, and then I goe:	Dido	4.3.6	Aeneas

GOE (cont.)

I faine would goe, yet beautie calles me backe:	Dido	4.3.46	Aeneas
Then let Aeneas goe abourd with us.	Dido	4.4.23	Achat
Thinkes Dido I will goe and leave him here?	Dido	4.4.30	Aeneas
Goe, bid my Nurse take yong Ascanius,	Dido	4.4.105	Dido
Aeneas will not goe without his sonne:	Dido	4.4.107	Dido
But though he goe, he stayes in Carthage still,	Dido	4.4.133	Dido
And told me that Aeneas ment to goe:	Dido	4.4.142	Dido
My Lord Ascanius, ye must goe with me.	Dido	4.5.1	Nurse
Whither must I goe? Ile stay with my mother.	Dido	4.5.2	Cupid
No, thou shalt goe with me unto my house,	Dido	4.5.3	Nurse
Now speake Ascanius, will ye goe or no?	Dido	4.5.12	Nurse
Come come, Ile goe, how farre hence is your house?	Dido	4.5.13	Cupid
How pretilie he laughs, goe ye wagge,	Dido	4.5.19	Nurse
Let some of those thy followers goe with me,	Dido	5.1.73	Iarbus
Aeneas, wherefore goe thy men abourd?	Dido	5.1.87	Dido
Not from my heart, for I can hardly goe,	Dido	5.1.103	Aeneas
Then let me goe and never say farewell?	Dido	5.1.109	Aeneas
Let me goe, farewell, I must from hence,	Dido	5.1.110	Dido
Then let me goe, and never say farewell?	Dido	5.1.124	Dido
Goe goe and spare not, seeke out Italy,	Dido	5.1.169	Dido
I but heele come againe, he cannot goe,	Dido	5.1.184	Dido
Once didst thou goe, and he came backe againe,	Dido	5.1.196	Dido
I goe faire sister, heavens graunt good successe.	Dido	5.1.211	Anna
Thou for some pettie guift hast let him goe,	Dido	5.1.218	Dido
How can ye goe when he hath all your fleete?	Dido	5.1.242	Anna
Goe Anna, bid my servants bring me fire.	Dido	5.1.278	Dido
Iarbus, talke not of Aeneas, let him goe,	Dido	5.1.283	Dido
You must be forced from me ere you goe:	1Tamb	1.2.120	Tamb
Goe on for me.	1Tamb	2.5.106	Therid
And where I goe be thus in triumph drawne:	1Tamb	4.2.86	Tamb
Shall lead him with us wheresoere we goe.	1Tamb	4.2.100	Tamb
straight goe charge a few of them/To chardge these Dames,	1Tamb	5.1.116	Tamb
But goe my Lords, put the rest to the sword.	1Tamb	5.1.134	Tamb
Goe to, my child, away, away, away.	1Tamb	5.1.312	P Zabina
Come let us goe and banquet in our tents:	2Tamb	1.1.160	Orcan
me my Lord, if I should goe, would you bee as good as your word?	2Tamb	1.2.62	P Almeda
Now goe I tc revenge my fathers death.	2Tamb	1.2.78	Callap
But Lady goe with us to Tamburlaine,	2Tamb	3.4.45	Therid
That you must goe with us, no remedy.	2Tamb	3.4.79	Therid
Goe villaine, cast thee headlong from a rock,	2Tamb	3.5.120	Tamb
Goe, goe tall stripling, fight you for us both,	2Tamb	4.1.33	Calyph
You wil not goe then?	2Tamb	4.1.40	Amyras
I goe into the field before I need?	2Tamb	4.1.51	Calyph
And should I goe and kill a thousand men,	2Tamb	4.1.53	Calyph
And should I goe and do nor harme nor good,	2Tamb	4.1.56	Calyph
Come, thou and I wil goe to cardes to drive away the time.	2Tamb	4.1.61	P Calyph
Shal we let goe these kings again my Lord/To gather greater	2Tamb	4.1.82	Amyras
Goe now and bind the Burghers hand and foot,	2Tamb	5.1.161	Tamb
In spight of death I will goe show my face.	2Tamb	5.3.114	Tamb
Why then goe bid them come ashore,/And bring with them their	Jew	1.1.55	Barab
Goe send 'um threescore Camels, thirty Mules,	Jew	1.1.59	Barab
Goe tell 'em the Jew of Malta sent thee, man:	Jew	1.1.66	Barab
I goe.	Jew	1.1.68	1Merch
[But] <by> goe, goe thou thy wayes, discharge thy Ship,	Jew	1.1.82	Barab
Well, goe/And bid the Merchants and my men dispatch	Jew	1.1.99	Barab
Come therefore let us goe to Barrabas;	Jew	1.1.141	2Jew
I know you will; well brethren let us goe.	Jew	1.1.174	1Jew
How ere the world goe, I'le make sure for one,	Jew	1.1.186	Barab
Goe one and call those Jewes of Malta hither:	Jew	1.2.34	Govnr
will give me leave once more, I trow,/To goe into my house.	Jew	1.2.253	Barab
Then father, goe with me.	Jew	1.2.300	Abigal
Seduced Daughter, Goe, forget not.	Jew	1.2.359	Barab
'Twere time well spent to goe and visit her:	Jew	1.2.389	Lodowk
And so will I too, or it shall goe hard.--	Jew	1.2.392	Lodowk
As good goe on, as sit so sadly thus.	Jew	2.1.40	Barab
Goe Officers and set them straight in shew.	Jew	2.2.43	Govnr
I, and his sonnes too, or it shall goe hard.	Jew	2.3.17	Barab
It shall goe hard but I will see your death.	Jew	2.3.94	Barab
Sometimes I goe about and poyson wells;	Jew	2.3.176	Barab
See 'em goe pinion'd along by my doore.	Jew	2.3.180	Barab
to see the cripples/Goe limping home to Christendome on stilts.	Jew	2.3.212	Ithimr
But goe you in, I'le thinke upon the account:	Jew	2.3.241	Barab
Well, let him goe.	Jew	2.3.336	Lodowk
Yes, you shall have him: Goe put her in.	Jew	2.3.362	Barab
So, now will I goe in to Lodowicke,	Jew	2.3.381	Barab
And I will have it or it shall goe hard.	Jew	3.1.15	Pilia
Goe to the new made Nunnery, and inquire/For any of the Fryars	Jew	3.3.27	Abigal
Come, shall we goe?	Jew	3.3.76	1Fryar
But let 'em goe:	Jew	3.4.28	Barab
Goe buy thee garments: but thou shalt not want:	Jew	3.4.47	Barab
But first goe fetch me in the pot of Rice/That for our supper	Jew	3.4.49	Barab
I goe Sir.	Jew	3.4.51	P Ithimr
There Ithimore must thou goe place this [pot] <plot>:	Jew	3.4.84	Barab
Well, master, I goe.	Jew	3.4.94	P Ithimr
this, then goe with me/And helpe me to exclaime against the Jew.	Jew	3.6.45	2Fryar
They weare no shirts, and they goe bare-foot too.	Jew	4.1.84	1Fryar
Rid him away, and goe you home with me.	Jew	4.1.89	Barab
Why goe, get you away.	Jew	4.1.93	2Fryar
I will not goe for thee.	Jew	4.1.94	1Fryar
Not? then I'le make thee, [rogue] <goe>.	Jew	4.1.95	2Fryar
Fryar Barnardine goe you with Ithimore.	Jew	4.1.99	Barab
Why does he goe to thy house? let him begone.	Jew	4.1.101	1Fryar

GOE (cont.)

Nor goe to bed, but sleepes in his owne clothes;	Jew	4.1.132	Ithimr
Away, I'de wish thee, and let me goe by:	Jew	4.1.170	1Fryar
Good Barabas let me goe.	Jew	4.1.184	1Fryar
Was up thus early; with intent to goe/Unto your Friery, because	Jew	4.1.191	Barab
goe whither he will, I'le be none of his followers in haste:	Jew	4.2.25	P Ithimr
I'le goe steale some mony from my Master to make me hansome:	Jew	4.2.49	P Ithimr
Pray pardon me, I must goe see a ship discharg'd.	Jew	4.2.51	P Ithimr
and such as--Goe to, no more, I'le make him send me half he has,	Jew	4.2.66	P Ithimr
Shall Ithimore my love goe in such rags?	Jew	4.2.85	Curtzn
Where Woods and Forrests goe in goodly greene,	Jew	4.2.93	Ithimr
Whither will I not goe with gentle Ithimore?	Jew	4.2.99	Curtzn
I will in some disguize goe see the slave,	Jew	4.3.67	Barab
Goe to, it shall be so.	Jew	4.4.3	Curtzn
Goe fetch him straight. I alwayes fear'd that Jew.	Jew	5.1.18	Govnr
I'le goe alone, dogs, do not hale me thus.	Jew	5.1.19	Barab
Goe walke about the City, see thy friends:	Jew	5.2.92	Barab
Tush, send not letters to 'em, goe thy selfe,	Jew	5.2.93	Barab
Goe swill in bowles of Sacke and Muscadine:	Jew	5.5.6	Barab
Besides, if we should let thee goe, all's one,	Jew	5.5.99	Govnr
Nay rather, Christians, let me goe to Turkey,	Jew	5.5.115	Calym
We think it good to goe and consumate/The rest, with hearing of	P 19	1.19	Charls
The rest that will not goe (my Lords) may stay:	P 23	1.23	Charls
Let us goe to honor this solemnitie.	P 25	1.25	Charls
Goe then, present them to the Queene Navarre:	P 79	2.22	Guise
betraide, come my Lords, and let us goe tell the King of this.	P 199	3.34	P Navrre
Your Majesty were best goe visite him,	P 249	4.47	QnMoth
Content, I will goe visite the Admirall.	P 251	4.49	Charls
And I will goe take order for his death.	P 252	4.50	Guise
Mountsorrell, goe shoote the ordinance of,	P 327	5.54	Guise
O let him goe, he is a catholick.	P 375	7.15	Retes
And he forsooth must goe and preach in Germany:	P 392	7.32	Guise
Goe place some men upon the bridge,	P 421	7.61	Dumain
Tis well advisde Dumain, goe see it strait be done.	P 424	7.64	Guise
Come let us goe tell the King.	P 440	7.80	Condy
Then come my Lords, lets goe.	P 481	8.31	Anjoy
I goe as whirl-windes rage before a storme.	P 511	9.30	Guise
Come my Lord [let] <lets> us goe.	P 527	9.46	QnMoth
Epernoune, goe see it presently be done,	P 558	11.23	QnMoth
goe sirra, worke no more,/Till this our Coronation day be past:	P 623	12.36	King
Lets goe my Lords, our dinner staies for us.	P 630	12.43	King
Come my [Lord] <Lords>, let us goe seek the Guise,	P 655	12.68	QnMoth
Goe fetch me pen and inke.	P 657	13.1	Duchss
But villaine he to whom these lines should goe,	P 696	13.40	Guise
But as report doth goe, the Duke of Joyeux/Hath made great sute	P 733	14.36	1Msngr
At thy request I am content thou goe,	P 746	15.4	King
Ile goe [take] <make> a walk/On purpose from the Court to meet	P 783	15.41	Mugern
come Epernoune/Lets goe seek the Duke and make them freends.	P 786	15.44	King
Pleshe, goe muster up our men with speed,	P 916	18.17	Navrre
I goe my Lord.	P 920	18.21	Pleshe
in the next roome, therefore good my Lord goe not foorth.	P 995	19.65	P 3Mur
Yet Caesar shall goe forth.	P 996	19.66	Guise
Thus Caesar did goe foorth, and thus he dyed.	P1015	19.85	Guise
Then stay a while and Ile goe call the King,	P1017	19.87	Capt
Goe fetch his sonne for to beholde his death:	P1021	19.91	King
Goe to the Governour of Orleance,	P1057	19.127	King
We will goe talke more of this within.	P1138	21.32	Dumain
Goe call a surgeon hether strait.	P1179	22.41	Navrre
Goe call the English Agent hether strait,	P1188	22.50	King
O that we might as well returne as goe.	Edw	1.4.143	Edward
Goe sit at home and eate your tenants beefe:	Edw	2.2.75	Gavstn
Goe, take the villaine, soldiers come away,	Edw	2.6.11	Warwck
For if they goe, the prince shall lose his right.	Edw	5.1.92	Leistr
Unpointed as it is, thus shall it goe,	Edw	5.4.13	Mortmr
That bootes not, therefore gentle madam goe.	Edw	5.6.91	2Lord
Goe fetche my fathers hearse, where it shall lie,	Edw	5.6.94	King
Faustus, I goe.	F 901	3.1.123	Mephst
But in dumbe silence let them come and goe.	F1252	4.1.98	Faust
Your Majesty may boldly goe and see.	F1269	4.1.115	Faust
He must needs goe that the Divell drives.	F1419	4.2.95	Fredrk
<I goe sweete Faustus, but with heavy cheare>,	F1737	(HC269)A	OldMan
goe and make cleane our bootes which lie foule upon our handes,	F App	p.234 32	P Robin
with you, I must yet have a goblet payde from you ere you goe.	F App	p.234 8	P Vintnr
Doctor, yet ere you goe, expect from me a bounteous reward.	F App	p.239 88	P Emper
what, wil you goe on horse backe, or on foote?	F App	p.239 95	P Mephst
Ile make you wake ere I goe.	F App	p.241 153	P HrsCsr
O Lord sir, let me goe, and Ile give you fortie dollers more.	F App	p.241 158	P HrsCsr
now through the world againe/I goe; o Phoebus shew me Neptunes	Lucan, First Booke		692
Strike backe the barre, night fast away doth goe.	Ovid's Elegies		1.6.32
One as a spy doth to his enemies goe,	Ovid's Elegies		1.9.17
Let him goe forth knowne, that unknowne did enter,	Ovid's Elegies		2.2.20
Let him goe see her though she doe not languish/And then report	Ovid's Elegies		2.2.21
O shun me not, but heare me ere you goe,	Hero and Leander		1.205

GOES

But Illioneus goes not in such robes.	Dido	2.1.48	Achat
So lovely is he that where ere he goes,	Dido	3.1.71	Anna
That doe pursue my peace where ere it goes.	Dido	4.2.51	Iarbus
And means to fire Turky as he goes:	2Tamb	1.1.18	Gazell
Looke where he goes, but see, he comes againe/Because I stay:	2Tamb	5.3.75	Tamb
Whither goes Don Mathias? stay a while.	Jew	2.3.251	Barab
I'le give him such a warning e're he goes/As he shall have	Jew	2.3.273	Barab
Or else I will confesse: I, there it goes:	Jew	4.3.4	Barab
And thus farre roundly goes the businesse:	Jew	5.2.110	Barab

GOES (cont.)			
Who goes there?	P 371	7.11	Gonzag
The Popedome cannot stand, all goes to wrack,	P1087	19.157	QnMoth
Which if I doe, the Papall Monarck goes/To wrack, and [his]	P1197	22.59	King
Whether goes my Lord of Coventrie so fast?	Edw	1.1.175	Edward
I there it goes, but yet I will not yeeld,	Edw	1.4.56	Edward
Whether goes my lord?	Edw	1.4.144	Queene
Whither goes this letter, to my lord the king?	Edw	5.2.68	Queene
The king must die, or Mortimer goes downe,	Edw	5.4.1	Mortmr
Goes to discover countries yet unknowne.	Edw	5.6.66	Mortmr
Whether goes my standarde?	Lucan, First Booke		193
Thy husband to a banquet goes with me,	Ovid's Elegies		1.4.1
Night goes away: the dores barre backeward strike.	Ovid's Elegies		1.6.24
Night goes away: I pray thee ope the dore.	Ovid's Elegies		1.6.48
The annuall pompe goes on the covered ground.	Ovid's Elegies		3.12.12
So on she goes, and in her idle flight,	Hero and Leander		2.10
Therefore unto him hastily she goes,	Hero and Leander		2.45
And drunke with gladnesse, to the dore she goes.	Hero and Leander		2.236
GOEST			
Now if thou goest, what canst thou leave behind,	Dido	5.1.151	Dido
And when thou goest, a golden Canapie/Enchac'd with pretious	2Tamb	1.2.48	Callap
Unhappie Gaveston, whether goest thou now.	Edw	2.5.110	Gavstn
GOETH			
and as constant report goeth, they intend to give king Edward	Edw	4.3.34	P Spencr
GOING			
They say Aeneas men are going abourd,	Dido	4.4.2	Dido
Pray for us Bajazeth, we are going.	1Tamb	5.1.213	Tamb
But need we not be spied going aboord?	2Tamb	1.2.56	Almeda
Oh they were going up to Sicily:	Jew	1.1.98	Barab
And intercept my going to the Jew;	Jew	4.1.167	1Fryar
going to the execution, a fellow met me with a muschatoes like	Jew	4.2.27	P Ithimr
That this your armie going severall waies,	Edw	2.4.42	Queene
My lord, be going, care not for these,	Edw	4.7.93	Rice
As I was going to Wittenberge t'other day, with a loade of Hay,	F1525	4.5.21	P Carter
Resembling faire Semiramis going to bed,	Ovid's Elegies		1.5.11
Going to sea, East windes he doth not chide/Nor to hoist saile	Ovid's Elegies		1.9.13
Going out againe passe forth the dore more wisely/And som-what	Ovid's Elegies		1.12.5
And in the midst thereof, set my soule going,	Ovid's Elegies		2.10.36
As loath to see Leander going out.	Hero and Leander		2.98
GOINGS			
Yes, and goings out too, you may see sir.	F 347	1.4.5	P Robin
I, and goings out too, you may see else.	F App	p.229 5	P Clown
GOINGS OUT			
I, and goings out too, you may see else.	F App	p.229 5	P Clown
GOLD (See also GOULD)			
Ile give thee tackling made of riveld gold,	Dido	3.1.116	Dido
But I had gold enough and cast him off:	Dido	3.1.162	Dido
I would have given Achates store of gold,	Dido	4.4.7	Dido
For tackling, let him take the chaines of gold,	Dido	4.4.161	Dido
Whose ransome made them martch in coates of gold,	1Tamb	1.1.143	Ceneus
Not all the Gold in Indias welthy armes,	1Tamb	1.2.85	Tamb
See how he raines down heaps of gold in showers,	1Tamb	1.2.182	Tamb
We have our Cammels laden all with gold:	1Tamb	2.2.62	Meandr
You fighting more for honor than for gold,	1Tamb	2.2.66	Meandr
Share equally the gold that bought their lives,	1Tamb	2.2.70	Meandr
What, thinkst thou Tamburlain esteems thy gold?	1Tamb	3.3.262	Tamb
The townes-men maske in silke and cloath of gold,	1Tamb	4.2.108	Tamb
Wagons of gold were set before my tent:	2Tamb	1.1.99	Orcan
Amongst so many crownes of burnisht gold,	2Tamb	1.2.30	Callap
Not lapt in lead but in a sheet of gold,	2Tamb	2.4.131	Tamb
As if a chaire of gold enamiled,	2Tamb	3.2.119	Tamb
And enter in, to seaze upon the gold:	2Tamb	3.3.8	Techel
The gold, the silver, and the pearle ye got,	2Tamb	3.4.88	Therid
And cloth'd in costly cloath of massy gold,	2Tamb	4.2.40	Therid
There lies more gold than Babylon is worth,	2Tamb	5.1.116	Govnr
Go thither some of you and take his gold,	2Tamb	5.1.123	Tamb
No, though Asphaltis lake were liquid gold,	2Tamb	5.1.155	Tamb
Pierce through the coffin and the sheet of gold,	2Tamb	5.3.226	Tamb
so richly pay/The things they traffique for with wedge of gold,	Jew	1.1.9	Barab
exceeding store/Of Persian silkes, of gold, and Orient Perle.	Jew	1.1.88	2Merch
My gold, my gold, and all my wealth is gone.	Jew	1.2.258	Barab
The gold and Jewels which I kept for thee.	Jew	1.2.298	Barab
Be close, my girle, for this must fetch my gold.	Jew	1.2.304	Barab
And thinke upon the Jewels and the gold,	Jew	1.2.349	Barab
And here behold (unseene) where I have found/The gold, the	Jew	2.1.23	Abigal
My gold, my fortune, my felicity;	Jew	2.1.48	Barab
Oh girle, oh gold, oh beauty, oh my blisse!	Jew	2.1.54	Barab
This truce we have is but in hope of gold,	Jew	2.2.26	1Knght
And buy it basely too for summes of gold?	Jew	2.2.29	Bosco
Therefore be rul'd by me, and keepe the gold:	Jew	2.2.39	Bosco
Proud-daring Calymath, instead of gold,	Jew	2.2.53	Govnr
Honor is bought with bloud and not with gold.	Jew	2.2.56	Govnr
Be true and secret, thou shalt want no gold.	Jew	2.3.216	Barab
I, but the Jew has gold,	Jew	3.1.14	Pilia
The wind that bloweth all the world besides,/Desire of gold.	Jew	3.5.4	Basso
Desire of gold, great Sir?	Jew	3.5.4	Govnr
Whole Chests of Gold, in Bullion, and in Coyne,	Jew	4.1.65	Barab
And bring his gold into our treasury.	Jew	4.1.163	1Fryar
hast thou the gold?	Jew	4.2.100	P Ithimr
Give me a Reame of paper, we'll have a kingdome of gold for't.	Jew	4.2.115	P Ithimr
Thus Bellamira esteemes of gold;	Jew	4.2.125	Curtzn
Jew, I must ha more gold.	Jew	4.3.18	P Pilia
the gold, or know Jew it is in my power to hang thee.	Jew	4.3.37	P Pilia

GOLD (cont.)			
Oh that I should part with so much gold!	Jew	4.3.51	Barab
And how the villaine revels with my gold.	Jew	4.3.68	Barab
And fit it should: but first let's ha more gold.	Jew	4.4.26	Curtzn
How liberally the villain gives me mine own gold.	Jew	4.4.48	P Barab
So did you when you stole my gold.	Jew	4.4.50	Barab
You run swifter when you threw my gold out of my Window.	Jew	4.4.52	P Barab
There, Carpenters, divide that gold amongst you:	Jew	5.5.5	Barab
Wants thou gold? go to my treasurie:	Edw	1.1.167	Edward
I trowe/The lords of Fraunce love Englands gold so well,	Edw	4.3.15	Edward
Be a Phisitian Faustus, heape up gold,	F 42	1.1.14	Faust
I'le have them flie to [India] <Indian> for gold;	F 109	1.1.81	Faust
The iterating of these lines brings gold;	F 544	2.1.156	Mephst
should turne to Gold, that I might locke you safe into <uppe	F 676	2.2.125	P Covet
and all the people in it were turnd> to Gold,	F 676	(HC263)A	P Covet
O my sweete Gold!	F 677	2.2.126	P Covet
And roof't aloft with curious worke in gold.	F 798	3.1.20	Faust
Who kils him shall have gold, and endlesse love.	F1349	4.2.25	Fredrk
Turne round thy gold-ring, as it were to ease thee.	Ovid's Elegies		1.4.26
The Poets God arayed in robes of gold,	Ovid's Elegies		1.8.59
Garments do weare, jewells and gold do wast,	Ovid's Elegies		1.10.61
[And] <The> banks ore which gold bearing Tagus flowes.	Ovid's Elegies		1.15.34
Chuf-like had I not gold, and could not use it?	Ovid's Elegies		3.6.50
Wit was some-times more pretious then gold,	Ovid's Elegies		3.7.3
His left hand whereon gold doth ill alight,	Ovid's Elegies		3.7.15
Jove being admonisht gold had soveraigne power,	Ovid's Elegies		3.7.29
Gold, silver, irons heavy weight, and brasse,	Ovid's Elegies		3.7.37
Gold from the earth in steade of fruits we pluck,	Ovid's Elegies		3.7.53
Jove turnes himselfe into a Swanne, or gold,	Ovid's Elegies		3.11.33
Jewels, and gold their Virgin tresses crowne,	Ovid's Elegies		3.12.25
Where sparrowes pearcht, of hollow pearle and gold,	Hero and Leander		1.33
Of two gold Ingots like in each respect.	Hero and Leander		1.172
Grosse gold, from them runs headlong to the boore.	Hero and Leander		1.472
sported with their loves/On heapes of heavie gold, and tooke	Hero and Leander		2.163
Than Dis, on heapes of gold fixing his looke.	Hero and Leander		2.326
With buckles of the purest gold.	Passionate Shepherd		16
GOLDE			
Lading their shippes with golde and pretious stones:	1Tamb	1.1.121	Cosroe
Their plumed helmes are wrought with beaten golde.	1Tamb	1.2.124	Souldr
their neckes/Hangs massie chaines of golde downe to the waste,	1Tamb	1.2.126	Souldr
To weare a Crowne enchac'd with pearle and golde,	1Tamb	2.5.60	Therid
That rooffes of golde, and sun-bright Pallaces,	1Tamb	4.2.62	Zabina
That meanes to fill your helmets full of golde:	1Tamb	4.4.7	Tamb
Fraughted with golde of rich America:	2Tamb	1.2.35	Callap
I, liquid golde when we have conquer'd him,	2Tamb	1.3.223	Tamb
as I doe a naked Lady in a net of golde, and for feare I should	2Tamb	4.1.69	P Calyph
Catholickes/Sends Indian golde to coyne me French ecues:	P 118	2.61	Guise
Come Ramus, more golde, or thou shalt have the stabbe.	P 376	7.16	Gonzag
Alas I am a scholler, how should I have golde?	P 377	7.17	Ramus
I, those are they that feed him with their golde,	P 845	17.40	King
This is the traitor that hath spent my golde,	P1028	19.98	King
Know you not Gaveston hath store of golde,	Edw	1.4.258	Mortmr
and thy selfe/Bedaubd with golde, rode laughing at the rest,	Edw	2.2.185	Mortmr
That suffered Jove to passe in showers of golde/To Danae, all	Edw	3.1.267	Spencr
Among the lords of France with Englands golde,	Edw	3.1.277	Levune
Yet gentle monkes, for treasure, golde nor fee,	Edw	4.7.24	Edward
and al the world/Ransackt for golde, which breeds the world	Lucan, First Booke		168
And Jasons Argos, and the fleece of golde?	Ovid's Elegies		1.15.22
GOLDEN			
And bind her hand and foote with golden cordes,	Dido	1.1.14	Jupitr
Virgins halfe dead dragged by their golden haire,	Dido	2.1.195	Aeneas
A silver girdle, and a golden purse,	Dido	2.1.306	Venus
Such bow, such quiver, and such golden shafts,	Dido	2.1.311	Venus
Convey this golden arrowe in thy sleeve,	Dido	3.1.3	Cupid
Ile make me bracelets of his golden haire,	Dido	3.1.85	Dido
And to a Scepter chaunge his golden shafts,	Dido	3.2.57	Venus
Faire Troian, hold my golden bowe awhile,	Dido	3.3.7	Dido
Whose golden Crowne might ballance my content:	Dido	3.4.36	Dido
These golden bracelets, and this wedding ring,	Dido	3.4.62	Dido
Whose golden fortunes clogd with courtly ease,	Dido	4.3.8	Aeneas
And beare this golden Scepter in my hand?	Dido	4.4.41	Aeneas
charme to keepe the windes/Within the closure of a golden ball,	Dido	4.4.100	Dido
From golden India Ganges will I fetch,	Dido	5.1.8	Aeneas
Lay out our golden wedges to the view,	1Tamb	1.2.139	Tamb
When she that rules in Rhamnis golden gates,	1Tamb	2.3.37	Cosroe
The golden stature of their feathered bird/That spreads her	1Tamb	4.2.105	Tamb
As was to Jason Colchos golden fleece.	1Tamb	4.4.9	Tamb
For all the wealth of Gehons golden waves.	1Tamb	5.1.123	Tamb
when thou goest, a golden Canapie/Enchac'd with pretious stones,	2Tamb	1.2.48	Callap
The golden balle of heavens eternal fire,	2Tamb	2.4.2	Tamb
Fame hovereth, sounding of her golden Trumpe:	2Tamb	3.4.63	Therid
Now in their glories shine the golden crownes/Of these proud	2Tamb	4.1.1	Amyras
and utterly consume/Your cities and your golden pallaces,	2Tamb	4.1.193	Tamb
The horse that guide the golden eie of heaven,	2Tamb	4.3.7	Tamb
Ile ride in golden armour like the Sun,	2Tamb	4.3.115	Tamb
Loe here my sonnes, are all the golden Mines,	2Tamb	5.3.151	Tamb
Give charge to Morpheus that he may dreame/A golden dreame, and	Jew	2.1.37	Abigal
And yet I'le give her many a golden crosse/With Christian	Jew	2.3.296	Barab
In Malta are no golden Minerals.	Jew	3.5.6	Govnr
I'le be thy Jason, thou my golden Fleece;	Jew	4.2.90	Ithimr
To rip the golden bowels of America.	P 854	17.49	Guise
Throwe of his golden miter, rend his stole,	Edw	1.1.187	Edward
Ile hang a golden tongue about thy neck,	Edw	1.4.328	Edward

GOLDEN (cont.)
the royall vine, whose golden leaves/Empale your princelie head, Edw 3.1.163 Herald
And glutted now <more> with learnings golden gifts, F 24 Prol.24 1Chor
And from America the Golden Fleece, ... F 158 1.1.130 Valdes
There saw we learned Maroes golden tombe: . . . . F 791 3.1.13 Faust
Adding this golden sentence to our praise; . . . F 917 3.1.139 Pope
Seven golden [keys] <seales> fast sealed with seven seales, F 933 3.1.155 Pope
and store of golden plate; besides two thousand duckets ready F1676 5.1.3 P Wagner
Ride golden Love in Chariots richly builded. . . . Ovid's Elegies 1.2.42
Not black, nor golden were they to our viewe, . . . Ovid's Elegies 1.14.9
lookes to my verse/Which golden love doth unto me rehearse. Ovid's Elegies 2.1.38
[A white wench thralles me, so doth golden yellowe], . Ovid's Elegies 2.4.39
Caried the famous golden-fleeced sheepe. . . . . . Ovid's Elegies 2.11.4
Is golden love hid in Mars mid alarmes. . . . . Ovid's Elegies 2.18.36
The shout is nigh; the golden pompe comes heere. . . Ovid's Elegies 3.2.44
Yet boorded I the golden Chie twise, ... Ovid's Elegies 3.6.23
To winne the maide came in a golden shewer. . . . Ovid's Elegies 3.7.30
Golden-hair'd Ceres crownd with eares of corne, . . Ovid's Elegies 3.9.3
Your golden ensignes [plucke] <pluckt> out of my field, . Ovid's Elegies 3.14.16
To hazard more, than for the golden Fleece. . . . Hero and Leander 1.58
Thence flew Loves arrow with the golden head, . . . Hero and Leander 1.161
Like untun'd golden strings all women are, ... Hero and Leander 1.229
his golden earth remains,/Which after his disceasse, some other Hero and Leander 1.245
Thus having swallow'd Cupids golden hooke, ... Hero and Leander 1.333
Whose sound allures the golden Morpheus, ... Hero and Leander 1.349
Saturne and Ops, began their golden raigne. . . . . Hero and Leander 1.456
describe, but hee/That puls or shakes it from the golden tree: Hero and Leander 2.300
By this Apollos golden harpe began, ... Hero and Leander 2.327

GOLDEN-FLEECED
Caried the famous golden-fleeced sheepe. . . . . . Ovid's Elegies 2.11.4

GOLDEN-HAIR'D
Golden-hair'd Ceres crownd with eares of corne, . . Ovid's Elegies 3.9.3

GOLD-RING
Turne round thy gold-ring, as it were to ease thee. . . Ovid's Elegies 1.4.26

GOLE
By which sweete path thou maist attaine the gole/That shall F App p.243 36 OldMan

GON
get ye gon. . . . . Jew 3.3.34 P Abigal
in the morning/We will discharge thee of thy charge, be gon. Edw 2.5.109 Penbrk
Away, tarrie no answer, but be gon. . . . . . . Edw 3.1.173 Edward
Be gon. . . . . Edw 3.1.255 Edward
Therefore be gon in hast, and with advice, ... Edw 3.1.264 Spencr
As good be gon, as stay and be benighted. . . . . Edw 4.7.86 Rice
Traitors be gon, and joine you with Mortimer, ... Edw 5.1.87 Edward
Thankes gentle Winchester: sirra, be gon. . . . . . Edw 5.2.27 Queene
If you mistrust me, ile be gon my lord. . . . . . Edw 5.5.97 Ltborn
And stay the messenger that would be gon: . . . . . Hero and Leander 2.82

GONE
But thou art gone and leav'st me here alone, ... Dido 1.1.247 Aeneas
We could have gone without your companie. . . . . . Dido 3.3.14 Dido
Twas time to runne, Aeneas had been gone, ... Dido 4.4.14 Anna
Your Nurse is gone with yong Ascanius, ... Dido 4.4.124 Lord
I have not power to stay thee: is he gone? . . . . Dido 5.1.183 Dido
But wheres Aeneas? ah hees gone hees gone! . . . . Dido 5.1.192 Dido
O Dido, your little sonne Ascanius/Is gone! . . . . Dido 5.1.213 Nurse
Death, whether art thou gone that both we live? . . . 2Tamb 3.4.11 Olymp
Are ye not gone ye villaines with your spoiles? . . . 2Tamb 4.3.84 Tamb
My gold, my gold, and all my wealth is gone. . . . . Jew 1.2.258 Barab
Forget me, see me not, and so be gone. . . . . . Jew 1.2.363 Barab
But now I must be gone to buy a slave. . . . . . Jew 2.3.95 Barab
I know not, but farewell, I must be gone. . . . . . Jew 2.3.322 Abigal
What, is he gone unto my mother? . . . . Jew 2.3.351 Mthias
I am gone. . . . . Jew 3.4.114 Ithimr
Oh he is gone to see the other Nuns. . . . . . . Jew 3.6.10 2Fryar
You heare your answer, and you may be gone. . . . . Jew 4.1.92 1Fryar
and now would I were gone, I am not worthy to looke upon her. Jew 4.2.36 P Ithimr
I'le be gone. . . . . Jew 4.2.39 P Ithimr
I am gone. . . . . Jew 4.2.122 P Pilia
Be gone my freend, present them to her straite. . . . P 82 2.25 Guise
Be gone, delay no time sweet Guise. . . . . . . P 509 9.28 QnMoth
But which way is he gone? . . . . P 783 15.41 Mugern
Bartus be gone, commend me to his grace, ... P 911 18.12 Navrre
Be gone I say, tis time that we were there. . . . . P 919 18.20 Navrre
I have no warre, and therefore sir be gone. . . . . Edw 1.1.36 Gavstn
Are gone towards Lambeth, there let them remaine. . . . Edw 1.3.5 Gavstn
Fawne not on me French strumpet, get thee gone. . . . Edw 1.4.145 Edward
he is gone. . . . . Edw 1.4.192 MortSr
Feare ye not Madam, now his minions gone, ... Edw 1.4.198 Lncstr
Hees gone, and for his absence thus I moorne, ... Edw 1.4.305 Edward
And when tis gone, our swordes shall purchase more. . . . Edw 2.2.197 Lncstr
Traitor be gone, whine thou with Mortimer. . . . . . Edw 2.2.214 Edward
Hees gone by water unto Scarborough, ... Edw 2.4.37 Queene
Be easilie supprest: and therefore be gone. . . . . Edw 2.4.45 Queene
And therefore gentle Mortimer be gone. . . . . . . Edw 2.4.56 Queene
hie thee, get thee gone,/Edward with fire and sword, followes Edw 3.1.179 Edward
all discontented and discomforted, is gone, whither if you aske, Edw 4.3.31 P Spencr
with them are gone lord Edmund, and the lord Mortimer, having Edw 4.3.32 P Spencr
With him is Edmund gone associate? . . . . Edw 4.3.39 Edward
Is with that smoothe toongd scholler Baldock gone, . . . Edw 4.6.57 Rice
O is he gone! . . . . Edw 4.7.100 Spencr
is noble Edward gone,/Parted from hence, never to see us more! Edw 4.7.100 Spencr
Earth melt to ayre, gone is my soveraigne, ... Edw 4.7.103 Spencr
Gone, gone alas, never to make returne. . . . . . Edw 4.7.104 Spencr

GONE (cont.)				
But what are kings, when regiment is gone,	Edw	5.1.26		Edward
So that he now is gone from Killingworth,	Edw	5.2.31		BshpWn
Gone, gone, and doe I remaine alive?	Edw	5.5.91		Edward
Into the councell chamber he is gone,	Edw	5.6.20		Queene
He now is gone to prove Cosmography,	F 773	2.3.52		2Chor
Away sweet Mephostophilis be gone,	F 975	3.1.197		Faust
My wine gone too?	F1055	3.2.75		Pope
Away be gone.	F1132	3.3.45		Mephst
Away, be gone.	F1273	4.1.119		Faust
if not, Faustus is gone to hell.	F1878	5.2.82	P	Faust
where is it now? 'tis gone.	F1943	5.2.147		Faust
Faustus is gone, regard his hellish fall,	F2005	5.3.23		4Chor
what, are they gone?	F App	p.230 51	P	Clown
sixe pence in your purse to pay for your supper, and be gone?	F App	p.235 42	P	Robin
thee into an Ape, and thee into a Dog, and so be gone.	F App	p.235 44	P	Mephst
Mephastophilis be gone.	F App	p.237 56	P	Faust
Nay, and you go to conjuring, Ile be gone.	F App	p.237 57	P	Knight
Be gone quickly.	F App	p.241 163	P	Mephst
What is he gone?	F App	p.241 164	P	Faust
Alas Madame, thats nothing, Mephastophilis, be gone.	F App	p.242 12	P	Faust
starre of Mars hath done thee harme,/Now Mars is gone:	Ovid's Elegies	1.8.30		
Now many guests were gone, the feast being done,	Ovid's Elegies	2.5.21		
My heate is heere, what moves my heate is gone.	Ovid's Elegies	2.16.12		
As she might straight have gone to church and praide:	Ovid's Elegies	3.6.54		
And to some corner secretly have gone,	Hero and Leander	2.311		
GONZAGO				
Dumaine, Gonzago, Retes, sweare by/The argent crosses in your	P 274	5.1		Guise
Gonzago conduct them thither, and then/Beset his house that not	P 288	5.15		Guise
Gonzago, what, is he dead?	P 304	5.31		Guise
Anjoy, Gonzago, Retes, if that you three,	P 322	5.49		Guise
Gonzago poste you to Orleance, Retes to Deep,	P 445	7.85		Guise
GOOD				
But first in bloud must his good fortune bud,	Dido	1.1.86		Jupitr
And chaunging heavens may those good daies returne,	Dido	1.1.150		Aeneas
Father I faint, good father give me meate.	Dido	1.1.163		Ascan
As to instruct us under what good heaven/We breathe as now, and	Dido	1.1.197		Aeneas
Wishing good lucke unto thy wandring steps.	Dido	1.1.239		Venus
Heres to thy better fortune and good starres.	Dido	2.1.98		Dido
Anna, good sister Anna goe for him,	Dido	3.1.75		Dido
Nor quit good turnes with double fee downe told:	Dido	3.2.15		Juno
Why wilt thou so betray thy sonnes good hap?	Dido	5.1.31		Hermes
Thankes good Iarbus for thy friendly ayde,	Dido	5.1.75		Aeneas
I goe faire sister, heavens graunt good successe.	Dido	5.1.211		Anna
Good brother tell the cause unto my Lords,	1Tamb	1.1.4		Mycet
Therefore tis good and meete for to be wise.	1Tamb	1.1.34		Mycet
And vow to weare it for my countries good:	1Tamb	1.1.158		Cosroe
But are they rich? And is their armour good?	1Tamb	1.2.123		Tamb
To be partaker of thy good or ill,	1Tamb	1.2.230		Therid
Therefore in pollicie I thinke it good/To hide it close:	1Tamb	2.4.10		Mycet
Thanks good Meander, then Cosroe raign/And governe Persea in	1Tamb	2.5.18		Cosroe
Now will i gratify your former good,	1Tamb	2.5.30		Cosroe
Nobly resolv'd, my good Ortygius.	1Tamb	2.6.24		Cosroe
If he think good, can from his garrisons,	1Tamb	3.3.21		Bassoe
Such good successe happen to Bajazeth.	1Tamb	3.3.116		Zabina
highnesse would let them be fed, it would doe them more good.	1Tamb	4.4.35	P	Therid
And place their chiefest good in earthly pompe:	1Tamb	5.1.353		Zenoc
my Lord, if I should goe, would you bee as good as your word?	2Tamb	1.2.62	P	Almeda
Thanks good Theridamas.	2Tamb	1.3.117		Tamb
Phisitions, wil no phisicke do her good?	2Tamb	2.4.38		Tamb
Ah good my Lord be patient, she is dead,	2Tamb	2.4.119		Therid
Come good my Lord, and let us haste from hence/Along the cave	2Tamb	3.4.1		Olymp
Give me your knife (good mother) or strike home:	2Tamb	3.4.28		Sonne
Good my Lord, let me take it.	2Tamb	3.5.133	P	Almeda
To think our helps will doe him any good.	2Tamb	4.1.21		Calyph
And should I goe and do nor harme nor good,	2Tamb	4.1.56		Calyph
which all the good I have/Join'd with my fathers crowne would	2Tamb	4.1.57		Calyph
Good my Lord, let him be forgiven for once,	2Tamb	4.1.101		Amyras
Stay good my Lord, and wil you save my honor,	2Tamb	4.2.55		Olymp
If Jove esteeming me too good for earth,	2Tamb	4.3.60		Tamb
I, good my Lord, let us in hast to Persea,	2Tamb	5.1.214		Therid
Ah good my Lord, leave these impatient words,	2Tamb	5.3.54		Therid
Let's take our leaves; Farewell good Barabas.	Jew	1.1.175		2Jew
And all good fortune wait on Calymath.	Jew	1.2.33		Govnr
Then good my Lord, to keepe your quiet still,	Jew	1.2.43		Barab
And better one want for a common good,	Jew	1.2.98		Govnr
Good Barabas be patient.	Jew	1.2.199		2Jew
As good dissemble that thou never mean'st/As first meane truth,	Jew	1.2.290		Barab
Now that my fathers fortune were so good/As but to be about	Jew	2.1.31		Abigal
As good goe on, as sit so sadly thus.	Jew	2.1.40		Barab
One that I love for his good fathers sake.	Jew	2.3.31		Barab
Pointed it is, good Sir,--but not for you.	Jew	2.3.60		Barab
Good Sir,/Your father has deserv'd it at my hands,	Jew	2.3.69		Barab
Are wondrous; and indeed doe no man good:	Jew	2.3.82		Barab
Good Barabas glance not at our holy Nuns.	Jew	2.3.86		Lodowk
In good time, father, here are letters come/From Ormus, and the	Jew	2.3.222		Abigal
Or though it wrought, it would have done no good,	Jew	4.1.5		Barab
Good master let me poyson all the Monks.	Jew	4.1.14		Ithimr
Oh good Barabas come to our house.	Jew	4.1.77		1Fryar
Oh no, good Barabas come to our house.	Jew	4.1.78		2Fryar
Good Barabas, come to me.	Jew	4.1.87		2Fryar
Good sirs I have don't, but no body knowes it but you two, I	Jew	4.1.180	P	1Fryar
Good Barabas let me goe.	Jew	4.1.184		1Fryar

GOOD (cont.)

Oh good words, Sir, and send it you, were best see; there's his	Jew	4.3.24	P	Pilia
And unto your good mistris as unknowne.	Jew	4.3.48		Barab
Here take 'em, fellow, with as good a will--	Jew	4.3.52		Barab
Yes, my good Lord, one that can spy a place/Where you may enter,	Jew	5.1.70		Barab
May all good fortune follow Calymath.	Jew	5.2.21		Barab
Governor, good words, be not so furious;	Jew	5.2.61		Barab
Will Barabas be good to Christians?	Jew	5.2.75		Govnr
till thy father hath made good/The ruines done to Malta and to	Jew	5.5.111		Govnr
Prince Condy, and my good Lord Admirall,	P 2	1.2		Charls
We think it good to goe and consumate/The rest, with hearing of	P 19	1.19		Charls
I will my good Lord.	P 22	1.22		QnMarg
Prince Condy and my good Lord Admiral,	P 27	1.27		Navrre
See where they be my good Lord, and he that smelles but to	P 73	2.16	P	Pothec
Thankes my good freend, I will requite thy love.	P 78	2.21		Guise
What glory is there in a common good,	P 97	2.40		Guise
Thanks my good freend, holde, take thou this reward.	P 168	3.3		OldQn
I my good Lord, shot through the arme.	P 198	3.33		Admral
And rather chuse to seek your countries good,	P 221	4.19		Guise
Ah my good Lord, these are the Guisians,	P 260	4.58		Admral
Assure your selfe my good Lord Admirall,	P 262	4.60		Charls
And so be pacient good Lord Admirall,	P 271	4.69		Charls
Oh good my Lord,/Wherein hath Ramus	P 383	7.23		Ramus
O good my Lord, let me but speak a word.	P 399	7.39		Ramus
that despiseth him, can nere/Be good in Logick or Philosophie.	P 410	7.50		Ramus
Hands of good fellow, I will be his baile/For this offence:	P 622	12.35		King
And tell him that tis for his Countries good,	P 646	12.59		Cardnl
Will laugh I feare me at their good aray.	P 673	13.17		Duchss
In honor of our God and countries good.	P 708	14.11		Navrre
My Lord, twere good to make them frends,	P 772	15.30		Eprnon
But we presume it is not for our good.	P 824	17.19		King
The Pope and King of Spaine are thy good frends,	P 843	17.38		Eprnon
It would be good the Guise were made away,	P 888	17.83		Eprnon
They be my good Lord.	P 948	19.18		Capt
Good morrow to your Majestie.	P 964	19.34		Guise
Good morrow to my loving Cousin of Guise.	P 965	19.35		King
And you good Cosin to imagine it.	P 970	19.40		King
in the next roome, therefore good my Lord goe not foorth.	P 995	19.65	P	3Mur
I my good Lord, and will dye therein.	P1165	22.27		Frier
He died a death too good, the devill of hell/Torture his wicked	P1218	22.80		Bartus
whom he vouchsafes/For vailing of his bonnet one good locke.	Edw	1.2.19		Lncstr
This will be good newes to the common sort.	Edw	1.4.92		Penbrk
They would not stir, were it to do me good:	Edw	1.4.95		Edward
Can this be true twas good to banish him,	Edw	1.4.245		Lncstr
Yet good my lord, heare what he can alledge.	Edw	1.4.250		Queene
To mend the king, and do our countrie good:	Edw	1.4.257		Mortmr
Seeing thou hast pleaded with so good successe.	Edw	1.4.329		Edward
a factious lord/Shall hardly do himselfe good, much lesse us,	Edw	2.1.7		Spencr
On whose good fortune Spencers hope depends.	Edw	2.1.11		Spencr
The winde is good, I wonder why he stayes,	Edw	2.2.1		Edward
Welcome is the good Earle of Cornewall.	Edw	2.2.66		Mortmr
Weel have him ransomd man, be of good cheere.	Edw	2.2.116		Lncstr
Yea my good lord, for Gaveston is dead.	Edw	3.1.90		Arundl
Souldiers, good harts, defend your soveraignes right,	Edw	3.1.182		Edward
Good Pierce of Gaveston my sweet favoret,	Edw	3.1.228		Edward
Till Edmund be arrivde for Englands good,	Edw	4.1.2		Kent
A good sir John of Henolt,/Never so cheereles, nor so farre	Edw	4.2.13		Queene
And lives t'advance your standard good my lord.	Edw	4.2.42		Mortmr
Prosper your happie motion good sir John.	Edw	4.2.75		Queene
Tell me good unckle, what Edward doe you meane?	Edw	4.6.32		Prince
Madam, tis good to looke to him betimes.	Edw	4.6.39		Mortmr
Shall do good service to her Majestie,	Edw	4.6.74		Mortmr
good father on thy lap/Lay I this head, laden with mickle care,	Edw	4.7.39		Edward
this drowsines/Betides no good, here even we are betraied.	Edw	4.7.45		Spencr
As good be gon, as stay and be benighted.	Edw	4.7.86		Rice
Be patient good my lord, cease to lament,	Edw	5.1.1		Leistr
Your grace mistakes, it is for Englands good,	Edw	5.1.38		BshpWn
And neither give him kinde word, nor good looke.	Edw	5.2.55		Mortmr
Feare not to kill the king tis good he die.	Edw	5.4.9		Mortmr
Kill not the king tis good to feare the worst.	Edw	5.4.12		Mortmr
Tis for your highnesse good, and for the realmes.	Edw	5.4.101		Mortmr
I my good Lord, I would it were undone.	Edw	5.6.2		Matrvs
must now performe/The forme of Faustus fortunes, good or bad,	F 8	Prol.8		1Chor
to have it well rosted, and good sauce to it, if I pay so deere,	F 352	1.4.10	P	Robin
that's good to kill Vermine:	F 358	1.4.16	P	Robin
I good Wagner, take away the devill then.	F 377	1.4.35	P	Robin
And tell me, what good will my soule do thy Lord?	F 428	2.1.40		Faust
I, take it, and the devill give thee good of it <on't>.	F 502	2.1.114		Faust
in every good towne and Citie>,	F 699	(HC264) A	P	Glutny
tell me, in good sadnesse Robin, is that a conjuring booke?	F 743	2.3.22	P	Dick
Having now my good Mephostophilis,	F 779	3.1.1		Faust
<Tut, tis no matter man>, wee'l be bold with his <good cheare>.	F 808	(HC265) A	P	Mephst
Make haste againe, my good Lord Cardinalls,	F 972	3.1.194		Pope
My good Lord Archbishop, heres a most daintie dish,	F1046	3.2.66		Pope
Come brethren, let's about our businesse with good devotion.	F1076	3.2.96	P	1Frier
Good Fredericke see the roomes be voyded straight,	F1157	4.1.3		Mrtino
good my Lord intreate for me:	F1306	4.1.152	P	Benvol
Then good Master Doctor,	F1308	4.1.154		Emper
thou canst not buy so good a horse, for so small a price:	F1459	4.4.3	P	Faust
more, take him, because I see thou hast a good minde to him.	F1461	4.4.5	P	Faust
I do thinke my selfe my good Lord, highly recompenced, in that	F1563	4.6.6	P	Faust
they should be good, for they come from a farre Country I can	F1576	4.6.19	P	Faust
us, he were as good commit with his father, as commit with us.	F1603	4.6.46	P	Dick

GOOD (cont.)				
They are good subject for a merriment.	F1606	4.6.49		Faust
Why, how now my [good] <goods> friends?	F1608	4.6.51		Faust
I, I, the house is good enough to drink in:	F1617	4.6.60	P	HrsCsr
Good Lord, that flesh and bloud should be so fraile with your	F1632	4.6.75	P	Carter
No in good sooth.	F1640	4.6.83	P	Faust
[Ah] <O> stay good Faustus, stay thy desperate steps.	F1729	5.1.56		OldMan
One thing good servant let me crave of thee,	F1759	5.1.86		Faust
And now poore soule must thy good Angell leave thee,	F1907	5.2.111		GdAngl
not so good friend, burladie I had neede have it wel roasted,	F App	p.229 11	P	Clown
have it wel roasted, and good sawce to it, if I pay so deere.	F App	p.229 12	P	Clown
crownes a man were as good have as many english counters,	F App	p.230 34	P	Clown
Come brethren, lets about our businesse with good devotion.	F App	p.232 29	P	Frier
Peccatum peccatorum, heeres thy goblet, good Vintner.	F App	p.235 28	P	Rafe
good divel forgive me now, and Ile never rob thy Library more.	F App	p.235 30	P	Robin
theres no haste but good, are you remembred how you crossed me	F App	p.238 76	P	Faust
Good Maister Doctor, at my intreaty release him, he hath done	F App	p.238 79	P	Emper
Now my good Lord having done my duety, I humbly take my leave.	F App	p.238 86	P	Faust
Thankes, good maister doctor.	F App	p.242 7	P	Duchss
hither, as ye see, how do you like them Madame, be they good?	F App	p.242 24	P	Faust
And laboring to approve his quarrell good.	Lucan, First Booke			267
Turne all to good, be Augury vaine, and Tages/Th'arts master	Lucan, First Booke			635
Good meaning, shame, and such as seeke loves wrack/Shall follow	Ovid's Elegies			1.2.31
And brings good fortune, a rich lover plants/His love on thee,	Ovid's Elegies			1.8.31
Brasse shines with use; good garments would be worne,	Ovid's Elegies			1.8.51
Oft to invade the sleeping foe tis good/And arm'd to shed	Ovid's Elegies			1.9.21
And doth constraind, what you do of good will.	Ovid's Elegies			1.10.24
Ill gotten goods good end will never have.	Ovid's Elegies			1.10.48
The number two no good divining bringes.	Ovid's Elegies			1.12.28
What good to me wil either Ajax bring?	Ovid's Elegies			2.1.30
Good forme there is, yeares apt to play togither,	Ovid's Elegies			2.3.13
A yong wench pleaseth, and an old is good,	Ovid's Elegies			2.4.45
Aye me poore soule, why is my cause so good.	Ovid's Elegies			2.5.8
In this sweete good, why hath a third to do?	Ovid's Elegies			2.5.32
I grieve least others should such good perceive,	Ovid's Elegies			2.5.53
There good birds rest (if we beleeve things hidden)/Whence	Ovid's Elegies			2.6.51
For which good turne my sweete reward repay,	Ovid's Elegies			2.8.21
Sythia, Cilicia, Brittaine are as good,	Ovid's Elegies			2.16.39
Egeria with just Numa had good sport,	Ovid's Elegies			2.17.18
For great revenews I good verses have,	Ovid's Elegies			2.17.27
Tis credible some [god-head] <good head> haunts the place.	Ovid's Elegies			3.1.2
Envious garments so good legges to hide,	Ovid's Elegies			3.2.27
her good wishes fade,/Let with strong hand the reine to bend be	Ovid's Elegies			3.2.71
Or in mine eyes good wench no paine transfuse.	Ovid's Elegies			3.3.48
And for a good verse drawe the first dart forth,	Ovid's Elegies			3.7.27
To Thracian Orpheus what did parents good?	Ovid's Elegies			3.8.21
When bad fates take good men, I am forbod,	Ovid's Elegies			3.8.35
Trust in good verse, Tibullus feeles deaths paines,	Ovid's Elegies			3.8.39
good growes by this griefe,/Oft bitter juice brings to the	Ovid's Elegies			3.10.7
Against my good they were an envious charme.	Ovid's Elegies			3.11.14
Such as confesse, have lost their good names by it.	Ovid's Elegies			3.13.6
Now he her favour and good will had wone.	Hero and Leander			2.54
GOOD-BY .(See BUY, GOD BUY)				
GOODE				
that I might locke you safe into <uppe in> my <goode> Chest:	F 676	2.2.125	P	Covet
GOODES				
For he hath given to me al his goodes,	F App	p.243 2		Wagner
GOODESSES				
And envious fates great [goddesses] <goodesses> assaile,	Ovid's Elegies			3.8.2
GOODLY				
a goodly Stratagem,/And far from any man that is a foole.	1Tamb	2.4.11		Mycet
them leave Madam, this speech is a goodly refreshing to them.	1Tamb	4.4.33	P	Techel
not the Turke and his wife make a goodly showe at a banquet?	1Tamb	4.4.58	P	Tamb
Sometimes the owner of a goodly house,	Jew	1.2.319		Abigal
Where Woods and Forrests goe in goodly greene,	Jew	4.2.93		Ithimr
Here's goodly 'parrell, is there not?	Jew	4.2.112		Ithimr
And both the Mortimers, two goodly men,	Edw	1.3.3		Gavstn
A goodly chauncelor, is he not my lord?	Edw	4.6.43		Queene
This is the goodly Palace of the Pope:	F 804	3.1.26		Mephst
Lost are the goodly lockes, which from their crowne/Phoebus and	Ovid's Elegies			1.14.31
Go goodly <godly> birdes, striking your breasts bewaile,	Ovid's Elegies			2.6.3
Turnes all the goodly <godly> birdes to what she please.	Ovid's Elegies			2.6.58
Her cheekes were scratcht, her goodly haires discheveld.	Ovid's Elegies			3.5.48
GOODNES				
That powres in lieu of all your goodnes showne,	Edw	3.1.44		Spencr
GOODS				
All that they have, their lands, their goods, their lives,	Dido	4.4.76		Dido
submit your selves/To leave your goods to their arbitrament?	Jew	1.2.80		Barab
Will you then steale my goods?	Jew	1.2.94		Barab
my Lord, we have seiz'd upon the goods/And wares of Barabas,	Jew	1.2.132		Offcrs
You have my goods, my mony, and my wealth,	Jew	1.2.138		Barab
and gather of these goods/The mony for this tribute of the	Jew	1.2.155		Govnr
Thou seest they have taken halfe our goods.	Jew	1.2.176		1Jew
What, Barabas, whose goods were lately seiz'd?	Jew	1.2.383		Lodowk
Here comes the Jew, had not his goods bin seiz'd,	Jew	2.3.5		1Offcr
be under colour of shaving, thou'lt cut my throat for my goods.	Jew	2.3.120	P	Barab
And shipping of our goods to Sicily,	Jew	3.5.15		Govnr
and I am resolv'd/You shall confesse me, and have all my goods.	Jew	4.1.86		Barab
men to suppose/That I will leave my house, my goods, and all,	Jew	4.1.123		Barab
Pull hard, I say, you would have had my goods.	Jew	4.1.149		Barab
And give my goods and substance to your house,	Jew	4.1.190		Barab
Take my goods too, and seize upon my lands:	Jew	5.1.66		Barab
Art thou that Jew whose goods we heard were sold/For	Jew	5.1.73		Calym

GOODS (cont.)			
said, within this Ile/In Malta here, that I have got my goods,	Jew	5.2.68	Barab
No, spare his life, but seaze upon his goods, ...	Edw	1.1.193	Edward
And take possession of his house and goods: . . .	Edw	1.1.203	Edward
And goods and body given to Gaveston.	Edw	1.2.2	Warwck
upon him, next/Himselfe imprisoned, and his goods asceasd,	Edw	1.2.37	ArchBp
[and] bloud, <or goods> into their habitation wheresoever.	F 498	2.1.110	P Faust
Why, how now my [good] <goods> friends?	F1608	4.6.51	Faust
his house, his goods, and store of golden plate; besides two	F1675	5.1.2	P Wagner
Ill gotten goods good end will never have. . . .	Ovid's Elegies		1.10.48
O let him change goods so ill got to dust. . . .	Ovid's Elegies		3.7.66
GOOSE			
As if a Goose should play the Porpintine, ...	Edw	1.1.40	Gavstn
GORDE			
in others and their sides/With their owne weapons gorde, .	Edw	4.4.8	Queene
But when the imperiall Lions flesh is gorde, ...	Edw	5.1.11	Edward
GORE (See also GOARE)			
And gore thy body with as many wounds.	1Tamb	5.1.216	Bajzth
If I be Englands king, in lakes of gore/Your headles trunkes,	Edw	3.1.135	Edward
In steed of red bloud wallowed venemous gore. . . .	Lucan, First Booke		614
GORGE			
But if I get him, Coupe de Gorge for that. . . .	Jew	4.3.5	Barab
GORGEOUS			
[The] <Whose> buildings faire, and gorgeous to the eye, .	F 788	3.1.10	Faust
And with my brand these gorgeous houses burne. . . .	Ovid's Elegies		1.6.58
GORGIOUS			
There Junoes bird displayes his gorgious feather, . .	Ovid's Elegies		2.6.55
GORGON (Homograph)			
were that Tamburlaine/As monsterous as Gorgon, prince of Hell,	1Tamb	4.1.18	Souldn
o per se, o, [demy] <deny> orgon, gorgon:	F 728	2.3.7	P Robin
GOSPEL			
And make his Gospel flourish in this land. . . .	P 57	1.57	Navrre
GOSPELL			
What I have done tis for the Gospell sake. . . .	P 826	17.21	Guise
GOST			
Whither gost thou hateful nimph?	Ovid's Elegies		1.13.31
GOT			
By this I got my father on my backe, ...	Dido	2.1.265	Aeneas
Then got we to our ships, and being abourd, ...	Dido	2.1.280	Aeneas
How got Aeneas to the fleete againe?	Dido	2.1.291	Iarbus
By this is he got to the water side, ...	Dido	5.1.188	Dido
The gold, the silver, and the pearle ye got, ...	2Tamb	3.4.88	Therid
Which mony was not got without my meanes.	Jew	Prol.32	Machvl
Warily garding that which I ha got.	Jew	1.1.188	Barab
Governour, it was not got so easily;	Jew	1.2.86	Barab
the Towne-seale might be got/To keepe him for his life time	Jew	2.3.103	Barab
Art thou againe got to the Nunnery?	Jew	3.4.4	Barab
said, within this Ile/In Malta here, that I have got my goods,	Jew	5.2.68	Barab
Now have we got the fatall stragling deere, ...	P 204	4.2	QnMoth
Your pardon is quicklie got of Isabell.	Edw	2.2.231	Queene
Whereof we got the name of Mortimer, ...	Edw	2.3.23	Mortmr
Flie, flie, my lords, the earles have got the holde, .	Edw	2.4.4	Edward
But hath your grace got shipping unto Fraunce? . . .	Edw	4.1.17	Mortmr
'Snayles, what hast thou got there, a book? . . .	F 730	2.3.9	P Dick
As soone as Caesar got unto the banke/And bounds of Italy;	Lucan, First Booke		225
And having once got head still shal he raigne? . . .	Lucan, First Booke		317
Is conquest got by civill war so hainous?	Lucan, First Booke		367
By verses horned Io got hir name, ...	Ovid's Elegies		1.3.21
By many hands great wealth is quickly got.	Ovid's Elegies		1.8.92
O care-got triumph hetherwards advance.	Ovid's Elegies		2.12.16
I wisht to be received in, <and> in I [get] <got> me, .	Ovid's Elegies		3.6.47
O let him change goods so ill got to dust. . . .	Ovid's Elegies		3.7.66
From him that yeelds the garland <palme> is quickly got, .	Ovid's Elegies		3.13.47
As if another Phaeton had got/The guidance of the sunnes rich	Hero and Leander		1.101
As soone as he his wished purpose got, ...	Hero and Leander		1.460
And therefore to her tower he got by stealth. . . .	Hero and Leander		2.18
And then he got him to a rocke aloft.	Hero and Leander		2.148
Till to the solitarie tower he got.	Hero and Leander		2.230
GOTE (Homograph)			
such exploits, gote such riches, subdued so many kingdomes,	F App	p.236 20	P Emper
Gote-footed Satyrs, and up-staring <upstarting> Fawnes, .	Hero and Leander		2.200
GOTE-FOOTED			
Gote-footed Satyrs, and up-staring <upstarting> Fawnes, .	Hero and Leander		2.200
GOT'ST			
And since by wrong thou got'st Authority, ...	Jew	5.2.35	Barab
GOTST			
But here in Malta, where thou gotst thy wealth, . .	Jew	1.2.101	Govnr
GOTTEN			
and the bordering Iles/Are gotten up by Nilus winding bankes:	Jew	1.1.43	Barab
Till thou hast gotten to be entertain'd.	Jew	1.2.288	Barab
That's to be gotten in the Westerne Inde:	Jew	3.5.5	Govnr
Thus hast thou gotten, by thy policie, ...	Jew	5.2.27	Barab
I have gotten one of Doctor Faustus conjuring bookes, and now	F 723	2.3.2	P Robin
Ill gotten goods good end will never have. . . .	Ovid's Elegies		1.10.48
GOULD			
Live where thou wilt, ile send thee gould enough, . .	Edw	1.4.113	Edward
GOVERN'D			
Force mastered right, the strongest govern'd all. . .	Lucan, First Booke		177
GOVERND			
And must be awde and governd like a child. . . .	Edw	3.1.31	Baldck
GOVERNE			
then Cosroe raign/And governe Persea in her former pomp: .	1Tamb	2.5.19	Cosroe
What star or state soever governe him, ...	1Tamb	2.6.18	Ortyg

GOVERNE (cont.)			
And scornes the Powers that governe Persea.	1Tamb	2.6.40	Cosroe
Ye Gods and powers that governe Persea,	1Tamb	3.3.189	Zenoc
Fal starres that governe his nativity,	2Tamb	5.3.2	Therid
And cause scme milder spirits governe you.	2Tamb	5.3.80	Phsitn
our Empire, fortune that made Roome/Governe the earth, the sea,	Lucan, First Booke		110
The Belgians apt to governe Brittish cars;	Lucan, First Booke		427
they governe fieldes, and lawes,/they manadge peace, and rawe	Ovid's Elegies		3.7.57
GOVERNED			
Now to be rulde and governed by a man,	1Tamb	1.1.12	Cosroe
Where all my youth I have bene governed,	1Tamb	1.2.13	Zenoc
health and majesty/Were strangely blest and governed by heaven,	2Tamb	5.3.25	Techel
GOVERNES			
What kind of people, and who governes them:	Dido	2.1.42	Aeneas
Now fals the star whose influence governes France,	P 944	19.14	Capt
GOVERNMENT			
Which will revolt from Persean government,	1Tamb	1.1.91	Cosroe
And languish in my brothers government:	1Tamb	1.1.156	Cosroe
Shal have a government in Medea:	1Tamb	2.2.33	Meandr
That doth assume the Papall government,	F 886	3.1.108	Pope
authority Apostolicall/Depose him from his Regall Government.	F 924	3.1.146	Pope
GOVERNOR			
Farewell great [Governor], and brave Knights of Malta.	Jew	1.2.32	Calym
Grave [Governor], list not to his exclames:	Jew	1.2.128	1Knght
Governor of Malta, hither am I bound;	Jew	2.2.4	Bosco
Perswade our Governor against the Turke;	Jew	2.2.25	1Knght
And be reveng'd upon the--Governor.	Jew	2.3.143	Barab
Because the Pryor <Governor> <Sire> dispossest thee once,/And	Jew	3.3.43	Abigal
Governor, since thou hast broke the league/By flat denyall of	Jew	3.5.19	Basso
This shall with me unto the Governor.	Jew	4.4.25	Pilia
Oh bring us to the Governor.	Jew	5.1.7	Curtzn
What e're I am, yet Governor heare me speake;	Jew	5.1.9	Curtzn
If this be true, I'le make thee Governor.	Jew	5.1.95	Calym
For thy desert we make thee Governor,	Jew	5.2.10	Calym
Now Governor--stand by there, wait within.--	Jew	5.2.50	Barab
Now tell me, Governor, and plainely too,	Jew	5.2.55	Barab
Governor, gcod words, be not so furious;	Jew	5.2.61	Barab
And now at length am growne your Governor,	Jew	5.2.70	Barab
me, Governor, to procure/A dissolution of the slavish Bands	Jew	5.2.76	Barab
Nay more, doe this, and live thou Governor still.	Jew	5.2.89	Govnr
Governor, I enlarge thee, live with me,	Jew	5.2.91	Barab
Governor, presently.	Jew	5.2.104	Barab
Malta's Governor, I bring/A message unto mighty Calymath;	Jew	5.3.13	Msngr
Selim, for that, thus saith the Governor,	Jew	5.3.26	Msngr
Well, tell the Governor we grant his suit,	Jew	5.3.40	Calym
Farewell grave Governor.	Jew	5.4.10	1Knght
And see he brings it: Now, Governor, the summe?	Jew	5.5.19	Barab
Governor, wel since it is no more/I'le satisfie my selfe with	Jew	5.5.21	Barab
No, Governor, I'le satisfie thee first,	Jew	5.5.44	Barab
Know, Governor, 'twas I that slew thy sonne;	Jew	5.5.81	Barab
Tush, Governor, take thou no care for that,	Jew	5.5.102	Calym
to stand gaping after the divels Governor, and can see nothing.	F1244	4.1.90	P Benvol
GOVERNOR'S			
Here comes Don Lodowicke the Governor's sonne,	Jew	2.3.30	Barab
GOVERNORS			
I have bought a house/As great and faire as is the Governors;	Jew	2.3.14	Barab
Barabas, thou know'st I am the Governors sonne.	Jew	2.3.40	Lodowk
Entertaine Lodowicke the Governors sonne/With all the curtesie	Jew	2.3.225	Barab
Pardon me though I weepe; the Governors sonne/Will, whether I	Jew	2.3.257	Barab
You knew Mathias and the Governors son; he and I kild 'em both,	Jew	4.4.17	P Ithimr
we may grace us best/To solemnize our Governors great feast.	Jew	5.3.45	Calym
There wanteth nothing but the Governors pelfe,	Jew	5.5.18	Barab
GOVERNOUR			
I doubt not but the Governour will yeeld,	1Tamb	4.2.113	Therid
of Egypt, the King of Arabia, and the Governour of Damascus.	1Tamb	4.4.114	P Tamb
As well for griefe our ruthlesse Governour/Have thus refusde	1Tamb	5.1.92	1Virgn
Are not so honoured in their Governour,	2Tamb	4.3.10	Tamb
Thou desperate Governour of Babylon,	2Tamb	5.1.49	Therid
Yeeld foolish Governour, we offer more/Than ever yet we did to	2Tamb	5.1.57	Techel
The sturdy Governour of Babylon,	2Tamb	5.1.81	Therid
So now he hangs like Bagdets Governour,	2Tamb	5.1.158	Tamb
I wish, grave [Governour], 'twere in my power/To favour you, but	Jew	1.2.10	Calym
Now [Governour], how are you resolv'd?	Jew	1.2.17	Calym
What respit aske you [Governour]?	Jew	1.2.27	Calym
No, Governour, I will be no convertite.	Jew	1.2.82	Barab
Governour, it was not got so easily;	Jew	1.2.86	Barab
For there I left the Governour placing Nunnes,	Jew	1.2.254	Abigal
The Governour feeds not as I doe.	Jew	4.4.63	P Barab
I hope to see the Governour a slave,	Jew	5.1.67	Barab
To prison with the Governour and these/Captaines, his consorts	Jew	5.2.23	Barab
I now am Governour of Malta; true,	Jew	5.2.29	Barab
and what boots it thee/Poore Barabas, to be the Governour,	Jew	5.2.32	Barab
And Governour, now partake my policy:	Jew	5.5.24	Barab
Governour, why stand you all so pittilesse?	Jew	5.5.71	Barab
Goe to the Governour of Orleance,	P1057	19.127	King
Hee wild the Governour of Orleance in his name,	P1117	21.11	Dumain
Be governour of Ireland in my stead,	Edw	1.4.125	Edward
Welcome Lord governour of the Ile of Man.	Edw	2.2.67	Warwck
GOWNE			
And all alone, comes walking in his gowne;	F1358	4.2.34	Fredrk
Yet this Ile see, but if thy gowne ought cover,	Ovid's Elegies		1.4.41
Then came Corinna in a long loose gowne,	Ovid's Elegies		1.5.9
I snatcht her gowne:	Ovid's Elegies		1.5.13

GOWNE (cont.)			
And slipt from bed cloth'd in a loose night-gowne,	Ovid's Elegies	3.1.51	
The more thou look'st, the more the gowne envide.	Ovid's Elegies	3.2.28	
With that her loose gowne on, from me she cast her,	Ovid's Elegies	3.6.81	
A gowne made of the finest wooll,	Passionate Shepherd	13	
GOWNES			
Raw soldiours lately prest; and troupes of gownes;	Lucan, First Booke	312	
least their gownes tosse thy haire,/To hide thee in my bosome	Ovid's Elegies	3.2.75	
GRACCHUS (See GRACHUS)			
GRAC'D			
That with their beauties grac'd the Memphion fields:	1Tamb	4.2.104	Tamb
Until with greater honors I be grac'd.	1Tamb	4.4.140	Tamb
And we are grac'd with wreathes of victory:	P 788	16.2	Navrre
[The fruitfull plot of Scholerisme grac'd],	F 16	Prol.16	1Chor
That shortly he was grac'd with Doctors name,	F 17	Prol.17	1Chor
In skipping out her naked feete much grac'd her.	Ovid's Elegies	3.6.82	
GRACE			
Grace my immortall beautie with this boone,	Dido	1.1.21	Ganimd
Thankes gentle Lord for such unlookt for grace.	Dido	1.2.44	Serg
May it please your grace to let Aeneas waite:	Dido	2.1.87	Aeneas
In all humilitie I thanke your grace.	Dido	2.1.99	Aeneas
Ile dye before a stranger have that grace:	Dido	3.3.11	Iarbus
Because I feard your grace would keepe me here.	Dido	4.4.20	Achat
For I will grace them with a fairer frame,	Dido	5.1.5	Aeneas
Your Grace hath taken order by Theridamas,	1Tamb	1.1.46	Meandr
But tell me Maddam, is your grace betroth'd?	1Tamb	1.2.32	Tamb
Must grace his bed that conquers Asia:	1Tamb	1.2.37	Tamb
And grace your calling with a greater sway.	1Tamb	2.5.31	Cosroe
Should have prepar'd to entertaine his Grace?	1Tamb	4.2.63	Zabina
we intreate/Grace to our words and pitie to our lookes,	1Tamb	5.1.51	2Virgn
One thought, one grace, one woonder at the least,	1Tamb	5.1.172	Tamb
Al sights of power to grace my victory:	1Tamb	5.1.474	Tamb
Then let me find no further time to grace/Her princely Temples	1Tamb	5.1.488	Tamb
Yet would I venture to conduct your Grace,	2Tamb	1.2.72	Almeda
But cals not then your Grace to memorie/The league we lately	2Tamb	2.1.27	Sgsmnd
Against the grace of our profession.	2Tamb	2.1.32	Sgsmnd
Assure your Grace tis superstition/To stand so strictly on	2Tamb	2.1.49	Fredrk
a souldier, and this wound/As great a grace and majesty to me,	2Tamb	3.2.118	Tamb
Ile give your Grace a present of such price,	2Tamb	4.2.56	Olymp
Wil get his pardon if your grace would send.	2Tamb	5.1.33	1Citzn
never sepulchre/Shall grace that base-borne Tyrant Tamburlaine.	2Tamb	5.2.18	Amasia
I crave but this, Grace him as he deserves,	Jew	Prol.33	Machvl
And meditate how we may grace us best/To solemnize our	Jew	5.3.44	Calym
The many favours which your grace hath showne,	P 9	1.9	Navrre
In what Queen Mother or your grace commands.	P 12	1.12	Navrre
I am my Lord, in what your grace commaundes till death.	P 76	2.19	P Pothec
Maddame, I beseech your grace to except this simple gift.	P 166	3.1	P Pothec
Doth not your grace know the man that gave them you?	P 172	3.7	Navrre
Your grace was ill advisde to take them then,	P 174	3.9	Admral
And it please your grace the Lord high Admirall,	P 243	4.41	Man
in that your grace,/Hath worne the Poland diadem, before	P 611	12.24	Mugern
How likes your grace my sonnes pleasantnes?	P 632	12.45	QnMoth
And so to quite your grace of all suspect.	P 889	17.84	Eprnon
And that Paris is revolted from his grace.	P 902	18.3	Navrre
Then hath your grace fit oportunitie,	P 903	18.4	Bartus
Bartus be gone, commend me to his grace,	P 911	18.12	Navrre
And please your grace the Duke of Guise doth crave/Accesse unto	P 959	19.29	Eprnon
the President of Paris, that craves accesse unto your grace.	P1157	22.19	P 1Msngr
The President of Paris greetes your grace,	P1168	22.30	Frier
God shield your grace from such a sodaine death:	P1178	22.40	Navrre
Pleaseth your grace to let the Surgeon search your wound.	P1191	22.53	Navrre
Here comes my lord of Canterburies grace.	Edw	1.2.33	Warwck
Your grace doth wel to place him by your side,	Edw	1.4.10	Lncstr
I meane not so, your grace must pardon me.	Edw	1.4.153	Gavstn
Madam, how fares your grace?	Edw	1.4.192	Mortmr
Slay me my lord, when I offend your grace.	Edw	1.4.349	Warwck
In this your grace hath highly honoured me,	Edw	1.4.364	MortSr
Then let his grace, whose youth is flexible,	Edw	1.4.398	MortSr
Or saying a long grace at a tables end,	Edw	2.1.37	Spencr
Nothing but Gaveston, what means your grace?	Edw	2.2.7	Mortmr
Mait please your grace to entertaine them now.	Edw	2.2.241	Neece
For my sake let him waite upon your grace,	Edw	2.2.250	Gavstn
me, for his sake/Ile grace thee with a higher stile ere long.	Edw	2.2.253	Edward
And if you gratifie his grace so farre,	Edw	2.5.39	Arundl
Then if you will not trust his grace in keepe,	Edw	2.5.65	Arundl
True, and it like your grace,/That powres in lieu of all your	Edw	3.1.43	Spencr
And bid me say as plainer to your grace,	Edw	3.1.158	Herald
Say they, and lovinglie advise your grace,	Edw	3.1.166	Herald
But hath your grace got shipping unto Fraunce?	Edw	4.1.17	Mortmr
will your grace with me to Henolt,/And there stay times	Edw	4.2.17	SrJohn
His grace I dare presume will welcome me,	Edw	4.2.33	Queene
we friends, assure your grace, in England/Would cast up cappes,	Edw	4.2.54	Mortmr
Your grace may sit secure, if none but wee/Doe wot of your	Edw	4.7.26	Monk
To let us take our farewell of his grace.	Edw	4.7.69	Spencr
Here humblie of your grace we take our leaves,	Edw	4.7.78	Baldck
Here is a Litter readie for your grace,	Edw	4.7.84	Leistr
Your grace mistakes, it is for Englands good,	Edw	5.1.38	BshpWn
Your grace must hence with mee to Bartley straight.	Edw	5.1.144	Bartly
And thinkes your grace that Bartley will bee cruell?	Edw	5.1.151	Bartly
In health sweete Mortimer, how fares your grace?	Edw	5.2.81	Kent
To keepe your grace in safetie,	Edw	5.3.14	Gurney
Sit downe, for weele be Barbars to your grace.	Edw	5.3.28	Matrvs
Long live king Edward, by the grace of God/King of England, and	Edw	5.4.73	ArchBp

GRACE (cont.)				
But hath your grace no other proofe then this?	Edw	5.6.43		Mortmr
Your Grace mistakes, you gave us no such charge.	F1024	3.2.44		1Card
Lord Raymond, I drink unto your grace.	F1053	3.2.73		Pope
I pledge your grace.	F1054	3.2.74		Faust
Will not his grace consort the Emperour?	F1162	4.1.8		Fredrk
For proofe whereof, if so your Grace be pleas'd,	F1221	4.1.67		Faust
To compasse whatsoere your grace commands.	F1226	4.1.72		Faust
Your grace demand no questions of the King,	F1251	4.1.97		Faust
grace to thinke but well of that which Faustus hath performed.	F1564	4.6.7	P	Faust
Please it your grace, the yeare is divided into two circles	F1581	4.6.24	P	Faust
I do beseech your grace let them come in,	F1605	4.6.48		Faust
I thanke your grace.	F1608	4.6.51		Faust
I'le gage my credit, 'twill content your grace.	F1622	4.6.65		Faust
I humbly thanke your grace: then fetch some Beere.	F1625	4.6.68		Faust
And with a vyoll full of pretious grace,	F1731	5.1.58		OldMan
Hell strives with grace for conquest in my breast:	F1741	5.1.68		Faust
[That from thy soule exclud'st the grace of heaven],	F1789	5.1.116A		OldMan
my Lord Ile drinke to your grace	F App	p.231 12	P	Pope
Ile pledge your grace.	F App	p.232 13	P	Faust
But if it like your Grace, it is not in my abilitie to present	F App	p.237 41	P	Faust
now theres a signe of grace in you, when you will confesse the	F App	p.237 44	P	Knight
shal appeare before your Grace, in that manner that they best	F App	p.237 47	P	Faust
If it like your grace, the yeere is divided into twoo circles	F App	p.242 19	P	Faust
I humbly thanke your Grace.	F App	p.243 32	P	Faust
easie grant men great estates,/But hardly grace to keepe them:	Lucan, First Booke	509		
What needes thou warre, I sue to thee for grace,	Ovid's Elegies	1.2.21		
Then seeing I grace thy show in following thee,	Ovid's Elegies	1.2.49		
Naked simplicitie, and modest grace.	Ovid's Elegies	1.3.14		
(O mischiefe) now for me obtaine small grace.	Ovid's Elegies	1.6.22		
Then with triumphant laurell will I grace them/And in the midst	Ovid's Elegies	1.11.25		
With Venus game who will a servant grace?	Ovid's Elegies	2.7.21		
By her footes blemish greater grace she tooke.	Ovid's Elegies	3.1.10		
She smilde, and with quicke eyes behight some grace:	Ovid's Elegies	3.2.83		
Least labour so shall winne great grace of any.	Ovid's Elegies	3.4.46		
And blush, and seeme as you were full of grace.	Ovid's Elegies	3.13.28		
Receives no blemish, but oft-times more grace,	Hero and Leander	1.217		
GRACED (See also GRAC'T)				
Yet was she graced with her ruffled hayre.	Ovid's Elegies	1.7.12		
What graced Kings, in me no shame I deeme.	Ovid's Elegies	2.8.14		
GRACES				
And on whose throne the holy Graces sit.	1Tamb	5.1.77		1Virgn
And by his graces councell it is thought,	P 465	8.15		Anjoy
Cannot but march with many graces more:	P 578	11.43		Pleshe
I kisse your graces hand, and take my leave,	P 868	17.63		Guise
[Is she attired, then shew her graces best].	Ovid's Elegies	2.4.38		
Wherein the liberall graces lock'd their wealth,	Hero and Leander	2.17		
GRACHUS				
The angry Senate urging Grachus deeds,	Lucan, First Booke	268		
GRACIOUS				
And gladly yeeld them to my gracious rule:	1Tamb	2.5.28		Cosroe
Now let me offer to my gracious Lord,	1Tamb	3.3.218		Zenoc
That hath betraied my gracious Soveraigne,	2Tamb	3.2.153		Usumc
O gracious God, what times are these?	P 188	3.23		Navrre
is massacred)/Infect thy gracious brest with fresh supply,	P 193	3.28		QnMarg
Humblye craving your gracious reply.	P1170	22.32		Frier
These gracious words, most royall Carolus,	F1217	4.1.63		Faust
My gracious Lord, you doe forget your selfe,	F1258	4.1.104		Faust
see, my gracious Lord, what strange beast is yon, that thrusts	F1274	4.1.120	P	Faust
My gracious Lord, not so much for injury done to me, as to	F1311	4.1.157	P	Faust
GRAC'T				
Benvolio's head was grac't with hornes to day?	F1331	4.2.7		Benvol
GRAECIA				
Passe into Graecia, as did Cyrus once.	1Tamb	1.1.130		Menaph
To overdare the pride of Graecia,	2Tamb	3.5.66		Tamb
I came at last to Graecia, and from thence/To Asia, where I	2Tamb	5.3.141		Tamb
GRAECINUS				
Graecinus (well I wot) thou touldst me once,	Ovid's Elegies	2.10.1		
GRAINE				
The graine-rich goddesse in high woods did stray,	Ovid's Elegies	3.9.35		
GRAINE-RICH				
The graine-rich goddesse in high woods did stray,	Ovid's Elegies	3.9.35		
GRAMERCIES				
Gramercies Wagner. Welcome gentlemen.	F1820	5.2.24		Faust
GRAMERCY				
Gramercy Mounsier.	Jew	4.4.34		Barab
GRAND (Homograph)				
Mounsier le Grand, a noble friend of yours,	Edw	4.2.47		Mortmr
Great grand-sires from their antient graves she chides/And with	Ovid's Elegies	1.8.17		
GRANDFATHER				
my father <grandfather> was a Gammon of Bacon, and my mother	F 696	2.2.145	P	Glutny
GRANDMOTHER				
and my mother <grandmother> was a Hogshead of Claret Wine.	F 697	2.2.146	P	Glutny
GRAND-SIRES				
Great grand-sires from their antient graves she chides/And with	Ovid's Elegies	1.8.17		
GRANSIRES				
Poore lover with thy gransires I exile thee.	Ovid's Elegies	1.8.66		
GRANT (See also GRAUNT)				
We grant a month, but see you keep your promise.	Jew	1.2.28		Calym
I have intreated her, and she will grant.	Jew	2.3.314		Barab
Well, tell the Governor we grant his suit,	Jew	5.3.40		Calym
grant unto them that foure and twentie yeares being expired,	F 495	2.1.107	P	Faust
And grant me my request, and then I go.	F 846	3.1.68		Faust

GRANT (cont.)			
O gods that easie grant men great estates,	Lucan, First Booke	508	
GRANTED			
They granted what he crav'd, and once againe,	Hero and Leander	1.455	
GRAPES			
I would request no better meate, then a dish of ripe grapes.	F1573	4.6.16	P Lady
is barren of his fruite, from whence you had these ripe grapes.	F1580	4.6.23	P Duke
spirit that I have, I had these grapes brought as you see.	F1586	4.6.29	P Faust
And trust me, they are the sweetest grapes that e're I tasted.	F1587	4.6.30	P Lady
I would desire no better meate then a dish of ripe grapes.	F App	p.242 11	P Duchss
in the month of January, how you shuld come by these grapes.	F App	p.242 18	P Duke
they be the best grapes that ere I tasted in my life before.	F App	p.242 25	P Duchss
Take clustred grapes from an ore-laden vine,	Ovid's Elegies	1.10.55	
Ascreus lives, while grapes with new wine swell,	Ovid's Elegies	1.15.11	
Why takest increasing grapes from Vine-trees full?	Ovid's Elegies	2.14.23	
By charmes maste drops from okes, from vines grapes fall,	Ovid's Elegies	3.6.33	
And with the other, wine from grapes out wroong.	Hero and Leander	1.140	
GRAPPELD			
And would have grappeld with Achilles sonne,	Dido	2.1.251	Aeneas
GRAPPLES			
Why grapples Rome, and makes war, having no foes?	Lucan, First Booke	681	
GRAS			
She knows with gras, with thrids on wrong wheeles spun/And what	Ovid's Elegies	1.8.7	
GRASHOPPERS			
Jew, he lives upon pickled Grashoppers, and sauc'd Mushrumbs.	Jew	4.4.62	P Ithimr
GRASPE			
A hand, that with a graspe may gripe the world,	P 159	2.102	Guise
GRASPT			
Wish in his hands graspt did Hippomenes.	Ovid's Elegies	3.2.30	
GRASSE			
Jacints, hard Topas, grasse-greene Emeraulds,	Jew	1.1.26	Barab
Bacchinall/That tyr'd doth rashly on the greene grasse fall.	Ovid's Elegies	1.14.22	
Whose earth doth not perpetuall greene-grasse lacke,	Ovid's Elegies	2.6.50	
And on the soft ground fertile greene grasse growe.	Ovid's Elegies	2.16.6	
Charmes change corne to grasse, and makes it dye,	Ovid's Elegies	3.6.31	
This was [their] <there> meate, the soft grasse was their bed.	Ovid's Elegies	3.9.10	
Which with the grasse of Tuscane fields are fed.	Ovid's Elegies	3.12.14	
And tumbling in the grasse, he often strayd/Beyond the bounds	Hero and Leander	1.406	
GRASSE-GREENE			
Jacints, hard Topas, grasse-greene Emeraulds,	Jew	1.1.26	Barab
GRASSIE			
A grassie turffe the moistened earth doth hide.	Ovid's Elegies	2.16.10	
GRATEFULL			
From dog-kept flocks come preys to woolves most gratefull.	Ovid's Elegies	1.8.56	
And for her skill to thee a gratefull maide.	Ovid's Elegies	2.7.24	
Who sayd with gratefull voyce perpetuall bee?	Ovid's Elegies	3.5.98	
GRATIFIE			
Then I may seeke to gratifie your love,	1Tamb	1.1.171	Cosroe
And if you gratifie his grace so farre,	Edw	2.5.39	Arundl
Arundell, we will gratifie the king/In other matters, he must	Edw	2.5.43	Warwck
Thus weele gratifie the king,	Edw	2.5.51	Mortmr
To gratifie the kings request therein,	Edw	2.5.75	Penbrk
GRATIFIED			
In this I count me highly gratified,	Edw	1.4.295	Mortmr
GRATIFY			
Now will i gratify your former good,	1Tamb	2.5.30	Cosroe
To gratify the <thee> sweet Zenocrate,	1Tamb	5.1.516	Tamb
And we will highly gratify thee for it.	F 653	2.2.102	Lucifr
GRATIOUS			
Doubt not my Lord and gratious Soveraigne,	1Tamb	1.1.70	Therid
Which gratious starres have promist at my birth.	1Tamb	1.2.92	Tamb
My gratious Lord, they have their mothers looks,	2Tamb	1.3.35	Zenoc
Let me accompany my gratious mother,	2Tamb	1.3.66	Calyph
issue, at whose byrth/Heaven did affoord a gratious aspect,	2Tamb	3.5.80	Tamb
Sit stil my gratious Lord, this griefe wil cease,	2Tamb	5.3.64	Techel
in whose gratious lookes/The blessednes of Gaveston remaines,	Edw	1.4.120	Gavstn
My gratious lord, I come to bring you newes.	Edw	1.4.320	Queene
That waite attendance for a gratious looke,	Edw	1.4.338	Queene
It shalbe done my gratious Lord.	Edw	1.4.372	Beamnt
I feare me he is slaine my gratious lord.	Edw	2.4.2	Spencr
Stand gratious gloomie night to his device.	Edw	4.1.11	Kent
Shall have me from my gratious mothers side,	Edw	4.2.23	Prince
I, my most gratious lord, so tis decreed.	Edw	5.1.138	Bartly
To murther you my most gratious lorde?	Edw	5.5.46	Ltborn
But gratious Lady, it may be, that you have taken no pleasure	F1565	4.6.8	P Faust
My gratious Soveraigne, though I must confesse my selfe farre	F App	p.236 12	P Faust
My gratious Lord, I am ready to accomplish your request, so	F App	p.237 37	P Faust
heere they are my gratious Lord.	F App	p.238 59	P Faust
My Gratious Lord, not so much for the injury hee offred me	F App	p.238 81	P Faust
My gratious Lord, I am glad it contents you so wel:	F App	p.242 3	P Faust
Forgive her gratious Gods this one delict,	Ovid's Elegies	2.14.43	
GRATIS			
Gratis thou maiest be free, give like for like,	Ovid's Elegies	1.6.23	
GRATITUDES			
I will requite your royall gratitudes/With all the benefits my	2Tamb	3.1.8	Callap
GRATULATE			
[Did gratulate his safetie with kinde words],	F1143	3.3.56A	3Chor
GRAUNT			
Tis not enough that thou doest graunt me love,	Dido	3.1.8	Iarbus
Let my Phenissa graunt, and then I goe:	Dido	4.3.6	Aeneas
Graunt she or no, Aeneas must away,	Dido	4.3.7	Aeneas
I goe faire sister, heavens graunt good successe.	Dido	5.1.211	Anna
But afterwards will Dido graunt me love?	Dido	5.1.288	Iarbus

GRAUNT (cont.)			
Graunt, though the traytors land in Italy, . . .	Dido	5.1.304	Dido
Graunt that these signes of victorie we yeeld/May bind the	1Tamb	5.1.55	2Virgn
Tell me Olympia, wilt thou graunt my suit? . . .	2Tamb	4.2.21	Therid
O graunt sweet God my daies may end with hers, . . .	P 189	3.24	Navrre
God graunt my neerest freends may prove no worse. . .	P 547	11.12	Charls
Graunt that our deeds may wel deserve your loves: . .	P 600	12.13	King
Will you not graunt me this?--	Edw	1.1.77	Edward
I yours, and therefore I would wish you graunt. . .	Edw	1.1.120	Edward
Ile rather loose his friendship I, then graunt. . .	Edw	1.4.237	Lncstr
On that condition Lancaster will graunt.	Edw	1.4.292	Lncstr
it is this life you aime at,/Yet graunt king Edward this.	Edw	2.5.49	Gavstn
Shalt thou appoint/What we shall graunt?	Edw	2.5.50	Mortmr
Heare me immortall Jove, and graunt it too.	Edw	5.1.143	Edward
I gladly graunt my parents given to save, ...	Ovid's Elegies	1.3.10	
Graunt Tragedie thy Poet times least tittle, . . .	Ovid's Elegies	3.1.67	
Let my new mistris graunt to be beloved:	Ovid's Elegies	3.2.57	
Insooth th'eternall powers graunt maides society/Falsely to	Ovid's Elegies	3.3.11	
Graunt this, that what you do I may not see, . . .	Ovid's Elegies	3.13.35	
And would be thought to graunt against her will. . .	Hero and Leander	1.336	
And neither would denie, nor graunt his sute. . . .	Hero and Leander	1.424	
GRAUNTED			
This graunted, they, their honors, and their lives, . .	Edw	3.1.170	Herald
GRAUNTING			
Shee, with a kind of graunting, put him by it, . . .	Hero and Leander	2.73	
GRAUNTS			
Who sees it, graunts some deity there is shrowded. . .	Ovid's Elegies	3.12.8	
GRAV'D			
Do but deserve gifts with this title grav'd. . . .	Ovid's Elegies	2.13.26	
GRAVE (Homograph)			
Will Dido raise old Priam forth his grave, . . .	Dido	4.3.39	Illion
A grave, and not a lover fits thy age:--	Dido	4.5.30	Nurse
A grave?	Dido	4.5.31	Nurse
I wish, grave [Governour], 'twere in my power/To favour you, but	Jew	1.2.10	Calym
Grave [Governor], list not to his exclames: . . .	Jew	1.2.128	1Knght
Grave Abbasse, and you happy Virgins guide, . . .	Jew	1.2.314	Abigal
Welcome grave Fryar; Ithamore begon, ...	Jew	3.3.52	Abigal
Farewell grave Governor.	Jew	5.4.10	1Knght
Grave Socrates, wilde Alcibiades:	Edw	1.4.397	MortSr
While at the councell table, grave enough, . . .	Edw	5.4.58	Mortmr
And with the rest accompanie him to his grave? . . .	Edw	5.6.88	Queene
<and see if hee by> his grave counsell may <can> reclaime him.	F 226	1.2.33	2Schol
Welcome grave Fathers, answere presently, ...	F 946	3.1.168	Pope
With all our Colledge of grave Cardinals, ...	F 968	3.1.190	Pope
his grave looke appeasd/The wrastling tumult, and right hand	Lucan, First Booke	298	
Tav'ron peering/(His grave broke open) did affright the Boores.	Lucan, First Booke	582	
That my dead bones may in their grave lie soft. . .	Ovid's Elegies	1.8.108	
None such the sister gives her brother grave, . . .	Ovid's Elegies	2.5.25	
A grave her bones hides, on her corps great <small> grave,	Ovid's Elegies	2.6.59	
Shee dyes, and with loose haires to grave is sent, . .	Ovid's Elegies	2.14.39	
Tis time to move grave things in lofty stile, . . .	Ovid's Elegies	3.1.23	
When you are up and drest, be sage and grave, . . .	Ovid's Elegies	3.13.19	
GRAVEL'D			
<Consissylogismes>/Gravel'd the Pastors of the Germane Church,	F 140	1.1.112	Faust
GRAVELY			
art thou aye gravely plaied?	Ovid's Elegies	3.1.36	
GRAVEN			
That by Characters graven in thy browes, ...	1Tamb	1.2.169	Tamb
Graven in the booke of Joves high firmament, . . .	F 756	2.3.35	2Chor
GRAVER			
Horned Bacchus graver furie doth distill, ...	Ovid's Elegies	3.14.17	
GRAVES			
armes in ure/With digging graves and ringing dead mens knels:	Jew	2.3.185	Barab
Soules quiet and appeas'd [sigh'd] <sight> from their graves,	Lucan, First Booke	566	
Great grand-sires from their antient graves she chides/And with	Ovid's Elegies	1.8.17	
GRAVEST			
I have the bravest, gravest, secret, subtil, bottle-nos'd knave	Jew	3.3.9	P Ithimr
They call th'Etrurian Augures, amongst whom/The gravest, Aruns, .	Lucan, First Booke	585	
GRAVISSIMUM			
Saying it is, onus quam gravissimum, ...	Edw	5.4.61	Mortmr
GRAY			
Shall make the morning hast her gray uprise, . . .	Dido	1.1.102	Jupitr
I'le not leave him worth a gray groat.	Jew	4.2.114	P Ithimr
GRAZ'D			
horsemen fought/Upon Mevanias plaine, where Buls are graz'd;	Lucan, First Booke	470	
GRAZING			
My men like Satyres grazing on the lawnes, . . .	Edw	1.1.59	Gavstn
GREAT			
Great Jupiter, still honourd maist thou be, . . .	Dido	1.1.137	Venus
For though my birth be great, my fortunes meane, . .	Dido	2.1.88	Aeneas
O let me live, great Neoptolemus.	Dido	2.1.239	Aeneas
Eternall Jove, great master of the Clowdes, . . .	Dido	4.2.4	Iarbus
For it requires a great and thundring speech: . . .	1Tamb	1.1.3	Mycet
at the spoile/Of great Darius and his wealthy hoast. .	1Tamb	1.1.154	Ceneus
Great Lord of Medea and Armenia:	1Tamb	1.1.163	Ortyg
May have the leading of so great an host, ...	1Tamb	1.2.48	Tamb
An ods too great, for us to stand against: . . .	1Tamb	1.2.122	Tamb
and strive to be retain'd/In such a great degree of amitie.	1Tamb	2.3.32	Therid
As great commander of this Easterne world, . . .	1Tamb	2.7.62	Tamb
Great Kings of Barbary, and my portly Bassoes, . .	1Tamb	3.1.1	Bajzth
Great King and conquerour of Grecia, ...	1Tamb	3.1.24	Bajzth
Most great and puisant Monarke of the earth, . . .	1Tamb	3.1.41	Bassoe
My Lord, the great Commander of the worlde, . . .	1Tamb	3.3.13	Bassoe

GREAT (cont.)

that am betroath'd/Unto the great and mighty Tamburlaine?	1Tamb	3.3.170	Zenoc
To Tamburlaine the great Tartarian thiefe?	1Tamb	3.3.171	Zabina
When thy great Bassoe-maister and thy selfe,	1Tamb	3.3.173	Zenoc
had the Turkish Emperour/So great a foile by any forraine foe.	1Tamb	3.3.235	Bajzth
And write my selfe great Lord of Affrica:	1Tamb	3.3.245	Tamb
And be the foot-stoole of great Tamburlain,	1Tamb	4.2.14	Tamb
Great Tamburlaine, great in my overthrow,	1Tamb	4.2.75	Bajzth
he persecutes/The noble Turke and his great Emperesse?	1Tamb	4.3.27	Arabia
But noble Lord of great Arabia,	1Tamb	4.3.29	Souldn
Great Emperours of Egypt and Arabia,	1Tamb	4.3.51	Capol
And leads with him the great Arabian King,	1Tamb	4.3.64	Souldn
Me thinks, tis a great deale better than a consort of musicke.	1Tamb	4.4.60	P Therid
Behold the Turke and his great Emperesse.	1Tamb	5.1.354	Zenoc
Behold the Turk and his great Emperesse.	1Tamb	5.1.357	Zenoc
Behold the Turke and his great Emperesse.	1Tamb	5.1.362	Zenoc
In this great Turk and haplesse Emperesse.	1Tamb	5.1.368	Zenoc
The Turk and his great Emperesse as it seems,	1Tamb	5.1.470	Tamb
With this great Turke and his faire Emperesse:	1Tamb	5.1.532	Tamb
of these Eastern parts/Plac'd by the issue of great Bajazeth,	2Tamb	1.1.2	Orcan
and Danes/[Feares] <feare> not Orcanes, but great Tamburlaine:	2Tamb	1.1.59	Orcan
Nor he but Fortune that hath made him great.	2Tamb	1.1.60	Orcan
Your Keeper under Tamburlaine the great,	2Tamb	1.2.68	Almeda
And not the issue of great Tamburlaine:	2Tamb	1.3.70	Tamb
My Lord the great and mighty Tamburlain,	2Tamb	1.3.113	Therid
where the mighty Christian Priest/Cal'd John the great, sits in	2Tamb	1.3.188	Techel
And if thou pitiest Tamburlain the great,	2Tamb	2.4.117	Tamb
Greek, is writ/This towne being burnt by Tamburlaine the great,	2Tamb	3.2.17	Calyph
Casemates to place the great Artillery,	2Tamb	3.2.78	Tamb
And worthy sonnes of Tamburlain the great.	2Tamb	3.2.92	Tamb
a souldier, and this wound/As great a grace and majesty to me,	2Tamb	3.2.118	Tamb
Fit for the followers of great Tamburlaine.	2Tamb	3.2.144	Tamb
Thou shalt with us to Tamburlaine the great,	2Tamb	3.4.39	Techel
Gods great lieftenant over all the world:	2Tamb	3.5.2	2Msngr
My royal army is as great as his,	2Tamb	3.5.10	Callap
your weapons point/That wil be blunted if the blow be great.	2Tamb	4.2.80	Olymp
And such a Coachman as great Tamburlaine?	2Tamb	4.3.4	Tamb
Where Belus, Ninus and great Alexander/Have rode in triumph,	2Tamb	5.1.69	Tamb
let this wound appease/The mortall furie of great Tamburlain.	2Tamb	5.1.154	Govnr
And here may we behold great Babylon,	2Tamb	5.2.4	Callap
not my Lord, I see great Mahomet/Clothed in purple clowdes,	2Tamb	5.2.31	Amasia
Captaine, the force of Tamburlaine is great,	2Tamb	5.2.42	Callap
<Hipostates>/Thick and obscure doth make your danger great,	2Tamb	5.3.83	Phsitn
where I tooke/The Turke and his great Empresse prisoners,	2Tamb	5.3.129	Tamb
H'had never bellowed in a brasen Bull/Of great ones envy; o'th	Jew	Prol.26	Machvl
And seildsene costly stones of so great price,	Jew	1.1.28	Barab
in perill of calamity/To ransome great Kings from captivity.	Jew	1.1.32	Barab
There's Kirriah Jairim, the great Jew of Greece,	Jew	1.1.124	Barab
Then give us leave, great Selim-Calymath.	Jew	1.2.13	Govnr
Farewell great [Governor], and brave Knights of Malta.	Jew	1.2.32	Calym
From the Emperour of Turkey is arriv'd/Great Selim-Calymath,	Jew	1.2.40	Govnr
And what's our aid against so great a Prince?	Jew	1.2.51	Barab
and all mens hatred/Inflict upon them, thou great Primus Motor.	Jew	1.2.164	Barab
Great injuries are not so soone forgot.	Jew	1.2.208	Barab
Ten thousand Portagues besides great Perles,	Jew	1.2.244	Barab
And seeme to them as if thy sinnes were great,	Jew	1.2.287	Barab
I have bought a house/As great and faire as is the Governors;	Jew	2.3.14	Barab
Pinning upon his breast a long great Scrowle/How I with	Jew	2.3.197	Barab
me in beleefe/Gives great presumption that she loves me not;	Jew	3.4.11	Barab
be it to her as the draught/Of which great Alexander drunke,	Jew	3.4.97	Barab
Welcome, great [Bashaw] <Bashaws>, how fares/Callymath,	Jew	3.5.1	Govnr
Desire of gold, great Sir?	Jew	3.5.4	Govnr
I must needs say that I have beene a great usurer.	Jew	4.1.39	Barab
Great summes of mony lying in the bancho;	Jew	4.1.74	Barab
'Twas sent me for a present from the great Cham.	Jew	4.4.68	Barab
Farewell brave Jew, farewell great Barabas.	Jew	5.2.20	Calym
privately procure/Great summes of mony for thy recompence:	Jew	5.2.88	Govnr
First to surprize great Selims souldiers,	Jew	5.2.118	Barab
To saile to Turkey, to great Ottoman,	Jew	5.3.16	Msngr
we may grace us best/To solemnize our Governors great feast.	Jew	5.3.45	Calym
Welcome great Calymath.	Jew	5.5.55	Barab
Of so great matter should be made the ground.	P 126	2.69	Guise
the Duke of Joyeux/Hath made great sute unto the King therfore.	P 734	14.37	1Msngr
To make his glory great upon the earth.	P 790	16.4	Navrre
That in the Court I bare so great a traine.	P 968	19.38	Guise
I have beene a great sinner in my dayes, and the deed is	P1133	21.27	P Frier
exhalatione/which our great sonn of fraunce cold not effecte	Paris	ms20,p390	Guise
Which whiles I have, I thinke my selfe as great,	Edw	1.1.172	Gavstn
Whose great atchivements in our forrain warre,	Edw	1.4.360	Edward
Great Alexander lovde Ephestion,	Edw	1.4.392	MortSr
Can get you any favour with great men.	Edw	2.1.41	Spencr
And dare not be revengde, for their power is great:	Edw	2.2.202	Edward
He that I list to favour shall be great:	Edw	2.2.263	Edward
the lovelie Elenor of Spaine,/Great Edward Longshankes issue:	Edw	3.1.12	Spencr
not lord and father, heavens great beames/On Atlas shoulder,	Edw	3.1.76	Prince
man, they say there is great execution/Done through the realme,	Edw	4.3.6	Edward
Thankes be heavens great architect and you.	Edw	4.6.22	Queene
Conjurer laureate]/[That canst commaund great Mephostophilis],	F 261	1.3.33A	Faust
I am a servant to great Lucifer,	F 268	1.3.40	Mephst
is great Mephostophilis so passionate/For being deprived of the	F 311	1.3.83	Faust
Go beare these <those> tydings to great Lucifer,	F 315	1.3.87	Faust
By him, I'le be great Emperour of the world,	F 332	1.3.104	Faust
Mephostophilis come/And bring glad tydings from great Lucifer.	F 416	2.1.28	Faust

GREAT (cont.)

For that security craves <great> Lucifer.	F 425	2.1.37		Mephst
As great as have the humane soules of men.	F 433	2.1.45		Mephst
at some certaine day/Great Lucifer may claime it as his owne,	F 440	2.1.52		Mephst
And then be thou as great as Lucifer.	F 441	2.1.53		Mephst
bloud/Assures his <assure my> soule to be great Lucifers,	F 444	2.1.56		Faust
and you have done me great injury to bring me from thence, let	F 705.1	2.2.155A	P	Sloth
<Great> Thankes mighty Lucifer:	F 719	2.2.171		Faust
Farewell great Lucifer: come Mephostophilis.	F 721	2.2.173		Faust
That we receive such great indignity?	F1050	3.2.70		Pope
flie amaine/Unto my Faustus to the great Turkes Court.	F1137	3.3.50		Mephst
And he intends to shew great Carolus,	F1167	4.1.13		Mrtino
Great Alexander, and his Paramour,	F1232	4.1.78		Emper
Great Alexander and his beauteous Paramour.	F1239	4.1.85		Faust
Shall I let slip so great an injury,	F1328	4.2.4		Benvol
I have no great need to sell him, but if thou likest him for	F1460	4.4.4	P	Faust
what did I but rid him into a great river, and when I came just	F1543	4.5.39	P	HrsCsr
great deserts in erecting that inchanted Castle in the Aire:	F1559	4.6.2	P	Duke
I have heard that great bellyed women, do long for things, are	F1568	4.6.11	P	Faust
His faith is great, I cannot touch his soule;	F1756	5.1.83		Mephst
blacke survey/Great Potentates do kneele with awful feare,	F App	p.235 35		Mephst
you have had a great journey, wil you take sixe pence in your	F App	p.235 40	P	Robin
attaine to that degree of high renowne and great authoritie,	F App	p.237 23	P	Emper
amongest which kings is Alexander the great, chiefe spectacle	F App	p.237 24	P	Emper
felow, and he has a great charge, neither wife nor childe.	F App	p.239 106	P	Mephst
that great bellied women do long for some dainties or other,	F App	p.242 5	P	Faust
this learned man for the great kindnes he hath shewd to you.	F App	p.243 29	P	Duke
Under great burdens fals are ever greevous;	Lucan, First Booke	71		
Roome was so great it could not beare it selfe:	Lucan, First Booke	72		
All great things crush themselves, such end the gods/Allot the	Lucan, First Booke	81		
Thou feard'st (great Pompey) that late deeds would dim/Olde	Lucan, First Booke	121		
Each side had great partakers; Caesars cause,	Lucan, First Booke	128		
even the same that wrack's all great [dominions] <dominion>.	Lucan, First Booke	160		
what ere thou be whom God assignes/This great effect, art hid.	Lucan, First Booke	420		
O gods that easie grant men great estates,	Lucan, First Booke	508		
Great store of strange and unknown stars were seene/Wandering	Lucan, First Booke	524		
to unfould/What you intend, great Jove is now displeas'd,	Lucan, First Booke	631		
Great are thy kingdomes, over strong and large,	Ovid's Elegies	1.1.17		
Over my Mistris is my right more great?	Ovid's Elegies	1.7.30		
Great grand-sires from their antient graves she chides/And with	Ovid's Elegies	1.8.17		
Within a while great heapes grow of a tittle.	Ovid's Elegies	1.8.90		
By many hands great wealth is quickly got.	Ovid's Elegies	1.8.92		
Great Agamemnon was, men say, amazed,	Ovid's Elegies	1.9.37		
should defend/Or great wealth from a judgement seate ascend.	Ovid's Elegies	1.10.40		
[Thy] <They> troubled haires, alas, endur'd great losse.	Ovid's Elegies	1.14.24		
I durst the great celestiall battells tell,	Ovid's Elegies	2.1.11		
A great reward:	Ovid's Elegies	2.1.35		
More he deserv'd, to both great harme he fram'd,	Ovid's Elegies	2.2.49		
I know no maister of so great hire sped.	Ovid's Elegies	2.5.62		
[Itis is] <It is as> great, but auntient cause of sorrowe.	Ovid's Elegies	2.6.10		
A grave her bones hides, on her corps great <small> grave,	Ovid's Elegies	2.6.59		
Loe how the miserable great eared Asse,	Ovid's Elegies	2.7.15		
Great Agamemnon lov'd his servant Chriseis.	Ovid's Elegies	2.8.12		
Hence with great laude thou maiest a triumph move.	Ovid's Elegies	2.9.16		
Great joyes by hope I inly shall conceive.	Ovid's Elegies	2.9.44		
Cupid by thee, Mars in great doubt doth trample,	Ovid's Elegies	2.9.47		
But if in so great feare I may advize thee,	Ovid's Elegies	2.13.27		
For great revenews I good verses have,	Ovid's Elegies	2.17.27		
And tender love hath great things hatefull made.	Ovid's Elegies	2.18.4		
Great gods what kisses, and how many gave she?	Ovid's Elegies	2.19.18		
We praise: great goddesse ayde my enterprize.	Ovid's Elegies	3.2.56		
Least labour so shall winne great grace of any.	Ovid's Elegies	3.4.46		
Great floods ought to assist young men in love,	Ovid's Elegies	3.5.23		
Great floods the force of it do often prove.	Ovid's Elegies	3.5.24		
If thy great fame in every region stood?	Ovid's Elegies	3.5.90		
I shame so great names to have usde so vainly:	Ovid's Elegies	3.5.102		
I thinke the great Gods greeved they had bestowde/This <The>	Ovid's Elegies	3.6.45		
Now poverty great barbarisme we hold.	Ovid's Elegies	3.7.4		
See a rich chuffe whose wounds great wealth inferr'd,	Ovid's Elegies	3.7.9		
And envious fates great [goddesses] <goodesses> assaile,	Ovid's Elegies	3.8.2		
That durst to so great wickednesse aspire.	Ovid's Elegies	3.8.44		
Our verse great Tityus a huge space out-spreads,	Ovid's Elegies	3.11.25		
A greater ground with great horse is to till.	Ovid's Elegies	3.14.18		
Came lovers home, from this great festivall.	Hero and Leander	1.96		
And many seeing great princes were denied,	Hero and Leander	1.129		
And few great lords in vertuous deeds shall joy,	Hero and Leander	1.479		
Yet when a token of great worth we send,	Hero and Leander	2.80		
their loves/On heapes of heavie gold, and tooke great pleasure,	Hero and Leander	2.163		

GREATE

He Citties greate, this thresholds lies before:	Ovid's Elegies	1.9.19		

GREATER

Thy fortune may be greater then thy birth,	Dido	2.1.90		Dido
pray you let him stay, a greater [task]/Fits Menaphon, than	1Tamb	1.1.87		Cosroe
Are countermanded by a greater man:	1Tamb	1.2.22		Tamb
And grace your calling with a greater sway.	1Tamb	2.5.31		Cosroe
The more he brings, the greater is the spoile,	1Tamb	3.3.23		Techel
Until with greater honors I be grac'd.	1Tamb	4.4.140		Tamb
And have a greater foe to fight against,	2Tamb	1.1.15		Gazell
With greater power than erst his pride hath felt,	2Tamb	2.2.10		Gazell
And thou shalt see a man greater than Mahomet,	2Tamb	3.4.46		Therid
kings again my Lord/To gather greater numbers gainst our power,	2Tamb	4.1.83		Amyras
Thou hast procur'd a greater enemie,	2Tamb	4.1.127		Tamb
But since I exercise a greater name,	2Tamb	4.1.153		Tamb

GREATER (cont.)

Have greater operation and more force/Than Cynthias in the	2Tamb	4.2.29	Therid
A greater Lamp than that bright eie of heaven,	2Tamb	4.2.88	Therid
His fortune greater, and the victories/Wherewith he hath so	2Tamb	5.2.43	Callap
Is greater far, than they can thus subdue.	2Tamb	5.3.39	Usumc
What greater gift can poore Mathias have?	Jew	2.3.346	Mthias
What greater misery could heaven inflict?	Jew	5.2.14	Govnr
If greater falshood ever has bin done.	Jew	5.5.50	Barab
For I will shew thee greater curtesie/Then Barabas would have	Jew	5.5.61	Govnr
What greater blisse can hap to Gaveston,	Edw	1.1.4	Gavstn
these may well suffice/For one of greater birth then Gaveston.	Edw	1.1.159	Kent
Kinde wordes, and mutuall talke, makes our greefe greater,	Edw	1.4.133	Edward
No greater titles happen unto me,	Edw	2.2.254	Spencr
For our behoofe will beare the greater sway/When as a kings	Edw	5.2.13	Mortmr
Affoords this Art no greater miracle?	F 37	1.1.9	Faust
A greater subject fitteth Faustus wit:	F 39	1.1.11	Faust
Their conference will be a greater helpe to me,	F 95	1.1.67	Faust
I Faustus, and do greater things then these.	F 476	2.1.88	Mephst
Hath Mephostophilis no greater skill?	F 601	2.2.50	Faust
Lest greater dangers <danger> do attend thy drift.	F1752	5.1.79	Mephst
were it a greater thing then this, so it would content you, you	F App	p.242 13 P	Faust
Who running long, fals in a greater floud,	Lucan, First Booke		401
their huge power made him bould/To mannage greater deeds; the	Lucan, First Booke		463
What he will give, with greater instance crave.	Ovid's Elegies		1.8.68
Her shut gates greater lightning then thyne brought.	Ovid's Elegies		2.1.20
Greater then these my selfe I not esteeme,	Ovid's Elegies		2.8.13
Small things with greater may be copulate.	Ovid's Elegies		2.17.14
By her footes blemish greater grace she tooke.	Ovid's Elegies		3.1.10
Long hast thou loyterd, greater workes compile.	Ovid's Elegies		3.1.24
Some greater worke will urge me on at last.	Ovid's Elegies		3.1.70
Greater then her, by her leave th'art, Ile say.	Ovid's Elegies		3.2.60
much (I crave)/Gifts then my promise greater thou shalt have.	Ovid's Elegies		3.5.66
A greater ground with great horse is to till.	Ovid's Elegies		3.14.18
For whom succeeding times make greater mone.	Hero and Leander		1.54

GREATEST

mightier Kings)/Hast had the greatest favours I could give:	Dido	3.1.13	Dido
With greatest pompe had crown'd thee Emperour.	1Tamb	2.5.5	Tamb
we wish for ought/The world affoords in greatest noveltie,	1Tamb	2.5.73	Tamb
The greatest Potentate of Affrica.	1Tamb	3.3.63	Bajzth
Natolia hath dismist the greatest part/Of all his armie, pitcht	2Tamb	2.1.16	Fredrk
Now crowch ye kings of greatest Asia,	2Tamb	4.3.98	Tamb
And make our greatest haste to Persea:	2Tamb	5.1.128	Tamb
Are greatest to discourage all our drifts,	2Tamb	5.2.45	Callap
The greatest warres within our Christian bounds,	P 460	8.10	Anjoy
With greatest [torments] <torment> that our hell affoords.	F1755	5.1.82	Faust
Poverty (who hatcht/Roomes greatest wittes) was loath'd, and al	Lucan, First Booke		167
men/Whom death the greatest of all feares affright not,	Lucan, First Booke		455
Now greatest spectacles the Praetor sends,	Ovid's Elegies		3.2.65
How small sc ere, Ile you for greatest praise.	Ovid's Elegies		3.14.14

GREATLY

I doe not greatly beleeve him, he lookes as like [a] conjurer	F1228	4.1.74	P Benvol

GREATNES

What thinks your greatnes best to be atchiev'd/In pursuit of	1Tamb	3.1.56	Fesse
Nay (mightie Souldan) did your greatnes see/The frowning lookes	1Tamb	4.1.12	2Msngr

GRECIA (See also GRAECIA, GRETIANS)

Great King and conquerour of Grecia,	1Tamb	3.1.24	Bajzth
Or spread his collours in Grecia,	1Tamb	3.1.29	Bajzth
footmen that have serv'd/In two set battels fought in Grecia:	1Tamb	3.3.19	Bassoe

GRECIAN

The Grecian souldiers tired with ten yeares warre,	Dido	2.1.126	Aeneas
And loade his speare with Grecian Princes heads,	Dido	3.3.43	Aeneas
As did Sir Paris with the Grecian Dame:	1Tamb	1.1.66	Mycet
from our dreadful siege/Of the famous Grecian Constantinople.	1Tamb	3.1.6	Bajzth
The Grecian virgins shall attend on thee,	2Tamb	1.2.36	Callap
As Hector did into the Grecian campe,	2Tamb	3.5.65	Tamb
About the Grecian Isles to rob and spoile:	2Tamb	3.5.94	Jrslem

GRECIANS

and be revengde/On these hard harted Grecians, which rejoyce	Dido	2.1.19	Aeneas
And after him a thousand Grecians more,	Dido	2.1.185	Aeneas
Troy is a fire, the Grecians have the towne.	Dido	2.1.208	Aeneas
But suddenly the Grecians followed us,	Dido	2.1.278	Aeneas
And thus the Grecians shall be conquered.	1Tamb	3.1.67	Bajzth
We have revclted Grecians, Albanees,	2Tamb	1.1.61	Orcan
Our fraught is Grecians, Turks, and Africk Moores.	Jew	2.2.9	Bosco

GREE

But weapons gree not with my tender yeares:	Dido	3.1.164	Dido

GREECE (Homograph)

We heare they led her captive into Greece.	Dido	2.1.295	Achat
I this in Greece when Paris stole faire Helen.	Dido	3.1.142	Aeneas
As if the Turke, the Pope, Affrike and Greece,	1Tamb	2.5.85	Tamb
Unpeopling Westerne Affrica and Greece:	1Tamb	3.3.34	Usumc
Affrik and Greece have garrisons enough/To make me Soveraigne	1Tamb	3.3.242	Bajzth
Affrica, and Greece/Follow my Standard and my thundring Drums:	2Tamb	1.1.158	Orcan
Hellen, whose beauty sommond Greece to armes,	2Tamb	2.4.87	Tamb
stay with me/Embalm'd with Cassia, Amber Greece and Myrre,	2Tamb	2.4.130	Tamb
That bought my Spanish Oyles, and Wines of Greece,	Jew	1.1.5	Barab
There's Kirriah Jairim, the great Jew of Greece,	Jew	1.1.124	Barab
And saile from hence to Greece, to lovely Greece,	Jew	4.2.89	Ithimr
that Hellen of Greece was the admirablest Lady that ever liv'd:	F1683	5.1.10	P 1Schol
as to let us see that peerelesse dame of Greece, whom all the	F1686	5.1.13	P 1Schol
You shall behold that peerelesse dame of Greece,	F1692	5.1.19	Faust
worth>/<Made Greece with ten yeares warres afflict poore Troy>?	F1696	(HC269)B	2Schol
Would have allur'd the vent'rous youth of Greece,	Hero and Leander		1.57

GREECE (cont.)
As Greece will thinke, if thus you live alone, — Hero and Leander 1.289

GREEDIE
These greedie lovers had, at their first meeting. — Hero and Leander 2.24

GREEDILY
Yet ever as he greedily assayd/To touch those dainties, she the — Hero and Leander 2.269

GREEDY
And either lanch his greedy thirsting throat, — 1Tamb 1.2.146 Tamb
All running headlong after greedy spoiles: — 1Tamb 2.2.45 Meandr
Shall massacre those greedy minded slaves. — 1Tamb 2.2.67 Meandr
dooth gastly death/With greedy tallents gripe my bleeding hart, — 1Tamb 2.7.49 Cosroe
And choakt with thorns, that greedy earth wants hinds, — Lucan, First Booke 29
Quarrels were rife, greedy desire stil poore/Did vild deeds, — Lucan, First Booke 174
Yet greedy Bauds command she curseth still, — Ovid's Elegies 1.10.23
The greedy spirits take the best things first, — Ovid's Elegies 2.6.39

GREEFE
To dye by Pesantes, what a greefe is this? — P1009 19.79 Guise
I cannot speak for greefe: when thou wast borne, — P1072 19.142 QnMoth
To live in greefe and balefull discontent, — Edw 1.2.48 Queene
Is all my hope turnd to this hell of greefe. — Edw 1.4.116 Gavstn
Kinde wordes, and mutuall talke, makes our greefe greater, — Edw 1.4.133 Edward
The greefe for his exile was not so much, — Edw 2.1.57 Neece
You will this greefe have ease and remedie, — Edw 3.1.160 Herald
Grone for this greefe, behold how thou art maimed. — Edw 3.1.251 Mortmr
Ah pardon me, greefe makes me lunatick. — Edw 5.1.114 Edward
Alas poore soule, would I could ease his greefe. — Edw 5.2.26 Queene
But amplifie his greefe with bitter words. — Edw 5.2.65 Mortmr
To ease his greefe, and worke his libertie: — Edw 5.2.71 Queene
The more my greefe. — Edw 5.2.84 Queene
I feele a hell of greefe: where is my crowne? — Edw 5.5.90 Edward
But that greefe keepes me waking, I shoulde sleepe, — Edw 5.5.93 Edward
Then come sweete death, and rid me of this greefe. — Edw 5.6.92 Queene
Be witnesse of my greefe and innocencie. — Edw 5.6.102 King
Greefe makes her pale, because she mooves not there. — Hero and Leander 1.60
went and came, as if he rewd/The greefe which Neptune felt. — Hero and Leander 2.215

GREEFES
Yet will the wisest note their proper greefes: — P 216 4.14 Anjoy
The greefes of private men are soone allayde, — Edw 5.1.8 Edward

GREEK
Greek, is writ/This towne being burnt by Tamburlaine the great, — 2Tamb 3.2.16 Calyph

GREEKE
Troianes destroy the Greeke wealth, while you may. — Ovid's Elegies 1.9.34
Such was the Greeke pompe, Agamemnon dead, — Ovid's Elegies 3.12.31

GREEKES
Come, come abourd, pursue the hatefull Greekes. — Dido 2.1.22 Aeneas
And we were round inviron'd with the Greekes: — Dido 2.1.269 Aeneas
The Greekes pursue me, stay and take me in. — Dido 2.1.282 Aeneas
And by this Sword that saved me from the Greekes, — Dido 3.4.48 Aeneas
And build the towne againe the Greekes did burne? — Dido 4.3.40 Illion
Will leade an hoste against the hatefull Greekes, — Dido 4.4.91 Aeneas
Which glided through the bowels of the Greekes. — 1Tamb 3.3.92 Argier
[No marvel tho the angry Greekes pursu'd]/[With tenne yeares — F1699 5.1.26A 3Schol

GREEKISH
causde the Greekish spyes/To hast to Tenedos and tell the — Dido 2.1.180 Aeneas
Kneeling for mercie to a Greekish lad, — Dido 2.1.198 Aeneas
Achilles horse/Drew him in triumph through the Greekish Campe, — Dido 2.1.206 Aeneas
Of Greekish wine now let us celebrate/Our happy conquest, — 2Tamb 2.3.46 Orcan
That like the Greekish strumpet traind to armes/And bloudie — Edw 2.5.15 Lncstr

GREEKS
As when my Emperour overthrew the Greeks: — 1Tamb 3.3.204 Zabina
Under my collors march ten thousand Greeks, — 2Tamb 1.3.118 Therid

GREENE
and in this grove/Amongst greene brakes Ile lay Ascanius, — Dido 2.1.317 Venus
Of [ever] <every> greene Selinus queintly dect/With bloomes — 2Tamb 4.3.121 Tamb
Jacints, hard Topas, grasse-greene Emeraulds, — Jew 1.1.26 Barab
Where Woods and Forrests goe in goodly greene, — Jew 4.2.93 Ithimr
Whom I respect as leaves of boasting greene, — P 720 14.23 Navrre
til I am past this faire and pleasant greene, ile walke on — F App p.239 96 P Faust
Bacchinall/That tyr'd doth rashly on the greene grasse fall. — Ovid's Elegies 1.14.22
Thou with thy quilles mightst make greene Emeralds darke, — Ovid's Elegies 2.6.21
Whose earth doth not perpetuall greene-grasse lacke, — Ovid's Elegies 2.6.50
addst thou starres to heaven, leaves to greene woods <wood>, — Ovid's Elegies 2.10.13
With cruell hand why doest greene Apples pull? — Ovid's Elegies 2.14.24
And on the soft ground fertile greene grasse growe. — Ovid's Elegies 2.16.6
Her wide sleeves greene, and bordered with a grove, — Hero and Leander 1.11
A livelie vine of greene sea agget spread; — Hero and Leander 1.138

GREENE-GRASSE
Whose earth doth not perpetuall greene-grasse lacke, — Ovid's Elegies 2.6.50

GREENLAND (See GRUNTLAND)

GREET
To greet his lordship with a poniard, — Edw 1.4.266 Mortmr

GREETE
Night runnes away; with open entrance greete them. — Ovid's Elegies 1.6.40
In white, with incense Ile thine Altars greete, — Ovid's Elegies 2.13.23
Jasons sad letter doth Hipsipile greete, — Ovid's Elegies 2.18.33
With Calvus learnd Catullus comes <come> and greete him. — Ovid's Elegies 3.8.62
Victorious wreathes at length my Temples greete. — Ovid's Elegies 3.10.6

GREETES
The President of Paris greetes your grace, — P1168 22.30 Frier
My lords, king Edward greetes you all by me. — Edw 2.5.33 Arundl
My lord protector greetes you. — Edw 5.5.14 Ltborn

GREETING
At last he came, O who can tell the greeting, — Hero and Leander 2.23

GREEV'D			
For much it greev'd her that the bright day-light,	Hero and Leander	2.303	
GREEVDE			
And like a burthen greevde the bed that mooved not.	Ovid's Elegies	3.6.4	
GREEVE			
And let her greeve her heart out if she will.	P1080	19.150	King
I shal be found, and then twil greeve me more.	Edw	1.4.132	Gavstn
My lord, it is in vaine to greeve or storme,	Edw	4.7.77	Baldck
Why should I greeve at my declining fall?	Edw	5.6.63	Mortmr
Was not one wench inough to greeve my heart?	Ovid's Elegies	2.10.12	
GREEVED			
I thinke the great Gods greeved they had bestowde/This <The>	Ovid's Elegies	3.6.45	
GREEVES			
To go from hence, greeves not poore Gaveston,	Edw	1.4.119	Gavstn
Unckle, his wanton humor greeves not me,	Edw	1.4.402	Mortmr
I, and it greeves me that I favoured him.	Edw	2.2.213	Kent
Ah nothing greeves me but my little boye,	Edw	4.3.48	Edward
GREEVOUS			
Under great burdens fals are ever greevous;	Lucan, First Booke	71	
GRESSES			
I have the [gesses] <gresses> that will pull you downe,	Edw	2.2.40	Edward
GRETIANS			
Nor raise our siege before the Gretians yeeld,	1Tamb	3.1.14	Bajzth
GREW			
Is this the wood that grew in Carthage plaines,	Dido	4.4.136	Dido
That sometime grew within this learned man:	F2004	5.3.22	4Chor
And then we grew licencious and rude,	Lucan, First Booke	162	
Grew pale, and in cold foords hot lecherous.	Ovid's Elegies	3.5.26	
Whereat the saphir visag'd god grew prowd,	Hero and Leander	2.155	
GRIDIRONS			
No, no, here take your gridirons againe.	F App	p.230 38 P	Clown
GRIDYRONS			
Gridyrons, what be they?	F App	p.230 31 P	Clown
GRIEFE (See also GREEFE, GRIFE)			
And drie with griefe was turnd into a stone,	Dido	2.1.5	Aeneas
And when we told her she would weepe for griefe,	Dido	2.1.67	Illion
Doe shame her worst, I will disclose my griefe:--	Dido	3.4.28	Dido
Better he frowne, then I should dye for griefe:	Dido	4.4.111	Dido
O then Aeneas, tis for griefe of thee:	Dido	5.1.116	Dido
Had I a sonne by thee, the griefe were lesse,	Dido	5.1.149	Dido
Then carelesly I rent my haire for griefe,	Dido	5.1.236	Anna
How long shall I with griefe consume my daies,	Dido	5.1.281	Iarbus
dye to expiate/The griefe that tires upon thine inward soule.	Dido	5.1.317	Iarbus
Declare the cause of my conceived griefe,	1Tamb	1.1.29	Mycet
Let griefe and furie hasten on revenge,	1Tamb	4.3.43	Arabia
As well for griefe our ruthlesse Governour/Have thus refusde	1Tamb	5.1.92	1Virgn
sparke of breath/Can quench or coole the torments of my griefe.	1Tamb	5.1.285	Zabina
Shake with their waight in signe of feare and griefe:	1Tamb	5.1.349	Zenoc
Your griefe and furie hurtes my second life:	2Tamb	2.4.68	Zenoc
If griefe, our murthered harts have straind forth blood.	2Tamb	2.4.123	Therid
With griefe and sorrow for my mothers death.	2Tamb	3.2.50	Amyras
Save griefe and sorrow which torment my heart,	2Tamb	4.2.24	Olymp
Sit stil my gratious Lord, this griefe wil cease,	2Tamb	5.3.64	Techel
bleeding harts/Wounded and broken with your Highnesse griefe,	2Tamb	5.3.162	Amyras
And now and then one hang himselfe for griefe,	Jew	2.3.196	Barab
Shee'll dye with griefe.	Jew	2.3.354	Mthias
Then of true griefe let us take equall share.	Jew	3.2.37	Govnr
But now experience, purchased with griefe,	Jew	3.3.61	Abigal
They'll dye with griefe.	Jew	4.1.16	Barab
Oh speake not of her, then I dye with griefe.	Jew	4.1.36	Barab
[Where such as beare <bare> his absence but with griefe],	F1141	3.3.54A	3Chor
We'le rather die with griefe, then live with shame.	F1456	4.3.26	Benvol
Faustus I leave thee, but with griefe of heart,	F1737	5.1.64	OldMan
Fond worldling, now his heart bloud dries with griefe;	F1808	5.2.12	Mephst
they, and none durst speake/And shew their feare, or griefe:	Lucan, First Booke	260	
But doubt thou not (revenge doth griefe appease)/With thy	Ovid's Elegies	1.7.63	
and too much his griefe doth favour/That seekes the conquest by	Ovid's Elegies	2.5.11	
Forbid thine anger to procure my griefe.	Ovid's Elegies	2.7.14	
Whom Ilia pleasd, though in her lookes griefe reveld,	Ovid's Elegies	3.5.47	
good growes by this griefe,/Oft bitter juice brings to the	Ovid's Elegies	3.10.7	
Laden with languishment and griefe he flies.	Hero and Leander	1.378	
GRIEFES			
And tell our griefes in more familiar termes:	Dido	1.1.246	Aeneas
So for a finall Issue to my griefes,	1Tamb	5.1.395	Zenoc
Thus will I end his griefes immediatly.	F1367	4.2.43	Benvol
GRIEFS			
Infecting all the Ghosts with curelesse griefs:	1Tamb	5.1.258	Bajzth
Accursed day infected with my griefs,	1Tamb	5.1.291	Bajzth
the cursed object/Whose Fortunes never mastered her griefs:	1Tamb	5.1.414	Zenoc
GRIESLY			
And griesly death, by running to and fro,	1Tamb	5.1.455	Tamb
GRIEV'D			
Oh leave to grieve me, I am griev'd enough.	Jew	3.2.17	Mater
GRIEVDE			
Or art thou grievde thy betters presse so nye?	Dido	3.3.18	Iarbus
GRIEVE (See also GREEVE)			
And have no gall at all to grieve my foes:	Dido	3.2.17	Juno
Would it not grieve a King to be so abusde,	1Tamb	2.2.5	Mycet
And therfore grieve not at your overthrow,	1Tamb	5.1.446	Tamb
Oh leave to grieve me, I am griev'd enough.	Jew	3.2.17	Mater
from hence/Ne're shall she grieve me more with her disgrace;	Jew	3.4.29	Barab
No, but I grieve because she liv'd so long.	Jew	4.1.18	Barab
<yet should I grieve for him>:	F 224	(HC258)A	2Schol

GRIEVE (cont.)

We grieve at this thy patience and delay: . . . . . Lucan, First Booke 362
live with thee, and die, or <ere> thou shalt <shall> grieve. Ovid's Elegies 1.3.18
The man did grieve, the woman was defam'd. . . . . Ovid's Elegies 2.2.50
I grieve least others should such good perceive, . . . Ovid's Elegies 2.5.53
One among many is to grieve thee tooke. . . . . Ovid's Elegies 2.7.4
Did not Pelides whom his Speare did grieve, ... Ovid's Elegies 2.9.7
Onely Ile signe nought, that may grieve me much. . . . Ovid's Elegies 2.15.18
Why grieve I? and of heaven reproches pen? . . . Ovid's Elegies 3.3.41

GRIEVED

And when my grieved heart sighes and sayes no, ... Dido 2.1.26 Aeneas
An uncouth paine torments my grieved soule, ... 1Tamb 2.7.7 Cosroe

GRIEVES

I know not, and that grieves me most of all. . . . . Jew 3.2.21 Govnr
I, and a Virgin too, that grieves me most: . . . . Jew 3.6.41 2Fryar
It grieves my soule I never saw the man: . . . . . F App p.237 28 Emper
This grieves me not, no joyned kisses spent, ... Ovid's Elegies 2.5.59
He is too clownish, whom a lewd wife grieves, ... Ovid's Elegies 3.4.37
And Venus grieves, Tibullus life being spent, ... Ovid's Elegies 3.8.15

GRIEVOUS (See also GREEVOUS)

That grievous image of ingratitude: . . . . . . 1Tamb 2.6.30 Cosroe
How are ye glutted with these grievous objects, . . . 1Tamb 5.1.341 Zenoc
In grievous memorie of his fathers shame, ... 2Tamb 3.1.25 Callap
And so revenge our latest grievous losse, ... 2Tamb 5.2.10 Callap
Wrinckles in beauty is a grievous fault. . . . . Ovid's Elegies 1.8.46
Ceres what sports to thee so grievous were, . . . Ovid's Elegies 3.9.43

GRIEVOUSLY

Are punisht with Bastones so grievously, ... 1Tamb 3.3.52 Tamb
I did offend high heaven so grievously, ... Jew 3.6.17 Abigal

GRIFE

This, and what grife inforc'd me say I say'd, ... Ovid's Elegies 2.5.33

GRIM

The Cyclops shelves, and grim Ceranias seate/Have you oregone, Dido 1.1.147 Aeneas
Then that which grim Atrides overthrew: . . . . . Dido 5.1.3 Aeneas
Made the grim monarch of infernall spirits, ... F1371 4.2.47 Fredrk

GRIN

Streching their monstrous pawes, grin with their teeth, . 2Tamb 3.5.28 Orcan
And when we grin we bite, yet are our lookes/As innocent and Jew 2.3.21 Barab

GRIND

Whose face has bin a grind-stone for mens swords, . . . Jew 4.3.9 Barab

GRIND-STONE

Whose face has bin a grind-stone for mens swords, . . . Jew 4.3.9 Barab

GRIPE

dooth gastly death/With greedy tallents gripe my bleeding hart, 1Tamb 2.7.49 Cosroe
Whose hands are made to gripe a warlike Lance, ... 1Tamb 3.3.106 Bajzth
A hand, that with a graspe may gripe the world, . . . P 159 2.102 Guise
Upon whose heart may all the furies gripe, ... P1101 20.11 Cardnl
And gripe the sorer being gript himselfe. . . . . . Edw 5.2.9 Mortmr
Base villaines, wherefore doe you gripe mee thus? . . . Edw 5.3.57 Kent

GRIPES

Sharp hunger bites upon and gripes the root, ... 1Tamb 5.1.273 Bajzth

GRIPING

with horror aie/Griping our bowels with retorqued thoughtes, 1Tamb 5.1.237 Bajzth
A griping paine hath ceasde upon my heart: . . . . P 537 11.2 Charls
Griping his false hornes with hir virgin hand: . . . Ovid's Elegies 1.3.24

GRIPT

And gripe the sorer being gript himselfe. . . . . . Edw 5.2.9 Mortmr

GRISLIE

And guarded with a thousand grislie ghosts, ... Dido 1.1.59 Venus

GRISLY (See also GRIESLY)

That when he speakes, drawes out his grisly beard, . . . Jew 4.3.7 Barab

GROANING (See also GRONING)

abroad a nights/And kill sicke people groaning under walls: Jew 2.3.175 Barab

GROAT

The needy groome that never fingred groat, ... Jew 1.1.12 Barab
I'le not leave him worth a gray groat. . . . . . Jew 4.2.114 P Ithimr

GROINE

As when the wilde boare Adons groine had rent. . . . Ovid's Elegies 3.8.16

GRONE

Grone for this greefe, behold how thou art maimed. . . . Edw 3.1.251 Mortmr
Grone you Master Doctor? . . . . F1365 4.2.41 Fredrk
Pharsalia grone with slaughter;/And Carthage soules be glutted Lucan, First Booke 38

GRONES

Where shaking ghosts with ever howling grones, . . . 1Tamb 5.1.245 Zabina
Breake may his heart with grones: deere Frederik see, . F1366 4.2.42 Benvol

GRONING

That earth-borne Atlas groning underprops: . . . . Dido 1.1.99 Jupitr
under Turkish yokes/Shall groning beare the burthen of our ire; Jew 5.2.8 Calym
And lame and poore, lie groning at the gates, ... Edw 2.2.163 Lncstr
Or fathers throate; or womens groning wombe; . . . Lucan, First Booke 378

GROOME

The needy groome that never fingred groat, ... Jew 1.1.12 Barab
Thinke me as base a groome as Gaveston. . . . . . Edw 1.4.291 Mortmr
Away base groome, robber of kings renowme, ... Edw 2.5.72 Mortmr
When every servile groome jeasts at my wrongs, ... F1329 4.2.5 Benvol

GROOMES

Humilitie belongs to common groomes. . . . . . . Dido 2.1.101 Dido
Proud Rome, that hatchest such imperiall groomes, . . . Edw 1.4.97 Edward
mainly throw the dart; wilt thou indure/These purple groomes? Lucan, First Booke 366

GROSSE

Lest their grosse eye-beames taint my lovers cheekes: . Dido 3.1.74 Dido
For he is grosse and like the massie earth, ... 1Tamb 2.7.31 Therid
And as grosse vapours perish by the sunne, ... Edw 1.4.341 Edward

GROSSE (cont.)			
Grosse gold, from them runs headlong to the boore.	Hero and Leander	1.472	
Would animate grosse clay, and higher set/The drooping thoughts	Hero and Leander	2.256	
GROUND			
Neoptolemus/Setting his speare upon the ground, leapt forth,	Dido	2.1.184	Aeneas
joyntly both/Beating their breasts and falling on the ground,	Dido	2.1.228	Aeneas
She crav'd a hide of ground to build a towne,	Dido	4.2.13	Iarbus
The ground is mine that gives them sustenance,	Dido	4.4.74	Dido
The ground is mantled with such multitudes.	1Tamb	3.1.53	Moroc
That leave no ground for thee to martch upon.	1Tamb	3.3.147	Bajzth
Steeds, disdainfully/With wanton paces trampling on the ground.	1Tamb	4.1.23	2Msngr
Unworthy to imbrace or touch the ground,	1Tamb	4.2.20	Tamb
chardg'd their quivering speares/Began to checke the ground,	1Tamb	5.1.333	Zenoc
And when the ground wheron my souldiers march/Shal rise aloft	2Tamb	1.3.13	Tamb
Ile have you learne to sleepe upon the ground,	2Tamb	3.2.55	Tamb
Looke here my boies, see what a world of ground,	2Tamb	5.3.145	Tamb
Is theft the ground of your Religion?	Jew	1.2.95	Barab
If 'twere above ground I could, and would have it; but hee	Jew	4.2.57	P Ithimr
Of so great matter should be made the ground.	P 126	2.69	Guise
and tyll the ground that he himself should occupy, which is his	P 811	17.6	P Souldr
This ground which is corrupted with their steps,	Edw	1.2.5	Lncstr
and enforce/The papall towers, to kisse the lowlie ground,	Edw	1.4.101	Edward
He is in Englands ground, our port-maisters/Are not so careles	Edw	4.3.22	Edward
And with a lowly conge to the ground,	Edw	5.4.49	Mortmr
The framing of this circle on the ground/Brings Thunder,	F 545	2.1.157	Mephst
unlesse <except> the ground be <were> perfum'd, and cover'd	F 670	2.2.119	P Pride
That underprop <underprops> the ground-worke of the same:	F 812	3.1.34	Mephst
and his owne waight/Keepe him within the ground, his armes al	Lucan, First Booke	140	
The ground which Curius and Camillus till'd,	Lucan, First Booke	170	
what store cf ground/For servitors to till?	Lucan, First Booke	344	
What wals thou wilt be leaveld with the ground,	Lucan, First Booke	384	
and the rest/Marcht not intirely, and yet hide the ground,	Lucan, First Booke	474	
And without ground, fear'd, what themselves had faind:	Lucan, First Booke	482	
No such voice-feigning bird was on the ground,	Ovid's Elegies	2.6.23	
And on the soft ground fertile greene grasse growe.	Ovid's Elegies	2.16.6	
But without thee, although vine-planted ground/Conteines me,	Ovid's Elegies	2.16.33	
Sterne was her front, her [cloake] <looke> on ground did lie.	Ovid's Elegies	3.1.12	
This thou wilt say to be a worthy ground.	Ovid's Elegies	3.1.26	
But on the ground thy cloathes too loosely lie,	Ovid's Elegies	3.2.25	
First to be throwne upon the untill'd ground.	Ovid's Elegies	3.5.16	
The ditcher no markes on the ground did leave.	Ovid's Elegies	3.7.42	
if Corcyras Ile/Had thee unknowne interr'd in ground most vile.	Ovid's Elegies	3.8.48	
And untild ground with crooked plough-shares broake.	Ovid's Elegies	3.9.14	
When well-toss'd mattocks did the ground prepare,	Ovid's Elegies	3.9.31	
And Juno like with Dis raignes under ground?	Ovid's Elegies	3.9.46	
The annuall pompe goes on the covered ground.	Ovid's Elegies	3.12.12	
Where little ground to be inclosd befalles,	Ovid's Elegies	3.14.12	
A greater ground with great horse is to till.	Ovid's Elegies	3.14.18	
From whence her vaile reacht to the ground beneath.	Hero and Leander	1.18	
Vaild to the ground, vailing her eie-lids close,	Hero and Leander	1.159	
As sheap-heards do, her on the ground hee layd,	Hero and Leander	1.405	
ringled bit, and with his hoves,/Checkes the submissive ground:	Hero and Leander	2.144	
him to the bottome, where the ground/Was strewd with pearle,	Hero and Leander	2.160	
GROUNDED			
And as a sure and grounded argument,	1Tamb	1.2.184	Tamb
He that is grounded in Astrology,	F 165	1.1.137	Cornel
Love deepely grounded, hardly is dissembled.	Hero and Leander	1.184	
GROUNDS			
In champion grounds, what figure serves you best,	2Tamb	3.2.63	Tamb
GROUND-WORKE			
That underprop <underprops> the ground-worke of the same:	F 812	3.1.34	Mephst
GROVE			
and in this grove/Amongst greene brakes Ile lay Ascanius,	Dido	2.1.316	Venus
One like Actaeon peeping through the grove,	Edw	1.1.67	Gavstn
That I may conjure in some bushy <lustie> Grove,	F 178	1.1.150	Faust
Then hast thee to some solitary Grove,	F 180	1.1.152	Valdes
Then gentle Fredericke hie thee to the grove,	F1340	4.2.16	Benvol
Come souldiers, follow me unto the grove,	F1348	4.2.24	Fredrk
Heere while I walke hid close in shadie grove,	Ovid's Elegies	3.1.5	
Her wide sleeves greene, and bordered with a grove,	Hero and Leander	1.11	
GROVELING			
Who groveling in the mire of Zanthus bankes,	Dido	2.1.150	Aeneas
To me and Peter, shalt thou groveling lie,	F 873	3.1.95	Pope
GROVES			
Thou in those Groves, by Dis above,	Jew	4.2.97	Ithimr
Whose bankes are set with Groves of fruitfull Vines.	F 786	3.1.8	Faust
In unfeld woods, and sacred groves you dwell,	Lucan, First Booke	448	
In woddie groves ist meete that Ceres Raigne,	Ovid's Elegies	1.1.13	
But woods and groves keepe your faults undetected.	Ovid's Elegies	3.5.84	
Ida the seate of groves did sing with corne,	Ovid's Elegies	3.9.39	
the ground/Was strewd with pearle, and in low corrall groves,	Hero and Leander	2.161	
That Vallies, groves, hills and fieldes,	Passionate Shepherd	3	
GROW			
Whether from earth, or hell, or heaven he grow.	1Tamb	2.6.23	Ortyg
Should by his soveraignes favour grow so pert,	Edw	1.4.404	Mortmr
Ye must not grow so passionate in speeches:	Edw	4.4.16	Mortmr
see al plants, hearbes and trees that grow upon the earth].	F 551.9	2.1.172A	P Faust
If sin by custome grow not into nature:	F1713	5.1.40	OldMan
Within a while great heapes grow of a tittle.	Ovid's Elegies	1.8.90	
Tis shame tc grow rich by bed merchandize,	Ovid's Elegies	1.10.41	
Of wealth and honour so shall grow thy heape,	Ovid's Elegies	2.2.39	
And I grow faint, as with some spirit haunted?	Ovid's Elegies	3.6.36	
GROWE			
If I be cruell, and growe tyrannous,	Edw	2.2.206	Edward

GROWE (cont.)			
But Leister leave to growe so passionate,	Edw	4.7.55	Leistr
He that will not growe slothfull let him love.	Ovid's Elegies		1.9.46
By thine owne hand and fault thy hurt doth growe,	Ovid's Elegies		1.14.43
And on the soft ground fertile greene grasse growe.	Ovid's Elegies		2.16.6
GROWES			
Since this Towne was besieg'd, my gaine growes cold:	Jew	3.1.1	Curtzn
That waites your pleasure, and the day growes old.	Edw	4.7.85	Leistr
He growes to prowd in his authority,	F 911	3.1.133	Pope
Thence growes the Judge, and knight of reputation.	Ovid's Elegies		3.7.56
good growes by this griefe,/Oft bitter juice brings to the	Ovid's Elegies		3.10.7
But love resisted once, growes passionate,	Hero and Leander		2.139
GROWEST			
if thou now growest penitent/Ile be thy ghostly father,	Edw	5.6.3	Mortmr
GROWNE			
How now Getulian, are ye growne so brave,	Dido	3.3.19	Dido
Thy victories are growne so violent,	2Tamb	4.1.140	Jrslem
And now at length am growne your Governor,	Jew	5.2.70	Barab
Am I growne olde, or is thy lust growne yong,	P 681	13.25	Guise
And that young Cardinall that is growne so proud?	P1056	19.126	King
And hew these knees that now are growne so stiffe.	Edw	1.1.95	Edward
But cannot brooke a night growne mushrump,	Edw	1.4.284	Mortmr
The yonger Mortimer is growne so brave,	Edw	2.2.232	Edward
<Belike he is growne into some sicknesse, by> being over	F1829	(HC270)A	P 3Schol
Cut is the branch that might have growne full straight,	F2002	5.3.20	4Chor
Can I but loath a husband growne a baude?	Ovid's Elegies		2.19.57
Floud with [reede-growne] <redde-growne> slime bankes, till I	Ovid's Elegies		3.5.1
'Tis so: by my witte her abuse is growne.	Ovid's Elegies		3.11.8
GRUDGE			
And if he grudge or crosse his Mothers will,	P 523	9.42	QnMoth
Nor lesse at mans prosperity any grudge.	Ovid's Elegies		3.9.6
GRUNT			
Anon you shal heare a hogge grunt, a calfe bleate, and an asse	F App	p.232 27	P Faust
GRUNTLAND			
Vast Gruntland compast with the frozen sea,	2Tamb	1.1.26	Orcan
GRUNTS			
grunts like a hog, and looks/Like one that is imploy'd in	Jew	4.3.11	Barab
GUALLATIA			
We have subdude the Southerne Guallatia,	2Tamb	1.3.178	Usumc
GUARD (See also GARD)			
And will my guard with Mauritanian darts,	Dido	4.4.68	Dido
Commaund my guard to slay for their offence:	Dido	4.4.72	Dido
Open the Males, yet guard the treasure sure,	1Tamb	1.2.138	Tamb
What if you sent the Bassoes of your guard,	1Tamb	3.1.17	Fesse
Bassoes and Janisaries of my Guard,	1Tamb	3.3.61	Bajzth
And guard the gates to entertaine his soule.	2Tamb	3.5.29	Orcan
and Barabas we give/To guard thy person, these our Janizaries:	Jew	5.2.16	Calym
[all] <call> the world/To rescue thee, so will we guard us now,	Jew	5.5.120	Govnr
Fearst thou thy person? thou shalt have a guard:	Edw	1.1.166	Edward
Wel, let that peevish Frenchman guard him sure,	Edw	1.2.7	Mortmr
Like Lyons shall they guard us when we please,	F 151	1.1.123	Valdes
She whom her husband, guard, and gate as foes,	Ovid's Elegies		2.12.3
hoping time would beate thee/To guard her well, that well I	Ovid's Elegies		2.19.50
By me Corinna learnes, cousening her guard,	Ovid's Elegies		3.1.49
Though thou her body guard, her minde is staind:	Ovid's Elegies		3.4.5
I have thy husband, guard, and fellow plaied.	Ovid's Elegies		3.10.18
GUARDE			
[Cossin] <Cosin> <Cousin>, take twenty of our strongest guarde,	P 266	4.64	Charls
[Cossin] <Cosin> <Cousin>, the Captaine of the Admirals guarde,	P 293	5.20	Anjoy
What should I doe but stand upon my guarde?	P 839	17.34	Guise
Now Captain of my guarde, are these murtherers ready?	P 947	19.17	King
Come follow me, and thou shalt have my guarde,	Edw	1.1.204	Edward
Nay more, the guarde upon his lordship waites:	Edw	1.2.21	Lncstr
That therewith all enchaunted like the guarde,	Edw	3.1.266	Spencr
Guarde the king sure, it is the earle of Kent.	Edw	5.3.50	Matrvs
GUARDED			
And guarded with a thousand grislie ghosts,	Dido	1.1.59	Venus
With armes or armed men I come not guarded,	Ovid's Elegies		1.6.33
GUARDIAN			
Then let some other be his guardian.	Edw	5.2.36	Queene
GUARDST			
Thou thunderer that guardst/Roomes mighty walles built on	Lucan, First Booke		197
GUELDER			
Praysing for me some unknowne Guelder dame,	Ovid's Elegies		1.14.49
GUERDON			
And reape no guerdon for my truest love?	Dido	5.1.282	Iarbus
Now shall I prove and guerdon to the ful,	P 68	2.11	Guise
And then Ile guerdon thee with store of crownes.	P 89	2.32	Guise
GUESSE			
And as I guesse will first arrive at Rome,	F 775	2.3.54	2Chor
What my old Guesse?	F1507	4.5.3	P Hostss
now you have sent away my guesse, I pray who shall pay me for	F1667	4.6.110	P Hostss
By speechlesse lookes we guesse at things succeeding.	Ovid's Elegies		1.11.18
GUEST			
Both happie that Aeneas is our guest:	Dido	2.1.82	Dido
To rob their mistresse of her Troian guest?	Dido	4.4.138	Dido
The Pope had never such a frolicke guest.	F1036	3.2.56	Faust
What my old Guest?	F1514	4.5.10	P Hostss
Shall I sit gazing as a bashfull guest,	Ovid's Elegies		1.4.3
And some guest viewing watry Sulmoes walles,	Ovid's Elegies		3.14.11
Thither resorted many a wandring guest,	Hero and Leander		1.94
GUESTS			
And cause we are no common guests,	F 805	3.1.27	Mephst

GUESTS (cont.)			
Now many guests were gone, the feast being done, . .	Ovid's Elegies		2.5.21
GUIDANCE			
Aspir'st unto the guidance of the sunne.	Edw	1.4.17	Warwck
Phaeton had got/The guidance of the sunnes rich chariot. .	Hero and Leander		1.102
GUIDE			
And now ye gods that guide the starrie frame, ...	Dido	5.1.302	Dido
Meander, you that were our brothers Guide, ...	1Tamb	2.5.10	Cosroe
The horse that guide the golden eie of heaven, ...	2Tamb	4.3.7	Tamb
Were woont to guide the seaman in the deepe, ...	2Tamb	5.1.65	Tamb
And guide this massy substance of the earthe, ...	2Tamb	5.3.18	Techel
As that which [Clymens] <Clymeus> brainsicke sonne did guide,	2Tamb	5.3.231	Tamb
chariot wil not beare/A guide of baser temper than my selfe,	2Tamb	5.3.243	Tamb
Grave Abbasse, and you happy Virgins guide, ...	Jew	1.2.314	Abigal
Thus God we see doth ever guide the right, ...	P 789	16.3	Navrre
To guide thy steps unto the way of life, ...	F App	p.243 35	OldMan
Undaunted though her former guide be chang'd. . . .	Lucan, First Booke		50
I guide and souldiour wunne the field and weare her, .	Ovid's Elegies		2.12.13
The bawde I play, lovers to her I guide:	Ovid's Elegies		3.11.11
GUIDER			
The guider of all crownes,/Graunt that our deeds may wel .	P 599	12.12	King
GUIDES			
their Spheares/That guides his steps and actions to the throne,	1Tamb	2.1.17	Menaph
What cursed power guides the murthering hands, . . .	1Tamb	5.1.403	Arabia
And guides my feete least stumbling falles they catch. .	Ovid's Elegies		1.6.8
That Paphos, and the floud-beate Cithera guides. . .	Ovid's Elegies		2.17.4
GUIDING			
Guiding thy chariot with thy Fathers hand.	2Tamb	5.3.229	Tamb
Guiding the harmelesse Pigeons with thy hand. . . .	Ovid's Elegies		1.2.26
GUIE			
With Guie of Warwick that redoubted knight, ...	Edw	1.3.4	Gavstn
GUIFT			
And be thou king of Libia, by my guift.	Dido	3.4.64	Dido
Thou for some pettie guift hast let him goe, ...	Dido	5.1.218	Dido
GUIFTS			
Thy woorth sweet friend is far above my guifts, . .	Edw	1.1.161	Edward
GUILDED			
With beautie of thy wings, thy faire haire guilded, . .	Ovid's Elegies		1.2.41
GUILDERS (See also GILDERS)			
Well sirra, leave your jesting, and take these Guilders. .	F 367	1.4.25	P Wagner
Here, take your Guilders [againe], I'le none of 'em. .	F 371	1.4.29	P Robin
GUILE			
Come Guise and see thy traiterous guile outreacht, . .	P 962	19.32	King
Who with incroching guile, keepes learning downe. . .	Hero and Leander		1.482
GUILT (Homograph)			
Surchargde with guilt of thousand massacres, ...	P1022	19.92	King
Whose bloud alone must wash away thy guilt. . . .	F App	p.243 45	OldMan
The lining, purple silke, with guilt starres drawne, .	Hero and Leander		1.10
GUILTIE			
hands of mine/Shall not be guiltie of so foule a crime. .	Edw	5.1.99	Edward
If you be guiltie, though I be your sonne, ...	Edw	5.6.81	King
On Hellespont guiltie of True-loves blood, ...	Hero and Leander		1.1
GUILTLES			
Our kinsmens [lives] <loves>, and thousand guiltles soules,	Dido	4.4.90	Aeneas
That seeke to massacre our guiltles lives.	P 261	4.59	Admral
GUILTLESLY			
And guiltlesly endure a cruell death.	1Tamb	5.1.329	Zenoc
GUILTLESSE			
(Too litle to defend our guiltlesse lives)/Sufficient to .	2Tamb	2.2.60	Orcan
To exercise upon such guiltlesse Dames, ...	2Tamb	4.3.79	Orcan
My diadem I meane, and guiltlesse life.	Edw	5.1.73	Edward
GUILTY (See also GILTY)			
Least I should thinke thee guilty of offence. . . .	Ovid's Elegies		1.4.50
Her teares, she silent, guilty did pronounce me. . .	Ovid's Elegies		1.7.22
Tis shame sculd tongues the guilty should defend/Or great	Ovid's Elegies		1.10.39
Feare to be guilty, then thou maiest desemble. . . .	Ovid's Elegies		2.2.18
A scarlet blush her guilty face arayed.	Ovid's Elegies		2.5.34
Doost me of new crimes alwayes guilty frame? . . .	Ovid's Elegies		2.7.1
GUISE (See also GUIZE, GUYSE)			
Now Guise may storme but doe us little hurt:	P 28	1.28	Navrre
My Lord I mervaile that th'aspiring Guise/Dares once adventure	P 36	1.36	Admral
My Lord you need not mervaile at the Guise, ...	P 39	1.39	Condy
That Guise hath slaine by treason of his heart, . . .	P 45	1.45	Navrre
And thats the cause that Guise so frowns at us, . . .	P 52	1.52	Navrre
The love thou bear'st unto the house of Guise: . . .	P 69	2.12	Guise
Now Guise, begins those deepe ingendred thoughts/To burst	P 91	2.34	Guise
Then Guise,/Since thou hast all the Cardes	P 145	2.88	Guise
The late suspition of the Duke of Guise, ...	P 178	3.13	Navrre
My noble sonne, and princely Duke of Guise, ...	P 203	4.1	QnMoth
And to my Nephew heere the Duke of Guise:	P 226	4.24	Charls
Thankes to my princely sonne, then tell me Guise, . .	P 228	4.26	QnMoth
Now Guise shall catholiques flourish once againe, . .	P 295	5.22	Anjoy
The Duke of Guise stampes on thy liveles bulke. . .	P 315	5.42	Guise
Mountsorrell from the Duke of Guise.	P 347	6.2	Mntsrl
down, heer's one would speak with you from the Duke of Guise.	P 349	6.4	P SrnsWf
Thou traitor Guise, lay of thy bloudy hands. . . .	P 439	7.79	Navrre
Beleeve me Guise he becomes the place so well, . . .	P 495	9.14	QnMoth
Doe so sweet Guise, let us delay no time, ...	P 505	9.24	QnMoth
Be gone, delay no time sweet Guise.	P 509	9.28	QnMoth
For the late nights worke which my Lord of Guise/Did make in	P 514	9.33	QnMoth
O Mounser de Guise, heare me but speake.	P 529	10.2	Prtsnt
For feare that Guise joyn'd with the King of Spaine, .	P 573	11.38	Navrre
Thy brother Guise and we may now provide, ...	P 636	12.49	QnMoth

GUISE (cont.)			
My brother Guise hath gathered a power of men,	P 642	12.55	Cardnl
Come my [Lord] <Lords>, let us goe seek the Guise,	P 655	12.68	QnMoth
And Guise usurpes it, cause I am his wife:	P 661	13.5	Duchss
I meane the Guise, the Pope, and King of Spaine,	P 701	14.4	Navrre
And Guise for Spaine hath now incenst the King,	P 711	14.14	Navrre
This is the Guise that hath incenst the King,	P 729	14.32	Navrre
I would the Guise in his steed might have come,	P 736	14.39	Navrre
Farwell to my Lord of Guise and Epernoune.	P 750	15.8	Joyeux
So kindely Cosin of Guise you and your wife/Doe both salute our	P 752	15.10	King
How now Mugeroun, metst thou not the Guise at the doore?	P 774	15.32	King
My Lord of Guise, we understand that you/Have gathered a power	P 821	17.16	King
What Peere in France but thou (aspiring Guise)/Durst be in	P 828	17.23	Eprnon
Thou shouldst perceive the Duke of Guise is mov'd.	P 832	17.27	Guise
Be patient Guise and threat not Epernoune,	P 833	17.28	King
Guise, weare our crowne, and be thou King of France,	P 859	17.54	King
Then farwell Guise, the King and thou are freends.	P 870	17.65	King
That the Guise durst stand in armes against the King,	P 877	17.72	Eprnon
It would be good the Guise were made away,	P 888	17.83	Eprnon
But as I live, so sure the Guise shall dye.	P 899	17.94	King
That the Guise hath taken armes against the King,	P 901	18.2	Navrre
For we must aide the King against the Guise.	P 918	18.19	Navrre
That wicked Guise I feare me much will be,	P 921	18.22	Navrre
Hating the life and honour of the Guise?	P 932	19.2	Capt
For anon the Guise will come.	P 941	19.11	Capt
Hating the life and honour of the Guise?	P 950	19.20	King
Then come proud Guise and heere disgordge thy brest,	P 952	19.22	King
I prethee tell him that the Guise is heere.	P 958	19.28	Guise
And please your grace the Duke of Guise doth crave/Accesse unto	P 959	19.29	Eprnon
Come Guise and see thy traiterous guile outreacht,	P 962	19.32	King
Good morrow to my loving Cousin of Guise.	P 965	19.35	King
Now sues the King for favour to the Guise,	P 978	19.48	Guise
O pardon me my Lord of Guise.	P 990	19.60	P 3Mur
Tut they are pesants, I am Duke of Guise:	P 998	19.68	Guise
My Lord, see where the Guise is slaine.	P1019	19.89	Capt
(As all the world shall know our Guise is dead)/Rest satisfied	P1042	19.112	King
These two will make one entire Duke of Guise,	P1060	19.130	King
I slew the Guise, because I would be King.	P1066	19.136	King
The Guise is slaine, and I rejoyce therefore:	P1078	19.148	King
Sweet Guise, would he had died so thou wert heere:	P1082	19.152	QnMoth
And all for thee my Guise: what may I doe?	P1088	19.158	QnMoth
For since the Guise is dead, I will not live.	P1090	19.160	QnMoth
Sweet Duke of Guise our prop to leane upon,	P1110	21.4	Dumain
That durst attempt to murder noble Guise.	P1121	21.15	Dumain
Trayterouse guise ah thow hast murthered me	Paris	ms17,p390	Minion
GUISES			
but did you mark the Cardinall/The Guises brother, and the Duke	P 48	1.48	Admral
Shall drive no plaintes into the Guises eares,	P 532	10.5	Guise
Is Guises glory but a clowdy mist,	P 686	13.30	Guise
Lye there the Kings delight, and Guises scorne.	P 818	17.13	Guise
For now that Paris takes the Guises parte,	P 896	17.91	King
For in thee is the Duke of Guises hope.	P 988	19.58	Guise
lye there the kinges delyght and guises scorne	Paris	ms22,p390	Guise
fondlie hast thow in censte the guises sowle	Paris	ms25,p391	Guise
GUISIANS			
These are the cursed Guisians that doe seeke our death.	P 201	3.36	Admral
Ah my good Lord, these are the Guisians,	P 260	4.58	Admral
I feare the Guisians have past the bridge,	P 363	7.3	Ramus
The Guisians are hard at thy doore,	P 367	7.7	Taleus
Against the Guisians and their complices.	P 910	18.11	Navrre
And make the Guisians stoup that are alive.	P1071	19.141	King
GUIZE (Homograph)			
And now the Guize is dead, is come from France/To view this	Jew	Prol.3	Machvl
Oh muse not at it, 'tis the Hebrewes guize,	Jew	2.3.325	Barab
GUL			
Hush, Ile gul him supernaturally:	F App	p.234 5	P Robin
GULFE			
I never vow'd at Aulis gulfe/The desolation of his native Troy,	Dido	5.1.202	Dido
And with their Cannons mouth'd like Orcus gulfe/Batter the	1Tamb	3.1.65	Bajzth
That yeerely saile to the Venetian gulfe,	1Tamb	3.3.249	Tamb
From thence I crost the Gulfe, call'd by the name/Mare magiore,	2Tamb	1.3.214	Therid
Shall lead his soule through Orcus burning gulfe:	2Tamb	2.3.25	Orcan
In what gulfe either Syrtes have their seate.	Ovid's Elegies		2.11.20
GULFES			
The Rockes and Sea-gulfes will performe at large,	Dido	5.1.171	Dido
Nor thy gulfes crooked Malea, would I feare.	Ovid's Elegies		2.16.24
GUM			
And Illioneus gum and Libian spice,	Dido	4.4.8	Dido
GUNNES			
[Gunnes] <Swords>, poyson, halters, and invenomb'd steele,	F 573	2.2.22	Faust
GUNPOWDER			
Bombards, whole Barrels full of Gunpowder,	Jew	5.5.28	Barab
GUNS			
[Faustus, thou art damn'd, then swords <guns> and knives],	F 572	2.2.21A	Faust
GURNEY			
Whose there? call hither Gurney and Matrevis.	Edw	5.2.38	Mortmr
That he resigne the king to thee and Gurney,	Edw	5.2.49	Mortmr
Gurney.	Edw	5.2.51	Mortmr
Deliver this to Gurney and Matrevis,	Edw	5.4.41	Mortmr
Gurney, I wonder the king dies not,	Edw	5.5.1	Matrvs
Gurney, it was left unpointed for the nonce,	Edw	5.5.16	Matrvs
Gurney, my lord, is fled, and will I feare,	Edw	5.6.7	Matrvs
False Gurney hath betraide me and himselfe.	Edw	5.6.45	Mortmr

GURNEYS			
And then thy heart, were it as Gurneys is,	Edw	5.5.53	Edward
GUSH			
Gush forth bloud in stead of teares, yea life and soule:	F1851	5.2.55	P Faust
GUSHEST			
And in thy foule deepe waters thicke thou [gushest] <rushest>.	Ovid's Elegies		3.5.8
GUSHING			
Like water gushing from consuming snowe.	Ovid's Elegies		1.7.58
GUSTS			
The carefull ship-man now feares angry gusts,	Ovid's Elegies		2.11.25
GUTS			
Play, Fidler, or I'le cut your cats guts into chitterlins.	Jew	4.4.44	P Ithimr
GUY (See also GUIE)			
Wherfore is Guy of Warwicke discontent?	Edw	1.2.10	Mortmr
GUYRONS			
Neere Guyrons head doth set his conquering feet,	2Tamb	1.1.17	Gazell
GUYSE			
And then shall we in this detested guyse,	1Tamb	5.1.235	Bajzth
GYANTS			
Gyants as big as hugie Polypheme:	2Tamb	1.1.28	Orcan
I had in hand/Which for his heaven fell on the Gyants band.	Ovid's Elegies		2.1.16
GYGES			
Hundred-hand Gyges, and had done it well,	Ovid's Elegies		2.1.12
GYRLE			
As faire as was Pigmalions Ivory gyrle,	2Tamb	1.2.38	Callap
GYRT			
Who meanes to gyrt Natolias walles with siege,	2Tamb	3.5.8	2Msngr
GYVES			
Hale them to prison, lade their limbes with gyves:	F1032	3.2.52	Pope
H'			
H'had never bellowed in a brasen Bull/Of great ones envy; o'th	Jew	Prol.25	Machvl
H.			
A per se, a, t. h. e. the:	F 728	2.3.7	P Robin
HA' (See also HA'T)			
Ha' you forgotten me?	F1664	4.6.107	P Robin
HA (Homograph)			
Ha, to the East? yes: See how stands the Vanes?	Jew	1.1.40	Barab
Warily garding that which I ha got.	Jew	1.1.188	Barab
They hop'd my daughter would ha bin a Nun;	Jew	2.3.12	Barab
I ha the poyson of the City for him,	Jew	2.3.53	Barab
Oh, Mistresse, ha ha ha.	Jew	3.3.5	P Ithimr
Ha.	Jew	3.3.8	Abigal
Why, a Turke could ha done no more.	Jew	4.1.198	P Ithimr
Jew, I must ha more gold.	Jew	4.3.18	P Pilia
Ha, to the Jew, and send me mony you were best.	Jew	4.4.12	P Ithimr
And fit it should: but first let's ha more gold.	Jew	4.4.26	Curtzn
Relent, ha, ha, I use much to relent.	Edw	5.4.27	Ltborn
ha, Stipendium, &c.	F 66	1.1.38	P Faust
him, stop him, stop him--ha, ha, ha, Faustus hath his leg againe	F1496	4.4.40	P Faust
stop him--ha, ha, ha, Faustus hath his leg againe, and the	F1496	4.4.40	P Faust
ha, ha, Faustus hath his leg againe, and the Horse-courser a	F1496	4.4.40	P Faust
Ha, ha, ha, dost heare him Dick, he has forgot his legge.	F1629	4.6.72	P Carter
here I ha stolne one of doctor Faustus conjuring books, and	F App	p.233 1	P Robin
HABIT			
If outward habit judge the inward man.	1Tamb	1.2.163	Tamb
Leanders amorous habit soone reveal'd.	Hero and Leander		2.104
HABITATION			
[and] bloud, <or goods> into their habitation wheresoever.	F 499	2.1.111	P Faust
HABUISSE			
Solamen miseris socios habuisse doloris.	F 431	2.1.43	Mephst
HACKT			
His hands are hackt, some fingers cut quite off;	Jew	4.3.10	Barab
HAD (See also AD, H'HAD)			
Had not the heavens conceav'd with hel-borne clowdes,	Dido	1.1.125	Venus
And had my being from thy bubling froth:	Dido	1.1.129	Venus
Had not such passions in her head as I.	Dido	2.1.6	Aeneas
Thinking the sea had swallowed up thy ships,	Dido	2.1.68	Illion
O had it never entred, Troy had stood.	Dido	2.1.172	Aeneas
and had not we/Fought manfully, I had not told this tale:	Dido	2.1.270	Aeneas
and had not we/Fought manfully, I had not told this tale:	Dido	2.1.271	Aeneas
O had that ticing strumpet nere been borne:	Dido	2.1.300	Dido
(And yet have I had many mightier Kings)/Hast had the greatest	Dido	3.1.12	Dido
mightier Kings)/Hast had the greatest favours I could give:	Dido	3.1.13	Dido
doe know no wanton thought/Had ever residence in Didos breast.	Dido	3.1.17	Dido
I had been wedded ere Aeneas came:	Dido	3.1.138	Dido
But I had gold enough and cast him off:	Dido	3.1.162	Dido
Had not my Doves discov'rd thy entent:	Dido	3.2.33	Venus
And wish that I had never wrongd him so:	Dido	3.2.48	Juno
And planted love where envie erst had sprong.	Dido	3.2.52	Juno
And rather had seeme faire [to] Sirens eyes,	Dido	3.4.39	Dido
When sleepe but newly had imbrast the night,	Dido	4.3.17	Aeneas
Twas time to runne, Aeneas had been gone,	Dido	4.4.14	Anna
O that I had a charme to keepe the windes/Within the closure of	Dido	4.4.99	Dido
Had I a sonne by thee, the griefe were lesse,	Dido	5.1.149	Dido
If Nature had not given me wisedomes lore?	1Tamb	2.4.7	Mycet
With greatest pompe had crown'd thee Emperour.	1Tamb	2.5.5	Tamb
Than if the Gods had held a Parliament:	1Tamb	2.7.66	Tamb
And might, if my extreams had full events,	1Tamb	3.2.16	Zenoc
The entertainment we have had of him,	1Tamb	3.2.37	Zenoc
That never fought but had the victorie:	1Tamb	3.3.153	Tamb
And never had the Turkish Emperour/So great a foile by any	1Tamb	3.3.234	Bajzth
So might your highnesse, had you time to sort/Your fighting men,	1Tamb	4.1.36	Capol
Had never bene erected as they bee,	1Tamb	5.1.32	1Virgn

HAD (cont.)

Had fed the feeling of their maisters thoughts,	1Tamb	5.1.162	Tamb
If these had made one Poems period/And all combin'd in Beauties	1Tamb	5.1.169	Tamb
If I had not bin wounded as I am.	1Tamb	5.1.421	Arabia
Which had ere this bin bathde in streames of blood,	1Tamb	5.1.438	Tamb
Whose power had share in this our victory:	2Tamb	2.3.35	Orcan
And had she liv'd before the siege of Troy,	2Tamb	2.4.86	Tamb
Had not bene nam'd in Homers Iliads:	2Tamb	2.4.89	Tamb
Her name had bene in every line he wrote:	2Tamb	2.4.90	Tamb
Or had those wanton Poets, for whose byrth/Olde Rome was proud,	2Tamb	2.4.91	Tamb
Nor Lesbia, nor Corrinna had bene nam'd,	2Tamb	2.4.93	Tamb
Zenocrate had bene the argument/Of every Epigram or Eligie.	2Tamb	2.4.94	Tamb
If I had wept a sea of teares for her,	2Tamb	3.2.47	Calyph
Ile make thee wish the earth had swallowed thee:	2Tamb	3.5.118	Tamb
He comes and findes his sonnes have had no shares/In all the	2Tamb	4.1.47	Amyras
Supposing amorous Jove had sent his sonne,	2Tamb	4.2.18	Therid
What right had Caesar to the [Empery] <Empire>?	Jew	Prol.19	Machvl
Which maxime had Phaleris observ'd,	Jew	Prol.24	Machvl
H'had never bellowed in a brasen Bull/Of great ones envy; o'th	Jew	Prol.25	Machvl
That had the Gallies of the Turke in chase.	Jew	1.1.97	2Merch
Rather had I a Jew be hated thus,	Jew	1.1.114	Barab
For to be short, amongst you 'tmust be had.	Jew	1.2.56	Govnr
he had seven thousand sheepe,/Three thousand Camels, and two	Jew	1.2.182	Barab
Had they beene valued at indifferent rate,	Jew	1.2.186	Barab
I had at home, and in mine Argosie/And other ships that came	Jew	1.2.187	Barab
For I had rather dye, then see her thus.	Jew	1.2.357	Barab
As had you seene her 'twould have mov'd your heart,	Jew	1.2.385	Mthias
Oh Abigal, Abigal, that I had thee here too,	Jew	2.1.51	Barab
Their creeping Gallyes had us in the chase:	Jew	2.2.12	Bosco
Here comes the Jew, had not his goods bin seiz'd,	Jew	2.3.5	1Offcr
Oh, Sir, your father had my Diamonds.	Jew	2.3.49	Barab
Seiz'd all I had, and thrust me out a doores,	Jew	2.3.76	Barab
as you went in at dores/You had bin stab'd, but not a word on't	Jew	2.3.338	Barab
a hundred of the Jewes Crownes that I had such a Concubine.	Jew	3.1.28	P Ithimr
bottle-nos'd knave to my Master, that ever Gentleman had.	Jew	3.3.10	P Ithimr
saies, he that eats with the devil had need of a long spoone.	Jew	3.4.59	P Ithimr
I was afraid the poyson had not wrought;	Jew	4.1.4	Barab
Pull hard, I say, you would have had my goods.	Jew	4.1.149	Barab
and when the Hangman had put on his hempen Tippet, he made such	Jew	4.2.23	P Ithimr
to his prayers, as if hee had had another Cure to serve; well,	Jew	4.2.24	P Ithimr
sort as if he had meant to make cleane my Boots with his lips;	Jew	4.2.30	P Ithimr
Sweet Bellamira, would I had my Masters wealth for thy sake.	Jew	4.2.55	P Ithimr
for your sake, and said what a faithfull servant you had bin.	Jew	4.2.110	P Pilia
I had not thought he had been so brave a man.	Jew	4.4.16	Curtzn
Had we but proofe of this--	Jew	5.1.15	Govnr
One dram of powder more had made all sure.	Jew	5.1.22	Barab
Now where's the hope you had of haughty Spaine?	Jew	5.2.3	Calym
had it not beene much better/To [have] kept thy promise then be	Jew	5.2.4	Calym
And in this City still have had successe,	Jew	5.2.69	Barab
And had I but escap'd this stratagem,	Jew	5.5.84	Barab
If that the King had given consent thereto,	P 33	1.33	Navrre
And had his alters deckt with duskie lightes:	P 59	2.2	Guise
Had late been pluckt from out faire Cupids wing:	P 668	13.12	Duchss
Not I my Lord, what if I had?	P 775	15.33	Mugern
Marry if thou hadst, thou mightst have had the stab,	P 776	15.34	King
For had your highnesse seene with what a pompe/He entred Paris,	P 872	17.67	Eprnon
I would that I had murdered thee my sonne.	P1073	19.143	QnMoth
Sweet Guise, would he had died so thou wert heere:	P1082	19.152	QnMoth
Ah, had your highnes let him live,	P1183	22.45	Eprnon
For which, had not his highnes lov'd him well,	Edw	1.1.112	Kent
Had chaungd my shape, or at the mariage day/The cup of Hymen	Edw	1.4.173	Queene
at the mariage day/The cup of Hymen had beene full of poyson,	Edw	1.4.174	Queene
I had beene stifled, and not lived to see,	Edw	1.4.176	Queene
Ah had some bloudlesse furie rose from hell,	Edw	1.4.316	Edward
The mightiest kings have had their minions,	Edw	1.4.391	MortSr
But I had thought the match had beene broke off,	Edw	2.1.25	Baldck
And that his banishment had changd her minde.	Edw	2.1.26	Baldck
Would Lancaster and he had both carroust,	Edw	2.2.237	Edward
Had power to mollifie his stonie hart,	Edw	2.4.20	Queene
That when I had him we might never part.	Edw	2.4.21	Queene
Hearing that you had taken Gaveston,	Edw	2.5.35	Arundl
him, but must we now/Leave him on had-I-wist, and let him go?	Edw	2.5.85	Warwck
and when they flatly had denyed,/Refusing to receive me pledge	Edw	3.1.106	Arundl
When we had sent our messenger to request/He might be spared to	Edw	3.1.234	Edward
A will be had ere long I doubt it not.	Edw	4.3.20	Spencr
I would he never had bin flattered more.	Edw	4.4.30	Kent
Thy speeches long agoe had easde my sorrowes,	Edw	5.1.6	Edward
As Leicester that had charge of him before.	Edw	5.2.35	BshpWn
Had Edmund liv'de, he would have sought thy death.	Edw	5.4.112	Queene
And had you lov'de him halfe so well as I,	Edw	5.6.35	King
Had I as many soules, as there be Starres,	F 330	1.3.102	Faust
I had need to have it well rosted, and good sauce to it,	F 352	1.4.10	P Robin
Had not sweete pleasure conquer'd deepe despaire.	F 576	2.2.25	Faust
I had neither father nor mother, I leapt out of a Lyons mouth	F 686	2.2.135	P Wrath
my selfe when I could get none <had no body> to fight withall:	F 689	2.2.138	P Wrath
you had best leave your foolery, for an my Maister come, he'le	F 734	2.3.13	P Dick
The Pope had never such a frolicke guest.	F1036	3.2.56	Faust
you have had a shroud journey of it, will it please you to take	F1120	3.3.33	P Robin
[When Faustus had with pleasure tane the view]/[Of rarest	F1138	3.3.51A	3Chor
Had on her necke a little wart, or mole;	F1267	4.1.113	Emper
And had you cut my body with your swords,	F1397	4.2.73	Faust
Yet in a minute had my spirit return'd,	F1399	4.2.75	Faust
And I had breath'd a man made free from harme.	F1400	4.2.76	Faust

HAD (cont.)

thinking some hidden mystery had beene in the horse, I had	F1485	4.4.29	P	HrsCsr
I had nothing under me but a little straw, and had much ado to	F1486	4.4.30	P	HrsCsr
me but a little straw, and had much ado to escape drowning:	F1486	4.4.30	P	HrsCsr
he never left eating, till he had eate up all my loade of hay.	F1531	4.5.27	P	Carter
so when I had my horse, Doctor Fauster bad me ride him night	F1539	4.5.35	P	HrsCsr
had had some [rare] quality that he would not have me know of,	F1542	4.5.38	P	HrsCsr
till I had pul'd me his leg quite off, and now 'tis at home in	F1551	4.5.47	P	HrsCsr
is barren of his fruite, from whence you had these ripe grapes.	F1580	4.6.23	P	Duke
spirit that I have, I had these grapes brought as you see.	F1586	4.6.29	P	Faust
O horrible, had the Doctor three legs?	F1658	4.6.101	P	All
chamber-fellow, had I liv'd with thee, then had I lived still,	F1824	5.2.28	P	Faust
thee, then had I lived still, but now must <I> dye eternally.	F1825	5.2.29	P	Faust
O would I had never seene Wittenberg <Wertenberge>, never read	F1841	5.2.45	P	Faust
Innumerable joyes had followed thee.	F1893	5.2.97		GdAngl
To want in hell, that had on earth such store.	F1898	5.2.102		BdAngl
Hell, or the Divell, had had no power on thee.	F1902	5.2.106		GdAngl
burladie I had neede have it wel roasted, and good sawce to it,	F App	p.229 11	P	Clown
with my flesh, as if they had payd for my meate and drinke.	F App	p.230 29	P	Clown
stand aside you had best, I charge you in the name of Belzabub:	F App	p.235 19	P	Robin
you have had a great journey, wil you take sixe pence in your	F App	p.235 40	P	Robin
how they had wonne by prowesse such exploits, gote such riches,	F App	p.236 19	P	Emper
this Lady while she liv'd had a wart or moale in her necke,	F App	p.238 60	P	Emper
if he had but the qualitie of hey ding, ding, hey, ding, ding,	F App	p.239 115	P	HrsCsr
had had some rare qualitie that he would not have had me knowne	F App	p.240 131	P	HrsCsr
had some rare qualitie that he would not have had me knowne of,	F App	p.240 131	P	HrsCsr
had some rare qualitie that he would not have had me knowne of,	F App	p.240 132	P	HrsCsr
swift spirit that I have, I had them brought hither, as ye see,	F App	p.242 23	P	Faust
Scythia and wilde Armenia had bin yoakt,	Lucan, First Booke	19		
Had fild Assirian Carras wals with bloud,	Lucan, First Booke	105		
had heaven given thee longer life/Thou hadst restrainde thy	Lucan, First Booke	115		
which of both/Had justest cause unlawful tis to judge:	Lucan, First Booke	127		
Each side had great partakers; Caesars cause,	Lucan, First Booke	128		
And then large limits had their butting lands,	Lucan, First Booke	169		
Which being broke the foot had easie passage.	Lucan, First Booke	224		
Now light had quite dissolv'd the mysty [night] <might>,	Lucan, First Booke	263		
Had forraine wars ill thriv'd; or wrathful France/Pursu'd us	Lucan, First Booke	308		
they had houses:	Lucan, First Booke	347		
And without ground, fear'd, what themselves had faind:	Lucan, First Booke	482		
You would have thought their houses had bin fierd/Or	Lucan, First Booke	490		
when by Junoes taske/He had before lookt Pluto in the face.	Lucan, First Booke	576		
While these thus in and out had circled Roome,	Lucan, First Booke	604		
Whose like Aegiptian Memphis never had/For skill in stars, and	Lucan, First Booke	639		
She nothing said, pale feare her tongue had tyed.	Ovid's Elegies	1.7.20		
Would of mine armes, my shoulders had beene scanted,	Ovid's Elegies	1.7.23		
To mine owne selfe have I had strength so furious?	Ovid's Elegies	1.7.25		
Then first I did perceive I had offended,	Ovid's Elegies	1.7.59		
Pleasure, and ease had mollifide my minde.	Ovid's Elegies	1.9.42		
for needfull uses/Ile prove had hands impure with all abuses.	Ovid's Elegies	1.12.16		
More fitly had [they] <thy> wrangling bondes contained/From	Ovid's Elegies	1.12.23		
Among day bookes and billes they had laine better/In which the	Ovid's Elegies	1.12.25		
But what had beene more faire had they beene kept?	Ovid's Elegies	1.14.3		
Beyond thy robes thy dangling [lockes] <lackes> had sweept.	Ovid's Elegies	1.14.4		
Hundred-hand Gyges, and had done it well,	Ovid's Elegies	2.1.12		
Jove and Joves thunderbolts I had in hand/Which for his heaven	Ovid's Elegies	2.1.15		
If ever wench had made luke-warme thy love:	Ovid's Elegies	2.3.6		
Rome if her strength the huge world had not fild,	Ovid's Elegies	2.9.17		
The Argos wrackt had deadly waters drunke.	Ovid's Elegies	2.11.6		
but for a Queene/Europe, and Asia in firme peace had beene.	Ovid's Elegies	2.12.18		
Had ancient Mothers this vile custome cherisht,	Ovid's Elegies	2.14.9		
All humaine kinde by their default had perisht.	Ovid's Elegies	2.14.10		
If watry Thetis had her childe fordone?	Ovid's Elegies	2.14.14		
In swelling wombe her twinnes had Ilia kilde?	Ovid's Elegies	2.14.15		
He had not beene that conquering Rome did build.	Ovid's Elegies	2.14.16		
Had Venus spoilde her bellies Troyane fruite,	Ovid's Elegies	2.14.17		
The earth of Caesars had beene destitute.	Ovid's Elegies	2.14.18		
If such a worke thy mother had assayed.	Ovid's Elegies	2.14.20		
My selfe that better dye with loving may/Had seene, my mother	Ovid's Elegies	2.14.22		
Had then swum over, but the way was blinde.	Ovid's Elegies	2.16.32		
Would I had beene my mistresse gentle prey,	Ovid's Elegies	2.17.5		
Egeria with just Numa had good sport,	Ovid's Elegies	2.17.18		
In brazen tower had not Danae dwelt,	Ovid's Elegies	2.19.27		
A mothers joy by Jove she had not felt.	Ovid's Elegies	2.19.28		
And yet remaines the face she had before.	Ovid's Elegies	3.3.2		
Sharpe eyes she had:	Ovid's Elegies	3.3.9		
But when her lover came, had she drawne backe,	Ovid's Elegies	3.3.39		
Argus had either way an hundred eyes,	Ovid's Elegies	3.4.19		
Now wish I those wings noble Perseus had,	Ovid's Elegies	3.5.13		
Troy had not yet beene ten yeares siege out-stander,	Ovid's Elegies	3.5.27		
My bones had beene, while yet I was a maide.	Ovid's Elegies	3.5.74		
Or she was not the wench I wisht t'have had.	Ovid's Elegies	3.6.2		
Yet like as if cold hemlocke I had drunke,	Ovid's Elegies	3.6.13		
And nine sweete bouts had we before day light.	Ovid's Elegies	3.6.26		
Even her I had, and she had me in vaine,	Ovid's Elegies	3.6.43		
I thinke the great Gods greeved they had bestowde/This <The>	Ovid's Elegies	3.6.45		
Chuf-like had I not gold, and could not use it?	Ovid's Elegies	3.6.50		
What sweete thought is there but I had the same?	Ovid's Elegies	3.6.63		
Jove being admonisht gold had soveraigne power,	Ovid's Elegies	3.7.29		
As when the wilde boare Adons groine had rent.	Ovid's Elegies	3.8.16		
if Corcyras Ile/Had thee unknowne interr'd in ground most vile.	Ovid's Elegies	3.8.48		
Yet this is lesse, then if he had seene me,	Ovid's Elegies	3.10.15		
With Muse oppos'd would I my lines had done,	Ovid's Elegies	3.11.17		
And Phoebus had forsooke my worke begun.	Ovid's Elegies	3.11.18		

HAD (cont.)

Upon their heads the holy mysteries had. . . . . . Ovid's Elegies 3.12.28
Had they beene cut, and unto Colchos borne, . . Hero and Leander 1.56
Had wilde Hippolitus, Leander seene, ... Hero and Leander 1.77
Enamoured of his beautie had he beene, ... Hero and Leander 1.78
To meet their loves; such as had none at all, . . Hero and Leander 1.95
As if another Phaeton had got/The guidance of the sunnes rich Hero and Leander 1.101
So faire a church as this, had Venus none, . . . Hero and Leander 1.135
I would my rude words had the influence, ... Hero and Leander 1.200
Compar'd with marriage, had you tried them both, . . Hero and Leander 1.263
The self-same day that he asleepe had layd/Inchaunted Argus, Hero and Leander 1.387
That she such lovelinesse and beautie had/As could provoke his Hero and Leander 1.422
Hermes had slept in hell with ignoraunce. . . . . Hero and Leander 1.468
As he had hope to scale the beauteous fort, . . . Hero and Leander 2.16
Had spread the boord, with roses strowed the roome, . . Hero and Leander 2.21
These greedie lovers had, at their first meeting. . . Hero and Leander 2.24
As if her name and honour had beene wrong'd, . . . Hero and Leander 2.35
Now he her favour and good will had wone. . . . Hero and Leander 2.54
Now had the morne espy'de her lovers steeds, . . . Hero and Leander 2.87
Leanders Father knew where hee had beene, ... Hero and Leander 2.136
Had left the heavens, therefore on him hee seaz'd. . . Hero and Leander 2.158

HAD-I-WIST

him, but must we now/Leave him on had-I-wist, and let him go? Edw 2.5.85 Warwck

HADST

O cursed tree, hadst thou but wit or sense, ... Dido 4.4.139 Dido
hadst thou perish'd by the Turke,/Wretched Ferneze might have Jew 3.2.13 Govnr
But wish thou hadst behav'd thee otherwise. . . . Jew 5.5.75 Govnr
Marry if thou hadst, thou mightst have had the stab, . P 776 15.34 King
O hadst thou ever beene a king, thy hart/Pierced deeply with Edw 4.7.9 Edward
Thou hadst not hatcht this monstrous treacherie! . . Edw 5.6.97 King
Oh <Ah> Faustus, if thou hadst given eare to me, . . F1892 5.2.96 GdAngl
Hadst thou affected sweet divinitie, ... F1901 5.2.105 GdAngl
Hadst thou kept on that way, Faustus behold, . . . F1903 5.2.107 GdAngl
In what resplendant glory thou hadst set/In yonder throne, like F1904 5.2.108 GdAngl
why I has thought thou hadst beene a batcheler, but now I see F App p.238 69 P Emper
longer life/Thou hadst restrainde thy headstrong husbands rage, Lucan, First Booke 116
But [heldst] <hadst> thou in thine armes some Caephalus, . Ovid's Elegies 1.13.39
Thou also, that wert borne faire, hadst decayed, . . Ovid's Elegies 2.14.19

HAEC

Oro, si quis [adhuc] <ad haec> precibus locus, exue mentem. Dido 5.1.138 Dido

HAEMUS (See HEMUS)

HAG

Out hatefull hag, thou wouldst have slaine my sonne, . Dido 3.2.32 Venus
Vile monster, borne of some infernal hag, ... 2Tamb 5.1.110 Govnr

HAGGE

O cursed hagge and false dissembling wretch! . . . Dido 5.1.216 Dido

HAGS

And hags howle for my death at Charons shore, . . . Edw 4.7.90 Edward

HAILD

It haild, it snowde, it lightned all at once. . . . Dido 4.1.8 Anna

HAILE (Homograph)

of the clowdes/And fall as thick as haile upon our heads, 2Tamb 2.2.15 Gazell
To haile the fatall Sisters by the haire, ... 2Tamb 2.4.99 Tamb
Weele haile him by the eares unto the block. . . . Edw 2.2.91 Lncstr

HAINAULT (See HENOLT)

HAINOUS

Murmures and hisses for his hainous sin. . . . . . 2Tamb 2.3.17 Orcan
the inward soule/With such flagitious crimes of hainous sinnes, F App p.243 42 OldMan
Is conquest got by civill war so hainous? . . . . Lucan, First Booke 367

HAIR'D

Golden-hair'd Ceres crownd with eares of corne, . . Ovid's Elegies 3.9.3

HAIRE (See also HAYRE, HEIRE)

By Saturnes soule, and this earth threatning [haire] <aire>, Dido 1.1.10 Jupitr
Yet shall the aged Sunne shed forth his [haire] <aire>, . Dido 1.1.159 Achat
Virgins halfe dead dragged by their golden haire, . . Dido 2.1.195 Aeneas
Her cheekes swolne with sighes, her haire all rent, . . Dido 2.1.276 Aeneas
Ile make me bracelets of his golden haire, . . . Dido 3.1.85 Dido
And strewe thy walkes with my discheveld haire. . . Dido 4.2.56 Anna
Then carelesly I rent my haire for griefe, . . . Dido 5.1.236 Anna
With haire discheweld wip'st thy watery cheeks: . . 1Tamb 5.1.139 Tamb
Their haire as white as milke and soft as Downe, . . 2Tamb 1.3.25 Tamb
To haile the fatall Sisters by the haire, ... 2Tamb 2.4.99 Tamb
here are Bugges/Wil make the haire stand upright on your heads, 2Tamb 3.5.148 Tamb
rebelling Jades/Wil take occasion by the slenderest haire, 2Tamb 5.3.239 Tamb
And rent their hearts with tearing of my haire, . . Jew 1.2.234 Abigal
To fast, to pray, and weare a shirt of haire, . . . Jew 4.1.61 Barab
With haire that gilds the water as it glides, . . . Edw 1.1.62 Gavstn
I, I, but he teares his haire, and wrings his handes, . Edw 5.6.18 Queene
Hell and the Furies forked haire, ... F1000 3.2.20 Mephst
Shaking her snakie haire and crooked pine/With flaming toppe, Lucan, First Booke 571
Yoke Venus Doves, put Mirtle on thy haire, . . . Ovid's Elegies 1.2.23
With beautie of thy wings, thy faire haire guilded, . . Ovid's Elegies 1.2.41
Now Germany shall captive haire-tyers send thee, . . Ovid's Elegies 1.14.45
And be heereafter seene with native haire. . . . Ovid's Elegies 1.14.56
If her white necke be shadowde with blacke haire, . . Ovid's Elegies 2.4.41
Cypassis that a thousand wayes trimst haire, . . . Ovid's Elegies 2.8.1
least their gownes tosse thy haire,/To hide thee in my bosome Ovid's Elegies 3.2.75
Scylla by us her fathers rich haire steales, . . . Ovid's Elegies 3.11.21
Like one start up your haire tost and displast, . . Ovid's Elegies 3.13.33
Whom young Apollo courted for her haire, ... Hero and Leander 1.6
Whose carelesse haire, in stead of pearle t'adorne it, . Hero and Leander 1.389

HAIRES

within whose silver haires/Honor and reverence evermore have 1Tamb 5.1.81 1Virgn

HAIRES (cont.)				
These silver haires will more adorne my court,	Edw	1.4.346		Edward
And on my haires a crowne of flowers remaine.	Ovid's Elegies	1.6.38		
But thou my crowne, from sad haires tane away,	Ovid's Elegies	1.6.67		
Put in their place thy keembed haires againe.	Ovid's Elegies	1.7.68		
In [skilfull] <skilfuld> gathering ruffled haires in order,	Ovid's Elegies	1.11.1		
Now hast thou left no haires at all to die.	Ovid's Elegies	1.14.2		
Oft in the morne her haires not yet digested,	Ovid's Elegies	1.14.19		
[Thy] <They> troubled haires, alas, endur'd great losse.	Ovid's Elegies	1.14.24		
I cryed, tis sinne, tis sinne, these haires to burne,	Ovid's Elegies	1.14.27		
Thy very haires will the hot bodkin teach.	Ovid's Elegies	1.14.30		
For wofull haires let piece-torne plumes abound,	Ovid's Elegies	2.6.5		
If I praise any, thy poore haires thou tearest,	Ovid's Elegies	2.7.7		
Shee dyes, and with loose haires to grave is sent,	Ovid's Elegies	2.14.39		
Elegia came with haires perfumed sweete,	Ovid's Elegies	3.1.7		
Her cheekes were scratcht, her goodly haires discheveld.	Ovid's Elegies	3.5.48		
Sad Elegia thy wofull haires unbinde:	Ovid's Elegies	3.8.3		
Her long haires eare-wrought garland fell away.	Ovid's Elegies	3.9.36		
Wee cause feete flie, wee mingle haires with snakes,	Ovid's Elegies	3.11.23		
HAIRE-TYERS				
Now Germany shall captive haire-tyers send thee,	Ovid's Elegies	1.14.45		
HALCIONS				
Into what corner peeres my Halcions bill?	Jew	1.1.39		Barab
HAL'D				
When as they would have hal'd thee from my sight:	Dido	1.1.27		Jupitr
HALDE				
Pean whither am I halde?	Lucan, First Booke	677		
HALE (See also HAILE)				
These hands did helpe to hale it to the gates,	Dido	2.1.170		Aeneas
looking out/When you should come and hale him from the doore.	Jew	2.3.265		Barab
Though womans modesty should hale me backe,	Jew	4.2.45		Curtzn
I'le goe alone, dogs, do not hale me thus.	Jew	5.1.19		Barab
Weele hale him from the bosome of the king,	Edw	1.2.29		Mortmr
And therefore soldiers whether will you hale me?	Edw	5.4.108		Kent
But new exploits do hale him out agen,	F 770	2.3.49		2Chor
Hale them to prison, lade their limbes with gyves:	F1032	3.2.52		Pope
And hale the stubborne Furies from their caves,	F1225	4.1.71		Faust
Ah often, that her [hale] <haole> head aked, she lying,	Ovid's Elegies	2.19.11		
HALED				
Our Phrigian [shepherds] <shepherd> haled within the gates,/And	Dido	2.1.153		Aeneas
HALESUS				
Which fact, and country wealth Halesus fled.	Ovid's Elegies	3.12.32		
HALF				
I'le make him send me half he has, and glad he scapes so too.	Jew	4.2.67	P	Ithimr
out of a Lyons mouth when I was scarce <half> an houre old,	F 687	2.2.136	P	Wrath
HALFE				
Virgins halfe dead dragged by their golden haire,	Dido	2.1.195		Aeneas
To be a King, is halfe to be a God.	1Tamb	2.5.56		Usumc
Halfe dead for feare before they feele my wrath:	1Tamb	4.4.4		Tamb
Ah were I now but halfe so eloquent/To paint in woords, what	2Tamb	1.2.9		Callap
Sweet Almeda, scarse halfe a league from hence.	2Tamb	1.2.55		Callap
For halfe the world shall perish in this fight:	2Tamb	1.3.171		Tamb
Go too sirha, take your crown, and make up the halfe dozen.	2Tamb	3.5.136	P	Tamb
much like so many suns/That halfe dismay the majesty of heaven:	2Tamb	4.1.3		Amyras
If halfe our campe should sit and sleepe with me,	2Tamb	4.1.18		Calyph
These Jades are broken winded, and halfe tyr'd,	2Tamb	5.1.129		Tamb
the Jewes, and each of them to pay one halfe of his estate.	Jew	1.2.69	P	Reader
Oh my Lord we will give halfe.	Jew	1.2.77		3Jews
Then pay thy halfe.	Jew	1.2.83		Govnr
Halfe of my substance is a Cities wealth.	Jew	1.2.85		Barab
Sir, halfe is the penalty of our decree,	Jew	1.2.88		Govnr
Corpo di dio stay, you shall have halfe,	Jew	1.2.90		Barab
And of the other we have seized halfe.	Jew	1.2.135		Offcrs
Thou seest they have taken halfe our goods.	Jew	1.2.176		1Jew
And whilst I live use halfe; spend as my selfe;	Jew	3.4.45		Barab
would he lov'd me/But halfe so much, then were I treble blest.	Edw	1.4.304		Queene
And had you lov'de him halfe so well as I,	Edw	5.6.35		King
I tell thee Faustus it is <tis> not halfe so faire/As thou, or	F 557	2.2.6		Mephst
Halfe smother'd in a Lake of mud and durt,	F1434	4.3.4		Mrtino
What ho, give's halfe a dosen of Beere here, and be hang'd.	F1612	4.6.55	P	Robin
One drop [would save my soule, halfe a drop, ah] my Christ.	F1940	5.2.144		Faust
[Ah] <O> halfe the houre is past:	F1957	5.2.161		Faust
That now the walles of houses halfe [rear'd] <reaer'd> totter,	Lucan, First Booke	24		
appear'd/A knob of flesh, whereof one halfe did looke/Dead, and	Lucan, First Booke	627		
I am no halfe horse, nor in woods I dwell,	Ovid's Elegies	1.4.9		
The gate halfe ope my bent side in will take.	Ovid's Elegies	1.6.4		
Her halfe dead joynts, and trembling limmes I sawe,	Ovid's Elegies	1.7.53		
Halfe sleeping on a purple bed she rested,	Ovid's Elegies	1.14.20		
halfe to weping framed,/Aye me she cries, to love, why art	Ovid's Elegies	2.18.7		
Since Heroes time, hath halfe the world beene blacke.	Hero and Leander	1.50		
Heav'd up her head, and halfe the world upon,	Hero and Leander	1.190		
Ere halfe this tale was done,/Aye me, Leander cryde,	Hero and Leander	2.201		
In such warres women use but halfe their strength.	Hero and Leander	2.296		
One halfe appear'd, the other halfe was hid.	Hero and Leander	2.316		
HALFE A DOSEN				
What ho, give's halfe a dosen of Beere here, and be hang'd.	F1612	4.6.55	P	Robin
HALFE DEAD				
Her halfe dead joynts, and trembling limmes I sawe,	Ovid's Elegies	1.7.53		
HALFE DOZEN				
Go too sirha, take your crown, and make up the halfe dozen.	2Tamb	3.5.136	P	Tamb
HALING				
Haling him headlong to the lowest hell.	2Tamb	4.3.42		Orcan
These hands are tir'd, with haling of my lord/From Gaveston,	Edw	2.4.26		Queene

HALL			
See where her servitors passe through the hall/Bearing a	Dido	2.1.70	Serg
Or banquet in bright honors burnisht hall,	Dido	4.3.10	Aeneas
His Majesty is comming to the Hall;	F1158	4.1.4	Mrtino
looke up into th'hall there ho.	F1519	4.5.15	P Hostss
HALLA			
Of Sorians from Halla is repair'd/And neighbor cities of your	2Tamb	3.5.46	Soria
HALLES			
As Monestaries, Priories, Abbyes and halles,	P 138	2.81	Guise
HALLOWED			
Unto the hallowed person of a prince,	1Tamb	4.3.40	Souldn
HALLOWING			
I kept a hallowing and whooping in his eares, but all could not	F1549	4.5.45	P HrsCsr
HALTER			
he was ready to leape off e're the halter was about his necke;	Jew	4.2.22	P Ithimr
HALTERS			
[Gunnes] <Swords>, poyson, halters, and invenomb'd steele,	F 573	2.2.22	Faust
HALTS			
With his stumpe-foote he halts ill-favouredly.	Ovid's Elegies		2.17.20
HAMMERS			
Which beates upon it like the Cyclops hammers,	Edw	1.4.313	Edward
HAND			
And bind her hand and foote with golden cordes,	Dido	1.1.14	Jupitr
And this right hand shall make thy Altars crack/With mountaine	Dido	1.1.201	Aeneas
Why talke we not together hand in hand?	Dido	1.1.245	Aeneas
And kisse his hand: O where is Hecuba?	Dido	2.1.12	Achat
Achates, see King Priam wags his hand,	Dido	2.1.29	Aeneas
Foulding his hand in hers, and joyntly both/Beating their	Dido	2.1.227	Aeneas
in mine armes, and by the hand/Led faire Creusa my beloved wife,	Dido	2.1.266	Aeneas
Who warne me of such daunger prest at hand,	Dido	3.2.22	Venus
how may I deserve/Such amourous favours at thy beautious hand?	Dido	3.2.65	Juno
Bearing his huntspeare bravely in his hand.	Dido	3.3.33	Anna
turne the hand of fate/Unto that happie day of my delight,	Dido	3.3.80	Iarbus
With this my hand I give to you my heart,	Dido	3.4.43	Aeneas
Hold, take these Jewels at thy Lovers hand,	Dido	3.4.61	Dido
That with thy gloomie hand corrects the heaven,	Dido	4.2.6	Iarbus
And beare this golden Scepter in my hand?	Dido	4.4.41	Aeneas
canst thou take her hand?	Dido	5.1.121	Dido
Thy hand and mine have plighted mutuall faith,	Dido	5.1.122	Dido
By this right hand, and by our spousall rites,	Dido	5.1.134	Dido
And, see the Sailers take him by the hand,	Dido	5.1.189	Dido
Then gan he wagge his hand, which yet held up,	Dido	5.1.229	Anna
Bearing his privie signet and his hand:	1Tamb	1.2.15	Zenoc
A thousand Persean horsmen are at hand,	1Tamb	1.2.111	Souldr
And with my hand turne Fortunes wheel about,	1Tamb	1.2.175	Tamb
And Jove himselfe will stretch his hand from heaven,	1Tamb	1.2.180	Tamb
Theridamas my friend, take here my hand,	1Tamb	1.2.232	Tamb
The King your Brother is now hard at hand,	1Tamb	2.3.45	Tamb
Even by the mighty hand of Tamburlaine,	1Tamb	2.5.3	Tamb
To dy by this resolved hand of thine,	1Tamb	3.2.98	Agidas
This hand shal set them on your conquering heads:	1Tamb	3.3.31	Tamb
starv'd, and he be provided for a moneths victuall before hand.	1Tamb	4.4.47	P Usumc
ruthlesse Governour/Have thus refusde the mercie of thy hand,	1Tamb	5.1.93	1Virgn
Whereto ech man of rule hath given his hand,	1Tamb	5.1.102	1Virgn
Brought up and propped by the hand of fame,	1Tamb	5.1.265	Bajzth
Since thy desired hand shall close mine eies.	1Tamb	5.1.432	Arabia
Though my right hand have thus enthralled thee,	1Tamb	5.1.435	Tamb
Mighty hath God and Mahomet made thy hand/(Renowmed Tamburlain)	1Tamb	5.1.479	Souldn
Even by this hand that shall establish them,	1Tamb	5.1.492	Tamb
My hand is ready to performe the deed,	1Tamb	5.1.503	Techel
Then here I sheath it, and give thee my hand,	2Tamb	1.1.127	Sgsmnd
And by the hand of Mahomet I sweare,	2Tamb	1.2.65	Callap
Holds out his hand in highest majesty/To entertaine divine	2Tamb	2.4.32	Tamb
Therefore die by thy loving mothers hand,	2Tamb	3.4.23	Olymp
Crown'd and invested by the hand of Jove,	2Tamb	4.1.151	Tamb
Goe now and bind the Burghers hand and foot,	2Tamb	5.1.161	Tamb
And threaten him whose hand afflicts my soul,	2Tamb	5.3.47	Tamb
Guiding thy chariot with thy Fathers hand.	2Tamb	5.3.229	Tamb
Abrahams off-spring; and direct the hand/Of Abigall this night;	Jew	2.1.14	Barab
Having Fernezes hand, whose heart I'le have;	Jew	2.3.16	Barab
I learn'd in Florence how to kisse my hand,	Jew	2.3.23	Barab
before your mother/Lest she mistrust the match that is in hand:	Jew	2.3.147	Barab
Nay on my life it is my Factors hand,	Jew	2.3.240	Barab
What, hand in hand, I cannot suffer this.	Jew	2.3.276	Mthias
let him have thy hand,/But keepe thy heart till Don Mathias	Jew	2.3.306	Barab
Oh, master, that I might have a hand in this.	Jew	2.3.368	Ithimr
Both held in hand, and flatly both beguil'd.	Jew	3.3.3	Ithimr
The time you tooke for respite, is at hand,	Jew	3.5.8	Basso
the Nuns, and he and I, snicle hand too fast, strangled a Fryar.	Jew	4.4.21	P Ithimr
Here is my hand that I'le set Malta free:	Jew	5.2.95	Barab
Here is my hand, beleeve me, Barabas,	Jew	5.2.102	Govnr
For this, this head, this heart, this hand and sworde,	P 109	2.52	Guise
A hand, that with a graspe may gripe the world,	P 159	2.102	Guise
This wrathfull hand should strike thee to the hart.	P 690	13.34	Guise
I kisse your graces hand, and take my leave,	P 868	17.63	Guise
First let us set our hand and seale to this,	P 890	17.85	King
O that his heart were leaping in my hand.	P 936	19.6	P 2Mur
Navarre, give me thy hand, I heere do sweare,	P1203	22.65	King
Farewell, and perish by a souldiers hand,	Edw	1.1.37	3PrMan
kis not my hand,/Embrace me Gaveston as I do thee:	Edw	1.1.140	Edward
Their downfall is at hand, their forces downe,	Edw	1.4.18	Mortmr
Tis done, and now accursed hand fall off.	Edw	1.4.88	Edward
Once more receive my hand, and let this be,	Edw	1.4.334	Edward

HAND (cont.)			
But whiles I have a sword, a hand, a hart,	Edw	1.4.422	Mortmr
Or holding of a napkin in your hand,	Edw	2.1.36	Spencr
In vaine I looke for love at Edwards hand,	Edw	2.4.61	Queene
And that the Mortimers are in hand withall,	Edw	3.1.54	Edward
By this right hand, and by my fathers sword,	Edw	3.1.130	Edward
And hart and hand to heavens immortall throne,	Edw	4.7.108	Baldck
To seeke for mercie at a tyrants hand.	Edw	5.3.36	Edward
Or else die by the hand of Mortimer.	Edw	5.6.6	Mortmr
Yes, if this be the hand of Mortimer.	Edw	5.6.44	King
Tis my hand, what gather you by this.	Edw	5.6.47	Mortmr
I have other matters in hand, let the horses walk themselves	F 727	2.3.6	P Robin
No bigger then my hand in quantity.	F 851	3.1.73	Faust
The sleepy Cardinals are hard at hand,	F 982	3.2.2	Mephst
Whilst on thy head I lay my hand,	F 995	3.2.15	Mephst
The Emperour is at hand, who comes to see/What wonders by	F1197	4.1.43	Mrtino
I saw him kneele, and kisse the Emperours hand,	F1344	4.2.20	Benvol
Close, close, the Conjurer is at hand,	F1357	4.2.33	Fredrk
Strike with a willing hand, his head is off.	F1368	4.2.44	Mrtino
He and his servant Wagner are at hand,	F1813	5.2.17	Mephst
All torne asunder by the hand of death.	F1989	5.3.7	2Schol
before you have him, ride him not into the water at any hand.	F App	p.239 109	P Faust
appeasd/The wrastling tumult, and right hand made silence:	Lucan, First Booke		299
This [band] <hand> that all behind us might be quail'd,	Lucan, First Booke		370
This hand (albeit unwilling) should performe it;	Lucan, First Booke		379
Wars radge draws neare; and to the swords strong hand,	Lucan, First Booke		665
Guiding the harmelesse Pigeons with thy hand.	Ovid's Elegies		1.2.26
Griping his false hornes with hir virgin hand:	Ovid's Elegies		1.3.24
Lines thou shalt read in wine by my hand writ.	Ovid's Elegies		1.4.20
My Mistresse weepes whom my mad hand did harme.	Ovid's Elegies		1.7.4
The rest my hand doth in my letters write.	Ovid's Elegies		1.11.14
What neede she [tyre] <try> her hand to hold the quill,	Ovid's Elegies		1.11.23
By thine owne hand and fault thy hurt doth growe,	Ovid's Elegies		1.14.43
Hundred-hand Gyges, and had done it well,	Ovid's Elegies		2.1.12
Jove and Joves thunderbolts I had in hand/Which for his heaven	Ovid's Elegies		2.1.15
Her trembling hand writ back she might not doo.	Ovid's Elegies		2.2.6
Thy dull hand stayes thy striving enemies harmes.	Ovid's Elegies		2.9.12
Heere thou hast strength, here thy right hand doth rest.	Ovid's Elegies		2.9.36
And with thy hand assist [the] <thy> swelling saile.	Ovid's Elegies		2.11.42
With cruell hand why doest greene Apples pull?	Ovid's Elegies		2.14.24
Blest ring thou in my mistris hand shalt lye,	Ovid's Elegies		2.15.7
And hide thy left hand underneath her lappe.	Ovid's Elegies		2.15.12
go small gift from hand,/Let her my faith with thee given	Ovid's Elegies		2.15.27
Her left hand held abroad a regal scepter,	Ovid's Elegies		3.1.13
Erre I? or mirtle in her right hand lies.	Ovid's Elegies		3.1.34
But spare my wench thou at her right hand seated,	Ovid's Elegies		3.2.21
That from thy fanne, mov'd by my hand may blow?	Ovid's Elegies		3.2.38
Let with strong hand the reine to bend be made.	Ovid's Elegies		3.2.72
At me Joves right-hand lightning hath to throwe.	Ovid's Elegies		3.3.30
Thou saiest broke with Alcides angry hand.	Ovid's Elegies		3.5.36
To take it in her hand and play with it.	Ovid's Elegies		3.6.74
But still droupt downe, regarding not her hand,	Ovid's Elegies		3.6.76
What man will now take liberall arts in hand,	Ovid's Elegies		3.7.1
His left hand whereon gold doth ill alight,	Ovid's Elegies		3.7.15
Canst touch that hand wherewith some one lie dead?	Ovid's Elegies		3.7.17
His fainting hand in death engrasped mee.	Ovid's Elegies		3.8.58
With strong hand striking wild-beasts brist'led hyde.	Ovid's Elegies		3.9.26
Or his Bulles hornes Europas hand doth hold.	Ovid's Elegies		3.11.34
Built walles high towred with a prosperous hand.	Ovid's Elegies		3.12.34
Jove might have sipt out Nectar from his hand.	Hero and Leander		1.62
Where by one hand, light headed Bacchus hoong,	Hero and Leander		1.139
He toucht her hand, in touching it she trembled,	Hero and Leander		1.183
Sad Hero wroong him by the hand, and wept,	Hero and Leander		2.95
The mace returning backe, his owne hand hit,	Hero and Leander		2.211
HANDE			
Yet stay a while, forbeare thy bloudie hande,	Edw	5.5.75	Edward
HANDES			
unto your majesty/May merit favour at your highnesse handes,	1Tamb	4.4.70	Zenoc
and our solemne othes/Sign'd with our handes, each shal retaine	2Tamb	1.1.144	Orcan
Away with him, cut of his head and handes,	P 316	5.43	Anjoy
Ile clippe his winges/Or ere he passe my handes, away with him.	P1053	19.123	King
What, will you fyle your handes with Churchmens bloud?	P1093	20.3	Cardnl
Confirme his banishment with our handes and seales.	Edw	1.2.71	ArchBp
Yet lustie lords I have escapt your handes,	Edw	2.5.1	Gavstn
These handes were never stainde with innocent bloud,	Edw	5.5.81	Ltborn
I, I, but he teares his haire, and wrings his handes,	Edw	5.6.18	Queene
goe and make cleane our bootes which lie foule upon our handes,	F App	p.234 33	P Robin
HANDFUL			
Was but a handful to that we will have.	1Tamb	2.3.17	Tamb
HANDFULL			
Being a handfull to a mighty hoste,	2Tamb	3.1.40	Orcan
HANDLE			
I will not tell thee how Ile handle thee,	1Tamb	3.3.84	Tamb
And then let me alone to handle him.	Edw	5.2.22	Mortmr
Men handle those, all manly hopes resigne,	Ovid's Elegies		2.3.9
HANDLED			
Shall talke how I have handled Bajazeth.	1Tamb	4.2.97	Tamb
Thus he determin'd to have handled thee,	Jew	5.5.93	Govnr
See how he must be handled for his labour,	Edw	5.5.23	Matrvs
nere was there any/So finely handled as this king shalbe.	Edw	5.5.40	Ltborn
Vessels of Brasse oft handled, brightly shine,	Hero and Leander		1.231
HANDLING			
hardly can we brooke/The cruell handling of our selves in this:	Jew	1.2.175	1Jew

HANDMAID

Those with sweet water oft her handmaid fils,	Hero and Leander	1.35	

HANDMAIDS

She is my Handmaids slave, and she shal looke/That these abuses	1Tamb	4.2.69	Zenoc

HANDS

Our hands are not prepar'd to lawles spoyle,	Dido	1.2.12	Illion
Lyes it in Didos hands to make thee blest,	Dido	2.1.103	Dido
His hands bound at his backe, and both his eyes/Turnd up to	Dido	2.1.151	Aeneas
These hands did helpe to hale it to the gates,	Dido	2.1.170	Aeneas
Ah, how could poore Aeneas scape their hands?	Dido	2.1.220	Dido
This butcher whil'st his hands were yet held up,	Dido	2.1.241	Aeneas
Treading upon his breast, strooke off his hands.	Dido	2.1.242	Aeneas
Forgetting both his want of strength and hands,	Dido	2.1.252	Aeneas
So much have I receiv'd at Didos hands,	Dido	3.1.103	Aeneas
Thou wouldst have leapt from out the Sailers hands,	Dido	4.4.141	Dido
And sheere ye all asunder with her hands:	Dido	4.4.156	Dido
In steed of oares, let him use his hands,	Dido	4.4.163	Dido
Lay to thy hands and helpe me make a fire,	Dido	5.1.284	Dido
Shall either perish by our warlike hands,	1Tamb	1.1.72	Therid
For when they perish by our warlike hands,	1Tamb	3.3.24	Techel
Whose hands are made to gripe a warlike Lance,	1Tamb	3.3.106	Bajzth
And in your hands bring hellish poison up,	1Tamb	4.4.19	Bajzth
What cursed power guides the murthering hands,	1Tamb	5.1.403	Arabia
Since I shall render all into your hands.	1Tamb	5.1.447	Tamb
Shal now, adjoining al their hands with mine,	1Tamb	5.1.493	Tamb
If peace, restore it to my hands againe:	2Tamb	1.1.84	Sgsmnd
Shot through the armes, cut overthwart the hands,	2Tamb	3.2.104	Tamb
And in my blood wash all your hands at once,	2Tamb	3.2.127	Tamb
by your highnesse hands)/All brandishing their brands of	2Tamb	3.5.26	Orcan
Shrowd any thought may holde my striving hands/From martiall	2Tamb	4.1.95	Tamb
Or hold our citie from the Conquerours hands.	2Tamb	5.1.5	Maxim
Yeeld speedily the citie to our hands,	2Tamb	5.1.51	Therid
Now Bassoes, what demand you at our hands?	Jew	1.2.1	Govnr
What at our hands demand ye?	Jew	1.2.6	Govnr
to staine our hands with blood/Is farre from us and our	Jew	1.2.144	Govnr
Your father has deserv'd it at my hands,	Jew	2.3.70	Barab
Which forc'd their hands divide united hearts:	Jew	3.2.35	Govnr
Though thou deservest hardly at my hands,	Jew	3.3.74	Abigal
His hands are hackt, some fingers cut quite off;	Jew	4.3.10	Barab
I was imprison'd, but escap'd their hands.	Jew	5.1.77	Barab
to fall into the hands/Of such a Traitor and unhallowed Jew!	Jew	5.2.12	Govnr
Knit in these hands, thus joyn'd in nuptiall rites,	P 4	1.4	Charls
Since thou hast all the Cardes within thy hands/To shuffle or	P 146	2.89	Guise
Thou traitor Guise, lay of thy bloudy hands.	P 439	7.79	Navrre
Hands of good fellow, I will be his baile/For this offence:	P 622	12.35	King
These bloudy hands shall teare his triple Crowne,	P1199	22.61	King
And in his sportfull hands an Olive tree,	Edw	1.1.64	Gavstn
Cosin, our hands I hope shall fence our heads,	Edw	1.1.123	Mortmr
Ah brother, lay not violent hands on him,	Edw	1.1.189	Kent
Then laide they violent hands upon him, next/Himselfe	Edw	1.2.36	ArchBp
Lay hands on that traitor Mortimer.	Edw	1.4.20	Edward
Lay hands on that traitor Gaveston.	Edw	1.4.21	MortSr
Nay, then lay violent hands upon your king,	Edw	1.4.35	Edward
Sits wringing of her hands, and beats her brest.	Edw	1.4.188	Lncstr
These hands are tir'd, with haling of my lord/From Gaveston,	Edw	2.4.26	Queene
Thou shalt have so much honor at our hands.	Edw	2.5.28	Warwck
Hath seazed Normandie into his hands.	Edw	3.1.64	Queene
And see him redelivered to your hands.	Edw	3.1.112	Arundl
in England/Would cast up cappes, and clap their hands for joy,	Edw	4.2.55	Mortmr
T'escape their hands that seeke to reave his life:	Edw	4.7.52	Leistr
these innocent hands of mine/Shall not be guiltie of so foule a	Edw	5.1.98	Edward
Lay hands upon the earle for this assault.	Edw	5.3.54	Gurney
What safetie may I looke for at his hands,	Edw	5.4.109	King
Long ere with Iron hands they punish men,	F 878	3.1.100	Pope
Faustus will have heads and hands,/I, [all] <I call> your	F1393	4.2.69	Faust
I would lift up my hands, but see they hold 'em <them>, they	F1853	5.2.57 P	Faust
Made all shake hands as once the Sabines did;	Lucan, First Booke	118	
These hands shall thrust the ram, and make them flie,	Lucan, First Booke	385	
And with their hands held up, all joyntly cryde/They'ill follow	Lucan, First Booke	388	
And hold my conquered hands for thee to tie.	Ovid's Elegies	1.2.20	
loves wrack/Shall follow thee, their hands tied at their backe.	Ovid's Elegies	1.2.32	
Who gardes [the] <thee> conquered with his conquering hands.	Ovid's Elegies	1.2.52	
Yet scarse my hands from thee containe I well.	Ovid's Elegies	1.4.10	
Say they are mine, and hands on thee impose.	Ovid's Elegies	1.4.40	
no darke night-flying spright/Nor hands prepar'd to slaughter,	Ovid's Elegies	1.6.14	
Binde fast my hands, they have deserved chaines,	Ovid's Elegies	1.7.1	
Deserved chaines these cursed hands shall fetter,	Ovid's Elegies	1.7.28	
My feared hands thrice back she did repell.	Ovid's Elegies	1.7.62	
(Anger will helpe thy hands though nere so weake).	Ovid's Elegies	1.7.66	
By many hands great wealth is quickly got.	Ovid's Elegies	1.8.92	
With much a do my hands I scarsely staide.	Ovid's Elegies	1.8.110	
The keepers hands and corps-dugard to passe/The souldiours, and	Ovid's Elegies	1.9.27	
for needfull uses/Ile prove had hands impure with all abuses.	Ovid's Elegies	1.12.16	
Thou setst their labouring hands to spin and card.	Ovid's Elegies	1.13.24	
painted stands/All naked holding in her wave-moist hands.	Ovid's Elegies	1.14.34	
My hands an unsheath'd shyning weapon have not.	Ovid's Elegies	2.2.64	
Thy hands agree not with the warlike speare.	Ovid's Elegies	2.3.8	
Who would not love those hands for their swift running?	Ovid's Elegies	2.4.28	
My lordly hands ile throwe upon my right.	Ovid's Elegies	2.5.30	
And their owne privie weapon'd hands destroy them.	Ovid's Elegies	2.14.4	
And rule so soone with private hands acquainted.	Ovid's Elegies	2.18.16	
And from my hands the reines will slip away.	Ovid's Elegies	3.2.14	
Wish in his hands graspt did Hippomenes.	Ovid's Elegies	3.2.30	

HANDS (cont.)

To thee Minerva turne the craftes-mens hands. Ovid's Elegies 3.2.52
Why letst discordant hands to armour fall? Ovid's Elegies 3.7.48
And knocks his bare brest with selfe-angry hands. Ovid's Elegies 3.8.10
Her gate by my hands is set open wide. Ovid's Elegies 3.11.12
for neither sunne nor wind/Would burne or parch her hands, Hero and Leander 1.28
for they tooke delite/To play upon those hands, they were so Hero and Leander 1.30
These lovers parled by the touch of hands, Hero and Leander 1.185
To expiat which sinne, kisse and shake hands, Hero and Leander 1.309
And hands so pure, so innocent, nay such, Hero and Leander 1.365
Looke how their hands, so were their hearts united, Hero and Leander 2.27
His hands he cast upon her like a snare, Hero and Leander 2.259
With both her hands she made the bed a tent, Hero and Leander 2.264
Even as a bird, which in our hands we wring, Hero and Leander 2.289

HANDSOME (See HANSOM)

HANG

To hang her meteor like twixt heaven and earth, Dido 1.1.13 Jupitr
Will Dido let me hang about her necke? Dido 3.1.30 Cupid
The Masts whereon thy swelling sailes shall hang, Dido 3.1.122 Dido
See where the pictures of my suiters hang, Dido 3.1.139 Dido
Ile hang ye in the chamber where I lye, Dido 4.4.128 Dido
Now let him hang my favours on his masts, Dido 4.4.159 Dido
Now hang our bloody collours by Damascus, 1Tamb 4.4.1 Tamb
Hang up your weapons on Alcides poste, 1Tamb 5.1.528 Tamb
Their armes to hang about a Ladies necke: 2Tamb 1.3.30 Tamb
Over my Zenith hang a blazing star, 2Tamb 3.2.6 Tamb
Hang in the aire as thicke as sunny motes, 2Tamb 3.2.101 Tamb
Ile hang a clogge about your necke for running away againe, you 2Tamb 3.5.100 P Tamb
let him hang a bunch of keies on his standerd, to put him in 2Tamb 3.5.139 P Tamb
Then hang out flagges (my Lord) of humble truce, 2Tamb 5.1.6 Maxim
Offer submission, hang up flags of truce, 2Tamb 5.1.26 1Citzn
Go bind the villaine, he shall hang in chaines, 2Tamb 5.1.84 Tamb
Hang him up in chaines upon the citie walles, 2Tamb 5.1.108 Tamb
Take them, and hang them both up presently. 2Tamb 5.1.132 Tamb
in distresse/Thinke me so mad as I will hang my selfe, Jew 1.2.263 Barab
And now and then one hang himselfe for griefe, Jew 2.3.196 Barab
So might my man and I hang with you for company. Jew 4.1.182 Barab
Hang him, Jew. Jew 4.2.81 P Ithimr
the gold, or know Jew it is in my power to hang thee. Jew 4.3.38 P Pilia
How stand the cords? How hang these hinges, fast? Jew 5.5.1 Barab
all doubts, be rulde by me, lets hang him heere upon this tree. P 491 9.10 P 2Atndt
For Mortimer will hang his armor up. Edw 1.1.89 Mortmr
And at the court gate hang the pessant up, Edw 1.2.30 Mortmr
Ile hang a golden tongue about thy neck, Edw 1.4.328 Edward
No other jewels hang about my neck/Then these my lord, nor let Edw 1.4.330 Queene
hang him at a bough. Edw 2.5.24 Warwck
me thinkes you hang the heads,/But weele advance them traitors, Edw 3.1.223 Edward
Hang him I say, and set his quarters up, Edw 5.6.53 King
next, like a Neckelace I hang about her Necke: F 666 2.2.115 P Pride
and let them hang/Within the window where he yoak'd me first, F1380 4.2.56 Benvol
There sat the hang-man for mens neckes to angle. Ovid's Elegies 1.12.18
Thy legges hang-downe: Ovid's Elegies 3.2.63
And stately robes to their gilt feete hang downe. Ovid's Elegies 3.12.26

HANG'D

Blame not us but the proverb, Confes and be hang'd. Jew 4.1.146 P Barab
As I wud see thee hang'd; oh, love stops my breath: Jew 4.3.53 Barab
he weares, Judas left under the Elder when he hang'd himselfe. Jew 4.4.67 P Ithimr
I do not doubt but to see you both hang'd the next Sessions. F 212 1.2.19 P Wagner
Why how now sir Knight, what, hang'd by the hornes? F1290 4.1.136 P Faust
What ho, give's halfe a dosen of Beere here, and be hang'd. F1613 4.6.56 P Robin

HANGD

Shall being dead, be hangd thereon in chaines. P 321 5.48 Anjoy

HANG-DOWNE

Thy legges hang-downe: Ovid's Elegies 3.2.63

HANGED

<No, Ile see thee hanged, thou wilt eate up all my victualls>. F 702 (HC264)A P Faust

HANGES

That hanges for every peasant to atchive? P 98 2.41 Guise
He claps his cheekes, and hanges about his neck, Edw 1.2.51 Queene

HANGING

And in his eyelids hanging by the nayles, Dido 2.1.245 Aeneas
With costlie jewels hanging at their eares, 1Tamb 1.1.144 Ceneus
With mournfull streamers hanging down their heads, 1Tamb 4.2.120 Tamb
Betwixt the hollow hanging of a hill/And crooked bending of a 2Tamb 1.2.57 Callap
That hanging here, wil draw the Gods from heaven: 2Tamb 3.2.28 Tamb
That heading is one, and hanging is the other, Edw 2.5.30 Gavstn
Her white necke hid with tresses hanging downe, Ovid's Elegies 1.5.10
from their crowne/Phoebus and Bacchus wisht were hanging downe. Ovid's Elegies 1.14.32
Nor hanging oares the troubled seas did sweepe, Ovid's Elegies 3.7.43

HANG-MAN

There sat the hang-man for mens neckes to angle. Ovid's Elegies 1.12.18

HANGMAN

tibi, cras mihi, and so I left him to the mercy of the Hangman: Jew 4.2.19 P Pilia
and when the Hangman had put on his hempen Tippet, he made such Jew 4.2.23 P Ithimr
What they intend, the hangman frustrates cleane. Edw 3.1.275 Baldck
and thee lewd hangman call. Ovid's Elegies 2.2.36

HANGS

Then Thetis hangs about Apolloes necke, Dido 3.1.132 Dido
their neckes/Hangs massie chaines of golde downe to the waste, 1Tamb 1.2.126 Souldr
About them hangs a knot of Amber heire, 1Tamb 2.1.23 Menaph
See now my Lord how brave the Captaine hangs. 2Tamb 5.1.149 Amyras
So now he hangs like Bagdets Governour, 2Tamb 5.1.158 Tamb
Under whose hoary rocks Gebenna hangs; Lucan, First Booke 436

HANNIBAL			
rageth now in armes/As if the Carthage Hannibal were neere;	Lucan, First Booke		305
HANNIBALL			
Fierce Pirhus, neither thou nor Hanniball/Art cause, no forraine	Lucan, First Booke		30
HANSOM			
Off with your girdle, make a hansom noose;	Jew	4.1.142	Barab
HANSOME			
I'le goe steale some mony from my Master to make me hansome:	Jew	4.2.50	P Ithimr
HAOLE			
Ah often, that her [hale] <haole> head aked, she lying,	Ovid's Elegies		2.19.11
HAP (See also HAPPE)			
Why wilt thou so betray thy sonnes good hap?	Dido	5.1.31	Hermes
Before such hap fall to Zenocrate.	1Tamb	3.2.20	Agidas
What greater blisse can hap to Gaveston,	Edw	1.1.4	Gavstn
But Mortimer reservde for better hap,	Edw	4.2.40	Mortmr
Because on him thy care doth hap to rest.	Ovid's Elegies		3.2.8
But victory, I thinke, will hap to love.	Ovid's Elegies		3.10.34
HAPLES			
But haples I, God wot, poore and unknowne,	Dido	1.1.227	Aeneas
Birdes haples glory, death thy life doth quench.	Ovid's Elegies		2.6.20
Haples is he that all the night lies quiet/And slumbring,	Ovid's Elegies		2.9.39
HAPLESSE			
In this great Turk and haplesse Emperesse.	1Tamb	5.1.368	Zenoc
Happily some haplesse man hath conscience,	Jew	1.1.119	Barab
The hopelesse daughter of a haplesse Jew,	Jew	1.2.317	Abigal
not a man surviv'd/To bring the haplesse newes to Christendome.	Jew	2.2.51	Bosco
But haplesse Edward, thou art fondly led,	Edw	5.1.76	Edward
Fearing the enemy <ruine> of thy haplesse <hopelesse> soule.	F1738	5.1.65	OldMan
When he appear'd to haplesse Semele:	F1784	5.1.111	Faust
HAPPE			
Aye me rare gifts unworthy such a happe.	Ovid's Elegies		1.14.54
to thee being cast do happe/Sharpe stripes, she sitteth in the	Ovid's Elegies		2.2.61
HAPPEN (See also HAP, HAPS)			
Such good successe happen to Bajazeth.	1Tamb	3.3.116	Zabina
For evils are apt to happen every day.	Jew	1.2.223	Barab
No greater titles happen unto me,	Edw	2.2.254	Spencr
Yet more will happen then I can unfold;	Lucan, First Booke		634
HAPPENED			
What happened to the Queene we cannot shewe,	Dido	2.1.294	Achat
HAPPIE			
Live happie in the height of all content,	Dido	1.1.195	Aeneas
Both happie that Aeneas is our guest:	Dido	2.1.82	Dido
O happie shall he be whom Dido loves.	Dido	3.1.168	Aeneas
turne the hand of fate/Unto that happie day of my delight,	Dido	3.3.81	Iarbus
O happie sand that made him runne aground:	Dido	4.4.95	Dido
We yeeld unto thee happie Tamburlaine.	1Tamb	1.2.257	Agidas
troopes)/Farewell Lord Regent, and his happie friends,	1Tamb	2.5.46	Cosroe
thou maist thinke thy selfe happie to be fed from my trencher.	1Tamb	4.4.92	P Tamb
of them, looking some happie power will pitie and inlarge us.	1Tamb	4.4.100	P Zabina
And happie is the man, whom he vouchsafes/For vailing of his	Edw	1.2.18	Lncstr
Happie were I, but now most miserable.	Edw	1.4.129	Edward
But see in happie time, my lord the king,	Edw	1.4.299	Queene
And may it proove more happie then the first.	Edw	1.4.336	Queene
Prosper your happie motion good sir John.	Edw	4.2.75	Queene
O happie newes, send for the prince my sonne.	Edw	5.2.29	Queene
Be thou the happie subject of my Bookes,	Ovid's Elegies		1.3.19
Hees happie who loves mutuall skirmish slayes <layes>,	Ovid's Elegies		2.10.29
HAPPIER			
Much happier then your friends in England do.	Edw	4.2.35	Kent
Delia departing, happier lov'd, she saith,	Ovid's Elegies		3.8.55
HAPPILIE			
But hath thy potion wrought so happilie?	Edw	4.1.14	Kent
HAPPILY			
And happily with full Natolian bowles/Of Greekish wine now let	2Tamb	2.3.45	Orcan
Happily some haplesse man hath conscience,	Jew	1.1.119	Barab
Happily for neither, but to passe along/Towards Venice by the	Jew	1.1.162	Barab
For happily we shall not tarry here:	Jew	1.2.16	Calym
Now have I happily espy'd a time/To search the plancke my	Jew	2.1.20	Abigal
no, but happily he stands in feare/Of that which you, I thinke,	Jew	2.3.282	Barab
For happily I shall be in distresse,	Jew	5.4.6	Govnr
HAPPINES			
That perill is the cheefest way to happines,	P 95	2.38	Guise
armes, by me salute/Your highnes, with long life and happines,	Edw	3.1.157	Herald
HAPPINESSE			
The comfort of my future happinesse/And hope to meet your	2Tamb	2.4.62	Zenoc
And herein was old Abrams happinesse:	Jew	1.1.106	Barab
Who hateth me but for my happinesse?	Jew	1.1.112	Barab
Then father here receive thy happinesse.	Jew	2.1.44	Abigal
And on that hope my happinesse is built:	Jew	3.4.17	Barab
Thou seest thy life, and Malta's happinesse,	Jew	5.2.52	Barab
Hath rob'd me of eternall happinesse.	F1884	5.2.88	Faust
O thou hast lost celestiall happinesse,	F1899	5.2.103	GdAngl
HAPPY			
In happy hower we have set the Crowne/Upon your kingly head,	1Tamb	2.1.50	Ortyg
Most happy Emperour in humblest tearms/I vow my service to your	1Tamb	2.5.15	Meandr
Even at the morning of my happy state,	1Tamb	2.7.4	Cosroe
Come bring them in, and for this happy conquest/Triumph, and	1Tamb	3.3.272	Tamb
Honor still waight on happy Tamburlaine:	1Tamb	4.4.85	Zenoc
You that have martcht with happy Tamburlaine,	1Tamb	4.4.121	Tamb
With happy looks of ruthe and lenity.	1Tamb	5.1.59	2Virgn
Most happy King and Emperour of the earth,	1Tamb	5.1.74	1Virgn
And wisht as worthy subjects happy meanes,	1Tamb	5.1.103	1Virgn
Thou that in conduct of thy happy stars,	1Tamb	5.1.358	Zenoc

HAPPY (cont.)				
With happy safty of my fathers life,	1Tamb	5.1.401		Zenoc
Come happy Father of Zenocrate,	1Tamb	5.1.433		Tamb
Of Greekish wine now let us celebrate/Our happy conquest, and	2Tamb	2.3.47		Orcan
By this my friendly keepers happy meanes,	2Tamb	3.1.34		Callap
The glorie of this happy day is yours:	2Tamb	3.5.161		Tamb
Grave Abbasse, and you happy Virgins guide,	Jew	1.2.314		Abigal
fortune were so good/As but to be about this happy place;	Jew	2.1.32		Abigal
As but to be about this happy place;/'Tis not so happy:	Jew	2.1.33		Abigal
This is the houre/Wherein I shall proceed; Oh happy houre,	Jew	4.1.161		1Fryar
The terrour of this happy victory,	P 791	16.5		Bartus
I see hell, and returne againe safe, how happy were I then.	F 714	2.2.166	P	Faust
Drinke to our late and happy victory.	F 980	3.1.202		Pope
sight <glorious deed>/Happy and blest be Faustus evermore.	F1705	5.1.32		1Schol
All beasts are happy, for when they die,	F1969	5.2.173		Faust
He's happy, that his love dares boldly credit,	Ovid's Elegies	2.5.9		
And he is happy whom the earth holds, say.	Ovid's Elegies	2.11.30		
To bring that happy time so soone as may be.	Ovid's Elegies	2.11.56		
First of thy minde the happy seedes I knewe,	Ovid's Elegies	3.1.59		
HAPS				
How haps Achates bid me not farewell?	Dido	4.4.19		Dido
What ever haps, by suffrance harme is done,	Ovid's Elegies	2.19.35		
What day was that, which all sad haps to bring,	Ovid's Elegies	3.11.1		
HARBENGER				
And ran before, as Harbenger of light,	Hero and Leander	2.331		
HARBOR				
While in the harbor ride thy ships unrigd.	Edw	2.2.169		Mortmr
Father, thy face should harbor no deceit,	Edw	4.7.8		Edward
not a thought so villanous/Can harbor in a man of noble birth.	Edw	5.1.132		Bartly
These lookes of thine can harbor nought but death.	Edw	5.5.73		Edward
HARBORD				
And I for pitie harbord in my bosome,	Dido	5.1.166		Dido
HARBORS				
Harbors revenge, war, death and cruelty:	2Tamb	1.3.78		Tamb
But that it harbors him I hold so deare,	Edw	1.1.13		Gavstn
HARBORST				
O if thou harborst murther in thy hart,	Edw	5.5.87		Edward
HARBOUR				
Forbids all hope to harbour neere our hearts.	Dido	1.2.16		Illion
This is the harbour that Aeneas seekes,	Dido	4.4.59		Aeneas
To harbour thoughts effeminate and faint?	1Tamb	5.1.177		Tamb
His house will harbour many holy Nuns.	Jew	1.2.130		1Knght
they Henries heart/Will not both harbour love and Majestie?	P 604	12.17		King
Gape earth; O no, it will not harbour me.	F1949	5.2.153		Faust
HARBOURD				
In hell were harbourd, here was found no masse.	Ovid's Elegies	3.7.38		
HARBOURS				
The Docke in harbours ships drawne from the flouds,	Ovid's Elegies	2.9.21		
HARD				
and be revengde/On these hard harted Grecians, which rejoyce	Dido	2.1.19		Aeneas
How now Iarbus, at your prayers so hard?	Dido	4.2.23		Anna
Hard hearted, wilt not deigne to heare me speake?	Dido	4.2.54		Anna
The King your Brother is now hard at hand,	1Tamb	2.3.45		Tamb
My vaines are pale, my sinowes hard and drie,	1Tamb	4.4.97		Bajzth
As blacke as Jeat, and hard as Iron or steel,	2Tamb	1.3.27		Tamb
Jacints, hard Topas, grasse-greene Emeraulds,	Jew	1.1.26		Barab
Since your hard conditions are such/That you will needs have	Jew	1.2.18		Govnr
And so will I too, or it shall goe hard.--	Jew	1.2.392		Lodowk
I, and his sonnes too, or it shall goe hard.	Jew	2.3.17		Barab
It shall goe hard but I will see your death.	Jew	2.3.94		Barab
And I will have it or it shall goe hard.	Jew	3.1.15		Pilia
Hard-hearted Father, unkind Barabas,	Jew	3.3.36		Abigal
But here's a royall Monastry hard by,	Jew	4.1.13		Ithimr
Hard harted to the poore, a covetous wretch,	Jew	4.1.52		Barab
Pull hard.	Jew	4.1.147	P	Barab
Pull hard, I say, you would have had my goods.	Jew	4.1.149		Barab
The Guisians are hard at thy doore,	P 367	7.7		Taleus
And when you see me in, then follow hard.	P 429	7.69		Anjoy
It will be hard for us to worke their deaths.	P 508	9.27		QnMoth
The choyse is hard, I must dissemble.	P 865	17.60		Guise
Twere hard with me if I should doubt my kinne,	P 971	19.41		King
He is hard hearted, therfore pull with violence.	P1105	20.15		1Mur
Shall bathe him in a spring, and there hard by,	Edw	1.1.66		Gavstn
Hard is the hart, that injures such a saint.	Edw	1.4.190		Penbrk
Tis hard for us to worke his overthrow.	Edw	1.4.262		Mortmr
How hard the nobles, how unkinde the king/Hath shewed himself:	Edw	4.2.49		Mortmr
Must! tis somwhat hard, when kings must go.	Edw	4.7.83		Edward
But not too hard, least that you bruse his body.	Edw	5.5.113		Ltborn
The reward of sin is death? that's hard:	F 67	1.1.39		Faust
The sleepy Cardinals are hard at hand,	F 982	3.2.2		Mephst
same cup, for the Vintners boy followes us at the hard heeles.	F1090	3.3.3	P	Dick
What makes my bed seem hard seeing it is soft?	Ovid's Elegies	1.2.1		
Nor thy soft foote with his hard foote combine.	Ovid's Elegies	1.4.44		
Strike, so againe hard chaines shall binde thee never,	Ovid's Elegies	1.6.25		
Hard-hearted Porter doest and wilt not heare?	Ovid's Elegies	1.6.27		
On this hard threshold till the morning lay.	Ovid's Elegies	1.6.68		
And dores conjoynd with an hard iron lock.	Ovid's Elegies	1.6.74		
Both of them watch: each on the hard earth sleepes:	Ovid's Elegies	1.9.7		
While bond-men cheat, fathers [be hard] <hoord>, bawds hoorish,	Ovid's Elegies	1.15.17		
Quickly soft words hard dores wide open strooke.	Ovid's Elegies	2.1.22		
Now let her flatter me, now chide me hard,	Ovid's Elegies	2.9.45		
Which is the loveliest it is hard to say:	Ovid's Elegies	2.10.6		
My hard way with my mistrisse would seeme soft.	Ovid's Elegies	2.16.20		

Headword / Line	Work	Reference	Speaker
HARD (cont.)			
Ah howe oft on hard doores hung I engrav'd,	Ovid's Elegies	3.1.53	
For shame presse not her backe with thy hard knee.	Ovid's Elegies	3.2.24	
Huge okes, hard Adamantes might she have moved,	Ovid's Elegies	3.6.57	
To lay my body on the hard moist floore.	Ovid's Elegies	3.10.10	
And Rams with hornes their hard heads wreathed back.	Ovid's Elegies	3.12.17	
And who have hard hearts, and obdurat minds,	Hero and Leander	2.217	
HARDEN			
Suffer, and harden:	Ovid's Elegies	3.10.7	
HARDER			
O harder then the dores thou gardest I prove thee.	Ovid's Elegies	1.6.62	
HARDEST			
His heart consists of flint, and hardest steele,	Ovid's Elegies	3.5.59	
HARD HARTED			
Hard harted to the poore, a covetous wretch,	Jew	4.1.52	Barab
HARD-HEARTED			
Hard-hearted Father, unkind Barabas,	Jew	3.3.36	Abigal
Hard-hearted Porter doest and wilt not heare?	Ovid's Elegies	1.6.27	
HARD HEARTED			
Hard hearted, wilt not deigne to heare me speake?	Dido	4.2.54	Anna
He is hard hearted, therfore pull with violence.	P1105	20.15	1Mur
HARDIE			
None be so hardie as to touche the King,	Edw	2.3.27	Lncstr
HARDINESSE			
Couragious and full of hardinesse:	1Tamb	4.3.55	Capol
HARDLY			
Not from my heart, for I can hardly goe,	Dido	5.1.103	Aeneas
as hardly can we brooke/The cruell handling of our selves in	Jew	1.2.174	1Jew
things past recovery/Are hardly cur'd with exclamations.	Jew	1.2.237	Barab
Though thou deservest hardly at my hands,	Jew	3.3.74	Abigal
Although my love to thee can hardly [suffer't] <suffer>,	P 747	15.5	King
That hardly art a gentleman by birth?	Edw	1.4.29	Mortmr
a factious lord/Shall hardly do himselfe good, much lesse us,	Edw	2.1.7	Spencr
hearing,/Mortimer hardly, Penbrooke and Lancaster/Spake least:	Edw	3.1.105	Arundl
way how hardly I can brooke/To loose my crowne and kingdome,	Edw	5.1.51	Edward
easie grant men great estates,/But hardly grace to keepe them:	Lucan, First Booke	509	
Can hardly blazon foorth the loves of men,	Hero and Leander	1.70	
Love deepely grounded, hardly is dissembled.	Hero and Leander	1.184	
HARDNED			
My heart is <hearts so> hardned, I cannot repent:	F 569	2.2.18	Faust
These hardned me, with what I keepe obscure,	Ovid's Elegies	3.10.27	
HARDST			
Why, hardst thou not the trumpet sound a charge?	Jew	5.5.105	Govnr
HARDY			
Thou knowest not (foolish hardy Tamburlaine)/What tis to meet	1Tamb	3.3.145	Bajzth
HAREBRAIND			
But vicious, harebraind, and illit'rat hinds?	Hero and Leander	2.218	
HARK (See also HEARK)			
but hark ye sir, if my horse be sick, or ill at ease, if I	F App	p.240 118	P HrsCsr
HARKE			
Harke to a motion of eternall league,	Dido	3.2.68	Juno
Harke, harke they come, Ile leap out at the window.	P 369	7.9	Taleus
Harke how he harpes upon his minion.	Edw	1.4.311	Queene
HARKEN			
Harken a while, and I will tell you why:	Hero and Leander	1.385	
HARKENING			
Harkening when he shall bid them plague the world.	2Tamb	3.4.60	Therid
HARLOT			
No charmed herbes of any harlot skathd thee,	Ovid's Elegies	1.14.39	
HARLOTS			
Then bring those Turkish harlots to my tent,	2Tamb	4.1.165	Tamb
meet not me/With troopes of harlots at your slouthful heeles.	2Tamb	4.3.82	Tamb
HARM			
you were his father too, Sir, that's al the harm I wish you:	Jew	2.3.41	P Barab
HARM'D			
Yet he harm'd lesse, whom I profess'd to love,	Ovid's Elegies	1.7.33	
I harm'd: a foe did Diomedes anger move.	Ovid's Elegies	1.7.34	
No sicknesse harm'd thee, farre be that a way,	Ovid's Elegies	1.14.41	
HARME			
To harme my sweete Ascanius lovely life.	Dido	3.2.23	Venus
To ward the blow, and shield me safe from harme.	1Tamb	1.2.181	Tamb
And feare to see thy kingly Fathers harme,	1Tamb	5.1.138	Tamb
And should I goe and do nor harme nor good,	2Tamb	4.1.56	Calyph
I might have harme, which all the good I have/Join'd with my	2Tamb	4.1.57	Calyph
Which if they were reveal'd, would doe him harme.	Jew	4.2.65	Pilia
Farre is it from my hart to do you harme,	Edw	5.5.47	Ltborn
And I had breath'd a man made free from harme.	F1400	4.2.76	Faust
being thin, the harme was small,/Yet strivde she to be covered	Ovid's Elegies	1.5.13	
My Mistresse weepes whom my mad hand did harme.	Ovid's Elegies	1.7.4	
Th'opposed starre of Mars hath done thee harme,	Ovid's Elegies	1.8.29	
Let thy tongue flatter, while thy minde harme-workes:	Ovid's Elegies	1.8.103	
Never to harme me made thy faith evasion.	Ovid's Elegies	1.11.6	
More he deserv'd, to both great harme he fram'd,	Ovid's Elegies	2.2.49	
Doest harme, and in thy tents why doest me wound?	Ovid's Elegies	2.9.4	
She secretly with me such harme attempted,	Ovid's Elegies	2.13.3	
What ever haps, by suffrance harme is done,	Ovid's Elegies	2.19.35	
Mars girts his deadly sword on for my harme:	Ovid's Elegies	3.3.27	
'Tis doubtfull whether verse availe, or harme,	Ovid's Elegies	3.11.13	
Now your credulity harme to me hath raisd.	Ovid's Elegies	3.11.44	
And swore the sea should never doe him harme.	Hero and Leander	2.180	
HARMEFULL			
Nor doth her tongue want harmefull eloquence.	Ovid's Elegies	1.8.20	
To plague your bodies with such harmefull strokes?	Ovid's Elegies	2.14.34	

HARMEFULL (cont.)			
Harmefull to beasts, and to the fields thou proves: . .	Ovid's Elegies	3.5.99	
HARMELESSE			
And harmelesse run among the deadly pikes. . . .	2Tamb	1.3.46	Tamb
yet are our lookes/As innocent and harmelesse as a Lambes.	Jew	2.3.22	Barab
Guiding the harmelesse Pigeons with thy hand. . . .	Ovid's Elegies	1.2.26	
There harmelesse Swans feed all abroad the river, . .	Ovid's Elegies	2.6.53	
HARMES			
Thy dull hand stayes thy striving enemies harmes. . .	Ovid's Elegies	2.9.12	
And thousand kisses gives, that worke my harmes: . .	Ovid's Elegies	2.18.10	
May spelles and droughs <drugges> do sillie soules such harmes?	Ovid's Elegies	3.6.28	
HARME-WORKES			
Let thy tongue flatter, while thy minde harme-workes: .	Ovid's Elegies	1.8.103	
HARMING			
As once I did for harming Hercules.	Dido	1.1.15	Jupitr
HARMLESSE			
Therefore, for these our harmlesse virgines sakes, . .	1Tamb	5.1.18	Govnr
HARMONY			
And speech more pleasant than sweet harmony:	1Tamb	3.3.121	Tamb
And in this sweet and currious harmony, ...	2Tamb	2.4.30	Tamb
For like Sea-nimphs inveigling harmony, ...	Hero and Leander	1.105	
And quite confound natures sweet harmony.	Hero and Leander	1.252	
HARNESSE			
His harnesse dropping bloud, and on his speare/The mangled head	Dido	2.1.214	Aeneas
And men in harnesse <armour> shall appeare to thee, . .	F 548	2.1.160	Mephst
HARNEST			
And harnest like my horses, draw my coch, ...	2Tamb	3.5.104	Tamb
HARPE			
O Anna, fetch [Arions] <Orions> Harpe, ...	Dido	5.1.248	Dido
walles of Thebes/With ravishing sound of his melodious Harpe,	F 580	2.2.29	Faust
While Mars doth take the Aonian harpe to play? . . .	Ovid's Elegies	1.1.16	
Then scarse can Phoebus say, this harpe is mine. . .	Ovid's Elegies	1.1.20	
Of his gilt Harpe the well tun'd strings doth hold. . .	Ovid's Elegies	1.8.60	
The Thracian Harpe with cunning to have strooke, . .	Ovid's Elegies	2.11.32	
Doth say, with her that lov'd the Aonian harpe. . .	Ovid's Elegies	2.18.26	
Sappho her vowed harpe laies at Phoebus feete. . . .	Ovid's Elegies	2.18.34	
father Phoebus layed/To sing with his unequald harpe is sayed.	Ovid's Elegies	3.8.24	
And sweet toucht harpe that to move stones was able? .	Ovid's Elegies	3.11.40	
By this Apollos golden harpe began, ...	Hero and Leander	2.327	
HARPES			
Harke how he harpes upon his minion.	Edw	1.4.311	Queene
HARPEY			
greedily assayd/To touch those dainties, she the Harpey playd,	Hero and Leander	2.270	
HARPIE			
Nor fowlest Harpie that shall swallow him. . . .	Edw	2.2.46	Edward
HARPYE			
And like a Harpyr <Harpye> tires on my life. . . .	1Tamb	2.7.50	Cosroe
HARPYR			
And like a Harpyr <Harpye> tires on my life. . . .	1Tamb	2.7.50	Cosroe
HARSH			
Peeres/Heare me, but yet with Mirmidons harsh eares, .	Dido	2.1.123	Aeneas
That slayest me with thy harsh and hellish tale, . .	Dido	5.1.217	Dido
Too harsh a subject for your dainty eares. . . .	1Tamb	3.2.46	Agidas
Whose cruelties are not so harsh as thine, ...	2Tamb	4.1.169	Jrslem
[Unpleasant, harsh, contemptible and vilde]:	F 136	1.1.108A	Faust
It may be this my exhortation/Seemes harsh, and all unpleasant;	F1718	5.1.45	OldMan
HARSHLY			
Which long time lie untoucht, will harshly jarre. . .	Hero and Leander	1.230	
HART (Homograph)			
dooth gastly death/With greedy tallents gripe my bleeding hart,	1Tamb	2.7.49	Cosroe
And in his eies the furie of his hart, ...	1Tamb	3.2.73	Agidas
Tamburlane) as I could willingly feed upon thy blood-raw hart.	1Tamb	4.4.12	P Bajzth
whose worthinesse/Deserves a conquest over every hart: .	1Tamb	5.1.208	Tamb
Ah wretched eies, the enemies of my hart, ...	1Tamb	5.1.340	Zenoc
But when they list, their conquering fathers hart: . .	2Tamb	1.3.36	Zenoc
How may my hart, thus fired with mine eies, . . .	2Tamb	4.1.93	Tamb
with what a broken hart/And damned spirit I ascend this seat,	2Tamb	5.3.206	Amyras
Like thy breath, sweet-hart, no violet like 'em. . .	Jew	4.4.40	Ithimr
This wrathfull hand should strike thee to the hart. . .	P 690	13.34	Guise
And running in the likenes of an Hart, ...	Edw	1.1.69	Gavstn
Therefore to equall it receive my hart.	Edw	1.1.162	Edward
What we have done, our hart bloud shall maintaine. . .	Edw	1.4.40	Mortmr
Rend not my hart with thy too piercing words, . . .	Edw	1.4.117	Edward
Witnesse this hart, that sighing for thee breakes, . .	Edw	1.4.165	Queene
Hard is the hart, that injures such a saint. . . .	Edw	1.4.190	Penbrk
But whiles I have a sword, a hand, a hart, . . .	Edw	1.4.422	Mortmr
My swelling hart for very anger breakes, ...	Edw	2.2.200	Edward
Had power to mollifie his stonie hart, ...	Edw	2.4.20	Queene
Oh my sweet hart, how do I mone thy wrongs, . . .	Edw	4.2.27	Queene
Edward, alas my hart relents for thee, ...	Edw	4.6.2	Kent
a king, thy hart/Pierced deeply with sence of my distresse,	Edw	4.7.9	Edward
O never more lift up this dying hart!	Edw	4.7.43	Edward
And hart and hand to heavens immortall throne, . . .	Edw	4.7.108	Baldck
To companie my hart with sad laments, ...	Edw	5.1.34	Edward
Well may I rent his name, that rends my hart. . . .	Edw	5.1.140	Edward
When will his hart be satisfied with bloud? . . .	Edw	5.3.9	Edward
Foh, heeres a place in deed with all my hart. . . .	Edw	5.5.41	Ltborn
Farre is it from my hart to do you harme, ...	Edw	5.5.47	Ltborn
O if thou harborst murther in thy hart, ...	Edw	5.5.87	Edward
this spectacle/Stroake Caesars hart with feare, his hayre	Lucan, First Booke	195	
Tooke out the shaft, ordaind my hart to shiver: . .	Ovid's Elegies	1.1.26	
Tis cruell love turmoyles my captive hart. . . .	Ovid's Elegies	1.2.8	
all, and everie part/Strove to resist the motions of her hart.	Hero and Leander	1.364	

HART (cont.)				
I, and shee wisht, albeit not from her hart,	Hero and Leander			2.37
HART BLOUD				
What we have done, our hart bloud shall maintaine.	Edw	1.4.40		Mortmr
HARTED				
and be revengde/On these hard harted Grecians, which rejoyce	Dido	2.1.19		Aeneas
Hard harted to the poore, a covetous wretch,	Jew	4.1.52		Barab
HARTEN				
Upon these Barons, harten up your men,	Edw	3.1.124		Spencr
HARTES				
with milke-white Hartes upon an Ivorie sled,	1Tamb	1.2.98		Tamb
HARTIE				
Their blubbered cheekes and hartie humble mones/Will melt his	1Tamb	5.1.21		Govnr
HARTILY				
you dine with me, Sir, and you shal be most hartily poyson'd.	Jew	4.3.30	P	Barab
HARTLESSE				
Compassion, love, vaine hope, and hartlesse feare,	Jew	2.3.170		Barab
HARTS				
And every sweetnes that inspir'd their harts,	1Tamb	5.1.163		Tamb
If griefe, our murthered harts have straind forth blood.	2Tamb	2.4.123		Therid
how should our bleeding harts/Wounded and broken with your	2Tamb	5.3.161		Amyras
Souldiers, good harts, defend your soveraignes right,	Edw	3.1.182		Edward
Romans if ye be,/And beare true harts, stay heare:	Lucan, First Booke			194
And love to Room (thogh slaughter steeld their harts/And minds	Lucan, First Booke			355
Thus while dum signs their yeelding harts entangled,	Hero and Leander			1.187
HARTY				
Health and harty farwell to my Lord Joyeux.	P 751	15.9		Guise
HARVEST				
That like a Foxe in midst of harvest time,	1Tamb	1.1.31		Mycet
I, but my Lord, the harvest is farre off:	Jew	2.3.79		Barab
Where Ceres went each place was harvest there.	Ovid's Elegies			3.9.38
HA'S				
be; for I have heard of one, that ha's eate a load of logges.	F1533	4.5.29	P	Robin
To please me, what faire termes and sweet words ha's shee,	Ovid's Elegies			2.19.17
HAS (See also HA)				
Lastly, he that denies this, shall absolutely lose al he has.	Jew	1.2.76	P	Reader
Oh what has made my lovely daughter sad?	Jew	1.2.225		Barab
Thy father has enough in store for thee.	Jew	1.2.227		Barab
For she has mortified her selfe.	Jew	1.2.341		1Fryar
sudden fall/Has humbled her and brought her downe to this:	Jew	1.2.368		Mthias
That has no further comfort for his maime.	Jew	2.1.11		Barab
Your father has deserv'd it at my hands,	Jew	2.3.70		Barab
Belike he has some new tricke for a purse;	Jew	2.3.101		Barab
And if he has, he is worth three hundred plats.	Jew	2.3.102		Barab
Because he is young and has more qualities.	Jew	2.3.110		1Offcr
For now by this has he kist Abigall;	Jew	2.3.246		Barab
He has my heart, I smile against my will.	Jew	2.3.287		Abigal
And so has she done you, even from a child.	Jew	2.3.289		Barab
The time has bin, that but for one bare night/A hundred Duckets	Jew	3.1.2		Curtzn
I, but the Jew has gold,	Jew	3.1.14		Pilia
Oh, my master has the bravest policy.	Jew	3.3.12	P	Ithimr
Has made me see the difference of things.	Jew	3.3.62		Abigal
What a blessing has he given't?	Jew	3.4.106	P	Ithimr
Why? what has he done?	Jew	3.6.47		1Fryar
What, has he crucified a child?	Jew	3.6.49		1Fryar
She has confest, and we are both undone,	Jew	4.1.46		Barab
I'le make him send me half he has, and glad he scapes so too.	Jew	4.2.67	P	Ithimr
Whose face has bin a grind-stone for mens swords,	Jew	4.3.9		Barab
The meaning has a meaning; come let's in:	Jew	4.4.80		Ithimr
In prison till the Law has past on him.	Jew	5.1.49		Govnr
For well has Barabas deserv'd of us.	Jew	5.3.25		Calym
intreat your Highnesse/Not to depart till he has feasted you.	Jew	5.3.33		Msngr
He will; and has commanded all his men/To come ashore, and march	Jew	5.5.14		Msngr
If greater falshood ever has bin done.	Jew	5.5.50		Barab
Then has <in> the white breasts of the Queene of love.	F 156	1.1.128		Valdes
Has not the Pope enough of conjuring yet?	F1189	4.1.35	P	Benvol
the Doctor has no skill,/No Art, no cunning, to present these	F1294	4.1.140		Faust
He has done penance now sufficently.	F1310	4.1.156		Emper
Murder or not murder, now he has but one leg, I'le out-run him,	F1494	4.4.38	P	HrsCsr
And has the Doctor but one leg then?	F1553	4.5.49	P	Dick
Ha, ha, ha, dost heare him Dick, he has forgot his legge.	F1629	4.6.72	P	Carter
to die shortly, he has made his will, and given me his wealth,	F1674	5.1.1	P	Wagner
hee has kild the divell, so I should be cald kill divell all	F App	p.230 48	P	Clown
all hee divels has hornes, and all shee divels has clifts and	F App	p.230 53	P	Clown
has hornes, and all shee divels has clifts and cloven feete.	F App	p.230 54	P	Clown
it, and she has sent me to looke thee out, prethee come away.	F App	p.233 8	P	Rafe
why I has thought thou hadst beene a batcheler, but now I see	F App	p.238 69	P	Emper
felow, and he has a great charge, neither wife nor childe.	F App	p.239 106	P	Mephst
on him; hee has a buttocke as slicke as an Ele; wel god buy sir,	F App	p.239 116	P	HrsCsr
has given me a purgation, has purg'd me of fortie Dollers,	F App	p.240 128	P	HrsCsr
has purg'd me of fortie Dollers, I shall never see them more:	F App	p.240 128	P	HrsCsr
I tell thee he has not slept this eight nights.	F App	p.240 144	P	Mephst
Faustus has his legge againe, and the Horsecourser I take it,	F App	p.241 164	P	Faust
HAST (Homograph)				
Shall make the morning hast her gray uprise,	Dido	1.1.102		Jupitr
A Gods name on and hast thee to the Court,	Dido	1.1.233		Venus
the Greekish spyes/To hast to Tenedos and tell the Campe:	Dido	2.1.181		Aeneas
mightier Kings)/Hast had the greatest favours I could give:	Dido	3.1.13		Dido
No, live Iarbus, what hast thou deserv'd,	Dido	3.1.41		Dido
Something thou hast deserv'd.--	Dido	3.1.43		Dido
Welcome sweet child, where hast thou been this long?	Dido	5.1.46		Aeneas
Hast thou forgot how many neighbour kings/Were up in armes, for	Dido	5.1.141		Dido
For though thou hast the heart to say farewell,	Dido	5.1.182		Dido

HAST (cont.)

Thou for some pettie guift hast let him goe,	Dido	5.1.218	Dido
that in former age/Hast bene the seat of mightie Conquerors,	1Tamb	1.1.7	Cosroe
But tell me, that hast seene him, Menaphon,	1Tamb	2.1.5	Cosroe
Wel hast thou pourtraid in thy tearms of life,	1Tamb	2.1.31	Cosroe
Capolin, hast thou survaid our powers?	1Tamb	4.3.50	Souldn
And now Bajazeth, hast thou any stomacke?	1Tamb	4.4.10	Tamb
Thou hast with honor usde Zenocrate.	1Tamb	5.1.484	Souldn
Viceroy of Byron, wisely hast thou said:	2Tamb	1.1.54	Orcan
Hast thou beheld a peale of ordinance strike/A ring of pikes,	2Tamb	3.2.98	Tamb
Hast thou not seene my horsmen charge the foe,	2Tamb	3.2.103	Tamb
Thou hast procur'd a greater enemie,	2Tamb	4.1.127	Tamb
I, good my Lord, let us in hast to Persea,	2Tamb	5.1.214	Therid
thou that hast seene/Millions of Turkes perish by Tamburlaine,	2Tamb	5.2.24	Callap
No, Jew, thou hast denied the Articles,	Jew	1.2.92	Govnr
Content thee, Barabas, thou hast nought but right.	Jew	1.2.152	Govnr
Till thou hast gotten to be entertain'd.	Jew	1.2.288	Barab
Hast thou't?	Jew	2.1.45	Barab
Here, Hast thou't?	Jew	2.1.46	P Abigal
What, hast the Philosophers stone?	Jew	2.3.111	P Barab
and thou hast, breake my head with it, I'le forgive thee.	Jew	2.3.111	P Barab
Tell me, hast thou thy health well?	Jew	2.3.121	P Barab
Thou hast thy Crownes, fellow, come let's away.	Jew	2.3.158	Mater
Hast thou no Trade?	Jew	2.3.167	Barab
But tell me now, How hast thou spent thy time?	Jew	2.3.201	Barab
Oh wretched Abigal, what hast [thou] <thee> done?	Jew	2.3.320	Abigal
False, and unkinde; what, hast thou lost thy father?	Jew	3.4.2	Barab
What, hast thou brought the Ladle with thee too?	Jew	3.4.57	Barab
go set it downe/And come againe so soone as thou hast done,	Jew	3.4.109	Barab
since thou hast broke the league/By flat denyall of the	Jew	3.5.19	Basso
Thou hast offended, therefore must be damn'd.	Jew	4.1.25	1Fryar
Barabas, thou hast--	Jew	4.1.28	2Fryar
I, that thou hast--	Jew	4.1.29	1Fryar
Thou hast committed--	Jew	4.1.40	2Fryar
Why, how now Jacomo, what hast thou done?	Jew	4.1.174	Barab
hast thou the gold?	Jew	4.2.100	P Ithimr
Musician, hast beene in Malta long?	Jew	4.4.54	Curtzn
Thus hast thou gotten, by thy policie,	Jew	5.2.27	Barab
gloves which I sent/To be poysoned, hast thou done them?	P 71	2.14	Guise
Since thou hast all the Cardes within thy hands/To shuffle or	P 146	2.89	Guise
Heere hast thou a country voide of feares,	P 591	12.4	QnMoth
Pardon thee, why what hast thou done?	P 991	19.61	Guise
Art thou King, and hast done this bloudy deed?	P1050	19.120	YngGse
Trayterouse guise ah thow hast murthered me	Paris	ms17,p390	Minion
fondlie hast thow in censte the guises sowle	Paris	ms25,p391	Guise
Then thou hast beene of me since thy exile.	Edw	1.1.145	Edward
The time is little that thou hast to stay,	Edw	1.4.138	Edward
Seeing thou hast pleaded with so good successe.	Edw	1.4.329	Edward
Ah furious Mortimer what hast thou done?	Edw	2.2.85	Queene
Complaines, that thou hast left her all forlorne.	Edw	2.2.173	Lncstr
Poore Gaveston, that hast no friend but me,	Edw	2.2.220	Edward
So well hast thou deserv'de sweete Mortimer.	Edw	2.4.59	Queene
We will in hast go certifie our Lord.	Edw	2.6.19	James
With all the hast we can dispatch him hence.	Edw	3.1.83	Edward
Therefore be gon in hast, and with advice,	Edw	3.1.264	Spencr
Vilde wretch, and why hast thou of all unkinde,	Edw	4.6.5	Kent
A litter hast thou, lay me in a hearse,	Edw	4.7.87	Edward
For kinde and loving hast thou alwaies beene:	Edw	5.1.7	Edward
And hast thou cast how to accomplish it?	Edw	5.4.24	Mortmr
At every ten miles end thou hast a horse.	Edw	5.4.42	Mortmr
Sweet Analitikes <Anulatikes>, tis thou hast ravisht me,	F 34	1.1.6	Faust
Then read no more, thou hast attain'd that <the> end;	F 38	1.1.10	Faust
Why Faustus, hast thou not attain'd that end?	F 46	1.1.18	Faust
Then hast thee to some solitary Grove,	F 180	1.1.152	Valdes
Seeing thou hast pray'd and sacrific'd to them.	F 235	1.3.7	Faust
Sirra, hast thou no commings in?	F 346	1.4.4	P Wagner
And give thee more then thou hast wit to aske.	F 436	2.1.48	Mephst
In which <wherein> thou hast given thy soule to Lucifer.	F 520	2.1.132	Mephst
Because thou hast depriv'd me of those Joyes.	F 554	2.2.3	Faust
'Tis thou hast damn'd distressed Faustus soule.	F 628	2.2.77	Faust
Now Faustus thou hast heard all my progeny, wilt thou bid me to	F 700	2.2.149	P Glutny
'Snayles, what hast thou got there, a book?	F 730	2.3.9	P Dick
Hast thou, as earst I did command,	F 801	3.1.23	Faust
Go hast thee gentle Mephostophilis,	F 891	3.1.113	Faust
And if this Bruno thou hast late redeem'd,	F1212	4.1.58	Emper
Make hast to help these noble Gentlemen,	F1421	4.2.97	1Soldr
more, take him, because I see thou hast a good minde to him.	F1461	4.4.5	P Faust
doubt of that, for me thinkes you make no hast to wipe it out.	F1517	4.5.13	P Hostss
Though thou hast now offended like a man,	F1710	5.1.37	OldMan
Yet, yet, thou hast an amiable soule,	F1712	5.1.39	OldMan
Where art thou Faustus? wretch, what hast thou done?	F1724	5.1.51	Faust
Accursed Faustus, <wretch what hast thou done>?	F1739	(HC270)B	Faust
Say Wagner, thou hast perus'd my will,	F1816	5.2.20	Faust
I, Faustus, now thou hast no hope of heaven,	F1880	5.2.84	Mephst
O thou hast lost celestiall happinesse,	F1899	5.2.103	GdAngl
that hast thou lost,/And now poore soule must thy good Angell	F1906	5.2.110	GdAngl
Now hast thou but one bare houre to live,	F1927	5.2.131	Faust
Or why is this immortall that thou hast?	F1965	5.2.169	Faust
Tel me sirra, hast thou any commings in?	F App	p.229 4	P Wagner
if thou hast any mind to Nan Spit our kitchin maide, then turn	F App	p.234 26	P Robin
thou hast no goblet.	F App	p.235 27	P Vintnr
they say thou hast a familiar spirit, by whome thou canst	F App	p.236 4	P Emper
but now I see thou hast a wife, that not only gives thee	F App	p.238 70	P Emper

HAST (cont.)			
Vilaine I say, undo what thou hast done.	F App	p.238 75	Knight
When thou hast tasted, I will take the cup,	Ovid's Elegies		1.4.31
Mistris thou knowest, thou hast a blest youth pleas'd,	Ovid's Elegies		1.8.23
When thou hast so much as he gives no more,	Ovid's Elegies		1.8.101
Jove that thou shouldst not hast but wait his leasure,	Ovid's Elegies		1.13.45
Now hast thou left no haires at all to die.	Ovid's Elegies		1.14.2
While thou hast time yet to bestowe that gift.	Ovid's Elegies		2.3.18
Heere thou hast strength, here thy right hand doth rest.	Ovid's Elegies		2.9.36
If any godly care of me thou hast,	Ovid's Elegies		2.16.47
Foole if to keepe thy wife thou hast no neede,	Ovid's Elegies		2.19.1
Long hast thou loyterd, greater workes compile.	Ovid's Elegies		3.1.24
Thou hast my gift, which she would from thee sue.	Ovid's Elegies		3.1.60
She gave me leave, soft loves in time make hast,	Ovid's Elegies		3.1.69
I to my mistris hast.	Ovid's Elegies		3.5.2
Thou hast no bridge, nor boate with ropes to throw,	Ovid's Elegies		3.5.3
What helpes my hast: what to have tane small rest?	Ovid's Elegies		3.5.9
To stay thy tresses white veyle hast thou none?	Ovid's Elegies		3.5.56
And I beleeve some wench thou hast affected:	Ovid's Elegies		3.5.83
Thou hast no name, but com'st from snowy mountaines;	Ovid's Elegies		3.5.91
No certaine house thou hast, nor any fountaines.	Ovid's Elegies		3.5.92
Ah now a name too true thou hast, I finde.	Ovid's Elegies		3.8.4
in vowing chastitie, hast sworne/To rob her name and honour,	Hero and Leander		1.304
But heale the heart, that thou hast wounded thus,	Hero and Leander		1.324
HASTE (See also HAST)			
Hermes awake, and haste to Neptunes realme,	Dido	1.1.114	Jupitr
Cloanthus, haste away, Aeneas calles.	Dido	4.3.14	Aeneas
Now will I haste unto Lavinian shoare,	Dido	5.1.78	Aeneas
Then haste Cosroe to be king alone,	1Tamb	2.3.42	Tamb
For presently Techelles here shal haste,	1Tamb	2.5.94	Tamb
Haste thee Techelles, we will follow thee.	1Tamb	2.5.104	Tamb
Then haste Agydas, and prevent the plagues:	1Tamb	3.2.100	Agidas
Thanks gentle Almeda, then let us haste,	2Tamb	1.2.74	Callap
And conquering that, made haste to Nubia,	2Tamb	1.3.202	Techel
let us haste and meete/Our Army and our brother of Jerusalem,	2Tamb	2.3.42	Orcan
and let us haste from hence/Along the cave that leads beyond	2Tamb	3.4.1	Olymp
And make our greatest haste to Persea:	2Tamb	5.1.128	Tamb
Theridamas, haste to the court of Jove,	2Tamb	5.3.61	Tamb
he made such haste to his prayers, as if hee had had another	Jew	4.2.24	P Ithimr
goe whither he will, I'le be none of his followers in haste:	Jew	4.2.26	P Ithimr
Hence will I haste to Killingworth castle,	Edw	5.2.119	Kent
Make haste againe, my good Lord Cardinalls,	F 972	3.1.194	Pope
theres no haste but good, are you remembred how you crossed me	F App	p.238 76	P Faust
Therefore sweet Mephastophilis, let us make haste to Wertenberge	F App	p.239 94	Faust
HASTEN			
Come Dido, let us hasten to the towne,	Dido	4.1.26	Aeneas
And hasten to remoove Damascus siege.	1Tamb	4.3.18	Souldn
Let griefe and furie hasten on revenge,	1Tamb	4.3.43	Arabia
HASTILY			
Therefore unto him hastily she goes,	Hero and Leander		2.45
HASTING			
Preserving life, by hasting cruell death.	1Tamb	4.4.96	Bajzth
And hasting to me, neither darkesome night,	Ovid's Elegies		2.11.51
HA'T			
I, I, for this Seroune, and thou shalt [ha't] <hate>.	P 351	6.6	Mntsrl
HAT			
And a fine brouch to put in my hat,	Dido	1.1.47	Ganimd
And sticke these spangled feathers in thy hat,	Dido	2.1.314	Venus
Pilia-borza, bid the Fidler give me the posey in his hat there.	Jew	4.4.36	P Curtzn
The Hat he weares, Judas left under the Elder when he hang'd	Jew	4.4.66	P Ithimr
HATCH			
To hatch forth treason gainst their naturall Queene?	P1032	19.102	King
HATCHES			
But he clapt under hatches saild away.	Dido	5.1.240	Anna
HATCHEST			
Proud Rome, that hatchest such imperiall groomes,	Edw	1.4.97	Edward
HATCHETH			
That hatcheth up such bloudy practises.	P1205	22.67	King
Fie on that love that hatcheth death and hate.	Edw	4.6.15	Kent
HATCHT			
Thou hadst not hatcht this monstrous treacherie!	Edw	5.6.97	King
women; Poverty (who hatcht/Roomes greatest wittes) was loath'd,	Lucan, First Booke		166
First he commands such monsters Nature hatcht/Against her kind	Lucan, First Booke		588
HATE (Homograph; See also HAT'ST)			
I was as farre from love, as they from hate.	Dido	3.1.167	Dido
not of it, for I love thee not,/And yet I hate thee not:--	Dido	3.1.172	Dido
Here lyes my hate, Aeneas cursed brat,	Dido	3.2.1	Juno
When for the hate of Troian Ganimed,	Dido	3.2.42	Juno
O love, O hate, O cruell womens hearts,	Dido	3.3.66	Iarbus
Be arm'd against the hate of such a foe,	1Tamb	2.6.22	Ortyg
The Scum of men, the hate and Scourge of God,	1Tamb	4.3.9	Souldn
As now when furie and incensed hate/Flings slaughtering terrour	1Tamb	5.1.71	Tamb
staid, with wrath and hate/Of our expreslesse band inflictions.	1Tamb	5.1.281	Bajzth
Nor yet imposd, with such a bitter hate.	2Tamb	4.1.170	Jrslem
Expell the hate wherewith he paines our soules.	2Tamb	4.1.173	Orcan
So for just hate, for shame, and to subdew/This proud contemner	2Tamb	4.3.39	Orcan
That his teare-thyrsty and unquenched hate,	2Tamb	5.3.222	Techel
Admir'd I am of those that hate me most:	Jew	Prol.9	Machvl
Both circumcized, we hate Christians both:	Jew	2.3.215	Barab
Those that hate me, will I learn to loath.	P 156	2.99	Guise
I, I, for this Seroune, and thou shalt [ha't] <hate>.	P 351	6.6	Mntsrl
But wherfore beares he me such deadly hate?	P 779	15.37	Mugern
I hope will make the King surcease his hate:	P 792	16.6	Bartus

HATE (cont.)

If you love us my lord, hate Gaveston.	Edw	1.1.80	MortSr
now breaks the kings hate forth,/And he confesseth that he	Edw	1.4.193	Queene
Spencer, thou knowest I hate such formall toies,	Edw	2.1.44	Baldck
Which all the other fishes deadly hate,	Edw	2.2.24	Lncstr
They love me not that hate my Gaveston.	Edw	2.2.37	Edward
But I respect neither their love nor hate.	Edw	2.2.261	Gavstn
Fie on that love that hatcheth death and hate.	Edw	4.6.15	Kent
Armes that pursue our lives with deadly hate.	Edw	4.7.32	Spencr
You say true, Ile hate.	F App	p.231 11 P	Faust
Nor then was land, or sea, to breed such hate,	Lucan, First Booke		96
I hate thee not, to thee my conquests stoope,	Lucan, First Booke		203
Either love, or cause that I may never hate:	Ovid's Elegies		1.3.2
Anger delaide doth oft to hate retire.	Ovid's Elegies		1.8.82
I hate faire Paper should writte matter lacke.	Ovid's Elegies		1.11.20
The lawier and the client <both do> hate thy view,	Ovid's Elegies		1.13.21
Keeper if thou be wise cease hate to cherish,	Ovid's Elegies		2.2.9
Please her, her hate makes others thee abhorre,	Ovid's Elegies		2.3.11
Crowes <crow> [survive] <survives> armes-bearing Pallas hate,	Ovid's Elegies		2.6.35
Now love, and hate my light brest each way move;	Ovid's Elegies		3.10.33
Ile hate, if I can; if not, love gainst my will:	Ovid's Elegies		3.10.35
Bulles hate the yoake, yet what they hate have still.	Ovid's Elegies		3.10.36
Her deeds gaine hate, her face entreateth love:	Ovid's Elegies		3.10.43
Then thee whom I must love I hate in vaine,	Ovid's Elegies		3.13.39
For faithfull love will never turne to hate.	Hero and Leander		1.128
It lies not in our power to love, or hate,	Hero and Leander		1.167
Then Hero hate me not, nor from me flie,	Hero and Leander		1.291
so much/As one poore word, their hate to him was such.	Hero and Leander		1.384
And nothing more than counsaile, lovers hate.	Hero and Leander		2.140

HATED

Rather had I a Jew be hated thus,	Jew	1.1.114	Barab
And he that living hated so the crosse,	P 320	5.47	Anjoy
And therfore hated of the Protestants.	P 838	17.33	Guise
And smite with death thy hated enterprise.	F 880	3.1.102	Pope
may adde more shame/To the blacke scandall of his hated name.	F1378	4.2.54	Fredrk
To sheild me from your hated treachery:	F1428	4.2.104	Faust
Onely the Goddesse hated Goate did lack,	Ovid's Elegies		3.12.18
Fearing her owne thoughts made her to be hated.	Hero and Leander		2.44

HATEFUL

Breake through the hedges of their hateful mouthes,	2Tamb	4.3.46	Therid
now Abigall, what mak'st thou/Amongst these hateful Christians?	Jew	1.2.339	Barab
and flying/Left hateful warre decreed to both the Consuls.	Lucan, First Booke		486
Whither gost thou hateful nimph?	Ovid's Elegies		1.13.31

HATEFULL

Come, come abourd, pursue the hatefull Greekes.	Dido	2.1.22	Aeneas
Out hatefull hag, thou wouldst have slaine my sonne,	Dido	3.2.32	Venus
Will leade an hoste against the hatefull Greekes,	Dido	4.4.91	Aeneas
With Eban Scepter strike this hatefull earth,	1Tamb	4.2.28	Bajzth
For my accurst and hatefull perjurie.	2Tamb	2.3.3	Sgsmnd
The towers and cities of these hatefull Turks,	2Tamb	3.2.148	Tamb
Searing thy hatefull flesh with burning yrons,	2Tamb	3.5.123	Tamb
Downe to the channels of your hatefull throats,	2Tamb	4.1.183	Tamb
wilt thou so defame/The hatefull fortunes of thy victory,	2Tamb	4.3.78	Orcan
How should I step or stir my hatefull feete,	2Tamb	5.3.195	Amyras
For through our sufferance of your hatefull lives,	Jew	1.2.63	Govnr
What wilt thou doe among these hatefull fiends?	Jew	1.2.345	Barab
And she is hatefull to my soule and me:	Jew	3.4.36	Barab
She cast her hatefull stomack to the earth.	P1154	22.16	King
Away I say with hatefull Gaveston.	Edw	1.4.33	Lncstr
Engirt the temples of his hatefull head,	Edw	5.1.46	Edward
Will hatefull Mortimer appoint no rest?	Edw	5.3.5	Edward
Thy hatefull and accursed head shall lie,	Edw	5.6.30	King
False Prelates, for this hatefull treachery,	F1033	3.2.53	Pope
Many to rob is more sure, and lesse hatefull,	Ovid's Elegies		1.8.55
And early mountest thy hatefull carriage:	Ovid's Elegies		1.13.38
And tender love hath great things hatefull made.	Ovid's Elegies		2.18.4

HATES

Knowing my father hates thy cowardise,	2Tamb	4.1.23	Amyras
And let your hates extended in his paines,	2Tamb	4.1.172	Orcan
But Malta hates me, and in hating me/My life's in danger, and	Jew	5.2.30	Barab
Why should you love him, whome the world hates so?	Edw	1.4.76	Mortmr

HATETH

Who hateth me but for my happinesse?	Jew	1.1.112	Barab

HATH

Since that religion hath no recompence.	Dido	1.1.81	Venus
Or force her smile that hetherto hath frownd:	Dido	1.1.88	Jupitr
Triton I know hath fild his trumpe with Troy,	Dido	1.1.130	Venus
To know what coast the winde hath driven us on,	Dido	1.1.176	Aeneas
Fortune hath favord thee what ere thou be,	Dido	1.1.231	Venus
Not one of them hath perisht in the storme,	Dido	1.1.236	Venus
Who for Troyes sake hath entertaind us all,	Dido	2.1.64	Illion
Oft hath she askt us under whom we serv'd,	Dido	2.1.66	Illion
Achates speake, sorrow hath tired me quite.	Dido	2.1.293	Aeneas
Troian, thy ruthfull tale hath made me sad:	Dido	2.1.301	Dido
I feare me Dido hath been counted light,	Dido	3.1.14	Dido
altar, where Ile offer up/As many kisses as the Sea hath sands,	Dido	3.1.88	Dido
That hath so many unresisted friends:	Dido	3.2.50	Juno
Whom casualtie of sea hath made such friends?	Dido	3.2.76	Juno
And dead to honour that hath brought me up.	Dido	3.3.45	Aeneas
And dead to scorne that hath pursued me so.	Dido	3.3.49	Iarbus
What, hath Iarbus angred her in ought?	Dido	3.4.13	Aeneas
Prometheus hath put on Cupids shape,	Dido	3.4.21	Dido
Hath summond me to fruitfull Italy:	Dido	4.3.4	Aeneas

HATH (cont.)

Till he hath furrowed Neptunes glassie fieldes,	Dido	4.3.11	Aeneas
Hath not the Carthage Queene mine onely sonne?	Dido	4.4.29	Aeneas
I have an Orchard that hath store of plums,	Dido	4.5.4	Nurse
If that all glorie hath forsaken thee,	Dido	5.1.36	Hermes
who ever since hath luld me in her armes.	Dido	5.1.48	Ascan
Yet hath she tane away my oares and masts,	Dido	5.1.60	Aeneas
Jove hath heapt on me such a desperate charge,	Dido	5.1.64	Aeneas
the time hath been/When Didos beautie [chaind] <chaungd> thine	Dido	5.1.113	Dido
How can ye goe when he hath all your fleete?	Dido	5.1.242	Anna
And he hath all [my] <thy> fleete, what shall I doe/But dye in	Dido	5.1.268	Dido
That hath dishonord her and Carthage both?	Dido	5.1.280	Iarbus
helpe Iarbus, Dido in these flames/Hath burnt her selfe, aye me,	Dido	5.1.315	Anna
Your Grace hath taken order by Theridamas,	1Tamb	1.1.46	Meandr
And by those steps that he hath scal'd the heavens,	1Tamb	1.2.200	Tamb
You see my Lord, what woorking woordes he hath.	1Tamb	2.3.25	Therid
Who entring at the breach thy sword hath made,	1Tamb	2.7.9	Cosroe
As hath the Ocean or the Terrene sea/Small drops of water, when	1Tamb	3.1.10	Bajzth
should be most)/Hath seem'd to be digested long agoe.	1Tamb	3.2.8	Agidas
As it hath chang'd my first conceiv'd disdaine.	1Tamb	3.2.12	Zenoc
see how right the man/Hath hit the meaning of my Lord the King.	1Tamb	3.2.108	Techel
Hath now in armes ten thousand Janisaries,	1Tamb	3.3.15	Bassoe
Hath spread his colours to our high disgrace:	1Tamb	4.1.7	Souldn
But speake, what power hath he?	1Tamb	4.1.20	Souldn
faire Arabian king/That hath bene disapointed by this slave,	1Tamb	4.1.69	Souldn
For Fame I feare hath bene too prodigall,	1Tamb	4.3.48	Arabia
belike he hath not bene watered to day, give him some drinke.	1Tamb	4.4.55	P Tamb
And since your highnesse hath so well vouchsaft,	1Tamb	4.4.130	Therid
Whereto ech man of rule hath given his hand,	1Tamb	5.1.102	1Virgn
That which hath [stoopt] <stopt> the tempest of the Gods,	1Tamb	5.1.184	Tamb
Hath Bajazeth bene fed to day?	1Tamb	5.1.192	Tamb
But such a Star hath influence in his sword,	1Tamb	5.1.232	Bajzth
whose moaning entercourse/Hath hetherto bin staid, with wrath	1Tamb	5.1.281	Bajzth
Ah Madam, this their slavery hath Enforc'd,	1Tamb	5.1.345	Anippe
Your love hath fortune so at his command,	1Tamb	5.1.373	Anippe
She that hath calmde the furie of my sword,	1Tamb	5.1.437	Tamb
With them Arabia too hath left his life,	1Tamb	5.1.473	Tamb
Mighty hath God and Mahomet made thy hand/(Renowmed Tamburlain)	1Tamb	5.1.479	Souldn
That long hath lingred for so high a seat.	1Tamb	5.1.502	Therid
Hath made our Poet pen his second part,	2Tamb	Prol.3	Prolog
Besides, king Sigismond hath brought from Christendome,	2Tamb	1.1.20	Uribas
Since Tamburlaine hath mustred all his men,	2Tamb	1.1.46	Gazell
Nor he but Fortune that hath made him great.	2Tamb	1.1.60	Orcan
Whose head hath deepest scarres, whose breast most woundes,	2Tamb	1.3.75	Tamb
Natolia hath dismist the greatest part/Of all his armie, pitcht	2Tamb	2.1.16	Fredrk
That God hath given to venge our Christians death/And scourge	2Tamb	2.1.52	Fredrk
And take the victorie our God hath given.	2Tamb	2.1.63	Sgsmnd
With greater power than erst his pride hath felt,	2Tamb	2.2.10	Gazell
And hath the power of his outstretched arme,	2Tamb	2.2.42	Orcan
And God hath thundered vengeance from on high,	2Tamb	2.3.2	Sgsmnd
And Christ or Mahomet hath bene my friend.	2Tamb	2.3.11	Orcan
And since this miscreant hath disgrac'd his faith,	2Tamb	2.3.36	Orcan
Hath suckt the measure of that vitall aire/That feeds the body	2Tamb	2.4.44	Zenoc
Her sacred beauty hath enchaunted heaven,	2Tamb	2.4.85	Tamb
For amorous Jove hath snatcht my love from hence,	2Tamb	2.4.107	Tamb
If woords might serve, our voice hath rent the aire,	2Tamb	2.4.121	Therid
Whose cursed fate hath so dismembred it,	2Tamb	3.1.13	Callap
not but your royall cares/Hath so provided for this cursed foe,	2Tamb	3.1.21	Callap
who hath followed long/The martiall sword of mighty	2Tamb	3.1.27	Callap
For so hath heaven provided my escape,	2Tamb	3.1.32	Callap
My mothers death hath mortified my mind,	2Tamb	3.2.51	Celeb
View me thy father that hath conquered kings,	2Tamb	3.2.110	Tamb
That hath betraied my gracious Soveraigne,	2Tamb	3.2.153	Usumc
In frame of which, Nature hath shewed more skill,	2Tamb	3.4.75	Techel
And oft hath warn'd thee to be stil in field,	2Tamb	4.1.24	Amyras
Turkes Concubines first, when my father hath conquered them.	2Tamb	4.1.65	P Calyph
Hath stain'd thy cheekes, and made thee look like death,	2Tamb	4.2.4	Olymp
Your Majesty already hath devisde/A meane, as fit as may be to	2Tamb	4.3.50	Usumc
the breach the enimie hath made/Gives such assurance of our	2Tamb	5.1.2	Maxim
Hath trode the Meisures, do my souldiers martch,	2Tamb	5.1.75	Tamb
That with his sword hath quail'd all earthly kings,	2Tamb	5.1.93	Tamb
<Affrica>/Which hath bene subject to the Persean king,	2Tamb	5.1.166	Tamb
My sword hath sent millions of Turks to hell,	2Tamb	5.1.180	Tamb
The Monster that hath drunke a sea of blood,	2Tamb	5.2.13	Amasia
and the victories/Wherewith he hath so sore dismaide the world,	2Tamb	5.2.44	Callap
hath nowe gathered a fresh Armie, and hearing your absence in	2Tamb	5.3.103	P 3Msngr
now, how Jove hath sent/A present medicine to recure my paine:	2Tamb	5.3.105	Tamb
And when my soule hath vertue of your sight,	2Tamb	5.3.225	Tamb
For earth hath spent the pride of all her fruit,	2Tamb	5.3.250	Amyras
And all his life time hath bin tired,	Jew	1.1.15	Barab
Happily some haplesse man hath conscience,	Jew	1.1.119	Barab
glide by night/About the place where Treasure hath bin hid:	Jew	2.1.27	Barab
My Lord and King hath title to this Isle,	Jew	2.2.37	Bosco
I, and take heed, for he hath sworne your death.	Jew	2.3.280	Barab
Now have I that for which my soule hath long'd.	Jew	2.3.318	Lodowk
alas, hath pac'd too long/The fatall Labyrinth of misbeleefe,	Jew	3.3.63	Abigal
A Fryar? false villaine, he hath done the deed.	Jew	3.4.22	Barab
Nor make enquiry who hath sent it them.	Jew	3.4.81	Barab
and invenome her/That like a fiend hath left her father thus.	Jew	3.4.105	Barab
slavish Bands/Wherein the Turke hath yoak'd your land and you?	Jew	5.2.78	Barab
For Callymath, when he hath view'd the Towne,	Jew	5.2.105	Barab
That he hath in store a Pearle so big,	Jew	5.3.27	Msngr
By treason hath delivered thee to us:	Jew	5.5.110	Govnr

HATH (cont.)

till thy father hath made good/The ruines done to Malta and to	Jew	5.5.111		Govnr
The many favours which your grace hath showne,	P 9	1.9		Navrre
That Guise hath slaine by treason of his heart,	P 45	1.45		Navrre
Which he hath pitcht within his deadly toyle.	P 54	1.54		Navrre
Hath often pleaded kindred to the King.	P 108	2.51		Guise
For this, hath heaven engendred me of earth,	P 113	2.56		Guise
My policye hath framde religion.	P 122	2.65		Guise
Paris hath full five hundred Colledges,	P 137	2.80		Guise
Anjoy hath well advisde/Your highnes to consider of the thing,	P 219	4.17		Guise
Hath he been hurt with villaines in the street?	P 254	4.52		Charls
Wherein hath Ramus been so offencious?	P 384	7.24		Ramus
As hath sufficient counsaile in himselfe,	P 456	8.6		Anjoy
And such a King whom practise long hath taught,	P 458	8.8		Anjoy
That hath blasphemde the holy Church of Rome,	P 531	10.4		Guise
A griping paine hath ceasde upon my heart:	P 537	11.2		Charls
All this and more hath Henry with his crowne.	P 596	12.9		QnMoth
Hath worne the Poland diadem, before/You were invested in the	P 612	12.25		Mugern
My brother Guise hath gathered a power of men,	P 642	12.55		Cardnl
Sweet Mugeroune, tis he that hath my heart,	P 660	13.4		Duchss
Or hath my love been so obscurde in thee,	P 682	13.26		Guise
And Guise for Spaine hath now incenst the King,	P 711	14.14		Navrre
This is the Guise that hath incenst the King,	P 729	14.32		Navrre
the Duke of Joyeux/Hath made great sute unto the King therfore.	P 734	14.37		1Msngr
For he hath solemnely sworne thy death.	P 777	15.35		King
That the Guise hath taken armes against the King,	P 901	18.2		Navrre
Then hath your grace fit oportunitie,	P 903	18.4		Bartus
This is the traitor that hath spent my golde,	P1028	19.98		King
Hath he not made me in the Popes defence,	P1036	19.106		King
My father slaine, who hath done this deed?	P1047	19.117		YngGse
What this detested Jacobin hath done.	P1195	22.57		King
Whom God hath blest for hating Papestry.	P1208	22.70		King
And may it never end in bloud as mine hath done.	P1233	22.95		King
A souldier, that hath serv'd against the Scot.	Edw	1.1.34		3PrMan
Barons and Earls, your pride hath made me mute,	Edw	1.1.107		Kent
Wilshire hath men enough to save our heads.	Edw	1.1.127		MortSr
And Northward Gaveston hath many friends.	Edw	1.1.129		Lncstr
no soule in hell/Hath felt more torment then poore Gaveston.	Edw	1.1.147		Gavstn
of Lancaster/That hath more earldomes then an asse can beare,	Edw	1.3.2		Gavstn
The king I feare hath ill intreated her.	Edw	1.4.189		Warwck
The angrie king hath banished me the court:	Edw	1.4.210		Queene
Know you not Gaveston hath store of golde,	Edw	1.4.258		Mortmr
Weele pull him from the strongest hould he hath.	Edw	1.4.289		Mortmr
In this your grace hath highly honoured me,	Edw	1.4.364		MortSr
But he that hath the favour of a king,	Edw	2.1.8		Spencr
And hath a speciall gift to forme a verbe.	Edw	2.1.55		Spencr
Your minion Gaveston hath taught you this.	Edw	2.2.149		Lncstr
The murmuring commons overstretched hath.	Edw	2.2.160		Mortmr
The king hath left him, and his traine is small.	Edw	2.4.39		Queene
How Gaveston hath robd me of his love:	Edw	2.4.67		Queene
In burying him, then he hath ever earned.	Edw	2.5.56		Lncstr
Your honor hath an adamant, of power/To drawe a prince.	Edw	2.5.105		Arundl
Because your highnesse hath beene slack in homage,	Edw	3.1.63		Queene
Hath seazed Normandie into his hands.	Edw	3.1.64		Queene
Edward this day hath crownd him king a new.	Edw	3.1.261		Edward
But hath thy potion wrought so happilie?	Edw	4.1.14		Kent
It hath my lord, the warders all a sleepe,	Edw	4.1.15		Mortmr
But hath your grace got shipping unto Fraunce?	Edw	4.1.17		Mortmr
Hath shaken off the thraldome of the tower,	Edw	4.2.41		Mortmr
How hard the nobles, how unkinde the king/Hath shewed himself:	Edw	4.2.50		Mortmr
A villaines, hath that Mortimer escapt?	Edw	4.3.38		Edward
Whose loosnes hath betrayed thy land to spoyle,	Edw	4.4.11		Queene
And for the open wronges and injuries/Edward hath done to us,	Edw	4.4.22		Mortmr
Your king hath wrongd your countrie and himselfe,	Edw	4.6.67		Mortmr
For friends hath Edward none, but these, and these,	Edw	4.7.91		Edward
That thus hath pent and mu'd me in a prison,	Edw	5.1.18		Edward
This poore revenge hath something easd my minde,	Edw	5.1.141		Edward
Mine enemie hath pitied my estate,	Edw	5.1.149		Edward
The king hath willingly resignde his crowne.	Edw	5.2.28		BshpWn
I heare of late he hath deposde himselfe.	Edw	5.2.83		Kent
My lord, he hath betraied the king his brother,	Edw	5.2.106		Mortmr
Mortimer shall know that he hath wrongde mee.	Edw	5.2.118		Kent
Not so my liege, the Queene hath given this charge,	Edw	5.3.13		Gurney
What hath he done?	Edw	5.4.83		King
He hath a body able to endure,	Edw	5.5.10		Matrvs
A Mortimer, the king my sonne hath news,	Edw	5.6.15		Queene
But hath your grace no other proofe then this?	Edw	5.6.43		Mortmr
False Gurney hath betraide me and himselfe.	Edw	5.6.45		Mortmr
He hath forgotten me, stay, I am his mother.	Edw	5.6.90		Queene
'Tis magick, magick, that hath ravisht me.	F 137	1.1.109		Faust
Hath all the Principles Magick doth require:	F 167	1.1.139		Cornel
So Faustus hath <I have> already done, and holds <hold> this	F 283	1.3.55		Faust
Seeing Faustus hath incur'd eternall death,	F 316	1.3.88		Faust
Already Faustus hath hazarded that for thee.	F 422	2.1.34		Faust
for love of thee/Faustus hath <I> cut his <mine> arme, and with	F 443	2.1.55		Faust
And Faustus hath bequeath'd his soule to Lucifer.	F 464	2.1.76		Faust
Hell hath no limits, nor is circumscrib'd,	F 510	2.1.122		Mephst
And hath not he that built the walles of Thebes/With ravishing	F 579	2.2.28		Faust
Hath Mephostophilis no greater skill?	F 601	2.2.50		Faust
hath every Spheare a Dominion, or Intelligentia <Inteligentij>?	F 607	2.2.56	P	Faust
Thou needst not do that, for my Mistresse hath done it.	F 739	2.3.18	P	Dick
Thus hitherto hath Faustus spent his time.	F 799	3.1.21		Faust
The sacred Sinod hath decreed for him,	F 885	3.1.107		Pope

HATH (cont.)			
hath Faustus justly requited this injurious knight, which being	F1312	4.1.158	P Faust
Sith blacke disgrace hath thus eclipst our fame,	F1455	4.3.25	Benvol
O help, help, the villaine hath murder'd me.	F1493	4.4.37	P Faust
Faustus hath his leg againe, and the Horse-courser a bundle of	F1496	4.4.40	P Faust
hath sent some of his men to attend you with provision fit for	F1501	4.4.45	P Wagner
grace to thinke but well of that which Faustus hath performed.	F1565	4.6.8	P Faust
A surfet of deadly sin, that hath damn'd both body and soule.	F1833	5.2.37	P Faust
for which Faustus hath lost both Germany and the world, yea	F1843	5.2.47	P Faust
On God, whom Faustus hath abjur'd?	F1849	5.2.53	P Faust
on God, whom Faustus hath blasphem'd?	F1850	5.2.54	P Faust
God forbade it indeed, but Faustus hath done it:	F1858	5.2.62	P Faust
and twenty yeares hath Faustus lost eternall joy and felicitie.	F1859	5.2.63	P Faust
Hath rob'd me of eternall happinesse.	F1884	5.2.88	Faust
Whose influence hath allotted death and hell;	F1951	5.2.155	Faust
[Yet for Christs sake, whose bloud hath ransom'd me],	F1959	5.2.163A	Faust
That hath depriv'd thee of the joies of heaven.	F1974	5.2.178	Faust
Wel, tone of you hath this goblet about you.	F App	p.235 16	P Vintnr
at my intreaty release him, he hath done penance sufficient.	F App	p.238 79	P Emper
hath Faustus worthily requited this injurious knight, which	F App	p.238 82	P Faust
Beleeve me maister Doctor, this merriment hath much pleased me.	F App	p.242 1	P Duke
this learned man for the great kindnes he hath shewd to you.	F App	p.243 29	P Duke
For he hath given to me al his goodes,	F App	p.243 2	Wagner
lust of warre/Hath made Barbarians drunke with Latin bloud?	Lucan, First Booke	9	
Italy many yeares hath lyen until'd,	Lucan, First Booke	28	
Let come their [leader] <leaders whom long peace hath quail'd;	Lucan, First Booke	311	
Hath with thee past the swelling Ocean;	Lucan, First Booke	371	
and Rhene, which he hath brought/From out their Northren parts,	Lucan, First Booke	478	
Kind Jupiter hath low declin'd himselfe;	Lucan, First Booke	660	
Which troopes hath alwayes bin on Cupids side:	Ovid's Elegies	1.2.36	
And Cupide who hath markt me for thy pray,	Ovid's Elegies	1.3.12	
Aye me, thy body hath no worthy weedes.	Ovid's Elegies	1.8.26	
Th'opposed starre of Mars hath done thee harme,	Ovid's Elegies	1.8.29	
All Lovers warre, and Cupid hath his tent,	Ovid's Elegies	1.9.1	
This cause hath thee from pleasing me debard.	Ovid's Elegies	1.10.12	
And hath no cloathes, but open doth remaine.	Ovid's Elegies	1.10.16	
He hath no bosome, where to hide base pelfe.	Ovid's Elegies	1.10.18	
Nape free-borne, whose cunning hath no border,	Ovid's Elegies	1.11.2	
And tis suppos'd Loves bowe hath wounded thee,	Ovid's Elegies	1.11.11	
This day denyall hath my sport adjourned.	Ovid's Elegies	1.12.2	
That with one worde hath nigh himselfe undone,	Ovid's Elegies	1.13.20	
Nor hath the needle, or the combes teeth reft them,	Ovid's Elegies	1.14.15	
what meanes learnd/Hath this same Poet my sad chaunce discernd?	Ovid's Elegies	2.1.10	
In this sweete good, why hath a third to do?	Ovid's Elegies	2.5.32	
Even such as by Aurora hath the skie,	Ovid's Elegies	2.5.35	
Envy hath rapt thee, no fierce warres thou movedst,	Ovid's Elegies	2.6.25	
Elisium hath a wood of holme trees black,	Ovid's Elegies	2.6.49	
In naked bones? love hath my bones left naked.	Ovid's Elegies	2.9.14	
The weary souldiour hath the conquerd fields,	Ovid's Elegies	2.9.19	
The Ocean hath no painted stones or shelles,	Ovid's Elegies	2.11.13	
The crooked Barque hath her swift sailes displayd.	Ovid's Elegies	2.11.24	
Nor in my act hath fortune mingled chance,	Ovid's Elegies	2.12.15	
Wearie Corinna hath her life in doubt.	Ovid's Elegies	2.13.2	
Shee oft hath serv'd thee upon certaine dayes,	Ovid's Elegies	2.13.17	
Oft dyes she that her paunch-wrapt child hath slaine.	Ovid's Elegies	2.14.38	
And tender love hath great things hatefull made.	Ovid's Elegies	2.18.4	
And Phillis hath to reade; if now she lives.	Ovid's Elegies	2.18.32	
Thy muse hath played what may milde girles content,	Ovid's Elegies	3.1.27	
My mistris hath her wish, my wish remaine:	Ovid's Elegies	3.2.81	
her selfe she hath forswore,/And yet remaines the face she had	Ovid's Elegies	3.3.1	
By which she perjurd oft hath lyed [to] <by> me.	Ovid's Elegies	3.3.10	
maides society/Falsely to sweare, their beauty hath some deity.	Ovid's Elegies	3.3.12	
At me Joves right-hand lightning hath to throwe.	Ovid's Elegies	3.3.30	
Th'Arcadian Virgins constant love hath wunne?	Ovid's Elegies	3.5.30	
With virgin waxe hath some imbast my joynts,	Ovid's Elegies	3.6.29	
Hath any rose so from a fresh yong maide,	Ovid's Elegies	3.6.53	
What ere he hath his body gaind in warres.	Ovid's Elegies	3.7.20	
Him the last day in black Averne hath drownd,	Ovid's Elegies	3.8.27	
What profit to us hath our pure life bred?	Ovid's Elegies	3.8.33	
Now your credulity harme to me hath raisd.	Ovid's Elegies	3.11.44	
She hath not trode <tred> awrie that doth denie it,	Ovid's Elegies	3.13.5	
Since Heroes time, hath halfe the world beene blacke.	Hero and Leander	1.50	
Such force and vertue hath an amorous looke.	Hero and Leander	1.166	
Nor hath it any place of residence,	Hero and Leander	1.272	
Of that which hath no being, doe not boast,	Hero and Leander	1.275	
HATING			
But Malta hates me, and in hating me/My life's in danger, and	Jew	5.2.30	Barab
Hating the life and honour of the Guise?	P 932	19.2	Capt
Hating the life and honour of the Guise?	P 950	19.20	King
Whom God hath blest for hating Papestry.	P1208	22.70	King
HATRED			
Earths barrennesse, and all mens hatred/Inflict upon them, thou	Jew	1.2.163	Barab
Even so let hatred with thy [soveraignes] <soveraigne> smile.	Edw	1.4.342	Edward
HAT'ST			
I cannot thinke but that thou hat'st my life.	Jew	3.4.38	Barab
HAUGHT			
This haught resolve becomes your majestie,	Edw	3.1.28	Baldck
HAUGHTIE			
Go take that haughtie Mortimer to the tower,	Edw	3.1.252	Edward
HAUGHTY (See also HAUTIE)			
sent a thousand armed men/To intercept this haughty enterprize,	2Tamb	1.2.71	Almeda
And let no basenesse in thy haughty breast,	2Tamb	5.3.30	Usumc
Now where's the hope you had of haughty Spaine?	Jew	5.2.3	Calym

HAUGHTY (cont.)			
But wee'le pul downe his haughty insolence:	F 914	3.1.136	Pope
So will we quell that haughty Schismatique;	F 922	3.1.144	Pope
Nor thunder in rough threatings haughty pride?	Ovid's Elegies		1.7.46
HAUNT			
And Helens rape doth haunt [ye] <thee> at the heeles.	Dido	1.1.144	Aeneas
Let him please, haunt the house, be kindly usd,	Ovid's Elegies		2.2.29
HAUNTED			
Shall I still be haunted thus?	Edw	2.2.154	Edward
Defend me heaven, shall I be haunted still?	F1439	4.3.9	Benvol
And I grow faint, as with some spirit haunted?	Ovid's Elegies		3.6.36
HAUNTS			
Tis credible some [god-head] <good head> haunts the place.	Ovid's Elegies		3.1.2
HAUTIE			
When made a victor in these hautie arms,	2Tamb	4.1.46	Amyras
I cannot brooke these hautie menaces:	Edw	1.1.134	Edward
The hautie Dane commands the narrow seas,	Edw	2.2.168	Mortmr
HAUTY			
Upon the hauty mountains of my brest:	P 718	14.21	Navrre
I cannot brook thy hauty insolence,	P 862	17.57	King
HAVE (See also HA, HA'T, HATE, HAV'T, THOU'ST)			
Have oft driven backe the horses of the night,	Dido	1.1.26	Jupitr
When as they would have hal'd thee from my sight:	Dido	1.1.27	Jupitr
I would have a jewell for mine eare,	Dido	1.1.46	Ganimd
And shall have Ganimed, if thou wilt be my love.	Dido	1.1.49	Jupitr
How many dangers have we over past?	Dido	1.1.145	Aeneas
and grim Ceranias seate/Have you oregone, and yet remaine	Dido	1.1.148	Aeneas
Till we have fire to dresse the meate we kild:	Dido	1.1.165	Aeneas
You shall have leaves and windfall bowes enow/Neere to these	Dido	1.1.172	Aeneas
And have not any coverture but heaven.	Dido	1.1.230	Aeneas
Thy mind Aeneas that would have it so/Deludes thy eye sight,	Dido	2.1.31	Achat
destinies/Have brought my sweete companions in such plight?	Dido	2.1.60	Aeneas
Ile have it so, Aeneas be content.	Dido	2.1.95	Dido
Then he alleag'd the Gods would have them stay,	Dido	2.1.141	Aeneas
Troy is a fire, the Grecians have the towne.	Dido	2.1.208	Aeneas
And would have grappeld with Achilles sonne,	Dido	2.1.251	Aeneas
Shall I have such a quiver and a bow?	Dido	2.1.310	Ascan
(And yet have I had many mightier Kings)/Hast had the greatest	Dido	3.1.12	Dido
What will you give me now? Ile have this Fanne.	Dido	3.1.32	Cupid
So much have I receiv'd at Didos hands,	Dido	3.1.103	Aeneas
Nor Sterne nor Anchor have our maimed Fleete,	Dido	3.1.109	Aeneas
Wherefore would Dido have Aeneas stay?	Dido	3.1.134	Aeneas
Have been most urgent suiters for my love,	Dido	3.1.151	Dido
Say Paris, now shall Venus have the ball?	Dido	3.2.12	Juno
And have no gall at all to grieve my foes:	Dido	3.2.17	Juno
Out hatefull hag, thou wouldst have slaine my sonne,	Dido	3.2.32	Venus
Is this then all the thankes that I shall have,	Dido	3.2.37	Juno
That would have kild him sleeping as he lay?	Dido	3.2.39	Juno
Be it as you will have [it] for this once,	Dido	3.2.97	Venus
The woods are wide, and we have store of game:	Dido	3.3.6	Dido
Ile dye before a stranger have that grace:	Dido	3.3.11	Iarbus
We could have gone without your companie.	Dido	3.3.14	Dido
men (Dido except)/Have taunted me in these opprobrious termes,	Dido	3.3.27	Iarbus
I would have either drunke his dying bloud,	Dido	3.3.28	Iarbus
Or els I would have given my life in gage.	Dido	3.3.29	Iarbus
And yet desire to have before I dye.	Dido	3.4.10	Dido
Something it was that now I have forgot.	Dido	3.4.30	Dido
But now that I have found what to effect,	Dido	3.4.37	Dido
In all this coyle, where have ye left the Queene?	Dido	4.1.14	Iarbus
I might have stakte them both unto the earth,	Dido	4.1.23	Iarbus
Whose emptie Altars have enlarg'd our illes.	Dido	4.2.3	Iarbus
Before my sorrowes tide have any stint.	Dido	4.2.42	Iarbus
For I have honey to present thee with:	Dido	4.2.53	Anna
So she may have Aeneas in her armes.	Dido	4.3.42	Illion
I would have given Achates store of gold,	Dido	4.4.7	Dido
All that they have, their lands, their goods, their lives,	Dido	4.4.76	Dido
Or impious traitors vowde to have my life,	Dido	4.4.114	Dido
So I may have Aeneas in mine armes.	Dido	4.4.135	Dido
Thou wouldst have leapt from out the Sailers hands,	Dido	4.4.141	Dido
I have an Orchard that hath store of plums,	Dido	4.5.4	Nurse
Ile have a husband, or els a lover.	Dido	4.5.23	Nurse
O what meane I to have such foolish thoughts!	Dido	4.5.25	Nurse
That have I not determinde with my selfe.	Dido	5.1.19	Aeneas
Nay, I will have it calde Anchisaeon,	Dido	5.1.22	Aeneas
Whom I have brought from Ida where he slept,	Dido	5.1.40	Hermes
Who have no sailes nor tackling for my ships?	Dido	5.1.56	Aeneas
What, would the Gods have me, Deucalion like,	Dido	5.1.57	Aeneas
And they shall have what thing so ere thou needst.	Dido	5.1.74	Iarbus
O thy lips have sworne/To stay with Dido:	Dido	5.1.120	Dido
Thy hand and mine have plighted mutuall faith,	Dido	5.1.122	Dido
Wherein have I offended Jupiter,	Dido	5.1.129	Dido
I have not power to stay thee: is he gone?	Dido	5.1.183	Dido
I thinke some Fairies have beguiled me.	Dido	5.1.215	Nurse
Made me suppose he would have heard me speake:	Dido	5.1.230	Anna
now have I found a meane/To rid me from these thoughts of	Dido	5.1.272	Dido
None in the world shall have my love but thou:	Dido	5.1.290	Dido
I know you have a better wit than I.	1Tamb	1.1.5	Mycet
Have triumpht over Affrike, and the bounds/Of Europe wher the	1Tamb	1.1.9	Cosroe
Oft have I heard your Majestie complain,	1Tamb	1.1.35	Meandr
Have sworne the death of wicked Tamburlaine.	1Tamb	1.1.64	Mycet
Unlesse they have a wiser king than you.	1Tamb	1.1.92	Cosroe
Unlesse they have a wiser king than you?	1Tamb	1.1.93	Mycet
Have swarm'd in troopes into the Easterne India:	1Tamb	1.1.120	Cosroe

HAVE (cont.)

That heretofore have fild Persepolis/With Affrike Captaines,	1Tamb	1.1.141	Ceneus
The jewels and the treasure we have tane/Shall be reserv'd, and	1Tamb	1.2.2	Tamb
Where all my youth I have bene governed,	1Tamb	1.2.13	Zenoc
Have past the armie of the mightie Turke:	1Tamb	1.2.14	Zenoc
And since we have arriv'd in Scythia,	1Tamb	1.2.17	Magnet
We have his highnesse letters to command/Aide and assistance if	1Tamb	1.2.19	Magnet
May have the leading of so great an host,	1Tamb	1.2.48	Tamb
Which graticus starres have promist at my birth.	1Tamb	1.2.92	Tamb
Such hope, such fortune have the thousand horse.	1Tamb	1.2.118	Tamb
Deserv'st to have the leading of an hoste?	1Tamb	1.2.171	Tamb
You shall have honors, as your merits be:	1Tamb	1.2.255	Tamb
In happy hower we have set the Crowne/Upon your kingly head,	1Tamb	2.1.50	Ortyg
and brave Theridamas/Have met us by the river Araris:	1Tamb	2.1.63	Cosroe
And have a thousand horsmen tane away?	1Tamb	2.2.6	Mycet
And which is worst to have his Diadem/Sought for by such scalde	1Tamb	2.2.7	Mycet
But I will have Cosroe by the head,	1Tamb	2.2.11	Mycet
Tell you the rest (Meander) I have said.	1Tamb	2.2.13	Mycet
Shal have a government in Medea:	1Tamb	2.2.33	Meandr
Have view'd the army of the Scythians,	1Tamb	2.2.41	Spy
And having thee, I have a jewell sure:	1Tamb	2.2.56	Mycet
We have our Cammels laden all with gold:	1Tamb	2.2.62	Meandr
Now worthy Tamburlaine, have I reposde,	1Tamb	2.3.1	Cosroe
For Fates and Oracles [of] heaven have sworne,	1Tamb	2.3.7	Tamb
Was but a handful to that we will have.	1Tamb	2.3.17	Tamb
we have discovered the enemie/Ready to chardge you with a	1Tamb	2.3.49	1Msngr
I marie am I: have you any suite to me?	1Tamb	2.4.24	Mycet
Such another word, and I will have thee executed.	1Tamb	2.4.30	Mycet
Wel, I meane you shall have it againe.	1Tamb	2.4.36	Tamb
Your Majestie shall shortly have your wish,	1Tamb	2.5.48	Menaph
To aske, and have: commaund, and be obeied.	1Tamb	2.5.62	Therid
And since we all have suckt one wholsome aire,	1Tamb	2.6.25	Cosroe
Doth teach us all to have aspyring minds:	1Tamb	2.7.20	Tamb
As many circumcised Turkes we have,	1Tamb	3.1.8	Bajzth
And if before the Sun have measured heaven/With triple circuit	1Tamb	3.1.36	Bajzth
As his exceding favours have deserv'd,	1Tamb	3.2.10	Zenoc
The entertainment we have had of him,	1Tamb	3.2.37	Zenoc
Than stay the torments he and heaven have sworne.	1Tamb	3.2.99	Agidas
Two hundred thousand footmen that have serv'd/In two set	1Tamb	3.3.18	Bassoe
those that lead my horse/Have to their names tytles of dignity,	1Tamb	3.3.70	Bajzth
Whom I have brought to see their overthrow.	1Tamb	3.3.81	Bajzth
I have of Turkes, Arabians, Moores and Jewes/Enough to cover	1Tamb	3.3.136	Bajzth
not endure to strike/So many blowes as I have heads for thee.	1Tamb	3.3.144	Bajzth
As these my followers willingly would have:	1Tamb	3.3.155	Tamb
We have their crownes, their bodies strowe the fielde.	1Tamb	3.3.215	Techel
The pillers that have bolstered up those tearmes,	1Tamb	3.3.229	Tamb
Ah faire Zabina, we have lost the field.	1Tamb	3.3.233	Bajzth
Affrik and Greece have garrisons enough/To make me Soveraigne	1Tamb	3.3.242	Bajzth
Have fetcht about the Indian continent:	1Tamb	3.3.254	Tamb
May have fresh warning to go war with us,	1Tamb	4.1.71	Souldn
Should have prepar'd to entertaine his Grace?	1Tamb	4.2.63	Zabina
Whose feet the kings of Affrica have kist.	1Tamb	4.2.65	Zabina
Or els I sweare to have you whipt stark nak'd.	1Tamb	4.2.74	Anippe
This is my minde, and I will have it so.	1Tamb	4.2.91	Tamb
Shall talke how I have handled Bajazeth.	1Tamb	4.2.97	Tamb
So shall he have his life, and all the rest.	1Tamb	4.2.115	Tamb
Yet would you have some pitie for my sake,	1Tamb	4.2.123	Zenoc
Not for the world Zenocrate, if I have sworn:	1Tamb	4.2.125	Tamb
have ye lately heard/The overthrow of mightie Bajazeth,	1Tamb	4.3.23	Arabia
I have, and sorrow for his bad successe:	1Tamb	4.3.28	Souldn
If thou wilt have a song, the Turke shall straine his voice:	1Tamb	4.4.63	P Tamb
And wouldst thou have me buy thy Fathers love/With such a	1Tamb	4.4.83	Tamb
Here Turk, wilt thou have a cleane trencher?	1Tamb	4.4.101	P Tamb
You that have martcht with happy Tamburlaine,	1Tamb	4.4.121	Tamb
higher meeds/Then erst our states and actions have retain'd,	1Tamb	4.4.132	Therid
We see his tents have now bene altered,	1Tamb	5.1.7	Govnr
Let us have hope that their unspotted praiers,	1Tamb	5.1.20	Govnr
some your children)/Might have intreated your obdurate breasts,	1Tamb	5.1.28	1Virgn
overweighing heavens/Have kept to qualifie these hot extreames,	1Tamb	5.1.46	Govnr
could they not as well/Have sent ye out, when first my	1Tamb	5.1.68	Tamb
For whome the Powers divine have made the world,	1Tamb	5.1.76	1Virgn
whose silver haires/Honor and reverence evermore have raign'd,	1Tamb	5.1.82	1Virgn
ruthlesse Gcvernour/Have thus refusde the mercie of thy hand,	1Tamb	5.1.93	1Virgn
They have refusde the offer of their lives,	1Tamb	5.1.126	Tamb
What, have your horsmen shewen the virgins Death?	1Tamb	5.1.129	Tamb
They have my Lord, and on Damascus wals/Have hoisted up their	1Tamb	5.1.130	Techel
on Damascus wals/Have hoisted up their slaughtered carcases.	1Tamb	5.1.131	Techel
Must needs have beauty beat on his conceites.	1Tamb	5.1.182	Tamb
Till we have made us ready for the field.	1Tamb	5.1.212	Tamb
And have no hope to end our extasies.	1Tamb	5.1.238	Bajzth
Then as the powers devine have preordainde,	1Tamb	5.1.400	Zenoc
accidents/Have chanc'd thy merits in this worthles bondage.	1Tamb	5.1.425	Arabia
Though my right hand have thus enthralled thee,	1Tamb	5.1.435	Tamb
Have swelling cloudes drawen from wide gasping woundes,	1Tamb	5.1.459	Tamb
That I have sent from sundry foughten fields,	1Tamb	5.1.466	Tamb
Have desperatly dispatcht their slavish lives:	1Tamb	5.1.472	Tamb
And have bene crown'd for prooved worthynesse:	1Tamb	5.1.491	Tamb
Now have we martcht from faire Natolia/Two hundred leagues, and	2Tamb	1.1.6	Orcan
And have a greater foe to fight against,	2Tamb	1.1.15	Gazell
And for that cause the Christians shall have peace.	2Tamb	1.1.57	Orcan
We have revolted Grecians, Albanees,	2Tamb	1.1.61	Orcan
Therefore Viceroies the Christians must have peace.	2Tamb	1.1.77	Orcan
Wee with our Peeres have crost Danubius stream/To treat of	2Tamb	1.1.79	Sgsmnd

HAVE (cont.)

Wilt thou have war, then shake this blade at me,	2Tamb	1.1.83	Sgsmnd
Forgetst thou, that to have me raise my siege,	2Tamb	1.1.98	Orcan
(For that's the style and tytle I have yet)/Although he sent a	2Tamb	1.2.69	Almeda
My gratious Lord, they have their mothers looks,	2Tamb	1.3.35	Zenoc
As I cried out for feare he should have falne.	2Tamb	1.3.42	Zenoc
Wel done my boy, thou shalt have shield and lance,	2Tamb	1.3.43	Tamb
Have under me as many kings as you,	2Tamb	1.3.55	Celeb
conquer all the world/And you have won enough for me to keep.	2Tamb	1.3.68	Calyph
Of all the provinces I have subdued/Thou shalt not have a foot,	2Tamb	1.3.71	Tamb
Of all the provinces I have subdued/Thou shalt not have a foot,	2Tamb	1.3.72	Tamb
For I have sworne by sacred Mahomet,	2Tamb	1.3.109	Tamb
My crowne, my selfe, and all the power I have,	2Tamb	1.3.115	Therid
All which have sworne to sacke Natolia:	2Tamb	1.3.121	Therid
I and my neighbor King of Fesse have brought/To aide thee in	2Tamb	1.3.130	Usumc
How have ye spent your absent time from me?	2Tamb	1.3.173	Tamb
our men of Barbary have martcht/Foure hundred miles with armour	2Tamb	1.3.174	Usumc
We have subdude the Southerne Guallatia,	2Tamb	1.3.178	Usumc
And I have martch'd along the river Nile,	2Tamb	1.3.186	Techel
Cookes shall have pensions to provide us cates,	2Tamb	1.3.219	Tamb
I, liquid golde when we have conquer'd him,	2Tamb	1.3.223	Tamb
They have nct long since massacred our Camp.	2Tamb	2.1.10	Fredrk
Have I not here the articles of peace,	2Tamb	2.2.30	Orcan
And solemne covenants we have both confirm'd,	2Tamb	2.2.31	Orcan
And make the power I have left behind/(Too litle to defend our	2Tamb	2.2.59	Orcan
If there be Christ, we shall have victorie.	2Tamb	2.2.64	Orcan
my Lords whose true nobilitie/Have merited my latest memorie:	2Tamb	2.4.74	Zenoc
If teares, our eies have watered all the earth:	2Tamb	2.4.122	Therid
If griefe, our murthered harts have straind forth blood.	2Tamb	2.4.123	Therid
We both will rest and have one Epitaph/Writ in as many severall	2Tamb	2.4.134	Tamb
As I have conquered kingdomes with my sword.	2Tamb	2.4.136	Tamb
I have a hundred thousand men in armes,	2Tamb	3.1.38	Orcan
That have nct past the Centers latitude,	2Tamb	3.2.31	Tamb
Ile have you learne to sleepe upon the ground,	2Tamb	3.2.55	Tamb
It must have privy ditches, countermines,	2Tamb	3.2.73	Tamb
It must have high Argins and covered waies/To keep the bulwark	2Tamb	3.2.75	Tamb
That we have sent before to fire the townes,	2Tamb	3.2.147	Tamb
Til fire and sword have found them at a bay.	2Tamb	3.2.151	Tamb
Thus have wee martcht Northwarde from Tamburlaine,	2Tamb	3.3.1	Therid
Where we will have [Gabions] <Galions> of sixe foot broad,/To	2Tamb	3.3.56	Therid
Killing my selfe, as I have done my sonne,	2Tamb	3.4.35	Olymp
Whose body with his fathers I have burnt,	2Tamb	3.4.36	Olymp
This Lady shall have twice so much againe,	2Tamb	3.4.90	Therid
But as for you (Viceroy) you shal have bits,	2Tamb	3.5.103	Tamb
Ile have you learne to feed on provander,	2Tamb	3.5.106	Tamb
And all have jointly sworne thy cruell death,	2Tamb	3.5.112	Soria
you knowe I shall have occasion shortly to journey you.	2Tamb	3.5.114 P	Tamb
wel to heare both you/Have won a heape of honor in the field,	2Tamb	4.1.37	Calyph
He comes and findes his sonnes have had no shares/In all the	2Tamb	4.1.47	Amyras
I might have harme, which all the good I have/Join'd with my	2Tamb	4.1.57	Calyph
which all the good I have/Join'd with my fathers crowne would	2Tamb	4.1.57	Calyph
with the meteors/Of blood and fire thy tyrannies have made,	2Tamb	4.1.142	Jrslem
Have greater operation and more force/Than Cynthias in the	2Tamb	4.2.29	Therid
What, have I slaine her? Villaine, stab thy selfe:	2Tamb	4.2.82	Therid
And have so proud a chariot at your heeles,	2Tamb	4.3.3	Tamb
Let me have coach my Lord, that I may ride,	2Tamb	4.3.27	Amyras
them for the funerall/They have bestowed on my abortive sonne.	2Tamb	4.3.66	Tamb
Have we not hope, for all our battered walles,	2Tamb	5.1.15	Govnr
And have no terrour but his threatning lookes?	2Tamb	5.1.23	Govnr
Ninus and great Alexander/Have rode in triumph, triumphs	2Tamb	5.1.70	Tamb
Whose chariot wheeles have burst th'Assirians bones,	2Tamb	5.1.71	Tamb
brave Assirian Dames/Have rid in pompe like rich Saturnia,	2Tamb	5.1.77	Tamb
Who have ye there my Lordes?	2Tamb	5.1.80	Tamb
But I have sent volleies of shot to you,	2Tamb	5.1.99	Tamb
Nor if my bcdy could have stopt the breach,	2Tamb	5.1.101	Govnr
Shouldst thou have entred, cruel Tamburlaine:	2Tamb	5.1.102	Govnr
Unharnesse them, and let me have fresh horse:	2Tamb	5.1.130	Tamb
Then have at him to begin withall.	2Tamb	5.1.152	Therid
Whom I have thought a God? they shal be burnt.	2Tamb	5.1.176	Tamb
Now Mahomet, if thou have any power,	2Tamb	5.1.187	Tamb
I have fulfil'd your highnes wil, my Lord,	2Tamb	5.1.203	Techel
Have made the water swell above the bankes,	2Tamb	5.1.205	Techel
For we have here the chiefe selected men/Of twenty severall	2Tamb	5.2.48	Callap
That have bene tearm'd the terrour of the world?	2Tamb	5.3.45	Tamb
Here have I purst their paltry [silverlings] <silverbings>.	Jew	1.1.6	Barab
and have sent me to know/Whether your selfe will come and	Jew	1.1.52	1Merch
but we have scambled up/More wealth by farre then those that	Jew	1.1.122	Barab
Oft have I heard tell, can be permanent.	Jew	1.1.133	Barab
I have no charge, nor many children,	Jew	1.1.136	Barab
And all I have is hers. But who comes here?	Jew	1.1.139	Barab
With whom they have attempted many times,	Jew	1.1.164	Barab
The Turkes have let increase to such a summe,	Jew	1.1.182	Barab
are such/That you will needs have ten yeares tribute past,	Jew	1.2.19	Govnr
We may have time to make collection/Amongst the Inhabitants of	Jew	1.2.20	Govnr
Where wee'll attend the respit you have tane,	Jew	1.2.30	Calym
Have you determin'd what to say to them?	Jew	1.2.37	1Knght
Your Lordship shall doe well to let them have it.	Jew	1.2.44	Barab
To what this ten yeares tribute will amount/That we have cast,	Jew	1.2.47	Govnr
Have strangers leave with us to get their wealth?	Jew	1.2.60	2Knght
Corpo di dio stay, you shall have halfe,	Jew	1.2.90	Barab
It shall be so: now Officers have you done?	Jew	1.2.131	Govnr
my Lord, we have seiz'd upon the goods/And wares of Barabas,	Jew	1.2.132	Offcrs
And of the other we have seized halfe.	Jew	1.2.135	Offcrs

HAVE (cont.)

You have my goods, my mony, and my wealth,	Jew	1.2.138	Barab
You have my wealth, the labour of my life,	Jew	1.2.149	Barab
That thus have dealt with me in my distresse.	Jew	1.2.168	Barab
Thou seest they have taken halfe our goods.	Jew	1.2.176	1Jew
And of me onely have they taken all.	Jew	1.2.179	Barab
As much as would have bought his beasts and him,	Jew	1.2.189	Barab
And yet have kept enough to live upon;	Jew	1.2.190	Barab
For onely I have toyl'd to inherit here/The months of vanity	Jew	1.2.196	Barab
And painefull nights have bin appointed me.	Jew	1.2.198	Barab
Who for the villaines have no wit themselves,	Jew	1.2.215	Barab
For they have seiz'd upon thy house and wares.	Jew	1.2.251	Abigal
You partiall heavens, have I deserv'd this plague?	Jew	1.2.259	Barab
Daughter, I have it:	Jew	1.2.270	Barab
the plight/Wherein these Christians have oppressed me:	Jew	1.2.271	Barab
it be to injure them/That have so manifestly wronged us,	Jew	1.2.275	Abigal
thus; thou toldst me they have turn'd my house/Into a Nunnery,	Jew	1.2.277	Barab
There have I hid close underneath the plancke/That runs along	Jew	1.2.296	Barab
Which they have now turn'd to a Nunnery.	Jew	1.2.320	Abigal
Noble Lodowicke, I have seene/The strangest sight, in my	Jew	1.2.375	Mthias
As had you seene her 'twould have mov'd your heart,	Jew	1.2.385	Mthias
pleasures of swift-footed time/Have tane their flight,	Jew	2.1.8	Barab
Till I have answer of my Abigall.	Jew	2.1.19	Barab
Now have I happily espy'd a time/To search the plancke my	Jew	2.1.20	Abigal
And here behold (unseene) where I have found/The gold, the	Jew	2.1.22	Abigal
Come and receive the Treasure I have found.	Jew	2.1.38	Abigal
Some have we fir'd, and many have we sunke;	Jew	2.2.15	Bosco
Martin del Bosco, I have heard of thee;	Jew	2.2.19	Govnr
This truce we have is but in hope of gold,	Jew	2.2.26	1Knght
and I have bought a house/As great and faire as is the	Jew	2.3.13	Barab
Having Fernezes hand, whose heart I'le have;	Jew	2.3.16	Barab
That I may have a sight of Abigall;	Jew	2.3.34	Lodowk
will I shew my selfe to have more of the Serpent then the Dove;	Jew	2.3.36	P Barab
Yet I have one left that will serve your turne:	Jew	2.3.50	Barab
but e're he shall have her	Jew	2.3.51	Barab
Your life and if you have it.--	Jew	2.3.64	Barab
I'le have a saying to that Nunnery.	Jew	2.3.90	Barab
I must have one that's sickly, and be but for sparing vittles:	Jew	2.3.123	P Barab
An hundred Crownes, I'le have him; there's the coyne.	Jew	2.3.130	Barab
All that I have shall be at your command.	Jew	2.3.137	Barab
But I have sworne to frustrate both their hopes,	Jew	2.3.142	Barab
When you have brought her home, come to my house;	Jew	2.3.148	Barab
As for the Comment on the Machabees/I have it, Sir, and 'tis at	Jew	2.3.154	Barab
Come, I have made a reasonable market,	Jew	2.3.161	1Offcr
I have as much coyne as will buy the Towne.	Jew	2.3.200	Barab
That I have laugh'd agood to see the cripples/Goe limping home	Jew	2.3.211	Ithimr
I have it for you, Sir; please you walke in with me:	Jew	2.3.220	Barab
I weigh it thus much; I have wealth enough.	Jew	2.3.245	Barab
Oh heaven forbid I should have such a thought.	Jew	2.3.256	Barab
the Governors sonne/Will, whether I will or no, have Abigall:	Jew	2.3.258	Barab
a warning e're he goes/As he shall have small hopes of Abigall.	Jew	2.3.274	Barab
Barabas, thou know'st I have lov'd thy daughter long.	Jew	2.3.288	Lodowk
This is thy Diamond, tell me, shall I have it?	Jew	2.3.292	Lodowk
And mine you have, yet let me talke to her;	Jew	2.3.300	Barab
let him have thy hand,/But keepe thy heart till Don Mathias	Jew	2.3.306	Barab
I have intreated her, and she will grant.	Jew	2.3.314	Barab
Now have I that for which my soule hath long'd.	Jew	2.3.318	Lodowk
So have not I, but yet I hope I shall.	Jew	2.3.319	Barab
Lodowicke, it is enough/That I have made thee sure to Abigal.	Jew	2.3.335	Barab
For this I'le have his heart.	Jew	2.3.344	Mthias
What greater gift can poore Mathias have?	Jew	2.3.346	Mthias
Father, why have you thus incenst them both?	Jew	2.3.356	Abigal
I will have Don Mathias, he is my love.	Jew	2.3.361	Abigal
Yes, you shall have him: Goe put her in.	Jew	2.3.362	Barab
Oh, master, that I might have a hand in this.	Jew	2.3.368	Ithimr
Till I have set 'em both at enmitie.	Jew	2.3.383	Barab
but for one bare night/A hundred Duckets have bin freely given:	Jew	3.1.3	Curtzn
And I will have it or it shall goe hard.	Jew	3.1.15	Pilia
Well, I have deliver'd the challenge in such sort,	Jew	3.1.29	Ithimr
So, now they have shew'd themselves to be tall fellowes.	Jew	3.2.7	Barab
Wretched Ferneze might have veng'd thy death.	Jew	3.2.14	Govnr
I have the bravest, gravest, secret, subtil, bottle-nos'd knave	Jew	3.3.9	P Ithimr
one; have not the Nuns fine sport with the Fryars now and then?	Jew	3.3.32	P Ithimr
For I have now no hope but even in thee;	Jew	3.4.16	Barab
All that I have is thine when I am dead,	Jew	3.4.44	Barab
I have brought you a Ladle.	Jew	3.4.59	P Ithimr
Assure thy selfe thou shalt have broth by the eye.	Jew	3.4.92	Barab
For I have other businesse for thee.	Jew	3.4.110	Barab
Bashaw, in briefe, shalt have no tribute here,	Jew	3.5.11	Govnr
So I have heard; pray therefore keepe it close.	Jew	3.6.37	Abigal
Or though it wrought, it would have done no good,	Jew	4.1.5	Barab
True, I have mony, what though I have?	Jew	4.1.30	Barab
I must needs say that I have beene a great usurer.	Jew	4.1.39	Barab
I Have beene zealous in the Jewish faith,	Jew	4.1.51	Barab
That would for Lucars sake have sold my soule.	Jew	4.1.53	Barab
A hundred for a hundred I have tane;	Jew	4.1.54	Barab
much weight in Pearle/Orient and round, have I within my house;	Jew	4.1.67	Barab
Have I debts owing; and in most of these,	Jew	4.1.73	Barab
I know that I have highly sinn'd,	Jew	4.1.80	Barab
You shall convert me, you shall have all my wealth.	Jew	4.1.81	Barab
and I am resolv'd/You shall confesse me, and have all my goods.	Jew	4.1.86	Barab
Now I have such a plot for both their lives,	Jew	4.1.117	Barab
The other knowes enough to have my life,	Jew	4.1.120	Barab

HAVE (cont.)

What, will you [have] <save> my life?	Jew	4.1.148	2Fryar
Pull hard, I say, you would have had my goods.	Jew	4.1.149	Barab
Why, stricken him that would have stroke at me.	Jew	4.1.175	1Fryar
Good sirs I have don't, but no body knowes it but you two, I	Jew	4.1.180	P 1Fryar
No, pardon me, the Law must have his course.	Jew	4.1.185	Barab
And you can have it, Sir, and if you please.	Jew	4.2.56	Pilia
and would have it; but hee hides and buries it up as Partridges	Jew	4.2.57	P Ithimr
I'le write unto him, we'le have mony strait.	Jew	4.2.69	P Ithimr
I have no husband, sweet, I'le marry thee.	Jew	4.2.87	Curtzn
Give me a Reame of paper, we'll have a kingdome of gold for't.	Jew	4.2.115	P Ithimr
No Sir; and therefore I must have five hundred more.	Jew	4.3.22	P Pilia
what hee writes for you, ye shall have streight.	Jew	4.3.27	P Barab
No god-a-mercy, shall I have these crownes?	Jew	4.3.31	Pilia
I cannot doe it, I have lost my keyes.	Jew	4.3.32	Barab
You know I have no childe, and unto whom/Should I leave all but	Jew	4.3.44	Barab
Speake, shall I have 'um, Sir?	Jew	4.3.49	Pilia
To have a shag-rag knave to come [demand]/Three hundred	Jew	4.3.61	Barab
I have it.	Jew	4.3.66	Barab
have at it; and doe you heare?	Jew	4.4.2	P Ithimr
Nay, I'le have all or none.	Jew	4.4.5	Curtzn
And he my bondman, let me have law,	Jew	5.1.38	Barab
Once more away with him; you shall have law.	Jew	5.1.40	Govnr
As these have spoke so be it to their soules:--	Jew	5.1.42	Barab
Whom have we there, a spy?	Jew	5.1.69	Calym
And since that time they have hir'd a slave my man/To accuse me	Jew	5.1.75	Barab
much better/To [have] kept thy promise then be thus surpriz'd?	Jew	5.2.5	Calym
Intreat them well, as we have used thee.	Jew	5.2.17	Calym
said, within this Ile/In Malta here, that I have got my goods,	Jew	5.2.68	Barab
And in this City still have had successe,	Jew	5.2.69	Barab
shut/His souldiers, till I have consum'd 'em all with fire?	Jew	5.2.82	Barab
Thus have we view'd the City, seene the sacke,	Jew	5.3.1	Calym
Have speciall care that no man sally forth/Till you shall heare	Jew	5.4.2	Govnr
Why now I see that you have Art indeed.	Jew	5.5.4	Barab
Then now are all things as my wish wud have 'em,	Jew	5.5.17	Barab
Here have I made a dainty Gallery,	Jew	5.5.33	Barab
thee greater curtesie/Then Barabas would have affoorded thee.	Jew	5.5.62	Govnr
I would have brought confusion on you all,	Jew	5.5.85	Barab
This traine he laid to have intrap'd thy life;	Jew	5.5.91	Govnr
Thus he determin'd to have handled thee,	Jew	5.5.93	Govnr
But I have rather chose to save thy life.	Jew	5.5.94	Govnr
Nay, Selim, stay, for since we have thee here,	Jew	5.5.97	Govnr
Have you not heard of late how he decreed,	P 32	1.32	Navrre
Should have been murdered the other night?	P 35	1.35	Navrre
Oft have I leveld, and at last have learnd,	P 94	2.37	Guise
For this have I a largesse from the Pope,	P 119	2.62	Guise
Me thinkes the gloves have a very strong perfume,	P 170	3.5	OldQn
Might well have moved your highnes to beware/How you did meddle	P 179	3.14	Navrre
Now have we got the fatall stragling deere,	P 204	4.2	QnMoth
To have some care for feare of enemies.	P 224	4.22	QnMoth
Then Ile have a peale of ordinance shot from the tower,	P 236	4.34	Guise
He mist him neer, but we have strook him now.	P 311	5.38	Guise
That they which have already set the street/May know their	P 328	5.55	Guise
I feare the Guisians have past the bridge,	P 363	7.3	Ramus
Come Ramus, more golde, or thou shalt have the stabbe.	P 376	7.16	Gonzag
Alas I am a scholler, how should I have golde?	P 377	7.17	Ramus
All that I have is but my stipend from the King,	P 378	7.18	Ramus
Who have you there?	P 380	7.20	Anjoy
In that I know the things that I have wrote,	P 403	7.43	Ramus
Which we have chaste into the river [Sene] <Rene>,	P 418	7.58	Guise
I have done what I could to stay this broile.	P 434	7.74	Anjoy
For Poland is as I have been enformde,	P 454	8.4	Anjoy
As I could long ere this have wisht him there.	P 496	9.15	QnMoth
My Lord of Loraine have you markt of late,/How Charles our	P 512	9.31	QnMoth
Madam, I have heard him solemnly vow,	P 516	9.35	Cardnl
For Katherine must have her will in France:	P 520	9.39	QnMoth
Comfort your selfe my Lord and have no doubt,	P 541	11.6	Navrre
I have deserv'd a scourge I must confesse,	P 544	11.9	Charls
Tush, all shall dye unles I have my will:	P 653	12.66	QnMoth
I would the Guise in his steed might have come,	P 736	14.39	Navrre
Even for your words that have incenst me so,	P 767	15.25	Guise
Whether he have dishonoured me or no.	P 769	15.27	Guise
Marry if thou hadst, thou mightst have had the stab,	P 776	15.34	King
How many noble men have lost their lives,	P 795	16.9	Navrre
have at ye sir.	P 816	17.11	P Souldr
of Guise, we understand that you/Have gathered a power of men.	P 822	17.17	King
What I have done tis for the Gospell sake.	P 826	17.21	Guise
Why this tis to have an army in the fielde.	P 980	19.50	Guise
the rest have taine their standings in the next roome,	P 994	19.64	P 3Mur
Oh I have my deaths wound, give me leave to speak.	P1003	19.73	Guise
Oh that I have not power to stay my life,	P1007	19.77	Guise
what, have you done?	P1016	19.86	Capt
Yours my Lord Cardinall, you should have saide.	P1103	20.13	1Mur
That I with speed should have beene put to death.	P1118	21.12	Dumain
I have beene a great sinner in my dayes, and the deed is	P1133	21.27	P Frier
Sancte [Jacobe] <Jacobus>, now have mercye upon me.	P1172	22.34	Frier
We might have punisht him to his deserts.	P1184	22.46	Eprnon
hes to have the choyce of his owne freeland | yf it be not to	Paris	ms 8,p390	P Souldr
yow are wellcome ser have at you	Paris	ms16,p390	P Souldr
the armye I have gathered now shall ayme/more at thie end then	Paris	ms28,p391	Guise
and when thow thinkst I have foregotten this	Paris	ms20,p391	Guise
Might have enforst me to have swum from France,	Edw	1.1.7	Gavstn
But I have no horses. What art thou?	Edw	1.1.28	Gavstn

HAVE (cont.)

And as I like your discoursing, ile have you.	Edw	1.1.32	Gavstn
I have no warre, and therefore sir be gone.	Edw	1.1.36	Gavstn
And yet I have not viewd my Lord the king,	Edw	1.1.45	Gavstn
I have some busines, leave me to my selfe.	Edw	1.1.48	Gavstn
I must have wanton Poets, pleasant wits,	Edw	1.1.51	Gavstn
Therefore ile have Italian maskes by night,	Edw	1.1.55	Gavstn
Ile have my will, and these two Mortimers,	Edw	1.1.78	Edward
I will have Gaveston, and you shall know,	Edw	1.1.96	Edward
Foure Earldomes have I besides Lancaster,	Edw	1.1.102	Lncstr
He should have lost his head, but with his looke,	Edw	1.1.113	Kent
I have my wish, in that I joy thy sight,	Edw	1.1.151	Edward
Fearst thou thy person? thou shalt have a guard:	Edw	1.1.166	Edward
Which whiles I have, I thinke my selfe as great,	Edw	1.1.172	Gavstn
Come follow me, and thou shalt have my guarde,	Edw	1.1.204	Edward
Go whether thou wilt seeing I have Gaveston.	Edw	1.2.54	Queene
The king shall lose his crowne, for we have power,	Edw	1.2.59	Mortmr
It is our pleasure, we will have it so.	Edw	1.4.9	Edward
What we have done, our hart bloud shall maintaine.	Edw	1.4.40	Mortmr
And see what we your councellers have done.	Edw	1.4.44	ArchBp
And either have our wils, or lose our lives.	Edw	1.4.46	Mortmr
Subscribe as we have done to his exile.	Edw	1.4.53	ArchBp
So I may have some nooke or corner left,	Edw	1.4.72	Edward
Give it me, ile have it published in the streetes.	Edw	1.4.89	Lncstr
The Legate of the Pope will have it so,	Edw	1.4.109	Edward
Wherein my lord, have I deservd these words?	Edw	1.4.163	Queene
But madam, would you have us cal him home?	Edw	1.4.208	Mortmr
What, would ye have me plead for Gaveston?	Edw	1.4.213	Mortmr
For howsoever we have borne it out,	Edw	1.4.280	Mortmr
So shall we have the people of our side,	Edw	1.4.282	Mortmr
That you have parled with your Mortimer?	Edw	1.4.321	Edward
about my neck/Then these my lord, nor let me have more wealth,	Edw	1.4.331	Queene
Weele have a generall tilt and turnament,	Edw	1.4.376	Edward
For wot you not that I have made him sure,	Edw	1.4.378	Edward
Let him without controulement have his will.	Edw	1.4.390	MortSr
The mightiest kings have had their minions,	Edw	1.4.391	MortSr
I have not seene a dapper jack so briske,	Edw	1.4.412	Mortmr
But whiles I have a sword, a hand, a hart,	Edw	1.4.422	Mortmr
And would have once preferd me to the king.	Edw	2.1.14	Spencr
My life for thine she will have Gaveston.	Edw	2.1.28	Spencr
For I have joyfull newes to tell thee of,	Edw	2.1.75	Neece
I knew the King would have him home againe.	Edw	2.1.78	Spencr
You have matters of more waight to thinke upon,	Edw	2.2.8	Mortmr
I have the [gesses] <gresses> that will pull you downe,	Edw	2.2.40	Edward
Yet have I words left to expresse my joy:	Edw	2.2.60	Gavstn
Ile have his bloud, or die in seeking it.	Edw	2.2.107	Warwck
Weel have him ransomd man, be of good cheere.	Edw	2.2.116	Lncstr
Who have we there, ist you?	Edw	2.2.140	Edward
Quiet your self, you shall have the broad seale,	Edw	2.2.147	Edward
Have drawne thy treasure drie, and made thee weake,	Edw	2.2.159	Mortmr
To Englands high disgrace, have made this Jig,	Edw	2.2.189	Lncstr
For your lemmons you have lost, at Bannocks borne,	Edw	2.2.191	Lncstr
So soone to have woone Scotland,	Edw	2.2.194	Lncstr
How oft have I beene baited by these peeres?	Edw	2.2.201	Edward
Why then weele have him privilie made away.	Edw	2.2.236	Gavstn
Have at the rebels, and their complices.	Edw	2.2.265	Edward
He is your brother, therefore have we cause/To cast the worst,	Edw	2.3.7	Warwck
I have enformd the Earle of Lancaster.	Edw	2.3.14	Kent
Flie, flie, my lords, the earles have got the holde,	Edw	2.4.4	Edward
Whose pining heart, her inward sighes have blasted,	Edw	2.4.24	Queene
As if he heare I have but talkt with you,	Edw	2.4.54	Queene
But yet I hope my sorrowes will have end,	Edw	2.4.68	Queene
Yet lustie lords I have escapt your handes,	Edw	2.5.1	Gavstn
Souldiers, have him away:	Edw	2.5.26	Warwck
Thou shalt have so much honor at our hands.	Edw	2.5.28	Warwck
is it not enough/That we have taken him, but must we now/Leave	Edw	2.5.84	Warwck
We that have prettie wenches to our wives,	Edw	2.5.102	Penbrk
Strive you no longer, I will have that Gaveston.	Edw	2.6.7	Warwck
Yea gentle Spencer, we have beene too milde,	Edw	3.1.24	Edward
Too kinde to them, but now have drawne our sword,	Edw	3.1.25	Edward
Thou shalt have crownes of us, t'out bid the Barons,	Edw	3.1.55	Edward
Ah traitors, have they put my friend to death?	Edw	3.1.91	Edward
I will this undertake, to have him hence,	Edw	3.1.111	Arundl
I will have heads, and lives, for him as many,	Edw	3.1.132	Edward
As I have manors, castels, townes, and towers:	Edw	3.1.133	Edward
You villaines that have slaine my Gaveston:	Edw	3.1.142	Edward
You will this greefe have ease and remedie,	Edw	3.1.160	Herald
And have old servitors in high esteeme,	Edw	3.1.168	Herald
So sir, you have spoke, away, avoid our presence.	Edw	3.1.232	Edward
Have you no doubts my lords, ile [clap so] <claps> close,/Among	Edw	3.1.276	Levune
Shall have me from my gratious mothers side,	Edw	4.2.23	Prince
And then have at the proudest Spencers head.	Edw	4.2.25	Prince
Yet have we friends, assure your grace, in England/Would cast	Edw	4.2.54	Mortmr
Have beene by thee restored and comforted.	Edw	4.2.80	Mortmr
the realme, my lord of Arundell/You have the note, have you not?	Edw	4.3.8	Edward
realme, my lord of Arundell/You have the note, have you not?	Edw	4.3.8	Edward
I pray let us see it, what have we there?	Edw	4.3.10	Edward
What now remaines, have you proclaimed, my lord,	Edw	4.3.17	Edward
My lord, we have, and if he be in England,	Edw	4.3.19	Spencr
I have according to instructions in that behalfe,	Edw	4.3.28	P Spencr
Our kindest friends in Belgia have we left,	Edw	4.4.3	Queene
Since then succesfully we have prevayled,	Edw	4.6.21	Queene
realme, and sith the fates/Have made his father so infortunate,	Edw	4.6.27	Queene

HAVE (cont.)

Madam, have done with care and sad complaint,	Edw	4.6.66		Mortmr
Meane while, have hence this rebell to the blocke,	Edw	4.6.69		Mortmr
Have you no doubt my Lorde, have you no feare,	Edw	4.7.1		Abbot
and fell invasion/Of such as have your majestie in chase,	Edw	4.7.5		Abbot
rule and emperie/Have not in life or death made miserable?	Edw	4.7.15		Edward
The gentle heavens have not to do in this.	Edw	4.7.76		Edward
You, and such as you are, have made wise worke in England.	Edw	4.7.114	P	Rice
That Mortimer and Isabell have done.	Edw	5.1.25		Edward
My lorde, the parlement must have present newes,	Edw	5.1.84		Trussl
Call thou them back, I have no power to speake.	Edw	5.1.93		Edward
and bid him rule/Better then I, yet how have I transgrest,	Edw	5.1.122		Edward
Faire Isabell, now have we our desire,	Edw	5.2.1		Mortmr
Have done their homage to the loftie gallowes,	Edw	5.2.3		Mortmr
And we have heard that Edmund laid a plot,	Edw	5.2.32		BshpWn
If he have such accesse unto the prince,	Edw	5.2.77		Mortmr
The more cause have I now to make amends.	Edw	5.2.103		Kent
Tis not the first time I have killed a man.	Edw	5.4.30		Ltborn
But yet I have a braver way then these.	Edw	5.4.37		Ltborn
What traitor have wee there with blades and billes?	Edw	5.4.82		Mortmr
A would have taken the king away perforce,	Edw	5.4.84		Souldr
Strike off his head, he shall have marshall lawe.	Edw	5.4.89		Mortmr
Had Edmund liv'de, he would have sought thy death.	Edw	5.4.112		Queene
Know you this token? I must have the king.	Edw	5.5.19		Ltborn
I, stay a while, thou shalt have answer straight.	Edw	5.5.20		Matrvs
let him have the king,/What else?	Edw	5.5.24		Matrvs
See that in the next roome I have a fier,	Edw	5.5.29		Ltborn
Yet will it melt, ere I have done my tale.	Edw	5.5.55		Edward
And there in mire and puddle have I stood,	Edw	5.5.59		Edward
And whether I have limmes or no, I know not.	Edw	5.5.65		Edward
One jewell have I left, receive thou this.	Edw	5.5.84		Edward
For not these ten daies have these eyes lids closd.	Edw	5.5.94		Edward
His fathers dead, and we have murdered him.	Edw	5.6.16		Queene
What if he have? the king is yet a childe.	Edw	5.6.17		Mortmr
Nay, to my death, for too long have I lived,	Edw	5.6.83		Queene
Could I have rulde thee then, as I do now,	Edw	5.6.96		King
Wherby whole Cities have escap't the plague,	F 49	1.1.21		Faust
If we say that we have no sinne we deceive our selves, and	F 69	1.1.41	P	Faust
I'le have them flie to [India] <Indian> for gold;	F 109	1.1.81		Faust
I'le have them read me strange Philosophy,	F 113	1.1.85		Faust
I'le have them wall all Germany with Brasse,	F 115	1.1.87		Faust
I'le have them fill the publique Schooles with [silke] <skill>,	F 117	1.1.89		Faust
Know that your words have won me at the last,	F 128	1.1.100		Faust
have with [concise] <subtle> Sillogismes <Consissylogismes>	F 139	1.1.111		Faust
And have these joies in full possession.	F 179	1.1.151		Faust
<Have you any witnesse on't>?	F 204	(HC258)A	P	Wagner
Then I feare that which I have long suspected:	F 220	1.2.27		1Schol
Now Faustus what wouldst thou have me do?	F 263	1.3.35		Mephst
So Faustus hath <I have> already done, and holds <hold> this	F 283	1.3.55		Faust
Now that I have obtain'd what I desir'd <desire>/I'le live in	F 340	1.3.112		Faust
have seene many boyes with [such pickadevaunts] <beards> I am	F 345	1.4.3	P	Robin
I had need to have it well rosted, and good sauce to it,	F 352	1.4.10	P	Robin
Why, have you any paine that torture other <tortures others>?	F 432	2.1.44		Faust
As great as have the humane soules of men.	F 433	2.1.45		Mephst
But tell me Faustus, shall I have thy soule?	F 434	2.1.46		Mephst
<off> this, let me have a wife, the fairest Maid in Germany,	F 529	2.1.141	P	Faust
<Nay sweete Mephastophilis fetch me one, for I will have one>.	F 530	(HC261)A	P	Faust
<Well thou wilt have one, sit there till I come,	F 531	(HC261)A	P	Mephst
Well Faustus, thou shalt have a wife.	F 531	2.1.143		Mephst
Now Faustus wilt thou have a wife?	F 533	2.1.145		Mephst
She whom thine eye shall like, thy heart shall have,	F 539	2.1.151		Mephst
have a booke wherein I might beholde al spels and incantations,	F 551.1	2.1.164A	P	Faust
have a booke where I might see al characters of <and> planets	F 551.4	2.1.167A	P	Faust
[Nay let me have one booke more, and then I have done, wherein	F 551.8	2.1.171A	P	Faust
booke more, and then I have done, wherein I might see al plants,	F 551.8	2.1.171A	P	Faust
long e're this, I should have done the deed <slaine my selfe>,	F 575	2.2.24		Faust
Have not I made blind Homer sing to me/Of Alexanders love, and	F 577	2.2.26		Faust
But <tell me> have they all/One motion, both situ et tempore?	F 595	2.2.44		Faust
Why are <have wee> not Conjunctions, Oppositions, Aspects,	F 615	2.2.64	P	Faust
all at one time, but in some years we have more, in some lesse?	F 616	2.2.65	P	Faust
Villaine, have I not bound thee to tell me any thing?	F 622	2.2.71	P	Faust
There's none but I have interest in the same.	F 637	2.2.86		Lucifr
I am Pride; I disdaine to have any parents:	F 664	2.2.113	P	Pride
bag; and might I now obtaine <have> my wish, this house,	F 675	2.2.124	P	Covet
have run up and downe the world with these <this> case of	F 688	2.2.137	P	Wrath
and the devill a peny they have left me, but a [bare] <small>	F 694	2.2.143	P	Glutny
[where I have laine ever since, and you have done me great	F 705.1	2.2.155A	P	Sloth
and you have done me great injury to bring me from thence, let	F 705.1	2.2.155A	P	Sloth
I have gotten one of Doctor Faustus conjuring bookes, and now	F 723	2.3.2	P	Robin
conjuring bookes, and now we'le have such knavery, as't passes.	F 724	2.3.3	P	Robin
I have other matters in hand, let the horses walk themselves	F 726	2.3.5	P	Robin
of us here, that have waded as deepe into matters, as other men,	F 740	2.3.19	P	Robin
Do but speake what thou't have me to do, and I'le do't:	F 745	2.3.24	P	Robin
I have my Faustus, and for proofe thereof,	F 803	3.1.25		Mephst
<Faustus I have, and because we wil not be unprovided,	F 805	(HC265)A	P	Mephst
I have taken up his holinesse privy chamber for our use>.	F 806	(HC265)A	P	Mephst
Pope Adrian let me have some right of Law,	F 904	3.1.126		Bruno
What have our holy Councell there decreed,	F 947	3.1.169		Pope
The Statutes Decretall have thus decreed,	F 961	3.1.183		Faust
Then wherefore would you have me view that booke?	F1023	3.2.43		Pope
I'le have that too.	F1048	3.2.68		Faust
I pray my Lords have patience at this troublesome banquet.	F1058	3.2.78		Pope
I am glad I have found you, you are a couple of fine	F1096	3.3.9	P	Vintnr

HAVE (cont.)

Never deny't, for I know you have it, and I'le search you.	F1101	3.3.14	P	Vintnr
life, Vintner you shall have your cup anon, say nothing Dick:	F1114	3.3.27	P	Robin
Constantinople have they brought me now <am I hither brought>,	F1118	3.3.31		Mephst
you have had a shroud journey of it, will it please you to take	F1120	3.3.33	P	Robin
let me have the carrying of him about to shew some trickes.	F1128	3.3.41	P	Robin
I have a charme in my head, shall controule him as well as the	F1202	4.1.48	P	Benvol
come not away quickly, you shall have me asleepe presently:	F1242	4.1.88	P	Benvol
to thinke I have beene such an Asse all this while, to stand	F1243	4.1.89	P	Benvol
That in mine armes I would have compast him.	F1262	4.1.108		Emper
I have heard it said,/That this faire Lady, whilest she liv'd	F1265	4.1.111		Emper
Till with my sword I have that Conjurer slaine.	F1333	4.2.9		Benvol
Who kils him shall have gold, and endlesse love.	F1349	4.2.25		Fredrk
For hornes he gave, Il'e have his head anone.	F1361	4.2.37		Benvol
Faustus will have heads and hands,/I, [all] <I call> your	F1393	4.2.69		Faust
Nay feare not man, we have no power to kill.	F1440	4.3.10		Mrtino
I have a Castle joyning neere these woods,	F1452	4.3.22		Benvol
I have no great need to sell him, but if thou likest him for	F1460	4.4.4	P	Faust
and have lost very much of late by horse flesh, and this	F1464	4.4.8	P	HrsCsr
I have puld off his leg.	F1492	4.4.36	P	HrsCsr
on the score, but say nothing, see if she have forgotten me.	F1512	4.5.8	P	Robin
heere's some on's have cause to know him; did he conjure thee	F1523	4.5.19	P	HrsCsr
be; for I have heard of one, that ha's eate a load of logges.	F1533	4.5.29	P	Robin
had had some [rare] quality that he would not have me know of,	F1543	4.5.39	P	HrsCsr
that you have taken no pleasure in those sights; therefor I	F1566	4.6.9	P	Faust
I pray you tell me, what is the thing you most desire to have?	F1567	4.6.10	P	Faust
I have heard that great bellyed women, do long for things, are	F1568	4.6.11	P	Faust
kind I will make knowne unto you what my heart desires to have,	F1571	4.6.14	P	Lady
that lye farre East, where they have fruit twice a yeare.	F1584	4.6.27	P	Faust
by meanes of a swift spirit that I have, I had these grapes	F1585	4.6.28	P	Faust
What rude disturbers have we at the gate?	F1588	4.6.31		Duke
And then demand of them, what they would have.	F1590	4.6.33		Duke
We have no reason for it, therefore a fig for him.	F1593	4.6.36	P	Dick
I hope sir, we have wit enough to be more bold then welcome.	F1595	4.6.38	P	HrsCsr
What would they have?	F1599	4.6.42		Duke
I have procur'd your pardons: welcome all.	F1610	4.6.53		Faust
Be not so furious: come you shall have Beere.	F1620	4.6.63		Faust
me thinkes you should have a wooden bedfellow of one of 'em.	F1653	4.6.96	P	Carter
But I have it againe now I am awake:	F1657	4.6.100	P	Faust
now you have sent away my guesse, I pray who shall pay me for	F1667	4.6.110	P	Hostss
we have determin'd with our selves, that Hellen of Greece was	F1682	5.1.9	P	1Schol
Now <Since> we have seene the pride of Natures worke <workes>,	F1702	5.1.29		1Schol
And so have hope, that this my kinde rebuke,	F1722	5.1.49		OldMan
That I may <might> have unto my paramour,	F1761	5.1.88		Faust
If it be so, wee'l have Physitians,	F1830	5.2.34		2Schol
remember that I have beene a student here these thirty yeares,	F1840	5.2.44	P	Faust
and what wonders I have done, all Germany can witnesse, yea all	F1842	5.2.46	P	Faust
tell us of this before, that Divines might have prayd for thee?	F1863	5.2.67	P	1Schol
Oft have I thought to have done so:	F1864	5.2.68	P	Faust
thou, and we will pray, that God may have mercie upon thee.	F1875	5.2.79	P	2Schol
O, I have seene enough to torture me.	F1921	5.2.125		Faust
[O God, if thou wilt not have mercy on my soule],	F1958	5.2.162A		Faust
Pray heaven the Doctor have escapt the danger.	F1987	5.3.5		1Schol
The devils whom Faustus serv'd have torne him thus:	F1990	5.3.8		3Schol
Cut is the branch that might have growne full straight,	F2002	5.3.20		4Chor
you have seene many boyes with such pickadevaunts as I have.	F App	p.229 2	P	Clown
you have seene many boyes with such pickadevaunts as I have.	F App	p.229 3	P	Clown
burladie I had neede have it wel roasted, and good sawce to it,	F App	p.229 11	P	Clown
crownes a man were as good have as many english counters,	F App	p.230 34	P	Clown
they have vilde long nailes, there was a hee divell and a shee	F App	p.230 51	P	Clown
theres a Gentleman tarries to have his horse, and he would have	F App	p.233 7	P	Rafe
his horse, and he would have his things rubd and made cleane:	F App	p.233 7	P	Rafe
O brave Robin, shal I have Nan Spit, and to mine owne use?	F App	p.234 29	P	Rafe
with you, I must yet have a goblet payde from you ere you goe.	F App	p.234 7	P	Vintnr
you have had a great journey, wil you take sixe pence in your	F App	p.235 40	P	Robin
Ile have fine sport with the boyes, Ile get nuts and apples	F App	p.236 45	P	Robin
have heard strange report of thy knowledge in the blacke Arte,	F App	p.236 1	P	Emper
be witnesses to confirme what mine eares have heard reported,	F App	p.236 7	P	Emper
my selfe farre inferior to the report men have published,	F App	p.236 13	P	Faust
I thinke I have met with you for it.	F App	p.238 78	P	Faust
I have beene al this day seeking one maister Fustian:	F App	p.239 98	P	HrsCsr
I have brought you forty dollers for your horse.	F App	p.239 101	P	HrsCsr
Alas sir, I have no more, I pray you speake for me.	F App	p.239 104	P	HrsCsr
I pray you let him have him, he is an honest felow, and he has	F App	p.239 105	P	Mephst
but I must tel you one thing before you have him, ride him not	F App	p.239 108	P	Faust
had some rare qualitie that he would not have had me knowne of,	F App	p.240 132	P	HrsCsr
and have my fortie dollers againe, or Ile make it the dearest	F App	p.240 136	P	HrsCsr
And he have not slept this eight weekes Ile speake with him.	F App	p.240 145	P	HrsCsr
I have none about me, come to my Oastrie, and Ile give them	F App	p.241 161	P	HrsCsr
have heard that great bellied women do long for some dainties	F App	p.242 4	P	Faust
tell me, and you shal have it.	F App	p.242 6	P	Faust
thing then this, so it would content you, you should have it	F App	p.242 14	P	Faust
and by means of a swift spirit that I have, I had them brought	F App	p.242 22	P	Faust
Might they have won whom civil broiles have slaine,	Lucan, First Booke	14		
all lands else/Have stable peace, here wars rage first begins,	Lucan, First Booke	252		
you that with me have borne/A thousand brunts, and tride me ful	Lucan, First Booke	300		
spread these flags that ten years space have conquer'd,	Lucan, First Booke	348		
Albeit the Citty thou wouldst have so ra'st/Be Roome it selfe.	Lucan, First Booke	386		
You would have thought their houses had bin fierd/Or	Lucan, First Booke	490		
And other Regions, I have seene Philippi:	Lucan, First Booke	693		
I have no mistris, nor no favorit,	Ovid's Elegies	1.1.23		
Then oxen which have drawne the plow before.	Ovid's Elegies	1.2.14		
I lately cought, will have a new made wound,	Ovid's Elegies	1.2.29		

HAVE (cont.)

Soone may you plow the little lands <land> I have,	Ovid's Elegies	1.3.9
If men have Faith, Ile live with thee for ever.	Ovid's Elegies	1.3.16
I have beene wanton, therefore am perplext,	Ovid's Elegies	1.4.45
Have care to walke in middle of the throng.	Ovid's Elegies	1.4.56
All have I spent:	Ovid's Elegies	1.6.61
Binde fast my hands, they have deserved chaines,	Ovid's Elegies	1.7.1
I might have then my parents deare misus'd,	Ovid's Elegies	1.7.5
Better I could part of my selfe have wanted.	Ovid's Elegies	1.7.24
To mine owne selfe have I had strength so furious?	Ovid's Elegies	1.7.25
(If I have faith) I sawe the starres drop bloud,	Ovid's Elegies	1.8.11
Faire women play, shee's chast whom none will have,	Ovid's Elegies	1.8.43
Who seekes, for being faire, a night to have,	Ovid's Elegies	1.8.67
hoary flieces/And riveld cheekes I would have puld a pieces.	Ovid's Elegies	1.8.112
Will you for gaine have Cupid sell himselfe?	Ovid's Elegies	1.10.17
Ill gotten goods good end will never have.	Ovid's Elegies	1.10.48
All for their Mistrisse, what they have, prepare.	Ovid's Elegies	1.10.58
My hands an unsheath'd shyning weapon have not.	Ovid's Elegies	2.2.64
If not, because shees simple I would have her.	Ovid's Elegies	2.4.18
[And nut-browne girles in doing have no fellowe].	Ovid's Elegies	2.4.40
But such kinde wenches let their lovers have.	Ovid's Elegies	2.5.26
All wasting years have that complaint [out] <not> worne.	Ovid's Elegies	2.6.8
The little stones these little verses have.	Ovid's Elegies	2.6.60
Doest joy to have thy hooked Arrowes shaked,	Ovid's Elegies	2.9.13
That have so oft serv'd pretty wenches dyet.	Ovid's Elegies	2.9.24
Let such as be mine enemies have none,	Ovid's Elegies	2.10.16
Though I am slender, I have store of pith,	Ovid's Elegies	2.10.23
Oft have I spent the night in wantonnesse,	Ovid's Elegies	2.10.27
O would that no Oares might in seas have suncke,	Ovid's Elegies	2.11.5
In what gulfe either Syrtes have their seate.	Ovid's Elegies	2.11.20
The Thracian Harpe with cunning to have strooke,	Ovid's Elegies	2.11.32
of me, or I am sure/I oft have done, what might as much procure.	Ovid's Elegies	2.13.6
To have this skirmish fought, let it suffice thee.	Ovid's Elegies	2.13.28
Who should have Priams wealthy substance wonne,	Ovid's Elegies	2.14.13
For great revenews I good verses have,	Ovid's Elegies	2.17.27
Long have I borne much, hoping time would beate thee/To guard	Ovid's Elegies	2.19.49
Such chaunce let me have:	Ovid's Elegies	3.2.9
Yet he attain'd by her support to have her,	Ovid's Elegies	3.2.17
The sea I use not: me my earth must have.	Ovid's Elegies	3.2.48
The Gods have eyes, and brests as well as men.	Ovid's Elegies	3.3.42
Few love, what others have unguarded left.	Ovid's Elegies	3.4.26
Thee I have pass'd, and knew thy streame none such,	Ovid's Elegies	3.5.5
What helpes my hast: what to have tane small rest?	Ovid's Elegies	3.5.9
much (I crave)/Gifts then my promise greater thou shalt have.	Ovid's Elegies	3.5.66
Shame, that should make me blush, I have no more.	Ovid's Elegies	3.5.78
I shame so great names to have usde so vainly:	Ovid's Elegies	3.5.102
Or she was not the wench I wisht t'have had.	Ovid's Elegies	3.6.2
As she might straight have gone to church and praide:	Ovid's Elegies	3.6.54
Huge okes, hard Adamantes might she have moved,	Ovid's Elegies	3.6.57
And with sweete words cause deafe rockes to have loved <moned>,	Ovid's Elegies	3.6.58
Romulus, temples brave/Bacchus, Alcides, and now Caesar have.	Ovid's Elegies	3.7.52
Souldiours by bloud to be inricht have lucke.	Ovid's Elegies	3.7.54
And some there be that thinke we have a deity.	Ovid's Elegies	3.8.18
What to have laine alone in empty bed?	Ovid's Elegies	3.8.34
And some, that she refrain'd teares, have deni'd.	Ovid's Elegies	3.8.46
Long have I borne much, mad thy faults me make:	Ovid's Elegies	3.10.1
Now have I freed my selfe, and fled the chaine,	Ovid's Elegies	3.10.3
And what I have borne, shame to beare againe.	Ovid's Elegies	3.10.4
I have sustainde so oft thrust from the dore,	Ovid's Elegies	3.10.9
When have not I fixt to thy side close layed?	Ovid's Elegies	3.10.17
I have thy husband, guard, and fellow plaied.	Ovid's Elegies	3.10.18
Bulles hate the yoake, yet what they hate have still.	Ovid's Elegies	3.10.36
Wilt have me willing, or to love by force?	Ovid's Elegies	3.10.50
Nor have their words true histories pretence,	Ovid's Elegies	3.11.42
And my wench ought to have seem'd falsely praisd,	Ovid's Elegies	3.11.43
Is said to have attempted flight forsooke.	Ovid's Elegies	3.12.20
Such as confesse, have lost their good names by it.	Ovid's Elegies	3.13.6
And in the bed hide all the faults you have,	Ovid's Elegies	3.13.20
My soule fleetes when I thinke what you have done,	Ovid's Elegies	3.13.37
Which I Pelignis foster-child have framde,	Ovid's Elegies	3.14.3
And there for honie, bees have sought in vaine,	Hero and Leander	1.23
And beat from thence, have lighted there againe.	Hero and Leander	1.24
Would have allur'd the vent'rous youth of Greece,	Hero and Leander	1.57
Jove might have sipt out Nectar from his hand.	Hero and Leander	1.62
And know that some have wrong'd Dianas name?	Hero and Leander	1.284
Yet for her sake whom you have vow'd to serve,	Hero and Leander	1.316
With that Leander stoopt, to have imbrac'd her,	Hero and Leander	1.341
As might have made heaven stoope to have a touch,	Hero and Leander	1.366
have concluded/That Midas brood shall sit in Honors chaire,	Hero and Leander	1.474
And would have turn'd againe, but was afrayd,	Hero and Leander	2.8
By nature have a mutuall appetence,	Hero and Leander	2.56
Love alwaies makes those eloquent that have it.	Hero and Leander	2.72
He would have chac'd away the swelling maine,	Hero and Leander	2.121
O none but gods have power their love to hide,	Hero and Leander	2.131
To have his head control'd, but breakes the raines,	Hero and Leander	2.142
Which mounted up, intending to have kist him,	Hero and Leander	2.173
And who have hard hearts, and obdurat minds,	Hero and Leander	2.217
And faine by stealth away she would have crept,	Hero and Leander	2.310
And to some corner secretly have gone,	Hero and Leander	2.311

HAVEN

or to what end/Launcht from the haven, lye they in the Rhode?	Dido 5.1.89	Dido
Than in the haven when the Pilot stands/And viewes a strangers	1Tamb 4.3.32	Souldn
The [haven] <heaven> touching barcke now nere the lea,	Ovid's Elegies	2.9.32

HAVEN (cont.)			
Now my ship in the wished haven crownd,	Ovid's Elegies	3.10.29	
HAVENS			
Deep rivers, havens, creekes, and litle seas,	2Tamb	3.2.87	Tamb
HAVING			
Having a quiver girded to her side,	Dido	1.1.185	Venus
And him, Epeus having made the horse,	Dido	2.1.147	Aeneas
Who having wrought her shame, is straight way fled:	Dido	4.2.18	Iarbus
Then having past Armenian desarts now,	1Tamb	2.2.14	Meandr
And having thee, I have a jewell sure:	1Tamb	2.2.56	Mycet
Having the power from the Emperiall heaven,	1Tamb	4.4.30	Tamb
lord, specially having so smal a walke, and so litle exercise.	1Tamb	4.4.105	P Therid
Having beheld devine Zenocrate,	1Tamb	5.1.418	Arabia
There having sackt Borno the Kingly seat,	2Tamb	1.3.203	Techel
Having as many bullets in his flesh,	2Tamb	5.1.159	Tamb
And having all, you can request no more;	Jew	1.2.140	Barab
Having Fernezes hand, whose heart I'le have;	Jew	2.3.16	Barab
of those Nuns/And holy Fryers, having mony for their paines,	Jew	2.3.81	Barab
For Calymath having hover'd here so long,	Jew	5.1.4	Govnr
Having the King, Queene Mother on our sides,	P 29	1.29	Navrre
Marry sir, in having a smack in all,	P 385	7.25	Guise
Having brought the Earle of Cornewall on his way,	Edw	1.4.300	Queene
And thinke I gaind, having bought so deare a friend.	Edw	1.4.310	Edward
Having the love of his renowned peeres.	Edw	1.4.367	Queene
Having read unto her since she was a childe.	Edw	2.1.30	Baldck
having in their company divers of your nation, and others,	Edw	4.3.33	P Spencr
Forgive my thought, for having such a thought,	Edw	5.5.83	Edward
Having commenc'd, be a Divine in shew,	F 31	1.1.3	Faust
Thus having triumpht over you, I will set my countenance like a	F 213	1.2.20	P Wagner
Having thee ever to attend on me,	F 321	1.3.93	Faust
Having now my good Mephostophilis,	F 779	3.1.1	Faust
thee not to sleepe much, having such a head of thine owne.	F1284	4.1.130	P Emper
and now sirs, having divided him, what shall the body doe?	F1389	4.2.65	P Mrtino
Now my good Lord having done my duety, I humbly take my leave.	F App	p.238 86	P Faust
rage increase, then having whiskt/His taile athwart his backe,	Lucan, First Booke	210	
The soldiours having won the market place,	Lucan, First Booke	238	
And having once got head still shal he raigne?	Lucan, First Booke	317	
[As] <A> brood of barbarous Tygars having lapt/The bloud of	Lucan, First Booke	327	
so Pompey thou having lickt/Warme goare from Syllas sword art	Lucan, First Booke	330	
Phoebe having fild/Her meeting hornes to match her brothers	Lucan, First Booke	535	
Why grapples Rome, and makes war, having no foes?	Lucan, First Booke	681	
So having conquerd Inde, was Bacchus hew,	Ovid's Elegies	1.2.47	
But cruelly her tresses having rent,	Ovid's Elegies	1.7.49	
So having vext she nourisht my warme fire,	Ovid's Elegies	2.19.15	
And having wandred now through sea and land,	Ovid's Elegies	3.12.33	
Thus having swallow'd Cupids golden hooke,	Hero and Leander	1.333	
So having paus'd a while, at last shee said:	Hero and Leander	1.337	
Having striv'ne in vaine, was now about to crie,	Hero and Leander	1.413	
Much more in subjects having intellect,	Hero and Leander	2.59	
Where having spy'de her tower, long star'd he on't,	Hero and Leander	2.149	
HAVOCK			
That make quick havock of the Christian blood.	1Tamb	3.3.58	Tamb
At al times charging home, and making havock;	Lucan, First Booke	148	
HAVOCKS			
That havocks Englands wealth and treasurie.	Edw	4.4.27	Mortmr
HAV'T			
Tell him I must hav't.	Jew	4.2.118	P Ithimr
I warrant your worship shall hav't.	Jew	4.2.119	P Pilia
HAY (See also HEY)			
Shall with their Goate feete daunce an antick hay.	Edw	1.1.60	Gavstn
for your horse is turned to a bottle of Hay,--Maister Doctor.	F1490	4.4.34	P HrsCsr
and the Horse-courser a bundle of hay for his forty Dollors.	F1497	4.4.41	P Faust
to Wittenberge t'other day, with a loade of Hay, he met me,	F1526	4.5.22	P Carter
me what he should give me for as much Hay as he could eate;	F1527	4.5.23	P Carter
he never left eating, till he had eate up all my loade of hay.	F1531	4.5.27	P Carter
O monstrous, eate a whole load of Hay!	F1532	4.5.28	P All
horse vanisht away, and I sate straddling upon a bottle of Hay.	F1545	4.5.41	P HrsCsr
our horses shal eate no hay as long as this lasts.	F App	p.234 3	P Robin
HAYRE			
spectacle/Stroake Caesars hart with feare, his hayre stoode up,	Lucan, First Booke	195	
Yet was she graced with her ruffled hayre.	Ovid's Elegies	1.7.12	
HAYRES			
Mourning appear'd, whose hoary hayres were torne,	Lucan, First Booke	189	
Pay vowes to Jove, engirt thy hayres with baies,	Ovid's Elegies	1.7.36	
HAZARD			
Will hazard that we might with surety hold.	2Tamb	1.1.24	Uribas
To hazard more, than for the golden Fleece.	Hero and Leander	1.58	
HAZARDED			
Already Faustus hath hazarded that for thee.	F 422	2.1.34	Faust
HE			
Before he be the Lord of Turnus towne,	Dido	1.1.87	Jupitr
Three winters shall he with the Rutiles warre,	Dido	1.1.89	Jupitr
And full three Sommers likewise shall he waste,	Dido	1.1.91	Jupitr
O Priamus is left and this is he,	Dido	2.1.21	Aeneas
He is alive, Troy is not overcome.	Dido	2.1.30	Aeneas
Sweete father leave to weepe, this is not he:	Dido	2.1.35	Ascan
For were it Priam he would smile on me.	Dido	2.1.36	Ascan
He [names] <meanes> Aeneas, let us kisse his feete.	Dido	2.1.51	Illion
is Aeneas, were he clad/In weedes as bad as ever Irus ware.	Dido	2.1.84	Dido
In whose defence he fought so valiantly:	Dido	2.1.119	Dido
And as he spoke, to further his entent/The windes did drive	Dido	2.1.138	Aeneas
Then he alleag'd the Gods would have them stay,	Dido	2.1.141	Aeneas
And therewithall he calde false Sinon forth,	Dido	2.1.143	Aeneas

HE (cont.)

To whom he used action so pitifull,	Dido	2.1.155	Aeneas
Then he unlockt the Horse, and suddenly/From out his entrailes,	Dido	2.1.182	Aeneas
All which hemd me about, crying, this is he.	Dido	2.1.219	Aeneas
He with his faulchions poynt raisde up at once,	Dido	2.1.229	Aeneas
Whereat he lifted up his bedred lims,	Dido	2.1.250	Aeneas
Which he disdaining whiskt his sword about,	Dido	2.1.253	Aeneas
Then from the navell to the throat at once,/He ript old Priam:	Dido	2.1.256	Aeneas
Yet he undaunted tooke his fathers flagge,	Dido	2.1.259	Aeneas
Through which he could not passe for slaughtred men:	Dido	2.1.262	Aeneas
So leaning on his sword he stood stone still,	Dido	2.1.263	Aeneas
As for Aeneas he swomme quickly backe,	Dido	2.1.296	Achat
Now is he fast asleepe, and in this grove/Amongst greene brakes	Dido	2.1.316	Venus
And he at last depart to Italy,	Dido	2.1.330	Venus
How lovely is Ascanius when he smiles?	Dido	3.1.29	Dido
Is he not eloquent in all his speech?	Dido	3.1.65	Dido
So lovely is he that where ere he goes,	Dido	3.1.71	Anna
You shall not hurt my father when he comes.	Dido	3.1.80	Cupid
O here he comes, love, love, give Dido leave/To be more modest	Dido	3.1.94	Dido
I know this face, he is a Persian borne,	Dido	3.1.144	Serg
and thought by words/To compasse me, but yet he was deceiv'd:	Dido	3.1.156	Dido
But playd he nere so sweet, I let him goe:	Dido	3.1.160	Dido
O happie shall he be whom Dido loves.	Dido	3.1.168	Aeneas
That would have kild him sleeping as he lay?	Dido	3.2.39	Juno
Then in one Cave the Queene and he shall meete,	Dido	3.2.92	Juno
Aeneas, be not movde at what he sayes,	Dido	3.3.23	Dido
For otherwhile he will be out of joynt.	Dido	3.3.24	Dido
I, and outface him to, doe what he can.	Dido	3.3.40	Cupid
How like his father speaketh he in all?	Dido	3.3.41	Anna
So doth he now, though not with equall gaine,	Dido	3.3.83	Iarbus
Who nere will cease to soare till he be slaine.	Dido	3.3.85	Iarbus
Who then of all so cruell may he be,	Dido	3.4.16	Aeneas
When as he buts his beames on Floras bed,	Dido	3.4.20	Dido
Aeneas, thou art he, what did I say?	Dido	3.4.29	Dido
Till he hath furrowed Neptunes glassie fieldes,	Dido	4.3.11	Aeneas
What willes our Lord, or wherefore did he call?	Dido	4.3.15	Achat
It may be he will steale away with them:	Dido	4.4.3	Dido
Which Circes sent Sicheus when he lived:	Dido	4.4.11	Dido
The sailes were hoysing up, and he abourd.	Dido	4.4.15	Anna
And Mercury to flye for what he calles?	Dido	4.4.47	Dido
I, but it may be he will leave my love,	Dido	4.4.97	Dido
That he might suffer shipwracke on my breast,	Dido	4.4.102	Dido
As oft as he attempts to hoyst up saile:	Dido	4.4.103	Dido
Yet lest he should, for I am full of feare,	Dido	4.4.108	Dido
Better he frowne, then I should dye for griefe:	Dido	4.4.111	Dido
If he forsake me not, I never dye,	Dido	4.4.121	Dido
But though he goe, he stayes in Carthage still,	Dido	4.4.133	Dido
How pretilie he laughs, goe ye wagge,	Dido	4.5.19	Nurse
Well, if he come a wooing he shall speede,	Dido	4.5.36	Nurse
Whom I have brought from Ida where he slept,	Dido	5.1.40	Hermes
With speede he bids me saile to Italy,	Dido	5.1.68	Aeneas
But here he is, now Dido trie thy wit.	Dido	5.1.86	Dido
Yet must he not gainsay the Gods behest.	Dido	5.1.127	Aeneas
That he should take Aeneas from mine armes?	Dido	5.1.130	Dido
Though thou nor he will pitie me a whit.	Dido	5.1.178	Dido
I have not power to stay thee: is he gone?.	Dido	5.1.183	Dido
I but heele come againe, he cannot goe,	Dido	5.1.184	Dido
He loves me to too well to serve me so:	Dido	5.1.185	Dido
Yet he that in my sight would not relent,	Dido	5.1.186	Dido
By this is he got to the water side,	Dido	5.1.188	Dido
But he shrinkes backe, and now remembring me,	Dido	5.1.190	Dido
Once didst thou goe, and he came backe againe,	Dido	5.1.196	Dido
I crave but this, he stay a tide or two,	Dido	5.1.207	Dido
If he depart thus suddenly, I dye:	Dido	5.1.209	Dido
he lay with me last night,/And in the morning he was stolne	Dido	5.1.213	Nurse
And in the morning he was stolne from me,	Dido	5.1.214	Nurse
Then gan he wagge his hand, which yet held up,	Dido	5.1.229	Anna
Made me suppose he would have heard me speake:	Dido	5.1.230	Anna
Yet he whose [hearts] <heart> of adamant or flint,	Dido	5.1.234	Anna
Which seene to all, though he beheld me not,	Dido	5.1.237	Anna
But he clapt under hatches saild away.	Dido	5.1.240	Anna
How can ye goe when he hath all your fleete?	Dido	5.1.242	Anna
Now is he come on shoare safe without hurt:	Dido	5.1.257	Dido
But he remembring me shrinkes backe againe:	Dido	5.1.260	Dido
See where he comes, welcome, welcome my love.	Dido	5.1.261	Dido
And he hath all [my] <thy> fleete, what shall I doe/But dye in	Dido	5.1.268	Dido
Here lye the Sword that in the darksome Cave/He drew, and swore	Dido	5.1.296	Dido
When first he came on shoare, perish thou to:	Dido	5.1.299	Dido
But ere he march in Asia, or display/His vagrant Ensigne in the	1Tamb	1.1.44	Meandr
That he may win the Babylonians hearts,	1Tamb	1.1.90	Cosroe
And he with frowning browes and fiery lookes,	1Tamb	1.2.56	Techel
his chaine shall serve/For Manackles, till he be ransom'd home.	1Tamb	1.2.148	Tamb
As if he now devis'd some Stratageme:	1Tamb	1.2.159	Therid
With what a majesty he rears his looks:--	1Tamb	1.2.165	Tamb
See how he raines down heaps of gold in showers,	1Tamb	1.2.182	Tamb
As if he meant to give my Souldiers pay,	1Tamb	1.2.183	Tamb
He sends this Souldans daughter rich and brave,	1Tamb	1.2.186	Tamb
And by those steps that he hath scal'd the heavens,	1Tamb	1.2.200	Tamb
What stature wields he, and what personage?	1Tamb	2.1.6	Cosroe
He that with Shepheards and a litle spoile,	1Tamb	2.1.54	Ceneus
What will he doe supported by a king?	1Tamb	2.1.57	Ceneus
And he that could with giftes and promises/Inveigle him that	1Tamb	2.2.25	Meandr
He that can take or slaughter Tamburlaine,	1Tamb	2.2.30	Meandr

HE (cont.)

His Highnesse pleasure is that he should live,	1Tamb	2.2.37	Meandr
He tells you true, my maisters, so he does.	1Tamb	2.2.74	Mycet
You see my Lord, what woorking woordes he hath.	1Tamb	2.3.25	Therid
Accurst be he that first invented war,	1Tamb	2.4.1	Mycet
I marveile much he stole it not away.	1Tamb	2.4.42	Mycet
Since he is yeelded to the stroke of War,	1Tamb	2.5.12	Cosroe
To bid him battaile ere he passe too farre,	1Tamb	2.5.95	Tamb
But as he thrust them underneath the hils,	1Tamb	2.6.5	Cosroe
For he was never sprong of humaine race,	1Tamb	2.6.11	Meandr
He dares so doubtlesly resolve of rule,	1Tamb	2.6.13	Meandr
Or of what mould or mettel he be made,	1Tamb	2.6.17	Ortyg
Whether from earth, or hell, or heaven he grow.	1Tamb	2.6.23	Ortyg
For he is grosse and like the massie earth,	1Tamb	2.7.31	Therid
Least he incurre the furie of my wrath.	1Tamb	3.1.30	Bajzth
Because I heare he beares a valiant mind.	1Tamb	3.1.32	Bajzth
He be so mad to manage Armes with me,	1Tamb	3.1.34	Bajzth
mornings next arise/For messenger, he will not be reclaim'd,	1Tamb	3.1.39	Bajzth
They say he is the King of Persea.	1Tamb	3.1.45	Argier
But if he dare attempt to stir your siege,	1Tamb	3.1.46	Argier
Twere requisite he should be ten times more,	1Tamb	3.1.47	Argier
He will with Tamburlaines destruction/Redeeme you from this	1Tamb	3.2.33	Agidas
And speake of Tamburlaine as he deserves.	1Tamb	3.2.36	Zenoc
Who when he shall embrace you in his armes,	1Tamb	3.2.42	Agidas
Will tell how many thousand men he slew.	1Tamb	3.2.43	Agidas
Now in his majesty he leaves those lookes,	1Tamb	3.2.61	Agidas
He bids you prophesie what it imports.	1Tamb	3.2.89	Techel
He needed not with words confirme my feare,	1Tamb	3.2.92	Agidas
Than stay the torments he and heaven have sworne.	1Tamb	3.2.99	Agidas
Wherewith he may excruciate thy soule.	1Tamb	3.2.104	Agidas
And since he was so wise and honorable,	1Tamb	3.2.110	Usumc
See how he comes?	1Tamb	3.3.3	Tamb
He meet me in the field and fetch thee hence?	1Tamb	3.3.5	Tamb
If he think good, can from his garrisons,	1Tamb	3.3.21	Bassoe
The more he brings, the greater is the spoile,	1Tamb	3.3.23	Techel
but some must stay/To rule the provinces he late subdude.	1Tamb	3.3.29	Bassoe
Even he that in a trice vanquisht two kings,	1Tamb	3.3.36	Therid
him assured hope/Of martiall triumph, ere he meete his foes:	1Tamb	3.3.43	Tamb
He cals me Bajazeth, whom you call Lord.	1Tamb	3.3.67	Bajzth
He shall be made a chast and lustlesse Eunuke,	1Tamb	3.3.77	Bajzth
When first he war'd against the Christians.	1Tamb	3.3.200	Zabina
Yet should he not perswade me otherwise,	1Tamb	3.3.210	Zenoc
But that he lives and will be Conquerour.	1Tamb	3.3.211	Zenoc
Though he be prisoner, he may be ransomed.	1Tamb	3.3.231	Zabina
But speake, what power hath he?	1Tamb	4.1.20	Souldn
Let him take all th'advantages he can,	1Tamb	4.1.40	Souldn
Whom he detaineth in despight of us,	1Tamb	4.1.44	Souldn
The first day when he pitcheth downe his tentes,	1Tamb	4.1.49	2Msngr
on his silver crest/A snowy Feather spangled white he beares,	1Tamb	4.1.51	2Msngr
He raceth all his foes with fire and sword.	1Tamb	4.1.63	2Msngr
Stoop villaine, stoope, stoope for so he bids,	1Tamb	4.2.22	Tamb
There whiles he lives, shal Bajazeth be kept,	1Tamb	4.2.85	Tamb
For he that gives him other food than this:	1Tamb	4.2.89	Tamb
So shall he have his life, and all the rest.	1Tamb	4.2.115	Tamb
But if he stay until the bloody flag/Be once advanc'd on my	1Tamb	4.2.116	Tamb
He dies, and those that kept us out so long.	1Tamb	4.2.118	Tamb
The slaverie wherewith he persecutes/The noble Turke and his	1Tamb	4.3.26	Arabia
Wherein he wrought such ignominious wrong,	1Tamb	4.3.39	Souldn
He stamps it under his feet my Lord.	1Tamb	4.4.42	P Therid
twere better he kild his wife, and then she shall be sure not	1Tamb	4.4.45	P Usumc
starv'd, and he be provided for a moneths victuall before hand.	1Tamb	4.4.46	P Usumc
Tis like he wil, when he cannot let it.	1Tamb	4.4.53	P Techel
belike he hath not bene watered to day, give him some drinke.	1Tamb	4.4.54	P Tamb
Which he observes as parcell of his fame,	1Tamb	5.1.14	Govnr
He now is seated on my horsmens speares,	1Tamb	5.1.114	Tamb
When he arrived last upon our stage,	2Tamb	Prol.2	Prolog
manie cities sacrifice/He celebrated her [sad] <said> funerall,	2Tamb	Prol.8	Prolog
And means to fire Turky as he goes:	2Tamb	1.1.18	Gazell
Nor he but Fortune that hath made him great.	2Tamb	1.1.60	Orcan
He brings a world of people to the field,	2Tamb	1.1.67	Orcan
forgetst thou I am he/That with the Cannon shooke Vienna	2Tamb	1.1.86	Orcan
Whose glorious body when he left the world,	2Tamb	1.1.139	Orcan
with my heart/Wish your release, but he whose wrath is death,	2Tamb	1.2.6	Almeda
Although he sent a thousand armed men/To intercept this haughty	2Tamb	1.2.70	Almeda
Which when he tainted with his slender rod,	2Tamb	1.3.40	Zenoc
He raign'd him straight and made him so curvet,	2Tamb	1.3.41	Zenoc
As I cried out for feare he should have falne.	2Tamb	1.3.42	Zenoc
Why may not I my Lord, as wel as he,	2Tamb	1.3.61	Amyras
For he shall weare the crowne of Persea,	2Tamb	1.3.74	Tamb
And he that meanes to place himselfe therin/Must armed wade up	2Tamb	1.3.83	Tamb
Were turnde to men, he should be overcome:	2Tamb	1.3.164	Tamb
He by his Christ, and I by Mahomet?	2Tamb	2.2.32	Orcan
If he be son to everliving Jove,	2Tamb	2.2.41	Orcan
If he be jealous of his name and honor,	2Tamb	2.2.43	Orcan
imperiall heaven/That he that sits on high and never sleeps,	2Tamb	2.2.49	Orcan
He bindes his temples with a frowning cloude,	2Tamb	2.4.6	Tamb
Her name had bene in every line he wrote:	2Tamb	2.4.90	Tamb
Who when he heares how resolute thou wert,	2Tamb	3.4.40	Techel
Harkening when he shall bid them plague the world.	2Tamb	3.4.60	Therid
Now, he that cals himself the scourge of Jove,	2Tamb	3.5.21	Orcan
Shal end the warlike progresse he intends,	2Tamb	3.5.23	Orcan
Where legions of devils (knowing he must die/Here in Natolia,	2Tamb	3.5.25	Orcan
Why, so he is Casane, I am here,	2Tamb	3.5.62	Tamb

HE (cont.)

By Mahomet he shal be tied in chaines,	2Tamb	3.5.92	Jrslem
Wel, in despight of thee he shall be king:	2Tamb	3.5.128	Callap
So he shal, and weare thy head in his Scutchion.	2Tamb	3.5.138	P Orcan
to put him in remembrance he was a Jailor, that when I take	2Tamb	3.5.140	P Tamb
I, my Lord, he was Calapines keeper.	2Tamb	3.5.152	P Therid
When he himselfe amidst the thickest troopes/Beats downe our	2Tamb	4.1.25	Amyras
He comes and findes his sonnes have had no shares/In all the	2Tamb	4.1.47	Amyras
sonnes have had no shares/In all the honors he proposde for us.	2Tamb	4.1.48	Amyras
And sooner far than he that never fights.	2Tamb	4.1.55	Calyph
Than he that darted mountaines at thy head,	2Tamb	4.1.128	Tamb
Expell the hate wherewith he paines our soules.	2Tamb	4.1.173	Orcan
How like his cursed father he begins,	2Tamb	4.3.55	Jrslem
I Turke, I tel thee, this same Boy is he,	2Tamb	4.3.57	Tamb
Wherein he spareth neither man nor child,	2Tamb	5.1.30	1Citzn
Whose state he ever pitied and reliev'd,	2Tamb	5.1.32	1Citzn
Go bind the villaine, he shall hang in chaines,	2Tamb	5.1.84	Tamb
So now he hangs like Bagdets Governour,	2Tamb	5.1.158	Tamb
He cannot heare the voice of Tamburlain,	2Tamb	5.1.199	Tamb
For he is God alone, and none but he.	2Tamb	5.1.202	Tamb
and the victories/Wherewith he hath so sore dismaide the world,	2Tamb	5.2.44	Callap
But if he die, your glories are disgrac'd,	2Tamb	5.3.15	Therid
For if he die, thy glorie is disgrac'd,	2Tamb	5.3.40	Usumc
Looke where he goes, but see, he comes againe/Because I stay:	2Tamb	5.3.75	Tamb
I crave but this, Grace him as he deserves,	Jew	Prol.33	Machvl
And let him not be entertain'd the worse/Because he favours me.	Jew	Prol.35	Machvl
But he whose steele-bard coffers are cramb'd full,	Jew	1.1.14	Barab
For he can counsell best in these affaires;	Jew	1.1.142	2Jew
For he can counsell best in these affaires;/And here he comes.	Jew	1.1.143	2Jew
To seize upon the Towne: I, that he seekes.	Jew	1.1.185	Barab
Lastly, he that denies this, shall absolutely lose al he has.	Jew	1.2.76	P Reader
he had seven thousand sheepe,/Three thousand Camels, and two	Jew	1.2.182	Barab
So that not he, but I may curse the day,	Jew	1.2.191	Barab
I have found/The gold, the perles, and Jewels which he hid.	Jew	2.1.23	Abigal
He said he wud attend me in the morne.	Jew	2.1.34	Abigal
Give charge to Morpheus that he may dreame/A golden dreame, and	Jew	2.1.36	Abigal
And with that summe he craves might we wage warre.	Jew	2.2.27	1Knght
And he meanes quickly to expell you hence;	Jew	2.2.38	Bosco
but e're he shall have her	Jew	2.3.51	Barab
But when he touches it, it will be foild:	Jew	2.3.57	Barab
What, can he steale that you demand so much?	Jew	2.3.100	Barab
Belike he has some new tricke for a purse;	Jew	2.3.101	Barab
And if he has, he is worth three hundred plats.	Jew	2.3.102	Barab
Because he is young and has more qualities.	Jew	2.3.110	1Offcr
I, marke him, you were best, for this is he	Jew	2.3.132	Barab
He loves my daughter, and she holds him deare:	Jew	2.3.141	Barab
This Moore is comeliest, is he not? speake son.	Jew	2.3.144	Mater
Converse not with him, he is cast off from heaven.	Jew	2.3.157	Mater
Use him as if he were a--Philistine.	Jew	2.3.228	Barab
He is not of the seed of Abraham.	Jew	2.3.230	Barab
For now by this has he kist Abigall;	Jew	2.3.246	Barab
So sure shall he and Don Mathias dye:	Jew	2.3.249	Barab
He sends her letters, bracelets, jewels, rings.	Jew	2.3.259	Barab
And when he comes, she lockes her selfe up fast;	Jew	2.3.262	Barab
Yet through the key-hole will he talke to her,	Jew	2.3.263	Barab
Even now as I came home, he slipt me in,	Jew	2.3.267	Barab
And I am sure he is with Abigall.	Jew	2.3.268	Barab
I'le give him such a warning e're he goes/As he shall have	Jew	2.3.273	Barab
a warning e're he goes/As he shall have small hopes of Abigall.	Jew	2.3.274	Barab
I, and take heed, for he hath sworne your death.	Jew	2.3.280	Barab
no, but happily he stands in feare/Of that which you, I thinke,	Jew	2.3.282	Barab
He has my heart, I smile against my will.	Jew	2.3.287	Abigal
What, is he gone unto my mother?	Jew	2.3.351	Mthias
I will have Don Mathias, he is my love.	Jew	2.3.361	Abigal
That he shall verily thinke it comes from him.	Jew	2.3.376	Ithimr
And he is very seldome from my house;	Jew	3.1.10	Curtzn
And here he comes.	Jew	3.1.11	Curtzn
And these my teares to blood, that he might live.	Jew	3.2.19	Govnr
A Fryar? false villaine, he hath done the deed.	Jew	3.4.22	Barab
ambles after wealth/Although he ne're be richer then in hope:	Jew	3.4.53	Barab
saies, he that eats with the devil had need of a long spoone.	Jew	3.4.58	P Ithimr
What a blessing has he given't?	Jew	3.4.106	P Ithimr
Oh he is gone to see the other Nuns.	Jew	3.6.10	2Fryar
Convert my father that he may be sav'd,	Jew	3.6.39	Abigal
Why? what has he done?	Jew	3.6.47	1Fryar
What, has he crucified a child?	Jew	3.6.49	1Fryar
You see I answer him, and yet he stayes;	Jew	4.1.88	Barab
Why does he goe to thy house? let him begone.	Jew	4.1.101	1Fryar
I never heard of any man but he/Malign'd the order of the	Jew	4.1.103	Barab
For he that shriv'd her is within my house.	Jew	4.1.115	Barab
One turn'd my daughter, therefore he shall dye;	Jew	4.1.119	Barab
Therefore 'tis not requisite he should live.	Jew	4.1.121	Barab
Doe what I can he will not strip himselfe,	Jew	4.1.131	Ithimr
I feare me he mistrusts what we intend.	Jew	4.1.133	Ithimr
Yet if he knew our meanings, could he scape?	Jew	4.1.135	Barab
No, none can heare him, cry he ne're so loud.	Jew	4.1.136	Ithimr
staffe; excellent, he stands as if he were begging of Bacon.	Jew	4.1.154	P Ithimr
He is slaine.	Jew	4.1.177	Barab
To be a Christian, I shut him out,/And there he sate:	Jew	4.1.189	Barab
And what think'st thou, will he come?	Jew	4.2.5	P Curtzn
reading of the letter, he look'd like a man of another world.	Jew	4.2.7	P Pilia
base slave as he should be saluted by such a tall man as I am,	Jew	4.2.9	P Pilia
And what said he?	Jew	4.2.11	P Curtzn

HE (cont.)

but the Exercise being done, see where he comes.	Jew	4.2.20	P	Pilia
he was ready to leape off e're the halter was about his necke;	Jew	4.2.22	P	Ithimr
he made such haste to his prayers, as if hee had had another	Jew	4.2.24	P	Ithimr
goe whither he will, I'le be none of his followers in haste:	Jew	4.2.25	P	Ithimr
and he gave me a letter from one Madam Bellamira, saluting me	Jew	4.2.29	P	Ithimr
sort as if he had meant to make cleane my Boots with his lips;	Jew	4.2.30	P	Ithimr
he flouts me, what gentry can be in a poore Turke of ten pence?	Jew	4.2.38	P	Ithimr
I'le make him send me half he has, and glad he scapes so too.	Jew	4.2.67	P	Ithimr
reading of the letter, he star'd and stamp'd, and turnd aside.	Jew	4.2.104	P	Pilia
told him he were best to send it; then he hug'd and imbrac'd	Jew	4.2.106	P	Pilia
him he were best to send it; then he hug'd and imbrac'd me.	Jew	4.2.106	P	Pilia
Then like a Jew he laugh'd and jeer'd, and told me he lov'd me	Jew	4.2.108	P	Pilia
and told me he lov'd me for your sake, and said what a	Jew	4.2.109	P	Pilia
The more villaine he to keep me thus:	Jew	4.2.111		Ithimr
To conclude, he gave me ten crownes.	Jew	4.2.113	P	Pilia
And if he aske why I demand so much, tell him, I scorne to	Jew	4.2.120	P	Ithimr
He was not wont to call me Barabas.	Jew	4.3.3		Barab
He sent a shaggy totter'd staring slave,	Jew	4.3.6		Barab
That when he speakes, drawes out his grisly beard,	Jew	4.3.7		Barab
Who when he speakes, grunts like a hog, and looks/Like one that	Jew	4.3.11		Barab
Well, my hope is, he will not stay there still;	Jew	4.3.16		Barab
And when he comes: Oh that he were but here!	Jew	4.3.17		Barab
Might he not as well come as send; pray bid him come and fetch	Jew	4.3.26	P	Barab
That he who knowes I love him as my selfe/Should write in this	Jew	4.3.42		Barab
his villany/He will tell all he knowes and I shall dye for't.	Jew	4.3.65		Barab
What wudst thou doe if he should send thee none?	Jew	4.4.13		Pilia
I had not thought he had been so brave a man.	Jew	4.4.16		Curtzn
son; he and I kild 'em both, and yet never touch'd 'em.	Jew	4.4.17	P	Ithimr
that poyson'd the Nuns, and he and I, snicle hand too fast,	Jew	4.4.20	P	Ithimr
Me thinkes he fingers very well.	Jew	4.4.49		Pilia
How swift he runnes.	Jew	4.4.51		Pilia
He knowes it already.	Jew	4.4.60	P	Barab
Jew, he lives upon pickled Grashoppers, and sauc'd Mushrumbs.	Jew	4.4.61	P	Ithimr
He never put on cleane shirt since he was circumcis'd.	Jew	4.4.64	P	Ithimr
The Hat he weares, Judas left under the Elder when he hang'd	Jew	4.4.66	P	Ithimr
he weares, Judas left under the Elder when he hang'd himselfe.	Jew	4.4.66	P	Ithimr
A masty <nasty> slave he is.	Jew	4.4.69		Pilia
And dye he shall, for we will never yeeld.	Jew	5.1.6		1Knght
Nay stay, my Lord, 'tmay be he will confesse.	Jew	5.1.25		1Knght
contracted unto Abigall; [he] forg'd a counterfeit challenge.	Jew	5.1.29	P	Ithimr
Marry, even he that strangled Bernardine, poyson'd the Nuns, and	Jew	5.1.33	P	Ithimr
Shee is a Curtezane and he a theefe,	Jew	5.1.37		Barab
And he my bondman, let me have law,	Jew	5.1.38		Barab
Be patient, gentle Madam, it was he,	Jew	5.1.46		Govnr
He forged the daring challenge made them fight.	Jew	5.1.47		Govnr
For he that liveth in Authority,	Jew	5.2.38		Barab
For Callymath, when he hath view'd the Towne,	Jew	5.2.105		Barab
And he from whom my most advantage comes,	Jew	5.2.113		Barab
He humbly would intreat your Majesty/To come and see his homely	Jew	5.3.17		Msngr
That he hath in store a Pearle so big,	Jew	5.3.27		Msngr
Therefore he humbly would intreat your Highnesse/Not to depart	Jew	5.3.32		Msngr
intreat your Highnesse/Not to depart till he has feasted you.	Jew	5.3.33		Msngr
Except he place his Tables in the streets.	Jew	5.3.35		Calym
There will he banquet them, but thee at home,	Jew	5.3.38		Msngr
Now sirra, what, will he come?	Jew	5.5.13		Barab
He will; and has commanded all his men/To come ashore, and	Jew	5.5.14		Msngr
And see he brings it: Now, Governor, the summe?	Jew	5.5.19		Barab
Here, hold that knife, and when thou seest he comes,	Jew	5.5.37		Barab
This traine he laid to have intrap'd thy life;	Jew	5.5.91		Govnr
Thus he determin'd to have handled thee,	Jew	5.5.93		Govnr
Was this the banquet he prepar'd for us?	Jew	5.5.95		Calym
For he that did by treason worke our fall,	Jew	5.5.109		Govnr
Have you not heard of late how he decreed,	P 32	1.32		Navrre
For what he doth the Pope will ratifie:	P 40	1.40		Condy
But he that sits and rules above the clowdes,	P 42	1.42		Navrre
Which he hath pitcht within his deadly toyle.	P 54	1.54		Navrre
they be my good Lord, and he that smelles but to them, dyes.	P 73	2.16	P	Pothec
If I repaire not what he ruinates:	P 129	2.72		Guise
So that for proofe, he barely beares the name:	P 131	2.74		Guise
I execute, and he sustaines the blame.	P 132	2.75		Guise
He that wantes these, and is suspected of heresie,	P 234	4.32		Guise
Shall dye, be he King or Emperour.	P 235	4.33		Guise
Hath he been hurt with villaines in the street?	P 254	4.52		Charls
Gonzago, what, is he dead?	P 304	5.31		Guise
It may be it is some other, and he escapte.	P 308	5.35		Anjoy
Cosin tis he, I know him by his look.	P 309	5.36		Guise
He mist him neer, but we have strook him now.	P 311	5.38		Guise
And he that living hated so the crosse,	P 320	5.47		Anjoy
To speek with me from such a man as he?	P 350	6.5		Seroun
O let him goe, he is a catholick.	P 375	7.15		Retes
He that will be a flat decotamest,	P 389	7.29		Guise
And he forsooth must goe and preach in Germany:	P 392	7.32		Guise
That he that despiseth him, can nere/Be good in Logick or	P 409	7.49		Ramus
Beleeve me Guise he becomes the place so well,	P 495	9.14		QnMoth
As I doe live, so surely shall he dye,	P 521	9.40		QnMoth
And if he grudge or crosse his Mothers will,	P 523	9.42		QnMoth
And he nor heares, nor sees us what we doe:	P 553	11.18		QnMoth
And whilste he sleepes securely thus in ease,	P 635	12.48		QnMoth
Which [are] <as> he saith, to kill the Puritans,	P 643	12.56		Cardnl
But tis the house of Burbon that he meanes.	P 644	12.57		Cardnl
And if he doe deny what I doe say,	P 650	12.63		QnMoth
Sweet Mugercune, tis he that hath my heart,	P 660	13.4		Duchss

HE (cont.)

That he may come and meet me in some place,	P 664	13.8	Duchss
But villaine he to whom these lines should goe,	P 696	13.40	Guise
Spaine is the place where he makes peace and warre,	P 710	14.13	Navrre
But he doth lurke within his drousie couch,	P 737	14.40	Navrre
So he be safe he cares not what becomes,	P 739	14.42	Navrre
Whether he have dishonoured me or no.	P 769	15.27	Guise
For he hath solemnely sworne thy death.	P 777	15.35	King
I may be stabd, and live till he be dead,	P 778	15.36	Mugern
But wherfore beares he me such deadly hate?	P 779	15.37	Mugern
But which way is he gone?	P 783	15.41	Mugern
and tyll the ground that he himself should occupy, which is his	P 812	17.7	P Souldr
For had your highnesse seene with what a pompe/He entred Paris,	P 873	17.68	Eprnon
Then meanes he present treason to our state.	P 880	17.75	King
Unles he meane to be betraide and dye:	P 898	17.93	King
tush, were he heere, we would kill him presently.	P 934	19.4	P 1Mur
But when will he come that we may murther him?	P 937	19.7	P 3Mur
Now must he fall and perish in his height.	P 946	19.16	Capt
And he shall follow my proud Chariots wheeles.	P 984	19.54	Guise
Stand close, he is comming, I know him by his voice.	P1000	19.70	P 1Mur
Thus Caesar did goe foorth, and thus he dyed.	P1015	19.85	Guise
But see where he comes.	P1018	19.88	Capt
Did he not draw a sorte of English priestes/From Doway to the	P1030	19.100	King
Did he not cause the King of Spaines huge fleete,	P1033	19.103	King
Did he not injure Mounser thats deceast?	P1035	19.105	King
Hath he not made me in the Popes defence,	P1036	19.106	King
Tush, to be short, he meant to make me Munke,	P1039	19.109	King
Ile clippe his winges/Or ere he passe my handes, away with him.	P1053	19.123	King
Nay he was King and countermanded me,	P1069	19.139	King
Sweet Guise, would he had died so thou wert heere:	P1082	19.152	QnMoth
He is hard hearted, therfore pull with violence.	P1105	20.15	1Mur
Whose service he may still commaund till death.	P1149	22.11	Navrre
Twere not amisse my Lord, if he were searcht.	P1160	22.22	Eprnon
He died a death too good, the devill of hell/Torture his wicked	P1218	22.80	Bartus
Ah curse him not sith he is dead.	P1220	22.82	King
For he is your lawfull King and my next heire:	P1230	22.92	King
He loves me not that sheds most teares,	P1239	22.101	King
But he that makes most lavish of his bloud.	P1240	22.102	King
displeases him | And fill up his rome that he shold occupie.	Paris	ms 5,p390	P Souldr
ser where he is your landlorde you take upon you to be his |	Paris	ms 9,p390	P Souldr
yett comminge upon you once unawares he frayde you out againe.	Paris	ms12,p390	P Souldr
And in the day when he shall walke abroad,	Edw	1.1.57	Gavstn
That he should nere returne into the realme:	Edw	1.1.84	Mortmr
Therefore if he be come, expell him straight.	Edw	1.1.106	Lncstr
He should have lost his head, but with his looke,	Edw	1.1.113	Kent
And Mowberie and he were reconcild:	Edw	1.1.115	Kent
He shall to prison, and there die in boults.	Edw	1.1.197	Gavstn
Unlesse his brest be sword proofe he shall die.	Edw	1.2.8	Mortmr
whom he vouchsafes/For vailing of his bonnet one good looke.	Edw	1.2.18	Lncstr
Thus arme in arme, the king and he dooth marche:	Edw	1.2.20	Lncstr
He nods, and scornes, and smiles at those that passe.	Edw	1.2.24	Warwck
His countenance bewraies he is displeasd.	Edw	1.2.34	Lncstr
He claps his cheekes, and hanges about his neck,	Edw	1.2.51	Queene
And when I come, he frownes, as who should say,	Edw	1.2.53	Queene
Is it not straunge, that he is thus bewitcht?	Edw	1.2.55	MortSr
Unlesse he be declinde from that base pesant.	Edw	1.4.7	Mortmr
Were he a peasant, being my minion,	Edw	1.4.30	Edward
if he refuse, and then may we/Depose him and elect an other	Edw	1.4.54	Mortmr
Because he loves me more then all the world:	Edw	1.4.77	Edward
Be it or no, he shall not linger here.	Edw	1.4.93	MortSr
For no where else seekes he felicitie.	Edw	1.4.122	Gavstn
So much as he on cursed Gaveston.	Edw	1.4.181	Queene
he is gone.	Edw	1.4.192	MortSr
And he confesseth that he loves me not.	Edw	1.4.194	Queene
he comes not back,/Unlesse the sea cast up his shipwrack body.	Edw	1.4.204	Lncstr
I Mortimer, for till he be restorde,	Edw	1.4.209	Queene
Plead for him he that will, I am resolvde.	Edw	1.4.214	MortSr
For tis against my will he should returne.	Edw	1.4.217	Queene
Yet good my lord, heare what he can alledge.	Edw	1.4.250	Queene
All that he speakes, is nothing, we are resolv'd.	Edw	1.4.251	Warwck
I would he were.	Edw	1.4.253	Penbrk
As he will front the mightiest of us all,	Edw	1.4.260	Mortmr
And whereas he shall live and be belovde,	Edw	1.4.261	Mortmr
But were he here, detested as he is,	Edw	1.4.264	Mortmr
He saith true.	Edw	1.4.271	Penbrk
Nay more, when he shall know it lies in us,	Edw	1.4.274	Mortmr
But how if he do not Nephew?	Edw	1.4.278	MortSr
Weele pull him from the strongest hould he hath.	Edw	1.4.289	Mortmr
I love him more/Then he can Gaveston, would he lov'd me/But	Edw	1.4.303	Queene
more/Then he can Gaveston, would he lov'd me/But halfe so much,	Edw	1.4.303	Queene
Harke how he harpes upon his minion.	Edw	1.4.311	Queene
Thou seest by nature he is milde and calme,	Edw	1.4.388	MortSr
He weares a lords revenewe on his back,	Edw	1.4.407	Mortmr
And Midas like he jets it in the court,	Edw	1.4.408	Mortmr
He weares a short Italian hooded cloake,	Edw	1.4.413	Mortmr
Whiles other walke below, the king and he/From out a window,	Edw	1.4.416	Mortmr
Because the king and he are enemies.	Edw	2.1.5	Spencr
But he that hath the favour of a king,	Edw	2.1.8	Spencr
No, his companion, for he loves me well,	Edw	2.1.13	Spencr
But he is banisht, theres small hope of him.	Edw	2.1.15	Baldck
Tis like enough, for since he was exild,	Edw	2.1.23	Baldck
Mine old lord whiles he livde, was so precise,	Edw	2.1.46	Baldck
That he would take exceptions at my buttons,	Edw	2.1.47	Baldck

HE (cont.)

He wils me to repaire unto the court,	Edw	2.1.67	Neece
Seeing that he talkes thus of my mariage day?	Edw	2.1.69	Neece
The winde is good, I wonder why he stayes,	Edw	2.2.1	Edward
I feare me he is wrackt upon the sea.	Edw	2.2.2	Edward
Looke Lancaster how passionate he is,	Edw	2.2.3	Queene
And threatenest death whether he rise or fall,	Edw	2.2.44	Edward
If in his absence thus he favors him,	Edw	2.2.47	Mortmr
What will he do when as he shall be present?	Edw	2.2.48	Mortmr
No more then I would answere were he slaine.	Edw	2.2.86	Mortmr
Yes more then thou canst answer though he live,	Edw	2.2.87	Edward
Moov'd may he be, and perish in his wrath.	Edw	2.2.101	Mortmr
He meanes to make us stoope by force of armes,	Edw	2.2.103	Lncstr
Seeing he is taken prisoner in his warres?	Edw	2.2.119	Mortmr
Cosin, and if he will not ransome him,	Edw	2.2.127	Mortmr
Why, so he may, but we will speake to him.	Edw	2.2.136	Lncstr
That to my face he threatens civill warres.	Edw	2.2.233	Edward
Would Lancaster and he had both carroust,	Edw	2.2.237	Edward
Two of my fathers servants whilst he liv'de,	Edw	2.2.240	Neece
His name is Spencer, he is well alied,	Edw	2.2.249	Gavstn
He that I list to favour shall be great:	Edw	2.2.263	Edward
He is your brother, therefore have we cause/To cast the worst,	Edw	2.3.7	Warwck
I feare me he is slaine my gratious lord.	Edw	2.4.2	Spencr
No, here he comes, now let them spoile and kill:	Edw	2.4.3	Edward
From my imbracements thus he breakes away,	Edw	2.4.16	Queene
I wonder how he scapt.	Edw	2.4.22	Lncstr
He turnes away, and smiles upon his minion.	Edw	2.4.29	Queene
Tell us where he remaines, and he shall die.	Edw	2.4.36	Lncstr
Pursue him quicklie, and he cannot scape,	Edw	2.4.38	Queene
How comes it, that the king and he is parted?	Edw	2.4.41	Mortmr
and with the power/That he intendeth presentlie to raise,	Edw	2.4.44	Queene
As if he heare I have but talkt with you,	Edw	2.4.54	Queene
But thinke of Mortimer as he deserves.	Edw	2.4.58	Mortmr
If he be straunge and not regarde my wordes,	Edw	2.4.64	Queene
Intreateth you by me, yet but he may/See him before he dies, for	Edw	2.5.36	Arundl
by me, yet but he may/See him before he dies, for why he saies,	Edw	2.5.37	Arundl
And sends you word, he knowes that die he shall,	Edw	2.5.38	Arundl
He will be mindfull of the curtesie.	Edw	2.5.40	Arundl
gratifie the king/In other matters, he must pardon us in this,	Edw	2.5.44	Warwck
bestow/His teares on that, for that is all he gets/Of Gaveston,	Edw	2.5.53	Mortmr
Not so my Lord, least he bestow more cost,	Edw	2.5.55	Lncstr
In burying him, then he hath ever earned.	Edw	2.5.56	Lncstr
And in the honor of a king he sweares,	Edw	2.5.58	Arundl
He will but talke with him and send him backe.	Edw	2.5.59	Arundl
We wot, he that the care of realme remits,	Edw	2.5.61	Warwck
For Gaveston, will if he [seaze] <zease> <sees> him once,	Edw	2.5.63	Warwck
the riches of my realme/Can ransome him, ah he is markt to die,	Edw	3.1.4	Edward
Tell me [Arundell] <Matre>, died he ere thou camst,	Edw	3.1.92	Edward
Neither my lord, for as he was surprizd,	Edw	3.1.94	Arundl
And promiseth he shall be safe returnd,	Edw	3.1.110	Arundl
Well, and how fortunes that he came not?	Edw	3.1.113	Edward
But ere he came, Warwick in ambush laie,	Edw	3.1.118	Arundl
to request/He might be spared to come to speake with us,	Edw	3.1.235	Edward
My lord, we have, and if he be in England,	Edw	4.3.19	Spencr
He is in Englands ground, our port-maisters/Are not so careles	Edw	4.3.22	Edward
Edward battell in England, sooner then he can looke for them:	Edw	4.3.35	P Spencr
I would he never had bin flattered more.	Edw	4.4.30	Kent
This way he fled, but I am come too late.	Edw	4.6.1	Kent
A goodly chauncelor, is he not my lord?	Edw	4.6.43	Queene
Rebell is he that fights against his prince,	Edw	4.6.71	SpncrP
Take him away, he prates. You Rice ap Howell,	Edw	4.6.73	Mortmr
But what is he, whome rule and emperie/Have not in life or	Edw	4.7.14	Edward
Alas, see where he sits, and hopes unseene,	Edw	4.7.51	Leistr
O is he gone!	Edw	4.7.100	Spencr
He rends and teares it with his wrathfull pawe,	Edw	5.1.12	Edward
If he be not, let him choose.	Edw	5.1.95	BshpWn
He of you all that most desires my bloud,	Edw	5.1.100	Edward
An other poast, what newes bringes he?	Edw	5.1.128	Leistr
And he himselfe lies in captivitie.	Edw	5.2.4	Mortmr
That if he slip will seaze upon us both,	Edw	5.2.8	Mortmr
So that he now is gone from Killingworth,	Edw	5.2.31	BshpWn
And none but we shall know where he lieth.	Edw	5.2.41	Mortmr
But Mortimer, as long as he survives/What safetie rests for us,	Edw	5.2.42	Queene
Speake, shall he presently be dispatch'd and die?	Edw	5.2.44	Mortmr
That he resigne the king to thee and Gurney,	Edw	5.2.49	Mortmr
Who now makes Fortunes wheele turne as he please,	Edw	5.2.53	Mortmr
[Till] <And> at the last, he come to Killingworth,	Edw	5.2.60	Mortmr
and in any case/Let no man comfort him, if he chaunce to weepe,	Edw	5.2.64	Mortmr
Some thing he whispers in his childish eares.	Edw	5.2.76	Queene
If he have such accesse unto the prince,	Edw	5.2.77	Mortmr
I heare of late he hath deposde himselfe.	Edw	5.2.83	Kent
Why, is he dead?	Edw	5.2.98	Prince
My lord, he hath betraied the king his brother,	Edw	5.2.106	Mortmr
Mortimer shall know that he hath wrongde mee.	Edw	5.2.118	Kent
Yet he that is the cause of Edwards death,	Edw	5.4.3	Mortmr
Feare not to kill the king tis good he die.	Edw	5.4.9	Mortmr
And by a secret token that he beares,	Edw	5.4.19	Mortmr
Shall he be murdered when the deed is done.	Edw	5.4.20	Mortmr
I, I, and none shall know which way he died.	Edw	5.4.25	Ltborn
What hath he done?	Edw	5.4.83	King
Mortimer, I did, he is our king,	Edw	5.4.87	Kent
Strike off his head, he shall have marshall lawe.	Edw	5.4.89	Mortmr
My lord, he is my unckle, and shall live.	Edw	5.4.91	King

HE (cont.)

My lord, he is your enemie, and shall die.	Edw		5.4.92		Mortmr
Had Edmund liv'de, he would have sought thy death.	Edw		5.4.112		Queene
He is a traitor, thinke not on him, come.	Edw		5.4.115		Queene
He hath a body able to endure,	Edw		5.5.10		Matrvs
See how he must be handled for his labour,	Edw		5.5.23		Matrvs
He sleepes.	Edw		5.5.100		Ltborn
What if he have? the king is yet a childe.	Edw		5.6.17		Mortmr
I, I, but he teares his haire, and wrings his handes,	Edw		5.6.18		Queene
Into the councell chamber he is gone,	Edw		5.6.20		Queene
Aye me, see where he comes, and they with him,	Edw		5.6.22		Queene
Forbid not me to weepe, he was my father,	Edw		5.6.34		King
A Mortimer, thou knowest that he is slaine,	Edw		5.6.50		King
And so shalt thou be too: why staies he heere?	Edw		5.6.51		King
He hath forgotten me, stay, I am his mother.	Edw		5.6.90		Queene
Now is he borne, of parents base of stocke,	F	11	Prol.11		1Chor
At <of> riper yeares to Wittenberg <Wertenberg> he went,	F	13	Prol.13		1Chor
So much <soone> he profits in Divinitie,	F	15	Prol.15		1Chor
That shortly he was grac'd with Doctors name,	F	17	Prol.17		1Chor
He surfets upon cursed Necromancie:	F	25	Prol.25		1Chor
Which he preferres before his chiefest blisse;	F	27	Prol.27		1Chor
as th'infernall spirits/On sweet Musaeus when he came to hell,	F	143	1.1.115		Faust
He that is grounded in Astrology,	F	165	1.1.137		Cornel
Go to sirra, leave your jesting, and tell us where he is.	F	201	1.2.8	P	1Schol
For is he not Corpus naturale?	F	207	1.2.14	P	Wagner
That thou art <he is> falne into that damned Art/For which they	F	221	1.2.28		1Schol
Were he a stranger, <and> not allyed to me,	F	223	1.2.30		2Schol
No more then he commands, must we performe.	F	270	1.3.42		Mephst
Did not he charge thee to appeare to me?	F	271	1.3.43		Faust
Nor will we come unlesse he use such meanes,	F	278	1.3.50		Mephst
Whereby he is in danger to be damn'd:	F	279	1.3.51		Mephst
For I confound <He confounds> hell in Elizium:	F	287	1.3.59		Faust
How comes it then that he is Prince of Devils?	F	294	1.3.66		Faust
Say he surrenders up to him his soule,	F	318	1.3.90		Faust
So he will spare him foure and twenty yeares,	F	319	1.3.91		Faust
that <I know> he would give his soule to the devill, for a	F	349	1.4.7	P	Wagner
[To God]? <Why> he loves thee not:	F	398	2.1.10		Faust
That I shall waite on Faustus whilst he lives,	F	420	2.1.32		Mephst
So he will buy my service with his soule.	F	421	2.1.33		Mephst
Is that the reason why he tempts us thus?	F	430	2.1.42		Faust
Fourthly, that he shall be in his chamber or house invisible.	F	490	2.1.102	P	Faust
at all times, in what shape [or] <and> forme soever he please.	F	492	2.1.104	P	Faust
And hath not he that built the walles of Thebes/With ravishing	F	579	2.2.28		Faust
Christ cannot save thy soule, for he is just,	F	636	2.2.85		Lucifr
He viewes the cloudes, the Planets, and the Starres,	F	760	2.3.39		2Chor
Not long he stayed within his quiet house,	F	768	2.3.47		2Chor
He now is gone to prove Cosmography,	F	773	2.3.52		2Chor
The way he cut, an English mile in length,	F	792	3.1.14		Faust
Both he and thou shalt stand excommunicate,	F	908	3.1.130		Pope
He growes to prowd in his authority,	F	911	3.1.133		Pope
Then he and thou, and all the world shall stoope,	F	937	3.1.159		Pope
He shall be streight condemn'd of heresie,	F	962	3.1.184		Faust
be he that stole [away] his holinesse meate from the Table.	F	1077	3.2.97		1Frier
Cursed be he that stroke his holinesse a blow [on] the face.	F	1079	3.2.99		1Frier
be he that strucke <tooke> fryer Sandelo a blow on the pate.	F	1081	3.2.101		1Frier
Cursed be he that disturbeth our holy Dirge.	F	1083	3.2.103		1Frier
Cursed be he that tooke away his holinesse wine.	F	1085	3.2.105		1Frier
let him come; an he follow us, I'le so conjure him, as he was	F	1091	3.3.4	P	Robin
him, as he was never conjur'd in his life, I warrant him:	F	1092	3.3.5	P	Robin
Yonder he comes:	F	1094	3.3.7	P	Dick
[What there he did in triall of his art],	F	1153	3.3.66A		3Chor
And he intends to shew great Carolus,	F	1167	4.1.13		Mrtino
He took his rouse with stopes of Rhennish wine,	F	1174	4.1.20		Mrtino
He was upon the devils backe late enough; and if he be so farre	F	1189	4.1.35	P	Benvol
and if he be so farre in love with him, I would he would post	F	1190	4.1.36	P	Benvol
love with him, I would he would post with him to Rome againe.	F	1191	4.1.37	P	Benvol
Bloud, he speakes terribly:	F	1227	4.1.73	P	Benvol
he lookes as like [a] conjurer as the Pope to a Coster-monger.	F	1228	4.1.74	P	Benvol
What, is he asleepe, or dead?	F	1279	4.1.125		Saxony
He sleeps my Lord, but dreames not of his hornes.	F	1280	4.1.126		Faust
He has done penance now sufficently.	F	1310	4.1.156		Emper
And kill that Doctor if he come this way.	F	1339	4.2.15		Fredrk
For hornes he gave, Il'e have his head anone.	F	1361	4.2.37		Benvol
See, see, he comes.	F	1362	4.2.38		Mrtino
and let them hang/Within the window where he yoak'd me first,	F	1381	4.2.57		Benvol
As he intended to dismember me.	F	1415	4.2.91		Faust
He must needs goe that the Divell drives.	F	1419	4.2.95		Fredrk
See where he comes, dispatch, and kill the slave.	F	1423	4.2.99		2Soldr
why will he not drink of all waters?	F	1470	4.4.14	P	HrsCsr
he will drinke of all waters, but ride him not into the water;	F	1472	4.4.16	P	Faust
Murder or not murder, now he has but one leg, I'le out-run him,	F	1494	4.4.38	P	HrsCsr
some on's have cause to know him; did he conjure thee too?	F	1524	4.5.20	P	HrsCsr
I'le tell you how he serv'd me:	F	1525	4.5.21	P	Carter
he met me, and asked me what he should give me for as much Hay	F	1526	4.5.22	P	Carter
me what he should give me for as much Hay as he could eate;	F	1527	4.5.23	P	Carter
bad him take as much as he would for three-farthings; so he	F	1529	4.5.25	P	Carter
so he presently gave me my mony, and fell to eating;	F	1529	4.5.25	P	Carter
he never left eating, till he had eate up all my loade of hay.	F	1530	4.5.26	P	Carter
he never left eating, till he had eate up all my loade of hay.	F	1531	4.5.27	P	Carter
Now sirs, you shall heare how villanously he serv'd mee:	F	1535	4.5.31	P	HrsCsr
and he would by no meanes sell him under forty Dollors; so sir,	F	1536	4.5.32	P	HrsCsr
no time; but, quoth he, in any case ride him not into the water.	F	1541	4.5.37	P	HrsCsr
had had some [rare] quality that he would not have me know of,	F	1542	4.5.38	P	HrsCsr

HE (cont.)

us, he were as good commit with his father, as commit with us.	F1603	4.6.46	P	Dick
Ha, ha, ha, dost heare him Dick, he has forgot his legge.	F1629	4.6.72	P	Carter
I, I, he does not stand much upon that.	F1630	4.6.73	P	HrsCsr
you remember you bid he should not ride [him] into the water?	F1636	4.6.79	P	Carter
to die shortly, he has made his will, and given me his wealth,	F1674	5.1.1	P	Wagner
I wonder what he meanes, if death were nie, he would not .	F1677	5.1.4	P	Wagner
what he meanes, if death were nie, he would not frolick thus:	F1677	5.1.4	P	Wagner
When he appear'd to haplesse Semele:	F1784	5.1.111		Faust
To marke him how he doth demeane himselfe. . . .	F1806	5.2.10		Belzeb
How should he, but in <with> desperate lunacie. . .	F1807	5.2.11		Mephst
He and his servant Wagner are at hand, ...	F1813	5.2.17		Mephst
Looke sirs, comes he not, comes he not?	F1826	5.2.30	P	Faust
He is not well with being over solitarie.	F1829	5.2.33		3Schol
<Belike he is growne into some sicknesse, by> being over	F1829	(HC270)A	P	3Schol
this is the time <the time wil come>, and he will fetch mee.	F1861	5.2.65	P	Faust
He that loves pleasure, must for pleasure fall. . .	F1923	5.2.127		BdAngl
Yet for he was a Scholler, once admired/For wondrous knowledge	F1997	5.3.15		2Schol
he would give his soule to the Divel for a shoulder of mutton,	F App	p.229 8	P	Wagner
God forgive me, he speakes Dutch fustian:	F App	p.231 72	P	Clown
Cursed be he that tooke Frier Sandelo a blow on the pate.	F App	p.232 35		Frier
Cursed be he that disturbeth our holy Dirge. . . .	F App	p.232 37		Frier
Cursed be he that tooke away his holinesse wine. . .	F App	p.233 39		Frier
his horse, and he would have his things rubd and made cleane:	F App	p.233 7	P	Rafe
he keepes such a chafing with my mistris about it, and she has	F App	p.233 8	P	Rafe
I can reade, he for his forehead, she for her private study,	F App	p.233 16	P	Robin
Ile feede thy divel with horse-bread as long as he lives,	F App	p.234 31	P	Rafe
Ifaith he lookes much like a conjurer.	F App	p.236 11	P	Knight
No sir, but when Acteon died, he left the hornes for you:	F App	p.237 55	P	Faust
at my intreaty release him, he hath done penance sufficient.	F App	p.238 79	P	Emper
masse see where he is, God save you maister doctor. . .	F App	p.239 99	P	HrsCsr
him have him, he is an honest felow, and he has a great charge,	F App	p.239 105	P	Mephst
felow, and he has a great charge, neither wife nor childe.	F App	p.239 106	P	Mephst
why sir, wil he not drinke of all waters?	F App	p.239 110	P	HrsCsr
he wil drinke of al waters, but ride him not into the water,	F App	p.239 111	P	Faust
if he had but the qualitie of hey ding, ding, hey, ding, ding,	F App	p.239 115	P	HrsCsr
by him, for he bade me I should ride him into no water; now,	F App	p.240 130	P	HrsCsr
had some rare qualitie that he would not have had me knowne of,	F App	p.240 132	P	HrsCsr
I tell thee he has not slept this eight nights. . .	F App	p.240 144	P	Mephst
And he have not slept this eight weekes Ile speake with him.	F App	p.240 145	P	HrsCsr
See where he is fast asleepe.	F App	p.241 147	P	Mephst
I, this is he, God save ye maister doctor, maister doctor,	F App	p.241 148	P	HrsCsr
Why, thou seest he heares thee not.	F App	p.241 151	P	Mephst
What is he gone?	F App	p.241 164	P	Faust
farwel he, Faustus has his legge againe, and the Horsecourser I	F App	p.241 164	P	Faust
this learned man for the great kindnes he hath shewd to you.	F App	p.243 29	P	Duke
For he hath given to me al his goodes, ...	F App	p.243 2		Wagner
He would not banquet, and carowse, and swill/Amongst the .	F App	p.243 4		Wagner
carowse, and swill/Amongst the Students, as even now he doth,	F App	p.243 5		Wagner
He liv'd secure boasting his former deeds, ...	Lucan, First Booke	135		
Yet he alone is held in reverence.	Lucan, First Booke	144		
Caesars renowne for war was lesse, he restles, . . .	Lucan, First Booke	145		
Shaming to strive but where he did subdue, ...	Lucan, First Booke	146		
His mind was troubled, and he aim'd at war, ...	Lucan, First Booke	186		
He thus cride out:	Lucan, First Booke	197		
He, he afflicts Roome that made me Roomes foe. . . .	Lucan, First Booke	205		
This said, he laying aside all lets of war, ...	Lucan, First Booke	206		
here, here (saith he)/An end of peace; here end polluted lawes;	Lucan, First Booke	226		
And some dim stars) he Arriminum enter'd:	Lucan, First Booke	234		
Caesar (said he) while eloquence prevail'd, ...	Lucan, First Booke	274		
Straight summon'd he his severall companies/Unto the standard:	Lucan, First Booke	297		
And thus he spake:	Lucan, First Booke	300		
(Whom from his youth he bribde) needs make him king? .	Lucan, First Booke	315		
And shal he triumph long before his time, ...	Lucan, First Booke	316		
And having once got head still shal he raigne? . . .	Lucan, First Booke	317		
now least age might waine his state, he casts/For civill warre,	Lucan, First Booke	324		
Caesar; he whom I heare thy trumpets charge/I hould no Romaine;	Lucan, First Booke	374		
held up, all joyntly cryde/They'll follow where he please:	Lucan, First Booke	389		
delay/Might crosse him, he withdrew his troupes from France,	Lucan, First Booke	395		
And ere he sees the sea looseth his name;	Lucan, First Booke	402		
the bordering townes/He garrison'd; and Italy he fild with	Lucan, First Booke	464		
townes/He garrison'd; and Italy he fild with soldiours. .	Lucan, First Booke	464		
(his vassals)/And that he lags behind with them of purpose,	Lucan, First Booke	477		
and Rhene, which he hath brought/From out their Northren parts,	Lucan, First Booke	478		
and that Roome/He looking on by these men should be sackt.	Lucan, First Booke	480		
when by Junoes taske/He had before lookt Pluto in the face.	Lucan, First Booke	576		
First he commands such monsters Nature hatcht/Against her kind	Lucan, First Booke	588		
on the Altar/He laies a ne're-yoakt Bull, and powers downe	Lucan, First Booke	608		
By these he seeing what myschiefes must ensue, . . .	Lucan, First Booke	629		
For these before the rest preferreth he:	Ovid's Elegies	1.1.2		
Oh woe is me, he never shootes but hits, ...	Ovid's Elegies	1.1.29		
Or lies he close, and shoots where none can spie him? .	Ovid's Elegies	1.2.6		
T'was so, he stroke me with a slender dart, ...	Ovid's Elegies	1.2.7		
let hir <he> that cought me late,/Either love, or cause that I	Ovid's Elegies	1.3.1		
About thy neck shall he at pleasure skippe?	Ovid's Elegies	1.4.6		
Lie with him gently, when his limbes he spread/Upon the bed, but	Ovid's Elegies	1.4.15		
What wine he fills thee, wisely will him drinke, . .	Ovid's Elegies	1.4.29		
And while he drinkes, to adde more do not misse, . .	Ovid's Elegies	1.4.52		
Then will he kisse thee, and not onely kisse/But force thee	Ovid's Elegies	1.4.63		
He shewes me how unheard to passe the watch, . . .	Ovid's Elegies	1.6.7		
Butcherd the flocks he found in spatious field, . . .	Ovid's Elegies	1.7.8		
And he who on his mother veng'd his sire, ...	Ovid's Elegies	1.7.9		
He first a Goddesse strooke; an other I.	Ovid's Elegies	1.7.32		

HE (cont.)

Yet he harm'd lesse, whom I profess'd to love,	Ovid's Elegies	1.7.33
He staide, and on thy lookes his gazes seaz'd.	Ovid's Elegies	1.8.24
Would he not buy thee thou for him shouldst care.	Ovid's Elegies	1.8.34
And therof many thousand he rehearses.	Ovid's Elegies	1.8.58
What he will give, with greater instance crave.	Ovid's Elegies	1.8.68
Dissemble so, as lov'd he may be thought,	Ovid's Elegies	1.8.71
And take heed least he gets that love for nought.	Ovid's Elegies	1.8.72
Receive him soone, least patient use he gaine,	Ovid's Elegies	1.8.75
Beware least he unrival'd loves secure,	Ovid's Elegies	1.8.95
If he gives nothing, let him from thee wend.	Ovid's Elegies	1.8.100
When thou hast so much as he gives no more,	Ovid's Elegies	1.8.101
Mounts, and raine-doubled flouds he passeth over,	Ovid's Elegies	1.9.11
East windes he doth not chide/Nor to hoist saile attends fit	Ovid's Elegies	1.9.13
He Citties greate, this thresholds lies before:	Ovid's Elegies	1.9.19
This breakes Towne gates, but he his Mistris dore.	Ovid's Elegies	1.9.20
On Priams loose-trest daughter when he gazed.	Ovid's Elegies	1.9.38
He that will not growe slothfull let him love.	Ovid's Elegies	1.9.46
He hath no bosome, where to hide base pelfe.	Ovid's Elegies	1.10.18
his rent discharg'd/From further duty he rests then inlarg'd.	Ovid's Elegies	1.10.46
He wants no gifts into thy lap to hurle.	Ovid's Elegies	1.10.54
O thou oft wilt blush/And say he likes me for my borrowed bush,	Ovid's Elegies	1.14.48
So shall Licoris whom he loved best:	Ovid's Elegies	1.15.30
Ile live, and as he puls me downe, mount higher.	Ovid's Elegies	1.15.42
Or he who war'd and wand'red twenty yeare?	Ovid's Elegies	2.1.31
But furiously he follow his loves fire/And [thinke] <thinkes>	Ovid's Elegies	2.2.13
His fauning wench with her desire he crownes.	Ovid's Elegies	2.2.34
More he deserv'd, to both great harme he fram'd,	Ovid's Elegies	2.2.49
If he loves not, deafe eares thou doest importune,	Ovid's Elegies	2.2.53
Or if he loves, thy tale breedes his misfortune.	Ovid's Elegies	2.2.54
he will lament/And say this blabbe shall suffer punnishment.	Ovid's Elegies	2.2.59
With selfe same woundes he gave, he ought to smart.	Ovid's Elegies	2.3.4
Yet should I curse a God, if he but said,	Ovid's Elegies	2.9.25
Haples is he that all the night lies quiet/And slumbring,	Ovid's Elegies	2.9.39
Even as he led his life, so did he die.	Ovid's Elegies	2.10.38
And he is happy whom the earth holds, say.	Ovid's Elegies	2.11.30
He had not beene that conquering Rome did build.	Ovid's Elegies	2.14.16
He being Judge, I am convinc'd of blame.	Ovid's Elegies	2.17.2
With his stumpe-foote he halts ill-favouredly.	Ovid's Elegies	2.17.20
Cruell is he, that loves whom none protect.	Ovid's Elegies	2.19.4
Jove liked her better then he did before.	Ovid's Elegies	2.19.30
To steale sands from the shore he loves alife,	Ovid's Elegies	2.19.45
And first [she] <he> sayd, when will thy love be spent,	Ovid's Elegies	3.1.15
And this is he whom fierce love burnes, they cry.	Ovid's Elegies	3.1.20
Hippodameias lockes while he beheld.	Ovid's Elegies	3.2.16
Yet he attain'd by her support to have her,	Ovid's Elegies	3.2.17
he shall subdue,/The horses seeme, as [thy] <they> desire they	Ovid's Elegies	3.2.67
Alas he runnes too farre about the ring,	Ovid's Elegies	3.2.69
He holdes the palme: my palme is yet to gaine.	Ovid's Elegies	3.2.82
Or if there be a God, he loves fine wenches,	Ovid's Elegies	3.3.25
When he perceivd the reines let slacke, he stayde,	Ovid's Elegies	3.4.15
He is too clownish, whom a lewd wife grieves,	Ovid's Elegies	3.4.37
This said he: shee her modest eyes held downe,	Ovid's Elegies	3.5.67
So in a spring thrives he that told so much,	Ovid's Elegies	3.6.51
And lookes uppon the fruits he cannot touch.	Ovid's Elegies	3.6.52
Now when he should not jette, he boults upright,	Ovid's Elegies	3.6.67
What ere he hath his body gaind in warres.	Ovid's Elegies	3.7.20
Perhaps he'ele tell howe oft he slewe a man,	Ovid's Elegies	3.7.21
How piteously with drouping wings he stands,	Ovid's Elegies	3.8.9
Faire-fac'd Iulus, he went forth thy court.	Ovid's Elegies	3.8.14
There, he who rules the worlds starre-spangled towers,	Ovid's Elegies	3.9.21
Yet this is lesse, then if he had seene me,	Ovid's Elegies	3.10.15
He to th'Hetrurians Junoes feast commended,	Ovid's Elegies	3.12.35
As he imagyn'd Hero was his mother.	Hero and Leander	1.40
Died ere he could enjoy the love of any.	Hero and Leander	1.76
Enamoured of his beautie had he beene,	Hero and Leander	1.78
Some swore he was a maid in mans attire,	Hero and Leander	1.83
And such as knew he was a man would say,	Hero and Leander	1.87
He whom she favours lives, the other dies.	Hero and Leander	1.124
Stone still he stood, and evermore he gazed,	Hero and Leander	1.163
He kneel'd, but unto her devoutly praid;	Hero and Leander	1.177
He started up, she blusht as one asham'd;	Hero and Leander	1.181
He toucht her hand, in touching it she trembled,	Hero and Leander	1.183
And alwaies cut him off as he replide.	Hero and Leander	1.196
With chearefull hope thus he accosted her.	Hero and Leander	1.198
As put thereby, yet might he hope for mo.	Hero and Leander	1.312
These arguments he us'de, and many more,	Hero and Leander	1.329
Her vowes above the emptie aire he flings:	Hero and Leander	1.370
All deepe enrag'd, his sinowie bow he bent,	Hero and Leander	1.371
And as she wept, her teares to pearle he turn'd,	Hero and Leander	1.375
Laden with languishment and griefe he flies.	Hero and Leander	1.378
The self-same day that he asleepe had layd/Inchaunted Argus,	Hero and Leander	1.387
The while upon a hillocke downe he lay,	Hero and Leander	1.400
Till in his twining armes he lockt her fast,	Hero and Leander	1.403
And then he woo'd with kisses, and at last,	Hero and Leander	1.404
in the grasse, he often strayd/Beyond the bounds of shame,	Hero and Leander	1.406
Herewith he stayd his furie, and began/To give her leave to	Hero and Leander	1.415
Still vowd he love, she wanting no excuse/To feed him with	Hero and Leander	1.425
As he ought not performe, nor yet she aske.	Hero and Leander	1.430
He readie to accomplish what she wil'd,	Hero and Leander	1.433
He inly storm'd, and waxt more furious,	Hero and Leander	1.437
he wandring here,/In mournfull tearmes, with sad and heavie	Hero and Leander	1.439
He wounds with love, and forst them equallie,	Hero and Leander	1.445

HE (cont.)

These he regarded not, but did intreat, ...	Hero and Leander	1.451	
They granted what he crav'd, and once againe, ...	Hero and Leander	1.455	
As soone as he his wished purpose got, ...	Hero and Leander	1.460	
He recklesse of his promise, did despise/The love of .	Hero and Leander	1.461	
That he and Povertie should alwaies kis.	Hero and Leander	1.470	
He kist her, and breath'd life into her lips, ...	Hero and Leander	2.3	
He being a novice, knew not what she meant, ...	Hero and Leander	2.13	
As he had hope to scale the beauteous fort, ...	Hero and Leander	2.16	
And therefore to her tower he got by stealth.	Hero and Leander	2.18	
And oft look't out, and mus'd he did not come.	Hero and Leander	2.22	
At last he came, O who can tell the greeting, ...	Hero and Leander	2.23	
He askt, she gave, and nothing was denied, ...	Hero and Leander	2.25	
And what he did, she willingly requited.	Hero and Leander	2.28	
That he would leave her turret and depart.	Hero and Leander	2.38	
To see how he this captive Nymph beguil'd.	Hero and Leander	2.40	
To slake his anger, if he were displeas'd, ...	Hero and Leander	2.49	
Like Aesops cocke, this jewell he enjoyed, ...	Hero and Leander	2.51	
Now he her favour and good will had wone.	Hero and Leander	2.54	
yet he suspected/Some amorous rites or other were neglected.	Hero and Leander	2.63	
Therefore unto his bodie, hirs he clung, ...	Hero and Leander	2.65	
As in plaine termes (yet cunningly) he crav'd it, . . .	Hero and Leander	2.71	
And ever as he thought himselfe most nigh it, ...	Hero and Leander	2.74	
And red for anger that he stayd so long, ...	Hero and Leander	2.89	
Long was he taking leave, and loath to go, ...	Hero and Leander	2.93	
Though it was morning, did he take his flight. . . .	Hero and Leander	2.102	
but he must weare/The sacred ring wherewith she was endow'd,	Hero and Leander	2.108	
Than he could saile, for incorporeal Fame, ...	Hero and Leander	2.113	
Home when he came, he seem'd not to be there, ...	Hero and Leander	2.117	
He would have chac'd away the swelling maine, ...	Hero and Leander	2.121	
The more he is restrain'd, the woorse he fares, . . .	Hero and Leander	2.145	
O Hero, Hero, thus he cry'de full oft, ...	Hero and Leander	2.147	
And then he got him to a rocke aloft.	Hero and Leander	2.148	
Where having spy'de her tower, long star'd he on't, . .	Hero and Leander	2.149	
And swore he never should returne to Jove.	Hero and Leander	2.168	
But when he knew it was not Ganimed, ...	Hero and Leander	2.169	
For under water he was almost dead, ...	Hero and Leander	2.170	
He heav'd him up, and looking on his face, ...	Hero and Leander	2.171	
He clapt his plumpe cheekes, with his tresses playd, .	Hero and Leander	2.181	
He watcht his armes, and as they opend wide, ...	Hero and Leander	2.183	
At every stroke, betwixt them would he slide, ...	Hero and Leander	2.184	
And as he turnd, cast many a lustfull glaunce, . . .	Hero and Leander	2.186	
And as he spake, upon the waves he springs.	Hero and Leander	2.206	
He flung at him his mace, but as it went, ...	Hero and Leander	2.209	
He cald it in, for love made him repent.	Hero and Leander	2.210	
went and came, as if he rewd/The greefe which Neptune felt.	Hero and Leander	2.214	
Thereon concluded that he was beloved.	Hero and Leander	2.220	
To the rich Ocean for gifts he flies.	Hero and Leander	2.224	
Breathlesse albeit he were, he rested not, ...	Hero and Leander	2.229	
Till to the solitarie tower he got.	Hero and Leander	2.230	
Unto her was he led, or rather drawne, ...	Hero and Leander	2.241	
The neerer that he came, the more she fled, ...	Hero and Leander	2.243	
His hands he cast upon her like a snare, ...	Hero and Leander	2.259	
Yet ever as he greedily assayd/To touch those dainties, she the	Hero and Leander	2.269	
For though the rising yv'rie mount he scal'd, ...	Hero and Leander	2.273	
Yet there with Sysiphus he toyld in vaine, ...	Hero and Leander	2.277	
Which so prevail'd, as he with small ado, ...	Hero and Leander	2.281	
(as men say)/But deaffe and cruell, where he meanes to pray.	Hero and Leander	2.288	
He on the suddaine cling'd her so about, ...	Hero and Leander	2.314	
But he the [days] <day> bright-bearing Car prepar'd. .	Hero and Leander	2.330	

HEAD

From forth her ashes shall advance her head, ...	Dido	1.1.94	Jupitr
Had not such passions in her head as I.	Dido	2.1.6	Aeneas
With sacrificing wreathes upon his head, ...	Dido	2.1.148	Aeneas
and on his speare/The mangled head of Priams yongest sonne,	Dido	2.1.215	Aeneas
Then touch her white breast with this arrow head, . .	Dido	2.1.326	Venus
And when she strokes thee softly on the head, ...	Dido	3.1.5	Cupid
But I will teare thy eyes fro forth thy head, ...	Dido	3.2.34	Venus
O how a Crowne becomes Aeneas head!	Dido	4.4.38	Dido
Shall overway his wearie witlesse head, ...	1Tamb	2.1.46	Cosroe
In happy hower we have set the Crowne/Upon your kingly head,	1Tamb	2.1.51	Ortyg
But I will have Cosroe by the head, ...	1Tamb	2.2.11	Mycet
Who brings that Traitors head Theridamas, ...	1Tamb	2.2.32	Meandr
And set it safe on my victorious head.	1Tamb	2.3.54	Cosroe
Then shalt thou see me pull it from thy head: . . .	1Tamb	2.4.39	Tamb
So, now it is more surer on my head, ...	1Tamb	2.7.65	Tamb
And on thy head weare my Emperiall crowne, ...	1Tamb	3.3.113	Bajzth
victorie we yeeld/May bind the temples of his conquering head,	1Tamb	5.1.56	2Virgn
And beat thy braines out of thy conquer'd head: . . .	1Tamb	5.1.287	Bajzth
That fights for honor to adorne your head.	1Tamb	5.1.376	Anippe
Then let us set the crowne upon her head, ...	1Tamb	5.1.501	Therid
Neere Guyrons head doth set his conquering feet, . . .	2Tamb	1.1.17	Gazell
Whose head hath deepest scarres, whose breast most woundes,	2Tamb	1.3.75	Tamb
Turkish Deputie/And all his Viceroies, snatch it from his head,	2Tamb	1.3.100	Tamb
Shall hide his head in Thetis watery lap, ...	2Tamb	1.3.169	Tamb
Their Spheares are mounted on the serpents head, . . .	2Tamb	2.4.53	Tamb
So he shal, and weare thy head in his Scutchion. . . .	2Tamb	3.5.138	P Orcan
Than he that darted mountaines at thy head, ...	2Tamb	4.1.128	Tamb
Will poure down blood and fire on thy head:	2Tamb	4.1.143	Jrslem
Or vengeance on the head of Tamburlain, ...	2Tamb	5.1.195	Tamb
clowdes, and on his head/A Chaplet brighter than Apollos crowne,	2Tamb	5.2.32	Amasia
To see thy foot-stoole set upon thy head, ...	2Tamb	5.3.29	Usumc
If your first curse fall heavy on thy head, ...	Jew	1.2.107	1Knght

HEAD (cont.)

and thou hast, breake my head with it, I'le forgive thee.	Jew	2.3.112	P Barab
Provided, that you keepe your Maiden-head.	Jew	2.3.227	Barab
I hold my head my master's hungry:	Jew	3.4.51	P Ithimr
For this, this head, this heart, this hand and sworde,	P 109	2.52	Guise
The sent whereof doth make my head to ake.	P 171	3.6	OldQn
the fatall poyson/Workes within my head, my brain pan breakes,	P 185	3.20	OldQn
The head being of, the members cannot stand.	P 296	5.23	Anjoy
Away with him, cut of his head and handes,	P 316	5.43	Anjoy
For if these straglers gather head againe,	P 506	9.25	QnMoth
Hence strumpet, hide thy head for shame,	P 691	13.35	Guise
My head shall be my counsell, they are false:	P 884	17.79	King
He should have lost his head, but with his looke,	Edw	1.1.113	Kent
To floate in bloud, and at thy wanton head,	Edw	1.1.132	Lncstr
The glozing head of thy base minion throwne.	Edw	1.1.133	Lncstr
Will to Newcastell heere, and gather head.	Edw	2.2.123	Warwck
The head-strong Barons shall not limit me.	Edw	2.2.262	Edward
souldiers take him hence, for by my sword,/His head shall off:	Edw	2.5.21	Warwck
Weele send his head by thee, let him bestow/His teares on that,	Edw	2.5.52	Mortmr
and in a trenche/Strake off his head, and marcht unto the	Edw	3.1.120	Arundl
whose golden leaves/Empale your princelie head, your diadem,	Edw	3.1.164	Herald
For which thy head shall over looke the rest,	Edw	3.1.239	Edward
And then have at the proudest Spencers head.	Edw	4.2.25	Prince
Raigne showers of vengeance on my cursed head/Thou God, to whom	Edw	4.6.7	Kent
Your lordship cannot priviledge your head.	Edw	4.6.70	Mortmr
good father on thy lap/Lay I this head, laden with mickle care,	Edw	4.7.40	Edward
Never againe lift up this drooping head,	Edw	4.7.42	Edward
No, tis for Mortimer, not Edwards head,	Edw	5.1.40	Edward
Engirt the temples of his hatefull head,	Edw	5.1.46	Edward
My head, the latest honor dew to it,	Edw	5.1.62	Edward
But that I feele the crowne upon my head,	Edw	5.1.82	Edward
Strike off his head, he shall have marshall lawe.	Edw	5.4.89	Mortmr
Strike of my head? base traitor I defie thee.	Edw	5.4.90	Kent
Thy hatefull and accursed head shall lie,	Edw	5.6.30	King
But bring his head back presently to me.	Edw	5.6.54	King
My lord, here is the head of Mortimer.	Edw	5.6.93	1Lord
accursed head,/Could I have rulde thee then, as I do now,	Edw	5.6.95	King
I offer up this wicked traitors head,	Edw	5.6.100	King
And heape Gods heavy wrath upon thy head.	F 99	1.1.71	GdAngl
no object, for my head]/[But ruminates on Negromantique skill].	F 131	1.1.103A	Faust
a paire of hornes on's head as e're thou sawest in thy life.	F 737	2.3.16	P Robin
Lifting his loftie head above the clouds,	F 912	3.1.134	Pope
Whilst on thy head I lay my hand,	F 995	3.2.15	Mephst
I am content for this once to thrust my head out at a window:	F1200	4.1.46	P Benvol
I have a charme in my head, shall controule him as well as the	F1202	4.1.48	P Benvol
beast is yon, that thrusts his head out at [the] window.	F1275	4.1.121	P Faust
hornes most strangely fastened/Upon the head of yong Benvolio.	F1278	4.1.124	Emper
thee not to sleepe much, having such a head of thine owne.	F1284	4.1.130	P Emper
The Emperour? where? O zounds my head.	F1287	4.1.133	Benvol
hold, tis no matter for thy head, for that's arm'd sufficiently.	F1288	4.1.134	P Emper
pull in your head for shame, let not all the world wonder at	F1291	4.1.137	P Faust
Benvolio's head was grac't with hornes to day?	F1331	4.2.7	Benvol
My head is lighter then it was by th'hornes,	F1350	4.2.26	Benvol
But yet my [heart's] <heart> more ponderous then my head,	F1351	4.2.27	Benvol
For hornes he gave, Il'e have his head anone.	F1361	4.2.37	Benvol
Strike with a willing hand, his head is off.	F1368	4.2.44	Mrtino
Was this that damned head, whose heart <art> conspir'd	F1373	4.2.49	Mrtino
I, that's the head, and here the body lies,	F1375	4.2.51	Benvol
First, on his head, in quittance of my wrongs,	F1379	4.2.55	Benvol
Give him his head for Gods sake.	F1392	4.2.68	P Fredrk
It is your owne you meane, feele on your head.	F1443	4.3.13	Fredrk
I see an Angell hover <hovers> ore thy head,	F1730	5.1.57	OldMan
Ifaith thy head will never be out of the potage pot.	F App	p.236 48	P Robin
thee hornes, but makes thee weare them, feele on thy head.	F App	p.238 71	P Emper
And on her Turret-bearing head disperst,	Lucan, First Booke	190	
And having once got head still shal he raigne?	Lucan, First Booke	317	
high; but headlong pitcht/Her burning head on bending Hespery.	Lucan, First Booke	545	
Or Atlas head; their saints and houshold gods/Sweate teares to	Lucan, First Booke	554	
And Marius head above cold Tav'ron peering/(His grave broke	Lucan, First Booke	581	
Nor [leane] <leave> thy soft head on his boistrous brest.	Ovid's Elegies	1.4.36	
Deny him oft, feigne now thy head doth ake:	Ovid's Elegies	1.8.73	
the drie fields strayed/When on her head a water pitcher laied.	Ovid's Elegies	1.10.6	
Thou mad'st thy head with compound poyson flow.	Ovid's Elegies	1.14.44	
While Rome of all the [conquered] <conquering> world is head.	Ovid's Elegies	1.15.26	
About my head be quivering Mirtle wound,	Ovid's Elegies	1.15.37	
Behold Cypassis wont to dresse thy head,	Ovid's Elegies	2.7.17	
Even as a head-strong courser beares away,	Ovid's Elegies	2.9.29	
Ah often, that her [hale] <haole> head aked, she lying,	Ovid's Elegies	2.19.11	
Tis credible some [god-head] <good head> haunts the place.	Ovid's Elegies	3.1.2	
And seaven [times] <time> shooke her head with thicke locks	Ovid's Elegies	3.1.32	
With lying lips my God-head to deceave,	Ovid's Elegies	3.3.44	
Bearing the head with dreadfull [Adders] <Arrowes> clad,	Ovid's Elegies	3.5.14	
Who so well keepes his waters head from knowing,	Ovid's Elegies	3.5.40	
It mocked me, hung down the head and suncke,	Ovid's Elegies	3.6.14	
Knowest not this head a helme was wont to beare,	Ovid's Elegies	3.7.13	
The ships, whose God-head in the sea now glisters?	Ovid's Elegies	3.11.38	
Upon her head she ware a myrtle wreath,	Hero and Leander	1.17	
And laid his childish head upon her brest,	Hero and Leander	1.43	
Thence flew Loves arrow with the golden head,	Hero and Leander	1.161	
Heav'd up her head, and halfe the world upon,	Hero and Leander	1.190	
To have his head control'd, but breakes the raines,	Hero and Leander	2.142	
This head was beat with manie a churlish billow,	Hero and Leander	2.251	

HEADDIE

Committing headdie ryots, incest, rapes:	Hero and Leander	1.144	

Line	Work	Reference	Speaker
HEADED			
Wun on the fiftie headed Vuolgas waves,	1Tamb	1.2.103	Tamb
[and] <To> pull the triple headed dog from hell.	1Tamb	1.2.161	Therid
The triple headed Cerberus would howle,	2Tamb	5.1.97	Tamb
Freely enjoy that vaine light-headed earle,	Edw	1.4.400	MortSr
Poore Pierce, and headed him against lawe of armes?	Edw	3.1.238	Edward
To dash the heavie headed Edmunds drift,	Edw	5.2.39	Mortmr
Where by one hand, light headed Bacchus hoong,	Hero and Leander	1.139	
HEADES			
A monster of five hundred thousand heades,	1Tamb	4.3.7	Souldn
To turne them al upon their proper heades.	1Tamb	4.4.31	Tamb
to clap hornes of honest mens heades o'this order,	F1317	4.1.163	P Benvol
HEADING			
That heading is one, and hanging is the other,	Edw	2.5.30	Gavstn
HEADLES			
Headles carkasses piled up in heapes,	Dido	2.1.194	Aeneas
in lakes of gore/Your headles trunkes, your bodies will I	Edw	3.1.136	Edward
headles darts, olde swords/With ugly teeth of blacke rust fouly	Lucan, First Booke	244	
HEADLESSE			
This headlesse trunke that lies on Nylus sande/I know:	Lucan, First Booke	684	
HEADLONG (See also HEDLONG)			
an hot alarme/Drive all their horses headlong down the hill.	1Tamb	1.2.135	Usumc
All running headlong after greedy spoiles:	1Tamb	2.2.45	Meandr
Goe villaine, cast thee headlong from a rock,	2Tamb	3.5.120	Tamb
Haling him headlong to the lowest hell.	2Tamb	4.3.42	Orcan
And cast them headlong in the cities lake:	2Tamb	5.1.162	Tamb
Our Turkish swords shal headlong send to hell,	2Tamb	5.2.15	Amasia
run to some rocke and throw my selfe headlong into the sea;	Jew	3.4.40	P Ithimr
Thence pitch them headlong to the lowest hell:	F1405	4.2.81	Faust
Then will I headlong run into the earth:	F1948	5.2.152	Faust
inconsiderate multitude/Thorough the Citty hurried headlong on,	Lucan, First Booke	493	
high; but headlong pitcht/Her burning head on bending Hespery.	Lucan, First Booke	544	
Grosse gold, from them runs headlong to the boore.	Hero and Leander	1.472	
All headlong throwes her selfe the clouds among/And now Leander	Hero and Leander	2.90	
HEADS			
And loade his speare with Grecian Princes heads,	Dido	3.3.43	Aeneas
And fire proude Lacedemon ore their heads.	Dido	4.4.92	Aeneas
All loden with the heads of killed men.	1Tamb	1.1.78	Mycet
Spurning their crownes from off their captive heads.	1Tamb	1.2.57	Techel
This hand shal set them on your conquering heads:	1Tamb	3.3.31	Tamb
And as the heads of Hydra, so my power/Subdued, shall stand as	1Tamb	3.3.140	Bajzth
not endure to strike/So many blowes as I have heads for thee.	1Tamb	3.3.144	Bajzth
With mournfull streamers hanging down their heads,	1Tamb	4.2.120	Tamb
Reflexing hewes of blood upon their heads,	1Tamb	4.4.2	Tamb
Shead from the heads and hearts of all our Sex,	1Tamb	5.1.26	1Virgn
Yet should ther hover in their restlesse heads,	1Tamb	5.1.171	Tamb
fethered steele/So thick upon the blink-ei'd Burghers heads,	2Tamb	1.1.93	Orcan
his fearefull arme/Be pour'd with rigour on our sinfull heads,	2Tamb	2.1.58	Fredrk
of the clowdes/And fall as thick as haile upon our heads,	2Tamb	2.2.15	Gazell
Hel and confusion light upon their heads,	2Tamb	2.2.33	Gazell
With apples like the heads of damned Feends.	2Tamb	2.3.23	Orcan
Will poure it downe in showers on our heads:	2Tamb	3.1.36	Callap
Upon the heads of all our enemies.	2Tamb	3.2.42	Tamb
here are Bugges/Wil make the haire stand upright on your heads,	2Tamb	3.5.148	Tamb
That we may venge their blood upon their heads.	Jew	3.2.28	Mater
Brother revenge it, and let these their heads,	Edw	1.1.117	Kent
O our heads?	Edw	1.1.119	Warwck
Cosin, our hands I hope shall fence our heads,	Edw	1.1.123	Mortmr
Wilshire hath men enough to save our heads.	Edw	1.1.127	MortSr
And being like pins heads, blame me for the bignesse,	Edw	2.1.48	Baldck
Looke to your owne heads, his is sure enough.	Edw	2.2.92	Edward
But if I live, ile tread upon their heads,	Edw	2.2.96	Edward
Strike off their heads, and let them preach on poles,	Edw	3.1.20	Spencr
I will have heads, and lives, for him as many,	Edw	3.1.132	Edward
For which ere long, their heads shall satisfie,	Edw	3.1.209	Edward
me thinkes you hang the heads,/But weele advance them traitors,	Edw	3.1.223	Edward
I charge you roundly off with both their heads,	Edw	3.1.247	Edward
These Barons lay their heads on blocks together,	Edw	3.1.274	Baldck
For we shall see them shorter by the heads.	Edw	4.7.94	Rice
Or clap huge hornes, upon the Cardinals heads:	F 864	3.1.86	Mephst
Faustus will have heads and hands,/I, [all] <I call> your	F1393	4.2.69	Faust
O hellish spite,/Your heads are all set with hornes.	F1442	4.3.12	Benvol
But managde horses heads are lightly borne,	Ovid's Elegies	1.2.16	
And in sad lovers heads let me be found.	Ovid's Elegies	1.15.38	
And gives the viper curled Dogge three heads.	Ovid's Elegies	3.11.26	
And Rams with hornes their hard heads wreathed back.	Ovid's Elegies	3.12.17	
Upon their heads the holy mysteries had.	Ovid's Elegies	3.12.28	
HEAD-STRONG			
The head-strong Barons shall not limit me.	Edw	2.2.262	Edward
Even as a head-strong courser beares away,	Ovid's Elegies	2.9.29	
HEADSTRONG			
The headstrong Jades of Thrace, Alcides tam'd,	2Tamb	4.3.12	Tamb
longer life/Thou hadst restrainde thy headstrong husbands rage,	Lucan, First Booke	116	
HEADY (See also HEADDIE)			
When yre, or hope provokt, heady, and bould,	Lucan, First Booke	147	
Their sway of fleight carries the heady rout/That in chain'd	Lucan, First Booke	488	
HEALE			
But heale the heart, that thou hast wounded thus,	Hero and Leander	1.324	
HEALTH			
My mother Venus jealous of my health,	Dido	2.1.221	Aeneas
of that vitall aire/That feeds the body with his dated health,	2Tamb	2.4.45	Zenoc
Whose heavenly presence beautified with health,	2Tamb	2.4.49	Tamb
health and majesty/Were strangely blest and governed by heaven,	2Tamb	5.3.24	Techel

HEALTH (cont.)
His byrth, his life, his health and majesty. | 2Tamb 5.3.27 | Techel
That thus invie the health of Tamburlaine. | 2Tamb 5.3.53 | Tamb
Tell me, hast thou thy health well? | Jew 2.3.121 | P Barab
But God will sure restore you to your health. | P 542 11.7 | Navrre
Health and harty farwell to my Lord Joyeux. | P 751 15.9 | Guise
A bowle of poison to each others health: | Edw 2.2.238 | Edward
In health madam, but full of pensivenes. | Edw 5.2.25 | Msngr
In health sweete Mortimer, how fares your grace? | Edw 5.2.81 | Kent
The end of Physicke is our bodies health: | F 45 1.1.17 | Faust
So kindly yesternight to Bruno's health, | F1175 4.1.21 | Mrtino
'faith Ile drinke a health to thy woodden leg for that word. | F1627 4.6.70 | P HrsCsr

HEALTHFULL
Healthfull Peligny I esteeme nought worth, | Ovid's Elegies | 2.16.37

HEAPE
But dares to heape up sorrowe to my heart: | Dido 4.4.152 | Dido
wel to heare both you/Have won a heape of honor in the field, | 2Tamb 4.1.37 | Calyph
And in his house heape pearle like pibble-stones, | Jew 1.1.23 | Barab
And said it was a heape of vanities? | P 388 7.28 | Guise
Be a Phisitian Faustus, heape up gold, | F 42 1.1.14 | Faust
And heape Gods heavy wrath upon thy head. | F 99 1.1.71 | GdAngl
Of wealth and honour so shall grow thy heape, | Ovid's Elegies | 2.2.39

HEAPES
Altars crack/With mountaine heapes of milke white Sacrifize. | Dido 1.1.202 | Aeneas
Headles carkasses piled up in heapes, | Dido 2.1.194 | Aeneas
And all the heapes of supersticious bookes, | 2Tamb 5.1.174 | Tamb
Make Englands civill townes huge heapes of stones, | Edw 3.1.215 | Edward
rampiers fallen down, huge heapes of stone/Lye in our townes, | Lucan, First Booke | 25
And on their faces heapes of Roses strow. | Ovid's Elegies | 1.2.40
Within a while great heapes grow of a tittle. | Ovid's Elegies | 1.8.90
And treades the deserts snowy heapes [do] <to> cover. | Ovid's Elegies | 1.9.12
sported with their loves/On heapes of heavie gold, and tooke | Hero and Leander | 2.163
Than Dis, on heapes of gold fixing his looke. | Hero and Leander | 2.326

HEAPING
In heaping up a masse of drossie pelfe, | Hero and Leander | 1.244

HEAPS
See how he raines down heaps of gold in showers, | 1Tamb 1.2.182 | Tamb
Beating in heaps against their Argoses, | 2Tamb 1.1.41 | Orcan
And kindle heaps of exhalations, | 2Tamb 3.2.3 | Tamb
Drawen with these kings on heaps of carkasses. | 2Tamb 5.1.72 | Tamb

HEAPT
Jove hath heapt on me such a desperate charge, | Dido 5.1.64 | Aeneas

HEAR
But do you hear? | F App p.230 56 | P Clown

HEARBES
see al plants, hearbes and trees that grow upon the earth]. | F 551.9 2.1.172A | P Faust

HEARBS
Affoords no hearbs, whose taste may poison thee, | 2Tamb 4.2.9 | Olymp

HEARD
I neither saw nor heard of any such: | Dido 1.1.187 | Aeneas
Made me suppose he would have heard me speake: | Dido 5.1.230 | Anna
Oft have I heard your Majestie complain, | 1Tamb 1.1.35 | Meandr
Thou art deceiv'd, I heard the Trumpets sound, | 1Tamb 3.3.203 | Zabina
have ye lately heard/The overthrow of mightie Bajazeth, | 1Tamb 4.3.23 | Arabia
As when an heard of lusty Cymbrian Buls, | 2Tamb 4.1.187 | Tamb
But this we heard some of our sea-men say, | Jew 1.1.78 | 1Merch
Oft have I heard tell, can be permanent. | Jew 1.1.133 | Barab
Martin del Bosco, I have heard of thee; | Jew 2.2.19 | Govnr
choyce, I heard a rumbling in the house; so I tooke onely this, | Jew 3.1.20 | P Pilia
So I have heard; pray therefore keepe it close. | Jew 3.6.37 | Abigal
I never heard of any man but he/Malign'd the order of the | Jew 4.1.103 | Barab
Art thou that Jew whose goods we heard were sold/For | Jew 5.1.73 | Calym
Have you not heard of late how he decreed, | P 32 1.32 | Navrre
Madam, I have heard him solemnly vow, | P 516 9.35 | Cardnl
I heard your Majestie was scarsely pleasde, | P 967 19.37 | Guise
And we have heard that Edmund laid a plot, | Edw 5.2.32 | BshpWn
<Yes sirre, I heard you>. | F 204 (HC258)A | P 1Schol
Now Faustus thou hast heard all my progeny, wilt thou bid me to | F 700 2.2.149 | P Glutny
I have heard it said,/That this faire Lady, whilest she liv'd | F1265 4.1.111 | Emper
I heard them parly with the Conjurer. | F1422 4.2.98 | 1Soldr
be; for I have heard of one, that ha's eate a load of logges. | F1533 4.5.29 | P Robin
I have heard that great bellyed women, do long for things, are | F1568 4.6.11 | P Faust
Such fearefull shrikes, and cries, were never heard, | F1986 5.3.4 | 1Schol
one, me thought/I heard him shreeke and call aloud for helpe: | F1992 5.3.10 | 3Schol
have heard strange report of thy knowledge in the blacke Arte, | F App p.236 1 | P Emper
be witnesses to confirme what mine eares have heard reported, | F App p.236 7 | P Emper
heard this Lady while she liv'd had a wart or moale in her | F App p.238 60 | P Emper
heard that great bellied women do long for some dainties or | F App p.242 4 | P Faust
of barbarous Tygars having lapt/The bloud of many a heard, | Lucan, First Booke | 328
Clashing of armes was heard, in untrod woods/Shrill voices | Lucan, First Booke | 567
Trumpets were heard to sound; and with what noise/An armed | Lucan, First Booke | 577
By chaunce I heard her talke, these words she sayd/While | Ovid's Elegies | 1.8.21
I chid no more, she blusht, and therefore heard me, | Ovid's Elegies | 1.13.47
Which watchfull Hesperus no sooner heard, | Hero and Leander | 2.329

HEARDES
Stretching their pawes, and threatning heardes of Beastes, | 1Tamb 1.2.53 | Techel

HEARDS
As sheap-heards do, her on the ground hee layd, | Hero and Leander | 1.405
And crave the helpe of sheap-heards that were nie. | Hero and Leander | 1.414

HEARE
I heare Aeneas voyce, but see him not, | Dido 2.1.45 | Illion
And Priam dead, yet how we heare no newes. | Dido 2.1.113 | Dido
And Dido and you Carthaginian Peeres/Heare me, but yet with | Dido 2.1.123 | Aeneas

HEARE (cont.)

O Hector who weepes not to heare thy name?	Dido	2.1.209	Dido
O end Aeneas, I can heare no more.	Dido	2.1.243	Dido
We heare they led her captive into Greece.	Dido	2.1.295	Achat
Sit in my lap and let me heare thee sing.	Dido	3.1.25	Dido
Yet must I heare that lothsome name againe?	Dido	3.1.78	Dido
In stead of musicke I will heare him speake,	Dido	3.1.89	Dido
What more then Delian musicke doe I heare,	Dido	3.4.52	Dido
Heare, heare, O heare Iarbus plaining prayers,	Dido	4.2.8	Iarbus
Hard hearted, wilt not deigne to heare me speake?	Dido	4.2.54	Anna
Come backe, come backe, I heare her crye a farre,	Dido	4.3.27	Aeneas
And stay a while to heare what I could say,	Dido	5.1.239	Anna
Where you shall heare the Scythian Tamburlaine,	1Tamb	Prol.4	Prolog
And as I heare, doth meane to pull my plumes.	1Tamb	1.1.33	Mycet
Then heare thy charge, valiant Theridamas,	1Tamb	1.1.57	Mycet
mated and amaz'd/To heare the king thus threaten like himselfe?	1Tamb	1.1.108	Menaph
I heare them come, shal we encounter them?	1Tamb	1.2.149	Techel
We heare, the Tartars and the Easterne theeves/Under the	1Tamb	3.1.2	Bajzth
Because I heare he beares a valiant mind.	1Tamb	3.1.32	Bajzth
Awake ye men of Memphis, heare the clange/Of Scythian trumpets,	1Tamb	4.1.1	Souldn
heare the clange/Of Scythian trumpets, heare the Basiliskes,	1Tamb	4.1.2	Souldn
Yet heare me speake my gentle Almeda.	2Tamb	1.2.13	Callap
Twill please my mind as wel to heare both you/Have won a heape	2Tamb	4.1.36	Calyph
And til by vision, or by speach I heare/Immortall Jove say,	2Tamb	4.1.198	Tamb
And tremble when ye heare this Scourge wil come,	2Tamb	4.3.99	Tamb
He cannot heare the voice of Tamburlain,	2Tamb	5.1.199	Tamb
I am asham'd to heare such fooleries.	Jew	Prol.17	Machvl
But who comes heare? How now.	Jew	1.1.48	Barab
I heare the wealthy Jew walked this way;	Jew	2.3.32	Lodowk
Give me the letters, daughter, doe you heare?	Jew	2.3.224	Barab
You heare your answer, and you may be gone.	Jew	4.1.92	1Fryar
No, none can heare him, cry he ne're so loud.	Jew	4.1.136	Ithimr
have at it; and doe you heare?	Jew	4.4.2	P Ithimr
A French Musician, come let's heare your skill?	Jew	4.4.30	Curtzn
What e're I am, yet Governor heare me speake;	Jew	5.1.9	Curtzn
you men of Malta, heare me speake;/Shee is a Curtezane and he a	Jew	5.1.36	Barab
Till you shall heare a Culverin discharg'd/By him that beares	Jew	5.4.3	Govnr
Doth heare and see the praiers of the just:	P 43	1.43	Navrre
An eare, to heare what my detractors say,	P 160	2.103	Guise
Which when they heare, they shall begin to kill:	P 239	4.37	Guise
Which as I heare one [Shekius] <Shekins> takes it ill,	P 404	7.44	Ramus
O Mounser de Guise, heare me but speake.	P 529	10.2	Prtsnt
Let Christian princes that shall heare of this,	P1041	19.111	King
see where she comes, as if she droupt/To heare these newes.	P1063	19.133	Eprnon
My lords, to eaze all this, but heare me speake.	Edw	1.2.68	ArchBp
My lord I heare it whispered every where,	Edw	1.4.106	Gavstn
Then thus, but none shal heare it but our selves.	Edw	1.4.229	Queene
Yet good my lord, heare what he can alledge.	Edw	1.4.250	Queene
Such newes we heare my lord.	Edw	1.4.380	Lncstr
Brother, doe you heare them?	Edw	2.2.69	Kent
As if he heare I have but talkt with you,	Edw	2.4.54	Queene
I long to heare an answer from the Barons/Touching my friend,	Edw	3.1.1	Edward
Because we heare Lord Bruse dooth sell his land,	Edw	3.1.53	Edward
I heare sweete lady of the kings unkindenes,	Edw	4.2.15	SrJohn
My lord of Gloster, do you heare the newes?	Edw	4.3.4	Edward
Heare me immortall Jove, and graunt it too.	Edw	5.1.143	Edward
First would I heare newes that hee were deposde,	Edw	5.2.21	Mortmr
rest, because we heare/That Edmund casts to worke his libertie,	Edw	5.2.57	Mortmr
I heare of late he hath deposde himselfe.	Edw	5.2.83	Kent
O wherefore sits thou heare?	Edw	5.5.96	Edward
For when we heare one racke the name of God,	F 275	1.3.47	Mephst
Then heare me read it Mephostophilis <them>.	F 483	2.1.95	Faust
Speak softly sir, least the devil heare you:	F1180	4.1.26	Mrtino
him o're hedge and ditch, and spare him not; but do you heare?	F1468	4.4.12	P Faust
Now sirs, you shall heare how villanously he serv'd mee:	F1535	4.5.31	P HrsCsr
But you shall heare how bravely I serv'd him for it; I went me	F1547	4.5.43	P HrsCsr
Ha, ha, ha, dost heare him Dick, he has forgot his legge.	F1629	4.6.72	P Carter
do you heare sir, did not I pull off one of your legs when you	F1655	4.6.98	P HrsCsr
heare you Maister Doctor, now you have sent away my guesse, I	F1666	4.6.109	P Hostss
heare [me] with patience, and tremble not at my speeches.	F1839	5.2.43	P Faust
and what noyse soever you <yee> heare, come not unto me, for	F1874	5.2.78	P Faust
Doe yee heare, I would be sorie to robbe you of your living.	F App	p.229 18	P Clown
Doe you heare sir?	F App	p.229 27	P Clown
wel, do you heare sirra?	F App	p.230 30	P Wagner
But doe you heare Wagner?	F App	p.231 66	P Clown
Anon you shal heare a hogge grunt, a calfe bleate, and an asse	F App	p.232 27	P Faust
As when I heare but motion made of him,	F App	p.237 27	Emper
Do you heare maister Doctor?	F App	p.237 51	P Knight
Do you heare sir?	F App	p.239 101	P HrsCsr
O yonder is his snipper snapper, do you heare?	F App	p.240 138	P HrsCsr
And joyed to heare his Theaters applause;	Lucan, First Booke	134	
Romans if ye be,/And beare true harts, stay heare:	Lucan, First Booke	194	
Caesar; he whom I heare thy trumpets charge/I hould no Romaine;	Lucan, First Booke	374	
Hard-hearted Porter doest and wilt not heare?	Ovid's Elegies	1.6.27	
or ist sleepe forbids thee heare,/Giving the windes my words	Ovid's Elegies	1.6.41	
Let him within heare bard out lovers prate.	Ovid's Elegies	1.8.78	
You are unapt my looser lines to heare.	Ovid's Elegies	2.1.4	
such faults are sad/Nor make they any man that heare them glad.	Ovid's Elegies	2.2.52	
Yet Love, if thou with thy faire mother heare,	Ovid's Elegies	2.9.51	
Nor, as use will not Poets record heare,	Ovid's Elegies	3.11.19	
Were I the saint hee worships, I would heare him,	Hero and Leander	1.179	
O shun me not, but heare me ere you goe,	Hero and Leander	1.205	
As she to heare his tale, left off her running.	Hero and Leander	1.418	

HEARE (cont.)			
Wherewith she wreath'd her largely spreading heare,	Hero and Leander		2.107
A kind of twilight breake, which through the heare,	Hero and Leander		2.319
HEARES			
So now the mighty Souldan heares of you,	1Tamb	3.2.31	Agidas
Who when he heares how resolute thou wert,	2Tamb	3.4.40	Techel
And he nor heares, nor sees us what we doe:	P 553	11.18	QnMoth
Why, thou seest he heares thee not.	F App	p.241 151	P Mephst
With joy heares Neptunes swelling waters sound.	Ovid's Elegies		3.10.30
HEARING			
and hearing your absence in the field, offers to set upon us	2Tamb	5.3.103	P 3Msngr
Hearing his Soveraigne was bound for Sea,	Jew	5.3.15	Msngr
to goe and consumate/The rest, with hearing of a holy Masse:	P 20	1.20	Charls
Hearing that you had taken Gaveston,	Edw	2.5.35	Arundl
The earle of Warwick would not bide the hearing,	Edw	3.1.104	Arundl
Love hearing it laugh'd with his tender mother/And smiling	Ovid's Elegies		1.6.11
Hearing her to be sicke, I thether ranne,	Ovid's Elegies		3.10.25
HEARK			
And I'le performe it Faustus: heark they come:	F 866	3.1.88	Mephst
HEARKE			
but hearke you Maister, will you teach me this conjuring	F 380	1.4.38	P Robin
Hearke you, we'le into another roome and drinke a while, and	F1556	4.5.52	P Robin
Nay, hearke you, can you tell me where you are?	F1614	4.6.57	Faust
HEARSE			
Now fetch the hearse of faire Zenocrate,	2Tamb	5.3.210	Tamb
A litter hast thou, lay me in a hearse,	Edw	4.7.87	Edward
And thou shalt die, and on his mournefull hearse,	Edw	5.6.29	King
Goe fetche my fathers hearse, where it shall lie,	Edw	5.6.94	King
Heere comes the hearse, helpe me to moorne, my lords:	Edw	5.6.98	King
HEARST			
Hearst thou Anippe, how thy drudge doth talk,	1Tamb	3.3.182	Zenoc
HEART (See also HART)			
Put thou about thy necke my owne sweet heart,	Dido	1.1.44	Jupitr
And when my grieved heart sighes and sayes no,	Dido	2.1.26	Aeneas
And the remainder weake and out of heart,	Dido	2.1.133	Aeneas
As every touch shall wound Queene Didos heart.	Dido	2.1.333	Cupid
Aeneas thoughts dare not ascend so high/As Didos heart, which	Dido	3.4.34	Aeneas
With this my hand I give to you my heart,	Dido	3.4.43	Aeneas
And dive into her heart by coloured lookes.	Dido	4.2.32	Iarbus
Whose yeelding heart may yeeld thee more reliefe.	Dido	4.2.36	Anna
onely Aeneas frowne/Is that which terrifies poore Didos heart:	Dido	4.4.116	Dido
But dares to heape up sorrowe to my heart:	Dido	4.4.152	Dido
These words proceed not from Aeneas heart.	Dido	5.1.102	Dido
Not from my heart, for I can hardly goe,	Dido	5.1.103	Aeneas
For though thou hast the heart to say farewell,	Dido	5.1.182	Dido
Yet he whose [hearts] <heart> of adamant or flint,	Dido	5.1.234	Anna
Thus shall my heart be still combinde with thine,	1Tamb	1.2.235	Tamb
Shal want my heart to be with gladnes pierc'd/To do you honor	1Tamb	1.2.250	Therid
I tel you true my heart is swolne with wrath,	1Tamb	2.2.2	Mycet
I, if I could with all my heart my Lord.	1Tamb	2.5.68	Techel
Direct my weapon to his barbarous heart,	1Tamb	2.6.38	Cosroe
Sackes every vaine and artier of my heart.	1Tamb	2.7.10	Cosroe
And sacrifice my heart to death and hell,	1Tamb	4.2.17	Bajzth
take it from my swords point, or Ile thrust it to thy heart.	1Tamb	4.4.41	P Tamb
Convey events of mercie to his heart:	1Tamb	5.1.54	2Virgn
That lingring paines may massacre his heart.	1Tamb	5.1.228	Zabina
That would with pity chear Zabinas heart,	1Tamb	5.1.271	Bajzth
Pierce through the center of my withered heart,	1Tamb	5.1.303	Bajzth
And rackt by dutie from my cursed heart:	1Tamb	5.1.387	Zenoc
Then shal I die with full contented heart,	1Tamb	5.1.417	Arabia
Depriv'd of care, my heart with comfort dies,	1Tamb	5.1.431	Arabia
My Lord I pitie it, and with my heart/Wish your release, but he	2Tamb	1.2.5	Almeda
Or treason in the fleshly heart of man,	2Tamb	2.2.37	Orcan
And vow to burne the villaines cruell heart.	2Tamb	3.1.56	Trebiz
As is that towne, so is my heart consum'd,	2Tamb	3.2.49	Amyras
Lies heavy on my heart, I cannot live.	2Tamb	3.4.5	Capt
Or rip thy bowels, and rend out thy heart,	2Tamb	3.5.121	Tamb
Wil send a deadly lightening to his heart.	2Tamb	4.1.10	Celeb
and of fire/Doth send such sterne affections to his heart.	2Tamb	4.1.176	Trebiz
vaine or Artier feed/The cursed substance of that cruel heart,	2Tamb	4.1.178	Soria
Save griefe and sorrow which torment my heart,	2Tamb	4.2.24	Olymp
My heart did never quake, or corrage faint.	2Tamb	5.1.106	Govnr
Cymerian spirits/Gives battile gainst the heart of Tamburlaine.	2Tamb	5.3.9	Therid
The lively spirits which the heart ingenders/Are partcht and	2Tamb	5.3.94	Phsitn
mortified lineaments/Should exercise the motions of my heart,	2Tamb	5.3.189	Amyras
Against the inward powers of my heart,	2Tamb	5.3.196	Amyras
As had you seene her 'twould have mov'd your heart,	Jew	1.2.385	Mthias
Having Fernezes hand, whose heart I'le have;	Jew	2.3.16	Barab
He has my heart, I smile against my will.	Jew	2.3.287	Abigal
But keepe thy heart till Don Mathias comes.	Jew	2.3.307	Barab
For this I'le have his heart.	Jew	2.3.344	Mthias
My heart misgives me, that to crosse your love,	Jew	2.3.349	Barab
Feare not, I'le so set his heart a fire,	Jew	2.3.375	Ithimr
Death seizeth on my heart:	Jew	3.6.38	Abigal
To stop the mallice of his envious heart,	P 30	1.30	Navrre
That Guise hath slaine by treason of his heart,	P 45	1.45	Navrre
For this, this head, this heart, this hand and sworde,	P 109	2.52	Guise
My heart doth faint, I dye.	P 186	3.21	OldQn
Besides my heart relentes that noble men,	P 211	4.9	Charls
To make the justice of my heart relent:	P 533	10.6	Guise
A griping paine hath ceasde upon my heart:	P 537	11.2	Charls
O say not so, thou kill'st thy mothers heart.	P 539	11.4	QnMoth
My heart doth break, I faint and dye.	P 550	11.15	Charls

HEART (cont.)			
think they Henries heart/Will not both harbour love and .	P 603	12.16	King
Sweet Mugercune, tis he that hath my heart, . . .	P 660	13.4	Duchss
That it might print these lines within his heart. . .	P 669	13.13	Duchss
no my Lord, a woman only must/Partake the secrets of my heart.	P 676	13.20	Duchss
O that his heart were leaping in my hand.	P 936	19.6	P 2Mur
And let her droup, my heart is light enough. . . .	P1064	19.134	King
And let her greeve her heart out if she will. . . .	P1080	19.150	King
Upon whose heart may all the furies gripe, . . .	P1101	20.11	Cardnl
Now is my heart at ease.	Edw	1.4.91	ArchBp
Did never sorrow go so neere my heart, ...	Edw	1.4.306	Edward
My heart is as an anvill unto sorrow, ...	Edw	1.4.312	Edward
This salutation overjoyes my heart.	Edw	1.4.344	Lncstr
I Isabell, nere was my heart so light.	Edw	1.4.368	Edward
When I forsake thee, death seaze on my heart, . . .	Edw	2.1.64	Neece
was thy parting hence/Bitter and irkesome to my sobbing heart.	Edw	2.2.58	Edward
Whose pining heart, her inward sighes have blasted, . .	Edw	2.4.24	Queene
And take my heart, in reskew of my friends. . . .	Edw	4.7.67	Edward
My heart with pittie earnes to see this sight, . . .	Edw	4.7.70	Abbot
I would those wordes proceeded from your heart. . .	Edw	5.2.100	Kent
And give my heart to Isabell and him, ...	Edw	5.3.11	Edward
My daily diet, is heart breaking sobs, ...	Edw	5.3.21	Edward
That almost rents the closet of my heart, ...	Edw	5.3.22	Edward
And then thy heart, were it as Gurneys is, ...	Edw	5.5.53	Edward
O speake no more my lorde, this breakes my heart. . .	Edw	5.5.71	Ltborn
She whom thine eye shall like, thy heart shall have, .	F 539	2.1.151	Mephst
My heart is <hearts so> hardned, I cannot repent: . .	F 569	2.2.18	Faust
let me be cloyd/With all things that delight the heart of man.	F 838	3.1.60	Faust
But yet my [heart's] <heart> more ponderous then my head,	F1351	4.2.27	Benvol
Breake may his heart with grones: deere Frederik see, .	F1366	4.2.42	Benvol
whose heart <art> conspir'd/Benvolio's shame before the	F1373	4.2.49	Mrtino
kind I will make knowne unto you what my heart desires to have,	F1571	4.6.14	P Lady
With all my heart kind Doctor, please thy selfe, . .	F1623	4.6.66	Duke
Faustus I leave thee, but with griefe of heart, . .	F1737	5.1.64	OldMan
Do it then Faustus <quickly>, with unfained heart, . .	F1751	5.1.78	Mephst
Fond worldling, now his heart bloud dries with griefe; .	F1808	5.2.12	Mephst
heart pant <pants> and quiver <quivers> to remember that I have	F1840	5.2.44	P Faust
Rend <Ah rend> not my heart, for naming of my Christ, .	F1941	5.2.145	Faust
end be such/As every Christian heart laments to thinke on:	F1996	5.3.14	2Schol
I wil not hide from you the thing my heart desires, and were it	F App	p.242 9	P Duchss
Breake heart, drop bloud, and mingle it with teares, .	F App	p.243 38	OldMan
Nor were the Commons only strooke to heart/With this vaine	Lucan, First Booke		483
The heart stird not, and from the gaping liver/Squis'd matter;	Lucan, First Booke		623
O boy that lyest so slothfull in my heart. . . .	Ovid's Elegies		2.9.2
Was not one wench inough to greeve my heart? . . .	Ovid's Elegies		2.10.12
Beauty gives heart, Corinnas lookes excell, . . .	Ovid's Elegies		2.17.7
His heart consists of flint, and hardest steele, . .	Ovid's Elegies		3.5.59
Both loves to whom my heart long time did yeeld, . .	Ovid's Elegies		3.14.15
Relenting Heroes gentle heart was strooke, . . .	Hero and Leander		1.165
But heale the heart, that thou hast wounded thus, . .	Hero and Leander		1.324
And in his heart revenging malice bare:	Hero and Leander		2.208
The longing heart of Hero much more joies/Then nymphs and	Hero and Leander		2.232
HEART BREAKING			
My daily diet, is heart breaking sobs, ...	Edw	5.3.21	Edward
HEARTED			
Hard hearted, wilt not deigne to heare me speake? . .	Dido	4.2.54	Anna
While you faint-hearted base Egyptians, ...	1Tamb	4.1.8	Souldn
Hard-hearted Father, unkind Barabas, ...	Jew	3.3.36	Abigal
He is hard hearted, therfore pull with violence. . .	P1105	20.15	1Mur
Hard-hearted Porter doest and wilt not heare? . . .	Ovid's Elegies		1.6.27
HEARTES			
for his vertues)/Revives the spirits of true Turkish heartes,	2Tamb	3.1.24	Callap
HEARTILY			
I pray you heartily sir; for wee cal'd you but in jeast I	F1123	3.3.36	P Dick
HEART'S			
But yet my [heart's] <heart> more ponderous then my head,	F1351	4.2.27	Benvol
HEARTS			
Pluck up your hearts, since fate still rests our friend, .	Dido	1.1.149	Aeneas
Forbids all hope to harbour neere our hearts. . . .	Dido	1.2.16	Illion
Whose short conclusion will seale up their hearts, . .	Dido	3.2.94	Juno
O love, O hate, O cruell womens hearts, ...	Dido	3.3.66	Iarbus
Yet he whose [hearts] <heart> of adamant or flint, . .	Dido	5.1.234	Anna
That he may win the Babylonians hearts, ...	1Tamb	1.1.90	Cosroe
a heavenly face/Should by hearts sorrow wax so wan and pale,	1Tamb	3.2.5	Agidas
Commandes the hearts of his associates, ...	1Tamb	4.1.15	2Msngr
Shead from the heads and hearts of all our Sex, . .	1Tamb	5.1.26	1Virgn
With knees and hearts submissive we intreate/Grace to our words	1Tamb	5.1.50	2Virgn
Whose cheekes and hearts so punisht with conceit, . .	1Tamb	5.1.87	1Virgn
That strikes a terrour to all Turkish hearts, . . .	2Tamb	2.1.15	Fredrk
tooles/Makes Earthquakes in the hearts of men and heaven.	2Tamb	2.2.8	Orcan
Worthy the worship of all faithfull hearts, ...	2Tamb	2.2.57	Orcan
My Lord, if ever you wil win our hearts, ...	2Tamb	5.1.38	2Citzn
A thousand deathes could not torment our hearts/More than the	2Tamb	5.1.144	Jrslem
Nor may our hearts all drown'd in teares of blood, . .	2Tamb	5.3.214	Usumc
Unlesse your unrelenting flinty hearts/Suppresse all pitty in	Jew	1.2.141	Barab
And rent their hearts with tearing of my haire, . .	Jew	1.2.234	Abigal
Which forc'd their hands divide united hearts: . . .	Jew	3.2.35	Govnr
That kindled first this motion in our hearts, . . .	P 7	1.7	Charls
My heart is <hearts so> hardned, I cannot repent: . .	F 569	2.2.18	Faust
I, [all] <I call> your hearts to recompence this deed. .	F1394	4.2.70	Faust
To glut the longing of my hearts desire, ...	F1760	5.1.87	Faust
one that knew/The hearts of beasts, and flight of wandring	Lucan, First Booke		587
Than she the hearts of those that neere her stood. . .	Hero and Leander		1.112

HEARTS (cont.)
Looke how their hands, so were their hearts united, . . Hero and Leander 2.27
And who have hard hearts, and obdurat minds, . . . Hero and Leander 2.217

HEAT
The heat and moisture which did feed each other, . . 1Tamb 2.7.46 Cosroe
My empty stomacke ful of idle heat, ... 1Tamb 4.4.94 Bajzth
And tempered every soule with lively heat, . . . 2Tamb 2.4.10 Tamb
Sustaine the scortching heat and freezing cold, . . 2Tamb 3.2.57 Tamb
remorsefull blood)/Drie up with anger, and consume with heat. 2Tamb 4.1.180 Soria
Your vaines are full of accidentall heat, ... 2Tamb 5.3.84 Phsitn
Make fires, heat irons, let the racke be fetch'd. . . Jew 5.1.24 Govnr
But now begins the extremity of heat/To pinch me with . Jew 5.5.87 Barab
Incenst with savage heat, gallop amaine, ... Hero and Leander 1.115
The more a gentle pleasing heat revived, ... Hero and Leander 2.68
Whose lively heat like fire from heaven fet, . . . Hero and Leander 2.255

HEATE
To make us live unto our former heate, ... Dido 1.1.160 Achat
sweat and dust/All chockt well neare, begin to faint for heate, Edw 3.1.192 SpncrP
And heaven tormented with thy chafing heate, . . . Lucan, First Booke 656
In summers heate, and midtime of the day, ... Ovid's Elegies 1.5.1
For when my loathing it of heate deprives me, . . . Ovid's Elegies 2.9.27
My heate is heere, what moves my heate is gone. . . Ovid's Elegies 2.16.12
Or is my heate, of minde, not of the skie? . . . Ovid's Elegies 3.2.39
Drye winters aye, and sunnes in heate extreame. . . Ovid's Elegies 3.5.106

HEATETH
And heateth kindly, shining lat'rally; . . . . . Hero and Leander 2.125

HEATHEN
If any heathen potentate or king/Invade Natolia, Sigismond will 2Tamb 1.1.152 Sgsmnd
If any Christian, Heathen, Turke, or Jew, ... Edw 5.4.75 Champn

HEATHENS
Nor shall the Heathens live upon our spoyle: . . . Jew 3.5.12 Govnr

HEATHNISH
These heathnish Turks and Pagans lately made, . . . 2Tamb 2.1.6 Fredrk

HEAV'D
having whiskt/His taile athwart his backe, and crest heav'd up, Lucan, First Booke 211
Heav'd up her head, and halfe the world upon, . . . Hero and Leander 1.190
He heav'd him up, and looking on his face, . . . Hero and Leander 2.171

HEAVE (See also HEAVING)
See see, the billowes heave him up to heaven, . . . Dido 5.1.252 Dido
Heave up my shoulders when they call me dogge, . . . Jew 2.3.24 Barab
With a heave and a ho, ... Edw 2.2.192 Lncstr

HEAVEN
To hang her meteor like twixt heaven and earth, . . Dido 1.1.13 Jupitr
And heaven and earth the bounds of thy delight? . . Dido 1.1.31 Jupitr
No bounds but heaven shall bound his Emperie, . . . Dido 1.1.100 Jupitr
And heaven and earth with his unrest acquaints. . . Dido 1.1.141 Venus
Doe thou but smile, and clowdie heaven will cleare, . . Dido 1.1.155 Achat
As to instruct us under what good heaven/We breathe as now, and Dido 1.1.197 Aeneas
And have not any coverture but heaven. . . . . . Dido 1.1.230 Aeneas
And heaven was darkned with tempestuous clowdes: . . Dido 2.1.140 Aeneas
and both his eyes/Turnd up to heaven as one resolv'd to dye, Dido 2.1.152 Aeneas
Yet how <here> <now> I sweare by heaven and him I love, . Dido 3.1.166 Dido
For here in spight of heaven Ile murder him, ... Dido 3.2.10 Juno
fond man, that were to warre gainst heaven,/And with one shaft Dido 3.3.71 Iarbus
O God of heaven, turne the hand of fate/Unto that happie day of Dido 3.3.80 Iarbus
By heaven and earth, and my faire brothers bowe, . . Dido 3.4.45 Aeneas
Come forth the Cave: can heaven endure this sight? . . Dido 4.1.17 Iarbus
That with thy gloomie hand corrects the heaven, . . Dido 4.2.6 Iarbus
Anna that doth admire thee more then heaven. . . . Dido 4.2.46 Anna
If there be any heaven in earth, tis love: . . . . Dido 4.5.27 Nurse
The king of Gods sent me from highest heaven, . . . Dido 5.1.32 Hermes
Witnes the Gods, and witnes heaven and earth, . . . Dido 5.1.80 Aeneas
See see, the billowes heave him up to heaven, . . . Dido 5.1.252 Dido
His looks do menace heaven and dare the Gods, . . . 1Tamb 1.2.157 Therid
And Jove himselfe will stretch his hand from heaven, . 1Tamb 1.2.180 Tamb
Which is as much as if I swore by heaven, ... 1Tamb 1.2.233 Tamb
A heaven of heavenly bodies in their Spheares/That guides his 1Tamb 2.1.16 Menaph
On which the breath of heaven delights to play, . . 1Tamb 2.1.25 Menaph
the man, ordain'd by heaven/To further every action to the best. 1Tamb 2.1.52 Ortyg
For Fates and Oracles [of] heaven have sworne, . . . 1Tamb 2.3.7 Tamb
Weel chase the Stars from heaven, and dim their eies/That stand 1Tamb 2.3.23 Tamb
As dooth the lightening, or the breath of heaven: . . 1Tamb 2.3.58 Tamb
I thinke the pleasure they enjoy in heaven/Can not compare with 1Tamb 2.5.58 Therid
To cast up hils against the face of heaven: . . . 1Tamb 2.6.3 Cosroe
Whether from earth, or hell, or heaven he grow. . . 1Tamb 2.6.23 Ortyg
And place himselfe in the Emperiall heaven, . . . 1Tamb 2.7.15 Tamb
And if before the Sun have measured heaven/With triple circuit 1Tamb 3.1.36 Bajzth
And might content the Queene of heaven as well, . . 1Tamb 3.2.11 Zenoc
Eternall heaven sooner be dissolv'd, ... 1Tamb 3.2.18 Agidas
Than stay the torments he and heaven have sworne. . . 1Tamb 3.2.99 Agidas
Whose eies are brighter than the Lamps of heaven, . . 1Tamb 3.3.120 Tamb
And make him raine down murthering shot from heaven/To dash the 1Tamb 3.3.196 Zabina
If Mahomet should come from heaven and sweare, . . . 1Tamb 3.3.208 Zenoc
Make heaven to frowne and every fixed starre/To sucke up poison 1Tamb 4.2.5 Bajzth
Will sooner burne the glorious frame of Heaven, . . 1Tamb 4.2.10 Tamb
And let the majestie of heaven beholde/Their Scourge and . 1Tamb 4.2.31 Tamb
That almost brent the Axeltree of heaven, ... 1Tamb 4.2.50 Tamb
A sacred vow to heaven and him I make, ... 1Tamb 4.3.36 Souldn
offences feele/Such plagues as heaven and we can poure on him. 1Tamb 4.3.45 Arabia
Having the power from the Emperiall heaven, ... 1Tamb 4.4.30 Tamb
As far as from the frozen [plage] <place> of heaven, . . 1Tamb 4.4.122 Tamb
Then here before the majesty of heaven, ... 1Tamb 5.1.48 2Virgn
Eies when that Ebena steps to heaven, ... 1Tamb 5.1.147 Tamb

HEAVEN (cont.)

Even from the fiery spangled vaile of heaven, . . .	1Tamb	5.1.185	Tamb
Blush heaven, that gave them honor at their birth, . .	1Tamb	5.1.350	Zenoc
To spread my fame through hell and up to heaven: . .	1Tamb	5.1.467	Tamb
I record heaven, her heavenly selfe is cleare: . . .	1Tamb	5.1.487	Tamb
Quiver about the Axeltree of heaven.	2Tamb	1.1.90	Orcan
And sweare in sight of heaven and by thy Christ. . .	2Tamb	1.1.132	Orcan
Whose beames illuminate the lamps of heaven, . . .	2Tamb	1.3.2	Tamb
When heaven shal cease to moove on both the poles/And when the	2Tamb	1.3.12	Tamb
and I might enter in/To see the state and majesty of heaven,	2Tamb	1.3.155	Tamb
tooles/Makes Earthquakes in the hearts of men and heaven.	2Tamb	2.2.8	Orcan
And make a passage from the imperiall heaven/That he that sits	2Tamb	2.2.48	Orcan
And died a traitor both to heaven and earth, ...	2Tamb	2.3.37	Orcan
Now walk the angels on the walles of heaven, ...	2Tamb	2.4.15	Tamb
Up to the pallace of th'imperiall heaven:	2Tamb	2.4.35	Tamb
Her sacred beauty hath enchaunted heaven, ...	2Tamb	2.4.85	Tamb
And with the cannon breake the frame of heaven, . .	2Tamb	2.4.104	Tamb
Meaning to make her stately Queene of heaven. . . .	2Tamb	2.4.108	Tamb
Come downe from heaven and live with me againe. . .	2Tamb	2.4.118	Tamb
For so hath heaven provided my escape, ...	2Tamb	3.1.32	Callap
Looke like the parti-coloured cloudes of heaven, . .	2Tamb	3.1.47	Jrslem
That may endure till heaven be dissolv'd, ...	2Tamb	3.2.7	Tamb
That hanging here, wil draw the Gods from heaven: . .	2Tamb	3.2.28	Tamb
Whose shattered lims, being tost as high as heaven, . .	2Tamb	3.2.100	Tamb
And when we enter in, not heaven it selfe/Shall ransome thee,	2Tamb	3.3.27	Therid
Intreat a pardon of the God of heaven, ...	2Tamb	3.4.32	Olymp
Which measureth the glorious frame of heaven, . . .	2Tamb	3.4.65	Therid
Drawing from it the shining Lamps of heaven. . . .	2Tamb	3.4.77	Techel
issue, at whose byrth/Heaven did affoord a gratious aspect,	2Tamb	3.5.80	Tamb
much like so many suns/That halfe dismay the majesty of heaven:	2Tamb	4.1.3	Amyras
That I might moove the turning Spheares of heaven, . .	2Tamb	4.1.118	Tamb
That shortly heaven, fild with the meteors/Of blood and fire	2Tamb	4.1.141	Jrslem
To scourge the pride of such as heaven abhors: . . .	2Tamb	4.1.149	Tamb
like armed men/Are seene to march upon the towers of heaven,	2Tamb	4.1.202	Tamb
A greater Lamp than that bright eie of heaven, . . .	2Tamb	4.2.88	Therid
The horse that guide the golden eie of heaven, . . .	2Tamb	4.3.7	Tamb
Above the threefold Astracisme of heaven, ...	2Tamb	4.3.62	Tamb
At every little breath that thorow heaven is blowen: .	2Tamb	4.3.124	Tamb
The God that sits in heaven, if any God, ...	2Tamb	5.1.201	Tamb
And sommon al the shining lamps of heaven/To cast their .	2Tamb	5.3.3	Therid
Earth droopes and saies, that hell in heaven is plac'd. .	2Tamb	5.3.16	Therid
health and majesty/Were strangely blest and governed by heaven,	2Tamb	5.3.25	Techel
So honour heaven til heaven dissolved be, ...	2Tamb	5.3.26	Techel
Blush heaven to loose the honor of thy name, . . .	2Tamb	5.3.28	Usumc
Earth droopes and saies that hel in heaven is plac'd. .	2Tamb	5.3.41	Usumc
Come let us march against the powers of heaven, . .	2Tamb	5.3.48	Tamb
That if I perish, heaven and earth may fade. . . .	2Tamb	5.3.60	Tamb
And that the spightfull influence of heaven, . . .	2Tamb	5.3.193	Amyras
And glut your longings with a heaven of joy. . . .	2Tamb	5.3.227	Tamb
Meet heaven and earth, and here let al things end, . .	2Tamb	5.3.249	Amyras
And heaven consum'd his choisest living fire. . . .	2Tamb	5.3.251	Amyras
Let earth and heaven his timelesse death deplore, . .	2Tamb	5.3.252	Amyras
What more may Heaven doe for earthly man/Then thus to powre out	Jew	1.1.107	Barab
Who stand accursed in the sight of heaven, ...	Jew	1.2.64	Govnr
The plagues of Egypt, and the curse of heaven, . . .	Jew	1.2.162	Barab
Converse not with him, he is cast off from heaven. . .	Jew	2.3.157	Mater
As sure as heaven rain'd Manna for the Jewes, . . .	Jew	2.3.248	Barab
Thou know'st, and heaven can witnesse it is true, . .	Jew	2.3.253	Barab
Oh heaven forbid I should have such a thought. . . .	Jew	2.3.256	Barab
I did offend high heaven so grievously, ...	Jew	3.6.17	Abigal
Heaven blesse me; what, a Fryar a murderer?	Jew	4.1.196	Barab
What greater misery could heaven inflict?	Jew	5.2.14	Govnr
Oh villaine, Heaven will be reveng'd on thee. . . .	Jew	5.2.25	Govnr
due praise be given/Neither to Fate nor Fortune, but to Heaven.	Jew	5.5.124	Govnr
If ever sunne stainde heaven with bloudy clowdes, . .	P 60	2.3	Guise
For this, hath heaven engendred me of earth, . . .	P 113	2.56	Guise
And all his heaven is to delight himselfe:	P 634	12.47	QnMoth
And heer by all the Saints in heaven I sweare, . . .	P 765	15.23	Guise
Sweet Epernoune all Rebels under heaven, ...	P1185	22.47	King
And witnesse heaven how deere thou art to me. . . .	Edw	1.4.167	Edward
By heaven, the abject villaine shall not live. . . .	Edw	2.2.106	Mortmr
The king of heaven perhaps, no other king, ...	Edw	2.6.16	Warwck
By heaven, and all the mooving orbes thereof, . . .	Edw	3.1.129	Edward
ragged stonie walles/Immure thy vertue that aspires to heaven?	Edw	3.1.257	Mortmr
Yea gentle brother, and the God of heaven, ...	Edw	4.2.74	Queene
Lords, sith that we are by sufferance of heaven, . .	Edw	4.4.17	Mortmr
Father, this life contemplative is heaven, ...	Edw	4.7.20	Edward
In heaven wee may, in earth never shall wee meete, . .	Edw	4.7.80	Edward
Rent sphere of heaven, and fier forsake thy orbe, . .	Edw	4.7.102	Spencr
Full often am I sowring up to heaven, ...	Edw	5.1.21	Edward
now sweete God of heaven,/Make me despise this transitorie	Edw	5.1.107	Edward
And sit for aye inthronized in heaven, ...	Edw	5.1.109	Edward
God in heaven knowes.	F 198	1.2.5	P Wagner
For which God threw him from the face of heaven. . .	F 296	1.3.68	Mephst
And tasted the eternall Joyes of heaven, ...	F 306	1.3.78	Mephst
so passionate/For being deprived of the Joyes of heaven? .	F 312	1.3.84	Faust
What bootes it then to thinke on <of> God or Heaven? .	F 391	2.1.3	Faust
O they are meanes to bring thee unto heaven. . . .	F 406	2.1.18	GdAngl
Sweet Faustus think of heaven, and heavenly things. . .	F 409	2.1.21	GdAngl
If unto [God] <heaven>, hee'le throw me <thee> downe to hell.	F 467	2.1.79	Faust
All places shall be hell that is not heaven.	F 515	2.1.127	Mephst
<why Faustus> think'st thou heaven is such a glorious thing?	F 556	2.2.5	Mephst
If Heaven was <it were> made for man, 'twas made for me: .	F 561	2.2.10	Faust

HEAVEN (cont.)

Scarce can I name salvation, faith, or heaven,	F 570	2.2.19	Faust
the seven Planets, the Firmament, and the Emperiall heaven.	F 611	2.2.60	P Mephst
And Faustus vowes never to looke to heaven,	F 648	2.2.97	Faust
We veiw'd the face of heaven, of earth and hell.	F 848	3.1.70	Faust
In token of our seven-fold power from heaven,	F 934	3.1.156	Pope
And mount aloft with them as high as heaven,	F1404	4.2.80	Faust
Defend me heaven, shall I be haunted still?	F1439	4.3.9	Benvol
I marry can I, we are under heaven.	F1615	4.6.58	P Carter
Then thou art banisht from the sight of heaven;	F1715	5.1.42	OldMan
Here will I dwell, for heaven is <be> in these lippes,	F1773	5.1.100	Faust
[That from thy soule exclud'st the grace of heaven],	F1789	5.1.116A	OldMan
Yet Faustus looke up to heaven, and remember [Gods] mercy is	F1835	5.2.39	P 2Schol
hath lost both Germany and the world, yea heaven it selfe:	F1844	5.2.48	P Faust
heaven the seate of God, the Throne of the Blessed, the	F1844	5.2.48	P Faust
I, Faustus, now thou hast no hope of heaven,	F1880	5.2.84	Mephst
'Twas I, that when thou wer't i'the way to heaven,	F1886	5.2.90	Mephst
Stand still you ever moving Spheares of heaven,	F1929	5.2.133	Faust
O I'le leape up to [my God] <heaven>: who puls me downe?	F1938	5.2.142	Faust
And hide me from the heavy wrath of [God] <heaven>.	F1946	5.2.150	Faust
[So that] my soule [may but] ascend to heaven.	F1956	5.2.160	Faust
<But let my soule mount and> ascend to heaven.	F1956	(HC271) B	Faust
That hath depriv'd thee of the joies of heaven.	F1974	5.2.178	Faust
[My God, my God] <O mercy heaven>, looke not so fierce on me;	F1979	5.2.183	Faust
Pray heaven the Doctor have escapt the danger.	F1987	5.3.5	1Schol
O help us heaven, see, here are Faustus limbs,	F1988	5.3.6	2Schol
As far as Titan springs where night dims heaven,	Lucan, First Booke	15	
nor Jove joide heaven/Untill the cruel Giants war was done)	Lucan, First Booke	35	
being old/Must shine a star) shal heaven (whom thou lovest),	Lucan, First Booke	46	
If any one part of vast heaven thou swayest,	Lucan, First Booke	56	
had heaven given thee longer life/Thou hadst restrainde thy	Lucan, First Booke	115	
the showts rent heaven,/As when against pine bearing Ossa's	Lucan, First Booke	389	
the deepe)/Puls them aloft, and makes the surge kisse heaven,	Lucan, First Booke	417	
And sundry fiery meteors blaz'd in heaven;	Lucan, First Booke	529	
Titan himselfe throand in the midst of heaven,	Lucan, First Booke	538	
And heaven tormented with thy chafing heate,	Lucan, First Booke	656	
is faint; swift Hermes retrograde;/Mars onely rules the heaven:	Lucan, First Booke	662	
Thy mother shall from heaven applaud this show,	Ovid's Elegies	1.2.39	
In heaven was never more notorious fable.	Ovid's Elegies	1.9.40	
Not one in heaven should be more base and vile.	Ovid's Elegies	1.13.36	
I had in hand/Which for his heaven fell on the Gyants band.	Ovid's Elegies	2.1.16	
The [haven] <heaven> touching barcke now nere the lea,	Ovid's Elegies	2.9.32	
Why addst thou starres to heaven, leaves to greene woods	Ovid's Elegies	2.10.13	
Let the bright day-starre cause in heaven this day be,	Ovid's Elegies	2.11.55	
In heaven without thee would I not be fixt.	Ovid's Elegies	2.16.14	
Why grieve I? and of heaven reproches pen?	Ovid's Elegies	3.3.41	
Heaven thou affects, with Romulus, temples brave/Bacchus,	Ovid's Elegies	3.7.51	
Live godly, thou shalt die, though honour heaven,	Ovid's Elegies	3.8.37	
Eternall heaven to burne, for so it seem'd,	Hero and Leander	1.100	
As thou in beautie doest exceed Loves mother/Nor heaven, nor	Hero and Leander	1.223	
As heaven preserves all things, so save thou one.	Hero and Leander	1.224	
All heaven would come to claime this legacie,	Hero and Leander	1.250	
As might have made heaven stoope to have a touch,	Hero and Leander	1.366	
fire filcht by Prometheus;/And thrusts him down from heaven:	Hero and Leander	1.439	
And those on whom heaven, earth, and hell relies,	Hero and Leander	1.443	
Will mount aloft, and enter heaven gate,	Hero and Leander	1.466	
For from the earth to heaven, is Cupid rais'd,	Hero and Leander	2.31	
As for his love, both earth and heaven pyn'd;	Hero and Leander	2.196	
Whose lively heat like fire from heaven fet,	Hero and Leander	2.255	

HEAVENLY

And Paris judgement of the heavenly ball,	Dido	3.2.44	Juno
But Lady, this faire face and heavenly hew,	1Tamb	1.2.36	Tamb
A heaven of heavenly bodies in their Spheares/That guides his	1Tamb	2.1.16	Menaph
That causde the eldest sonne of heavenly Ops,	1Tamb	2.7.13	Tamb
Tis more then pitty such a heavenly face/Should by hearts	1Tamb	3.2.4	Agidas
Ye holy Priests of heavenly Mahomet,	1Tamb	4.2.2	Bajzth
is compriz'd the Sum/Of natures Skill and heavenly majestie.	1Tamb	5.1.79	1Virgn
If all the heavenly Quintessence they still/From their	1Tamb	5.1.165	Tamb
the Sun-bright troope/Of heavenly vyrgins and unspotted maides,	1Tamb	5.1.325	Zenoc
I record heaven, her heavenly selfe is cleare:	1Tamb	5.1.487	Tamb
Whose heavenly presence beautified with health,	2Tamb	2.4.49	Tamb
Intends our Muse to vaunt <daunt> his heavenly verse;	F 6	Prol.6	1Chor
sweete delight's] dispute/In th'heavenly matters of Theologie,	F 19	Prol.19	1Chor
And Negromantick bookes are heavenly.	F 77	1.1.49	Faust
I see there's vertue in my heavenly words.	F 255	1.3.27	Faust
Sweet Faustus think of heaven, and heavenly things.	F 409	2.1.21	GdAngl
[Whose heavenly beauty passeth all compare].	F1701	5.1.28A	3Schol
That heavenly Hellen, which I saw of late,	F1762	5.1.89	Faust
To practise more then heavenly power permits.	F2009	5.3.27	4Chor
And only gods and heavenly powers you know,	Lucan, First Booke	449	
But Figulus more seene in heavenly mysteries,	Lucan, First Booke	638	
That heavenly path, with many a curious dint,	Hero and Leander	1.68	
A heavenly Nimph, belov'd of humane swaines,	Hero and Leander	1.216	

HEAVENS

Drawne through the heavens by Steedes of Boreas brood,	Dido	1.1.55	Venus
Had not the heavens conceav'd with hel-borne clowdes,	Dido	1.1.125	Venus
And chaunging heavens may those good daies returne,	Dido	1.1.150	Aeneas
There was such hurly burly in the heavens:	Dido	4.1.10	Achat
Heavens envious of our joyes is waxen pale,	Dido	4.4.52	Dido
I goe faire sister, heavens graunt good successe.	Dido	5.1.211	Anna
And by those steps that he hath scal'd the heavens,	1Tamb	1.2.200	Tamb
wel then, by heavens I sweare,/Aurora shall not peepe out of	1Tamb	2.2.9	Mycet
with winged Steads/All sweating, tilt about the watery heavens,	1Tamb	3.2.79	Agidas

HEAVENS (cont.)			
Lifting his prayers to the heavens for aid,	1Tamb	3.2.83	Agidas
Or be the meanes the overweighing heavens/Have kept to qualifie	1Tamb	5.1.45	Govnr
and prevent their soules/From heavens of comfort, yet their age	1Tamb	5.1.90	1Virgn
The heavens may frowne, the earth for anger quake,	1Tamb	5.1.231	Bajzth
And shut the windowes of the lightsome heavens.	1Tamb	5.1.293	Bajzth
The golden balle of heavens eternal fire,	2Tamb	2.4.2	Tamb
no more, but deck the heavens/To entertaine divine Zenocrate.	2Tamb	2.4.20	Tamb
happinesse/And hope to meet your highnesse in the heavens,	2Tamb	2.4.63	Zenoc
in] <resisting> me/The power of heavens eternall majesty.	2Tamb	4.1.158	Tamb
the flames that beat against the clowdes/Incense the heavens,	2Tamb	4.1.195	Tamb
Whose shyning Turrets shal dismay the heavens,	2Tamb	4.3.112	Tamb
Weepe heavens, and vanish into liquid teares,	2Tamb	5.3.1	Therid
And made his state an honor to the heavens,	2Tamb	5.3.12	Therid
Heavens witnes me, with what a broken hart/And damned spirit I	2Tamb	5.3.206	Amyras
More then heavens coach, the pride of Phaeton.	2Tamb	5.3.244	Tamb
You partiall heavens, have I deserv'd this plague?	Jew	1.2.259	Barab
But rather let the brightsome heavens be dim,	Jew	2.3.330	Lodowk
And with my prayers pierce [th']impartiall heavens,	Jew	3.2.33	Govnr
Wonder not at it, Sir, the heavens are just:	Jew	5.1.55	Govnr
The heavens forbid your highnes such mishap.	P 177	3.12	QnMarg
Heavens can witnesse, I love none but you.	Edw	2.4.15	Queene
not lord and father, heavens great beames/On Atlas shoulder,	Edw	3.1.76	Prince
Thankes be heavens great architect and you.	Edw	4.6.22	Queene
We must my lord, so will the angry heavens.	Edw	4.7.74	Spencr
The gentle heavens have not to do in this.	Edw	4.7.76	Edward
And hart and hand to heavens immortall throne,	Edw	4.7.108	Baldck
Heavens turne it to a blaze of quenchelesse fier,	Edw	5.1.44	Edward
But what the heavens appoint, I must obaye,	Edw	5.1.56	Edward
I might, but heavens and earth conspire/To make me miserable:	Edw	5.1.96	Edward
And melting, heavens conspir'd his over-throw:	F 22	Prol.22	1Chor
Figures of every adjunct to the heavens,	F 239	1.3.11	Faust
Under the heavens.	F 506	2.1.118	Mephst
I might see al characters of <and> planets of the heavens,	F 551.5	2.1.168A	P Faust
When I behold the heavens then I repent/And curse thee wicked	F 552	2.2.1	Faust
<Tel me>, are there many Spheares <heavens> above the Moone?	F 586	2.2.35	Faust
As are the elements, such are the heavens <spheares>,/Even from	F 589	2.2.38	Mephst
How many Heavens, or Spheares, are there?	F 609	2.2.58	P Faust
[Ambitious fiends, see how the heavens smiles]/[At your repulse,	F1794	5.1.121A	OldMan
Untill the cruel Giants war was done)/We plaine not heavens,	Lucan, First Booke		37
That drawes the day from heavens cold axletree.	Ovid's Elegies		1.13.2
Yet when old Saturne heavens rule possest,	Ovid's Elegies		3.7.35
Heavens winged herrald, Jove-borne Mercury,	Hero and Leander		1.386
Had left the heavens, therefore on him hee seaz'd.	Hero and Leander		2.158
HEAVIE			
Burdening their bodies with your heavie chaines,	1Tamb	3.3.48	Tamb
What other heavie news now brings Philemus?	1Tamb	5.1.377	Zenoc
a heavie case,/When force to force is knit, and sword and	Edw	4.4.4	Queene
To dash the heavie headed Edmunds drift,	Edw	5.2.39	Mortmr
tearmes, with sad and heavie cheare/Complaind to Cupid;	Hero and Leander		1.440
sported with their loves/On heapes of heavie gold, and tooke	Hero and Leander		2.163
HEAVIE HEADED			
To dash the heavie headed Edmunds drift,	Edw	5.2.39	Mortmr
HEAVINESSE			
Teares falling from repentant heavinesse/Of thy most vilde and	F App	p.243 39	OldMan
HEAVING			
Blood-quaffing Mars, heaving the yron net,	Hero and Leander		1.151
HEAV'N			
But we must part, when heav'n with black night lowers.	Ovid's Elegies		1.4.60
When she will, cloudes the darckned heav'n obscure,	Ovid's Elegies		1.8.9
Why seek'st not heav'n the third realme to frequent?	Ovid's Elegies		3.7.50
Heav'n starre Electra that bewaild her sisters?	Ovid's Elegies		3.11.37
HEAVY			
Lies heavy on my heart, I cannot live.	2Tamb	3.4.5	Capt
If your first curse fall heavy on thy head,	Jew	1.2.107	1Knght
For that will be most heavy to thy soule.	Jew	3.3.71	1Fryar
the burthen of my sinnes/Lye heavy on my soule; then pray you	Jew	4.1.49	Barab
Let not this heavy chaunce my dearest Lord,	P 191	3.26	QnMarg
And heape Gods heavy wrath upon thy head.	F 99	1.1.71	GdAngl
To light as heavy as the paines of hell.	F 939	3.1.161	Pope
<I goe sweete Faustus, but with heavy cheare>,	F1737	(HC269)A	OldMan
And hide me from the heavy wrath of [God] <heaven>.	F1946	5.2.150	Faust
Shall waite upon his heavy funerall.	F2001	5.3.19	2Schol
Whose bodies with their heavy burthens ake.	Ovid's Elegies		2.13.20
Gold, silver, irons heavy weight, and brasse,	Ovid's Elegies		3.7.37
HEBE			
Made Hebe to direct her ayrie wheeles/Into the windie countrie	Dido	1.1.56	Venus
Stole some from Hebe (Hebe, Joves cup fil'd),	Hero and Leander		1.434
HEBES			
That was advanced by my Hebes shame,	Dido	3.2.43	Juno
HEBON			
The jouyce of Hebon, and Cocitus breath,	Jew	3.4.101	Barab
HEBREW			
Where in Arabian, Hebrew, Greek, is writ/This towne being burnt	2Tamb	3.2.16	Calyph
An Hebrew borne, and would become a Christian?	Jew	4.1.19	Barab
The Hebrew Psalter, and new Testament;	F 182	1.1.154	Valdes
HEBREWES			
Of Hebrewes, three score thousand fighting men/Are come since	2Tamb	3.5.33	Jrslem
Oh muse not at it, 'tis the Hebrewes guize,	Jew	2.3.325	Barab
HEBREWS			
Yes, give me leave, and Hebrews now come neare.	Jew	1.2.38	Govnr
Oh earth-mettall'd villaines, and no Hebrews born!	Jew	1.2.78	Barab
HECAT'S			
Pluto's blew fire, and Hecat's tree,	F 997	3.2.21	Mephst

Text	Work	Reference		Speaker
HECTOR				
O Hector who weepes not to heare thy name?	Dido	2.1.209		Dido
As Hector did into the Grecian campe,	2Tamb	3.5.65		Tamb
For if I should as Hector did Achilles,	2Tamb	3.5.70		Tamb
The conquering [Hercules] <Hector> for Hilas wept,	Edw	1.4.393		MortSr
Hector to armes went from his wives embraces,	Ovid's Elegies			1.9.35
Or wofull Hector whom wilde jades did teare?	Ovid's Elegies			2.1.32
And Hector dyed his brothers yet alive.	Ovid's Elegies			2.6.42
HECTORS				
Thus in stoute Hectors race three hundred yeares,	Dido	1.1.104		Jupitr
And thinking to goe downe, came Hectors ghost/With ashie visage,	Dido	2.1.201		Aeneas
HECUBA				
And kisse his hand: O where is Hecuba?	Dido	2.1.12		Achat
O Priamus, O Troy, oh Hecuba!	Dido	2.1.105		Aeneas
About whose withered necke hung Hecuba,	Dido	2.1.226		Aeneas
O what became of aged Hecuba?	Dido	2.1.290		Anna
HE'D				
He'd joyne long Asses eares to these huge hornes,	F1449	4.3.19		Benvol
HE'DE				
He'de give us present mony for them all.	Jew	2.3.6		1Offcr
HEDGE				
that you may ride him o're hedge and ditch, and spare him not;	F1467	4.4.11	P	Faust
not into the water; o're hedge and ditch, or where thou wilt,	F1473	4.4.17	P	Faust
such a horse, as would run over hedge and ditch, and never tyre,	F1538	4.5.34	P	HrsCsr
the water, ride him over hedge or ditch, or where thou wilt,	F App	p.239 112	P	Faust
HEDGES				
Breake through the hedges of their hateful mouthes,	2Tamb	4.3.46		Therid
we wil break the hedges of their mouths/And pul their kicking	2Tamb	4.3.48		Techel
HEDLONG				
And traveile hedlong to the lake of hell:	2Tamb	3.5.24		Orcan
a point, to which when men aspire,/They tumble hedlong downe:	Edw	5.6.61		Mortmr
HEE				
Wel, now you see hee is a king, looke to him Theridamas, when we	2Tamb	3.5.153	P	Tamb
least hee hide his crowne as the foolish king of Persea did.	2Tamb	3.5.154	P	Tamb
hee shall not be put to that exigent, I warrant thee.	2Tamb	3.5.156	P	Soria
hee that denies to pay, shal straight become a Christian.	Jew	1.2.73	P	Reader
And she vowes love to him, and hee to her.	Jew	2.3.247		Barab
to his prayers, as if hee had had another Cure to serve; well,	Jew	4.2.24	P	Ithimr
but hee hides and buries it up as Partridges doe their egges,	Jew	4.2.58	P	Ithimr
what hee writes for you, ye shall have streight.	Jew	4.3.27	P	Barab
[Sanctus] <Sancta> Jacobus hee was my Saint, pray to him.	P 358	6.13		Mntsrl
and whereas hee is your Landlord, you will take upon you to be	P 810	17.5	P	Souldr
Hee wild the Governour of Orleance in his name,	P1117	21.11		Dumain
Till hee pay deerely for their companie.	Edw	3.1.198		Lncstr
First would I heare newes that hee were deposde,	Edw	5.2.21		Mortmr
I would hee were, so it were not by my meanes.	Edw	5.2.45		Queene
But hee repents, and sorrowes for it now.	Edw	5.2.108		Prince
<and see if hee by> his grave counsell may <can> reclaime him.	F 226	1.2.33		2Schol
that hee shall appeare to the said John Faustus, at all times,	F 491	2.1.103	P	Faust
[Hee stayde his course, and so returned home],	F1140	3.3.53A		3Chor
oh hee stayes my tongue:	F1852	5.2.56	P	Faust
hee has kild the divell, so I should be cald kill divell all	F App	p.230 48	P	Clown
there was a hee divell and a shee divell, Ile tell you how you	F App	p.230 52	P	Clown
all hee divels has hornes, and all shee divels has clifts and	F App	p.230 53	P	Clown
Cursed be hee that stole away his holinesse meate from/the	F App	p.232 31		Frier
Cursed be hee that strooke his holinesse a blowe on the face.	F App	p.232 33		Frier
so much for the injury hee offred me heere in your presence,	F App	p.238 81	P	Faust
on him; hee has a buttocke as slicke as an Ele; wel god buy sir,	F App	p.239 116	P	HrsCsr
If hee gives thee what first himselfe did tast,	Ovid's Elegies			1.4.33
If hee lyes downe with Wine and sleepe opprest,	Ovid's Elegies			1.4.53
Were I the saint hee worships, I would heare him,	Hero and Leander			1.179
Hee thus replide:	Hero and Leander			1.299
As sheap-heards do, her on the ground hee layd,	Hero and Leander			1.405
Wide open stood the doore, hee need not clime,	Hero and Leander			2.19
For hitherto hee did but fan the fire,	Hero and Leander			2.41
Leanders Father knew where hee had beene,	Hero and Leander			2.136
so hee that loves,/The more he is restrain'd, the woorse he	Hero and Leander			2.144
To part in twaine, that hee might come and go,	Hero and Leander			2.151
With that hee stript him to the yv'rie skin,	Hero and Leander			2.153
Had left the heavens, therefore on him hee seaz'd.	Hero and Leander			2.158
And when hee sported in the fragrant lawnes,	Hero and Leander			2.199
Neptune was angrie that hee gave no eare,	Hero and Leander			2.207
describe, but hee/That puls or shakes it from the golden tree:	Hero and Leander			2.299
HEED				
I, and take heed, for he hath sworne your death.	Jew	2.3.280		Barab
In any case, take heed of childish feare,	Edw	5.2.6		Mortmr
now Friers take heed,/Lest Faustus make your shaven crownes to	F1006	3.2.26		Faust
take heed what you say, we looke not like cup-stealers I can	F1099	3.3.12	P	Robin
And take heed least he gets that love for nought.	Ovid's Elegies			1.8.72
let either heed/What please them, and their eyes let either	Ovid's Elegies			3.2.5
HEEDLESSE				
Tell me, to whom mad'st thou that heedlesse oath?	Hero and Leander			1.294
HEE'L				
zounds hee'l raise up a kennell of Divels I thinke anon:	F1305	4.1.151	P	Benvol
HE'ELE				
Perhaps he'ele tell howe oft he slewe a man,	Ovid's Elegies			3.7.21
HEE'LE				
If unto [God] <heaven>, hee'le throw me <thee> downe to hell.	F 467	2.1.79		Faust
HEELE (Homograph)				
What if I sinke his ships? O heele frowne:	Dido	4.4.110		Dido
And heele make me immortall with a kisse.	Dido	4.4.123		Dido
I but heele come againe, he cannot goe,	Dido	5.1.184		Dido
For heele complaine unto the sea of Rome.	Edw	1.1.190		Kent

HEELE (cont.)				
And war must be the meanes, or heele stay stil.	Edw	1.2.63		Warwck
And yet heele ever dote on Gaveston,	Edw	1.4.185		Queene
And yet I love in vaine, heele nere love me.	Edw	1.4.197		Queene
your right eye be alwaies Diametrally fixt upon my left heele,	F 387	1.4.45	P	Wagner
Yea, I will wound Achilles in the heele,	F1779	5.1.106		Faust
and let thy left eye be diametarily fixt upon my right heele,	F App	p.231 70	P	Wagner
Though himselfe see; heele credit her denyall,	Ovid's Elegies	2.2.57		
HEELES				
And Helens rape doth haunt [ye] <thee> at the heeles.	Dido	1.1.144		Aeneas
Thongs at his heeles, by which Achilles horse/Drew him in	Dido	2.1.205		Aeneas
At last the souldiers puld her by the heeles,	Dido	2.1.247		Aeneas
And have so proud a chariot at your heeles,	2Tamb	4.3.3		Tamb
meet not me/With troopes of harlots at your slothful heeles.	2Tamb	4.3.82		Tamb
Oh how I long to see him shake his heeles.	Jew	4.1.140		Ithimr
Ile make her shake off love with her heeles.	P 782	15.40		Mugern
With base outlandish cullions at his heeles,	Edw	1.4.409		Mortmr
Edward with fire and sword, followes at thy heeles.	Edw	3.1.180		Edward
same cup, for the Vintners boy followes us at the hard heeles.	F1090	3.3.3	P	Dick
And at his heeles a thousand furies waite,	F1182	4.1.28		Mrtino
Through which the Furies drag'd me by the heeles.	F1435	4.3.5		Mrtino
HEER				
That linke you in mariage with our daughter heer:	P 14	1.14		QnMoth
For that let me alone, Cousin stay you heer,	P 428	7.68		Anjoy
O let me stay and rest me heer a while,	P 536	11.1		Charls
And heer by all the Saints in heaven I sweare,	P 765	15.23		Guise
our Guise is dead)/Rest satisfied with this that heer I sweare,	P1043	19.113		King
My Lord heer is his sonne.	P1045	19.115		Eprnon
HEERE				
My Mother poysoned heere before my face:	P 187	3.22		Navrre
And to my Nephew heere the Duke of Guise:	P 226	4.24		Charls
all doubts, be rulde by me, lets hang him heere upon this tree.	P 492	9.11	P	2Atndt.
Heere hast thou a country voide of feares,	P 591	12.4		QnMoth
O would to God this quill that heere doth write,	P 667	13.11		Duchss
Ah base Epernoune, were not his highnes heere,	P 831	17.26		Guise
Heere is no staying for the King of France,	P 897	17.92		King
tush, were he heere, we would kill him presently.	P 934	19.4	P	1Mur
Then come proud Guise and heere disgordge thy brest,	P 952	19.22		King
I prethee tell him that the Guise is heere.	P 958	19.28		Guise
And heere in presence of you all I sweare,	P1026	19.96		King
Sweet Guise, would he had died so thou wert heere:	P1082	19.152		QnMoth
Now thou art dead, heere is no stay for us:	P1111	21.5		Dumain
Then heere wee'l lye before [Lutetia] <Lucrecia> walles,	P1151	22.13		King
your Majestie heere is a Frier of the order of the Jacobins,	P1155	22.17	P	1Msngr
Navarre, give me thy hand, I heere do sweare,	P1203	22.65		King
And heere protest eternall love to thee,	P1206	22.68		King
We will wait heere about the court.	Edw	1.1.49		Omnes
Heere comes the king and the nobles/From the parlament, ile	Edw	1.1.72		Gavstn
Mine unckle heere, this Earle, and I my selfe,	Edw	1.1.82		Mortmr
I heere create thee Lord high Chamberlaine,	Edw	1.1.154		Edward
What? are you mov'd that Gaveston sits heere?	Edw	1.4.8		Edward
O might I keepe thee heere, as I doe this,	Edw	1.4.128		Edward
I make thee heere lord Marshall of the realme.	Edw	1.4.356		Edward
Heere, here <King>.	Edw	2.2.81		Penbrk
Will to Newcastell heere, and gather head.	Edw	2.2.123		Warwck
Nay, now you are heere alone, ile speake my minde.	Edw	2.2.155		Mortmr
Heere comes she thats cause of all these jarres.	Edw	2.2.224		Edward
Heere in the river rides a Flemish hoie,	Edw	2.4.46		Mortmr
[King] <Kind> Edward is not heere to buckler thee.	Edw	2.5.18		Lncstr
Spencer, I heere create thee earle of Wilshire,	Edw	3.1.49		Edward
Spencer, sweet Spencer, I adopt thee heere,	Edw	3.1.144		Edward
Heere come the rebels.	Edw	3.1.194		Spencr
the newes was heere my lord,/That you were dead, or very neare	Edw	4.2.37		Queene
To this distressed Queene his sister heere,	Edw	4.2.63		SrJohn
Heere for our countries cause sweare we to him/All homage,	Edw	4.4.19		Mortmr
We heere create our welbeloved sonne,	Edw	4.6.24		Queene
heere receive my crowne.	Edw	5.1.97		Edward
Yet stay, for rather then I will looke on them,/Heere, heere:	Edw	5.1.107		Edward
Heere comes the yong prince, with the Earle of Kent.	Edw	5.2.75		Mortmr
Where is the court but heere, heere is the king,	Edw	5.3.59		Kent
Whats heere? I know not how to conster it.	Edw	5.5.15		Gurney
Heere is the keyes, this is the lake,/Doe as you are commaunded	Edw	5.5.25		Matrvs
And so shalt thou be too: why staies he heere?	Edw	5.6.51		King
Heere comes the hearse, helpe me to moorne, my lords:	Edw	5.6.98		King
Sweete father heere, unto thy murdered ghost,	Edw	5.6.99		King
I see it plaine, even heere <in this place> is writ/Homo fuge:	F 469	2.1.81		Faust
[Heere they are too].	F 551.7	2.1.170A	P	Mephst
But fye, what a smell <scent> is heere?	F 669	2.2.118	P	Pride
looke you heere sir.	F1657	4.6.100	P	Faust
heere they are my gratious Lord.	F App	p.238 58	P	Faust
so much for the injury hee offred me heere in your presence,	F App	p.238 82	P	Faust
that when it is heere winter with us, in the contrary circle it	F App	p.242 20	P	Faust
Heere I display my lewd and loose behaviour.	Ovid's Elegies	2.4.4		
Heere thou hast strength, here thy right hand doth rest.	Ovid's Elegies	2.9.36		
My heate is heere, what moves my heate is gone.	Ovid's Elegies	2.16.12		
Heere while I walke hid close in shadie grove,	Ovid's Elegies	3.1.5		
The shout is nigh; the golden pompe comes heere.	Ovid's Elegies	3.2.44		
Pay it not heere, but in an other place.	Ovid's Elegies	3.2.84		
Where's thy attire? why wand'rest heere alone?	Ovid's Elegies	3.5.55		
I heere and there go witty with dishonour.	Ovid's Elegies	3.7.8		
Part of her sorrowe heere thy sister bearing,	Ovid's Elegies	3.8.51		
A worke, that after my death, heere shall dwell	Ovid's Elegies	3.14.20		
HEEREAFTER				
And be heereafter seene with native haire.	Ovid's Elegies	1.14.56		

HEERE'S			
heere's some on's have cause to know him; did he conjure thee	F1523	4.5.19	P HrsCsr
Heere's no body, if it like your Holynesse.	F App	p.231 4	P Frier
HEERES			
Heeres channell water, as our charge is given.	Edw	5.3.27	Matrvs
Champion, heeres to thee.	Edw	5.4.80	King
Heeres a light to go into the dungeon.	Edw	5.5.37	Gurney
Foh, heeres a place in deed with all my hart.	Edw	5.5.41	Ltborn
heeres a simple purchase for horse-keepers, our horses shal	F App	p.234 2	P Robin
Peccatum peccatorum, heeres thy goblet, good Vintner.	F App	p.235 28	P Rafe
HEERETOFORE			
Then heeretofore the Delphian <Dolphian> Oracle.	F 170	1.1.142	Cornel
HEER'S			
down, heer's one would speak with you from the Duke of Guise.	P 348	6.3	P SrnsWf
HEERS			
For heers no saftie in the Realme for me,	P 568	11.33	Navrre
Come sir, give me my buttons and heers your eare.	P 620	12.33	Mugern
Saying, Poet heers a worke beseeming thee.	Ovid's Elegies		1.1.28
HEE'S			
Hee's with your mother, therefore after him.	Jew	2.3.350	Barab
hee's now at supper with the schollers, where ther's such	F1678	5.1.5	P Wagner
Why hee's fast asleepe, come some other time.	F App	p.240 141	P Mephst
HEES			
But wheres Aeneas? ah hees gone hees gone!	Dido	5.1.192	Dido
Hees gone, and for his absence thus I moorne,	Edw	1.4.305	Edward
That hees repeald, and sent for back againe,	Edw	2.1.18	Spencr
Hees gone by water unto Scarborough,	Edw	2.4.37	Queene
For hees a lambe, encompassed by Woolves,	Edw	5.1.41	Edward
Thou leav'st his bed, because hees faint through age,	Ovid's Elegies		1.13.37
Hees happie who loves mutuall skirmish slayes <layes>,	Ovid's Elegies		2.10.29
HEIFER			
I saw how Bulls for a white Heifer strive,	Ovid's Elegies		2.12.25
HEIFERS			
White Heifers by glad people forth are led,	Ovid's Elegies		3.12.13
HEIGHT			
Live happie in the height of all content,	Dido	1.1.195	Aeneas
And with the Jacobs staffe measure the height/And distance of	2Tamb	3.3.50	Techel
And yeeld your thoughts to height of my desertes.	P 602	12.15	King
Now must he fall and perish in his height.	P 946	19.16	Capt
Even to the height of Primum Mobile:	F 763	2.3.42	2Chor
such end the gods/Allot the height of honor, men so strong/By	Lucan, First Booke		82
HEINOUS (See HAINOUS)			
HEIRE (Homograph)			
The heire of [fame] <furie>, the favorite of the [fates]	Dido	3.2.3	Juno
About them hangs a knot of Amber heire,	1Tamb	2.1.23	Menaph
son and successive heire to the late mighty Emperour Bajazeth,	2Tamb	3.1.2	P Orcan
That since the heire of mighty Bajazeth/(An Emperour so	2Tamb	3.1.22	Callap
Shee is thy wife, and thou shalt be mine heire.	Jew	2.3.328	Barab
I here adopt thee for mine onely heire,	Jew	3.4.43	Barab
That thou mayst freely live to be my heire.	Jew	3.4.63	Barab
For he is your lawfull King and my next heire:	P1230	22.92	King
Unto our cosin, the earle of Glosters heire.	Edw	1.4.379	Edward
neece, the onely heire/Unto the Earle of Gloster late deceased.	Edw	2.2.258	Edward
Sound Trumpets then, for thus Saint Peters Heire,	F 875	3.1.97	Pope
were wont/In large spread heire to exceed the rest of France;	Lucan, First Booke		439
am I by such wanton toyes defamde)/Heire of an antient house,	Ovid's Elegies		3.14.5
To which the Muses sonnes are only heire:	Hero and Leander		1.476
HEIRES			
That Peters heires should tread on Emperours,	F 918	3.1.140	Pope
HEL			
Had not the heavens conceav'd with hel-borne clowdes,	Dido	1.1.125	Venus
Hel, death, Tamburlain, Hell.	1Tamb	5.1.316	P Zabina
Hel and confusion light upon their heads,	2Tamb	2.2.33	Gazell
More strong than are the gates of death or hel?	2Tamb	5.1.20	Govnr
Fall to the earth, and pierce the pit of Hel,	2Tamb	5.1.44	Govnr
Earth droopes and saies that hel in heaven is plac'd.	2Tamb	5.3.41	Usumc
[My faith, vile hel, shall triumph over thee],	F1793	5.1.120A	OldMan
[Hence hel, for hence I flie unto my God].	F1796	5.1.123A	OldMan
Monarch of hel, under whose blacke survey/Great Potentates do	F App	p.235 34	Mephst
HEL-BORNE			
Had not the heavens conceav'd with hel-borne clowdes,	Dido	1.1.125	Venus
HELD			
And held the cloath of pleasance whiles you dranke,	Dido	1.1.6	Ganimd
This butcher whil'st his hands were yet held up,	Dido	2.1.241	Aeneas
Then gan he wagge his hand, which yet held up,	Dido	5.1.229	Anna
Than if the Gods had held a Parliament:	1Tamb	2.7.66	Tamb
If all the pens that ever poets held,	1Tamb	5.1.161	Tamb
Though this be held his last daies dreadfull siege,	2Tamb	5.1.29	1Citzn
'tis a custome held with us,/That when we speake with Gentiles	Jew	2.3.44	Barab
Faith is not to be held with Heretickes;	Jew	2.3.311	Barab
Both held in hand, and flatly both beguil'd.	Jew	3.3.3	Ithimr
Mathias was the man that I held deare,	Jew	3.6.24	Abigal
This day is held through Rome and Italy,	F 834	3.1.56	Mephst
What by the holy Councell held at Trent,	F 884	3.1.106	Pope
and the Germane Emperour/Be held as Lollords, and bold	F 955	3.1.177	Faust
Yet he alone is held in reverence.	Lucan, First Booke		144
And with their hands held up, all joyntly cryde/They'ill follow	Lucan, First Booke		388
As loath to leave Roome whom they held so deere,	Lucan, First Booke		506
Her left hand held abroad a regal scepter,	Ovid's Elegies		3.1.13
If I a lover bee by thee held back.	Ovid's Elegies		3.5.22
shee her modest eyes held downe,/Her wofull bosome a warme	Ovid's Elegies		3.5.67
Tis said the slippery streame held up her brest,	Ovid's Elegies		3.5.81
She held her lap ope to receive the same.	Ovid's Elegies		3.7.34

HELD (cont.)				
When carefull Rome in doubt their prowesse held.	Ovid's Elegies	3.14.10		
(For his sake whom their goddesse held so deare,	Hero and Leander	1.92		
would not yeeld/So soone to part from that she deerely held.	Hero and Leander	2.84		
HELDE				
Is all my love forgot which helde thee deare?	P 684	13.28		Guise
HELDST				
But [heldst] <hadst> thou in thine armes some Caephalus,	Ovid's Elegies	1.13.39		
HE'LE				
your foolery, for an my Maister come, he'le conjure you 'faith.	F 735	2.3.14	P	Dick
HELEN (See also HELLEN)				
But how scapt Helen, she that causde this warre?	Dido	2.1.292		Dido
My cosin Helen taught it me in Troy.	Dido	3.1.28		Cupid
I this in Greece when Paris stole faire Helen.	Dido	3.1.142		Aeneas
And all the world calles me a second Helen,	Dido	5.1.144		Dido
HELENA				
And Helena betraied Deiphobus,	Dido	2.1.297		Achat
And I be calde a second Helena.	Dido	5.1.148		Dido
And all is drosse that is not Helena.	F1774	5.1.101		Faust
HELENS				
O how would I with Helens brother laugh,	Dido	1.1.17		Ganimd
And Helens rape doth haunt [ye] <thee> at the heeles.	Dido	1.1.144		Aeneas
There Paris is, and Helens crymes record,	Ovid's Elegies	2.18.37		
HE'LL				
now at my lodging/That was his Agent, he'll confesse it all.	Jew	5.1.17		Curtzn
HELL (See also HEL'S, HEL, HELS)				
and with this sword/Sent many of their savadge ghosts to hell.	Dido	2.1.212		Aeneas
[and] <To> pull the triple headed dog from hell.	1Tamb	1.2.161		Therid
So will I send this monstrous slave to hell,	1Tamb	2.6.7		Cosroe
Whether from earth, or hell, or heaven he grow.	1Tamb	2.6.23		Ortyg
My soule begins to take her flight to hell:	1Tamb	2.7.44		Cosroe
Remooved from the Torments and the hell:	1Tamb	3.2.103		Agidas
were that Tamburlaine/As monsterous as Gorgon, prince of Hell,	1Tamb	4.1.18		Souldn
And Jetty Feathers menace death and hell.	1Tamb	4.1.61		2Msngr
And sacrifice my heart to death and hell,	1Tamb	4.2.17		Bajzth
Feends looke on me, and thou dread God of hell,	1Tamb	4.2.27		Bajzth
And madnesse send his damned soule to hell.	1Tamb	5.1.229		Zabina
Which fils the nookes of Hell with standing aire,	1Tamb	5.1.257		Bajzth
Hel, death, Tamburlain, Hell.	1Tamb	5.1.317	P	Zabina
Hell and Elisian swarme with ghosts of men,	1Tamb	5.1.465		Tamb
To spread my fame through hell and up to heaven:	1Tamb	5.1.467		Tamb
Should pierce the blacke circumference of hell,	2Tamb	1.3.145		Techel
And feeds upon the banefull tree of hell,	2Tamb	2.3.19		Orcan
And throw them in the triple mote of Hell,	2Tamb	2.4.100		Tamb
And traveile hedlong to the lake of hell:	2Tamb	3.5.24		Orcan
O damned monster, nay a Feend of Hell,	2Tamb	4.1.168		Jrslem
Now Hell is fairer than Elisian,	2Tamb	4.2.87		Therid
Haling him headlong to the lowest hell.	2Tamb	4.3.42		Orcan
And cast the fame of Ilions Tower to hell.	2Tamb	4.3.113		Tamb
Should I but touch the rusty gates of hell,	2Tamb	5.1.96		Tamb
And sent from hell to tyrannise on earth,	2Tamb	5.1.111		Govnr
My sword hath sent millions of Turks to hell,	2Tamb	5.1.180		Tamb
Wel souldiers, Mahomet remaines in hell,	2Tamb	5.1.198		Tamb
Our Turkish swords shal headlong send to hell,	2Tamb	5.2.15		Amasia
For hell and darknesse pitch their pitchy tentes,	2Tamb	5.3.7		Therid
Earth droopes and saies, that hell in heaven is plac'd.	2Tamb	5.3.16		Therid
And Angels dive into the pooles of hell.	2Tamb	5.3.33		Usumc
And weary Death with bearing soules to hell.	2Tamb	5.3.77		Tamb
unrelenting eares/Of death and hell be shut against my praiers,	2Tamb	5.3.192		Amyras
And night made semblance of the hue of hell,	P 63	2.6		Guise
Although my downfall be the deepest hell.	P 104	2.47		Guise
Stab him I say and send him to his freends in hell.	P 415	7.55		Guise
Mounser of Loraine sinke away to hell,	P1023	19.93		King
And with their pawes drench his black soule in hell.	P1102	20.12		Cardnl
No, let the villaine dye, and feele in hell,	P1174	22.36		King
a death too good, the devill of hell/Torture his wicked soule.	P1218	22.80		Bartus
no soule in hell/Hath felt more torment then poore Gaveston.	Edw	1.1.146		Gavstn
Let him complaine unto the sea of hell,	Edw	1.1.191		Gavstn
Is all my hope turnd to this hell of greefe.	Edw	1.4.116		Gavstn
Ah had some bloudlesse furie rose from hell,	Edw	1.4.316		Edward
Nay so will hell, and cruell Mortimer,	Edw	4.7.75		Edward
And to the gates of hell convay me hence,	Edw	4.7.88		Edward
I feele a hell of greefe: where is my crowne?	Edw	5.5.90		Edward
as th'infernall spirits/On sweet Musaeus when he came to hell,	F 143	1.1.115		Faust
And pray devoutely to the Prince of hell.	F 282	1.3.54		Mephst
For I confound <He confounds> hell in Elizium:	F 287	1.3.59		Faust
In hell.	F 302	1.3.74		Mephst
How comes it then that thou art out of hell?	F 303	1.3.75		Faust
Why this is hell: nor am I out of it.	F 304	1.3.76		Mephst
If thou deny it I must <wil> backe to hell.	F 426	2.1.38		Mephst
If unto [God] <heaven>, hee'le throw me <thee> downe to hell.	F 467	2.1.79		Faust
Faustus, I sweare by Hell and Lucifer,	F 481	2.1.93		Mephst
First, I will question [with] thee about hell:	F 504	2.1.116		Faust
Tell me, where is the place that men call Hell?	F 505	2.1.117		Faust
Hell hath no limits, nor is circumscrib'd,	F 510	2.1.122		Mephst
but <for> where we are is hell,/And where hell is there must we	F 511	2.1.123		Mephst
And where hell is there must we ever be.	F 512	2.1.124		Mephst
All places shall be hell that is not heaven.	F 515	2.1.127		Mephst
For I tell thee I am damn'd, and <am> now in hell.	F 526	2.1.138		Mephst
<How? now in hell? nay>	F 527	2.1.139		Faust
Nay, and this be hell, I'le willingly be damn'd <damned here>.	F 527	2.1.139		Faust
<Thinke thou on hell Faustus, for thou art damnd>.	F 624	(HC262)A		Mephst
Thou art damn'd, think thou of hell>.	F 624	2.2.73	P	Mephst

HELL (cont.)
I, go accursed spirit to ugly hell: F 627 2.2.76 Faust
And this is my companion Prince in hell. F 640 2.2.89 Lucifr
we are come from hell in person to shew thee some pastime: F 654 2.2.103 P Belzeb
I was borne in hell, and look to it, for some of you shall be F 690 2.2.139 P Wrath
Away to hell, away: on piper. F 711 2.2.163 Lucifr
[Tut] <But> Faustus, in hell is all manner of delight. F 713 2.2.165 Lucifr
O might I see hell, and returne againe safe, how happy were I F 714 2.2.166 P Faust
We veiw'd the face of heaven, of earth and hell. F 848 3.1.70 Faust
To light as heavy as the paines of hell. F 939 3.1.161 Pope
Hell and the Furies forked haire, F1000 3.2.20 Mephst
Forward and backward, to curse Faustus to hell. F1075 3.2.95 Faust
that shall pierce through/The Ebon gates of ever-burning hell, F1224 4.1.70 Faust
O were that damned Hell-hound but in place, F1355 4.2.31 Benvol
Hell take his soule, his body thus must fall. F1363 4.2.39 Benvol
Thence pitch them headlong to the lowest hell: F1405 4.2.81 Faust
And hell shall after plague their treacherie. F1407 4.2.83 Faust
This Magicke, that will charme thy soule to hell, F1708 5.1.35 OldMan
No mortall can expresse the paines of hell. F1716 5.1.43 OldMan
Hell claimes his <calls for> right, and with a roaring voyce, F1726 5.1.53 Faust
Hell strives with grace for conquest in my breast: F1741 5.1.68 Faust
With greatest [torments] <torment> that our hell affoords. F1755 5.1.82 Faust
Those soules which sinne seales the blacke sonnes of hell, F1799 5.2.3 Lucifr
the Kingdome of Joy, and must remaine in hell for ever. F1846 5.2.50 P Faust
Hell, [ah] <O> hell for ever. F1846 5.2.50 P Faust
friends, what shall become of Faustus being in hell for ever? F1847 5.2.51 P Faust
if not, Faustus is gone to hell. F1878 5.2.82 P Faust
Therefore despaire, thinke onely upon hell; F1881 5.2.85 Mephst
Fooles that will laugh on earth, [must] <most> weepe in hell. F1891 5.2.95 Mephst
To want in hell, that had on earth such store. F1898 5.2.102 BdAngl
Hell, or the Divell, had had no power on thee. F1902 5.2.106 GdAngl
like those bright shining Saints,/And triumpht over hell: F1906 5.2.110 GdAngl
The jawes of hell are open to receive thee. F1908 5.2.112 GdAngl
Whose influence hath allotted death and hell; F1951 5.2.155 Faust
Let Faustus live in hell a thousand yeares, F1961 5.2.165 Faust
But mine must live still to be plagu'd in hell. F1971 5.2.175 Faust
Or Lucifer will beare thee quicke to hell. F1976 5.2.180 Faust
Ugly hell gape not; come not Lucifer, F1981 5.2.185 Faust
Forward and backward, to curse Faustus to hell. F App p.232 26 Faust
Bare downe to hell her sonne, the pledge of peace, Lucan, First Booke 113
In hell were harbourd, here was found no masse. Ovid's Elegies 3.7.38
And those on whom heaven, earth, and hell relies, Hero and Leander 1.443
Might presently be banisht into hell, Hero and Leander 1.453
Hermes had slept in hell with ignoraunce. Hero and Leander 1.468
Dang'd downe to hell her loathsome carriage. Hero and Leander 2.334

HELLEN
Hellen, whose beauty sommond Greece to armes, 2Tamb 2.4.87 Tamb
that Hellen of Greece was the admirablest Lady that ever liv'd: F1683 5.1.10 P 1Schol
<Was this faire Hellen, whose admired worth>/<Made Greece with F1696 (HC269)B 2Schol
That heavenly Hellen, which I saw of late, F1762 5.1.89 Faust
Sweet Hellen make me immortall with a kisse: F1770 5.1.97 Faust
Come Hellen, come, give me my soule againe, F1772 5.1.99 Faust
And then returne to Hellen for a kisse. F1780 5.1.107 Faust

HELLES
The god put Helles bracelet on his arme, Hero and Leander 2.179

HELLESPONT
On Hellespont guiltie of True-loves blood, Hero and Leander 1.1
And pray'd the narrow toyling Hellespont, Hero and Leander 2.150

HELL-HOUND
O were that damned Hell-hound but in place, F1355 4.2.31 Benvol

HELLISH
That slayest me with thy harsh and hellish tale, Dido 5.1.217 Dido
And in your hands bring hellish poison up, 1Tamb 4.4.19 Bajzth
her latest breath/All dasled with the hellish mists of death. 2Tamb 2.4.14 Tamb
Curst be your soules to hellish misery. F1034 3.2.54 Pope
O hellish spite,/Your heads are all set with hornes. F1441 4.3.11 Benvol
Faustus is gone, regard his hellish fall, F2005 5.3.23 4Chor
much like that hellish fiend/Which made the sterne Lycurgus Lucan, First Booke 572

HELME (Homograph)
Armour of proofe, horse, helme, and Curtle-axe, 2Tamb 1.3.44 Tamb
And in my helme a triple plume shal spring, 2Tamb 4.3.116 Tamb
The Pilot from the helme leapes in the sea; Lucan, First Booke 499
Knowest not this head a helme was wont to beare, Ovid's Elegies 3.7.13

HELMES
Their plumed helmes are wrought with beaten golde. 1Tamb 1.2.124 Souldr

HELMET (See also HELME)
on a Lions backe)/Rhamnusia beares a helmet ful of blood, 2Tamb 3.4.57 Therid
And on Andromache his helmet laces. Ovid's Elegies 1.9.36

HELMETS
That meanes to fill your helmets full of golde: 1Tamb 4.4.7 Tamb

HELP
For they are friends that help to weane my state, 1Tamb 1.2.29 Tamb
Till men and kingdomes help to strengthen it: 1Tamb 1.2.30 Tamb
And here's the crown my Lord, help set it on. 1Tamb 5.1.505 Usumc
Help me (my Lords) to make my last remoove. 2Tamb 5.3.180 Tamb
Pray doe, and let me help you, master. Jew 3.4.86 P Ithimr
Help sonne Navarre, I am poysoned. P 176 3.11 OldQn
O I am slaine, help me my Lords: F1068 3.2.88 Pope
O come and help to beare my body hence: F1069 3.2.89 Pope
Make hast to help these noble Gentlemen, F1421 4.2.97 1Soldr
O help me gentle friend; where is Martino? F1432 4.3.2 Fredrk
O help, help, the villaine hath murder'd me. F1493 4.4.37 P Faust
O help us heaven, see, here are Faustus limbs, F1988 5.3.6 2Schol

HELPE			
These hands did helpe to hale it to the gates,	Dido	2.1.170	Aeneas
Lay to thy hands and helpe me make a fire,	Dido	5.1.284	Dido
O helpe Iarbus, Dido in these flames/Hath burnt her selfe, aye	Dido	5.1.314	Anna
Well, Barabas, canst helpe me to a Diamond?	Jew	2.3.48	Lodowk
That by my helpe shall doe much villanie.	Jew	2.3.133	Barab
And Physicke will not helpe them; they must dye.	Jew	3.6.2	1Fryar
First helpe to bury this, then goe with me/And helpe me to	Jew	3.6.45	2Fryar
then goe with me/And helpe me to exclaime against the Jew.	Jew	3.6.46	2Fryar
Come Ithimore, let's helpe to take him hence.	Jew	4.1.200	Barab
I'le helpe to slay their children and their wives,	Jew	5.1.64	Barab
Helpe, helpe me, Christians, helpe.	Jew	5.5.65	Barab
Oh helpe me, Selim, helpe me, Christians.	Jew	5.5.70	Barab
You will not helpe me then?	Jew	5.5.76	Barab
And villaines, know you cannot helpe me now.	Jew	5.5.77	Barab
Especially with our olde mothers helpe.	P1061	19.131	King
Or who will helpe to builde Religion?	P1084	19.154	QnMoth
their sides/With their owne weapons gorde, but whats the helpe?	Edw	4.4.8	Queene
Helpe unckle Kent, Mortimer will wrong me.	Edw	5.2.113	Prince
O gentle brother, helpe to rescue me.	Edw	5.3.51	Edward
Yet be not farre off, I shall need your helpe,	Edw	5.5.28	Ltborn
Heere comes the hearse, helpe me to moorne, my lords:	Edw	5.6.98	King
Their conference will be a greater helpe to me,	F 95	1.1.67	Faust
Helpe <seeke> to save distressed Faustus soule.	F 635	2.2.84	Faust
one, me thought/I heard him shreeke and call aloud for helpe:	F1992	5.3.10	3Schol
my legge, helpe Mephastophilis, call the Officers, my legge,	F App	p.241 155 P	Faust
I shall not need/To crave Apolloes ayde, or Bacchus helpe;	Lucan, First Booke		65
(Anger will helpe thy hands though nere so weake).	Ovid's Elegies		1.7.66
Being requirde, with speedy helpe relieve?	Ovid's Elegies		2.9.8
Request milde Zephires helpe for thy availe,	Ovid's Elegies		2.11.41
Nor can an other say his helpe I tooke.	Ovid's Elegies		2.12.12
toyes defamde)/Heire of an antient house, if helpe that can,	Ovid's Elegies		3.14.5
And crave the helpe of sheap-heards that were nie.	Hero and Leander		1.414
HELPES			
What helpes it me of fierce Achill to sing?	Ovid's Elegies		2.1.29
What helpes it thou wert given to please my wench,	Ovid's Elegies		2.6.19
What helpes it Woman to be free from warre?	Ovid's Elegies		2.14.1
What helpes my hast: what to have tane small rest?	Ovid's Elegies		3.5.9
HELPING			
Under pretence of helping Charles the fifth,	Jew	2.3.188	Barab
And waters force, force helping Gods to faile,	Ovid's Elegies		2.16.28
HELPS			
Confusion light on him that helps thee thus.	1Tamb	4.2.84	Bajzth
Nor you depend on such weake helps as we.	1Tamb	5.1.33	1Virgn
To think our helps will doe him any good.	2Tamb	4.1.21	Calyph
HEL'S			
<Come>, I thinke Hel's a fable.	F 516	2.1.128	Faust
HELS			
Am not tormented with ten thousand hels,	F 307	1.3.79	Mephst
And now must taste hels paines perpetually.	F1895	5.2.99	BdAngl
HEM			
I, and tis likewise thought you favour him <them> <'em> <hem>.	Edw	2.2.226	Edward
HEM'D			
Till I may see thee hem'd with armed men.	1Tamb	2.4.38	Tamb
Twas his troupe hem'd in Milo being accusde;	Lucan, First Booke		323
HEMD			
All which hemd me about, crying, this is he.	Dido	2.1.219	Aeneas
HEMI			
When Phoebus leaping from his Hemi-Spheare,	2Tamb	1.2.51	Callap
As Pilgrimes traveile to our Hemi-spheare,	2Tamb	3.2.32	Tamb
HEMI-SPHEARE			
When Phoebus leaping from his Hemi-Spheare,	2Tamb	1.2.51	Callap
As Pilgrimes traveile to our Hemi-spheare,	2Tamb	3.2.32	Tamb
HEMLOCKE			
Yet like as if cold hemlocke I had drunke,	Ovid's Elegies		3.6.13
HEMLOCKS			
Which I thinke gather'd from cold hemlocks flower/Wherein bad	Ovid's Elegies		1.12.9
HEMPEN			
whom I saluted with an old hempen proverb, Hodie tibi,	Jew	4.2.18	P Pilia
and when the Hangman had put on his hempen Tippet, he made such	Jew	4.2.23	P Ithimr
HEMUS			
With hoarie toppe, and under Hemus mount/Philippi plaines;	Lucan, First Booke		679
HENCE			
But are arived safe not farre from hence:	Dido	1.1.237	Venus
Till I returne and take thee hence againe.	Dido	2.1.339	Venus
O foolish Troians that would steale from hence,	Dido	4.4.5	Dido
Packt with the windes to beare Aeneas hence?	Dido	4.4.127	Dido
Come come, Ile goe, how farre hence is your house?	Dido	4.5.13	Cupid
Sergestus, beare him hence unto our ships,	Dido	5.1.49	Aeneas
Aeneas will not faine with his deare love,/I must from hence:	Dido	5.1.93	Aeneas
Let me goe, farewell, I must from hence,	Dido	5.1.110	Dido
It is Aeneas calles Aeneas hence,	Dido	5.1.132	Dido
Not farre from hence/There is a woman famoused for arts,	Dido	5.1.274	Dido
are in readines/Ten thousand horse to carie you from hence,	1Tamb	1.1.185	Ortyg
Let us afford him now the bearing hence.	1Tamb	3.2.111	Usumc
He meet me in the field and fetch thee hence?	1Tamb	3.3.5	Tamb
I will dispatch chiefe of my army hence/To faire Natolia, and	2Tamb	1.1.161	Orcan
I know thou wouldst depart from hence with me.	2Tamb	1.2.11	Callap
How far hence lies the Galley, say you?	2Tamb	1.2.54	Almeda
Sweet Almeda, scarse halfe a league from hence.	2Tamb	1.2.55	Callap
For taking hence my faire Zenocrate.	2Tamb	2.4.101	Tamb
For amorous Jove hath snatcht my love from hence,	2Tamb	2.4.107	Tamb
and let us haste from hence/Along the cave that leads beyond	2Tamb	3.4.1	Olymp

HENCE (cont.)

Line	Work	Ref.	Speaker
The winged Hermes, to convay thee hence:	2Tamb	4.2.19	Therid
Away with him hence, let him speake no more:	2Tamb	5.1.125	Tamb
Hence comes it, that a strong built Citadell/Commands much more	Jew	Prol.22	Machvl
And he meanes quickly to expell you hence;	Jew	2.2.38	Bosco
Then marke him, Sir, and take him hence.	Jew	2.3.131	1Offcr
from hence/Ne're shall she grieve me more with her disgrace;	Jew	3.4.28	Barab
Then will nct Jacomo be long from hence.	Jew	4.1.159	Barab
Come Ithimore, let's helpe to take him hence.	Jew	4.1.200	Barab
And saile from hence to Greece, to lovely Greece,	Jew	4.2.89	Ithimr
Let's hence, lest further mischiefe be pretended.	Jew	5.5.96	Calym
For with thy Gallyes couldst thou not get hence,	Jew	5.5.100	Govnr
Come my Lords let us beare her body hence,	P 195	3.30	Admral
Murder the Hugonets, take those pedantes hence.	P 438	7.78	Guise
For if th'almighty take my brother hence,	P 469	8.19	Anjoy
Come let us take his body hence.	P 564	11.29	QnMoth
Hence strumpet, hide thy head for shame,	P 691	13.35	Guise
Take hence that damned villaine from my sight.	P1182	22.44	King
And since I went from hence, no soule in hell/Hath felt more	Edw	1.1.146	Gavstn
Then beare the ship that shall transport thee hence:	Edw	1.1.153	Edward
Why post we not from hence to levie men?	Edw	1.2.16	Mortmr
No, but weele lift Gaveston from hence.	Edw	1.2.62	Lncstr
But I long more to see him banisht hence.	Edw	1.4.5	Warwck
And thou must hence, or I shall be deposd,	Edw	1.4.110	Edward
To go from hence, greeves not poore Gaveston,	Edw	1.4.119	Gavstn
Thou shalt not hence, ile hide thee Gaveston.	Edw	1.4.131	Edward
See that my coache be readie, I must hence.	Edw	2.1.71	Neece
then was thy parting hence/Bitter and irkesome to my sobbing	Edw	2.2.57	Edward
Convey hence Gaveston, thaile murder him.	Edw	2.2.82	Edward
The wind that bears him hence, wil fil our sailes,	Edw	2.4.48	Lncstr
Go souldiers take him hence, for by my sword,	Edw	2.5.20	Warwck
My house is not farre hence, out of the way/A little, but our	Edw	2.5.100	Penbrk
With all the hast we can dispatch him hence.	Edw	3.1.83	Edward
I will this undertake, to have him hence,	Edw	3.1.111	Arundl
Meane while, have hence this rebell to the blocke,	Edw	4.6.69	Mortmr
And to the gates of hell convay me hence,	Edw	4.7.88	Edward
Hence fained weeds, unfained are my woes,	Edw	4.7.97	Edward
Parted from hence, never to see us more!	Edw	4.7.101	Spencr
Spencer, I see our soules are fleeted hence,	Edw	4.7.105	Baldck
Your grace must hence with mee to Bartley straight.	Edw	5.1.144	Bartly
Hence will I haste to Killingworth castle,	Edw	5.2.119	Kent
How often shall I bid you beare him hence?	Edw	5.4.102	Mortmr
Hence with the traitor, with the murderer.	Edw	5.6.58	King
Thus madam, tis the kings will you shall hence.	Edw	5.6.89	2Lord
To censure Bruno, that is posted hence,	F 983	3.2.3	Mephst
O come and help to beare my body hence:	F1069	3.2.89	Pope
Go Belimothe, and take this caitife hence,	F1408	4.2.84	Faust
Fly hence, dispatch my charge immediatly.	F1416	4.2.92	Faust
[Hence hel, for hence I flie unto my God].	F1796	5.1.123A	OldMan
for Julia/Snatcht hence by cruel fates with ominous howles,	Lucan, First Booke		112
Hence came it that th'edicts were overrul'd,	Lucan, First Booke		178
Hence interest and devouring usury sprang,	Lucan, First Booke		183
Faiths breach, and hence came war to most men welcom.	Lucan, First Booke		184
Hence leagues, and covenants; Fortune thee I follow,	Lucan, First Booke		228
Now while their part is weake, and feares, march hence,	Lucan, First Booke		281
thence/To the pine bearing hils, hence to the mounts/Pirene,	Lucan, First Booke		688
Do not thou so, but throw thy mantle hence,	Ovid's Elegies		1.4.49
Time flying slides hence closely, and deceaves us,	Ovid's Elegies		1.8.49
Nor let my words be with the windes hence blowne,	Ovid's Elegies		1.8.106
Hence luck-lesse tables, funerall wood be flying/And thou the	Ovid's Elegies		1.12.7
So Cupid wills, farre hence be the severe,	Ovid's Elegies		2.1.3
Hence with great laude thou maiest a triumph move.	Ovid's Elegies		2.9.16
But if my words with winged stormes hence slip,	Ovid's Elegies		2.11.33
Which as it seemes, hence winde and sea bereaves.	Ovid's Elegies		2.16.46
When you fleet hence, can be bequeath'd to none.	Hero and Leander		1.248
HENCEFORTH			
Dido is thine, henceforth Ile call thee Lord:	Dido	4.4.84	Dido
Henceforth you shall be our Carthage Gods:	Dido	4.4.96	Dido
And henceforth wish for an eternall night,	Jew	1.2.193	Barab
And henceforth parle with our naked swords.	Edw	1.1.126	Mortmr
Nor will [I] <Faustus> henceforth:	F 647	2.2.96	Faust
HENOLT			
A good sir John of Henolt,/Never so cheereles, nor so farre	Edw	4.2.13	Queene
will your grace with me to Henolt,/And there stay times	Edw	4.2.17	SrJohn
Will we with thee to Henolt, so we will.	Edw	4.2.31	Queene
distressed Queene his sister heere,/Go you with her to Henolt:	Edw	4.2.64	SrJohn
Sir John of Henolt, pardon us I pray,	Edw	4.2.71	Kent
Sir John of Henolt, be it thy renowne,	Edw	4.2.78	Mortmr
if you aske, with sir John of Henolt, brother to the Marquesse,	Edw	4.3.31	P Spencr
And will sir John of Henolt lead the round?	Edw	4.3.40	Edward
HENOLTS			
That Englands peeres may Henolts welcome see.	Edw	4.2.82	SrJohn
HENRIES			
the speed we can, provide/For Henries coronation from Polonie:	P 563	11.28	QnMoth
think they Henries heart/Will not both harbour love and	P 603	12.16	King
And rulde in France by Henries fatall death.	P1250	22.112	Navrre
HENRY			
And Henry then shall weare the diadem.	P 522	9.41	QnMoth
despatch Embassadours/To Poland, to call Henry back againe,	P 556	11.21	QnMoth
And now that Henry is cal'd from Polland,	P 569	11.34	Navrre
welcome from Poland Henry once agayne,	P 589	12.2	QnMoth
All this and more hath Henry with his crowne.	P 596	12.9	QnMoth
And long may Henry enjoy all this and more.	P 597	12.10	Cardnl

HENRY (cont.)			
Revenge it Henry as thou list or dare,	P 819	17.14	Guise
Henry thy King wipes cf these childish teares,	P1236	22.98	King
And tell her Henry dyes her faithfull freend.	P1244	22.106	King
revenge it henry yf thow liste or darst	Paris	ms23,p391	Guise
HEPHAESTION (See EPHESTION)			
HER (See alsc HIR, HIRS)			
That will nct shield me from her shrewish blowes:	Dido	1.1.4	Ganimd
To hang her meteor like twixt heaven and earth,	Dido	1.1.13	Jupitr
And bind her hand and foote with golden cordes,	Dido	1.1.14	Jupitr
From Junos bird Ile pluck her spotted pride,	Dido	1.1.34	Jupitr
My Juno ware upon her marriage day,	Dido	1.1.43	Jupitr
Juno, false Juno in her Chariots pompe,	Dido	1.1.54	Venus
Made Hebe tc direct her ayrie wheeles/Into the windie countrie	Dido	1.1.56	Venus
Or force her smile that hetherto hath frownd:	Dido	1.1.88	Jupitr
From forth her ashes shall advance her head,	Dido	1.1.94	Jupitr
Shall make the morning hast her gray uprise,	Dido	1.1.102	Jupitr
To feede her eyes with his engraven fame.	Dido	1.1.103	Jupitr
Which Pergama did vaunt in all her pride.	Dido	1.1.151	Aeneas
Bequeath her young ones to our scanted foode.	Dido	1.1.162	Achat
Having a quiver girded to her side,	Dido	1.1.185	Venus
Where Dido will receive ye with her smiles:	Dido	1.1.234	Venus
I know her by the movings of her feete:	Dido	1.1.241	Aeneas
Who for her sonnes death wept out life and breath,	Dido	2.1.4	Aeneas
Had not such passions in her head as I.	Dido	2.1.6	Aeneas
And when we told her she would weepe for griefe,	Dido	2.1.67	Illion
See where her servitors passe through the hall/Bearing a	Dido	2.1.70	Serg
Looke where she comes: Aeneas [view] <viewd> her well.	Dido	2.1.72	Illion
Well may I view her, but she sees not me.	Dido	2.1.73	Aeneas
A little while prolong'd her husbands life:	Dido	2.1.246	Aeneas
At last the souldiers puld her by the heeles,	Dido	2.1.247	Aeneas
And swong her howling in the emptie ayre,	Dido	2.1.248	Aeneas
Her cheekes swolne with sighes, her haire all rent,	Dido	2.1.276	Aeneas
And I alas, was forst to let her lye.	Dido	2.1.279	Aeneas
Moved with her voyce, I lept into the sea,	Dido	2.1.283	Aeneas
Thinking to beare her on my backe abourd,	Dido	2.1.284	Aeneas
We heare they led her captive into Greece.	Dido	2.1.295	Achat
Her Lover after Alexander dyed,	Dido	2.1.298	Achat
in stead of him/Will set thee on her lap and play with thee:	Dido	2.1.325	Venus
Then touch her white breast with this arrow head,	Dido	2.1.326	Venus
Then shall I touch her breast and conquer her.	Dido	3.1.6	Cupid
No Dido will not take me in her armes,	Dido	3.1.22	Cupid
I shall not be her sonne, she loves me not.	Dido	3.1.23	Cupid
Will Dido let me hang about her necke?	Dido	3.1.30	Cupid
I wagge, and give thee leave to kisse her to.	Dido	3.1.31	Dido
And if my mother goe, Ile follow her.	Dido	3.1.38	Cupid
give Dido leave/To be more modest then her thoughts admit,	Dido	3.1.95	Dido
We will account her author of our lives.	Dido	3.1.112	Aeneas
Troy shall nc more call him her second hope,	Dido	3.2.8	Juno
Say vengeance, now shall her Ascanius dye?	Dido	3.2.13	Juno
And feedes his eyes with favours of her Court,	Dido	3.2.71	Juno
She likewise in admyring spends her time,	Dido	3.2.72	Juno
Darts forth her light to Lavinias shoare.	Dido	3.2.84	Venus
Bearing her bowe and quiver at her backe.	Dido	3.3.55	Achat
Revenge me on Aeneas, or on her:	Dido	3.3.70	Iarbus
On her?	Dido	3.3.71	Iarbus
But time will discontinue her content,	Dido	3.3.78	Iarbus
And mould her minde unto newe fancies shapes:	Dido	3.3.79	Iarbus
What, hath Iarbus angred her in ought?	Dido	3.4.13	Aeneas
Doe shame her worst, I will disclose my griefe:--	Dido	3.4.28	Dido
Never to like or love any but her.	Dido	3.4.51	Aeneas
Yeelds up her beautie to a strangers bed,	Dido	4.2.17	Iarbus
Who having wrought her shame, is straight way fled:	Dido	4.2.18	Iarbus
And dive into her heart by coloured lookes.	Dido	4.2.32	Iarbus
For her that so delighteth in thy paine:	Dido	4.2.34	Anna
Yet Dido casts her eyes like anchors out,	Dido	4.3.25	Aeneas
Come backe, come backe, I heare her crye a farre,	Dido	4.3.27	Aeneas
So she may have Aeneas in her armes.	Dido	4.3.42	Illion
To leave her so and not once say farewell,	Dido	4.3.47	Aeneas
Her silver armes will coll me round about,	Dido	4.3.51	Aeneas
And beare him in the countrey to her house,	Dido	4.4.106	Dido
To rob their mistresse of her Troian guest?	Dido	4.4.138	Dido
Why did it suffer thee to touch her breast,	Dido	4.4.145	Dido
And sheere ye all asunder with her hands:	Dido	4.4.156	Dido
Carthage shall vaunt her pettie walles no more,	Dido	5.1.4	Aeneas
And clad her in a Chrystall liverie,	Dido	5.1.6	Aeneas
Whose wealthie streames may waite upon her towers,	Dido	5.1.9	Aeneas
And triple wise intrench her round about:	Dido	5.1.10	Aeneas
And plant our pleasant suburbes with her fumes.	Dido	5.1.15	Aeneas
Who ever since hath luld me in her armes.	Dido	5.1.48	Ascan
been/When Didos beautie [chaind] <chaungd> thine eyes to her:	Dido	5.1.114	Dido
canst thou take her hand?	Dido	5.1.121	Dido
Desires Aeneas to remaine with her:	Dido	5.1.135	Dido
Away with her to prison presently,	Dido	5.1.220	Dido
Away with her, suffer her not to speake.	Dido	5.1.224	Dido
My sister comes, I like not her sad lookes.	Dido	5.1.225	Dido
That hath dishonord her and Carthage both?	Dido	5.1.280	Iarbus
helpe Iarbus, Dido in these flames/Hath burnt her selfe, aye me,	Dido	5.1.315	Anna
And mixe her bloud with thine, this shall I doe,	Dido	5.1.326	Anna
Before the Moone renew her borrowed light,	1Tamb	1.1.69	Therid
Where her betrothed Lord Alcidamus,	1Tamb	1.2.78	Agidas
Expects th'arrivall of her highnesse person.	1Tamb	1.2.79	Agidas
Aurora shall not peepe out of her doores,	1Tamb	2.2.10	Mycet

HER (cont.)

Fortune her selfe dooth sit upon our Crests.	1Tamb	2.2.73	Meandr
then Cosroe raign/And governe Persea in her former pomp:	1Tamb	2.5.19	Cosroe
My soule begins to take her flight to hell:	1Tamb	2.7.44	Cosroe
when the Moon begins/To joine in one her semi-circled hornes:	1Tamb	3.1.12	Bajzth
Or when the morning holds him in her armes:	1Tamb	3.2.48	Zenoc
And makes my soule devine her overthrow.	1Tamb	3.2.87	Agidas
Sit downe by her:	1Tamb	3.3.124	Tamb
And manage words with her as we will armes.	1Tamb	3.3.131	Tamb
Then Victorie begins to take her flight,	1Tamb	3.3.160	Tamb
Resting her selfe upon my milk-white Tent:	1Tamb	3.3.161	Tamb
How lik'st thou her Ebea, will she serve?	1Tamb	3.3.178	Zabina
But I shall turne her into other weedes,	1Tamb	3.3.180	Ebea
And make her daintie fingers fall to woorke.	1Tamb	3.3.181	Ebea
And how my slave, her mistresse menaceth.	1Tamb	3.3.183	Zenoc
And made my lordly Love her worthy King:	1Tamb	3.3.190	Zenoc
Nay take the Turkish Crown from her, Zenocrate,	1Tamb	3.3.220	Tamb
Give her the Crowne Turkesse, you wer best.	1Tamb	3.3.224	Therid
Not now Theridamas, her time is past:	1Tamb	3.3.228	Tamb
And be reveng'd for her disparadgement.	1Tamb	4.1.72	Souldn
and she shal looke/That these abuses flow not from her tongue:	1Tamb	4.2.70	Zenoc
Chide her Anippe.	1Tamb	4.2.71	Zenoc
feathered bird/That spreads her wings upon the citie wals,	1Tamb	4.2.106	Tamb
dispatch her while she is fat, for if she live but a while	1Tamb	4.4.48	P Tamb
flags/Through which sweet mercie threw her gentle beams,	1Tamb	5.1.69	Tamb
And like to Flora in her mornings pride,	1Tamb	5.1.140	Tamb
Shaking her silver tresses in the aire,	1Tamb	5.1.141	Tamb
And comments vollumes with her Yvory pen,	1Tamb	5.1.145	Tamb
Let ugly darknesse with her rusty coach/Engyrt with tempests	1Tamb	5.1.294	Bajzth
And let her horses from their nostrels breathe/Rebellious winds	1Tamb	5.1.297	Bajzth
I, even I speake to her.	1Tamb	5.1.314	P Zabina
Whose lives were dearer to Zenocrate/Than her owne life, or	1Tamb	5.1.338	Zenoc
That she shall stay and turne her wheele no more,	1Tamb	5.1.374	Anippe
eies beholde/That as for her thou bearst these wretched armes,	1Tamb	5.1.409	Arabia
Even so for her thou diest in these armes:	1Tamb	5.1.410	Arabia
the cursed object/Whose Fortunes never mastered her griefs:	1Tamb	5.1.414	Zenoc
Behold her wounded in conceit for thee,	1Tamb	5.1.415	Zenoc
Her state and person wants no pomp you see,	1Tamb	5.1.485	Tamb
I record heaven, her heavenly selfe is cleare:	1Tamb	5.1.487	Tamb
time to grace/Her princely Temples with the Persean crowne:	1Tamb	5.1.489	Tamb
Invest her here my Queene of Persea.	1Tamb	5.1.494	Tamb
and protestations/Of endlesse honor to thee for her love.	1Tamb	5.1.497	Souldn
Then let us set the crowne upon her head,	1Tamb	5.1.501	Therid
For now her mariage time shall worke us rest.	1Tamb	5.1.504	Techel
That darted mountaines at her brother Jove:	1Tamb	5.1.511	Tamb
shadowing in her browes/Triumphes and Trophees for my	1Tamb	5.1.512	Tamb
manie cities sacrifice/He celebrated her [sad] <said> funerall,	2Tamb	Prol.8	Prolog
And make faire Europe mounted on her bull,	2Tamb	1.1.42	Orcan
Stampt with the princely Foule that in her wings/Caries the	2Tamb	1.1.100	Orcan
She lies so close that none can find her out.	2Tamb	1.2.60	Callap
Plac'd by her side, looke on their mothers face.	2Tamb	1.3.20	Tamb
Yet flourisheth as Flora in her pride,	2Tamb	2.3.22	Orcan
Drawes in the comfort of her latest breath/All dasled with the	2Tamb	2.4.13	Tamb
Phisitions, wil no phisicke do her good?	2Tamb	2.4.38	Tamb
Her sacred beauty hath enchaunted heaven,	2Tamb	2.4.85	Tamb
Her name had bene in every line he wrote:	2Tamb	2.4.90	Tamb
for whose byrth/Olde Rome was proud, but gasde a while on her,	2Tamb	2.4.92	Tamb
Meaning to make her stately Queene of heaven.	2Tamb	2.4.108	Tamb
And all this raging cannot make her live,	2Tamb	2.4.120	Therid
And feed my mind that dies for want of her:	2Tamb	2.4.128	Tamb
Where ere her soule be, thou shalt stay with me/Embalm'd with	2Tamb	2.4.129	Tamb
And here will I set up her stature <statue>/And martch about it	2Tamb	2.4.140	Tamb
Will now retaine her olde inconstancie,	2Tamb	3.1.29	Callap
This Piller plac'd in memorie of her,	2Tamb	3.2.15	Calyph
this table as a Register/Of all her vertues and perfections.	2Tamb	3.2.24	Celeb
To shew her beautie, which the world admyr'd,	2Tamb	3.2.26	Tamb
If I had wept a sea of teares for her,	2Tamb	3.2.47	Calyph
And Eagles wings join'd to her feathered breast,	2Tamb	3.4.62	Therid
Fame hovereth, sounding of her golden Trumpe:	2Tamb	3.4.63	Therid
That humbly craves upon her knees to stay,	2Tamb	3.4.70	Olymp
And cast her bodie in the burning flame,	2Tamb	3.4.71	Olymp
That feeds upon her sonnes and husbands flesh.	2Tamb	3.4.72	Olymp
turrets of my Court/Sit like to Venus in her chaire of state,	2Tamb	4.2.42	Therid
What, have I slaine her? Villaine, stab thy selfe:	2Tamb	4.2.82	Therid
For every Fury gazeth on her lookes:	2Tamb	4.2.92	Therid
Inventing maskes and stately showes for her,	2Tamb	4.2.94	Therid
For love, for honor, and to make her Queene,	2Tamb	4.3.38	Orcan
The pride and beautie of her princely seat,	2Tamb	4.3.109	Tamb
As there be breaches in her battered wall.	2Tamb	5.1.160	Tamb
Denie my soule fruition of her joy,	2Tamb	5.3.194	Amyras
For earth hath spent the pride of all her fruit,	2Tamb	5.3.250	Amyras
Tush, they are wise; I know her and her strength:	Jew	1.1.81	Barab
Hinder her not, thou man of little faith,	Jew	1.2.340	1Fryar
For she has mortified her selfe.	Jew	1.2.341	1Fryar
For I had rather dye, then see her thus.	Jew	1.2.357	Barab
her fathers sudden fall/Has humbled her and brought her downe	Jew	1.2.367	Mthias
sudden fall/Has humbled her and brought her downe to this:	Jew	1.2.368	Mthias
As had you seene her 'twould have mov'd your heart,	Jew	1.2.385	Mthias
'Twere time well spent to goe and visit her:	Jew	1.2.389	Lodowk
Raven that tolls/The sicke mans passeport in her hollow beake,	Jew	2.1.2	Barab
of the silent night/Doth shake contagion from her sable wings;	Jew	2.1.4	Barab
That I may hover with her in the Ayre,	Jew	2.1.62	Barab
Singing ore these, as she does ore her young.	Jew	2.1.63	Barab

HER (cont.)

but e're he shall have her	Jew	2.3.51	Barab
I'le sacrifice her on a pile of wood.	Jew	2.3.52	Barab
When you have brought her home, come to my house;	Jew	2.3.148	Barab
And she vowes lcve to him, and hee to her.	Jew	2.3.247	Barab
He sends her letters, bracelets, jewels, rings.	Jew	2.3.259	Barab
And when he comes, she lockes her selfe up fast;	Jew	2.3.262	Barab
Yet through the key-hole will he talke to her,	Jew	2.3.263	Barab
Doth she not with her smiling answer you?	Jew	2.3.286	Barab
And yet I'le give her many a golden crosse/With Christian	Jew	2.3.296	Barab
'Tis not thy wealth, but her that I esteeme,	Jew	2.3.298	Lodowk
And mine you have, yet let me talke to her;	Jew	2.3.300	Barab
I have intreated her, and she will grant.	Jew	2.3.314	Barab
Stay her,--but let her not speake one word more.	Jew	2.3.323	Barab
Trouble her not, sweet Lodowicke depart:	Jew	2.3.327	Barab
Nay, if you will, stay till she comes her selfe.	Jew	2.3.352	Barab
Yes, you shall have him: Goe put her in.	Jew	2.3.362	Barab
I, I'le put her in.	Jew	2.3.363	Ithimr
I know she is a Curtezane by her attire:	Jew	3.1.27	P Ithimr
now Abigall shall see/Whether Mathias holds her deare or no.	Jew	3.2.2	Mthias
from hence/Ne're shall she grieve me more with her disgrace;	Jew	3.4.29	Barab
Ithimore, intreat not for her, I am mov'd,	Jew	3.4.35	Barab
master, wil you poison her with a messe of rice [porredge]?	Jew	3.4.64	P Ithimr
make her round and plump, and batten more then you are aware.	Jew	3.4.65	P Ithimr
As fatall be it to her as the draught/Of which great Alexander	Jew	3.4.96	Barab
And with her let it worke like Borgias wine,	Jew	3.4.98	Barab
and invenome her/That like a fiend hath left her father thus.	Jew	3.4.104	Barab
and invenome her/That like a fiend hath left her father thus.	Jew	3.4.105	Barab
I'le to her lodging; hereabouts she lyes.	Jew	3.6.6	1Fryar
Oh speake nct of her, then I dye with griefe.	Jew	4.1.36	Barab
For he that shriv'd her is within my house.	Jew	4.1.115	Barab
with his lips; the effect was, that I should come to her house.	Jew	4.2.32	P Ithimr
here's her house, and here she comes, and now would I were	Jew	4.2.35	P Ithimr
and now would I were gone, I am not worthy to looke upon her.	Jew	4.2.36	P Ithimr
But came it freely, did the Cow give down her milk freely?	Jew	4.2.102	P Ithimr
Away with her, she is a Curtezane.	Jew	5.1.8	Govnr
My Lord, the Curtezane and her man are dead;	Jew	5.1.50	1Offcr
Be gone my freend, present them to her straite.	P 82	2.25	Guise
Rifling the bowels of her treasurie,	P 135	2.78	Guise
Too late it is my Lord if that be true/To blame her highnes,	P 182	3.17	QnMarg
but I hope it be/Only some naturall passion makes her sicke.	P 183	3.18	QnMarg
That I with her may dye and live againe.	P 190	3.25	Navrre
Come my Lords let us beare her body hence,	P 195	3.30	Admral
For Katherine must have her will in France:	P 520	9.39	QnMoth
Your Majestie her rightfull Lord and Soveraigne.	P 583	11.48	Pleshe
Her eyes and lookes sow'd seeds of perjury,	P 695	13.39	Guise
Shall buy her love even with his dearest bloud.	P 697	13.41	Guise
Plaies with her goary coulours of revenge,	P 719	14.22	Navrre
And her chosen freend?	P 756	15.14	King
If that be all, the next time that I meet her,	P 781	15.39	Mugern
Ile make her shake off love with her heeles.	P 782	15.40	Mugern
And let her droup, my heart is light enough.	P1064	19.134	King
And let her greeve her heart out if she will.	P1080	19.150	King
She cast her hatefull stomack to the earth.	P1154	22.16	King
And give her warning of her trecherous foes.	P1190	22.52	King
Tell her for all this that I hope to live,	P1196	22.58	King
And tell her Henry dyes her faithfull freend.	P1244	22.106	King
And dart her plumes, thinking to pierce my brest,	Edw	1.1.41	Gavstn
Speake not unto her, let her droope and pine.	Edw	1.4.162	Edward
Sits wringing of her hands, and beats her brest.	Edw	1.4.188	Lncstr
The king I feare hath ill intreated her.	Edw	1.4.189	Warwck
Then let her live abandond and forlorne.	Edw	1.4.298	Queene
It is about her lover Gaveston.	Edw	2.1.22	Spencr
And that his banishment had changd her minde.	Edw	2.1.26	Baldck
Then hope I by her meanes to be preferd,	Edw	2.1.29	Baldck
Having read unto her since she was a childe.	Edw	2.1.30	Baldck
Desirde her more, and waxt outragious,	Edw	2.2.55	Edward
Complaines, that thou hast left her all forlorne.	Edw	2.2.173	Lncstr
My lord, dissemble with her, speake her faire.	Edw	2.2.229	Gavstn
Whose pining heart, her inward sighes have blasted,	Edw	2.4.24	Queene
France/Makes friends, to crosse the seas with her yong sonne,	Edw	3.1.270	Spencr
That Isabell shall make her plaints in vaine,	Edw	3.1.278	Levune
And Fraunce shall be obdurat with her teares.	Edw	3.1.279	Levune
distressed Queene his sister heere,/Go you with her to Henolt:	Edw	4.2.64	SrJohn
queene in peace may reposesse/Her dignities and honors,	Edw	4.4.25	Mortmr
Her friends doe multiply and yours doe fayle,	Edw	4.5.2	Spencr
Tis not in her controulment, nor in ours,	Edw	4.6.35	Mortmr
God save Queene Isabell, and her princely sonne.	Edw	4.6.46	Rice
Shall do good service to her Majestie,	Edw	4.6.74	Mortmr
When for her sake I ran at tilt in Fraunce,	Edw	5.5.69	Edward
I doe not thinke her so unnaturall.	Edw	5.6.76	King
Awaye with her, her wordes inforce these teares,	Edw	5.6.85	King
And I shall pitie her if she speake againe.	Edw	5.6.86	King
And dyms the Welkin, with her pitchy breathe:	F 232	1.3.4	Faust
Be it to make the Moone drop from her Sphere,	F 266	1.3.38	Faust
<A plague on her for a hote whore>.	F 534	(HC261)A	P Faust
Sometimes, like a Perriwig, I sit upon her Brow:	F 666	2.2.115	P Pride
next, like a Neckelace I hang about her Necke:	F 667	2.2.116	P Pride
I kisse her [lippes]; And then turning my selfe to a wrought	F 667	2.2.116	P Pride
Gentlewoman, her name was <mistress> Margery March-beere:	F 699	2.2.148	P Glutny
thought you did not sneake up and downe after her for nothing.	F 743	2.3.22	P Dick
That threates the starres with her aspiring top,	F 796	3.1.18	Faust
Had on her necke a little wart, or mole;	F1267	4.1.113	Emper

HER (cont.)

Then when sir Paris crost the seas with <for> her,	F1694	5.1.21	Faust
Too simple is my wit to tell her worth <praise>,/Whom all the	F1697	5.1.24	2Schol
Her lips sucke <suckes> forth my soule, see where it flies.	F1771	5.1.98	Faust
she for her private study, shee's borne to beare with me,	F App	p.233 16 P	Robin
then turn her and wind hir to thy owne use, as often as thou	F App	p.234 27 P	Robin
this Lady while she liv'd had a wart or moale in her necke,	F App	p.238 61 P	Emper
Undaunted though her former guide be chang'd.	Lucan, First Booke	50	
Bare downe to hell her sonne, the pledge of peace,	Lucan, First Booke	113	
And on her Turret-bearing head disperst,	Lucan, First Booke	190	
battailes fought with prosperous successe/May bring her downe,	Lucan, First Booke	286	
successe/May bring her downe, and with her all the world;	Lucan, First Booke	286	
having fild/Her meeting hornes to match her brothers light,	Lucan, First Booke	536	
high; but headlong pitcht/Her burning head on bending Hespery.	Lucan, First Booke	545	
Shaking her snakie haire and crooked pine/With flaming toppe,	Lucan, First Booke	571	
Against her kind (the barren Mules loth'd issue)/To be cut	Lucan, First Booke	589	
Her white necke hid with tresses hanging downe,	Ovid's Elegies	1.5.10	
I snatcht her gowne:	Ovid's Elegies	1.5.13	
Betrayde her selfe, and yeelded at the last.	Ovid's Elegies	1.5.16	
Not one wen in her bodie could I spie,	Ovid's Elegies	1.5.18	
How apt her breasts were to be prest by me,	Ovid's Elegies	1.5.20	
How smoothe a bellie, under her waste sawe I,	Ovid's Elegies	1.5.21	
I clinged her naked bodie, downe she fell,	Ovid's Elegies	1.5.24	
Now frosty night her flight beginnes to take,	Ovid's Elegies	1.6.65	
Could I therefore her comely tresses teare?	Ovid's Elegies	1.7.11	
Yet was she graced with her ruffled hayre.	Ovid's Elegies	1.7.12	
when she bewayles/Her perjur'd Theseus flying vowes and sayles,	Ovid's Elegies	1.7.16	
She nothing said, pale feare her tongue had tyed.	Ovid's Elegies	1.7.20	
But secretlie her lockes with checks did trounce mee,	Ovid's Elegies	1.7.21	
Her teares, she silent, guilty did pronounce me.	Ovid's Elegies	1.7.22	
lockes spred/On her white necke but for hurt cheekes be led.	Ovid's Elegies	1.7.40	
Meeter it were her lips were blewe with kissing/And on her	Ovid's Elegies	1.7.41	
with kissing/And on her necke a wantons marke not missing.	Ovid's Elegies	1.7.42	
Nor shamefully her coate pull ore her crowne,	Ovid's Elegies	1.7.47	
Which to her wast her girdle still kept downe.	Ovid's Elegies	1.7.48	
But cruelly her tresses having rent,	Ovid's Elegies	1.7.49	
My nayles to scratch her lovely cheekes I bent.	Ovid's Elegies	1.7.50	
her bloodlesse white lookes shewed/Like marble from the Parian	Ovid's Elegies	1.7.51	
Her halfe dead joynts, and trembling limmes I sawe,	Ovid's Elegies	1.7.53	
And downe her cheekes, the trickling teares did flow,	Ovid's Elegies	1.7.57	
My bloud, the teares were that from her descended.	Ovid's Elegies	1.7.60	
Before her feete thrice prostrate downe I fell,	Ovid's Elegies	1.7.61	
Her name comes from the thing:	Ovid's Elegies	1.8.3	
Her I suspect among nights spirits to fly,	Ovid's Elegies	1.8.13	
And her old body in birdes plumes to lie.	Ovid's Elegies	1.8.14	
Fame saith as I suspect, and in her eyes/Two eye-balles shine,	Ovid's Elegies	1.8.15	
Nor doth her tongue want harmefull eloquence.	Ovid's Elegies	1.8.20	
By chaunce I heard her talke, these words she sayd/While	Ovid's Elegies	1.8.21	
And Venus rules in her Aeneas Citty.	Ovid's Elegies	1.8.42	
Or, but for bashfulnesse her selfe would crave.	Ovid's Elegies	1.8.44	
Penelope in bowes her youths strength tride,	Ovid's Elegies	1.8.47	
But her bleare eyes, balde scalpes [thin] <thine> hoary flieces	Ovid's Elegies	1.8.111	
Her valiant lover followes without end.	Ovid's Elegies	1.9.10	
And to her tentes wild me my selfe addresse.	Ovid's Elegies	1.9.44	
the drie fields strayed/When on her head a water pitcher laied.	Ovid's Elegies	1.10.6	
each mans mony/And seekes vild wealth by selling of her Cony,	Ovid's Elegies	1.10.22	
Farmes out her-self on nights for what she can.	Ovid's Elegies	1.10.30	
Making her joy according to her hire.	Ovid's Elegies	1.10.32	
The sonne slew her, that forth to meete him went,	Ovid's Elegies	1.10.51	
give her my writ/But see that forth-with shee peruseth it.	Ovid's Elegies	1.11.15	
I charge thee marke her eyes and front in reading,	Ovid's Elegies	1.11.17	
Straight being read, will her to write much backe,	Ovid's Elegies	1.11.19	
Let her make verses, and some blotted letter/On the last edge	Ovid's Elegies	1.11.21	
What neede she [tyre] <try> her hand to hold the quill,	Ovid's Elegies	1.11.23	
Subscribing that to her I consecrate/My faithfull tables being	Ovid's Elegies	1.11.27	
Now on <ore> the sea from her old love comes shee,	Ovid's Elegies	1.13.1	
Now in her tender armes I sweetly bide,	Ovid's Elegies	1.13.5	
foote drawes out/Fastning her light web some old beame about.	Ovid's Elegies	1.14.8	
Snatching the combe, to beate the wench out drive <drave> her.	Ovid's Elegies	1.14.18	
Oft in the morne her haires not yet digested,	Ovid's Elegies	1.14.19	
painted stands/All naked holding in her wave-moist hands.	Ovid's Elegies	1.14.34	
Alas she almost weepes, and her white cheekes,	Ovid's Elegies	1.14.51	
She holds, and viewes her old lockes in her lappe,	Ovid's Elegies	1.14.53	
My wench her dore shut, Joves affares I left,	Ovid's Elegies	2.1.17	
Her shut gates greater lightning then thyne brought.	Ovid's Elegies	2.1.20	
Shee pleas'd me, soone I sent, and did her woo,	Ovid's Elegies	2.2.5	
Her trembling hand writ back she might not doo.	Ovid's Elegies	2.2.6	
Nor is her husband wise, what needes defence/When	Ovid's Elegies	2.2.11	
fire/And [thinke] <thinkes> her chast whom many doe desire.	Ovid's Elegies	2.2.14	
Which giving her, she may give thee againe.	Ovid's Elegies	2.2.16	
Wilt thou her fault learne, she may make thee tremble,	Ovid's Elegies	2.2.17	
Thinke when she reades, her mother letters sent her,	Ovid's Elegies	2.2.19	
Let him goe see her though she doe not languish/And then report	Ovid's Elegies	2.2.21	
doe not languish/And then report her sicke and full of anguish.	Ovid's Elegies	2.2.22	
Knowing her scapes thine honour shall encrease,	Ovid's Elegies	2.2.27	
When most her husband bends the browes and frownes,	Ovid's Elegies	2.2.33	
His fauning wench with her desire he crownes.	Ovid's Elegies	2.2.34	
But yet sometimes to chide thee let her fall/Counterfet teares:	Ovid's Elegies	2.2.35	
She safe by favour of her judge doth rest.	Ovid's Elegies	2.2.56	
Though himselfe see; heele credit her denyall,	Ovid's Elegies	2.2.57	
Please her, her hate makes others thee abhorre,	Ovid's Elegies	2.3.11	
Shee may deceive thee, though thou her protect,	Ovid's Elegies	2.3.15	
Though her sowre looks a Sabines browe resemble,	Ovid's Elegies	2.4.15	

HER (cont.)

If she be learned, then for her skill I crave her,	Ovid's Elegies	2.4.17
If not, because shees simple I would have her.	Ovid's Elegies	2.4.18
Yet would I lie with her if that I might.	Ovid's Elegies	2.4.22
To quaver on her lippes even in her song,	Ovid's Elegies	2.4.26
And she <her> I like that with a majestie,	Ovid's Elegies	2.4.29
Foldes up her armes, and makes low curtesie.	Ovid's Elegies	2.4.30
[Is she attired, then shew her graces best].	Ovid's Elegies	2.4.38
If her white necke be shadowde with blacke haire,	Ovid's Elegies	2.4.41
This for her looks, that for her woman-hood:	Ovid's Elegies	2.4.46
doth favour/That seekes the conquest by her loose behaviour.	Ovid's Elegies	2.5.12
None such the sister gives her brother grave,	Ovid's Elegies	2.5.25
But Venus often to her Mars such brought.	Ovid's Elegies	2.5.28
A scarlet blush her guilty face arayed.	Ovid's Elegies	2.5.34
To these, or some of these like was her colour,	Ovid's Elegies	2.5.41
By chaunce her beauty never shined fuller.	Ovid's Elegies	2.5.42
She viewed the earth: the earth to viewe, beseem'd her.	Ovid's Elegies	2.5.43
She looked sad: sad, comely I esteem'd her.	Ovid's Elegies	2.5.44
Even kembed as they were, her lockes to rend,	Ovid's Elegies	2.5.45
And scratch her faire soft cheekes I did intend.	Ovid's Elegies	2.5.46
Seeing her face, mine upreard armes discended,	Ovid's Elegies	2.5.47
With her owne armor was my wench defended.	Ovid's Elegies	2.5.48
Lay her whole tongue hid, mine in hers she dips.	Ovid's Elegies	2.5.58
Is dead, al-fowles her exequies frequent.	Ovid's Elegies	2.6.2
But what availde this faith? her rarest hue?	Ovid's Elegies	2.6.17
A grave her bones hides, on her corps great <small> grave,	Ovid's Elegies	2.6.59
Is charg'd to violate her mistresse bed.	Ovid's Elegies	2.7.18
And for her skill to thee a gratefull maide.	Ovid's Elegies	2.7.24
Should I sollicit her that is so just:	Ovid's Elegies	2.7.25
To take repulse, and cause her shew my lust?	Ovid's Elegies	2.7.26
But when on thee her angry eyes did rush,	Ovid's Elegies	2.8.15
Rome if her strength the huge world had not fild,	Ovid's Elegies	2.9.17
With strawie cabins now her courts should build.	Ovid's Elegies	2.9.18
Now let her flatter me, now chide me hard,	Ovid's Elegies	2.9.45
Let [me] <her> enjoy [her] <me> oft, oft be debard.	Ovid's Elegies	2.9.46
Nor want I strength, but weight to presse her with:	Ovid's Elegies	2.10.24
The crooked Barque hath her swift sailes displayd.	Ovid's Elegies	2.11.24
Yet Galatea favour thou her ship.	Ovid's Elegies	2.11.34
And say it brings her that preserveth me;	Ovid's Elegies	2.11.44
She whom her husband, guard, and gate as foes,	Ovid's Elegies	2.12.3
Least Arte should winne her, firmely did inclose.	Ovid's Elegies	2.12.4
I guide and souldiour wunne the field and weare her,	Ovid's Elegies	2.12.13
While rashly her wombes burthen she casts out,	Ovid's Elegies	2.13.1
Wearie Corinna hath her life in doubt.	Ovid's Elegies	2.13.2
Worthy she is, thou shouldst in mercy save her.	Ovid's Elegies	2.13.22
If watry Thetis had her childe fordone?	Ovid's Elegies	2.14.14
In swelling wombe her twinnes had Ilia kilde?	Ovid's Elegies	2.14.15
Had Venus spoilde her bellies Troyane fruite,	Ovid's Elegies	2.14.17
Nor dares the Lyonesse her young whelpes kill.	Ovid's Elegies	2.14.36
Oft dyes she that her paunch-wrapt child hath slaine.	Ovid's Elegies	2.14.38
And who ere see her, worthily lament.	Ovid's Elegies	2.14.40
Forgive her gratious Gods this one delict,	Ovid's Elegies	2.14.43
Be welcome to her, gladly let her take thee,	Ovid's Elegies	2.15.3
And her small joynts incircling round hoope make thee.	Ovid's Elegies	2.15.4
Fit her so well, as she is fit for me:	Ovid's Elegies	2.15.5
And of just compasse for her knuckles bee.	Ovid's Elegies	2.15.6
And hide thy left hand underneath her lappe.	Ovid's Elegies	2.15.12
And in her bosome strangely fall at last.	Ovid's Elegies	2.15.14
Then I, that I may seale her privy leaves,	Ovid's Elegies	2.15.15
But in lesse compasse her small fingers knit.	Ovid's Elegies	2.15.20
Let her my faith with thee given understand.	Ovid's Elegies	2.15.28
With her I durst the Lybian Syrtes breake through,	Ovid's Elegies	2.16.21
Aye me why is it knowne to her so well?	Ovid's Elegies	2.17.8
But by her glasse disdainefull pride she learnes,	Ovid's Elegies	2.17.9
Nor she her selfe but first trim'd up discernes.	Ovid's Elegies	2.17.10
I know a wench reports her selfe Corinne,	Ovid's Elegies	2.17.29
Then wreathes about my necke her winding armes,	Ovid's Elegies	2.18.9
Or Phillis teares that her [Demophoon] <Domoophon> misses,/What	Ovid's Elegies	2.18.22
And what poore Dido with her drawne sword sharpe,	Ovid's Elegies	2.18.25
Doth say, with her that lov'd the Aonian harpe.	Ovid's Elegies	2.18.26
Sappho her vowed harpe laies at Phoebus feete.	Ovid's Elegies	2.18.34
With Laodameia mate to her dead Lord.	Ovid's Elegies	2.18.38
Keepe her for me, my more desire to breede.	Ovid's Elegies	2.19.2
Ah often, that her [hale] <haole> head aked, she lying,	Ovid's Elegies	2.19.11
Jove liked her better then he did before.	Ovid's Elegies	2.19.30
Her lover let her mocke, that long will raigne,	Ovid's Elegies	2.19.33
Now I forewarne, unlesse to keepe her stronger,	Ovid's Elegies	2.19.47
hoping time would beate thee/To guard her well, that well I	Ovid's Elegies	2.19.50
And one, I thinke, was longer, of her feete.	Ovid's Elegies	3.1.8
By her footes blemish greater grace she tooke.	Ovid's Elegies	3.1.10
Sterne was her front, her [cloake] <looke> on ground did lie.	Ovid's Elegies	3.1.12
Her left hand held abroad a regal scepter,	Ovid's Elegies	3.1.13
The Lydian buskin [in] fit [paces] <places> kept her.	Ovid's Elegies	3.1.14
This saied, she mov'd her buskins gaily varnisht,	Ovid's Elegies	3.1.31
And seaven [times] <time> shooke her head with thicke locks	Ovid's Elegies	3.1.32
Erre I? or mirtle in her right hand lies.	Ovid's Elegies	3.1.34
By me Corinna learnes, cousening her guard,	Ovid's Elegies	3.1.49
To move her feete unheard in [setting] <sitting> downe.	Ovid's Elegies	3.1.52
The maide to hide me in her bosome let not.	Ovid's Elegies	3.1.56
What gift with me was on her birth day sent,	Ovid's Elegies	3.1.57
But cruelly by her was drown'd and rent.	Ovid's Elegies	3.1.58
Yet he attain'd by her support to have her,	Ovid's Elegies	3.2.17
But spare my wench thou at her right hand seated,	Ovid's Elegies	3.2.21

HER (cont.)

For shame presse not her backe with thy hard knee.	Ovid's Elegies	3.2.24
Which lie hid under her thinne veile supprest.	Ovid's Elegies	3.2.36
While thus I speake, blacke dust her white robes ray:	Ovid's Elegies	3.2.41
Foule dust, from her faire body, go away.	Ovid's Elegies	3.2.42
Greater then her, by her leave th'art, Ile say.	Ovid's Elegies	3.2.60
her good wishes fade,/Let with strong hand the reine to bend be	Ovid's Elegies	3.2.71
My mistris hath her wish, my wish remaine:	Ovid's Elegies	3.2.81
her selfe she hath forswore,/And yet remaines the face she had	Ovid's Elegies	3.3.1
How long her lockes were, ere her oath she tooke:	Ovid's Elegies	3.3.3
So long they be, since she her faith forsooke.	Ovid's Elegies	3.3.4
Now shine her lookes pure white and red betwixt.	Ovid's Elegies	3.3.6
Her foote was small: her footes forme is most fit:	Ovid's Elegies	3.3.7
By her eyes I remember late she swore,	Ovid's Elegies	3.3.13
For her ill-beautious Mother judgd to slaughter?	Ovid's Elegies	3.3.18
But by my paine to purge her perjuries,	Ovid's Elegies	3.3.21
Her owne request to her owne torment turnd.	Ovid's Elegies	3.3.38
But when her lover came, had she drawne backe,	Ovid's Elegies	3.3.39
Though thou her body guard, her minde is staind:	Ovid's Elegies	3.4.5
Nor canst by watching keepe her minde from sinne.	Ovid's Elegies	3.4.7
Penelope, though no watch look'd unto her,	Ovid's Elegies	3.4.23
Nor doth her face please, but her husbands love;	Ovid's Elegies	3.4.27
Thy feare is, then her body, valued more.	Ovid's Elegies	3.4.30
What day and night to travaile in her quest?	Ovid's Elegies	3.5.10
Whom Ilia pleasd, though in her lookes griefe reveld,	Ovid's Elegies	3.5.47
Her cheekes were scratcht, her goodly haires discheveld.	Ovid's Elegies	3.5.48
She wailing Mars sinne, and her uncles crime,	Ovid's Elegies	3.5.49
Her, from his swift waves, the bold floud perceav'd,	Ovid's Elegies	3.5.51
shee her modest eyes held downe,/Her wofull bosome a warme	Ovid's Elegies	3.5.67
Her wofull bosome a warme shower did drowne.	Ovid's Elegies	3.5.68
Yet rending with enraged thumbe her tresses,	Ovid's Elegies	3.5.71
Her trembling mouth these unmeete sounds expresses.	Ovid's Elegies	3.5.72
her coate hood-winckt her fearefull eyes,/And into water	Ovid's Elegies	3.5.79
Tis said the slippery streame held up her brest,	Ovid's Elegies	3.5.81
And kindly gave her, what she liked best.	Ovid's Elegies	3.5.82
Either she was foule, or her attire was bad,	Ovid's Elegies	3.6.1
Idly I lay with her, as if I lovde <her> not,	Ovid's Elegies	3.6.3
She on my necke her Ivorie armes did throw,	Ovid's Elegies	3.6.7
That were as white as is <Her armes farre whiter, then> the	Ovid's Elegies	3.6.8
And eagerlie she kist me with her tongue,	Ovid's Elegies	3.6.9
And under mine her wanton thigh she flong,	Ovid's Elegies	3.6.10
Or one that with her tender brother lies,	Ovid's Elegies	3.6.22
My idle thoughts delighted her no more,	Ovid's Elegies	3.6.39
Yet might her touch make youthfull Pilius fire,	Ovid's Elegies	3.6.41
Even her I had, and she had me in vaine,	Ovid's Elegies	3.6.43
To kisse, I kisse, to lie with her shee let me.	Ovid's Elegies	3.6.48
To take it in her hand and play with it.	Ovid's Elegies	3.6.74
But still droupt downe, regarding not her hand,	Ovid's Elegies	3.6.76
With that her loose gowne on, from me she cast her,	Ovid's Elegies	3.6.81
In skipping out her naked feete much grac'd her.	Ovid's Elegies	3.6.82
And least her maide should know of this disgrace,	Ovid's Elegies	3.6.83
She prais'd me, yet the gate shutt fast upon her,	Ovid's Elegies	3.7.7
Till then, rough was her father, she severe,	Ovid's Elegies	3.7.31
She held her lap ope to receive the same.	Ovid's Elegies	3.7.34
One [her] <she> commands, who many things can give.	Ovid's Elegies	3.7.62
Eryx bright Empresse turnd her lookes aside,	Ovid's Elegies	3.8.45
Nor did thy ashes her last offrings lose.	Ovid's Elegies	3.8.50
Part of her sorrowe heere thy sister bearing,	Ovid's Elegies	3.8.51
Comes forth her [unkeembd] <unkeembe> locks a sunder tearing.	Ovid's Elegies	3.8.52
Who thinkes her to be glad at lovers smart,	Ovid's Elegies	3.9.15
A clowne, nor no love from her warme brest yeelds.	Ovid's Elegies	3.9.18
things feigne)/Crete proud that Jove her nourcery maintaine.	Ovid's Elegies	3.9.20
She sawe, and as her marrowe tooke the flame,	Ovid's Elegies	3.9.27
Her long haires eare-wrought garland fell away.	Ovid's Elegies	3.9.36
What should I tell her vaine tongues filthy lyes,	Ovid's Elegies	3.10.21
What secret becks in banquets with her youths,	Ovid's Elegies	3.10.23
Hearing her to be sicke, I thether ranne,	Ovid's Elegies	3.10.25
I flie her lust, but follow beauties creature;	Ovid's Elegies	3.10.37
I loath her manners, love her bodies feature.	Ovid's Elegies	3.10.38
Her deeds gaine hate, her face entreateth love:	Ovid's Elegies	3.10.43
Ah, she doth more worth then her vices prove.	Ovid's Elegies	3.10.44
'Tis so: by my witte her abuse is growne.	Ovid's Elegies	3.11.8
And justly: for her praise why did I tell?	Ovid's Elegies	3.11.9
The bawde I play, lovers to her I guide:	Ovid's Elegies	3.11.11
Her gate by my hands is set open wide.	Ovid's Elegies	3.11.12
Scylla by us her fathers rich haire steales,	Ovid's Elegies	3.11.21
Bird-changed Progne doth her Itys teare.	Ovid's Elegies	3.11.32
Heav'n starre Electra that bewaild her sisters?	Ovid's Elegies	3.11.37
And she her vestall virgin Priests doth follow.	Ovid's Elegies	3.12.30
Whom young Apollo courted for her haire,	Hero and Leander	1.6
The outside of her garments were of lawne,	Hero and Leander	1.9
Her wide sleeves greene, and bordered with a grove,	Hero and Leander	1.11
Where Venus in her naked glory strove,	Hero and Leander	1.12
Of proud Adonis that before her lies.	Hero and Leander	1.14
Her kirtle blew, whereon was many a staine,	Hero and Leander	1.15
Upon her head she ware a myrtle wreath,	Hero and Leander	1.17
From whence her vaile reacht to the ground beneath.	Hero and Leander	1.18
Her vaile was artificiall flowers and leaves,	Hero and Leander	1.19
When t'was the odour which her breath foorth cast.	Hero and Leander	1.22
About her necke hung chaines of peble stone,	Hero and Leander	1.25
Which lightned by her necke, like Diamonds shone.	Hero and Leander	1.26
for neither sunne nor wind/Would burne or parch her hands,	Hero and Leander	1.28
sunne nor wind/Would burne or parch her hands, but to her mind,	Hero and Leander	1.28

HER (cont.)

Those with sweet water oft her handmaid fils,	Hero and Leander	1.35
Some say, for her the fairest Cupid pyn'd,	Hero and Leander	1.37
And looking in her face, was strooken blind.	Hero and Leander	1.38
And oftentimes into her bosome flew,	Hero and Leander	1.41
About her naked necke his bare armes threw.	Hero and Leander	1.42
And laid his childish head upon her brest,	Hero and Leander	1.43
Because she tooke more from her than she left,	Hero and Leander	1.47
And of such wondrous beautie her bereft:	Hero and Leander	1.48
Therefore in signe her treasure suffred wracke,	Hero and Leander	1.49
Faire Cinthia wisht, his armes might be her spheare,	Hero and Leander	1.59
Greefe makes her pale, because she mooves not there.	Hero and Leander	1.60
So was her beautie to the standers by.	Hero and Leander	1.106
(When yawning dragons draw her thirling carre,	Hero and Leander	1.108
Than she the hearts of those that neere her stood.	Hero and Leander	1.112
So ran the people foorth to gaze upon her,	Hero and Leander	1.117
And all that view'd her, were enamour'd on her.	Hero and Leander	1.118
So at her presence all surpris'd and tooken,	Hero and Leander	1.122
Await the sentence of her scornefull eies:	Hero and Leander	1.123
Pyn'd as they went, and thinking on her died.	Hero and Leander	1.130
Went Hero thorow Sestos, from her tower/To Venus temple, [where]	Hero and Leander	1.132
Vaild to the ground, vailing her eie-lids close,	Hero and Leander	1.159
He kneel'd, but unto her devoutly praid;	Hero and Leander	1.177
Chast Hero to her selfe thus softly said:	Hero and Leander	1.178
He toucht her hand, in touching it she trembled,	Hero and Leander	1.183
Heav'd up her head, and halfe the world upon,	Hero and Leander	1.190
With cheerefull hope thus he accosted her.	Hero and Leander	1.198
footsteps bending)/Doth testifie that you exceed her farre,	Hero and Leander	1.211
Why should you worship her?	Hero and Leander	1.213
her you surpasse,/As much as sparkling Diamonds flaring glasse.	Hero and Leander	1.213
of liquid pearle, which downe her face/Made milk-white paths,	Hero and Leander	1.297
hast sworne/To rob her name and honour, and thereby/Commit'st a	Hero and Leander	1.305
Even sacrilege against her Deitie,	Hero and Leander	1.307
And her in humble manner thus beseech.	Hero and Leander	1.314
Yet for her sake whom you have vow'd to serve,	Hero and Leander	1.316
Heroes lookes yeelded, but her words made warre,	Hero and Leander	1.331
And would be thought to graunt against her will.	Hero and Leander	1.336
With that Leander stoopt, to have imbrac'd her,	Hero and Leander	1.341
But from his spreading armes away she cast her,	Hero and Leander	1.342
Come thither; As she spake this, her toong tript,	Hero and Leander	1.357
For unawares (Come thither) from her slipt,	Hero and Leander	1.358
And sodainly her former colour chang'd,	Hero and Leander	1.359
And here and there her eies through anger rang'd.	Hero and Leander	1.360
all, and everie part/Strove to resist the motions of her hart.	Hero and Leander	1.364
Cupid beats downe her praiers with his wings,	Hero and Leander	1.369
Her vowes above the emptie aire he flings:	Hero and Leander	1.370
And as she wept, her teares to pearle he turn'd,	Hero and Leander	1.375
And wound them on his arme, and for her mourn'd.	Hero and Leander	1.376
Her breath as fragrant as the morning rose,	Hero and Leander	1.391
Her mind pure, and her toong untaught to glose.	Hero and Leander	1.392
And silver tincture of her cheekes, that drew/The love of	Hero and Leander	1.396
On her, this god/Enamoured was, and with his snakie rod,	Hero and Leander	1.397
Did charme her nimble feet, and made her stay,	Hero and Leander	1.399
And with smooth speech, her fancie to assay,	Hero and Leander	1.402
Till in his twining armes he lockt her fast,	Hero and Leander	1.403
As sheap-heards do, her on the ground hee layd,	Hero and Leander	1.405
Whose only dower was her chastitie,	Hero and Leander	1.412
he stayd his furie, and began/To give her leave to rise:	Hero and Leander	1.416
As she to heare his tale, left off her running.	Hero and Leander	1.418
And knowing Hermes courted her, was glad/That she such	Hero and Leander	1.421
Impos'd upon her lover such a taske,	Hero and Leander	1.429
He kist her, and breath'd life into her lips,	Hero and Leander	2.3
So on she goes, and in her idle flight,	Hero and Leander	2.10
Her painted fanne of curled plumes let fall,	Hero and Leander	2.11
But stayd, and after her a letter sent.	Hero and Leander	2.14
And therefore to her tower he got by stealth.	Hero and Leander	2.18
And she her selfe before the pointed time,	Hero and Leander	2.20
And turn'd aside, and to her selfe lamented.	Hero and Leander	2.34
As if her name and honour had beene wrong'd,	Hero and Leander	2.35
I, and shee wisht, albeit not from her hart,	Hero and Leander	2.37
That he would leave her turret and depart.	Hero and Leander	2.38
Fearing her owne thoughts made her to be hated.	Hero and Leander	2.44
And like light Salmacis, her body throes/Upon his bosome, where	Hero and Leander	2.46
She offers up her selfe a sacrifice,	Hero and Leander	2.48
Now he her favour and good will had wone.	Hero and Leander	2.54
And seeming lavish, sav'de her maydenhead.	Hero and Leander	2.76
Now had the morne espy'de her lovers steeds,	Hero and Leander	2.87
Whereat she starts, puts on her purple weeds,	Hero and Leander	2.88
All headlong throwes her selfe the clouds among/And now Leander	Hero and Leander	2.90
Imbrast her sodainly, tooke leave, and kist,	Hero and Leander	2.92
Wherewith she wreath'd her largely spreading heare,	Hero and Leander	2.107
Whose waight consists in nothing but her name,	Hero and Leander	2.114
That him from her unjustly did detaine.	Hero and Leander	2.122
Where having spy'de her tower, long star'd he on't,	Hero and Leander	2.149
She stayd not for her robes, but straight arose,	Hero and Leander	2.235
And ran into the darke her selfe to hide,	Hero and Leander	2.239
Unto her was he led, or rather drawne,	Hero and Leander	2.241
And seeking refuge, slipt into her bed.	Hero and Leander	2.244
And in her luke-warme place Leander lay.	Hero and Leander	2.254
His hands he cast upon her like a snare,	Hero and Leander	2.259
Like chast Diana, when Acteon spyde her,	Hero and Leander	2.261
Being sodainly betraide, dyv'd downe to hide her.	Hero and Leander	2.262
And as her silver body downeward went,	Hero and Leander	2.263

HER (cont.)				
With both her hands she made the bed a tent,	Hero and Leander	2.264		
And in her owne mind thought her selfe secure,	Hero and Leander	2.265		
And now she lets him whisper in her eare,	Hero and Leander	2.267		
Wherein Leander on her quivering brest,	Hero and Leander	2.279		
Inclos'd her in his armes and kist her to.	Hero and Leander	2.282		
And everie kisse to her was as a charme,	Hero and Leander	2.283		
Foorth plungeth, and oft flutters with her wing,	Hero and Leander	2.290		
Treason was in her thought,/And cunningly to yeeld her selfe	Hero and Leander	2.293		
And cunningly to yeeld her selfe she sought.	Hero and Leander	2.294		
For much it greev'd her that the bright day-light,	Hero and Leander	2.303		
Againe she knew not how to frame her looke,	Hero and Leander	2.307		
But as her naked feet were whipping out,	Hero and Leander	2.313		
He on the suddaine cling'd her so about,	Hero and Leander	2.314		
And from her countenance behold ye might,	Hero and Leander	2.318		
And her all naked to his sight displayd.	Hero and Leander	2.324		
Dang'd downe to hell her loathsome carriage.	Hero and Leander	2.334		
HERALD (See also HERRALD)				
Aeneas stay, Joves Herald bids thee stay.	Dido	5.1.24		Hermes
HERALDRIE				
and my gentrie/Is fetcht from Oxford, not from Heraldrie.	Edw	2.2.244		Baldck
HERALDS				
Now send our Heralds to defie the King,	Edw	2.2.110		Lncstr
HERBE (See also HEARBES, HEARBS)				
being strucke/Runnes to an herbe that closeth up the wounds,	Edw	5.1.10		Edward
HERBES				
No charmed herbes of any harlot skathd thee,	Ovid's Elegies	1.14.39		
And by the rising herbes, where cleare springs slide,	Ovid's Elegies	2.16.9		
HERCULES				
As once I did for harming Hercules.	Dido	1.1.15		Jupitr
Than Hercules, that in his infancie/Did pash the jawes of	1Tamb	3.3.104		Bajzth
Not Hilas was more mourned of Hercules,	Edw	1.1.144		Edward
The conquering [Hercules] <Hector> for Hilas wept,	Edw	1.4.393		MortSr
Leander now like Theban Hercules,	Hero and Leander	2.297		
HERE (Homograph; See also HEER, HEERE)				
Hold here my little love:	Dido	1.1.42		Jupitr
Here in this bush disguised will I stand,	Dido	1.1.139		Venus
men, saw you as you came/Any of all my Sisters wandring here?	Dido	1.1.184		Venus
But thou art gone and leav'st me here alone,	Dido	1.1.247		Aeneas
And every Troian be as welcome here,	Dido	1.2.40		Iarbus
Here she was wont to sit, but saving ayre/Is nothing here, and	Dido	2.1.13		Achat
but saving ayre/Is nothing here, and what is this but stone?	Dido	2.1.14		Achat
Aeneas see, here come the Citizens,	Dido	2.1.37		Achat
And here Queene Dido weares th'imperiall Crowne,	Dido	2.1.63		Illion
Here let him sit, be merrie lovely child.	Dido	2.1.93		Dido
Troy is invincible, why stay we here?	Dido	2.1.128		Aeneas
Nay leave not here, resolve me of the rest.	Dido	2.1.160		Dido
Why staiest thou here? thou art no love of mine.	Dido	3.1.39		Dido
Mother, looke here.	Dido	3.1.47		Cupid
O here he comes, love, love, give Dido leave/To be more modest	Dido	3.1.94		Dido
but now thou art here, tell me in sooth/In what might Dido	Dido	3.1.101		Dido
Take what ye will, but leave Aeneas here.	Dido	3.1.127		Dido
Yet how <here> <now> I sweare by heaven and him I love,	Dido	3.1.166		Dido
Here lyes my hate, Aeneas cursed brat,	Dido	3.2.1		Juno
For here in spight of heaven Ile murder him,	Dido	3.2.10		Juno
Juno, my mortall foe, what make you here?	Dido	3.2.24		Venus
What makes Iarbus here of all the rest?	Dido	3.3.13		Dido
As I remember, here you shot the Deere,	Dido	3.3.51		Achat
And here we met faire Venus virgine like,	Dido	3.3.54		Achat
I thinke some fell Inchantresse dwelleth here,	Dido	4.1.3		Iarbus
Servants, come fetch these emptie vessels here,	Dido	4.2.49		Iarbus
And not stand lingering here for amorous lookes:	Dido	4.3.38		Illion
We will not stay a minute longer here.	Dido	4.3.44		Cloan
Because I feard your grace would keepe me here.	Dido	4.4.20		Achat
I charge thee put to sea and stay not here.	Dido	4.4.22		Dido
Thinkes Dido I will goe and leave him here?	Dido	4.4.30		Aeneas
Stay here Aeneas, and commaund as King.	Dido	4.4.39		Dido
O that the Clowdes were here wherein thou [fledst] <fleest>,	Dido	4.4.50		Dido
Then here in me shall flourish Priams race,	Dido	4.4.87		Aeneas
Here will Aeneas build a statelier Troy,	Dido	5.1.2		Aeneas
Shall here unburden their exhaled sweetes,	Dido	5.1.14		Aeneas
Why cosin, stand you building Cities here,	Dido	5.1.27		Hermes
Vaine man, what Monarky expectst thou here?	Dido	5.1.34		Hermes
But here he is, now Dido trie thy wit.	Dido	5.1.86		Dido
For lingering here, neglecting Italy.	Dido	5.1.97		Aeneas
Here lye the Sword that in the darksome Cave/He drew, and swore	Dido	5.1.295		Dido
Here lye the garment which I cloath'd him in,	Dido	5.1.298		Dido
Well here I sweare by this my royal seat--	1Tamb	1.1.97		Mycet
We here doo crowne thee Monarch of the East,	1Tamb	1.1.161		Ortyg
Lie here ye weedes that I disdaine to weare,	1Tamb	1.2.41		Tamb
Theridamas my friend, take here my hand,	1Tamb	1.2.232		Tamb
Least if we let them lynger here a while,	1Tamb	2.2.20		Meandr
Here will I hide it in this simple hole.	1Tamb	2.4.15		Mycet
Here take it for a while, I lend it thee,	1Tamb	2.4.37		Tamb
For presently Techelles here shal haste,	1Tamb	2.5.94		Tamb
Sit here upon this royal chaire of state,	1Tamb	3.3.112		Bajzth
Here Madam, you are Empresse, she is none.	1Tamb	3.3.227		Therid
here, eat sir, take it from my swords point, or Ile thrust it	1Tamb	4.4.40	P	Tamb
Here is my dagger, dispatch her while she is fat, for if she	1Tamb	4.4.48	P	Tamb
Here at Damascus will I make the Point/That shall begin the	1Tamb	4.4.81		Tamb
Here Turk, wilt thou have a cleane trencher?	1Tamb	4.4.101	P	Tamb
Casane, here are the cates you desire to finger, are they not?	1Tamb	4.4.107	P	Tamb
Wel, here is now to the Souldane of Egypt, the King of Arabia,	1Tamb	4.4.113	P	Tamb

HERE (cont.)

I crowne you here (Theridamas) King of Argier:	1Tamb	4.4.116	P	Tamb
Then here before the majesty of heaven,	1Tamb	5.1.48		2Virgn
Here let him stay my maysters from the tents,	1Tamb	5.1.211		Tamb
Here, here, here.	1Tamb	5.1.315	P	Zabina
Thy princely daughter here shall set thee free.	1Tamb	5.1.436		Tamb
And here in Affrick where it seldom raines,	1Tamb	5.1.457		Tamb
But here these kings that on my fortunes wait,	1Tamb	5.1.490		Tamb
Invest her here my Queene of Persea.	1Tamb	5.1.494		Tamb
And here we crowne thee Queene of Persea,	1Tamb	5.1.507		Tamb
for as the Romans usde/I here present thee with a naked sword.	2Tamb	1.1.82		Sgsmnd
Here is his sword, let peace be ratified/On these conditions	2Tamb	1.1.124		Orcan
Then here I sheath it, and give thee my hand,	2Tamb	1.1.127		Sgsmnd
Yet here detain'd by cruell Tamburlaine.	2Tamb	1.2.4		Callap
Then here I sweare, as I am Almeda,	2Tamb	1.2.67		Almeda
Now rest thee here on faire Larissa Plaines,	2Tamb	1.3.5		Tamb
Arch-Monarke of the world, I offer here,	2Tamb	1.3.114		Therid
I here present thee with the crowne of Fesse,	2Tamb	1.3.140		Techel
Thanks king of Fesse, take here thy crowne again.	2Tamb	1.3.150		Tamb
Have I not here the articles of peace,	2Tamb	2.2.30		Orcan
Take here these papers as our sacrifice/And witnesse of thy	2Tamb	2.2.45		Orcan
See here the perjur'd traitor Hungary,	2Tamb	2.3.12		Gazell
which here appeares as full/As raies of Cynthia to the clearest	2Tamb	2.3.29		Orcan
Behold me here divine Zenocrate,	2Tamb	2.4.111		Tamb
And here will I set up her stature <statue>/And martch about it	2Tamb	2.4.140		Tamb
And here this mournful streamer shal be plac'd/Wrought with the	2Tamb	3.2.19		Amyras
And here this table as a Register/Of all her vertues and	2Tamb	3.2.23		Celeb
And here the picture of Zenocrate,	2Tamb	3.2.25		Tamb
That hanging here, wil draw the Gods from heaven:	2Tamb	3.2.28		Tamb
pearle of welthie India/Were mounted here under a Canapie:	2Tamb	3.2.122		Tamb
Here father, cut it bravely as you did your own.	2Tamb	3.2.135	P	Celeb
And for his sake here will I end my daies.	2Tamb	3.4.44		Olymp
Here at Alepo with an hoste of men/Lies Tamburlaine, this king	2Tamb	3.5.3		2Msngr
Where legions of devils (knowing he must die/Here in Natolia,	2Tamb	3.5.26		Orcan
Why, so he is Casane, I am here,	2Tamb	3.5.62		Tamb
I here invest thee king of Ariadan,	2Tamb	3.5.130		Callap
Here, take it.	2Tamb	3.5.134	P	Callap
here are Bugges/Wil make the haire stand upright on your heads,	2Tamb	3.5.147		Tamb
And take my other toward brother here,	2Tamb	4.1.34		Calyph
Here my Lord.	2Tamb	4.1.60	P	Perdic
Here Jove, receive his fainting soule againe,	2Tamb	4.1.111		Tamb
whose weeping eies/Since thy arrivall here beheld no Sun,	2Tamb	4.2.2		Olymp
Here then Olympia.	2Tamb	4.2.81		Therid
To Byron here where thus I honor you?	2Tamb	4.3.6		Tamb
Here my Lord.	2Tamb	4.3.69		Soldrs
Yet are there Christians of Georgia here,	2Tamb	5.1.31		1Citzn
Here they are my Lord.	2Tamb	5.1.177		Usumc
To some high hill about <above> the citie here.	2Tamb	5.1.216		Therid
And here may we behold great Babylon,	2Tamb	5.2.4		Callap
For we have here the chiefe selected men/Of twenty severall	2Tamb	5.2.48		Callap
Here I began to martch towards Persea,	2Tamb	5.3.126		Tamb
And here not far from Alexandria,	2Tamb	5.3.131		Tamb
Looke here my boies, see what a world of ground,	2Tamb	5.3.145		Tamb
Loe here my sonnes, are all the golden Mines,	2Tamb	5.3.151		Tamb
Here lovely boies, what death forbids my life,	2Tamb	5.3.159		Tamb
Meet heaven and earth, and here let al things end,	2Tamb	5.3.249		Amyras
To reade a lecture here in [Britanie] <Britaine>,	Jew	Prol.29		Machvl
Here have I purst their paltry [silverlings] <silverbings>.	Jew	1.1.6		Barab
And all I have is hers. But who comes here?	Jew	1.1.139		Barab
For he can counsell best in these affaires;/And here he comes.	Jew	1.1.143		2Jew
For happily we shall not tarry here:	Jew	1.2.16		Calym
They were, my Lord, and here they come.	Jew	1.2.36		Offcrs
Now then here know that it concerneth us--	Jew	1.2.42		Govnr
How, a Christian? Hum, what's here to doe?	Jew	1.2.75		Barab
But here in Malta, where thou gotst thy wealth,	Jew	1.2.101		Govnr
And here upon my knees, striking the earth,	Jew	1.2.165		Barab
For onely I have toyl'd to inherit here/The months of vanity	Jew	1.2.196		Barab
But here they come; be cunning Abigall.	Jew	1.2.299		Barab
It may be so: but who comes here?	Jew	1.2.313		Abbass
And here behold (unseene) where I have found/The gold, the	Jew	2.1.22		Abigal
For whilst I live, here lives my soules sole hope,	Jew	2.1.29		Barab
And when I dye, here shall my spirit walke.	Jew	2.1.30		Barab
Then father here receive thy happinesse.	Jew	2.1.44		Abigal
Here, Hast thou't?	Jew	2.1.46	P	Abigal
Oh Abigal, Abigal, that I had thee here too,	Jew	2.1.51		Barab
Of whom we would make sale in Malta here.	Jew	2.2.18		Bosco
and you were stated here/To be at deadly enmity with Turkes.	Jew	2.2.32		Bosco
This is the Market-place, here let 'em stand:	Jew	2.3.1		1Offcr
Here comes the Jew, had not his goods bin seiz'd,	Jew	2.3.5		1Offcr
Here comes Don Lodowicke the Governor's sonne,	Jew	2.3.30		Barab
Seeme not to know me here before your mother/Lest she mistrust	Jew	2.3.146		Barab
But stand aside, here comes Don Lodowicke.	Jew	2.3.217		Barab
father, here are letters come/From Ormus, and the Post stayes	Jew	2.3.222		Abigal
are letters come/From Ormus, and the Post stayes here within.	Jew	2.3.223		Abigal
Away, for here they come.	Jew	2.3.275		Barab
My daughter here, a paltry silly girle.	Jew	2.3.284		Barab
Here must no speeches passe, nor swords be drawne.	Jew	2.3.339		Barab
Doe so; loe here I give thee Abigall.	Jew	2.3.345		Barab
And here he comes.	Jew	3.1.11		Curtzn
But here comes cursed Ithimore with the Fryar.	Jew	3.3.49		Abigal
Now here she writes, and wils me to repent.	Jew	3.4.5		Barab
But who comes here?	Jew	3.4.13		Barab
I here adopt thee for mine onely heire,	Jew	3.4.43		Barab

HERE (cont.)

Here take my keyes, I'le give 'em thee anon:	Jew	3.4.46	Barab
Here 'tis, Master.	Jew	3.4.55	P Ithimr
This Even they use in Malta here ('tis call'd/Saint Jaques	Jew	3.4.75	Barab
Bashaw, in briefe, shalt have no tribute here,	Jew	3.5.11	Govnr
Look, look, master, here come two religious Caterpillers.	Jew	4.1.21	P Ithimr
Stands here a purpose, meaning me some wrong,	Jew	4.1.166	1Fryar
here's her house, and here she comes, and now would I were gone,	Jew	4.2.35	P Ithimr
And when he comes: Oh that he were but here!	Jew	4.3.17	Barab
Sir, here they are.	Jew	4.3.50	Barab
Here take 'em, fellow, with as good a will--	Jew	4.3.52	Barab
For Calymath having hover'd here so long,	Jew	5.1.4	Govnr
Dead, my Lord, and here they bring his body.	Jew	5.1.53	1Offcr
The Jew is here, and rests at your command.	Jew	5.1.83	Barab
Feare not, my Lord, for here, against the [sluice] <Truce>,/The	Jew	5.1.86	Barab
Within [there] <here>.	Jew	5.2.47	Barab
said, within this Ile/In Malta here, that I have got my goods,	Jew	5.2.68	Barab
Here is my hand that I'le set Malta free:	Jew	5.2.95	Barab
Here is my hand, beleeve me, Barabas,	Jew	5.2.102	Govnr
Here have I made a dainty Gallery,	Jew	5.5.33	Barab
Here, hold that knife, and when thou seest he comes,	Jew	5.5.37	Barab
here, hold thee, Barabas,/I trust thy word, take what I	Jew	5.5.42	Govnr
Stand close, for here they come:	Jew	5.5.46	Barab
Nay, Selim, stay, for since we have thee here,	Jew	5.5.97	Govnr
To keepe me here will nought advantage you.	Jew	5.5.117	Calym
Content thee, Calymath, here thou must stay,	Jew	5.5.118	Govnr
My Lord, here me but speak.	P1129	21.23	P Frier
I give him thee, here use him as thou wilt.	Edw	1.1.196	Edward
Here comes my lord of Canterburies grace.	Edw	1.2.33	Warwck
Here is the forme of Gavestons exile:	Edw	1.4.1	Lncstr
Here Mortimer, sit thou in Edwards throne,	Edw	1.4.36	Edward
Be it or no, he shall not linger here.	Edw	1.4.93	MortSr
Here take my picture, and let me weare thine,	Edw	1.4.127	Edward
Theres none here, but would run his horse to death.	Edw	1.4.207	Warwck
But were he here, detested as he is,	Edw	1.4.264	Mortmr
Nephue, I must to Scotland, thou staiest here.	Edw	1.4.386	MortSr
Leave of this jesting, here my lady comes.	Edw	2.1.56	Baldck
But rest thee here where Gaveston shall sleepe.	Edw	2.1.65	Neece
And come not here to scoffe at Gaveston,	Edw	2.2.76	Gavstn
Heere, here <King>.	Edw	2.2.81	Penbrk
And therefore let us jointlie here protest,	Edw	2.2.104	Lncstr
Do what they can, weele live in Tinmoth here,	Edw	2.2.221	Edward
And here in Tinmoth frollicks with the king.	Edw	2.3.17	Lncstr
No, here he comes, now let them spoile and kill:	Edw	2.4.3	Edward
Madam, stay you within this castell here.	Edw	2.4.50	Mortmr
Upon my weapons point here shouldst thou fall,	Edw	2.5.13	Mortmr
cause,/That here severelie we will execute/Upon thy person:	Edw	2.5.23	Warwck
My lord, here comes the Queene.	Edw	3.1.58	Spencr
My lord, [here] is <heres> a messenger from the Barons,/Desires	Edw	3.1.148	Spencr
and then a Fig/For all my unckles frienship here in Fraunce.	Edw	4.2.5	Prince
Being of countenance in your countrey here,	Edw	4.6.75	Mortmr
and here to pine in feare/Of Mortimer and his confederates.	Edw	4.7.35	Baldck
this drowsines/Betides no good, here even we are betraied.	Edw	4.7.45	Spencr
I arrest you of high treason here,	Edw	4.7.57	Leistr
Here man, rip up this panting brest of mine,	Edw	4.7.66	Edward
Here humblie of your grace we take our leaves,	Edw	4.7.78	Baldck
Here is a Litter readie for your grace,	Edw	4.7.84	Leistr
And that you lay for pleasure here a space,	Edw	5.1.3	Leistr
In which extreame my minde here murthered is:	Edw	5.1.55	Edward
Here, take my crowne, the life of Edward too,	Edw	5.1.57	Edward
By Mortimer, whose name is written here,	Edw	5.1.139	Edward
Let me alone, here is the privie seale,	Edw	5.2.37	Mortmr
My lord, here is the head of Mortimer.	Edw	5.6.93	1Lord
god>,/Here <Faustus> tire my <trie thy> braines to get a Deity.	F .90	1.1.62	Faust
That shall we presently know, <for see> here comes his boy.	F 196	1.2.3	2Schol
Here, take your Guilders [againe], I'le none of 'em.	F 371	1.4.29	P Robin
and Belcher come here, I'le belch him:	F 374	1.4.32	P Robin
Veiw here this <the> bloud that trickles from mine arme,	F 446	2.1.58	Faust
See <come> Faustus, here is <heres> fire, set it on.	F 459	2.1.71	Mephst
<Here Mephastophilis> receive this scrole,	F 477	(HC260) A	Faust
Nay, and this be hell, I'le willingly be damn'd <damned here>.	F 527	2.1.139	Faust
[Hold] <Here>, take this booke, <and> peruse it [thoroughly]	F 543	2.1.155	Mephst
[Here they are in this booke].	F 551.3	2.1.166A	P Mephst
[Here they be].	F 551.11	2.1.174A	P Mephst
an my Maister come here, I'le clap as faire a paire of hornes	F 737	2.3.16	P Robin
I, there be of us here, that have waded as deepe into matters,	F 740	2.3.19	P Robin
Whilst I am here on earth let me be cloyd/With all things that	F 837	3.1.59	Faust
here, take him to your charge,/And beare him streight to Ponte	F 964	3.1.186	Pope
Here, take his triple Crowne along with you,	F 970	3.1.192	Pope
Sweet Mephostophilis so charme me here,	F 991	3.2.11	Faust
weare this girdle, then appeare/Invisible to all are here:	F 998	3.2.18	Mephst
we all are witnesses/That Bruno here was late delivered you,	F1026	3.2.46	Raymnd
Here 'tis:	F1094	3.3.7	P Dick
O, are you here?	F1096	3.3.9	P Vintnr
here will Benvolio die,/But Faustus death shall quit my	F1336	4.2.12	Benvol
Here will we stay to bide the first assault,	F1354	4.2.30	Benvol
I, that's the head, and here the body lies,	F1375	4.2.51	Benvol
What's here? an ambush to betray my life:	F1424	4.2.100	Faust
Here, what Frederick, ho.	F1431	4.3.1	Benvol
Deere Frederick here,	F1433	4.3.3	Mrtino
Here, now taste yee these, they should be good, for they come	F1576	4.6.19	P Faust
What ho, give's halfe a dosen of Beere here, and be hang'd.	F1613	4.6.56	P Robin
Here will I dwell, for heaven is <be> in these lippes,	F1773	5.1.100	Faust

HERE (cont.)				
Here in this roome will wretched Faustus be.	F1804	5.2.8		Mephst
And here wee'l stay,	F1805	5.2.9		Belzeb
remember that I have beene a student here these thirty yeares,	F1841	5.2.45	P	Faust
O help us heaven, see, here are Faustus limbs,	F1988	5.3.6		2Schol
No, no, here take your gridirons againe.	F App	p.230 38	P	Clown
Let your Balio and your Belcher come here, and Ile knocke them,	F App	p.230 45	P	Clown
that I may be here and there and every where, O Ile tickle the	F App	p.231 62	P	Clown
here is a daintie dish was sent me from the Bishop of Millaine.	F App	p.231 5	P	Pope
here I ha stolne one of doctor Faustus conjuring books, and	F App	p.233 1	P	Robin
But Robin, here comes the vintner.	F App	p.234 4	P	Rafe
and here I sweare to thee, by the honor of mine Imperial	F App	p.236 8	P	Emper
send for the knight that was so pleasent with me here of late?	F App	p.238 67	P	Faust
here they be madam, wilt please you taste on them.	F App	p.242 15	P	Faust
And bounds of Italy; here, here (saith he)/An end of peace;	Lucan, First Booke			226
here, here (saith he)/An end of peace; here end polluted lawes;	Lucan, First Booke			226
here, here (saith he)/An end of peace; here end polluted lawes;	Lucan, First Booke			227
all lands else/Have stable peace, here wars rage first begins,	Lucan, First Booke			252
As oft as Roome was sackt, here gan the spoile:	Lucan, First Booke			258
Here every band applauded,/And with their hands held up, all	Lucan, First Booke			387
Heere thou hast strength, here thy right hand doth rest.	Ovid's Elegies			2.9.36
Here of themselves thy shafts come, as if shot,	Ovid's Elegies			2.9.37
Hether the windes blowe, here the spring-tide rore.	Ovid's Elegies			2.11.40
I sit not here the noble horse to see,	Ovid's Elegies			3.2.1
Goddesse come here, make my love conquering.	Ovid's Elegies			3.2.46
If standing here I can by no meanes get,	Ovid's Elegies			3.5.11
Who bad thee lie downe here against thy will?	Ovid's Elegies			3.6.78
In hell were harbourd, here was found no masse.	Ovid's Elegies			3.7.38
Thy dying eyes here did thy mother close,	Ovid's Elegies			3.8.49
Here when the Pipe with solemne tunes doth sound,	Ovid's Elegies			3.12.11
Why vowest thou then to live in Sestos here,	Hero and Leander			1.227
And here and there her eies through anger rang'd.	Hero and Leander			1.360
he wandring here,/In mournfull tearmes, with sad and heavie	Hero and Leander			1.439
For here the stately azure pallace stood,	Hero and Leander			2.165
As from an orient cloud, glymse <glimps'd> here and there.	Hero and Leander			2.320
HEREABOUTS				
I'le to her lodging; hereabouts she lyes.	Jew	3.6.6		1Fryar
HEREAFTER				
And we wil force him to the field hereafter.	2Tamb	4.1.102		Amyras
As I behave my selfe in this, imploy me hereafter.	Jew	2.3.379		Ithimr
him; and hereafter sir, looke you speake well of Schollers.	F1315	4.1.161	P	Faust
or they that shal hereafter possesse our throne, shal (I feare	F App	p.236 21	P	Emper
and sir knight, hereafter speake well of Scholers:	F App	p.238 85	P	Faust
HEREBY				
But hereby child, we shall get thither straight.	Dido	4.5.14		Nurse
And wish hereby them all unknowne to leave.	Ovid's Elegies			2.5.54
HEREIN				
And herein was old Abrams happinesse:	Jew	1.1.106		Barab
Herein ser you forestalle the markett and sett upe your	Paris	ms 5,p390	P	Souldr
HEREOF				
Now then my Lord, advantage take hereof,	2Tamb	2.1.22		Fredrk
And for a present easie proofe hereof,	2Tamb	4.2.75		Olymp
HERE'S				
There Zanthus streame, because here's Priamus,	Dido	2.1.8		Aeneas
And here's the crown my Lord, help set it on.	1Tamb	5.1.505		Usumc
then, here's the marketplace; whats the price of this slave,	Jew	2.3.97	P	Barab
Here's a leaner, how like you him?	Jew	2.3.126	P	1Offcr
Mute a the sudden; here's a sudden change.	Jew	2.3.324		Lodowk
but here's the Jews man.	Jew	3.1.21	P	Pilia
Here's a drench to poyson a whole stable of Flanders mares:	Jew	3.4.111	P	Ithimr
But here's a royall Monastry hard by,	Jew	4.1.13		Ithimr
'Tis neatly done, Sir, here's no print at all.	Jew	4.1.151		Ithimr
here's her house, and here she comes, and now would I were	Jew	4.2.35	P	Ithimr
Here's goodly 'parrell, is there not?	Jew	4.2.112		Ithimr
Here's many words but no crownes; the crownes.	Jew	4.3.46	P	Pilia
Of that condition I wil drink it up; here's to thee.	Jew	4.4.4	P	Ithimr
French-man, here's to thee with a--pox on this drunken hick-up.	Jew	4.4.32	P	Ithimr
My sences are deceiv'd, here's nothing writ:	F 468	2.1.80		Faust
for here's the scrowle/In which <Wherein> thou hast given thy	F 519	2.1.131		Mephst
Here's a hot whore indeed; no, I'le no wife.	F 534	2.1.146		Faust
HERES				
Heres to thy better fortune and good starres.	Dido	2.1.98		Dido
And heres Aeneas tackling, oares and sailes.	Dido	4.4.125		Lord
My lord, [here] is <heres> a messenger from the Barons,/Desires	Edw	3.1.148		Spencr
See <come> Faustus, here is <heres> fire, set it on.	F 459	2.1.71		Mephst
My good Lord Archbishop, heres a most daintie dish,	F1046	3.2.66		Pope
HERESIE				
that thou leave/These divels, and their damned heresie.	Jew	1.2.347		Barab
He that wantes these, and is suspected of heresie,	P 234	4.32		Guise
To kill all that you suspect of heresie.	P 276	5.3		Guise
He shall be streight condemn'd of heresie,	F 962	3.1.184		Faust
HERESIES				
That makes these upstart heresies in Fraunce:	P 81	2.24		Guise
Are you a preacher of these heresies?	P 340	5.67		Guise
In spite of Spaine and all his heresies.	P 716	14.19		Bartus
HERESY				
unto Roan, and spare not one/That you suspect of heresy.	P 447	7.87		Guise
HERETICK				
Why let us burne him for an heretick.	P 483	9.2	P	2Atndt
HERETICKES				
Faith is not to be held with Heretickes;	Jew	2.3.311		Barab
HERETICKS				
But all are Hereticks that are not Jewes;	Jew	2.3.312		Barab

HERETICKS (cont.)			
That with a rablement of his hereticks, ...	P 151	2.94	Guise
Then pittie or releeve these upstart hereticks. . .	P 222	4.20	Guise
HERETOFORE			
That heretofore have fild Persepolis/With Affrike Captaines,	1Tamb	1.1.141	Ceneus
HEREWITH			
Herewith he stayd his furie, and began/To give her leave to	Hero and Leander		1.415
Herewith afrighted Hero shrunke away, ...	Hero and Leander		2.253
HERICINAS			
queintly dect/With blcomes more white than Hericinas browes,	2Tamb	4.3.122	Tamb
HERMES			
Hermes no more shall shew the world his wings, ...	Dido	1.1.38	Jupitr
Hermes awake, and haste to Neptunes realme, ...	Dido	1.1.114	Jupitr
Whose ticing tongue was made of Hermes pipe, ...	Dido	2.1.145	Aeneas
Hermes this night descending in a dreame, ...	Dido	4.3.3	Aeneas
Not Hermes Prolocutor to the Gods, ...	1Tamb	1.2.210	Therid
The winged Hermes, to convay thee hence:	2Tamb	4.2.19	Therid
Venus is faint; swift Hermes retrograde;	Lucan, First Booke		661
And knowing Hermes courted her, was glad/That she such .	Hero and Leander		1.421
Hermes had slept in hell with ignoraunce.	Hero and Leander		1.468
To venge themselves on Hermes, have concluded/That Midas brood	Hero and Leander		1.474
HERMOSO			
Hermoso Placer de los Dineros.	Jew	2.1.64	Barab
HERO			
The youth oft swimming to his Hero kinde, ...	Ovid's Elegies		2.16.31
At Sestos, Hero dwelt; Hero the faire, ...	Hero and Leander		1.5
As he imagyn'd Hero was his mother.	Hero and Leander		1.40
So lovely faire was Hero, Venus Nun, ...	Hero and Leander		1.45
But far above the loveliest, Hero shin'd, ...	Hero and Leander		1.103
Went Hero thorow Sestos, from her tower/To Venus temple, .	Hero and Leander		1.132
There Hero sacrificing turtles blood, ...	Hero and Leander		1.158
Chast Hero to her selfe thus softly said:	Hero and Leander		1.178
Ah simple Hero, learne thy selfe to cherish, ...	Hero and Leander		1.241
Beleeve me Hero, honour is not wone, ...	Hero and Leander		1.281
Then Hero hate me not, nor from me flie, ...	Hero and Leander		1.291
Love Hero then, and be not tirannous, ...	Hero and Leander		1.323
By this, sad Hero, with love unacquainted, ...	Hero and Leander		2.1
Which joyfull Hero answered in such sort, ...	Hero and Leander		2.15
Long dallying with Hero, nothing saw/That might delight him	Hero and Leander		2.62
Than Hero this inestimable gemme.	Hero and Leander		2.78
though Hero would not yeeld/So soone to part from that she	Hero and Leander		2.83
Sad Hero wroong him by the hand, and wept, ...	Hero and Leander		2.95
O Hero, Herc, thus he cry'de full oft, ...	Hero and Leander		2.147
O let mee viste Hero ere I die.	Hero and Leander		2.178
The longing heart of Hero much more joies/Then nymphs and	Hero and Leander		2.232
Herewith afrighted Hero shrunke away, ...	Hero and Leander		2.253
So Heroes ruddie cheeke, Hero betrayd, ...	Hero and Leander		2.323
HEROES (Homograph)			
Heroes, O <cf> famous names/Farewel, your favour nought my	Ovid's Elegies		2.1.35
Since Heroes time, hath halfe the world beene blacke. .	Hero and Leander		1.50
Relenting Heroes gentle heart was strooke, ...	Hero and Leander		1.165
Which like sweet musicke entred Heroes eares, ...	Hero and Leander		1.194
Heroes lookes yeelded, but her words made warre, . . .	Hero and Leander		1.331
Descends upon my radiant Heroes tower.	Hero and Leander		2.204
So Heroes ruddie cheeke, Hero betrayd, ...	Hero and Leander		2.323
HEROICKE			
With shorter numbers the heroicke sit.	Ovid's Elegies		2.17.22
HERRALD			
Heavens winged herrald, Jove-borne Mercury, ...	Hero and Leander		1.386
HERRALDS			
Sent Herralds out, which basely on their knees/In all your	2Tamb	1.1.96	Orcan
HERRING			
Peter Pickeld-herring <Pickle-herring>, and Martin . .	F 698	2.2.147	P Glutny
HERS			
Foulding his hand in hers, and joyntly both/Beating their	Dido	2.1.227	Aeneas
And all I have is hers. But who comes here?	Jew	1.1.139	Barab
O graunt sweet God my daies may end with hers, ...	P 189	3.24	Navrre
Lay her whole tongue hid, mine in hers she dips. . . .	Ovid's Elegies		2.5.58
this strife of hers (like that/Which made the world) another	Hero and Leander		2.291
HER-SELF			
Farmes out her-self on nights for what she can. . .	Ovid's Elegies		1.10.30
HER SELFE			
helpe Iarbus, Dido in these flames/Hath burnt her selfe, aye me,	Dido	5.1.315	Anna
Fortune her selfe dooth sit upon our Crests.	1Tamb	2.2.73	Meandr
Resting her selfe upon my milk-white Tent:	1Tamb	3.3.161	Tamb
For she has mortified her selfe.	Jew	1.2.341	1Fryar
And when he comes, she lockes her selfe up fast; . . .	Jew	2.3.262	Barab
Nay, if you will, stay till she comes her selfe. . . .	Jew	2.3.352	Barab
Betrayde her selfe, and yeelded at the last.	Ovid's Elegies		1.5.16
Or, but for bashfulnesse her selfe would crave. . . .	Ovid's Elegies		1.8.44
Nor she her selfe but first trim'd up discernes. . . .	Ovid's Elegies		2.17.10
I know a wench reports her selfe Corinne, ...	Ovid's Elegies		2.17.29
her selfe she hath forswore,/And yet remaines the face she had	Ovid's Elegies		3.3.1
Chast Hero to her selfe thus softly said:	Hero and Leander		1.178
And she her selfe before the pointed time, ...	Hero and Leander		2.20
And turn'd aside, and to her selfe lamented.	Hero and Leander		2.34
She offers up her selfe a sacrifice, ...	Hero and Leander		2.48
All headlong throwes her selfe the clouds among/And now Leander	Hero and Leander		2.90
And ran intc the darke her selfe to hide, ...	Hero and Leander		2.239
And in her cwne mind thought her selfe secure, ...	Hero and Leander		2.265
And cunningly to yeeld her selfe she sought.	Hero and Leander		2.294
HE'S			
For your sake and his own he's welcome hither. . . .	Jew	2.3.233	Abigal

HE'S (cont.)			
I, master, he's slain; look how his brains drop out on's nose.	Jew	4.1.178	P Ithimr
He's a murderer.	Jew	4.4.15	P Ithimr
was> made for man; then he's <therefore is man> more excellent.	F 560	2.2.9	Mephst
warre, wherein through use he's known/To exceed his maister,	Lucan, First Booke		325
And that he's much chang'd, looking wild and big, . .	Lucan, First Booke		475
He's happy, that his love dares boldly credit, . . .	Ovid's Elegies		2.5.9
He's cruell, and too much his griefe doth favour/That seekes	Ovid's Elegies		2.5.11
HES			
hes to have the choyce of his owne freeland | yf it be not to	Paris	ms 8,p390	P Souldr
HESPERIA			
There is a place Hesperia term'd by us, ...	Dido	1.2.20	Cloan
HESPERIDES (See also ESPERIDES)			
Daughter unto the Nimphs Hesperides, ...	Dido	5.1.276	Dido
HESPERUS			
Which watchfull Hesperus no sooner heard, ...	Hero and Leander		2.329
HESPERY			
high; but headlong pitcht/Her burning head on bending Hespery.	Lucan, First Booke		545
HEST			
And try if devils will obey thy Hest, ...	F 234	1.3.6	Faust
HESUS			
And where to Hesus, and fell Mercury <(Jove)>/They offer humane	Lucan, First Booke		440
HETHER			
Will him to send Apollo hether straight, ...	2Tamb	5.3.62	Tamb
Goe call a surgeon hether strait.	P1179	22.41	Navrre
Goe call the English Agent hether strait, ...	P1188	22.50	King
Come hether James,/I do commit this Gaveston to thee, .	Edw	2.5.106	Penbrk
No, I came now hether of mine owne accord. . . .	F 272	1.3.44	Mephst
Whose blast may hether strongly be inclinde, . . .	Ovid's Elegies		2.11.38
Hether the windes blowe, here the spring-tide rore. . .	Ovid's Elegies		2.11.40
Turne thy lookes hether, and in one spare twaine, . .	Ovid's Elegies		2.13.15
To sit, and talke with thee I hether came, . . .	Ovid's Elegies		3.2.3
HETHERTO			
Or force her smile that hetherto hath frownd: . . .	Dido	1.1.88	Jupitr
whose moaning entercourse/Hath hetherto bin staid, with wrath	1Tamb	5.1.281	Bajzth
HETHERWARDS			
O care-got triumph hetherwards advance.	Ovid's Elegies		2.12.16
HETRURIANS			
He to th'Hetrurians Junoes feast commended, . . .	Ovid's Elegies		3.12.35
HEW (Homograph)			
But Lady, this faire face and heavenly hew, ...	1Tamb	1.2.36	Tamb
White is their hew, and on his silver crest/A snowy Feather	1Tamb	4.1.50	2Msngr
With terrours to the last and cruelst hew: . . .	1Tamb	5.1.8	Govnr
or with a Curtle-axe/To hew thy flesh and make a gaping wound?	2Tamb	3.2.97	Tamb
Will hew us peecemeale, put us to the wheele, ...	2Tamb	3.4.21	Olymp
Lay waste the Iland, hew the Temples downe, . . .	Jew	3.5.14	Govnr
And hew these knees that now are growne so stiffe. . .	Edw	1.1.95	Edward
So having conquerd Inde, was Bacchus hew, ...	Ovid's Elegies		1.2.47
HEW'D			
Or hew'd this flesh and bones as small as sand, . .	F1398	4.2.74	Faust
And him that hew'd you out for needfull uses/Ile prove had	Ovid's Elegies		1.12.15
HEWED			
Thy Anchors shall be hewed from Christall Rockes, . .	Dido	3.1.120	Dido
lookes shewed/Like marble from the Parian Mountaines hewed.	Ovid's Elegies		1.7.52
HEWES			
Reflexing hewes of blood upon their heads, ...	1Tamb	4.4.2	Tamb
HEWNE			
Or as Matrevis, hewne from the Caucasus, ...	Edw	5.5.54	Edward
HEY (Homograph)			
Hey Rivo Castiliano, a man's a man.	Jew	4.4.10	P Ithimr
Holla verlete, hey: Epernoune, where is the King? . .	P 956	19.26	Guise
Hey ho; I am Sloth:	F 705	2.2.154	P Sloth
hey ho: I'le not speake an other word.	F 706	2.2.158	P Sloth
you thinke to carry it away with your Hey-passe, and Re-passe:	F1665	4.6.108	P Robin
if he had but the qualitie of hey ding, ding, hey, ding, ding,	F App	p.239 115	P HrsCsr
and I sat upon a bottle of hey, never so neare drowning in my	F App	p.240 135	P HrsCsr
you, hey, passe, where's your maister?	F App	p.240 138	P HrsCsr
Fustian, fortie dollers, fortie dollers for a bottle of hey.	F App	p.241 150	P HrsCsr
the Horsecourser I take it, a bottle of hey for his labour; wel,	F App	p.241 165	P Faust
HEY-PASSE			
you thinke to carry it away with your Hey-passe, and Re-passe:	F1665	4.6.108	P Robin
H'HAD			
H'had never bellowed in a brasen Bull/Of great ones envy; o'th	Jew	Prol.25	Machvl
HICK			
here's to thee with a--pox on this drunken hick-up. . .	Jew	4.4.33	P Ithimr
HICK-UP			
here's to thee with a--pox on this drunken hick-up. . .	Jew	4.4.33	P Ithimr
HID			
Which when the citie was besieg'd I hid, ...	2Tamb	5.1.117	Govnr
I closely hid.	Jew	1.2.247	Barab
There have I hid close underneath the plancke/That runs along	Jew	1.2.296	Barab
As much I hope as all I hid is worth.	Jew	1.2.336	Barab
I have found/The gold, the perles, and Jewels which he hid.	Jew	2.1.23	Abigal
glide by night/About the place where Treasure hath bin hid:	Jew	2.1.27	Barab
Breath out that life wherein my death was hid, . . .	P 954	19.24	King
I feard as much, murther cannot be hid.	Edw	5.6.46	Queene
Yea <I> all the wealth that our fore-fathers hid, . .	F 173	1.1.145	Cornel
what ere thou be whom God assignes/This great effect, art hid.	Lucan, First Booke		420
Her white necke hid with tresses hanging downe, . .	Ovid's Elegies		1.5.10
words she sayd/While closely hid betwixt two dores I layed.	Ovid's Elegies		1.8.22
Lay her whole tongue hid, mine in hers she dips. . .	Ovid's Elegies		2.5.58
Why with hid irons are your bowels torne?	Ovid's Elegies		2.14.27
Is golden love hid in Mars mid alarmes.	Ovid's Elegies		2.18.36

HID (cont.)
Heere while I walke hid close in shadie grove, ... Ovid's Elegies 3.1.5
Which lie hid under her thinne veile supprest. . . . . Ovid's Elegies 3.2.36
Which being knowne (as what is hid from Jove)? . . . . Hero and Leander 1.436
One halfe appear'd, the other halfe was hid. . . . . Hero and Leander 2.316

HIDDEN
thinking some hidden mystery had beene in the horse, I had F1485 4.4.29 P HrsCsr
There good birds rest (if we beleeve things hidden)/Whence Ovid's Elegies 2.6.51
[And] <Or> hidden secrets openlie to bewray? . . . Ovid's Elegies 3.13.8
Some hidden influence breeds like effect. . . . . Hero and Leander 2.60
The light of hidden fire it selfe discovers, . . . Hero and Leander 2.133

HIDE (Homograph; See also HYDE)
She crav'd a hide of ground to build a towne, ... Dido 4.2.13 Iarbus
Therefore in pollicie I thinke it good/To hide it close: . 1Tamb 2.4.11 Mycet
Here will I hide it in this simple hole. . . . . . 1Tamb 2.4.15 Mycet
To hide the folded furrowes of his browes, ... 1Tamb 5.1.57 2Virgn
Hide now thy stained face in endles night, ... 1Tamb 5.1.292 Bajzth
Shall hide his head in Thetis watery lap, ... 2Tamb 1.3.169 Tamb
And Parapets to hide the Muscatters: . . . . . . 2Tamb 3.2.77 Tamb
least hee hide his crowne as the foolish king of Persea did. 2Tamb 3.5.154 P Tamb
And hide these extreme sorrowes from mine eyes: . . . Jew 1.2.195 Barab
Hide the bagge. . . . . Jew 3.1.23 Curtzn
Hence strumpet, hide thy head for shame, ... P 691 13.35 Guise
To hide those parts which men delight to see, ... Edw 1.1.65 Gavstn
Thou shalt not hence, ile hide thee Gaveston. . . . . Edw 1.4.131 Edward
What may we do, that we may hide our shames? . . . . F1447 4.3.17 Fredrk
And hide me from the heavy wrath of [God] <heaven>. . . . F1946 5.2.150 Faust
I wil not hide from you the thing my heart desires, and were it F App p.242 8 P Duchss
and the rest/Marcht not intirely, and yet hide the ground, Lucan, First Booke 474
He hath no bosome, where to hide base pelfe. . . . . Ovid's Elegies 1.10.18
Died red with shame, to hide from shame she seekes. . . . Ovid's Elegies 1.14.52
Vaine causes faine of him the true to hide, ... Ovid's Elegies 2.2.31
And hide thy left hand underneath her lappe. . . . . Ovid's Elegies 2.15.12
A grassie turffe the moistened earth doth hide. . . . Ovid's Elegies 2.16.10
The maide to hide me in her bosome let not. . . . . Ovid's Elegies 3.1.56
Now would I slacke the reines, now lash their hide, . . . Ovid's Elegies 3.2.11
Envious garments so good legges to hide, ... Ovid's Elegies 3.2.27
To hide thee in my bosome straight repaire. . . . . Ovid's Elegies 3.2.76
They say Peneus neere Phthias towne did hide. . . . . Ovid's Elegies 3.5.32
And in the bed hide all the faults you have, ... Ovid's Elegies 3.13.20
O none but gods have power their love to hide, ... Hero and Leander 2.131
And ran into the darke her selfe to hide, ... Hero and Leander 2.239
Being sodainly betraide, dyv'd downe to hide her. . . . Hero and Leander 2.262

HIDEOUS
And hoyst aloft on Neptunes hideous hilles, ... Dido 3.3.47 Iarbus
Whose hideous ecchoes make the welkin howle, ... Dido 4.2.9 Iarbus
Surpriz'd with feare of hideous revenge, ... 1Tamb 3.2.68 Agidas
For when their hideous force environ'd Rhodes, ... Jew 2.2.48 Bosco
With cracke of riven ayre and hideous sound, ... Lucan, First Booke 153
Which makes the maine saile fal with hideous sound; . . . Lucan, First Booke 498

HIDES
That hides these plaines, and seems as vast and wide, . . 2Tamb 1.1.107 Sgsmnd
I, Daughter, for Religion/Hides many mischiefes from suspition. Jew 1.2.282 Barab
but hee hides and buries it up as Partridges doe their egges, Jew 4.2.58 P Ithimr
A grave her bones hides, on her corps great <small> grave, Ovid's Elegies 2.6.59
Let me be slandered, while my fire she hides, ... Ovid's Elegies 2.17.3
The subject hides thy wit, mens acts resound, ... Ovid's Elegies 3.1.25

HID'ST
Whereat thou trembling hid'st thee in the aire, . . . 2Tamb 4.1.130 Tamb

HIE (See also HYE)
Hie thee my Bassoe fast to Persea, ... 1Tamb 3.1.21 Bajzth
Villaine away, and hie thee to the field, ... 2Tamb 5.3.72 Tamb
hie thee, get thee gone,/Edward with fire and sword, followes Edw 3.1.179 Edward
Then gentle Fredericke hie thee to the grove, ... F1340 4.2.16 Benvol

HIER
And kept it downe that it might mount the hier. . . . Hero and Leander 2.42

HIGH
And Proteus raising hils of flouds on high, ... Dido 1.1.76 Venus
And wrong my deitie with high disgrace: . . . . . Dido 3.2.5 Juno
Aeneas thoughts dare not ascend so high/As Didos heart, which Dido 3.4.33 Aeneas
And order all things at your high dispose, ... Dido 5.1.303 Dido
Threatning the world with high astounding tearms/And scourging 1Tamb Prol.5 Prolog
Whose foming galle with rage and high disdaine, . . . 1Tamb 1.1.63 Mycet
The high and highest Monarke of the world, ... 1Tamb 3.1.26 Bajzth
Hath spread his collours to our high disgrace: . . . . 1Tamb 4.1.7 Souldn
a blemish to the Majestie/And high estate of mightie Emperours, 1Tamb 4.3.20 Souldn
Making thee mount as high as Eagles soare. . . . . 1Tamb 5.1.224 Bajzth
So high within the region of the aire, ... 1Tamb 5.1.250 Zabina
That long hath lingred for so high a seat. . . . . 1Tamb 5.1.502 Therid
If all the christall gates of Joves high court/Were opened 2Tamb 1.3.153 Tamb
imperiall heaven/That he that sits on high and never sleeps, 2Tamb 2.2.49 Orcan
And God hath thundered vengeance from on high, ... 2Tamb 2.3.2 Sgsmnd
And raise our honors to as high a pitch/In this our strong and 2Tamb 3.1.30 Callap
Counterscarps/Narrow and steepe, the wals made high and broad, 2Tamb 3.2.69 Tamb
It must have high Argins and covered waies/To keep the bulwark 2Tamb 3.2.75 Tamb
Whose shattered lims, being tost as high as heaven, . . . 2Tamb 3.2.100 Tamb
In whose high lookes is much more majesty/Than from the Concave 2Tamb 3.4.47 Therid
Like to an almond tree ymounted high, ... 2Tamb 4.3.119 Tamb
To some high hill about <above> the citie here. . . . 2Tamb 5.1.216 Therid
As much too high for this disdainfull earth. . . . . 2Tamb 5.3.122 Tamb
I did offend high heaven so grievously, ... Jew 3.6.17 Abigal
Set me to scale the high Peramides, ... P 100 2.43 Guise
What are you hurt my Lord high Admiral? . . . . . P 197 3.32 Condy

HIGH (cont.)			
And it please your grace the Lord high Admirall,	P 243	4.41	Man
How fares it with my Lord high Admiral,	P 253	4.51	Charls
And that high minded earle of Lancaster,	Edw	1.1.150	Edward
I heere create thee Lord high Chamberlaine,	Edw	1.1.154	Edward
Thou Lancaster, high admirall of our fleete,	Edw	1.4.66	Edward
And you the Eagles, sore ye nere so high,	Edw	2.2.39	Edward
That thinke with high lookes thus to tread me down.	Edw	2.2.97	Edward
To Englands high disgrace, have made this Jig,	Edw	2.2.189	Lncstr
And have old servitors in high esteeme,	Edw	3.1.168	Herald
I arrest you of high treason here,	Edw	4.7.57	Leistr
Graven in the booke of Joves high firmament,	F 756	2.3.35	2Chor
Beside <Besides> the gates, and high Pyramydes,	F 823	3.1.45	Mephst
The which this day with high solemnity,	F 833	3.1.55	Mephst
So high our Dragons soar'd into the aire,	F 849	3.1.71	Faust
In recompence of this thy high desert,	F1322	4.1.168	Emper
And mount aloft with them as high as heaven,	F1404	4.2.80	Faust
attaine to that degree of high renowne and great authoritie,	F App	p.236 22 P	Emper
The fates are envious, high seats quickly perish,	Lucan, First Booke		70
Which flamed not on high; but headlong pitcht/Her burning head	Lucan, First Booke		544
The Ocean swell'd, as high as Spanish Calpe,	Lucan, First Booke		553
Aie me how high that gale did lift my hope!	Ovid's Elegies		1.6.52
As evill wood throwne in the high-waies lie,	Ovid's Elegies		1.12.13
For ever lasts high Sophocles proud vaine,	Ovid's Elegies		1.15.15
With earthes revenge and how Olimpus toppe/High Ossa bore,	Ovid's Elegies		2.1.14
The lofty Pine from high mount Pelion raught/Ill waies by rough	Ovid's Elegies		2.11.1
But though I apt were for such high deseignes,	Ovid's Elegies		2.18.14
With scepters, and high buskins th'one would dresse me,	Ovid's Elegies		3.1.63
The graine-rich goddesse in high woods did stray,	Ovid's Elegies		3.9.35
By whom disclosd, she in the high woods tooke,	Ovid's Elegies		3.12.19
Built walles high towred with a prosperous hand.	Ovid's Elegies		3.12.34
paths, wheron the gods might trace/To Joves high court.	Hero and Leander		1.299
HIGHER (See also HIER)			
And higher would I reare my estimate,	1Tamb	3.2.53	Zenoc
If we deserve them not with higher meeds/Then erst our states	1Tamb	4.4.131	Therid
A title higher than thy Souldans name:	1Tamb	5.1.434	Tamb
Raise Cavalieros higher than the cloudes,	2Tamb	2.4.103	Tamb
shall raise a hill/Of earth and fagots higher than thy Fort,	2Tamb	3.3.22	Therid
That must (advaunst in higher pompe than this)/Rifle the	2Tamb	4.3.58	Tamb
Whose lofty Pillers, higher than the cloudes,	2Tamb	5.1.64	Tamb
That meane t'invest me in a higher throane,	2Tamb	5.3.121	Tamb
And bankes raisd higher with their sepulchers:	Edw	1.4.103	Edward
me, for his sake/Ile grace thee with a higher stile ere long.	Edw	2.2.253	Edward
And seeing there was no place to mount up higher,	Edw	5.6.62	Mortmr
dore more wisely/And som-what higher beare thy foote precisely.	Ovid's Elegies		1.12.6
Ile live, and as he puls me downe, mount higher.	Ovid's Elegies		1.15.42
and higher set/The drooping thoughts of base declining soules,	Hero and Leander		2.256
HIGHEST			
The king of Gods sent me from highest heaven,	Dido	5.1.32	Hermes
And stuft with treasure for his highest thoughts?	1Tamb	2.1.59	Ceneus
by princely deeds/Doth meane to soare above the highest sort.	1Tamb	2.7.33	Therid
The high and highest Monarke of the world,	1Tamb	3.1.26	Bajzth
Than Juno sister to the highest God,	1Tamb	3.2.54	Zenoc
in a myrrour we perceive/The highest reaches of a humaine wit:	1Tamb	5.1.168	Tamb
O highest Lamp of everliving Jove,	1Tamb	5.1.290	Bajzth
So surely will the vengeance of the highest/And jealous anger	2Tamb	2.1.56	Fredrk
Whose shape is figure of the highest God?	2Tamb	2.2.38	Orcan
Holds out his hand in highest majesty/To entertaine divine	2Tamb	2.4.32	Tamb
Flame to the highest region of the aire:	2Tamb	3.2.2	Tamb
Thus am I right the Scourge of highest Jove,	2Tamb	4.3.24	Tamb
Nor yet thy selfe, the anger of the highest,	2Tamb	5.1.104	Govnr
And gets unto the highest bough of all,	Edw	2.2.19	Mortmr
HIGHLY			
here, tell me in sooth/In what might Dido highly pleasure thee.	Dido	3.1.102	Dido
How highly I doe prize this amitie,	Dido	3.2.67	Juno
His royall Crowne againe, so highly won.	1Tamb	3.3.219	Zenoc
I know that I have highly sinn'd,	Jew	4.1.80	Barab
Lord Percie of the North being highly mov'd,	Edw	1.1.110	Kent
In this I count me highly gratified,	Edw	1.4.295	Mortmr
In this your grace hath highly honoured me,	Edw	1.4.364	MortSr
[And] highly scorning, that the lowly earth/Should drinke his	Edw	5.1.13	Edward
And we will highly gratify thee for it.	F 653	2.2.102	Lucifr
The which <That to> this day is highly solemnized.	F 778	2.3.57	2Chor
highly recompenced, in that it pleaseth your grace to thinke	F1563	4.6.6 P	Faust
Virginitie, albeit some highly prise it,	Hero and Leander		1.262
For as a hote prowd horse highly disdaines,	Hero and Leander		2.141
HIGH MINDED			
And that high minded earle of Lancaster,	Edw	1.1.150	Edward
HIGHNES			
I have fulfil'd your highnes wil, my Lord,	2Tamb	5.1.203	Techel
Shall binde me ever to your highnes will,	P 11	1.11	Navrre
The heavens forbid your highnes such mishap.	P 177	3.12	QnMarg
Might well have moved your highnes to beware/How you did meddle	P 179	3.14	Navrre
Too late it is my Lord if that be true/To blame her highnes,	P 182	3.17	QnMarg
Anjoy hath well advisde/Your highnes to consider of the thing,	P 220	4.18	Guise
All this and more your highnes shall commaund,	P 479	8.29	Lord
And meanes to meet your highnes in the field.	P 727	14.30	1Msngr
Ah base Epernoune, were not his highnes heere,	P 831	17.26	Guise
Your highnes needs not feare mine armies force,	P 857	17.52	Guise
grace the Duke of Guise doth crave/Accesse unto your highnes.	P 960	19.30	Eprnon
What, is your highnes hurt?	P1176	22.38	Navrre
Ah, had your highnes let him live,	P1183	22.45	Eprnon
To see your highnes in this vertuous minde.	P1210	22.72	Navrre

HIGHNES (cont.)
Alas my Lord, your highnes cannot live. P1223 22.85 Srgeon
For which, had not his highnes lov'd him well, Edw 1.1.112 Kent
Your highnes knowes, it lies not in my power. Edw 1.4.158 Queene
In this, or ought, your highnes shall commaund us. Edw 1.4.384 Warwck
His highnes is disposde to be alone. Edw 2.2.135 Guard
As though your highnes were a schoole boy still, Edw 3.1.30 Baldck
Bound to your highnes everlastinglie, Edw 3.1.41 SpncrP
I did your highnes message to them all, Edw 3.1.96 Arundl
That I would undertake to carrie him/Unto your highnes, and to Edw 3.1.100 Arundl
armes, by me salute/Your highnes, with long life and happines, Edw 3.1.157 Herald
I warrant you, ile winne his highnes quicklie, Edw 4.2.6 Prince
To do your highnes service and devoire, Edw 5.1.133 Bartly
Your highnes may boldly go and see. F App p.238 63 P Faust
highnes now to send for the knight that was so pleasent with me F App p.238 66 P Faust

HIGHNESSE
I understand your highnesse sent for me. Dido 3.1.100 Aeneas
to apprehend/And bring him Captive to your Highnesse throne. 1Tamb 1.1.48 Meandr
Or plead for mercie at your highnesse feet. 1Tamb 1.1.73 Therid
This should intreat your highnesse to rejoice, 1Tamb 1.1.123 Menaph
We will invest your Highnesse Emperour: 1Tamb 1.1.151 Ceneus
We have his highnesse letters to command/Aide and assistance if 1Tamb 1.2.19 Magnet
Expects th'arrivall of her highnesse person. 1Tamb 1.2.79 Agidas
His Highnesse pleasure is that he should live, 1Tamb 2.2.37 Meandr
Your Highnesse needs not doubt but in short time, 1Tamb 3.2.32 Agidas
Such as his Highnesse please, but some must stay/To rule the 1Tamb 3.3.28 Bassoe
Yet somtimes let your highnesse send for them/To do the work my 1Tamb 3.3.187 Anippe
So might your highnesse, had you time to sort/Your fighting 1Tamb 4.1.36 Capol
But if his highnesse would let them be fed, it would doe them 1Tamb 4.4.34 P Therid
unto your majesty/May merit favour at your highnesse handes, 1Tamb 4.4.70 Zenoc
And since your highnesse hath so well vouchsaft, 1Tamb 4.4.130 Therid
Your Highnesse knowes for Tamburlaines repaire, 2Tamb 2.1.14 Fredrk
happinesse/And hope to meet your highnesse in the heavens, 2Tamb 2.4.63 Zenoc
And bring him captive to your highnesse feet. 2Tamb 3.1.62 Soria
quyvering leaves/Of Idas forrest, where your highnesse hounds, 2Tamb 3.5.6 2Msngr
by your highnesse hands)/All brandishing their brands of 2Tamb 3.5.26 Orcan
Halla is repair'd/And neighbor cities of your highnesse land, 2Tamb 3.5.47 Soria
Let al of us intreat your highnesse pardon. 2Tamb 4.1.98 Tec&Us
To sue for mercie at your highnesse feete. 2Tamb 5.2.41 Amasia
I joy my Lord, your highnesse is so strong, 2Tamb 5.3.110 Usumc
bleeding harts/Wounded and broken with your Highnesse griefe, 2Tamb 5.3.162 Amyras
I hope your Highnesse will consider us. Jew 1.2.9 Govnr
of Turkey is arriv'd/Great Selim-Calymath, his Highnesse sonne, Jew 1.2.40 Govnr
Therefore he humbly would intreat your Highnesse/Not to depart Jew 5.3.32 Msngr
That holdes it from your highnesse wrongfully: P 582 11.47 Pleshe
For had your highnesse seene with what a pompe/He entred Paris, P 872 17.67 Eprnon
And there salute his highnesse in our name, P 908 18.9 Navrre
Or else be banisht from his highnesse presence. Edw 1.4.203 Queene
Because your highnesse hath beene slack in homage, Edw 3.1.63 Queene
Are to your highnesse vowd and consecrate. Edw 3.1.171 Herald
But bee content, seeing it his highnesse pleasure. Edw 5.2.94 Queene
Tis for your highnesse good, and for the realmes. Edw 5.4.101 Mortmr
What meanes your highnesse to mistrust me thus? Edw 5.5.79 Ltborn

HIGHT
a bawde aright/Give eare, there is an old trot Dipsas hight. Ovid's Elegies 1.8.2
The one Abydos, the other Sestos hight. Hero and Leander 1.4

HIGH-WAIES
As evill wood throwne in the high-waies lie, Ovid's Elegies 1.12.13

HILAS
Not Hilas was more mourned of Hercules, Edw 1.1.144 Edward
The conquering [Hercules] <Hector> for Hilas wept, Edw 1.4.393 MortSr

HILL
Epeus horse, to Aetnas hill transformd, Dido 1.1.66 Venus
Me thinkes that towne there should be Troy, yon Idas hill, Dido 2.1.7 Aeneas
an hot alarme/Drive all their horses headlong down the hill. 1Tamb 1.2.135 Usumc
Betwixt the hollow hanging of a hill/And crooked bending of a 2Tamb 1.2.57 Callap
Even in the cannons face shall raise a hill/Of earth and fagots 2Tamb 3.3.21 Therid
To some high hill about <above> the citie here. 2Tamb 5.1.216 Therid
rites and Latian Jove advanc'd/On Alba hill o Vestall flames, Lucan, First Booke 201
I see Pangeus hill,/With hoarie toppe, and under Hemus mount Lucan, First Booke 678
Each little hill shall for a table stand: Ovid's Elegies 2.11.48
With snow thaw'd from the next hill now thou rushest, Ovid's Elegies 3.5.7
Upon a rocke, and underneath a hill, Hero and Leander 1.345

HILLES
And hoyst aloft on Neptunes hideous hilles, Dido 3.3.47 Iarbus
And cut a passage through his toples hilles: Dido 4.3.12 Aeneas
And [pitcht] <pitch> our tents under the Georgean hilles, 1Tamb 2.2.15 Meandr

HILLOCKE
The while upon a hillocke downe he lay, Hero and Leander 1.400

HILLS
That Vallies, groves, hills and fieldes, Passionate Shepherd 3

HILLY
Such as in hilly Idas watry plaines, Ovid's Elegies 1.14.11
Though thether leades a rough steepe hilly way. Ovid's Elegies 3.12.6

HILS
And Proteus raising hils of floods on high, Dido 1.1.76 Venus
Fairer than whitest snow on Scythian hils, 1Tamb 1.2.89 Tamb
To cast up hils against the face of heaven: 1Tamb 2.6.3 Cosroe
But as he thrust them underneath the hils, 1Tamb 2.6.5 Cosroe
Brave horses, bred on the white Tartarian hils: 1Tamb 3.3.151 Tamb
Covers the hils, the valleies and the plaines. 2Tamb 3.5.13 Callap
I'le joyne the Hils that bind the Affrick shore, F 335 1.3.107 Faust
Know that this City stands upon seven hils, F 811 3.1.33 Mephst

HILS (cont.)			
Mountaines and Hils, come, come, and fall on me, . . .	F1945	5.2.149	Faust
where swift Rhodanus/Drives Araris to sea; They neere the hils,	Lucan, First Booke		435
from thence/To the pine bearing hils, hence to the mounts	Lucan, First Booke		688
HILT			
and a Dagger with a hilt like a warming-pan, and he gave me a	Jew	4.2.29	P Ithimr
HIM			
But as this one Ile teare them all from him, ...	Dido	1.1.40	Jupitr
She humbly did beseech him for our bane, ...	Dido	1.1.60	Venus
And charg'd him drowne my sonne with all his traine. .	Dido	1.1.61	Venus
Entends ere long to sport him in the skie. . . .	Dido	1.1.77	Venus
In those faire walles I promist him of yore: . . .	Dido	1.1.85	Jupitr
Charge him from me to turne his stormie powers, . .	Dido	1.1.117	Jupitr
For my sake pitie him Oceanus, ...	Dido	1.1.127	Venus
To succour him in this extremitie.	Dido	1.1.133	Venus
And plaine to him the summe of your distresse. . . .	Dido	1.2.2	Illion
I heare Aeneas voyce, but see him not, ...	Dido	2.1.45	Illion
Here let him sit, be merrie lovely child.	Dido	2.1.93	Dido
And him, Epeus having made the horse, ...	Dido	2.1.147	Aeneas
Kist him, imbrast him, and unloosde his bands, . . .	Dido	2.1.158	Aeneas
Made him to thinke Epeus pine-tree Horse/A sacrifize t'appease	Dido	2.1.162	Aeneas
And after him a thousand Grecians more, ...	Dido	2.1.185	Aeneas
Achilles horse/Drew him in triumph through the Greekish Campe,	Dido	2.1.206	Aeneas
And after him his band of Mirmidons, ...	Dido	2.1.216	Aeneas
And strewe him with sweete smelling Violets, ...	Dido	2.1.318	Venus
Who if that any seeke to doe him hurt, ...	Dido	2.1.321	Venus
who in stead of him/Will set thee on her lap and play with	Dido	2.1.324	Venus
Victuall his Souldiers, give him wealthie gifts, . .	Dido	2.1.329	Venus
The people swarme to gaze him in the face. . . .	Dido	3.1.72	Anna
But tell them none shall gaze on him but I, . . .	Dido	3.1.73	Dido
Anna, good sister Anna goe for him, ...	Dido	3.1.75	Dido
Runne for Aeneas, or Ile flye to him.	Dido	3.1.79	Dido
In stead of musicke I will heare him speake, . . .	Dido	3.1.89	Dido
I traveld with him to Aetolia.	Dido	3.1.145	Serg
But playd he nere so sweet, I let him goe:	Dido	3.1.160	Dido
But I had gold enough and cast him off:	Dido	3.1.162	Dido
Yet how <here> <now> I sweare by heaven and him I love,	Dido	3.1.166	Dido
Troy shall no more call him her second hope, . . .	Dido	3.2.8	Juno
For here in spight of heaven Ile murder him, . . .	Dido	3.2.10	Juno
For saving him from Snakes and Serpents stings, . .	Dido	3.2.38	Juno
That would have kild him sleeping as he lay? . . .	Dido	3.2.39	Juno
And wrought him mickle woe on sea and land, . . .	Dido	3.2.41	Juno
And wish that I had never wrongd him so:	Dido	3.2.48	Juno
And cannot talke nor thinke of ought but him: . . .	Dido	3.2.73	Juno
And couch him in Adonis purple downe.	Dido	3.2.100	Venus
But love and duetie led him on perhaps, ...	Dido	3.3.15	Aeneas
I, and outface him to, doe what he can.	Dido	3.3.40	Cupid
And mought I live to see him sacke rich Thebes, . .	Dido	3.3.42	Aeneas
But Dido that now holdeth him so deare, ...	Dido	3.3.76	Iarbus
Then to the Carthage Queene that dyes for him. . . .	Dido	3.4.40	Dido
and warne him to his ships/That now afflicts me with his .	Dido	4.2.21	Iarbus
Thinkes Dido I will goe and leave him here? . . .	Dido	4.4.30	Aeneas
let him ride/As Didos husband through the Punicke streetes,	Dido	4.4.66	Dido
To waite upon him as their soveraigne Lord. . . .	Dido	4.4.69	Dido
O blessed tempests that did drive him in, ...	Dido	4.4.94	Dido
O happie sand that made him runne aground:	Dido	4.4.95	Dido
I must prevent him, wishing will not serve:	Dido	4.4.104	Dido
And beare him in the countrey to her house, ...	Dido	4.4.106	Dido
I cannot see him frowne, it may not be:	Dido	4.4.112	Dido
O Dido, blame not him, but breake his oares, . . .	Dido	4.4.149	Dido
These were the instruments that launcht him forth, . .	Dido	4.4.150	Dido
Now let him hang my favours on his masts, ...	Dido	4.4.159	Dido
For tackling, let him take the chaines of gold, . . .	Dido	4.4.161	Dido
In steed of oares, let him use his hands, ...	Dido	4.4.163	Dido
O how unwise was I to say him nay!	Dido	4.5.37	Nurse
Sergestus, beare him hence unto our ships, ...	Dido	5.1.49	Aeneas
Lest Dido spying him keepe him for a pledge. . . .	Dido	5.1.50	Aeneas
And, see the Sailers take him by the hand, ...	Dido	5.1.189	Dido
Now bring him backe, and thou shalt be a Queene, . . .	Dido	5.1.197	Dido
And I will live a private life with him.	Dido	5.1.198	Dido
Call him not wicked, sister, speake him faire, . . .	Dido	5.1.200	Dido
And looke upon him with a Mermaides eye, ...	Dido	5.1.201	Dido
Tell him, I never vow'd at Aulis gulfe/The desolation of his	Dido	5.1.202	Dido
Nor ever violated faith to him:	Dido	5.1.205	Dido
Request him gently (Anna) to returne, ...	Dido	5.1.206	Dido
Thou for some pettie guift hast let him goe, ...	Dido	5.1.218	Dido
They gan to move him to redresse my ruth, ...	Dido	5.1.238	Anna
O Anna, Anna, I will follow him.	Dido	5.1.241	Dido
That I may swim to him like Tritons neece:	Dido	5.1.247	Dido
See see, the billowes heave him up to heaven, ...	Dido	5.1.252	Dido
But see, Achates wils him put to sea, ...	Dido	5.1.258	Dido
Must I make ships for him to saile away?	Dido	5.1.266	Dido
Nothing can beare me to him but a ship, ...	Dido	5.1.267	Dido
Iarbus, talke not of Aeneas, let him goe, ...	Dido	5.1.283	Dido
Here lye the garment which I cloath'd him in, ...	Dido	5.1.298	Dido
to apprehend/And bring him Captive to your Highnesse throne.	1Tamb	1.1.48	Meandr
Nay, pray you let him stay, a greater [task]/Fits Menaphon, than	1Tamb	1.1.87	Cosroe
Create him Prorex of [Assiria] <Affrica>, ...	1Tamb	1.1.89	Cosroe
Or take him prisoner, and his chaine shall serve/For Manackles,	1Tamb	1.2.147	Tamb
His deep affections make him passionate.	1Tamb	1.2.164	Techel
Techelles, and Casane, welcome him.	1Tamb	1.2.238	Tamb
But tell me, that hast seene him, Menaphon, ...	1Tamb	2.1.5	Cosroe
wrought in him with passion,/Thirsting with soverainty, with	1Tamb	2.1.19	Menaph

HIM (cont.)

To make him famous in accomplisht woorth:	1Tamb	2.1.34		Cosroe
And well his merits show him to be made/His Fortunes maister,	1Tamb	2.1.35		Cosroe
his Diadem/Sought for by such scalde knaves as love him not?	1Tamb	2.2.8		Mycet
giftes and promises/Inveigle him that lead a thousand horse,	1Tamb	2.2.26		Meandr
And make him false his faith unto his King,	1Tamb	2.2.27		Meandr
Beside the spoile of him and all his traine:	1Tamb	2.2.34		Meandr
And bid him battell for his novell Crowne?	1Tamb	2.5.88		Techel
To bid him battaile ere he passe too farre,	1Tamb	2.5.95		Tamb
And bid him turne [him] <his> back to war with us,	1Tamb	2.5.100		Tamb
That onely made him King to make us sport.	1Tamb	2.5.101		Tamb
We will not steale upon him cowardly,	1Tamb	2.5.102		Tamb
But give him warning and more warriours.	1Tamb	2.5.103		Tamb
What star or state soever governe him,	1Tamb	2.6.18		Ortyg
Let's cheere our souldiers to incounter him,	1Tamb	2.6.29		Cosroe
And burne him in the fury of that flame,	1Tamb	2.6.32		Cosroe
That thus opposeth him against the Gods,	1Tamb	2.6.39		Cosroe
To charge him to remaine in Asia.	1Tamb	3.1.18		Fesse
Tell him thy Lord the Turkish Emperour,	1Tamb	3.1.22		Bajzth
Tell him, I am content to take a truce,	1Tamb	3.1.31		Bajzth
Then stay thou with him, say I bid thee so.	1Tamb	3.1.35		Bajzth
And meane to fetch thee in despight of him.	1Tamb	3.1.40		Bajzth
The entertainment we have had of him,	1Tamb	3.2.37		Zenoc
Or when the morning holds him in her armes:	1Tamb	3.2.48		Zenoc
Let us afford him now the bearing hence.	1Tamb	3.2.111		Usumc
Agreed Casane, we wil honor him.	1Tamb	3.2.113		Techel
I meane to meet him in Bithynia:	1Tamb	3.3.2		Tamb
Withdraw as many more to follow him.	1Tamb	3.3.22		Bassoe
Let him bring millions infinite of men,	1Tamb	3.3.33		Usumc
Shall rouse him out of Europe, and pursue/His scattered armie	1Tamb	3.3.38		Therid
Whose smiling stars gives him assured hope/Of martiall triumph,	1Tamb	3.3.42		Tamb
Triumphing over him and these his kings,	1Tamb	3.3.128		Tamb
Now strengthen him against the Turkish Bajazeth,	1Tamb	3.3.191		Zenoc
That I may see him issue Conquerour.	1Tamb	3.3.194		Zenoc
And make him raine down murthering shot from heaven/To dash the	1Tamb	3.3.196		Zabina
That dare to manage armes with him,	1Tamb	3.3.198		Zabina
The Souldane would not start a foot from him.	1Tamb	4.1.19		Souldn
Let him take all th'advantages he can,	1Tamb	4.1.40		Souldn
This arme should send him downe to Erebus,	1Tamb	4.1.45		Souldn
And treading him beneath thy loathsome feet,	1Tamb	4.2.64		Zabina
Put him in againe.	1Tamb	4.2.82		Tamb
Confusion light on him that helps thee thus.	1Tamb	4.2.84		Bajzth
And thou his wife shalt feed him with the scraps/My servitures	1Tamb	4.2.87		Tamb
For he that gives him other food than this:	1Tamb	4.2.89		Tamb
Shall sit by him and starve to death himselfe.	1Tamb	4.2.90		Tamb
Shall ransome him, or take him from his cage.	1Tamb	4.2.94		Tamb
These Mores that drew him from Bythinia,	1Tamb	4.2.98		Tamb
Shall lead him with us wheresoere we goe.	1Tamb	4.2.100		Tamb
A sacred vow to heaven and him I make,	1Tamb	4.3.36		Souldn
offences feele/Such plagues as heaven and we can poure on him.	1Tamb	4.3.45		Arabia
And leads with him the great Arabian King,	1Tamb	4.3.64		Souldn
O let him alone:	1Tamb	4.4.40	P	Tamb
belike he hath not bene watered to day, give him some drinke.	1Tamb	4.4.55	P	Tamb
Yet give me leave to plead for him my Lord.	1Tamb	4.4.86		Zenoc
Whose honors and whose lives relie on him:	1Tamb	5.1.19		Govnr
But I am pleasde you shall not see him there:	1Tamb	5.1.113		Tamb
Bring him forth, and let us know if the towne be ransackt.	1Tamb	5.1.194	P	Tamb
Here let him stay my maysters from the tents,	1Tamb	5.1.211		Tamb
Give him his liquor?	1Tamb	5.1.310	P	Zabina
and fire, and my blood I bring him againe, teare me in peeces,	1Tamb	5.1.311	P	Zabina
Downe with him, downe with him.	1Tamb	5.1.312	P	Zabina
Ah, save that Infant, save him, save him.	1Tamb	5.1.313	P	Zabina
Ah, save that Infant, save him, save him.	1Tamb	5.1.314	P	Zabina
Fearing my power should pull him from his throne.	1Tamb	5.1.453		Tamb
When men presume to manage armes with him.	1Tamb	5.1.478		Tamb
Or crosse the streame, and meet him in the field?	2Tamb	1.1.12		Orcan
Gainst him my Lord must you addresse your power.	2Tamb	1.1.19		Gazell
Nor he but Fortune that hath made him great.	2Tamb	1.1.60		Orcan
By him that made the world and sav'd my soule,	2Tamb	1.1.133		Sgsmnd
He raign'd him straight and made him so curvet,	2Tamb	1.3.41		Zenoc
If any man will hold him, I will strike,	2Tamb	1.3.102		Calyph
And cleave him to the channell with my sword.	2Tamb	1.3.103		Calyph
Hold him, and cleave him too, or Ile cleave thee,	2Tamb	1.3.104		Tamb
And made him sweare obedience to my crowne.	2Tamb	1.3.190		Techel
I took the king, and lead him bound in chaines/Unto Damasco,	2Tamb	1.3.204		Techel
I, liquid golde when we have conquer'd him,	2Tamb	1.3.223		Tamb
An hundred kings by scores wil bid him armes,	2Tamb	2.2.11		Gazell
Be able to withstand and conquer him.	2Tamb	2.2.19		Gazell
But in their deeds deny him for their Christ:	2Tamb	2.2.40		Orcan
Zenocrate that gave him light and life,	2Tamb	2.4.8		Tamb
And bring him captive to your highnesse feet.	2Tamb	3.1.62		Soria
To keep my promise, and to make him king,	2Tamb	3.1.71		Callap
And see him lance his flesh to teach you all.	2Tamb	3.2.114		Tamb
For think ye I can live, and see him dead?	2Tamb	3.4.27		Sonne
Least cruell Scythians should dismember him.	2Tamb	3.4.37		Olymp
And him faire Lady shall thy eies behold.	2Tamb	3.4.67		Therid
And turne him to his ancient trade againe.	2Tamb	3.5.95		Jrslem
Doost thou aske him leave?	2Tamb	3.5.134	P	Callap
let him hang a bunch of keies on his standerd, to put him in	2Tamb	3.5.139	P	Tamb
to put him in remembrance he was a Jailor, that when I take	2Tamb	3.5.140	P	Tamb
that when I take him, I may knocke out his braines with them,	2Tamb	3.5.140	P	Tamb
hee is a king, looke to him Theridamas, when we are fighting,	2Tamb	3.5.153	P	Tamb
For if my father misse him in the field,	2Tamb	4.1.8		Celeb

HIM (cont.)

To think our helps will doe him any good.	2Tamb	4.1.21	Calyph
Yet pardon him I pray your Majesty.	2Tamb	4.1.97	Therid
Good my Lord, let him be forgiven for once,	2Tamb	4.1.101	Amyras
And we wil force him to the field hereafter.	2Tamb	4.1.102	Amyras
Ile dispose them as it likes me best,/Meane while take him in.	2Tamb	4.1.167	Tamb
pitie him, in whom thy looks/Have greater operation and more	2Tamb	4.2.28	Therid
If you loved him, and it so precious?	2Tamb	4.2.72	Therid
Haling him headlong to the lowest hell.	2Tamb	4.3.42	Orcan
Shall mount the milk-white way and meet him there.	2Tamb	4.3.132	Tamb
Wel, now Ile make it quake, go draw him up,	2Tamb	5.1.107	Tamb
Hang him up in chaines upon the citie walles,	2Tamb	5.1.108	Tamb
Up with him then, his body shalbe scard.	2Tamb	5.1.114	Tamb
Away with him hence, let him speake no more:	2Tamb	5.1.125	Tamb
Then have at him to begin withall.	2Tamb	5.1.152	Therid
Yet shouldst thou die, shoot at him all at once.	2Tamb	5.1.157	Tamb
Whose Scourge I am, and him will I obey.	2Tamb	5.1.185	Tamb
Wee may lie ready to encounter him,	2Tamb	5.2.8	Callap
Doubt not my lord, but we shal conquer him.	2Tamb	5.2.12	Amasia
And make him after all these overthrowes,	2Tamb	5.2.29	Callap
let us lie in wait for him/And if we find him absent from his	2Tamb	5.2.56	Callap
lie in wait for him/And if we find him absent from his campe,	2Tamb	5.2.57	Callap
And threaten him whose hand afflicts my soul,	2Tamb	5.3.47	Tamb
Will him to send Apollo hether straight,	2Tamb	5.3.62	Tamb
To cure me, or Ile fetch him downe my selfe.	2Tamb	5.3.63	Tamb
Be warn'd by him then, learne with awfull eie/To sway a throane	2Tamb	5.3.234	Tamb
For both their woorths wil equall him no more.	2Tamb	5.3.253	Amyras
I crave but this, Grace him as he deserves,	Jew	Prol.33	Machvl
And let him not be entertain'd the worse/Because he favours me.	Jew	Prol.34	Machvl
easily in a day/Tell that which may maintaine him all his life.	Jew	1.1.11	Barab
why then let every man/Provide him, and be there for	Jew	1.1.171	Barab
As much as would have bought his beasts and him,	Jew	1.2.189	Barab
But give him liberty at least to mourne,	Jew	1.2.202	Barab
Come, let us leave him in his irefull mood,	Jew	1.2.209	1Jew
my fingers take/A kisse from him that sends it from his soule.	Jew	2.1.59	Barab
'Tis true, my Lord, therefore intreat him well.	Jew	2.2.8	1Knght
I'le seeke him out, and so insinuate,	Jew	2.3.33	Lodowk
I ha the poyson of the City for him,	Jew	2.3.53	Barab
might be got/To keepe him for his life time from the gallowes.	Jew	2.3.104	Barab
Here's a leaner, how like you him?	Jew	2.3.126	P 1Offcr
An hundred Crownes, I'le have him; there's the coyne.	Jew	2.3.130	Barab
Then marke him, Sir, and take him hence.	Jew	2.3.131	1Offcr
I, marke him, you were best, for this is he	Jew	2.3.132	Barab
He loves my daughter, and she holds him deare:	Jew	2.3.141	Barab
and my talke with him was [but]/About the borrowing of a booke	Jew	2.3.155	Mthias
Converse not with him, he is cast off from heaven.	Jew	2.3.157	Mater
breast a long great Scrowle/How I with interest tormented him.	Jew	2.3.198	Barab
Use him as if he were a--Philistine.	Jew	2.3.228	Barab
Dissemble, sweare, protest, vow to love him,	Jew	2.3.229	Barab
Abigall, bid him welcome for my sake.	Jew	2.3.232	Barab
Daughter, a word more; kisse him, speake him faire,	Jew	2.3.234	Barab
yet I say make love to him;/Doe, it is requisite it should be	Jew	2.3.238	Barab
And she vowes love to him, and hee to her.	Jew	2.3.247	Barab
looking out/When you should come and hale him from the doore.	Jew	2.3.265	Barab
I'le rouze him thence.	Jew	2.3.269	Mthias
But steale you in, and seeme to see him not;	Jew	2.3.272	Barab
I'le give him such a warning e're he goes/As he shall have	Jew	2.3.273	Barab
let him have thy hand,/But keepe thy heart till Don Mathias	Jew	2.3.306	Barab
Well, let him goe.	Jew	2.3.336	Lodowk
Suffer me, Barabas, but to follow him.	Jew	2.3.340	Mthias
Revenge it on him when you meet him next.	Jew	2.3.343	Barab
Hee's with your mother, therefore after him.	Jew	2.3.350	Barab
I cannot take my leave of him for teares:	Jew	2.3.355	Abigal
Yes, you shall have him: Goe put her in.	Jew	2.3.362	Barab
And tell him that it comes from Lodowicke.	Jew	2.3.371	Barab
That he shall verily thinke it comes from him.	Jew	2.3.376	Ithimr
Looke not towards him, let's away:	Jew	3.1.24	Pilia
And so did Lodowicke him.	Jew	3.2.22	Govnr
That's no lye, for she sent me for him.	Jew	3.4.25	P Ithimr
I sent for him, but seeing you are come/Be you my ghostly	Jew	3.6.11	Abigal
First to Don Lodowicke, him I never lov'd;	Jew	3.6.23	Abigal
But I must to the Jew and exclaime on him,	Jew	3.6.42	2Fryar
And make him stand in feare of me.	Jew	3.6.43	2Fryar
You see I answer him, and yet he stayes;	Jew	4.1.88	Barab
Rid him away, and goe you home with me.	Jew	4.1.89	Barab
You know my mind, let me alone with him.	Jew	4.1.100	Barab
Why does he goe to thy house? let him begone.	Jew	4.1.101	1Fryar
I'le give him something and so stop his mouth.	Jew	4.1.102	Barab
What if I murder'd him e're Jacomo comes?	Jew	4.1.116	Barab
No, none can heare him, cry he ne're so loud.	Jew	4.1.136	Ithimr
Why true, therefore did I place him there:	Jew	4.1.137	Barab
Oh how I long to see him shake his heeles.	Jew	4.1.140	Ithimr
Then is it as it should be, take him up.	Jew	4.1.152	Barab
so, let him leane upon his staffe; excellent, he stands as if he	Jew	4.1.153	P Ithimr
Why, stricken him that would have stroke at me.	Jew	4.1.175	1Fryar
No, let us beare him to the Magistrates.	Jew	4.1.183	Ithimr
by this Bernardine/To be a Christian, I shut him out,	Jew	4.1.188	Barab
Come Ithimore, let's helpe to take him hence.	Jew	4.1.200	Barab
and so I left him, being driven to a non-plus at the critical	Jew	4.2.13	P Pilia
And where didst meet him?	Jew	4.2.15	P Curtzn
tibi, cras mihi, and so I left him to the mercy of the Hangman:	Jew	4.2.19	P Pilia
Let me alone, doe but you speake him faire:	Jew	4.2.63	Pilia
Which if they were reveal'd, would doe him harme.	Jew	4.2.65	Pilia

HIM (cont.)

I'le make him send me half he has, and glad he scapes so too.	Jew	4.2.67	P Ithimr
I'le write unto him, we'le have mony strait.	Jew	4.2.69	P Ithimr
Write not so submissively, but threatning him.	Jew	4.2.72	P Pilia
Tell him you will confesse.	Jew	4.2.77	P Pilia
Let me alone, I'le use him in his kinde.	Jew	4.2.80	Pilia
Hang him, Jew.	Jew	4.2.81	P Ithimr
Send to the Merchant, bid him bring me silkes,	Jew	4.2.84	Curtzn
I tooke him by the [beard] <sterd>, and look'd upon him thus;	Jew	4.2.105	P Pilia
and look'd upon him thus; told him he were best to send it;	Jew	4.2.105	P Pilia
told him he were best to send it; then he hug'd and imbrac'd	Jew	4.2.106	P Pilia
I'le not leave him worth a gray groat.	Jew	4.2.114	P Ithimr
Tell him I must hav't.	Jew	4.2.118	P Ithimr
tell him, I scorne to write a line under a hundred crownes.	Jew	4.2.120	P Ithimr
But if I get him, Coupe de Gorge for that.	Jew	4.3.5	Barab
And I by him must send three hundred crownes.	Jew	4.3.15	Barab
he not as well come as send; pray bid him come and fetch it:	Jew	4.3.26	P Barab
That he who knowes I love him as my selfe/Should write in this	Jew	4.3.42	Barab
Commend me to him, Sir, most humbly,	Jew	4.3.47	Barab
Give him a crowne, and fill me out more wine.	Jew	4.4.46	Ithimr
I scorne the Peasant, tell him so.	Jew	4.4.59	P Ithimr
now; Bid him deliver thee a thousand Crownes, by the same token,	Jew	4.4.75	P Ithimr
Goe fetch him straight. I alwayes fear'd that Jew.	Jew	5.1.18	Govnr
Away with him, his sight is death to me.	Jew	5.1.35	Govnr
Once more away with him; you shall have law.	Jew	5.1.40	Govnr
Ferneze, 'twas thy sonne that murder'd him.	Jew	5.1.45	Mater
In prison till the Law has past on him.	Jew	5.1.49	Govnr
Away, no more, let him not trouble me.	Jew	5.2.26	Barab
And neither gets him friends, nor fils his bags,	Jew	5.2.39	Barab
What will you give him that procureth this?	Jew	5.2.83	Barab
And banquet with him e're thou leav'st the Ile.	Jew	5.3.19	Msngr
To banquet with him in his Citadell?	Jew	5.3.20	Calym
Wee'll in this Summer Evening feast with him.	Jew	5.3.41	Calym
heare a Culverin discharg'd/By him that beares the Linstocke,	Jew	5.4.4	Govnr
Let us salute him. Save thee, Barabas.	Jew	5.5.54	Calym
How the slave jeeres at him?	Jew	5.5.56	Govnr
Him as a childe I dayly winne with words,	P 130	2.73	Guise
Him will we--but first lets follow those in France,	P 153	2.96	Guise
<humble> intreates your Majestie/To visite him sick in his bed.	P 246	4.44	Man
Messenger, tell him I will see him straite.	P 247	4.45	Charls
Your Majesty were best goe visite him,	P 249	4.47	QnMoth
Then throw him down.	P 306	5.33	Guise
Now cosin view him well,	P 307	5.34	Anjoy
Cosin tis he, I know him by his look.	P 309	5.36	Guise
See where my Souldier shot him through the arm.	P 310	5.37	Guise
He mist him neer, but we have strook him now.	P 311	5.38	Guise
Away with him, cut of his head and handes,	P 316	5.43	Anjoy
And thou a traitor to thy soule and him.	P 342	5.69	Lorein
Come dragge him away and throw him in a ditch.	P 345	5.72	Guise
[Sanctus] <Sancta> Jacobus hee was my Saint, pray to him.	P 358	6.13	Mntsrl
O let him goe, he is a catholick.	P 375	7.15	Retes
Stab him.	P 382	7.22	Guise
kill him.	P 398	7.38	Guise
That he that despiseth him, can nere/Be good in Logick or	P 409	7.49	Ramus
Stab him I say and send him to his freends in hell.	P 415	7.55	Guise
That are tutors to him and the prince of Condy--	P 427	7.67	Guise
And so convey him closely to his bed.	P 450	7.90	Guise
Why let us turne him for an heretick.	P 483	9.2	P 2Atndt
and the fire the aire, and so we shall be poysoned with him.	P 485	9.4	P 1Atndt
Lets throw him into the river.	P 487	9.6	P 1Atndt
Then throw him into the ditch.	P 490	9.9	P 1Atndt
all doubts, be rulde by me, lets hang him heere upon this tree.	P 491	9.10	P 2Atndt
As I could long ere this have wisht him there.	P 496	9.15	QnMoth
Sirs, take him away and throw him in some ditch.	P 499	9.18	Guise
Madam, I have heard him solemnly vow,	P 516	9.35	Cardnl
Ile disinherite him and all the rest:	P 524	9.43	QnMoth
And bid him come without delay to us.	P 559	11.24	QnMoth
Sirra, take him away.	P 621	12.34	Guise
And tell him that tis for his Countries good,	P 646	12.59	Cardnl
Tush man, let me alone with him,	P 648	12.61	QnMoth
Ile dispatch him with his brother presently,	P 651	12.64	QnMoth
Faine would I finde some means to speak with him/But cannot,	P 662	13.6	Duchss
<make> a walk/On purpose from the Court to meet with him.	P 784	15.42	Mugern
yet you put in that which displeaseth him, and so forestall his	P 809	17.4	P Souldr
I, those are they that feed him with their golde,	P 845	17.40	King
But trust him not my Lord,	P 871	17.66	Eprnon
With gifts and shewes did entertaine him/And promised to be at	P 874	17.69	Eprnon
Did they of Paris entertaine him so?	P 879	17.74	King
Offering him aide against his enemies,	P 905	18.6	Bartus
Assure him all the aide we can provide,	P 909	18.10	Navrre
And tell him ere it be long, Ile visite him.	P 912	18.13	Navrre
Wee'l beat him back, and drive him to his death,	P 929	18.30	Navrre
What, will you not feare when you see him come?	P 933	19.3	Capt
Feare him said you?	P 934	19.4	P 1Mur
tush, were he heere, we would kill him presently.	P 934	19.4	P 1Mur
But when will he come that we may murther him?	P 937	19.7	P 3Mur
I prethee tell him that the Guise is heere.	P 958	19.28	Guise
Let him come in.	P 961	19.31	King
Stand close, he is comming, I know him by his voice.	P1000	19.70	P 1Mur
Downe with him, downe with him.	P1002	19.72	P AllMur
Trouble me not, I neare offended him,	P1005	19.75	Guise
Sirra twas I that slew him, and will slay/Thee too, and thou	P1048	19.118	King
Away to prison with him, Ile clippe his winges/Or ere he passe	P1052	19.122	King

HIM (cont.)

Ile clippe his winges/Or ere he passe my handes, away with him.	P1053	19.123	King
And will him in my name to kill the Duke.	P1058	19.128	King
Come take him away.	P1106	20.16	1Mur
Let him come in.	P1158	22.20	King
O my Lord, let him live a while.	P1173	22.35	Eprnon
Ah, had your highnes let him live,	P1183	22.45	Eprnon
We might have punisht him to his deserts.	P1184	22.46	Eprnon
That we might torture him with some new found death.	P1217	22.79	Eprnon
Ah curse him not sith he is dead.	P1220	22.82	King
yett you putt in that displeases him | And fill up his rome	Paris	ms 4,p390 P	Souldr
But you will saye you leave him rome enoughe besides:	Paris	ms 7,p390 P	Souldr
But that it harbors him I hold so deare,	Edw	1.1.13	Gavstn
Shall bathe him in a spring, and there hard by,	Edw	1.1.66	Gavstn
Therefore if he be come, expell him straight.	Edw	1.1.106	Lncstr
For which, had not his highnes lov'd him well,	Edw	1.1.112	Kent
All Warwickshire will love him for my sake.	Edw	1.1.128	Warwck
And in the channell christen him a new.	Edw	1.1.188	Edward
Ah brother, lay not violent hands on him,	Edw	1.1.189	Kent
Let him complaine unto the sea of hell,	Edw	1.1.191	Gavstn
Ile be revengd on him for my exile.	Edw	1.1.192	Gavstn
And make him serve thee as thy chaplaine,	Edw	1.1.195	Edward
I give him thee, here use him as thou wilt.	Edw	1.1.196	Edward
Wel, let that peevish Frenchman guard him sure,	Edw	1.2.7	Mortmr
And all the court begins to flatter him.	Edw	1.2.22	Lncstr
All stomack him, but none dare speake a word.	Edw	1.2.26	Lncstr
Weele hale him from the bosome of the king,	Edw	1.2.29	Mortmr
Then laide they violent hands upon him, next/Himselfe	Edw	1.2.36	ArchBp
Then let him stay, for rather then my lord/Shall be opprest by	Edw	1.2.64	Queene
And let him frollick with his minion.	Edw	1.2.67	Queene
Then may we lawfully revolt from him.	Edw	1.2.73	Mortmr
But I long more to see him banisht hence.	Edw	1.4.5	Warwck
Your grace doth wel to place him by your side,	Edw	1.4.10	Lncstr
We know our duties, let him know his peeres.	Edw	1.4.23	Warwck
Whether will you beare him, stay or ye shall die.	Edw	1.4.24	Edward
Ile make the prowdest of you stoope to him.	Edw	1.4.31	Edward
And with the earle of Kent that favors him.	Edw	1.4.34	MortSr
Curse him, if he refuse, and then may we/Depose him and elect	Edw	1.4.54	Mortmr
he refuse, and then may we/Depose him and elect an other king.	Edw	1.4.55	Mortmr
Either banish him that was the cause thereof,	Edw	1.4.60	ArchBp
Why should you love him, whome the world hates so?	Edw	1.4.76	Mortmr
You that be noble borne should pitie him.	Edw	1.4.80	Edward
You that are princely borne should shake him off,	Edw	1.4.81	Warwck
Urge him, my lord.	Edw	1.4.83	MortSr
Are you content to banish him the realme?	Edw	1.4.84	ArchBp
Ile see him presently dispatched away.	Edw	1.4.90	Mortmr
How fast they run to banish him I love,	Edw	1.4.94	Edward
I must entreat him, I must speake him faire,	Edw	1.4.183	Queene
Crie quittance Madam then, and love not him.	Edw	1.4.195	Mortmr
But madam, would you have us cal him home?	Edw	1.4.208	Mortmr
Plead for him he that will, I am resolvde.	Edw	1.4.214	MortSr
O Lancaster, let him diswade the king,	Edw	1.4.216	Queene
Then speake not for him, let the pesant go.	Edw	1.4.218	Warwck
Tis for my selfe I speake, and not for him.	Edw	1.4.219	Queene
Which being caught, strikes him that takes it dead,	Edw	1.4.222	Mortmr
Feare not, the queens words cannot alter him.	Edw	1.4.233	Penbrk
Can this be true twas good to banish him,	Edw	1.4.245	Lncstr
And is this true to call him home againe?	Edw	1.4.246	Lncstr
Which may in Ireland purchase him such friends,	Edw	1.4.259	Mortmr
But rather praise him for that brave attempt,	Edw	1.4.268	Mortmr
To banish him, and then to call him home,	Edw	1.4.275	Mortmr
Twill make him vaile the topflag of his pride,	Edw	1.4.276	Mortmr
Weele pull him from the strongest hould he hath.	Edw	1.4.289	Mortmr
Is new returnd, this newes will glad him much,	Edw	1.4.301	Queene
I love him more/Then he can Gaveston, would he lov'd me	Edw	1.4.302	Queene
And could my crownes revenew bring him back,	Edw	1.4.308	Edward
For wot you not that I have made him sure,	Edw	1.4.378	Edward
That day, if not for him, yet for my sake,	Edw	1.4.381	Edward
Let him without controulement have his will.	Edw	1.4.390	MortSr
For riper yeares will weane him from such toyes.	Edw	1.4.401	MortSr
Then so am I, and live to do him service,	Edw	1.4.421	Mortmr
But he is banisht, theres small hope of him.	Edw	2.1.15	Baldck
I knew the King would have him home againe.	Edw	2.1.78	Spencr
A trifle, weele expell him when we please:	Edw	2.2.10	Edward
Though thou comparst him to a flying Fish,	Edw	2.2.43	Edward
Nor fowlest Harpie that shall swallow him.	Edw	2.2.46	Edward
If in his absence thus he favors him,	Edw	2.2.47	Mortmr
Salute him? yes: welcome Lord Chamberlaine.	Edw	2.2.65	Lncstr
Convey hence Gaveston, thaile murder him.	Edw	2.2.82	Edward
Weele haile him by the eares unto the block.	Edw	2.2.91	Lncstr
Looke to your owne crowne, if you back him thus.	Edw	2.2.93	Warwck
Cosin it is no dealing with him now,	Edw	2.2.102	Lncstr
And make the people sweare to put him downe.	Edw	2.2.111	Lncstr
Weel have him ransomd man, be of good cheere.	Edw	2.2.116	Lncstr
Cosin, and if he will not ransome him,	Edw	2.2.127	Mortmr
Why, so he may, but we will speake to him.	Edw	2.2.136	Lncstr
Then ransome him.	Edw	2.2.143	Edward
Twas in your wars, you should ransome him.	Edw	2.2.144	Lncstr
And you shall ransome him, or else--	Edw	2.2.145	Mortmr
What Mortimer, you will not threaten him?	Edw	2.2.146	Kent
To gather for him thoroughout the realme.	Edw	2.2.148	Edward
And therefore brother banish him for ever.	Edw	2.2.211	Kent
I, and it greeves me that I favoured him.	Edw	2.2.213	Kent

HIM (cont.)

And so I walke with him about the walles,	Edw	2.2.222	Edward
I, and tis likewise thought you favour him <them> <'em> <hem>.	Edw	2.2.226	Edward
Why do you not commit him to the tower?	Edw	2.2.234	Gavstn
I dare not, for the people love him well.	Edw	2.2.235	Edward
Why then weele have him privilie made away.	Edw	2.2.236	Gavstn
Knowest thou him Gaveston?	Edw	2.2.248	Edward
For my sake let him waite upon your grace,	Edw	2.2.250	Gavstn
But whats the reason you should leave him now?	Edw	2.3.13	Penbrk
That I might pull him to me where I would,	Edw	2.4.18	Queene
That when I had him we might never part.	Edw	2.4.21	Queene
And all in vaine, for when I speake him faire,	Edw	2.4.28	Queene
What would you with the king, ist him you seek?	Edw	2.4.31	Queene
Pursue him quicklie, and he cannot scape,	Edw	2.4.38	Queene
The king hath left him, and his traine is small.	Edw	2.4.39	Queene
Lets all abcord, and follow him amaine.	Edw	2.4.47	Mortmr
The wind that bears him hence, wil fil our sailes,	Edw	2.4.48	Lncstr
Yet once more ile importune him with praiers,	Edw	2.4.63	Queene
Upon him souldiers, take away his weapons.	Edw	2.5.8	Warwck
Go souldiers take him hence, for by my sword,	Edw	2.5.20	Warwck
hang him at a bough.	Edw	2.5.24	Warwck
Souldiers, have him away:	Edw	2.5.26	Warwck
by me, yet but he may/See him before he dies, for why he saies,	Edw	2.5.37	Arundl
Souldiers away with him.	Edw	2.5.45	Warwck
Souldiers away with him:	Edw	2.5.50	Mortmr
Weele send his head by thee, let him bestow/His teares on that,	Edw	2.5.52	Mortmr
In burying him, then he hath ever earned.	Edw	2.5.56	Lncstr
He will but talke with him and send him backe.	Edw	2.5.59	Arundl
For Gaveston, will if he [seaze] <zease> <sees> him once,	Edw	2.5.63	Warwck
Violate any promise to possesse him.	Edw	2.5.64	Warwck
I will upon mine honor undertake/To carrie him, and bring him	Edw	2.5.80	Penbrk
mine honor undertake/To carrie him, and bring him back againe,	Edw	2.5.80	Penbrk
is it not enough/That we have taken him, but must we now/Leave	Edw	2.5.84	Warwck
him, but must we now/Leave him on had-I-wist, and let him go?	Edw	2.5.85	Warwck
Upon mine oath I will returne him back.	Edw	2.5.88	Penbrk
Why I say, let him go on Penbrookes word.	Edw	2.5.90	Lncstr
Then give him me.	Edw	2.5.94	Penbrk
My lord of Penbrooke, we deliver him you,	Edw	2.5.97	Mortmr
Returne him on your honor. Sound, away.	Edw	2.5.98	Mortmr
to your maister/My friend, and tell him that I watcht it well.	Edw	2.6.13	Warwck
not the riches of my realme/Can ransome him, ah he is markt to	Edw	3.1.4	Edward
For favors done in him, unto us all.	Edw	3.1.42	SpncrP
With all the hast we can dispatch him hence.	Edw	3.1.83	Edward
Demanding him of them, entreating rather,	Edw	3.1.97	Arundl
That I would undertake to carrie him/Unto your highnes, and to	Edw	3.1.99	Arundl
to carrie him/Unto your highnes, and to bring him back.	Edw	3.1.100	Arundl
Refusing to receive me pledge for him,	Edw	3.1.107	Arundl
My lords, because our soveraigne sends for him,	Edw	3.1.109	Arundl
I will this undertake, to have him hence,	Edw	3.1.111	Arundl
And see him redelivered to your hands.	Edw	3.1.112	Arundl
The earle of Warwick seazde him on his way,	Edw	3.1.115	Arundl
And bare him to his death, and in a trenche/Strake off his	Edw	3.1.119	Arundl
I will have heads, and lives, for him as many,	Edw	3.1.132	Edward
Admit him neere.	Edw	3.1.150	Edward
And there let him bee,	Edw	3.1.197	Lncstr
A rebels, recreants, you made him away.	Edw	3.1.229	Edward
Poore Pierce, and headed him against lawe of armes?	Edw	3.1.238	Edward
There see him safe bestowed, and for the rest,	Edw	3.1.253	Edward
Edward this day hath crownd him king a new.	Edw	3.1.261	Edward
With him is Edmund gone associate?	Edw	4.3.39	Edward
Heere for our countries cause sweare we to him/All homage,	Edw	4.4.19	Mortmr
Edward will thinke we come to flatter him.	Edw	4.4.29	SrJohn
O fly him then, but Edmund calme this rage,	Edw	4.6.11	Kent
Nephew, your father, I dare not call him king.	Edw	4.6.33	Kent
Madam, tis good to looke to him betimes.	Edw	4.6.39	Mortmr
Take him away, he prates. You Rice ap Howell,	Edw	4.6.73	Mortmr
If he be not, let him choose.	Edw	5.1.95	BshpWn
Commend me to my sonne, and bid him rule/Better then I, yet how	Edw	5.1.121	Edward
Favor him my lord, as much as lieth in you.	Edw	5.1.147	Leistr
Even so betide my soule as I use him.	Edw	5.1.148	Bartly
And that I be protector over him,	Edw	5.2.12	Mortmr
And then let me alone to handle him.	Edw	5.2.22	Mortmr
As Leicester that had charge of him before.	Edw	5.2.35	BshpWn
Seeke all the meanes thou canst to make him droope,	Edw	5.2.54	Mortmr
And neither give him kinde word, nor good looke.	Edw	5.2.55	Mortmr
Remoove him still from place to place by night,	Edw	5.2.59	Mortmr
And by the way to make him fret the more,	Edw	5.2.62	Mortmr
Speake curstlie to him, and in any case/Let no man comfort him,	Edw	5.2.63	Mortmr
and in any case/Let no man comfort him, if he chaunce to weepe,	Edw	5.2.64	Mortmr
And tell him, that I labour all in vaine,	Edw	5.2.70	Queene
And beare him this, as witnesse of my love.	Edw	5.2.72	Queene
But she that gave him life, I meane the Queene?	Edw	5.2.91	Kent
Let him be king, I am too yong to raigne.	Edw	5.2.93	Prince
Let me but see him first, and then I will.	Edw	5.2.95	Prince
Inconstant Edmund, doost thou favor him,	Edw	5.2.101	Mortmr
And therefore trust him not.	Edw	5.2.107	Mortmr
Sister, Edward is my charge, redeeme him.	Edw	5.2.116	Kent
Edward is my sonne, and I will keepe him.	Edw	5.2.117	Queene
And give my heart to Isabell and him,	Edw	5.3.11	Edward
Souldiers, let me but talke to him one worde.	Edw	5.3.53	Kent
Binde him, and so convey him to the court.	Edw	5.3.58	Gurney
And I will visit him, why stay you me?	Edw	5.3.60	Kent
The commons now begin to pitie him,	Edw	5.4.2	Mortmr

HIM (cont.)

I am the Champion that will combate him!	Edw	5.4.78	Champn
Lord Mortimer, now take him to your charge.	Edw	5.4.81	Queene
As we were bringing him to Killingworth.	Edw	5.4.85	Souldr
Sweete mother, if I cannot pardon him, ...	Edw	5.4.94	King
But seeing I cannot, ile entreate for him:	Edw	5.4.98	King
How often shall I bid you beare him hence?	Edw	5.4.102	Mortmr
At our commaund, once more away with him.	Edw	5.4.104	Mortmr
He is a traitor, thinke not on him, come.	Edw	5.4.115	Queene
yesternight/I opened but the doore to throw him meate,/And I	Edw	5.5.8	Gurney
Send for him out thence, and I will anger him.	Edw	5.5.13	Gurney
let him have the king,/What else?	Edw	5.5.24	Matrvs
His fathers dead, and we have murdered him.	Edw	5.6.16	Queene
Aye me, see where he comes, and they with him, . . .	Edw	5.6.22	Queene
And had you lov'de him halfe so well as I, ...	Edw	5.6.35	King
Who is the man dare say I murdered him?	Edw	5.6.40	Mortmr
And plainely saith, twas thou that murdredst him. . . .	Edw	5.6.42	King
Bring him unto a hurdle, drag him foorth, ...	Edw	5.6.52	King
Hang him I say, and set his quarters up, ...	Edw	5.6.53	King
And with the rest accompanie him to his grave?	Edw	5.6.88	Queene
Whereas his kinsmen chiefly brought him up;	F 14	Prol.14	1Chor
Nothing so sweet as Magicke is to him, ...	F 26	Prol.26	1Chor
Whose [shadows] made all Europe honour him.	F 145	1.1.117	Faust
Valdes, first let him know the words of Art, ...	F 185	1.1.157	Cornel
<yet should I grieve for him>:	F 224	(HC258)A	2Schol
<and see if hee by> his grave counsell may <can> reclaime him.	F 226	1.2.33	2Schol
<O but> I feare me, nothing will <can> reclaime him now. .	F 227	1.2.34	1Schol
This word Damnation, terrifies not me <him>, ...	F 286	1.3.58	Faust
For which God threw him from the face of heaven. . . .	F 296	1.3.68	Mephst
Say he surrenders up to him his soule, ...	F 318	1.3.90	Faust
So he will spare him foure and twenty yeares, ...	F 319	1.3.91	Faust
Letting him live in all voluptuousnesse, ...	F 320	1.3.92	Faust
By him, I'le be great Emperour of the world, ...	F 332	1.3.104	Faust
and Belcher come here, I'le belch him:	F 374	1.4.32	P Robin
To him, I'le build an Altar and a Church, ...	F 401	2.1.13	Faust
I Mephostophilis, I'le <I> give it him <thee>.	F 437	2.1.49	Faust
I'le fetch him somewhat to delight his minde.	F 471	2.1.83	Mephst
shall be his servant, and be by him commanded <at his command>.	F 486	2.1.98	P Faust
that Mephostophilis shall doe for him, and bring him .	F 488	2.1.100	P Faust
Mephostophilis shall doe for him, and bring him whatsoever.	F 488	2.1.100	P Faust
pardon [me] <him> for <in> this,/And Faustus vowes never to	F 647	2.2.96	Faust
[Never to name God, or to pray to him], ...	F 649	2.2.98A	Faust
Did mount him up <himselfe> to scale Olimpus top. . . .	F 757	2.3.36	2Chor
And in eight daies did bring him home againe.	F 767	2.3.46	2Chor
But new exploits do hale him out agen, ...	F 770	2.3.49	2Chor
The sacred Sinod hath decreed for him, ...	F 885	3.1.107	Pope
And beare him to the States of Germany.	F 900	3.1.122	Faust
And curse the people that submit to him;	F 907	3.1.129	Pope
authority Apostolicall/Depose him from his Regall Government.	F 924	3.1.146	Pope
For him, and the succeeding Popes of Rome, ...	F 926	3.1.148	Bruno
here, take him to your charge,/And beare him streight to Ponte	F 964	3.1.186	Pope
And beare him streight to Ponte Angelo, ...	F 965	3.1.187	Pope
And in the strongest Tower inclose him fast.	F 966	3.1.188	Pope
'Tis no matter, let him come; an he follow us, I'le so conjure	F1091	3.3.4	P Robin
us, I'le so conjure him, as he was never conjur'd in his life,	F1092	3.3.5	P Robin
him, as he was never conjur'd in his life, I warrant him:	F1092	3.3.5	P Robin
let me have the carrying of him about to shew some trickes.	F1129	3.3.42	P Robin
be thou transformed to/A dog, and carry him upon thy backe;	F1131	3.3.44	Mephst
And with him comes the Germane Conjurer, ...	F1164	4.1.10	Mrtino
See, see his window's ope, we'l call to him.	F1177	4.1.23	Fredrk
and if he be so farre in love with him, I would he would post	F1191	4.1.37	P Benvol
love with him, I would he would post with him to Rome againe.	F1191	4.1.37	P Benvol
drunke over night, the Divell cannot hurt him in the morning:	F1201	4.1.47	P Benvol
shall controule him as well as the Conjurer, I warrant you.	F1203	4.1.49	P Benvol
I doe not greatly beleeve him, he lookes as like [a] conjurer	F1228	4.1.74	P Benvol
That in mine armes I would have compast him.	F1262	4.1.108	Emper
This sport is excellent: wee'l call and wake him. . . .	F1281	4.1.127	Emper
Il'e raise a kennell of Hounds shall hunt him so, . . .	F1301	4.1.147	Faust
Mephostophilis, transforme him; and hereafter sir, looke you	F1314	4.1.160	P Faust
I saw him kneele, and kisse the Emperours hand, . . .	F1344	4.2.20	Benvol
Who kils him shall have gold, and endlesse love. . . .	F1349	4.2.25	Fredrk
and now sirs, having divided him, what shall the body doe?	F1389	4.2.65	P Mrtino
Give him his head for Gods sake.	F1392	4.2.68	P Fredrk
And hurle him in some lake of mud and durt:	F1409	4.2.85	Faust
Take thou this other, dragge him through the woods, . . .	F1410	4.2.86	Faust
If we should follow him to worke revenge, ...	F1448	4.3.18	Benvol
I have no great need to sell him, but if thou likest him for	F1460	4.4.4	P Faust
sell him; but if thou likest him for ten Dollors more, take him,	F1460	4.4.4	P Faust
more, take him, because I see thou hast a good minde to him.	F1461	4.4.5	P Faust
more, take him, because I see thou hast a good minde to him.	F1462	4.4.6	P Faust
that you may ride him o're hedge and ditch, and spare him not;	F1467	4.4.11	P Faust
him o're hedge and ditch, and spare him not; but do you heare?	F1468	4.4.12	P Faust
in any case, ride him not into the water.	F1469	4.4.13	P Faust
waters, but ride him not into the water; o're hedge and ditch,	F1472	4.4.16	P Faust
Go bid the Hostler deliver him unto you, and remember what I	F1474	4.4.18	P Faust
Well I'le go rouse him, and make him give me my forty Dollors	F1487	4.4.31	P HrsCsr
go rouse him, and make him give me my forty Dollors againe.	F1488	4.4.32	P HrsCsr
I'le out-run him, and cast this leg into some ditch or other.	F1495	4.4.39	P HrsCsr
Stop him, stop him, stop him--ha, ha, ha, Faustus hath his leg	F1496	4.4.40	P Faust
I, a plague take him, heere's some on's have cause to know him;	F1523	4.5.19	P HrsCsr
heere's some on's have cause to know him; did he conjure thee	F1524	4.5.20	P HrsCsr
bad him take as much as he would for three-farthings; so he	F1528	4.5.24	P Carter
I went to him yesterday to buy a horse of him, and he would by	F1536	4.5.32	P HrsCsr

HIM (cont.)

and he would by no meanes sell him under forty Dollors; so sir,	F1537	4.5.33	P HrsCsr
because I knew him to be such a horse, as would run over hedge	F1538	4.5.34	P HrsCsr
and never tyre, I gave him his money; so when I had my horse,	F1539	4.5.35	P HrsCsr
Doctor Fauster bad me ride him night and day, and spare him no	F1540	4.5.36	P HrsCsr
bad me ride him night and day, and spare him no time; but,	F1540	4.5.36	P HrsCsr
time; but, quoth he, in any case ride him not into the water.	F1541	4.5.37	P HrsCsr
what did I but rid him into a great river, and when I came just	F1543	4.5.39	P HrsCsr
But you shall heare how bravely I serv'd him for it; I went me	F1547	4.5.43	P HrsCsr
and there I found him asleepe; I kept a hallowing and whooping	F1548	4.5.44	P HrsCsr
and whooping in his eares, but all could not wake him:	F1550	4.5.46	P HrsCsr
I seeing that, tooke him by the leg, and never rested pulling,	F1550	4.5.46	P HrsCsr
We have no reason for it, therefore a fig for him.	F1593	4.6.36	P Dick
I, and we will speake with him.	F1601	4.6.44	Carter
Ha, ha, ha, dost heare him Dick, he has forgot his legge.	F1629	4.6.72	P Carter
you remember you bid he should not ride [him] into the water?	F1636	4.6.79	P Carter
deny/The just [requests] <request> of those that wish him well,	F1691	5.1.18	Faust
I do repent I ere offended him,	F1746	5.1.73	Faust
To marke him how he doth demeane himselfe.	F1806	5.2.10	Belzeb
<to cure him, tis but a surffet, never feare man>.	F1831	(HC270)A	P 2Schol
but let us into the next roome, and [there] pray for him.	F1872	5.2.76	P 1Schol
Yet will I call on him: O spare me Lucifer.	F1942	5.2.146	Faust
The devils whom Faustus serv'd have torne him thus:	F1990	5.3.8	3Schol
one, me thought/I heard him shreeke and call aloud for helpe:	F1992	5.3.10	3Schol
I, I thought that was al the land his father left him:	F App	p.229 18	P Clown
Beare witnesse I gave them him.	F App	p.230 41	P Wagner
well, Ile folow him, Ile serve him, thats flat.	F App	p.231 73	P Clown
Hush, Ile gul him supernaturally:	F App	p.234 5	P Robin
As when I heare but motion made of him,	F App	p.237 27	Emper
And bring with him his beauteous Paramour,	F App	p.237 32	Emper
One of you call him foorth.	F App	p.238 68	P Emper
at my intreaty release him, he hath done penance sufficient.	F App	p.238 79	P Emper
being all I desire, I am content to release him of his hornes:	F App	p.238 84	P Faust
Mephastophilis, transforme him strait.	F App	p.238 85	P Faust
I cannot sel him so:	F App	p.239 103	P Faust
if thou likst him for fifty, take him.	F App	p.239 103	P Faust
I pray you let him have him, he is an honest felow, and he has	F App	p.239 105	P Mephst
Wel, come give me your money, my boy wil deliver him to you:	F App	p.239 108	P Faust
but I must tel you one thing before you have him, ride him not	F App	p.239 108	P Faust
before you have him, ride him not into the water at any hand.	F App	p.239 109	P Faust
but ride him not into the water, ride him over hedge or ditch,	F App	p.239 111	P Faust
the water, ride him over hedge or ditch, or where thou wilt,	F App	p.239 112	P Faust
Ide make a brave living on him; hee has a buttocke as slicke as	F App	p.239 116	P HrsCsr
slicke as an Ele; wel god buy sir, your boy wil deliver him me:	F App	p.240 117	P HrsCsr
I would not be ruled by him, for he bade me I should ride him	F App	p.240 130	P HrsCsr
by him, for he bade me I should ride him into no water; now,	F App	p.240 131	P HrsCsr
rid him into the deepe pond at the townes ende, I was no sooner	F App	p.240 133	P HrsCsr
you cannot speake with him.	F App	p.240 139	P Mephst
But I wil speake with him.	F App	p.240 140	P HrsCsr
Ile speake with him now, or Ile breake his glasse-windowes	F App	p.240 142	P HrsCsr
And he have not slept this eight weekes Ile speake with him.	F App	p.240 146	P HrsCsr
his labour; wel, this tricke shal cost him fortie dollers more.	F App	p.241 166	P Faust
niggard of my cunning, come Mephastophilis, let's away to him.	F App	p.241 172	P Faust
And thought his name sufficient to uphold him,	Lucan, First Booke	136	
and his owne waight/Keepe him within the ground, his armes al	Lucan, First Booke	140	
And glad when bloud, and ruine made him way:	Lucan, First Booke	151	
But gods and fortune prickt him to this war,	Lucan, First Booke	265	
(Whom from his youth he bribde) needs make him king?	Lucan, First Booke	315	
And by him kept of purpose for a dearth?	Lucan, First Booke	319	
least sloth and long delay/Might crosse him, he withdrew his	Lucan, First Booke	395	
come, their huge power made him bould/To mannage greater deeds;	Lucan, First Booke	462	
hornes/The quick priest pull'd him on his knees and slew him:	Lucan, First Booke	612	
The very cullor scard him; a dead blacknesse/Ranne through the	Lucan, First Booke	617	
Were Love the cause, it's like I shoulde descry him,	Ovid's Elegies	1.2.5	
Or lies he close, and shoots where none can spie him?	Ovid's Elegies	1.2.6	
Yeelding or striving <strugling> doe we give him might,	Ovid's Elegies	1.2.9	
Thee Pompous birds and him two tygres drew.	Ovid's Elegies	1.2.48	
Accept him that will serve thee all his youth,	Ovid's Elegies	1.3.5	
Accept him that will love with spotlesse truth:	Ovid's Elegies	1.3.6	
Wilt lying under him his bosome clippe?	Ovid's Elegies	1.4.5	
though I not see/What may be done, yet there before him bee.	Ovid's Elegies	1.4.14	
Lie with him gently, when his limbes he spread/Upon the bed,	Ovid's Elegies	1.4.15	
What wine he fills thee, wisely will him drinke,	Ovid's Elegies	1.4.29	
Thy bosomes Roseat buds let him not finger,	Ovid's Elegies	1.4.37	
not onely kisse/But force thee give him my stolne honey blisse.	Ovid's Elegies	1.4.64	
To him I pray it no delight may bring,	Ovid's Elegies	1.4.67	
would, I cannot him cashiere/Before I be divided from my geere.	Ovid's Elegies	1.6.35	
Would he not buy thee thou for him shouldst care.	Ovid's Elegies	1.8.34	
Deny him oft, feigne now thy head doth ake:	Ovid's Elegies	1.8.73	
Receive him soone, least patient use he gaine,	Ovid's Elegies	1.8.75	
Let him within heare bard out lovers prate.	Ovid's Elegies	1.8.78	
And sister, Nurse, and mother spare him not,	Ovid's Elegies	1.8.91	
On all the [bed mens] <beds men> tumbling let him viewe/And thy	Ovid's Elegies	1.8.97	
Chiefely shew him the gifts, which others send:	Ovid's Elegies	1.8.99	
If he gives nothing, let him from thee wend.	Ovid's Elegies	1.8.100	
Pray him to lend what thou maist nere restore.	Ovid's Elegies	1.8.102	
Let him surcease: love tries wit best of all.	Ovid's Elegies	1.9.32	
He that will not growe slothfull let him love.	Ovid's Elegies	1.9.46	
The sonne slew her, that forth to meete him went,	Ovid's Elegies	1.10.51	
And him that hew'd you out for needfull uses/Ile prove had	Ovid's Elegies	1.12.15	
Who can indure, save him with whom none lies?	Ovid's Elegies	1.13.26	
[Doest] punish <ye >me, because yeares make him waine?	Ovid's Elegies	1.13.41	
Let him goe forth knowne, that unknowne did enter,	Ovid's Elegies	2.2.20	

HIM (cont.)

Let him goe see her though she doe not languish/And then report	Ovid's Elegies	2.2.21
Let him please, haunt the house, be kindly usd,	Ovid's Elegies	2.2.29
Vaine causes faine of him the true to hide,	Ovid's Elegies	2.2.31
Him timelesse death tooke, she was deifide.	Ovid's Elegies	2.2.46
To prove him foolish did I ere contend?	Ovid's Elegies	2.8.10
His rider vainely striving him to stay,	Ovid's Elegies	2.9.30
And with the waters sees death neere him thrusts,	Ovid's Elegies	2.11.26
Because on him thy care doth hap to rest.	Ovid's Elegies	3.2.8
One slowe we favour, Romans him revoke:	Ovid's Elegies	3.2.73
They call him backe:	Ovid's Elegies	3.2.75
Foole canst thou him in thy white armes embrace?	Ovid's Elegies	3.7.11
Confessing this, why doest thou touch him than?	Ovid's Elegies	3.7.22
O let him change goods so ill got to dust.	Ovid's Elegies	3.7.66
Him the last day in black Averne hath drownd,	Ovid's Elegies	3.8.27
Their <Your> youthfull browes with Ivie girt to meete him,/With	Ovid's Elegies	3.8.61
With Calvus learnd Catullus comes <come> and greete him.	Ovid's Elegies	3.8.62
And give to him that the first wound imparts.	Ovid's Elegies	3.12.22
From him that yeelds the garland <palme> is quickly got,	Ovid's Elegies	3.13.47
Musaeus soong)/Dwelt at Abidus; since him, dwelt there none,	Hero and Leander	1.53
Was moov'd with him, and for his favour sought.	Hero and Leander	1.82
Were I the saint hee worships, I would heare him,	Hero and Leander	1.179
And as shee spake those words, came somewhat nere him.	Hero and Leander	1.180
And alwaies cut him off as he replide.	Hero and Leander	1.196
Thereat she smild, and did denie him so	Hero and Leander	1.311
Which makes him quickly re-enforce his speech,	Hero and Leander	1.313
his spreading armes away she cast her,/And thus bespake him:	Hero and Leander	1.343
And shot a shaft that burning from him went,	Hero and Leander	1.372
so much/As one poore word, their hate to him was such.	Hero and Leander	1.384
she wanting no excuse/To feed him with delaies, as women use:	Hero and Leander	1.426
fire filcht by Prometheus;/And thrusts him down from heaven:	Hero and Leander	1.439
They offred him the deadly fatall knife,	Hero and Leander	1.447
They seeing it, both Love and him abhor'd,	Hero and Leander	1.463
By being possest of him for whom she long'd:	Hero and Leander	2.36
Therefore unto him hastily she goes,	Hero and Leander	2.45
nothing saw/That might delight him more, yet he suspected/Some	Hero and Leander	2.63
Which taught him all that elder lovers know,	Hero and Leander	2.69
Shee, with a kind of graunting, put him by it,	Hero and Leander	2.73
Sad Hero wroong him by the hand, and wept,	Hero and Leander	2.95
That him from her unjustly did detaine.	Hero and Leander	2.122
And then he got him to a rocke aloft.	Hero and Leander	2.148
With that hee stript him to the yv'rie skin,	Hero and Leander	2.153
Had left the heavens, therefore on him hee seaz'd.	Hero and Leander	2.158
Leander striv'd, the waves about him wound,	Hero and Leander	2.159
And puld him to the bottome, where the ground/Was strewd with	Hero and Leander	2.160
The lustie god imbrast him, cald him love,	Hero and Leander	2.167
He heav'd him up, and looking on his face,	Hero and Leander	2.171
Which mounted up, intending to have kist him,	Hero and Leander	2.173
And fell in drops like teares, because they mist him.	Hero and Leander	2.174
And looking backe, saw Neptune follow him.	Hero and Leander	2.176
And swore the sea should never doe him harme.	Hero and Leander	2.180
And [throw] <threw> him gawdie toies to please his eie,	Hero and Leander	2.187
And up againe, and close beside him swim,	Hero and Leander	2.190
Least water-nymphs should pull him from the brinke.	Hero and Leander	2.198
and up-staring <upstarting> Fawnes,/Would steale him thence.	Hero and Leander	2.201
He flung at him his mace, but as it went,	Hero and Leander	2.209
He cald it in, for love made him repent.	Hero and Leander	2.210
The god seeing him with pittie to be moved,	Hero and Leander	2.219
And now she lets him whisper in her eare,	Hero and Leander	2.267
Or speake to him who in a moment tooke,	Hero and Leander	2.308

HIMSELF

Now, he that cals himself the scourge of Jove,	2Tamb	3.5.21	Orcan
Approove the difference twixt himself and you.	2Tamb	4.1.137	Tamb
and tyll the ground that he himself should occupy, which is his	P 812	17.7	P Souldr
How hard the nobles, how unkinde the king/Hath shewed himself:	Edw	4.2.50	Mortmr

HIMSELFE

Whiles my Aeneas spends himselfe in plaints,	Dido	1.1.140	Venus
To see my sweet Iarbus slay himselfe?	Dido	5.1.324	Anna
To make himselfe the Monarch of the East:	1Tamb	1.1.43	Meandr
mated and amaz'd/To heare the king thus threaten like himselfe?	1Tamb	1.1.108	Menaph
And Jove himselfe will stretch his hand from heaven,	1Tamb	1.2.180	Tamb
Will quickly win such as are like himselfe.	1Tamb	2.2.28	Meandr
And place himselfe in the Emperiall heaven,	1Tamb	2.7.15	Tamb
Though Mars himselfe the angrie God of armes,	1Tamb	2.7.58	Tamb
Now Mahomet, solicit God himselfe,	1Tamb	3.3.195	Zabina
Shall sit by him and starve to death himselfe.	1Tamb	4.2.90	Tamb
Himselfe in presence shal unfold at large.	2Tamb	Prol.9	Prolog
And he that meanes to place himselfe therin/Must armed wade up	2Tamb	1.3.83	Tamb
Brothers to holy Mahomet himselfe,	2Tamb	3.3.36	Capt
When he himselfe amidst the thickest troopes/Beats downe our	2Tamb	4.1.25	Amyras
Where men report, thou sitt'st by God himselfe,	2Tamb	5.1.194	Tamb
Though God himselfe and holy Mahomet,	2Tamb	5.2.37	Amasia
Before himselfe or his be conquered.	2Tamb	5.2.53	Callap
May be upon himselfe reverberate.	2Tamb	5.3.223	Techel
And for a pound to sweat himselfe to death:	Jew	1.1.18	Barab
Doth see his souldiers slaine, himselfe disarm'd,	Jew	1.2.204	Barab
And now and then one hang himselfe for griefe,	Jew	2.3.196	Barab
For Selim-Calymath shall come himselfe,	Jew	3.5.23	Basso
Doe what I can he will not strip himselfe,	Jew	4.1.131	Ithimr
he weares, Judas left under the Elder when he hang'd himselfe.	Jew	4.4.67	P Ithimr
policy for Barabas/To dispossesse himselfe of such a place?	Jew	5.2.66	Barab
As hath sufficient counsaile in himselfe,	P 456	8.6	Anjoy
To please himselfe with mannage of the warres,	P 459	8.9	Anjoy

HIMSELFE (cont.)			
And all his heaven is to delight himselfe:	P 634	12.47	QnMoth
hands upon him, next/Himselfe imprisoned, and his goods asceasd,	Edw	1.2.37	ArchBp
What neede I, God himselfe is up in armes,	Edw	1.2.40	ArchBp
a factious lord/Shall hardly do himselfe good, much lesse us,	Edw	2.1.7	Spencr
Your king hath wrongd your countrie and himselfe,	Edw	4.6.67	Mortmr
And he himselfe lies in captivitie.	Edw	5.2.4	Mortmr
And gripe the sorer being gript himselfe.	Edw	5.2.9	Mortmr
I heare of late he hath deposde himselfe.	Edw	5.2.83	Kent
False Gurney hath betraide me and himselfe.	Edw	5.6.45	Mortmr
Faustus may try his cunning by himselfe.	F 187	1.1.159	Cornel
To whom Faustus doth dedicate himselfe.	F 285	1.3.57	Faust
Did mount him up <himselfe> to scale Olimpus top.	F 757	2.3.36	2Chor
Who's this, that stands so solemnly by himselfe:	F1513	4.5.9	P Hostss
To marke him how he doth demeane himselfe.	F1806	5.2.10	Belzeb
Titan himselfe throand in the midst of heaven,	Lucan, First Booke		538
Kind Jupiter hath low declin'd himselfe;	Lucan, First Booke		660
If hee gives thee what first himselfe did tast,	Ovid's Elegies		1.4.33
Will you for gaine have Cupid sell himselfe?	Ovid's Elegies		1.10.17
That with one worde hath nigh himselfe undone,	Ovid's Elegies		1.13.20
Even Jove himselfe out off my wit was reft.	Ovid's Elegies		2.1.18
Though himselfe see; heele credit her denyall,	Ovid's Elegies		2.2.57
lies quiet/And slumbring, thinkes himselfe much blessed by it.	Ovid's Elegies		2.9.40
Jove turnes himselfe into a Swanne, or gold,	Ovid's Elegies		3.11.33
Lesse sinnes the poore rich man that starves himselfe,	Hero and Leander		1.243
And ever as he thought himselfe most nigh it,	Hero and Leander		2.74
HINDE			
The painfull Hinde by thee to field is sent,	Ovid's Elegies		1.13.15
HINDER			
Hinder her not, thou man of little faith,	Jew	1.2.340	1Fryar
That hinder our possession to the crowne:	P 154	2.97	Guise
HINDES			
Though Hindes in brookes the running waters bring,	Ovid's Elegies		2.16.35
HINDRED			
The spring is hindred by your smoothering host,	1Tamb	3.1.50	Moroc
HINDS			
And choakt with thorns, that greedy earth wants hinds,	Lucan, First Booke		29
Was stretcht unto the fields of hinds unknowne;	Lucan, First Booke		171
But vicious, harebraind, and illit'rat hinds?	Hero and Leander		2.218
HINGES			
How stand the cords? How hang these hinges, fast?	Jew	5.5.1	Barab
The earth went off hir hinges; And the Alpes/Shooke the old	Lucan, First Booke		551
or do the turned hinges sound,/And opening dores with creaking	Ovid's Elegies		1.6.49
HIPOLITE			
Phedra, and Hipolite may read, my care is,	Ovid's Elegies		2.18.24
HIPOSTASIS			
and the [Hipostasis] <Hipostates>/Thick and obscure doth make	2Tamb	5.3.82	Phsitn
HIPOSTATES			
and the [Hipostasis] <Hipostates>/Thick and obscure doth make	2Tamb	5.3.82	Phsitn
HIPPOCRAS (See IPOCRASE)			
HIPPODAMEIAS			
Hippodameias lookes while he beheld.	Ovid's Elegies		3.2.16
HIPPOLITUS (See also HYPPOLITUS)			
Had wilde Hippolitus, Leander seene,	Hero and Leander		1.77
HIPPOLYTA (See HIPOLITE)			
HIPPOMENES			
Wish in his hands graspt did Hippomenes.	Ovid's Elegies		3.2.30
HIPSIPILE			
Jasons sad letter doth Hipsipile greete,	Ovid's Elegies		2.18.33
HIR			
then turn her and wind hir to thy owne use, as often as thou	F App	p.234 27 P	Robin
The earth went off hir hinges; And the Alpes/Shooke the old	Lucan, First Booke		551
let hir <he> that cought me late,/Either love, or cause that I	Ovid's Elegies		1.3.1
I aske too much, would she but let me love hir,	Ovid's Elegies		1.3.3
Love <Jove> knowes with such like praiers, I dayly move hir:	Ovid's Elegies		1.3.4
I love but one, and hir I love change never,	Ovid's Elegies		1.3.15
By verses horned Io got hir name,	Ovid's Elegies		1.3.21
Griping his false hornes with hir virgin hand:	Ovid's Elegies		1.3.24
HIRCANIA			
And Tygers of Hircania gave thee sucke:	Dido	5.1.159	Dido
whilst with their dams/They kennel'd in Hircania, evermore/Wil	Lucan, First Booke		329
HIR'D			
And since that time they have hir'd a slave my man/To accuse me	Jew	5.1.75	Barab
HIRE (See also HYR'D)			
Well I remember when I first did hire thee,	Ovid's Elegies		1.6.43
Servants fit for thy purpose thou must hire/To teach thy lover,	Ovid's Elegies		1.8.87
Making her joy according to her hire.	Ovid's Elegies		1.10.32
I know no maister of so great hire sped.	Ovid's Elegies		2.5.62
HIRER			
The hirer payeth al, his rent discharg'd/From further duty he	Ovid's Elegies		1.10.45
HIRS			
Therefore unto his bodie, hirs he clung,	Hero and Leander		2.65
HIS (See also HYS, ON'S)			
Hermes no more shall shew the world his wings,	Dido	1.1.38	Jupitr
If that thy fancie in his feathers dwell,	Dido	1.1.39	Jupitr
And charg'd him drowne my sonne with all his traine.	Dido	1.1.61	Venus
sounds/The surges, his fierce souldiers, to the spoyle:	Dido	1.1.69	Venus
But first in bloud must his good fortune bud,	Dido	1.1.86	Jupitr
And in the end subdue them with his sword,	Dido	1.1.90	Jupitr
Shall build his throne amidst those starrie towers,	Dido	1.1.98	Jupitr
No bounds but heaven shall bound his Emperie,	Dido	1.1.100	Jupitr
Whose azured gates enchased with his name,	Dido	1.1.101	Jupitr
To feede her eyes with his engraven fame.	Dido	1.1.103	Jupitr

HIS (cont.)

pooles, refraines/To taint his tresses in the Tyrrhen maine?	Dido	1.1.112	Venus
Charge him from me to turne his stormie powers,	Dido	1.1.117	Jupitr
Vaild his resplendant glorie from your view.	Dido	1.1.126	Venus
Triton I know hath fild his trumpe with Troy,	Dido	1.1.130	Venus
And therefore will take pitie on his toyle,	Dido	1.1.131	Venus
And heaven and earth with his unrest acquaints.	Dido	1.1.141	Venus
Yet shall the aged Sunne shed forth his [haire] <aire>,	Dido	1.1.159	Achat
Which now we call Italia of his name,	Dido	1.2.23	Cloan
And kisse his hand: O where is Hecuba?	Dido	2.1.12	Achat
it life, that under his conduct/We might saile backe to Troy,	Dido	2.1.17	Aeneas
Achates, see King Priam wags his hand,	Dido	2.1.29	Aeneas
Aeneas see, Sergestus or his ghost.	Dido	2.1.50	Achat
He [names] <meanes> Aeneas, let us kisse his feete.	Dido	2.1.51	Illion
Why turnes Aeneas from his trustie friends?	Dido	2.1.57	Cloan
Summoned the Captaines to his princely tent,	Dido	2.1.130	Aeneas
to further his entent/The windes did drive huge billowes to the	Dido	2.1.138	Aeneas
With sacrificing wreathes upon his head,	Dido	2.1.148	Aeneas
His hands bound at his backe, and both his eyes/Turnd up to	Dido	2.1.151	Aeneas
and both his eyes/Turnd up to heaven as one resolv'd to dye,	Dido	2.1.151	Aeneas
Kist him, imbrast him, and unloosde his bands,	Dido	2.1.158	Aeneas
for that one Laocoon/Breaking a speare upon his hollow breast,	Dido	2.1.165	Aeneas
and suddenly/From out his entrailes, Neoptolemus/Setting his	Dido	2.1.183	Aeneas
Neoptolemus/Setting his speare upon the ground, leapt forth,	Dido	2.1.184	Aeneas
His armes torne from his shoulders, and his breast/Furrowd with	Dido	2.1.203	Aeneas
torne from his shoulders, and his breast/Furrowd with wounds,	Dido	2.1.203	Aeneas
Thongs at his heeles, by which Achilles horse/Drew him in	Dido	2.1.205	Aeneas
His harnesse dropping bloud, and on his speare/The mangled head	Dido	2.1.214	Aeneas
and on his speare/The mangled head of Priams yongest sonne,	Dido	2.1.214	Aeneas
And after him his band of Mirmidons,	Dido	2.1.216	Aeneas
Foulding his hand in hers, and joyntly both/Beating their	Dido	2.1.227	Aeneas
He with his faulchions poynt raisde up at once,	Dido	2.1.229	Aeneas
Not mov'd at all, but smiling at his teares,	Dido	2.1.240	Aeneas
This butcher whil'st his hands were yet held up,	Dido	2.1.241	Aeneas
Treading upon his breast, strooke off his hands.	Dido	2.1.242	Aeneas
At which the franticke Queene leapt on his face,	Dido	2.1.244	Aeneas
And in his eyelids hanging by the nayles,	Dido	2.1.245	Aeneas
Whereat he lifted up his bedred lims,	Dido	2.1.250	Aeneas
Forgetting both his want of strength and hands,	Dido	2.1.252	Aeneas
Which he disdaining whiskt his sword about,	Dido	2.1.253	Aeneas
Yet he undaunted tooke his fathers flagge,	Dido	2.1.259	Aeneas
So leaning on his sword he stood stone still,	Dido	2.1.263	Aeneas
These milke white Doves shall be his Centronels:	Dido	2.1.320	Venus
And by that meanes repaire his broken ships,	Dido	2.1.328	Venus
Victuall his Souldiers, give him wealthie gifts,	Dido	2.1.329	Venus
Or els in Carthage make his kingly throne.	Dido	2.1.331	Venus
Because his lothsome sight offends mine eye,	Dido	3.1.57	Dido
Is he not eloquent in all his speech?	Dido	3.1.65	Dido
Ile make me bracelets of his golden haire,	Dido	3.1.85	Dido
His glistering eyes shall be my looking glasse,	Dido	3.1.86	Dido
His lips an altar, where Ile offer up/As many kisses as the Sea	Dido	3.1.87	Dido
His lookes shall be my only Librarie,	Dido	3.1.90	Dido
But his fantastick humours pleasde not me:	Dido	3.1.158	Dido
As for Achates, and his followers.	Dido	3.1.176	Dido
Nor Venus triumph in his tender youth:	Dido	3.2.9	Juno
And feede infection with his [let] <left> out life:	Dido	3.2.11	Juno
But lustfull Jove and his adulterous child,	Dido	3.2.18	Juno
I mustred all the windes unto his wracke,	Dido	3.2.45	Juno
And urg'd each Element to his annoy:	Dido	3.2.46	Juno
Yet now I doe repent me of his ruth,	Dido	3.2.47	Juno
Cupid shall lay his arrowes in thy lap,	Dido	3.2.56	Venus
And to a Scepter chaunge his golden shafts,	Dido	3.2.57	Venus
And feedes his eyes with favours of her Court,	Dido	3.2.71	Juno
I would have either drunke his dying bloud,	Dido	3.3.28	Iarbus
Sister, see see Ascanius in his pompe,	Dido	3.3.32	Anna
Bearing his huntspeare bravely in his hand.	Dido	3.3.33	Anna
How like his father speaketh he in all?	Dido	3.3.41	Anna
And loade his speare with Grecian Princes heads,	Dido	3.3.43	Aeneas
Will dye with very tidings of his death:	Dido	3.3.77	Iarbus
Aeneas no, although his eyes doe pearce.	Dido	3.4.12	Dido
And will she be avenged on his life?	Dido	3.4.14	Aeneas
That should detaine thy eye in his defects?	Dido	3.4.17	Aeneas
When as he buts his beames on Floras bed,	Dido	3.4.20	Dido
And I must perish in his burning armes.	Dido	3.4.22	Dido
That calles my soule from forth his living seate,	Dido	3.4.53	Dido
and warne him to his ships/That now afflicts me with his	Dido	4.2.21	Iarbus
him to his ships/That now afflicts me with his flattering eyes.	Dido	4.2.22	Iarbus
And cut a passage through his toples hilles:	Dido	4.3.12	Aeneas
Will Dido raise old Priam forth his grave,	Dido	4.3.39	Illion
O where is Ganimed to hold his cup,	Dido	4.4.46	Dido
Aeneas for his parentage deserves/As large a kingdome as is	Dido	4.4.79	Achat
For Troy, for Priam, for his fiftie sonnes,	Dido	4.4.89	Aeneas
Aeneas will not goe without his sonne:	Dido	4.4.107	Dido
Bring me his oares, his tackling, and his sailes:	Dido	4.4.109	Dido
What if I sinke his ships? O heele frowne:	Dido	4.4.110	Dido
For in his lookes I see eternitie,	Dido	4.4.122	Dido
Why should I blame Aeneas for his flight?	Dido	4.4.148	Dido
O Dido, blame not him, but breake his oares,	Dido	4.4.149	Dido
Now let him hang my favours on his masts,	Dido	4.4.159	Dido
Which I bestowd upon his followers:	Dido	4.4.162	Dido
In steed of oares, let him use his hands,	Dido	4.4.163	Dido
Wherewith his burning beames like labouring Bees,	Dido	5.1.12	Aeneas
If it be so, his father meanes to flye:	Dido	5.1.85	Dido

HIS (cont.)

Aeneas will not faine with his deare love,	Dido	5.1.92	Aeneas
Sent from his father Jove, appeard to me,	Dido	5.1.95	Aeneas
And in his name rebukt me bitterly,	Dido	5.1.96	Aeneas
But yet Aeneas will not leave his love?	Dido	5.1.98	Dido
That I might see Aeneas in his face:	Dido	5.1.150	Dido
I never vow'd at Aulis gulfe/The desolation of his native Troy,	Dido	5.1.203	Dido
Then gan he wagge his hand, which yet held up,	Dido	5.1.229	Anna
And ore his ships will soare unto the Sunne,	Dido	5.1.244	Dido
That they may melt and I fall in his armes:	Dido	5.1.245	Dido
And ride upon his backe unto my love:	Dido	5.1.250	Dido
Theile breake his ships, O Proteus, Neptune, Jove,	Dido	5.1.255	Dido
Who wild me sacrifize his ticing relliques:	Dido	5.1.277	Dido
Thou shalt burne first, thy crime is worse then his:	Dido	5.1.297	Dido
By plowing up his Countries with the Sword:	Dido	5.1.308	Dido
tearms/And scourging kingdoms with his conquering sword.	1Tamb	Prol.6	Prolog
View but his picture in this tragicke glasse,	1Tamb	Prol.7	Prolog
And then applaud his fortunes if you please.	1Tamb	Prol.8	Prolog
denied/To shed [their] <his> influence in his fickle braine,	1Tamb	1.1.15	Cosroe
And in your confines with his lawlesse traine,	1Tamb	1.1.39	Meandr
in Asia, or display/His vagrant Ensigne in the Persean fields,	1Tamb	1.1.45	Meandr
These are his words, Meander set them downe.	1Tamb	1.1.94	Mycet
Ah Menaphon, I passe not for his threates,	1Tamb	1.1.109	Cosroe
at the spoile/Of great Darius and his wealthy hoast.	1Tamb	1.1.154	Ceneus
Bearing his privie signet and his hand:	1Tamb	1.2.15	Zenoc
We have his highnesse letters to command/Aide and assistance if	1Tamb	1.2.19	Magnet
Must grace his bed that conquers Asia:	1Tamb	1.2.37	Tamb
Measuring the limits of his Emperie/By East and west, as	1Tamb	1.2.39	Tamb
of his Emperie/By East and west, as Phoebus doth his course:	1Tamb	1.2.40	Tamb
So in his Armour looketh Tamburlaine:	1Tamb	1.2.54	Techel
Me thinks I see kings kneeling at his feet,	1Tamb	1.2.55	Techel
And either lanch his greedy thirsting throat,	1Tamb	1.2.146	Tamb
Or take him prisoner, and his chaine shall serve/For Manackles,	1Tamb	1.2.147	Tamb
His looks do menace heaven and dare the Gods,	1Tamb	1.2.157	Therid
His fierie eies are fixt upon the earth,	1Tamb	1.2.158	Therid
His deep affections make him passionate.	1Tamb	1.2.164	Techel
With what a majesty he rears his looks:--	1Tamb	1.2.165	Tamb
And sooner shall the Sun fall from his Spheare,	1Tamb	1.2.176	Tamb
And Jove himselfe will stretch his hand from heaven,	1Tamb	1.2.180	Tamb
As far as Boreas claps his brazen wings,	1Tamb	1.2.206	Tamb
Or faire Bootes sends his cheerefull light,	1Tamb	1.2.207	Tamb
And sit with Tamburlaine in all his majestie.	1Tamb	1.2.209	Tamb
We are his friends, and if the Persean king/Should offer	1Tamb	1.2.214	Techel
Than dooth the King of Persea in his Crowne:	1Tamb	1.2.242	Tamb
The man that in the forhead of his fortune,	1Tamb	2.1.3	Cosroe
Like his desire, lift upwards and divine,	1Tamb	2.1.8	Menaph
So large of lims, his joints so strongly knit,	1Tamb	2.1.9	Menaph
Twixt his manly pitch,/A pearle more worth, then all the world	1Tamb	2.1.11	Menaph
Are fixt his piercing instruments of sight:	1Tamb	2.1.14	Menaph
their Spheares/That guides his steps and actions to the throne,	1Tamb	2.1.17	Menaph
His lofty browes in foldes, do figure death,	1Tamb	2.1.21	Menaph
His armes and fingers long and [sinowy] <snowy>,	1Tamb	2.1.27	Menaph
Nature doth strive with Fortune and his stars,	1Tamb	2.1.33	Cosroe
And well his merits show him to be made/His Fortunes maister,	1Tamb	2.1.35	Cosroe
And well his merits show him to be made/His Fortunes maister,	1Tamb	2.1.36	Cosroe
With reasons of his valour and his life,	1Tamb	2.1.38	Cosroe
Proud is his fortune if we pierce it not.	1Tamb	2.1.44	Cosroe
Shall overway his wearie witlesse head,	1Tamb	2.1.46	Cosroe
Defend his freedome gainst a Monarchie:	1Tamb	2.1.56	Ceneus
And stuft with treasure for his highest thoughts?	1Tamb	2.1.59	Ceneus
And which is worst to have his Diadem/Sought for by such scalde	1Tamb	2.2.7	Mycet
And make him false his faith unto his King,	1Tamb	2.2.27	Meandr
Beside the spoile of him and all his traine:	1Tamb	2.2.34	Meandr
His Highnesse pleasure is that he should live,	1Tamb	2.2.37	Meandr
And make them blest that share in his attemptes.	1Tamb	2.3.9	Tamb
But when you see his actions [top] <stop> his speech,	1Tamb	2.3.26	Therid
Your speech will stay, or so extol his worth,	1Tamb	2.3.27	Therid
and excusde/For turning my poore charge to his direction.	1Tamb	2.3.29	Therid
And these his two renowmed friends my Lord,	1Tamb	2.3.30	Therid
And chiefest Counsailor in all his acts,	1Tamb	2.5.11	Cosroe
troopes)/Farewell Lord Regent, and his happie friends,	1Tamb	2.5.46	Cosroe
And bid him battell for his novell Crowne?	1Tamb	2.5.88	Techel
Nay quickly then, before his roome be hot.	1Tamb	2.5.89	Usumc
And bid him turne [him] <his> back to war with us,	1Tamb	2.5.100	Tamb
Where flames shall ever feed upon his soule.	1Tamb	2.6.8	Cosroe
or els infernall, mixt/Their angry seeds at his conception:	1Tamb	2.6.10	Meandr
Since with the spirit of his fearefull pride,	1Tamb	2.6.12	Meandr
Direct my weapon to his barbarous heart,	1Tamb	2.6.38	Cosroe
To thrust his doting father from his chaire,	1Tamb	2.7.14	Tamb
(for say not I intreat)/Not once to set his foot in Affrica,	1Tamb	3.1.28	Bajzth
Or spread his collours in Grecia,	1Tamb	3.1.29	Bajzth
But if presuming on his silly power,	1Tamb	3.1.33	Bajzth
We meane to take his mornings next arise/For messenger, he will	1Tamb	3.1.38	Bajzth
Nor Sun reflexe his vertuous beames thereon,	1Tamb	3.1.52	Moroc
As his exceding favours have deserv'd,	1Tamb	3.2.10	Zenoc
Ah, life and soule still hover in his Breast,	1Tamb	3.2.21	Zenoc
Or els unite you to his life and soule,	1Tamb	3.2.23	Zenoc
Being supposde his worthlesse Concubine,	1Tamb	3.2.29	Agidas
Who when he shall embrace you in his armes,	1Tamb	3.2.42	Agidas
Will rattle foorth his facts of war and blood.	1Tamb	3.2.45	Agidas
His talke much sweeter than the Muses song,	1Tamb	3.2.50	Zenoc
After your rescue to enjoy his choise.	1Tamb	3.2.58	Agidas
Now in his majesty he leaves those lookes,	1Tamb	3.2.61	Agidas

HIS (cont.)

Fearing his love through my unworthynesse.	1Tamb	3.2.65	Zenoc
but most astonied/To see his choller shut in secrete thoughtes,	1Tamb	3.2.70	Agidas
And wrapt in silence of his angry soule.	1Tamb	3.2.71	Agidas
Upon his browes was pourtraid ugly death,	1Tamb	3.2.72	Agidas
And in his eies the furie of his hart,	1Tamb	3.2.73	Agidas
And casts a pale complexion on his cheeks.	1Tamb	3.2.75	Agidas
strike flames of lightening)/All fearefull foldes his sailes,	1Tamb	3.2.82	Agidas
Lifting his prayers to the heavens for aid,	1Tamb	3.2.83	Agidas
And crave his triple worthy buriall.	1Tamb	3.2.112	Usumc
Alas (poore Turke) his fortune is to weake,	1Tamb	3.3.6	Tamb
And cannot terrefie his mightie hoste.	1Tamb	3.3.12	Bassoe
If he think good, can from his garrisons,	1Tamb	3.3.21	Bassoe
Such as his Highnesse please, but some must stay/To rule the	1Tamb	3.3.28	Bassoe
Europe, and pursue/His scattered armie til they yeeld or die.	1Tamb	3.3.39	Therid
him assured hope/Of martiall triumph, ere he meete his foes:	1Tamb	3.3.43	Tamb
And all his Captaines that thus stoutly stand,	1Tamb	3.3.79	Bajzth
that in his infancie/Did pash the jawes of Serpents venomous:	1Tamb	3.3.104	Bajzth
And all his Captains bound in captive chaines.	1Tamb	3.3.115	Bajzth
Triumphing over him and these his kings,	1Tamb	3.3.128	Tamb
The field is ours, the Turk, his wife and all.	1Tamb	3.3.163	Tamb
Must plead for mercie at his kingly feet,	1Tamb	3.3.174	Zenoc
And let his foes like flockes of fearfull Roes,	1Tamb	3.3.192	Zenoc
Pursude by hunters, flie his angrie lookes,	1Tamb	3.3.193	Zenoc
His royall Crowne againe, so highly won.	1Tamb	3.3.219	Zenoc
Shall Tamburlain extend his puisant arme.	1Tamb	3.3.247	Tamb
The Souldans daughter for his Concubine,	1Tamb	4.1.5	Souldn
Hath spread his collours to our high disgrace:	1Tamb	4.1.7	Souldn
That with his terrour and imperious eies,	1Tamb	4.1.14	2Msngr
Commandes the hearts of his associates,	1Tamb	4.1.15	2Msngr
Yet would the Souldane by his conquering power,	1Tamb	4.1.33	Souldn
So scatter and consume them in his rage,	1Tamb	4.1.34	Souldn
To shroud his shame in darknes of the night.	1Tamb	4.1.46	Souldn
His resolution far exceedeth all:	1Tamb	4.1.48	2Msngr
The first day when he pitcheth downe his tentes,	1Tamb	4.1.49	2Msngr
and on his silver crest/A snowy Feather spangled white he	1Tamb	4.1.50	2Msngr
To signify the mildnesse of his minde:	1Tamb	4.1.52	2Msngr
As red as scarlet is his furniture,	1Tamb	4.1.55	2Msngr
Then must his kindled wrath bee quencht with blood:	1Tamb	4.1.56	2Msngr
Black are his collours, blacke Pavilion,	1Tamb	4.1.59	2Msngr
His speare, his shield, his horse, his armour, plumes,	1Tamb	4.1.60	2Msngr
He raceth all his foes with fire and sword.	1Tamb	4.1.63	2Msngr
Pillage and murder are his usuall trades.	1Tamb	4.1.66	Souldn
Of my faire daughter, and his princely Love:	1Tamb	4.1.70	Souldn
Staining his Altars with your purple blood:	1Tamb	4.2.4	Bajzth
My sword stroke fire from his coat of steele,	1Tamb	4.2.41	Tamb
Being thy Captive, thus abuse his state,	1Tamb	4.2.60	Zabina
Keeping his kingly body in a Cage,	1Tamb	4.2.61	Zabina
Should have prepar'd to entertaine his Grace?	1Tamb	4.2.63	Zabina
And thou his wife shalt feed him with the scraps/My servitures	1Tamb	4.2.87	Tamb
Shall ransome him, or take him from his cage.	1Tamb	4.2.94	Tamb
So shall he have his life, and all the rest.	1Tamb	4.2.115	Tamb
he persecutes/The noble Turke and his great Emperesse?	1Tamb	4.3.27	Arabia
I have, and sorrow for his bad successe:	1Tamb	4.3.28	Souldn
that the Souldan is/No more dismaide with tidings of his fall,	1Tamb	4.3.31	Souldn
Yet in compassion of his wretched state,	1Tamb	4.3.35	Souldn
As Concubine I feare, to feed his lust.	1Tamb	4.3.42	Souldn
Let Tamburlaine for his offences feele/Such plagues as heaven	1Tamb	4.3.44	Arabia
I long to breake my speare upon his crest,	1Tamb	4.3.46	Arabia
And proove the waight of his victorious arme:	1Tamb	4.3.47	Arabia
In sounding through the world his partiall praise.	1Tamb	4.3.49	Arabia
That fed upon the substance of his child.	1Tamb	4.4.25	Zabina
But if his highnesse would let them be fed, it would doe them	1Tamb	4.4.34	P Therid
He stamps it under his feet my Lord.	1Tamb	4.4.42	P Therid
twere better he kild his wife, and then she shall be sure not	1Tamb	4.4.45	P Usumc
not the Turke and his wife make a goodly showe at a banquet?	1Tamb	4.4.57	P Tamb
If thou wilt have a song, the Turke shall straine his voice:	1Tamb	4.4.64	P Tamb
Content thy selfe, his person shall be safe,	1Tamb	4.4.87	Tamb
We see his tents have now bene altered,	1Tamb	5.1.7	Govnr
His cole-blacke collours every where advaunst,	1Tamb	5.1.9	Govnr
Offer our safeties to his clemencie,	1Tamb	5.1.12	Govnr
I feare the custome proper to his sword,	1Tamb	5.1.13	Govnr
Which he observes as parcell of his fame,	1Tamb	5.1.14	Govnr
and hartie humble mones/Will melt his furie into some remorse:	1Tamb	5.1.22	Govnr
Convey events of mercie to his heart:	1Tamb	5.1.54	2Virgn
victorie we yeeld/May bind the temples of his conquering head,	1Tamb	5.1.56	2Virgn
To hide the folded furrowes of his browes,	1Tamb	5.1.57	2Virgn
And shadow his displeased countenance,	1Tamb	5.1.58	2Virgn
bed, where many a Lord/In prime and glorie of his loving joy,	1Tamb	5.1.84	1Virgn
The jealous bodie of his fearfull wife,	1Tamb	5.1.86	1Virgn
Whereto ech man of rule hath given his hand,	1Tamb	5.1.102	1Virgn
Keeping his circuit by the slicing edge.	1Tamb	5.1.112	Tamb
And on their points his fleshlesse bodie feedes.	1Tamb	5.1.115	Tamb
His life that so consumes Zenocrate,	1Tamb	5.1.154	Tamb
Must needs have beauty beat on his conceites.	1Tamb	5.1.182	Tamb
For faire Zenocrate, that so laments his state.	1Tamb	5.1.205	Therid
Stick in his breast, as in their proper roomes.	1Tamb	5.1.226	Zabina
That lingring paines may massacre his heart.	1Tamb	5.1.228	Zabina
And madnesse send his damned soule to hell.	1Tamb	5.1.229	Zabina
Ah faire Zabina, we may curse his power,	1Tamb	5.1.230	Bajzth
But such a Star hath influence in his sword,	1Tamb	5.1.232	Bajzth
May styl excruciat his tormented thoughts.	1Tamb	5.1.301	Bajzth
His Skul al rivin in twain, his braines dasht out?	1Tamb	5.1.306	Zabina

HIS (cont.)

Give him his liquor?	1Tamb	5.1.310	P Zabina
Fling the meat in his face.	1Tamb	5.1.315	P Zabina
To breake his sword, and mildly treat of love,	1Tamb	5.1.327	Zenoc
Behold the Turke and his great Emperesse.	1Tamb	5.1.354	Zenoc
Behold the Turk and his great Emperesse.	1Tamb	5.1.357	Zenoc
Behold the Turke and his great Emperesse.	1Tamb	5.1.362	Zenoc
Pardon my Love, oh pardon his contempt,	1Tamb	5.1.364	Zenoc
ruthlesly pursewde/Be equally against his life incenst,	1Tamb	5.1.367	Zenoc
Your love hath fortune so at his command,	1Tamb	5.1.373	Anippe
As long as life maintaines his mighty arme,	1Tamb	5.1.375	Anippe
The God of war resignes his roume to me,	1Tamb	5.1.450	Tamb
Fearing my power should pull him from his throne.	1Tamb	5.1.453	Tamb
The Turk and his great Emperesse as it seems,	1Tamb	5.1.470	Tamb
With them Arabia too hath left his life,	1Tamb	5.1.473	Tamb
His honor, that consists in sheading blood,	1Tamb	5.1.477	Tamb
Affrick to the banks/Of Ganges, shall his mighty arme extend.	1Tamb	5.1.521	Tamb
With this great Turke and his faire Emperesse:	1Tamb	5.1.532	Tamb
Hath made our Poet pen his second part,	2Tamb	Prol.3	Prolog
Wher death cuts off the progres of his pomp,	2Tamb	Prol.4	Prolog
And murdrous Fates throwes al his triumphs down.	2Tamb	Prol.5	Prolog
Which kept his father in an yron cage:	2Tamb	1.1.5	Orcan
Neere Guyrons head doth set his conquering feet,	2Tamb	1.1.17	Gazell
More then his Camp of stout Hungarians,	2Tamb	1.1.21	Uribas
Shall carie wrapt within his scarlet waves,	2Tamb	1.1.34	Orcan
Since Tamburlaine hath mustred all his men,	2Tamb	1.1.46	Gazell
Marching from Cairon northward with his camp,	2Tamb	1.1.47	Gazell
Lantchidol/Beates on the regions with his boysterous blowes,	2Tamb	1.1.70	Orcan
Here is his sword, let peace be ratified/On these conditions	2Tamb	1.1.124	Orcan
When Phoebus leaping from his Hemi-Spheare,	2Tamb	1.2.51	Callap
Which when he tainted with his slender rod,	2Tamb	1.3.40	Zenoc
Which being wroth, sends lightning from his eies,	2Tamb	1.3.76	Tamb
And in the furrowes of his frowning browes,	2Tamb	1.3.77	Tamb
For if his chaire were in a sea of blood,	2Tamb	1.3.89	Celeb
When we shall meet the Turkish Deputie/And all his Viceroies,	2Tamb	1.3.100	Tamb
Turkish Deputie/And all his Viceroies, snatch it from his head,	2Tamb	1.3.100	Tamb
And cleave his Pericranion with thy sword.	2Tamb	1.3.101	Tamb
And millions of his strong tormenting spirits:	2Tamb	1.3.147	Techel
With all his viceroies shall be so affraide,	2Tamb	1.3.162	Tamb
That Jove shall send his winged Messenger/To bid me sheath my	2Tamb	1.3.166	Tamb
Shall hide his head in Thetis watery lap,	2Tamb	1.3.169	Tamb
And leave his steeds to faire Boetes charge:	2Tamb	1.3.170	Tamb
Natolia hath dismist the greatest part/Of all his armie, pitcht	2Tamb	2.1.17	Fredrk
And jealous anger of his feareful arme/Be pour'd with rigour	2Tamb	2.1.57	Fredrk
And with the thunder of his martial tooles/Makes Earthquakes in	2Tamb	2.2.7	Orcan
And now come we to make his sinowes shake,	2Tamb	2.2.9	Gazell
With greater power than erst his pride hath felt,	2Tamb	2.2.10	Gazell
He by his Christ, and I by Mahomet?	2Tamb	2.2.32	Orcan
And hath the power of his outstretched arme,	2Tamb	2.2.42	Orcan
If he be jealous of his name and honor,	2Tamb	2.2.43	Orcan
With strange infusion of his sacred vigor,	2Tamb	2.2.52	Orcan
May in his endlesse power and puritie/Behold and venge this	2Tamb	2.2.53	Orcan
Bloody and breathlesse for his villany.	2Tamb	2.3.13	Gazell
Now shall his barbarous body be a pray/To beasts and foules,	2Tamb	2.3.14	Orcan
Murmures and hisses for his hainous sin.	2Tamb	2.3.17	Orcan
Now scaldes his soule in the Tartarian streames,	2Tamb	2.3.18	Orcan
Shall lead his soule through Orcus burning gulfe:	2Tamb	2.3.25	Orcan
What saiest thou yet Gazellus to his foile:	2Tamb	2.3.27	Orcan
Which we referd to justice of his Christ,	2Tamb	2.3.28	Orcan
And to his power, which here appeares as full/As raies of	2Tamb	2.3.29	Orcan
And since this miscreant hath disgrac'd his faith,	2Tamb	2.3.36	Orcan
We wil both watch and ward shall keepe his trunke/Amidst these	2Tamb	2.3.38	Orcan
now let us celebrate/Our happy conquest, and his angry fate.	2Tamb	2.3.47	Orcan
Now wants the fewell that enflamde his beames:	2Tamb	2.4.4	Tamb
He bindes his temples with a frowning cloude,	2Tamb	2.4.6	Tamb
Holds out his hand in highest majesty/To entertaine divine	2Tamb	2.4.32	Tamb
of that vitall aire/That feeds the body with his dated health,	2Tamb	2.4.45	Zenoc
Or els discended to his winding traine:	2Tamb	2.4.54	Tamb
What God so ever holds thee in his armes,	2Tamb	2.4.109	Tamb
by the aid of God and his friend Mahomet, Emperour of Natolia,	2Tamb	3.1.3	P Orcan
and thirty Kingdomes late contributory to his mighty father.	2Tamb	3.1.5	P Orcan
(An Emperour so honoured for his vertues)/Revives the spirits	2Tamb	3.1.23	Callap
In grievous memorie of his fathers shame,	2Tamb	3.1.25	Callap
And with his hoste [martcht] <martch> round about the earth,	2Tamb	3.2.111	Tamb
And see him lance his flesh to teach you all.	2Tamb	3.2.114	Tamb
I long to pierce his bowels with my sword,	2Tamb	3.2.152	Usumc
That we may tread upon his captive necke,	2Tamb	3.2.157	Tamb
And treble all his fathers slaveries.	2Tamb	3.2.158	Tamb
That with his ruine fils up all the trench.	2Tamb	3.3.26	Therid
And carie both our soules, where his remaines.	2Tamb	3.4.17	Olymp
Whose body with his fathers I have burnt,	2Tamb	3.4.36	Olymp
And for his sake here will I end my daies.	2Tamb	3.4.44	Olymp
That treadeth Fortune underneath his feete,	2Tamb	3.4.52	Therid
And makes the mighty God of armes his slave:	2Tamb	3.4.53	Therid
My royal army is as great as his,	2Tamb	3.5.10	Callap
Phrigia to the sea/Which washeth Cyprus with his brinish waves,	2Tamb	3.5.12	Callap
His sonnes, his Captaines and his followers,	2Tamb	3.5.16	Callap
And guard the gates to entertaine his soule.	2Tamb	3.5.29	Orcan
And set his warlike person to the view/Of fierce Achilles,	2Tamb	3.5.67	Tamb
person to the view/Of fierce Achilles, rivall of his fame.	2Tamb	3.5.68	Tamb
To false his service to his Soveraigne,	2Tamb	3.5.88	Tamb
And turne him to his ancient trade againe.	2Tamb	3.5.95	Jrslem
That most may vex his body and his soule.	2Tamb	3.5.99	Callap

HIS (cont.)

So he shal, and weare thy head in his Scutchion.	2Tamb	3.5.138	P	Orcan
let him hang a bunch of keies on his standerd, to put him in	2Tamb	3.5.139	P	Tamb
I may knocke out his braines with them, and lock you in the	2Tamb	3.5.141	P	Tamb
least hee hide his crowne as the foolish king of Persea did.	2Tamb	3.5.154	P	Tamb
And cuts down armies with his [conquering] <conquerings> wings.	2Tamb	4.1.6		Amyras
Wrath kindled in the furnace of his breast,	2Tamb	4.1.9		Celeb
Wil send a deadly lightening to his heart.	2Tamb	4.1.10		Celeb
You doo dishonor to his majesty,	2Tamb	4.1.20		Calyph
He comes and findes his sonnes have had no shares/In all the	2Tamb	4.1.47		Amyras
Embracing thee with deepest of his love,	2Tamb	4.1.109		Tamb
Here Jove, receive his fainting soule againe,	2Tamb	4.1.111		Tamb
And by the state of his supremacie,	2Tamb	4.1.136		Tamb
Souldier shall defile/His manly fingers with so faint a boy.	2Tamb	4.1.164		Tamb
And let your hates extended in his paines,	2Tamb	4.1.172		Orcan
May never day give vertue to his eies,	2Tamb	4.1.174		Trebiz
and of fire/Doth send such sterne affections to his heart.	2Tamb	4.1.176		Trebiz
teares of Mahomet/For hot consumption of his countries pride:	2Tamb	4.1.197		Tamb
Rather than yeeld to his detested suit,	2Tamb	4.2.6		Olymp
Supposing amorous Jove had sent his sonne,	2Tamb	4.2.18		Therid
But was prevented by his sodaine end.	2Tamb	4.2.74		Olymp
Opening the doores of his rich treasurie,	2Tamb	4.2.95		Therid
Come once in furie and survay his pride,	2Tamb	4.3.41		Orcan
How like his cursed father he begins,	2Tamb	4.3.55		Jrslem
Mounted his shining [chariot] <chariots>, gilt with fire,	2Tamb	4.3.126		Tamb
When all the Gods stand gazing at his pomp:	2Tamb	4.3.129		Tamb
To live secure, and keep his forces out,	2Tamb	5.1.16		Govnr
that falles/Into the liquid substance of his streame,	2Tamb	5.1.19		Govnr
And have no terrour but his threatning lookes?	2Tamb	5.1.23		Govnr
Though this be held his last daies dreadfull siege,	2Tamb	5.1.29		1Citzn
Wil get his pardon if your grace would send.	2Tamb	5.1.33		1Citzn
That with his sword hath quail'd all earthly kings,	2Tamb	5.1.93		Tamb
Up with him then, his body shalbe scard.	2Tamb	5.1.114		Tamb
Go thither some of you and take his gold,	2Tamb	5.1.123		Tamb
Having as many bullets in his flesh,	2Tamb	5.1.159		Tamb
Slew all his Priests, his kinsmen, and his friends,	2Tamb	5.1.181		Tamb
That shakes his sword against thy majesty,	2Tamb	5.1.196		Tamb
Where Tamburlaine with all his armie lies,	2Tamb	5.2.6		Callap
Before his hoste be full from Babylon,	2Tamb	5.2.9		Callap
And yet gapes stil for more to quench his thirst,	2Tamb	5.2.14		Amasia
To be reveng'd of all his Villanie.	2Tamb	5.2.23		Callap
clowdes, and on his head/A Chaplet brighter than Apollos crowne,	2Tamb	5.2.32		Amasia
And pull proud Tamburlaine upon his knees,	2Tamb	5.2.40		Amasia
His fortune greater, and the victories/Wherewith he hath so	2Tamb	5.2.43		Callap
She waines againe, and so shall his I hope,	2Tamb	5.2.47		Callap
Before himselfe or his be conquered.	2Tamb	5.2.53		Callap
lie in wait for him/And if we find him absent from his campe,	2Tamb	5.2.57		Callap
Fal starres that governe his nativity,	2Tamb	5.3.2		Therid
Your sacred vertues pour'd upon his throne,	2Tamb	5.3.11		Therid
And made his state an honor to the heavens,	2Tamb	5.3.12		Therid
Triumphing in his fall whom you advaunst,	2Tamb	5.3.23		Techel
But as his birth, life, health and majesty/Were strangely blest	2Tamb	5.3.24		Techel
His byrth, his life, his health and majesty.	2Tamb	5.3.27		Techel
Come let us chardge our speares and pierce his breast,	2Tamb	5.3.58		Tamb
Stands aiming at me with his murthering dart,	2Tamb	5.3.69		Tamb
where I tooke/The Turke and his great Empresse prisoners,	2Tamb	5.3.129		Tamb
Must part, imparting his impressions,	2Tamb	5.3.170		Tamb
My Lord, you must obey his majesty,	2Tamb	5.3.204		Therid
His anguish and his burning agony.	2Tamb	5.3.209		Amyras
And therefore stil augments his cruelty.	2Tamb	5.3.219		Tamb
Then let some God oppose his holy power,	2Tamb	5.3.220		Techel
That his teare-thyrsty and unquenched hate,	2Tamb	5.3.222		Techel
learne with awfull eie/To sway a throane as dangerous as his:	2Tamb	5.3.235		Tamb
And heaven consum'd his choisest living fire.	2Tamb	5.3.251		Amyras
Let earth and heaven his timelesse death deplore,	2Tamb	5.3.252		Amyras
Yet was his soule but flowne beyond the Alpes,	Jew	Prol.2		Machvl
from France/To view this Land, and frolicke with his friends.	Jew	Prol.4		Machvl
Who smiles to see how full his bags are cramb'd,	Jew	Prol.31		Machvl
easily in a day/Tell that which may maintaine him all his life.	Jew	1.1.11		Barab
And all his life time hath bin tired,	Jew	1.1.15		Barab
Wearying his fingers ends with telling it,	Jew	1.1.16		Barab
Would in his age be loath to labour so,	Jew	1.1.17		Barab
the Easterne rockes/Without controule can picke his riches up,	Jew	1.1.22		Barab
And in his house heape pearle like pibble-stones,	Jew	1.1.23		Barab
Where Nilus payes his tribute to the maine,	Jew	1.1.75		Barab
And bid my Factor bring his loading in.	Jew	1.1.83		Barab
Or who is honour'd now but for his wealth?	Jew	1.1.113		Barab
And for his conscience lives in beggery.	Jew	1.1.120		Barab
Daughter, whom I hold as deare/As Agamemnon did his Iphegen:	Jew	1.1.138		Barab
of Turkey is arriv'd/Great Selim-Calymath, his Highnesse sonne,	Jew	1.2.40		Govnr
the Jewes, and each of them to pay one halfe of his estate.	Jew	1.2.69	P	Reader
Grave [Governor], list not to his exclames:	Jew	1.2.128		1Knght
Convert his mansion to a Nunnery,	Jew	1.2.129		1Knght
His house will harbour many holy Nuns.	Jew	1.2.130		1Knght
I wot his wealth/Was written thus:	Jew	1.2.181		Barab
As much as would have bought his beasts and him,	Jew	1.2.189		Barab
That in a field amidst his enemies,	Jew	1.2.203		Barab
Doth see his souldiers slaine, himselfe disarm'd,	Jew	1.2.204		Barab
And knowes no meanes of his recoverie:	Jew	1.2.205		Barab
Come, let us leave him in his irefull mood,	Jew	1.2.209		1Jew
Our words will but increase his extasie.	Jew	1.2.210		1Jew
A reaching thought will search his deepest wits,	Jew	1.2.221		Barab
That has no further comfort for his maime.	Jew	2.1.11		Barab

HIS (cont.)

Then, gentle sleepe, where e're his bodie rests,	Jew	2.1.35	Abigal
my fingers take/A kisse from him that sends it from his soule.	Jew	2.1.59	Barab
I'le write unto his Majesty for ayd,	Jew	2.2.40	Bosco
Every ones price is written on his backe,	Jew	2.3.3	2Offcr
Here comes the Jew, had not his goods bin seiz'd,	Jew	2.3.5	1Offcr
I, and his sonnes too, or it shall goe hard.	Jew	2.3.17	Barab
One that I love for his good fathers sake.	Jew	2.3.31	Barab
I wud you were his father too, Sir, that's al the harm I wish	Jew	2.3.41	P Barab
Sir, that's his price.	Jew	2.3.99	1Offcr
might be got/To keepe him for his life time from the gallowes.	Jew	2.3.104	Barab
Pinning upon his breast a long great Scrowle/How I with	Jew	2.3.197	Barab
For your sake and his own he's welcome hither.	Jew	2.3.233	Abigal
His father was my chiefest enemie.	Jew	2.3.250	Barab
For this I'le have his heart.	Jew	2.3.344	Mthias
Feare not, I'le so set his heart a fire,	Jew	2.3.375	Ithimr
Thy sonne slew mine, and I'le revenge his death.	Jew	3.2.15	Mater
Admit thou lov'dst not Lodowicke for his [sire] <sinne>,	Jew	3.3.40	Abigal
And couldst not venge it, but upon his sonne,	Jew	3.3.44	Abigal
Nor on his sonne, but by Mathias meanes;	Jew	3.3.45	Abigal
my bitter curse/Like Cain by Adam, for his brother's death.	Jew	3.4.33	Barab
Whereof his sire, the Pope, was poysoned.	Jew	3.4.99	Barab
And for his sake did I become a Nunne.	Jew	3.6.25	Abigal
I'le give him something and so stop his mouth.	Jew	4.1.102	Barab
But doe you thinke that I beleeve his words?	Jew	4.1.105	Barab
Nor goe to bed, but sleepes in his owne clothes;	Jew	4.1.132	Ithimr
Oh how I long to see him shake his heeles.	Jew	4.1.140	Ithimr
so, let him leane upon his staffe; excellent, he stands as if he	Jew	4.1.154	P Ithimr
And bring his gold into our treasury.	Jew	4.1.163	1Fryar
I, master, he's slain; look how his brains drop out on's nose.	Jew	4.1.178	P Ithimr
No, pardon me, the Law must have his course.	Jew	4.1.185	Barab
conning his neck-verse I take it, looking of a Fryars	Jew	4.2.17	P Pilia
I never knew a man take his death so patiently as this Fryar;	Jew	4.2.21	P Ithimr
he was ready to leape off e're the halter was about his necke;	Jew	4.2.22	P Ithimr
and when the Hangman had put on his hempen Tippet, he made such	Jew	4.2.23	P Ithimr
he made such haste to his prayers, as if hee had had another	Jew	4.2.24	P Ithimr
goe whither he will, I'le be none of his followers in haste:	Jew	4.2.25	P Ithimr
sort as if he had meant to make cleane my Boots with his lips;	Jew	4.2.31	P Ithimr
Let me alone, I'le use him in his kinde.	Jew	4.2.80	Pilia
That when he speakes, drawes out his grisly beard,	Jew	4.3.7	Barab
And winds it twice or thrice about his eare;	Jew	4.3.8	Barab
His hands are hackt, some fingers cut quite off;	Jew	4.3.10	Barab
No; but three hundred will not serve his turne.	Jew	4.3.20	P Pilia
Not serve his turne, Sir?	Jew	4.3.21	P Barab
words, Sir, and send it you, were best see; there's his letter.	Jew	4.3.25	P Pilia
for in his villany/He will tell all he knowes and I shall dye	Jew	4.3.64	Barab
Pilia-borza, bid the Fidler give me the posey in his hat there.	Jew	4.4.36	P Curtzn
Very mush, Mounsier, you no be his man?	Jew	4.4.57	P Barab
His man?	Jew	4.4.58	P Pilia
lov'd Rice, that Fryar Bernardine slept in his owne clothes.	Jew	4.4.76	P Ithimr
poyson'd his owne daughter and the Nuns, strangled a Fryar,	Jew	5.1.13	P Pilia
my Lord, his man's now at my lodging/That was his Agent, he'll	Jew	5.1.16	Curtzn
his man's now at my lodging/That was his Agent, he'll confesse	Jew	5.1.17	Curtzn
strangled Bernardine, poyson'd the Nuns, and his owne daughter.	Jew	5.1.34	P Ithimr
Away with him, his sight is death to me.	Jew	5.1.35	Govnr
Dead, my Lord, and here they bring his body.	Jew	5.1.53	1Offcr
This sudden death of his is very strange.	Jew	5.1.54	Bosco
Governour and these/Captaines, his consorts and confederates.	Jew	5.2.24	Barab
And neither gets him friends, nor fils his bags,	Jew	5.2.39	Barab
Arbitrament; and Barabas/At his discretion may dispose of both:	Jew	5.2.54	Barab
give me if I render you/The life of Calymath, surprize his men,	Jew	5.2.80	Barab
And in an out-house of the City shut/His souldiers, till I have	Jew	5.2.82	Barab
Will take his leave and saile toward Ottoman.	Jew	5.2.106	Barab
Hearing his Soveraigne was bound for Sea,	Jew	5.3.15	Msngr
would intreat your Majesty/To come and see his homely Citadell,	Jew	5.3.18	Msngr
To banquet with him in his Citadell?	Jew	5.3.20	Calym
serve to entertaine/Selim and all his souldiers for a month;	Jew	5.3.31	Msngr
Except he place his Tables in the streets.	Jew	5.3.35	Calym
Well, tell the Governor we grant his suit,	Jew	5.3.40	Calym
He will; and has commanded all his men/To come ashore, and march	Jew	5.5.14	Msngr
First, for his Army, they are sent before,	Jew	5.5.25	Barab
Now as for Calymath and his consorts,	Jew	5.5.32	Barab
And with his Bashawes shall be blithely set,	Jew	5.5.38	Barab
busie Barrabas is there above/To entertaine us in his Gallery;	Jew	5.5.53	Calym
See his end first, and flye then if thou canst.	Jew	5.5.69	Govnr
To stop the mallice of his envious heart,	P 30	1.30	Navrre
That Guise hath slaine by treason of his heart,	P 45	1.45	Navrre
And beates his braines to catch us in his trap,	P 53	1.53	Navrre
Which he hath pitcht within his deadly toyle.	P 54	1.54	Navrre
And make his Gospel flourish in this land.	P 57	1.57	Navrre
And had his alters deckt with duskie lightes:	P 59	2.2	Guise
Discharge thy musket and perfourme his death:	P 88	2.31	Guise
Weakneth his body, and will waste his Realme,	P 128	2.71	Guise
That with a rablement of his hereticks,	P 151	2.94	Guise
As Caesar to his souldiers, so say I:	P 155	2.98	Guise
<humble> intreates your Majestie/To visite him sick in his bed.	P 246	4.44	Man
And I will goe take order for his death.	P 252	4.50	Guise
Be murdered in his bed.	P 287	5.14	Guise
them thither, and then/Beset his house that not a man may live.	P 289	5.16	Guise
Plac'd by my brother, will betray his Lord:	P 294	5.21	Anjoy
And slay his servants that shall issue out.	P 299	5.26	Anjoy
Cosin tis he, I know him by his look.	P 309	5.36	Guise
Away with him, cut of his head and handes,	P 316	5.43	Anjoy

HIS (cont.)

Unto mount Faucon will we dragge his coarse:	P	319	5.46	Anjoy
That frightes poore Ramus sitting at his book?	P	362	7.2	Ramus
Because my places being but three, contains all his:	P	405	7.45	Ramus
Stab him I say and send him to his freends in hell.	P	415	7.55	Guise
Now every man put of his burgonet,	P	449	7.89	Guise
And so convey him closely to his bed.	P	450	7.90	Guise
And by his graces councell it is thought,	P	465	8.15	Anjoy
O no, his bodye will infect the fire, and the fire the aire, and	P	484	9.3	P 1Atndt
And if he grudge or crosse his Mothers will,	P	523	9.42	QnMoth
O no, his soule is fled from out his breast,	P	552	11.17	QnMoth
To weare his brcthers crowne and dignity.	P	557	11.22	QnMoth
Come let us take his body hence.	P	564	11.29	QnMoth
Will shew his mercy and preserve us still.	P	576	11.41	Navrre
And true profession of his holy word:	P	586	11.51	Navrre
All this and more hath Henry with his crowne.	P	596	12.9	QnMoth
Shall slacke my loves affection from his bent.	P	607	12.20	King
Hands of good fellow, I will be his baile/For this offence:	P	622	12.35	King
His minde you see runnes on his minions,	P	633	12.46	QnMoth
And all his heaven is to delight himselfe:	P	634	12.47	QnMoth
And tell him that tis for his Countries good,	P	646	12.59	Cardnl
Ile dispatch him with his brother presently,	P	651	12.64	QnMoth
And Guise usurpes it, cause I am his wife:	P	661	13.5	Duchss
That it might print these lines within his heart.	P	669	13.13	Duchss
Shall buy her love even with his dearest bloud.	P	697	13.41	Guise
To send his power to meet us in the field.	P	712	14.15	Navrre
In spite of Spaine and all his heresies.	P	716	14.19	Bartus
It will not countervaile his paines I hope,	P	735	14.38	Navrre
I would the Guise in his steed might have come,	P	736	14.39	Navrre
But he doth lurke within his drousie couch,	P	737	14.40	Navrre
And makes his footstoole on securitie:	P	738	14.41	Navrre
Shall buy that strumpets favour with his blood,	P	768	15.26	Guise
For his othes are seldome spent in vaine.	P	773	15.31	Eprnon
Because his wife beares thee such kindely love.	P	780	15.38	King
The Duke is slaine and all his power dispearst,	P	787	16.1	Navrre
To make his glory great upon the earth.	P	790	16.4	Navrre
I hope will make the King surcease his hate:	P	792	16.6	Bartus
and use a ccunterfeite key to his privie Chamber doore:	P	807	17.2	P Souldr
and so forestall his market, and set up your standing where you	P	809	17.4	P Souldr
you will take upon you to be his, and tyll the ground that he	P	811	17.6	P Souldr
that he himself should occupy, which is his own free land.	P	812	17.7	P Souldr
Ah base Epernoune, were not his highnes heere,	P	831	17.26	Guise
And know my Lord, the Pope will sell his triple crowne,	P	851	17.46	Guise
Ere I shall want, will cause his Indians,	P	853	17.48	Guise
Navarre that cloakes them underneath his wings,	P	855	17.50	Guise
Shall feele the house of Lorayne is his foe:	P	856	17.51	Guise
shewes did entertaine him/And promised to be at his commaund:	P	875	17.70	Eprnon
For not effecting of his holines will.	P	878	17.73	Eprnon
And that Paris is revolted from his grace.	P	902	18.3	Navrre
Offering him aide against his enemies,	P	905	18.6	Bartus
And there salute his highnesse in our name,	P	908	18.9	Navrre
Bartus be gone, commend me to his grace,	P	911	18.12	Navrre
For his aspiring thoughts aime at the crowne,	P	923	18.24	Navrre
And takes his vantage on Religion,	P	924	18.25	Navrre
Wee'l beat him back, and drive him to his death,	P	929	18.30	Navrre
That basely seekes the ruine of his Realme.	P	930	18.31	Navrre
O that his heart were leaping in my hand.	P	936	19.6	P 2Mur
Now must he fall and perish in his height.	P	946	19.16	Capt
Mounted his royall Cabonet.	P	957	19.27	Eprnon
And all his Minions stoup when I commaund:	P	979	19.49	Guise
Stand close, he is comming, I know him by his voice.	P	1000	19.70	P 1Mur
The wicked branch of curst Valois his line.	P	1013	19.83	Guise
Goe fetch his sonne for to beholde his death:	P	1021	19.91	King
My Lord heer is his sonne.	P	1045	19.115	Eprnon
with him, Ile clippe his winges/Or ere he passe my handes,	P	1052	19.122	King
When Duke Dumaine his brother is alive,	P	1055	19.125	King
And with their pawes drench his black soule in hell.	P	1102	20.12	Cardnl
And roote Valoys his line from forth of France,	P	1113	21.7	Dumain
And beate proud Burbon to his native home,	P	1114	21.8	Dumain
Whose murderous thoughts will be his overthrow.	P	1116	21.10	Dumain
Hee wild the Governour of Orleance in his name,	P	1117	21.11	Dumain
But thats prevented, for to end his life,	P	1119	21.13	Dumain
And sends <send> his dutie by these speedye lines,	P	1169	22.31	Frier
Just torments for his trechery.	P	1175	22.37	King
We might have punisht him to his deserts.	P	1184	22.46	Eprnon
Shall take example by [his] <their> punishment,	P	1186	22.48	King
Monarck goes/To wrack, and [his] antechristian kingdome falles.	P	1198	22.60	King
These bloudy hands shall teare his triple Crowne,	P	1199	22.61	King
And fire accursed Rome about his eares.	P	1200	22.62	King
Ile fire his crased buildings and [inforse] <incense>/The	P	1201	22.63	King
a death too good, the devill of hell/Torture his wicked soule.	P	1219	22.81	Bartus
But he that makes most lavish of his bloud.	P	1240	22.102	King
And then I vow for to revenge his death,	P	1247	22.109	Navrre
duke a cuckolde and use a counterfeyt key to his privy chamber	Paris	ms 2,	p390	P Souldr
displeases him | And fill up his rome that he shold occupie.	Paris	ms 4,	p390	P Souldr
hes to have the choyce of his owne freeland | yf it be not to	Paris	ms 8,	p390	P Souldr
ser where he is your landlorde you take upon you to be his |	Paris	ms10,	p390	P Souldr
I, I, these wordes of his move me as much,	Edw		1.1.39	Gavstn
Musicke and poetrie is his delight,	Edw		1.1.54	Gavstn
Crownets of pearle about his naked armes,	Edw		1.1.63	Gavstn
And in his sportfull hands an Olive tree,	Edw		1.1.64	Gavstn
Such things as these best please his majestie,	Edw		1.1.71	Gavstn
That villaine Mortimer, ile be his death.	Edw		1.1.81	Gavstn

HIS (cont.)

Were sworne to your father at his death,	Edw	1.1.83	Mortmr
For Mortimer will hang his armor up.	Edw	1.1.89	Mortmr
For which, had not his highnes lov'd him well,	Edw	1.1.112	Kent
He should have lost his head, but with his looke,	Edw	1.1.113	Kent
Yet dare you brave the king unto his face.	Edw	1.1.116	Kent
And strike off his that makes you threaten us.	Edw	1.1.124	Mortmr
With captive kings at his triumphant Carre.	Edw	1.1.174	Gavstn
That wert the onely cause of his exile.	Edw	1.1.179	Edward
Throwe of his golden miter, rend his stole,	Edw	1.1.187	Edward
No, spare his life, but seaze upon his goods,	Edw	1.1.193	Edward
Be thou lord bishop, and receive his rents,	Edw	1.1.194	Edward
And take possession of his house and goods:	Edw	1.1.203	Edward
A prison may beseeme his holinesse.	Edw	1.1.207	Gavstn
Unlesse his brest be sword proofe he shall die.	Edw	1.2.8	Mortmr
whom he vouchsafes/For vailing of his bonnet one good looke.	Edw	1.2.19	Lncstr
Nay more, the guarde upon his lordship waites:	Edw	1.2.21	Lncstr
His countenance bewraies he is displeasd.	Edw	1.2.34	Lncstr
First were his sacred garments rent and torne,	Edw	1.2.35	ArchBp
upon him, next/Himselfe imprisoned, and his goods asceasd,	Edw	1.2.37	ArchBp
Then wil you joine with us that be his peeres/To banish or	Edw	1.2.42	Mortmr
The Bishoprick of Coventrie is his.	Edw	1.2.45	ArchBp
He claps his cheekes, and hanges about his neck,	Edw	1.2.51	Queene
Smiles in his face, and whispers in his eares,	Edw	1.2.52	Queene
The king shall lose his crowne, for we have power,	Edw	1.2.59	Mortmr
And let him frollick with his minion.	Edw	1.2.67	Queene
We and the rest that are his counsellers,	Edw	1.2.69	ArchBp
Confirme his banishment with our handes and seales.	Edw	1.2.71	ArchBp
We know our duties, let him know his peeres.	Edw	1.4.23	Warwck
Subscribe as we have done to his exile.	Edw	1.4.53	ArchBp
Yong Mortimer and his unckle shalbe earles,	Edw	1.4.67	Edward
The king is love-sick for his minion.	Edw	1.4.87	Mortmr
And art a bawd to his affections,	Edw	1.4.151	Queene
But that will more exasperate his wrath,	Edw	1.4.182	Queene
Feare ye not Madam, now his minions gone,	Edw	1.4.198	Lncstr
His wanton humor will be quicklie left.	Edw	1.4.199	Lncstr
To sue unto you all for his repeale:	Edw	1.4.201	Queene
Or else be banisht from his highnesse presence.	Edw	1.4.203	Queene
For his repeale, Madam!	Edw	1.4.204	Lncstr
Unlesse the sea cast up his shipwrack body.	Edw	1.4.205	Lncstr
Theres none here, but would run his horse to death.	Edw	1.4.207	Warwck
As thou wilt soone subscribe to his repeale.	Edw	1.4.227	Queene
And see how coldly his lookes make deniall.	Edw	1.4.235	Lncstr
She smiles, now for my life his mind is changd.	Edw	1.4.236	Warwck
Ile rather loose his friendship I, then graunt.	Edw	1.4.237	Lncstr
And therefore though I pleade for his repeall,	Edw	1.4.241	Mortmr
Tis not for his sake, but for our availe:	Edw	1.4.242	Mortmr
Tis hard for us to worke his overthrow.	Edw	1.4.262	Mortmr
To greet his lordship with a poniard,	Edw	1.4.266	Mortmr
And in the Chronicle, enrowle his name,	Edw	1.4.269	Mortmr
Twill make him vaile the topflag of his pride,	Edw	1.4.276	Mortmr
Which for his fathers sake leane to the king,	Edw	1.4.283	Mortmr
Having brought the Earle of Cornewall on his way,	Edw	1.4.300	Queene
Hees gone, and for his absence thus I moorne,	Edw	1.4.305	Edward
I would freelie give it to his enemies,	Edw	1.4.309	Edward
Harke how he harpes upon his minion.	Edw	1.4.311	Queene
Having the love of his renowned peeres.	Edw	1.4.367	Queene
And then his mariage shalbe solemnized,	Edw	1.4.377	Edward
And seeing his minde so dotes on Gaveston,	Edw	1.4.389	MortSr
Let him without controulement have his will.	Edw	1.4.390	MortSr
Then let his grace, whose youth is flexible,	Edw	1.4.398	MortSr
Unckle, his wanton humor greeves not me,	Edw	1.4.402	Mortmr
Should by his soveraignes favour grow so pert,	Edw	1.4.404	Mortmr
He weares a lords revenewe on his back,	Edw	1.4.407	Mortmr
With base outlandish cullions at his heeles,	Edw	1.4.409	Mortmr
and in his tuskan cap/A jewell of more value then the crowne.	Edw	1.4.414	Mortmr
Not Mortimer, nor any of his side,	Edw	2.1.4	Spencr
What, meane you then to be his follower?	Edw	2.1.12	Baldck
No, his companion, for he loves me well,	Edw	2.1.13	Spencr
And that his banishment had changd her minde.	Edw	2.1.26	Baldck
The greefe for his exile was not so much,	Edw	2.1.57	Neece
As is the joy of his returning home.	Edw	2.1.58	Neece
And still his minde runs on his minion.	Edw	2.2.4	Queene
If in his absence thus he favors him,	Edw	2.2.47	Mortmr
That shall wee see, looke where his lordship comes.	Edw	2.2.49	Lncstr
Looke to your owne heads, his is sure enough.	Edw	2.2.92	Edward
Moov'd may he be, and perish in his wrath.	Edw	2.2.101	Mortmr
Ile have his bloud, or die in seeking it.	Edw	2.2.107	Warwck
They rate his ransome at five thousand pound.	Edw	2.2.117	Mortmr
Seeing he is taken prisoner in his warres?	Edw	2.2.119	Mortmr
Ile thunder such a peale into his eares,	Edw	2.2.128	Mortmr
As never subject did unto his King.	Edw	2.2.129	Mortmr
His highnes is disposde to be alone.	Edw	2.2.135	Guard
His name is Spencer, he is well alied,	Edw	2.2.249	Gavstn
me, for his sake/Ile grace thee with a higher stile ere long.	Edw	2.2.252	Edward
never was Plantagenet/False of his word, and therefore trust we	Edw	2.3.12	Mortmr
But neither spare you Gaveston, nor his friends.	Edw	2.3.28	Lncstr
Had power to mollifie his stonie hart,	Edw	2.4.20	Queene
He turnes away, and smiles upon his minion.	Edw	2.4.29	Queene
To offer violence to his soveraigne,	Edw	2.4.34	Lncstr
The king hath left him, and his traine is small.	Edw	2.4.39	Queene
How Gaveston hath robd me of his love:	Edw	2.4.67	Queene
against your king)/To see his royall soveraigne once againe.	Edw	2.5.7	Gavstn

HIS (cont.)

Upon him souldiers, take away his weapons.	Edw	2.5.8	Warwck
souldiers take him hence, for by my sword,/His head shall off:	Edw	2.5.21	Warwck
His majesty,/Hearing that you had taken Gaveston,	Edw	2.5.34	Arundl
And if you gratifie his grace so farre,	Edw	2.5.39	Arundl
Weele send his head by thee, let him bestow/His teares on that,	Edw	2.5.52	Mortmr
let him bestow/His teares on that, for that is all he gets/Of	Edw	2.5.53	Mortmr
that is all he gets/Of Gaveston, or else his sencelesse trunck.	Edw	2.5.54	Mortmr
My lords, it is his majesties request,	Edw	2.5.57	Arundl
And drives his nobles to these exigents/For Gaveston, will if	Edw	2.5.62	Warwck
Then if you will not trust his grace in keepe,	Edw	2.5.65	Arundl
My lords, I will be pledge for his returne.	Edw	2.5.66	Arundl
Because his majestie so earnestlie/Desires to see the man	Edw	2.5.77	Penbrk
majestie so earnestlie/Desires to see the man before his death,	Edw	2.5.78	Penbrk
Be thou this night his keeper, in the morning/We will discharge	Edw	2.5.108	Penbrk
His life, my lord, before your princely feete.	Edw	3.1.45	Spencr
Because we heare Lord Bruse dooth sell his land,	Edw	3.1.53	Edward
Hath seazed Normandie into his hands.	Edw	3.1.64	Queene
Or didst thou see my friend to take his death?	Edw	3.1.93	Edward
The earle of Warwick seazde him on his way,	Edw	3.1.115	Arundl
Their lord rode home, thinking his prisoner safe,	Edw	3.1.117	Arundl
And bare him to his death, and in a trenche/Strake off his	Edw	3.1.119	Arundl
and in a trenche/Strake off his head, and marcht unto the	Edw	3.1.120	Arundl
Thou comst from Mortimer and his complices,	Edw	3.1.153	Edward
Rebels, will they appoint their soveraigne/His sports, his	Edw	3.1.175	Edward
their soveraigne/His sports, his pleasures, and his companie:	Edw	3.1.175	Edward
Yonder is Edward among his flatterers.	Edw	3.1.196	Mortmr
And Penbrooke undertooke for his returne,	Edw	3.1.236	Edward
Mortimers hope surmounts his fortune farre.	Edw	3.1.259	Mortmr
And step into his fathers regiment.	Edw	3.1.271	Spencr
Stand gratious gloomie night to his device.	Edw	4.1.11	Kent
I warrant you, ile winne his highnes quicklie,	Edw	4.2.6	Prince
His grace I dare presume will welcome me,	Edw	4.2.33	Queene
The king will nere forsake his flatterers.	Edw	4.2.60	Mortmr
To this distressed Queene his sister heere,	Edw	4.2.63	SrJohn
Triumpheth Englands Edward with his friends,	Edw	4.3.2	Edward
And triumph Edward with his friends uncontrould.	Edw	4.3.3	Edward
behalfe, dealt with the king of Fraunce his lords, and effected,	Edw	4.3.29	P Spencr
and injuries/Edward hath done to us, his Queene and land,	Edw	4.4.22	Mortmr
To them that fight in right and feare his wrath:	Edw	4.6.20	Queene
Of love and care unto his royall person,	Edw	4.6.25	Queene
realme, and sith the fates/Have made his father so infortunate,	Edw	4.6.27	Queene
How will you deale with Edward in his fall?	Edw	4.6.31	Kent
Rebell is he that fights against his prince,	Edw	4.6.71	SpncrP
and here to pine in feare/Of Mortimer and his confederates.	Edw	4.7.36	Baldck
T'escape their hands that seeke to reave his life:	Edw	4.7.52	Leistr
To let us take our farewell of his grace.	Edw	4.7.69	Spencr
He rends and teares it with his wrathfull pawe,	Edw	5.1.12	Edward
that the lowly earth/Should drinke his bloud, mounts up into	Edw	5.1.14	Edward
Which in a moment will abridge his life:	Edw	5.1.42	Edward
Engirt the temples of his hatefull head,	Edw	5.1.46	Edward
For if they goe, the prince shall lose his right.	Edw	5.1.92	Leistr
is there in a Tigers jawes,/[Then] <This> his imbrasements:	Edw	5.1.117	Edward
Well may I rent his name, that rends my hart.	Edw	5.1.140	Edward
So may his limmes be torne, as is this paper,	Edw	5.1.142	Edward
Conclude against his father what thou wilt,	Edw	5.2.19	Queene
Alas poore soule, would I could ease his greefe.	Edw	5.2.26	Queene
The king hath willingly resignde his crowne.	Edw	5.2.28	BshpWn
To set his brother free, no more but so.	Edw	5.2.33	BshpWn
Then let some other be his guardian.	Edw	5.2.36	Queene
rest, because we heare/That Edmund casts to worke his libertie,	Edw	5.2.58	Mortmr
But amplifie his greefe with bitter words.	Edw	5.2.65	Mortmr
Commend me humblie to his Majestie,	Edw	5.2.69	Queene
To ease his greefe, and worke his libertie:	Edw	5.2.71	Queene
Some thing he whispers in his childish eares.	Edw	5.2.76	Queene
Thou being his unckle, and the next of bloud,	Edw	5.2.88	Mortmr
But bee content, seeing it his highnesse pleasure.	Edw	5.2.94	Queene
That wast a cause of his imprisonment?	Edw	5.2.102	Mortmr
My lord, he hath betraied the king his brother,	Edw	5.2.106	Mortmr
Brother Edmund, strive not, we are his friends,	Edw	5.2.114	Queene
And rescue aged Edward from his foes,	Edw	5.2.120	Kent
When will the furie of his minde asswage?	Edw	5.3.8	Edward
When will his hart be satisfied with bloud?	Edw	5.3.9	Edward
Is sure to pay for it when his sonne is of age,	Edw	5.4.4	Mortmr
Containes his death, yet bids them save his life.	Edw	5.4.7	Mortmr
But at his lookes Lightborne thou wilt relent.	Edw	5.4.26	Mortmr
sleepe, to take a quill/And blowe a little powder in his eares,	Edw	5.4.35	Ltborn
Or open his mouth, and powre quick silver downe,	Edw	5.4.36	Ltborn
And will avouche his saying with the sworde,	Edw	5.4.77	Champn
Did you attempt his rescue, Edmund speake?	Edw	5.4.86	Mortmr
Strike off his head, he shall have marshall lawe.	Edw	5.4.89	Mortmr
Intreate my lord Protector for his life.	Edw	5.4.95	King
Either my brother or his sonne is king,	Edw	5.4.106	Kent
What safetie may I looke for at his hands,	Edw	5.4.109	King
Let us assaile his minde another while.	Edw	5.5.12	Matrvs
Thats his meaning.	Edw	5.5.18	Matrvs
See how he must be handled for his labour,	Edw	5.5.23	Matrvs
But not too hard, least that you bruse his body.	Edw	5.5.113	Ltborn
Lets see who dare impeache me for his death?	Edw	5.6.14	Mortmr
His fathers dead, and we have murdered him.	Edw	5.6.16	Queene
I, I, but he teares his haire, and wrings his handes,	Edw	5.6.18	Queene
To crave the aide and succour of his peeres.	Edw	5.6.21	Queene
And thou shalt die, and on his mournefull hearse,	Edw	5.6.29	King

HIS (cont.)

His kingly body was too soone interrde.	Edw	5.6.32	King
You could not beare his death thus patiently,	Edw	5.6.36	King
Hang him I say, and set his quarters up,	Edw	5.6.53	King
But bring his head back presently to me.	Edw	5.6.54	King
I spill his bloud? no.	Edw	5.6.72	Queene
Mother, you are suspected for his death,	Edw	5.6.78	King
And with the rest accompanie him to his grave?	Edw	5.6.88	Queene
He hath forgotten me, stay, I am his mother.	Edw	5.6.90	Queene
Intends our Muse to vaunt <daunt> his heavenly verse;	F 6	Prol.6	1Chor
And speake for Faustus in his infancie.	F 10	Prol.10	1Chor
Whereas his kinsmen chiefly brought him up;	F 14	Prol.14	1Chor
His waxen wings did mount above his reach,	F 21	Prol.21	1Chor
And melting, heavens conspir'd his over-throw:	F 22	Prol.22	1Chor
Which he preferres before his chiefest blisse;	F 27	Prol.27	1Chor
And this the man that in his study sits.	F 28	Prol.28	1Chor
This <His> study fits a Mercenarie drudge,	F 61	1.1.33	Faust
But his dominion that exceeds <excells> in this,	F 87	1.1.59	Faust
Faustus may try his cunning by himselfe.	F 187	1.1.159	Cornel
That shall we presently know, <for see> here comes his boy.	F 196	1.2.3	2Schol
The danger of his soule would make me mourne:	F 224	1.2.31	2Schol
<and see if hee by> his grave counsell may <can> reclaime him.	F 226	1.2.33	2Schol
And may not follow thee without his leave;	F 269	1.3.41	Mephst
Abjure the Scriptures, and his Saviour Christ;	F 276	1.3.48	Mephst
We flye in hope to get his glorious soule:	F 277	1.3.49	Mephst
My <His> Ghost be with the old Phylosophers.	F 288	1.3.60	Faust
Say he surrenders up to him his soule,	F 318	1.3.90	Faust
see how poverty jests in his nakednesse, I know the Villaines	F 348	1.4.6	P Wagner
that <I know> he would give his soule to the devill, for a	F 350	1.4.8	P Wagner
So he will buy my service with his soule.	F 421	2.1.33	Mephst
Enlarge his Kingdome.	F 429	2.1.41	Mephst
at some certaine day/Great Lucifer may claime it as his owne,	F 440	2.1.52	Mephst
for love of thee/Faustus hath <I> cut his <mine> arme, and with	F 443	2.1.55	Faust
and with his <my> proper bloud/Assures his <assure my> soule to	F 443	2.1.55	Faust
bloud/Assures his <assure my> soule to be great Lucifers,	F 444	2.1.56	Faust
Faustus gives to thee his soule: [ah] <O> there it staid.	F 456	2.1.68	Faust
Then write againe: Faustus gives to thee his soule.	F 458	2.1.70	Faust
What will not I do to obtaine his soule?	F 462	2.1.74	Mephst
And Faustus hath bequeath'd his soule to Lucifer.	F 464	2.1.76	Faust
I'le fetch him somewhat to delight his minde.	F 471	2.1.83	Mephst
that Mephostophilis shall be his servant, and be by him	F 486	2.1.98	P Faust
shall be his servant, and be by him commanded <at his command>.	F 487	2.1.99	P Faust
Fourthly, that he shall be in his chamber or house invisible.	F 490	2.1.102	P Faust
and his Minister Mephostophilis, and furthermore grant unto	F 494	2.1.106	P Faust
Saba, or as beautifull/As was bright Lucifer before his fall.	F 542	2.1.154	Mephst
walles of Thebes/With ravishing sound of his melodious Harpe,	F 580	2.2.29	Faust
And <of> his dam <dame> to.	F 646	2.2.95	Belzeb
[To burne his Scriptures, slay his Ministers],	F 650	2.2.99A	Faust
[And make my spirites pull his churches downe].	F 651	2.2.100A	Faust
me, as Paradise was to Adam the first day of his creation.	F 658	2.2.107	P Faust
From East to West his Dragons swiftly glide,	F 766	2.3.45	2Chor
Not long he stayed within his quiet house,	F 768	2.3.47	2Chor
To rest his bones after his weary toyle,	F 769	2.3.48	2Chor
That with his wings did part the subtle aire,	F 772	2.3.51	2Chor
To see the Pope and manner of his Court,	F 776	2.3.55	2Chor
Thus hitherto hath Faustus spent his time.	F 799	3.1.21	Faust
I chuse his privy chamber for our use.	F 806	3.1.28	Mephst
I have taken up his holinesse privy chamber for our use>.	F 806	(HC265)A	P Mephst
I hope his Holinesse will bid us welcome.	F 807	3.1.29	Faust
All's one, for wee'l be bold with his Venison.	F 808	3.1.30	Mephst
<Tut, tis no matter man>, wee'l be bold with his <good cheare>.	F 808	(HC265)A	P Mephst
To make his Monkes and Abbots stand like Apes,	F 861	3.1.83	Mephst
And point like Antiques at his triple Crowne:	F 862	3.1.84	Mephst
Whilst on thy backe his hollinesse ascends/Saint Peters Chaire	F 869	3.1.91	Raymnd
And in despite of all his Holinesse/Restore this Bruno to his	F 898	3.1.120	Faust
despite of all his Holinesse/Restore this Bruno to his liberty,	F 899	3.1.121	Faust
He growes to prowd in his authority,	F 911	3.1.133	Pope
Lifting his loftie head above the clouds,	F 912	3.1.134	Pope
But wee'le pul downe his haughty insolence:	F 914	3.1.136	Pope
authority Apostolicall/Depose him from his Regall Government.	F 924	3.1.146	Pope
And therefore none of his Decrees can stand.	F 929	3.1.151	Pope
Let us salute his reverend Father-hood.	F 944	3.1.166	Faust
And if that Bruno by his owne assent,	F 957	3.1.179	Faust
We will determine of his life or death.	F 969	3.1.191	Pope
Here, take his triple Crowne along with you,	F 970	3.1.192	Pope
That slept both Bruno and his crowne away.	F 988	3.2.8	Faust
But now, that Faustus may delight his minde,	F 989	3.2.9	Faust
And there determine of his punishment?	F1018	3.2.38	Pope
With his rich triple crowne to be reserv'd,	F1027	3.2.47	Raymnd
Purgatory, and now is come unto your holinesse for his pardon.	F1061	3.2.81	P Archbp
be he that stole [away] his holinesse meate from the Table.	F1077	3.2.97	1Frier
Cursed be he that stroke his holinesse a blow [on] the face.	F1079	3.2.99	1Frier
Cursed be he that tooke away his holinesse wine.	F1085	3.2.105	1Frier
him, as he was never conjur'd in his life, I warrant him:	F1092	3.3.5	P Robin
[Hee stayde his course, and so returned home],	F1140	3.3.53A	3Chor
[Where such as beare <bare> his absence but with griefe],	F1141	3.3.54A	3Chor
[I meane his friends and nearest companions],	F1142	3.3.55A	3Chor
[Did gratulate his safetie with kinde words],	F1143	3.3.56A	3Chor
[Touching his journey through the world and ayre],	F1145	3.3.58A	3Chor
[As they admirde and wondred at his wit].	F1148	3.3.61A	3Chor
[Now is his fame spread forth in every land],	F1149	3.3.62A	3Chor
at whose pallace now]/[Faustus is feasted mongst his noblemen].	F1152	3.3.65A	3Chor
[What there he did in triall of his art],	F1153	3.3.66A	3Chor

HIS (cont.)

His Majesty is comming to the Hall;	F1158	4.1.4		Mrtino
Will not his grace consort the Emperour?	F1162	4.1.8		Fredrk
The race of all his stout progenitors;	F1168	4.1.14		Mrtino
And bring in presence of his Majesty,	F1169	4.1.15		Mrtino
and warlike semblances/Of Alexander and his beauteous Paramour.	F1171	4.1.17		Mrtino
He took his rouse with stopes of Rhennish wine,	F1174	4.1.20		Mrtino
That all this day the sluggard keepes his bed.	F1176	4.1.22		Mrtino
See, see his window's ope, we'l call to him.	F1177	4.1.23		Fredrk
And at his heeles a thousand furies waite,	F1182	4.1.28		Mrtino
thine, in setting Bruno free/From his and our professed enemy,	F1207	4.1.53		Emper
Shall make poore Faustus to his utmost power,	F1218	4.1.64		Faust
And lay his life at holy Bruno's feet.	F1220	4.1.66		Faust
To cast his Magicke charmes, that shall pierce through/The Ebon	F1223	4.1.69		Faust
Great Alexander, and his Paramour,	F1232	4.1.78		Emper
Great Alexander and his beauteous Paramour.	F1239	4.1.85		Faust
present the royall shapes/Of Alexander and his Paramour,	F1250	4.1.96		Faust
and thou bring Alexander and his Paramour before the Emperour,	F1255	4.1.101	P	Benvol
beast is yon, that thrusts his head out at [the] window.	F1275	4.1.121	P	Faust
He sleeps my Lord, but dreames not of his hornes.	F1280	4.1.126		Faust
As all his footmanship shall scarce prevaile,	F1302	4.1.148		Faust
To keepe his Carkasse from their bloudy phangs.	F1303	4.1.149		Faust
Let me intreate you to remove his hornes,	F1309	4.1.155		Emper
which being all I desire, I am content to remove his hornes.	F1314	4.1.160	P	Faust
And take his leave, laden with rich rewards.	F1345	4.2.21		Benvol
And all alone, comes walking in his gowne;	F1358	4.2.34		Fredrk
For hornes he gave, Il'e have his head anone.	F1361	4.2.37		Benvol
Hell take his soule, his body thus must fall.	F1363	4.2.39		Benvol
Breake may his heart with grones: deere Frederik see,	F1366	4.2.42		Benvol
Thus will I end his griefes immediatly.	F1367	4.2.43		Benvol
Strike with a willing hand, his head is off.	F1368	4.2.44		Mrtino
Tremble and quake at his commanding charmes?	F1372	4.2.48		Fredrk
Justly rewarded for his villanies.	F1376	4.2.52		Benvol
may adde more shame/To the blacke scandall of his hated name.	F1378	4.2.54		Fredrk
First, on his head, in quittance of my wrongs,	F1379	4.2.55		Benvol
What use shall we put his beard to?	F1383	4.2.59	P	Mrtino
What shall [his] eyes doe?	F1386	4.2.62	P	Fredrk
Wee'l put out his eyes, and they shall serve for buttons to his	F1387	4.2.63	P	Benvol
and they shall serve for buttons to his lips, to keepe his	F1388	4.2.64	P	Benvol
buttons to his lips, to keepe his tongue from catching cold.	F1388	4.2.64	P	Benvol
Give him his head for Gods sake.	F1392	4.2.68	P	Fredrk
I have puld off his leg.	F1492	4.4.36	P	HrsCsr
Faustus hath his leg againe, and the Horse-courser a bundle of	F1497	4.4.41	P	Faust
and the Horse-courser a bundle of hay for his forty Dollors.	F1497	4.4.41	P	Faust
of his men to attend you with provision fit for your journey.	F1501	4.4.45	P	Wagner
I thinking that a little would serve his turne, bad him take as	F1528	4.5.24	P	Carter
and never tyre, I gave him his money; so when I had my horse,	F1539	4.5.35	P	HrsCsr
it; I went me home to his house, and there I found him asleepe;	F1548	4.5.44	P	HrsCsr
I kept a hallowing and whooping in his eares, but all could not	F1549	4.5.45	P	HrsCsr
till I had pul'd me his leg quite off, and now 'tis at home in	F1551	4.5.47	P	HrsCsr
one of his devils turn'd me into the likenesse of an Apes face.	F1554	4.5.50	P	Dick
when every Tree is barren of his fruite, from whence you had	F1579	4.6.22	P	Duke
us, he were as good commit with his father, as commit with us.	F1603	4.6.46	P	Dick
Ha, ha, ha, dost heare him Dick, he has forgot his legge.	F1629	4.6.72	P	Carter
His Artfull sport, drives all sad thoughts away.	F1673	4.6.116		Duke
to die shortly, he has made his will, and given me his wealth,	F1675	5.1.2	P	Wagner
he has made his will, and given me his wealth, his house, his	F1675	5.1.2	P	Wagner
and given me his wealth, his house, his goods, and store of	F1675	5.1.2	P	Wagner
his house, his goods, and store of golden plate; besides two	F1675	5.1.2	P	Wagner
such belly-cheere, as Wagner in his life nere saw the like:	F1679	5.1.6	P	Wagner
Hell claimes his <calls for> right, and with a roaring voyce,	F1726	5.1.53		Faust
His faith is great, I cannot touch his soule;	F1756	5.1.83		Mephst
But what I may afflict his body with,	F1757	5.1.84		Mephst
[And fliest the throne of his tribunall seate],	F1790	5.1.117A		OldMan
[Sathan begins to sift me with his pride]:	F1791	5.1.118A		OldMan
Fond worldling, now his heart bloud dries with griefe;	F1808	5.2.12		Mephst
His conscience kils it, and his labouring braine,	F1809	5.2.13		Mephst
His store of pleasures must be sauc'd with paine.	F1812	5.2.16		Mephst
He and his servant Wagner are at hand,	F1813	5.2.17		Mephst
That Faustus may repent, and save his soule.	F1934	5.2.138		Faust
And see [where God]/[Stretcheth out his Arme, and bends his	F1944	5.2.148A		Faust
God]/[Stretcheth out his Arme, and bends his irefull Browes]:	F1944	5.2.148A		Faust
We'll give his mangled limbs due buryall:	F1999	5.3.17		2Schol
Shall waite upon his heavy funerall.	F2001	5.3.19		2Schol
Faustus is gone, regard his hellish fall,	F2005	5.3.23		4Chor
see how poverty jesteth in his nakednesse, the vilaine is bare,	F App	p.229 6	P	Wagner
he would give his soule to the Divel for a shoulder of mutton,	F App	p.229 8	P	Wagner
I, I thought that was al the land his father left him:	F App	p.229 17	P	Clown
Cursed be hee that stole away his holinesse meate from/the	F App	p.232 31		Frier
Cursed be hee that strooke his holinesse a blowe on the face.	F App	p.232 33		Frier
Cursed be he that tooke away his holinesse wine.	F App	p.233 39		Frier
theres a Gentleman tarries to have his horse, and he would have	F App	p.233 7	P	Rafe
his horse, and he would have his things rubd and made cleane:	F App	p.233 7	P	Rafe
I can reade, he for his forehead, she for her private study,	F App	p.233 16	P	Robin
glorious actes/Lightens the world with his reflecting beames,	F App	p.237 26		Emper
And bring with him his beauteous Paramour,	F App	p.237 32		Emper
spirites as can lively resemble Alexander and his Paramour,	F App	p.237 46	P	Faust
you bring Alexander and his paramour before the emperor?	F App	p.237 52	P	Knight
being all I desire, I am content to release him of his hornes:	F App	p.238 84	P	Faust
at ease, if I bring his water to you, youle tel me what it is?	F App	p.240 118	P	HrsCsr
O yonder is his snipper snapper, do you heare?	F App	p.240 137	P	HrsCsr
him now, or Ile breake his glasse-windowes about his eares.	F App	p.240 142	P	HrsCsr
him now, or Ile breake his glasse-windowes about his eares.	F App	p.240 143	P	HrsCsr

HIS (cont.)

Faustus has his legge againe, and the Horsecourser I take it,	F App	p.241 164 P Faust
the Horsecourser I take it, a bottle of hey for his labour: wel,	F App	p.241 165 P Faust
For he hath given to me al his goodes,	F App	p.243 2 Wagner
As Wagner nere beheld in all his life.	F App	p.243 7 Wagner
and Phoebe's waine/Chace Phoebus and inrag'd affect his place,	Lucan, First Booke	78
His losse made way for Roman outrages.	Lucan, First Booke	106
And joyed to heare his Theaters applause;	Lucan, First Booke	134
He liv'd secure boasting his former deeds,	Lucan, First Booke	135
And thought his name sufficient to uphold him,	Lucan, First Booke	136
Who though his root be weake, and his owne waight/Keepe him	Lucan, First Booke	139
root be weake, and his owne waight/Keepe him within the ground,	Lucan, First Booke	139
his owne waight/Keepe him within the ground, his armes al bare,	Lucan, First Booke	140
His body (not his boughs) send forth a shade;	Lucan, First Booke	141
Urging his fortune, trusting in the gods,	Lucan, First Booke	149
Destroying what withstood his proud desires,	Lucan, First Booke	150
His mind was troubled, and he aim'd at war,	Lucan, First Booke	186
spectacle/Stroake Caesars hart with feare, his hayre stoode up,	Lucan, First Booke	195
And faintnes numm'd his steps there on the brincke:	Lucan, First Booke	196
then having whiskt/His taile athwart his backe, and crest	Lucan, First Booke	211
(Albeit the Moores light Javelin or his speare/Sticks in his	Lucan, First Booke	213
or his speare/Sticks in his side) yet runs upon the hunter.	Lucan, First Booke	214
And laboring to approve his quarrell good.	Lucan, First Booke	267
Straight summon'd he his severall companies/Unto the standard:	Lucan, First Booke	297
his grave looke appeasd/The wrastling tumult, and right hand	Lucan, First Booke	298
(Whom from his youth he bribde) needs make him king?	Lucan, First Booke	315
And shal he triumph long before his time,	Lucan, First Booke	316
Twas his troupe hem'd in Milo being accusde;	Lucan, First Booke	323
And now least age might waine his state, he casts/For civill	Lucan, First Booke	324
wherein through use he's known/To exceed his maister, that	Lucan, First Booke	326
Must Pompey as his last foe plume on me,	Lucan, First Booke	338
me,/Because at his commaund I wound not up/My conquering Eagles?	Lucan, First Booke	339
When Caesar saw his army proane to war,	Lucan, First Booke	393
delay/Might crosse him, he withdrew his troupes from France,	Lucan, First Booke	395
And ere he sees the sea looseth his name;	Lucan, First Booke	402
One sweares his troupes of daring horsemen fought/Upon Mevanias	Lucan, First Booke	469
And that his owne ten ensignes, and the rest/Marcht not	Lucan, First Booke	473
And far more barbarous then the French (his vassals)/And that	Lucan, First Booke	476
Thus in his fright did each man strengthen Fame,	Lucan, First Booke	481
His burning chariot plung'd in sable cloudes,	Lucan, First Booke	539
hellish fiend/Which made the sterne Lycurgus wound his thigh,	Lucan, First Booke	573
Tav'ron peering/(His grave broke open) did affright the Boores.	Lucan, First Booke	582
Then crams salt levin on his crooked knife;	Lucan, First Booke	609
hornes/The quick priest pull'd him on his knees and slew him:	Lucan, First Booke	612
Scorpion with the burning taile/And fier'st his cleyes.	Lucan, First Booke	659
Thus I complaind, but Love unlockt his quiver,	Ovid's Elegies	1.1.25
And bent his sinewy bow upon his knee,	Ovid's Elegies	1.1.27
Who gardes [the] <thee> conquered with his conquering hands.	Ovid's Elegies	1.2.52
Accept him that will serve thee all his youth,	Ovid's Elegies	1.3.5
Griping his false hornes with hir virgin hand:	Ovid's Elegies	1.3.24
Pray God it may his latest supper be,	Ovid's Elegies	1.4.2
Wilt lying under him his bosome clippe?	Ovid's Elegies	1.4.5
Lie with him gently, when his limbes he spread/Upon the bed, but	Ovid's Elegies	1.4.15
Even in his face his offered [Gobbets] <Goblets> cast.	Ovid's Elegies	1.4.34
Let not thy necke by his vile armes be prest,	Ovid's Elegies	1.4.35
Nor [leane] <leave> thy soft head on his boistrous brest.	Ovid's Elegies	1.4.36
Chiefely on thy lips let not his lips linger.	Ovid's Elegies	1.4.38
Mingle not thighes, nor to his legge joyne thine,	Ovid's Elegies	1.4.43
Nor thy soft foote with his hard foote combine.	Ovid's Elegies	1.4.44
Love hearing it laugh'd with his tender mother/And smiling	Ovid's Elegies	1.6.11
And he who on his mother veng'd his sire,	Ovid's Elegies	1.7.9
He staide, and on thy lookes his gazes seaz'd.	Ovid's Elegies	1.8.24
a rich lover plants/His love on thee, and can supply thy wants.	Ovid's Elegies	1.8.32
Such is his forme as may with thine compare,	Ovid's Elegies	1.8.33
Each one according to his gifts respect.	Ovid's Elegies	1.8.38
Of his gilt Harpe the well tun'd strings doth hold.	Ovid's Elegies	1.8.60
Or least his love oft beaten backe should waine.	Ovid's Elegies	1.8.76
Thy fault with his fault so repuls'd will vanish.	Ovid's Elegies	1.8.80
All Lovers warre, and Cupid hath his tent,	Ovid's Elegies	1.9.1
His Mistris dores this; that his Captaines keepes.	Ovid's Elegies	1.9.8
One as a spy doth to his enemies goe,	Ovid's Elegies	1.9.17
The other eyes his rivall as his foe.	Ovid's Elegies	1.9.18
This breakes Towne gates, but he his Mistris dore.	Ovid's Elegies	1.9.20
Hector to armes went from his wives embraces,	Ovid's Elegies	1.9.35
And on Andromache his helmet laces.	Ovid's Elegies	1.9.36
Love is a naked boy, his yeares saunce staine,	Ovid's Elegies	1.10.15
his rent discharg'd/From further duty he rests then inlarg'd.	Ovid's Elegies	1.10.45
better/In which the Merchant wayles his banquerout debter.	Ovid's Elegies	1.12.26
Memnon the elfe/Received his cole-blacke colour from thy selfe.	Ovid's Elegies	1.13.32
Thou leav'st his bed, because hees faint through age,	Ovid's Elegies	1.13.37
Jove that thou shouldst not hast but wait his leasure,	Ovid's Elegies	1.13.45
Made two nights one to finish up his pleasure.	Ovid's Elegies	1.13.46
The Cedar tall spoyld of his barke retaines.	Ovid's Elegies	1.14.12
[His Arte excelld, although his witte was weake].	Ovid's Elegies	1.15.14
loves bowe/His owne flames best acquainted signes may knowe,	Ovid's Elegies	2.1.8
I had in hand/Which for his heaven fell on the Gyants band.	Ovid's Elegies	2.1.16
But furiously he follow his loves fire/And [thinke] <thinkes>	Ovid's Elegies	2.2.13
His fauning wench with her desire he crownes.	Ovid's Elegies	2.2.34
flying touch/Tantalus seekes, his long tongues gaine is such.	Ovid's Elegies	2.2.44
By whom the husband his wives incest knewe.	Ovid's Elegies	2.2.48
Or if he loves, thy tale breedes his misfortune.	Ovid's Elegies	2.2.54
Condemne his eyes, and say there is no tryall.	Ovid's Elegies	2.2.58
Spying his mistrisse teares, he will lament/And say this blabbe	Ovid's Elegies	2.2.59

HIS (cont.)

He's happy, that his love dares boldly credit,	Ovid's Elegies	2.5.9
To whom his wench can say, I never did it.	Ovid's Elegies	2.5.10
and too much his griefe doth favour/That seekes the conquest by	Ovid's Elegies	2.5.11
as might make/Wrath-kindled Jove away his thunder shake.	Ovid's Elegies	2.5.52
And Hector dyed his brothers yet alive.	Ovid's Elegies	2.6.42
There Junoes bird displayes his gorgious feather,	Ovid's Elegies	2.6.55
Great Agamemnon lov'd his servant Chriseis.	Ovid's Elegies	2.8.12
Did not Pelides whom his Speare did grieve,	Ovid's Elegies	2.9.7
His sword layed by, safe, though rude places yeelds.	Ovid's Elegies	2.9.20
His rider vainely striving him to stay,	Ovid's Elegies	2.9.30
And purple Love resumes his dartes againe.	Ovid's Elegies	2.9.34
Let souldiour <souldiours> chase his <their> enemies amaine,	Ovid's Elegies	2.10.31
And with his <their> bloud eternall honour gaine,	Ovid's Elegies	2.10.32
Even as he led his life, so did he die.	Ovid's Elegies	2.10.38
Nor can an other say his helpe I tooke.	Ovid's Elegies	2.12.12
Cupid commands to move his ensignes further.	Ovid's Elegies	2.12.28
And where swift Nile in his large channell slipping <skipping>,	Ovid's Elegies	2.13.9
The youth oft swimming to his Hero kinde,	Ovid's Elegies	2.16.31
With his stumpe-foote he halts ill-favouredly.	Ovid's Elegies	2.17.20
And Love triumpheth ore his buskind Poet.	Ovid's Elegies	2.18.18
Ah Pelops from his coach was almost feld,	Ovid's Elegies	3.2.15
Wish in his hands graspt did Hippomenes.	Ovid's Elegies	3.2.30
Applaud you Neptune, that dare trust his wave,	Ovid's Elegies	3.2.47
And each give signes by casting up his cloake.	Ovid's Elegies	3.2.74
Mars girts his deadly sword on for my harme:	Ovid's Elegies	3.3.27
At me Apollo bends his pliant bowe:	Ovid's Elegies	3.3.29
Jove throwes downe woods, and Castles with his fire:	Ovid's Elegies	3.3.35
But bids his darts from perjurd girles retire.	Ovid's Elegies	3.3.36
Like lightning go, his strugling mouth being checkt.	Ovid's Elegies	3.4.14
And on his loose mane the loose bridle laide.	Ovid's Elegies	3.4.16
Where Mars his sonnes not without fault did breed,	Ovid's Elegies	3.4.39
Who so well keepes his waters head from knowing,	Ovid's Elegies	3.5.40
As his deepe whirle-pooles could not quench the same.	Ovid's Elegies	3.5.42
Flye backe his [streame] <shame> chargd, the streame chargd,	Ovid's Elegies	3.5.44
Her, from his swift waves, the bold floud perceav'd,	Ovid's Elegies	3.5.51
And from the mid foord his hoarse voice upheav'd,	Ovid's Elegies	3.5.52
His heart consists of flint, and hardest steele,	Ovid's Elegies	3.5.59
And Tithon livelier then his yeeres require.	Ovid's Elegies	3.6.42
And craves his taske, and seekes to be at fight.	Ovid's Elegies	3.6.68
Foole canst thou lie in his enfolding space?	Ovid's Elegies	3.7.12
His left hand whereon gold doth ill alight,	Ovid's Elegies	3.7.15
A target bore: bloud sprinckled was his right.	Ovid's Elegies	3.7.16
Behold the signes of antient fight, his skarres,	Ovid's Elegies	3.7.19
What ere he hath his body gaind in warres.	Ovid's Elegies	3.7.20
Burnes his dead body in the funerall flame.	Ovid's Elegies	3.8.6
Loe Cupid brings his quiver spoyled quite,	Ovid's Elegies	3.8.7
His broken bowe, his fire-brand without light.	Ovid's Elegies	3.8.8
And knocks his bare brest with selfe-angry hands.	Ovid's Elegies	3.8.10
The locks spred on his necke receive his teares,	Ovid's Elegies	3.8.11
And shaking sobbes his mouth for speeches beares.	Ovid's Elegies	3.8.12
Where Linus by his father Phoebus layed/To sing with his	Ovid's Elegies	3.8.23
father Phoebus layed/To sing with his unequald harpe is sayed.	Ovid's Elegies	3.8.24
The one his first love, th'other his new care.	Ovid's Elegies	3.8.32
His fainting hand in death engrasped mee.	Ovid's Elegies	3.8.58
His side past service, and his courage spent.	Ovid's Elegies	3.10.14
Or his Bulles hornes Europas hand doth hold.	Ovid's Elegies	3.11.34
And offred as a dower his burning throne,	Hero and Leander	1.7
As he imagyn'd Hero was his mother.	Hero and Leander	1.40
About her naked necke his bare armes threw.	Hero and Leander	1.42
And laid his childish head upon her brest,	Hero and Leander	1.43
And with still panting rockt, there tooke his rest.	Hero and Leander	1.44
His dangling tresses that were never shorne,	Hero and Leander	1.55
Faire Cinthia wisht, his armes might be her spheare,	Hero and Leander	1.59
His bodie was as straight as Circes wand,	Hero and Leander	1.61
Jove might have sipt out Nectar from his hand.	Hero and Leander	1.62
So was his necke in touching, and surpast/The white of Pelops	Hero and Leander	1.64
How smooth his brest was, and how white his bellie,	Hero and Leander	1.66
That runs along his backe, but my rude pen,	Hero and Leander	1.69
and lippes, exceeding his/That leapt into the water for a kis	Hero and Leander	1.73
That leapt into the water for a kis/Of his owne shadow, and	Hero and Leander	1.75
Enamoured of his beautie had he beene,	Hero and Leander	1.78
His presence made the rudest paisant melt,	Hero and Leander	1.79
Was moov'd with him, and for his favour sought.	Hero and Leander	1.82
For in his lookes were all that men desire,	Hero and Leander	1.84
(For his sake whom their goddesse held so deare,	Hero and Leander	1.92
Jove, slylie stealing from his sisters bed,	Hero and Leander	1.147
And for his love Europa, bellowing loud,	Hero and Leander	1.149
Which limping Vulcan and his Cyclops set:	Hero and Leander	1.152
Till with the fire that from his count'nance blazed,	Hero and Leander	1.164
Then shouldst thou bee his prisoner who is thine.	Hero and Leander	1.202
A Diamond set in lead his worth retaines,	Hero and Leander	1.215
his golden earth remains,/Which after his disceasse, some other	Hero and Leander	1.245
Which after his disceasse, some other gains.	Hero and Leander	1.246
Some one or other keepes you as his owne.	Hero and Leander	1.290
Which makes him quickly re-enforce his speech,	Hero and Leander	1.313
But from his spreading armes away she cast her,	Hero and Leander	1.342
Cupid beats downe her praiers with his wings,	Hero and Leander	1.369
All deepe enrag'd, his sinowie bow he bent,	Hero and Leander	1.371
As made Love sigh, to see his tirannie.	Hero and Leander	1.374
And wound them on his arme, and for her mourn'd.	Hero and Leander	1.376
On her, this god/Enamoured was, and with his snakie rod,/Did	Hero and Leander	1.398
And sweetly on his pipe began to play,	Hero and Leander	1.401

HIS (cont.)

Till in his twining armes he lockt her fast,	Hero and Leander		1.403
Boasting his parentage, would needs discover/The way to new	Hero and Leander		1.410
Herewith he stayd his furie, and began/To give her leave to	Hero and Leander		1.415
As she to heare his tale, left off her running.	Hero and Leander		1.418
such lovelinesse and beautie had/As could provoke his liking,	Hero and Leander		1.423
And neither would denie, nor graunt his sute.	Hero and Leander		1.424
And gave it to his simple rustike love,	Hero and Leander		1.435
sad and heavie cheare/Complaind to Cupid; Cupid for his sake,	Hero and Leander		1.441
At his faire feathered feet, the engins layd,	Hero and Leander		1.449
That Jove, usurper of his fathers seat,	Hero and Leander		1.452
As soone as he his wished purpose got,	Hero and Leander		1.460
He recklesse of his promise, did despise/The love of	Hero and Leander		1.461
And Jupiter unto his place restor'd.	Hero and Leander		1.464
Now waxt she jealous, least his love abated,	Hero and Leander		2.43
her body throes/Upon his bosome, where with yeelding eyes,	Hero and Leander		2.47
To slake his anger, if he were displeas'd,	Hero and Leander		2.49
And as a brother with his sister toyed,	Hero and Leander		2.52
Therefore unto his bodie, hirs he clung,	Hero and Leander		2.65
Ne're king more sought to keepe his diademe,	Hero and Leander		2.77
Though it was morning, did he take his flight.	Hero and Leander		2.102
With Cupids myrtle was his bonet crownd,	Hero and Leander		2.105
About his armes the purple riband wound,	Hero and Leander		2.106
Which made his love through Sestos to bee knowne,	Hero and Leander		2.111
But like exiled aire thrust from his sphere,	Hero and Leander		2.118
So to his mind was yoong Leanders looke.	Hero and Leander		2.130
His secret flame apparantly was seene,	Hero and Leander		2.135
And for the same mildly rebuk't his sonne,	Hero and Leander		2.137
To have his head control'd, but breakes the raines,	Hero and Leander		2.142
Spits foorth the ringled bit, and with his hoves,	Hero and Leander		2.143
And made his capring Triton sound alowd,	Hero and Leander		2.156
Where kingly Neptune and his traine abode.	Hero and Leander		2.166
He heav'd him up, and looking on his face,	Hero and Leander		2.171
Beat downe the bold waves with his triple mace,	Hero and Leander		2.172
The god put Helles bracelet on his arme,	Hero and Leander		2.179
He clapt his plumpe cheekes, with his tresses playd,	Hero and Leander		2.181
And smiling wantonly, his love bewrayd.	Hero and Leander		2.182
He watcht his armes, and as they opend wide,	Hero and Leander		2.183
And [throw] <threw> him gawdie toies to please his eie,	Hero and Leander		2.187
dive into the water, and there prie/Upon his brest, his thighs,	Hero and Leander		2.189
and there prie/Upon his brest, his thighs, and everie lim,	Hero and Leander		2.189
As for his love, both earth and heaven pyn'd;	Hero and Leander		2.196
And in his heart revenging malice bare:	Hero and Leander		2.208
He flung at him his mace, but as it went,	Hero and Leander		2.209
The mace returning backe, his owne hand hit,	Hero and Leander		2.211
His colour went and came, as if he rewd/The greefe which	Hero and Leander		2.214
Cast downe his wearie feet, and felt the sand.	Hero and Leander		2.228
His hands he cast upon her like a snare,	Hero and Leander		2.259
Inclos'd her in his armes and kist her to.	Hero and Leander		2.282
(Poore sillie maiden) at his mercie was.	Hero and Leander		2.286
And her all naked to his sight displayd.	Hero and Leander		2.324
Whence his admiring eyes more pleasure tooke,	Hero and Leander		2.325
Than Dis, on heapes of gold fixing his looke.	Hero and Leander		2.326
And with his flaring beames mockt ougly night,	Hero and Leander		2.332

HISSE

And hisse at Dido for preserving thee?	Dido	5.1.168	Dido

HISSES

Murmures and hisses for his hainous sin.	2Tamb	2.3.17	Orcan

HISTORIE

My love alludes to everie historie:	Ovid's Elegies		2.4.44

HISTORIES

Nor have their words true histories pretence,	Ovid's Elegies		3.11.42

HIT

How those were hit by pelting Cannon shot,	1Tamb	2.4.3	Mycet
see how right the man/Hath hit the meaning of my Lord the King.	1Tamb	3.2.108	Techel
You hit it right,/It is your owne you meane, feele on your	F1442	4.3.12	Fredrk
I would not out, might I in one place hit,	Ovid's Elegies		2.15.19
The mace returning backe, his owne hand hit,	Hero and Leander		2.211

HITHER (See also HETHER)

Goe one and call those Jewes of Malta hither:	Jew	1.2.34	Govnr
Governor of Malta, hither am I bound;	Jew	2.2.4	Bosco
For your sake and his own he's welcome hither.	Jew	2.3.233	Abigal
And bid the Jeweller come hither too.	Jew	4.2.86	Ithimr
So wish not they Iwis that sent thee hither,	Edw	3.1.152	Edward
Whose there? call hither Gurney and Matrevis.	Edw	5.2.38	Mortmr
Sweete sonne come hither, I must talke with thee.	Edw	5.2.87	Queene
Come hither sirra boy.	F 343	1.4.1	P Wagner
Constantinople have they brought me now <am I hither brought>,	F1118	3.3.31	Mephst
Sirra boy, come hither.	F App	p.229 1	P Wagner
From Constantinople am I hither come,	F App	p.235 38	Mephst
swift spirit that I have, I had them brought hither, as ye see,	F App	p.242 23	P Faust
or wrathful France/Pursu'd us hither, how were we bestead/When	Lucan, First Booke		309

HITHERTO (See also HETHERTO)

Thus hitherto hath Faustus spent his time.	F 799	3.1.21	Faust
For hitherto hee did but fan the fire,	Hero and Leander		2.41

HITS

Oh woe is me, he never shootes but hits,	Ovid's Elegies		1.1.29

HIVES

A garden where are Bee hives full of honey,	Dido	4.5.7	Nurse

HMM (See HUM, UMH)

HO (Homograph)

Brother, ho, what, given so much to sleep/You cannot leave it,	2Tamb	4.1.11	Amyras
What, ho, Abigall; open the doore I say.	Jew	2.3.221	Barab

HO (cont.)
With a heave and a ho, Edw 2.2.192 Lncstr
Hey ho; I am Sloth: F 705 2.2.154 P Sloth
hey ho: I'le not speake an other word. F 706 2.2.158 P Sloth
What ho, Officers, Gentlemen, F1155 4.1.1 Mrtino
What ho, Benvolio. F1282 4.1.128 Emper
Ho, Belimoth, Argiron, Asteroth. F1304 4.1.150 Faust
What ho, Benvolio. F1431 4.3.1 Mrtino
Here, what Frederick, ho. F1431 4.3.1 Benvol
Ho sirra Doctor, you cosoning scab; Maister Doctor awake, and F1488 4.4.32 P HrsCsr
I'le bring you to the best beere in Europe, what ho, Hostis; F1506 4.5.2 P Carter
looke up into th'hall there ho. F1519 4.5.15 P Hostss
What ho, give's halfe a dosen of Beere here, and be hang'd. F1612 4.6.55 P Robin
scab, do you remember how you cosened me with <of> a ho-- F1663 4.6.106 P HrsCsr
So, ho, ho: F App p.241 152 P HrsCsr
so, ho, ho. F App p.241 152 P HrsCsr

HOARCE
Cry out, exclaime, houle till thy throat be hoarce, P1077 19.147 King

HOARD (See HOORD)

HOARIE
With hoarie toppe, and under Hemus mount/Philippi plaines; Lucan, First Booke 679

HOARSE
To hoarse scrich-owles foule shadowes it allowes, Ovid's Elegies 1.12.19
And from the mid foord his hoarse voice upheav'd, Ovid's Elegies 3.5.52

HOARY
Mourning appear'd, whose hoary hayres were torne, Lucan, First Booke 189
Under whose hoary rocks Gebenna hangs; Lucan, First Booke 436
balde scalpes [thin] <thine> hoary flieces/And riveld cheekes I Ovid's Elegies 1.8.111
Suffring much cold by hoary nights frost bred. Ovid's Elegies 2.19.22

HOAST
at the spoile/Of great Darius and his wealthy hoast. 1Tamb 1.1.154 Ceneus
And being able, Ile keep an hoast in pay. P 840 17.35 Guise
Thou able to maintaine an hoast in pay, P 841 17.36 Eprnon
nights deawie hoast/March fast away: Ovid's Elegies 1.6.55

HODIE
I saluted with an old hempen proverb, Hodie tibi, cras mihi, Jew 4.2.18 P Pilia

HOE
Hoe yong men, saw you as you came/Any of all my Sisters Dido 1.1.183 Venus
What hoe, Benvolio. F1178 4.1.24 Mrtino

HOG
grunts like a hog, and looks/Like one that is imploy'd in Jew 4.3.11 Barab
And little Piggs, base Hog-sties sacrifice, Ovid's Elegies 3.12.16

HOGGE
Anon you shal heare a hogge grunt, a calfe bleate, and an asse F App p.232 27 P Faust

HOGS
the slave looks like a hogs cheek new sindg'd. Jew 2.3.42 P Barab

HOGSHEAD
and my mother <grandmother> was a Hogshead of Claret Wine. F 697 2.2.146 P Glutny

HOG-STIES
And little Piggs, base Hog-sties sacrifice, Ovid's Elegies 3.12.16

HOIE
Heere in the river rides a Flemish hoie, Edw 2.4.46 Mortmr

HOIST (See also HOYST)
Which when I come aboord will hoist up saile, 2Tamb 1.2.24 Callap
he doth not chide/Nor to hoist saile attends fit time and tyde. Ovid's Elegies 1.9.14
Rather Ile hoist up saile, and use the winde, Ovid's Elegies 3.10.51

HOISTED
on Damascus wals/Have hoisted up their slaughtered carcases. 1Tamb 5.1.131 Techel
On horsmens Lances to be hoisted up, 1Tamb 5.1.328 Zenoc

HOKE
Foh, me thinkes they stinke like a Holly-Hoke. Jew 4.4.41 Pilia

HOLBARD
Muffes, and Danes/That with the Holbard, Lance, and murthering 2Tamb 1.1.23 Uribas

HOLD (See also HOULD)
Hold here my little love: Dido 1.1.42 Jupitr
Hold, take this candle and goe light a fire, Dido 1.1.171 Aeneas
Faire Troian, hold my golden bowe awhile, Dido 3.3.7 Dido
And yet Ile speake, and yet Ile hold my peace, Dido 3.4.27 Dido
Hold, take these Jewels at thy Lovers hand, Dido 3.4.61 Dido
O where is Ganimed to hold his cup, Dido 4.4.46 Dido
Aeneas could not choose but hold thee deare, Dido 5.1.126 Aeneas
I hold the Fates bound fast in yron chaines, 1Tamb 1.2.174 Tamb
Will hazard that we might with surety hold. 2Tamb 1.1.24 Uribas
If any man will hold him, I will strike, 2Tamb 1.3.102 Calyph
Hold him, and cleave him too, or Ile cleave thee, 2Tamb 1.3.104 Tamb
And this is Balsera their chiefest hold, 2Tamb 3.3.3 Therid
Captaine, that thou yeeld up thy hold to us. 2Tamb 3.3.16 Therid
Shal play upon the bulwarks of thy hold/Volleies of ordinance 2Tamb 3.3.24 Therid
And souldiers play the men, the [hold] <holds> is yours. 2Tamb 3.3.63 Techel
No hope is left to save this conquered hold. 2Tamb 3.4.3 Olymp
By which I hold my name and majesty. 2Tamb 4.3.26 Tamb
Hold ye tal souldiers, take ye Queens apeece/(I meane such 2Tamb 4.3.70 Tamb
Or hold our citie from the Conquerours hands. 2Tamb 5.1.5 Maxim
To hold the fiery spirit it containes, 2Tamb 5.3.169 Tamb
And hold there is no sinne but Ignorance. Jew Prol.15 Machvl
Daughter, whom I hold as deare/As Agamemnon did his Iphegen: Jew 1.1.137 Barab
And now I can no longer hold my minde. Jew 2.3.290 Lodowk
For they themselves hold it a principle, Jew 2.3.310 Barab
Hold thee, wench, there's something for thee to spend. Jew 3.1.12 Pilia
Hold, let's inquire the causers of their deaths, Jew 3.2.27 Mater
I hold my head my master's hungry: Jew 3.4.51 P Ithimr
Upon mine owne free-hold within fortie foot of the gallowes, Jew 4.2.16 P Pilia
I can with-hold no longer; welcome sweet love. Jew 4.2.46 Curtzn

HOLD (cont.)

Here, hold that knife, and when thou seest he comes,	Jew	5.5.37	Barab
here, hold thee, Barabas,/I trust thy word, take what I promis'd	Jew	5.5.42	Govnr
Hold thee tale soldier take the this and flye	Paris	ms18,p390	Guise
But that it harbors him I hold so deare,	Edw	1.1.13	Gavstn
Will you be resolute and hold with me?	Edw	1.4.231	Lncstr
Was borne I see to be our anchor hold.	Edw	4.2.77	Mortmr
hath <I have> already done, and holds <hold> this principle,	F 283	1.3.55	Faust
[Hold] <Here>, take this booke, <and> peruse it [thoroughly]	F 543	2.1.155	Mephst
hold belly hold, and wee'le not pay one peny for it.	F 749	2.3.28	P Robin
To hold the Emperours their lawfull Lords.	F 927	3.1.149	Bruno
hold the cup Dick, come, come, search me, search me.	F1102	3.3.15	P Robin
do, hold the cup Robin, I feare not your searching; we scorne to	F1105	3.3.18	P Dick
Nay, and thy hornes hold, tis no matter for thy head, for that's	F1288	4.1.134	P Emper
Hold, hold: zounds hee'l raise up a kennel of Divels	F1305	4.1.151	P Benvol
up my hands, but see they hold 'em <them>, they hold 'em <them>.	F1853	5.2.57	P Faust
my hands, but see they hold 'em <them>, they hold 'em <them>.	F1853	5.2.57	P Faust
For you hold/That soules passe not to silent Erebus	Lucan, First Booke		450
And hold my conquered hands for thee to tie.	Ovid's Elegies		1.2.20
Of his gilt Harpe the well tun'd strings doth hold.	Ovid's Elegies		1.8.60
What neede she [tyre] <try> her hand to hold the quill,	Ovid's Elegies		1.11.23
Hold in thy rosie horses that they move not.	Ovid's Elegies		1.13.10
And what lesse labour then to hold thy peace?	Ovid's Elegies		2.2.28
And what she likes, let both hold ratifide.	Ovid's Elegies		2.2.32
Least to the waxe the hold-fast drye gemme cleaves,	Ovid's Elegies		2.15.16
Now poverty great barbarisme we hold.	Ovid's Elegies		3.7.4
Or his Bulles hornes Europas hand doth hold.	Ovid's Elegies		3.11.34
Ile not sift much, but hold thee soone excusde,	Ovid's Elegies		3.13.41

HOLDE

Holde thee Cosroe, weare two imperiall Crownes.	1Tamb	2.5.1	Tamb
the plaines/To spie what force comes to relieve the holde.	2Tamb	3.3.48	Techel
Shrowd any thought may holde my striving hands/From martiall	2Tamb	4.1.95	Tamb
and Calor, which some holde/Is not a parcell of the Elements,	2Tamb	5.3.86	Phsitn
Thanks my good freend, holde, take thou this reward.	P 168	3.3	OldQn
Which in the woods doe holde their synagogue:	P 502	9.21	Guise
O holde me up, my sight begins to faile,	P 548	11.13	Charls
yet I meane to keepe you out, which I will if this geare holde:	P 815	17.10	P Souldr
Holde thee tall Souldier, take thee this and flye.	P 817	17.12	Guise
Holde Sworde,	P 987	19.57	Guise
Of such as holde them of the holy church?	P1181	22.43	King
Flie, flie, my lords, the earles have got the holde,	Edw	2.4.4	Edward
holde, take these gilders.	F App	p.230 30	P Wagner

HOLDES

That holdes it from your highnesse wrongfully:	P 582	11.47	Pleshe
I know none els but holdes them in disgrace:	P 764	15.22	Guise
He holdes the palme: my palme is yet to gaine.	Ovid's Elegies		3.2.82

HOLDETH

But Dido that now holdeth him so deare,	Dido	3.3.76	Iarbus

HOLD-FAST

Least to the waxe the hold-fast drye gemme cleaves,	Ovid's Elegies		2.15.16

HOLDING

Or holding of a napkin in your hand,	Edw	2.1.36	Spencr
painted stands/All naked holding in her wave-moist hands.	Ovid's Elegies		1.14.34

HOLDS

That holds us up, and foiles our neighbour foes.	1Tamb	1.1.61	Mycet
That holds you from your father in despight,	1Tamb	3.2.27	Agidas
Or when the morning holds him in her armes:	1Tamb	3.2.48	Zenoc
The rogue of Volga holds Zenocrate,	1Tamb	4.1.4	Souldn
Holds out his hand in highest majesty/To entertaine divine	2Tamb	2.4.32	Tamb
What God so ever holds thee in his armes,	2Tamb	2.4.109	Tamb
And souldiers play the men, the [hold] <holds> is yours.	2Tamb	3.3.63	Techel
He loves my daughter, and she holds him deare:	Jew	2.3.141	Barab
now Abigall shall see/Whether Mathias holds her deare or no.	Jew	3.2.2	Mthias
hath <I have> already done, and holds <hold> this principle,	F 283	1.3.55	Faust
She holds, and viewes her old lockes in her lappe,	Ovid's Elegies		1.14.53
And he is happy whom the earth holds, say.	Ovid's Elegies		2.11.30

HOLE

Here will I hide it in this simple hole.	1Tamb	2.4.15	Mycet
Yet through the key-hole will he talke to her,	Jew	2.3.263	Barab

HOLES

Oares of massie Ivorie full of holes,	Dido	3.1.118	Dido
And marche to fire them from their starting holes.	Edw	3.1.127	Spencr

HOLINES

For not effecting of his holines will.	P 878	17.73	Eprnon

HOLINESSE

If you retaine desert of holinesse,	2Tamb	5.3.19	Techel
but be thou so precise/As they may thinke it done of Holinesse.	Jew	1.2.285	Barab
A prison may beseeme his holinesse.	Edw	1.1.207	Gavstn
I have taken up his holinesse privy chamber for our use>.	F 806	(HC265) A	P Mephst
I hope his Holinesse will bid us welcome.	F 807	3.1.29	Faust
And in despite of all his Holinesse/Restore this Bruno to his	F 898	3.1.120	Faust
So Faustus, now for all their holinesse,	F1004	3.2.24	Mephst
First, may it please your sacred Holinesse,	F1013	3.2.33	1Card
I thanke your Holinesse.	F1038	3.2.58	Archbp
Please it your holinesse, I thinke it be some Ghost crept out	F1059	3.2.79	P Archbp
Purgatory, and now is come unto your holinesse for his pardon.	F1060	3.2.80	P Archbp
be he that stole [away] his holinesse meate from the Table.	F1077	3.2.97	1Frier
Cursed be he that stroke his holinesse a blow [on] the face.	F1079	3.2.99	1Frier
Cursed be he that tooke away his holinesse wine.	F1085	3.2.105	1Frier
out of Purgatory come to begge a pardon of your holinesse.	F App	p.232 15	P Lorein
Cursed be hee that stole away his holinesse meate from/the	F App	p.232 31	Frier
Cursed be hee that strooke his holinesse a blowe on the face.	F App	p.232 33	Frier
Cursed be he that tooke away his holinesse wine.	F App	p.233 39	Frier

HOLLA			
Holla, ye pampered Jades of Asia:	2Tamb	4.3.1	Tamb
Holla verlete, hey: Epernoune, where is the King?	P 956	19.26	Guise
Content, ile beare my part, holla whose there?	Edw	2.2.130	Lncstr
Holla, who walketh there, ist you my lord?	Edw	4.1.12	Mortmr
HOLLER (See HALLOWING, HOLLOW)			
HOLLINESSE			
Whilst on thy backe his hollinesse ascends/Saint Peters Chaire	F 869	3.1.91	Raymnd
What Lollards do attend our Hollinesse,	F1049	3.2.69	Pope
HOLLO (See HALLOWING)			
HOLLOW (Homograph; See also HALLOWING)			
for that one Laocoon/Breaking a speare upon his hollow breast,	Dido	2.1.165	Aeneas
Hollow Pyramides of silver plate:	Dido	3.1.123	Dido
Betwixt the hollow hanging of a hill/And crooked bending of a	2Tamb	1.2.57	Callap
Under a hollow bank, right opposite/Against the Westerne gate	2Tamb	5.1.121	Govnr
Raven that tolls/The sicke mans passeport in her hollow beake,	Jew	2.1.2	Barab
The rocke is hollow, and of purpose digg'd,	Jew	5.1.87	Barab
Canst raise this man from hollow vaults below,	F App	p.237 30	Emper
whose seas/Eate hollow rocks, and where the north-west wind/Nor	Lucan, First Booke		407
Io, a strong man conquerd this Wench, hollow.	Ovid's Elegies		1.7.38
Nor passe I thee, who hollow rocks downe tumbling,	Ovid's Elegies		3.5.45
Apples, and hony in oakes hollow boughes.	Ovid's Elegies		3.7.40
When the chiefe pompe comes, lowd the people hollow,	Ovid's Elegies		3.12.29
Where sparrowes pearcht, of hollow pearle and gold,	Hero and Leander		1.33
HOLLY			
Foh, me thinkes they stinke like a Holly-Hoke.	Jew	4.4.41	Pilia
HOLLY-HOKE			
Foh, me thinkes they stinke like a Holly-Hoke.	Jew	4.4.41	Pilia
HOLME			
Elisium hath a wood of holme trees black,	Ovid's Elegies		2.6.49
HOLY			
All this is true as holy Mahomet,	1Tamb	3.1.54	Bajzth
And by the holy Alcaron I sweare,	1Tamb	3.3.76	Bajzth
Ye holy Priests of heavenly Mahomet,	1Tamb	4.2.2	Bajzth
Confirming it with Ibis holy name,	1Tamb	4.3.37	Souldn
Theridamas, when holy Fates/Shall stablish me in strong Egyptia,	1Tamb	4.4.134	Tamb
And holy Patrones <Patrons> of Egyptia,	1Tamb	5.1.49	2Virgn
And on whose throne the holy Graces sit.	1Tamb	5.1.77	1Virgn
Ah myghty Jove and holy Mahomet,	1Tamb	5.1.363	Zenoc
Whose holy Alcaron remaines with us,	2Tamb	1.1.138	Orcan
The holy lawes of Christendome injoine:	2Tamb	2.1.36	Baldwn
As is our holy prophet Mahomet,	2Tamb	2.2.44	Orcan
The Cherubins and holy Seraphins/That sing and play before the	2Tamb	2.4.26	Tamb
Then let some holy trance convay my thoughts,	2Tamb	2.4.34	Tamb
Brothers to holy Mahomet himselfe,	2Tamb	3.3.36	Capt
Though God himselfe and holy Mahomet,	2Tamb	5.2.37	Amasia
Then let some God oppose his holy power,	2Tamb	5.3.220	Techel
His house will harbour many holy Nuns.	Jew	1.2.130	1Knght
And yet I know the prayers of those Nuns/And holy Fryers,	Jew	2.3.81	Barab
Good Barabas glance not at our holy Nuns.	Jew	2.3.86	Lodowk
Know, holy Sir, I am bold to sollicite thee.	Jew	3.3.53	Abigal
And then thou didst not like that holy life.	Jew	3.3.58	1Fryar
Oh holy Fryars, the burthen of my sinnes/Lye heavy on my soule;	Jew	4.1.48	Barab
when holy Friars turne devils and murder one another.	Jew	4.1.194	P Ithimr
to goe and consumate/The rest, with hearing of a holy Masse:	P 20	1.20	Charls
That hath blasphemde the holy Church of Rome,	P 531	10.4	Guise
And true profession of his holy word:	P 586	11.51	Navrre
To punish those that doe prophane this holy feast.	P 617	12.30	Mugern
I am a juror in the holy league,	P 837	17.32	Guise
Now by the holy sacrament I sweare,	P 981	19.51	Guise
Sweete Epernoune, our Friers are holy men,	P1161	22.23	King
Of such as holde them of the holy church?	P1181	22.43	King
<incense>/The papall towers to kisse the [lowly] <holy> earth.	P1202	22.64	King
Th'abreviated <breviated> names of holy Saints,	F 238	1.3.10	Faust
That holy shape becomes a devill best.	F 254	1.3.26	Faust
And take some part of holy Peters feast,	F 777	2.3.56	2Chor
<faine> see the Pope/And take some part of holy Peters feast,	F 832	3.1.54	Mephst
Go forth-with to our holy Consistory,	F 882	3.1.104	Pope
What by the holy Councell held at Trent,	F 884	3.1.106	Pope
And all society of holy men:	F 910	3.1.132	Pope
and two such Cardinals/Ne're serv'd a holy Pope, as we shall	F 942	3.1.164	Faust
What have our holy Councell there decreed,	F 947	3.1.169	Pope
By full consent of all the [reverend] <holy> Synod/Of Priests	F 952	3.1.174	Faust
Were by the holy Councell both condemn'd/For lothed Lollords,	F1021	3.2.41	Pope
By holy Paul we saw them not.	F1029	3.2.49	BthCrd
Cursed be he that disturbeth our holy Dirge.	F1083	3.2.103	1Frier
And lay his life at holy Bruno's feet.	F1220	4.1.66	Faust
bleate, and an asse braye, because it is S. Peters holy day.	F App	p.232 28	P Faust
Cursed be he that disturbeth our holy Dirge.	F App	p.232 37	Frier
Crownes fell from holy statues, ominous birds/Defil'd the day,	Lucan, First Booke		556
Or holy gods with cruell strokes abus'd.	Ovid's Elegies		1.7.6
too dearely wunne/That unto death did presse the holy Nunne.	Ovid's Elegies		1.10.50
Outrageous death profanes all holy things/And on all creatures	Ovid's Elegies		3.8.19
The holy gods gilt temples they might fire,	Ovid's Elegies		3.8.43
Upon their heads the holy mysteries had.	Ovid's Elegies		3.12.28
And now begins Leander to display/Loves holy fire, with words,	Hero and Leander		1.193
Thee as a holy Idiot doth she scorne,	Hero and Leander		1.303
HOLYNESSE			
Heere's no body, if it like your Holynesse.	F App	p.231 4	P Frier
HOMAG			
To doo their ceassles homag to my sword:	1Tamb	5.1.456	Tamb
HOMAGE			
Because your highnesse hath beene slack in homage,	Edw	3.1.63	Queene

HOMAGE (cont.)			
Heere for our countries cause sweare we to him/All homage,	Edw	4.4.20	Mortmr
Have done their homage to the loftie gallowes,	Edw	5.2.3	Mortmr
So of both people shalt thou homage gaine.	Ovid's Elegies		2.9.54
HOME			
Go frowning foorth, but come thou smyling home,	1Tamb	1.1.65	Mycet
And cause them to withdraw their forces home,	1Tamb	1.1.131	Menaph
his chaine shall serve/For Manackles, till he be ransom'd home.	1Tamb	1.2.148	Tamb
As martiall presents to our friends at home,	2Tamb	1.1.35	Orcan
kings and more/Upon their knees, all bid me welcome home.	2Tamb	1.2.29	Callap
Give me your knife (good mother) or strike home:	2Tamb	3.4.28	Sonne
Nor plowman, Priest, nor Merchant staies at home,	2Tamb	5.2.50	Callap
I had at home, and in mine Argosie/And other ships that came	Jew	1.2.187	Barab
But she's at home, and I have bought a house/As great and faire	Jew	2.3.13	Barab
Come home and there's no price shall make us part,	Jew	2.3.92	Barab
When you have brought her home, come to my house;	Jew	2.3.148	Barab
to see the cripples/Goe limping home to Christendome on stilts.	Jew	2.3.212	Ithimr
Even now as I came home, he slipt me in,	Jew	2.3.267	Barab
Oh bravely fought, and yet they thrust not home.	Jew	3.2.5	Barab
Rid him away, and goe you home with me.	Jew	4.1.89	Barab
There will he banquet them, but thee at home,	Jew	5.3.38	Msngr
on me, then with your leaves/I may retire me to my native home.	P 474	8.24	Anjoy
To steale from France, and hye me to my home.	P 567	11.32	Navrre
And beate proud Burbon to his native home,	P1114	21.8	Dumain
I know it, brother welcome home my friend.	Edw	1.1.148	Edward
No, threaten not my lord, but pay them home.	Edw	1.4.26	Gavstn
And there abide till fortune call thee home.	Edw	1.4.126	Edward
And be a meanes to call home Gaveston:	Edw	1.4.184	Queene
But madam, would you have us cal him home?	Edw	1.4.208	Mortmr
And is this true to call him home againe?	Edw	1.4.246	Lncstr
To banish him, and then to call him home,	Edw	1.4.275	Mortmr
As is the joy of his returning home.	Edw	2.1.58	Neece
I knew the King would have him home againe.	Edw	2.1.78	Spencr
Goe sit at home and eate your tenants beefe:	Edw	2.2.75	Gavstn
And go in peace, leave us in warres at home.	Edw	3.1.85	Edward
Their lord rode home, thinking his prisoner safe,	Edw	3.1.117	Arundl
friends in Belgia have we left,/To cope with friends at home:	Edw	4.4.4	Queene
And in eight daies did bring him home againe.	F 767	2.3.46	2Chor
[Hee stayde his course, and so returned home],	F1140	3.3.53A	3Chor
now sword strike home,/For hornes he gave, Il'e have his head	F1360	4.2.36	Benvol
it; I went me home to his house, and there I found him asleepe;	F1548	4.5.44	P HrsCsr
me his leg quite off, and now 'tis at home in mine Hostry.	F1551	4.5.47	P HrsCsr
At al times charging home, and making havock;	Lucan, First Booke		148
let thy sword bring us home.	Lucan, First Booke		280
Sit safe at home and chaunt sweet Poesie.	Lucan, First Booke		445
I pay them home with that they most desire:	Ovid's Elegies		2.10.26
And see at home much, that thou nere broughtst thether.	Ovid's Elegies		3.4.48
With famous pageants, and their home-bred beasts.	Ovid's Elegies		3.12.4
Came lovers home, from this great festivall.	Hero and Leander		1.96
Home when he came, he seem'd not to be there,	Hero and Leander		2.117
HOME-BRED			
With famous pageants, and their home-bred beasts.	Ovid's Elegies		3.12.4
HOMELY			
would intreat your Majesty/To come and see his homely Citadell,	Jew	5.3.18	Msngr
To ascend our homely stayres?	Jew	5.5.58	Barab
A homely one my lord, not worth the telling.	Edw	2.2.13	Mortmr
HOMER			
Have not I made blind Homer sing to me/Of Alexanders love, and	F 577	2.2.26	Faust
Let Homer yeeld to such as presents bring,	Ovid's Elegies		1.8.61
Homer shall live while Tenedos stands and Ide,	Ovid's Elegies		1.15.9
Homer without this shall be nothing worth.	Ovid's Elegies		3.7.28
See Homer from whose fountaine ever fild,	Ovid's Elegies		3.8.25
HOMERS			
Had not bene nam'd in Homers Iliads:	2Tamb	2.4.89	Tamb
HOMEWARDS			
When to go homewards we rise all along,	Ovid's Elegies		1.4.55
HOMO			
Homo fuge: whether should I flye?	F 466	2.1.78	Faust
I see it plaine, even heere <in this place> is writ/Homo fuge:	F 470	2.1.82	Faust
HONEST			
to clap hornes of honest mens heades o'this order,	F1317	4.1.163	P Benvol
you may be ashamed to burden honest men with a matter of truth.	F App	p.234 15	P Rafe
sirra you, Ile teach ye to impeach honest men:	F App	p.235 18	P Robin
him have him, he is an honest felow, and he has a great charge,	F App	p.239 105	P Mephst
She must be honest to thy servants credit.	Ovid's Elegies		3.4.36
Will you make shipwracke of your honest name,	Ovid's Elegies		3.13.11
But with your robes, put on an honest face,	Ovid's Elegies		3.13.27
Whom liberty to honest armes compeld,	Ovid's Elegies		3.14.9
HONEY (See also HONY)			
on the sand/Assayd with honey words to turne them backe:	Dido	2.1.137	Aeneas
For I have honey to present thee with:	Dido	4.2.53	Anna
To be partakers of our honey talke.	Dido	4.4.54	Dido
A garden where are Bee hives full of honey,	Dido	4.5.7	Nurse
not onely kisse/But force thee give him my stolne honey blisse.	Ovid's Elegies		1.4.64
HONEYS			
That loade their thighes with Hyblas honeys spoyles,	Dido	5.1.13	Aeneas
HONIE			
And there for honie, bees have sought in vaine,	Hero and Leander		1.23
HONOR			
Aeneas, thinke not but I honor thee,	Dido	3.3.1	Dido
But Anna now shall honor thee in death,	Dido	5.1.325	Anna
admyre me not)/And when my name and honor shall be spread,	1Tamb	1.2.205	Tamb
Besides the honor in assured conquestes:	1Tamb	1.2.219	Usumc

HONOR (cont.)			
heart to be with gladnes pierc'd/To do you honor and securitie.	1Tamb	1.2.251	Therid
Where honor sits invested royally:	1Tamb	2.1.18	Menaph
set the Crowne/Upon your kingly head, that seeks our honor,	1Tamb	2.1.51	Ortyg
You fighting more for honor than for gold,	1Tamb	2.2.66	Meandr
And sought your state all honor it deserv'd,	1Tamb	2.5.33	Ortyg
In love of honor and defence of right,	1Tamb	2.6.21	Ortyg
They sung for honor gainst Pierides,	1Tamb	3.2.51	Zenoc
More honor and lesse paine it may procure,	1Tamb	3.2.97	Agidas
Agreed Casane, we wil honor him.	1Tamb	3.2.113	Techel
That beares the honor of my royall waight.	1Tamb	4.2.21	Tamb
Honor still waight on happy Tamburlaine:	1Tamb	4.4.85	Zenoc
For vertue is the fount whence honor springs.	1Tamb	4.4.128	Tamb
Our love of honor loth to be enthral'd/To forraine powers, and	1Tamb	5.1.35	Govnr
Image of Honor and Nobilitie.	1Tamb	5.1.75	1Virgn
whose silver haires/Honor and reverence evermore have raign'd,	1Tamb	5.1.82	1Virgn
to prevent/That which mine honor sweares shal be perform'd:	1Tamb	5.1.107	Tamb
That sees my crowne, my honor and my name,	1Tamb	5.1.260	Bajzth
Blush heaven, that gave them honor at their birth,	1Tamb	5.1.350	Zenoc
That fights for honor to adorne your head.	1Tamb	5.1.376	Anippe
Conclude a league of honor to my hope.	1Tamb	5.1.399	Zenoc
His honor, that consists in sheading blood,	1Tamb	5.1.477	Tamb
Thou hast with honor usde Zenocrate.	1Tamb	5.1.484	Souldn
and protestations/Of endlesse honor to thee for her love.	1Tamb	5.1.497	Souldn
Shall we with honor (as beseemes) entombe,	1Tamb	5.1.531	Tamb
If he be jealous of his name and honor,	2Tamb	2.2.43	Orcan
Do us such honor and supremacie,	2Tamb	3.1.16	Callap
I doe you honor in the simile,	2Tamb	3.5.69	Tamb
wel to heare both you/Have won a heape of honor in the field,	2Tamb	4.1.37	Calyph
Take you the honor, I will take my ease,	2Tamb	4.1.49	Calyph
For honor of my woondrous victories.	2Tamb	4.1.205	Tamb
Stay good my Lord, and wil you save my honor,	2Tamb	4.2.55	Olymp
To Byron here where thus I honor you?	2Tamb	4.3.6	Tamb
For love, for honor, and to make her Queene,	2Tamb	4.3.38	Orcan
Than honor of thy countrie or thy name?	2Tamb	5.1.11	Govnr
And but one hoste is left to honor thee:	2Tamb	5.2.27	Callap
And made his state an honor to the heavens,	2Tamb	5.3.12	Therid
Blush heaven to loose the honor of thy name,	2Tamb	5.3.28	Usumc
Let not thy love exceed thyne honor sonne,	2Tamb	5.3.199	Tamb
Honor is bought with bloud and not with gold.	Jew	2.2.56	Govnr
Let us goe to honor this solemnitie.	P 25	1.25	Charls
Ladies of honor, Knightes and Gentlemen,	P 213	4.11	Charls
In honor of our God and countries good.	P 708	14.11	Navrre
But thou must call mine honor thus in question?	Edw	1.4.152	Queene
And saying, trulie ant may please your honor,	Edw	2.1.40	Spencr
Mine honor shalbe hostage of my truth,	Edw	2.3.9	Kent
Thou shalt have so much honor at our hands.	Edw	2.5.28	Warwck
And in the honor of a king he sweares,	Edw	2.5.58	Arundl
I will upon mine honor undertake/To carrie him, and bring him	Edw	2.5.79	Penbrk
Returne him on your honor. Sound, away.	Edw	2.5.98	Mortmr
Your honor hath an adamant, of power/To drawe a prince.	Edw	2.5.105	Arundl
And in this place of honor and of trust,	Edw	3.1.143	Edward
For Englands honor, peace, and quietnes.	Edw	4.2.58	Kent
My dutie to your honor [premised] <promised>, &c. I have	Edw	4.3.28	P Spencr
And in this bed of [honor] <honors> die with fame.	Edw	4.5.7	Edward
My head, the latest honor dew to it,	Edw	5.1.62	Edward
by the honor of mine Imperial crowne, that what ever thou	F App	p.236 8	P Emper
and nothing answerable to the honor of your Imperial majesty,	F App	p.236 14	P Faust
such end the gods/Allot the height of honor, men so strong/By	Lucan, First Booke		82
Take these away, where is thy <thine> honor then?	Ovid's Elegies		1.2.38
HONORABLE			
How like you this, my honorable Lords?	1Tamb	1.1.54	Mycet
And since he was so wise and honorable,	1Tamb	3.2.110	Usumc
I thinke it requisite and honorable,	2Tamb	3.1.70	Callap
And wrong our lord, your honorable friend.	Edw	2.6.9	James
How fares my honorable lord of Kent?	Edw	5.2.80	Mortmr
HONORED			
Be honored with your love, but for necessity.	1Tamb	3.2.30	Agidas
HONORS			
That crave such favour at your honors feete,	Dido	1.2.5	Illion
Or banquet in bright honors burnisht hall,	Dido	4.3.10	Aeneas
You shall have honors, as your merits be:	1Tamb	1.2.255	Tamb
And keeps you from the honors of a Queene,	1Tamb	3.2.28	Agidas
Until with greater honors I be grac'd.	1Tamb	4.4.140	Tamb
Whose honors and whose lives relie on him:	1Tamb	5.1.19	Govnr
Your honors, liberties and lives were weigh'd/In equall care	1Tamb	5.1.41	Govnr
that thus defame/Their faiths, their honors, and their religion,	2Tamb	2.1.45	Sgsmnd
And raise our honors to as high a pitch/In this our strong and	2Tamb	3.1.30	Callap
sonnes have had no shares/In all the honors he proposde for us.	2Tamb	4.1.48	Amyras
Blush, blush faire citie, at thine honors foile,	2Tamb	4.1.107	Tamb
And resolution honors fairest aime.	P 96	2.39	Guise
With all the honors and affections,	P1145	22.7	King
I hope your honors make no question,	Edw	1.4.240	Mortmr
My lords, I will not over wooe your honors,	Edw	2.5.86	Penbrk
And all the honors longing to my crowne,	Edw	3.1.131	Edward
This graunted, they, their honors, and their lives,	Edw	3.1.170	Herald
Your honors in all service, [Levune] <Lewne>.	Edw	4.3.37	P Spencr
queene in peace may reposesse/Her dignities and honors,	Edw	4.4.25	Mortmr
And in this bed of [honor] <honors> die with fame.	Edw	4.5.7	Edward
may be won/With farre lesse toile, and yet the honors more;	Lucan, First Booke		284
Wars dustie <rustie> honors are refused being yong,	Ovid's Elegies		1.15.4
have concluded/That Midas brood shall sit in Honors chaire,	Hero and Leander		1.475
HONOUR			
Such honour, stranger, doe I not affect:	Dido	1.1.203	Venus

HONOUR (cont.)

Such honour, stranger, doe I not affect:	Dido	1.1.203	Venus
And cause the souldiers that thus honour me,	1Tamb	1.1.172	Cosroe
and vallours be advaunst/To roomes of honour and Nobilitie.	1Tamb	2.3.41	Cosroe
Lost long before you knew what honour meant.	2Tamb	4.3.87	Tamb
So, now their best is done to honour me,	2Tamb	5.1.131	Tamb
So honour heaven til heaven dissolved be,	2Tamb	5.3.26	Techel
Come to my house and I will giv't your honour--	Jew	2.3.66	Barab
Hating the life and honour of the Guise?	P 932	19.2	Capt
Hating the life and honour of the Guise?	P 950	19.20	King
That naturally would love and honour you,	Edw	1.1.100	Lncstr
Ile give thee more, for but to honour thee,	Edw	1.1.164	Edward
Mine honour will be cald in question,	Edw	2.4.55	Queene
And said, upon the honour of my name,	Edw	3.1.98	Arundl
Thither shall your honour go, and so farewell.	Edw	5.3.62	Matrvs
I humblie thanke your honour.	Edw	5.6.10	Matrvs
Of power, of honour, and <of> omnipotence,	F 81	1.1.53	Faust
Whose [shadows] made all Europe honour him.	F 145	1.1.117	Faust
No Faustus, thinke of honour and of wealth.	F 410	2.1.22	BdAngl
In honour of the Popes triumphant victory.	F 835	3.1.57	Mephst
Mine be that honour then:	F1360	4.2.36	Benvol
about the honour of mine auncestors, how they had wonne by	F App	p.236 19 P	Emper
Knowing her scapes thine honour shall encrease,	Ovid's Elegies		2.2.27
Of wealth and honour so shall grow thy heape,	Ovid's Elegies		2.2.39
And with his <their> bloud eternall honour gaine,	Ovid's Elegies		2.10.32
Honour what friends thy wife gives, sheele give many:	Ovid's Elegies		3.4.45
Live godly, thou shalt die, though honour heaven,	Ovid's Elegies		3.8.37
Much lesse can honour bee ascrib'd thereto,	Hero and Leander		1.279
Honour is purchac'd by the deedes wee do.	Hero and Leander		1.280
Beleeve me Hero, honour is not wone,	Hero and Leander		1.281
hast sworne/To rob her name and honour, and thereby/Commit'st a	Hero and Leander		1.305
As if her name and honour had beene wrong'd,	Hero and Leander		2.35

HONOURABLE

Even for your Honourable fathers sake.	Jew	2.3.93	Barab
Prince of Navarre my honourable brother,	P 1	1.1	Charls
It is honourable in thee to offer this,	Edw	2.5.67	Mortmr
A noble attempt, and honourable deed,	Edw	3.1.206	SpncrP
The Duke of Vanholt's an honourable Gentleman, and one to whom	F1503	4.4.47 P	Faust
an honourable gentleman, to whom I must be no niggard of my	F App	p.241 170 P	Faust
Untill some honourable deed be done.	Hero and Leander		1.282

HONOURABLY

That we may see it honourably interde:	P1246	22.108	Navrre

HONOUR'D

Or who is honour'd now but for his wealth?	Jew	1.1.113	Barab
And honour'd of the Germane Emperour.	F1216	4.1.62	Emper

HONOURD

Great Jupiter, still honourd maist thou be,	Dido	1.1.137	Venus

HONOURED

Yet in my thoughts shall Christ be honoured,	2Tamb	2.3.33	Orcan
(An Emperour so honoured for his vertues)/Revives the spirits	2Tamb	3.1.23	Callap
Are not so honoured in their Governour,	2Tamb	4.3.10	Tamb
And see it honoured with just solemnitie.	P 196	3.31	Admral
In this your grace hath highly honoured me,	Edw	1.4.364	MortSr

HONOURS

O pity us my Lord, and save our honours.	2Tamb	4.3.83	Ladies
Save your honours?	2Tamb	4.3.86	Tamb

HONOUR'ST

Delbosco, as thou lovest and honour'st us,	Jew	2.2.24	1Knght

HONY

Under sweete hony deadly poison lurkes.	Ovid's Elegies		1.8.104
cold hemlocks flower/Wherein bad hony Corsicke Bees did power.	Ovid's Elegies		1.12.10
Apples, and hony in oakes hollow boughes.	Ovid's Elegies		3.7.40

HOOD (Homograph)

And is admitted to the Sister-hood.	Jew	1.2.343	1Fryar
Although unworthy of that Sister-hood.	Jew	3.3.69	Abigal
Let us salute his reverend Father-hood.	F 944	3.1.166	Faust
This for her looks, that for her woman-hood:	Ovid's Elegies		2.4.46
her coate hood-winckt her fearefull eyes,/And into water	Ovid's Elegies		3.5.79
And that slowe webbe nights fals-hood did unframe.	Ovid's Elegies		3.8.30

HOODED

He weares a short Italian hooded cloake,	Edw	1.4.413	Mortmr

HOOD-WINCKT

her coate hood-winckt her fearefull eyes,/And into water	Ovid's Elegies		3.5.79

HOOFES (See also HOV'D)

And from their knees, even to their hoofes below,	1Tamb	1.1.79	Mycet

HOOFFES

Trampling their bowels with our horses hooffes:	1Tamb	3.3.150	Tamb

HOOKE

Thus having swallow'd Cupids golden hooke,	Hero and Leander		1.333

HOOKED

Doest joy to have thy hooked Arrowes shaked,	Ovid's Elegies		2.9.13

HOOKES

On mooved hookes set ope the churlish dore.	Ovid's Elegies		1.6.2

HOOKS

and in the night I clamber'd up with my hooks, and as I was	Jew	3.1.20 P	Pilia

HOONG

Where by one hand, light headed Bacchus hoong,	Hero and Leander		1.139

HOOPE

And her small joynts incircling round hoope make thee.	Ovid's Elegies		2.15.4

HOORD

While bond-men cheat, fathers [be hard] <hoord>, bawds hoorish,	Ovid's Elegies		1.15.17

HOORISH

While bond-men cheat, fathers [be hard] <hoord>, bawds hoorish,	Ovid's Elegies		1.15.17

HOOVES (See also HOOFES)			
Stead/That stampt on others with their thundring hooves,	1Tamb	5.1.331	Zenoc
HOP'D			
They hop'd my daughter would ha bin a Nun;	Jew	2.3.12	Barab
HOPE (See also HOP'ST)			
Forbids all hope to harbour neere our hearts.	Dido	1.2.16	Illion
Then would we hope to quite such friendly turnes,	Dido	1.2.46	Serg
Troy shall no more call him her second hope,	Dido	3.2.8	Juno
I hope that that which love forbids me doe,	Dido	5.1.170	Dido
The hope of Persea, and the verie legges/Whereon our state doth	1Tamb	1.1.59	Mycet
I hope our Ladies treasure and our owne,	1Tamb	1.2.74	Agidas
How say you Lordings, Is not this your hope?	1Tamb	1.2.116	Tamb
We hope your selfe wil willingly restore them.	1Tamb	1.2.117	Agidas
Such hope, such fortune have the thousand horse.	1Tamb	1.2.118	Tamb
In thy approoved Fortunes all my hope,	1Tamb	2.3.2	Cosroe
same proportion of Elements/Resolve, I hope we are resembled,	1Tamb	2.6.27	Cosroe
So do we hope to raign in Asia,	1Tamb	2.7.38	Usumc
But let the yong Arabian live in hope,	1Tamb	3.2.57	Agidas
Whose smiling stars gives him assured hope/Of martiall triumph,	1Tamb	3.3.42	Tamb
Or hope of rescue from the Souldans power,	1Tamb	5.1.4	Govnr
Let us have hope that their unspotted praiers,	1Tamb	5.1.20	Govnr
Before all hope of rescue were denied,	1Tamb	5.1.38	Govnr
You hope of libertie and restitution:	1Tamb	5.1.210	Tamb
And have no hope to end our extasies.	1Tamb	5.1.238	Bajzth
Fortune, nor no hope of end/To our infamous monstrous slaveries?	1Tamb	5.1.240	Zabina
Conclude a league of honor to my hope.	1Tamb	5.1.399	Zenoc
happinesse/And hope to meet your highnesse in the heavens,	2Tamb	2.4.63	Zenoc
No hope is left to save this conquered hold.	2Tamb	3.4.3	Olymp
That litle hope is left to save our lives,	2Tamb	5.1.4	Maxim
Have we not hope, for all our battered walles,	2Tamb	5.1.15	Govnr
She waines againe, and so shall his I hope,	2Tamb	5.2.47	Callap
Your paines do pierce our soules, no hope survives,	2Tamb	5.3.166	Celeb
Joy any hope of your recovery?	2Tamb	5.3.215	Usumc
why then I hope my ships/I sent for Egypt and the bordering	Jew	1.1.41	Barab
I hope our credit in the Custome-house/Will serve as well as I	Jew	1.1.57	Barab
I hope your Highnesse will consider us.	Jew	1.2.9	Govnr
The comfort of mine age, my childrens hope,	Jew	1.2.150	Barab
As much I hope as all I hid is worth.	Jew	1.2.336	Barab
For whilst I live, here lives my soules sole hope,	Jew	2.1.29	Barab
This truce we have is but in hope of gold,	Jew	2.2.26	1Knght
Compassion, love, vaine hope, and hartlesse feare,	Jew	2.3.170	Barab
So have not I, but yet I hope I shall.	Jew	2.3.319	Barab
For I have now no hope but even in thee;	Jew	3.4.16	Barab
And on that hope my happinesse is built:	Jew	3.4.17	Barab
ambles after wealth/Although he ne're be richer then in hope:	Jew	3.4.53	Barab
Well, my hope is, he will not stay there still;	Jew	4.3.16	Barab
I hope the poyson'd flowers will worke anon.	Jew	5.1.43	Barab
I hope to see the Governour a slave,	Jew	5.1.67	Barab
Now where's the hope you had of haughty Spaine?	Jew	5.2.3	Calym
Nor hope of thee but extreme cruelty,	Jew	5.2.59	Govnr
And in my love entombes the hope of Fraunce:	P 134	2.77	Guise
but I hope it be/Only some naturall passion makes her sicke.	P 182	3.17	QnMarg
I hope these reasons may serve my princely Sonne,	P 223	4.21	QnMoth
That durst presume for hope of any gaine,	P 258	4.56	Charls
it may prejudice their hope/Of my inheritance to the crowne of	P 467	8.17	Anjoy
Of whose encrease I set some longing hope,	P 689	13.33	Guise
It will not countervaile his paines I hope,	P 735	14.38	Navrre
I hope will make the King surcease his hate:	P 792	16.6	Bartus
For in thee is the Duke of Guises hope.	P 988	19.58	Guise
Yes Navarre, but not to death I hope.	P1177	22.39	King
Tell her for all this that I hope to live,	P1196	22.58	King
Ile flatter these, and make them live in hope:	Edw	1.1.43	Gavstn
But now ile speake, and to the proofe I hope:	Edw	1.1.108	Kent
Cosin, our hands I hope shall fence our heads,	Edw	1.1.123	Mortmr
Is all my hope turnd to this hell of greefe.	Edw	1.4.116	Gavstn
That now I hope flotes on the Irish seas.	Edw	1.4.224	Mortmr
I hope your honors make no question,	Edw	1.4.240	Mortmr
On whose good fortune Spencers hope depends.	Edw	2.1.11	Spencr
But he is banisht, theres small hope of him.	Edw	2.1.15	Baldck
Then hope I by her meanes to be preferd,	Edw	2.1.29	Baldck
If all things sort out, as I hope they will,	Edw	2.1.79	Neece
But yet I hope my sorrowes will have end,	Edw	2.4.68	Queene
Breathing, in hope (malgrado all your beards,	Edw	2.5.5	Gavstn
Mortimers hope surmounts his fortune farre.	Edw	3.1.259	Mortmr
Yet triumphe in the hope of thee my joye?	Edw	4.2.28	Queene
We flye in hope to get his glorious soule:	F 277	1.3.49	Mephst
I hope his Holinesse will bid us welcome.	F 807	3.1.29	Faust
I hope my score stands still.	F1515	4.5.11	P Robin
I hope sir, we have wit enough to be more bold then welcome.	F1595	4.6.38	P HrsCsr
And so have hope, that this my kinde rebuke,	F1722	5.1.49	OldMan
I, Faustus, now thou hast no hope of heaven,	F1880	5.2.84	Mephst
hope you have seene many boyes with such pickadevaunts as I	F App	p.229 2	P Clown
Drawer, I hope al is payd, God be with you, come Rafe.	F App	p.234 5	P Robin
When yre, or hope provokt, heady, and bould,	Lucan, First Booke		147
the only hope (that did remaine/To their afflictions) were	Lucan, First Booke		494
Now evermore least some one hope might ease/The Commons	Lucan, First Booke		520
Aie me how high that gale did lift my hope!	Ovid's Elegies		1.6.52
If, what I do, she askes, say hope for night,	Ovid's Elegies		1.11.13
Great joyes by hope I inly shall conceive.	Ovid's Elegies		2.9.44
Let us both lovers hope, and feare a like,	Ovid's Elegies		2.19.5
With chearefull hope thus he accosted her.	Hero and Leander		1.198
Which makes me hope, although I am but base,	Hero and Leander		1.218
As put thereby, yet might he hope for mo.	Hero and Leander		1.312

HOPE (cont.)
As he had hope to scale the beauteous fort, ... Hero and Leander 2.16
With follie and false hope deluding us). . . . . . Hero and Leander 2.222
HOPELESSE
The hopelesse daughter of a haplesse Jew, ... Jew 1.2.317 Abigal
Fearing the enemy <ruine> of thy haplesse <hopelesse> soule. F1738 5.1.65 OldMan
HOPES
And makes our hopes survive to [coming] <cunning> joyes: . Dido 1.1.154 Achat
And quell those hopes that thus employ your [cares] <eares>. Dido 4.1.35 Dido
But I have sworne to frustrate both their hopes, . . Jew 2.3.142 Barab
a warning e're he goes/As he shall have small hopes of Abigall. Jew 2.3.274 Barab
Will not these delaies beget my hopes? . . . . . Edw 2.5.47 Gavstn
Alas, see where he sits, and hopes unseene, ... Edw 4.7.51 Leistr
Men handle those, all manly hopes resigne, ... Ovid's Elegies 2.3.9
The plough-mans hopes were frustrate at the last. . . Ovid's Elegies 3.9.34
HOPING
Hoping (misled by dreaming prophesies)/To raigne in Asia, and 1Tamb 1.1.41 Meandr
Hoping by some means I shall be releast, ... 2Tamb 1.2.23 Callap
Hoping to see them starve upon a stall, ... Jew 2.3.26 Barab
Hoping ere long to set the house a fire; . . . . . Jew 2.3.88 Barab
I borne much, hoping time would beate thee/To guard her well, Ovid's Elegies 2.19.49
Who hoping to imbrace thee, cherely swome. . . . . Hero and Leander 2.250
HOPS
That hops about the chamber where I lie, ... Hero and Leander 1.354
HOP'ST
Even as thou hop'st to be eternized, ... 1Tamb 1.2.72 Zenoc
HORIZON (See ORIZON, TH'ORIZON)
HORND
And in thy pompe hornd Apis with thee keepe, ... Ovid's Elegies 2.13.14
HORNE
Of horne the bowe was that approv'd their side. . . Ovid's Elegies 1.8.48
HORNED
my souldiers march/Shal rise aloft and touch the horned Moon, 2Tamb 1.3.14 Tamb
From the bright circle of the horned Moone, ... F 762 2.3.41 2Chor
By verses horned Io got hir name, ... Ovid's Elegies 1.3.21
Verses [deduce] <reduce> the horned bloudy moone/And call the Ovid's Elegies 2.1.23
Horned Bacchus graver furie doth distill, ... Ovid's Elegies 3.14.17
HORNES
when the Moon begins/To joine in one her semi-circled hornes: 1Tamb 3.1.12 Bajzth
Whose hornes shall sprinkle through the tainted aire, . 2Tamb 3.1.66 Orcan
a paire of hornes on's head as e're thou sawest in thy life. F 737 2.3.16 P Robin
Or clap huge hornes, upon the Cardinals heads: . . . F 864 3.1.86 Mephst
And Il'e play Diana, and send you the hornes presently. . F1257 4.1.103 P Faust
Two spreading hornes most strangely fastened/Upon the head of F1277 4.1.123 Emper
He sleeps my Lord, but dreames not of his hornes. . . F1280 4.1.126 Faust
Nay, and thy hornes hold, tis no matter for thy head, for that's F1288 4.1.134 P Emper
Why how now sir Knight, what, hang'd by the hornes? . . F1290 4.1.136 P Faust
Let me intreate you to remove his hornes, ... F1309 4.1.155 Emper
which being all I desire, I am content to remove his hornes. F1314 4.1.160 P Faust
to clap hornes of honest mens heades o'this order, . . F1317 4.1.163 P Benvol
Benvolio's head was grac't with hornes to day? . . . F1331 4.2.7 Benvol
My head is lighter then it was by th'hornes, ... F1350 4.2.26 Benvol
For hornes he gave, Il'e have his head anone. . . . F1361 4.2.37 Benvol
Il'e naile huge forked hornes, and let them hang/Within the F1380 4.2.56 Benvol
Martino see,/Benvolio's hornes againe. . . . . . F1437 4.3.7 Fredrk
O hellish spite,/Your heads are all set with hornes. . F1442 4.3.12 Benvol
'Zons, hornes againe. . . . . F1444 4.3.14 Benvol
He'd joyne long Asses eares to these huge hornes, . . F1449 4.3.19 Benvol
all hee divels has hornes, and all shee divels has clifts and F App p.230 53 P Clown
No sir, but when Acteon died, he left the hornes for you: F App p.237 55 P Faust
that not only gives thee hornes, but makes thee weare them, F App p.238 71 P Emper
being all I desire, I am content to release him of his hornes: F App p.238 84 P Faust
having fild/Her meeting hornes to match her brothers light, Lucan, First Booke 536
but by the hornes/The quick priest pull'd him on his knees and Lucan, First Booke 611
Griping his false hornes with hir virgin hand: . . . . Ovid's Elegies 1.3.24
While Juno Io keepes when hornes she wore, ... Ovid's Elegies 2.19.29
If Achelous, I aske where thy hornes stand, ... Ovid's Elegies 3.5.35
Or his Bulles hornes Europas hand doth hold. . . . . Ovid's Elegies 3.11.34
And Rams with hornes their hard heads wreathed back. . Ovid's Elegies 3.12.17
HORRIBLE
this [is] most horrible: . . . . F1291 4.1.137 P Faust
O horrible, had the Doctor three legs? . . . . . F1658 4.6.101 P All
HORRID
thou shalt see/Ten thousand tortures that more horrid be. F1920 5.2.124 BdAngl
HORROR
and with horror aie/Griping our bowels with retorqued . 1Tamb 5.1.236 Bajzth
Now Faustus let thine eyes with horror stare/Into that vaste F1909 5.2.113 BdAngl
With dreadfull horror of these damned fiends. . . . F1994 5.3.12 3Schol
and every vaine/Did threaten horror from the host of Caesar; Lucan, First Booke 621
HORSE (See also HO)
Epeus horse, to Aetnas hill transformd, ... Dido 1.1.66 Venus
And him, Epeus having made the horse, ... Dido 2.1.147 Aeneas
Made him to thinke Epeus pine-tree Horse/A sacrifize t'appease Dido 2.1.162 Aeneas
Then he unlockt the Horse, and suddenly/From out his entrailes, Dido 2.1.182 Aeneas
by which Achilles horse/Drew him in triumph through the . Dido 2.1.205 Aeneas
Chardg'd with a thousand horse, to apprehend/And bring him 1Tamb 1.1.47 Meandr
To send my thousand horse incontinent, ... 1Tamb 1.1.52 Mycet
Thou shalt be leader of this thousand horse, ... 1Tamb 1.1.62 Mycet
are in readines/Ten thousand horse to carie you from hence, 1Tamb 1.1.185 Ortyg
Such hope, such fortune have the thousand horse. . . 1Tamb 1.2.118 Tamb
Art thou but Captaine of a thousand horse, ... 1Tamb 1.2.168 Tamb
And lead thy thousand horse with my conduct, ... 1Tamb 1.2.189 Tamb
Those thousand horse shall sweat with martiall spoile/Of . 1Tamb 1.2.191 Tamb

HORSE (cont.)				
I yeeld my selfe, my men and horse to thee:	1Tamb	1.2.229		Therid
giftes and promises/Inveigle him that lead a thousand horse,	1Tamb	2.2.26		Meandr
Techelles, take a thousand horse with thee,	1Tamb	2.5.99		Tamb
Two thousand horse shall forrage up and downe,	1Tamb	3.1.61		Bajzth
those that lead my horse/Have to their names tytles of dignity,	1Tamb	3.3.69		Bajzth
And know thou Turke, that those which lead my horse,	1Tamb	3.3.72		Tamb
His speare, his shield, his horse, his armour, plumes,	1Tamb	4.1.60		2Msngr
A hundred and fifty thousand horse,	1Tamb	4.3.53		Capol
Sharpe forked arrowes light upon thy horse:	1Tamb	5.1.217		Bajzth
will send/A hundred thousand horse train'd to the war,	2Tamb	1.1.154		Sgsmnd
Armour of proofe, horse, helme, and Curtle-axe,	2Tamb	1.3.44		Tamb
ordinance strike/A ring of pikes, mingled with shot and horse,	2Tamb	3.2.99		Tamb
A hundred horse shall scout about the plaines/To spie what	2Tamb	3.3.47		Techel
Came forty thousand warlike foot and horse,	2Tamb	3.5.38		Orcan
Ten thousand horse, and thirty thousand foot,	2Tamb	3.5.48		Soria
The horse that guide the golden eie of heaven,	2Tamb	4.3.7		Tamb
to restraine/These coltish coach-horse tongues from blasphemy.	2Tamb	4.3.52		Usumc
Unharnesse them, and let me have fresh horse:	2Tamb	5.1.130		Tamb
First let thy Scythyan horse teare both our limmes/Rather then	2Tamb	5.1.138		Orcan
And the horse pestilence to boot; away.	Jew	3.4.113		Barab
Theres none here, but would run his horse to death.	Edw	1.4.207		Warwck
And this retire refresheth horse and man.	Edw	3.1.193		SpncrP
Give me my horse and lets r'enforce our troupes:	Edw	4.5.6		Edward
At every ten miles end thou hast a horse.	Edw	5.4.42		Mortmr
And therefore let us take horse and away.	Edw	5.5.115		Matrvs
Go horse these traytors on your fiery backes,	F1403	4.2.79		Faust
thou canst not buy so good a horse, for so small a price:	F1459	4.4.3	P	Faust
and have lost very much of late by horse flesh, and this	F1464	4.4.8	P	HrsCsr
I riding my horse into the water, thinking some hidden mystery	F1485	4.4.29	P	HrsCsr
thinking some hidden mystery had beene in the horse, I had	F1486	4.4.30	P	HrsCsr
for your horse is turned to a bottle of Hay,--Maister Doctor.	F1490	4.4.34	P	HrsCsr
and the Horse-courser a bundle of hay for his forty Dollors.	F1497	4.4.41	P	Faust
I went to him yesterday to buy a horse of him, and he would by	F1536	4.5.32	P	HrsCsr
because I knew him to be such a horse, as would run over hedge	F1538	4.5.34	P	HrsCsr
so when I had my horse, Doctor Fauster bad me ride him night	F1539	4.5.35	P	HrsCsr
horse had had some [rare] quality that he would not have me	F1542	4.5.38	P	HrsCsr
and when I came just in the midst my horse vanisht away, and I	F1544	4.5.40	P	HrsCsr
do not you remember a Horse-courser you sold a horse to?	F1633	4.6.76	P	Carter
do not you remember a Horse-courser you sold a horse to?	F1634	4.6.77	P	Carter
Yes, I remember I sold one a horse.	F1635	4.6.78		Faust
theres a Gentleman tarries to have his horse, and he would have	F App	p.233 7	P	Rafe
Ile feede thy divel with horse-bread as long as he lives,	F App	p.234 30	P	Rafe
heeres a simple purchase for horse-keepers, our horses shal	F App	p.234 3	P	Robin
what, wil you goe on horse backe, or on foote?	F App	p.239 95	P	Mephst
What horse-courser, you are wel met.	F App	p.239 100	P	Faust
I have brought you forty dollers for your horse.	F App	p.239 102	P	HrsCsr
Now am I made man for ever, Ile not leave my horse for fortie:	F App	p.239 115	P	HrsCsr
but hark ye sir, if my horse be sick, or ill at ease, if I bring	F App	p.240 118	P	HrsCsr
what, doost thinke I am a horse-doctor?	F App	p.240 120	P	Faust
horse had had some rare qualitie that he would not have had me	F App	p.240 131	P	HrsCsr
pond, but my horse vanisht away, and I sat upon a bottle of hey,	F App	p.240 134	P	HrsCsr
my fortie dollers againe, or Ile make it the dearest horse:	F App	p.240 137	P	HrsCsr
The thunder hov'd horse in a crooked line,	Lucan, First Booke	222		
Cornets of horse are mustered for the field;	Lucan, First Booke	306		
I am no halfe horse, nor in woods I dwell,	Ovid's Elegies	1.4.9		
The Mare askes not the Horse, the Cowe the Bull,	Ovid's Elegies	1.10.27		
Horse freed from service range abroad the woods.	Ovid's Elegies	2.9.22		
I was both horse-man, foote-man, standard bearer.	Ovid's Elegies	2.12.14		
I sit not here the noble horse to see,	Ovid's Elegies	3.2.1		
What horse-driver thou favourst most is best,	Ovid's Elegies	3.2.7		
I saw a horse against the bitte stiffe-neckt,	Ovid's Elegies	3.4.13		
A greater ground with great horse is to till.	Ovid's Elegies	3.14.18		
For as a hote prowd horse highly disdaines,	Hero and Leander	2.141		
HORSE BACKE				
what, wil you goe on horse backe, or on foote?	F App	p.239 95	P	Mephst
HORSE-BREAD				
Ile feede thy divel with horse-bread as long as he lives,	F App	p.234 30	P	Rafe
HORSE-COURSER				
and the Horse-courser a bundle of hay for his forty Dollors.	F1497	4.4.41	P	Faust
do not you remember a Horse-courser you sold a horse to?	F1633	4.6.76	P	Carter
What horse-courser, you are wel met.	F App	p.239 100	P	Faust
HORSECOURSER				
and the Horsecourser I take it, a bottle of hey for his labour;	F App	p.241 165	P	Faust
HORSED				
That should be horsed on fower mightie kings.	1Tamb	4.2.78		Bajzth
HORSE-DOCTOR				
what, doost thinke I am a horse-doctor?	F App	p.240 120	P	Faust
HORSE-DRIVER				
What horse-driver thou favourst most is best,	Ovid's Elegies	3.2.7		
HORSE-KEEPERS				
heeres a simple purchase for horse-keepers, our horses shal	F App	p.234 3	P	Robin
HORSE-MAN				
I was both horse-man, foote-man, standard bearer.	Ovid's Elegies	2.12.14		
HORSEMEN				
One sweares his troupes of daring horsemen fought/Upon Mevanias	Lucan, First Booke	469		
pleace <please> Pollux, Castor [love] <loves> horsemen more.	Ovid's Elegies	3.2.54		
HORSEMENS				
Like Almaine Rutters with their horsemens staves,	F 152	1.1.124		Valdes
HORSES				
Have oft driven backe the horses of the night,	Dido	1.1.26		Jupitr
an hot alarme/Drive all their horses headlong down the hill.	1Tamb	1.2.135		Usumc
Trampling their bowels with our horses hooffes:	1Tamb	3.3.150		Tamb

HORSES (cont.)				
Brave horses, bred on the white Tartarian hils:	1Tamb	3.3.151		Tamb
And let her horses from their nostrels breathe/Rebellious winds	1Tamb	5.1.297		Bajzth
And harnest like my horses, draw my coch,	2Tamb	3.5.104		Tamb
But I have no horses. What art thou?	Edw	1.1.28		Gavstn
What Dick, looke to the horses there till I come againe.	F 722	2.3.1	P	Robin
What Robin, you must come away and walk the horses.	F 725	2.3.4	P	Dick
I walke the horses, I scorn't 'faith, I have other matters in	F 726	2.3.5	P	Robin
matters in hand, let the horses walk themselves and they will.	F 727	2.3.6	P	Robin
our horses shal eate no hay as long as this lasts.	F App	p.234 3	P	Robin
But managde horses heads are lightly borne,	Ovid's Elegies			1.2.16
Sees not the morne on rosie horses rise.	Ovid's Elegies			1.8.4
And with swift horses the swift yeare soone leaves us.	Ovid's Elegies			1.8.50
Rhesus fell/And Captive horses bad their Lord fare-well.	Ovid's Elegies			1.9.24
Hold in thy rosie horses that they move not.	Ovid's Elegies			1.13.10
And call the sunnes white horses [backe] <blacke> at noone.	Ovid's Elegies			2.1.24
Fower chariot-horses from the lists even ends.	Ovid's Elegies			3.2.66
The horses seeme, as [thy] <they> desire they knewe.	Ovid's Elegies			3.2.68
And forth the gay troupes on swift horses flie.	Ovid's Elegies			3.2.78
HORSMEN				
A thousand Persean horsmen are at hand,	1Tamb	1.2.111		Souldr
A thousand horsmen? We five hundred foote?	1Tamb	1.2.121		Tamb
And have a thousand horsmen tane away?	1Tamb	2.2.6		Mycet
An hundred horsmen of my company/Scowting abroad upon these	1Tamb	2.2.39		Spy
What, have your horsmen shewen the virgins Death?	1Tamb	5.1.129		Tamb
Hast thou not seene my horsmen charge the foe,	2Tamb	3.2.103		Tamb
My horsmen brandish their unruly blades.	2Tamb	5.1.79		Tamb
HORSMENS				
He now is seated on my horsmens speares,	1Tamb	5.1.114		Tamb
On horsmens Lances to be hoisted up,	1Tamb	5.1.328		Zenoc
HORSSE				
This certifie the Pope, away, take horsse.	Edw	1.2.38		ArchBp
HOSPITALITIE				
And vow by all the Gods of Hospitalitie,	Dido	3.4.44		Aeneas
HOSPITALL				
That wouldst reward them with an hospitall.	Edw	1.1.38		3PrMan
HOSPITALS				
And with young Orphans planted Hospitals,	Jew	2.3.194		Barab
Why there are hospitals for such as you,	Edw	1.1.35		Gavstn
HOST (Homograph; See also HOAST)				
Carthage, my friendly host adue,	Dido	4.3.1		Aeneas
May have the leading of so great an host,	1Tamb	1.2.48		Tamb
The host of Xerxes, which by fame is said/To drinke the mightie	1Tamb	2.3.15		Tamb
The spring is hindred by your smoothering host,	1Tamb	3.1.50		Moroc
and every vaine/Did threaten horror from the host of Caesar;	Lucan, First Booke			621
HOSTAGE				
Mine honor shalbe hostage of my truth,	Edw	2.3.9		Kent
HOSTE				
Will leade an hoste against the hatefull Greekes,	Dido	4.4.91		Aeneas
The chiefest Captaine of Mycetes hoste,	1Tamb	1.1.58		Mycet
How easely may you with a mightie hoste,	1Tamb	1.1.129		Menaph
Deserv'st to have the leading of an hoste?	1Tamb	1.2.171		Tamb
And cannot terrefie his mightie hoste.	1Tamb	3.3.12		Bassoe
Your threefold armie and my hugie hoste,	1Tamb	3.3.94		Bajzth
My Campe is like to Julius Caesars Hoste,	1Tamb	3.3.152		Tamb
time to sort/Your fighting men, and raise your royall hoste.	1Tamb	4.1.37		Capol
Since I arriv'd with my triumphant hoste,	1Tamb	5.1.458		Tamb
Our warlike hoste in compleat armour rest,	2Tamb	1.1.8		Orcan
But now Orcanes, view my royall hoste,	2Tamb	1.1.106		Sgsmnd
And with an hoste of Moores trainde to the war,	2Tamb	1.3.141		Techel
Giving commandement to our generall hoste,	2Tamb	2.1.61		Sgsmnd
That nigh Larissa swaies a mighty hoste,	2Tamb	2.2.6		Orcan
With unacquainted power of our hoste.	2Tamb	2.2.23		Uribas
Discomfited is all the Christian hoste,	2Tamb	2.3.1		Sgsmnd
Being a handfull to a mighty hoste,	2Tamb	3.1.40		Orcan
And with his hoste [martcht] <martch> round about the earth,	2Tamb	3.2.111		Tamb
Here at Alepo with an hoste of men/Lies Tamburlaine, this king	2Tamb	3.5.3		2Msngr
The common souldiers of our mighty hoste/Shal bring thee bound	2Tamb	3.5.110		Trebiz
King of Amasia, now our mighty hoste,	2Tamb	5.2.1		Callap
Before his hoste be full from Babylon,	2Tamb	5.2.9		Callap
And but one hoste is left to honor thee:	2Tamb	5.2.27		Callap
Yet might your mighty hoste incounter all,	2Tamb	5.2.39		Amasia
HOSTELRY (See OASTRIE, OSTRY)				
HOSTES				
And hostes of souldiers stand amaz'd at us,	1Tamb	1.2.221		Usumc
The world will strive with hostes of men at armes,	1Tamb	2.3.13		Tamb
The number of your hostes united is,	1Tamb	4.3.52		Capol
Larissa plaines/With hostes apeece against this Turkish crue,	2Tamb	1.3.108		Tamb
HOSTESSE				
Why Hostesse, I say, fetch us some Beere.	F1518	4.5.14	P	Dick
Come sirs, what shall we do now till mine Hostesse comes?	F1520	4.5.16	P	Dick
Some more drinke Hostesse.	F1555	4.5.51	P	Carter
HOSTILE				
Why enviest me, this hostile [denne] <dende> unbarre,	Ovid's Elegies			1.6.17
HOSTIS				
best beere in Europe, what ho, Hostis; where be these Whores?	F1506	4.5.2	P	Carter
HOSTISSE				
O Hostisse how do you?	F1515	4.5.11	P	Robin
HOSTLER				
One time I was an Hostler in an Inne,	Jew	2.3.205		Ithimr
keepe further from me O thou illiterate, and unlearned Hostler.	F 729	2.3.8	P	Robin
Go bid the Hostler deliver him unto you, and remember what I	F1474	4.4.18	P	Faust
HOSTRY (See also CASTRIE)				
me his leg quite off, and now 'tis at home in mine Hostry.	F1548	4.4.48	P	Horse-

HOT

And with a sodaine and an hot alarme/Drive all their horses	1Tamb	1.2.134	Usumc
Nay quickly then, before his roome be hot.	1Tamb	2.5.89	Usumc
Nor in Pharsalia was there such hot war,	1Tamb	3.3.154	Tamb
overweighing heavens/Have kept to qualifie these hot extreames,	1Tamb	5.1.46	Govnr
And save our forces for the hot assaults/Proud Tamburlaine	2Tamb	1.1.52	Gazell
Or cease one day from war and hot alarms,	2Tamb	1.3.183	Usumc
teares of Mahomet/For hot consumption of his countries pride:	2Tamb	4.1.197	Tamb
Here's a hot whore indeed; no, I'le no wife.	F 534	2.1.146	Faust
Or Scythia; or hot Libiaes thirsty sands.	Lucan, First Booke		369
Now all feare with my mindes hot love abates,	Ovid's Elegies		1.10.9
How patiently hot irons they did take/In crooked [tramells]	Ovid's Elegies		1.14.25
Thy very haires will the hot bodkin teach.	Ovid's Elegies		1.14.30
Let Mayles whom hot desire to husbands leade,	Ovid's Elegies		2.1.5
Grew pale, and in cold foords hot lecherous.	Ovid's Elegies		3.5.26
I blush, [that] <and> being youthfull, hot, and lustie,	Ovid's Elegies		3.6.19

HOTE

that of it self was hote enoughe to worke/thy Just degestione	Paris	ms26,p391	Guise
Your threats, your larums, and your hote pursutes,	Edw	2.5.2	Gavstn
And get me a spit, and let it be red hote.	Edw	5.5.30	Ltborn
<A plague on her for a hote whore>.	F 534	(HC261)A	P Faust
For as a hote prowd horse highly disdaines,	Hero and Leander		2.141

HOULD

Weele pull him from the strongest hould he hath.	Edw	1.4.289	Mortmr
For now we hould an old Wolfe by the eares,	Edw	5.2.7	Mortmr
Caesar; he whom I heare thy trumpets charge/I hould no Romaine;	Lucan, First Booke		375
and would hould/The world (were it together) is by cowards	Lucan, First Booke		510
Fierce Mastives hould; the vestall fires went out,	Lucan, First Booke		547

HOULE

Cry out, exclaime, houle till thy throat be hoarce,	P1077	19.147	King

HOUND

O were that damned Hell-hound but in place,	F1355	4.2.31	Benvol

HOUNDS

quyvering leaves/Of Idas forrest, where your highnesse hounds,	2Tamb	3.5.6	2Msngr
By yelping hounds puld downe, and seeme to die.	Edw	1.1.70	Gavstn
Il'e raise a kennell of Hounds shall hunt him so,	F1301	4.1.147	Faust

HOURE (See also HOWER, HOWRES)

This is the houre/Wherein I shall proceed; Oh happy houre,	Jew	4.1.160	1Fryar
This is the houre/Wherein I shall proceed; Oh happy houre,	Jew	4.1.161	1Fryar
This day, this houre, this fatall night,	P 64	2.7	Guise
But in my latter houre to purge my selfe,	P 402	7.42	Ramus
I nere was King of France untill this houre:	P1027	19.97	King
out of a Lyons mouth when I was scarce <half> an houre old,	F 687	2.2.136	P Wrath
Saies Faustus come, thine houre is almost come,	F1727	5.1.54	Faust
Now hast thou but one bare houre to live,	F1927	5.2.131	Faust
or let this houre be but/A yeare, a month, a weeke, a naturall	F1932	5.2.136	Faust
[Ah] <O> halfe the houre is past:	F1957	5.2.161	Faust
Loftie Lucretius shall live that houre,	Ovid's Elegies		1.15.23

HOURES

yet not appeare/In forty houres after it is tane.	Jew	3.4.72	Barab
Come, come aboord, tis but an houres sailing.	Edw	2.4.49	Lncstr
West, in foure and twenty houres, upon the poles of the world,	F 598	2.2.47	P Mephst
For twixt the houres of twelve and one, me thought/I heard him	F1991	5.3.9	3Schol
houres warning whensoever or wheresoever the divell shall fetch	F App	p.230 36	P Wagner

HOUSE

As Jupiter to sillie [Baucis] <Vausis> house:	Dido	1.2.41	Iarbus
You to the vallies, thou unto the house.	Dido	3.3.62	Dido
Cannot ascend to Fames immortall house,	Dido	4.3.9	Aeneas
And beare him in the countrey to her house,	Dido	4.4.106	Dido
Drive if you can my house to Italy:	Dido	4.4.129	Dido
No, thou shalt goe with me unto my house,	Dido	4.5.3	Nurse
Come come, Ile goe, how farre hence is your house?	Dido	4.5.13	Cupid
And every house is as a treasurie.	1Tamb	4.2.109	Tamb
Thou doost dishonor manhood, and thy house.	2Tamb	4.1.32	Celeb
And in his house heape pearle like pibble-stones,	Jew	1.1.23	Barab
I hope our credit in the Custome-house/Will serve as well as I	Jew	1.1.57	Barab
And they this day sit in the Counsell-house/To entertaine them	Jew	1.1.148	1Jew
But there's a meeting in the Senate-house,	Jew	1.1.167	2Jew
His house will harbour many holy Nuns.	Jew	1.2.130	1Knght
With fierce exclaimes run to the Senate-house,	Jew	1.2.232	Abigal
In my house, my girle.	Jew	1.2.249	Barab
For they have seiz'd upon thy house and wares.	Jew	1.2.251	Abigal
will give me leave once more, I trow,/To goe into my house.	Jew	1.2.253	Barab
Displacing me; and of thy house they meane/To make a Nunnery,	Jew	1.2.255	Abigal
thus; thou toldst me they have turn'd my house/Into a Nunnery,	Jew	1.2.277	Barab
But, Madam, this house/And waters of this new made Nunnery	Jew	1.2.310	1Fryar
Sometimes the owner of a goodly house,	Jew	1.2.319	Abigal
and I have bought a house/As great and faire as is the	Jew	2.3.13	Barab
Come to my house and I will giv't your honour--	Jew	2.3.66	Barab
And made my house a place for Nuns most chast.	Jew	2.3.77	Barab
Hoping ere long to set the house a fire;	Jew	2.3.88	Barab
I pray, Sir, be no stranger at my house,	Jew	2.3.136	Barab
When you have brought her home, come to my house;	Jew	2.3.148	Barab
If you love me, no quarrels in my house;	Jew	2.3.271	Barab
And he is very seldome from my house;	Jew	3.1.10	Curtzn
up to the Jewes counting-house where I saw some bags of mony,	Jew	3.1.18	P Pilia
choyce, I heard a rumbling in the house; so I tooke onely this,	Jew	3.1.21	P Pilia
The Abbasse of the house/Whose zealous admonition I embrace:	Jew	3.3.66	Abigal
That in this house I liv'd religiously,	Jew	3.6.13	Abigal
much weight in Pearle/Orient and round, have I within my house;	Jew	4.1.67	Barab
All this I'le give to some religious house/So I may be baptiz'd	Jew	4.1.75	Barab
Oh good Barabas come to our house.	Jew	4.1.77	1Fryar
Oh no, good Barabas come to our house.	Jew	4.1.78	2Fryar

HOUSE (cont.)

Come to my house at one a clocke this night. Jew 4.1.91 Barab
Why does he goe to thy house? let him begone. Jew 4.1.101 1Fryar
For he that shriv'd her is within my house. Jew 4.1.115 Barab
not both these wise men to suppose/That I will leave my house, Jew 4.1.123 Barab
And give my goods and substance to your house, Jew 4.1.190 Barab
with his lips; the effect was, that I should come to her house. Jew 4.2.32 P Ithimr
here's her house, and here she comes, and now would I were Jew 4.2.35 P Ithimr
Or climbe up to my Counting-house window: Jew 4.3.34 P Barab
enough, and therfore talke not to me of your Counting-house: Jew 4.3.37 P Pilia
Pray when, Sir, shall I see you at my house? Jew 4.3.56 Barab
And in an out-house of the City shut/His souldiers, till I have Jew 5.2.81 Barab
is a monastery/Which standeth as an out-house to the Towne; Jew 5.3.37 Msngr
And fire the house; say, will not this be brave? Jew 5.5.41 Barab
Why, then the house was fir'd,/Blowne up, and all thy souldiers Jew 5.5.106 Govnr
Because the house of Burbon now comes in, P 50 1.50 Admral
The love thou bear'st unto the house of Guise: P 69 2.12 Guise
Away then, break into the Admirals house. P 282 5.9 Guise
them thither, and then/Beset his house that not a man may live. P 289 5.16 Guise
But look my Lord, ther's some in the Admirals house. P 297 5.24 Retes
But tis the house of Burbon that he meanes. P 644 12.57 Cardnl
Shall feele the house of Lorayne is his foe: P 856 17.51 Guise
Now let the house of Bourbon weare the crowne, P1232 22.94 King
And take possession of his house and goods: Edw 1.1.203 Edward
What should a priest do with so faire a house? Edw 1.1.206 Gavstn
My house is not farre hence, out of the way/A little, but our Edw 2.5.100 Penbrk
Fourthly, that he shall be in his chamber or house invisible. F 490 2.1.102 P Faust
<I would desire, that this house, F 675 (HC263)A P Covet
and might I now obtaine <have> my wish, this house, you and all, F 675 2.2.124 P Covet
Not long he stayed within his quiet house, F 768 2.3.47 2Chor
it; I went me home to his house, and there I found him asleepe; F1548 4.5.44 P HrsCsr
I, I, the house is good enough to drink in: F1617 4.6.60 P HrsCsr
or we'll breake all the barrels in the house, and dash out all F1618 4.6.61 P HrsCsr
and given me his wealth, his house, his goods, and store of F1675 5.1.2 P Wagner
with horror stare/Into that vaste perpetuall torture-house, F1910 5.2.114 BdAngl
At which selfe time the house seem'd all on fire, F1993 5.3.11 3Schol
Se impious warre defiles the Senat house, Lucan, First Booke 690
The gods send thee no house, a poore old age, Ovid's Elegies 1.8.113
Let him please, haunt the house, be kindly usd, Ovid's Elegies 2.2.29
(Their reines let loose) right soone my house approach. Ovid's Elegies 2.16.50
Beginne to shut thy house at evening sure. Ovid's Elegies 2.19.38
No certaine house thou hast, nor any fountaines. Ovid's Elegies 3.5.92
If I should give, both would the house forbeare. Ovid's Elegies 3.7.64
am I by such wanton toyes defamde)/Heire of an antient house, Ovid's Elegies 3.14.5

HOUSES

The houses burnt, wil looke as if they mourn'd, 2Tamb 2.4.139 Tamb
Ware-houses stuft with spices and with drugs, Jew 4.1.64 Barab
To fire the Churches, pull their houses downe, Jew 5.1.65 Barab
The Northren borderers seeing [their] <the> houses burnt,/Their Edw 2.2.179 Lncstr
That now the walles of houses halfe [rear'd] <reaer'd> totter, Lucan, First Booke 24
heapes of stone/Lye in our townes, that houses are abandon'd, Lucan, First Booke 26
Men tooke delight in Jewels, houses, plate, Lucan, First Booke 164
wars,/We from our houses driven, most willingly/Suffered exile: Lucan, First Booke 279
they had houses: Lucan, First Booke 347
You would have thought their houses had bin fierd/Or Lucan, First Booke 490
And with my brand these gorgeous houses burne. Ovid's Elegies 1.6.58
Houses not dwelt in, are with filth forlorne. Ovid's Elegies 1.8.52
Small doores unfitting for large houses are. Ovid's Elegies 3.1.40
Lone women like to emptie houses perish. Hero and Leander 1.242

HOUSHOLD

Or steale your houshold lares from their shrines: Dido 1.2.11 Illion
And snatcht armes neer their houshold gods hung up/Such as Lucan, First Booke 242
their houshold gods/And love to Room (thogh slaughter steeld Lucan, First Booke 354
their saints and houshold gods/Sweate teares to shew the Lucan, First Booke 554

HOUSHOULD

Their houshould gods restrain them not, none lingered, Lucan, First Booke 505

HOV'D

The thunder hov'd horse in a crooked line, Lucan, First Booke 222

HOVER

Ten thousand Cupids hover in the ayre, Dido 4.4.48 Dido
Ah, life and soule still hover in his Breast, 1Tamb 3.2.21 Zenoc
And hover in the straightes for Christians wracke, 1Tamb 3.3.250 Tamb
Yet should ther hover in their restlesse heads, 1Tamb 5.1.171 Tamb
Hover about the ugly Ferriman, 1Tamb 5.1.246 Zabina
That I may hover with her in the Ayre, Jew 2.1.62 Barab
I see an Angell hover <hovers> ore thy head, F1730 5.1.57 OldMan
Suspitious feare in all my veines will hover, Ovid's Elegies 1.4.42

HOVER'D

For Calymath having hover'd here so long, Jew 5.1.4 Govnr

HOVERETH

Fame hovereth, sounding of her golden Trumpe: 2Tamb 3.4.63 Therid

HOVERING

Hovering betwixt our armies, light on me, 2Tamb 3.5.163 Tamb

HOVERS

I see an Angell hover <hovers> ore thy head, F1730 5.1.57 OldMan
The ravenous vulture lives, the Puttock hovers/Around the aire, Ovid's Elegies 2.6.33

HOVES

Spits foorth the ringled bit, and with his hoves, Hero and Leander 2.143

HOW

O how would I with Helens brother laugh, Dido 1.1.17 Ganimd
See how the night Ulysses-like comes forth, Dido 1.1.70 Venus
How may I credite these thy flattering termes, Dido 1.1.109 Venus
Venus, how art thou compast with content, Dido 1.1.135 Venus

HOW (cont.)

How many dangers have we over past?	Dido	1.1.145		Aeneas
How neere my sweet Aeneas art thou driven?	Dido	1.1.170		Venus
And now she sees thee how will she rejoyce?	Dido	2.1.69		Illion
And truely to, how Troy was overcome:	Dido	2.1.107		Dido
And Priam dead, yet how we heare no newes.	Dido	2.1.113		Dido
Ah, how could poore Aeneas scape their hands?	Dido	2.1.220		Dido
How got Aeneas to the fleete againe?	Dido	2.1.291		Iarbus
But how scapt Helen, she that causde this warre?	Dido	2.1.292		Dido
How long faire Dido shall I pine for thee?	Dido	3.1.7		Iarbus
Looke sister how Aeneas little sonne/Playes with your garments	Dido	3.1.20		Anna
How lovely is Ascanius when he smiles?	Dido	3.1.29		Dido
O Anna, didst thou know how sweet love were,	Dido	3.1.59		Dido
Achates, how doth Carthage please your Lord?	Dido	3.1.97		Dido
Yet how <here> <now> I sweare by heaven and him I love,	Dido	3.1.166		Dido
how may I deserve/Such amourous favours at thy beautious hand?	Dido	3.2.64		Juno
How highly I doe prize this amitie,	Dido	3.2.67		Juno
How now Getulian, are ye growne so brave,	Dido	3.3.19		Dido
How like his father speaketh he in all?	Dido	3.3.41		Anna
O how these irksome labours now delight,	Dido	3.3.56		Aeneas
Tell me deare love, how found you out this Cave?	Dido	3.4.3		Dido
Faire Anna, how escapt you from the shower?	Dido	4.1.29		Aeneas
How now Iarbus, at your prayers so hard?	Dido	4.2.23		Anna
No no, she cares not how we sinke or swimme,	Dido	4.3.41		Illion
See where they come, how might I doe to chide?	Dido	4.4.13		Dido
How haps Achates bid me not farewell?	Dido	4.4.19		Dido
O how a Crowne becomes Aeneas head!	Dido	4.4.38		Dido
How vaine am I to weare this Diadem,	Dido	4.4.40		Aeneas
To measure how I prize Aeneas love,	Dido	4.4.140		Dido
Come come, Ile goe, how farre hence is your house?	Dido	4.5.13		Cupid
How pretilie he laughs, goe ye wagge,	Dido	4.5.19		Nurse
O how unwise was I to say him nay!	Dido	4.5.37		Nurse
How should I put into the raging deepe,	Dido	5.1.55		Aeneas
How now Aeneas, sad, what meanes these dumpes?	Dido	5.1.62		Iarbus
As how I pray, may I entreate you tell.	Dido	5.1.67		Iarbus
How loth I am to leave these Libian bounds,	Dido	5.1.81		Aeneas
Aeneas, say, how canst thou take thy leave?	Dido	5.1.119		Dido
Hast thou forgot how many neighbour kings/Were up in armes, for	Dido	5.1.141		Dido
How Carthage did rebell, Iarbus storme,	Dido	5.1.143		Dido
How can ye goe when he hath all your fleete?	Dido	5.1.242		Anna
How long will Dido mourne a strangers flight,	Dido	5.1.279		Iarbus
How long shall I with griefe consume my daies,	Dido	5.1.281		Iarbus
How like you this, my honorable Lords?	1Tamb	1.1.54		Mycet
How now my Lord, what, mated and amaz'd/To heare the king thus	1Tamb	1.1.107		Menaph
How easely may you with a mightie hoste,	1Tamb	1.1.129		Menaph
How now, what's the matter?	1Tamb	1.2.110		Tamb
How now my Lords of Egypt and Zenocrate?	1Tamb	1.2.113		Tamb
How say you Lordings, Is not this your hope?	1Tamb	1.2.116		Tamb
See how he raines down heaps of gold in showers,	1Tamb	1.2.182		Tamb
How those were hit by pelting Cannon shot,	1Tamb	2.4.3		Mycet
I know not how to take their tyrannies.	1Tamb	2.7.41		Cosroe
How can you fancie one that lookes so fierce,	1Tamb	3.2.40		Agidas
Will tell how many thousand men he slew.	1Tamb	3.2.43		Agidas
See you Agidas how the King salutes you.	1Tamb	3.2.88		Techel
see how right the man/Hath hit the meaning of my Lord the King.	1Tamb	3.2.107		Techel
See how he comes?	1Tamb	3.3.3		Tamb
I will not tell thee how Ile handle thee,	1Tamb	3.3.84		Tamb
How can ye suffer these indignities?	1Tamb	3.3.90		Moroc
How lik'st thou her Ebea, will she serve?	1Tamb	3.3.178		Zabina
Hearst thou Anippe, how thy drudge doth talk,	1Tamb	3.3.182		Zenoc
And how my slave, her mistresse menaceth.	1Tamb	3.3.183		Zenoc
How dare you thus abuse my Majesty?	1Tamb	3.3.226		Zabina
How you abuse the person of the king:	1Tamb	4.2.73		Anippe
Shall talke how I have handled Bajazeth.	1Tamb	4.2.97		Tamb
how can you suffer these outragious curses by these slaves of	1Tamb	4.4.26	P	Zenoc
How now Zenccrate, dooth not the Turke and his wife make a	1Tamb	4.4.57	P	Tamb
How can it but afflict my verie soule?	1Tamb	4.4.67		Zenoc
How say you to this (Turke) these are not your contributorie	1Tamb	4.4.117	P	Tamb
But how unseemly is it for my Sex,	1Tamb	5.1.174		Tamb
How are ye glutted with these grievous objects,	1Tamb	5.1.341		Zenoc
And with how manie cities sacrifice/He celebrated her [sad]	2Tamb	Prol.7		Prolog
How canst thou think of this and offer war?	2Tamb	1.1.102		Orcan
How far hence lies the Galley, say you?	2Tamb	1.2.54		Almeda
And I will teach thee how to charge thy foe,	2Tamb	1.3.45		Tamb
How have ye spent your absent time from me?	2Tamb	1.3.173		Tamb
How through the midst of Verna and Bulgaria/And almost to the	2Tamb	2.1.8		Fredrk
Me thinks I see how glad the christian King/Is made, for joy of	2Tamb	2.2.20		Uribas
Tell me, how fares my faire Zenocrate?	2Tamb	2.4.41		Tamb
Ile teach you how to make the water mount,	2Tamb	3.2.85		Tamb
How say ye Souldiers, Shal we not?	2Tamb	3.3.9		Techel
How now Madam, what are you doing?	2Tamb	3.4.34		Therid
Who when he heares how resolute thou wert,	2Tamb	3.4.40		Techel
How now Casane?	2Tamb	3.5.58		Tamb
I see how fearfully ye would refuse,	2Tamb	3.5.73		Tamb
See father, how Almeda the Jaylor lookes upon us.	2Tamb	3.5.116		Celeb
How now ye pety kings, loe, here are Bugges/Wil make the haire	2Tamb	3.5.147		Tamb
I smile to think, how when this field is fought,	2Tamb	3.5.165		Techel
How may my hart, thus fired with mine eies,	2Tamb	4.1.93		Tamb
How like you that sir king? why speak you not?	2Tamb	4.3.53		Celeb
How like his cursed father he begins,	2Tamb	4.3.55		Jrslem
How is my soule environed,	2Tamb	5.1.34		Govnr
See now my Lord how brave the Captaine hangs.	2Tamb	5.1.149		Amyras
now, how Jove hath sent/A present medicine to recure my paine:	2Tamb	5.3.105		Tamb

HOW (cont.)

then let me see how much/Is left for me to conquer all the	2Tamb	5.3.123	Tamb
how should our bleeding harts/Wounded and broken with your	2Tamb	5.3.161	Amyras
let me see how well/Thou wilt become thy fathers majestie.	2Tamb	5.3.183	Tamb
How should I step or stir my hatefull feete,	2Tamb	5.3.195	Amyras
Who smiles to see how full his bags are cramb'd,	Jew	Prol.31	Machvl
But now how stands the wind?	Jew	1.1.38	Barab
Ha, to the East? yes: See how stands the Vanes?	Jew	1.1.40	Barab
But who comes heare? How now.	Jew	1.1.48	Barab
They wondred how you durst with so much wealth/Trust such a	Jew	1.1.79	1Merch
How chance you came not with those other ships/That sail'd by	Jew	1.1.89	Barab
Why, how now Countrymen?	Jew	1.1.143	Barab
How ere the world goe, I'le make sure for one,	Jew	1.1.186	Barab
Now [Governour], how are you resolv'd?	Jew	1.2.17	Calym
How, my Lord, my mony?	Jew	1.2.55	Barab
How, equally?	Jew	1.2.62	Barab
How, a Christian? Hum, what's here to doe?	Jew	1.2.75	Barab
Christians; what, or how can I multiply?	Jew	1.2.103	Barab
How, as a Nunne?	Jew	1.2.281	Abigal
Why how now Abigall, what mak'st thou/Amongst these hateful	Jew	1.2.338	Barab
How, mortified!	Jew	1.2.342	Barab
Why how now Don Mathias, in a dump?	Jew	1.2.374	Lodowk
How say you, shall we?	Jew	1.2.390	Lodowk
I learn'd in Florence how to kisse my hand,	Jew	2.3.23	Barab
How showes it by night?	Jew	2.3.62	Lodowk
Here's a leaner, how like you him?	Jew	2.3.126	P 1Offcr
breast a long great Scrowle/How I with interest tormented him.	Jew	2.3.198	Barab
But marke how I am blest for plaguing them,	Jew	2.3.199	Barab
But tell me now, How hast thou spent thy time?	Jew	2.3.201	Barab
Now tell me, Ithimore, how lik'st thou this?	Jew	2.3.364	Barab
Tell me, how cam'st thou by this?	Jew	3.1.16	Curtzn
Why, how now Ithimore, why laugh'st thou so?	Jew	3.3.4	Abigal
Thy father's, how?	Jew	3.3.72	1Fryar
How, Sir?	Jew	3.4.23	P Ithimr
How master?	Jew	3.4.73	P Ithimr
How so?	Jew	3.4.82	P Ithimr
Welcome, great [Bashaw] <Bashaws>, how fares/Callymath,	Jew	3.5.1	Govnr
So, say how was their end?	Jew	3.6.26	2Fryar
How sweet the Bels ring now the Nuns are dead/That sound at	Jew	4.1.2	Barab
How can it if we two be secret.	Jew	4.1.9	Barab
Besides I know not how much weight in Pearle/Orient and round,	Jew	4.1.66	Barab
How, dost call me rogue?	Jew	4.1.96	1Fryar
Oh how I long to see him shake his heeles.	Jew	4.1.140	Ithimr
Why, how now Jacomo, what hast thou done?	Jew	4.1.174	Barab
I, master, he's slain; look how his brains drop out on's nose.	Jew	4.1.178	P Ithimr
And ye did but know how she loves you, Sir.	Jew	4.2.53	Pilia
Nay, I care not how much she loves me; Sweet Bellamira, would I	Jew	4.2.54	P Ithimr
How now?	Jew	4.2.100	P Ithimr
And how the villaine revels with my gold.	Jew	4.3.68	Barab
How sweet, my Ithimore, the flowers smell.	Jew	4.4.39	Curtzn
How liberally the villain gives me mine own gold.	Jew	4.4.48	P Barab
How swift he runnes.	Jew	4.4.51	Pilia
so, or how else,/The Jew is here, and rests at your command.	Jew	5.1.82	Barab
And how secure this conquer'd Iland stands/Inviron'd with the	Jew	5.3.6	Calym
I wonder how it could be conquer'd thus?	Jew	5.3.12	Calym
And meditate how we may grace us best/To solemnize our	Jew	5.3.44	Calym
How stand the cords? How hang these hinges, fast?	Jew	5.5.1	Barab
How busie Barrabas is there above/To entertaine us in his	Jew	5.5.52	Calym
How the slave jeeres at him?	Jew	5.5.56	Govnr
How now, what means this?	Jew	5.5.64	Calym
Have you not heard of late how he decreed,	P 32	1.32	Navrre
How they did storme at these your nuptiall rites,	P 49	1.49	Admral
Fye, I am ashamde, how ever that I seeme,	P 124	2.67	Guise
to beware/How you did meddle with such dangerous giftes.	P 180	3.15	Navrre
How now fellow, what newes?	P 242	4.40	Charls
How fares it with my Lord high Admiral,	P 253	4.51	Charls
Alas I am a scholler, how should I have golde?	P 377	7.17	Ramus
How answere you that?	P 397	7.37	Guise
How may we doe? I feare me they will live.	P 420	7.60	Guise
How now my Lords, how fare you?	P 430	7.70	Anjoy
Now Madame, how like you our lusty Admirall?	P 494	9.13	Guise
How Charles our sonne begins for to lament/For the late nights	P 513	9.32	QnMoth
How meanst thou that?	P 618	12.31	King
How likes your grace my sonnes pleasantnes?	P 632	12.45	QnMoth
How now sirra, what newes?	P 723	14.26	Navrre
How now my Lord, faith this is more then need,	P 757	15.15	Guise
They should know how I scornde them and their mockes.	P 762	15.20	Guise
How now Mugeroun, metst thou not the Guise at the doore?	P 774	15.32	King
How many noble men have lost their lives,	P 795	16.9	Navrre
Else all France knowes how poor a Duke thou art.	P 844	17.39	Eprnon
and how the Citizens/With gifts and shewes did entertaine him	P 873	17.68	Eprnon
How fares it this morning with your excellence?	P 966	19.36	King
Mother, how like you this device of mine?	P1065	19.135	King
But how wilt thou get opportunitye?	P1135	21.29	Dumain
How they beare armes against their soveraigne.	P1187	22.49	King
But how now, what are these?	Edw	1.1.24	Gavstn
How now, why droops the earle of Lancaster?	Edw	1.2.9	MortSr
Remember how the Bishop was abusde,	Edw	1.4.59	ArchBp
How fast they run to banish him I love,	Edw	1.4.94	Edward
How deare my lord is to poore Isabell.	Edw	1.4.166	Queene
And witnesse heaven how deere thou art to me.	Edw	1.4.167	Edward
Madam, how fares your grace?	Edw	1.4.192	Mortmr
No? doe but marke how earnestly she pleads.	Edw	1.4.234	Warwck

HOW (cont.)

And see how coldly his lookes make deniall.	Edw	1.4.235	Lncstr
How easilie might some base slave be subbornd,	Edw	1.4.265	Mortmr
I, but how chance this was not done before?	Edw	1.4.272	Lncstr
But how if he do not Nephew?	Edw	1.4.278	MortSr
Harke how he harpes upon his minion.	Edw	1.4.311	Queene
O how a kisse revives poore Isabell.	Edw	1.4.333	Queene
Looke Lancaster how passionate he is,	Edw	2.2.3	Queene
How now, what newes, is Gaveston arrivde?	Edw	2.2.6	Edward
Why how now cosin, how fares all our friends?	Edw	2.2.114	Lncstr
How now, what noise is this?	Edw	2.2.139	Edward
How oft have I beene baited by these peeres?	Edw	2.2.201	Edward
I wonder how he scapt.	Edw	2.4.22	Lncstr
How comes it, that the king and he is parted?	Edw	2.4.41	Mortmr
How Gaveston hath robd me of his love:	Edw	2.4.67	Queene
How now my lord of Arundell?	Edw	2.5.32	Lncstr
How now?	Edw	2.5.41	Warwck
Renowmed Edward, how thy name/Revives poore Gaveston.	Edw	2.5.41	Gavstn
How meanst thou Mortimer? that is over base.	Edw	2.5.71	Gavstn
How say you my lord of Warwick?	Edw	2.5.92	Mortmr
Nay, do your pleasures, I know how twill proove.	Edw	2.5.93	Warwck
Well, and how fortunes that he came not?	Edw	3.1.113	Edward
Yet ere thou go, see how I do devorce	Edw	3.1.176	Edward
My [lords] <lord>, perceive you how these rebels swell:	Edw	3.1.181	Edward
Grone for this greefe, behold how thou art maimed.	Edw	3.1.251	Mortmr
How say you my Lord, will you go with your friends,	Edw	4.2.19	SrJohn
Oh my sweet hart, how do I mone thy wrongs,	Edw	4.2.27	Queene
How meane you, and the king my father lives?	Edw	4.2.43	Prince
How hard the nobles, how unkinde the king/Hath shewed himself:	Edw	4.2.49	Mortmr
How say yong Prince, what thinke you of the match?	Edw	4.2.67	SrJohn
How now, what newes with thee, from whence come these?	Edw	4.3.24	Edward
How will you deale with Edward in his fall?	Edw	4.6.31	Kent
How Baldocke, Spencer, and their complices,	Edw	4.6.78	Mortmr
way how hardly I can brooke/To loose my crowne and kingdome,	Edw	5.1.51	Edward
and bid him rule/Better then I, yet how have I transgrest,	Edw	5.1.122	Edward
How fares my lord the king?	Edw	5.2.24	Queene
How fares my honorable lord of Kent?	Edw	5.2.80	Mortmr
In health sweete Mortimer, how fares your grace?	Edw	5.2.81	Kent
How now, who comes there?	Edw	5.3.49	Gurney
And hast thou cast how to accomplish it?	Edw	5.4.24	Mortmr
I learnde in Naples how to poison flowers,	Edw	5.4.31	Ltborn
I care not how it is, so it be not spide:	Edw	5.4.40	Mortmr
How often shall I bid you beare him hence?	Edw	5.4.102	Mortmr
Whats heere? I know not how to conster it.	Edw	5.5.15	Gurney
See how he must be handled for his labour,	Edw	5.5.23	Matrvs
The Queene sent me, to see how you were used,	Edw	5.5.48	Ltborn
How now my Lorde.	Edw	5.5.102	Ltborn
How now my lord?	Edw	5.6.26	Mortmr
How am I glutted with conceipt of this?	F 105	1.1.77	Faust
How now sirra, where's thy Maister?	F 197	1.2.4	P 1Schol
How pliant is this Mephostophilis?	F 257	1.3.29	Faust
How comes it then that he is Prince of Devils?	F 294	1.3.66	Faust
How comes it then that thou art out of hell?	F 303	1.3.75	Faust
see how poverty jests in his nakednesse, I know the Villaines	F 348	1.4.6	P Wagner
How now sir, will you serve me now?	F 376	1.4.34	P Wagner
<How? now in hell: nay>	F 527	2.1.139	Faust
<How, a wife: I prithee Faustus talke not of a wife>.	F 530	(HC261) A	P Mephst
<Tel Faustus, how dost thou like thy wife>?	F 533	(HC261) A	P Mephst
How prov'st thou that?	F 559	2.2.8	Faust
How many Heavens, or Spheares, are there?	F 609	2.2.58	P Faust
live along, then thou should'st see how fat I'de <I would> be.	F 683	2.2.132	P Envy
<Now Faustus, how dost thou like this>?	F 711	(HC264) A	Lucifr
O how this sight doth delight <this feedes> my soule.	F 712	2.2.164	Faust
I see hell, and returne againe safe, how happy were I then.	F 714	2.2.166	P Faust
How now? who snatch't the meat from me!	F1044	3.2.64	Pope
How now?	F1065	3.2.85	Faust
How, how?	F1099	3.3.12	P Robin
How am I vexed by these villaines Charmes?	F1117	3.3.30	Mephst
How may I prove that saying to be true?	F1268	4.1.114	Emper
Why how now sir Knight, what, hang'd by the hornes?	F1290	4.1.136	P Faust
let's devise how we may adde more shame/To the blacke scandall	F1377	4.2.53	Fredrk
How now Benvolio?	F1438	4.3.8	Mrtino
How sir, not into the water?	F1470	4.4.14	P HrsCsr
How now Wagner what newes with thee?	F1499	4.4.43	P Faust
How now, what lacke you?	F1507	4.5.3	P Hostss
O Hostisse how do you?	F1515	4.5.11	P Robin
I'le tell you the bravest tale how a Conjurer serv'd me; you	F1521	4.5.17	P Carter
I'le tell you how he serv'd me:	F1525	4.5.21	P Carter
Now sirs, you shall heare how villanously he serv'd mee:	F1535	4.5.31	P HrsCsr
But you shall heare how bravely I serv'd him for it; I went me	F1547	4.5.43	P HrsCsr
how sufficiently to recompence your great deserts in erecting	F1559	4.6.2	P Duke
Why how now Maisters, what a coyle is there?	F1591	4.6.34	Servnt
Why, how now my [good] <goods> friends?	F1608	4.6.51	Faust
Do you remember sir, how you cosened me and eat up my load of--	F1659	4.6.102	P Carter
Do you remember how you made me weare an Apes--	F1661	4.6.104	P Dick
scab, do you remember how you cosened me with <of> a ho--	F1663	4.6.106	P HrsCsr
[Ambitious fiends, see how the heavens smiles]/[At your repulse,	F1794	5.1.121A	OldMan
To marke him how he doth demeane himselfe.	F1806	5.2.10	Belzeb
How should he, but in <with> desperate lunacie.	F1807	5.2.11	Mephst
Say Wagner, thou hast perus'd my will,/How dost thou like it?	F1817	5.2.21	Faust
How, boy?	F App	p.229 2	P Clown
see how poverty jesteth in his nakednesse, the vilaine is bare,	F App	p.229 6	P Wagner
How, my soule to the Divel for a shoulder of mutton though	F App	p.229 10	P Clown

HOW (cont.)

How, in verse?	F App	p.229 15	P	Clown
how, how, knaves acre?	F App	p.229 17	P	Clown
Ile tell you how you shall know them, all hee divels has	F App	p.230 53	P	Clown
How? a Christian fellow to a dogge or catte,	F App	p.231 60	P	Clown
How Balioll and Belcher.	F App	p.231 67	P	Wagner
How now, whose that which spake?	F App	p.231 3	P	Pope
How now, whose that which snatcht the meate from me?	F App	p.231 8	P	Pope
How? bell, booke, and candle,	F App	p.232 25		Faust
How say you now?	F App	p.234 12	P	Robin
How am I vexed with these vilaines charmes?	F App	p.235 37		Mephst
How, from Constantinople?	F App	p.235 40	P	Robin
How, into an Ape?	F App	p.236 45	P	Robin
how that none in my Empire, nor in the whole world can compare	F App	p.236 2	P	Emper
how they had wonne by prowesse such exploits, gote such riches,	F App	p.236 19	P	Emper
How then sir?	F App	p.237 53	P	Faust
or moale in her necke, how shal I know whether it be so or no?	F App	p.238 61	P	Emper
How now sir Knight?	F App	p.238 69	P	Emper
How darst thou thus abuse a Gentleman?	F App	p.238 74		Knight
how you crossed me in my conference with the emperour?	F App	p.238 77	P	Faust
How now Wagner, what's the newes with thee?	F App	p.241 167	P	Faust
in the month of January, how you shuld come by these grapes.	F App	p.242 18	P	Duke
hither, as ye see, how do you like them Madame, be they good?	F App	p.242 23	P	Faust
See how they quit our [bloud shed] <bloudshed> in the North;	Lucan, First Booke	302		
Pursu'd us hither, how were we bestead/When comming conqueror,	Lucan, First Booke	309		
Looke how when stormy Auster from the breach/Of Libian Syrtes	Lucan, First Booke	496		
But how thou shouldst behave thy selfe now know;	Ovid's Elegies	1.4.11		
How apt her breasts were to be prest by me,	Ovid's Elegies	1.5.20		
How smoothe a bellie, under her waste sawe I,	Ovid's Elegies	1.5.21		
How large a legge, and what a lustie thigh?	Ovid's Elegies	1.5.22		
He shewes me how unheard to passe the watch,	Ovid's Elegies	1.6.7		
See how the gates with my teares wat'red are.	Ovid's Elegies	1.6.18		
Excludst a lover, how wouldst use a foe?	Ovid's Elegies	1.6.31		
Aie me how high that gale did lift my hope!	Ovid's Elegies	1.6.52		
She may perceive how we the time did wast:	Ovid's Elegies	1.6.70		
How oft wisht I night would not give thee place,	Ovid's Elegies	1.13.27		
How oft, that either wind would breake thy coche,	Ovid's Elegies	1.13.29		
How patiently hot irons they did take/In crooked [tramells]	Ovid's Elegies	1.14.25		
With earthes revenge and how Olimpus toppe/High Ossa bore,	Ovid's Elegies	2.1.13		
Oh how the burthen irkes, that we should shun.	Ovid's Elegies	2.4.6		
Behould how quailes among their battailes live,	Ovid's Elegies	2.6.27		
Loe how the miserable great eared Asse,	Ovid's Elegies	2.7.15		
By Venus Deity how did I protest.	Ovid's Elegies	2.8.18		
How oft, and by what meanes we did agree.	Ovid's Elegies	2.8.28		
Let others tell how winds fierce battailes wage,	Ovid's Elegies	2.11.17		
How Scyllaes and Caribdis waters rage.	Ovid's Elegies	2.11.18		
How almost wrackt thy ship in maine seas fell.	Ovid's Elegies	2.11.50		
I saw how Bulls for a white Heifer strive,	Ovid's Elegies	2.12.25		
And thou my light accept me how so ever,	Ovid's Elegies	2.17.23		
Ah oft how much she might she feignd offence;	Ovid's Elegies	2.19.13		
Great gods what kisses, and how many gave she?	Ovid's Elegies	2.19.18		
How long her lockes were, ere her oath she tooke:	Ovid's Elegies	3.3.3		
How to attaine, what is denyed, we thinke,	Ovid's Elegies	3.4.17		
How wouldst thou flowe wert thou a noble floud,	Ovid's Elegies	3.5.89		
How piteously with drouping wings he stands,	Ovid's Elegies	3.8.9		
How such a Poet could you bring forth, sayes,	Ovid's Elegies	3.14.13		
How small sc ere, Ile you for greatest praise.	Ovid's Elegies	3.14.14		
How smooth his brest was, and how white his bellie,	Hero and Leander	1.66		
Looke how their hands, so were their hearts united,	Hero and Leander	2.27		
To see how he this captive Nymph beguil'd.	Hero and Leander	2.40		
How that a sheapheard sitting in a vale,	Hero and Leander	2.194		
Againe she knew not how to frame her looke,	Hero and Leander	2.307		

HOWE

Ah howe thy lot is above my lot blest:	Ovid's Elegies	1.6.46
Or voice that howe to change the wilde notes knew?	Ovid's Elegies	2.6.18
Ah howe oft on hard doores hung I engrav'd,	Ovid's Elegies	3.1.53
Perhaps he'ele tell howe oft he slewe a man,	Ovid's Elegies	3.7.21

HOWELL

Take him away, he prates. You Rice ap Howell,	Edw	4.6.73	Mortmr

HOWER

In happy hower we have set the Crowne/Upon your kingly head,	1Tamb	2.1.50	Ortyg
That Tamburlaine shall rue the day, the hower,	1Tamb	4.3.38	Souldn
Unto the watry mornings ruddy [bower] <hower>,	1Tamb	4.4.123	Tamb
And every hower I will visite you.	P 272	4.70	Charls
On this feast day, O cursed day and hower,	Hero and Leander	1.131	

HOWERS

Would lend an howers license to my tongue:	1Tamb	5.1.423	Arabia
Aye me I warne what profits some few howers,	Ovid's Elegies	1.4.59	

HOW EVER

Fye, I am ashamde, how ever that I seeme,	P 124	2.67	Guise

HOWLE (See also HOULLE)

Whose hideous ecchoes make the welkin howle,	Dido	4.2.9	Iarbus
The triple headed Cerberus would howle,	2Tamb	5.1.97	Tamb
And hags howle for my death at Charons shore,	Edw	4.7.90	Edward
Curling their bloudy lockes, howle dreadfull things,	Lucan, First Booke	565	

HOWLES

for Julia/Snatcht hence by cruel fates with ominous howles,	Lucan, First Booke	112

HOWLING

And swong her howling in the emptie ayre,	Dido	2.1.248	Aeneas
Where shaking ghosts with ever howling grones,	1Tamb	5.1.245	Zabina

HOWRES

So, now thou art to bee at an howres warning, whensoever, and	F 369	1.4.27	P Wagner

HOW SO EVER

And thou my light accept me how so ever,	Ovid's Elegies	2.17.23

HOWSOEVER			
For howsoever we have borne it out, ...	Edw	1.4.280	Mortmr
HOY (See HOIE)			
HOYSED			
Was it not you that hoysed up these sailes?	Dido	4.4.153	Dido
HOYSING			
The sailes were hoysing up, and he abourd. . . .	Dido	4.4.15	Anna
HOYST			
And hoyst aloft on Neptunes hideous hilles, . . .	Dido	3.3.47	Iarbus
As oft as he attempts to hoyst up saile:	Dido	4.4.103	Dido
And spying me, hoyst up the sailes amaine: . . .	Dido	5.1.227	Anna
HUE (See alsc HEW)			
And night made semblance of the hue of hell, ...	P 63	2.6	Guise
Yet although [neither] <either>, mixt of eithers hue, .	Ovid's Elegies		1.14.10
But what availde this faith? her rarest hue? . . .	Ovid's Elegies		2.6.17
HUG'D			
him he were best to send it; then he hug'd and imbrac'd me.	Jew	4.2.106	P Pilia
HUGE			
his entent/The windes did drive huge billowes to the shoare,	Dido	2.1.139	Aeneas
Through which it could not enter twas so huge. . . .	Dido	2.1.171	Aeneas
with Russian stems/Plow up huge furrowes in the Caspian sea,	1Tamb	1.2.195	Tamb
For she is that huge blemish in our eye, ...	P 80	2.23	Guise
Did he not cause the King of Spaines huge fleete, . .	P1033	19.103	King
Make Englands civill townes huge heapes of stones, . .	Edw	3.1.215	Edward
As for my selfe, I stand as Joves huge tree, ...	Edw	5.6.11	Mortmr
From <For> Venice shall they drag <dregge> huge Argosies,/And	F 157	1.1.129	Valdes
Or clap huge hornes, upon the Cardinals heads: . . .	F 864	3.1.86	Mephst
Il'e naile huge forked hornes, and let them hang/Within the	F1380	4.2.56	Benvol
He'd joyne long Asses eares to these huge hornes, . .	F1449	4.3.19	Benvol
what huge lust of warre/Hath made Barbarians drunke with Latin	Lucan, First Booke		8
rampiers fallen down, huge heapes of stone/Lye in our townes,	Lucan, First Booke		25
come, their huge power made him bould/To mannage greater deeds;	Lucan, First Booke		462
Rome if her strength the huge world had not fild, . .	Ovid's Elegies		2.9.17
By seaven huge mouthes into the sea is [skipping] <slipping>,	Ovid's Elegies		2.13.10
Then with huge steps came violent Tragedie, . . .	Ovid's Elegies		3.1.11
Huge okes, hard Adamantes might she have moved, . .	Ovid's Elegies		3.6.57
Our verse great Tityus a huge space out-spreads, . .	Ovid's Elegies		3.11.25
HUGEST			
Tis not the hugest monster of the sea, ...	Edw	2.2.45	Edward
HUGGE			
And then Ile hugge with you an hundred times. . . .	Dido	1.1.48	Ganimd
HUGH			
Spencer, the father of Hugh Spencer there, ...	Edw	3.1.40	SpncrP
HUGIE			
Your threefold armie and my hugie hoste, ...	1Tamb	3.3.94	Bajzth
Gyants as big as hugie Polypheme:	2Tamb	1.1.28	Orcan
HUGONET			
There shall not a Hugonet breath in France. . . .	P 324	5.51	Guise
HUGONETS			
Let none escape, murder the Hugonets.	P 337	5.64	Guise
Murder the Hugonets, take those pedantes hence. . .	P 438	7.78	Guise
There are a hundred Hugonets and more, ...	P 501	9.20	Guise
Vive la messe, perish Hugonets, ...	P1014	19.84	Guise
HUGONITES			
which my Lord of Guise/Did make in Paris amongst the Hugonites?	P 515	9.34	QnMoth
Downe with the Hugonites, murder them.	P 528	10.1	Guise
HUM (See also UMH)			
How, a Christian? Hum, what's here to doe?	Jew	1.2.75	Barab
HUMAINE			
Nor speech bewraies ought humaine in thy birth, . . .	Dido	1.1.190	Aeneas
that Dido may desire/And not obtaine, be it in humaine power?	Dido	3.4.8	Aeneas
For he was never sprong of humaine race, ...	1Tamb	2.6.11	Meandr
in a myrrour we perceive/The highest reaches of a humaine wit:	1Tamb	5.1.168	Tamb
That King Egeus fed with humaine flesh, ...	2Tamb	4.3.13	Tamb
And fishes [fed] <feed> by humaine carkasses, ...	2Tamb	5.1.206	Techel
All humaine kinde by their default had perisht. . .	Ovid's Elegies		2.14.10
HUMANE			
As great as have the humane soules of men.	F 433	2.1.45	Mephst
and fell Mercury <(Jove)>/They offer humane flesh, and where	Lucan, First Booke		441
Cattell were seene that muttered humane speech: . .	Lucan, First Booke		559
A heavenly Nimph, belov'd of humane swaines, . . .	Hero and Leander		1.216
We humane creatures should enjoy that blisse. . . .	Hero and Leander		1.254
That sheares the slender threads of humane life, . .	Hero and Leander		1.448
HUMBLE			
Their blubbered cheekes and hartie humble mones/Will melt his	1Tamb	5.1.21	Govnr
If humble suites or imprecations, ...	1Tamb	5.1.24	1Virgn
Then hang out flagges (my Lord) of humble truce, . .	2Tamb	5.1.6	Maxim
And most [humbly] <humble> intreates your Majestie/To visite	P 245	4.43	Man
As in all humble dutie, I do yeeld/My life and lasting service	F1818	5.2.22	Wagner
And her in humble manner thus beseech.	Hero and Leander		1.314
HUMBLED			
sudden fall/Has humbled her and brought her downe to this:	Jew	1.2.368	Mthias
HUMBLEST			
Most happy Emperour in humblest tearms/I vow my service to your	1Tamb	2.5.15	Meandr
HUMBLIE			
I humblie thanke your majestie.	Edw	2.2.247	Baldck
Here humblie of your grace we take our leaves, . . .	Edw	4.7.78	Baldck
Commend me humblie to his Majestie, ...	Edw	5.2.69	Queene
I humblie thanke your honour.	Edw	5.6.10	Matrvs
And to those sterne nymphs humblie made request, . .	Hero and Leander		1.379
HUMBLY			
She humbly did beseech him for our bane, ...	Dido	1.1.60	Venus
Then now my Lord, I humbly take my leave.	1Tamb	1.1.81	Therid

HUMBLY (cont.)

That humbly craves upon her knees to stay, . . . 2Tamb 3.4.70 Olymp
thou shalt kneele to us/And humbly crave a pardon for thy life. 2Tamb 3.5.109 Orcan
Commend me to him, Sir, most humbly, ... Jew 4.3.47 Barab
He humbly would intreat your Majesty/To come and see his homely Jew 5.3.17 Msngr
Therefore he humbly would intreat your Highnesse/Not to depart Jew 5.3.32 Msngr
I humbly thank your Majestie. . . . . P 169 3.4 P Pothec
And most [humbly] <humble> intreates your Majestie/To visite P 245 4.43 Man
I humbly thank your royall Majestie. . . . . . P 273 4.71 Admral
I humbly thanke your Ladieship. . . . . . . Edw 2.1.81 Spencr
And thus, most humbly do we take our leave. . . . Edw 5.1.124 Trussl
I humbly thanke your grace: then fetch some Beere. . . F1625 4.6.68 Faust
Now my good Lord having done my duety, I humbly take my leave. F App p.238 86 P Faust
I humbly thanke your Grace. . . . . F App p.243 32 P Faust
I that ere-while was fierce, now humbly sue, . . . Ovid's Elegies 2.5.49

HUMBLYE

Humblye craving your gracious reply. . . . . . . P1170 22.32 Frier

HUMIDUM

The Humidum and Calor, which some holde/Is not a parcell of the 2Tamb 5.3.86 Phsitn

HUMILITIE

In all humilitie I thanke your grace. . . . . Dido 2.1.99 Aeneas
Humilitie belongs to common groomes. . . . . . Dido 2.1.101 Dido
My Lord, in token of my true humilitie, ... P 866 17.61 Guise

HUMILITY

Full of obedience and humility, ... F 258 1.3.30 Faust

HUMOR

And in this humor is Achates to, ... Dido 2.1.10 Achat
His wanton humor will be quicklie left. . . . . Edw 1.4.199 Lncstr
Unckle, his wanton humor greeves not me, ... Edw 1.4.402 Mortmr

HUMORS

Such humors stirde them up; but this warrs seed, . . Lucan, First Booke 159

HUMOUR

I goe to feed the humour of my Love, ... Dido 3.1.50 Iarbus
wheeles spun/And what with Mares ranck humour may be done. Ovid's Elegies 1.8.8

HUMOURS

But his fantastick humours pleasde not me: . . . Dido 3.1.158 Dido
Drawes bloody humours from my feeble partes, . . . 1Tamb 4.4.95 Bajzth

HUNC

Hunc dies vidit fugiens jacentem. . . . . . . Edw 4.7.54 Leistr

HUNDRED

And then Ile hugge with you an hundred times. . . . Dido 1.1.48 Ganimd
Thus in stoute Hectors race three hundred yeares, . . Dido 1.1.104 Jupitr
To force an hundred watchfull eyes to sleepe: . . . Dido 2.1.146 Aeneas
why, I may live a hundred yeares,/Fourescore is but a girles Dido 4.5.31 Nurse
A hundreth <hundred> Tartars shall attend on thee, . . 1Tamb 1.2.93 Tamb
My martiall prises with five hundred men, ... 1Tamb 1.2.102 Tamb
A thousand horsmen? We five hundred foote? . . . 1Tamb 1.2.121 Tamb
Weele fight five hundred men at armes to one, . . . 1Tamb 1.2.143 Tamb
An hundred horsmen of my company/Scowting abroad upon these 1Tamb 2.2.39 Spy
Two hundred thousand footmen that have serv'd/In two set . 1Tamb 3.3.18 Bassoe
Three hundred thousand men in armour clad, ... 1Tamb 4.1.21 2Msngr
Five hundred thousand footmen threatning shot, . . . 1Tamb 4.1.24 2Msngr
A monster of five hundred thousand heades, ... 1Tamb 4.3.7 Souldn
A hundred and fifty thousand horse, ... 1Tamb 4.3.53 Capol
Two hundred thousand foot, brave men at armes, . . . 1Tamb 4.3.54 Capol
Now have we martcht from faire Natolia/Two hundred leagues, and 2Tamb 1.1.7 Orcan
will send/A hundred thousand horse train'd to the war, . 2Tamb 1.1.154 Sgsmnd
Then shalt thou see a hundred kings and more/Upon their knees, 2Tamb 1.2.28 Callap
A hundred Bassoes cloath'd in crimson silk/Shall ride before 2Tamb 1.2.46 Callap
Five hundred Briggandines are under saile, ... 2Tamb 1.3.122 Therid
A hundred thousand expert souldiers: . . . . . . 2Tamb 1.3.132 Usumc
have martcht/Foure hundred miles with armour on their backes, 2Tamb 1.3.175 Usumc
An hundred kings by scores wil bid him armes, . . . 2Tamb 2.2.11 Gazell
And hundred thousands subjects to each score: . . . 2Tamb 2.2.12 Gazell
hundred and thirty Kingdomes late contributory to his mighty 2Tamb 3.1.5 P Orcan
I have a hundred thousand men in armes, ... 2Tamb 3.1.38 Orcan
A hundred horse shall scout about the plaines/To spie what 2Tamb 3.3.47 Techel
royall is esteem'd/Six hundred thousand valiant fighting men. 2Tamb 3.5.51 Soria
Being distant lesse than ful a hundred leagues, . . . 2Tamb 5.3.133 Tamb
Three thousand Camels, and two hundred yoake/Of labouring Oxen, Jew 1.2.183 Barab
hundred yoake/Of labouring Oxen, and five hundred/Shee Asses: Jew 1.2.184 Barab
A hundred thousand Crownes. . . . . Jew 2.2.36 Govnr
marketplace; whats the price of this slave, two hundred Crowns? Jew 2.3.98 P Barab
And if he has, he is worth three hundred plats. . . Jew 2.3.102 Barab
Ratest thou this Moore but at two hundred plats? . . Jew 2.3.107 Lodowk
An hundred Crownes, I'le have him; there's the coyne. . Jew 2.3.130 Barab
word a Merchant's fled/That owes me for a hundred Tun of Wine: Jew 2.3.244 Barab
but for one bare night/A hundred Duckets have bin freely given: Jew 3.1.3 Curtzn
a hundred of the Jewes Crownes that I had such a Concubine. Jew 3.1.27 P Ithimr
A hundred for a hundred I have tane; . . . . . . Jew 4.1.54 Barab
Send for a hundred Crownes at least. . . . . . . Jew 4.2.70 P Pilia
Ten hundred thousand crownes,--Master Barabas. . . . Jew 4.2.71 P Ithimr
Sirra Barabas, send me a hundred crownes. . . . . Jew 4.2.73 P Ithimr
Put in two hundred at least. . . . . Jew 4.2.74 P Pilia
I charge thee send me three hundred by this bearer, and this Jew 4.2.75 P Ithimr
Write for five hundred Crownes. . . . . Jew 4.2.116 P Pilia
as you love your life send me five hundred crowns, and give the Jew 4.2.117 P Ithimr
send me five hundred crowns, and give the Bearer one hundred. Jew 4.2.118 P Ithimr
tell him, I scorne to write a line under a hundred crownes. Jew 4.2.121 P Ithimr
Barabas send me three hundred Crownes. . . . . . Jew 4.3.1 Barab
crosbiting, such a Rogue/As is the husband to a hundred whores: Jew 4.3.14 Barab
And I by him must send three hundred crownes. . . . Jew 4.3.15 Barab
No; but three hundred will not serve his turne. . . Jew 4.3.20 P Pilia

HUNDRED (cont.)
No Sir; and therefore I must have five hundred more. — Jew 4.3.22 P Pilia
'Tis not five hundred Crownes that I esteeme, — Jew 4.3.40 Barab
have a shag-rag knave to come [demand]/Three hundred Crownes, — Jew 4.3.62 Barab
[demand]/Three hundred Crownes, and then five hundred Crownes? — Jew 4.3.62 Barab
I'le lead five hundred souldiers through the Vault, — Jew 5.1.91 Barab
With free consent a hundred thousand pounds. — Jew 5.5.20 Govnr
Paris hath full five hundred Colledges, — P 137 2.80 Guise
Five hundred fatte Franciscan Fryers and priestes. — P 142 2.85 Guise
My Lord of Anjoy, there are a hundred Protestants, — P 417 7.57 Guise
There are a hundred Hugonets and more, — P 501 9.20 Guise
Browne bils, and targetiers, foure hundred strong, — Edw 3.1.37 SpncrP
A hundred thousand, and at last be sav'd. — F1962 5.2.166 Faust
Ad <And> they were apt to curle an hundred waies, — Ovid's Elegies 1.14.13
Hundred-hand Gyges, and had done it well, — Ovid's Elegies 2.1.12
A hundred reasons makes <make> me ever love. — Ovid's Elegies 2.4.10
Argus had either way an hundred eyes, — Ovid's Elegies 3.4.19

HUNDRED-HAND
Hundred-hand Gyges, and had done it well, — Ovid's Elegies 2.1.12

HUNDRETH
A hundreth <hundred> Tartars shall attend on thee, — 1Tamb 1.2.93 Tamb
Thou ore a hundreth Nimphes, or more shalt raigne: — Ovid's Elegies 3.5.63

HUNG (See also HOONG)
About whose withered necke hung Hecuba, — Dido 2.1.226 Aeneas
And hung on stately Mecas Temple roofe, — 2Tamb 1.1.141 Orcan
And cloath of Arras hung about the walles, — 2Tamb 1.2.44 Callap
Where womens favors hung like labels downe. — Edw 2.2.187 Mortmr
Are not thy bils hung up as monuments, — F 48 1.1.20 Faust
And snatcht armes neer their houshold gods hung up/Such as — Lucan, First Booke 242
Ah howe oft on hard doores hung I engrav'd, — Ovid's Elegies 3.1.53
It mocked me, hung down the head and suncke, — Ovid's Elegies 3.6.14
About her necke hung chaines of peble stone, — Hero and Leander 1.25

HUNGAR
with hungar, and with horror aie/Griping our bowels with — 1Tamb 5.1.236 Bajzth

HUNGARIANS
More then his Camp of stout Hungarians, — 2Tamb 1.1.21 Uribas

HUNGARIE
Kings of Natolia and of Hungarie, — 2Tamb 1.1.114 Gazell

HUNGARY
Where Sigismond the king of Hungary/Should meet our person to — 2Tamb 1.1.9 Orcan
to parle for a peace/With Sigismond the king of Hungary: — 2Tamb 1.1.51 Gazell
Freend Sigismond, and peeres of Hungary, — 2Tamb 1.1.164 Orcan
See here the perjur'd traitor Hungary, — 2Tamb 2.3.12 Gazell
And with Lord Raymond, King of Hungary, — F 979 3.1.201 Pope

HUNGER (See also HUNGAR)
Faste and welcome sir, while hunger make you eat. — 1Tamb 4.4.56 P Tamb
Sharp hunger bites upon and gripes the root, — 1Tamb 5.1.273 Bajzth
Hunger and [thirst] <cold>, right adjuncts of the war. — 2Tamb 3.2.58 Tamb
And let their lives bloud slake thy furies hunger: — Edw 2.2.205 Edward

HUNGRY
I hold my head my master's hungry: — Jew 3.4.51 P Ithimr
and so hungry, that <I know> he would give his soule to the — F 349 1.4.7 P Wagner
and so hungry, that I know he would give his soule to the Divel — F App p.229 7 P Wagner

HUNT
That thus in person goe with thee to hunt: — Dido 3.3.2 Dido
And hunt that Coward, faintheart runaway, — 2Tamb 3.2.149 Tamb
Il'e raise a kennell of Hounds shall hunt him so, — F1301 4.1.147 Faust

HUNTER
or his speare/Sticks in his side) yet runs upon the hunter. — Lucan, First Booke 214

HUNTERS
Pursude by hunters, flie his angrie lookes, — 1Tamb 3.3.193 Zenoc
As frolike as the hunters in the chace/Of savage beastes amid — 1Tamb 4.3.56 Capol
Who seeing hunters pauseth till fell wrath/And kingly rage — Lucan, First Booke 209
Hunters leave taken beasts, pursue the chase, — Ovid's Elegies 2.9.9
With Augures Phoebus, Phoebe with hunters standes, — Ovid's Elegies 3.2.51

HUNTING
We two will goe a hunting in the woods, — Dido 3.1.174 Dido
This day they both a hunting forth will ride/Into these woods, — Dido 3.2.87 Juno
Come sonne, weele ride a hunting in the parke. — Edw 5.4.113 Queene

HUNTS
When strong wilde beasts, she stronger hunts to strike them. — Ovid's Elegies 3.2.32

HUNTSMEN
Huntsmen, why pitch you not your toyles apace, — Dido 3.3.30 Dido

HUNTSPEARE
Bearing his huntspeare bravely in his hand. — Dido 3.3.33 Anna

HURDLE
Bring him unto a hurdle, drag him foorth, — Edw 5.6.52 King

HURL'D
Where painted Carpets o're the meads are hurl'd, — Jew 4.2.91 Ithimr

HURLD
[Or] <On> stones, our stockes originall, should be hurld, — Ovid's Elegies 2.14.11

HURLE
And hurle him in some lake of mud and durt: — F1409 4.2.85 Faust
He wants no gifts into thy lap to hurle. — Ovid's Elegies 1.10.54

HURLY
There was such hurly burly in the heavens: — Dido 4.1.10 Achat

HURLY BURLY
There was such hurly burly in the heavens: — Dido 4.1.10 Achat

HURRIED
inconsiderate multitude/Thorough the Citty hurried headlong on, — Lucan, First Booke 493

HURT
Who if that any seeke to doe him hurt, — Dido 2.1.321 Venus
You shall not hurt my father when he comes. — Dido 3.1.80 Cupid

HURT (cont.)

Tut, I am simple, without [minde] <made> to hurt, . . Dido 3.2.16 Juno
Now is he come on shoare safe without hurt: . . . . Dido 5.1.257 Dido
I beleeve there will be some hurt done anon amongst them. 2Tamb 4.1.74 P Calyph
No; so shall I, if any hurt be done, ... 2Tamb... Jew 2.3.341 Barab

Now Guise may storme but doe us little hurt: . . . . P 28 1.28 Navrre
What are you hurt my Lord high Admiral? . . . . P 197 3.32 Condy
Hath he been hurt with villaines in the street? . . P 254 4.52 Charls
To hurt the noble man their soveraign loves. . . . P 259 4.57 Charls
What, is your highnes hurt? . . . . P1176 22.38 Navrre
shall stand by me,/What [god] <power> can hurt me <thee>? F 414 2.1.26 Faust
drunke over night, the Divell cannot hurt him in the morning: F1201 4.1.47 P Benvol
But thy fiers hurt not; Mars, 'tis thou enflam'st/The . Lucan, First Booke 657
Forbeare to hurt thy selfe in spoyling mee. . . . . Ovid's Elegies 1.2.50
lockes spred/On her white necke but for hurt cheekes be led. Ovid's Elegies 1.7.40
By thine owne hand and fault thy hurt doth growe, . . . Ovid's Elegies 1.14.43
That some youth hurt as I am with loves bowe/His owne flames Ovid's Elegies 2.1.7

HURTES

Your griefe and furie hurtes my second life: . . . . 2Tamb 2.4.68 Zenoc

HURTS

Where men are ready, lingering ever hurts: . . . . Lucan, First Booke 282

HUS

Sooth Lovers watch till sleepe the hus-band charmes, . Ovid's Elegies 1.9.25

HUS-BAND

Sooth Lovers watch till sleepe the hus-band charmes, . Ovid's Elegies 1.9.25

HUSBAND

Wherewith my husband woo'd me yet a maide, ... Dido 3.4.63 Dido
let him ride/As Didos husband through the Punicke streetes, Dido 4.4.67 Dido
Ile have a husband, or els a lover. . . . . Dido 4.5.23 Nurse
A husband and no teeth! . . . . Dido 4.5.24 Cupid
Before thou met my husband in the field, ... 1Tamb 4.2.59 Zabina
What do mine eies behold, my husband dead? . . . . 1Tamb 5.1.305 Zabina
O Bajazeth, my husband and my Lord, ... 1Tamb 5.1.308 Zabina
And meet my husband and my loving sonne. . . . . . 2Tamb 4.2.36 Olymp
Nothing, but stil thy husband and thy sonne? . . . . 2Tamb 4.2.37 Therid
Why gave you not your husband some of it, ... 2Tamb 4.2.71 Therid
I have no husband, sweet, I'le marry thee. . . . . Jew 4.2.87 Curtzn
crosbiting, such a Rogue/As is the husband to a hundred whores: Jew 4.3.14 Barab
Husband come down, heer's one would speak with you from the P 348 6.3 P SrnsWf
On whom but on my husband should I fawne? . . . . . Edw 1.4.146 Queene
Sweete husband be content, they all love you. . . . Edw 2.2.36 Queene
Thy husband to a banquet goes with me, ... Ovid's Elegies 1.4.1
Before thy husband come, though I not see/What may be done, yet Ovid's Elegies 1.4.13
When thou doest wish thy husband at the devill. . . . Ovid's Elegies 1.4.28
Entreat thy husband drinke, but do not kisse, ... Ovid's Elegies 1.4.51
At night thy husband clippes thee, I will weepe/And to the Ovid's Elegies 1.4.61
Nor is her husband wise, what needes defence/When . . Ovid's Elegies 2.2.11
When most her husband bends the browes and frownes, . . Ovid's Elegies 2.2.33
By whom the husband his wives incest knewe. . . . . Ovid's Elegies 2.2.48
She whom her husband, guard, and gate as foes, . . . Ovid's Elegies 2.12.3
Thou suffrest what no husband can endure, ... Ovid's Elegies 2.19.51
Can I but loath a husband growne a baude? . . . . . Ovid's Elegies 2.19.57
For me, she doth keeper, and husband feare, ... Ovid's Elegies 3.7.63
Rude husband-men bak'd not their corne before, . . . Ovid's Elegies 3.9.7
I have thy husband, guard, and fellow plaied. . . . Ovid's Elegies 3.10.18

HUSBANDES

My Lord and husbandes death, with my sweete sons, . . 2Tamb 4.2.22 Olymp

HUSBAND-MEN

Rude husband-men bak'd not their corne before, . . . Ovid's Elegies 3.9.7

HUSBANDS

A little while prolong'd her husbands life: . . . . Dido 2.1.246 Aeneas
That feeds upon her sonnes and husbands flesh. . . . 2Tamb 3.4.72 Olymp
longer life/Thou hadst restrainde thy headstrong husbands rage, Lucan, First Booke 116
parents/Keep back their sons, or womens teares their husbands; Lucan, First Booke 503
Such as the cause was of two husbands warre, ... Ovid's Elegies 1.10.1
Let Maydes whom hot desire to husbands leade, ... Ovid's Elegies 2.1.5
Trust me all husbands for such faults are sad/Nor make they any Ovid's Elegies 2.2.51
Or maides that their betrothed husbands spie. . . . Ovid's Elegies 2.5.36
Their wedlocks pledges veng'd their husbands bad. . . Ovid's Elegies 2.14.32
Nor doth her face please, but her husbands love; . . Ovid's Elegies 3.4.27
Looke gently, and rough husbands lawes despise. . . . Ovid's Elegies 3.4.44

HUSH

Hush, Ile gul him supernaturally: . . . . F App p.234 5 P Robin

HUSH'T

But hush't. . . . . Jew 3.4.54 Barab

HYACINTHE

Blushing Roses, purple Hyacinthe: . . . . Dido 2.1.319 Venus

HYADES

As when the Sea-man sees the Hyades/Gather an armye of Cemerian 1Tamb 3.2.76 Agidas

HYBLAS

That loade their thighes with Hyblas honeys spoyles, . Dido 5.1.13 Aeneas

HYDE

With strong hand striking wild-beasts brist'led hyde. . Ovid's Elegies 3.9.26

HYDRA

And as the heads of Hydra, so my power/Subdued, shall stand as 1Tamb 3.3.140 Bajzth
In few, the blood of Hydra, Lerna's bane; . . . . . Jew 3.4.100 Barab

HYE

To steale from France, and hye me to my home. . . . P 567 11.32 Navrre
Hye to the presence to attend the Emperour. . . . F1156 4.1.2 Mrtino

HYLAS (See HILAS)

HYMEN

If ever Hymen lowr'd at marriage rites, ... P 58 2.1 Guise
at the mariage day/The cup of Hymen had beene full of poyson, Edw 1.4.174 Queene

HYMEN (cont.)			
Though never-singling Hymen couple thee.	Hero and Leander		1.258
HYPOCRISIE			
A counterfet profession is better/Then unseene hypocrisie.	Jew	1.2.293	Barab
And use them but of meere hypocrisie.	Edw	2.1.45	Baldck
HYPOSTASIS (See HIPOSTASIS)			
HYPOSTATES (See HIPOSTATES)			
HYPPOLITUS			
And draw thee peecemeale like Hyppolitus,	2Tamb	5.3.240	Tamb
The stepdame read Hyppolitus lustlesse line.	Ovid's Elegies		2.18.30
HYPSIPYLE (See HIPSIPILE)			
HYR'D			
For beds ill hyr'd we are indebted nought.	Ovid's Elegies		1.10.44
HYS			
These cowards invisiblie assaile hys soule,	2Tamb	5.3.13	Therid
I'			
But take it to you i'th devils name.	Jew	1.2.154	Barab
And rise with them i'th middle of the Towne,	Jew	5.1.92	Barab
To morrow we would sit i'th Consistory,	F1017	3.2.37	Pope
I, and I fall not asleepe i'th meane time.	F1196	4.1.42	Benvol
'Twas I, that when thou wer't i'the way to heaven,	F1886	5.2.90	Mephst
I (Homograph; See also IDE, ILE)			
I love thee well, say Juno what she will.	Dido	1.1.2	Jupitr
I am much better for your worthles love,	Dido	1.1.3	Ganimd
To day when as I fild into your cups,	Dido	1.1.5	Ganimd
She reacht me such a rap for that I spilde,	Dido	1.1.7	Ganimd
I vow, if she but once frowne on thee more,	Dido	1.1.12	Jupitr
As once I did for harming Hercules.	Dido	1.1.15	Jupitr
Might I but see that pretie sport a foote,	Dido	1.1.16	Ganimd
O how would I with Helens brother laugh,	Dido	1.1.17	Ganimd
Sweet Jupiter, if ere I pleasde thine eye,	Dido	1.1.19	Ganimd
And I will spend my time in thy bright armes.	Dido	1.1.22	Ganimd
What ist sweet wagge I should deny thy youth?	Dido	1.1.23	Jupitr
As I exhal'd with thy fire darting beames,	Dido	1.1.25	Jupitr
I would have a jewell for mine eare,	Dido	1.1.46	Ganimd
I, this is it, you can sit toying there,	Dido	1.1.50	Venus
What shall I doe to save thee my sweet boy?	Dido	1.1.74	Venus
In those faire walles I promist him of yore:	Dido	1.1.85	Jupitr
How may I credite these thy flattering termes,	Dido	1.1.109	Venus
I will take order for that presently:	Dido	1.1.113	Jupitr
Triton I know hath fild his trumpe with Troy,	Dido	1.1.130	Venus
What? doe I see my sonne now come on shoare:	Dido	1.1.134	Venus
Here in this bush disguised will I stand,	Dido	1.1.139	Venus
Father I faint, good father give me meate.	Dido	1.1.163	Ascan
Whiles I with my Achates roave abroad,	Dido	1.1.175	Aeneas
Yet much I marvell that I cannot finde,	Dido	1.1.180	Achat
I neither saw nor heard of any such:	Dido	1.1.187	Aeneas
But what may I faire Virgin call your name?	Dido	1.1.188	Aeneas
Such honour, stranger, doe I not affect:	Dido	1.1.203	Venus
Of Troy am I, Aeneas is my name,	Dido	1.1.216	Aeneas
With twise twelve Phrigian ships I plowed the deepe,	Dido	1.1.220	Aeneas
But haples I, God wot, poore and unknowne,	Dido	1.1.227	Aeneas
And so I leave thee to thy fortunes lot,	Dido	1.1.238	Venus
I know her by the movings of her feete:	Dido	1.1.241	Aeneas
I but the barbarous sort doe threat our ships,	Dido	1.2.34	Serg
Where am I now? these should be Carthage walles.	Dido	2.1.1	Aeneas
Had not such passions in her head as I.	Dido	2.1.6	Aeneas
And when I know it is not, then I dye.	Dido	2.1.9	Aeneas
I cannot choose but fall upon my knees,	Dido	2.1.11	Achat
O were I not at all so thou mightst be.	Dido	2.1.28	Aeneas
I heare Aeneas voyce, but see him not,	Dido	2.1.45	Illion
You are Achates, or I [am] deciv'd.	Dido	2.1.49	Serg
Achates, speake, for I am overjoyed.	Dido	2.1.54	Aeneas
Blest be the time I see Achates face.	Dido	2.1.56	Illion
O tell me, for I long to be resolv'd.	Dido	2.1.61	Aeneas
Well may I view her, but she sees not me.	Dido	2.1.73	Aeneas
Sometime I was a Troian, mightie Queene:	Dido	2.1.75	Aeneas
But Troy is not, what shall I say I am?	Dido	2.1.76	Aeneas
And if this be thy sonne as I suppose,	Dido	2.1.92	Dido
And so I will sweete child:	Dido	2.1.97	Dido
In all humilitie I thanke your grace.	Dido	2.1.99	Aeneas
May I entreate thee to discourse at large,	Dido	2.1.106	Dido
In which unhappie worke was I employd,	Dido	2.1.169	Aeneas
Frighted with this confused noyse, I rose,	Dido	2.1.191	Aeneas
Then buckled I mine armour, drew my sword,	Dido	2.1.200	Aeneas
Yet flung I forth, and desperate of my life,	Dido	2.1.210	Aeneas
So I escapt the furious Pirrhus wrath:	Dido	2.1.223	Aeneas
Achilles sonne, remember what I was,	Dido	2.1.233	Aeneas
O end Aeneas, I can heare no more.	Dido	2.1.243	Dido
By this I got my father on my backe,	Dido	2.1.265	Aeneas
O there I lost my wife:	Dido	2.1.270	Aeneas
and had not we/Fought manfully, I had not told this tale:	Dido	2.1.271	Aeneas
Whom I tooke up to beare unto our ships:	Dido	2.1.277	Aeneas
And I alas, was forst to let her lye.	Dido	2.1.279	Aeneas
Moved with her voyce, I lept into the sea,	Dido	2.1.283	Aeneas
And as I swomme, she standing on the shoare,	Dido	2.1.286	Aeneas
I dye with melting ruth, Aeneas leave.	Dido	2.1.289	Dido
I, and my mother gave me this fine bow.	Dido	2.1.309	Cupid
Shall I have such a quiver and a bow?	Dido	2.1.310	Ascan
For Didos sake I take thee in my armes,	Dido	2.1.313	Venus
Eate Comfites in mine armes, and I will sing.	Dido	2.1.315	Venus
I will faire mother, and so play my part,	Dido	2.1.332	Cupid
Till I returne and take thee hence againe.	Dido	2.1.339	Venus

I (cont.)

Then shall I touch her breast and conquer her.	Dido	3.1.6	Cupid
How long faire Dido shall I pine for thee?	Dido	3.1.7	Iarbus
But that I may enjoy what I desire:	Dido	3.1.9	Iarbus
(And yet have I had many mightier Kings)/Hast had the greatest	Dido	3.1.12	Dido
mightier Kings)/Hast had the greatest favours I could give:	Dido	3.1.13	Dido
I feare me Dido hath been counted light,	Dido	3.1.14	Dido
But Dido is the favour I request.	Dido	3.1.18	Iarbus
I shall not be her sonne, she loves me not.	Dido	3.1.23	Cupid
I wagge, and give thee leave to kisse her to.	Dido	3.1.31	Dido
That I should say thou art no love of mine?	Dido	3.1.42	Dido
Away I say,/Depart from Carthage, come not in my sight.	Dido	3.1.43	Dido
Am I not King of rich Getulia?	Dido	3.1.45	Iarbus
Am not I Queen of Libia? then depart.	Dido	3.1.49	Dido
I goe to feed the humour of my Love,	Dido	3.1.50	Iarbus
No, but I charge thee never looke on me.	Dido	3.1.54	Dido
Poore soule I know too well the sower of love,	Dido	3.1.61	Anna
But tell them none shall gaze on him but I,	Dido	3.1.73	Dido
Lest with these sweete thoughts I melt cleane away.	Dido	3.1.76	Dido
Yet must I heare that lothsome name againe?	Dido	3.1.78	Dido
In stead of musicke I will heare him speake,	Dido	3.1.89	Dido
In whose faire bosome I will locke more wealth,	Dido	3.1.92	Dido
Lest I be made a wonder to the world.	Dido	3.1.96	Dido
I understand your highnesse sent for me.	Dido	3.1.100	Aeneas
So much have I receiv'd at Didos hands,	Dido	3.1.103	Aeneas
As without blushing I can aske no more:	Dido	3.1.104	Aeneas
I had been wedded ere Aeneas came:	Dido	3.1.138	Dido
I saw this man at Troy ere Troy was sackt.	Dido	3.1.141	Achat
I this in Greece when Paris stole faire Helen.	Dido	3.1.142	Aeneas
This man and I were at Olympus games.	Dido	3.1.143	Illion
I know this face, he is a Persian borne,	Dido	3.1.144	Serg
I traveld with him to Aetolia.	Dido	3.1.145	Serg
And I in Athens with this gentleman,	Dido	3.1.146	Cloan
Unlesse I be deceiv'd disputed once.	Dido	3.1.147	Cloan
All these and others which I never sawe,	Dido	3.1.150	Dido
Yet none obtaind me, I am free from all.--	Dido	3.1.153	Dido
But playd he nere so sweet, I let him goe:	Dido	3.1.160	Dido
But I had gold enough and cast him off:	Dido	3.1.162	Dido
Yet how <here> <now> I sweare by heaven and him I love,	Dido	3.1.166	Dido
I was as farre from love, as they from hate.	Dido	3.1.167	Dido
Yet boast not of it, for I love thee not,	Dido	3.1.171	Dido
not of it, for I love thee not,/And yet I hate thee not:--	Dido	3.1.172	Dido
O if I speake/I shall betray my selfe:--	Dido	3.1.172	Dido
O if I speake/I shall betray my selfe:--	Dido	3.1.173	Dido
But I will take another order now,	Dido	3.2.6	Juno
O no God wot, I cannot watch my time,	Dido	3.2.14	Juno
Tut, I am simple, without [minde] <made> to hurt,	Dido	3.2.16	Juno
But I will teare thy eyes fro forth thy head,	Dido	3.2.34	Venus
Is this then all the thankes that I shall have,	Dido	3.2.37	Juno
What though I was offended with thy sonne,	Dido	3.2.40	Juno
I mustred all the windes unto his wracke,	Dido	3.2.45	Juno
Yet now I doe repent me of his ruth,	Dido	3.2.47	Juno
And wish that I had never wrongd him so:	Dido	3.2.48	Juno
Bootles I sawe it was to warre with fate,	Dido	3.2.49	Juno
Wherefore I [chaungd] <chaunge> my counsell with the time,	Dido	3.2.51	Juno
how may I deserve/Such amourous favours at thy beautious hand?	Dido	3.2.64	Juno
How highly I doe prize this amitie,	Dido	3.2.67	Juno
Which I will make in quittance of thy love:	Dido	3.2.69	Juno
Well could I like this reconcilements meanes,	Dido	3.2.81	Venus
But much I feare my sonne will nere consent,	Dido	3.2.82	Venus
Faire Queene of love, I will devorce these doubts,	Dido	3.2.85	Juno
Sister, I see you savour of my wiles,	Dido	3.2.96	Venus
Whom I will beare to Ida in mine armes,	Dido	3.2.99	Venus
Aeneas, thinke not but I honor thee,	Dido	3.3.1	Dido
Untill I gird my quiver to my side:	Dido	3.3.8	Dido
Why, man of Troy, doe I offend thine eyes?	Dido	3.3.17	Iarbus
And meddle not with any that I love:	Dido	3.3.22	Dido
I would have either drunke his dying bloud,	Dido	3.3.28	Iarbus
Or els I would have given my life in gage.	Dido	3.3.29	Iarbus
I mother, I shall one day be a man,	Dido	3.3.35	Cupid
Which I will breake betwixt a Lyons jawes.	Dido	3.3.38	Cupid
I, and outface him to, doe what he can.	Dido	3.3.40	Cupid
And mought I live to see him sacke rich Thebes,	Dido	3.3.42	Aeneas
Then would I wish me with Anchises Tombe,	Dido	3.3.44	Aeneas
And might I live to see thee shipt away,	Dido	3.3.46	Iarbus
Then would I wish me in faire Didos armes,	Dido	3.3.48	Iarbus
As I remember, here you shot the Deere,	Dido	3.3.51	Achat
I, this it is which wounds me to the death,	Dido	3.3.63	Iarbus
What shall I doe thus wronged with disdaine?	Dido	3.3.69	Iarbus
And yet I am not free, oh would I were.	Dido	3.4.6	Dido
The thing that I will dye before I aske,	Dido	3.4.9	Dido
And yet desire to have before I dye.	Dido	3.4.10	Dido
The man that I doe eye where ere I am,	Dido	3.4.18	Dido
And I must perish in his burning armes.	Dido	3.4.22	Dido
I must conceale/The torment, that it bootes me not reveale,	Dido	3.4.25	Dido
Doe shame her worst, I will disclose my griefe:--	Dido	3.4.28	Dido
Aeneas, thou art he, what did I say?	Dido	3.4.29	Dido
Something it was that now I have forgot.	Dido	3.4.30	Dido
It was because I saw no King like thee,	Dido	3.4.35	Dido
But now that I have found what to effect,	Dido	3.4.37	Dido
I followe one that loveth fame for me,	Dido	3.4.38	Dido
With this my hand I give to you my heart,	Dido	3.4.43	Aeneas
What more then Delian musicke doe I heare,	Dido	3.4.52	Dido

I (cont.)

I thinke some fell Inchantresse dwelleth here,	Dido	4.1.3	Iarbus
In all my life I never knew the like,	Dido	4.1.7	Anna
I thinke it was the divels revelling night,	Dido	4.1.9	Achat
I might have stakte them both unto the earth,	Dido	4.1.23	Iarbus
I see Aeneas sticketh in your minde,	Dido	4.1.33	Dido
But I will soone put by that stumbling blocke,	Dido	4.1.34	Dido
That I may pacifie that gloomie Jove,	Dido	4.2.2	Iarbus
I Anna, is there ought you would with me?	Dido	4.2.24	Iarbus
I would be thankfull for such curtesie.	Dido	4.2.29	Anna
Anna, against this Troian doe I pray,	Dido	4.2.30	Iarbus
And I will either move the thoughtles flint,	Dido	4.2.40	Iarbus
I will not leave Iarbus whom I love,	Dido	4.2.43	Anna
I may nor will list to such loathsome chaunge,	Dido	4.2.47	Iarbus
For I will flye from these alluring eyes,	Dido	4.2.50	Iarbus
For I have honey to present thee with:	Dido	4.2.53	Anna
Let my Phenissa graunt, and then I goe:	Dido	4.3.6	Aeneas
Come backe, come backe, I heare her crye a farre,	Dido	4.3.27	Aeneas
Troians abourd, and I will follow you,	Dido	4.3.45	Aeneas
I faine would goe, yet beautie calles me backe:	Dido	4.3.46	Aeneas
But if I use such ceremonious thankes,	Dido	4.3.49	Aeneas
I may not dure this female drudgerie,	Dido	4.3.55	Aeneas
I would have given Achates store of gold,	Dido	4.4.7	Dido
See where they come, how might I doe to chide?	Dido	4.4.13	Dido
I went to take my farewell of Achates.	Dido	4.4.18	Aeneas
Because I feard your grace would keepe me here.	Dido	4.4.20	Achat
I charge thee put to sea and stay not here.	Dido	4.4.22	Dido
Thinkes Dido I will goe and leave him here?	Dido	4.4.30	Aeneas
me, for I forgot/That yong Ascanius lay with me this night:	Dido	4.4.31	Dido
How vaine am I to weare this Diadem,	Dido	4.4.40	Aeneas
That thou and I unseene might sport our selves:	Dido	4.4.51	Dido
When I leave thee, death be my punishment,	Dido	4.4.56	Aeneas
Shall vulgar pesants storme at what I doe?	Dido	4.4.73	Dido
And I the Goddesse of all these, commaund/Aeneas ride as	Dido	4.4.77	Dido
I, and unlesse the destinies be false,	Dido	4.4.81	Aeneas
I shall be planted in as rich a land.	Dido	4.4.82	Aeneas
Doe as I bid thee sister, leade the way,	Dido	4.4.85	Dido
And thou and I Achates, for revenge,	Dido	4.4.88	Aeneas
I, but it may be he will leave my love,	Dido	4.4.97	Dido
O that I had a charme to keepe the windes/Within the closure of	Dido	4.4.99	Dido
I must prevent him, wishing will not serve:	Dido	4.4.104	Dido
Yet lest he should, for I am full of feare,	Dido	4.4.108	Dido
What if I sinke his ships? O heele frowne:	Dido	4.4.110	Dido
Better he frowne, then I should dye for griefe:	Dido	4.4.111	Dido
I cannot see him frowne, it may not be:	Dido	4.4.112	Dido
If he forsake me not, I never dye,	Dido	4.4.121	Dido
For in his lookes I see eternitie,	Dido	4.4.122	Dido
Ile hang ye in the chamber where I lye,	Dido	4.4.128	Dido
So I may have Aeneas in mine armes.	Dido	4.4.135	Dido
To measure how I prize Aeneas love,	Dido	4.4.140	Dido
And yet I blame thee not, thou art but wood.	Dido	4.4.143	Dido
Why should I blame Aeneas for his flight?	Dido	4.4.148	Dido
Which I bestowd upon his followers:	Dido	4.4.162	Dido
Whither must I goe? Ile stay with my mother.	Dido	4.5.2	Cupid
I have an Orchard that hath store of plums,	Dido	4.5.4	Nurse
Nurse I am wearie, will you carrie me?	Dido	4.5.15	Cupid
I, so youle dwell with me and call me mother.	Dido	4.5.16	Nurse
So youle love me, I care not if I doe.	Dido	4.5.17	Cupid
That I might live to see this boy a man,	Dido	4.5.18	Nurse
Say Dido what she will I am not old,	Dido	4.5.21	Nurse
Ile be no more a widowe, I am young,	Dido	4.5.22	Nurse
O what meane I to have such foolish thoughts!	Dido	4.5.25	Nurse
Why, I may live a hundred yeares,/Fourescore is but a girles	Dido	4.5.31	Nurse
Why doe I thinke of love now I should dye?	Dido	4.5.34	Nurse
O how unwise was I to say him nay!	Dido	4.5.37	Nurse
For I will grace them with a fairer frame,	Dido	5.1.5	Aeneas
From golden India Ganges will I fetch,	Dido	5.1.8	Aeneas
That have I not determinde with my selfe.	Dido	5.1.19	Aeneas
Nay, I will have it calde Anchisaeon,	Dido	5.1.22	Aeneas
Whom doe I see, Joves winged messenger?	Dido	5.1.25	Aeneas
Whom I have brought from Ida where he slept,	Dido	5.1.40	Hermes
And givest not eare unto the charge I bring?	Dido	5.1.52	Hermes
I tell thee thou must straight to Italy,	Dido	5.1.53	Hermes
How should I put into the raging deepe,	Dido	5.1.55	Aeneas
Iarbus, I am cleane besides my selfe,	Dido	5.1.63	Aeneas
Nor I devise by what meanes to contrive.	Dido	5.1.66	Aeneas
As how I pray, may I entreate you tell.	Dido	5.1.67	Iarbus
When as I want both rigging for my fleete,	Dido	5.1.69	Aeneas
For I will furnish thee with such supplies:	Dido	5.1.72	Iarbus
Whil'st I rest thankfull for this curtesie.	Dido	5.1.77	Aeneas
Now will I haste unto Lavinian shoare,	Dido	5.1.78	Aeneas
How loth I am to leave these Libian bounds,	Dido	5.1.81	Aeneas
I feare I sawe Aeneas little sonne,	Dido	5.1.83	Dido
Pardon me though I aske, love makes me aske.	Dido	5.1.90	Dido
O pardon me, if I resolve thee why:	Dido	5.1.91	Aeneas
Aeneas will not faine with his deare love,/I must from hence:	Dido	5.1.93	Aeneas
swift Mercury/When I was laying a platforme for these walles,	Dido	5.1.94	Aeneas
I am commaunded by immortall Jove,	Dido	5.1.99	Aeneas
Not from my heart, for I can hardly goe,	Dido	5.1.103	Aeneas
And yet I may not stay, Dido farewell.	Dido	5.1.104	Aeneas
I dye, if my Aeneas say farewell.	Dido	5.1.108	Dido
Let me goe, farewell, I must from hence,	Dido	5.1.110	Dido
Am I lesse faire then when thou sawest me first?	Dido	5.1.115	Dido

I (cont.)

Wherein have I offended Jupiter,	Dido	5.1.129	Dido
And I be calde a second Helena.	Dido	5.1.148	Dido
Had I a sonne by thee, the griefe were lesse,	Dido	5.1.149	Dido
That I might see Aeneas in his face:	Dido	5.1.150	Dido
If words might move me I were overcome.	Dido	5.1.154	Aeneas
Repairde not I thy ships, made thee a King,	Dido	5.1.163	Dido
And I for pitie harbord in my bosome,	Dido	5.1.166	Dido
I hope that that which love forbids me doe,	Dido	5.1.170	Dido
I traytor, and the waves shall cast thee up,	Dido	5.1.174	Dido
I have not power to stay thee: is he gone?	Dido	5.1.183	Dido
I but heele come againe, he cannot goe,	Dido	5.1.184	Dido
And I will live a private life with him.	Dido	5.1.198	Dido
I never vow'd at Aulis gulfe/The desolation of his native Troy,	Dido	5.1.202	Dido
I crave but this, he stay a tide or two,	Dido	5.1.207	Dido
That I may learne to beare it patiently,	Dido	5.1.208	Dido
If he depart thus suddenly, I dye:	Dido	5.1.209	Dido
I goe faire sister, heavens graunt good successe.	Dido	5.1.211	Anna
I thinke some Fairies have beguiled me.	Dido	5.1.215	Nurse
And I am thus deluded of my boy:	Dido	5.1.219	Dido
I know not what you meane by treason, I,	Dido	5.1.222	Nurse
I am as true as any one of yours.	Dido	5.1.223	Nurse
My sister comes, I like not her sad lookes.	Dido	5.1.225	Dido
Before I came, Aeneas was abourd,	Dido	5.1.226	Anna
But I cride out, Aeneas, false Aeneas stay.	Dido	5.1.228	Anna
Which when I viewd, I cride, Aeneas stay,	Dido	5.1.232	Anna
Then carelesly I rent my haire for griefe,	Dido	5.1.236	Anna
And stay a while to heare what I could say,	Dido	5.1.239	Anna
O Anna, Anna, I will follow him.	Dido	5.1.241	Dido
That they may melt and I fall in his armes:	Dido	5.1.245	Dido
That I may swim to him like Tritons neece:	Dido	5.1.247	Dido
That I may tice a Dolphin to the shoare,	Dido	5.1.249	Dido
Dido I am, unlesse I be deceiv'd,	Dido	5.1.264	Dido
And must I rave thus for a runnagate?	Dido	5.1.265	Dido
Must I make ships for him to saile away?	Dido	5.1.266	Dido
fleete, what shall I doe/But dye in furie of this oversight?	Dido	5.1.268	Dido
I, I must be the murderer of my selfe:	Dido	5.1.270	Dido
No but I am not, yet I will be straight.	Dido	5.1.271	Dido
now have I found a meane/To rid me from these thoughts of	Dido	5.1.272	Dido
How long shall I with griefe consume my daies,	Dido	5.1.281	Iarbus
For I entend a private Sacrifize,	Dido	5.1.286	Dido
I, I, Iarbus, after this is done,	Dido	5.1.289	Dido
Here lye the garment which I cloath'd him in,	Dido	5.1.298	Dido
Dido I come to thee, aye me Aeneas.	Dido	5.1.318	Iarbus
And mixe her bloud with thine, this shall I doe,	Dido	5.1.326	Anna
Now sweet Iarbus stay, I come to thee.	Dido	5.1.329	Anna
Brother Cosroe, I find my selfe agreev'd,	1Tamb	1.1.1	Mycet
I know you have a better wit than I.	1Tamb	1.1.5	Mycet
Brother, I see your meaning well enough.	1Tamb	1.1.18	Mycet
And thorough your Planets I perceive you thinke,	1Tamb	1.1.19	Mycet
I am not wise enough to be a kinge,	1Tamb	1.1.20	Mycet
But I refer me to my noble men,	1Tamb	1.1.21	Mycet
I might command you to be slaine for this,	1Tamb	1.1.23	Mycet
Meander, might I not?	1Tamb	1.1.24	Mycet
I meane it not, but yet I know I might,	1Tamb	1.1.26	Mycet
And as I heare, doth meane to pull my plumes.	1Tamb	1.1.33	Mycet
Oft have I heard your Majestie complain,	1Tamb	1.1.35	Meandr
Whom I may tearme a Damon for thy love.	1Tamb	1.1.50	Mycet
I long to see thee backe returne from thence,	1Tamb	1.1.76	Mycet
That I may view these milk-white steeds of mine,	1Tamb	1.1.77	Mycet
Then now my Lord, I humbly take my leave.	1Tamb	1.1.81	Therid
Well here I sweare by this my royal seat--	1Tamb	1.1.97	Mycet
What, shall I call thee brother?	1Tamb	1.1.103	Mycet
Meander come, I am abus'd Meander.	1Tamb	1.1.106	Mycet
Ah Menaphon, I passe not for his threates,	1Tamb	1.1.109	Cosroe
Wel, since I see the state of Persea droope,	1Tamb	1.1.155	Cosroe
I willingly receive th'emperiall crowne,	1Tamb	1.1.157	Cosroe
Then I may seeke to gratifie your love,	1Tamb	1.1.171	Cosroe
I doubt not shortly but to raigne sole king,	1Tamb	1.1.175	Cosroe
I know it wel my Lord, and thanke you all.	1Tamb	1.1.187	Cosroe
Where all my youth I have bene governed,	1Tamb	1.2.13	Zenoc
But since I love to live at liberty,	1Tamb	1.2.26	Tamb
I am (my Lord), for so you do import.	1Tamb	1.2.33	Zenoc
I am a Lord, for so my deeds shall proove,	1Tamb	1.2.34	Tamb
Lie here ye weedes that I disdaine to weare,	1Tamb	1.2.41	Tamb
Me thinks I see kings kneeling at his feet,	1Tamb	1.2.55	Techel
I hope our Ladies treasure and our owne,	1Tamb	1.2.74	Agidas
Thinke you I way this treasure more than you?	1Tamb	1.2.84	Tamb
But this is she with whom I am in love.	1Tamb	1.2.108	Tamb
And I that triumpht so be overcome.	1Tamb	1.2.115	Tamb
Or looke you, I should play the Orator?	1Tamb	1.2.129	Tamb
I heare them come, shal we encounter them?	1Tamb	1.2.149	Techel
Whom seekst thou Persean? I am Tamburlain.	1Tamb	1.2.153	Tamb
I see the folly of thy Emperour:	1Tamb	1.2.167	Tamb
I hold the Fates bound fast in yron chaines,	1Tamb	1.2.174	Tamb
That I shall be the Monark of the East,	1Tamb	1.2.185	Tamb
(I cal it meane, because being yet obscure,	1Tamb	1.2.203	Tamb
But shall I proove a Traitor to my King?	1Tamb	1.2.226	Therid
I yeeld my selfe, my men and horse to thee:	1Tamb	1.2.229	Therid
Which is as much as if I swore by heaven,	1Tamb	1.2.233	Tamb
These are my friends in whom I more rejoice,	1Tamb	1.2.241	Tamb
Before I crowne you kings in Asia.	1Tamb	1.2.246	Tamb
For you then Maddam, I am out of doubt.	1Tamb	1.2.258	Tamb

I (cont.)

I must be pleasde perforce, wretched Zenocrate.	1Tamb	1.2.259	Zenoc
I will my Lord.	1Tamb	2.1.69	Menaph
I tel you true my heart is swolne with wrath,	1Tamb	2.2.2	Mycet
I thinke it would:	1Tamb	2.2.9	Mycet
wel then, by heavens I sweare,/Aurora shall not peepe out of	1Tamb	2.2.9	Mycet
But I will have Cosroe by the head,	1Tamb	2.2.11	Mycet
Tell you the rest (Meander) I have said.	1Tamb	2.2.13	Mycet
And having thee, I have a jewell sure:	1Tamb	2.2.56	Mycet
Go on my Lord, and give your charge I say,	1Tamb	2.2.57	Mycet
Now worthy Tamburlaine, have I reposde,	1Tamb	2.3.1	Cosroe
I take thy doome for satisfaction.	1Tamb	2.3.5	Cosroe
To swarme unto the Ensigne I support.	1Tamb	2.3.14	Tamb
As I shall be commended and excusde/For turning my poore charge	1Tamb	2.3.28	Therid
Which I esteeme as portion of my crown.	1Tamb	2.3.35	Cosroe
That I with these my friends and all my men,	1Tamb	2.3.43	Tamb
In what a lamentable case were I,	1Tamb	2.4.6	Mycet
Therefore in pollicie I thinke it good/To hide it close:	1Tamb	2.4.10	Mycet
So shall not I be knowen, or if I bee,	1Tamb	2.4.13	Mycet
Here will I hide it in this simple hole.	1Tamb	2.4.15	Mycet
Away, I am the King: go, touch me not.	1Tamb	2.4.20	Mycet
I marie am I: have you any suite to me?	1Tamb	2.4.24	Mycet
I would intreat you to speak but three wise wordes.	1Tamb	2.4.25	Tamb
So I can when I see my time.	1Tamb	2.4.26	Mycet
I, Didst thou ever see a fairer?	1Tamb	2.4.28	Mycet
Such another word, and I will have thee executed.	1Tamb	2.4.30	Mycet
No, I tooke it prisoner.	1Tamb	2.4.32	Tamb
You lie, I gave it you.	1Tamb	2.4.33	Mycet
No, I meane, I let you keep it.	1Tamb	2.4.35	Mycet
Wel, I meane you shall have it againe.	1Tamb	2.4.36	Tamb
Here take it for a while, I lend it thee,	1Tamb	2.4.37	Tamb
Till I may see thee hem'd with armed men.	1Tamb	2.4.38	Tamb
I marveile much he stole it not away.	1Tamb	2.4.42	Mycet
So do I thrice renowmed man at armes,	1Tamb	2.5.6	Cosroe
Thee doo I make my Regent of Persea,	1Tamb	2.5.8	Cosroe
Emperour in humblest tearms/I vow my service to your Majestie,	1Tamb	2.5.16	Meandr
Now will I gratify your former good,	1Tamb	2.5.30	Cosroe
I will not thank thee (sweet Ortigius)/Better replies shall	1Tamb	2.5.36	Cosroe
my brothers Campe/I leave to thee, and to Theridamas,	1Tamb	2.5.39	Cosroe
I long to sit upon my brothers throne.	1Tamb	2.5.47	Cosroe
I thinke the pleasure they enjoy in heaven/Can not compare with	1Tamb	2.5.58	Therid
Nay, though I praise it, I can live without it.	1Tamb	2.5.66	Therid
I, if I could with all my heart my Lord.	1Tamb	2.5.68	Techel
Why, that's wel said Techelles, so would I,	1Tamb	2.5.69	Tamb
Me thinks we should not, I am strongly moov'd,	1Tamb	2.5.75	Tamb
That if I should desire the Persean Crowne,	1Tamb	2.5.76	Tamb
I could attaine it with a woondrous ease,	1Tamb	2.5.77	Tamb
I know they would with our perswasions.	1Tamb	2.5.80	Therid
And if I prosper, all shall be as sure,	1Tamb	2.5.84	Tamb
I judge the purchase more important far.	1Tamb	2.5.92	Therid
So will I send this monstrous slave to hell,	1Tamb	2.6.7	Cosroe
same proportion of Elements/Resolve, I hope we are resembled,	1Tamb	2.6.27	Cosroe
I know not how to take their tyrannies.	1Tamb	2.7.41	Cosroe
Theridamas and Tamburlaine, I die,	1Tamb	2.7.51	Cosroe
Yet will I weare it in despight of them,	1Tamb	2.7.61	Tamb
Wils and commands (for say not I intreat)/Not once to set his	1Tamb	3.1.27	Bajzth
Tell him, I am content to take a truce,	1Tamb	3.1.31	Bajzth
Because I heare he beares a valiant mind.	1Tamb	3.1.32	Bajzth
Then stay thou with him, say I bid thee so.	1Tamb	3.1.35	Bajzth
I wil the captive Pioners of Argier,	1Tamb	3.1.58	Bajzth
may I presume/To know the cause of these unquiet fits:	1Tamb	3.2.1	Agidas
That I may live and die with Tamburlaine.	1Tamb	3.2.24	Zenoc
And higher would I reare my estimate,	1Tamb	3.2.53	Zenoc
If I were matcht with mightie Tamburlaine.	1Tamb	3.2.55	Zenoc
Surpriz'd with feare of hideous revenge,/I stand agast:	1Tamb	3.2.69	Agidas
I prophecied before and now I proove,	1Tamb	3.2.90	Agidas
I meane to meet him in Bithynia:	1Tamb	3.3.2	Tamb
I that am tearm'd the Scourge and Wrath of God,	1Tamb	3.3.44	Tamb
But as I live that towne shall curse the time/That Tamburlaine	1Tamb	3.3.59	Tamb
I meane t'incounter with that Bajazeth.	1Tamb	3.3.65	Tamb
I tell thee villaine, those that lead my horse/Have to their	1Tamb	3.3.69	Bajzth
And by the holy Alcaron I sweare,	1Tamb	3.3.76	Bajzth
Whom I have brought to see their overthrow.	1Tamb	3.3.81	Bajzth
I will not tell thee how Ile handle thee,	1Tamb	3.3.84	Tamb
I long to see those crownes won by our swords,	1Tamb	3.3.98	Therid
I speake it, and my words are oracles.	1Tamb	3.3.102	Tamb
Untill I bring this sturdy Tamburlain,	1Tamb	3.3.114	Bajzth
Which I will bring as Vassals to thy feete.	1Tamb	3.3.129	Tamb
I have of Turkes, Arabians, Moores and Jewes/Enough to cover	1Tamb	3.3.136	Bajzth
not endure to strike/So many blowes as I have heads for thee.	1Tamb	3.3.144	Bajzth
I tell thee shamelesse girle,/Thou shalt be Landresse to my	1Tamb	3.3.176	Zabina
But I shall turne her into other weedes,	1Tamb	3.3.180	Ebea
That I may see him issue Conquerour.	1Tamb	3.3.194	Zenoc
Thou art deceiv'd, I heard the Trumpets sound,	1Tamb	3.3.203	Zabina
Straight will I use thee as thy pride deserves:	1Tamb	3.3.206	Zabina
But ere I die those foule Idolaters/Shall make me bonfires with	1Tamb	3.3.239	Bajzth
Those walled garrisons wil I subdue,	1Tamb	3.3.244	Tamb
Ile make the kings of India ere I die,	1Tamb	3.3.263	Tamb
I tell thee, were that Tamburlaine/As monsterous as Gorgon,	1Tamb	4.1.17	Souldn
That I may rise into my royall throne.	1Tamb	4.2.15	Tamb
Before I yeeld to such a slavery.	1Tamb	4.2.18	Bajzth
Then as I look downe to the damned Feends,	1Tamb	4.2.26	Bajzth
For I the chiefest Lamp of all the earth,	1Tamb	4.2.36	Tamb

I (cont.)

Even in Bythinia, when I took this Turke:				
But ere I martch to wealthy Persea,	1Tamb	4.2.42		Tamb
It shall be said, I made it red my selfe,	1Tamb	4.2.47		Tamb
Or els I sweare to have you whipt stark nak'd.	1Tamb	4.2.54		Tamb
And where I goe be thus in triumph drawne:	1Tamb	4.2.74		Anippe
This is my minde, and I will have it so.	1Tamb	4.2.86		Tamb
Shall talke how I have handled Bajazeth.	1Tamb	4.2.91		Tamb
I doubt not but the Governour will yeeld,	1Tamb	4.2.97		Tamb
Not for the world Zenocrate, if I have sworn:	1Tamb	4.2.113		Therid
I have, and sorrow for his bad successe:	1Tamb	4.2.125		Tamb
A sacred vow to heaven and him I make,	1Tamb	4.3.28		Souldn
As Concubine I feare, to feed his lust.	1Tamb	4.3.36		Souldn
I long to breake my speare upon his crest,	1Tamb	4.3.42		Souldn
For Fame I feare hath bene too prodigall,	1Tamb	4.3.46		Arabia
I, such a stomacke (cruel Tamburlane) as I could willingly feed	1Tamb	4.3.48		Arabia
Tamburlane) as I could willingly feed upon thy blood-raw hart.	1Tamb	4.4.11	P	Bajzth
them see (divine Zenocrate)/I glorie in the curses of my foes,	1Tamb	4.4.11	P	Bajzth
I pray you give them leave Madam, this speech is a goodly	1Tamb	4.4.29		Tamb
I will make thee slice the brawnes of thy armes into	1Tamb	4.4.32	P	Techel
Yet would I with my sword make Jove to stoope.	1Tamb	4.4.43	P	Tamb
I will confute those blind Geographers/That make a triple	1Tamb	4.4.74		Tamb
Excluding Regions which I meane to trace,	1Tamb	4.4.75		Tamb
Here at Damascus will I make the Point/That shall begin the	1Tamb	4.4.77		Tamb
My jointes benumb'd, unlesse I eat, I die.	1Tamb	4.4.81		Tamb
I Tyrant, and more meat.	1Tamb	4.4.98		Bajzth
I (my Lord) but none save kinges must feede with these.	1Tamb	4.4.102	P	Bajzth
I crowne you here (Theridamas) King of Argier:	1Tamb	4.4.109	P	Therid
Nor shall they long be thine, I warrant them.	1Tamb	4.4.116	P	Tamb
Deserve these tytles I endow you with,	1Tamb	4.4.119		Bajzth
Zenocrate, I will not crowne thee yet,	1Tamb	4.4.125		Tamb
Until with greater honors I be grac'd.	1Tamb	4.4.139		Tamb
I feare the custome proper to his sword,	1Tamb	4.4.140		Tamb
But I am pleasde you shall not see him there:	1Tamb	5.1.13		Govnr
Away with them I say and shew them death.	1Tamb	5.1.113		Tamb
I will not spare these proud Egyptians,	1Tamb	5.1.120		Tamb
A sight as banefull to their soules I think/As are Thessalian	1Tamb	5.1.121		Tamb
I thus conceiving and subduing both:	1Tamb	5.1.132		Tamb
I, my Lord.	1Tamb	5.1.183		Tamb
No more there is not I warrant thee Techelles.	1Tamb	5.1.193	P	Attend
And now my footstoole, if I loose the field,	1Tamb	5.1.202		Tamb
I may poure foorth my soule into thine armes,	1Tamb	5.1.209		Tamb
Sweet Bajazeth, I will prolong thy life,	1Tamb	5.1.279		Bajzth
Not I, bring milk and fire, and my blood I bring him againe,	1Tamb	5.1.283		Zabina
and fire, and my blood I bring him againe, teare me in peeces,	1Tamb	5.1.310	P	Zabina
I, even I speake to her.	1Tamb	5.1.310	P	Zabina
Make ready my Coch, my chaire, my jewels, I come, I come, I come	1Tamb	5.1.314	P	Zabina
ready my Coch, my chaire, my jewels, I come, I come, I come.	1Tamb	5.1.317	P	Zabina
Whom should I wish the fatall victory,	1Tamb	5.1.318	P	Zabina
Wherin the change I use condemns my faith,	1Tamb	5.1.385		Zenoc
Then shal I die with full contented heart,	1Tamb	5.1.390		Zenoc
If I had not bin wounded as I am.	1Tamb	5.1.417		Arabia
Ah that the deadly panges I suffer now,	1Tamb	5.1.421		Arabia
And that I might be privy to the state,	1Tamb	5.1.422		Arabia
Twas I my lord that gat the victory,	1Tamb	5.1.426		Arabia
Since I shall render all into your hands.	1Tamb	5.1.445		Tamb
Where ere I come the fatall sisters sweat,	1Tamb	5.1.447		Tamb
Since I arriv'd with my triumphant hoste,	1Tamb	5.1.454		Tamb
That I have sent from sundry foughten fields,	1Tamb	5.1.458		Tamb
And I am pleasde with this my overthrow,	1Tamb	5.1.466		Tamb
I record heaven, her heavenly selfe is cleare:	1Tamb	5.1.482		Souldn
I yeeld with thanks and protestations/Of endlesse honor to thee	1Tamb	5.1.487		Tamb
Then doubt I not but faire Zenocrate/Will soone consent to	1Tamb	5.1.496		Souldn
Els should I much forget my self, my Lord.	1Tamb	5.1.498		Tamb
for as the Romans usde/I here present thee with a naked sword.	1Tamb	5.1.500		Zenoc
And I wil sheath it to confirme the same.	2Tamb	1.1.82		Sgsmnd
forgetst thou I am he/That with the Cannon shooke Vienna	2Tamb	1.1.85		Sgsmnd
Forgetst thou that I sent a shower of dartes/Mingled with	2Tamb	1.1.86		Orcan
Vienna was besieg'd, and I was there,	2Tamb	1.1.91		Orcan
And tell me whether I should stoope so low,	2Tamb	1.1.103		Sgsmnd
Then here I sheath it, and give thee my hand,	2Tamb	1.1.112		Sgsmnd
But whilst I live will be at truce with thee.	2Tamb	1.1.127		Sgsmnd
Sweet Jesus Christ, I sollemnly protest,	2Tamb	1.1.130		Sgsmnd
I sweare to keepe this truce inviolable:	2Tamb	1.1.135		Sgsmnd
So am I fear'd among all Nations.	2Tamb	1.1.142		Orcan
I thank thee Sigismond, but when I war/All Asia Minor, Affrica,	2Tamb	1.1.151		Orcan
I will dispatch chiefe of my army hence/To faire Natolia, and	2Tamb	1.1.157		Orcan
My Lord I pitie it, and with my heart/Wish your release, but he	2Tamb	1.1.161		Orcan
Ah were I now but halfe so eloquent/To paint in woords, what	2Tamb	1.2.5		Almeda
I know thou wouldst depart from hence with me.	2Tamb	1.2.9		Callap
No talke of running, I tell you sir.	2Tamb	1.2.11		Callap
Hoping by some means I shall be releast,	2Tamb	1.2.16		Almeda
Which when I come aboord will hoist up saile,	2Tamb	1.2.23		Callap
Gallies mann'd with Christian slaves/I freely give thee,	2Tamb	1.2.24		Callap
And more than this, for all I cannot tell.	2Tamb	1.2.33		Callap
I like that well:	2Tamb	1.2.53		Callap
me my Lord, if I should goe, would you bee as good as your word?	2Tamb	1.2.61	P	Almeda
Shall I be made a king for my labour?	2Tamb	1.2.61	P	Almeda
As I am Callapine the Emperour,	2Tamb	1.2.62	P	Almeda
And by the hand of Mahomet I sweare,	2Tamb	1.2.64		Callap
Then here I sweare, as I am Almeda,	2Tamb	1.2.65		Callap
(For that's the style and tytle I have yet)/Although he sent a	2Tamb	1.2.67		Almeda
Yet would I venture to conduct your Grace,	2Tamb	1.2.69		Almeda
	2Tamb	1.2.72		Almeda

I (cont.)

And die before I brought you backe again.	2Tamb	1.2.73	Almeda
When you will my Lord, I am ready.	2Tamb	1.2.76	Almeda
Now goe I to revenge my fathers death.	2Tamb	1.2.78	Callap
in mine eies/Than all the wealthy kingdomes I subdewed:	2Tamb	1.3.19	Tamb
But that I know they issued from thy wombe,	2Tamb	1.3.33	Tamb
As I cried out for feare he should have falne.	2Tamb	1.3.42	Zenoc
And I will teach thee how to charge thy foe,	2Tamb	1.3.45	Tamb
Yes father, you shal see me if I live,	2Tamb	1.3.54	Celeb
When I am old and cannot mannage armes,	2Tamb	1.3.59	Tamb
Why may not I my Lord, as wel as he,	2Tamb	1.3.61	Amyras
Of all the provinces I have subdued/Thou shalt not have a foot,	2Tamb	1.3.71	Tamb
I would prepare a ship and saile to it,	2Tamb	1.3.90	Celeb
Ere I would loose the tytle of a king.	2Tamb	1.3.91	Celeb
And I would strive to swim through pooles of blood,	2Tamb	1.3.92	Amyras
Ere I would loose the tytle of a king.	2Tamb	1.3.95	Amyras
If any man will hold him, I will strike,	2Tamb	1.3.102	Calyph
For I have sworne by sacred Mahomet,	2Tamb	1.3.109	Tamb
Arch-Monarke of the world, I offer here,	2Tamb	1.3.114	Therid
My crowne, my selfe, and all the power I have,	2Tamb	1.3.115	Therid
I and my neighbor King of Fesse have brought/To aide thee in	2Tamb	1.3.130	Usumc
Which with my crowne I gladly offer thee.	2Tamb	1.3.136	Usumc
I here present thee with the crowne of Fesse,	2Tamb	1.3.140	Techel
and I might enter in/To see the state and majesty of heaven,	2Tamb	1.3.154	Tamb
Such lavish will I make of Turkish blood,	2Tamb	1.3.165	Tamb
And I have martch'd along the river Nile,	2Tamb	1.3.186	Techel
Whose triple Myter I did take by force,	2Tamb	1.3.189	Techel
From thence unto Cazates did I martch,	2Tamb	1.3.191	Techel
With whom (being women) I vouchsaft a league,	2Tamb	1.3.193	Techel
The Westerne part of Affrike, where I view'd/The Ethiopian sea,	2Tamb	1.3.195	Techel
Therfore I tooke my course to Manico:	2Tamb	1.3.198	Techel
Where unresisted I remoov'd my campe.	2Tamb	1.3.199	Techel
I came to Cubar, where the Negros dwell,	2Tamb	1.3.201	Techel
I took the king, and lead him bound in chaines/Unto Damasco,	2Tamb	1.3.204	Techel
lead him bound in chaines/Unto Damasco, where I staid before.	2Tamb	1.3.205	Techel
I left the confines and the bounds of Affrike/And made a voyage	2Tamb	1.3.207	Therid
Where by the river Tyros I subdew'd/Stoka, Padalia, and	2Tamb	1.3.209	Therid
Which in despight of them I set on fire:	2Tamb	1.3.213	Therid
From thence I crost the Gulfe, call'd by the name/Mare magiore,	2Tamb	1.3.214	Therid
I, liquid golde when we have conquer'd him,	2Tamb	1.3.223	Tamb
Your Majesty remembers I am sure/What cruell slaughter of our	2Tamb	2.1.4	Fredrk
Though I confesse the othes they undertake,	2Tamb	2.1.42	Sgsmnd
Me thinks I see how glad the christian King/Is made, for joy of	2Tamb	2.2.20	Uribas
Have I not here the articles of peace,	2Tamb	2.2.30	Orcan
He by his Christ, and I by Mahomet?	2Tamb	2.2.32	Orcan
And make the power I have left behind/(Too litle to defend our	2Tamb	2.2.59	Orcan
Let the dishonor of the paines I feele,	2Tamb	2.3.5	Sgsmnd
And let this death wherein to sinne I die,	2Tamb	2.3.8	Sgsmnd
I will my Lord.	2Tamb	2.3.41	Uribas
I fare my Lord, as other Emperesses,	2Tamb	2.4.42	Zenoc
transfourme my love/In whose sweet being I repose my life,	2Tamb	2.4.48	Tamb
For should I but suspect your death by mine,	2Tamb	2.4.61	Zenoc
Yet let me kisse my Lord before I die,	2Tamb	2.4.69	Zenoc
with which I burst/The rusty beames of Janus Temple doores,	2Tamb	2.4.113	Tamb
And till I die thou shalt not be interr'd.	2Tamb	2.4.132	Tamb
As I have conquered kingdomes with my sword.	2Tamb	2.4.136	Tamb
This cursed towne will I consume with fire,	2Tamb	2.4.137	Tamb
And here will I set up her stature <statue>/And martch about it	2Tamb	2.4.140	Tamb
I will requite your royall gratitudes/With all the benefits my	2Tamb	3.1.8	Callap
And now I doubt not but your royall cares/Hath so provided for	2Tamb	3.1.20	Callap
I have a hundred thousand men in armes,	2Tamb	3.1.38	Orcan
And I as many from Jerusalem,	2Tamb	3.1.44	Jrslem
And I as many bring from Trebizon,	2Tamb	3.1.49	Trebiz
I march to meet and aide my neigbor kings,	2Tamb	3.1.60	Soria
I thinke it requisite and honorable,	2Tamb	3.1.70	Callap
That is a Gentleman (I know) at least.	2Tamb	3.1.72	Callap
Then wil I shortly keep my promise Almeda.	2Tamb	3.1.78	P Callap
Why, I thank your Majesty.	2Tamb	3.1.79	P Almeda
At every towne and castle I besiege,	2Tamb	3.2.36	Tamb
And when I meet an armie in the field,	2Tamb	3.2.38	Tamb
If I had wept a sea of teares for her,	2Tamb	3.2.47	Calyph
It would not ease the sorrow I sustaine.	2Tamb	3.2.48	Calyph
Now look I like a souldier, and this wound/As great a grace and	2Tamb	3.2.117	Tamb
And I sat downe, cloth'd with the massie robe,	2Tamb	3.2.123	Tamb
Whom I brought bound unto Damascus walles.	2Tamb	3.2.125	Tamb
While I sit smiling to behold the sight.	2Tamb	3.2.128	Tamb
I know not what I should think of it.	2Tamb	3.2.130	P Calyph
I long to pierce his bowels with my sword,	2Tamb	3.2.152	Usumc
I would not yeeld it: therefore doo your worst.	2Tamb	3.3.37	Capt
Yet I am resolute, and so farewell.	2Tamb	3.3.40	Capt
Pioners away, and where I stuck the stake,	2Tamb	3.3.41	Therid
Intrench with those dimensions I prescribed:	2Tamb	3.3.42	Therid
Lies heavy on my heart, I cannot live.	2Tamb	3.4.5	Capt
I feele my liver pierc'd and all my vaines,	2Tamb	3.4.6	Capt
Farewell sweet wife, sweet son farewell, I die.	2Tamb	3.4.10	Capt
For think ye I can live, and see him dead?	2Tamb	3.4.27	Sonne
Sweet mother strike, that I may meet my father.	2Tamb	3.4.30	Sonne
Killing my selfe, as I have done my sonne,	2Tamb	3.4.35	Olymp
Whose body with his fathers I have burnt,	2Tamb	3.4.36	Olymp
And for his sake here will I end my daies.	2Tamb	3.4.44	Olymp
Madam, I am so far in love with you,	2Tamb	3.4.78	Therid
Then carie me I care not where you will,	2Tamb	3.4.80	Olymp
Why, so he is Casane, I am here,	2Tamb	3.5.62	Tamb

I (cont.)

Ye petty kings of Turkye I am come,	2Tamb	3.5.64		Tamb
I doe you honor in the simile,	2Tamb	3.5.69		Tamb
For if I should as Hector did Achilles,	2Tamb	3.5.70		Tamb
I see how fearfully ye would refuse,	2Tamb	3.5.73		Tamb
I shall now revenge/My fathers vile abuses and mine owne.	2Tamb	3.5.90		Callap
you knowe I shall have occasion shortly to journey you.	2Tamb	3.5.114	P	Tamb
I here invest thee king of Ariadan,	2Tamb	3.5.130		Callap
that when I take him, I may knocke out his braines with them,	2Tamb	3.5.140	P	Tamb
I may knocke out his braines with them, and lock you in the	2Tamb	3.5.141	P	Tamb
I, my Lord, he was Calapines keeper.	2Tamb	3.5.152	P	Therid
hee shall not be put to that exigent, I warrant thee.	2Tamb	3.5.156	P	Soria
I smile to think, how when this field is fought,	2Tamb	3.5.165		Techel
I know sir, what it is to kil a man,	2Tamb	4.1.27		Calyph
I take no pleasure to be murtherous,	2Tamb	4.1.29		Calyph
As if I lay with you for company.	2Tamb	4.1.39		Calyph
I would not bide the furie of my father:	2Tamb	4.1.45		Amyras
Take you the honor, I will take my ease,	2Tamb	4.1.49		Calyph
I goe into the field before I need?	2Tamb	4.1.51		Calyph
And should I goe and kill a thousand men,	2Tamb	4.1.53		Calyph
I were as soone rewarded with a shot,	2Tamb	4.1.54		Calyph
And should I goe and do nor harme nor good,	2Tamb	4.1.56		Calyph
I might have harme, which all the good I have/Join'd with my	2Tamb	4.1.57		Calyph
which all the good I have/Join'd with my fathers crowne would	2Tamb	4.1.57		Calyph
Come, thou and I wil goe to cardes to drive away the time.	2Tamb	4.1.61	P	Calyph
They say I am a coward, (Perdicas) and I feare as litle their	2Tamb	4.1.67	P	Calyph
(Perdicas) and I feare as litle their tara, tantaras, their	2Tamb	4.1.67	P	Calyph
as I doe a naked Lady in a net of golde, and for feare I should	2Tamb	4.1.68	P	Calyph
and for feare I should be affraid, would put it off and come to	2Tamb	4.1.69	P	Calyph
I would my father would let me be put in the front of such a	2Tamb	4.1.72	P	Calyph
I beleeve there will be some hurt done anon amongst them.	2Tamb	4.1.74	P	Calyph
Yet pardon him I pray your Majesty.	2Tamb	4.1.97		Therid
Stand up my boyes, and I wil teach ye arms,	2Tamb	4.1.103		Tamb
O Samarcanda, where I breathed first,	2Tamb	4.1.105		Tamb
That I might moove the turning Spheares of heaven,	2Tamb	4.1.118		Tamb
By Mahomet, thy mighty friend I sweare,	2Tamb	4.1.121		Tamb
(If tyrannies wars justice ye repute)/I execute, enjoin'd me	2Tamb	4.1.148		Tamb
Nor am I made Arch-monark of the world,	2Tamb	4.1.150		Tamb
But since I exercise a greater name,	2Tamb	4.1.153		Tamb
I must apply my selfe to fit those tearmes,	2Tamb	4.1.155		Tamb
I will with Engines, never exercisde,	2Tamb	4.1.191		Tamb
And til by vision, or by speach I heare/Immortall Jove say,	2Tamb	4.1.198		Tamb
I will persist a terrour to the world,	2Tamb	4.1.200		Tamb
Wel met Olympia, I sought thee in my tent,	2Tamb	4.2.14		Therid
But when I saw the place obscure and darke,	2Tamb	4.2.15		Therid
Enrag'd I ran about the fields for thee,	2Tamb	4.2.17		Therid
But now I finde thee, and that feare is past.	2Tamb	4.2.20		Therid
With whom I buried al affections,	2Tamb	4.2.23		Olymp
And I will cast off armes and sit with thee,	2Tamb	4.2.44		Therid
I cannot love to be an Emperesse.	2Tamb	4.2.49		Olymp
I must and wil be pleasde, and you shall yeeld:	2Tamb	4.2.53		Therid
To proove it, I wil noint my naked throat,	2Tamb	4.2.68		Olymp
That I dissemble not, trie it on me.	2Tamb	4.2.76		Olymp
I wil Olympia, and will keep it for/The richest present of this	2Tamb	4.2.77		Therid
What, have I slaine her? Villaine, stab thy selfe:	2Tamb	4.2.82		Therid
But from Asphaltis, where I conquer'd you,	2Tamb	4.3.5		Tamb
To Byron here where thus I honor you?	2Tamb	4.3.6		Tamb
Thus am I right the Scourge of highest Jove,	2Tamb	4.3.24		Tamb
By which I hold my name and majesty.	2Tamb	4.3.26		Tamb
Let me have coach my Lord, that I may ride,	2Tamb	4.3.27		Amyras
I Turke, I tel thee, this same Boy is he,	2Tamb	4.3.57		Tamb
pompe than this)/Rifle the kingdomes I shall leave unsackt,	2Tamb	4.3.59		Tamb
Before I conquere all the triple world.	2Tamb	4.3.63		Tamb
I will prefer them for the funerall/They have bestowed on my	2Tamb	4.3.65		Tamb
(I meane such Queens as were kings Concubines)/Take them,	2Tamb	4.3.71		Tamb
Brawle not (I warne you) for your lechery,	2Tamb	4.3.75		Tamb
So will I ride through Samarcanda streets,	2Tamb	4.3.130		Tamb
For I wil cast my selfe from off these walles,	2Tamb	5.1.40		2Citzn
Before I bide the wrath of Tamburlaine.	2Tamb	5.1.42		2Citzn
I care not, nor the towne will never yeeld/As long as any life	2Tamb	5.1.47		Govnr
Tyrant, I turne the traitor in thy throat,	2Tamb	5.1.54		Govnr
down to the earth/Could not affright you, no, nor I my selfe,	2Tamb	5.1.91		Tamb
villaine I say,/Should I but touch the rusty gates of hell,	2Tamb	5.1.95		Tamb
Should I but touch the rusty gates of hell,	2Tamb	5.1.96		Tamb
But I have sent volleies of shot to you,	2Tamb	5.1.99		Tamb
Which when the citie was besieg'd I hid,	2Tamb	5.1.117		Govnr
Save but my life and I wil give it thee.	2Tamb	5.1.118		Govnr
I think I make your courage something quaile.	2Tamb	5.1.126		Tamb
I will my Lord.	2Tamb	5.1.135		Therid
That I may sheath it in this breast of mine,	2Tamb	5.1.143		Jrslem
And to command the citie, I will build/A Cytadell, that all	2Tamb	5.1.164		Tamb
I will about it straight, come Souldiers.	2Tamb	5.1.172		Techel
Whom I have thought a God? they shal be burnt.	2Tamb	5.1.176		Tamb
In vaine I see men worship Mahomet,	2Tamb	5.1.179		Tamb
And yet I live untoucht by Mahomet:	2Tamb	5.1.182		Tamb
Whose Scourge I am, and him will I obey.	2Tamb	5.1.185		Tamb
I have fulfil'd your highnes wil, my Lord,	2Tamb	5.1.203		Techel
I, good my Lord, let us in hast to Persea,	2Tamb	5.1.214		Therid
But stay, I feele my selfe distempered sudainly.	2Tamb	5.1.218		Tamb
Something Techelles, but I know not what,	2Tamb	5.1.220		Tamb
When I record my Parents slavish life,	2Tamb	5.2.19		Callap
Me thinks I could sustaine a thousand deaths,	2Tamb	5.2.22		Callap
not my Lord, I see great Mahomet/Clothed in purple clowdes,	2Tamb	5.2.31		Amasia

I (cont.)

She waines againe, and so shall his I hope,	2Tamb	5.2.47	Callap
Ah friends, what shal I doe, I cannot stand,	2Tamb	5.3.51	Tamb
Why, shal I sit and languish in this paine?	2Tamb	5.3.56	Tamb
That if I perish, heaven and earth may fade.	2Tamb	5.3.60	Tamb
Not last Techelles, no, for I shall die.	2Tamb	5.3.66	Tamb
Who flies away at every glance I give,	2Tamb	5.3.70	Tamb
And when I look away, comes stealing on:	2Tamb	5.3.71	Tamb
I and myne armie come to lode thy barke/With soules of thousand	2Tamb	5.3.73	Tamb
Looke where he goes, but see, he comes againe/Because I stay:	2Tamb	5.3.76	Tamb
I view'd your urine, and the [Hipostasis] <Hipostates>/Thick	2Tamb	5.3.82	Phsitn
Then will I comfort all my vital parts,	2Tamb	5.3.100	Tamb
My looks shall make them flie, and might I follow,	2Tamb	5.3.107	Tamb
I joy my Lord, your highnesse is so strong,	2Tamb	5.3.110	Usumc
I know it wil Casane:	2Tamb	5.3.113	Tamb
In spight of death I will goe show my face.	2Tamb	5.3.114	Tamb
And could I but a while pursue the field,	2Tamb	5.3.117	Tamb
But I perceive my martial strength is spent,	2Tamb	5.3.119	Tamb
In vaine I strive and raile against those powers,	2Tamb	5.3.120	Tamb
Here I began to martch towards Persea,	2Tamb	5.3.126	Tamb
where I tooke/The Turke and his great Empresse prisoners,	2Tamb	5.3.128	Tamb
Then martcht I into Egypt and Arabia,	2Tamb	5.3.130	Tamb
I meant to cut a channell to them both,	2Tamb	5.3.134	Tamb
I conquered all as far as Zansibar.	2Tamb	5.3.139	Tamb
I came at last to Graecia, and from thence/To Asia, where I	2Tamb	5.3.141	Tamb
Graecia, and from thence/To Asia, where I stay against my will,	2Tamb	5.3.142	Tamb
Which is from Scythia, where I first began,	2Tamb	5.3.143	Tamb
And shall I die, and this unconquered?	2Tamb	5.3.150	Tamb
And shal I die, and this unconquered?	2Tamb	5.3.158	Tamb
Shal still retaine my spirit, though I die,	2Tamb	5.3.173	Tamb
me, that I may resigne/My place and proper tytle to my sonne:	2Tamb	5.3.175	Tamb
That I may see thee crown'd before I die.	2Tamb	5.3.179	Tamb
With what a flinty bosome should I joy,	2Tamb	5.3.185	Amyras
How should I step or stir my hatefull feete,	2Tamb	5.3.195	Amyras
with what a broken hart/And damned spirit I ascend this seat,	2Tamb	5.3.207	Amyras
And let them know that I am Machevill,	Jew	Prol.7	Machvl
Admir'd I am of those that hate me most:	Jew	Prol.9	Machvl
I count Religion but a childish Toy,	Jew	Prol.14	Machvl
I am asham'd to heare such fooleries.	Jew	Prol.17	Machvl
But whither am I bound, I come not, I,	Jew	Prol.28	Machvl
I crave but this, Grace him as he deserves,	Jew	Prol.33	Machvl
Here have I purst their paltry [silverlings] <silverbings>.	Jew	1.1.6	Barab
why then I hope my ships/I sent for Egypt and the bordering	Jew	1.1.41	Barab
I sent for Egypt and the bordering Iles/Are gotten up by Nilus	Jew	1.1.42	Barab
I hope our credit in the Custome-house/Will serve as well as I	Jew	1.1.57	Barab
the Custome-house/Will serve as well as I were present there.	Jew	1.1.58	Barab
I goe.	Jew	1.1.68	1Merch
I neither saw them, nor inquir'd of them.	Jew	1.1.77	1Merch
Tush, they are wise; I know her and her strength:	Jew	1.1.81	Barab
And yet I wonder at this Argosie.	Jew	1.1.84	Barab
Rather had I a Jew be hated thus,	Jew	1.1.114	Barab
For I can see no fruits in all their faith,	Jew	1.1.116	Barab
I cannot tell, but we have scambled up/More wealth by farre	Jew	1.1.122	Barab
I, wealthier farre then any Christian.	Jew	1.1.128	Barab
I must confesse we come not to be Kings:	Jew	1.1.129	Barab
Oft have I heard tell, can be permanent.	Jew	1.1.133	Barab
I have no charge, nor many children,	Jew	1.1.136	Barab
Daughter, whom I hold as deare/As Agamemnon did his Iphegen:	Jew	1.1.137	Barab
And all I have is hers. But who comes here?	Jew	1.1.139	Barab
I feare their comming will afflict us all.	Jew	1.1.156	2Jew
I, like enough, why then let every man/Provide him, and be	Jew	1.1.170	Barab
I know you will; well brethren let us goe.	Jew	1.1.174	1Jew
Which Tribute all in policie, I feare,	Jew	1.1.181	Barab
To seize upon the Towne: I, that he seekes.	Jew	1.1.185	Barab
Warily garding that which I ha got.	Jew	1.1.188	Barab
I hope your Highnesse will consider us.	Jew	1.2.9	Govnr
I wish, grave [Governour], 'twere in my power/To favour you,	Jew	1.2.10	Calym
Wherein I may not, nay I dare not dally.	Jew	1.2.12	Calym
No, Governour, I will be no convertite.	Jew	1.2.82	Barab
Nor will I part so slightly therewithall.	Jew	1.2.87	Barab
Christians; what, or how can I multiply?	Jew	1.2.103	Barab
But say the Tribe that I descended of/Were all in generall cast	Jew	1.2.113	Barab
Shall I be tryed by their transgression?	Jew	1.2.115	Barab
I, but theft is worse:	Jew	1.2.125	Barab
I must be forc'd to steale and compasse more.	Jew	1.2.127	Barab
I, my Lord, we have seiz'd upon the goods/And wares of Barabas,	Jew	1.2.132	Offcrs
My ships, my store, and all that I enjoy'd;	Jew	1.2.139	Barab
Why I esteeme the injury farre lesse,	Jew	1.2.146	Barab
I, policie?	Jew	1.2.160	Barab
I banne their soules to everlasting paines/And extreme tortures	Jew	1.2.166	Barab
Why pine not I, and dye in this distresse?	Jew	1.2.173	Barab
You were a multitude, and I but one,	Jew	1.2.178	Barab
I wot his wealth/Was written thus:	Jew	1.2.181	Barab
I had at home, and in mine Argosie/And other ships that came	Jew	1.2.187	Barab
So that not he, but I may curse the day,	Jew	1.2.191	Barab
For onely I have toyl'd to inherit here/The months of vanity	Jew	1.2.196	Barab
I, I,/Pray leave me in my patience.	Jew	1.2.199	Barab
I, let me sorrow for this sudden chance,	Jew	1.2.206	Barab
'Tis in the trouble of my spirit I speake;	Jew	1.2.207	Barab
I, fare you well.	Jew	1.2.213	Barab
But I will learne to leave these fruitlesse teares,	Jew	1.2.230	Abigal
I closely hid.	Jew	1.2.247	Barab
But they will give me leave once more, I trow,	Jew	1.2.252	Barab

I (cont.)

For there I left the Governour placing Nunnes,	Jew	1.2.254		Abigal
You partiall heavens, have I deserv'd this plague?	Jew	1.2.259		Barab
in distresse/Thinke me so mad as I will hang my selfe,	Jew	1.2.263		Barab
That I may vanish ore the earth in ayre,	Jew	1.2.264		Barab
And leave no memory that e're I was.	Jew	1.2.265		Barab
No, I will live; nor loath I this my life:	Jew	1.2.266		Barab
Daughter, I have it:	Jew	1.2.270		Barab
I did.	Jew	1.2.279		Abigal
I, Daughter, for Religion/Hides many mischiefes from suspition.	Jew	1.2.281		Barab
I, but father they will suspect me there.	Jew	1.2.283		Abigal
Thus father shall I much dissemble.	Jew	1.2.289		Abigal
Well father, say I be entertain'd,	Jew	1.2.294		Abigal
There have I hid close underneath the plancke/That runs along	Jew	1.2.296		Barab
The gold and Jewels which I kept for thee.	Jew	1.2.298		Barab
No, Abigall, in this/It is not necessary I be seene.	Jew	1.2.302		Barab
For I will seeme offended with thee for't.	Jew	1.2.303		Barab
I, and of a moving spirit too, brother; but come,	Jew	1.2.328		2Fryar
And let me lodge where I was wont to lye.	Jew	1.2.333		Abigal
I doe not doubt by your divine precepts/And mine owne industry,	Jew	1.2.334		Abigal
As much I hope as all I hid is worth.	Jew	1.2.336		Barab
I charge thee on my blessing that thou leave/These divels, and	Jew	1.2.346		Barab
Blind, Fryer, I wrecke not thy perswasions.	Jew	1.2.355		Barab
For I had rather dye, then see her thus.	Jew	1.2.357		Barab
Noble Lodowicke, I have seene/The strangest sight, in my	Jew	1.2.375		Mthias
The strangest sight, in my opinion,/That ever I beheld.	Jew	1.2.377		Mthias
What wast I prethe?	Jew	1.2.377		Lodowk
I must and will, Sir, there's no remedy.	Jew	1.2.391		Mthias
And so will I too, or it shall goe hard.--	Jew	1.2.392		Lodowk
Till I have answer of my Abigall.	Jew	2.1.19		Barab
Now have I happily espy'd a time/To search the plancke my	Jew	2.1.20		Abigal
And here behold (unseene) where I have found/The gold, the	Jew	2.1.22		Abigal
Now I remember those old womens words,	Jew	2.1.24		Barab
And now me thinkes that I am one of those:	Jew	2.1.28		Barab
For whilst I live, here lives my soules sole hope,	Jew	2.1.29		Barab
And when I dye, here shall my spirit walke.	Jew	2.1.30		Barab
Come and receive the Treasure I have found.	Jew	2.1.38		Abigal
Peace, Abigal, 'tis I.	Jew	2.1.43		Barab
Oh Abigal, Abigal, that I had thee here too,	Jew	2.1.51		Barab
But I will practise thy enlargement thence:	Jew	2.1.53		Barab
That I may hover with her in the Ayre,	Jew	2.1.62		Barab
Governor of Malta, hither am I bound;	Jew	2.2.4		Bosco
And so am I, Delbosco is my name;	Jew	2.2.6		Bosco
Martin del Bosco, I have heard of thee;	Jew	2.2.19		Govnr
And not depart untill I see you free.	Jew	2.2.41		Bosco
and Vespasian conquer'd us)/Am I become as wealthy as I was:	Jew	2.3.11		Barab
and I have bought a house/As great and faire as is the	Jew	2.3.13		Barab
And there in spite of Malta will I dwell:	Jew	2.3.15		Barab
I, and his sonnes too, or it shall goe hard.	Jew	2.3.17		Barab
I am not of the Tribe of Levy, I,	Jew	2.3.18		Barab
I learn'd in Florence how to kisse my hand,	Jew	2.3.23		Barab
Even for charity I may spit intoo't.	Jew	2.3.29		Barab
One that I love for his good fathers sake.	Jew	2.3.31		Barab
I heare the wealthy Jew walked this way;	Jew	2.3.32		Lodowk
That I may have a sight of Abigall;	Jew	2.3.34		Lodowk
will I shew my selfe to have more of the Serpent then the Dove;	Jew	2.3.36	P	Barab
I, I, no doubt but shee's at your command.	Jew	2.3.39		Barab
Barabas, thou know'st I am the Governors sonne.	Jew	2.3.40		Lodowk
I wud you were his father too, Sir, that's al the harm I wish	Jew	2.3.41	P	Barab
you were his father too, Sir, that's al the harm I wish you:	Jew	2.3.41	P	Barab
Yet I have one left that will serve your turne:	Jew	2.3.50		Barab
I meane my daughter:--	Jew	2.3.51		Barab
I ha the poyson of the City for him,	Jew	2.3.53		Barab
The Diamond that I talke of, ne'r was foild:	Jew	2.3.56		Barab
I like it much the better.	Jew	2.3.61		Lodowk
So doe I too.	Jew	2.3.61		Barab
Come to my house and I will giv't your honour--	Jew	2.3.66		Barab
No, Barabas, I will deserve it first.	Jew	2.3.68		Lodowk
Against my will, and whether I would or no,	Jew	2.3.75		Barab
Seiz'd all I had, and thrust me out a doores,	Jew	2.3.76		Barab
I, but my Lord, the harvest is farre off:	Jew	2.3.79		Barab
And yet I know the prayers of those Nuns/And holy Fryers,	Jew	2.3.80		Barab
I meane in fulnesse of perfection.	Jew	2.3.85		Barab
No, but I doe it through a burning zeale,	Jew	2.3.87		Barab
As for the Diamond, Sir, I told you of,	Jew	2.3.91		Barab
It shall goe hard but I will see your death.	Jew	2.3.94		Barab
But now I must be gone to buy a slave.	Jew	2.3.95		Barab
No Sir, I can cut and shave.	Jew	2.3.113	P	Slave
Alas, Sir, I am a very youth.	Jew	2.3.115	P	Slave
I will serve you, Sir.	Jew	2.3.118	P	Slave
I, passing well.	Jew	2.3.122	P	Slave
I must have one that's sickly, and be but for sparing vittles:	Jew	2.3.123	P	Barab
I, marke him, you were best, for this is he	Jew	2.3.132		Barab
I pray, Sir, be no stranger at my house,	Jew	2.3.136		Barab
All that I have shall be at your command.	Jew	2.3.137		Barab
I feare me 'tis about faire Abigall.	Jew	2.3.139		Mthias
But I have sworne to frustrate both their hopes,	Jew	2.3.142		Barab
As for the Comment on the Machabees/I have it, Sir, and 'tis at	Jew	2.3.154		Barab
Marry will I, Sir.	Jew	2.3.160		Barab
Come, I have made a reasonable market,	Jew	2.3.161		1Offcr
And I will teach [thee] that shall sticke by thee:	Jew	2.3.168		Barab
Oh brave, master, I worship your nose for this.	Jew	2.3.173		Ithimr
I walke abroad a nights/And kill sicke people groaning under	Jew	2.3.174		Barab

I (cont.)

Sometimes I goe about and poyson wells;	Jew	2.3.176	Barab
I am content to lose some of my Crownes;	Jew	2.3.178	Barab
That I may, walking in my Gallery,	Jew	2.3.179	Barab
Being young I studied Physicke, and began/To practise first	Jew	2.3.181	Barab
There I enrich'd the Priests with burials,	Jew	2.3.183	Barab
And after that I was an Engineere,	Jew	2.3.186	Barab
Then after that was I an Usurer,	Jew	2.3.190	Barab
I fill'd the Jailes with Bankrouts in a yeare,	Jew	2.3.193	Barab
breast a long great Scrowle/How I with interest tormented him.	Jew	2.3.198	Barab
But marke how I am blest for plaguing them,	Jew	2.3.199	Barab
I have as much coyne as will buy the Towne.	Jew	2.3.200	Barab
One time I was an Hostler in an Inne,	Jew	2.3.205	Ithimr
And in the night time secretly would I steale/To travellers	Jew	2.3.206	Ithimr
I strowed powder on the Marble stones,	Jew	2.3.209	Ithimr
That I have laugh'd agood to see the cripples/Goe limping home	Jew	2.3.211	Ithimr
I have it for you, Sir; please you walke in with me:	Jew	2.3.220	Barab
What, ho, Abigall; open the doore I say.	Jew	2.3.221	Barab
I am a little busie, Sir, pray pardon me.	Jew	2.3.231	Barab
I know it:	Jew	2.3.238	Barab
yet I say make love to him;/Doe, it is requisite it should be	Jew	2.3.238	Barab
I weigh it thus much; I have wealth enough.	Jew	2.3.245	Barab
That I intend my daughter shall be thine.	Jew	2.3.254	Barab
I, Barabas, or else thou wrong'st me much.	Jew	2.3.255	Mthias
Oh heaven forbid I should have such a thought.	Jew	2.3.256	Barab
Pardon me though I weepe; the Governors sonne/Will, whether I	Jew	2.3.257	Barab
the Governors sonne/Will, whether I will or no, have Abigall:	Jew	2.3.258	Barab
Even now as I came home, he slipt me in,	Jew	2.3.267	Barab
And I am sure he is with Abigall.	Jew	2.3.268	Barab
What, hand in hand, I cannot suffer this.	Jew	2.3.276	Mthias
I, and take heed, for he hath sworne your death.	Jew	2.3.280	Barab
stands in feare/Of that which you, I thinke, ne're dreame upon,	Jew	2.3.283	Barab
He has my heart, I smile against my will.	Jew	2.3.287	Abigal
Barabas, thou know'st I have lov'd thy daughter long.	Jew	2.3.288	Lodowk
And now I can no longer hold my minde.	Jew	2.3.290	Lodowk
Nor I the affection that I beare to you.	Jew	2.3.291	Barab
This is thy Diamond, tell me, shall I have it?	Jew	2.3.292	Lodowk
Oh but I know your Lordship wud disdaine/To marry with the	Jew	2.3.294	Barab
'Tis not thy wealth, but her that I esteeme,	Jew	2.3.298	Lodowk
Yet crave I thy consent.	Jew	2.3.299	Lodowk
This gentle Magot, Lodowicke I meane,	Jew	2.3.305	Barab
What, shall I be betroth'd to Lodowicke?	Jew	2.3.308	Abigal
I have intreated her, and she will grant.	Jew	2.3.314	Barab
I cannot chuse, seeing my father bids:--	Jew	2.3.316	Abigal
Now have I that for which my soule hath long'd.	Jew	2.3.318	Lodowk
So have not I, but yet I hope I shall.	Jew	2.3.319	Barab
I know not, but farewell, I must be gone.	Jew	2.3.322	Abigal
Oh, is't the custome, then I am resolv'd:	Jew	2.3.329	Lodowk
Lodowicke, it is enough/That I have made thee sure to Abigal.	Jew	2.3.335	Barab
No; so shall I, if any hurt be done,	Jew	2.3.341	Barab
Doe so; loe here I give thee Abigall.	Jew	2.3.345	Barab
I cannot stay; for if my mother come,	Jew	2.3.353	Mthias
I cannot take my leave of him for teares:	Jew	2.3.355	Abigal
I will have Don Mathias, he is my love.	Jew	2.3.361	Abigal
I, I'le put her in.	Jew	2.3.363	Ithimr
Faith Master, I thinke by this/You purchase both their lives; is	Jew	2.3.365	Ithimr
Oh, master, that I might have a hand in this.	Jew	2.3.368	Ithimr
I, so thou shalt, 'tis thou must doe the deed:	Jew	2.3.369	Barab
I cannot choose but like thy readinesse:	Jew	2.3.377	Barab
As I behave my selfe in this, imploy me hereafter.	Jew	2.3.379	Ithimr
So, now will I goe in to Lodowicke,	Jew	2.3.381	Barab
Till I have set 'em both at enmitie.	Jew	2.3.383	Barab
But now against my will I must be chast.	Jew	3.1.4	Curtzn
And yet I know my beauty doth not faile.	Jew	3.1.5	Curtzn
Schollers I meane, learned and liberall;	Jew	3.1.8	Curtzn
'Tis silver, I disdaine it.	Jew	3.1.13	Curtzn
I, but the Jew has gold,	Jew	3.1.14	Pilia
And I will have it or it shall goe hard.	Jew	3.1.15	Pilia
I chanc'd to cast mine eye up to the Jewes counting-house where	Jew	3.1.18	P Pilia
up to the Jewes counting-house where I saw some bags of mony,	Jew	3.1.19	P Pilia
and in the night I clamber'd up with my hooks, and as I was	Jew	3.1.19	P Pilia
and as I was taking my choyce, I heard a rumbling in the house;	Jew	3.1.20	P Pilia
choyce, I heard a rumbling in the house; so I tooke onely this,	Jew	3.1.20	P Pilia
rumbling in the house; so I tooke onely this, and runne my way:	Jew	3.1.21	P Pilia
O the sweetest face that ever I beheld!	Jew	3.1.26	P Ithimr
I know she is a Curtezane by her attire:	Jew	3.1.26	P Ithimr
I give a hundred of the Jewes Crownes that I had such a	Jew	3.1.27	P Ithimr
a hundred of the Jewes Crownes that I had such a Concubine.	Jew	3.1.28	P Ithimr
Well, I have deliver'd the challenge in such sort,	Jew	3.1.29	Ithimr
I did it, and revenge it if thou dar'st.	Jew	3.2.4	Mthias
I, part 'em now they are dead: Farewell, farewell.	Jew	3.2.9	Barab
Oh leave to grieve me, I am griev'd enough.	Jew	3.2.17	Mater
I know not, and that grieves me most of all.	Jew	3.2.21	Govnr
Upon which Altar I will offer up/My daily sacrifice of sighes	Jew	3.2.31	Govnr
I have the bravest, gravest, secret, subtil, bottle-nos'd knave	Jew	3.3.9	P Ithimr
my master writ it, and I carried it, first to Lodowicke, and	Jew	3.3.19	P Ithimr
Am I Ithimore?	Jew	3.3.23	P Ithimr
So sure did your father write, and I cary the chalenge.	Jew	3.3.25	P Ithimr
And say, I pray them come and speake with me.	Jew	3.3.29	Abigal
I pray, mistris, wil you answer me to one question?	Jew	3.3.30	P Ithimr
I will forsooth, Mistris.	Jew	3.3.35	P Ithimr
But I perceive there is no love on earth,	Jew	3.3.47	Abigal
Know, holy Sir, I am bold to sollicite thee.	Jew	3.3.53	Abigal

I (cont.)

Abigal it is not yet long since/That I did labour thy admition,	Jew	3.3.57	1Fryar
And I was chain'd to follies of the world:	Jew	3.3.60	Abigal
The Abbasse of the house/Whose zealous admonition I embrace:	Jew	3.3.67	Abigal
Abigal I will, but see thou change no more,	Jew	3.3.70	1Fryar
I feare she knowes ('tis so) of my device/In Don Mathias and	Jew	3.4.7	Barab
For I have now no hope but even in thee;	Jew	3.4.16	Barab
Ithimore, intreat not for her, I am mov'd,	Jew	3.4.35	Barab
And [less] <least> thou yeeld to this that I intreat,	Jew	3.4.37	Barab
I cannot thinke but that thou hat'st my life.	Jew	3.4.38	Barab
Who I, master?	Jew	3.4.39	P Ithimr
I here adopt thee for mine onely heire,	Jew	3.4.43	Barab
All that I have is thine when I am dead,	Jew	3.4.44	Barab
And whilst I live use halfe; spend as my selfe;	Jew	3.4.45	Barab
I hold my head my master's hungry:	Jew	3.4.51	P Ithimr
I goe Sir.	Jew	3.4.51	P Ithimr
I have brought you a Ladle.	Jew	3.4.59	P Ithimr
And for thy sake, whom I so dearely love,	Jew	3.4.61	Barab
I but Ithimore seest thou this?	Jew	3.4.67	Barab
It is a precious powder that I bought/Of an Italian in Ancona	Jew	3.4.68	Barab
Saint Jaques Even) and then I say they use/To send their Almes	Jew	3.4.76	Barab
Well, master, I goe.	Jew	3.4.94	P Ithimr
What shall I doe with it?	Jew	3.4.107	P Ithimr
For I have other businesse for thee.	Jew	3.4.110	Barab
I am gone.	Jew	3.4.114	Ithimr
And for the Tribute-mony I am sent.	Jew	3.5.10	Basso
And I shall dye too, for I feele death comming.	Jew	3.6.8	Abigal
I sent for him, but seeing you are come/Be you my ghostly	Jew	3.6.11	Abigal
That in this house I liv'd religiously,	Jew	3.6.13	Abigal
But e're I came--	Jew	3.6.15	Abigal
I did offend high heaven so grievously,	Jew	3.6.17	Abigal
As I am almost desperate for my sinnes:	Jew	3.6.18	Abigal
First to Don Lodowicke, him I never lov'd;	Jew	3.6.23	Abigal
Mathias was the man that I held deare,	Jew	3.6.24	Abigal
And for his sake did I become a Nunne.	Jew	3.6.25	Abigal
To worke my peace, this I confesse to thee;	Jew	3.6.31	Abigal
So I have heard; pray therefore keepe it close.	Jew	3.6.37	Abigal
And witnesse that I dye a Christian.	Jew	3.6.40	Abigal
I, and a Virgin too, that grieves me most:	Jew	3.6.41	2Fryar
But I must to the Jew and exclaime on him,	Jew	3.6.42	2Fryar
I was afraid the poyson had not wrought;	Jew	4.1.4	Barab
I'de cut thy throat if I did.	Jew	4.1.11	Barab
No, but I grieve because she liv'd so long.	Jew	4.1.18	Barab
I smelt 'em e're they came.	Jew	4.1.22	Barab
Stay wicked Jew, repent, I say, and stay.	Jew	4.1.24	2Fryar
I feare they know we sent the poyson'd broth.	Jew	4.1.26	Barab
And so doe I, master, therfore speake 'em faire.	Jew	4.1.27	Ithimr
I, that thou hast--	Jew	4.1.29	1Fryar
True, I have mony, what though I have?	Jew	4.1.30	Barab
I, that thou art a--	Jew	4.1.32	1Fryar
What needs all this? I know I am a Jew.	Jew	4.1.33	Barab
I, thy daughter--	Jew	4.1.35	1Fryar
Oh speake not of her, then I dye with griefe.	Jew	4.1.36	Barab
I, remember that--	Jew	4.1.38	1Fryar
I must needs say that I have beene a great usurer.	Jew	4.1.39	Barab
I, but Barabas, remember Mathias and Don Lodowick.	Jew	4.1.43	P 2Fryar
I will not say that by a forged challenge they met.	Jew	4.1.45	P 2Fryar
My bosome [inmate] <inmates> <intimates>, but I must dissemble.	Jew	4.1.47	Barab
I have beene zealous in the Jewish faith,	Jew	4.1.51	Barab
A hundred for a hundred I have tane;	Jew	4.1.54	Barab
And now for store of wealth may I compare/With all the Jewes in	Jew	4.1.55	Barab
I am a Jew, and therefore am I lost.	Jew	4.1.57	Barab
I could afford to whip my selfe to death.	Jew	4.1.59	Barab
And so could I; but pennance will not serve.	Jew	4.1.60	Ithimr
Besides I know not how much weight in Pearle/Orient and round,	Jew	4.1.66	Barab
much weight in Pearle/Orient and round, have I within my house;	Jew	4.1.67	Barab
Have I debts owing; and in most of these,	Jew	4.1.73	Barab
to some religious house/So I may be baptiz'd and live therein.	Jew	4.1.76	Barab
I know that I have highly sinn'd,	Jew	4.1.80	Barab
I know they are, and I will be with you.	Jew	4.1.83	Barab
Then 'tis not for me; and I am resolv'd/You shall confesse me,	Jew	4.1.85	Barab
You see I answer him, and yet he stayes;	Jew	4.1.88	Barab
I will not goe for thee.	Jew	4.1.94	1Fryar
I never heard of any man but he/Malign'd the order of the	Jew	4.1.103	Barab
But doe you thinke that I beleeve his words?	Jew	4.1.105	Barab
And I am bound in charitie to requite it,	Jew	4.1.107	Barab
And so I will, oh Jacomo, faile not but come.	Jew	4.1.108	Barab
I warrant thee, Barabas.	Jew	4.1.113	1Fryar
So, now the feare is past, and I am safe:	Jew	4.1.114	Barab
What if I murder'd him e're Jacomo comes?	Jew	4.1.116	Barab
Now I have such a plot for both their lives,	Jew	4.1.117	Barab
not both these wise men to suppose/That I will leave my house,	Jew	4.1.123	Barab
Now Fryar Bernardine I come to you,	Jew	4.1.125	Barab
And after that, I and my trusty Turke--	Jew	4.1.127	Barab
Yes; and I know not what the reason is:	Jew	4.1.130	Ithimr
Doe what I can he will not strip himselfe,	Jew	4.1.131	Ithimr
I feare me he mistrusts what we intend.	Jew	4.1.133	Ithimr
Why true, therefore did I place him there:	Jew	4.1.137	Barab
Oh how I long to see him shake his heeles.	Jew	4.1.140	Ithimr
Pull hard, I say, you would have had my goods.	Jew	4.1.149	Barab
I, and our lives too, therfore pull amaine.	Jew	4.1.150	Ithimr
This is the houre/Wherein I shall proceed; Oh happy houre,	Jew	4.1.161	1Fryar
Wherein I shall convert an Infidell,	Jew	4.1.162	1Fryar

I (cont.)

And understanding I should come this way,	Jew	4.1.165		1Fryar
thou think'st I see thee not;/Away, I'de wish thee, and let me	Jew	4.1.169		1Fryar
I, master, he's slain; look how his brains drop out on's nose.	Jew	4.1.178	P	Ithimr
Good sirs I have don't, but no body knowes it but you two, I	Jew	4.1.180	P	1Fryar
I have don't, but no body knowes it but you two, I may escape.	Jew	4.1.181	P	1Fryar
So might my man and I hang with you for company.	Jew	4.1.182		Barab
I must be forc'd to give in evidence,	Jew	4.1.186		Barab
by this Bernardine/To be a Christian, I shut him out,	Jew	4.1.188		Barab
now I to keepe my word,/And give my goods and substance to your	Jew	4.1.189		Barab
Villaines, I am a sacred person, touch me not.	Jew	4.1.201		1Fryar
'Las I could weepe at your calamity.	Jew	4.1.203		Barab
I did.	Jew	4.2.2	P	Pilia
I did.	Jew	4.2.4	P	Pilia
I think so, and yet I cannot tell, for at the reading of the	Jew	4.2.6	P	Pilia
so, and yet I cannot tell, for at the reading of the letter,	Jew	4.2.6	P	Pilia
base slave as he should be saluted by such a tall man as I am,	Jew	4.2.10	P	Pilia
and so I left him, being driven to a non-plus at the critical	Jew	4.2.13	P	Pilia
conning his neck-verse I take it, looking of a Fryars	Jew	4.2.17	P	Pilia
whom I saluted with an old hempen proverb, Hodie tibi,	Jew	4.2.18	P	Pilia
tibi, cras mihi, and so I left him to the mercy of the Hangman:	Jew	4.2.19	P	Pilia
I never knew a man take his death so patiently as this Fryar;	Jew	4.2.21	P	Ithimr
And now I thinke on't, going to the execution, a fellow met me	Jew	4.2.27	P	Ithimr
with his lips; the effect was, that I should come to her house.	Jew	4.2.31	P	Ithimr
I wonder what the reason is.	Jew	4.2.32	P	Ithimr
It may be she sees more in me than I can find in my selfe:	Jew	4.2.33	P	Ithimr
and now would I were gone, I am not worthy to looke upon her.	Jew	4.2.36	P	Ithimr
I did Sir, and from this Gentlewoman, who as my selfe, and the	Jew	4.2.43	P	Pilia
I can with-hold no longer; welcome sweet love.	Jew	4.2.46		Curtzn
Now am I cleane, or rather fouly out of the way.	Jew	4.2.47	P	Ithimr
Pray pardon me, I must goe see a ship discharg'd.	Jew	4.2.51	P	Ithimr
Nay, I care not how much she loves me; Sweet Bellamira, would I	Jew	4.2.54	P	Ithimr
Sweet Bellamira, would I had my Masters wealth for thy sake.	Jew	4.2.55	P	Ithimr
If 'twere above ground I could, and would have it; but hee	Jew	4.2.57	P	Ithimr
I, and such as--Goe to, no more, I'le make him send me half he	Jew	4.2.66	P	Ithimr
I charge thee send me three hundred by this bearer, and this	Jew	4.2.75	P	Ithimr
I have no husband, sweet, I'le marry thee.	Jew	4.2.87		Curtzn
Whither will I not goe with gentle Ithimore?	Jew	4.2.99		Curtzn
I tooke him by the [beard] <sterd>, and look'd upon him thus;	Jew	4.2.105	P	Pilia
Tell him I must hav't.	Jew	4.2.118	P	Ithimr
I warrant your worship shall hav't.	Jew	4.2.119	P	Pilia
And if he aske why I demand so much, tell him, I scorne to	Jew	4.2.120	P	Ithimr
tell him, I scorne to write a line under a hundred crownes.	Jew	4.2.120	P	Ithimr
I am gone.	Jew	4.2.122	P	Pilia
'Tis not thy mony, but thy selfe I weigh:	Jew	4.2.124		Curtzn
Or else I will confesse: I, there it goes:	Jew	4.3.4		Barab
But if I get him, Coupe de Gorge for that.	Jew	4.3.5		Barab
And I by him must send three hundred crownes.	Jew	4.3.15		Barab
Jew, I must ha more gold.	Jew	4.3.18	P	Pilia
No Sir; and therefore I must have five hundred more.	Jew	4.3.22	P	Pilia
I, and the rest too, or else--	Jew	4.3.28	P	Pilia
I must make this villaine away:	Jew	4.3.29	P	Barab
No god-a-mercy, shall I have these crownes?	Jew	4.3.31		Pilia
I cannot doe it, I have lost my keyes.	Jew	4.3.32		Barab
Oh, if that be all, I can picke ope your locks.	Jew	4.3.33		Pilia
I know enough, and therfore talke not to me of your	Jew	4.3.36	P	Pilia
I am betraid.--	Jew	4.3.39		Barab
'Tis not five hundred Crownes that I esteeme,	Jew	4.3.40		Barab
five hundred Crownes that I esteeme,/I am not mov'd at that:	Jew	4.3.41		Barab
That he who knowes I love him as my selfe/Should write in this	Jew	4.3.42		Barab
You know I have no childe, and unto whom/Should I leave all but	Jew	4.3.44		Barab
no childe, and unto whom/Should I leave all but unto Ithimore?	Jew	4.3.45		Barab
Speake, shall I have 'um, Sir?	Jew	4.3.49		Pilia
Oh that I should part with so much gold!	Jew	4.3.51		Barab
As I wud see thee hang'd; oh, love stops my breath:	Jew	4.3.53		Barab
Never lov'd man servant as I doe Ithimore.	Jew	4.3.54		Barab
I know it, Sir.	Jew	4.3.55		Pilia
Pray when, Sir, shall I see you at my house?	Jew	4.3.56		Barab
Was ever Jew tormented as I am?	Jew	4.3.60		Barab
Well, I must seeke a meanes to rid 'em all,	Jew	4.3.63		Barab
his villany/He will tell all he knowes and I shall dye for't.	Jew	4.3.65		Barab
I have it.	Jew	4.3.66		Barab
I will in some disguize goe see the slave,	Jew	4.3.67		Barab
Of that condition I wil drink it up; here's to thee.	Jew	4.4.4	P	Ithimr
nothing; but I know what I know.	Jew	4.4.14	P	Ithimr
I had not thought he had been so brave a man.	Jew	4.4.16		Curtzn
son; he and I kild 'em both, and yet never touch'd 'em.	Jew	4.4.17	P	Ithimr
I carried the broth that poyson'd the Nuns, and he and I,	Jew	4.4.20	P	Ithimr
that poyson'd the Nuns, and he and I, snicle hand too fast,	Jew	4.4.21	P	Ithimr
Whilst I in thy incony lap doe tumble.	Jew	4.4.29		Ithimr
So, now I am reveng'd upon 'em all.	Jew	4.4.42		Barab
The scent thereof was death, I poyson'd it.	Jew	4.4.43		Barab
I scorne the Peasant, tell him so.	Jew	4.4.59	P	Ithimr
The Governour feeds not as I doe.	Jew	4.4.63	P	Barab
Oh raskall! I change my selfe twice a day.	Jew	4.4.65		Barab
Let me alone to urge it now I know the meaning.	Jew	4.4.79		Pilia
What e're I am, yet Governor heare me speake;	Jew	5.1.9		Curtzn
I bring thee newes by whom thy sonne was slaine:	Jew	5.1.10		Curtzn
Nuns, strangled a Fryar, and I know not what mischiefe beside.	Jew	5.1.14	P	Pilia
Goe fetch him straight. I alwayes fear'd that Jew.	Jew	5.1.18		Govnr
Nor me neither, I cannot out-run you Constable, oh my belly.	Jew	5.1.20	P	Ithimr
What a damn'd slave was I?	Jew	5.1.23		Barab
I confesse; your sonne and Mathias were both contracted unto	Jew	5.1.28	P	Ithimr

I (cont.)

I carried it, I confesse, but who writ it?	Jew		5.1.32	P Ithimr
Devils doe your worst, [I'le] <I> live in spite of you.	Jew		5.1.41	Barab
I hope the poyson'd flowers will worke anon.	Jew		5.1.43	Barab
I hope to see the Governour a slave,	Jew		5.1.67	Barab
My name is Barabas; I am a Jew.	Jew		5.1.72	Barab
I was imprison'd, but escap'd their hands.	Jew		5.1.77	Barab
I dranke of Poppy and cold mandrake juyce;	Jew		5.1.80	Barab
What should I say? we are captives and must yeeld.	Jew		5.2.6	Govnr
I, villains, you must yeeld, and under Turkish yokes/Shall	Jew		5.2.7	Calym
I now am Governour of Malta; true,	Jew		5.2.29	Barab
I, Lord, thus slaves will learne.	Jew		5.2.49	Barab
This is the reason that I sent for thee;	Jew		5.2.51	Barab
I see no reason but of Malta's wracke,	Jew		5.2.58	Govnr
Nor feare I death, nor will I flatter thee.	Jew		5.2.60	Govnr
said, within this Ile/In Malta here, that I have got my goods,	Jew		5.2.68	Barab
What will you give me if I render you/The life of Calymath,	Jew		5.2.79	Barab
shut/His souldiers, till I have consum'd 'em all with fire?	Jew		5.2.82	Barab
And I will send amongst the Citizens/And by my letters	Jew		5.2.86	Govnr
Governor, I enlarge thee, live with me,	Jew		5.2.91	Barab
To a solemne feast/I will invite young Selim-Calymath,/Where be	Jew		5.2.97	Barab
And I will warrant Malta free for ever.	Jew		5.2.101	Barab
I will be there, and doe as thou desirest;	Jew		5.2.103	Govnr
Then will I, Barabas, about this coyne,	Jew		5.2.107	Govnr
Thus loving neither, will I live with both,	Jew		5.2.111	Barab
I know; and they shall witnesse with their lives.	Jew		5.2.123	Barab
And now I see the Scituation,	Jew		5.3.5	Calym
I wonder how it could be conquer'd thus?	Jew		5.3.12	Calym
Malta's Governor, I bring/A message unto mighty Calymath;	Jew		5.3.13	Msngr
I feare me, Messenger, to feast my traine/Within a Towne of	Jew		5.3.21	Calym
Yet would I gladly visit Barabas,	Jew		5.3.24	Calym
I cannot feast my men in Malta wals,	Jew		5.3.34	Calym
I shall, my Lord.	Jew		5.3.42	Msngr
For happily I shall be in distresse,	Jew		5.4.6	Govnr
Why now I see that you have Art indeed.	Jew		5.5.4	Barab
For so I live, perish may all the world.	Jew		5.5.10	Barab
returne me word/That thou wilt come, and I am satisfied.	Jew		5.5.12	Barab
For if I keepe not promise, trust not me.	Jew		5.5.23	Barab
Here have I made a dainty Gallery,	Jew		5.5.33	Barab
I trust thy word, take what I promis'd thee.	Jew		5.5.43	Govnr
Companion-Bashawes, see I pray/How busie Barrabas is there above	Jew		5.5.51	Calym
I, Barabas, come Bashawes, attend.	Jew		5.5.59	Calym
For I will shew thee greater curtesie/Then Barabas would have	Jew		5.5.61	Govnr
Should I in pitty of thy plaints or thee,	Jew		5.5.72	Govnr
Know, Governor, 'twas I that slew thy sonne;	Jew		5.5.81	Barab
I fram'd the challenge that did make them meet:	Jew		5.5.82	Barab
Know, Calymath, I aym'd thy overthrow,	Jew		5.5.83	Barab
And had I but escap'd this stratagem,	Jew		5.5.84	Barab
I would have brought confusion on you all,	Jew		5.5.85	Barab
But I have rather chose to save thy life.	Jew		5.5.94	Govnr
I wishe this union and religious league,	P	3	1.3	Charls
Sister, I think your selfe will beare us company.	P	21	1.21	Charls
I will my good Lord.	P	22	1.22	QnMarg
My Lord I mervaile that th'aspiring Guise/Dares once adventure	P	36	1.36	Admral
Now shall I prove and guerdon to the ful,	P	68	2.11	Guise
Where are those perfumed gloves which I sent/To be poysoned,	P	70	2.13	Guise
I am my Lord, in what your grace commaundes till death.	P	76	2.19	P Pothec
Thankes my good freend, I will requite thy love.	P	78	2.21	Guise
I will my Lord.	P	90	2.33	P Souldr
Oft have I leveld, and at last have learnd,	P	94	2.37	Guise
That like I best that flyes beyond my reach.	P	99	2.42	Guise
For this, I wake, when others think I sleepe,	P	105	2.48	Guise
For this, I waite, that scornes attendance else:	P	106	2.49	Guise
For this, my quenchles thirst whereon I builde,	P	107	2.50	Guise
For this have I a largesse from the Pope,	P	119	2.62	Guise
Fye, I am ashamde, how ever that I seeme,	P	124	2.67	Guise
If I repaire not what he ruinates:	P	129	2.72	Guise
Him as a childe I dayly winne with words,	P	130	2.73	Guise
I execute, and he sustaines the blame.	P	132	2.75	Guise
I but, Navarre, Navarre.	P	149	2.92	Guise
As Caesar to his souldiers, so say I:	P	155	2.98	Guise
Those that hate me, will I learn to loath.	P	156	2.99	Guise
Give me a look, that when I bend the browes,	P	157	2.100	Guise
Maddame, I beseech your grace to except this simple gift.	P	166	3.1	P Pothec
I humbly thank your Majestie.	P	169	3.4	P Pothec
Help sonne Navarre, I am poysoned.	P	176	3.11	OldQn
but I hope it be/Only some naturall passion makes her sicke.	P	182	3.17	QnMarg
My heart doth faint, I dye.	P	186	3.21	OldQn
That I with her may dye and live againe.	P	190	3.25	Navrre
I my good Lord, shot through the arme.	P	198	3.33	Admral
I hope these reasons may serve my princely Sonne,	P	223	4.21	QnMoth
Well Madam, I referre it to your Majestie,	P	225	4.23	Charls
What you determine, I will ratifie.	P	227	4.25	Charls
Messenger, tell him I will see him straite.	P	247	4.45	Charls
Content, I will goe visite the Admirall.	P	251	4.49	Charls
And I will goe take order for his death.	P	252	4.50	Guise
I vow and sweare as I am King of France,	P	255	4.53	Charls
I deepely sorrow for your trecherous wrong:	P	263	4.61	Charls
And that I am not more secure my selfe,	P	264	4.62	Charls
Then I am carefull you should be preserved.	P	265	4.63	Charls
And every hower I will visite you.	P	272	4.70	Charls
I humbly thank your royall Majestie.	P	273	4.71	Admral
I sweare by this to be unmercifull.	P	277	5.4	Dumain

I (cont.)

I am disguisde and none knows who I am,	P 278	5.5	Anjoy
And therfore meane to murder all I meet.	P 279	5.6	Anjoy
And so will I.	P 280	5.7	Gonzag
And I.	P 281	5.8	Retes
I let the Admirall be first dispatcht.	P 283	5.10	Retes
O let me pray before I dye.	P 301	5.28	Admral
I my Lord.	P 305	5.32	Gonzag
Cosin tis he, I know him by his look.	P 309	5.36	Guise
Will be as resolute as I and Dumaine:	P 323	5.50	Guise
I sweare by this crosse, wee'l not be partiall,	P 325	5.52	Anjoy
I will my Lord.	P 331	5.58	Mntsrl
I am a preacher of the word of God,	P 341	5.68	Lorein
I, I, for this Seroune, and thou shalt [ha't] <hate>.	P 351	6.6	Mntsrl
O let me pray before I take my death.	P 352	6.7	Seroun
I feare the Guisians have past the bridge,	P 363	7.3	Ramus
Tell me Taleus, wherfore should I flye?	P 366	7.6	Ramus
I am as Ramus is, a Christian.	P 374	7.14	Taleus
Alas I am a scholler, how should I have golde?	P 377	7.17	Ramus
All that I have is but my stipend from the King,	P 378	7.18	Ramus
To contradict which, I say Ramus shall dye:	P 396	7.36	Guise
Not for my life doe I desire this pause,	P 401	7.41	Ramus
In that I know the things that I have wrote,	P 403	7.43	Ramus
Which as I heare one [Shekius] <Shekins> takes it ill,	P 404	7.44	Ramus
I knew the Organon to be confusde,	P 406	7.46	Ramus
And I reduc'd it into better forme.	P 407	7.47	Ramus
And this for Aristotle will I say,	P 408	7.48	Ramus
Stab him I say and send him to his freends in hell.	P 415	7.55	Guise
How may we doe? I feare me they will live.	P 420	7.60	Guise
I, so they are, but yet what remedy:	P 433	7.73	Anjoy
I have done what I could to stay this broile.	P 434	7.74	Anjoy
Who I? you are deceived, I rose but now.	P 437	7.77	Anjoy
My Lords of Poland I must needs confesse,	P 451	8.1	Anjoy
For Poland is as I have been enformde,	P 454	8.4	Anjoy
I meane our warres against the Muscovites:	P 461	8.11	Anjoy
That if I undertake to weare the crowne/Of Poland, it may	P 466	8.16	Anjoy
With Poland therfore must I covenant thus,	P 471	8.21	Anjoy
on me, then with your leaves/I may retire me to my native home.	P 474	8.24	Anjoy
I thankfully shall undertake the charge/Of you and yours, and	P 476	8.26	Anjoy
As I could long ere this have wisht him there.	P 496	9.15	QnMoth
And now Madam as I understand,	P 500	9.19	Guise
And thither will I to put them to the sword.	P 504	9.23	Guise
I goe as whirl-windes rage before a storme.	P 511	9.30	Guise
Madam, I have heard him solemnly vow,	P 516	9.35	Cardnl
I, but my Lord let me alone for that,	P 519	9.38	QnMoth
As I doe live, so surely shall he dye,	P 521	9.40	QnMoth
And if they storme, I then may pull them downe.	P 526	9.45	QnMoth
I must say so, paine forceth me complaine.	P 540	11.5	Charls
I have deserv'd a scourge I must confesse,	P 544	11.9	Charls
My heart doth break, I faint and dye.	P 550	11.15	Charls
Madam, I will.	P 560	11.25	Eprnon
And therefore as speedily as I can perfourme,	P 571	11.36	Navrre
As I entend to labour for the truth,	P 585	11.50	Navrre
I tell thee Mugeroun we will be freends,	P 614	12.27	King
Hands of good fellow, I will be his baile/For this offence:	P 622	12.35	King
Madam, as in secrecy I was tolde,	P 641	12.54	Cardnl
And if he doe deny what I doe say,	P 650	12.63	QnMoth
Tush, all shall dye unles I have my will:	P 653	12.66	QnMoth
I will Madam.	P 658	13.2	Maid
That I may write unto my dearest Lord.	P 659	13.3	Duchss
And Guise usurpes it, cause I am his wife:	P 661	13.5	Duchss
Faine would I finde some means to speak with him/But cannot,	P 662	13.6	Duchss
I prethee say to whome thou writes?	P 671	13.15	Guise
Will laugh I feare me at their good aray.	P 673	13.17	Duchss
I pray thee let me see.	P 674	13.18	Guise
But Madam I must see.	P 677	13.21	Guise
Am I growne olde, or is thy lust growne yong,	P 681	13.25	Guise
I, dearer then the apple of mine eye?	P 685	13.29	Guise
Of whose encrease I set some longing hope,	P 689	13.33	Guise
Now doe I see that from the very first,	P 694	13.38	Guise
I meane the Guise, the Pope, and King of Spaine,	P 701	14.4	Navrre
Whom I respect as leaves of boasting greene,	P 720	14.23	Navrre
When I shall vaunt as victor in revenge.	P 722	14.25	Navrre
It will not countervaile his paines I hope,	P 735	14.38	Navrre
I would the Guise in his steed might have come,	P 736	14.39	Navrre
My sweet Joyeux, I make thee Generall,	P 743	15.1	King
At thy request I am content thou goe,	P 746	15.4	King
Thanks to your Majestie, and so I take my leave.	P 749	15.7	Joyeux
Am I thus to be jested at and scornde?	P 758	15.16	Guise
They should know how I scornde them and their mockes.	P 762	15.20	Guise
I love your Minions?	P 763	15.21	Guise
I know none els but holdes them in disgrace:	P 764	15.22	Guise
And heer by all the Saints in heaven I sweare,	P 765	15.23	Guise
That villain for whom I beare this deep disgrace,	P 766	15.24	Guise
Not I my Lord, what if I had?	P 775	15.33	Mugern
I may be stabd, and live till he be dead,	P 778	15.36	Mugern
If that be all, the next time that I meet her,	P 781	15.39	Mugern
I like not this, come Epernoune/Lets goe seek the Duke and make	P 785	15.43	King
I hope will make the King surcease his hate:	P 792	16.6	Bartus
I come not to take possession (as I would I might) yet I meane	P 813	17.8	P Souldr
possession (as I would I might) yet I meane to keepe you out,	P 814	17.9	P Souldr
yet I meane to keepe you out, which I will if this geare holde:	P 815	17.10	P Souldr
I did it only in despite of thee.	P 820	17.15	Guise

I (cont.)

Why I am no traitor to the crowne of France.	P 825	17.20		Guise
What I have done tis for the Gospell sake.	P 826	17.21		Guise
I challenge thee for treason in the cause.	P 830	17.25		Eprnon
I am a Prince of the Valoyses line,/Therfore an enemy to the	P 835	17.30		Guise
I am a juror in the holy league,	P 837	17.32		Guise
What should I doe but stand upon my guarde?	P 839	17.34		Guise
I, those are they that feed him with their golde,	P 845	17.40		King
I meane to muster all the power I can,	P 849	17.44		Guise
I, and the catholick Philip King of Spaine,	P 852	17.47		Guise
Ere I shall want, will cause his Indians,	P 853	17.48		Guise
Whilste I cry placet like a Senator.	P 861	17.56		King
I cannot brook thy hauty insolence,	P 862	17.57		King
The choyse is hard, I must dissemble.	P 865	17.60		Guise
I kisse your graces hand, and take my leave,	P 868	17.63		Guise
And Epernoune I will be rulde by thee.	P 885	17.80		King
I think for safety of your royall person,	P 887	17.82		Eprnon
And then Ile tell thee what I meane to doe.	P 891	17.86		King
And Epernoune though I seeme milde and calme,	P 893	17.88		King
Thinke not but I am tragicall within:	P 894	17.89		King
But as I live, so sure the Guise shall dye.	P 899	17.94		King
My Lord, I am advertised from France,	P 900	18.1		Navrre
I will my Lord.	P 913	18.14		Bartus
Be gone I say, tis time that we were there.	P 919	18.20		Navrre
I goe my Lord.	P 920	18.21		Pleshe
That wicked Guise I feare me much will be,	P 921	18.22		Navrre
Well then, I see you are resolute.	P 938	19.8		Capt
Let us alone, I warrant you.	P 939	19.9	P	1Mur
I, I, feare not: stand close, so, be resolute:	P 943	19.13		Capt
I warrant ye my Lord.	P 951	19.21		Capt
I prethee tell him that the Guise is heere.	P 958	19.28		Guise
I heard your Majestie was scarsely pleasde,	P 967	19.37		Guise
That in the Court I bare so great a traine.	P 968	19.38		Guise
They were to blame that said I was displeasde,	P 969	19.39		King
Twere hard with me if I should doubt my kinne,	P 971	19.41		King
Cousin, assure you I am resolute,	P 973	19.43		King
And all his Minions stoup when I commaund:	P 979	19.49		Guise
Now by the holy sacrament I sweare,	P 981	19.51		Guise
So will I triumph over this wanton King,	P 983	19.53		Guise
Now doe I but begin to look about,	P 985	19.55		Guise
O my Lord, I am one of them that is set to murder you.	P 992	19.62	P	3Mur
I my Lord, the rest have taine their standings in the next	P 994	19.64	P	3Mur
Tut they are pesants, I am Duke of Guise:	P 998	19.68		Guise
Stand close, he is comming, I know him by his voice.	P1000	19.70	P	1Mur
Oh I have my deaths wound, give me leave to speak.	P1003	19.73		Guise
Trouble me not, I neare offended him,	P1005	19.75		Guise
Nor will I aske forgivenes of the King.	P1006	19.76		Guise
Oh that I have not power to stay my life,	P1007	19.77		Guise
Philip and Parma, I am slaine for you:	P1011	19.81		Guise
And heere in presence of you all I sweare,	P1026	19.96		King
I nere was King of France untill this houre:	P1027	19.97		King
our Guise is dead)/Rest satisfied with this that heer I sweare,	P1043	19.113		King
Nere was there King of France so yoakt as I.	P1044	19.114		King
Sirra twas I that slew him, and will slay/Thee too, and thou	P1048	19.118		King
I slew the Guise, because I would be King.	P1066	19.136		King
But now I will be King and rule my selfe,	P1070	19.140		King
I cannot speak for greefe: when thou wast borne,	P1072	19.142		QnMoth
I would that I had murdered thee my sonne.	P1073	19.143		QnMoth
I curse thee and exclaime thee miscreant,	P1075	19.145		QnMoth
The Guise is slaine, and I rejoyce therefore:	P1078	19.148		King
And now will I to armes, come Epernoune:	P1079	19.149		King
To whom shall I bewray my secrets now,	P1083	19.153		QnMoth
And all for thee my Guise: what may I doe?	P1088	19.158		QnMoth
For since the Guise is dead, I will not live.	P1090	19.160		QnMoth
Murder me not, I am a Cardenall.	P1091	20.1		Cardnl
Then there is no remedye but I must dye?	P1096	20.6		Cardnl
Oh what may I doe, for to revenge thy death?	P1108	21.2		Dumain
I am thy brother, and ile revenge thy death,	P1112	21.6		Dumain
That I with speed should have beene put to death.	P1118	21.12		Dumain
I come to bring you newes, that your brother the Cardinall of	P1122	21.16	P	Frier
My brother Cardenall slaine and I alive?	P1125	21.19		Dumain
I am a Frier of the order of the Jacobyns, that for my	P1130	21.24	P	Frier
I have beene a great sinner in my dayes, and the deed is	P1133	21.27	P	Frier
Brother of Navarre, I sorrow much,	P1139	22.1		King
That ever I was prov'd your enemy,	P1140	22.2		King
I vow as I am lawfull King of France,	P1143	22.5		King
That ever I vouchsafte my dearest freends.	P1146	22.8		King
I like not this Friers look.	P1159	22.21		Eprnon
I my good Lord, and will dye therein.	P1165	22.27		Frier
Yes Navarre, but not to death I hope.	P1177	22.39		King
The wound I warrant ye is deepe my Lord,	P1192	22.54		King
Tell her for all this that I hope to live,	P1196	22.58		King
Which if I doe, the Papall Monarck goes/To wrack, and [his]	P1197	22.59		King
Navarre, give me thy hand, I heere do sweare,	P1203	22.65		King
Tell me Surgeon, shall I live?	P1211	22.73		King
Tell me Surgeon and flatter not, may I live?	P1222	22.84		King
I dye Navarre, come beare me to my Sepulchre.	P1242	22.104		King
And then I vow for to revenge his death,	P1247	22.109		Navrre
And thoughe I come nct to keep possessione as I wold I mighte	Paris	ms14,p390	P	Souldr
And thoughe I come not to keep possessione as I wold I mighte	Paris	ms15,p390	P	Souldr
yet I come to keepe you out ser.	Paris	ms15,p390	P	Souldr
I did it onely in dispight of thee	Paris	ms24,p391		Guise
the armye I have gathered now shall ayme/more at thie end then	Paris	ms28,p391		Guise

I (cont.)

and when thow thinkst I have foregotten this	Paris	ms20,p391	Guise
then will I wake thee from thie folishe dreame/and lett thee	Paris	ms32,p391	Guise
Sweete prince I come, these these thy amorous lines,	Edw	1.1.6	Gavstn
Not that I love the citie or the men,	Edw	1.1.12	Gavstn
But that it harbors him I hold so deare,	Edw	1.1.13	Gavstn
I can ride.	Edw	1.1.27	1PrMan
But I have no horses. What art thou?	Edw	1.1.28	Gavstn
And as I like your discoursing, ile have you.	Edw	1.1.32	Gavstn
I have no warre, and therefore sir be gone.	Edw	1.1.36	Gavstn
I, I, these wordes of his move me as much,	Edw	1.1.39	Gavstn
You know that I came lately out of France,	Edw	1.1.44	Gavstn
And yet I have not viewd my Lord the king,	Edw	1.1.45	Gavstn
If I speed well, ile entertaine you all.	Edw	1.1.46	Gavstn
I have some busines, leave me to my selfe.	Edw	1.1.48	Gavstn
I must have wanton Poets, pleasant wits,	Edw	1.1.51	Gavstn
of a string/May draw the pliant king which way I please:	Edw	1.1.53	Gavstn
That Earle of Lancaster do I abhorre.	Edw	1.1.76	Gavstn
That crosse me thus, shall know I am displeasd.	Edw	1.1.79	Edward
Mine unckle heere, this Earle, and I my selfe,	Edw	1.1.82	Mortmr
And know my lord, ere I will breake my oath,	Edw	1.1.85	Mortmr
I will have Gaveston, and you shall know,	Edw	1.1.96	Edward
Foure Earldomes have I besides Lancaster,	Edw	1.1.102	Lncstr
These will I sell to give my souldiers paye,	Edw	1.1.104	Lncstr
But now ile speake, and to the proofe I hope:	Edw	1.1.108	Kent
I do remember in my fathers dayes,	Edw	1.1.109	Kent
I yours, and therefore I would wish you graunt.	Edw	1.1.120	Edward
I cannot, nor I will not, I must speake.	Edw	1.1.122	Mortmr
Cosin, our hands I hope shall fence our heads,	Edw	1.1.123	Mortmr
I cannot brooke these hautie menaces:	Edw	1.1.134	Edward
Am I a king and must be over rulde?	Edw	1.1.135	Edward
I can no longer keepe me from my lord.	Edw	1.1.139	Gavstn
Embrace me Gaveston as I do thee:	Edw	1.1.141	Edward
Why shouldst thou kneele, knowest thou not who I am?	Edw	1.1.142	Edward
And since I went from hence, no soule in hell/Hath felt more	Edw	1.1.146	Gavstn
I know it, brother welcome home my friend.	Edw	1.1.148	Edward
I have my wish, in that I joy thy sight,	Edw	1.1.151	Edward
I heere create thee Lord high Chamberlaine,	Edw	1.1.154	Edward
Cease brother, for I cannot brooke these words:	Edw	1.1.160	Edward
Which whiles I have, I thinke my selfe as great,	Edw	1.1.172	Gavstn
I priest, and lives to be revengd on thee,	Edw	1.1.178	Edward
I did no more then I was bound to do,	Edw	1.1.182	BshpCv
As then I did incense the parlement,	Edw	1.1.184	BshpCv
So will I now, and thou shalt back to France.	Edw	1.1.185	BshpCv
I give him thee, here use him as thou wilt.	Edw	1.1.196	Edward
I, to the tower, the fleete, or where thou wilt.	Edw	1.1.198	Edward
I, and besides, lord Chamberlaine of the realme,	Edw	1.2.13	Warwck
What neede I, God himselfe is up in armes,	Edw	1.2.40	ArchBp
And when I come, he frownes, as who should say,	Edw	1.2.53	Queene
Go whether thou wilt seeing I have Gaveston.	Edw	1.2.54	Queene
I wil endure a melancholie life,	Edw	1.2.66	Queene
I, if words will serve, if not, I must.	Edw	1.2.83	Mortmr
Quick quick my lorde, I long to write my name.	Edw	1.4.4	Lncstr
But I long more to see him banisht hence.	Edw	1.4.5	Warwck
Were I a king--	Edw	1.4.27	Gavstn
Away I say with hatefull Gaveston.	Edw	1.4.33	Lncstr
Was ever king thus over rulde as I?	Edw	1.4.38	Edward
You know that I am legate to the Pope,	Edw	1.4.51	ArchBp
I there it goes, but yet I will not yeeld,	Edw	1.4.56	Edward
Or I will presentlie discharge these lords,	Edw	1.4.61	ArchBp
It bootes me not to threat, I must speake faire,	Edw	1.4.63	Edward
So I may have some nooke or corner left,	Edw	1.4.72	Edward
I see I must, and therefore am content.	Edw	1.4.85	Edward
How fast they run to banish him I love,	Edw	1.4.94	Edward
If I be king, not one of them shall live.	Edw	1.4.105	Edward
My lord I heare it whispered every where,	Edw	1.4.106	Gavstn
That I am banishd, and must flie the land.	Edw	1.4.107	Gavstn
And thou must hence, or I shall be deposd,	Edw	1.4.110	Edward
But I will raigne to be reveng'd of them,	Edw	1.4.111	Edward
Thou from this land, I from my selfe am banisht.	Edw	1.4.118	Edward
That whether I will or no thou must depart:	Edw	1.4.124	Edward
O might I keepe thee heere, as I doe this,	Edw	1.4.128	Edward
Happie were I, but now most miserable.	Edw	1.4.129	Edward
I shal be found, and then twil greeve me more.	Edw	1.4.132	Gavstn
Stay Gaveston, I cannot leave thee thus.	Edw	1.4.135	Edward
Seeing I must go, do not renew my sorrow.	Edw	1.4.137	Gavstn
I passe not for their anger, come lets go.	Edw	1.4.142	Edward
On whom but on my husband should I fawne?	Edw	1.4.146	Queene
I say no more, judge you the rest my lord.	Edw	1.4.148	Gavstn
I meane not so, your grace must pardon me.	Edw	1.4.153	Gavstn
But I would wish thee reconcile the lords,	Edw	1.4.156	Edward
Wherein my lord, have I deservd these words?	Edw	1.4.163	Queene
Would when I left sweet France and was imbarkt,	Edw	1.4.171	Queene
I had beene stifled, and not lived to see,	Edw	1.4.176	Queene
Like frantick Juno will I fill the earth,	Edw	1.4.178	Queene
I must entreat him, I must speake him faire,	Edw	1.4.183	Queene
And so am I for ever miserable.	Edw	1.4.186	Queene
The king I feare hath ill intreated her.	Edw	1.4.189	Warwck
I know tis long of Gaveston she weepes.	Edw	1.4.191	Mortmr
No, rather will I die a thousand deaths,	Edw	1.4.196	Queene
And yet I love in vaine, heele nere love me.	Edw	1.4.197	Queene
I am injoynde,/To sue unto you all for his repeale:	Edw	1.4.200	Queene
This wils my lord, and this must I performe,	Edw	1.4.202	Queene

I (cont.)

I Mortimer, for till he be restorde,	Edw	1.4.209	Queene
Plead for him he that will, I am resolvde.	Edw	1.4.214	MortSr
And so am I my lord, diswade the Queene.	Edw	1.4.215	Lncstr
Tis for my selfe I speake, and not for him.	Edw	1.4.219	Queene
I meane that vile Torpedo, Gaveston,	Edw	1.4.223	Mortmr
That now I hope flotes on the Irish seas.	Edw	1.4.224	Mortmr
And I will tell thee reasons of such waighte,	Edw	1.4.226	Queene
Not I against my nephew.	Edw	1.4.232	MortSr
Ile rather loose his friendship I, then graunt.	Edw	1.4.237	Lncstr
My Lords, that I abhorre base Gaveston,	Edw	1.4.239	Mortmr
I hope your honors make no question,	Edw	1.4.240	Mortmr
And therefore though I pleade for his repeall,	Edw	1.4.241	Mortmr
I would he were.	Edw	1.4.253	Penbrk
This which I urge, is of a burning zeale,	Edw	1.4.256	Mortmr
I, but how chance this was not done before?	Edw	1.4.272	Lncstr
My lords, if to performe this I be slack,	Edw	1.4.290	Mortmr
And so will Penbrooke and I.	Edw	1.4.293	Warwck
And I.	Edw	1.4.294	MortSr
In this I count me highly gratified,	Edw	1.4.295	Mortmr
I love him more/Then he can Gaveston, would he lov'd me	Edw	1.4.302	Queene
would he lov'd me/But halfe so much, then were I treble blest.	Edw	1.4.304	Queene
Hees gone, and for his absence thus I moorne,	Edw	1.4.305	Edward
I would freelie give it to his enemies,	Edw	1.4.309	Edward
And thinke I gaind, having bought so deare a friend.	Edw	1.4.310	Edward
When I was forst to leave my Gaveston.	Edw	1.4.318	Edward
My gratious lord, I come to bring you newes.	Edw	1.4.320	Queene
Then I may fetch from this ritch treasurie:	Edw	1.4.332	Queene
Chide me sweete Warwick, if I go astray.	Edw	1.4.348	Edward
Slay me my lord, when I offend your grace.	Edw	1.4.349	Warwck
I make thee heere lord Marshall of the realme.	Edw	1.4.356	Edward
I Isabell, nere was my heart so light.	Edw	1.4.368	Edward
For wot you not that I have made him sure,	Edw	1.4.378	Edward
Nephue, I must to Scotland, thou staiest here.	Edw	1.4.386	MortSr
But this I scorne, that one so baselie borne,	Edw	1.4.403	Mortmr
I have not seene a dapper jack so briske,	Edw	1.4.412	Mortmr
Then so am I, and live to do him service,	Edw	1.4.421	Mortmr
But whiles I have a sword, a hand, a hart,	Edw	1.4.422	Mortmr
I will not yeeld to any such upstart.	Edw	1.4.423	Mortmr
I for a while, but Baldock marke the end,	Edw	2.1.16	Spencr
But I had thought the match had beene broke off,	Edw	2.1.25	Baldck
Then hope I by her meanes to be preferd,	Edw	2.1.29	Baldck
Spencer, thou knowest I hate such formall toies,	Edw	2.1.44	Baldck
I am none of these common [pedants] <pendants> I,	Edw	2.1.52	Baldck
I know thou couldst not come and visit me.	Edw	2.1.61	Neece
I will not long be from thee though I die:	Edw	2.1.62	Neece
When I forsake thee, death seaze on my heart,	Edw	2.1.64	Neece
why do I stay,/Seeing that he talkes thus of my mariage day?	Edw	2.1.68	Neece
See that my coache be readie, I must hence.	Edw	2.1.71	Neece
For I have joyfull newes to tell thee of,	Edw	2.1.75	Neece
I knew the King would have him home againe.	Edw	2.1.78	Spencr
If all things sort out, as I hope they will,	Edw	2.1.79	Neece
I humbly thanke your Ladieship.	Edw	2.1.81	Spencr
Come lead the way, I long till I am there.	Edw	2.1.82	Neece
The winde is good, I wonder why he stayes,	Edw	2.2.1	Edward
I feare me he is wrackt upon the sea.	Edw	2.2.2	Edward
this fish my lord I beare,/The motto this:	Edw	2.2.27	Lncstr
I am that Cedar, shake me not too much,	Edw	2.2.38	Edward
I have the [gesses] <gresses> that will pull you downe,	Edw	2.2.40	Edward
Yet have I words left to expresse my joy:	Edw	2.2.60	Gavstn
Then I doe to behold your Majestie.	Edw	2.2.63	Gavstn
My Lord I cannot brooke these injuries.	Edw	2.2.71	Gavstn
Yet I disdaine not to doe this for you.	Edw	2.2.79	Lncstr
Villaine thy life, unlesse I misse mine aime.	Edw	2.2.84	Mortmr
No more then I would answere were he slaine.	Edw	2.2.86	Mortmr
But if I live, ile tread upon their heads,	Edw	2.2.96	Edward
I warrant you.	Edw	2.2.126	Warwck
I marry, such a garde as this dooth well.	Edw	2.2.131	Mortmr
Nay, stay my lord, I come to bring you newes,	Edw	2.2.141	Mortmr
Shall I still be haunted thus?	Edw	2.2.154	Edward
And so will I, and then my lord farewell.	Edw	2.2.156	Lncstr
I meane the peeres, whom thou shouldst dearly love:	Edw	2.2.176	Mortmr
How oft have I beene baited by these peeres?	Edw	2.2.201	Edward
If I be cruell, and growe tyrannous,	Edw	2.2.206	Edward
My lord, I see your love to Gaveston,	Edw	2.2.208	Kent
I, and it greeves me that I favoured him.	Edw	2.2.213	Kent
So will I, rather then with Gaveston.	Edw	2.2.215	Kent
When I thy brother am rejected thus.	Edw	2.2.218	Kent
And so I walke with him about the walles,	Edw	2.2.222	Edward
What care I though the Earles begirt us round?	Edw	2.2.223	Edward
I, and tis likewise thought you favour him <them> <'em> <hem>.	Edw	2.2.226	Edward
Pardon me sweet, I forgot my selfe.	Edw	2.2.230	Edward
I dare not, for the people love him well.	Edw	2.2.235	Edward
I humblie thanke your majestie.	Edw	2.2.247	Baldck
I my lord,/His name is Spencer, he is well alied,	Edw	2.2.248	Gavstn
And Gaveston, thinke that I love thee well,	Edw	2.2.257	Edward
I know my lord, many will stomack me,	Edw	2.2.260	Gavstn
But I respect neither their love nor hate.	Edw	2.2.261	Gavstn
He that I list to favour shall be great:	Edw	2.2.263	Edward
I come to joine with you, and leave the king,	Edw	2.3.2	Kent
I feare me you are sent of pollicie,	Edw	2.3.5	Lncstr
I have enformd the Earle of Lancaster.	Edw	2.3.14	Kent
Will I advaunce upon this castell walles,	Edw	2.3.24	Mortmr

I (cont.)

I feare me he is slaine my gratious lord.	Edw	2.4.2	Spencr
Spencer and I will post away by land.	Edw	2.4.6	Edward
I will not trust them, Gaveston away.	Edw	2.4.8	Edward
Heavens can witnesse, I love none but you.	Edw	2.4.15	Queene
That I might pull him to me where I would,	Edw	2.4.18	Queene
That when I had him we might never part.	Edw	2.4.21	Queene
I wonder how he scapt.	Edw	2.4.22	Lncstr
I Mortimer, the miserable Queene,	Edw	2.4.23	Queene
And all in vaine, for when I speake him faire,	Edw	2.4.28	Queene
As if he heare I have but talkt with you,	Edw	2.4.54	Queene
Madam, I cannot stay to answer you,	Edw	2.4.57	Mortmr
In vaine I looke for love at Edwards hand,	Edw	2.4.61	Queene
My sonne and I will over into France,	Edw	2.4.65	Queene
But yet I hope my sorrowes will have end,	Edw	2.4.68	Queene
Yet lustie lords I have escapt your handes,	Edw	2.5.1	Gavstn
I thanke you all my lords, then I perceive,	Edw	2.5.29	Gavstn
I know it lords, it is this life you aime at,	Edw	2.5.48	Gavstn
My lords, I will be pledge for his returne.	Edw	2.5.66	Arundl
I will upon mine honor undertake/To carrie him, and bring him	Edw	2.5.79	Penbrk
him, but must we now/Leave him on had-I-wist, and let him go?	Edw	2.5.85	Warwck
My lords, I will not over wooe your honors,	Edw	2.5.86	Penbrk
Upon mine oath I will returne him back.	Edw	2.5.88	Penbrk
Why I say, let him go on Penbrookes word.	Edw	2.5.90	Lncstr
Nay, do your pleasures, I know how twill proove.	Edw	2.5.93	Warwck
Sweete soveraigne, yet I come/To see thee ere I die.	Edw	2.5.94	Gavstn
Sweete soveraigne, yet I come/To see thee ere I die.	Edw	2.5.95	Gavstn
I do commit this Gaveston to thee,	Edw	2.5.107	Penbrk
I see it is your life these armes pursue.	Edw	2.6.2	James
Weaponles must I fall and die in bands,	Edw	2.6.3	Gavstn
Strive you no longer, I will have that Gaveston.	Edw	2.6.7	Warwck
No James, it is my countries cause I follow.	Edw	2.6.10	Warwck
to your maister/My friend, and tell him that I watcht it well.	Edw	2.6.13	Warwck
Treacherous earle, shall I not see the king?	Edw	2.6.15	Gavstn
I long to heare an answer from the Barons/Touching my friend,	Edw	3.1.1	Edward
I know the malice of the yonger Mortimer,	Edw	3.1.5	Edward
Warwick I know is roughe, and Lancaster/Inexorable, and I shall	Edw	3.1.6	Edward
Lancaster/Inexorable, and I shall never see/My lovely Pierce,	Edw	3.1.7	Edward
Were I king Edward, Englands soveraigne,	Edw	3.1.10	Spencr
would I beare/These braves, this rage, and suffer uncontrowld	Edw	3.1.12	Spencr
I come in person to your majestie,	Edw	3.1.39	SpncrP
Spencer, I heere create thee earle of Wilshire,	Edw	3.1.49	Edward
Sib, if this be all/Valoys and I will soone be friends againe.	Edw	3.1.67	Edward
shall I never see,/Never behold thee now?	Edw	3.1.68	Edward
things of more waight/Then fits a prince so yong as I to beare,	Edw	3.1.75	Prince
God end them once, my lord I take my leave,	Edw	3.1.87	Queene
I did your highnes message to them all,	Edw	3.1.96	Arundl
That I would undertake to carrie him/Unto your highnes, and to	Edw	3.1.99	Arundl
I found them at the first inexorable,	Edw	3.1.103	Arundl
I will this undertake, to have him hence,	Edw	3.1.111	Arundl
O shall I speake, or shall I sigh and die!	Edw	3.1.122	Edward
I will have heads, and lives, for him as many,	Edw	3.1.132	Edward
As I have manors, castels, townes, and towers:	Edw	3.1.133	Edward
If I be Englands king, in lakes of gore/Your headles trunkes,	Edw	3.1.135	Edward
lakes of gore/Your headles trunkes, your bodies will I traile,	Edw	3.1.136	Edward
Spencer, sweet Spencer, I adopt thee heere,	Edw	3.1.144	Edward
Yet ere thou go, see how I do devorce	Edw	3.1.176	Edward
And tell them I will come to chastise them,	Edw	3.1.178	Edward
This day I shall powre vengeance with my sword/On those proud	Edw	3.1.186	Edward
I doubt it not my lord, right will prevaile.	Edw	3.1.189	Spencr
I traitors all, rather then thus be bravde,	Edw	3.1.214	Edward
Tyrant, I scorne thy threats and menaces,	Edw	3.1.241	Warwck
I charge you roundly off with both their heads,	Edw	3.1.247	Edward
Mortimer I stay thy sweet escape,	Edw	4.1.10	Kent
Mortimer tis I,	Edw	4.1.13	Kent
I thanke them, gave me leave to passe in peace:	Edw	4.1.16	Mortmr
I warrant you, ile winne his highnes quicklie,	Edw	4.2.6	Prince
I heare sweete lady of the kings unkindenes,	Edw	4.2.15	SrJohn
Till I be strong enough to breake a staffe,	Edw	4.2.24	Prince
Oh my sweet hart, how do I mone thy wrongs,	Edw	4.2.27	Queene
His grace I dare presume will welcome me,	Edw	4.2.33	Queene
No my lord Mortimer, not I, I trow.	Edw	4.2.44	Prince
I would it were no worse,/But gentle lords, friendles we are in	Edw	4.2.45	Queene
I thinke king Edward will out-run us all.	Edw	4.2.68	Prince
Sir John of Henolt, pardon us I-pray,	Edw	4.2.71	Kent
Was borne I see to be our anchor hold.	Edw	4.2.77	Mortmr
I pray let us see it, what have we there?	Edw	4.3.10	Edward
I trowe/The lords of Fraunce love Englands gold so well,	Edw	4.3.14	Edward
A will be had ere long I doubt it not.	Edw	4.3.20	Spencr
I have according to instructions in that behalfe,	Edw	4.3.28	P Spencr
Betweene you both, shorten the time I pray,	Edw	4.3.45	Edward
That I may see that most desired day,	Edw	4.3.46	Edward
I would he never had bin flattered more.	Edw	4.4.30	Kent
What, was I borne to flye and runne away,	Edw	4.5.4	Edward
This way he fled, but I am come too late.	Edw	4.6.1	Kent
Madam, without offence if I may aske,	Edw	4.6.30	Kent
Nephew, your father, I dare not call him king.	Edw	4.6.33	Kent
I like not this relenting moode in Edmund,	Edw	4.6.38	Mortmr
They shalbe started thence I doubt it not.	Edw	4.6.60	Mortmr
Shall I not see the king my father yet?	Edw	4.6.61	Prince
I rue my lords ill fortune, but alas,	Edw	4.6.64	Queene
Whilom I was, powerfull and full of pompe,	Edw	4.7.13	Edward
O that I might this life in quiet lead,	Edw	4.7.21	Edward

I (cont.)

Not one alive, but shrewdly I suspect,	Edw	4.7.28	Spencr
And all the land I know is up in armes,	Edw	4.7.31	Spencr
good father on thy lap/Lay I this head, laden with mickle care,	Edw	4.7.40	Edward
O might I never open these eyes againe,	Edw	4.7.41	Edward
my lord I pray be short,/A faire commission warrants what we	Edw	4.7.47	Rice
I arrest you of high treason here,	Edw	4.7.57	Leistr
Our lots are cast, I feare me so is thine.	Edw	4.7.79	Baldck
And go I must, life farewell with my friends.	Edw	4.7.99	Edward
Spencer, I see our soules are fleeted hence,	Edw	4.7.105	Baldck
Your worship I trust will remember me?	Edw	4.7.117	Mower
Full often am I sowring up to heaven,	Edw	5.1.21	Edward
But when I call to minde I am a king,	Edw	5.1.23	Edward
Me thinkes I should revenge me of the wronges,	Edw	5.1.24	Edward
My nobles rule, I beare the name of king,	Edw	5.1.28	Edward
I weare the crowne, but am contrould by them,	Edw	5.1.29	Edward
Whilst I am lodgd within this cave of care,	Edw	5.1.32	Edward
But tell me, must I now resigne my crowne,	Edw	5.1.36	Edward
way how hardly I can brooke/To loose my crowne and kingdome,	Edw	5.1.51	Edward
But what the heavens appoint, I must obaye,	Edw	5.1.56	Edward
That I may gaze upon this glittering crowne,	Edw	5.1.60	Edward
And needes I must resigne my wished crowne.	Edw	5.1.70	Edward
My diadem I meane, and guiltlesse life.	Edw	5.1.73	Edward
And in this torment, comfort finde I none,	Edw	5.1.81	Edward
But that I feele the crowne upon my head,	Edw	5.1.82	Edward
Ile not resigne, but whilst I live, [be king].	Edw	5.1.86	Edward
Call thou them back, I have no power to speake.	Edw	5.1.93	Edward
O would I might, but heavens and earth conspire/To make me	Edw	5.1.96	Edward
Yet stay, for rather then I will looke on them,	Edw	5.1.106	Edward
Or if I live, let me forget my selfe.	Edw	5.1.111	Edward
and bid him rule/Better then I, yet how have I transgrest,	Edw	5.1.122	Edward
Farewell, I know the next newes that they bring,	Edw	5.1.125	Edward
Such newes as I expect, come Bartley, come,	Edw	5.1.129	Edward
That I resigne my charge.	Edw	5.1.136	Leistr
I, my most gratious lord, so tis decreed.	Edw	5.1.138	Bartly
Well may I rent his name, that rends my hart.	Edw	5.1.140	Edward
Even so betide my soule as I use him.	Edw	5.1.148	Bartly
And thats the cause that I am now remoovde.	Edw	5.1.150	Edward
I know not, but of this am I assured,	Edw	5.1.152	Edward
That death ends all, and I can die but once.	Edw	5.1.153	Edward
And that I be protector over him,	Edw	5.2.12	Mortmr
Be thou perswaded, that I love thee well,	Edw	5.2.16	Queene
Whome I esteeme as deare as these mine eyes,	Edw	5.2.18	Queene
And I my selfe will willinglie subscribe.	Edw	5.2.20	Queene
First would I heare newes that hee were deposde,	Edw	5.2.21	Mortmr
Alas poore soule, would I could ease his greefe.	Edw	5.2.26	Queene
I would hee were, so it were not by my meanes.	Edw	5.2.45	Queene
I warrant you my lord.	Edw	5.2.56	Gurney
And tell him, that I labour all in vaine,	Edw	5.2.70	Queene
I will madam.	Edw	5.2.73	Matrvs
I heare of late he hath deposde himselfe.	Edw	5.2.83	Kent
Sweete sonne come hither, I must talke with thee.	Edw	5.2.87	Queene
Not I my lord:	Edw	5.2.90	Kent
But she that gave him life, I meane the Queene?	Edw	5.2.91	Kent
Let him be king, I am too yong to raigne.	Edw	5.2.93	Prince
Let me but see him first, and then I will.	Edw	5.2.95	Prince
I, do sweete Nephew.	Edw	5.2.96	Kent
I would those wordes proceeded from your heart.	Edw	5.2.100	Kent
The more cause have I now to make amends.	Edw	5.2.103	Kent
I tell thee tis not meet, that one so false/Should come about	Edw	5.2.104	Mortmr
With you I will, but not with Mortimer.	Edw	5.2.110	Prince
Then I will carrie thee by force away.	Edw	5.2.112	Mortmr
Edward is my sonne, and I will keepe him.	Edw	5.2.117	Queene
Hence will I haste to Killingworth castle,	Edw	5.2.119	Kent
Must I be vexed like the nightly birde,	Edw	5.3.6	Edward
Where I am sterv'd for want of sustenance,	Edw	5.3.20	Edward
But all in vaine, so vainely do I strive,	Edw	5.3.35	Edward
O Gaveston, it is for thee that I am wrongd,	Edw	5.3.41	Edward
And I will visit him, why stay you me?	Edw	5.3.60	Kent
I, lead me whether you will, even to my death,	Edw	5.3.66	Kent
And therefore will I do it cunninglie.	Edw	5.4.5	Mortmr
I, I, and none shall know which way he died.	Edw	5.4.25	Ltborn
Relent, ha, ha, I use much to relent.	Edw	5.4.27	Ltborn
Tis not the first time I have killed a man.	Edw	5.4.30	Ltborn
I learnde in Naples how to poison flowers,	Edw	5.4.31	Ltborn
But yet I have a braver way then these.	Edw	5.4.37	Ltborn
I care not how it is, so it be not spide:	Edw	5.4.40	Mortmr
That will I quicklie do, farewell my lord.	Edw	5.4.47	Ltborn
The prince I rule, the queene do I commaund,	Edw	5.4.48	Mortmr
The proudest lords salute me as I passe,	Edw	5.4.50	Mortmr
I seale, I cancell, I do what I will,	Edw	5.4.51	Mortmr
Feard am I more then lov'd, let me be feard,	Edw	5.4.52	Mortmr
And when I frowne, make all the court looke pale,	Edw	5.4.53	Mortmr
I view the prince with Aristarchus eyes,	Edw	5.4.54	Mortmr
And sue to me for that that I desire,	Edw	5.4.57	Mortmr
First I complaine of imbecilitie,	Edw	5.4.60	Mortmr
And to conclude, I am Protector now,	Edw	5.4.64	Mortmr
Mine enemies will I plague, my friends advance,	Edw	5.4.67	Mortmr
And what I list commaund, who dare controwle?	Edw	5.4.68	Mortmr
The trumpets sound, I must go take my place.	Edw	5.4.72	Mortmr
I am the Champion that will combate him!	Edw	5.4.78	Champn
Mortimer, I did, he is our king,	Edw	5.4.87	Kent
Strike of my head? base traitor I defie thee.	Edw	5.4.90	Kent

I (cont.)

Sweete mother, if I cannot pardon him,	Edw	5.4.94	King
Sonne, be content, I dare not speake a worde.	Edw	5.4.96	Queene
Nor I, and yet me thinkes I should commaund,	Edw	5.4.97	King
But seeing I cannot, ile entreate for him:	Edw	5.4.98	King
I will requite it when I come to age.	Edw	5.4.100	King
How often shall I bid you beare him hence?	Edw	5.4.102	Mortmr
Art thou king, must I die at thy commaund?	Edw	5.4.103	Kent
Let me but stay and speake, I will not go,	Edw	5.4.105	Kent
What safetie may I looke for at his hands,	Edw	5.4.109	King
Gurney, I wonder the king dies not,	Edw	5.5.1	Matrvs
And so do I, Matrevis:	Edw	5.5.7	Gurney
yesternight/I opened but the doore to throw him meate,/And I	Edw	5.5.8	Gurney
And I was almost stifeled with the savor.	Edw	5.5.9	Gurney
Send for him out thence, and I will anger him.	Edw	5.5.13	Gurney
Whats heere? I know not how to conster it.	Edw	5.5.15	Gurney
Know you this token? I must have the king.	Edw	5.5.19	Ltborn
I, stay a while, thou shalt have answer straight.	Edw	5.5.20	Matrvs
I thought as much.	Edw	5.5.22	Gurney
I know what I must do, get you away,	Edw	5.5.27	Ltborn
Yet be not farre off, I shall need your helpe,	Edw	5.5.28	Ltborn
See that in the next roome I have a fier,	Edw	5.5.29	Ltborn
I, I, so: when I call you, bring it in.	Edw	5.5.35	Ltborn
So,/Now must I about this geare, nere was there any/So finely	Edw	5.5.39	Ltborn
Villaine, I know thou comst to murther me.	Edw	5.5.45	Edward
Yet will it melt, ere I have done my tale.	Edw	5.5.55	Edward
And there in mire and puddle have I stood,	Edw	5.5.59	Edward
This ten dayes space, and least that I should sleepe,	Edw	5.5.60	Edward
And whether I have limmes or no, I know not.	Edw	5.5.65	Edward
Tell Isabell the Queene, I lookt not thus,	Edw	5.5.68	Edward
When for her sake I ran at tilt in Fraunce,	Edw	5.5.69	Edward
I see my tragedie written in thy browes,	Edw	5.5.74	Edward
That <and> even then when I shall lose my life,	Edw	5.5.77	Edward
One jewell have I left, receive thou this.	Edw	5.5.84	Edward
Still feare I, and I know not whats the cause,	Edw	5.5.85	Edward
But everie jointe shakes as I give it thee:	Edw	5.5.86	Edward
Know that I am a king, oh at that name,	Edw	5.5.89	Edward
I feele a hell of greefe: where is my crowne?	Edw	5.5.90	Edward
Gone, gone, and doe I remaine alive?	Edw	5.5.91	Edward
But that greefe keepes me waking, I shoulde sleepe,	Edw	5.5.93	Edward
Now as I speake they fall, and yet with feare/Open againe.	Edw	5.5.95	Edward
And tels me, if I sleepe I never wake,	Edw	5.5.104	Edward
I am too weake and feeble to resist,	Edw	5.5.108	Edward
I feare mee that this crie will raise the towne,	Edw	5.5.114	Matrvs
I my good Lord, I would it were undone.	Edw	5.6.2	Matrvs
Gurney, my lord, is fled, and will I feare,	Edw	5.6.7	Matrvs
I humblie thanke your honour.	Edw	5.6.10	Matrvs
As for my selfe, I stand as Joves huge tree,	Edw	5.6.11	Mortmr
All tremble at my name, and I feare none,	Edw	5.6.13	Mortmr
I, I, but he teares his haire, and wrings his handes,	Edw	5.6.18	Queene
Thinke not that I am frighted with thy words,	Edw	5.6.27	King
And had you lov'de him halfe so well as I,	Edw	5.6.35	King
But you I feare, conspirde with Mortimer.	Edw	5.6.37	King
Because I thinke scorne to be accusde,	Edw	5.6.39	Mortmr
Who is the man dare say I murdered him?	Edw	5.6.40	Mortmr
I feard as much, murther cannot be hid.	Edw	5.6.46	Queene
What murtherer? bring foorth the man I sent.	Edw	5.6.49	Mortmr
Hang him I say, and set his quarters up,	Edw	5.6.53	King
Madam, intreat not, I will rather die,	Edw	5.6.56	Mortmr
Base fortune, now I see, that in thy wheele/There is a point, to	Edw	5.6.59	Mortmr
that point I touchte,/And seeing there was no place to mount up	Edw	5.6.61	Mortmr
Why should I greeve at my declining fall?	Edw	5.6.63	Mortmr
I spill his bloud? no.	Edw	5.6.72	Queene
I, madam, you, for so the rumor runnes.	Edw	5.6.73	King
I doe not thinke her so unnaturall.	Edw	5.6.76	King
My lord, I feare me it will proove too true.	Edw	5.6.77	2Lord
If you be guiltie, though I be your sonne,	Edw	5.6.81	King
Nay, to my death, for too long have I lived,	Edw	5.6.83	Queene
And I shall pitie her if she speake againe.	Edw	5.6.86	King
Shall I not moorne for my beloved lord,	Edw	5.6.87	Queene
He hath forgotten me, stay, I am his mother.	Edw	5.6.90	Queene
Could I have rulde thee then, as I do now,	Edw	5.6.96	King
I offer up this wicked traitors head,	Edw	5.6.100	King
I, we must die, an everlasting death.	F 73	1.1.45	Faust
I these are those that Faustus most desires.	F 79	1.1.51	Faust
I will sir.	F 94	1.1.66	Wagner
Then all my labours, plod I ne're so fast.	F 96	1.1.68	Faust
How am I glutted with conceipt of this?	F 105	1.1.77	Faust
Shall I make spirits fetch me what I please?	F 106	1.1.78	Faust
Performe what desperate enterprise I will?	F 108	1.1.80	Faust
And I, that have with [concise] <subtle> Sillogismes	F 139	1.1.111	Faust
Valdes, as resolute am I in this,	F 161	1.1.133	Faust
Yea <I> all the wealth that our fore-fathers hid,	F 173	1.1.145	Cornel
That I may conjure in some bushy <lustie> Grove,	F 178	1.1.150	Faust
And then wilt thou be perfecter then I.	F 189	1.1.161	Valdes
For e're I sleep, I'le try what I can do:	F 192	1.1.164	Faust
This night I'le conjure tho I die therefore.	F 193	1.1.165	Faust
I wonder what's become of Faustus that/Was wont to make our	F 194	1.2.1	1Schol
Yes, I know, but that followes not.	F 200	1.2.7	P Wagner
<Yes sirre, I heard you>.	F 204	(HC258) A	P 1Schol
<Aske my fellow if I be a thiefe>.	F 204	(HC258) A	P Wagner
You are deceiv'd, for <Yes sir>, I will tell you:	F 206	1.2.13	P Wagner
But that I am by nature flegmatique, slow to wrath, and prone	F 209	1.2.16	P Wagner

I (cont.)

I would say) it were not for you to come within fortie foot of	F 210	1.2.17	P	Wagner
I do not doubt but to see you both hang'd the next Sessions.	F 212	1.2.19	P	Wagner
I will set my countenance like a Precisian, and begin to speake	F 213	1.2.20	P	Wagner
Then I feare that which I have long suspected:	F 220	1.2.27		1Schol
<yet should I grieve for him>:	F 224	(HC258) A		2Schol
<O but> I feare me, nothing will <can> reclaime him now.	F 227	1.2.34		1Schol
I charge thee to returne, and change thy shape,	F 251	1.3.23		Faust
I see there's vertue in my heavenly words.	F 255	1.3.27		Faust
I charge thee waite upon me whilst I live/To do what ever	F 264	1.3.36		Faust
I am a servant to great Lucifer,	F 268	1.3.40		Mephst
No, I came now hether of mine owne accord.	F 272	1.3.44		Mephst
So Faustus hath <I have> already done, and holds <hold> this	F 283	1.3.55		Faust
For I confound <He confounds> hell in Elizium:	F 287	1.3.59		Faust
Why this is hell: nor am I out of it.	F 304	1.3.76		Mephst
Think'st thou that I [who] saw the face of God,	F 305	1.3.77		Mephst
To give me whatsoever I shall aske:	F 322	1.3.94		Faust
To tell me whatsoever I demand:	F 323	1.3.95		Faust
I will Faustus.	F 329	1.3.101		Mephst
Had I as many soules, as there be Starres,	F 330	1.3.102		Faust
Now that I have obtain'd what I desir'd <desire>/I'le live in	F 340	1.3.112		Faust
seene many boyes with [such pickadevaunts] <beards> I am sure.	F 345	1.4.3	P	Robin
nakednesse, I know the Villaines out of service, and so hungry,	F 349	1.4.7	P	Wagner
that <I know> he would give his soule to the devill, for a	F 349	1.4.7	P	Wagner
I had need to have it well rosted, and good sauce to it,	F 352	1.4.10	P	Robin
rosted, and good sauce to it, if I pay so deere, I can tell you.	F 353	1.4.11	P	Robin
and good sauce to it, if I pay so deere, I can tell you.	F 353	1.4.11	P	Robin
and I will make thee go, like Qui mihi discipulus.	F 354	1.4.12	P	Wagner
then belike if I serve you, I shall be lousy.	F 358	1.4.16	P	Robin
then belike if I serve you, I shall be lousy.	F 359	1.4.17	P	Robin
me, as if they payd for their meate and drinke, I can tell you.	F 365	1.4.23	P	Robin
Yes marry sir, and I thanke you to.	F 368	1.4.26	P	Robin
Not I, thou art Prest, prepare thy selfe, for I will presently	F 372	1.4.30	P	Wagner
for I will presently raise up two devils to carry thee away:	F 372	1.4.30	P	Wagner
I am not afraid of a devill.	F 374	1.4.32	P	Robin
I good Wagner, take away the devill then.	F 377	1.4.35	P	Robin
I will sir; but hearke you Maister, will you teach me this	F 380	1.4.38	P	Robin
I sirra, I'le teach thee to turne thy selfe to a Dog, or a Cat,	F 382	1.4.40	P	Wagner
Well sir, I warrant you.	F 388	1.4.46	P	Robin
[I and Faustus will turne to God againe].	F 397	2.1.9A		Faust
That I shall waite on Faustus whilst he lives,	F 420	2.1.32		Mephst
If thou deny it I must <wil> backe to hell.	F 426	2.1.38		Mephst
But tell me Faustus, shall I have thy soule?	F 434	2.1.46		Mephst
And I will be thy slave and waite on thee,	F 435	2.1.47		Mephst
I Mephostophilis, I'le <I> give it him <thee>.	F 437	2.1.49		Faust
for love of thee/Faustus hath <I> cut his <mine> arme, and with	F 443	2.1.55		Faust
I so I do <will>; but Mephostophilis,	F 450	2.1.62		Faust
My bloud congeales, and I can write no more.	F 451	2.1.63		Faust
Is it unwilling I should write this byll?	F 454	2.1.66		Faust
Why streames it not, that I may write a fresh?	F 455	2.1.67		Faust
Now will I make an end immediately.	F 461	2.1.73		Faust
What will not I do to obtaine his soule?	F 462	2.1.74		Mephst
Homo fuge: whether should I flye?	F 466	2.1.78		Faust
I see it plaine, even heere <in this place> is writ/Homo fuge:	F 469	2.1.81		Faust
But may I raise such <up> spirits when I please?	F 475	2.1.87		Faust
I Faustus, and do greater things then these.	F 476	2.1.88		Mephst
Faustus, I sweare by Hell and Lucifer,	F 481	2.1.93		Mephst
I John Faustus of Wittenberg <Wertenberge>, Doctor, by these	F 493	2.1.105	P	Faust
I, take it, and the devill give thee good of it <on't>.	F 502	2.1.114		Faust
First, I will question [with] thee about hell:	F 504	2.1.116		Faust
I, so are all things else; but whereabouts <where about>?	F 507	2.1.119		Faust
<Come>, I thinke Hel's a fable.	F 516	2.1.128		Faust
I, thinke so still, till experience change thy mind.	F 517	2.1.129		Mephst
I, of necessity, for here's the scrowle/In which <Wherein> thou	F 519	2.1.131		Mephst
I, and body too, but what of that:	F 521	2.1.133		Faust
But <Faustus> I am an instance to prove the contrary:	F 525	2.1.137		Mephst
For I tell thee I am damn'd, and <am> now in hell.	F 526	2.1.138		Mephst
for I am wanton and lascivious, and cannot live without a wife.	F 530	2.1.142	P	Faust
<How, a wife? I prithee Faustus talke not of a wife>.	F 530	(HC261) A	P	Mephst
<Nay sweete Mephastophilis fetch me one, for I will have one>.	F 530	(HC261) A	P	Faust
<Well thou wilt have one, sit there till I come,	F 531	(HC261) A	P	Mephst
This will I keepe, as chary as my life.	F 551	2.1.163		Faust
I have a booke wherein I might beholde al spels and	F 551.1	2.1.164A	P	Faust
have a booke wherein I might beholde al spels and incantations,	F 551.1	2.1.164A	P	Faust
and incantations, that I might raise up spirits when I please].	F 551.2	2.1.165A	P	Faust
I have a booke where I might see al characters of <and> planets	F 551.4	2.1.167A	P	Faust
I might see al characters of <and> planets of the heavens,	F 551.4	2.1.167A	P	Faust
heavens, that I might knowe their motions and dispositions].	F 551.5	2.1.168A	P	Faust
booke more, and then I have done, wherein I might see al plants,	F 551.8	2.1.171A	P	Faust
wherein I might see al plants, hearbes and trees that grow upon	F 551.9	2.1.172A	P	Faust
[Tut I warrant thee].	F 551.13	2.1.176A	P	Mephst
When I behold the heavens then I repent/And curse thee wicked	F 552	2.2.1		Faust
I tell thee Faustus it is <tis> not halfe so faire/As thou, or	F 557	2.2.6		Mephst
I will renounce this Magicke and repent.	F 562	2.2.11		Faust
Who buzzeth in mine eares I am a spirit?	F 565	2.2.14		Faust
Be I a devill yet God may pitty me,	F 566	2.2.15		Faust
Yea <I>, God will pitty me if I repent.	F 567	2.2.16		Faust
I, but Faustus never shall repent.	F 568	2.2.17		BdAngl
My heart is <hearts so> hardned, I cannot repent:	F 569	2.2.18		Faust
Scarce can I name salvation, faith, or heaven,	F 570	2.2.19		Faust
long e're this, I should have done the deed <slaine my selfe>,	F 575	2.2.24		Faust
Have not I made blind Homer sing to me/Of Alexanders love, and	F 577	2.2.26		Faust
Why should I die then, or basely despaire?	F 582	2.2.31		Faust

I (cont.)

I am resolv'd, Faustus shall not <nere> repent.	F 583	2.2.32		Faust
I.	F 608	2.2.57	P	Mephst
Well, I am answer'd:	F 618	2.2.67	P	Faust
I will not.	F 619	2.2.68	P	Mephst
Move me not Faustus <for I will not tell thee>.	F 621	2.2.70	P	Mephst
Villaine, have I not bound thee to tell me any thing?	F 622	2.2.71	P	Faust
I, that is not against our Kingdome:	F 623	2.2.72	P	Mephst
I, go accursed spirit to ugly hell:	F 627	2.2.76		Faust
There's none but I have interest in the same.	F 637	2.2.86		Lucifr
I am Lucifer,	F 639	2.2.88		Lucifr
Nor will [I] <Faustus> henceforth:	F 647	2.2.96		Faust
That shall I soone: What art thou the first?	F 663	2.2.112		Faust
I am Pride; I disdaine to have any parents:	F 664	2.2.113	P	Pride
I am like to Ovids Flea, I can creepe into every corner of a	F 664	2.2.113	P	Pride
like to Ovids Flea, I can creepe into every corner of a Wench:	F 665	2.2.114	P	Pride
Sometimes, like a Perriwig, I sit upon her Brow:	F 666	2.2.115	P	Pride
next, like a Neckelace I hang about her Necke:	F 666	2.2.115	P	Pride
I kisse her [lippes]; And then turning my selfe to a wrought	F 667	2.2.116	P	Pride
<indeede I doe, what doe I not>?	F 668	(HC263)A	P	Pride
And then turning my selfe to a wrought Smocke do what I list.	F 668	2.2.117	P	Pride
I am Covetousnesse:	F 674	2.2.123	P	Covet
<I would desire, that this house,	F 675	(HC263)A	P	Covet
bag; and might I now obtaine <have> my wish, this house,	F 675	2.2.124	P	Covet
that I might locke you safe into <uppe in> my <goode> Chest:	F 676	2.2.125	P	Covet
I am Envy, begotten of a Chimney-sweeper, and an Oyster-wife:	F 679	2.2.128	P	Envy
I cannot read, and therefore wish all books burn'd <were	F 680	2.2.129	P	Envy
I am leane with seeing others eate:	F 681	2.2.130	P	Envy
and I live along, then thou should'st see how fat I'de <I	F 682	2.2.131	P	Envy
live along, then thou should'st see how fat I'de <I would> be.	F 683	2.2.132	P	Envy
but must thou sit, and I stand?	F 683	2.2.132	P	Envy
I am Wrath:	F 686	2.2.135	P	Wrath
I had neither father nor mother, I leapt out of a Lyons mouth	F 686	2.2.135	P	Wrath
I leapt out of a Lyons mouth when I was scarce <half> an houre	F 686	2.2.135	P	Wrath
out of a Lyons mouth when I was scarce <half> an houre old,	F 687	2.2.136	P	Wrath
<I> have run up and downe the world with these <this> case of	F 688	2.2.137	P	Wrath
my selfe when I could get none <had no body> to fight withall:	F 689	2.2.138	P	Wrath
I was borne in hell, and look to it, for some of you shall be	F 690	2.2.139	P	Wrath
I <who I sir, I> am Gluttony; my parents are all dead, and the	F 693	2.2.142	P	Glutny
I <O I> come of a Royall Pedigree <parentage>, my father	F 696	2.2.145	P	Glutny
Not I.	F 702	2.2.151	P	Faust
Hey ho; I am Sloth:	F 705	2.2.154	P	Sloth
I was begotten on a sunny bank:	F 705	2.2.154	P	Sloth
[where I have laine ever since, and you have done me great	F 705.1	2.2.155A	P	Sloth
Who I <I I> sir?	F 708	2.2.160	P	Ltchry
I am one that loves an inch of raw Mutton, better then an ell	F 708	2.2.160	P	Ltchry
O might I see hell, and returne againe safe, how happy were I	F 714	2.2.166	P	Faust
I see hell, and returne againe safe, how happy were I then.	F 715	2.2.167	P	Faust
Faustus, thou shalt, at midnight I will send for thee;	F 716	2.2.168		Lucifr
[This will I keepe as chary as my life].	F 719.1	2.2.172		Faust
What Dick, looke to the horses there till I come againe.	F 722	2.3.1	P	Robin
I have gotten one of Doctor Faustus conjuring bookes, and now	F 723	2.3.2	P	Robin
I walke the horses, I scorn't 'faith, I have other matters in	F 726	2.3.5	P	Robin
the horses, I scorn't 'faith, I have other matters in hand,	F 726	2.3.5	P	Robin
I have other matters in hand, let the horses walk themselves	F 726	2.3.5	P	Robin
circle, I say, least I send you into the Ostry with a vengeance.	F 732	2.3.11	P	Robin
I say, least I send you into the Ostry with a vengeance.	F 733	2.3.12	P	Robin
I, there be of us here, that have waded as deepe into matters,	F 740	2.3.19	P	Robin
I thought you did not sneake up and downe after her for	F 742	2.3.21	P	Dick
But I prethee tell me, in good sadnesse Robin, is that a	F 743	2.3.22	P	Dick
brave, prethee let's to it presently, for I am as dry as a dog.	F 751	2.3.30	P	Dick
And as I guesse will first arrive at Rome,	F 775	2.3.54		2Chor
Hast thou, as earst I did command,	F 801	3.1.23		Faust
I have my Faustus, and for proofe thereof,	F 803	3.1.25		Mephst
<Faustus I have, and because we wil not be unprovided,	F 805	(HC265)A	P	Mephst
I chuse his privy chamber for our use.	F 806	3.1.28		Mephst
I have taken up his holinesse privy chamber for our use>.	F 806	(HC265)A	P	Mephst
I hope his Holinesse will bid us welcome.	F 807	3.1.29		Faust
Of ever-burning Phlegeton, I sweare,	F 827	3.1.49		Faust
That I do long to see the Monuments/And situation of bright	F 828	3.1.50		Faust
I know you'd <faine> see the Pope/And take some part of holy	F 831	3.1.53		Mephst
Whilst I am here on earth let me be cloyd/With all things that	F 837	3.1.59		Faust
And grant me my request, and then I go.	F 846	3.1.68		Faust
And what might please mine eye, I there beheld.	F 853	3.1.75		Faust
But thus I fall to Peter, not to thee.	F 872	3.1.94		Bruno
Thy selfe and I, may parly with this Pope:	F 896	3.1.118		Faust
Faustus, I goe.	F 901	3.1.123		Mephst
I was elected by the Emperour.	F 905	3.1.127		Bruno
<Well, I am content, to compasse then some sport>,	F 989	(HC266)A		Faust
<Then charme me that I may be invisible>,	F 991	(HC266)A		Faust
That I may walke invisible to all,	F 992	3.2.12		Faust
And doe what ere I please, unseene of any.	F 993	3.2.13		Faust
<to do what I please unseene of any whilst I stay in Rome>.	F 993	(HC266)A	P	Faust
Whilst on thy head I lay my hand,	F 995	3.2.15		Mephst
Did I not tell you,/To morrow we would sit i'th Consistory,	F1016	3.2.36		Pope
I thanke your Holinesse.	F1038	3.2.58		Archbp
Raymond pray fall too, I am beholding/To the Bishop of Millaine,	F1041	3.2.61		Pope
I thanke you sir.	F1043	3.2.63		Faust
I, pray do, for Faustus is a dry.	F1052	3.2.72		Faust
Lord Raymond, I drink unto your grace.	F1053	3.2.73		Pope
I pledge your grace.	F1054	3.2.74		Faust
I pray my Lords have patience at this troublesome banquet.	F1058	3.2.78		Pope
I thinke it be some Ghost crept out of Purgatory, and now is	F1059	3.2.79	P	Archbp

I (cont.)

O I am slaine, help me my Lords:	F1068	3.2.88	Pope
for I can tell you, you'le be curst with Bell, Booke, and	F1072	3.2.92	P Mephst
him, as he was never conjur'd in his life, I warrant him:	F1092	3.3.5	P Robin
I am glad I have found you, you are a couple of fine	F1096	3.3.9	P Vintnr
what you say, we looke not like cup-stealers I can tell you.	F1100	3.3.13	P Robin
Never deny't, for I know you have it, and I'le search you.	F1101	3.3.14	P Vintnr
I and spare not:	F1102	3.3.15	P Robin
I, I, do, do, hold the cup Robin, I feare not your searching;	F1105	3.3.18	P Dick
I feare not your searching; we scorne to steale your cups I can	F1105	3.3.18	P Dick
your searching; we scorne to steale your cups I can tell you.	F1106	3.3.19	P Dick
plague take you, I thought 'twas your knavery to take it away:	F1110	3.3.23	P Vintnr
I much:	F1112	3.3.25	P Robin
How am I vexed by these villaines Charmes?	F1117	3.3.30	Mephst
Constantinople have they brought me now <am I hither brought>,	F1118	3.3.31	Mephst
I, I pray you heartily sir; for wee cal'd you but in jeast I	F1123	3.3.36	P Dick
I pray you heartily sir; for wee cal'd you but in jeast I	F1123	3.3.36	P Dick
you heartily sir; for wee cal'd you but in jeast I promise you.	F1124	3.3.37	P Dick
I pray sir, let me have the carrying of him about to shew some	F1128	3.3.41	P Robin
[I meane his friends and nearest companions],	F1142	3.3.55A	3Chor
[I leave untold, your eyes shall see performd].	F1154	3.3.67A	3Chor
Fast a sleepe I warrant you,	F1173	4.1.19	Mrtino
love with him, I would he would post with him to Rome againe.	F1191	4.1.37	P Benvol
Not I.	F1194	4.1.40	P Benvol
I, and I fall not asleepe i'th meane time.	F1196	4.1.42	Benvol
I am content for this once to thrust my head out at a window:	F1199	4.1.45	P Benvol
I have a charme in my head, shall controule him as well as the	F1202	4.1.48	P Benvol
shall controule him as well as the Conjurer, I warrant you.	F1203	4.1.49	P Benvol
I doe not greatly beleeve him, he lookes as like [a] conjurer	F1227	4.1.73	P Benvol
Faustus I will.	F1240	4.1.86	Mephst
zounds I could eate my selfe for anger, to thinke I have beene	F1242	4.1.88	P Benvol
to thinke I have beene such an Asse all this while, to stand	F1243	4.1.89	P Benvol
My Lord, I must forewarne your Majesty,	F1248	4.1.94	Faust
I, I, and I am content too:	F1254	4.1.100	P Benvol
That in mine armes I would have compast him.	F1262	4.1.108	Emper
But Faustus, since I may not speake to them,	F1263	4.1.109	Emper
I have heard it said,/That this faire Lady, whilest she liv'd	F1265	4.1.111	Emper
How may I prove that saying to be true?	F1268	4.1.114	Emper
Faustus I see it plaine,	F1270	4.1.116	Emper
Then if I gain'd another Monarchie.	F1272	4.1.118	Emper
I blame thee not to sleepe much, having such a head of thine	F1284	4.1.130	P Emper
zounds hee'l raise up a kennell of Divels I thinke anon:	F1306	4.1.152	P Benvol
'sbloud I am never able to endure these torments.	F1306	4.1.152	P Benvol
which being all I desire, I am content to remove his hornes.	F1313	4.1.159	P Faust
But an I be not reveng'd for this, would I might be turn'd to a	F1319	4.1.165	P Benvol
would I might be turn'd to a gaping Oyster, and drinke nothing	F1319	4.1.165	P Benvol
Shall I let slip so great an injury,	F1328	4.2.4	Benvol
Till with my sword I have that Conjurer slaine.	F1333	4.2.9	Benvol
By this (I know) the Conjurer is neere,	F1343	4.2.19	Benvol
I saw him kneele, and kisse the Emperours hand,	F1344	4.2.20	Benvol
And pants untill I see that Conjurer dead.	F1352	4.2.28	Benvol
Thus will I end his griefes immediatly.	F1367	4.2.43	Benvol
I, that's the head, and here the body lies,	F1375	4.2.51	Benvol
it will weare out ten birchin broomes I warrant you.	F1385	4.2.61	P Benvol
I, [all] <I call> your hearts to recompence this deed.	F1394	4.2.70	Faust
you not Traytors, I was limitted/For foure and twenty yeares,	F1395	4.2.71	Faust
And I had breath'd a man made free from harme.	F1400	4.2.76	Faust
But wherefore doe I dally my revenge?	F1401	4.2.77	Faust
I heard them parly with the Conjurer.	F1422	4.2.98	1Soldr
Defend me heaven, shall I be haunted still?	F1439	4.3.9	Benvol
I have a Castle joyning neere these woods,	F1452	4.3.22	Benvol
I beseech your Worship accept of these forty Dollors.	F1457	4.4.1	P HrsCsr
I have no great need to sell him, but if thou likest him for	F1460	4.4.4	P Faust
more, take him, because I see thou hast a good minde to him.	F1461	4.4.5	P Faust
I beseech you sir accept of this; I am a very poore man, and	F1463	4.4.7	P HrsCsr
I am a very poore man, and have lost very much of late by horse	F1463	4.4.7	P HrsCsr
Well, I will not stand with thee, give me the money:	F1466	4.4.10	P Faust
now sirra I must tell you, that you may ride him o're hedge and	F1467	4.4.11	P Faust
bid the Hostler deliver him unto you, and remember what I say.	F1475	4.4.19	P Faust
I warrant you sir; O joyfull day:	F1476	4.4.20	P HrsCsr
Now am I a made man for ever.	F1476	4.4.20	P HrsCsr
I riding my horse into the water, thinking some hidden mystery	F1484	4.4.28	P HrsCsr
I had nothing under me but a little straw, and had much ado to	F1486	4.4.30	P HrsCsr
Alas I am undone, what shall I do?	F1492	4.4.36	P HrsCsr
I have puld off his leg.	F1492	4.4.36	P HrsCsr
and one to whom I must be no niggard of my cunning; Come,	F1504	4.4.48	P Faust
Sirra Dick, dost thou know why I stand so mute?	F1509	4.5.5	P Robin
I am eighteene pence on the score, but say nothing, see if she	F1511	4.5.7	P Robin
I hope my score stands still.	F1515	4.5.11	P Robin
I there's no doubt of that, for me thinkes you make no hast to	F1516	4.5.12	P Hostss
Why Hostesse, I say, fetch us some Beere.	F1518	4.5.14	P Dick
I, a plague take him, heere's some on's have cause to know him;	F1523	4.5.19	P HrsCsr
As I was going to Wittenberge t'other day, with a loade of Hay,	F1525	4.5.21	P Carter
I thinking that a little would serve his turne, bad him take as	F1528	4.5.24	P Carter
fell to eating; and as I am a cursen man, he never left eating,	F1530	4.5.26	P Carter
be; for I have heard of one, that ha's eate a load of logges.	F1533	4.5.29	P Robin
I went to him yesterday to buy a horse of him, and he would by	F1536	4.5.32	P HrsCsr
because I knew him to be such a horse, as would run over hedge	F1537	4.5.33	P HrsCsr
and never tyre, I gave him his money; so when I had my horse,	F1539	4.5.35	P HrsCsr
so when I had my horse, Doctor Fauster bad me ride him night	F1539	4.5.35	P HrsCsr
I thinking the horse had had some [rare] quality that he would	F1542	4.5.38	P HrsCsr
what did I but rid him into a great river, and when I came just	F1543	4.5.39	P HrsCsr
and when I came just in the midst my horse vanisht away, and I	F1544	4.5.40	P HrsCsr

I (cont.)

horse vanisht away, and I sate straddling upon a bottle of Hay.	F1544	4.5.40	P	HrsCsr
But you shall heare how bravely I serv'd him for it; I went me	F1547	4.5.43	P	HrsCsr
it; I went me home to his house, and there I found him asleepe;	F1548	4.5.44	P	HrsCsr
and there I found him asleepe; I kept a hallowing and whooping	F1548	4.5.44	P	HrsCsr
I kept a hallowing and whooping in his eares, but all could not	F1548	4.5.44	P	HrsCsr
I seeing that, tooke him by the leg, and never rested pulling,	F1550	4.5.46	P	HrsCsr
till I had pul'd me his leg quite off, and now 'tis at home in	F1551	4.5.47	P	HrsCsr
I how sufficiently to recompence your great deserts in erecting	F1559	4.6.2	P	Duke
I do thinke my selfe my good Lord, highly recompenced, in that	F1563	4.6.6	P	Faust
therefor I pray you tell me, what is the thing you most desire	F1566	4.6.9	P	Faust
I have heard that great bellyed women, do long for things, are	F1568	4.6.11	P	Faust
I finde you so kind I will make knowne unto you what my heart	F1570	4.6.13	P	Lady
kind I will make knowne unto you what my heart desires to have,	F1570	4.6.13	P	Lady
I would request no better meate, then a dish of ripe grapes.	F1572	4.6.15	P	Lady
Madam, I will do more then this for your content.	F1575	4.6.18	P	Faust
be good, for they come from a farre Country I can tell you.	F1577	4.6.20	P	Faust
by meanes of a swift spirit that I have, I had these grapes	F1585	4.6.28	P	Faust
spirit that I have, I had these grapes brought as you see.	F1585	4.6.28	P	Faust
And trust me, they are the sweetest grapes that e're I tasted.	F1587	4.6.30	P	Lady
I hope sir, we have wit enough to be more bold then welcome.	F1595	4.6.38	P	HrsCsr
I, and we will speake with him.	F1601	4.6.44		Carter
I do beseech your grace let them come in,	F1605	4.6.48		Faust
Do as thou wilt Faustus, I give thee leave.	F1607	4.6.50		Duke
I thanke your grace.	F1608	4.6.51		Faust
I have procur'd your pardons: welcome all.	F1610	4.6.53		Faust
I marry can I, we are under heaven.	F1615	4.6.58	P	Carter
I but sir sauce box, know you in what place?	F1616	4.6.59		Servnt
I, I, the house is good enough to drink in:	F1617	4.6.60	P	HrsCsr
I humbly thanke your grace: then fetch some Beere.	F1625	4.6.68		Faust
I mary, there spake a Doctor indeed, and 'faith Ile drinke a	F1626	4.6.69	P	HrsCsr
I, I, he does not stand much upon that.	F1630	4.6.73	P	HrsCsr
Yes, I remember I sold one a horse.	F1635	4.6.78		Faust
Yes, I do verie well remember that.	F1638	4.6.81	P	Faust
Then I pray remember your curtesie.	F1641	4.6.84	P	Carter
I thank you sir.	F1642	4.6.85	P	Faust
'Tis not so much worth; I pray you tel me one thing.	F1643	4.6.86	P	Carter
sir, I would make nothing of you, but I would faine know that.	F1648	4.6.91	P	Carter
Then I assure thee certainelie they are.	F1650	4.6.93		Faust
I thanke you, I am fully satisfied.	F1651	4.6.94	P	Carter
sir, did not I pull off one of your legs when you were asleepe?	F1655	4.6.98	P	HrsCsr
But I have it againe now I am awake:	F1657	4.6.100	P	Faust
have sent away my guesse, I pray who shall pay me for my A--	F1667	4.6.110	P	Hostss
I think my Maister means to die shortly, he has made his will,	F1674	5.1.1	P	Wagner
I wonder what he meanes, if death were nie, he would not	F1676	5.1.3	P	Wagner
For that I know your friendship is unfain'd,	F1689	5.1.16		Faust
Gentlemen farewell: the same wish I to you.	F1706	5.1.33		Faust
For gentle sonne, I speake it not in wrath,	F1719	5.1.46		OldMan
I see an Angell hover <hovers> ore thy head,	F1730	5.1.57		OldMan
I feele thy words to comfort my distressed soule,	F1735	5.1.62		Faust
<I goe sweete Faustus, but with heavy cheare>,	F1737	(HC269)A		OldMan
Faustus I leave thee, but with griefe of heart,	F1737	5.1.64		OldMan
I do repent, and yet I doe despaire,	F1740	5.1.67		Faust
What shall I doe to shun the snares of death?	F1742	5.1.69		Faust
Thou traytor Faustus, I arrest thy soule,	F1743	5.1.70		Mephst
I do repent I ere offended him,	F1746	5.1.73		Faust
And with my bloud againe I will confirme/The <My> former vow I	F1749	5.1.76		Faust
againe I will confirme/The <My> former vow I made to Lucifer.	F1750	5.1.77		Faust
His faith is great, I cannot touch his soule;	F1756	5.1.83		Mephst
But what I may afflict his body with,	F1757	5.1.84		Mephst
I will attempt, which is but little worth.	F1758	5.1.85		Mephst
That I may <might> have unto my paramour,	F1761	5.1.88		Faust
That heavenly Hellen, which I saw of late,	F1762	5.1.89		Faust
And keepe [mine oath] <my vow> I made to Lucifer.	F1765	5.1.92		Faust
Here will I dwell, for heaven is <be> in these lippes,	F1773	5.1.100		Faust
I will be Paris <Pacis>, and for love of thee,	F1775	5.1.102		Faust
And I will combat with weake Menelaus,	F1777	5.1.104		Faust
Yea, I will wound Achilles in the heele,	F1779	5.1.106		Faust
[Hence hel, for hence I flie unto my God].	F1796	5.1.123A		OldMan
dutie, I do yeeld/My life and lasting service for your love.	F1818	5.2.22		Wagner
chamber-fellow, had I liv'd with thee, then had I lived still,	F1824	5.2.28	P	Faust
thee, then had I lived still, but now must <I> dye eternally.	F1825	5.2.29	P	Faust
remember that I have beene a student here these thirty yeares,	F1840	5.2.44	P	Faust
O would I had never seene Wittenberg <Wertenberge>, never read	F1841	5.2.45	P	Faust
and what wonders I have done, all Germany can witnesse, yea all	F1842	5.2.46	P	Faust
<O> my God, I would weepe, but the Divell drawes in my teares.	F1850	5.2.54	P	Faust
I would lift up my hands, but see they hold 'em <them>, they	F1852	5.2.56	P	Faust
[Ah] <O> gentlemen, I gave them my soule for my cunning.	F1856	5.2.60		Faust
I writ them a bill with mine owne bloud, the date is expired:	F1860	5.2.64	P	Faust
Oft have I thought to have done so:	F1864	5.2.68	P	Faust
but the Divel threatned to teare me in peeces if I nam'd God:	F1865	5.2.69	P	Faust
me <both> body and soule, if I once gave eare to Divinitie:	F1866	5.2.70	P	Faust
God will strengthen me, I will stay with Faustus.	F1870	5.2.74	P	3Schol
I, pray for me, pray for me:	F1873	5.2.77	P	Faust
if I live till morning, Il'e visit you:	F1877	5.2.81	P	Faust
I, Faustus, now thou hast no hope of heaven,	F1880	5.2.84		Mephst
I doe confesse it Faustus, and rejoyce;	F1885	5.2.89		Mephst
'Twas I, that when thou wer't i'the way to heaven,	F1886	5.2.90		Mephst
view the Scriptures, then I turn'd the leaves/And led thine eye.	F1888	5.2.92		Mephst
O, I have seene enough to torture me.	F1921	5.2.125		Faust
And so I leave thee Faustus till anon,	F1924	5.2.128		BdAngl
Yet will I call on him: O spare me Lucifer.	F1942	5.2.146		Faust
Then will I headlong run into the earth:	F1948	5.2.152		Faust

I (cont.)

flie from me, and I be chang'd/[Unto] <Into> some brutish beast.	F1967	5.2.171		Faust
one, me thought/I heard him shreeke and call aloud for helpe:	F1992	5.3.10		3Schol
I hope you have seene many boyes with such pickadevaunts as I	F App	p.229 2	P	Clown
you have seene many boyes with such pickadevaunts as I have.	F App	p.229 3	P	Clown
I, and goings out too, you may see else.	F App	p.229 5	P	Clown
I know he would give his soule to the Divel for a shoulder of	F App	p.229 8	P	Wagner
burladie I had neede have it wel roasted, and good sawce to it,	F App	p.229 11	P	Clown
have it wel roasted, and good sawce to it, if I pay so deere.	F App	p.229 12	P	Clown
I, I thought that was al the land his father left him:	F App	p.229 17	P	Clown
Doe yee heare, I would be sorie to robbe you of your living.	F App	p.229 18	P	Clown
Sirra, I say in staves acre.	F App	p.229 20	P	Wagner
why then belike, if I were your man, I should be ful of vermine.	F App	p.229 21	P	Clown
then belike, if I were your man, I should be ful of vermine.	F App	p.229 22	P	Clown
have as many english counters, and what should I do with these?	F App	p.230 34	P	Clown
Beare witnesse I gave them him.	F App	p.230 41	P	Wagner
Beare witnesse I give them you againe.	F App	p.230 42	P	Clown
I will cause two divels presently to fetch thee away Baliol and	F App	p.230 43	P	Wagner
divels, say I should kill one of them, what would folkes say?	F App	p.230 46	P	Clown
divell, so I should be cald kill divell all the parish over.	F App	p.230 48	P	Clown
if I should serve you, would you teach me to raise up Banios	F App	p.230 56	P	Clown
I will teach thee to turne thy selfe to anything, to a dogge,	F App	p.231 58	P	Wagner
that I may be here and there and every where, O Ile tickle the	F App	p.231 62	P	Clown
O Lord I pray sir, let Banio and Belcher go sleepe.	F App	p.231 68	P	Clown
I thanke you sir.	F App	p.231 7	P	Faust
Well use that tricke no more, I would advise you.	F App	p.232 19		Faust
the second time, aware the third, I give you faire warning.	F App	p.232 20	P	Faust
Nay I know not, we shalbe curst with bell, booke, and candle.	F App	p.232 23	P	Mephst
here I ha stolne one of doctor Faustus conjuring books, and	F App	p.233 1	P	Robin
and ifaith I meane to search some circles for my owne use:	F App	p.233 2	P	Robin
I make al the maidens in our parish dance at my pleasure starke	F App	p.233 3	P	Robin
and so by that meanes I shal see more then ere I felt, or saw	F App	p.233 4	P	Robin
and so by that meanes I shal see more then ere I felt, or saw	F App	p.233 5	P	Robin
Rafe, keepe out, for I am about a roaring peece of worke.	F App	p.233 11	P	Robin
my maister and mistris shal finde that I can reade, he for his	F App	p.233 15	P	Robin
I can do al these things easily with it:	F App	p.234 22	P	Robin
I can make thee druncke with ipocrase at any taberne in Europe	F App	p.234 22	P	Robin
O brave Robin, shal I have Nan Spit, and to mine owne use?	F App	p.234 29	P	Rafe
did not I tell thee, we were for ever made by this doctor	F App	p.234 1	P	Robin
Drawer, I hope al is payd, God be with you, come Rafe.	F App	p.234 5	P	Robin
with you, I must yet have a goblet payde from you ere you goe.	F App	p.234 7	P	Vintnr
I a goblet Rafe, I a goblet?	F App	p.234 9	P	Robin
I scorne you:	F App	p.234 9	P	Robin
I a goblet?	F App	p.234 10	P	Robin
I meane so sir with your favor.	F App	p.234 11	P	Vintnr
I must say somewhat to your felow, you sir.	F App	p.234 13	P	Vintnr
stand aside you had best, I charge you in the name of Belzabub:	F App	p.235 19	P	Robin
Ile tel you what I meane.	F App	p.235 22	P	Robin
Misericordia pro nobis, what shal I doe?	F App	p.235 30	P	Robin
How am I vexed with these vilaines charmes?	F App	p.235 37		Mephst
From Constantinople am I hither come,	F App	p.235 38		Mephst
presumption, I transforme thee into an Ape, and thee into a Dog,	F App	p.235 43	P	Mephst
And I must be a Dogge.	F App	p.236 47	P	Rafe
I have heard strange report of thy knowledge in the blacke	F App	p.236 1	P	Emper
and here I sweare to thee, by the honor of mine Imperial	F App	p.236 8	P	Emper
I must confesse my selfe farre inferior to the report men have	F App	p.236 12	P	Faust
I am content to do whatsoever your majesty shall command me.	F App	p.236 15	P	Faust
Faustus, marke what I shall say, As I was sometime solitary set,	F App	p.236 17	P	Emper
I shall say, As I was sometime solitary set, within my Closet,	F App	p.236 17	P	Emper
(I feare me) never attaine to that degree of high renowne and	F App	p.236 22	P	Emper
As when I heare but motion made of him,	F App	p.237 27		Emper
It grieves my soule I never saw the man:	F App	p.237 28		Emper
And give me cause to praise thee whilst I live.	F App	p.237 36		Emper
I am ready to accomplish your request, so farre forth as by art	F App	p.237 37	P	Faust
forth as by art and power of my spirit I am able to performe.	F App	p.237 38	P	Faust
I mary master doctor, now theres a signe of grace in you, when	F App	p.237 44	P	Knight
I doubt not shal sufficiently content your Imperiall majesty.	F App	p.237 48	P	Faust
I heard this Lady while she liv'd had a wart or moale in her	F App	p.238 60	P	Emper
or moale in her necke, how shal I know whether it be so or no?	F App	p.238 61	P	Emper
why I has thought thou hadst beene a batcheler, but now I see	F App	p.238 69	P	Emper
but now I see thou hast a wife, that not only gives thee	F App	p.238 70	P	Emper
Vilaine I say, undo what thou hast done.	F App	p.238 75		Knight
I thinke I have met with you for it.	F App	p.238 78	P	Faust
which being all I desire, I am content to release him of his	F App	p.238 84	P	Faust
being all I desire, I am content to release him of his hornes:	F App	p.238 84	P	Faust
Now my good Lord having done my duety, I humbly take my leave.	F App	p.238 86	P	Faust
til I am past this faire and pleasant greene, ile walke on	F App	p.239 96	P	Faust
I have beene al this day seeking one maister Fustian:	F App	p.239 98	P	HrsCsr
I have brought you forty dollers for your horse.	F App	p.239 101	P	HrsCsr
I cannot sel him so:	F App	p.239 103	P	Faust
Alas sir, I have no more, I pray you speake for me.	F App	p.239 104	P	HrsCsr
I pray you let him have him, he is an honest felow, and he has	F App	p.239 105	P	Mephst
but I must tel you one thing before you have him, ride him not	F App	p.239 108	P	Faust
Now am I made man for ever, Ile not leave my horse for fortie:	F App	p.239 114	P	HrsCsr
at ease, if I bring his water to you, youle tel me what it is?	F App	p.240 118	P	HrsCsr
what, doost thinke I am a horse-doctor?	F App	p.240 120	P	Faust
has purg'd me of fortie Dollers, I shall never see them more:	F App	p.240 129	P	HrsCsr
but yet like an asse as I was, I would not be ruled by him, for	F App	p.240 130	P	HrsCsr
I would not be ruled by him, for he bade me I should ride him	F App	p.240 130	P	HrsCsr
by him, for he bade me I should ride him into no water; now,	F App	p.240 131	P	HrsCsr
I thinking my horse had had some rare qualitie that he would	F App	p.240 131	P	HrsCsr
I like a ventrous youth, rid him into the deepe pond at the	F App	p.240 132	P	HrsCsr
I was no sooner in the middle of the pond, but my horse vanisht	F App	p.240 134	P	HrsCsr

I (cont.)

and I sat upon a bottle of hey, never so neare drowning in my	F App	p.240 135 P HrsCsr
But I wil speake with him.	F App	p.240 140 P HrsCsr
I tell thee he has not slept this eight nights.	F App	p.240 144 P Mephst
I, this is he, God save ye maister doctor, maister doctor,	F App	p.241 148 P HrsCsr
Ile make you wake ere I goe.	F App	p.241 153 P HrsCsr
Alas, I am undone, what shall I do:	F App	p.241 154 P HrsCsr
I have none about me, come to my Oastrie, and Ile give them	F App	p.241 161 P HrsCsr
and the Horsecourser I take it, a bottle of hey for his labour;	F App	p.241 165 P Faust
to whom I must be no niggard of my cunning, come	F App	p.241 171 P Faust
My gratious Lord, I am glad it contents you so wel:	F App	p.242 3 P Faust
I have heard that great bellied women do long for some dainties	F App	p.242 4 P Faust
And for I see your curteous intent to pleasure me, I wil not	F App	p.242 8 P Duchss
I wil not hide from you the thing my heart desires, and were it	F App	p.242 8 P Duchss
I would desire no better meate then a dish of ripe grapes.	F App	p.242 10 P Duchss
and by means of a swift spirit that I have, I had them brought	F App	p.242 22 P Faust
swift spirit that I have, I had them brought hither, as ye see,	F App	p.242 23 P Faust
they be the best grapes that ere I tasted in my life before.	F App	p.242 26 P Duchss
I am glad they content you so Madam.	F App	p.242 27 P Faust
And so I wil my Lord, and whilst I live, Rest beholding for	F App	p.243 30 P Duchss
my Lord, and whilst I live, Rest beholding for this curtesie.	F App	p.243 30 P Duchss
I humbly thanke your Grace.	F App	p.243 32 P Faust
I thinke my maister meanes to die shortly,	F App	p.243 1 Wagner
Ah Doctor Faustus, that I might prevaile,	F App	p.243 34 OldMan
I to the Torrid Zone where midday burnes,	Lucan, First Booke	16
Thee if I invocate, I shall not need/To crave Apolloes ayde, or	Lucan, First Booke	64
The causes first I purpose to unfould/Of these garboiles,	Lucan, First Booke	67
I hate thee not, to thee my conquests stoope,	Lucan, First Booke	203
Hence leagues, and covenants; Fortune thee I follow,	Lucan, First Booke	228
or blustring south were cause/I know not, but the cloudy ayre	Lucan, First Booke	237
And I might pleade, and draw the Commons minds/To favour thee,	Lucan, First Booke	275
Five yeeres I lengthned thy commaund in France:	Lucan, First Booke	277
What should I talke of mens corne reapt by force,	Lucan, First Booke	318
me,/Because at his commaund I wound not up/My conquering Eagles?	Lucan, First Booke	339
say I merit nought,/Yet for long service done, reward these	Lucan, First Booke	340
So be I may be bold to speake a truth,	Lucan, First Booke	361
Love over-rules my will, I must obay thee,	Lucan, First Booke	373
Caesar; he whom I heare thy trumpets charge/I hould no Romaine;	Lucan, First Booke	374
Caesar; he whom I heare thy trumpets charge/I hould no Romaine;	Lucan, First Booke	375
I tremble to unfould/What you intend, great Jove is now	Lucan, First Booke	630
Yet more will happen then I can unfold;	Lucan, First Booke	634
Pean whither am I halde?	Lucan, First Booke	677
where shall I fall,/Thus borne aloft?	Lucan, First Booke	677
I see Pangeus hill,/With hoarie toppe, and under Hemus mount	Lucan, First Booke	678
Whither turne I now?	Lucan, First Booke	682
This headlesse trunke that lies on Nylus sande/I know:	Lucan, First Booke	685
now throughout the aire I flie,/To doubtfull Sirtes and drie	Lucan, First Booke	685
now through the world againe/I goe; o Phoebus shew me Neptunes	Lucan, First Booke	692
And other Regions, I have seene Philippi:	Lucan, First Booke	693
Muse upreard <prepar'd> I [meant] <meane> to sing of armes,	Ovid's Elegies	1.1.5
When in this [workes] <worke> first verse I trod aloft,	Ovid's Elegies	1.1.21
[Love] <I> slackt my Muse, and made my [numbers] <number> soft.	Ovid's Elegies	1.1.22
I have no mistris, nor no favorit,	Ovid's Elegies	1.1.23
Thus I complaind, but Love unlockt his quiver,	Ovid's Elegies	1.1.25
I burne, love in my idle bosome sits.	Ovid's Elegies	1.1.30
Although the nights be long, I sleepe not tho,	Ovid's Elegies	1.2.3
Were Love the cause, it's like I shoulde descry him,	Ovid's Elegies	1.2.5
I saw a brandisht fire increase in strength,	Ovid's Elegies	1.2.11
Which being not shakt <slackt>, I saw it die at length.	Ovid's Elegies	1.2.12
Loe I confesse, I am thy captive I,	Ovid's Elegies	1.2.19
What needes thou warre, I sue to thee for grace,	Ovid's Elegies	1.2.21
I lately cought, will have a new made wound,	Ovid's Elegies	1.2.29
Unlesse I erre, full many shalt thou burne,	Ovid's Elegies	1.2.43
Then seeing I grace thy show in following thee,	Ovid's Elegies	1.2.49
I aske but right:	Ovid's Elegies	1.3.1
Either love, or cause that I may never hate:	Ovid's Elegies	1.3.2
I aske too much, would she but let me love hir,	Ovid's Elegies	1.3.3
Love <Jove> knowes with such like praiers, I dayly move hir:	Ovid's Elegies	1.3.4
Soone may you plow the little lands <land> I have,	Ovid's Elegies	1.3.9
I gladly graunt my parents given to save,	Ovid's Elegies	1.3.10
I love but one, and hir I love change never,	Ovid's Elegies	1.3.15
That I may write things worthy thy faire lookes:	Ovid's Elegies	1.3.20
Shall I sit gazing as a bashfull guest,	Ovid's Elegies	1.4.3
While others touch the damsell I love best?	Ovid's Elegies	1.4.4
I am no halfe horse, nor in woods I dwell,	Ovid's Elegies	1.4.9
Yet scarse my hands from thee containe I well.	Ovid's Elegies	1.4.10
Before thy husband come, though I not see/What may be done, yet	Ovid's Elegies	1.4.13
When I (my light) do or say ought that please thee,	Ovid's Elegies	1.4.25
When thou hast tasted, I will take the cup,	Ovid's Elegies	1.4.31
And where thou drinkst, on that part I will sup.	Ovid's Elegies	1.4.32
If thou givest kisses, I shall all disclose,	Ovid's Elegies	1.4.39
I have beene wanton, therefore am perplext,	Ovid's Elegies	1.4.45
I and my wench oft under clothes did lurke,	Ovid's Elegies	1.4.47
Least I should thinke thee guilty of offence.	Ovid's Elegies	1.4.50
There will I finde thee, or be found by thee,	Ovid's Elegies	1.4.57
Aye me I warne what profits some few howers,	Ovid's Elegies	1.4.59
I will weepe/And to the dores sight of thy selfe [will] keepe:	Ovid's Elegies	1.4.61
To him I pray it no delight may bring,	Ovid's Elegies	1.4.67
To rest my limbes, uppon a bedde I lay,	Ovid's Elegies	1.5.2
I snatcht her gowne:	Ovid's Elegies	1.5.13
Not one wen in her bodie could I spie,	Ovid's Elegies	1.5.18
What armes and shoulders did I touch and see,	Ovid's Elegies	1.5.19
How smoothe a bellie, under her waste sawe I,	Ovid's Elegies	1.5.21

I (cont.)

I clinged her naked bodie, downe she fell,	Ovid's Elegies	1.5.24
Little I aske, a little entrance make,	Ovid's Elegies	1.6.3
But in times past I fear'd vaine shades, and night,	Ovid's Elegies	1.6.9
Thee feare I too much:	Ovid's Elegies	1.6.15
only thee I flatter,/Thy lightning can my life in pieces	Ovid's Elegies	1.6.15
For thee I did thy mistris faire entreate.	Ovid's Elegies	1.6.20
With armes or armed men I come not guarded,	Ovid's Elegies	1.6.33
I am alone, were furious Love discarded.	Ovid's Elegies	1.6.34
Although I would, I cannot him cashiere/Before I be divided	Ovid's Elegies	1.6.35
would, I cannot him cashiere/Before I be divided from my geere.	Ovid's Elegies	1.6.35
would, I cannot him cashiere/Before I be divided from my geere.	Ovid's Elegies	1.6.36
Well I remember when I first did hire thee,	Ovid's Elegies	1.6.43
Night goes away: I pray thee ope the dore.	Ovid's Elegies	1.6.48
Or I more sterne then fire or sword will turne,	Ovid's Elegies	1.6.57
All have I spent:	Ovid's Elegies	1.6.61
O harder then the dores thou gardest I prove thee.	Ovid's Elegies	1.6.62
I might have then my parents deare misus'd,	Ovid's Elegies	1.7.5
Could I therefore her comely tresses teare?	Ovid's Elegies	1.7.11
That I was mad, and barbarous all men cried,	Ovid's Elegies	1.7.19
Better I could part of my selfe have wanted.	Ovid's Elegies	1.7.24
To mine owne selfe have I had strength so furious?	Ovid's Elegies	1.7.25
And to my selfe could I be so injurious?	Ovid's Elegies	1.7.26
Punisht I am, if I a Romaine beat,	Ovid's Elegies	1.7.29
He first a Goddesse strooke; an other I.	Ovid's Elegies	1.7.32
Yet he harm'd lesse, whom I profess'd to love,	Ovid's Elegies	1.7.33
I harm'd: a foe did Diomedes anger move.	Ovid's Elegies	1.7.34
But though I like a swelling floud was driven,	Ovid's Elegies	1.7.43
My nayles to scratch her lovely cheekes I bent.	Ovid's Elegies	1.7.50
Her halfe dead joynts, and trembling limmes I sawe,	Ovid's Elegies	1.7.53
Then first I did perceive I had offended,	Ovid's Elegies	1.7.59
Before her feete thrice prostrate downe I fell,	Ovid's Elegies	1.7.61
(If I have faith) I sawe the starres drop bloud,	Ovid's Elegies	1.8.11
Her I suspect among nights spirits to fly,	Ovid's Elegies	1.8.13
Fame saith as I suspect, and in her eyes/Two eye-balles shine,	Ovid's Elegies	1.8.15
By chaunce I heard her talke, these words she sayd/While	Ovid's Elegies	1.8.21
words she sayd/While closely hid betwixt two dores I layed.	Ovid's Elegies	1.8.22
Poore lover with thy gransires I exile thee.	Ovid's Elegies	1.8.66
With much a do my hands I scarsely staide.	Ovid's Elegies	1.8.110
hoary flieces/And riveld cheekes I would have puld a pieces.	Ovid's Elegies	1.8.112
and I fear'd the Bull and Eagle/And what ere love made Jove	Ovid's Elegies	1.10.7
Ask'st why I chaunge? because thou crav'st reward:	Ovid's Elegies	1.10.11
While thou wert plaine, I lov'd thy minde and face:	Ovid's Elegies	1.10.13
Why should I loose, and thou gaine by the pleasure/Which man	Ovid's Elegies	1.10.35
And whom I like eternize by mine art.	Ovid's Elegies	1.10.60
To give I love, but to be ask't disdayne,	Ovid's Elegies	1.10.63
Leave asking, and Ile give what I refraine.	Ovid's Elegies	1.10.64
If, what I do, she askes, say hope for night,	Ovid's Elegies	1.11.13
Time passeth while I speake, give her my writ/But see that	Ovid's Elegies	1.11.15
I charge thee marke her eyes and front in reading,	Ovid's Elegies	1.11.17
I hate faire Paper should writte matter lacke.	Ovid's Elegies	1.11.20
Then with triumphant laurell will I grace them/And in the midst	Ovid's Elegies	1.11.25
Subscribing that to her I consecrate/My faithfull tables being	Ovid's Elegies	1.11.27
Which I thinke gather'd from cold hemlocks flower/Wherein bad	Ovid's Elegies	1.12.9
To these my love I foolishly committed/And then with sweete	Ovid's Elegies	1.12.21
I pray that rotten age you wrackes/And sluttish white-mould	Ovid's Elegies	1.12.29
Now in her tender armes I sweetly bide,	Ovid's Elegies	1.13.5
[All] <This> could I beare, but that the wench should rise,/Who	Ovid's Elegies	1.13.25
How oft wisht I night would not give thee place,	Ovid's Elegies	1.13.27
I did not bid thee wed an aged swaine.	Ovid's Elegies	1.13.42
I chid no more, she blusht, and therefore heard me,	Ovid's Elegies	1.13.47
Leave colouring thy tresses I did cry,	Ovid's Elegies	1.14.1
I cryed, tis sinne, tis sinne, these haires to burne,	Ovid's Elegies	1.14.27
But I remember when it was my fame.	Ovid's Elegies	1.14.50
Or that unlike the line from whence I [sprong] <come>,	Ovid's Elegies	1.15.3
Nor that I studie not the brawling lawes,	Ovid's Elegies	1.15.5
I Ovid Poet of [my] <thy> wantonnesse,	Ovid's Elegies	2.1.1
That some youth hurt as I am with loves bowe/His owne flames	Ovid's Elegies	2.1.7
I durst the great celestiall battells tell,	Ovid's Elegies	2.1.11
Jove and Joves thunderbolts I had in hand/Which for his heaven	Ovid's Elegies	2.1.15
My wench her dore shut, Joves affares I left,	Ovid's Elegies	2.1.17
Toyes, and light Elegies my darts I tooke,	Ovid's Elegies	2.1.21
But when I praise a pretty wenches face/Shee in requitall doth	Ovid's Elegies	2.1.33
While I speake some fewe, yet fit words be idle.	Ovid's Elegies	2.2.2
I sawe the damsell walking yesterday/There where the porch doth	Ovid's Elegies	2.2.3
Shee pleas'd me, soone I sent, and did her woo,	Ovid's Elegies	2.2.5
I saw ones legges with fetters blacke and blewe,	Ovid's Elegies	2.2.47
I meane not to defend the scapes of any,	Ovid's Elegies	2.4.1
For I confesse, if that might merite favour,	Ovid's Elegies	2.4.3
Heere I display my lewd and loose behaviour.	Ovid's Elegies	2.4.4
I loathe, yet after that I loathe, I runne:	Ovid's Elegies	2.4.5
I cannot rule my selfe, but where love please/[Am] <And> driven	Ovid's Elegies	2.4.7
I [burne] <blushe>, and by that blushfull [glance] <glasse> am	Ovid's Elegies	2.4.12
And she thats coy I like for being no clowne,	Ovid's Elegies	2.4.13
I thinke sheele doe, but deepely can dissemble.	Ovid's Elegies	2.4.16
If she be learned, then for her skill I crave her,	Ovid's Elegies	2.4.17
If not, because shees simple I would have her.	Ovid's Elegies	2.4.18
Another railes at me, and that I write,	Ovid's Elegies	2.4.21
Yet would I lie with her if that I might.	Ovid's Elegies	2.4.22
And when one sweetely sings, then straight I long,	Ovid's Elegies	2.4.25
And she <her> I like that with a majestie,	Ovid's Elegies	2.4.29
Both short and long please me, for I love both:	Ovid's Elegies	2.4.36
[I thinke what one undeckt would be, being drest];	Ovid's Elegies	2.4.37

I (cont.)

[Amber] <Yellow> trest is shee, then on the morne thinke I,/My	Ovid's Elegies	2.4.43
Minding thy fault, with death I wish to revill,	Ovid's Elegies	2.5.3
To whom his wench can say, I never did it.	Ovid's Elegies	2.5.10
[wretch] <wench> I sawe when thou didst thinke I slumbred,	Ovid's Elegies	2.5.13
Not drunke, your faults [in] <on> the spilt wine I numbred.	Ovid's Elegies	2.5.14
I sawe your nodding eye-browes much to speake,	Ovid's Elegies	2.5.15
I knew your speech (what do not lovers see)?	Ovid's Elegies	2.5.19
I sawe you then unlawfull kisses joyne,	Ovid's Elegies	2.5.23
What doest, I cryed, transportst thou my delight?	Ovid's Elegies	2.5.29
This, and what grife inforc'd me say I say'd,	Ovid's Elegies	2.5.33
She looked sad: sad, comely I esteem'd her.	Ovid's Elegies	2.5.44
And scratch her faire soft cheekes I did intend.	Ovid's Elegies	2.5.46
I that ere-while was fierce, now humbly sue,	Ovid's Elegies	2.5.49
I grieve least others should such good perceive,	Ovid's Elegies	2.5.53
Also much better were they then I tell,	Ovid's Elegies	2.5.55
Bewaile I onely, though I them lament.	Ovid's Elegies	2.5.60
I know no maister of so great hire sped.	Ovid's Elegies	2.5.62
My wenches vowes for thee what should I show,	Ovid's Elegies	2.6.43
This tombe approoves, I pleasde my mistresse well,	Ovid's Elegies	2.6.61
To over-come, so oft to fight I shame.	Ovid's Elegies	2.7.2
If on the Marble Theater I looke,	Ovid's Elegies	2.7.3
If I praise any, thy poore haires thou tearest,	Ovid's Elegies	2.7.7
If I looke well, thou thinkest thou doest not move,	Ovid's Elegies	2.7.9
If ill, thou saiest I die for others love.	Ovid's Elegies	2.7.10
Would I were culpable of some offence,	Ovid's Elegies	2.7.11
Should I sollicit her that is so just:	Ovid's Elegies	2.7.25
I sweare by Venus, and the wingd boyes bowe,	Ovid's Elegies	2.7.27
My selfe unguilty of this crime I know.	Ovid's Elegies	2.7.28
Whence knowes Corinna that with thee I playde?	Ovid's Elegies	2.8.6
Yet blusht I not, nor usde I any saying,	Ovid's Elegies	2.8.7
To prove him foolish did I ere contend?	Ovid's Elegies	2.8.10
Greater then these my selfe I not esteeme,	Ovid's Elegies	2.8.13
What graced Kings, in me no shame I deeme.	Ovid's Elegies	2.8.14
By Venus Deity how did I protest.	Ovid's Elegies	2.8.18
Telling thy mistresse, where I was with thee,	Ovid's Elegies	2.8.27
Yet should I curse a God, if he but said,	Ovid's Elegies	2.9.25
I know not whether my mindes whirle-wind drives me.	Ovid's Elegies	2.9.28
Strike boy, I offer thee my naked brest,	Ovid's Elegies	2.9.35
Better then I their quiver knowes them not.	Ovid's Elegies	2.9.38
Great joyes by hope I inly shall conceive.	Ovid's Elegies	2.9.44
Graecinus (well I wot) thou touldst me once,	Ovid's Elegies	2.10.1
I could not be in love with twoo at once,	Ovid's Elegies	2.10.2
By thee deceived, by thee surprisde am I,	Ovid's Elegies	2.10.3
For now I love two women equallie:	Ovid's Elegies	2.10.4
Though I am slender, I have store of pith,	Ovid's Elegies	2.10.23
Nor want I strength, but weight to presse her with:	Ovid's Elegies	2.10.24
I pay them home with that they most desire:	Ovid's Elegies	2.10.26
Oft have I spent the night in wantonnesse,	Ovid's Elegies	2.10.27
But when I die, would I might droope with doing,	Ovid's Elegies	2.10.35
I from the shore thy knowne ship first will see,	Ovid's Elegies	2.11.43
But I no partner of my glory brooke,	Ovid's Elegies	2.12.11
Nor can an other say his helpe I tooke.	Ovid's Elegies	2.12.12
I guide and souldiour wunne the field and weare her,	Ovid's Elegies	2.12.13
I was both horse-man, foote-man, standard bearer.	Ovid's Elegies	2.12.14
I saw how Bulls for a white Heifer strive,	Ovid's Elegies	2.12.25
Angry I was, but feare my wrath exempted.	Ovid's Elegies	2.13.4
But she conceiv'd of me, or I am sure/I oft have done, what	Ovid's Elegies	2.13.5
of me, or I am sure/I oft have done, what might as much procure.	Ovid's Elegies	2.13.6
By fear'd Anubis visage I thee pray,	Ovid's Elegies	2.13.11
My wench, Lucina, I intreat thee favour,	Ovid's Elegies	2.13.21
But if in so great feare I may advize thee,	Ovid's Elegies	2.13.27
I could my selfe by secret Magicke shift.	Ovid's Elegies	2.15.10
Then would I wish thee touch my mistris pappe,	Ovid's Elegies	2.15.11
I would get off though straight, and sticking fast,	Ovid's Elegies	2.15.13
Then I, that I may seale her privy leaves,	Ovid's Elegies	2.15.15
I would not out, might I in one place hit,	Ovid's Elegies	2.15.19
My life, that I will shame thee never feare,	Ovid's Elegies	2.15.21
But seeing thee, I thinke my thing will swell,	Ovid's Elegies	2.15.25
Vaine things why wish I?	Ovid's Elegies	2.15.27
Pollux and Castor, might I stand betwixt,	Ovid's Elegies	2.16.13
In heaven without thee would I not be fixt.	Ovid's Elegies	2.16.14
Then on the rough Alpes should I tread aloft,	Ovid's Elegies	2.16.19
With her I durst the Lybian Syrtes breake through,	Ovid's Elegies	2.16.21
Nor thy gulfes crooked Malea, would I feare.	Ovid's Elegies	2.16.24
So sweete a burthen I will beare with eaze.	Ovid's Elegies	2.16.30
Healthfull Peligny I esteeme nought worth,	Ovid's Elegies	2.16.37
Nor do I like the country of my birth.	Ovid's Elegies	2.16.38
He being Judge, I am convinc'd of blame.	Ovid's Elegies	2.17.2
Would I had beene my mistresse gentle prey,	Ovid's Elegies	2.17.5
Since some faire one I should of force obey.	Ovid's Elegies	2.17.6
For great revenews I good verses have,	Ovid's Elegies	2.17.27
I know a wench reports her selfe Corinne,	Ovid's Elegies	2.17.29
Often at length, my wench depart, I bid,	Ovid's Elegies	2.18.5
I sayd it irkes me:	Ovid's Elegies	2.18.7
I yeeld, and back my wit from battells bring,	Ovid's Elegies	2.18.11
But though I apt were for such high deseignes,	Ovid's Elegies	2.18.14
Unlesse I erre to these thou more incline,	Ovid's Elegies	2.18.39
What should I do with fortune that nere failes me?	Ovid's Elegies	2.19.7
Nothing I love, that at all times availes me.	Ovid's Elegies	2.19.8
What flies, I followe, what followes me I shunne.	Ovid's Elegies	2.19.36
Now I forewarne, unlesse to keepe her stronger,	Ovid's Elegies	2.19.47
Long have I borne much, hoping time would beate thee/To guard	Ovid's Elegies	2.19.49

I (cont.)

beate thee/To guard her well, that well I might entreate thee.	Ovid's Elegies	2.19.50
Shall I poore soule be never interdicted?	Ovid's Elegies	2.19.53
In sleeping shall I fearelesse drawe my breath?	Ovid's Elegies	2.19.55
Wilt nothing do, why I should wish thy death?	Ovid's Elegies	2.19.56
Can I but loath a husband growne a baude?	Ovid's Elegies	2.19.57
Heere while I walke hid close in shadie grove,	Ovid's Elegies	3.1.5
To finde, what worke my muse might move, I strove.	Ovid's Elegies	3.1.6
And one, I thinke, was longer, of her feete.	Ovid's Elegies	3.1.8
The other smilde, (I wot) with wanton eyes,	Ovid's Elegies	3.1.33
Erre I? or mirtle in her right hand lies.	Ovid's Elegies	3.1.34
Thy lofty stile with mine I not compare,	Ovid's Elegies	3.1.39
Light am I, and with me, my care, light love,	Ovid's Elegies	3.1.41
Not stronger am I, then the thing I move.	Ovid's Elegies	3.1.42
And I deserve more then thou canst in verity,	Ovid's Elegies	3.1.47
Ah howe oft on hard doores hung I engrav'd,	Ovid's Elegies	3.1.53
But till the [keeper] <keepes> went forth, I forget not,	Ovid's Elegies	3.1.55
First of thy minde the happy seedes I knewe,	Ovid's Elegies	3.1.59
She left; I say'd, you both I must beseech,	Ovid's Elegies	3.1.61
I sit not here the noble horse to see,	Ovid's Elegies	3.2.1
To sit, and talke with thee I hether came,	Ovid's Elegies	3.2.3
Thou viewst the course, I thee:	Ovid's Elegies	3.2.5
I would bravely runne,/On swift steedes mounted till the race	Ovid's Elegies	3.2.9
Now would I slacke the reines, now lash their hide,	Ovid's Elegies	3.2.11
In running if I see thee, I shall stay,	Ovid's Elegies	3.2.13
Gather them up, or lift them loe will I.	Ovid's Elegies	3.2.26
Ere these were seene, I burnt: what will these do?	Ovid's Elegies	3.2.33
By these I judge, delight me may the rest,	Ovid's Elegies	3.2.35
While thus I speake, blacke dust her white robes ray:	Ovid's Elegies	3.2.41
The sea I use not: me my earth must have.	Ovid's Elegies	3.2.48
I see whom thou affectest:	Ovid's Elegies	3.2.67
By her eyes I remember late she swore,	Ovid's Elegies	3.3.13
For others faults, why do I losse receive?	Ovid's Elegies	3.3.16
Couzend, I am the couzeners sacrifice.	Ovid's Elegies	3.3.22
Why grieve I? and of heaven reproches pen?	Ovid's Elegies	3.3.41
Were I a God, I should give women leave,	Ovid's Elegies	3.3.43
And I would be none of the Gods severe.	Ovid's Elegies	3.3.46
I saw a horse against the bitte stiffe-neckt,	Ovid's Elegies	3.4.13
I know not, what men thinke should thee so move.	Ovid's Elegies	3.4.28
She pleaseth best, I feare, if any say.	Ovid's Elegies	3.4.32
Because the keeper may come say, I did it,	Ovid's Elegies	3.4.35
<redde-growne> slime bankes, till I be past/Thy waters stay:	Ovid's Elegies	3.5.1
I to my mistris hast.	Ovid's Elegies	3.5.2
Thee I have pass'd, and knew thy streame none such,	Ovid's Elegies	3.5.5
If standing here I can by no meanes get,	Ovid's Elegies	3.5.11
Now wish I those wings noble Perseus had,	Ovid's Elegies	3.5.13
I speake old Poets wonderfull inventions,	Ovid's Elegies	3.5.17
If I a lover bee by thee held back.	Ovid's Elegies	3.5.22
What should I name Aesope, that Thebe lov'd,	Ovid's Elegies	3.5.33
If Achelous, I aske where thy hornes stand,	Ovid's Elegies	3.5.35
Nor passe I thee, who hollow rocks downe tumbling,	Ovid's Elegies	3.5.45
Nor Romane stocke scorne me so much (I crave)/Gifts then my	Ovid's Elegies	3.5.65
My bones had beene, while yet I was a maide.	Ovid's Elegies	3.5.74
Why being a vestall am I wooed to wed,	Ovid's Elegies	3.5.75
Why stay I?	Ovid's Elegies	3.5.77
Shame, that should make me blush, I have no more.	Ovid's Elegies	3.5.78
And I beleeve some wench thou hast affected:	Ovid's Elegies	3.5.83
While thus I speake, the waters more abounded:	Ovid's Elegies	3.5.85
To this I fondly loves of flouds told plainly:	Ovid's Elegies	3.5.101
I shame so great names to have usde so vainly:	Ovid's Elegies	3.5.102
I know not what expecting, I ere while/Nam'd Achelaus, Inachus,	Ovid's Elegies	3.5.103
But for thy merits I wish thee, white streame,	Ovid's Elegies	3.5.105
Or she was not the wench I wisht t'have had.	Ovid's Elegies	3.6.2
Idly I lay with her, as if I lovde <her> not,	Ovid's Elegies	3.6.3
Yet could I not cast ancor where I meant,	Ovid's Elegies	3.6.6
Yet like as if cold hemlocke I had drunke,	Ovid's Elegies	3.6.13
Like a dull Cipher, or rude blocke I lay,	Ovid's Elegies	3.6.15
Or shade, or body was [I] <Io>, who can say?	Ovid's Elegies	3.6.16
What will my age do, age I cannot shunne,	Ovid's Elegies	3.6.17
I blush, [that] <and> being youthfull, hot, and lustie,	Ovid's Elegies	3.6.19
I prove neither youth nor man, but old and rustie.	Ovid's Elegies	3.6.20
Yet boorded I the golden Chie twise,	Ovid's Elegies	3.6.23
And I grow faint, as with some spirit haunted?	Ovid's Elegies	3.6.36
Even her I had, and she had me in vaine,	Ovid's Elegies	3.6.43
What might I crave more if I aske againe?	Ovid's Elegies	3.6.44
I thinke the great Gods greeved they had bestowde/This <The>	Ovid's Elegies	3.6.45
they had bestowde/This <The> benefite, which lewdly I forslowd:	Ovid's Elegies	3.6.46
I wisht to be received in, <and> in I [get] <got> me,	Ovid's Elegies	3.6.47
To kisse, I kisse, to lie with her shee let me.	Ovid's Elegies	3.6.48
Why was I blest?	Ovid's Elegies	3.6.49
Chuf-like had I not gold, and could not use it?	Ovid's Elegies	3.6.50
Well, I beleeve she kist not as she should,	Ovid's Elegies	3.6.55
But neither was I man, nor lived then.	Ovid's Elegies	3.6.60
What sweete thought is there but I had the same?	Ovid's Elegies	3.6.63
Thou [cousenst] <cousendst> mee, by thee surprizde am I,	Ovid's Elegies	3.6.71
I might not go, whether my papers went.	Ovid's Elegies	3.7.6
I heere and there go witty with dishonour.	Ovid's Elegies	3.7.8
I the pure priest of Phoebus and the muses,	Ovid's Elegies	3.7.23
If I should give, both would the house forbeare.	Ovid's Elegies	3.7.64
Ah now a name too true thou hast, I finde.	Ovid's Elegies	3.8.4
When bad fates take good men, I am forbod,	Ovid's Elegies	3.8.35
Was I: thou liv'dst, while thou esteemdst my faith.	Ovid's Elegies	3.8.56
Thy bones I pray may in the urne safe rest,	Ovid's Elegies	3.8.67

I (cont.)

Ceres, I thinke, no knowne fault will deny.	Ovid's Elegies	3.9.24
Why am I sad, when Proserpine is found,	Ovid's Elegies	3.9.45
Long have I borne much, mad thy faults me make:	Ovid's Elegies	3.10.1
Now have I freed my selfe, and fled the chaine,	Ovid's Elegies	3.10.3
And what I have borne, shame to beare againe.	Ovid's Elegies	3.10.4
I have sustainde so oft thrust from the dore,	Ovid's Elegies	3.10.9
I know not whom thou lewdly didst imbrace,	Ovid's Elegies	3.10.11
When I to watch supplyed a servants place.	Ovid's Elegies	3.10.12
I saw when forth a tyred lover went,	Ovid's Elegies	3.10.13
When have not I fixt to thy side close layed?	Ovid's Elegies	3.10.17
I have thy husband, guard, and fellow plaied.	Ovid's Elegies	3.10.18
What should I tell her vaine tongues filthy lyes,	Ovid's Elegies	3.10.21
Hearing her to be sicke, I thether ranne,	Ovid's Elegies	3.10.25
These hardned me, with what I keepe obscure,	Ovid's Elegies	3.10.27
I am not as I was before, unwise.	Ovid's Elegies	3.10.32
But victory, I thinke, will hap to love.	Ovid's Elegies	3.10.34
Ile hate, if I can; if not, love gainst my will:	Ovid's Elegies	3.10.35
I flie her lust, but follow beauties creature;	Ovid's Elegies	3.10.37
I loath her manners, love her bodies feature.	Ovid's Elegies	3.10.38
Nor with thee, nor without thee can I live,	Ovid's Elegies	3.10.39
That I may love yet, though against my minde.	Ovid's Elegies	3.10.52
Or is I thinke my wish against the [starres] <starre>?	Ovid's Elegies	3.11.3
Or shall I plaine some God against me warres?	Ovid's Elegies	3.11.4
Who mine was cald, whom I lov'd more then any,	Ovid's Elegies	3.11.5
I feare with me is common now to many.	Ovid's Elegies	3.11.6
Erre I? or by my [bookes] <lookes> is she so knowne?	Ovid's Elegies	3.11.7
And justly: for her praise why did I tell?	Ovid's Elegies	3.11.9
The bawde I play, lovers to her I guide:	Ovid's Elegies	3.11.11
With Muse oppos'd would I my lines had done,	Ovid's Elegies	3.11.17
Would I my words would any credit beare.	Ovid's Elegies	3.11.20
Proteus what should I name? teeth, Thebes first seed?	Ovid's Elegies	3.11.35
Seeing thou art faire, I barre not thy false playing,	Ovid's Elegies	3.13.1
Nor do I give thee counsaile to live chaste,	Ovid's Elegies	3.13.3
And I shall thinke you chaste, do what you can.	Ovid's Elegies	3.13.14
Deceive all, let me erre, and thinke I am right,	Ovid's Elegies	3.13.29
Why see I lines so oft receivde and given,	Ovid's Elegies	3.13.31
Graunt this, that what you do I may not see,	Ovid's Elegies	3.13.35
My soule fleetes when I thinke what you have done,	Ovid's Elegies	3.13.37
Then thee whom I must love I hate in vaine,	Ovid's Elegies	3.13.39
And I see when you ope the two leavde booke:	Ovid's Elegies	3.13.44
Sweare I was blinde, yeeld not <deny>, if you be wise,	Ovid's Elegies	3.13.45
And I will trust your words more then mine eies.	Ovid's Elegies	3.13.46
Teach but your tongue to say, I did it not,	Ovid's Elegies	3.13.48
two words, thinke/The cause acquits you not, but I that winke.	Ovid's Elegies	3.13.50
Which I Pelignis foster-child have framde,	Ovid's Elegies	3.14.3
(Nor am I by such wanton toyes defamde)/Heire of an antient	Ovid's Elegies	3.14.4
I could tell ye,/How smooth his brest was, and how white his	Hero and Leander	1.65
Were I the saint hee worships, I would heare him,	Hero and Leander	1.179
I would my rude words had the influence,	Hero and Leander	1.200
God knowes I cannot force love, as you doe.	Hero and Leander	1.206
Which makes me hope, although I am but base,	Hero and Leander	1.218
And I in dutie will excell all other,	Hero and Leander	1.221
Aye me, such words as these should I abhor,	Hero and Leander	1.339
And yet I like them for the Orator.	Hero and Leander	1.340
youth forbeare/To touch the sacred garments which I weare.	Hero and Leander	1.344
and there God knowes I play/With Venus swannes and sparrowes	Hero and Leander	1.351
That hops about the chamber where I lie,	Hero and Leander	1.354
Harken a while, and I will tell you why:	Hero and Leander	1.385
I mean the Adamantine Destinies,	Hero and Leander	1.444
I, and shee wisht, albeit not from her hart,	Hero and Leander	2.37
And crying, Love I come, leapt lively in.	Hero and Leander	2.154
O let mee viste Hero ere I die.	Hero and Leander	2.178
You are deceav'd, I am no woman I.	Hero and Leander	2.192
Much like a globe, (a globe may I tearme this,	Hero and Leander	2.275
And I will make thee beds of Roses,	Passionate Shepherd	9

IARBUS

Iarbus, know that thou of all my wooers/(And yet have I had	Dido	3.1.11	Dido
In being too familiar with Iarbus:	Dido	3.1.15	Dido
Feare not Iarbus, Dido may be thine.	Dido	3.1.19	Dido
O stay Iarbus, and Ile goe with thee.	Dido	3.1.37	Dido
Iarbus dye, seeing she abandons thee.	Dido	3.1.40	Iarbus
No, live Iarbus, what hast thou deserv'd,	Dido	3.1.41	Dido
Iarbus pardon me, and stay a while.	Dido	3.1.46	Dido
Iarbus.	Dido	3.1.52	Dido
Wherefore doth Dido bid Iarbus goe?	Dido	3.1.56	Anna
O that Iarbus could but fancie me.	Dido	3.1.62	Anna
Yes, and Iarbus foule and favourles.	Dido	3.1.64	Anna
Yes, and Iarbus rude and rusticall.	Dido	3.1.66	Anna
Name not Iarbus, but sweete Anna say,	Dido	3.1.67	Dido
Then sister youle abjure Iarbus love?	Dido	3.1.77	Anna
Ungentle, can she wrong Iarbus so?	Dido	3.3.10	Iarbus
What makes Iarbus here of all the rest?	Dido	3.3.13	Dido
And then, what then? Iarbus shall but love:	Dido	3.3.82	Iarbus
What, hath Iarbus angred her in ought?	Dido	3.4.13	Aeneas
Iarbus, curse that unrevenging Jove,	Dido	4.1.18	Iarbus
But where were you Iarbus all this while?	Dido	4.1.31	Dido
Heare, heare, O heare Iarbus plaining prayers,	Dido	4.2.8	Iarbus
How now Iarbus, at your prayers so hard?	Dido	4.2.23	Anna
I will not leave Iarbus whom I love,	Dido	4.2.43	Anna
Iarbus stay, loving Iarbus stay,	Dido	4.2.52	Anna
Iarbus, I am cleane besides my selfe,	Dido	5.1.63	Aeneas
Thankes good Iarbus for thy friendly ayde,	Dido	5.1.75	Aeneas

IARBUS (cont.)			
How Carthage did rebell, Iarbus storme,	Dido	5.1.143	Dido
Iarbus, talke not of Aeneas, let him goe,	Dido	5.1.283	Dido
I, I, Iarbus, after this is done,	Dido	5.1.289	Dido
O helpe Iarbus, Dido in these flames/Hath burnt her selfe, aye	Dido	5.1.314	Anna
Cursed Iarbus, dye to expiate/The griefe that tires upon thine	Dido	5.1.316	Iarbus
Iarbus slaine, Iarbus my deare love,	Dido	5.1.321	Anna
O sweet Iarbus, Annas sole delight,	Dido	5.1.322	Anna
To see my sweet Iarbus slay himselfe?	Dido	5.1.324	Anna
Now sweet Iarbus stay, I come to thee.	Dido	5.1.329	Anna
IASION			
The goddesse sawe Iasion on Candyan Ide,	Ovid's Elegies		3.9.25
IBI			
[Seeing ubi desinit philosophus, ibi incipit medicus].	F 41	1.1.13A	Faust
IBIS			
Confirming it with Ibis holy name,	1Tamb	4.3.37	Souldn
ICARIAN			
And the Icarian froward Dog-starre shine,	Ovid's Elegies		2.16.4
ICARUS			
Ile frame me wings of waxe like Icarus,	Dido	5.1.243	Dido
ICE (See also YCE, YSIE)			
Shall water be conjeal'd and turn'd to ice?	Lucan, First Booke		647
ICY			
With Icy Boreas, and the Southerne gale:	Ovid's Elegies		2.11.10
IDA (See also IDE)			
Whom I will beare to Ida in mine armes,	Dido	3.2.99	Venus
Whom I have brought from Ida where he slept,	Dido	5.1.40	Hermes
Ida the seate of groves did sing with corne,	Ovid's Elegies		3.9.39
IDAEAN			
Ilia, sprung from Idaean Laomedon?	Ovid's Elegies		3.5.54
IDALIAN			
To dallie with Idalian Ganimed:	Hero and Leander		1.148
IDAS			
Me thinkes that towne there should be Troy, yon Idas hill,	Dido	2.1.7	Aeneas
In number more than are the quyvering leaves/Of Idas forrest,	2Tamb	3.5.6	2Msngr
Such as in hilly Idas watry plaines,	Ovid's Elegies		1.14.11
I'DE			
I'de passe away my life in penitence,	Jew	1.2.324	Abigal
I'de cut thy throat if I did.	Jew	4.1.11	Barab
Away, I'de wish thee, and let me goe by:	Jew	4.1.170	1Fryar
I'de give them all for Mephostophilis.	F 331	1.3.103	Faust
live along, then thou should'st see how fat I'de <I would> be.	F 683	2.2.132 P	Envy
IDE (Homograph)			
Ide make a brave living on him; hee has a buttocke as slicke as	F App	p.239 116 P	HrsCsr
Homer shall live while Tenedos stands and Ide,	Ovid's Elegies		1.15.9
The goddesse sawe Iasion on Candyan Ide,	Ovid's Elegies		3.9.25
IDIOT			
Thee as a holy Idiot doth she scorne,	Hero and Leander		1.303
IDLE			
Ah sister, leave these idle fantasies,	Dido	5.1.262	Anna
Now living idle in the walled townes,	1Tamb	1.1.146	Ceneus
My empty stomacke ful of idle heat,	1Tamb	4.4.94	Bajzth
And thus be drawen with these two idle kings.	2Tamb	4.3.28	Amyras
Let us not be idle then my Lord,	2Tamb	4.3.95	Techel
And seeing they are not idle, but still doing,	Jew	2.3.83	Barab
The idle triumphes, maskes, lascivious showes/And prodigall	Edw	2.2.157	Mortmr
Begets a world of idle fantasies,	F1810	5.2.14	Mephst
I burne, love in my idle bosome sits.	Ovid's Elegies		1.1.30
And tearmes <termst> [my] <our> works fruits of an idle quill?	Ovid's Elegies		1.15.2
While I speake some fewe, yet fit words be idle.	Ovid's Elegies		2.2.2
My idle thoughts delighted her no more,	Ovid's Elegies		3.6.39
So on she goes, and in her idle flight,	Hero and Leander		2.10
IDLENESSE			
But follie, sloth, and damned idlenesse:	2Tamb	4.1.126	Tamb
Strike them with sloth, and drowsy idlenesse;	F 894	3.1.116	Faust
IDLY			
Idly I lay with her, as if I lovde <her> not,	Ovid's Elegies		3.6.3
IDOLATERS			
But ere I die those foule Idolaters/Shall make me bonfires with	1Tamb	3.3.239	Bajzth
IDOLL			
This idoll which you terme Virginitie,	Hero and Leander		1.269
IF (See also AN, ANT, YF)			
I vow, if she but once frowne on thee more,	Dido	1.1.12	Jupitr
Sweet Jupiter, if ere I pleasde thine eye,	Dido	1.1.19	Ganimd
If that thy fancie in his feathers dwell,	Dido	1.1.39	Jupitr
And shall have Ganimed, if thou wilt be my love.	Dido	1.1.49	Jupitr
But tell me Troians, Troians if you be,	Dido	1.2.17	Iarbus
And if this be thy sonne as I suppose,	Dido	2.1.92	Dido
Who if that any seeke to doe him hurt,	Dido	2.1.321	Venus
And if my mother goe, Ile follow her.	Dido	3.1.38	Cupid
Which piteous wants if Dido will supplie,	Dido	3.1.111	Aeneas
Which if thou lose shall shine above the waves:	Dido	3.1.121	Dido
For if that any man could conquer me,	Dido	3.1.137	Dido
O if I speake/I shall betray my selfe:--	Dido	3.1.172	Dido
If thou but lay thy fingers on my boy.	Dido	3.2.36	Venus
Sister of Jove, if that thy love be such,	Dido	3.2.53	Venus
If that your majestie can looke so lowe,	Dido	3.4.41	Aeneas
Now if thou beest a pitying God of power,	Dido	4.2.19	Iarbus
Yet if you would partake with me the cause/Of this devotion	Dido	4.2.27	Anna
But if I use such ceremonious thankes,	Dido	4.3.49	Aeneas
What if the Citizens repine thereat?	Dido	4.4.70	Anna
What if I sinke his ships? O heele frowne:	Dido	4.4.110	Dido
If he forsake me not, I never dye,	Dido	4.4.121	Dido

IF (cont.)

Drive if you can my house to Italy:	Dido	4.4.129	Dido
And see if those will serve in steed of sailes:	Dido	4.4.160	Dido
So youle love me, I care not if I doe.	Dido	4.5.17	Cupid
If there be any heaven in earth, tis love:	Dido	4.5.27	Nurse
Well, if he come a wooing he shall speede,	Dido	4.5.36	Nurse
If that all glorie hath forsaken thee,	Dido	5.1.36	Hermes
If that be all, then cheare thy drooping lookes,	Dido	5.1.71	Iarbus
If it be so, his father meanes to flye:	Dido	5.1.85	Dido
O pardon me, if I resolve thee why:	Dido	5.1.91	Aeneas
I dye, if my Aeneas say farewell.	Dido	5.1.108	Dido
Now if thou goest, what canst thou leave behind,	Dido	5.1.151	Dido
If words might move me I were overcome.	Dido	5.1.154	Aeneas
Which if it chaunce, Ile give ye buriall,	Dido	5.1.176	Dido
if thou wilt stay,/Leape in mine armes, mine armes are open	Dido	5.1.179	Dido
If not, turne from me, and Ile turne from thee:	Dido	5.1.181	Dido
If he depart thus suddenly, I dye:	Dido	5.1.209	Dido
And then applaud his fortunes if you please.	1Tamb	Prol.8	Prolog
Therefore tis best, if so it lik you all,	1Tamb	1.1.51	Mycet
Or if they would, there are in readines/Ten thousand horse to	1Tamb	1.1.184	Ortyg
Than if you were arriv'd in Siria,	1Tamb	1.2.4	Tamb
(If as thou seem'st, thou art so meane a man)/And seeke not to	1Tamb	1.2.8	Zenoc
letters to command/Aide and assistance if we stand in need.	1Tamb	1.2.20	Magnet
If you intend to keep your treasure safe.	1Tamb	1.2.25	Tamb
But if they offer word or violence,	1Tamb	1.2.142	Tamb
As if he now devis'd some Stratageme:	1Tamb	1.2.159	Therid
If outward habit judge the inward man.	1Tamb	1.2.163	Tamb
As if he meant to give my Souldiers pay,	1Tamb	1.2.183	Tamb
If thou wilt stay with me, renowmed man,	1Tamb	1.2.188	Tamb
and if the Persean king/Should offer present Dukedomes to our	1Tamb	1.2.214	Techel
Which is as much as if I swore by heaven,	1Tamb	1.2.233	Tamb
If you will willingly remaine with me,	1Tamb	1.2.254	Tamb
Proud is his fortune if we pierce it not.	1Tamb	2.1.44	Cosroe
Least if we let them lynger here a while,	1Tamb	2.2.20	Meandr
But if Cosroe (as our Spials say,	1Tamb	2.2.35	Meandr
If wealth or riches may prevaile with them,	1Tamb	2.2.61	Meandr
And doubt you not, but if you favour me,	1Tamb	2.3.10	Tamb
If Nature had not given me wisedomes lore?	1Tamb	2.4.7	Mycet
So shall not I be knowen, or if I bee,	1Tamb	2.4.13	Mycet
As if as many kinges as could encompasse thee,	1Tamb	2.5.4	Tamb
I, if I could with all my heart my Lord.	1Tamb	2.5.68	Techel
That if I should desire the Persean Crowne,	1Tamb	2.5.76	Tamb
If we should aime at such a dignitie?	1Tamb	2.5.79	Tamb
And if I prosper, all shall be as sure,	1Tamb	2.5.84	Tamb
As if the Turke, the Pope, Affrike and Greece,	1Tamb	2.5.85	Tamb
If Tamburlain be plac'd in Persea.	1Tamb	2.7.39	Usumc
If you but say that Tamburlaine shall raigne.	1Tamb	2.7.63	Tamb
Than if the Gods had held a Parliament:	1Tamb	2.7.66	Tamb
What if you sent the Bassoes of your guard,	1Tamb	3.1.17	Fesse
But if presuming on his silly power,	1Tamb	3.1.33	Bajzth
And if before the Sun have measured heaven/With triple circuit	1Tamb	3.1.36	Bajzth
But if he dare attempt to stir your siege,	1Tamb	3.1.46	Argier
And might, if my extreams had full events,	1Tamb	3.2.16	Zenoc
If I were matcht with mightie Tamburlaine.	1Tamb	3.2.55	Zenoc
and my souldiers looke/As if they meant to conquer Affrica.	1Tamb	3.3.10	Tamb
If he think good, can from his garrisons,	1Tamb	3.3.21	Bassoe
As if thou wert the Empresse of the world.	1Tamb	3.3.125	Tamb
If they should yeeld their necks unto the sword,	1Tamb	3.3.142	Bajzth
If Mahomet should come from heaven and sweare,	1Tamb	3.3.208	Zenoc
But if these threats moove not submission,	1Tamb	4.1.58	2Msngr
If they would lay their crownes before my feet,	1Tamb	4.2.93	Tamb
But if he stay until the bloody flag/Be once advanc'd on my	1Tamb	4.2.116	Tamb
Not for the world Zenocrate, if I have sworn:	1Tamb	4.2.125	Tamb
But if his highnesse would let them be fed, it would doe them	1Tamb	4.4.34	P Therid
for if she live but a while longer, shee will fall into a	1Tamb	4.4.49	P Tamb
If thou wilt have a song, the Turke shall straine his voice:	1Tamb	4.4.63	P Tamb
If any love remaine in you my Lord,	1Tamb	4.4.68	Zenoc
Or if my love unto your majesty/May merit favour at your	1Tamb	4.4.69	Zenoc
If with their lives they will be pleasde to yeeld,	1Tamb	4.4.89	Tamb
If we deserve them not with higher meeds/Then erst our states	1Tamb	4.4.131	Therid
And if we should with common rites of Armes,	1Tamb	5.1.11	Govnr
If humble suites or imprecations,	1Tamb	5.1.24	1Virgn
If all the pens that ever poets held,	1Tamb	5.1.161	Tamb
If all the heavenly Quintessence they still/From their	1Tamb	5.1.165	Tamb
If these had made one Poems period/And all combin'd in Beauties	1Tamb	5.1.169	Tamb
Bring him forth, and let us know if the towne be ransackt.	1Tamb	5.1.194	P Tamb
As if there were no way but one with us.	1Tamb	5.1.201	Techel
And now my footstoole, if I loose the field,	1Tamb	5.1.209	Tamb
See, se Anippe if they breathe or no.	1Tamb	5.1.343	Zenoc
If I had not bin wounded as I am.	1Tamb	5.1.421	Arabia
If as beseemes a person of thy state,	1Tamb	5.1.483	Souldn
If peace, restore it to my hands againe:	2Tamb	1.1.84	Sgsmnd
Which if your General refuse or scorne,	2Tamb	1.1.119	Fredrk
So prest are we, but yet if Sigismond/Speake as a friend, and	2Tamb	1.1.122	Orcan
if any Christian King/Encroche upon the confines of thy realme,	2Tamb	1.1.146	Orcan
If any heathen potentate or king/Invade Natolia, Sigismond will	2Tamb	1.1.152	Sgsmnd
me my Lord, if I should goe, would you bee as good as your word?	2Tamb	1.2.61	P Almeda
If thou wilt love the warres and follow me,	2Tamb	1.3.47	Tamb
If thou exceed thy elder Brothers worth,	2Tamb	1.3.50	Tamb
Yes father, you shal see me if I live,	2Tamb	1.3.54	Celeb
For if his chaire were in a sea of blood,	2Tamb	1.3.89	Celeb
And sirha, if you meane to weare a crowne,	2Tamb	1.3.98	Tamb
If any man will hold him, I will strike,	2Tamb	1.3.102	Calyph

IF (cont.)

as if infernall Jove/Meaning to aid [thee] <them> in this	2Tamb	1.3.143	Techel
If all the christall gates of Joves high court/Were opened	2Tamb	1.3.153	Tamb
If we neglect this offered victory.	2Tamb	2.1.59	Fredrk
Which if a shower of wounding thunderbolts/Should breake out	2Tamb	2.2.13	Gazell
Then if there be a Christ, as Christians say,	2Tamb	2.2.39	Orcan
If he be son to everliving Jove,	2Tamb	2.2.41	Orcan
If he be jealous of his name and honor,	2Tamb	2.2.43	Orcan
If thou wilt proove thy selfe a perfect God,	2Tamb	2.2.56	Orcan
If there be Christ, we shall have victorie.	2Tamb	2.2.64	Orcan
And if she passe this fit, the worst is past.	2Tamb	2.4.40	1Phstn
And if thou pitiest Tamburlain the great,	2Tamb	2.4.117	Tamb
If woords might serve, our voice hath rent the aire,	2Tamb	2.4.121	Therid
If teares, our eies have watered all the earth:	2Tamb	2.4.122	Therid
If griefe, our murthered harts have straind forth blood.	2Tamb	2.4.123	Therid
The houses burnt, wil looke as if they mourn'd,	2Tamb	2.4.139	Tamb
As if Bellona, Goddesse of the war/Threw naked swords and	2Tamb	3.2.40	Tamb
If I had wept a sea of teares for her,	2Tamb	3.2.47	Calyph
As if a chaire of gold enamiled,	2Tamb	3.2.119	Tamb
Then let us see if coward Calapine/Dare levie armes against our	2Tamb	3.2.155	Tamb
If thou withstand the friends of Tamburlain.	2Tamb	3.3.19	Techel
That we may know if our artillery/Will carie full point blancke	2Tamb	3.3.52	Techel
Ah sacred Mahomet, if this be sin,	2Tamb	3.4.31	Olymp
Sitting as if they were a telling ridles.	2Tamb	3.5.59	Tamb
Poore soules they looke as if their deaths were neere.	2Tamb	3.5.61	Usumc
For if I should as Hector did Achilles,	2Tamb	3.5.70	Tamb
For if thou livest, not any Element/Shal shrowde thee from the	2Tamb	3.5.126	Tamb
For if my father misse him in the field,	2Tamb	4.1.8	Celeb
If halfe our campe should sit and sleepe with me,	2Tamb	4.1.18	Calyph
As if I lay with you for company.	2Tamb	4.1.39	Calyph
and tel me if the warres/Be not a life that may illustrate	2Tamb	4.1.78	Tamb
tyrannies/(If tyrannies wars justice ye repute)/I execute,	2Tamb	4.1.147	Tamb
As if they were the teares of Mahomet/For hot consumption of	2Tamb	4.1.196	Tamb
Nay Lady, then if nothing wil prevaile,	2Tamb	4.2.50	Therid
With which if you but noint your tender Skin,	2Tamb	4.2.65	Olymp
If you loved him, and it so precious?	2Tamb	4.2.72	Therid
your weapons point/That wil be blunted if the blow be great.	2Tamb	4.2.80	Olymp
If you can live with it, then live, and draw/My chariot swifter	2Tamb	4.3.20	Tamb
If not, then dy like beasts, and fit for nought/But perches for	2Tamb	4.3.22	Tamb
If Jove esteeming me too good for earth,	2Tamb	4.3.60	Tamb
My Lord, if ever you did deed of ruth,	2Tamb	5.1.24	1Citzn
Wil get his pardon if your grace would send.	2Tamb	5.1.33	1Citzn
My Lord, if ever you wil win our hearts,	2Tamb	5.1.38	2Citzn
Which threatned more than if the region/Next underneath the	2Tamb	5.1.87	Tamb
Nor if my body could have stopt the breach,	2Tamb	5.1.101	Govnr
They will talk still my Lord, if you doe not bridle them.	2Tamb	5.1.146	P Amyras
Now Mahomet, if thou have any power,	2Tamb	5.1.187	Tamb
The God that sits in heaven, if any God,	2Tamb	5.1.201	Tamb
If God or Mahomet send any aide.	2Tamb	5.2.11	Callap
lie in wait for him/And if we find him absent from his campe,	2Tamb	5.2.57	Callap
But if he die, your glories are disgrac'd,	2Tamb	5.3.15	Therid
If you retaine desert of holinesse,	2Tamb	5.3.19	Techel
For if he die, thy glorie is disgrac'd,	2Tamb	5.3.40	Usumc
That if I perish, heaven and earth may fade.	2Tamb	5.3.60	Tamb
Yet if your majesty may escape this day,	2Tamb	5.3.98	Phsitn
If not resolv'd into resolved paines,	2Tamb	5.3.187	Amyras
if the unrelenting eares/Of death and hell be shut against my	2Tamb	5.3.191	Amyras
For if thy body thrive not full of thoughtes/As pure and fiery	2Tamb	5.3.236	Tamb
If any thing shall there concerne our state/Assure your selves	Jew	1.1.172	Barab
Live still; and if thou canst, get more.	Jew	1.2.102	Govnr
If your first curse fall heavy on thy head,	Jew	1.2.107	1Knght
As if we knew not thy profession?	Jew	1.2.120	Govnr
If thou rely upon thy righteousnesse,	Jew	1.2.121	Govnr
For that is theft; and if you rob me thus,	Jew	1.2.126	Barab
For if we breake our day, we breake the league,	Jew	1.2.158	1Knght
And seeme to them as if thy sinnes were great,	Jew	1.2.287	Barab
No come not at me, if thou wilt be damn'd,	Jew	1.2.362	Barab
And if she be so faire as you report,	Jew	1.2.388	Lodowk
The Loadstarre of my life, if Abigall.	Jew	2.1.42	Barab
Your life and if you have it.--	Jew	2.3.64	Barab
And if he has, he is worth three hundred plats.	Jew	2.3.102	Barab
I'le buy you, and marry you to Lady vanity, if you doe well.	Jew	2.3.117	P Barab
Use him as if he were a--Philistine.	Jew	2.3.228	Barab
If you love me, no quarrels in my house;	Jew	2.3.271	Barab
No; so shall I, if any hurt be done,	Jew	2.3.341	Barab
Nay, if you will, stay till she comes her selfe.	Jew	2.3.352	Barab
I cannot stay; for if my mother come,	Jew	2.3.353	Mthias
I did it, and revenge it if thou dar'st.	Jew	3.2.4	Mthias
If so, 'tis time that it be seene into:	Jew	3.4.9	Barab
Thou know'st 'tis death and if it be reveal'd.	Jew	3.6.51	2Fryar
How can it if we two be secret.	Jew	4.1.9	Barab
I'de cut thy throat if I did.	Jew	4.1.11	Barab
What if I murder'd him e're Jacomo comes?	Jew	4.1.116	Barab
Yet if he knew our meanings, could he scape?	Jew	4.1.135	Barab
staffe; excellent, he stands as if he were begging of Bacon.	Jew	4.1.154	P Ithimr
to his prayers, as if hee had had another Cure to serve; well,	Jew	4.2.24	P Ithimr
sort as if he had meant to make cleane my Boots with his lips;	Jew	4.2.30	P Ithimr
And you can have it, Sir, and if you please.	Jew	4.2.56	Pilia
If 'twere above ground I could, and would have it; but hee	Jew	4.2.57	P Ithimr
Which if they were reveal'd, would doe him harme.	Jew	4.2.65	Pilia
and this shall be your warrant; if you doe not, no more but so.	Jew	4.2.76	P Ithimr
And if he aske why I demand so much, tell him, I scorne to	Jew	4.2.120	P Ithimr
But if I get him, Coupe de Gorge for that.	Jew	4.3.5	Barab

IF (cont.)

Oh, if that be all, I can picke ope your locks.	Jew	4.3.33	Pilia
Nay [to] thine owne cost, villaine, if thou com'st.	Jew	4.3.59	Barab
There, if thou lov'st me doe not leave a drop.	Jew	4.4.6	P Ithimr
What wudst thou doe if he should send thee none?	Jew	4.4.13	Pilia
If this be true, I'le make thee Governor.	Jew	5.1.95	Calym
And if it be not true, then let me dye.	Jew	5.1.96	Barab
What will you give me if I render you/The life of Calymath,	Jew	5.2.79	Barab
And if you like them, drinke your fill and dye:	Jew	5.5.9	Barab
For if I keepe not promise, trust not me.	Jew	5.5.23	Barab
If greater falshood ever has bin done.	Jew	5.5.50	Barab
See his end first, and flye then if thou canst.	Jew	5.5.69	Govnr
Besides, if we should let thee goe, all's one,	Jew	5.5.99	Govnr
If that the King had given consent thereto,	P 33	1.33	Navrre
If ever Hymen lowr'd at marriage rites,	P 58	2.1	Guise
If ever sunne stainde heaven with bloudy clowdes,	P 60	2.3	Guise
If ever day were turnde to ugly night,	P 62	2.5	Guise
If I repaire not what he ruinates:	P 129	2.72	Guise
All this and more, if more may be comprisde,	P 143	2.86	Guise
Too late it is my Lord if that be true/To blame her highnes,	P 181	3.16	QnMarg
And make a shew as if all were well.	P 250	4.48	QnMoth
Anjoy, Gonzago, Retes, if that you three,	P 322	5.49	Guise
Flye Ramus flye, if thou wilt save thy life.	P 365	7.5	Taleus
That if I undertake to weare the crowne/Of Poland, it may	P 466	8.16	Anjoy
For if th'almighty take my brother hence,	P 469	8.19	Anjoy
That if by death of Charles, the diadem/Of France be cast on	P 472	8.22	Anjoy
If your commission serve to warrant this,	P 475	8.25	Anjoy
For if these straglers gather head againe,	P 506	9.25	QnMoth
And if he grudge or crosse his Mothers will,	P 523	9.42	QnMoth
And if they storme, I then may pull them downe.	P 526	9.45	QnMoth
And so they shall, if fortune speed my will,	P 601	12.14	King
And if he doe deny what I doe say,	P 650	12.63	QnMoth
And fly my presence if thou looke to live.	P 692	13.36	Guise
And sure if all the proudest Kings/In Christendome, should	P 760	15.18	Guise
Not I my Lord, what if I had?	P 775	15.33	Mugern
Marry if thou hadst, thou mightst have had the stab,	P 776	15.34	King
If that be all, the next time that I meet her,	P 781	15.39	Mugern
If it be not too free there's the question:	P 812	17.7	P Souldr
yet I meane to keepe you out, which I will if this geare holde:	P 815	17.10	P Souldr
But if that God doe prosper mine attempts,	P 927	18.28	Navrre
Twere hard with me if I should doubt my kinne,	P 971	19.41	King
see where she comes, as if she droupt/To heare these newes.	P1062	19.132	Eprnon
And let her greeve her heart out if she will.	P1080	19.150	King
It is enough if that Navarre may be/Esteemed faithfull to the	P1147	22.9	Navrre
Twere not amisse my Lord, if he were searcht.	P1160	22.22	Eprnon
Which if I doe, the Papall Monarck goes/To wrack, and [his]	P1197	22.59	King
As if a Goose should play the Porpintine,	Edw	1.1.40	Gavstn
If I speed well, ile entertaine you all.	Edw	1.1.46	Gavstn
If you love us my lord, hate Gaveston.	Edw	1.1.80	MortSr
Therefore if he be come, expell him straight.	Edw	1.1.106	Lncstr
If for these dignities thou be envied,	Edw	1.1.163	Edward
I, if words will serve, if not, I must.	Edw	1.2.83	Mortmr
if he refuse, and then may we/Depose him and elect an other	Edw	1.4.54	Mortmr
if this content you not,/Make severall kingdomes of this	Edw	1.4.69	Edward
If I be king, not one of them shall live.	Edw	1.4.105	Edward
And long thou shalt not stay, or if thou doost,	Edw	1.4.114	Edward
But how if he do not Nephew?	Edw	1.4.278	MortSr
My lords, if to performe this I be slack,	Edw	1.4.290	Mortmr
But will you love me, if you finde it so?	Edw	1.4.324	Queene
If it be so, what will not Edward do?	Edw	1.4.325	Edward
For thee faire Queene, if thou lovest Gaveston,	Edw	1.4.327	Edward
Chide me sweete Warwick, if I go astray.	Edw	1.4.348	Edward
Or if that loftie office like thee not,	Edw	1.4.355	Edward
That day, if not for him, yet for my sake,	Edw	1.4.381	Edward
As if that Proteus god of shapes appearde.	Edw	1.4.411	Mortmr
If all things sort out, as I hope they will,	Edw	2.1.79	Neece
If in his absence thus he favors him,	Edw	2.2.47	Mortmr
Looke to your owne crowne, if you back him thus.	Edw	2.2.93	Warwck
But if I live, ile tread upon their heads,	Edw	2.2.96	Edward
Cosin, and if he will not ransome him,	Edw	2.2.127	Mortmr
If ye be moov'de, revenge it as you can,	Edw	2.2.198	Lncstr
If I be cruell, and growe tyrannous,	Edw	2.2.206	Edward
If that will not suffice, farwell my lords.	Edw	2.3.10	Kent
As if he heare I have but talkt with you,	Edw	2.4.54	Queene
If he be straunge and not regarde my wordes,	Edw	2.4.64	Queene
And if you gratifie his grace so farre,	Edw	2.5.39	Arundl
For Gaveston, will if he [seaze] <zease> <sees> him once,	Edw	2.5.63	Warwck
Then if you will not trust his grace in keepe,	Edw	2.5.65	Arundl
But if you dare trust Penbrooke with the prisoner,	Edw	2.5.87	Penbrk
If Warwickes wit and policie prevaile.	Edw	2.5.96	Warwck
And if they send me not my Gaveston,	Edw	3.1.26	Edward
Sib, if this be all/Valoys and I will soone be friends againe.	Edw	3.1.66	Edward
If I be Englands king, in lakes of gore/Your headles trunkes,	Edw	3.1.135	Edward
That if without effusion of bloud,	Edw	3.1.159	Herald
My lord, we have, and if he be in England,	Edw	4.3.19	Spencr
If, doost thou say?	Edw	4.3.21	Edward
is gone, whither if you aske, with sir John of Henolt, brother	Edw	4.3.31	P Spencr
Nay madam, if you be a warriar,	Edw	4.4.15	Mortmr
Madam, without offence if I may aske,	Edw	4.6.30	Kent
grace may sit secure, if none but wee/Doe wot of your abode.	Edw	4.7.26	Monk
Leister, if gentle words might comfort me,	Edw	5.1.5	Edward
But if proud Mortimer do weare this crowne,	Edw	5.1.43	Edward
For if they goe, the prince shall lose his right.	Edw	5.1.92	Leistr

IF (cont.)

If he be not, let him choose.	Edw	5.1.95		BshpWn
Or if I live, let me forget my selfe.	Edw	5.1.111		Edward
If with the sight thereof she be not mooved,	Edw	5.1.119		Edward
That if he slip will seaze upon us both,	Edw	5.2.8		Mortmr
and in any case/Let no man comfort him, if he chaunce to weepe,	Edw	5.2.64		Mortmr
If he have such accesse unto the prince,	Edw	5.2.77		Mortmr
Use Edmund friendly, as if all were well.	Edw	5.2.79		Queene
Well, if my Lorde your brother were enlargde.	Edw	5.2.82		Queene
If mine will serve, unbowell straight this brest,	Edw	5.3.10		Edward
That being dead, if it chaunce to be found,	Edw	5.4.14		Mortmr
If any Christian, Heathen, Turke, or Jew,	Edw	5.4.75		Champn
Sweete mother, if I cannot pardon him,	Edw	5.4.94		King
My lord, if you will let my unckle live,	Edw	5.4.99		King
If that my Unckle shall be murthered thus?	Edw	5.4.110		King
O if thou harborst murther in thy hart,	Edw	5.5.87		Edward
If you mistrust me, ile be gon my lord.	Edw	5.5.97		Ltborn
No, no, for if thou meanst to murther me,	Edw	5.5.98		Edward
And tels me, if I sleepe I never wake,	Edw	5.5.104		Edward
if thou now growest penitent/Ile be thy ghostly father,	Edw	5.6.3		Mortmr
What if he have? the king is yet a childe.	Edw	5.6.17		Mortmr
Yes, if this be the hand of Mortimer.	Edw	5.6.44		King
If you be guiltie, though I be your sonne,	Edw	5.6.81		King
And I shall pitie her if she speake againe.	Edw	5.6.86		King
If we say that we have no sinne we deceive our selves, and	F 69	1.1.41	P	Faust
If learned Faustus will be resolute.	F 160	1.1.132		Valdes
<Aske my fellow if I be a thiefe>.	F 204	(HC258)A	P	Wagner
yet if you were not dunces, you would never aske me such a	F 206	1.2.13	P	Wagner
this wine, if it could speake, <it> would informe your Worships:	F 216	1.2.23	P	Wagner
<and see if hee by> his grave counsell may <can> reclaime him.	F 226	1.2.33		2Schol
And try if devils will obey thy Hest,	F 234	1.3.6		Faust
rosted, and good sauce to it, if I pay so deere, I can tell you.	F 353	1.4.11	P	Robin
then belike if I serve you, I shall be lousy.	F 358	1.4.16	P	Robin
if thou dost not presently bind thy selfe to me for seven	F 361	1.4.19	P	Wagner
me, as if they payd for their meate and drinke, I can tell you.	F 365	1.4.23	P	Robin
If thou deny it I must <wil> backe to hell.	F 426	2.1.38		Mephst
If unto [God] <heaven>, hee'le throw me <thee> downe to hell.	F 467	2.1.79		Faust
And if thou lovest me thinke no more of it.	F 536	2.1.148		Mephst
If Heaven was <it were> made for man, 'twas made for me:	F 561	2.2.10		Faust
Yea <I>, God will pitty me if I repent.	F 567	2.2.16		Faust
Never too late, if Faustus will <can> repent.	F 631	2.2.80		GdAngl
If thou repent, devils will <shall> teare thee in peeces.	F 632	2.2.81		BdAngl
into matters, as other men, if they were disposed to talke.	F 741	2.3.20	P	Robin
If thou't dance naked, put off thy cloathes, and I'le conjure	F 746	2.3.25	P	Robin
Or if thou't go but to the Taverne with me, I'le give thee	F 747	2.3.26	P	Robin
And if that Bruno by his owne assent,	F 957	3.1.179		Faust
and if he be so farre in love with him, I would he would post	F1190	4.1.36	P	Benvol
if a man be drunke over night, the Divell cannot hurt him in	F1200	4.1.46	P	Benvol
if that bee true, I have a charme in my head, shall controule	F1202	4.1.48	P	Benvol
Then if by powerfull Necromantick spels,	F1209	4.1.55		Emper
And if this Bruno thou hast late redeem'd,	F1212	4.1.58		Emper
For proofe whereof, if so your Grace be pleas'd,	F1221	4.1.67		Faust
Il'e make you feele something anon, if my Art faile me not.	F1246	4.1.92	P	Faust
Then if I gain'd another Monarchie.	F1272	4.1.118		Emper
If Faustus do it, you are streight resolv'd,	F1298	4.1.144		Faust
If you will aid me in this enterprise,	F1334	4.2.10		Benvol
If not, depart:	F1336	4.2.12		Benvol
And kill that Doctor if he come this way.	F1339	4.2.15		Fredrk
Then Souldiers boldly fight; if Faustus die,	F1346	4.2.22		Benvol
If we should follow him to worke revenge,	F1448	4.3.18		Benvol
sell him, but if thou likest him for ten Dollors more, take him,	F1460	4.4.4	P	Faust
If it please you, the Duke of Vanholt doth earnestly entreate	F1500	4.4.44	P	Wagner
on the score, but say nothing, see if she have forgotten me.	F1512	4.5.8	P	Robin
what he meanes, if death were nie, he would not frolick thus:	F1677	5.1.4	P	Wagner
if you will doe us so much <that> favour, as to let us see that	F1684	5.1.11	P	1Schol
If sin by custome grow not into nature:	F1713	5.1.40		OldMan
If it be so, wee'l have Physitians,	F1830	5.2.34		2Schol
but the Divel threatned to teare me in peeces if I nam'd God:	F1865	5.2.69	P	Faust
me <both> body and soule, if I once gave eare to Divinitie:	F1866	5.2.70	P	Faust
if I live till morning, Il'e visit you:	F1877	5.2.81	P	Faust
if not, Faustus is gone to hell.	F1878	5.2.82	P	Faust
Oh <Ah> Faustus, if thou hadst given eare to me,	F1892	5.2.96		GdAngl
<O, if my soule must suffer for my sinne>,	F1958	(HC271)B		Faust
[O God, if thou wilt not have mercy on my soule],	F1958	5.2.162A		Faust
have it wel roasted, and good sawce to it, if I pay so deere.	F App	p.229 12	P	Clown
why then belike, if I were your man, I should be ful of vermine.	F App	p.229 21	P	Clown
with my flesh, as if they had payd for my meate and drinke.	F App	p.230 29	P	Clown
if I should serve you, would you teach me to raise up Banios	F App	p.230 56	P	Clown
if you turne me into any thing, let it be in the likenesse of a	F App	p.231 61	P	Clown
Heere's no body, if it like your Holynesse.	F App	p.231 4	P	Frier
if thou hast any mind to Nan Spit our kitchin maide, then turn	F App	p.234 26	P	Robin
If therefore thou, by cunning of thine Art,	F App	p.237 29		Emper
But if it like your Grace, it is not in my abilitie to present	F App	p.237 41	P	Faust
if thou likst him for fifty, take him.	F App	p.239 103	P	Faust
if he had but the qualitie of hey ding, ding, hey, ding, ding,	F App	p.239 115	P	HrsCsr
but hark ye sir, if my horse be sick, or ill at ease, if I bring	F App	p.240 118	P	HrsCsr
at ease, if I bring his water to you, youle tel me what it is?	F App	p.240 118	P	HrsCsr
If it like your grace, the yeere is divided into twoo circles	F App	p.242 19	P	Faust
And yet me thinkes, if that death were neere,	F App	p.243 3		Wagner
And they of Nilus mouth (if there live any).	Lucan, First Booke			20
Roome, if thou take delight in impious warre,	Lucan, First Booke			21
But if for Nero (then unborne) the fates/Would find no other	Lucan, First Booke			33
If any one part of vast heaven thou swayest,	Lucan, First Booke			56

IF (cont.)

Thee if I invocate, I shall not need/To crave Apolloes ayde, or	Lucan, First Booke	64
Romans if ye be,/And beare true harts, stay heare:	Lucan, First Booke	193
rageth now in armes/As if the Carthage Hannibal were neere;	Lucan, First Booke	305
If to incampe on Thuscan Tybers streames,	Lucan, First Booke	382
so (if truth you sing)/Death brings long life.	Lucan, First Booke	453
As if, the cnly hope (that did remaine/To their afflictions)	Lucan, First Booke	494
Or if Fate rule them, Rome thy Cittizens/Are neere some plague:	Lucan, First Booke	643
If cold noysome Saturne/were now exalted, and with blew beames	Lucan, First Booke	650
If reading five thou plainst of tediousnesse,	Ovid's Elegies	1.1.3
[What] <That> if thy Mother take Dianas bowe,	Ovid's Elegies	1.1.11
If loftie titles cannot make me thine,	Ovid's Elegies	1.3.7
If men have Faith, Ile live with thee for ever.	Ovid's Elegies	1.3.16
If ought of me thou speak'st in inward thought,	Ovid's Elegies	1.4.23
If hee gives thee what first himselfe did tast,	Ovid's Elegies	1.4.33
If thou givest kisses, I shall all disclose,	Ovid's Elegies	1.4.39
Yet this Ile see, but if thy gowne ought cover,	Ovid's Elegies	1.4.41
If hee lyes downe with Wine and sleepe opprest,	Ovid's Elegies	1.4.53
Or if it do, to thee no joy thence spring:	Ovid's Elegies	1.4.68
Wondring if any walked without light.	Ovid's Elegies	1.6.10
If Boreas beares Orithyas rape in minde,	Ovid's Elegies	1.6.53
Punisht I am, if I a Romaine beat,	Ovid's Elegies	1.7.29
(If I have faith) I sawe the starres drop bloud,	Ovid's Elegies	1.8.11
red shame becomes white cheekes, but this/If feigned, doth well;	Ovid's Elegies	1.8.36
but this/If feigned, doth well; if true it doth amisse.	Ovid's Elegies	1.8.36
Nor, if thou couzenst one, dread to for-sweare,	Ovid's Elegies	1.8.85
If he gives nothing, let him from thee wend.	Ovid's Elegies	1.8.100
If this thou doest, to me by long use knowne,	Ovid's Elegies	1.8.105
If, what I do, she askes, say hope for night,	Ovid's Elegies	1.11.13
Yet as if mixt with red leade thou wert ruddy,	Ovid's Elegies	1.12.11
If ever, now well lies she by my side.	Ovid's Elegies	1.13.6
Keeper if thou be wise cease hate to cherish,	Ovid's Elegies	2.2.9
If long she stayes, to thinke the time more short/Lay downe thy	Ovid's Elegies	2.2.23
If he loves not, deafe eares thou doest importune,	Ovid's Elegies	2.2.53
Or if he loves, thy tale breedes his misfortune.	Ovid's Elegies	2.2.54
If ever wench had made luke-warme thy love:	Ovid's Elegies	2.3.6
If she discardes thee, what use servest thou for?	Ovid's Elegies	2.3.12
For I confesse, if that might merite favour,	Ovid's Elegies	2.4.3
If any eie mee with a modest looke,	Ovid's Elegies	2.4.11
If she be learned, then for her skill I crave her,	Ovid's Elegies	2.4.17
If not, because shees simple I would have her.	Ovid's Elegies	2.4.18
Yet would I lie with her if that I might.	Ovid's Elegies	2.4.22
Or if one touch the lute with art and cunning,	Ovid's Elegies	2.4.27
If she be tall, shees like an Amazon,	Ovid's Elegies	2.4.33
If short, she lies the rounder:	Ovid's Elegies	2.4.35
If her white necke be shadowde with blacke haire,	Ovid's Elegies	2.4.41
There good birds rest (if we beleeve things hidden)/Whence	Ovid's Elegies	2.6.51
If on the Marble Theater I looke,	Ovid's Elegies	2.7.3
If some faire wench me secretly behold,	Ovid's Elegies	2.7.5
If I praise any, thy poore haires thou tearest,	Ovid's Elegies	2.7.7
If blame, dissembling of my fault thou fearest.	Ovid's Elegies	2.7.8
If I looke well, thou thinkest thou doest not move,	Ovid's Elegies	2.7.9
If ill, thou saiest I die for others love.	Ovid's Elegies	2.7.10
What if a man with bond-women offend,	Ovid's Elegies	2.8.9
If thou deniest foole, Ile our deeds expresse,	Ovid's Elegies	2.8.25
Rome if her strength the huge world had not fild,	Ovid's Elegies	2.9.17
Yet should I curse a God, if he but said,	Ovid's Elegies	2.9.25
Here of themselves thy shafts come, as if shot,	Ovid's Elegies	2.9.37
Yet Love, if thou with thy faire mother heare,	Ovid's Elegies	2.9.51
If one can doote, if not, two everie night,	Ovid's Elegies	2.10.22
But if that Triton tosse the troubled floud,	Ovid's Elegies	2.11.27
But if my wcrds with winged stormes hence slip,	Ovid's Elegies	2.11.33
But if in sc great feare I may advize thee,	Ovid's Elegies	2.13.27
If without battell selfe-wrought wounds annoy them,	Ovid's Elegies	2.14.3
If watry Thetis had her childe fordone?	Ovid's Elegies	2.14.14
If such a worke thy mother had assayed.	Ovid's Elegies	2.14.20
yong-mens mates, to go/If they determine to persever so.	Ovid's Elegies	2.16.18
But if sterne Neptunes windie powre prevaile,	Ovid's Elegies	2.16.27
If any godly care of me thou hast,	Ovid's Elegies	2.16.47
To serve a wench if any thinke it shame,	Ovid's Elegies	2.17.1
And Phillis hath to reade; if now she lives.	Ovid's Elegies	2.18.32
Foole if to keepe thy wife thou hast no neede,	Ovid's Elegies	2.19.1
In running if I see thee, I shall stay,	Ovid's Elegies	3.2.13
thou maiest, if that be best,/[A] <Or> while thy tiptoes on the	Ovid's Elegies	3.2.63
if she unpunisht you deceive,/For others faults, why do I losse	Ovid's Elegies	3.3.15
Or if there be a God, he loves fine wenches,	Ovid's Elegies	3.3.25
She pleaseth best, I feare, if any say.	Ovid's Elegies	3.4.32
Cannot a faire one, if not chast, please thee?	Ovid's Elegies	3.4.41
Kindly thy mistris use, if thou be wise.	Ovid's Elegies	3.4.43
If standing here I can by no meanes get,	Ovid's Elegies	3.5.11
If I a lover bee by thee held back.	Ovid's Elegies	3.5.22
If Achelous, I aske where thy hornes stand,	Ovid's Elegies	3.5.35
If thy great fame in every region stood?	Ovid's Elegies	3.5.90
Idly I lay with her, as if I lovde <her> not,	Ovid's Elegies	3.6.3
Yet like as if cold hemlocke I had drunke,	Ovid's Elegies	3.6.13
What might I crave more if I aske againe?	Ovid's Elegies	3.6.44
Tis well, if some wench for the poore remaine.	Ovid's Elegies	3.7.60
If I should give, both would the house forbeare.	Ovid's Elegies	3.7.64
If of scornd lovers god be venger just,	Ovid's Elegies	3.7.65
If Thetis, and the morne their sonnes did waile,	Ovid's Elegies	3.8.1
then if Corcyras Ile/Had thee unknowne interr'd in ground most	Ovid's Elegies	3.8.47
If ought remaines of us but name, and spirit,	Ovid's Elegies	3.8.59
And thou, if falsely charged to wrong thy friend,	Ovid's Elegies	3.8.63

IF (cont.)			
With these thy soule walkes, soules if death release,	Ovid's Elegies	3.8.65	
Yet this is lesse, then if he had seene me,	Ovid's Elegies	3.10.15	
Ile hate, if I can; if not, love gainst my will:	Ovid's Elegies	3.10.35	
If you wey not ill speeches, yet wey mee:	Ovid's Elegies	3.13.36	
Sweare I was blinde, yeeld not <deny>, if you be wise,	Ovid's Elegies	3.13.45	
toyes defamde)/Heire of an antient house, if helpe that can,	Ovid's Elegies	3.14.5	
As if another Phaeton had got/The guidance of the sunnes rich	Hero and Leander	1.101	
Neither themselves nor others, if not worne.	Hero and Leander	1.238	
Or if it could, downe from th'enameld skie,	Hero and Leander	1.249	
Whose name is it, if she be false or not,	Hero and Leander	1.285	
As Greece will thinke, if thus you live alone,	Hero and Leander	1.289	
The richest corne dies, if it be not reapt,	Hero and Leander	1.327	
As if her name and honour had beene wrong'd,	Hero and Leander	2.35	
To slake his anger, if he were displeas'd,	Hero and Leander	2.49	
went and came, as if he rewd/The greefe which Neptune felt.	Hero and Leander	2.214	
If not for love, yet love for pittie sake,	Hero and Leander	2.247	
And if these pleasures may thee <things thy minde may> move,	Passionate Shepherd	19	
If these delights thy minde may move;	Passionate Shepherd	23	
IFAITH (See also 'FAITH, YFAITH)			
Each man a crown? why kingly fought ifaith.	1Tamb	3.3.216	Tamb
tickle the pretie wenches plackets Ile be amongst them ifaith.	F App	p.231 64	P Clown
and ifaith I meane to search some circles for my owne use:	F App	p.233 2	P Robin
Ifaith thy head will never be out of the potage pot.	F App	p.236 48	P Robin
Ifaith he lookes much like a conjurer.	F App	p.236 11	P Knight
Ifaith thats just nothing at all.	F App	p.237 40	P Knight
Ifaith thats as true as Diana turned me to a stag.	F App	p.237 54	P Knight
IGNEI			
valeat numen triplex Jehovae, Ignei, Aerii, [Aquatici]	F 244	1.3.16	P Faust
IGNEUM			
But is there not Coelum igneum, [and] <&> <et> Christalinum?	F 612	2.2.61	P Faust
IGNOBLE			
Ignoble vassaile that like Phaeton,	Edw	1.4.16	Warwck
IGNOMINIOUS			
Wherein he wrought such ignominious wrong,	1Tamb	4.3.39	Souldn
abject our princely mindes/To vile and ignominious servitude.	2Tamb	5.1.141	Orcan
IGNORANCE			
And hold there is no sinne but Ignorance.	Jew	Prol.15	Machvl
IGNORANT			
Tell us, O tell us that are ignorant,	Dido	1.1.200	Aeneas
Mercilesse villaine, Pesant ignorant,	1Tamb	4.1.64	Souldn
IGNORAUNCE			
Hermes had slept in hell with ignoraunce.	Hero and Leander	1.468	
IL			
Par [le] <la> mor du, Il mora.	P 770	15.28	Guise
ILAND			
Lay waste the Iland, hew the Temples downe,	Jew	3.5.14	Govnr
And how secure this conquer'd Iland stands/Inviron'd with the	Jew	5.3.6	Calym
I'LE			
shall there concerne our state/Assure your selves I'le looke--	Jew	1.1.173	Barab
How ere the world goe, I'le make sure for one,	Jew	1.1.186	Barab
I'le rouse my senses, and awake my selfe.	Jew	1.2.269	Barab
To morrow early I'le be at the doore.	Jew	1.2.361	Barab
I'le write unto his Majesty for ayd,	Jew	2.2.40	Bosco
Having Fernezes hand, whose heart I'le have;	Jew	2.3.16	Barab
I'le seeke him out, and so insinuate,	Jew	2.3.33	Lodowk
I'le sacrifice her on a pile of wood.	Jew	2.3.52	Barab
I'le have a saying to that Nunnery.	Jew	2.3.90	Barab
And, Barabas, I'le beare thee company.	Jew	2.3.96	Lodowk
and thou hast, breake my head with it, I'le forgive thee.	Jew	2.3.112	P Barab
I'le buy you, and marry you to Lady vanity, if you doe well.	Jew	2.3.116	P Barab
An hundred Crownes, I'le have him; there's the coyne.	Jew	2.3.130	Barab
But goe you in, I'le thinke upon the account:	Jew	2.3.241	Barab
I'le rouze him thence.	Jew	2.3.269	Mthias
I'le give him such a warning e're he goes/As he shall have	Jew	2.3.273	Barab
And yet I'le give her many a golden crosse/With Christian	Jew	2.3.296	Barab
There comes the villaine, now I'le be reveng'd.	Jew	2.3.333	Lodowk
For this I'le have his heart.	Jew	2.3.344	Mthias
I'le make 'em friends againe.	Jew	2.3.357	Abigal
I, I'le put her in.	Jew	2.3.363	Ithimr
Feare not, I'le so set his heart a fire,	Jew	2.3.375	Ithimr
Thy sonne slew mine, and I'le revenge his death.	Jew	3.2.15	Mater
I'le run to some rocke and throw my selfe headlong into the	Jew	3.4.39	P Ithimr
into the sea; why I'le doe any thing for your sweet sake.	Jew	3.4.40	P Ithimr
Here take my keyes, I'le give 'em thee anon:	Jew	3.4.46	Barab
I'le carry't to the Nuns with a powder.	Jew	3.4.112	P Ithimr
I'le to her lodging; hereabouts she lyes.	Jew	3.6.6	1Fryar
All this I'le give to some religious house/So I may be baptiz'd	Jew	4.1.75	Barab
I'le be with you to night.	Jew	4.1.90	2Fryar
Not? then I'le make thee, [rogue] <goe>.	Jew	4.1.95	2Fryar
I'le give him something and so stop his mouth.	Jew	4.1.102	Barab
To fast and be well whipt; I'le none of that.	Jew	4.1.124	Barab
I'le feast you, lodge you, give you faire words,	Jew	4.1.126	Barab
nay then I'le force my way;/And see, a staffe stands ready for	Jew	4.1.171	1Fryar
No, for this example I'le remaine a Jew:	Jew	4.1.195	Barab
goe whither he will, I'le be none of his followers in haste:	Jew	4.2.25	P Ithimr
I'le be gone.	Jew	4.2.39	P Ithimr
I'le goe steale some mony from my Master to make me hansome:	Jew	4.2.49	P Ithimr
I'le make him send me half he has, and glad he scapes so too.	Jew	4.2.67	P Ithimr
I'le write unto him, we'le have mony strait.	Jew	4.2.69	P Ithimr
Otherwise I'le confesse all:--	Jew	4.2.78	P Ithimr
Let me alone, I'le use him in his kinde.	Jew	4.2.80	Pilia
I have no husband, sweet, I'le marry thee.	Jew	4.2.87	Curtzn

I'LE (cont.)

I'le be thy Jason, thou my golden Fleece;	Jew	4.2.90		Ithimr
I'le be Adonis, thou shalt be Loves Queene.	Jew	4.2.94		Ithimr
I'le not leave him worth a gray groat.	Jew	4.2.114	P	Ithimr
I'le rather--	Jew	4.3.23	P	Barab
I'le pledge thee, love, and therefore drinke it off.	Jew	4.4.1		Curtzn
Nay, I'le have all or none.	Jew	4.4.5		Curtzn
Three and fifty dozen, I'le pledge thee.	Jew	4.4.8	P	Ithimr
Play, Fidler, or I'le cut your cats guts into chitterlins.	Jew	4.4.44	P	Ithimr
I'le send by word of mouth now; Bid him deliver thee a thousand	Jew	4.4.74	P	Ithimr
I'le goe alone, dogs, do not hale me thus.	Jew	5.1.19		Barab
Devils doe your worst, [I'le] <I> live in spite of you.	Jew	5.1.41		Barab
I'le be reveng'd on this accursed Towne;	Jew	5.1.62		Barab
I'le helpe to slay their children and their wives,	Jew	5.1.64		Barab
I'le lead five hundred souldiers through the Vault,	Jew	5.1.91		Barab
If this be true, I'le make thee Governor.	Jew	5.1.95		Calym
I'le reare up Malta now remedilesse.	Jew	5.2.73		Barab
Here is my hand that I'le set Malta free:	Jew	5.2.95		Barab
onely to performe/One stratagem that I'le impart to thee,	Jew	5.2.99		Barab
wel since it is no more/I'le satisfie my selfe with that; nay,	Jew	5.5.22		Barab
No, Governor, I'le satisfie thee first,	Jew	5.5.44		Barab
No, thus I'le see thy treachery repaid,	Jew	5.5.74		Govnr
I'le have them flie to [India] <Indian> for gold;	F 109	1.1.81		Faust
I'le have them read me strange Philosophy,	F 113	1.1.85		Faust
I'le have them wall all Germany with Brasse,	F 115	1.1.87		Faust
I'le have them fill the publique Schooles with [silke] <skill>,	F 117	1.1.89		Faust
I'le leavy souldiers with the coyne they bring,	F 119	1.1.91		Faust
I'le make my servile spirits to invent.	F 124	1.1.96		Faust
First I'le instruct thee in the rudiments,	F 188	1.1.160		Valdes
For e're I sleep, I'le try what I can do:	F 192	1.1.164		Faust
This night I'le conjure tho I die therefore.	F 193	1.1.165		Faust
By him, I'le be great Emperour of the world,	F 332	1.3.104		Faust
I'le joyne the Hils that bind the Affrick shore,	F 335	1.3.107		Faust
I'le live in speculation of this Art/Till Mephostophilis	F 341	1.3.113		Faust
I'le turne all the lice about thee into Familiars, and make	F 362	1.4.20	P	Wagner
Here, take your Guilders [againe], I'le none of 'em.	F 371	1.4.29	P	Robin
and Belcher come here, I'le belch him:	F 374	1.4.32	P	Robin
I sirra, I'le teach thee to turne thy selfe to a Dog, or a Cat,	F 382	1.4.40	P	Wagner
To him, I'le build an Altar and a Church,	F 401	2.1.13		Faust
I Mephostophilis, I'le <I> give it him <thee>.	F 437	2.1.49		Faust
I'le fetch thee fire to dissolve it streight.	F 452	2.1.64		Mephst
I'le fetch him somewhat to delight his minde.	F 471	2.1.83		Mephst
Nay, and this be hell, I'le willingly be damn'd <damned here>.	F 527	2.1.139		Faust
Here's a hot whore indeed; no, I'le no wife.	F 534	2.1.146		Faust
I'le cull thee out the fairest Curtezans,	F 537	2.1.149		Mephst
I'le not speake a word more for a Kings ransome <an other	F 669	2.2.118	P	Pride
I'le not speake <an other word for a King's raunsome>.	F 706	(HC264)A	P	Sloth
I'le not speake <a word more for a kings ransome>.	F 706	(HC264)B	P	Sloth
I'le not speake [an other] word.	F 706	2.2.158	P	Sloth
I'le tell thee what, an my Maister come here, I'le clap as	F 736	2.3.15	P	Robin
I'le clap as faire a paire of hornes on's head as e're thou	F 737	2.3.16	P	Robin
Do but speake what thou't have me to do, and I'le do't:	F 745	2.3.24	P	Robin
put off thy cloathes, and I'le conjure thee about presently:	F 746	2.3.25	P	Robin
but to the Taverne with me, I'le give thee white wine, red wine,	F 747	2.3.26	P	Robin
yeares of liberty/I'le spend in pleasure and in daliance,	F 840	3.1.62		Faust
And I'le performe it Faustus: heark they come:	F 866	3.1.88		Mephst
I'le have that too.	F1048	3.2.68		Faust
us, I'le so conjure him, as he was never conjur'd in his life,	F1091	3.3.4	P	Robin
Never deny't, for I know you have it, and I'le search you.	F1101	3.3.14	P	Vintnr
to their porridge-pots, for I'le into the Kitchin presently:	F1134	3.3.47	P	Robin
I'le wing my selfe and forth-with flie amaine/Unto my Faustus	F1136	3.3.49		Mephst
Well I'le go rouse him, and make him give me my forty Dollors	F1487	4.4.31	P	HrsCsr
I'le out-run him, and cast this leg into some ditch or other.	F1495	4.4.39	P	HrsCsr
Maisters, I'le bring you to the best beere in Europe, what ho,	F1505	4.5.1	P	Carter
I'le tell you the bravest tale how a Conjurer serv'd me; you	F1521	4.5.17	P	Carter
I'le tell you how he serv'd me:	F1525	4.5.21	P	Carter
I'le gage my credit, 'twill content your grace.	F1622	4.6.65		Faust
Revolt, or I'le in peece-meale teare thy flesh.	F1745	5.1.72		Mephst
O I'le leape up to [my God] <heaven>: who puls me downe?	F1938	5.2.142		Faust
I'le burne my bookes; [ah] <oh> Mephostophilis.	F1982	5.2.186		Faust

IL'E

Il'e make you feele something anon, if my Art faile me not.	F1246	4.1.92	P	Faust
the Emperour, Il'e be Acteon, and turne my selfe to a Stagge.	F1255	4.1.101	P	Benvol
And Il'e play Diana, and send you the hornes presently.	F1257	4.1.103	P	Faust
Il'e raise a kennell of Hounds shall hunt him so,	F1301	4.1.147		Faust
order, Il'e nere trust smooth faces, and small ruffes more.	F1318	4.1.164	P	Benvol
For hornes he gave, Il'e have his head anone.	F1361	4.2.37		Benvol
Il'e naile huge forked hornes, and let them hang/Within the	F1380	4.2.56		Benvol
if I live till morning, Il'e visit you:	F1877	5.2.81	P	Faust

ILE (Homograph)

From Junos bird Ile pluck her spotted pride,	Dido	1.1.34		Jupitr
But as this one Ile teare them all from him,	Dido	1.1.40		Jupitr
And then Ile hugge with you an hundred times.	Dido	1.1.48		Ganimd
Come in with me, Ile bring you to my Queene,	Dido	1.2.42		Iarbus
Ile have it so, Aeneas be content.	Dido	2.1.95		Dido
Ile give thee Sugar-almonds, sweete Conserves,	Dido	2.1.305		Venus
and in this grove/Amongst greene brakes Ile lay Ascanius,	Dido	2.1.317		Venus
What will you give me now? Ile have this Fanne.	Dido	3.1.32		Cupid
O stay Iarbus, and Ile goe with thee.	Dido	3.1.37		Dido
And if my mother goe, Ile follow her.	Dido	3.1.38		Cupid
Runne for Aeneas, or Ile flye to him.	Dido	3.1.79		Dido
No, for thy sake Ile love thy father well.	Dido	3.1.81		Dido
Ile make me bracelets of his golden haire,	Dido	3.1.85		Dido

ILE (cont.)

altar, where Ile offer up/As many kisses as the Sea hath sands,	Dido	3.1.87		Dido
Aeneas, Ile repaire thy Troian ships,	Dido	3.1.113		Dido
Ile give thee tackling made of riveld gold,	Dido	3.1.116		Dido
For here in spight of heaven Ile murder him,	Dido	3.2.10		Juno
Ile make the Clowdes dissolve their watrie workes,	Dido	3.2.90		Juno
Ile dye befcre a stranger have that grace:	Dido	3.3.11		Iarbus
And yet Ile speake, and yet Ile hold my peace,	Dido	3.4.27		Dido
Ile follow thee with outcryes nere the lesse,	Dido	4.2.55		Anna
Dido is thine, henceforth Ile call thee Lord:	Dido	4.4.84		Dido
And from a turret Ile behold my love.	Dido	4.4.86		Dido
Ile hang ye in the chamber where I lye,	Dido	4.4.128		Dido
Ile set the casement open that the windes/May enter in, and	Dido	4.4.130		Dido
And swim to Italy, Ile keepe these sure:	Dido	4.4.164		Dido
Whither must I goe? Ile stay with my mother.	Dido	4.5.2		Cupid
Come come, Ile goe, how farre hence is your house?	Dido	4.5.13		Cupid
Ile be no more a widowe, I am young,	Dido	4.5.22		Nurse
Ile have a husband, or els a lover.	Dido	4.5.23		Nurse
And bore yong Cupid unto Cypresse Ile.	Dido	5.1.41		Hermes
Which if it chaunce, Ile give ye buriall,	Dido	5.1.176		Dido
If not, turne from me, and Ile turne from thee:	Dido	5.1.181		Dido
Ile frame me wings of waxe like Icarus,	Dido	5.1.243		Dido
Or els Ile make a prayer unto the waves,	Dido	5.1.246		Dido
Why then Theridamas, Ile first assay,	1Tamb	2.5.81		Tamb
I will not tell thee how Ile handle thee,	1Tamb	3.3.84		Tamb
And by this meanes Ile win the world at last.	1Tamb	3.3.260		Tamb
Ile make the kings of India ere I die,	1Tamb	3.3.263		Tamb
take it from my swords point, or Ile thrust it to thy heart.	1Tamb	4.4.41	P	Tamb
so eloquent/To paint in woords, what Ile perfourme in deeds,	2Tamb	1.2.10		Callap
Hold him, and cleave him too, or Ile cleave thee,	2Tamb	1.3.104		Tamb
Ile have you learne to sleepe upon the ground,	2Tamb	3.2.55		Tamb
Ile teach ycu how to make the water mount,	2Tamb	3.2.85		Tamb
Mother dispatch me, or Ile kil my selfe,	2Tamb	3.4.26		Sonne
But yet Ile save their lives and make them slaves.	2Tamb	3.5.63		Tamb
Ile hang a clogge about your necke for running away againe, you	2Tamb	3.5.100	P	Tamb
Ile have you learne to feed on provander,	2Tamb	3.5.106		Tamb
Ile make thee wish the earth had swallowed thee:	2Tamb	3.5.118		Tamb
T'appease my wrath, or els Ile torture thee,	2Tamb	3.5.122		Tamb
as the battaile is done, Ile ride in triumph through the Camp.	2Tamb	3.5.145	P	Tamb
Ile to cardes: Perdicas.	2Tamb	4.1.59		Calyph
And Ile dispose them as it likes me best,	2Tamb	4.1.166		Tamb
Ile bridle al your tongues/And bind them close with bits of	2Tamb	4.1.181		Tamb
Ile make ye roare, that earth may eccho foorth/The far	2Tamb	4.1.185		Tamb
Ile use some other means to make you yeeld,	2Tamb	4.2.51		Therid
Ile give your Grace a present of such price,	2Tamb	4.2.56		Olymp
Ile ride in golden armour like the Sun,	2Tamb	4.3.115		Tamb
Wel, now Ile make it quake, go draw him up,	2Tamb	5.1.107		Tamb
To cure me, or Ile fetch him downe my selfe.	2Tamb	5.3.63		Tamb
The Christian Ile of Rhodes, from whence you came,	Jew	2.2.31		Bosco
Ile pay thee with a vengeance Ithamore.	Jew	3.4.116		Barab
as once you said, within this Ile/In Malta here, that I have got	Jew	5.2.67		Barab
And banquet with him e're thou leav'st the Ile.	Jew	5.3.19		Msngr
Which Ile desolve with bloud and crueltie.	P 26	1.26		QnMoth
And then Ile guerdon thee with store of crownes.	P 89	2.32		Guise
Ile either rend it with my nayles to naught,	P 102	2.45		Guise
And with this wait Ile counterpoise a Crowne,	P 115	2.58		Guise
Then Ile have a peale of ordinance shot from the tower,	P 236	4.34		Guise
Harke, harke they come, Ile leap out at the window.	P 369	7.9		Taleus
Come sirs, Ile whip you to death with my punniards point.	P 441	7.81		Guise
Ile disinherite him and all the rest:	P 524	9.43		QnMoth
For Ile rule France, but they shall weare the crowne:	P 525	9.44		QnMoth
Ile muster up an army secretly,	P 572	11.37		Navrre
Ile dispatch him with his brother presently,	P 651	12.64		QnMoth
Ile make her shake off love with her heeles.	P 782	15.40		Mugern
Ile goe [take] <make> a walk/On purpose from the Court to meet	P 783	15.41		Mugern
Which Ile maintaine so long as life doth last:	P 800	16.14		Navrre
And being able, Ile keep an hoast in pay.	P 840	17.35		Guise
And Ile subscribe my name and seale it straight.	P 883	17.78		King
And then Ile tell thee what I meane to doe.	P 891	17.86		King
Ile secretly convay me unto Bloyse,	P 895	17.90		King
And tell him ere it be long, Ile visite him.	P 912	18.13		Navrre
Then stay a while and Ile goe call the King,	P1017	19.87		Capt
Ile be revengde.	P1051	19.121		YngGse
with him, Ile clippe his winges/Or ere he passe my handes,	P1052	19.122		King
I am thy brcther, and ile revenge thy death,	P1112	21.6		Dumain
Ile read them Frier, and then Ile answere thee.	P1171	22.33		King
Ile send my sister England newes of this,	P1189	22.51		King
Ile fire his crased buildings and [inforse] <incense>/The	P1201	22.63		King
Ile [fawne] <fanne> first on the winde,/That glaunceth at my	Edw	1.1.22		Gavstn
And as I like your discoursing, ile have you.	Edw	1.1.32		Gavstn
Ile flatter these, and make them live in hope:	Edw	1.1.43		Gavstn
If I speed well, ile entertaine you all.	Edw	1.1.46		Gavstn
Therefore ile have Italian maskes by night,	Edw	1.1.55		Gavstn
the king and the nobles/From the parlament, ile stand aside.	Edw	1.1.73		Gavstn
Ile have my will, and these two Mortimers,	Edw	1.1.78		Edward
That villaine Mortimer, ile be his death.	Edw	1.1.81		Gavstn
Well Mortimer, ile make thee rue these words,	Edw	1.1.91		Edward
But now ile speake, and to the proofe I hope:	Edw	1.1.108		Kent
Ile bandie with the Barons and the Earles,	Edw	1.1.137		Edward
Ile give thee more, for but to honour thee,	Edw	1.1.164		Edward
Ile be revengd on him for my exile.	Edw	1.1.192		Gavstn
And in the meane time ile intreat you all,	Edw	1.2.77		ArchBp
Ile make the prowdest of you stoope to him.	Edw	1.4.31		Edward

ILE (cont.)

This Ile shall fleete upon the Ocean,	Edw	1.4.49		Edward
In steede of inke, ile write it with my teares.	Edw	1.4.86		Edward
Give it me, ile have it published in the streetes.	Edw	1.4.89		Lncstr
Ile see him presently dispatched away.	Edw	1.4.90		Mortmr
Ile fire thy crased buildings, and enforce/The papall towers,	Edw	1.4.100		Edward
Live where thou wilt, ile send thee gould enough,	Edw	1.4.113		Edward
Ile come to thee, my love shall neare decline.	Edw	1.4.115		Edward
Thou shalt not hence, ile hide thee Gaveston.	Edw	1.4.131		Edward
But come sweete friend, ile beare thee on thy way.	Edw	1.4.140		Edward
Ile rather loose his friendship I, then graunt.	Edw	1.4.237		Lncstr
Ile hang a golden tongue about thy neck,	Edw	1.4.328		Edward
My lord, ile marshall so your enemies,	Edw	1.4.357		Mortmr
Welcome Lord governour of the Ile of Man.	Edw	2.2.67		Warwck
Returne it to their throtes, ile be thy warrant.	Edw	2.2.73		Edward
Ile not be barde the court for Gaveston.	Edw	2.2.90		Mortmr
But if I live, ile tread upon their heads,	Edw	2.2.96		Edward
Ile have his bloud, or die in seeking it.	Edw	2.2.107		Warwck
Ile to the King.	Edw	2.2.120		Mortmr
Do cosin, and ile beare thee companie.	Edw	2.2.121		Lncstr
Ile thunder such a peale into his eares,	Edw	2.2.128		Mortmr
Content, ile beare my part, holla whose there?	Edw	2.2.130		Lncstr
Nay, now you are heere alone, ile speake my minde.	Edw	2.2.155		Mortmr
Waite on me, and ile see thou shalt not want.	Edw	2.2.246		Edward
me, for his sake/Ile grace thee with a higher stile ere long.	Edw	2.2.253		Edward
Ile give the onset.	Edw	2.3.20		Mortmr
And ile follow thee.	Edw	2.3.20		Warwck
O that mine armes could close this Ile about,	Edw	2.4.17		Queene
No Mortimer, ile to my lord the king.	Edw	2.4.51		Queene
Yet once more ile importune him with praiers,	Edw	2.4.63		Queene
Have you no doubts my lords, ile [clap so] <claps> close,/Among	Edw	3.1.276		Levune
But ile to Fraunce, and cheere the wronged Queene,	Edw	4.1.6		Kent
I warrant you, ile winne his highnes quicklie,	Edw	4.2.6		Prince
See monsters see, ile weare my crowne againe,	Edw	5.1.74		Edward
Ile not resigne, but whilst I live, [be king].	Edw	5.1.86		Edward
Not yet my lorde, ile beare you on your waye.	Edw	5.1.155		Leistr
And for your sakes, a thousand wronges ile take,	Edw	5.3.43		Edward
Wish well to mine, then tush, for them ile die.	Edw	5.3.45		Edward
But seeing I cannot, ile entreate for him:	Edw	5.4.98		King
Feare not sweete boye, ile garde thee from thy foes,	Edw	5.4.111		Queene
If you mistrust me, ile be gon my lord.	Edw	5.5.97		Ltborn
if thou now growest penitent/Ile be thy ghostly father,	Edw	5.6.4		Mortmr
Ile fetch thee a wife in the divels name>.	F 531	(HC261)A	P	Mephst
<No, Ile see thee hanged, thou wilt eate up all my victualls>.	F 702	(HC264)A	P	Faust
'faith Ile drinke a health to thy wooden leg for that word.	F1626	4.6.69	P	HrsCsr
thou serve me, and Ile make thee go like Qui mihi discipulus?	F App	p.229 13	P	Wagner
or Ile turne al the lice about thee into familiars, and they	F App	p.229 25	P	Wagner
Truly Ile none of them.	F App	p.230 39	P	Wagner
and Ile knocke them, they were never so knocht since they were	F App	p.230 45	P	Clown
Ile tell you how you shall know them, all hee divels has	F App	p.230 52	P	Clown
Ile tickle the pretie wenches plackets Ile be amongst them	F App	p.231 63	P	Clown
tickle the pretie wenches plackets Ile be amongst them ifaith.	F App	p.231 63	P	Clown
well, Ile folow him, Ile serve him, thats flat.	F App	p.231 72	P	Clown
well, Ile folow him, Ile serve him, thats flat.	F App	p.231 73	P	Clown
You say true, Ile hate.	F App	p.231 11	P	Faust
my Lord Ile drinke to your grace	F App	p.231 12	P	Pope
Ile pledge your grace.	F App	p.232 13	P	Faust
Ile feede thy divel with horse-bread as long as he lives,	F App	p.234 30	P	Rafe
Hush, Ile gul him supernaturally:	F App	p.234 5	P	Robin
sirra you, Ile teach ye to impeach honest men:	F App	p.235 17	P	Robin
stand by, Ile scowre you for a goblet, stand aside you had best,	F App	p.235 18	P	Robin
Ile tel you what I meane.	F App	p.235 22	P	Robin
nay Ile tickle you Vintner, looke to the goblet Rafe,	F App	p.235 23	P	Robin
good divel forgive me now, and Ile never rob thy Library more.	F App	p.235 31	P	Robin
Ile have fine sport with the boyes, Ile get nuts and apples	F App	p.236 45	P	Robin
have fine sport with the boyes, Ile get nuts and apples enow.	F App	p.236 46	P	Robin
Nay, and you go to conjuring, Ile be gone.	F App	p.237 57	P	Knight
Ile meete with you anone for interrupting me so:	F App	p.238 58	P	Faust
I am past this faire and pleasant greene, ile walke on foote.	F App	p.239 96	P	Faust
Now am I made man for ever, Ile not leave my horse for fortie:	F App	p.239 114	P	HrsCsr
but Ile seeke out my Doctor, and have my fortie dollers againe,	F App	p.240 136	P	HrsCsr
my fortie dollers againe, or Ile make it the dearest horse:	F App	p.240 137	P	HrsCsr
Ile speake with him now, or Ile breake his glasse-windowes	F App	p.240 142	P	HrsCsr
him now, or Ile breake his glasse-windowes about his eares.	F App	p.240 142	P	HrsCsr
And he have not slept this eight weekes Ile speake with him.	F App	p.240 145	P	HrsCsr
Ile make you wake ere I goe.	F App	p.241 153	P	HrsCsr
O Lord sir, let me goe, and Ile give you fortie dollers more.	F App	p.241 158	P	HrsCsr
have none about me, come to my Oastrie, and Ile give them you.	F App	p.241 161	P	HrsCsr
Ile bouldly quarter out the fields of Rome;	Lucan, First Booke	383		
If men have Faith, Ile live with thee for ever.	Ovid's Elegies	1.3.16		
that fatall destenie shall give,/Ile live with thee, and die,	Ovid's Elegies	1.3.18		
Yet this Ile see, but if thy gowne ought cover,	Ovid's Elegies	1.4.41		
Leave asking, and Ile give what I refraine.	Ovid's Elegies	1.10.64		
for needfull uses/Ile prove had hands impure with all abuses.	Ovid's Elegies	1.12.16		
Ile live, and as he puls me downe, mount higher.	Ovid's Elegies	1.15.42		
My lordly hands ile throwe upon my right.	Ovid's Elegies	2.5.30		
If thou deniest foole, Ile our deeds expresse,	Ovid's Elegies	2.8.25		
Ile clip and kisse thee with all contentation,	Ovid's Elegies	2.11.45		
Ile thinke all true, though it be feigned matter.	Ovid's Elegies	2.11.53		
In white, with incense Ile thine Altars greete,	Ovid's Elegies	2.13.23		
Onely Ile signe nought, that may grieve me much.	Ovid's Elegies	2.15.18		
But absent is my fire, lyes ile tell none,	Ovid's Elegies	2.16.11		
Greater then her, by her leave th'art, Ile say.	Ovid's Elegies	3.2.60		

ILE (cont.)			
I ere while/Nam'd Achelaus, Inachus, and [Nile] <Ile>,	Ovid's Elegies	3.5.104	
then if Corcyras Ile/Had thee unknowne interr'd in ground most	Ovid's Elegies	3.8.47	
Ile hate, if I can; if not, love gainst my will:	Ovid's Elegies	3.10.35	
Rather Ile hoist up saile, and use the winde,	Ovid's Elegies	3.10.51	
Ile not sift much, but hold thee soone excusde,	Ovid's Elegies	3.13.41	
How small sc ere, Ile you for greatest praise.	Ovid's Elegies	3.14.14	
ILES			
I sent for Egypt and the bordering Iles/Are gotten up by Nilus	Jew	1.1.42	Barab
and those other Iles/That lye betwixt the Mediterranean seas.	Jew	1.2.3	Basso
What's Cyprus, Candy, and those other Iles/To us, or Malta?	Jew	1.2.5	Govnr
Strong contermin'd <countermur'd> with other petty Iles;	Jew	5.3.8	Calym
ILIA			
In swelling wombe her twinnes had Ilia kilde?	Ovid's Elegies	2.14.15	
Whom Ilia pleasd, though in her lookes griefe reveld,	Ovid's Elegies	3.5.47	
Ilia, sprung from Idaean Laomedon?	Ovid's Elegies	3.5.54	
There shalt be lov'd: Ilia lay feare aside.	Ovid's Elegies	3.5.62	
ILIADS			
Had not bene nam'd in Homers Iliads:	2Tamb	2.4.89	Tamb
ILIAN			
faine themselves/The Romanes brethren, sprung of Ilian race;	Lucan, First Booke	429	
ILIAS			
Remus and Romulus, Ilias twinne-borne seed.	Ovid's Elegies	3.4.40	
ILION			
Viewing the fire wherewith rich Ilion burnt.	Dido	2.1.264	Aeneas
ILIONS			
And cast the fame of Ilions Tower to hell.	2Tamb	4.3.113	Tamb
ILIUM			
And burnt the toplesse Towers of Ilium?	F1769	5.1.96	Faust
ILL (See alsc ILS)			
To be partaker of thy good or ill,	1Tamb	1.2.230	Therid
But 'twas ill done of you to come so farre/Without the ayd or	Jew	1.1.93	Barab
Your grace was ill advisde to take them then,	P 174	3.9	Admral
Which as I heare one [Shekius] <Shekins> takes it ill,	P 404	7.44	Ramus
The king I feare hath ill intreated her.	Edw	1.4.189	Warwck
Warwicke, these words do ill beseeme thy years.	Edw	2.2.94	Kent
I rue my lords ill fortune, but alas,	Edw	4.6.64	Queene
my horse be sick, or ill at ease, if I bring his water to you,	F App	p.240 118 P	HrsCsr
Had forraine wars ill thriv'd; or wrathful France/Pursu'd us	Lucan, First Booke	308	
held up, all joyntly cryde/They'll follow where he please:	Lucan, First Booke	389	
And which (aie me) ever pretendeth ill,	Lucan, First Booke	625	
For beds ill hyr'd we are indebted nought.	Ovid's Elegies	1.10.44	
Ill gotten goods good end will never have.	Ovid's Elegies	1.10.48	
Why doest thy ill kembd tresses losse lament?	Ovid's Elegies	1.14.35	
Envie, why carpest thou my time is spent so ill,	Ovid's Elegies	1.15.1	
Tis ill they pleas'd so much, for in my lips,	Ovid's Elegies	2.5.57	
If ill, thou saiest I die for others love.	Ovid's Elegies	2.7.10	
Live without love, so sweete ill is a maide.	Ovid's Elegies	2.9.26	
raught/Ill waies by rough seas wondring waves first taught,	Ovid's Elegies	2.11.2	
Armenian Tygers never did so ill,	Ovid's Elegies	2.14.35	
With his stumpe-foote he halts ill-favouredly.	Ovid's Elegies	2.17.20	
By thy sides touching ill she is entreated.	Ovid's Elegies	3.2.22	
For her ill-beautious Mother judgd to slaughter?	Ovid's Elegies	3.3.18	
Who may offend, sinnes least; power to do ill,	Ovid's Elegies	3.4.9	
Why mockst thou me she cried, or being ill,	Ovid's Elegies	3.6.77	
His left hand whereon gold doth ill alight,	Ovid's Elegies	3.7.15	
O let him change goods so ill got to dust.	Ovid's Elegies	3.7.66	
Beauty with lewdnesse doth right ill agree.	Ovid's Elegies	3.10.42	
If you wey not ill speeches, yet wey mee:	Ovid's Elegies	3.13.36	
ILL-BEAUTIOUS			
For her ill-beautious Mother judgd to slaughter?	Ovid's Elegies	3.3.18	
ILLES			
Whose emptie Altars have enlarg'd our illes.	Dido	4.2.3	Iarbus
Adde, Caesar, tc these illes Perusian famine;	Lucan, First Booke	41	
ILL-FAVOUREDLY			
With his stumpe-foote he halts ill-favouredly.	Ovid's Elegies	2.17.20	
ILL GOTTEN			
Ill gotten goods good end will never have.	Ovid's Elegies	1.10.48	
ILLIBERALL			
Too servile <The devill> and illiberall for mee.	F 63	1.1.35	Faust
ILLICIANS			
[Illirians] <Illicians>, Thracians, and Bythinians,	2Tamb	1.1.64	Orcan
ILLIONEUS			
Like Illioneus speakes this Noble man,	Dido	2.1.47	Achat
But Illioneus goes not in such robes.	Dido	2.1.48	Achat
O Illioneus, art thou yet alive?	Dido	2.1.55	Achat
Sergestus, Illioneus and the rest,	Dido	2.1.58	Aeneas
Achates come forth, Sergestus, Illioneus,	Dido	4.3.13	Aeneas
And Illioneus gum and Libian spice,	Dido	4.4.8	Dido
ILLIRIANS			
[Illirians] <Illicians>, Thracians, and Bythinians,	2Tamb	1.1.64	Orcan
ILLITERATE			
keepe further from me O thou illiterate, and unlearned Hostler.	F 729	2.3.8 P	Robin
ILLIT'RAT			
But vicious, harebraind, and illit'rat hinds?	Hero and Leander	2.218	
ILLUMINATE			
Whose beames illuminate the lamps of heaven,	2Tamb	1.3.2	Tamb
ILLUMINATES			
The christall springs whose taste illuminates/Refined eies with	2Tamb	2.4.22	Tamb
ILLUSIONS			
Rather illusions, fruits of lunacy,	F 407	2.1.19	BdAngl
ILLUSTRATE			
tel me if the warres/Be not a life that may illustrate Gods,	2Tamb	4.1.79	Tamb

ILLYRIA (See also ILLIRIANS)
Illyria, Carmonia and al the hundred and thirty Kingdomes late — 2Tamb 3.1.4 P Orcan

ILS
Is thus misled to countenance their ils. — Edw 4.3.49 Edward

I'M
Troth master, I'm loth such a pot of pottage should be spoyld. — Jew 3.4.89 P Ithimr

IMAGE
That grievous image of ingratitude: — 1Tamb 2.6.30 Cosroe
Image of Honor and Nobilitie. — 1Tamb 5.1.75 1Virgn
Image of sloth, and picture of a slave, — 2Tamb 4.1.91 Tamb
Dead is that speaking image of mans voice, — Ovid's Elegies 2.6.37
Foole, what is sleepe but image of cold death, — Ovid's Elegies 2.9.41

IMAGINE
Lest she imagine thou art Venus sonne: — Dido 3.1.4 Cupid
And you good Cosin to imagine it. — P 970 19.40 King
Imagine Killingworth castell were your court, — Edw 5.1.2 Leistr
[Quin redis <regis> Mephostophilis fratris imagine]. — F 262 1.3.34A Faust
Think'st thou that Faustus, is so fond to imagine, — F 522 2.1.134 Faust

IMAGINES
Contrives, imagines and fully executes/Matters of importe, aimed — P 110 2.53 Guise

IMAGINING
Imagining, that Ganimed displeas'd, — Hero and Leander 2.157

IMAGYN'D
As he imagyn'd Hero was his mother. — Hero and Leander 1.40

IMBARKT
Would when I left sweet France and was imbarkt, — Edw 1.4.171 Queene
We were imbarkt for Ireland, wretched we, — Edw 4.7.33 Baldck

IMBAST
With virgin waxe hath some imbast my joynts, — Ovid's Elegies 3.6.29

IMBECILITIE
First I complaine of imbecilitie, — Edw 5.4.60 Mortmr

IMBELLISHED
A Scythian Shepheard, so imbellished/With Natures pride, and — 1Tamb 1.2.155 Therid

IMBRAC'D
him he were best to send it; then he hug'd and imbrac'd me. — Jew 4.2.106 P Pilia
With that Leander stoopt, to have imbrac'd her, — Hero and Leander 1.341

IMBRACE
Unworthy to imbrace or touch the ground, — 1Tamb 4.2.20 Tamb
Couragious Lancaster, imbrace thy king, — Edw 1.4.340 Edward
Where Tarbels winding shoares imbrace the sea, — Lucan, First Booke 422
a pretty wenches face/Shee in requitall doth me oft imbrace. — Ovid's Elegies 2.1.34
Or any back made rough with stripes imbrace? — Ovid's Elegies 2.7.22
I know not whom thou lewdly didst imbrace, — Ovid's Elegies 3.10.11
Who hoping to imbrace thee, cherely swome. — Hero and Leander 2.250

IMBRACEMENT
Therefore with dum imbracement let us part. — Edw 1.4.134 Edward

IMBRACEMENTS
From my imbracements thus he breakes away, — Edw 2.4.16 Queene
(Sweet are the kisses, the imbracements sweet, — Hero and Leander 2.29

IMBRACETH
little sonne/Playes with your garments and imbraceth you. — Dido 3.1.21 Anna

IMBRACINGS
sweet embraces <imbracings> may extinguish cleare <cleane>, — F1763 5.1.90 Faust

IMBRASEMENTS
is there in a Tigers jawes,/[Then] <This> his imbrasements: — Edw 5.1.117 Edward

IMBRAST
Kist him, imbrast him, and unloosde his bands, — Dido 2.1.158 Aeneas
When sleepe but newly had imbrast the night, — Dido 4.3.17 Aeneas
Imbrast her sodainly, tooke leave, and kist, — Hero and Leander 2.92
The lustie god imbrast him, cald him love, — Hero and Leander 2.167

IMBRODERED
The common souldiers rich imbrodered coates, — Dido 4.4.9 Dido

IMBROTHERIE
Then gaudie silkes, or rich imbrotherie. — Edw 1.4.347 Edward

IMBROYDRED
Imbroydred all with leaves of Mirtle. — Passionate Shepherd 12

IMITATE
That imitate the Moone in every chaunge, — Dido 3.3.67 Iarbus
So shall you imitate those you succeed: — Jew 2.2.47 Bosco

IMMEDIATELY
Now will I make an end immediately. — F 461 2.1.73 Faust
come then stand by me/And thou shalt see them come immediately. — F 844 3.1.66 Mephst

IMMEDIATLY
You shall be princes all immediatly: — 2Tamb 3.5.168 Tamb
Unlesse you bring them forth immediatly: — F1031 3.2.51 Pope
Thus will I end his griefes immediatly. — F1367 4.2.43 Benvol
Fly hence, dispatch my charge immediatly. — F1416 4.2.92 Faust

IMMENSE
Poets large power is boundlesse, and immense, — Ovid's Elegies 3.11.41

IMMODEST
And before folke immodest speeches shunne, — Ovid's Elegies 3.13.16

IMMORTAL
(and gods not sleightly/Purchase immortal thrones; nor Jove — Lucan, First Booke 35
whose immortal pens/Renowne the valiant soules slaine in your — Lucan, First Booke 443

IMMORTALITIE
Nor immortalitie to be reveng'd: — P1008 19.78 Guise
Or thirsting after immortalitie, — Hero and Leander 1.427

IMMORTALL
Grace my immortall beautie with this boone, — Dido 1.1.21 Ganimd
Cannot ascend to Fames immortall house, — Dido 4.3.9 Aeneas
Now lookes Aeneas like immortall Jove, — Dido 4.4.45 Dido
And heele make me immortall with a kisse. — Dido 4.4.123 Dido
I am commaunded by immortall Jove, — Dido 5.1.99 Aeneas

IMMORTALL (cont.)			
May we become immortall like the Gods.	1Tamb	1.2.201	Tamb
Quintessence they still/From their immortall flowers of Poesy,	1Tamb	5.1.166	Tamb
As Centinels to warne th'immortall soules,	2Tamb	2.4.16	Tamb
And scourge the Scourge of the immortall God:	2Tamb	2.4.80	Tamb
or by speach I heare/Immortall Jove say, Cease my Tamburlaine,	2Tamb	4.1.199	Tamb
And hart and hand to heavens immortall throne,	Edw	4.7.108	Baldck
Heare me immortall Jove, and graunt it too.	Edw	5.1.143	Edward
Immortall powers, that knowes the painfull cares,	Edw	5.3.37	Edward
Sweet Hellen make me immortall with a kisse:	F1770	5.1.97	Faust
Or why is this immortall that thou hast?	F1965	5.2.169	Faust
Verse is immortall, and shall nere decay.	Ovid's Elegies		1.15.32
And whose immortall fingars did imprint,	Hero and Leander		1.67
Seeke you for chastitie, immortall fame,	Hero and Leander		1.283
IMMORTALLIE			
bloudie colours may suggest/Remembrance of revenge immortallie,	Edw	3.1.140	Edward
IMMORTALLY			
And live in all your seedes immortally:	2Tamb	5.3.174	Tamb
IMMURE			
ragged stonie walles/Immure thy vertue that aspires to heaven?	Edw	3.1.257	Mortmr
IMP (See alsc IMPE)			
Ambitious Imp, why seekst thou further charge?	Ovid's Elegies		1.1.18
IMPALE (See EMPALE)			
IMPART			
onely to performe/One stratagem that I'le impart to thee,	Jew	5.2.99	Barab
IMPARTIALL			
And with my prayers pierce [th']impartiall heavens,	Jew	3.2.33	Govnr
IMPARTING			
Must part, imparting his impressions,	2Tamb	5.3.170	Tamb
IMPARTS			
And give to him that the first wound imparts.	Ovid's Elegies		3.12.22
IMPATIENT			
But Priamus impatient of delay,	Dido	2.1.173	Aeneas
Raving, impatient, desperate and mad,	2Tamb	2.4.112	Tamb
Ah good my Lord, leave these impatient words,	2Tamb	5.3.54	Therid
And knowing me impatient in distresse/Thinke me so mad as I	Jew	1.2.262	Barab
Unckle, tis this that makes me impatient.	Edw	1.4.419	Mortmr
IMPE			
That ugly impe that shall outweare my wrath,	Dido	3.2.4	Juno
IMPEACH			
sirra you, Ile teach ye to impeach honest men:	F App	p.235 18 P	Robin
IMPEACHE			
Lets see whc dare impeache me for his death?	Edw	5.6.14	Mortmr
IMPERFETT			
thus fall Imperfett exhalatione/which our great sonn of fraunce	Paris	ms19,p390	Guise
IMPERIAL (See also EMPERIALL)			
by the honor of mine Imperial crowne, that what ever thou	F App	p.236 8 P	Emper
and nothing answerable to the honor of your Imperial majesty,	F App	p.236 14 P	Faust
IMPERIALL			
And here Queene Dido weares th'imperiall Crowne,	Dido	2.1.63	Illion
Holde thee Cosroe, weare two imperiall Crownes.	1Tamb	2.5.1	Tamb
The strength and sinewes of the imperiall seat.	2Tamb	1.1.156	Sgsmnd
And make a passage from the imperiall heaven/That he that sits	2Tamb	2.2.48	Orcan
Up to tne pallace of th'imperiall heaven:	2Tamb	2.4.35	Tamb
And were the sinowes of th'imperiall seat/So knit and	2Tamb	3.1.10	Callap
Of Joves vast pallace the imperiall Orbe,	2Tamb	3.4.49	Therid
First take my Scourge and my imperiall Crowne,	2Tamb	5.3.177	Tamb
Proud Rome, that hatchest such imperiall groomes,	Edw	1.4.97	Edward
But when the imperiall Lions flesh is gorde,	Edw	5.1.11	Edward
I doubt not shal sufficiently content your Imperiall majesty.	F App	p.237 49 P	Faust
IMPERIOUS (See also EMPERIOUS)			
That with his terrour and imperious eies,	1Tamb	4.1.14	2Msngr
to be enthral'd/Tc forraine powers, and rough imperious yokes:	1Tamb	5.1.36	Govnr
For there sits Death, there sits imperious Death,	1Tamb	5.1.111	Tamb
I love him as my selfe/Should write in this imperious vaine!	Jew	4.3.43	Barab
IMPIOUS			
Or impious traitors vowde to have my life,	Dido	4.4.114	Dido
Roome, if thcu take delight in impious warre,	Lucan, First Booke		21
Se impious warre defiles the Senat house,	Lucan, First Booke		690
IMPLOY			
As I behave my selfe in this, imploy me hereafter.	Jew	2.3.379	Ithimr
IMPLOY'D			
and looks/Like one that is imploy'd in Catzerie/And crosbiting,	Jew	4.3.12	Barab
IMPORT			
Nay, no such waightie busines of import,	Dido	4.2.25	Anna
I am (my Lord), fcr so you do import.	1Tamb	1.2.33	Zenoc
And see my Lord, a sight of strange import,	1Tamb	5.1.468	Tamb
built Citadell/Commands much more then letters can import:	Jew	Prol.23	Machvl
this is all the newes of import.	Edw	4.3.36 P	Spencr
IMPORTANT			
I judge the purchase more important far.	1Tamb	2.5.92	Therid
IMPORTE			
Contrives, imagines and fully executes/Matters of importe,	P 111	2.54	Guise
IMPORTS			
He bids you prophesie what it imports.	1Tamb	3.2.89	Techel
Which being the cause of life, imports your death.	2Tamb	5.3.90	Phsitn
Thinke therefore madam that imports [us] <as> much,	Edw	5.2.10	Mortmr
O my deere Faustus what imports this feare?	F1827	5.2.31	1Schol
IMPORTUN'D			
That being importun'd by this Bernardine/To be a Christian, I	Jew	4.1.187	Barab
IMPORTUNE			
Yet once more ile importune him with praiers,	Edw	2.4.63	Queene
If he loves not, deafe eares thou doest importune,	Ovid's Elegies		2.2.53

IMPOS'D
Impos'd upon her lover such a taske, ... Hero and Leander 1.429
IMPOSD
Nor yet imposd, with such a bitter hate. . . . . 2Tamb 4.1.170 Jrslem
IMPOSE
Impose some end to my incessant paine: . . . . F1960 5.2.164 Faust
Say they are mine, and hands on thee impose. . . . Ovid's Elegies 1.4.40
IMPOSSIBLE
It is impossible, but speake your minde. . . . . Edw 1.4.228 Mortmr
Brother, you know it is impossible. . . . . . Edw 5.2.97 Queene
IMPRECATIONS
If humble suites or imprecations, ... 1Tamb 5.1.24 1Virgn
IMPRECOR
Littora littoribus contraria, fluctibus undas/Imprecor: . Dido 5.1.311 Dido
IMPRESSION
Even so for mens impression do we you. . . . . Hero and Leander 1.266
IMPRESSIONS
Must part, imparting his impressions, ... 2Tamb 5.3.170 Tamb
IMPRIMIS
and I carried it, first to Lodowicke, and imprimis to Mathias. Jew 3.3.19 P Ithimr
IMPRINT
And whose immortall fingars did imprint, ... Hero and Leander 1.67
IMPRINTED
No steps of men imprinted in the earth. . . . . Dido 1.1.181 Achat
IMPRISON'D
I was imprison'd, but escap'd their hands. . . . . Jew 5.1.77 Barab
IMPRISONED
hands upon him, next/Himselfe imprisoned, and his goods asceasd, Edw 1.2.37 ArchBp
IMPRISONMENT
That wast a cause of his imprisonment? . . . . Edw 5.2.102 Mortmr
IMPURE
for neeifull uses/Ile prove had hands impure with all abuses. Ovid's Elegies 1.12.16
INACHUS
In mid Bithynia 'tis said Inachus, ... Ovid's Elegies 3.5.25
I ere while/Nam'd Achelaus, Inachus, and [Nile] <Ile>, . Ovid's Elegies 3.5.104
INAMOURD
To be inamourd of thy brothers lookes, ... Dido 3.1.2 Cupid
INARTIFICIALE
<testimonis> est [inartificiale] <in arte fetiales>. . P 395 7.35 Guise
INASPIRING
And fruitfull wits that in aspiring <inaspiring> are, . Hero and Leander 1.477
INCAMPE
If to incampe on Thuscan Tybers streames, ... Lucan, First Booke 382
INCAMPES
The power of vengeance now incampes it selfe, . . . P 717 14.20 Navrre
INCANTATIONS
Faustus, begin thine Incantations, ... F 233 1.3.5 Faust
have a booke wherein I might beholde al spels and incantations, F 551.2 2.1.165A P Faust
INCENDERE
Desine meque tuis incendere teque querelis, ... Dido 5.1.139 Aeneas
INCENSE
the flames that beat against the clowdes/Incense the heavens, 2Tamb 4.1.195 Tamb
Ile fire his crased buildings and [inforse] <incense>/The P1201 22.63 King
My lord, why do you thus incense your peeres, . . . Edw 1.1.99 Lncstr
As then I did incense the parlement, ... Edw 1.1.184 BshpCv
In white, with incense Ile thine Altars greete, . . . Ovid's Elegies 2.13.23
An Altar takes mens incense, and oblation, ... Ovid's Elegies 3.12.9
INCENSED
As now when furie and incensed hate/Flings slaughtering terrour 1Tamb 5.1.71 Tamb
INCENST
ruthlesly pursewde/Be equally against his life incenst, . 1Tamb 5.1.367 Zenoc
Father, why have you thus incenst them both? . . . Jew 2.3.356 Abigal
And Guise for Spaine hath now incenst the King, . . P 711 14.14 Navrre
This is the Guise that hath incenst the King, . . . P 729 14.32 Navrre
Even for your words that have incenst me so, . . . P 767 15.25 Guise
to warre,/Was so incenst as are Eleius steedes/With clamors: Lucan, First Booke 294
Incenst with savage heat, gallop amaine, ... Hero and Leander 1.115
IN CENSTE
fondlie hast thow in censte the guises sowle . . . Paris ms25,p391 Guise
INCERTAINE
The incertaine pleasures of swift-footed time/Have tane their Jew 2.1.7 Barab
INCESSANT
Impose some end to my incessant paine: . . . . F1960 5.2.164 Faust
INCEST
By whom the husband his wives incest knewe. . . . Ovid's Elegies 2.2.48
Committing headdie ryots, incest, rapes: . . . . Hero and Leander 1.144
INCH
I am one that loves an inch of raw Mutton, better then an ell F 708 2.2.160 P Ltchry
INCHANTED
great deserts in erecting that inchanted Castle in the Aire: F1560 4.6.3 P Duke
Why might not then my sinews be inchanted, ... Ovid's Elegies 3.6.35
INCHANTRESSE
I thinke some fell Inchantresse dwelleth here, . . . Dido 4.1.3 Iarbus
INCHASTITY
And for all blot of foule inchastity, ... 1Tamb 5.1.486 Tamb
INCHAUNTED
And stole away th'inchaunted gazers mind, ... Hero and Leander 1.104
The self-same day that he asleepe had layd/Inchaunted Argus, Hero and Leander 1.388
INCHAUNTING
O th'inchaunting words of that base slave, ... Dido 2.1.161 Aeneas
INCIPIT
[Seeing ubi desinit philosophus, ibi incipit medicus]. . F 41 1.1.13A Faust
INCIRCLING
And her small joynts incircling round hoope make thee. . Ovid's Elegies 2.15.4

INCITE			
Marveile not though the faire Bride did incite/The drunken	Ovid's Elegies	1.4.7	
INCITES			
Whome trumpets clang incites, and those that dwel/By Cyngas	Lucan, First Booke	433	
INCIVILL			
Daily commits incivill outrages, ...	1Tamb	1.1.40	Meandr
INCLINDE			
Thy Rosie cheekes be to thy thombe inclinde. . . .	Ovid's Elegies	1.4.22	
My selfe was dull, and faint, to sloth inclinde, . .	Ovid's Elegies	1.9.41	
Bee not to see with wonted eyes inclinde, ...	Ovid's Elegies	1.14.37	
Whose blast may hether strongly be inclinde, . . .	Ovid's Elegies	2.11.38	
INCLINE			
Although the sunne to rive the earth incline, . . .	Ovid's Elegies	2.16.3	
Unlesse I erre to these thou more incline, . . .	Ovid's Elegies	2.18.39	
INCLOS'D			
Inclos'd her in his armes and kist her to. . . .	Hero and Leander	2.282	
INCLOSD			
Where little ground to be inclosd befalles, . . .	Ovid's Elegies	3.14.12	
INCLOSE			
Wealth increaseth, so inclose/Infinite riches in a little roome.	Jew	1.1.36	Barab
That clouds of darkenesse may inclose my flesh, . .	Jew	1.2.194	Barab
And in the strongest Tower inclose him fast. . . .	F 966	3.1.188	Pope
Least Arte should winne her, firmely did inclose. . .	Ovid's Elegies	2.12.4	
INCLOSED			
Wilt thou thy wombe-inclosed off-spring wracke? . .	Ovid's Elegies	2.14.8	
INCLUDED			
God deluded/In snowe-white plumes of a false swanne included.	Ovid's Elegies	1.10.4	
INCONSIDERATE			
So rusht the inconsiderate multitude/Thorough the City hurried	Lucan, First Booke	492	
INCONSTANCIE			
Will now retaine her olde inconstancie, ...	2Tamb	3.1.29	Callap
INCONSTANT			
Yet be not so inconstant in your love, ...	1Tamb	3.2.56	Agidas
Be not inconstant, carelesse of your fame, ...	2Tamb	5.3.21	Techel
False, credulous, inconstant Abigall!	Jew	3.4.27	Barab
Inconstant Edmund, doost thou favor him, ...	Edw	5.2.101	Mortmr
INCONTINENCE			
She drawes chast women to incontinence, ...	Ovid's Elegies	1.8.19	
INCONTINENT			
To send my thousand horse incontinent, ...	1Tamb	1.1.52	Mycet
Behold an Army comes incontinent.	F1430	4.2.106	Faust
INCONY			
Whilst I in thy incony lap doe tumble.	Jew	4.4.29	Ithimr
INCORPORAT			
Whose matter is incorporat in your flesh.	2Tamb	5.3.165	Amyras
INCORPOREAL			
Than he could saile, for incorporeal Fame, . . .	Hero and Leander	2.113	
INCORPOREALL			
Wherein an incorporeall spirit mooves, ...	2Tamb	4.1.114	Tamb
INCOUNTER			
Let's cheere our souldiers to incounter him, . . .	1Tamb	2.6.29	Cosroe
T'incounter with the strength of Tamburlaine. . . .	1Tamb	3.3.7	Tamb
I meane t'incounter with that Bajazeth.	1Tamb	3.3.65	Tamb
T'incounter with the cruell Tamburlain, ...	2Tamb	2.2.5	Orcan
Yet might your mighty hoste incounter all, ...	2Tamb	5.2.39	Amasia
being worne away/They both burst out, and each incounter other:	Lucan, First Booke	103	
untrod woods/Shrill voices schright, and ghoasts incounter men.	Lucan, First Booke	568	
INCOUNTRING			
Let us put on our meet incountring mindes, . . .	1Tamb	2.6.19	Ortyg
INCREASE (See also ENCREASE)			
The Turkes have let increase to such a summe, . . .	Jew	1.1.182	Barab
Then let the rich increase your portions.	Jew	1.2.58	Govnr
Be patient and thy riches will increase.	Jew	1.2.122	Govnr
Our words will but increase his extasie.	Jew	1.2.210	1Jew
For though they doe a while increase and multiply, . .	Jew	2.3.89	Barab
Your passions make your dolours to increase. . . .	Edw	5.3.15	Gurney
This usage makes my miserie increase.	Edw	5.3.16	Edward
hunters pauseth till fell wrath/And kingly rage increase,	Lucan, First Booke	210	
I saw a brandisht fire increase in strength, . . .	Ovid's Elegies	1.2.11	
Fruites ripe will fall, let springing things increase, .	Ovid's Elegies	2.14.25	
The godly, sweete Tibullus doth increase.	Ovid's Elegies	3.8.66	
INCREASETH			
And as their wealth increaseth, so inclose/Infinite riches in a	Jew	1.1.36	Barab
INCREASING			
Why takest increasing grapes from Vine-trees full? . .	Ovid's Elegies	2.14.23	
INCREAST			
Vaine fame increast true feare, and did invade/The peoples	Lucan, First Booke	465	
INCROCHING			
Who with incroching guile, keepes learning downe. . .	Hero and Leander	1.482	
INCUR'D			
Seeing Faustus hath incur'd eternall death, . . .	F 316	1.3.88	Faust
INCURRE			
Least he incurre the furie of my wrath.	1Tamb	3.1.30	Bajzth
INDAMAGED			
thou doest, thou shalt be no wayes prejudiced or indamaged.	F App	p.236 10 P	Emper
INDE			
From Barbary unto the Westerne Inde, ...	1Tamb	5.1.518	Tamb
That's to be gotten in the Westerne Inde:	Jew	3.5.5	Govnr
And wander to the unfrequented Inde.	Edw	1.4.50	Edward
So having conquerd Inde, was Bacchus hew, ...	Ovid's Elegies	1.2.47	
INDEBTED			
For beds ill hyr'd we are indebted nought. . . .	Ovid's Elegies	1.10.44	
IN DEED			
Foh, heeres a place in deed with all my hart. . . .	Edw	5.5.41	Ltborn

INDEED				
twere but time indeed,/Lost long before you knew what honour	2Tamb	4.3.86		Tamb
Tis brave indeed my boy, wel done,	2Tamb	5.1.150		Tamb
Are wondrous; and indeed doe no man good:	Jew	2.3.82		Barab
Why now I see that you have Art indeed.	Jew	5.5.4		Barab
Here's a hot whore indeed; no, I'le no wife.	F 534	2.1.146		Faust
Thou art a proud knave indeed:	F 672	2.2.121	P	Faust
there spake a Doctor indeed, and 'faith Ile drinke a health to	F1626	4.6.69	P	HrsCsr
God forbade it indeed, but Faustus hath done it:	F1858	5.2.62	P	Faust
INDEEDE				
<indeede I doe, what doe I not>?	F 668	(HC263)A	P	Pride
INDEVOR				
Indevor to preserve and prosper it.	1Tamb	2.5.35		Ortyg
INDEX				
Therefore even as an Index to a booke,	Hero and Leander			2.129
INDIA (See also INDE)				
From golden India Ganges will I fetch,	Dido	5.1.8		Aeneas
Have swarm'd in troopes into the Easterne India:	1Tamb	1.1.120		Cosroe
East India and the late discovered Isles,	1Tamb	1.1.166		Ortyg
Ile make the kings of India ere I die,	1Tamb	3.3.263		Tamb
From Scythia to the Orientall Plage/Of India, wher raging	2Tamb	1.1.69		Orcan
And fairest pearle of welthie India/Were mounted here under a	2Tamb	3.2.121		Tamb
That men might quickly saile to India.	2Tamb	5.3.135		Tamb
I'le have them flie to [India] <Indian> for gold;	F 109	1.1.81		Faust
circle it is likewise Summer with them, as in India, Saba,	F1583	4.6.26	P	Faust
the contrary circle it is summer with them, as in India, Saba,	F App	p.242 21	P	Faust
The parrat from east India to me sent,	Ovid's Elegies			2.6.1
INDIAES				
Then twentie thousand Indiaes can affoord:	Dido	3.1.93		Dido
INDIAN				
Then will we march to all those Indian Mines,	1Tamb	2.5.41		Cosroe
Have fetcht about the Indian continent:	1Tamb	3.3.254		Tamb
Give me the Merchants of the Indian Mynes,	Jew	1.1.19		Barab
Catholickes/Sends Indian golde to coyne me French ecues:	P 118	2.61		Guise
I'le have them flie to [India] <Indian> for gold;	F 109	1.1.81		Faust
As Indian Moores, obey their Spanish Lords,	F 148	1.1.120		Valdes
INDIANS				
Ere I shall want, will cause his Indians,	P 853	17.48		Guise
INDIAS				
Not all the Gold in Indias welthy armes,	1Tamb	1.2.85		Tamb
INDIES (See INDE)				
INDIFFERENT				
Had they beene valued at indifferent rate,	Jew	1.2.186		Barab
INDIFFERENTLY				
View well my Camp, and speake indifferently,	1Tamb	3.3.8		Tamb
As one of them indifferently rated,	Jew	1.1.29		Barab
As be it valued but indifferently,	Jew	5.3.29		Msngr
INDIGNITIES				
How can ye suffer these indignities?	1Tamb	3.3.90		Moroc
INDIGNITY				
That we receive such great indignity?	F1050	3.2.70		Pope
INDUE				
Least with worse kisses she should me indue.	Ovid's Elegies			2.5.50
INDURE				
Can not indure by argument of art.	2Tamb	5.3.97		Phsitn
mainly throw the dart; wilt thou indure/These purple groomes?	Lucan, First Booke			365
Who can indure, save him with whom none lies?	Ovid's Elegies			1.13.26
INDUSTRY				
I doe not doubt by your divine precepts/And mine owne industry,	Jew	1.2.335		Abigal
INESTIMABLE				
Inestimable drugs and precious stones,	2Tamb	5.3.152		Tamb
Than Hero this inestimable gemme.	Hero and Leander			2.78
INEXCELLENCE				
Sustaine a shame of such inexcellence:	2Tamb	5.3.31		Usumc
INEXORABLE				
and Lancaster/Inexorable, and I shall never see/My lovely	Edw	3.1.7		Edward
I found them at the first inexorable,	Edw	3.1.103		Arundl
INFAMIE				
Then live in infamie under such a king.	Edw	3.1.244		Lncstr
Who spots my nuptiall bed with infamie,	Edw	5.1.31		Edward
But Faustus death shall quit my infamie.	F1337	4.2.13		Benvol
And bide sore losse, with endlesse infamie.	Ovid's Elegies			3.6.72
To follow swiftly blasting infamie.	Hero and Leander			1.292
INFAMIES				
blot our dignities/Out of the booke of base borne infamies.	2Tamb	3.1.19		Callap
INFAMOUS				
nor no hope of end/To our infamous monstrous slaveries?	1Tamb	5.1.241		Zabina
And makes my deeds infamous through the world.	1Tamb	5.1.391		Zenoc
Of this infamous Tyrants souldiers,	1Tamb	5.1.404		Arabia
damned Art/For which they two are infamous through the world.	F 222	1.2.29		1Schol
INFANCIE				
that in his infancie/Did pash the jawes of Serpents venomous:	1Tamb	3.3.104		Bajzth
And speake for Faustus in his infancie.	F 10	Prol.10		1Chor
INFANT				
Ah, save that Infant, save him, save him.	1Tamb	5.1.313	P	Zabina
Roomes infant walles were steept in brothers bloud;	Lucan, First Booke			95
INFANTS				
might behold/Young infants swimming in their parents bloud,	Dido	2.1.193		Aeneas
For us, for infants, and for all our bloods,	1Tamb	5.1.97		1Virgn
Who unborne infants first to slay invented,	Ovid's Elegies			2.14.5
INFECT				
Contagious smels, and vapors to infect thee,	2Tamb	4.2.11		Olymp
Whose operation is to binde, infect,	Jew	3.4.70		Barab

INFECT (cont.)			
is massacred)/Infect thy gracious brest with fresh supply,	P 193	3.28	QnMarg
O no, his bodye will infect the fire, and the fire the aire, and	P 484	9.3	P 1Atndt
INFECTED			
Accursed day infected with my griefs,	1Tamb	5.1.291	Bajzth
INFECTING			
Infecting all the Ghosts with curelesse griefs:	1Tamb	5.1.258	Bajzth
INFECTION			
And feede infection with his [let] <left> out life:	Dido	3.2.11	Juno
INFERIOR			
my selfe farre inferior to the report men have published,	F App	p.236 13	P Faust
INFERIOUR			
Whose lookes make this inferiour world to quake,	2Tamb	1.3.139	Techel
Next, an inferiour troupe, in tuckt up vestures,	Lucan, First Booke		595
The vaine name of inferiour slaves despize.	Ovid's Elegies		1.8.64
INFERNAL			
Vile monster, borne of some infernal hag,	2Tamb	5.1.110	Govnr
INFERNALL			
or els infernall, mixt/Their angry seeds at his conception:	1Tamb	2.6.9	Meandr
and let the Feends infernall view/As are the blasted banks of	1Tamb	5.1.242	Zabina
In this obscure infernall servitude?	1Tamb	5.1.254	Zabina
as if infernall Jove/Meaning to aid [thee] <them> in this	2Tamb	1.3.143	Techel
And we discend into th'infernall vaults,	2Tamb	2.4.98	Tamb
Infernall Dis is courting of my Love,	2Tamb	4.2.93	Therid
O mercilesse infernall cruelty.	2Tamb	4.3.85	Jrslem
as th'infernall spirits/On sweet Musaeus when he came to hell,	F 142	1.1.114	Faust
Now by the Kingdomes of Infernall Rule,	F 825	3.1.47	Faust
You Princely Legions of infernall Rule,	F1116	3.3.29	Mephst
Made the grim monarch of infernall spirits,	F1371	4.2.47	Fredrk
Thus from infernall Dis do we ascend/To view the subjects of	F1797	5.2.1	Lucifr
the brest of this slaine Bull are crept,/Th'infernall powers.	Lucan, First Booke		633
INFERNI			
[Lucifer], Belzebub inferni ardentis monarcha, et Demogorgon,	F 246	1.3.18	P Faust
INFERR'D			
See a rich chuffe whose wounds great wealth inferr'd,	Ovid's Elegies		3.7.9
INFIDELL			
Wherein I shall convert an Infidell,	Jew	4.1.162	1Fryar
INFIDELS			
And worke revenge upon these Infidels:	2Tamb	2.1.13	Fredrk
for with such Infidels,/In whom no faith nor true religion	2Tamb	2.1.33	Baldwn
No, Jew, like infidels.	Jew	1.2.62	Govnr
Damn'd Christians, dogges, and Turkish Infidels;	Jew	5.5.86	Barab
INFINIT			
Suppose they be in number infinit,	1Tamb	2.2.43	Meandr
And numbers more than infinit of men,	2Tamb	2.2.18	Gazell
INFINITE			
Still climing after knowledge infinite,	1Tamb	2.7.24	Tamb
Let him bring millions infinite of men,	1Tamb	3.3.33	Usumc
increaseth, so inclose/Infinite riches in a little roome.	Jew	1.1.37	Barab
Rich costly Jewels, and Stones infinite,	Jew	1.2.245	Barab
to heaven, and remember [Gods] mercy is <mercies are> infinite.	F1836	5.2.40	P 2Schol
And give woundes infinite at everie turne.	Ovid's Elegies		1.2.44
INFIRMITIES			
Yet those infirmities that thus defame/Their faiths, their	2Tamb	2.1.44	Sgsmnd
INFLAM'D (See also ENFLAMDE)			
Wherewith Leander much more was inflam'd.	Hero and Leander		1.182
INFLAMES			
What motion is it that inflames your thoughts,	2Tamb	2.1.2	Sgsmnd
famous names/Farewel, your favour nought my minde inflames.	Ovid's Elegies		2.1.36
Fires and inflames objects remooved farre,	Hero and Leander		2.124
INFLICT (See also ENFLICT)			
And with the paines my rigour shall inflict,	2Tamb	4.1.184	Tamb
and all mens hatred/Inflict upon them, thou great Primus Motor.	Jew	1.2.164	Barab
What greater misery could heaven inflict?	Jew	5.2.14	Govnr
Tis but temporall that thou canst inflict.	Edw	3.1.242	Warwck
And on the next fault punishment inflict.	Ovid's Elegies		2.14.44
INFLICTIONS			
staid, with wrath and hate/Of our expreslesse band inflictions.	1Tamb	5.1.282	Bajzth
INFLUENCE			
denied/To shed [their] <his> influence in his fickle braine,	1Tamb	1.1.15	Cosroe
But such a Star hath influence in his sword,	1Tamb	5.1.232	Bajzth
[Those] <Whose> looks will shed such influence in my campe,/As	2Tamb	3.2.39	Tamb
And shed their feble influence in the aire.	2Tamb	5.3.5	Therid
And that the spightfull influence of heaven,	2Tamb	5.3.193	Amyras
Now fals the star whose influence governes France,	P 944	19.14	Capt
Whose influence hath allotted death and hell;	F1951	5.2.155	Faust
I would my rude words had the influence,	Hero and Leander		1.200
Some hidden influence breeds like effect.	Hero and Leander		2.60
INFORC'D			
By which the spirits are inforc'd to rise:	F 241	1.3.13	Faust
This, and what grife inforc'd me say I say'd,	Ovid's Elegies		2.5.33
INFORCE			
Awaye with her, her wordes inforce these teares,	Edw	5.6.85	King
INFORCEMENT			
Without inforcement of the German Peeres,	F 958	3.1.180	Faust
INFORME (See also ENFORMD)			
We will informe thee e're our conference cease.	F 184	1.1.156	Valdes
wine, if it could speake, <it> would informe your Worships:	F 216	1.2.23	P Wagner
But come, let us go, and informe the Rector:	F 225	1.2.32	2Schol
INFORMETH			
Informeth us, by letters and by words,	Edw	3.1.61	Queene
INFORSE			
Ile fire his crased buildings and [inforse] <incense>/The	P1201	22.63	King

INFORST			
Inforst a wide breach in that rampierd wall, ...	Dido	2.1.174	Aeneas
Being three daies old inforst the floud to swell, . .	Lucan, First Booke		220
INFORTUNATE			
realme, and sith the fates/Have made his father so infortunate,	Edw	4.6.27	Queene
INFRINGE			
So what we vow to them should not infringe/Our liberty of armes	2Tamb	2.1.40	Baldwn
INFRINGING			
Infringing all excuse of modest shame, ...	Lucan, First Booke		266
INFUSION			
With strange infusion of his sacred vigor, . . .	2Tamb	2.2.52	Orcan
INGENDER			
And princes with their lookes ingender feare. . . .	P 999	19.69	Guise
INGENDERS			
The lively spirits which the heart ingenders/Are partcht and	2Tamb	5.3.94	Phsitn
INGENDRED			
Guise, begins those deepe ingendred thoughts/To burst abroad,	P 91	2.34	Guise
Curst be the parents that ingendred me;	F1972	5.2.176	Faust
INGLORIOUS			
To race and scatter thy inglorious crue, ...	1Tamb	4.3.67	Souldn
INGOTS			
Of two gold Ingots like in each respect.	Hero and Leander		1.172
INGRAFT			
That in the midst of fire is ingraft, ...	2Tamb	2.3.21	Orcan
INGRATE (See UNGRATE)			
INGRATITUDE			
That grievous image of ingratitude:	1Tamb	2.6.30	Cosroe
INHABIT			
Tartars and Perseans shall inhabit there, ...	2Tamb	5.1.163	Tamb
INHABITANTES			
the Gulfe, call'd by the name/Mare magiore, of th'inhabitantes:	2Tamb	1.3.215	Therid
INHABITANTS			
Death and destruction to th'inhabitants.	2Tamb	3.2.5	Tamb
time to make collection/Amongst the Inhabitants of Malta for't.	Jew	1.2.21	Govnr
INHABITE			
Or whether men or beasts inhabite it.	Dido	1.1.177	Aeneas
INHABITED			
Inhabited with stragling Runnagates, ...	1Tamb	3.3.57	Tamb
Inhabited with tall and sturdy men, ...	2Tamb	1.1.27	Orcan
Those that inhabited the suburbe fieldes/Fled, fowle Erinnis	Lucan, First Booke		569
INHABITS			
vouchsafe of ruth/To tell us who inhabits this faire towne,	Dido	2.1.41	Aeneas
INHERENT			
'Tis not our fault, but thy inherent sinne.	Jew	1.2.109	1Knght
INHERIT			
For onely I have toyl'd to inherit here/The months of vanity	Jew	1.2.196	Barab
Ne're shall she live to inherit ought of mine, ...	Jew	3.4.30	Barab
Which without bloud-shed doth the pray inherit. . .	Ovid's Elegies		2.12.6
Tibullus doth Elysiums joy inherit.	Ovid's Elegies		3.8.60
INHERITANCE			
prejudice their hope/Of my inheritance to the crowne of France:	P 468	8.18	Anjoy
INHUMAINE			
Inhumaine creatures, nurst with Tigers milke, ...	Edw	5.1.71	Edward
INJOINE			
The holy lawes of Christendome injoine:	2Tamb	2.1.36	Baldwn
INJOY			
Now eies, injoy your latest benefite, ...	2Tamb	5.3.224	Tamb
Where we may one injoy the others sight.	P 665	13.9	Duchss
share the world thou canst not;/Injoy it all thou maiest:	Lucan, First Booke		292
INJOYNDE			
I am injoynde,/To sue unto you all for his repeale: . .	Edw	1.4.200	Queene
INJURE			
To injure or suppresse your woorthy tytle.	1Tamb	1.1.183	Ortyg
what e're it be to injure them/That have so manifestly wronged	Jew	1.2.274	Abigal
Did he not injure Mounser thats deceast?	P1035	19.105	King
O stay my lord, they will not injure you.	Edw	2.4.7	Gavstn
We are come to tell thee thou dost injure us. . . .	F 642	2.2.91	Belzeb
INJURED			
Seeing in their loves, the Fates were injured. . . .	Hero and Leander		1.484
INJURES			
Hard is the hart, that injures such a saint. . . .	Edw	1.4.190	Penbrk
INJURIE			
Not dooing Mahomet an injurie, ...	2Tamb	2.3.34	Orcan
INJURIES			
Great injuries are not so soone forgot.	Jew	1.2.208	Barab
My Lord I cannot brooke these injuries.	Edw	2.2.71	Gavstn
And for the open wronges and injuries/Edward hath done to us,	Edw	4.4.21	Mortmr
INJURIOUS			
Injurious villaines, thieves, runnagates, ...	1Tamb	3.3.225	Zabina
Injurious tyrant, wilt thou so defame/The hatefull fortunes of	2Tamb	4.3.77	Orcan
Was ever troubled with injurious warres:	P1142	22.4	King
As you injurious were to beare them foorth.	Edw	4.3.52	Edward
hath Faustus justly requited this injurious knight, which being	F1313	4.1.159	P Faust
hath Faustus worthily requited this injurious knight, which	F App	p.238 83	P Faust
And to my selfe could I be so injurious?	Ovid's Elegies		1.7.26
INJUROUSLY			
Say but thou wert injurously accusde.	Ovid's Elegies		3.13.42
INJURY			
Why I esteeme the injury farre lesse, ...	Jew	1.2.146	Barab
That can so soone forget an injury.	Jew	2.3.19	Barab
and you have done me great injury to bring me from thence, let	F 705.1	2.2.155A	P Sloth
not so much for injury done to me, as to delight your Majesty	F1311	4.1.157	P Faust
Shall I let slip so great an injury, ...	F1328	4.2.4	Benvol

INJURY (cont.)
so much for the injury hee offred me heere in your presence, F App p.238 81 P Faust
INKE
Pen and Inke: . . . . Jew 4.2.68 P Ithimr
Goe fetch me pen and inke. . . . . P 657 13.1 Duchss
In steede of inke, ile write it with my teares. . . Edw 1.4.86 Edward
INLARG'D
his rent discharg'd/From further duty he rests then inlarg'd. Ovid's Elegies 1.10.46
INLARGE
subdue the Turke, and then inlarge/Those Christian Captives, 1Tamb 3.3.46 Tamb
of them, locking some happie power will pitie and inlarge us. 1Tamb 4.4.100 P Zabina
INLY
Great joyes by hope I inly shall conceive. . . . Ovid's Elegies 2.9.44
He inly storm'd, and waxt more furious, ... Hero and Leander 1.437
INMATE
My bosome [inmate] <inmates> <intimates>, but I must dissemble. Jew 4.1.47 Barab
INMATES
My bosome [inmate] <inmates> <intimates>, but I must dissemble. Jew 4.1.47 Barab
INNE
One time I was an Hostler in an Inne, ... Jew 2.3.205 Ithimr
INNOCENCE
Then dye Aeneas in thine innocence, ... Dido 1.1.80 Venus
And doing wrong made shew of innocence. . . . . . Ovid's Elegies 2.19.14
INNOCENCIE
Be witnesse of my greefe and innocencie. . . . . . Edw 5.6.102 King
INNOCENT
The Gods, defenders of the innocent, ... 1Tamb 1.2.68 Zenoc
yet are our lookes/As innocent and harmelesse as a Lambes. Jew 2.3.22 Barab
these innocent hands of mine/Shall not be guiltie of so foule a Edw 5.1.98 Edward
These handes were never stainde with innocent bloud, . Edw 5.5.81 Ltborn
And hands so pure, so innocent, nay such, ... Hero and Leander 1.365
INNOCENTS
And will revenge the bloud of innocents, ... P 44 1.44 Navrre
INNOVATION
By any innovation or remorse, ... 1Tamb 5.1.16 Govnr
INNUMERABLE
Innumerable joyes had followed thee. . . . . . . F1893 5.2.97 GdAngl
INOUGH
Inough. . . . . Edw 5.2.46 Mortmr
<Then theres inough for a thousand soules>, . . . F 477 (HC260) A Faust
Was not one wench inough to greeve my heart? . . . Ovid's Elegies 2.10.12
INQUIR'D
I neither saw them, nor inquir'd of them. . . . . . Jew 1.1.77 1Merch
INQUIRE (See also ENQUIRE)
Hold, let's inquire the causers of their deaths, . . . Jew 3.2.27 Mater
and inquire/For any of the Fryars of Saint [Jaques] <Jaynes>, Jew 3.3.27 Abigal
INQUIRY (See ENQUIRY)
INRAG'D
and Phoebe's waine/Chace Phoebus and inrag'd affect his place, Lucan, First Booke 78
INRICH
thou art so meane a man)/And seeke not to inrich thy followers, 1Tamb 1.2.9 Zenoc
And still inrich the loftie servile clowne, ... Hero and Leander 1.481
INRICH'D
And thus are wee on every side inrich'd: . . . . . Jew 1.1.104 Barab
INRICHT
Inricht with tongues, well seene in Minerals, ... F 166 1.1.138 Cornel
Souldiours by bloud to be inricht have lucke. . . . Ovid's Elegies 3.7.54
INSATIATE
Bloody and insatiate Tamburlain. . . . . 1Tamb 2.7.11 Cosroe
INSCRIPTION
But what is this Inscription on mine Arme? . . . . F 465 2.1.77 Faust
INSINUATE
I'le seeke him out, and so insinuate, ... Jew 2.3.33 Lodowk
Now Madam must you insinuate with the King, ... P 645 12.58 Cardnl
INSISTERE
left heele, that thou maist, Quasi vestigiis nostris insistere. F 387 1.4.45 P Wagner
upon my right heele, with quasi vestigias nostras insistere. F App p.231 71 P Wagner
INSOLENCE
I cannot brook thy hauty insolence, ... P 862 17.57 King
by aspiring pride and insolence,/For which God threw him from F 295 1.3.67 Mephst
But wee'le pul downe his haughty insolence: . . . . F 914 3.1.136 Pope
INSOLENT
And like an insolent commaunding lover, ... Hero and Leander 1.409
INSOOTH
Insooth th'eternall powers graunt maides society/Falsely to Ovid's Elegies 3.3.11
INSPIR'D
And every sweetnes that inspir'd their harts, ... 1Tamb 5.1.163 Tamb
INSPIRES
Thy power inspires the Muze that sings this war. . . Lucan, First Booke 66
INSTALL
Elect, conspire, install, do what you will, ... Edw 5.1.88 Edward
INSTANCE
But <Faustus> I am an instance to prove the contrary: . F 525 2.1.137 Mephst
What he will give, with greater instance crave. . . . Ovid's Elegies 1.8.68
INSTANT
That at one instant all things may be done, ... Jew 5.2.120 Barab
Thou Caesar at this instant art my God, ... Lucan, First Booke 63
At one selfe instant, she poore soule assaies, . . . Hero and Leander 1.362
IN STEAD
who in stead of him/Will set thee on her lap and play with Dido 2.1.324 Venus
In stead of musicke I will heare him speake, ... Dido 3.1.89 Dido
In stead of Troy shall Wittenberg <Wertenberge> be sack't,/And F1776 5.1.103 Faust
Gush forth bloud in stead of teares, yea life and soule: . F1851 5.2.55 P Faust

IN STEAD (cont.)

Whose carelesse haire, in stead of pearle t'adorne it,	Hero and Leander	1.389	

INSTEAD

Proud-daring Calymath, instead of gold,	Jew	2.2.53	Govnr
Instead of Sedge and Reed, beare Sugar Canes:	Jew	4.2.96	Ithimr

IN STEADE

Gold from the earth in steade of fruits we pluck,	Ovid's Elegies	3.7.53	

IN STEED

And see if those will serve in steed of sailes:	Dido	4.4.160	Dido
In steed of oares, let him use his hands,	Dido	4.4.163	Dido
In steed of red bloud wallowed venemous gore.	Lucan, First Booke	614	

IN STEEDE

In steede of inke, ile write it with my teares.	Edw	1.4.86	Edward

INSTINCT

With whose instinct the soule of man is toucht,	1Tamb	5.1.179	Tamb

INSTITUTE

Such is the subject of the Institute,	F 59	1.1.31	Faust

INSTRUCT

As to instruct us under what good heaven/We breathe as now, and	Dido	1.1.197	Aeneas
As your supreame estates instruct our thoughtes,	2Tamb	5.3.20	Techel
First I'le instruct thee in the rudiments,	F 188	1.1.160	Valdes

INSTRUCTIONS

Taking instructions from thy flowing eies:	1Tamb	5.1.146	Tamb
I have according to instructions in that behalfe,	Edw	4.3.28	P Spencr
You shall not need to give instructions,	Edw	5.4.29	Ltborn

INSTRUMENT

And so came in this fatall instrument:	Dido	2.1.176	Aeneas
Let this invention be the instrument.	2Tamb	4.2.13	Olymp
Thy instrument and note of Majesty,	2Tamb	5.3.38	Usumc

INSTRUMENTS

These were the instruments that launcht him forth,	Dido	4.4.150	Dido
Are fixt his piercing instruments of sight:	1Tamb	2.1.14	Menaph
Use all their voices and their instruments/To entertaine divine	2Tamb	2.4.28	Tamb
Slaughter and mischiefs instruments, no better,	Ovid's Elegies	1.7.27	

INSUE

what mischiefe shall insue?	Lucan, First Booke	644	

INSUFFICIENT

Yet insufficient to expresse the same:	1Tamb	1.1.2	Mycet

INSULTE

The Protestants will glory and insulte,	P1085	19.155	QnMoth

IN'T

Tut, tut, there is some other matter in't.	Jew	1.1.160	Barab
Belike there is some Ceremony in't.	Jew	3.4.83	Barab

INTANGLED

And yet God knowes intangled unto one.--	Dido	3.1.154	Dido
For being intangled by a strangers lookes:	Dido	5.1.145	Dido

INTELIGENTIJ

hath every Spheare a Dominion, or Intelligentia <Inteligentij>?	F 607	2.2.56	P Faust

INTELLECT

Much more in subjects having intellect,	Hero and Leander	2.59	

INTELLIGENTIA

hath every Spheare a Dominion, or Intelligentia <Inteligentij>?	F 607	2.2.56	P Faust

INTEMPERATE

Become intemperate? shall the earth be barraine?	Lucan, First Booke	646	

INTEND (See also ENTEND)

If you intend to keep your treasure safe.	1Tamb	1.2.25	Tamb
That I intend my daughter shall be thine.	Jew	2.3.254	Barab
I feare me he mistrusts what we intend.	Jew	4.1.133	Ithimr
What they intend, the hangman frustrates cleane.	Edw	3.1.275	Baldck
they intend to give king Edward battell in England, sooner then	Edw	4.3.34	P Spencr
I tremble to unfould/What you intend, great Jove is now	Lucan, First Booke	631	
And scratch her faire soft cheekes I did intend.	Ovid's Elegies	2.5.46	
Rome did send/The Sabine Fathers, who sharpe warres intend.	Ovid's Elegies	2.12.24	
And feare those, that to feare them least intend.	Ovid's Elegies	3.3.32	

INTENDED

Will never prosper your intended driftes,	1Tamb	1.2.69	Zenoc
As he intended to dismember me.	F1415	4.2.91	Faust

INTENDEST

As thou intendest to rise by Mortimer,	Edw	5.2.52	Mortmr

INTENDETH

and with the power/That he intendeth presentlie to raise,	Edw	2.4.44	Queene

INTENDING

Intending your investion so neere/The residence of your	1Tamb	1.1.180	Ortyg
Intending but to rase my charmed skin:	1Tamb	1.2.179	Tamb
Intending so to terrifie the world:	1Tamb	5.1.15	Govnr
Intending to dislodge my campe with speed.	P 869	17.64	Guise
Which mounted up, intending to have kist him,	Hero and Leander	2.173	

INTENDS

forces for the hot assaults/Proud Tamburlaine intends Natolia.	2Tamb	1.1.53	Gazell
Shal end the warlike progresse he intends,	2Tamb	3.5.23	Orcan
Intends our Muse to vaunt <daunt> his heavenly verse;	F 6	Prol.6	1Chor
And he intends to shew great Carolus,	F1167	4.1.13	Mrtino

INTENT (See also ENTENT)

And we from Europe to the same intent,	2Tamb	1.1.118	Fredrk
Was up thus early; with intent to goe/Unto your Friery, because	Jew	4.1.191	Barab
What your intent is yet we cannot learn,	P 823	17.18	King
And for I see your curteous intent to pleasure me, I wil not	F App	p.242 8	P Duchss
Though both of us performd our true intent,	Ovid's Elegies	3.6.5	

INTERCEPT

sent a thousand armed men/To intercept this haughty enterprize,	2Tamb	1.2.71	Almeda
And seeke in time to intercept the worst,	Jew	1.1.187	Barab
And intercept my going to the Jew;	Jew	4.1.167	1Fryar

INTERCEPTED

No intercepted lines thy deedes display,	Ovid's Elegies	2.5.5	

INTERCEPTS			
And intercepts the day as Dolon erst:	Dido	1.1.71	Venus
That intercepts the course of my desire:	Dido	4.2.48	Iarbus
INTERCESSION			
Without the intercession of some Saint?	P 357	6.12	Mntsrl
INTERCHANGEABLY			
And interchangeably discourse their thoughts,	Dido	3.2.93	Juno
INTERCOURSE (See ENTERCOURSE)			
INTERDE			
That we may see it honourably interde:	P1246	22.108	Navrre
INTERDICT			
And from the first earth interdict our feete.	Dido	1.2.37	Serg
And interdict from Churches priviledge,	F 909	3.1.131	Pope
INTERDICTED			
Shall I poore soule be never interdicted?	Ovid's Elegies		2.19.53
INTEREST			
breast a long great Scrowle/How I with interest tormented him.	Jew	2.3.198	Barab
There's none but I have interest in the same.	F 637	2.2.86	Lucifr
Hence interest and devouring usury sprang,	Lucan, First Booke		183
INTERR'D			
And till I die thou shalt not be interr'd.	2Tamb	2.4.132	Tamb
and let them be interr'd/Within one sacred monument of stone;	Jew	3.2.29	Govnr
if Corcyras Ile/Had thee unknowne interr'd in ground most vile.	Ovid's Elegies		3.8.48
INTERRDE			
His kingly body was too soone interrde.	Edw	5.6.32	King
INTERRUPT			
And nothing interrupt thy quiet sleepe,	Dido	2.1.338	Venus
INTERRUPTED			
Till being interrupted by my friends,	Edw	5.4.62	Mortmr
INTERRUPTING			
Ile meete with you anone for interrupting me so:	F App	p.238 58 P	Faust
INTERS			
blasted, Aruns takes/And it inters with murmurs dolorous,	Lucan, First Booke		606
INTESTINE			
And with intestine broiles the world destroy,	Hero and Leander		1.251
INTHRALLD			
And men inthralld by Mermaids singing charmes.	Ovid's Elegies		3.11.28
INTHRONIZED			
And sit for aye inthronized in heaven,	Edw	5.1.109	Edward
INTICE			
Whose deepnesse doth intice such forward wits,	F2008	5.3.26	4Chor
INTIMATES			
My bosome [inmate] <inmates> <intimates>, but I must dissemble.	Jew	4.1.47	Barab
INTIMATEST			
Deale truly with us as thou intimatest,	Jew	5.2.85	Govnr
INTIRELY			
and the rest/Marcht not intirely, and yet hide the ground,	Lucan, First Booke		474
IN TO			
Come bring them in to our Pavilion.	2Tamb	4.1.206	Tamb
INTO (See also INTOO'T)			
To day when as I fild into your cups,	Dido	1.1.5	Ganimd
her ayrie wheeles/Into the windie countrie of the clowdes,	Dido	1.1.57	Venus
And led our ships into the shallow sands,	Dido	1.2.27	Cloan
And drie with griefe was turnd into a stone,	Dido	2.1.5	Aeneas
we were commanded straight/With reverence to draw it into Troy.	Dido	2.1.168	Aeneas
And through the breach did march into the streetes,	Dido	2.1.189	Aeneas
And then in triumph ran into the streetes,	Dido	2.1.261	Aeneas
Moved with her voyce, I lept into the sea,	Dido	2.1.283	Aeneas
For all our ships were launcht into the deepe:	Dido	2.1.285	Aeneas
We heare they led her captive into Greece.	Dido	2.1.295	Achat
This day they both a hunting forth will ride/Into these woods,	Dido	3.2.88	Juno
And dive into blacke tempests treasurie,	Dido	4.1.5	Iarbus
And dive into her heart by coloured lookes.	Dido	4.2.32	Iarbus
We may as one saile into Italy.	Dido	4.3.30	Aeneas
How should I put into the raging deepe,	Dido	5.1.55	Aeneas
Then gan they drive into the Ocean,	Dido	5.1.231	Anna
And now downe falles the keeles into the deepe:	Dido	5.1.253	Dido
Go Menaphon, go into Scythia,	1Tamb	1.1.85	Mycet
And that which might resolve me into teares,	1Tamb	1.1.118	Cosroe
Have swarm'd in troopes into the Easterne India:	1Tamb	1.1.120	Cosroe
Passe into Graecia, as did Cyrus once.	1Tamb	1.1.130	Menaph
That we may traveile into Siria,	1Tamb	1.2.77	Agidas
whet thy winged sword/And lift thy lofty arme into the cloudes,	1Tamb	2.3.52	Cosroe
But I shall turne her into other weedes,	1Tamb	3.3.180	Ebea
And led them Captive into Affrica.	1Tamb	3.3.205	Zabina
Deliver them into my treasurie.	1Tamb	3.3.217	Tamb
That I may rise into my royall throne.	1Tamb	4.2.15	Tamb
will make thee slice the brawnes of thy armes into carbonadoes,	1Tamb	4.4.44 P	Tamb
shee will fall into a consumption with freatting, and then she	1Tamb	4.4.49 P	Tamb
and hartie humble mones/Will melt his furie into some remorse:	1Tamb	5.1.22	Govnr
Which into words no vertue can digest:	1Tamb	5.1.173	Tamb
And sink not quite into my tortur'd soule.	1Tamb	5.1.263	Bajzth
I may poure foorth my soule into thine armes,	1Tamb	5.1.279	Bajzth
Armed with lance into the Egyptian fields,	1Tamb	5.1.381	Philem
Since I shall render all into your hands.	1Tamb	5.1.447	Tamb
And soon put foorth into the Terrene sea:	2Tamb	1.2.25	Callap
and the bounds of Affrike/And made a voyage into Europe,	2Tamb	1.3.208	Therid
And we discend into th'infernall vaults,	2Tamb	2.4.98	Tamb
bringing of our ordinance/Along the trench into the battery,	2Tamb	3.3.55	Therid
As Hector did into the Grecian campe,	2Tamb	3.5.65	Tamb
Turn'd into pearle and proffered for my stay,	2Tamb	4.1.44	Amyras
I goe into the field before I need?	2Tamb	4.1.51	Calyph
that falles/Into the liquid substance of his streame,	2Tamb	5.1.19	Govnr

INTO (cont.)

Weepe heavens, and vanish into liquid teares,	2Tamb	5.3.1		Therid
And Angels dive into the pooles of hell.	2Tamb	5.3.33		Usumc
Then martcht I into Egypt and Arabia,	2Tamb	5.3.130		Tamb
By equall portions into both your breasts:	2Tamb	5.3.171		Tamb
If not resolv'd into resolved paines,	2Tamb	5.3.187		Amyras
Into what corner peeres my Halcions bill?	Jew	1.1.39		Barab
from Egypt, or by Caire/But at the entry there into the sea,	Jew	1.1.74		Barab
will give me leave once more, I trow,/To goe into my house.	Jew	1.2.253		Barab
thou toldst me they have turn'd my house/Into a Nunnery, and	Jew	1.2.278		Barab
We turne into the Ayre to purge our selves:	Jew	2.3.46		Barab
if so, 'tis time that it be seene into:	Jew	3.4.9		Barab
run to some rocke and throw my selfe headlong into the sea;	Jew	3.4.40	P	Ithimr
fares Callymath, What wind drives you thus into Malta rhode?	Jew	3.5.2	P	Govnr
And bring his gold into our treasury.	Jew	4.1.163		1Fryar
Play, Fidler, or I'le cut your cats guts into chitterlins.	Jew	4.4.44	P	Ithimr
to fall into the hands/Of such a Traitor and unhallowed Jew!	Jew	5.2.12		Govnr
No, Barabas, this must be look'd into;	Jew	5.2.34		Barab
asunder; so that it doth sinke/Into a deepe pit past recovery.	Jew	5.5.36		Barab
Away then, break into the Admirals house.	P 282	5.9		Guise
And I reduc'd it into better forme.	P 407	7.47		Ramus
Which we have chaste into the river [Sene] <Rene>,	P 418	7.58		Guise
Lets throw him into the river.	P 487	9.6	P	1Atndt
Then throw him into the ditch.	P 490	9.9	P	1Atndt
Shall drive no plaintes into the Guises eares,	P 532	10.5		Guise
That he should nere returne into the realme:	Edw	1.1.84		Mortmr
Ile thunder such a peale into his eares,	Edw	2.2.128		Mortmr
My sonne and I will over into France,	Edw	2.4.65		Queene
Hath seazed Normandie into his hands.	Edw	3.1.64		Queene
And step into his fathers regiment.	Edw	3.1.271		Spencr
sir John of Henolt, brother to the Marquesse, into Flaunders:	Edw	4.3.32	P	Spencr
Proud Mortimer pries neare into thy walkes.	Edw	4.6.18		Kent
lowly earth/Should drinke his bloud, mounts up into the ayre:	Edw	5.1.14		Edward
Heeres a light to go into the dungeon.	Edw	5.5.37		Gurney
Into the councell chamber he is gone,	Edw	5.6.20		Queene
That thou art <he is> falne into that damned Art/For which they	F 221	1.2.28		1Schol
I'le turne all the lice about thee into Familiars, and make	F 362	1.4.20	P	Wagner
[and] bloud, <or goods> into their habitation wheresoever.	F 498	2.1.110	P	Faust
like to Ovids Flea, I can creepe into every corner of a Wench:	F 665	2.2.114	P	Pride
that I might locke you safe into <uppe in> my <goode> Chest:	F 676	2.2.125	P	Covet
And thou shalt turne thy selfe into what shape thou wilt.	F 718	2.2.170		Lucifr
I say, least I send you into the Ostry with a vengeance.	F 733	2.3.12	P	Robin
of us here, that have waded as deepe into matters, as other men,	F 740	2.3.19	P	Robin
We saw the River Maine, fall into Rhine <Rhines>,	F 785	3.1.7		Faust
So high our Dragons soar'd into the aire,	F 849	3.1.71		Faust
And put into the Churches treasury.	F1028	3.2.48		Raymnd
to their porridge-pots, for I'le into the Kitchin presently:	F1134	3.3.47	P	Robin
in any case, ride him not into the water.	F1469	4.4.13	P	Faust
How sir, not into the water?	F1470	4.4.14	P	HrsCsr
waters, but ride him not into the water; o're hedge and ditch,	F1472	4.4.16	P	Faust
hedge and ditch, or where thou wilt, but not into the water:	F1473	4.4.17	P	Faust
Despaire doth drive distrust into my thoughts.	F1480	4.4.24		Faust
I riding my horse into the water, thinking some hidden mystery	F1485	4.4.29	P	HrsCsr
I'le out-run him, and cast this leg into some ditch or other.	F1495	4.4.39	P	HrsCsr
looke up into th'hall there ho.	F1519	4.5.15	P	Hostss
time; but, quoth he, in any case ride him not into the water.	F1541	4.5.37	P	HrsCsr
what did I but rid him into a great river, and when I came just	F1543	4.5.39	P	HrsCsr
one of his devils turn'd me into the likenesse of an Apes face.	F1554	4.5.50	P	Dick
we'le into another roome and drinke a while, and then we'le go	F1556	4.5.52	P	Robin
the yeare is divided into two circles over the whole world, so	F1581	4.6.24	P	Faust
you remember you bid he should not ride [him] into the water?	F1637	4.6.80	P	Carter
If sin by custome grow not into nature:	F1713	5.1.40		OldMan
Offers to poure the same into thy soule,	F1732	5.1.59		OldMan
<Belike he is growne into some sicknesse, by> being over	F1829	(HC270)A	P	3Schol
but let us into the next roome, and [there] pray for him.	F1871	5.2.75	P	1Schol
with horror stare/Into that vaste perpetuall torture-house,	F1910	5.2.114		BdAngl
Then will I headlong run into the earth:	F1948	5.2.152		Faust
Into the entrals of yon labouring cloud,	F1953	5.2.157		Faust
That when you vomite forth into the aire,	F1954	5.2.158		Faust
from me, and I be chang'd/[Unto] <Into> some brutish beast.	F1968	5.2.172		Faust
O soule be chang'd into <to> [little] <small> water drops,	F1977	5.2.181		Faust
And fall into the Ocean, ne're be found.	F1978	5.2.182		Faust
or Ile turne al the lice about thee into familiars, and they	F App	p.229 25	P	Wagner
if you turne me into any thing, let it be in the likenesse of a	F App	p.231 61	P	Clown
presumption, I transforme thee into an Ape, and thee into a Dog,	F App	p.235 44	P	Mephst
thee into an Ape, and thee into a Dog, and so be gone.	F App	p.235 44	P	Mephst
How, into an Ape?	F App	p.236 45	P	Robin
before you have him, ride him not into the water at any hand.	F App	p.239 109	P	Faust
but ride him not into the water, ride him over hedge or ditch,	F App	p.239 111	P	Faust
hedge or ditch, or where thou wilt, but not into the water.	F App	p.239 113	P	Faust
by him, for he bade me I should ride him into no water; now,	F App	p.240 131	P	HrsCsr
rid him into the deepe pond at the townes ende, I was no sooner	F App	p.240 133	P	HrsCsr
the yeere is divided into twoo circles over the whole worlde,	F App	p.242 19	P	Faust
bands were spread/Along Nar floud that into Tiber fals,	Lucan, First Booke	472		
He wants no gifts into thy lap to hurle.	Ovid's Elegies	1.10.54		
Or [into] <to the> sea swift Symois [doth] <shall> slide.	Ovid's Elegies	1.15.10		
Which stormie South-windes into sea did blowe?	Ovid's Elegies	2.6.44		
The Parrat into wood receiv'd with these,	Ovid's Elegies	2.6.57		
Or as a sodaine gale thrustes into sea,	Ovid's Elegies	2.9.31		
By seaven huge mouthes into the sea is [skipping] <slipping>,	Ovid's Elegies	2.13.10		
O would that sodainly into my gift,	Ovid's Elegies	2.15.9		
Flames into flame, flouds thou powrest seas into.	Ovid's Elegies	3.2.34		
And into water desperately she flies.	Ovid's Elegies	3.5.80		

INTO (cont.)
Men kept the shoare, and sailde not into deepe. . . . Ovid's Elegies 3.7.44
Jove turnes himselfe into a Swanne, or gold, ... Ovid's Elegies 3.11.33
And oftentimes into her bosome flew, ... Hero and Leander 1.41
his/That leapt into the water for a kis/Of his owne shadow, Hero and Leander 1.74
for the lovely boy/That now is turn'd into a Cypres tree, Hero and Leander 1.155
Might presently be banisht into hell, ... Hero and Leander 1.453
Shall discontent run into regions farre; . . . . . Hero and Leander 1.478
He kist her, and breath'd life into her lips, ... Hero and Leander 2.3
And dive into the water, and there prie/Upon his brest, his Hero and Leander 2.188
And ran into the darke her selfe to hide, ... Hero and Leander 2.239
And seeking refuge, slipt into her bed. . . . . . Hero and Leander 2.244
INTOLERABLE
Malta to a wildernesse/For these intolerable wrongs of yours; Jew 3.5.26 Basso
the extremity of heat/To pinch me with intolerable pangs: Jew 5.5.88 Barab
INTOLLERABLE
intollerable booke for conjuring that ere was invented by any F App p.233 19 P Robin
INTOLLORABLE
Proud furie and intollorable fit, ... 2Tamb 2.4.78 Tamb
That Tamburlains intollorable wrath/May be suppresst by our 2Tamb 5.1.8 Maxim
INTOMBDE
where lies intombde this famous Conquerour, ... F App p.237 31 Emper
INTOMBE
thou bid me/Intombe my sword within my brothers bowels; . Lucan, First Booke 377
There in your rosie lippes my tongue intombe, ... Ovid's Elegies 3.13.23
INTOO'T
Even for charity I may spit intoo't. . . . . Jew 2.3.29 Barab
INTRAILES
No barking Dogs that Syllaes intrailes beare, ... Ovid's Elegies 2.16.23
INTRALLS
liver/Squis'd matter; through the cal, the intralls pearde, Lucan, First Booke 624
INTRAP
Then noble souldiors, to intrap these theeves, ... 1Tamb 2.2.59 Meandr
INTRAP'D
This traine he laid to have intrap'd thy life; . . . . Jew 5.5.91 Govnr
INTREAT
This should intreat your highnesse to rejoice, ... 1Tamb 1.1.123 Menaph
I would intreat you to speak but three wise wordes. . . 1Tamb 2.4.25 Tamb
Wils and commands (for say not I intreat)/Not once to set his 1Tamb 3.1.27 Bajzth
Intreat a pardon of the God of heaven, ... 2Tamb 3.4.32 Olymp
Let al of us intreat your highnesse pardon. . . . . 2Tamb 4.1.98 Tec&Us
That thus intreat their shame and servitude? . . . . 2Tamb 5.1.37 Govnr
there must my girle/Intreat the Abbasse to be entertain'd. Jew 1.2.280 Barab
Intreat 'em faire, and give them friendly speech, . . . Jew 1.2.286 Barab
Let us intreat she may be entertain'd. . . . . . Jew 1.2.329 2Fryar
'Tis true, my Lord, therefore intreat him well. . . . Jew 2.2.8 1Knght
Ithimore, intreat not for her, I am mov'd, ... Jew 3.4.35 Barab
And [less] <least> thou yeeld to this that I intreat, . Jew 3.4.37 Barab
Intreat them well, as we have used thee. . . . . . Jew 5.2.17 Calym
He humbly would intreat your Majesty/To come and see his homely Jew 5.3.17 Msngr
Therefore he humbly would intreat your Highnesse/Not to depart Jew 5.3.32 Msngr
And in the meane time ile intreat you all, ... Edw 1.2.77 ArchBp
Madam, intreat not, I will rather die, ... Edw 5.6.56 Mortmr
intreat thy Lord/To pardon my unjust presumption, . . . F1747 5.1.74 Faust
My wench, Lucina, I intreat thee favour, ... Ovid's Elegies 2.13.21
These he regarded not, but did intreat, ... Hero and Leander 1.451
Flatter, intreat, promise, protest and sweare, ... Hero and Leander 2.268
INTREATE
With knees and hearts submissive we intreate/Grace to our words 1Tamb 5.1.50 2Virgn
Intreate my lord Protector for his life. . . . . . Edw 5.4.95 King
Els would you not intreate for Mortimer. . . . . . Edw 5.6.71 King
good my Lord intreate for me: . . . . F1306 4.1.152 P Benvol
Let me intreate you to remove his hornes, ... F1309 4.1.155 Emper
INTREATED
some your children)/Might have intreated your obdurate breasts, 1Tamb 5.1.28 1Virgn
I have intreated her, and she will grant. . . . . . Jew 2.3.314 Barab
The king I feare hath ill intreated her. . . . . . Edw 1.4.189 Warwck
INTREATES
And most [humbly] <humble> intreates your Majestie/To visite P 245 4.43 Man
INTREATETH
Intreateth you by me, yet but he may/See him before he dies, Edw 2.5.36 Arundl
INTREATY
at my intreaty release him, he hath done penance sufficient. F App p.238 79 P Emper
INTRENCH
And triple wise intrench her round about: . . . . . Dido 5.1.10 Aeneas
Raise mounts, batter, intrench, and undermine, ... 2Tamb 3.3.38 Capt
Intrench with those dimensions I prescribed: . . . . 2Tamb 3.3.42 Therid
Both we (Theridamas) wil intrench our men, ... 2Tamb 3.3.49 Techel
INTRENCHED
With wals of Flint, and deepe intrenched Lakes, . . . F 782 3.1.4 Faust
INTRENCHT
Where finding Aeolus intrencht with stormes, ... Dido 1.1.58 Venus
INTRUSIONE
therefore your entrye is mere Intrusione . . . . . Paris ms13,p390 P Souldr
INUR'D
Daily inur'd to broyles and Massacres, ... Dido 2.1.124 Aeneas
Effeminate our mindes inur'd to warre. . . . . . Dido 4.3.36 Achat
INVADE
If any heathen potentate or king/Invade Natolia, Sigismond will 2Tamb 1.1.153 Sgsmnd
fame increast true feare, and did invade/The peoples minds, Lucan, First Booke 465
Oft to invade the sleeping foe tis good/And arm'd to shed Ovid's Elegies 1.9.21
INVASION
and fell invasion/Of such as have your majestie in chase, Edw 4.7.4 Abbot

INVEGLE			
Bull and Eagle/And what ere love made Jove should thee invegle.	Ovid's Elegies	1.10.8	
INVEIGLE			
giftes and promises/Inveigle him that lead a thousand horse,	1Tamb	2.2.26	Meandr
INVEIGLING			
That slie inveigling Frenchman weele exile,	Edw	1.2.57	Mortmr
For like Sea-nimphs inveigling harmony,	Hero and Leander	1.105	
INVENOMB'D			
[Gunnes] <Swords>, poyson, halters, and invenomb'd steele,	F 573	2.2.22	Faust
INVENOME			
and invenome her/That like a fiend hath left her father thus.	Jew	3.4.104	Barab
INVENT			
Or els invent some torture worse than that.	2Tamb	3.4.22	Olymp
And sit in councell to invent some paine,	2Tamb	3.5.98	Callap
I'le make my servile spirits to invent.	F 124	1.1.96	Faust
INVENTED			
Accurst be he that first invented war,	1Tamb	2.4.1	Mycet
Why the devil invented a challenge, my master writ it, and I	Jew	3.3.18	P Ithimr
for conjuring that ere was invented by any brimstone divel.	F App	p.233 20	P Robin
Who unborne infants first to slay invented,	Ovid's Elegies	2.14.5	
INVENTING			
Inventing maskes and stately showes for her,	2Tamb	4.2.94	Therid
INVENTION			
Let this invention be the instrument.	2Tamb	4.2.13	Olymp
INVENTIONS			
But to defend their strange inventions,	P 705	14.8	Navrre
I speake old Poets wonderfull inventions,	Ovid's Elegies	3.5.17	
INVEST			
We will invest your Highnesse Emperour:	1Tamb	1.1.151	Ceneus
Both may invest you Empresse of the East:	1Tamb	1.2.46	Tamb
Invest her here my Queene of Persea.	1Tamb	5.1.494	Tamb
I here invest thee king of Ariadan,	2Tamb	3.5.130	Callap
That meane t'invest me in a higher throane,	2Tamb	5.3.121	Tamb
INVESTED			
Where honor sits invested royally:	1Tamb	2.1.18	Menaph
Thinke thee invested now as royally,	1Tamb	2.5.2	Tamb
Crown'd and invested by the hand of Jove,	2Tamb	4.1.151	Tamb
diadem, before/You were invested in the crowne of France.	P 613	12.26	Mugern
INVESTERS			
To be investers of thy royall browes,	1Tamb	5.1.104	1Virgn
INVESTETH			
And they are worthy she investeth kings.	1Tamb	4.4.129	Tamb
INVESTION			
Intending your investion so neere/The residence of your	1Tamb	1.1.180	Ortyg
INVIE			
That thus invie the health of Tamburlaine.	2Tamb	5.3.53	Tamb
INVINCIBLE			
Troy is invincible, why stay we here?	Dido	2.1.128	Aeneas
You know our Armie is invincible:	1Tamb	3.1.7	Bajzth
a foot, unlesse thou beare/A mind corragious and invincible:	2Tamb	1.3.73	Tamb
Invincible by nature of the place.	2Tamb	3.2.90	Tamb
INVIOLABLE			
And vow to keepe this peace inviolable.	2Tamb	1.1.136	Sgsmnd
I sweare to keepe this truce inviolable:	2Tamb	1.1.142	Orcan
INVIOLATE			
Religious, righteous, and inviolate.	2Tamb	2.1.48	Sgsmnd
above written being inviolate, full power to fetch or carry the	F 497	2.1.109	P Faust
INVIRON'D			
And we were round inviron'd with the Greekes:	Dido	2.1.269	Aeneas
For when their hideous force inviron'd Rhodes,	Jew	2.2.48	Bosco
conquer'd Iland stands/Inviron'd with the mediterranean Sea,	Jew	5.3.7	Calym
INVIRONED			
Invironed round with airy mountaine tops,	F 781	3.1.3	Faust
INVISIBLE			
Ye Furies that can maske invisible,	1Tamb	4.4.17	Bajzth
Fourthly, that he shall be in his chamber or house invisible.	F 490	2.1.102	P Faust
<Then charme me that I may be invisible>,	F 991	(HC266)A	Faust
That I may walke invisible to all,	F 992	3.2.12	Faust
weare this girdle, then appeare/Invisible to all are here:	F 998	3.2.18	Mephst
INVISIBLIE			
These cowards invisiblie assaile hys soule,	2Tamb	5.3.13	Therid
INVITE			
To a solemne feast/I will invite young Selim-Calymath,/Where be	Jew	5.2.97	Barab
INVOCATE			
Thee if I invocate, I shall not need/To crave Apolloes ayde, or	Lucan, First Booke	64	
INVOLVING			
Involving all, did Aruns darkly sing.	Lucan, First Booke	637	
INWARD			
dye to expiate/The griefe that tires upon thine inward soule.	Dido	5.1.317	Iarbus
If outward habit judge the inward man.	1Tamb	1.2.163	Tamb
Against the inward powers of my heart,	2Tamb	5.3.196	Amyras
Whose pining heart, her inward sighes have blasted,	Edw	2.4.24	Queene
The stench whereof corrupts the inward soule/With such	F App	p.243 41	OldMan
If ought of me thou speak'st in inward thought,	Ovid's Elegies	1.4.23	
Now inward faults thy outward forme disgrace.	Ovid's Elegies	1.10.14	
With wheeles bent inward now the ring-turne ride.	Ovid's Elegies	3.2.12	
INWARDLY			
Though inwardly licentious enough,	Edw	2.1.50	Baldck
IO			
Or lovely Io metamorphosed.	2Tamb	1.2.39	Callap
Io, triumphing shall thy people sing.	Ovid's Elegies	1.2.34	
By verses horned Io got hir name,	Ovid's Elegies	1.3.21	
Io, a strong man conquerd this Wench, hollow.	Ovid's Elegies	1.7.38	

IO (cont.)
While Junos watch-man Io too much eyde, Ovid's Elegies 2.2.45
While Juno Io keepes when hornes she wore, Ovid's Elegies 2.19.29
Or shade, or body was [I] <Io>, who can say? Ovid's Elegies 3.6.16

IONIAN
Betwixt the Aegean and the Ionian sea, Lucan, First Booke 101

IOVE
And in my thoughts is shrin'd another [love] <Iove>: Dido 3.1.58 Dido

IPHEGEN
Daughter, whom I hold as deare/As Agamemnon did his Iphegen: Jew 1.1.138 Barab

IPOCRASE
druncke with ipocrase at any taberne in Europe for nothing, F App p.234 23 P Robin

IPSE
And ipse dixi with this quidditie, P 394 7.34 Guise
per vota nostra ipse nunc surgat nobis dicatus Mephostophilis. F 250 1.3.22 P Faust

IPSIQUE
pugnent ipsique nepotes: Dido 5.1.311 Dido

IRE (Homograph; See also YRE)
At last came Pirrhus fell and full of ire, Dido 2.1.213 Aeneas
Sic sic juvat ire sub umbras. Dido 5.1.313 Dido
under Turkish yokes/Shall groning beare the burthen of our ire; Jew 5.2.8 Calym
But never give a spatious time to ire, Ovid's Elegies 1.8.81

IREFULL
Come, let us leave him in his irefull mood, Jew 1.2.209 1Jew
God]/[Stretcheth out his Arme, and bends his irefull Browes]: F1944 5.2.148A Faust

IRELAND
Be governour of Ireland in my stead, Edw 1.4.125 Edward
Which may in Ireland purchase him such friends, Edw 1.4.259 Mortmr
the crowne, direct our warrant forth,/For Gaveston to Ireland: Edw 1.4.370 Edward
Shape we our course to Ireland there to breath. Edw 4.5.3 Spencr
And shipt but late for Ireland with the king. Edw 4.6.58 Rice
We were imbarkt for Ireland, wretched we, Edw 4.7.33 Baldck
by the grace of God/King of England, and lorde of Ireland. Edw 5.4.74 ArchBp

IRIS
As fast as Iris, or Joves Mercurie. Edw 1.4.371 Edward

IRISH
That now I hope flotes on the Irish seas. Edw 1.4.224 Mortmr
The wilde Oneyle, with swarmes of Irish Kernes, Edw 2.2.164 Lncstr

IRKES
Oh how the burthen irkes, that we should shun. Ovid's Elegies 2.4.6
I sayd it irkes me: Ovid's Elegies 2.18.7

IRKESOME
was thy parting hence/Bitter and irkesome to my sobbing heart. Edw 2.2.58 Edward
That meane to travaile some long irkesome way. Ovid's Elegies 2.16.16

IRKSOME
O how these irksome labours now delight, Dido 3.3.56 Aeneas

IRON (See also YRON)
As blacke as Jeat, and hard as Iron or steel, 2Tamb 1.3.27 Tamb
And duskie night, in rustie iron carre: Edw 4.3.44 Edward
Long ere with Iron hands they punish men, F 878 3.1.100 Pope
And boult the brazen gates with barres of Iron. Lucan, First Booke 62
And dores conjoynd with an hard iron lock. Ovid's Elegies 1.6.74
nor iron, are in thy soft brest/But pure simplicity in thee Ovid's Elegies 1.11.9
The posts of brasse, the walles of iron were. Ovid's Elegies 3.7.32

IRONS
Make fires, heat irons, let the racke be fetch'd. Jew 5.1.24 Govnr
How patiently hot irons they did take/In crooked [tramells] Ovid's Elegies 1.14.25
Why with hid irons are your bowels torne? Ovid's Elegies 2.14.27
Gold, silver, irons heavy weight, and brasse, Ovid's Elegies 3.7.37

IRRATIONALL
Take from irrationall beasts a president, Ovid's Elegies 1.10.25

IRRELIGEOUS
What irreligeous Pagans partes be these, P1180 22.42 King

IRREVERENT (See UNREVEREND)

IRREVOCABLE
Th'irrevocable people flie in troupes. Lucan, First Booke 507

IRUS
is Aeneas, were he clad/In weedes as bad as ever Irus ware. Dido 2.1.85 Dido

IS (See also IS'T, IST)
I, this is it, you can sit toying there, Dido 1.1.50 Venus
What? is not pietie exempt from woe? Dido 1.1.79 Venus
Since thy Aeneas wandring fate is firme, Dido 1.1.83 Jupitr
The ayre is pleasant, and the soyle most fit/For Cities, and Dido 1.1.178 Achat
Now is the time for me to play my part: Dido 1.1.182 Venus
good heaven/We breathe as now, and what this world is calde, Dido 1.1.198 Aeneas
It is the use for [Tirien] <Turen> maides to weare/Their bowe Dido 1.1.204 Venus
It is the Punick kingdome rich and strong, Dido 1.1.210 Venus
Of Troy am I, Aeneas is my name, Dido 1.1.216 Aeneas
Achates, tis my mother that is fled, Dido 1.1.240 Aeneas
Such force is farre from our unweaponed thoughts, Dido 1.2.14 Illion
There is a place Hesperia term'd by us, Dido 1.2.20 Cloan
And when I know it is not, then I dye. Dido 2.1.9 Aeneas
And in this humor is Achates to, Dido 2.1.10 Achat
And kisse his hand: O where is Hecuba? Dido 2.1.12 Achat
but saving ayre/Is nothing here, and what is this but stone? Dido 2.1.14 Achat
Grecians, which rejoyce/That nothing now is left of Priamus: Dido 2.1.20 Aeneas
O Priamus is left and this is he, Dido 2.1.21 Aeneas
Achates though mine eyes say this is stone, Dido 2.1.24 Aeneas
Yet thinkes my minde that this is Priamus: Dido 2.1.25 Aeneas
He is alive, Troy is not overcome. Dido 2.1.30 Aeneas
that would have it so/Deludes thy eye sight, Priamus is dead. Dido 2.1.32 Achat
Sweete father leave to weepe, this is not he: Dido 2.1.35 Ascan
It is our Captaine, see Ascanius. Dido 2.1.52 Cloan

IS (cont.)

passe through the hall/Bearing a banket, Dido is not farre.	Dido	2.1.71	Serg
But Troy is not, what shall I say I am?	Dido	2.1.76	Aeneas
Both happie that Aeneas is our guest:	Dido	2.1.82	Dido
Aeneas is Aeneas, were he clad/In weedes as bad as ever Irus	Dido	2.1.84	Dido
This is no seate for one thats comfortles,	Dido	2.1.86	Aeneas
And who so miserable as Aeneas is?	Dido	2.1.102	Aeneas
But all in this that Troy is overcome,	Dido	2.1.112	Dido
Troy is invincible, why stay we here?	Dido	2.1.128	Aeneas
Troy is a fire, the Grecians have the towne.	Dido	2.1.208	Aeneas
All which hemd me about, crying, this is he.	Dido	2.1.219	Aeneas
King of this Citie, but my Troy is fired,	Dido	2.1.236	Aeneas
Now is he fast asleepe, and in this grove/Amongst greene brakes	Dido	2.1.316	Venus
That love is childish which consists in words.	Dido	3.1.10	Iarbus
But Dido is the favour I request.	Dido	3.1.18	Iarbus
How lovely is Ascanius when he smiles?	Dido	3.1.29	Dido
Ungentle Queene, is this thy love to me?	Dido	3.1.36	Iarbus
And in my thoughts is shrin'd another [love] <Iove>:	Dido	3.1.58	Dido
Is not Aeneas faire and beautifull?	Dido	3.1.63	Dido
Is he not eloquent in all his speech?	Dido	3.1.65	Dido
Is not Aeneas worthie Didos love?	Dido	3.1.68	Dido
So lovely is he that where ere he goes,	Dido	3.1.71	Anna
Aeneas, thinke not Dido is in love:	Dido	3.1.136	Dido
I know this face, he is a Persian borne,	Dido	3.1.144	Serg
Why is it then displeasure should disjoyne,	Dido	3.2.30	Juno
Is this then all the thankes that I shall have,	Dido	3.2.37	Juno
Love my Aeneas, and desire is thine,	Dido	3.2.60	Venus
I, this it is which wounds me to the death,	Dido	3.3.63	Iarbus
Why, what is it that Dido may desire/And not obtaine, be it in	Dido	3.4.7	Aeneas
It is not ought Aeneas may atchieve?	Dido	3.4.11	Aeneas
What ailes my Queene, is she falne sicke of late?	Dido	3.4.24	Aeneas
Doubtles Apollos Axeltree is crackt,	Dido	4.1.11	Achat
Nay, where is my warlike father, can you tell?	Dido	4.1.15	Cupid
The ayre is cleere, and Southerne windes are whist,	Dido	4.1.25	Aeneas
Who having wrought her shame, is straight way fled:	Dido	4.2.18	Iarbus
I Anna, is there ought you would with me?	Dido	4.2.24	Iarbus
Mine eye is fixt where fancie cannot start,	Dido	4.2.37	Iarbus
This is no life for men at armes to live,	Dido	4.3.33	Achat
Is this thy love to me?	Dido	4.4.16	Dido
The sea is rough, the windes blow to the shoare.	Dido	4.4.25	Aeneas
O false Aeneas, now the sea is rough,	Dido	4.4.26	Dido
O where is Ganimed to hold his cup,	Dido	4.4.46	Dido
Heavens envious of our joyes is waxen pale,	Dido	4.4.52	Dido
This is the harbour that Aeneas seekes,	Dido	4.4.59	Aeneas
The ground is mine that gives them sustenance,	Dido	4.4.74	Dido
for his parentage deserves/As large a kingdome as is Libia.	Dido	4.4.80	Achat
Speake of no other land, this land is thine,	Dido	4.4.83	Dido
Dido is thine, henceforth Ile call thee Lord:	Dido	4.4.84	Dido
onely Aeneas frowne/Is that which terrifies poore Didos heart:	Dido	4.4.116	Dido
It is Aeneas frowne that ends my daies:	Dido	4.4.120	Dido
Your Nurse is gone with yong Ascanius,	Dido	4.4.124	Lord
Is this the wood that grew in Carthage plaines,	Dido	4.4.136	Dido
The water is an Element, no Nimph,	Dido	4.4.147	Dido
Come come, Ile goe, how farre hence is your house?	Dido	4.5.13	Cupid
Foolish is love, a toy.--	Dido	4.5.26	Nurse
Fourescore is but a girles age, love is sweete:--	Dido	4.5.32	Nurse
While Italy is cleane out of thy minde?	Dido	5.1.29	Hermes
But here he is, now Dido trie thy wit.	Dido	5.1.86	Dido
Farewell: is this the mends for Didos love?	Dido	5.1.105	Dido
It is Aeneas calles Aeneas hence,	Dido	5.1.132	Dido
I have not power to stay thee: is he gone?	Dido	5.1.183	Dido
By this is he got to the water side,	Dido	5.1.188	Dido
O Anna, my Aeneas is abourd,	Dido	5.1.194	Dido
O Dido, your little sonne Ascanius/Is gone!	Dido	5.1.213	Nurse
Now is he come on shoare safe without hurt:	Dido	5.1.257	Dido
Not farre from hence/There is a woman famoused for arts,	Dido	5.1.275	Dido
I, I, Iarbus, after this is done,	Dido	5.1.289	Dido
Thou shalt burne first, thy crime is worse then his:	Dido	5.1.297	Dido
Dido is dead,	Dido	5.1.320	Anna
Which is (God knowes) about that Tamburlaine,	1Tamb	1.1.30	Mycet
Is it not a kingly resolution?	1Tamb	1.1.55	Mycet
Our life is fraile, and we may die to day.	1Tamb	1.1.68	Mycet
O where is dutie and allegeance now?	1Tamb	1.1.101	Mycet
The plot is laid by Persean Noble men,	1Tamb	1.1.110	Cosroe
But this it is that doth excruciate/The verie substance of my	1Tamb	1.1.113	Cosroe
But tell me Maddam, is your grace betroth'd?	1Tamb	1.2.32	Tamb
Brighter than is the silver [Rhodope] <Rhodolfe>,	1Tamb	1.2.88	Tamb
Thy person is more woorth to Tamburlaine,	1Tamb	1.2.90	Tamb
But this is she with whom I am in love.	1Tamb	1.2.108	Tamb
How say you Lordings, Is not this your hope?	1Tamb	1.2.116	Tamb
But are they rich? And is their armour good?	1Tamb	1.2.123	Tamb
Looke for orations when the foe is neere.	1Tamb	1.2.131	Techel
Where is this Scythian Tamburlaine?	1Tamb	1.2.152	Therid
Which is as much as if I swore by heaven,	1Tamb	1.2.233	Tamb
A pearle more worth, then all the world is plaste:	1Tamb	2.1.12	Menaph
Proud is his fortune if we pierce it not.	1Tamb	2.1.44	Cosroe
That now is marching neer to Parthia:	1Tamb	2.1.65	Cosroe
I tel you true my heart is swolne with wrath,	1Tamb	2.2.2	Mycet
And which is worst to have his Diadem/Sought for by such scalde	1Tamb	2.2.7	Mycet
His Highnesse pleasure is that he should live,	1Tamb	2.2.37	Meandr
And when their scattered armie is subdu'd,	1Tamb	2.2.68	Meandr
which by fame is said/To drinke the mightie Parthian Araris,	1Tamb	2.3.15	Tamb
The King your Brother is now hard at hand,	1Tamb	2.3.45	Tamb

IS (cont.)

See where it is, the keenest Cutle-axe <curtle-axe>,/That ere	1Tamb	2.3.55		Tamb
And far from any man that is a foole.	1Tamb	2.4.12		Mycet
Is this your Crowne?	1Tamb	2.4.27		Tamb
O Gods, is this Tamburlaine the thiefe,	1Tamb	2.4.41		Mycet
Since he is yeelded to the stroke of War,	1Tamb	2.5.12		Cosroe
And let them know the Persean King is chang'd:	1Tamb	2.5.21		Cosroe
Is it not brave to be a King, Techelles?	1Tamb	2.5.51		Tamb
Is it not passing brave to be a King,	1Tamb	2.5.53		Tamb
To be a King, is halfe to be a God.	1Tamb	2.5.56		Usumc
A God is not so glorious as a King:	1Tamb	2.5.57		Therid
For he is grosse and like the massie earth,	1Tamb	2.7.31		Therid
Is drie and cold, and now dooth gastly death/With greedy	1Tamb	2.7.48		Cosroe
Who thinke you now is king of Persea?	1Tamb	2.7.56		Tamb
So, now it is more surer on my head,	1Tamb	2.7.65		Tamb
You know our Armie is invincible:	1Tamb	3.1.7		Bajzth
They say he is the King of Persea.	1Tamb	3.1.45		Argier
The spring is hindred by your smoothering host,	1Tamb	3.1.50		Moroc
The ground is mantled with such multitudes.	1Tamb	3.1.53		Moroc
All this is true as holy Mahomet,	1Tamb	3.1.54		Bajzth
Is far from villanie or servitude.	1Tamb	3.2.38		Zenoc
Alas (poore Turke) his fortune is to weake,	1Tamb	3.3.6		Tamb
The more he brings, the greater is the spoile,	1Tamb	3.3.23		Techel
My Campe is like to Julius Caesars Hoste,	1Tamb	3.3.152		Tamb
The field is ours, the Turk, his wife and all.	1Tamb	3.3.163		Tamb
Madame, she thinks perhaps she is too fine.	1Tamb	3.3.179		Ebea
lie weltring in their blood/And Tamburlaine is Lord of Affrica.	1Tamb	3.3.202		Zenoc
My royall Lord is slaine or conquered,	1Tamb	3.3.209		Zenoc
Now king of Bassoes, who is Conqueror?	1Tamb	3.3.212		Tamb
Here Madam, you are Empresse, she is none.	1Tamb	3.3.227		Therid
Not now Theridamas, her time is past:	1Tamb	3.3.228		Tamb
White is their hew, and on his silver crest/A snowy Feather	1Tamb	4.1.50		2Msngr
As red as scarlet is his furniture,	1Tamb	4.1.55		2Msngr
She is my Handmaids slave, and she shal looke/That these abuses	1Tamb	4.2.69		Zenoc
Is this a place for mighty Bajazeth?	1Tamb	4.2.83		Bajzth
This is my minde, and I will have it so.	1Tamb	4.2.91		Tamb
And every house is as a treasurie.	1Tamb	4.2.109		Tamb
The men, the treasure, and the towne is ours.	1Tamb	4.2.110		Tamb
Because it is my countries, and my Fathers.	1Tamb	4.2.124		Zenoc
My Lord it is the bloody Tamburlaine,	1Tamb	4.3.11		Souldn
It is a blemish to the Majestie/And high estate of mightie	1Tamb	4.3.19		Souldn
that the Souldan is/No more dismaide with tidings of his fall,	1Tamb	4.3.30		Souldn
The number of your hostes united is,	1Tamb	4.3.52		Capol
Nay, thine owne is easier to come by, plucke out that, and twil	1Tamb	4.4.13	P	Tamb
them leave Madam, this speech is a goodly refreshing to them.	1Tamb	4.4.32	P	Techel
Here is my dagger, dispatch her while she is fat, for if she	1Tamb	4.4.48	P	Tamb
dispatch her while she is fat, for if she live but a while	1Tamb	4.4.48	P	Tamb
but why is it?	1Tamb	4.4.64	P	Tamb
Wel, here is now to the Souldane of Egypt, the King of Arabia,	1Tamb	4.4.113	P	Tamb
For vertue is the fount whence honor springs.	1Tamb	4.4.128		Tamb
In whose sweete person is compriz'd the Sum/Of natures Skill	1Tamb	5.1.78		1Virgn
He now is seated on my horsmens speares,	1Tamb	5.1.114		Tamb
Faire is too foule an Epithite for thee,	1Tamb	5.1.136		Tamb
What is beauty, saith my sufferings then?	1Tamb	5.1.160		Tamb
But how unseemly is it for my Sex,	1Tamb	5.1.174		Tamb
With whose instinct the soule of man is toucht,	1Tamb	5.1.179		Tamb
And every warriour that is rapt with love/Of fame, of valour,	1Tamb	5.1.180		Tamb
That Vertue solely is the sum of glorie,	1Tamb	5.1.189		Tamb
The town is ours my Lord, and fresh supply/Of conquest, and of	1Tamb	5.1.196		Techel
and fresh supply/Of conquest, and of spoile is offered us.	1Tamb	5.1.197		Techel
No more there is not I warrant thee Techelles.	1Tamb	5.1.202		Tamb
We know the victorie is ours my Lord,	1Tamb	5.1.203		Therid
Then is there left no Mahomet, no God,	1Tamb	5.1.239		Zabina
As much as thy faire body is for me.	1Tamb	5.1.416		Zenoc
I record heaven, her heavenly selfe is cleare:	1Tamb	5.1.487		Tamb
My hand is ready to performe the deed,	1Tamb	5.1.503		Techel
All Asia is in Armes with Tamburlaine.	2Tamb	1.1.72		Orcan
All Affrike is in Armes with Tamburlaine.	2Tamb	1.1.76		Orcan
Here is his sword, let peace be ratified/On these conditions	2Tamb	1.1.124		Orcan
with my heart/Wish your release, but he whose wrath is death,	2Tamb	1.2.6		Almeda
<superfluities>/Is covered with a liquid purple veile,	2Tamb	1.3.80		Tamb
Is Barbary unpeopled for thy sake,	2Tamb	1.3.134		Usumc
All Barbary is unpeopled for thy sake.	2Tamb	1.3.149		Techel
What motion is it that inflames your thoughts,	2Tamb	2.1.2		Sgsmnd
faith which they prophanely plight/Is not by necessary pollycy,	2Tamb	2.1.38		Baldwn
Me thinks I see how glad the christian King/Is made, for joy of	2Tamb	2.2.21		Uribas
Whose shape is figure of the highest God?	2Tamb	2.2.38		Orcan
As is our holy prophet Mahomet,	2Tamb	2.2.44		Orcan
Nor in one place is circumscriptible,	2Tamb	2.2.50		Orcan
Discomfited is all the Christian hoste,	2Tamb	2.3.1		Sgsmnd
That in the midst of fire is ingraft,	2Tamb	2.3.21		Orcan
Whose power is often proov'd a myracle.	2Tamb	2.3.32		Gazell
Blacke is the beauty of the brightest day,	2Tamb	2.4.1		Tamb
And if she passe this fit, the worst is past.	2Tamb	2.4.40		1Phstn
But since my life is lengthened yet a while,	2Tamb	2.4.71		Zenoc
What, is she dead?	2Tamb	2.4.96		Tamb
Ah good my Lord be patient, she is dead,	2Tamb	2.4.119		Therid
Nothing prevailes, for she is dead my Lord.	2Tamb	2.4.124		Therid
For she is dead? thy words doo pierce my soule.	2Tamb	2.4.125		Tamb
That is a Gentleman (I know) at least.	2Tamb	3.1.72		Callap
them seeme as black/As is the Island where the Furies maske,	2Tamb	3.2.12		Tamb
Because my deare Zenocrate is dead.	2Tamb	3.2.14		Tamb
Greek, is writ/This towne being burnt by Tamburlaine the great,	2Tamb	3.2.16		Calyph

IS (cont.)

As is that towne, so is my heart consum'd,	2Tamb	3.2.49		Amyras
For [which] <with> the quinque-angle fourme is meet:	2Tamb	3.2.64		Tamb
And sharpest where th'assault is desperate.	2Tamb	3.2.67		Tamb
When this is learn'd for service on the land,	2Tamb	3.2.83		Tamb
When this is done, then are ye souldiers,	2Tamb	3.2.91		Tamb
My Lord, but this is dangerous to be done,	2Tamb	3.2.93		Calyph
A wound is nothing be it nere so deepe,	2Tamb	3.2.115		Tamb
Blood is the God of Wars rich livery.	2Tamb	3.2.116		Tamb
And this is Balsera their chiefest hold,	2Tamb	3.3.3		Therid
Wherein is all the treasure of the land.	2Tamb	3.3.4		Therid
And souldiers play the men, the [hold] <holds> is yours.	2Tamb	3.3.63		Techel
No hope is left to save this conquered hold.	2Tamb	3.4.3		Olymp
In whose high lookes is much more majesty/Than from the Concave	2Tamb	3.4.47		Therid
The name of mightie Tamburlain is spread:	2Tamb	3.4.66		Therid
Who by this time is at Natolia,	2Tamb	3.4.86		Therid
My royal army is as great as his,	2Tamb	3.5.10		Callap
And what our Army royall is esteem'd.	2Tamb	3.5.31		Callap
Of Sorians from Halla is repair'd/And neighbor cities of your	2Tamb	3.5.46		Soria
So that the Army royall is esteem'd/Six hundred thousand	2Tamb	3.5.50		Soria
Why, so he is Casane, I am here,	2Tamb	3.5.62		Tamb
So famous as is mighty Tamburlain:	2Tamb	3.5.84		Tamb
For as soone as the battaile is done, Ile ride in triumph	2Tamb	3.5.145	P	Tamb
Wel, now you see hee is a king, looke to him Theridamas, when we	2Tamb	3.5.153	P	Tamb
The glorie of this happy day is yours:	2Tamb	3.5.161		Tamb
I smile to think, how when this field is fought,	2Tamb	3.5.165		Techel
I know sir, what it is to kil a man,	2Tamb	4.1.27		Calyph
That they may say, it is not chance doth this,	2Tamb	4.1.84		Amyras
Whose matter is the flesh of Tamburlain,	2Tamb	4.1.113		Tamb
Whose drift is onely to dishonor thee.	2Tamb	4.2.7		Olymp
But now I finde thee, and that feare is past.	2Tamb	4.2.20		Therid
No such discourse is pleasant in mine eares,	2Tamb	4.2.46		Olymp
Such is the sodaine fury of my love,	2Tamb	4.2.52		Therid
What is it?	2Tamb	4.2.58		Therid
Now Hell is fairer than Elisian,	2Tamb	4.2.87		Therid
Infernall Dis is courting of my Love,	2Tamb	4.2.93		Therid
I Turke, I tel thee, this same Boy is he,	2Tamb	4.3.57		Tamb
At every little breath that thorow heaven is blowen:	2Tamb	4.3.124		Tamb
That little hope is left to save our lives,	2Tamb	5.1.4		Maxim
Is not my life and state as deere to me,	2Tamb	5.1.12		Govnr
How is my soule environed,	2Tamb	5.1.34		Govnr
the towne will never yeeld/As long as any life is in my breast.	2Tamb	5.1.48		Govnr
There lies more gold than Babylon is worth,	2Tamb	5.1.116		Govnr
When this is done, we'll martch from Babylon,	2Tamb	5.1.127		Tamb
So, now their best is done to honour me,	2Tamb	5.1.131		Tamb
There is a God full of revenging wrath,	2Tamb	5.1.183		Tamb
For he is God alone, and none but he.	2Tamb	5.1.202		Tamb
What is it dares distemper Tamburlain?	2Tamb	5.1.219		Techel
And but one hoste is left to honor thee:	2Tamb	5.2.27		Callap
Captaine, the force of Tamburlaine is great,	2Tamb	5.2.42		Callap
Yet when the pride of Cynthia is at full,	2Tamb	5.2.46		Callap
All Turkie is in armes with Callapine.	2Tamb	5.2.51		Callap
This is the time that must eternize me,	2Tamb	5.2.54		Callap
Earth droopes and saies, that hell in heaven is plac'd.	2Tamb	5.3.16		Therid
And though they think their painfull date is out,	2Tamb	5.3.34		Usumc
And that their power is puissant as Joves,	2Tamb	5.3.35		Usumc
Is greater far, than they can thus subdue.	2Tamb	5.3.39		Usumc
For if he die, thy glorie is disgrac'd,	2Tamb	5.3.40		Usumc
Earth droopes and saies that hel in heaven is plac'd.	2Tamb	5.3.41		Usumc
And cannot last, it is so violent.	2Tamb	5.3.65		Techel
Whereby the moisture of your blood is dried,	2Tamb	5.3.85		Phsitn
and Calor, which some holde/Is not a parcell of the Elements,	2Tamb	5.3.87		Phsitn
Is almost cleane extinguished and spent,	2Tamb	5.3.89		Phsitn
Besides my Lord, this day is Critical,	2Tamb	5.3.91		Phsitn
Dangerous to those, whose Chrisis is as yours:	2Tamb	5.3.92		Phsitn
I joy my Lord, your highnesse is so strong,	2Tamb	5.3.110		Usumc
But I perceive my martial strength is spent,	2Tamb	5.3.119		Tamb
let me see how much/Is left for me to conquer all the world,	2Tamb	5.3.124		Tamb
Which is from Scythia, where I first began,	2Tamb	5.3.143		Tamb
Whose matter is incorporat in your flesh.	2Tamb	5.3.165		Amyras
As precious is the charge thou undertak'st/As that which	2Tamb	5.3.230		Tamb
Albeit the world thinke Machevill is dead,	Jew	Prol.1		Machvl
And now the Guize is dead, is come from France/To view this	Jew	Prol.3		Machvl
now the Guize is dead, is come from France/To view this Land,	Jew	Prol.3		Machvl
To some perhaps my name is odious,	Jew	Prol.5		Machvl
And hold there is no sinne but Ignorance.	Jew	Prol.15		Machvl
of judgement frame/This is the ware wherein consists my wealth:	Jew	1.1.33		Barab
And is thy credit not enough for that?	Jew	1.1.62		Barab
Or who is honour'd now but for his wealth?	Jew	1.1.113		Barab
And all I have is hers. But who comes here?	Jew	1.1.139		Barab
Tut, tut, there is some other matter in't.	Jew	1.1.160		Barab
Alas, my Lord, the summe is overgreat,	Jew	1.2.8		Govnr
That's more then is in our Commission.	Jew	1.2.22		Basso
Let's know their time, perhaps it is not long;	Jew	1.2.24		Calym
From the Emperour of Turkey is arriv'd/Great Selim-Calymath,	Jew	1.2.39		Govnr
Halfe of my substance is a Cities wealth.	Jew	1.2.85		Barab
Sir, halfe is the penalty of our decree,	Jew	1.2.88		Govnr
Is theft the ground of your Religion?	Jew	1.2.95		Barab
Of nought is nothing made.	Jew	1.2.104		Barab
Excesse of wealth is cause of covetousnesse:	Jew	1.2.123		Govnr
I, but theft is worse:	Jew	1.2.125		Barab
For that is theft; and if you rob me thus,	Jew	1.2.126		Barab
our hands with blood/Is farre from us and our profession.	Jew	1.2.145		Govnr

IS (cont.)

No, Barabas is borne to better chance,	Jew	1.2.218	Barab
My gold, my gold, and all my wealth is gone.	Jew	1.2.258	Barab
it,/A counterfet profession is better/Then unseene hypocrisie.	Jew	1.2.292	Barab
No, Abigall, in this/It is not necessary I be seene.	Jew	1.2.302	Barab
Well, daughter, say, what is thy suit with us?	Jew	1.2.321	Abbass
As much I hope as all I hid is worth.	Jew	1.2.336	Barab
And is admitted to the Sister-hood.	Jew	1.2.343	1Fryar
The boord is marked thus that covers it.	Jew	1.2.350	Barab
The boord is marked thus that covers it,	Jew	1.2.356	Barab
Is she so faire?	Jew	1.2.384	Lodowk
Whence is thy ship that anchors in our Rhoad?	Jew	2.2.2	Govnr
My Ship, the flying Dragon, is of Spaine,	Jew	2.2.5	Bosco
And so am I, Delbosco is my name;	Jew	2.2.6	Bosco
Our fraught is Grecians, Turks, and Africk Moores.	Jew	2.2.9	Bosco
This truce we have is but in hope of gold,	Jew	2.2.26	1Knght
Captaine we know it, but our force is small.	Jew	2.2.34	Govnr
What is the summe that Calymath requires?	Jew	2.2.35	Bosco
Honor is bought with bloud and not with gold.	Jew	2.2.56	Govnr
This is the Market-place, here let 'em stand:	Jew	2.3.1	1Offcr
Every ones price is written on his backe,	Jew	2.3.3	2Offcr
I have bought a house/As great and faire as is the Governors;	Jew	2.3.14	Barab
For Don Mathias tels me she is faire.	Jew	2.3.35	Lodowk
of the Serpent then the Dove; that is, more knave than foole.	Jew	2.3.37	P Barab
Is it square or pointed, pray let me know.	Jew	2.3.59	Lodowk
Pointed it is, good Sir,--but not for you.	Jew	2.3.60	Barab
I, but my Lord, the harvest is farre off:	Jew	2.3.79	Barab
And if he has, he is worth three hundred plats.	Jew	2.3.102	Barab
The Sessions day is criticall to theeves,	Jew	2.3.105	Barab
Because he is young and has more qualities.	Jew	2.3.110	1Offcr
I, marke him, you were best, for this is he	Jew	2.3.132	Barab
This Moore is comeliest, is he not? speake son.	Jew	2.3.144	Mater
No, this is the better, mother, view this well.	Jew	2.3.145	Mthias
before your mother/Lest she mistrust the match that is in hand:	Jew	2.3.147	Barab
Tell me, Mathias, is not that the Jew?	Jew	2.3.152	Mater
Converse not with him, he is cast off from heaven.	Jew	2.3.157	Mater
Faith, Sir, my birth is but meane, my name's Ithimor,	Jew	2.3.165	Ithimr
Why this is something:	Jew	2.3.213	Barab
Where is the Diamond you told me of?	Jew	2.3.219	Lodowk
He is not of the seed of Abraham.	Jew	2.3.230	Barab
O father, Don Mathias is my love.	Jew	2.3.237	Abigal
Doe, it is requisite it should be so.	Jew	2.3.239	Barab
Nay on my life it is my Factors hand,	Jew	2.3.240	Barab
The account is made, for [Lodovico] <Lodowicke> dyes.	Jew	2.3.242	Barab
Thou know'st, and heaven can witnesse it is true,	Jew	2.3.253	Barab
And I am sure he is with Abigall.	Jew	2.3.268	Barab
Barabas, is not that the widowes sonne?	Jew	2.3.279	Lodowk
My death? what, is the base borne peasant mad?	Jew	2.3.281	Lodowk
This is thy Diamond, tell me, shall I have it?	Jew	2.3.292	Lodowk
Win it, and weare it, it is yet [unfoyl'd] <unsoyl'd>.	Jew	2.3.293	Barab
Nor our Messias that is yet to come,	Jew	2.3.304	Barab
Faith is not to be held with Heretickes;	Jew	2.3.311	Barab
Why on the sudden is your colour chang'd?	Jew	2.3.321	Lodowk
Shee is thy wife, and thou shalt be mine heire.	Jew	2.3.328	Barab
Lodowicke, it is enough/That I have made thee sure to Abigal.	Jew	2.3.334	Barab
My life is not so deare as Abigall.	Jew	2.3.348	Mthias
What, is he gone unto my mother?	Jew	2.3.351	Mthias
I will have Don Mathias, he is my love.	Jew	2.3.361	Abigal
I thinke by this/You purchase both their lives; is it not so?	Jew	2.3.366	Ithimr
'Tis poyson'd, is it not?	Jew	2.3.372	Ithimr
It is a challenge feign'd from Lodowicke.	Jew	2.3.374	Barab
And he is very seldome from my house;	Jew	3.1.10	Curtzn
I know she is a Curtezane by her attire:	Jew	3.1.26	P Ithimr
This is the place, now Abigall shall see/Whether Mathias holds	Jew	3.2.1	Mthias
What sight is this? my [Lodovico] <Lodowicke> slaine!	Jew	3.2.10	Govnr
Who is this? my sonne Mathias slaine!	Jew	3.2.12	Mater
Go to, sirra sauce, is this your question?	Jew	3.3.34	P Abigal
But I perceive there is no love on earth,	Jew	3.3.47	Abigal
Why Abigal it is not yet long since/That I did labour thy	Jew	3.3.56	1Fryar
And on that hope my happinesse is built:	Jew	3.4.17	Barab
And she is hatefull to my soule and me:	Jew	3.4.36	Barab
All that I have is thine when I am dead,	Jew	3.4.44	Barab
It is a precious powder that I bought/Of an Italian in Ancona	Jew	3.4.68	Barab
Whose operation is to binde, infect,	Jew	3.4.70	Barab
yet not appeare/In forty houres after it is tane.	Jew	3.4.72	Barab
Belike there is some Ceremony in't.	Jew	3.4.83	Barab
My purse, my Coffer, and my selfe is thine.	Jew	3.4.93	Barab
Pay me my wages for my worke is done.	Jew	3.4.115	Ithimr
The time you tooke for respite, is at hand,	Jew	3.5.8	Basso
For by this Answer, broken is the league,	Jew	3.5.34	Govnr
And nought is to be look'd for now but warres,	Jew	3.5.35	Govnr
And nought to us more welcome is then wars.	Jew	3.5.36	Govnr
Where is the Fryar that converst with me?	Jew	3.6.9	Abigal
Oh he is gone to see the other Nuns.	Jew	3.6.10	2Fryar
And by my father's practice, which is there/Set downe at large,	Jew	3.6.28	Abigal
There is no musicke to a Christians knell:	Jew	4.1.1	Barab
And besides, the Wench is dead.	Jew	4.1.42	Barab
may I compare/With all the Jewes in Malta; but what is wealth?	Jew	4.1.56	Barab
This is meere frailty, brethren, be content.	Jew	4.1.98	Barab
So, now the feare is past, and I am safe:	Jew	4.1.114	Barab
For he that shriv'd her is within my house.	Jew	4.1.115	Barab
Ithimore, tell me, is the Fryar asleepe?	Jew	4.1.129	Barab
Yes; and I know not what the reason is:	Jew	4.1.130	Ithimr

IS (cont.)

Then is it as it should be, take him up.	Jew	4.1.152	Barab
This is the houre/Wherein I shall proceed; Oh happy houre,	Jew	4.1.160	1Fryar
But sort, is not this Bernardine?	Jew	4.1.164	1Fryar
it is;/And understanding I should come this way,	Jew	4.1.164	1Fryar
Who is it?	Jew	4.1.176	Barab
He is slaine.	Jew	4.1.177	Barab
To morrow is the Sessions; you shall to it.	Jew	4.1.199	Barab
as who shold say, Is it even so; and so I left him, being driven	Jew	4.2.13	P Pilia
I wonder what the reason is.	Jew	4.2.32	P Ithimr
This is the Gentleman you writ to.	Jew	4.2.37	P Pilia
Here's goodly 'parrell, is there not?	Jew	4.2.112	Ithimr
and looks/Like one that is imploy'd in Catzerie/And crosbiting,	Jew	4.3.12	Barab
crosbiting, such a Rogue/As is the husband to a hundred whores:	Jew	4.3.14	Barab
Well, my hope is, he will not stay there still;	Jew	4.3.16	Barab
the gold, or know Jew it is in my power to hang thee.	Jew	4.3.37	P Pilia
A masty <nasty> slave he is.	Jew	4.4.69	Pilia
To undoe a Jew is charity, and not sinne.	Jew	4.4.81	Ithimr
Away with her, she is a Curtezane.	Jew	5.1.8	Govnr
Away with him, his sight is death to me.	Jew	5.1.35	Govnr
Shee is a Curtezane and he a theefe,	Jew	5.1.37	Barab
Where is the Jew, where is that murderer?	Jew	5.1.48	Mater
So is the Turke, and Barabas the Jew.	Jew	5.1.51	1Offcr
This sudden death of his is very strange.	Jew	5.1.54	Bosco
My name is Barabas; I am a Jew.	Jew	5.1.72	Barab
The Jew is here, and rests at your command.	Jew	5.1.83	Barab
The rocke is hollow, and of purpose digg'd,	Jew	5.1.87	Barab
And by this meanes the City is your owne.	Jew	5.1.94	Barab
This is the reason that I sent for thee;	Jew	5.2.51	Barab
Here is my hand that I'le set Malta free:	Jew	5.2.95	Barab
Here is my hand, beleeve me, Barabas,	Jew	5.2.102	Govnr
I will be there, and doe as thou desirest;/When is the time?	Jew	5.2.104	Govnr
This is the life we Jewes are us'd to lead;	Jew	5.2.115	Barab
that there is a monastery/Which standeth as an out-house to the	Jew	5.3.36	Msngr
wel since it is no more/I'le satisfie my selfe with that;	Jew	5.5.21	Barab
Why, is not this/A kingly kinde of trade	Jew	5.5.46	Barab
How busie Barrabas is there above/To entertaine us in his	Jew	5.5.52	Calym
For she is that huge blemish in our eye,	P 80	2.23	Guise
That perill is the cheefest way to happines,	P 95	2.38	Guise
What glory is there in a common good,	P 97	2.40	Guise
The plot is laide, and things shall come to passe,	P 164	2.107	Guise
Too late it is my Lord if that be true/To blame her highnes,	P 181	3.16	QnMarg
(For whose effects my soule is massacred)/Infect thy gracious	P 192	3.27	QnMarg
He that wantes these, and is suspected of heresie,	P 234	4.32	Guise
That charge is mine.	P 290	5.17	Anjoy
Where is the Admirall?	P 300	5.27	Gonzag
Gonzago, what, is he dead?	P 304	5.31	Guise
It may be it is some other, and he escapte.	P 308	5.35	Anjoy
And when this just revenge is finished,	P 318	5.45	Anjoy
Who is that which knocks there?	P 346	6.1	P SrnsWf
I am as Ramus is, a Christian.	P 374	7.14	Taleus
O let him goe, he is a catholick.	P 375	7.15	Retes
All that I have is but my stipend from the King,	P 378	7.18	Ramus
Which is no sooner receiv'd but it is spent.	P 379	7.19	Ramus
Is in your judgment thought a learned man.	P 391	7.31	Guise
For Poland is as I have been enformde,	P 454	8.4	Anjoy
And by his graces councell it is thought,	P 465	8.15	Anjoy
By due discent the Regall seat is mine.	P 470	8.20	Anjoy
Yet is [their] <there> pacience of another sort,	P 545	11.10	Charls
O no, his soule is fled from out his breast,	P 552	11.17	QnMoth
And now that Henry is cal'd from Polland,	P 569	11.34	Navrre
It is my due by just succession:	P 570	11.35	Navrre
And all his heaven is to delight himselfe:	P 634	12.47	QnMoth
Am I growne olde, or is thy lust growne yong,	P 681	13.25	Guise
Is all my love forgot which helde thee deare?	P 684	13.28	Guise
Is Guises glory but a clowdy mist,	P 686	13.30	Guise
But for you know our quarrell is no more,	P 704	14.7	Navrre
Spaine is the counsell chamber of the pope,	P 709	14.12	Navrre
Spaine is the place where he makes peace and warre,	P 710	14.13	Navrre
This is the Guise that hath incenst the King,	P 729	14.32	Navrre
But canst thou tell who is their generall?	P 731	14.34	Navrre
How now my Lord, faith this is more then need,	P 757	15.15	Guise
But which way is he gone?	P 783	15.41	Mugern
The Duke is slaine and all his power dispearst,	P 787	16.1	Navrre
Is ruth and almost death to call to minde:	P 797	16.11	Navrre
Come my Lords, now that this storme is overpast,	P 804	16.18	Navrre
and whereas hee is your Landlord, you will take upon you to be	P 810	17.5	P Souldr
that he himself should occupy, which is his own free land.	P 812	17.7	P Souldr
What your intent is yet we cannot learn,	P 823	17.18	King
But we presume it is not for our good.	P 824	17.19	King
Thou shouldst perceive the Duke of Guise is mov'd.	P 832	17.27	Guise
My Lord, to speak more plainely, thus it is:	P 847	17.42	Guise
Shall feele the house of Lorayne is his foe:	P 856	17.51	Guise
The choyse is hard, I must dissemble.	P 865	17.60	Guise
Heere is no staying for the King of France,	P 897	17.92	King
And that Paris is revolted from his grace.	P 902	18.3	Navrre
Holla verlete, hey: Epernoune, where is the King?	P 956	19.26	Guise
I prethee tell him that the Guise is heere.	P 958	19.28	Guise
For in thee is the Duke of Guises hope.	P 988	19.58	Guise
O my Lord, I am one of them that is set to murder you.	P 992	19.62	P 3Mur
Stand close, he is comming, I know him by his voice.	P1000	19.70	P 1Mur
To dye by Pesantes, what a greefe is this?	P1009	19.79	Guise
My Lord, see where the Guise is slaine.	P1019	19.89	Capt

IS (cont.)

Ah this sweet sight is phisick to my soule,	P1020	19.90	King
This is the traitor that hath spent my golde,	P1028	19.98	King
(As all the world shall know our Guise is dead)/Rest satisfied	P1042	19.112	King
My Lord heer is his sonne.	P1045	19.115	Eprnon
When Duke Dumaine his brother is alive,	P1055	19.125	King
And that young Cardinall that is growne so proud?	P1056	19.126	King
And let her droup, my heart is light enough.	P1064	19.134	King
Pray God thou be a King now this is done.	P1068	19.138	QnMoth
The Guise is slaine, and I rejoyce therefore:	P1078	19.148	King
For since the Guise is dead, I will not live.	P1090	19.160	QnMoth
Then there is no remedye but I must dye?	P1096	20.6	Cardnl
He is hard hearted, therfore pull with violence.	P1105	20.15	1Mur
Now thou art dead, heere is no stay for us:	P1111	21.5	Dumain
of Loraine by the Kings consent is lately strangled unto death.	P1123	21.17	P Frier
beene a great sinner in my dayes, and the deed is meritorious.	P1134	21.28	P Frier
It is enough if that Navarre may be/Esteemed faithfull to the	P1147	22.9	Navrre
your Majestie heere is a Frier of the order of the Jacobins,	P1155	22.17	P 1Msngr
What, is your highnes hurt?	P1176	22.38	Navrre
The wound I warrant ye is deepe my Lord,	P1192	22.54	King
Alas my Lord, the wound is dangerous,	P1212	22.74	Srgeon
Ah curse him not sith he is dead.	P1220	22.82	King
For he is your lawfull King and my next heire:	P1230	22.92	King
Ah Epernoune, is this thy love to me?	P1235	22.97	King
ser where he is your landlorde you take upon you to be his |	Paris	ms 9,p390	P Souldr
therefore your entrye is mere Intrusione	Paris	ms13,p390	P Souldr
this is againste the lawe ser:	Paris	ms14,p390	P Souldr
My father is deceast, come Gaveston,	Edw	1.1.1	Gavstn
Is as Elizium to a new come soule.	Edw	1.1.11	Gavstn
But yet it is no paine to speake men faire,	Edw	1.1.42	Gavstn
Musicke and poetrie is his delight,	Edw	1.1.54	Gavstn
Thy woorth sweet friend is far above my guifts,	Edw	1.1.161	Edward
Is Edward pleazd with kinglie regiment.	Edw	1.1.165	Edward
But is that wicked Gaveston returnd?	Edw	1.1.177	BshpCv
Tis true, the Bishop is in the tower,	Edw	1.2.1	Warwck
This ground which is corrupted with their steps,	Edw	1.2.5	Lncstr
Wherfore is Guy of Warwicke discontent?	Edw	1.2.10	Mortmr
That villaine Gaveston is made an Earle.	Edw	1.2.11	Lncstr
And happie is the man, whom he vouchsafes/For vailing of his	Edw	1.2.18	Lncstr
His countenance bewraies he is displeasd.	Edw	1.2.34	Lncstr
What neede I, God himselfe is up in armes,	Edw	1.2.40	ArchBp
When violence is offered to the church.	Edw	1.2.41	ArchBp
The Bishoprick of Coventrie is his.	Edw	1.2.45	ArchBp
Is it not straunge, that he is thus bewitcht?	Edw	1.2.55	MortSr
Here is the forme of Gavestons exile:	Edw	1.4.1	Lncstr
It is our pleasure, we will have it so.	Edw	1.4.9	Edward
For no where else the new earle is so safe.	Edw	1.4.11	Lncstr
Their downfall is at hand, their forces downe,	Edw	1.4.18	Mortmr
Is this the dutie that you owe your king?	Edw	1.4.22	Kent
The king is love-sick for his minion.	Edw	1.4.87	Mortmr
Now is my heart at ease.	Edw	1.4.91	ArchBp
And so is mine.	Edw	1.4.91	Warwck
Is all my hope turnd to this hell of greefe.	Edw	1.4.116	Gavstn
The time is little that thou hast to stay,	Edw	1.4.138	Edward
And by thy meanes is Gaveston exilde.	Edw	1.4.155	Edward
How deare my lord is to poore Isabell.	Edw	1.4.166	Queene
Hard is the hart, that injures such a saint.	Edw	1.4.190	Penbrk
he is gone.	Edw	1.4.192	MortSr
It is impossible, but speake your minde.	Edw	1.4.228	Mortmr
She smiles, now for my life his mind is changd.	Edw	1.4.236	Warwck
And is this true to call him home againe?	Edw	1.4.246	Lncstr
All that he speakes, is nothing, we are resolv'd.	Edw	1.4.251	Warwck
This which I urge, is of a burning zeale,	Edw	1.4.256	Mortmr
But were he here, detested as he is,	Edw	1.4.264	Mortmr
Such a one as my Lord of Cornewall is,	Edw	1.4.285	Mortmr
Is new returnd, this newes will glad him much,	Edw	1.4.301	Queene
My heart is as an anvill unto sorrow,	Edw	1.4.312	Edward
Repeald, the newes is too sweet to be true.	Edw	1.4.323	Edward
Now is the king of England riche and strong,	Edw	1.4.366	Queene
Thou seest by nature he is milde and calme,	Edw	1.4.388	MortSr
Then let his grace, whose youth is flexible,	Edw	1.4.398	MortSr
But nephew, now you see the king is changd.	Edw	1.4.420	MortSr
The liberall earle of Cornewall is the man,	Edw	2.1.10	Spencr
But he is banisht, theres small hope of him.	Edw	2.1.15	Baldck
It is about her lover Gaveston.	Edw	2.1.22	Spencr
Our Ladies first love is not wavering,	Edw	2.1.27	Spencr
As is the joy of his returning home.	Edw	2.1.58	Neece
My lord of Cornewall is a comming over,	Edw	2.1.76	Neece
The winde is good, I wonder why he stayes,	Edw	2.2.1	Edward
I feare me he is wrackt upon the sea.	Edw	2.2.2	Edward
Looke Lancaster how passionate he is,	Edw	2.2.3	Queene
How now, what newes, is Gaveston arrivde?	Edw	2.2.6	Edward
But seeing you are so desirous, thus it is:	Edw	2.2.15	Mortmr
And what is yours my lord of Lancaster?	Edw	2.2.21	Edward
Plinie reports, there is a flying Fish,	Edw	2.2.23	Lncstr
No sooner is it up, but thers a foule,	Edw	2.2.26	Lncstr
Is this the love you beare your soveraigne?	Edw	2.2.30	Edward
Is this the fruite your reconcilement beares?	Edw	2.2.31	Edward
and now thy sight/Is sweeter farre, then was thy parting hence	Edw	2.2.57	Edward
Welcome is the good Earle of Cornewall.	Edw	2.2.66	Mortmr
Looke to your owne heads, his is sure enough.	Edw	2.2.92	Edward
Lets to our castels, for the king is moovde.	Edw	2.2.100	Warwck
Cosin it is no dealing with him now,	Edw	2.2.102	Lncstr

IS (cont.)

Seeing he is taken prisoner in his warres?	Edw	2.2.119	Mortmr
His highnes is disposde to be alone.	Edw	2.2.135	Guard
How now, what noise is this?	Edw	2.2.139	Edward
Thy court is naked, being bereft of those,	Edw	2.2.174	Mortmr
And dare not be revengde, for their power is great:	Edw	2.2.202	Edward
Your pardon is quicklie got of Isabell.	Edw	2.2.231	Queene
The yonger Mortimer is growne so brave,	Edw	2.2.232	Edward
Tell me, where wast thou borne? What is thine armes?	Edw	2.2.242	Edward
My name is Baldock, and my gentrie/Is fetcht from Oxford, not	Edw	2.2.243	Baldck
and my gentrie/Is fetcht from Oxford, not from Heraldrie.	Edw	2.2.244	Baldck
His name is Spencer, he is well alied,	Edw	2.2.249	Gavstn
He is your brother, therefore have we cause/To cast the worst,	Edw	2.3.7	Warwck
That Gaveston is secretlie arrivde,	Edw	2.3.16	Lncstr
O tell me Spencer, where is Gaveston?	Edw	2.4.1	Edward
I feare me he is slaine my gratious lord.	Edw	2.4.2	Spencr
The king hath left him, and his traine is small.	Edw	2.4.39	Queene
How comes it, that the king and he is parted?	Edw	2.4.41	Mortmr
You know the king is so suspitious,	Edw	2.4.53	Queene
[King] <Kind> Edward is not heere to buckler thee.	Edw	2.5.18	Lncstr
it is our countries cause,/That here severelie we will execute	Edw	2.5.22	Warwck
That heading is one, and hanging is the other,	Edw	2.5.30	Gavstn
And death is all.	Edw	2.5.31	Gavstn
I know it lords, it is this life you aime at,	Edw	2.5.48	Gavstn
bestow/His teares on that, for that is all he gets/Of Gaveston,	Edw	2.5.53	Mortmr
My lords, it is his majesties request,	Edw	2.5.57	Arundl
It is honourable in thee to offer this,	Edw	2.5.67	Mortmr
How meanst thou Mortimer? that is over base.	Edw	2.5.71	Gavstn
is it not enough/That we have taken him, but must we now	Edw	2.5.83	Warwck
My house is not farre hence, out of the way/A little, but our	Edw	2.5.100	Penbrk
I see it is your life these armes pursue.	Edw	2.6.2	James
No James, it is my countries cause I follow.	Edw	2.6.10	Warwck
the riches of my realme/Can ransome him, ah he is markt to die,	Edw	3.1.4	Edward
Warwick I know is roughe, and Lancaster/Inexorable, and I shall	Edw	3.1.6	Edward
Yea my good lord, for Gaveston is dead.	Edw	3.1.90	Arundl
My lord, [here] is <heres> a messenger from the Barons,/Desires	Edw	3.1.148	Spencr
Yonder is Edward among his flatterers.	Edw	3.1.196	Mortmr
Is it not, trowe ye, to assemble aide,	Edw	3.1.207	SpncrP
But justice of the quarrell and the cause,/Vaild is your pride:	Edw	3.1.223	Edward
The worst is death, and better die to live,	Edw	3.1.243	Lncstr
And certifie what Edwards loosenes is.	Edw	4.1.7	Kent
The Marques is a noble Gentleman,	Edw	4.2.32	Queene
man, they say there is great execution/Done through the realme,	Edw	4.3.6	Edward
He is in Englands ground, our port-maisters/Are not so careles	Edw	4.3.22	Edward
all discontented and discomforted, is gone, whither if you aske,	Edw	4.3.30	P Spencr
this is all the newes of import.	Edw	4.3.36	P Spencr
With him is Edmund gone associate?	Edw	4.3.39	Edward
Is thus misled to countenance their ils.	Edw	4.3.49	Edward
When force to force is knit, and sword and gleave/In civill	Edw	4.4.5	Queene
Fly, fly, my Lord, the Queene is over strong,	Edw	4.5.1	Spencr
Bristow to Longshankes blood/Is false, be not found single for	Edw	4.6.17	Kent
Baldock is with the king,/A goodly chauncelor, is he not my	Edw	4.6.42	Queene
A goodly chauncelor, is he not my lord?	Edw	4.6.43	Queene
This, Edward, is the ruine of the realme.	Edw	4.6.45	Kent
Is with that smoothe toongd scholler Baldock gone,	Edw	4.6.57	Rice
[Unhappie] <Unhappies> <Unhappy is> Edward, chaste from	Edw	4.6.62	Kent
Rebell is he that fights against his prince,	Edw	4.6.71	SpncrP
But what is he, whome rule and emperie/Have not in life or	Edw	4.7.14	Edward
Father, this life contemplative is heaven,	Edw	4.7.20	Edward
And all the land I know is up in armes,	Edw	4.7.31	Spencr
Too true it is, quem dies vidit veniens superbum,	Edw	4.7.53	Leistr
My lord, it is in vaine to greeve or storme,	Edw	4.7.77	Baldck
Our lots are cast, I feare me so is thine.	Edw	4.7.79	Baldck
Here is a Litter readie for your grace,	Edw	4.7.84	Leistr
O is he gone!	Edw	4.7.100	Spencr
is noble Edward gone,/Parted from hence, never to see us more!	Edw	4.7.100	Spencr
Earth melt to ayre, gone is my soveraigne,	Edw	4.7.103	Spencr
But when the imperiall Lions flesh is gorde,	Edw	5.1.11	Edward
But what are kings, when regiment is gone,	Edw	5.1.26	Edward
Your grace mistakes, it is for Englands good,	Edw	5.1.38	BshpWn
In which extreame my minde here murthered is:	Edw	5.1.55	Edward
My lord, the king is willing to resigne.	Edw	5.1.94	Leistr
More safetie is there in a Tigers jawes,	Edw	5.1.116	Edward
To wretched men death is felicitie.	Edw	5.1.127	Edward
By Mortimer, whose name is written here,	Edw	5.1.139	Edward
So may his limmes be torne, as is this paper,	Edw	5.1.142	Edward
And every earth is fit for buriall.	Edw	5.1.146	Edward
So that he now is gone from Killingworth,	Edw	5.2.31	BshpWn
The lord of Bartley is so pitifull,	Edw	5.2.34	BshpWn
Let me alone, here is the privie seale,	Edw	5.2.37	Mortmr
Brother, you know it is impossible.	Edw	5.2.97	Queene
Why, is he dead?	Edw	5.2.98	Prince
Isabell is neerer then the earle of Kent.	Edw	5.2.115	Queene
Sister, Edward is my charge, redeeme him.	Edw	5.2.116	Kent
Edward is my sonne, and I will keepe him.	Edw	5.2.117	Queene
Whose sight is loathsome to all winged fowles?	Edw	5.3.7	Edward
It is the chiefest marke they levell at.	Edw	5.3.12	Edward
Within a dungeon Englands king is kept,	Edw	5.3.19	Edward
My daily diet, is heart breaking sobs,	Edw	5.3.21	Edward
Heeres channell water, as our charge is given.	Edw	5.3.27	Matrvs
Why strive you thus? your labour is in vaine.	Edw	5.3.33	Matrvs
O Gaveston, it is for thee that I am wrongd,	Edw	5.3.41	Edward
Guarde the king sure, it is the earle of Kent.	Edw	5.3.50	Matrvs

IS (cont.)

Where is the court but heere, heere is the king,	Edw		5.3.59		Kent
The court is where lord Mortimer remaines,	Edw		5.3.61		Matrvs
O miserable is that commonweale,	Edw		5.3.63		Kent
Yet he that is the cause of Edwards death,	Edw		5.4.3		Mortmr
Is sure to pay for it when his sonne is of age,	Edw		5.4.4		Mortmr
Unpointed as it is, thus shall it goe,	Edw		5.4.13		Mortmr
Within this roome is lockt the messenger,	Edw		5.4.17		Mortmr
Shall he be murdered when the deed is done.	Edw		5.4.20		Mortmr
Or whilst one is a sleepe, to take a quill/And blowe a little	Edw		5.4.34		Ltborn
I care not how it is, so it be not spide:	Edw		5.4.40		Mortmr
Saying it is, onus quam gravissimum,	Edw		5.4.61		Mortmr
Now is all sure, the Queene and Mortimer/Shall rule the realme,	Edw		5.4.65		Mortmr
Mortimer, I did, he is our king,	Edw		5.4.87		Kent
My lord, he is my unckle, and shall live.	Edw		5.4.91		King
My lord, he is your enemie, and shall die.	Edw		5.4.92		Mortmr
Either my brother or his sonne is king,	Edw		5.4.106		Kent
He is a traitor, thinke not on him, come.	Edw		5.4.115		Queene
Heere is the keyes, this is the lake,/Doe as you are commaunded	Edw		5.5.25		Matrvs
Whose there, what light is that, wherefore comes thou?	Edw		5.5.42		Edward
Farre is it from my hart to do you harme,	Edw		5.5.47		Ltborn
And then thy heart, were it as Gurneys is,	Edw		5.5.53		Edward
This dungeon where they keepe me, is the sincke,	Edw		5.5.56		Edward
I feele a hell of greefe: where is my crowne?	Edw		5.5.90		Edward
This feare is that which makes me tremble thus,	Edw		5.5.105		Edward
Gurney, my lord, is fled, and will I feare,	Edw		5.6.7		Matrvs
What if he have? the king is yet a childe.	Edw		5.6.17		Mortmr
Into the councell chamber he is gone,	Edw		5.6.20		Queene
Who is the man dare say I murdered him?	Edw		5.6.40		Mortmr
A Mortimer, thou knowest that he is slaine,	Edw		5.6.50		King
that in thy wheele/There is a point, to which when men aspire,	Edw		5.6.60		Mortmr
That rumor is untrue, for loving thee,	Edw		5.6.74		Queene
Is this report raisde on poore Isabell.	Edw		5.6.75		Queene
My lord, here is the head of Mortimer.	Edw		5.6.93		1Lord
of love/In Courts of Kings, where state is over-turn'd,	F	4	Prol.4		1Chor
Now is he borne, of parents base of stocke,	F	11	Prol.11		1Chor
Nothing so sweet as Magicke is to him,	F	26	Prol.26		1Chor
Is to dispute well Logickes chiefest end?	F	36	1.1.8		Faust
The end of Physicke is our bodies health:	F	45	1.1.17		Faust
[Is not thy common talke sound Aphorismes]?	F	47	1.1.19A		Faust
Physicke farewell: where is Justinian?	F	55	1.1.27		Faust
Such is the subject of the Institute,	F	59	1.1.31		Faust
When all is done, Divinitie is best:	F	64	1.1.36		Faust
The reward of sin is death? that's hard:	F	67	1.1.39		Faust
we deceive our selves, and there is <theres> no truth in us.	F	70	1.1.42	P	Faust
Is promised to the Studious Artizan?	F	82	1.1.54		Faust
A sound Magitian is a Demi-god <mighty god>,	F	89	1.1.61		Faust
Reade, reade the Scriptures: that is blasphemy.	F	100	1.1.72		GdAngl
Art/Wherein all natures [treasury] <treasure> is contain'd:	F	102	1.1.74		BdAngl
Be thou on earth as Jove is in the skye,	F	103	1.1.75		BdAngl
Philosophy is odious and obscure,	F	133	1.1.105		Faust
[Divinitie is basest of the three],	F	135	1.1.107A		Faust
He that is grounded in Astrology,	F	165	1.1.137		Cornel
And whatsoever else is requisite,	F	183	1.1.155		Valdes
Go to sirra, leave your jesting, and tell us where he is.	F	201	1.2.8	P	1Schol
For is he not Corpus naturale?	F	207	1.2.14	P	Wagner
and is not that Mobile?	F	208	1.2.15	P	Wagner
my Maister is within at dinner, with Valdes and Cornelius,	F	215	1.2.22	P	Wagner
That thou art <he is> falne into that damned Art/For which they	F	221	1.2.28		1Schol
Within this circle is Jehova's Name,	F	236	1.3.8		Faust
How pliant is this Mephostophilis?	F	257	1.3.29		Faust
Such is the force of Magicke, and my spels.	F	259	1.3.31		Faust
Whereby he is in danger to be damn'd:	F	279	1.3.51		Mephst
conjuring/Is stoutly to abjure [the Trinity] <all godlinesse>,	F	281	1.3.53		Mephst
There is no chiefe but onely Beelzebub:	F	284	1.3.56		Faust
Tell me, what is that Lucifer, thy Lord?	F	290	1.3.62		Faust
How comes it then that he is Prince of Devils?	F	294	1.3.66		Faust
Why this is hell: nor am I out of it.	F	304	1.3.76		Mephst
is great Mephostophilis so passionate/For being deprived of the	F	311	1.3.83		Faust
The god thou serv'st is thine owne appetite,	F	399	2.1.11		Faust
Wherein is fixt the love of Belzebub,	F	400	2.1.12		Faust
Is that the reason why he tempts us thus?	F	430	2.1.42		Faust
Is it unwilling I should write this byll?	F	454	2.1.66		Faust
Why shouldst thou not? is not thy soule thine owne?	F	457	2.1.69		Faust
See <come> Faustus, here is <heres> fire, set it on.	F	459	2.1.71		Mephst
this byll is ended,/And Faustus hath bequeath'd his soule to	F	463	2.1.75		Faust
But what is this Inscription on mine Arme?	F	465	2.1.77		Faust
I see it plaine, even heere <in this place> is writ/Homo fuge:	F	469	2.1.81		Faust
Tell me, where is the place that men call Hell?	F	505	2.1.117		Faust
Hell hath no limits, nor is circumscrib'd,	F	510	2.1.122		Mephst
but <for> where we are is hell,/And where hell is there must we	F	511	2.1.123		Mephst
And where hell is there must we ever be.	F	512	2.1.124		Mephst
All places shall be hell that is not heaven.	F	515	2.1.127		Mephst
Think'st thou that Faustus, is so fond to imagine,	F	522	2.1.134		Faust
That after this life there is any paine?	F	523	2.1.135		Faust
What sight is this?	F	532	2.1.144		Faust
<Tut Faustus>, Marriage is but a ceremoniall toy,	F	535	2.1.147		Mephst
<why Faustus> think'st thou heaven is such a glorious thing?	F	556	2.2.5		Mephst
I tell thee Faustus it is <tis> not halfe so faire/As thou, or	F	557	2.2.6		Mephst
was> made for man; then he's <therefore is man> more excellent.	F	560	2.2.9		Mephst
My heart is <hearts so> hardned, I cannot repent:	F	569	2.2.18		Faust
As is the substance of this centricke earth?	F	588	2.2.37		Faust
Whose termine <terminine>, is tearmed the worlds wide Pole.	F	593	2.2.42		Mephst

IS (cont.)

That the first is finisht in a naturall day?	F 603	2.2.52		Faust
But is there not Coelum igneum, [and] <&> <et> Christalinum?	F 612	2.2.61	P	Faust
I, that is not against our kingdome: <but> this is.	F 623	2.2.72	P	Mephst
Christ cannot save thy soule, for he is just,	F 636	2.2.85		Lucifr
And this is my companion Prince in hell.	F 640	2.2.89		Lucifr
But fye, what a smell <scent> is heere?	F 669	2.2.118	P	Pride
and that buyes me <is> thirty meales a day, and ten Beavers:	F 694	2.2.143	P	Glutny
[Tut] <But> Faustus, in hell is all manner of delight.	F 713	2.2.165		Lucifr
tell me, in good sadnesse Robin, is that a conjuring booke?	F 744	2.3.23	P	Dick
He now is gone to prove Cosmography,	F 773	2.3.52		2Chor
The which <That to> this day is highly solemnized.	F 778	2.3.57		2Chor
Whose frame is paved with sundry coloured stones,	F 797	3.1.19		Faust
But tell me now, what resting place is this?	F 800	3.1.22		Faust
This is the goodly Palace of the Pope:	F 804	3.1.26		Mephst
Erected is a Castle passing strong,	F 818	3.1.40		Mephst
This day is held through Rome and Italy,	F 834	3.1.56		Mephst
<Whose summum bonum is in belly-cheare>.	F 834	(HC265) A		Mephst
Is not all power on earth bestowed on us?	F 930	3.1.152		Pope
Behold this Silver Belt whereto is fixt/Seven golden [keys]	F 932	3.1.154		Pope
<holy> Synod/Of Priests and Prelates, it is thus decreed:	F 953	3.1.175		Faust
It is enough:	F 964	3.1.186		Pope
To censure Bruno, that is posted hence,	F 983	3.2.3		Mephst
I, pray do, for Faustus is a dry.	F1052	3.2.72		Faust
Purgatory, and now is come unto your holinesse for his pardon.	F1060	3.2.80	P	Archbp
me for the matter, for sure the cup is betweene you two.	F1107	3.3.20	P	Vintnr
[Now is his fame spread forth in every land],	F1149	3.3.62A		3Chor
[Amongst the rest the Emperour is one],	F1150	3.3.63A		3Chor
at whose pallace now]/[Faustus is feasted mongst his noblemen].	F1152	3.3.65A		3Chor
His Majesty is comming to the Hall;	F1158	4.1.4		Mrtino
But where is Bruno our elected Pope,	F1160	4.1.6		Fredrk
Where is Benvolio?	F1172	4.1.18		Fredrk
For Faustus at the Court is late arriv'd,	F1181	4.1.27		Mrtino
The Emperour is at hand, who comes to see/What wonders by	F1197	4.1.43		Mrtino
what strange beast is yon, that thrusts his head out at [the]	F1274	4.1.120	P	Faust
What, is he asleepe, or dead?	F1279	4.1.125		Saxony
This sport is excellent: wee'l call and wake him.	F1281	4.1.127		Emper
this [is] most horrible:	F1291	4.1.137	P	Faust
Zounds Doctor, is this your villany?	F1293	4.1.139	P	Benvol
By this (I know) the Conjurer is neere,	F1343	4.2.19		Benvol
My head is lighter then it was by th'hornes,	F1350	4.2.26		Benvol
Close, close, the Conjurer is at hand,	F1357	4.2.33		Fredrk
Strike with a willing hand, his head is off.	F1368	4.2.44		Mrtino
O help me gentle friend; where is Martino?	F1432	4.3.2		Fredrk
It is your owne you meane, feele on your head.	F1443	4.3.13		Fredrk
for your horse is turned to a bottle of Hay,--Maister Doctor.	F1490	4.4.34	P	HrsCsr
I pray you tell me, what is the thing you most desire to have?	F1567	4.6.10	P	Faust
were it now Summer, as it is January, a dead time of the Winter,	F1572	4.6.15	P	Lady
This is but a small matter:	F1574	4.6.17	P	Faust
when every Tree is barren of his fruite, from whence you had	F1579	4.6.22	P	Duke
the yeare is divided into two circles over the whole world, so	F1581	4.6.24	P	Faust
so that when it is Winter with us, in the contrary circle it is	F1582	4.6.25	P	Faust
in the contrary circle it is likewise Summer with them, as in	F1583	4.6.26	P	Faust
Why how now Maisters, what a coyle is there?	F1591	4.6.34		Servnt
What is the reason you disturbe the Duke?	F1592	4.6.35		Servnt
I, I, the house is good enough to drink in:	F1617	4.6.60	P	HrsCsr
and see where they come, belike the feast is done.	F1680	5.1.7	P	Wagner
For that I know your friendship is unfain'd,	F1689	5.1.16		Faust
<It is not Faustus custome> to deny	F1690	(HC269) B		Faust
[And] Faustus custome is not to deny/The just [requests]	F1690	5.1.17		Faust
Be silent then, for danger is in words.	F1696	5.1.23		Faust
Too simple is my wit to tell her worth <praise>,/Whom all the	F1697	5.1.24		2Schol
Saies Faustus come, thine houre is almost come,	F1727	5.1.54		Faust
Accursed Faustus, [where is mercy now]?	F1739	5.1.66		Faust
His faith is great, I cannot touch his soule;	F1756	5.1.83		Mephst
I will attempt, which is but little worth.	F1758	5.1.85		Mephst
Here will I dwell, for heaven is <be> in these lippes,	F1773	5.1.100		Faust
And all is drosse that is not Helena.	F1774	5.1.101		Faust
To wait upon thy soule; the time is come/Which makes it forfeit.	F1802	5.2.6		Lucifr
Is all our pleasure turn'd to melancholy?	F1828	5.2.32		2Schol
He is not well with being over solitarie.	F1829	5.2.33		3Schol
<Belike he is growne into some sicknesse, by> being over	F1829	(HC270) A	P	3Schol
to heaven, and remember [Gods] mercy is <mercies are> infinite.	F1836	5.2.40	P	2Schol
I writ them a bill with mine owne bloud, the date is expired:	F1861	5.2.65	P	Faust
this is the time <the time wil come>, and he will fetch mee.	F1861	5.2.65	P	Faust
if not, Faustus is gone to hell.	F1878	5.2.82	P	Faust
Is for ore-tortur'd soules to rest them in.	F1915	5.2.119		BdAngl
Where is it now?	F1943	5.2.147		Faust
[Ah] <O> halfe the houre is past:	F1957	5.2.161		Faust
<O> No end is limited to damned soules.	F1963	5.2.167		Faust
Or why is this immortall that thou hast?	F1965	5.2.169		Faust
Cut is the branch that might have growne full straight,	F2002	5.3.20		4Chor
And burned is Apollo's Lawrell bough,	F2003	5.3.21		4Chor
Faustus is gone, regard his hellish fall,	F2005	5.3.23		4Chor
in his nakednesse, the vilaine is bare, and out of service,	F App	p.229 7	P	Wagner
here is a daintie dish was sent me from the Bishop of Millaine.	F App	p.231 5	P	Pope
bleate, and an asse braye, because it is S. Peters holy day.	F App	p.232 28	P	Faust
O this is admirable!	F App	p.233 1	P	Robin
Why Robin what booke is that?	F App	p.233 18	P	Rafe
Drawer, I hope al is payd, God be with you, come Rafe.	F App	p.234 5	P	Robin
this therefore is my request, that thou let me see some proofe	F App	p.236 5	P	Emper
amongest which kings is Alexander the great, chiefe spectacle	F App	p.237 23	P	Emper

IS (cont.)

it is not in my abilitie to present before your eyes, the true	F App	p.237 41 P Faust
masse see where he is, God save you maister doctor.	F App	p.239 99 P HrsCsr
him have him, he is an honest felow, and he has a great charge,	F App	p.239 105 P Mephst
at ease, if I bring his water to you, youle tel me what it is?	F App	p.240 119 P HrsCsr
O yonder is his snipper snapper, do you heare?	F App	p.240 137 P HrsCsr
See where he is fast asleepe.	F App	p.241 147 P Mephst
I, this is he, God save ye maister doctor, maister doctor,	F App	p.241 148 P HrsCsr
What is he gone?	F App	p.241 164 P Faust
women do long for some dainties or other, what is it Madame?	F App	p.242 5 P Faust
nowe summer, as it is January, and the dead time of the winter,	F App	p.242 10 P Duchss
the yeere is divided into twoo circles over the whole worlde,	F App	p.242 19 P Faust
that when it is heere winter with us, in the contrary circle it	F App	p.242 20 P Faust
us, in the contrary circle it is summer with them, as in India,	F App	p.242 21 P Faust
See where they come: belike the feast is ended.	F App	p.243 8 Wagner
Yet Room is much bound to these civil armes,	Lucan, First Booke	44
The midst is best; that place is pure, and bright,	Lucan, First Booke	58
Yet he alone is held in reverence.	Lucan, First Booke	144
Caesar is thine, so please it thee, thy soldier;	Lucan, First Booke	204
Which issues from a small spring, is but shallow,	Lucan, First Booke	216
Now while their part is weake, and feares, march hence,	Lucan, First Booke	281
Is conquest got by civill war so hainous?	Lucan, First Booke	367
And frontier Varus that the campe is farre,	Lucan, First Booke	405
Which is nor sea, nor land, but oft times both,	Lucan, First Booke	411
And shame to spare life which being lost is wonne.	Lucan, First Booke	458
The world (were it together) is by cowards/Left as a pray now	Lucan, First Booke	511
At that bunch where the liver is, appear'd/A knob of flesh,	Lucan, First Booke	626
to unfould/What you intend, great Jove is now displeas'd,	Lucan, First Booke	631
The worlds swift course is lawlesse/And casuall; all the	Lucan, First Booke	641
Venus is faint; swift Hermes retrograde;	Lucan, First Booke	661
under Hemus mount/Philippi plaines; Phoebus what radge is this?	Lucan, First Booke	680
Then scarse can Phoebus say, this harpe is mine.	Ovid's Elegies	1.1.20
Oh woe is me, he never shootes but hits,	Ovid's Elegies	1.1.29
What makes my bed seem hard seeing it is soft?	Ovid's Elegies	1.2.1
Lets yeeld, a burden easly borne is light.	Ovid's Elegies	1.2.10
With armes to conquer armlesse men is base,	Ovid's Elegies	1.2.22
Take these away, where is thy <thine> honor then?	Ovid's Elegies	1.2.38
Ah howe thy lot is above my lot blest:	Ovid's Elegies	1.6.46
Silent the Cittie is:	Ovid's Elegies	1.6.55
The carefull prison is more meete for thee.	Ovid's Elegies	1.6.64
While rage is absent, take some friend the paynes.	Ovid's Elegies	1.7.2
Over my Mistris is my right more great?	Ovid's Elegies	1.7.30
There is, who ere will knowe a bawde aright/Give eare, there is	Ovid's Elegies	1.8.1
a bawde aright/Give eare, there is an old trot Dipsas hight.	Ovid's Elegies	1.8.2
starre of Mars hath done thee harme,/Now Mars is gone:	Ovid's Elegies	1.8.30
Such is his forme as may with thine compare,	Ovid's Elegies	1.8.33
Wrinckles in beauty is a grievous fault.	Ovid's Elegies	1.8.46
Beauty not exercisde with age is spent,	Ovid's Elegies	1.8.53
Many to rob is more sure, and lesse hatefull,	Ovid's Elegies	1.8.55
(Trust me) to give, it is a witty thing.	Ovid's Elegies	1.8.62
By many hands great wealth is quickly got.	Ovid's Elegies	1.8.92
Who but a souldiour or a lover is bould/To suffer storme mixt	Ovid's Elegies	1.9.15
Doubtfull is warre and love, the vanquisht rise/And who thou	Ovid's Elegies	1.9.29
Love is a naked boy, his yeares saunce staine,	Ovid's Elegies	1.10.15
Thy service for nights scapes is knowne commodious/And to give	Ovid's Elegies	1.11.3
commodious/And to give signes dull wit to thee is odious.	Ovid's Elegies	1.11.4
Bewaile my chaunce, the sad booke is returned,	Ovid's Elegies	1.12.1
The aire is colde, and sleepe is sweetest now,	Ovid's Elegies	1.13.7
The painfull Hinde by thee to field is sent,	Ovid's Elegies	1.13.15
Then thinkest thou thy loose life is not showne?	Ovid's Elegies	1.13.34
Envie, why carpest thou my time is spent so ill,	Ovid's Elegies	1.15.1
Thy scope is mortall, mine eternall fame,	Ovid's Elegies	1.15.7
While Rome of all the [conquered] <conquering> world is head.	Ovid's Elegies	1.15.26
Verse is immortall, and shall nere decay.	Ovid's Elegies	1.15.32
Nor is her husband wise, what needes defence/When	Ovid's Elegies	2.2.11
defence/When [un-protected] <un-protested> ther is no expence?	Ovid's Elegies	2.2.12
flying touch/Tantalus seekes, his long tongues gaine is such.	Ovid's Elegies	2.2.44
Nor is it easily prov'd though manifest,	Ovid's Elegies	2.2.55
Condemne his eyes, and say there is no tryall.	Ovid's Elegies	2.2.58
Good forme there is, yeares apt to play togither,	Ovid's Elegies	2.3.13
Unmeete is beauty without use to wither.	Ovid's Elegies	2.3.14
[Is she attired, then shew her graces best].	Ovid's Elegies	2.4.38
[Amber] <Yellow> trest is shee, then on the morne thinke I,/My	Ovid's Elegies	2.4.43
A yong wench pleaseth, and an old is good,	Ovid's Elegies	2.4.45
Nay what is she that any Romane loves,	Ovid's Elegies	2.4.47
No love is so dere (quiverd Cupid flie)/That my chiefe wish	Ovid's Elegies	2.5.1
Alas a wench is a perpetuall evill.	Ovid's Elegies	2.5.4
Aye me poore soule, why is my cause so good.	Ovid's Elegies	2.5.8
Such blisse is onely common to us two,	Ovid's Elegies	2.5.31
Is dead, al-fowles her exequies frequent.	Ovid's Elegies	2.6.2
[Itis is] <It is as> great, but auntient cause of sorrowe.	Ovid's Elegies	2.6.10
Dead is that speaking image of mans voice,	Ovid's Elegies	2.6.37
One among many is to grieve thee tooke.	Ovid's Elegies	2.7.4
Is charg'd to violate her mistresse bed.	Ovid's Elegies	2.7.18
Should I sollicit her that is so just:	Ovid's Elegies	2.7.25
Live without love, so sweete ill is a maide.	Ovid's Elegies	2.9.26
Haples is he that all the night lies quiet/And slumbring,	Ovid's Elegies	2.9.39
Foole, what is sleepe but image of cold death,	Ovid's Elegies	2.9.41
Which is the loveliest it is hard to say:	Ovid's Elegies	2.10.6
Yet this is better farre then lie alone,	Ovid's Elegies	2.10.15
And he is happy whom the earth holds, say.	Ovid's Elegies	2.11.30
It is more safe to sleepe, to read a booke,	Ovid's Elegies	2.11.31
Nor is my warres cause new, but for a Queene/Europe, and Asia	Ovid's Elegies	2.12.17

IS (cont.)

By seaven huge mouthes into the sea is [skipping] <slipping>,	Ovid's Elegies	2.13.10
Worthy she is, thou shouldst in mercy save her.	Ovid's Elegies	2.13.22
Life is no light price of a small surcease.	Ovid's Elegies	2.14.26
Shee dyes, and with loose haires to grave is sent,	Ovid's Elegies	2.14.39
Wherein is seene the givers loving minde:	Ovid's Elegies	2.15.2
Fit her so well, as she is fit for me:	Ovid's Elegies	2.15.5
But absent is my fire, lyes ile tell none,	Ovid's Elegies	2.16.11
My heate is heere, what moves my heate is gone.	Ovid's Elegies	2.16.12
Aye me why is it knowne to her so well?	Ovid's Elegies	2.17.8
Love-snarde Calypso is supposde to pray,	Ovid's Elegies	2.17.15
This kinde of verse is not alike, yet fit,	Ovid's Elegies	2.17.21
What lawfull is, or we professe Loves art,	Ovid's Elegies	2.18.19
Phedra, and Hipolite may read, my care is,	Ovid's Elegies	2.18.24
Is golden love hid in Mars mid alarmes.	Ovid's Elegies	2.18.36
There Paris is, and Helens crymes record,	Ovid's Elegies	2.18.37
Cruell is he, that loves whom none protect.	Ovid's Elegies	2.19.4
What ever haps, by suffrance harme is done,	Ovid's Elegies	2.19.35
And this is he whom fierce love burnes, they cry.	Ovid's Elegies	3.1.20
And by those numbers is thy first youth spent.	Ovid's Elegies	3.1.28
What horse-driver thou favourst most is best,	Ovid's Elegies	3.2.7
By thy sides touching ill she is entreated.	Ovid's Elegies	3.2.22
Or is my heate, of minde, not of the skie?	Ovid's Elegies	3.2.39
The shout is nigh; the golden pompe comes heere.	Ovid's Elegies	3.2.44
First Victory is brought with large spred wing,	Ovid's Elegies	3.2.45
Peace pleaseth me, and in mid peace is love.	Ovid's Elegies	3.2.50
He holdes the palme: my palme is yet to gaine.	Ovid's Elegies	3.2.82
Her foote was small: her footes forme is most fit:	Ovid's Elegies	3.3.7
God is a name, no substance, feard in vaine,	Ovid's Elegies	3.3.23
Who, without feare, is chaste, is chast in sooth:	Ovid's Elegies	3.4.3
Though thou her body guard, her minde is staind:	Ovid's Elegies	3.4.5
All being shut out, th'adulterer is within.	Ovid's Elegies	3.4.8
How to attaine, what is denyed, we thinke,	Ovid's Elegies	3.4.17
She is not chaste, that's kept, but a deare whore:	Ovid's Elegies	3.4.29
Thy feare is, then her body, valued more.	Ovid's Elegies	3.4.30
Although thou chafe, stolne pleasure is sweet play,	Ovid's Elegies	3.4.31
He is too clownish, whom a lewd wife grieves,	Ovid's Elegies	3.4.37
Is by Evadne thought to take such flame,	Ovid's Elegies	3.5.41
That were as white as is <Her armes farre whiter, then> the	Ovid's Elegies	3.6.8
Seeing <when> in my prime my force is spent and done?	Ovid's Elegies	3.6.18
What sweete thought is there but I had the same?	Ovid's Elegies	3.6.63
Ah whether is [thy] <they> brests soft nature [fled] <sled>?	Ovid's Elegies	3.7.18
father Phoebus layed/To sing with his unequald harpe is sayed.	Ovid's Elegies	3.8.24
Pierian deawe to Poets is distild.	Ovid's Elegies	3.8.26
By secreat thoughts to thinke there is a god.	Ovid's Elegies	3.8.36
Nor is she, though she loves the fertile fields,	Ovid's Elegies	3.9.17
Why am I sad, when Proserpine is found,	Ovid's Elegies	3.9.45
Yet this is lesse, then if he had seene me,	Ovid's Elegies	3.10.15
Or is I thinke my wish against the [starres] <starre>?	Ovid's Elegies	3.11.3
I feare with me is common now to many.	Ovid's Elegies	3.11.6
Erre I? or by my [bookes] <lookes> is she so knowne?	Ovid's Elegies	3.11.7
'Tis so: by my witte her abuse is growne.	Ovid's Elegies	3.11.8
The wench by my fault is set forth to sell.	Ovid's Elegies	3.11.10
Her gate by my hands is set open wide.	Ovid's Elegies	3.11.12
Poets large power is boundlesse, and immense,	Ovid's Elegies	3.11.41
Who sees it, graunts some deity there is shrowded.	Ovid's Elegies	3.12.8
Is said to have attempted flight forsooke.	Ovid's Elegies	3.12.20
Now is the goat brought through the boyes with darts,	Ovid's Elegies	3.12.21
As is the use, the Nunnes in white veyles clad,	Ovid's Elegies	3.12.27
The bed is for lascivious toyings meete,	Ovid's Elegies	3.13.17
From him that yeelds the garland <palme> is quickly got,	Ovid's Elegies	3.13.47
This last end to my Elegies is set,	Ovid's Elegies	3.14.2
A greater ground with great horse is to till.	Ovid's Elegies	3.14.18
But this is true, so like was one the other,	Hero and Leander	1.39
Even as delicious meat is to the tast,	Hero and Leander	1.63
for the lovely boy/That now is turn'd into a Cypres tree,	Hero and Leander	1.155
For will in us is over-rul'd by fate.	Hero and Leander	1.168
What we behold is censur'd by our eies.	Hero and Leander	1.174
Where both deliberat, the love is slight,	Hero and Leander	1.175
Love deepely grounded, hardly is dissembled.	Hero and Leander	1.184
True love is mute, and oft amazed stands.	Hero and Leander	1.186
Breath'd darkenesse forth (darke night is Cupids day).	Hero and Leander	1.191
Then shouldst thou bee his prisoner who is thine.	Hero and Leander	1.202
Then treasure is abus'de,/When misers keepe it; being put to	Hero and Leander	1.234
Well therefore by the gods decreed it is,	Hero and Leander	1.253
One is no number, mayds are nothing then,	Hero and Leander	1.255
Is neither essence subject to the eie,	Hero and Leander	1.270
What vertue is it that is borne with us?	Hero and Leander	1.278
Honour is purchac'd by the deedes wee do.	Hero and Leander	1.280
Beleeve me Hero, honour is not wone,	Hero and Leander	1.281
Whose name is it, if she be false or not,	Hero and Leander	1.285
Beautie alone is lost, too warily kept.	Hero and Leander	1.328
Far from the towne (where all is whist and still,	Hero and Leander	1.346
that dwels/In tow'red courts, is oft in sheapheards cels).	Hero and Leander	1.394
Wherewith the king of Gods and men is feasted.	Hero and Leander	1.432
Which being knowne (as what is hid from Jove)?	Hero and Leander	1.436
And to this day is everie scholler poore,	Hero and Leander	1.471
For from the earth to heaven, is Cupid rais'd,	Hero and Leander	2.31
Where fancie is in equall ballance pais'd).	Hero and Leander	2.32
Is swifter than the wind, whose tardie plumes,	Hero and Leander	2.115
Affection by the count'nance is descride.	Hero and Leander	2.132
And love that is conceal'd, betraies poore lovers.	Hero and Leander	2.134
The more he is restrain'd, the woorse he fares,	Hero and Leander	2.145

IS (cont.)			
What is it now, but mad Leander dares?	Hero and Leander	2.146	
(Love is too full of faith, too credulous,	Hero and Leander	2.221	
Which is with azure circling lines empal'd,	Hero and Leander	2.274	
Love is not ful of pittie (as men say)/But deaffe and cruell,	Hero and Leander	2.287	
ISABELL			
How deare my lord is to poore Isabell.	Edw	1.4.166	Queene
And when this favour Isabell forgets,	Edw	1.4.297	Queene
For Gaveston, but not for Isabell.	Edw	1.4.326	Queene
O how a kisse revives poore Isabell.	Edw	1.4.333	Queene
I Isabell, nere was my heart so light.	Edw	1.4.368	Edward
Your pardon is quicklie got of Isabell.	Edw	2.2.231	Queene
No farewell, to poore Isabell, thy Queene?	Edw	2.4.13	Queene
As Isabell could live with thee for ever.	Edw	2.4.60	Queene
all aide may be denied/To Isabell the Queene, that now in	Edw	3.1.269	Spencr
That Isabell shall make her plaints in vaine,	Edw	3.1.278	Levune
Unhappie Isabell, when Fraunce rejects,	Edw	4.2.11	Queene
As Isabella <Isabell> gets no aide from thence.	Edw	4.3.16	Edward
diest, for Mortimer/And Isabell doe kisse while they conspire,	Edw	4.6.13	Kent
God save Queene Isabell, and her princely sonne.	Edw	4.6.46	Rice
Tis in the name of Isabell the Queene:	Edw	4.7.59	Leistr
And that unnaturall Queene false Isabell,	Edw	5.1.17	Edward
That Mortimer and Isabell have done.	Edw	5.1.25	Edward
Then send for unrelenting Mortimer/And Isabell, whose eyes	Edw	5.1.104	Edward
Faire Isabell, now have we our desire,	Edw	5.2.1	Mortmr
Sweet Mortimer, the life of Isabell,	Edw	5.2.15	Queene
Isabell is neerer then the earle of Kent.	Edw	5.2.115	Queene
And give my heart to Isabell and him,	Edw	5.3.11	Edward
It pleaseth me, and Isabell the Queene.	Edw	5.4.71	Mortmr
Tell Isabell the Queene, I lookt not thus,	Edw	5.5.68	Edward
Is this report raisde on poore Isabell.	Edw	5.6.75	Queene
ISABELLA			
Witnesse the teares that Isabella sheds,	Edw	1.4.164	Queene
As Isabella <Isabell> gets no aide from thence.	Edw	4.3.16	Edward
ISABELLAS			
Comes Leister then in Isabellas name,	Edw	4.7.64	Edward
ISARA			
And many came from shallow Isara,	Lucan, First Booke	400	
ISIS			
And Isis now will shew what scuse to make.	Ovid's Elegies	1.8.74	
Enquire not what with Isis may be done/Nor feare least she to	Ovid's Elegies	2.2.25	
ISLAND (See also ILAND)			
them seeme as black/As is the Island where the Furies maske,	2Tamb	3.2.12	Tamb
ISLE (See also ILE, ILES)			
Shall lie at anchor in the Isle Asant,	1Tamb	3.3.251	Tamb
My Lord and King hath title to this Isle,	Jew	2.2.37	Bosco
ISLES			
[Trading] <Treading> by land unto the Westerne Isles,	1Tamb	1.1.38	Meandr
East India and the late discovered Isles,	1Tamb	1.1.166	Ortyg
Where twixt the Isles of Cyprus and of Creete,	2Tamb	1.2.26	Callap
About the Grecian Isles to rob and spoile:	2Tamb	3.5.94	Jrslem
ISRAEL			
piller led'st/The sonnes of Israel through the dismall shades,	Jew	2.1.13	Barab
ISSUE			
That I may see him issue Conquerour.	1Tamb	3.3.194	Zenoc
So for a finall Issue to my griefes,	1Tamb	5.1.395	Zenoc
To see the king my Father issue safe,	1Tamb	5.1.441	Zenoc
of these Eastern parts/Plac'd by the issue of great Bajazeth,	2Tamb	1.1.2	Orcan
and thy seed/Shall issue crowned from their mothers wombe.	2Tamb	1.1.134	Sgsmnd
And not the issue of great Tamburlaine:	2Tamb	1.3.53	Tamb
And issue sodainly upon the rest:	2Tamb	1.3.70	Tamb
Then arme my Lords, and issue sodainly,	2Tamb	2.1.23	Fredrk
Nor [any] issue foorth, but they shall die:	2Tamb	2.1.60	Sgsmnd
But Shepheards issue, base borne Tamburlaine,	2Tamb	3.3.33	Techel
the shepheards issue, at whose byrth/Heaven did affoord a	2Tamb	3.5.77	Orcan
In sending to my issue such a soule,	2Tamb	3.5.79	Tamb
Then issue out and come to rescue me,	2Tamb	4.1.122	Tamb
At which they all shall issue out and set the streetes.	Jew	5.4.5	Govnr
And slay his servants that shall issue out.	P 237	4.35	Guise
the lovelie Elenor of Spaine,/Great Edward Longshankes issue:	P 299	5.26	Anjoy
My limbes may issue from your smoky mouthes,	Edw	3.1.12	Spencr
Against her kind (the barren Mules loth'd issue)/To be cut	F1955	5.2.159	Faust
	Lucan, First Booke	589	
ISSUED			
That erst-while issued from thy watrie loynes,	Dido	1.1.128	Venus
But that I knew they issued from thy wombe,	2Tamb	1.3.33	Tamb
ISSUES			
From whence the issues of my thoughts doe breake:	1Tamb	5.1.274	Bajzth
Which issues from a small spring, is but shallow,	Lucan, First Booke	216	
ISSUINGS			
And secret issuings to defend the ditch.	2Tamb	3.2.74	Tamb
IS'T			
Oh, is't the custome, then I am resolv'd:	Jew	2.3.329	Lodowk
Well, sirra, what is't?	Jew	3.3.31	Abigal
Is't not too late now to turne Christian?	Jew	4.1.50	Barab
What time a night is't now, sweet Ithimore?	Jew	4.1.157	Barab
Is't not a sweet fac'd youth, Pilia?	Jew	4.2.40	P Curtzn
And is't not possible to find it out?	Jew	4.2.60	Pilia
No Robin, why is't?	F1510	4.5.6	P Dick
Nor is't of earth or mold celestiall,	Hero and Leander	1.273	
IST			
What ist sweet wagge I should deny thy youth?	Dido	1.1.23	Jupitr
Ist not enough, that thou corrupts my lord,	Edw	1.4.150	Queene

IST (cont.)			
Who have we there, ist you?	Edw	2.2.140	Edward
What would you with the king, ist him you seek?	Edw	2.4.31	Queene
Holla, who walketh there, ist you my lord?	Edw	4.1.12	Mortmr
Ist done, Matrevis, and the murtherer dead?	Edw	5.6.1	Mortmr
Ist not midnight? come Mephostophilis <Mephastophilis>.	F 417	2.1.29	Faust
Ist not too late?	F 629	2.2.78	Faust
In wooddie groves ist meete that Ceres Raigne,	Ovid's Elegies		1.1.13
or ist sleepe forbids thee heare,/Giving the windes my words	Ovid's Elegies		1.6.41
Ist womens love my captive brest doth frie?	Ovid's Elegies		3.2.40
Yet better ist, then if Corcyras Ile/Had thee unknowne interr'd	Ovid's Elegies		3.8.47
What madnesse ist to tell night <nights> prankes by day,	Ovid's Elegies		3.13.7
ISTAM			
et istam/Oro, si quis [adhuc] <ad haec> precibus locus,	Dido	5.1.137	Dido
ISTE			
See how he must be handled for his labour,/Pereat iste:	Edw	5.5.24	Matrvs
ISTHMOS			
even as the slender Isthmos,/Betwixt the Aegean and the Ionian	Lucan, First Booke		100
IT			
I, this is it, you can sit toying there,	Dido	1.1.50	Venus
Or whether men or beasts inhabite it.	Dido	1.1.177	Aeneas
It is the use for [Tirien] <Turen> maides to weare/Their bowe	Dido	1.1.204	Venus
It is the Punick kingdome rich and strong,	Dido	1.1.210	Venus
And when I know it is not, then I dye.	Dido	2.1.9	Aeneas
And would my prayers (as Pigmalions did)/Could give it life,	Dido	2.1.17	Aeneas
Then would it leape out to give Priam life:	Dido	2.1.27	Aeneas
Thy mind Aeneas that would have it so/Deludes thy eye sight,	Dido	2.1.31	Achat
For were it Priam he would smile on me.	Dido	2.1.36	Ascan
It is our Captaine, see Ascanius.	Dido	2.1.52	Cloan
May it please your grace to let Aeneas waite:	Dido	2.1.87	Aeneas
Ile have it so, Aeneas be content.	Dido	2.1.95	Dido
Lyes it in Didos hands to make thee blest,	Dido	2.1.103	Dido
We were commanded straight/With reverence to draw it into Troy.	Dido	2.1.168	Aeneas
These hands did helpe to hale it to the gates,	Dido	2.1.170	Aeneas
Through which it could not enter twas so huge.	Dido	2.1.171	Aeneas
O had it never entred, Troy had stood.	Dido	2.1.172	Aeneas
And dipt it in the old Kings chill cold bloud,	Dido	2.1.260	Aeneas
My cosin Helen taught it me in Troy.	Dido	3.1.28	Cupid
Take it Ascanius, for thy fathers sake.	Dido	3.1.33	Dido
No Madame, but it seemes that these are Kings.	Dido	3.1.149	Aeneas
Because it may be thou shalt be my love:	Dido	3.1.170	Dido
Yet boast not of it, for I love thee not,	Dido	3.1.171	Dido
Shall finde it written on confusions front,	Dido	3.2.19	Juno
Why is it then displeasure should disjoyne,	Dido	3.2.30	Juno
Bootles I sawe it was to warre with fate,	Dido	3.2.49	Juno
Be it as you will have [it] for this once,	Dido	3.2.97	Venus
I, this it is which wounds me to the death,	Dido	3.3.63	Iarbus
Why, what is it that Dido may desire/And not obtaine, be it in	Dido	3.4.7	Aeneas
that Dido may desire/And not obtaine, be it in humaine power?	Dido	3.4.8	Aeneas
It is not ought Aeneas may atchieve?	Dido	3.4.11	Aeneas
I must conceale/The torment, that it bootes me not reveale,/And	Dido	3.4.26	Dido
Something it was that now I have forgot.	Dido	3.4.30	Dido
It was because I sawe no King like thee,	Dido	3.4.35	Dido
It haild, it snowde, it lightned all at once.	Dido	4.1.8	Anna
I thinke it was the divels revelling night,	Dido	4.1.9	Achat
That doe pursue my peace where ere it goes.	Dido	4.2.51	Iarbus
Jove wils it so, my mother wils it so:	Dido	4.3.5	Aeneas
It may be he will steale away with them:	Dido	4.4.3	Dido
And fanne it in Aeneas lovely face,	Dido	4.4.49	Dido
I, but it may be he will leave my love,	Dido	4.4.97	Dido
I cannot see him frowne, it may not be:	Dido	4.4.112	Dido
It is Aeneas frowne that ends my daies:	Dido	4.4.120	Dido
Why did it suffer thee to touch her breast,	Dido	4.4.145	Dido
Was it not you that hoysed up these sailes?	Dido	4.4.153	Dido
But what shall it be calde, Troy as before?	Dido	5.1.18	Illion
Let it be term'd Aenea by your name.	Dido	5.1.20	Cloan
Nay, I will have it calde Anchisaeon,	Dido	5.1.22	Aeneas
If it be so, his father meanes to flye:	Dido	5.1.85	Dido
It is Aeneas calles Aeneas hence,	Dido	5.1.132	Dido
Which if it chaunce, Ile give ye buriall,	Dido	5.1.176	Dido
That I may learne to beare it patiently,	Dido	5.1.208	Dido
For it requires a great and thundring speech:	1Tamb	1.1.3	Mycet
I meane it not, but yet I know I might,	1Tamb	1.1.26	Mycet
Yet live, yea, live, Mycetes wils it so:	1Tamb	1.1.27	Mycet
Therefore tis best, if so it lik you all,	1Tamb	1.1.51	Mycet
Is it not a kingly resolution?	1Tamb	1.1.55	Mycet
It cannot choose, because it comes from you.	1Tamb	1.1.56	Cosroe
You may doe well to kisse it then.	1Tamb	1.1.98	Cosroe
But this it is that doth excruciate/The verie substance of my	1Tamb	1.1.113	Cosroe
And vow to weare it for my countries good:	1Tamb	1.1.158	Cosroe
I know it wel my Lord, and thanke you all.	1Tamb	1.1.187	Cosroe
Till men and kingdomes help to strengthen it:	1Tamb	1.2.30	Tamb
(I cal it meane, because being yet obscure,	1Tamb	1.2.203	Tamb
We thinke it losse to make exchange for that/We are assured of	1Tamb	1.2.216	Techel
Making it daunce with wanton majestie:	1Tamb	2.1.26	Menaph
Proud is his fortune if we pierce it not.	1Tamb	2.1.44	Cosroe
Would it not grieve a King to be so abusde,	1Tamb	2.2.5	Mycet
I thinke it would:	1Tamb	2.2.9	Mycet
Which make reports it far exceeds the Kings.	1Tamb	2.2.42	Spy
And while the base borne Tartars take it up,	1Tamb	2.2.65	Meandr
That it may reach the King of Perseas crowne,	1Tamb	2.3.53	Cosroe
And set it safe on my victorious head.	1Tamb	2.3.54	Cosroe
See where it is, the keenest Cutle-axe <curtle-axe>,/That ere	1Tamb	2.3.55	Tamb

IT (cont.)

These are the wings shall make it flie as swift,	1Tamb	2.3.57		Tamb
And kill as sure as it swiftly flies.	1Tamb	2.3.59		Tamb
Therefore in pollicie I thinke it good/To hide it close:	1Tamb	2.4.10		Mycet
Therefore in pollicie I thinke it good/To hide it close:	1Tamb	2.4.11		Mycet
Here will I hide it in this simple hole.	1Tamb	2.4.15		Mycet
You will not sell it, wil ye?	1Tamb	2.4.29		Tamb
Come give it me.	1Tamb	2.4.31		Mycet
No, I tooke it prisoner.	1Tamb	2.4.32		Tamb
You lie, I gave it you.	1Tamb	2.4.33		Mycet
No, I meane, I let you keep it.	1Tamb	2.4.35		Mycet
Wel, I meane you shall have it againe.	1Tamb	2.4.36		Tamb
Here take it for a while, I lend it thee,	1Tamb	2.4.37		Tamb
Then shalt thou see me pull it from thy head:	1Tamb	2.4.39		Tamb
I marveile much he stole it not away.	1Tamb	2.4.42		Mycet
And sought your state all honor it deserv'd,	1Tamb	2.5.33		Ortyg
Indevor to preserve and prosper it.	1Tamb	2.5.35		Ortyg
Is it not brave to be a King, Techelles?	1Tamb	2.5.51		Tamb
Is it not passing brave to be a King,	1Tamb	2.5.53		Tamb
Whose vertues carie with it life and death,	1Tamb	2.5.61		Therid
Nay, though I praise it, I can live without it.	1Tamb	2.5.66		Therid
I could attaine it with a woondrous ease,	1Tamb	2.5.77		Tamb
Yet will I weare it in despight of them,	1Tamb	2.7.61		Tamb
So, now it is more surer on my head,	1Tamb	2.7.65		Tamb
Although it be digested long agoe,	1Tamb	3.2.9		Zenoc
As it hath chang'd my first conceiv'd disdaine.	1Tamb	3.2.12		Zenoc
He bids you prophesie what it imports.	1Tamb	3.2.89		Techel
It saies, Agydas, thou shalt surely die,	1Tamb	3.2.95		Agidas
More honor and lesse paine it may procure,	1Tamb	3.2.97		Agidas
Faith, and Techelles, it was manly done:	1Tamb	3.2.109		Usumc
I speake it, and my words are oracles.	1Tamb	3.3.102		Tamb
It might amaze your royall majesty.	1Tamb	4.1.16		2Msngr
And poure it in this glorious Tyrants throat.	1Tamb	4.2.7		Bajzth
Then it should so conspire my overthrow.	1Tamb	4.2.11		Tamb
And make it swallow both of us at once.	1Tamb	4.2.29		Bajzth
It shall be said, I made it red my selfe,	1Tamb	4.2.54		Tamb
That will maintaine it against a world of Kings.	1Tamb	4.2.81		Tamb
This is my minde, and I will have it so.	1Tamb	4.2.91		Tamb
Shall not defend it from our battering shot.	1Tamb	4.2.107		Tamb
Because it is my countries, and my Fathers.	1Tamb	4.2.124		Zenoc
My Lord it is the bloody Tamburlaine,	1Tamb	4.3.11		Souldn
It is a blemish to the Majestie/And high estate of mightie	1Tamb	4.3.19		Souldn
Confirming it with Ibis holy name,	1Tamb	4.3.37		Souldn
And squease it in the cup of Tamburlain.	1Tamb	4.4.20		Bajzth
highnesse would let them be fed, it would doe them more good.	1Tamb	4.4.34	P	Therid
take it from my swords point, or Ile thrust it to thy heart.	1Tamb	4.4.40	P	Tamb
take it from my swords point, or Ile thrust it to thy heart.	1Tamb	4.4.41	P	Tamb
He stamps it under his feet my Lord.	1Tamb	4.4.42	P	Therid
Take it up Villaine, and eat it, or I will make thee slice the	1Tamb	4.4.43	P	Tamb
and eat it, or I will make thee slice the brawnes of thy armes	1Tamb	4.4.43	P	Tamb
Tis like he wil, when he cannot let it.	1Tamb	4.4.53	P	Techel
but why is it?	1Tamb	4.4.64	P	Tamb
How can it but afflict my verie soule?	1Tamb	4.4.67		Zenoc
So it would my lord, specially having so smal a walke, and so	1Tamb	4.4.105	P	Therid
But how unseemly is it for my Sex,	1Tamb	5.1.174		Tamb
in peeces, give me the sworde with a ball of wildefire upon it.	1Tamb	5.1.312	P	Zabina
As now it bringeth sweetnesse to my wound,	1Tamb	5.1.420		Arabia
And here in Affrick where it seldom raines,	1Tamb	5.1.457		Tamb
And make it quake at every drop it drinks:	1Tamb	5.1.462		Tamb
The Turk and his great Emperesse as it seems,	1Tamb	5.1.470		Tamb
And here's the crown my Lord, help set it on.	1Tamb	5.1.505		Usumc
If peace, restore it to my hands againe:	2Tamb	1.1.84		Sgsmnd
And I wil sheath it to confirme the same.	2Tamb	1.1.85		Sgsmnd
And made it dance upon the Continent:	2Tamb	1.1.88		Orcan
Then here I sheath it, and give thee my hand,	2Tamb	1.1.127		Sgsmnd
Never to draw it out, or manage armes/Against thy selfe or thy	2Tamb	1.1.128		Sgsmnd
But (Sigismond) confirme it with an oath,	2Tamb	1.1.131		Orcan
My Lord I pitie it, and with my heart/Wish your release, but he	2Tamb	1.2.5		Almeda
do cleare the clowdy aire/And cloath it in a christall liverie,	2Tamb	1.3.4		Tamb
I would prepare a ship and saile to it,	2Tamb	1.3.90		Celeb
Turkish Deputie/And all his Viceroies, snatch it from his head,	2Tamb	1.3.100		Tamb
To make it parcel of my Empery.	2Tamb	1.3.110		Tamb
It could not more delight me than your sight.	2Tamb	1.3.156		Tamb
What motion is it that inflames your thoughts,	2Tamb	2.1.2		Sgsmnd
It resteth now then that your Majesty/Take all advantages of	2Tamb	2.1.11		Fredrk
Go Uribassa, give it straight in charge.	2Tamb	2.3.40		Orcan
And wound the earth, that it may cleave in twaine,	2Tamb	2.4.97		Tamb
stature <statue>/And martch about it with my mourning campe,	2Tamb	2.4.141		Tamb
Whose cursed fate hath so dismembred it,	2Tamb	3.1.13		Callap
Will poure it downe in showers on our heads:	2Tamb	3.1.36		Callap
I thinke it requisite and honorable,	2Tamb	3.1.70		Callap
Forbids the world to build it up againe.	2Tamb	3.2.18		Calyph
It would not ease the sorrow I sustaine.	2Tamb	3.2.48		Calyph
It must have privy ditches, countermines,	2Tamb	3.2.73		Tamb
It must have high Argins and covered waies/To keep the bulwark	2Tamb	3.2.75		Tamb
A wound is nothing be it nere so deepe,	2Tamb	3.2.115		Tamb
I know not what I should think of it.	2Tamb	3.2.130	P	Calyph
Here father, cut it bravely as you did your own.	2Tamb	3.2.135	P	Celeb
It shall suffice thou darst abide a wound.	2Tamb	3.2.136		Tamb
Yes, my Lord, yes, come lets about it.	2Tamb	3.3.10		Soldrs
It may be they will yeeld it quietly,	2Tamb	3.3.12		Therid
To you? Why, do you thinke me weary of it?	2Tamb	3.3.17		Capt
And when we enter in, not heaven it selfe/Shall ransome thee,	2Tamb	3.3.27		Therid

IT (cont.)

And therefore Captaine, yeeld it quietly.	2Tamb	3.3.34		Techel
I would not yeeld it: therefore doo your worst.	2Tamb	3.3.37		Capt
Which til it may defend you, labour low:	2Tamb	3.3.44		Therid
And purge my soule before it come to thee.	2Tamb	3.4.33		Olymp
Drawing from it the shining Lamps of heaven.	2Tamb	3.4.77		Techel
What, take it man.	2Tamb	3.5.132	P	Orcan
Good my Lord, let me take it.	2Tamb	3.5.133	P	Almeda
Here, take it.	2Tamb	3.5.134	P	Callap
given so much to sleep/You cannot leave it, when our enemies	2Tamb	4.1.12		Amyras
I know sir, what it is to kil a man,	2Tamb	4.1.27		Calyph
It works remorse of conscience in me,	2Tamb	4.1.28		Calyph
I should be affraid, would put it off and come to bed with me.	2Tamb	4.1.70	P	Calyph
That they may say, it is not chance doth this,	2Tamb	4.1.84		Amyras
And glut it not with stale and daunted foes.	2Tamb	4.1.88		Tamb
Although it shine as brightly as the Sun.	2Tamb	4.1.134		Tamb
And Ile dispose them as it likes me best,	2Tamb	4.1.166		Tamb
Revenge it Radamanth and Eacus,	2Tamb	4.1.171		Orcan
What is it?	2Tamb	4.2.58		Therid
To proove it, I wil noint my naked throat,	2Tamb	4.2.68		Olymp
Why gave you not your husband some of it,	2Tamb	4.2.71		Therid
If you loved him, and it so precious?	2Tamb	4.2.72		Therid
My purpose was (my Lord) to spend it so,	2Tamb	4.2.73		Olymp
That I dissemble not, trie it on me.	2Tamb	4.2.76		Olymp
and will keep it for/The richest present of this Easterne	2Tamb	4.2.77		Therid
If you can live with it, then live, and draw/My chariot swifter	2Tamb	4.3.20		Tamb
It seemes they meant to conquer us my Lord,	2Tamb	4.3.88		Therid
But presently be prest to conquer it.	2Tamb	4.3.96		Techel
And wil defend it in despight of thee.	2Tamb	5.1.55		Govnr
Wel, now Ile make it quake, go draw him up,	2Tamb	5.1.107		Tamb
Save but my life and I wil give it thee.	2Tamb	5.1.118		Govnr
Where about lies it?	2Tamb	5.1.120		Tamb
That I may sheath it in this breast of mine,	2Tamb	5.1.143		Jrslem
I will about it straight, come Souldiers.	2Tamb	5.1.172		Techel
Let it be so, about it souldiers:	2Tamb	5.1.217		Tamb
What is it dares distemper Tamburlain?	2Tamb	5.1.219		Techel
But foorth ye vassals, what so ere it be,	2Tamb	5.1.221		Tamb
Or that it be rejoin'd again at full,	2Tamb	5.2.58		Callap
Assaile it and be sure of victorie.	2Tamb	5.2.59		Callap
And cannot last, it is so violent.	2Tamb	5.3.65		Techel
that the soule/Wanting those Organnons by which it mooves,	2Tamb	5.3.96		Phsitn
I know it wil Casane:	2Tamb	5.3.113		Tamb
To hold the fiery spirit it containes,	2Tamb	5.3.169		Tamb
Let it be plac'd by this my fatall chaire,	2Tamb	5.3.211		Tamb
Hence comes it, that a strong built Citadell/Commands much more	Jew	Prol.22		Machvl
Wearying his fingers ends with telling it,	Jew	1.1.16		Barab
Were it for confirmation of a League,	Jew	1.1.154		1Jew
And very wisely sayd, it may be so.	Jew	1.1.166		3Jew
Let's know their time, perhaps it is not long;	Jew	1.2.24		Calym
Now then here know that it concerneth us--	Jew	1.2.42		Govnr
Your Lordship shall doe well to let them have it.	Jew	1.2.44		Barab
we have cast, but cannot compasse it/By reason of the warres,	Jew	1.2.47		Govnr
Governour, it was not got so easily;	Jew	1.2.86		Barab
And now it cannot be recall'd.	Jew	1.2.93		Govnr
It shall be so: now Officers have you done?	Jew	1.2.131		Govnr
But take it to you i'th devils name.	Jew	1.2.154		Barab
Fearing the worst of this before it fell,	Jew	1.2.246		Barab
Daughter, I have it:	Jew	1.2.270		Barab
what e're it be to injure them/That have so manifestly wronged	Jew	1.2.274		Abigal
but be thou so precise/As they may thinke it done of Holinesse.	Jew	1.2.285		Barab
thou never mean'st/As first meane truth, and then dissemble it,	Jew	1.2.291		Barab
No, Abigall, in this/It is not necessary I be seene.	Jew	1.2.302		Barab
It may be so: but who comes here?	Jew	1.2.313		Abbass
The boord is marked thus that covers it.	Jew	1.2.350		Barab
Becomes it Jewes to be so credulous,	Jew	1.2.360		Barab
And so will I too, or it shall goe hard.--	Jew	1.2.392		Lodowk
Father, it draweth towards midnight now,	Jew	2.1.55		Abigal
my fingers take/A kisse from him that sends it from his soule.	Jew	2.1.59		Barab
And buy it basely too for summes of gold?	Jew	2.2.29		Bosco
Captaine we know it, but our force is small.	Jew	2.2.34		Govnr
They fought it out, and not a man surviv'd/To bring the	Jew	2.2.50		Bosco
So will we fight it out; come, let's away:	Jew	2.2.52		Govnr
I, and his sonnes too, or it shall goe hard.	Jew	2.3.17		Barab
What sparkle does it give without a foile?	Jew	2.3.55		Lodowk
But when he touches it, it will be foild:	Jew	2.3.57		Barab
Lord Lodowicke, it sparkles bright and faire.	Jew	2.3.58		Barab
Is it square or pointed, pray let me know.	Jew	2.3.59		Lodowk
Pointed it is, good Sir,--but not for you.	Jew	2.3.60		Barab
I like it much the better.	Jew	2.3.61		Lodowk
How showes it by night?	Jew	2.3.62		Lodowk
You'le like it better farre a nights than dayes.	Jew	2.3.63		Barab
Your life and if you have it.--	Jew	2.3.64		Barab
No, Barabas, I will deserve it first.	Jew	2.3.68		Lodowk
Your father has deserv'd it at my hands,	Jew	2.3.70		Barab
And as it were in Catechising sort,	Jew	2.3.73		Barab
No doubt your soule shall reape the fruit of it.	Jew	2.3.78		Lodowk
No, but I doe it through a burning zeale,	Jew	2.3.87		Barab
It shall goe hard but I will see your death.	Jew	2.3.94		Barab
and thou hast, breake my head with it, I'le forgive thee.	Jew	2.3.112	P	Barab
It may be under colour of shaving, thou'lt cut my throat for my	Jew	2.3.119	P	Barab
As for the Diamond it shall be yours;	Jew	2.3.135		Barab
As for the Comment on the Machabees/I have it, Sir, and 'tis at	Jew	2.3.154		Barab
I have it for you, Sir; please you walke in with me:	Jew	2.3.220		Barab

IT (cont.)

I know it:			
Doe, it is requisite it should be so.	Jew	2.3.238	Barab
Nay on my life it is my Factors hand,	Jew	2.3.239	Barab
I weigh it thus much; I have wealth enough.	Jew	2.3.240	Barab
Thou know'st, and heaven can witnesse it is true,	Jew	2.3.245	Barab
Well, let it passe, another time shall serve.	Jew	2.3.253	Barab
This is thy Diamond, tell me, shall I have it?	Jew	2.3.278	Mthias
Win it, and weare it, it is yet [unfoyl'd] <unsoyl'd>.	Jew	2.3.292	Lodowk
For they themselves hold it a principle,	Jew	2.3.293	Barab
Oh muse not at it, 'tis the Hebrewes guize,	Jew	2.3.310	Barab
Lodowicke, it is enough/That I have made thee sure to Abigal.	Jew	2.3.325	Barab
Revenge it on him when you meet him next.	Jew	2.3.334	Barab
I thinke by this/You purchase both their lives; is it not so?	Jew	2.3.343	Barab
True; and it shall be cunningly perform'd.	Jew	2.3.366	Ithimr
Take this and beare it to Mathias streight,	Jew	2.3.367	Barab
And tell him that it comes from Lodowicke.	Jew	2.3.370	Barab
'Tis poyson'd, is it not?	Jew	2.3.371	Barab
No, no, and yet it might be done that way:	Jew	2.3.372	Ithimr
It is a challenge feign'd from Lodowicke.	Jew	2.3.373	Barab
That he shall verily thinke it comes from him.	Jew	2.3.374	Barab
'Tis silver, I disdaine it.	Jew	2.3.376	Ithimr
And I will have it or it shall goe hard.	Jew	3.1.13	Curtzn
I did it, and revenge it if thou dar'st.	Jew	3.1.15	Pilia
And it shall murder me.	Jew	3.2.4	Mthias
No, what was it?	Jew	3.2.24	Mater
devil invented a challenge, my master writ it, and I carried it,	Jew	3.3.17	Abigal
my master writ it, and I carried it, first to Lodowicke, and	Jew	3.3.18	P Ithimr
And couldst not venge it, but upon his sonne,	Jew	3.3.19	P Ithimr
Why Abigal it is not yet long since/That I did labour thy	Jew	3.3.44	Abigal
If so, 'tis time that it be seene into:	Jew	3.3.56	1Fryar
It is a precious powder that I bought/Of an Italian in Ancona	Jew	3.4.9	Barab
yet not appeare/In forty houres after it is tane.	Jew	3.4.68	Barab
Among the rest beare this, and set it there;	Jew	3.4.72	Barab
There's a darke entry where they take it in,	Jew	3.4.78	Barab
Nor make enquiry who hath sent it them.	Jew	3.4.79	Barab
Stay, let me spice it first.	Jew	3.4.81	Barab
Stay, first let me stirre it Ithimore.	Jew	3.4.85	Barab
As fatall be it to her as the draught/Of which great Alexander	Jew	3.4.95	Barab
And with her let it worke like Borgias wine,	Jew	3.4.96	Barab
what shall I doe with it?	Jew	3.4.98	Barab
Oh my sweet Ithimore go set it downe/And come againe so soone	Jew	3.4.107	P Ithimr
Shall overflow it with their refluence.	Jew	3.4.108	Barab
Reveale it not, for then my father dyes.	Jew	3.5.18	Govnr
The Canon Law forbids it, and the Priest/That makes it knowne,	Jew	3.6.32	Abigal
it, and the Priest/That makes it knowne, being degraded first,	Jew	3.6.34	2Fryar
So I have heard; pray therefore keepe it close.	Jew	3.6.35	2Fryar
Thou know'st 'tis death and if it be reveal'd.	Jew	3.6.37	Abigal
Or though it wrought, it would have done no good,	Jew	3.6.51	2Fryar
That's brave, master, but think you it wil not be known?	Jew	4.1.5	Barab
How can it if we two be secret.	Jew	4.1.8	P Ithimr
And I am bound in charitie to requite it,	Jew	4.1.9	Barab
No more but so: it must and shall be done.	Jew	4.1.107	Barab
Then is it as it should be, take him up.	Jew	4.1.128	Barab
it is;/And understanding I should come this way,	Jew	4.1.152	Barab
Who is it?	Jew	4.1.164	1Fryar
I have don't, but no body knowes it but you two, I may escape.	Jew	4.1.176	Barab
To morrow is the Sessions; you shall to it.	Jew	4.1.180	P 1Fryar
as who shold say, Is it even so; and so I left him, being driven	Jew	4.1.199	Barab
conning his neck-verse I take it, looking of a Fryars	Jew	4.2.13	P Pilia
It may be she sees more in me than I can find in my selfe:	Jew	4.2.17	P Pilia
And you can have it, Sir, and if you please.	Jew	4.2.32	P Ithimr
and would have it; but hee hides and buries it up as Partridges	Jew	4.2.56	Pilia
but hee hides and buries it up as Partridges doe their egges,	Jew	4.2.57	P Ithimr
And is't not possible to find it out?	Jew	4.2.58	P Ithimr
But came it freely, did the Cow give down her milk freely?	Jew	4.2.60	Pilia
told him he were best to send it; then he hug'd and imbrac'd	Jew	4.2.102	P Ithimr
Take thou the mony, spend it for my sake.	Jew	4.2.106	P Pilia
It twinckles like a Starre.	Jew	4.2.123	Ithimr
Or else I will confesse: I, there it goes:	Jew	4.2.128	P Ithimr
And winds it twice or thrice about his eare;	Jew	4.3.4	Barab
words, Sir, and send it you, were best see; there's his letter.	Jew	4.3.8	Barab
he not as well come as send; pray bid him come and fetch it:	Jew	4.3.24	P Pilia
I cannot doe it, I have lost my keyes.	Jew	4.3.27	P Barab
the gold, or know Jew it is in my power to hang thee.	Jew	4.3.32	Barab
I know it, Sir.	Jew	4.3.37	P Pilia
I have it.	Jew	4.3.55	Pilia
I'le pledge thee, love, and therefore drinke it off.	Jew	4.3.66	Barab
have at it; and doe you heare?	Jew	4.4.1	Curtzn
Goe to, it shall be so.	Jew	4.4.2	P Ithimr
Of that condition I wil drink it up; here's to thee.	Jew	4.4.3	Curtzn
And fit it should: but first let's ha more gold.	Jew	4.4.4	P Ithimr
The scent thereof was death, I poyson'd it.	Jew	4.4.26	Curtzn
He knowes it already.	Jew	4.4.43	Barab
Prethe sweet love, one more, and write it sharp.	Jew	4.4.60	P Barab
Any of 'em will doe it.	Jew	4.4.73	Curtzn
Let me alone to urge it now I know the meaning.	Jew	4.4.78	P Ithimr
And it behoves you to be resolute;	Jew	4.4.79	Pilia
Mathias did it not, it was the Jew.	Jew	5.1.3	Govnr
now at my lodging/That was his Agent, he'll confesse it all.	Jew	5.1.11	Curtzn
I carried it, I confesse, but who writ it?	Jew	5.1.17	Curtzn
As these have spoke so be it to their soules:--	Jew	5.1.32	P Ithimr
Be patient, gentle Madam, it was he,	Jew	5.1.42	Barab
	Jew	5.1.46	Govnr

IT (cont.)

Wonder not at it, Sir, the heavens are just:	Jew	5.1.55	Govnr
And if it be not true, then let me dye.	Jew	5.1.96	Barab
Thou'st doom'd thy selfe, assault it presently.	Jew	5.1.97	Calym
had it not beene much better/To [have] kept thy promise then be	Jew	5.2.4	Calym
me/My life's in danger, and what boots it thee/Poore Barabas,	Jew	5.2.31	Barab
Maintaine it bravely by firme policy,	Jew	5.2.36	Barab
At least unprofitably lose it not:	Jew	5.2.37	Barab
And leaves it off to snap on Thistle tops:	Jew	5.2.42	Barab
too late/Thou seek'st for much, but canst not compasse it.	Jew	5.2.46	Barab
What thinkst thou shall become of it and thee?	Jew	5.2.56	Barab
Your selves shall see it shall not be forgot:	Jew	5.2.71	Barab
And thus we cast it:	Jew	5.2.96	Barab
And bring it with me to thee in the evening.	Jew	5.2.108	Govnr
I wonder how it could be conquer'd thus?	Jew	5.3.12	Calym
As be it valued but indifferently,	Jew	5.3.29	Msngr
And see he brings it: Now, Governor, the summe?	Jew	5.5.19	Barab
wel since it is no more/I'le satisfie my selfe with that;	Jew	5.5.21	Barab
no more/I'le satisfie my selfe with that; nay, keepe it still,	Jew	5.5.22	Barab
That on the sudden shall dissever it,	Jew	5.5.29	Barab
asunder; so that it doth sinke/Into a deepe pit past recovery.	Jew	5.5.35	Barab
We think it good to goe and consumate/The rest, with hearing of	P 19	1.19	Charls
And made it look with terrour on the worlde:	P 61	2.4	Guise
Ile either rend it witn my nayles to naught,	P 102	2.45	Guise
Too late it is my Lord if that be true/To blame her highnes,	P 181	3.16	QnMarg
but I hope it be/Only some naturall passion makes her sicke.	P 182	3.17	QnMarg
And see it honoured with just solemnitie.	P 196	3.31	Admral
Madam, it wilbe noted through the world,	P 207	4.5	Charls
Well Madam, I referre it to your Majestie,	P 225	4.23	Charls
And it please your grace the Lord high Admirall,	P 243	4.41	Man
How fares it with my Lord high Admiral,	P 253	4.51	Charls
It may be it is some other, and he escapte.	P 308	5.35	Anjoy
Which is no sooner receiv'd but it is spent.	P 379	7.19	Ramus
Was it not thou that scoftes the Organon,	P 387	7.27	Guise
And said it was a heape of vanities?	P 388	7.28	Guise
Which as I heare one [Shekius] <Shekins> takes it ill,	P 404	7.44	Ramus
And I reduc'd it into better forme.	P 407	7.47	Ramus
Tis well advisde Dumain, goe see it strait be done.	P 424	7.64	Guise
And by his graces councell it is thought,	P 465	8.15	Anjoy
it may prejudice their hope/Of my inheritance to the crowne of	P 467	8.17	Anjoy
It will be hard for us to worke their deaths.	P 508	9.27	QnMoth
Epernoune, goe see it presently be done,	P 558	11.23	QnMoth
It is my due by just succession:	P 570	11.35	Navrre
That holdes it from your highnesse wrongfully:	P 582	11.47	Pleshe
Then may it please your Majestie to give me leave,	P 616	12.29	Mugern
And Guise usurpes it, cause I am his wife:	P 661	13.5	Duchss
So, set it down and leave me to my selfe.	P 666	13.10	Duchss
That it might print these lines within his heart.	P 669	13.13	Duchss
The power of vengeance now incampes it selfe,	P 717	14.20	Navrre
It will not countervaile his paines I hope,	P 735	14.38	Navrre
If it be not too free there's the question:	P 812	17.7	P Souldr
Revenge it Henry as thou list or dare,	P 819	17.14	Guise
I did it only in despite of thee.	P 820	17.15	Guise
But we presume it is not for our good.	P 824	17.19	King
My Lord, to speak more plainely, thus it is:	P 847	17.42	Guise
And Ile subscribe my name and seale it straight.	P 883	17.78	King
It would be good the Guise were made away,	P 888	17.83	Eprnon
Bartus, it shall be so, poast then to Fraunce,	P 907	18.8	Navrre
And tell him ere it be long, Ile visite him.	P 912	18.13	Navrre
And binde it wholy to the Sea of Rome:	P 926	18.27	Navrre
How fares it this morning with your excellence?	P 966	19.36	King
And you good Cosin to imagine it.	P 970	19.40	King
The Kings alone, it cannot satisfie.	P1109	21.3	Dumain
It is enough if that Navarre may be/Esteemed faithfull to the	P1147	22.9	Navrre
it please your Majestie heere is a Frier of the order of the	P1155	22.17	P 1Msngr
And may it never end in bloud as mine hath done.	P1233	22.95	King
That it may keenly slice the Catholicks.	P1238	22.100	King
That we may see it honourably interde:	P1246	22.108	Navrre
yf it be not to free theres the questione | now ser where he is	Paris	ms 8,p390	P Souldr
revenge it henry yf thow liste or darst	Paris	ms23,p391	Guise
I did it onely in dispight of thee	Paris	ms24,p391	Guise
that of it self was hote enoughe to worke/thy Just degestione	Paris	ms26,p391	Guise
But that it harbors him I hold so deare,	Edw	1.1.13	Gavstn
But yet it is no paine to speake men faire,	Edw	1.1.42	Gavstn
With haire that gilds the water as it glides,	Edw	1.1.62	Gavstn
Beseemes it thee to contradict thy king?	Edw	1.1.92	Edward
Brother revenge it, and let these their heads,	Edw	1.1.117	Kent
I know it, brother welcome home my friend.	Edw	1.1.148	Edward
Therefore to equall it receive my hart.	Edw	1.1.162	Edward
It shall suffice me to enjoy your love,	Edw	1.1.171	Gavstn
To see it done, and bring thee safe againe.	Edw	1.1.205	Edward
What els my lords, for it concernes me neere,	Edw	1.2.44	ArchBp
Is it not straunge, that he is thus bewitcht?	Edw	1.2.55	MortSr
May it please your lordship to subscribe your name.	Edw	1.4.2	Lncstr
It is our pleasure, we will have it so.	Edw	1.4.9	Edward
I there it goes, but yet I will not yeeld,	Edw	1.4.56	Edward
Then linger not my lord but do it straight.	Edw	1.4.58	Lncstr
It bootes me not to threat, I must speake faire,	Edw	1.4.63	Edward
And share it equally amongst you all,	Edw	1.4.71	Edward
In steede of inke, ile write it with my teares.	Edw	1.4.86	Edward
Give it me, ile have it published in the streetes.	Edw	1.4.89	Lncstr
Be it or no, he shall not linger here.	Edw	1.4.93	MortSr
They would not stir, were it to do me good:	Edw	1.4.95	Edward

IT (cont.)

My lord I heare it whispered every where,	Edw	1.4.106	Gavstn
Tis true sweete Gaveston, oh were it false.	Edw	1.4.108	Edward
The Legate of the Pope will have it so,	Edw	1.4.109	Edward
And therefore sweete friend, take it patiently,	Edw	1.4.112	Edward
Your highnes knowes, it lies not in my power.	Edw	1.4.158	Queene
Which being caught, strikes him that takes it dead,	Edw	1.4.222	Mortmr
It is impossible, but speake your minde.	Edw	1.4.228	Mortmr
Then thus, but none shal heare it but our selves.	Edw	1.4.229	Queene
Well of necessitie it must be so.	Edw	1.4.238	Mortmr
Because my lords, it was not thought upon:	Edw	1.4.273	Mortmr
Nay more, when he shall know it lies in us,	Edw	1.4.274	Mortmr
For howsoever we have borne it out,	Edw	1.4.280	Mortmr
I would freelie give it to his enemies,	Edw	1.4.309	Edward
Which beates upon it like the Cyclops hammers,	Edw	1.4.313	Edward
But will you love me, if you finde it so?	Edw	1.4.324	Queene
If it be so, what will not Edward do?	Edw	1.4.325	Edward
And may it proove more happie then the first.	Edw	1.4.336	Queene
It shalbe done my gratious Lord.	Edw	1.4.372	Beamnt
Now let us in, and feast it roiallie:	Edw	1.4.374	Edward
And riote it with the treasure of the realme,	Edw	1.4.405	Mortmr
And Midas like he jets it in the court,	Edw	1.4.408	Mortmr
It is about her lover Gaveston.	Edw	2.1.22	Spencr
And learne to court it like a Gentleman,	Edw	2.1.32	Spencr
It shall be done madam.	Edw	2.1.72	Baldck
Prethee let me know it.	Edw	2.2.14	Edward
But seeing you are so desirous, thus it is:	Edw	2.2.15	Mortmr
And therefore being pursued, it takes the aire:	Edw	2.2.25	Lncstr
No sooner is it up, but thers a foule,	Edw	2.2.26	Lncstr
No sooner is it up, but thers a foule,/That seaseth it:	Edw	2.2.27	Lncstr
Desirde her more, and waxt outragious,/So did it sure with me:	Edw	2.2.56	Edward
Returne it to their throtes, ile be thy warrant.	Edw	2.2.73	Edward
Cosin it is no dealing with him now,	Edw	2.2.102	Lncstr
Ile have his bloud, or die in seeking it.	Edw	2.2.107	Warwck
About it then, and we will follow you.	Edw	2.2.124	Mortmr
And thereof came it, that the fleering Scots,	Edw	2.2.188	Lncstr
If ye be moov'de, revenge it as you can,	Edw	2.2.198	Lncstr
I, and it greeves me that I favoured him.	Edw	2.2.213	Kent
And it sufficeth:	Edw	2.3.15	Lncstr
Farre be it from the thought of Lancaster,	Edw	2.4.33	Lncstr
How comes it, that the king and he is parted?	Edw	2.4.41	Mortmr
Base flatterer, yeeld, and were it not for shame,	Edw	2.5.11	Mortmr
it is our countries cause,/That here severelie we will execute	Edw	2.5.22	Warwck
No, it needeth not.	Edw	2.5.42	Warwck
I know it lords, it is this life you aime at,	Edw	2.5.48	Gavstn
My lords, it is his majesties request,	Edw	2.5.57	Arundl
It is honourable in thee to offer this,	Edw	2.5.67	Mortmr
is it not enough/That we have taken him, but must we now	Edw	2.5.83	Warwck
I see it is your life these armes pursue.	Edw	2.6.2	James
No James, it is my countries cause I follow.	Edw	2.6.10	Warwck
to your maister/My friend, and tell him that I watcht it well.	Edw	2.6.13	Warwck
Come fellowes, it booted not for us to strive,	Edw	2.6.18	James
Weele steele it on their crest, and powle their tops.	Edw	3.1.27	Edward
True, and it like your grace,/That powres in lieu of all your	Edw	3.1.43	Spencr
And Spencer, spare them not, but lay it on.	Edw	3.1.56	Edward
I doubt it not my lord, right will prevaile.	Edw	3.1.189	Spencr
Is it not, trowe ye, to assemble aide,	Edw	3.1.207	SpncrP
Then Edward, thou wilt fight it to the last,	Edw	3.1.211	Mortmr
No Edward, Englands scourge, it may not be,	Edw	3.1.258	Mortmr
Thats it these Barons and the subtill Queene,	Edw	3.1.272	Levune
It hath my lord, the warders all a sleepe,	Edw	4.1.15	Mortmr
Feare it not.	Edw	4.1.18	Kent
So pleaseth the Queene my mother, me it likes.	Edw	4.2.21	Prince
I would it were no worse,/But gentle lords, friendles we are in	Edw	4.2.45	Queene
But by the sword, my lord, it must be deserv'd.	Edw	4.2.59	Mortmr
Sir John of Henolt, be it thy renowne,	Edw	4.2.78	Mortmr
I pray let us see it, what have we there?	Edw	4.3.10	Edward
Read it Spencer.	Edw	4.3.11	Edward
A will be had ere long I doubt it not.	Edw	4.3.20	Spencr
We come in armes to wrecke it with the [sword] <swords>:	Edw	4.4.23	Mortmr
to whom in justice it belongs/To punish this unnaturall revolt:	Edw	4.6.8	Kent
They shalbe started thence I doubt it not.	Edw	4.6.60	Mortmr
And we must seeke to right it as we may,	Edw	4.6.68	Mortmr
Too true it is, quem dies vidit veniens superbum,	Edw	4.7.53	Leistr
It may become thee yet,/To let us take our farewell of his	Edw	4.7.68	Spencr
My lord, it is in vaine to greeve or storme,	Edw	4.7.77	Baldck
He rends and teares it with his wrathfull pawe,	Edw	5.1.12	Edward
And so it fares with me, whose dauntlesse minde/The ambitious	Edw	5.1.15	Edward
Your grace mistakes, it is for Englands good,	Edw	5.1.38	BshpWn
Heavens turne it to a blaze of quenchelesse fier,	Edw	5.1.44	Edward
My head, the latest honor dew to it,	Edw	5.1.62	Edward
And therefore let me weare it yet a while.	Edw	5.1.83	Edward
Receive it?	Edw	5.1.98	Edward
Take it: what are you moovde, pitie you me?	Edw	5.1.102	Edward
Returne it backe and dip it in my bloud.	Edw	5.1.120	Edward
Unlesse it be with too much clemencie?	Edw	5.1.123	Edward
Will be my death, and welcome shall it be,	Edw	5.1.126	Edward
Heare me immortall Jove, and graunt it too.	Edw	5.1.143	Edward
I would hee were, so it were not by my meanes.	Edw	5.2.45	Queene
It shall be done my lord.	Edw	5.2.51	Matrvs
But bee content, seeing it his highnesse pleasure.	Edw	5.2.94	Queene
Brother, you know it is impossible.	Edw	5.2.97	Queene
But hee repents, and sorrowes for it now.	Edw	5.2.108	Prince

IT (cont.)

It is the chiefest marke they levell at.	Edw	5.3.12	Edward
O Gaveston, it is for thee that I am wrongd,	Edw	5.3.41	Edward
Guarde the king sure, it is the earle of Kent.	Edw	5.3.50	Matrvs
Is sure to pay for it when his sonne is of age,	Edw	5.4.4	Mortmr
And therefore will I do it cunninglie.	Edw	5.4.5	Mortmr
But read it thus, and thats an other sence:	Edw	5.4.10	Mortmr
Unpointed as it is, thus shall it goe,	Edw	5.4.13	Mortmr
That being dead, if it chaunce to be found,	Edw	5.4.14	Mortmr
And we be quit that causde it to be done:	Edw	5.4.16	Mortmr
That shall conveie it, and performe the rest,	Edw	5.4.18	Mortmr
And hast thou cast how to accomplish it?	Edw	5.4.24	Mortmr
Well, do it bravely, and be secret.	Edw	5.4.28	Mortmr
I care not how it is, so it be not spide:	Edw	5.4.40	Mortmr
Saying it is, onus quam gravissimum,	Edw	5.4.61	Mortmr
Suscepi that provinciam as they terme it,	Edw	5.4.63	Mortmr
It pleaseth me, and Isabell the Queene.	Edw	5.4.71	Mortmr
I will requite it when I come to age.	Edw	5.4.100	King
Whats heere? I know not how to conster it.	Edw	5.5.15	Gurney
Gurney, it was left unpointed for the nonce,	Edw	5.5.16	Matrvs
And get me a spit, and let it be red hote.	Edw	5.5.30	Ltborn
I, I, so: when I call you, bring it in.	Edw	5.5.35	Ltborn
Farre is it from my hart to do you harme,	Edw	5.5.47	Ltborn
And then thy heart, were it as Gurneys is,	Edw	5.5.53	Edward
Yet will it melt, ere I have done my tale.	Edw	5.5.55	Edward
And let me see the stroke before it comes,	Edw	5.5.76	Edward
But everie jointe shakes as I give it thee:	Edw	5.5.86	Edward
So, lay the table downe, and stampe on it,	Edw	5.5.112	Ltborn
Tell me sirs, was it not bravelie done?	Edw	5.5.116	Ltborn
I my good Lord, I would it were undone.	Edw	5.6.2	Matrvs
My lord, I feare me it will proove too true.	Edw	5.6.77	2Lord
Goe fetche my fathers hearse, where it shall lie,	Edw	5.6.94	King
Jeromes Bible Faustus, view it well:	F 65	1.1.37	Faust
And gaze not on it least it tempt thy soule,	F 98	1.1.70	GdAngl
As thou to live, therefore object it not.	F 162	1.1.134	Faust
it were not for you to come within fortie foot of the place of	F 210	1.2.17	P Wagner
this wine, if it could speake, <it> would informe your Worships:	F 216	1.2.23	P Wagner
wine, if it could speake, <it> would informe your Worships:	F 216	1.2.23	P Wagner
It may be <and see if hee by> his grave counsell may <can>	F 226	1.2.33	2Schol
Be it to make the Moone drop from her Sphere,	F 266	1.3.38	Faust
How comes it then that he is Prince of Devils?	F 294	1.3.66	Faust
How comes it then that thou art out of hell?	F 303	1.3.75	Faust
Why this is hell: nor am I out of it.	F 304	1.3.76	Mephst
to the devill, for a shoulder of Mutton, tho it were bloud raw.	F 350	1.4.8	P Wagner
I had need to have it well rosted, and good sauce to it,	F 352	1.4.10	P Robin
to have it well rosted, and good sauce to it, if I pay so deere,	F 353	1.4.11	P Robin
Why so thou shalt be, whether thou dost it or no:	F 360	1.4.18	P Wagner
What bootes it then to thinke on <of> God or Heaven?	F 391	2.1.3	Faust
But now <Faustus> thou must bequeath it solemnly,	F 423	2.1.35	Mephst
If thou deny it I must <wil> backe to hell.	F 426	2.1.38	Mephst
I Mephostophilis, I'le <I> give it him <thee>.	F 437	2.1.49	Faust
at some certaine day/Great Lucifer may claime it as his owne,	F 440	2.1.52	Mephst
And let it be propitious for my wish.	F 447	2.1.59	Faust
But Faustus/<thou must> Write it in manner of a Deed of Gift.	F 449	2.1.61	Mephst
I'le fetch thee fire to dissolve it streight.	F 452	2.1.64	Mephst
Is it unwilling I should write this byll?	F 454	2.1.66	Faust
Why streames it not, that I may write a fresh?	F 455	2.1.67	Faust
Faustus gives to thee his soule: [ah] <O> there it staid.	F 456	2.1.68	Faust
See <come> Faustus, here is <heres> fire, set it on.	F 459	2.1.71	Mephst
I see it plaine, even heere <in this place> is writ/Homo fuge:	F 469	2.1.81	Faust
Then heare me read it Mephostophilis <them>.	F 483	2.1.95	Faust
I, take it, and the devill give thee good of it <on't>.	F 502	2.1.114	Faust
And if thou lovest me thinke no more of it.	F 536	2.1.148	Mephst
<Here>, take this booke, <and> peruse it [thoroughly] <well>:	F 543	2.1.155	Mephst
I tell thee Faustus it is <tis> not halfe so faire/As thou, or	F 557	2.2.6	Mephst
'Twas <It was> made for man; then he's <therefore is man> more	F 560	2.2.9	Mephst
If Heaven was <it were> made for man, 'twas made for me:	F 561	2.2.10	Faust
And we will highly gratify thee for it.	F 653	2.2.102	Lucifr
and all the people in it were turnd> to Gold,	F 676	(HC263) A	P Covet
in hell, and look to it, for some of you shall be my father.	F 690	2.2.139	P Wrath
Meane while peruse this booke, and view it throughly,	F 717	2.2.169	Lucifr
<in mean time take this booke, peruse it throwly>,	F 717	(HC264) A	Lucifr
Thou needst not do that, for my Mistresse hath done it.	F 739	2.3.18	P Dick
hold belly hold, and wee'le not pay one peny for it.	F 750	2.3.29	P Robin
brave, prethee let's to it presently, for I am as dry as a dog.	F 751	2.3.30	P Dick
With winding bankes that cut it in two parts;	F 814	3.1.36	Mephst
Let it be so my Faustus, but first stay,	F 856	3.1.78	Mephst
And I'le performe it Faustus: heark they come:	F 866	3.1.88	Mephst
Dispatch it soone,	F 902	3.1.124	Faust
<holy> Synod/Of Priests and Prelates, it is thus decreed:	F 953	3.1.175	Faust
It is enough:	F 964	3.1.186	Pope
And leave it in the Churches treasury.	F 971	3.1.193	Pope
First, may it please your sacred Holinesse,	F1013	3.2.33	1Card
You brought us word even now, it was decreed,	F1019	3.2.39	Pope
Deny it not, we all are witnesses/That Bruno here was late	F1025	3.2.45	Raymnd
Please it your holinesse, I thinke it be some Ghost crept out	F1059	3.2.79	P Archbp
I thinke it be some Ghost crept out of Purgatory, and now is	F1059	3.2.79	P Archbp
It may be so:	F1062	3.2.82	Pope
Never deny't, for I know you have it, and I'le search you.	F1101	3.3.14	P Vintnr
plague take you, I thought 'twas your knavery to take it away:	F1111	3.3.24	P Vintnr
Come, give it me againe.	F1111	3.3.24	P Vintnr
you have had a shroud journey of it, will it please you to take	F1120	3.3.33	P Robin
will it please you to take a shoulder of Mutton to supper, and	F1120	3.3.33	P Robin

IT (cont.)

Wilt thou stand in thy Window, and see it then? . .	F1195	4.1.41		Mrtino
Be it as Faustus please, we are content.	F1253	4.1.99		Emper
I have heard it said,/That this faire Lady, whilest she liv'd	F1265	4.1.111		Emper
Faustus I see it plaine, ...	F1270	4.1.116		Emper
If Faustus do it, you are streight resolv'd, . . .	F1298	4.1.144		Faust
My head is lighter then it was by th'hornes, . . .	F1350	4.2.26		Benvol
Wee'l sell it to a Chimny-sweeper:	F1384	4.2.60	P	Benvol
it will weare out ten birchin broomes I warrant you. .	F1384	4.2.60	P	Benvol
Nay keepe it:	F1393	4.2.69		Faust
You hit it right,/It is your owne you meane, feele on your	F1442	4.3.12		Fredrk
It is your owne you meane, feele on your head. . . .	F1443	4.3.13		Fredrk
If it please you, the Duke of Vanholt doth earnestly entreate	F1500	4.4.44	P	Wagner
doubt of that, for me thinkes you make no hast to wipe it out.	F1517	4.5.13	P	Hostss
But you shall heare how bravely I serv'd him for it; I went me	F1547	4.5.43	P	HrsCsr
it pleaseth your grace to thinke but well of that which Faustus	F1564	4.6.7	P	Faust
it may be, that you have taken no pleasure in those sights;	F1565	4.6.8	P	Faust
be it in the world, it shall be yours:	F1567	4.6.10	P	Faust
heart desires to have, and were it now Summer, as it is January,	F1572	4.6.15	P	Lady
were it now Summer, as it is January, a dead time of the Winter,	F1572	4.6.15	P	Lady
Please it your grace, the yeare is divided into two circles	F1581	4.6.24	P	Faust
so that when it is Winter with us, in the contrary circle it is	F1582	4.6.25	P	Faust
in the contrary circle it is likewise Summer with them, as in	F1583	4.6.26	P	Faust
Go pacifie their fury, set it ope, ...	F1589	4.6.32		Duke
We have no reason for it, therefore a fig for him. . .	F1593	4.6.36	P	Dick
It appeares so, pray be bold else-where, ...	F1597	4.6.40		Servnt
But I have it againe now I am awake:	F1657	4.6.100	P	Faust
you thinke to carry it away with your Hey-passe, and Re-passe:	F1664	4.6.107	P	Robin
<It is not Faustus custome> to deny	F1690	(HC269)B		Faust
Doe not persever in it like a Divell;	F1711	5.1.38		OldMan
It may be this my exhortation/Seemes harsh, and all unpleasant;	F1717	5.1.44		OldMan
my exhortation/Seemes harsh, and all unpleasant; let it not,	F1718	5.1.45		OldMan
For gentle sonne, I speake it not in wrath, . . .	F1719	5.1.46		OldMan
Do it then Faustus <quickly>, with unfained heart, . .	F1751	5.1.78		Mephst
Her lips sucke <suckes> forth my soule, see where it flies.	F1771	5.1.98		Faust
wait upon thy soule; the time is come/Which makes it forfeit.	F1803	5.2.7		Lucifr
His conscience kils it, and his labouring braine, . .	F1809	5.2.13		Mephst
Say Wagner, thou hast perus'd my will,/How dost thou like it?	F1817	5.2.21		Faust
If it be so, wee'l have Physitians, ...	F1830	5.2.34		2Schol
hath lost both Germany and the world, yea heaven it selfe:	F1844	5.2.48	P	Faust
God forbade it indeed, but Faustus hath done it: . .	F1858	5.2.62	P	Faust
I doe confesse it Faustus, and rejoyce;	F1885	5.2.89		Mephst
Where is it now?	F1943	5.2.147		Faust
Gape earth; O no, it will not harbour me.	F1949	5.2.153		Faust
<O> It strikes, it strikes; now body turne to aire, . .	F1975	5.2.179		Faust
the Divel for a shoulder of mutton, though it were blood rawe.	F App	p.229 9	P	Wagner
burladie I had neede have it wel roasted, and good sawce to it,	F App	p.229 11	P	Clown
have it wel roasted, and good sawce to it, if I pay so deere.	F App	p.229 12	P	Clown
let it be in the likenesse of a little pretie frisking flea,	F App	p.231 61	P	Clown
Heere's no body, if it like your Holynesse. . . .	F App	p.231 4	P	Frier
it may be some ghost newly crept out of Purgatory come to begge	F App	p.232 14	P	Lorein
It may be so, Friers prepare a dirge to lay the fury of this	F App	p.232 16	P	Pope
bleate, and an asse braye, because it is S. Peters holy day.	F App	p.232 28	P	Faust
he keepes such a chafing with my mistris about it, and she has	F App	p.233 8	P	Rafe
Canst thou conjure with it?	F App	p.233 21	P	Rafe
I can do al these things easily with it:	F App	p.234 22	P	Robin
It grieves my soule I never saw the man:	F App	p.237 28		Emper
But if it like your Grace, it is not in my abilitie to present	F App	p.237 41	P	Faust
it is not in my abilitie to present before your eyes, the true	F App	p.237 41	P	Faust
or moale in her necke, how shal I know whether it be so or no?	F App	p.238 61	P	Emper
I thinke I have met with you for it.	F App	p.238 78	P	Faust
at ease, if I bring his water to you, youle tel me what it is?	F App	p.240 119	P	HrsCsr
my fortie dollers againe, or Ile make it the dearest horse:	F App	p.240 137	P	HrsCsr
and the Horsecourser I take it, a bottle of hey for his labour;	F App	p.241 165	P	Faust
My gratious Lord, I am glad it contents you so wel: . .	F App	p.242 3	P	Faust
but it may be Madame, you take no delight in this, I have heard	F App	p.242 4	P	Faust
women do long for some dainties or other, what is it Madame?	F App	p.242 5	P	Faust
tell me, and you shal have it.	F App	p.242 6	P	Faust
my heart desires, and were it nowe summer, as it is January,	F App	p.242 9	P	Duchss
nowe summer, as it is January, and the dead time of the winter,	F App	p.242 9	P	Duchss
were it a greater thing then this, so it would content you, you	F App	p.242 13	P	Faust
thing then this, so it would content you, you should have it	F App	p.242 14	P	Faust
If it like your grace, the yeere is divided into twoo circles	F App	p.242 19	P	Faust
that when it is heere winter with us, in the contrary circle it	F App	p.242 20	P	Faust
us, in the contrary circle it is summer with them, as in India,	F App	p.242 21	P	Faust
Breake heart, drop bloud, and mingle it with teares, .	F App	p.243 38		OldMan
What God it please thee be, or where to sway: . . .	Lucan, First Booke			52
Roome was so great it could not beare it selfe: . .	Lucan, First Booke			72
Affording it no shoare, and Phoebe's waine/Chace Phoebus and	Lucan, First Booke			77
that made Rome/Governe the earth, the sea, the world it selfe,	Lucan, First Booke			110
Though every blast it nod, and seeme to fal, . . .	Lucan, First Booke			142
shoots/Alongst the ayre and [nought] <not> resisting it/Falls,	Lucan, First Booke			157
resisting it/Falls, and returnes, and shivers where it lights.	Lucan, First Booke			158
Hence came it that th'edicts were overrul'd, . . .	Lucan, First Booke			178
Caesar is thine, so please it thee, thy soldier; . .	Lucan, First Booke			204
share the world thou canst not;/Injoy it all thou maiest:	Lucan, First Booke			292
This hand (albeit unwilling) should performe it; . .	Lucan, First Booke			379
Albeit the Citty thou wouldst have so ra'st/Be Roome it selfe.	Lucan, First Booke			387
Mild Atax glad it beares not Roman [boats] <bloats>; .	Lucan, First Booke			404
humane flesh, and where [Jove] <it> seemes/Bloudy like Dian,	Lucan, First Booke			441
The world (were it together) is by cowards/Left as a pray now	Lucan, First Booke			511
blasted, Aruns takes/And it inters with murmurs dolorous,	Lucan, First Booke			606
Ranne through the bloud, that turn'd it all to gelly, .	Lucan, First Booke			618

IT (cont.)

What makes my bed seem hard seeing it is soft?	Ovid's Elegies	1.2.1
Which being not shakt <slackt>, I saw it die at length.	Ovid's Elegies	1.2.12
Pray God it may his latest supper be,	Ovid's Elegies	1.4.2
Turne round thy gold-ring, as it were to ease thee.	Ovid's Elegies	1.4.26
Constrain'd against thy will give it the pezant,	Ovid's Elegies	1.4.65
To him I pray it no delight may bring,	Ovid's Elegies	1.4.67
Or if it do, to thee no joy thence spring:	Ovid's Elegies	1.4.68
But though this night thy fortune be to trie it,	Ovid's Elegies	1.4.69
To me to morrow constantly deny it.	Ovid's Elegies	1.4.70
Love hearing it laugh'd with his tender mother/And smiling	Ovid's Elegies	1.6.11
Though it be so, shut me not out therefore,	Ovid's Elegies	1.6.47
Meeter it were her lips were blewe with kissing/And on her	Ovid's Elegies	1.7.41
but this/If feigned, doth well; if true it doth amisse.	Ovid's Elegies	1.8.36
(Trust me) to give, it is a witty thing.	Ovid's Elegies	1.8.62
The sport being such, as both alike sweete try it,	Ovid's Elegies	1.10.33
Why should one sell it, and the other buy it?	Ovid's Elegies	1.10.34
give her my writ/But see that forth-with shee peruseth it.	Ovid's Elegies	1.11.16
To hoarse scrich-owles foule shadowes it allowes,	Ovid's Elegies	1.12.19
But I remember when it was my fame.	Ovid's Elegies	1.14.50
Hundred-hand Gyges, and had done it well,	Ovid's Elegies	2.1.12
What helpes it me of fierce Achill to sing?	Ovid's Elegies	2.1.29
Nor is it easily prov'd though manifest,	Ovid's Elegies	2.2.55
Trips she, it likes me well, plods she, what than?	Ovid's Elegies	2.4.23
To whom his wench can say, I never did it.	Ovid's Elegies	2.5.10
(Such with my tongue it likes me to purloyne).	Ovid's Elegies	2.5.24
[Itis is] <It is as> great, but auntient cause of sorrowe.	Ovid's Elegies	2.6.10
What helpes it thou wert given to please my wench,	Ovid's Elegies	2.6.19
And time it was for me to live in quiet,	Ovid's Elegies	2.9.23
For when my loathing it of heate deprives me,	Ovid's Elegies	2.9.27
lies quiet/And slumbring, thinkes himselfe much blessed by it.	Ovid's Elegies	2.9.40
Which is the loveliest it is hard to say:	Ovid's Elegies	2.10.6
It is more safe to sleepe, to read a booke,	Ovid's Elegies	2.11.31
And say it brings her that preserveth me;	Ovid's Elegies	2.11.44
Ile thinke all true, though it be feigned matter.	Ovid's Elegies	2.11.53
To have this skirmish fought, let it suffice thee.	Ovid's Elegies	2.13.28
What helpes it Woman to be free from warre?	Ovid's Elegies	2.14.1
But tender Damsels do it, though with paine,	Ovid's Elegies	2.14.37
Which as it seemes, hence winde and sea bereaves.	Ovid's Elegies	2.16.46
To serve a wench if any thinke it shame,	Ovid's Elegies	2.17.1
Aye me why is it knowne to her so well?	Ovid's Elegies	2.17.8
I sayd it irkes me:	Ovid's Elegies	2.18.7
My Mistris deity also drewe me fro it,	Ovid's Elegies	2.18.17
That to deceits it may me forward pricke.	Ovid's Elegies	2.19.44
But of my love it will an end procure.	Ovid's Elegies	2.19.52
Pay it not heere, but in an other place.	Ovid's Elegies	3.2.84
Because the keeper may come say, I did it,	Ovid's Elegies	3.4.35
Great flouds the force of it do often prove.	Ovid's Elegies	3.5.24
It mocked me, hung down the head and suncke,	Ovid's Elegies	3.6.14
Corinna cravde it in a summers night,	Ovid's Elegies	3.6.25
Charmes change corne to grasse, and makes it dye,	Ovid's Elegies	3.6.31
To this ad shame, shame to performe it quaild mee,	Ovid's Elegies	3.6.37
Why made king [to refuse] <and refusde> it?	Ovid's Elegies	3.6.49
Chuf-like had I not gold, and could not use it?	Ovid's Elegies	3.6.50
Yet notwithstanding, like one dead it lay,	Ovid's Elegies	3.6.65
To take it in her hand and play with it.	Ovid's Elegies	3.6.74
But when she saw it would by no meanes stand,	Ovid's Elegies	3.6.75
To cover it, spilt water in <on> the place.	Ovid's Elegies	3.6.84
But better things it gave, corne without ploughes,	Ovid's Elegies	3.7.39
And corne with least part of it selfe returnd.	Ovid's Elegies	3.9.30
Who sees it, graunts some deity there is shrowded.	Ovid's Elegies	3.12.8
Let me, and them by it be aye be-friended.	Ovid's Elegies	3.12.36
She hath not trode <tred> awrie that doth denie it,	Ovid's Elegies	3.13.5
Such as confesse, have lost their good names by it.	Ovid's Elegies	3.13.6
Slippe still, onely denie it when tis done,	Ovid's Elegies	3.13.15
Teach but your tongue to say, I did it not,	Ovid's Elegies	3.13.48
Let it suffise,/That my slacke muse, sings of Leanders eies,	Hero and Leander	1.71
Eternall heaven to burne, for so it seem'd,	Hero and Leander	1.100
The towne of Sestos cal'd it Venus glasse.	Hero and Leander	1.142
It lies not in our power to love, or hate,	Hero and Leander	1.167
The reason no man knowes, let it suffise,	Hero and Leander	1.173
He toucht her hand, in touching it she trembled,	Hero and Leander	1.183
When misers keepe it; being put to lone,	Hero and Leander	1.235
In time it will returne us two for one.	Hero and Leander	1.236
Shall see it ruinous and desolate.	Hero and Leander	1.240
Or if it could, downe from th'enameld skie,	Hero and Leander	1.249
Well therefore by the gods decreed it is,	Hero and Leander	1.253
But they that dayly tast neat wine, despise it.	Hero and Leander	1.261
Virginitie, albeit some highly prise it,	Hero and Leander	1.262
Nor hath it any place of residence,	Hero and Leander	1.272
Men foolishly doe call it vertuous,	Hero and Leander	1.277
What vertue is it that is borne with us?	Hero and Leander	1.278
Whose name is it, if she be false or not,	Hero and Leander	1.285
The richest corne dies, if it be not reapt,	Hero and Leander	1.327
Whose carelesse haire, in stead of pearle t'adorne it,	Hero and Leander	1.389
Glist'red with deaw, as one that seem'd to skorne it:	Hero and Leander	1.390
And gave it to his simple rustike love,	Hero and Leander	1.435
They seeing it, both Love and him abhor'd,	Hero and Leander	1.463
And to the seat of Jove it selfe advaunce,	Hero and Leander	1.467
And kept it downe that it might mount the hier.	Hero and Leander	2.42
As in plaine termes (yet cunningly) he crav'd it,	Hero and Leander	2.71
Love alwaies makes those eloquent that have it.	Hero and Leander	2.72
Shee, with a kind of graunting, put him by it,	Hero and Leander	2.73

IT (cont.)			
And ever as he thought himselfe most nigh it,	Hero and Leander		2.74
We often kisse it, often looke thereon,	Hero and Leander		2.81
Though it was morning, did he take his flight.	Hero and Leander		2.102
Burnes where it cherisht, murders where it loved.	Hero and Leander		2.128
The light of hidden fire it selfe discovers,	Hero and Leander		2.133
What is it now, but mad Leander dares?	Hero and Leander		2.146
But when he knew it was not Ganimed,	Hero and Leander		2.169
He flung at him his mace, but as it went,	Hero and Leander		2.209
He cald it in, for love made him repent.	Hero and Leander		2.210
As meaning to be veng'd for darting it.	Hero and Leander		2.212
And therefore let it rest upon thy pillow.	Hero and Leander		2.252
describe, but hee/That puls or shakes it from the golden tree:	Hero and Leander		2.300
For much it greev'd her that the bright day-light,	Hero and Leander		2.303
ITALIA			
Which now we call Italia of his name,	Dido	1.2.23	Cloan
ITALIAM			
Italiam non sponte sequor.	Dido	5.1.140	Aeneas
ITALIAN			
studied Physicke, and began/To practise first upon the Italian;	Jew	2.3.182	Barab
a precious powder that I bought/Of an Italian in Ancona once,	Jew	3.4.69	Barab
Therefore ile have Italian maskes by night,	Edw	1.1.55	Gavstn
He weares a short Italian hooded cloake,	Edw	1.4.413	Mortmr
ITALY			
Put sailes to sea to seeke out Italy,	Dido	1.1.218	Aeneas
And he at last depart to Italy,	Dido	2.1.330	Venus
And let Achates saile to Italy:	Dido	3.1.115	Dido
Stoute love in mine armes make thy Italy,	Dido	3.4.57	Dido
Hath summond me to fruitfull Italy:	Dido	4.3.4	Aeneas
We may as one saile into Italy.	Dido	4.3.30	Aeneas
To Italy, sweete friends to Italy,	Dido	4.3.43	Cloan
To sea Aeneas, finde out Italy.	Dido	4.3.56	Aeneas
And seeke a forraine land calde Italy:	Dido	4.4.98	Dido
Drive if you can my house to Italy:	Dido	4.4.129	Dido
And swim to Italy, Ile keepe these sure:	Dido	4.4.164	Dido
While Italy is cleane out of thy minde?	Dido	5.1.29	Hermes
I tell thee thou must straight to Italy,	Dido	5.1.53	Hermes
With speede he bids me saile to Italy,	Dido	5.1.68	Aeneas
For lingering here, neglecting Italy.	Dido	5.1.97	Aeneas
To leave this towne and passe to Italy,	Dido	5.1.100	Aeneas
Goe goe and spare not, seeke out Italy,	Dido	5.1.169	Dido
And leaving me will saile to Italy.	Dido	5.1.195	Dido
Graunt, though the traytors land in Italy,	Dido	5.1.304	Dido
The wandring Sailers of proud Italy,	2Tamb	1.1.39	Orcan
My selfe in Malta, some in Italy,	Jew	1.1.126	Barab
This day is held through Rome and Italy,	F 834	3.1.56	Mephst
Thou shalt be famous through all Italy,	F1215	4.1.61	Emper
Italy many yeares hath lyen until'd,	Lucan, First Booke		28
vales, deviding just/The bounds of Italy, from Cisalpin Fraunce;	Lucan, First Booke		218
As soone as Caesar got unto the banke/And bounds of Italy;	Lucan, First Booke		226
townes/He garrison'd; and Italy he fild with soldiours.	Lucan, First Booke		464
ITERATING			
The iterating of these lines brings gold;	F 544	2.1.156	Mephst
I'TH			
But take it to you i'th devils name.	Jew	1.2.154	Barab
And rise with them i'th middle of the Towne,	Jew	5.1.92	Barab
To morrow we would sit i'th Consistory,	F1017	3.2.37	Pope
I, and I fall not asleepe i'th meane time.	F1196	4.1.42	Benvol
ITHAMORE (See also ITHIMORE)			
Welcome grave Fryar; Ithamore begon,	Jew	3.3.52	Abigal
Ile pay thee with a vengeance Ithamore.	Jew	3.4.116	Barab
I'THE			
'Twas I, that when thou wer't i'the way to heaven,	F1886	5.2.90	Mephst
ITHIMOR			
Faith, Sir, my birth is but meane, my name's Ithimor,	Jew	2.3.165	Ithimr
ITHIMORE			
Now tell me, Ithimore, how lik'st thou this?	Jew	2.3.364	Barab
Why, how now Ithimore, why laugh'st thou so?	Jew	3.3.4	Abigal
Am I Ithimore?	Jew	3.3.23	P Ithimr
Well, Ithimore, let me request thee this,	Jew	3.3.26	Abigal
But here comes cursed Ithimore with the Fryar.	Jew	3.3.49	Abigal
Oh Ithimore come neere;/Come neere, my love, come neere, thy	Jew	3.4.13	Barab
And Ithimore, from hence/Ne're shall she grieve me more with	Jew	3.4.28	Barab
Ithimore, intreat not for her, I am mov'd,	Jew	3.4.35	Barab
Oh trusty Ithimore; no servant, but my friend;	Jew	3.4.42	Barab
Well said, Ithimore;	Jew	3.4.56	Barab
Very well, Ithimore, then now be secret;	Jew	3.4.60	Barab
I but Ithimore seest thou this?	Jew	3.4.67	Barab
Thus Ithimore:	Jew	3.4.74	Barab
There Ithimore must thou goe place this [pot] <plot>:	Jew	3.4.84	Barab
Peace, Ithimore, 'tis better so then spar'd.	Jew	3.4.91	Barab
Stay, first let me stirre it Ithimore.	Jew	3.4.95	Barab
Oh my sweet Ithimore go set it downe/And come againe so soone	Jew	3.4.108	Barab
Fryar Barnardine goe you with Ithimore.	Jew	4.1.99	Barab
Ithimore, tell me, is the Fryar asleepe?	Jew	4.1.129	Barab
What time a night is't now, sweet Ithimore?	Jew	4.1.157	Barab
Come Ithimore, let's helpe to take him hence.	Jew	4.1.200	Barab
Pilia-borza, didst thou meet with Ithimore?	Jew	4.2.1	P Curtzn
Now, gentle Ithimore, lye in my lap.	Jew	4.2.82	Curtzn
Shall Ithimore my love goe in such rags?	Jew	4.2.85	Curtzn
Whither will I not goe with gentle Ithimore?	Jew	4.2.99	Curtzn
no childe, and unto whom/Should I leave all but unto Ithimore?	Jew	4.3.45	Barab
Never lov'd man servant as I doe Ithimore.	Jew	4.3.54	Barab

ITHIMORE (cont.)			
Come gentle Ithimore, lye in my lap.	Jew	4.4.27	Curtzn
How sweet, my Ithimore, the flowers smell.	Jew	4.4.39	Curtzn
ITIS			
[Itis is] <It is as> great, but auntient cause of sorrowe.	Ovid's Elegies		2.6.10
And mother-murtherd Itis [they] <thee> bewaile,	Ovid's Elegies		2.14.30
IT'S			
It's no sinne to deceive a Christian;	Jew	2.3.309	Barab
Were Love the cause, it's like I shoulde descry him,	Ovid's Elegies		1.2.5
IT SELF			
that of it self was hote enoughe to worke/thy Just degestione	Paris	ms26,p391	Guise
IT SELFE			
And when we enter in, not heaven it selfe/Shall ransome thee,	2Tamb	3.3.27	Therid
The power of vengeance now incampes it selfe,	P 717	14.20	Navrre
hath lost both Germany and the world, yea heaven it selfe:	F1844	5.2.48 P	Faust
Roome was so great it could not beare it selfe:	Lucan, First Booke		72
that made Rcome/Governe the earth, the sea, the world it selfe,	Lucan, First Booke		110
Albeit the Citty thou wouldst have so ra'st/Be Roome it selfe.	Lucan, First Booke		387
And corne with least part of it selfe returnd.	Ovid's Elegies		3.9.30
And to the seat of Jove it selfe advaunce,	Hero and Leander		1.467
The light of hidden fire it selfe discovers,	Hero and Leander		2.133
ITYS (See also ITIS)			
Bird-changed Progne doth her Itys teare.	Ovid's Elegies		3.11.32
IULUS			
And yong Iulus more then thousand yeares,	Dido	5.1.39	Hermes
Ye gods of Phrigia and Iulus line,	Lucan, First Booke		199
Faire-fac'd Iulus, he went forth thy court.	Ovid's Elegies		3.8.14
IVIE			
Their <Your> youthfull browes with Ivie girt to meete him,/With	Ovid's Elegies		3.8.61
A belt of straw, and Ivie buds,	Passionate Shepherd		17
IVORIE			
Oares of massie Ivorie full of holes,	Dido	3.1.118	Dido
With milke-white Hartes upon an Ivorie sled,	1Tamb	1.2.98	Tamb
She on my necke her Ivorie armes did throw,	Ovid's Elegies		3.6.7
IVORY (See also YVORY)			
As faire as was Pigmalions Ivory gyrle,	2Tamb	1.2.38	Callap
Whose eies shot fire from their Ivory bowers,	2Tamb	2.4.9	Tamb
Who gently now wil lance thy Ivory throat,	2Tamb	3.4.24	Olymp
When wandring Phoebes Ivory cheeks were scortcht/And all the	2Tamb	5.3.232	Tamb
Arachne staynes Assyrian ivory.	Ovid's Elegies		2.5.40
IVY (See IVIE)			
IWIS			
So wish not they Iwis that sent thee hither,	Edw	3.1.152	Edward
IXIONS			
Wretched Ixions shaggie footed race,	Hero and Leander		1.114
JACENTEM			
Hunc dies vidit fugiens jacentem.	Edw	4.7.54	Leistr
JACINTS			
Jacints, hard Topas, grasse-greene Emeraulds,	Jew	1.1.26	Barab
JACK			
I have not seene a dapper jack so briske,	Edw	1.4.412	Mortmr
JACOBE			
Sancte [Jacobe] <Jacobus>, now have mercye upon me.	P1172	22.34	Frier
JACOBIN			
What this detested Jacobin hath done.	P1195	22.57	King
JACOBINES			
heard of any man but he/Malign'd the order of the Jacobines:	Jew	4.1.104	Barab
JACOBINS			
your Majestie heere is a Frier of the order of the Jacobins,	P1156	22.18 P	1Msngr
JACOBS			
And with the Jacobs staffe measure the height/And distance of	2Tamb	3.3.50	Techel
JACOBUS			
[Sanctus] <Sancta> Jacobus hee was my Saint, pray to him.	P 358	6.13	Mntsrl
Sancte [Jacobe] <Jacobus>, now have mercye upon me.	P1172	22.34	Frier
JACOBYNS			
I am a Frier of the order of the Jacobyns, that for my	P1130	21.24 P	Frier
JACOMO			
Oh therefore, Jacomo, let me be one,	Jew	3.3.68	Abigal
And so I will, oh Jacomo, faile not but come.	Jew	4.1.108	Barab
What if I murder'd him e're Jacomo comes?	Jew	4.1.116	Barab
Then will not Jacomo be long from hence.	Jew	4.1.159	Barab
Why, how now Jacomo, what hast thou done?	Jew	4.1.174	Barab
JADED			
And jaded king of Pontus poisoned slaine,	Lucan, First Booke		337
Or jaded camst thou from some others bed.	Ovid's Elegies		3.6.80
JADES			
Holla, ye pampered Jades of Asia:	2Tamb	4.3.1	Tamb
The headstrong Jades of Thrace, Alcides tam'd,	2Tamb	4.3.12	Tamb
That like unruly never broken Jades,	2Tamb	4.3.45	Therid
We wil Techelles, forward then ye Jades:	2Tamb	4.3.97	Tamb
These Jades are broken winded, and halfe tyr'd,	2Tamb	5.1.129	Tamb
Bridle the steeled stomackes of those Jades.	2Tamb	5.3.203	Tamb
The nature of these proud rebelling Jades/Wil take occasion by	2Tamb	5.3.238	Tamb
And rough jades mouths with stubburn bits are torne,	Ovid's Elegies		1.2.15
Or wofull Hector whom wilde jades did teare?	Ovid's Elegies		2.1.32
JAERTIS			
And shame of nature [which] <with> Jaertis streame,	2Tamb	4.1.108	Tamb
city Samarcanda/And christall waves of fresh Jaertis streame,	2Tamb	4.3.108	Tamb
JAILES			
I fill'd the Jailes with Bankrouts in a yeare,	Jew	2.3.193	Barab
JAILOR (See also JAYLOR)			
to put him in remembrance he was a Jailor, that when I take	2Tamb	3.5.140 P	Tamb
JAIRIM			
There's Kirriah Jairim, the great Jew of Greece,	Jew	1.1.124	Baraba

JAMES
Come hether James,/I do commit this Gaveston to thee, . Edw. 2.5.106 Penbrk
No James, it is my countries cause I follow. . . . Edw 2.6.10 Warwck
JANGLING
least some one hope might ease/The Commons jangling minds, Lucan, First Booke 521
JANISARIES
Hath now in armes ten thousand Janisaries, . . . 1Tamb 3.3.15 Bassoe
Bassoes and Janisaries of my Guard, ... 1Tamb 3.3.61 Bajzth
JANISARS
And rifle all those stately Janisars. . . . . 1Tamb 3.3.26 Techel
JANIZARIES
and Barabas we give/To guard thy person, these our Janizaries: Jew 5.2.16 Calym
JANUARY
were it now Summer, as it is January, a dead time of the Winter, F1572 4.6.15 P Lady
nowe summer, as it is January, and the dead time of the winter, F App p.242 10 P Duchss
and in the month of January, how you shuld come by these . F App p.242 18 P Duke
JANUS
with which I burst/The rusty beames of Janus Temple doores, 2Tamb 2.4.114 Tamb
Peace through the world from Janus Phane shal flie, . . Lucan, First Booke 61
JAQUES
and inquire/For any of the Fryars of Saint [Jaques] <Jaynes>, Jew 3.3.28 Abigal
Saint Jaques Even) and then I say they use/To send their Almes Jew 3.4.76 Barab
JARARTES (See JAERTIS)
JARRE
Oh my Lord we will not jarre about the price; . . . Jew 2.3.65 Barab
Aye me poore soule when these begin to jarre. . . . Edw 2.2.72 Queene
that we can yet be tun'd together,/No, no, we jarre too farre. Edw 4.2.10 Queene
Seeing she likes my bookes, why should we jarre? . . Ovid's Elegies 2.4.20
Which long time lie untoucht, will harshly jarre. . . Hero and Leander 1.230
Women are woon when they begin to jarre. . . . . Hero and Leander 1.332
JARRES
Heere comes she thats cause of all these jarres. . . Edw 2.2.224 Edward
JARRING
Caesars, and Pompeys jarring love soone ended, . . . Lucan, First Booke 98
JASON
As was to Jason Colchos golden fleece. . . . . 1Tamb 4.4.9 Tamb
I'le be thy Jason, thou my golden Fleece; . . . . Jew 4.2.90 Ithimr
What Tereus, what Jason you provokes, ... Ovid's Elegies 2.14.33
What thanklesse Jason, Macareus, and Paris, . . . Ovid's Elegies 2.18.23
JASONS
And Jasons Argos, and the fleece of golde? . . . Ovid's Elegies 1.15.22
Jasons sad letter doth Hipsipile greete, ... Ovid's Elegies 2.18.33
JASPER
The wals were of discoloured Jasper stone, . . . Hero and Leander 1.136
JAVELIN
(Albeit the Moores light Javelin or his speare/Sticks in his Lucan, First Booke 213
JAWES
Which I will breake betwixt a Lyons jawes. . . . Dido 3.3.38 Cupid
And prest out fire from their burning jawes: . . . 1Tamb 2.6.6 Cosroe
that in his infancie/Did pash the jawes of Serpents venomous: 1Tamb 3.3.105 Bajzth
More safetie is there in a Tigers jawes, ... Edw 5.1.116 Edward
The jawes of hell are open to receive thee. . . . F1908 5.2.112 GdAngl
With jawes wide open ghastly roaring out; . . . . Lucan, First Booke 212
Jawes flesht with bloud continue murderous. . . . Lucan, First Booke 332
they manadge peace, and rawe warres bloudy jawes, . . Ovid's Elegies 3.7.58
JAYLOR
See father, how Almeda the Jaylor lookes upon us. . . 2Tamb 3.5.116 Celeb
JAYNES
and inquire/For any of the Fryars of Saint [Jaques] <Jaynes>, Jew 3.3.28 Abigal
JEALOUS
My mother Venus jealous of my health, ... Dido 2.1.221 Aeneas
Love made me jealous, but to make amends, ... Dido 4.4.33 Dido
The jealous bodie of his fearfull wife, ... 1Tamb 5.1.86 1Virgn
And jealous anger of his fearefull arme/Be pour'd with rigour 2Tamb 2.1.57 Fredrk
If he be jealous of his name and honor, ... 2Tamb 2.2.43 Orcan
Both jealous of my love, envied each other: . . . Jew 3.6.27 Abigal
Now waxt she jealous, least his love abated, . . . Hero and Leander 2.43
JEALOUSIE
Threatned with frowning wrath and jealousie, . . . 1Tamb 3.2.67 Agidas
The killing frownes of jealousie and love. . . . 1Tamb 3.2.91 Agidas
Whose jealousie admits no second Mate, ... 2Tamb 2.4.12 Tamb
And what the jealousie of warres must doe. . . . 2Tamb 4.1.104 Tamb
JEAST
you heartily sir; for wee cal'd you but in jeast I promise you. F1123 3.3.36 P Dick
JEASTING
And make us jeasting Pageants for their Trulles. . . 2Tamb 4.3.89 Therid
JEASTS
When every servile groome jeasts at my wrongs, . . . F1329 4.2.5 Benvol
JEAT
As blacke as Jeat, and hard as Iron or steel, . . . 2Tamb 1.3.27 Tamb
JEBUSITE
yet let me talke to her;/This off-spring of Cain, this Jebusite Jew 2.3.301 Barab
JEER'D
Then like a Jew he laugh'd and jeer'd, and told me he lov'd me Jew 4.2.108 P Pilia
JEERES (See also FLEERING)
How the slave jeeres at him? . . . . Jew 5.5.56 Govnr
JEHOVAE
Dei Acherontis propitii, valeat numen triplex Jehovae, Ignei, F 244 1.3.16 P Faust
JEHOVAM
[Quid tu moraris] <quod tumeraris>; per Jehovam, Gehennam, et F 248 1.3.20 P Faust
JEHOVA'S
Within this circle is Jehova's Name, ... F 236 1.3.8 Faust
JELLY (See GELLY)

JEM			
But this faire jem, sweet in the losse alone,	Hero and Leander	1.247	
JEROMES			
Jeromes Bible Faustus, view it well:	F 65	1.1.37	Faust
JERUSALEM			
To aid the kings of Soria and Jerusalem.	2Tamb	2.1.21	Fredrk
let us haste and meete/Our Army and our brother of Jerusalem,	2Tamb	2.3.43	Orcan
friend Mahomet, Emperour of Natolia, Jerusalem, Trebizon, Soria,	2Tamb	3.1.4	P Orcan
And I as many from Jerusalem,	2Tamb	3.1.44	Jrslem
From Palestina and Jerusalem,	2Tamb	3.5.32	Jrslem
Once at Jerusalem, where the pilgrims kneel'd,	Jew	2.3.208	Ithimr
And on my knees creepe to Jerusalem.	Jew	4.1.62	Barab
JESSES (See GESSES)			
JEST (See also JEAST)			
Twil proove a pretie jest (in faith) my friends.	1Tamb	2.5.90	Tamb
A jest to chardge on twenty thousand men?	1Tamb	2.5.91	Therid
Make but a jest to win the Persean crowne.	1Tamb	2.5.98	Tamb
And common souldiers jest with all their Truls.	2Tamb	4.3.91	Tamb
Beleeve me this jest bites sore.	P 771	15.29	King
And floute our traine, and jest at our attire:	Edw	1.4.418	Mortmr
JESTED			
Am I thus to be jested at and scornde?	P 758	15.16	Guise
JESTETH			
see how poverty jesteth in his nakednesse, the vilaine is bare,	F App	p.229 6	P Wagner
JESTING			
Leave of this jesting, here my lady comes.	Edw	2.1.56	Baldck
Go to sirra, leave your jesting, and tell us where he is.	F 201	1.2.8	P 1Schol
Well sirra, leave your jesting, and take these Guilders.	F 367	1.4.25	P Wagner
leave your jesting, and binde your selfe presently unto me for	F App	p.229 24	P Wagner
JESTS			
see how poverty jests in his nakednesse, I know the Villaines	F 348	1.4.6	P Wagner
JESUS			
Sweet Jesus Christ, I sollemnly protest,	2Tamb	1.1.135	Sgsmnd
JETS			
And Midas like he jets it in the court,	Edw	1.4.408	Mortmr
JETTE (See also JEAT)			
Now when he should not jette, he boults upright,	Ovid's Elegies	3.6.67	
JETTY			
And Jetty Feathers menace death and hell.	1Tamb	4.1.61	2Msngr
JEW			
But to present the Tragedy of a Jew,	Jew	Prol.30	Machvl
Goe tell 'em the Jew of Malta sent thee, man:	Jew	1.1.66	Barab
Rather had I a Jew be hated thus,	Jew	1.1.114	Barab
There's Kirriah Jairim, the great Jew of Greece,	Jew	1.1.124	Barab
Tut, Jew, we know thou art no souldier;	Jew	1.2.52	1Knght
No, Jew, like infidels.	Jew	1.2.62	Govnr
No, Jew, thou hast denied the Articles,	Jew	1.2.92	Govnr
Jew, we take particularly thine/To save the ruine of a	Jew	1.2.96	Govnr
The hopelesse daughter of a haplesse Jew,	Jew	1.2.317	Abigal
The Jew of Malta, wretched Barabas;	Jew	1.2.318	Abigal
Here comes the Jew, had not his goods bin seiz'd,	Jew	2.3.5	1Offcr
I heare the wealthy Jew walked this way;	Jew	2.3.32	Lodowk
Yond walks the Jew, now for faire Abigall.	Jew	2.3.38	Lodowk
What makes the Jew and Lodowicke so private?	Jew	2.3.138	Mthias
Tell me, Mathias, is not that the Jew?	Jew	2.3.152	Mater
Sirra, Jew, remember the booke.	Jew	2.3.159	Mthias
And like a cunning Jew so cast about,	Jew	2.3.235	Barab
your Lordship wud disdaine/To marry with the daughter of a Jew:	Jew	2.3.295	Barab
I, but the Jew has gold,	Jew	3.1.14	Pilia
But I must to the Jew and exclaime on him,	Jew	3.6.42	2Fryar
then goe with me/And helpe me to exclaime against the Jew.	Jew	3.6.46	2Fryar
Stay wicked Jew, repent, I say, and stay.	Jew	4.1.24	2Fryar
What needs all this? I know I am a Jew.	Jew	4.1.33	Barab
I am a Jew, and therefore am I lost.	Jew	4.1.57	Barab
As never Jew nor Christian knew the like:	Jew	4.1.118	Barab
And intercept my going to the Jew;	Jew	4.1.167	1Fryar
No, for this example I'le remaine a Jew:	Jew	4.1.195	Barab
When shall you see a Jew commit the like?	Jew	4.1.197	Barab
But you know some secrets of the Jew,	Jew	4.2.64	Pilia
Hang him, Jew.	Jew	4.2.81	P Ithimr
Then like a Jew he laugh'd and jeer'd, and told me he lov'd me	Jew	4.2.108	P Pilia
Sirra Jew, as you love your life send me five hundred crowns,	Jew	4.2.117	P Ithimr
Jew, I must ha more gold.	Jew	4.3.18	P Pilia
the gold, or know Jew it is in my power to hang thee.	Jew	4.3.37	P Pilia
Was ever Jew tormented as I am?	Jew	4.3.60	Barab
Now to the Jew.	Jew	4.4.11	Curtzn
Ha, to the Jew, and send me mony you were best.	Jew	4.4.12	P Ithimr
Dost not know a Jew, one Barabas?	Jew	4.4.56	P Ithimr
'Tis a strange thing of that Jew, he lives upon pickled	Jew	4.4.61	P Ithimr
Farewell Fidler: One letter more to the Jew.	Jew	4.4.72	Pilia
To undoe a Jew is charity, and not sinne.	Jew	4.4.81	Ithimr
Mathias did it not, it was the Jew.	Jew	5.1.11	Curtzn
Goe fetch him straight. I alwayes fear'd that Jew.	Jew	5.1.18	Govnr
Was my Mathias murder'd by the Jew?	Jew	5.1.44	Mater
Where is the Jew, where is that murderer?	Jew	5.1.48	Mater
So is the Turke, and Barabas the Jew.	Jew	5.1.51	1Offcr
My name is Barabas; I am a Jew.	Jew	5.1.72	Barab
Art thou that Jew whose goods we heard were sold/For	Jew	5.1.73	Calym
The Jew is here, and rests at your command.	Jew	5.1.83	Barab
to fall into the hands/Of such a Traitor and unhallowed Jew!	Jew	5.2.13	Govnr
Farewell brave Jew, farewell great Barabas.	Jew	5.2.20	Calym
Accursed Barabas, base Jew, relent?	Jew	5.5.73	Govnr
If any Christian, Heathen, Turke, or Jew,	Edw	5.4.75	Champn

JEWELL (See also JUELLES)
I would have a jewell for mine eare, ... Dido 1.1.46 Ganimd
And having thee, I have a jewell sure: . . . . . 1Tamb 2.2.56 Mycet
and in his tuskan cap/A jewell of more value then the crowne. Edw 1.4.415 Mortmr
One jewell have I left, receive thou this. . . . Edw 5.5.84 Edward
Like Aesops cocke, this jewell he enjoyed, . . . Hero and Leander 2.51

JEWELLER
And bid the Jeweller come hither too. . . . . . Jew 4.2.86 Ithimr

JEWELLS
Garments do weare, jewells and gold do wast, . . . Ovid's Elegies 1.10.61

JEWELS
Hold, take these Jewels at thy Lovers hand, ... Dido 3.4.61 Dido
With costlie jewels hanging at their eares, ... 1Tamb 1.1.144 Ceneus
The jewels and the treasure we have tane/Shall be reserv'd, and 1Tamb 1.2.2 Tamb
Now must your jewels be restor'd againe: . . . . . 1Tamb 1.2.114 Tamb
That offered jewels to thy sacred shrine, ... 1Tamb 3.3.199 Zabina
Make ready my Coch, my chaire, my jewels, I come, I come, I come 1Tamb 5.1.317 P Zabina
kings Concubines)/Take them, devide them and their jewels too, 2Tamb 4.3.72 Tamb
Rich costly Jewels, and Stones infinite, ... Jew 1.2.245 Barab
The gold and Jewels which I kept for thee. . . . Jew 1.2.298 Barab
And thinke upon the Jewels and the gold, ... Jew 1.2.349 Barab
I have found/The gold, the perles, and Jewels which he hid. Jew 2.1.23 Abigal
He sends her letters, bracelets, jewels, rings. . . Jew 2.3.259 Barab
No other jewels hang about my neck/Then these my lord, nor let Edw 1.4.330 Queene
Men tooke delight in Jewels, houses, plate, ... Lucan, First Booke 164
Jewels, and gold their Virgin tresses crowne, . . . Ovid's Elegies 3.12.25
Jewels being lost are found againe, this never, . . Hero and Leander 2.85
Rich jewels in the darke are soonest spide. . . . Hero and Leander 2.240

JEWES
Turkes, Arabians, Moores and Jewes/Enough to cover all Bythinia. 1Tamb 3.3.136 Bajzth
Cicilians, Jewes, Arabians, Turks, and Moors, . . . 2Tamb 1.1.62 Orcan
These are the Blessings promis'd to the Jewes, . . . Jew 1.1.105 Barab
What accident's betided to the Jewes? . . . . . . Jew 1.1.145 Barab
And all the Jewes in Malta must be there. . . . . . Jew 1.1.168 2Jew
Umh; All the Jewes in Malta must be there? . . . . Jew 1.1.169 Barab
Goe one and call those Jewes of Malta hither: . . . Jew 1.2.34 Govnr
mony of the Turkes shall all be levyed amongst the Jewes, Jew 1.2.69 P Reader
Some Jewes are wicked, as all Christians are: . . . Jew 1.2.112 Barab
Becomes it Jewes to be so credulous, ... Jew 1.2.360 Barab
Faire Abigall the rich Jewes daughter/Become a Nun? . . Jew 1.2.366 Mthias
Why, the rich Jewes daughter. . . . . Jew 1.2.382 Mthias
We Jewes can fawne like Spaniels when we please; . . Jew 2.3.20 Barab
As sure as heaven rain'd Manna for the Jewes, . . . Jew 2.3.248 Barab
But all are Hereticks that are not Jewes; . . . . . Jew 2.3.312 Barab
Are there not Jewes enow in Malta, ... Jew 2.3.359 Barab
up to the Jewes counting-house where I saw some bags of mony, Jew 3.1.18 P Pilia
a hundred of the Jewes Crownes that I had such a Concubine. Jew 3.1.27 P Ithimr
Pitty in Jewes, nor piety in Turkes. . . . . Jew 3.3.48 Abigal
for store of wealth may I compare/With all the Jewes in Malta; Jew 4.1.56 Barab
For the Jewes body, throw that o're the wals, . . . Jew 5.1.58 Govnr
This is the life we Jewes are us'd to lead; . . . . Jew 5.2.115 Barab
Now Selim note the unhallowed deeds of Jewes: . . . . Jew 5.5.92 Govnr
A Jewes curtesie: . . . . Jew 5.5.108 Govnr

JEWISH
I have beene zealous in the Jewish faith, ... Jew 4.1.51 Barab

JEWS
but here's the Jews man. . . . . Jew 3.1.22 P Pilia

JIG (See also JYGGING)
To Englands high disgrace, have made this Jig, . . . Edw 2.2.189 Lncstr

JOB
Yet brother Barabas remember Job. . . . . Jew 1.2.180 1Jew
What tell you me of Job? . . . . Jew 1.2.181 Barab

JOHN
where the mighty Christian Priest/Cal'd John the great, sits in 2Tamb 1.3.188 Techel
A good sir John of Henolt,/Never so cheereles, nor so farre Edw 4.2.13 Queene
Ah sweete sir John, even to the utmost verge/Of Europe, or the Edw 4.2.29 Queene
Sir John of Henolt, pardon us I pray, ... Edw 4.2.71 Kent
Prosper your happie motion good sir John. . . . . . Edw 4.2.75 Queene
Sir John of Henolt, be it thy renowne, ... Edw 4.2.78 Mortmr
if you aske, with sir John of Henolt, brother to the Marquesse, Edw 4.3.31 P Spencr
And will sir John of Henolt lead the round? . . . . Edw 4.3.40 Edward
that hee shall appeare to the said John Faustus, at all times, F 491 2.1.103 P Faust
I John Faustus of Wittenberg <Wertenberge>, Doctor, by these F 493 2.1.105 P Faust
full power to fetch or carry the said John Faustus, body and F 498 2.1.110 P Faust
By me John Faustus. . . . . F 500 2.1.112 P Faust

JOIDE
nor Jove joide heaven/Untill the cruel Giants war was done) Lucan, First Booke 35

JOIES
And have these joies in full possession. . . . . . F 179 1.1.151 Faust
That hath depriv'd thee of the joies of heaven. . . F1974 5.2.178 Faust
Flint-brested Pallas joies in single life, ... Hero and Leander 1.321
The longing heart of Hero much more joies/Then nymphs and Hero and Leander 2.232

JOIFUL
O sight thrice welcome to my joiful soule, ... 1Tamb 5.1.440 Zenoc

JOIN'D
Then when our powers in points of swords are join'd, . 1Tamb 2.1.40 Cosroe
And Eagles wings join'd to her feathered breast, . . . 2Tamb 3.4.62 Therid
And join'd those stars that shall be opposite, ... 2Tamb 3.5.81 Tamb
the good I have/Join'd with my fathers crowne would never cure. 2Tamb 4.1.58 Calyph

JOINDE
At whose byrth-day Cynthia with Saturne joinde, . . . 1Tamb 1.1.13 Cosroe

JOINE (See also JOYNE)
Forsake thy king and do but joine with me/And we will triumph 1Tamb 1.2.172 Tamb

JOINE (cont.)
Joine with me now in this my meane estate, 1Tamb 1.2.202 Tamb
And that made me to joine with Tamburlain, 1Tamb 2.7.30 Therid
when the Moon begins/To joine in one her semi-circled hornes: 1Tamb 3.1.12 Bajzth
Where they shall meete, and joine their force in one, 1Tamb 3.3.257 Tamb
Joine your Arabians with the Souldans power: 1Tamb 4.3.16 Souldn
All which will joine against this Tamburlain, 2Tamb 3.1.61 Soria
To joine with you against this Tamburlaine. 2Tamb 5.2.35 Amasia
Then wil you joine with us that be his peeres/To banish or Edw 1.2.42 Mortmr
I come to joine with you, and leave the king, Edw 2.3.2 Kent
Traitors be gon, and joine you with Mortimer, Edw 5.1.87 Edward
Why joine you force to share the world betwixt you? Lucan, First Booke 88
JOINES
and with what noise/An armed battaile joines, such and more Lucan, First Booke 578
JOINTE
But everie jointe shakes as I give it thee: Edw 5.5.86 Edward
JOINTES
My jointes benumb'd, unlesse I eat, I die. 1Tamb 4.4.98 Bajzth
Thy streetes strowed with dissevered jointes of men, 1Tamb 5.1.322 Zenoc
Prodigious birthes with more and ugly jointes/Then nature Lucan, First Booke 560
JOINTLIE
And therefore let us jointlie here protest, Edw 2.2.104 Lncstr
JOINTLY
And all have jointly sworne thy cruell death, 2Tamb 3.5.112 Soria
And <Faustus all> jointly move upon one Axle-tree, F 592 2.2.41 Mephst
JOINTS
So large of lims, his joints so strongly knit, 1Tamb 2.1.9 Menaph
Or roaring Cannons sever all thy joints, 1Tamb 5.1.223 Bajzth
while all thy joints/Be rackt and beat asunder with the wheele, 2Tamb 3.5.124 Tamb
JOLLY
<a jolly gentlewoman, and welbeloved F 699 (HC264)A P Glutny
JOURNEY
And let the end of this my fatall journey, 2Tamb 3.4.81 Olymp
you knowe I shall have occasion shortly to journey you. 2Tamb 3.5.115 P Tamb
you have had a shroud journey of it, will it please you to take F1120 3.3.33 P Robin
[Touching his journey through the world and ayre], F1145 3.3.58A 3Chor
of his men to attend you with provision fit for your journey. F1502 4.4.46 P Wagner
you have had a great journey, wil you take sixe pence in your F App p.235 41 P Robin
Clowne, from my journey why doest me deterre? Ovid's Elegies 3.5.88
JOUYCE
The jouyce of Hebon, and Cocitus breath, Jew 3.4.101 Barab
JOVE (See also IOVE)
And my divine descent from sceptred Jove: Dido 1.1.219 Aeneas
But lustfull Jove and his adulterous child, Dido 3.2.18 Juno
Sister of Jove, if that thy love be such, Dido 3.2.53 Venus
Iarbus, curse that unrevenging Jove, Dido 4.1.18 Iarbus
That I may pacifie that gloomie Jove, Dido 4.2.2 Iarbus
Eternall Jove, great master of the Clowdes, Dido 4.2.4 Iarbus
Jove wils it so, my mother wils it so: Dido 4.3.5 Aeneas
Now lookes Aeneas like immortall Jove, Dido 4.4.45 Dido
Or els abide the wrath of frowning Jove. Dido 5.1.54 Hermes
Jove hath heapt on me such a desperate charge, Dido 5.1.64 Aeneas
Sent from his father Jove, appeard to me, Dido 5.1.95 Aeneas
I am commaunded by immortall Jove, Dido 5.1.99 Aeneas
Theile breake his ships, O Proteus, Neptune, Jove, Dido 5.1.255 Dido
And Jove, the Sun and Mercurie denied/To shed [their] <his> 1Tamb 1.1.14 Cosroe
And Jove may never let me longer live, 1Tamb 1.1.170 Cosroe
Zenocrate, lovelier than the Love of Jove, 1Tamb 1.2.87 Tamb
And Jove himselfe will stretch his hand from heaven, 1Tamb 1.2.180 Tamb
Jove sometime masked in a Shepheards weed, 1Tamb 1.2.199 Tamb
What better president than mightie Jove? 1Tamb 2.7.17 Tamb
For as when Jove did thrust old Saturn down, 1Tamb 2.7.36 Usumc
Yet would I with my sword make Jove to stoope. 1Tamb 4.4.74 Tamb
O highest Lamp of everliving Jove, 1Tamb 5.1.290 Bajzth
Ah myghty Jove and holy Mahomet, 1Tamb 5.1.363 Zenoc
Jove viewing me in armes, lookes pale and wan, 1Tamb 5.1.452 Tamb
That darted mountaines at her brother Jove: 1Tamb 5.1.511 Tamb
that in her wings/Caries the fearfull thunderbolts of Jove. 2Tamb 1.1.101 Orcan
as if infernall Jove/Meaning to aid [thee] <them> in this 2Tamb 1.3.143 Techel
That Jove shall send his winged Messenger/To bid me sheath my 2Tamb 1.3.166 Tamb
If he be son to everliving Jove, 2Tamb 2.2.41 Orcan
For amorous Jove hath snatcht my love from hence, 2Tamb 2.4.107 Tamb
That Jove surchardg'd with pity of our wrongs, 2Tamb 3.1.35 Callap
Now, he that cals himself the scourge of Jove, 2Tamb 3.5.21 Orcan
Who now with Jove opens the firmament, 2Tamb 3.5.56 Callap
Here Jove, receive his fainting soule againe, 2Tamb 4.1.111 Tamb
Crown'd and invested by the hand of Jove, 2Tamb 4.1.151 Tamb
or by speach I heare/Immortall Jove say, Cease my Tamburlaine, 2Tamb 4.1.199 Tamb
Supposing amorous Jove had sent his sonne, 2Tamb 4.2.18 Therid
Thus am I right the Scourge of highest Jove, 2Tamb 4.3.24 Tamb
And art a king as absolute as Jove, 2Tamb 4.3.33 Orcan
If Jove esteeming me too good for earth, 2Tamb 4.3.60 Tamb
The wrathfull messenger of mighty Jove, 2Tamb 5.1.92 Tamb
And wake blacke Jove to crouch and kneele to me, 2Tamb 5.1.98 Tamb
Theridamas, haste to the court of Jove, 2Tamb 5.3.61 Tamb
now, how Jove hath sent/A present medicine to recure my paine: 2Tamb 5.3.105 Tamb
For never doted Jove on Ganimed, Edw 1.4.180 Queene
That suffered Jove to passe in showers of golde/To Danae, all Edw 3.1.267 Spencr
Heare me immortall Jove, and graunt it too. Edw 5.1.143 Edward
Be thou on earth as Jove is in the skye, F 103 1.1.75 BdAngl
nor Jove joide heaven/Untill the cruel Giants war was done) Lucan, First Booke 35
Quirinus rites and Latian Jove advanc'd/On Alba hill o Vestall Lucan, First Booke 200
These troupes should soone pull down the church of Jove. Lucan, First Booke 381

JOVE (cont.)
to Hesus, and fell Mercury <(Jove)>/They offer humane flesh, Lucan, First Booke 440
humane flesh, and where [Jove] <it> seemes/Bloudy like Dian, Lucan, First Booke 441
The flame in Alba consecrate to Jove, Lucan, First Booke 548
to unfould/What you intend, great Jove is now displeas'd, Lucan, First Booke 631
Love <Jove> knowes with such like praiers, I dayly move hir: Ovid's Elegies 1.3.4
And she to whom in shape of [Swanne] <Bull> Jove came. Ovid's Elegies 1.3.22
Jove send me more such afternoones as this. Ovid's Elegies 1.5.26
Pay vowes to Jove, engirt thy hayres with baies, Ovid's Elegies 1.7.36
Bull and Eagle/And what ere love made Jove should thee invegle. Ovid's Elegies 1.10.8
Jove that thou shouldst not hast but wait his leasure, Ovid's Elegies 1.13.45
Jove and Joves thunderbolts I had in hand/Which for his heaven Ovid's Elegies 2.1.15
Even Jove himselfe out off my wit was reft. Ovid's Elegies 2.1.18
Pardon me Jove, thy weapons ayde me nought, Ovid's Elegies 2.1.19
as might make/Wrath-kindled Jove away his thunder shake. Ovid's Elegies 2.5.52
A mothers joy by Jove she had not felt. Ovid's Elegies 2.19.28
Jove liked her better then he did before. Ovid's Elegies 2.19.30
Jove throwes downe woods, and Castles with his fire: Ovid's Elegies 3.3.35
Jove being admonisht gold had soveraigne power, Ovid's Elegies 3.7.29
things feigne)/Crete proud that Jove her nourcery maintaine. Ovid's Elegies 3.9.20
Jove turnes himselfe into a Swanne, or gold, Ovid's Elegies 3.11.33
Jove might have sipt out Nectar from his hand. Hero and Leander 1.62
Jove, slylie stealing from his sisters bed, Hero and Leander 1.147
Heavens winged herrald, Jove-borne Mercury, Hero and Leander 1.386
Which being knowne (as what is hid from Jove)? Hero and Leander 1.436
To be reveng'd on Jove, did undertake, Hero and Leander 1.442
That Jove, usurper of his fathers seat, Hero and Leander 1.452
Were with Jove clos'd in Stigian Emperie. Hero and Leander 1.458
And to the seat of Jove it selfe advaunce, Hero and Leander 1.467
And swore he never should returne to Jove. Hero and Leander 2.168

JOVE-BORNE
Heavens winged herrald, Jove-borne Mercury, Hero and Leander 1.386

JOVES
And at Joves Altar finding Priamus, Dido 2.1.225 Aeneas
at whose latter gaspe/Joves marble statue gan to bend the brow, Dido 2.1.257 Aeneas
Aeneas stay, Joves Herald bids thee stay. Dido 5.1.24 Hermes
Whom doe I see, Joves winged messenger? Dido 5.1.25 Aeneas
And bullets like Joves dreadfull Thunderbolts, 1Tamb 2.3.19 Tamb
Zenocrate, were Egypt Joves owne land, 1Tamb 4.4.73 Tamb
If all the christall gates of Joves high court/Were opened 2Tamb 1.3.153 Tamb
Of Joves vast pallace the imperiall Orbe, 2Tamb 3.4.49 Therid
And that their power is puissant as Joves, 2Tamb 5.3.35 Usumc
As fast as Iris, or Joves Mercurie. Edw 1.4.371 Edward
As for my selfe, I stand as Joves huge tree, Edw 5.6.11 Mortmr
By desperate thoughts against Joves Deity: F 317 1.3.89 Faust
Graven in the booke of Joves high firmament, F 756 2.3.35 2Chor
Apolloes southsayers; and Joves feasting priests; Lucan, First Booke 601
Jove and Joves thunderbolts I had in hand/Which for his heaven Ovid's Elegies 2.1.15
My wench her dore shut, Joves affares I left, Ovid's Elegies 2.1.17
At me Joves right-hand lightning hath to throwe. Ovid's Elegies 3.3.30
Faith to the witnesse Joves praise doth apply, Ovid's Elegies 3.9.23
paths, wheron the gods might trace/To Joves high court. Hero and Leander 1.299
Stole some from Hebe (Hebe, Joves cup fil'd), Hero and Leander 1.434

JOY (See also JOIES)
And all the Sailers merrie make for joy, Dido 5.1.259 Dido
Whereat the Souldiers will conceive more joy, 1Tamb 1.1.152 Ceneus
Ringing with joy their superstitious belles: 1Tamb 3.3.237 Bajzth
bed, where many a Lord/In prime and glorie of his loving joy, 1Tamb 5.1.84 1Virgn
Whose sight with joy would take away my life, 1Tamb 5.1.419 Arabia
Since Death denies me further cause of joy, 1Tamb 5.1.430 Arabia
friends and fellow kings)/Makes me to surfet in conceiving joy. 2Tamb 1.3.152 Tamb
the christian King/Is made, for joy of your admitted truce: 2Tamb 2.2.21 Uribas
No Madam, but the beginning of your joy, 2Tamb 3.4.83 Techel
I joy my Lord, your highnesse is so strong, 2Tamb 5.3.110 Usumc
Retaine a thought of joy, or sparke of life? 2Tamb 5.3.163 Amyras
With what a flinty bosome should I joy, 2Tamb 5.3.185 Amyras
Pierc'd with the joy of any dignity? 2Tamb 5.3.190 Amyras
Denie my soule fruition of her joy, 2Tamb 5.3.194 Amyras
Joy any hope of your recovery? 2Tamb 5.3.215 Usumc
And glut your longings with a heaven of joy. 2Tamb 5.3.227 Tamb
Farewell my joy, and by my fingers take/A kisse from him that Jew 2.1.58 Barab
I have my wish, in that I joy thy sight, Edw 1.1.151 Edward
As is the joy of his returning home. Edw 2.1.58 Neece
Yet have I words left to expresse my joy: Edw 2.2.60 Gavstn
in England/Would cast up cappes, and clap their hands for joy, Edw 4.2.55 Mortmr
Blessed, the Kingdome of Joy, and must remaine in hell for ever. F1845 5.2.49 P Faust
and twenty yeares hath Faustus lost eternall joy and felicitie. F1860 5.2.64 P Faust
Or if it do, to thee no joy thence spring: Ovid's Elegies 1.4.68
Making her joy according to her hire. Ovid's Elegies 1.10.32
Doest joy to have thy hooked Arrowes shaked, Ovid's Elegies 2.9.13
My stay no crime, my flight no joy shall breede, Ovid's Elegies 2.17.25
A mothers joy by Jove she had not felt. Ovid's Elegies 2.19.28
That seeing thy teares can any joy then feele. Ovid's Elegies 3.5.60
Tibullus doth Elysiums joy inherit. Ovid's Elegies 3.8.60
With joy heares Neptunes swelling waters sound. Ovid's Elegies 3.10.30
And few great lords in vertuous deeds shall joy, Hero and Leander 1.479
Which made the world) another world begat,/Of unknowne joy. Hero and Leander 2.293

JOY'D
And joy'd the fire of this martiall flesh, 2Tamb 4.1.106 Tamb

JOYE
Yet triumphe in the hope of thee my joye? Edw 4.2.28 Queene

JOYED
And joyed to heare his Theaters applause; Lucan, First Booke 134

JOYES			
The while thine eyes attract their sought for joyes:	Dido	1.1.136	Venus
And makes our hopes survive to [coming] <cunning> joyes:	Dido	1.1.154	Achat
Heavens envious of our joyes is waxen pale,	Dido	4.4.52	Dido
enjoy in heaven/Can not compare with kingly joyes in earth.	1Tamb	2.5.59	Therid
For with thy view my joyes are at the full,	2Tamb	4.2.31	Therid
Beare not the burthen of your enemies joyes,	2Tamb	5.3.22	Techel
And tasted the eternall Joyes of heaven,	F 306	1.3.78	Mephst
so passionate/For being deprived of the Joyes of heaven?	F 312	1.3.84	Faust
And scorne those Joyes thou never shalt possesse.	F 314	1.3.86	Faust
Because thou hast depriv'd me of those Joyes.	F 554	2.2.3	Faust
Innumerable joyes had followed thee.	F1893	5.2.97	GdAngl
Great joyes by hope I inly shall conceive.	Ovid's Elegies		2.9.44
Joyes with uncertaine faith thou takest and brings.	Ovid's Elegies		2.9.50
By thy default thou doest our joyes defraude.	Ovid's Elegies		2.19.58
Mad streame, why doest our mutuall joyes deferre?	Ovid's Elegies		3.5.87
In Virgil Mantua joyes:	Ovid's Elegies		3.14.7
JOYEUX			
the Duke of Joyeux/Hath made great sute unto the King therfore.	P 733	14.36	1Msngr
My sweet Joyeux, I make thee Generall,	P 743	15.1	King
Health and harty farwell to my Lord Joyeux.	P 751	15.9	Guise
JOYFULL (See also JOIFUL)			
For I have joyfull newes to tell thee of,	Edw	2.1.75	Neece
To comfort you, and bring you joyfull newes.	Edw	5.5.43	Ltborn
I warrant you sir; O joyfull day:	F1476	4.4.20	P HrsCsr
Which joyfull Hero answered in such sort,	Hero and Leander		2.15
JOYING			
Joying the fruit of Ceres garden plot,	2Tamb	4.3.37	Orcan
JOYN'D			
Knit in these hands, thus joyn'd in nuptiall rites,	P 4	1.4	Charls
For feare that Guise joyn'd with the King of Spaine,	P 573	11.38	Navrre
O faintly joyn'd friends with ambition blind,	Lucan, First Booke		87
JOYNDE			
Put of that feare, they are already joynde,	P 605	12.18	King
JOYNE			
Why should not they then joyne in marriage,	Dido	3.2.74	Juno
And with the Queene of England joyne my force,	P 801	16.15	Navrre
That basely seekes to joyne with such a King,	P1115	21.9	Dumain
And when the commons and the nobles joyne,	Edw	1.4.287	Mortmr
Provided this, that you my lord of Arundell/Will joyne with me.	Edw	2.5.82	Penbrk
I'le joyne the Hils that bind the Affrick shore,	F 335	1.3.107	Faust
He'd joyne long Asses eares to these huge hornes,	F1449	4.3.19	Benvol
At Munda let the dreadfull battailes joyne;	Lucan, First Booke		40
Mingle not thighes, nor to his legge joyne thine,	Ovid's Elegies		1.4.43
I sawe you then unlawfull kisses joyne,	Ovid's Elegies		2.5.23
Nemesis and thy first wench joyne their kisses,	Ovid's Elegies		3.8.53
JOYNED			
This grieves me not, no joyned kisses spent,	Ovid's Elegies		2.5.59
JOYNES			
And joynes your linnage to the crowne of France?	P 51	1.51	Admral
JOYNING			
In joyning with the man, ordain'd by heaven/To further every	1Tamb	2.1.52	Ortyg
I have a Castle joyning neere these woods,	F1452	4.3.22	Benvol
JOYNT			
For otherwhile he will be out of joynt.	Dido	3.3.24	Dido
Or aged Atlas shoulder out of joynt,	Dido	4.1.12	Achat
JOYNTLY			
and joyntly both/Beating their breasts and falling on the	Dido	2.1.227	Aeneas
And joyntly both yeeld up their wished right.	Edw	5.1.63	Edward
All <joyntly> move from East to West, in foure and twenty	F 597	2.2.46	P Mephst
held up, all joyntly cryde/They'ill follow where he please:	Lucan, First Booke		388
JOYNTS			
Her halfe dead joynts, and trembling limmes I sawe,	Ovid's Elegies		1.7.53
And her small joynts incircling round hoope make thee.	Ovid's Elegies		2.15.4
With virgin waxe hath some imbast my joynts,	Ovid's Elegies		3.6.29
JUBALTER			
And thence unto the straightes of Jubalter:	1Tamb	3.3.256	Tamb
JUDAEA			
Judaea, Gaza, and Scalonians bounds,	2Tamb	3.1.45	Jrslem
JUDAS			
he weares, Judas left under the Elder when he hang'd himselfe.	Jew	4.4.66	P Ithimr
JUDGD			
For her ill-beautious Mother judgd to slaughter?	Ovid's Elegies		3.3.18
JUDGE			
If outward habit judge the inward man.	1Tamb	1.2.163	Tamb
I judge the purchase more important far.	1Tamb	2.5.92	Therid
Judge by thy selfe Theridamas, not me,	1Tamb	2.5.93	Tamb
I say no more, judge you the rest my lord.	Edw	1.4.148	Gavstn
To binde or loose, lock fast, condemne, or judge,	F 935	3.1.157	Pope
which of both/Had justest cause unlawful tis to judge:	Lucan, First Booke		127
Who sees not warre sit by the quivering Judge;	Lucan, First Booke		320
Judge you the rest, being tyrde <tride> she bad me kisse.	Ovid's Elegies		1.5.25
The unjust Judge for bribes becomes a stale.	Ovid's Elegies		1.10.38
She safe by favour of her judge doth rest.	Ovid's Elegies		2.2.56
He being Judge, I am convinc'd of blame.	Ovid's Elegies		2.17.2
By these I judge, delight me may the rest,	Ovid's Elegies		3.2.35
Thence growes the Judge, and knight of reputation.	Ovid's Elegies		3.7.56
Thee, goddesse, bountifull all nations judge,	Ovid's Elegies		3.9.5
JUDGEMENT			
And Paris judgement of the heavenly ball,	Dido	3.2.44	Juno
And thus me thinkes should men of judgement frame/This is the	Jew	1.1.34	Barab
In sight and judgement of thy lustfull eye?	P 687	13.31	Guise
should defend/Or great wealth from a judgement seate ascend.	Ovid's Elegies		1.10.40

JUDGEMENTS			
And now <so> to patient judgements we appeale <our plaude>,	F 9	Prol.9	1Chor
JUDGES			
cast do happe/Sharpe stripes, she sitteth in the judges lappe.	Ovid's Elegies		2.2.62
JUDGMENT			
Is in your judgment thought a learned man.	P 391	7.31	Guise
JUELLES			
Enchast with precious juelles of mine owne:	1Tamb	1.2.96	Tamb
JUICE (See also JOUYCE, JUYCE)			
Oft bitter juice brings to the sicke reliefe.	Ovid's Elegies		3.10.8
JULIA			
for Julia/Snatcht hence by cruel fates with ominous howles,	Lucan, First Booke		111
Julia, had heaven given thee longer life/Thou hadst restrainde	Lucan, First Booke		115
JULIUS			
My Campe is like to Julius Caesars Hoste,	1Tamb	3.3.152	Tamb
That <which> Julius caesar brought from Affrica.	F 824	3.1.46	Mephst
Pope Julius swore to Princely Sigismond,	F 925	3.1.147	Bruno
Pope Julius did abuse the Churches Rites,	F 928	3.1.150	Pope
JUNO			
I love thee well, say Juno what she will.	Dido	1.1.2	Jupitr
My Juno ware upon her marriage day,	Dido	1.1.43	Jupitr
Juno, false Juno in her Chariots pompe,	Dido	1.1.54	Venus
That onely Juno rules in Rhamnuse towne.	Dido	3.2.20	Juno
Juno, my mortall foe, what make you here?	Dido	3.2.24	Venus
Than Juno sister to the highest God,	1Tamb	3.2.54	Zenoc
As Juno, when the Giants were supprest,	1Tamb	5.1.510	Tamb
Like frantick Juno will I fill the earth,	Edw	1.4.178	Queene
While Juno Io keepes when hornes she wore,	Ovid's Elegies		2.19.29
And Juno like with Dis raignes under ground?	Ovid's Elegies		3.9.46
The Priests to Juno did prepare chaste feasts,	Ovid's Elegies		3.12.3
Where Juno comes, each youth, and pretty maide,	Ovid's Elegies		3.12.23
JUNOES			
when by Junoes taske/He had before lookt Pluto in the face.	Lucan, First Booke		575
There Junoes bird displayes his gorgious feather,	Ovid's Elegies		2.6.55
He to th'Hetrurians Junoes feast commended,	Ovid's Elegies		3.12.35
JUNOS			
From Junos bird Ile pluck her spotted pride,	Dido	1.1.34	Jupitr
Whiles Dido lives and rules in Junos towne,	Dido	3.4.50	Aeneas
While Junos watch-man Io too much eyde,	Ovid's Elegies		2.2.45
JUPITER			
Sweet Jupiter, if ere I pleasde thine eye,	Dido	1.1.19	Ganimd
False Jupiter, rewardst thou vertue so?	Dido	1.1.78	Venus
Great Jupiter, still honourd maist thou be,	Dido	1.1.137	Venus
As Jupiter to sillie [Baucis] <Vausis> house:	Dido	1.2.41	Iarbus
But that eternall Jupiter commands.	Dido	5.1.82	Aeneas
Wherein have I offended Jupiter,	Dido	5.1.129	Dido
And dare the force of angrie Jupiter.	1Tamb	2.6.4	Cosroe
And calme the rage of thundring Jupiter:	1Tamb	3.3.123	Tamb
Strooke with the voice of thundring Jupiter.	1Tamb	4.2.25	Tamb
Nor are the names of Saturne, Mars, or Jupiter,	F 594	2.2.43	Mephst
<as> Saturne in thirty yeares, Jupiter in twelve, Mars in four,	F 604	2.2.53	P Faust
Brighter art thou then flaming Jupiter,	F1783	5.1.110	Faust
Kind Jupiter hath low declin'd himselfe;	Lucan, First Booke		660
And Jupiter unto his place restor'd.	Hero and Leander		1.464
JUROR			
I am a juror in the holy league,	P 837	17.32	Guise
JUST			
Save onely that in Beauties just applause,	1Tamb	5.1.178	Tamb
O just and dreadfull punisher of sinne,	2Tamb	2.3.4	Sgsmnd
So for just hate, for shame, and to subdew/This proud contemner	2Tamb	4.3.39	Orcan
Wonder not at it, Sir, the heavens are just:	Jew	5.1.55	Govnr
Doth heare and see the praiers of the just:	P 43	1.43	Navrre
And see it honoured with just solemnitie.	P 196	3.31	Admral
And when this just revenge is finished,	P 318	5.45	Anjoy
It is my due by just succession:	P 570	11.35	Navrre
My Lords, sith in a quarrell just and right,	P 698	14.1	Navrre
Just torments for his trechery.	P1175	22.37	King
enoughe to worke/thy Just degestione with extreamest shame	Paris	ms27,p391	Guise
Christ cannot save thy soule, for he is just,	F 636	2.2.85	Lucifr
Just through the midst runnes flowing Tybers streame,	F 813	3.1.35	Mephst
That all the world may see my just revenge.	F1382	4.2.58	Benvol
and when I came just in the midst my horse vanisht away, and I	F1544	4.5.40	P HrsCsr
deny/The just [requests] <request> of those that wish him well,	F1691	5.1.18	Faust
Thou shalt both satisfie my just desire,	F App	p.237 35	Emper
Ifaith thats just nothing at all.	F App	p.237 40	P Knight
And creepes along the vales, deviding just/The bounds of Italy,	Lucan, First Booke		217
Should I sollicit her that is so just:	Ovid's Elegies		2.7.25
new to enter/Warres, just Latinus, in thy kingdomes center:	Ovid's Elegies		2.12.22
And of just compasse for her knuckles bee.	Ovid's Elegies		2.15.6
Egeria with just Numa had good sport,	Ovid's Elegies		2.17.18
If of scornd lovers god be venger just,	Ovid's Elegies		3.7.65
JUSTEST			
which of both/Had justest cause unlawful tis to judge:	Lucan, First Booke		127
JUSTICE			
Which we referd to justice of his Christ,	2Tamb	2.3.28	Orcan
my striving hands/From martiall justice on thy wretched soule.	2Tamb	4.1.96	Tamb
tyrannies/(If tyrannies wars justice ye repute)/I execute,	2Tamb	4.1.147	Tamb
To make the justice of my heart relent:	P 533	10.6	Guise
But justice of the quarrell and the cause,	Edw	3.1.222	Edward
to whom in justice it belongs/To punish this unnaturall revolt:	Edw	4.6.8	Kent
JUSTIFIE			
Sham'st thou not thus to justifie thy selfe,	Jew	1.2.119	Govnr
Or justifie my vices being many,	Ovid's Elegies		2.4.2

JUSTIFIED
And being justified by two words, thinke/The cause acquits you   Ovid's Elegies   3.13.49
JUSTINIAN
Physicke farewell: where is Justinian? . . . . .   F 55   1.1.27   Faust
JUSTLY
They justly challenge their protection: . . . . . .   P 210   4.8   Charls
hath Faustus justly requited this injurious knight, which being   F1312   4.1.158   P Faust
Justly rewarded for his villanies. . . . . . .   F1376   4.2.52   Benvol
And justly: for her praise why did I tell? . . .   Ovid's Elegies   3.11.9
JUVAT
Sic sic juvat ire sub umbras. . . . .   Dido   5.1.313   Dido
JUYCE
I dranke of Poppy and cold mandrake juyce; . . . .   Jew   5.1.80   Barab
JYGGING
From jygging vaines of riming mother wits, ...   1Tamb   Prol.1   Prolog
KATHERIN
Looke, Katherin, looke, thy sonne gave mine these wounds.   Jew   3.2.16   Govnr
KATHERINA
Come, Katherina, our losses equall are, ...   Jew   3.2.36   Govnr
KATHERINE
For Katherine must have her will in France: . . . .   P 520   9.39   QnMoth
For while she lives Katherine will be Queene. . . . .   P 654   12.67   QnMoth
KEELE
keele at [Antwerpe] <Anwerpe> <Antwarpes> <Antwerpes> bridge,   F 123   1.1.95   Faust
And Marriners, albeit the keele be sound, ...   Lucan, First Booke   500
KEELES
And now downe falles the keeles into the deepe: . .   Dido   5.1.253   Dido
KEEMBE (See also UNKEEMBE)
Worthy to keembe none but a Goddesse faire, ...   Ovid's Elegies   2.8.2
KEEMBED
Put in their place thy keembed haires againe. . . .   Ovid's Elegies   1.7.68
KEEND
Traytoresse too [keene] <keend> <kind> and cursed Sorceresse.   Dido   5.1.221   Dido
KEENE
Traytoresse too [keene] <keend> <kind> and cursed Sorceresse.   Dido   5.1.221   Dido
KEENEST
See where it is, the keenest Cutle-axe <curtle-axe>,/That ere   1Tamb   2.3.55   Tamb
KEENLY
That it may keenly slice the Catholicks. . . . . .   P1238   22.100   King
KEEP
If you intend to keep your treasure safe. . . . . .   1Tamb   1.2.25   Tamb
Keep all your standings, and not stir a foote, ...   1Tamb   1.2.150   Tamb
No, I meane, I let you keep it. . . . .   1Tamb   2.4.35   Mycet
inlarge/Those Christian Captives, which you keep as slaves,   1Tamb   3.3.47   Tamb
Nor fortune keep them selves from victory. . . . .   1Tamb   5.1.406   Arabia
conquer all the world/And you have won enough for me to keep.   2Tamb   1.3.68   Calyph
To keep my promise, and to make him king, ...   2Tamb   3.1.71   Callap
Then wil I shortly keep my promise Almeda. . . . .   2Tamb   3.1.78   P Callap
But keep within the circle of mine armes. . . . . .   2Tamb   3.2.35   Tamb
and covered waies/To keep the bulwark fronts from battery,   2Tamb   3.2.76   Tamb
and will keep it for/The richest present of this Easterne   2Tamb   4.2.77   Therid
To live secure, and keep his forces out, ...   2Tamb   5.1.16   Govnr
We grant a month, but see you keep your promise. . . .   Jew   1.2.28   Calym
The more villaine he to keep me thus: . . . . .   Jew   4.2.111   Ithimr
And under your direction see they keep/All trecherous violence   P 267   4.65   Charls
In lucky time, come let us keep this lane, ...   P 298   5.25   Anjoy
And keep those relicks from our countries coastes. . . .   P 803   16.17   Navrre
And being able, Ile keep an hoast in pay. . . . . .   P 840   17.35   Guise
And thoughe I come not to keep possessione as I wold I mighte   Paris   ms15,p390   P Souldr
keep out of the circle, I say, least I send you into the Ostry   F 732   2.3.11   P Robin
Keepe out, keep out, or else you are blowne up, you are .   F App   p.233 10   P Robin
nor could the bed-rid parents/Keep back their sons, or womens   Lucan, First Booke   503
Defend the fort, and keep the foe-man out. . . . .   Hero and Leander   2.272
KEEPE
Because I feard your grace would keepe me here. . . .   Dido   4.4.20   Achat
O keepe them still, and let me gaze my fill: . . . .   Dido   4.4.44   Dido
O that I had a charme to keepe the windes/Within the closure of   Dido   4.4.99   Dido
And swim to Italy, Ile keepe these sure: . . . . .   Dido   4.4.164   Dido
Lest Dido spying him keepe him for a pledge. . . . .   Dido   5.1.50   Aeneas
And none shall keepe the crowne but Tamburlaine: . . .   1Tamb   2.5.7   Cosroe
And vow to keepe this peace inviolable. . . . . .   2Tamb   1.1.136   Sgsmnd
I sweare to keepe this truce inviolable: . . . . .   2Tamb   1.1.142   Orcan
We wil both watch and ward shall keepe his trunke/Amidst these   2Tamb   2.3.38   Orcan
What a coyle they keepe, I beleeve there will be some hurt done   2Tamb   4.1.74   P Calyph
And send to keepe our Gallies under-saile, ...   Jew   1.2.15   Calym
Then good my Lord, to keepe your quiet still, ...   Jew   1.2.43   Barab
Therefore be rul'd by me, and keepe the gold: . . . .   Jew   2.2.39   Bosco
might be got/To keepe him for his life time from the gallowes.   Jew   2.3.104   Barab
Provided, that you keepe your Maiden-head. . . . .   Jew   2.3.227   Barab
But keepe thy heart till Don Mathias comes. . . . .   Jew   2.3.307   Barab
So I have heard; pray therefore keepe it close. . . .   Jew   3.6.37   Abigal
now I to keepe my word,/And give my goods and substance to your   Jew   4.1.189   Barab
no more/I'le satisfie my selfe with that; nay, keepe it still,   Jew   5.5.22   Barab
For if I keepe not promise, trust not me. . . . . .   Jew   5.5.23   Barab
To keepe me here will nought advantage you. . . . .   Jew   5.5.117   Calym
Swizers keepe you the streetes,/And at ech corner shall the   P 290   5.17   Anjoy
possession (as I would I might) yet I meane to keepe you out,   P 814   17.9   P Souldr
yet I come to keepe you out ser. . . . .   Paris   ms16,p390   P Souldr
I can no longer keepe me from my lord. . . . . .   Edw   1.1.139   Gavstn
O might I keepe thee heere, as I doe this, ...   Edw   1.4.128   Edward
Then if you will not trust his grace in keepe, ...   Edw   2.5.65   Arundl
To keepe your royall person safe with us, ...   Edw   4.7.3   Abbot
keepe these preachments till you come to the place appointed.   Edw   4.7.113   P Rice

KEEPE (cont.)

And who must keepe mee now, must you my lorde?	Edw	5.1.137		Edward
Edward is my sonne, and I will keepe him.	Edw	5.2.117		Queene
To keepe your grace in safetie,	Edw	5.3.14		Gurney
Keepe them a sunder, thrust in the king.	Edw	5.3.52		Matrvs
Where lords keepe courts, and kings are lockt in prison!	Edw	5.3.64		Kent
This dungeon where they keepe me, is the sincke,	Edw	5.5.56		Edward
you, and keepe you, my deere brethren <my deare brethren>.	F 217	1.2.24	P	Wagner
This will I keepe, as chary as my life.	F 551	2.1.163		Faust
[This will I keepe as chary as my life].	F 719.1	2.2.172		Faust
keepe further from me O thou illiterate, and unlearned Hostler.	F 728	2.3.7	P	Robin
To keepe his Carkasse from their bloudy phangs.	F1303	4.1.149		Faust
buttons to his lips, to keepe his tongue from catching cold.	F1388	4.2.64	P	Benvol
Nay keepe it:	F1393	4.2.69		Faust
And keepe [mine oath] <my vow> I made to Lucifer.	F1765	5.1.92		Faust
Keepe out, keep out, or else you are blowne up, you are	F App	p.233 10	P	Robin
Rafe, keepe out, for I am about a roaring peece of worke.	F App	p.233 11	P	Robin
and his owne waight/Keepe him within the ground, his armes al	Lucan, First Booke	140		
easie grant men great estates,/But hardly grace to keepe them:	Lucan, First Booke	509		
then, they that keepe, and read/Sybillas secret works, and	Lucan, First Booke	598		
I will weepe/And to the dores sight of thy selfe [will] keepe:	Ovid's Elegies	1.4.62		
That this, or that man may thy cheekes moist keepe.	Ovid's Elegies	1.8.84		
Pure waters moisture thirst away did keepe.	Ovid's Elegies	2.6.32		
And in thy pompe hornd Apis with thee keepe,	Ovid's Elegies	2.13.14		
Foole if to keepe thy wife thou hast no neede,	Ovid's Elegies	2.19.1		
Keepe her for me, my more desire to breede.	Ovid's Elegies	2.19.2		
Now I forewarne, unlesse to keepe her stronger,	Ovid's Elegies	2.19.47		
Nor canst by watching keepe her minde from sinne.	Ovid's Elegies	3.4.7		
But woods and groves keepe your faults undetected.	Ovid's Elegies	3.5.84		
These hardned me, with what I keepe obscure,	Ovid's Elegies	3.10.27		
When misers keepe it; being put to lone,	Hero and Leander	1.235		
Ne're king more sought to keepe his diademe,	Hero and Leander	2.77		

KEEPER

Your Keeper under Tamburlaine the great,	2Tamb	1.2.68		Almeda
I, my Lord, he was Calapines keeper.	2Tamb	3.5.152	P	Therid
Be thou this night his keeper, in the morning/We will discharge	Edw	2.5.108		Penbrk
No pritty wenches keeper maist thou bee:	Ovid's Elegies	1.6.63		
Keeper if thou be wise cease hate to cherish,	Ovid's Elegies	2.2.9		
But till the [keeper] <keepes> went forth, I forget not,	Ovid's Elegies	3.1.55		
Because the keeper may come say, I did it,	Ovid's Elegies	3.4.35		
For me, she doth keeper, and husband feare,	Ovid's Elegies	3.7.63		

KEEPERS

By this my friendly keepers happy meanes,	2Tamb	3.1.34		Callap
heeres a simple purchase for horse-keepers, our horses shal	F App	p.234 3	P	Robin
The keepers hands and corps-dugard to passe/The souldiours, and	Ovid's Elegies	1.9.27		
Rude man, 'tis vaine, thy damsell to commend/To keepers trust:	Ovid's Elegies	3.4.2		

KEEPES

And such conceits as clownage keepes in pay,	1Tamb	Prol.2		Prolog
But that greefe keepes me waking, I shoulde sleepe,	Edw	5.5.93		Edward
That all this day the sluggard keepes his bed.	F1176	4.1.22		Mrtino
he keepes such a chafing with my mistris about it, and she has	F App	p.233 8	P	Rafe
Keepes each from other, but being worne away/They both burst	Lucan, First Booke	102		
His Mistris dores this; that his Captaines keepes.	Ovid's Elegies	1.9.8		
Aye me an Eunuch keepes my mistrisse chaste,	Ovid's Elegies	2.3.1		
While Juno Io keepes when hornes she wore,	Ovid's Elegies	2.19.29		
But till the [keeper] <keepes> went forth, I forget not,	Ovid's Elegies	3.1.55		
Who so well keepes his waters head from knowing,	Ovid's Elegies	3.5.40		
Some one or other keepes you as his owne.	Hero and Leander	1.290		
Who with incroching guile, keepes learning downe.	Hero and Leander	1.482		

KEEPING

Keeping in aw the Bay of Portingale:	1Tamb	3.3.258		Tamb
Keeping his kingly body in a Cage,	1Tamb	4.2.61		Zabina
Keeping his circuit by the slicing edge.	1Tamb	5.1.112		Tamb
Keeping in yron cages Emperours.	2Tamb	1.3.49		Tamb
By keeping of thy birth make but a shift.	Ovid's Elegies	1.8.94		

KEEPS

And keeps you from the honors of a Queene,	1Tamb	3.2.28		Agidas
of my knowledge in one cloyster keeps,/Five hundred fatte	P 141	2.84		Guise

KEEP'ST

Zoon's what a looking thou keep'st, thou'lt betraye's anon.	Jew	3.1.25		Pilia

KEIES

let him hang a bunch of keies on his standerd, to put him in	2Tamb	3.5.139	P	Tamb

KEMBD (See also KEEMBE, UNKEEMBE)

The maide that kembd them ever safely left them.	Ovid's Elegies	1.14.16		
Why doest thy ill kembd tresses losse lament?	Ovid's Elegies	1.14.35		

KEMBED

Even kembed as they were, her lockes to rend,	Ovid's Elegies	2.5.45		

KENNEL'D

whilst with their dams/They kennel'd in Hircania, evermore/Wil	Lucan, First Booke	329		

KENNELL

Il'e raise a kennell of Hounds shall hunt him so,	F1301	4.1.147		Faust
zounds hee'l raise up a kennell of Divels I thinke anon:	F1305	4.1.151	P	Benvol

KENT

And with the earle of Kent that favors him.	Edw	1.4.34		MortSr
My lord of Kent, what needes these questions?	Edw	4.6.34		Mortmr
Heere comes the yong prince, with the Earle of Kent.	Edw	5.2.75		Mortmr
How fares my honorable lord of Kent?	Edw	5.2.80		Mortmr
Helpe unckle Kent, Mortimer will wrong me.	Edw	5.2.113		Prince
Isabell is neerer then the earle of Kent.	Edw	5.2.115		Queene
Guarde the king sure, it is the earle of Kent.	Edw	5.3.50		Matrvs
Edmund the Earle of Kent.	Edw	5.4.83		Souldr

KEPT

They shall be kept our forced followers,	1Tamb	1.2.66		Tamb

KEPT (cont.)
There whiles he lives, shal Bajazeth be kept, ... 1Tamb 4.2.85 Tamb
He dies, and those that kept us out so long. . . . . 1Tamb 4.2.118 Tamb
Or kept the faire Zenocrate so long, ... 1Tamb 4.3.41 Souldn
overweighing heavens/Have kept to qualifie these hot extreames, 1Tamb 5.1.46 Govnr
Which kept his father in an yron cage: . . . . . 2Tamb 1.1.5 Orcan
We kept the narrow straight of Gibralter, ... 2Tamb 1.3.180 Usumc
And yet have kept enough to live upon; . . . . . Jew 1.2.190 Barab
The gold and Jewels which I kept for thee. . . . . Jew 1.2.298 Barab
Small though the number was that kept the Towne, . . . Jew 2.2.49 Bosco
And alwayes kept the Sexton's armes in ure/With digging graves Jew 2.3.184 Barab
much better/To [have] kept thy promise then be thus surpriz'd? Jew 5.2.5 Calym
Within a dungeon Englands king is kept, ... Edw 5.3.19 Edward
I kept a hallowing and whooping in his eares, but all could not F1549 4.5.45 P HrsCsr
Hadst thou kept on that way, Faustus behold, ... F1903 5.2.107 GdAngl
And by him kept of purpose for a dearth? . . . . Lucan, First Booke 319
Which to her wast her girdle still kept downe. . . . . Ovid's Elegies 1.7.48
From dog-kept flocks come preys to woolves most gratefull. Ovid's Elegies 1.8.56
But what had beene more faire had they beene kept? . . Ovid's Elegies 1.14.3
The Lydian buskin [in] fit [paces] <places> kept her. . Ovid's Elegies 3.1.14
What's kept, we covet more: the care makes theft: . . Ovid's Elegies 3.4.25
She is not chaste, that's kept, but a deare whore: . . Ovid's Elegies 3.4.29
Men kept the shoare, and sailde not into deepe. . . . Ovid's Elegies 3.7.44
Rose-cheekt Adonis) kept a solemne feast. . . . . Hero and Leander 1.93
Beautie alone is lost, too warily kept. . . . . Hero and Leander 1.328
And kept it downe that it might mount the hier. . . . Hero and Leander 2.42
Saying, let your vowes and promises be kept. . . . Hero and Leander 2.96
That which so long so charily she kept, ... Hero and Leander 2.309

KERNES
The wilde Oneyle, with swarmes of Irish Kernes, . . . Edw 2.2.164 Lncstr

KEY (See also KEIES)
Yet through the key-hole will he talke to her, ... Jew 2.3.263 Barab
and use a counterfeite key to his privie Chamber doore: . P 807 17.2 P Souldr
duke a cuckolde and use a counterfeyt key to his privy chamber Paris ms 2,p390 P Souldr

KEYES
Here take my keyes, I'le give 'em thee anon: . . . . Jew 3.4.46 Barab
I cannot doe it, I have lost my keyes. . . . . . Jew 4.3.32 Barab
Heere is the keyes, this is the lake,/Doe as you are commaunded Edw 5.5.25 Matrvs

KEY-HOLE
Yet through the key-hole will he talke to her, ... Jew 2.3.263 Barab

KEYS
Seven golden [keys] <seales> fast sealed with seven seales, F 933 3.1.155 Pope

KICKING
their mouths/And pul their kicking colts out of their pastures. 2Tamb 4.3.49 Techel

KIL
Mother dispatch me, or Ile kil my selfe, ... 2Tamb 3.4.26 Sonne
I know sir, what it is to kil a man, ... 2Tamb 4.1.27 Calyph

KILD
Till we have fire to dresse the meate we kild: . . . . Dido 1.1.165 Aeneas
That would have kild him sleeping as he lay? . . . . Dido 3.2.39 Juno
twere better he kild his wife, and then she shall be sure not 1Tamb 4.4.45 P Usumc
son; he and I kild 'em both, and yet never touch'd 'em. . Jew 4.4.18 P Ithimr
hee has kild the divell, so I should be cald kill divell all F App p.230 48 P Clown

KILDE
In swelling wombe her twinnes had Ilia kilde? . . . . Ovid's Elegies 2.14.15

KILL
Where meeting with the rest, kill kill they cryed. . . . Dido 2.1.190 Aeneas
And kill proud Tamburlaine with point of sword. . . . 1Tamb 2.2.12 Mycet
And kill as sure as it swiftly flies. . . . . . . 1Tamb 2.3.59 Tamb
That would not kill and curse at Gods command, . . . 2Tamb 2.1.55 Fredrk
And should I goe and kill a thousand men, ... 2Tamb 4.1.53 Calyph
Nay let 'em combat, conquer, and kill all, ... Jew 1.1.152 Barab
abroad a nights/And kill sicke people groaning under walls: Jew 2.3.175 Barab
Lend me that weapon that did kill my sonne, ... Jew 3.2.23 Mater
Which when they heare, they shall begin to kill: . . . P 239 4.37 Guise
To kill all that you suspect of heresie. . . . . . P 276 5.3 Guise
Kill them, kill them. . . . . P 338 5.65 Anjoy
kill him. . . . . P 398 7.38 Guise
Which [are] <as> he saith, to kill the Puritans, ... P 643 12.56 Cardnl
tush, were he heere, we would kill him presently. . . . P 934 19.4 P 1Mur
But are they resolute and armde to kill, ... P 949 19.19 King
And will him in my name to kill the Duke. . . . . . P1058 19.128 King
O wordes of power to kill a thousand men. . . . . . P1126 21.20 Dumain
the Jacobyns, that for my conscience sake will kill the King. P1131 21.25 P Frier
No, here he comes, now let them spoile and kill: . . . Edw 2.4.3 Edward
Feare not to kill the king tis good he die. . . . . Edw 5.4.9 Mortmr
Kill not the king tis good to feare the worst. . . . . Edw 5.4.12 Mortmr
that's good to kill Vermine: . . . . F 358 1.4.16 P Robin
And kill that Doctor if he come this way. . . . . . F1339 4.2.15 Fredrk
See where he comes, dispatch, and kill the slave. . . . F1423 4.2.99 2Soldr
Nay feare not man, we have no power to kill. . . . . F1440 4.3.10 Mrtino
divels, say I should kill one of them, what would folkes say? F App p.230 47 P Clown
divell, so I should be cald kill divell all the parish over. F App p.230 48 P Clown
Nor dares the Lyonesse her young whelpes kill. . . . . Ovid's Elegies 2.14.36
The fainting seedes of naughtinesse doth kill. . . . . Ovid's Elegies 3.4.10

KILL'D
Wounded with shame, and kill'd with discontent, . . . 2Tamb 4.1.94 Tamb

KILL DIVELL
divell, so I should be cald kill divell all the parish over. F App p.230 48 P Clown

KILLED
All loden with the heads of killed men. . . . . . 1Tamb 1.1.78 Mycet
Tis not the first time I have killed a man. . . . . Edw 5.4.30 Ltborn

KILLING
And closde in compasse of the killing bullet, ... 1Tamb 2.1.41 Cosroe

KILLING (cont.)

The killing frownes of jealousie and love. . . . . 1Tamb 3.2.91 Agidas
Killing my selfe, as I have done my sonne, . . . 2Tamb 3.4.35 Olymp
And fearelesse spurne the killing Basiliske: . . . F 921 3.1.143 Pope
with loving may/Had seene, my mother killing me, [no] <to> day. Ovid's Elegies 2.14.22

KILLINGWORTH

Your majestie must go to Killingworth. . . . . Edw 4.7.82 Leistr
Imagine Killingworth castell were your court, . . . Edw 5.1.2 Leistr
From Killingworth my lorde. . . . . . . Edw 5.2.23 2Msngr
So that he now is gone from Killingworth, . . . Edw 5.2.31 BshpWn
[Till] <And> at the last, he come to Killingworth, . . Edw 5.2.60 Mortmr
Hence will I haste to Killingworth castle, . . . Edw 5.2.119 Kent
Weele enter in by darkenes to Killingworth. . . . Edw 5.3.48 Matrvs
As we were bringing him to Killingworth. . . . . Edw 5.4.85 Souldr

KILL'ST

O say not so, thou kill'st thy mothers heart. . . . P 539 11.4 QnMoth

KILS

Who kils him shall have gold, and endlesse love. . . F1349 4.2.25 Fredrk
His conscience kils it, and his labouring braine, . . F1809 5.2.13 Mephst

KIN (See also KINNE)

In civill broiles makes kin and country men/Slaughter . Edw 4.4.6 Queene

KIND

Nor armed to offend in any kind: . . . . . . Dido 1.2.13 Illion
What kind of people, and who governes them: . . . Dido 2.1.42 Aeneas
Who would not undergoe all kind of toyle, ... Dido 3.3.58 Aeneas
Kind clowdes that sent forth such a curteous storme, . Dido 3.4.55 Dido
Traytoresse too [keene] <keend> <kind> and cursed Sorceresse. Dido 5.1.221 Dido
Thy words assure me of kind successe: . . . . . 1Tamb 2.3.60 Cosroe
[King] <Kind> Edward is not heere to buckler thee. . . Edw 2.5.18 Lncstr
kind I will make knowne unto you what my heart desires to have, F1570 4.6.13 P Lady
With all my heart kind Doctor, please thy selfe, . . F1623 4.6.66 Duke
Against her kind (the barren Mules loth'd issue)/To be cut Lucan, First Booke 589
Kind Jupiter hath low declin'd himselfe; . . . . Lucan, First Booke 660
Shee, with a kind of graunting, put him by it, . . . Hero and Leander 2.73
Playd with a boy so faire and [so] kind, ... Hero and Leander 2.195
A kind of twilight breake, which through the heare, . . Hero and Leander 2.319

KINDE

Let me alone, I'le use him in his kinde. . . . . . Jew 4.2.80 Pilia
A kingly kinde of trade to purchase Townes/By treachery, and Jew 5.5.47 Barab
Kinde wordes, and mutuall talke, makes our greefe greater, Edw 1.4.133 Edward
And apt for any kinde of villanie. . . . . . . Edw 2.1.51 Baldck
Too kinde to them, but now have drawne our sword, . . Edw 3.1.25 Edward
For kinde and loving hast thou alwaies beene: . . . Edw 5.1.7 Edward
And neither give him kinde word, nor good looke. . . Edw 5.2.55 Mortmr
[Did gratulate his safetie with kinde words], . . . F1143 3.3.56A 3Chor
And so have hope, that this my kinde rebuke, . . . F1722 5.1.49 OldMan
In verse to praise kinde Wenches tis my part, . . . Ovid's Elegies 1.10.59
To kinde requests thou wouldst more gentle prove, . . Ovid's Elegies 2.3.5
But such kinde wenches let their lovers have. . . . Ovid's Elegies 2.5.26
All humaine kinde by their default had perisht. . . . Ovid's Elegies 2.14.10
The youth oft swimming to his Hero kinde, ... Ovid's Elegies 2.16.31
This kinde of verse is not alike, yet fit, ... Ovid's Elegies 2.17.21

KINDELY

So kindely Cosin of Guise you and your wife/Doe both salute our P 752 15.10 King
Because his wife beares thee such kindely love. . . P 780 15.38 King

KINDENES

Binde us in kindenes all at your commaund. . . . . Edw 4.2.73 Kent

KINDEST

Our kindest friends in Belgia have we left, ... Edw 4.4.3 Queene

KINDLE

And kindle heaps of exhalations, ... 2Tamb 3.2.3 Tamb
Forbeare to kindle vice by prohibition, ... Ovid's Elegies 3.4.11

KINDLED

Then must his kindled wrath bee quencht with blood: . . 1Tamb 4.1.56 2Msngr
Whose courages are kindled with the flames, . . . 2Tamb 3.1.54 Trebiz
Wrath kindled in the furnace of his breast, ... 2Tamb 4.1.9 Celeb
discharg'd/By him that beares the Linstocke, kindled thus; Jew 5.4.4 Govnr
That kindled first this motion in our hearts, . . . P 7 1.7 Charls
as might make/Wrath-kindled Jove away his thunder shake. . Ovid's Elegies 2.5.52

KINDLIE

Tis verie kindlie spoke my lord of Penbrooke, . . . Edw 2.5.104 Arundl

KINDLING

Love kindling fire, to burne such townes as Troy, . . Hero and Leander 1.153

KINDLY

Sweet unckle speake more kindly to the queene. . . . Edw 2.2.228 Neece
So kindly yesternight to Bruno's health, ... F1175 4.1.21 Mrtino
Let him please, haunt the house, be kindly usd, . . Ovid's Elegies 2.2.29
Kindly thy mistris use, if thou be wise. . . . . Ovid's Elegies 3.4.43
And kindly gave her, what she liked best. . . . . Ovid's Elegies 3.5.82
And heateth kindly, shining lat'rally; . . . . . Hero and Leander 2.125

KINDNES

Spencer, this love, this kindnes to thy King, . . . Edw 3.1.47 Edward
this learned man for the great kindnes he hath shewd to you. F App p.243 29 P Duke

KINDNESSE

we will recompence/With all the love and kindnesse that we may. F1672 4.6.115 Duke
Sooner shall kindnesse gaine thy wills fruition. . . . Ovid's Elegies 3.4.12

KINDRED

Whom kindred and acquaintance counites? . . . . . Dido 3.2.31 Juno
Hath often pleaded kindred to the King. . . . . . P 108 2.51 Guise

KING

Achates, see King Priam wags his hand, ... Dido 2.1.29 Aeneas
Who then ran to the pallace of the King, ... Dido 2.1.224 Aeneas
To whom the aged King thus trembling spoke: . . . . Dido 2.1.232 Aeneas

KING (cont.)

King of this Citie, but my Troy is fired,	Dido	2.1.236		Aeneas
And now am neither father, Lord, nor King:	Dido	2.1.239		Aeneas
Which sent an eccho to the wounded King:	Dido	2.1.249		Aeneas
And with the [wind] <wound> thereof the King fell downe:	Dido	2.1.254		Aeneas
Am I not King of rich Getulia?	Dido	3.1.45		Iarbus
This was the wealthie King of Thessaly,	Dido	3.1.161		Dido
It was because I sawe no King like thee,	Dido	3.4.35		Dido
The King of Carthage, not Anchises sonne:	Dido	3.4.60		Dido
And be thou king of Libia, by my guift.	Dido	3.4.64		Dido
Alas poore King that labours so in vaine,	Dido	4.2.33		Anna
Stay here Aeneas, and command as King.	Dido	4.4.39		Dido
of all these, commaund/Aeneas ride as Carthaginian King.	Dido	4.4.78		Dido
The king of Gods sent me from highest heaven,	Dido	5.1.32		Hermes
Repairde not I thy ships, made thee a King,	Dido	5.1.163		Dido
Unlesse they have a wiser king than you.	1Tamb	1.1.92		Cosroe
Unlesse they have a wiser king than you?	1Tamb	1.1.93		Mycet
to them, that all Asia/Lament to see the follie of their King.	1Tamb	1.1.96		Cosroe
mated and amaz'd/To heare the king thus threaten like himselfe?	1Tamb	1.1.108		Menaph
And openly exclaime against the King.	1Tamb	1.1.149		Ceneus
I doubt not shortly but to raigne sole king,	1Tamb	1.1.175		Cosroe
Sound up the trumpets then, God save the King.	1Tamb	1.1.188		Ortyg
Sent from the King to overcome us all.	1Tamb	1.2.112		Souldr
Forsake thy king and do but joine with me/And we will triumph	1Tamb	1.2.172		Tamb
and if the Persean king/Should offer present Dukedomes to our	1Tamb	1.2.214		Techel
But shall I proove a Traitor to my King?	1Tamb	1.2.226		Therid
Than dooth the King of Persea in his Crowne:	1Tamb	1.2.242		Tamb
show him to be made/His Fortunes maister, and the king of men,	1Tamb	2.1.36		Cosroe
noble Tamburlaine/Shall be my Regent, and remaine as King.	1Tamb	2.1.49		Cosroe
What will he doe supported by a king?	1Tamb	2.1.57		Ceneus
And all conjoin'd to meet the witlesse King,	1Tamb	2.1.64		Cosroe
Would it not grieve a King to be so abusde,	1Tamb	2.2.5		Mycet
And make him false his faith unto his King,	1Tamb	2.2.27		Meandr
Then haste Cosroe to be king alone,	1Tamb	2.3.42		Tamb
The King your Brother is now hard at hand,	1Tamb	2.3.45		Tamb
That it may reach the King of Perseas crowne,	1Tamb	2.3.53		Cosroe
go before and charge/The fainting army of that foolish King.	1Tamb	2.3.62		Cosroe
Away, I am the King: go, touch me not.	1Tamb	2.4.20		Mycet
And cry me mercie, noble King.	1Tamb	2.4.22		Mycet
Are you the witty King of Persea?	1Tamb	2.4.23		Tamb
And let them know the Persean King is chang'd:	1Tamb	2.5.21		Cosroe
From one that knew not what a King should do,	1Tamb	2.5.22		Cosroe
Is it not brave to be a King, Techelles?	1Tamb	2.5.51		Tamb
Is it not passing brave to be a King,	1Tamb	2.5.53		Tamb
To be a King, is halfe to be a God.	1Tamb	2.5.56		Usumc
A God is not so glorious as a King:	1Tamb	2.5.57		Therid
Why say Theridamas, wilt thou be a king?	1Tamb	2.5.65		Tamb
Then shall we send to this triumphing King,	1Tamb	2.5.87		Techel
That onely made him King to make us sport.	1Tamb	2.5.101		Tamb
To save your King and country from decay:	1Tamb	2.6.35		Cosroe
To lift our swords against the Persean King.	1Tamb	2.7.35		Techel
Who thinke you now is king of Persea?	1Tamb	2.7.56		Tamb
And all pronounst me king of Persea.	1Tamb	2.7.67		Tamb
Great King and conquerour of Grecia,	1Tamb	3.1.24		Bajzth
They say he is the King of Persea.	1Tamb	3.1.45		Argier
You see though first the King of Persea/(Being a Shepheard)	1Tamb	3.2.59		Agidas
See you Agidas how the King salutes you.	1Tamb	3.2.88		Techel
see how right the man/Hath hit the meaning of my Lord the King.	1Tamb	3.2.108		Techel
And may my Love, the king of Persea,	1Tamb	3.3.132		Zenoc
And made my lordly Love her worthy King:	1Tamb	3.3.190		Zenoc
Now king of Bassoes, who is Conqueror?	1Tamb	3.3.212		Tamb
the faire Arabian king/That hath bene disapointed by this	1Tamb	4.1.68		Souldn
Unworthy king, that by thy crueltie,	1Tamb	4.2.56		Zabina
How you abuse the person of the king:	1Tamb	4.2.73		Anippe
That such a base usurping vagabond/Should brave a king, or	1Tamb	4.3.22		Souldn
And leads with him the great Arabian King,	1Tamb	4.3.64		Souldn
As Prognes to th'adulterous Thracian King,	1Tamb	4.4.24		Zabina
of Egypt, the King of Arabia, and the Governour of Damascus.	1Tamb	4.4.114	P	Tamb
I crowne you here (Theridamas) King of Argier:	1Tamb	4.4.116	P	Tamb
Techelles King of Fesse, and Usumcasane King of Morocus.	1Tamb	4.4.116	P	Tamb
Techelles King of Fesse, and Usumcasane King of Morocus.	1Tamb	4.4.117	P	Tamb
Most happy King and Emperour of the earth,	1Tamb	5.1.74		1Virgn
The Souldan and the Arabian king together/Martch on us with	1Tamb	5.1.199		Techel
Madam, your father and th'Arabian king,	1Tamb	5.1.378		Philem
Ready for battaile gainst my Lord the King.	1Tamb	5.1.382		Philem
To see the king my Father issue safe,	1Tamb	5.1.441		Zenoc
Where Sigismond the king of Hungary/Should meet our person to	2Tamb	1.1.9		Orcan
King of Natolia, let us treat of peace,	2Tamb	1.1.13		Gazell
Besides, king Sigismond hath brought from Christendome,	2Tamb	1.1.20		Uribas
to parle for a peace/With Sigismond the king of Hungary:	2Tamb	1.1.51		Gazell
The king of Boheme, and the Austrich Duke,	2Tamb	1.1.95		Orcan
Then County-Pallatine, but now a king:	2Tamb	1.1.104		Sgsmnd
Or treat of peace with the Natolian king?	2Tamb	1.1.113		Sgsmnd
if any Christian King/Encroche upon the confines of thy realme,	2Tamb	1.1.146		Orcan
If any heathen potentate or king/Invade Natolia, Sigismond will	2Tamb	1.1.152		Sgsmnd
Shall I be made a king for my labour?	2Tamb	1.2.62	P	Almeda
Thou shalt be crown'd a king and be my mate.	2Tamb	1.2.66		Callap
Thou shalt be made a King and raigne with me,	2Tamb	1.3.48		Tamb
Thou shalt be king before them, and thy seed/Shall issue	2Tamb	1.3.52		Tamb
Ere I would loose the tytle of a king.	2Tamb	1.3.91		Celeb
Ere I would loose the tytle of a king.	2Tamb	1.3.95		Amyras
Welcome Theridamas, king of Argier.	2Tamb	1.3.112		Tamb
I and my neighbor King of Fesse have brought/To aide thee in	2Tamb	1.3.130		Usumc

KING (cont.)

Thanks king of Morocus, take your crown again.	2Tamb	1.3.137	Tamb
Thanks king of Fesse, take here thy crowne again.	2Tamb	1.3.150	Tamb
I took the king, and lead him bound in chaines/Unto Damasco,	2Tamb	1.3.204	Techel
Grace to memorie/The league we lately made with king Orcanes,	2Tamb	2.1.28	Sgsmnd
Me thinks I see how glad the christian King/Is made, for joy of	2Tamb	2.2.20	Uribas
and holy Seraphins/That sing and play before the king of kings,	2Tamb	2.4.27	Tamb
This proud usurping king of Persea,	2Tamb	3.1.15	Callap
To keep my promise, and to make him king,	2Tamb	3.1.71	Callap
matter sir, for being a king, for Tamburlain came up of nothing.	2Tamb	3.1.73	P Almeda
Wil match thee with a viceroy or a king.	2Tamb	3.4.41	Techel
Than any Viceroy, King or Emperour.	2Tamb	3.4.43	Olymp
with an hoste of men/Lies Tamburlaine, this king of Persea:	2Tamb	3.5.4	2Msngr
Wel, in despight of thee he shall be king:	2Tamb	3.5.128	Callap
I here invest thee king of Ariadan,	2Tamb	3.5.130	Callap
So sirha, now you are a king you must give armes.	2Tamb	3.5.137	P Tamb
See ye this rout, and know ye this same king?	2Tamb	3.5.151	Tamb
Wel, now you see hee is a king, looke to him Theridamas, when we	2Tamb	3.5.153	P Tamb
least hee hide his crowne as the foolish king of Persea did.	2Tamb	3.5.155	P Tamb
That King Egeus fed with humaine flesh,	2Tamb	4.3.13	Tamb
And art a king as absolute as Jove,	2Tamb	4.3.33	Orcan
How like you that sir king? why speak you not?	2Tamb	4.3.53	Celeb
<Affrica>/Which hath bene subject to the Persean king,	2Tamb	5.1.166	Tamb
King of Amasia, now our mighty hoste,	2Tamb	5.2.1	Callap
Vizadmirall unto the Catholike King.	Jew	2.2.7	Bosco
My Lord and King hath title to this Isle,	Jew	2.2.37	Bosco
Having the King, Queene Mother on our sides,	P 29	1.29	Navrre
If that the King had given consent thereto,	P 33	1.33	Navrre
Hath often pleaded kindred to the King.	P 108	2.51	Guise
The gentle King whose pleasure uncontrolde,	P 127	2.70	Guise
That right or wrong, thou deale thy selfe a King.	P 148	2.91	Guise
Sufficient yet for such a pettie King:	P 150	2.93	Guise
betraide, come my Lords, and let us goe tell the King of this.	P 200	3.35	P Navrre
Shall dye, be he King or Emperour.	P 235	4.33	Guise
I vow and sweare as I am King of France,	P 255	4.53	Charls
All that I have is but my stipend from the King,	P 378	7.18	Ramus
To get those pedantes from the King Navarre,	P 426	7.66	Guise
Come let us goe tell the King.	P 440	7.80	Condy
A martiall people, worthy such a King,	P 455	8.5	Anjoy
And such a King whom practise long hath taught,	P 458	8.8	Anjoy
Yet by my brother Charles our King of France,	P 464	8.14	Anjoy
With the rebellious King of Navarre,	P 517	9.36	Cardnl
Then to misdoe the welfare of their King:	P 546	11.11	Charls
For feare that Guise joyn'd with the King of Spaine,	P 573	11.38	Navrre
And all things that a King may wish besides:	P 595	12.8	QnMoth
Remooveles from the favours of your King.	P 609	12.22	King
Now Madam must you insinuate with the King,	P 645	12.58	Cardnl
I meane the Guise, the Pope, and King of Spaine,	P 701	14.4	Navrre
And Guise for Spaine hath now incenst the King,	P 711	14.14	Navrre
This is the Guise that hath incenst the King,	P 729	14.32	Navrre
the Duke of Joyeux/Hath made great sute unto the King therfore.	P 734	14.37	1Msngr
Of King or Country, no not for them both.	P 740	14.43	Navrre
To march against the rebellious King Navarre:	P 745	15.3	King
I hope will make the King surcease his hate:	P 792	16.6	Bartus
Least thou perceive the King of France be mov'd.	P 834	17.29	King
The Pope and King of Spaine are thy good frends,	P 843	17.38	Eprnon
I, and the catholick Philip King of Spaine,	P 852	17.47	Guise
Guise, weare our crowne, and be thou King of France,	P 859	17.54	King
Then farwell Guise, the King and thou are freends.	P 870	17.65	King
That the Guise durst stand in armes against the King,	P 877	17.72	Eprnon
Heere is no staying for the King of France,	P 897	17.92	King
That the Guise hath taken armes against the King,	P 901	18.2	Navrre
To shew your love unto the King of France:	P 904	18.5	Bartus
For we must aide the King against the Guise.	P 918	18.19	Navrre
Holla verlete, hey: Epernoune, where is the King?	P 956	19.26	Guise
Now sues the King for favour to the Guise,	P 978	19.48	Guise
So will I triumph over this wanton King,	P 983	19.53	Guise
Then pray to God, and aske forgivenes of the King.	P1004	19.74	P 2Mur
Nor will I aske forgivenes of the King.	P1006	19.76	Guise
Ah Sextus, be reveng'd upon the King,	P1010	19.80	Guise
Then stay a while and Ile goe call the King,	P1017	19.87	Capt
I nere was King of France untill this houre:	P1027	19.97	King
Did he not cause the King of Spaines huge fleete,	P1033	19.103	King
Or else to murder me, and so be King.	P1040	19.110	King
Nere was there King of France so yoakt as I.	P1044	19.114	King
Art thou King, and hast done this bloudy deed?	P1050	19.120	YngGse
I slew the Guise, because I would be King.	P1066	19.136	King
King, why so thou wert before.	P1067	19.137	QnMoth
Pray God thou be a King now this is done.	P1068	19.138	QnMoth
Nay he was King and countermanded me,	P1069	19.139	King
But now I will be King and rule my selfe,	P1070	19.140	King
To revenge our deaths upon that cursed King,	P1100	20.10	Cardnl
My noble brother murthered by the King,	P1107	21.1	Dumain
That basely seekes to joyne with such a King,	P1115	21.9	Dumain
the Jacobyns, that for my conscience sake will kill the King.	P1131	21.25	P Frier
I vow as I am lawfull King of France,	P1143	22.5	King
that Navarre may be/Esteemed faithfull to the King of France:	P1148	22.10	Navrre
And will not offer violence to their King,	P1162	22.24	King
Frier, thou dost acknowledge me thy King?	P1164	22.26	King
what, shall the French king dye,/Wounded and poysoned, both at	P1214	22.76	King
Surgeon, why saist thou so? the King may live.	P1224	22.86	Navrre
Oh no Navarre, thou must be King of France.	P1225	22.87	King
Long may you live, and still be King of France.	P1226	22.88	Navrre

KING (cont.)

Sweet Epernoune thy King must dye.	P1228	22.90	King
For he is your lawfull King and my next heire:	P1230	22.92	King
Henry thy King wipes of these childish teares,	P1236	22.98	King
Come Lords, take up the body of the King,	P1245	22.107	Navrre
Shall curse the time that ere Navarre was King,	P1249	22.111	Navrre
Then live and be the favorit of a king?	Edw	1.1.5	Gavstn
The king, upon whose bosome let me die,	Edw	1.1.14	Gavstn
My knee shall bowe to none but to the king.	Edw	1.1.19	Gavstn
And yet I have not viewd my Lord the king,	Edw	1.1.45	Gavstn
of a string/May draw the pliant king which way I please:	Edw	1.1.53	Gavstn
Heere comes the king and the nobles/From the parlament, ile	Edw	1.1.72	Gavstn
Beseemes it thee to contradict thy king?	Edw	1.1.92	Edward
What danger tis to stand against your king.	Edw	1.1.97	Edward
Brav'd Mowberie in presence of the king,	Edw	1.1.111	Kent
Yet dare you brave the king unto his face.	Edw	1.1.116	Kent
Come unckle, let us leave the brainsick king,	Edw	1.1.125	Mortmr
Am I a king and must be over rulde?	Edw	1.1.135	Edward
Earle of Cornewall, king and lord of Man.	Edw	1.1.156	Edward
Ah wicked king, accurssed Gaveston,	Edw	1.2.4	Lncstr
Thus arme in arme, the king and he dooth marche:	Edw	1.2.20	Lncstr
Thus leaning on the shoulder of the king,	Edw	1.2.23	Warwck
Weele hale him from the bosome of the king,	Edw	1.2.29	Mortmr
My lord, will you take armes against the king?	Edw	1.2.39	Lncstr
For now my lord the king regardes me not,	Edw	1.2.49	Queene
The king shall lose his crowne, for we have power,	Edw	1.2.59	Mortmr
But yet lift not your swords against the king.	Edw	1.2.61	ArchBp
What we confirme the king will frustrate.	Edw	1.2.72	Lncstr
Forbeare to levie armes against the king.	Edw	1.2.82	Queene
The name of Mortimer shall fright the king,	Edw	1.4.6	Mortmr
Is this the dutie that you owe your king?	Edw	1.4.22	Kent
Were I a king--	Edw	1.4.27	Gavstn
Thou villaine, wherfore talkes thou of a king,	Edw	1.4.28	Mortmr
Nay, then lay violent hands upon your king,	Edw	1.4.35	Edward
Was ever king thus over rulde as I?	Edw	1.4.38	Edward
he refuse, and then may we/Depose him and elect an other king.	Edw	1.4.55	Mortmr
The king is love-sick for his minion.	Edw	1.4.87	Mortmr
Why should a king be subject to a priest?	Edw	1.4.96	Edward
If I be king, not one of them shall live.	Edw	1.4.105	Edward
Tis something to be pitied of a king.	Edw	1.4.130	Gavstn
The king my lord thus to abandon me:	Edw	1.4.177	Queene
Looke where the sister of the king of Fraunce,	Edw	1.4.187	Lncstr
The king I feare hath ill intreated her.	Edw	1.4.189	Warwck
The angrie king hath banished me the court:	Edw	1.4.210	Queene
O Lancaster, let him diswade the king,	Edw	1.4.216	Queene
To mend the king, and do our countrie good:	Edw	1.4.257	Mortmr
Tis treason to be up against the king.	Edw	1.4.281	Mortmr
Which for his fathers sake leane to the king,	Edw	1.4.283	Mortmr
Tis not the king can buckler Gaveston,	Edw	1.4.288	Mortmr
But see in happie time, my lord the king,	Edw	1.4.299	Queene
Couragious Lancaster, imbrace thy king,	Edw	1.4.340	Edward
Penbrooke shall beare the sword before the king.	Edw	1.4.351	Edward
Now is the king of England riche and strong,	Edw	1.4.366	Queene
Leave now to oppose thy selfe against the king,	Edw	1.4.387	MortSr
Whiles other walke below, the king and he/From out a window,	Edw	1.4.416	Mortmr
But nephew, now you see the king is changd.	Edw	1.4.420	MortSr
Because the king and he are enemies.	Edw	2.1.5	Spencr
But he that hath the favour of a king,	Edw	2.1.8	Spencr
And would have once preferd me to the king.	Edw	2.1.14	Spencr
With letters to our ladie from the King,	Edw	2.1.20	Spencr
Now to the letter of my Lord the King,	Edw	2.1.66	Neece
I knew the King would have him home againe.	Edw	2.1.78	Spencr
The King of Fraunce sets foote in Normandie.	Edw	2.2.9	Mortmr
Sweet Lord and King, your speech preventeth mine,	Edw	2.2.59	Gavstn
Heere, here <King>.	Edw	2.2.81	Penbrk
Lets to our castels, for the king is moovde.	Edw	2.2.100	Warwck
Now send our Heralds to defie the King,	Edw	2.2.110	Lncstr
Who should defray the money, but the King,	Edw	2.2.118	Mortmr
Ile to the King.	Edw	2.2.120	Mortmr
As never subject did unto his King.	Edw	2.2.129	Mortmr
Whither else but to the King.	Edw	2.2.134	Mortmr
That makes a king seeme glorious to the world,	Edw	2.2.175	Mortmr
What weeneth the king of England,	Edw	2.2.193	Lncstr
I come to joine with you, and leave the king,	Edw	2.3.2	Kent
And here in Tinmoth frollicks with the king.	Edw	2.3.17	Lncstr
None be so hardie as to touche the King,	Edw	2.3.27	Lncstr
Cease to lament, and tell us wheres the king?	Edw	2.4.30	Mortmr
What would you with the king, ist him you seek?	Edw	2.4.31	Queene
The king hath left him, and his traine is small.	Edw	2.4.39	Queene
How comes it, that the king and he is parted?	Edw	2.4.41	Mortmr
No Mortimer, ile to my lord the king.	Edw	2.4.51	Queene
You know the king is so suspitious,	Edw	2.4.53	Queene
And to the king my brother there complaine,	Edw	2.4.66	Queene
And though devorsed from king Edwards eyes,	Edw	2.5.3	Gavstn
That muster rebels thus against your king)/To see his royall	Edw	2.5.6	Gavstn
Corrupter of thy king, cause of these broiles,	Edw	2.5.10	Mortmr
[King] <Kind> Edward is not heere to buckler thee.	Edw	2.5.18	Lncstr
But for thou wert the favorit of a King,	Edw	2.5.27	Warwck
My lords, king Edward greetes you all by me.	Edw	2.5.33	Arundl
Arundell, we will gratifie the king/In other matters, he must	Edw	2.5.43	Warwck
it is this life you aime at,/Yet graunt king Edward this.	Edw	2.5.49	Gavstn
Thus weele gratifie the king,	Edw	2.5.51	Mortmr
And in the honor of a king he sweares,	Edw	2.5.58	Arundl

KING (cont.)

And yee be men,/Speede to the king.	Edw	2.6.6	Gavstn
Come, let thy shadow parley with king Edward.	Edw	2.6.14	Warwck
Treacherous earle, shall I not see the king?	Edw	2.6.15	Gavstn
The king of heaven perhaps, no other king,	Edw	2.6.16	Warwck
Were I king Edward, Englands soveraigne,	Edw	3.1.10	Spencr
And learne obedience to their lawfull king.	Edw	3.1.23	Spencr
Sworne to defend king Edwards royall right,	Edw	3.1.38	SpncrP
Spencer, this love, this kindnes to thy King,	Edw	3.1.47	Edward
That lord Valoyes our brother, king of Fraunce,	Edw	3.1.62	Queene
You shall go parley with the king of Fraunce.	Edw	3.1.71	Edward
Boye, see you beare you bravelie to the king,	Edw	3.1.72	Edward
Unnatural wars, where subjects brave their king,	Edw	3.1.86	Queene
If I be Englands king, in lakes of gore/Your headles trunkes,	Edw	3.1.135	Edward
Long live king Edward, Englands lawful lord.	Edw	3.1.151	Herald
And do confront and countermaund their king.	Edw	3.1.188	Edward
And levie armes against your lawfull king?	Edw	3.1.208	SpncrP
T'appeaze the wrath of their offended king.	Edw	3.1.210	Edward
Saint George for England, and king Edwards right.	Edw	3.1.220	Edward
Then live in infamie under such a king.	Edw	3.1.244	Lncstr
Edward this day hath crownd him king a new.	Edw	3.1.261	Edward
Begets the quiet of king Edwards land,	Edw	3.1.263	Spencr
Proclaime king Edwards warres and victories.	Edw	3.1.281	Spencr
Unnaturall king, to slaughter noble men/And cherish flatterers:	Edw	4.1.8	Kent
The lords are cruell, and the king unkinde,	Edw	4.2.2	Queene
The king of England, nor the court of Fraunce,	Edw	4.2.22	Prince
How meane you, and the king my father lives?	Edw	4.2.43	Prince
How hard the nobles, how unkinde the king/Hath shewed himself:	Edw	4.2.49	Mortmr
The king will nere forsake his flatterers.	Edw	4.2.60	Mortmr
sith the ungentle king/Of Fraunce refuseth to give aide of	Edw	4.2.61	SrJohn
men, and friends/Ere long, to bid the English king a base.	Edw	4.2.66	SrJohn
I thinke king Edward will out-run us all.	Edw	4.2.68	Prince
behalfe, dealt with the king of Fraunce his lords, and effected,	Edw	4.3.29	P Spencr
they intend to give king Edward battell in England, sooner then	Edw	4.3.34	P Spencr
and withall/We may remoove these flatterers from the king,	Edw	4.4.26	Mortmr
thou chase/Thy lawfull king thy soveraigne with thy sword?	Edw	4.6.4	Kent
Borne armes against thy brother and thy king?	Edw	4.6.6	Kent
Nephew, your father, I dare not call him king.	Edw	4.6.33	Kent
Baldock is with the king,/A goodly chauncelor, is he not my	Edw	4.6.42	Queene
But wheres the king and the other Spencer fled?	Edw	4.6.55	Mortmr
And shipt but late for Ireland with the king.	Edw	4.6.58	Rice
Shall I not see the king my father yet?	Edw	4.6.61	Prince
Your king hath wrongd your countrie and himselfe,	Edw	4.6.67	Mortmr
O hadst thou ever beene a king, thy hart/Pierced deeply with	Edw	4.7.9	Edward
Why do you lowre unkindly on a king?	Edw	4.7.63	Edward
A king to beare these words and proud commaunds.	Edw	4.7.71	Abbot
But when I call to minde I am a king,	Edw	5.1.23	Edward
My nobles rule, I beare the name of king,	Edw	5.1.28	Edward
To make usurping Mortimer a king?	Edw	5.1.37	Edward
But stay a while, let me be king till night,	Edw	5.1.59	Edward
That Edward may be still faire Englands king:	Edw	5.1.68	Edward
What, feare you not the furie of your king?	Edw	5.1.75	Edward
But seekes to make a new elected king,	Edw	5.1.78	Edward
Ile not resigne, but whilst I live, [be king].	Edw	5.1.86	Edward
My lord, the king is willing to resigne.	Edw	5.1.94	Leistr
And will be called the murtherer of a king,	Edw	5.1.101	Edward
The proud corrupters of the light-brainde king,	Edw	5.2.2	Mortmr
How fares my lord the king?	Edw	5.2.24	Queene
The king hath willingly resignde his crowne.	Edw	5.2.28	BshpWn
Bartley shall be dischargd, the king remoovde,	Edw	5.2.40	Mortmr
That he resigne the king to thee and Gurney,	Edw	5.2.49	Mortmr
Whither goes this letter, to my lord the king?	Edw	5.2.68	Queene
Let him be king, I am too yong to raigne.	Edw	5.2.93	Prince
My lord, he hath betraied the king his brother,	Edw	5.2.106	Mortmr
Within a dungeon Englands king is kept,	Edw	5.3.19	Edward
That wronges their liege and soveraigne, Englands king.	Edw	5.3.40	Edward
Guarde the king sure, it is the earle of Kent.	Edw	5.3.50	Matrvs
Keepe them a sunder, thrust in the king.	Edw	5.3.52	Matrvs
Lay downe your weapons, traitors, yeeld the king.	Edw	5.3.55	Kent
Where is the court but heere, heere is the king,	Edw	5.3.59	Kent
The king must die, or Mortimer goes downe,	Edw	5.4.1	Mortmr
Feare not to kill the king tis good he die.	Edw	5.4.9	Mortmr
Kill not the king tis good to feare the worst.	Edw	5.4.12	Mortmr
and Mortimer/Shall rule the realme, the king, and none rule us,	Edw	5.4.66	Mortmr
Long live king Edward, by the grace of God/King of England, and	Edw	5.4.73	ArchBp
by the grace of God/King of England, and lorde of Ireland.	Edw	5.4.74	ArchBp
Dares but affirme, that Edwards not true king,	Edw	5.4.76	Champn
A would have taken the king away perforce,	Edw	5.4.84	Souldr
Mortimer, I did, he is our king,	Edw	5.4.87	Kent
Art thou king, must I die at thy commaund?	Edw	5.4.103	Kent
Either my brother or his sonne is king,	Edw	5.4.106	Kent
Gurney, I wonder the king dies not,	Edw	5.5.1	Matrvs
Much more a king brought up so tenderlie.	Edw	5.5.6	Matrvs
Know you this token? I must have the king.	Edw	5.5.19	Ltborn
This villain's sent to make away the king.	Edw	5.5.21	Matrvs
let him have the king,/What else?	Edw	5.5.24	Matrvs
nere was there any/So finely handled as this king shalbe.	Edw	5.5.40	Ltborn
To see a king in this most pittious state?	Edw	5.5.51	Ltborn
They give me bread and water being a king,	Edw	5.5.62	Edward
Know that I am a king, oh at that name,	Edw	5.5.89	Edward
A Mortimer, the king my sonne hath news,	Edw	5.6.15	Queene
What if he have? the king is yet a childe.	Edw	5.6.17	Mortmr
Feare not my lord, know that you are a king.	Edw	5.6.24	1Lord

KING (cont.)			
Why speake you not unto my lord the king?	Edw	5.6.38	1Lord
And raigne sole King of all [our] Provinces.	F 121	1.1.93	Faust
And with Lord Raymond, King of Hungary,	F 979	3.1.201	Pope
Your grace demand no questions of the King,	F1251	4.1.97	Faust
Receive with shouts; where thou wilt raigne as King,	Lucan, First Booke		47
(Whom from his youth he bribde) needs make him king?	Lucan, First Booke		315
And jaded king of Pontus poisoned slaine,	Lucan, First Booke		337
Thee all shall feare and worship as a King,	Ovid's Elegies		1.2.33
why made king [to refuse] <and refusde> it?	Ovid's Elegies		3.6.49
Wherewith the king of Gods and men is feasted.	Hero and Leander		1.432
Ne're king more sought to keepe his diademe,	Hero and Leander		2.77
KINGDOM			
And share the kingdom with thy deerest friend.	Edw	1.1.2	Gavstn
Neither spoile, nor kingdom seeke we by these armes,	Lucan, First Booke		351
soules passe not to silent Erebus/Or Plutoes bloodles kingdom,	Lucan, First Booke		452
KINGDOME			
It is the Punick kingdome rich and strong,	Dido	1.1.210	Venus
Whose Crowne and kingdome rests at thy commande:	Dido	3.4.58	Dido
for his parentage deserves/As large a kingdome as is Libia.	Dido	4.4.80	Achat
To get the Persean Kingdome to my selfe:	1Tamb	2.5.82	Tamb
the fiery Element/Dissolve, and make your kingdome in the Sky,	2Tamb	2.4.59	Zenoc
Tis nought for your majesty to give a kingdome.	2Tamb	3.1.77	Jrslem
with all the pompe/The treasure of my kingdome may affoord.	2Tamb	4.2.98	Therid
poysons of the Stygian poole/Breake from the fiery kingdome;	Jew	3.4.103	Barab
Give me a Reame of paper, we'll have a kingdome of gold for't.	Jew	4.2.115	P Ithimr
Monarck goes/To wrack, and [his] antechristian kingdome falles.	P1198	22.60	King
way how hardly I can brooke/To loose my crowne and kingdome,	Edw	5.1.52	Edward
Enlarge his Kingdome.	F 429	2.1.41	Mephst
I, that is not against our Kingdome:	F 623	2.2.72	P Mephst
Blessed, the Kingdome of Joy, and must remaine in hell for ever.	F1845	5.2.49	P Faust
Dire league of partners in a kingdome last not.	Lucan, First Booke		86
KINGDOMES			
Till men and kingdomes help to strengthen it:	1Tamb	1.2.30	Tamb
horse shall sweat with martiall spoile/Of conquered kingdomes,	1Tamb	1.2.192	Tamb
And kingdomes at the least we all expect,	1Tamb	1.2.218	Usumc
And all the kingdomes and dominions/That late the power of	1Tamb	5.1.508	Tamb
That purchac'd kingdomes by your martiall deeds,	1Tamb	5.1.523	Tamb
in mine eies/Than all the wealthy kingdomes I subdewed:	2Tamb	1.3.19	Tamb
As I have conquered kingdomes with my sword.	2Tamb	2.4.136	Tamb
and thirty Kingdomes late contributory to his mighty father.	2Tamb	3.1.5	P Orcan
pompe than this)/Rifle the kingdomes I shall leave unsackt,	2Tamb	4.3.59	Tamb
Kingdomes made waste, brave cities sackt and burnt,	2Tamb	5.2.26	Callap
chiefe selected men/Of twenty severall kingdomes at the least:	2Tamb	5.2.49	Callap
maintaine/The wealth and safety of your kingdomes right.	P 478	8.28	Anjoy
Make severall kingdomes of this monarchie,	Edw	1.4.70	Edward
That measures costs, and kingdomes of the earth:	F 774	2.3.53	2Chor
Now by the Kingdomes of Infernall Rule,	F 825	3.1.47	Faust
There did we view the Kingdomes of the world,	F 852	3.1.74	Faust
such riches, subdued so many kingdomes, as we that do succeede,	F App	p.236 20	P Emper
Great are thy kingdomes, over strong and large,	Ovid's Elegies		1.1.17
new to enter/Warres, just Latinus, in thy kingdomes center:	Ovid's Elegies		2.12.22
KINGDOMS			
tearms/And scourging kingdoms with his conquering sword.	1Tamb	Prol.6	Prolog
Armies alied, the kingdoms league uprooted,	Lucan, First Booke		4
And Commets that presage the fal of kingdoms.	Lucan, First Booke		527
KINGE			
I am not wise enough to be a kinge,	1Tamb	1.1.20	Mycet
KINGES			
And making thee and me Techelles, kinges,	1Tamb	1.2.58	Usumc
As if as many kinges as could encompasse thee,	1Tamb	2.5.4	Tamb
I (my Lord) but none save kinges must feede with these.	1Tamb	4.4.109	P Therid
lye there the kinges delyght and guises scorne	Paris	ms22,p390	Guise
KINGLIE			
Is Edward pleazd with kinglie regiment.	Edw	1.1.165	Edward
Can kinglie Lions fawne on creeping Ants?	Edw	1.4.15	Penbrk
And with my kinglie scepter stroke me dead,	Edw	1.4.317	Edward
On whose top-branches Kinglie Eagles pearch,	Edw	2.2.17	Mortmr
KINGLY			
Besiege the ofspring of our kingly loynes,	Dido	1.1.116	Jupitr
The kingly seate of Southerne Libia,	Dido	1.1.212	Venus
Or els in Carthage make his kingly throne.	Dido	2.1.331	Venus
Is it not a kingly resolution?	1Tamb	1.1.55	Mycet
In happy hower we have set the Crowne/Upon your kingly head,	1Tamb	2.1.51	Ortyg
enjoy in heaven/Can not compare with kingly joyes in earth.	1Tamb	2.5.59	Therid
Must plead for mercie at his kingly feet,	1Tamb	3.3.174	Zenoc
Each man a crown? why kingly fought ifaith.	1Tamb	3.3.216	Tamb
Keeping his kingly body in a Cage,	1Tamb	4.2.61	Zabina
And feare to see thy kingly Fathers harme,	1Tamb	5.1.138	Tamb
In all affection at thy kingly feet.	2Tamb	1.3.116	Therid
There having sackt Borno the Kingly seat,	2Tamb	1.3.203	Techel
Thy youth forbids such ease my kingly boy,	2Tamb	4.3.29	Tamb
And 'tis more Kingly to obtaine by peace/Then to enforce	Jew	1.2.25	Calym
A kingly kinde of trade to purchase Townes/By treachery, and	Jew	5.5.47	Barab
For Polands crowne and kingly diadem.	P 480	8.30	Lord
Tis more then kingly or Emperious.	P 759	15.17	Guise
Thankes to my Kingly Brother of Navarre.	P1150	22.12	King
His kingly body was too soone Interrde.	Edw	5.6.32	King
hunters pauseth till fell wrath/And kingly rage increase,	Lucan, First Booke		210
Let Kings give place to verse, and kingly showes,	Ovid's Elegies		1.15.33
Where kingly Neptune and his traine abode.	Hero and Leander		2.166
KING'S			
I'le not speake <an other word for a King's raunsome>.	F 706	(HC264)A	P Sloth

KINGS

And dipt it in the old Kings chill cold bloud,	Dido	2.1.260		Aeneas
(And yet have I had many mightier Kings)/Hast had the greatest	Dido	3.1.12		Dido
No Madame, but it seemes that these are Kings.	Dido	3.1.149		Aeneas
And bring forth mightie Kings to Carthage towne,	Dido	3.2.75		Juno
Hast thou forgot how many neighbour kings/Were up in armes, for	Dido	5.1.141		Dido
Me thinks I see kings kneeling at his feet,	1Tamb	1.2.55		Techel
And mightie kings shall be our Senators.	1Tamb	1.2.198		Tamb
Where kings shall crouch unto our conquering swords,	1Tamb	1.2.220		Usumc
Before I crowne you kings in Asia.	1Tamb	1.2.246		Tamb
Which make reports it far exceeds the Kings.	1Tamb	2.2.42		Spy
For Kings are clouts that every man shoots at,	1Tamb	2.4.8		Mycet
from the camp/When Kings themselves are present in the field?	1Tamb	2.4.17		Tamb
Now send Ambassage to thy neighbor Kings,	1Tamb	2.5.20		Cosroe
What saies my other friends, wil you be kings?	1Tamb	2.5.67		Tamb
Great Kings of Barbary, and my portly Bassoes,	1Tamb	3.1.1		Bajzth
Besides fifteene contributorie kings,	1Tamb	3.3.14		Bassoe
But wil those Kings accompany your Lord?	1Tamb	3.3.27		Tamb
Even he that in a trice vanquisht two kings,	1Tamb	3.3.36		Therid
Kings of Fesse, Moroccus and Argier,	1Tamb	3.3.66		Bajzth
Wel said my stout contributory kings,	1Tamb	3.3.93		Bajzth
That we may raigne as kings of Affrica.	1Tamb	3.3.99		Therid
Fight all couragiously and be you kings.	1Tamb	3.3.101		Tamb
Triumphing over him and these his kings,	1Tamb	3.3.128		Tamb
Come Kings and Bassoes, let us glut our swords/That thirst to	1Tamb	3.3.164		Bajzth
Where are your stout contributorie kings?	1Tamb	3.3.214		Tamb
Ile make the kings of India ere I die,	1Tamb	3.3.263		Tamb
Whose feet the kings of Affrica have kist.	1Tamb	4.2.65		Zabina
That should be horsed on fower mightie kings.	1Tamb	4.2.78		Bajzth
That will maintaine it against a world of Kings.	1Tamb	4.2.81		Tamb
Not all the Kings and Emperours of the Earth:	1Tamb	4.2.92		Tamb
these three crownes, and pledge me, my contributorie Kings.	1Tamb	4.4.115	P	Tamb
say you to this (Turke) these are not your contributorie kings.	1Tamb	4.4.118	P	Tamb
Kings of Argier, Morocus, and of Fesse,	1Tamb	4.4.120		Tamb
And they are worthy she investeth kings.	1Tamb	4.4.129		Tamb
Emperours and kings lie breathlesse at my feet.	1Tamb	5.1.469		Tamb
(Renowmed Tamburlain) to whom all kings/Of force must yeeld	1Tamb	5.1.480		Souldn
But here these kings that on my fortunes wait,	1Tamb	5.1.490		Tamb
Kings of Natolia and of Hungarie,	2Tamb	1.1.114		Gazell
Then shalt thou see a hundred kings and more/Upon their knees,	2Tamb	1.2.28		Callap
Have under me as many kings as you,	2Tamb	1.3.55		Celeb
Kings of Morocus and of Fesse, welcome.	2Tamb	1.3.128		Tamb
Your presence (loving friends and fellow kings)/Makes me to	2Tamb	1.3.151		Tamb
And made Canarea cal us kings and Lords,	2Tamb	1.3.181		Usumc
To aid the kings of Soria and Jerusalem.	2Tamb	2.1.21		Fredrk
where our neighbour kings/Expect our power and our royall	2Tamb	2.2.3		Orcan
An hundred kings by scores wil bid him armes,	2Tamb	2.2.11		Gazell
and holy Seraphins/That sing and play before the king of kings,	2Tamb	2.4.27		Tamb
Thrice worthy kings of Natolia, and the rest,	2Tamb	3.1.7		Callap
I march to meet and aide my neigbor kings,	2Tamb	3.1.60		Soria
View me thy father that hath conquered kings,	2Tamb	3.2.110		Tamb
Knowing two kings, the [friends] <friend> to Tamburlain,	2Tamb	3.3.13		Therid
See a knot of kings,/Sitting as if they were a telling ridles.	2Tamb	3.5.58		Tamb
Ye petty kings of Turkye I am come,	2Tamb	3.5.64		Tamb
How now ye pety kings, loe, here are Bugges/Wil make the haire	2Tamb	3.5.147		Tamb
Shal we let goe these kings again my Lord/To gather greater	2Tamb	4.1.82		Amyras
And thus be drawen with these two idle kings.	2Tamb	4.3.28		Amyras
While these their fellow kings may be refresht.	2Tamb	4.3.31		Tamb
(I meane such Queens as were kings Concubines)/Take them,	2Tamb	4.3.71		Tamb
Now crowch ye kings of greatest Asia,	2Tamb	4.3.98		Tamb
Thorow the streets with troops of conquered kings,	2Tamb	4.3.114		Tamb
Drawen with these kings on heaps of carkasses.	2Tamb	5.1.72		Tamb
Courted by kings and peeres of Asia,	2Tamb	5.1.74		Tamb
That with his sword hath quail'd all earthly kings,	2Tamb	5.1.93		Tamb
And that vile Carkasse drawne by warlike kings,	2Tamb	5.2.16		Amasia
Might first made Kings, and Lawes were then most sure/When like	Jew	Prol.20		Machvl
in perill of calamity/To ransome great Kings from captivity.	Jew	1.1.32		Barab
I must confesse we come not to be Kings:	Jew	1.1.129		Barab
Give us a peacefull rule, make Christians Kings,	Jew	1.1.134		Barab
Guise/Dares once adventure without the Kings consent,	P 37	1.37		Admral
And at ech corner shall the Kings garde stand.	P 291	5.18		Anjoy
Tis Ramus, the Kings professor of Logick.	P 381	7.21		Retes
And sure if all the proudest Kings/In Christendome, should	P 760	15.18		Guise
Lye there the Kings delight, and Guises scorne.	P 818	17.13		Guise
(aspiring Guise)/Durst be in armes without the Kings consent?	P 829	17.24		Eprnon
The Kings alone, it cannot satisfie.	P1109	21.3		Dumain
of Loraine by the Kings consent is lately strangled unto death.	P1123	21.17	P	Frier
With captive kings at his triumphant Carre.	Edw	1.1.174		Gavstn
now breaks the kings hate forth,/And he confesseth that he	Edw	1.4.193		Queene
Nay, for the realms behoofe and for the kings.	Edw	1.4.243		Mortmr
The mightiest kings have had their minions,	Edw	1.4.391		MortSr
And not kings onelie, but the wisest men,	Edw	1.4.395		MortSr
Away base groome, robber of kings renowme,	Edw	2.5.72		Mortmr
To gratifie the kings request therein,	Edw	2.5.75		Penbrk
I heare sweete lady of the kings unkindenes,	Edw	4.2.15		SrJohn
our port-maisters/Are not so careles of their kings commaund.	Edw	4.3.23		Edward
Misgoverned kings are cause of all this wrack,	Edw	4.4.9		Queene
Succesfull battells gives the God of kings,	Edw	4.6.19		Queene
Must! tis somwhat hard, when kings must go.	Edw	4.7.83		Edward
The greefes of private men are soone allayde,/But not of kings:	Edw	5.1.9		Edward
But what are kings, when regiment is gone,	Edw	5.1.26		Edward
Two kings in England cannot raigne at once:	Edw	5.1.58		Edward
the greater sway/When as a kings name shall be under writ.	Edw	5.2.14		Mortmr

KINGS (cont.)
Where lords keepe courts, and kings are lockt in prison! — Edw 5.3.64 Kent
Nor shall they now be tainted with a kings. — Edw 5.5.82 Ltborn
And beare the kings to Mortimer our lord, — Edw 5.5.119 Gurney
Thus madam, tis the kings will you shall hence. — Edw 5.6.89 2Lord
Nor sporting in the dalliance of love/In Courts of Kings, where — F 4 Prol.4 1Chor
Emperors and Kings,/Are but obey'd in their severall Provinces: — F 84 1.1.56 Faust
And tell the secrets of all forraine Kings: — F 114 1.1.86 Faust
not speake a word more for a Kings ransome <an other worde>, — F 670 2.2.119 P Pride
I'le not speake <a word more for a kings ransome>. — F 706 (HC264)B P Sloth
tane the view]/[Of rarest things, and royal courts of kings], — F1139 3.3.52A 3Chor
amongest which kings is Alexander the great, chiefe spectacle — F App p.237 23 P Emper
Shall never faith be found in fellow kings. — Lucan, First Booke 92
Let Kings give place to verse, and kingly showes, — Ovid's Elegies 1.15.33
What graced Kings, in me no shame I deeme. — Ovid's Elegies 2.8.14

KINNE
Twere hard with me if I should doubt my kinne, — P 971 19.41 King

KINSMANS
That durst thus proudly wrong our kinsmans peace. — Dido 1.1.119 Jupitr
By Mahomet, my Kinsmans sepulcher, — 1Tamb 3.3.75 Bajzth
Beholde thy kinsmans Caesars prosperous bandes, — Ovid's Elegies 1.2.51

KINSMEN
Slew all his Priests, his kinsmen, and his friends, — 2Tamb 5.1.181 Tamb
Whereas his kinsmen chiefly brought him up; — F 14 Prol.14 1Chor

KINSMENS
Our kinsmens [lives] <loves>, and thousand guiltles soules, — Dido 4.4.90 Aeneas

KIRRIAH
There's Kirriah Jairim, the great Jew of Greece, — Jew 1.1.124 Barab

KIRTLE
Her kirtle blew, whereon was many a staine, — Hero and Leander 1.15
A cap of flowers, and a kirtle, — Passionate Shepherd 11

KIS
kis not my hand,/Embrace me Gaveston as I do thee: — Edw 1.1.140 Edward
his/That leapt into the water for a kis/Of his owne shadow, — Hero and Leander 1.74
That he and Povertie should alwaies kis. — Hero and Leander 1.470

KISSE
And kisse his hand: O where is Hecuba? — Dido 2.1.12 Achat
He [names] <meanes> Aeneas, let us kisse his feete. — Dido 2.1.51 Illion
I wagge, and give thee leave to kisse her to. — Dido 3.1.31 Dido
And every speech be ended with a kisse: — Dido 4.3.54 Aeneas
This kisse shall be faire Didos punishment. — Dido 4.4.37 Aeneas
And heele make me immortall with a kisse. — Dido 4.4.123 Dido
Wilt thou kisse Dido? — Dido 5.1.120 Dido
You may doe well to kisse it then. — 1Tamb 1.1.98 Cosroe
(Whose scepter Angels kisse, and Furies dread)/As for their — 1Tamb 5.1.94 1Virgn
Yet let me kisse my Lord before I die, — 2Tamb 2.4.69 Zenoc
Who shal kisse the fairest of the Turkes Concubines first, when — 2Tamb 4.1.64 P Calyph
my fingers take/A kisse from him that sends it from his soule. — Jew 2.1.59 Barab
I learn'd in Florence how to kisse my hand, — Jew 2.3.23 Barab
Daughter, a word more; kisse him, speake him faire, — Jew 2.3.234 Barab
That kisse againe; she runs division of my lips. — Jew 4.2.127 P Ithimr
Then pray unto our Ladye, kisse this crosse. — P 302 5.29 Gonzag
I kisse your graces hand, and take my leave, — P 868 17.63 Guise
<incense>/The papall towers to kisse the [lowly] <holy> earth. — P1202 22.64 King
and enforce/The papall towers, to kisse the lowlie ground, — Edw 1.4.101 Edward
O how a kisse revives poore Isabell. — Edw 1.4.333 Queene
diest, for Mortimer/And Isabell doe kisse while they conspire, — Edw 4.6.13 Kent
I kisse her [lippes]; And then turning my selfe to a wrought — F 667 2.2.116 P Pride
I saw him kneele, and kisse the Emperours hand, — F1344 4.2.20 Benvol
Sweet Hellen make me immortall with a kisse: — F1770 5.1.97 Faust
And then returne to Hellen for a kisse. — F1780 5.1.107 Faust
the deepe)/Puls them aloft, and makes the surge kisse heaven, — Lucan, First Booke 417
Entreat thy husband drinke, but do not kisse, — Ovid's Elegies 1.4.51
Then will he kisse thee, and not onely kisse/But force thee — Ovid's Elegies 1.4.63
and not onely kisse/But force thee give him my stolne honey — Ovid's Elegies 1.4.63
Judge you the rest, being tyrde <tride> she bad me kisse. — Ovid's Elegies 1.5.25
Thou art as faire as shee, then kisse and play. — Ovid's Elegies 1.13.44
And loving Doves kisse eagerly together. — Ovid's Elegies 2.6.56
Ile clip and kisse thee with all contentation, — Ovid's Elegies 2.11.45
To kisse, I kisse, to lie with her shee let me. — Ovid's Elegies 3.6.48
To expiat which sinne, kisse and shake hands, — Hero and Leander 1.309
We often kisse it, often looke thereon, — Hero and Leander 2.81
And steale a kisse, and then run out and daunce, — Hero and Leander 2.185
And everie kisse to her was as a charme, — Hero and Leander 2.283

KISSED
and kissed so sweetely as might make/Wrath-kindled Jove away — Ovid's Elegies 2.5.51

KISSES
altar, where Ile offer up/As many kisses as the Sea hath sands, — Dido 3.1.88 Dido
If thou givest kisses, I shall all disclose, — Ovid's Elegies 1.4.39
I sawe you then unlawfull kisses joyne, — Ovid's Elegies 2.5.23
Least with worse kisses she should me indue. — Ovid's Elegies 2.5.50
This grieves me not, no joyned kisses spent, — Ovid's Elegies 2.5.59
And thousand kisses gives, that worke my harmes: — Ovid's Elegies 2.18.10
Great gods what kisses, and how many gave she? — Ovid's Elegies 2.19.18
Nemesis and thy first wench joyne their kisses, — Ovid's Elegies 3.8.53
And then he woo'd with kisses, and at last, — Hero and Leander 1.404
(Sweet are the kisses, the imbracements sweet, — Hero and Leander 2.29

KISSING
And let me die with kissing of my Lord. — 2Tamb 2.4.70 Zenoc
Meeter it were her lips were blewe with kissing/And on her — Ovid's Elegies 1.7.41

KIST
Kist him, imbrast him, and unloosde his bands, — Dido 2.1.158 Aeneas
Whose feet the kings of Affrica have kist. — 1Tamb 4.2.65 Zabina

KIST (cont.)
For now by this has he kist Abigall; Jew 2.3.246 Barab
And eagerlie she kist me with her tongue, Ovid's Elegies 3.6.9
Well, I beleeve she kist not as she should, Ovid's Elegies 3.6.55
He kist her, and breath'd life into her lips, Hero and Leander 2.3
Imbrast her sodainly, tooke leave, and kist, Hero and Leander 2.92
And kist againe, as lovers use to do. Hero and Leander 2.94
Which mounted up, intending to have kist him, Hero and Leander 2.173
Inclos'd her in his armes and kist her to. Hero and Leander 2.282

KITCHIN
to their porridge-pots, for I'le into the Kitchin presently: F1134 3.3.47 P Robin
if thou hast any mind to Nan Spit our kitchin maide, then turn F App p.234 27 P Robin

KNAVE
of the Serpent then the Dove; that is, more knave than foole. Jew 2.3.37 P Barab
bottle-nos'd knave to my Master, that ever Gentleman had. Jew 3.3.10 P Ithimr
Say, knave, why rail'st upon my father thus? Jew 3.3.11 Abigal
To have a shag-rag knave to come [demand]/Three hundred Jew 4.3.61 Barab
Thou art a proud knave indeed: F 672 2.2.121 P Faust

KNAVELY
Knavely spoke, and like a Knight at Armes. Jew 4.4.9 Pilia

KNAVERY
conjuring bookes, and now we'le have such knavery, as't passes. F 724 2.3.3 P Robin
plague take you, I thought 'twas your knavery to take it away: F1110 3.3.23 P Vintnr

KNAVES
his Diadem/Sought for by such scalde knaves as love him not? 1Tamb 2.2.8 Mycet
how, how, knaves acre? F App p.229 17 P Clown

KNEE
Sit on my knee, and call for thy content, Dido 1.1.28 Jupitr
My knee shall bowe to none but to the king. Edw 1.1.19 Gavstn
And bent his sinewy bow upon his knee, Ovid's Elegies 1.1.27
For shame presse not her backe with thy hard knee. Ovid's Elegies 3.2.24
And brancht with blushing corall to the knee; Hero and Leander 1.32

KNEEL'D
Once at Jerusalem, where the pilgrims kneel'd, Jew 2.3.208 Ithimr
He kneel'd, but unto her devoutly praid; Hero and Leander 1.177

KNEELE
Thou breakst the law of Armes unlesse thou kneele, 1Tamb 2.4.21 Mycet
make no period/Untill Natolia kneele before your feet. 2Tamb 1.3.217 Therid
first thou shalt kneele to us/And humbly crave a pardon for thy 2Tamb 3.5.108 Orcan
And wake blacke Jove to crouch and kneele to me, 2Tamb 5.1.98 Tamb
And kneele for mercy to your conquering foe: Jew 5.2.2 Calym
Why shouldst thou kneele, knowest thou not who I am? Edw 1.1.142 Edward
Faustus thou shalt, then kneele downe presently, F 994 3.2.14 Mephst
I saw him kneele, and kisse the Emperours hand, F1344 4.2.20 Benvol
blacke survey/Great Potentates do kneele with awful feare, F App p.235 35 Mephst

KNEELING
Kneeling for mercie to a Greekish lad, Dido 2.1.198 Aeneas
Me thinks I see kings kneeling at his feet, 1Tamb 1.2.55 Techel

KNEES
I cannot choose but fall upon my knees, Dido 2.1.11 Achat
And from their knees, even to their hoofes below, 1Tamb 1.1.79 Mycet
With knees and hearts submissive we intreate/Grace to our words 1Tamb 5.1.50 2Virgn
which basely on their knees/In all your names desirde a truce 2Tamb 1.1.96 Orcan
Then shalt thou see a hundred kings and more/Upon their knees, 2Tamb 1.2.29 Callap
That humbly craves upon her knees to stay, 2Tamb 3.4.70 Olymp
And pull proud Tamburlaine upon his knees, 2Tamb 5.2.40 Amasia
And here upon my knees, striking the earth, Jew 1.2.165 Barab
And therewithall their knees wouldranckle, so/That I have Jew 2.3.210 Ithimr
And on my knees creepe to Jerusalem. Jew 4.1.62 Barab
And hew these knees that now are growne so stiffe. Edw 1.1.95 Edward
And on their knees salute your majestie. Edw 1.4.339 Queene
Being in a vault up to the knees in water, Edw 5.5.2 Matrvs
hornes/The quick priest pull'd him on his knees and slew him: Lucan, First Booke 612

KNELL
There is no musicke to a Christians knell: Jew 4.1.1 Barab
And ring aloude the knell of Gaveston. Edw 2.3.26 Mortmr
Let Plutos bels ring out my fatall knell, Edw 4.7.89 Edward

KNELS
armes in ure/With digging graves and ringing dead mens knels: Jew 2.3.185 Barab

KNEW
In all my life I never knew the like, Dido 4.1.7 Anna
We knew my Lord, before we brought the crowne, 1Tamb 1.1.179 Ortyg
They knew not, ah, they knew not simple men, 1Tamb 2.4.2 Mycet
From one that knew not what a King should do, 1Tamb 2.5.22 Cosroe
And made so wanton that they knew their strengths, 2Tamb 4.3.14 Tamb
Lost long before you knew what honour meant. 2Tamb 4.3.87 Tamb
As if we knew not thy profession? Jew 1.2.120 Govnr
You knew Mathias and Don Lodowicke? Jew 3.6.20 Abigal
As never Jew nor Christian knew the like: Jew 4.1.118 Barab
Yet if he knew our meanings, could he scape? Jew 4.1.135 Barab
I never knew a man take his death so patiently as this Fryar; Jew 4.2.21 P Ithimr
You knew Mathias and the Governors son; he and I kild 'em both, Jew 4.4.17 P Ithimr
I knew the Organon to be confusde, P 406 7.46 Ramus
I knew the King would have him home againe. Edw 2.1.78 Spencr
To whome right well you knew our soule was knit, Edw 3.1.227 Edward
Knew you not Traytors, I was limitted/For foure and twenty F1395 4.2.71 Faust
because I knew him to be such a horse, as would run over hedge F1538 4.5.34 P HrsCsr
Well skild in Pyromancy; one that knew/The hearts of beasts, and Lucan, First Booke 586
I knew your speech (what do not lovers see)? Ovid's Elegies 2.5.19
Or voice that howe to change the wilde notes knew? Ovid's Elegies 2.6.18
Thee I have pass'd, and knew thy streame none such, Ovid's Elegies 3.5.5
And such as knew he was a man would say, Hero and Leander 1.87
And too too well the faire vermilion knew, Hero and Leander 1.395

KNEW (cont.)

He being a novice, knew not what she meant, ... Hero and Leander 2.13
Leanders Father knew where hee had beene, ... Hero and Leander 2.136
But when he knew it was not Ganimed, ... Hero and Leander 2.169
Againe she knew not how to frame her looke, . . . Hero and Leander 2.307

KNEWE

By whom the husband his wives incest knewe. . . . Ovid's Elegies 2.2.48
White-cheekt Penelope knewe Ulisses signe, . . . Ovid's Elegies 2.18.29
First of thy minde the happy seedes I knewe, . . . Ovid's Elegies 3.1.59
The horses seeme, as [thy] <they> desire they knewe. . Ovid's Elegies 3.2.68
Not what we slouthfull [knowe] <knewe>, let wise men learne, Ovid's Elegies 3.7.25

KNEWST

<Why, didst thou not say thou knewst>? . . . . . F 204 (HC258)A P 2Schol

KNIFE

Give me your knife (good mother) or strike home: . . 2Tamb 3.4.28 Sonne
Here, hold that knife, and when thou seest he comes, . Jew 5.5.37 Barab
For you are stricken with a poysoned knife. . . . P1213 22.75 Srgeon
A poysoned knife? . . . . P1214 22.76 King
Then crams salt levin on his crooked knife; . . . Lucan, First Booke 609
They offred him the deadly fatall knife, ... Hero and Leander 1.447

KNIGHT

(The worthiest knight that ever brandisht sword)/Challenge in 2Tamb 3.5.71 Tamb
Knavely spoke, and like a Knight at Armes. . . . Jew 4.4.9 Pilia
With Guie of Warwick that redoubted knight, . . . Edw 1.3.4 Gavstn
Why how now sir Knight, what, hang'd by the hornes? . . F1290 4.1.136 P Faust
hath Faustus justly requited this injurious knight, which being F1313 4.1.159 P Faust
send for the knight that was so pleasent with me here of late? F App p.238 66 P Faust
How now sir Knight? . . . . F App p.238 69 P Emper
hath Faustus worthily requited this injurious knight, which F App p.238 83 P Faust
and sir knight, hereafter speake well of Scholers: . . F App p.238 84 P Faust
Thence growes the Judge, and knight of reputation. . . Ovid's Elegies 3.7.56

KNIGHTED

For bloudshed knighted, before me preferr'd. . . . Ovid's Elegies 3.7.10

KNIGHTES

Environed with brave Argolian knightes, ... 1Tamb 4.3.2 Souldn
Ladies of honor, Knightes and Gentlemen, ... P 213 4.11 Charls

KNIGHTLY

That am descended but of knightly line, ... Ovid's Elegies 1.3.8

KNIGHTS

Know Knights of Malta, that we came from Rhodes, . . Jew 1.2.2 Basso
Stand all aside, and let the Knights determine, . . Jew 1.2.14 Calym
Farewell great [Governor], and brave Knights of Malta. . Jew 1.2.32 Calym
Will Knights of Malta be in league with Turkes, . . . Jew 2.2.28 Bosco
We and our warlike Knights will follow thee/Against these Jew 2.2.45 Govnr
traind to armes/And bloudie warres, so many valiant knights, Edw 2.5.16 Lncstr
Knights of the post of perjuries make saile, . . . Ovid's Elegies 1.10.37

KNIT

So large of lims, his joints so strongly knit, . . . 1Tamb 2.1.9 Menaph
were the sinowes of th'imperiall seat/So knit and strengthned, 2Tamb 3.1.11 Callap
Knit in these hands, thus joyn'd in nuptiall rites, . . P 4 1.4 Charls
To whome right well you knew our soule was knit, . . Edw 3.1.227 Edward
When force to force is knit, and sword and gleave/In civill Edw 4.4.5 Queene
But in lesse compasse her small fingers knit. . . . Ovid's Elegies 2.15.20

KNITT

On tell-tales neckes thou seest the linke-knitt chaines, . Ovid's Elegies 2.2.41

KNIVES

[Faustus, thou art damn'd, then swords <guns> and knives], F 572 2.2.21A Faust

KNOB

is, appear'd/A knob of flesh, whereof one halfe did looke/Dead, Lucan, First Booke 627

KNOCHT

they were never so knocht since they were divels, say I should F App p.230 46 P Clown

KNOCKE

I may knocke out his braines with them, and lock you in the 2Tamb 3.5.141 P Tamb
and Ile knocke them, they were never so knocht since they were F App p.230 45 P Clown
My flatt'ring speeches soone wide open knocke. . . . Ovid's Elegies 3.1.46

KNOCKS

Who is that which knocks there? . . . . P 346 6.1 P SrnsWf
Search at the dore who knocks oft in the darke, . . Ovid's Elegies 2.19.39
And knocks his bare brest with selfe-angry hands. . . Ovid's Elegies 3.8.10

KNOCKST

And fiercely knockst thy brest that open lyes? . . . Ovid's Elegies 3.5.58

KNOCKT

And knockt and cald, at which celestiall noise, . . . Hero and Leander 2.231

KNOT

About them hangs a knot of Amber heire, ... 1Tamb 2.1.23 Menaph
See a knot of kings,/Sitting as if they were a telling ridles. 2Tamb 3.5.58 Tamb

KNOTS

For this will Dido tye ye full of knots, ... Dido 4.4.155 Dido

KNOW

Triton I know hath fild his trumpe with Troy, . . . Dido 1.1.130 Venus
To know what coast the winde hath driven us on, . . . Dido 1.1.176 Aeneas
I know her by the movings of her feete: . . . . Dido 1.1.241 Aeneas
And when I know it is not, then I dye. . . . . Dido 2.1.9 Aeneas
And scarcely know within what Clime we are. . . . Dido 2.1.44 Aeneas
know that thou of all my wooers/(And yet have I had many Dido 3.1.11 Dido
Albeit the Gods doe know no wanton thought/Had ever residence Dido 3.1.16 Dido
O Anna, didst thou know how sweet love were, . . . Dido 3.1.59 Dido
Poore soule I know too well the sower of love, . . . Dido 3.1.61 Anna
I know this face, he is a Persian borne, ... Dido 3.1.144 Serg
But speake Aeneas, know you none of these? . . . . Dido 3.1.148 Dido
Stoute friend Achates, doest thou know this wood? . . Dido 3.3.50 Aeneas
I know not what you meane by treason, I, ... Dido 5.1.222 Nurse
I know you have a better wit than I. . . . . . 1Tamb 1.1.5 Mycet

KNOW (cont.)

I meane it not, but yet I know I might,	1Tamb	1.1.26		Mycet
I know it wel my Lord, and thanke you all.	1Tamb	1.1.187		Cosroe
And as we know) remaines with Tamburlaine,	1Tamb	2.2.36		Meandr
And let them know the Persean King is chang'd:	1Tamb	2.5.21		Cosroe
I know they would with our perswasions.	1Tamb	2.5.80		Therid
I know not how to take their tyrannies.	1Tamb	2.7.41		Cosroe
You know our Armie is invincible:	1Tamb	3.1.7		Bajzth
may I presume/To know the cause of these unquiet fits:	1Tamb	3.2.2		Agidas
And know thou Turke, that those which lead my horse,	1Tamb	3.3.72		Tamb
They know my custome:	1Tamb	5.1.67		Tamb
And know my customes are as peremptory/As wrathfull Planets,	1Tamb	5.1.127		Tamb
Bring him forth, and let us know if the towne be ransackt.	1Tamb	5.1.194	P	Tamb
We know the victorie is ours my Lord,	1Tamb	5.1.203		Therid
I know thou wouldst depart from hence with me.	2Tamb	1.2.11		Callap
But that I know they issued from thy wombe,	2Tamb	1.3.33		Tamb
That is a Gentleman (I know) at least.	2Tamb	3.1.72		Callap
I know not what I should think of it.	2Tamb	3.2.130	P	Calyph
That we may know if our artillery/Will carie full point blancke	2Tamb	3.3.52		Techel
See ye this rout, and know ye this same king?	2Tamb	3.5.151		Tamb
I know sir, what it is to kil a man,	2Tamb	4.1.27		Calyph
Know ye not yet the argument of Armes?	2Tamb	4.1.100		Tamb
Something Techelles, but I know not what,	2Tamb	5.1.220		Tamb
I know it wil Casane:	2Tamb	5.3.113		Tamb
And let them know that I am Machevill,	Jew	Prol.7		Machvl
and have sent me to know/Whether your selfe will come and	Jew	1.1.52		1Merch
Tush, they are wise; I know her and her strength:	Jew	1.1.81		Barab
Know Barabas, doth ride in Malta Rhode,	Jew	1.1.86		2Merch
I know you will; well brethren let us goe.	Jew	1.1.174		1Jew
Know Knights of Malta, that we came from Rhodes,	Jew	1.2.2		Basso
Let's know their time, perhaps it is not long;	Jew	1.2.24		Calym
Now then here know that it concerneth us--	Jew	1.2.42		Govnr
Tut, Jew, we know thou art no souldier;	Jew	1.2.52		1Knght
Why know you what you did by this device?	Jew	1.2.84		Barab
Captaine we know it, but our force is small.	Jew	2.2.34		Govnr
Is it square or pointed, pray let me know.	Jew	2.3.59		Lodowk
And yet I know the prayers of those Nuns/And holy Fryers,	Jew	2.3.80		Barab
Seeme not to know me here before your mother/Lest she mistrust	Jew	2.3.146		Barab
Now let me know thy name, and therewithall/Thy birth,	Jew	2.3.163		Barab
I know it:	Jew	2.3.238		Barab
Oh but I know your Lordship wud disdaine/To marry with the	Jew	2.3.294		Barab
I know not, but farewell, I must be gone.	Jew	2.3.322		Abigal
And yet I know my beauty doth not faile.	Jew	3.1.5		Curtzn
I know she is a Curtezane by her attire:	Jew	3.1.26	P	Ithimr
I know not, and that grieves me most of all.	Jew	3.2.21		Govnr
Why, know you not?	Jew	3.3.14	P	Ithimr
Know you not of Mathias and Don Lodowickes disaster?	Jew	3.3.16	P	Ithimr
Know, holy Sir, I am bold to sollicite thee.	Jew	3.3.53		Abigal
Onely know this, that thus thou art to doe:	Jew	3.4.48		Barab
seeing you are come/Be you my ghostly father; and first know,	Jew	3.6.12		Abigal
Know that Confession must not be reveal'd,	Jew	3.6.33		2Fryar
I feare they know we sent the poyson'd broth.	Jew	4.1.26		Barab
What needs all this? I know I am a Jew.	Jew	4.1.33		Barab
Besides I know not how much weight in Pearle/Orient and round,	Jew	4.1.66		Barab
And Barabas, you know--	Jew	4.1.79		2Fryar
I know that I have highly sinn'd,	Jew	4.1.80		Barab
I know they are, and I will be with you.	Jew	4.1.83		Barab
You know my mind, let me alone with him.	Jew	4.1.100		Barab
Yes; and I know not what the reason is:	Jew	4.1.130		Ithimr
And ye did but know how she loves you, Sir.	Jew	4.2.53		Pilia
But you know some secrets of the Jew,	Jew	4.2.64		Pilia
you know my meaning.	Jew	4.3.34	P	Barab
I know enough, and therfore talke not to me of your	Jew	4.3.36	P	Pilia
the gold, or know Jew it is in my power to hang thee.	Jew	4.3.37	P	Pilia
You know I have no childe, and unto whom/Should I leave all but	Jew	4.3.44		Barab
I know it, Sir.	Jew	4.3.55		Pilia
nothing; but I know what I know.	Jew	4.4.14	P	Ithimr
Dost not know a Jew, one Barabas?	Jew	4.4.56	P	Ithimr
Let me alone to urge it now I know the meaning.	Jew	4.4.79		Pilia
Nuns, strangled a Fryar, and I know not what mischiefe beside.	Jew	5.1.14	P	Pilia
I know; and they shall witnesse with their lives.	Jew	5.2.123		Barab
Know, Selim, that there is a monastery/Which standeth as an	Jew	5.3.36		Msngr
And villaines, know you cannot helpe me now.	Jew	5.5.77		Barab
Know, Governor, 'twas I that slew thy sonne;	Jew	5.5.81		Barab
Know, Calymath, I aym'd thy overthrow,	Jew	5.5.83		Barab
Know therefore, till thy father hath made good/The ruines done	Jew	5.5.111		Govnr
And as you know, our difference in Religion/Might be a meanes	P 15	1.15		QnMoth
Doth not your grace know the man that gave them you?	P 172	3.7		Navrre
Cosin tis he, I know him by his look.	P 309	5.36		Guise
which have already set the street/May know their watchword,	P 329	5.56		Guise
In that I know the things that I have wrote,	P 403	7.43		Ramus
We know that noble mindes change not their thoughts/For wearing	P 610	12.23		Mugern
Are these your secrets that no man must know?	P 678	13.22		Guise
But for you know our quarrell is no more,	P 704	14.7		Navrre
They should know how I scornde them and their mockes.	P 762	15.20		Guise
I know none els but holdes them in disgrace:	P 764	15.22		Guise
But God we know will alwaies put them downe,	P 798	16.12		Navrre
And know my Lord, the Pope will sell his triple crowne,	P 851	17.46		Guise
Stand close, he is comming, I know him by his voice.	P1000	19.70	P	1Mur
(As all the world shall know our Guise is dead)/Rest satisfied	P1042	19.112		King
You know that I came lately out of France,	Edw	1.1.44		Gavstn
That crosse me thus, shall know I am displeasd.	Edw	1.1.79		Edward
And know my lord, ere I will breake my oath,	Edw	1.1.85		Mortmr

KNOW (cont.)

I will have Gaveston, and you shall know,	Edw	1.1.96		Edward
I know it, brother welcome home my friend.	Edw	1.1.148		Edward
We know our duties, let him know his peeres.	Edw	1.4.23		Warwck
You know that I am legate to the Pope,	Edw	1.4.51		ArchBp
I know tis long of Gaveston she weepes.	Edw	1.4.191		Mortmr
Know you not Gaveston hath store of golde,	Edw	1.4.258		Mortmr
Nay more, when he shall know it lies in us,	Edw	1.4.274		Mortmr
You know my minde, come unckle lets away.	Edw	1.4.424		Mortmr
I know thou couldst not come and visit me.	Edw	2.1.61		Neece
Prethee let me know it.	Edw	2.2.14		Edward
I know my lcrd, many will stomack me,	Edw	2.2.260		Gavstn
now my lords know this,/That Gaveston is secretlie arrivde,	Edw	2.3.15		Lncstr
You know the king is so suspitious,	Edw	2.4.53		Queene
I know it lcrds, it is this life you aime at,	Edw	2.5.48		Gavstn
But for we know thou art a noble gentleman,	Edw	2.5.68		Mortmr
Nay, do your pleasures, I know how twill proove.	Edw	2.5.93		Warwck
I know the malice of the yonger Mortimer,	Edw	3.1.5		Edward
Warwick I know is roughe, and Lancaster/Inexorable, and I shall	Edw	3.1.6		Edward
And all the land I know is up in armes,	Edw	4.7.31		Spencr
Farewell, I know the next newes that they bring,	Edw	5.1.125		Edward
I know not, but of this am I assured,	Edw	5.1.152		Edward
And none but we shall know where he lieth.	Edw	5.2.41		Mortmr
Brother, you know it is impossible.	Edw	5.2.97		Queene
Mortimer shall know that he hath wrongde mee.	Edw	5.2.118		Kent
I, I, and none shall know which way he died.	Edw	5.4.25		Ltborn
Whats heere? I know not how to conster it.	Edw	5.5.15		Gurney
Know you this token? I must have the king.	Edw	5.5.19		Ltborn
I know what I must do, get you away,	Edw	5.5.27		Ltborn
Villaine, I know thou comst to murther me.	Edw	5.5.45		Edward
And whether I have limmes or no, I know not.	Edw	5.5.65		Edward
Still feare I, and I know not whats the cause,	Edw	5.5.85		Edward
Know that I am a king, oh at that name,	Edw	5.5.89		Edward
Feare not my lord, know that you are a king.	Edw	5.6.24		1Lord
Know that your words have won me at the last,	F 128	1.1.100		Faust
Valdes, first let him know the words of Art,	F 185	1.1.157		Cornel
That shall we presently know, <for see> here comes his boy.	F 196	1.2.3		2Schol
Why, dost not thou know then?	F 199	1.2.6	P	2Schol
Yes, I know, but that followes not.	F 200	1.2.7	P	Wagner
nakednesse, I know the Villaines out of service, and so hungry,	F 349	1.4.7	P	Wagner
that <I know> he would give his soule to the devill, for a	F 349	1.4.7	P	Wagner
Learned Faustus/To find <know> the secrets of Astronomy,/Graven	F 755	2.3.34		2Chor
Know that this City stands upon seven hils,	F 811	3.1.33		Mephst
I know you'd <faine> see the Pope/And take some part of holy	F 831	3.1.53		Mephst
Never deny't, for I know you have it, and I'le search you.	F1101	3.3.14	P	Vintnr
By this (I know) the Conjurer is neere,	F1343	4.2.19		Benvol
Sirra Dick, dost thou know why I stand so mute?	F1509	4.5.5	P	Robin
bravest tale how a Conjurer serv'd me; you know Doctor Fauster?	F1522	4.5.18	P	Carter
heere's some on's have cause to know him; did he conjure thee	F1524	4.5.20	P	HrsCsr
had had some [rare] quality that he would not have me know of,	F1543	4.5.39	P	HrsCsr
know I how sufficiently to recompence your great deserts in	F1559	4.6.2	P	Duke
I but sir sauce box, know you in what place?	F1616	4.6.59		Servnt
sir, I would make nothing of you, but I would faine know that.	F1649	4.6.92	P	Carter
For that I know your friendship is unfain'd,	F1689	5.1.16		Faust
know he would give his soule to the Divel for a shoulder of	F App	p.229 8	P	Wagner
Ile tell you how you shall know them, all hee divels has	F App	p.230 53	P	Clown
Nay I know not, we shalbe curst with bell, booke, and candle.	F App	p.232 23	P	Mephst
or moale in her necke, how shal I know whether it be so or no?	F App	p.238 61	P	Emper
or blustring south were cause/I know not, but the cloudy ayre	Lucan, First Booke			237
And only gods and heavenly powers you know,	Lucan, First Booke			449
gods and heavenly powers you know,/Or only know you nothing.	Lucan, First Booke			450
This headlesse trunke that lies on Nylus sande/I know:	Lucan, First Booke			685
But how thou shouldst behave thy selfe now know;	Ovid's Elegies			1.4.11
She magick arts and Thessale charmes doth know,	Ovid's Elegies			1.8.5
I know no maister of so great hire sped.	Ovid's Elegies			2.5.62
My selfe unguilty of this crime I know.	Ovid's Elegies			2.7.28
I know not whether my mindes whirle-wind drives me.	Ovid's Elegies			2.9.28
Loe country Gods, and [known] <know> bed to forsake,	Ovid's Elegies			2.11.7
I know a wench reports her selfe Corinne,	Ovid's Elegies			2.17.29
That thou maiest know with love thou mak'st me flame.	Ovid's Elegies			3.2.4
I know not, what men thinke should thee so move.	Ovid's Elegies			3.4.28
I know not what expecting, I ere while/Nam'd Achelaus, Inachus,	Ovid's Elegies			3.5.103
And least her maide should know of this disgrace,	Ovid's Elegies			3.6.83
I know not whom thou lewdly didst imbrace,	Ovid's Elegies			3.10.11
To know their rites, well recompenc'd my stay,	Ovid's Elegies			3.12.5
But let not mee poore soule know of thy straying.	Ovid's Elegies			3.13.2
For know, that underneath this radiant floure,	Hero and Leander			1.145
And know that some have wrong'd Dianas name?	Hero and Leander			1.284
But know you not that creatures wanting sence,	Hero and Leander			2.55
Which taught him all that elder lovers know,	Hero and Leander			2.69
Should know the pleasure of this blessed night,	Hero and Leander			2.304

KNOWE

That know my wit, and can be witnesses:	1Tamb	1.1.22		Mycet
you knowe I shall have occasion shortly to journey you.	2Tamb	3.5.114	P	Tamb
You knowe not sir:	2Tamb	3.5.158		Tamb
Nay, you shall pardon me, none shall knowe my trickes.	Edw	5.4.39		Ltborn
heavens, that I might knowe their motions and dispositions].	F 551.5	2.1.168A	P	Faust
There is, who ere will knowe a bawde aright/Give eare, there is	Ovid's Elegies			1.8.1
loves bowe/His owne flames best acquainted signes may knowe,	Ovid's Elegies			2.1.8
Not what we slouthfull [knowe] <knewe>, let wise men learne,	Ovid's Elegies			3.7.25

KNOWEN

So shall not I be knowen, or if I bee,	1Tamb	2.4.13		Mycet

KNOWES

Since Carthage knowes to entertaine distresse.	Dido	1.2.33		Iarbus

KNOWES (cont.)

And yet God knowes intangled unto one.--	Dido	3.1.154	Dido
The rest are such as all the world well knowes,	Dido	3.1.165	Dido
Which is (God knowes) about that Tamburlaine,	1Tamb	1.1.30	Mycet
Bassoe, by this thy Lord and maister knowes,	1Tamb	3.3.1	Tamb
Your Highnesse knowes for Tamburlaines repaire,	2Tamb	2.1.14	Fredrk
That fighting, knowes not what retreat doth meane,	2Tamb	3.5.43	Trebiz
Tush, who amongst 'em knowes not Barrabas?	Jew	1.1.67	Barab
And knowes no meanes of his recoverie:	Jew	1.2.205	Barab
I feare she knowes ('tis so) of my device/In Don Mathias and	Jew	3.4.7	Barab
The other knowes enough to have my life,	Jew	4.1.120	Barab
I have don't, but no body knowes it but you two, I may escape.	Jew	4.1.180	P 1Fryar
That he who knowes I love him as my selfe/Should write in this	Jew	4.3.42	Barab
his villany/He will tell all he knowes and I shall dye for't.	Jew	4.3.65	Barab
He knowes it already.	Jew	4.4.60	P Barab
Else all France knowes how poor a Duke thou art.	P 844	17.39	Eprnon
Your highnes knowes, it lies not in my power.	Edw	1.4.158	Queene
And sends you word, he knowes that die he shall,	Edw	2.5.38	Arundl
Immortall powers, that knowes the painfull cares,	Edw	5.3.37	Edward
God in heaven knowes.	F 198	1.2.5	P Wagner
Who knowes not the double motion of the Planets?	F 602	2.2.51	Faust
Love <Jove> knowes with such like praiers, I dayly move hir:	Ovid's Elegies		1.3.4
Whence knowes Corinna that with thee I playde?	Ovid's Elegies		2.8.6
Better then I their quiver knowes them not.	Ovid's Elegies		2.9.38
And craftily knowes by what meanes to winne me.	Ovid's Elegies		2.19.10
The reason no man knowes, let it suffise,	Hero and Leander		1.173
God knowes I cannot force love, as you doe.	Hero and Leander		1.206
and there God knowes I play/With Venus swannes and sparrowes	Hero and Leander		1.351

KNOWEST

ships, thou knowest/We sawe Cassandra sprauling in the streetes,	Dido	2.1.273	Aeneas
Thy sonne thou knowest with Dido now remaines,	Dido	3.2.70	Juno
Thou knowest not (foolish hardy Tamburlaine)/What tis to meet	1Tamb	3.3.145	Bajzth
Villain, knowest thou to whom thou speakest?	1Tamb	4.4.39	P Usumc
Why shouldst thou kneele, knowest thou not who I am?	Edw	1.1.142	Edward
Spencer, thou knowest I hate such formall toies,	Edw	2.1.44	Baldck
Knowest thou him Gaveston?	Edw	2.2.248	Edward
A Mortimer, thou knowest that he is slaine,	Edw	5.6.50	King
Mistris thou knowest, thou hast a blest youth pleas'd,	Ovid's Elegies		1.8.23
Knowest not this head a helme was wont to beare,	Ovid's Elegies		3.7.13

KNOWING

And shrunke not backe, knowing my love was there?	Dido	4.4.146	Dido
Knowing two kings, the [friends] <friend> to Tamburlain,	2Tamb	3.3.13	Therid
Where legions of devils (knowing he must die/Here in Natolia,	2Tamb	3.5.25	Orcan
Knowing my father hates thy cowardise,	2Tamb	4.1.23	Amyras
And knowing me impatient in distresse/Thinke me so mad as I	Jew	1.2.262	Barab
Knowing her scapes thine honour shall encrease,	Ovid's Elegies		2.2.27
Who so well keepes his waters head from knowing,	Ovid's Elegies		3.5.40
And knowing Hermes courted her, was glad/That she such	Hero and Leander		1.421

KNOWLEDGE

Still climing after knowledge infinite,	1Tamb	2.7.24	Tamb
To give thee knowledge when to cut the cord,	Jew	5.5.40	Barab
of my knowledge in one cloyster keeps,/Five hundred fatte	P 141	2.84	Guise
once admired/For wondrous knowledge in our Germane schooles,	F1998	5.3.16	2Schol
have heard strange report of thy knowledge in the blacke Arte,	F App	p.236 2	P Emper

KNOWN (See also KNOWEN)

That's brave, master, but think you it wil not be known?	Jew	4.1.8	P Ithimr
But seeing white Eagles, and Roomes flags wel known,	Lucan, First Booke		246
warre, wherein through use he's known/To exceed his maister,	Lucan, First Booke		325
Loe country Gods, and [known] <know> bed to forsake,	Ovid's Elegies		2.11.7

KNOWNE

it, and the Priest/That makes it knowne, being degraded first,	Jew	3.6.35	2Fryar
Law wils that each particular be knowne.	Jew	4.1.205	Barab
We two, and 'twas never knowne, nor never shall be for me.	Jew	4.4.23	P Ithimr
For as a friend not knowne, but in distresse,	Jew	5.2.72	Barab
Least you be knowne, and so be rescued.	Edw	5.3.32	Gurney
kind I will make knowne unto you what my heart desires to have,	F1571	4.6.14	P Lady
had some rare qualitie that he would not have had me knowne of,	F App	p.240 132	P HrsCsr
If this thou doest, to me by long use knowne,	Ovid's Elegies		1.8.105
Thy service for nights scapes is knowne commodious/And to give	Ovid's Elegies		1.11.3
Say that thy love with Caephalus were not knowne,	Ovid's Elegies		1.13.33
And Gallus shall be knowne from East to West,	Ovid's Elegies		1.15.29
Let him goe forth knowne, that unknowne did enter,	Ovid's Elegies		2.2.20
I from the shore thy knowne ship first will see,	Ovid's Elegies		2.11.43
Aye me why is it knowne to her so well?	Ovid's Elegies		2.17.8
And this townes well knowne customes not beleeves,	Ovid's Elegies		3.4.38
Nor on the earth was knowne the name of floore.	Ovid's Elegies		3.9.8
Ceres, I thinke, no knowne fault will deny.	Ovid's Elegies		3.9.24
Erre I? or by my [bookes] <lookes> is she so knowne?	Ovid's Elegies		3.11.7
Which being knowne (as what is hid from Jove)?	Hero and Leander		1.436
Which made his love through Sestos to bee knowne,	Hero and Leander		2.111

KNOWS

I am disguisde and none knows who I am,	P 278	5.5	Anjoy
My lord, the Maior of Bristow knows our mind.	Edw	4.6.40	Queene
She knows with gras, with thrids on wrong wheeles spun/And what	Ovid's Elegies		1.8.7

KNOW'ST

Barabas, thou know'st I am the Governors sonne.	Jew	2.3.40	Lodowk
Thou know'st, and heaven can witnesse it is true,	Jew	2.3.253	Barab
Barabas, thou know'st I have lov'd thy daughter long.	Jew	2.3.288	Lodowk
Thou know'st 'tis death and if it be reveal'd.	Jew	3.6.51	2Fryar
Thou know'st within the compasse of eight daies,	F 847	3.1.69	Faust

KNUCKLES

And of just compasse for her knuckles bee.	Ovid's Elegies		2.15.6

KORAN (See ALCARON)

LA
Vive [le] <la> Roy, vive [le] <la> Roy. — P 588 12.1 All
Vive [le] <la> Roy, vive [le] <la> Roy. — P 598 12.11 All
Par [le] <la> mor du, Il mora. — P 770 15.28 Guise
Vive la messe, perish Hugonets, — P1014 19.84 Guise

LABELS
Where womens favors hung like labels downe. — Edw 2.2.187 Mortmr

LABENTIS
fuit aut tibi quidquam/Dulce meum, miserere domus labentis: — Dido 5.1.137 Dido

LABOR
And lose more labor than the gaine will quight. — 1Tamb 2.5.96 Tamb
Two tane away, thy labor will be lesse: — Ovid's Elegies 1.1.4

LABORING
And laboring to approve his quarrell good. — Lucan, First Booke 267

LABOUR
in vaine ye labour to prevent/That which mine honor sweares — 1Tamb 5.1.106 Tamb
Shall I be made a king for my labour? — 2Tamb 1.2.63 P Almeda
Which til it may defend you, labour low: — 2Tamb 3.3.44 Therid
To save thy life, and us a litle labour, — 2Tamb 5.1.50 Therid
That made us all the labour for the towne, — 2Tamb 5.1.82 Therid
Would in his age be loath to labour so, — Jew 1.1.17 Barab
You have my wealth, the labour of my life, — Jew 1.2.149 Barab
Abigal it is not yet long since/That I did labour thy admition, — Jew 3.3.57 1Fryar
As I entend to labour for the truth, — P 585 11.50 Navrre
And tell him, that I labour all in vaine, — Edw 5.2.70 Queene
Why strive you thus? your labour is in vaine. — Edw 5.3.33 Matrvs
See how he must be handled for his labour, — Edw 5.5.23 Matrvs
you may save your selfe a labour, for they are as familiar with — F 364 1.4.22 P Robin
you may save that labour, they are too familiar with me — F App p.229 27 P Clown
the Horsecourser I take it, a bottle of hey for his labour; wel, — F App p.241 165 P Faust
And what lesse labour then to hold thy peace? — Ovid's Elegies 2.2.28
Thy labour ever lasts, she askes but little. — Ovid's Elegies 3.1.68
Least labour so shall winne great grace of any. — Ovid's Elegies 3.4.46

LABOURING
Wherewith his burning beames like labouring Bees, — Dido 5.1.12 Aeneas
and two hundred yoake/Of labouring Oxen, and five hundred/Shee — Jew 1.2.184 Barab
To make attonement for my labouring soule. — Jew 1.2.326 Abigal
His conscience kils it, and his labouring braine, — F1809 5.2.13 Mephst
Into the entrals of yon labouring cloud, — F1953 5.2.157 Faust
Thou setst their labouring hands to spin and card. — Ovid's Elegies 1.13.24
On labouring women thou doest pitty take, — Ovid's Elegies 2.13.19

LABOURS
O how these irksome labours now delight, — Dido 3.3.56 Aeneas
Alas poore King that labours so in vaine, — Dido 4.2.33 Anna
That labours with a load of bread and wine, — Jew 5.2.41 Barab
Then all my labours, plod I ne're so fast. — F 96 1.1.68 Faust
The worke of Poets lasts Troyes labours fame, — Ovid's Elegies 3.8.29

LABYRINTH
alas, hath pac'd too long/The fatall Labyrinth of misbeleefe, — Jew 3.3.64 Abigal

LACE
And a rich neck-lace caus'd that punnishment. — Ovid's Elegies 1.10.52

LACEDEMON
And fire proude Lacedemon ore their heads. — Dido 4.4.92 Aeneas

LACES
And on Andromache his helmet laces. — Ovid's Elegies 1.9.36

LACHRIMA
Lachrima Christi and Calabrian wines/Shall common Souldiers — 2Tamb 1.3.221 Tamb

LACK
(Trust me) land-streame thou shalt no envie lack, — Ovid's Elegies 3.5.21
Onely the Goddesse hated Goate did lack, — Ovid's Elegies 3.12.18

LACKE
How now, what lacke you? — F1507 4.5.3 P Hostss
I hate faire Paper should writte matter lacke. — Ovid's Elegies 1.11.20
Whose earth doth not perpetuall greene-grasse lacke, — Ovid's Elegies 2.6.50
Because thy belly should rough wrinckles lacke, — Ovid's Elegies 2.14.7
The fathers thigh should unborne Bacchus lacke. — Ovid's Elegies 3.3.40

LACKES
Beyond thy robes thy dangling [lockes] <lackes> had sweept. — Ovid's Elegies 1.14.4

LAD
Kneeling for mercie to a Greekish lad, — Dido 2.1.198 Aeneas

LADE
Hale them to prison, lade their limbes with gyves: — F1032 3.2.52 Pope

LADEN (See also LOADEN, LODEN)
We have our Cammels laden all with gold: — 1Tamb 2.2.62 Meandr
Laden with riches, and exceeding store/Of Persian silkes, of — Jew 1.1.87 2Merch
good father on thy lap/Lay I this head, laden with mickle care, — Edw 4.7.40 Edward
And take his leave, laden with rich rewards. — F1345 4.2.21 Benvol
Take clustred grapes from an ore-laden vine, — Ovid's Elegies 1.10.55
Laden with languishment and griefe he flies. — Hero and Leander 1.378

LADIE
With letters to our ladie from the King, — Edw 2.1.20 Spencr
Ladie, farewell. — Edw 2.4.10 Edward

LADIES
I hope our Ladies treasure and our owne, — 1Tamb 1.2.74 Agidas
Their armes to hang about a Ladies necke: — 2Tamb 1.3.30 Tamb
Take pitie of a Ladies ruthfull teares, — 2Tamb 3.4.69 Olymp
Ladies of honor, Knightes and Gentlemen, — P 213 4.11 Charls
Our Ladies first love is not wavering, — Edw 2.1.27 Spencr
since our conference about faire Ladies, which was the — F1682 5.1.9 P 1Schol

LADIESHIP
I humbly thanke your Ladieship. — Edw 2.1.81 Spencr

LADING
Lading their shippes with golde and pretious stones: — 1Tamb 1.1.121 Cosroe

LADLE
What, hast thou brought the Ladle with thee too? Jew 3.4.57 Barab
I have brought you a Ladle. Jew 3.4.59 P Ithimr

LADY (See also BURLADIE, LADIE)
Come lady, let not this appal your thoughts. 1Tamb 1.2.1 Tamb
But Lady, this faire face and heavenly hew, 1Tamb 1.2.36 Tamb
But Lady goe with us to Tamburlaine, 2Tamb 3.4.45 Therid
And him faire Lady shall thy eies behold. 2Tamb 3.4.67 Therid
This Lady shall have twice so much againe, 2Tamb 3.4.90 Therid
as I doe a naked Lady in a net of golde, and for feare I should 2Tamb 4.1.69 P Calyph
Nay Lady, then if nothing wil prevaile, 2Tamb 4.2.50 Therid
I'le buy you, and marry you to Lady vanity, if you doe well. Jew 2.3.116 P Barab
Leave of this jesting, here my lady comes. Edw 2.1.56 Baldck
I heare sweete lady of the kings unkindenes, Edw 4.2.15 SrJohn
Lady, the last was truest of the twaine, Edw 4.2.39 Mortmr
By Lady sir, you have had a shroud journey of it, will it F1120 3.3.33 P Robin
That this faire Lady, whilest she liv'd on earth, F1266 4.1.112 Emper
But gratious Lady, it may be, that you have taken no pleasure F1565 4.6.8 P Faust
that Hellen of Greece was the admirablest Lady that ever liv'd: F1684 5.1.11 P 1Schol
this Lady while she liv'd had a wart or moale in her necke, F App p.238 60 P Emper

LADYE
Then pray unto our Ladye, kisse this crosse. P 302 5.29 Gonzag

LAEDAS
Then wilt thou Laedas noble twinne-starres pray, Ovid's Elegies 2.11.29

LAELIUS
then Laelius/The chiefe Centurion crown'd with Oaken leaves, Lucan, First Booke 357

LAGS
(his vassals)/And that he lags behind with them of purpose, Lucan, First Booke 477

LAID
The plot is laid by Persean Noble men, 1Tamb 1.1.110 Cosroe
This traine he laid to have intrap'd thy life; Jew 5.5.91 Govnr
And we have heard that Edmund laid a plot, Edw 5.2.32 BshpWn
Are laid before me to dispatch my selfe: F 574 2.2.23 Faust
And laid his childish head upon her brest, Hero and Leander 1.43

LAIDE
The plot is laide, and things shall come to passe, P 164 2.107 Guise
Then laide they violent hands upon him, next/Himselfe Edw 1.2.36 ArchBp
peoples minds, and laide before their eies/Slaughter to come, Lucan, First Booke 466
Venus with Vulcan, though smiths tooles laide by, Ovid's Elegies 2.17.19
And on his loose mane the loose bridle laide. Ovid's Elegies 3.4.16

LAIE
But ere he came, Warwick in ambush laie, Edw 3.1.118 Arundl

LAIED
the drie fields strayed/When on her head a water pitcher laied. Ovid's Elegies 1.10.6

LAIES (Homograph)
Skilful in musicke and in amorous laies: 2Tamb 1.2.37 Callap
on the Altar/He laies a ne're-yoakt Bull, and powers downe Lucan, First Booke 608
Elegian Muse, that warblest amorous laies, Ovid's Elegies 1.1.33
Sappho her vowed harpe laies at Phoebus feete. Ovid's Elegies 2.18.34

LAIN (See LAYD)

LAINE
And laine in leagre fifteene moneths and more, 2Tamb 1.3.176 Usumc
[where I have laine ever since, and you have done me great F 705.1 2.2.155A P Sloth
Among day bookes and billes they had laine better/In which the Ovid's Elegies 1.12.25
What to have laine alone in empty bed? Ovid's Elegies 3.8.34

LAIRE
And rowse the light foote Deere from forth their laire? Dido 3.3.31 Dido

LAIS (See LAYIS)

LAISIE
Call foorth our laisie brother from the tent, 2Tamb 4.1.7 Celeb

LAKE
And of the ever raging Caspian Lake: 1Tamb 1.1.168 Ortyg
Shall vaile to us, as Lords of all the Lake. 1Tamb 1.2.196 Tamb
Furies from the blacke Cocitus lake, 1Tamb 5.1.218 Bajzth
And traveile hedlong to the lake of hell: 2Tamb 3.5.24 Orcan
When this our famous lake of Limnasphaltis/Makes walles a fresh 2Tamb 5.1.17 Govnr
Now fil the mouth of Limnasphaltes lake, 2Tamb 5.1.67 Tamb
But Tamburlain, in Lymnasphaltis lake, 2Tamb 5.1.115 Govnr
No, though Asphaltis lake were liquid gold, 2Tamb 5.1.155 Tamb
And cast them headlong in the cities lake: 2Tamb 5.1.162 Tamb
Thousands of men drown'd in Asphaltis Lake, 2Tamb 5.1.204 Techel
Circled about with Limnasphaltis Lake, 2Tamb 5.2.5 Callap
From thence to Nubia neere Borno Lake, 2Tamb 5.3.136 Tamb
Heere is the keyes, this is the lake,/Doe as you are commaunded Edw 5.5.25 Matrvs
Of Stix, of Acheron, and the fiery Lake, F 826 3.1.48 Faust
And hurle him in some lake of mud and durt: F1409 4.2.85 Faust
Halfe smother'd in a Lake of mud and durt, F1434 4.3.4 Mrtino

LAKES
of Affrike, where I view'd/The Ethiopian sea, rivers and lakes: 2Tamb 1.3.196 Techel
That you may dryfoot martch through lakes and pooles, 2Tamb 3.2.86 Tamb
If I be Englands king, in lakes of gore/Your headles trunkes, Edw 3.1.135 Edward
With wals of Flint, and deepe intrenched Lakes, F 782 3.1.4 Faust

LAMBE
For hees a lambe, encompassed by Woolves, Edw 5.1.41 Edward

LAMBES
yet are our lookes/As innocent and harmelesse as a Lambes. Jew 2.3.22 Barab
Which from our pretty Lambes we pull, Passionate Shepherd 14

LAMBETH
To crosse to Lambeth, and there stay with me. Edw 1.2.78 ArchBp
Are gone towards Lambeth, there let them remaine. Edw 1.3.5 Gavstn

LAME
And lame and poore, lie groning at the gates, Edw 2.2.163 Lncstr

LAMENT
Leave to lament lest they laugh at our feares. Dido 2.1.38 Achat

LAMENT (cont.)			
to them, that all Asia/Lament to see the follie of their King.	1Tamb	1.1.96	Cosroe
How Charles our sonne begins for to lament/For the late nights	P 513	9.32	QnMoth
Cease to lament, and tell us wheres the king?	Edw	2.4.30	Mortmr
Be patient good my lord, cease to lament,	Edw	5.1.1	Leistr
Why doest thy ill kemba tresses losse lament?	Ovid's Elegies		1.14.35
he will lament/And say this blabbe shall suffer punnishment.	Ovid's Elegies		2.2.59
Bewaile I onely, though I them lament.	Ovid's Elegies		2.5.60
And who ere see her, worthily lament.	Ovid's Elegies		2.14.40
LAMENTABLE			
In what a lamentable case were I,	1Tamb	2.4.6	Mycet
LAMENTED			
And turn'd aside, and to her selfe lamented.	Hero and Leander		2.34
LAMENTETH			
Father, for thee lamenteth Abigaile:	Jew	1.2.229	Abigal
LAMENTS			
For faire Zenocrate, that so laments his state.	1Tamb	5.1.205	Therid
Why stand you thus unmov'd with my laments?	Jew	1.2.171	Barab
To companie my hart with sad laments,	Edw	5.1.34	Edward
end be such/As every Christian heart laments to thinke on:	F1996	5.3.14	2Schol
LAMP			
For I the chiefest Lamp of all the earth,	1Tamb	4.2.36	Tamb
O highest Lamp of everliving Jove,	1Tamb	5.1.290	Bajzth
A greater Lamp than that bright eie of heaven,	2Tamb	4.2.88	Therid
LAMPS			
Whose eies are brighter than the Lamps of heaven,	1Tamb	3.3.120	Tamb
of that Spheare/Enchac'd with thousands ever shining lamps,	1Tamb	4.2.9	Tamb
And dim the brightnesse of their neighbor Lamps:	1Tamb	4.2.34	Tamb
Whose beames illuminate the lamps of heaven,	2Tamb	1.3.2	Tamb
and the ceaslesse lamps/That gently look'd upon this loathsome	2Tamb	2.4.18	Tamb
Drawing from it the shining Lamps of heaven.	2Tamb	3.4.77	Techel
And sommon al the shining lamps of heaven/To cast their	2Tamb	5.3.3	Therid
that shine as bright/As all the Lamps that beautifie the Sky,	2Tamb	5.3.157	Tamb
LANCASTER			
Lancaster.	Edw	1.1.74	Edward
That Earle of Lancaster do I abhorre.	Edw	1.1.76	Gavstn
Frownst thou thereat, aspiring Lancaster,	Edw	1.1.93	Edward
Foure Earldomes have I besides Lancaster,	Edw	1.1.102	Lncstr
And that high minded earle of Lancaster,	Edw	1.1.150	Edward
How now, why droops the earle of Lancaster?	Edw	1.2.9	MortSr
Ah that bewraies their basenes Lancaster,	Edw	1.2.27	Mortmr
the mightie prince of Lancaster/That hath more earldomes then	Edw	1.3.1	Gavstn
Warwicke and Lancaster, weare you my crowne,	Edw	1.4.37	Edward
Thou Lancaster, high admirall of our fleete,	Edw	1.4.66	Edward
O never Lancaster!	Edw	1.4.200	Queene
O Lancaster, let him diswade the king,	Edw	1.4.216	Queene
My Lord of Lancaster, marke the respect.	Edw	1.4.248	Mortmr
Marke you but that my lord of Lancaster.	Edw	1.4.263	Warwck
On that condition Lancaster will graunt.	Edw	1.4.292	Lncstr
Couragious Lancaster, imbrace thy king,	Edw	1.4.340	Edward
Looke Lancaster how passionate he is,	Edw	2.2.3	Queene
And what is yours my lord of Lancaster?	Edw	2.2.21	Edward
Proud Mortimer, ungentle Lancaster,	Edw	2.2.29	Edward
And so doth Lancaster:	Edw	2.2.109	Lncstr
Would Lancaster and he had both carroust,	Edw	2.2.237	Edward
I have enformd the Earle of Lancaster.	Edw	2.3.14	Kent
Farre be it from the thought of Lancaster,	Edw	2.4.33	Lncstr
Forslowe no time, sweet Lancaster lets march.	Edw	2.4.40	Warwck
Lancaster, why talkst thou to the slave?	Edw	2.5.19	Warwck
My lord of Lancaster, what say you in this?	Edw	2.5.89	Arundl
Warwick I know is roughe, and Lancaster/Inexorable, and I shall	Edw	3.1.6	Edward
hearing,/Mortimer hardly, Penbrooke and Lancaster/Spake least:	Edw	3.1.105	Arundl
Looke Lancaster,/Yonder is Edward among his flatterers.	Edw	3.1.195	Mortmr
Traitor on thy face, rebellious Lancaster.	Edw	3.1.204	Spencr
These lustie leaders Warwicke and Lancaster,	Edw	3.1.246	Edward
and though a many friends/Are made away, as Warwick, Lancaster,	Edw	4.2.52	Mortmr
LANCE (See also LANCH, LAUNCE)			
Whose hands are made to gripe a warlike Lance,	1Tamb	3.3.106	Bajzth
Armed with lance into the Egyptian fields,	1Tamb	5.1.381	Philem
and Danes/That with the Holbard, Lance, and murthering Axe,	2Tamb	1.1.23	Uribas
Wel done my boy, thou shalt have shield and lance,	2Tamb	1.3.43	Tamb
Breaking my steeled lance, with which I burst/The rusty beames	2Tamb	2.4.113	Tamb
And see him lance his flesh to teach you all.	2Tamb	3.2.114	Tamb
Who gently now wil lance thy Ivory throat,	2Tamb	3.4.24	Olymp
Thinke of thy end, this sword shall lance thy throat.	2Tamb	3.5.78	Orcan
Nor Pistol, Sword, nor Lance can pierce your flesh.	2Tamb	4.2.66	Olymp
LANCERES			
And backt by stout Lanceres of Germany,	2Tamb	1.1.155	Sgsmnd
LANCES			
Our quivering Lances shaking in the aire,	1Tamb	2.3.18	Tamb
Leave words and let them feele your lances pointes,	1Tamb	3.3.91	Argier
So shall our swords, our lances and our shot,	1Tamb	4.2.51	Tamb
Let all the swords and Lances in the field,	1Tamb	5.1.225	Zabina
On horsmens Lances to be hoisted up,	1Tamb	5.1.328	Zenoc
Dieng their lances with their streaming blood,	2Tamb	3.2.105	Tamb
And breake their burning Lances in the aire,	2Tamb	4.1.204	Tamb
LANCH			
And either lanch his greedy thirsting throat,	1Tamb	1.2.146	Tamb
Their carelesse swords shal lanch their fellowes throats/And	1Tamb	2.2.49	Meandr
Now lanch our Gallies backe againe to Sea,	Jew	1.2.29	Calym
LANCHING			
That lanching from Argier to Tripoly,	2Tamb	1.3.124	Therid
LAND (See also FREELAND, LAWNDES)			
But for the land whereof thou doest enquire,	Dido	1.1.209	Venus

LAND (cont.)
From thence a fewe of us escapt to land, ... Dido 1.2.30 Cloan
And wrought him mickle woe on sea and land, . . . Dido 3.2.41 Juno
With whom we did devide both lawes and land, . . . Dido 4.2.14 Iarbus
I shall be planted in as rich a land. . . . . Dido 4.4.82 Aeneas
Speake of no other land, this land is thine, . . . Dido 4.4.83 Dido
And seeke a forraine land calde Italy: . . . . Dido 4.4.98 Dido
Graunt, though the traytors land in Italy, . . . Dido 5.1.304 Dido
Betwixt this land and that be never league, . . . Dido 5.1.309 Dido
[Trading] <Treading> by land unto the Westerne Isles, . 1Tamb 1.1.38 Meandr
Affrike and Europe bordering on your land, . . . 1Tamb 1.1.127 Menaph
That no reliefe or succour come by Land. . . . . 1Tamb 3.1.62 Bajzth
Zenocrate, were Egypt Joves owne land, ... 1Tamb 4.4.73 Tamb
And thence by land unto the Torrid Zone, ... 1Tamb 4.4.124 Tamb
Meaning to make a conquest of our land: . . . . 2Tamb 1.1.49 Gazell
And all the land unto the coast of Spaine. . . . 2Tamb 1.3.179 Usumc
But neither man nor child in al the land: . . . . 2Tamb 1.3.197 Techel
Threatning a death <dearth> and famine to this land, . 2Tamb 3.2.9 Tamb
When this is learn'd for service on the land, . . . 2Tamb 3.2.83 Tamb
Wherein is all the treasure of the land. . . . . 2Tamb 3.3.4 Therid
Fire the towne and overrun the land. 2Tamb 3.5.9 2Msngr
and the bounds/Of that sweet land, whose brave Metropolis 2Tamb 3.5.36 Orcan
Halla is repair'd/And neighbor cities of your highnesse land, 2Tamb 3.5.47 Soria
Survaieng all the glories of the land: . . . . . 2Tamb 4.3.35 Orcan
Eastward behold/As much more land, which never was descried, 2Tamb 5.3.155 Tamb
is come from France/To view this Land, and frolicke with his Jew Prol.4 Machvl
Thus trowles our fortune in by land and Sea, . . . Jew 1.1.103 Barab
Nor e're shall see the land of Canaan, ... Jew 2.3.303 Barab
Content, but we will leave this paltry land, . . . Jew 4.2.88 Ithimr
slavish Bands/Wherein the Turke hath yoak'd your land and you? Jew 5.2.78 Barab
And make his Gospel flourish in this land. . . . P 57 1.57 Navrre
And rent our true religion from this land: . . . P 703 14.6 Navrre
Which are already mustered in the land, ... P 726 14.29 1Msngr
that he himself should occupy, which is his own free land. P 812 17.7 P Souldr
To spend the treasure that should strength my land, . . P1037 19.107 King
And sooner shall the sea orewhelme my land, . . . Edw 1.1.152 Edward
That I am banishd, and must flie the land. . . . Edw 1.4.107 Gavstn
Thou from this land, I from my selfe am banisht. . . Edw 1.4.118 Edward
the Mortimers/Are not so poore, but would they sell their land, Edw 2.2.151 Mortmr
My lords, of love to this our native land, . . . Edw 2.3.1 Kent
Spencer and I will post away by land. . . . . Edw 2.4.6 Edward
suffer uncontrowld/These Barons thus to beard me in my land, Edw 3.1.14 Spencr
Because we heare Lord Bruse dooth sell his land, . . . Edw 3.1.53 Edward
Brother, in regard of thee and of thy land, . . . Edw 3.1.230 Kent
Begets the quiet of king Edwards land, ... Edw 3.1.263 Spencr
Whose loosnes hath betrayed thy land to spoyle, . . . Edw 4.4.11 Queene
and injuries/Edward hath done to us, his Queene and land, Edw 4.4.22 Mortmr
And all the land I know is up in armes, ... Edw 4.7.31 Spencr
And chase the Prince of Parma from our Land, . . . F 120 1.1.92 Faust
And make that Country <land>, continent to Spaine, . . F 336 1.3.108 Faust
May be admired through the furthest Land. . . . F 842 3.1.64 Faust
[Now is his fame spread forth in every land], . . . F1149 3.3.62A 3Chor
I, I thought that was al the land his father left him: . F App p.229 17 P Clown
Ay me, O what a world of land and sea, ... Lucan, First Booke 13
Allot the height of honor, men so strong/By land, and sea, no Lucan, First Booke 83
Nor then was land, or sea, to breed such hate, . . . Lucan, First Booke 96
Or sea far from the land, so all were whist. . . . Lucan, First Booke 262
Woods turn'd to ships; both land and sea against us: . Lucan, First Booke 307
Which is nor sea, nor land, but oft times both, . . Lucan, First Booke 411
Soone may you plow the little lands <land> I have, . . Ovid's Elegies 1.3.9
And she that on a faind Bull swamme to land, . . . Ovid's Elegies 1.3.23
(Trust me) land-streame thou shalt no envie lack, . . Ovid's Elegies 3.5.21
And having wandred now through sea and land, . . . Ovid's Elegies 3.12.33
Sends foorth a ratling murmure to the land, . . . Hero and Leander 1.348
By this Leander being nere the land, ... Hero and Leander 2.227

LANDLORD
and whereas hee is your Landlord, you will take upon you to be P 811 17.6 P Souldr

LANDLORDE
ser where he is your landlorde you take upon you to be his | Paris ms10,p390 P Souldr

LANDRESSE
Thou shalt be Landresse to my waiting maid. . . . 1Tamb 3.3.177 Zabina

LANDS
All that they have, their lands, their goods, their lives, Dido 4.4.76 Dido
Take my goods too, and seize upon my lands: . . . Jew 5.1.66 Barab
To beat the papall Monarck from our lands, . . . P 802 16.16 Navrre
And then large limits had their butting lands, . . . Lucan, First Booke 169
Predestinate to ruine; all lands else/Have stable peace, here Lucan, First Booke 251
Soone may you plow the little lands <land> I have, . . Ovid's Elegies 1.3.9
As soone as from strange lands Sabinus came, . . . Ovid's Elegies 2.18.27
not Alpheus in strange lands to runne,/Th'Arcadian Virgins Ovid's Elegies 3.5.29

LAND-STREAME
(Trust me) land-streame thou shalt no envie lack, . . Ovid's Elegies 3.5.21

LANE
In lucky time, come let us keep this lane, . . . P 298 5.25 Anjoy

LANES
lanes through the Gardens I chanc'd to cast mine eye up to the Jew 3.1.17 P Pilia
The Meads, the Orchards, and the Primrose lanes, . . Jew 4.2.95 Ithimr

LANGUAGES
rest and have one Epitaph/Writ in as many severall languages, 2Tamb 2.4.135 Tamb

LANGUISH
And languish in my brothers government: . . . . 1Tamb 1.1.156 Cosroe
Why, shal I sit and languish in this paine? . . . 2Tamb 5.3.56 Tamb
Let him goe see her though she doe not languish/And then report Ovid's Elegies 2.2.21

LANGUISHMENT			
Laden with languishment and griefe he flies.	Hero and Leander	1.378	
LANTCHIDOL			
wher raging Lantchidol/Beates on the regions with his	2Tamb	1.1.69	Orcan
LAOCOON			
The rather for that one Laocoon/Breaking a speare upon his	Dido	2.1.164	Aeneas
LAODAMEIA			
With Laodameia mate to her dead Lord.	Ovid's Elegies	2.18.38	
LAOMEDON			
Ilia, sprung from Idaean Laomedon?	Ovid's Elegies	3.5.54	
LAP (See also LEP)			
in stead of him/Will set thee on her lap and play with thee:	Dido	2.1.325	Venus
Sit in my lap and let me heare thee sing.	Dido	3.1.25	Dido
Cupid shall lay his arrowes in thy lap,	Dido	3.2.56	Venus
As made disdaine to flye to fancies lap:	Dido	3.4.56	Dido
Shall hide his head in Thetis watery lap,	2Tamb	1.3.169	Tamb
Now, gentle Ithimore, lye in my lap.	Jew	4.2.82	Curtzn
Come gentle Ithimore, lye in my lap.	Jew	4.4.27	Curtzn
Whilst I in thy incony lap doe tumble.	Jew	4.4.29	Ithimr
good father on thy lap/Lay I this head, laden with mickle care,	Edw	4.7.39	Edward
He wants no gifts into thy lap to hurle.	Ovid's Elegies	1.10.54	
the time more short/Lay downe thy forehead in thy lap to snort.	Ovid's Elegies	2.2.24	
Shee in my lap sits still as earst she did.	Ovid's Elegies	2.18.6	
She held her lap ope to receive the same.	Ovid's Elegies	3.7.34	
LAPHITHES			
The Laphithes, and the Centaures for a woman,	Ovid's Elegies	2.12.19	
LAPLAND			
Or Lapland Giants trotting by our sides:	F 153	1.1.125	Valdes
LAPPE			
When on thy lappe thine eyes thou dost deject,	Ovid's Elegies	1.8.37	
She holds, and viewes her old lockes in her lappe,	Ovid's Elegies	1.14.53	
cast do happe/Sharpe stripes, she sitteth in the judges lappe.	Ovid's Elegies	2.2.62	
And hide thy left hand underneath her lappe.	Ovid's Elegies	2.15.12	
LAPS			
for earthly man/Then thus to powre out plenty in their laps,	Jew	1.1.108	Barab
the Alpes/Shooke the old snow from off their trembling laps.	Lucan, First Booke	552	
LAPT (Homograph)			
Not lapt in lead but in a sheet of gold,	2Tamb	2.4.131	Tamb
[As] <A> brood of barbarous Tygars having lapt/The bloud of	Lucan, First Booke	327	
LARDED			
Larded with pearle, and in his tuskan cap/A jewell of more	Edw	1.4.414	Mortmr
LARES			
Or steale your houshold lares from their shrines:	Dido	1.2.11	Illion
LARGE			
May I entreate thee to discourse at large,	Dido	2.1.106	Dido
for his parentage deserves/As large a kingdome as is Libia.	Dido	4.4.80	Achat
The Rockes and Sea-gulfes will performe at large,	Dido	5.1.171	Dido
So large of lims, his joints so strongly knit,	1Tamb	2.1.9	Menaph
Their lims more large and of a bigger size/Than all the brats	1Tamb	3.3.108	Bajzth
Himselfe in presence shal unfold at large.	2Tamb	Prol.9	Prolog
The Bulwarks and the rampiers large and strong,	2Tamb	3.2.70	Tamb
which is there/Set downe at large, the Gallants were both	Jew	3.6.29	Abigal
And then large limits had their butting lands,	Lucan, First Booke	169	
were wont/In large spread heire to exceed the rest of France;	Lucan, First Booke	439	
Great are thy kingdomes, over strong and large,	Ovid's Elegies	1.1.17	
How large a legge, and what a lustie thigh?	Ovid's Elegies	1.5.22	
And makes large streams back to their fountaines flow,	Ovid's Elegies	1.8.6	
And where swift Nile in his large channell slipping <skipping>,	Ovid's Elegies	2.13.9	
Small doores unfitting for large houses are.	Ovid's Elegies	3.1.40	
First Victory is brought with large spred wing,	Ovid's Elegies	3.2.45	
Rather thou large banke over-flowing river,	Ovid's Elegies	3.5.19	
And seedes were equally in large fields cast,	Ovid's Elegies	3.9.33	
Poets large power is boundlesse, and immense,	Ovid's Elegies	3.11.41	
Shew large wayes with their garments there displayed.	Ovid's Elegies	3.12.24	
LARGELY			
And in the midst their bodies largely spread:	Ovid's Elegies	2.10.18	
Wherewith she wreath'd her largely spreading heare,	Hero and Leander	2.107	
LARGESSE			
For this have I a largesse from the Pope,	P 119	2.62	Guise
LARGIS			
Souldiers a largis, and thrice welcome all.	Edw	3.1.57	Edward
LARISSA			
Now rest thee here on faire Larissa Plaines,	2Tamb	1.3.5	Tamb
Promist to meet me on Larissa plaines/With hostes apeece	2Tamb	1.3.107	Tamb
That nigh Larissa swaies a mighty hoste,	2Tamb	2.2.6	Orcan
Thou shalt not beautifie Larissa plaines,	2Tamb	3.2.34	Tamb
And let the burning of Larissa wals,	2Tamb	3.2.141	Tamb
LARKE			
And for the Raven wake the morning Larke,	Jew	2.1.61	Barab
LARUMS			
Your threats, your larums, and your hote pursutes,	Edw	2.5.2	Gavstn
'LAS			
'Las I could weepe at your calamity.	Jew	4.1.203	Barab
LASCIVIOUS			
lascivious showes/And prodigall gifts bestowed on Gaveston,	Edw	2.2.157	Mortmr
for I am wanton and lascivious, and cannot live without a wife.	F 530	2.1.142	P Faust
When our lascivious toyes come in thy minde,	Ovid's Elegies	1.4.21	
let him viewe/And thy neck with lascivious markes made blew.	Ovid's Elegies	1.8.98	
The bed is for lascivious toyings meete,	Ovid's Elegies	3.13.17	
LASH			
Now would I slacke the reines, now lash their hide,	Ovid's Elegies	3.2.11	
LASHES			
dost betray them/To Pedants, that with cruell lashes pay them.	Ovid's Elegies	1.13.18	

LASHT

And when ye stay, be lasht with whips of wier:	2Tamb	3.5.105	Tamb

LAST (Homograph; See also LATTER)

At last came Pirrhus fell and full of ire,	Dido	2.1.213	Aeneas
At last the souldiers puld her by the heeles,	Dido	2.1.247	Aeneas
And he at last depart to Italy,	Dido	2.1.330	Venus
he lay with me last night,/And in the morning he was stolne	Dido	5.1.213	Nurse
And by this meanes Ile win the world at last.	1Tamb	3.3.260	Tamb
With terrours to the last and cruelst hew:	1Tamb	5.1.8	Govnr
When he arrived last upon our stage,	2Tamb	Prol.2	Prolog
And by the coast of Byather at last,	2Tamb	1.3.200	Techel
fighting men/Are come since last we shewed your majesty.	2Tamb	3.5.34	Jrslem
Since last we numbred to your Majesty.	2Tamb	3.5.39	Orcan
Since last we numbred to your majesty.	2Tamb	3.5.45	Trebiz
Since last we numbred to your majestie:	2Tamb	3.5.49	Soria
Though this be held his last daies dreadfull siege,	2Tamb	5.1.29	1Citzn
Thou seest us prest to give the last assault,	2Tamb	5.1.60	Techel
And cannot last, it is so violent.	2Tamb	5.3.65	Techel
Not last Techelles, no, for I shall die.	2Tamb	5.3.66	Tamb
I came at last to Graecia, and from thence/To Asia, where I	2Tamb	5.3.141	Tamb
Help me (my Lords) to make my last remoove.	2Tamb	5.3.180	Tamb
and in mine Argosie/And other ships that came from Egypt last,	Jew	1.2.188	Barab
yet when we parted last,/He said he wud attend me in the morne.	Jew	2.1.33	Abigal
Oft have I leveld, and at last have learnd,	P 94	2.37	Guise
And now Navarre whilste that these broiles doe last,	P 565	11.30	Navrre
Which Ile maintaine so long as life doth last:	P 800	16.14	Navrre
Then Edward, thou wilt fight it to the last,	Edw	3.1.211	Mortmr
Lady, the last was truest of the twaine,	Edw	4.2.39	Mortmr
the last of all my blisse on earth,/Center of all misfortune.	Edw	4.7.61	Edward
So shall my eyes receive their last content,	Edw	5.1.61	Edward
[Till] <And> at the last, he come to Killingworth,	Edw	5.2.60	Mortmr
Know that your words have won me at the last,	F 128	1.1.100	Faust
And what are you Mistris Minkes, the seventh and last?	F 707	2.2.159	Faust
A hundred thousand, and at last be sav'd.	F1962	5.2.166	Faust
Dire league of partners in a kingdome last not.	Lucan, First Booke		86
At last learne wretch to leave thy monarchy;	Lucan, First Booke		335
Must Pompey as his last foe plume on me,	Lucan, First Booke		338
And Flamins last, with networke wollen vailes.	Lucan, First Booke		603
Many a yeare these [furious] <firious> broiles let last,	Lucan, First Booke		667
Let my first verse be sixe, my last five feete,	Ovid's Elegies		1.1.31
Betrayde her selfe, and yeelded at the last.	Ovid's Elegies		1.5.16
The fame that verse gives doth for ever last.	Ovid's Elegies		1.10.62
blotted letter/On the last edge to stay mine eyes the better.	Ovid's Elegies		1.11.22
And in her bosome strangely fall at last.	Ovid's Elegies		2.15.14
Adde deeds unto thy promises at last.	Ovid's Elegies		2.16.48
Some greater worke will urge me on at last.	Ovid's Elegies		3.1.70
Him the last day in black Averne hath drownd,	Ovid's Elegies		3.8.27
Nor did thy ashes her last offrings lose.	Ovid's Elegies		3.8.50
With thine, nor this last fire their presence misses.	Ovid's Elegies		3.8.54
The plough-mans hopes were frustrate at the last.	Ovid's Elegies		3.9.34
This last end to my Elegies is set,	Ovid's Elegies		3.14.2
At last, like to a bold sharpe Sophister,	Hero and Leander		1.197
So having paus'd a while, at last shee said:	Hero and Leander		1.337
And then he woo'd with kisses, and at last,	Hero and Leander		1.404
At last he came, O who can tell the greeting,	Hero and Leander		2.23

LASTING

Bringing with us lasting damnation,	F1801	5.2.5	Lucifr
dutie, I do yeeld/My life and lasting service for your love.	F1819	5.2.23	Wagner
Perpetuall thirst, and winters lasting rage.	Ovid's Elegies		1.8.114

LASTLY

Lastly, he that denies this, shall absolutely lose al he has.	Jew	1.2.76	P Reader
Lastly, that hee shall appeare to the said John Faustus, at all	F 491	2.1.103	P Faust

LASTS

our horses shal eate no hay as long as this lasts.	F App	p.234 3	P Robin
For ever lasts high Sophocles proud vaine,	Ovid's Elegies		1.15.15
Thy labour ever lasts, she askes but little.	Ovid's Elegies		3.1.68
The worke of Poets lasts Troyes labours fame,	Ovid's Elegies		3.8.29

LATE

What ailes my Queene, is she falne sicke of late?	Dido	3.4.24	Aeneas
East India and the late discovered Isles,	1Tamb	1.1.166	Ortyg
So fares Agydas for the late felt frownes/That sent a tempest	1Tamb	3.2.85	Agidas
but some must stay/To rule the provinces he late subdude.	1Tamb	3.3.29	Bassoe
And tels for trueth, submissions comes too late.	1Tamb	5.1.73	Tamb
and dominions/That late the power of Tamburlaine subdewed:	1Tamb	5.1.509	Tamb
son and successive heire to the late mighty Emperour Bajazeth,	2Tamb	3.1.2	P Orcan
and thirty Kingdomes late contributory to his mighty father.	2Tamb	3.1.5	P Orcan
That late adorn'd the Affrike Potentate,	2Tamb	3.2.124	Tamb
For late upon the coast of Corsica,	Jew	2.2.10	Bosco
Is't not too late now to turne Christian?	Jew	4.1.50	Barab
not thine opportunity, for feare too late/Thou seek'st for much,	Jew	5.2.45	Barab
Have you not heard of late how he decreed,	P 32	1.32	Navrre
The late suspition of the Duke of Guise,	P 178	3.13	Navrre
Too late it is my Lord if that be true/To blame her highnes,	P 181	3.16	QnMarg
And as we late decreed we may perfourme.	P 206	4.4	QnMoth
My Lord of Loraine have you markt of late,/How Charles our	P 512	9.31	QnMoth
For the late nights worke which my Lord of Guise/Did make in	P 514	9.33	QnMoth
Had late been pluckt from out faire Cupids wing:	P 668	13.12	Duchss
Now let them thanke themselves, and rue too late.	Edw	2.2.207	Edward
neece, the onely heire/Unto the Earle of Gloster late deceased.	Edw	2.2.259	Edward
This way he fled, but I am come too late.	Edw	4.6.1	Kent
And shipt but late for Ireland with the king.	Edw	4.6.58	Rice
They passe not for thy frownes as late they did,	Edw	5.1.77	Edward
I heare of late he hath deposde himselfe.	Edw	5.2.83	Kent

LATE (cont.)
Ist not too late? . . . . F 629 2.2.78 Faust
Too late. . . . . F 630 2.2.79 BdAngl
Never too late, if Faustus will <can> repent. . . . . F 631 2.2.80 GdAngl
In quittance of their late conspiracie/Against our State, and F 949 3.1.171 Pope
Drinke to our late and happy victory. . . . . . F 980 3.1.202 Pope
we all are witnesses/That Bruno here was late delivered you, F1026 3.2.46 Raymnd
For Faustus at the Court is late arriv'd, ... F1181 4.1.27 Mrtino
He was upon the devils backe late enough; and if he be so farre F1190 4.1.36 P Benvol
And if this Bruno thou hast late redeem'd, ... F1212 4.1.58 Emper
Then Faustus as thou late didst promise us, ... F1230 4.1.76 Emper
and have lost very much of late by horse flesh, and this . F1464 4.4.8 P HrsCsr
Then Faustus, will repentance come too late, ... F1714 5.1.41 OldMan
That heavenly Hellen, which I saw of late, ... F1762 5.1.89 Faust
and now ['tis] <'ts> too late. . . . . F1866 5.2.70 P Faust
'tis too late, despaire, farewell,/Fooles that will laugh on F1890 5.2.94 Mephst
send for the knight that was so pleasent with me here of late? F App p.238 67 P Faust
Thou feard'st (great Pompey) that late deeds would dim/Olde Lucan, First Booke 121
And you late shorne Ligurians, who were wont/In large spread Lucan, First Booke 438
let hir <he> that cought me late,/Either love, or cause that I Ovid's Elegies 1.3.1
to her I consecrate/My faithfull tables being vile maple late. Ovid's Elegies 1.11.28
Too late you looke back, when with anchors weighd, . . Ovid's Elegies 2.11.23
A woman against late-built Rome did send/The Sabine Fathers, Ovid's Elegies 2.12.23
Thou also that late tookest mine eyes away, ... Ovid's Elegies 2.19.19
By her eyes I remember late she swore, ... Ovid's Elegies 3.3.13
passions to asswage)/Compile sharpe satyrs, but alas too late, Hero and Leander 1.127

LATE-BUILT
A woman against late-built Rome did send/The Sabine Fathers, Ovid's Elegies 2.12.23

LATELY
Which lately made all Europe quake for feare: . . . . 1Tamb 3.3.135 Bajzth
have ye lately heard/The overthrow of mightie Bajazeth, . 1Tamb 4.3.23 Arabia
These heathnish Turks and Pagans lately made, ... 2Tamb 2.1.6 Fredrk
Grace to memorie/The league we lately made with king Orcanes, 2Tamb 2.1.28 Sgsmnd
yong Callapine that lately fled from your majesty, hath nowe 2Tamb 5.3.102 P 3Msngr
What, Barabas, whose goods were lately seiz'd? . . . Jew 1.2.383 Lodowk
Was lately lost, and you were stated here/To be at deadly Jew 2.2.32 Bosco
to feast my traine/Within a Towne of warre so lately pillag'd, Jew 5.3.22 Calym
of Loraine by the Kings consent is lately strangled unto death. P1123 21.17 P Frier
You know that I came lately out of France, ... Edw 1.1.44 Gavstn
Raw soldiours lately prest; and troupes of gownes; . . Lucan, First Booke 312
I lately cought, will have a new made wound, . . . Ovid's Elegies 1.2.29

LATERALLY (See LAT'RALLY)

LATEST
Drawes in the comfort of her latest breath/All dasled with the 2Tamb 2.4.13 Tamb
my Lords whose true nobilitie/Have merited my latest memorie: 2Tamb 2.4.74 Zenoc
And so revenge our latest grievous losse, ... 2Tamb 5.2.10 Callap
Now eies, injoy your latest benefite, ... 2Tamb 5.3.224 Tamb
Then Barabas breath forth thy latest fate, ... Jew 5.5.78 Barab
My head, the latest honor dew to it, ... Edw 5.1.62 Edward
Both come from drawing Faustus latest will. . . . . F1814 5.2.18 Mephst
Calls for the payment of my latest yeares, ... F App p.239 93 Faust
Pray God it may his latest supper be, ... Ovid's Elegies 1.4.2

LATIAN
Quirinus rites and Latian Jove advanc'd/On Alba hill o Vestall Lucan, First Booke 200

LATIN
lust of warre/Hath made Barbarians drunke with Latin bloud? Lucan, First Booke 9

LATINUS
new to enter/Warres, just Latinus, in thy kingdomes center: Ovid's Elegies 2.12.22

LATITUDE
That have not past the Centers latitude, ... 2Tamb 3.2.31 Tamb

LATMUS
From Latmus mount up to the glomie skie, ... Hero and Leander 1.109

LATONAS
Or as Latonas daughter bent to armes, ... 1Tamb 5.1.514 Tamb

LAT'RALLY
And heateth kindly, shining lat'rally; . . . . . Hero and Leander 2.125

LATTER
at whose latter gaspe/Joves marble statue gan to bend the brow, Dido 2.1.256 Aeneas
But in my latter houre to purge my selfe, ... P 402 7.42 Ramus

LAUDE
Hence with great laude thou maiest a triumph move. . . Ovid's Elegies 2.9.16

LAUGH
O how would I with Helens brother laugh, ... Dido 1.1.17 Ganimd
Leave to lament lest they laugh at our feares. . . . Dido 2.1.38 Achat
That all the world will see and laugh to scorne, . . . 1Tamb 5.1.252 Zabina
Will laugh I feare me at their good aray. . . . . . P 673 13.17 Duchss
below, the king and he/From out a window, laugh at such as we, Edw 1.4.417 Mortmr
The Divel's dead, the Furies now may laugh. . . . . F1369 4.2.45 Benvol
Fooles that will laugh on earth, [must] <most> weepe in hell. F1891 5.2.95 Mephst

LAUGH'D
That I have laugh'd agood to see the cripples/Goe limping home Jew 2.3.211 Ithimr
Then like a Jew he laugh'd and jeer'd, and told me he lov'd me Jew 4.2.108 P Pilia
Love hearing it laugh'd with his tender mother/And smiling Ovid's Elegies 1.6.11

LAUGHED
Love laughed at my cloak, and buskines painted, . . . Ovid's Elegies 2.18.15

LAUGHING
Vulcan shall daunce to make thee laughing sport, . . . Dido 1.1.32 Jupitr
and thy selfe/Bedaubd with golde, rode laughing at the rest, Edw 2.2.185 Mortmr
And make us laughing stockes to all the world. . . . F1450 4.3.20 Benvol
A laughing stocke thou art to all the citty, ... Ovid's Elegies 3.1.21

LAUGHS
How pretilie he laughs, goe ye wagge, ... Dido 4.5.19 Nurse
Now sits and laughs our regiment to scorne: . . . . 1Tamb 1.1.117 Cosroe

LAUGHS (cont.)			
smiles]/[At your repulse, and laughs your state to scorne],	F1795	5.1.122A	OldMan
LAUGH'ST			
Why, how now Ithimore, why laugh'st thou so?	Jew	3.3.4	Abigal
LAUGHT			
And laught to see the poore starve at their gates:	F1918	5.2.122	BdAngl
She laught, and kissed so sweetely as might make/Wrath-kindled	Ovid's Elegies		2.5.51
LAUNCE			
Pallas launce strikes me with unconquerd arme.	Ovid's Elegies		3.3.28
LAUNCHT (See also LANCH)			
For all our ships were launcht into the deepe:	Dido	2.1.285	Aeneas
These were the instruments that launcht him forth,	Dido	4.4.150	Dido
or to what end/Launcht from the haven, lye they in the Rhode?	Dido	5.1.89	Dido
Was this the face that Launcht a thousand ships,	F1768	5.1.95	Faust
We sing, whose conquering swords their own breasts launcht,	Lucan, First Booke		3
LAUNDRESS (See LANDRESSE)			
LAUREATE			
thou art Conjurer laureate]/[That canst commaund great	F 260	1.3.32A	Faust
LAURELL (See also LAWRELL)			
Then with triumphant laurell will I grace them/And in the midst	Ovid's Elegies		1.11.25
LAVINIA			
Prevented Turnus of Lavinia,	1Tamb	5.1.393	Zenoc
LAVINIAN			
Now will I haste unto Lavinian shoare,	Dido	5.1.78	Aeneas
LAVINIAS			
Darts forth her light to Lavinias shoare.	Dido	3.2.84	Venus
LAVISH			
Thou wilt repent these lavish words of thine,	1Tamb	3.3.172	Zenoc
To make these captives reine their lavish tongues.	1Tamb	4.2.67	Techel
Such lavish will I make of Turkish blood,	2Tamb	1.3.165	Tamb
But he that makes most lavish of his bloud.	P1240	22.102	King
And seeming lavish, sav'de her maydenhead.	Hero and Leander		2.76
LAW			
Thou breakst the law of Armes unlesse thou kneele,	1Tamb	2.4.21	Mycet
The Canon Law forbids it, and the Priest/That makes it knowne,	Jew	3.6.34	2Fryar
No, pardon me, the Law must have his course.	Jew	4.1.185	Barab
The Law shall touch you, we'll but lead you, we:	Jew	4.1.202	Barab
Law wils that each particular be knowne.	Jew	4.1.205	Barab
And he my bondman, let me have law,	Jew	5.1.38	Barab
Once more away with him; you shall have law.	Jew	5.1.40	Govnr
In prison till the Law has past on him.	Jew	5.1.49	Govnr
A bloudie part, flatly against law of armes.	Edw	3.1.121	Spencr
And universall body of the law <Church>.	F 60	1.1.32	Faust
Both Law and Physicke are for petty wits:	F 134	1.1.106	Faust
Pope Adrian let me have some right of Law,	F 904	3.1.126	Bruno
And outrage strangling law and people strong,	Lucan, First Booke		2
But law being put to silence by the wars,	Lucan, First Booke		278
Lay in the mid bed, there be my law giver.	Ovid's Elegies		2.17.24
Law-giving Minos did such yeares desire;	Ovid's Elegies		3.9.41
LAWE			
this is againste the lawe ser:	Paris	ms14,p390 P	Souldr
Poore Pierce, and headed him against lawe of armes?	Edw	3.1.238	Edward
Strike off his head, he shall have marshall lawe.	Edw	5.4.89	Mortmr
LAWES			
With whom we did devide both lawes and land,	Dido	4.2.14	Iarbus
Were to transgresse against all lawes of love:	Dido	4.3.48	Aeneas
And there make lawes to rule your provinces:	1Tamb	5.1.527	Tamb
The holy lawes of Christendome injoine:	2Tamb	2.1.36	Baldwn
And spurns the Abstracts of thy foolish lawes.	2Tamb	5.1.197	Tamb
and Lawes were then most sure/When like the [Dracos] <Drancus>	Jew	Prol.20	Machvl
Novice learne to frame/My solitary life to your streight lawes,	Jew	1.2.332	Abigal
Oh Barabas, their Lawes are strict.	Jew	4.1.82	1Fryar
A watchfull Senate for ordaining lawes,	P 593	12.6	QnMoth
That lawes were broake, Tribunes with Consuls strove,	Lucan, First Booke		179
here, here (saith he)/An end of peace; here end polluted lawes;	Lucan, First Booke		227
And lawes assailde, and arm'd men in the Senate?	Lucan, First Booke		322
Let all Lawes yeeld, sinne beare the name of vertue,	Lucan, First Booke		666
Nor that I studie not the brawling lawes,	Ovid's Elegies		1.15.5
To fill my lawes thy wanton spirit frame.	Ovid's Elegies		3.1.30
The places lawes this benefit allowe.	Ovid's Elegies		3.2.20
Looke gently, and rough husbands lawes despise.	Ovid's Elegies		3.4.44
they governe fieldes, and lawes,/they manadge peace, and rawe	Ovid's Elegies		3.7.57
LAWFUL			
Long live King Edward, Englands lawful lord.	Edw	3.1.151	Herald
LAWFULL			
Of lawfull armes, or martiall discipline:	1Tamb	4.1.65	Souldn
I vow as I am lawfull King of France,	P1143	22.5	King
For he is your lawfull King and my next heire:	P1230	22.92	King
And learne obedience to their lawfull king.	Edw	3.1.23	Spencr
And levie armes against your lawfull king?	Edw	3.1.208	SpncrP
thou chase/Thy lawfull king thy soveraigne with thy sword?	Edw	4.6.4	Kent
To hold the Emperours their lawfull Lords.	F 927	3.1.149	Bruno
What lawfull is, or we professe Loves art,	Ovid's Elegies		2.18.19
Wee skorne things lawfull, stolne sweetes we affect,	Ovid's Elegies		2.19.3
Who covets lawfull things takes leaves from woods,	Ovid's Elegies		2.19.31
LAWFULLY			
Then may we lawfully revolt from him.	Edw	1.2.73	Mortmr
LAW GIVER			
Lay in the mid bed, there be my law giver.	Ovid's Elegies		2.17.24
LAW-GIVING			
Law-giving Minos did such yeares desire;	Ovid's Elegies		3.9.41
LAWIER			
The lawier and the client <both do> hate thy view,	Ovid's Elegies		1.13.21

LAWLES			
Our hands are not prepar'd to lawles spoyle,	Dido	1.2.12	Illion
That like the lawles Catiline of Rome,	Edw	4.6.51	Rice
LAWLESSE			
And in your confines with his lawlesse traine,	1Tamb	1.1.39	Meandr
By lawlesse rapine from a silly maide.	1Tamb	1.2.10	Zenoc
That live by rapine and by lawlesse spoile,	1Tamb	2.2.23	Meandr
The worlds swift course is lawlesse/And casuall; all the	Lucan, First Booke		641
LAWNDES			
That they may trip more lightly ore the lawndes,	Dido	1.1.207	Venus
LAWNE			
The sailes of foulded Lawne, where shall be wrought/The warres	Dido	3.1.124	Dido
To strangle with a lawne thrust through the throte,	Edw	5.4.32	Ltborn
The outside of her garments were of lawne,	Hero and Leander		1.9
By those white limmes, which sparckled through the lawne.	Hero and Leander		2.242
LAWNES			
My men like Satyres grazing on the lawnes,	Edw	1.1.59	Gavstn
And when hee sported in the fragrant lawnes,	Hero and Leander		2.199
LAWRELL			
Loden with Lawrell wreathes to crowne us all.	2Tamb	3.5.164	Tamb
And burned is Apollo's Lawrell bough,	F2003	5.3.21	4Chor
LAWYER (See also LAWIER)			
Thou makste the suretie to the lawyer runne,	Ovid's Elegies		1.13.19
LAY (See also LAIE)			
Disquiet Seas lay downe your swelling lookes,	Dido	1.1.122	Venus
and in this grove/Amongst greene brakes Ile lay Ascanius,	Dido	2.1.317	Venus
If thou but lay thy fingers on my boy.	Dido	3.2.36	Venus
That would have kild him sleeping as he lay?	Dido	3.2.39	Juno
Cupid shall lay his arrowes in thy lap,	Dido	3.2.56	Venus
me, for I forgot/That yong Ascanius lay with me this night:	Dido	4.4.32	Dido
he lay with me last night,/And in the morning he was stolne	Dido	5.1.213	Nurse
Lay to thy hands and helpe me make a fire,	Dido	5.1.284	Dido
Lay out our golden wedges to the view,	1Tamb	1.2.139	Tamb
If they would lay their crownes before my feet,	1Tamb	4.2.93	Tamb
Whose sorrowes lay more siege unto my soule,	1Tamb	5.1.155	Tamb
As if I lay with you for company.	2Tamb	4.1.39	Calyph
Lay waste the Iland, hew the Temples downe,	Jew	3.5.14	Govnr
Thou traitor Guise, lay of thy bloudy hands.	P 439	7.79	Navrre
Ah brother, lay not violent hands on him,	Edw	1.1.189	Kent
Lay hands on that traitor Mortimer.	Edw	1.4.20	Edward
Lay hands on that traitor Gaveston.	Edw	1.4.21	MortSr
Nay, then lay violent hands upon your king,	Edw	1.4.35	Edward
And Spencer, spare them not, but lay it on.	Edw	3.1.56	Edward
These Barons lay their heads on blocks together,	Edw	3.1.274	Baldck
good father on thy lap/Lay I this head, laden with mickle care,	Edw	4.7.40	Edward
A litter hast thou, lay me in a hearse,	Edw	4.7.87	Edward
And that you lay for pleasure here a space,	Edw	5.1.3	Leistr
Lay hands upon the earle for this assault.	Edw	5.3.54	Gurney
Lay downe your weapons, traitors, yeeld the king.	Edw	5.3.55	Kent
So, lay the table downe, and stampe on it,	Edw	5.5.112	Ltborn
O Faustus, lay that damned booke aside,	F 97	1.1.69	GdAngl
Whilst on thy head I lay my hand,	F 995	3.2.15	Mephst
To lay the fury of this same troublesome ghost.	F1064	3.2.84	Pope
And lay his life at holy Bruno's feet.	F1220	4.1.66	Faust
Friers prepare a dirge to lay the fury of this ghost, once	F App	p.232 16 P	Pope
To rest my limbes, uppon a bedde I lay,	Ovid's Elegies		1.5.2
On this hard threshold till the morning lay.	Ovid's Elegies		1.6.68
Make a small price, while thou thy nets doest lay,	Ovid's Elegies		1.8.69
the time more short/Lay downe thy forehead in thy lap to snort.	Ovid's Elegies		2.2.24
Lay her whole tongue hid, mine in hers she dips.	Ovid's Elegies		2.5.58
Upon the cold earth pensive let them lay,	Ovid's Elegies		2.16.15
Lay in the mid bed, there be my law giver.	Ovid's Elegies		2.17.24
There shalt be lov'd: Ilia lay feare aside.	Ovid's Elegies		3.5.62
Idly I lay with her, as if I lovde <her> not,	Ovid's Elegies		3.6.3
Like a dull Cipher, or rude blocke I lay,	Ovid's Elegies		3.6.15
Yet notwithstanding, like one dead it lay,	Ovid's Elegies		3.6.65
To lay my body on the hard moist floore.	Ovid's Elegies		3.10.10
The while upon a hillocke downe he lay,	Hero and Leander		1.400
And in her luke-warme place Leander lay.	Hero and Leander		2.254
LAYD			
My princely robes thou seest are layd aside,	Dido	3.3.3	Dido
The self-same day that he asleepe had layd/Inchaunted Argus,	Hero and Leander		1.387
As sheap-heards do, her on the ground hee layd,	Hero and Leander		1.405
At his faire feathered feet, the engins layd,	Hero and Leander		1.449
Both in each others armes chaind as they layd.	Hero and Leander		2.306
LAYDE			
O would in my fore-fathers tombe deepe layde,	Ovid's Elegies		3.5.73
LAYED			
words she sayd/While closely hid betwixt two dores I layed.	Ovid's Elegies		1.8.22
His sword layed by, safe, though rude places yeelds.	Ovid's Elegies		2.9.20
Where Linus by his father Phoebus layed/To sing with his	Ovid's Elegies		3.8.23
When have not I fixt to thy side close layed?	Ovid's Elegies		3.10.17
LAYES			
Hees happie who loves mutuall skirmish slayes <layes>,	Ovid's Elegies		2.10.29
Conquer'd Corinna in my bosome layes.	Ovid's Elegies		2.12.2
LAYING			
swift Mercury/When I was laying a platforme for these walles,	Dido	5.1.94	Aeneas
This said, he laying aside all lets of war,	Lucan, First Booke		206
LAYIS			
Or Layis of a thousand [wooers] <lovers> [sped] <spread>.	Ovid's Elegies		1.5.12
LAZY (See LAISIE)			
LE			
Vive [le] <la> Roy, vive [le] <la> Roy.	P 588	12.1	All

LE (cont.)
Vive [le] <la> Roy, vive [le] <la> Roy. . . . . . P 598 12.11 All
Par [le] <la> mor du, Il mora. . . . . P 770 15.28 Guise
Mounsier le Grand, a noble friend of yours, . . . Edw 4.2.47 Mortmr
LEA
The [haven] <heaven> touching barcke now nere the lea, . Ovid's Elegies 2.9.32
LEACHERY
be carried thither againe by Gluttony and Letchery <Leachery>], F 705.3 2.2.157A P Sloth
the first letter of my name begins with Letchery <leachery>. F 710 2.2.162 P Ltchry
LEAD (Homograph)
And lead thy thousand horse with my conduct, ... 1Tamb 1.2.189 Tamb
giftes and promises/Inveigle him that lead a thousand horse, 1Tamb 2.2.26 Meandr
those that lead my horse/Have to their names tytles of dignity, 1Tamb 3.3.69 Bajzth
And know thou Turke, that those which lead my horse, . 1Tamb 3.3.72 Tamb
Shall lead thee Captive thorow Affrica. . . . . . 1Tamb 3.3.73 Tamb
Come bind them both and one lead in the Turke. . . . 1Tamb 3.3.266 Tamb
The Turkesse let my Loves maid lead away. . . . . 1Tamb 3.3.267 Tamb
Shall lead him with us wheresoere we goe. . . . . 1Tamb 4.2.100 Tamb
I took the king, and lead him bound in chaines/Unto Damasco, 2Tamb 1.3.204 Techel
Shall lead his soule through Orcus burning gulfe: . . 2Tamb 2.3.25 Orcan
Not lapt in lead but in a sheet of gold, ... 2Tamb 2.4.131 Tamb
And drops of scalding lead, while all thy joints/Be rackt and 2Tamb 3.5.124 Tamb
The Law shall touch you, we'll but lead you, we: . . Jew 4.1.202 Barab
I'le lead five hundred souldiers through the Vault, . . Jew 5.1.91 Barab
This is the life we Jewes are us'd to lead; . . . Jew 5.2.115 Barab
Come lead the way, I long till I am there. . . . Edw 2.1.82 Neece
Lead on the way. . . . . Edw 2.2.132 Lncstr
And will sir John of Henolt lead the round? . . . Edw 4.3.40 Edward
O that I might this life in quiet lead, ... Edw 4.7.21 Edward
I, lead me whether you will, even to my death, . . . Edw 5.3.66 Kent
On burning forkes: their bodies [boyle] <broyle> in lead. F1912 5.2.116 BdAngl
Yong men and women, shalt thou lead as thrall, . . . Ovid's Elegies 1.2.27
To lead thy thoughts, as thy faire lookes doe mine, . . Hero and Leander 1.201
A Diamond set in lead his worth retaines, ... Hero and Leander 1.215
LEADE (Homograph)
Faire sister Anna leade my lover forth, ... Dido 4.4.65 Dido
Doe as I bid thee sister, leade the way, ... Dido 4.4.85 Dido
Will leade an hoste against the hatefull Greekes, . . . Dido 4.4.91 Aeneas
Weele leade you to the stately tent of War: . . . . 1Tamb Prol.3 Prolog
Well, leade us then to Syrtes desart shoare; . . . . Lucan, First Booke 368
Yet as if mixt with red leade thou wert ruddy, . . . Ovid's Elegies 1.12.11
Faire Phoebus leade me to the Muses springs. . . . Ovid's Elegies 1.15.36
Let Maydes whom hot desire to husbands leade, . . . Ovid's Elegies 2.1.5
LEADEN
that by leaden pipes/Runs to the citie from the mountain . 1Tamb 3.1.59 Bajzth
Captaine, these Moores shall cut the leaden pipes, . . 2Tamb 3.3.29 Techel
Base leaden Earles that glorie in your birth, . . . Edw 2.2.74 Gavstn
LEADER
Thou shalt be leader of this thousand horse, ... 1Tamb 1.1.62 Mycet
Let come their [leader] <leaders whom long peace hath quail'd; Lucan, First Booke 311
chiefe leader of Rooms force,/So be I may be bold to speake a Lucan, First Booke 360
LEADERS
These lustie leaders Warwicke and Lancaster, ... Edw 3.1.246 Edward
Let come their [leader] <leaders whom long peace hath quail'd; Lucan, First Booke 311
LEADES
where/A fury leades the Emathian bandes, from thence/To the Lucan, First Booke 687
Though thether leades a rough steepe hilly way. . . Ovid's Elegies 3.12.6
LEADING
May have the leading of so great an host, ... 1Tamb 1.2.48 Tamb
Deserv'st to have the leading of an hoste? . . . 1Tamb 1.2.171 Tamb
Leading a troope of Gentlemen and Lords, ... 1Tamb 2.1.58 Ceneus
Leading a life that onely strives to die, ... 2Tamb 5.3.197 Amyras
LEADS
That leads to Pallace of my brothers life, ... 1Tamb 2.1.43 Cosroe
And leads with him the great Arabian King, ... 1Tamb 4.3.64 Souldn
us haste from hence/Along the cave that leads beyond the foe, 2Tamb 3.4.2 Olymp
pride/And leads your glories <bodies> sheep-like to the sword. 2Tamb 4.1.77 Tamb
LEAD'ST
thou lead'st me toward th'east,/Where Nile augmenteth the Lucan, First Booke 682
LEAFE (See also LEAVY)
Stand staggering like a quivering Aspen leafe, . . . 1Tamb 2.4.4 Mycet
LEAGRE
And laine in leagre fifteene moneths and more, . . . 2Tamb 1.3.176 Usumc
LEAGUE (Homograph)
Harke to a motion of eternall league, ... Dido 3.2.68 Juno
Betwixt this land and that be never league, . . . Dido 5.1.309 Dido
Conclude a league of honor to my hope. . . . . 1Tamb 5.1.399 Zenoc
We came from Turky to confirme a league, ... 2Tamb 1.1.115 Gazell
As memorable witnesse of our league. . . . . . 2Tamb 1.1.145 Orcan
of Natolia/Confirm'd this league beyond Danubius streame, 2Tamb 1.1.149 Orcan
Sweet Almeda, scarse halfe a league from hence. . . 2Tamb 1.2.55 Callap
With whom (being women) I vouchsaft a league, . . . 2Tamb 1.3.193 Techel
Grace to memorie/The league we lately made with king Orcanes, 2Tamb 2.1.28 Sgsmnd
by a Spanish Fleet/That never left us till within a league, Jew 1.1.96 2Merch
Were it for confirmation of a League, ... Jew 1.1.154 1Jew
What need they treat of peace that are in league? . . Jew 1.1.158 Barab
The Turkes and those of Malta are in league. . . . Jew 1.1.159 Barab
For if we breake our day, we breake the league, . . . Jew 1.2.158 1Knght
nay we dare not give consent/By reason of a Tributary league. Jew 2.2.23 Govnr
Will Knights of Malta be in league with Turkes, . . . Jew 2.2.28 Bosco
since thou hast broke the league/By flat denyall of the . Jew 3.5.19 Basso
For by this Answer, broken is the league, ... Jew 3.5.34 Govnr
I wishe this union and religious league, ... P 3 1.3 Charls

LEAGUE (cont.)
I am a juror in the holy league, — P 837 17.32 Guise
Armies allied, the kingdoms league uprooted, — Lucan, First Booke 4
Then men from war shal bide in league, and ease, — Lucan, First Booke 60
Dire league of partners in a kingdome last not. — Lucan, First Booke 86

LEAGUES (Homograph)
Now have we martcht from faire Natolia/Two hundred leagues, and — 2Tamb 1.1.7 Orcan
Being distant lesse than ful a hundred leagues, — 2Tamb 5.3.133 Tamb
Backeward and forwards nere five thousand leagues. — 2Tamb 5.3.144 Tamb
Hence leagues, and covenants; Fortune thee I follow, — Lucan, First Booke 228

LEANDER
And like Leander gaspt upon the sande, — Edw 1.1.8 Gavstn
Amorous Leander, beautifull and yoong, — Hero and Leander 1.51
Had wilde Hippolitus, Leander seene, — Hero and Leander 1.77
Leander, thou art made for amorous play: — Hero and Leander 1.88
And thus Leander was enamoured. — Hero and Leander 1.162
Wherewith Leander much more was inflam'd. — Hero and Leander 1.182
And now begins Leander to display/Loves holy fire, with words, — Hero and Leander 1.192
With that Leander stoopt, to have imbrac'd her, — Hero and Leander 1.341
Thinking to traine Leander therewithall. — Hero and Leander 2.12
Albeit Leander rude in love, and raw, — Hero and Leander 2.61
her selfe the clouds among/And now Leander fearing to be mist, — Hero and Leander 2.91
As loath to see Leander going out. — Hero and Leander 2.98
What is it now, but mad Leander dares? — Hero and Leander 2.146
Leander striv'd, the waves about him wound, — Hero and Leander 2.159
Leander being up, began to swim, — Hero and Leander 2.175
Leander made replie,/You are deceav'd, I am no woman I. — Hero and Leander 2.191
Aye me, Leander cryde, th'enamoured sunne, — Hero and Leander 2.202
When this fresh bleeding wound Leander viewd, — Hero and Leander 2.213
By this Leander being nere the land, — Hero and Leander 2.227
Whereon Leander sitting, thus began, — Hero and Leander 2.245
And in her luke-warme place Leander lay. — Hero and Leander 2.254
Wherein Leander on her quivering brest, — Hero and Leander 2.279
And to Leander as a fresh alarme. — Hero and Leander 2.284
Leander now like Theban Hercules, — Hero and Leander 2.297
Leaving Leander in the bed alone. — Hero and Leander 2.312

LEANDERS
That my slacke muse, sings of Leanders eies, — Hero and Leander 1.72
Viewing Leanders face, fell downe and fainted. — Hero and Leander 2.2
Leanders amorous habit soone reveal'd. — Hero and Leander 2.104
So to his mind was yoong Leanders looke. — Hero and Leander 2.130
Leanders Father knew where hee had beene, — Hero and Leander 2.136
Wherefore Leanders fancie to surprize, — Hero and Leander 2.223

LEANE (Homograph)
and the verie legges/Whereon our state doth leane, as on a — 1Tamb 1.1.60 Mycet
so, let him leane upon his staffe; excellent, he stands as if he — Jew 4.1.153 P Ithimr
Sweet Duke of Guise our prop to leane upon, — P1110 21.4 Dumain
Which for his fathers sake leane to the king, — Edw 1.4.283 Mortmr
I am leane with seeing others eate: — F 681 2.2.130 P Envy
Over the which [foure] <two> stately Bridges leane, — F 815 3.1.37 Mephst
did looke/Dead, and discoulour'd; th'other leane and thinne. — Lucan, First Booke 628
Nor [leane] <leave> thy soft head on his boistrous brest. — Ovid's Elegies 1.4.36

LEANER
you in these chops; let me see one that's somewhat leaner. — Jew 2.3.125 P Barab
Here's a leaner, how like you him? — Jew 2.3.126 P 1Offcr

LEANING
So leaning on his sword he stood stone still, — Dido 2.1.263 Aeneas
Thus leaning on the shoulder of the king, — Edw 1.2.23 Warwck

LEAP (See also LEP, LEPT)
Harke, harke they come, Ile leap out at the window. — P 369 7.9 Taleus

LEAPE
Then would it leape out to give Priam life: — Dido 2.1.27 Aeneas
Where thou shalt see the red gild fishes leape, — Dido 4.5.10 Nurse
Leape in mine armes, mine armes are open wide: — Dido 5.1.180 Dido
he was ready to leape off e're the halter was about his necke; — Jew 4.2.22 P Ithimr
O I'le leape up to [my God] <heaven>: who puls me downe? — F1938 5.2.142 Faust
Snakes leape by verse from caves of broken mountaines/And — Ovid's Elegies 2.1.25

LEAPES
Leapes from th'Antarticke world unto the skie, — F 231 1.3.3 Faust
Filling the world, leapes out and throwes forth fire, — Lucan, First Booke 154
The Pilot from the helme leapes in the sea; — Lucan, First Booke 499

LEAPING
When Phoebus leaping from his Hemi-Spheare, — 2Tamb 1.2.51 Callap
O that his heart were leaping in my hand. — P 936 19.6 P 2Mur

LEAPT
Neoptolemus/Setting his speare upon the ground, leapt forth, — Dido 2.1.184 Aeneas
At which the franticke Queene leapt on his face, — Dido 2.1.244 Aeneas
Thou wouldst have leapt from out the Sailers hands, — Dido 4.4.141 Dido
leapt out of a Lyons mouth when I was scarce <half> an houre — F 686 2.2.135 P Wrath
The fathers selves leapt from their seats; and flying/Left — Lucan, First Booke 485
his/That leapt into the water for a kis/Of his owne shadow, — Hero and Leander 1.74
And crying, Love I come, leapt lively in. — Hero and Leander 2.154

LEARN
Those that hate me, will I learn to loath. — P 156 2.99 Guise
What your intent is yet we cannot learn, — P 823 17.18 King

LEARN'D
When this is learn'd for service on the land, — 2Tamb 3.2.83 Tamb
I learn'd in Florence how to kisse my hand, — Jew 2.3.23 Barab
And then all other ceremonies learn'd, — F 186 1.1.158 Cornel

LEARND
Oft have I leveld, and at last have learnd, — P 94 2.37 Guise
And long admiring say by what meanes learnd/Hath this same Poet — Ovid's Elegies 2.1.9
With Calvus learnd Catullus comes <come> and greete him. — Ovid's Elegies 3.8.62

LEARNDE

I learnde in Naples how to poison flowers,	Edw	5.4.31	Ltborn

LEARNDST

And tell me where [learndst] <learnst> thou this pretie song?	Dido	3.1.27	Dido

LEARNE

That I may learne to beare it patiently,	Dido	5.1.208	Dido
Ile have you learne to sleepe upon the ground,	2Tamb	3.2.55	Tamb
We may be slaine or wounded ere we learne.	2Tamb	3.2.94	Calyph
Ile have you learne to feed on provander,	2Tamb	3.5.106	Tamb
learne with awfull eie/To sway a throane as dangerous as his:	2Tamb	5.3.234	Tamb
But I will learne to leave these fruitlesse teares,	Jew	1.2.230	Abigal
First let me as a Novice learne to frame/My solitary life to	Jew	1.2.331	Abigal
I, Lord, thus slaves will learne.	Jew	5.2.49	Barab
Learne then to rule us better and the realme.	Edw	1.4.39	Lncstr
learne this of me, a factious lord/Shall hardly do himselfe	Edw	2.1.6	Spencr
And learne to court it like a Gentleman,	Edw	2.1.32	Spencr
And learne obedience to their lawfull king.	Edw	3.1.23	Spencr
Learne thou of Faustus manly fortitude,	F 313	1.3.85	Faust
At last learne wretch to leave thy monarchy;	Lucan, First Booke	335	
And let thine eyes constrained learne to weepe,	Ovid's Elegies	1.8.83	
Wilt thou her fault learne, she may make thee tremble,	Ovid's Elegies	2.2.17	
Not what we slouthfull [knowe] <knewe>, let wise men learne,	Ovid's Elegies	3.7.25	
Ah simple Hero, learne thy selfe to cherish,	Hero and Leander	1.241	

LEARNED

In whom the learned Rabies of this age,	2Tamb	4.2.84	Therid
Schollers I meane, learned and liberall;	Jew	3.1.8	Curtzn
Is in your judgment thought a learned man.	P 391	7.31	Guise
If learned Faustus will be resolute.	F 160	1.1.132	Valdes
Learned Faustus/To find <know> the secrets of Astronomy,	F 754	2.3.33	2Chor
There saw we learned Maroes golden tombe:	F 791	3.1.13	Faust
[Which Faustus answered with such learned skill],	F1147	3.3.60A	3Chor
The learned Faustus, fame of Wittenberge,	F1165	4.1.11	Mrtino
Thrice learned Faustus, welcome to our Court.	F1205	4.1.51	Emper
We are much beholding to this learned man.	F1670	4.6.113	Lady
That sometime grew within this learned man:	F2004	5.3.22	4Chor
this learned man for the great kindnes he hath shewd to you.	F App	p.243 29 P	Duke
Next learned Augures follow;/Apolloes southsayers; and Joves	Lucan, First Booke	600	
If she be learned, then for her skill I crave her,	Ovid's Elegies	2.4.17	

LEARNES

But by her glasse disdainefull pride she learnes,	Ovid's Elegies	2.17.9	
By me Corinna learnes, cousening her guard,	Ovid's Elegies	3.1.49	

LEARNING

And but that Learning, in despight of Fate,	Hero and Leander	1.465	
Who with incroching guile, keepes learning downe.	Hero and Leander	1.482	

LEARNINGS

And glutted now <more> with learnings golden gifts,	F 24	Prol.24	1Chor

LEARNST

And tell me where [learndst] <learnst> thou this pretie song?	Dido	3.1.27	Dido

LEAST

Least you subdue the pride of Christendome?	1Tamb	1.1.132	Menaph
Therefore at least admit us libertie,	1Tamb	1.2.71	Zenoc
And kingdomes at the least we all expect,	1Tamb	1.2.218	Usumc
Least if we let them lynger here a while,	1Tamb	2.2.20	Meandr
Least he incurre the furie of my wrath.	1Tamb	3.1.30	Bajzth
And of extremities elect the least.	1Tamb	3.2.96	Agidas
One thought, one grace, one woonder at the least,	1Tamb	5.1.172	Tamb
Least time be past, and lingring let us both.	2Tamb	1.2.75	Callap
That is a Gentleman (I know) at least.	2Tamb	3.1.72	Callap
Least cruell Scythians should dismember him.	2Tamb	3.4.37	Olymp
least hee hide his crowne as the foolish king of Persea did.	2Tamb	3.5.154 P	Tamb
chiefe selected men/Of twenty severall kingdomes at the least:	2Tamb	5.2.49	Callap
But give him liberty at least to mourne,	Jew	1.2.202	Barab
Or at the least to pitty.	Jew	1.2.387	Mthias
And [less] <least> thou yeeld to this that I intreat,	Jew	3.4.37	Barab
Send for a hundred Crownes at least.	Jew	4.2.70 P	Pilia
Put in two hundred at least.	Jew	4.2.74 P	Pilia
At least unprofitably lose it not:	Jew	5.2.37	Barab
Least thou perceive the King of France be mov'd.	P 834	17.29	King
the least of these may well suffice/For one of greater birth	Edw	1.1.158	Kent
Not so my Lord, least he bestow more cost,	Edw	2.5.55	Lncstr
Mortimer hardly, Penbrooke and Lancaster/Spake least:	Edw	3.1.106	Arundl
A boye, thou art deceivde at least in this,	Edw	4.2.8	Queene
Least you be knowne, and so be rescued.	Edw	5.3.32	Gurney
This ten dayes space, and least that I should sleepe,	Edw	5.5.60	Edward
But not too hard, least that you bruse his body.	Edw	5.5.113	Ltborn
And gaze not on it least it tempt thy soule,	F 98	1.1.70	GdAngl
I say, least I send you into the Ostry with a vengeance.	F 733	2.3.12 P	Robin
Speak softly sir, least the devil heare you:	F1180	4.1.26	Mrtino
Gentlemen away, least you perish with me.	F1867	5.2.71 P	Faust
And now least age might waine his state, he casts/For civill	Lucan, First Booke	324	
And fates so bent, least sloth and long delay/Might crosse him,	Lucan, First Booke	394	
Now evermore least some one hope might ease/The Commons	Lucan, First Booke	520	
Least I should thinke thee guilty of offence.	Ovid's Elegies	1.4.50	
And guides my feete least stumbling falles they catch.	Ovid's Elegies	1.6.8	
And least the sad signes of my crime remaine,	Ovid's Elegies	1.7.67	
Least they should fly, being tane, the tirant play.	Ovid's Elegies	1.8.70	
And take heed least he gets that love for nought.	Ovid's Elegies	1.8.72	
Receive him soone, least patient use he gaine,	Ovid's Elegies	1.8.75	
Or least his love oft beaten backe should waine.	Ovid's Elegies	1.8.76	
Beware least he unrival'd loves secure,	Ovid's Elegies	1.8.95	
Isis may be done/Nor feare least she to th'theater's runne.	Ovid's Elegies	2.2.26	
Or such, as least long yeares should turne the die,	Ovid's Elegies	2.5.39	
Least with worse kisses she should me indue.	Ovid's Elegies	2.5.50	

LEAST (cont.)
I grieve least others should such good perceive, — Ovid's Elegies 2.5.53
Least Arte should winne her, firmely did inclose. — Ovid's Elegies 2.12.4
Least to the waxe the hold-fast drye gemme cleaves, — Ovid's Elegies 2.15.16
Graunt Tragedie thy Poet times least tittle, — Ovid's Elegies 3.1.67
least their gownes tosse thy haire,/To hide thee in my bosome — Ovid's Elegies 3.2.75
At least now conquer, and out-runne the rest: — Ovid's Elegies 3.2.79
And feare those, that to feare them least intend. — Ovid's Elegies 3.3.32
Nor, least she will, can any be restrainde. — Ovid's Elegies 3.4.6
Who may offend, sinnes least; power to do ill, — Ovid's Elegies 3.4.9
Least labour so shall winne great grace of any. — Ovid's Elegies 3.4.46
And least her maide should know of this disgrace, — Ovid's Elegies 3.6.83
And corne with least part of it selfe returnd. — Ovid's Elegies 3.9.30
Now waxt she jealous, least his love abated, — Hero and Leander 2.43
Least water-nymphs should pull him from the brinke. — Hero and Leander 2.198
At least vouchsafe these armes some little roome, — Hero and Leander 2.249

LEASURE
Jove that thou shouldst not hast but wait his leasure, — Ovid's Elegies 1.13.45

LEATHER
of an old Churle in a <an olde> leather <leatherne> bag; — F 675 2.2.124 P Covet

LEATHERNE
of an old Churle in a <an olde> leather <leatherne> bag; — F 675 2.2.124 P Covet
gods hung up/Such as peace yeelds; wormeaten leatherne targets, — Lucan, First Booke 243

LEAVDE
And I see when you ope the two leavde booke: — Ovid's Elegies 3.13.44

LEAVE (Homograph)
And so I leave thee to thy fortunes lot, — Dido 1.1.238 Venus
Sweete father leave to weepe, this is not he: — Dido 2.1.35 Ascan
Leave to lament lest they laugh at our feares. — Dido 2.1.38 Achat
Nay leave nct here, resolve me of the rest. — Dido 2.1.160 Dido
I dye with melting ruth, Aeneas leave. — Dido 2.1.289 Dido
I wagge, and give thee leave to kisse her to. — Dido 3.1.31 Dido
Come Dido, leave Ascanius, let us walke. — Dido 3.1.34 Iarbus
love, give Dido leave/To be more modest then her thoughts admit, — Dido 3.1.94 Dido
Take what ye will, but leave Aeneas here. — Dido 3.1.127 Dido
Aeneas, leave these dumpes and lets away, — Dido 3.3.60 Dido
Never to leave these newe upreared walles, — Dido 3.4.49 Aeneas
O leave me, leave me to my silent thoughts, — Dido 4.2.38 Iarbus
I will not leave Iarbus whom I love, — Dido 4.2.43 Anna
Commaunds me leave these unrenowmed [reames] <beames>, — Dido 4.3.18 Aeneas
To leave her so and not once say farewell, — Dido 4.3.47 Aeneas
O princely Dido, give me leave to speake, — Dido 4.4.17 Aeneas
Thinkes Didc I will goe and leave him here? — Dido 4.4.30 Aeneas
When I leave thee, death be my punishment, — Dido 4.4.56 Aeneas
I, but it may be he will leave my love, — Dido 4.4.97 Dido
How loth I am to leave these Libian bounds, — Dido 5.1.81 Aeneas
But yet Aeneas will nct leave his love? — Dido 5.1.98 Dido
To leave this towne and passe to Italy, — Dido 5.1.100 Aeneas
Aeneas, say, how canst thou take thy leave? — Dido 5.1.119 Dido
Now if thou goest, what canst thou leave behind, — Dido 5.1.151 Dido
Ah sister, leave these idle fantasies, — Dido 5.1.262 Anna
So, leave me now, let none approach this place. — Dido 5.1.291 Dido
Then now my Lord, I humbly take my leave. — 1Tamb 1.1.81 Therid
And they will never leave thee till the death. — 1Tamb 1.2.248 Tamb
my brothers Campe/I leave to thee, and to Theridamas, — 1Tamb 2.5.39 Cosroe
Shall make me leave so rich a prize as this: — 1Tamb 2.7.54 Tamb
And leave my body senceless as the earth. — 1Tamb 3.2.22 Zenoc
[Agidas], leave to wound me with these words: — 1Tamb 3.2.35 Zenoc
Leave words and let them feele your lances pointes, — 1Tamb 3.3.91 Argier
That leave no ground for thee to martch upon. — 1Tamb 3.3.147 Bajzth
Or leave Damascus and th'Egyptian fields, — 1Tamb 4.2.48 Tamb
And leave your venoms in this Tyrants dish. — 1Tamb 4.4.22 Bajzth
I pray you give them leave Madam, this speech is a goodly — 1Tamb 4.4.32 P Techel
Yet give me leave tc plead for him my Lord. — 1Tamb 4.4.86 Zenoc
Leave us my Lord, and loving countrimen, — 1Tamb 5.1.60 2Virgn
for the love of Venus, would she leave/The angrie God of Armes, — 1Tamb 5.1.124 Tamb
when wilt thou leave these armes/And save thy sacred person — 2Tamb 1.3.9 Zenoc
Messenger/To bid me sheath my sword, and leave the field: — 2Tamb 1.3.167 Tamb
And leave his steeds to faire Boetes charge: — 2Tamb 1.3.170 Tamb
Let me take leave of these my loving sonnes, — 2Tamb 2.4.72 Zenoc
Boyes leave to mourne, this towne shall ever mourne, — 2Tamb 3.2.45 Tamb
But now my boies, leave off, and list to me, — 2Tamb 3.2.53 Tamb
Doost thou aske him leave? — 2Tamb 3.5.134 P Callap
given so much to sleep/You cannot leave it, when our enemies — 2Tamb 4.1.12 Amyras
Leave this my Love, and listen more to me. — 2Tamb 4.2.38 Therid
pompe than this)/Rifle the kingdomes I shall leave unsackt, — 2Tamb 4.3.59 Tamb
Leave not a Babylonian in the towne. — 2Tamb 5.1.171 Tamb
But that we leave sufficient garrison/And presently depart to — 2Tamb 5.1.211 Tamb
Ah good my Lord, leave these impatient words, — 2Tamb 5.3.54 Therid
Then give us leave, great Selim-Calymath. — Jew 1.2.13 Govnr
Yes, give me leave, and Hebrews now come neare. — Jew 1.2.38 Govnr
Have strangers leave with us to get their wealth? — Jew 1.2.60 2Knght
submit your selves/To leave your goods to their arbitrament? — Jew 1.2.80 Barab
I, I,/Pray leave me in my patience. — Jew 1.2.200 Barab
Come, let us leave him in his irefull mood, — Jew 1.2.209 1Jew
But I will learne to leave these fruitlesse teares, — Jew 1.2.230 Abigal
But they will give me leave once more, I trow, — Jew 1.2.252 Barab
And leave no memory that e're I was. — Jew 1.2.265 Barab
And since ycu leave me in the Ocean thus/To sinke or swim, and — Jew 1.2.267 Barab
I charge thee on my blessing that thou leave/These divels, and — Jew 1.2.346 Barab
And why thou cam'st ashore without our leave? — Jew 2.2.3 Govnr
I cannot take my leave of him for teares: — Jew 2.3.355 Abigal
Oh leave to grieve me, I am griev'd enough. — Jew 3.2.17 Mater

LEAVE (cont.)

not both these wise men to suppose/That I will leave my house,	Jew	4.1.123	Barab
Canst thou be so unkind to leave me thus?	Jew	4.2.52	Curtzn
Content, but we will leave this paltry land, . . .	Jew	4.2.88	Ithimr
I'le not leave him worth a gray groat.	Jew	4.2.114	P Ithimr
no childe, and unto whom/Should I leave all but unto Ithimore?	Jew	4.3.45	Barab
There, if thou lov'st me doe not leave a drop. . . .	Jew	4.4.6	P Ithimr
Will take his leave and saile toward Ottoman. . . .	Jew	5.2.106	Barab
Leave nothing loose, all leveld to my mind. . . .	Jew	5.5.3	Barab
Then may it please your Majestie to give me leave, . .	P 616	12.29	Mugern
So, set it down and leave me to my selfe.	P 666	13.10	Duchss
Thanks to your Majestie, and so I take my leave. . .	P 749	15.7	Joyeux
I kisse your graces hand, and take my leave, . . .	P 868	17.63	Guise
Oh I have my deaths wound, give me leave to speak. . .	P1003	19.73	Guise
Away, leave me alone to meditate.	P1081	19.151	QnMoth
But you will saye you leave him rome enoughe besides: .	Paris	ms 7,p390	P Souldr
I have some busines, leave me to my selfe. . . .	Edw	1.1.48	Gavstn
Come unckle, let us leave the brainsick king, . . .	Edw	1.1.125	Mortmr
Stay Gaveston, I cannot leave thee thus.	Edw	1.4.135	Edward
And therefore give me leave to looke my fill, . . .	Edw	1.4.139	Edward
Why then my lord, give me but leave to speak. . . .	Edw	1.4.254	Mortmr
When I was forst to leave my Gaveston.	Edw	1.4.318	Edward
Lord Mortimer, we leave you to your charge: . . .	Edw	1.4.373	Edward
Leave now to oppose thy selfe against the king, . .	Edw	1.4.387	MortSr
Leave of this jesting, here my lady comes. . . .	Edw	2.1.56	Baldck
I come to joine with you, and leave the king, . . .	Edw	2.3.2	Kent
But whats the reason you should leave him now? . . .	Edw	2.3.13	Penbrk
him, but must we now/Leave him on had-I-wist, and let him go?	Edw	2.5.85	Warwck
And go in peace, leave us in warres at home. . . .	Edw	3.1.85	Edward
God end them once, my lord I take my leave, . . .	Edw	3.1.87	Queene
I thanke them, gave me leave to passe in peace: . .	Edw	4.1.16	Mortmr
And leave the Mortimers conquerers behind? . . .	Edw	4.5.5	Edward
But Leister leave to growe so passionate, ...	Edw	4.7.55	Leistr
And thus, most humbly do we take our leave. . . .	Edw	5.1.124	Trussl
Go to sirra, leave your jesting, and tell us where he is.	F 201	1.2.8	P 1Schol
And may not follow thee without his leave; . . .	F 269	1.3.41	Mephst
O Faustus leave these frivolous demandes, ...	F 309	1.3.81	Mephst
The Emperour shall not live, but by my leave, . . .	F 338	1.3.110	Faust
Well sirra, leave your jesting, and take these Guilders. .	F 367	1.4.25	P Wagner
Sweete Faustus leave that execrable Art.	F 404	2.1.16	GdAngl
you had best leave your foolery, for an my Maister come, he'le	F 734	2.3.13	P Dick
And leave it in the Churches treasury.	F 971	3.1.193	Pope
[I leave untold, your eyes shall see performd]. . .	F1154	3.3.67A	3Chor
Come leave thy chamber first, and thou shalt see/This Conjurer	F1185	4.1.31	Mrtino
And take his leave, laden with rich rewards. . . .	F1345	4.2.21	Benvol
Take you the wealth, leave us the victorie. . . .	F1347	4.2.23	Benvol
Do as thou wilt Faustus, I give thee leave. . . .	F1607	4.6.50	Duke
My Lord, beseech you give me leave a while, . . .	F1621	4.6.64	Faust
O gentle Faustus leave this damned Art, ...	F1707	5.1.34	OldMan
Leave me a while, to ponder on my sinnes. . . .	F1736	5.1.63	Faust
Faustus I leave thee, but with griefe of heart, . . .	F1737	5.1.64	OldMan
And now poore soule must thy good Angell leave thee, .	F1907	5.2.111	GdAngl
And so I leave thee Faustus till anon, ...	F1924	5.2.128	BdAngl
leave your jesting, and binde your selfe presently unto me for	F App	p.229 24	P Wagner
Now my good Lord having done my duety, I humbly take my leave.	F App	p.238 87	P Faust
Now am I made man for ever, Ile not leave my horse for fortie:	F App	p.239 114	P HrsCsr
At last learne wretch to leave thy monarchy; . . .	Lucan, First Booke		335
As loath to leave Roome whom they held so deere, . .	Lucan, First Booke		506
Nor [leane] <leave> thy soft head on his boistrous brest.	Ovid's Elegies		1.4.36
To leave the rest, all likt me passing well, . . .	Ovid's Elegies		1.5.23
Leave asking, and Ile give what I refraine. . . .	Ovid's Elegies		1.10.64
Leave colouring thy tresses I did cry, ...	Ovid's Elegies		1.14.1
To leave my selfe, that am in love [with all] <withall>, .	Ovid's Elegies		2.4.31
And wish hereby them all unknowne to leave. . . .	Ovid's Elegies		2.5.54
Hunters leave taken beasts, pursue the chase, . . .	Ovid's Elegies		2.9.9
She gave me leave, soft loves in time make hast, . .	Ovid's Elegies		3.1.69
Greater then her, by her leave th'art, Ile say. . .	Ovid's Elegies		3.2.60
Were I a God, I should give women leave, ...	Ovid's Elegies		3.3.43
The ditcher no markes on the ground did leave. . .	Ovid's Elegies		3.7.42
Leave thy once powerfull words, and flatteries, . .	Ovid's Elegies		3.10.31
he stayd his furie, and began/To give her leave to rise: .	Hero and Leander		1.416
That he would leave her turret and depart. . . .	Hero and Leander		2.38
Imbrast her sodainly, tooke leave, and kist, . . .	Hero and Leander		2.92
Long was he taking leave, and loath to go, . . .	Hero and Leander		2.93

LEAVELD

What wais thou wilt be leaveld with the ground, . .	Lucan, First Booke		384

LEAVEN (See LEVIN)

LEAVES (Homograph)

You shall have leaves and windfall bowes enow/Neere to these	Dido	1.1.172	Aeneas
Or whisking of these leaves, all shall be still, . .	Dido	2.1.337	Venus
Now in his majesty he leaves those lookes, . . .	1Tamb	3.2.61	Agidas
Or withered leaves that Autume shaketh downe: . . .	1Tamb	4.1.32	Souldn
shall breath/Through shady leaves of every senceless tree,	2Tamb	2.3.16	Orcan
In number more than are the quyvering leaves/Of Idas forrest,	2Tamb	3.5.5	2Msngr
Let's take our leaves; Farewell good Barabas. . . .	Jew	1.1.175	2Jew
And leaves it off to snap on Thistle tops: . . .	Jew	5.2.42	Barab
on me, then with your leaves/I may retire me to my native home.	P 473	8.23	Anjoy
As not a man may live without our leaves.	P 638	12.51	QnMoth
Whom I respect as leaves of boasting greene, . . .	P 720	14.23	Navrre
the royall vine, whose golden leaves/Empale your princelie head,	Edw	3.1.163	Herald
Here humblie of your grace we take our leaves, . . .	Edw	4.7.78	Baldck
<Wee'l take our leaves>, and for this blessed sight . .	F1704	(HC269)B	1Schol
view the Scriptures, then I turn'd the leaves/And led thine eye.	F1888	5.2.92	Mephst

LEAVES (cont.)			
then Laelius/The chiefe Centurion crown'd with Oaken leaves,	Lucan, First Booke	358	
Like Popler leaves blowne with a stormy flawe,	Ovid's Elegies	1.7.54	
And with swift horses the swift yeare soone leaves us.	Ovid's Elegies	1.8.50	
addst thou starres to heaven, leaves to greene woods <wood>,	Ovid's Elegies	2.10.13	
Then I, that I may seale her privy leaves,	Ovid's Elegies	2.15.15	
Maides words more vaine and light then falling leaves,	Ovid's Elegies	2.16.45	
Who covets lawfull things takes leaves from woods,	Ovid's Elegies	2.19.31	
Her vaile was artificiall flowers and leaves,	Hero and Leander	1.19	
Imbroydred all with leaves of Mirtle.	Passionate Shepherd	12	
LEAVING			
And leaving me will saile to Italy.	Dido	5.1.195	Dido
Leaving thy blood for witnesse of thy love.	1Tamb	5.1.411	Arabia
But leaving these vaine trifles of mens soules,	F 289	1.3.61	Faust
But leaving <off> this, let me have a wife, the fairest Maid in	F 529	2.1.141	P Faust
fierce men of Rhene/Leaving your countrey open to the spoile.	Lucan, First Booke	461	
Leaving the woods, lodge in the streetes of Rome.	Lucan, First Booke	558	
Leaving Leander in the bed alone.	Hero and Leander	2.312	
LEAV'ST			
But thou art gone and leav'st me here alone,	Dido	1.1.247	Aeneas
And banquet with him e're thou leav'st the Ile.	Jew	5.3.19	Msngr
Thou leav'st his bed, because hees faint through age,	Ovid's Elegies	1.13.37	
LEAVY (Homograph)			
To leavy armes and make these civill broyles:	P 730	14.33	Navrre
Come let us away and leavy men,	P1127	21.21	Dumain
I'le leavy souldiers with the coyne they bring,	F 119	1.1.91	Faust
And coole gales shake the tall trees leavy spring,	Ovid's Elegies	2.16.36	
LECHEROUS			
Grew pale, and in cold foords hot lecherous.	Ovid's Elegies	3.5.26	
LECHERY (See also LEACHERY, LETCHERIE)			
Brawle not (I warne you) for your lechery,	2Tamb	4.3.75	Tamb
LECTURE			
To reade a lecture here in [Britanie] <Britaine>,	Jew	Prol.29	Machvl
LED			
And made that way my mother Venus led:	Dido	1.1.221	Aeneas
And led our ships into the shallow sands,	Dido	1.2.27	Cloan
mine armes, and by the hand/Led faire Creusa my beloved wife,	Dido	2.1.267	Aeneas
We heare they led her captive into Greece.	Dido	2.1.295	Achat
But love and duetie led him on perhaps,	Dido	3.3.15	Aeneas
Led by Achates to the Troian fleete:	Dido	5.1.84	Dido
And led them Captive into Affrica.	1Tamb	3.3.205	Zabina
But haplesse Edward, thou art fondly led,	Edw	5.1.76	Edward
the Scriptures, then I turn'd the leaves/And led thine eye.	F1889	5.2.93	Mephst
lockes spred/On her white necke but for hurt cheekes be led.	Ovid's Elegies	1.7.40	
Even as he led his life, so did he die.	Ovid's Elegies	2.10.38	
White Heifers by glad people forth are led,	Ovid's Elegies	3.12.13	
Unto her was he led, or rather drawne,	Hero and Leander	2.241	
LEDA (See also LAEDAS)			
Such as was Leda, whom the God deluded/In snowe-white plumes of	Ovid's Elegies	1.10.3	
Why so was Ledas, yet was Leda faire.	Ovid's Elegies	2.4.42	
LEDAS			
Why so was Ledas, yet was Leda faire.	Ovid's Elegies	2.4.42	
LED'ST			
Oh thou that with a fiery piller led'st/The sonnes of Israel	Jew	2.1.12	Barab
LEEFEST			
Save, save Aeneas, Didos leefest love!	Dido	5.1.256	Dido
LEFT (Homograph)			
Grecians, which rejoyce/That nothing now is left of Priamus:	Dido	2.1.20	Aeneas
O Priamus is left and this is he,	Dido	2.1.21	Aeneas
And feede infection with his [let] <left> out life:	Dido	3.2.11	Juno
In all this coyle, where have ye left the Queene?	Dido	4.1.14	Iarbus
And left me neither saile nor sterne abourd.	Dido	5.1.61	Aeneas
That shall consume all that this stranger left,	Dido	5.1.285	Dido
Then is there left no Mahomet, no God,	1Tamb	5.1.239	Zabina
Left to themselves while we were at the fight,	1Tamb	5.1.471	Tamb
With them Arabia too hath left his life,	1Tamb	5.1.473	Tamb
Whose glorious body when he left the world,	2Tamb	1.1.139	Orcan
For since we left you at the Souldans court,	2Tamb	1.3.177	Usumc
I left the confines and the bounds of Affrike/And made a voyage	2Tamb	1.3.207	Therid
And make the power I have left behind/(Too litle to defend our	2Tamb	2.2.59	Orcan
No hope is left to save this conquered hold.	2Tamb	3.4.3	Olymp
And left your slender carkasses behind,	2Tamb	4.1.38	Calyph
That litle hope is left to save our lives,	2Tamb	5.1.4	Maxim
And but one hoste is left to honor thee:	2Tamb	5.2.27	Callap
let me see how much/Is left for me to conquer all the world,	2Tamb	5.3.124	Tamb
by a Spanish Fleet/That never left us till within a league,	Jew	1.1.96	2Merch
For there I left the Governour placing Nunnes,	Jew	1.2.254	Abigal
time/Have tane their flight, and left me in despaire;	Jew	2.1.8	Barab
And then we [luft] <left>, and [tackt] <tooke>, and fought at	Jew	2.2.14	Bosco
Yet I have one left that will serve your turne:	Jew	2.3.50	Barab
and invenome her/That like a fiend hath left her father thus.	Jew	3.4.105	Barab
and so I left him, being driven to a non-plus at the critical	Jew	4.2.13	P Pilia
tibi, cras mihi, and so I left him to the mercy of the Hangman:	Jew	4.2.19	P Pilia
he weares, Judas left under the Elder when he hang'd himselfe.	Jew	4.4.66	P Ithimr
So I may have some nooke or corner left,	Edw	1.4.72	Edward
Would when I left sweet France and was imbarkt,	Edw	1.4.171	Queene
His wanton humor will be quicklie left.	Edw	1.4.199	Lncstr
Yet have I words left to expresse my joy:	Edw	2.2.60	Gavstn
Complaines, that thou hast left her all forlorne.	Edw	2.2.173	Lncstr
The king hath left him, and his traine is small.	Edw	2.4.39	Queene
Our kindest friends in Belgia have we left,	Edw	4.4.3	Queene
Gurney, it was left unpointed for the nonce,	Edw	5.5.16	Matrvs
One jewell have I left, receive thou this.	Edw	5.5.84	Edward

LEFT (cont.)

your right eye be alwaies Diametrally fixt upon my left heele, F 387 1.4.45 P Wagner
and the devill a peny they have left me, but a [bare] <small> F 694 2.2.143 P Glutny
he never left eating, till he had eate up all my loade of hay. F1530 4.5.26 P Carter
I, I thought that was al the land his father left him: F App p.229 18 P Clown
and let thy left eye be diametarily fixt upon my right heele, F App p.231 69 P Wagner
No sir, but when Acteon died, he left the hornes for you: F App p.237 55 P Faust
The people started; young men left their beds, Lucan, First Booke 241
The yellow Ruthens left their garrisons; Lucan, First Booke 403
and flying/Left hateful warre decreed to both the Consuls. Lucan, First Booke 486
even so the Citty left,/All rise in armes; nor could the Lucan, First Booke 501
is by cowards/Left as a pray now Caesar doth approach: Lucan, First Booke 512
Tydides left worst signes of villanie, Ovid's Elegies 1.7.31
Now hast thou left no haires at all to die. Ovid's Elegies 1.14.2
The maide that kembd them ever safely left them. Ovid's Elegies 1.14.16
My wench her dore shut, Joves affares I left, Ovid's Elegies 2.1.17
In naked bones? love hath my bones left naked. Ovid's Elegies 2.9.14
And hide thy left hand underneath her lappe. Ovid's Elegies 2.15.12
Her left hand held abroad a regal scepter, Ovid's Elegies 3.1.13
She left; I say'd, you both I must beseech, Ovid's Elegies 3.1.61
Few love, what others have unguarded left. Ovid's Elegies 3.4.26
His left hand whereon gold doth ill alight, Ovid's Elegies 3.7.15
Because she tooke more from her than she left, Hero and Leander 1.47
As she to heare his tale, left off her running. Hero and Leander 1.418
Had left the heavens, therefore on him hee seaz'd. Hero and Leander 2.158

LEG

I have puld off his leg. F1492 4.4.36 P HrsCsr
Murder or not murder, now he has but one leg, I'le out-run him, F1494 4.4.38 P HrsCsr
I'le out-run him, and cast this leg into some ditch or other. F1495 4.4.39 P HrsCsr
Faustus hath his leg againe, and the Horse-courser a bundle of F1497 4.4.41 P Faust
I seeing that, tooke him by the leg, and never rested pulling, F1550 4.5.46 P HrsCsr
till I had pul'd me his leg quite off, and now 'tis at home in F1551 4.5.47 P HrsCsr
And has the Doctor but one leg then? F1553 4.5.49 P Dick
'faith Ile drinke a health to thy wooden leg for that word. F1627 4.6.70 P HrsCsr
My wooden leg? what dost thou meane by that? F1628 4.6.71 Faust
No faith, not much upon a wooden leg. F1631 4.6.74 Faust
And do you remember nothing of your leg? F1639 4.6.82 P Carter

LEGACIE

All heaven would come to claime this legacie, Hero and Leander 1.250

LEGACIES

A petty <pretty> case of paltry Legacies: F 57 1.1.29 Faust

LEGATE

As fits the Legate of the stately Turk. 1Tamb 3.1.44 Bassoe
You know that I am legate to the Pope, Edw 1.4.51 ArchBp
The Legate of the Pope will be obayd: Edw 1.4.64 Edward
The Legate of the Pope will have it so, Edw 1.4.109 Edward

LEGATES

Orcanes (as our Legates promist thee)/Wee with our Peeres have 2Tamb 1.1.78 Sgsmnd

LEGATS

Some came in person, others sent their Legats: Dido 3.1.152 Dido

LEGATUR

Si una eademque res legatur duobus, alter rem, alter valorem F 56 1.1.28 P Faust

LEGEND

Are both in Fames eternall legend writ. Ovid's Elegies 1.15.20

LEGGE

Ha, ha, ha, dost heare him Dick, he has forgot his legge. F1629 4.6.72 P Carter
O my legge, my legge, helpe Mephastophilis, call the Officers, F App p.241 155 P Faust
helpe Mephastophilis, call the Officers, my legge, my legge. F App p.241 156 P Faust
Faustus has his legge againe, and the Horsecourser I take it, F App p.241 164 P Faust
Mingle not thighes, nor to his legge joyne thine, Ovid's Elegies 1.4.43
How large a legge, and what a lustie thigh? Ovid's Elegies 1.5.22

LEGGES

of Persea, and the verie legges/Whereon our state doth leane, 1Tamb 1.1.59 Mycet
I sawe ones legges with fetters blacke and blewe, Ovid's Elegies 2.2.47
Envious garments so good legges to hide, Ovid's Elegies 3.2.27
Swift Atalantas flying legges like these, Ovid's Elegies 3.2.29
Coate-tuckt Dianas legges are painted like them, Ovid's Elegies 3.2.31
Thy legges hang-downe: Ovid's Elegies 3.2.63

LEGIONS

Legions of Spirits fleeting in the [aire], 1Tamb 3.3.156 Tamb
First legions of devils shall teare thee in peeces. 1Tamb 4.4.38 P Bajzth
Where legions of devils (knowing he must die/Here in Natolia, 2Tamb 3.5.25 Orcan
That legions of tormenting spirits may vex/Your slavish bosomes 2Tamb 5.1.45 Govnr
You Princely Legions of infernall Rule, F1116 3.3.29 Mephst

LEGS

Their legs to dance and caper in the aire: 2Tamb 1.3.31 Tamb
Or making lowe legs to a noble man, Edw 2.1.38 Spencr
Be both your legs bedfellowes every night together? F1645 4.6.88 P Carter
sir, did not I pull off one of your legs when you were asleepe? F1656 4.6.99 P HrsCsr
O horrible, had the Doctor three legs? F1658 4.6.101 P All

LEICESTER

Darbie, Salsburie, Lincolne, Leicester, Edw 1.1.103 Lncstr
Leicester, farewell. Edw 5.1.154 Edward
As Leicester that had charge of him before. Edw 5.2.35 BshpWn

LEISTER

But Leister leave to growe so passionate, Edw 4.7.55 Leistr
Comes Leister then in Isabellas name, Edw 4.7.64 Edward
And Leister say, what shall become of us? Edw 4.7.81 Edward
Leister, thou staist for me,/And go I must, life farewell with Edw 4.7.98 Edward
Leister, if gentle words might comfort me, Edw 5.1.5 Edward
Ah Leister, way how hardly I can brooke/To loose my crowne and Edw 5.1.51 Edward

LEISURE (See LEASURE)

LEMANNUS

They by Lemannus nooke forsooke their tents; Lucan, First Booke 397

LEMMONS			
For your lemmons you have lost, at Bannocks borne,	Edw	2.2.191	Lncstr
LEND			
Here take it for a while, I lend it thee,	1Tamb	2.4.37	Tamb
Would lend an howers license to my tongue:	1Tamb	5.1.423	Arabia
Rather lend me thy weapon Tamburlain,	2Tamb	5.1.142	Jrslem
Lend me that weapon that did kill my sonne,	Jew	3.2.23	Mater
Pray him to lend what thou maist nere restore.	Ovid's Elegies	1.8.102	
And vanquisht people curious dressings lend thee,	Ovid's Elegies	1.14.46	
LENDES			
Venus to mockt men lendes a sencelesse eare.	Ovid's Elegies	1.8.86	
LENGTH			
What length or bredth shal this brave towne containe?	Dido	5.1.16	Achat
And now at length am growne your Governor,	Jew	5.2.70	Barab
And at the length in Pampelonia crowne,	P 580	11.45	Pleshe
The way he cut, an English mile in length,	F 792	3.1.14	Faust
Which being not shakt <slackt>, I saw it die at length.	Ovid's Elegies	1.2.12	
Often at length, my wench depart, I bid,	Ovid's Elegies	2.18.5	
Victorious wreathes at length my Temples greete.	Ovid's Elegies	3.10.6	
Seeming not woon, yet woon she was at length,	Hero and Leander	2.295	
LENGTHENED			
But since my life is lengthened yet a while,	2Tamb	2.4.71	Zenoc
LENGTHNED			
Five yeeres I lengthned thy commaund in France:	Lucan, First Booke	277	
LENITIE			
And be reclaim'd with princely lenitie.	1Tamb	2.2.38	Meandr
LENITY			
With happy looks of ruthe and lenity.	1Tamb	5.1.59	2Virgn
LENTE			
O lente lente currite noctis equi:	F1935	5.2.139	Faust
LEOPARDS			
And cloathed in a spotted Leopards skin.	Dido	1.1.186	Venus
LEP			
Mov'd by Loves force, unto ech other lep?	Hero and Leander	2.58	
LEPROSIE			
And the white leprosie.	Jew	2.3.54	Barab
LEPT			
Moved with her voyce, I lept into the sea,	Dido	2.1.283	Aeneas
LERNA			
Or winged snakes of Lerna cast your stings,	1Tamb	4.4.21	Bajzth
LERNA'S			
In few, the blood of Hydra, Lerna's bane;	Jew	3.4.100	Barab
LESBIA			
Nor Lesbia, nor Corrinna had bene nam'd,	2Tamb	2.4.93	Tamb
LESS			
And [less] <least> thou yeeld to this that I intreat,	Jew	3.4.37	Barab
LESSE			
Ile follow thee with outcryes nere the lesse,	Dido	4.2.55	Anna
Am I lesse faire then when thou sawest me first?	Dido	5.1.115	Dido
Had I a sonne by thee, the griefe were lesse,	Dido	5.1.149	Dido
More honor and lesse paine it may procure,	1Tamb	3.2.97	Agidas
From Trebizon in Asia the lesse,	2Tamb	3.5.40	Trebiz
Being distant lesse than ful a hundred leagues,	2Tamb	5.3.133	Tamb
Why I esteeme the injury farre lesse,	Jew	1.2.146	Barab
a factious lord/Shall hardly do himselfe good, much lesse us,	Edw	2.1.7	Spencr
all at one time, but in some years we have more, in some lesse?	F 616	2.2.65 P	Faust
Caesars renowne for war was lesse, he restles,	Lucan, First Booke	145	
Roome may be won/With farre lesse toile, and yet the honors	Lucan, First Booke	284	
Two tane away, thy labor will be lesse:	Ovid's Elegies	1.1.4	
Yet he harm'd lesse, whom I profess'd to love,	Ovid's Elegies	1.7.33	
Many to rob is more sure, and lesse hatefull,	Ovid's Elegies	1.8.55	
Hence luck-lesse tables, funerall wood be flying/And thou the	Ovid's Elegies	1.12.7	
And what lesse labour then to hold thy peace?	Ovid's Elegies	2.2.28	
But in lesse compasse her small fingers knit.	Ovid's Elegies	2.15.20	
What doest? thy wagon in lesse compasse bring.	Ovid's Elegies	3.2.70	
Nor lesse at mans prosperity any grudge.	Ovid's Elegies	3.9.6	
Yet this is lesse, then if he had seene me,	Ovid's Elegies	3.10.15	
Or lesse faire, or lesse lewd would thou mightst bee,	Ovid's Elegies	3.10.41	
blazon foorth the loves of men,/Much lesse of powerfull gods.	Hero and Leander	1.71	
Lesse sinnes the poore rich man that starves himselfe,	Hero and Leander	1.243	
Much lesse can honour bee ascrib'd thereto,	Hero and Leander	1.279	
LESSER			
Might be of lesser force, and with the power/That he intendeth	Edw	2.4.43	Queene
The lesser stars/Which wont to run their course through empty	Lucan, First Booke	533	
LESSONS			
No doubt, such lessons they will teach the rest,	Edw	3.1.21	Spencr
Reduce we all our lessons unto this,	Edw	4.7.110	Baldck
LEST			
Leave to lament lest they laugh at our feares.	Dido	2.1.38	Achat
Lest you be mov'd too much with my sad tale.	Dido	2.1.125	Aeneas
Lest she imagine thou art Venus sonne:	Dido	3.1.4	Cupid
Lest their grosse eye-beames taint my lovers cheekes:	Dido	3.1.74	Dido
Lest with these sweete thoughts I melt cleane away.	Dido	3.1.76	Dido
Lest I be made a wonder to the world.	Dido	3.1.96	Dido
Yet lest he should, for I am full of feare,	Dido	4.4.108	Dido
Lest Dido spying him keepe him for a pledge.	Dido	5.1.50	Aeneas
before your mother/Lest she mistrust the match that is in hand:	Jew	2.3.147	Barab
Let's hence, lest further mischiefe be pretended.	Jew	5.5.96	Calym
Lest Faustus make your shaven crownes to bleed.	F1007	3.2.27	Faust
Lest greater dangers <danger> do attend thy drift.	F1752	5.1.79	Mephst
LET (Homograph; See also LETTS)			
And will not let us lodge upon the sands:	Dido	1.2.35	Serg
He [names] <meanes> Aeneas, let us kisse his feete.	Dido	2.1.51	Illion

LET (cont.)

May it please your grace to let Aeneas waite:	Dido	2.1.87	Aeneas
Here let him sit, be merrie lovely child.	Dido	2.1.93	Dido
Began to crye, let us unto our ships,	Dido	2.1.127	Aeneas
O let me live, great Neoptolemus.	Dido	2.1.239	Aeneas
And I alas, was forst to let her lye.	Dido	2.1.279	Aeneas
Come let us thinke upon some pleasing sport,	Dido	2.1.302	Dido
Sit in my lap and let me heare thee sing.	Dido	3.1.25	Dido
Will Dido let me hang about her necke?	Dido	3.1.30	Cupid
Come Dido, leave Ascanius, let us walke.	Dido	3.1.34	Iarbus
Then pull out both mine eyes, or let me dye.	Dido	3.1.55	Iarbus
And let Achates saile to Italy:	Dido	3.1.115	Dido
But playd he nere so sweet, I let him goe:	Dido	3.1.160	Dido
And feede infection with his [let] <left> out life:	Dido	3.2.11	Juno
And Venus, let there be a match confirmd/Betwixt these two,	Dido	3.2.77	Juno
Come Dido, let us hasten to the towne,	Dido	4.1.26	Aeneas
Let my Phenissa graunt, and then I goe:	Dido	4.3.6	Aeneas
And let me linke [thy] <my> bodie to my <thy> lips,	Dido	4.3.28	Aeneas
Why, let us build a Citie of our owne,	Dido	4.3.37	Illion
And not let Dido understand their drift:	Dido	4.4.6	Dido
Then let Aeneas goe abourd with us.	Dido	4.4.23	Achat
O keepe them still, and let me gaze my fill:	Dido	4.4.44	Dido
let him ride/As Didos husband through the Punicke streetes,	Dido	4.4.66	Dido
And let rich Carthage fleete upon the seas,	Dido	4.4.134	Dido
Now let him hang my favours on his masts,	Dido	4.4.159	Dido
For tackling, let him take the chaines of gold,	Dido	4.4.161	Dido
In steed of oares, let him use his hands,	Dido	4.4.163	Dido
Let it be term'd Aenea by your name.	Dido	5.1.20	Cloan
Let some of those thy followers goe with me,	Dido	5.1.73	Iarbus
Then let me goe and never say farewell?	Dido	5.1.109	Aeneas
Let me goe, farewell, I must from hence,	Dido	5.1.110	Dido
Then let me goe, and never say farewell?	Dido	5.1.124	Dido
Thou for some pettie guift hast let him goe,	Dido	5.1.218	Dido
Iarbus, talke not of Aeneas, let him goe,	Dido	5.1.283	Dido
So, leave me now, let none approach this place.	Dido	5.1.291	Dido
And from mine ashes let a Conquerour rise,	Dido	5.1.306	Dido
Nay, pray you let him stay, a greater [task]/Fits Menaphon, than	1Tamb	1.1.87	Cosroe
And Jove may never let me longer live,	1Tamb	1.1.170	Cosroe
Come lady, let not this appal your thoughts.	1Tamb	1.2.1	Tamb
Come let us meet them at the mountain foot,	1Tamb	1.2.133	Usumc
Come let us martch.	1Tamb	1.2.136	Techel
Come my Meander, let us to this geere,	1Tamb	2.2.1	Mycet
Least if we let them lynger here a while,	1Tamb	2.2.20	Meandr
And let my Fortunes and my valour sway,	1Tamb	2.3.11	Tamb
No, I meane, I let you keep it.	1Tamb	2.4.35	Mycet
And let them know the Persean King is chang'd:	1Tamb	2.5.21	Cosroe
Let us put on our meet incountring mindes,	1Tamb	2.6.19	Ortyg
Let not a man so vile and barbarous,	1Tamb	3.2.26	Agidas
But let the yong Arabian live in hope,	1Tamb	3.2.57	Agidas
And let Agidas by Agidas die,	1Tamb	3.2.105	Agidas
Let us afford him now the bearing hence.	1Tamb	3.2.111	Usumc
Let him bring millions infinite of men,	1Tamb	3.3.33	Usumc
Leave words and let them feele your lances pointes,	1Tamb	3.3.91	Argier
Let thousands die, their slaughtered Carkasses/Shall serve for	1Tamb	3.3.138	Bajzth
But come my Lords, to weapons let us fall.	1Tamb	3.3.162	Tamb
let us glut our swords/That thirst to drinke the feble Perseans	1Tamb	3.3.164	Bajzth
Yet somtimes let your highnesse send for them/To do the work my	1Tamb	3.3.187	Anippe
And let his foes like flockes of fearfull Roes,	1Tamb	3.3.192	Zenoc
Now let me offer to my gracious Lord,	1Tamb	3.3.218	Zenoc
The Turkesse let my Loves maid lead away.	1Tamb	3.3.267	Tamb
Let him take all th'advantages he can,	1Tamb	4.1.40	Souldn
And let the majestie of heaven beholde/Their Scourge and	1Tamb	4.2.31	Tamb
Let these be warnings for you then my slave,	1Tamb	4.2.72	Anippe
Let us unite our royall bandes in one,	1Tamb	4.3.17	Souldn
Let griefe and furie hasten on revenge,	1Tamb	4.3.43	Arabia
Let Tamburlaine for his offences feele/Such plagues as heaven	1Tamb	4.3.44	Arabia
let your sounding Drummes/Direct our Souldiers to Damascus	1Tamb	4.3.61	Souldn
Then let us freely banquet and carouse/Full bowles of wine unto	1Tamb	4.4.5	Tamb
To let them see (divine Zenocrate)/I glorie in the curses of my	1Tamb	4.4.28	Tamb
But if his highnesse would let them be fed, it would doe them	1Tamb	4.4.34	P Therid
O let him alone:	1Tamb	4.4.40	P Tamb
Tis like he wil, when he cannot let it.	1Tamb	4.4.53	P Techel
Let us live in spite of them, looking some happie power will	1Tamb	4.4.99	P Zabina
Let us have hope that their unspotted praiers,	1Tamb	5.1.20	Govnr
Bring him forth, and let us know if the towne be ransackt.	1Tamb	5.1.194	P Tamb
But let us save the reverend Souldans life,	1Tamb	5.1.204	Therid
Here let him stay my maysters from the tents,	1Tamb	5.1.211	Tamb
Let all the swords and Lances in the field,	1Tamb	5.1.225	Zabina
At every pore let blood comme dropping foorth,	1Tamb	5.1.227	Zabina
and let the Feends infernall view/As are the blasted banks of	1Tamb	5.1.242	Zabina
Let ugly darknesse with her rusty coach/Engyrt with tempests	1Tamb	5.1.294	Bajzth
And let her horses from their nostrels breathe/Rebellious winds	1Tamb	5.1.297	Bajzth
Then let the stony dart of sencelesse colde,	1Tamb	5.1.302	Bajzth
Let the souldiers be buried.	1Tamb	5.1.316	P Zabina
And let them die a death so barbarous.	1Tamb	5.1.351	Zenoc
And let not conquest ruthlesly pursewde/Be equally against his	1Tamb	5.1.366	Zenoc
And let Zenocrates faire eies beholde/That as for her thou	1Tamb	5.1.408	Arabia
Then let me find no further time to grace/Her princely Temples	1Tamb	5.1.488	Tamb
Then let us set the crowne upon her head,	1Tamb	5.1.501	Therid
King of Natolia, let us treat of peace,	2Tamb	1.1.13	Gazell
let peace be ratified/On these conditions specified before,	2Tamb	1.1.124	Orcan
Come let us goe and banquet in our tents:	2Tamb	1.1.160	Orcan
but tel me my Lord, if I should let you goe,	2Tamb	1.2.61	P Callap

LET (cont.)

Thanks gentle Almeda, then let us haste,	2Tamb	1.2.74	Callap
Least time be past, and lingring let us both.	2Tamb	1.2.75	Callap
Let me accompany my gratious mother,	2Tamb	1.3.66	Calyph
But now my friends, let me examine ye,	2Tamb	1.3.172	Tamb
And therefore let them rest a while my Lord.	2Tamb	1.3.184	Usumc
Come let us banquet and carrouse the whiles.	2Tamb	1.3.225	Tamb
To armes my Lords, on Christ still let us crie,	2Tamb	2.2.63	Orcan
Let the dishonor of the paines I feele,	2Tamb	2.3.5	Sgsmnd
And let this death wherein to sinne I die,	2Tamb	2.3.8	Sgsmnd
let us haste and meete/Our Army and our brother of Jerusalem,	2Tamb	2.3.42	Orcan
Of Greekish wine now let us celebrate/Our happy conquest,	2Tamb	2.3.46	Orcan
Then let some holy trance convay my thoughts,	2Tamb	2.4.34	Tamb
Live still my Lord, O let my soveraigne live,	2Tamb	2.4.57	Zenoc
And sooner let the fiery Element/Dissolve, and make your	2Tamb	2.4.58	Zenoc
But let me die my Love, yet let me die,	2Tamb	2.4.66	Zenoc
With love and patience let your true love die,	2Tamb	2.4.67	Zenoc
Yet let me kisse my Lord before I die,	2Tamb	2.4.69	Zenoc
And let me die with kissing of my Lord.	2Tamb	2.4.70	Zenoc
Let me take leave of these my loving sonnes,	2Tamb	2.4.72	Zenoc
Though she be dead, yet let me think she lives,	2Tamb	2.4.127	Tamb
And let the burning of Larissa wals,	2Tamb	3.2.141	Tamb
Usumcasane now come let us martch/Towards Techelles and	2Tamb	3.2.145	Tamb
Then let us see if coward Calapine/Dare levie armes against our	2Tamb	3.2.155	Tamb
Then let us bring our light Artilery,	2Tamb	3.3.5	Techel
and let us haste from hence/Along the cave that leads beyond	2Tamb	3.4.1	Olymp
And let the end of this my fatall journey,	2Tamb	3.4.81	Olymp
Souldiers now let us meet the Generall,	2Tamb	3.4.85	Therid
Come puissant Viceroies, let us to the field,	2Tamb	3.5.53	Callap
Good my Lord, let me take it.	2Tamb	3.5.133	P Almeda
let him hang a bunch of keies on his standerd, to put him in	2Tamb	3.5.139	P Tamb
Away, let us to the field, that the villaine may be slaine.	2Tamb	3.5.143	P Trebiz
would let me be put in the front of such a battaile once,	2Tamb	4.1.72	P Calyph
Shal we let goe these kings again my Lord/To gather greater	2Tamb	4.1.82	Amyras
Let al of us intreat your highnesse pardon.	2Tamb	4.1.98	Tec&Us
Good my Lord, let him be forgiven for once,	2Tamb	4.1.101	Amyras
And let your hates extended in his paines,	2Tamb	4.1.172	Orcan
Let this invention be the instrument.	2Tamb	4.2.13	Olymp
Let me have coach my Lord, that I may ride,	2Tamb	4.3.27	Amyras
And let them equally serve all your turnes.	2Tamb	4.3.73	Tamb
Let them take pleasure soundly in their spoiles,	2Tamb	4.3.92	Tamb
Let us not be idle then my Lord,	2Tamb	4.3.95	Techel
And let my souldiers shoot the slave to death.	2Tamb	5.1.109	Tamb
Away with him hence, let him speake no more:	2Tamb	5.1.125	Tamb
Unharnesse them, and let me have fresh horse:	2Tamb	5.1.130	Tamb
First let thy Scythyan horse teare both our limmes/Rather then	2Tamb	5.1.138	Orcan
Bridle them, and let me to my coach.	2Tamb	5.1.148	Tamb
and let this wound appease/The mortall furie of great	2Tamb	5.1.153	Govnr
Wel said, let there be a fire presently.	2Tamb	5.1.178	Tamb
I, good my Lord, let us in hast to Persea,	2Tamb	5.1.214	Therid
And let this Captaine be remoov'd the walles,	2Tamb	5.1.215	Therid
Let it be so, about it souldiers:	2Tamb	5.1.217	Tamb
let us lie in wait for him/And if we find him absent from his	2Tamb	5.2.56	Callap
And let no basenesse in thy haughty breast,	2Tamb	5.3.30	Usumc
Come let us march against the powers of heaven,	2Tamb	5.3.48	Tamb
Come let us chardge our speares and pierce his breast,	2Tamb	5.3.58	Tamb
Techelles let us march,/And weary Death with bearing soules to	2Tamb	5.3.76	Tamb
then let me see how much/Is left for me to conquer all the	2Tamb	5.3.123	Tamb
That let your lives commaund in spight of death.	2Tamb	5.3.160	Tamb
let me see how well/Thou wilt become thy fathers majestie.	2Tamb	5.3.183	Tamb
Let not thy love exceed thyne honor sonne,	2Tamb	5.3.199	Tamb
Let it be plac'd by this my fatall chaire,	2Tamb	5.3.211	Tamb
Then let some God oppose his holy power,	2Tamb	5.3.220	Techel
Meet heaven and earth, and here let al things end,	2Tamb	5.3.249	Amyras
Let earth and heaven his timelesse death deplore,	2Tamb	5.3.252	Amyras
And let them know that I am Machevill,	Jew	Prol.7	Machvl
Let me be envy'd and not pittied!	Jew	Prol.27	Machvl
And let him not be entertain'd the worse/Because he favours me.	Jew	Prol.34	Machvl
Come therefore let us goe to Barrabas;	Jew	1.1.141	2Jew
Why let 'em come, so they come not to warre;	Jew	1.1.150	Barab
Or let 'em warre, so we be conquerors:	Jew	1.1.151	Barab
Nay let 'em combat, conquer, and kill all,	Jew	1.1.152	Barab
like enough, why then let every man/Provide him, and be there	Jew	1.1.170	Barab
I know you will; well brethren let us goe.	Jew	1.1.174	1Jew
The Turkes have let increase to such a summe,	Jew	1.1.182	Barab
Why let 'em enter, let 'em take the Towne.	Jew	1.1.190	Barab
Stand all aside, and let the Knights determine,	Jew	1.2.14	Calym
Your Lordship shall doe well to let them have it.	Jew	1.2.44	Barab
Then let the rich increase your portions.	Jew	1.2.58	Govnr
Then let them with us contribute.	Jew	1.2.61	2Knght
Let me be us'd but as my brethren are.	Jew	1.2.91	Barab
let us in, and gather of these goods/The mony for this tribute	Jew	1.2.155	Govnr
I, let me sorrow for this sudden chance,	Jew	1.2.206	Barab
Come, let us leave him in his irefull mood,	Jew	1.2.209	1Jew
Let 'em suspect, but be thou so precise/As they may thinke it	Jew	1.2.284	Barab
Let us intreat she may be entertain'd.	Jew	1.2.329	2Fryar
First let me as a Novice learne to frame/My solitary life to	Jew	1.2.331	Abigal
And let me lodge where I was wont to lye.	Jew	1.2.333	Abigal
Yet let thy daughter be no longer blinde.	Jew	1.2.354	1Fryar
night; or let the day/Turne to eternall darkenesse after this:	Jew	2.1.15	Barab
To shun suspition, therefore, let us part.	Jew	2.1.57	Abigal
This is the Market-place, here let 'em stand:	Jew	2.3.1	1Offcr
Is it square or pointed, pray let me know.	Jew	2.3.59	Lodowk

LET (cont.)

Let me see, sirra, are you not an old shaver?	Jew	2.3.114	P Barab
you in these chops; let me see one that's somewhat leaner.	Jew	2.3.125	P Barab
Yonder comes Don Mathias, let us stay;	Jew	2.3.140	Barab
Now let me know thy name, and therewithall/Thy birth, .	Jew	2.3.163	Barab
Well, let it passe, another time shall serve. . . .	Jew	2.3.278	Mthias
And mine you have, yet let me talke to her; . . .	Jew	2.3.300	Barab
let him have thy hand,/But keepe thy heart till Don Mathias	Jew	2.3.306	Barab
Stay her,--but let her not speake one word more. . .	Jew	2.3.323	Barab
But rather let the brightsome heavens be dim, . . .	Jew	2.3.330	Lodowk
Well, let him goe.	Jew	2.3.336	Lodowk
and let them be interr'd/Within one sacred monument of stone;	Jew	3.2.29	Govnr
Then of true griefe let us take equall share. . . .	Jew	3.2.37	Govnr
Well, Ithimore, let me request thee this, ...	Jew	3.3.26	Abigal
Oh therefore, Jacomo, let me be one, ...	Jew	3.3.68	Abigal
But let 'em goe:	Jew	3.4.28	Barab
Stay, let me spice it first.	Jew	3.4.85	Barab
Pray doe, and let me help you, master.	Jew	3.4.86	P Ithimr
Pray let me taste first.	Jew	3.4.86	P Ithimr
Stay, first let me stirre it Ithimore.	Jew	3.4.95	Barab
And with her let it worke like Borgias wine, . . .	Jew	3.4.98	Barab
Good master let me poyson all the Monks.	Jew	4.1.14	Ithimr
You know my mind, let me alone with him.	Jew	4.1.100	Barab
Why does he goe to thy house? let him begone. . . .	Jew	4.1.101	1Fryar
so, let him leane upon his staffe; excellent, he stands as if he	Jew	4.1.153	P Ithimr
Away, I'de wish thee, and let me goe by:	Jew	4.1.170	1Fryar
No, let us beare him to the Magistrates.	Jew	4.1.183	Ithimr
Good Barabas let me goe.	Jew	4.1.184	1Fryar
Let me alone, doe but you speake him faire:	Jew	4.2.63	Pilia
Let me alone, I'le use him in his kinde.	Jew	4.2.80	Pilia
Love me little, love me long, let musicke rumble, . .	Jew	4.4.28	Ithimr
Let me alone to urge it now I know the meaning. . .	Jew	4.4.79	Pilia
Make fires, heat irons, let the racke be fetch'd. . .	Jew	5.1.24	Govnr
And he my bondman, let me have law, ...	Jew	5.1.38	Barab
Since they are dead, let them be buried.	Jew	5.1.57	Govnr
And if it be not true, then let me dye.	Jew	5.1.96	Barab
Away, no more, let him not trouble me.	Jew	5.2.26	Barab
And let me see what mony thou canst make;	Jew	5.2.94	Barab
And now, bold Bashawes, let us to our Tents, . . .	Jew	5.3.43	Calym
Let us salute him. Save thee, Barabas.	Jew	5.5.54	Calym
We will not let thee part so suddenly:	Jew	5.5.98	Govnr
Besides, if we should let thee goe, all's one, . . .	Jew	5.5.99	Govnr
Nay rather, Christians, let me goe to Turkey, . . .	Jew	5.5.115	Calym
away, and let due praise be given/Neither to Fate nor Fortune,	Jew	5.5.123	Govnr
Well Madam, let that rest:	P 17	1.17	Charls
Let us goe to honor this solemnitie.	P 25	1.25	Charls
Let not this heavy chaunce my dearest Lord, ...	P 191	3.26	QnMarg
Come my Lords let us beare her body hence.	P 195	3.30	Admral
betraide, come my Lords, and let us goe tell the King of this.	P 199	3.34	P Navrre
I let the Admirall be first dispatcht.	P 283	5.10	Retes
In lucky time, come let us keep this lane, ...	P 298	5.25	Anjoy
O let me pray before I dye.	P 301	5.28	Admral
And now my Lords let us closely to our busines. . .	P 332	5.59	Guise
Let none escape, murder the Hugonets.	P 337	5.64	Guise
Stay my Lord, let me begin the psalme.	P 344	5.71	Anjoy
O let me pray before I take my death.	P 352	6.7	Seroun
O let me pray unto my God.	P 359	6.14	Seroun
O let him goe, he is a catholick.	P 375	7.15	Retes
O good my Lord, let me but speak a word.	P 399	7.39	Ramus
For that let me alone, Cousin stay you heer, . . .	P 428	7.68	Anjoy
Come let us goe tell the King.	P 440	7.80	Condy
And now sirs for this night let our fury stay. . . .	P 443	7.83	Guise
Why let us burne him for an heretick.	P 483	9.2	P 2Atndt
Doe so sweet Guise, let us delay no time, ...	P 505	9.24	QnMoth
I, but my Lord let me alone for that, ...	P 519	9.38	QnMoth
Come my Lord [let] <lets> us goe.	P 527	9.46	QnMoth
Tue, tue, tue, let none escape:	P 534	10.7	Guise
O let me stay and rest me heer a while, ...	P 536	11.1	Charls
Come let us take his body hence.	P 564	11.29	QnMoth
Tush man, let me alone with him, ...	P 648	12.61	QnMoth
Come my [Lord] <Lords>, let us goe seek the Guise, . .	P 655	12.68	QnMoth
I pray thee let me see.	P 674	13.18	Guise
In Gods name, let them come.	P 728	14.31	Navrre
But come my Lords, let us away with speed, ...	P 741	14.44	Navrre
Let us away with triumph to our tents.	P 805	16.19	Navrre
Well, let me alone, whose within there?	P 881	17.76	King
First let us set our hand and seale to this, ...	P 890	17.85	King
And let them march away to France amaine:	P 917	18.18	Navrre
Let us alone, I warrant you.	P 939	19.9	P 1Mur
Let him come in.	P 961	19.31	King
Let mean consaits, and baser men feare death, . . .	P 997	19.67	Guise
Let Christian princes that shall heare of this, . . .	P1041	19.111	King
And let her droup, my heart is light enough. . . .	P1064	19.134	King
And let her greeve her heart out if she will. . . .	P1080	19.150	King
Come let us away and leavy men, ...	P1127	21.21	Dumain
Tush my Lord, let me alone for that.	P1136	21.30	P Frier
Let him come in.	P1158	22.20	King
O my Lord, let him live a while.	P1173	22.35	Eprnon
No, let the villaine dye, and feele in hell, ...	P1174	22.36	King
Ah, had your highnes let him live, ...	P1183	22.45	Eprnon
Pleaseth your grace to let the Surgeon search your wound.	P1191	22.53	Navrre
Now let the house of Bourbon weare the crowne, . . .	P1232	22.94	King
The king, upon whose bosome let me die, ...	Edw	1.1.14	Gavstn

LET (cont.)

Let me see, thou wouldst do well/To waite at my trencher, and	Edw	1.1.30	Gavstn
Brother revenge it, and let these their heads,	Edw	1.1.117	Kent
Come unckle, let us leave the brainsick king,	Edw	1.1.125	Mortmr
Now let the treacherous Mortimers conspire,	Edw	1.1.149	Edward
Let him complaine unto the sea of hell,	Edw	1.1.191	Gavstn
Wel, let that peevish Frenchman guard him sure,	Edw	1.2.7	Mortmr
Then let him stay, for rather then my lord/Shall be opprest by	Edw	1.2.64	Queene
And let him frollick with his minion.	Edw	1.2.67	Queene
Are gone towards Lambeth, there let them remaine.	Edw	1.3.5	Gavstn
We know our duties, let him know his peeres.	Edw	1.4.23	Warwck
My lords, now let us all be resolute,	Edw	1.4.45	Mortmr
For shame subscribe, and let the lowne depart.	Edw	1.4.82	Warwck
Here take my picture, and let me weare thine,	Edw	1.4.127	Edward
Therefore with dum imbracement let us part.	Edw	1.4.134	Edward
Speake not unto her, let her droope and pine.	Edw	1.4.162	Edward
O Lancaster, let him diswade the king,	Edw	1.4.216	Queene
Then speake not for him, let the pesant go.	Edw	1.4.218	Warwck
Then let her live abandond and forlorne.	Edw	1.4.298	Queene
about my neck/Then these my lord, nor let me have more wealth,	Edw	1.4.331	Queene
Once more receive my hand, and let this be,	Edw	1.4.334	Edward
Even so let hatred with thy [soveraignes] <soveraigne> smile.	Edw	1.4.342	Edward
Now let us in, and feast it roiallie:	Edw	1.4.374	Edward
Let him without controulement have his will.	Edw	1.4.390	MortSr
Then let his grace, whose youth is flexible,	Edw	1.4.398	MortSr
Prethee let me know it.	Edw	2.2.14	Edward
And therefore let us jointlie here protest,	Edw	2.2.104	Lncstr
And let their lives bloud slake thy furies hunger:	Edw	2.2.205	Edward
Now let them thanke themselves, and rue too late.	Edw	2.2.207	Edward
But let them go, and tell me what are these.	Edw	2.2.239	Edward
For my sake let him waite upon your grace,	Edw	2.2.250	Gavstn
Let us with these our followers scale the walles,	Edw	2.3.18	Lncstr
No, here he comes, now let them spoile and kill:	Edw	2.4.3	Edward
Weele send his head by thee, let him bestow/His teares on that,	Edw	2.5.52	Mortmr
him, but must we now/Leave him on had-I-wist, and let him go?	Edw	2.5.85	Warwck
Why I say, let him go on Penbrookes word.	Edw	2.5.90	Lncstr
Come, let thy shadow parley with king Edward.	Edw	2.6.14	Warwck
Strike off their heads, and let them preach on poles,	Edw	3.1.20	Spencr
Let them not unrevengd murther your friends,	Edw	3.1.125	Spencr
And there let him bee,	Edw	3.1.197	Lncstr
I pray let us see it, what have we there?	Edw	4.3.10	Edward
Sound trumpets my lord and forward let us martch,	Edw	4.4.28	SrJohn
To let us take our farewell of his grace.	Edw	4.7.69	Spencr
Let Plutos bels ring out my fatall knell,	Edw	4.7.89	Edward
But stay a while, let me be king till night,	Edw	5.1.59	Edward
Let never silent night possesse this clime,	Edw	5.1.65	Edward
And therefore let me weare it yet a while.	Edw	5.1.83	Edward
If he be not, let him choose.	Edw	5.1.95	BshpWn
Or if I live, let me forget my selfe.	Edw	5.1.111	Edward
Let not that Mortimer protect my sonne,	Edw	5.1.115	Edward
And then let me alone to handle him.	Edw	5.2.22	Mortmr
Then let some other be his guardian.	Edw	5.2.36	Queene
Let me alone, here is the privie seale,	Edw	5.2.37	Mortmr
and in any case/Let no man comfort him, if he chaunce to weepe,	Edw	5.2.64	Mortmr
Let him be king, I am too yong to raigne.	Edw	5.2.93	Prince
Let me but see him first, and then I will.	Edw	5.2.95	Prince
Souldiers, let me but talke to him one worde.	Edw	5.3.53	Kent
Feard am I more then lov'd, let me be feard,	Edw	5.4.52	Mortmr
My lord, if you will let my unckle live,	Edw	5.4.99	King
Let me but stay and speake, I will not go,	Edw	5.4.105	Kent
Let us assaile his minde another while.	Edw	5.5.12	Matrvs
let him have the king,/What else?	Edw	5.5.24	Matrvs
And get me a spit, and let it be red hote.	Edw	5.5.30	Ltborn
And let me see the stroke before it comes,	Edw	5.5.76	Edward
Let this gift change thy minde, and save thy soule,	Edw	5.5.88	Edward
O let me not die yet, stay, O stay a while.	Edw	5.5.101	Edward
And therefore let us take horse and away.	Edw	5.5.115	Matrvs
Come let us cast the body in the mote,	Edw	5.5.118	Gurney
Betray us both, therefore let me flie.	Edw	5.6.8	Matrvs
And let these teares distilling from mine eyes,	Edw	5.6.101	King
Valdes, first let him know the words of Art,	F 185	1.1.157	Cornel
But come, let us go, and informe the Rector:	F 225	1.2.32	2Schol
Yet let us see <trie> what we can do.	F 228	1.2.35	2Schol
let your right eye be alwaies Diametrally fixt upon my left	F 386	1.4.44	P Wagner
And let it be propitious for my wish.	F 447	2.1.59	Faust
And let thee see <shewe thee> what Magicke can performe.	F 474	2.1.86	Mephst
<off> this, let me have a wife, the fairest Maid in Germany,	F 529	2.1.141	P Faust
[Nay let me have one booke more, and then I have done, wherein	F 551.8	2.1.171A	P Faust
Come Mephostophilis let us dispute againe,	F 584	2.2.33	Faust
let me be carried thither againe by Gluttony and Letchery	F 705.2	2.2.156A	P Sloth
matters in hand, let the horses walk themselves and they will.	F 727	2.3.6	P Robin
Whilst I am here on earth let me be cloyd/With all things that	F 837	3.1.59	Faust
Then in this shew let me an Actor be,	F 854	3.1.76	Faust
Let it be so my Faustus, but first stay,	F 856	3.1.78	Mephst
Pope Adrian let me have some right of Law,	F 904	3.1.126	Bruno
Let us salute his reverend Father-hood.	F 944	3.1.166	Faust
'Tis no matter, let him come; an he follow us, I'le so conjure	F1091	3.3.4	P Robin
let me see the cup.	F1093	3.3.6	P Robin
Come on sirra, let me search you now.	F1104	3.3.17	P Vintnr
let me have the carrying of him about to shew some trickes.	F1128	3.3.41	P Robin
let the Maids looke well to their porridge-pots, for I'le into	F1133	3.3.46	P Robin
But in dumbe silence let them come and goe.	F1252	4.1.98	Faust
To satisfie my longing thoughts at full,/Let me this tell thee:	F1265	4.1.111	Emper

LET (cont.)

A plague upcn you, let me sleepe a while.	F1283	4.1.129		Benvol
in your head for shame, let not all the world wonder at you.	F1291	4.1.137	P	Faust
Let me intreate you to remove his hornes,	F1309	4.1.155		Emper
let us sway thy thoughts/From this attempt against the	F1325	4.2.1		Mrtino
Shall I let slip so great an injury,	F1328	4.2.4		Benvol
and let them hang/Within the window where he yoak'd me first,	F1380	4.2.56		Benvol
I do beseech your grace let them come in,	F1605	4.6.48		Faust
as to let us see that peerelesse dame of Greece, whom all the	F1685	5.1.12	P	1Schol
[Let us depart], and for this blessed sight <glorious deed>	F1704	5.1.31		1Schol
my exhortation/Seemes harsh, and all unpleasant; let it not,	F1718	5.1.45		OldMan
One thing gcod servant let me crave of thee,	F1759	5.1.86		Faust
but let us into the next roome, and [there] pray for him.	F1871	5.2.75	P	1Schol
Now Faustus let thine eyes with horror stare/Into that vaste	F1909	5.2.113		BdAngl
or let this houre be but/A yeare, a month, a weeke, a naturall	F1932	5.2.136		Faust
<But let my soule mount and> ascend to heaven.	F1956	(HC271)B		Faust
Let Faustus live in hell a thousand yeares,	F1961	5.2.165		Faust
Adders and serpents, let me breathe a while:	F1980	5.2.184		Faust
Come Gentlemen, let us go visit Faustus,	F1983	5.3.1		1Schol
Let your Balio and your Belcher come here, and Ile knocke them,	F App	p.230 45	P	Clown
let it be in the likenesse of a little pretie frisking flea,	F App	p.231 61	P	Clown
O Lord I pray sir, let Banio and Belcher go sleepe.	F App	p.231 68	P	Clown
and let thy left eye be diametarily fixt upon my right heele,	F App	p.231 69	P	Wagner
that thou let me see some proofe of thy skil, that mine eies	F App	p.236 6	P	Emper
Go to maister Doctor, let me see them presently.	F App	p.237 50	P	Emper
Therefore sweet Mephastophilis, let us make haste to Wertenberge	F App	p.239 94		Faust
I pray you let him have him, he is an honest felow, and he has	F App	p.239 105	P	Mephst
O Lord sir, let me goe, and Ile give you fortie dollers more.	F App	p.241 158	P	HrsCsr
let us in, where you must wel reward this learned man for the	F App	p.243 28	P	Duke
At Munda let the dreadfull battailes joyne;	Lucan, First Booke	40		
let thy sword bring us home.	Lucan, First Booke	280		
Let come their [leader] <leaders whom long peace hath quail'd;	Lucan, First Booke	311		
Let all Lawes yeeld, sinne beare the name of vertue,	Lucan, First Booke	666		
Many a yeare these [furious] <firious> broiles let last,	Lucan, First Booke	667		
Let my first verse be sixe, my last five feete,	Ovid's Elegies	1.1.31		
let hir <he> that cought me late,/Either love, or cause that I	Ovid's Elegies	1.3.1		
I aske too much, would she but let me love hir,	Ovid's Elegies	1.3.3		
Nor let the windes away my warnings blowe.	Ovid's Elegies	1.4.12		
Let thy soft finger to thy eare be brought.	Ovid's Elegies	1.4.24		
Let not thy necke by his vile armes be prest,	Ovid's Elegies	1.4.35		
Thy bosomes Roseat buds let him not finger,	Ovid's Elegies	1.4.37		
Chiefely on thy lips let not his lips linger.	Ovid's Elegies	1.4.38		
And let the troupes which shall thy Chariot follow,	Ovid's Elegies	1.7.37		
Let the sad captive formost with lockes spred/On her white	Ovid's Elegies	1.7.39		
Let Homer yeeld to such as presents bring,	Ovid's Elegies	1.8.61		
Nor let the armes of antient [lines] <lives> beguile thee,	Ovid's Elegies	1.8.65		
Let him within heare bard out lovers prate.	Ovid's Elegies	1.8.78		
And let thine eyes constrained learne to weepe,	Ovid's Elegies	1.8.83		
Let them aske some-what, many asking little,	Ovid's Elegies	1.8.89		
On all the [bed mens] <beds men> tumbling let him viewe/And thy	Ovid's Elegies	1.8.97		
If he gives nothing, let him from thee wend.	Ovid's Elegies	1.8.100		
Let thy tongue flatter, while thy minde harme-workes:	Ovid's Elegies	1.8.103		
Nor let my words be with the windes hence blowne,	Ovid's Elegies	1.8.106		
Let him surcease: love tries wit best of all.	Ovid's Elegies	1.9.32		
He that will not growe slothfull let him love.	Ovid's Elegies	1.9.46		
Let poore men show their service, faith, and care;	Ovid's Elegies	1.10.57		
Be sedulous, let no stay cause thee tarry.	Ovid's Elegies	1.11.8		
Let her make verses, and some blotted letter/On the last edge	Ovid's Elegies	1.11.21		
Let this word, come, alone the tables fill.	Ovid's Elegies	1.11.24		
Let Kings give place to verse, and kingly showes,	Ovid's Elegies	1.15.33		
Let base conceited wits admire vilde things,	Ovid's Elegies	1.15.35		
And in sad lovers heads let me be found.	Ovid's Elegies	1.15.38		
Let Maydes whom hot desire to husbands leade,	Ovid's Elegies	2.1.5		
Let him goe forth knowne, that unknowne did enter,	Ovid's Elegies	2.2.20		
Let him goe see her though she doe not languish/And then report	Ovid's Elegies	2.2.21		
Let him please, haunt the house, be kindly usd,	Ovid's Elegies	2.2.29		
Enjoy the wench, let all else be refusd.	Ovid's Elegies	2.2.30		
And what she likes, let both hold ratifide.	Ovid's Elegies	2.2.32		
But yet sometimes to chide thee let her fall/Counterfet teares:	Ovid's Elegies	2.2.35		
But such kinde wenches let their lovers have.	Ovid's Elegies	2.5.26		
For wofull haires let piece-torne plumes abound,	Ovid's Elegies	2.6.5		
For long shrild trumpets let your notes resound.	Ovid's Elegies	2.6.6		
Thy tunes let this rare birdes sad funerall borrowe,	Ovid's Elegies	2.6.9		
Let me lie with thee browne Cypasse to day.	Ovid's Elegies	2.8.22		
But me let crafty damsells words deceive,	Ovid's Elegies	2.9.43		
Now let her flatter me, now chide me hard,	Ovid's Elegies	2.9.45		
Let [me] <her> enjoy [her] <me> oft, oft be debard.	Ovid's Elegies	2.9.46		
Let such as be mine enemies have none,	Ovid's Elegies	2.10.16		
Yea, let my foes sleepe in an emptie bed,	Ovid's Elegies	2.10.17		
And from my mistris bosome let me rise:	Ovid's Elegies	2.10.20		
Let one wench cloy me with sweete lcves delight,	Ovid's Elegies	2.10.21		
Let souldiour <souldiours> chase his <their> enemies amaine,	Ovid's Elegies	2.10.31		
Let marchants seeke wealth, [and] with perjured lips,	Ovid's Elegies	2.10.33		
Let others tell how winds fierce battailes wage,	Ovid's Elegies	2.11.17		
Let others tell this, and what each one speakes/Beleeve, no	Ovid's Elegies	2.11.21		
Let Nereus bend the waves unto this shore,	Ovid's Elegies	2.11.39		
Let the bright day-starre cause in heaven this day be,	Ovid's Elegies	2.11.55		
To have this skirmish fought, let it suffice thee.	Ovid's Elegies	2.13.28		
Fruites ripe will fall, let springing things increase,	Ovid's Elegies	2.14.25		
But in the ayre let these words come to nought,	Ovid's Elegies	2.14.41		
Be welcome to her, gladly let her take thee,	Ovid's Elegies	2.15.3		
And through the gemme let thy lost waters pash.	Ovid's Elegies	2.15.24		
Let her my faith with thee given understand.	Ovid's Elegies	2.15.28		

LET (cont.)

Upon the cold earth pensive let them lay,	Ovid's Elegies	2.16.15		
(Their reines let loose) right soone my house approach.	Ovid's Elegies	2.16.50		
Let me be slandered, while my fire she hides,	Ovid's Elegies	2.17.3		
Let us both lovers hope, and feare a like,	Ovid's Elegies	2.19.5		
And on thy thre-shold let me lie dispred,	Ovid's Elegies	2.19.21		
Her lover let her mocke, that long will raigne,	Ovid's Elegies	2.19.33		
Aye me, let not my warnings cause my paine.	Ovid's Elegies	2.19.34		
Let this care some-times bite thee to the quick,	Ovid's Elegies	2.19.43		
The maide to hide me in her bosome let not.	Ovid's Elegies	3.1.56		
let either heed/What please them, and their eyes let either	Ovid's Elegies	3.2.5		
either heed/What please them, and their eyes let either feede.	Ovid's Elegies	3.2.6		
Such chaunce let me have:	Ovid's Elegies	3.2.9		
Let us all conquer by our mistris favour.	Ovid's Elegies	3.2.18		
Now comes the pompe; themselves let all men cheere:	Ovid's Elegies	3.2.43		
Let my new mistris graunt to be beloved:	Ovid's Elegies	3.2.57		
Let with strong hand the reine to bend be made.	Ovid's Elegies	3.2.72		
When he perceivd the reines let slacke, he stayde,	Ovid's Elegies	3.4.15		
To kisse, I kisse, to lie with her shee let me.	Ovid's Elegies	3.6.48		
Not what we slouthfull [knowe] <knewe>, let wise men learne,	Ovid's Elegies	3.7.25		
Onely our loves let not such rich churles gaine,	Ovid's Elegies	3.7.59		
O let him change goods so ill got to dust.	Ovid's Elegies	3.7.66		
Let me, and them by it be aye be-friended.	Ovid's Elegies	3.12.36		
But let not mee poore soule know of thy straying.	Ovid's Elegies	3.13.2		
And let the world be witnesse of the same?	Ovid's Elegies	3.13.12		
And with your pastime let the bedsted creake,	Ovid's Elegies	3.13.26		
Deceive all, let me erre, and thinke I am right,	Ovid's Elegies	3.13.29		
Let it suffise,/That my slacke muse, sings of Leanders eies,	Hero and Leander	1.71		
The reason no man knowes, let it suffise,	Hero and Leander	1.173		
Faire creature, let me speake without offence,	Hero and Leander	1.199		
Her painted fanne of curled plumes let fall,	Hero and Leander	2.11		
Saying, let your vowes and promises be kept.	Hero and Leander	2.96		
O let mee viste Hero ere I die.	Hero and Leander	2.178		
And therefore let it rest upon thy pillow.	Hero and Leander	2.252		

LETCHERIE

letcherie (to love I would say) it were not for you to come	F 210	1.2.17	P	Wagner

LETCHERY

be carried thither againe by Gluttony and Letchery <Leachery>],	F 705.3	2.2.157A	P	Sloth
the first letter of my name begins with Letchery <leachery>.	F 710	2.2.162	P	Ltchry

LETHE

Compast with Lethe, Styx, and Phlegeton,	2Tamb	3.2.13		Tamb

LET'S

Let's cheere our souldiers to incounter him,	1Tamb	2.6.29		Cosroe
Let's take our leaves; Farewell good Barabas.	Jew	1.1.175		2Jew
Let's know their time, perhaps it is not long;	Jew	1.2.24		Calym
So will we fight it out; come, let's away:	Jew	2.2.52		Govnr
Thou hast thy Crownes, fellow, come let's away.	Jew	2.3.158		Mater
Looke not towards him, let's away:	Jew	3.1.24		Pilia
Hold, let's inquire the causers of their deaths,	Jew	3.2.27		Mater
And let's provide to welcome Calymath:	Jew	3.5.30		Govnr
Oh brother, all the Nuns are dead, let's bury them.	Jew	3.6.44		1Fryar
Come let's away.	Jew	3.6.52		2Fryar
God-a-mercy nose; come let's begone.	Jew	4.1.23		Ithimr
Come Ithimore, let's helpe to take him hence.	Jew	4.1.200		Barab
Come my deare love, let's in and sleepe together.	Jew	4.2.129		Curtzn
And fit it should: but first let's ha more gold.	Jew	4.4.26		Curtzn
A French Musician, come let's heare your skill?	Jew	4.4.30		Curtzn
The meaning has a meaning; come let's in:	Jew	4.4.80		Ithimr
Let's hence, lest further mischiefe be pretended.	Jew	5.5.96		Calym
brave, prethee let's to it presently, for I am as dry as a dog.	F 751	2.3.30	P	Dick
Come then let's away.	F 753	2.3.32	P	Robin
Come therefore, let's away.	F 830	3.1.52		Faust
Come brethren, let's about our businesse with good devotion.	F1076	3.2.96	P	1Frier
let's devise how we may adde more shame/To the blacke scandall	F1377	4.2.53		Fredrk
niggard of my cunning, come Mephastophilis, let's away to him.	F App	p.241 171	P	Faust

LETS (Homograph)

Aeneas, leave these dumpes and lets away,	Dido	3.3.60		Dido
Lets see what tempests can anoy me now.	Dido	4.4.60		Aeneas
Yes, my Lord, yes, come lets about it.	2Tamb	3.3.10		Soldrs
Lets away.	Jew	2.3.162		1Offcr
Come my Lords lets go to the Church and pray,	P 55	1.55		Navrre
Him will we--but first lets follow those in France,	P 153	2.96		Guise
And so lets forward to the Massacre.	P 330	5.57		Guise
Come then, lets away.	P 335	5.62		Guise
Then come my Lords, lets goe.	P 481	8.31		Anjoy
Lets throw him into the river.	P 487	9.6	P	1Atndt
all doubts, be rulde by me, lets hang him heere upon this tree.	P 491	9.10	P	2Atndt
But come lets walke aside, th'airs not very sweet.	P 497	9.16		QnMoth
Come my Lord [let] <lets> us goe.	P 527	9.46		QnMoth
Come Pleshe, lets away whilste time doth serve.	P 587	11.52		Navrre
Lets goe my Lords, our dinner staies for us.	P 630	12.43		King
come Epernoune/Lets goe seek the Duke and make them freends.	P 786	15.44		King
Come then lets away.	Edw	1.2.79		Lncstr
I passe not for their anger, come lets go.	Edw	1.4.142		Edward
Thankes gentle Warwick, come lets in and revell.	Edw	1.4.385		Edward
You know my minde, come unckle lets away.	Edw	1.4.424		Mortmr
Come Edmund lets away, and levie men,	Edw	2.2.98		Edward
Lets to our castels, for the king is moovde.	Edw	2.2.100		Warwck
Come lets away, and when the mariage ends,	Edw	2.2.264		Edward
Forslowe no time, sweet Lancaster lets march.	Edw	2.4.40		Warwck
Lets all aboord, and follow him amaine.	Edw	2.4.47		Mortmr
Give me my horse and lets r'enforce our troupes:	Edw	4.5.6		Edward
Lets see who dare impeache me for his death?	Edw	5.6.14		Mortmr

LETS (cont.)
Come brethren, lets about our businesse with good devotion. F App p.232 29 P Frier
This said, he laying aside all lets of war, Lucan, First Booke 206
Lets use our tried force, they that now thwart right/In wars Lucan, First Booke 349
Lets yeeld, a burden easly borne is light. Ovid's Elegies 1.2.10
And lets what both delight, what both desire, Ovid's Elegies 1.10.31
And now she lets him whisper in her eare, Hero and Leander 2.267

LETST
Why letst discordant hands to armour fall? Ovid's Elegies 3.7.48

LETT
thie folishe dreame/and lett thee see thie selfe my prysoner Paris ms33,p391 Guise

LETTER
And didst thou deliver my letter? Jew 4.2.3 P Curtzn
for at the reading of the letter, he look'd like a man of Jew 4.2.7 P Pilia
and he gave me a letter from one Madam Bellamira, saluting me Jew 4.2.29 P Ithimr
sweet youth; did not you, Sir, bring the sweet youth a letter? Jew 4.2.42 P Ithimr
At reading of the letter, he star'd and stamp'd, and turnd Jew 4.2.104 P Pilia
words, Sir, and send it you, were best see; there's his letter. Jew 4.3.25 P Pilia
Farewell Fidler: One letter more to the Jew. Jew 4.4.72 Pilia
Remember you the letter gentle sir, P 754 15.12 King
This letter came from my sweete Gaveston, Edw 2.1.59 Neece
Now to the letter of my Lord the King, Edw 2.1.66 Neece
Further, or this letter was sealed, Lord Bartley came, Edw 5.2.30 BshpWn
write a letter presently/Unto the Lord of Bartley from Edw 5.2.47 Mortmr
Whither goes this letter, to my lord the king? Edw 5.2.68 Queene
This letter written by a friend of ours, Edw 5.4.6 Mortmr
the first letter of my name begins with Letchery <leachery>. F 709 2.2.161 P Ltchry
and some blotted letter/On the last edge to stay mine eyes the Ovid's Elegies 1.11.21
Jasons sad letter doth Hipsipile greete, Ovid's Elegies 2.18.33
But stayd, and after her a letter sent. Hero and Leander 2.14

LETTERS
These letters, lines, and perjurd papers all, Dido 5.1.300 Dido
We have his highnesse letters to command/Aide and assistance if 1Tamb 1.2.19 Magnet
But now you see these letters and commandes, 1Tamb 1.2.21 Tamb
you must expect/Letters of conduct from my mightinesse, 1Tamb 1.2.24 Tamb
built Citadell/Commands much more then letters can import: Jew Prol.23 Machvl
father, here are letters come/From Ormus, and the Post stayes Jew 2.3.222 Abigal
Give me the letters, daughter, doe you heare? Jew 2.3.224 Barab
He sends her letters, bracelets, jewels, rings. Jew 2.3.259 Barab
And by my letters privately procure/Great summes of mony for Jew 5.2.87 Govnr
Tush, send not letters to 'em, goe thy selfe, Jew 5.2.93 Barab
With letters to our ladie from the King, Edw 2.1.20 Spencr
Letters, from whence? Edw 2.2.112 Mortmr
Informeth us, by letters and by words, Edw 3.1.61 Queene
These be the letters, this the messenger. Edw 3.1.65 Queene
Letters my lord, and tidings foorth of Fraunce, Edw 4.3.25 Post
Letters, from whence? Edw 5.2.23 Mortmr
Lines, Circles, [Signes], Letters, [and] Characters, F 78 1.1.50 Faust
The rest my hand doth in my letters write. Ovid's Elegies 1.11.14
Thinke when she reades, her mother letters sent her, Ovid's Elegies 2.2.19

LETTING
Letting out death and tyrannising war, 2Tamb 2.4.115 Tamb
Letting him live in all voluptuousnesse, F 320 1.3.92 Faust

LETTS
letts goe and make cleane our bootes which lie foule upon our F App p.234 32 P Robin

LEUCA (Homograph)
The Mutin toyles; the fleet at Leuca suncke; Lucan, First Booke 42
And they of Rhene and Leuca, cunning darters, Lucan, First Booke 425
whom/The gravest, Aruns, dwelt in forsaken Leuca <or Luna>, Lucan, First Booke 585

LEUDNESSE
Why Philomele doest Tereus leudnesse mourne? Ovid's Elegies 2.6.7

LEVELD
Leave nothing loose, all leveld to my mind. Jew 5.5.3 Barab
Oft have I leveld, and at last have learnd, P 94 2.37 Guise
these Barons and the subtill Queene,/Long [leveld] <levied> at. Edw 3.1.273 Levune

LEVELL (See also LEAVELD)
It is the chiefest marke they levell at. Edw 5.3.12 Edward
O levell all your lookes upon these daring men, Edw 5.3.39 Edward
Yet levell at the end of every Art, F 32 1.1.4 Faust

LEVI (See LEVY)

LEVIE
see if coward Calapine/Dare levie armes against our puissance, 2Tamb 3.2.156 Tamb
Ready to levie power against thy throne, 2Tamb 4.1.117 Tamb
To levie of us ten yeares tribute past, Jew 1.2.41 Govnr
Why post we not from hence to levie men? Edw 1.2.16 Mortmr
Forbeare to levie armes against the king. Edw 1.2.82 Queene
Come Edmund lets away, and levie men, Edw 2.2.98 Edward
Would levie men enough to anger you. Edw 2.2.152 Mortmr
And levie armes against your lawfull king? Edw 3.1.208 SpncrP

LEVIED
Be you the generall of the levied troopes, Edw 1.4.362 Edward
these Barons and the subtill Queene,/Long [leveld] <levied> at. Edw 3.1.273 Levune

LEVIN
Then crams salt levin on his crooked knife; Lucan, First Booke 609

LEVUNE
Our friend [Levune] <Lewne>, faithfull and full of trust, Edw 3.1.60 Queene
Welcome [Levune] <Lewne>, tush Sib, if this be all/Valoys and I Edw 3.1.66 Edward
And this our sonne, [Levune] <Lewne> shall follow you, Edw 3.1.82 Edward
[Levune] <Lewne>, the trust that we repose in thee,/Begets the Edw 3.1.262 Spencr
Yea, but [Levune] <Lewne> thou seest,/These Barons lay their Edw 3.1.273 Baldck
Then make for Fraunce amaine, [Levune] <Lewne> away,/Proclaime Edw 3.1.280 Spencr
To you my lord of Gloster from [Levune] <Lewne>. Edw 4.3.26 Post
Your honors in all service, [Levune] <Lewne>. Edw 4.3.37 P Spencr

LEVY (See also LEVIE, LEAVY)
I am not of the Tribe of Levy, I, ... Jew 2.3.18 Barab
LEVYED
mony of the Turkes shall all be levyed amongst the Jewes, Jew 1.2.68 P Reader
LEWD
and thee lewd hangman call. . . . . . . Ovid's Elegies 2.2.36
Heere I display my lewd and loose behaviour. . . . Ovid's Elegies 2.4.4
He is too clownish, whom a lewd wife grieves, . . . Ovid's Elegies 3.4.37
Or lesse faire, or lesse lewd would thou mightst bee, . Ovid's Elegies 3.10.41
LEWDLY
they had bestowde/This <The> benefite, which lewdly I forslowd: Ovid's Elegies 3.6.46
I know not whom thou lewdly didst imbrace, ... Ovid's Elegies 3.10.11
LEWDNESSE (See also LEUDNESSE)
While without shame thou singst thy lewdnesse ditty. . Ovid's Elegies 3.1.22
Beauty with lewdnesse doth right ill agree. . . . Ovid's Elegies 3.10.42
LEWNE
Our friend [Levune] <Lewne>, faithfull and full of trust, Edw 3.1.60 Queene
Welcome [Levune] <Lewne>, tush Sib, if this be all/Valoys and I Edw 3.1.66 Edward
And this our sonne, [Levune] <Lewne> shall follow you, . Edw 3.1.82 Edward
[Levune] <Lewne>, the trust that we repose in thee,/Begets the Edw 3.1.262 Spencr
Yea, but [Levune] <Lewne> thou seest,/These Barons lay their Edw 3.1.273 Baldck
Then make for Fraunce amaine, [Levune] <Lewne> away,/Proclaime Edw 3.1.280 Spencr
To you my lord of Gloster from [Levune] <Lewne>. . . . Edw 4.3.26 Post
Your honors in all service, [Levune] <Lewne>. . . . Edw 4.3.37 P Spencr
LIBAS
And Libas, and the white cheek'de Pitho thrise, . . Ovid's Elegies 3.6.24
LIBELLING
What call you this but private libelling, ... Edw 2.2.34 Edward
LIBELS
Libels are cast againe thee in the streete, . . . Edw 2.2.177 Mortmr
LIBERAL
And being popular sought by liberal gifts, . . . Lucan, First Booke 132
LIBERALL
Schollers I meane, learned and liberall; . . . . Jew 3.1.8 Curtzn
The liberall earle of Cornewall is the man, . . . Edw 2.1.10 Spencr
What man will now take liberall arts in hand, . . . Ovid's Elegies 3.7.1
Wherein the liberall graces lock'd their wealth, . . Hero and Leander 2.17
LIBERALLY
How liberally the villain gives me mine own gold. . . Jew 4.4.48 P Barab
LIBERTIE
Therefore at least admit us libertie, ... 1Tamb 1.2.71 Zenoc
on whose safe return/Depends our citie, libertie, and lives. 1Tamb 5.1.63 Govnr
You hope of libertie and restitution: . . . . 1Tamb 5.1.210 Tamb
rest, because we heare/That Edmund casts to worke his libertie, Edw 5.2.58 Mortmr
To ease his greefe, and worke his libertie: . . . Edw 5.2.71 Queene
LIBERTIES
May serve for ransome to our liberties: . . . . 1Tamb 1.2.75 Agidas
liberties and lives were weigh'd/In equall care and ballance 1Tamb 5.1.41 Govnr
and Furies dread)/As for their liberties, their loves or lives. 1Tamb 5.1.95 1Virgn
LIBERTY
But since I love to live at liberty, ... 1Tamb 1.2.26 Tamb
Forbids you further liberty than this. . . . . 2Tamb 1.2.8 Almeda
to them should not infringe/Our liberty of armes and victory. 2Tamb 2.1.41 Baldwn
But give him liberty at least to mourne, ... Jew 1.2.202 Barab
My foure and twenty yeares of liberty/I'le spend in pleasure F 839 3.1.61 Faust
despite of all his Holinesse/Restore this Bruno to his liberty, F 899 3.1.121 Faust
Stolne liberty she may by thee obtaine, ... Ovid's Elegies 2.2.15
Whom liberty to honest armes compeld, ... Ovid's Elegies 3.14.9
LIBIA
The kingly seate of Southerne Libia, ... Dido 1.1.212 Venus
Am not I Queen of Libia? then depart. . . . . Dido 3.1.49 Dido
And be thou king of Libia, by my guift. . . . . Dido 3.4.64 Dido
Weare the emperiall Crowne of Libia, ... Dido 4.4.34 Dido
for his parentage deserves/As large a kingdome as is Libia. Dido 4.4.80 Achat
Or with what thought sleepst thou in Libia shoare? . . Dido 5.1.35 Hermes
LIBIAES
Or Scythia; or hot Libiaes thirsty sands. . . . . Lucan, First Booke 369
LIBIAN
Doe trace these Libian deserts all despisde, . . . Dido 1.1.228 Aeneas
We come not we to wrong your Libian Gods, ... Dido 1.2.10 Illion
And Illioneus gum and Libian spice, ... Dido 4.4.8 Dido
How loth I am to leave these Libian bounds, . . . Dido 5.1.81 Aeneas
Wast thou not wrackt upon this Libian shoare, . . . Dido 5.1.161 Dido
from the breach/Of Libian Syrtes roules a monstrous wave, Lucan, First Booke 497
LIBRARIE
His lookes shall be my only Librarie, ... Dido 3.1.90 Dido
LIBRARY
good divel forgive me now, and Ile never rob thy Library more. F App p.235 31 P Robin
LIBYA (See LIBIA, LYBIAN)
LICE
I'le turne all the lice about thee into Familiars, and make F 362 1.4.20 P Wagner
or Ile turne al the lice about thee into familiars, and they F App p.229 25 P Wagner
LICENCIOUS
And then we grew licencious and rude, ... Lucan, First Booke 162
LICENSE
Would lend an howers license to my tongue: . . . 1Tamb 5.1.423 Arabia
LICENTIATE
<that> you, being Licentiats <licentiate>, should stand upon; F 203 1.2.10 P Wagner
LICENTIATS
<that> you, being Licentiats <licentiate>, should stand upon; F 203 1.2.10 P Wagner
LICENTIOUS
Though inwardly licentious enough, ... Edw 2.1.50 Baldck
LICKT
so Pompey thou having lickt/Warme goare from Syllas sword art Lucan, First Booke 330

Text	Work	Location	Speaker
LICORIS			
So shall Licoris whom he loved best:	Ovid's Elegies	1.15.30	
LIDS			
Now Phoebus ope the eye-lids of the day,	Jew	2.1.60	Barab
Or looking downeward, with your eye lids close,	Edw	2.1.39	Spencr
For not these ten daies have these eyes lids closd.	Edw	5.5.94	Edward
O may these eye-lids never close againe,	F1332	4.2.8	Benvol
Vaild to the ground, vailing her eie-lids close,	Hero and Leander	1.159	
LIE (Homograph; See also LYE)			
Lie here ye weedes that I disdaine to weare,	1Tamb	1.2.41	Tamb
That lie in ambush, waiting for a pray:	1Tamb	2.2.17	Meandr
Base villaine, darst thou give the lie?	1Tamb	2.4.19	Tamb
You lie, I gave it you.	1Tamb	2.4.33	Mycet
Or breathles lie before the citie walles.	1Tamb	3.1.15	Bajzth
Then shall our footmen lie within the trench,	1Tamb	3.1.64	Bajzth
That they lie panting on the Gallies side,	1Tamb	3.3.53	Tamb
By this the Turks lie weltring in their blood/And Tamburlaine	1Tamb	3.3.201	Zenoc
Shall lie at anchor in the Isle Asant,	1Tamb	3.3.251	Tamb
Lie slumbering on the flowrie bankes of Nile,	1Tamb	4.1.9	Souldn
Would she leave/The angrie God of Armes, and lie with me.	1Tamb	5.1.125	Tamb
Emperours and kings lie breathlesse at my feet.	1Tamb	5.1.469	Tamb
Now lie the Christians bathing in their bloods,	2Tamb	2.3.10	Orcan
And lie in trench before thy castle walles,	2Tamb	3.3.31	Techel
And in a stable lie upon the planks.	2Tamb	3.5.107	Tamb
Wee may lie ready to encounter him,	2Tamb	5.2.8	Callap
let us lie in wait for him/And if we find him absent from his	2Tamb	5.2.56	Callap
And lame and poore, lie groning at the gates,	Edw	2.2.163	Lncstr
great beames/On Atlas shoulder, shall not lie more safe,	Edw	3.1.77	Prince
Lie on this bed, and rest your selfe a while.	Edw	5.5.72	Ltborn
Your overwatchde my lord, lie downe and rest.	Edw	5.5.92	Ltborn
Thy hatefull and accursed head shall lie,	Edw	5.6.30	King
Goe fetche my fathers hearse, where it shall lie,	Edw	5.6.94	King
To me and Peter, shalt thou groveling lie,	F 873	3.1.95	Pope
Nay there you lie, 'tis beyond us both.	F1109	3.3.22	P Robin
goe and make cleane our bootes which lie foule upon our handes,	F App	p.234 33	P Robin
You lie Drawer, tis afore me:	F App	p.235 17	P Robin
Upon whose altars thousand soules do lie,	F App	p.235 36	Mephst
Lie with him gently, when his limbes he spread/Upon the bed,	Ovid's Elegies	1.4.15	
And her old body in birdes plumes to lie.	Ovid's Elegies	1.8.14	
That my dead bones may in their grave lie soft.	Ovid's Elegies	1.8.108	
As evill wood throwne in the high-waies lie,	Ovid's Elegies	1.12.13	
Yet would I lie with her if that I might.	Ovid's Elegies	2.4.22	
Let me lie with thee browne Cypasse to day.	Ovid's Elegies	2.8.22	
Yet this is better farre then lie alone,	Ovid's Elegies	2.10.15	
And on thy thre-shold let me lie dispred,	Ovid's Elegies	2.19.21	
Sterne was her front, her [cloake] <looke> on ground did lie.	Ovid's Elegies	3.1.12	
But on the ground thy cloathes too loosely lie,	Ovid's Elegies	3.2.25	
Which lie hid under her thinne veile supprest.	Ovid's Elegies	3.2.36	
To kisse, I kisse, to lie with her shee let me.	Ovid's Elegies	3.6.48	
Lie downe with shame, and see thou stirre no more,	Ovid's Elegies	3.6.69	
Who bad thee lie downe here against thy will?	Ovid's Elegies	3.6.78	
Foole canst thou lie in his enfolding space?	Ovid's Elegies	3.7.12	
Canst touch that hand wherewith some one lie dead?	Ovid's Elegies	3.7.17	
Which long time lie untoucht, will harshly jarre.	Hero and Leander	1.230	
That hops about the chamber where I lie,	Hero and Leander	1.354	
LIEF (See LEEFEST)			
LIEFTENANT			
And Generall Lieftenant of my Armies.	1Tamb	2.5.9	Cosroe
Gods great lieftenant over all the world:	2Tamb	3.5.2	2Msngr
LIEGE			
Tis not amisse my liege for eyther part,	Edw	3.1.190	SpncrP
Not so my liege, the Queene hath given this charge,	Edw	5.3.13	Gurney
That wronges their liege and soveraigne, Englands king.	Edw	5.3.40	Edward
LIES (Homograph)			
wherin at anchor lies/A Turkish Gally of my royall fleet,	2Tamb	1.2.20	Callap
How far hence lies the Galley, say you?	2Tamb	1.2.54	Almeda
She lies so close that none can find her out.	2Tamb	1.2.60	Callap
Lies heavy on my heart, I cannot live.	2Tamb	3.4.5	Capt
Here at Alepo with an hoste of men/Lies Tamburlaine, this king	2Tamb	3.5.4	2Msngr
There lies more gold than Babylon is worth,	2Tamb	5.1.116	Govnr
Where about lies it?	2Tamb	5.1.120	Tamb
Where Tamburlaine with all his armie lies,	2Tamb	5.2.6	Callap
Lies westward from the midst of Cancers line,	2Tamb	5.3.146	Tamb
well/To waite at my trencher, and tell me lies at dinner time,	Edw	1.1.31	Gavstn
Your highnes knowes, it lies not in my power.	Edw	1.4.158	Queene
Nay more, when he shall know it lies in us,	Edw	1.4.274	Mortmr
And he himselfe lies in captivitie.	Edw	5.2.4	Mortmr
I, that's the head, and here the body lies,	F1375	4.2.51	Benvol
where lies intombde this famous Conquerour,	F App	p.237 31	Emper
bringing newes/Of present war, made many lies and tales.	Lucan, First Booke	468	
This headlesse trunke that lies on Nylus sande/I know:	Lucan, First Booke	684	
Or lies he close, and shoots where none can spie him?	Ovid's Elegies	1.2.6	
He Citties greate, this thresholds lies before:	Ovid's Elegies	1.9.19	
rise/And who thou never think'st should fall downe lies.	Ovid's Elegies	1.9.30	
If ever, now well lies she by my side.	Ovid's Elegies	1.13.6	
Who can indure, save him with whom none lies?	Ovid's Elegies	1.13.26	
And therefore filles the bed she lies uppon:	Ovid's Elegies	2.4.34	
If short, she lies the rounder:	Ovid's Elegies	2.4.35	
Haples is he that all the night lies quiet/And slumbring,	Ovid's Elegies	2.9.39	
Erre I? or mirtle in her right hand lies.	Ovid's Elegies	3.1.34	
Or one that with her tender brother lies,	Ovid's Elegies	3.6.22	
In emptie bed alone my mistris lies.	Ovid's Elegies	3.9.2	
Of proud Adonis that before her lies.	Hero and Leander	1.14	

LIES (cont.)			
It lies not in our power to love, or hate,	Hero and Leander	1.167	
LIEST			
Thou liest.	1Tamb	2.4.18	Mycet
LIETH			
Favor him my lord, as much as lieth in you.	Edw	5.1.147	Leistr
And none but we shall know where he lieth.	Edw	5.2.41	Mortmr
LIEU			
That powres in lieu of all your goodnes showne,	Edw	3.1.44	Spencr
LIEUTENANT (See also LIEFTENANT)			
From the lieutenant of the tower my lord.	Edw	4.3.9	Arundl
LIFE			
Who for her sonnes death wept out life and breath,	Dido	2.1.4	Aeneas
And would my prayers (as Pigmalions did)/Could give it life,	Dido	2.1.17	Aeneas
Then would it leape out to give Priam life:	Dido	2.1.27	Aeneas
Yet flung I forth, and desperate of my life,	Dido	2.1.210	Aeneas
A little while prolong'd her husbands life:	Dido	2.1.246	Aeneas
Full soone wouldst thou abjure this single life.	Dido	3.1.60	Dido
And feede infection with his [let] <left> out life:	Dido	3.2.11	Juno
To harme my sweete Ascanius lovely life.	Dido	3.2.23	Venus
Or els I would have given my life in gage.	Dido	3.3.29	Iarbus
And will she be avenged on his life?	Dido	3.4.14	Aeneas
In all my life I never knew the like,	Dido	4.1.7	Anna
This is no life for men at armes to live,	Dido	4.3.33	Achat
Or impious traitors vowde to have my life,	Dido	4.4.114	Dido
againe conspire/Against the life of me poore Carthage Queene:	Dido	4.4.132	Dido
And I will live a private life with him.	Dido	5.1.198	Dido
And rue our ends senceles of life or breath:	Dido	5.1.328	Anna
Our life is fraile, and we may die to day.	1Tamb	1.1.68	Mycet
And must maintaine my life exempt from servitude.	1Tamb	1.2.31	Tamb
As long as life maintaines Theridamas.	1Tamb	1.2.231	Therid
And in their smoothnesse, amitie and life:	1Tamb	2.1.22	Menaph
Wel hast thou pourtraid in thy tearms of life,	1Tamb	2.1.31	Cosroe
With reasons of his valour and his life,	1Tamb	2.1.38	Cosroe
That leads to Pallace of my brothers life,	1Tamb	2.1.43	Cosroe
Whose vertues carie with it life and death,	1Tamb	2.5.61	Therid
Vowing our loves to equall death and life.	1Tamb	2.6.28	Cosroe
the Starres that make/The loathsome Circle of my dated life,	1Tamb	2.6.37	Cosroe
Thus to deprive me of my crowne and life.	1Tamb	2.7.2	Cosroe
And with my blood my life slides through my wound,	1Tamb	2.7.43	Cosroe
And like a Harpyr <Harpye> tires on my life.	1Tamb	2.7.50	Cosroe
Ah, life and soule still hover in his Breast,	1Tamb	3.2.21	Zenoc
Or els unite you to his life and soule,	1Tamb	3.2.23	Zenoc
And strive for life at every stroke they give.	1Tamb	3.3.54	Tamb
So shall he have his life, and all the rest.	1Tamb	4.2.115	Tamb
Preserving life, by hasting cruell death.	1Tamb	4.4.96	Bajzth
For Egypts freedom and the Souldans life:	1Tamb	5.1.153	Tamb
His life that so consumes Zenocrate,	1Tamb	5.1.154	Tamb
But let us save the reverend Souldans life,	1Tamb	5.1.204	Therid
O life more loathsome to my vexed thoughts,	1Tamb	5.1.255	Bajzth
That in the shortned sequel of my life,	1Tamb	5.1.278	Bajzth
Sweet Bajazeth, I will prolong thy life,	1Tamb	5.1.283	Zabina
And make a passage for my loathed life.	1Tamb	5.1.304	Bajzth
And wounded bodies gasping yet for life.	1Tamb	5.1.323	Zenoc
Whose lives were dearer to Zenocrate/Than her owne life, or	1Tamb	5.1.338	Zenoc
ruthlesly pursewde/Be equally against his life incenst,	1Tamb	5.1.367	Zenoc
As long as life maintaines his mighty arme,	1Tamb	5.1.375	Anippe
Must fight against my life and present love:	1Tamb	5.1.389	Zenoc
With happy safty of my fathers life,	1Tamb	5.1.401	Zenoc
Whose sight with joy would take away my life,	1Tamb	5.1.419	Arabia
With them Arabia too hath left his life,	1Tamb	5.1.473	Tamb
Conceive a second life in endlesse mercie.	2Tamb	2.3.9	Sgsmnd
Zenocrate that gave him light and life,	2Tamb	2.4.8	Tamb
That this my life may be as short to me/As are the daies of	2Tamb	2.4.36	Tamb
transfourme my love/In whose sweet being I repose my life,	2Tamb	2.4.48	Tamb
Live still my Love and so conserve my life,	2Tamb	2.4.55	Tamb
Your griefe and furie hurtes my second life:	2Tamb	2.4.68	Zenoc
But since my life is lengthened yet a while,	2Tamb	2.4.71	Zenoc
Nay Captain, thou art weary of thy life,	2Tamb	3.3.18	Techel
And quickly rid thee both of paine and life.	2Tamb	3.4.25	Olymp
Be likewise end to my accursed life.	2Tamb	3.4.82	Olymp
thou shalt kneele to us/And humbly crave a pardon for thy life.	2Tamb	3.5.109	Orcan
tel me if the warres/Be not a life that may illustrate Gods,	2Tamb	4.1.79	Tamb
Devise some meanes to rid thee of thy life,	2Tamb	4.2.5	Olymp
Spending my life in sweet discourse of love.	2Tamb	4.2.45	Therid
Villaine, respects thou more thy slavish life,	2Tamb	5.1.10	Govnr
Is not my life and state as deere to me,	2Tamb	5.1.12	Govnr
the towne will never yeeld/As long as any life is in my breast.	2Tamb	5.1.48	Govnr
To save thy life, and us a litle labour,	2Tamb	5.1.50	Therid
Save but my life and I wil give it thee.	2Tamb	5.1.118	Govnr
Then for all your valour, you would save your life.	2Tamb	5.1.119	Tamb
Yet save my life, and let this wound appease/The mortall furie	2Tamb	5.1.153	Govnr
And offer'd me as ransome for thy life,	2Tamb	5.1.156	Tamb
When I record my Parents slavish life,	2Tamb	5.2.19	Callap
life, health and majesty/Were strangely blest and governed by	2Tamb	5.3.24	Techel
His byrth, his life, his health and majesty.	2Tamb	5.3.27	Techel
Which being the cause of life, imports your death.	2Tamb	5.3.90	Phsitn
Here lovely boies, what death forbids my life,	2Tamb	5.3.159	Tamb
Retaine a thought of joy, or sparke of life?	2Tamb	5.3.163	Amyras
For by your life we entertaine our lives.	2Tamb	5.3.167	Celeb
The breath of life, and burthen of my soule,	2Tamb	5.3.186	Amyras
Leading a life that onely strives to die,	2Tamb	5.3.197	Amyras
easily in a day/Tell that which may maintaine him all his life.	Jew	1.1.11	Barab

LIFE (cont.)

And all his life time hath bin tired,	Jew	1.1.15	Barab
And now shall move you to bereave my life.	Jew	1.2.143	Barab
You have my wealth, the labour of my life,	Jew	1.2.149	Barab
No, I will live; nor loath I this my life:	Jew	1.2.266	Barab
I'de passe away my life in penitence,	Jew	1.2.324	Abigal
Novice learne to frame/My solitary life to your streight lawes,	Jew	1.2.332	Abigal
The Loadstarre of my life, if Abigall.	Jew	2.1.42	Barab
Your life and if you have it.--	Jew	2.3.64	Barab
might be got/To keepe him for his life time from the gallowes.	Jew	2.3.104	Barab
Nay on my life it is my Factors hand,	Jew	2.3.240	Barab
My life is not so deare as Abigall.	Jew	2.3.348	Barab
And then thou didst not like that holy life.	Jew	3.3.58	Mthias
Farre from the Sonne that gives eternall life.	Jew	3.3.65	1Fryar
Yet never shall these lips bewray thy life.	Jew	3.3.75	Abigal
Come neere, my love, come neere, thy masters life,	Jew	3.4.14	Abigal
My trusty servant, nay, my second [selfe] <life>;	Jew	3.4.15	Barab
I cannot thinke but that thou hat'st my life.	Jew	3.4.38	Barab
that wil preserve life, make her round and plump, and batten	Jew	3.4.65	Barab
The other knowes enough to have my life,	Jew	4.1.120	P Ithimr
What, will you [have] <save> my life?	Jew	4.1.148	Barab
as you love your life send me five hundred crowns, and give the	Jew	4.2.117	2Fryar
For none of this can prejudice my life.	Jew	5.1.39	P Ithimr
When as thy life shall be at their command?	Jew	5.2.33	Barab
Thou seest thy life, and Malta's happinesse,	Jew	5.2.52	Barab
'Tis not thy life which can availe me ought,	Jew	5.2.62	Barab
What will you give me if I render you/The life of Calymath,	Jew	5.2.80	Barab
Wherein no danger shall betide thy life,	Jew	5.2.100	Barab
This is the life we Jewes are us'd to lead;	Jew	5.2.115	Barab
fury of thy torments, strive/To end thy life with resolution:	Jew	5.5.80	Barab
Dye life, flye soule, tongue curse thy fill and dye.	Jew	5.5.89	Barab
This traine he laid to have intrap'd thy life;	Jew	5.5.91	Govnr
But I have rather chose to save thy life.	Jew	5.5.94	Govnr
Flye Ramus flye, if thou wilt save thy life.	P 365	7.5	Taleus
Not for my life doe I desire this pause,	P 401	7.41	Ramus
Regarding still the danger of thy life.	P 748	15.6	King
Which Ile maintaine so long as life doth last:	P 800	16.14	Navrre
Hating the life and honour of the Guise?	P 932	19.2	Capt
Hating the life and honour of the Guise?	P 950	19.20	King
Breath out that life wherein my death was hid,	P 954	19.24	King
Oh that I have not power to stay my life,	P1007	19.77	Guise
But thats prevented, for to end his life,	P1119	21.13	Dumain
No, spare his life, but seaze upon his goods,	Edw	1.1.193	Edward
I wil endure a melancholie life,	Edw	1.2.66	Queene
She smiles, now for my life his mind is changd.	Edw	1.4.236	Warwck
My life for thine she will have Gaveston.	Edw	2.1.28	Spencr
The life of thee shall salve this foule disgrace.	Edw	2.2.83	Gavstn
Villaine thy life, unlesse I misse mine aime.	Edw	2.2.84	Mortmr
Will be the first that shall adventure life.	Edw	2.3.4	Kent
I know it lords, it is this life you aime at,	Edw	2.5.48	Gavstn
I see it is your life these armes pursue.	Edw	2.6.2	James
O must this day be period of my life,	Edw	2.6.4	Gavstn
His life, my lord, before your princely feete.	Edw	3.1.45	Spencr
armes, by me salute/Your highnes, with long life and happines,	Edw	3.1.157	Herald
Now on my life, theile neither barke nor bite.	Edw	4.3.13	Edward
Edward, this Mortimer aimes at thy life:	Edw	4.6.10	Kent
rule and emperie/Have not in life or death made miserable?	Edw	4.7.15	Edward
Father, this life contemplative is heaven,	Edw	4.7.20	Edward
O that I might this life in quiet lead,	Edw	4.7.21	Edward
Upon my life, those be the men ye seeke.	Edw	4.7.46	Mower
T'escape their hands that seeke to reave his life:	Edw	4.7.52	Leistr
To take my life, my companie from me?	Edw	4.7.65	Edward
And go I must, life farewell with my friends.	Edw	4.7.99	Edward
We are deprivde the sun-shine of our life,	Edw	4.7.106	Baldck
Make for a new life man, throw up thy eyes,	Edw	4.7.107	Baldck
Which in a moment will abridge his life:	Edw	5.1.42	Edward
Here, take my crowne, the life of Edward too,	Edw	5.1.57	Edward
My diadem I meane, and guiltlesse life.	Edw	5.1.73	Edward
Sweet Mortimer, the life of Isabell,	Edw	5.2.15	Queene
But she that gave him life, I meane the Queene?	Edw	5.2.91	Kent
But can my ayre of life continue long,	Edw	5.3.17	Edward
Containes his death, yet bids them save his life.	Edw	5.4.7	Mortmr
Intreate my lord Protector for his life.	Edw	5.4.95	King
That <and> even then when I shall lose my life,	Edw	5.5.77	Edward
To rid thee of thy life. Matrevis come.	Edw	5.5.107	Ltborn
Then sue for life unto a paltrie boye.	Edw	5.6.57	Mortmr
As thou receivedst thy life from me,	Edw	5.6.68	Queene
Or being dead, raise them to life againe,	F 53	1.1.25	Faust
That after this life there is any paine?	F 523	2.1.135	Faust
This will I keepe, as chary as my life.	F 551	2.1.163	Faust
[This will I keepe as chary as my life].	F 719.1	2.2.172	Faust
a paire of hornes on's head as e're thou sawest in thy life.	F 738	2.3.17	P Robin
We will determine of his life or death.	F 969	3.1.191	Pope
him, as he was never conjur'd in his life, I warrant him:	F1092	3.3.5	P Robin
and stir not for thy life, Vintner you shall have your cup	F1113	3.3.26	P Robin
And lay his life at holy Bruno's feet.	F1220	4.1.66	Faust
What's here? an ambush to betray my life:	F1424	4.2.100	Faust
such belly-cheere, as Wagner in his life nere saw the like:	F1679	5.1.6	P Wagner
dutie, I do yeeld/My life and lasting service for your love.	F1819	5.2.23	Wagner
Gush forth bloud in stead of teares, yea life and soule:	F1852	5.2.56	P Faust
and attire/They usde to weare during their time of life,	F App	p.237 34	Emper
Shortning my dayes and thred of vitall life,	F App	p.239 92	Faust
I sat upon a bottle of hey, never so neare drowning in my life:	F App	p.240 136	P HrsCsr

LIFE (cont.)			
they be the best grapes that ere I tasted in my life before.	F App	p.242 26 P	Duchss
As Wagner nere beheld in all his life.	F App	p.243 7	Wagner
To guide thy steps unto the way of life,	F App	p.243 35	OldMan
had heaven given thee longer life/Thou hadst restrainde thy	Lucan, First Booke	115	
so (if truth you sing)/Death brings long life.	Lucan, First Booke	454	
And shame tc spare life which being lost is wonne.	Lucan, First Booke	458	
My spotlesse life, which but to Gods [gives] <give> place,	Ovid's Elegies	1.3.13	
Thy lightning can my life in pieces batter.	Ovid's Elegies	1.6.16	
Then thinkest thou thy loose life is not showne?	Ovid's Elegies	1.13.34	
Birdes haples glory, death thy life doth quench.	Ovid's Elegies	2.6.20	
Whose life nine ages scarce bring out of date.	Ovid's Elegies	2.6.36	
Even as he led his life, so did he die.	Ovid's Elegies	2.10.38	
Wearie Corinna hath her life in doubt.	Ovid's Elegies	2.13.2	
Thou givest my mistris life, she mine againe.	Ovid's Elegies	2.13.16	
Life is no light price of a small surcease.	Ovid's Elegies	2.14.26	
My life, that I will shame thee never feare,	Ovid's Elegies	2.15.21	
And Venus grieves, Tibullus life being spent,	Ovid's Elegies	3.8.15	
What profit to us hath our pure life bred?	Ovid's Elegies	3.8.33	
Yet shall thy life be forcibly bereaven.	Ovid's Elegies	3.8.38	
Gallus that [car'dst] <carst> not bloud, and life to spend.	Ovid's Elegies	3.8.64	
Flint-brested Pallas joies in single life,	Hero and Leander	1.321	
That sheares the slender threads of humane life,	Hero and Leander	1.448	
He kist her, and breath'd life into her lips,	Hero and Leander	2.3	
Above our life we love a stedfast friend,	Hero and Leander	2.79	
LIFELESS (See LIVELES)			
LIFE'S			
and in hating me/My life's in danger, and what boots it thee	Jew	5.2.31	Barab
LIFE TIME			
might be got/To keepe him for his life time from the gallowes.	Jew	2.3.104	Barab
LIFT			
And gainst the Generall we will lift our swords,	1Tamb	1.2.145	Tamb
Like his desire, lift upwards and divine,	1Tamb	2.1.8	Menaph
whet thy winged sword/And lift thy lofty arme into the cloudes,	1Tamb	2.3.52	Cosroe
To lift our swords against the Persean King.	1Tamb	2.7.35	Techel
That lift themselves against the perfect truth,	P 799	16.13	Navrre
But yet lift not your swords against the king.	Edw	1.2.61	ArchBp
No, but weele lift Gaveston from hence.	Edw	1.2.62	Lncstr
Never againe lift up this drooping head,	Edw	4.7.42	Edward
O never more lift up this dying hart!	Edw	4.7.43	Edward
I would lift up my hands, but see they hold 'em <them>, they	F1852	5.2.56 P	Faust
Aie me how high that gale did lift my hope!	Ovid's Elegies	1.6.52	
Gather them up, or lift them loe will I.	Ovid's Elegies	3.2.26	
LIFTED			
Whereat he lifted up his bedred lims,	Dido	2.1.250	Aeneas
LIFTING			
Lifting his prayers to the heavens for aid,	1Tamb	3.2.83	Agidas
Lifting his loftie head above the clouds,	F 912	3.1.134	Pope
LIGHT (Homograph)			
Hold, take this candle and goe light a fire,	Dido	1.1.171	Aeneas
I feare me Dido hath been counted light,	Dido	3.1.14	Dido
Darts forth her light to Lavinias shoare.	Dido	3.2.84	Venus
And rowse the light foote Deere from forth their laire?	Dido	3.3.31	Dido
Before the Moone renew her borrowed light,	1Tamb	1.1.69	Therid
Or faire Bootes sends his cheerefull light,	1Tamb	1.2.207	Tamb
And fearefull vengeance light upon you both.	1Tamb	2.7.52	Cosroe
Disdaine to borrow light of Cynthia,	1Tamb	4.2.35	Tamb
And cause the Sun to borrowe light of you.	1Tamb	4.2.40	Tamb
Confusion light on him that helps thee thus.	1Tamb	4.2.84	Bajzth
The Moone, the Planets, and the Meteors light.	1Tamb	5.1.150	Tamb
Sharpe forked arrowes light upon thy horse:	1Tamb	5.1.217	Bajzth
Hel and confusion light upon their heads,	2Tamb	2.2.33	Gazell
Zenocrate that gave him light and life,	2Tamb	2.4.8	Tamb
Gives light to Phoebus and the fixed stars,	2Tamb	2.4.50	Tamb
Then let us bring our light Artilery,	2Tamb	3.3.5	Techel
Hovering betwixt our armies, light on me,	2Tamb	3.5.163	Tamb
Which with thy beauty thou wast woont to light,	2Tamb	4.2.16	Therid
From whence the starres doo borrow all their light,	2Tamb	4.2.89	Therid
Light Abrahams off-spring; and direct the hand/Of Abigall this	Jew	2.1.14	Barab
Whose light was deadly to the Protestants:	P 945	19.15	Capt
And let her droup, my heart is light enough.	P1064	19.134	King
What neede the artick people love star-light,	Edw	1.1.16	Gavstn
I Isabell, nere was my heart so light.	Edw	1.4.368	Edward
Freely enjoy that vaine light-headed earle,	Edw	1.4.400	MortSr
The proud corrupters of the light-brainde king,	Edw	5.2.2	Mortmr
Heeres a light to go into the dungeon.	Edw	5.5.37	Gurney
Whose there, what light is that, wherefore comes thou?	Edw	5.5.42	Edward
To light as heavy as the paines of hell.	F 939	3.1.161	Pope
To gaine the light unstable commons love,	Lucan, First Booke	133	
and ware robes/Too light for women; Poverty (who hatcht/Roomes	Lucan, First Booke	166	
(Albeit the Moores light Javelin or his speare/Sticks in his	Lucan, First Booke	213	
Now light had quite dissolv'd the mysty [night] <might>,	Lucan, First Booke	263	
Those of Bituriges and light Axon pikes;	Lucan, First Booke	424	
having fild/Her meeting hornes to match her brothers light,	Lucan, First Booke	536	
Lets yeeld, a burden easly borne is light.	Ovid's Elegies	1.2.10	
When I (my light) do or say ought that please thee,	Ovid's Elegies	1.4.25	
Which gave such light, as twincles in a wood,	Ovid's Elegies	1.5.4	
Such light to shamefaste maidens must be showne,	Ovid's Elegies	1.5.7	
Wondring if any walked without light.	Ovid's Elegies	1.6.10	
her eyes/Two eye-balles shine, and double light thence flies.	Ovid's Elegies	1.8.16	
foote drawes out/Fastning her light web some old beame about.	Ovid's Elegies	1.14.8	
Toyes, and light Elegies my darts I tooke,	Ovid's Elegies	2.1.21	
Light art thou, and more windie then thy winges,	Ovid's Elegies	2.9.49	

LIGHT (cont.)			
Life is no light price of a small surcease.	Ovid's Elegies	2.14.26	
Maides words more vaine and light then falling leaves,	Ovid's Elegies	2.16.45	
And thou my light accept me how so ever,	Ovid's Elegies	2.17.23	
Light am I, and with me, my care, light love,	Ovid's Elegies	3.1.41	
And nine sweete bouts had we before day light.	Ovid's Elegies	3.6.26	
His broken bowe, his fire-brand without light.	Ovid's Elegies	3.8.8	
Now love, and hate my light brest each way move;	Ovid's Elegies	3.10.33	
Where crown'd with blazing light and majestie,	Hero and Leander	1.110	
Where by one hand, light headed Bacchus hoong,	Hero and Leander	1.139	
In offring parlie, to be counted light.	Hero and Leander	2.9	
And like light Salmacis, her body throes/Upon his bosome, where	Hero and Leander	2.46	
The light of hidden fire it selfe discovers,	Hero and Leander	2.133	
For much it greev'd her that the bright day-light,	Hero and Leander	2.303	
And ran before, as Harbenger of light,	Hero and Leander	2.331	
LIGHTBORN			
Lightborn,/Come forth.	Edw	5.4.21	Mortmr
LIGHTBORNE			
But at his lookes Lightborne thou wilt relent.	Edw	5.4.26	Mortmr
LIGHT-BRAINDE			
The proud corrupters of the light-brainde king,	Edw	5.2.2	Mortmr
LIGHTED			
And beat from thence, have lighted there againe.	Hero and Leander	1.24	
LIGHTEN (See also LIGHTNED)			
And lighten our extreames with this one boone,	Dido	1.1.196	Aeneas
To lighten doubts and frustrate subtile foes.	P 457	8.7	Anjoy
LIGHTENING			
As dooth the lightening, or the breath of heaven:	1Tamb	2.3.58	Tamb
And from their shieldes strike flames of lightening)/All	1Tamb	3.2.81	Agidas
Wil send a deadly lightening to his heart.	2Tamb	4.1.10	Celeb
LIGHTENS			
glorious actes/Lightens the world with his reflecting beames,	F App	p.237 26	Emper
LIGHTER			
My head is lighter then it was by th'hornes,	F1350	4.2.26	Benvol
LIGHTES			
And had his alters deckt with duskie lightes:	P 59	2.2	Guise
LIGHT FOOTE			
And rowse the light foote Deere from forth their laire?	Dido	3.3.31	Dido
LIGHT-HEADED			
Freely enjoy that vaine light-headed earle,	Edw	1.4.400	MortSr
LIGHT HEADED			
Where by one hand, light headed Bacchus hoong,	Hero and Leander	1.139	
LIGHTLY			
That they may trip more lightly ore the lawndes,	Dido	1.1.207	Venus
But managde horses heads are lightly borne,	Ovid's Elegies	1.2.16	
LIGHTNED			
It haild, it snowde, it lightned all at once.	Dido	4.1.8	Anna
Which lightned by her necke, like Diamonds shone.	Hero and Leander	1.26	
LIGHTNING (See also LIGHTENING)			
And casts a flash of lightning to the earth.	1Tamb	4.2.46	Tamb
Which being wroth, sends lightning from his eies,	2Tamb	1.3.76	Tamb
Flieng Dragons, lightning, fearfull thunderclaps,	2Tamb	3.2.10	Tamb
From whom the thunder and the lightning breaks,	2Tamb	5.1.184	Tamb
Brings Thunder, Whirle-winds, Storme <tempests> and Lightning:	F 546	2.1.158	Mephst
Lightning in silence, stole forth without clouds,	Lucan, First Booke	531	
Looke what the lightning blasted, Aruns takes/And it inters	Lucan, First Booke	605	
Thy lightning can my life in pieces batter.	Ovid's Elegies	1.6.16	
Her shut gates greater lightning then thyne brought.	Ovid's Elegies	2.1.20	
At me Joves right-hand lightning hath to throwe.	Ovid's Elegies	3.3.30	
Like lightning go, his strugling mouth being checkt.	Ovid's Elegies	3.4.14	
LIGHTS			
resisting it/Falls, and returnes, and shivers where it lights.	Lucan, First Booke	158	
LIGHTSOME			
And shut the windowes of the lightsome heavens.	1Tamb	5.1.293	Bajzth
LIGURIANS			
And you late shorne Ligurians, who were wont/In large spread	Lucan, First Booke	438	
LIK			
Therefore tis best, if so it lik you all,	1Tamb	1.1.51	Mycet
LIKE (Homograph)			
To hang her meteor like twixt heaven and earth,	Dido	1.1.13	Jupitr
And Aeolus like Agamemnon sounds/The surges, his fierce	Dido	1.1.68	Venus
See how the night Ulysses-like comes forth,	Dido	1.1.70	Venus
the Starres supprisde like Rhesus Steedes,/Are drawne by	Dido	1.1.72	Venus
Like Illioneus speakes this Noble man,	Dido	2.1.47	Achat
Remember who thou art, speake like thy selfe,	Dido	2.1.100	Dido
Whose memorie like pale deaths stony mace,	Dido	2.1.115	Aeneas
Well could I like this reconcilements meanes,	Dido	3.2.81	Venus
Pesant, goe seeke companions like thy selfe,	Dido	3.3.21	Dido
How like his father speaketh he in all?	Dido	3.3.41	Anna
And here we met faire Venus virgine like,	Dido	3.3.54	Achat
And like the Planets ever love to raunge:	Dido	3.3.68	Iarbus
Whose amorous face like Pean sparkles fire,	Dido	3.4.19	Dido
It was because I sawe no King like thee,	Dido	3.4.35	Dido
Never to like or love any but her.	Dido	3.4.51	Aeneas
In all my life I never knew the like,	Dido	4.1.7	Anna
Yet Dido casts her eyes like anchors out,	Dido	4.3.25	Aeneas
Now lookes Aeneas like immortall Jove,	Dido	4.4.45	Dido
Speakes not Aeneas like a Conqueror?	Dido	4.4.93	Dido
Wherewith his burning beames like labouring Bees,	Dido	5.1.12	Aeneas
What, would the Gods have me, Deucalion like,	Dido	5.1.57	Aeneas
O speake like my Aeneas, like my love:	Dido	5.1.112	Dido
And cam'st to Dido like a Fisher swaine?	Dido	5.1.162	Dido
My sister comes, I like not her sad lookes.	Dido	5.1.225	Dido

LIKE (cont.)

Ile frame me wings of waxe like Icarus,	Dido	5.1.243	Dido
That I may swim to him like Tritons neece:	Dido	5.1.247	Dido
That like a Foxe in midst of harvest time,	1Tamb	1.1.31	Mycet
Ful true thcu speakst, and like thy selfe my lord,	1Tamb	1.1.49	Mycet
How like you this, my honorable Lords?	1Tamb	1.1.54	Mycet
mated and amaz'd/To heare the king thus threaten like himselfe?	1Tamb	1.1.108	Menaph
May we become immortall like the Gods.	1Tamb	1.2.201	Tamb
Like his desire, lift upwards and divine,	1Tamb	2.1.8	Menaph
In every part proportioned like the man,	1Tamb	2.1.29	Menaph
And fall like mellowed fruit, with shakes of death,	1Tamb	2.1.47	Cosroe
Will quickly win such as are like himselfe.	1Tamb	2.2.28	Meandr
Like to the cruell brcthers of the earth,	1Tamb	2.2.47	Meandr
And live like Gentlemen in Persea.	1Tamb	2.2.71	Meandr
And bullets like Joves dreadfull Thunderbolts,	1Tamb	2.3.19	Tamb
Stand staggering like a quivering Aspen leafe,	1Tamb	2.4.4	Mycet
For he is grosse and like the massie earth,	1Tamb	2.7.31	Therid
And like a Harpyr <Harpye> tires on my life.	1Tamb	2.7.50	Cosroe
And with their Cannons mouth'd like Orcus gulfe/Batter the	1Tamb	3.1.65	Bajzth
My Campe is like to Julius Caesars Hoste,	1Tamb	3.3.152	Tamb
And let his foes like flockes of fearfull Roes,	1Tamb	3.3.192	Zenoc
Or scattered like the lofty Cedar trees,	1Tamb	4.2.24	Tamb
Like to the shadowes of Pyramides,	1Tamb	4.2.103	Tamb
Tis like he wil, when he cannot let it.	1Tamb	4.4.53	P Techel
And use us like a loving Conquerour.	1Tamb	5.1.23	Govnr
And like to Flora in her mornings pride,	1Tamb	5.1.140	Tamb
In feare and feeling of the like distresse,	1Tamb	5.1.361	Zenoc
Send like defence of faire Arabia.	1Tamb	5.1.402	Zenoc
I like that well:	2Tamb	1.2.61	P Almeda
Sit up and rest thee like a lovely Queene.	2Tamb	1.3.16	Tamb
Which should be like the quilles of Porcupines,	2Tamb	1.3.26	Tamb
Should not give us presumption to the like.	2Tamb	2.1.46	Sgsmnd
With apples like the heads of damned Feends.	2Tamb	2.3.23	Orcan
Like tried silver runs through Paradice/To entertaine divine	2Tamb	2.4.24	Tamb
Looke like the parti-coloured cloudes of heaven,	2Tamb	3.1.47	Jrslem
Now look I like a souldier, and this wound/As great a grace and	2Tamb	3.2.117	Tamb
Twas bravely done, and like a souldiers wife.	2Tamb	3.4.38	Techel
Like lovely Thetis in a Christall robe:	2Tamb	3.4.51	Therid
That like a roguish runnaway, suborn'd/That villaine there,	2Tamb	3.5.86	Tamb
And harnest like my horses, draw my coch,	2Tamb	3.5.104	Tamb
Fight as you ever did, like Conquerours,	2Tamb	3.5.160	Tamb
much like sc many suns/That halfe dismay the majesty of heaven:	2Tamb	4.1.2	Amyras
For person like to proove a second Mars.	2Tamb	4.1.35	Calyph
pride/And leads your glories <bodies> sheep-like to the sword.	2Tamb	4.1.77	Tamb
that like armed men/Are seene to march upon the towers of	2Tamb	4.1.201	Tamb
Hath stain'd thy cheekes, and made thee look like death,	2Tamb	4.2.4	Olymp
turrets of my Court/Sit like to Venus in her chaire of state,	2Tamb	4.2.42	Therid
As all the world cannct affoord the like.	2Tamb	4.2.57	Olymp
then dy like beasts, and fit for nought/But perches for the	2Tamb	4.3.22	Tamb
That like unruly never broken Jades,	2Tamb	4.3.45	Therid
How like you that sir king? why speak you not?	2Tamb	4.3.53	Celeb
How like his cursed father he begins,	2Tamb	4.3.55	Jrslem
souldiers now that fought/So Lion-like upon Asphaltis plaines?	2Tamb	4.3.68	Tamb
Ile ride in golden armour like the Sun,	2Tamb	4.3.115	Tamb
Like to an almond tree ymounted high,	2Tamb	4.3.119	Tamb
Then in my coach like Saturnes royal son,	2Tamb	4.3.125	Tamb
And use us like a loving Conquerour.	2Tamb	5.1.28	1Citzn
brave Assirian Dames/Have rid in pompe like rich Saturnia,	2Tamb	5.1.77	Tamb
And like base slaves abject our princely mindes/To vile and	2Tamb	5.1.140	Orcan
So now he hangs like Bagdets Governour,	2Tamb	5.1.158	Tamb
Like Summers vapours, vanisht by the Sun.	2Tamb	5.3.116	Tamb
were scortcht/And all the earth like Aetna breathing fire:	2Tamb	5.3.233	Tamb
And draw thee peecemeale like Hyppolitus,	2Tamb	5.3.240	Tamb
sure/When like the [Dracos] <Drancus> they were writ in blood.	Jew	Prol.21	Machvl
And in his house heape pearle like pibble-stones,	Jew	1.1.23	Barab
I, like enough, why then let every man/Provide him, and be there	Jew	1.1.170	Barab
No, Jew, like infidels.	Jew	1.2.62	Govnr
Thus like the sad presaging Raven that tolls/The sicke mans	Jew	2.1.1	Barab
rests no more/But bare remembrance; like a souldiers skarre,	Jew	2.1.10	Barab
We Jewes can fawne like Spaniels when we please;	Jew	2.3.20	Barab
the slave lccks like a hogs cheek new sindg'd.	Jew	2.3.42	P Barab
That when we speake with Gentiles like to you,	Jew	2.3.45	Barab
I like it much the better.	Jew	2.3.61	Lodowk
You'le like it better farre a nights than dayes.	Jew	2.3.63	Barab
Here's a leaner, how like you him?	Jew	2.3.126	P 1Offcr
And like a cunning Jew so cast about,	Jew	2.3.235	Barab
I cannot choose but like thy readinesse:	Jew	2.3.377	Barab
And like a cunning spirit feigne some lye,	Jew	2.3.382	Barab
And then thcu didst not like that holy life.	Jew	3.3.58	1Fryar
But perish underneath my bitter curse/Like Cain by Adam, for	Jew	3.4.33	Barab
And with her let it worke like Borgias wine,	Jew	3.4.98	Barab
and invenome her/That like a fiend hath left her father thus.	Jew	3.4.105	Barab
the Nuns are dead/That sound at other times like Tinkers pans?	Jew	4.1.3	Barab
As never Jew nor Christian knew the like:	Jew	4.1.118	Barab
When shall you see a Jew commit the like?	Jew	4.1.197	Barab
reading of the letter, he look'd like a man of another world.	Jew	4.2.7	P Pilia
a fellow met me with a muschatoes like a Ravens wing, and a	Jew	4.2.28	P Ithimr
and a Dagger with a hilt like a warming-pan, and he gave me a	Jew	4.2.29	P Ithimr
Then like a Jew he laugh'd and jeer'd, and told me he lov'd me	Jew	4.2.108	P Pilia
It twinckles like a Starre.	Jew	4.2.128	P Ithimr
grunts like a hog, and looks/Like one that is imploy'd in	Jew	4.3.11	Barab
and looks/Like one that is imploy'd in Catzerie/And crosbiting,	Jew	4.3.12	Barab
Knavely spoke, and like a Knight at Armes.	Jew	4.4.9	Pilia

LIKE (cont.)

Like thy breath, sweet-hart, no violet like 'em.	Jew	4.4.40		Ithimr
Foh, me thinkes they stinke like a Holly-Hoke.	Jew	4.4.41		Pilia
Their deaths were like their lives, then think not of 'em;	Jew	5.1.56		Govnr
Lives like the Asse that Aesope speaketh of,	Jew	5.2.40		Barab
And reason too, for Christians doe the like:	Jew	5.2.116		Barab
And if you like them, drinke your fill and dye:	Jew	5.5.9		Barab
That like I best that flyes beyond my reach.	P 99	2.42		Guise
Now Madame, how like you our lusty Admirall?	P 494	9.13		Guise
And like disportes, such as doe fit the Court?	P 629	12.42		King
I like not this, come Epernoune/Lets goe seek the Duke and make	P 785	15.43		King
Whilste I cry placet like a Senator.	P 861	17.56		King
Mother, how like you this device of mine?	P1065	19.135		King
I like not this Friers look.	P1159	22.21		Eprnon
And like Leander gaspt upon the sande,	Edw	1.1.8		Gavstn
And as I like your discoursing, ile have you.	Edw	1.1.32		Gavstn
Like Sylvian <Sylvan> Nimphes my pages shall be clad,	Edw	1.1.58		Gavstn
My men like Satyres grazing on the lawnes,	Edw	1.1.59		Gavstn
One like Actaeon peeping through the grove,	Edw	1.1.67		Gavstn
Ignoble vassaile that like Phaeton,	Edw	1.4.16		Warwck
Like frantick Juno will I fill the earth,	Edw	1.4.178		Queene
Which beates upon it like the Cyclops hammers,	Edw	1.4.313		Edward
Or if that loftie office like thee not,	Edw	1.4.355		Edward
And Midas like he jets it in the court,	Edw	1.4.408		Mortmr
Tis like enough, for since he was exild,	Edw	2.1.23		Baldck
And learne to court it like a Gentleman,	Edw	2.1.32		Spencr
And being like pins heads, blame me for the bignesse,	Edw	2.1.48		Baldck
Which made me curate-like in mine attire,	Edw	2.1.49		Baldck
The like oath Penbrooke takes.	Edw	2.2.108		Penbrk
But once, and then thy souldiers marcht like players,	Edw	2.2.183		Mortmr
Where womens favors hung like labels downe.	Edw	2.2.187		Mortmr
That like the Greekish strumpet traind to armes/And bloudie	Edw	2.5.15		Lncstr
And must be awde and governd like a child.	Edw	3.1.31		Baldck
True, and it like your grace,/That powres in lieu of all your	Edw	3.1.43		Spencr
That therewith all enchaunted like the guarde,	Edw	3.1.266		Spencr
I like not this relenting moode in Edmund,	Edw	4.6.38		Mortmr
That like the lawles Catiline of Rome,	Edw	4.6.51		Rice
Or like the snakie wreathe of Tisiphon,	Edw	5.1.45		Edward
That like a mountaine overwhelmes my blisse,	Edw	5.1.54		Edward
Must I be vexed like the nightly birde,	Edw	5.3.6		Edward
Like Lyons shall they guard us when we please,	F 151	1.1.123		Valdes
Like Almaine Rutters with their horsemens staves,	F 152	1.1.124		Valdes
Sometimes like women or unwedded Maides,	F 154	1.1.126		Valdes
I will set my countenance like a Precisian, and begin to speake	F 214	1.2.21	P	Wagner
and I will make thee go, like Qui mihi discipulus.	F 355	1.4.13	P	Wagner
<Tel Faustus, how dost thou like thy wife>?	F 533	(HC261) A	P	Mephst
She whom thine eye shall like, thy heart shall have,	F 539	2.1.151		Mephst
I am like to Ovids Flea, I can creepe into every corner of a	F 664	2.2.113	P	Pride
Sometimes, like a Perriwig, I sit upon her Brow:	F 666	2.2.115	P	Pride
next, like a Neckelace I hang about her Necke:	F 666	2.2.115	P	Pride
Then <or>, like a Fan of Feathers, I kisse her [lippes]; And	F 667	2.2.116	P	Pride
<Now Faustus, how dost thou like this>?	F 711	(HC264) A		Lucifr
That's like, 'faith:	F 734	2.3.13	P	Dick
To make his Monkes and Abbots stand like Apes,	F 861	3.1.83		Mephst
And point like Antiques at his triple Crowne:	F 862	3.1.84		Mephst
And like a Steeple over-peeres the Church.	F 913	3.1.135		Pope
what you say, we looke not like cup-stealers I can tell you.	F1100	3.3.13	P	Robin
he lookes as like [a] conjurer as the Pope to a Coster-monger.	F1228	4.1.74	P	Benvol
such belly-cheere, as Wagner in his life nere saw the like:	F1679	5.1.6	P	Wagner
Though thou hast now offended like a man,	F1710	5.1.37		OldMan
Doe not persever in it like a Divell;	F1711	5.1.38		OldMan
Say Wagner, thou hast perus'd my will,/How dost thou like it?	F1817	5.2.21		Faust
hadst set/In yonder throne, like those bright shining Saints,	F1905	5.2.109		GdAngl
Now draw up Faustus like a foggy mist,	F1952	5.2.156		Faust
thou serve me, and Ile make thee go like Qui mihi discipulus?	F App	p.229 13	P	Wagner
Heere's no body, if it like your Holynesse.	F App	p.231 4	P	Frier
Vanish vilaines, th'one like an Ape, an other like a Beare, the	F App	p.235 32	P	Mephst
th'one like an Ape, an other like a Beare, the third an Asse,	F App	p.235 32	P	Mephst
Ifaith he lookes much like a conjurer.	F App	p.236 11	P	Knight
But if it like your Grace, it is not in my abilitie to present	F App	p.237 41	P	Faust
but yet like an asse as I was, I would not be ruled by him, for	F App	p.240 129	P	HrsCsr
I like a ventrous youth, rid him into the deepe pond at the	F App	p.240 132	P	HrsCsr
If it like your grace, the yeere is divided into twoo circles	F App	p.242 19	P	Faust
hither, as ye see, how do you like them Madame, be they good?	F App	p.242 23	P	Faust
Trumpets and drums, like deadly threatning other,	Lucan, First Booke	6		
Like to a tall oake in a fruitfull field,	Lucan, First Booke	137		
Like to a Lyon of scortcht desart Affricke,	Lucan, First Booke	208		
And Vangions who like those of Sarmata,	Lucan, First Booke	431		
and where [Jove] <it> seemes/Bloudy like Dian, whom the	Lucan, First Booke	442		
Now spearlike, long; now like a spreading torch:	Lucan, First Booke	530		
a double point/Rose like the Theban brothers funerall fire;	Lucan, First Booke	550		
much like that hellish fiend/Which made the sterne Lycurgus	Lucan, First Booke	572		
Or fierce Agave mad; or like Megaera/That scar'd Alcides, when	Lucan, First Booke	574		
The skipping Salii with shields like wedges;	Lucan, First Booke	602		
long struggled, as being like to prove/An aukward sacrifice,	Lucan, First Booke	610		
Whose like Aegiptian Memphis never had/For skill in stars, and	Lucan, First Booke	639		
Were Love the cause, it's like I shoulde descry him,	Ovid's Elegies	1.2.5		
And captive like be manacled and bound.	Ovid's Elegies	1.2.30		
Love <Jove> knowes with such like praiers, I dayly move hir:	Ovid's Elegies	1.3.4		
Strike on the boord like them that pray for evill,	Ovid's Elegies	1.4.27		
And with mistrust of the like measure vext.	Ovid's Elegies	1.4.46		
Like twilight glimps at setting of the sunne,	Ovid's Elegies	1.5.5		
<make> slender/And to get out doth like apt members render.	Ovid's Elegies	1.6.6		

LIKE (cont.)

Gratis thou maiest be free, give like for like, Ovid's Elegies 1.6.23
What ere thou art, farewell, be like me paind, Ovid's Elegies 1.6.71
But though I like a swelling floud was driven, Ovid's Elegies 1.7.43
lookes shewed/Like marble from the Parian Mountaines hewed. Ovid's Elegies 1.7.52
Like Popler leaves blowne with a stormy flawe, Ovid's Elegies 1.7.54
Like water gushing from consuming snowe. Ovid's Elegies 1.7.58
And whom I like eternize by mine art. Ovid's Elegies 1.10.60
Your name approves you made for such like things, Ovid's Elegies 1.12.27
fine and thinne/Like to the silke the curious Seres spinne, Ovid's Elegies 1.14.6
Yet seemely like a Thracian Bacchinall/That tyr'd doth rashly Ovid's Elegies 1.14.21
When they were slender, and like downy mosse, Ovid's Elegies 1.14.23
love please/[Am] <And> driven like a ship upon rough seas, Ovid's Elegies 2.4.8
And she thats coy I like for being no clowne, Ovid's Elegies 2.4.13
And she <her> I like that with a majestie, Ovid's Elegies 2.4.29
If she be tall, shees like an Amazon, Ovid's Elegies 2.4.33
To these, or some of these like was her colour, Ovid's Elegies 2.5.41
To like a base wench of despisd condition. Ovid's Elegies 2.7.20
Nor do I like the country of my birth. Ovid's Elegies 2.16.38
Let us both lovers hope, and feare a like, Ovid's Elegies 2.19.5
Swift Atalantas flying legges like these, Ovid's Elegies 3.2.29
Coate-tuckt Dianas legges are painted like them, Ovid's Elegies 3.2.31
radiant like starres they be,/By which she perjurd oft hath Ovid's Elegies 3.3.9
Like lightning go, his strugling mouth being checkt. Ovid's Elegies 3.4.14
And like a burthen greevde the bed that mooved not. Ovid's Elegies 3.6.4
Yet like as if cold hemlocke I had drunke, Ovid's Elegies 3.6.13
Like a dull Cipher, or rude blocke I lay, Ovid's Elegies 3.6.15
Pure rose shee, like a Nun to sacrifice, Ovid's Elegies 3.6.21
Chur-like had I not gold, and could not use it? Ovid's Elegies 3.6.50
Yet notwithstanding, like one dead it lay, Ovid's Elegies 3.6.65
Now, Sabine-like, though chast she seemes to live, Ovid's Elegies 3.7.61
And Juno like with Dis raignes under ground? Ovid's Elegies 3.9.46
And like a wittall thinke thee voyde of slight. Ovid's Elegies 3.13.30
Like one start up your haire tost and displast, Ovid's Elegies 3.13.33
Which lightned by her necke, like Diamonds shone. Hero and Leander 1.26
But this is true, so like was one the other, Hero and Leander 1.39
For everie street like to a Firmament/Glistered with breathing Hero and Leander 1.97
For like Sea-nimphs inveigling harmony, Hero and Leander 1.105
Of two gold Ingots like in each respect. Hero and Leander 1.172
Which like sweet musicke entred Heroes eares, Hero and Leander 1.194
At last, like to a bold sharpe Sophister, Hero and Leander 1.197
Like untun'd golden strings all women are, Hero and Leander 1.229
for both not us'de,/Are of like worth. Hero and Leander 1.234
Lone women like to emptie houses perish. Hero and Leander 1.242
And yet I like them for the Orator. Hero and Leander 1.340
And like a planet, mooving severall waies, Hero and Leander 1.361
And like an insolent commaunding lover, Hero and Leander 1.409
When like desires and affections meet, Hero and Leander 2.30
And like light Salmacis, her body throes/Upon his bosome, where Hero and Leander 2.46
Like Aesops cocke, this jewell he enjoyed, Hero and Leander 2.51
Some hidden influence breeds like effect. Hero and Leander 2.60
Like to the tree of Tantalus she fled, Hero and Leander 2.75
But like exiled aire thrust from his sphere, Hero and Leander 2.118
Alcides like, by mightie violence, Hero and Leander 2.120
Like as the sunne in a Dyameter, Hero and Leander 2.123
And fell in drops like teares, because they mist him. Hero and Leander 2.174
Whose lively heat like fire from heaven fet, Hero and Leander 2.255
His hands he cast upon her like a snare, Hero and Leander 2.259
Like chast Diana, when Acteon spyde her, Hero and Leander 2.261
Much like a globe, (a globe may I tearme this, Hero and Leander 2.275
this strife of hers (like that/Which made the world) another Hero and Leander 2.291
Leander now like Theban Hercules, Hero and Leander 2.297
And [them] <then> like Mars and Ericine displayd, Hero and Leander 2.305
That Meremaid-like unto the floore she slid, Hero and Leander 2.315

LIKED

Jove liked her better then he did before. Ovid's Elegies 2.19.30
And kindly gave her, what she liked best. Ovid's Elegies 3.5.82

LIKELY

'Tis likely they in time may reape some fruit, Jew 2.3.84 Barab

LIKENES

And running in the likenes of an Hart, Edw 1.1.69 Gavstn

LIKENESSE

appeare to thee in their owne proper shapes and likenesse. F 656 2.2.105 P Belzeb
one of his devils turn'd me into the likenesse of an Apes face. F1554 4.5.50 P Dick
let it be in the likenesse of a little pretie frisking flea, F App p.231 62 P Clown

LIKES

And Ile dispose them as it likes me best, 2Tamb 4.1.166 Tamb
How likes your grace my sonnes pleasantnes? P 632 12.45 QnMoth
What so thy minde affectes or fancie likes. Edw 1.1.170 Edward
So pleaseth the Queene my mother, me it likes. Edw 4.2.21 Prince
O thou oft wilt blush/And say he likes me for my borrowed bush, Ovid's Elegies 1.14.48
And what she likes, let both hold ratifide. Ovid's Elegies 2.2.32
No one face likes me best, all faces moove, Ovid's Elegies 2.4.9
Seeing she likes my bookes, why should we jarre? Ovid's Elegies 2.4.20
Trips she, it likes me well, plods she, what than? Ovid's Elegies 2.4.23
(Such with my tongue it likes me to purloyne). Ovid's Elegies 2.5.24

LIKEST

sell him, but if thou likest him for ten Dollors more, take him, F1460 4.4.4 P Faust

LIKEWISE

And full three Sommers likewise shall he waste, Dido 1.1.91 Jupitr
She likewise in admyring spends her time, Dido 3.2.72 Juno
Be likewise end to my accursed life. 2Tamb 3.4.82 Olymp
I, and tis likewise thought you favour him <them> <'em> <hem>. Edw 2.2.226 Edward

LIKEWISE (cont.)
in the contrary circle it is likewise Summer with them, as in — F1583 4.6.26 P Faust
You likewise that repulst the Caicke foe, ... — Lucan, First Booke 459
So likewise we will through the world be rung, . . . — Ovid's Elegies 1.3.25
Thy mistrisse enseignes must be likewise thine. . . — Ovid's Elegies 2.3.10
Likewise the angrie sisters thus deluded, ... — Hero and Leander 1.473
LIKING
such lovelinesse and beautie had/As could provoke his liking, — Hero and Leander 1.423
LIK'ST
How lik'st thou her Ebea, will she serve? . . . . . — 1Tamb 3.3.178 Zabina
Now tell me, Ithimore, how lik'st thou this? . . . — Jew 2.3.364 Barab
As thou lik'st that, stop me another time. . . . — Jew 4.1.173 1Fryar
LIKST
if thou likst him for fifty, take him. . . . . — F App p.239 103 P Faust
LIKT
The gods abetted; Cato likt the other; . . . . . — Lucan, First Booke 129
To leave the rest, all likt me passing well, . . . — Ovid's Elegies 1.5.23
LILLY
Such as a rose mixt with a lilly breedes, ... — Ovid's Elegies 2.5.37
LIM
and there prie/Upon his brest, his thighs, and everie lim, — Hero and Leander 2.189
And every lim did as a soldier stout, ... — Hero and Leander 2.271
LIMBES
Hale them to prison, lade their limbes with gyves: . . — F1032 3.2.52 Pope
My limbes may issue from your smoky mouthes, . . . — F1955 5.2.159 Faust
Lie with him gently, when his limbes he spread/Upon the bed, but — Ovid's Elegies 1.4.15
To rest my limbes, uppon a bedde I lay, ... — Ovid's Elegies 1.5.2
LIMBS (See also LIMMES, LIMS)
O help us heaven, see, here are Faustus limbs, . . . — F1988 5.3.6 2Schol
We'll give his mangled limbs due buryall: . . . . — F1999 5.3.17 2Schol
What, wast my limbs through some Thesalian charms, . . — Ovid's Elegies 3.6.27
LIMIT
The head-strong Barons shall not limit me. . . . . — Edw 2.2.262 Edward
LIMITED
<O> No end is limited to damned soules. . . . . — F1963 5.2.167 Faust
LIMITS
Measuring the limits of his Emperie/By East and west, as . — 1Tamb 1.2.39 Tamb
Hell hath no limits, nor is circumscrib'd, ... — F 510 2.1.122 Mephst
And then large limits had their butting lands, . . . — Lucan, First Booke 169
LIMITTED
you not Traytors, I was limitted/For foure and twenty yeares, — F1395 4.2.71 Faust
LIMMES
First let thy Scythyan horse teare both our limmes/Rather then — 2Tamb 5.1.138 Orcan
So may his limmes be torne, as is this paper, ... — Edw 5.1.142 Edward
And whether I have limmes or no, I know not. . . . — Edw 5.5.65 Edward
Her halfe dead joynts, and trembling limmes I sawe, . . — Ovid's Elegies 1.7.53
By those white limmes, which sparckled through the lawne. — Hero and Leander 2.242
LIMNASPHALTES
Now fil the mouth of Limnasphaltes lake, ... — 2Tamb 5.1.67 Tamb
LIMNASPHALTIS (See also LYMNASPHALTIS)
When this our famous lake of Limnasphaltis/Makes walles a fresh — 2Tamb 5.1.17 Govnr
Circled about with Limnasphaltis Lake, ... — 2Tamb 5.2.5 Callap
LIMPING
to see the cripples/Goe limping home to Christendome on stilts. — Jew 2.3.212 Ithimr
Which limping Vulcan and his Cyclops set: . . . . . — Hero and Leander 1.152
LIMS
Whose wearie lims shall shortly make repose, ... — Dido 1.1.84 Jupitr
Ascanius, goe and drie thy drenched lims, ... — Dido 1.1.174 Aeneas
Whereat he lifted up his bedred lims, ... — Dido 2.1.250 Aeneas
So large of lims, his joints so strongly knit, ... — 1Tamb 2.1.9 Menaph
Their lims more large and of a bigger size/Than all the brats — 1Tamb 3.3.108 Bajzth
Whose shattered lims, being tost as high as heaven, . . — 2Tamb 3.2.100 Tamb
They shooke for feare, and cold benumm'd their lims, . — Lucan, First Booke 248
LINCOLNE
Darbie, Salsburie, Lincolne, Leicester, ... — Edw 1.1.103 Lncstr
LINE (See also LYNE)
Men from the farthest Equinoctiall line, ... — 1Tamb 1.1.119 Cosroe
But fixed now in the Meridian line, ... — 1Tamb 4.2.38 Tamb
Millions of Souldiers cut the Artick line, ... — 2Tamb 1.1.29 Orcan
Her name had bene in every line he wrote: . . . . . — 2Tamb 2.4.90 Tamb
That to the adverse poles of that straight line, . . . — 2Tamb 3.4.64 Therid
And every line begins with death againe: . . . . . — 2Tamb 4.2.48 Olymp
Cutting the Tropicke line of Capricorne, ... — 2Tamb 5.3.138 Tamb
Lies westward from the midst of Cancers line, ... — 2Tamb 5.3.146 Tamb
tell him, I scorne to write a line under a hundred crownes. — Jew 4.2.121 P Ithimr
I am a Prince of the Valoyses line,/Therfore an enemy to the — P 835 17.30 Guise
The wicked branch of curst Valois his line. . . . . — P1013 19.83 Guise
And roote Valoys his line from forth of France, . . . — P1113 21.7 Dumain
Ye gods of Phrigia and Iulus line, ... — Lucan, First Booke 199
The thunder hov'd horse in a crooked line, ... — Lucan, First Booke 222
Rash boy, who gave thee power to change a line? . . . — Ovid's Elegies 1.1.9
That am descended but of knightly line, ... — Ovid's Elegies 1.3.8
Or that unlike the line from whence I [sprong] <come>, . — Ovid's Elegies 1.15.3
the boord with wine/Was scribled, and thy fingers writ a line. — Ovid's Elegies 2.5.18
The stepdame read Hyppolitus lustlesse line. . . . . — Ovid's Elegies 2.18.30
LINEAGE (See LINNAGE)
LINEAMENTS
My bodies mortified lineaments/Should exercise the motions of — 2Tamb 5.3.188 Amyras
LINED
Fayre lined slippers for the cold: . . . . . . — Passionate Shepherd 15
LINEN (See LINNEN)
LINES
These letters, lines, and perjurd papers all, ... — Dido 5.1.300 Dido

LINES (cont.)		
That it might print these lines within his heart.	P 669 13.13	Duchss
To such a one my Lord, as when she reads my lines,	P 672 13.16	Duchss
Thou trothles and unjust, what lines are these?	P 680 13.24	Guise
But villaine he to whom these lines should goe,	P 696 13.40	Guise
And sends <send> his dutie by these speedye lines,	P1169 22.31	Frier
Sweete prince I come, these these thy amorous lines,	Edw 1.1.6	Gavstn
Lines, Circles, [Signes], Letters, [and] Characters,	F 78 1.1.50	Faust
The iterating of these lines brings gold;	F 544 2.1.156	Mephst
Lines thou shalt read in wine by my hand writ.	Ovid's Elegies	1.4.20
Nor let the armes of antient [lines] <lives> beguile thee,	Ovid's Elegies	1.8.65
Receive these lines, them to my Mistrisse carry,	Ovid's Elegies	1.11.7
You are unapt my looser lines to heare.	Ovid's Elegies	2.1.4
No intercepted lines thy deedes display,	Ovid's Elegies	2.5.5
Yet tragedies, and scepters fild my lines,	Ovid's Elegies	2.18.13
Whether the subtile maide lines bringes and carries,	Ovid's Elegies	2.19.41
Thou deignst unequall lines should thee rehearse,	Ovid's Elegies	3.1.37
With Muse oppos'd would I my lines had done,	Ovid's Elegies	3.11.17
Why see I lines so oft receivde and given,	Ovid's Elegies	3.13.31
Which is with azure circling lines empal'd,	Hero and Leander	2.274
LINGER (See also LYNGER)		
Then linger not my lord but do it straight.	Edw 1.4.58	Lncstr
Be it or no, he shall not linger here.	Edw 1.4.93	MortSr
Chiefely on thy lips let not his lips linger.	Ovid's Elegies	1.4.38
To linger by the way, and once she stayd,	Hero and Leander	2.7
LINGERED		
Their houshould gods restrain them not, none lingered,	Lucan, First Booke	505
Yet lingered not the day, but morning scard me.	Ovid's Elegies	1.13.48
LINGERING		
And not stand lingering here for amorous lookes:	Dido 4.3.38	Illion
For lingering here, neglecting Italy.	Dido 5.1.97	Aeneas
Where men are ready, lingering ever hurts:	Lucan, First Booke	282
LINGONES		
They whom the Lingones foild with painted speares,	Lucan, First Booke	398
LINGRED		
That long hath lingred for so high a seat.	1Tamb 5.1.502	Therid
LINGRING		
That lingring paines may massacre his heart.	1Tamb 5.1.228	Zabina
Least time be past, and lingring let us both.	2Tamb 1.2.75	Callap
LINING		
The lining, purple silke, with guilt starres drawne,	Hero and Leander	1.10
LINKE		
And let me linke [thy] <my> bodie to my <thy> lips,	Dido 4.3.28	Aeneas
That linke you in mariage with our daughter heer:	P 14 1.14	QnMoth
On tell-tales neckes thou seest the linke-knitt chaines,	Ovid's Elegies	2.2.41
LINKED		
these linked gems,/My Juno ware	Dido 1.1.42	Jupitr
LINKE-KNITT		
On tell-tales neckes thou seest the linke-knitt chaines,	Ovid's Elegies	2.2.41
LINNAGE		
And joynes your linnage to the crowne of France?	P 51 1.51	Admral
LINNEN		
And tye white linnen scarfes about their armes.	P 233 4.31	Guise
LINSTOCKE		
heare a Culverin discharg'd/By him that beares the Linstocke,	Jew 5.4.4	Govnr
LINUS		
Where Linus by his father Phoebus layed/To sing with his	Ovid's Elegies	3.8.23
LION (See also LYON)		
souldiers now that fought/So Lion-like upon Asphaltis plaines?	2Tamb 4.3.68	Tamb
Yet, shall the crowing of these cockerels,/Affright a Lion?	Edw 2.2.204	Edward
LIONESS (See LYONESSE)		
LION-LIKE		
souldiers now that fought/So Lion-like upon Asphaltis plaines?	2Tamb 4.3.68	Tamb
LIONS		
As princely Lions when they rouse themselves,	1Tamb 1.2.52	Techel
Before whom (mounted on a Lions backe)/Rhamnusia beares a	2Tamb 3.4.56	Therid
Can kinglie Lions fawne on creeping Ants?	Edw 1.4.15	Penbrk
But when the imperiall Lions flesh is gorde,	Edw 5.1.11	Edward
The Wrenne may strive against the Lions strength,	Edw 5.3.34	Edward
LIPPES		
I kisse her [lippes]; And then turning my selfe to a wrought	F 667 2.2.116	P Pride
Here will I dwell, for heaven is <be> in these lippes,	F1773 5.1.100	Faust
To quaver on her lippes even in her song,	Ovid's Elegies	2.4.26
There in your rosie lippes my tongue intombe,	Ovid's Elegies	3.13.23
Those orient cheekes and lippes, exceeding his/That leapt into	Hero and Leander	1.73
LIPS		
His lips an altar, where Ile offer up/As many kisses as the Sea	Dido 3.1.87	Dido
And let me linke [thy] <my> bodie to my <thy> lips,	Dido 4.3.28	Aeneas
O thy lips have sworne/To stay with Dido:	Dido 5.1.120	Dido
Yet never shall these lips bewray thy life.	Jew 3.3.75	Abigal
sort as if he had meant to make cleane my Boots with his lips;	Jew 4.2.31	P Ithimr
That kisse againe; she runs division of my lips.	Jew 4.2.127	P Ithimr
That glaunceth at my lips and flieth away:	Edw 1.1.23	Gavstn
Sir, must not come so neare and balke their lips.	Edw 2.5.103	Penbrk
and they shall serve for buttons to his lips, to keepe his	F1388 4.2.64	P Benvol
Her lips sucke <suckes> forth my soule, see where it flies.	F1771 5.1.98	Faust
Chiefely on thy lips let not his lips linger.	Ovid's Elegies	1.4.38
Meeter it were her lips were blewe with kissing/And on her	Ovid's Elegies	1.7.41
bondes contained/From barbarous lips of some Atturney strained.	Ovid's Elegies	1.12.24
Tis ill they pleas'd so much, for in my lips,	Ovid's Elegies	2.5.57
Let marchants seeke wealth, [and] with perjured lips,	Ovid's Elegies	2.10.33
Would first my beautious wenches moist lips touch,	Ovid's Elegies	2.15.17
With lying lips my God-head to deceave,	Ovid's Elegies	3.3.44

Line	Work	Ref	Speaker
LIPS (cont.)			
He kist her, and breath'd life into her lips,	Hero and Leander		2.3
LIQUED			
Pelignian fields [with] <which> liqued rivers flowe,	Ovid's Elegies		2.16.5
LIQUID			
And my pin'd soule resolv'd in liquid [ayre] <ay>,	1Tamb	5.1.300	Bajzth
<superfluities>/Is covered with a liquid purple veile,	2Tamb	1.3.80	Tamb
I, liquid golde when we have conquer'd him,	2Tamb	1.3.223	Tamb
that falles/Into the liquid substance of his streame,	2Tamb	5.1.19	Govnr
No, though Asphaltis lake were liquid gold,	2Tamb	5.1.155	Tamb
Weepe heavens, and vanish into liquid teares,	2Tamb	5.3.1	Therid
A streame of liquid pearle, which downe her face/Made	Hero and Leander		1.297
LIQUOR			
Give him his liquor?	1Tamb	5.1.310	P Zabina
LIST (Homograph)			
I may nor will list to such loathsome chaunge,	Dido	4.2.47	Iarbus
But when they list, their conquering fathers hart:	2Tamb	1.3.36	Zenoc
But now my boies, leave off, and list to me,	2Tamb	3.2.53	Tamb
The bullets fly at random where they list.	2Tamb	4.1.52	Calyph
Grave [Governor], list not to his exclames:	Jew	1.2.128	1Knght
Revenge it Henry as thou list or dare,	P 819	17.14	Guise
He that I list to favour shall be great:	Edw	2.2.263	Edward
And what I list commaund, who dare controwle?	Edw	5.4.68	Mortmr
list a while to me,/And then thy heart, were it as Gurneys is,	Edw	5.5.52	Edward
And then turning my selfe to a wrought Smocke do what I list.	F 668	2.2.117	P Pride
by whome thou canst accomplish what thou list, this therefore	F App	p.236 5	P Emper
LISTE			
revenge it henry yf thow liste or darst	Paris	ms23,p391	Guise
LISTEN (See also LIST)			
Leave this my Love, and listen more to me.	2Tamb	4.2.38	Therid
then listen to my words,/And I will teach [thee] that shall	Jew	2.3.167	Barab
LISTS			
Fower chariot-horses from the lists even ends.	Ovid's Elegies		3.2.66
LITLE			
He that with Shepheards and a litle spoile,	1Tamb	2.1.54	Ceneus
With litle slaughter take Meanders course,	1Tamb	2.5.27	Cosroe
lord, specially having so smal a walke, and so litle exercise.	1Tamb	4.4.106	P Therid
A litle further, gentle Almeda.	2Tamb	1.2.17	Callap
Breed litle strength to our securitie,	2Tamb	2.1.43	Sgsmnd
And cares so litle for their prophet Christ.	2Tamb	2.2.35	Gazell
(Too litle to defend our guiltlesse lives)/Sufficient to	2Tamb	2.2.60	Orcan
Deep rivers, havens, creekes, and litle seas,	2Tamb	3.2.87	Tamb
(Perdicas) and I feare as litle their tara, tantaras, their	2Tamb	4.1.67	P Calyph
That litle hope is left to save our lives,	2Tamb	5.1.4	Maxim
To save thy life, and us a litle labour,	2Tamb	5.1.50	Therid
LITTER			
Here is a Litter readie for your grace,	Edw	4.7.84	Leistr
A litter hast thou, lay me in a hearse,	Edw	4.7.87	Edward
LITTLE			
Hold here my little love:	Dido	1.1.42	Jupitr
A little while prolong'd her husbands life:	Dido	2.1.246	Aeneas
Looke sister how Aeneas little sonne/Playes with your garments	Dido	3.1.20	Anna
Yea little sonne, are you so forward now?	Dido	3.3.34	Dido
As in the Sea are little water drops:	Dido	4.4.63	Dido
Rather Ascania by your little sonne.	Dido	5.1.21	Serg
Spendst thou thy time about this little boy,	Dido	5.1.51	Hermes
I feare I sawe Aeneas little sonne,	Dido	5.1.83	Dido
O Dido, your little sonne Ascanius/Is gone!	Dido	5.1.212	Nurse
At every little breath that thorow heaven is blowen:	2Tamb	4.3.124	Tamb
increaseth, so inclose/Infinite riches in a little roome.	Jew	1.1.37	Barab
What Callapine, a little curtesie.	Jew	1.2.23	Calym
From nought at first thou camst to little welth,	Jew	1.2.105	1Knght
From little unto more, from more to most:	Jew	1.2.106	1Knght
What, woman, moane not for a little losse:	Jew	1.2.226	Barab
Hinder her not, thou man of little faith,	Jew	1.2.340	1Fryar
I am a little busie, Sir, pray pardon me.	Jew	2.3.231	Barab
master, be rul'd by me a little; so, let him leane upon his	Jew	4.1.153	P Ithimr
Love me little, love me long, let musicke rumble,	Jew	4.4.28	Ithimr
Now Guise may storme but doe us little hurt:	P 28	1.28	Navrre
The time is little that thou hast to stay,	Edw	1.4.138	Edward
Tis not a black coate and a little band,	Edw	2.1.33	Spencr
hence, out of the way/A little, but our men shall go along.	Edw	2.5.101	Penbrk
Madam in this matter/We will employ you and your little sonne,	Edw	3.1.70	Edward
Ah nothing greeves me but my little boye,	Edw	4.3.48	Edward
sleepe, to take a quill/And blowe a little powder in his eares,	Edw	5.4.35	Ltborn
Had on her necke a little wart, or mole;	F1267	4.1.113	Emper
I had nothing under me but a little straw, and had much ado to	F1486	4.4.30	P HrsCsr
I thinking that a little would serve his turne, bad him take as	F1528	4.5.24	P Carter
I will attempt, which is but little worth.	F1758	5.1.85	Mephst
O soule be chang'd into <to> [little] <small> water drops,	F1977	5.2.181	Faust
let it be in the likenesse of a little pretie frisking flea,	F App	p.231 62	P Clown
Soone may you plow the little lands <land> I have,	Ovid's Elegies		1.3.9
Little I aske, a little entrance make,	Ovid's Elegies		1.6.3
Let them aske some-what, many asking little,	Ovid's Elegies		1.8.89
A little fild thee, and for love of talke,	Ovid's Elegies		2.6.29
The little stones these little verses have.	Ovid's Elegies		2.6.60
Each little hill shall for a table stand:	Ovid's Elegies		2.11.48
No little ditched townes, no lowlie walles,	Ovid's Elegies		2.12.7
And with swift Naggs drawing thy little Coach,	Ovid's Elegies		2.16.49
To get the dore with little noise unbard.	Ovid's Elegies		3.1.50
Thy labour ever lasts, she askes but little.	Ovid's Elegies		3.1.68
A little boy druncke teate-distilling showers.	Ovid's Elegies		3.9.22
And little Piggs, base Hog-sties sacrifice,	Ovid's Elegies		3.12.16

LITTLE (cont.)				
Where little ground to be inclosd befalles,	Ovid's Elegies	3.14.12		
At least vouchsafe these armes some little roome,	Hero and Leander	2.249		
LITTORA				
league,/Littora littoribus contraria, fluctibus undas/Imprecor:	Dido	5.1.310		Dido
LITTORIBUS				
league,/Littora littoribus contraria, fluctibus undas/Imprecor:	Dido	5.1.310		Dido
LIV'D				
And had she liv'd before the siege of Troy,	2Tamb	2.4.86		Tamb
That in this house I liv'd religiously,	Jew	3.6.13		Abigal
No, but I grieve because she liv'd so long.	Jew	4.1.18		Barab
Who would not thinke but that this Fryar liv'd?	Jew	4.1.156		Barab
That this faire Lady, whilest she liv'd on earth,	F1266	4.1.112		Emper
that Hellen of Greece was the admirablest Lady that ever liv'd:	F1684	5.1.11	P	1Schol
chamber-fellow, had I liv'd with thee, then had I lived still,	F1824	5.2.28	P	Faust
in that manner that they best liv'd in, in their most	F App	p.237 48	P	Faust
this Lady while she liv'd had a wart or moale in her necke,	F App	p.238 60	P	Emper
He liv'd secure boasting his former deeds,	Lucan, First Booke	135		
LIV'DE				
Two of my fathers servants whilst he liv'de,	Edw	2.2.240		Neece
Had Edmund liv'de, he would have sought thy death.	Edw	5.4.112		Queene
LIVDE				
Mine old lord whiles he livde, was so precise,	Edw	2.1.46		Baldck
LIV'DST				
Was I: thou liv'dst, while thou esteemdst my faith.	Ovid's Elegies	3.8.56		
LIVE				
To make us live unto our former heate,	Dido	1.1.160		Achat
Live happie in the height of all content,	Dido	1.1.195		Aeneas
Live long Aeneas and Ascanius.	Dido	2.1.53		Serg
Yet who so wretched but desires to live?	Dido	2.1.238		Aeneas
O let me live, great Neoptolemus.	Dido	2.1.239		Aeneas
No, live Iarbus, what hast thou deserv'd,	Dido	3.1.41		Dido
Fancie and modestie shall live as mates,	Dido	3.2.58		Venus
And mought I live to see him sacke rich Thebes,	Dido	3.3.42		Aeneas
And might I live to see thee shipt away,	Dido	3.3.46		Iarbus
This is no life for men at armes to live,	Dido	4.3.33		Achat
That I might live to see this boy a man,	Dido	4.5.18		Nurse
why, I may live a hundred yeares,/Fourescore is but a girles	Dido	4.5.31		Nurse
And I will live a private life with him.	Dido	5.1.198		Dido
Live false Aeneas, truest Dido dyes,	Dido	5.1.312		Dido
Yet live, yea, live, Mycetes wils it so:	1Tamb	1.1.27		Mycet
Long live Cosroe mighty Emperour.	1Tamb	1.1.169		Ortyg
And Jove may never let me longer live,	1Tamb	1.1.170		Cosroe
But since I love to live at liberty,	1Tamb	1.2.26		Tamb
Disdaines Zenocrate to live with me?	1Tamb	1.2.82		Tamb
That live by rapine and by lawlesse spoile,	1Tamb	2.2.23		Meandr
His Highnesse pleasure is that he should live,	1Tamb	2.2.37		Meandr
That live confounded in disordered troopes,	1Tamb	2.2.60		Meandr
And live like Gentlemen in Persea.	1Tamb	2.2.71		Meandr
Nay, though I praise it, I can live without it.	1Tamb	2.5.66		Therid
Long live Tamburlaine, and raigne in Asia.	1Tamb	2.7.64		All
That I may live and die with Tamburlaine.	1Tamb	3.2.24		Zenoc
But let the yong Arabian live in hope,	1Tamb	3.2.57		Agidas
But as I live that towne shall curse the time/That Tamburlaine	1Tamb	3.3.59		Tamb
Prepare thy selfe to live and die my slave.	1Tamb	3.3.207		Zabina
That not a man should live to rue their fall.	1Tamb	4.1.35		Souldn
for if she live but a while longer, shee will fall into a	1Tamb	4.4.49	P	Tamb
Let us live in spite of them, looking some happie power will	1Tamb	4.4.99	P	Zabina
Why should we live, O wretches, beggars, slaves,	1Tamb	5.1.248		Zabina
Why live we Bajazeth, and build up neasts,	1Tamb	5.1.249		Zabina
That in this terrour Tamburlaine may live.	1Tamb	5.1.299		Bajzth
To see them live so long in misery:	1Tamb	5.1.370		Zenoc
But whilst I live will be at truce with thee.	2Tamb	1.1.130		Sgsmnd
Yes father, you shal see me if I live,	2Tamb	1.3.54		Celeb
Live still my Love and so conserve my life,	2Tamb	2.4.55		Tamb
Live still my Lord, O let my soveraigne live,	2Tamb	2.4.57		Zenoc
Come downe from heaven and live with me againe.	2Tamb	2.4.118		Tamb
And all this raging cannot make her live,	2Tamb	2.4.120		Therid
Long live Callepinus, Emperour of Turky.	2Tamb	3.1.6	P	Orcan
Lies heavy on my heart, I cannot live.	2Tamb	3.4.5		Capt
Death, whether art thou gone that both we live?	2Tamb	3.4.11		Olymp
For think ye I can live, and see him dead?	2Tamb	3.4.27		Sonne
By Mahomet not one of them shal live.	2Tamb	3.5.17		Callap
If you can live with it, then live, and draw/My chariot swifter	2Tamb	4.3.20		Tamb
then live, and draw/My chariot swifter than the racking	2Tamb	4.3.20		Tamb
Live [continent] <content> then (ye slaves) and meet not me	2Tamb	4.3.81		Tamb
To live secure, and keep his forces out,	2Tamb	5.1.16		Govnr
And yet I live untoucht by Mahomet:	2Tamb	5.1.182		Tamb
And live in spight of death above a day.	2Tamb	5.3.101		Tamb
of all the villaines power/Live to give offer of another fight.	2Tamb	5.3.109		Tamb
And live in all your seedes immortally:	2Tamb	5.3.174		Tamb
Live still; and if thou canst, get more.	Jew	1.2.102		Govnr
The man that dealeth righteously shall live:	Jew	1.2.116		Barab
And yet have kept enough to live upon;	Jew	1.2.190		Barab
No, I will live; nor loath I this my life:	Jew	1.2.266		Barab
For whilst I live, here lives my soules sole hope,	Jew	2.1.29		Barab
And these my teares to blood, that he might live.	Jew	3.2.19		Govnr
Ne're shall she live to inherit ought of mine,	Jew	3.4.30		Barab
And whilst I live use halfe; spend as my selfe;	Jew	3.4.45		Barab
That thou mayst freely live to be my heire.	Jew	3.4.63		Barab
Nor shall the Heathens live upon our spoyle:	Jew	3.5.12		Govnr
For every yeare they swell, and yet they live;	Jew	4.1.6		Barab
to some religious house/So I may be baptiz'd and live therein.	Jew	4.1.76		Barab

LIVE (cont.)

Therefore 'tis not requisite he should live.	Jew	4.1.121		Barab
Shalt live with me and be my love.	Jew	4.2.98		Ithimr
Devils doe your worst, [I'le] <I> live in spite of you.	Jew	5.1.41		Barab
Yet you doe live, and live for me you shall:	Jew	5.2.63		Barab
Nay more, doe this, and live thou Governor still.	Jew	5.2.89		Govnr
Governor, I enlarge thee, live with me,	Jew	5.2.91		Barab
Thus loving neither, will I live with both,	Jew	5.2.111		Barab
Rather then thus to live as Turkish thrals,	Jew	5.4.8		1Knght
For so I live, perish may all the world.	Jew	5.5.10		Barab
Thou shalt not live in doubt of any thing.	Jew	5.5.45		Barab
And live in Malta prisoner; for come [all] <call> the world/To	Jew	5.5.119		Govnr
That I with her may dye and live againe.	P 190	3.25		Navrre
them thither, and then/Beset his house that not a man may live.	P 289	5.16		Guise
How may we doe? I feare me they will live.	P 420	7.60		Guise
As I doe live, so surely shall he dye,	P 521	9.40		QnMoth
As not a man may live without our leaves.	P 638	12.51		QnMoth
And fly my presence if thou looke to live.	P 692	13.36		Guise
I may be stabd, and live till he be dead,	P 778	15.36		Mugern
But as I live, so sure the Guise shall dye.	P 899	17.94		King
For since the Guise is dead, I will not live.	P1090	19.160		QnMoth
O my Lord, let him live a while.	P1173	22.35		Eprnon
Ah, had your highnes let him live,	P1183	22.45		Eprnon
Tell her for all this that I hope to live,	P1196	22.58		King
Tell me Surgeon, shall I live?	P1211	22.73		King
Tell me Surgeon and flatter not, may I live?	P1222	22.84		King
Alas my Lord, your highnes cannot live.	P1223	22.85		Srgeon
Surgeon, why saist thou so? the King may live.	P1224	22.86		Navrre
Long may you live, and still be King of France.	P1226	22.88		Navrre
Then live and be the favorit of a king?	Edw	1.1.5		Gavstn
Ile flatter these, and make them live in hope:	Edw	1.1.43		Gavstn
And eyther die, or live with Gaveston.	Edw	1.1.138		Edward
To live in greefe and balefull discontent,	Edw	1.2.48		Queene
If I be king, not one of them shall live.	Edw	1.4.105		Edward
Live where thou wilt, ile send thee gould enough,	Edw	1.4.113		Edward
And whereas he shall live and be belovde,	Edw	1.4.261		Mortmr
Then let her live abandond and forlorne.	Edw	1.4.298		Queene
Live thou with me as my companion.	Edw	1.4.343		Edward
Then so am I, and live to do him service,	Edw	1.4.421		Mortmr
May with one word, advaunce us while we live:	Edw	2.1.9		Spencr
Yes more then thou canst answer though he live,	Edw	2.2.87		Edward
But if I live, ile tread upon their heads,	Edw	2.2.96		Edward
By heaven, the abject villaine shall not live.	Edw	2.2.106		Mortmr
Do what they can, weele live in Tinmoth here,	Edw	2.2.221		Edward
As Isabell could live with thee for ever.	Edw	2.4.60		Queene
Long live my soveraigne the noble Edward,	Edw	3.1.32		SpncrP
Long live king Edward, Englands lawful lord.	Edw	3.1.151		Herald
The worst is death, and better die to live,	Edw	3.1.243		Lncstr
Then live in infamie under such a king.	Edw	3.1.244		Lncstr
Madam, long may you live,	Edw	4.2.34		Kent
To die sweet Spencer, therefore live wee all,	Edw	4.7.111		Baldck
Spencer, all live to die, and rise to fall.	Edw	4.7.112		Baldck
Ile not resigne, but whilst I live, [be king].	Edw	5.1.86		Edward
Or if I live, let me forget my selfe.	Edw	5.1.111		Edward
Men are ordaind to live in miserie,	Edw	5.3.2		Matrvs
Long live king Edward, by the grace of God/King of England, and	Edw	5.4.73		ArchBp
My lord, he is my unckle, and shall live.	Edw	5.4.91		King
My lord, if you will let my unckle live,	Edw	5.4.99		King
And live and die in Aristotles workes.	F 33	1.1.5		Faust
Couldst <Wouldst> thou make men <man> to live eternally,	F 52	1.1.24		Faust
As thou to live, therefore object it not.	F 162	1.1.134		Faust
I charge thee waite upon me whilst I live/To do what ever	F 264	1.3.36		Faust
And what are you that live with Lucifer?	F 297	1.3.69		Faust
Unhappy spirits that [fell] <live> with Lucifer,	F 298	1.3.70		Mephst
Letting him live in all voluptuousnesse,	F 320	1.3.92		Faust
The Emperour shall not live, but by my leave,	F 338	1.3.110		Faust
I'le live in speculation of this Art/Till Mephostophilis	F 341	1.3.113		Faust
for I am wanton and lascivious, and cannot live without a wife.	F 530	2.1.142	P	Faust
and I live along, then thou should'st see how fat I'de <I	F 682	2.2.131	P	Envy
And live belov'd of mightie Carolus.	F1324	4.1.170		Emper
And thither wee'le repaire and live obscure,	F1453	4.3.23		Benvol
We'le rather die with griefe, then live with shame.	F1456	4.3.26		Benvol
if I live till morning, Il'e visit you:	F1877	5.2.81	P	Faust
There are live quarters broyling on the coles,	F1913	5.2.117		BdAngl
Now hast thou but one bare houre to live,	F1927	5.2.131		Faust
Let Faustus live in hell a thousand yeares,	F1961	5.2.165		Faust
But mine must live still to be plagu'd in hell.	F1971	5.2.175		Faust
And give me cause to praise thee whilst I live.	F App	p.237 36		Emper
my Lord, and whilst I live, Rest beholding for this curtesie.	F App	p.243 30	P	Duchss
And they of Nilus mouth (if there live any).	Lucan, First Booke	20		
And few live that behold their ancient seats;	Lucan, First Booke	27		
If men have Faith, Ile live with thee for ever.	Ovid's Elegies	1.3.16		
Ile live with thee, and die, or <ere> thou shalt <shall>	Ovid's Elegies	1.3.18		
Oft thou wilt say, live well, thou wilt pray oft,	Ovid's Elegies	1.8.107		
Homer shall live while Tenedos stands and Ide,	Ovid's Elegies	1.15.9		
Loftie Lucretius shall live that houre,	Ovid's Elegies	1.15.23		
Ile live, and as he puls me downe, mount higher.	Ovid's Elegies	1.15.42		
Behould how quailes among their battailes live,	Ovid's Elegies	2.6.27		
And time it was for me to live in quiet,	Ovid's Elegies	2.9.23		
Live without love, so sweete ill is a maide.	Ovid's Elegies	2.9.26		
Now, Sabine-like, though chast she seemes to live,	Ovid's Elegies	3.7.61		
Live godly, thou shalt die, though honour heaven,	Ovid's Elegies	3.8.37		
Nor with thee, nor without thee can I live,	Ovid's Elegies	3.10.39		

LIVE (cont.)
Nor do I give thee counsaile to live chaste, — Ovid's Elegies 3.13.3
Why vowest thou then to live in Sestos here, — Hero and Leander 1.227
Wilt thou live single still? — Hero and Leander 1.257
As Greece will thinke, if thus you live alone, — Hero and Leander 1.289
Come live with mee, and be my love, — Passionate Shepherd 1
Come <Then> live with mee, and be my love. — Passionate Shepherd 20
Then live with mee, and be my love. — Passionate Shepherd 24

LIVED
Which Circes sent Sicheus when he lived: — Dido 4.4.11 Dido
I had beene stifled, and not lived to see, — Edw 1.4.176 Queene
Nay, to my death, for too long have I lived, — Edw 5.6.83 Queene
thee, then had I lived still, but now must <I> dye eternally. — F1825 5.2.29 P Faust
But neither was I man, nor lived then. — Ovid's Elegies 3.6.60

LIVELES
And weepe upon your liveles carcases, — Dido 5.1.177 Dido
The Duke of Guise stampes on thy liveles bulke. — P 315 5.42 Guise

LIVELESSE
Which dies my lockes so livelesse as they are. — 1Tamb 3.2.15 Zenoc

LIVELIE
A livelie vine of greene sea agget spread; — Hero and Leander 1.138

LIVELIER
And Tithon livelier then his yeeres require. — Ovid's Elegies 3.6.42

LIVELY
And tempered every soule with lively heat, — 2Tamb 2.4.10 Tamb
The lively spirits which the heart ingenders/Are partcht and — 2Tamb 5.3.94 Phsitn
Oh that my sighs could turne to lively breath; — Jew 3.2.18 Govnr
spirites as can lively resemble Alexander and his Paramour, — F App p.237 46 P Faust
even nowe when youthfull bloud/Pricks forth our lively bodies, — Lucan, First Booke 364
And in the morne beene lively nerethelesse. — Ovid's Elegies 2.10.28
And crying, Love I come, leapt lively in. — Hero and Leander 2.154
Whose lively heat like fire from heaven fet, — Hero and Leander 2.255

LIVER
I feele my liver pierc'd and all my vaines, — 2Tamb 3.4.6 Capt
The liver swell'd with filth, and every vaine/Did threaten — Lucan, First Booke 620
The heart stird not, and from the gaping liver/Squis'd matter; — Lucan, First Booke 623
At that bunch where the liver is, appear'd/A knob of flesh, — Lucan, First Booke 626
And pierst my liver with sharpe needle poynts <needles>? — Ovid's Elegies 3.6.30

LIVERIE
And clad her in a Chrystall liverie, — Dido 5.1.6 Aeneas
do cleare the clowdy aire/And cloath it in a christall liverie, — 2Tamb 1.3.4 Tamb

LIVERIES
With naked swords and scarlet liveries: — 2Tamb 3.4.55 Therid
Whose proud fantastick liveries make such show, — Edw 1.4.410 Mortmr

LIVERY
Blood is the God of Wars rich livery. — 2Tamb 3.2.116 Tamb

LIVES
And spare our lives whom every spite pursues. — Dido 1.2.9 Illion
We will account her author of our lives. — Dido 3.1.112 Aeneas
That sav'd your famisht souldiers lives from death, — Dido 3.3.52 Achat
Whiles Dido lives and rules in Junos towne, — Dido 3.4.50 Aeneas
O Dido, patronesse of all our lives, — Dido 4.4.55 Aeneas
All that they have, their lands, their goods, their lives, — Dido 4.4.76 Dido
Our kinsmens [lives] <loves>, and thousand guiltles soules, — Dido 4.4.90 Aeneas
Share equally the gold that bought their lives, — 1Tamb 2.2.70 Meandr
So will we with our powers and our lives, — 1Tamb 2.5.34 Ortyg
Why stay we thus prolonging all their lives? — 1Tamb 3.3.97 Techel
But that he lives and will be Conquerour. — 1Tamb 3.3.211 Zenoc
There whiles he lives, shal Bajazeth be kept, — 1Tamb 4.2.85 Tamb
If with their lives they will be pleasde to yeeld, — 1Tamb 4.4.89 Tamb
And make us desperate of our threatned lives: — 1Tamb 5.1.6 Govnr
Whose honors and whose lives relie on him: — 1Tamb 5.1.19 Govnr
liberties and lives were weigh'd/In equall care and ballance — 1Tamb 5.1.41 Govnr
on whose safe return/Depends our citie, libertie, and lives. — 1Tamb 5.1.63 Govnr
and Furies dread)/As for their liberties, their loves or lives. — 1Tamb 5.1.95 1Virgn
They have refusde the offer of their lives, — 1Tamb 5.1.126 Tamb
Whose lives were dearer to Zenocrate/Than her owne life, or — 1Tamb 5.1.337 Zenoc
Have desperatly dispatcht their slavish lives: — 1Tamb 5.1.472 Tamb
Who lives in Egypt, prisoner to that slave, — 2Tamb 1.1.4 Orcan
To bid us battaile for our dearest lives. — 2Tamb 2.2.28 1Msngr
(Too litle to defend our guiltlesse lives)/Sufficient to — 2Tamb 2.2.60 Orcan
And in your lives your fathers excellency. — 2Tamb 2.4.76 Zenoc
Though she be dead, yet let me think she lives, — 2Tamb 2.4.127 Tamb
But yet Ile save their lives and make them slaves. — 2Tamb 3.5.63 Tamb
That litle hope is left to save our lives, — 2Tamb 5.1.4 Maxim
And now will work a refuge to our lives, — 2Tamb 5.1.25 1Citzn
That let your lives commaund in spight of death. — 2Tamb 5.3.160 Tamb
For by your life we entertaine our lives. — 2Tamb 5.3.167 Celeb
And for his conscience lives in beggery. — Jew 1.1.120 Barab
For through our sufferance of your hatefull lives, — Jew 1.2.63 Govnr
To take the lives of miserable men, — Jew 1.2.147 Barab
For whilst I live, here lives my soules sole hope, — Jew 2.1.29 Barab
I thinke by this/You purchase both their lives; is it not so? — Jew 2.3.366 Ithimr
Now I have such a plot for both their lives, — Jew 4.1.117 Barab
I, and our lives too, therfore pull amaine. — Jew 4.1.150 Ithimr
Jew, he lives upon pickled Grashoppers, and sauc'd Mushrumbs. — Jew 4.4.61 P Ithimr
Their deaths were like their lives, then think not of 'em; — Jew 5.1.56 Govnr
Lives like the Asse that Aesope speaketh of, — Jew 5.2.40 Barab
I know; and they shall witnesse with their lives. — Jew 5.2.123 Barab
May not desolve, till death desolve our lives, — P 5 1.5 Charls
That seeke to massacre our guiltles lives. — P 261 4.59 Admral
That swim about and so preserve their lives: — P 419 7.59 Guise
For while she lives Katherine will be Queene. — P 654 12.67 QnMoth

LIVES (cont.)			
How many noble men have lost their lives,	P 795	16.9	Navrre
Yet lives/My brother Duke Dumaine, and many moe:	P1098	20.8	Cardnl
I priest, and lives to be revengd on thee,	Edw	1.1.178	Edward
That slie inveigling Frenchman weele exile,/Or lose our lives:	Edw	1.2.58	Mortmr
And either have our wils, or lose our lives.	Edw	1.4.46	Mortmr
Lives uncontroulde within the English pale,	Edw	2.2.165	Lncstr
And let their lives bloud slake thy furies hunger:	Edw	2.2.205	Edward
I will have heads, and lives, for him as many,	Edw	3.1.132	Edward
This graunted, they, their honors, and their lives,	Edw	3.1.170	Herald
And lives t'advance your standard good my lord.	Edw	4.2.42	Mortmr
How meane you, and the king my father lives?	Edw	4.2.43	Prince
Your lives and my dishonor they pursue,	Edw	4.7.23	Edward
Armes that pursue our lives with deadly hate.	Edw	4.7.32	Spencr
Therefore come, dalliance dangereth our lives.	Edw	5.3.3	Matrvs
Thus lives old Edward not reliev'd by any,	Edw	5.3.23	Edward
That I shall waite on Faustus whilst he lives,	F 420	2.1.32	Mephst
Come Faustus while the Emperour lives.	F1321	4.1.167	Emper
Pitie us gentle Faustus, save our lives.	F1417	4.2.93	Fredrk
Ile feede thy divel with horse-bread as long as he lives,	F App	p.234 31	P Rafe
Nor let the armes of antient [lines] <lives> beguile thee,	Ovid's Elegies	1.8.65	
Ascreus lives, while grapes with new wine swell,	Ovid's Elegies	1.15.11	
Full concord all your lives was you betwixt,	Ovid's Elegies	2.6.13	
The ravenous vulture lives, the Puttock hovers/Around the aire,	Ovid's Elegies	2.6.33	
There lives the Phoenix one alone bird ever.	Ovid's Elegies	2.6.54	
And Phillis hath to reade; if now she lives.	Ovid's Elegies	2.18.32	
He whom she favours lives, the other dies.	Hero and Leander	1.124	
LIVEST			
Wretched Zenocrate, that livest to see,	1Tamb	5.1.319	Zenoc
For if thou livest, not any Element/Shal shrowde thee from the	2Tamb	3.5.126	Tamb
That livest by forraine exhibition?	P 842	17.37	Eprnon
LIVETH			
For he that liveth in Authority,	Jew	5.2.38	Barab
Yet liveth Pierce of Gaveston unsurprizd,	Edw	2.5.4	Gavstn
LIVING			
That calles my soule from forth his living seate,	Dido	3.4.53	Dido
Now living idle in the walled townes,	1Tamb	1.1.146	Ceneus
By living Asias mightie Emperour.	1Tamb	1.2.73	Zenoc
By living long in this oppression,	1Tamb	5.1.251	Zabina
And heaven consum'd his choisest living fire.	2Tamb	5.3.251	Amyras
And he that living hated so the crosse,	P 320	5.47	Anjoy
Doe yee heare, I would be sorie to robbe you of your living.	F App	p.229 19	P Clown
Ide make a brave living on him; hee has a buttocke as slicke as	F App	p.239 116	P HrsCsr
The living, not the dead can envie bite,	Ovid's Elegies	1.15.39	
The aire with sparkes of living fire was spangled,	Hero and Leander	1.188	
LO (See LOE)			
LOAD (See also LODE)			
That labours with a load of bread and wine,	Jew	5.2.41	Barab
O monstrous, eate a whole load of Hay!	F1532	4.5.28	P All
be; for I have heard of one, that ha's eate a load of logges.	F1534	4.5.30	P Robin
Do you remember sir, how you cosened me and eat up my load of--	F1660	4.6.103	P Carter
LOADE			
And all of them unburdened of their loade,	Dido	1.1.225	Aeneas
And loade his speare with Grecian Princes heads,	Dido	3.3.43	Aeneas
That loade their thighes with Hyblas honeys spoyles,	Dido	5.1.13	Aeneas
to Wittenberge t'other day, with a loade of Hay, he met me,	F1526	4.5.22	P Carter
he never left eating, till he had eate up all my loade of hay.	F1531	4.5.27	P Carter
Or [be] a loade thou shouldst refuse to beare.	Ovid's Elegies	2.15.22	
LOADEN			
Loaden with Spice and Silkes, now under saile,	Jew	1.1.45	Barab
LOADING			
And bid my Factor bring his loading in.	Jew	1.1.83	Barab
LOADSTARRE			
The Loadstarre of my life, if Abigall.	Jew	2.1.42	Barab
LOAM (See LOME)			
LOAN (See LONE)			
LOATH (See also LOTH)			
Would in his age be loath to labour so,	Jew	1.1.17	Barab
No, I will live; nor loath I this my life:	Jew	1.2.266	Barab
Those that hate me, will I learn to loath.	P 156	2.99	Guise
As loath to leave Roome whom they held so deere,	Lucan, First Booke	506	
Can I but loath a husband growne a baude?	Ovid's Elegies	2.19.57	
I loath her manners, love her bodies feature.	Ovid's Elegies	3.10.38	
Perhaps, thy sacred Priesthood makes thee loath,	Hero and Leander	1.293	
Long was he taking leave, and loath to go,	Hero and Leander	2.93	
As loath to see Leander going out.	Hero and Leander	2.98	
LOATH'D			
Poverty (who hatcht/Roomes greatest wittes) was loath'd, and al	Lucan, First Booke	167	
LOATHE			
I loathe, yet after that I loathe, I runne:	Ovid's Elegies	2.4.5	
LOATHED			
O dreary Engines of my loathed sight,	1Tamb	5.1.259	Bajzth
And make a passage for my loathed life.	1Tamb	5.1.304	Bajzth
LOATHING			
For when my loathing it of heate deprives me,	Ovid's Elegies	2.9.27	
LOATHSOME			
I may nor will list to such loathsome chaunge,	Dido	4.2.47	Iarbus
the Starres that make/The loathsome Circle of my dated life,	1Tamb	2.6.37	Cosroe
And treading him beneath thy loathsome feet,	1Tamb	4.2.64	Zabina
O life more loathsome to my vexed thoughts,	1Tamb	5.1.255	Bajzth
ceaslesse lamps/That gently look'd upon this loathsome earth,	2Tamb	2.4.19	Tamb
Whose sight is loathsome to all winged fowles?	Edw	5.3.7	Edward
heavinesse/Of thy most vilde and loathsome filthinesse,	F App	p.243 40	OldMan

LOATHSOME (cont.)
Dang'd downe to hell her loathsome carriage. — Hero and Leander 2.334

LOCK
and lock you in the stable, when you shall come sweating from — 2Tamb 3.5.141 P Tamb
To binde or loose, lock fast, condemne, or judge, — F 935 3.1.157 Pope
And dores conjoynd with an hard iron lock. — Ovid's Elegies 1.6.74

LOCK'D
Wherein the liberall graces lock'd their wealth, — Hero and Leander 2.17

LOCKE
In whose faire bosome I will locke more wealth, — Dido 3.1.92 Dido
that I might locke you safe into <uppe in> my <goode> Chest: — F 676 2.2.125 P Covet
A free-borne wench, no right 'tis up to locke: — Ovid's Elegies 3.4.33

LOCKES (Homograph)
And when he comes, she lockes her selfe up fast; — Jew 2.3.262 Barab
Curling their bloudy lockes, howle dreadfull things, — Lucan, First Booke 565
Let the sad captive formost with lockes spred/On her white — Ovid's Elegies 1.7.39
Bescratch mine eyes, spare not my lockes to breake, — Ovid's Elegies 1.7.65
Beyond thy robes thy dangling [lockes] <lackes> had sweept. — Ovid's Elegies 1.14.4
Lost are the goodly lockes, which from their crowne/Phoebus and — Ovid's Elegies 1.14.31
No envious tongue wrought thy thicke lockes decay. — Ovid's Elegies 1.14.42
She holds, and viewes her old lockes in her lappe, — Ovid's Elegies 1.14.53
Verses ope dores, and lockes put in the poast/Although of oake, — Ovid's Elegies 2.1.27
Even kembed as they were, her lockes to rend, — Ovid's Elegies 2.5.45
How long her lockes were, ere her oath she tooke: — Ovid's Elegies 3.3.3

LOCKS (Homograph)
Oh, if that be all, I can picke ope your locks. — Jew 4.3.33 Pilia
Adde she was diligent thy locks to braide, — Ovid's Elegies 2.7.23
And seaven [times] <time> shooke her head with thicke locks — Ovid's Elegies 3.1.32
The locks spred on his necke receive his teares, — Ovid's Elegies 3.8.11
Comes forth her [unkeembd] <unkeembe> locks a sunder tearing. — Ovid's Elegies 3.8.52

LOCKT
When she was lockt up in a brasen tower, — Edw 2.2.54 Edward
Where lords keepe courts, and kings are lockt in prison! — Edw 5.3.64 Kent
Within this roome is lockt the messenger, — Edw 5.4.17 Mortmr
who though lockt and chaind in stalls,/Souse downe the wals, — Lucan, First Booke 295
Till in his twining armes he lockt her fast, — Hero and Leander 1.403

LOCUS
Oro, si quis [adhuc] <ad haec> precibus locus, exue mentem. — Dido 5.1.138 Dido

LODE
I and myne armie come to lode thy barke/With soules of thousand — 2Tamb 5.3.73 Tamb

LODEN
All loden with the heads of killed men. — 1Tamb 1.1.78 Mycet
Loden with Lawrell wreathes to crowne us all. — 2Tamb 3.5.164 Tamb
Shal al be loden with the martiall spoiles/We will convay with — 2Tamb 4.3.105 Tamb

LODESTAR (See LOADSTARRE)

LODGD
Whilst I am lodgd within this cave of care, — Edw 5.1.32 Edward

LODGE
And will not let us lodge upon the sands: — Dido 1.2.35 Serg
And roome within to lodge sixe thousand men. — 2Tamb 3.2.72 Tamb
And let me lodge where I was wont to lye. — Jew 1.2.333 Abigal
I'le feast you, lodge you, give you faire words, — Jew 4.1.126 Barab
Leaving the woods, lodge in the streetes of Rome. — Lucan, First Booke 558

LODGING
I'le to her lodging; hereabouts she lyes. — Jew 3.6.6 1Fryar
my Lord, his man's now at my lodging/That was his Agent, he'll — Jew 5.1.16 Curtzn

LODOVICO
The account is made, for [Lodovico] <Lodowicke> dyes. — Jew 2.3.242 Barab
What sight is this? my [Lodovico] <Lodowicke> slaine! — Jew 3.2.10 Govnr

LODOVICOES
('tis so) of my device/In Don Mathias and Lodovicoes deaths: — Jew 3.4.8 Barab

LODOWICK
But wherefore talk'd Don Lodowick with you? — Jew 2.3.150 Mthias
I, but Barabas, remember Mathias and Don Lodowick. — Jew 4.1.43 P 2Fryar

LODOWICKE
Beleeve me, Noble Lodowicke, I have seene/The strangest sight, — Jew 1.2.375 Mthias
Farewell Lodowicke. — Jew 1.2.393 Mthias
Here comes Don Lodowicke the Governor's sonne, — Jew 2.3.30 Barab
Lord Lodowicke, it sparkles bright and faire. — Jew 2.3.58 Barab
What makes the Jew and Lodowicke so private? — Jew 2.3.138 Mthias
But stand aside, here comes Don Lodowicke. — Jew 2.3.217 Barab
Entertaine Lodowicke the Governors sonne/With all the curtesie — Jew 2.3.225 Barab
The account is made, for [Lodovico] <Lodowicke> dyes. — Jew 2.3.242 Barab
Oh treacherous Lodowicke! — Jew 2.3.266 Mthias
This gentle Magot, Lodowicke I meane, — Jew 2.3.305 Barab
What, shall I be betroth'd to Lodowicke? — Jew 2.3.308 Abigal
Trouble her not, sweet Lodowicke depart: — Jew 2.3.327 Barab
Be quiet Lodowicke, it is enough/That I have made thee sure to — Jew 2.3.334 Barab
Shall Lodowicke rob me of so faire a love? — Jew 2.3.347 Mthias
And tell him that it comes from Lodowicke. — Jew 2.3.371 Barab
It is a challenge feign'd from Lodowicke. — Jew 2.3.374 Barab
So, now will I goe in to Lodowicke, — Jew 2.3.381 Barab
Now Lodowicke, now Mathias, so; — Jew 3.2.6 Barab
What sight is this? my [Lodovico] <Lodowicke> slaine! — Jew 3.2.10 Govnr
Oh Lodowicke! — Jew 3.2.13 Govnr
And so did Lodowicke him. — Jew 3.2.22 Govnr
and I carried it, first to Lodowicke, and imprimis to Mathias. — Jew 3.3.19 P Ithimr
Admit thou lov'dst not Lodowicke for his [sire] <sinne>, — Jew 3.3.40 Abigal
You knew Mathias and Don Lodowicke? — Jew 3.6.20 Abigal
First to Don Lodowicke, him I never lov'd; — Jew 3.6.23 Abigal

LODOWICKES
Know you not of Mathias and Don Lodowickes disaster? — Jew 3.3.16 P Ithimr

LOE
loe, here are Bugges/Wil make the haire stand upright on your — 2Tamb 3.5.147 Tamb

LOE (cont.)
Loe here my sonnes, are all the golden Mines, 2Tamb 5.3.151 Tamb
Doe so; loe here I give thee Abigall. Jew 2.3.345 Barab
Loe, with a band of bowmen and of pikes, Edw 3.1.36 SpncrP
Loe Mephostophilis, for love of thee/Faustus hath <I> cut his F 442 2.1.54 Faust
For loe these Trees remove at my command, F1426 4.2.102 Faust
Loe I confesse, I am thy captive I, Ovid's Elegies 1.2.19
Loe how the miserable great eared Asse, Ovid's Elegies 2.7.15
Loe country Gods, and [known] <know> bed to forsake, Ovid's Elegies 2.11.7
Gather them up, or lift them loe will I. Ovid's Elegies 3.2.26
Loe Cupid brings his quiver spoyled quite, Ovid's Elegies 3.8.7

LOFTIE
And shining stones upon their loftie Crestes: 1Tamb 1.1.145 Ceneus
Or if that loftie office like thee not, Edw 1.4.355 Edward
A loftie Cedar tree faire flourishing, Edw 2.2.16 Mortmr
Have done their homage to the loftie gallowes, Edw 5.2.3 Mortmr
Lifting his loftie head above the clouds, F 912 3.1.134 Pope
If loftie titles cannot make me thine, Ovid's Elegies 1.3.7
Loftie Lucretius shall live that houre, Ovid's Elegies 1.15.23
prowd she was, (for loftie pride that dwels/In tow'red courts, Hero and Leander 1.393
And still inrich the loftie servile clowne, Hero and Leander 1.481

LOFTY
And scale the ysie mountaines lofty tops: 1Tamb 1.2.100 Tamb
Both we wil walke upon the lofty clifts, 1Tamb 1.2.193 Tamb
His lofty browes in foldes, do figure death, 1Tamb 2.1.21 Menaph
whet thy winged sword/And lift thy lofty arme into the cloudes, 1Tamb 2.3.52 Cosroe
Or scattered like the lofty Cedar trees, 1Tamb 4.2.24 Tamb
Now may we see Damascus lofty towers, 1Tamb 4.2.102 Tamb
Desart of Arabia/To those that stand on Badgeths lofty Tower, 2Tamb 1.1.109 Sgsmnd
Were all the lofty mounts of Zona mundi, 2Tamb 4.1.42 Amyras
Upon the lofty and celestiall mount, 2Tamb 4.3.120 Tamb
Whose lofty Pillers, higher than the cloudes, 2Tamb 5.1.64 Tamb
Two lofty Turrets that command the Towne. Jew 5.3.11 Calym
And lofty Caesar in the thickest throng, Lucan, First Booke 247
The lofty Pine from high mount Pelion raught/Ill waies by rough Ovid's Elegies 2.11.1
Tis time to move grave things in lofty stile, Ovid's Elegies 3.1.23
With lofty wordes stout Tragedie (she sayd)/Why treadst me Ovid's Elegies 3.1.35
Thy lofty stile with mine I not compare, Ovid's Elegies 3.1.39

LOGGES
be; for I have heard of one, that ha's eate a load of logges. F1534 4.5.30 P Robin

LOGICES
Bene disserere est finis logices. F 35 1.1.7 Faust

LOGICK
Tis Ramus, the Kings professor of Logick. P 381 7.21 Retes
that despiseth him, can nere/Be good in Logick or Philosophie. P 410 7.50 Ramus

LOGICKES
Is to dispute well Logickes chiefest end? F 36 1.1.8 Faust

LOINES
Ah cruel Brat, sprung from a tyrants loines, 2Tamb 4.3.54 Jrslem

LOINS (See also LOYNES)
of a bigger size/Than all the brats ysprong from Typhons loins: 1Tamb 3.3.109 Bajzth
Bastardly boy, sprong from some cowards loins, 2Tamb 1.3.69 Tamb

LOITER (See LOYTER)

LOLLARDS
What Lollards do attend our Hollinesse, F1049 3.2.69 Pope

LOLLORDS
and the Germane Emperour/Be held as Lollords, and bold F 955 3.1.177 Faust
Were by the holy Councell both condemn'd/For lothed Lollords, F1022 3.2.42 Pope

LOME
[May] <Many> bounteous [lome] <love> Alcinous fruite resigne. Ovid's Elegies 1.10.56

LONDON
In Florence, Venice, Antwerpe, London, Civill, Jew 4.1.71 Barab
The sight of London to my exiled eyes, Edw 1.1.10 Gavstn

LONE (Homograph)
When misers keepe it; being put to lone, Hero and Leander 1.235
Lone women like to emptie houses perish. Hero and Leander 1.242

LONG (Homograph)
Entends ere long to sport him in the skie. Dido 1.1.77 Venus
Which once performd, poore Troy so long supprest, Dido 1.1.93 Jupitr
That in such peace long time did rule the same: Dido 1.2.24 Cloan
Live long Aeneas and Ascanius. Dido 2.1.53 Serg
O tell me, for I long to be resolv'd. Dido 2.1.61 Aeneas
How long faire Dido shall I pine for thee? Dido 3.1.7 Iarbus
Welcome sweet child, where hast thou been this long? Dido 5.1.46 Aeneas
Ah foolish Dido to forbeare this long! Dido 5.1.160 Dido
How long will Dido mourne a strangers flight, Dido 5.1.279 Iarbus
How long shall I with griefe consume my daies, Dido 5.1.281 Iarbus
I long to see thee backe returne from thence, 1Tamb 1.1.76 Mycet
Long live Cosroe mighty Emperour. 1Tamb 1.1.169 Ortyg
As long as life maintaines Theridamas. 1Tamb 1.2.231 Therid
Long may Theridamas remaine with us. 1Tamb 1.2.240 Usumc
His armes and fingers long and [sinowy] <snowy>, 1Tamb 2.1.27 Menaph
May triumph in our long expected Fate. 1Tamb 2.3.44 Tamb
I long to sit upon my brothers throne. 1Tamb 2.5.47 Cosroe
Long live Tamburlaine, and raigne in Asia. 1Tamb 2.7.64 All
should be most)/Hath seem'd to be digested long agoe. 1Tamb 3.2.8 Agidas
Although it be digested long agoe, 1Tamb 3.2.9 Zenoc
I long to see those crownes won by our swords, 1Tamb 3.3.98 Therid
He dies, and those that kept us out so long. 1Tamb 4.2.118 Tamb
Or kept the faire Zenocrate so long, 1Tamb 4.3.41 Souldn
I long to breake my speare upon his crest, 1Tamb 4.3.46 Arabia
Nor shall they long be thine, I warrant them. 1Tamb 4.4.119 Bajzth
By living long in this oppression, 1Tamb 5.1.251 Zabina

LONG (cont.)

As long as any blood or sparke of breath/Can quench or coole	1Tamb	5.1.284	Zabina
To see them live so long in misery:	1Tamb	5.1.370	Zenoc
As long as life maintaines his mighty arme,	1Tamb	5.1.375	Anippe
That long hath lingred for so high a seat.	1Tamb	5.1.502	Therid
Not long agoe bestrid a Scythian Steed:	2Tamb	1.3.38	Zenoc
They have not long since massacred our Camp.	2Tamb	2.1.10	Fredrk
Long live Callepinus, Emperour of Turky.	2Tamb	3.1.6	P Orcan
who hath followed long/The martiall sword of mighty	2Tamb	3.1.27	Callap
I long to pierce his bowels with my sword,	2Tamb	3.2.152	Usumc
Lost long before you knew what honour meant.	2Tamb	4.3.87	Tamb
the towne will never yeeld/As long as any life is in my breast.	2Tamb	5.1.48	Govnr
Long to the Turke did Malta contribute;	Jew	1.1.180	Barab
Let's know their time, perhaps it is not long;	Jew	1.2.24	Calym
'Tis thirtie winters long since some of us/Did stray so farre	Jew	1.2.308	Abbass
Hoping ere long to set the house a fire;	Jew	2.3.88	Barab
Pinning upon his breast a long great Scrowle/How I with	Jew	2.3.197	Barab
Barabas, thou know'st I have lov'd thy daughter long.	Jew	2.3.288	Lodowk
Why Abigal it is not yet long since/That I did labour thy	Jew	3.3.56	1Fryar
alas, hath pac'd too long/The fatall Labyrinth of misbeleefe,	Jew	3.3.63	Abigal
saies, he that eats with the devil had need of a long spoone.	Jew	3.4.59	P Ithimr
No, but I grieve because she liv'd so long.	Jew	4.1.18	Barab
Oh how I long to see him shake his heeles.	Jew	4.1.140	Ithimr
Then will not Jacomo be long from hence.	Jew	4.1.159	Barab
Love me little, love me long, let musicke rumble,	Jew	4.4.28	Ithimr
Musician, hast beene in Malta long?	Jew	4.4.54	Curtzn
For Calymath having hover'd here so long,	Jew	5.1.4	Govnr
And such a King whom practise long hath taught,	P 458	8.8	Anjoy
As I could long ere this have wisht him there.	P 496	9.15	QnMoth
And long may Henry enjoy all this and more.	P 597	12.10	Cardnl
Which Ile maintaine so long as life doth last:	P 800	16.14	Navrre
And tell him ere it be long, Ile visite him.	P 912	18.13	Navrre
Long may you live, and still be King of France.	P1226	22.88	Navrre
Quick quick my lorde, I long to write my name.	Edw	1.4.4	Lncstr
But I long more to see him banisht hence.	Edw	1.4.5	Warwck
And long thou shalt not stay, or if thou doost,	Edw	1.4.114	Edward
I know tis long of Gaveston she weepes.	Edw	1.4.191	Mortmr
Or saying a long grace at a tables end,	Edw	2.1.37	Spencr
I will not long be from thee though I die:	Edw	2.1.62	Neece
Come lead the way, I long till I am there.	Edw	2.1.82	Neece
me, for his sake/Ile grace thee with a higher stile ere long.	Edw	2.2.253	Edward
I long to heare an answer from the Barons/Touching my friend,	Edw	3.1.1	Edward
Long live my soveraigne the noble Edward,	Edw	3.1.32	SpncrP
Long live king Edward, Englands lawful lord.	Edw	3.1.151	Herald
armes, by me salute/Your highnes, with long life and happines,	Edw	3.1.157	Herald
For which ere long, their heads shall satisfie,	Edw	3.1.209	Edward
these Barons and the subtill Queene,/Long [leveld] <levied> at.	Edw	3.1.273	Levune
Madam, long may you live,	Edw	4.2.34	Kent
men, and friends/Ere long, to bid the English king a base.	Edw	4.2.66	SrJohn
A will be had ere long I doubt it not.	Edw	4.3.20	Spencr
A gave a long looke after us my lord,	Edw	4.7.30	Spencr
Thy speeches long agoe had easde my sorrowes,	Edw	5.1.6	Edward
But Mortimer, as long as he survives/What safetie rests for us,	Edw	5.2.42	Queene
But can my ayre of life continue long,	Edw	5.3.17	Edward
Long live king Edward, by the grace of God/King of England, and	Edw	5.4.73	ArchBp
Nay, to my death, for too long have I lived,	Edw	5.6.83	Queene
Then I feare that which I have long suspected:	F 220	1.2.27	1Schol
And long e're this, I should have done the deed <slaine	F 575	2.2.24	Faust
Not long he stayed within his quiet house,	F 768	2.3.47	2Chor
That I do long to see the Monuments/And situation of bright	F 828	3.1.50	Faust
Long ere with Iron hands they punish men,	F 878	3.1.100	Pope
He'd joyne long Asses eares to these huge hornes,	F1449	4.3.19	Benvol
great bellyed women, do long for things, are rare and dainty.	F1568	4.6.11	P Faust
they have vilde long nailes, there was a hee divell and a shee	F App	p.230 52	P Clown
Ile feede thy divel with horse-bread as long as he lives,	F App	p.234 30	P Rafe
our horses shal eate no hay as long as this lasts.	F App	p.234 3	P Robin
two deceased princes which long since are consumed to dust.	F App	p.237 43	P Faust
that great bellied women do long for some dainties or other,	F App	p.242 5	P Faust
Of these garboiles, whence springs [a long] <along> discourse,	Lucan, First Booke	68	
And by long rest forgot to manage armes,	Lucan, First Booke	131	
Let come their [leader] <leaders whom long peace hath quail'd;	Lucan, First Booke	311	
And shal he triumph long before his time,	Lucan, First Booke	316	
Speake, when shall this thy long usurpt power end?	Lucan, First Booke	333	
Yet for long service done, reward these men,	Lucan, First Booke	341	
And fates so bent, least sloth and long delay/Might crosse him,	Lucan, First Booke	394	
Who running long, fals in a greater floud,	Lucan, First Booke	401	
so (if truth you sing)/Death brings long life.	Lucan, First Booke	454	
Now spearlike, long; now like a spreading torch:	Lucan, First Booke	530	
The beast long struggled, as being like to prove/An aukward	Lucan, First Booke	610	
Although the nights be long, I sleepe not tho,	Ovid's Elegies	1.2.3	
Then came Corinna in a long loose gowne,	Ovid's Elegies	1.5.9	
Long Love my body to such use [makes] <make> slender/And to get	Ovid's Elegies	1.6.5	
she chides/And with long charmes the solide earth divides.	Ovid's Elegies	1.8.18	
If this thou doest, to me by long use knowne,	Ovid's Elegies	1.8.105	
And long admiring say by what meanes learnd/Hath this same Poet	Ovid's Elegies	2.1.9	
If long she stayes, to thinke the time more short/Lay downe thy	Ovid's Elegies	2.2.23	
flying touch/Tantalus seekes, his long tongues gaine is such.	Ovid's Elegies	2.2.44	
And when one sweetely sings, then straight I long,	Ovid's Elegies	2.4.25	
Both short and long please me, for I love both:	Ovid's Elegies	2.4.36	
Or such, as least long yeares should turne the die,	Ovid's Elegies	2.5.39	
For long shrild trumpets let your notes resound.	Ovid's Elegies	2.6.6	
Long shalt thou rest when Fates expire thy breath.	Ovid's Elegies	2.9.42	
That meane to travaile some long irkesome way.	Ovid's Elegies	2.16.16	

LONG (cont.)			
Her lover let her mocke, that long will raigne,	Ovid's Elegies		2.19.33
Long have I borne much, hoping time would beate thee/To guard	Ovid's Elegies		2.19.49
An old wood, stands uncut of long yeares space,	Ovid's Elegies		3.1.1
Long hast thou loyterd, greater workes compile.	Ovid's Elegies		3.1.24
Come therefore, and to long verse shorter frame.	Ovid's Elegies		3.1.66
How long her lockes were, ere her oath she tooke:	Ovid's Elegies		3.3.3
So long they be, since she her faith forsooke.	Ovid's Elegies		3.3.4
Her long haires eare-wrought garland fell away.	Ovid's Elegies		3.9.36
And wisht the goddesse long might feele loves fire.	Ovid's Elegies		3.9.42
Long have I borne much, mad thy faults me make:	Ovid's Elegies		3.10.1
Both loves to whom my heart long time did yeeld,	Ovid's Elegies		3.14.15
When two are stript, long ere the course begin,	Hero and Leander		1.169
Which long time lie untoucht, will harshly jarre.	Hero and Leander		1.230
But long this blessed time continued not;	Hero and Leander		1.459
Long dallying with Hero, nothing saw/That might delight him	Hero and Leander		2.62
And red for anger that he stayd so long,	Hero and Leander		2.89
Long was he taking leave, and loath to go,	Hero and Leander		2.93
Where having spy'de her tower, long star'd he on't,	Hero and Leander		2.149
That which so long so charily she kept,	Hero and Leander		2.309
LONG'D			
Now have I that for which my soule hath long'd.	Jew	2.3.318	Lodowk
By being possest of him for whom she long'd:	Hero and Leander		2.36
LONGER			
We will not stay a minute longer here.	Dido	4.3.44	Cloan
And Jove may never let me longer live,	1Tamb	1.1.170	Cosroe
for if she live but a while longer, shee will fall into a	1Tamb	4.4.49	P Tamb
And to resist with longer stubbornesse,	1Tamb	5.1.3	Govnr
To coole and comfort me with longer date,	1Tamb	5.1.277	Bajzth
Yet let thy daughter be no longer blinde.	Jew	1.2.354	1Fryar
And now I can no longer hold my minde.	Jew	2.3.290	Lodowk
I can with-hold no longer; welcome sweet love.	Jew	4.2.46	Curtzn
I can no longer keepe me from my lord.	Edw	1.1.139	Gavstn
Strive you no longer, I will have that Gaveston.	Edw	2.6.7	Warwck
had heaven given thee longer life/Thou hadst restrainde thy	Lucan, First Booke		115
Thou doest beginne, she shall be mine no longer.	Ovid's Elegies		2.19.48
And one, I thinke, was longer, of her feete.	Ovid's Elegies		3.1.8
LONGING			
Of whose encrease I set some longing hope,	P 689	13.33	Guise
And all the honors longing to my crowne,	Edw	3.1.131	Edward
Longing to view Orions drisling looke <looks>,	F 230	1.3.2	Faust
To satisfie my longing thoughts at full,	F1264	4.1.110	Emper
To glut the longing of my hearts desire,	F1760	5.1.87	Faust
The longing heart of Hero much more joies/Then nymphs and	Hero and Leander		2.232
LONGINGS			
And glut your longings with a heaven of joy.	2Tamb	5.3.227	Tamb
LONGS			
To one that can commaund what longs thereto:	1Tamb	2.5.23	Cosroe
Soft Barabas, there's more longs too't than so.	Jew	1.2.45	Govnr
LONGSHANKES			
the lovelie Elenor of Spaine,/Great Edward Longshankes issue:	Edw	3.1.12	Spencr
Edmund away, Bristow to Longshankes blood/Is false, be not found	Edw	4.6.16	Kent
LOOK			
Then as I look downe to the damned Feends,	1Tamb	4.2.26	Bajzth
Now look I like a souldier, and this wound/As great a grace and	2Tamb	3.2.117	Tamb
Hath stain'd thy cheekes, and made thee look like death,	2Tamb	4.2.4	Olymp
And when I look away, comes stealing on:	2Tamb	5.3.71	Tamb
Look, look, master, here come two religious Caterpillers.	Jew	4.1.21	P Ithimr
I, master, he's slain; look how his brains drop out on's nose.	Jew	4.1.178	P Ithimr
And made it look with terrour on the worlde:	P 61	2.4	Guise
Give me a look, that when I bend the browes,	P 157	2.100	Guise
But look my Lord, ther's some in the Admirals house.	P 297	5.24	Retes
Cosin tis he, I know him by his look.	P 309	5.36	Guise
Now doe I but begin to look about,	P 985	19.55	Guise
Villaine, why dost thou look so gastly? speake.	P 989	19.59	Guise
As pale as ashes, nay then tis time to look about.	P1001	19.71	Guise
Boy, look where your father lyes.	P1046	19.116	King
I like not this Friers look.	P1159	22.21	Eprnon
in hell, and look to it, for some of you shall be my father.	F 690	2.2.139	P Wrath
yee Lubbers look about/And find the man that doth this villany,	F1055	3.2.75	Pope
LOOK'D			
That never look'd on man but Tamburlaine.	2Tamb	1.3.34	Tamb
ceaslesse lamps/That gently look'd upon this loathsome earth,	2Tamb	2.4.19	Tamb
'Tis necessary that be look'd unto:	Jew	1.2.157	1Knght
And nought is to be look'd for now but warres,	Jew	3.5.35	Govnr
reading of the letter, he look'd like a man of another world.	Jew	4.2.7	P Pilia
and look'd upon him thus; told him he were best to send it;	Jew	4.2.105	P Pilia
No, Barabas, this must be look'd into;	Jew	5.2.34	Barab
Penelope, though no watch look'd unto her,	Ovid's Elegies		3.4.23
wherewith she strooken, look'd so dolefully,	Hero and Leander		1.373
Yet as she went, full often look'd behind,	Hero and Leander		2.5
LOOKE			
Looke where she comes: Aeneas [view] <viewd> her well.	Dido	2.1.72	Illion
Looke up and speake.	Dido	2.1.120	Dido
Looke sister how Aeneas little sonne/Playes with your garments	Dido	3.1.20	Anna
Mother, looke here.	Dido	3.1.47	Cupid
No, but I charge thee never looke on me.	Dido	3.1.54	Dido
What, darest thou looke a Lyon in the face?	Dido	3.3.39	Dido
If that your majestie can looke so lowe,	Dido	3.4.41	Aeneas
And looke upon him with a Mermaides eye,	Dido	5.1.201	Dido
Looke sister, looke lovely Aeneas ships,	Dido	5.1.251	Dido
Or looke you, I should play the Orator?	1Tamb	1.2.129	Tamb
Looke for orations when the foe is neere.	1Tamb	1.2.131	Techel

LOOKE (cont.)

And looke we friendly on them when they come:	1Tamb	1.2.141		Tamb
And when you looke for amorous discourse,	1Tamb	3.2.44		Agidas
Doo not my captaines and my souldiers looke/As if they meant to	1Tamb	3.3.9		Tamb
Feends looke on me, and thou dread God of hell,	1Tamb	4.2.27		Bajzth
Zenocrate, looke better to your slave.	1Tamb	4.2.68		Tamb
and she shal looke/That these abuses flow not from her tongue:	1Tamb	4.2.69		Zenoc
Plac'd by her side, looke on their mothers face.	2Tamb	1.3.20		Tamb
The houses burnt, wil looke as if they mourn'd,	2Tamb	2.4.139		Tamb
Looke like the parti-coloured cloudes of heaven,	2Tamb	3.1.47		Jrslem
Poore soules they looke as if their deaths were neere.	2Tamb	3.5.61		Usumc
hee is a king, looke to him Theridamas, when we are fighting,	2Tamb	3.5.153	P	Tamb
Which when you stab, looke on your weapons point,	2Tamb	4.2.69		Olymp
Looke where he goes, but see, he comes againe/Because I stay:	2Tamb	5.3.75		Tamb
Looke here my boies, see what a world of ground,	2Tamb	5.3.145		Tamb
shall there concerne our state/Assure your selves I'le looke--	Jew	1.1.173		Barab
Looke not towards him, let's away:	Jew	3.1.24		Pilia
Looke, Katherin, looke, thy sonne gave mine these wounds.	Jew	3.2.16		Govnr
And now you men of Malta looke about,	Jew	3.5.29		Govnr
and now would I were gone, I am not worthy to looke upon her.	Jew	4.2.36	P	Ithimr
And fly my presence if thou looke to live.	P 692	13.36		Guise
He should have lost his head, but with his looke,	Edw	1.1.113		Kent
Or looke to see the throne where you should sit,	Edw	1.1.131		Lncstr
whom he vouchsafes/For vailing of his bonnet one good looke.	Edw	1.2.19		Lncstr
See what a scornfull looke the pesant casts.	Edw	1.4.14		MortSr
For every looke, my lord, drops downe a teare,	Edw	1.4.136		Gavstn
And therefore give me leave to looke my fill,	Edw	1.4.139		Edward
Looke where the sister of the king of Fraunce,	Edw	1.4.187		Lncstr
That waite attendance for a gratious looke,	Edw	1.4.338		Queene
Looke Lancaster how passionate he is,	Edw	2.2.3		Queene
That shall wee see, looke where his lordship comes.	Edw	2.2.49		Lncstr
As to bestow a looke on such as you.	Edw	2.2.78		Gavstn
Looke to your owne heads, his is sure enough.	Edw	2.2.92		Edward
Looke to your owne crowne, if you back him thus.	Edw	2.2.93		Warwck
Looke for rebellion, looke to be deposde,	Edw	2.2.161		Lncstr
Looke next to see us with our ensignes spred.	Edw	2.2.199		Lncstr
In vaine I looke for love at Edwards hand,	Edw	2.4.61		Queene
Looke for no other fortune wretch then death,	Edw	2.5.17		Lncstr
Looke Lancaster,/Yonder is Edward among his flatterers.	Edw	3.1.195		Mortmr
For which thy head shall over looke the rest,	Edw	3.1.239		Edward
Edward battell in England, sooner then he can looke for them:	Edw	4.3.35	P	Spencr
Madam, tis good to looke to him betimes.	Edw	4.6.39		Mortmr
A gave a long looke after us my lord,	Edw	4.7.30		Spencr
Looke up my lord.	Edw	4.7.44		Spencr
Yet stay, for rather then I will looke on them,	Edw	5.1.106		Edward
And neither give him kinde word, nor good looke.	Edw	5.2.55		Mortmr
Doe looke to be protector over the prince?	Edw	5.2.89		Mortmr
And when I frowne, make all the court looke pale,	Edw	5.4.53		Mortmr
What safetie may I looke for at his hands,	Edw	5.4.109		King
Longing to view Orions drisling looke <looks>,	F 230	1.3.2		Faust
And Faustus vowes never to looke to heaven,	F 648	2.2.97		Faust
What Dick, looke to the horses there till I come againe.	F 722	2.3.1	P	Robin
Who's that spoke? Friers looke about.	F1040	3.2.60		Pope
looke that your devill can answere the stealing of this same	F1088	3.3.1	P	Dick
what you say, we looke not like cup-stealers I can tell you.	F1100	3.3.13	P	Robin
let the Maids looke well to their porridge-pots, for I'le into	F1133	3.3.46	P	Robin
Looke up Benvolio, tis the Emperour calls.	F1286	4.1.132		Saxony
him; and hereafter sir, looke you speake well of Schollers.	F1315	4.1.161	P	Faust
looke up into th'hall there ho.	F1519	4.5.15	P	Hostss
looke you heere sir.	F1657	4.6.100	P	Faust
Looke sirs, comes he not, comes he not?	F1826	5.2.30	P	Faust
Yet Faustus looke up to heaven, and remember [Gods] mercy is	F1835	5.2.39	P	2Schol
[My God, my God] <O mercy heaven>, looke not so fierce on me;	F1979	5.2.183		Faust
Friers looke about.	F App	p.231 3	P	Pope
will no man looke?	F App	p.231 9	P	Pope
it, and she has sent me to looke thee out, prethee come away.	F App	p.233 9	P	Rafe
looke to the goblet Rafe.	F App	p.235 19	P	Robin
looke to the goblet Rafe, Polypragmos Belseborams framanto	F App	p.235 24	P	Robin
his grave looke appeasd/The wrastling tumult, and right hand	Lucan, First Booke			298
Philosophers looke you, for unto me/Thou cause, what ere thou	Lucan, First Booke			418
Looke how when stormy Auster from the breach/Of Libian Syrtes	Lucan, First Booke			496
Looke what the lightning blasted, Aruns takes/And it inters	Lucan, First Booke			605
appear'd/A knob of flesh, whereof one halfe did looke/Dead, and	Lucan, First Booke			627
Why in thy glasse doest looke being discontent?	Ovid's Elegies			1.14.36
If any eie mee with a modest looke,	Ovid's Elegies			2.4.11
If on the Marble Theater I looke,	Ovid's Elegies			2.7.3
If I looke well, thou thinkest thou doest not move,	Ovid's Elegies			2.7.9
Too late you looke back, when with anchors weighd,	Ovid's Elegies			2.11.23
A decent forme, thinne robe, a lovers looke,	Ovid's Elegies			3.1.9
Sterne was her front, her [cloake] <looke> on ground did lie.	Ovid's Elegies			3.1.12
Looke gently, and rough husbands lawes despise.	Ovid's Elegies			3.4.44
Such force and vertue hath an amorous looke.	Hero and Leander			1.166
Looke how their hands, so were their hearts united,	Hero and Leander			2.27
We often kisse it, often looke thereon,	Hero and Leander			2.81
So to his mind was yoong Leanders looke.	Hero and Leander			2.130
Againe she knew not how to frame her looke,	Hero and Leander			2.307
Than Dis, on heapes of gold fixing his looke.	Hero and Leander			2.326

LOOKED

She looked sad: sad, comely I esteem'd her.	Ovid's Elegies			2.5.44

LOOKES

Disquiet Seas lay downe your swelling lookes,	Dido	1.1.122		Venus
Whose lookes set forth no mortall forme to view,	Dido	1.1.189		Aeneas
Lookes so remorcefull, vowes so forcible,	Dido	2.1.156		Aeneas

LOOKES (cont.)

To be inamourd of thy brothers lookes, ... Dido 3.1.2 Cupid
His lookes shall be my only Librarie, ... Dido 3.1.90 Dido
And dive into her heart by coloured lookes. . . . . Dido 4.2.32 Iarbus
And not stand lingering here for amorous lookes: . . Dido 4.3.38 Illion
Now lookes Aeneas like immortall Jove, ... Dido 4.4.45 Dido
For in his lookes I see eternitie, ... Dido 4.4.122 Dido
If that be all, then cheare thy drooping lookes, . . . Dido 5.1.71 Iarbus
For being intangled by a strangers lookes: . . . . Dido 5.1.145 Dido
My sister comes, I like not her sad lookes. . . . . Dido 5.1.225 Dido
And with thy lookes thou conquerest all thy foes: . . 1Tamb 1.1.75 Mycet
And he with frowning browes and fiery lookes, . . . 1Tamb 1.2.56 Techel
When looks breed love, with lookes to gaine the prize. . 1Tamb 2.5.63 Therid
True (Argier) and tremble at my lookes. . . . . . 1Tamb 3.1.49 Bajzth
Which dies my lookes so livelesse as they are. . . . 1Tamb 3.2.15 Zenoc
How can you fancie one that lookes so fierce, . . . 1Tamb 3.2.40 Agidas
So lookes my Lordly love, faire Tamburlaine. . . . 1Tamb 3.2.49 Zenoc
Now in his majesty he leaves those lookes, ... 1Tamb 3.2.61 Agidas
That with thy lookes canst cleare the darkened Sky: . . 1Tamb 3.3.122 Tamb
Pursude by hunters, flie his angrie lookes, ... 1Tamb 3.3.193 Zenoc
did your greatnes see/The frowning lookes of fiery Tamburlaine, 1Tamb 4.1.13 2Msngr
And bring us pardon in your chearfull lookes. . . . 1Tamb 5.1.47 Govnr
we intreate/Grace to our words and pitie to our lookes, . 1Tamb 5.1.51 2Virgn
Whose lookes might make the angry God of armes, . . 1Tamb 5.1.326 Zenoc
Gazing upon the beautie of their lookes: . . . . . 1Tamb 5.1.334 Zenoc
Jove viewing me in armes, lookes pale and wan, . . . 1Tamb 5.1.452 Tamb
So lookes my Love, shadowing in her browes/Triumphes and . 1Tamb 5.1.512 Tamb
Whose lookes make this inferiour world to quake, . . 2Tamb 1.3.139 Techel
In whose high lookes is much more majesty/Than from the Concave 2Tamb 3.4.47 Therid
See father, how Almeda the Jaylor lookes upon us. . . 2Tamb 3.5.116 Celeb
For every Fury gazeth on her lookes: . . . . . . 2Tamb 4.2.92 Therid
And have no terrour but his threatning lookes? . . . 2Tamb 5.1.23 Govnr
bite, yet are our lookes/As innocent and harmelesse as a Lambes. Jew 2.3.21 Barab
Her eyes and lookes sow'd seeds of perjury, ... P 695 13.39 Guise
And princes with their lookes ingender feare. . . . P 999 19.69 Guise
in whose gratious lookes/The blessednes of Gaveston remaines, Edw 1.4.120 Gavstn
And see how coldly his lookes make deniall. . . . . Edw 1.4.235 Lncstr
That thinke with high lookes thus to tread me down. . . Edw 2.2.97 Edward
O levell all your lookes upon these daring men, . . . Edw 5.3.39 Edward
But at his lookes Lightborne thou wilt relent. . . . Edw 5.4.26 Mortmr
Whose lookes were as a breeching to a boye. . . . . Edw 5.4.55 Mortmr
Small comfort findes poore Edward in thy lookes, . . . Edw 5.5.44 Edward
These lookes of thine can harbor nought but death. . . Edw 5.5.73 Edward
he lookes as like [a] conjurer as the Pope to a Coster-monger. F1228 4.1.74 P Benvol
Ifaith he lookes much like a conjurer. . . . . . F App p.236 11 P Knight
That I may write things worthy thy faire lookes: . . . Ovid's Elegies 1.3.20
But secretlie her lookes with checks did trounce mee, . . Ovid's Elegies 1.7.21
her bloodlesse white lookes shewed/Like marble from the Parian Ovid's Elegies 1.7.51
He staide, and on thy lookes his gazes seaz'd. . . . Ovid's Elegies 1.8.24
By speechlesse lookes we guesse at things succeeding. . . Ovid's Elegies 1.11.18
Wenches apply your faire lookes to my verse/Which golden love Ovid's Elegies 2.1.37
Turne thy lookes hether, and in one spare twaine, . . Ovid's Elegies 2.13.15
Beauty gives heart, Corinnas lookes excell, ... Ovid's Elegies 2.17.7
Hippodameias lookes while he beheld. . . . . . . Ovid's Elegies 3.2.16
Now shine her lookes pure white and red betwixt. . . . Ovid's Elegies 3.3.6
When nimph-Neaera rapt thy lookes Scamander. . . . . Ovid's Elegies 3.5.28
Whom Ilia pleasd, though in her lookes griefe reveld, . . Ovid's Elegies 3.5.47
And lookes uppon the fruits he cannot touch. . . . . Ovid's Elegies 3.6.52
Eryx bright Empresse turnd her lookes aside, ... Ovid's Elegies 3.8.45
Erre I? or by my [bookes] <lookes> is she so knowne? . . Ovid's Elegies 3.11.7
For in his lookes were all that men desire, ... Hero and Leander 1.84
To lead thy thoughts, as thy faire lookes doe mine, . . Hero and Leander 1.201
Heroes lookes yeelded, but her words made warre, . . . Hero and Leander 1.331

LOOKETH

So in his Armour looketh Tamburlaine: . . . . . 1Tamb 1.2.54 Techel

LOOKING

Who looking on the scarres we Troians gave, ... Dido 2.1.131 Aeneas
And looking from a turret, might behold/Young infants swimming Dido 2.1.192 Aeneas
His glistering eyes shall be my looking glasse, . . . Dido 3.1.86 Dido
of them, looking some happie power will pitie and inlarge us. 1Tamb 4.4.99 P Zabina
While she runs to the window looking out/When you should come Jew 2.3.264 Barab
Zoon's what a looking thou keep'st, thou'lt betraye's anon. Jew 3.1.25 Pilia
looking of a Fryars Execution, whom I saluted with an old Jew 4.2.17 P Pilia
Or looking downeward, with your eye lids close, . . . Edw 2.1.39 Spencr
That looking downe the earth appear'd to me, ... F 850 3.1.72 Faust
And that he's much chang'd, looking wild and big, . . . Lucan, First Booke 475
and that Rome/He looking on by these men should be sackt. Lucan, First Booke 480
Shee looking on them did more courage give. . . . . Ovid's Elegies 2.12.26
And looking in her face, was strooken blind. . . . . Hero and Leander 1.38
He heav'd him up, and looking on his face, ... Hero and Leander 2.171
And looking backe, saw Neptune follow him. . . . . Hero and Leander 2.176

LOOKS

His looks do menace heaven and dare the Gods, ... 1Tamb 1.2.157 Therid
With what a majesty he rears his looks:-- . . . . . 1Tamb 1.2.165 Tamb
Won with thy words, and conquered with thy looks, . . . 1Tamb 1.2.228 Therid
When looks breed love, with lookes to gaine the prize. . 1Tamb 2.5.63 Therid
As looks the sun through Nilus flowing stream, ... 1Tamb 3.2.47 Zenoc
With happy looks of ruthe and lenity. 1Tamb 5.1.59 2Virgn
Whose chearful looks do cleare the clowdy aire/And cloath it in 2Tamb 1.3.3 Tamb
But yet me thinks their looks are amorous, ... 2Tamb 1.3.21 Tamb
My gratious Lord, they have their mothers looks, . . . 2Tamb 1.3.35 Zenoc
[Those] <Whose> looks will shed such influence in my campe,/As 2Tamb 3.2.39 Tamb
Seest thou not death within my wrathfull looks? . . . 2Tamb 3.5.119 Tamb

LOOKS (cont.)
him, in whom thy looks/Have greater operation and more force — 2Tamb 4.2.28 Therid
My looks shall make them flie, and might I follow, — 2Tamb 5.3.107 Tamb
the slave looks like a hogs cheek new sindg'd. — Jew 2.3.42 P Barab
like a hog, and looks/Like one that is imploy'd in Catzerie — Jew 4.3.11 Barab
Longing to view Orions drisling looke <looks>, — F 230 1.3.2 Faust
Now worthy Faustus: me thinks your looks are chang'd. — F1821 5.2.25 1Schol
Though her sowre looks a Sabines browe resemble, — Ovid's Elegies 2.4.15
This for her looks, that for her woman-hood: — Ovid's Elegies 2.4.46

LOOK'ST
Why look'st thou toward the sea? — Dido 5.1.113 Dido
O what art thou that look'st so [terrible] <terribly>. — F 638 2.2.87 Faust
The more thou look'st, the more the gowne envide. — Ovid's Elegies 3.2.28

LOOK'T
And oft look't out, and mus'd he did not come. — Hero and Leander 2.22

LOOKT
Tell Isabell the Queene, I lookt not thus, — Edw 5.5.68 Edward
when by Junces taske/He had before lookt Pluto in the face. — Lucan, First Booke 576

LOON (See LOWNE)

LOOSE (Homograph)
Why, that was in a net, where we are loose, — Dido 3.4.5 Dido
And now my footstoole, if I loose the field, — 1Tamb 5.1.209 Tamb
Ere I would loose the tytle of a king. — 2Tamb 1.3.91 Celeb
Ere I would loose the tytle of a king. — 2Tamb 1.3.95 Amyras
My boy, Thou shalt not loose a drop of blood, — 2Tamb 3.2.137 Tamb
Blush heaven to loose the honor of thy name, — 2Tamb 5.3.28 Usumc
Leave nothing loose, all leveld to my mind. — Jew 5.5.3 Barab
Ile rather loose his friendship I, then graunt. — Edw 1.4.237 Lncstr
way how hardly I can brooke/To loose my crowne and kingdome, — Edw 5.1.52 Edward
To binde or loose, lock fast, condemne, or judge, — F 935 3.1.157 Pope
Then came Corinna in a long loose gowne, — Ovid's Elegies 1.5.9
On Priams loose-trest daughter when he gazed. — Ovid's Elegies 1.9.38
Why should I loose, and thou gaine by the pleasure/Which man — Ovid's Elegies 1.10.35
Then thinkest thou thy loose life is not showne? — Ovid's Elegies 1.13.34
Heere I display my lewd and loose behaviour. — Ovid's Elegies 2.4.4
doth favour/That seekes the conquest by her loose behaviour. — Ovid's Elegies 2.5.12
Shee dyes, and with loose haires to grave is sent, — Ovid's Elegies 2.14.39
(Their reines let loose) right soone my house approach. — Ovid's Elegies 2.16.50
And slipt from bed cloth'd in a loose night-gowne, — Ovid's Elegies 3.1.51
And on his loose mane the loose bridle laide. — Ovid's Elegies 3.4.16
With that her loose gowne on, from me she cast her, — Ovid's Elegies 3.6.81
We wish that one should loose, the other win. — Hero and Leander 1.170

LOOSELY
But on the ground thy cloathes too loosely lie, — Ovid's Elegies 3.2.25

LOOSENES
And certifie what Edwards loosenes is. — Edw 4.1.7 Kent

LOOSER
You are unapt my looser lines to heare. — Ovid's Elegies 2.1.4

LOOSETH
And ere he sees the sea looseth his name; — Lucan, First Booke 402

LOOSE-TREST
On Priams loose-trest daughter when he gazed. — Ovid's Elegies 1.9.38

LOOSING
To stay my Fleete from loosing forth the Bay: — Dido 4.3.26 Aeneas

LOOSNES
Whose loosnes hath betrayed thy land to spoyle, — Edw 4.4.11 Queene

LOPUS
mas Doctor Lopus was never such a Doctor, has given me a — F App p.240 127 P HrsCsr

LORAINE
My Lord of Loraine have you markt of late,/How Charles our — P 512 9.31 QnMoth
My Lord Cardinall of Loraine, tell me, — P 631 12.44 QnMoth
Mounser of Loraine sinke away to hell, — P1023 19.93 King
of Loraine by the Kings consent is lately strangled unto death. — P1123 21.17 P Frier

LORAYNE
Shall feele the house of Lorayne is his foe: — P 856 17.51 Guise

LORD
Before he be the Lord of Turnus towne, — Dido 1.1.87 Jupitr
Follow ye Troians, follow this brave Lord, — Dido 1.2.1 Illion
Thankes gentle Lord for such unlookt for grace. — Dido 1.2.44 Serg
Lord of my fortune, but my fortunes turnd, — Dido 2.1.235 Aeneas
And now am neither father, Lord, nor King: — Dido 2.1.239 Aeneas
Achates, how doth Carthage please your Lord? — Dido 3.1.97 Dido
What willes our Lord, or wherefore did he call? — Dido 4.3.15 Achat
To waite upon him as their soveraigne Lord. — Dido 4.4.69 Dido
Dido is thine, henceforth Ile call thee Lord: — Dido 4.4.84 Dido
My Lord Ascanius, ye must goe with me. — Dido 4.5.1 Nurse
Not for so small a fault my soveraigne Lord. — 1Tamb 1.1.25 Meandr
Ful true thou speakst, and like thy selfe my lord, — 1Tamb 1.1.49 Mycet
Doubt not my Lord and gratious Soveraigne, — 1Tamb 1.1.70 Therid
Then now my Lord, I humbly take my leave. — 1Tamb 1.1.81 Therid
How now my Lord, what, mated and amaz'd/To heare the king thus — 1Tamb 1.1.107 Menaph
Behold, my Lord, Ortigius and the rest, — 1Tamb 1.1.134 Menaph
Great Lord of Medea and Armenia: — 1Tamb 1.1.163 Ortyg
Chiefe Lord of all the wide vast Euxine sea, — 1Tamb 1.1.167 Ortyg
We knew my Lord, before we brought the crowne, — 1Tamb 1.1.179 Ortyg
The [Lords] <Lord> would not be too exasperate, — 1Tamb 1.1.182 Ortyg
I know it wel my Lord, and thanke you all. — 1Tamb 1.1.187 Cosroe
I am (my Lord), for so you do import. — 1Tamb 1.2.33 Zenoc
I am a Lord, for so my deeds shall proove, — 1Tamb 1.2.34 Tamb
Where her betrothed Lord Alcidamus, — 1Tamb 1.2.78 Agidas
I will my Lord. — 1Tamb 2.1.69 Menaph
So Poets say, my Lord. — 1Tamb 2.2.53 Meandr
Go on my Lord, and give your charge I say, — 1Tamb 2.2.57 Mycet

LORD (cont.)

And so mistake you not a whit my Lord.	1Tamb	2.3.6		Tamb
You see my Lord, what woorking woordes he hath.	1Tamb	2.3.25		Therid
And these his two renowmed friends my Lord,	1Tamb	2.3.30		Therid
My Lord, we have discovered the enemie/Ready to chardge you	1Tamb	2.3.49		1Msngr
And now Lord Tamburlaine, my brothers Campe/I leave to thee,	1Tamb	2.5.38		Cosroe
to order all the scattered troopes)/Farewell Lord Regent,	1Tamb	2.5.46		Cosroe
O my Lord, tis sweet and full of pompe.	1Tamb	2.5.55		Techel
I, if I could with all my heart my Lord.	1Tamb	2.5.68		Techel
What then my Lord?	1Tamb	2.5.71		Usumc
Tell him thy Lord the Turkish Emperour,	1Tamb	3.1.22		Bajzth
Dread Lord of Affrike, Europe and Asia,	1Tamb	3.1.23		Bajzth
see how right the man/Hath hit the meaning of my Lord the King.	1Tamb	3.2.108		Techel
Bassoe, by this thy Lord and maister knowes,	1Tamb	3.3.1		Tamb
My Lord, the great Commander of the worlde,	1Tamb	3.3.13		Bassoe
But wil those Kings accompany your Lord?	1Tamb	3.3.27		Tamb
Attend upon the person of your Lord,	1Tamb	3.3.62		Bajzth
He cals me Bajazeth, whom you call Lord.	1Tamb	3.3.67		Bajzth
lie weltring in their blood/And Tamburlaine is Lord of Affrica.	1Tamb	3.3.202		Zenoc
My royall Lord is slaine or conquered,	1Tamb	3.3.209		Zenoc
Now let me offer to my gracious Lord,	1Tamb	3.3.218		Zenoc
Thou shalt not yet be Lord of Affrica.	1Tamb	3.3.223		Zabina
And write my selfe great Lord of Affrica:	1Tamb	3.3.245		Tamb
Mightie Lord,/Three hundred thousand men in armour clad,	1Tamb	4.1.20		2Msngr
You must devise some torment worsse, my Lord,	1Tamb	4.2.66		Techel
My Lord it is the bloody Tamburlaine,	1Tamb	4.3.11		Souldn
But noble Lord of great Arabia,	1Tamb	4.3.29		Souldn
My Lord, how can you suffer these outragious curses by these	1Tamb	4.4.26	P	Zenoc
He stamps it under his feet my Lord.	1Tamb	4.4.42	P	Therid
Yes, my Lord.	1Tamb	4.4.59	P	Zenoc
My lord, to see my fathers towne besieg'd,	1Tamb	4.4.65		Zenoc
If any love remaine in you my Lord,	1Tamb	4.4.68		Zenoc
Yet give me leave to plead for him my Lord.	1Tamb	4.4.86		Zenoc
So it would my lord, specially having so smal a walke, and so	1Tamb	4.4.105	P	Therid
I (my Lord) but none save kinges must feede with these.	1Tamb	4.4.109	P	Therid
Leave us my Lord, and loving countrimen,	1Tamb	5.1.60		2Virgn
bed, where many a Lord/In prime and glorie of his loving joy,	1Tamb	5.1.83		1Virgn
Nothing but feare and fatall steele my Lord.	1Tamb	5.1.109		1Virgn
They have my Lord, and on Damascus wals/Have hoisted up their	1Tamb	5.1.130		Techel
I, my Lord.	1Tamb	5.1.193	P	Attend
The town is ours my Lord, and fresh supply/Of conquest, and of	1Tamb	5.1.196		Techel
We know the victorie is ours my Lord,	1Tamb	5.1.203		Therid
The braines of Bajazeth, my Lord and Soveraigne?	1Tamb	5.1.307		Zabina
O Bajazeth, my husband and my Lord,	1Tamb	5.1.308		Zabina
Ready for battaile gainst my Lord the King.	1Tamb	5.1.382		Philem
Too deare a witnesse for such love my Lord.	1Tamb	5.1.412		Zenoc
Twas I my lord that gat the victory,	1Tamb	5.1.445		Tamb
And see my Lord, a sight of strange import,	1Tamb	5.1.468		Tamb
Els should I much forget my self, my Lord.	1Tamb	5.1.500		Zenoc
And here's the crown my Lord, help set it on.	1Tamb	5.1.505		Usumc
And sacred Lord, the mighty Calapine:	2Tamb	1.1.3		Orcan
Gainst him my Lord must you addresse your power.	2Tamb	1.1.19		Gazell
My Lord I pitie it, and with my heart/Wish your release, but he	2Tamb	1.2.5		Almeda
My soveraigne Lord, renowmed Tamburlain,	2Tamb	1.2.7		Almeda
but tel me my Lord, if I should goe, would you bee as good as	2Tamb	1.2.61	P	Almeda
When you will my Lord, I am ready.	2Tamb	1.2.76		Almeda
My gratious Lord, they have their mothers looks,	2Tamb	1.3.35		Zenoc
Why may not I my Lord, as wel as he,	2Tamb	1.3.61		Amyras
But while my brothers follow armes my lord,	2Tamb	1.3.65		Calyph
My Lord, such speeches to our princely sonnes,	2Tamb	1.3.85		Zenoc
My Lord the great and mighty Tamburlain,	2Tamb	1.3.113		Therid
Meet for your service on the sea, my Lord,	2Tamb	1.3.123		Therid
My Lord, our men of Barbary have martcht/Foure hundred miles	2Tamb	1.3.174		Usumc
And therefore let them rest a while my Lord.	2Tamb	1.3.184		Usumc
Now then my Lord, advantage take hereof,	2Tamb	2.1.22		Fredrk
No whit my Lord:	2Tamb	2.1.33		Baldwn
Tis but the fortune of the wars my Lord,	2Tamb	2.3.31		Gazell
I will my Lord.	2Tamb	2.3.41		Uribas
My Lord, your Majesty shall soone perceive:	2Tamb	2.4.39		1Phstn
I fare my Lord, as other Emperesses,	2Tamb	2.4.42		Zenoc
Live still my Lord, O let my soveraigne live,	2Tamb	2.4.57		Zenoc
Yet let me kisse my Lord before I die,	2Tamb	2.4.69		Zenoc
And let me die with kissing of my Lord.	2Tamb	2.4.70		Zenoc
Some musicke, and my fit wil cease my Lord.	2Tamb	2.4.77		Zenoc
Ah good my Lord be patient, she is dead,	2Tamb	2.4.119		Therid
Nothing prevailes, for she is dead my Lord.	2Tamb	2.4.124		Therid
as when Bajazeth/My royall Lord and father fild the throne,	2Tamb	3.1.12		Callap
My Lord, but this is dangerous to be done,	2Tamb	3.2.93		Calyph
And me another my Lord.	2Tamb	3.2.133	P	Amyras
Yes, my Lord, yes, come lets about it.	2Tamb	3.3.10		Soldrs
We will my Lord.	2Tamb	3.3.46		Pionrs
Come good my Lord, and let us haste from hence/Along the cave	2Tamb	3.4.1		Olymp
My Lord deceast, was dearer unto me,	2Tamb	3.4.42		Olymp
My Lord, your presence makes them pale and wan.	2Tamb	3.5.60		Usumc
Good my Lord, let me take it.	2Tamb	3.5.133	P	Almeda
I, my Lord, he was Calapines keeper.	2Tamb	3.5.152	P	Therid
Here my Lord.	2Tamb	4.1.60	P	Perdic
Content my Lord, but what shal we play for?	2Tamb	4.1.63	P	Perdic
Such a feare (my Lord) would never make yee retire.	2Tamb	4.1.71	P	Perdic
Shal we let goe these kings again my Lord/To gather greater	2Tamb	4.1.82		Amyras
Good my Lord, let him be forgiven for once,	2Tamb	4.1.101		Amyras
We will my Lord.	2Tamb	4.1.167		Soldrs
My Lord and husbandes death, with my sweete sons,	2Tamb	4.2.22		Olymp

LORD (cont.)

Ah, pity me my Lord, and draw your sword,	2Tamb	4.2.33	Olymp
Stay good my Lord, and wil you save my honor,	2Tamb	4.2.55	Olymp
My purpose was (my Lord) to spend it so,	2Tamb	4.2.73	Olymp
Now stab my Lord, and mark your weapons point/That wil be	2Tamb	4.2.79	Olymp
Let me have coach my Lord, that I may ride,	2Tamb	4.3.27	Amyras
Here my Lord.	2Tamb	4.3.69	Soldrs
O pity us my Lord, and save our honours.	2Tamb	4.3.83	Ladies
It seemes they meant to conquer us my Lord,	2Tamb	4.3.88	Therid
Let us not be idle then my Lord,	2Tamb	4.3.95	Techel
My Lord, the breach the enimie hath made/Gives such assurance	2Tamb	5.1.2	Maxim
Then hang out flagges (my Lord) of humble truce,	2Tamb	5.1.6	Maxim
My Lord, if ever you did deed of ruth,	2Tamb	5.1.24	1Citzn
My Lord, if ever you wil win our hearts,	2Tamb	5.1.38	2Citzn
I will my Lord.	2Tamb	5.1.135	Therid
They will talk still my Lord, if you doe not bridle them.	2Tamb	5.1.146	P Amyras
See now my Lord how brave the Captaine hangs.	2Tamb	5.1.149	Amyras
Shoot first my Lord, and then the rest shall follow.	2Tamb	5.1.151	Tamb
What shal be done with their wives and children my Lord.	2Tamb	5.1.169	P Techel
Here they are my Lord.	2Tamb	5.1.177	Usumc
I have fulfil'd your highnes wil, my Lord,	2Tamb	5.1.203	Techel
I, good my Lord, let us in hast to Persea,	2Tamb	5.1.214	Therid
Doubt not my lord, but we shal conquer him.	2Tamb	5.2.12	Amasia
Feare not my Lord, I see great Mahomet/Clothed in purple	2Tamb	5.2.31	Amasia
Ah good my Lord, leave these impatient words,	2Tamb	5.3.54	Therid
Sit stil my gratious Lord, this griefe wil cease,	2Tamb	5.3.64	Techel
Besides my Lord, this day is Criticall,	2Tamb	5.3.91	Phsitn
My lord, yong Callapine that lately fled from your majesty,	2Tamb	5.3.102	P 3Msngr
I joy my Lord, your highnesse is so strong,	2Tamb	5.3.110	Usumc
Alas my Lord, how should our bleeding harts/Wounded and broken	2Tamb	5.3.161	Amyras
A woful change my Lord, that daunts our thoughts,	2Tamb	5.3.181	Therid
My Lord, you must obey his majesty,	2Tamb	5.3.204	Therid
Alas, my Lord, the summe is overgreat,	Jew	1.2.8	Govnr
They were, my Lord, and here they come.	Jew	1.2.36	Offcrs
Then good my Lord, to keepe your quiet still,	Jew	1.2.43	Barab
Alas, my Lord, we are no souldiers:	Jew	1.2.50	Barab
How, my Lord, my mony?	Jew	1.2.55	Barab
Alas, my Lord, the most of us are poore!	Jew	1.2.57	1Jew
Oh my Lord we will give halfe.	Jew	1.2.77	3Jews
I, my Lord, we have seiz'd upon the goods/And wares of Barabas,	Jew	1.2.132	Offcrs
Well then my Lord, say, are you satisfied?	Jew	1.2.137	Barab
'Tis true, my Lord, therefore intreat him well.	Jew	2.2.8	1Knght
My Lord, Remember that to Europ's shame,	Jew	2.2.30	Bosco
My Lord and King hath title to this Isle,	Jew	2.2.37	Bosco
Lord Lodowicke, it sparkles bright and faire.	Jew	2.3.58	Barab
Oh my Lord we will not jarre about the price;	Jew	2.3.65	Barab
I, but my Lord, the harvest is farre off:	Jew	2.3.79	Barab
No more, my Lord.	Jew	2.3.108	1Offcr
My Lord farewell: Come Sirra you are mine.	Jew	2.3.134	Barab
proofe, my Lord, his man's now at my lodging/That was his Agent,	Jew	5.1.16	Curtzn
Nay stay, my Lord, 'tmay be he will confesse.	Jew	5.1.25	1Knght
Gilty, my Lord, I confesse; your sonne and Mathias were both	Jew	5.1.28	P Ithimr
My Lord, the Curtezane and her man are dead;	Jew	5.1.50	1Offcr
Dead, my Lord, and here they bring his body.	Jew	5.1.53	1Offcr
Yes, my good Lord, one that can spy a place/Where you may enter,	Jew	5.1.70	Barab
The very same, my Lord:	Jew	5.1.74	Barab
Feare not, my Lord, for here, against the [sluice] <Truce>,/The	Jew	5.1.86	Barab
Thankes, my Lord.	Jew	5.2.11	Barab
My Lord?	Jew	5.2.48	Govnr
I, Lord, thus slaves will learne.	Jew	5.2.49	Barab
I shall, my Lord.	Jew	5.3.42	Msngr
We shall, my Lord, and thanke you.	Jew	5.5.8	Crpntr
Prince Condy, and my good Lord Admirall,	P 2	1.2	Charls
I will my good Lord.	P 22	1.22	QnMarg
Prince Condy and my good Lord Admiral,	P 27	1.27	Navrre
My Lord I mervaile that th'aspiring Guise/Dares once adventure	P 36	1.36	Admral
My Lord you need not mervaile at the Guise,	P 39	1.39	Condy
My Lord, but did you mark the Cardinall/The Guises brother, and	P 47	1.47	Admral
My Lord.	P 67	2.10	Pothec
See where they be my good Lord, and he that smelles but to	P 73	2.16	P Pothec
I am my Lord, in what your grace commaundes till death.	P 76	2.19	P Pothec
My Lord.	P 84	2.27	P Souldr
I will my Lord.	P 90	2.33	P Souldr
Too late it is my Lord if that be true/To blame her highnes,	P 181	3.16	QnMarg
Let not this heavy chaunce my dearest Lord,	P 191	3.26	QnMarg
What are you hurt my Lord high Admiral?	P 197	3.32	Condy
I my good Lord, shot through the arme.	P 198	3.33	Admral
Me thinkes my Lord, Anjoy hath well advisde/Your highnes to	P 219	4.17	Guise
And it please your grace the Lord high Admirall,	P 243	4.41	Man
How fares it with my Lord high Admiral,	P 253	4.51	Charls
Ah my good Lord, these are the Guisians,	P 260	4.58	Admral
Assure your selfe my good Lord Admirall,	P 262	4.60	Charls
And so be pacient good Lord Admirall,	P 271	4.69	Charls
Plac'd by my brother, will betray his Lord:	P 294	5.21	Anjoy
But look my Lord, ther's some in the Admirals house.	P 297	5.24	Retes
I my Lord.	P 305	5.32	Gonzag
I will my Lord.	P 331	5.58	Mntsrl
Stay my Lord, let me begin the psalme.	P 344	5.71	Anjoy
Oh good my Lord,/Wherein hath Ramus	P 383	7.23	Ramus
O good my Lord, let me but speak a word.	P 399	7.39	Ramus
My Lord of Anjoy, there are a hundred Protestants,	P 417	7.57	Guise
And in the mean time my Lord, could we devise,	P 425	7.65	Guise
My Lord, they say/That all the protestants are massacred.	P 431	7.71	Navrre

LORD (cont.)

But yet my Lord the report doth run,	P 435	7.75		Navrre
My Lord of Loraine have you markt of late,/How Charles our	P 512	9.31		QnMoth
For the late nights worke which my Lord of Guise/Did make in	P 514	9.33		QnMoth
I, but my Lord let me alone for that,	P 519	9.38		QnMoth
Come my Lord [let] <lets> us goe.	P 527	9.46		QnMoth
Comfort your selfe my Lord and have no doubt,	P 541	11.6		Navrre
Your Majestie her rightfull Lord and Soveraigne.	P 583	11.48		Pleshe
O Lord, mine eare.	P 619	12.32		Cutprs
My Lord Cardinall of Loraine, tell me,	P 631	12.44		QnMoth
Come my [Lord] <Lords>, let us goe seek the Guise,	P 655	12.68		QnMoth
That I may write unto my dearest Lord.	P 659	13.3		Duchss
To such a one my Lord, as when she reads my lines,	P 672	13.16		Duchss
O no my Lord, a woman only must/Partake the secrets of my	P 675	13.19		Duchss
O pardon me my Lord.	P 679	13.23		Duchss
My Lord, as by our scoutes we understande,	P 724	14.27		1Msngr
Not yet my Lord, for thereon doe they stay:	P 732	14.35		1Msngr
Farwell to my Lord of Guise and Epernoune.	P 750	15.8		Joyeux
Health and harty farwell to my Lord Joyeux.	P 751	15.9		Guise
How now my Lord, faith this is more then need,	P 757	15.15		Guise
My Lord, twere good to make them frends,	P 772	15.30		Eprnon
Not I my Lord, what if I had?	P 775	15.33		Mugern
My Lord of Guise, we understand that you/Have gathered a power	P 821	17.16		King
My Lord, to speak more plainely, thus it is:	P 847	17.42		Guise
And know my Lord, the Pope will sell his triple crowne,	P 851	17.46		Guise
My Lord, in token of my true humilitie,	P 866	17.61		Guise
But trust him not my Lord,	P 871	17.66		Eprnon
My Lord,/I think for safety of your royall person,	P 886	17.81		Eprnon
My Lord, I am advertised from France,	P 900	18.1		Navrre
I will my Lord.	P 913	18.14		Bartus
My Lord.	P 915	18.16		Pleshe
I goe my Lord.	P 920	18.21		Pleshe
They be my good Lord.	P 948	19.18		Capt
I warrant ye my Lord.	P 951	19.21		Capt
O pardon me my Lord of Guise.	P 990	19.60	P	3Mur
O my Lord, I am one of them that is set to murder you.	P 992	19.62	P	3Mur
I my Lord, the rest have taine their standings in the next	P 994	19.64	P	3Mur
in the next roome, therefore good my Lord goe not foorth.	P 995	19.65	P	3Mur
My Lord, see where the Guise is slaine.	P1019	19.89		Capt
My Lord heer is his sonne.	P1045	19.115		Eprnon
My Lord, see where she comes, as if she droupt/To heare these	P1062	19.132		Eprnon
O Lord no: for we entend to strangle you.	P1095	20.5		2Mur
Yours my Lord Cardinall, you should have saide.	P1103	20.13		1Mur
My Lord, I come to bring you newes, that your brother the	P1122	21.16	P	Frier
My Lord, here me but speak.	P1129	21.23	P	Frier
O my Lord, I have beene a great sinner in my dayes, and the	P1133	21.27	P	Frier
Tush my Lord, let me alone for that.	P1136	21.30	P	Frier
Twere not amisse my Lord, if he were searcht.	P1160	22.22		Eprnon
I my good Lord, and will dye therein.	P1165	22.27		Frier
My Lord,/The President of Paris greets your grace,	P1167	22.29		Frier
O my Lord, let him live a while.	P1173	22.35		Eprnon
The wound I warrant ye is deepe my Lord,	P1192	22.54		King
Alas my Lord, the wound is dangerous,	P1212	22.74		Srgeon
Alas my Lord, your highnes cannot live.	P1223	22.85		Srgeon
And yet I have not viewd my Lord the king,	Edw	1.1.45		Gavstn
Such things as these best please his majestie,/My lord.	Edw	1.1.72		Gavstn
If you love us my lord, hate Gaveston.	Edw	1.1.80		MortSr
And know my lord, ere I will breake my oath,	Edw	1.1.85		Mortmr
My lord, why do you thus incense your peeres,	Edw	1.1.99		Lncstr
Lord Percie of the North being highly mov'd,	Edw	1.1.110		Kent
Adew my Lord, and either change your minde,	Edw	1.1.130		Lncstr
I can no longer keepe me from my lord.	Edw	1.1.139		Gavstn
I heere create thee Lord high Chamberlaine,	Edw	1.1.154		Edward
Earle of Cornewall, king and lord of Man.	Edw	1.1.156		Edward
My lord, these titles far exceed my worth.	Edw	1.1.157		Gavstn
Whether goes my Lord of Coventrie so fast?	Edw	1.1.175		Edward
Be thou lord bishop, and receive his rents,	Edw	1.1.194		Edward
I, and besides, lord Chamberlaine of the realme,	Edw	1.2.13		Warwck
And secretary to, and lord of Man.	Edw	1.2.14		Warwck
My lord of Cornewall now, at every worde,	Edw	1.2.17		Lncstr
Here comes my lord of Canterburies grace.	Edw	1.2.33		Warwck
My lord, will you take armes against the king?	Edw	1.2.39		Lncstr
For now my lord the king regardes me not,	Edw	1.2.49		Queene
for rather then my lord/Shall be opprest by civill mutinies,	Edw	1.2.64		Queene
But say my lord, where shall this meeting bee?	Edw	1.2.74		Warwck
No, threaten not my lord, but pay them home.	Edw	1.4.26		Gavstn
My lord, you may not thus disparage us,	Edw	1.4.32		Lncstr
Why are you moov'd, be patient my lord,	Edw	1.4.43		ArchBp
Then linger not my lord but do it straight.	Edw	1.4.58		Lncstr
My lord, you shalbe Chauncellor of the realme,	Edw	1.4.65		Edward
And you lord Warwick, president of the North,	Edw	1.4.68		Edward
Urge him, my lord.	Edw	1.4.83		MortSr
My lord I heare it whispered every where,	Edw	1.4.106		Gavstn
For every looke, my lord, drops downe a teare,	Edw	1.4.136		Gavstn
Whether goes my lord?	Edw	1.4.144		Queene
I say no more, judge you the rest my lord.	Edw	1.4.148		Gavstn
Ist not enough, that thou corrupts my lord,	Edw	1.4.150		Queene
Villaine, tis thou that robst me of my lord.	Edw	1.4.160		Queene
Madam, tis you that rob me of my lord.	Edw	1.4.161		Gavstn
Wherein my lord, have I deservd these words?	Edw	1.4.163		Queene
How deare my lord is to poore Isabell.	Edw	1.4.166		Queene
The king my lord thus to abandon me:	Edw	1.4.177		Queene
This wils my lord, and this must I performe,	Edw	1.4.202		Queene

LORD (cont.)

And so am I my lord, diswade the Queene.	Edw	1.4.215	Lncstr
My Lord of Lancaster, marke the respect.	Edw	1.4.248	Mortmr
Yet good my lord, heare what he can alledge.	Edw	1.4.250	Queene
Why then my lord, give me but leave to speak.	Edw	1.4.254	Mortmr
Marke you but that my lord of Lancaster.	Edw	1.4.263	Warwck
Such a one as my Lord of Cornewall is,	Edw	1.4.285	Mortmr
But see in happie time, my lord the king,	Edw	1.4.299	Queene
My gratious lord, I come to bring you newes.	Edw	1.4.320	Queene
That Gaveston, my Lord, shalbe repeald.	Edw	1.4.322	Queene
No other jewels hang about my neck/Then these my lord, nor let	Edw	1.4.331	Queene
My gentle lord, bespeake these nobles faire,	Edw	1.4.337	Queene
Slay me my lord, when I offend your grace.	Edw	1.4.349	Warwck
I make thee heere lord Marshall of the realme.	Edw	1.4.356	Edward
My lord, ile marshall so your enemies,	Edw	1.4.357	Mortmr
And as for you, lord Mortimer of Chirke,	Edw	1.4.359	Edward
It shalbe done my gratious Lord.	Edw	1.4.372	Beamnt
Lord Mortimer, we leave you to your charge:	Edw	1.4.373	Edward
Such newes we heare my lord.	Edw	1.4.380	Lncstr
Seeing that our Lord th'earle of Glosters dead,	Edw	2.1.2	Baldck
this of me, a factious lord/Shall hardly do himselfe good,	Edw	2.1.6	Spencr
Mine old lord whiles he livde, was so precise,	Edw	2.1.46	Baldck
This argues the entire love of my Lord.	Edw	2.1.63	Neece
Now to the letter of my Lord the King,	Edw	2.1.66	Neece
My lord of Cornewall is a comming over,	Edw	2.1.76	Neece
My Lord.	Edw	2.2.5	Lncstr
A homely one my lord, not worth the telling.	Edw	2.2.13	Mortmr
And what is yours my lord of Lancaster?	Edw	2.2.21	Edward
My lord, mines more obscure then Mortimers.	Edw	2.2.22	Lncstr
this fish my lord I beare,/The motto this:	Edw	2.2.27	Lncstr
Sweet Lord and King, your speech preventeth mine,	Edw	2.2.59	Gavstn
Salute him? yes: welcome Lord Chamberlaine.	Edw	2.2.65	Lncstr
Welcome Lord governour of the Ile of Man.	Edw	2.2.67	Warwck
My Lord I cannot brooke these injuries.	Edw	2.2.71	Gavstn
From Scotland my lord.	Edw	2.2.113	1Msngr
Meane time my lord of Penbrooke and my selfe,	Edw	2.2.122	Warwck
You may not in, my lord.	Edw	2.2.137	Guard
Nay, stay my lord, I come to bring you newes,	Edw	2.2.141	Mortmr
My lord, the familie of the Mortimers/Are not so poore, but	Edw	2.2.150	Mortmr
And so will I, and then my lord farewell.	Edw	2.2.156	Lncstr
My lord, I see your love to Gaveston,	Edw	2.2.208	Kent
My lord, tis thought, the Earles are up in armes.	Edw	2.2.225	Queene
My lord, dissemble with her, speake her faire.	Edw	2.2.229	Gavstn
I my lord,/His name is Spencer, he is well alied,	Edw	2.2.248	Gavstn
I know my lord, many will stomack me,	Edw	2.2.260	Gavstn
I feare me he is slaine my gratious lord.	Edw	2.4.2	Spencr
O stay my lord, they will not injure you.	Edw	2.4.7	Gavstn
Farewell my Lord.	Edw	2.4.9	Gavstn
These hands are tir'd, with haling of my lord/From Gaveston,	Edw	2.4.26	Queene
No Mortimer, ile to my lord the king.	Edw	2.4.51	Queene
My Lord!	Edw	2.5.25	Gavstn
How now my lord of Arundell?	Edw	2.5.32	Lncstr
Why my Lord of Warwicke,	Edw	2.5.46	Gavstn
Not so my Lord, least he bestow more cost,	Edw	2.5.55	Lncstr
My lord Mortimer, and you my lords each one,	Edw	2.5.74	Penbrk
Provided this, that you my lord of Arundell/Will joyne with me.	Edw	2.5.81	Penbrk
My lord of Lancaster, what say you in this?	Edw	2.5.89	Arundl
And you lord Mortimer?	Edw	2.5.91	Penbrk
How say you my lord of Warwick?	Edw	2.5.92	Mortmr
My lord of Penbrooke, we deliver him you,	Edw	2.5.97	Mortmr
My Lord, you shall go with me,	Edw	2.5.99	Penbrk
Tis verie kindlie spoke my lord of Penbrooke,	Edw	2.5.104	Arundl
So my lord.	Edw	2.5.106	Penbrk
My lord, weele quicklie be at Cobham.	Edw	2.5.111	HrsBoy
My lord of Penbrookes men,	Edw	2.6.6	Warwck
And wrong our lord, your honorable friend.	Edw	2.6.9	James
We will in hast go certifie our Lord.	Edw	2.6.19	James
my lord pardon my speeche,/Did you retaine your fathers	Edw	3.1.15	Spencr
His life, my lord, before your princely feete.	Edw	3.1.45	Spencr
Because we heare Lord Bruse dooth sell his land,	Edw	3.1.53	Edward
My lord, here comes the Queene.	Edw	3.1.58	Spencr
Newes of dishonor lord, and discontent,	Edw	3.1.59	Queene
That lord Valoyes our brother, king of Fraunce,	Edw	3.1.62	Queene
And feare not lord and father, heavens great beames/On Atlas	Edw	3.1.76	Prince
God end them once, my lord I take my leave,	Edw	3.1.87	Queene
What lord [Arundell] <Matre>, dost thou come alone?	Edw	3.1.89	Edward
Yea my good lord, for Gaveston is dead.	Edw	3.1.90	Arundl
Neither my lord, for as he was surprizd,	Edw	3.1.94	Arundl
Their lord rode home, thinking his prisoner safe,	Edw	3.1.117	Arundl
My lord, referre your vengeance to the sword,	Edw	3.1.123	Spencr
love we do create thee/Earle of Gloster, and lord Chamberlaine,	Edw	3.1.146	Edward
My lord, [here] is <heres> a messenger from the Barons,/Desires	Edw	3.1.148	Spencr
Long live king Edward, Englands lawful lord.	Edw	3.1.151	Herald
My [lords] <lord>, perceive you how these rebels swell:	Edw	3.1.181	Edward
I doubt it not my lord, right will prevaile.	Edw	3.1.189	Spencr
my lord of Winchester,/These lustie leaders Warwicke and	Edw	3.1.245	Edward
Holla, who walketh there, ist you my lord?	Edw	4.1.12	Mortmr
It hath my lord, the warders all a sleepe,	Edw	4.1.15	Mortmr
How say you my Lord, will you go with your friends,	Edw	4.2.19	SrJohn
Well said my lord.	Edw	4.2.26	SrJohn
Lord Edmund and lord Mortimer alive?	Edw	4.2.36	Queene
the newes was heere my lord,/That you were dead, or very neare	Edw	4.2.37	Queene
And lives t'advance your standard good my lord.	Edw	4.2.42	Mortmr

LORD (cont.)

No my lord Mortimer, not I, I trow.	Edw	4.2.44	Prince
But by the sword, my lord, it must be deserv'd.	Edw	4.2.59	Mortmr
Madam along, and you my lord, with me,	Edw	4.2.81	SrJohn
My lord of Gloster, do you heare the newes?	Edw	4.3.4	Edward
What newes my lord?	Edw	4.3.5	Spencr
Done through the realme, my lord of Arundell/You have the note,	Edw	4.3.7	Edward
From the lieutenant of the tower my lord.	Edw	4.3.9	Arundl
What now remaines, have you proclaimed, my lord,	Edw	4.3.17	Edward
My lord, we have, and if he be in England,	Edw	4.3.19	Spencr
Letters my lord, and tidings foorth of Fraunce,	Edw	4.3.25	Post
To you my lord of Gloster from [Levune] <Lewne>.	Edw	4.3.26	Post
With them are gone lord Edmund, and the lord Mortimer, having	Edw	4.3.32	P Spencr
and the lord Mortimer, having in their company divers of your	Edw	4.3.33	P Spencr
Sound trumpets my lord and forward let us martch,	Edw	4.4.28	SrJohn
Fly, fly, my Lord, the Queene is over strong,	Edw	4.5.1	Spencr
O no my lord, this princely resolution/Fits not the time, away,	Edw	4.5.8	Baldck
Lord warden of the realme, and sith the fates/Have made his	Edw	4.6.26	Queene
My lord of Kent, what needes these questions?	Edw	4.6.34	Mortmr
My lord, the Maior of Bristow knows our mind.	Edw	4.6.40	Queene
A goodly chauncelor, is he not my lord?	Edw	4.6.43	Queene
A gave a long looke after us my lord,	Edw	4.7.30	Spencr
Looke up my lord.	Edw	4.7.44	Spencr
my lord I pray be short,/A faire commission warrants what we	Edw	4.7.47	Rice
My lord, why droope you thus?	Edw	4.7.60	Leistr
We must my lord, so will the angry heavens.	Edw	4.7.74	Spencr
My lord, it is in vaine to greeve or storme,	Edw	4.7.77	Baldck
My lord, be going, care not for these,	Edw	4.7.93	Rice
Be patient good my lord, cease to lament,	Edw	5.1.1	Leistr
My lord, why waste you thus the time away,	Edw	5.1.49	Leistr
My lord, the king is willing to resigne.	Edw	5.1.94	Leistr
My lord, thinke not a thought so villanous/Can harbor in a man	Edw	5.1.131	Bartly
I, my most gratious lord, so tis decreed.	Edw	5.1.138	Bartly
Favor him my lord, as much as lieth in you.	Edw	5.1.147	Leistr
How fares my lord the king?	Edw	5.2.24	Queene
Further, or this letter was sealed, Lord Bartley came,	Edw	5.2.30	BshpWn
The lord of Bartley is so pitifull,	Edw	5.2.34	BshpWn
a letter presently/Unto the Lord of Bartley from our selfe,	Edw	5.2.48	Mortmr
It shall be done my lord.	Edw	5.2.51	Matrvs
I warrant you my lord.	Edw	5.2.56	Gurney
Feare not my Lord, weele do as you commaund.	Edw	5.2.66	Matrvs
Whither goes this letter, to my lord the king?	Edw	5.2.68	Queene
How fares my honorable lord of Kent?	Edw	5.2.80	Mortmr
Not I my lord:	Edw	5.2.90	Kent
My lord, he hath betraied the king his brother,	Edw	5.2.106	Mortmr
My lord, be not pensive, we are your friends.	Edw	5.3.1	Matrvs
The court is where lord Mortimer remaines,	Edw	5.3.61	Matrvs
What else my lord? and farre more resolute.	Edw	5.4.23	Ltborn
That will I quicklie do, farewell my lord.	Edw	5.4.47	Ltborn
Lord Mortimer, now take him to your charge.	Edw	5.4.81	Queene
My lord, he is my unckle, and shall live.	Edw	5.4.91	King
My lord, he is your enemie, and shall die.	Edw	5.4.92	Mortmr
Intreate my lord Protector for his life.	Edw	5.4.95	King
My lord, if you will let my unckle live,	Edw	5.4.99	King
My lord protector greetes you.	Edw	5.5.14	Ltborn
Doe as you are commaunded by my lord.	Edw	5.5.26	Matrvs
Your overwatchde my lord, lie downe and rest.	Edw	5.5.92	Ltborn
If you mistrust me, ile be gon my lord.	Edw	5.5.97	Ltborn
And beare the kings to Mortimer our lord,	Edw	5.5.119	Gurney
I my good Lord, I would it were undone.	Edw	5.6.2	Matrvs
Gurney, my lord, is fled, and will I feare,	Edw	5.6.7	Matrvs
Feare not my lord, know that you are a king.	Edw	5.6.24	1Lord
How now my lord?	Edw	5.6.26	Mortmr
Why speake you not unto my lord the king?	Edw	5.6.38	1Lord
My lord, I feare me it will proove too true.	Edw	5.6.77	2Lord
Shall I not moorne for my beloved lord,	Edw	5.6.87	Queene
My lord, here is the head of Mortimer.	Edw	5.6.93	1Lord
Lord and Commander of these elements.	F 104	1.1.76	BdAngl
and so the Lord blesse you, preserve you, and keepe you, my	F 217	1.2.24	P Wagner
Tell me, what is that Lucifer, thy Lord?	F 290	1.3.62	Faust
Now tell me what saith <sayes> Lucifer thy Lord.	F 419	2.1.31	Faust
And tell me, what good will my soule do thy Lord?	F 428	2.1.40	Faust
Chiefe Lord and Regent of perpetuall night.	F 445	2.1.57	Faust
Lord Cardinals of France and Padua,	F 881	3.1.103	Pope
We go my Lord.	F 889	3.1.111	1Card
Lord Raymond--	F 890	3.1.112	Pope
Behold my Lord, the Cardinals are return'd.	F 945	3.1.167	Raymnd
Make haste againe, my good Lord Cardinalls,	F 972	3.1.194	Pope
And with Lord Raymond, King of Hungary,	F 979	3.1.201	Pope
Welcome Lord Cardinals: come sit downe.	F1009	3.2.29	Pope
Lord Raymond, take your seate, Friers attend,	F1010	3.2.30	Pope
Lord Archbishop of Reames, sit downe with us.	F1037	3.2.57	Pope
Lord Raymond pray fall too, I am beholding/To the Bishop of	F1041	3.2.61	Pope
My good Lord Archbishop, heres a most daintie dish,	F1046	3.2.66	Pope
Lord Raymond, I drink unto your grace.	F1053	3.2.73	Pope
My Lord, I must forewarne your Majesty,	F1248	4.1.94	Faust
My gracious Lord, you doe forget your selfe,	F1258	4.1.104	Faust
see, my gracious Lord, what strange beast is yon, that thrusts	F1274	4.1.120	P Faust
He sleeps my Lord, but dreames not of his hornes.	F1280	4.1.126	Faust
And therefore my Lord, so please your Majesty,	F1300	4.1.146	Faust
good my Lord intreate for me:	F1306	4.1.152	P Benvol
My gracious Lord, not so much for injury done to me, as to	F1311	4.1.157	P Faust
I do thinke my selfe my good Lord, highly recompenced, in that	F1563	4.6.6	P Faust

LORD (cont.)				
My Lord, beseech you give me leave a while,	F1621	4.6.64		Faust
Good Lord, that flesh and bloud should be so fraile with your	F1632	4.6.75	P	Carter
My Lord,/we are much beholding to this learned man.	F1669	4.6.112		Lady
For disobedience to my soveraigne Lord,	F1744	5.1.71		Mephst
intreat thy Lord/To pardon my unjust presumption,	F1747	5.1.74		Faust
O Lord I pray sir, let Banio and Belcher go sleepe.	F App	p.231 68	P	Clown
My Lord of Lorraine, wilt please you draw neare.	F App	p.231 1	P	Pope
My Lord, here is a daintie dish was sent me from the Bishop of	F App	p.231 5	P	Pope
My Lord, this dish was sent me from the Cardinall of Florence.	F App	p.231 9	P	Pope
my Lord Ile drinke to your grace	F App	p.231 12	P	Pope
My Lord, it may be some ghost newly crept out of Purgatory come	F App	p.232 14	P	Lorein
to lay the fury of this ghost, once again my Lord fall too.	F App	p.232 17	P	Pope
My gratious Lord, I am ready to accomplish your request, so	F App	p.237 37	P	Faust
heere they are my gratious Lord.	F App	p.238 59	P	Faust
My Gratious Lord, not so much for the injury hee offred me	F App	p.238 81	P	Faust
Now my good Lord having done my duety, I humbly take my leave.	F App	p.238 86	P	Faust
O Lord sir, let me goe, and Ile give you fortie dollers more.	F App	p.241 158	P	HrsCsr
My gratious Lord, I am glad it contents you so wel:	F App	p.242 3	P	Faust
And so I wil my Lord, and whilst I live, Rest beholding for	F App	p.243 30	P	Duchss
Rhesus fell/And Captive horses bad their Lord fare-well.	Ovid's Elegies	1.9.24		
A mortall nimphes refusing Lord to stay.	Ovid's Elegies	2.17.16		
With Laodameia mate to her dead Lord.	Ovid's Elegies	2.18.38		
LORDE				
My Lorde.	Edw	1.1.75		Lncstr
Quick quick my lorde, I long to write my name.	Edw	1.4.4		Lncstr
Have you no doubt my Lorde, have you no feare,	Edw	4.7.1		Abbot
My lorde, the parlement must have present newes,	Edw	5.1.84		Trussl
Call them againe my lorde, and speake them faire,	Edw	5.1.91		Leistr
My lorde--	Edw	5.1.112		Bishop
Call me not lorde, away, out of my sight:	Edw	5.1.113		Edward
My lorde, the counsell of the Queene commaunds,	Edw	5.1.135		Leistr
And who must keepe mee now, must you my lorde?	Edw	5.1.137		Edward
Not yet my lorde, ile beare you on your waye.	Edw	5.1.155		Leistr
From Killingworth my lorde.	Edw	5.2.23		2Msngr
My Lorde.	Edw	5.2.51		Gurney
Well, if my Lorde your brother were enlargde.	Edw	5.2.82		Queene
Come sonne, and go with this gentle Lorde and me.	Edw	5.2.109		Queene
by the grace of God/King of England, and lorde of Ireland.	Edw	5.4.74		ArchBp
To murther you my most gratious lorde?	Edw	5.5.46		Ltborn
O speake no more my lorde, this breakes my heart.	Edw	5.5.71		Ltborn
How now my Lorde.	Edw	5.5.102		Ltborn
LORDES				
Or you my Lordes to be my followers?	1Tamb	1.2.83		Tamb
Who have ye there my Lordes?	2Tamb	5.1.80		Tamb
Wel then my friendly Lordes, what now remaines/But that we	2Tamb	5.1.210		Tamb
Ere farther we proceede my noble lordes,	Edw	4.6.23		Queene
LORDINGS				
How say you Lordings, Is not this your hope?	1Tamb	1.2.116		Tamb
LORDLY				
So lookes my Lordly love, faire Tamburlaine.	1Tamb	3.2.49		Zenoc
And made my lordly Love her worthy King:	1Tamb	3.3.190		Zenoc
Farewell base stooping to the lordly peeres,	Edw	1.1.18		Gavstn
My lordly hands ile throwe upon my right.	Ovid's Elegies	2.5.30		
LORDS				
Lords of this towne, or whatsoever stile/Belongs unto your	Dido	2.1.39		Aeneas
Lords goe before, we two must talke alone.	Dido	3.3.9		Dido
Good brother tell the cause unto my Lords,	1Tamb	1.1.4		Mycet
How like you this, my honorable Lords?	1Tamb	1.1.54		Mycet
Whether we presently will flie (my Lords)/To rest secure	1Tamb	1.1.177		Cosroe
The [Lords] <Lord> would not be too exasperate,	1Tamb	1.1.182		Ortyg
Who traveiling with these Medean Lords/To Memphis, from my	1Tamb	1.2.11		Zenoc
These Lords (perhaps) do scorne our estimates,	1Tamb	1.2.61		Tamb
How now my Lords of Egypt and Zenocrate?	1Tamb	1.2.113		Tamb
Soft ye my Lords and sweet Zenocrate.	1Tamb	1.2.119		Tamb
Shall vaile to us, as Lords of all the Lake.	1Tamb	1.2.196		Tamb
And now faire Madam, and my noble Lords,	1Tamb	1.2.253		Tamb
Leading a troope of Gentlemen and Lords,	1Tamb	2.1.58		Ceneus
The Lords and Captaines of my brothers campe,	1Tamb	2.5.26		Cosroe
Resolve my Lords and loving souldiers now,	1Tamb	2.6.34		Cosroe
But come my Lords, to weapons let us fall.	1Tamb	3.3.162		Tamb
But goe my Lords, put the rest to the sword.	1Tamb	5.1.134		Tamb
And now my Iords and loving followers,	1Tamb	5.1.522		Tamb
And made Canarea cal us kings and Lords,	2Tamb	1.3.181		Usumc
Now say my Lords of Buda and Bohemia,	2Tamb	2.1.1		Sgsmnd
Then arme my Lords, and issue sodainly,	2Tamb	2.1.60		Sgsmnd
Arme dread Soveraign and my noble Lords.	2Tamb	2.2.24		1Msngr
To armes my Lords, on Christ still let us crie,	2Tamb	2.2.63		Orcan
And of my Lords whose true nobilitie/Have merited my latest	2Tamb	2.4.73		Zenoc
Wel then my noble Lords, for this my friend,	2Tamb	3.1.68		Callap
And now my Lords, advance your speares againe,	2Tamb	3.2.43		Tamb
To Babylon my Lords, to Babylon.	2Tamb	4.3.133		Tamb
Help me (my Lords) to make my last remoove.	2Tamb	5.3.180		Tamb
Confesse; what meane you, Lords, who should confesse?	Jew	5.1.26		Barab
And now my Lords the mariage rites perfourm'd,	P 18	1.18		Charls
The rest that will not goe (my Lords) may stay:	P 23	1.23		Charls
Come my Lords lets go to the Church and pray,	P 55	1.55		Navrre
Come my Lords let us beare her body hence,	P 195	3.30		Admral
betraide, come my Lords, and let us goe tell the King of this.	P 199	3.34	P	Navrre
And now my Lords let us closely to our busines.	P 332	5.59		Guise
How now my Lords, how fare you?	P 430	7.70		Anjoy
My Lords of Poland I must needs confesse,	P 451	8.1		Anjoy
Then come my Lords, lets goe.	P 481	8.31		Anjoy

LORDS (cont.)

My Lords, what resteth there now for to be done?	P 554	11.19	QnMoth
And now my lords after these funerals be done,	P 561	11.26	QnMoth
Lets goe my Lords, our dinner staies for us.	P 630	12.43	King
Come my [Lord] <Lords>, let us goe seek the Guise,	P 655	12.68	QnMoth
My Lords, sith in a quarrell just and right,	P 698	14.1	Navrre
But come my Lords, let us away with speed,	P 741	14.44	Navrre
Come my Lords, now that this storme is overpast,	P 804	16.18	Navrre
As ancient Romanes over their Captive Lords,	P 982	19.52	Guise
My Lords,/Fight in the quarrell of this valiant Prince,	P1228	22.90	King
Come Lords, take up the body of the King,	P1245	22.107	Navrre
What els my lords, for it concernes me neere,	Edw	1.2.44	ArchBp
My lords, to eaze all this, but heare me speake.	Edw	1.2.68	ArchBp
My lords, now let us all be resolute,	Edw	1.4.45	Mortmr
Or I will presentlie discharge these lords,	Edw	1.4.61	ArchBp
But I would wish thee reconcile the lords,	Edw	1.4.156	Edward
My Lords, albeit the Queen winne Mortimer,	Edw	1.4.230	Lncstr
My Lords, that I abhorre base Gaveston,	Edw	1.4.239	Mortmr
Because my lords, it was not thought upon:	Edw	1.4.273	Mortmr
My lords, if to performe this I be slack,	Edw	1.4.290	Mortmr
He weares a lords revenewe on his back,	Edw	1.4.407	Mortmr
My lords, of love to this our native land,	Edw	2.3.1	Kent
If that will not suffice, farwell my lords.	Edw	2.3.10	Kent
now my lords know this,/That Gaveston is secretlie arrivde,	Edw	2.3.15	Lncstr
Flie, flie, my lords, the earles have got the holde,	Edw	2.4.4	Edward
Yet lustie lcrds I have escapt your handes,	Edw	2.5.1	Gavstn
I thanke you all my lcrds, then I perceive,	Edw	2.5.29	Gavstn
My lords, king Edward greetes you all by me.	Edw	2.5.33	Arundl
I know it lcrds, it is this life you aime at,	Edw	2.5.48	Gavstn
My lords, it is his majesties request,	Edw	2.5.57	Arundl
My lords, I will be pledge for his returne.	Edw	2.5.66	Arundl
My lord Mortimer, and you my lords each one,	Edw	2.5.74	Penbrk
My lords, I will not over wooe your honors,	Edw	2.5.86	Penbrk
Choose of our lcrds to beare you companie,	Edw	3.1.84	Edward
My lords, because our soveraigne sends for him,	Edw	3.1.109	Arundl
now get thee to thy lords,/And tell them I will come to	Edw	3.1.177	Edward
My [lords] <lord>, perceive you how these rebels swell:	Edw	3.1.181	Edward
upon them lords,/This day I shall powre vengeance with my sword	Edw	3.1.185	Edward
Now lustie lcrds, now not by chance of warre,	Edw	3.1.221	Edward
Bestowe that treasure on the lords of Fraunce,	Edw	3.1.265	Spencr
Have you no doubts my lords, ile [clap so] <claps> close,/Among	Edw	3.1.276	Levune
Among the lcrds of France with Englands golde,	Edw	3.1.277	Levune
The lords are cruell, and the king unkinde,	Edw	4.2.2	Queene
But gentle lords, friendles we are in Fraunce.	Edw	4.2.46	Queene
My Lords of England, sith the ungentle king/Of Fraunce refuseth	Edw	4.2.61	SrJohn
I trowe/The lords of Fraunce love Englands gold so well,	Edw	4.3.15	Edward
behalfe, dealt with the king of Fraunce his lords, and effected,	Edw	4.3.29	P Spencr
Now lords, our loving friends and countrimen,	Edw	4.4.1	Queene
Lords, sith that we are by sufferance of heaven,	Edw	4.4.17	Mortmr
Deale you my lords in this, my loving lords,	Edw	4.6.28	Queene
I rue my lords ill fortune, but alas,	Edw	4.6.64	Queene
Where lords keepe courts, and kings are lockt in prison!	Edw	5.3.64	Kent
The proudest lords salute me as I passe,	Edw	5.4.50	Mortmr
Heere comes the hearse, helpe me to moorne, my lords:	Edw	5.6.98	King
As Indian Mcores, obey their Spanish Lords,	F 148	1.1.120	Valdes
To hold the Emperours their lawfull Lords.	F 927	3.1.149	Bruno
I pray my Lords have patience at this troublesome banquet.	F1058	3.2.78	Pope
O I am slaine, help me my Lords:	F1068	3.2.88	Pope
No Art, no cunning, to present these Lords,	F1295	4.1.141	Faust
earth, the sea, the world it selfe,/Would not admit two Lords:	Lucan, First Booke		111
When fortune made us lords of all, wealth flowed,	Lucan, First Booke		161
And few great lords in vertuous deeds shall joy,	Hero and Leander		1.479

LORDSHIP

Your Lordship shall doe well to let them have it.	Jew	1.2.44	Barab
Oh but I knew your Lordship wud disdaine/To marry with the	Jew	2.3.294	Barab
Nay more, the guarde upon his lordship waites:	Edw	1.2.21	Lncstr
May it please your lordship to subscribe your name.	Edw	1.4.2	Lncstr
To greet his lordship with a poniard,	Edw	1.4.266	Mortmr
That shall wee see, looke where his lordship comes.	Edw	2.2.49	Lncstr
Your lordship doth dishonor to your selfe,	Edw	2.6.8	James
Your lordship cannot priviledge your head.	Edw	4.6.70	Mortmr

LCRDSHIPS

Whither will your lordships?	Edw	2.2.133	Guard
Will your Lcrdships away?	Edw	4.7.116	Rice

LORE

If Nature had not given me wisedomes lore?	1Tamb	2.4.7	Mycet

LOREINE

Loreine, Loreine, fcllow Loreine.	P 339	5.66	Guise

LORRAINE (See also LORAINE, LOREINE)

My Lord of Lorraine, wilt please you draw neare.	F App	p.231 1	P Pope

LCS

Hermoso Placer de los Dineros.	Jew	2.1.64	Barab

LCSE (See also LOOSE, LOOSETH)

which if thcu lose shall shine above the waves:	Dido	3.1.121	Dido
And lose more labor than the gaine will quight.	1Tamb	2.5.96	Tamb
And should we lose the opportunity/That God hath given to venge	2Tamb	2.1.51	Fredrk
Lastly, he that denies this, shall absolutely lose al he has.	Jew	1.2.76	P Reader
I am content to lcse some of my Crownes;	Jew	2.3.178	Barab
At least unprofitably lose it not:	Jew	5.2.37	Barab
That slie inveigling Frenchman weele exile,/Or lose our lives:	Edw	1.2.58	Mortmr
The king shall lose his crowne, for we have power,	Edw	1.2.59	Mortmr
And either have our wils, or lose our lives.	Edw	1.4.46	Mortmr
For if they goe, the prince shall lcse his right.	Edw	5.1.92	Leistr

LOSE (cont.)			
That <and> even then when I shall lose my life,	Edw	5.5.77	Edward
Nor did thy ashes her last offrings lose.	Ovid's Elegies		3.8.50
LOSSE			
whatsoever you esteeme/Of this successe, and losse unvallued,	1Tamb	1.2.45	Tamb
We thinke it losse to make exchange for that/We are assured of	1Tamb	1.2.216	Techel
wouldst thou have me buy thy Fathers love/With such a losse?	1Tamb	4.4.84	Tamb
Though with the losse of Egypt and my Crown.	1Tamb	5.1.444	Souldn
And so revenge our latest grievous losse,	2Tamb	5.2.10	Callap
toyl'd to inherit here/The months of vanity and losse of time,	Jew	1.2.197	Barab
What, woman, moane not for a little losse:	Jew	1.2.226	Barab
Will Barabas recover Malta's losse?	Jew	5.2.74	Govnr
His losse made way for Roman outrages.	Lucan, First Booke		106
[Thy] <They> troubled haires, alas, endur'd great losse.	Ovid's Elegies		1.14.24
Why doest thy ill kembd tresses losse lament?	Ovid's Elegies		1.14.35
Cheere up thy selfe, thy losse thou maiest repaire,	Ovid's Elegies		1.14.55
The losse of such a wench much blame will gather,	Ovid's Elegies		2.11.35
For others faults, why do I losse receive?	Ovid's Elegies		3.3.16
Perchance these, others, me mine owne losse mooves.	Ovid's Elegies		3.5.100
And bide sore losse, with endlesse infamie.	Ovid's Elegies		3.6.72
And to thine owne losse was thy wit swift running.	Ovid's Elegies		3.7.46
Nemesis answeares, what's my losse to thee?	Ovid's Elegies		3.8.57
And to my losse God-wronging perjuries?	Ovid's Elegies		3.10.22
But this faire jem, sweet in the losse alone,	Hero and Leander		1.247
LOSSES			
Come, Katherina, our losses equall are,	Jew	3.2.36	Govnr
LOST			
And for thy ships which thou supposest lost,	Dido	1.1.235	Venus
O there I lost my wife:	Dido	2.1.270	Aeneas
My Oares broken, and my Tackling lost,	Dido	3.1.107	Aeneas
My witlesse brother to the Christians lost:	1Tamb	2.5.42	Cosroe
Ah faire Zabina, we have lost the field.	1Tamb	3.3.233	Bajzth
For though the glorie of this day be lost,	1Tamb	3.3.241	Bajzth
the Center of our Empery/Once lost, All Turkie would be	2Tamb	1.1.56	Orcan
That by the warres lost not a dram of blood,	2Tamb	3.2.113	Tamb
Lost long before you knew what honour meant.	2Tamb	4.3.87	Tamb
Was lately lost, and you were stated here/To be at deadly	Jew	2.2.32	Bosco
False, and unkinde; what, hast thou lost thy father?	Jew	3.4.2	Barab
I am a Jew, and therefore am I lost.	Jew	4.1.57	Barab
I cannot doe it, I have lost my keyes.	Jew	4.3.32	Barab
How many noble men have lost their lives,	P 795	16.9	Navrre
He should have lost his head, but with his looke,	Edw	1.1.113	Kent
For your lemmons you have lost, at Bannocks borne,	Edw	2.2.191	Lncstr
and have lost very much of late by horse flesh, and this	F1464	4.4.8	P HrsCsr
for which Faustus hath lost both Germany and the world, yea	F1843	5.2.47	P Faust
and twenty yeares hath Faustus lost eternall joy and felicitie.	F1859	5.2.63	P Faust
O thou hast lost celestiall happinesse,	F1899	5.2.103	GdAngl
that hast thou lost,/And now poore soule must thy good Angell	F1906	5.2.110	GdAngl
And shame to spare life which being lost is wonne.	Lucan, First Booke		458
Lost are the goodly lockes, which from their crowne/Phoebus and	Ovid's Elegies		1.14.31
And through the gemme let thy lost waters pash.	Ovid's Elegies		2.15.24
Such as confesse, have lost their good names by it.	Ovid's Elegies		3.13.6
Things that are not at all, are never lost.	Hero and Leander		1.276
Beautie alone is lost, too warily kept.	Hero and Leander		1.328
Jewels being lost are found againe, this never,	Hero and Leander		2.85
T'is lost but once, and once lost, lost for ever.	Hero and Leander		2.86
LOT			
And so I leave thee to thy fortunes lot,	Dido	1.1.238	Venus
Ah howe thy lot is above my lot blest:	Ovid's Elegies		1.6.46
LOTH			
How loth I am to leave these Libian bounds,	Dido	5.1.81	Aeneas
Our love of honor loth to be enthral'd/To forraine powers, and	1Tamb	5.1.35	Govnr
Troth master, I'm loth such a pot of pottage should be spoyld.	Jew	3.4.89	P Ithimr
LOTH'D			
Against her kind (the barren Mules loth'd issue)/To be cut	Lucan, First Booke		589
LOTHED			
Were by the holy Councell both condemn'd/For lothed Lollords,	F1022	3.2.42	Pope
LOTHING			
As lothing Pirrhus for this wicked act:	Dido	2.1.258	Aeneas
LOTHSOME			
Because his lothsome sight offends mine eye,	Dido	3.1.57	Dido
Yet must I heare that lothsome name againe?	Dido	3.1.78	Dido
And stain'd the bowels with darke lothsome spots:	Lucan, First Booke		619
LOTS			
Our lots are cast, I feare me so is thine.	Edw	4.7.79	Baldck
LOUD (See also LOWD)			
No, none can heare him, cry he ne're so loud.	Jew	4.1.136	Ithimr
And for his love Europa, bellowing loud,	Hero and Leander		1.149
LOUR (See LOWERS, LOWR'D)			
LOUSY			
then belike if I serve you, I shall be lousy.	F 359	1.4.17	P Robin
LOV'D			
Barabas, thou know'st I have lov'd thy daughter long.	Jew	2.3.288	Lodowk
My sonne lov'd thine.	Jew	3.2.22	Mater
First to Don Lodowicke, him I never lov'd;	Jew	3.6.23	Abigal
and told me he lov'd me for your sake, and said what a	Jew	4.2.109	P Pilia
Never lov'd man servant as I doe Ithimore.	Jew	4.3.54	Barab
that the Nuns lov'd Rice, that Fryar Bernardine slept in his	Jew	4.4.76	P Ithimr
For which, had not his highnes lov'd him well,	Edw	1.1.112	Kent
more/Then he can Gaveston, would he lov'd me/But halfe so much,	Edw	1.4.303	Queene
Feard am I more then lov'd, let me be feard,	Edw	5.4.52	Mortmr
Yes Faustus, and most deerely lov'd of God.	F 293	1.3.65	Mephst
were gluttons, and lov'd only delicates,	F1917	5.2.121	BdAngl

LOV'D (cont.)			
Dissemble sc, as lov'd he may be thought,	Ovid's Elegies	1.8.71	
While thou wert plaine, I lov'd thy minde and face:	Ovid's Elegies	1.10.13	
Great Agamemnon lov'd his servant Chriseis.	Ovid's Elegies	2.8.12	
Doth say, with her that lov'd the Aonian harpe.	Ovid's Elegies	2.18.26	
What should I name Aesope, that Thebe lov'd,	Ovid's Elegies	3.5.33	
There shalt be lov'd: Ilia lay feare aside.	Ovid's Elegies	3.5.62	
Delia departing, happier lov'd, she saith,	Ovid's Elegies	3.8.55	
Who mine was cald, whom I lov'd more then any,	Ovid's Elegies	3.11.5	
Why art thou not in love, and lov'd of all?	Hero and Leander	1.89	
Who ever lov'd, that lov'd not at first sight?	Hero and Leander	1.176	
LOV'DE			
And had you lov'de him halfe so well as I,	Edw	5.6.35	King
LOVDE			
Wouldst thou be lovde and fearde?	Edw	1.1.168	Edward
Great Alexander lovde Ephestion,	Edw	1.4.392	MortSr
Idly I lay with her, as if I lovde <her> not,	Ovid's Elegies	3.6.3	
LOV'DST			
Admit thou lov'dst not Lodowicke for his [sire] <sinne>,	Jew	3.3.40	Abigal
LOVE			
I love thee well, say Juno what she will.	Dido	1.1.2	Jupitr
I am much better for your worthles love,	Dido	1.1.3	Ganimd
Hold here my little love:	Dido	1.1.42	Jupitr
And shall have Ganimed, if thou wilt be my love.	Dido	1.1.49	Jupitr
That she may dote upon Aeneas love:	Dido	2.1.327	Venus
Tis not enough that thou doest graunt me love,	Dido	3.1.8	Iarbus
That love is childish which consists in words.	Dido	3.1.10	Iarbus
Ungentle Queene, is this thy love to me?	Dido	3.1.36	Iarbus
Why staiest thou here? thou art no love of mine.	Dido	3.1.39	Dido
That I should say thou art no love of mine?	Dido	3.1.42	Dido
I goe to feed the humour of my Love,	Dido	3.1.50	Iarbus
And in my thoughts is shrin'd another [love] <Iove>:	Dido	3.1.58	Dido
O Anna, didst thou know how sweet love were,	Dido	3.1.59	Dido
Poore soule I know too well the sower of love,	Dido	3.1.61	Anna
Is not Aeneas worthie Didos love?	Dido	3.1.68	Dido
Aeneas well deserves to be your love,	Dido	3.1.70	Anna
Then sister youle abjure Iarbus love?	Dido	3.1.77	Anna
No, for thy sake Ile love thy father well.	Dido	3.1.81	Dido
O here he ccmes, love, love, give Dido leave/To be more modest	Dido	3.1.94	Dido
love, give Dido leave/To be more modest then her thoughts	Dido	3.1.94	Dido
Aeneas, thinke not Dido is in love:	Dido	3.1.136	Dido
Have been most urgent suiters for my love,	Dido	3.1.151	Dido
Yet how <here> <now> I sweare by heaven and him I love,	Dido	3.1.166	Dido
I was as farre from love, as they from hate.	Dido	3.1.167	Dido
Because it may be thou shalt be my love:	Dido	3.1.170	Dido
Yet boast nct of it, for I love thee not,	Dido	3.1.171	Dido
And planted love where envie erst had sprong.	Dido	3.2.52	Juno
Sister of Jove, if that thy love be such,	Dido	3.2.53	Venus
Love my Aeneas, and desire is thine,	Dido	3.2.60	Venus
Which I will make in quittance of thy love:	Dido	3.2.69	Juno
Faire Queene of love, I will devorce these doubts,	Dido	3.2.85	Juno
But love and duetie led him on perhaps,	Dido	3.3.15	Aeneas
And meddle not with any that I love:	Dido	3.3.22	Dido
Women may wrcng by priviledge of love:	Dido	3.3.25	Iarbus
O love, O hate, O cruell womens hearts,	Dido	3.3.66	Iarbus
And like the Planets ever love to raunge:	Dido	3.3.68	Iarbus
And make love drunken with thy sweete desire:	Dido	3.3.75	Iarbus
And then, what then? Iarbus shall but love:	Dido	3.3.82	Iarbus
Tell me deare love, how found you out this Cave?	Dido	3.4.3	Dido
Not sicke my love, but sicke:--	Dido	3.4.25	Dido
Never to like or love any but her.	Dido	3.4.51	Aeneas
Stoute love in mine armes make thy Italy,	Dido	3.4.57	Dido
Who seekes to rob me of thy Sisters love,	Dido	4.2.31	Iarbus
Be rul'd by me, and seeke some other love,	Dido	4.2.35	Anna
I will not leave Iarbus whom I love,	Dido	4.2.43	Anna
Were to transgresse against all lawes of love:	Dido	4.3.48	Aeneas
Is this thy love to me?	Dido	4.4.16	Dido
Love made me jealous, but to make amends,	Dido	4.4.33	Dido
And now to make experience of my love,	Dido	4.4.64	Dido
And from a turret Ile behold my love.	Dido	4.4.86	Dido
I, but it may be he will leave my lcve,	Dido	4.4.97	Dido
To measure how I prize Aeneas love,	Dido	4.4.140	Dido
And shrunke not backe, knowing my lcve was there?	Dido	4.4.146	Dido
So youle love me, I care not if I doe.	Dido	4.5.17	Cupid
Foolish is love, a toy.--	Dido	4.5.26	Nurse
O sacred love,/If there be any heaven in earth, tis love:	Dido	4.5.26	Nurse
If there be any heaven in earth, tis love:	Dido	4.5.27	Nurse
Blush blush for shame, why shouldst thou thinke of love?	Dido	4.5.29	Nurse
Fourescore is but a girles age, love is sweete:--	Dido	4.5.32	Nurse
Why doe I thinke of love now I should dye?	Dido	4.5.34	Nurse
No marvell Dido though thou be in love,	Dido	5.1.44	Aeneas
Pardon me though I aske, love makes me aske.	Dido	5.1.90	Dido
Aeneas will not faine with his deare love,	Dido	5.1.92	Aeneas
But yet Aeneas will not leave his love?	Dido	5.1.98	Dido
Farewell: is this the mends for Didos love?	Dido	5.1.105	Dido
O speake like my Aeneas, like my love:	Dido	5.1.112	Dido
many neighbour kings/Were up in armes, for making thee my love?	Dido	5.1.142	Dido
In vaine my lcve thou spendst thy fainting breath,	Dido	5.1.153	Aeneas
I hope that that which love forbids me doe,	Dido	5.1.170	Dido
Returnes amaine: welcome, welcome my love:	Dido	5.1.191	Dido
And ride upcn his backe unto my love:	Dido	5.1.250	Dido
Save, save Aeneas, Didos leefest love!	Dido	5.1.256	Dido
See where he comes, welcome, welcome my love.	Dido	5.1.261	Dido

LOVE (cont.)

And reape nc guerdon for my truest love?	Dido	5.1.282	Iarbus
To cure my minde that melts for unkind love.	Dido	5.1.287	Dido
But afterwards will Dido graunt me love?	Dido	5.1.288	Iarbus
None in the world shall have my love but thou:	Dido	5.1.290	Dido
Iarbus slaine, Iarbus my deare love,	Dido	5.1.321	Anna
Whom I may tearme a Damon for thy love.	1Tamb	1.1.50	Mycet
Then I may seeke to gratifie your love,	1Tamb	1.1.171	Cosroe
But since I love to live at liberty,	1Tamb	1.2.26	Tamb
Zenocrate, lovelier than the Love of Jove,	1Tamb	1.2.87	Tamb
What now? In love?	1Tamb	1.2.106	Techel
But this is she with whom I am in love.	1Tamb	1.2.108	Tamb
And by the love of Pylladés and Orestes,	1Tamb	1.2.243	Tamb
Thirsting with soverainty, with love of armes:	1Tamb	2.1.20	Menaph
his Diadem/Sought for by such scalde knaves as love him not?	1Tamb	2.2.8	Mycet
when looks breed love, with lookes to gaine the prize.	1Tamb	2.5.63	Therid
In love or honor and defence of right,	1Tamb	2.6.21	Ortyg
Be honored with your love, but for necessity.	1Tamb	3.2.30	Agidas
So lookes my Lordly lcve, faire Tamburlaine.	1Tamb	3.2.49	Zenoc
Yet be not so inconstant in your love,	1Tamb	3.2.56	Agidas
the King of Persea/(Being a Shepheard) seem'd to love you much,	1Tamb	3.2.60	Agidas
Fearing his love through my unworthynesse.	1Tamb	3.2.65	Zenoc
Betraide by fortune and suspitious love,	1Tamb	3.2.66	Agidas
The killing frownes of jealousie and love.	1Tamb	3.2.91	Agidas
And may my Love, the king of Persea,	1Tamb	3.3.132	Zenoc
And made my lordly Love her worthy King:	1Tamb	3.3.190	Zenoc
Of my faire daughter, and his princely Love:	1Tamb	4.1.70	Souldn
If any love remaine in you my Lord,	1Tamb	4.4.68	Zenoc
Or if my love unto your majesty/May merit favour at your	1Tamb	4.4.69	Zenoc
And wouldst thou have me buy thy Fathers love/With such a	1Tamb	4.4.83	Tamb
Our love of honor loth to be enthral'd/To forraine powers, and	1Tamb	5.1.35	Govnr
Or for the love of Venus, would she leave/The angrie God of	1Tamb	5.1.124	Tamb
That in thy passion for thy countries love,	1Tamb	5.1.137	Tamb
And every warriour that is rapt with love/Of fame, of valour,	1Tamb	5.1.180	Tamb
may poure foorth my soule into thine armes,/With words of love:	1Tamb	5.1.280	Bajzth
To breake his sword, and mildly treat of love,	1Tamb	5.1.327	Zenoc
the cause of this/That tearm'st Zenocrate thy dearest love?	1Tamb	5.1.336	Zenoc
to Zenocrate/Than her owne life, or ought save thine owne love.	1Tamb	5.1.338	Zenoc
Ah Tamburlaine, my love, sweet Tamburlaine,	1Tamb	5.1.355	Zenoc
Pardon my Love, oh pardon his contempt,	1Tamb	5.1.364	Zenoc
Your love hath fortune so at his command,	1Tamb	5.1.373	Anippe
love and feare presents/A thousand sorrowes to my martyred	1Tamb	5.1.383	Zenoc
My father and my first betrothed love,	1Tamb	5.1.388	Zenoc
Must fight against my life and present love:	1Tamb	5.1.389	Zenoc
And fatally enricht Eneas love.	1Tamb	5.1.394	Zenoc
To pacifie my countrie and my love,	1Tamb	5.1.396	Zenoc
Leaving thy blood for witnesse of thy love.	1Tamb	5.1.411	Arabia
Too deare a witnesse for such love my Lord.	1Tamb	5.1.412	Zenoc
Of thy deserv'd contentment and thy love:	1Tamb	5.1.427	Arabia
From dangerous battel of my conquering Love.	1Tamb	5.1.442	Zenoc
and protestations/Of endlesse honor to thee for her love.	1Tamb	5.1.497	Souldn
So lookes my Love, shadowing in her browes/Triumphes and	1Tamb	5.1.512	Tamb
Thy first betrothed Love, Arabia,	1Tamb	5.1.530	Tamb
If thou wilt love the warres and follow me,	2Tamb	1.3.47	Tamb
May never such a change transfourme my love/In whose sweet	2Tamb	2.4.47	Tamb
Live still my Love and so conserve my life,	2Tamb	2.4.55	Tamb
But let me die my Love, yet let me die,	2Tamb	2.4.66	Zenoc
With love and patience let your true love die,	2Tamb	2.4.67	Zenoc
That dares torment the body of my Love,	2Tamb	2.4.79	Tamb
Wounding the world with woonder and with love,	2Tamb	2.4.82	Tamb
For amorous Jove hath snatcht my love from hence,	2Tamb	2.4.107	Tamb
Because this place bereft me of my Love:	2Tamb	2.4.138	Tamb
Madam, I am so far in love with you,	2Tamb	3.4.78	Therid
Embracing thee with deepest of his love,	2Tamb	4.1.109	Tamb
Forbids my mind to entertaine a thought/That tends to love, but	2Tamb	4.2.26	Olymp
Leave this my Love, and listen more to me.	2Tamb	4.2.38	Therid
Spending my life in sweet discourse of love.	2Tamb	4.2.45	Therid
I cannot love to be an Emperesse.	2Tamb	4.2.49	Olymp
Such is the sodaine fury of my love,	2Tamb	4.2.52	Therid
Cut off this arme that murthered my Love:	2Tamb	4.2.83	Therid
Infernall Dis is courting of my Love,	2Tamb	4.2.93	Therid
For love, for honor, and to make her Queene,	2Tamb	4.3.38	Orcan
Now in defiance of that woonted love,	2Tamb	5.3.10	Therid
Let not thy love exceed thyne honor sonne,	2Tamb	5.3.199	Tamb
But such as love me, gard me from their tongues,	Jew	Prol.6	Machvl
The better; for we love not to be seene:	Jew	1.2.307	Abbass
she were fitter for a tale of love/Then to be tired out with	Jew	1.2.369	Mthias
Tho countermin'd <countermur'd> with walls of brasse, to love,	Jew	1.2.386	Mthias
One that I love for his good fathers sake.	Jew	2.3.31	Barab
Compassion, love, vaine hope, and hartlesse feare,	Jew	2.3.170	Barab
Dissemble, sweare, protest, vow to love him,	Jew	2.3.229	Barab
O father, Don Mathias is my love.	Jew	2.3.237	Abigal
yet I say make love to him;/Doe, it is requisite it should be	Jew	2.3.238	Barab
And she vowes lcve to him, and hee to her.	Jew	2.3.247	Barab
Whither but to my faire love Abigall?	Jew	2.3.252	Mthias
If you love me, no quarrels in my house;	Jew	2.3.271	Barab
Nothing but death shall part my love and me.	Jew	2.3.317	Abigal
Shall Lodowicke rob me of so faire a love?	Jew	2.3.347	Mthias
My heart misgives me, that to crosse your love,	Jew	2.3.349	Barab
I will have Don Mathias, he is my love.	Jew	2.3.361	Abigal
But I perceive there is no love on earth,	Jew	3.3.47	Abigal
Come neere, my love, come neere, thy masters life,	Jew	3.4.14	Barab
And for thy sake, whcm I so dearely love,	Jew	3.4.61	Barab

LOVE (cont.)

Both jealous of my love, envied each other:	Jew	3.6.27		Abigal
me ever since she saw me, and who would not requite such love?	Jew	4.2.35	P	Ithimr
I can with-hold no longer; welcome sweet love.	Jew	4.2.46		Curtzn
Shall Ithimore my love goe in such rags?	Jew	4.2.85		Curtzn
Shalt live with me and be my love.	Jew	4.2.98		Ithimr
Rather for feare then love.	Jew	4.2.107	P	Ithimr
as you love your life send me five hundred crowns, and give the	Jew	4.2.117	P	Ithimr
Come my deare love, let's in and sleepe together.	Jew	4.2.129		Curtzn
That he who knowes I love him as my selfe/Should write in this	Jew	4.3.42		Barab
As I wud see thee hang'd; oh, love stops my breath:	Jew	4.3.53		Barab
I'le pledge thee, love, and therefore drinke it off.	Jew	4.4.1		Curtzn
Love thee, fill me three glasses.	Jew	4.4.7		Curtzn
Love me little, love me long, let musicke rumble,	Jew	4.4.28		Ithimr
Prethe sweet love, one more, and write it sharp.	Jew	4.4.73		Curtzn
And that the native sparkes of princely love,	P 6	1.6		Charls
Thanks sonne Navarre, you see we love you well,	P 13	1.13		QnMoth
in Religion/Might be a meanes to crosse you in your love.	P 16	1.16		QnMoth
The love thou bear'st unto the house of Guise:	P 69	2.12		Guise
Thankes my good freend, I will requite thy love.	P 78	2.21		Guise
And in my love entombes the hope of Fraunce:	P 134	2.77		Guise
they Henries heart/Will not both harbour love and Majestie?	P 604	12.17		King
What, all alone my love, and writing too:	P 670	13.14		Guise
Or hath my love been so obscurde in thee,	P 682	13.26		Guise
Is all my love forgot which helde thee deare?	P 684	13.28		Guise
Shall buy her love even with his dearest bloud.	P 697	13.41		Guise
Although my love to thee can hardly [suffer't] <suffer>,	P 747	15.5		King
I love your Minions?	P 763	15.21		Guise
Because his wife beares thee such kindely love.	P 780	15.38		King
Ile make her shake off love with her heeles.	P 782	15.40		Mugern
To shew your love unto the King of France:	P 904	18.5		Bartus
To recompence your reconciled love,	P1144	22.6		King
And heere protest eternall love to thee,	P1206	22.68		King
Ah Epernoune, is this thy love to me?	P1235	22.97		King
Not that I love the citie or the men,	Edw	1.1.12		Gavstn
What neede the artick people love star-light,	Edw	1.1.16		Gavstn
If you love us my lord, hate Gaveston.	Edw	1.1.80		MortSr
That naturally would love and honour you,	Edw	1.1.100		Lncstr
All Warwickshire will love him for my sake.	Edw	1.1.128		Warwck
It shall suffice me to enjoy your love,	Edw	1.1.171		Gavstn
But dotes upon the love of Gaveston.	Edw	1.2.50		Queene
Why should you love him, whome the world hates so?	Edw	1.4.76		Mortmr
The king is love-sick for his minion.	Edw	1.4.87		Mortmr
How fast they run to banish him I love,	Edw	1.4.94		Edward
Ile come to thee, my love shall neare decline.	Edw	1.4.115		Edward
Crie quittance Madam then, and love not him.	Edw	1.4.195		Mortmr
And yet I love in vaine, heele nere love me.	Edw	1.4.197		Queene
I love him more/Then he can Gaveston, would he lov'd me	Edw	1.4.302		Queene
But will you love me, if you finde it so?	Edw	1.4.324		Queene
Having the love of his renowned peeres.	Edw	1.4.367		Queene
Spare for no cost, we will requite your love.	Edw	1.4.383		Edward
Our Ladies first love is not wavering,	Edw	2.1.27		Spencr
What needst thou, love, thus to excuse thy selfe?	Edw	2.1.60		Neece
This argues the entire love of my Lord.	Edw	2.1.63		Neece
Is this the love you beare your soveraigne?	Edw	2.2.30		Edward
Sweete husband be content, they all love you.	Edw	2.2.36		Queene
They love me not that hate my Gaveston.	Edw	2.2.37		Edward
I meane the peeres, whom thou shouldst dearly love:	Edw	2.2.176		Mortmr
My lord, I see your love to Gaveston,	Edw	2.2.208		Kent
I dare not, for the people love him well.	Edw	2.2.235		Edward
And Gaveston, thinke that I love thee well,	Edw	2.2.257		Edward
But I respect neither their love nor hate.	Edw	2.2.261		Gavstn
My lords, of love to this our native land,	Edw	2.3.1		Kent
To undermine us with a showe of love.	Edw	2.3.6		Lncstr
Heavens can witnesse, I love none but you.	Edw	2.4.15		Queene
In vaine I looke for love at Edwards hand,	Edw	2.4.61		Queene
How Gaveston hath robd me of his love:	Edw	2.4.67		Queene
Spencer, this love, this kindnes to thy King,	Edw	3.1.47		Edward
Beside, the more to manifest our love,	Edw	3.1.52		Edward
And meerely of our love we do create thee/Earle of Gloster, and	Edw	3.1.145		Edward
I trowe/The lords of Fraunce love Englands gold so well,	Edw	4.3.15		Edward
And yet she beares a face of love forsooth:	Edw	4.6.14		Kent
Fie on that love that hatcheth death and hate.	Edw	4.6.15		Kent
Of love and care unto his royall person,	Edw	4.6.25		Queene
In signe of love and dutie to this presence,	Edw	4.6.48		Rice
Be thou perswaded, that I love thee well,	Edw	5.2.16		Queene
And beare him this, as witnesse of my love.	Edw	5.2.72		Queene
Nor sporting in the dalliance of love/In Courts of Kings, where	F 3	Prol.3		1Chor
Then has <in> the white breasts of the Queene of love.	F 156	1.1.128		Valdes
love I would say) it were not for you to come within fortie	F 210	1.2.17	P	Wagner
wherein is fixt the love of Belzebub,	F 400	2.1.12		Faust
for love of thee/Faustus hath <I> cut his <mine> arme,	F 442	2.1.54		Faust
Have not I made blind Homer sing to me/Of Alexanders love, and	F 578	2.2.27		Faust
and if he be so farre in love with him, I would he would post	F1191	4.1.37	P	Benvol
Both love and serve the Germane Emperour,	F1219	4.1.65		Faust
Away, you love me not, to urge me thus,	F1327	4.2.3		Benvol
Who kils him shall have gold, and endlesse love.	F1349	4.2.25		Fredrk
we will recompence/With all the love and kindnesse that we may.	F1672	4.6.115		Duke
Or envy of thee, but in tender love,	F1720	5.1.47		OldMan
I will be Paris <Pacis>, and for love of thee,	F1775	5.1.102		Faust
dutie, I do yeeld/My life and lasting service for your love.	F1819	5.2.23		Wagner
But thou didst love the world.	F1894	5.2.98		GdAngl
yet for that love and duety bindes me thereunto, I am content	F App	p.236 15	P	Faust

LOVE (cont.)

Caesars, and Pompeys jarring love soone ended,	Lucan, First Booke	98
To gaine the light unstable commons love,	Lucan, First Booke	133
And love to Room (thogh slaughter steeld their harts/And minds	Lucan, First Booke	355
prone) restrain'd them; but wars love/And Caesars awe dasht all:	Lucan, First Booke	356
Love over-rules my will, I must obay thee,	Lucan, First Booke	373
The Santons that rejoyce in Caesars love,	Lucan, First Booke	423
Both verses were alike till Love (men say)/Began to smile and	Ovid's Elegies	1.1.7
Shall Dian fanne when love begins to glowe?	Ovid's Elegies	1.1.12
[Love] <I> slackt my Muse, and made my [numbers] <number> soft.	Ovid's Elegies	1.1.22
Thus I complaind, but Love unlockt his quiver,	Ovid's Elegies	1.1.25
I burne, love in my idle bosome sits.	Ovid's Elegies	1.1.30
Were Love the cause, it's like I shoulde descry him,	Ovid's Elegies	1.2.5
Tis cruell love turmoyles my captive hart.	Ovid's Elegies	1.2.8
Unwilling Lovers, love doth more torment,	Ovid's Elegies	1.2.17
Ride golden Love in Chariots richly builded.	Ovid's Elegies	1.2.42
Either love, or cause that I may never hate:	Ovid's Elegies	1.3.2
I aske too much, would she but let me love hir,	Ovid's Elegies	1.3.3
Love <Jove> knowes with such like praiers, I dayly move hir:	Ovid's Elegies	1.3.4
Accept him that will love with spotlesse truth:	Ovid's Elegies	1.3.6
I love but one, and hir I love change never,	Ovid's Elegies	1.3.15
While others touch the damsell I love best?	Ovid's Elegies	1.4.4
Long Love my body to such use [makes] <make> slender/And to get	Ovid's Elegies	1.6.5
Love hearing it laugh'd with his tender mother/And smiling	Ovid's Elegies	1.6.11
Forth-with Love came, no darke night-flying spright/Nor hands	Ovid's Elegies	1.6.13
I am alone, were furious Love discarded.	Ovid's Elegies	1.6.34
See Love with me, wine moderate in my braine,	Ovid's Elegies	1.6.37
Night, Love, and wine to all extreames perswade:	Ovid's Elegies	1.6.59
Night shamelesse, wine and Love are fearelesse made.	Ovid's Elegies	1.6.60
Yet he harm'd lesse, whom I profess'd to love,	Ovid's Elegies	1.7.33
a rich lover plants/His love on thee, and can supply thy wants.	Ovid's Elegies	1.8.32
To yeeld their love to more then one disdainde.	Ovid's Elegies	1.8.40
And take heed least he gets that love for nought.	Ovid's Elegies	1.8.72
Or least his love oft beaten backe should waine.	Ovid's Elegies	1.8.76
Take strife away, love doth not well endure.	Ovid's Elegies	1.8.96
Tis shame for eld in warre or love to be.	Ovid's Elegies	1.9.4
Doubtfull is warre and love, the vanquisht rise/And who thou	Ovid's Elegies	1.9.29
Therefore who ere love sloathfulnesse doth call,	Ovid's Elegies	1.9.31
Let him surcease: love tries wit best of all.	Ovid's Elegies	1.9.32
He that will not growe slothfull let him love.	Ovid's Elegies	1.9.46
Bull and Eagle/And what ere love made Jove should thee invegle.	Ovid's Elegies	1.10.8
Now all feare with my mindes hot love abates,	Ovid's Elegies	1.10.9
Love is a naked boy, his yeares saunce staine,	Ovid's Elegies	1.10.15
Love and Loves sonne are with fierce armes to oddes;	Ovid's Elegies	1.10.19
[May] <Many> bounteous [lome] <love> Alcinous fruite resigne.	Ovid's Elegies	1.10.56
To give I love, but to be ask't disdayne,	Ovid's Elegies	1.10.63
To these my love I foolishly committed/And then with sweete	Ovid's Elegies	1.12.21
Now on <ore> the sea from her old love comes shee,	Ovid's Elegies	1.13.1
Whither runst thou, that men, and women, love not?	Ovid's Elegies	1.13.9
Say that thy love with Caephalus were not knowne,	Ovid's Elegies	1.13.33
And rude boyes toucht with unknowne love me reade,	Ovid's Elegies	2.1.6
lookes to my verse/Which golden love doth unto me rehearse.	Ovid's Elegies	2.1.38
Wee seeke that through thee safely love we may,	Ovid's Elegies	2.2.65
If ever wench had made luke-warme thy love:	Ovid's Elegies	2.3.6
but where love please/[Am] <And> driven like a ship upon rough	Ovid's Elegies	2.4.7
A hundred reasons makes <make> me ever love.	Ovid's Elegies	2.4.10
Who would not love those hands for their swift running?	Ovid's Elegies	2.4.28
To leave my selfe, that am in love [with all] <withall>,	Ovid's Elegies	2.4.31
Both short and long please me, for I love both:	Ovid's Elegies	2.4.36
My love alludes to everie historie:	Ovid's Elegies	2.4.44
No love is so dere (quiverd Cupid flie)/That my chiefe wish	Ovid's Elegies	2.5.1
He's happy, that his love dares boldly credit,	Ovid's Elegies	2.5.9
A little fild thee, and for love of talke,	Ovid's Elegies	2.6.29
If ill, thou saiest I die for others love.	Ovid's Elegies	2.7.10
In naked bones? love hath my bones left naked.	Ovid's Elegies	2.9.14
So many men and maidens without love,	Ovid's Elegies	2.9.15
Live without love, so sweete ill is a maide.	Ovid's Elegies	2.9.26
And purple Love resumes his dartes againe.	Ovid's Elegies	2.9.34
Yet Love, if thou with thy faire mother heare,	Ovid's Elegies	2.9.51
I could not be in love with twoo at once,	Ovid's Elegies	2.10.2
For now I love two women equallie:	Ovid's Elegies	2.10.4
So with this love and that, wavers my minde.	Ovid's Elegies	2.10.10
But may soft love rowse up my drowsie eies,	Ovid's Elegies	2.10.19
Elmes love the Vines, the Vines with Elmes abide,	Ovid's Elegies	2.16.41
Love-snarde Calypso is supposde to pray,	Ovid's Elegies	2.17.15
Nor of our love to be asham'd we need,	Ovid's Elegies	2.17.26
And tender love hath great things hatefull made.	Ovid's Elegies	2.18.4
Aye me she cries, to love, why art a shamed?	Ovid's Elegies	2.18.8
Love laughed at my cloak, and buskines painted,	Ovid's Elegies	2.18.15
And Love triumpheth ore his buskind Poet.	Ovid's Elegies	2.18.18
Is golden love hid in Mars mid alarmes.	Ovid's Elegies	2.18.36
Nothing I love, that at all times availes me.	Ovid's Elegies	2.19.8
So shall my love continue many yeares,	Ovid's Elegies	2.19.23
Fat love, and too much fulsome me annoyes,	Ovid's Elegies	2.19.25
But of my love it will an end procure.	Ovid's Elegies	2.19.52
And first [she] <he> sayd, when will thy love be spent,	Ovid's Elegies	3.1.15
And this is he whom fierce love burnes, they cry.	Ovid's Elegies	3.1.20
Light am I, and with me, my care, light love,	Ovid's Elegies	3.1.41
The other gives my love a conquering name,	Ovid's Elegies	3.1.65
That thou maiest know with love thou mak'st me flame.	Ovid's Elegies	3.2.4
Ist womens love my captive brest doth frie?	Ovid's Elegies	3.2.40
Goddesse come here, make my love conquering.	Ovid's Elegies	3.2.46
Peace pleaseth me, and in mid peace is love.	Ovid's Elegies	3.2.50

LOVE (cont.)

pleace <please> Pollux, Castor [love] <loves> horsemen more.	Ovid's Elegies	3.2.54	
Yet by deceit Love did them all surprize.	Ovid's Elegies	3.4.20	
Few love, what others have unguarded left.	Ovid's Elegies	3.4.26	
Nor doth her face please, but her husbands love;	Ovid's Elegies	3.4.27	
Great flouds ought to assist young men in love,	Ovid's Elegies	3.5.23	
Th'Arcadian Virgins constant love hath wunne?	Ovid's Elegies	3.5.30	
The one his first love, th'other his new care.	Ovid's Elegies	3.8.32	
A clowne, nor no love from her warme brest yeelds.	Ovid's Elegies	3.9.18	
Was divers waies distract with love, and shame.	Ovid's Elegies	3.9.28	
Love conquer'd shame, the furrowes dry were burnd,	Ovid's Elegies	3.9.29	
Dishonest love my wearied brest forsake,	Ovid's Elegies	3.10.2	
We vanquish, and tread tam'd love under feete,	Ovid's Elegies	3.10.5	
My love was cause that more mens love she seazd.	Ovid's Elegies	3.10.20	
Now love, and hate my light brest each way move;	Ovid's Elegies	3.10.33	
But victory, I thinke, will hap to love.	Ovid's Elegies	3.10.34	
Ile hate, if I can; if not, love gainst my will:	Ovid's Elegies	3.10.35	
I loath her manners, love her bodies feature.	Ovid's Elegies	3.10.38	
Her deeds gaine hate, her face entreateth love:	Ovid's Elegies	3.10.43	
Wilt have me willing, or to love by force?	Ovid's Elegies	3.10.50	
That I may love yet, though against my minde.	Ovid's Elegies	3.10.52	
Then thee whom I must love I hate in vaine,	Ovid's Elegies	3.13.39	
Died ere he could enjoy the love of any.	Hero and Leander	1.76	
A brow for Love to banquet roiallye,	Hero and Leander	1.86	
Why art thou not in love, and lov'd of all?	Hero and Leander	1.89	
For faithfull love will never turne to hate.	Hero and Leander	1.128	
And for his love Europa, bellowing loud,	Hero and Leander	1.149	
Love kindling fire, to burne such townes as Troy,	Hero and Leander	1.153	
Under whose shade the Wood-gods love to bee.	Hero and Leander	1.156	
It lies not in our power to love, or hate,	Hero and Leander	1.167	
Where both deliberat, the love is slight,	Hero and Leander	1.175	
Love deepely grounded, hardly is dissembled.	Hero and Leander	1.184	
True love is mute, and oft amazed stands.	Hero and Leander	1.186	
God knowes I cannot force love, as you doe.	Hero and Leander	1.206	
Dutifull service may thy love procure,	Hero and Leander	1.220	
Love Hero then, and be not tirannous,	Hero and Leander	1.323	
not to love at all, and everie part/Strove to resist the	Hero and Leander	1.363	
As made Love sigh, to see his tirannie.	Hero and Leander	1.374	
They answered Love, nor would vouchsafe so much/As one poore	Hero and Leander	1.383	
tincture of her cheekes, that drew/The love of everie swaine:	Hero and Leander	1.397	
Still vowd he love, she wanting no excuse/To feed him with	Hero and Leander	1.425	
And gave it to his simple rustike love,	Hero and Leander	1.435	
He wounds with love, and forst them equallie,	Hero and Leander	1.445	
his promise, did despise/The love of th'everlasting Destinies.	Hero and Leander	1.462	
They seeing it, both Love and him abhor'd,	Hero and Leander	1.463	
By this, sad Hero, with love unacquainted,	Hero and Leander	2.1	
Now waxt she jealous, least his love abated,	Hero and Leander	2.43	
Albeit Leander rude in love, and raw,	Hero and Leander	2.61	
Love alwaies makes those eloquent that have it.	Hero and Leander	2.72	
Above our life we love a stedfast friend,	Hero and Leander	2.79	
Which made his love through Sestos to bee knowne,	Hero and Leander	2.111	
O none but gods have power their love to hide,	Hero and Leander	2.131	
And love that is conceal'd, betraies poore lovers.	Hero and Leander	2.134	
But love resisted once, growes passionate,	Hero and Leander	2.139	
And crying, Love I come, leapt lively in.	Hero and Leander	2.154	
The lustie god imbrast him, cald him love,	Hero and Leander	2.167	
And smiling wantonly, his love bewrayd.	Hero and Leander	2.182	
And up againe, and close beside him swim,/And talke of love:	Hero and Leander	2.191	
As for his love, both earth and heaven pyn'd;	Hero and Leander	2.196	
He cald it in, for love made him repent.	Hero and Leander	2.210	
(Love is too full of faith, too credulous,	Hero and Leander	2.221	
If not for love, yet love for pittie sake,	Hero and Leander	2.247	
By which love sailes to regions full of blis),	Hero and Leander	2.276	
Love is not ful of pittie (as men say)/But deaffe and cruell,	Hero and Leander	2.287	
Come live with mee, and be my love,	Passionate Shepherd	1	
Come <Then> live with mee, and be my love.	Passionate Shepherd	20	
Then live with mee, and be my love.	Passionate Shepherd	24	

LOVED

If you loved him, and it so precious?	2Tamb	4.2.72	Therid
The Romaine Tullie loved Octavius,	Edw	1.4.396	MortSr
So shall Licoris whom he loved best:	Ovid's Elegies	1.15.30	
And with sweete words cause deafe rockes to have loved <moned>,	Ovid's Elegies	3.6.58	
Burnes where it cherisht, murders where it loved.	Hero and Leander	2.128	

LOVEDST

Vaine babling speech, and pleasant peace thou lovedst.	Ovid's Elegies	2.6.26	

LOVELIE

Sometime a lovelie boye in Dians shape,	Edw	1.1.61	Gavstn
Sonne to the lovelie Elenor of Spaine,	Edw	3.1.11	Spencr

LOVELIER

Zenocrate, lovelier than the Love of Jove,	1Tamb	1.2.87	Tamb

LOVELIEST

Zenocrate, the loveliest Maide alive,	1Tamb	3.3.117	Tamb
Which is the loveliest it is hard to say:	Ovid's Elegies	2.10.6	
But far above the loveliest, Hero shin'd,	Hero and Leander	1.103	

LOVELINESSE

That she such lovelinesse and beautie had/As could provoke his	Hero and Leander	1.422	

LOVELY

Lovely Aeneas, these are Carthage walles,	Dido	2.1.62	Illion
Here let him sit, be merrie lovely child.	Dido	2.1.93	Dido
How lovely is Ascanius when he smiles?	Dido	3.1.29	Dido
So lovely is he that where ere he goes,	Dido	3.1.71	Anna
To harme my sweete Ascanius lovely life.	Dido	3.2.23	Venus
And fanne it in Aeneas lovely face,	Dido	4.4.49	Dido

LOVELY (cont.)			
White Swannes, and many lovely water fowles:	Dido	4.5.11	Nurse
Looke sister, looke lovely Aeneas ships, ...	Dido	5.1.251	Dido
Wel, lovely Virgins, think our countries care, ...	1Tamb	5.1.34	Govnr
To feele the lovely warmth of shepheards flames, . . .	1Tamb	5.1.186	Tamb
Or lovely Ic metamorphosed.	2Tamb	1.2.39	Callap
Sit up and rest thee like a lovely Queene. . . .	2Tamb	1.3.16	Tamb
This lovely boy the yongest of the three, ...	2Tamb	1.3.37	Zenoc
Wel lovely boies, you shal be Emperours both, . . .	2Tamb	1.3.96	Tamb
Whose lovely faces never any viewed, ...	2Tamb	3.2.30	Tamb
Like lovely Thetis in a Christall robe:	2Tamb	3.4.51	Therid
Here lovely boies, what death forbids my life, . . .	2Tamb	5.3.159	Tamb
Oh what has made my lovely daughter sad?	Jew	1.2.225	Barab
And saile from hence to Greece, to lovely Greece, . .	Jew	4.2.89	Ithimr
of Guise you and your wife/Doe both salute our lovely Minions.	P 753	15.11	King
Inexorable, and I shall never see/My lovely Pierce, my Gaveston	Edw	3.1.8	Edward
More lovely then the Monarch of the sky, ...	F1785	5.1.112	Faust
My nayles tc scratch her lovely cheekes I bent. . .	Ovid's Elegies		1.7.50
So lovely faire was Hero, Venus Nun, ...	Hero and Leander		1.45
Sylvanus weeping for the lovely boy/That now is turn'd into a	Hero and Leander		1.154
LOVER			
Her Lover after Alexander dyed, ...	Dido	2.1.298	Achat
Faire sister Anna leade my lover forth, ...	Dido	4.4.65	Dido
Ile have a husband, or els a lover.	Dido	4.5.23	Nurse
A grave, and not a lover fits thy age:--	Dido	4.5.30	Nurse
It is about her lover Gaveston.	Edw	2.1.22	Spencr
Excludst a lover, how wouldst use a foe?	Ovid's Elegies		1.6.31
And brings good fortune, a rich lover plants/His love on thee,	Ovid's Elegies		1.8.31
Poore lover with thy gransires I exile thee. . . .	Ovid's Elegies		1.8.66
Servants fit for thy purpose thou must hire/To teach thy lover,	Ovid's Elegies		1.8.88
Her valiant lover followes without end.	Ovid's Elegies		1.9.10
Who but a souldiour or a lover is bould/To suffer storme mixt	Ovid's Elegies		1.9.15
Her lover let her mocke, that long will raigne, . . .	Ovid's Elegies		2.19.33
But when her lover came, had she drawne backe, . . .	Ovid's Elegies		3.3.39
If I a lover bee by thee held back.	Ovid's Elegies		3.5.22
I saw when forth a tyred lover went, ...	Ovid's Elegies		3.10.13
And like an insolent commaunding lover, ...	Hero and Leander		1.409
Impos'd upon her lover such a taske, ...	Hero and Leander		1.429
LOVERS			
Lest their grosse eye-beames taint my lovers cheekes: .	Dido	3.1.74	Dido
Hold, take these Jewels at thy Lovers hand, ...	Dido	3.4.61	Dido
Doe Troians use to quit their Lovers thus?	Dido	5.1.106	Dido
O no, the Gcds wey not what Lovers doe, ...	Dido	5.1.131	Dido
she farre become a bed/Embraced in a friendly lovers armes,	Jew	1.2.372	Mthias
For as the lovers of faire Danae, ...	Edw	2.2.53	Edward
Yes, yes, fcr Mortimer your lovers sake.	Edw	2.4.14	Edward
Unwilling Lovers, love doth more torment, ...	Ovid's Elegies		1.2.17
Or Layis of a thousand [wooers] <lovers> [sped] <spread>.	Ovid's Elegies		1.5.12
Let him within heare bard out lovers prate. . . .	Ovid's Elegies		1.8.78
All Lovers warre, and Cupid hath his tent, ...	Ovid's Elegies		1.9.1
Atticke, all lovers are to warre farre sent. . . .	Ovid's Elegies		1.9.2
Those in their lovers, pretty maydes desire. . . .	Ovid's Elegies		1.9.6
Sooth Lovers watch till sleepe the hus-band charmes, . .	Ovid's Elegies		1.9.25
to passe/The souldiours, and poore lovers worke ere was.	Ovid's Elegies		1.9.28
And in sad lovers heads let me be found.	Ovid's Elegies		1.15.38
I knew your speech (what do not lovers see)? . . .	Ovid's Elegies		2.5.19
But such kinde wenches let their lovers have. . . .	Ovid's Elegies		2.5.26
Let us both lovers hope, and feare a like, ...	Ovid's Elegies		2.19.5
A decent forme, thinne robe, a lovers looke, . . .	Ovid's Elegies		3.1.9
If of scornd lovers god be venger just, ...	Ovid's Elegies		3.7.65
Who thinkes her to be glad at lovers smart, ...	Ovid's Elegies		3.9.15
White birdes to lovers did not alwayes sing. . . .	Ovid's Elegies		3.11.2
The bawde I play, lovers to her I guide:	Ovid's Elegies		3.11.11
Made with the blood of wretched Lovers slaine. . . .	Hero and Leander		1.16
Came lovers home, frcm this great festivall. . . .	Hero and Leander		1.96
These lovers parled by the touch of hands, ...	Hero and Leander		1.185
These greedie lovers had, at their first meeting. . .	Hero and Leander		2.24
Which taught him all that elder lovers know, ...	Hero and Leander		2.69
Now had the morne espy'de her lovers steeds, . . .	Hero and Leander		2.87
And kist againe, as lovers use to do.	Hero and Leander		2.94
As pittying these lovers, downeward creepes. . . .	Hero and Leander		2.100
And love that is conceal'd, betraies poore lovers. . .	Hero and Leander		2.134
And nothing more than counsaile, lovers hate. . . .	Hero and Leander		2.140
LOVES			
I shall not be her sonne, she loves me not.	Dido	3.1.23	Cupid
O happie shall he be whom Dido loves.	Dido	3.1.168	Aeneas
a match confirmd/Betwixt these two, whose loves are so alike,	Dido	3.2.78	Juno
Nay, nothing, but Aeneas loves me not.	Dido	3.4.32	Dido
Scorning our loves and royall marriage rites, ...	Dido	4.2.16	Iarbus
Our kinsmens [lives] <loves>, and thousand guiltles soules,	Dido	4.4.90	Aeneas
He loves me to too well to serve me so:	Dido	5.1.185	Dido
Vowing our loves to equall death and life.	1Tamb	2.6.28	Cosroe
The Turkesse let my Loves maid lead away.	1Tamb	3.3.267	Tamb
and Furies dread)/As for their liberties, their loves or lives.	1Tamb	5.1.95	1Virgn
He loves my daughter, and she holds him deare:	Jew	2.3.141	Barab
Why, loves she Don Mathias?	Jew	2.3.285	Lodowk
me in beleefe/Gives great presumption that she loves me not;	Jew	3.4.11	Barab
that she loves me ever since she saw me, and who would not	Jew	4.2.34	P Ithimr
And ye did but know how she loves you, Sir.	Jew	4.2.53	Pilia
Nay, I care not how much she loves me; Sweet Bellamira, would I	Jew	4.2.54	P Ithimr
I'le be Adonis, thou shalt be Loves Queene.	Jew	4.2.94	Ithimr
To hurt the noble man their soveraign loves.	P 259	4.57	Charls
Graunt that our deeds may wel deserve your loves: . . .	P 600	12.13	King

LOVES (cont.)			
Shall slacke my loves affection from his bent.	P 607	12.20	King
He loves me not that sheds most teares,	P1239	22.101	King
Because he loves me more then all the world:	Edw	1.4.77	Edward
And he confesseth that he loves me not.	Edw	1.4.194	Queene
No, his companion, for he loves me well,	Edw	2.1.13	Spencr
Who loves thee? but a sort of flatterers.	Edw	2.2.171	Mortmr
A loves me better than a thousand Spencers.	Edw	4.2.7	Prince
[To God]? <Why> he loves thee not:	F 398	2.1.10	Faust
I am one that loves an inch of raw Mutton, better then an ell	F 708	2.2.160	P Ltchry
He that loves pleasure, must for pleasure fall.	F1923	5.2.127	BdAngl
shame, and such as seeke loves wrack/Shall follow thee, their	Ovid's Elegies		1.2.31
Beware least he unrival'd loves secure,	Ovid's Elegies		1.8.95
Love and Loves sonne are with fierce armes to oddes;	Ovid's Elegies		1.10.19
And tis suppos'd Loves bowe hath wounded thee,	Ovid's Elegies		1.11.11
That some youth hurt as I am with loves bowe/His owne flames	Ovid's Elegies		2.1.7
But furiously he follow his loves fire/And [thinke] <thinkes>	Ovid's Elegies		2.2.13
If he loves not, deafe eares thou doest importune,	Ovid's Elegies		2.2.53
Or if he loves, thy tale breedes his misfortune.	Ovid's Elegies		2.2.54
Nay what is she that any Romane loves,	Ovid's Elegies		2.4.47
Let one wench cloy me with sweete loves delight,	Ovid's Elegies		2.10.21
Hees happie who loves mutuall skirmish slayes <layes>,	Ovid's Elegies		2.10.29
What lawfull is, or we professe Loves art,	Ovid's Elegies		2.18.19
Cruell is he, that loves whom none protect.	Ovid's Elegies		2.19.4
To steale sands from the shore he loves alife,	Ovid's Elegies		2.19.45
She gave me leave, soft loves in time make hast,	Ovid's Elegies		3.1.69
pleace <please> Pollux, Castor [love] <loves> horsemen more.	Ovid's Elegies		3.2.54
Or if there be a God, he loves fine wenches,	Ovid's Elegies		3.3.25
To this I fondly loves of flouds told plainly:	Ovid's Elegies		3.5.101
Onely our loves let not such rich churles gaine,	Ovid's Elegies		3.7.59
Nor is she, though she loves the fertile fields,	Ovid's Elegies		3.9.17
And wisht the goddesse long might feele loves fire.	Ovid's Elegies		3.9.42
Tender loves Mother a new Poet get,	Ovid's Elegies		3.14.1
Both loves to whom my heart long time did yeeld,	Ovid's Elegies		3.14.15
On Hellespont guiltie of True-loves blood,	Hero and Leander		1.1
Can hardly blazon foorth the loves of men,	Hero and Leander		1.70
To meet their loves; such as had none at all,	Hero and Leander		1.95
Thence flew Loves arrow with the golden head,	Hero and Leander		1.161
And now begins Leander to display/Loves holy fire, with words,	Hero and Leander		1.193
As thou in beautie doest exceed Loves mother/Nor heaven, nor	Hero and Leander		1.222
Who on Loves seas more glorious wouldst appeare?	Hero and Leander		1.228
The rites/In which Loves beauteous Empresse most delites,/Are	Hero and Leander		1.300
The gentle queene of Loves sole enemie.	Hero and Leander		1.318
Seeing in their loves, the Fates were injured.	Hero and Leander		1.484
Mov'd by Loves force, unto ech other lep?	Hero and Leander		2.58
so hee that loves,/The more he is restrain'd, the woorse he	Hero and Leander		2.144
Meremaids, sported with their loves/On heapes of heavie gold,	Hero and Leander		2.162
LOVE-SICK			
The king is love-sick for his minion.	Edw	1.4.87	Mortmr
LOVE-SNARDE			
Love-snarde Calypso is supposde to pray,	Ovid's Elegies		2.17.15
LOVEST			
Delbosco, as thou lovest and honour'st us,	Jew	2.2.24	1Knght
And therefore as thou lovest and tendrest me,	Edw	1.4.211	Queene
For thee faire Queene, if thou lovest Gaveston,	Edw	1.4.327	Edward
And if thou lovest me thinke no more of it.	F 536	2.1.148	Mephst
being old/Must shine a star) shal heaven (whom thou lovest),	Lucan, First Booke		46
LOVETH			
I followe one that loveth fame for me,	Dido	3.4.38	Dido
LOVING			
Iarbus stay, loving Iarbus stay,	Dido	4.2.52	Anna
Resolve my Lords and loving souldiers now,	1Tamb	2.6.34	Cosroe
Techelles, and my loving followers,	1Tamb	4.2.101	Tamb
And use us like a loving Conquerour.	1Tamb	5.1.23	Govnr
Leave us my Lord, and loving countrimen,	1Tamb	5.1.60	2Virgn
bed, where many a Lord/In prime and glorie of his loving joy,	1Tamb	5.1.84	1Virgn
And now my Lords and loving followers,	1Tamb	5.1.522	Tamb
Your presence (loving friends and fellow kings)/Makes me to	2Tamb	1.3.151	Tamb
Let me take leave of these my loving sonnes,	2Tamb	2.4.72	Zenoc
Therefore die by thy loving mothers hand,	2Tamb	3.4.23	Olymp
But now my followers and my loving friends,	2Tamb	3.5.159	Tamb
And meet my husband and my loving sonne.	2Tamb	4.2.36	Olymp
And use us like a loving Conquerour.	2Tamb	5.1.28	1Citzn
Or loving, doth dislike of something done.	Jew	3.4.12	Barab
Thus loving neither, will I live with both,	Jew	5.2.111	Barab
O no, my loving brother of Navarre.	P 543	11.8	Charls
A loving mother to preserve thy state,	P 594	12.7	QnMoth
Good morrow to my loving Cousin of Guise.	P 965	19.35	King
Now lords, our loving friends and countrimen,	Edw	4.4.1	Queene
Deale you my lords in this, my loving lords,	Edw	4.6.28	Queene
Your loving care in this,/Deserveth princelie favors and	Edw	4.6.53	Mortmr
For kinde and loving hast thou alwaies beene:	Edw	5.1.7	Edward
Traitor, in me my loving father speakes,	Edw	5.6.41	King
That rumor is untrue, for loving thee,	Edw	5.6.74	Queene
And loving Doves kisse eagerly together.	Ovid's Elegies		2.6.56
My selfe that better dye with loving may/Had seene, my mother	Ovid's Elegies		2.14.21
Wherein is seene the givers loving minde:	Ovid's Elegies		2.15.2
Loving, not to love at all, and everie part/Strove to resist	Hero and Leander		1.363
LOVINGLIE			
Say they, and lovinglie advise your grace,	Edw	3.1.166	Herald
LOV'ST			
Mathias, as thou lov'st me, not a word.	Jew	2.3.277	Barab
There, if thou lov'st me doe not leave a drop.	Jew	4.4.6	P Ithimr

Entry	Work	Reference	Speaker
LOW			
Ambitious pride shall make thee fall as low,	1Tamb	4.2.76	Bajzth
And tell me whether I should stoope so low,	2Tamb	1.1.112	Sgsmnd
Which til it may defend you, labour low:	2Tamb	3.3.44	Therid
And ducke as low as any bare-foot Fryar,	Jew	2.3.25	Barab
Whose mounting thoughts did never creepe so low,	Edw	2.2.77	Gavstn
Kind Jupiter hath low declin'd himselfe;	Lucan, First Booke		660
Foldes up her armes, and makes low curtesie.	Ovid's Elegies		2.4.30
the ground/Was strewd with pearle, and in low corrall groves,	Hero and Leander		2.161
LOWD			
When the chiefe pompe comes, lowd the people hollow,	Ovid's Elegies		3.12.29
LOWE			
If that your majestie can looke so lowe,	Dido	3.4.41	Aeneas
Fall prostrate on the lowe disdainefull earth.	1Tamb	4.2.13	Tamb
Or making lowe legs to a noble man,	Edw	2.1.38	Spencr
LOWERS			
But we must part, when heav'n with black night lowers.	Ovid's Elegies		1.4.60
LOWEST			
Haling him headlong to the lowest hell.	2Tamb	4.3.42	Orcan
Thence pitch them headlong to the lowest hell:	F1405	4.2.81	Faust
LOWLIE			
and enforce/The papall towers, to kisse the lowlie ground,	Edw	1.4.101	Edward
No little ditched townes, no lowlie walles,	Ovid's Elegies		2.12.7
LOWLY			
<incense>/The papall towers to kisse the [lowly] <holy> earth.	P1202	22.64	King
highly scorning, that the lowly earth/Should drinke his bloud,	Edw	5.1.13	Edward
And with a lowly conge to the ground,	Edw	5.4.49	Mortmr
LOWNE			
For shame subscribe, and let the lowne depart.	Edw	1.4.82	Warwck
LOWR'D			
If ever Hymen lowr'd at marriage rites,	P 58	2.1	Guise
LOWRE			
Why do you lowre unkindly on a king?	Edw	4.7.63	Edward
LOYNES			
Besiege the ofspring of our kingly loynes,	Dido	1.1.116	Jupitr
That erst-while issued from thy watrie loynes,	Dido	1.1.128	Venus
LOYTER			
You loyter, master, wherefore stay [we] <me> thus?	Jew	4.1.139	Ithimr
LOYTERD			
Long hast thou loyterd, greater workes compile.	Ovid's Elegies		3.1.24
LUBBERS			
yee Lubbers look about/And find the man that doth this villany,	F1055	3.2.75	Pope
LUBECKE			
Frankeford, Lubecke, Mosco, and where not,	Jew	4.1.72	Barab
LUCA (See LEUCA)			
LUCARS			
That would for Lucars sake have sold my soule.	Jew	4.1.53	Barab
LUCIFER			
Orientis Princeps [Lucifer], Belzebub inferni ardentis	F 245	1.3.17	P Faust
I am a servant to great Lucifer,	F 268	1.3.40	Mephst
Tell me, what is that Lucifer, thy Lord?	F 290	1.3.62	Faust
Was not that Lucifer an Angell once?	F 292	1.3.64	Faust
And what are you that live with Lucifer?	F 297	1.3.69	Faust
Unhappy spirits that [fell] <live> with Lucifer,	F 298	1.3.70	Mephst
Conspir'd against our God with Lucifer,	F 299	1.3.71	Mephst
And are for ever damn'd with Lucifer.	F 300	1.3.72	Mephst
Go beare these <those> tydings to great Lucifer,	F 315	1.3.87	Faust
Go, and returne to mighty Lucifer,	F 326	1.3.98	Faust
Mephostophilis come/And bring glad tydings from great Lucifer.	F 416	2.1.28	Faust
Now tell me what saith <sayes> Lucifer thy Lord.	F 419	2.1.31	Faust
For that security craves <great> Lucifer.	F 425	2.1.37	Mephst
at some certaine day/Great Lucifer may claime it as his owne,	F 440	2.1.52	Mephst
And then be thou as great as Lucifer.	F 441	2.1.53	Mephst
And Faustus hath bequeath'd his soule to Lucifer.	F 464	2.1.76	Faust
Faustus, I sweare by Hell and Lucifer,	F 481	2.1.93	Mephst
by these presents doe give both body and soule to Lucifer,	F 494	2.1.106	P Faust
In which <Wherein> thou hast given thy soule to Lucifer.	F 520	2.1.132	Mephst
Saba, or as beautifull/As was bright Lucifer before his fall.	F 542	2.1.154	Mephst
I am Lucifer,	F 639	2.2.88	Lucifr
<Great> Thankes mighty Lucifer:	F 719	2.2.171	Faust
Farewell great Lucifer: come Mephostophilis.	F 721	2.2.173	Faust
Proud Lucifer, that State belongs to me:	F 871	3.1.93	Bruno
againe I will confirme/The <My> former vow I made to Lucifer.	F1750	5.1.77	Faust
That durst disswade me from thy Lucifer,	F1754	5.1.81	Faust
And keepe [mine oath] <my vow> I made to Lucifer.	F1765	5.1.92	Faust
Why, Lucifer and Mephostophilis:	F1855	5.2.59	Faust
Yet will I call on him: O spare me Lucifer.	F1942	5.2.146	Faust
No Faustus, curse thy selfe, curse Lucifer,	F1973	5.2.177	Faust
Or Lucifer will beare thee quicke to hell.	F1976	5.2.180	Faust
Ugly hell gape not; come not Lucifer,	F1981	5.2.185	Faust
shoot) marcht on/And then (when Lucifer did shine alone,	Lucan, First Booke		233
LUCIFERS			
bloud/Assures his <assure my> soule to be great Lucifers,	F 444	2.1.56	Faust
LUCINA			
My wench, Lucina, I intreat thee favour,	Ovid's Elegies		2.13.21
LUCK			
Hence luck-lesse tables, funerall wood be flying/And thou the	Ovid's Elegies		1.12.7
LUCKE			
Wishing good lucke unto thy wandring steps.	Dido	1.1.239	Venus
Souldiours by bloud to be inricht have lucke.	Ovid's Elegies		3.7.54
LUCK-LESSE			
Hence luck-lesse tables, funerall wood be flying/And thou the	Ovid's Elegies		1.12.7
LUCKLESSE			
What, will you thus oppose me, lucklesse Starres,	Jew	1.2.260	Baraba

LUCKY
In lucky time, come let us keep this lane, ... P 298 5.25 Anjoy
LUCRE (See LUCARS)
LUCRECIA
Then heere wee'l lye before [Lutetia] <Lucrecia> walles, . P1151 22.13 King
LUCRETIUS
Loftie Lucretius shall live that houre, ... Ovid's Elegies 1.15.23
LUFT
And then we [luft] <left>, and [tackt] <tooke>, and fought at Jew 2.2.14 Bosco
LUKE
And offer luke-warme bloud, of new borne babes. . . F 402 2.1.14 Faust
If ever wench had made luke-warme thy love: . . . Ovid's Elegies 2.3.6
And in her luke-warme place Leander lay. . . . . Hero and Leander 2.254
LUKE-WARME
And offer luke-warme bloud, of new borne babes. . . F 402 2.1.14 Faust
If ever wench had made luke-warme thy love: . . . Ovid's Elegies 2.3.6
And in her luke-warme place Leander lay. . . . . Hero and Leander 2.254
LULD
Who ever since hath luld me in her armes. . . . . Dido 5.1.48 Ascan
LUMPE
Thinke me to be a senselesse lumpe of clay/That will with every Jew 1.2.216 Barab
LUNA
whom/The gravest, Aruns, dwelt in forsaken Leuca <or Luna>, Lucan, First Booke 585
LUNACIE
have I found a meane/To rid me from these thoughts of Lunacie: Dido 5.1.273 Dido
How should he, but in <with> desperate lunacie. . . . F1807 5.2.11 Mephst
LUNACY
Rather illusions, fruits of lunacy, ... F 407 2.1.19 BdAngl
LUNATICK
Ah pardon me, greefe makes me lunatick. . . . . Edw 5.1.114 Edward
LURE
make our <ycur> strokes to wound the sencelesse [aire] <lure>. 1Tamb 3.3.158 Tamb
LURKE
But he doth lurke within his drousie couch, . . . P 737 14.40 Navrre
Fire Paris where these trecherous rebels lurke. . . P1241 22.103 King
I and my wench oft under clothes did lurke, . . . Ovid's Elegies 1.4.47
LURKES
Under sweete hony deadly poison lurkes. . . . . Ovid's Elegies 1.8.104
LUST
As Concubine I feare, to feed his lust. . . . . . 1Tamb 4.3.42 Souldn
The violence of thy common Souldiours lust? . . . 2Tamb 4.3.80 Orcan
Am I growne olde, or is thy lust growne yong, . . . P 681 13.25 Guise
what huge lust of warre/Hath made Barbarians drunke with Latin Lucan, First Booke 8
To take repulse, and cause her shew my lust? . . . Ovid's Elegies 2.7.26
I flie her lust, but follow beauties creature; . . . Ovid's Elegies 3.10.37
Murder, rape, warre, lust and trecherie, ... Hero and Leander 1.457
LUSTFULL
But lustfull Jove and his adulterous child, . . . Dido 3.2.18 Juno
In sight and judgement of thy lustfull eye? . . . P 687 13.31 Guise
Pleasure addes fuell to my lustfull fire, ... Ovid's Elegies 2.10.25
And as he turnd, cast many a lustfull glaunce, . . Hero and Leander 2.186
LUSTIE
Or Cephalus with lustie Thebane youths, ... 1Tamb 4.3.4 Souldn
Yet lustie lords I have escapt your handes, . . . Edw 2.5.1 Gavstn
Now lustie lords, now not by chance of warre, . . . Edw 3.1.221 Edward
These lustie leaders Warwicke and Lancaster, . . . Edw 3.1.246 Edward
That I may conjure in some bushy <lustie> Grove, . . F 178 1.1.150 Faust
How large a legge, and what a lustie thigh? . . . Ovid's Elegies 1.5.22
I blush, [that] <and> being youthfull, hot, and lustie, . Ovid's Elegies 3.6.19
The lustie god imbrast him, cald him love, . . . Hero and Leander 2.167
LUSTLESSE
He shall be made a chast and lustlesse Eunuke, . . . 1Tamb 3.3.77 Bajzth
The stepdame read Hyppolitus lustlesse line. . . . Ovid's Elegies 2.18.30
LUSTRATION
the sacred priests/That with divine lustration purg'd the wals, Lucan, First Booke 593
LUSTY
Mounted on lusty Mauritanian Steeds, ... 1Tamb 3.3.16 Bassoe
Me thinks the slave should make a lusty theefe. . . 2Tamb 3.5.96 Jrslem
As when an heard of lusty Cymbrian Buls, ... 2Tamb 4.1.187 Tamb
Now Madame, how like you our lusty Admirall? . . . P 494 9.13 Guise
LUTE
Their fingers made to quaver on a Lute, ... 2Tamb 1.3.29 Tamb
Must tuna my Lute for sound, twang twang first. . . Jew 4.4.31 Barab
Or if one touch the lute with art and cunning, . . . Ovid's Elegies 2.4.27
LUTETIA
Then heere wee'l lye before [Lutetia] <Lucrecia> walles, . P1151 22.13 King
LUTHERANES
Cheefe standard bearer to the Lutheranes, ... P 285 5.12 Guise
Cheef standard bearer to the Lutheranes, ... P 313 5.40 Guise
LYBIAN
With her I durst the Lybian Syrtes breake through, . . Ovid's Elegies 2.16.21
LYCORIS (See LICORIS)
LYCURGUS
hellish fiend/Which made the sterne Lycurgus wound his thigh, Lucan, First Booke 573
LYDIAN
The Lydian buskin [in] fit [paces] <places> kept her. . Ovid's Elegies 3.1.14
LYE (Homograph)
And I alas, was forst to let her lye. . . . . Dido 2.1.279 Aeneas
Ile hang ye in the chamber where I lye, ... Dido 4.4.128 Dido
or to what end/Launcht from the haven, lye they in the Rhode? Dido 5.1.89 Dido
Here lye the Sword that in the darksome Cave/He drew, and swore Dido 5.1.295 Dido
Here lye the garment which I cloath'd him in, . . . Dido 5.1.298 Dido
Lye down Arabia, wounded to the death, ... 1Tamb 5.1.407 Arabia

Context	Work	Reference	Speaker
LYE (cont.)			
Are come from Turkey, and lye in our Rhode:	Jew	1.1.147	1Jew
and those other Iles/That lye betwixt the Mediterranean seas.	Jew	1.2.4	Basso
And let me lodge where I was wont to lye.	Jew	1.2.333	Abigal
And like a cunning spirit feigne some lye,	Jew	2.3.382	Barab
That's no lye, for she sent me for him.	Jew	3.4.25	P Ithimr
the burthen of my sinnes/Lye heavy on my soule; then pray you	Jew	4.1.49	Barab
Now, gentle Ithimore, lye in my lap.	Jew	4.2.82	Curtzn
Come gentle Ithimore, lye in my lap.	Jew	4.4.27	Curtzn
Lye there the Kings delight, and Guises scorne.	P 818	17.13	Guise
Then heere wee'l lye before [Lutetia] <Lucrecia> walles,	P1151	22.13	King
lye there the kinges delyght and guises scorne	Paris	ms22,p390	Guise
and such Countries that lye farre East, where they have fruit	F1584	4.6.27	P Faust
huge heapes of stone/Lye in our townes, that houses are	Lucan, First Booke	26	
Blest ring thou in my mistris hand shalt lye,	Ovid's Elegies	2.15.7	
But now againe the barriers open lye;	Ovid's Elegies	3.2.77	
LYED			
By which she perjurd oft hath lyed [to] <by> me.	Ovid's Elegies	3.3.10	
LYEN			
Italy many yeares hath lyen until'd,	Lucan, First Booke	28	
LYES (Homograph)			
Lyes it in Didos hands to make thee blest,	Dido	2.1.103	Dido
Here lyes my hate, Aeneas cursed brat,	Dido	3.2.1	Juno
I'le to her lodging; hereabouts she lyes.	Jew	3.6.6	1Fryar
Boy, look where your father lyes.	P1046	19.116	King
If hee lyes downe with Wine and sleepe opprest,	Ovid's Elegies	1.4.53	
But absent is my fire, lyes ile tell none,	Ovid's Elegies	2.16.11	
And fiercely knockst thy brest that open lyes?	Ovid's Elegies	3.5.58	
What should I tell her vaine tongues filthy lyes,	Ovid's Elegies	3.10.21	
LYEST			
O boy that lyest so slothfull in my heart.	Ovid's Elegies	2.9.2	
LYING (Homograph)			
Great summes of mony lying in the bancho;	Jew	4.1.74	Barab
Wilt lying under him his bosome clippe?	Ovid's Elegies	1.4.5	
She would be nimbler, lying with a man.	Ovid's Elegies	2.4.24	
Ah often, that her [hale] <haole> head aked, she lying,	Ovid's Elegies	2.19.11	
With lying lips my God-head to deceave,	Ovid's Elegies	3.3.44	
And worshipt by their paine, and lying apart?	Ovid's Elegies	3.9.16	
LYMNASPHALTIS			
But Tamburlain, in Lymnasphaltis lake,	2Tamb	5.1.115	Govnr
LYNE			
Valoyses lyne ends in my tragedie.	P1231	22.93	King
LYNGER			
Least if we let them lynger here a while,	1Tamb	2.2.20	Meandr
LYON			
What, darest thou looke a Lyon in the face?	Dido	3.3.39	Dido
Treading the Lyon, and the Dragon downe,	F 920	3.1.142	Pope
Like to a Lyon of scortcht desart Affricke,	Lucan, First Booke	208	
LYONESSE			
Nor dares the Lyonesse her young whelpes kill.	Ovid's Elegies	2.14.36	
LYONS			
Which I will breake betwixt a Lyons jawes.	Dido	3.3.38	Cupid
Like Lyons shall they guard us when we please,	F 151	1.1.123	Valdes
out of a Lyons mouth when I was scarce <half> an houre old,	F 687	2.2.136	P Wrath
MACAREUS			
What thanklesse Jason, Macareus, and Paris,	Ovid's Elegies	2.18.23	
MACCABEES (See MACHABEES)			
MACE			
Whose memorie like pale deaths stony mace,	Dido	2.1.115	Aeneas
Beat downe the bold waves with his triple mace,	Hero and Leander	2.172	
He flung at him his mace, but as it went,	Hero and Leander	2.209	
The mace returning backe, his owne hand hit,	Hero and Leander	2.211	
MACEDONIANS			
Then did the Macedonians at the spoile/Of great Darius and his	1Tamb	1.1.153	Ceneus
MACER			
Wee Macer sit in Venus slothfull shade,	Ovid's Elegies	2.18.3	
Nor of thee Macer that resoundst forth armes,	Ovid's Elegies	2.18.35	
MACHABEES			
As for the Comment on the Machabees/I have it, Sir, and 'tis at	Jew	2.3.153	Barab
MACHDA			
To Machda, where the mighty Christian Priest/Cal'd John the	2Tamb	1.3.187	Techel
MACHEVILL			
Albeit the world thinke Machevill is dead,	Jew	Prol.1	Machvl
And let them know that I am Machevill,	Jew	Prol.7	Machvl
MAD			
He be so mad to manage Armes with me,	1Tamb	3.1.34	Bajzth
Raving, impatient, desperate and mad,	2Tamb	2.4.112	Tamb
in distresse/Thinke me so mad as I will hang my selfe,	Jew	1.2.263	Barab
And every Moone made some or other mad,	Jew	2.3.195	Barab
My death? what, is the base borne peasant mad?	Jew	2.3.281	Lodowk
Or fierce Agave mad; or like Megaera/That scar'd Alcides, when	Lucan, First Booke	574	
My Mistresse weepes whom my mad hand did harme.	Ovid's Elegies	1.7.4	
That I was mad, and barbarous all men cried,	Ovid's Elegies	1.7.19	
Mad streame, why doest our mutuall joyes deferre?	Ovid's Elegies	3.5.87	
Long have I borne much, mad thy faults me make:	Ovid's Elegies	3.10.1	
And Scyllaes wombe mad raging dogs conceales.	Ovid's Elegies	3.11.22	
What is it now, but mad Leander dares?	Hero and Leander	2.146	
MADAM			
And now faire Madam, and my noble Lords,	1Tamb	1.2.253	Tamb
Here Madam, you are Empresse, she is none.	1Tamb	3.3.227	Therid
I pray you give them leave Madam, this speech is a goodly	1Tamb	4.4.32	P Techel
Ah Madam, this their slavery hath Enforc'd,	1Tamb	5.1.345	Anippe
Madam content your self and be resolv'd,	1Tamb	5.1.372	Anippe

MADAM (cont.)

Madam, your father and th'Arabian king,	1Tamb	5.1.378	Philem
No Madam, these are speeches fit for us,	2Tamb	1.3.88	Celeb
How now Madam, what are you doing?	2Tamb	3.4.34	Therid
Madam, sooner shall fire consume us both,	2Tamb	3.4.73	Techel
Madam, I am so far in love with you,	2Tamb	3.4.78	Therid
No Madam, but the beginning of your joy,	2Tamb	3.4.83	Techel
Why Madam, thinke ye to mocke me thus palpably?	2Tamb	4.2.67	Therid
But, Madam, this house/And waters of this new made Nunnery	Jew	1.2.310	1Fryar
Madam, and my talke with him was [but]/About the borrowing of a	Jew	2.3.155	Mthias
Nay Madam stay, that weapon was my son's,	Jew	3.2.25	Govnr
and he gave me a letter from one Madam Bellamira, saluting me	Jew	4.2.30	P Ithimr
A voustre cõmandemente Madam.	Jew	4.4.38	Barab
Two, three, foure month Madam.	Jew	4.4.55	P Barab
Be patient, gentle Madam, it was he,	Jew	5.1.46	Govnr
Well Madam, let that rest:	P 17	1.17	Charls
Madam, it wilbe noted through the world,	P 207	4.5	Charls
Well Madam, I referre it to your Majestie,	P 225	4.23	Charls
No by my faith Madam.	P 498	9.17	Guise
And now Madam as I understand,	P 500	9.19	Guise
Madam,/I goe as whirl-windes rage before a storme.	P 510	9.29	Guise
Madam, I have heard him solemnly vow,	P 516	9.35	Cardnl
Madam, I will.	P 560	11.25	Eprnon
Madam, as in secrecy I was tolde,	P 641	12.54	Cardnl
Now Madam must you insinuate with the King,	P 645	12.58	Cardnl
I will Madam.	P 658	13.2	Maid
But Madam I must see.	P 677	13.21	Guise
Madam, whether walks your majestie so fast?	Edw	1.2.46	Mortmr
Madam, returne unto the court againe:	Edw	1.2.56	Mortmr
Madam farewell.	Edw	1.2.80	Mortmr
Madam, tis you that rob me of my lord.	Edw	1.4.161	Gavstn
Madam, how fares your grace?	Edw	1.4.192	Mortmr
Crie quittance Madam then, and love not him.	Edw	1.4.195	Mortmr
Feare ye not Madam, now his minions gone,	Edw	1.4.198	Lncstr
For his repeale, Madam!	Edw	1.4.204	Lncstr
But madam, would you have us cal him home?	Edw	1.4.208	Mortmr
It shall be done madam.	Edw	2.1.72	Baldck
No madam, but that cursed Gaveston.	Edw	2.4.32	Lncstr
Madam, stay you within this castell here.	Edw	2.4.50	Mortmr
Madam, I cannot stay to answer you,	Edw	2.4.57	Mortmr
Madam, what newes?	Edw	3.1.58	Edward
Madam in this matter/We will employ you and your little sonne,	Edw	3.1.69	Edward
Madam, we will that you with speed be shipt,	Edw	3.1.81	Edward
Madam, returne to England,/And please my father well, and then	Edw	4.2.3	Prince
Madam, what cheere?	Edw	4.2.13	SrJohn
But droope not madam, noble mindes contemne/Despaire:	Edw	4.2.16	SrJohn
Madam, long may you live,	Edw	4.2.34	Kent
but madam, right makes roome,/Where weapons want, and though a	Edw	4.2.50	Mortmr
Madam along, and you my lord, with me,	Edw	4.2.81	SrJohn
Welcome a Gods name Madam and your sonne,	Edw	4.3.41	Edward
Nay madam, if you be a warriar,	Edw	4.4.15	Mortmr
Madam, without offence if I may aske,	Edw	4.6.30	Kent
Madam, tis good to looke to him betimes.	Edw	4.6.39	Mortmr
Yea madam, and they scape not easilie,	Edw	4.6.41	Mortmr
Madam, the Maior and Citizens of Bristow,	Edw	4.6.47	Rice
Madam, what resteth, why stand ye in a muse?	Edw	4.6.63	SrJohn
Madam, have done with care and sad complaint,	Edw	4.6.66	Mortmr
We in meane while madam, must take advise,	Edw	4.6.77	Mortmr
Thinke therefore madam that imports [us] <as> much,	Edw	5.2.10	Mortmr
In health madam, but full of pensivenes.	Edw	5.2.25	Msngr
I will madam.	Edw	5.2.73	Matrvs
Madam, intreat not, I will rather die,	Edw	5.6.56	Mortmr
I, madam, you, for so the rumor runnes.	Edw	5.6.73	King
Thus madam, tis the kings will you shall hence.	Edw	5.6.89	2Lord
That bootes not, therefore gentle madam goe.	Edw	5.6.91	2Lord
Madam, I will do more then this for your content.	F1575	4.6.18	P Faust
So are we Madam, which we will recompence/With all the love and	F1671	4.6.114	Duke
here they be madam, wilt please you taste on them.	F App	p.242 15	P Faust
I am glad they content you so Madam.	F App	p.242 27	P Faust

MADAME

Madame, you shall be my mother.	Dido	2.1.96	Ascan
No Madame, but it seemes that these are Kings.	Dido	3.1.149	Aeneas
Madame Zenocrate, may I presume/To know the cause of these	1Tamb	3.2.1	Agidas
Madame, she thinks perhaps she is too fine.	1Tamb	3.3.179	Ebea
Thus Madame.	P 230	4.28	Guise
Now Madame, how like you our lusty Admirall?	P 494	9.13	Guise
but it may be Madame, you take no delight in this, I have heard	F App	p.242 4	P Faust
women do long for some dainties or other, what is it Madame?	F App	p.242 6	P Faust
Alas Madame, thats nothing, Mephastophilis, be gone.	F App	p.242 12	P Faust
hither, as ye see, how do you like them Madame, be they good?	F App	p.242 23	P Faust
Come, Madame, let us in, where you must wel reward this learned	F App	p.243 28	P Duke

MADDAM

But tell me Maddam, is your grace betroth'd?	1Tamb	1.2.32	Tamb
And Maddam, whatsoever you esteeme/Of this successe, and losse	1Tamb	1.2.44	Tamb
For you then Maddam, I am out of doubt.	1Tamb	1.2.258	Tamb

MADDAME

Maddame, I beseech your grace to except this simple gift.	P 166	3.1	P Pothec

MADDING

And what made madding people shake off peace.	Lucan, First Booke		69

MADE

As made the bloud run downe about mine eares.	Dido	1.1.8	Ganimd
Made Hebe to direct her ayrie wheeles/Into the windie countrie	Dido	1.1.56	Venus
And made that way my mother Venus led:	Dido	1.1.221	Aeneas

MADE (cont.)

Thither made we,	Dido	1.2.25	Cloan
Whose ticing tongue was made of Hermes pipe,	Dido	2.1.145	Aeneas
And him, Epeus having made the horse,	Dido	2.1.147	Aeneas
Made him to thinke Epeus pine-tree Horse/A sacrifize t'appease	Dido	2.1.162	Aeneas
his breast/Furrowd with wounds, and that which made me weepe,	Dido	2.1.204	Aeneas
Which made the funerall flame that burnt faire Troy:	Dido	2.1.218	Aeneas
Troian, thy ruthfull tale hath made me sad:	Dido	2.1.301	Dido
Lest I be made a wonder to the world.	Dido	3.1.96	Dido
Ile give thee tackling made of riveld gold,	Dido	3.1.116	Dido
Tut, I am simple, without [minde] <made> to hurt,	Dido	3.2.16	Juno
Whom casualtie of sea hath made such friends?	Dido	3.2.76	Juno
As made disdaine to flye to fancies lap:	Dido	3.4.56	Dido
Love made me jealous, but to make amends,	Dido	4.4.33	Dido
O happie sand that made him runne aground:	Dido	4.4.95	Dido
And made me take my brother for my sonne?	Dido	5.1.43	Aeneas
Repairde not I thy ships, made thee a King,	Dido	5.1.163	Dido
Made me suppose he would have heard me speake:	Dido	5.1.230	Anna
And made their spoiles from all our provinces.	1Tamb	1.1.122	Cosroe
Whose ransome made them martch in coates of gold,	1Tamb	1.1.143	Ceneus
Thy Garments shall be made of Medean silke,	1Tamb	1.2.95	Tamb
And well his merits show him to be made/His Fortunes maister,	1Tamb	2.1.35	Cosroe
Though straight the passage and the port be made,	1Tamb	2.1.42	Cosroe
That ere made passage thorow Persean Armes.	1Tamb	2.3.56	Tamb
That onely made him King to make us sport.	1Tamb	2.5.101	Tamb
Or of what mould or mettel he be made,	1Tamb	2.6.17	Ortyg
Who entring at the breach thy sword hath made,	1Tamb	2.7.9	Cosroe
And that made me to joine with Tamburlain,	1Tamb	2.7.30	Therid
And that made us, the friends of Tamburlaine,	1Tamb	2.7.34	Techel
The strangest men that ever nature made,	1Tamb	2.7.40	Cosroe
That made me Emperour of Asia.	1Tamb	3.3.32	Tamb
He shall be made a chast and lustlesse Eunuke,	1Tamb	3.3.77	Bajzth
Whose hands are made to gripe a warlike Lance,	1Tamb	3.3.106	Bajzth
Which lately made all Europe quake for feare:	1Tamb	3.3.135	Bajzth
And made my lordly Love her worthy King:	1Tamb	3.3.190	Zenoc
It shall be said, I made it red my selfe,	1Tamb	4.2.54	Tamb
Some made your wives, and some your children)/Might have	1Tamb	5.1.27	1Virgn
For whome the Powers divine have made the world,	1Tamb	5.1.76	1Virgn
If these had made one Poems period/And all combin'd in Beauties	1Tamb	5.1.169	Tamb
Till we have made us ready for the field.	1Tamb	5.1.212	Tamb
Mighty hath God and Mahomet made thy hand/(Renowmed Tamburlain)	1Tamb	5.1.479	Souldn
Hath made our Poet pen his second part,	2Tamb	Prol.3	Prolog
Nor he but Fortune that hath made him great.	2Tamb	1.1.60	Orcan
And made it dance upon the Continent:	2Tamb	1.1.88	Orcan
By him that made the world and sav'd my soule,	2Tamb	1.1.133	Sgsmnd
Shall I be made a king for my labour?	2Tamb	1.2.62	P Almeda
Their fingers made to quaver on a Lute,	2Tamb	1.3.29	Tamb
He raign'd him straight and made him so curvet,	2Tamb	1.3.41	Zenoc
Thou shalt be made a King and raigne with me,	2Tamb	1.3.48	Tamb
And made Canarea cal us kings and Lords,	2Tamb	1.3.181	Usumc
And made him sweare obedience to my crowne.	2Tamb	1.3.190	Techel
And conquering that, made haste to Nubia,	2Tamb	1.3.202	Techel
and the bounds of Affrike/And made a voyage into Europe,	2Tamb	1.3.208	Therid
These heathnish Turks and Pagans lately made,	2Tamb	2.1.6	Fredrk
Grace to memorie/The league we lately made with king Orcanes,	2Tamb	2.1.28	Sgsmnd
Me thinks I see how glad the christian King/Is made, for joy of	2Tamb	2.2.21	Uribas
Counterscarps/Narrow and steepe, the wals made high and broad,	2Tamb	3.2.69	Tamb
of thy hold/Volleies of ordinance til the breach be made,	2Tamb	3.3.25	Therid
When made a victor in these hautie arms,	2Tamb	4.1.46	Amyras
Made of the mould whereof thy selfe consists,	2Tamb	4.1.115	Tamb
with the meteors/Of blood and fire thy tyrannies have made,	2Tamb	4.1.142	Jrslem
Nor am I made Arch-monark of the world,	2Tamb	4.1.150	Tamb
Hath stain'd thy cheekes, and made thee look like death,	2Tamb	4.2.4	Olymp
And made so wanton that they knew their strengths,	2Tamb	4.3.14	Tamb
the breach the enimie hath made/Gives such assurance of our	2Tamb	5.1.2	Maxim
That made us all the labour for the towne,	2Tamb	5.1.82	Therid
Yet could not enter till the breach was made.	2Tamb	5.1.100	Tamb
Have made the water swell above the bankes,	2Tamb	5.1.205	Techel
Kingdomes made waste, brave cities sackt and burnt,	2Tamb	5.2.26	Callap
And made his state an honor to the heavens,	2Tamb	5.3.12	Therid
Might first made Kings, and Lawes were then most sure/When like	Jew	Prol.20	Machvl
So that of thus much that returne was made:	Jew	1.1.1	Barab
Of nought is nothing made.	Jew	1.2.104	Barab
Oh what has made my lovely daughter sad?	Jew	1.2.225	Barab
We now are almost at the new made Nunnery.	Jew	1.2.306	1Fryar
And waters of this new made Nunnery/Will much delight you.	Jew	1.2.311	1Fryar
And made my house a place for Nuns most chast.	Jew	2.3.77	Barab
Come, I have made a reasonable market,	Jew	2.3.161	1Offcr
And every Moone made some or other mad,	Jew	2.3.195	Barab
That ye be both made sure e're you come out.	Jew	2.3.236	Barab
The account is made, for [Lodovico] <Lodowicke> dyes.	Jew	2.3.242	Barab
Lodowicke, it is enough/That I have made thee sure to Abigal.	Jew	2.3.335	Barab
Be made an accessary of your deeds;	Jew	2.3.342	Barab
Who made them enemies?	Jew	3.2.20	Mater
Goe to the new made Nunnery, and inquire/For any of the Fryars	Jew	3.3.27	Abigal
Has made me see the difference of things.	Jew	3.3.62	Abigal
Why, made mine Abigall a Nunne.	Jew	3.4.24	Barab
he made such haste to his prayers, as if hee had had another	Jew	4.2.24	P Ithimr
One dram of powder more had made all sure.	Jew	5.1.22	Barab
He forged the daring challenge made them fight.	Jew	5.1.47	Govnr
walke about/The ruin'd Towne, and see the wracke we made:	Jew	5.2.19	Calym
Here have I made a dainty Gallery,	Jew	5.5.33	Barab
till thy father hath made good/The ruines done to Malta and to	Jew	5.5.111	Govnr

MADE (cont.)

And made it look with terrour on the worlde:	P 61	2.4	Guise
And night made semblance of the hue of hell,	P 63	2.6	Guise
Of so great matter should be made the ground.	P 126	2.69	Guise
That you were one that made this Massacre.	P 436	7.76	Navrre
the Duke of Joyeux/Hath made great sute unto the King therfore.	P 734	14.37	1Msngr
It would be good the Guise were made away,	P 888	17.83	Eprnon
Hath he not made me in the Popes defence,	P1036	19.106	King
Barons and Earls, your pride hath made me mute,	Edw	1.1.107	Kent
That villaine Gaveston is made an Earle.	Edw	1.2.11	Lncstr
For wot you not that I have made him sure,	Edw	1.4.378	Edward
Which made me curate-like in mine attire,	Edw	2.1.49	Baldck
Thy absence made me droope, and pine away,	Edw	2.2.52	Edward
Have drawne thy treasure drie, and made thee weake,	Edw	2.2.159	Mortmr
Unto the walles of Yorke the Scots made rode,	Edw	2.2.166	Lncstr
Ballads and rimes, made of thy overthrow.	Edw	2.2.178	Mortmr
To Englands high disgrace, have made this Jig,	Edw	2.2.189	Lncstr
Why then weele have him privilie made away.	Edw	2.2.236	Gavstn
A rebels, recreants, you made him away.	Edw	3.1.229	Edward
want, and though a many friends/Are made away, as Warwick,	Edw	4.2.52	Mortmr
And made the channels overflow with blood,	Edw	4.4.12	Queene
realme, and sith the fates/Have made his father so infortunate,	Edw	4.6.27	Queene
rule and emperie/Have not in life or death made miserable?	Edw	4.7.15	Edward
You, and such as you are, have made wise worke in England.	Edw	4.7.114	P Rice
Till further triall may be made thereof.	Edw	5.6.80	King
And made the flowring pride of Wittenberg <Wertenberge>	F 141	1.1.113	Faust
Whose [shadows] made all Europe honour him.	F 145	1.1.117	Faust
To effect all promises betweene us [made] <both>.	F 482	2.1.94	Mephst
'Twas <It was> made for man; then he's <therefore is man> more	F 560	2.2.9	Mephst
If Heaven was <it were> made for man, 'twas made for me:	F 561	2.2.10	Faust
Have not I made blind Homer sing to me/Of Alexanders love, and	F 577	2.2.26	Faust
Made musicke with my Mephostophilis?	F 581	2.2.30	Faust
now tell me who made the world?	F 618	2.2.67	P Faust
Thinke Faustus upon God, that made the world.	F 625	2.2.74	P Faust
Made the grim monarch of infernall spirits,	F1371	4.2.47	Fredrk
And I had breath'd a man made free from harme.	F1400	4.2.76	Faust
Now am I a made man for ever.	F1477	4.4.21	P HrsCsr
Do you remember how you made me weare an Apes--	F1661	4.6.104	P Dick
to die shortly, he has made his will, and given me his wealth,	F1674	5.1.1	P Wagner
worth>/<Made Greece with ten yeares warres afflict poore Troy>?	F1696	(HC269)B	2Schol
againe I will confirme/The <My> former vow I made to Lucifer.	F1750	5.1.77	Faust
And keepe [mine oath] <my vow> I made to Lucifer.	F1765	5.1.92	Faust
his horse, and he would have his things rubd and made cleane:	F App	p.233 7	P Rafe
tell thee, we were for ever made by this doctor Faustus booke?	F App	p.234 1	P Robin
As when I heare but motion made of him,	F App	p.237 27	Emper
Now am I made man for ever, Ile not leave my horse for fortie:	F App	p.239 114	P HrsCsr
lust of warre/Hath made Barbarians drunke with Latin bloud?	Lucan, First Booke		9
Which made thee Emperor; thee (seeing thou being old/Must shine	Lucan, First Booke		45
And what made madding people shake off peace.	Lucan, First Booke		69
His losse made way for Roman outrages.	Lucan, First Booke		106
share our Empire, fortune that made Roome/Governe the earth,	Lucan, First Booke		109
Made all shake hands as once the Sabines did;	Lucan, First Booke		118
And glad when bloud, and ruine made him way:	Lucan, First Booke		151
When fortune made us lords of all, wealth flowed,	Lucan, First Booke		161
Sale made of offices, and peoples voices/Bought by themselves	Lucan, First Booke		180
He, he afflicts Roome that made me Roomes foe.	Lucan, First Booke		205
appeasd/The wrastling tumult, and right hand made silence:	Lucan, First Booke		299
none answer'd, but a murmuring buz/Th'unstable people made:	Lucan, First Booke		354
come, their huge power made him bould/To mannage greater deeds;	Lucan, First Booke		462
bringing newes/Of present war, made many lies and tales.	Lucan, First Booke		468
hellish fiend/Which made the sterne Lycurgus wound his thigh,	Lucan, First Booke		573
These direful signes made Aruns stand amaz'd,	Lucan, First Booke		615
[Love] <I> slackt my Muse, and made my [numbers] <number> soft.	Ovid's Elegies		1.1.22
I lately cought, will have a new made wound,	Ovid's Elegies		1.2.29
Night shamelesse, wine and Love are fearelesse made.	Ovid's Elegies		1.6.60
let him viewe/And thy neck with lascivious markes made blew.	Ovid's Elegies		1.8.98
Bull and Eagle/And what ere love made Jove should thee invegle.	Ovid's Elegies		1.10.8
Never to harme me made thy faith evasion.	Ovid's Elegies		1.11.6
Your name approves you made for such like things,	Ovid's Elegies		1.12.27
Made two nights one to finish up his pleasure.	Ovid's Elegies		1.13.46
If ever wench had made luke-warme thy love:	Ovid's Elegies		2.3.6
Or any back made rough with stripes imbrace?	Ovid's Elegies		2.7.22
And tender love hath great things hatefull made.	Ovid's Elegies		2.18.4
And doing wrong made shew of innocence.	Ovid's Elegies		2.19.14
Let with strong hand the reine to bend be made.	Ovid's Elegies		3.2.72
Why made king [to refuse] <and refusde> it?	Ovid's Elegies		3.6.49
An Altar made after the ancient fashion.	Ovid's Elegies		3.12.10
This bed, and that by tumbling made uneven,	Ovid's Elegies		3.13.32
Not onely by warres rage made Gentleman.	Ovid's Elegies		3.14.6
Made with the blood of wretched Lovers slaine.	Hero and Leander		1.16
His presence made the rudest paisant melt,	Hero and Leander		1.79
Leander, thou art made for amorous play:	Hero and Leander		1.88
Loves mother/Nor heaven, nor thou, were made to gaze upon,	Hero and Leander		1.223
which downe her face/Made milk-white paths, wheron the gods	Hero and Leander		1.298
Heroes lookes yeelded, but her words made warre,	Hero and Leander		1.331
As might have made heaven stoope to have a touch,	Hero and Leander		1.366
As made Love sigh, to see his tirannie.	Hero and Leander		1.374
And to those sterne nymphs humblie made request,	Hero and Leander		1.379
Did charme her nimble feet, and made her stay,	Hero and Leander		1.399
Fearing her owne thoughts made her to be hated.	Hero and Leander		2.44
Which made his love through Sestos to bee knowne,	Hero and Leander		2.111
And made his capring Triton sound alowd,	Hero and Leander		2.156
Leander made replie,/You are deceav'd, I am no woman I.	Hero and Leander		2.191

MADE (cont.)			
He cald it in, for love made him repent.	Hero and Leander	2.210	
With both her hands she made the bed a tent,	Hero and Leander	2.264	
of hers (like that/Which made the world) another world begat,	Hero and Leander	2.292	
A gowne made of the finest wooll,	Passionate Shepherd	13	
MADNES			
what madnes, what huge lust of warre/Hath made Barbarians	Lucan, First Booke	8	
MADNESSE			
And madnesse send his damned soule to hell.	1Tamb	5.1.229	Zabina
What madnesse ist to tell night <nights> prankes by day,	Ovid's Elegies	3.13.7	
MADRIGALLS			
Melodious byrds [sing] <sings> Madrigalls.	Passionate Shepherd	8	
MAD'ST			
When thou Achates with thy sword mad'st way,	Dido	2.1.268	Aeneas
Nature, why mad'st me not some poysonous beast,	Dido	4.1.21	Iarbus
And perish in the pit thou mad'st for me.	P 963	19.33	King
Thou mad'st thy head with compound poyson flow.	Ovid's Elegies	1.14.44	
Tell me, to whom mad'st thou that heedlesse oath?	Hero and Leander	1.294	
MAENAS			
As [Maenas] <Maenus> full of wine on Pindus raves,	Lucan, First Booke	674	
MAENUS			
As [Maenas] <Maenus> full of wine on Pindus raves,	Lucan, First Booke	674	
MAGICALL			
Come, shew me some demonstrations Magicall,	F 177	1.1.149	Faust
MAGICIAN (See also MAGITIAN)			
What devill attends this damn'd Magician,	F1445	4.3.15	Benvol
MAGICK			
'Tis magick, magick, that hath ravisht me.	F 137	1.1.109	Faust
The miracles that magick will performe,	F 163	1.1.135	Cornel
Hath all the Principles Magick doth require:	F 167	1.1.139	Cornel
The wonder of the world for Magick Art;	F1166	4.1.12	Mrtino
She magick arts and Thessale charmes doth know,	Ovid's Elegies	1.8.5	
MAGICKE			
And Spels of magicke from the mouthes of spirits,	2Tamb	4.2.64	Olymp
Nothing so sweet as Magicke is to him,	F 26	Prol.26	1Chor
To practise Magicke and concealed Arts.	F 129	1.1.101	Faust
resolute/And try the utmost <uttermost> Magicke can performe.	F 243	1.3.15	Faust
Such is the force of Magicke, and my spels.	F 259	1.3.31	Faust
Abjure this Magicke, turne to God againe.	F 396	2.1.8	Faust
And let thee see <shewe thee> what Magicke can performe.	F 474	2.1.86	Mephst
I will renounce this Magicke and repent.	F 562	2.2.11	Faust
And charme thee with this Magicke wand,	F 996	3.2.16	Mephst
With Magicke spels so compasse thee,	F1002	3.2.22	Mephst
To cast his Magicke charmes, that shall pierce through/The Ebon	F1223	4.1.69	Faust
This Magicke, that will charme thy soule to hell,	F1708	5.1.35	OldMan
world can compare with thee, for the rare effects of Magicke:	F App	p.236 4	P Emper
I could my selfe by secret Magicke shift.	Ovid's Elegies	2.15.10	
MAGIORE			
the Gulfe, call'd by the name/Mare magiore, of th'inhabitantes:	2Tamb	1.3.215	Therid
MAGISTRATES			
No, let us beare him to the Magistrates.	Jew	4.1.183	Ithimr
MAGITIAN			
A sound Magitian is a Demi-god <mighty god>,	F 89	1.1.61	Faust
Wonder of men, renown'd Magitian,	F1204	4.1.50	Emper
MAGITIANS			
These Metaphisicks of Magitians,	F 76	1.1.48	Faust
MAGNANIMITIE			
Nor bar thy mind that magnanimitie,	2Tamb	5.3.200	Tamb
Did you retaine your fathers magnanimitie,	Edw	3.1.16	Spencr
MAGNANIMITY			
By [valure] <value and by magnanimity.	1Tamb	4.4.126	Tamb
But matchlesse strength and magnanimity?	2Tamb	4.1.85	Amyras
MAGNIFICALL			
So will thy [triumph] <triumphs> seeme magnificall.	Ovid's Elegies	1.2.28	
MAGNIFICENCE			
For all flesh quakes at your magnificence.	1Tamb	3.1.48	Argier
MAGNIFICENT			
Magnificent and mightie Prince Cosroe,	1Tamb	1.1.136	Ortyg
Magnificent and peerlesse Tamburlaine,	2Tamb	1.3.129	Usumc
MAGOT			
This gentle Magot, Lodowicke I meane,	Jew	2.3.305	Barab
MAHOMET			
All this is true as holy Mahomet,	1Tamb	3.1.54	Bajzth
By Mahomet, my Kinsmans sepulcher,	1Tamb	3.3.75	Bajzth
Now Mahomet, solicit God himselfe,	1Tamb	3.3.195	Zabina
If Mahomet should come from heaven and sweare,	1Tamb	3.3.208	Zenoc
O Mahomet, Oh sleepie Mahomet.	1Tamb	3.3.269	Bajzth
O cursed Mahomet that makest us thus/The slaves to Scythians	1Tamb	3.3.270	Zabina
Ye holy Priests of heavenly Mahomet,	1Tamb	4.2.2	Bajzth
Doost thou think that Mahomet wil suffer this?	1Tamb	4.4.52	P Therid
Then is there left no Mahomet, no God,	1Tamb	5.1.239	Zabina
Ah myghty Jove and holy Mahomet,	1Tamb	5.1.363	Zenoc
Mighty hath God and Mahomet made thy hand/(Renowmed Tamburlain)	1Tamb	5.1.479	Souldn
By sacred Mahomet, the friend of God,	2Tamb	1.1.137	Orcan
And by the hand of Mahomet I sweare,	2Tamb	1.2.65	Callap
For I have sworne by sacred Mahomet,	2Tamb	1.3.109	Tamb
He by his Christ, and I by Mahomet?	2Tamb	2.2.32	Orcan
As is our holy prophet Mahomet,	2Tamb	2.2.44	Orcan
And Christ or Mahomet hath bene my friend.	2Tamb	2.3.11	Orcan
Not dooing Mahomet an injurie,	2Tamb	2.3.34	Orcan
by the aid of God and his friend Mahomet, Emperour of Natolia,	2Tamb	3.1.3	P Orcan
Brothers to holy Mahomet himselfe,	2Tamb	3.3.36	Capt
Ah sacred Mahomet, if this be sin,	2Tamb	3.4.31	Olymp

MAHOMET (cont.)
And thou shalt see a man greater than Mahomet, 2Tamb 3.4.46 Therid
By Mahomet not one of them shal live. 2Tamb 3.5.17 Callap
and sacrifice/Mountaines of breathlesse men to Mahomet, 2Tamb 3.5.55 Callap
By Mahomet he shal be tied in chaines, 2Tamb 3.5.92 Jrslem
By Mahomet, thy mighty friend I sweare, 2Tamb 4.1.121 Tamb
As if they were the teares of Mahomet/For hot consumption of 2Tamb 4.1.196 Tamb
Found in the Temples of that Mahomet, 2Tamb 5.1.175 Tamb
In vaine I see men worship Mahomet, 2Tamb 5.1.179 Tamb
And yet I live untoucht by Mahomet: 2Tamb 5.1.182 Tamb
Now Mahomet, if thou have any power, 2Tamb 5.1.187 Tamb
Wel souldiers, Mahomet remaines in hell, 2Tamb 5.1.198 Tamb
If God or Mahomet send any aide. 2Tamb 5.2.11 Callap
Ah sacred Mahomet, thou that hast seene/Millions of Turkes 2Tamb 5.2.24 Callap
not my Lord, I see great Mahomet/Clothed in purple clowdes, 2Tamb 5.2.31 Amasia
Though God himselfe and holy Mahomet, 2Tamb 5.2.37 Amasia

MAID (See also MAYD)
Thou shalt be Landresse to my waiting maid. 1Tamb 3.3.177 Zabina
send for them/To do the work my chamber maid disdaines. 1Tamb 3.3.188 Anippe
The Turkesse let my Loves maid lead away. 1Tamb 3.3.267 Tamb
Pitty the state of a distressed Maid. Jew 1.2.315 Abigal
A faire young maid scarce fourteene yeares of age, Jew 1.2.378 Mthias
the fairest Maid in Germany, for I am wanton and lascivious, F 529 2.1.141 P Faust
Some swore he was a maid in mans attire, Hero and Leander 1.83
Who taught thee Rhethoricke to deceive a maid? Hero and Leander 1.338

MAIDE
Faire child stay thou with Didos waiting maide, Dido 2.1.304 Venus
Wherewith my husband woo'd me yet a maide, Dido 3.4.63 Dido
Eating sweet Comfites with Queene Didos maide, Dido 5.1.47 Ascan
By lawlesse rapine from a silly maide. 1Tamb 1.2.10 Zenoc
Zenocrate, the loveliest Maide alive, 1Tamb 3.3.117 Tamb
if thou hast any mind to Nan Spit our kitchin maide, then turn F App p.234 27 P Robin
The maide that kembd them ever safely left them. Ovid's Elegies 1.14.16
And for her skill to thee a gratefull maide. Ovid's Elegies 2.7.24
Live without love, so sweete ill is a maide. Ovid's Elegies 2.9.26
Whether the subtile maide lines bringes and carries, Ovid's Elegies 2.19.41
The maide to hide me in her bosome let not. Ovid's Elegies 3.1.56
Came forth a mother, though a maide there put. Ovid's Elegies 3.4.22
My bones had beene, while yet I was a maide. Ovid's Elegies 3.5.74
Hath any rose so from a fresh yong maide, Ovid's Elegies 3.6.53
And least her maide should know of this disgrace, Ovid's Elegies 3.6.83
To winne the maide came in a golden shewer. Ovid's Elegies 3.7.30
Where Juno comes, each youth, and pretty maide, Ovid's Elegies 3.12.23

MAIDEN
Provided, that you keepe your Maiden-head. Jew 2.3.227 Barab
And new sworne souldiours maiden armes retainst, Ovid's Elegies 2.18.2
Me in thy bed and maiden bosome take, Hero and Leander 2.248
(Poore sillie maiden) at his mercie was. Hero and Leander 2.286

MAIDEN-HEAD (See also MAYDENHEAD)
Provided, that you keepe your Maiden-head. Jew 2.3.227 Barab

MAIDENS
That maidens new betroth'd should weepe a while: Jew 2.3.326 Barab
maidens in our parish dance at my pleasure starke naked before F App p.233 3 P Robin
Such light to shamefaste maidens must be showne, Ovid's Elegies 1.5.7
So many men and maidens without love, Ovid's Elegies 2.9.15
Or els will maidens, yong-mens mates, to go/If they determine Ovid's Elegies 2.16.17

MAIDES
It is the use for [Tirien] <Turen> maides to weare/Their bowe Dido 1.1.204 Venus
the Sun-bright troope/Of heavenly vyrgins and unspotted maides, 1Tamb 5.1.325 Zenoc
Sometimes like women or unwedded Maides, F 154 1.1.126 Valdes
A faire maides care expeld this sluggishnesse, Ovid's Elegies 1.9.43
Or maides that their betrothed husbands spie. Ovid's Elegies 2.5.36
Maides on the shore, with marble white feete tread, Ovid's Elegies 2.11.15
Maides words more vaine and light then falling leaves, Ovid's Elegies 2.16.45
Insooth th'eternall powers graunt maides society/Falsely to Ovid's Elegies 3.3.11

MAIDS (See also MAYDES)
Where are my Maids? Jew 4.2.83 Curtzn
Maids of England, sore may you moorne, Edw 2.2.190 Lncstr
let the Maids looke well to their porridge-pots, for I'le into F1133 3.3.46 P Robin
Maids are not woon by brutish force and might, Hero and Leander 1.419
Such sights as this, to tender maids are rare. Hero and Leander 2.238

MAIEST
share the world thou canst not;/Injoy it all thou maiest: Lucan, First Booke 292
Gratis thou maiest be free, give like for like, Ovid's Elegies 1.6.23
Cheere up thy selfe, thy losse thou maiest repaire, Ovid's Elegies 1.14.55
Feare to be guilty, then thou maiest desemble. Ovid's Elegies 2.2.18
Well maiest thou one thing for thy Mistresse use. Ovid's Elegies 2.8.24
Hence with great laude thou maiest a triumph move. Ovid's Elegies 2.9.16
That thou maiest know with love thou mak'st me flame. Ovid's Elegies 3.2.4
thou maiest, if that be best,/[A] <Or> while thy tiptoes on the Ovid's Elegies 3.2.63

MAIL (See MAIES)

MAIME
That has no further comfort for his maime. Jew 2.1.11 Barab

MAIMED
Nor Sterne nor Anchor have our maimed Fleete, Dido 3.1.109 Aeneas
By curing of this maimed Emperie. 1Tamb 1.1.126 Menaph
Grone for this greefe, behold how thou art maimed. Edw 3.1.251 Mortmr

MAIN
The Terrene main wherin Danubius fals, 2Tamb 1.1.37 Orcan

MAINE (Homograph)
pooles, refraines/To taint his tresses in the Tyrrhen maine? Dido 1.1.112 Venus
And with maine force flung on a ring of pikes, Dido 2.1.196 Aeneas
Fled to the Caspean or the Ocean maine? 1Tamb 1.1.102 Mycet

MAINE (cont.)

All fearefull foldes his sailes, and sounds the maine,	1Tamb	3.2.82		Agidas
Where Nilus payes his tribute to the maine,	Jew	1.1.75		Barab
We saw the River Maine, fall into Rhine <Rhines>,	F 785	3.1.7		Faust
Or that the wandring maine follow the moone;	Lucan, First Booke			415
Which makes the maine saile fal with hideous sound;	Lucan, First Booke			498
How almost wrackt thy ship in maine seas fell.	Ovid's Elegies			2.11.50
He would have chac'd away the swelling maine,	Hero and Leander			2.121

MAINELY

Such breadth of shoulders as might mainely beare/Olde Atlas	1Tamb	2.1.10		Menaph

MAINE SAILE

Which makes the maine saile fal with hideous sound;	Lucan, First Booke			498

MAINLY

and strong armes/Can mainly throw the dart; wilt thou indure	Lucan, First Booke			365

MAINTAINE

And must maintaine my life exempt from servitude.	1Tamb	1.2.31		Tamb
That will maintaine it against a world of Kings.	1Tamb	4.2.81		Tamb
easily in a day/Tell that which may maintaine him all his life.	Jew	1.1.11		Barab
nct a stone of beef a day will maintaine you in these chops;	Jew	2.3.124	P	Barab
Maintaine it bravely by firme policy,	Jew	5.2.36		Barab
and carefully maintaine/The wealth and safety of your kingdomes	P 477	8.27		Anjoy
A warlike people to maintaine thy right,	P 592	12.5		QnMoth
Which Ile maintaine so long as life doth last:	P 800	16.14		Navrre
Thou able tc maintaine an hoast in pay,	P 841	17.36		Eprnon
What we have done, our hart bloud shall maintaine.	Edw	1.4.40		Mortmr
things feigne)/Crete proud that Jove her nourcery maintaine.	Ovid's Elegies			3.9.20

MAINTAINES

As long as life maintaines Theridamas.	1Tamb	1.2.231		Therid
As long as life maintaines his mighty arme,	1Tamb	5.1.375		Anippe

MAIOR

My lord, the Maior of Bristow knows our mind.	Edw	4.6.40		Queene
Madam, the Maior and Citizens of Bristow,	Edw	4.6.47		Rice

MAIST

Great Jupiter, still honourd maist thou be,	Dido	1.1.137		Venus
But that thcu maist more easilie perceive,	Dido	3.2.66		Juno
thou maist thinke thy selfe happie to be fed from my trencher.	1Tamb	4.4.92	P	Tamb
That thou maist feast them in thy Citadell.	Jew	5.5.16		Msngr
left heele, that thou maist, Quasi vestigiis nostris insistere.	F 387	1.4.45	P	Wagner
But <And> now my Faustus, that thou maist perceive,	F 809	3.1.31		Mephst
By which sweete path thou maist attaine the gole/That shall	F App	p.243 36		OldMan
No pritty wenches keeper maist thou bee:	Ovid's Elegies			1.6.63
Nor, so thou maist obtaine a wealthy prize,	Ovid's Elegies			1.8.63
Pray him to lend what thou maist nere restore.	Ovid's Elegies			1.8.102
Since maist thou see me watch and night warres move:	Ovid's Elegies			1.9.45

MAISTER

And well his merits show him to be made/His Fortunes maister,	1Tamb	2.1.36		Cosroe
Bassoe, by this thy Lord and maister knowes,	1Tamb	3.3.1		Tamb
When thy great Bassoe-maister and thy selfe,	1Tamb	3.3.173		Zenoc
Welcome maister secretarie.	Edw	2.2.68		Penbrk
Weel make quick worke, commend me to your maister/My friend, and	Edw	2.6.12		Warwck
How now sirra, where's thy Maister?	F 197	1.2.4	P	1Schol
my Maister is within at dinner, with Valdes and Cornelius,	F 215	1.2.22	P	Wagner
but hearke you Maister, will you teach me this conjuring	F 380	1.4.38	P	Robin
call me Maister Wagner, and see that you walke attentively,	F 385	1.4.43	P	Wagner
your foolery, for an my Maister come, he'le conjure you 'faith.	F 735	2.3.14	P	Dick
My Maister conjure me?	F 736	2.3.15	P	Robin
an my Maister come here, I'le clap as faire a paire of hornes	F 736	2.3.15	P	Robin
you cosoning scab; Maister Doctor awake, and rise, and give me	F1489	4.4.33	P	HrsCsr
for your horse is turned to a bottle of Hay,--Maister Doctor.	F1490	4.4.34	P	HrsCsr
Thankes Maister Doctor, for these pleasant sights, nor know I	F1558	4.6.1	P	Duke
True Maister Doctor, and since I finde you so kind I will make	F1570	4.6.13	P	Lady
heare you Maister Doctor, now you have sent away my guesse, I	F1666	4.6.109	P	Hostss
I think my Maister means to die shortly, he has made his will,	F1674	5.1.1	P	Wagner
call me Maister Wagner, and let thy left eye be diametarily	F App	p.231 69	P	Wagner
my maister and mistris shal finde that I can reade, he for his	F App	p.233 15	P	Robin
Our maister Parson sayes thats nothing.	F App	p.234 25	P	Rafe
Maister doctor Faustus, I have heard strange report of thy	F App	p.236 1	P	Emper
Go to maister Doctor, let me see them presently.	F App	p.237 50	P	Emper
Do you heare maister Doctor?	F App	p.237 51	P	Knight
Maister Doctor, I heard this Lady while she liv'd had a wart or	F App	p.238 60	P	Emper
Good Maister Doctor, at my intreaty release him, he hath done	F App	p.238 79	P	Emper
Farewel maister Doctor, yet ere you goe, expect from me a	F App	p.239 88	P	Emper
I have beene al this day seeking one maister Fustian:	F App	p.239 98	P	HrsCsr
masse see where he is, God save you maister doctor.	F App	p.239 99	P	HrsCsr
you, hey, passe, where's your maister?	F App	p.240 138	P	HrsCsr
this is he, God save ye maister doctor, maister doctor, maister	F App	p.241 148	P	HrsCsr
save ye maister doctor, maister doctor, maister doctor Fustian,	F App	p.241 148	P	HrsCsr
maister doctor, maister doctor Fustian, fortie dollers, fortie	F App	p.241 149	P	HrsCsr
Beleeve me maister Doctor, this merriment hath much pleased me.	F App	p.242 1	P	Duke
Thankes, good maister doctor.	F App	p.242 7	P	Duchss
Beleeve me Maister doctor, they be the best grapes that ere I	F App	p.242 25	P	Duchss
Come, maister Doctor follow us, and receive your reward.	F App	p.243 33	P	Duke
I thinke my maister meanes to die shortly,	F App	p.243 1		Wagner
wherein through use he's known/To exceed his maister, that	Lucan, First Booke			326
Ajax, maister of the seven-fould shield,/Butcherd the flocks he	Ovid's Elegies			1.7.7
I know no maister of so great hire sped.	Ovid's Elegies			2.5.62

MAISTERS

He tells you true, my maisters, so he does.	1Tamb	2.2.74		Mycet
And so would you my maisters, would you not?	1Tamb	2.5.70		Tamb
Had fed the feeling of their maisters thoughts,	1Tamb	5.1.162		Tamb
What requier you my maisters?	2Tamb	3.3.15		Capt
our port-maisters/Are not so careles of their kings commaund.	Edw	4.3.22		Edward
And then resolve me of thy Maisters mind.	F 328	1.3.100		Faust

MAISTERS (cont.)
Come my Maisters, I'le bring you to the best beere in Europe, F1505 4.5.1 P Carter
Why how now Maisters, what a coyle is there? . . . . F1591 4.6.34 Servnt

MAIT
Mait please your grace to entertaine them now. . . . . Edw 2.2.241 Neece

MAJESTICALL
In their true shapes, and state Majesticall, ... F1233 4.1.79 Emper
The Ocean maketh more majesticall: . . . . Hero and Leander 1.226

MAJESTIE
That will Aeneas shewe your majestie. . . . . . Dido 3.1.98 Achat
Preferd before a man of majestie: . . . . . . Dido 3.3.65 Iarbus
If that your majestie can looke so lowe, ... Dido 3.4.41 Aeneas
Oft have I heard your Majestie complain, ... 1Tamb 1.1.35 Meandr
And sit with Tamburlaine in all his majestie. . . . . 1Tamb 1.2.209 Tamb
Making it daunce with wanton majestie: . . . . . . 1Tamb 2.1.26 Menaph
Emperour in humblest tearms/I vow my service to your Majestie, 1Tamb 2.5.16 Meandr
Your Majestie shall shortly have your wish, ... 1Tamb 2.5.48 Menaph
And let the majestie of heaven beholde/Their Scourge and . 1Tamb 4.2.31 Tamb
It is a blemish to the Majestie/And high estate of mightie 1Tamb 4.3.19 Souldn
is compriz'd the Sum/Of natures Skill and heavenly majestie. 1Tamb 5.1.79 1Virgn
So, now she sits in pompe and majestie: . . . . . 2Tamb 1.3.17 Tamb
Since last we numbred to your majestie: . . . . . 2Tamb 3.5.49 Soria
let me see how well/Thou wilt become thy fathers majestie. 2Tamb 5.3.184 Tamb
I humbly thank your Majestie. . . . . P 169 3.4 P Pothec
Well Madam, I referre it to your Majestie, ... P 225 4.23 Charls
And most [humbly] <humble> intreates your Majestie/To visite P 245 4.43 Man
I humbly thank your royall Majestie. . . . . . . P 273 4.71 Admral
Your Majestie her rightfull Lord and Soveraigne. . . . P 583 11.48 Pleshe
they Henries heart/Will not both harbour love and Majestie? P 604 12.17 King
Then may it please your Majestie to give me leave, . . . P 616 12.29 Mugern
Thanks to your Majestie, and so I take my leave. . . . P 749 15.7 Joyeux
And simple meaning to your Majestie, ... P 867 17.62 Guise
Good morrow to your Majestie. . . . . P 964 19.34 Guise
I heard your Majestie was scarsely pleasde, ... P 967 19.37 Guise
your Majestie heere is a Frier of the order of the Jacobins, P1155 22.17 P 1Msngr
Such things as these best please his majestie, ... Edw 1.1.71 Gavstn
Madam, whether walks your majestie so fast? . . . . Edw 1.2.46 Mortmr
And on their knees salute your majestie. . . . . . Edw 1.4.339 Queene
Then I doe to behold your Majestie. . . . . . . Edw 2.2.63 Gavstn
I humblie thanke your majestie. . . . . Edw 2.2.247 Baldck
Then to be favoured of your majestie. . . . . . . Edw 2.2.255 Spencr
Because his majestie so earnestlie/Desires to see the man Edw 2.5.77 Penbrk
You would not suffer thus your majestie/Be counterbuft of your Edw 3.1.17 Spencr
This haught resolve becomes your majestie, ... Edw 3.1.28 Baldck
I come in person to your majestie, ... Edw 3.1.39 SpncrP
And do your message with a majestie. . . . . . . Edw 3.1.73 Edward
Desires accesse unto your majestie. . . . . . . Edw 3.1.149 Spencr
Shall do good service to her Majestie, ... Edw 4.6.74 Mortmr
and fell invasion/Of such as have your majestie in chase, Edw 4.7.5 Abbot
Your majestie must go to Killingworth. . . . . . Edw 4.7.82 Leistr
Commend me humblie to his Majestie, ... Edw 5.2.69 Queene
And she <her> I like that with a majestie, ... Ovid's Elegies 2.4.29
Where crown'd with blazing light and majestie, ... Hero and Leander 1.110

MAJESTIES
My lords, it is his majesties request, ... Edw 2.5.57 Arundl

MAJESTY
With what a majesty he rears his looks:-- . . . . . 1Tamb 1.2.165 Tamb
Now in his majesty he leaves those lookes, ... 1Tamb 3.2.61 Agidas
How dare you thus abuse my Majesty? . . . . . . 1Tamb 3.3.226 Zabina
It might amaze your royall majesty. 1Tamb 4.1.16 2Msngr
Offering Damascus to your Majesty. . . . . . . 1Tamb 4.2.114 Therid
Or if my love unto your majesty/May merit favour at your . 1Tamb 4.4.69 Zenoc
Then here before the majesty of heaven, ... 1Tamb 5.1.48 2Virgn
and I might enter in/To see the state and majesty of heaven, 2Tamb 1.3.155 Tamb
Your Majesty remembers I am sure/What cruell slaughter of our 2Tamb 2.1.4 Fredrk
It resteth now then that your Majesty/Take all advantages of 2Tamb 2.1.11 Fredrk
Holds out his hand in highest majesty/To entertaine divine 2Tamb 2.4.32 Tamb
My Lord, your Majesty shall soone perceive: 2Tamb 2.4.39 1Phstn
Than this base earth should shroud your majesty: . . . 2Tamb 2.4.60 Zenoc
Your Majesty may choose some pointed time, ... 2Tamb 3.1.75 Jrslem
Tis nought for your majesty to give a kingdome. . . . 2Tamb 3.1.77 Jrslem
Why, I thank your Majesty. . . . . 2Tamb 3.1.79 P Almeda
a souldier, and this wound/As great a grace and majesty to me, 2Tamb 3.2.118 Tamb
In whose high lookes is much more majesty/Than from the Concave 2Tamb 3.4.47 Therid
fighting men/Are come since last we shewed your majesty. . 2Tamb 3.5.34 Jrslem
Since last we numbred to your Majesty. . . . . . 2Tamb 3.5.39 Orcan
Since last we numbred to your majesty. . . . . . 2Tamb 3.5.45 Trebiz
much like so many suns/That halfe dismay the majesty of heaven: 2Tamb 4.1.3 Amyras
You doo dishonor to his majesty, ... 2Tamb 4.1.20 Calyph
But traitor to my name and majesty. . . . . . . 2Tamb 4.1.90 Tamb
Yet pardon him I pray your Majesty. . . . . . . 2Tamb 4.1.97 Therid
in] <resisting> me/The power of heavens eternall majesty. . 2Tamb 4.1.158 Tamb
By which I hold my name and majesty. . . . . . . 2Tamb 4.3.26 Tamb
Your Majesty must get some byts for these, ... 2Tamb 4.3.43 Therid
Your Majesty already hath devisde/A meane, as fit as may be to 2Tamb 4.3.50 Usumc
We thank your majesty. . . . . 2Tamb 4.3.74 Soldrs
And usde such slender reckning of [your] <you> majesty. . 2Tamb 5.1.83 Therid
That shakes his sword against thy majesty, ... 2Tamb 5.1.196 Tamb
health and majesty/Were strangely blest and governed by heaven, 2Tamb 5.3.24 Techel
His byrth, his life, his health and majesty. . . . . 2Tamb 5.3.27 Techel
Thy instrument and note of Majesty, ... 2Tamb 5.3.38 Usumc
Pleaseth your Majesty to drink this potion, ... 2Tamb 5.3.78 Phsitn
Yet if your majesty may escape this day, ... 2Tamb 5.3.98 Phsitn

MAJESTY (cont.)				
yong Callapine that lately fled from your majesty, hath nowe	2Tamb	5.3.103	P	3Msngr
My Lord, you must obey his majesty,	2Tamb	5.3.204		Therid
Then feeles your majesty no sovereraigne ease,	2Tamb	5.3.213		Usumc
I'le write unto his Majesty for ayd,	Jew	2.2.40		Bosco
He humbly would intreat your Majesty/To come and see his homely	Jew	5.3.17		Msngr
Your Majesty were best goe visite him,	P 249	4.47		QnMoth
His majesty,/Hearing that you had taken Gaveston,	Edw	2.5.34		Arundl
His Majesty is comming to the Hall;	F1158	4.1.4		Mrtino
And bring in presence of his Majesty,	F1169	4.1.15		Mrtino
Your Majesty shall see them presently.	F1235	4.1.81		Faust
My Lord, I must forewarne your Majesty,	F1248	4.1.94		Faust
Your Majesty may boldly goe and see.	F1269	4.1.115		Faust
And therefore my Lord, so please your Majesty,	F1300	4.1.146		Faust
as to delight your Majesty with some mirth, hath Faustus justly	F1312	4.1.158	P	Faust
whom all the world admires for Majesty, we should thinke	F1686	5.1.13	P	1Schol
No [otherwaies] <otherwise> for pompe or <and> Majesty,	F1693	5.1.20		Faust
whom all the world admires for majesty.	F1698	5.1.25		2Schol
and nothing answerable to the honor of your Imperial majesty,	F App	p.236 14	P	Faust
I am content to do whatsoever your majesty shall command me.	F App	p.236 16	P	Faust
I doubt not shal sufficiently content your Imperiall majesty.	F App	p.237 49	P	Faust
MAJOR				
All bordring on the Mare-major sea:	2Tamb	3.1.51		Trebiz
Marcheth in Asia major, where the streames,	2Tamb	5.2.2		Callap
Major sum quam cui possit fortuna nocere.	Edw	5.4.69		Mortmr
MAJORE (See MAGIORE)				
MAKE				
Vulcan shall daunce to make thee laughing sport,	Dido	1.1.32		Jupitr
To make thee fannes wherewith to coole thy face,	Dido	1.1.35		Jupitr
Whose wearie lims shall shortly make repose,	Dido	1.1.84		Jupitr
Shall make the morning hast her gray uprise,	Dido	1.1.102		Jupitr
Whose beautious burden well might make you proude,	Dido	1.1.124		Venus
To make us live unto our former heate,	Dido	1.1.160		Achat
That we may make a fire to warme us with,	Dido	1.1.167		Aeneas
And this right hand shall make thy Altars crack/With mountaine	Dido	1.1.201		Aeneas
O yet this stone doth make Aeneas weepe,	Dido	2.1.15		Aeneas
Lyes it in Didos hands to make thee blest,	Dido	2.1.103		Dido
Or els in Carthage make his kingly throne.	Dido	2.1.331		Venus
Ile make me bracelets of his golden haire,	Dido	3.1.85		Dido
Juno, my mortall foe, what make you here?	Dido	3.2.24		Venus
Which I will make in quittance of thy love:	Dido	3.2.69		Juno
Ile make the Clowdes dissolve their watrie workes,	Dido	3.2.90		Juno
And make love drunken with thy sweete desire:	Dido	3.3.75		Iarbus
Stoute love in mine armes make thy Italy,	Dido	3.4.57		Dido
Whose hideous ecchoes make the welkin howle,	Dido	4.2.9		Iarbus
Love made me jealous, but to make amends,	Dido	4.4.33		Dido
And now to make experience of my love,	Dido	4.4.64		Dido
And heele make me immortall with a kisse.	Dido	4.4.123		Dido
Or els Ile make a prayer unto the waves,	Dido	5.1.246		Dido
And all the Sailers merrie make for joy,	Dido	5.1.259		Dido
Must I make ships for him to saile away?	Dido	5.1.266		Dido
Lay to thy hands and helpe me make a fire,	Dido	5.1.284		Dido
And make Aeneas famous through the world,	Dido	5.1.293		Dido
To make himselfe the Monarch of the East:	1Tamb	1.1.43		Meandr
Bringing the Crowne to make you Emperour.	1Tamb	1.1.135		Menaph
As with their waight shall make the mountains quake,	1Tamb	1.2.49		Tamb
His deep affections make him passionate.	1Tamb	1.2.164		Techel
We thinke it losse to make exchange for that/We are assured of	1Tamb	1.2.216		Techel
Make much of them gentle Theridamas,	1Tamb	1.2.247		Tamb
Should make the world subdued to Tamburlaine.	1Tamb	2.1.30		Menaph
To make him famous in accomplisht woorth:	1Tamb	2.1.34		Cosroe
And make him false his faith unto his King,	1Tamb	2.2.27		Meandr
Which make reports it far exceeds the Kings.	1Tamb	2.2.42		Spy
their fellowes throats/And make us triumph in their overthrow.	1Tamb	2.2.50		Meandr
Thy wit will make us Conquerors to day.	1Tamb	2.2.58		Mycet
And make them blest that share in his attemptes.	1Tamb	2.3.9		Tamb
Would make one thrust and strive to be retain'd/In such a great	1Tamb	2.3.31		Therid
Shall make me solely Emperour of Asia:	1Tamb	2.3.39		Cosroe
These are the wings shall make it flie as swift,	1Tamb	2.3.57		Tamb
And more than needes to make an Emperour.	1Tamb	2.3.65		Tamb
Thee doo I make my Regent of Persea,	1Tamb	2.5.8		Cosroe
Make but a jest to win the Persean crowne.	1Tamb	2.5.98		Tamb
That onely made him King to make us sport.	1Tamb	2.5.101		Tamb
and all the Starres that make/The loathsome Circle of my dated	1Tamb	2.6.36		Cosroe
Shall make me leave so rich a prize as this:	1Tamb	2.7.54		Tamb
Make me the gastly counterfeit of death.	1Tamb	3.2.17		Zenoc
That make quick havock of the Christian blood.	1Tamb	3.3.58		Tamb
Thy fall shall make me famous through the world:	1Tamb	3.3.83		Tamb
make our <your> strokes to wound the sencelesse [aire] <lure>.	1Tamb	3.3.158		Tamb
And make her daintie fingers fall to woorke.	1Tamb	3.3.181		Ebea
And make him raine down murthering shot from heaven/To dash the	1Tamb	3.3.196		Zabina
foule Idolaters/Shall make me bonfires with their filthy bones,	1Tamb	3.3.240		Bajzth
garrisons enough/To make me Soveraigne of the earth againe.	1Tamb	3.3.243		Bajzth
Ile make the kings of India ere I die,	1Tamb	3.3.263		Tamb
Make heaven to frowne and every fixed starre/To sucke up poison	1Tamb	4.2.5		Bajzth
And make it swallow both of us at once.	1Tamb	4.2.29		Bajzth
Fighting for passage, [makes] <make> the Welkin cracke,	1Tamb	4.2.45		Tamb
To make me think of nought but blood and war.	1Tamb	4.2.55		Tamb
To make these captives reine their lavish tongues.	1Tamb	4.2.67		Techel
Ambitious pride shall make thee fall as low,	1Tamb	4.2.76		Bajzth
A sacred vow to heaven and him I make,	1Tamb	4.3.36		Souldn
And make Damascus spoiles as rich to you,	1Tamb	4.4.8		Tamb
will make thee slice the brawnes of thy armes into carbonadoes,	1Tamb	4.4.43	P	Tamb

MAKE (cont.)

Faste and welcome sir, while hunger make you eat.	1Tamb	4.4.56	P	Tamb
not the Turke and his wife make a goodly showe at a banquet?	1Tamb	4.4.57	P	Tamb
Yet would I with my sword make Jove to stoope.	1Tamb	4.4.74		Tamb
those blind Geographers/That make a triple region in the world,	1Tamb	4.4.76		Tamb
Here at Damascus will I make the Point/That shall begin the	1Tamb	4.4.81		Tamb
Or may be forc'd, to make me Emperour.	1Tamb	4.4.90		Tamb
sir, you must be dieted, too much eating will make you surfeit.	1Tamb	4.4.104	P	Tamb
Take them away againe and make us slaves.	1Tamb	4.4.133		Therid
And make us desperate of our threatned lives:	1Tamb	5.1.6		Govnr
And make our soules resolve in ceasles teares:	1Tamb	5.1.272		Bajzth
And make a passage for my loathed life.	1Tamb	5.1.304		Bajzth
Make ready my Coch, my chaire, my jewels, I come, I come, I	1Tamb	5.1.317	P	Zabina
Whose lookes might make the angry God of armes,	1Tamb	5.1.326		Zenoc
To make discourse of some sweet accidents/Have chanc'd thy	1Tamb	5.1.424		Arabia
Meaning to make me Generall of the world,	1Tamb	5.1.451		Tamb
And make it quake at every drop it drinks:	1Tamb	5.1.462		Tamb
And there make lawes to rule your provinces:	1Tamb	5.1.527		Tamb
And make this champion mead a bloody Fen.	2Tamb	1.1.32		Orcan
And make faire Europe mounted on her bull,	2Tamb	1.1.42		Orcan
Meaning to make a conquest of our land:	2Tamb	1.1.49		Gazell
Would make me thinke them Bastards, not my sons,	2Tamb	1.3.32		Tamb
Or make a bridge of murthered Carcases,	2Tamb	1.3.93		Amyras
To make it parcel of my Empery.	2Tamb	1.3.110		Tamb
Whose lookes make this inferiour world to quake,	2Tamb	1.3.139		Techel
Whose coleblacke faces make their foes retire,	2Tamb	1.3.142		Techel
Such lavish will I make of Turkish blood,	2Tamb	1.3.165		Tamb
Yet shall my souldiers make no period/Untill Natolia kneele	2Tamb	1.3.216		Therid
And now come we to make his sinowes shake,	2Tamb	2.2.9		Gazell
And make a passage from the imperiall heaven/That he that sits	2Tamb	2.2.48		Orcan
And make the power I have left behind/(Too litle to defend our	2Tamb	2.2.59		Orcan
Whose absence make the sun and Moone as darke/As when opposde	2Tamb	2.4.51		Tamb
the fiery Element/Dissolve, and make your kingdome in the Sky,	2Tamb	2.4.59		Zenoc
Meaning to make her stately Queene of heaven.	2Tamb	2.4.108		Tamb
And all this raging cannot make her live,	2Tamb	2.4.120		Therid
To keep my promise, and to make him king,	2Tamb	3.1.71		Callap
and make them seeme as black/As is the Island where the Furies	2Tamb	3.2.11		Tamb
And make whole cyties caper in the aire.	2Tamb	3.2.61		Tamb
Ile teach you how to make the water mount,	2Tamb	3.2.85		Tamb
And make a Fortresse in the raging waves,	2Tamb	3.2.88		Tamb
or with a Curtle-axe/To hew thy flesh and make a gaping wound?	2Tamb	3.2.97		Tamb
the Ecchoe and the souldiers crie/Make deafe the aire, and dim	2Tamb	3.3.61		Therid
But yet Ile save their lives and make them slaves.	2Tamb	3.5.63		Tamb
And never meant to make a Conquerour,	2Tamb	3.5.83		Tamb
Me thinks the slave should make a lusty theefe.	2Tamb	3.5.96		Jrslem
Ile make thee wish the earth had swallowed thee:	2Tamb	3.5.118		Tamb
Go too sirha, take your crown, and make up the halfe dozen.	2Tamb	3.5.135	P	Tamb
here are Bugges/Wil make the haire stand upright on your heads,	2Tamb	3.5.148		Tamb
My sterne aspect shall make faire Victory,	2Tamb	3.5.162		Tamb
Such a feare (my Lord) would never make yee retire.	2Tamb	4.1.71	P	Perdic
Ile make ye roare, that earth may eccho foorth/The far	2Tamb	4.1.185		Tamb
the clowdes/Incense the heavens, and make the starres to melt,	2Tamb	4.1.195		Tamb
Ile use some other means to make you yeeld,	2Tamb	4.2.51		Therid
To make you fierce, and fit my appetite,	2Tamb	4.3.17		Tamb
For love, for honor, and to make her Queene,	2Tamb	4.3.38		Orcan
And make us jeasting Pageants for their Trulles.	2Tamb	4.3.89		Therid
And now themselves shal make our Pageant,	2Tamb	4.3.90		Tamb
Whether we next make expedition.	2Tamb	4.3.94		Tamb
And make a bridge unto the battered walles.	2Tamb	5.1.68		Tamb
Tis not thy bloody tents can make me yeeld,	2Tamb	5.1.103		Govnr
Wel, now Ile make it quake, go draw him up,	2Tamb	5.1.107		Tamb
I think I make your courage something quaile.	2Tamb	5.1.126		Tamb
And make our greatest haste to Persea:	2Tamb	5.1.128		Tamb
And make him after all these overthrowes,	2Tamb	5.2.29		Callap
Yet make them feele the strength of Tamburlain,	2Tamb	5.3.37		Usumc
<Hipostates>/Thick and obscure doth make your danger great,	2Tamb	5.3.83		Phsitn
My looks shall make them flie, and might I follow,	2Tamb	5.3.107		Tamb
Help me (my Lords) to make my last remoove.	2Tamb	5.3.180		Tamb
Would make a miracle of thus much coyne:	Jew	1.1.13		Barab
Give us a peacefull rule, make Christians Kings,	Jew	1.1.134		Barab
How ere the world goe, I'le make sure for one,	Jew	1.1.186		Barab
We may have time to make collection/Amongst the Inhabitants of	Jew	1.2.20		Govnr
And make thee poore and scorn'd of all the world,	Jew	1.2.108		1Knght
and of thy house they meane/To make a Nunnery, where none but	Jew	1.2.256		Abigal
To make me desperate in my poverty?	Jew	1.2.261		Barab
by me, for in extremitie/We ought to make barre of no policie.	Jew	1.2.273		Barab
To make attonement for my labouring soule.	Jew	1.2.326		Abigal
Of whom we would make sale in Malta here.	Jew	2.2.18		Bosco
To make me mindfull of my mortall sinnes,	Jew	2.3.74		Barab
Come home and there's no price shall make us part,	Jew	2.3.92		Barab
make account of me/As of thy fellow; we are villaines both:	Jew	2.3.213		Barab
yet I say make love to him;/Doe, it is requisite it should be	Jew	2.3.238		Barab
I'le make 'em friends againe.	Jew	2.3.357		Abigal
You'll make 'em friends?	Jew	2.3.358		Barab
To make me shew them favour severally,	Jew	3.3.38		Abigal
make her round and plump, and batten more then you are aware.	Jew	3.4.65	P	Ithimr
Nor make enquiry who hath sent it them.	Jew	3.4.81		Barab
And make him stand in feare of me.	Jew	3.6.43		2Fryar
Not? then I'le make thee, [rogue] <goe>.	Jew	4.1.95		2Fryar
Off with your girdle, make a hansom noose;	Jew	4.1.142		Barab
sort as if he had meant to make cleane my Boots with his lips;	Jew	4.2.31	P	Ithimr
I'le goe steale some mony from my Master to make me hansome:	Jew	4.2.49	P	Ithimr
I'le make him send me half he has, and glad he scapes so too.	Jew	4.2.67	P	Ithimr

MAKE (cont.)

You'd make a rich Poet, Sir.	Jew	4.2.122	P Pilia
I must make this villaine away:	Jew	4.3.29	P Barab
Make fires, heat irons, let the racke be fetch'd.	Jew	5.1.24	Govnr
Canst thou, as thou reportest, make Malta ours?	Jew	5.1.85	Calym
To make a passage for the running streames/And common channels	Jew	5.1.88	Barab
If this be true, I'le make thee Governor.	Jew	5.1.95	Calym
For thy desert we make thee Governor,	Jew	5.2.10	Calym
And let me see what mony thou canst make;	Jew	5.2.94	Barab
And then to make provision for the feast,	Jew	5.2.119	Barab
I fram'd the challenge that did make them meet:	Jew	5.5.82	Barab
And make his Gospel flourish in this land.	P 57	1.57	Navrre
The sent whereof doth make my head to ake.	P 171	3.6	OldQn
And make a shew as if all were well.	P 250	4.48	QnMoth
which my Lord of Guise/Did make in Paris amongst the Hugonites?	P 515	9.34	QnMoth
To make the justice of my heart relent:	P 533	10.6	Guise
To leavy armes and make these civill broyles:	P 730	14.33	Navrre
My sweet Joyeux, I make thee Generall,	P 743	15.1	King
My Lord, twere good to make them frends,	P 772	15.30	Eprnon
Ile make her shake off love with her heeles.	P 782	15.40	Mugern
Ile goe [take] <make> a walk/On purpose from the Court to meet	P 783	15.41	Mugern
come Epernoune/Lets goe seek the Duke and make them freends.	P 786	15.44	King
To make his glory great upon the earth.	P 790	16.4	Navrre
I hope will make the King surcease his hate:	P 792	16.6	Bartus
that dares make the Duke a cuckolde, and use a counterfeite key	P 806	17.1	P Souldr
And as Dictator make or warre or peace,	P 860	17.55	King
Make a discharge of all my counsell straite,	P 882	17.77	King
Tush, to be short, he meant to make me Munke,	P1039	19.109	King
These two will make one entire Duke of Guise,	P1060	19.130	King
And make the Guisians stoup that are alive.	P1071	19.141	King
make a duke a cuckolde and use a counterfeyt key to his	Paris	ms 1,p390	P Souldr
Ah words that make me surfet with delight:	Edw	1.1.3	Gavstn
Ile flatter these, and make them live in hope:	Edw	1.1.43	Gavstn
Well Mortimer, ile make thee rue these words,	Edw	1.1.91	Edward
And make him serve thee as thy chaplaine,	Edw	1.1.195	Edward
Ile make the prowdest of you stoope to him.	Edw	1.4.31	Edward
Make severall kingdomes of this monarchie,	Edw	1.4.70	Edward
With slaughtered priests [make] <may> Tibers channell swell,	Edw	1.4.102	Edward
And see how coldly his lookes make deniall.	Edw	1.4.235	Lncstr
I hope your honors make no question,	Edw	1.4.240	Mortmr
Such reasons make white blacke, and darke night day.	Edw	1.4.247	Lncstr
Twill make him vaile the topflag of his pride,	Edw	1.4.276	Mortmr
I make thee heere lord Marshall of the realme.	Edw	1.4.356	Edward
Whose proud fantastick liveries make such show,	Edw	1.4.410	Mortmr
Can you in words make showe of amitie,	Edw	2.2.32	Edward
He meanes to make us stoope by force of armes,	Edw	2.2.103	Lncstr
And make the people sweare to put him downe.	Edw	2.2.111	Lncstr
To make away a true man for a theefe.	Edw	2.5.70	Mortmr
Weel make quick worke, commend me to your maister/My friend,	Edw	2.6.12	Warwck
To make my preparation for Fraunce.	Edw	3.1.88	Queene
For now, even now, we marche to make them stoope,	Edw	3.1.183	Edward
Make Englands civill townes huge heapes of stones,	Edw	3.1.215	Edward
That Isabell shall make her plaints in vaine,	Edw	3.1.278	Levune
Then make for Fraunce amaine, [Levune] <Lewne> away,/Proclaime	Edw	3.1.280	Spencr
Come friends to Bristow, there to make us strong,	Edw	4.3.50	Edward
Make triall now of that philosophie,	Edw	4.7.17	Edward
Gone, gone alas, never to make returne.	Edw	4.7.104	Spencr
Make for a new life man, throw up thy eyes,	Edw	4.7.107	Baldck
To make usurping Mortimer a king?	Edw	5.1.37	Edward
But seekes to make a new elected king,	Edw	5.1.78	Edward
I might, but heavens and earth conspire/To make me miserable:	Edw	5.1.97	Edward
Make me despise this transitorie pompe,	Edw	5.1.108	Edward
Seeke all the meanes thou canst to make him droope,	Edw	5.2.54	Mortmr
And by the way to make him fret the more,	Edw	5.2.62	Mortmr
The more cause have I now to make amends.	Edw	5.2.103	Kent
Your passions make your dolours to increase.	Edw	5.3.15	Gurney
And when I frowne, make all the court looke pale,	Edw	5.4.53	Mortmr
This villain's sent to make away the king.	Edw	5.5.21	Matrvs
Couldst <Wouldst> thou make men <man> to live eternally,	F 52	1.1.24	Faust
Shall I make spirits fetch me what I please?	F 106	1.1.78	Faust
And make swift Rhine, circle faire Wittenberge <Wertenberge>:	F 116	1.1.88	Faust
I'le make my servile spirits to invent.	F 124	1.1.96	Faust
And make me blest with your sage conference.	F 126	1.1.98	Faust
Shall make all Nations to Canonize us:	F 147	1.1.119	Valdes
Will make thee vow to study nothing else.	F 164	1.1.136	Cornel
become of Faustus that/Was wont to make our schooles ring,	F 195	1.2.2	1Schol
The danger of his soule would make me mourne:	F 224	1.2.31	2Schol
Be it to make the Moone drop from her Sphere,	F 266	1.3.38	Faust
And make a bridge, thorough the moving Aire,	F 333	1.3.105	Faust
And make that Country <land>, continent to Spaine,	F 336	1.3.108	Faust
and I will make thee go, like Qui mihi discipulus.	F 355	1.4.13	P Wagner
about thee into Familiars, and make them tare thee in peeces.	F 362	1.4.20	P Wagner
[makes men] <make them> foolish that do use <trust> them most.	F 408	2.1.20	BdAngl
Now will I make an end immediately.	F 461	2.1.73	Faust
[And make my spirites pull his churches downe].	F 651	2.2.100A	Faust
That make <makes> safe passage, to each part of Rome.	F 816	3.1.38	Mephst
To make his Monkes and Abbots stand like Apes,	F 861	3.1.83	Mephst
This day shall make thee be admir'd in Rome.	F 867	3.1.89	Mephst
And make them sleepe so sound, that in their shapes,	F 895	3.1.117	Faust
Make haste againe, my good Lord Cardinalls,	F 972	3.1.194	Pope
And by their folly make some <us> merriment,	F 990	3.2.10	Faust
Lest Faustus make your shaven crownes to bleed.	F1007	3.2.27	Faust
Dick, make me a circle, and stand close at my backe, and stir	F1112	3.3.25	P Robin

MAKE (cont.)

Shall make poore Faustus to his utmost power, . . .	F1218	4.1.64		Faust
Il'e make you feele something anon, if my Art faile me not.	F1246	4.1.92	P	Faust
Make hast to help these noble Gentlemen, ...	F1421	4.2.97		1Soldr
And make us laughing stockes to all the world. . . .	F1450	4.3.20		Benvol
go rouse him, and make him give me my forty Dollors againe.	F1487	4.4.31	P	HrsCsr
doubt of that, for me thinkes you make no hast to wipe it out.	F1516	4.5.12	P	Hostss
kind I will make knowne unto you what my heart desires to have,	F1571	4.6.14	P	Lady
Wouldst thou make a Colossus of me, that thou askest me such	F1646	4.6.89	P	Faust
sir, I would make nothing of you, but I would faine know that.	F1648	4.6.91	P	Carter
Sweet Hellen make me immortall with a kisse: . . .	F1770	5.1.97		Faust
Faire natures eye, rise, rise againe and make/Perpetuall day:	F1931	5.2.135		Faust
thou serve me, and Ile make thee go like Qui mihi discipulus?	F App	p.229 13	P	Wagner
make al the maidens in our parish dance at my pleasure starke	F App	p.233 3	P	Robin
make thee druncke with ipocrase at any taberne in Europe for	F App	p.234 22	P	Robin
goe and make cleane our bootes which lie foule upon our handes,	F App	p.234 32	P	Robin
Therefore sweet Mephastophilis, let us make haste to Wertenberge	F App	p.239 94		Faust
Ide make a brave living on him; hee has a buttocke as slicke as	F App	p.239 116	P	HrsCsr
my fortie dollers againe, or Ile make it the dearest horse:	F App	p.240 137	P	HrsCsr
Ile make you wake ere I goe.	F App	p.241 153	P	HrsCsr
Souse downe the wals, and make a passage forth: . .	Lucan, First Booke			296
(Whom from his youth he bribde) needs make him king? .	Lucan, First Booke			315
These hands shall thrust the ram, and make them flie, .	Lucan, First Booke			385
snatcht up/Would make them sleepe securely in their tents.	Lucan, First Booke			516
out the date/Of slaughter; onely civill broiles make peace.	Lucan, First Booke			671
If loftie titles cannot make me thine, ...	Ovid's Elegies			1.3.7
Little I aske, a little entrance make, ...	Ovid's Elegies			1.6.3
Long Love my body to such use [makes] <make> slender/And to get	Ovid's Elegies			1.6.5
Make a small price, while thou thy nets doest lay, . .	Ovid's Elegies			1.8.69
And Isis now will shew what scuse to make.	Ovid's Elegies			1.8.74
By keeping of thy birth make but a shift.	Ovid's Elegies			1.8.94
Knights of the post of perjuries make saile, . . .	Ovid's Elegies			1.10.37
Let her make verses, and some blotted letter/On the last edge	Ovid's Elegies			1.11.21
And souldiours make them ready to the fight, . . .	Ovid's Elegies			1.13.14
[Doest] punish <ye >me, because yeares make him waine? .	Ovid's Elegies			1.13.41
take/In crooked [tramells] <trannels> crispy curles to make.	Ovid's Elegies			1.14.26
Wilt thou her fault learne, she may make thee tremble, .	Ovid's Elegies			2.2.17
such faults are sad/Nor make they any man that heare them glad.	Ovid's Elegies			2.2.52
A hundred reasons makes <make> me ever love. . . .	Ovid's Elegies			2.4.10
Some one of these might make the chastest fall. . .	Ovid's Elegies			2.4.32
and kissed so sweetely as might make/Wrath-kindled Jove away	Ovid's Elegies			2.5.51
Thou with thy quilles mightst make greene Emeralds darke,	Ovid's Elegies			2.6.21
For thee the East and West winds make me pale, . . .	Ovid's Elegies			2.11.9
And her small joynts incircling round hoope make thee. .	Ovid's Elegies			2.15.4
Not though thy face in all things make thee raigne, . .	Ovid's Elegies			2.17.11
She gave me leave, soft loves in time make hast, . .	Ovid's Elegies			3.1.69
Goddesse come here, make my love conquering. . . .	Ovid's Elegies			3.2.46
Shame, that should make me blush, I have no more. . .	Ovid's Elegies			3.5.78
Yet might her touch make youthfull Pilius fire, . .	Ovid's Elegies			3.6.41
Long have I borne much, mad thy faults me make: . .	Ovid's Elegies			3.10.1
We make Enceladus use a thousand armes, ...	Ovid's Elegies			3.11.27
Niobe flint, Callist we make a Beare, ...	Ovid's Elegies			3.11.31
Will you make shipwracke of your honest name, . . .	Ovid's Elegies			3.13.11
For whom succeeding times make greater mone. . . .	Hero and Leander			1.54
And I will make thee beds of Roses, ...	Passionate Shepherd			9

MAKERS

Cuckold-makers to clap hornes of honest mens heades o'this	F1317	4.1.163	P	Benvol

MAKES

That shaken thrise, makes Natures buildings quake, . .	Dido	1.1.11		Jupitr
And makes our hopes survive to [coming] <cunning> joyes: .	Dido	1.1.154		Achat
And makes Aeneas sinke at Didos feete.	Dido	2.1.117		Aeneas
What makes Iarbus here of all the rest?	Dido	3.3.13		Dido
Pardon me though I aske, love makes me aske. . . .	Dido	5.1.90		Dido
Besmer'd with blood, that makes a dainty show. . . .	1Tamb	1.1.80		Mycet
And makes a passage for all prosperous Armes, . . .	1Tamb	2.3.38		Cosroe
And makes my soule devine her overthrow.	1Tamb	3.2.87		Agidas
Fighting for passage, [makes] <make> the Welkin cracke, .	1Tamb	4.2.45		Tamb
And makes my deeds infamous through the world. . . .	1Tamb	5.1.391		Zenoc
friends and fellow kings)/Makes me to surfet in conceiving joy.	2Tamb	1.3.152		Tamb
tooles/Makes Earthquakes in the hearts of men and heaven.	2Tamb	2.2.8		Orcan
And makes the mighty God of armes his slave: . . .	2Tamb	3.4.53		Therid
My Lord, your presence makes them pale and wan. . . .	2Tamb	3.5.60		Usumc
Which makes me valiant, proud, ambitious, ...	2Tamb	4.1.116		Tamb
Makes walles a fresh with every thing that falles/Into the	2Tamb	5.1.18		Govnr
Which makes them fleet aloft and gaspe for aire. . .	2Tamb	5.1.209		Techel
Which makes them manage armes against thy state, . .	2Tamb	5.3.36		Usumc
What makes the Jew and Lodowicke so private? . . .	Jew	2.3.138		Mthias
it, and the Priest/That makes it knowne, being degraded first,	Jew	3.6.35		2Fryar
A thing that makes me tremble to unfold.	Jew	3.6.48		2Fryar
That makes these upstart heresies in Fraunce: . . .	P 81	2.24		Guise
but I hope it be/Only some naturall passion makes her sicke.	P 183	3.18		QnMarg
Spaine is the place where he makes peace and warre, .	P 710	14.13		Navrre
And makes his footstoole on securitie:	P 738	14.41		Navrre
But he that makes most lavish of his bloud. . . .	P1240	22.102		King
And strike off his that makes you threaten us. . . .	Edw	1.1.124		Mortmr
Kinde wordes, and mutuall talke, makes our greefe greater,	Edw	1.4.133		Edward
And makes me frantick for my Gaveston:	Edw	1.4.315		Edward
Unckle, tis this that makes me impatient.	Edw	1.4.419		Mortmr
And as she red, she smild, which makes me thinke, . .	Edw	2.1.21		Spencr
That makes a king seeme glorious to the world, . . .	Edw	2.2.175		Mortmr
this towardnes makes thy mother feare/Thou art not markt to	Edw	3.1.79		Queene
that now in France/Makes friends, to crosse the seas with her	Edw	3.1.270		Spencr
but madam, right makes roome,/Where weapons want, and though a	Edw	4.2.50		Mortmr

MAKES (cont.)
In civill broiles makes kin and country men/Slaughter . Edw 4.4.6 Queene
Ah pardon me, greefe makes me lunatick. . . . . . Edw 5.1.114 Edward
Who now makes Fortunes wheele turne as he please, . . Edw 5.2.53 Mortmr
This usage makes my miserie increase. . . . . Edw 5.3.16 Edward
This feare is that which makes me tremble thus, . . Edw 5.5.105 Edward
[makes men] <make them> foolish that do use <trust> them most. F 408 2.1.20 BdAngl
That make <makes> safe passage, to each part of Rome. . F 816 3.1.38 Mephst
This makes me wonder more then all the rest, that at this time F1578 4.6.21 P Duke
wait upon thy soule; the time is come/Which makes it forfeit. F1803 5.2.7 Lucifr
gives thee hornes, but makes thee weare them, feele on thy head. F App p.238 71 P Emper
this makes me wonder above the rest, that being in the dead F App p.242 16 P Duke
the deepe)/Puls them aloft, and makes the surge kisse heaven, Lucan, First Booke 417
this makes them/Run on the swords point and desire to die, Lucan, First Booke 456
Which makes the maine saile fal with hideous sound; . . Lucan, First Booke 498
Why grapples Rome, and makes war, having no foes? . . Lucan, First Booke 681
what makes my bed seem hard seeing it is soft? . . . Ovid's Elegies 1.2.1
Long Love my body to such use [makes] <make> slender/And to get Ovid's Elegies 1.6.5
And makes large streams back to their fountaines flow, . Ovid's Elegies 1.8.6
Please her, her hate makes others thee abhorre, . . Ovid's Elegies 2.3.11
A hundred reasons makes <make> me ever love. . . . Ovid's Elegies 2.4.10
Foldes up her armes, and makes low curtesie. . . . Ovid's Elegies 2.4.30
What's kept, we covet more: the care makes theft: . . Ovid's Elegies 3.4.25
Charmes change corne to grasse, and makes it dye, . . Ovid's Elegies 3.6.31
Greefe makes her pale, because she mooves not there. . Hero and Leander 1.60
Which makes me hope, although I am but base, . . . Hero and Leander 1.218
Perhaps, thy sacred Priesthood makes thee loath, . . Hero and Leander 1.293
Which makes him quickly re-enforce his speech, . . . Hero and Leander 1.313
Love alwaies makes those eloquent that have it. . . Hero and Leander 2.72

MAKEST
O cursed Mahomet that makest us thus/The slaves to Scythians 1Tamb 3.3.270 Zabina

MAKETH
The Ocean maketh more majesticall: . . . . . . Hero and Leander 1.226

MAKING
many neighbour kings/Were up in armes, for making thee my love? Dido 5.1.142 Dido
And making thee and me Techelles, kinges, ... 1Tamb 1.2.58 Usumc
Making it daunce with wanton majestie: . . . . . 1Tamb 2.1.26 Menaph
And making bonfires for my overthrow. . . . . . 1Tamb 3.3.238 Bajzth
Making the mantle of the richest night, ... 1Tamb 5.1.149 Tamb
Making thee mount as high as Eagles soare. . . . . 1Tamb 5.1.224 Bajzth
But making now a vertue of thy sight, ... 1Tamb 5.1.428 Arabia
Making them burie this effeminate brat, ... 2Tamb 4.1.162 Tamb
Making the Meteors, that like armed men/Are seene to march upon 2Tamb 4.1.201 Tamb
Making a passage for my troubled soule, ... 2Tamb 4.2.34 Olymp
Making their fiery gate above the cloudes, ... 2Tamb 4.3.9 Tamb
Making the Sea their [servant] <servants>, and the winds/To Jew 1.1.110 Barab
Making a profit of my policie; . . . . Jew 5.2.112 Barab
In making forraine warres and civile broiles. . . . P1029 19.99 King
Or making lowe legs to a noble man, ... Edw 2.1.38 Spencr
At al times charging home, and making havock; . . . . Lucan, First Booke 148
And whelm'd the world in darknesse, making men/Dispaire of day; Lucan, First Booke 540
Making her joy according to her hire. . . . . . Ovid's Elegies 1.10.32

MAK'ST
now Abigall, what mak'st thou/Amongst these hateful Christians? Jew 1.2.338 Barab
That thou maiest know with love thou mak'st me flame. . Ovid's Elegies 3.2.4

MAKSTE
Thou makste the suretie to the lawyer runne, ... Ovid's Elegies 1.13.19

MALADIES (See also MALLADIE)
And thousand desperate maladies beene cur'd <eas'd>? . F 50 1.1.22 Faust

MALE
Quam male conveniunt: . . . . Edw 1.4.13 MortSr
male, &c. . . . . F App p.232 36 Frier
male, &c. . . . . F App p.232 38 Frier

MALEA
Nor thy gulfes crooked Malea, would I feare. . . . Ovid's Elegies 2.16.24

MALEDICAT (See also MALE)
Maledicat Dominus. F1078 3.2.98 1Frier
Maledicat Dominus. F1080 3.2.100 1Frier
Maledicat Dominus. F1082 3.2.102 1Frier
Maledicat Dominus. F1084 3.2.104 1Frier
Maledicat Dominus. F1086 3.2.106 1Frier
maledicat dominus. . . . . F App p.232 32 Frier
maledicat dominus. . . . . F App p.232 34 Frier
maledicat dominus. . . . . F App p.233 40 Frier

MALES
Open the Males, yet guard the treasure sure, . . . 1Tamb 1.2.138 Tamb

MALGRADO
Breathing, in hope (malgrado all your beards, . . . Edw 2.5.5 Gavstn

MALICE
In spight of them shall malice my estate. . . . . 1Tamb 1.1.159 Cosroe
Endure as we the malice of our stars, ... 1Tamb 5.1.43 Govnr
Now by the malice of the angry Skies, ... 2Tamb 2.4.11 Tamb
But malice, falshood, and excessive pride, ... Jew 1.1.117 Barab
I know the malice of the yonger Mortimer, ... Edw 3.1.5 Edward
And in his heart revenging malice bare: . . . . . Hero and Leander 2.208

MALIGN'D
heard of any man but he/Malign'd the order of the Jacobines: Jew 4.1.104 Barab

MALLADIE
Which ad much danger to your malladie. . . . . . 2Tamb 5.3.55 Therid

MALLICE
To stop the mallice of his envious heart, ... P 30 1.30 Navrre

MALMESEY
Muskadine, Malmesey and Whippincrust, hold belly hold, and F 749 2.3.28 P Robin

MALTA			
Are smoothly gliding downe by Candie shoare/To Malta, through	Jew	1.1.47	Barab
Thy ships are safe, riding in Malta Rhode:	Jew	1.1.50	1Merch
Goe tell 'em the Jew of Malta sent thee, man:	Jew	1.1.66	Barab
Know Barabas, doth ride in Malta Rhode,	Jew	1.1.86	2Merch
My selfe in Malta, some in Italy,	Jew	1.1.126	Barab
The Turkes and those of Malta are in league.	Jew	1.1.159	Barab
And all the Jewes in Malta must be there.	Jew	1.1.168	2Jew
Umh; All the Jewes in Malta must be there?	Jew	1.1.169	Barab
Long to the Turke did Malta contribute;	Jew	1.1.180	Barab
As all the wealth of Malta cannot pay;	Jew	1.1.183	Barab
Know Knights of Malta, that we came from Rhodes,	Jew	1.2.2	Basso
What's Cyprus, Candy, and those other Iles/To us, or Malta?	Jew	1.2.6	Govnr
time to make collection/Amongst the Inhabitants of Malta for't.	Jew	1.2.21	Govnr
Farewell great [Governor], and brave Knights of Malta.	Jew	1.2.32	Calym
Goe one and call those Jewes of Malta hither:	Jew	1.2.34	Govnr
But here in Malta, where thou gotst thy wealth,	Jew	1.2.101	Govnr
which being valued/Amount to more then all the wealth in Malta.	Jew	1.2.134	Offcrs
The Jew of Malta, wretched Barabas;	Jew	1.2.318	Abigal
Governor of Malta, hither am I bound;	Jew	2.2.4	Bosco
Of whom we would make sale in Malta here.	Jew	2.2.18	Bosco
Welcome to Malta, and to all of us;	Jew	2.2.20	Govnr
Will Knights of Malta be in league with Turkes,	Jew	2.2.28	Bosco
And there in spite of Malta will I dwell:	Jew	2.3.15	Barab
Not for all Malta, therefore sheath your sword;	Jew	2.3.270	Barab
Are there not Jewes enow in Malta,	Jew	2.3.359	Barab
This Even they use in Malta here ('tis call'd/Saint Jaques	Jew	3.4.75	Barab
fares Callymath, What wind drives you thus into Malta rhode?	Jew	3.5.2	P Govnr
In Malta are no golden Minerals.	Jew	3.5.6	Govnr
To you of Malta thus saith Calymath:	Jew	3.5.7	Basso
And turne proud Malta to a wildernesse/For these intolerable	Jew	3.5.25	Basso
And now you men of Malta looke about,	Jew	3.5.29	Govnr
for store of wealth may I compare/With all the Jewes in Malta;	Jew	4.1.56	Barab
Musician, hast beene in Malta long?	Jew	4.4.54	Curtzn
And see that Malta be well fortifi'd;	Jew	5.1.2	Govnr
you men of Malta, heare me speake;/Shee is a Curtezane and he a	Jew	5.1.36	Barab
Canst thou, as thou reportest, make Malta ours?	Jew	5.1.85	Calym
I now am Governour of Malta; true,	Jew	5.2.29	Barab
But Malta hates me, and in hating me/My life's in danger, and	Jew	5.2.30	Barab
said, within this Ile/In Malta here, that I have got my goods,	Jew	5.2.68	Barab
I'le reare up Malta now remedilesse.	Jew	5.2.73	Barab
Here is my hand that I'le set Malta free:	Jew	5.2.95	Barab
And I will warrant Malta free for ever.	Jew	5.2.101	Barab
I cannot feast my men in Malta wals,	Jew	5.3.34	Calym
all his men/To come ashore, and march through Malta streets,	Jew	5.5.15	Msngr
thy father hath made good/The ruines done to Malta and to us,	Jew	5.5.112	Govnr
for Malta shall be freed,/Or Selim ne're returne to Ottoman.	Jew	5.5.113	Govnr
And live in Malta prisoner; for come [all] <call> the world/To	Jew	5.5.119	Govnr
Then conquer Malta, or endanger us.	Jew	5.5.122	Govnr
MALTA'S			
Bosco, thou shalt be Malta's Generall;	Jew	2.2.44	Govnr
Thou seest thy life, and Malta's happinesse,	Jew	5.2.52	Barab
I see no reason but of Malta's wracke,	Jew	5.2.58	Govnr
And as for Malta's ruine, thinke you not/'Twere slender policy	Jew	5.2.64	Barab
Will Barabas recover Malta's losse?	Jew	5.2.74	Govnr
Malta's Governor, I bring/A message unto mighty Calymath;	Jew	5.3.13	Msngr
MAN (Homograph)			
Like Illioneus speakes this Noble man,	Dido	2.1.47	Achat
be merrie man,/Heres to thy better fortune and good starres.	Dido	2.1.97	Dido
A man compact of craft and perjurie,	Dido	2.1.144	Aeneas
As therewithall the old man overcome,	Dido	2.1.157	Aeneas
For if that any man could conquer me,	Dido	3.1.137	Dido
I saw this man at Troy ere Troy was sackt.	Dido	3.1.141	Achat
This man and I were at Olympus games.	Dido	3.1.143	Illion
Why, man of Troy, doe I offend thine eyes?	Dido	3.3.17	Iarbus
But should that man of men (Dido except)/Have taunted me in	Dido	3.3.26	Iarbus
I mother, I shall one day be a man,	Dido	3.3.35	Cupid
Preferd before a man of majestie:	Dido	3.3.65	Iarbus
fond man, that were to warre gainst heaven,/And with one shaft	Dido	3.3.71	Iarbus
The man that I doe eye where ere I am,	Dido	3.4.18	Dido
That I might live to see this boy a man,	Dido	4.5.18	Nurse
Vaine man, what Monarky expectst thou here?	Dido	5.1.34	Hermes
Thy mother was no Goddesse perjurd man,	Dido	5.1.156	Dido
Now to be rulde and governed by a man,	1Tamb	1.1.12	Cosroe
thou art so meane a man)/And seeke not to inrich thy followers,	1Tamb	1.2.8	Zenoc
Are countermanded by a greater man:	1Tamb	1.2.22	Tamb
If outward habit judge the inward man.	1Tamb	1.2.163	Tamb
In thee (thou valiant man of Persea)	1Tamb	1.2.166	Tamb
Draw foorth thy sword, thou mighty man at Armes,	1Tamb	1.2.178	Tamb
If thou wilt stay with me, renowmed man,	1Tamb	1.2.188	Tamb
And valiant Tamburlaine, the man of fame,	1Tamb	2.1.2	Cosroe
The man that in the forhead of his fortune,	1Tamb	2.1.3	Cosroe
In every part proportioned like the man,	1Tamb	2.1.29	Menaph
The face and personage of a woondrous man:	1Tamb	2.1.32	Cosroe
In joyning with the man, ordain'd by heaven/To further every	1Tamb	2.1.52	Ortyg
What thinkst thou man, shal come of our attemptes?	1Tamb	2.3.3	Cosroe
For Kings are clouts that every man shoots at,	1Tamb	2.4.8	Mycet
And far from any man that is a foole.	1Tamb	2.4.12	Mycet
So do I thrice renowmed man at armes,	1Tamb	2.5.6	Cosroe
Let not a man so vile and barbarous,	1Tamb	3.2.26	Agidas
As when the Sea-man sees the Hyades/Gather an armye of Cemerian	1Tamb	3.2.76	Agidas
see how right the man/Hath hit the meaning of my Lord the King.	1Tamb	3.2.107	Techel
Each man a crown? why kingly fought ifaith.	1Tamb	3.3.216	Tamb

MAN (cont.)

That not a man should live to rue their fall.	1Tamb	4.1.35		Souldn
Stil dooth this man or rather God of war,	1Tamb	5.1.1		Govnr
Whereto ech man of rule hath given his hand,	1Tamb	5.1.102		1Virgn
With whose instinct the soule of man is toucht,	1Tamb	5.1.179		Tamb
That never sea-man yet discovered:	2Tamb	1.1.71		Orcan
That never look'd on man but Tamburlaine.	2Tamb	1.3.34		Tamb
If any man will hold him, I will strike,	2Tamb	1.3.102		Calyph
But neither man nor child in al the land:	2Tamb	1.3.197		Techel
Or treason in the fleshly heart of man,	2Tamb	2.2.37		Orcan
And thou shalt see a man greater than Mahomet,	2Tamb	3.4.46		Therid
What, take it man.	2Tamb	3.5.132	P	Orcan
I know sir, what it is to kil a man,	2Tamb	4.1.27		Calyph
For every man that so offends shall die.	2Tamb	4.3.76		Tamb
Wherein he spareth neither man nor child,	2Tamb	5.1.30		1Citzn
Techelles, Drowne them all, man, woman, and child,	2Tamb	5.1.170		Tamb
Shall sicknesse proove me now to be a man,	2Tamb	5.3.44		Tamb
Whereof a man may easily in a day/Tell that which may maintaine	Jew	1.1.10		Barab
Goe tell 'em the Jew of Malta sent thee, man:	Jew	1.1.66		Barab
What more may Heaven doe for earthly man/Then thus to powre out	Jew	1.1.107		Barab
Happily some haplesse man hath conscience,	Jew	1.1.119		Barab
like enough, why then let every man/Provide him, and be there	Jew	1.1.170		Barab
Thou art a Merchant, and a monied man,	Jew	1.2.53		1Knght
Then many perish for a private man:	Jew	1.2.99		Govnr
The man that dealeth righteously shall live:	Jew	1.2.116		Barab
but trust me 'tis a misery/To see a man in such affliction:	Jew	1.2.212		2Jew
Hinder her not, thou man of little faith,	Jew	1.2.340		1Fryar
and not a man surviv'd/To bring the haplesse newes to	Jew	2.2.50		Bosco
Are wondrous; and indeed doe no man good:	Jew	2.3.82		Barab
Tush man, we talk'd of Diamonds, not of Abigal.	Jew	2.3.151		Barab
but here's the Jews man.	Jew	3.1.22	P	Pilia
Mathias was the man that I held deare,	Jew	3.6.24		Abigal
I never heard of any man but he/Malign'd the order of the	Jew	4.1.103		Barab
So might my man and I hang with you for company.	Jew	4.1.182		Barab
reading of the letter, he look'd like a man of another world.	Jew	4.2.7	P	Pilia
base slave as he should be saluted by such a tall man as I am,	Jew	4.2.10	P	Pilia
I never knew a man take his death so patiently as this Fryar;	Jew	4.2.21	P	Ithimr
Never lov'd man servant as I doe Ithimore.	Jew	4.3.54		Barab
Hey Rivo Castiliano, a man's a man.	Jew	4.4.10	P	Ithimr
I had not thought he had been so brave a man.	Jew	4.4.16		Curtzn
Wilt drinke French-man, here's to thee with a--pox on this	Jew	4.4.32	P	Ithimr
Very mush, Mounsier, you no be his man?	Jew	4.4.57	P	Barab
His man?	Jew	4.4.58	P	Pilia
My Lord, the Curtezane and her man are dead;	Jew	5.1.50		1Offcr
And since that time they have hir'd a slave my man/To accuse me	Jew	5.1.75		Barab
Have speciall care that no man sally forth/Till you shall heare	Jew	5.4.2		Govnr
Doth not your grace know the man that gave them you?	P 172	3.7		Navrre
Not wel, but do remember such a man.	P 173	3.8		OldQn
To finde and to repay the man with death:	P 256	4.54		Charls
To hurt the noble man their soveraign loves.	P 259	4.57		Charls
them thither, and then/Beset his house that not a man may live.	P 289	5.16		Guise
To speek with me from such a man as he?	P 350	6.5		Seroun
Is in your judgment thought a learned man.	P 391	7.31		Guise
Now every man put of his burgonet,	P 449	7.89		Guise
As not a man may live without our leaves.	P 638	12.51		QnMoth
Tush man, let me alone with him,	P 648	12.61		QnMoth
Are these your secrets that no man must know?	P 678	13.22		Guise
Earle of Cornewall, king and lord of Man.	Edw	1.1.156		Edward
And secretary to, and lord of Man.	Edw	1.2.14		Warwck
And happie is the man, whom he vouchsafes/For vailing of his	Edw	1.2.18		Lncstr
Doth no man take exceptions at the slave?	Edw	1.2.25		MortSr
What man of noble birth can brooke this sight?	Edw	1.4.12		MortSr
And feare to offend the meanest noble man.	Edw	1.4.277		Mortmr
The liberall earle of Cornewall is the man,	Edw	2.1.10		Spencr
Or making lowe legs to a noble man,	Edw	2.1.38		Spencr
Welcome Lord governour of the Ile of Man.	Edw	2.2.67		Warwck
Weel have him ransomd man, be of good cheere.	Edw	2.2.116		Lncstr
Scarce shall you finde a man of more desart.	Edw	2.2.251		Gavstn
To make away a true man for a theefe.	Edw	2.5.70		Mortmr
majestie so earnestlie/Desires to see the man before his death,	Edw	2.5.78		Penbrk
Welcome old man, comst thou in Edwards aide?	Edw	3.1.34		Edward
Welcome ten thousand times, old man againe.	Edw	3.1.46		Edward
And this retire refresheth horse and man.	Edw	3.1.193		SpncrP
Why man, they say there is great execution/Done through the	Edw	4.3.6		Edward
Who wounds me with the name of Mortimer/That bloudy man?	Edw	4.7.39		Edward
Here man, rip up this panting brest of mine,	Edw	4.7.66		Edward
Make for a new life man, throw up thy eyes,	Edw	4.7.107		Baldck
not a thought so villanous/Can harbor in a man of noble birth.	Edw	5.1.132		Bartly
and in any case/Let no man comfort him, if he chaunce to weepe,	Edw	5.2.64		Mortmr
Tis not the first time I have killed a man.	Edw	5.4.30		Ltborn
That were enough to poison any man,	Edw	5.5.5		Matrvs
Who is the man dare say I murdered him?	Edw	5.6.40		Mortmr
What murtherer? bring foorth the man I sent.	Edw	5.6.49		Mortmr
And this the man that in his study sits.	F 28	Prol.28		1Chor
Yet art thou still but Faustus, and a man.	F 51	1.1.23		Faust
Couldst <Wouldst> thou make men <man> to live eternally,	F 52	1.1.24		Faust
Stretcheth as farre as doth the mind of man:	F 88	1.1.60		Faust
Sirra, wilt thou be my man and waite on me?	F 354	1.4.12	P	Wagner
faire/As thou, or any man that [breathes] <breathe> on earth.	F 558	2.2.7		Mephst
'Twas <It was> made for man; then he's <therefore is man> more	F 560	2.2.9		Mephst
was> made for man; then he's <therefore is man> more excellent.	F 560	2.2.9		Mephst
If Heaven was <it were> made for man, 'twas made for me:	F 561	2.2.10		Faust
<Tut, tis no matter man>, wee'l be bold with his <good cheare>.	F 808	(HC265)A	P	Mephst

MAN (cont.)
let me be cloyd/With all things that delight the heart of man. F 838 3.1.60 Faust
yee Lubbers look about/And find the man that doth this villany, F1056 3.2.76 Pope
if a man be drunke over night, the Divell cannot hurt him in F1201 4.1.47 P Benvol
And I had breath'd a man made free from harme. F1400 4.2.76 Faust
Nay feare nct man, we have no power to kill. F1440 4.3.10 Mrtino
Nay chafe not man, we all are sped. F1444 4.3.14 Mrtino
I am a very poore man, and have lost very much of late by horse F1464 4.4.8 P HrsCsr
Now am I a made man for ever. F1477 4.4.21 P HrsCsr
What art thou Faustus but a man condemn'd to die? F1478 4.4.22 Faust
fell to eating; and as I am a cursen man, he never left eating, F1530 4.5.26 P Carter
We are much beholding to this learned man. F1670 4.6.113 Lady
Though thou hast now offended like a man, F1710 5.1.37 OldMan
Torment sweet friend, that base and [crooked age] <aged man>, F1753 5.1.80 Faust
[Accursed Faustus, miserable man], F1788 5.1.115A OldMan
<to cure him, tis but a surffet, never feare man>. F1831 (HC270)A P 2Schol
That sometime grew within this learned man: F2004 5.3.22 4Chor
why then belike, if I were your man, I should be ful of vermine. F App p.229 22 P Clown
crownes a man were as good have as many english counters, F App p.230 33 P Clown
will no man looke? F App p.231 9 P Pope
It grieves my soule I never saw the man: F App p.237 28 Emper
Canst raise this man from hollow vaults below, F App p.237 30 Emper
Now am I made man for ever, Ile not leave my horse for fortie: F App p.239 114 P HrsCsr
what art thou Faustus but a man condemnd to die? F App p.240 121 P Faust
this learned man for the great kindnes he hath shewd to you. F App p.243 29 P Duke
Thus in his fright did each man strengthen Fame, Lucan, First Booke 481
Io, a strong man conquerd this Wench, hollow. Ovid's Elegies 1.7.38
That this, or that man may thy cheekes moist keepe. Ovid's Elegies 1.8.84
Only a Woman gets spoiles from a Man, Ovid's Elegies 1.10.29
by the pleasure/Which man and woman reape in equall measure? Ovid's Elegies 1.10.36
There sat the hang-man for mens neckes to angle. Ovid's Elegies 1.12.18
While Junos watch-man Io too much eyde, Ovid's Elegies 2.2.45
The man did grieve, the woman was defam'd. Ovid's Elegies 2.2.50
such faults are sad/Nor make they any man that heare them glad. Ovid's Elegies 2.2.52
She would be nimbler, lying with a man. Ovid's Elegies 2.4.24
What if a man with bond-women offend, Ovid's Elegies 2.8.9
The carefull ship-man now feares angry gusts, Ovid's Elegies 2.11.25
I was both horse-man, foote-man, standard bearer. Ovid's Elegies 2.12.14
Rude man, 'tis vaine, thy damsell to commend/To keepers trust: Ovid's Elegies 3.4.1
I prove neither youth nor man, but old and rustie. Ovid's Elegies 3.6.20
But neither was I man, nor lived then. Ovid's Elegies 3.6.60
What man will now take liberall arts in hand, Ovid's Elegies 3.7.1
Perhaps he'ele tell howe oft he slewe a man, Ovid's Elegies 3.7.21
With strong plough shares no man the earth did cleave, Ovid's Elegies 3.7.41
Whose workmanship both man and beast deceaves. Hero and Leander 1.20
And such as knew he was a man would say, Hero and Leander 1.87
The reason no man knowes, let it suffise, Hero and Leander 1.173
Lesse sinnes the poore rich man that starves himselfe, Hero and Leander 1.243
Where seeing a naked man, she scriecht for feare, Hero and Leander 2.237
Defend the fort, and keep the foe-man out. Hero and Leander 2.272

MANACKLES
and his chaine shall serve/For Manackles, till he be ransom'd 1Tamb 1.2.148 Tamb

MANACLED
And captive like be manacled and bound. Ovid's Elegies 1.2.30

MANADGE
they manadge peace, and rawe warres bloudy jawes, Ovid's Elegies 3.7.58

MANAGDE
But managde horses heads are lightly borne, Ovid's Elegies 1.2.16

MANAGE (See also MANNAGE)
Moov'd me tc manage armes against thy state. 1Tamb 2.7.16 Tamb
He be so mad to manage Armes with me, 1Tamb 3.1.34 Bajzth
And manage words with her as we will armes. 1Tamb 3.3.131 Tamb
That dare to manage armes with him, 1Tamb 3.3.198 Zabina
Not sparing any that can manage armes. 1Tamb 4.1.57 2Msngr
When men presume to manage armes with him. 1Tamb 5.1.478 Tamb
it out, or manage armes/Against thy selfe or thy confederates: 2Tamb 1.1.128 Sgsmnd
Which makes them manage armes against thy state, 2Tamb 5.3.36 Usumc
And by long rest forgct to manage armes, Lucan, First Booke 131
And Sequana that well could manage steeds; Lucan, First Booke 426

MANDRAKE
I dranke of Poppy and cold mandrake juyce; Jew 5.1.80 Barab

MANE
And on his loose mane the loose bridle laide. Ovid's Elegies 3.4.16

MANER
Our battaile then in martiall maner pitcht, 2Tamb 3.1.63 Orcan

MANFULLY
and had not we/Fought manfully, I had not told this tale: Dido 2.1.271 Aeneas

MANGLE
Meaning to mangle all thy Provinces. 1Tamb 1.1.17 Cosroe
Whet all your swords to mangle Tamburlain, 2Tamb 3.5.15 Callap

MANGLED
and on his speare/The mangled head of Priams yongest sonne, Dido 2.1.215 Aeneas
Mangled and torne, and all my entrals bath'd/In blood that 2Tamb 3.4.8 Capt
to lode thy barke/With soules of thousand mangled carkasses. 2Tamb 5.3.74 Tamb
We'll give his mangled limbs due buryall: F1999 5.3.17 2Schol

MANHOOD
Yet manhood would not serve, of force we fled, Dido 2.1.272 Aeneas
Thou doost dishonor manhood, and thy house. 2Tamb 4.1.32 Celeb

MANICO
Therfore I tooke my course to Manico: 2Tamb 1.3.198 Techel

MANIE
And with how manie cities sacrifice/He celebrated her [sad] 2Tamb Prol.7 Prolog

MANIE (cont.)
This head was beat with manie a churlish billow, . . — Hero and Leander 2.251

MANIFEST
Beside, the more to manifest our love, — Edw 3.1.52 Edward
Nor is it easily prov'd though manifest, — Ovid's Elegies 2.2.55

MANIFESTLY
it be to injure them/That have so manifestly wronged us, — Jew 1.2.275 Abigal

MANLY
Achates, thou shalt be so [manly] <meanly> clad, — Dido 3.1.128 Dido
Twixt his manly pitch,/A pearle more worth, then all the world — 1Tamb 2.1.11 Menaph
Or Monster turned to a manly shape, — 1Tamb 2.6.16 Ortyg
Faith, and Techelles, it was manly done: — 1Tamb 3.2.109 Usumc
Will batter Turrets with their manly fists. — 1Tamb 3.3.111 Bajzth
you wil be thought/More childish valourous than manly wise: — 2Tamb 4.1.17 Calyph
Souldier shall defile/His manly fingers with so faint a boy. — 2Tamb 4.1.164 Tamb
Learne thou of Faustus manly fortitude, — F 313 1.3.85 Faust
Men handle those, all manly hopes resigne, — Ovid's Elegies 2.3.9

MANNA
As sure as heaven rain'd Manna for the Jewes, — Jew 2.3.248 Barab

MANNAGE
When I am old and cannot mannage armes, — 2Tamb 1.3.59 Tamb
To please himselfe with mannage of the warres, — P 459 8.9 Anjoy
We undertake to mannage these our warres/Against the proud — P 699 14.2 Navrre
And either never mannage army more, — P 793 16.7 Bartus
their huge power made him bould/To mannage greater deeds; the — Lucan, First Booke 463

MANNAGING
In mannaging those fierce barbarian mindes: — Dido 1.1.92 Jupitr

MANN'D
A thousand Gallies mann'd with Christian slaves/I freely give — 2Tamb 1.2.32 Callap

MANNER (See also MANER)
They would not come in warlike manner thus. — Jew 1.1.155 1Jew
But Faustus/<thou must> Write it in manner of a Deed of Gift. — F 449 2.1.61 Mephst
[Tut] <But> Faustus, in hell is all manner of delight. — F 713 2.2.165 Lucifr
To see the Pope and manner of his Court, — F 776 2.3.55 2Chor
in that manner that they best liv'd in, in their most — F App p.237 47 P Faust
troupe, in tuckt up vestures,/After the Gabine manner: — Lucan, First Booke 596
And her in humble manner thus beseech. — Hero and Leander 1.314

MANNERS
I loath her manners, love her bodies feature. — Ovid's Elegies 3.10.38

MANORS
As I have manors, castels, townes, and towers: — Edw 3.1.133 Edward

MAN'S
Hey Rivo Castiliano, a man's a man. — Jew 4.4.10 P Ithimr
my Lord, his man's now at my lodging/That was his Agent, he'll — Jew 5.1.16 Curtzn

MANS
Raven that tolls/The sicke mans passeport in her hollow beake, — Jew 2.1.2 Barab
The whore stands to be bought for each mans mony/And seekes — Ovid's Elegies 1.10.21
Dead is that speaking image of mans voice, — Ovid's Elegies 2.6.37
And even the ring performe a mans part well. — Ovid's Elegies 2.15.26
From no mans reading fearing to be sav'd. — Ovid's Elegies 3.1.54
Against thy selfe, mans nature, thou wert cunning, — Ovid's Elegies 3.7.45
Nor lesse at mans prosperity any grudge. — Ovid's Elegies 3.9.6
The plough-mans hopes were frustrate at the last. — Ovid's Elegies 3.9.34
Some swore he was a maid in mans attire, — Hero and Leander 1.83

MANSION
Convert his mansion to a Nunnery, — Jew 1.2.129 1Knght
For that must be thy mansion, there to dwell. — F1882 5.2.86 Mephst

MANTLE
Making the mantle of the richest night, — 1Tamb 5.1.149 Tamb
Do not thou so, but throw thy mantle hence, — Ovid's Elegies 1.4.49

MANTLED
The ground is mantled with such multitudes. — 1Tamb 3.1.53 Moroc

MANTUA
In Virgil Mantua joyes: — Ovid's Elegies 3.14.7

MANY (See also MANIE)
How many dangers have we over past? — Dido 1.1.145 Aeneas
For many tales goe of that Cities fall, — Dido 2.1.108 Dido
and with this sword/Sent many of their savadge ghosts to hell. — Dido 2.1.212 Aeneas
(And yet have I had many mightier Kings)/Hast had the greatest — Dido 3.1.12 Dido
altar, where Ile offer up/As many kisses as the Sea hath sands, — Dido 3.1.88 Dido
That hath so many unresisted friends: — Dido 3.2.50 Juno
Aeneas may commaund as many Moores, — Dido 4.4.62 Dido
White Swannes, and many lovely water fowles: — Dido 4.5.11 Nurse
Hast thou forgot how many neighbour kings/Were up in armes, for — Dido 5.1.141 Dido
To triumph over many Provinces. — 1Tamb 1.1.173 Cosroe
As if as many kinges as could encompasse thee, — 1Tamb 2.5.4 Tamb
As many circumcised Turkes we have, — 1Tamb 3.1.8 Bajzth
Will tell how many thousand men he slew. — 1Tamb 3.2.43 Agidas
Withdraw as many more to follow him. — 1Tamb 3.3.22 Bassoe
not endure to strike/So many blowes as I have heads for thee. — 1Tamb 3.3.144 Bajzth
bed, where many a Lord/In prime and glorie of his loving joy, — 1Tamb 5.1.83 1Virgn
And gore thy body with as many wounds. — 1Tamb 5.1.216 Bajzth
Amongst so many crownes of burnisht gold, — 2Tamb 1.2.30 Callap
Have under me as many kings as you, — 2Tamb 1.3.55 Celeb
rest and have one Epitaph/Writ in as many severall languages, — 2Tamb 2.4.135 Tamb
And I as many from Jerusalem, — 2Tamb 3.1.44 Jrslem
And I as many bring from Trebizon, — 2Tamb 3.1.49 Trebiz
much like so many suns/That halfe dismay the majesty of heaven: — 2Tamb 4.1.2 Amyras
Might find as many woondrous myracles, — 2Tamb 4.2.85 Therid
Having as many bullets in his flesh, — 2Tamb 5.1.159 Tamb
Many will talke of Title to a Crowne: — Jew Prol.18 Machvl
comes to more/Then many Merchants of the Towne are worth, — Jew 1.1.64 1Merch
Many in France, and wealthy every one: — Jew 1.1.127 Barab

MANY (cont.)

I have no charge, nor many children,	Jew	1.1.136		Barab
With whom they have attempted many times,	Jew	1.1.164		Barab
Then many perish for a private man:	Jew	1.2.99		Govnr
His house will harbour many holy Nuns.	Jew	1.2.130		1Knght
I, Daughter, for Religion/Hides many mischiefes from suspition.	Jew	1.2.282		Barab
Some have we fir'd, and many have we sunke;	Jew	2.2.15		Bosco
And yet I'le give her many a golden crosse/With Christian	Jew	2.3.296		Barab
Here's many words but no crownes; the crownes.	Jew	4.3.46	P	Pilia
The many favours which your grace hath showne,	P 9	1.9		Navrre
and fully executes/Matters of importe, aimed at by many,	P 111	2.54		Guise
But slay as many as we can come neer.	P 326	5.53		Anjoy
Cannot but march with many graces more:	P 578	11.43		Pleshe
How many noble men have lost their lives,	P 795	16.9		Navrre
Yet lives/My brother Duke Dumaine, and many moe:	P1099	20.9		Cardnl
And Northward Gaveston hath many friends.	Edw	1.1.129		Lncstr
I know my lord, many will stomack me,	Edw	2.2.260		Gavstn
traind to armes/And bloudie warres, so many valiant knights,	Edw	2.5.16		Lncstr
thy mother feare/Thou art not markt to many daies on earth.	Edw	3.1.80		Queene
I will have heads, and lives, for him as many,	Edw	3.1.132		Edward
Where weapons want, and though a many friends/Are made away, as	Edw	4.2.51		Mortmr
Thus after many threats of wrathfull warre,	Edw	4.3.1		Edward
And so must die, though pitied by many.	Edw	5.3.24		Edward
Had I as many soules, as there be Starres,	F 330	1.3.102		Faust
seene many boyes with [such pickadevaunts] <beards> I am sure.	F 345	1.4.3	P	Robin
<Tel me>, are there many Spheares <heavens> above the Moone?	F 586	2.2.35		Faust
How many Heavens, or Spheares, are there?	F 609	2.2.58	P	Faust
you have seene many boyes with such pickadevaunts as I have.	F App	p.229 2	P	Clown
crownes a man were as good have as many english counters,	F App	p.230 34	P	Clown
such riches, subdued so many kingdomes, as we that do succeede,	F App	p.236 20	P	Emper
Italy many yeares hath lyen until'd,	Lucan, First Booke	28		
of barbarous Tygars having lapt/The bloud of many a heard,	Lucan, First Booke	328		
And many came from shallow Isara,	Lucan, First Booke	400		
bringing newes/Of present war, made many lies and tales.	Lucan, First Booke	468		
the death of many men/Meetes in one period.	Lucan, First Booke	649		
Many a yeare these [furious] <firious> broiles let last,	Lucan, First Booke	667		
Unlesse I erre, full many shalt thou burne,	Ovid's Elegies	1.2.43		
Many to rob is more sure, and lesse hatefull,	Ovid's Elegies	1.8.55		
And therof many thousand he rehearses.	Ovid's Elegies	1.8.58		
Let them aske some-what, many asking little,	Ovid's Elegies	1.8.89		
By many hands great wealth is quickly got.	Ovid's Elegies	1.8.92		
[May] <Many> bounteous [lome] <love> Alcinous fruite resigne.	Ovid's Elegies	1.10.56		
fire/And [thinke] <thinkes> her chast whom many doe desire.	Ovid's Elegies	2.2.14		
Or justifie my vices being many,	Ovid's Elegies	2.4.2		
Now many guests were gone, the feast being done,	Ovid's Elegies	2.5.21		
Thy mouth to taste of many meates did balke.	Ovid's Elegies	2.6.30		
One among many is to grieve thee tooke.	Ovid's Elegies	2.7.4		
So many men and maidens without love,	Ovid's Elegies	2.9.15		
There wine being fild, thou many things shalt tell,	Ovid's Elegies	2.11.49		
With the Atrides many gainde renowne.	Ovid's Elegies	2.12.10		
And me with many, but yet me without murther,	Ovid's Elegies	2.12.27		
And many by me to get glory crave.	Ovid's Elegies	2.17.28		
Great gods what kisses, and how many gave she?	Ovid's Elegies	2.19.18		
So shall my love continue many yeares,	Ovid's Elegies	2.19.23		
Poore Semele, among so many burn'd;	Ovid's Elegies	3.3.37		
Honour what friends thy wife gives, sheele give many:	Ovid's Elegies	3.4.45		
One [her] <she> commands, who many things can give.	Ovid's Elegies	3.7.62		
I feare with me is common now to many.	Ovid's Elegies	3.11.6		
Her kirtle blew, whereon was many a staine,	Hero and Leander	1.15		
Many would praise the sweet smell as she past,	Hero and Leander	1.21		
That heavenly path, with many a curious dint,	Hero and Leander	1.68		
the water for a kis/Of his owne shadow, and despising many,	Hero and Leander	1.75		
Thither resorted many a wandring guest,	Hero and Leander	1.94		
And many seeing great princes were denied,	Hero and Leander	1.129		
These arguments he us'de, and many more,	Hero and Leander	1.329		
And many poore excuses did she find,	Hero and Leander	2.6		
And as he turnd, cast many a lustfull glaunce,	Hero and Leander	2.186		

MAP

And rest the map of weatherbeaten woe:	Dido	1.1.158	Achat
And with this pen reduce them to a Map,	1Tamb	4.4.78	Tamb
Give me a Map, then let me see how much/Is left for me to	2Tamb	5.3.123	Tamb

MAPLE

to her I consecrate/My faithfull tables being vile maple late.	Ovid's Elegies	1.11.28

MARBLE

at whose latter gaspe/Joves marble statue gan to bend the brow,	Dido	2.1.257	Aeneas
Upon the marble turrets of my Court/Sit like to Venus in her	2Tamb	4.2.41	Therid
In which the essentiall fourme of Marble stone,	2Tamb	4.2.62	Olymp
I strowed powder on the Marble stones,	Jew	2.3.209	Ithimr
lookes shewed/Like marble from the Parian Mountaines hewed.	Ovid's Elegies	1.7.52	
If on the Marble Theater I looke,	Ovid's Elegies	2.7.3	
Maides on the shore, with marble white feete tread,	Ovid's Elegies	2.11.15	

MARCELLUS

Brabbling Marcellus; Cato whom fooles reverence;	Lucan, First Booke	313

MARCH (Homograph; See also MARTCH)

And through the breach did march into the streetes,	Dido	2.1.189	Aeneas
But ere he march in Asia, or display/His vagrant Ensigne in the	1Tamb	1.1.44	Meandr
And you march on their slaughtered carkasses:	1Tamb	2.2.69	Meandr
and with our Sun-bright armour as we march,	1Tamb	2.3.221	Tamb
Then will we march to all those Indian Mines,	1Tamb	2.5.41	Cosroe
marshal us the way/We use to march upon the slaughtered foe:	1Tamb	3.3.149	Tamb
And when they see me march in black aray.	1Tamb	4.2.119	Tamb
And when the ground wheron my souldiers march/Shal rise aloft	2Tamb	1.3.13	Tamb
Under my collors march ten thousand Greeks,	2Tamb	1.3.118	Therid

MARCH (cont.)			
And with my power did march to Zansibar,	2Tamb	1.3.194	Techel
Now will we march from proud Orminius mount/To faire Natolia,	2Tamb	2.2.2	Orcan
I march to meet and aide my neigbor kings,	2Tamb	3.1.60	Soria
March in your armour thorowe watery Fens,	2Tamb	3.2.56	Tamb
like armed men/Are seene to march upon the towers of heaven,	2Tamb	4.1.202	Tamb
Come let us march against the powers of heaven,	2Tamb	5.3.48	Tamb
Techelles let us march,/And weary Death with bearing soules to	2Tamb	5.3.76	Tamb
all his men/To come ashore, and march through Malta streets,	Jew	5.5.15	Msngr
So march away, and let due praise be given/Neither to Fate nor	Jew	5.5.123	Govnr
Cannot but march with many graces more:	P 578	11.43	Pleshe
To march against the rebellious King Navarre:	P 745	15.3	King
And let them march away to France amaine:	P 917	18.18	Navrre
And underneath thy banners march who will,	Edw	1.1.88	Mortmr
Forslowe no time, sweet Lancaster lets march.	Edw	2.4.40	Warwck
Gentlewoman, her name was <mistress> Margery March-beere:	F 700	2.2.149	P Glutny
Now while their part is weake, and feares, march hence,	Lucan, First Booke		281
March towards Roome; and you fierce men of Rhene/Leaving your	Lucan, First Booke		460
nights deawie hoast/March fast away:	Ovid's Elegies		1.6.56
MARCHANTS			
Let marchants seeke wealth, [and] with perjured lips,	Ovid's Elegies		2.10.33
MARCH-BEERE			
Gentlewoman, her name was <mistress> Margery March-beere:	F 700	2.2.149	P Glutny
MARCHE			
Thus arme in arme, the king and he dooth marche:	Edw	1.2.20	Lncstr
And marche to fire them from their starting holes.	Edw	3.1.127	Spencr
For now, even now, we marche to make them stoope,	Edw	3.1.183	Edward
Sound drums and trumpets, marche with me my friends,	Edw	3.1.260	Edward
MARCHETH			
Marcheth in Asia major, where the streames,	2Tamb	5.2.2	Callap
MARCHING			
That now is marching neer to Parthia:	1Tamb	2.1.65	Cosroe
Marching from Cairon northward with his camp,	2Tamb	1.1.47	Gazell
And sent them marching up to Belgasar,	2Tamb	2.1.19	Fredrk
Comes marching on us, and determines straight,	2Tamb	2.2.27	1Msngr
Marching about the ayer with armed men,	2Tamb	5.2.34	Amasia
Not marching <now> in the fields of Thrasimen,	F 1	Prol.1	1Chor
MARCHT			
And so in troopes all marcht to Tenedos:	Dido	2.1.135	Aeneas
But once, and then thy souldiers marcht like players,	Edw	2.2.183	Mortmr
in a trenche/Strake off his head, and marcht unto the campe.	Edw	3.1.120	Arundl
Or darts which Parthians backward shoot) marcht on/And then	Lucan, First Booke		232
and the rest/Marcht not intirely, and yet hide the ground,	Lucan, First Booke		474
MARE (Homograph)			
the Gulfe, call'd by the name/Mare magiore, of th'inhabitantes:	2Tamb	1.3.215	Therid
All bordring on the Mare-major sea:	2Tamb	3.1.51	Trebiz
Bordering on Mare Roso neere to Meca.	2Tamb	3.5.131	Callap
The Mare askes not the Horse, the Cowe the Bull,	Ovid's Elegies		1.10.27
MARE-MAJOR			
All bordring on the Mare-major sea:	2Tamb	3.1.51	Trebiz
MARES			
Here's a drench to poyson a whole stable of Flanders mares:	Jew	3.4.112	P Ithimr
wheeles spun/And what with Mares ranck humour may be done.	Ovid's Elegies		1.8.8
MARGARET			
O no, sweet Margaret, the fatall poyson/Workes within my head,	P 184	3.19	OldQn
MARGERY			
Gentlewoman, her name was <mistress> Margery March-beere:	F 700	2.2.149	P Glutny
MARIA			
And so did faire Maria send for me:	Jew	3.6.5	1Fryar
MARIAGE			
Pitie the mariage bed, where many a Lord/In prime and glorie of	1Tamb	5.1.83	1Virgn
For now her mariage time shall worke us rest.	1Tamb	5.1.504	Techel
We wil our celebrated rites of mariage solemnize.	1Tamb	5.1.534	Tamb
That linke you in mariage with our daughter heer:	P 14	1.14	QnMoth
And now my lords the mariage rites perfourm'd,	P 18	1.18	Charls
Oh fatall was this mariage to us all.	P 202	3.37	Admral
or at the mariage day/The cup of Hymen had beene full of	Edw	1.4.173	Queene
A second mariage twixt thy selfe and me.	Edw	1.4.335	Edward
And then his mariage shalbe solemnized,	Edw	1.4.377	Edward
Seeing that he talkes thus of my mariage day?	Edw	2.1.69	Neece
Cosin, this day shalbe your mariage feast,	Edw	2.2.256	Edward
Come lets away, and when the mariage ends,	Edw	2.2.264	Edward
MARIE			
I marie am I: have you any suite to me?	1Tamb	2.4.24	Mycet
MARINER (See MARRINERS)			
MARIUS			
And Marius head above cold Tav'ron peering/(His grave broke	Lucan, First Booke		581
MARK			
and mark your weapons point/That wil be blunted if the blow be	2Tamb	4.2.79	Olymp
My Lord, but did you mark the Cardinall/The Guises brother, and	P 47	1.47	Admral
MARKE (Homograph)			
Then marke him, Sir, and take him hence.	Jew	2.3.131	1Offcr
I, marke him, you were best, for this is he	Jew	2.3.132	Barab
But marke how I am blest for plaguing them,	Jew	2.3.199	Barab
No? doe but marke how earnestly she pleads.	Edw	1.4.234	Warwck
My Lord of Lancaster, marke the respect.	Edw	1.4.248	Mortmr
Marke you but that my lord of Lancaster.	Edw	1.4.263	Warwck
I for a while, but Baldock marke the end,	Edw	2.1.16	Spencr
It is the chiefest marke they levell at.	Edw	5.3.12	Edward
not of Paradice or <nor> Creation, but marke the <this> shew.	F 659	2.2.108	P Lucifr
To marke him how he doth demeane himselfe.	F1806	5.2.10	Belzeb
Faustus, marke what I shall say, As I was sometime solitary set,	F App	p.236 17	P Emper
with kissing/And on her necke a wantons marke not missing.	Ovid's Elegies		1.7.42

MARKE (cont.)
I charge thee marke her eyes and front in reading, — Ovid's Elegies 1.11.17
And passe our scarlet of red saffrons marke. — Ovid's Elegies 2.6.22
MARKED
The boord is marked thus that covers it. — Jew 1.2.350 Barab
The boord is marked thus that covers it, — Jew 1.2.356 Barab
MARKES
let him viewe/And thy neck with lascivious markes made blew. — Ovid's Elegies 1.8.98
And words that seem'd for certaine markes to be. — Ovid's Elegies 2.5.20
Thou arguest she doth secret markes unfold. — Ovid's Elegies 2.7.6
The ditcher no markes on the ground did leave. — Ovid's Elegies 3.7.42
MARKET
This is the Market-place, here let 'em stand: — Jew 2.3.1 1Offcr
Come, I have made a reasonable market, — Jew 2.3.161 1Offcr
and so forestall his market, and set up your standing where you — P 809 17.4 P Souldr
The souldiours having won the market place, — Lucan, First Booke 238
MARKET-PLACE
This is the Market-place, here let 'em stand: — Jew 2.3.1 1Offcr
MARKETPLACE
then, here's the marketplace; whats the price of this slave, — Jew 2.3.97 P Barab
MARKETT
the markett and sett upe your standinge where you shold not: — Paris ms 5,p390 P Souldr
MARKT
My Lord of Loraine have you markt of late,/How Charles our — P 512 9.31 QnMoth
the riches of my realme/Can ransome him, ah he is markt to die, — Edw 3.1.4 Edward
thy mother feare/Thou art not markt to many daies on earth. — Edw 3.1.80 Queene
And Cupide who hath markt me for thy pray, — Ovid's Elegies 1.3.12
MAROES
There saw we learned Maroes golden tombe: — F 791 3.1.13 Faust
MARQUES
The Marques is a noble Gentleman, — Edw 4.2.32 Queene
MARQUESSE
sir John of Henolt, brother to the Marquesse, into Flaunders: — Edw 4.3.32 P Spencr
MARRIAGE (See also MARIAGE)
My Juno ware upon her marriage day, — Dido 1.1.43 Jupitr
Why should not they then joyne in marriage, — Dido 3.2.74 Juno
Scorning our loves and royall marriage rites, — Dido 4.2.16 Iarbus
If ever Hymen lowr'd at marriage rites, — P 58 2.1 Guise
<Tut Faustus>, Marriage is but a ceremoniall toy, — F 535 2.1.147 Mephst
Compar'd with marriage, had you tried them both, — Hero and Leander 1.263
MARRINERS
And Marriners, albeit the keele be sound, — Lucan, First Booke 500
MARROWE
She sawe, and as her marrowe tooke the flame, — Ovid's Elegies 3.9.27
MARRY (Homograph; See also MARIE, MARY)
I'le buy you, and marry you to Lady vanity, if you doe well. — Jew 2.3.116 P Barab
Marry will I, Sir. — Jew 2.3.160 Barab
your Lordship wud disdaine/To marry with the daughter of a Jew: — Jew 2.3.295 Barab
Marry the Turke shall be one of my godfathers, — Jew 4.1.111 Barab
I have no husband, sweet, I'le marry thee. — Jew 4.2.87 Curtzn
Marry, even he that strangled Bernardine, poyson'd the Nuns, — Jew 5.1.33 P Ithimr
Marry sir, in having a smack in all, — P 385 7.25 Guise
Marry if thou hadst, thou mightst have had the stab, — P 776 15.34 King
I marry, such a garde as this dooth well. — Edw 2.2.131 Mortmr
Yes marry sir, and I thanke you to. — F 368 1.4.26 P Robin
Marry sir, I'le tell you the bravest tale how a Conjurer serv'd — F1521 4.5.17 P Carter
I marry can I, we are under heaven. — F1615 4.6.58 P Carter
MARS (See also HESUS)
Till that a Princesse priest conceav'd by Mars, — Dido 1.1.106 Jupitr
By chance sweete Queene, as Mars and Venus met. — Dido 3.4.4 Aeneas
Though Mars himselfe the angrie God of armes, — 1Tamb 2.7.58 Tamb
For person like to proove a second Mars. — 2Tamb 4.1.35 Calyph
Where Mars did mate the warlicke Carthagens <Carthaginians>, — F 2 Prol.2 1Chor
Nor are the names of Saturne, Mars, or Jupiter, — F 594 2.2.43 Mephst
thirty yeares, Jupiter in twelve, Mars in four, the Sun, Venus, — F 604 2.2.53 P Faust
and every yeare/Frauds and corruption in the field of Mars; — Lucan, First Booke 182
Mars, 'tis thou enflam'st/The threatning Scorpion with the — Lucan, First Booke 657
is faint; swift Hermes retrograde;/Mars onely rules the heaven: — Lucan, First Booke 662
While Mars doth take the Aonian harpe to play? — Ovid's Elegies 1.1.16
Th'opposed starre of Mars hath done thee harme, — Ovid's Elegies 1.8.29
starre of Mars hath done thee harme,/Now Mars is gone: — Ovid's Elegies 1.8.30
Now Mars doth rage abroad without all pitty, — Ovid's Elegies 1.8.41
What age fits Mars, with Venus doth agree, — Ovid's Elegies 1.9.3
Mars in the deed the black-smithes net did stable, — Ovid's Elegies 1.9.39
But Venus often to her Mars such brought. — Ovid's Elegies 2.5.28
Cupid by thee, Mars in great doubt doth trample, — Ovid's Elegies 2.9.47
Is golden love hid in Mars mid alarmes. — Ovid's Elegies 2.18.36
Souldiour applaud thy Mars: — Ovid's Elegies 3.2.49
Mars girts his deadly sword on for my harme: — Ovid's Elegies 3.3.27
Where Mars his sonnes not without fault did breed, — Ovid's Elegies 3.4.39
She wailing Mars sinne, and her uncles crime, — Ovid's Elegies 3.5.49
Blood-quaffing Mars, heaving the yron net, — Hero and Leander 1.151
Then drerie Mars, carowsing Nectar boules. — Hero and Leander 2.258
And [them] <then> like Mars and Ericine displayd, — Hero and Leander 2.305
MARSHAL
Our conquering swords shall marshal us the way/We use to march — 1Tamb 3.3.148 Tamb
MARSHALL
I make thee heere lord Marshall of the realme. — Edw 1.4.356 Edward
My lord, ile marshall so your enemies, — Edw 1.4.357 Mortmr
Strike off his head, he shall have marshall lawe. — Edw 5.4.89 Mortmr
MARTCH
Whose ransome made them martch in coates of gold, — 1Tamb 1.1.143 Ceneus
Come let us martch. — 1Tamb 1.2.136 Techel

MARTCH (cont.)			
Strike up the Drum and martch corragiously,	1Tamb	2.2.72	Meandr
untill thou see/Me martch victoriously with all my men,	1Tamb	3.3.127	Tamb
That leave no ground for thee to martch upon.	1Tamb	3.3.147	Bajzth
But ere I martch to wealthy Persea,	1Tamb	4.2.47	Tamb
Me thinks we martch as Meliager did,	1Tamb	4.3.1	Souldn
And martch in cottages of strowed weeds:	1Tamb	5.1.187	Tamb
Arabian King together/Martch on us with such eager violence,	1Tamb	5.1.200	Techel
And martch with such a multitude of men,	2Tamb	1.3.56	Celeb
For we will martch against them presently.	2Tamb	1.3.105	Tamb
And after martch to Turky with our Campe,	2Tamb	1.3.158	Tamb
From thence unto Cazates did I martch,	2Tamb	1.3.191	Techel
To martch with me under this bloody flag:	2Tamb	2.4.116	Tamb
stature <statue>/And martch about it with my mourning campe,	2Tamb	2.4.141	Tamb
That you may dryfoot martch through lakes and pooles,	2Tamb	3.2.86	Tamb
And with his hoste [martcht] <martch> round about the earth,	2Tamb	3.2.111	Tamb
Usumcasane now come let us martch/Towards Techelles and	2Tamb	3.2.145	Tamb
Till we prepare our martch to Babylon,	2Tamb	4.3.93	Tamb
Hath trode the Meisures, do my souldiers martch,	2Tamb	5.1.75	Tamb
When this is done, we'll martch from Babylon,	2Tamb	5.1.127	Tamb
Here I began to martch towards Persea,	2Tamb	5.3.126	Tamb
Sound trumpets my lord and forward let us martch,	Edw	4.4.28	SrJohn
MARTCH'D			
And I have martch'd along the river Nile,	2Tamb	1.3.186	Techel
MARTCHT			
You that have martcht with happy Tamburlaine,	1Tamb	4.4.121	Tamb
Now have we martcht from faire Natolia/Two hundred leagues, and	2Tamb	1.1.6	Orcan
our men of Barbary have martcht/Foure hundred miles with armour	2Tamb	1.3.174	Usumc
And with his hoste [martcht] <martch> round about the earth,	2Tamb	3.2.111	Tamb
Thus have wee martcht Northwarde from Tamburlaine,	2Tamb	3.3.1	Therid
Then martcht I into Egypt and Arabia,	2Tamb	5.3.130	Tamb
MARTIAL			
Engins and munition/Exceed the forces of their martial men.	1Tamb	4.1.29	2Msngr
And with the thunder of his martial tooles/Makes Earthquakes in	2Tamb	2.2.7	Orcan
But I perceive my martial strength is spent,	2Tamb	5.3.119	Tamb
MARTIALL			
Wanting both pay and martiall discipline,	1Tamb	1.1.147	Ceneus
My martiall prises with five hundred men,	1Tamb	1.2.102	Tamb
And by thy martiall face and stout aspect,	1Tamb	1.2.170	Tamb
Those thousand horse shall sweat with martiall spoile/Of	1Tamb	1.2.191	Tamb
Yet being void of Martiall discipline,	1Tamb	2.2.44	Meandr
To some direction in your martiall deeds,	1Tamb	2.3.12	Tamb
Onelie disposed to martiall Stratagems?	1Tamb	3.2.41	Agidas
Whose smiling stars gives him assured hope/Of martiall triumph,	1Tamb	3.3.43	Tamb
this happy conquest/Triumph, and solemnize a martiall feast.	1Tamb	3.3.273	Tamb
Of lawfull armes, or martiall discipline:	1Tamb	4.1.65	Souldn
Nor change my Martiall observations,	1Tamb	5.1.122	Tamb
That purchac'd kingdomes by your martiall deeds,	1Tamb	5.1.523	Tamb
As martiall presents to our friends at home,	2Tamb	1.1.35	Orcan
Not martiall as the sons of Tamburlaine.	2Tamb	1.3.22	Tamb
hath followed long/The martiall sword of mighty Tamburlaine,	2Tamb	3.1.28	Callap
Our battaile then in martiall maner pitcht,	2Tamb	3.1.63	Orcan
my striving hands/From martiall justice on thy wretched soule.	2Tamb	4.1.96	Tamb
And joy'd the fire of this martiall flesh,	2Tamb	4.1.106	Tamb
Shal al be loden with the martiall spoiles/We will convay with	2Tamb	4.3.105	Tamb
A martiall people, worthy such a King,	P 455	8.5	Anjoy
MARTIN			
Martin del Bosco, I have heard of thee;	Jew	2.2.19	Govnr
Pickeld-herring <Pickle-herring>, and Martin Martlemasse-beefe:	F 698	2.2.147	P Glutny
MARTINO			
O help me gentle friend; where is Martino?	F1432	4.3.2	Fredrk
Martino see,/Benvolio's hornes againe.	F1436	4.3.6	Fredrk
MARTLEMASSE			
Pickeld-herring <Pickle-herring>, and Martin Martlemasse-beefe:	F 698	2.2.147	P Glutny
MARTLEMASSE-BEEFE			
Pickeld-herring <Pickle-herring>, and Martin Martlemasse-beefe:	F 698	2.2.147	P Glutny
MARTYRED			
and feare presents/A thousand sorrowes to my martyred soule:	1Tamb	5.1.384	Zenoc
Which thoughts are martyred with endles torments.	Edw	5.1.80	Edward
MARVEILE			
I marveile much he stole it not away.	1Tamb	2.4.42	Mycet
Marveile not though the faire Bride did incite/The drunken	Ovid's Elegies		1.4.7
MARVEL (See also MERVAILE)			
[No marvel tho the angry Greekes pursu'd]/[With tenne yeares	F1699	5.1.26A	3Schol
MARVELL			
Yet much I marvell that I cannot finde,	Dido	1.1.180	Achat
No marvell Dido though thou be in love,	Dido	5.1.44	Aeneas
No marvell though thou scorne thy noble peeres,	Edw	2.2.217	Kent
No marvell then, though Hero would not yeeld/So soone to part	Hero and Leander		2.83
MARY			
I mary, there spake a Doctor indeed, and 'faith Ile drinke a	F1626	4.6.69	P HrsCsr
I mary master doctor, now theres a signe of grace in you, when	F App	p.237 44	P Knight
MAS			
Mas but for the name of french crownes a man were as good have	F App	p.230 33	P Clown
mas Doctor Lopus was never such a Doctor, has given me a	F App	p.240 127	P HrsCsr
MASKE			
When as she meanes to maske the world with clowdes.	Dido	4.1.6	Iarbus
The townes-men maske in silke and cloath of gold,	1Tamb	4.2.108	Tamb
Ye Furies that can maske invisible,	1Tamb	4.4.17	Bajzth
them seeme as black/As is the Island where the Furies maske,	2Tamb	3.2.12	Tamb
MASKED			
Jove sometime masked in a Shepheards weed,	1Tamb	1.2.199	Tamb
MASKES			
inventing maskes and stately showes for her,	2Tamb	4.2.94	Therid

MASKES (cont.)
Therefore ile have Italian maskes by night, . . . Edw 1.1.55 Gavstn
maskes, lascivious showes/And prodigall gifts bestowed on Edw 2.2.157 Mortmr
Plaies, maskes, and all that stern age counteth evill. . Hero and Leander 1.302

MASSACRE
Shall massacre those greedy minded slaves. . . . . 1Tamb 2.2.67 Meandr
That lingring paines may massacre his heart. . . . . 1Tamb 5.1.228 Zabina
What order wil you set downe for the Massacre? . . . P 229 4.27 QnMoth
They that shalbe actors in this Massacre, ... P 231 4.29 Guise
That seeke to massacre our guiltles lives. . . . . P 261 4.59 Admral
Shall in the entrance of this Massacre, ... P 286 5.13 Guise
And so lets forward to the Massacre. . . . . . P 330 5.57 Guise
That you were one that made this Massacre. . . . . P 436 7.76 Navrre
Yet will we not that the Massacre shall end: . . . . P 444 7.84 Guise

MASSACRED
They have not long since massacred our Camp. . . . . 2Tamb 2.1.10 Fredrk
Blowne up, and all thy souldiers massacred. . . . . Jew 5.5.107 Govnr
(For whose effects my soule is massacred)/Infect thy gracious P 192 3.27 QnMarg
My Lord, they say/That all the protestants are massacred. P 432 7.72 Navrre

MASSACRES
Daily inur'd to broyles and Massacres, ... Dido 2.1.124 Aeneas
Surchargde with guilt of thousand massacres, ... P1022 19.92 King

MASSE (Homograph; See also MAS, MESSE)
Then rise at midnight to a solemne masse. . . . . Jew 1.2.373 Mthias
to goe and consumate/The rest, with hearing of a holy Masse: P 20 1.20 Charls
masse see where he is, God save you maister doctor. . . F App p.239 99 P HrsCsr
In hell were harbourd, here was found no masse. . . . Ovid's Elegies 3.7.38
In heaping up a masse of drossie pelfe, ... Hero and Leander 1.244

MASSIE
Oares of massie Ivorie full of holes, ... Dido 3.1.118 Dido
their neckes/Hangs massie chaines of golde downe to the waste, 1Tamb 1.2.126 Souldr
For he is grosse and like the massie earth, ... 1Tamb 2.7.31 Therid
And I sat downe, cloth'd with the massie robe, . . . 2Tamb 3.2.123 Tamb

MASSY
As when the massy substance of the earth, ... 2Tamb 1.1.89 Orcan
Created of the massy dregges of earth, ... 2Tamb 4.1.123 Tamb
And cloth'd in costly cloath of massy gold, ... 2Tamb 4.2.40 Therid
And guide this massy substance of the earthe, ... 2Tamb 5.3.18 Techel
Within the massy entrailes of the earth: . . . . . F 174 1.1.146 Cornel

MAST (Homograph)
The sailes wrapt up, the mast and tacklings downe, . . . 2Tamb 1.2.59 Callap
On mast of oakes, first oracles, men fed, ... Ovid's Elegies 3.9.9

MASTE
By charmes maste drops from okes, from vines grapes fall, Ovid's Elegies 3.6.33

MASTER (See also MAISTER, MAYSTERS)
Eternall Jove, great master of the Clowdes, ... Dido 4.2.4 Iarbus
But art thou master in a ship of mine, ... Jew 1.1.61 Barab
Sirra, which of my ships art thou Master of? . . . . Jew 1.1.70 Barab
Oh brave, master, I worship your nose for this. . . . Jew 2.3.173 Ithimr
Faith, Master,/In setting Christian villages on fire, . . Jew 2.3.202 Ithimr
Faith Master, I thinke by this/You purchase both their lives; Jew 2.3.365 Ithimr
Oh, master, that I might have a hand in this. . . . Jew 2.3.368 Ithimr
Oh my master. . . . . Jew 3.3.7 P Ithimr
bottle-nos'd knave to my Master, that ever Gentleman had. Jew 3.3.10 P Ithimr
Oh, my master has the bravest policy. . . . . . . Jew 3.3.12 P Ithimr
devil invented a challenge, my master writ it, and I carried it, Jew 3.3.18 P Ithimr
Oh master. . . . . Jew 3.4.34 P Ithimr
Who I, master? . . . . Jew 3.4.39 P Ithimr
Here 'tis, Master. . . . . Jew 3.4.55 P Ithimr
master, wil you poison her with a messe of rice [porredge]? Jew 3.4.64 P Ithimr
How master? . . . . Jew 3.4.73 P Ithimr
Pray doe, and let me help you, master. . . . . . . Jew 3.4.86 P Ithimr
Troth master, I'm loth such a pot of pottage should be spoyld. Jew 3.4.89 P Ithimr
Well, master, I goe. . . . . Jew 3.4.94 P Ithimr
That's brave, master, but think you it wil not be known? . Jew 4.1.8 P Ithimr
Good master let me poyson all the Monks. . . . . . Jew 4.1.14 Ithimr
Look, look, master, here come two religious Caterpillers. . Jew 4.1.21 P Ithimr
And so doe I, master, therfore speake 'em faire. . . . Jew 4.1.27 Ithimr
Part 'em, master, part 'em. . . . . Jew 4.1.97 P Ithimr
You loyter, master, wherefore stay [we] <me> thus? . . . Jew 4.1.139 Ithimr
Nay, master, be rul'd by me a little; so, let him leane upon Jew 4.1.153 P Ithimr
I, master, he's slain; look how his brains drop out on's nose. Jew 4.1.178 P Ithimr
Fie upon 'em, master, will you turne Christian, when holy Jew 4.1.193 P Ithimr
I'le goe steale some mony from my Master to make me hansome: Jew 4.2.49 P Ithimr
Ten hundred thousand crownes,--Master Barabas. . . . Jew 4.2.71 P Ithimr
Well Master Doctor, an your Divels come not away quickly, you F1241 4.1.87 P Benvol
Then good Master Doctor, ... F1308 4.1.154 Emper
Grone you Master Doctor? . . . . F1365 4.2.41 Fredrk
Master Doctor Faustus, since our conference about faire Ladies, F1681 5.1.8 P 1Schol
therefore Master Doctor, if you will doe us so much <that> F1684 5.1.11 P 1Schol
I mary master doctor, now theres a signe of grace in you, when F App p.237 44 P Knight
Beleeve me master Doctor, this makes me wonder above the rest, F App p.242 16 P Duke
all to good, be Augury vaine, and Tages/Th'arts master falce. Lucan, First Booke 636

MASTERED
the cursed object/Whose Fortunes never mastered her griefs: 1Tamb 5.1.414 Zenoc
Force mastered right, the strongest govern'd all. . . . Lucan, First Booke 177

MASTER'S
I hold my head my master's hungry: . . . . Jew 3.4.51 P Ithimr

MASTERS
Come neere, my love, come neere, thy masters life, . . . Jew 3.4.14 Barab
Sweet Bellamira, would I had my Masters wealth for thy sake. Jew 4.2.55 P Ithimr

MASTIFF (See MASTIVES)

MASTIVES
Fierce Mastives hould; the vestall fires went out, . . . Lucan, First Booke 547

MASTS			
Our Masts the furious windes strooke over bourd:	Dido	3.1.110	Aeneas
The Masts whereon thy swelling sailes shall hang,	Dido	3.1.122	Dido
Now let him hang my favours on his masts,	Dido	4.4.159	Dido
Yet hath she tane away my oares and masts,	Dido	5.1.60	Aeneas
MASTY			
A masty <nasty> slave he is.	Jew	4.4.69	Pilia
MATCH			
And Venus, let there be a match confirmd/Betwixt these two,	Dido	3.2.77	Juno
Thou art no match for mightie Tamburlaine.	1Tamb	2.4.40	Tamb
Wil match thee with a viceroy or a king.	2Tamb	3.4.41	Techel
Raise me to match the faire Aldeboran,	2Tamb	4.3.61	Tamb
before your mother/Lest she mistrust the match that is in hand:	Jew	2.3.147	Barab
But I had thought the match had beene broke off,	Edw	2.1.25	Baldck
How say yong Prince, what thinke you of the match?	Edw	4.2.67	SrJohn
Do [match] <watch> the number of the daies contain'd,	F 821	3.1.43	Mephst
<As match the dayes within one compleate yeare>,	F 821	(HC265)A	Mephst
having fild/Her meeting hornes to match her brothers light,	Lucan, First Booke		536
MATCHLESSE			
But matchlesse strength and magnanimity?	2Tamb	4.1.85	Amyras
And matchlesse beautifull;/As had you seene her 'twould have	Jew	1.2.384	Mthias
MATCHT			
If I were matcht with mightie Tamburlaine.	1Tamb	3.2.55	Zenoc
MATE			
Thou shalt be crown'd a king and be my mate.	2Tamb	1.2.66	Callap
Whose jealousie admits no second Mate,	2Tamb	2.4.12	Tamb
Where Mars did mate the warlicke Carthagens <Carthaginians>,	F 2	Prol.2	1Chor
to detaine)/Thou oughtst therefore to scorne me for thy mate,	Ovid's Elegies		2.17.13
With Laodameia mate to her dead Lord.	Ovid's Elegies		2.18.38
MATED			
mated and amaz'd/To heare the King thus threaten like himselfe?	1Tamb	1.1.107	Menaph
MATES			
Fancie and modestie shall live as mates,	Dido	3.2.58	Venus
The dreames (brave mates) that did beset my bed,	Dido	4.3.16	Aeneas
Triumph, my mates, our travels are at end,	Dido	5.1.1	Aeneas
Question with thy companions and thy mates.	Edw	2.5.73	Mortmr
yong-mens mates, to go/If they determine to persever so.	Ovid's Elegies		2.16.17
MATHIAS			
Why how now Don Mathias, in a dump?	Jew	1.2.374	Lodowk
Farewell Mathias.	Jew	1.2.393	Lodowk
For Don Mathias tels me she is faire.	Jew	2.3.35	Lodowk
Yonder comes Don Mathias, let us stay;	Jew	2.3.140	Barab
Tell me, Mathias, is not that the Jew?	Jew	2.3.152	Mater
O father, Don Mathias is my love.	Jew	2.3.237	Abigal
So sure shall he and Don Mathias dye:	Jew	2.3.249	Barab
Whither goes Don Mathias? stay a while.	Jew	2.3.251	Barab
No, Mathias, no, but sends them backe,/And when he comes, she	Jew	2.3.261	Barab
Mathias, as thou lov'st me, not a word.	Jew	2.3.277	Barab
Why, loves she Don Mathias?	Jew	2.3.285	Lodowk
But keepe thy heart till Don Mathias comes.	Jew	2.3.307	Barab
What greater gift can poore Mathias have?	Jew	2.3.346	Mthias
I will have Don Mathias, he is my love.	Jew	2.3.361	Abigal
Take this and beare it to Mathias streight,	Jew	2.3.370	Barab
now Abigall shall see/Whether Mathias holds her deare or no.	Jew	3.2.2	Mthias
Now Lodowicke, now Mathias, so;	Jew	3.2.6	Barab
Who is this? my sonne Mathias slaine!	Jew	3.2.12	Mater
Know you not of Mathias and Don Lodowickes disaster?	Jew	3.3.16	P Ithimr
and I carried it, first to Lodowicke, and imprimis to Mathias.	Jew	3.3.19	P Ithimr
Yet Don Mathias ne're offended thee:	Jew	3.3.41	Abigal
Nor on his sonne, but by Mathias meanes;	Jew	3.3.45	Abigal
Nor on Mathias, but by murdering me.	Jew	3.3.46	Abigal
('tis so) of my device/In Don Mathias and Lodovicoes deaths:	Jew	3.4.8	Barab
You knew Mathias and Don Lodowicke?	Jew	3.6.20	Abigal
Mathias was the man that I held deare,	Jew	3.6.24	Abigal
I, but Barabas, remember Mathias and Don Lodowick.	Jew	4.1.43	P 2Fryar
You knew Mathias and the Governors son; he and I kild 'em both,	Jew	4.4.17	P Ithimr
Mathias did it not, it was the Jew.	Jew	5.1.11	Curtzn
your sonne and Mathias were both contracted unto Abigall; [he]	Jew	5.1.28	P Ithimr
Was my Mathias murder'd by the Jew?	Jew	5.1.44	Mater
MATINS (See MATTINS)			
MATRE			
What lord [Arundell] <Matre>, dost thou come alone?	Edw	3.1.89	Edward
Tell me [Arundell] <Matre>, died he ere thou camst,	Edw	3.1.92	Edward
MATREVIS (See also MATRE)			
Whose there? call hither Gurney and Matrevis.	Edw	5.2.38	Mortmr
Matrevis, write a letter presently/Unto the Lord of Bartley	Edw	5.2.47	Mortmr
Matrevis and the rest may beare the blame,	Edw	5.4.15	Mortmr
Deliver this to Gurney and Matrevis,	Edw	5.4.41	Mortmr
And so do I, Matrevis:	Edw	5.5.7	Gurney
Or as Matrevis, hewne from the Caucasus,	Edw	5.5.54	Edward
To rid thee of thy life. Matrevis come.	Edw	5.5.107	Ltborn
Ist done, Matrevis, and the murtherer dead?	Edw	5.6.1	Mortmr
Matrevis, if thou now growest penitent/Ile be thy ghostly	Edw	5.6.3	Mortmr
MATRON			
then the Nunnes/And their vaild Matron, who alone might view	Lucan, First Booke		597
So runnes a Matron through th'amazed streetes,	Lucan, First Booke		675
MATTER			
How now, what's the matter?	1Tamb	1.2.110	Tamb
That's no matter sir, for being a king, for Tamburlain came up	2Tamb	3.1.73	P Almeda
Whose matter is the flesh of Tamburlain,	2Tamb	4.1.113	Tamb
Whose matter is incorporat in your flesh.	2Tamb	5.3.165	Amyras
Tut, tut, there is some other matter in't.	Jew	1.1.160	Barab
These silly men mistake the matter cleane.	Jew	1.1.179	Barab

MATTER (cont.)			
Of so great matter should be made the ground.	P 126	2.69	Guise
Madam in this matter/We will employ you and your little sonne,	Edw	3.1.69	Edward
<Tut, tis no matter man>, wee'l be bold with his <good cheare>.	F 808	(HC265)A	P Mephst
'Tis no matter, let him come; an he follow us, I'le so conjure	F1091	3.3.4	P Robin
Never out face me for the matter, for sure the cup is betweene	F1107	3.3.20	P Vintnr
hold, tis no matter for thy head, for that's arm'd sufficiently.	F1288	4.1.134	P Emper
This is but a small matter:	F1574	4.6.17	P Faust
you may be ashamed to burden honest men with a matter of truth.	F App	p.234 15	P Rafe
not, and from the gaping liver/Squis'd matter; through the cal,	Lucan, First Booke	624	
Being fittest matter for a wanton wit,	Ovid's Elegies	1.1.24	
I hate faire Paper should writte matter lacke.	Ovid's Elegies	1.11.20	
Ile thinke all true, though it be feigned matter.	Ovid's Elegies	2.11.53	
Thou doest alone give matter to my wit.	Ovid's Elegies	2.17.34	
MATTERS			
Contrives, imagines and fully executes/Matters of importe,	P 111	2.54	Guise
You have matters of more waight to thinke upon,	Edw	2.2.8	Mortmr
Arundell, we will gratifie the king/In other matters, he must	Edw	2.5.44	Warwck
sweete delight's] dispute/In th'heavenly matters of Theologie,	F 19	Prol.19	1Chor
I have other matters in hand, let the horses walk themselves	F 726	2.3.5	P Robin
of us here, that have waded as deepe into matters, as other men,	F 741	2.3.20	P Robin
MATTINS			
And now stay/That bel that to the devils mattins rings.	P 448	7.88	Guise
MATTOCKS			
When well-toss'd mattocks did the ground prepare,	Ovid's Elegies	3.9.31	
MAURITANIAN			
And will my guard with Mauritanian darts,	Dido	4.4.68	Dido
Mounted on lusty Mauritanian Steeds,	1Tamb	3.3.16	Bassoe
MAUSOLUS			
Then in as rich a tombe as Mausolus,	2Tamb	2.4.133	Tamb
MAXIME			
Which maxime had Phaleris observ'd,	Jew	Prol.24	Machvl
MAXIMUS			
What saith Maximus?	2Tamb	5.1.1	Govnr
MAY (Homograph; See also 'TMAY, MAIEST, MAIST, MAIT, MOUGHT)			
How may I credite these thy flattering termes,	Dido	1.1.109	Venus
And chaunging heavens may those good daies returne,	Dido	1.1.150	Aeneas
That we may make a fire to warme us with,	Dido	1.1.167	Aeneas
But what may I faire Virgin call your name?	Dido	1.1.188	Aeneas
That they may trip more lightly ore the lawndes,	Dido	1.1.207	Venus
Whence may you come, or whither will you goe?	Dido	1.1.215	Venus
As poore distressed miserie may pleade:	Dido	1.2.6	Illion
Well may I view her, but she sees not me.	Dido	2.1.73	Aeneas
May it please your grace to let Aeneas waite:	Dido	2.1.87	Aeneas
Thy fortune may be greater then thy birth,	Dido	2.1.90	Dido
May I entreate thee to discourse at large,	Dido	2.1.106	Dido
That she may dote upon Aeneas love:	Dido	2.1.327	Venus
But that I may enjoy what I desire:	Dido	3.1.9	Iarbus
Feare not Iarbus, Dido may be thine.	Dido	3.1.19	Dido
So that Aeneas may but stay with me.	Dido	3.1.133	Dido
And are not these as faire as faire may be?	Dido	3.1.140	Dido
Because it may be thou shalt be my love:	Dido	3.1.170	Dido
how may I deserve/Such amourous favours at thy beautious hand?	Dido	3.2.64	Juno
Women may wrong by priviledge of love:	Dido	3.3.25	Iarbus
Why, what is it that Dido may desire/And not obtaine, be it in	Dido	3.4.7	Aeneas
It is not ought Aeneas may atchieve?	Dido	3.4.11	Aeneas
Who then of all so cruell may he be,	Dido	3.4.16	Aeneas
That I may pacifie that gloomie Jove,	Dido	4.2.2	Iarbus
But may be slackt untill another time:	Dido	4.2.26	Anna
Whose yeelding heart may yeeld thee more reliefe.	Dido	4.2.36	Anna
I may nor will list to such loathsome chaunge,	Dido	4.2.47	Iarbus
On whom the nimble windes may all day waight,	Dido	4.3.23	Aeneas
We may as one saile into Italy.	Dido	4.3.30	Aeneas
So she may have Aeneas in her armes.	Dido	4.3.42	Illion
I may not dure this female drudgerie,	Dido	4.3.55	Aeneas
It may be he will steale away with them:	Dido	4.4.3	Dido
Aeneas may commaund as many Moores,	Dido	4.4.62	Dido
I, but it may be he will leave my love,	Dido	4.4.97	Dido
I cannot see him frowne, it may not be:	Dido	4.4.112	Dido
Ile set the casement open that the windes/May enter in, and	Dido	4.4.131	Dido
So I may have Aeneas in mine armes.	Dido	4.4.135	Dido
Why, I may live a hundred yeares,/Fourescore is but a girles	Dido	4.5.31	Nurse
Wherein the day may evermore delight:	Dido	5.1.7	Aeneas
Whose wealthie streames may waite upon her towers,	Dido	5.1.9	Aeneas
Which neither art nor reason may atchieve,	Dido	5.1.65	Aeneas
As how I pray, may I entreate you tell.	Dido	5.1.67	Iarbus
And yet I may not stay, Dido farewell.	Dido	5.1.104	Aeneas
Fare well may Dido, so Aeneas stay,	Dido	5.1.107	Dido
That I may learne to beare it patiently,	Dido	5.1.208	Dido
That they may melt and I fall in his armes:	Dido	5.1.245	Dido
That I may swim to him like Tritons neece:	Dido	5.1.247	Dido
That I may tice a Dolphin to the shoare,	Dido	5.1.249	Dido
They may be still tormented with unrest,	Dido	5.1.305	Dido
That may revenge this treason to a Queene,	Dido	5.1.307	Dido
That Gods and men may pitie this my death,	Dido	5.1.327	Anna
Whom I may tearme a Damon for thy love.	1Tamb	1.1.50	Mycet
Our life is fraile, and we may die to day.	1Tamb	1.1.68	Mycet
That I may view these milk-white steeds of mine,	1Tamb	1.1.77	Mycet
That he may win the Babylonians hearts,	1Tamb	1.1.90	Cosroe
You may doe well to kisse it then.	1Tamb	1.1.98	Cosroe
How easely may you with a mightie hoste,	1Tamb	1.1.129	Menaph
And Jove may never let me longer live,	1Tamb	1.1.170	Cosroe
Then I may seeke to gratifie your love,	1Tamb	1.1.171	Cosroe

MAY (cont.)

As easely may you get the Souldans crowne,	1Tamb	1.2.27	Tamb
Both may invest you Empresse of the East:	1Tamb	1.2.46	Tamb
May have the leading of so great an host,	1Tamb	1.2.48	Tamb
May serve for ransome to our liberties:	1Tamb	1.2.75	Agidas
That we may travelle into Siria,	1Tamb	1.2.77	Agidas
That their reflexions may amaze the Perseans.	1Tamb	1.2.140	Tamb
May we become immortall like the Gods.	1Tamb	1.2.201	Tamb
Long may Theridamas remaine with us.	1Tamb	1.2.240	Usumc
If wealth or riches may prevaile with them,	1Tamb	2.2.61	Meandr
May triumph in our long expected Fate.	1Tamb	2.3.44	Tamb
That it may reach the King of Perseas crowne,	1Tamb	2.3.53	Cosroe
Till I may see thee hem'd with armed men.	1Tamb	2.4.38	Tamb
may I presume/To know the cause of these unquiet fits:	1Tamb	3.2.1	Agidas
That I may live and die with Tamburlaine.	1Tamb	3.2.24	Zenoc
More honor and lesse paine it may procure,	1Tamb	3.2.97	Agidas
Which thy prolonged Fates may draw on thee:	1Tamb	3.2.101	Agidas
Wherewith he may excruciate thy soule.	1Tamb	3.2.104	Agidas
That we may raigne as kings of Affrica.	1Tamb	3.3.99	Therid
And may my Love, the king of Persea,	1Tamb	3.3.132	Zenoc
That I may see him issue Conquerour.	1Tamb	3.3.194	Zenoc
Though he be prisoner, he may be ransomed.	1Tamb	3.3.231	Zabina
May have fresh warning to go war with us,	1Tamb	4.1.71	Souldn
That I may rise into my royall throne.	1Tamb	4.2.15	Tamb
That may command thee peecemeale to be torne,	1Tamb	4.2.23	Tamb
Now may we see Damascus lofty towers,	1Tamb	4.2.102	Tamb
Fall to, and never may your meat digest.	1Tamb	4.4.16	Bajzth
And may this banquet proove as omenous,	1Tamb	4.4.23	Zabina
unto your majesty/May merit favour at your highnesse handes,	1Tamb	4.4.70	Zenoc
Or may be forc'd, to make me Emperour.	1Tamb	4.4.90	Tamb
That this devise may proove propitious,	1Tamb	5.1.52	2Virgn
victorie we yeeld/May bind the temples of his conquering head,	1Tamb	5.1.56	2Virgn
What simple Virgins may perswade, we will.	1Tamb	5.1.61	2Virgn
That lingring paines may massacre his heart.	1Tamb	5.1.228	Zabina
Ah faire Zabina, we may curse his power,	1Tamb	5.1.230	Bajzth
The heavens may frowne, the earth for anger quake,	1Tamb	5.1.231	Bajzth
I may poure foorth my soule into thine armes,	1Tamb	5.1.279	Bajzth
That may be ministers of my decay.	1Tamb	5.1.289	Bajzth
That in this terrour Tamburlaine may live.	1Tamb	5.1.299	Bajzth
May styl excruciat his tormented thoughts.	1Tamb	5.1.301	Bajzth
Ah what may chance to thee Zenocrate?	1Tamb	5.1.371	Zenoc
That no escape may save their enemies:	1Tamb	5.1.405	Arabia
Wherein as in a mirrour may be seene,	1Tamb	5.1.476	Tamb
We quickly may in Turkish seas arrive.	2Tamb	1.2.27	Callap
Why may not I my Lord, as wel as he,	2Tamb	1.3.61	Amyras
We may discourage all the pagan troope,	2Tamb	2.1.25	Fredrk
May in his endlesse power and puritie/Behold and venge this	2Tamb	2.2.53	Orcan
That this my life may be as short to me/As are the daies of	2Tamb	2.4.36	Tamb
May never such a change transfourme my love/In whose sweet	2Tamb	2.4.47	Tamb
And wound the earth, that it may cleave in twaine,	2Tamb	2.4.97	Tamb
Your Majesty may choose some pointed time,	2Tamb	3.1.75	Jrslem
That being fiery meteors, may presage,	2Tamb	3.2.4	Tamb
That may endure till heaven be dissolv'd,	2Tamb	3.2.7	Tamb
Because the corners there may fall more flat,	2Tamb	3.2.65	Tamb
Whereas the Fort may fittest be assailde,	2Tamb	3.2.66	Tamb
from every flanke/May scoure the outward curtaines of the Fort,	2Tamb	3.2.80	Tamb
That you may dryfoot martch through lakes and pooles,	2Tamb	3.2.86	Tamb
We may be slaine or wounded ere we learne.	2Tamb	3.2.94	Calyph
That we may tread upon his captive necke,	2Tamb	3.2.157	Tamb
It may be they will yeeld it quietly,	2Tamb	3.3.12	Therid
Which til it may defend you, labour low:	2Tamb	3.3.44	Therid
That we may know if our artillery/Will carie full point blancke	2Tamb	3.3.52	Techel
Sweet mother strike, that I may meet my father.	2Tamb	3.4.30	Sonne
That most may vex his body and his soule.	2Tamb	3.5.99	Callap
I may knocke out his braines with them, and lock you in the	2Tamb	3.5.141	P Tamb
Away, let us to the field, that the villaine may be slaine.	2Tamb	3.5.143	P Trebiz
tel me if the warres/Be not a life that may illustrate Gods,	2Tamb	4.1.79	Tamb
That they may say, it is not chance doth this,	2Tamb	4.1.84	Amyras
How may my hart, thus fired with mine eies,	2Tamb	4.1.93	Tamb
Shrowd any thought may holde my striving hands/From martiall	2Tamb	4.1.95	Tamb
May never day give vertue to his eies,	2Tamb	4.1.174	Trebiz
May never spirit, vaine or Artier feed/The cursed substance of	2Tamb	4.1.177	Soria
that earth may eccho foorth/The far resounding torments ye	2Tamb	4.1.185	Tamb
Affoords no hearbs, whose taste may poison thee,	2Tamb	4.2.9	Olymp
with all the pompe/The treasure of my kingdome may affoord.	2Tamb	4.2.98	Therid
Let me have coach my Lord, that I may ride,	2Tamb	4.3.27	Amyras
While these their fellow kings may be refresht.	2Tamb	4.3.31	Tamb
as fit as may be to restraine/These coltish coach-horse tongues	2Tamb	4.3.51	Usumc
intollorable wrath/May be suppresst by our submission.	2Tamb	5.1.9	Maxim
That Tamburlaine may pitie our distresse,	2Tamb	5.1.27	1Citzn
That legions of tormenting spirits may vex/Your slavish bosomes	2Tamb	5.1.45	Govnr
That I may sheath it in this breast of mine,	2Tamb	5.1.143	Jrslem
And here may we behold great Babylon,	2Tamb	5.2.4	Callap
Wee may lie ready to encounter him,	2Tamb	5.2.8	Callap
That if I perish, heaven and earth may fade.	2Tamb	5.3.60	Tamb
Yet if your majesty may escape this day,	2Tamb	5.3.98	Phsitn
That these my boies may finish all my wantes.	2Tamb	5.3.125	Tamb
me, that I may resigne/My place and proper tytle to my sonne:	2Tamb	5.3.175	Tamb
That I may see thee crown'd before I die.	2Tamb	5.3.179	Tamb
Nor may our hearts all drown'd in teares of blood,	2Tamb	5.3.214	Usumc
May be upon himselfe reverberate.	2Tamb	5.3.223	Techel
Whereof a man may easily in a day/Tell that which may maintaine	Jew	1.1.10	Barab
easily in a day/Tell that which may maintaine him all his life.	Jew	1.1.11	Barab

MAY (cont.)

May serve in perill of calamity/To ransome great Kings from	Jew	1.1.31		Barab
What more may Heaven doe for earthly man/Then thus to powre out	Jew	1.1.107		Barab
And very wisely sayd, it may be so.	Jew	1.1.166		3Jew
Wherein I may not, nay I dare not dally.	Jew	1.2.12		Calym
We may have time to make collection/Amongst the Inhabitants of	Jew	1.2.20		Govnr
So that not he, but I may curse the day,	Jew	1.2.191		Barab
That clouds of darkenesse may inclose my flesh,	Jew	1.2.194		Barab
And time may yeeld us an occasion/Which on the sudden cannot	Jew	1.2.239		Barab
That may they not:	Jew	1.2.253		Abigal
That I may vanish ore the earth in ayre,	Jew	1.2.264		Barab
but be thou so precise/As they may thinke it done of Holinesse.	Jew	1.2.285		Barab
It may be so: but who comes here?	Jew	1.2.313		Abbass
Let us intreat she may be entertain'd.	Jew	1.2.329		2Fryar
Give charge to Morpheus that he may dreame/A golden dreame, and	Jew	2.1.36		Abigal
That I may hover with her in the Ayre,	Jew	2.1.62		Barab
But to admit a sale of these thy Turkes/We may not, nay we dare	Jew	2.2.22		Govnr
Even for charity I may spit intoo't.	Jew	2.3.29		Barab
That I may have a sight of Abigall;	Jew	2.3.34		Lodowk
'Tis likely they in time may reape some fruit,	Jew	2.3.84		Barab
It may be under colour of shaving, thou'lt cut my throat for my	Jew	2.3.119	P	Barab
That I may, walking in my Gallery,	Jew	2.3.179		Barab
That we may venge their blood upon their heads.	Jew	3.2.28		Mater
Convert my father that he may be sav'd,	Jew	3.6.39		Abigal
And now for store of wealth may I compare/With all the Jewes in	Jew	4.1.55		Barab
to some religious house/So I may be baptiz'd and live therein.	Jew	4.1.76		Barab
You heare your answer, and you may be gone.	Jew	4.1.92		1Fryar
I have don't, but no body knowes it but you two, I may escape.	Jew	4.1.181	P	1Fryar
It may be she sees more in me than I can find in my selfe:	Jew	4.2.32	P	Ithimr
one that can spy a place/Where you may enter, and surprize the	Jew	5.1.71		Barab
May all good fortune follow Calymath.	Jew	5.2.21		Barab
Arbitrament; and Barabas/At his discretion may dispose of both:	Jew	5.2.54		Barab
That at one instant all things may be done,	Jew	5.2.120		Barab
And meditate how we may grace us best/To solemnize our	Jew	5.3.44		Calym
For so I live, perish may all the world.	Jew	5.5.10		Barab
May not desolve, till death desolve our lives,	P 5	1.5		Charls
May still be feweld in our progenye.	P 8	1.8		Charls
The rest that will not goe (my Lords) may stay:	P 23	1.23		Charls
Now Guise may storme but doe us little hurt:	P 28	1.28		Navrre
That God may still defend the right of France:	P 56	1.56		Navrre
All this and more, if more may be comprisde,	P 143	2.86		Guise
Pale death may walke in furrowes of my face:	P 158	2.101		Guise
A hand, that with a graspe may gripe the world,	P 159	2.102		Guise
they may become/As men that stand and gase against the Sunne.	P 162	2.105		Guise
O graunt sweet God my daies may end with hers,	P 189	3.24		Navrre
That I with her may dye and live againe.	P 190	3.25		Navrre
And as we late decreed we may perfourme.	P 206	4.4		QnMoth
I hope these reasons may serve my princely Sonne,	P 223	4.21		QnMoth
them thither, and then/Beset his house that not a man may live.	P 289	5.16		Guise
It may be it is some other, and he escapte.	P 308	5.35		Anjoy
which have already set the street/May know their watchword,	P 329	5.56		Guise
How may we doe? I feare me they will live.	P 420	7.60		Guise
it may prejudice their hope/Of my inheritance to the crowne of	P 467	8.17		Anjoy
on me, then with your leaves/I may retire me to my native home.	P 474	8.24		Anjoy
And if they storme, I then may pull them downe.	P 526	9.45		QnMoth
God graunt my neerest freends may prove no worse.	P 547	11.12		Charls
My opportunity may serve me fit,	P 566	11.31		Navrre
And all things that a King may wish besides:	P 595	12.8		QnMoth
And long may Henry enjoy all this and more.	P 597	12.10		Cardnl
Graunt that our deeds may wel deserve your loves:	P 600	12.13		King
Then may it please your Majestie to give me leave,	P 616	12.29		Mugern
Thy brother Guise and we may now provide,	P 636	12.49		QnMoth
As not a man may live without our leaves.	P 638	12.51		QnMoth
That I may write unto my dearest Lord.	P 659	13.3		Duchss
That he may come and meet me in some place,	P 664	13.8		Duchss
Where we may one injoy the others sight.	P 665	13.9		Duchss
Then in this bloudy brunt they may beholde,	P 713	14.16		Bartus
I may be stabd, and live till he be dead,	P 778	15.36		Mugern
But when will he come that we may murther him?	P 937	19.7	P	3Mur
And all for thee my Guise: what may I doe?	P1088	19.158		QnMoth
Upon whose heart may all the furies gripe,	P1101	20.11		Cardnl
Oh what may I doe, for to revenge thy death?	P1108	21.2		Dumain
It is enough if that Navarre may be/Esteemed faithfull to the	P1147	22.9		Navrre
Whose service he may still commaund till death.	P1149	22.11		Navrre
Tell me Surgeon and flatter not, may I live?	P1222	22.84		King
Surgeon, why saist thou so? the King may live.	P1224	22.86		Navrre
Long may you live, and still be King of France.	P1226	22.88		Navrre
And may it never end in bloud as mine hath done.	P1233	22.95		King
That it may keenly slice the Catholicks.	P1238	22.100		King
That we may see it honourably interde:	P1246	22.108		Navrre
of a string/May draw the pliant king which way I please:	Edw	1.1.53		Gavstn
the least of these may well suffice/For one of greater birth	Edw	1.1.158		Kent
A prison may beseeme his holinesse.	Edw	1.1.207		Gavstn
We may not, nor we will not suffer this.	Edw	1.2.15		MortSr
Then may we lawfully revolt from him.	Edw	1.2.73		Mortmr
May it please your lordship to subscribe your name.	Edw	1.4.2		Lncstr
My lord, you may not thus disparage us,	Edw	1.4.32		Lncstr
he refuse, and then may we/Depose him and elect an other king.	Edw	1.4.54		Mortmr
So I may have some nooke or corner left,	Edw	1.4.72		Edward
With slaughtered priests [make] <may> Tibers channell swell,	Edw	1.4.102		Edward
Which may in Ireland purchase him such friends,	Edw	1.4.259		Mortmr
Then may we with some colour rise in armes,	Edw	1.4.279		Mortmr
Then I may fetch from this ritch treasurie:	Edw	1.4.332		Queene

MAY (cont.)

And may it proove more happie then the first.	Edw	1.4.336		Queene
May with one word, advaunce us while we live:	Edw	2.1.9		Spencr
And saying, trulie ant may please your honor,	Edw	2.1.40		Spencr
Moov'd may he be, and perish in his wrath.	Edw	2.2.101		Mortmr
Why, so he may, but we will speake to him.	Edw	2.2.136		Lncstr
You may not in, my lord.	Edw	2.2.137		Guard
May we not?	Edw	2.2.138		Mortmr
Maids of England, sore may you moorne,	Edw	2.2.190		Lncstr
Intreateth you by me, yet but he may/See him before he dies, for	Edw	2.5.36		Arundl
That you may drinke your fill, and quaffe in bloud,	Edw	3.1.137		Edward
That so my bloudie colours may suggest/Remembrance of revenge	Edw	3.1.139		Edward
No Edward, Englands scourge, it may not be,	Edw	3.1.258		Mortmr
of golde/To Danae, all aide may be denied/To Isabell the Queene,	Edw	3.1.268		Spencr
Madam, long may you live,	Edw	4.2.34		Kent
That Englands peeres may Henolts welcome see.	Edw	4.2.82		SrJohn
That I may see that most desired day,	Edw	4.3.46		Edward
When we may meet these traitors in the field.	Edw	4.3.47		Edward
That Englands queene in peace may reposesse/Her dignities and	Edw	4.4.24		Mortmr
and withall/We may remoove these flatterers from the king,	Edw	4.4.26		Mortmr
Madam, without offence if I may aske,	Edw	4.6.30		Kent
And we must seeke to right it as we may,	Edw	4.6.68		Mortmr
May in their fall be followed to their end.	Edw	4.6.79		Mortmr
Your grace may sit secure, if none but wee/Doe wot of your	Edw	4.7.26		Monk
It may become thee yet,/To let us take our farewell of his	Edw	4.7.68		Spencr
In heaven wee may, in earth never shall wee meete,	Edw	4.7.80		Edward
That I may gaze upon this glittering crowne,	Edw	5.1.60		Edward
That Edward may be still faire Englands king:	Edw	5.1.68		Edward
Well may I rent his name, that rends my hart.	Edw	5.1.140		Edward
So may his limmes be torne, as is this paper,	Edw	5.1.142		Edward
To erect your sonne with all the speed we may,	Edw	5.2.11		Mortmr
The Wrenne may strive against the Lions strength,	Edw	5.3.34		Edward
Matrevis and the rest may beare the blame,	Edw	5.4.15		Mortmr
What safetie may I looke for at his hands,	Edw	5.4.109		King
My minde may be more stedfast on my God.	Edw	5.5.78		Edward
Till further triall may be made thereof.	Edw	5.6.80		King
That I may conjure in some bushy <lustie> Grove,	F 178	1.1.150		Faust
Faustus may try his cunning by himselfe.	F 187	1.1.159		Cornel
may be <and see if hee by> his grave counsell may <can>	F 226	1.2.33		2Schol
<and see if hee by> his grave counsell may <can> reclaime him.	F 226	1.2.33		2Schol
And may not follow thee without his leave;	F 269	1.3.41		Mephst
Yes, and goings out too, you may see sir.	F 347	1.4.5	P	Robin
you may save your selfe a labour, for they are as familiar with	F 364	1.4.22	P	Robin
at some certaine day/Great Lucifer may claime it as his owne,	F 440	2.1.52		Mephst
Why streames it not, that I may write a fresh?	F 455	2.1.67		Faust
But may I raise such <up> spirits when I please?	F 475	2.1.87		Faust
First, that Faustus may be a spirit in forme and substance.	F 485	2.1.97	P	Faust
Be I a devill yet God may pitty me,	F 566	2.2.15		Faust
May be admired through the furthest Land.	F 842	3.1.64		Faust
be,/That this proud Pope may Faustus [cunning] <comming> see.	F 855	3.1.77		Faust
Thy selfe and I, may parly with this Pope:	F 896	3.1.118		Faust
That we may solemnize Saint Peters feast,	F 978	3.1.200		Pope
But now, that Faustus may delight his minde,	F 989	3.2.9		Faust
<Then charme me that I may be invisible>,	F 991	(HC266) A		Faust
That I may walke invisible to all,	F 992	3.2.12		Faust
That no eye may thy body see.	F1003	3.2.23		Mephst
First, may it please your sacred Holinesse,	F1013	3.2.33		1Card
It may be so:	F1062	3.2.82		Pope
who comes to see/What wonders by blacke spels may compast be.	F1198	4.1.44		Mrtino
That we may wonder at their excellence.	F1234	4.1.80		Emper
But Faustus, since I may not speake to them,	F1263	4.1.109		Emper
How may I prove that saying to be true?	F1268	4.1.114		Emper
Your Majesty may boldly goe and see.	F1269	4.1.115		Faust
O may these eye-lids never close againe,	F1332	4.2.8		Benvol
Nay, we will stay with thee, betide what may,	F1338	4.2.14		Fredrk
Breake may his heart with grones: deere Frederik see,	F1366	4.2.42		Benvol
The Divel's dead, the Furies now may laugh.	F1369	4.2.45		Benvol
let's devise how we may adde more shame/To the blacke scandall	F1377	4.2.53		Fredrk
That all the world may see my just revenge.	F1382	4.2.58		Benvol
That rowling downe, may breake the villaines bones,	F1414	4.2.90		Faust
What may we do, that we may hide our shames?	F1447	4.3.17		Fredrk
that you may ride him o're hedge and ditch, and spare him not;	F1467	4.4.11	P	Faust
yes, that may be; for I have heard of one, that ha's eate a load	F1533	4.5.29	P	Robin
it may be, that you have taken no pleasure in those sights;	F1565	4.6.8	P	Faust
we will recompence/With all the love and kindnesse that we may.	F1672	4.6.115		Duke
It may be this my exhortation/Seemes harsh, and all unpleasant;	F1717	5.1.44		OldMan
Checking thy body, may amend thy soule.	F1723	5.1.50		OldMan
But what I may afflict his body with,	F1757	5.1.84		Mephst
That I may <might> have unto my paramour,	F1761	5.1.88		Faust
sweet embraces <imbracings> may extinguish cleare <cleane>,	F1763	5.1.90		Faust
the serpent that tempted Eve may be saved, but not Faustus.	F1838	5.2.42	P	Faust
O what may <shal> we do to save Faustus?	F1868	5.2.72	P	2Schol
thou, and we will pray, that God may have mercie upon thee.	F1875	5.2.79	P	2Schol
That time may cease, and midnight never come.	F1930	5.2.134		Faust
That Faustus may repent, and save his soule.	F1934	5.2.138		Faust
My limbes may issue from your smoky mouthes,	F1955	5.2.159		Faust
[So that] my soule [may but] ascend to heaven.	F1956	5.2.160		Faust
Whose fiendfull fortune may exhort the wise/Onely to wonder at	F2006	5.3.24		4Chor
I, and goings out too, you may see else.	F App	p.229 5	P	Clown
you may save that labour, they are too familiar with me	F App	p.229 27	P	Clown
that I may be here and there and every where, O Ile tickle the	F App	p.231 62	P	Clown
may be some ghost newly crept out of Purgatory come to begge a	F App	p.232 14	P	Lorein
It may be so, Friers prepare a dirge to lay the fury of this	F App	p.232 16	P	Pope

MAY (cont.)

you may be ashamed to burden honest men with a matter of truth. F App p.234 14 P Rafe
may be witnesses to confirme what mine eares have heard . F App p.236 6 P Emper
Your highnes may boldly go and see. . . . . . . F App p.238 63 P Faust
but it may be Madame, you take no delight in this, I have heard F App p.242 4 P Faust
As no commiseration may expel, ... F App p.243 43 OldMan
wonst thou France; Roome may be won/With farre lesse toile, Lucan, First Booke 283
battailes fought with prosperous successe/May bring her downe, Lucan, First Booke 286
So be I may be bold to speake a truth, ... Lucan, First Booke 361
Either love, or cause that I may never hate: . . . . Ovid's Elegies 1.3.2
Soone may you plow the little lands <land> I have, . . . Ovid's Elegies 1.3.9
Apollo, Bacchus, and the Muses may, ... Ovid's Elegies 1.3.11
That I may write things worthy thy faire lookes: . . . Ovid's Elegies 1.3.20
Pray God it may his latest supper be, ... Ovid's Elegies 1.4.2
though I not see/What may be done, yet there before him bee. Ovid's Elegies 1.4.14
To him I pray it no delight may bring, ... Ovid's Elegies 1.4.67
Where they may sport, and seeme to be unknowne. . . . Ovid's Elegies 1.5.8
She may perceive how we the time did wast: . . . . Ovid's Elegies 1.6.70
wheeles spun/And what with Mares ranck humour may be done. Ovid's Elegies 1.8.8
Such is his forme as may with thine compare, ... Ovid's Elegies 1.8.33
Dissemble so, as lov'd he may be thought, ... Ovid's Elegies 1.8.71
That this, or that man may thy cheekes moist keepe. . . Ovid's Elegies 1.8.84
That my dead bones may in their grave lie soft. . . . Ovid's Elegies 1.8.108
Troianes destroy the Greeke wealth, while you may. . . Ovid's Elegies 1.9.34
[May] <Many> bounteous [lome] <love> Alcinous fruite resigne. Ovid's Elegies 1.10.56
Farre off be force, no fire to them may reach, . . . Ovid's Elegies 1.14.29
That all the world [may] <might> ever chaunt my name. . Ovid's Elegies 1.15.8
loves bowe/His owne flames best acquainted signes may knowe, Ovid's Elegies 2.1.8
Stolne liberty she may by thee obtaine, ... Ovid's Elegies 2.2.15
Which giving her, she may give thee againe. . . . . Ovid's Elegies 2.2.16
Wilt thou her fault learne, she may make thee tremble, . . Ovid's Elegies 2.2.17
Enquire not what with Isis may be done/Nor feare least she to Ovid's Elegies 2.2.25
Object thou then what she may well excuse, ... Ovid's Elegies 2.2.37
Wee seeke that through thee safely love we may, . . . Ovid's Elegies 2.2.65
Shee may deceive thee, though thou her protect, . . . Ovid's Elegies 2.3.15
But may soft love rowse up my drowsie eies, ... Ovid's Elegies 2.10.19
That at my funeralles some may weeping crie, ... Ovid's Elegies 2.10.37
Whose blast may hether strongly be inclinde, ... Ovid's Elegies 2.11.38
To bring that happy time so soone as may be. . . . . Ovid's Elegies 2.11.56
But if in so great feare I may advize thee, ... Ovid's Elegies 2.13.27
My selfe that better dye with loving may/Had seene, my mother Ovid's Elegies 2.14.21
Then I, that I may seale her privy leaves, ... Ovid's Elegies 2.15.15
Onely Ile signe nought, that may grieve me much. . . . Ovid's Elegies 2.15.18
Small things with greater may be copulate. . . . . Ovid's Elegies 2.17.14
Phedra, and Hipolite may read, my care is, ... Ovid's Elegies 2.18.24
And may repulse place for our wishes strike. . . . . Ovid's Elegies 2.19.6
That to deceits it may me forward pricke. . . . . Ovid's Elegies 2.19.44
Some other seeke that may in patience strive with thee, . Ovid's Elegies 2.19.59
Thy muse hath played what may milde girles content, . . Ovid's Elegies 3.1.27
To empty aire may go my fearefull speech. . . . . Ovid's Elegies 3.1.62
Yet whom thou favourst, pray may conquerour be. . . . Ovid's Elegies 3.2.2
By these I judge, delight me may the rest, ... Ovid's Elegies 3.2.35
That from thy fanne, mov'd by my hand may blow? . . . Ovid's Elegies 3.2.38
Who may offend, sinnes least; power to do ill, . . . Ovid's Elegies 3.4.9
Because the keeper may come say, I did it, ... Ovid's Elegies 3.4.35
That may transport me without oares to rowe. . . . . Ovid's Elegies 3.5.4
May spelles and droughs <drugges> do sillie soules such harmes? Ovid's Elegies 3.6.28
Thy bones I pray may in the urne safe rest, ... Ovid's Elegies 3.8.67
And may th'earths weight thy ashes nought molest. . . . Ovid's Elegies 3.8.68
May that shame fall mine enemies chance to be. . . . Ovid's Elegies 3.10.16
That I may love yet, though against my minde. . . . Ovid's Elegies 3.10.52
Graunt this, that what you do I may not see, ... Ovid's Elegies 3.13.35
Dutifull service may thy love procure, ... Hero and Leander 1.220
Though neither gods nor men may thee deserve, ... Hero and Leander 1.315
Much like a globe, (a globe may I tearme this, ... Hero and Leander 2.275
And if these pleasures may thee <things thy minde may> move, Passionate Shepherd 19
For thy delight each May-morning. . . . . . . Passionate Shepherd 22
If these delights thy minde may move; . . . . . Passionate Shepherd 23

MAYD

The sonne of God and issue of a Mayd, ... 2Tamb 1.1.134 Sgsmnd
he asleepe had layd/Inchaunted Argus, spied a countrie mayd, Hero and Leander 1.388

MAYDENHEAD

And seeming lavish, sav'de her maydenhead. . . . . Hero and Leander 2.76

MAYDES

Those in their lovers, pretty maydes desire. . . . . Ovid's Elegies 1.9.6
Let Maydes whom hot desire to husbands leade, ... Ovid's Elegies 2.1.5

MAYDS

One is no number, mayds are nothing then, ... Hero and Leander 1.255

MAY-MORNING

For thy delight each May-morning. . . . . . . Passionate Shepherd 22

MAYOR (See MAIOR)

MAY'ST

[There] <Their> Caesar may'st thou shine and no cloud dim thee; Lucan, First Booke 59

MAYST

That thou mayst freely live to be my heire. . . . . Jew 3.4.63 Barab

MAYSTERS

Here let him stay my maysters from the tents, ... 1Tamb 5.1.211 Tamb

ME (Homograph; See also MEE)

Come gentle Ganimed and play with me, ... Dido 1.1.1 Jupitr
That will not shield me from her shrewish blowes: . . . Dido 1.1.4 Ganimd
She reacht me such a rap for that I spilde, ... Dido 1.1.7 Ganimd
Doe thou but say their colour pleaseth me. . . . . Dido 1.1.41 Jupitr
Ay me! . . . . Dido 1.1.72 Venus

ME (cont.)

Charge him from me tc turne his stormie powers,	Dido	1.1.117	Jupitr
Father I faint, good father give me meate.	Dido	1.1.163	Ascan
Now is the time fcr me to play my part:	Dido	1.1.182	Venus
But what are you that aske of me these things?	Dido	1.1.214	Venus
Too cruell, why wilt thou forsake me thus?	Dido	1.1.243	Aeneas
But thou art gone and leav'st me here alone,	Dido	1.1.247	Aeneas
But tell me Troians, Troians if you be,	Dido	1.2.17	Iarbus
Come in with me, Ile bring you to my Queene,	Dido	1.2.42	Iarbus
Me thinkes that towne there should be Troy, yon Idas hill,	Dido	2.1.7	Aeneas
For were it Priam he would smile on me.	Dido	2.1.36	Ascan
Your sight amazde me, O what destinies/Have brought my sweete	Dido	2.1.59	Aeneas
O tell me, for I long to be resolv'd.	Dido	2.1.61	Aeneas
Well may I view her, but she sees not me.	Dido	2.1.73	Aeneas
What stranger art thou that doest eye me thus?	Dido	2.1.74	Dido
Brave Prince, welcome to Carthage and to me,	Dido	2.1.81	Dido
This place beseemes me not, O pardon me.	Dido	2.1.94	Aeneas
And Dido and you Carthaginian Peeres/Heare me, but yet with	Dido	2.1.123	Aeneas
And then--O Dido, pardon me.	Dido	2.1.159	Aeneas
Nay leave nct here, resolve me of the rest.	Dido	2.1.160	Dido
his breast/Furrowd with wounds, and that which made me weepe,	Dido	2.1.204	Aeneas
All which hemd me about, crying, this is he.	Dido	2.1.219	Aeneas
Convaid me from their crooked nets and bands:	Dido	2.1.222	Aeneas
O let me live, great Neoptolemus.	Dido	2.1.239	Aeneas
The Greekes pursue me, stay and take me in.	Dido	2.1.282	Aeneas
Achates speake, sorrow hath tired me quite.	Dido	2.1.293	Aeneas
Troian, thy ruthfull tale hath made me sad:	Dido	2.1.301	Dido
To rid me from these melancholly thoughts.	Dido	2.1.303	Dido
I, and my mcther gave me this fine bow.	Dido	2.1.309	Cupid
Tis not enough that thou doest graunt me love,	Dido	3.1.8	Iarbus
I feare me Dido hath been counted light,	Dido	3.1.14	Dido
No Dido will not take me in her armes,	Dido	3.1.22	Cupid
I shall not be her sonne, she loves me not.	Dido	3.1.23	Cupid
Sit in my lap and let me heare thee sing.	Dido	3.1.25	Dido
And tell me where [learndst] <learnst> thou this pretie song?	Dido	3.1.27	Dido
My cosin Helen taught it me in Troy.	Dido	3.1.28	Cupid
Will Dido let me hang about her necke?	Dido	3.1.30	Cupid
What will ycu give me now? Ile have this Fanne.	Dido	3.1.32	Cupid
Ungentle Queene, is this thy love to me?	Dido	3.1.36	Iarbus
Iarbus pardcn me, and stay a while.	Dido	3.1.46	Dido
What telst thou me of rich Getulia?	Dido	3.1.48	Dido
Doth Dido call me backe?	Dido	3.1.53	Iarbus
No, but I charge thee never looke on me.	Dido	3.1.54	Dido
Then pull out both mine eyes, or let me dye.	Dido	3.1.55	Iarbus
O that Iarbus could but fancie me.	Dido	3.1.62	Anna
Ile make me bracelets of his golden haire,	Dido	3.1.85	Dido
I understand your highnesse sent for me.	Dido	3.1.100	Aeneas
here, tell me in sooth/In what might Dido highly pleasure thee.	Dido	3.1.101	Dido
Conditionally that thou wilt stay with me,	Dido	3.1.114	Dido
So that Aeneas may but stay with me.	Dido	3.1.133	Dido
For if that any man could conquer me,	Dido	3.1.137	Dido
Yet none obtaind me, I am free from all.--	Dido	3.1.153	Dido
and thought by words/To compasse me, but yet he was deceiv'd:	Dido	3.1.156	Dido
But his fantastick humours pleasde not me:	Dido	3.1.158	Dido
Who warne me of such daunger prest at hand,	Dido	3.2.22	Venus
Yet now I dce repent me of his ruth,	Dido	3.2.47	Juno
More then melodious are these words to me,	Dido	3.2.62	Juno
men (Dido except)/Have taunted me in these opprobrious termes,	Dido	3.3.27	Iarbus
Then would I wish me with Anchises Tombe,	Dido	3.3.44	Aeneas
And dead to honour that hath brought me up.	Dido	3.3.45	Aeneas
Then would I wish me in faire Didos armes,	Dido	3.3.48	Iarbus
And dead to scorne that hath pursued me so.	Dido	3.3.49	Iarbus
I, this it is which wounds me to the death,	Dido	3.3.63	Iarbus
Revenge me on Aeneas, or on her:	Dido	3.3.70	Iarbus
Tell me deare love, how found you out this Cave?	Dido	3.4.3	Dido
Not angred me, except in angring thee.	Dido	3.4.15	Dido
I must conceale/The torment, that it bootes me not reveale,/And	Dido	3.4.26	Dido
Nay, nothing, but Aeneas loves me not.	Dido	3.4.32	Dido
I followe one that loveth fame for me,	Dido	3.4.38	Dido
And by this Sword that saved me from the Greekes,	Dido	3.4.48	Aeneas
Wherewith my husband woo'd me yet a maide,	Dido	3.4.63	Dido
Nature, why mad'st me not some poysonous beast,	Dido	4.1.21	Iarbus
him to his ships/That now afflicts me with his flattering eyes.	Dido	4.2.22	Iarbus
I Anna, is there ought you would with me?	Dido	4.2.24	Iarbus
Yet if you would partake with me the cause/Of this devotion	Dido	4.2.27	Anna
Who seekes to rob me of thy Sisters love,	Dido	4.2.31	Iarbus
Be rul'd by me, and seeke some other love,	Dido	4.2.35	Anna
O leave me, leave me to my silent thoughts,	Dido	4.2.38	Iarbus
Hard hearted, wilt not deigne to heare me speake?	Dido	4.2.54	Anna
Since destinie doth call me from [thy] <the> shoare:	Dido	4.3.2	Aeneas
Hath summond me to fruitfull Italy:	Dido	4.3.4	Aeneas
Commaunds me leave these unrenowmed [reames] <beames>,	Dido	4.3.18	Aeneas
And let me linke [thy] <my> bodie to my <thy> lips,	Dido	4.3.28	Aeneas
I faine would goe, yet beautie calles me backe:	Dido	4.3.46	Aeneas
Her silver armes will coll me round about,	Dido	4.3.51	Aeneas
Stay not to answere me, runne Anna runne.	Dido	4.4.4	Dido
Is this thy love to me?	Dido	4.4.16	Dido
O princely Dido, give me leave to speake,	Dido	4.4.17	Aeneas
How haps Achates bid me not farewell?	Dido	4.4.19	Dido
Because I feard your grace would keepe me here.	Dido	4.4.20	Achat
Aeneas pardon me, for I forgot/That yong Ascanius lay with me	Dido	4.4.31	Dido
me, for I forgot/That yong Ascanius lay with me this night:	Dido	4.4.32	Dido
Love made me jealous, but to make amends,	Dido	4.4.33	Dido

ME (cont.)

And punish me Aeneas for this crime.	Dido	4.4.36	Dido
O keepe them still, and let me gaze my fill:	Dido	4.4.44	Dido
Lets see what tempests can anoy me now.	Dido	4.4.60	Aeneas
Then here in me shall flourish Priams race,	Dido	4.4.87	Aeneas
Bring me his oares, his tackling, and his sailes:	Dido	4.4.109	Dido
Affright me not, onely Aeneas frowne/Is that which terrifies	Dido	4.4.115	Dido
If he forsake me not, I never dye,	Dido	4.4.121	Dido
And heele make me immortall with a kisse.	Dido	4.4.123	Dido
Are these the sailes that in despight of me,	Dido	4.4.126	Dido
againe conspire/Against the life of me poore Carthage Queene:	Dido	4.4.132	Dido
And told me that Aeneas ment to goe:	Dido	4.4.142	Dido
My Lord Ascanius, ye must goe with me.	Dido	4.5.1	Nurse
No, thou shalt goe with me unto my house,	Dido	4.5.3	Nurse
Nurse I am wearie, will you carrie me?	Dido	4.5.15	Cupid
I, so youle dwell with me and call me mother.	Dido	4.5.16	Nurse
So youle love me, I care not if I doe.	Dido	4.5.17	Cupid
The king of Gods sent me from highest heaven,	Dido	5.1.32	Hermes
And made me take my brother for my sonne:	Dido	5.1.43	Aeneas
Who ever since hath luld me in her armes.	Dido	5.1.48	Ascan
What, would the Gods have me, Deucalion like,	Dido	5.1.57	Aeneas
Though she repairde my fleete and gave me ships,	Dido	5.1.59	Aeneas
And left me neither saile nor sterne abourd.	Dido	5.1.61	Aeneas
Jove hath heapt on me such a desperate charge,	Dido	5.1.64	Aeneas
With speede he bids me saile to Italy,	Dido	5.1.68	Aeneas
Let some of those thy followers goe with me,	Dido	5.1.73	Iarbus
Pardon me though I aske, love makes me aske.	Dido	5.1.90	Dido
O pardon me, if I resolve thee why:	Dido	5.1.91	Aeneas
Sent from his father Jove, appeard to me,	Dido	5.1.95	Aeneas
And in his name rebukt me bitterly,	Dido	5.1.96	Aeneas
Then let me goe and never say farewell?	Dido	5.1.109	Aeneas
Let me goe, farewell, I must from hence,	Dido	5.1.110	Dido
Am I lesse faire then when thou sawest me first?	Dido	5.1.115	Dido
Then let me goe, and never say farewell?	Dido	5.1.124	Dido
And all the world calles me a second Helen,	Dido	5.1.144	Dido
If words might move me I were overcome.	Dido	5.1.154	Aeneas
Wilt thou now slay me with thy venomed sting,	Dido	5.1.167	Dido
I hope that that which love forbids me doe,	Dido	5.1.170	Dido
Though thou nor he will pitie me a whit.	Dido	5.1.178	Dido
If not, turne from me, and Ile turne from thee:	Dido	5.1.181	Dido
He loves me to too well to serve me so:	Dido	5.1.185	Dido
But he shrinkes backe, and now remembring me,	Dido	5.1.190	Dido
And leaving me will saile to Italy.	Dido	5.1.195	Dido
Run Anna, run, stay not to answere me.	Dido	5.1.210	Dido
he lay with me last night,/And in the morning he was stolne	Dido	5.1.213	Nurse
And in the morning he was stolne from me,	Dido	5.1.214	Nurse
I thinke some Fairies have beguiled me.	Dido	5.1.215	Nurse
That slayest me with thy harsh and hellish tale,	Dido	5.1.217	Dido
And spying me, hoyst up the sailes amaine:	Dido	5.1.227	Anna
Made me suppose he would have heard me speake:	Dido	5.1.230	Anna
Which seene to all, though he beheld me not,	Dido	5.1.237	Anna
Ile frame me wings of waxe like Icarus,	Dido	5.1.243	Dido
But he remembring me shrinkes backe againe:	Dido	5.1.260	Dido
Nothing can beare me to him but a ship,	Dido	5.1.267	Dido
have I found a meane/To rid me from these thoughts of Lunacie:	Dido	5.1.273	Dido
Who wild me sacrifize his ticing relliques:	Dido	5.1.277	Dido
Goe Anna, bid my servants bring me fire.	Dido	5.1.278	Dido
Lay to thy hands and helpe me make a fire,	Dido	5.1.284	Dido
But afterwards will Dido graunt me love?	Dido	5.1.288	Iarbus
So, leave me now, let none approach this place.	Dido	5.1.291	Dido
in the darksome Cave/He drew, and swore by to be true to me,	Dido	5.1.296	Dido
Dido in these flames/Hath burnt her selfe, aye me, unhappie me!	Dido	5.1.315	Anna
Dido I come to thee, aye me Aeneas.	Dido	5.1.318	Iarbus
What can my teares or cryes prevaile me now?	Dido	5.1.319	Anna
What fatall destinie envies me thus,	Dido	5.1.323	Anna
But I refer me to my noble men,	1Tamb	1.1.21	Mycet
To crowne me Emperour of Asia.	1Tamb	1.1.112	Cosroe
And that which might resolve me into teares,	1Tamb	1.1.118	Cosroe
And Jove may never let me longer live,	1Tamb	1.1.170	Cosroe
And cause the souldiers that thus honour me,	1Tamb	1.1.172	Cosroe
But tell me Maddam, is your grace betroth'd?	1Tamb	1.2.32	Tamb
Me thinks I see kings kneeling at his feet,	1Tamb	1.2.55	Techel
And making thee and me Techelles, kinges,	1Tamb	1.2.58	Usumc
Disdaines Zenocrate to live with me?	1Tamb	1.2.82	Tamb
You must be forced from me ere you goe:	1Tamb	1.2.120	Tamb
Forsake thy king and do but joine with me/And we will triumph	1Tamb	1.2.172	Tamb
To ward the blow, and shield me safe from harme.	1Tamb	1.2.181	Tamb
If thou wilt stay with me, renowmed man,	1Tamb	1.2.188	Tamb
Joine with me now in this my meane estate,	1Tamb	1.2.202	Tamb
The Nations far remoov'd admyre me not)/And when my name and	1Tamb	1.2.204	Tamb
Then shalt thou be Competitor with me,	1Tamb	1.2.208	Tamb
Thy selfe and them shall never part from me,	1Tamb	1.2.245	Tamb
If you will willingly remaine with me,	1Tamb	1.2.254	Tamb
But tell me, that hast seene him, Menaphon,	1Tamb	2.1.5	Cosroe
To seeke revenge on me and Tamburlaine.	1Tamb	2.1.67	Cosroe
To whom sweet Menaphon, direct me straight.	1Tamb	2.1.68	Cosroe
And doubt you not, but if you favour me,	1Tamb	2.3.10	Tamb
Shall make me solely Emperour of Asia:	1Tamb	2.3.39	Cosroe
Thy words assure me of kind successe:	1Tamb	2.3.60	Cosroe
If Nature had not given me wisedomes lore?	1Tamb	2.4.7	Mycet
They cannot take away my crowne from me.	1Tamb	2.4.14	Mycet
Away, I am the King: go, touch me not.	1Tamb	2.4.20	Mycet
And cry me mercie, noble King.	1Tamb	2.4.22	Mycet

ME (cont.)

I marie am I: have ycu any suite to me?	1Tamb	2.4.24		Mycet
Come give it me.	1Tamb	2.4.31		Mycet
Then shalt thou see me pull it from thy head:	1Tamb	2.4.39		Tamb
To follow me to faire Persepolis.	1Tamb	2.5.40		Cosroe
And till thou overtake me Tamburlaine,	1Tamb	2.5.44		Cosroe
Me thinks we should nct, I am strongly moov'd,	1Tamb	2.5.75		Tamb
Judge by thy selfe Theridamas, not me,	1Tamb	2.5.93		Tamb
Goe on for me.	1Tamb	2.5.106		Therid
Thus to deprive me of my crowne and life.	1Tamb	2.7.2		Cosroe
Moov'd me tc manage armes against thy state.	1Tamb	2.7.16		Tamb
And that made me to joine with Tamburlain,	1Tamb	2.7.30		Therid
Shall make me leave so rich a prize as this:	1Tamb	2.7.54		Tamb
To dispossesse me of this Diadem:	1Tamb	2.7.60		Tamb
And all pronounst me king of Persea.	1Tamb	2.7.67		Tamb
He be so mad to manage Armes with me,	1Tamb	3.1.34		Bajzth
Make me the gastly ccunterfeit of death.	1Tamb	3.2.17		Zenoc
[Agidas], leave to wound me with these words:	1Tamb	3.2.35		Zenoc
He meet me in the field and fetch thee hence?	1Tamb	3.3.5		Tamb
That made me Emperour of Asia.	1Tamb	3.3.32		Tamb
He cals me Bajazeth, whom you call Lord.	1Tamb	3.3.67		Bajzth
And dar'st thou bluntly call me Bajazeth?	1Tamb	3.3.71		Bajzth
And dar'st thou bluntly call me Tamburlaine?	1Tamb	3.3.74		Tamb
Thy fall shall make me famous through the world:	1Tamb	3.3.83		Tamb
untill thou see/Me martch victoriously with all my men,	1Tamb	3.3.127		Tamb
hardy Tamburlaine)/What tis to meet me in the open field,	1Tamb	3.3.146		Bajzth
must thou be plac'd by me/That am the Empresse of the mighty	1Tamb	3.3.166		Zabina
Cal'st thou me Concubine that am betroath'd/Unto the great and	1Tamb	3.3.169		Zenoc
And sue to me tc be your Advocates.	1Tamb	3.3.175		Zenoc
Yet should he not perswade me otherwise,	1Tamb	3.3.210		Zenoc
Now let me cffer to my gracious Lord,	1Tamb	3.3.218		Zenoc
And crowne me Emperour of Affrica.	1Tamb	3.3.221		Tamb
foule Idolaters/Shall make me bonfires with their filthy bones,	1Tamb	3.3.240		Bajzth
garrisons enough/To make me Soveraigne of the earth againe.	1Tamb	3.3.243		Bajzth
Yet set a ransome on me Tamburlaine.	1Tamb	3.3.261		Bajzth
Offer their mines (to sew for peace) to me,	1Tamb	3.3.264		Tamb
But Villaine, thou that wishest this to me,	1Tamb	4.2.12		Tamb
Feends looke on me, and thou dread God of hell,	1Tamb	4.2.27		Bajzth
To make me think of nought but blood and war.	1Tamb	4.2.55		Tamb
Are fled from Bajazeth, and remaine with me,	1Tamb	4.2.80		Tamb
And when they see me march in black aray.	1Tamb	4.2.119		Tamb
Me thinks we martch as Meliager did,	1Tamb	4.3.1		Souldn
Me thinks, tis a great deale better than a consort of musicke.	1Tamb	4.4.60	P	Therid
And wouldst thou have me buy thy Fathers love/With such a	1Tamb	4.4.83		Tamb
Tell me Zenccrate?	1Tamb	4.4.84		Tamb
Yet give me leave to plead for him my Lord.	1Tamb	4.4.86		Zenoc
Or may be forc'd, to make me Emperour.	1Tamb	4.4.90		Tamb
take these three crownes, and pledge me, my contributorie Kings.	1Tamb	4.4.115	P	Tamb
when holy Fates/Shall stablish me in strong Egyptia,	1Tamb	4.4.135		Tamb
would she leave/The angrie God of Armes, and lie with me.	1Tamb	5.1.125		Tamb
Fetch me some water for my burning breast,	1Tamb	5.1.276		Bajzth
To coole and comfort me with longer date,	1Tamb	5.1.277		Bajzth
Since other meanes are all forbidden me,	1Tamb	5.1.288		Bajzth
teare me in peeces, give me the sworde with a ball of wildefire	1Tamb	5.1.311	P	Zabina
in peeces, give me the sworde with a ball of wildefire upon it.	1Tamb	5.1.311	P	Zabina
And pardon me that was not moov'd with ruthe,	1Tamb	5.1.369		Zenoc
As much as thy faire body is for me.	1Tamb	5.1.416		Zenoc
Since Death denies me further cause of joy,	1Tamb	5.1.430		Arabia
The God of war resignes his roume to me,	1Tamb	5.1.450		Tamb
Meaning to make me Generall of the world,	1Tamb	5.1.451		Tamb
Jove viewing me in armes, lookes pale and wan,	1Tamb	5.1.452		Tamb
Then let me find no further time to grace/Her princely Temples	1Tamb	5.1.488		Tamb
Wilt thou have war, then shake this blade at me,	2Tamb	1.1.83		Sgsmnd
basely on their knees/In all your names desirde a truce of me?	2Tamb	1.1.97		Orcan
Forgetst thou, that to have me raise my siege,	2Tamb	1.1.98		Orcan
And tell me whether I should stoope so low,	2Tamb	1.1.112		Sgsmnd
I know thou wouldst depart from hence with me.	2Tamb	1.2.11		Callap
Not for all Affrike, therefore moove me not.	2Tamb	1.2.12		Almeda
Yet heare me speake my gentle Almeda.	2Tamb	1.2.13		Callap
kings and mcre/Upon their knees, all bid me welcome home.	2Tamb	1.2.29		Callap
but tel me my Lord, if I should goe, would you bee as good as	2Tamb	1.2.61	P	Almeda
But yet me thinks their looks are amorous,	2Tamb	1.3.21		Tamb
Would make me thinke them Bastards, not my sons,	2Tamb	1.3.32		Tamb
If thou wilt love the warres and follow me,	2Tamb	1.3.47		Tamb
Thou shalt be made a King and raigne with me,	2Tamb	1.3.48		Tamb
Yes father, you shal see me if I live,	2Tamb	1.3.54		Celeb
Have under me as many kings as you,	2Tamb	1.3.55		Celeb
These words assure me boy, thou art my sonne,	2Tamb	1.3.58		Tamb
Let me accompany my gratious mother,	2Tamb	1.3.66		Calyph
conquer all the world/And you have won enough for me to keep.	2Tamb	1.3.68		Calyph
Promist to meet me on Larissa plaines/With hostes apeece	2Tamb	1.3.107		Tamb
And all the men in armour under me,	2Tamb	1.3.135		Usumc
friends and fellow kings)/Makes me to surfet in conceiving joy.	2Tamb	1.3.152		Tamb
It could not more delight me than your sight.	2Tamb	1.3.156		Tamb
Jove shall send his winged Messenger/To bid me sheath my sword,	2Tamb	1.3.167		Tamb
But now my friends, let me examine ye,	2Tamb	1.3.172		Tamb
How have ye spent your absent time from me?	2Tamb	1.3.173		Tamb
Wher Amazonians met me in the field:	2Tamb	1.3.192		Techel
Me thinks I see how glad the christian King/Is made, for joy of	2Tamb	2.2.20		Uribas
That this my life may be as short to me/As are the daies of	2Tamb	2.4.36		Tamb
Tell me, how fares my faire Zenocrate?	2Tamb	2.4.41		Tamb
But let me die my Love, yet let me die,	2Tamb	2.4.66		Zenoc
Yet let me kisse my Lord before I die,	2Tamb	2.4.69		Zenoc

ME (cont.)

And let me die with kissing of my Lord.	2Tamb	2.4.70	Zenoc
Let me take leave of these my loving sonnes,	2Tamb	2.4.72	Zenoc
Sweet sons farewell, in death resemble me,	2Tamb	2.4.75	Zenoc
Behold me here divine Zenocrate,	2Tamb	2.4.111	Tamb
To martch with me under this bloody flag:	2Tamb	2.4.116	Tamb
Come downe from heaven and live with me againe.	2Tamb	2.4.118	Tamb
Though she be dead, yet let me think she lives,	2Tamb	2.4.127	Tamb
her soule be, thou shalt stay with me/Embalm'd with Cassia,	2Tamb	2.4.129	Tamb
Because this place bereft me of my Love:	2Tamb	2.4.138	Tamb
That freed me from the bondage of my foe:	2Tamb	3.1.69	Callap
But now my boies, leave off, and list to me,	2Tamb	3.2.53	Tamb
View me thy father that hath conquered kings,	2Tamb	3.2.110	Tamb
a souldier, and this wound/As great a grace and majesty to me,	2Tamb	3.2.118	Tamb
Me thinks tis a pitifull sight.	2Tamb	3.2.130	P Calyph
give me a wound father.	2Tamb	3.2.132	P Celeb
And me another my Lord.	2Tamb	3.2.133	P Amyras
Come sirra, give me your arme.	2Tamb	3.2.134	P Tamb
To you? Why, do you thinke me weary of it?	2Tamb	3.3.17	Capt
Tell me sweet boie, art thou content to die?	2Tamb	3.4.18	Olymp
Mother dispatch me, or Ile kil my selfe,	2Tamb	3.4.26	Sonne
Give me your knife (good mother) or strike home:	2Tamb	3.4.28	Sonne
The Scythians shall not tyrannise on me.	2Tamb	3.4.29	Sonne
My Lord deceast, was dearer unto me,	2Tamb	3.4.42	Olymp
Then carie me I care not where you will,	2Tamb	3.4.80	Olymp
Tell me Viceroies the number of your men,	2Tamb	3.5.30	Callap
Me thinks the slave should make a lusty theefe.	2Tamb	3.5.96	Jrslem
againe, you shall not trouble me thus to come and fetch you.	2Tamb	3.5.101	P Tamb
Come Almeda, receive this crowne of me,	2Tamb	3.5.129	Callap
Good my Lord, let me take it.	2Tamb	3.5.133	P Almeda
Hovering betwixt our armies, light on me,	2Tamb	3.5.163	Tamb
Away ye fools, my father needs not me,	2Tamb	4.1.15	Calyph
If halfe our campe should sit and sleepe with me,	2Tamb	4.1.18	Calyph
It works remorse of conscience in me,	2Tamb	4.1.28	Calyph
I should be affraid, would put it off and come to bed with me.	2Tamb	4.1.70	P Calyph
would let me be put in the front of such a battaile once,	2Tamb	4.1.72	P Calyph
and tel me if the warres/Be not a life that may illustrate	2Tamb	4.1.78	Tamb
Which makes me valiant, proud, ambitious,	2Tamb	4.1.116	Tamb
wars justice ye repute)/I execute, enjoin'd me from above,	2Tamb	4.1.148	Tamb
And plague such Pesants as [resist in] <resisting> me/The power	2Tamb	4.1.157	Tamb
And Ile dispose them as it likes me best,	2Tamb	4.1.166	Tamb
Tell me Olympia, wilt thou graunt my suit?	2Tamb	4.2.21	Therid
And eb againe, as thou departst from me.	2Tamb	4.2.32	Therid
Ah, pity me my Lord, and draw your sword,	2Tamb	4.2.33	Olymp
Leave this my Love, and listen more to me.	2Tamb	4.2.38	Therid
Why Madam, thinke ye to mocke me thus palpably?	2Tamb	4.2.67	Therid
That I dissemble not, trie it on me.	2Tamb	4.2.76	Olymp
Let me have coach my Lord, that I may ride,	2Tamb	4.3.27	Amyras
If Jove esteeming me too good for earth,	2Tamb	4.3.60	Tamb
Raise me to match the faire Aldeboran,	2Tamb	4.3.61	Tamb
Now fetch me out the Turkish Concubines,	2Tamb	4.3.64	Tamb
Live [continent] <content> then (ye slaves) and meet not me	2Tamb	4.3.81	Tamb
To note me Emperour of the three fold world:	2Tamb	4.3.118	Tamb
Is not my life and state as deere to me,	2Tamb	5.1.12	Govnr
And wake blacke Jove to crouch and kneele to me,	2Tamb	5.1.98	Tamb
Tis not thy bloody tents can make me yeeld,	2Tamb	5.1.103	Govnr
Unharnesse them, and let me have fresh horse:	2Tamb	5.1.130	Tamb
So, now their best is done to honour me,	2Tamb	5.1.131	Tamb
Rather lend me thy weapon Tamburlain,	2Tamb	5.1.142	Jrslem
Bridle them, and let me to my coach.	2Tamb	5.1.148	Tamb
And offer'd me as ransome for thy life,	2Tamb	5.1.156	Tamb
Shall pay me tribute for, in Babylon.	2Tamb	5.1.167	Tamb
Sicknes or death can never conquer me.	2Tamb	5.1.222	Tamb
Me thinks I could sustaine a thousand deaths,	2Tamb	5.2.22	Callap
This is the time that must eternize me,	2Tamb	5.2.54	Callap
Shall sicknesse proove me now to be a man,	2Tamb	5.3.44	Tamb
Come carie me to war against the Gods,	2Tamb	5.3.52	Tamb
To cure me, or Ile fetch him downe my selfe.	2Tamb	5.3.63	Tamb
Stands aiming at me with his murthering dart,	2Tamb	5.3.69	Tamb
Tel me, what think you of my sicknes now?	2Tamb	5.3.81	Tamb
That meane t'invest me in a higher throane,	2Tamb	5.3.121	Tamb
Give me a Map, then let me see how much/Is left for me to	2Tamb	5.3.123	Tamb
then let me see how much/Is left for me to conquer all the	2Tamb	5.3.123	Tamb
let me see how much/Is left for me to conquer all the world,	2Tamb	5.3.124	Tamb
Then now remoove me, that I may resigne/My place and proper	2Tamb	5.3.175	Tamb
Help me (my Lords) to make my last remoove.	2Tamb	5.3.180	Tamb
let me see how well/Thou wilt become thy fathers majestie.	2Tamb	5.3.183	Tamb
Heavens witnes me, with what a broken hart/And damned spirit I	2Tamb	5.3.206	Amyras
Cannot behold the teares ye shed for me,	2Tamb	5.3.218	Tamb
But such as love me, gard me from their tongues,	Jew	Prol.6	Machvl
Admir'd I am of those that hate me most:	Jew	Prol.9	Machvl
Yet will they reade me, and thereby attaine/To Peters Chayre:	Jew	Prol.11	Machvl
And when they cast me off,/Are poyson'd by my climing	Jew	Prol.12	Machvl
Let me be envy'd and not pittied!	Jew	Prol.27	Machvl
And let him not be entertain'd the worse/Because he favours me.	Jew	Prol.35	Machvl
Give me the Merchants of the Indian Mynes,	Jew	1.1.19	Barab
And thus me thinkes should men of judgement frame/This is the	Jew	1.1.34	Barab
and have sent me to know/Whether your selfe will come and	Jew	1.1.52	1Merch
Who hateth me but for my happinesse?	Jew	1.1.112	Barab
Which me thinkes fits not their profession.	Jew	1.1.118	Barab
Tush, tell not me 'twas done of policie.	Jew	1.1.140	1Jew
Why flocke you thus to me in multitudes?	Jew	1.1.144	Barab
So they spare me, my daughter, and my wealth.	Jew	1.1.153	Barab

ME (cont.)

Yes, give me leave, and Hebrews now come neare.	Jew	1.2.38		Govnr
Let me be us'd but as my brethren are.	Jew	1.2.91		Barab
Preach me not out of my possessions.	Jew	1.2.111		Barab
And which of you can charge me otherwise?	Jew	1.2.117		Barab
tush, take not from me then,/For that is theft; and if you rob	Jew	1.2.125		Barab
For that is theft; and if you rob me thus,	Jew	1.2.126		Barab
Your extreme right does me exceeding wrong:	Jew	1.2.153		Barab
That thus have dealt with me in my distresse.	Jew	1.2.168		Barab
And of me onely have they taken all.	Jew	1.2.179		Barab
What tell you me of Job?	Jew	1.2.181		Barab
And painefull nights have bin appointed me.	Jew	1.2.198		Barab
I, I,/Pray leave me in my patience.	Jew	1.2.200		Barab
I, let me sorrow for this sudden chance,	Jew	1.2.206		Barab
but trust me 'tis a misery/To see a man in such affliction:	Jew	1.2.211		2Jew
Thinke me to be a senselesse lumpe of clay/That will with every	Jew	1.2.216		Barab
thinke me not all so fond/As negligently to forgoe so much	Jew	1.2.241		Barab
to forgoe so much/Without provision for thy selfe and me.	Jew	1.2.243		Barab
But they will give me leave once more, I trow,	Jew	1.2.252		Barab
Displacing me; and of thy house they meane/To make a Nunnery,	Jew	1.2.255		Abigal
what, will you thus oppose me, lucklesse Starres,	Jew	1.2.260		Barab
To make me desperate in my poverty?	Jew	1.2.261		Barab
And knowing me impatient in distresse/Thinke me so mad as I	Jew	1.2.262		Barab
in distresse/Thinke me so mad as I will hang my selfe,	Jew	1.2.263		Barab
And since you leave me in the Ocean thus/To sinke or swim, and	Jew	1.2.267		Barab
me in the Ocean thus/To sinke or swim, and put me to my shifts,	Jew	1.2.268		Barab
the plight/Wherein these Christians have oppressed me:	Jew	1.2.271		Barab
Be rul'd by me, for in extremitie/We ought to make barre of no	Jew	1.2.272		Barab
thus; thou toldst me they have turn'd my house/Into a Nunnery,	Jew	1.2.277		Barab
I, but father they will suspect me there.	Jew	1.2.283		Abigal
Then father, goe with me.	Jew	1.2.300		Abigal
First let me as a Novice learne to frame/My solitary life to	Jew	1.2.331		Abigal
And let me lodge where I was wont to lye.	Jew	1.2.333		Abigal
Father, give me--	Jew	1.2.348		Abigal
No come not at me, if thou wilt be damn'd,	Jew	1.2.362		Barab
Forget me, see me not, and so be gone.	Jew	1.2.363		Barab
Beleeve me, Noble Lodowicke, I have seene/The strangest sight,	Jew	1.2.375		Mthias
time/Have tane their flight, and left me in despaire;	Jew	2.1.8		Barab
Who in my wealth wud tell me winters tales,	Jew	2.1.25		Barab
And now me thinkes that I am one of those:	Jew	2.1.28		Barab
He said he wud attend me in the morne.	Jew	2.1.34		Abigal
Therefore be rul'd by me, and keepe the gold:	Jew	2.2.39		Bosco
Heave up my shoulders when they call me dogge,	Jew	2.3.24		Barab
That when the offering-Bason comes to me,	Jew	2.3.28		Barab
For Don Mathias tels me she is faire.	Jew	2.3.35		Lodowk
Well, Barabas, canst helpe me to a Diamond?	Jew	2.3.48		Lodowk
Is it square or pointed, pray let me know.	Jew	2.3.59		Lodowk
To bring me to religious purity,	Jew	2.3.72		Barab
To make me mindfull of my mortall sinnes,	Jew	2.3.74		Barab
Seiz'd all I had, and thrust me out a doores,	Jew	2.3.76		Barab
Let me see, sirra, are you not an old shaver?	Jew	2.3.114	P	Barab
Tell me, hast thou thy health well?	Jew	2.3.121	P	Barab
you in these chops; let me see one that's somewhat leaner.	Jew	2.3.125	P	Barab
I feare me 'tis about faire Abigall.	Jew	2.3.139		Mthias
Seeme not to know me here before your mother/Lest she mistrust	Jew	2.3.146		Barab
Thinke of me as thy father; Sonne farewell.	Jew	2.3.149		Barab
Tell me, Mathias, is not that the Jew?	Jew	2.3.152		Mater
Now let me know thy name, and therewithall/Thy birth,	Jew	2.3.163		Barab
But tell me now, How hast thou spent thy time?	Jew	2.3.201		Barab
make account of me/As of thy fellow; we are villaines both:	Jew	2.3.213		Barab
Where is the Diamond you told me of?	Jew	2.3.219		Lodowk
I have it for you, Sir; please you walke in with me:	Jew	2.3.220		Barab
Give me the letters, daughter, doe you heare?	Jew	2.3.224		Barab
I am a little busie, Sir, pray pardon me.	Jew	2.3.231		Barab
My Factor sends me word a Merchant's fled/That owes me for a	Jew	2.3.243		Barab
word a Merchant's fled/That owes me for a hundred Tun of Wine:	Jew	2.3.244		Barab
I, Barabas, or else thou wrong'st me much.	Jew	2.3.255		Mthias
Pardon me though I weepe; the Governors sonne/Will, whether I	Jew	2.3.257		Barab
Even now as I came home, he slipt me in,	Jew	2.3.267		Barab
If you love me, no quarrels in my house;	Jew	2.3.271		Barab
Mathias, as thou lov'st me, not a word.	Jew	2.3.277		Barab
This is thy Diamond, tell me, shall I have it?	Jew	2.3.292		Lodowk
And mine you have, yet let me talke to her;	Jew	2.3.300		Barab
Then gentle Abigal plight thy faith to me.	Jew	2.3.315		Lodowk
Nothing but death shall part my love and me.	Jew	2.3.317		Abigal
Then my faire Abigal should frowne on me.	Jew	2.3.332		Lodowk
Well, but for me, as you went in at dores/You had bin stab'd,	Jew	2.3.337		Barab
Suffer me, Barabas, but to follow him.	Jew	2.3.340		Mthias
Shall Lodowicke rob me of so faire a love?	Jew	2.3.347		Mthias
My heart misgives me, that to crosse your love,	Jew	2.3.349		Barab
Now tell me, Ithimore, how lik'st thou this?	Jew	2.3.364		Barab
As I behave my selfe in this, imploy me hereafter.	Jew	2.3.379		Ithimr
Tell me, how cam'st thou by this?	Jew	3.1.16		Curtzn
Oh leave to grieve me, I am griev'd enough.	Jew	3.2.17		Mater
I know not, and that grieves me most of all.	Jew	3.2.21		Govnr
Lend me that weapon that did kill my sonne,	Jew	3.2.23		Mater
And it shall murder me.	Jew	3.2.24		Mater
Well, Ithimore, let me request thee this,	Jew	3.3.26		Abigal
And say, I pray them come and speake with me.	Jew	3.3.29		Abigal
I pray, mistris, wil you answer me to one question?	Jew	3.3.30	P	Ithimr
To make me shew them favour severally,	Jew	3.3.38		Abigal
Nor on Mathias, but by murdering me.	Jew	3.3.46		Abigal
To get me be admitted for a Nun.	Jew	3.3.55		Abigal

ME (cont.)

Has made me see the difference of things.	Jew	3.3.62	Abigal
Oh therefore, Jacomo, let me be one,	Jew	3.3.68	Abigal
Nay, you shall pardon me:	Jew	3.3.73	Abigal
And all unknowne, and unconstrain'd of me,	Jew	3.4.3	Barab
Now here she writes, and wils me to repent.	Jew	3.4.5	Barab
For she that varies from me in beleefe/Gives great presumption	Jew	3.4.10	Barab
me in beleefe/Gives great presumption that she loves me not;	Jew	3.4.11	Barab
That's no lye, for she sent me for him.	Jew	3.4.25	P Ithimr
from hence/Ne're shall she grieve me more with her disgrace;	Jew	3.4.29	Barab
Be blest of me, nor come within my gates,	Jew	3.4.31	Barab
And she is hatefull to my soule and me:	Jew	3.4.36	Barab
But first goe fetch me in the pot of Rice/That for our supper	Jew	3.4.49	Barab
Stay, let me spice it first.	Jew	3.4.85	Barab
Pray doe, and let me help you, master.	Jew	3.4.86	P Ithimr
Pray let me taste first.	Jew	3.4.86	P Ithimr
Stay, first let me stirre it Ithimore.	Jew	3.4.95	Barab
Pay me my wages for my worke is done.	Jew	3.4.115	Ithimr
The Abbasse sent for me to be confest:	Jew	3.6.3	2Fryar
And so did faire Maria send for me:	Jew	3.6.5	1Fryar
Where is the Fryar that converst with me?	Jew	3.6.9	Abigal
And one offence torments me more then all.	Jew	3.6.19	Abigal
My father did contract me to 'em both:	Jew	3.6.22	Abigal
I, and a Virgin too, that grieves me most:	Jew	3.6.41	2Fryar
And make him stand in feare of me.	Jew	3.6.43	2Fryar
this, then goe with me/And helpe me to exclaime against the Jew.	Jew	3.6.45	2Fryar
then goe with me/And helpe me to exclaime against the Jew.	Jew	3.6.46	2Fryar
A thing that makes me tremble to unfold.	Jew	3.6.48	2Fryar
'twas told me in shrift,/Thou know'st 'tis death and if it be	Jew	3.6.50	2Fryar
Good master let me poyson all the Monks.	Jew	4.1.14	Ithimr
of my sinnes/Lye heavy on my soule; then pray you tell me,	Jew	4.1.49	Barab
You shall convert me, you shall have all my wealth.	Jew	4.1.81	Barab
Then 'tis not for me; and I am resolv'd/You shall confesse me,	Jew	4.1.85	Barab
and I am resolv'd/You shall confesse me, and have all my goods.	Jew	4.1.86	Barab
Good Barabas, come to me.	Jew	4.1.87	2Fryar
Rid him away, and goe you home with me.	Jew	4.1.89	Barab
How, dost call me rogue?	Jew	4.1.96	1Fryar
You know my mind, let me alone with him.	Jew	4.1.100	Barab
Ithimore, tell me, is the Fryar asleepe?	Jew	4.1.129	Barab
I feare me he mistrusts what we intend.	Jew	4.1.133	Ithimr
You loyter, master, wherefore stay [we] <me> thus?	Jew	4.1.139	Ithimr
What, doe you meane to strangle me?	Jew	4.1.144	2Fryar
master, be rul'd by me a little; so, let him leane upon his	Jew	4.1.153	P Ithimr
Stands here a purpose, meaning me some wrong,	Jew	4.1.166	1Fryar
Away, I'de wish thee, and let me goe by:	Jew	4.1.170	1Fryar
As thou lik'st that, stop me another time.	Jew	4.1.173	1Fryar
Why, stricken him that would have stroke at me.	Jew	4.1.175	1Fryar
Good Barabas let me goe.	Jew	4.1.184	1Fryar
No, pardon me, the Law must have his course.	Jew	4.1.185	Barab
Heaven blesse me; what, a Fryar a murderer?	Jew	4.1.196	Barab
Villaines, I am a sacred person, touch me not.	Jew	4.1.201	1Fryar
Not a wise word, only gave me a nod, as who shold say, Is it	Jew	4.2.12	P Pilia
a fellow met me with a muschatoes like a Ravens wing, and a	Jew	4.2.27	P Ithimr
and he gave me a letter from one Madam Bellamira, saluting me	Jew	4.2.29	P Ithimr
me in such sort as if he had meant to make cleane my Boots with	Jew	4.2.30	P Ithimr
It may be she sees more in me than I can find in my selfe:	Jew	4.2.33	P Ithimr
that she loves me ever since she saw me, and who would not	Jew	4.2.34	P Ithimr
he flouts me, what gentry can be in a poore Turke of ten pence?	Jew	4.2.38	P Ithimr
Though womans modesty should hale me backe,	Jew	4.2.45	Curtzn
I'le goe steale some mony from my Master to make me hansome:	Jew	4.2.50	P Ithimr
Pray pardon me, I must goe see a ship discharg'd.	Jew	4.2.51	P Ithimr
Canst thou be so unkind to leave me thus?	Jew	4.2.52	Curtzn
Nay, I care not how much she loves me; Sweet Bellamira, would I	Jew	4.2.54	P Ithimr
Let me alone, doe but you speake him faire:	Jew	4.2.63	Pilia
I'le make him send me half he has, and glad he scapes so too.	Jew	4.2.67	P Ithimr
Sirra Barabas, send me a hundred crownes.	Jew	4.2.73	P Ithimr
I charge thee send me three hundred by this bearer, and this	Jew	4.2.75	P Ithimr
Let me alone, I'le use him in his kinde.	Jew	4.2.80	Pilia
Send to the Merchant, bid him bring me silkes,	Jew	4.2.84	Curtzn
Shalt live with me and be my love.	Jew	4.2.98	Ithimr
him he were best to send it; then he hug'd and imbrac'd me.	Jew	4.2.106	P Pilia
and told me he lov'd me for your sake, and said what a	Jew	4.2.108	P Pilia
and told me he lov'd me for your sake, and said what a	Jew	4.2.109	P Pilia
The more villaine he to keep me thus:	Jew	4.2.111	Ithimr
To conclude, he gave me ten crownes.	Jew	4.2.113	P Pilia
Give me a Reame of paper, we'll have a kingdome of gold for't.	Jew	4.2.114	P Ithimr
as you love your life send me five hundred crowns, and give the	Jew	4.2.117	P Ithimr
What an eye she casts on me?	Jew	4.2.128	P Ithimr
Barabas send me three hundred Crownes.	Jew	4.3.1	Barab
He was not wont to call me Barabas.	Jew	4.3.3	Barab
please you dine with me, Sir, and you shal be most hartily	Jew	4.3.29	P Barab
enough, and therfore talke not to me of your Counting-house:	Jew	4.3.36	P Pilia
this angers me,/That he who knowes I love him as my selfe	Jew	4.3.41	Barab
Commend me to him, Sir, most humbly,	Jew	4.3.47	Barab
Saist thou me so?	Jew	4.4.2	P Ithimr
There, if thou lov'st me doe not leave a drop.	Jew	4.4.6	P Ithimr
Love thee, fill me three glasses.	Jew	4.4.7	Curtzn
Ha, to the Jew, and send me mony you were best.	Jew	4.4.12	P Ithimr
We two, and 'twas never knowne, nor never shall be for me.	Jew	4.4.24	P Ithimr
This shall with me unto the Governor.	Jew	4.4.25	Pilia
Love me little, love me long, let musicke rumble,	Jew	4.4.28	Ithimr
Pilia-borza, bid the Fidler give me the posey in his hat there.	Jew	4.4.35	P Curtzn
Foh, me thinkes they stinke like a Holly-Hoke.	Jew	4.4.41	Pilia

ME (cont.)

Give him a crowne, and fill me out more wine.	Jew	4.4.46	Ithimr
How liberally the villain gives me mine own gold.	Jew	4.4.48	P Barab
Me thinkes he fingers very well.	Jew	4.4.49	Pilia
'Twas sent me for a present from the great Cham.	Jew	4.4.68	Barab
Pardona moy, Mounsier, [me] <we> be no well.	Jew	4.4.71	Barab
Let me alone to urge it now I know the meaning.	Jew	4.4.79	Pilia
What e're I am, yet Governor heare me speake;	Jew	5.1.9	Curtzn
I'le goe alone, dogs, do not hale me thus.	Jew	5.1.19	Barab
Nor me neither, I cannot out-run you Constable, oh my belly.	Jew	5.1.20	P Ithimr
Away with him, his sight is death to me.	Jew	5.1.35	Govnr
you men of Malta, heare me speake;/Shee is a Curtezane and he a	Jew	5.1.36	Barab
And he my bondman, let me have law,	Jew	5.1.38	Barab
have hir'd a slave my man/To accuse me of a thousand villanies:	Jew	5.1.76	Barab
And being asleepe, belike they thought me dead,	Jew	5.1.81	Barab
belike they thought me dead,/And threw me o're the wals:	Jew	5.1.82	Barab
but tell me, Barabas,/Canst thou, as thou reportest, make Malta	Jew	5.1.84	Calym
And if it be not true, then let me dye.	Jew	5.1.96	Barab
Away, no more, let him not trouble me.	Jew	5.2.26	Barab
But Malta hates me, and in hating me/My life's in danger, and	Jew	5.2.30	Barab
Now tell me, Governor, and plainely too,	Jew	5.2.55	Barab
'Tis not thy life which can availe me ought,	Jew	5.2.62	Barab
Yet you doe live, and live for me you shall:	Jew	5.2.63	Barab
What wilt thou give me, Governor, to procure/A dissolution of	Jew	5.2.76	Barab
What will you give me if I render you/The life of Calymath,	Jew	5.2.79	Barab
Governor, I enlarge thee, live with me,	Jew	5.2.91	Barab
And let me see what mony thou canst make;	Jew	5.2.94	Barab
Here is my hand, beleeve me, Barabas,	Jew	5.2.102	Govnr
And bring it with me to thee in the evening.	Jew	5.2.108	Govnr
I feare me, Messenger, to feast my traine/Within a Towne of	Jew	5.3.21	Calym
In this, my Countrimen, be rul'd by me,	Jew	5.4.1	Govnr
Then issue out and come to rescue me,	Jew	5.4.5	Govnr
Now Selim-Calymath, returne me word/That thou wilt come, and I	Jew	5.5.11	Barab
For if I keepe not promise, trust not me.	Jew	5.5.23	Barab
Now tell me, worldlings, underneath the [sunne] <summe>,	Jew	5.5.49	Barab
Helpe, helpe me, Christians, helpe.	Jew	5.5.65	Barab
Oh helpe me, Selim, helpe me, Christians.	Jew	5.5.70	Barab
You will not helpe me then?	Jew	5.5.76	Barab
And villaines, know you cannot helpe me now.	Jew	5.5.77	Barab
the extremity of heat/To pinch me with intolerable pangs:	Jew	5.5.88	Barab
Tell me, you Christians, what doth this portend?	Jew	5.5.90	Calym
Nay rather, Christians, let me goe to Turkey,	Jew	5.5.115	Calym
To keepe me here will nought advantage you.	Jew	5.5.117	Calym
Shall binde me ever to your highnes will,	P 11	1.11	Navrre
Set me to scale the high Peramides,	P 100	2.43	Guise
For this, hath heaven engendred me of earth,	P 113	2.56	Guise
Catholickes/Sends Indian golde to coyne me French ecues:	P 118	2.61	Guise
Those that hate me, will I learn to loath.	P 156	2.99	Guise
Give me a look, that when I bend the browes,	P 157	2.100	Guise
Me thinkes the gloves have a very strong perfume,	P 170	3.5	OldQn
Me thinkes my Lord, Anjoy hath well advisde/Your highnes to	P 219	4.17	Guise
Thankes to my princely sonne, then tell me Guise,	P 228	4.26	QnMoth
Come sirs follow me.	P 292	5.19	Gonzag
O let me pray before I dye.	P 301	5.28	Admral
Stay my Lord, let me begin the psalme.	P 344	5.71	Anjoy
To speek with me from such a man as he?	P 350	6.5	Seroun
O let me pray before I take my death.	P 352	6.7	Seroun
O let me pray unto my God.	P 359	6.14	Seroun
And meane once more to menace me.	P 364	7.4	Ramus
Tell me Taleus, wherfore should I flye?	P 366	7.6	Ramus
O good my Lord, let me but speak a word.	P 399	7.39	Ramus
How may we doe? I feare me they will live.	P 420	7.60	Guise
For that let me alone, Cousin stay you heer,	P 428	7.68	Anjoy
And when you see me in, then follow hard.	P 429	7.69	Anjoy
the diadem/Of France be cast on me, then with your leaves/I may	P 473	8.23	Anjoy
on me, then with your leaves/I may retire me to my native home.	P 474	8.24	Anjoy
all doubts, be rulde by me, lets hang him heere upon this tree.	P 491	9.10	P 2Atndt
Beleeve me Guise he becomes the place so well,	P 495	9.14	QnMoth
I, but my Lord let me alone for that,	P 519	9.38	QnMoth
O Mounser de Guise, heare me but speake.	P 529	10.2	Prtsnt
O let me stay and rest me heer a while,	P 536	11.1	Charls
I must say so, paine forceth me complaine.	P 540	11.5	Charls
O holde me up, my sight begins to faile,	P 548	11.13	Charls
My opportunity may serve me fit,	P 566	11.31	Navrre
To steale from France, and hye me to my home.	P 567	11.32	Navrre
For heers no saftie in the Realme for me,	P 568	11.33	Navrre
Might seeme <seek> to crosse me in mine enterprise.	P 574	11.39	Navrre
Truth Pleshe, and God so prosper me in all,	P 584	11.49	Navrre
Then may it please your Majestie to give me leave,	P 616	12.29	Mugern
Come sir, give me my buttons and heers your eare.	P 620	12.33	Mugern
My Lord Cardinall of Loraine, tell me,	P 631	12.44	QnMoth
Tush man, let me alone with him,	P 648	12.61	QnMoth
Goe fetch me pen and inke.	P 657	13.1	Duchss
That he may come and meet me in some place,	P 664	13.8	Duchss
So, set it down and leave me to my selfe.	P 666	13.10	Duchss
Will laugh I feare me at their good aray.	P 673	13.17	Duchss
I pray thee let me see.	P 674	13.18	Guise
O pardon me my Lord.	P 679	13.23	Duchss
proudest Kings/In Christendome, should beare me such derision,	P 761	15.19	Guise
Even for your words that have incenst me so,	P 767	15.25	Guise
Whether he have dishonoured me or no.	P 769	15.27	Guise
Beleeve me this jest bites sore.	P 771	15.29	King
But wherfore beares he me such deadly hate?	P 779	15.37	Mugern

ME (cont.)

Well, let me alone, whose within there?	P 881	17.76	King
Ile secretly convay me unto Bloyse,	P 895	17.90	King
Bartus be gone, commend me to his grace,	P 911	18.12	Navrre
That wicked Guise I feare me much will be,	P 921	18.22	Navrre
And perish in the pit thou mad'st for me.	P 963	19.33	King
Twere hard with me if I should doubt my kinne,	P 971	19.41	King
O pardon me my Lord of Guise.	P 990	19.60	P 3Mur
To murder me, villaine?	P 993	19.63	Guise
Oh I have my deaths wound, give me leave to speak.	P1003	19.73	Guise
Trouble me not, I neare offended him,	P1005	19.75	Guise
To which thou didst alure me being alive:	P1025	19.95	King
To threaten England and to menace me?	P1034	19.104	King
Hath he not made me in the Popes defence,	P1036	19.106	King
In civill broiles between Navarre and me?	P1038	19.108	King
Tush, to be short, he meant to make me Munke,	P1039	19.109	King
Or else to murder me, and so be King.	P1040	19.110	King
Nay he was King and countermanded me,	P1069	19.139	King
Away, leave me alone to meditate.	P1081	19.151	QnMoth
Murder me not, I am a Cardenall.	P1091	20.1	Cardnl
My Lord, here me but speak.	P1129	21.23	P Frier
Tush my Lord, let me alone for that.	P1136	21.30	P Frier
Frier come with me,	P1137	21.31	Dumain
Frier, thou dost acknowledge me thy King?	P1164	22.26	King
Sancte [Jacobe] <Jacobus>, now have mercye upon me.	P1172	22.34	Frier
Search Surgeon and resolve me what thou seest.	P1193	22.55	King
Navarre, give me thy hand, I heere do sweare,	P1203	22.65	King
These words revive my thoughts and comforts me,	P1209	22.71	Navrre
Tell me Surgeon, shall I live?	P1211	22.73	King
Tell me Surgeon and flatter not, may I live?	P1222	22.84	King
Ah Epernoune, is this thy love to me?	P1235	22.97	King
He loves me not that sheds most teares,	P1239	22.101	King
I dye Navarre, come beare me to my Sepulchre.	P1242	22.104	King
Trayterouse guise ah thow hast murthered me	Paris	ms17,p390	Minion
Ah words that make me surfet with delight:	Edw	1.1.3	Gavstn
Might have enforst me to have swum from France,	Edw	1.1.7	Gavstn
Sc thou wouldst smile and take me in thy <thine> armes.	Edw	1.1.9	Gavstn
The king, upon whose bosome let me die,	Edw	1.1.14	Gavstn
Let me see, thou wouldst do well/To waite at my trencher, and	Edw	1.1.30	Gavstn
well/To waite at my trencher, and tell me lies at dinner time,	Edw	1.1.31	Gavstn
I, I, these wordes of his move me as much,	Edw	1.1.39	Gavstn
I have some busines, leave me to my selfe.	Edw	1.1.48	Gavstn
these are not men for me,/I must have wanton Poets, pleasant	Edw	1.1.50	Gavstn
Will you not graunt me this?--	Edw	1.1.77	Edward
That crosse me thus, shall know I am displeasd.	Edw	1.1.79	Edward
Barons and Earls, your pride hath made me mute,	Edw	1.1.107	Kent
I can no longer keepe me from my lord.	Edw	1.1.139	Gavstn
Embrace me Gaveston as I do thee:	Edw	1.1.141	Edward
Then thou hast beene of me since thy exile.	Edw	1.1.145	Edward
Cheefe Secretarie to the state and me,	Edw	1.1.155	Edward
It shall suffice me to enjoy your love,	Edw	1.1.171	Gavstn
Saving your reverence, you must pardon me.	Edw	1.1.186	Gavstn
Come follow me, and thou shalt have my guarde,	Edw	1.1.204	Edward
What els my lords, for it concernes me neere,	Edw	1.2.44	ArchBp
For now my lord the king regardes me not,	Edw	1.2.49	Queene
My lords, to eaze all this, but heare me speake.	Edw	1.2.68	ArchBp
To crosse to Lambeth, and there stay with me.	Edw	1.2.78	ArchBp
Give me the paper.	Edw	1.4.3	ArchBp
Ere my sweete Gaveston shall part from me,	Edw	1.4.48	Edward
Curse me, depose me, doe the worst you can.	Edw	1.4.57	Edward
It bootes me not to threat, I must speake faire,	Edw	1.4.63	Edward
Because he loves me more then all the world:	Edw	1.4.77	Edward
Give it me, ile have it published in the streetes.	Edw	1.4.89	Lncstr
They would not stir, were it to do me good:	Edw	1.4.95	Edward
Here take my picture, and let me weare thine,	Edw	1.4.127	Edward
I shal be found, and then twil greeve me more.	Edw	1.4.132	Gavstn
And therefore give me leave to looke my fill,	Edw	1.4.139	Edward
Fawne not on me French strumpet, get thee gone.	Edw	1.4.145	Edward
In saying this, thou wrongst me Gaveston,	Edw	1.4.149	Queene
I meane not sc, your grace must pardon me.	Edw	1.4.153	Gavstn
Or thou shalt nere be reconcild to me.	Edw	1.4.157	Edward
Away then, touch me not, come Gaveston.	Edw	1.4.159	Edward
Villaine, tis thou that robst me of my lord.	Edw	1.4.160	Queene
Madam, tis you that rob me of my lord.	Edw	1.4.161	Gavstn
And witnesse heaven how deere thou art to me.	Edw	1.4.167	Edward
The king my lord thus to abandon me:	Edw	1.4.177	Queene
And he confesseth that he loves me not.	Edw	1.4.194	Queene
And yet I lcve in vaine, heele nere love me.	Edw	1.4.197	Queene
The angrie king hath banished me the court:	Edw	1.4.210	Queene
And therefore as thou lovest and tendrest me,	Edw	1.4.211	Queene
What, would ye have me plead for Gaveston?	Edw	1.4.213	Mortmr
Sweete Mortimer, sit downe by me a while,	Edw	1.4.225	Queene
Will you be resolute and hold with me?	Edw	1.4.231	Lncstr
Why then my lcrd, give me but leave to speak.	Edw	1.4.254	Mortmr
Thinke me as base a groome as Gaveston.	Edw	1.4.291	Mortmr
In this I ccunt me highly gratified,	Edw	1.4.295	Mortmr
returnd, this newes will glad him much,/Yet not so much as me.	Edw	1.4.302	Queene
more/Then he can Gaveston, would he lov'd me/But halfe so much,	Edw	1.4.303	Queene
And makes me frantick for my Gaveston:	Edw	1.4.315	Edward
And with my kinglie scepter stroke me dead,	Edw	1.4.317	Edward
But will you love me, if you finde it so?	Edw	1.4.324	Queene
about my neck/Then these my lord, nor let me have more wealth,	Edw	1.4.331	Queene
A second mariage twixt thy selfe and me.	Edw	1.4.335	Edward

ME (cont.)

Live thou with me as my companion.	Edw	1.4.343	Edward
Chide me sweete Warwick, if I go astray.	Edw	1.4.348	Edward
Slay me my lord, when I offend your grace.	Edw	1.4.349	Warwck
In this your grace hath highly honoured me,	Edw	1.4.364	MortSr
Unckle, his wanton humor greeves not me,	Edw	1.4.402	Mortmr
Unckle, tis this that makes me impatient.	Edw	1.4.419	Mortmr
learne this of me, a factious lord/Shall hardly do himselfe	Edw	2.1.6	Spencr
No, his companion, for he loves me well,	Edw	2.1.13	Spencr
And would have once preferd me to the king.	Edw	2.1.14	Spencr
A friend of mine told me in secrecie,	Edw	2.1.17	Spencr
And as she red, she smild, which makes me thinke,	Edw	2.1.21	Spencr
And being like pins heads, blame me for the bignesse,	Edw	2.1.48	Baldck
Which made me curate-like in mine attire,	Edw	2.1.49	Baldck
I know thou couldst not come and visit me.	Edw	2.1.61	Neece
He wils me to repaire unto the court,	Edw	2.1.67	Neece
And meete me at the parke pale presentlie:	Edw	2.1.73	Neece
Spencer, stay you and beare me companie,	Edw	2.1.74	Neece
I feare me he is wrackt upon the sea.	Edw	2.2.2	Edward
But tell me Mortimer, whats thy devise,	Edw	2.2.11	Edward
Prethee let me know it.	Edw	2.2.14	Edward
And by the barke a canker creepes me up,	Edw	2.2.18	Mortmr
They love me not that hate my Gaveston.	Edw	2.2.37	Edward
I am that Cedar, shake me not too much,	Edw	2.2.38	Edward
Thy absence made me droope, and pine away,	Edw	2.2.52	Edward
Desirde her more, and waxt outragious,/So did it sure with me:	Edw	2.2.56	Edward
Stil wil these Earles and Barrons use me thus?	Edw	2.2.70	Edward
Aye me poore soule when these begin to jarre.	Edw	2.2.72	Queene
Nay all of them conspire to crosse me thus,	Edw	2.2.95	Edward
That thinke with high lookes thus to tread me down.	Edw	2.2.97	Edward
I, and it greeves me that I favoured him.	Edw	2.2.213	Kent
Out of my sight, and trouble me no more.	Edw	2.2.216	Edward
Poore Gaveston, that hast no friend but me,	Edw	2.2.220	Edward
Thus do you still suspect me without cause.	Edw	2.2.227	Queene
Pardon me sweet, I forgot my selfe.	Edw	2.2.230	Edward
But let them go, and tell me what are these.	Edw	2.2.239	Edward
Tell me, where wast thou borne? What is thine armes?	Edw	2.2.242	Edward
Waite on me, and ile see thou shalt not want.	Edw	2.2.246	Edward
Then Spencer waite upon me, for his sake/Ile grace thee with a	Edw	2.2.252	Edward
No greater titles happen unto me,	Edw	2.2.254	Spencr
I know my lord, many will stomack me,	Edw	2.2.260	Gavstn
The head-strong Barons shall not limit me.	Edw	2.2.262	Edward
I feare me you are sent of pollicie,	Edw	2.3.5	Lncstr
O tell me Spencer, where is Gaveston?	Edw	2.4.1	Edward
I feare me he is slaine my gratious lord.	Edw	2.4.2	Spencr
That I might pull him to me where I would,	Edw	2.4.18	Queene
How Gaveston hath robd me of his love:	Edw	2.4.67	Queene
My lords, king Edward greetes you all by me.	Edw	2.5.33	Arundl
Intreateth you by me, yet but he may/See him before he dies,	Edw	2.5.36	Arundl
Provided this, that you my lord of Arundell/Will joyne with me.	Edw	2.5.82	Penbrk
Then give him me.	Edw	2.5.94	Penbrk
My Lord, you shall go with me,	Edw	2.5.99	Penbrk
Weel make quick worke, commend me to your maister/My friend, and	Edw	2.6.12	Warwck
The Barons overbeare me with their pride.	Edw	3.1.9	Edward
suffer uncontrowld/These Barons thus to beard me in my land,	Edw	3.1.14	Spencr
And if they send me not my Gaveston,	Edw	3.1.26	Edward
Tell me [Arundell] <Matre>, died he ere thou camst,	Edw	3.1.92	Edward
And tell me, would the rebels denie me that?	Edw	3.1.101	Edward
Refusing to receive me pledge for him,	Edw	3.1.107	Arundl
The Barons up in armes, by me salute/Your highnes, with long	Edw	3.1.156	Herald
And bid me say as plainer to your grace,	Edw	3.1.158	Herald
see how I do devorce/Spencer from me:	Edw	3.1.177	Edward
me thinkes you hang the heads,/But weele advance them traitors,	Edw	3.1.223	Edward
Sound drums and trumpets, marche with me my friends,	Edw	3.1.260	Edward
Proud Edward, doost thou banish me thy presence?	Edw	4.1.5	Kent
I thanke them, gave me leave to passe in peace:	Edw	4.1.16	Mortmr
A loves me better than a thousand Spencers.	Edw	4.2.7	Prince
will your grace with me to Henolt,/And there stay times	Edw	4.2.17	SrJohn
So pleaseth the Queene my mother, me it likes.	Edw	4.2.21	Prince
Shall have me from my gratious mothers side,	Edw	4.2.23	Prince
His grace I dare presume will welcome me,	Edw	4.2.33	Queene
Madam along, and you my lord, with me,	Edw	4.2.81	SrJohn
Ah nothing greeves me but my little boye,	Edw	4.3.48	Edward
Give me my horse and lets r'enforce our troupes:	Edw	4.5.6	Edward
Tell me good unckle, what Edward doe you meane?	Edw	4.6.32	Prince
Present by me this traitor to the state,	Edw	4.6.49	Rice
Care of my countrie cald me to this warre.	Edw	4.6.65	Queene
Come Spencer, come Baldocke, come sit downe by me,	Edw	4.7.16	Edward
Who wounds me with the name of Mortimer/That bloudy man?	Edw	4.7.38	Edward
To take my life, my companie from me?	Edw	4.7.65	Edward
Our lots are cast, I feare me so is thine.	Edw	4.7.79	Baldck
A litter hast thou, lay me in a hearse,	Edw	4.7.87	Edward
And to the gates of hell convay me hence,	Edw	4.7.88	Edward
Leister, thou staist for me,/And go I must, life farewell with	Edw	4.7.98	Edward
Your worship I trust will remember me?	Edw	4.7.117	Mower
Follow me to the towne.	Edw	4.7.119	Rice
Leister, if gentle words might comfort me,	Edw	5.1.5	Edward
And so it fares with me, whose dauntlesse minde/The ambitious	Edw	5.1.15	Edward
That thus hath pent and mu'd me in a prison,	Edw	5.1.18	Edward
To plaine me to the gods against them both:	Edw	5.1.22	Edward
Me thinkes I should revenge me of the wronges,	Edw	5.1.24	Edward
That bleedes within me for this strange exchange.	Edw	5.1.35	Edward
But tell me, must I now resigne my crowne,	Edw	5.1.36	Edward

ME (cont.)

But stay a while, let me be king till night,	Edw	5.1.59	Edward
And therefore let me weare it yet a while.	Edw	5.1.83	Edward
I might, but heavens and earth conspire/To make me miserable:	Edw	5.1.97	Edward
Take it: what are you moovde, pitie you me?	Edw	5.1.102	Edward
Make me despise this transitorie pompe,	Edw	5.1.108	Edward
Or if I live, let me forget my selfe.	Edw	5.1.111	Edward
Call me not lorde, away, out of my sight:	Edw	5.1.113	Edward
Ah pardon me, greefe makes me lunatick.	Edw	5.1.114	Edward
Commend me to my sonne, and bid him rule/Better then I, yet how	Edw	5.1.121	Edward
Heare me immortall Jove, and graunt it too.	Edw	5.1.143	Edward
Be rulde by me, and we will rule the realme,	Edw	5.2.5	Mortmr
And then let me alone to handle him.	Edw	5.2.22	Mortmr
Let me alone, here is the privie seale,	Edw	5.2.37	Mortmr
Commend me humblie to his Majestie,	Edw	5.2.69	Queene
Mother, perswade me not to weare the crowne,	Edw	5.2.92	Prince
Let me but see him first, and then I will.	Edw	5.2.95	Prince
Come sonne, and go with this gentle Lorde and me.	Edw	5.2.109	Queene
Helpe unckle Kent, Mortimer will wrong me.	Edw	5.2.113	Prince
Traitors away, what will you murther me,	Edw	5.3.29	Edward
For me, both thou, and both the Spencers died,	Edw	5.3.42	Edward
O gentle brother, helpe to rescue me.	Edw	5.3.51	Edward
Souldiers, let me but talke to him one worde.	Edw	5.3.53	Kent
And I will visit him, why stay you me?	Edw	5.3.60	Kent
I, lead me whether you will, even to my death,	Edw	5.3.66	Kent
Nay, you shall pardon me, none shall knowe my trickes.	Edw	5.4.39	Ltborn
Take this, away, and never see me more.	Edw	5.4.43	Mortmr
Unlesse thou bring me newes of Edwards death.	Edw	5.4.46	Mortmr
The proudest lords salute me as I passe,	Edw	5.4.50	Mortmr
Feard am I more then lov'd, let me be feard,	Edw	5.4.52	Mortmr
They thrust upon me the Protectorship,	Edw	5.4.56	Mortmr
And sue to me for that that I desire,	Edw	5.4.57	Mortmr
It pleaseth me, and Isabell the Queene.	Edw	5.4.71	Mortmr
Nor I, and yet me thinkes I should commaund,	Edw	5.4.97	King
Let me but stay and speake, I will not go,	Edw	5.4.105	Kent
And therefore soldiers whether will you hale me?	Edw	5.4.108	Kent
And get me a spit, and let it be red hote.	Edw	5.5.30	Ltborn
Villaine, I know thou comst to murther me.	Edw	5.5.45	Edward
The Queene sent me, to see how you were used,	Edw	5.5.48	Ltborn
list a while to me,/And then thy heart, were it as Gurneys is,	Edw	5.5.52	Edward
This dungeon where they keepe me, is the sincke,	Edw	5.5.56	Edward
They give me bread and water being a king,	Edw	5.5.62	Edward
And let me see the stroke before it comes,	Edw	5.5.76	Edward
What meanes your highnesse to mistrust me thus?	Edw	5.5.79	Ltborn
What meanes thou to dissemble with me thus?	Edw	5.5.80	Edward
But that greefe keepes me waking, I shoulde sleepe,	Edw	5.5.93	Edward
If you mistrust me, ile be gon my lord.	Edw	5.5.97	Ltborn
No, no, for if thou meanst to murther me,	Edw	5.5.98	Edward
O let me not die yet, stay, O stay a while.	Edw	5.5.101	Edward
And tels me, if I sleepe I never wake,	Edw	5.5.104	Edward
This feare is that which makes me tremble thus,	Edw	5.5.105	Edward
And therefore tell me, wherefore art thou come?	Edw	5.5.106	Edward
Assist me sweete God, and receive my soule.	Edw	5.5.109	Edward
O spare me, or dispatche me in a trice.	Edw	5.5.111	Edward
Tell me sirs, was it not bravelie done?	Edw	5.5.116	Ltborn
Betray us both, therefore let me flie.	Edw	5.6.8	Matrvs
And others are but shrubs compard to me,	Edw	5.6.12	Mortmr
Lets see who dare impeache me for his death?	Edw	5.6.14	Mortmr
Aye me, see where he comes, and they with him,	Edw	5.6.22	Queene
Forbid not me to weepe, he was my father,	Edw	5.6.34	King
Traitor, in me my loving father speakes,	Edw	5.6.41	King
False Gurney hath betraide me and himselfe.	Edw	5.6.45	Mortmr
But bring his head back presently to me.	Edw	5.6.54	King
As thou receivedst thy life from me,	Edw	5.6.68	Queene
My lord, I feare me it will proove too true.	Edw	5.6.77	2Lord
Thinke not to finde me slack or pitifull.	Edw	5.6.82	King
He hath forgotten me, stay, I am his mother.	Edw	5.6.90	Queene
Then come sweete death, and rid me of this greefe.	Edw	5.6.92	Queene
Heere comes the hearse, helpe me to moorne, my lords:	Edw	5.6.98	King
Sweet Analitikes <Anulatikes>, tis thou hast ravisht me,	F 34	1.1.6	Faust
Bid [on kai me on] <Oncaymaeon> farewell, <and> Galen come:	F 40	1.1.12	Faust
Wagner, commend me to me deerest friends,	F 91	1.1.63	Faust
Request them earnestly to visit me.	F 93	1.1.65	Faust
Their conference will be a greater helpe to me,	F 95	1.1.67	Faust
Shall I make spirits fetch me what I please?	F 106	1.1.78	Faust
Resolve me of all ambiguities?	F 107	1.1.79	Faust
I'le have them read me strange Philosophy,	F 113	1.1.85	Faust
And make me blest with your sage conference.	F 126	1.1.98	Faust
Know that your words have won me at the last,	F 128	1.1.100	Faust
'Tis magick, magick, that hath ravisht me.	F 137	1.1.109	Faust
Then gentle friends aid me in this attempt,	F 138	1.1.110	Faust
The spirits tell me they can dry the sea,	F 171	1.1.143	Cornel
Then tell me Faustus what shall we three want?	F 175	1.1.147	Cornel
Come, shew me some demonstrations Magicall,	F 177	1.1.149	Faust
Then come and dine with me, and after meate/We'le canvase every	F 190	1.1.162	Faust
you were not dunces, you would never aske me such a question:	F 207	1.2.14	P Wagner
Then wherefore should you aske me such a question?	F 209	1.2.16	P Wagner
Were he a stranger, <and> not allyed to me,	F 223	1.2.30	2Schol
The danger of his soule would make me mourne:	F 224	1.2.31	2Schol
<O but> I feare me, nothing will <can> reclaime him now.	F 227	1.2.34	1Schol
Thou art too ugly to attend on me:	F 252	1.3.24	Faust
Now Faustus what wouldst thou have me do?	F 263	1.3.35	Mephst
I charge thee waite upon me whilst I live/To do what ever	F 264	1.3.36	Faust

ME (cont.)

Did not he charge thee to appeare to me?	F 271	1.3.43		Faust
This word Damnation, terrifies not me <him>,	F 286	1.3.58		Faust
Tell me, what is that Lucifer, thy Lord?	F 290	1.3.62		Faust
Having thee ever to attend on me,	F 321	1.3.93		Faust
To give me whatsoever I shall aske;	F 322	1.3.94		Faust
To tell me whatsoever I demand:	F 323	1.3.95		Faust
And meet me in my Study, at Midnight,	F 327	1.3.99		Faust
And then resolve me of thy Maisters mind.	F 328	1.3.100		Faust
Sirra, wilt thou be my man and waite on me?	F 354	1.4.12	P	Wagner
thou dost not presently bind thy selfe to me for seven yeares,	F 361	1.4.19	P	Wagner
for they are as familiar with me, as if they payd for their	F 365	1.4.23	P	Robin
How now sir, will you serve me now?	F 376	1.4.34	P	Wagner
Now sirra follow me.	F 379	1.4.37	P	Wagner
you Maister, will you teach me this conjuring Occupation?	F 380	1.4.38	P	Robin
call me Maister Wagner, and see that you walke attentively,	F 385	1.4.43	P	Wagner
When Mephostophilis shall stand by me,	F 413	2.1.25		Faust
shall stand by me,/What [god] <power> can hurt me <thee>?	F 414	2.1.26		Faust
Now tell me what saith <sayes> Lucifer thy Lord.	F 419	2.1.31		Faust
Stay Mephostophilis/And tell me, what good will my soule do thy	F 428	2.1.40		Faust
But tell me Faustus, shall I have thy soule?	F 434	2.1.46		Mephst
If unto [God] <heaven>, hee'le throw me <thee> downe to hell.	F 467	2.1.79		Faust
Then heare me read it Mephostophilis <them>.	F 483	2.1.95		Faust
By me John Faustus.	F 500	2.1.112	P	Faust
So, now Faustus aske me what thou wilt.	F 503	2.1.115		Mephst
Tell me, where is the place that men call Hell?	F 505	2.1.117		Faust
<off> this, let me have a wife, the fairest Maid in Germany,	F 529	2.1.141	P	Faust
<Nay sweete Mephastophilis fetch me one, for I will have one>.	F 530	(HC261)A	P	Faust
And if thou lovest me thinke no more of it.	F 536	2.1.148		Mephst
[Nay let me have one booke more, and then I have done, wherein	F 551.8	2.1.171A	P	Faust
Because thou hast depriv'd me of those Joyes.	F 554	2.2.3		Faust
If Heaven was <it were> made for man, 'twas made for me:	F 561	2.2.10		Faust
Be I a devill yet God may pitty me,	F 566	2.2.15		Faust
Yea <I>, God will pitty me if I repent.	F 567	2.2.16		Faust
Are laid before me to dispatch my selfe:	F 574	2.2.23		Faust
Have not I made blind Homer sing to me/Of Alexanders love, and	F 577	2.2.26		Faust
Speake <Tel me>, are there many Spheares <heavens> above the	F 586	2.2.35		Faust
But <tell me> have they all/One motion, both situ et tempore?	F 595	2.2.44		Faust
But tell me, hath every Spheare a Dominion, or Intelligentia	F 607	2.2.56	P	Faust
<Well>, Resolve me then in this one question:	F 614	2.2.63	P	Faust
now tell me who made the world?	F 618	2.2.67	P	Faust
Sweet Mephostophilis tell me.	F 620	2.2.69	P	Faust
Move me not Faustus <for I will not tell thee>.	F 621	2.2.70	P	Mephst
Villaine, have I not bound thee to tell me any thing?	F 622	2.2.71	P	Faust
pardon [me] <him> for <in> this,/And Faustus vowes never to	F 647	2.2.96		Faust
That sight will be as pleasant to <pleasing unto> me, as	F 657	2.2.106	P	Faust
and the devill a peny they have left me, but a [bare] <small>	F 694	2.2.143	P	Glutny
and that buyes me <is> thirty meales a day, and ten Beavers:	F 694	2.2.143	P	Glutny
thou hast heard all my progeny, wilt thou bid me to supper?	F 701	2.2.150	P	Glutny
and you have done me great injury to bring me from thence, let	F 705.1	2.2.155A	P	Sloth
and you have done me great injury to bring me from thence, let	F 705.2	2.2.156A	P	Sloth
me be carried thither againe by Gluttony and Letchery	F 705.2	2.2.156A	P	Sloth
Keepe further from me O thou illiterate, and unlearned Hostler.	F 728	2.3.7	P	Robin
My Maister conjure me?	F 736	2.3.15	P	Robin
But I prethee tell me, in good sadnesse Robin, is that a	F 743	2.3.22	P	Dick
Do but speake what thou't have me to do, and I'le do't:	F 745	2.3.24	P	Robin
Or if thou't go but to the Taverne with me, I'le give thee	F 747	2.3.26	P	Robin
But tell me now, what resting place is this?	F 800	3.1.22		Faust
Conducted me within the walles of Rome?	F 802	3.1.24		Faust
Sweete Mephostophilis, thou pleasest me:	F 836	3.1.58		Faust
Whilst I am here on earth let me be cloyd/With all things that	F 837	3.1.59		Faust
come then stand by me/And thou shalt see them come immediately.	F 843	3.1.65		Mephst
And grant me my request, and then I go.	F 846	3.1.68		Faust
That looking downe the earth appear'd to me,	F 850	3.1.72		Faust
Then in this shew let me an Actor be,	F 854	3.1.76		Faust
Proud Lucifer, that State belongs to me:	F 871	3.1.93		Bruno
To me and Peter, shalt thou groveling lie,	F 873	3.1.95		Pope
Pope Adrian let me have some right of Law,	F 904	3.1.126		Bruno
Now tell me Faustus, are we not fitted well?	F 940	3.1.162		Mephst
<Then charme me that I may be invisible>,	F 991	(HC266)A		Faust
Sweet Mephostophilis so charme me here,	F 991	3.2.11		Faust
Then wherefore would you have me view that booke?	F1023	3.2.43		Pope
How now? who snatch't the meat from me!	F1044	3.2.64		Pope
Was sent me from a Cardinall in France.	F1047	3.2.67		Pope
Fetch me some wine.	F1051	3.2.71		Pope
O I am slaine, help me my Lords:	F1068	3.2.88		Pope
let me see the cup.	F1093	3.3.6	P	Robin
Search me?	F1102	3.3.15	P	Robin
hold the cup Dick, come, come, search me, search me.	F1103	3.3.16	P	Robin
Come on sirra, let me search you now.	F1104	3.3.17	P	Vintnr
Never out face me for the matter, for sure the cup is betweene	F1107	3.3.20	P	Vintnr
Come, give it me againe.	F1111	3.3.24	P	Vintnr
Dick, make me a circle, and stand close at my backe, and stir	F1112	3.3.25	P	Robin
Constantinople have they brought me now <am I hither brought>,	F1118	3.3.31		Mephst
let me have the carrying of him about to shew some trickes.	F1128	3.3.41	P	Robin
come not away quickly, you shall have me asleepe presently:	F1242	4.1.88	P	Benvol
Il'e make you feele something anon, if my Art faile me not.	F1246	4.1.92	P	Faust
O pardon me, my thoughts are ravished so/With sight of this	F1260	4.1.106		Emper
To satisfie my longing thoughts at full,/Let me this tell thee:	F1265	4.1.111		Emper
And in this sight thou better pleasest me,	F1271	4.1.117		Emper
A plague upon you, let me sleepe a while.	F1283	4.1.129		Benvol
good my Lord intreate for me:	F1306	4.1.152	P	Benvol
Let me intreate you to remove his hornes,	F1309	4.1.155		Emper

ME (cont.)

not so much for injury done to me, as to delight your Majesty	F1311	4.1.157	P	Faust
Away, you love me not, to urge me thus,	F1327	4.2.3		Benvol
If you will aid me in this enterprise,	F1334	4.2.10		Benvol
Come souldiers, follow me unto the grove,	F1348	4.2.24		Fredrk
Thou soone shouldst see me quit my foule disgrace.	F1356	4.2.32		Benvol
and let them hang/Within the window where he yoak'd me first,	F1381	4.2.57		Benvol
As he intended to dismember me.	F1415	4.2.91		Faust
And stand as Bulwarkes twixt your selves and me,	F1427	4.2.103		Faust
To sheild me from your hated treachery:	F1428	4.2.104		Faust
O help me gentle friend; where is Martino?	F1432	4.3.2		Fredrk
Through which the Furies drag'd me by the heeles.	F1435	4.3.5		Mrtino
Defend me heaven, shall I be haunted still?	F1439	4.3.9		Benvol
late by horse flesh, and this bargaine will set me up againe.	F1465	4.4.9	P	HrsCsr
Well, I will not stand with thee, give me the money:	F1466	4.4.10	P	Faust
I had nothing under me but a little straw, and had much ado to	F1486	4.4.30	P	HrsCsr
go rouse him, and make him give me my forty Dollors againe.	F1488	4.4.32	P	HrsCsr
and give me my mony againe, for your horse is turned to a	F1489	4.4.33	P	HrsCsr
O help, help, the villaine hath murder'd me.	F1493	4.4.37	P	Faust
on the score, but say nothing, see if she have forgotten me.	F1512	4.5.8	P	Robin
doubt of that, for me thinkes you make no hast to wipe it out.	F1516	4.5.12	P	Hostss
I'le tell you the bravest tale how a Conjurer serv'd me; you	F1522	4.5.18	P	Carter
I'le tell you how he serv'd me:	F1525	4.5.21	P	Carter
he met me, and asked me what he should give me for as much Hay	F1526	4.5.22	P	Carter
me what he should give me for as much Hay as he could eate;	F1526	4.5.22	P	Carter
me what he should give me for as much Hay as he could eate;	F1527	4.5.23	P	Carter
so he presently gave me my mony, and fell to eating;	F1529	4.5.25	P	Carter
Doctor Fauster bad me ride him night and day, and spare him no	F1540	4.5.36	P	HrsCsr
had had some [rare] quality that he would not have me know of,	F1543	4.5.39	P	HrsCsr
it; I went me home to his house, and there I found him asleepe;	F1548	4.5.44	P	HrsCsr
till I had pul'd me his leg quite off, and now 'tis at home in	F1551	4.5.47	P	HrsCsr
one of his devils turn'd me into the likenesse of an Apes face.	F1554	4.5.50	P	Dick
the sight whereof so delighted me, as nothing in the world	F1561	4.6.4	P	Duke
so delighted me, as nothing in the world could please me more.	F1561	4.6.4	P	Duke
therefor I pray you tell me, what is the thing you most desire	F1566	4.6.9	P	Faust
This makes me wonder more then all the rest, that at this time	F1578	4.6.21	P	Duke
And trust me, they are the sweetest grapes that e're I tasted.	F1587	4.6.30	P	Lady
Nay, hearke you, can you tell me where you are?	F1614	4.6.57		Faust
My Lord, beseech you give me leave a while,	F1621	4.6.64		Faust
'Tis not so much worth; I pray you tel me one thing.	F1643	4.6.86	P	Carter
Wouldst thou make a Colossus of me, that thou askest me such	F1646	4.6.89	P	Faust
thou make a Colossus of me, that thou askest me such questions?	F1647	4.6.90	P	Faust
me thinkes you should have a wooden bedfellow of one of 'em.	F1653	4.6.96	P	Carter
Do you remember sir, how you cosened me and eat up my load of--	F1659	4.6.102	P	Carter
Do you remember how you made me weare an Apes--	F1661	4.6.104	P	Dick
scab, do you remember how you cosened me with <of> a ho--	F1663	4.6.106	P	HrsCsr
Ha' you forgotten me?	F1664	4.6.107	P	Robin
have sent away my guesse, I pray who shall pay me for my A--	F1667	4.6.110	P	Hostss
he has made his will, and given me his wealth, his house, his	F1675	5.1.2	P	Wagner
Leave me a while, to ponder on my sinnes.	F1736	5.1.63		Faust
That durst disswade me from thy Lucifer,	F1754	5.1.81		Faust
One thing good servant let me crave of thee,	F1759	5.1.86		Faust
Those <These> thoughts that do disswade me from my vow,	F1764	5.1.91		Faust
Sweet Hellen make me immortall with a kisse:	F1770	5.1.97		Faust
Come Hellen, come, give me my soule againe,	F1772	5.1.99		Faust
[Sathan begins to sift me with his pride]:	F1791	5.1.118A		OldMan
Now worthy Faustus: me thinks your looks are chang'd.	F1821	5.2.25		1Schol
heare [me] with patience, and tremble not at my speeches.	F1839	5.2.43	P	Faust
but the Divel threatned to teare me in peeces if I nam'd God:	F1865	5.2.69	P	Faust
to fetch me <both> body and soule, if I once gave eare to	F1865	5.2.69	P	Faust
Gentlemen away, least you perish with me.	F1867	5.2.71	P	Faust
Talke not of me, but save your selves and depart.	F1869	5.2.73	P	Faust
God will strengthen me, I will stay with Faustus.	F1870	5.2.74	P	3Schol
I, pray for me, pray for me:	F1873	5.2.77	P	Faust
you <yee> heare, come not unto me, for nothing can rescue me.	F1874	5.2.78	P	Faust
Hath rob'd me of eternall happinesse.	F1884	5.2.88		Faust
Oh <Ah> Faustus, if thou hadst given eare to me,	F1892	5.2.96		GdAngl
Gave eare to me,/And now must taste hels paines perpetually.	F1894	5.2.98		BdAngl
O, I have seene enough to torture me.	F1921	5.2.125		Faust
O I'le leape up to [my God] <heaven>: who puls me downe?	F1938	5.2.142		Faust
One drop <of bloud will save me; oh> my Christ.	F1940	(HC271)B		Faust
Yet will I call on him: O spare me Lucifer.	F1942	5.2.146		Faust
Mountaines and Hils, come, come, and fall on me,	F1945	5.2.149		Faust
And hide me from the heavy wrath of [God] <heaven>.	F1946	5.2.150		Faust
Gape earth; O no, it will not harbour me.	F1949	5.2.153		Faust
[Yet for Christs sake, whose bloud hath ransom'd me],	F1959	5.2.163A		Faust
This soule should flie from me, and I be chang'd/[Unto] <Into>	F1967	5.2.171		Faust
Curst be the parents that ingendred me;	F1972	5.2.176		Faust
[My God, my God] <O mercy heaven>, looke not so fierce on me;	F1979	5.2.183		Faust
Adders and serpents, let me breathe a while:	F1980	5.2.184		Faust
one, me thought/I heard him shreeke and call aloud for helpe:	F1991	5.3.9		3Schol
Tel me sirra, hast thou any commings in?	F App	p.229 4	P	Wagner
wilt thou serve me, and Ile make thee go like Qui mihi	F App	p.229 13	P	Wagner
So thou shalt, whether thou beest with me, or no:	F App	p.229 22	P	Wagner
and binde your selfe presently unto me for seaven yeeres, or	F App	p.229 24	P	Wagner
they are too familiar with me already, swowns they are as bolde	F App	p.230 28	P	Clown
Well sirra follow me.	F App	p.230 55	P	Wagner
serve you, would you teach me to raise up Banios and Belcheos?	F App	p.230 57	P	Clown
if you turne me into any thing, let it be in the likenesse of a	F App	p.231 61	P	Clown
call me Maister Wagner, and let thy left eye be diametarily	F App	p.231 69	P	Wagner
God forgive me, he speakes Dutch fustian:	F App	p.231 72	P	Clown
here is a daintie dish was sent me from the Bishop of Millaine.	F App	p.231 5	P	Pope
How now, whose that which snatcht the meate from me?	F App	p.231 8	P	Pope

ME (cont.)

Line	Work	Reference		Speaker
My Lord, this dish was sent me from the Cardinall of Florence.	F App	p.231 9	P	Pope
in our parish dance at my pleasure starke naked before me,	F App	p.233 4	P	Robin
it, and she has sent me to looke thee out, prethee come away.	F App	p.233 9	P	Rafe
study, shee's borne to beare with me, or else my Art failes.	F App	p.233 17	P	Robin
search me.	F App	p.234 10	P	Robin
me sir, me sir, search your fill:	F App	p.234 14	P	Rafe
You lie Drawer, tis afore me:	F App	p.235 17	P	Robin
good divel forgive me now, and Ile never rob thy Library more.	F App	p.235 31	P	Robin
that thou let me see some proofe of thy skil, that mine eies	F App	p.236 6	P	Emper
yet for that love and duety bindes me thereunto, I am content	F App	p.236 15	P	Faust
I am content to do whatsoever your majesty shall command me.	F App	p.236 16	P	Faust
me) never attaine to that degree of high renowne and great	F App	p.236 22	P	Emper
And give me cause to praise thee whilst I live.	F App	p.237 36		Emper
Go to maister Doctor, let me see them presently.	F App	p.237 50	P	Emper
Ifaith thats as true as Diana turned me to a stag.	F App	p.237 54	P	Knight
Ile meete with you anone for interrupting me so:	F App	p.238 58	P	Faust
send for the knight that was so pleasent with me here of late?	F App	p.238 67	P	Faust
how you crossed me in my conference with the emperour?	F App	p.238 77	P	Faust
so much for the injury hee offred me heere in your presence,	F App	p.238 82	P	Faust
Doctor, yet ere you goe, expect from me a bounteous reward.	F App	p.239 89	P	Emper
Alas sir, I have no more, I pray you speake for me.	F App	p.239 104	P	HrsCsr
Wel, come give me your money, my boy wil deliver him to you:	F App	p.239 107	P	Faust
slicke as an Ele; wel god buy sir, your boy wil deliver him me:	F App	p.240 117	P	HrsCsr
at ease, if I bring his water to you, youle tel me what it is?	F App	p.240 119	P	HrsCsr
has given me a purgation, has purg'd me of fortie Dollers,	F App	p.240 128	P	HrsCsr
has purg'd me of fortie Dollers, I shall never see them more:	F App	p.240 129	P	HrsCsr
by him, for he bade me I should ride him into no water; now,	F App	p.240 130	P	HrsCsr
had some rare qualitie that he would not have had me knowne of,	F App	p.240 132	P	HrsCsr
O Lord sir, let me goe, and Ile give you fortie dollers more.	F App	p.241 158	P	HrsCsr
I have none about me, come to my Oastrie, and Ile give them	F App	p.241 161	P	HrsCsr
Beleeve me maister Doctor, this merriment hath much pleased me.	F App	p.242 1	P	Duke
Beleeve me maister Doctor, this merriment hath much pleased me.	F App	p.242 2	P	Duke
tell me, and you shal have it.	F App	p.242 6	P	Faust
And for I see your curteous intent to pleasure me, I wil not	F App	p.242 8	P	Duchss
Beleeve me master Doctor, this makes me wonder above the rest,	F App	p.242 16	P	Duke
this makes me wonder above the rest, that being in the dead	F App	p.242 16	P	Duke
Beleeve me Maister doctor, they be the best grapes that ere I	F App	p.242 25	P	Duchss
For he hath given to me al his goodes,	F App	p.243 2		Wagner
And yet me thinkes, if that death were neere,	F App	p.243 3		Wagner
Ay me, O what a world of land and sea,	Lucan, First Booke	13		
He, he afflicts Roome that made me Roomes foe.	Lucan, First Booke	205		
you that with me have borne/A thousand brunts, and tride me ful	Lucan, First Booke	300		
me have borne/A thousand brunts, and tride me ful ten yeeres,	Lucan, First Booke	301		
were we bestead/When comming conqueror, Roome afflicts me thus?	Lucan, First Booke	310		
Must Pompey as his last foe plume on me,	Lucan, First Booke	338		
shouldst thou bid me/Intombe my sword within my brothers	Lucan, First Booke	376		
Philosophers looke you, for unto me/Thou cause, what ere thou be	Lucan, First Booke	418		
And which (aie me) ever pretendeth ill,	Lucan, First Booke	625		
thou lead'st me toward th'east,/Where Nile augmenteth the	Lucan, First Booke	682		
the world againe/I goe; o Phoebus shew me Neptunes shore,	Lucan, First Booke	692		
Oh woe is me, he never shootes but hits,	Ovid's Elegies	1.1.29		
T'was so, he stroke me with a slender dart,	Ovid's Elegies	1.2.7		
let hir <he> that cought me late,/Either love, or cause that I	Ovid's Elegies	1.3.1		
I aske too much, would she but let me love hir,	Ovid's Elegies	1.3.3		
If loftie titles cannot make me thine,	Ovid's Elegies	1.3.7		
And Cupide who hath markt me for thy pray,	Ovid's Elegies	1.3.12		
Thy husband to a banquet goes with me,	Ovid's Elegies	1.4.1		
View me, my becks, and speaking countenance:	Ovid's Elegies	1.4.17		
If ought of me thou speak'st in inward thought,	Ovid's Elegies	1.4.23		
Aye me I warne what profits some few howers,	Ovid's Elegies	1.4.59		
To me to morrow constantly deny it.	Ovid's Elegies	1.4.70		
How apt her breasts were to be prest by me,	Ovid's Elegies	1.5.20		
To leave the rest, all likt me passing well,	Ovid's Elegies	1.5.23		
Judge you the rest, being tyrde <tride> she bad me kisse.	Ovid's Elegies	1.5.25		
Jove send me more such afternoones as this.	Ovid's Elegies	1.5.26		
He shewes me how unheard to passe the watch,	Ovid's Elegies	1.6.7		
spright/Nor hands prepar'd to slaughter, me affright.	Ovid's Elegies	1.6.14		
Why enviest me, this hostile [denne] <dende> unbarre,	Ovid's Elegies	1.6.17		
(O mischiefe) now for me obtaine small grace.	Ovid's Elegies	1.6.22		
See Love with me, wine moderate in my braine,	Ovid's Elegies	1.6.37		
Though it be so, shut me not out therefore,	Ovid's Elegies	1.6.47		
Aie me how high that gale did lift my hope!	Ovid's Elegies	1.6.52		
What ere thou art, farewell, be like me paind,	Ovid's Elegies	1.6.71		
Her teares, she silent, guilty did pronounce me.	Ovid's Elegies	1.7.22		
Aye me, thy body hath no worthy weedes.	Ovid's Elegies	1.8.26		
(Trust me) to give, it is a witty thing.	Ovid's Elegies	1.8.62		
If this thou doest, to me by long use knowne,	Ovid's Elegies	1.8.105		
As thus she spake, my shadow me betraide,	Ovid's Elegies	1.8.109		
And to her tentes wild me my selfe addresse.	Ovid's Elegies	1.9.44		
Since maist thou see me watch and night warres move:	Ovid's Elegies	1.9.45		
This cause hath thee from pleasing me debard.	Ovid's Elegies	1.10.12		
Corinna clips me oft by thy perswasion,	Ovid's Elegies	1.11.5		
Never to harme me made thy faith evasion.	Ovid's Elegies	1.11.6		
[Doest] punish <ye >me, because yeares make him waine?	Ovid's Elegies	1.13.41		
I chid no more, she blusht, and therefore heard me,	Ovid's Elegies	1.13.47		
Yet lingered not the day, but morning scard me.	Ovid's Elegies	1.13.48		
O thou oft wilt blush/And say he likes me for my borrowed bush,	Ovid's Elegies	1.14.48		
Praysing for me some unknowne Guelder dame,	Ovid's Elegies	1.14.49		
Aye me rare gifts unworthy such a happe.	Ovid's Elegies	1.14.54		
Faire Phoebus leade me to the Muses springs.	Ovid's Elegies	1.15.36		
And in sad lovers heads let me be found.	Ovid's Elegies	1.15.38		
Ile live, and as he puls me downe, mount higher.	Ovid's Elegies	1.15.42		

ME (cont.)

And rude boyes toucht with unknowne love me reade,	Ovid's Elegies	2.1.6
Pardon me Jove, thy weapons ayde me nought,	Ovid's Elegies	2.1.19
What helpes it me of fierce Achill to sing?	Ovid's Elegies	2.1.29
What good to me wil either Ajax bring?	Ovid's Elegies	2.1.30
a pretty wenches face/Shee in requitall doth me oft imbrace.	Ovid's Elegies	2.1.34
lookes to my verse/Which golden love doth unto me rehearse.	Ovid's Elegies	2.1.38
Shee pleas'd me, soone I sent, and did her woo,	Ovid's Elegies	2.2.5
Beleeve me, whom we feare, we wish to perish.	Ovid's Elegies	2.2.10
Trust me all husbands for such faults are sad/Nor make they any	Ovid's Elegies	2.2.51
Aye me an Eunuch keepes my mistrisse chaste,	Ovid's Elegies	2.3.1
No one face likes me best, all faces moove,	Ovid's Elegies	2.4.9
A hundred reasons makes <make> me ever love.	Ovid's Elegies	2.4.10
Me thinkes she should <would> be nimble when shees downe.	Ovid's Elegies	2.4.14
Before Callimachus one preferres me farre,	Ovid's Elegies	2.4.19
Another railes at me, and that I write,	Ovid's Elegies	2.4.21
Trips she, it likes me well, plods she, what than?	Ovid's Elegies	2.4.23
Both short and long please me, for I love both:	Ovid's Elegies	2.4.36
[A white wench thralles me, so doth golden yellowe],	Ovid's Elegies	2.4.39
Aye me poore soule, why is my cause so good.	Ovid's Elegies	2.5.8
(Such with my tongue it likes me to purloyne).	Ovid's Elegies	2.5.24
This, and what grife inforc'd me say I say'd,	Ovid's Elegies	2.5.33
Least with worse kisses she should me indue.	Ovid's Elegies	2.5.50
This grieves me not, no joyned kisses spent,	Ovid's Elegies	2.5.59
The parrat from east India to me sent,	Ovid's Elegies	2.6.1
The Parrat given me, the farre [worlds] <words> best choice.	Ovid's Elegies	2.6.38
Doost me of new crimes alwayes guilty frame?	Ovid's Elegies	2.7.1
If some faire wench me secretly behold,	Ovid's Elegies	2.7.5
The Gods from this sinne rid me of suspition,	Ovid's Elegies	2.7.19
Apt to thy mistrisse, but more apt to me.	Ovid's Elegies	2.8.4
What graced Kings, in me no shame I deeme.	Ovid's Elegies	2.8.14
Let me lie with thee browne Cypasse to day.	Ovid's Elegies	2.8.22
Why me that alwayes was thy souldiour found,	Ovid's Elegies	2.9.3
Doest harme, and in thy tents why doest me wound?	Ovid's Elegies	2.9.4
And time it was for me to live in quiet,	Ovid's Elegies	2.9.23
For when my loathing it of heate deprives me,	Ovid's Elegies	2.9.27
I know not whether my mindes whirle-wind drives me.	Ovid's Elegies	2.9.28
So wavering Cupid bringes me backe amaine,	Ovid's Elegies	2.9.33
But me let crafty damsells words deceive,	Ovid's Elegies	2.9.43
Now let her flatter me, now chide me hard,	Ovid's Elegies	2.9.45
Let [me] <her> enjoy [her] <me> oft, oft be debard.	Ovid's Elegies	2.9.46
Graecinus (well I wot) thou touldst me once,	Ovid's Elegies	2.10.1
[And] this doth please me most, and so doth she.	Ovid's Elegies	2.10.8
And from my mistris bosome let me rise:	Ovid's Elegies	2.10.20
Let one wench cloy me with sweete loves delight,	Ovid's Elegies	2.10.21
For thee the East and West winds make me pale,	Ovid's Elegies	2.11.9
And say it brings her that preserveth me;	Ovid's Elegies	2.11.44
And hasting to me, neither darkesome night,	Ovid's Elegies	2.11.51
And me with many, but yet me without murther,	Ovid's Elegies	2.12.27
She secretly with me such harme attempted,	Ovid's Elegies	2.13.3
But she conceiv'd of me, or I am sure/I oft have done, what	Ovid's Elegies	2.13.5
with loving may/Had seene, my mother killing me, [no] <to> day.	Ovid's Elegies	2.14.22
Fit her so well, as she is fit for me:	Ovid's Elegies	2.15.5
Onely Ile signe nought, that may grieve me much.	Ovid's Elegies	2.15.18
Weare me, when warmest showers thy members wash,	Ovid's Elegies	2.15.23
Sulmo, Pelignies third part me containes,	Ovid's Elegies	2.16.1
although vine-planted ground/Conteines me, though the streames	Ovid's Elegies	2.16.34
Why doth my mistresse from me oft devide?	Ovid's Elegies	2.16.42
By me, and by my starres, thy radiant eyes.	Ovid's Elegies	2.16.44
If any godly care of me thou hast,	Ovid's Elegies	2.16.47
Let me be slandered, while my fire she hides,	Ovid's Elegies	2.17.3
Aye me why is it knowne to her so well?	Ovid's Elegies	2.17.8
to detaine)/Thou oughtst therefore to scorne me for thy mate,	Ovid's Elegies	2.17.13
And thou my light accept me how so ever,	Ovid's Elegies	2.17.23
And many by me to get glory crave.	Ovid's Elegies	2.17.28
I sayd it irkes me:	Ovid's Elegies	2.18.7
Aye me she cries, to love, why art a shamed?	Ovid's Elegies	2.18.8
My Mistris deity also drewe me fro it,	Ovid's Elegies	2.18.17
Keepe her for me, my more desire to breede.	Ovid's Elegies	2.19.2
What should I do with fortune that nere failes me?	Ovid's Elegies	2.19.7
Nothing I love, that at all times availes me.	Ovid's Elegies	2.19.8
Wily Corinna sawe this blemish in me,	Ovid's Elegies	2.19.9
And craftily knowes by what meanes to winne me.	Ovid's Elegies	2.19.10
Wild me, whose slowe feete sought delay, be flying.	Ovid's Elegies	2.19.12
To please me, what faire termes and sweet words ha's shee,	Ovid's Elegies	2.19.17
Oft couzen me, oft being wooed say nay.	Ovid's Elegies	2.19.20
And on thy thre-shold let me lie dispred,	Ovid's Elegies	2.19.21
This doth delight me, this my courage cheares.	Ovid's Elegies	2.19.24
Fat love, and too much fulsome me annoyes,	Ovid's Elegies	2.19.25
Aye me, let not my warnings cause my paine.	Ovid's Elegies	2.19.34
What flies, I followe, what followes me I shunne.	Ovid's Elegies	2.19.36
That to deceits it may me forward pricke.	Ovid's Elegies	2.19.44
To pleasure me, for-bid me to corive with thee.	Ovid's Elegies	2.19.60
lofty wordes stout Tragedie (she sayd)/Why treadst me downe?	Ovid's Elegies	3.1.36
Thou fightst against me using mine owne verse.	Ovid's Elegies	3.1.38
Light am I, and with me, my care, light love,	Ovid's Elegies	3.1.41
Venus without me should be rusticall,	Ovid's Elegies	3.1.43
This goddesse company doth to me befall.	Ovid's Elegies	3.1.44
By me Corinna learnes, cousening her guard,	Ovid's Elegies	3.1.49
The maide to hide me in her bosome let not.	Ovid's Elegies	3.1.56
What gift with me was on her birth day sent,	Ovid's Elegies	3.1.57
With scepters, and high buskins th'one would dresse me,	Ovid's Elegies	3.1.63
So through the world shold bright renown expresse me.	Ovid's Elegies	3.1.64

ME (cont.)			
She gave me leave, soft loves in time make hast,	Ovid's Elegies	3.1.69	
Some greater worke will urge me on at last.	Ovid's Elegies	3.1.70	
That thou maiest know with love thou mak'st me flame.	Ovid's Elegies	3.2.4	
Such chaunce let me have:	Ovid's Elegies	3.2.9	
By these I judge, delight me may the rest,	Ovid's Elegies	3.2.35	
The sea I use not: me my earth must have.	Ovid's Elegies	3.2.48	
Peace pleaseth me, and in mid peace is love.	Ovid's Elegies	3.2.50	
The Gods, and their rich pompe witnesse with me,	Ovid's Elegies	3.2.61	
By which she perjurd oft hath lyed [to] <by> me.	Ovid's Elegies	3.3.10	
And unrevengd mockt Gods with me doth scoffe.	Ovid's Elegies	3.3.20	
Pallas launce strikes me with unconquerd arme.	Ovid's Elegies	3.3.28	
At me Apollo bends his pliant bowe:	Ovid's Elegies	3.3.29	
At me Joves right-hand lightning hath to throwe.	Ovid's Elegies	3.3.30	
That may transport me without oares to rowe.	Ovid's Elegies	3.5.4	
(Trust me) land-streame thou shalt no envie lack,	Ovid's Elegies	3.5.21	
Nor Romane stocke scorne me so much (I crave)/Gifts then my	Ovid's Elegies	3.5.65	
men point at me for a whore,/Shame, that should make me blush,	Ovid's Elegies	3.5.77	
Shame, that should make me blush, I have no more.	Ovid's Elegies	3.5.78	
Clowne, from my journey why doest me deterre?	Ovid's Elegies	3.5.88	
Perchance these, others, me mine owne losse mooves.	Ovid's Elegies	3.5.100	
And eagerlie she kist me with her tongue,	Ovid's Elegies	3.6.9	
Yea, and she soothde me up, and calde me sir <sire>,	Ovid's Elegies	3.6.11	
It mocked me, hung down the head and suncke,	Ovid's Elegies	3.6.14	
Even her I had, and she had me in vaine,	Ovid's Elegies	3.6.43	
I wisht to be received in, <and> in I [get] <got> me,	Ovid's Elegies	3.6.47	
To kisse, I kisse, to lie with her shee let me.	Ovid's Elegies	3.6.48	
Seeing now thou wouldst deceive me as before:	Ovid's Elegies	3.6.70	
Why mockst thou me she cried, or being ill,	Ovid's Elegies	3.6.77	
With that her loose gowne on, from me she cast her,	Ovid's Elegies	3.6.81	
She prais'd me, yet the gate shutt fast upon her,	Ovid's Elegies	3.7.7	
For bloudshed knighted, before me preferr'd.	Ovid's Elegies	3.7.10	
For me, she doth keeper, and husband feare,	Ovid's Elegies	3.7.63	
Long have I borne much, mad thy faults me make:	Ovid's Elegies	3.10.1	
Yet this is lesse, then if he had seene me,	Ovid's Elegies	3.10.15	
These hardned me, with what I keepe obscure,	Ovid's Elegies	3.10.27	
Spare me, O by our fellow bed, by all/The Gods who by thee to	Ovid's Elegies	3.10.45	
And by thy face to me a powre divine,	Ovid's Elegies	3.10.47	
Wilt have me willing, or to love by force?	Ovid's Elegies	3.10.50	
Or shall I plaine some God against me warres?	Ovid's Elegies	3.11.4	
I feare with me is common now to many.	Ovid's Elegies	3.11.6	
Now your credulity harme to me hath raisd.	Ovid's Elegies	3.11.44	
When fruite fild Tuscia should a wife give me,	Ovid's Elegies	3.12.1	
Let me, and them by it be aye be-friended.	Ovid's Elegies	3.12.36	
Deceive all, let me erre, and thinke I am right,	Ovid's Elegies	3.13.29	
Of me Pelignis nation boasts alone,	Ovid's Elegies	3.14.8	
Faire creature, let me speake without offence,	Hero and Leander	1.199	
O shun me not, but heare me ere you goe,	Hero and Leander	1.205	
Which makes me hope, although I am but base,	Hero and Leander	1.218	
Beleeve me Hero, honour is not wone,	Hero and Leander	1.281	
But you are faire (aye me) so wondrous faire,	Hero and Leander	1.287	
Then Hero hate me not, nor from me flie,	Hero and Leander	1.291	
Tell me, to whom mad'st thou that heedlesse oath?	Hero and Leander	1.294	
Aye me, such words as these should I abhor,	Hero and Leander	1.339	
A dwarfish beldame beares me companie,	Hero and Leander	1.353	
Aye me, Leander cryde, th'enamoured sunne,	Hero and Leander	2.202	
Me in thy bed and maiden bosome take,	Hero and Leander	2.248	
MEAD			
And make this champion mead a bloody Fen.	2Tamb	1.1.32	Orcan
MEADE			
A gloomie fellow in a meade belowe,	Edw	4.7.29	Spencr
MEADS			
Where painted Carpets o're the meads are hurl'd,	Jew	4.2.91	Ithimr
The Meads, the Orchards, and the Primrose lanes,	Jew	4.2.95	Ithimr
MEALE			
Revolt, or I'le in peece-meale teare thy flesh.	F1745	5.1.72	Mephst
MEALES			
and that buyes me <is> thirty meales a day, and ten Beavers:	F 695	2.2.144	P Glutny
MEAN (Homograph)			
And in the mean time my Lord, could we devise,	P 425	7.65	Guise
Let mean consaits, and baser men feare death,	P 997	19.67	Guise
<in mean time take this booke, peruse it throwly>,	F 717	(HC264)A	Lucifr
I mean the Adamantine Destinies,	Hero and Leander	1.444	
MEANDER			
Meander, might I not?	1Tamb	1.1.24	Mycet
Meander, thou my faithfull Counsellor,	1Tamb	1.1.28	Mycet
These are his words, Meander set them downe.	1Tamb	1.1.94	Mycet
Meander come, I am abus'd Meander.	1Tamb	1.1.106	Mycet
Come my Meander, let us to this geere,	1Tamb	2.2.1	Mycet
Tell you the rest (Meander) I have said.	1Tamb	2.2.13	Mycet
Was there such brethren, sweet Meander, say,	1Tamb	2.2.51	Mycet
Wel, wel (Meander) thou art deeply read:	1Tamb	2.2.55	Mycet
Drums, why sound ye not when Meander speaks.	1Tamb	2.2.75	Mycet
Meander, you that were our brothers Guide,	1Tamb	2.5.10	Cosroe
Thanks good Meander, then Cosroe raign/And governe Persea in	1Tamb	2.5.18	Cosroe
MEANDERS			
With litle slaughter take Meanders course,	1Tamb	2.5.27	Cosroe
MEANE (Homograph)			
For though my birth be great, my fortunes meane,	Dido	2.1.88	Aeneas
Too meane to be companion to a Queene.	Dido	2.1.89	Aeneas
What should this meane?	Dido	3.2.21	Venus
Meane time, Ascanius shall be my charge,	Dido	3.2.98	Venus
Meane time these wanton weapons serve my warre,	Dido	3.3.37	Cupid

MEANE (cont.)

O what meane I to have such foolish thoughts!	Dido	4.5.25	Nurse
I know not what you meane by treason, I,	Dido	5.1.222	Nurse
now have I found a meane/To rid me from these thoughts of	Dido	5.1.272	Dido
I meane it not, but yet I know I might,	1Tamb	1.1.26	Mycet
And as I heare, doth meane to pull my plumes.	1Tamb	1.1.33	Mycet
thou art so meane a man)/And seeke not to inrich thy followers,	1Tamb	1.2.8	Zenoc
But since they measure our deserts so meane,	1Tamb	1.2.63	Tamb
Joine with me now in this my meane estate,	1Tamb	1.2.202	Tamb
(I cal it meane, because being yet obscure,	1Tamb	1.2.203	Tamb
No, I meane, I let you keep it.	1Tamb	2.4.35	Mycet
Wel, I meane you shall have it againe.	1Tamb	2.4.36	Tamb
by princely deeds/Doth meane to soare above the highest sort.	1Tamb	2.7.33	Therid
We meane to take his mornings next arise/For messenger, he will	1Tamb	3.1.38	Bajzth
And meane to fetch thee in despight of him.	1Tamb	3.1.40	Bajzth
I meane to meet him in Bithynia:	1Tamb	3.3.2	Tamb
We meane to seate our footmen on their Steeds,	1Tamb	3.3.25	Techel
I meane t'incounter with that Bajazeth.	1Tamb	3.3.65	Tamb
Excluding Regions which I meane to trace,	1Tamb	4.4.77	Tamb
We meane to traveile to th'Antartique Pole,	1Tamb	4.4.136	Tamb
And sirha, if you meane to weare a crowne,	2Tamb	1.3.98	Tamb
That meane to teach you rudiments of war:	2Tamb	3.2.54	Tamb
That fighting, knowes not what retreat doth meane,	2Tamb	3.5.43	Trebiz
Ile dispose them as it likes me best,/Meane while take him in.	2Tamb	4.1.167	Tamb
Your Majesty already hath devisde/A meane, as fit as may be to	2Tamb	4.3.51	Usumc
(I meane such Queens as were Kings Concubines)/Take them,	2Tamb	4.3.71	Tamb
That meane t'invest me in a higher throane,	2Tamb	5.3.121	Tamb
Displacing me; and of thy house they meane/To make a Nunnery,	Jew	1.2.255	Abigal
As good dissemble that thou never mean'st/As first meane truth,	Jew	1.2.291	Barab
I meane my daughter:--	Jew	2.3.51	Barab
I meane in fulnesse of perfection.	Jew	2.3.85	Barab
Faith, Sir, my birth is but meane, my name's Ithimor,	Jew	2.3.165	Ithimr
This gentle Magot, Lodowicke I meane,	Jew	2.3.305	Barab
Schollers I meane, learned and liberall;	Jew	3.1.8	Curtzn
What, doe you meane to strangle me?	Jew	4.1.144	2Fryar
Confesse; what meane you, Lords, who should confesse?	Jew	5.1.26	Barab
And therfore meane to murder all I meet.	P 279	5.6	Anjoy
And meane once more to menace me.	P 364	7.4	Ramus
And meane to murder us:	P 368	7.8	Taleus
I meane our warres against the Muscovites:	P 461	8.11	Anjoy
I meane the Guise, the Pope, and King of Spaine,	P 701	14.4	Navrre
possession (as I would I might) yet I meane to keepe you out,	P 814	17.9	P Souldr
I meane to muster all the power I can,	P 849	17.44	Guise
And then Ile tell thee what I meane to doe.	P 891	17.86	King
Unles he meane to be betraide and dye:	P 898	17.93	King
But in the meane time Gaveston away,	Edw	1.1.202	Edward
And in the meane time ile intreat you all,	Edw	1.2.77	ArchBp
I meane not so, your grace must pardon me.	Edw	1.4.153	Gavstn
I meane that vile Torpedo, Gaveston,	Edw	1.4.223	Mortmr
Deserves no common place, nor meane reward:	Edw	1.4.361	Edward
Which of the nobles dost thou meane to serve?	Edw	2.1.3	Baldck
What, meane you then to be his follower?	Edw	2.1.12	Baldck
Meane time my lord of Penbrooke and my selfe,	Edw	2.2.122	Warwck
I meane the peeres, whom thou shouldst dearly love:	Edw	2.2.176	Mortmr
How meane you, and the king my father lives?	Edw	4.2.43	Prince
Tell me good unckle, what Edward doe you meane?	Edw	4.6.32	Prince
Meane while, have hence this rebell to the blocke,	Edw	4.6.69	Mortmr
We in meane while madam, must take advise,	Edw	4.6.77	Mortmr
My diadem I meane, and guiltlesse life.	Edw	5.1.73	Edward
But she that gave him life, I meane the Queene?	Edw	5.2.91	Kent
Meane while peruse this booke, and view it throughly,	F 717	2.2.169	Lucifr
[I meane his friends and nearest companions],	F1142	3.3.55A	3Chor
I, and I fall not asleepe i'th meane time.	F1196	4.1.42	Benvol
It is your owne you meane, feele on your head.	F1443	4.3.13	Fredrk
My woodden leg? what dost thou meane by that?	F1628	4.6.71	Faust
and ifaith I meane to search some circles for my owne use:	F App	p.233 2	P Robin
I meane so sir with your favor.	F App	p.234 11	P Vintnr
what meane you sirra?	F App	p.235 21	P Vintnr
Ile tel you what I meane.	F App	p.235 22	P Robin
with what plague/Meane ye to radge?	Lucan, First Booke		649
Muse upreard <prepar'd> I [meant] <meane> to sing of armes,	Ovid's Elegies		1.1.5
I meane not to defend the scapes of any,	Ovid's Elegies		2.4.1
That meane to travaile some long irkesome way.	Ovid's Elegies		2.16.16
Yet in the meane time wilt small windes bestowe,	Ovid's Elegies		3.2.37

MEANES (Homograph)

What meanes Aeneas?	Dido	2.1.23	Achat
He [names] <meanes> Aeneas, let us kisse his feete.	Dido	2.1.51	Illion
And by that meanes repaire his broken ships,	Dido	2.1.328	Venus
Well could I like this reconcilements meanes,	Dido	3.2.81	Venus
What meanes faire Dido by this doubtfull speech?	Dido	3.4.31	Aeneas
When as she meanes to maske the world with clowdes.	Dido	4.1.6	Iarbus
Get you abourd, Aeneas meanes to stay.	Dido	4.4.24	Dido
How now Aeneas, sad, what meanes these dumpes?	Dido	5.1.62	Iarbus
Nor I devise by what meanes to contrive.	Dido	5.1.66	Aeneas
If it be so, his father meanes to flye:	Dido	5.1.85	Dido
What meanes my sister thus to rave and crye?	Dido	5.1.193	Anna
And meanes to be a terrour to the world,	1Tamb	1.2.38	Tamb
What meanes the mighty Turkish Emperor/To talk with one so base	1Tamb	3.3.87	Fesse
And by this meanes Ile win the world at last.	1Tamb	3.3.260	Tamb
That meanes to fill your helmets full of golde:	1Tamb	4.4.7	Tamb
And wisht as worthy subjects happy meanes,	1Tamb	5.1.103	1Virgn
Since other meanes are all forbidden me,	1Tamb	5.1.288	Bajzth
And he that meanes to place himselfe therin/Must armed wade up	2Tamb	1.3.83	Tamb

MEANES (cont.)			
By this my friendly keepers happy meanes, ...	2Tamb	3.1.34	Callap
Who meanes to gyrt Natolias walles with siege, ...	2Tamb	3.5.8	2Msngr
Devise some meanes to rid thee of thy life, ...	2Tamb	4.2.5	Olymp
Which mony was not got without my meanes.	Jew	Prol.32	Machvl
Their meanes of traffique from the vulgar trade, . . .	Jew	1.1.35	Barab
And knowes no meanes of his recoverie:	Jew	1.2.205	Barab
And he meanes quickly to expell you hence;	Jew	2.2.38	Bosco
Nor on his sonne, but by Mathias meanes;	Jew	3.3.45	Abigal
By no meanes possible.	Jew	4.2.61	P Ithimr
Well, I must seeke a meanes to rid 'em all, ...	Jew	4.3.63	Barab
For by my meanes Calymath shall enter in.	Jew	5.1.63	Barab
And by this meanes the City is your owne.	Jew	5.1.94	Barab
in Religion/Might be a meanes to crosse you in your love.	P 16	1.16	QnMoth
But tis the house of Burbon that he meanes.	P 644	12.57	Cardnl
And meanes to meet your highnes in the field. . . .	P 727	14.30	1Msngr
Then meanes he present treason to our state.	P 880	17.75	King
And war must be the meanes, or heele stay stil. . . .	Edw	1.2.63	Warwck
And by thy meanes is Gaveston exilde.	Edw	1.4.155	Edward
And be a meanes to call home Gaveston:	Edw	1.4.184	Queene
Then hope I by her meanes to be preferd, ...	Edw	2.1.29	Baldck
He meanes to make us stoope by force of armes, ...	Edw	2.2.103	Lncstr
I would hee were, so it were not by my meanes.	Edw	5.2.45	Queene
Seeke all the meanes thou canst to make him droope, . .	Edw	5.2.54	Mortmr
What meanes your highnesse to mistrust me thus? . . .	Edw	5.5.79	Ltborn
What meanes thou to dissemble with me thus?	Edw	5.5.80	Edward
To witnesse to the world, that by thy meanes, ...	Edw	5.6.31	King
Nor will we come unlesse he use such meanes, ...	F 278	1.3.50	Mephst
O they are meanes to bring thee unto heaven.	F 406	2.1.18	GdAngl
What meanes this shew? speake Mephostophilis.	F 472	2.1.84	Faust
and he would by no meanes sell him under forty Dollors; so sir,	F1537	4.5.33	P HrsCsr
by meanes of a swift spirit that I have, I had these grapes	F1585	4.6.28	P Faust
I wonder what he meanes, if death were nie, he would not .	F1677	5.1.4	P Wagner
<what meanes Faustus>?	F1827	(HC270)A	P 2Schol
and so by that meanes I shal see more then ere I felt, or saw	F App	p.233 4	P Robin
I thinke my maister meanes to die shortly, ...	F App	p.243 1	Wagner
for Nero (then unborne) the fates/Would find no other meanes,	Lucan, First Booke		34
By thy meanes women of their rest are bard, ...	Ovid's Elegies		1.13.23
And long admiring say by what meanes learnd/Hath this same Poet	Ovid's Elegies		2.1.9
How oft, and by what meanes we did agree.	Ovid's Elegies		2.8.28
Corinna meanes, and dangerous wayes to take.	Ovid's Elegies		2.11.8
And craftily knowes by what meanes to winne me. . . .	Ovid's Elegies		2.19.10
Who, because meanes want, doeth not, she doth. . . .	Ovid's Elegies		3.4.4
Never can these by any meanes agree.	Ovid's Elegies		3.4.42
If standing here I can by no meanes get, ...	Ovid's Elegies		3.5.11
But when she saw it would by no meanes stand, ...	Ovid's Elegies		3.6.75
Why are our pleasures by thy meanes forborne?	Ovid's Elegies		3.9.4
(as men say)/But deaffe and cruell, where he meanes to pray.	Hero and Leander		2.288
MEANEST			
Shall buy the meanest souldier in my traine.	1Tamb	1.2.86	Tamb
And feare to offend the meanest noble man.	Edw	1.4.277	Mortmr
MEANE TIME			
Meane time, Ascanius shall be my charge, ...	Dido	3.2.98	Venus
Meane time these wanton weapons serve my warre, . . .	Dido	3.3.37	Cupid
But in the meane time Gaveston away, ...	Edw	1.1.202	Edward
And in the meane time ile intreat you all, ...	Edw	1.2.77	ArchBp
Meane time my lord of Penbrooke and my selfe, ...	Edw	2.2.122	Warwck
I, and I fall not asleepe i'th meane time.	F1196	4.1.42	Benvol
Yet in the meane time wilt small windes bestowe, . . .	Ovid's Elegies		3.2.37
MEANE WHILE			
Ile dispose them as it likes me best,/Meane while take him in.	2Tamb	4.1.167	Tamb
Meane while, have hence this rebell to the blocke, . . .	Edw	4.6.69	Mortmr
We in meane while madam, must take advise, ...	Edw	4.6.77	Mortmr
Meane while peruse this booke, and view it throughly, .	F 717	2.2.169	Lucifr
MEANING			
Meaning to mangle all thy Provinces.	1Tamb	1.1.17	Cosroe
Brother, I see your meaning well enough.	1Tamb	1.1.18	Mycet
see how right the man/Hath hit the meaning of my Lord the King.	1Tamb	3.2.108	Techel
Meaning to make me Generall of the world, ...	1Tamb	5.1.451	Tamb
Meaning to make a conquest of our land:	2Tamb	1.1.49	Gazell
Meaning to aid [thee] <them> in this <these> Turkish armes,	2Tamb	1.3.144	Techel
Meaning to make her stately Queene of heaven.	2Tamb	2.4.108	Tamb
Stands here a purpose, meaning me some wrong, ...	Jew	4.1.166	1Fryar
you know my meaning.	Jew	4.3.35	P Barab
Let me alone to urge it now I know the meaning. . . .	Jew	4.4.79	Pilia
The meaning has a meaning; come let's in:	Jew	4.4.80	Ithimr
And simple meaning to your Majestie, ...	P 867	17.62	Guise
Thats his meaning.	Edw	5.5.18	Matrvs
Good meaning, shame, and such as seeke loves wrack/Shall follow	Ovid's Elegies		1.2.31
As meaning to be veng'd for darting it.	Hero and Leander		2.212
MEANINGS			
Yet if he knew our meanings, could he scape?	Jew	4.1.135	Barab
MEANLY			
Achates, thou shalt be so [manly] <meanly> clad, . . .	Dido	3.1.128	Dido
MEANS (Homograph)			
But Menaphon, what means this trumpets sound?	1Tamb	1.1.133	Cosroe
What means this divelish shephgard to aspire/With such a .	1Tamb	2.6.1	Cosroe
Or be the means the overweighing heavens/Have kept to qualifie	1Tamb	5.1.45	Govnr
And means to fire Turky as he goes:	2Tamb	1.1.18	Gazell
Hoping by some means I shall be releast, ...	2Tamb	1.2.23	Callap
Ile use some other means to make you yeeld, ...	2Tamb	4.2.51	Therid
How now, what means this?	Jew	5.5.64	Calym
Faine would I finde some means to speak with him/But cannot,	P 662	13.6	Duchss

MEANS (cont.)
Nothing but Gaveston, what means your grace? — Edw 2.2.7 — Mortmr
I think my Maister means to die shortly, he has made his will, — F1674 5.1.1 — P Wagner
and by means of a swift spirit that I have, I had them brought — F App p.242 22 — P Faust

MEAN'ST
As good dissemble that thou never mean'st/As first meane truth, — Jew 1.2.290 — Barab
And staring, thus bespoke: what mean'st thou Caesar? — Lucan, First Booke — 192

MEANST
How meanst thou that? — P 618 12.31 — King
How meanst thou Mortimer? that is over base. — Edw 2.5.71 — Gavstn
No, no, for if thou meanst to murther me, — Edw 5.5.98 — Edward
O nomine Domine, what meanst thou Robin? — F App p.235 26 — P Vintnr

MEANT (See also MENT)
Or meant to pierce Avernus darksome vaults, — 1Tamb 1.2.160 — Therid
As if he meant to give my Souldiers pay, — 1Tamb 1.2.183 — Tamb
and my souldiers looke/As if they meant to conquer Affrica. — 1Tamb 3.3.10 — Tamb
And never meant to make a Conquerour, — 2Tamb 3.5.83 — Tamb
Lost long before you knew what honour meant. — 2Tamb 4.3.87 — Tamb
It seemes they meant to conquer us my Lord, — 2Tamb 4.3.88 — Therid
I meant to cut a channell to them both, — 2Tamb 5.3.134 — Tamb
sort as if he had meant to make cleane my Boots with his lips; — Jew 4.2.30 — P Ithimr
Tush, to be short, he meant to make me Munke, — P1039 19.109 — King
Muse upreard <prepar'd> I [meant] <meane> to sing of armes, — Ovid's Elegies — 1.1.5
Yet could I not cast ancor where I meant, — Ovid's Elegies — 3.6.6
He being a novice, knew not what she meant, — Hero and Leander — 2.13

MEAN TIME
And in the mean time my Lord, could we devise, — P 425 7.65 — Guise
<in mean time take this booke, peruse it throwly>, — F 717 (HC264)A — Lucifr

MEASURE (See also MEISURES)
To measure how I prize Aeneas love, — Dido 4.4.140 — Dido
But since they measure our deserts so meane, — 1Tamb 1.2.63 — Tamb
And measure every wandring plannets course: — 1Tamb 2.7.23 — Tamb
Hath suckt the measure of that vitall aire/That feeds the body — 2Tamb 2.4.44 — Zenoc
And with the Jacobs staffe measure the height/And distance of — 2Tamb 3.3.50 — Techel
That measure nought but by the present time. — Jew 1.2.220 — Barab
And with mistrust of the like measure vext. — Ovid's Elegies — 1.4.46
by the pleasure/Which man and woman reape in equall measure? — Ovid's Elegies — 1.10.36

MEASURED
And if before the Sun have measured heaven/With triple circuit — 1Tamb 3.1.36 — Bajzth

MEASURES
To move unto the measures of delight: — Dido 3.4.54 — Dido
That measures costs, and kingdomes of the earth: — F 774 2.3.53 — 2Chor

MEASURETH
Which measureth the glorious frame of heaven, — 2Tamb 3.4.65 — Therid

MEASURING
Measuring the limits of his Emperie/By East and west, as — 1Tamb 1.2.39 — Tamb

MEAT
To dresse the common souldiers meat and drink. — 1Tamb 3.3.185 — Zenoc
Fall to, and never may your meat digest. — 1Tamb 4.4.16 — Bajzth
Go to, fal to your meat: — 1Tamb 4.4.54 — P Tamb
I Tyrant, and more meat. — 1Tamb 4.4.102 — P Bajzth
Fling the meat in his face. — 1Tamb 5.1.315 — P Zabina
How now? who snatch't the meat from me! — F1044 3.2.64 — Pope
Even as delicious meat is to the tast, — Hero and Leander — 1.63

MEATE
Father I faint, good father give me meate. — Dido 1.1.163 — Ascan
Till we have fire to dresse the meate we kild: — Dido 1.1.165 — Aeneas
bowes enow/Neere to these woods, to rost your meate withall: — Dido 1.1.173 — Aeneas
yesternight/I opened but the doore to throw him meate,/And I — Edw 5.5.8 — Gurney
with me, and after meate/We'le canvase every quidditie thereof: — F 190 1.1.162 — Faust
me, as if they payd for their meate and drinke, I can tell you. — F 365 1.4.23 — P Robin
be he that stole [away] his holinesse meate from the Table. — F1077 3.2.97 — 1Frier
I would request no better meate, then a dish of ripe grapes. — F1573 4.6.16 — P Lady
with my flesh, as if they had payd for my meate and drinke. — F App p.230 29 — P Clown
How now, whose that which snatcht the meate from me? — F App p.231 8 — P Pope
Cursed be hee that stole away his holinesse meate from/the — F App p.232 31 — Frier
I would desire no better meate then a dish of ripe grapes. — F App p.242 11 — P Duchss
Even as sweete meate a glutted stomacke cloyes. — Ovid's Elegies — 2.19.26
This was [their] <there> meate, the soft grasse was their bed. — Ovid's Elegies — 3.9.10

MEATES
Thy mouth to taste of many meates did balke. — Ovid's Elegies — 2.6.30

MECA
Bordering on Mare Roso neere to Meca. — 2Tamb 3.5.131 — Callap

MECAS
And hung on stately Mecas Temple roofe, — 2Tamb 1.1.141 — Orcan

MEDDLE
And meddle not with any that I love: — Dido 3.3.22 — Dido
To meddle or attempt such dangerous things. — P 38 1.38 — Admral
to beware/How you did meddle with such dangerous giftes. — P 180 3.15 — Navrre

MEDEA
Great Lord of Medea and Armenia: — 1Tamb 1.1.163 — Ortyg
these Medean Lords/To Memphis, from my uncles country of Medea, — 1Tamb 1.2.12 — Zenoc
Shal have a government in Medea: — 1Tamb 2.2.33 — Meandr
Then thou for Parthia, they for Scythia and Medea. — 1Tamb 2.5.83 — Tamb

MEDEAN
And Captaines of the Medean garrisons, — 1Tamb 1.1.111 — Cosroe
Who traveiling with these Medean Lords/To Memphis, from my — 1Tamb 1.2.11 — Zenoc
Thy Garments shall be made of Medean silke, — 1Tamb 1.2.95 — Tamb

MEDIATE
In person there to [mediate] <meditate> your peace; — Jew 5.5.116 — Calym

MEDICINAE
Summum bonum medicinae sanitas, — F 44 1.1.16 — Faust

MEDICINE
now, how Jove hath sent/A present medicine to recure my paine: — 2Tamb 5.3.106 — Tamb

MEDICUS
[Seeing ubi desinit philosophus, ibi incipit medicus]. . F 41 1.1.13A Faust
MEDITATE
entertaine a thought/That tends to love, but meditate on death, 2Tamb 4.2.26 Olymp
And meditate how we may grace us best/To solemnize our . Jew 5.3.44 Calym
In person there to [mediate] <meditate> your peace; . . Jew 5.5.116 Calym
Away, leave me alone to meditate. . . . . . . P1081 19.151 QnMoth
MEDITERRANEAN (See also TERRENE, TERREN)
downe by Candie shoare/To Malta, through our Mediterranean sea. Jew 1.1.47 Barab
and those other Iles/That lye betwixt the Mediterranean seas. Jew 1.2.4 Basso
conquer'd Iland stands/Inviron'd with the mediterranean Sea, Jew 5.3.7 Calym
MEE
Wilt thou forsake mee too in my distresse, ... Jew 1.2.358 Barab
And who must keepe mee now, must you my lorde? . . . . Edw 5.1.137 Edward
Your grace must hence with mee to Bartley straight. . . Edw 5.1.144 Bartly
Mortimer shall know that he hath wrongde mee. . . . Edw 5.2.118 Kent
Base villaines, wherefore doe you gripe mee thus? . . Edw 5.3.57 Kent
I feare mee that this crie will raise the towne, . . Edw 5.5.114 Matrvs
Too servile <The devill> and illiberall for mee. . . F 63 1.1.35 Faust
Now sirs, you shall heare how villanously he serv'd mee: . F1536 4.5.32 P HrsCsr
this is the time <the time wil come>, and he will fetch mee. F1861 5.2.65 P Faust
Forbeare to hurt thy selfe in spoyling mee. . . . . Ovid's Elegies 1.2.50
There touch what ever thou canst touch of mee. . . . Ovid's Elegies 1.4.58
But secretlie her lookes with checks did trounce mee, . Ovid's Elegies 1.7.21
Defend the ensignes of thy warre in mee. . . . . . Ovid's Elegies 1.11.12
If any eie mee with a modest looke, ... Ovid's Elegies 2.4.11
This seemes the fairest, so doth that to mee, . . . Ovid's Elegies 2.10.7
To this ad shame, shame to performe it quaild mee, . . Ovid's Elegies 3.6.37
And was the second cause why vigor failde mee: . . . Ovid's Elegies 3.6.38
Thou [cousenst] <cousendst> mee, by thee surprizde am I, . Ovid's Elegies 3.6.71
His fainting hand in death engrasped mee. . . . . Ovid's Elegies 3.8.58
But let not mee poore soule know of thy straying. . . Ovid's Elegies 3.13.2
If you wey not ill speeches, yet wey mee: . . . . . Ovid's Elegies 3.13.36
O let mee viste Hero ere I die. . . . . . . Hero and Leander 2.178
Come live with mee, and be my love, ... Passionate Shepherd 1
Come <Then> live with mee, and be my love. . . . . Passionate Shepherd 20
Then live with mee, and be my love. . . . . . . Passionate Shepherd 24
MEEDS
Then shall your meeds and vallours be advaunst/To roomes of 1Tamb 2.3.40 Cosroe
If we deserve them not with higher meeds/Then erst our states 1Tamb 4.4.131 Therid
MEERE
Who of meere charity and Christian ruth, ... Jew 2.3.71 Barab
This is meere frailty, brethren, be content. . . . . Jew 4.1.98 Barab
And use them but of meere hypocrisie. . . . . . Edw 2.1.45 Baldck
[Tush] <No>, these are trifles, and meere old wives Tales. F 524 2.1.136 Faust
MEERELY
And meerely of our love we do create thee/Earle of Gloster, and Edw 3.1.145 Edward
MEET (Homograph; See also METST)
Come let us meet them at the mountain foot, ... 1Tamb 1.2.133 Usumc
And all conjoin'd to meet the witlesse King, ... 1Tamb 2.1.64 Cosroe
Let us put on our meet incountring mindes, ... 1Tamb 2.6.19 Ortyg
I meane to meet him in Bithynia: . . . . 1Tamb 3.3.2 Tamb
He meet me in the field and fetch thee hence? . . . . 1Tamb 3.3.5 Tamb
hardy Tamburlaine)/What tis to meet me in the open field, 1Tamb 3.3.146 Bajzth
the king of Hungary/Should meet our person to conclude a truce. 2Tamb 1.1.10 Orcan
Or crosse the streame, and meet him in the field? . . 2Tamb 1.1.12 Orcan
Shall meet those Christians fleeting with the tyde, . . 2Tamb 1.1.40 Orcan
When we shall meet the Turkish Deputie/And all his Viceroies, 2Tamb 1.3.99 Tamb
Promist to meet me on Larissa plaines/With hostes apeece . 2Tamb 1.3.107 Tamb
Meet for your service on the sea, my Lord, ... 2Tamb 1.3.123 Therid
happinesse/And hope to meet your highnesse in the heavens, 2Tamb 2.4.63 Zenoc
I march to meet and aide my neigbor kings, ... 2Tamb 3.1.60 Soria
And when I meet an armie in the field, ... 2Tamb 3.2.38 Tamb
For [which] <with> the quinque-angle fourme is meet: . 2Tamb 3.2.64 Tamb
Before we meet the armie of the Turke. . . . . . 2Tamb 3.2.138 Tamb
Sweet mother strike, that I may meet my father. . . . 2Tamb 3.4.30 Sonne
Souldiers now let us meet the Generall, ... 2Tamb 3.4.85 Therid
Nay, when the battaile ends, al we wil meet, ... 2Tamb 3.5.97 Callap
No, we wil meet thee slavish Tamburlain. . . . . . 2Tamb 3.5.170 Orcan
A Forme not meet to give that subject essence, . . . 2Tamb 4.1.112 Tamb
And meet my husband and my loving sonne. . . . . . 2Tamb 4.2.36 Olymp
Live [continent] <content> then (ye slaves) and meet not me 2Tamb 4.3.81 Tamb
Shall mount the milk-white way and meet him there. . . 2Tamb 4.3.132 Tamb
Whereas the Terren and the red sea meet, ... 2Tamb 5.3.132 Tamb
Meet heaven and earth, and here let al things end, . . 2Tamb 5.3.249 Amyras
Revenge it on him when you meet him next. . . . . . Jew 2.3.343 Barab
As meet they will, and fighting dye; brave sport. . . . Jew 3.1.30 Ithimr
Pilia-borza, didst thou meet with Ithimore? . . . . Jew 4.2.1 P Curtzn
And where didst meet him? . . . . Jew 4.2.15 P Curtzn
I fram'd the challenge that did make them meet: . . . Jew 5.5.82 Barab
And therfore meane to murder all I meet. . . . . . P 279 5.6 Anjoy
And dayly meet about this time of day, ... P 503 9.22 Guise
That he may come and meet me in some place, ... P 664 13.8 Duchss
To send his power to meet us in the field. . . . . P 712 14.15 Navrre
And meanes to meet your highnes in the field. . . . P 727 14.30 1Msngr
If that be all, the next time that I meet her, . . . P 781 15.39 Mugern
<make> a walk/On purpose from the Court to meet with him. P 784 15.42 Mugern
When we may meet these traitors in the field. . . . . Edw 4.3.47 Edward
I tell thee tis not meet, that one so false/Should come about Edw 5.2.104 Mortmr
And meet me in my Study, at Midnight, ... F 327 1.3.99 Faust
To meet their loves; such as had none at all, ... Hero and Leander 1.95
When like desires and affections meet, ... Hero and Leander 2.30
MEETE (Homograph)
Then in one Cave the Queene and he shall meete, . . . Dido 3.2.92 Juno

MEETE (cont.)
Therefore tis good and meete for to be wise. 1Tamb 1.1.34 Mycet
Meete with the foole, and rid your royall shoulders/Of such a 1Tamb 2.3.46 Tamb
him assured hope/Of martiall triumph, ere he meete his foes: 1Tamb 3.3.43 Tamb
Where they shall meete, and joine their force in one, 1Tamb 3.3.257 Tamb
let us haste and meete/Our Army and our brother of Jerusalem, 2Tamb 2.3.42 Orcan
Will meete, and with a generall consent, Edw 1.2.70 ArchBp
Meete you for this, proud overdaring peeres? Edw 1.4.47 Edward
He wils me to repaire unto the court,/And meete my Gaveston: Edw 2.1.68 Neece
And meete me at the parke pale presentlie: Edw 2.1.73 Neece
Farewell sweete unckle till we meete againe. Edw 2.4.11 Neece
In heaven wee may, in earth never shall wee meete, Edw 4.7.80 Edward
Ile meete with you anone for interrupting me so: F App p.238 58 P Faust
Confused stars shal meete, celestiall fire/Fleete on the Lucan, First Booke 75
In wooddie groves ist meete that Ceres Raigne, Ovid's Elegies 1.1.13
Fare well sterne warre, for blunter Poets meete. Ovid's Elegies 1.1.32
Who feares these armes? who wil not go to meete them? Ovid's Elegies 1.6.39
The carefull prison is more meete for thee. Ovid's Elegies 1.6.64
The sonne slew her, that forth to meete him went, Ovid's Elegies 1.10.51
To meete for poyson or vilde facts we crave not, Ovid's Elegies 2.2.63
Their <Your> youthfull browes with Ivie girt to meete him,/With Ovid's Elegies 3.8.61
These gifts are meete to please the powers divine. Ovid's Elegies 3.9.48
The bed is for lascivious toyings meete, Ovid's Elegies 3.13.17
MEETER
Meeter it were her lips were blewe with kissing/And on her Ovid's Elegies 1.7.41
MEETES
the death of many men/Meetes in one period. Lucan, First Booke 650
MEETING
Where meeting with the rest, kill kill they cryed. Dido 2.1.190 Aeneas
But there's a meeting in the Senate-house, Jew 1.1.167 2Jew
But say my lord, where shall this meeting bee? Edw 1.2.74 Warwck
having fild/Her meeting hornes to match her brothers light, Lucan, First Booke 536
These greedie lovers had, at their first meeting. Hero and Leander 2.24
MEGAERA
Or fierce Agave mad; or like Megaera/That scar'd Alcides, when Lucan, First Booke 574
MEGERAS
And with Megeras eyes stared in their face, Dido 2.1.230 Aeneas
MEISURES
Hath trode the Meisures, do my souldiers martch, 2Tamb 5.1.75 Tamb
MELANCHOLIE
I wil endure a melancholie life, Edw 1.2.66 Queene
Frighted the melancholie earth, which deem'd, Hero and Leander 1.99
MELANCHOLLY
To rid me from these melancholly thoughts. Dido 2.1.303 Dido
MELANCHOLY
Is all our pleasure turn'd to melancholy? F1828 5.2.32 2Schol
MELEAGERS
This Meleagers sonne, a warlike Prince, Dido 3.1.163 Dido
MELIAGER
Me thinks we martch as Meliager did, 1Tamb 4.3.1 Souldn
MELLOWED
And fall like mellowed fruit, with shakes of death, 1Tamb 2.1.47 Cosroe
MELODIOUS
More then melodious are these words to me, Dido 3.2.62 Juno
walles of Thebes/With ravishing sound of his melodious Harpe, F 580 2.2.29 Faust
Melodious byrds [sing] <sings> Madrigalls. Passionate Shepherd 8
MELT
Lest with these sweete thoughts I melt cleane away. Dido 3.1.76 Dido
That they may melt and I fall in his armes: Dido 5.1.245 Dido
and hartie humble mones/Will melt his furie into some remorse: 1Tamb 5.1.22 Govnr
the clowdes/Incense the heavens, and make the starres to melt, 2Tamb 4.1.195 Tamb
Earth melt to ayre, gone is my soveraigne, Edw 4.7.103 Spencr
Yet will it melt, ere I have done my tale. Edw 5.5.55 Edward
His presence made the rudest paisant melt, Hero and Leander 1.79
MELTED
Thy springs are nought but raine and melted snowe: Ovid's Elegies 3.5.93
MELTING
I dye with melting ruth, Aeneas leave. Dido 2.1.289 Dido
And melting, heavens conspir'd his over-throw: F 22 Prol.22 1Chor
MELTS
To cure my minde that melts for unkind love. Dido 5.1.287 Dido
MEMBERS
The head being of, the members cannot stand. P 296 5.23 Anjoy
<make> slender/And to get out doth like apt members render. Ovid's Elegies 1.6.6
Weare me, when warmest showers thy members wash, Ovid's Elegies 2.15.23
MEMNON
And birds for <from> Memnon yearly shall be slaine. Ovid's Elegies 1.13.4
Memnon the elfe/Received his cole-blacke colour from thy selfe. Ovid's Elegies 1.13.31
MEMORABLE
As memorable witnesse of our league. 2Tamb 1.1.145 Orcan
MEMORIE
Whose memorie like pale deaths stony mace, Dido 2.1.115 Aeneas
But cals not then your Grace to memorie/The league we lately 2Tamb 2.1.27 Sgsmnd
my Lords whose true nobilitie/Have merited my latest memorie: 2Tamb 2.4.74 Zenoc
In grievous memorie of his fathers shame, 2Tamb 3.1.25 Callap
This Piller plac'd in memorie of her, 2Tamb 3.2.15 Calyph
In memorie of this our victory. 2Tamb 3.5.20 Callap
MEMORY
And leave no memory that e're I was. Jew 1.2.265 Barab
MEMPHION
That with their beauties grac'd the Memphion fields: 1Tamb 4.2.104 Tamb
MEMPHIS
Who traveiling with these Medean Lords/To Memphis, from my 1Tamb 1.2.12 Zenoc

MEMPHIS (cont.)

Awake ye men of Memphis, heare the clange/Of Scythian trumpets,	1Tamb	4.1.1	Souldn
Whose like Aegiptian Memphis never had/For skill in stars, and	Lucan, First Booke		639
Memphis, and Pharos that sweete date trees yeelds,	Ovid's Elegies		2.13.8

MEN

And Neptunes waves be envious men of warre,	Dido	1.1.65	Venus
Or whether men or beasts inhabite it.	Dido	1.1.177	Aeneas
No steps of men imprinted in the earth.	Dido	1.1.181	Achat
Hoe yong men, saw you as you came/Any of all my Sisters	Dido	1.1.183	Venus
Brave men at armes, abandon fruitles feares,	Dido	1.2.32	Iarbus
Your men and you shall banquet in our Court,	Dido	1.2.39	Iarbus
Seeing the number of their men decreast,	Dido	2.1.132	Aeneas
Old men with swords thrust through their aged sides,	Dido	2.1.197	Aeneas
Through which he could not passe for slaughtred men:	Dido	2.1.262	Aeneas
But should that man of men (Dido except)/Have taunted me in	Dido	3.3.26	Iarbus
Did ever men see such a sudden storme?	Dido	4.1.1	Achat
This is no life for men at armes to live,	Dido	4.3.33	Achat
They say Aeneas men are going abourd,	Dido	4.4.2	Dido
And also furniture for these my men.	Dido	5.1.70	Aeneas
Aeneas, wherefore goe thy men abourd?	Dido	5.1.87	Dido
That Gods and men may pitie this my death,	Dido	5.1.327	Anna
But I refer me to my noble men,	1Tamb	1.1.21	Mycet
All loden with the heads of killed men.	1Tamb	1.1.78	Mycet
When other men prease forward for renowne:	1Tamb	1.1.84	Mycet
The plot is laid by Persean Noble men,	1Tamb	1.1.110	Cosroe
Men from the farthest Equinoctiall line,	1Tamb	1.1.119	Cosroe
Till men and kingdomes help to strengthen it:	1Tamb	1.2.30	Tamb
My martiall prises with five hundred men,	1Tamb	1.2.102	Tamb
Weele fight five hundred men at armes to one,	1Tamb	1.2.143	Tamb
shall confesse/Theise are the men that all the world admires.	1Tamb	1.2.223	Usumc
I yeeld my selfe, my men and horse to thee:	1Tamb	1.2.229	Therid
show him to be made/His Fortunes maister, and the king of men,	1Tamb	2.1.36	Cosroe
This countrie swarmes with vile outragious men,	1Tamb	2.2.22	Meandr
The world will strive with hostes of men at armes,	1Tamb	2.3.13	Tamb
That I with these my friends and all my men,	1Tamb	2.3.43	Tamb
They knew not, ah, they knew not simple men,	1Tamb	2.4.2	Mycet
Till I may see thee hem'd with armed men.	1Tamb	2.4.38	Tamb
A jest to chardge on twenty thousand men?	1Tamb	2.5.91	Therid
The strangest men that ever nature made,	1Tamb	2.7.40	Cosroe
Will tell how many thousand men he slew.	1Tamb	3.2.43	Agidas
Your men are valiant but their number few,	1Tamb	3.3.11	Bassoe
Brought to the war by men of Tripoly:	1Tamb	3.3.17	Bassoe
Let him bring millions infinite of men,	1Tamb	3.3.33	Usumc
Ye Moores and valiant men of Barbary,	1Tamb	3.3.89	Moroc
untill thou see/Me martch victoriously with all my men,	1Tamb	3.3.127	Tamb
Untill the Persean Fleete and men of war,	1Tamb	3.3.252	Tamb
Awake ye men of Memphis, heare the clange/Of Scythian trumpets,	1Tamb	4.1.1	Souldn
Three hundred thousand men in armour clad,	1Tamb	4.1.21	2Msngr
Engins and munition/Exceed the forces of their martial men.	1Tamb	4.1.29	2Msngr
had you time to sort/Your fighting men, and raise your royall	1Tamb	4.1.37	Capol
The townes-men maske in silke and cloath of gold,	1Tamb	4.2.108	Tamb
The men, the treasure, and the towne is ours.	1Tamb	4.2.110	Tamb
The Scum of men, the hate and Scourge of God,	1Tamb	4.3.9	Souldn
Two hundred thousand foot, brave men at armes,	1Tamb	4.3.54	Capol
my spirit doth foresee/The utter ruine of thy men and thee.	1Tamb	4.3.60	Arabia
And fashions men with true nobility.	1Tamb	5.1.190	Tamb
Millions of men encompasse thee about,	1Tamb	5.1.215	Bajzth
Thy streetes strowed with dissevered jointes of men,	1Tamb	5.1.322	Zenoc
Hell and Elisian swarme with ghosts of men,	1Tamb	5.1.465	Tamb
When men presume to manage armes with him.	1Tamb	5.1.478	Tamb
Egyptians, Moores and men of Asia,	1Tamb	5.1.517	Tamb
Environed with troopes of noble men,	1Tamb	5.1.526	Tamb
Inhabited with tall and sturdy men,	2Tamb	1.1.27	Orcan
Since Tamburlaine hath mustred all his men,	2Tamb	1.1.46	Gazell
Our Tents are pitcht, our men stand in array,	2Tamb	1.1.120	Fredrk
Although he sent a thousand armed men/To intercept this haughty	2Tamb	1.2.70	Almeda
And martch with such a multitude of men,	2Tamb	1.3.56	Celeb
And sprinkled with the braines of slaughtered men,	2Tamb	1.3.81	Tamb
frontier townes/Twise twenty thousand valiant men at armes,	2Tamb	1.3.120	Therid
And all the men in armour under me,	2Tamb	1.3.135	Usumc
Were turnde to men, he should be overcome:	2Tamb	1.3.164	Tamb
our men of Barbary have martcht/Foure hundred miles with armour	2Tamb	1.3.174	Usumc
tooles/Makes Earthquakes in the hearts of men and heaven.	2Tamb	2.2.8	Orcan
And numbers more than infinit of men,	2Tamb	2.2.18	Gazell
I have a hundred thousand men in armes,	2Tamb	3.1.38	Orcan
Then next, the way to fortifie your men,	2Tamb	3.2.62	Tamb
And roome within to lodge sixe thousand men.	2Tamb	3.2.72	Tamb
That bring fresh water to thy men and thee:	2Tamb	3.3.30	Techel
Both we (Theridamas) wil intrench our men,	2Tamb	3.3.49	Techel
And souldiers play the men, the [hold] <holds> is yours.	2Tamb	3.3.63	Techel
And strowes the way with braines of slaughtered men:	2Tamb	3.4.58	Therid
Here at Alepo with an hoste of men/Lies Tamburlaine, this king	2Tamb	3.5.3	2Msngr
Viceroies and Peeres of Turky play the men,	2Tamb	3.5.14	Callap
Tell me Viceroies the number of your men,	2Tamb	3.5.30	Callap
three score thousand fighting men/Are come since last we shewed	2Tamb	3.5.33	Jrslem
royall is esteem'd/Six hundred thousand valiant fighting men.	2Tamb	3.5.51	Soria
and sacrifice/Mountaines of breathlesse men to Mahomet,	2Tamb	3.5.55	Callap
our men shall sweat/With carrieng pearle and treasure on their	2Tamb	3.5.166	Techel
And should I goe and kill a thousand men,	2Tamb	4.1.53	Calyph
that like armed men/Are seene to march upon the towers of	2Tamb	4.1.201	Tamb
In vaine I see men worship Mahomet,	2Tamb	5.1.179	Tamb
Where men report, thou sitt'st by God himselfe,	2Tamb	5.1.194	Tamb
Thousands of men drown'd in Asphaltis Lake,	2Tamb	5.1.204	Techel

MEN (cont.)

Marching about the ayer with armed men,	2Tamb	5.2.34		Amasia
For we have here the chiefe selected men/Of twenty severall	2Tamb	5.2.48		Callap
That men might quickly saile to India.	2Tamb	5.3.135		Tamb
And weigh not men, and therefore not mens words.	Jew	Prol.8		Machvl
As for those [Samnites] <Samintes>, and the men of Uzz,/That	Jew	1.1.4		Barab
And thus me thinkes should men of judgement frame/This is the	Jew	1.1.34		Barab
But this we heard some of our sea-men say,	Jew	1.1.78		1Merch
goe/And bid the Merchants and my men dispatch/And come ashore,	Jew	1.1.100		Barab
Fond men, what dreame you of their multitudes?	Jew	1.1.157		Barab
These silly men mistake the matter cleane.	Jew	1.1.179		Barab
To take the lives of miserable men,	Jew	1.2.147		Barab
And fram'd of finer mold then common men,	Jew	1.2.219		Barab
none but their owne sect/Must enter in; men generally barr'd.	Jew	1.2.257		Abigal
And now you men of Malta looke about,	Jew	3.5.29		Govnr
But are not both these wise men to suppose/That I will leave my	Jew	4.1.122		Barab
you men of Malta, heare me speake;/Shee is a Curtezane and he a	Jew	5.1.36		Barab
give me if I render you/The life of Calymath, surprize his men,	Jew	5.2.80		Barab
I cannot feast my men in Malta wals,	Jew	5.3.34		Calym
He will; and has commanded all his men/To come ashore, and march	Jew	5.5.14		Msngr
Without fresh men to rigge and furnish them.	Jew	5.5.101		Govnr
My men are all aboord,	Jew	5.5.103		Calym
Wherein are thirtie thousand able men,	P 139	2.82		Guise
they may become/As men that stand and gase against the Sunne.	P 163	2.106		Guise
Besides my heart relentes that noble men,	P 211	4.9		Charls
Goe place some men upon the bridge,	P 421	7.61		Dumain
My brother Guise hath gathered a power of men,	P 642	12.55		Cardnl
How many noble men have lost their lives,	P 795	16.9		Navrre
of Guise, we understand that you/Have gathered a power of men.	P 822	17.17		King
Pleshe, goe muster up our men with speed,	P 916	18.17		Navrre
Let mean consaits, and baser men feare death,	P 997	19.67		Guise
O wordes of power to kill a thousand men.	P1126	21.20		Dumain
Come let us away and leavy men,	P1127	21.21		Dumain
Sweete Epernoune, our Friers are holy men,	P1161	22.23		King
Not that I love the citie or the men,	Edw	1.1.12		Gavstn
But yet it is no paine to speake men faire,	Edw	1.1.42		Gavstn
these are not men for me,/I must have wanton Poets, pleasant	Edw	1.1.50		Gavstn
My men like Satyres grazing on the lawnes,	Edw	1.1.59		Gavstn
To hide those parts which men delight to see,	Edw	1.1.65		Gavstn
Wilshire hath men enough to save our heads.	Edw	1.1.127		MortSr
Why post we not from hence to levie men?	Edw	1.2.16		Mortmr
And both the Mortimers, two goodly men,	Edw	1.3.3		Gavstn
Ah none but rude and savage minded men,	Edw	1.4.78		Edward
And not kings onelie, but the wisest men,	Edw	1.4.395		MortSr
Can get you any favour with great men.	Edw	2.1.41		Spencr
Come Edmund lets away, and levie men,	Edw	2.2.98		Edward
Would levie men enough to anger you.	Edw	2.2.152		Mortmr
Monster of men,/That like the Greekish strumpet traind to armes	Edw	2.5.14		Lncstr
hence, out of the way/A little, but our men shall go along.	Edw	2.5.101		Penbrk
And yee be men,/Speede to the king.	Edw	2.6.5		Gavstn
My lord of Penbrookes men,	Edw	2.6.6		Warwck
For being delivered unto Penbrookes men,	Edw	3.1.116		Arundl
Upon these Barons, harten up your men,	Edw	3.1.124		Spencr
a while, our men with sweat and dust/All chockt well neare,	Edw	3.1.191		SpncrP
Unnaturall king, to slaughter noble men/And cherish flatterers:	Edw	4.1.8		Kent
money, men, and friends/Ere long, to bid the English king a	Edw	4.2.65		SrJohn
In civill broiles makes kin and country men/Slaughter	Edw	4.4.6		Queene
Upon my life, those be the men ye seeke.	Edw	4.7.46		Mower
The greefes of private men are soone allayde,	Edw	5.1.8		Edward
To wretched men death is felicitie.	Edw	5.1.127		Edward
Men are ordaind to live in miserie,	Edw	5.3.2		Matrvs
O levell all your lookes upon these daring men,	Edw	5.3.39		Edward
that in thy wheele/There is a point, to which when men aspire,	Edw	5.6.60		Mortmr
Couldst <Wouldst> thou make men <man> to live eternally,	F 52	1.1.24		Faust
To passe the Ocean with a band of men,	F 334	1.3.106		Faust
[makes men] <make them> foolish that do use <trust> them most.	F 408	2.1.20		BdAngl
As great as have the humane soules of men.	F 433	2.1.45		Mephst
Tell me, where is the place that men call Hell?	F 505	2.1.117		Faust
And men in harnesse <armour> shall appeare to thee,	F 548	2.1.160		Mephst
into matters, as other men, if they were disposed to talke.	F 741	2.3.20	P	Robin
Long ere with Iron hands they punish men,	F 878	3.1.100		Pope
And all society of holy men:	F 910	3.1.132		Pope
Wonder of men, renown'd Magitian,	F1204	4.1.50		Emper
of his men to attend you with provision fit for your journey.	F1501	4.4.45	P	Wagner
you may be ashamed to burden honest men with a matter of truth.	F App	p.234 15	P	Rafe
sirra you, Ile teach ye to impeach honest men:	F App	p.235 18	P	Robin
my selfe farre inferior to the report men have published,	F App	p.236 13	P	Faust
Then men from war shal bide in league, and ease,	Lucan, First Booke			60
end the gods/Allot the height of honor, men so strong/By land,	Lucan, First Booke			82
Affrights poore fearefull men, and blasts their eyes/With	Lucan, First Booke			155
Men tooke delight in Jewels, houses, plate,	Lucan, First Booke			164
Faiths breach, and hence came war to most men welcom.	Lucan, First Booke			184
The people started; young men left their beds,	Lucan, First Booke			241
Where men are ready, lingering ever hurts:	Lucan, First Booke			282
And lawes assailde, and arm'd men in the Senate?	Lucan, First Booke			322
Yet for long service done, reward these men,	Lucan, First Booke			341
And in all quarters musters men for Roome.	Lucan, First Booke			396
Doubtles these northren men/Whom death the greatest of all	Lucan, First Booke			454
and you fierce men of Rhene/Leaving your countrey open to the	Lucan, First Booke			460
and that Roome/He looking on by these men should be sackt.	Lucan, First Booke			480
O gods that easie grant men great estates,	Lucan, First Booke			508
And whelm'd the world in darknesse, making men/Dispaire of day;	Lucan, First Booke			540
untrod woods/Shrill voices schright, and ghoasts incounter men.	Lucan, First Booke			568

MEN (cont.)

the death of many men/Meetes in one period. — Lucan, First Booke 649
Both verses were alike till Love (men say)/Began to smile and — Ovid's Elegies 1.1.7
With armes to conquer armlesse men is base, — Ovid's Elegies 1.2.22
Yong men and women, shalt thou lead as thrall, — Ovid's Elegies 1.2.27
Thou with these souldiers conquerest gods and men, — Ovid's Elegies 1.2.37
If men have Faith, Ile live with thee for ever. — Ovid's Elegies 1.3.16
With armes or armed men I come not guarded, — Ovid's Elegies 1.6.33
That I was mad, and barbarous all men cried, — Ovid's Elegies 1.7.19
Nor one or two men are sufficient. — Ovid's Elegies 1.8.54
Venus to mockt men lendes a sencelesse eare. — Ovid's Elegies 1.8.86
On all the [bed mens] <beds men> tumbling let him viewe/And thy — Ovid's Elegies 1.8.97
Great Agamemnon was, men say, amazed, — Ovid's Elegies 1.9.37
Let poore men show their service, faith, and care; — Ovid's Elegies 1.10.57
Whither runst thou, that men, and women, love not? — Ovid's Elegies 1.13.9
Or men with crooked sickles corne downe fell. — Ovid's Elegies 1.15.12
While bond-men cheat, fathers [be hard] <hoord>, bawds hoorish, — Ovid's Elegies 1.15.17
For after death all men receive their right: — Ovid's Elegies 1.15.40
Men handle those, all manly hopes resigne, — Ovid's Elegies 2.3.9
So many men and maidens without love, — Ovid's Elegies 2.9.15
At Colchis stain'd with childrens bloud men raile, — Ovid's Elegies 2.14.29
Now comes the pompe; themselves let all men cheere: — Ovid's Elegies 3.2.43
Ceres and Bacchus Country-men adore, — Ovid's Elegies 3.2.53
Tut, men should not their courage so consume. — Ovid's Elegies 3.3.34
The Gods have eyes, and brests as well as men. — Ovid's Elegies 3.3.42
I know not, what men thinke should thee so move. — Ovid's Elegies 3.4.28
Great flouds ought to assist young men in love, — Ovid's Elegies 3.5.23
men point at me for a whore,/Shame, that should make me blush, — Ovid's Elegies 3.5.77
Worthy she was to move both Gods and men, — Ovid's Elegies 3.6.59
Not what we slouthfull [knowe] <knewe>, let wise men learne, — Ovid's Elegies 3.7.25
Men kept the shoare, and sailde not into deepe. — Ovid's Elegies 3.7.44
So at Aeneas buriall men report, — Ovid's Elegies 3.8.13
The gods care we are cald, and men of piety, — Ovid's Elegies 3.8.17
When bad fates take good men, I am forbod, — Ovid's Elegies 3.8.35
Rude husband-men bak'd not their corne before, — Ovid's Elegies 3.9.7
On mast of cakes, first oracles, men fed, — Ovid's Elegies 3.9.9
And men inthralld by Mermaids singing charmes. — Ovid's Elegies 3.11.28
Where she should sit for men to gaze upon. — Hero and Leander 1.8
Can hardly blazon foorth the loves of men, — Hero and Leander 1.70
For in his lookes were all that men desire, — Hero and Leander 1.84
The men of wealthie Sestos, everie yeare, — Hero and Leander 1.91
Without the sweet societie of men. — Hero and Leander 1.256
Men foolishly doe call it vertuous, — Hero and Leander 1.277
Though neither gods nor men may thee deserve, — Hero and Leander 1.315
Wherewith the king of Gods and men is feasted. — Hero and Leander 1.432
Love is not ful of pittie (as men say)/But deaffe and cruell, — Hero and Leander 2.287

MENACE

His looks do menace heaven and dare the Gods, — 1Tamb 1.2.157 Therid
are ful of brags/And menace more than they can wel performe: — 1Tamb 3.3.4 Tamb
And Jetty Feathers menace death and hell. — 1Tamb 4.1.61 2Msngr
And meane once more to menace me. — P 364 7.4 Ramus
To threaten England and to menace me? — P1034 19.104 King

MENACES

I cannot brooke these hautie menaces: — Edw 1.1.134 Edward
Tyrant, I scorne thy threats and menaces, — Edw 3.1.241 Warwck

MENACETH

And how my slave, her mistresse menaceth. — 1Tamb 3.3.183 Zenoc

MENACING

That shine as Comets, menacing revenge, — 1Tamb 3.2.74 Agidas

MENANDER

And strumpets flatter, shall Menander flourish. — Ovid's Elegies 1.15.18

MENAPHON

Ah, Menaphon, why staiest thou thus behind, — 1Tamb 1.1.83 Mycet
Go Menaphon, go into Scythia, — 1Tamb 1.1.85 Mycet
a greater [task]/Fits Menaphon, than warring with a Thiefe: — 1Tamb 1.1.88 Cosroe
Ah Menaphon, I passe not for his threates, — 1Tamb 1.1.109 Cosroe
But Menaphon, what means this trumpets sound? — 1Tamb 1.1.133 Cosroe
But tell me, that hast seene him, Menaphon, — 1Tamb 2.1.5 Cosroe
To whom sweet Menaphon, direct me straight. — 1Tamb 2.1.68 Cosroe
Ortigius and Menaphon, my trustie friendes, — 1Tamb 2.5.29 Cosroe

MEN AT ARMES

This is no life for men at armes to live, — Dido 4.3.33 Achat
The world will strive with hostes of men at armes, — 1Tamb 2.3.13 Tamb
Two hundred thousand foot, brave men at armes, — 1Tamb 4.3.54 Capol
frontier townes/Twise twenty thousand valiant men at armes, — 2Tamb 1.3.120 Therid

MEND

To mend the king, and do our countrie good: — Edw 1.4.257 Mortmr

MENDS

Farewell: is this the mends for Didos love? — Dido 5.1.105 Dido

MENELAUS

And so was reconcil'd to Menelaus. — Dido 2.1.299 Achat
And I will combat with weake Menelaus, — F1777 5.1.104 Faust

MEN OF WAR

Untill the Persean Fleete and men of war, — 1Tamb 3.3.252 Tamb

MEN OF WARRE

And Neptunes waves be envious men of warre, — Dido 1.1.65 Venus

MENS

And weigh not men, and therefore not mens words. — Jew Prol.8 Machvl
Earths barrennesse, and all mens hatred/Inflict upon them, thou — Jew 1.2.163 Barab
armes in ure/With digging graves and ringing dead mens knels: — Jew 2.3.185 Barab
Whose face has bin a grind-stone for mens swords, — Jew 4.3.9 Barab
But leaving these vaine trifles of mens soules, — F 289 1.3.61 Faust
[Tush], these are fresh mens [suppositions] <questions>: — F 606 2.2.55 P Faust

MENS (cont.)
to clap hornes of honest mens heades o'this order, F1317 4.1.163 P Benvol
Thy selfe thus shivered out to three mens shares: Lucan, First Booke 85
What should I talke of mens corne reapt by force, Lucan, First Booke 318
On all the [bed mens] <beds men> tumbling let him viewe/And thy Ovid's Elegies 1.8.97
There sat the hang-man for mens neckes to angle. Ovid's Elegies 1.12.18
yong-mens mates, to go/If they determine to persever so. Ovid's Elegies 2.16.17
The subject hides thy wit, mens acts resound, Ovid's Elegies 3.1.25
To thee Minerva turne the craftes-mens hands. Ovid's Elegies 3.2.52
My love was cause that more mens love she seazd. Ovid's Elegies 3.10.20
An Altar takes mens incense, and oblation, Ovid's Elegies 3.12.9
Even so for mens impression do we you. Hero and Leander 1.266

MENT
Thou and Achates ment to saile away. Dido 4.4.28 Dido
And told me that Aeneas ment to goe: Dido 4.4.142 Dido

MENTEM
Oro, si quis [adhuc] <ad haec> precibus locus, exue mentem. Dido 5.1.138 Dido

MENTIONS (See also MOTION)
Nere was, nor shall be, what my verse mentions. Ovid's Elegies 3.5.18

MEPHASTOPHILIS
Ist not midnight? come Mephostophilis <Mephastophilis>. F 417 2.1.29 Faust
<Here Mephastophilis> receive this scrole, F 477 (HC260)A Faust
<Nay sweete Mephastophilis fetch me one, for I will have one>. F 530 (HC261)A P Faust
Come on Mephastophilis, what shall we do? F App p.232 22 P Faust
Belseborams framanto pacostiphos tostu Mephastophilis, F App p.235 25 P Robin
Mephastophilis be gone. F App p.237 56 P Faust
Mephastophilis, transforme him strait. F App p.238 85 P Faust
Now Mephastophilis, the restlesse course that time doth runne F App p.239 90 P Faust
Therefore sweet Mephastophilis, let us make haste to Wertenberge F App p.239 94 Faust
my legge, helpe Mephastophilis, call the Officers, my legge, F App p.241 155 P Faust
niggard of my cunning, come Mephastophilis, let's away to him. F App p.241 171 P Faust
Alas Madame, thats nothing, Mephastophilis, be gone. F App p.242 12 P Faust

MEPHOSTOPHILE
Veni veni Mephostophile. F 418 2.1.30 Faust

MEPHOSTOPHILIS
propitiamus vos, ut appareat, et surgat Mephostophilis. F 247 1.3.19 P Faust
per vota nostra ipse nunc surgat nobis dicatus Mephostophilis. F 250 1.3.22 P Faust
How pliant is this Mephostophilis? F 257 1.3.29 Faust
Conjurer laureate]/[That canst commaund great Mephostophilis], F 261 1.3.33A Faust
[Quin redis <regis> Mephostophilis fratris imagine]. F 262 1.3.34A Faust
is great Mephostophilis so passionate/For being deprived of the F 311 1.3.83 Faust
I'de give them all for Mephostophilis. F 331 1.3.103 Faust
in speculation of this Art/Till Mephostophilis returne againe. F 342 1.3.114 Faust
When Mephostophilis shall stand by me, F 413 2.1.25 Faust
Mephostophilis come/And bring glad tydings from great Lucifer. F 415 2.1.27 Faust
Ist not midnight? come Mephostophilis <Mephastophilis>. F 417 2.1.29 Faust
Stay Mephostophilis/And tell me, what good will my soule do thy F 427 2.1.39 Faust
I Mephostophilis, I'le <I> give it him <thee>. F 437 2.1.49 Faust
Loe Mephostophilis, for love of thee/Faustus hath <I> cut his F 442 2.1.54 Faust
I so I do <will>; but Mephostophilis, F 450 2.1.62 Faust
What meanes this shew? speake Mephostophilis. F 472 2.1.84 Faust
Then Mephostophilis receive this scrole, F 477 2.1.89 Faust
Then heare me read it Mephostophilis <them>. F 483 2.1.95 Faust
that Mephostophilis shall be his servant, and be by him F 486 2.1.98 P Faust
that Mephostophilis shall doe for him, and bring him F 488 2.1.100 P Faust
and his Minister Mephostophilis, and furthermore grant unto F 495 2.1.107 P Faust
Thankes Mephostophilis for this sweete booke. F 550 2.1.162 Faust
the heavens then I repent/And curse thee wicked Mephostophilis, F 553 2.2.2 Faust
Made musicke with my Mephostophilis? F 581 2.2.30 Faust
Come Mephostophilis let us dispute againe, F 584 2.2.33 Faust
Hath Mephostophilis no greater skill? F 601 2.2.50 Faust
Sweet Mephostophilis tell me. F 620 2.2.69 P Faust
Go Mephostophilis, fetch them in. F 660 2.2.109 P Lucifr
Farewell great Lucifer: come Mephostophilis. F 721 2.2.173 Faust
Having now my good Mephostophilis, F 779 3.1.1 Faust
Sweete Mephostophilis, thou pleasest me: F 836 3.1.58 Faust
Nay stay my gentle Mephostophilis, F 845 3.1.67 Faust
Go hast thee gentle Mephostophilis, F 891 3.1.113 Faust
Yes Mephostophilis, and two such Cardinals/Ne're serv'd a holy F 941 3.1.163 Faust
Away sweet Mephostophilis be gone, F 975 3.1.197 Faust
Sweet Mephostophilis so charme me here, F 991 3.2.11 Faust
Thankes Mephostophilis: F1006 3.2.26 Faust
O per se o, demogorgon, Belcher and Mephostophilis. F1115 3.3.28 P Robin
Mephostophilis away, F1236 4.1.82 Faust
Mephostophilis, transforme him; and hereafter sir, looke you F1314 4.1.160 P Faust
Asteroth, Belimoth, Mephostophilis, F1402 4.2.78 Faust
Whilst with my gentle Mephostophilis, F1412 4.2.88 Faust
Go Mephostophilis, away. F1574 4.6.17 P Faust
Sweet Mephostophilis, intreat thy Lord/To pardon my unjust F1747 5.1.74 Faust
Why, Lucifer and Mephostophilis: F1855 5.2.59 Faust
I'le burne my bookes; [ah] <oh> Mephostophilis. F1982 5.2.186 Faust

MEQUE
Desine meque tuis incendere teque querelis, Dido 5.1.139 Aeneas

MERCENARIE
This <His> study fits a Mercenarie drudge, F 61 1.1.33 Faust

MERCHANDIZE
And all the Merchants with other Merchandize/Are safe arriv'd, Jew 1.1.51 1Merch
At Alexandria, Merchandize unsold: Jew 4.1.68 Barab
Tis shame to grow rich by bed merchandize, Ovid's Elegies 1.10.41

MERCHANT
Nor plowman, Priest, nor Merchant staies at home, 2Tamb 5.2.50 Callap
Thou art a Merchant, and a monied man, Jew 1.2.53 1Knght

MERCHANT (cont.)			
Send to the Merchant, bid him bring me silkes,	Jew	4.2.84	Curtzn
better/In which the Merchant wayles his banquerout debter.	Ovid's Elegies		1.12.26
MERCHANT'S			
My Factor sends me word a Merchant's fled/That owes me for a	Jew	2.3.243	Barab
MERCHANTS			
That robs your merchants of Persepolis,	1Tamb	1.1.37	Meandr
And Christian Merchants that with Russian stems/Plow up huge	1Tamb	1.2.194	Tamb
Give me the Merchants of the Indian Mynes,	Jew	1.1.19	Barab
And all the Merchants with other Merchandize/Are safe arriv'd,	Jew	1.1.51	1Merch
comes to more/Then many Merchants of the Towne are worth,	Jew	1.1.64	1Merch
goe/And bid the Merchants and my men dispatch/And come ashore,	Jew	1.1.100	Barab
From Venice Merchants, and from Padua/Were wont to come	Jew	3.1.6	Curtzn
MERCIE			
Kneeling for mercie to a Greekish lad,	Dido	2.1.198	Aeneas
Or plead for mercie at your highnesse feet.	1Tamb	1.1.73	Therid
And cry me mercie, noble King.	1Tamb	2.4.22	Mycet
Must plead for mercie at his kingly feet,	1Tamb	3.3.174	Zenoc
Convey events of mercie to his heart:	1Tamb	5.1.54	2Virgn
flags/Through which sweet mercie threw her gentle beams,	1Tamb	5.1.69	Tamb
ruthlesse Governour/Have thus refusde the mercie of thy hand,	1Tamb	5.1.93	1Virgn
Conceive a second life in endlesse mercie.	2Tamb	2.3.9	Sgsmnd
To sue for mercie at your highnesse feete.	2Tamb	5.2.41	Amasia
To seeke for mercie at a tyrants hand.	Edw	5.3.36	Edward
thou, and we will pray, that God may have mercie upon thee.	F1875	5.2.79	P 2Schol
But mercie Faustus of thy Saviour sweete,	F App	p.243 44	OldMan
(Poore sillie maiden) at his mercie was.	Hero and Leander		2.286
MERCIES			
to heaven, and remember [Gods] mercy is <mercies are> infinite.	F1836	5.2.40	P 2Schol
MERCILESSE			
Mercilesse villaine, Pesant ignorant,	1Tamb	4.1.64	Souldn
O mercilesse infernall cruelty.	2Tamb	4.3.85	Jrslem
MERCURIE			
the Sun and Mercurie denied/To shed [their] <his> influence in	1Tamb	1.1.14	Cosroe
As fast as Iris, or Joves Mercurie.	Edw	1.4.371	Edward
After went Mercurie, who us'd such cunning,	Hero and Leander		1.417
To dote upon deceitfull Mercurie.	Hero and Leander		1.446
MERCURY			
And Mercury to flye for what he calles?	Dido	4.4.47	Dido
this day swift Mercury/When I was laying a platforme for these	Dido	5.1.93	Aeneas
Venus, and Mercury in a yeare; the Moone in twenty eight daies.	F 605	2.2.54	P Faust
to Hesus, and fell Mercury <(Jove)>/They offer humane flesh,	Lucan, First Booke		440
Heavens winged herrald, Jove-borne Mercury,	Hero and Leander		1.386
MERCY (See also MERCIE)			
God-a-mercy nose; come let's begone.	Jew	4.1.23	Ithimr
tibi, cras mihi, and so I left him to the mercy of the Hangman:	Jew	4.2.19	P Pilia
No god-a-mercy, shall I have these crownes?	Jew	4.3.31	Pilia
And kneele for mercy to your conquering foe:	Jew	5.2.2	Calym
Will shew his mercy and preserve us still.	P 576	11.41	Navrre
Then call for mercy, and avoyd despaire.	F1733	5.1.60	OldMan
Accursed Faustus, [where is mercy now]?	F1739	5.1.66	Faust
to heaven, and remember [Gods] mercy is <mercies are> infinite.	F1836	5.2.40	P 2Schol
[O God, if thou wilt not have mercy on my soule],	F1958	5.2.162A	Faust
[My God, my God] <O mercy heaven>, looke not so fierce on me;	F1979	5.2.183	Faust
Worthy she is, thou shouldst in mercy save her.	Ovid's Elegies		2.13.22
MERCYE			
Sancte [Jacobe] <Jacobus>, now have mercye upon me.	P1172	22.34	Frier
MERE (See also MEERE)			
therefore your entrye is mere Intrusione	Paris	ms13,p390	P Souldr
MEREMAID			
That Meremaid-like unto the floore she slid,	Hero and Leander		2.315
MEREMAID-LIKE			
That Meremaid-like unto the floore she slid,	Hero and Leander		2.315
MEREMAIDS			
Sweet singing Meremaids, sported with their loves/On heapes of	Hero and Leander		2.162
MERIDIAN			
But fixed now in the Meridian line,	1Tamb	4.2.38	Tamb
MERIT			
unto your majesty/May merit favour at your highnesse handes,	1Tamb	4.4.70	Zenoc
say I merit nought,/Yet for long service done, reward these	Lucan, First Booke		340
That victory doth chiefely triumph merit,	Ovid's Elegies		2.12.5
MERITE			
For I confesse, if that might merite favour,	Ovid's Elegies		2.4.3
MERITED			
my Lords whose true nobilitie/Have merited my latest memorie:	2Tamb	2.4.74	Zenoc
MERITORIOUS			
beene a great sinner in my dayes, and the deed is meritorious.	P1134	21.28	P Frier
MERITS			
You shall have honors, as your merits be:	1Tamb	1.2.255	Tamb
And well his merits show him to be made/His Fortunes maister,	1Tamb	2.1.35	Cosroe
accidents/Have chanc'd thy merits in this worthles bondage.	1Tamb	5.1.425	Arabia
But for thy merits I wish thee, white streame,	Ovid's Elegies		3.5.105
MERMAIDES			
And wanton Mermaides court thee with sweete songs,	Dido	3.1.130	Dido
And looke upon him with a Mermaides eye,	Dido	5.1.201	Dido
MERMAIDS (See also MEREMAID)			
And men inthralld by Mermaids singing charmes.	Ovid's Elegies		3.11.28
MERRIE			
Here let him sit, be merrie lovely child.	Dido	2.1.93	Dido
be merrie man,/Heres to thy better fortune and good starres.	Dido	2.1.97	Dido
And all the Sailers merrie make for joy,	Dido	5.1.259	Dido
MERRIMENT			
And by their folly make some <us> merriment,	F 990	3.2.10	Faust

MERRIMENT (cont.)
They are good subject for a merriment. F1606 4.6.49 Faust
Beleeve me maister Doctor, this merriment hath much pleased me. F App p.242 1 P Duke
might be better spent)/In vaine discourse, and apish merriment. Hero and Leander 1.356
MERUI
Si bene quid de te merui, fuit aut tibi quidquam/Dulce meum, Dido 5.1.136 Dido
MERVAILE
My Lord I mervaile that th'aspiring Guise/Dares once adventure P 36 1.36 Admral
My Lord you need not mervaile at the Guise, P 39 1.39 Condy
MESOPOTAMIA
Mesopotamia and of Parthia, 1Tamb 1.1.165 Ortyg
MESSAGE
To sound this angrie message in thine eares. Dido 5.1.33 Hermes
Malta's Governor, I bring/A message unto mighty Calymath; Jew 5.3.14 Msngr
Arundell, say your message. Edw 2.5.34 Warwck
And do your message with a majestie. Edw 3.1.73 Edward
I did your highnes message to them all, Edw 3.1.96 Arundl
Well, say thy message. Edw 3.1.155 Edward
And tell thy message to my naked brest. Edw 5.1.130 Edward
MESSE (Homograph)
master, wil you poison her with a messe of rice [porredge]? Jew 3.4.64 P Ithimr
Vive la messe, perish Hugonets, P1014 19.84 Guise
MESSENGER
Whom doe I see, Joves winged messenger? Dido 5.1.25 Aeneas
We meane to take his mornings next arise/For messenger, he will 1Tamb 3.1.39 Bajzth
That Jove shall send his winged Messenger/To bid me sheath my 2Tamb 1.3.166 Tamb
Wel, this must be the messenger for thee. 2Tamb 3.4.15 Olymp
The wrathfull messenger of mighty Jove, 2Tamb 5.1.92 Tamb
And for the mony send our messenger. Jew 1.2.31 Calym
Where they must neither see the messenger, Jew 3.4.80 Barab
Messenger, to feast my traine/Within a Towne of warre so lately Jew 5.3.21 Calym
Messenger, tell him I will see him straite. P 247 4.45 Charls
A sodaine pang, the messenger of death. P 538 11.3 Charls
These be the letters, this the messenger. Edw 3.1.65 Queene
My lord, [here] is <heres> a messenger from the Barons,/Desires Edw 3.1.148 Spencr
When we had sent our messenger to request/He might be spared to Edw 3.1.234 Edward
Within this roome is lockt the messenger, Edw 5.4.17 Mortmr
And stay the messenger that would be gon: Hero and Leander 2.82
MESSIAS
Nor our Messias that is yet to come, Jew 2.3.304 Barab
MET
And here we met faire Venus virgine like, Dido 3.3.54 Achat
By chance sweete Queene, as Mars and Venus met. Dido 3.4.4 Aeneas
Achates and Ascanius, well met. Dido 4.1.28 Dido
and brave Theridamas/Have met us by the river Araris: 1Tamb 2.1.63 Cosroe
Before thou met my husband in the field, 1Tamb 4.2.59 Zabina
Wel met my only deare Zenocrate, 1Tamb 5.1.443 Souldn
Wher Amazonians met me in the field: 2Tamb 1.3.192 Techel
Wel met Olympia, I sought thee in my tent, 2Tamb 4.2.14 Therid
Oh Barabas well met; Jew 2.3.218 Lodowk
And then they met, [and] as the story sayes, Jew 3.3.20 Ithimr
I will not say that by a forged challenge they met. Jew 4.1.45 P 2Fryar
a fellow met me with a muschatoes like a Ravens wing, and a Jew 4.2.27 P Ithimr
he met me, and asked me what he should give me for as much Hay F1526 4.5.22 P Carter
I thinke I have met with you for it. F App p.238 78 P Faust
What horse-courser, you are wel met. F App p.239 100 P Faust
METAMORPHIS'D
And strangely metamorphis'd Nun. Jew 1.2.381 Mthias
METAMORPHOSED
Or lovely Io metamorphosed. 2Tamb 1.2.39 Callap
METAPHISICALL
Tempered by science metaphisicall, 2Tamb 4.2.63 Olymp
METAPHISICKS
These Metaphisicks of Magitians, F 76 1.1.48 Faust
METEM SU COSSIS
[Ah] <Oh> Pythagoras Metemsycosis <metem su cossis>; were that F1966 5.2.170 Faust
METEMSYCOSIS
[Ah] <Oh> Pythagoras Metemsycosis <metem su cossis>; were that F1966 5.2.170 Faust
METEOR
To hang her meteor like twixt heaven and earth, Dido 1.1.13 Jupitr
A meteor that might terrify the earth, 1Tamb 5.1.461 Tamb
a fyery meteor in the fermament Paris ms21,p390 Guise
METEORS
For freezing meteors and conjealed colde: 1Tamb 1.1.11 Cosroe
Fill all the aire with fiery meteors. 1Tamb 4.2.52 Tamb
The Moone, the Planets, and the Meteors light. 1Tamb 5.1.150 Tamb
That being fiery meteors, may presage, 2Tamb 3.2.4 Tamb
fild with the meteors/Of blood and fire thy tyrannies have 2Tamb 4.1.141 Jrslem
Making the Meteors, that like armed men/Are seene to march upon 2Tamb 4.1.201 Tamb
And sundry fiery meteors blaz'd in heaven; Lucan, First Booke 529
ME THINKES
Me thinkes that towne there should be Troy, yon Idas hill, Dido 2.1.7 Aeneas
And thus me thinkes should men of judgement frame/This is the Jew 1.1.34 Barab
Which me thinkes fits not their profession. Jew 1.1.118 Barab
And now me thinkes that I am one of those: Jew 2.1.28 Barab
Foh, me thinkes they stinke like a Holly-Hoke. Jew 4.4.41 Pilia
Me thinkes he fingers very well. Jew 4.4.49 Pilia
Me thinkes the gloves have a very strong perfume, P 170 3.5 OldQn
Me thinkes my Lord, Anjoy hath well advisde/Your highnes to P 219 4.17 Guise
me thinkes you hang the heads,/But weele advance them traitors, Edw 3.1.223 Edward
Me thinkes I should revenge me of the wronges, Edw 5.1.24 Edward
Nor I, and yet me thinkes I should commaund, Edw 5.4.97 King
doubt of that, for me thinkes you make no hast to wipe it out. F1516 4.5.12 P Hostss

ME THINKES (cont.)
me thinkes you should have a wooden bedfellow of one of 'em. F1653 4.6.96 P Carter
And yet me thinkes, if that death were neere, . . . F App p.243 3 Wagner
Me thinkes she should <would> be nimble when shees downe. Ovid's Elegies 2.4.14

ME THINKS
Me thinks I see kings kneeling at his feet, . . . 1Tamb 1.2.55 Techel
Me thinks we should not, I am strongly moov'd, . . . 1Tamb 2.5.75 Tamb
Me thinks we martch as Meliager did, ... 1Tamb 4.3.1 Souldn
Me thinks, tis a great deale better than a consort of musicke. 1Tamb 4.4.60 P Therid
But yet me thinks their looks are amorous, . . . 2Tamb 1.3.21 Tamb
Me thinks I see how glad the christian King/Is made, for joy of 2Tamb 2.2.20 Uribas
Me thinks tis a pitifull sight. . . . . 2Tamb 3.2.130 P Calyph
Me thinks the slave should make a lusty theefe. . . 2Tamb 3.5.96 Jrslem
Me thinks I could sustaine a thousand deaths, . . . 2Tamb 5.2.22 Callap
Now worthy Faustus: me thinks your looks are chang'd. . F1821 5.2.25 1Schol

ME THOUGHT
one, me thought/I heard him shreeke and call aloud for helpe: F1991 5.3.9 3Schol

METROPOLIS
land, whose brave Metropolis/Reedified the faire Semyramis, 2Tamb 3.5.36 Orcan

METST
How now Mugeroun, metst thou not the Guise at the doore? . P 774 15.32 King

METTALL
That trade in mettall of the purest mould; . . . Jew 1.1.20 Barab

METTALL'D
Oh earth-mettall'd villaines, and no Hebrews born! . . Jew 1.2.78 Barab

METTEL
Or of what mould or mettel he be made, ... 1Tamb 2.6.17 Ortyg

MEUM
fuit aut tibi quidquam/Dulce meum, miserere domus labentis: Dido 5.1.137 Dido

MEVANIAS
his troupes of daring horsemen fought/Upon Mevanias plaine, Lucan, First Booke 470

MEW (See MU'D)

MEXICO
Even from Persepolis to Mexico, ... 1Tamb 3.3.255 Tamb

MI
Bien para todos mi ganado no es: . . . . . . Jew 2.1.39 Barab

MICKLE
And wrought him mickle woe on sea and land, . . . Dido 3.2.41 Juno
good father on thy lap/Lay I this head, laden with mickle care, Edw 4.7.40 Edward

MID
Watching till after mid-night did not tire thee. . . Ovid's Elegies 1.6.44
Lay in the mid bed, there be my law giver. . . . Ovid's Elegies 2.17.24
Is golden love hid in Mars mid alarmes. . . . . Ovid's Elegies 2.18.36
Peace pleaseth me, and in mid peace is love. . . . Ovid's Elegies 3.2.50
In mid Bithynia 'tis said Inachus, ... Ovid's Elegies 3.5.25
And from the mid foord his hoarse voice upheav'd, . . Ovid's Elegies 3.5.52
Either th'art muddy in mid winter tide: . . . . Ovid's Elegies 3.5.95
And blabbing Tantalus in mid-waters put. . . . . Ovid's Elegies 3.11.30

MIDAS
And Midas like he jets it in the court, ... Edw 1.4.408 Mortmr
have concluded/That Midas brood shall sit in Honors chaire, Hero and Leander 1.475

MIDDAY
I to the Torrid Zone where midday burnes, ... Lucan, First Booke 16

MIDDLE
And rise with them i'th middle of the Towne, ... Jew 5.1.92 Barab
I was no sooner in the middle of the pond, but my horse vanisht F App p.240 134 P HrsCsr
Have care to walke in middle of the throng. . . . Ovid's Elegies 1.4.56

MID-NIGHT
Watching till after mid-night did not tire thee. . . Ovid's Elegies 1.6.44

MIDNIGHT
Then rise at midnight to a solemne masse. . . . . Jew 1.2.373 Mthias
Father, it draweth towards midnight now, ... Jew 2.1.55 Abigal
And meet me in my Study, at Midnight, ... F 327 1.3.99 Faust
Ist not midnight? come Mephostophilis <Mephastophilis>. . F 417 2.1.29 Faust
Faustus, thou shalt, at midnight I will send for thee; . F 716 2.2.168 Lucifr
That time may cease, and midnight never come. . . . F1930 5.2.134 Faust
hir to thy owne use, as often as thou wilt, and at midnight. F App p.234 28 P Robin
Are banquets, Dorick musicke, midnight-revell, . . . Hero and Leander 1.301

MIDNIGHT-REVELL
Are banquets, Dorick musicke, midnight-revell, . . . Hero and Leander 1.301

MIDST
When in the midst of all their gamesome sports, . . Dido 3.2.89 Juno
And in the midst doth run a silver streame, . . . Dido 4.5.9 Nurse
That like a Foxe in midst of harvest time, . . . 1Tamb 1.1.31 Mycet
Even from the midst of fiery Cancers Tropick, . . . 2Tamb 1.1.73 Orcan
How through the midst of Verna and Bulgaria/And almost to the 2Tamb 2.1.8 Fredrk
That in the midst of fire is ingraft, ... 2Tamb 2.3.21 Orcan
That fill the midst of farthest Tartary, ... 2Tamb 4.1.43 Amyras
Lies westward from the midst of Cancers line, . . . 2Tamb 5.3.146 Tamb
In [midst] <one> of which a sumptuous Temple stands, . F 795 3.1.17 Faust
Just through the midst runnes flowing Tybers streame, . F 813 3.1.35 Mephst
and when I came just in the midst my horse vanisht away, and I F1544 4.5.40 P HrsCsr
The midst is best; that place is pure, and bright, . . Lucan, First Booke 58
Titan himselfe throand in the midst of heaven, . . . Lucan, First Booke 538
In midst of peace why art of armes afraide? . . . Ovid's Elegies 1.6.30
will I grace them/And in the midst of Venus temple place them. Ovid's Elegies 1.11.26
And in the midst their bodies largely spread: . . . Ovid's Elegies 2.10.18
And in the midst thereof, set my soule going, . . . Ovid's Elegies 2.10.36
In midst thereof a stone-pav'd sacred spring, . . . Ovid's Elegies 3.1.3
And in the midst a silver altar stood, ... Hero and Leander 1.157

MIDTIME
In summers heate, and midtime of the day, ... Ovid's Elegies 1.5.1

MID-WATERS
And blabbing Tantalus in mid-waters put. . . . . Ovid's Elegies 3.11.30

MID WINTER

Either th'art muddy in mid winter tide:	Ovid's Elegies	3.5.95	

MIGHT (Homograph; See also MOUGHT)

Might I but see that pretie sport a foote,	Dido	1.1.16	Ganimd
Whose beautious burden well might make you proude,	Dido	1.1.124	Venus
Might we but once more see Aeneas face,	Dido	1.2.45	Serg
that under his conduct/We might saile backe to Troy, and be	Dido	2.1.18	Aeneas
might behold/Young infants swimming in their parents bloud,	Dido	2.1.192	Aeneas
here, tell me in sooth/In what might Dido highly pleasure thee.	Dido	3.1.102	Dido
And might I live to see thee shipt away,	Dido	3.3.46	Iarbus
ascend so high/As Didos heart, which Monarkes might not scale.	Dido	3.4.34	Aeneas
Whose golden Crowne might ballance my content:	Dido	3.4.36	Dido
I might have stakte them both unto the earth,	Dido	4.1.23	Iarbus
See where they come, how might I doe to chide?	Dido	4.4.13	Dido
That thou and I unseene might sport our selves:	Dido	4.4.51	Dido
That he might suffer shipwracke on my breast,	Dido	4.4.102	Dido
That I might live to see this boy a man,	Dido	4.5.18	Nurse
Would, as faire Troy was, Carthage might be sackt,	Dido	5.1.147	Dido
That I might see Aeneas in his face:	Dido	5.1.150	Dido
If words might move me I were overcome.	Dido	5.1.154	Aeneas
I might command you to be slaine for this,	1Tamb	1.1.23	Mycet
Meander, might I not?	1Tamb	1.1.24	Mycet
I meane it not, but yet I know I might,	1Tamb	1.1.26	Mycet
And that which might resolve me into teares,	1Tamb	1.1.118	Cosroe
Such breadth of shoulders as might mainely beare/Olde Atlas	1Tamb	2.1.10	Menaph
And might content the Queene of heaven as well,	1Tamb	3.2.11	Zenoc
And might, if my extreams had full events,	1Tamb	3.2.16	Zenoc
And might in noble minds be counted princely.	1Tamb	3.2.39	Zenoc
It might amaze your royall majesty.	1Tamb	4.1.16	2Msngr
So might your highnesse, had you time to sort/Your fighting	1Tamb	4.1.36	Capol
some your children)/Might have intreated your obdurate breasts,	1Tamb	5.1.28	1Virgn
soules/From heavens of comfort, yet their age might beare,	1Tamb	5.1.90	1Virgn
Whose lookes might make the angry God of armes,	1Tamb	5.1.326	Zenoc
And that I might be privy to the state,	1Tamb	5.1.426	Arabia
A meteor that might terrify the earth,	1Tamb	5.1.461	Tamb
Will hazard that we might with surety hold.	2Tamb	1.1.24	Uribas
A friendly parle might become ye both.	2Tamb	1.1.117	Gazell
and I might enter in/To see the state and majesty of heaven,	2Tamb	1.3.154	Tamb
If woords might serve, our voice hath rent the aire,	2Tamb	2.4.121	Therid
I might have harme, which all the good I have/Join'd with my	2Tamb	4.1.57	Calyph
That I might moove the turning Spheares of heaven,	2Tamb	4.1.118	Tamb
Might find as many woondrous myracles,	2Tamb	4.2.85	Therid
Yet might your mighty hoste incounter all,	2Tamb	5.2.39	Amasia
My looks shall make them flie, and might I follow,	2Tamb	5.3.107	Tamb
That men might quickly saile to India.	2Tamb	5.3.135	Tamb
Might first made Kings, and Lawes were then most sure/When like	Jew	Prol.20	Machvl
And with that summe he craves might we wage warre.	Jew	2.2.27	1Knght
the Towne-seale might be got/To keepe him for his life time	Jew	2.3.103	Barab
Oh, master, that I might have a hand in this.	Jew	2.3.368	Ithimr
No, no, and yet it might be done that way:	Jew	2.3.373	Barab
Wretched Ferneze might have veng'd thy death.	Jew	3.2.14	Govnr
And these my teares to blood, that he might live.	Jew	3.2.19	Govnr
So might my man and I hang with you for company.	Jew	4.1.182	Barab
That wee might sleepe seven yeeres together afore we wake.	Jew	4.2.131	Ithimr
Might he not as well come as send; pray bid him come and fetch	Jew	4.3.26	P Barab
in Religion/Might be a meanes to crosse you in your love.	P 16	1.16	QnMoth
Might well have moved your highnes to beware/How you did meddle	P 179	3.14	Navrre
Might seeme <seek> to crosse me in mine enterprise.	P 574	11.39	Navrre
That it might print these lines within his heart.	P 669	13.13	Duchss
I would the Guise in his steed might have come,	P 736	14.39	Navrre
possession (as I would I might) yet I meane to keepe you out,	P 814	17.9	P Souldr
We might have punisht him to his deserts.	P1184	22.46	Eprnon
That we might torture him with some new found death.	P1217	22.79	Eprnon
Might have enforst me to have swum from France,	Edw	1.1.7	Gavstn
O might I keepe thee heere, as I doe this,	Edw	1.4.128	Edward
O that we might as well returne as goe.	Edw	1.4.143	Edward
How easilie might some base slave be subbornd,	Edw	1.4.265	Mortmr
That I might pull him to me where I would,	Edw	2.4.18	Queene
That when I had him we might never part.	Edw	2.4.21	Queene
Might be of lesser force, and with the power/That he intendeth	Edw	2.4.43	Queene
to request/He might be spared to come to speake with us,	Edw	3.1.235	Edward
O that I might this life in quiet lead,	Edw	4.7.21	Edward
O might I never open these eyes againe,	Edw	4.7.41	Edward
Leister, if gentle words might comfort me,	Edw	5.1.5	Edward
O would I might, but heavens and earth conspire/To make me	Edw	5.1.96	Edward
What might the staying of my bloud portend?	F 453	2.1.65	Faust
have a booke wherein I might beholde al spels and incantations,	F 551.1	2.1.164A	P Faust
and incantations, that I might raise up spirits when I please].	F 551.2	2.1.165A	P Faust
I might see al characters of <and> planets of the heavens,	F 551.4	2.1.167A	P Faust
heavens, that I might knowe their motions and dispositions].	F 551.5	2.1.168A	P Faust
wherein I might see al plants, hearbes and trees that grow upon	F 551.9	2.1.172A	P Faust
bag; and might I now obtaine <have> my wish, this house,	F 675	2.2.124	P Covet
that I might locke you safe into <uppe in> my <goode> Chest:	F 676	2.2.125	P Covet
<through> all the world, that all might die, and I live along,	F 682	2.2.131	P Envy
O might I see hell, and returne againe safe, how happy were I	F 714	2.2.166	P Faust
And what might please mine eye, I there beheld.	F 853	3.1.75	Faust
would I might be turn'd to a gaping Oyster, and drinke nothing	F1319	4.1.165	P Benvol
That I may <might> have unto my paramour,	F1761	5.1.88	Faust
tell us of this before, that Divines might have prayd for thee?	F1863	5.2.67	P 1Schol
Cut is the branch that might have growne full straight,	F2002	5.3.20	4Chor
Ah Doctor Faustus, that I might prevaile,	F App	p.243 34	OldMan
Might they have won whom civil broiles have slaine,	Lucan, First Booke	14	
Them freedome without war might not suffice,	Lucan, First Booke	173	

MIGHT (cont.)

We bide the first brunt, safer might we dwel, ... Lucan, First Booke 253
Now light had quite dissolv'd the mysty [night] <might>, . Lucan, First Booke 263
And I might pleade, and draw the Commons minds/To favour thee, Lucan, First Booke 275
And now least age might waine his state, he casts/For civill Lucan, First Booke 324
This [band] <hand> that all behind us might be quail'd, . Lucan, First Booke 370
least sloth and long delay/Might crosse him, he withdrew his Lucan, First Booke 395
Wel might these feare, when Pompey fear'd and fled. . . Lucan, First Booke 519
Now evermore least some one hope might ease/The Commons Lucan, First Booke 520
And their vaild Matron, who alone might view/Minervas statue; Lucan, First Booke 597
Yeelding or striving <strugling> doe we give him might, . Ovid's Elegies 1.2.9
I might have then my parents deare misus'd, ... Ovid's Elegies 1.7.5
Or steeds might fal forcd with thick clouds approch. . Ovid's Elegies 1.13.30
Would Tithon might but talke of thee a while, . . . Ovid's Elegies 1.13.35
That all the world [may] <might> ever chaunt my name. . Ovid's Elegies 1.15.8
Her trembling hand writ back she might not doo. . . Ovid's Elegies 2.2.6
For I confesse, if that might merite favour, . . . Ovid's Elegies 2.4.3
Yet would I lie with her if that I might. . . . . Ovid's Elegies 2.4.22
Some one of these might make the chastest fall. . . Ovid's Elegies 2.4.32
O would my proofes as vaine might be withstood, . . Ovid's Elegies 2.5.7
and kissed so sweetely as might make/Wrath-kindled Jove away Ovid's Elegies 2.5.51
That might be urg'd to witnesse our false playing. . . Ovid's Elegies 2.8.8
But being present, might that worke the best, . . . Ovid's Elegies 2.8.17
But when I die, would I might droope with doing, . . Ovid's Elegies 2.10.35
O would that no Oares might in seas have suncke, . . Ovid's Elegies 2.11.5
me, or I am sure/I oft have done, what might as much procure. Ovid's Elegies 2.13.6
I would not out, might I in one place hit, ... Ovid's Elegies 2.15.19
Pollux and Castor, might I stand betwixt, ... Ovid's Elegies 2.16.13
Ah oft how much she might she feignd offence; . . . Ovid's Elegies 2.19.13
beate thee/To guard her well, that well I might entreate thee. Ovid's Elegies 2.19.50
To finde, what worke my muse might move, I strove. . . Ovid's Elegies 3.1.6
And usde all speech that might provoke and stirre. . . Ovid's Elegies 3.6.12
Why might not then my sinews be inchanted, . . . Ovid's Elegies 3.6.35
Yet might her touch make youthfull Pilius fire, . . Ovid's Elegies 3.6.41
What might I crave more if I aske againe? . . . . Ovid's Elegies 3.6.44
As she might straight have gone to church and praide: . Ovid's Elegies 3.6.54
Huge okes, hard Adamantes might she have moved, . . Ovid's Elegies 3.6.57
I might not go, whether my papers went. . . . . Ovid's Elegies 3.7.6
The holy gods gilt temples they might fire, . . . Ovid's Elegies 3.8.43
And wisht the goddesse long might feele loves fire. . . Ovid's Elegies 3.9.42
[Seaborderers] <Seaborders>, disjoin'd by Neptunes might: Hero and Leander 1.3
Faire Cinthia wisht, his armes might be her spheare, . Hero and Leander 1.59
Jove might have sipt out Nectar from his hand. . . . Hero and Leander 1.62
There might you see one sigh, another rage, . . . Hero and Leander 1.125
There might you see the gods in sundrie shapes, . . Hero and Leander 1.143
paths, wheron the gods might trace/To Joves high court. . Hero and Leander 1.298
As put thereby, yet might he hope for mo. . . . . Hero and Leander 1.312
And spends the night (that might be better spent)/In vaine Hero and Leander 1.355
As might have made heaven stoope to have a touch, . . Hero and Leander 1.366
Both might enjoy ech other, and be blest. . . . . Hero and Leander 1.380
Maids are not woon by brutish force and might, . . . Hero and Leander 1.419
Might presently be banisht into hell, ... Hero and Leander 1.453
And kept it downe that it might mount the hier. . . Hero and Leander 2.42
nothing saw/That might delight him more, yet he suspected/Some Hero and Leander 2.63
To part in twaine, that hee might come and go, . . . Hero and Leander 2.151
And from her countenance behold ye might, ... Hero and Leander 2.318

MIGHTE

And thoughe I come not to keep possessione as I wold I mighte Paris ms15,p390 P Souldr

MIGHTIE

Sometime I was a Troian, mightie Queene: . . . . . Dido 2.1.75 Aeneas
And bring forth mightie Kings to Carthage towne, . . . Dido 3.2.75 Juno
that in former age/Hast bene the seat of mightie Conquerors, 1Tamb 1.1.7 Cosroe
How easely may you with a mightie hoste, ... 1Tamb 1.1.129 Menaph
Magnificent and mightie Prince Cosroe, ... 1Tamb 1.1.136 Ortyg
And commons of this mightie Monarchie, ... 1Tamb 1.1.138 Ortyg
The mightie Souldan of Egyptia. . . . . 1Tamb 1.2.6 Tamb
Have past the armie of the mightie Turke: . . . . 1Tamb 1.2.14 Zenoc
By living Asias mightie Emperour. . . . . . . 1Tamb 1.2.73 Zenoc
And mightie kings shall be our Senators. . . . . . 1Tamb 1.2.198 Tamb
which by fame is said/To drinke the mightie Parthian Araris, 1Tamb 2.3.16 Tamb
Thou art no match for mightie Tamburlaine. . . . . 1Tamb 2.4.40 Tamb
What better president than mightie Jove? . . . . 1Tamb 2.7.17 Tamb
If I were matcht with mightie Tamburlaine. . . . . 1Tamb 3.2.55 Zenoc
And cannot terrefie his mightie hoste. . . . . . 1Tamb 3.3.12 Bassoe
Nay (mightie Souldan) did your greatnes see/The frowning lookes 1Tamb 4.1.12 2Msngr
Mightie Lord,/Three hundred thousand men in armour clad, . 1Tamb 4.1.20 2Msngr
That should be horsed on fower mightie kings. . . . 1Tamb 4.2.78 Bajzth
a blemish to the Majestie/And high estate of mightie Emperours, 1Tamb 4.3.20 Souldn
have ye lately heard/The overthrow of mightie Bajazeth, . 1Tamb 4.3.24 Arabia
Now Tamburlaine, the mightie Souldane comes, ... 1Tamb 4.3.63 Souldn
The name of mightie Tamburlain is spread: . . . . . 2Tamb 3.4.66 Therid
the mightie prince of Lancaster/That hath more earldomes then Edw 1.3.1 Gavstn
Or bring before this royall Emperour/The mightie Monarch, F1297 4.1.143 Faust
And live belov'd of mightie Carolus. . . . . . . F1324 4.1.170 Emper
Alcides like, by mightie violence, ... Hero and Leander 2.120

MIGHTIER

(And yet have I had many mightier Kings)/Hast had the greatest Dido 3.1.12 Dido

MIGHTIEST

As he will front the mightiest of us all, ... Edw 1.4.260 Mortmr
The mightiest kings have had their minions, ... Edw 1.4.391 MortSr

MIGHTINES

The former triumphes of our mightines, ... 1Tamb 5.1.253 Zabina

MIGHTINESSE

you must expect/Letters of conduct from my mightinesse, . 1Tamb 1.2.24 Tamb

MIGHTINESSE (cont.)
Pleaseth your mightinesse to understand, ... 1Tamb 4.1.47 2Msngr
MIGHTST
O were I not at all so thou mightst be. . . . . . Dido 2.1.28 Aeneas
Marry if thou hadst, thou mightst have had the stab, . P 776 15.34 King
Wert thou the Pope thou mightst not scape from us. . . P1092 20.2 1Mur
Thou with thy quilles mightst make greene Emeralds darke, Ovid's Elegies 2.6.21
The seventh day came, none following mightst thou see, . Ovid's Elegies 2.6.45
Or lesse faire, or lesse lewd would thou mightst bee, . Ovid's Elegies 3.10.41
MIGHTY (See also MYGHTY)
Long live Cosroe mighty Emperour. . . . . . . 1Tamb 1.1.169 Ortyg
Draw foorth thy sword, thou mighty man at Armes, . . . 1Tamb 1.2.178 Tamb
discovered the enemie/Ready to chardge you with a mighty armie. 1Tamb 2.3.50 1Msngr
Even by the mighty hand of Tamburlaine, ... 1Tamb 2.5.3 Tamb
Renowmed Emperour, and mighty Generall, ... 1Tamb 3.1.16 Fesse
As from the mouth of mighty Bajazeth. . . . . . 1Tamb 3.1.20 Fesse
So now the mighty Souldan heares of you, ... 1Tamb 3.2.31 Agidas
More mighty than the Turkish Emperour: . . . . . 1Tamb 3.3.37 Therid
What meanes the mighty Turkish Emperor/To talk with one so base 1Tamb 3.3.87 Fesse
Puissant, renowmed and mighty Tamburlain, ... 1Tamb 3.3.96 Techel
of Hydra, so my power/Subdued, shall stand as mighty as before: 1Tamb 3.3.141 Bajzth
thou be plac'd by me/That am the Empresse of the mighty Turke? 1Tamb 3.3.167 Zabina
that am betroath'd/Unto the great and mighty Tamburlaine? 1Tamb 3.3.170 Zenoc
Is this a place for mighty Bajazeth? . . . . . . 1Tamb 4.2.83 Bajzth
As long as life maintaines his mighty arme, ... 1Tamb 5.1.375 Anippe
Mighty hath God and Mahomet made thy hand/(Renowmed Tamburlain) 1Tamb 5.1.479 Souldn
Affrick to the banks/Of Ganges, shall his mighty arme extend. 1Tamb 5.1.521 Tamb
And sacred Lord, the mighty Calapine: . . . . . 2Tamb 1.1.3 Orcan
My Lord the great and mighty Tamburlain, ... 2Tamb 1.3.113 Therid
And mighty Tamburlaine, our earthly God, ... 2Tamb 1.3.138 Techel
Machda, where the mighty Christian Priest/Cal'd John the great, 2Tamb 1.3.187 Techel
That nigh Larissa swaies a mighty hoste, ... 2Tamb 2.2.6 Orcan
son and successive heire to the late mighty Emperour Bajazeth, 2Tamb 3.1.2 P Orcan
and thirty Kingdomes late contributory to his mighty father. 2Tamb 3.1.6 P Orcan
That since the heire of mighty Bajazeth/(An Emperour so . 2Tamb 3.1.22 Callap
hath followed long/The martiall sword of mighty Tamburlaine, 2Tamb 3.1.28 Callap
Being a handfull to a mighty hoste, ... 2Tamb 3.1.40 Orcan
Stand at the walles, with such a mighty power. . . . 2Tamb 3.3.14 Therid
And makes the mighty God of armes his slave: . . . . 2Tamb 3.4.53 Therid
Renowmed Emperour, mighty Callepine, ... 2Tamb 3.5.1 2Msngr
So famous as is mighty Tamburlain: . . . . . . 2Tamb 3.5.84 Tamb
The common souldiers of our mighty hoste/Shal bring thee bound 2Tamb 3.5.110 Trebiz
By Mahomet, thy mighty friend I sweare, ... 2Tamb 4.1.121 Tamb
Shaking the burthen mighty Atlas beares: . . . . . 2Tamb 4.1.129 Tamb
As you (ye slaves) in mighty Tamburlain. . . . . . 2Tamb 4.3.11 Tamb
The wrathfull messenger of mighty Jove, ... 2Tamb 5.1.92 Tamb
King of Amasia, now our mighty hoste, ... 2Tamb 5.2.1 Callap
Renowmed Generall mighty Callapine, ... 2Tamb 5.2.36 Amasia
Yet might your mighty hoste incounter all, ... 2Tamb 5.2.39 Amasia
And seeks to conquer mighty Tamburlaine, ... 2Tamb 5.3.43 Tamb
Malta's Governor, I bring/A message unto mighty Calymath; Jew 5.3.14 Msngr
Will't please thee, mighty Selim-Calymath, ... Jew 5.5.57 Barab
Rich Princes both, and mighty Emperours: . . . . . P 463 8.13 Anjoy
A mighty army comes from France with speed: . . . . P 725 14.28 1Msngr
A sound Magitian is a Demi-god <mighty god>, . . . F 89 1.1.61 Faust
Go, and returne to mighty Lucifer, ... F 326 1.3.98 Faust
<Great> Thankes mighty Lucifer: . . . . F 719 2.2.171 Faust
that guardst/Roomes mighty walles built on Tarpeian rocke, Lucan, First Booke 198
MIHI
tibi, cras mihi, and so I left him to the mercy of the Hangman: Jew 4.2.19 P Pilia
Sint mihi Dei Acherontis propitii, valeat numen triplex . F 244 1.3.16 P Faust
and I will make thee go, like Qui mihi discipulus. . . F 355 1.4.13 P Wagner
thou serve me, and Ile make thee go like Qui mihi discipulus? F App p.229 14 P Wagner
MIHIMET
Ego mihimet sum semper proximus. . . . . . . Jew 1.1.189 Barab
MILAN (See MILLAINE)
MILD
Mild Atax glad it beares not Roman [boats] <bloats>; . Lucan, First Booke 404
MILDE
Noble and milde this Persean seemes to be, ... 1Tamb 1.2.162 Tamb
First rising in the East with milde aspect, ... 1Tamb 4.2.37 Tamb
And Epernoune though I seeme milde and calme, . . . P 893 17.88 King
Thou seest by nature he is milde and calme, ... Edw 1.4.388 MortSr
Yea gentle Spencer, we have beene too milde, . . . Edw 3.1.24 Edward
Nor the milde Ewe gifts from the Ramme doth pull. . . Ovid's Elegies 1.10.28
Request milde Zephires helpe for thy availe, . . . Ovid's Elegies 2.11.41
Thy muse hath played what may milde girles content, . . Ovid's Elegies 3.1.27
MILDER
And cause some milder spirits governe you. . . . . 2Tamb 5.3.80 Phsitn
MILDLIE
The earle of Penbrooke mildlie thus bespake. . . . . Edw 3.1.108 Arundl
MILDLY
To breake his sword, and mildly treat of love, . . . 1Tamb 5.1.327 Zenoc
And for the same mildly rebuk't his sonne, ... Hero and Leander 2.137
MILDNESSE
To signify the mildnesse of his minde: 1Tamb 4.1.52 2Msngr
MILE
The way he cut, an English mile in length, ... F 792 3.1.14 Faust
MILES
have martcht/Foure hundred miles with armour on their backes, 2Tamb 1.3.175 Usumc
What, can ye draw but twenty miles a day, ... 2Tamb 4.3.2 Tamb
At every ten miles end thou hast a horse. . . . . . Edw 5.4.42 Mortmr
MILK
That I may view these milk-white steeds of mine, . . . 1Tamb 1.1.77 Mycete

MILK (cont.)			
Resting her selfe upon my milk-white Tent:	1Tamb	3.3.161	Tamb
Not I, bring milk and fire, and my blood I bring him againe,	1Tamb	5.1.310	P Zabina
Priest/Cal'd John the great, sits in a milk-white robe,	2Tamb	1.3.188	Techel
Shall mount the milk-white way and meet him there.	2Tamb	4.3.132	Tamb
But came it freely, did the Cow give down her milk freely?	Jew	4.2.102	P Ithimr
which downe her face/Made milk-white paths, wheron the gods	Hero and Leander		1.298
MILKE			
Altars crack/With mountaine heapes of milke white Sacrifize.	Dido	1.1.202	Aeneas
These milke white Doves shall be his Centronels:	Dido	2.1.320	Venus
With milke-white Hartes upon an Ivorie sled,	1Tamb	1.2.98	Tamb
Their haire as white as milke and soft as Downe,	2Tamb	1.3.25	Tamb
Inhumaine creatures, nurst with Tigers milke,	Edw	5.1.71	Edward
MILKE-WHITE			
With milke-white Hartes upon an Ivorie sled,	1Tamb	1.2.98	Tamb
MILKE WHITE			
Altars crack/With mountaine heapes of milke white Sacrifize.	Dido	1.1.202	Aeneas
MILK-WHITE			
That I may view these milk-white steeds of mine,	1Tamb	1.1.77	Mycet
Resting her selfe upon my milk-white Tent:	1Tamb	3.3.161	Tamb
Priest/Cal'd John the great, sits in a milk-white robe,	2Tamb	1.3.188	Techel
Shall mount the milk-white way and meet him there.	2Tamb	4.3.132	Tamb
which downe her face/Made milk-white paths, wheron the gods	Hero and Leander		1.298
MILKWHITE			
when first my milkwhite flags/Through which sweet mercie threw	1Tamb	5.1.68	Tamb
MILLAINE			
I am beholding/To the Bishop of Millaine, for this so rare a	F1042	3.2.62	Pope
here is a daintie dish was sent me from the Bishop of Millaine.	F App	p.231 6	P Pope
MILLIONS			
Let him bring millions infinite of men,	1Tamb	3.3.33	Usumc
Millions of men encompasse thee about,	1Tamb	5.1.215	Bajzth
Millions of soules sit on the bankes of Styx,	1Tamb	5.1.463	Tamb
Millions of Souldiers cut the Artick line,	2Tamb	1.1.29	Orcan
And millions of his strong tormenting spirits:	2Tamb	1.3.147	Techel
My sword hath sent millions of Turks to hell,	2Tamb	5.1.180	Tamb
thou that hast seene/Millions of Turkes perish by Tamburlaine,	2Tamb	5.2.25	Callap
MILO			
Twas his troupe hem'd in Milo being accusde;	Lucan, First Booke		323
MIND			
Thy mind Aeneas that would have it so/Deludes thy eye sight,	Dido	2.1.31	Achat
Because I heare he beares a valiant mind.	1Tamb	3.1.32	Bajzth
My mind presageth fortunate successe,	1Tamb	4.3.58	Arabia
Adding more courage to my conquering mind.	1Tamb	5.1.515	Tamb
a foot, unlesse thou beare/A mind corragious and invincible:	2Tamb	1.3.73	Tamb
And feed my mind that dies for want of her:	2Tamb	2.4.128	Tamb
My mothers death hath mortified my mind,	2Tamb	3.2.51	Celeb
Twill please my mind as wel to heare both you/Have won a heape	2Tamb	4.1.36	Calyph
Forbids my mind to entertaine a thought/That tends to love, but	2Tamb	4.2.25	Olymp
Nor bar thy mind that magnanimitie,	2Tamb	5.3.200	Tamb
You know my mind, let me alone with him.	Jew	4.1.100	Barab
Leave nothing loose, all leveld to my mind.	Jew	5.5.3	Barab
She smiles, now for my life his mind is changd.	Edw	1.4.236	Warwck
My lord, the Maior of Bristow knows our mind.	Edw	4.6.40	Queene
Which fils my mind with strange despairing thoughts,	Edw	5.1.79	Edward
Stretcheth as farre as doth the mind of man:	F 88	1.1.60	Faust
And then resolve me of thy Maisters mind.	F 328	1.3.100	Faust
Nothing Faustus but to delight thy mind <withall>,/And let thee	F 473	2.1.85	Mephst
I, thinke so still, till experience change thy mind.	F 517	2.1.129	Mephst
if thou hast any mind to Nan Spit our kitchin maide, then turn	F App	p.234 26	P Robin
His mind was troubled, and he aim'd at war,	Lucan, First Booke		186
And Caesars mind unsetled musing stood;	Lucan, First Booke		264
and whose tongue/Could tune the people to the Nobles mind:	Lucan, First Booke		273
But my ambitious ranging mind approoves?	Ovid's Elegies		2.4.48
sunne nor wind/Would burne or parch her hands, but to her mind,	Hero and Leander		1.28
And stole away th'inchaunted gazers mind,	Hero and Leander		1.104
Her mind pure, and her toong untaught to glose.	Hero and Leander		1.392
So to his mind was yoong Leanders looke.	Hero and Leander		2.130
And in her owne mind thought her selfe secure,	Hero and Leander		2.265
MINDE			
Yet thinkes my minde that this is Priamus:	Dido	2.1.25	Aeneas
Tut, I am simple, without [minde] <made> to hurt,	Dido	3.2.16	Juno
And mould her minde unto newe fancies shapes:	Dido	3.3.79	Iarbus
I see Aeneas sticketh in your minde,	Dido	4.1.33	Dido
While Italy is cleane out of thy minde?	Dido	5.1.29	Hermes
To cure my minde that melts for unkind love.	Dido	5.1.287	Dido
To signify the mildnesse of his minde:	1Tamb	4.1.52	2Msngr
This is my minde, and I will have it so.	1Tamb	4.2.91	Tamb
Torture or paine can daunt my dreadlesse minde.	2Tamb	5.1.113	Govnr
And now I can no longer hold my minde.	Jew	2.3.290	Lodowk
His minde you see runnes on his minions,	P 633	12.46	QnMoth
Is ruth and almost death to call to minde:	P 797	16.11	Navrre
And that the sweet and princely minde you beare,	P1141	22.3	King
To see your highnes in this vertuous minde.	P1210	22.72	Navrre
Adew my Lord, and either change your minde,	Edw	1.1.130	Lncstr
What so thy minde affectes or fancie likes.	Edw	1.1.170	Edward
Were all the Earles and Barons of my minde,	Edw	1.2.28	Mortmr
It is impossible, but speake your minde.	Edw	1.4.228	Mortmr
And seeing his minde so dotes on Gaveston,	Edw	1.4.389	MortSr
You know my minde, come unckle lets away.	Edw	1.4.424	Mortmr
And that his banishment had changd her minde.	Edw	2.1.26	Baldck
And still his minde runs on his minion.	Edw	2.2.4	Queene
Nay, now you are heere alone, ile speake my minde.	Edw	2.2.155	Mortmr
Argues thy noble minde and disposition:	Edw	3.1.48	Edward

MINDE (cont.)
whose dauntlesse minde/The ambitious Mortimer would seeke to   Edw 5.1.15 Edward
But when I call to minde I am a king,   Edw 5.1.23 Edward
In which extreame my minde here murthered is: Edw 5.1.55 Edward
This poore revenge hath something easd my minde,   Edw 5.1.141 Edward
When will the furie of his minde asswage?   Edw 5.3.8 Edward
Let us assaile his minde another while.   Edw 5.5.12 Matrvs
My minde may be more stedfast on my God.   Edw 5.5.78 Edward
Let this gift change thy minde, and save thy soule,   Edw 5.5.88 Edward
I'le fetch him somewhat to delight his minde.   F 471 2.1.83 Mephst
And then devise what best contents thy minde,   F 858 3.1.80 Mephst
But now, that Faustus may delight his minde,   F 989 3.2.9 Faust
more, take him, because I see thou hast a good minde to him.   F1461 4.4.5 P Faust
When our lascivious toyes come in thy minde,   Ovid's Elegies 1.4.21
If Boreas beares Orithyas rape in minde,   Ovid's Elegies 1.6.53
Let thy tongue flatter, while thy minde harme-workes: Ovid's Elegies 1.8.103
Pleasure, and ease had mollifide my minde.   Ovid's Elegies 1.9.42
While thou wert plaine, I lov'd thy minde and face: Ovid's Elegies 1.10.13
To please thy selfe, thy selfe put out of minde.   Ovid's Elegies 1.14.38
famous names/Farewel, your favour nought my minde inflames.   Ovid's Elegies 2.1.36
So with this love and that, wavers my minde.   Ovid's Elegies 2.10.10
Wherein is seene the givers loving minde: Ovid's Elegies 2.15.2
First of thy minde the happy seedes I knewe,   Ovid's Elegies 3.1.59
Or is my heate, of minde, not of the skie?   Ovid's Elegies 3.2.39
Though thou her body guard, her minde is staind: Ovid's Elegies 3.4.5
Nor canst by watching keepe her minde from sinne.   Ovid's Elegies 3.4.7
That I may love yet, though against my minde.   Ovid's Elegies 3.10.52
And if these pleasures may thee <things thy minde may> move,   Passionate Shepherd 19
If these delights thy minde may move;   Passionate Shepherd 23

MINDED
Shall massacre those greedy minded slaves.   1Tamb 2.2.67 Meandr
And that high minded earle of Lancaster,   Edw 1.1.150 Edward
Ah none but rude and savage minded men,   Edw 1.4.78 Edward

MINDES
In mannaging those fierce barbarian mindes: Dido 1.1.92 Jupitr
Effeminate our mindes inur'd to warre.   Dido 4.3.36 Achat
Therefore cheere up your mindes, prepare to fight,   1Tamb 2.2.29 Meandr
Let us put on our meet incountring mindes,   1Tamb 2.6.19 Ortyg
Dismaies their mindes before they come to proove/The wounding   2Tamb 1.3.86 Zenoc
And like base slaves abject our princely mindes/To vile and   2Tamb 5.1.140 Orcan
Though gentle mindes should pittie others paines,   P 215 4.13 Anjoy
We know that noble mindes change not their thoughts/For wearing   P 610 12.23 Mugern
We must with resolute mindes resolve to fight,   P 707 14.10 Navrre
But droope not madam, noble mindes contemne/Despaire: Edw 4.2.16 SrJohn
My mindes distempered, and my bodies numde,   Edw 5.5.64 Edward
Now all feare with my mindes hot love abates,   Ovid's Elegies 1.10.9
I know not whether my mindes whirle-wind drives me.   Ovid's Elegies 2.9.28

MINDFULL
To make me mindfull of my mortall sinnes,   Jew 2.3.74 Barab
He will be mindfull of the curtesie.   Edw 2.5.40 Arundl

MINDING
Minding thy fault, with death I wish to revill,   Ovid's Elegies 2.5.3
Go, minding to returne with prosperous winde,   Ovid's Elegies 2.11.37

MINDS
Doth teach us all to have aspyring minds: 1Tamb 2.7.20 Tamb
And might in noble minds be counted princely.   1Tamb 3.2.39 Zenoc
Your fearfull minds are thicke and mistie then,   1Tamb 5.1.110 Tamb
Their minds, and muses on admyred theames: 1Tamb 5.1.164 Tamb
Teach you my boyes to beare couragious minds,   2Tamb 3.2.143 Tamb
And in your shields display your rancorous minds?   Edw 2.2.33 Edward
And I might pleade, and draw the Commons minds/To favour thee,   Lucan, First Booke 275
steeld their harts/And minds were prone) restrain'd them;   Lucan, First Booke 356
and did invade/The peoples minds, and laide before their eies   Lucan, First Booke 466
least some one hope might ease/The Commons jangling minds,   Lucan, First Booke 521
And who have hard hearts, and obdurat minds,   Hero and Leander 2.217

MINE (Homograph; See also MYNE)
As made the bloud run downe about mine eares.   Dido 1.1.8 Ganimd
Whose face reflects such pleasure to mine eyes,   Dido 1.1.24 Jupitr
I would have a jewell for mine eare,   Dido 1.1.46 Ganimd
Or in these shades deceiv'st mine eye so oft?   Dido 1.1.244 Aeneas
Achates though mine eyes say this is stone,   Dido 2.1.24 Aeneas
Then buckled I mine armour, drew my sword,   Dido 2.1.200 Aeneas
This young boy in mine armes, and by the hand/Led faire Creusa   Dido 2.1.266 Aeneas
Eate Comfites in mine armes, and I will sing.   Dido 2.1.315 Venus
Why staiest thou here? thou art no love of mine.   Dido 3.1.39 Dido
That I should say thou art no love of mine?   Dido 3.1.42 Dido
Then pull out both mine eyes, or let me dye.   Dido 3.1.55 Iarbus
Because his lothsome sight offends mine eye,   Dido 3.1.57 Dido
Whom I will beare to Ida in mine armes,   Dido 3.2.99 Venus
Stoute love in mine armes make thy Italy,   Dido 3.4.57 Dido
Mine eye is fixt where fancie cannot start,   Dido 4.2.37 Iarbus
Or drop out both mine eyes in drisling teares,   Dido 4.2.41 Iarbus
Hath not the Carthage Queene mine onely sonne?   Dido 4.4.29 Aeneas
Not all the world can take thee from mine armes,   Dido 4.4.61 Dido
The ground is mine that gives them sustenance,   Dido 4.4.74 Dido
Or that the Tyrrhen sea were in mine armes,   Dido 4.4.101 Dido
So I may have Aeneas in mine armes.   Dido 4.4.135 Dido
Thy hand and mine have plighted mutuall faith,   Dido 5.1.122 Dido
That he should take Aeneas from mine armes?   Dido 5.1.130 Dido
Leape in mine armes, mine armes are open wide: Dido 5.1.180 Dido
And from mine ashes let a Conquerour rise,   Dido 5.1.306 Dido
That I may view these milk-white steeds of mine,   1Tamb 1.1.77 Mycet
Enchast with precious juelles of mine owne: 1Tamb 1.2.96 Tamb

MINE (cont.)

Then tis mine.	1Tamb	2.4.34		Tamb
For Egypt and Arabia must be mine.	1Tamb	4.4.91		Tamb
to prevent/That which mine honor sweares shal be perform'd:	1Tamb	5.1.107		Tamb
What do mine eies behold, my husband dead?	1Tamb	5.1.305		Zabina
Since thy desired hand shall close mine eies.	1Tamb	5.1.432		Arabia
Shal now, adjoining al their hands with mine,	1Tamb	5.1.493		Tamb
more precious in mine eies/Than all the wealthy kingdomes I	2Tamb	1.3.18		Tamb
For should I but suspect your death by mine,	2Tamb	2.4.61		Zenoc
But keep within the circle of mine armes.	2Tamb	3.2.35		Tamb
I shall now revenge/My fathers vile abuses and mine owne.	2Tamb	3.5.91		Callap
How may my hart, thus fired with mine eies,	2Tamb	4.1.93		Tamb
No such discourse is pleasant in mine eares,	2Tamb	4.2.46		Olymp
Than you by this unconquered arme of mine.	2Tamb	4.3.16		Tamb
That I may sheath it in this breast of mine,	2Tamb	5.1.143		Jrslem
Their cruel death, mine owne captivity,	2Tamb	5.2.20		Callap
Mine Argosie from Alexandria,	Jew	1.1.44		Barab
But art thou master in a ship of mine,	Jew	1.1.61		Barab
And saw'st thou not/Mine Argosie at Alexandria?	Jew	1.1.72		Barab
The comfort of mine age, my childrens hope,	Jew	1.2.150		Barab
and in mine Argosie/And other ships that came from Egypt last,	Jew	1.2.187		Barab
And hide these extreme sorrowes from mine eyes:	Jew	1.2.195		Barab
I doe not doubt by your divine precepts/And mine owne industry,	Jew	1.2.335		Abigal
Strength to my soule, death to mine enemy;	Jew	2.1.49		Barab
My Lord farewell: Come Sirra you are mine.	Jew	2.3.134		Barab
And mine you have, yet let me talke to her;	Jew	2.3.300		Barab
Shee is thy wife, and thou shalt be mine heire.	Jew	2.3.328		Barab
mine eye up to the Jewes counting-house where I saw some bags	Jew	3.1.18	P	Pilia
These armes of mine shall be thy Sepulchre.	Jew	3.2.11		Govnr
Thy sonne slew mine, and I'le revenge his death.	Jew	3.2.15		Mater
Looke, Katherin, looke, thy sonne gave mine these wounds.	Jew	3.2.16		Govnr
Why, made mine Abigall a Nunne.	Jew	3.4.24		Barab
Ne're shall she live to inherit ought of mine,	Jew	3.4.30		Barab
I here adopt thee for mine onely heire,	Jew	3.4.43		Barab
Upon mine owne free-hold within fortie foot of the gallowes,	Jew	4.2.16	P	Pilia
How liberally the villain gives me mine own gold.	Jew	4.4.48	P	Barab
That charge is mine.	P 290	5.17		Anjoy
By due discent the Regall seat is mine.	P 470	8.20		Anjoy
Might seeme <seek> to crosse me in mine enterprise.	P 574	11.39		Navrre
O Lord, mine eare.	P 619	12.32		Cutprs
I, dearer then the apple of mine eye?	P 685	13.29		Guise
Your highnes needs not feare mine armies force,	P 857	17.52		Guise
But if that God doe prosper mine attempts,	P 927	18.28		Navrre
Whatsoever any whisper in mine eares,	P 974	19.44		King
Mother, how like you this device of mine?	P1065	19.135		King
And may it never end in bloud as mine hath done.	P1233	22.95		King
Mine unckle heere, this Earle, and I my selfe,	Edw	1.1.82		Mortmr
This sword of mine that should offend your foes,	Edw	1.1.86		Mortmr
Shall be their timeles sepulcher, or mine.	Edw	1.2.6		Lncstr
And so is mine.	Edw	1.4.91		Warwck
But thou must call mine honor thus in question?	Edw	1.4.152		Queene
A friend of mine told me in secrecie,	Edw	2.1.17		Spencr
Mine old lord whiles he livde, was so precise,	Edw	2.1.46		Baldck
Which made me curate-like in mine attire,	Edw	2.1.49		Baldck
Sweet Lord and King, your speech preventeth mine,	Edw	2.2.59		Gavstn
Villaine thy life, unlesse I misse mine aime.	Edw	2.2.84		Mortmr
Mine unckles taken prisoner by the Scots.	Edw	2.2.142		Mortmr
Mine honor shalbe hostage of my truth,	Edw	2.3.9		Kent
O that mine armes could close this Ile about,	Edw	2.4.17		Queene
Or that these teares that drissell from mine eyes,	Edw	2.4.19		Queene
Mine honour will be cald in question,	Edw	2.4.55		Queene
I will upon mine honor undertake/To carrie him, and bring him	Edw	2.5.79		Penbrk
Upon mine oath I will returne him back.	Edw	2.5.88		Penbrk
These Barons thus to beard me in my land,/In mine owne realme?	Edw	3.1.15		Spencr
Here man, rip up this panting brest of mine,	Edw	4.7.66		Edward
these innocent hands of mine/Shall not be guiltie of so foule a	Edw	5.1.98		Edward
Mine enemie hath pitied my estate,	Edw	5.1.149		Edward
Whome I esteeme as deare as these mine eyes,	Edw	5.2.18		Queene
And mine.	Edw	5.2.85		Mortmr
If mine will serve, unbowell straight this brest,	Edw	5.3.10		Edward
Wish well to mine, then tush, for them ile die.	Edw	5.3.45		Edward
Mine enemies will I plague, my friends advance,	Edw	5.4.67		Mortmr
Something still busseth in mine eares,	Edw	5.5.103		Edward
And let these teares distilling from mine eyes,	Edw	5.6.101		King
[Yet not your words onely, but mine owne fantasie],	F 130	1.1.102A		Faust
No, I came now hether of mine owne accord.	F 272	1.3.44		Mephst
To slay mine enemies, and aid my friends,	F 324	1.3.96		Faust
O something soundeth in mine [eares] <eare>,/Abjure this	F 395	2.1.7		Faust
Why, the Signory of Embden shall be mine:	F 412	2.1.24		Faust
for love of thee/Faustus hath <I> cut his <mine> arme, and with	F 443	2.1.55		Faust
Veiw here this <the> bloud that trickles from mine arme,	F 446	2.1.58		Faust
But what is this Inscription on mine Arme?	F 465	2.1.77		Faust
Who buzzeth in mine eares I am a spirit?	F 565	2.2.14		Faust
[But feareful ecchoes thunder <thunders> in mine eares],	F 571	2.2.20A		Faust
And what might please mine eye, I there beheld.	F 853	3.1.75		Faust
That in mine armes I would have compast him.	F1262	4.1.108		Emper
Mine be that honour then:	F1360	4.2.36		Benvol
Come sirs, what shall we do now till mine Hostesse comes?	F1520	4.5.16	P	Dick
me his leg quite off, and now 'tis at home in mine Hostry.	F1551	4.5.47	P	HrsCsr
And keepe [mine oath] <my vow> I made to Lucifer.	F1765	5.1.92		Faust
I writ them a bill with mine owne bloud, the date is expired:	F1860	5.2.64	P	Faust
But mine must live still to be plagu'd in hell.	F1971	5.2.175		Faust
O brave Robin, shal I have Nan Spit, and to mine owne use?	F App	p.234 29	P	Rafe

MINE (cont.)

Line	Work	Reference	Speaker
mine eies may be witnesses to confirme what mine eares have	F App	p.236 6 P	Emper
be witnesses to confirme what mine eares have heard reported,	F App	p.236 7 P	Emper
by the honor of mine Imperial crowne, that what ever thou	F App	p.236 8 P	Emper
about the honour of mine auncestors, how they had wonne by	F App	p.236 19 P	Emper
My thoughts sole goddes, aide mine enterprise,	Lucan, First Booke	202	
Then scarse can Phoebus say, this harpe is mine.	Ovid's Elegies	1.1.20	
Say they are mine, and hands on thee impose.	Ovid's Elegies	1.4.40	
Starke naked as she stood before mine eie,	Ovid's Elegies	1.5.17	
Would of mine armes, my shoulders had beene scanted,	Ovid's Elegies	1.7.23	
To mine owne selfe have I had strength so furious?	Ovid's Elegies	1.7.25	
Bescratch mine eyes, spare not my lockes to breake,	Ovid's Elegies	1.7.65	
No more this beauty mine eyes captivates.	Ovid's Elegies	1.10.10	
And whom I like eternize by mine art.	Ovid's Elegies	1.10.60	
blotted letter/On the last edge to stay mine eyes the better.	Ovid's Elegies	1.11.22	
Oft was she drest before mine eyes, yet never,	Ovid's Elegies	1.14.17	
Thy scope is mortall, mine eternall fame,	Ovid's Elegies	1.15.7	
Seeing her face, mine upreard armes discended,	Ovid's Elegies	2.5.47	
Lay her whole tongue hid, mine in hers she dips.	Ovid's Elegies	2.5.58	
And as a traitour mine owne fault confesse.	Ovid's Elegies	2.8.26	
Let such as be mine enemies have none,	Ovid's Elegies	2.10.16	
Mine owne desires why should my selfe not flatter?	Ovid's Elegies	2.11.54	
Thou givest my mistris life, she mine againe.	Ovid's Elegies	2.13.16	
My selfe poore wretch mine owne gifts now envie.	Ovid's Elegies	2.15.8	
(O face most cunning mine eyes to detaine)/Thou oughtst	Ovid's Elegies	2.17.12	
Domesticke acts, and mine owne warres to sing.	Ovid's Elegies	2.18.12	
Then warres, and from thy tents wilt come to mine.	Ovid's Elegies	2.18.40	
Thou also that late tookest mine eyes away,	Ovid's Elegies	2.19.19	
Thou doest beginne, she shall be mine no longer.	Ovid's Elegies	2.19.48	
Thou fightst against me using mine owne verse.	Ovid's Elegies	3.1.38	
Thy lofty stile with mine I not compare,	Ovid's Elegies	3.1.39	
And by mine eyes, and mine were pained sore.	Ovid's Elegies	3.3.14	
Or in mine eyes good wench no paine transfuse.	Ovid's Elegies	3.3.48	
Perchance these, others, me mine owne losse mooves.	Ovid's Elegies	3.5.100	
And under mine her wanton thigh she flong,	Ovid's Elegies	3.6.10	
May that shame fall mine enemies chance to be.	Ovid's Elegies	3.10.16	
And by thine eyes whose radiance burnes out mine.	Ovid's Elegies	3.10.48	
What ere thou art mine art thou:	Ovid's Elegies	3.10.49	
Who mine was cald, whom I lov'd more then any,	Ovid's Elegies	3.11.5	
And mingle thighs, yours ever mine to beare.	Ovid's Elegies	3.13.22	
And I will trust your words more then mine eies.	Ovid's Elegies	3.13.46	
To lead thy thoughts, as thy faire lookes doe mine,	Hero and Leander	1.201	
What difference betwixt the richest mine/And basest mold, but	Hero and Leander	1.232	
O that these tardie armes of mine were wings,	Hero and Leander	2.205	

MINERALS

Line	Work	Reference	Speaker
And simplest extracts of all Minerals,	2Tamb	4.2.61	Olymp
In Malta are no golden Minerals.	Jew	3.5.6	Govnr
Inricht with tongues, well seene in Minerals,	F 166	1.1.138	Cornel

MINERVA

Line	Work	Reference	Speaker
Or when Minerva did with Neptune strive.	1Tamb	3.2.52	Zenoc
So chast Minerva did Cassandra fall,	Ovid's Elegies	1.7.17	
To thee Minerva turne the craftes-mens hands.	Ovid's Elegies	3.2.52	

MINERVAS

Line	Work	Reference	Speaker
Epeus pine-tree Horse/A sacrifize t'appease Minervas wrath:	Dido	2.1.163	Aeneas
their vaild Matron, who alone might view/Minervas statue; then,	Lucan, First Booke	598	

MINES (Homograph)

Line	Work	Reference	Speaker
Then will we march to all those Indian Mines,	1Tamb	2.5.41	Cosroe
Offer their mines (to sew for peace) to me,	1Tamb	3.3.264	Tamb
Loe here my sonnes, are all the golden Mines,	2Tamb	5.3.151	Tamb
My lord, mines more obscure then Mortimers.	Edw	2.2.22	Lncstr

MINGLE

Line	Work	Reference	Speaker
Breake heart, drop bloud, and mingle it with teares,	F App	p.243 38	OldMan
Mingle not thighes, nor to his legge joyne thine,	Ovid's Elegies	1.4.43	
Wee cause feete flie, wee mingle haires with snakes,	Ovid's Elegies	3.11.23	
And mingle thighs, yours ever mine to beare.	Ovid's Elegies	3.13.22	

MINGLED

Line	Work	Reference	Speaker
Mingled with powdered shot and fethered steele/So thick upon	2Tamb	1.1.92	Orcan
Mingled with corrall and with [orient] <orientall> pearle:	2Tamb	1.3.224	Tamb
ordinance strike/A ring of pikes, mingled with shot and horse,	2Tamb	3.2.99	Tamb
Nor in my act hath fortune mingled chance,	Ovid's Elegies	2.12.15	

MINION

Line	Work	Reference	Speaker
Which your wife writ to my deare Minion,	P 755	15.13	King
The glozing head of thy base minion throwne.	Edw	1.1.133	Lncstr
And let him frollick with his minion.	Edw	1.2.67	Queene
Were he a peasant, being my minion,	Edw	1.4.30	Edward
The king is love-sick for his minion.	Edw	1.4.87	Mortmr
Harke how he harpes upon his minion.	Edw	1.4.311	Queene
And still his minde runs on his minion.	Edw	2.2.4	Queene
Your minion Gaveston hath taught you this.	Edw	2.2.149	Lncstr
He turnes away, and smiles upon his minion.	Edw	2.4.29	Queene

MINIONS

Line	Work	Reference	Speaker
Minions, Fauknets, and Sakars to the trench,	2Tamb	3.3.6	Techel
What saies our Minions, think they Henries heart/Will not both	P 603	12.16	King
His minde you see runnes on his minions,	P 633	12.46	QnMoth
of Guise you and your wife/Doe both salute our lovely Minions.	P 753	15.11	King
I love your Minions?	P 763	15.21	Guise
And all his Minions stoup when I commaund:	P 979	19.49	Guise
Feare ye not Madam, now his minions gone,	Edw	1.4.198	Lncstr
The mightiest kings have had their minions,	Edw	1.4.391	MortSr

MINISTER

Line	Work	Reference	Speaker
and his Minister Mephostophilis, and furthermore grant unto	F 495	2.1.107 P	Faust

MINISTERS

Line	Work	Reference	Speaker
That may be ministers of my decay.	1Tamb	5.1.289	Bajzth

MINISTERS (cont.)			
[To burne his Scriptures, slay his Ministers], ...	F 650	2.2.99A	Faust
MINKES			
And what are you Mistris Minkes, the seventh and last? .	F 707	2.2.159	Faust
MINOR			
I thank thee Sigismond, but when I war/All Asia Minor, Affrica,	2Tamb	1.1.158	Orcan
MINOS			
Law-giving Minos did such yeares desire;	Ovid's Elegies		3.9.41
MINUTE			
We will not stay a minute longer here.	Dido	4.3.44	Cloan
One minute end our daies, and one sepulcher/Containe our .	2Tamb	3.4.13	Olymp
Yet in a minute had my spirit return'd, ...	F1399	4.2.75	Faust
MIRACLE (See also MYRACLE)			
Would make a miracle of thus much coyne:	Jew	1.1.13	Barab
Affoords this Art no greater miracle?	F 37	1.1.9	Faust
MIRACLES			
The miracles that magick will performe, ...	F 163	1.1.135	Cornel
MIRE			
Who groveling in the mire of Zanthus bankes, ...	Dido	2.1.150	Aeneas
And there in mire and puddle have I stood, ...	Edw	5.5.59	Edward
MIRMIDONS			
Peeres/Heare me, but yet with Mirmidons harsh eares, .	Dido	2.1.123	Aeneas
And after him his band of Mirmidons, ...	Dido	2.1.216	Aeneas
Was by the cruell Mirmidons surprizd, ...	Dido	2.1.287	Aeneas
MIRROUR (See also MYRROUR)			
Wherein as in a mirrour may be seene, ...	1Tamb	5.1.476	Tamb
MIRTH			
Now Faustus, come prepare thy selfe for mirth, ...	F 981	3.2.1	Mephst
as to delight your Majesty with some mirth, hath Faustus justly	F1312	4.1.158	P Faust
as to delight you with some mirth, hath Faustus worthily .	F App	p.238 82	P Faust
MIRTHFULL			
The mirthfull God of amorous pleasure smil'd, ...	Hero and Leander		2.39
MIRTLE			
Girt my shine browe with sea banke mirtle praise <sprays>.	Ovid's Elegies		1.1.34
Yoke Venus Doves, put Mirtle on thy haire, ...	Ovid's Elegies		1.2.23
About my head be quivering Mirtle wound, ...	Ovid's Elegies		1.15.37
Erre I? or mirtle in her right hand lies.	Ovid's Elegies		3.1.34
Imbroydred all with leaves of Mirtle.	Passionate Shepherd		12
MIS			
Barabas, although thou art in mis-beleefe, ...	Jew	1.2.352	1Fryar
will follow thee/Against these barbarous mis-beleeving Turkes.	Jew	2.2.46	Govnr
MIS-BELEEFE			
Barabas, although thou art in mis-beleefe, ...	Jew	1.2.352	1Fryar
MISBELEEFE			
alas, hath pac'd too long/The fatall Labyrinth of misbeleefe,	Jew	3.3.64	Abigal
MIS-BELEEVING			
will follow thee/Against these barbarous mis-beleeving Turkes.	Jew	2.2.46	Govnr
MISCHEEFE			
In murder, mischeefe, or in tiranny.	P 41	1.41	Condy
MISCHIEFE (See also MYSCHIEFES)			
Nuns, strangled a Fryar, and I know not what mischiefe beside.	Jew	5.1.14	P Pilia
Let's hence, lest further mischiefe be pretended. . .	Jew	5.5.96	Calym
What end of mischiefe?	Lucan, First Booke		334
what mischiefe shall insue?	Lucan, First Booke		644
o Rome continue/The course of mischiefe, and stretch out the	Lucan, First Booke		670
(O mischiefe) now for me obtaine small grace. . . .	Ovid's Elegies		1.6.22
MISCHIEFES			
I, Daughter, for Religion/Hides many mischiefes from suspition.	Jew	1.2.282	Barab
MISCHIEFS			
Slaughter and mischiefs instruments, no better, . . .	Ovid's Elegies		1.7.27
MISCREANT			
And since this miscreant hath disgrac'd his faith, . .	2Tamb	2.3.36	Orcan
I curse thee and exclaime thee miscreant, ...	P1075	19.145	QnMoth
MISCREANTS			
Now will the Christian miscreants be glad, ...	1Tamb	3.3.236	Bajzth
MISDOE			
Then to misdoe the welfare of their King:	P 546	11.11	Charls
MISERABLE			
And who so miserable as Aeneas is?	Dido	2.1.102	Aeneas
Then be assured thou art not miserable.	Dido	2.1.104	Dido
Then never say that thou art miserable, ...	Dido	3.1.169	Dido
souldier of my Camp/Shall smile to see thy miserable state.	1Tamb	3.3.86	Tamb
To take the lives of miserable men, ...	Jew	1.2.147	Barab
Happie were I, but now most miserable.	Edw	1.4.129	Edward
O miserable and distressed Queene!	Edw	1.4.170	Queene
And so am I for ever miserable.	Edw	1.4.186	Queene
I Mortimer, the miserable Queene, ...	Edw	2.4.23	Queene
rule and emperie/Have not in life or death made miserable?	Edw	4.7.15	Edward
I might, but heavens and earth conspire/To make me miserable:	Edw	5.1.97	Edward
O miserable is that commonweale, ...	Edw	5.3.63	Kent
[Accursed Faustus, miserable man], ...	F1788	5.1.115A	OldMan
Loe how the miserable great eared Asse, ...	Ovid's Elegies		2.7.15
MISERERE			
fuit aut tibi quidquam/Dulce meum, miserere domus labentis:	Dido	5.1.137	Dido
MISERICORDIA			
Misericordia pro nobis, what shal I doe?	F App	p.235 30	P Robin
MISERIE			
Though we be now in extreame miserie, ...	Dido	1.1.157	Achat
As poore distressed miserie may pleade:	Dido	1.2.6	Illion
To agravate our sodaine miserie.	P 194	3.29	QnMarg
Men are ordaind to live in miserie, ...	Edw	5.3.2	Matrvs
This usage makes my miserie increase.	Edw	5.3.16	Edward
For she relents at this your miserie.	Edw	5.5.49	Ltborn

MISERIE (cont.)			
Yet stay, the world shall see their miserie,	F1406	4.2.82	Faust
And pitty of thy future miserie.	F1721	5.1.48	OldMan
MISERIS			
Solamen miseris socios habuisse doloris.	F 431	2.1.43	Mephst
MISERS			
When misers keepe it; being put to lone,	Hero and Leander		1.235
MISERY			
And Villanesse to shame, disdaine, and misery:	1Tamb	5.1.269	Bajzth
To see them live so long in misery:	1Tamb	5.1.370	Zenoc
Then be the causers of their misery.	Jew	1.2.148	Barab
but trust me 'tis a misery/To see a man in such affliction:	Jew	1.2.211	2Jew
What greater misery could heaven inflict?	Jew	5.2.14	Govnr
Curst be your soules to hellish misery.	F1034	3.2.54	Pope
O misery.	F1437	4.3.7	Mrtino
MISFORTUNE			
Priams misfortune followes us by sea,	Dido	1.1.143	Aeneas
Center of all misfortune. O my starres!	Edw	4.7.62	Edward
Or if he loves, thy tale breedes his misfortune.	Ovid's Elegies		2.2.54
MISGIVES			
My heart misgives me, that to crosse your love,	Jew	2.3.349	Barab
MISGOVERNED			
Misgoverned kings are cause of all this wrack,	Edw	4.4.9	Queene
MISHAP			
The heavens forbid your highnes such mishap.	P 177	3.12	QnMarg
MISHAPEN			
faire, mishapen stuffe/Are of behaviour boisterous and ruffe.	Hero and Leander		1.203
MISLED			
Hoping (misled by dreaming prophesies)/To raigne in Asia, and	1Tamb	1.1.41	Meandr
Is thus misled to countenance their ils.	Edw	4.3.49	Edward
MISSE (See also MIST)			
For if my father misse him in the field,	2Tamb	4.1.8	Celeb
Run mourning round about the Femals misse,	2Tamb	4.1.188	Tamb
Villaine thy life, unlesse I misse mine aime.	Edw	2.2.84	Mortmr
And while he drinkes, to adde more do not misse,	Ovid's Elegies		1.4.52
MISSES			
Or Phillis teares that her [Demophoon] <Domoophon> misses,/What	Ovid's Elegies		2.18.22
With thine, nor this last fire their presence misses.	Ovid's Elegies		3.8.54
MISSING			
with kissing/And on her necke a wantons marke not missing.	Ovid's Elegies		1.7.42
MIST (Homograph; See also MYSTY)			
He mist him neer, but we have strook him now.	P 311	5.38	Guise
Is Guises glory but a clowdy mist,	P 686	13.30	Guise
Now draw up Faustus like a foggy mist,	F1952	5.2.156	Faust
her selfe the clouds among/And now Leander fearing to be mist,	Hero and Leander		2.91
And fell in drops like teares, because they mist him.	Hero and Leander		2.174
MISTAKE			
And so mistake you not a whit my Lord.	1Tamb	2.3.6	Tamb
These silly men mistake the matter cleane.	Jew	1.1.179	Barab
MISTAKES			
Your grace mistakes, it is for Englands good,	Edw	5.1.38	BshpWn
Your Grace mistakes, you gave us no such charge.	F1024	3.2.44	1Card
MISTES			
Enrolde in flames and fiery smoldering mistes,	1Tamb	2.3.20	Tamb
Smother the earth with never fading mistes:	1Tamb	5.1.296	Bajzth
MISTIE			
Your fearfull minds are thicke and mistie then,	1Tamb	5.1.110	Tamb
MISTRES			
Agent for England, send thy mistres word,	P1194	22.56	King
MISTRESS			
Gentlewoman, her name was <mistress> Margery March-beere:	F 700	2.2.149	P Glutny
MISTRESSE			
To rob their mistresse of her Troian guest?	Dido	4.4.138	Dido
And how my slave, her mistresse menaceth.	1Tamb	3.3.183	Zenoc
Oh, Mistresse, ha ha ha.	Jew	3.3.5	P Ithimr
Thou needst not do that, for my Mistresse hath done it.	F 739	2.3.18	P Dick
That when my mistresse there beholds thee cast,	Ovid's Elegies		1.6.69
My Mistresse weepes whom my mad hand did harme.	Ovid's Elegies		1.7.4
Because [thy] <they> care too much thy Mistresse troubled.	Ovid's Elegies		2.2.8
This tombe approoves, I pleasde my mistresse well,	Ovid's Elegies		2.6.61
Is charg'd to violate her mistresse bed.	Ovid's Elegies		2.7.18
Well maiest thou one thing for thy Mistresse use.	Ovid's Elegies		2.8.24
Telling thy mistresse, where I was with thee,	Ovid's Elegies		2.8.27
Why doth my mistresse from me oft devide?	Ovid's Elegies		2.16.42
Would I had beene my mistresse gentle prey,	Ovid's Elegies		2.17.5
But Pallas and your mistresse are at strife.	Hero and Leander		1.322
MISTRIS			
Oh Mistris!	Jew	3.3.9	P Ithimr
I pray, mistris, wil you answer me to one question?	Jew	3.3.30	P Ithimr
I will forsooth, Mistris.	Jew	3.3.35	P Ithimr
And unto your good mistris as unknowne.	Jew	4.3.48	Barab
Sirra, you must give my mistris your posey.	Jew	4.4.37	Pilia
And what are you Mistris Minkes, the seventh and last?	F 707	2.2.159	Faust
he keepes such a chafing with my mistris about it, and she has	F App	p.233 8	P Rafe
my maister and mistris shal finde that I can reade, he for his	F App	p.233 15	P Robin
I have no mistris, nor no favorit,	Ovid's Elegies		1.1.23
For thee I did thy mistris faire entreate.	Ovid's Elegies		1.6.20
Over my Mistris is my right more great?	Ovid's Elegies		1.7.30
Mistris thou knowest, thou hast a blest youth pleas'd,	Ovid's Elegies		1.8.23
His Mistris dores this; that his Captaines keepes.	Ovid's Elegies		1.9.8
This breakes Towne gates, but he his Mistris dore.	Ovid's Elegies		1.9.20
And from my mistris bosome let me rise:	Ovid's Elegies		2.10.20
Thou givest my mistris life, she mine againe.	Ovid's Elegies		2.13.16

MISTRIS (cont.)
Blest ring thou in my mistris hand shalt lye,	•	Ovid's Elegies	2.15.7
Then would I wish thee touch my mistris pappe,	• •	Ovid's Elegies	2.15.11
My Mistris deity also drewe me fro it,	• •	Ovid's Elegies	2.18.17
Let us all conquer by our mistris favour.	•	Ovid's Elegies	3.2.18
Let my new mistris graunt to be beloved:	•	Ovid's Elegies	3.2.57
For evermore thou shalt my mistris be.	•	Ovid's Elegies	3.2.62
My mistris wish confirme with my request.	•	Ovid's Elegies	3.2.80
My mistris hath her wish, my wish remaine:	•	Ovid's Elegies	3.2.81
Kindly thy mistris use, if thou be wise.	•	Ovid's Elegies	3.4.43
I to my mistris hast.	•	Ovid's Elegies	3.5.2
When our bookes did my mistris faire content,	•	Ovid's Elegies	3.7.5
In emptie bed alone my mistris lies.	•	Ovid's Elegies	3.9.2

MISTRISSE
All for their Mistrisse, what they have, prepare.	•	Ovid's Elegies	1.10.58
Receive these lines, them to my Mistrisse carry,	•	Ovid's Elegies	1.11.7
committed/And then with sweete words to my Mistrisse fitted.		Ovid's Elegies	1.12.22
Bagous whose care doth thy Mistrisse bridle,		Ovid's Elegies	2.2.1
Spying his mistrisse teares, he will lament/And say this blabbe		Ovid's Elegies	2.2.59
Aye me an Eunuch keepes my mistrisse chaste,	•	Ovid's Elegies	2.3.1
Thy mistrisse enseignes must be likewise thine.	•	Ovid's Elegies	2.3.10
Apt to thy mistrisse, but more apt to me.	•	Ovid's Elegies	2.8.4
My hard way with my mistrisse would seeme soft.	•	Ovid's Elegies	2.16.20

MISTRUST
before your mother/Lest she mistrust the match that is in hand:		Jew	2.3.147	Barab
What meanes your highnesse to mistrust me thus?	•	Edw	5.5.79	Ltborn
If you mistrust me, ile be gon my lord.	• •	Edw	5.5.97	Ltborn
And with mistrust of the like measure vext.	• •	Ovid's Elegies	1.4.46	

MISTRUSTS
I feare me he mistrusts what we intend.	• •	Jew	4.1.133	Ithimr

MISTS
her latest breath/All dasled with the hellish mists of death.		2Tamb	2.4.14	Tamb

MISUS'D
I might have then my parents deare misus'd,	• •	Ovid's Elegies	1.7.5

MITER (See also MYTER)
Throwe of his golden miter, rend his stole,		Edw	1.1.187	Edward

MITHRADATE
to their soules I think/As are Thessalian drugs or Mithradate.		1Tamb	5.1.133	Tamb

MIXE
And mixe her bloud with thine, this shall I doe,	•	Dido	5.1.326	Anna

MIXT
or els infernall, mixt/Their angry seeds at his conception:		1Tamb	2.6.9	Meandr
is bould/To suffer storme mixt snowes with nights sharpe cold?		Ovid's Elegies	1.9.16	
Yet as if mixt with red leade thou wert ruddy,		Ovid's Elegies	1.12.11	
Yet although [neither] <either>, mixt of eithers hue,	•	Ovid's Elegies	1.14.10	
Such as a rose mixt with a lilly breedes,	• •	Ovid's Elegies	2.5.37	

MO
As put thereby, yet might he hope for mo.	• •	Hero and Leander	1.312	

MOALE
this Lady while she liv'd had a wart or moale in her necke,		F App	p.238 61	P Emper

MOANE (See also MONE)
To dull the ayre with my discoursive moane.	•	Dido	1.1.248	Aeneas
What, woman, moane not for a little losse:	•	Jew	1.2.226	Barab
But to thy selfe smile when the Christians moane.	•	Jew	2.3.172	Barab

MOANING
whose moaning entercourse/Hath hetherto bin staid, with wrath		1Tamb	5.1.280	Bajzth

MOAT (See MOTE)

MOBILE
and is not that Mobile?	•	F 208	1.2.15	P Wagner
Even to the height of Primum Mobile:	•	F 763	2.3.42	2Chor

MOCKE
That dar'st presume thy Soveraigne for to mocke.	•	1Tamb	1.1.105	Mycet
Why Madam, thinke ye to mocke me thus palpably?	•	2Tamb	4.2.67	Therid
Her lover let her mocke, that long will raigne,		Ovid's Elegies	2.19.33	

MOCKED
It mocked me, hung down the head and suncke,	•	Ovid's Elegies	3.6.14

MOCKES
They should know how I scornde them and their mockes.	•	P 762	15.20	Guise

MOCKST
Why mockst thou me she cried, or being ill,		Ovid's Elegies	3.6.77

MOCKT
Venus to mockt men lendes a sencelesse eare.	•	Ovid's Elegies	1.8.86	
And unrevengd mockt Gods with me doth scoffe.	• •	Ovid's Elegies	3.3.20	
And with his flaring beames mockt ougly night,	•	Hero and Leander	2.332	

MODERATE
See Love with me, wine moderate in my braine,	•	Ovid's Elegies	1.6.37

MODERATELY
But yet their gift more moderately use,	• •	Ovid's Elegies	3.3.47

MODEST
maides to weare/Their bowe and quiver in this modest sort,		Dido	1.1.205	Venus
give Dido leave/To be more modest then her thoughts admit,		Dido	3.1.95	Dido
Infringing all excuse of modest shame,	•	Lucan, First Booke	266	
Naked simplicitie, and modest grace.	•	Ovid's Elegies	1.3.14	
If any eie mee with a modest looke,	•	Ovid's Elegies	2.4.11	
shee her modest eyes held downe,/Her wofull bosome a warme		Ovid's Elegies	3.5.67	

MODESTIE
Fancie and modestie shall live as mates,	•	Dido	3.2.58	Venus

MODESTLY
And modestly they opened as she rose:		Hero and Leander	1.160	

MODESTY
Though womans modesty should hale me backe,	• •	Jew	4.2.45	Curtzn

MOE
Yet lives/My brother Duke Dumaine, and many moe:	•	P1099	20.9	Cardnl

MOHAMMED (See MAHOMET)

MOIST

That this, or that man may thy cheekes moist keepe. . . Ovid's Elegies 1.8.84
painted stands/All naked holding in her wave-moist hands. Ovid's Elegies 1.14.34
Would first my beautious wenches moist lips touch, . . . Ovid's Elegies 2.15.17
To lay my body on the hard moist floore. . . . . . Ovid's Elegies 3.10.10

MOISTENED

A grassie turffe the moistened earth doth hide. . . Ovid's Elegies 2.16.10

MOISTURE

The heat and moisture which did feed each other, . . 1Tamb 2.7.46 Cosroe
But (wanting moisture and remorsefull blood)/Drie up with 2Tamb 4.1.179 Soria
Whereby the moisture of your blood is dried, ... 2Tamb 5.3.85 Phsitn
Pure waters moisture thirst away did keepe. . . . Ovid's Elegies 2.6.32

MOLD (Homograph; See also MOULD)

And fram'd of finer mold then common men, ... Jew 1.2.219 Barab
What difference betwixt the richest mine/And basest mold, but Hero and Leander 1.233
Nor is't of earth or mold celestiall, ... Hero and Leander 1.273

MOLE (See also MOALE)

Had on her necke a little wart, or mole; . . . . . F1267 4.1.113 Emper

MOLEST

And may th'earths weight thy ashes nought molest. . . Ovid's Elegies 3.8.68

MOLLIFIDE

Pleasure, and ease had mollifide my minde. . . . Ovid's Elegies 1.9.42

MOLLIFIE

My teares nor plaints could mollifie a whit: . . . . Dido 5.1.235 Anna
Had power to mollifie his stonie hart, ... Edw 2.4.20 Queene

MOMENT

Which in a moment will abridge his life: . . . . . Edw 5.1.42 Edward
Or speake to him who in a moment tooke, ... Hero and Leander 2.308

MONARCH

To make himselfe the Monarch of the East: . . . . . 1Tamb 1.1.43 Meandr
We here doo crowne thee Monarch of the East, ... 1Tamb 1.1.161 Ortyg
Born to be Monarch of the Western world: . . . . . 2Tamb 1.2.3 Callap
Or bring before this royall Emperour/The mightie Monarch, F1297 4.1.143 Faust
Made the grim monarch of infernall spirits, ... F1371 4.2.47 Fredrk
More lovely then the Monarch of the sky, ... F1785 5.1.112 Faust
Monarch of hel, under whose blacke survey/Great Potentates do F App p.235 34 Mephst

MONARCHA

[Lucifer], Belzebub inferni ardentis monarcha, et Demogorgon, F 246 1.3.18 P Faust

MONARCHIE

And commons of this mightie Monarchie, ... 1Tamb 1.1.138 Ortyg
Defend his freedome gainst a Monarchie: . . . . . 1Tamb 2.1.56 Ceneus
Make severall kingdomes of this monarchie, ... Edw 1.4.70 Edward
Then if I gain'd another Monarchie. . . . . . . F1272 4.1.118 Emper

MONARCHY

Dis do we ascend/To view the subjects of our Monarchy, . F1798 5.2.2 Lucifr
At last learne wretch to leave thy monarchy; . . . Lucan, First Booke 335

MONARCK

To beat the papall Monarck from our lands, ... P 802 16.16 Navrre
Which if I doe, the Papall Monarck goes/To wrack, and [his] P1197 22.59 King

MONARK

That I shall be the Monark of the East, ... 1Tamb 1.2.185 Tamb
Nor am I made Arch-monark of the world, ... 2Tamb 4.1.150 Tamb

MONARKE

The high and highest Monarke of the world, ... 1Tamb 3.1.26 Bajzth
Most great and puisant Monarke of the earth, ... 1Tamb 3.1.41 Bassoe
Arch-Monarke of the world, I offer here, ... 2Tamb 1.3.114 Therid
And wife unto the Monarke of the East. . . . . . 2Tamb 3.2.22 Amyras
Casane no, the Monarke of the earth, ... 2Tamb 5.3.216 Tamb

MONARKES

ascend so high/As Didos heart, which Monarkes might not scale. Dido 3.4.34 Aeneas
were woont to quake/And tremble at the Persean Monarkes name, 1Tamb 1.1.116 Cosroe

MONARKY

Vaine man, what Monarky expectst thou here? . . . Dido 5.1.34 Hermes

MONASTERY

that there is a monastery/Which standeth as an out-house to the Jew 5.3.36 Msngr
Enter'd the Monastery, and underneath/In severall places are Jew 5.5.26 Barab

MONASTRY

But here's a royall Monastry hard by, ... Jew 4.1.13 Ithimr

MONE

Oh my sweet hart, how do I mone thy wrongs, ... Edw 4.2.27 Queene
For whom succeeding times make greater mone. . . . Hero and Leander 1.54

MONED

And with sweete words cause deafe rockes to have loved <moned>, Ovid's Elegies 3.6.58

MONES

Their blubbered cheekes and hartie humble mones/Will melt his 1Tamb 5.1.21 Govnr

MONESTARIES

As Monestaries, Priories, Abbyes and halles, . . . P 138 2.81 Guise

MONETHS

starv'd, and he be provided for a moneths victuall before hand. 1Tamb 4.4.46 P Usumc
And laine in leagre fifteene moneths and more, . . . 2Tamb 1.3.176 Usumc

MONEY (See also MONY)

You will give us our money? . . . . P 942 19.12 P AllMur
Who should defray the money, but the King, ... Edw 2.2.118 Mortmr
We will finde comfort, money, men, and friends/Ere long, to bid Edw 4.2.65 SrJohn
Well, I will not stand with thee, give me the money: . F1466 4.4.10 P Faust
and never tyre, I gave him his money; so when I had my horse, F1539 4.5.35 P HrsCsr
Wel, come give me your money, my boy wil deliver him to you: F App p.239 107 P Faust

'MONG

'Mong which as chiefe, Faustus we come to thee, . . F1800 5.2.4 Lucifr

MONGER

he lookes as like [a] conjurer as the Pope to a Coster-monger. F1229 4.1.75 P Benvol

MONGST

at whose pallace now]/[Faustus is feasted amongst his noblemen]. F1148 3.3.65A 3Chor

MONIED				
Thou art a Merchant, and a monied man,	Jew	1.2.53		1Knght
MONKES				
Yet gentle monkes, for treasure, golde nor fee,	Edw	4.7.24		Edward
To make his Monkes and Abbots stand like Apes,	F 861	3.1.83		Mephst
MONKS (See also MUNKE)				
Good master let me poyson all the Monks.	Jew	4.1.14		Ithimr
MONSTER				
Monster of Nature, shame unto thy stocke,	1Tamb	1.1.104		Mycet
Or Monster turned to a manly shape,	1Tamb	2.6.16		Ortyg
A monster of five hundred thousand heades,	1Tamb	4.3.7		Souldn
O damned monster, nay a Feend of Hell,	2Tamb	4.1.168		Jrslem
Vile monster, borne of some infernal hag,	2Tamb	5.1.110		Govnr
The Monster that hath drunke a sea of blood,	2Tamb	5.2.13		Amasia
where my slave, the uglie monster death/Shaking and quivering,	2Tamb	5.3.67		Tamb
And eielesse Monster that torments my soule,	2Tamb	5.3.217		Tamb
Tis not the hugest monster of the sea,	Edw	2.2.45		Edward
Monster of men,/That like the Greekish strumpet traind to armes	Edw	2.5.14		Lncstr
MONSTEROUS				
were that Tamburlaine/As monsterous as Gorgon, prince of Hell,	1Tamb	4.1.18		Souldn
MONSTERS				
See monsters see, ile weare my crowne againe,	Edw	5.1.74		Edward
First he commands such monsters Nature hatcht/Against her kind	Lucan, First Booke			588
MONSTROUS				
So will I send this monstrous slave to hell,	1Tamb	2.6.7		Cosroe
nor no hope of end/To our infamous monstrous slaveries?	1Tamb	5.1.241		Zabina
Fenc'd with the concave of a monstrous rocke,	2Tamb	3.2.89		Tamb
Streching their monstrous pawes, grin with their teeth,	2Tamb	3.5.28		Orcan
And covetousnesse, oh 'tis a monstrous sinne.	Jew	1.2.124		Govnr
Oh monstrous villany.	Jew	3.6.30		2Fryar
Oh monstrous treason!	Jew	5.5.108		Calym
Thou hadst not hatcht this monstrous treacherie!	Edw	5.6.97		King
O monstrous, eate a whole load of Hay!	F1532	4.5.28	P	All
Bred in the concave of some monstrous rocke:	F App	p.238 73		Knight
from the breach/Of Libian Syrtes roules a monstrous wave,	Lucan, First Booke			497
MONTH (See also MONETHS)				
But a month.	Jew	1.2.27		Govnr
We grant a month, but see you keep your promise.	Jew	1.2.28		Calym
Two, three, foure month Madam.	Jew	4.4.55	P	Barab
serve to entertaine/Selim and all his souldiers for a month;	Jew	5.3.31		Msngr
Why so, they barkt a pace a month agoe,	Edw	4.3.12		Edward
or let this houre be but/A yeare, a month, a weeke, a naturall	F1933	5.2.137		Faust
and in the month of January, how you shuld come by these	F App	p.242 17	P	Duke
MONTHS				
toyl'd to inherit here/The months of vanity and losse of time,	Jew	1.2.197		Barab
MONUMENT				
and let them be interr'd/Within one sacred monument of stone;	Jew	3.2.30		Govnr
MONUMENTS				
Are not thy bils hung up as monuments,	F 48	1.1.20		Faust
That I do long to see the Monuments/And situation of bright	F 828	3.1.50		Faust
Bearing old spoiles and conquerors monuments,	Lucan, First Booke			138
MONY				
Which mony was not got without my meanes.	Jew	Prol.32		Machvl
And for the mony send our messenger.	Jew	1.2.31		Calym
And 'tis thy mony, Barabas, we seeke.	Jew	1.2.54		1Knght
How, my Lord, my mony?	Jew	1.2.55		Barab
mony of the Turkes shall all be levyed amongst the Jewes,	Jew	1.2.68	P	Reader
You have my goods, my mony, and my wealth,	Jew	1.2.138		Barab
gather of these goods/The mony for this tribute of the Turke.	Jew	1.2.156		Govnr
He'de give us present mony for them all.	Jew	2.3.6		1Offcr
of those Nuns/And holy Fryers, having mony for their paines,	Jew	2.3.81		Barab
up to the Jewes counting-house where I saw some bags of mony,	Jew	3.1.19	P	Pilia
And for the Tribute-mony I am sent.	Jew	3.5.10		Basso
True, I have mony, what though I have?	Jew	4.1.30		Barab
Great summes of mony lying in the bancho;	Jew	4.1.74		Barab
I'le goe steale some mony from my Master to make me hansome:	Jew	4.2.49	P	Ithimr
I'le write unto him, we'le have mony strait.	Jew	4.2.69	P	Ithimr
Take thou the mony, spend it for my sake.	Jew	4.2.123		Ithimr
'Tis not thy mony, but thy selfe I weigh:	Jew	4.2.124		Curtzn
Ha, to the Jew, and send me mony you were best.	Jew	4.4.12	P	Ithimr
thou that Jew whose goods we heard were sold/For Tribute-mony?	Jew	5.1.74		Calym
privately procure/Great summes of mony for thy recompence:	Jew	5.2.88		Govnr
And let me see what mony thou canst make;	Jew	5.2.94		Barab
and give me my mony againe, for your horse is turned to a	F1490	4.4.34	P	HrsCsr
so he presently gave me my mony, and fell to eating;	F1530	4.5.26	P	Carter
we will be wellcome for our mony, and we will pay for what we	F1611	4.6.54	P	Robin
The whore stands to be bought for each mans mony/And seekes	Ovid's Elegies			1.10.21
MOOD				
Wel said Theridamas, speake in that mood,	1Tamb	3.3.40		Tamb
Come, let us leave him in his irefull mood,	Jew	1.2.209		1Jew
MOODE				
I like not this relenting moode in Edmund,	Edw	4.6.38		Mortmr
MOON				
when the Moon begins/To joine in one her semi-circled hornes:	1Tamb	3.1.11		Bajzth
my souldiers march/Shal rise aloft and touch the horned Moon,	2Tamb	1.3.14		Tamb
MOONE				
That imitate the Moone in every chaunge,	Dido	3.3.67		Iarbus
Before the Moone renew her borrowed light,	1Tamb	1.1.69		Therid
The Moone, the Planets, and the Meteors light.	1Tamb	5.1.150		Tamb
Whose absence make the sun and Moone as darke/As when opposde	2Tamb	2.4.51		Tamb
ancient use, shall beare/The figure of the semi-circled Moone:	2Tamb	3.1.65		Orcan
And every Moone made some or other mad,	Jew	2.3.195		Barab
Be it to make the Moone drop from her Sphere,	F 266	1.3.38		Faust

MOONE (cont.)			
<Tel me>, are there many Spheares <heavens> above the Moone?	F 586	2.2.35	Faust
Even from the Moone unto the Emperiall Orbe,	F 590	2.2.39	Mephst
Venus, and Mercury in a yeare; the Moone in twenty eight daies.	F 605	2.2.54	P Faust
From the bright circle of the horned Moone,	F 762	2.3.41	2Chor
But now the winters wrath and wat'ry moone,	Lucan, First Booke		219
Or that the wandring maine follow the moone;	Lucan, First Booke		415
The purple moone with sanguine visage stood.	Ovid's Elegies		1.8.12
The Moone sleepes with Endemion everie day,	Ovid's Elegies		1.13.43
With sunne and moone Aratus shall remaine.	Ovid's Elegies		1.15.16
Verses [deduce] <reduce> the horned bloudy moone/And call the	Ovid's Elegies		2.1.23
Or when the Moone travailes with charmed steedes.	Ovid's Elegies		2.5.38
MOORE (See also MORES)			
The wealthy Moore, that in the Easterne rockes/Without	Jew	1.1.21	Barab
Ratest thou this Moore but at two hundred plats?	Jew	2.3.107	Lodowk
Why should this Turke be dearer then that Moore?	Jew	2.3.109	Barab
This Moore is comeliest, is he not? speake son.	Jew	2.3.144	Mater
MOORES			
Aeneas may commaund as many Moores,	Dido	4.4.62	Dido
Ye Moores and valiant men of Barbary,	1Tamb	3.3.89	Moroc
Turkes, Arabians, Moores and Jewes/Enough to cover all Bythinia.	1Tamb	3.3.136	Bajzth
Egyptians, Moores and men of Asia,	1Tamb	5.1.517	Tamb
And with an hoste of Moores trainde to the war,	2Tamb	1.3.141	Techel
Captaine, these Moores shall cut the leaden pipes,	2Tamb	3.3.29	Techel
And Moores, in whom was never pitie found,	2Tamb	3.4.20	Olymp
Our fraught is Grecians, Turks, and Africk Moores.	Jew	2.2.9	Bosco
As Indian Moores, obey their Spanish Lords,	F 148	1.1.120	Valdes
(Albeit the Moores light Javelin or his speare/Sticks in his	Lucan, First Booke		213
And furious Cymbrians and of Carthage Moores,	Lucan, First Booke		257
MOORISH			
every fixed starre/To sucke up poison from the moorish Fens,	1Tamb	4.2.6	Bajzth
MOORNE			
Hees gone, and for his absence thus I moorne,	Edw	1.4.305	Edward
Maids of England, sore may you moorne,	Edw	2.2.190	Lncstr
Shall I not moorne for my beloved lord,	Edw	5.6.87	Queene
Heere comes the hearse, helpe me to moorne, my lords:	Edw	5.6.98	King
MOORNING			
And body with continuall moorning wasted:	Edw	2.4.25	Queene
MOORS			
Cicilians, Jewes, Arabians, Turks, and Moors,	2Tamb	1.1.62	Orcan
MOOV'D			
Me thinks we should not, I am strongly moov'd,	1Tamb	2.5.75	Tamb
Moov'd me to manage armes against thy state.	1Tamb	2.7.16	Tamb
And pardon me that was not moov'd with ruthe,	1Tamb	5.1.369	Zenoc
Why are you moov'd, be patient my lord,	Edw	1.4.43	ArchBp
Moov'd may he be, and perish in his wrath.	Edw	2.2.101	Mortmr
The barbarous Thratian soldier moov'd with nought,	Hero and Leander		1.81
Was moov'd with him, and for his favour sought.	Hero and Leander		1.82
MOOV'DE			
If ye be moov'de, revenge it as you can,	Edw	2.2.198	Lncstr
MOOVDE			
Lets to our castels, for the king is moovde.	Edw	2.2.100	Warwck
Take it: what are you moovde, pitie you me?	Edw	5.1.102	Edward
MOOVE			
But if these threats moove not submission,	1Tamb	4.1.58	2Msngr
Not for all Affrike, therefore moove me not.	2Tamb	1.2.12	Almeda
When heaven shal cease to moove on both the poles/And when the	2Tamb	1.3.12	Tamb
That I might moove the turning Spheares of heaven,	2Tamb	4.1.118	Tamb
No one face likes me best, all faces moove,	Ovid's Elegies		2.4.9
MOOVED			
If with the sight thereof she be not mooved,	Edw	5.1.119	Edward
On mooved hookes set ope the churlish dore.	Ovid's Elegies		1.6.2
And like a burthen greevde the bed that mooved not.	Ovid's Elegies		3.6.4
MOOVER			
first moover of that Spheare/Enchac'd with thousands ever	1Tamb	4.2.8	Tamb
MOOVES			
That mooves not upwards, nor by princely deeds/Doth meane to	1Tamb	2.7.32	Therid
Wherein an incorporeall spirit mooves,	2Tamb	4.1.114	Tamb
that the soule/Wanting those Organnons by which it mooves,	2Tamb	5.3.96	Phsitn
Perchance these, others, me mine owne losse mooves.	Ovid's Elegies		3.5.100
Greefe makes her pale, because she mooves not there.	Hero and Leander		1.60
MOOVING			
And alwaies mooving as the restles Spheares,	1Tamb	2.7.25	Tamb
By heaven, and all the mooving orbes thereof,	Edw	3.1.129	Edward
And like a planet, mooving severall waies,	Hero and Leander		1.361
MOR (Homograph)			
And tell my soule mor tales of bleeding ruth?	1Tamb	5.1.342	Zenoc
Mor du, wert <were> not the fruit within thy wombe,	P 688	13.32	Guise
Par [le] <la> mor du, Il mora.	P 770	15.28	Guise
MORA			
Par [le] <la> mor du, Il mora.	P 770	15.28	Guise
MORARIS			
[Quid tu moraris] <quod tumeraris>; per Jehovam, Gehennam, et	F 248	1.3.20	P Faust
MORE (See also MO, MOE, MOR)			
I vow, if she but once frowne on thee more,	Dido	1.1.12	Jupitr
Hermes no more shall shew the world his wings,	Dido	1.1.38	Jupitr
That they may trip more lightly ore the lawndes,	Dido	1.1.207	Venus
And tell our griefes in more familiar termes:	Dido	1.1.246	Aeneas
Might we but once more see Aeneas face,	Dido	1.2.45	Serg
And after him a thousand Grecians more,	Dido	2.1.185	Aeneas
O end Aeneas, I can heare no more.	Dido	2.1.243	Dido
No more my child, now talke another while,	Dido	3.1.26	Dido
In whose faire bosome I will locke more wealth,	Dido	3.1.92	Dido

MORE (cont.)

give Dido leave/To be more modest then her thoughts admit,	Dido	3.1.95	Dido
As without blushing I can aske no more:	Dido	3.1.104	Aeneas
Flinging in favours of more soveraigne worth,	Dido	3.1.131	Dido
Troy shall no more call him her second hope,	Dido	3.2.8	Juno
More then melodious are these words to me,	Dido	3.2.62	Juno
But that thou maist more easilie perceive,	Dido	3.2.66	Juno
What more then Delian musicke doe I heare,	Dido	3.4.52	Dido
Whose yeelding heart may yeeld thee more reliefe.	Dido	4.2.36	Anna
Anna that doth admire thee more then heaven.	Dido	4.2.46	Anna
Ye shall no more offend the Carthage Queene.	Dido	4.4.158	Dido
Ile be no more a widowe, I am young,	Dido	4.5.22	Nurse
Carthage shall vaunt her pettie walles no more,	Dido	5.1.4	Aeneas
And yong Iulus more then thousand yeares,	Dido	5.1.39	Hermes
Whereat the Souldiers will conceive more joy,	1Tamb	1.1.152	Ceneus
and this curtle-axe/Are adjuncts more beseeming Tamburlaine.	1Tamb	1.2.43	Tamb
Thinke you I way this treasure more than you?	1Tamb	1.2.84	Tamb
Thy person is more woorth to Tamburlaine,	1Tamb	1.2.90	Tamb
More rich and valurous than Zenocrates.	1Tamb	1.2.97	Tamb
Could use perswasions more patheticall.	1Tamb	1.2.211	Therid
Nor are Apollos Oracles more true,	1Tamb	1.2.212	Tamb
These are my friends in whom I more rejoice,	1Tamb	1.2.241	Tamb
A pearle more worth, then all the world is plaste:	1Tamb	2.1.12	Menaph
And more regarding gaine than victory:	1Tamb	2.2.46	Meandr
You fighting more for honor than for gold,	1Tamb	2.2.66	Meandr
Shall threat the Gods more than Cyclopian warres,	1Tamb	2.3.21	Tamb
And more than needes to make an Emperour.	1Tamb	2.3.65	Tamb
I judge the purchase more important far.	1Tamb	2.5.92	Therid
And lose more labor than the gaine will quight.	1Tamb	2.5.96	Tamb
But give him warning and more warriours.	1Tamb	2.5.103	Tamb
So, now it is more surer on my head,	1Tamb	2.7.65	Tamb
Twere requisite he should be ten times more,	1Tamb	3.1.47	Argier
Tis more then pitty such a heavenly face/Should by hearts	1Tamb	3.2.4	Agidas
And gives no more than common courtesies.	1Tamb	3.2.63	Agidas
More honor and lesse paine it may procure,	1Tamb	3.2.97	Agidas
are ful of brags/And menace more than they can wel performe:	1Tamb	3.3.4	Tamb
Withdraw as many more to follow him.	1Tamb	3.3.22	Bassoe
The more he brings, the greater is the spoile,	1Tamb	3.3.23	Techel
More mighty than the Turkish Emperour:	1Tamb	3.3.37	Therid
Their lims more large and of a bigger size/Than all the brats	1Tamb	3.3.108	Bajzth
And speech more pleasant than sweet harmony:	1Tamb	3.3.121	Tamb
that the Souldan is/No more dismaide with tidings of his fall,	1Tamb	4.3.31	Souldn
highnesse would let them be fed, it would doe them more good.	1Tamb	4.4.35	P Therid
I Tyrant, and more meat.	1Tamb	4.4.102	P Bajzth
These more than dangerous warrants of our death,	1Tamb	5.1.31	1Virgn
Whose sorrowes lay more siege unto my soule,	1Tamb	5.1.155	Tamb
No more there is not I warrant thee Techelles.	1Tamb	5.1.202	Tamb
More than Cymerian Stix or Distinie.	1Tamb	5.1.234	Bajzth
O life more loathsome to my vexed thoughts,	1Tamb	5.1.255	Bajzth
That she shall stay and turne her wheele no more,	1Tamb	5.1.374	Anippe
And ad more strength to your dominions/Than ever yet confirm'd	1Tamb	5.1.448	Tamb
Adding more courage to my conquering mind.	1Tamb	5.1.515	Tamb
More then his Camp of stout Hungarians,	2Tamb	1.1.21	Uribas
Then shalt thou see a hundred kings and more/Upon their knees,	2Tamb	1.2.28	Callap
And more than this, for all I cannot tell.	2Tamb	1.2.53	Callap
more precious in mine eies/Than all the wealthy kingdomes I	2Tamb	1.3.18	Tamb
And shine in compleat vertue more than they,	2Tamb	1.3.51	Tamb
It could not more delight me than your sight.	2Tamb	1.3.156	Tamb
In number more than are the drops that fall/When Boreas rents a	2Tamb	1.3.159	Tamb
And laine in leagre fifteene moneths and more,	2Tamb	1.3.176	Usumc
And numbers more than infinit of men,	2Tamb	2.2.18	Gazell
Shine downwards now no more, but deck the heavens/To entertaine	2Tamb	2.4.20	Tamb
Ah sweet Theridamas, say so no more,	2Tamb	2.4.126	Tamb
Sorrow no more my sweet Casane now:	2Tamb	3.2.44	Tamb
Because the corners there may fall more flat,	2Tamb	3.2.65	Tamb
In whose high lookes is much more majesty/Than from the Concave	2Tamb	3.4.47	Therid
In frame of which, Nature hath shewed more skill,	2Tamb	3.4.75	Techel
In number more than are the quyvering leaves/Of Idas forrest,	2Tamb	3.5.5	2Msngr
and stout Bythinians/Came to my bands full fifty thousand more,	2Tamb	3.5.42	Trebiz
you wil be thought/More childish valourous than manly wise:	2Tamb	4.1.17	Calyph
Have greater operation and more force/Than Cynthias in the	2Tamb	4.2.29	Therid
Leave this my Love, and listen more to me.	2Tamb	4.2.38	Therid
Were not subdew'd with valour more divine,	2Tamb	4.3.15	Tamb
queintly dect/With bloomes more white than Hericinas browes,	2Tamb	4.3.122	Tamb
Villaine, respects thou more thy slavish life,	2Tamb	5.1.10	Govnr
More strong than are the gates of death or hel?	2Tamb	5.1.20	Govnr
More exquisite than ever Traitor felt.	2Tamb	5.1.53	Therid
we offer more/Than ever yet we did to such proud slaves,	2Tamb	5.1.57	Techel
And that shal bide no more regard of parlie.	2Tamb	5.1.61	Techel
Which threatned more than if the region/Next underneath the	2Tamb	5.1.87	Tamb
There lies more gold than Babylon is worth,	2Tamb	5.1.116	Govnr
Away with him hence, let him speake no more:	2Tamb	5.1.125	Tamb
our hearts/More than the thought of this dooth vexe our soules.	2Tamb	5.1.145	Jrslem
And yet gapes stil for more to quench his thirst,	2Tamb	5.2.14	Amasia
But of a substance more divine and pure,	2Tamb	5.3.88	Phsitn
More worth than Asia, and the world beside,	2Tamb	5.3.153	Tamb
Eastward behold/As much more land, which never was descried,	2Tamb	5.3.155	Tamb
More than the ruine of our proper soules.	2Tamb	5.3.182	Therid
Through rocks more steepe and sharp than Caspian cliftes.	2Tamb	5.3.241	Tamb
More then heavens coach, the pride of Phaeton.	2Tamb	5.3.244	Tamb
For both their woorths wil equall him no more.	2Tamb	5.3.253	Amyras
built Citadell/Commands much more then letters can import:	Jew	Prol.23	Machvl
The very Custome barely comes to more/Then many Merchants of	Jew	1.1.63	1Merch

MORE (cont.)

What more may Heaven doe for earthly man/Then thus to powre out	Jew	1.1.107	Barab
scambled up/More wealth by farre then those that brag of faith.	Jew	1.1.123	Barab
That's more then is in our Commission.	Jew	1.2.22	Basso
And 'tis more Kingly to obtaine by peace/Then to enforce	Jew	1.2.25	Calym
Soft Barabas, there's more longs too't than so.	Jew	1.2.45	Govnr
Live still; and if thou canst, get more.	Jew	1.2.102	Govnr
From little unto more, from more to most:	Jew	1.2.106	1Knght
I must be forc'd to steale and compasse more.	Jew	1.2.127	Barab
which being valued/Amount to more then all the wealth in Malta.	Jew	1.2.134	Offcrs
And having all, you can request no more;	Jew	1.2.140	Barab
But they will give me leave once more, I trow,	Jew	1.2.252	Barab
And of my former riches rests no more/But bare remembrance;	Jew	2.1.9	Barab
There's more, and more, and more.	Jew	2.1.46	P Abigal
will I shew my selfe to have more of the Serpent then the Dove;	Jew	2.3.36	P Barab
of the Serpent then the Dove; that is, more knave than foole.	Jew	2.3.37	P Barab
No more, my Lord.	Jew	2.3.108	1Offcr
Because he is young and has more qualities.	Jew	2.3.110	1Offcr
Daughter, a word more; kisse him, speake him faire,	Jew	2.3.234	Barab
Stay her,--but let her not speake one word more.	Jew	2.3.323	Barab
Abigal I will, but see thou change no more,	Jew	3.3.70	1Fryar
from hence/Ne're shall she grieve me more with her disgrace;	Jew	3.4.29	Barab
make her round and plump, and batten more then you are aware.	Jew	3.4.66	P Ithimr
And nought to us more welcome is then wars.	Jew	3.5.36	Govnr
And one offence torments me more then all.	Jew	3.6.19	Abigal
No more but so: it must and shall be done.	Jew	4.1.128	Barab
Why, a Turke could ha done no more.	Jew	4.1.198	P Ithimr
It may be she sees more in me than I can find in my selfe:	Jew	4.2.33	P Ithimr
Goe to, no more, I'le make him send me half he has, and glad he	Jew	4.2.66	P Ithimr
and this shall be your warrant; if you doe not, no more but so.	Jew	4.2.76	P Ithimr
The more villaine he to keep me thus:	Jew	4.2.111	Ithimr
Jew, I must ha more gold.	Jew	4.3.18	P Pilia
No Sir; and therefore I must have five hundred more.	Jew	4.3.22	P Pilia
And fit it should: but first let's ha more gold.	Jew	4.4.26	Curtzn
Give him a crowne, and fill me out more wine.	Jew	4.4.46	Ithimr
Farewell Fidler: One letter more to the Jew.	Jew	4.4.72	Pilia
Prethe sweet love, one more, and write it sharp.	Jew	4.4.73	Curtzn
One dram of powder more had made all sure.	Jew	5.1.22	Barab
Once more away with him; you shall have law.	Jew	5.1.40	Govnr
Away, no more, let him not trouble me.	Jew	5.2.26	Barab
But Barabas will be more circumspect.	Jew	5.2.43	Barab
Nay more, doe this, and live thou Governor still.	Jew	5.2.89	Govnr
wel since it is no more/I'le satisfie my selfe with that;	Jew	5.5.21	Barab
Besides a thousand sturdy student Catholicks,/And more:	P 141	2.84	Guise
All this and more, if more may be comprisde,	P 143	2.86	Guise
And that I am not more secure my selfe,	P 264	4.62	Charls
And meane once more to menace me.	P 364	7.4	Ramus
Come Ramus, more golde, or thou shalt have the stabbe.	P 376	7.16	Gonzag
All this and more your highnes shall commaund,	P 479	8.29	Lord
There are a hundred Hugonets and more,	P 501	9.20	Guise
Cannot but march with many graces more:	P 578	11.43	Pleshe
All this and more hath Henry with his crowne.	P 596	12.9	QnMoth
And long may Henry enjoy all this and more.	P 597	12.10	Cardnl
goe sirra, worke no more,/Till this our Coronation day be past:	P 623	12.36	King
But for you know our quarrell is no more,	P 704	14.7	Navrre
How now my Lord, faith this is more then need,	P 757	15.15	Guise
Tis more then kingly or Emperious.	P 759	15.17	Guise
And either never mannage army more,	P 793	16.7	Bartus
My Lord, to speak more plainely, thus it is:	P 847	17.42	Guise
We will goe talke more of this within.	P1138	21.32	Dumain
gathered now shall ayme/more at thie end then exterpatione	Paris	ms29,p391	Guise
Not Hilas was more mourned of Hercules,	Edw	1.1.144	Edward
no soule in hell/Hath felt more torment then poore Gaveston.	Edw	1.1.147	Gavstn
Ile give thee more, for but to honour thee,	Edw	1.1.164	Edward
I did no more then I was bound to do,	Edw	1.1.182	BshpCv
Nay more, the guarde upon his lordship waites:	Edw	1.2.21	Lncstr
of Lancaster/That hath more earldomes then an asse can beare,	Edw	1.3.2	Gavstn
But I long more to see him banisht hence.	Edw	1.4.5	Warwck
Because he loves me more then all the world:	Edw	1.4.77	Edward
I shal be found, and then twil greeve me more.	Edw	1.4.132	Gavstn
I say no more, judge you the rest my lord.	Edw	1.4.148	Gavstn
But that will more exasperate his wrath,	Edw	1.4.182	Queene
Nay more, when he shall know it lies in us,	Edw	1.4.274	Mortmr
I love him more/Then he can Gaveston, would he lov'd me	Edw	1.4.302	Queene
about my neck/Then these my lord, nor let me have more wealth,	Edw	1.4.331	Queene
Once more receive my hand, and let this be,	Edw	1.4.334	Edward
And may it proove more happie then the first.	Edw	1.4.336	Queene
These silver haires will more adorne my court,	Edw	1.4.346	Edward
and in his tuskan cap/A jewell of more value then the crowne.	Edw	1.4.415	Mortmr
You have matters of more waight to thinke upon,	Edw	2.2.8	Mortmr
My lord, mines more obscure then Mortimers.	Edw	2.2.22	Lncstr
Desirde her more, and waxt outragious,	Edw	2.2.55	Edward
Frolicks not more to see the paynted springe,	Edw	2.2.62	Gavstn
No more then I would answere were he slaine.	Edw	2.2.86	Mortmr
Yes more then thou canst answer though he live,	Edw	2.2.87	Edward
And when tis gone, our swordes shall purchase more.	Edw	2.2.197	Lncstr
Out of my sight, and trouble me no more.	Edw	2.2.216	Edward
Sweet unckle speake more kindly to the queene.	Edw	2.2.228	Neece
Scarce shall you finde a man of more desart.	Edw	2.2.251	Gavstn
Yet once more ile importune him with praiers,	Edw	2.4.63	Queene
Not so my Lord, least he bestow more cost,	Edw	2.5.55	Lncstr
Cause yet more bloudshed:	Edw	2.5.83	Warwck

MORE (cont.)

Beside, the more to manifest our love,	Edw	3.1.52		Edward
Commit not to my youth things of more waight/Then fits a prince	Edw	3.1.74		Prince
great beames/On Atlas shoulder, shall not lie more safe,	Edw	3.1.77		Prince
I would he never had bin flattered more.	Edw	4.4.30		Kent
O never more lift up this dying hart!	Edw	4.7.43		Edward
Parted from hence, never to see us more!	Edw	4.7.101		Spencr
More safetie is there in a Tigers jawes,	Edw	5.1.116		Edward
To set his brother free, no more but so.	Edw	5.2.33		BshpWn
And by the way to make him fret the more,	Edw	5.2.62		Mortmr
The more my greefe.	Edw	5.2.84		Queene
The more cause have I now to make amends.	Edw	5.2.103		Kent
What else my lord? and farre more resolute.	Edw	5.4.23		Ltborn
Take this, away, and never see me more.	Edw	5.4.43		Mortmr
Feard am I more then lov'd, let me be feard,	Edw	5.4.52		Mortmr
At our commaund, once more away with him.	Edw	5.4.104		Mortmr
Much more a king brought up so tenderlie.	Edw	5.5.6		Matrvs
More then we can enflict, and therefore now,	Edw	5.5.11		Matrvs
O speake no more my lorde, this breakes my heart.	Edw	5.5.71		Ltborn
My minde may be more stedfast on my God.	Edw	5.5.78		Edward
And glutted now <more> with learnings golden gifts,	F 24	Prol.24		1Chor
Then read no more, thou hast attain'd that <the> end;	F 38	1.1.10		Faust
Shadowing more beauty in their Airie browes,	F 155	1.1.127		Valdes
And more frequented for this mysterie,	F 169	1.1.141		Cornel
No more then he commands, must we performe.	F 270	1.3.42		Mephst
Cast no more doubts; Mephostophilis come/And bring glad tydings	F 415	2.1.27		Faust
And give thee more then thou hast wit to aske.	F 436	2.1.48		Mephst
My bloud congeales, and I can write no more.	F 451	2.1.63		Faust
And if thou lovest me thinke no more of it.	F 536	2.1.148		Mephst
[Nay let me have one booke more, and then I have done, wherein	F 551.8	2.1.171A	P	Faust
was> made for man; then he's <therefore is man> more excellent.	F 560	2.2.9		Mephst
all at one time, but in some years we have more, in some lesse?	F 616	2.2.65	P	Faust
not speake a word more for a Kings ransome <an other worde>,	F 669	2.2.118	P	Pride
I'le not speake <a word more for a kings ransome>.	F 706	(HC264)B	P	Sloth
Faustus no more: see where the Cardinals come.	F1008	3.2.28		Mephst
Shall adde more excellence unto thine Art,	F1208	4.1.54		Emper
order, I'le nere trust smooth faces, and small ruffes more.	F1318	4.1.164	P	Benvol
But yet my [heart's] <heart> more ponderous then my head,	F1351	4.2.27		Benvol
let's devise how we may adde more shame/To the blacke scandall	F1377	4.2.53		Fredrk
sell him, but if thou likest him for ten Dollors more, take him,	F1461	4.4.5	P	Faust
Some more drinke Hostesse.	F1555	4.5.51	P	Carter
so delighted me, as nothing in the world could please me more.	F1562	4.6.5	P	Duke
Madam, I will do more then this for your content.	F1575	4.6.18	P	Faust
This makes me wonder more then all the rest, that at this time	F1578	4.6.21	P	Duke
I hope sir, we have wit enough to be more bold then welcome.	F1595	4.6.38	P	HrsCsr
More lovely then the Monarch of the sky,	F1785	5.1.112		Faust
Nothing but vexe thee more,/To want in hell, that had on earth	F1897	5.2.101		BdAngl
thou shalt see/Ten thousand tortures that more horrid be.	F1920	5.2.124		BdAngl
To practise more then heavenly power permits.	F2009	5.3.27		4Chor
Well use that tricke no more, I would advise you.	F App	p.232 19		Faust
and so by that meanes I shal see more then ere I felt, or saw	F App	p.233 5	P	Robin
and more Rafe, if thou hast any mind to Nan Spit our kitchin	F App	p.234 26	P	Robin
No more sweete Rafe, letts goe and make cleane our bootes which	F App	p.234 32	P	Robin
good divel forgive me now, and Ile never rob thy Library more.	F App	p.235 31	P	Robin
Alas sir, I have no more, I pray you speake for me.	F App	p.239 104	P	HrsCsr
has purg'd me of fortie Dollers, I shall never see them more:	F App	p.240 129	P	HrsCsr
O Lord sir, let me goe, and Ile give you fortie dollers more.	F App	p.241 159	P	HrsCsr
his labour; wel, this tricke shal cost him fortie dollers more.	F App	p.241 166	P	Faust
Parthians y'afflict us more then ye suppose,	Lucan, First Booke	107		
may be won/With farre lesse toile, and yet the honors more;	Lucan, First Booke	284		
And far more barbarous then the French (his vassals)/And that	Lucan, First Booke	476		
Prodigious birthes with more and ugly jointes/Then nature	Lucan, First Booke	560		
such and more strange/Blacke night brought forth in secret:	Lucan, First Booke	578		
Yet more will happen then I can unfold;	Lucan, First Booke	634		
But Figulus more seene in heavenly mysteries,	Lucan, First Booke	638		
Yong oxen newly yokt are beaten more,	Ovid's Elegies	1.2.13		
Unwilling Lovers, love doth more torment,	Ovid's Elegies	1.2.17		
And while he drinkes, to adde more do not misse,	Ovid's Elegies	1.4.52		
Jove send me more such afternoones as this.	Ovid's Elegies	1.5.26		
Or I more sterne then fire or sword will turne,	Ovid's Elegies	1.6.57		
The carefull prison is more meete for thee.	Ovid's Elegies	1.6.64		
Over my Mistris is my right more great?	Ovid's Elegies	1.7.30		
To yeeld their love to more then one disdainde.	Ovid's Elegies	1.8.40		
Many to rob is more sure, and lesse hatefull,	Ovid's Elegies	1.8.55		
When thou hast so much as he gives no more,	Ovid's Elegies	1.8.101		
In heaven was never more notorious fable.	Ovid's Elegies	1.9.40		
No more this beauty mine eyes captivates.	Ovid's Elegies	1.10.10		
Tis shame their wits should be more excelent.	Ovid's Elegies	1.10.26		
Going out againe passe forth the dore more wisely/And som-what	Ovid's Elegies	1.12.5		
More fitly had [they] <thy> wrangling bondes contained/From	Ovid's Elegies	1.12.23		
Not one in heaven should be more base and vile.	Ovid's Elegies	1.13.36		
I chid no more, she blusht, and therefore heard me,	Ovid's Elegies	1.13.47		
But what had beene more faire had they beene kept?	Ovid's Elegies	1.14.3		
Borne at Peligny, to write more addresse.	Ovid's Elegies	2.1.2		
to thinke the time more short/Lay downe thy forehead in thy lap	Ovid's Elegies	2.2.23		
More he deserv'd, to both great harme he fram'd,	Ovid's Elegies	2.2.49		
To kinde requests thou wouldst more gentle prove,	Ovid's Elegies	2.3.5		
Apt to thy mistrisse, but more apt to me.	Ovid's Elegies	2.8.4		
More glory by thy vanquisht foes assends.	Ovid's Elegies	2.9.6		
Light art thou, and more windie then thy winges,	Ovid's Elegies	2.9.49		
It is more safe to sleepe, to read a booke,	Ovid's Elegies	2.11.31		
Shee looking on them did more courage give.	Ovid's Elegies	2.12.26		
With corne the earth abounds, with vines much more,	Ovid's Elegies	2.16.7		

MORE (cont.)

Maides words more vaine and light then falling leaves,	Ovid's Elegies	2.16.45	
Unlesse I erre to these thou more incline,	Ovid's Elegies	2.18.39	
Keepe her for me, my more desire to breede.	Ovid's Elegies	2.19.2	
And I deserve more then thou canst in verity,	Ovid's Elegies	3.1.47	
The more thou look'st, the more the gowne envide.	Ovid's Elegies	3.2.28	
pleace <please> Pollux, Castor [love] <loves> horsemen more.	Ovid's Elegies	3.2.54	
But yet their gift more moderately use,	Ovid's Elegies	3.3.47	
What's kept, we covet more: the care makes theft:	Ovid's Elegies	3.4.25	
Thy feare is, then her body, valued more.	Ovid's Elegies	3.4.30	
One Deianira was more worth then these.	Ovid's Elegies	3.5.38	
Thou ore a hundreth Nimphes, or more shalt raigne:	Ovid's Elegies	3.5.63	
For five score Nimphes, or more our flouds conteine.	Ovid's Elegies	3.5.64	
Shame, that should make me blush, I have no more.	Ovid's Elegies	3.5.78	
While thus I speake, the waters more abounded:	Ovid's Elegies	3.5.85	
My idle thoughts delighted her no more,	Ovid's Elegies	3.6.39	
Then did the robe or garment which she wore <more>,	Ovid's Elegies	3.6.40	
What might I crave more if I aske againe?	Ovid's Elegies	3.6.44	
Drouping more then a Rose puld yesterday:	Ovid's Elegies	3.6.66	
Lie downe with shame, and see thou stirre no more,	Ovid's Elegies	3.6.69	
Nay more, the wench did not disdaine a whit,	Ovid's Elegies	3.6.73	
Wit was some-times more pretious then gold,	Ovid's Elegies	3.7.3	
My love was cause that more mens love she seazd.	Ovid's Elegies	3.10.20	
Ah, she doth more worth then her vices prove.	Ovid's Elegies	3.10.44	
Who mine was cald, whom I lov'd more then any,	Ovid's Elegies	3.11.5	
Be more advisde, walke as a puritane,	Ovid's Elegies	3.13.13	
And I will trust your words more then mine eies.	Ovid's Elegies	3.13.46	
Because she tooke more from her than she left,	Hero and Leander	1.47	
To hazard more, than for the golden Fleece.	Hero and Leander	1.58	
She proudly sits) more over-rules the flood,	Hero and Leander	1.111	
Wherewith Leander much more was inflam'd.	Hero and Leander	1.182	
Receives no blemish, but oft-times more grace,	Hero and Leander	1.217	
The Ocean maketh more majesticall:	Hero and Leander	1.226	
Who on Loves seas more glorious wouldst appeare?	Hero and Leander	1.228	
These arguments he us'de, and many more,	Hero and Leander	1.329	
The more she striv'd, the deeper was she strooke.	Hero and Leander	1.334	
He inly storm'd, and waxt more furious,	Hero and Leander	1.437	
Much more in subjects having intellect,	Hero and Leander	2.59	
nothing saw/That might delight him more, yet he suspected/Some	Hero and Leander	2.63	
the more she strived,/The more a gentle pleasing heat revived,	Hero and Leander	2.67	
The more a gentle pleasing heat revived,	Hero and Leander	2.68	
Ne're king more sought to keepe his diademe,	Hero and Leander	2.77	
And nothing more than counsaile, lovers hate.	Hero and Leander	2.140	
The more he is restrain'd, the woorse he fares,	Hero and Leander	2.145	
The longing heart of Hero much more joies/Then nymphs and	Hero and Leander	2.232	
The neerer that he came, the more she fled,	Hero and Leander	2.243	
Whence his admiring eyes more pleasure tooke,	Hero and Leander	2.325	

MORES

These Mores that drew him from Bythinia,	1Tamb	4.2.98	Tamb

MORNE

That shew faire weather to the neighbor morne.	2Tamb	3.1.48	Jrslem
He said he wud attend me in the morne.	Jew	2.1.34	Abigal
Sees not the morne on rosie horses rise.	Ovid's Elegies	1.8.4	
Oft in the morne her haires not yet digested,	Ovid's Elegies	1.14.19	
[Amber] <Yellow> trest is shee, then on the morne thinke I,/My	Ovid's Elegies	2.4.43	
And in the morne beene lively nerethelesse.	Ovid's Elegies	2.10.28	
If Thetis, and the morne their sonnes did waile,	Ovid's Elegies	3.8.1	
Now had the morne espy'de her lovers steeds,	Hero and Leander	2.87	
And round about the chamber this false morne,	Hero and Leander	2.321	

MORNING

Shall make the morning hast her gray uprise,	Dido	1.1.102	Jupitr
And in the morning he was stolne from me,	Dido	5.1.214	Nurse
Even at the morning of my happy state,	1Tamb	2.7.4	Cosroe
Or when the morning holds him in her armes:	1Tamb	3.2.48	Zenoc
And blow the morning from their nosterils,	2Tamb	4.3.8	Tamb
Farewell, Remember to morrow morning.	Jew	1.2.364	Barab
And for the Raven wake the morning Larke,	Jew	2.1.61	Barab
How fares it this morning with your excellence?	P 966	19.36	King
his keeper, in the morning/We will discharge thee of thy charge,	Edw	2.5.108	Penbrk
And bring them every morning to thy bed:	F 538	2.1.150	Mephst
drunke over night, the Divell cannot hurt him in the morning:	F1202	4.1.48	P Benvol
if I live till morning, Il'e visit you:	F1877	5.2.81	P Faust
On this hard threshold till the morning lay.	Ovid's Elegies	1.6.68	
Nor morning starres shunne thy uprising face.	Ovid's Elegies	1.13.28	
Yet lingered not the day, but morning scard me.	Ovid's Elegies	1.13.48	
Her breath as fragrant as the morning rose,	Hero and Leander	1.391	
Though it was morning, did he take his flight.	Hero and Leander	2.102	
For thy delight each May-morning.	Passionate Shepherd	22	

MORNINGS

We meane to take his mornings next arise/For messenger, he will	1Tamb	3.1.38	Bajzth
Unto the watry mornings ruddy [bower] <hower>,	1Tamb	4.4.123	Tamb
And like to Flora in her mornings pride,	1Tamb	5.1.140	Tamb

MOROCCUS

Kings of Fesse, Moroccus and Argier,	1Tamb	3.3.66	Bajzth

MOROCUS

Techelles King of Fesse, and Usumcasane King of Morocus.	1Tamb	4.4.117	P Tamb
Kings of Argier, Morocus, and of Fesse,	1Tamb	4.4.120	Tamb
Kings of Morocus and of Fesse, welcome.	2Tamb	1.3.128	Tamb
Thanks king of Morocus, take your crown again.	2Tamb	1.3.137	Tamb

MORPHEUS

Give charge to Morpheus that he may dreame/A golden dreame, and	Jew	2.1.36	Abigal
Whose sound allures the golden Morpheus,	Hero and Leander	1.349	

MORROW

They shall to morrow draw my chariot,	2Tamb	4.3.30	Tamb

MORROW (cont.)			
To morrow early I'le be at the doore.	Jew	1.2.361	Barab
Farewell, Remember to morrow morning.	Jew	1.2.364	Barab
To morrow is the Sessions; you shall to it.	Jew	4.1.199	Barab
Good morrow to your Majestie.	P 964	19.34	Guise
Good morrow to my loving Cousin of Guise.	P 965	19.35	King
To morrow, sitting in our Consistory,	F 967	3.1.189	Pope
To morrow we would sit i'th Consistory,	F1017	3.2.37	Pope
To me to morrow constantly deny it.	Ovid's Elegies		1.4.70
MORS			
The motto this: Undique mors est.	Edw	2.2.28	Lncstr
Stipendium peccati mors est:	F 66	1.1.38	P Faust
MORT (See also MOR)			
Mort dieu.	Edw	1.1.90	Gavstn
MORTALL			
Whose lookes set forth no mortall forme to view,	Dido	1.1.189	Aeneas
Juno, my mortall foe, what make you here?	Dido	3.2.24	Venus
In this my mortall well deserved wound,	2Tamb	2.3.6	Sgsmnd
let this wound appease/The mortall furie of great Tamburlain.	2Tamb	5.1.154	Govnr
To make me mindfull of my mortall sinnes,	Jew	2.3.74	Barab
No mortall can expresse the paines of hell.	F1716	5.1.43	OldMan
Thy scope is mortall, mine eternall fame,	Ovid's Elegies		1.15.7
A mortall nimphes refusing Lord to stay.	Ovid's Elegies		2.17.16
MORTIFIED			
My mothers death hath mortified my mind,	2Tamb	3.2.51	Celeb
My bodies mortified lineaments/Should exercise the motions of	2Tamb	5.3.188	Amyras
For she has mortified her selfe.	Jew	1.2.341	1Fryar
How, mortified!	Jew	1.2.342	Barab
MORTIMER			
That villaine Mortimer, ile be his death.	Edw	1.1.81	Gavstn
For Mortimer will hang his armor up.	Edw	1.1.89	Mortmr
Well Mortimer, ile make thee rue these words,	Edw	1.1.91	Edward
Bridle thy anger gentle Mortimer.	Edw	1.1.121	Warwck
Unto the forrest gentle Mortimer,	Edw	1.2.47	Queene
Farewell sweet Mortimer, and for my sake,	Edw	1.2.81	Queene
The name of Mortimer shall fright the king,	Edw	1.4.6	Mortmr
Lay hands on that traitor Mortimer.	Edw	1.4.20	Edward
Here Mortimer, sit thou in Edwards throne,	Edw	1.4.36	Edward
Yong Mortimer and his unckle shalbe earles,	Edw	1.4.67	Edward
On Mortimer, with whom ungentle Queene--	Edw	1.4.147	Gavstn
Thou art too familiar with that Mortimer,	Edw	1.4.154	Edward
Ah Mortimer!	Edw	1.4.193	Queene
I Mortimer, for till he be restorde,	Edw	1.4.209	Queene
Sweete Mortimer, sit downe by me a while,	Edw	1.4.225	Queene
My Lords, albeit the Queen winne Mortimer,	Edw	1.4.230	Lncstr
Fie Mortimer, dishonor not thy selfe,	Edw	1.4.244	Lncstr
And Mortimer will rest at your commaund.	Edw	1.4.296	Mortmr
That you have parled with your Mortimer?	Edw	1.4.321	Edward
But wherefore walkes yong Mortimer aside?	Edw	1.4.353	Edward
And as for you, lord Mortimer of Chirke,	Edw	1.4.359	Edward
Lord Mortimer, we leave you to your charge:	Edw	1.4.373	Edward
Not Mortimer, nor any of his side,	Edw	2.1.4	Spencr
But tell me Mortimer, whats thy devise,	Edw	2.2.11	Edward
Proud Mortimer, ungentle Lancaster,	Edw	2.2.29	Edward
Ah furious Mortimer what hast thou done?	Edw	2.2.85	Queene
What Mortimer, you will not threaten him?	Edw	2.2.146	Kent
Traitor be gone, whine thou with Mortimer.	Edw	2.2.214	Edward
The yonger Mortimer is growne so brave,	Edw	2.2.232	Edward
Whereof we got the name of Mortimer,	Edw	2.3.23	Mortmr
Yes, yes, for Mortimer your lovers sake.	Edw	2.4.14	Edward
I Mortimer, the miserable Queene,	Edw	2.4.23	Queene
No Mortimer, ile to my lord the king.	Edw	2.4.51	Queene
And therefore gentle Mortimer be gone.	Edw	2.4.56	Queene
But thinke of Mortimer as he deserves.	Edw	2.4.58	Mortmr
So well hast thou deserv'de sweete Mortimer.	Edw	2.4.59	Queene
How meanst thou Mortimer? that is over base.	Edw	2.5.71	Gavstn
My lord Mortimer, and you my lords each one,	Edw	2.5.74	Penbrk
And you lord Mortimer?	Edw	2.5.91	Penbrk
I know the malice of the yonger Mortimer,	Edw	3.1.5	Edward
hearing,/Mortimer hardly, Penbrooke and Lancaster/Spake least:	Edw	3.1.105	Arundl
Tretcherous Warwicke, traiterous Mortimer,	Edw	3.1.134	Edward
Thou comst from Mortimer and his complices,	Edw	3.1.153	Edward
Sweete Mortimer farewell.	Edw	3.1.249	Lncstr
Go take that haughtie Mortimer to the tower,	Edw	3.1.252	Edward
What Mortimer?	Edw	3.1.256	Mortmr
Mortimer I stay thy sweet escape,	Edw	4.1.10	Kent
Mortimer tis I,	Edw	4.1.13	Kent
Lord Edmund and lord Mortimer alive?	Edw	4.2.36	Queene
But Mortimer reservde for better hap,	Edw	4.2.40	Mortmr
No my lord Mortimer, not I, I trow.	Edw	4.2.44	Prince
Reward for them can bring in Mortimer?	Edw	4.3.18	Edward
and the lord Mortimer, having in their company divers of your	Edw	4.3.33	P Spencr
A villaines, hath that Mortimer escapt?	Edw	4.3.38	Edward
Proud traytor Mortimer why doost thou chase/Thy lawfull king	Edw	4.6.3	Kent
Edward, this Mortimer aimes at thy life:	Edw	4.6.10	Kent
diest, for Mortimer/And Isabell doe kisse while they conspire,	Edw	4.6.12	Kent
Proud Mortimer pries neare into thy walkes.	Edw	4.6.18	Kent
and here to pine in feare/Of Mortimer and his confederates.	Edw	4.7.36	Baldck
Mortimer, who talkes of Mortimer,	Edw	4.7.37	Edward
Who wounds me with the name of Mortimer/That bloudy man?	Edw	4.7.38	Edward
The Queenes commission, urgd by Mortimer,	Edw	4.7.49	Leistr
What cannot gallant Mortimer with the Queene?	Edw	4.7.50	Leistr
Nay so will hell, and cruell Mortimer,	Edw	4.7.75	Edward

MORTIMER (cont.)			
dauntlesse minde/The ambitious Mortimer would seeke to curbe,	Edw	5.1.16	Edward
That Mortimer and Isabell have done.	Edw	5.1.25	Edward
By Mortimer, and my unconstant Queene,	Edw	5.1.30	Edward
To make usurping Mortimer a king?	Edw	5.1.37	Edward
No, tis for Mortimer, not Edwards head,	Edw	5.1.40	Edward
But if proud Mortimer do weare this crowne,	Edw	5.1.43	Edward
To give ambitious Mortimer my right,	Edw	5.1.53	Edward
Traitors be gon, and joine you with Mortimer,	Edw	5.1.87	Edward
Then send for unrelenting Mortimer/And Isabell, whose eyes	Edw	5.1.103	Edward
Let not that Mortimer protect my sonne,	Edw	5.1.115	Edward
By Mortimer, whose name is written here,	Edw	5.1.139	Edward
Sweet Mortimer, the life of Isabell,	Edw	5.2.15	Queene
But Mortimer, as long as he survives/What safetie rests for us,	Edw	5.2.42	Queene
As thou intendest to rise by Mortimer,	Edw	5.2.52	Mortmr
In health sweete Mortimer, how fares your grace?	Edw	5.2.81	Kent
With you I will, but not with Mortimer.	Edw	5.2.110	Prince
Why yongling, s'dainst thou so of Mortimer.	Edw	5.2.111	Mortmr
Helpe unckle Kent, Mortimer will wrong me.	Edw	5.2.113	Prince
Mortimer shall know that he hath wrongde mee.	Edw	5.2.118	Kent
To be revengde on Mortimer and thee.	Edw	5.2.121	Kent
Will hatefull Mortimer appoint no rest?	Edw	5.3.5	Edward
The court is where lord Mortimer remaines,	Edw	5.3.61	Matrvs
The king must die, or Mortimer goes downe,	Edw	5.4.1	Mortmr
Now is all sure, the Queene and Mortimer/Shall rule the realme,	Edw	5.4.65	Mortmr
Lord Mortimer, now take him to your charge.	Edw	5.4.81	Queene
Mortimer, I did, he is our king,	Edw	5.4.87	Kent
And beare the kings to Mortimer our lord,	Edw	5.5.119	Gurney
Or else die by the hand of Mortimer.	Edw	5.6.6	Mortmr
A Mortimer, the king my sonne hath news,	Edw	5.6.15	Queene
Now Mortimer begins our tragedie.	Edw	5.6.23	Queene
But you I feare, conspirde with Mortimer.	Edw	5.6.37	King
Yes, if this be the hand of Mortimer.	Edw	5.6.44	King
A Mortimer, thou knowest that he is slaine,	Edw	5.6.50	King
For my sake sweete sonne pittie Mortimer.	Edw	5.6.55	Queene
Farewell faire Queene, weepe not for Mortimer,	Edw	5.6.64	Mortmr
Spill not the bloud of gentle Mortimer.	Edw	5.6.69	Queene
Els would you not intreate for Mortimer.	Edw	5.6.71	King
My lord, here is the head of Mortimer.	Edw	5.6.93	1Lord
MORTIMERS			
Ile have my will, and these two Mortimers,	Edw	1.1.78	Edward
Now let the treacherous Mortimers conspire,	Edw	1.1.149	Edward
And both the Mortimers, two goodly men,	Edw	1.3.3	Gavstn
My lord, mines more obscure then Mortimers.	Edw	2.2.22	Lncstr
My lord, the familie of the Mortimers/Are not so poore, but	Edw	2.2.150	Mortmr
And that the Mortimers are in hand withall,	Edw	3.1.54	Edward
Mortimers hope surmounts his fortune farre.	Edw	3.1.259	Mortmr
And leave the Mortimers conquerers behind?	Edw	4.5.5	Edward
MOSCO			
Frankeford, Lubecke, Mosco, and where not,	Jew	4.1.72	Barab
MOSCOVITE (See MUSCOVITES)			
MOSSE			
When they were slender, and like downy mosse,	Ovid's Elegies		1.14.23
MOST			
The ayre is pleasant, and the soyle most fit/For Cities, and	Dido	1.1.178	Achat
Have been most urgent suiters for my love,	Dido	3.1.151	Dido
Not past foure thousand paces at the most.	Dido	5.1.17	Aeneas
Most happy Emperour in humblest tearms/I vow my service to your	1Tamb	2.5.15	Meandr
Most great and puisant Monarke of the earth,	1Tamb	3.1.41	Bassoe
(Which of your whole displeasures should be most)/Hath seem'd	1Tamb	3.2.7	Agidas
but most astonied/To see his choller shut in secrete thoughtes,	1Tamb	3.2.69	Agidas
Most happy King and Emperour of the earth,	1Tamb	5.1.74	1Virgn
But most accurst, to see the Sun-bright troope/Of heavenly	1Tamb	5.1.324	Zenoc
Whose head hath deepest scarres, whose breast most woundes,	2Tamb	1.3.75	Tamb
That most may vex his body and his soule.	2Tamb	3.5.99	Callap
Admir'd I am of those that hate me most:	Jew	Prol.9	Machvl
and Lawes were then most sure/When like the [Dracos] <Drancus>	Jew	Prol.20	Machvl
Alas, my Lord, the most of us are poore!	Jew	1.2.57	1Jew
From little unto more, from more to most:	Jew	1.2.106	1Knght
And made my house a place for Nuns most chast.	Jew	2.3.77	Barab
I know not, and that grieves me most of all.	Jew	3.2.21	Govnr
For that will be most heavy to thy soule.	Jew	3.3.71	1Fryar
I, and a Virgin too, that grieves me most:	Jew	3.6.41	2Fryar
Have I debts owing; and in most of these,	Jew	4.1.73	Barab
you dine with me, Sir, and you shal be most hartily poyson'd.	Jew	4.3.30	P Barab
Commend me to him, Sir, most humbly,	Jew	4.3.47	Barab
And he from whom my most advantage comes,	Jew	5.2.113	Barab
And most [humbly] <humble> intreates your Majestie/To visite	P 245	4.43	Man
He loves me not that sheds most teares,	P1239	22.101	King
But he that makes most lavish of his bloud.	P1240	22.102	King
and that thow most reposest one my faythe	Paris	ms31,p391	Guise
Happie were I, but now most miserable.	Edw	1.4.129	Edward
That I may see that most desired day,	Edw	4.3.46	Edward
He of you all that most desires my bloud,	Edw	5.1.100	Edward
And thus, most humbly do we take our leave.	Edw	5.1.124	Trussl
I, my most gratious lord, so tis decreed.	Edw	5.1.138	Bartly
To murther you my most gratious lorde?	Edw	5.5.46	Ltborn
To see a king in this most pittious state?	Edw	5.5.51	Ltborn
I these are those that Faustus most desires.	F 79	1.1.51	Faust
Yes Faustus, and most deerely lov'd of God.	F 293	1.3.65	Mephst
[makes men] <make them> foolish that do use <trust> them most.	F 408	2.1.20	BdAngl
Most sacred Patron of the Church of Rome,	F 951	3.1.173	Faust
My good Lord Archbishop, heres a most daintie dish,	F1046	3.2.66	Pope

MOST (cont.)

These gracicus words, most royall Carolus,	F1217	4.1.63		Faust
Two spreading hornes most strangely fastened/Upon the head of this [is] most horrible:	F1277	4.1.123		Emper
I pray you tell me, what is the thing you most desire to have?	F1291	4.1.137	P	Faust
Fooles that will laugh on earth, [must] <most> weepe in hell.	F1567	4.6.10	P	Faust
most intollerable booke for conjuring that ere was invented by	F1891	5.2.95		Mephst
in their most florishing estate, which I doubt not shal	F App	p.233 19	P	Robin
heavinesse/Cf thy most vilde and loathsome filthinesse,	F App	p.237 48	P	Faust
Faiths breach, and hence came war to most men welcom.	F App	p.243 40		OldMan
wars,/We from our houses driven, most willingly/Suffered exile:	Lucan, First Booke			184
When she will, day shines every where most pure.	Lucan, First Booke			279
From dog-kept flocks come preys to woolves most gratefull.	Ovid's Elegies			1.8.10
When most her husband bends the browes and frownes,	Ovid's Elegies			1.8.56
But most thou friendly turtle-dove, deplore.	Ovid's Elegies			2.2.33
[And] this doth please me most, and so doth she.	Ovid's Elegies			2.6.12
I pay them home with that they most desire:	Ovid's Elegies			2.10.8
(O face most cunning mine eyes to detaine)/Thou oughtst	Ovid's Elegies			2.10.26
And was againe most apt to my desire.	Ovid's Elegies			2.17.12
Where round about small birdes most sweetely sing.	Ovid's Elegies			2.19.16
What horse-driver thou favourst most is best,	Ovid's Elegies			3.1.4
Her foote was small: her footes forme is most fit:	Ovid's Elegies			3.2.7
if Corcyras Ile/Had thee unknowne interr'd in ground most vile.	Ovid's Elegies			3.3.7
The rites/In which Loves beauteous Empresse most delites,/Are	Ovid's Elegies			3.8.48
Then shall you most resemble Venus Nun,	Hero and Leander			1.300
And ever as he thought himselfe most nigh it,	Hero and Leander			1.319
	Hero and Leander			2.74

MOTE

And throw them in the triple mote of Hell,	2Tamb	2.4.100		Tamb
Come let us cast the body in the mote,	Edw	5.5.118		Gurney

MOTES

Hang in the aire as thicke as sunny motes,	2Tamb	3.2.101		Tamb

MOTHER

And made that way my mother Venus led:	Dido	1.1.221		Aeneas
Achates, tis my mother that is fled,	Dido	1.1.240		Aeneas
Madame, you shall be my mother.	Dido	2.1.96		Ascan
My mother Venus jealous of my health,	Dido	2.1.221		Aeneas
I, and my mother gave me this fine bow.	Dido	2.1.309		Cupid
I will faire mother, and so play my part,	Dido	2.1.332		Cupid
And if my mother goe, Ile follow her.	Dido	3.1.38		Cupid
Mother, looke here.	Dido	3.1.47		Cupid
I mother, I shall one day be a man,	Dido	3.3.35		Cupid
From whence my radiant mother did descend,	Dido	3.4.47		Aeneas
Jove wils it so, my mother wils it so:	Dido	4.3.5		Aeneas
Whither must I goe? Ile stay with my mother.	Dido	4.5.2		Cupid
I, so youle dwell with me and call me mother.	Dido	4.5.16		Nurse
This was my mother that beguild the Queene,	Dido	5.1.42		Aeneas
Thy mother was no Goddesse perjurd man,	Dido	5.1.156		Dido
From jygging vaines of riming mother wits,	1Tamb	Prol.1		Prolog
Zabina, mother of three braver boies,	1Tamb	3.3.103		Bajzth
Wher Beauty, mother to the Muses sits,	1Tamb	5.1.144		Tamb
Let me accompany my gratious mother,	2Tamb	1.3.66		Calyph
Mother dispatch me, or Ile kil my selfe,	2Tamb	3.4.26		Sonne
Give me your knife (good mother) or strike home:	2Tamb	3.4.28		Sonne
Sweet mother strike, that I may meet my father.	2Tamb	3.4.30		Sonne
No, this is the better, mother, view this well.	Jew	2.3.145		Mthias
Seeme not to know me here before your mother/Lest she mistrust	Jew	2.3.146		Barab
Hee's with your mother, therefore after him.	Jew	2.3.350		Barab
What, is he gone unto my mother?	Jew	2.3.351		Mthias
I cannot stay; for if my mother come,	Jew	2.3.353		Mthias
In what Queen Mother or your grace commands.	P 12	1.12		Navrre
Come Mother,/Let us goe to honor this solemnitie.	P 24	1.24		Charls
Having the King, Queene Mother on our sides,	P 29	1.29		Navrre
The Mother Queene workes wonders for my sake,	P 133	2.76		Guise
My Mother poysoned heere before my face:	P 187	3.22		Navrre
What art thou dead, sweet sonne speak to thy Mother.	P 551	11.16		QnMoth
A loving mother to preserve thy state,	P 594	12.7		QnMoth
Mother, how like you this device of mine?	P1065	19.135		King
this towardnes makes thy mother feare/Thou art not markt to	Edw	3.1.79		Queene
By earth, the common mother of us all,	Edw	3.1.128		Edward
So pleaseth the Queene my mother, me it likes.	Edw	4.2.21		Prince
Mother, perswade me not to weare the crowne,	Edw	5.2.92		Prince
Sweete mother, if I cannot pardon him,	Edw	5.4.94		King
Mother, you are suspected for his death,	Edw	5.6.78		King
He hath forgotten me, stay, I am his mother.	Edw	5.6.90		Queene
I had neither father nor mother, I leapt out of a Lyons mouth	F 686	2.2.135	P	Wrath
and my mother <grandmother> was a Hogshead of Claret Wine.	F 697	2.2.146	P	Glutny
ugly jointes/Then nature gives, whose sight appauls the mother,	Lucan, First Booke			561
[What] <That> if thy Mother take Dianas bowe,	Ovid's Elegies			1.1.11
Thy mother shall from heaven applaud this show,	Ovid's Elegies			1.2.39
Love hearing it laugh'd with his tender mother/And smiling	Ovid's Elegies			1.6.11
And he who on his mother veng'd his sire,	Ovid's Elegies			1.7.9
And sister, Nurse, and mother spare him not,	Ovid's Elegies			1.8.91
Thinke when she reades, her mother letters sent her,	Ovid's Elegies			2.2.19
Yet Love, if thou with thy faire mother heare,	Ovid's Elegies			2.9.51
If such a worke thy mother had assayed.	Ovid's Elegies			2.14.20
with loving may/Had seene, my mother killing me, [no] <to> day.	Ovid's Elegies			2.14.22
And mother-murtherd Itis [they] <thee> bewaile,	Ovid's Elegies			2.14.30
For her ill-beautious Mother judgd to slaughter?	Ovid's Elegies			3.3.18
Came forth a mother, though a maide there put.	Ovid's Elegies			3.4.22
Thebe who Mother of five Daughters prov'd?	Ovid's Elegies			3.5.34
Thy dying eyes here did thy mother close,	Ovid's Elegies			3.8.49
Tender loves Mother a new Poet get,	Ovid's Elegies			3.14.1
As he imagyn'd Hero was his mother.	Hero and Leander			1.40

MOTHER (cont.)			
As thou in beautie doest exceed Loves mother/Nor heaven, nor	Hero and Leander		1.222
MOTHER-MURTHERD			
And mother-murtherd Itis [they] <thee> bewaile,	Ovid's Elegies		2.14.30
MOTHER QUEENE			
The Mother Queene workes wonders for my sake,	P 133	2.76	Guise
MOTHERS			
Plac'd by her side, looke on their mothers face.	2Tamb	1.3.20	Tamb
My gratious Lord, they have their mothers looks,	2Tamb	1.3.35	Zenoc
and thy seed/Shall issue crowned from their mothers wombe.	2Tamb	1.3.53	Tamb
Being burnt to cynders for your mothers death.	2Tamb	3.2.46	Tamb
With griefe and sorrow for my mothers death.	2Tamb	3.2.50	Amyras
My mothers death hath mortified my mind,	2Tamb	3.2.51	Celeb
Therefore die by thy loving mothers hand,	2Tamb	3.4.23	Olymp
And if he grudge or crosse his Mothers will,	P 523	9.42	QnMoth
O say not so, thou kill'st thy mothers heart.	P 539	11.4	QnMoth
Especially with our olde mothers helpe.	P1061	19.131	King
Shall have me from my gratious mothers side,	Edw	4.2.23	Prince
Had ancient Mothers this vile custome cherisht,	Ovid's Elegies		2.14.9
A mothers joy by Jove she had not felt.	Ovid's Elegies		2.19.28
MOTHER WITS			
From jygging vaines of riming mother wits,	1Tamb	Prol.1	Prolog
MOTION (Homograph)			
Harke to a motion of eternall league,	Dido	3.2.68	Juno
The motion was so over violent.	Dido	4.1.13	Achat
No breath nor sence, nor motion in them both.	1Tamb	5.1.344	Anippe
What motion is it that inflames your thoughts,	2Tamb	2.1.2	Sgsmnd
That kindled first this motion in our hearts,	P 7	1.7	Charls
Prosper your happie motion good sir John.	Edw	4.2.75	Queene
But <tell me> have they all/One motion, both situ et tempore?	F 596	2.2.45	Faust
in their motions <motion> upon the poles of the Zodiacke.	F 598	2.2.47	P Mephst
Who knowes not the double motion of the Planets?	F 602	2.2.51	Faust
As when I heare but motion made of him,	F App	p.237 27	Emper
MOTIONS			
And wanton motions of alluring eyes,	Dido	4.3.35	Achat
mortified lineaments/Should exercise the motions of my heart,	2Tamb	5.3.189	Amyras
heavens, that I might knowe their motions and dispositions].	F 551.5	2.1.168A	P Faust
in their motions <motion> upon the poles of the Zodiacke.	F 598	2.2.47	P Mephst
all, and everie part/Strove to resist the motions of her hart.	Hero and Leander		1.364
MOTOR			
and all mens hatred/Inflict upon them, thou great Primus Motor.	Jew	1.2.164	Barab
MOTTO			
The motto: Aeque tandem.	Edw	2.2.20	Mortmr
The motto this: Undique mors est.	Edw	2.2.28	Lncstr
MOUGHT			
And mought I live to see him sacke rich Thebes,	Dido	3.3.42	Aeneas
MOULD (Homograph; See also MOLD)			
And mould her minde unto newe fancies shapes:	Dido	3.3.79	Iarbus
Or of what mould or mettel he be made,	1Tamb	2.6.17	Ortyg
Made of the mould whereof thy selfe consists,	2Tamb	4.1.115	Tamb
That trade in mettall of the purest mould;	Jew	1.1.20	Barab
age you wrackes/And sluttish white-mould overgrowe the waxe.	Ovid's Elegies		1.12.30
MOUNSER			
O Mounser de Guise, heare me but speake.	P 529	10.2	Prtsnt
And then shall Mounser weare the diadem.	P 652	12.65	QnMoth
Mounser of Loraine sinke away to hell,	P1023	19.93	King
Did he not injure Mounser thats deceast?	P1035	19.105	King
MOUNSIER			
Gramercy Mounsier.	Jew	4.4.34	Barab
Very mush, Mounsier, you no be his man?	Jew	4.4.57	P Barab
Pardona moy, Mounsier, [me] <we> be no well.	Jew	4.4.71	Barab
Mounsier le Grand, a noble friend of yours,	Edw	4.2.47	Mortmr
MOUNT (Homograph; See also YMOUNTED)			
Making thee mount as high as Eagles soare.	1Tamb	5.1.224	Bajzth
Mount up your royall places of estate,	1Tamb	5.1.525	Tamb
pitcht against our power/Betwixt Cutheia and Orminius mount:	2Tamb	2.1.18	Fredrk
Now will we march from proud Orminius mount/To faire Natolia,	2Tamb	2.2.2	Orcan
That on mount Sinay with their ensignes spread,	2Tamb	3.1.46	Jrslem
Ile teach you how to make the water mount,	2Tamb	3.2.85	Tamb
Upon the lofty and celestiall mount,	2Tamb	4.3.120	Tamb
Shall mount the milk-white way and meet him there.	2Tamb	4.3.132	Tamb
To see the devils mount in Angels throanes,	2Tamb	5.3.32	Usumc
And mount my royall chariot of estate,	2Tamb	5.3.178	Tamb
Or mount the top with my aspiring winges,	P 103	2.46	Guise
Unto mount Faucon will we dragge his coarse:	P 319	5.46	Anjoy
And seeing there was no place to mount up higher,	Edw	5.6.62	Mortmr
His waxen wings did mount above his reach,	F 21	Prol.21	1Chor
Did mount him up <himselfe> to scale Olimpus top.	F 757	2.3.36	2Chor
And mount aloft with them as high as heaven,	F1404	4.2.80	Faust
<But let my soule mount and> ascend to heaven.	F1956	(HC271)B	Faust
Or mount the sunnes flame bearing <plume bearing> charriot,	Lucan, First Booke		48
With hoarie toppe, and under Hemus mount/Philippi plaines;	Lucan, First Booke		679
Ile live, and as he puls me downe, mount higher.	Ovid's Elegies		1.15.42
how Olimpus toppe/High Ossa bore, mount Pelion up to proppe.	Ovid's Elegies		2.1.14
The lofty Pine from high mount Pelion raught/Ill waies by rough	Ovid's Elegies		2.11.1
From Latmus mount up to the glomie skie,	Hero and Leander		1.109
Will mount aloft, and enter heaven gate,	Hero and Leander		1.466
And kept it downe that it might mount the hier.	Hero and Leander		2.42
For though the rising yv'rie mount he scal'd,	Hero and Leander		2.273
MOUNTAIN			
Come let us meet them at the mountain foot,	1Tamb	1.2.133	Usumc
by leaden pipes/Runs to the citie from the mountain Carnon.	1Tamb	3.1.60	Bajzth
MOUNTAINE			
Altars crack/With mountaine heapes of milke white Sacrifize.	Dido	1.1.202	Aeneas

MOUNTAINE (cont.)			
That like a mountaine overwhelmes my blisse,	Edw	5.1.54	Edward
Invironed round with airy mountaine tops,	F 781	3.1.3	Faust
Woods, or steepie mountaine yeeldes.	Passionate Shepherd		4
MOUNTAINES			
Some to the mountaines, some unto the soyle,	Dido	3.3.61	Dido
And scale the ysie mountaines lofty tops:	1Tamb	1.2.100	Tamb
That darted mountaines at her brother Jove:	1Tamb	5.1.511	Tamb
and sacrifice/Mountaines of breathlesse men to Mahomet,	2Tamb	3.5.55	Callap
Than he that darted mountaines at thy head,	2Tamb	4.1.128	Tamb
Mountaines and Hils, come, come, and fall on me,	F1945	5.2.149	Faust
lookes shewed/Like marble from the Parian Mountaines hewed.	Ovid's Elegies		1.7.52
Snakes leape by verse from caves of broken mountaines/And	Ovid's Elegies		2.1.25
Thou hast no name, but com'st from snowy mountaines;	Ovid's Elegies		3.5.91
MOUNTAINS			
As with their waight shall make the mountains quake,	1Tamb	1.2.49	Tamb
Upon the hauty mountains of my brest:	P 718	14.21	Navrre
From steepe Pine-bearing mountains to the plaine:	Hero and Leander		1.116
MOUNTED			
Mounted on Steeds, swifter than Pegasus.	1Tamb	1.2.94	Tamb
Mounted on lusty Mauritanian Steeds,	1Tamb	3.3.16	Bassoe
And make faire Europe mounted on her bull,	2Tamb	1.1.42	Orcan
Closde in a coffyn mounted up the aire,	2Tamb	1.1.140	Orcan
Their Spheares are mounted on the serpents head,	2Tamb	2.4.53	Tamb
pearle of welthie India/Were mounted here under a Canapie:	2Tamb	3.2.122	Tamb
Before whom (mounted on a Lions backe)/Rhamnusia beares a	2Tamb	3.4.56	Therid
Mounted his shining [chariot] <chariots>, gilt with fire,	2Tamb	4.3.126	Tamb
Mounted his royall Cabonet.	P 957	19.27	Eprnon
And mounted then upon a Dragons backe,	F 771	2.3.50	2Chor
On swift steedes mounted till the race were done.	Ovid's Elegies		3.2.10
Which mounted up, intending to have kist him,	Hero and Leander		2.173
MOUNTEST			
And early mountest thy hatefull carriage:	Ovid's Elegies		1.13.38
MOUNTING			
Whose mounting thoughts did never creepe so low,	Edw	2.2.77	Gavstn
MOUNTS (Homograph)			
But when Aurora mounts the second time,	1Tamb	4.1.54	2Msngr
Raise mounts, batter, intrench, and undermine,	2Tamb	3.3.38	Capt
Were all the lofty mounts of Zona mundi,	2Tamb	4.1.42	Amyras
lowly earth/Should drinke his bloud, mounts up into the ayre:	Edw	5.1.14	Edward
thence/To the pine bearing hils, hence to the mounts/Pirene,	Lucan, First Booke		688
Mounts, and raine-doubled flouds he passeth over,	Ovid's Elegies		1.9.11
But when she comes, [you] <your> swelling mounts sinck downe,	Ovid's Elegies		2.16.51
MOUNTSORRELL			
Mountsorrell, goe shoote the ordinance of,	P 327	5.54	Guise
Mountsorrell from the Duke of Guise.	P 347	6.2	Mntsrl
Mountsorrell unto Roan, and spare not one/That you suspect of	P 446	7.86	Guise
MOURN'D			
The houses burnt, wil looke as if they mourn'd,	2Tamb	2.4.139	Tamb
And wound them on his arme, and for her mourn'd.	Hero and Leander		1.376
MOURNE (See also MOORNE)			
How long will Dido mourne a strangers flight,	Dido	5.1.279	Iarbus
Boyes leave to mourne, this towne shall ever mourne,	2Tamb	3.2.45	Tamb
But give him liberty at least to mourne,	Jew	1.2.202	Barab
The danger of his soule would make me mourne:	F 224	1.2.31	2Schol
Why Philomele doest Tereus leudnesse mourne?	Ovid's Elegies		2.6.7
MOURNED			
Not Hilas was more mourned of Hercules,	Edw	1.1.144	Edward
MOURNEFULL			
And thou shalt die, and on his mournefull hearse,	Edw	5.6.29	King
MOURNFUL			
And here this mournful streamer shal be plac'd/Wrought with the	2Tamb	3.2.19	Amyras
MOURNFULL			
With mournfull streamers hanging down their heads,	1Tamb	4.2.120	Tamb
In mournfull tearmes, with sad and heavie cheare/Complaind to	Hero and Leander		1.440
MOURNING (See also MOORNING)			
Alight and weare a woful mourning weed.	2Tamb	1.1.44	Orcan
stature <statue>/And martch about it with my mourning campe,	2Tamb	2.4.141	Tamb
Run mourning round about the Femals misse,	2Tamb	4.1.188	Tamb
And all the Students clothed in mourning blacke,	F2000	5.3.18	2Schol
Mourning appear'd, whose hoary hayres were torne,	Lucan, First Booke		189
MOURRA (See MORA)			
MOUSE			
thy selfe to a Dog, or a Cat, or a Mouse, or a Rat, or any thing	F 383	1.4.41	P Wagner
A Dog, or a Cat, or a Mouse, or a Rat?	F 384	1.4.42	P Robin
to a dogge, or a catte, or a mouse, or a ratte, or any thing.	F App	p.231 59	P Wagner
a Christian fellow to a dogge or a catte, a mouse or a ratte?	F App	p.231 60	P Clown
MOUSTACHE (See MUSCHATOES)			
MOUTH			
Should ere defile so faire a mouth as thine:	Dido	3.2.27	Juno
Banish that ticing dame from forth your mouth,	Dido	4.3.31	Achat
As from the mouth of mighty Bajazeth.	1Tamb	3.1.20	Fesse
Now fil the mouth of Limnasphaltes lake,	2Tamb	5.1.67	Tamb
I'le give him something and so stop his mouth.	Jew	4.1.102	Barab
I'le send by word of mouth now; Bid him deliver thee a thousand	Jew	4.4.74	P Ithimr
Or open his mouth, and powre quick silver downe,	Edw	5.4.36	Ltborn
out of a Lyons mouth when I was scarce <half> an houre old,	F 687	2.2.136	P Wrath
And they of Nilus mouth (if there live any).	Lucan, First Booke		20
Thy mouth to taste of many meates did balke.	Ovid's Elegies		2.6.30
My mouth in speaking did all birds excell.	Ovid's Elegies		2.6.62
Like lightning go, his strugling mouth being checkt.	Ovid's Elegies		3.4.14
Her trembling mouth these unmeete sounds expresses.	Ovid's Elegies		3.5.72
And shaking sobbes his mouth for speeches beares.	Ovid's Elegies		3.8.12

MOUTH'D
And with their Cannons mouth'd like Orcus gulfe/Batter the 1Tamb 3.1.65 Bajzth
MOUTHES
And Spels of magicke from the mouthes of spirits, 2Tamb 4.2.64 Olymp
Breake through the hedges of their hateful mouthes, 2Tamb 4.3.46 Therid
My limbes may issue from your smoky mouthes, F1955 5.2.159 Faust
By seaven huge mouthes into the sea is [skipping] <slipping>, Ovid's Elegies 2.13.10
Rich Nile by seaven mouthes to the vast sea flowing, Ovid's Elegies 3.5.39
Oxen in whose mouthes burning flames did breede? Ovid's Elegies 3.11.36
MOUTHS
we wil break the hedges of their mouths/And pul their kicking 2Tamb 4.3.48 Techel
And rough jades mouths with stubburn bits are torne, Ovid's Elegies 1.2.15
MOV'D
Lest you be mov'd too much with my sad tale. Dido 2.1.125 Aeneas
Not mov'd at all, but smiling at his teares, Dido 2.1.240 Aeneas
And wilt thou not be mov'd with Didos words? Dido 5.1.155 Dido
As had you seene her 'twould have mov'd your heart, Jew 1.2.385 Mthias
Be mov'd at nothing, see thou pitty none, Jew 2.3.171 Barab
Ithimore, intreat not for her, I am mov'd, Jew 3.4.35 Barab
five hundred Crownes that I esteeme,/I am not mov'd at that: Jew 4.3.41 Barab
Thou shouldst perceive the Duke of Guise is mov'd. P 832 17.27 Guise
Least thou perceive the King of France be mov'd. P 834 17.29 King
Lord Percie of the North being highly mov'd, Edw 1.1.110 Kent
What? are you mov'd that Gaveston sits heere? Edw 1.4.8 Edward
When pleasure mov'd us to our sweetest worke. Ovid's Elegies 1.4.48
For rage against my wench mov'd my rash arme, Ovid's Elegies 1.7.3
This saied, she mov'd her buskins gaily varnisht, Ovid's Elegies 3.1.31
That from thy fanne, mov'd by my hand may blow? Ovid's Elegies 3.2.38
Mov'd by Loves force, unto ech other lep? Hero and Leander 2.58
MOVDE
Aeneas, be not movde at what he sayes, Dido 3.3.23 Dido
MOVE (See also MOOVE)
To move unto the measures of delight: Dido 3.4.54 Dido
And I will either move the thoughtles flint, Dido 4.2.40 Iarbus
If words might move me I were overcome. Dido 5.1.154 Aeneas
They gan to move him to redresse my ruth, Dido 5.1.238 Anna
And now shall move you to bereave my life. Jew 1.2.143 Barab
But what doth move thee above the rest to doe the deed? P1132 21.26 P Dumain
I, I, these wordes of his move me as much, Edw 1.1.39 Gavstn
All things that move betweene the quiet Poles/Shall be at my F 83 1.1.55 Faust
And <Faustus all> jointly move upon one Axle-tree, F 592 2.2.41 Mephst
All <joyntly> move from East to West, in foure and twenty F 597 2.2.46 P Mephst
Move me not Faustus <for I will not tell thee>. F 621 2.2.70 P Mephst
The Stars move still, Time runs, the Clocke will strike, F1936 5.2.140 Faust
Love <Jove> knowes with such like praiers, I dayly move hir: Ovid's Elegies 1.3.4
no threats or prayers move thee,/O harder then the dores thou Ovid's Elegies 1.6.61
I harm'd: a foe did Diomedes anger move. Ovid's Elegies 1.7.34
Since maist thou see me watch and night warres move: Ovid's Elegies 1.9.45
Hold in thy rosie horses that they move not. Ovid's Elegies 1.13.10
Our prayers move thee to assist our drift, Ovid's Elegies 2.3.17
If I looke well, thou thinkest thou doest not move, Ovid's Elegies 2.7.9
Hence with great laude thou maiest a triumph move. Ovid's Elegies 2.9.16
Cupid commands to move his ensignes further. Ovid's Elegies 2.12.28
To finde, what worke my muse might move, I strove. Ovid's Elegies 3.1.6
Tis time to move grave things in lofty stile, Ovid's Elegies 3.1.23
Not stronger am I, then the thing I move. Ovid's Elegies 3.1.42
To move her feete unheard in [setting] <sitting> downe. Ovid's Elegies 3.1.52
no warres we move,/Peace pleaseth me, and in mid peace is love. Ovid's Elegies 3.2.49
I know not, what men thinke should thee so move. Ovid's Elegies 3.4.28
Worthy she was to move both Gods and men, Ovid's Elegies 3.6.59
Now love, and hate my light brest each way move; Ovid's Elegies 3.10.33
And sweet toucht harpe that to move stones was able? Ovid's Elegies 3.11.40
And if these pleasures may thee <things thy minde may> move, Passionate Shepherd 19
If these delights thy minde may move; Passionate Shepherd 23
MOVED
Moved with her voyce, I lept into the sea, Dido 2.1.283 Aeneas
Might well have moved your highnes to beware/How you did meddle P 179 3.14 Navrre
She beckt, and prosperous signes gave as she moved. Ovid's Elegies 3.2.58
Huge okes, hard Adamantes might she have moved, Ovid's Elegies 3.6.57
The god seeing him with pittie to be moved, Hero and Leander 2.219
MOVEDST
Envy hath rapt thee, no fierce warres thou movedst, Ovid's Elegies 2.6.25
MOVES
And they whom fierce Bellonaes fury moves/To wound their armes, Lucan, First Booke 563
My heate is heere, what moves my heate is gone. Ovid's Elegies 2.16.12
Alone Corinna moves my wanton wit. Ovid's Elegies 3.11.16
MOVING
I, and of a moving spirit too, brother; but come, Jew 1.2.328 2Fryar
And make a bridge, thorough the moving Aire, F 333 1.3.105 Faust
Stand still you ever moving Spheares of heaven, F1929 5.2.133 Faust
MOVINGS
I know her by the movings of her feete: Dido 1.1.241 Aeneas
MOWBERIE
Brav'd Mowberie in presence of the king, Edw 1.1.111 Kent
And Mowberie and he were reconcild: Edw 1.1.115 Kent
MOY
Pardona moy, be no in tune yet; so, now, now all be in. Jew 4.4.45 P Barab
Pardona moy, Mounsier, [me] <we> be no well. Jew 4.4.71 Barab
MUCH
I am much better for your worthles love, Dido 1.1.3 Ganimd
Yet much I marvell that I cannot finde, Dido 1.1.180 Achat
Lest you be mov'd too much with my sad tale. Dido 2.1.125 Aeneas
So much have I receiv'd at Didos hands, Dido 3.1.103 Aeneas

MUCH (cont.)

But not so much for thee, thou art but one, ...	Dido	3.1.175		Dido
But much I feare my sonne will nere consent, ...	Dido	3.2.82		Venus
Theres not so much as this base tackling too, ...	Dido	4.4.151		Dido
Which is as much as if I swore by heaven, ...	1Tamb	1.2.233		Tamb
Make much of them gentle Theridamas, ...	1Tamb	1.2.247		Tamb
I marveile much he stole it not away.	1Tamb	2.4.42		Mycet
His talke much sweeter than the Muses song, ...	1Tamb	3.2.50		Zenoc
the King of Persea/(Being a Shepheard) seem'd to love you much,	1Tamb	3.2.60		Agidas
sir, you must be dieted, too much eating will make you surfeit.	1Tamb	4.4.103	P	Tamb
Would not with too much cowardize or feare, ...	1Tamb	5.1.37		Govnr
So much by much, as dooth Zenocrate.	1Tamb	5.1.159		Tamb
As much as thy faire body is for me.	1Tamb	5.1.416		Zenoc
Els should I much forget my self, my Lord.	1Tamb	5.1.500		Zenoc
In whose high lockes is much more majesty/Than from the Concave	2Tamb	3.4.47		Therid
This Lady shall have twice so much againe, ...	2Tamb	3.4.90		Therid
much like so many suns/That halfe dismay the majesty of heaven:	2Tamb	4.1.2		Amyras
what, given so much to sleep/You cannot leave it, when our	2Tamb	4.1.11		Amyras
which ad much danger to your malladie.	2Tamb	5.3.55		Therid
As much too high for this disdainfull earth.	2Tamb	5.3.122		Tamb
then let me see how much/Is left for me to conquer all the	2Tamb	5.3.123		Tamb
Eastward behold/As much more land, which never was descried,	2Tamb	5.3.155		Tamb
built Citadell/Commands much more then letters can import:	Jew	Prol.23		Machvl
So that of thus much that returne was made:	Jew	1.1.1		Barab
Would make a miracle of thus much coyne:	Jew	1.1.13		Barab
They wondred how you durst with so much wealth/Trust such a	Jew	1.1.79		1Merch
That thirst so much for Principality.	Jew	1.1.135		Barab
As much as would have bought his beasts and him, . . .	Jew	1.2.189		Barab
As negligently to forgoe so much/Without provision for .	Jew	1.2.242		Barab
Thus father shall I much dissemble.	Jew	1.2.289		Abigal
And waters of this new made Nunnery/Will much delight you.	Jew	1.2.312		1Fryar
divine precepts/And mine owne industry, but to profit much.	Jew	1.2.335		Abigal
As much I hope as all I hid is worth.	Jew	1.2.336		Barab
And so much must they yeeld or not be sold.	Jew	2.3.4		2Offcr
I like it much the better.	Jew	2.3.61		Lodowk
Do the [Turkes] <Turke> weigh so much?	Jew	2.3.98	P	Barab
What, can he steale that you demand so much?	Jew	2.3.100		Barab
So much the worse; I must have one that's sickly, and be but	Jew	2.3.123	P	Barab
So much the better, thou art for my turne.	Jew	2.3.129		Barab
That by my helpe shall doe much villanie.	Jew	2.3.133		Barab
I have as much coyne as will buy the Towne.	Jew	2.3.200		Barab
I weigh it thus much; I have wealth enough.	Jew	2.3.245		Barab
I, Barabas, or else thou wrong'st me much.	Jew	2.3.255		Mthias
Chast, and devout, much sorrowing for my sinnes, . . .	Jew	3.6.14		Abigal
Besides I know not how much weight in Pearle/Orient and round,	Jew	4.1.66		Barab
Nay, I care not how much she loves me; Sweet Bellamira, would I	Jew	4.2.54	P	Ithimr
And if he aske why I demand so much, tell him, I scorne to	Jew	4.2.120	P	Ithimr
Oh that I should part with so much gold!	Jew	4.3.51		Barab
had it not beene much better/To [have] kept thy promise then be	Jew	5.2.4		Calym
for feare too late/Thou seek'st for much, but canst not .	Jew	5.2.46		Barab
[Sorbonests] <thorbonest>/Attribute as much unto their workes,	P 412	7.52		Ramus
That wicked Guise I feare me much will be, ...	P 921	18.22		Navrre
Brother of Navarre, I sorrow much, ...	P1139	22.1		King
I, I, these wordes of his move me as much, ...	Edw	1.1.39		Gavstn
So much as he on cursed Gaveston.	Edw	1.4.181		Queene
And none so much as blame the murtherer, ...	Edw	1.4.267		Mortmr
Is new returnd, this newes will glad him much, ...	Edw	1.4.301		Queene
returnd, this newes will glad him much,/Yet not so much as me.	Edw	1.4.302		Queene
would he lov'd me/But halfe so much, then were I treble blest.	Edw	1.4.304		Queene
And promiseth as much as we can wish, ...	Edw	1.4.399		MortSr
a factious lord/Shall hardly do himselfe good, much lesse us,	Edw	2.1.7		Spencr
The greefe for his exile was not so much, ...	Edw	2.1.57		Neece
I am that Cedar, shake me not too much, ...	Edw	2.2.38		Edward
Thou shalt have so much honor at our hands.	Edw	2.5.28		Warwck
As by their preachments they will profit much, ...	Edw	3.1.22		Spencr
As much as thou in rage out wentst the rest.	Edw	3.1.240		Edward
Much happier then your friends in England do.	Edw	4.2.35		Kent
Unlesse it be with too much clemencie?	Edw	5.1.123		Edward
Favor him my lord, as much as lieth in you.	Edw	5.1.147		Leistr
Thinke therefore madam that imports [us] <as> much, . . .	Edw	5.2.10		Mortmr
Relent, ha, ha, I use much to relent.	Edw	5.4.27		Ltborn
Much more a king brought up so tenderlie.	Edw	5.5.6		Matrvs
I thought as much.	Edw	5.5.22		Gurney
I feard as much, murther cannot be hid.	Edw	5.6.46		Queene
So much <soone> he profits in Divinitie, ...	F 15	Prol.15		1Chor
I much:	F1112	3.3.25	P	Robin
I blame thee not to sleepe much, having such a head of thine	F1284	4.1.130	P	Emper
not so much for injury done to me, as to delight your Majesty	F1311	4.1.157	P	Faust
and have lost very much of late by horse flesh, and this .	F1464	4.4.8	P	HrsCsr
me but a little straw, and had much ado to escape drowning:	F1487	4.4.31	P	HrsCsr
me what he should give me for as much Hay as he could eate;	F1527	4.5.23	P	Carter
bad him take as much as he would for three-farthings; so he	F1529	4.5.25	P	Carter
I, I, he does not stand much upon that.	F1630	4.6.73	P	HrsCsr
No faith, not much upon a woodden leg.	F1631	4.6.74		Faust
'Tis not so much worth; I pray you tel me one thing. . .	F1643	4.6.86	P	Carter
We are much beholding to this learned man.	F1670	4.6.113		Lady
if you will doe us so much <that> favour, as to let us see that	F1685	5.1.12	P	1Schol
Majesty, we should thinke our selves much beholding unto you.	F1687	5.1.14	P	1Schol
Ifaith he lookes much like a conjurer.	F App	p.236 11	P	Knight
so much for the injury hee offred me heere in your presence,	F App	p.238 81	P	Faust
Beleeve me maister Doctor, this merriment hath much pleased me.	F App	p.242 1	P	Duke
Yet Room is much bound to these civil armes, ...	Lucan, First Booke	44		
Both differ'd much, Pompey was strooke in yeares, . . .	Lucan, First Booke	130		

MUCH (cont.)			
And muttering much, thus to themselves complain'd:	Lucan, First Booke		249
And that he's much chang'd, looking wild and big,	Lucan, First Booke		475
much like that hellish fiend/Which made the sterne Lycurgus	Lucan, First Booke		572
I aske too much, would she but let me love hir,	Ovid's Elegies		1.3.3
Thee feare I too much:	Ovid's Elegies		1.6.15
When thou hast so much as he gives no more,	Ovid's Elegies		1.8.101
With much a do my hands I scarsely staide.	Ovid's Elegies		1.8.110
Straight being read, will her to write much backe,	Ovid's Elegies		1.11.19
Because [thy] <they> care too much thy Mistresse troubled.	Ovid's Elegies		2.2.8
While Junos watch-man Io too much eyde,	Ovid's Elegies		2.2.45
and too much his griefe doth favour/That seekes the conquest by	Ovid's Elegies		2.5.11
I sawe your nodding eye-browes much to speake,	Ovid's Elegies		2.5.15
Also much better were they then I tell,	Ovid's Elegies		2.5.55
Tis ill they pleas'd so much, for in my lips,	Ovid's Elegies		2.5.57
Duld with much beating slowly forth doth passe.	Ovid's Elegies		2.7.16
lies quiet/And slumbring, thinkes himselfe much blessed by it.	Ovid's Elegies		2.9.40
The losse of such a wench much blame will gather,	Ovid's Elegies		2.11.35
me, or I am sure/I oft have done, what might as much procure.	Ovid's Elegies		2.13.6
Onely Ile signe nought, that may grieve me much.	Ovid's Elegies		2.15.18
With corne the earth abounds, with vines much more,	Ovid's Elegies		2.16.7
Ah oft how much she might she feignd offence;	Ovid's Elegies		2.19.13
Suffring much cold by hoary nights frost bred.	Ovid's Elegies		2.19.22
Fat love, and too much fulsome me annoyes,	Ovid's Elegies		2.19.25
Long have I borne much, hoping time would beate thee/To guard	Ovid's Elegies		2.19.49
Each crosse waies corner doth as much expresse.	Ovid's Elegies		3.1.18
By suffring much not borne by thy severity.	Ovid's Elegies		3.1.48
And all things too much in their sole power drenches.	Ovid's Elegies		3.3.26
And see at home much, that thou nere broughtst thether.	Ovid's Elegies		3.4.48
Nor Romane stocke scorne me so much (I crave)/Gifts then my	Ovid's Elegies		3.5.65
So in a spring thrives he that told so much,	Ovid's Elegies		3.6.51
In skipping out her naked feete much grac'd her.	Ovid's Elegies		3.6.82
Long have I borne much, mad thy faults me make:	Ovid's Elegies		3.10.1
Ile not sift much, but hold thee soone excusde,	Ovid's Elegies		3.13.41
blazon foorth the loves of men,/Much lesse of powerfull gods.	Hero and Leander		1.71
Wherewith Leander much more was inflam'd.	Hero and Leander		1.182
As much as sparkling Diamonds flaring glasse.	Hero and Leander		1.214
Differs as much, as wine and water doth.	Hero and Leander		1.264
Much lesse can honour bee ascrib'd thereto,	Hero and Leander		1.279
answered Love, nor would vouchsafe so much/As one poore word,	Hero and Leander		1.383
Much more in subjects having intellect,	Hero and Leander		2.59
'Tis wisedome to give much, a gift prevailes,	Hero and Leander		2.225
The longing heart of Hero much more joies/Then nymphs and	Hero and Leander		2.232
Much like a globe, (a globe may I tearme this,	Hero and Leander		2.275
For much it greev'd her that the bright day-light,	Hero and Leander		2.303
MU'D			
That thus hath pent and mu'd me in a prison,	Edw	5.1.18	Edward
MUD			
And hurle him in some lake of mud and durt:	F1409	4.2.85	Faust
Halfe smother'd in a Lake of mud and durt,	F1434	4.3.4	Mrtino
MUDDY			
Either th'art muddy in mid winter tide:	Ovid's Elegies		3.5.95
MUFFES			
Rutters>, Muffes, and Danes/That with the Holbard, Lance,	2Tamb	1.1.22	Uribas
Rutters>, Muffes, and Danes/[Feares] <feare> not Orcanes, but	2Tamb	1.1.58	Orcan
MUFFLE			
Muffle your beauties with eternall clowdes,	2Tamb	5.3.6	Therid
MUGEROUN			
I tell thee Mugeroun we will be freends,	P 614	12.27	King
How now Mugeroun, metst thou not the Guise at the doore?	P 774	15.32	King
MUGEROUNE			
Sweet Mugeroune, tis he that hath my heart,	P 660	13.4	Duchss
MULCIBER			
Fierce Mulciber unbarred Aetna's gate,	Lucan, First Booke		543
MULES			
Returne our Mules and emptie Camels backe,	1Tamb	1.2.76	Agidas
Goe send 'um threescore Camels, thirty Mules,	Jew	1.1.59	Barab
Against her kind (the barren Mules loth'd issue)/To be cut	Lucan, First Booke		589
MULTIPLY			
Christians; what, or how can I multiply?	Jew	1.2.103	Barab
For though they doe a while increase and multiply,	Jew	2.3.89	Barab
Her friends doe multiply and yours doe fayle,	Edw	4.5.2	Spencr
MULTITUDE			
And martch with such a multitude of men,	2Tamb	1.3.56	Celeb
we take particularly thine/To save the ruine of a multitude:	Jew	1.2.97	Govnr
You were a multitude, and I but one,	Jew	1.2.178	Barab
long since some of us/Did stray so farre amongst the multitude.	Jew	1.2.309	Abbass
As for the multitude that are but sparkes,	Edw	1.1.20	Gavstn
So rusht the inconsiderate multitude/Thorough the Citty hurried	Lucan, First Booke		492
MULTITUDES			
In multitudes they swarme unto the shoare,	Dido	1.2.36	Serg
The ground is mantled with such multitudes.	1Tamb	3.1.53	Moroc
Why flocke you thus to me in multitudes?	Jew	1.1.144	Barab
Fond men, what dreame you of their multitudes?	Jew	1.1.157	Barab
MUNDA			
At Munda let the dreadfull battailes joyne;	Lucan, First Booke		40
MUNDI			
Were all the lofty mounts of Zona mundi,	2Tamb	4.1.42	Amyras
MUNITION			
Their warlike Engins and munition/Exceed the forces of their	1Tamb	4.1.28	2Msngr
MUNKE			
Tush, to be short, he meant to make me Munke,	P1039	19.109	King

MURDER (cont.)			
Pillage and murder are his usuall trades.	1Tamb	4.1.66	Souldn
By murder raised to the Persean Crowne,	1Tamb	4.3.13	Souldn
And it shall murder me.	Jew	3.2.24	Mater
when holy Friars turne devils and murder one another.	Jew	4.1.194	P Ithimr
That seekes to murder all the Protestants:	P 31	1.31	Navrre
In murder, mischeefe, or in tiranny.	P 41	1.41	Condy
And brought by murder to their timeles ends.	P 46	1.46	Navrre
And therfore meane to murder all I meet.	P 279	5.6	Anjoy
Let none escape, murder the Hugonets.	P 337	5.64	Guise
And meane to murder us:	P 368	7.8	Taleus
Murder the Hugonets, take those pedantes hence.	P 438	7.78	Guise
Downe with the Hugonites, murder them.	P 528	10.1	Guise
O my Lord, I am one of them that is set to murder you.	P 992	19.62	P 3Mur
To murder me, villaine?	P 993	19.63	Guise
Or else to murder me, and so be King.	P1040	19.110	King
Murder me not, I am a Cardenall.	P1091	20.1	Cardnl
That durst attempt to murder noble Guise.	P1121	21.15	Dumain
Convey hence Gaveston, thaile murder him.	Edw	2.2.82	Edward
Murder or not murder, now he has but one leg, I'le out-run him,	F1494	4.4.38	P HrsCsr
Murder, rape, warre, lust and trecherie,	Hero and Leander		1.457
MURDER'D			
What if I murder'd him e're Jacomo comes?	Jew	4.1.116	Barab
Was my Mathias murder'd by the Jew?	Jew	5.1.44	Mater
Ferneze, 'twas thy sonne that murder'd him.	Jew	5.1.45	Mater
O help, help, the villaine hath murder'd me.	F1493	4.4.37	P Faust
MURDERED			
Should have been murdered the other night?	P 35	1.35	Navrre
Be murdered in his bed.	P 287	5.14	Guise
I would that I had murdered thee my sonne.	P1073	19.143	QnMoth
Shall he be murdered when the deed is done.	Edw	5.4.20	Mortmr
His fathers dead, and we have murdered him.	Edw	5.6.16	Queene
My father's murdered through thy treacherie,	Edw	5.6.28	King
Who is the man dare say I murdered him?	Edw	5.6.40	Mortmr
Sweete father heere, unto thy murdered ghost,	Edw	5.6.99	King
MURDERER			
I, I must be the murderer of my selfe:	Dido	5.1.270	Dido
Heaven blesse me; what, a Fryar a murderer?	Jew	4.1.196	Barab
He's a murderer.	Jew	4.4.15	P Ithimr
Where is the Jew, where is that murderer?	Jew	5.1.48	Mater
Hence with the traitor, with the murderer.	Edw	5.6.58	King
MURDERING			
With balles of wilde fire in their murdering pawes,	Dido	2.1.217	Aeneas
Nor on Mathias, but by murdering me.	Jew	3.3.46	Abigal
MURDEROUS			
Whose murderous thoughts will be his overthrow.	P1116	21.10	Dumain
Jawes flesht with bloud continue murderous.	Lucan, First Booke		332
MURDERS			
Birds of the Aire will tell of murders past;	Jew	Prol.16	Machvl
And when the murders done,/See how he must be handled for his	Edw	5.5.22	Matrvs
Burnes where it cherisht, murders where it loved.	Hero and Leander		2.128
MURDREDST			
And plainely saith, twas thou that murdredst him.	Edw	5.6.42	King
MURDROUS			
And murdrous Fates throwes al his triumphs down.	2Tamb	Prol.5	Prolog
MURMURE			
Free from the murmure of these running streames,	Dido	2.1.335	Venus
With gastlie murmure of my sighes and cries,	Edw	1.4.179	Queene
Sends foorth a ratling murmure to the land,	Hero and Leander		1.348
MURMURES			
Murmures and hisses for his hainous sin.	2Tamb	2.3.17	Orcan
MURMURING			
The murmuring commons overstretched hath.	Edw	2.2.160	Mortmr
none answer'd, but a murmuring buz/Th'unstable people made:	Lucan, First Booke		353
MURMURS			
blasted, Aruns takes/And it inters with murmurs dolorous,	Lucan, First Booke		606
MURTHER			
Murther the Foe and save [the] <their> walles from breach.	2Tamb	3.2.82	Tamb
Nor thy close Cave a sword to murther thee,	2Tamb	4.2.12	Olymp
But when will he come that we may murther him?	P 937	19.7	P 3Mur
Let them not unrevengd murther your friends,	Edw	3.1.125	Spencr
And for the murther of my deerest friend,	Edw	3.1.226	Edward
Traitors away, what will you murther me,	Edw	5.3.29	Edward
Villaine, I know thou comst to murther me.	Edw	5.5.45	Edward
To murther you my most gratious lorde?	Edw	5.5.46	Ltborn
O if thou harborst murther in thy hart,	Edw	5.5.87	Edward
No, no, for if thou meanst to murther me,	Edw	5.5.98	Edward
I feard as much, murther cannot be hid.	Edw	5.6.46	Queene
And me with many, but yet me without murther,	Ovid's Elegies		2.12.27
MURTHERD			
And mother-murtherd Itis [they] <thee> bewaile,	Ovid's Elegies		2.14.30
MURTHERED			
Or make a bridge of murthered Carcases,	2Tamb	1.3.93	Amyras
If griefe, our murthered harts have straind forth blood.	2Tamb	2.4.123	Therid
Cut off this arme that murthered my Love:	2Tamb	4.2.83	Therid
My noble brother murthered by the King,	P1107	21.1	Dumain
Trayterouse guise ah thow hast murthered me	Paris	ms17,p390	Minion
In which extreame my minde here murthered is:	Edw	5.1.55	Edward
If that my Unckle shall be murthered thus?	Edw	5.4.110	King
MURTHERER			
And none so much as blame the murtherer,	Edw	1.4.267	Mortmr
And will be called the murtherer of a king,	Edw	5.1.101	Edward
Ist done, Matrevis, and the murtherer dead?	Edw	5.6.1	Mortmr

MURTHERER (cont.)
That thither thou didst send a murtherer. . . . . . Edw 5.6.48 King
What murtherer? bring foorth the man I sent. . . . Edw 5.6.49 Mortmr
MURTHERERS
Now Captain of my guarde, are these murtherers ready? . P 947 19.17 King
MURTHERING
And make him raine down murthering shot from heaven/To dash the 1Tamb 3.3.196 Zabina
What cursed power guides the murthering hands, . . . 1Tamb 5.1.403 Arabia
and Danes/That with the Holbard, Lance, and murthering Axe, 2Tamb 1.1.23 Uribas
Stands aiming at me with his murthering dart, . . . 2Tamb 5.3.69 Tamb
them I will come to chastise them,/For murthering Gaveston: Edw 3.1.179 Edward
MURTHEROUS
I take no pleasure to be murtherous, ... 2Tamb 4.1.29 Calyph
MUSAEUS
as th'infernall spirits/On sweet Musaeus when he came to hell, F 143 1.1.115 Faust
(Whose tragedie divine Musaeus soong)/Dwelt at Abidus; since Hero and Leander 1.52
MUSCADELL (See also MUSCADINE, MUSKADINE)
And drinke in pailes the strongest Muscadell: . . . . 2Tamb 4.3.19 Tamb
MUSCADINE
Goe swill in bowles of Sacke and Muscadine: . . . Jew 5.5.6 Barab
MUSCATTERS
And Parapets to hide the Muscatters: . . . . . . 2Tamb 3.2.77 Tamb
MUSCHATOES
a fellow met me with a muschatoes like a Ravens wing, and a Jew 4.2.28 P Ithimr
MUSCOVITES
I meane our warres against the Muscovites: . . . . P 461 8.11 Anjoy
MUS'D
And oft look't out, and mus'd he did not come. . . . . Hero and Leander 2.22
MUSE (Homograph; See also MUZE)
and dim their eies/That stand and muse at our admyred armes. 1Tamb 2.3.24 Tamb
Oh muse not at it, 'tis the Hebrewes guize, ... Jew 2.3.325 Barab
Madam, what resteth, why stand ye in a muse? . . . Edw 4.6.63 SrJohn
Intends our Muse to vaunt <daunt> his heavenly verse; . F 6 Prol.6 1Chor
Muse upreard <prepar'd> I [meant] <meane> to sing of armes, Ovid's Elegies 1.1.5
[Love] <I> slackt my Muse, and made my [numbers] <number> soft. Ovid's Elegies 1.1.22
Elegian Muse, that warblest amorous laies, ... Ovid's Elegies 1.1.33
To finde, what worke my muse might move, I strove. . . Ovid's Elegies 3.1.6
Thy muse hath played what may milde girles content, . . Ovid's Elegies 3.1.27
With Muse oppos'd would I my lines had done, . . . Ovid's Elegies 3.11.17
Weake Elegies, delightfull Muse farewell; . . . . . Ovid's Elegies 3.14.19
That my slacke muse, sings of Leanders eies, . . . Hero and Leander 1.72
Then muse not, Cupids sute no better sped, . . . Hero and Leander 1.483
MUSES (Homograph)
His talke much sweeter than the Muses song, ... 1Tamb 3.2.50 Zenoc
Wher Beauty, mother to the Muses sits, ... 1Tamb 5.1.144 Tamb
Their minds, and muses on admyred theames: . . . . 1Tamb 5.1.164 Tamb
We are the Muses prophets, none of thine. . . . . Ovid's Elegies 1.1.10
Are all things thine? the Muses Tempe <Temple> thine? . Ovid's Elegies 1.1.19
Apollo, Bacchus, and the Muses may, ... Ovid's Elegies 1.3.11
Faire Phoebus leade me to the Muses springs. . . . Ovid's Elegies 1.15.36
I the pure priest of Phoebus and the muses, ... Ovid's Elegies 3.7.23
To which the Muses sonnes are only heire: . . . . Hero and Leander 1.476
MUSH
Very mush, Mounsier, you no be his man? . . . . . Jew 4.4.57 P Barab
MUSHROOM (See MUSHRUMBS, MUSHRUMP)
MUSHRUMBS
Jew, he lives upon pickled Grashoppers, and sauc'd Mushrumbs. Jew 4.4.62 P Ithimr
MUSHRUMP
But cannot brooke a night growne mushrump, ... Edw 1.4.284 Mortmr
MUSICIAN (See also MUSITION)
A French Musician, come let's heare your skill? . . . Jew 4.4.30 Curtzn
Musician, hast beene in Malta long? . . . . . . Jew 4.4.54 Curtzn
MUSICKE
In stead of musicke I will heare him speake, ... Dido 3.1.89 Dido
What more then Delian musicke doe I heare, ... Dido 3.4.52 Dido
Me thinks, tis a great deale better than a consort of musicke. 1Tamb 4.4.61 P Therid
Yet musicke woulde doe well to cheare up Zenocrate: . . 1Tamb 4.4.62 P Tamb
Skilful in musicke and in amorous laies: . . . . . 2Tamb 1.2.37 Callap
The God that tunes this musicke to our soules, . . . 2Tamb 2.4.31 Tamb
Some musicke, and my fit wil cease my Lord. . . . . 2Tamb 2.4.77 Zenoc
There is no musicke to a Christians knell: . . . . Jew 4.1.1 Barab
Love me little, love me long, let musicke rumble, . . Jew 4.4.28 Ithimr
Musicke and poetrie is his delight, ... Edw 1.1.54 Gavstn
Made musicke with my Mephostophilis? . . . . . . F 581 2.2.30 Faust
Which like sweet musicke entred Heroes eares, ... Hero and Leander 1.194
Are banquets, Dorick musicke, midnight-revell, . . . Hero and Leander 1.301
To sound foorth musicke to the Ocean, ... Hero and Leander 2.328
MUSING
And Caesars mind unsetled musing stood; . . . . . Lucan, First Booke 264
MUSITIANS
Musitians, that with touching of a string/May draw the pliant Edw 1.1.52 Gavstn
MUSITION
This was Alcion, a Musition, ... Dido 3.1.159 Dido
MUSK
Musk-roses, and a thousand sort of flowers, ... Dido 4.5.8 Nurse
MUSKADINE
Sacke, Muskadine, Malmesey and Whippincrust, hold belly hold, F 748 2.3.27 P Robin
MUSKET
To save our Cannoniers from musket shot, ... 2Tamb 3.3.57 Therid
Discharge thy musket and perfourme his death: . . . P 88 2.31 Guise
MUSKETEER (See MUSCATTERS)
MUSK-ROSES
Musk-roses, and a thousand sort of flowers, ... Dido 4.5.8 Nurse

MUST (See also 'IMUST)

Poore Troy must now be sackt upon the Sea,	Dido	1.1.64		Venus
But first in bloud must his good fortune bud,	Dido	1.1.86		Jupitr
Come Ganimed, we must about this geare.	Dido	1.1.121		Jupitr
Alas sweet boy, thou must be still a while,	Dido	1.1.164		Aeneas
Yet must I heare that lothsome name againe?	Dido	3.1.78		Dido
Lords goe before, we two must talke alone.	Dido	3.3.9		Dido
And I must perish in his burning armes.	Dido	3.4.22		Dido
I must conceale/The torment, that it bootes me not reveale,	Dido	3.4.25		Dido
Graunt she or no, Aeneas must away,	Dido	4.3.7		Aeneas
I must prevent him, wishing will not serve:	Dido	4.4.104		Dido
My Lord Ascanius, ye must goe with me.	Dido	4.5.1		Nurse
Whither must I goe? Ile stay with my mother.	Dido	4.5.2		Cupid
I tell thee thou must straight to Italy,	Dido	5.1.53		Hermes
Aeneas will not faine with his deare love,/I must from hence:	Dido	5.1.93		Aeneas
And therefore must of force.	Dido	5.1.101		Aeneas
Let me goe, farewell, I must from hence,	Dido	5.1.110		Dido
Therefore unkind Aeneas, must thou say,	Dido	5.1.123		Dido
Yet must he not gainsay the Gods behest.	Dido	5.1.127		Aeneas
And must I rave thus for a runnagate?	Dido	5.1.265		Dido
Must I make ships for him to saile away?	Dido	5.1.266		Dido
I, I must be the murderer of my selfe:	Dido	5.1.270		Dido
And through my provinces you must expect/Letters of conduct	1Tamb	1.2.23		Tamb
And must maintaine my life exempt from servitude.	1Tamb	1.2.31		Tamb
Must grace his bed that conquers Asia:	1Tamb	1.2.37		Tamb
Techelles, women must be flatered.	1Tamb	1.2.107		Tamb
Now must your jewels be restor'd againe:	1Tamb	1.2.114		Tamb
You must be forced from me ere you goe:	1Tamb	1.2.120		Tamb
I must be pleasde perforce, wretched Zenocrate.	1Tamb	1.2.259		Zenoc
But some must stay/To rule the provinces he late subdude.	1Tamb	3.3.28		Bassoe
must thou be plac'd by me/That am the Empresse of the mighty	1Tamb	3.3.166		Zabina
Must plead for mercie at his kingly feet,	1Tamb	3.3.174		Zenoc
Then must his kindled wrath bee quencht with blood:	1Tamb	4.1.56		2Msngr
You must devise some torment worsse, my Lord,	1Tamb	4.2.66		Techel
For Egypt and Arabia must be mine.	1Tamb	4.4.91		Tamb
sir, you must be dieted, too much eating will make you surfeit.	1Tamb	4.4.103	P	Tamb
I (my Lord) but none save kinges must feede with these.	1Tamb	4.4.109	P	Therid
must you be first shal feele/The sworne destruction of	1Tamb	5.1.65		Tamb
Must needs have beauty beat on his conceites.	1Tamb	5.1.182		Tamb
Must fight against my life and present love:	1Tamb	5.1.389		Zenoc
Must Tamburlaine by their resistlesse powers,	1Tamb	5.1.397		Zenoc
whom all kings/Of force must yeeld their crownes and Emperies:	1Tamb	5.1.481		Souldn
Gainst him my Lord must you addresse your power.	2Tamb	1.1.19		Gazell
Therefore Viceroies the Christians must have peace.	2Tamb	1.1.77		Orcan
place himselfe therin/Must armed wade up to the chin in blood.	2Tamb	1.3.84		Tamb
Our faiths are sound, and must be [consumate] <consinuate>,	2Tamb	2.1.47		Sgsmnd
The ditches must be deepe, the Counterscarps/Narrow and steepe,	2Tamb	3.2.68		Tamb
It must have privy ditches, countermines,	2Tamb	3.2.73		Tamb
It must have high Argins and covered waies/To keep the bulwark	2Tamb	3.2.75		Tamb
Wel, this must be the messenger for thee.	2Tamb	3.4.15		Olymp
That you must goe with us, no remedy.	2Tamb	3.4.79		Therid
Where legions of devils (knowing he must die/Here in Natolia,	2Tamb	3.5.25		Orcan
So sirha, now you are a king you must give armes.	2Tamb	3.5.137	P	Tamb
And what the jealousie of warres must doe.	2Tamb	4.1.104		Tamb
I must apply my selfe to fit those tearmes,	2Tamb	4.1.155		Tamb
I must and wil be pleasde, and you shall yeeld:	2Tamb	4.2.53		Therid
Your Majesty must get some byts for these,	2Tamb	4.3.43		Therid
That must (advaunst in higher pompe than this)/Rifle the	2Tamb	4.3.58		Tamb
This is the time that must eternize me,	2Tamb	5.2.54		Callap
Must part, imparting his impressions,	2Tamb	5.3.170		Tamb
That nobly must admit necessity:	2Tamb	5.3.201		Tamb
My Lord, you must obey his majesty,	2Tamb	5.3.204		Therid
For Tamburlaine, the Scourge of God must die.	2Tamb	5.3.248		Tamb
Thou needs must saile by Alexandria.	Jew	1.1.76		Barab
I must confesse we come not to be Kings:	Jew	1.1.129		Barab
And all the Jewes in Malta must be there.	Jew	1.1.168		2Jew
Umh; All the Jewes in Malta must be there?	Jew	1.1.169		Barab
I must be forc'd to steale and compasse more.	Jew	1.2.127		Barab
where none but their owne sect/Must enter in; men generally	Jew	1.2.257		Abigal
there must my girle/Intreat the Abbasse to be entertain'd.	Jew	1.2.279		Barab
Be close, my girle, for this must fetch my gold.	Jew	1.2.304		Barab
I must and will, Sir, there's no remedy.	Jew	1.2.391		Mthias
And so much must they yeeld or not be sold.	Jew	2.3.4		2Offcr
But now I must be gone to buy a slave.	Jew	2.3.95		Barab
I must have one that's sickly, and be but for sparing vittles:	Jew	2.3.123	P	Barab
This gentle Magot, Lodowicke I meane,/Must be deluded:	Jew	2.3.306		Barab
I know not, but farewell, I must be gone.	Jew	2.3.322		Abigal
Here must no speeches passe, nor swords be drawne.	Jew	2.3.339		Barab
But thou must dote upon a Christian?	Jew	2.3.360		Barab
I, so thou shalt, 'tis thou must doe the deed:	Jew	2.3.369		Barab
But now against my will I must be chast.	Jew	3.1.4		Curtzn
Where they must neither see the messenger,	Jew	3.4.80		Barab
There Ithimore must thou goe place this [pot] <plot>:	Jew	3.4.84		Barab
And Physicke will not helpe them; they must dye.	Jew	3.6.2		1Fryar
Know that Confession must not be reveal'd,	Jew	3.6.33		2Fryar
But I must to the Jew and exclaime on him,	Jew	3.6.42		2Fryar
Thou hast offended, therefore must be damn'd.	Jew	4.1.25		1Fryar
I must needs say that I have beene a great usurer.	Jew	4.1.39		Barab
My bosome [inmate] <inmates> <intimates>, but I must dissemble.	Jew	4.1.47		Barab
No more but so: it must and shall be done.	Jew	4.1.128		Barab
No, pardon me, the Law must have his course.	Jew	4.1.185		Barab
I must be forc'd to give in evidence,	Jew	4.1.186		Barab
Take in the staffe too, for that must be showne:	Jew	4.1.204		Barab

MUST (cont.)

Pray pardon me, I must goe see a ship discharg'd.	Jew	4.2.51	P Ithimr
Tell him I must hav't.	Jew	4.2.118	P Ithimr
And I by him must send three hundred crownes.	Jew	4.3.15	Barab
Jew, I must ha more gold.	Jew	4.3.18	P Pilia
No Sir; and therefore I must have five hundred more.	Jew	4.3.22	P Pilia
I must make this villaine away:	Jew	4.3.29	P Barab
Well, I must seeke a meanes to rid 'em all,	Jew	4.3.63	Barab
Must tuna my Lute for sound, twang twang first.	Jew	4.4.31	Barab
Sirra, you must give my mistris your posey.	Jew	4.4.37	Pilia
What should I say? we are captives and must yeeld.	Jew	5.2.6	Govnr
you must yeeld, and under Turkish yokes/Shall groning beare the	Jew	5.2.7	Calym
No, Barabas, this must be look'd into;	Jew	5.2.34	Barab
Content thee, Calymath, here thou must stay,	Jew	5.5.118	Govnr
And he forsooth must goe and preach in Germany:	P 392	7.32	Guise
My Lords of Poland I must needs confesse,	P 451	8.1	Anjoy
With Poland therfore must I covenant thus,	P 471	8.21	Anjoy
For Katherine must have her will in France:	P 520	9.39	QnMoth
I must say so, paine forceth me complaine.	P 540	11.5	Charls
I have deserv'd a scourge I must confesse,	P 544	11.9	Charls
Now Madam must you insinuate with the King,	P 645	12.58	Cardnl
O no my Lord, a woman only must/Partake the secrets of my heart.	P 675	13.19	Duchss
But Madam I must see.	P 677	13.21	Guise
Are these your secrets that no man must know?	P 678	13.22	Guise
We must with resolute mindes resolve to fight,	P 707	14.10	Navrre
The choyse is hard, I must dissemble.	P 865	17.60	Guise
For we must aide the King against the Guise.	P 918	18.19	Navrre
Now must he fall and perish in his height.	P 946	19.16	Capt
Then there is no remedye but I must dye?	P1096	20.6	Cardnl
Tis warre that must asswage this tyrantes pride.	P1128	21.22	Dumain
Oh no Navarre, thou must be King of France.	P1225	22.87	King
Sweet Epernoune thy King must dye.	P1228	22.90	King
I must have wanton Poets, pleasant wits,	Edw	1.1.51	Gavstn
I cannot, nor I will not, I must speake.	Edw	1.1.122	Mortmr
Am I a king and must be over rulde?	Edw	1.1.135	Edward
Saving your reverence, you must pardon me.	Edw	1.1.186	Gavstn
And war must be the meanes, or heele stay stil.	Edw	1.2.63	Warwck
I, if words will serve, if not, I must.	Edw	1.2.83	Mortmr
It bootes me not to threat, I must speake faire,	Edw	1.4.63	Edward
I see I must, and therefore am content.	Edw	1.4.85	Edward
That I am banishd, and must flie the land.	Edw	1.4.107	Gavstn
And thou must hence, or I shall be deposd,	Edw	1.4.110	Edward
That whether I will or no thou must depart:	Edw	1.4.124	Edward
Seeing I must go, do not renew my sorrow.	Edw	1.4.137	Gavstn
But thou must call mine honor thus in question?	Edw	1.4.152	Queene
I meane not so, your grace must pardon me.	Edw	1.4.153	Gavstn
I must entreat him, I must speake him faire,	Edw	1.4.183	Queene
This wils my lord, and this must I performe,	Edw	1.4.202	Queene
Well of necessitie it must be so.	Edw	1.4.238	Mortmr
Nephue, I must to Scotland, thou staiest here.	Edw	1.4.386	MortSr
Then Balduck, you must cast the scholler off,	Edw	2.1.31	Spencr
You must be proud, bold, pleasant, resolute,	Edw	2.1.42	Spencr
See that my coache be readie, I must hence.	Edw	2.1.71	Neece
Tis warre that must abate these Barons pride.	Edw	2.2.99	Edward
gratifie the king/In other matters, he must pardon us in this,	Edw	2.5.44	Warwck
That we have taken him, but must we now/Leave him on had-I-wist,	Edw	2.5.84	Warwck
Sir, must not come so neare and balke their lips.	Edw	2.5.103	Penbrk
Weaponles must I fall and die in bands,	Edw	2.6.3	Gavstn
O must this day be period of my life,	Edw	2.6.4	Gavstn
And must be awde and governd like a child.	Edw	3.1.31	Baldck
But by the sword, my lord, it must be deserv'd.	Edw	4.2.59	Mortmr
and you must not discourage/Your friends that are so forward in	Edw	4.2.69	Queene
Ye must not grow so passionate in speeches:	Edw	4.4.16	Mortmr
And we must seeke to right it as we may,	Edw	4.6.68	Mortmr
We in meane while madam, must take advise,	Edw	4.6.77	Mortmr
A sweet Spencer, thus then must we part.	Edw	4.7.73	Edward
We must my lord, so will the angry heavens.	Edw	4.7.74	Spencr
Your majestie must go to Killingworth.	Edw	4.7.82	Leistr
Must! tis somwhat hard, when kings must go.	Edw	4.7.83	Edward
And these must die under a tyrants sword.	Edw	4.7.92	Edward
part we must,/Sweete Spencer, gentle Baldocke, part we must.	Edw	4.7.95	Edward
Sweete Spencer, gentle Baldocke, part we must.	Edw	4.7.96	Edward
And go I must, life farewell with my friends.	Edw	4.7.99	Edward
But tell me, must I now resigne my crowne,	Edw	5.1.36	Edward
But what the heavens appoint, I must obaye,	Edw	5.1.56	Edward
And needes I must resigne my wished crowne.	Edw	5.1.70	Edward
My lorde, the parlement must have present newes,	Edw	5.1.84	Trussl
And who must keepe mee now, must you my lorde?	Edw	5.1.137	Edward
Your grace must hence with mee to Bartley straight.	Edw	5.1.144	Bartly
Sweete sonne come hither, I must talke with thee.	Edw	5.2.87	Queene
Friends, whither must unhappie Edward go,	Edw	5.3.4	Edward
Must I be vexed like the nightly birde,	Edw	5.3.6	Edward
And so must die, though pitied by many.	Edw	5.3.24	Edward
The king must die, or Mortimer goes downe,	Edw	5.4.1	Mortmr
The trumpets sound, I must go take my place.	Edw	5.4.72	Mortmr
Art thou king, must I die at thy commaund?	Edw	5.4.103	Kent
Know you this token? I must have the king.	Edw	5.5.19	Ltborn
See how he must be handled for his labour,	Edw	5.5.23	Matrvs
I know what I must do, get you away,	Edw	5.5.27	Ltborn
So,/Now must I about this geare, nere was there any/So finely	Edw	5.5.39	Ltborn
We must now performe/The forme of Faustus fortunes, good or	F 7	Prol.7	1Chor
Why then belike/We must sinne, and so consequently die,/I, we	F 72	1.1.44	Faust
I, we must die, an everlasting death.	F 73	1.1.45	Faust

MUST (cont.)

No more then he commands, must we performe.	F 270	1.3.42		Mephst
Now Faustus, must thou needs be damn'd,	F 389	2.1.1		Faust
But now <Faustus> thou must bequeath it solemnly,	F 423	2.1.35		Mephst
If thou deny it I must <wil> backe to hell.	F 426	2.1.38		Mephst
But Faustus/<thou must> Write it in manner of a Deed of Gift.	F 449	2.1.61		Mephst
And where hell is there must we ever be.	F 512	2.1.124		Mephst
but must thou sit, and I stand?	F 683	2.2.132	P	Envy
What Robin, you must come away and walk the horses.	F 725	2.3.4	P	Dick
Must every bit be spiced with a Crosse?	F1066	3.2.86		Faust
My Lord, I must forewarne your Majesty,	F1248	4.1.94		Faust
Hell take his soule, his body thus must fall.	F1363	4.2.39		Benvol
He must needs goe that the Divell drives.	F1419	4.2.95		Fredrk
now sirra I must tell you, that you may ride him o're hedge and	F1467	4.4.11	P	Faust
and one to whom I must be no niggard of my cunning; Come,	F1504	4.4.48	P	Faust
His store of pleasures must be sauc'd with paine.	F1812	5.2.16		Mephst
thee, then had I lived still, but now must <I> dye eternally.	F1825	5.2.29	P	Faust
the Kingdome of Joy, and must remaine in hell for ever.	F1845	5.2.49	P	Faust
For that must be thy mansion, there to dwell.	F1882	5.2.86		Mephst
Fooles that will laugh on earth, [must] <most> weepe in hell.	F1891	5.2.95		Mephst
And now must taste hels paines perpetually.	F1895	5.2.99		BdAngl
And now poore soule must thy good Angell leave thee,	F1907	5.2.111		GdAngl
Nay, thou must feele them, taste the smart of all:	F1922	5.2.126		BdAngl
He that loves pleasure, must for pleasure fall.	F1923	5.2.127		BdAngl
And then thou must be damn'd perpetually.	F1928	5.2.132		Faust
The devill will come, and Faustus must be damn'd.	F1937	5.2.141		Faust
<O, if my soule must suffer for my sinne>,	F1958	(HC271)B		Faust
But mine must live still to be plagu'd in hell.	F1971	5.2.175		Faust
with you, I must yet have a goblet payde from you ere you goe.	F App	p.234 7	P	Vintnr
I must say somewhat to your felow, you sir.	F App	p.234 13	P	Vintnr
And I must be a Dogge.	F App	p.236 47	P	Rafe
must confesse my selfe farre inferior to the report men have	F App	p.236 12	P	Faust
but I must tel you one thing before you have him, ride him not	F App	p.239 108	P	Faust
to whom I must be no niggard of my cunning, come	F App	p.241 171	P	Faust
must wel reward this learned man for the great kindnes he hath	F App	p.243 28	P	Duke
Whose bloud alone must wash away thy guilt.	F App	p.243 45		OldMan
being old/Must shine a star) shal heaven (whom thou lovest),	Lucan, First Booke			46
denies all, with thy bloud must thou/Abie thy conquest past:	Lucan, First Booke			289
Must Pompeis followers with strangers ayde,	Lucan, First Booke			314
Must Pompey as his last foe plume on me,	Lucan, First Booke			338
Love over-rules my will, I must obay thee,	Lucan, First Booke			373
By these he seeing what myschiefes must ensue,	Lucan, First Booke			629
But we must part, when heav'n with black night lowers.	Ovid's Elegies			1.4.60
Such light to shamefaste maidens must be showne,	Ovid's Elegies			1.5.7
Servants fit for thy purpose thou must hire/To teach thy lover,	Ovid's Elegies			1.8.87
Souldiers must travaile farre:	Ovid's Elegies			1.9.9
Thy mistrisse enseignes must be likewise thine.	Ovid's Elegies			2.3.10
She left; I say'd, you both I must beseech,	Ovid's Elegies			3.1.61
The sea I use not: me my earth must have.	Ovid's Elegies			3.2.48
She must be honest to thy servants credit.	Ovid's Elegies			3.4.36
Then thee whom I must love I hate in vaine,	Ovid's Elegies			3.13.39
but he must weare/The sacred ring wherewith she was endow'd,	Hero and Leander			2.108

MUSTER

Ile muster up an army secretly,	P 572	11.37		Navrre
I meane to muster all the power I can,	P 849	17.44		Guise
Pleshe, goe muster up our men with speed,	P 916	18.17		Navrre
That muster rebels thus against your king)/To see his royall	Edw	2.5.6		Gavstn

MUSTERED

Which are already mustered in the land,	P 726	14.29		1Msngr
Cornets of horse are mustered for the field;	Lucan, First Booke			306
to run their course through empty night/At noone day mustered,	Lucan, First Booke			535

MUSTERS

And in all quarters musters men for Roome.	Lucan, First Booke			396

MUSTRED

I mustred all the windes unto his wracke,	Dido	3.2.45		Juno
Since Tamburlaine hath mustred all his men,	2Tamb	1.1.46		Gazell

MUTE

Mute a the sudden; here's a sudden change.	Jew	2.3.324		Lodowk
Barons and Earls, your pride hath made me mute,	Edw	1.1.107		Kent
Sirra Dick, dost thou know why I stand so mute?	F1509	4.5.5	P	Robin
True love is mute, and oft amazed stands.	Hero and Leander			1.186
and beautie had/As could provoke his liking, yet was mute,	Hero and Leander			1.423

MUTIN

The Mutin toyles; the fleet at Leuca suncke;	Lucan, First Booke			42

MUTINIE

While souldiers mutinie for want of paie.	Edw	1.4.406		Mortmr

MUTINIES

Therefore to stay all sodaine mutinies,	1Tamb	1.1.150		Ceneus
for rather then my lord/Shall be opprest by civill mutinies,	Edw	1.2.65		Queene

MUTTERED

Cattell were seene that muttered humane speech:	Lucan, First Booke			559

MUTTERING

And muttering much, thus to themselves complain'd:	Lucan, First Booke			249

MUTTON

to the devill, for a shoulder of Mutton, tho it were bloud raw.	F 350	1.4.8	P	Wagner
I am one that loves an inch of raw Mutton, better then an ell	F 708	2.2.160	P	Ltchry
will it please you to take a shoulder of Mutton to supper, and	F1121	3.3.34	P	Robin
he would give his soule to the Divel for a shoulder of mutton,	F App	p.229 9	P	Wagner
to the Divel for a shoulder of mutton though twere blood rawe?	F App	p.229 10	P	Clown

MUTUALL

Thy hand and mine have plighted mutuall faith,	Dido	5.1.122		Dido
Kinde wordes, and mutuall talke, makes our greefe greater,	Edw	1.4.133		Edward
That cannot Venus mutuall pleasure taste.	Ovid's Elegies			2.3.2

MUTUALL (cont.)			
Hees happie who loves mutuall skirmish slayes <layes>,	Ovid's Elegies	2.10.29	
Mad streame, why doest our mutuall joyes deferre?	Ovid's Elegies	3.5.87	
By nature have a mutuall appetence,	Hero and Leander	2.56	
MUTUALLY			
Mutually folded in each others Spheares <orbe>,	F 591	2.2.40	Mephst
MUZE			
Thy power inspires the Muze that sings this war.	Lucan, First Booke	66	
MY			
What? dares she strike the darling of my thoughts?	Dido	1.1.9	Jupitr
Grace my immortall beautie with this boone,	Dido	1.1.21	Ganimd
And I will spend my time in thy bright armes.	Dido	1.1.22	Ganimd
When as they would have hal'd thee from my sight:	Dido	1.1.27	Jupitr
Sit on my knee, and call for thy content,	Dido	1.1.28	Jupitr
And my nine Daughters sing when thou art sad,	Dido	1.1.33	Jupitr
Hold here my little love:	Dido	1.1.42	Jupitr
My Juno ware upon her marriage day,	Dido	1.1.43	Jupitr
Put thou about thy necke my owne sweet heart,	Dido	1.1.44	Jupitr
And tricke thy armes and shoulders with my theft.	Dido	1.1.45	Jupitr
And a fine brouch to put in my hat,	Dido	1.1.47	Ganimd
And shall have Ganimed, if thou wilt be my love.	Dido	1.1.49	Jupitr
Whiles my Aeneas wanders on the Seas,	Dido	1.1.52	Venus
And charg'd him drowne my sonne with all his traine.	Dido	1.1.61	Venus
What shall I doe to save thee my sweet boy?	Dido	1.1.74	Venus
For my sake pitie him Oceanus,	Dido	1.1.127	Venus
And had my being from thy bubling froth:	Dido	1.1.129	Venus
What? doe I see my sonne now come on shoare:	Dido	1.1.134	Venus
Whiles my Aeneas spends himselfe in plaints,	Dido	1.1.140	Venus
You sonnes of care, companions of my course,	Dido	1.1.142	Aeneas
How neere my sweet Aeneas art thou driven?	Dido	1.1.170	Venus
Whiles I with my Achates roave abroad,	Dido	1.1.175	Aeneas
Now is the time for me to play my part:	Dido	1.1.182	Venus
men, saw you as you came/Any of all my Sisters wandring here?	Dido	1.1.184	Venus
Of Troy am I, Aeneas is my name,	Dido	1.1.216	Aeneas
Who driven by warre from forth my native world,	Dido	1.1.217	Aeneas
And my divine descent from sceptred Jove:	Dido	1.1.219	Aeneas
And made that way my mother Venus led:	Dido	1.1.221	Aeneas
Achates, tis my mother that is fled,	Dido	1.1.240	Aeneas
To dull the ayre with my discoursive moane.	Dido	1.1.248	Aeneas
My selfe will see they shall not trouble ye,	Dido	1.2.38	Iarbus
Come in with me, Ile bring you to my Queene,	Dido	1.2.42	Iarbus
Who shall confirme my words with further deedes.	Dido	1.2.43	Iarbus
Why stands my sweete Aeneas thus amazde?	Dido	2.1.2	Achat
O my Achates, Theban Niobe,	Dido	2.1.3	Aeneas
I cannot choose but fall upon my knees,	Dido	2.1.11	Achat
And would my prayers (as Pigmalions did)/Could give it life,	Dido	2.1.16	Aeneas
Yet thinkes my minde that this is Priamus:	Dido	2.1.25	Aeneas
And when my grieved heart sighes and sayes no,	Dido	2.1.26	Aeneas
destinies/Have brought my sweete companions in such plight?	Dido	2.1.60	Aeneas
For though my birth be great, my fortunes meane,	Dido	2.1.88	Aeneas
Madame, you shall be my mother.	Dido	2.1.96	Ascan
Beates forth my senses from this troubled soule,	Dido	2.1.116	Aeneas
Lest you be mov'd too much with my sad tale.	Dido	2.1.125	Aeneas
Then buckled I mine armour, drew my sword,	Dido	2.1.200	Aeneas
Yet flung I forth, and desperate of my life,	Dido	2.1.210	Aeneas
My mother Venus jealous of my health,	Dido	2.1.221	Aeneas
Lord of my fortune, but my fortunes turnd,	Dido	2.1.235	Aeneas
King of this Citie, but my Troy is fired,	Dido	2.1.236	Aeneas
By this I got my father on my backe,	Dido	2.1.265	Aeneas
mine armes, and by the hand/Led faire Creusa my beloved wife,	Dido	2.1.267	Aeneas
O there I lost my wife:	Dido	2.1.270	Aeneas
Thinking to beare her on my backe abourd,	Dido	2.1.284	Aeneas
I, and my mother gave me this fine bow.	Dido	2.1.309	Cupid
For Didos sake I take thee in my armes,	Dido	2.1.313	Venus
I will faire mother, and so play my part,	Dido	2.1.332	Cupid
Sleepe my sweete nephew in these cooling shades,	Dido	2.1.334	Venus
know that thou of all my wooers/(And yet have I had many	Dido	3.1.11	Dido
Sit in my lap and let me heare thee sing.	Dido	3.1.25	Dido
No more my child, now talke another while,	Dido	3.1.26	Dido
My cosin Helen taught it me in Troy.	Dido	3.1.28	Cupid
And if my mother goe, Ile follow her.	Dido	3.1.38	Cupid
Depart from Carthage, come not in my sight.	Dido	3.1.44	Dido
I goe to feed the humour of my Love,	Dido	3.1.50	Iarbus
And in my thoughts is shrin'd another [love] <Iove>:	Dido	3.1.58	Dido
Lest their grosse eye-beames taint my lovers cheekes:	Dido	3.1.74	Dido
You shall not hurt my father when he comes.	Dido	3.1.80	Cupid
His glistering eyes shall be my looking glasse,	Dido	3.1.86	Dido
His lookes shall be my only Librarie,	Dido	3.1.90	Dido
Yet Queene of Affricke, are my ships unrigd,	Dido	3.1.105	Aeneas
My Sailes all rent in sunder with the winde,	Dido	3.1.106	Aeneas
My Oares broken, and my Tackling lost,	Dido	3.1.107	Aeneas
Yea all my Navie split with Rockes and Shelfes:	Dido	3.1.108	Aeneas
To warre against my bordering enemies:	Dido	3.1.135	Dido
See where the pictures of my suiters hang,	Dido	3.1.139	Dido
Have been most urgent suiters for my love,	Dido	3.1.151	Dido
But weapons gree not with my tender yeares:	Dido	3.1.164	Dido
Because it may be thou shalt be my love:	Dido	3.1.170	Dido
O if I speake/I shall betray my selfe:--	Dido	3.1.173	Dido
Here lyes my hate, Aeneas cursed brat,	Dido	3.2.1	Juno
That ugly impe that shall outweare my wrath,	Dido	3.2.4	Juno
And wrong my deitie with high disgrace:	Dido	3.2.5	Juno
O no God wot, I cannot watch my time,	Dido	3.2.14	Juno
And have no gall at all to grieve my foes:	Dido	3.2.17	Juno

MY (cont.)

my Doves are back returnd,/Who warne me of such daunger prest	Dido	3.2.21	Venus
To harme my sweete Ascanius lovely life.	Dido	3.2.23	Venus
Juno, my mortall foe, what make you here?	Dido	3.2.24	Venus
Avaunt old witch and trouble not my wits.	Dido	3.2.25	Venus
Out hatefull hag, thou wouldst have slaine my sonne,	Dido	3.2.32	Venus
Had not my Doves discov'rd thy entent:	Dido	3.2.33	Venus
If thou but lay thy fingers on my boy.	Dido	3.2.36	Venus
That was advanced by my Hebes shame,	Dido	3.2.43	Juno
Wherefore I [chaungd] <chaunge> my counsell with the time,	Dido	3.2.51	Juno
And thy faire peacockes by my pigeons pearch:	Dido	3.2.59	Venus
Love my Aeneas, and desire is thine,	Dido	3.2.60	Venus
The day, the night, my Swannes, my sweetes are thine.	Dido	3.2.61	Venus
That overcloy my soule with their content:	Dido	3.2.63	Juno
But much I feare my sonne will nere consent,	Dido	3.2.82	Venus
Sister, I see you savour of my wiles,	Dido	3.2.96	Venus
Meane time, Ascanius shall be my charge,	Dido	3.2.98	Venus
My princely robes thou seest are layd aside,	Dido	3.3.3	Dido
Faire Troian, hold my golden bowe awhile,	Dido	3.3.7	Dido
Untill I gird my quiver to my side:	Dido	3.3.8	Dido
Or els I would have given my life in gage.	Dido	3.3.29	Iarbus
Meane time these wanton weapons serve my warre,	Dido	3.3.37	Cupid
And overjoy my thoughts with their escape:	Dido	3.3.57	Aeneas
turne the hand of fate/Unto that happie day of my delight,	Dido	3.3.81	Iarbus
What ailes my Queene, is she falne sicke of late?	Dido	3.4.24	Aeneas
Not sicke my love, but sicke:--	Dido	3.4.25	Dido
And yet Ile speake, and yet Ile hold my peace,	Dido	3.4.27	Dido
Doe shame her worst, I will disclose my griefe:--	Dido	3.4.28	Dido
Whose golden Crowne might ballance my content:	Dido	3.4.36	Dido
As my despised worths, that shun all praise,	Dido	3.4.42	Aeneas
With this my hand I give to you my heart,	Dido	3.4.43	Aeneas
By heaven and earth, and my faire brothers bowe,	Dido	3.4.45	Aeneas
From whence my radiant mother did descend,	Dido	3.4.47	Aeneas
That calles my soule from forth his living seate,	Dido	3.4.53	Dido
Wherewith my husband woo'd me yet a maide,	Dido	3.4.63	Dido
And be thou king of Libia, by my guift.	Dido	3.4.64	Dido
In all my life I never knew the like,	Dido	4.1.7	Anna
Nay, where is my warlike father, can you tell?	Dido	4.1.15	Cupid
That with the sharpnes of my edged sting,	Dido	4.1.22	Iarbus
O leave me, leave me to my silent thoughts,	Dido	4.2.38	Iarbus
That register the numbers of my ruth,	Dido	4.2.39	Iarbus
Before my sorrowes tide have any stint.	Dido	4.2.42	Iarbus
That intercepts the course of my desire:	Dido	4.2.48	Iarbus
That doe pursue my peace where ere it goes.	Dido	4.2.51	Iarbus
And strewe thy walkes with my discheveld haire.	Dido	4.2.56	Anna
Carthage, my friendly host adue,	Dido	4.3.1	Aeneas
Jove wils it so, my mother wils it so:	Dido	4.3.5	Aeneas
Let my Phenissa graunt, and then I goe:	Dido	4.3.6	Aeneas
The dreames (brave mates) that did beset my bed,	Dido	4.3.16	Aeneas
To stay my Fleete from loosing forth the Bay:	Dido	4.3.26	Aeneas
And let me linke [thy] <my> bodie to my <thy> lips,	Dido	4.3.28	Aeneas
I went to take my farewell of Achates.	Dido	4.4.18	Aeneas
Sway thou the Punike Scepter in my steede,	Dido	4.4.35	Dido
And beare this golden Scepter in my hand?	Dido	4.4.41	Aeneas
O keepe them still, and let me gaze my fill:	Dido	4.4.44	Dido
When I leave thee, death be my punishment,	Dido	4.4.56	Aeneas
And now to make experience of my love,	Dido	4.4.64	Dido
Faire sister Anna leade my lover forth,	Dido	4.4.65	Dido
And seated on my Gennet, let him ride/As Didos husband through	Dido	4.4.66	Dido
And will my guard with Mauritanian darts,	Dido	4.4.68	Dido
Commaund my guard to slay for their offence:	Dido	4.4.72	Dido
And from a turret Ile behold my love.	Dido	4.4.86	Dido
I, but it may be he will leave my love,	Dido	4.4.97	Dido
That he might suffer shipwracke on my breast,	Dido	4.4.102	Dido
Goe, bid my Nurse take yong Ascanius,	Dido	4.4.105	Dido
Or impious traitors vowde to have my life,	Dido	4.4.114	Dido
Presage the downfall of my Emperie,	Dido	4.4.118	Dido
It is Aeneas frowne that ends my daies:	Dido	4.4.120	Dido
Drive if you can my house to Italy:	Dido	4.4.129	Dido
And shrunke not backe, knowing my love was there?	Dido	4.4.146	Dido
But dares to heape up sorrowe to my heart:	Dido	4.4.152	Dido
Now let him hang my favours on his masts,	Dido	4.4.159	Dido
My Lord Ascanius, ye must goe with me.	Dido	4.5.1	Nurse
Whither must I goe? Ile stay with my mother.	Dido	4.5.2	Cupid
No, thou shalt goe with me unto my house,	Dido	4.5.3	Nurse
My vaines are withered, and my sinewes drie,	Dido	4.5.33	Nurse
Triumph, my mates, our travels are at end,	Dido	5.1.1	Aeneas
That have I not determinde with my selfe.	Dido	5.1.19	Aeneas
Of my old fathers name.	Dido	5.1.23	Aeneas
This was my mother that beguild the Queene,	Dido	5.1.42	Aeneas
And made me take my brother for my sonne:	Dido	5.1.43	Aeneas
Who have no sailes nor tackling for my ships?	Dido	5.1.56	Aeneas
Though she repairde my fleete and gave me ships,	Dido	5.1.59	Aeneas
Yet hath she tane away my oares and masts,	Dido	5.1.60	Aeneas
Iarbus, I am cleane besides my selfe,	Dido	5.1.63	Aeneas
When as I want both rigging for my fleete,	Dido	5.1.69	Aeneas
And also furniture for these my men.	Dido	5.1.70	Aeneas
Not from my heart, for I can hardly goe,	Dido	5.1.103	Aeneas
I dye, if my Aeneas say farewell.	Dido	5.1.108	Dido
O speake like my Aeneas, like my love:	Dido	5.1.112	Dido
Say thou wilt stay in Carthage with [thy] <my> Queene,	Dido	5.1.117	Dido
The Gods, what Gods be those that seeke my death?	Dido	5.1.128	Dido
many neighbour kings/were up in armes, for making thee my love?	Dido	5.1.142	Dido

MY (cont.)

But rather will augment then ease my woe?	Dido	5.1.152	Dido
In vaine my love thou spendst thy fainting breath,	Dido	5.1.153	Aeneas
And I for pitie harbord in my bosome,	Dido	5.1.166	Dido
Why star'st thou in my face?	Dido	5.1.179	Dido
Yet he that in my sight would not relent,	Dido	5.1.186	Dido
Returnes amaine: welcome, welcome my love:	Dido	5.1.191	Dido
What meanes my sister thus to rave and crye?	Dido	5.1.193	Anna
O Anna, my Aeneas is abourd,	Dido	5.1.194	Dido
And I am thus deluded of my boy:	Dido	5.1.219	Dido
My sister comes, I like not her sad lookes.	Dido	5.1.225	Dido
My teares nor plaints could mollifie a whit:	Dido	5.1.235	Anna
Then carelesly I rent my haire for griefe,	Dido	5.1.236	Anna
They gan to move him to redresse my ruth,	Dido	5.1.238	Anna
And ride upon his backe unto my love:	Dido	5.1.250	Dido
See where he comes, welcome, welcome my love.	Dido	5.1.261	Dido
And he hath all [my] <thy> fleete, what shall I doe/But dye in	Dido	5.1.268	Dido
I, I must be the murderer of my selfe:	Dido	5.1.270	Dido
Goe Anna, bid my servants bring me fire.	Dido	5.1.278	Dido
How long shall I with griefe consume my daies,	Dido	5.1.281	Iarbus
And reape no guerdon for my truest love?	Dido	5.1.282	Iarbus
To cure my minde that melts for unkind love.	Dido	5.1.287	Dido
None in the world shall have my love but thou:	Dido	5.1.290	Dido
What can my teares or cryes prevaile me now?	Dido	5.1.319	Anna
Iarbus slaine, Iarbus my deare love,	Dido	5.1.321	Anna
To see my sweet Iarbus slay himselfe?	Dido	5.1.324	Anna
That Gods and men may pitie this my death,	Dido	5.1.327	Anna
Brother Cosroe, I find my selfe agreev'd,	1Tamb	1.1.1	Mycet
Good brother tell the cause unto my Lords,	1Tamb	1.1.4	Mycet
But I refer me to my noble men,	1Tamb	1.1.21	Mycet
That knowe my wit, and can be witnesses:	1Tamb	1.1.22	Mycet
Not for so small a fault my soveraigne Lord.	1Tamb	1.1.25	Meandr
Meander, thou my faithfull Counsellor,	1Tamb	1.1.28	Mycet
Declare the cause of my conceived griefe,	1Tamb	1.1.29	Mycet
Dooth pray uppon my flockes of Passengers,	1Tamb	1.1.32	Mycet
And as I heare, doth meane to pull my plumes.	1Tamb	1.1.33	Mycet
Ful true thou speakst, and like thy selfe my lord,	1Tamb	1.1.49	Mycet
To send my thousand horse incontinent,	1Tamb	1.1.52	Mycet
How like you this, my honorable Lords?	1Tamb	1.1.54	Mycet
Doubt not my Lord and gratious Soveraigne,	1Tamb	1.1.70	Therid
Then now my Lord, I humbly take my leave.	1Tamb	1.1.81	Therid
Well here I sweare by this my royal seat--	1Tamb	1.1.97	Mycet
Embost with silke as best beseemes my state,	1Tamb	1.1.99	Mycet
How now my Lord, what, mated and amaz'd/To heare the king thus	1Tamb	1.1.107	Menaph
is that doth excruciate/The verie substance of my vexed soule:	1Tamb	1.1.114	Cosroe
Behold, my Lord, Ortigius and the rest,	1Tamb	1.1.134	Menaph
And languish in my brothers government:	1Tamb	1.1.156	Cosroe
And vow to weare it for my countries good:	1Tamb	1.1.158	Cosroe
In spight of them shall malice my estate.	1Tamb	1.1.159	Cosroe
Whether we presently will flie (my Lords)/To rest secure	1Tamb	1.1.177	Cosroe
will flie (my Lords)/To rest secure against my brothers force.	1Tamb	1.1.178	Cosroe
We knew my Lord, before we brought the crowne,	1Tamb	1.1.179	Ortyg
I know it wel my Lord, and thanke you all.	1Tamb	1.1.187	Cosroe
Ah Shepheard, pity my distressed plight,	1Tamb	1.2.7	Zenoc
these Medean Lords/To Memphis, from my uncles country of Medea,	1Tamb	1.2.12	Zenoc
Where all my youth I have bene governed,	1Tamb	1.2.13	Zenoc
And through my provinces you must expect/Letters of conduct	1Tamb	1.2.23	Tamb
you must expect/Letters of conduct from my mightinesse,	1Tamb	1.2.24	Tamb
As any prizes out of my precinct.	1Tamb	1.2.28	Tamb
For they are friends that help to weane my state,	1Tamb	1.2.29	Tamb
And must maintaine my life exempt from servitude.	1Tamb	1.2.31	Tamb
I am (my Lord), for so you do import.	1Tamb	1.2.33	Zenoc
I am a Lord, for so my deeds shall proove,	1Tamb	1.2.34	Tamb
And yet a shepheard by my Parentage:	1Tamb	1.2.35	Tamb
Or you my Lordes to be my followers?	1Tamb	1.2.83	Tamb
Shall buy the meanest souldier in my traine.	1Tamb	1.2.86	Tamb
Which graticus starres have promist at my birth.	1Tamb	1.2.92	Tamb
My martiall prises with five hundred men,	1Tamb	1.2.102	Tamb
And then my selfe to faire Zenocrate.	1Tamb	1.2.105	Tamb
How now my Lords of Egypt and Zenocrate?	1Tamb	1.2.113	Tamb
Soft ye my Lords and sweet Zenocrate.	1Tamb	1.2.119	Tamb
My selfe will bide the danger of the brunt.	1Tamb	1.2.151	Tamb
And with my hand turne Fortunes wheel about,	1Tamb	1.2.175	Tamb
Intending but to rase my charmed skin:	1Tamb	1.2.179	Tamb
As if he meant to give my Souldiers pay,	1Tamb	1.2.183	Tamb
To be my Queen and portly Emperesse.	1Tamb	1.2.187	Tamb
And lead thy thousand horse with my conduct,	1Tamb	1.2.189	Tamb
Joine with me now in this my meane estate,	1Tamb	1.2.202	Tamb
admyre me nct)/And when my name and honor shall be spread,	1Tamb	1.2.205	Tamb
Then thou shalt find my vaunts substantiall.	1Tamb	1.2.213	Tamb
What stronge enchantments tice my yeelding soule?	1Tamb	1.2.224	Therid
But shall I proove a Traitor to my King?	1Tamb	1.2.226	Therid
I yeeld my selfe, my men and horse to thee:	1Tamb	1.2.229	Therid
Theridamas my friend, take here my hand,	1Tamb	1.2.232	Tamb
And call'd the Gods to witnesse of my vow,	1Tamb	1.2.234	Tamb
Thus shall my heart be still combinde with thine,	1Tamb	1.2.235	Tamb
These are my friends in whom I more rejoice,	1Tamb	1.2.241	Tamb
Shal want my heart to be with gladnes pierc'd/To do you honor	1Tamb	1.2.250	Therid
And now faire Madam, and my noble Lords,	1Tamb	1.2.253	Tamb
That leads to Pallace of my brothers life,	1Tamb	2.1.43	Cosroe
In faire Persea noble Tamburlaine/Shall be my Regent, and	1Tamb	2.1.49	Cosroe
I will my Lord.	1Tamb	2.1.69	Menaph
Come my Meander, let us to this geere,	1Tamb	2.2.1	Mycet

MY (cont.)

I tel you true my heart is swolne with wrath,	1Tamb	2.2.2	Mycet
And of that false Cosroe, my traiterous brother.	1Tamb	2.2.4	Mycet
An hundred horsmen of my company/Scowting abroad upon these	1Tamb	2.2.39	Spy
So Poets say, my Lord.	1Tamb	2.2.53	Meandr
Go on my Lord, and give your charge I say,	1Tamb	2.2.57	Mycet
He tells you true, my maisters, so he does.	1Tamb	2.2.74	Mycet
In thy approoved Fortunes all my hope,	1Tamb	2.3.2	Cosroe
And so mistake you not a whit my Lord.	1Tamb	2.3.6	Tamb
And let my Fortunes and my valour sway,	1Tamb	2.3.11	Tamb
You see my Lord, what woorking woordes he hath.	1Tamb	2.3.25	Therid
and excusde/For turning my poore charge to his direction.	1Tamb	2.3.29	Therid
And these his two renowmed friends my Lord,	1Tamb	2.3.30	Therid
Which I esteeme as portion of my crown.	1Tamb	2.3.35	Cosroe
That I with these my friends and all my men,	1Tamb	2.3.43	Tamb
My Lord, we have discovered the enemie/Ready to chardge you	1Tamb	2.3.49	1Msngr
And set it safe on my victorious head.	1Tamb	2.3.54	Cosroe
They cannot take away my crowne from me.	1Tamb	2.4.14	Mycet
So I can when I see my time.	1Tamb	2.4.26	Mycet
Thee doo I make my Regent of Persea,	1Tamb	2.5.8	Cosroe
And Generall Lieftenant of my Armies.	1Tamb	2.5.9	Cosroe
Emperour in humblest tearms/I vow my service to your Majestie,	1Tamb	2.5.16	Meandr
With utmost vertue of my faith and dutie.	1Tamb	2.5.17	Meandr
The Lords and Captaines of my brothers campe,	1Tamb	2.5.26	Cosroe
And gladly yeeld them to my gracious rule:	1Tamb	2.5.28	Cosroe
Ortigius and Menaphon, my trustie friendes,	1Tamb	2.5.29	Cosroe
thee (sweet Ortigius)/Better replies shall proove my purposes.	1Tamb	2.5.37	Cosroe
And now Lord Tamburlaine, my brothers Campe/I leave to thee, and	1Tamb	2.5.38	Cosroe
My witlesse brother to the Christians lost:	1Tamb	2.5.42	Cosroe
I long to sit upon my brothers throne.	1Tamb	2.5.47	Cosroe
O my Lord, tis sweet and full of pompe.	1Tamb	2.5.55	Techel
What saies my other friends, wil you be kings?	1Tamb	2.5.67	Tamb
I, if I could with all my heart my Lord.	1Tamb	2.5.68	Techel
And so would you my maisters, would you not?	1Tamb	2.5.70	Tamb
What then my Lord?	1Tamb	2.5.71	Usumc
To get the Persean Kingdome to my selfe:	1Tamb	2.5.82	Tamb
Twil proove a pretie jest (in faith) my friends.	1Tamb	2.5.90	Tamb
Nobly resolv'd, my good Ortygius.	1Tamb	2.6.24	Cosroe
Resolve my Lords and loving souldiers now,	1Tamb	2.6.34	Cosroe
the Starres that make/The loathsome Circle of my dated life,	1Tamb	2.6.37	Cosroe
Direct my weapon to his barbarous heart,	1Tamb	2.6.38	Cosroe
Thus to deprive me of my crowne and life.	1Tamb	2.7.2	Cosroe
Even at the morning of my happy state,	1Tamb	2.7.4	Cosroe
Scarce being seated in my royall throne,	1Tamb	2.7.5	Cosroe
To worke my downfall and untimely end.	1Tamb	2.7.6	Cosroe
An uncouth paine torments my grieved soule,	1Tamb	2.7.7	Cosroe
And death arrests the organe of my voice,	1Tamb	2.7.8	Cosroe
Sackes every vaine and artier of my heart.	1Tamb	2.7.10	Cosroe
My bloodlesse body waxeth chill and colde,	1Tamb	2.7.42	Cosroe
And with my blood my life slides through my wound,	1Tamb	2.7.43	Cosroe
My soule begins to take her flight to hell:	1Tamb	2.7.44	Cosroe
And sommons all my sences to depart.	1Tamb	2.7.45	Cosroe
dooth gastly death/With greedy tallents gripe my bleeding hart,	1Tamb	2.7.49	Cosroe
And like a Harpyr <Harpye> tires on my life.	1Tamb	2.7.50	Cosroe
So, now it is more surer on my head,	1Tamb	2.7.65	Tamb
Great Kings of Barbary, and my portly Bassoes,	1Tamb	3.1.1	Bajzth
Hie thee my Bassoe fast to Persea,	1Tamb	3.1.21	Bajzth
Least he incurre the furie of my wrath.	1Tamb	3.1.30	Bajzth
True (Argier) and tremble at my lookes.	1Tamb	3.1.49	Bajzth
And all the sea my Gallies countermaund.	1Tamb	3.1.63	Bajzth
As it hath chang'd my first conceiv'd disdaine.	1Tamb	3.2.12	Zenoc
Yet since a farther passion feeds my thoughts,	1Tamb	3.2.13	Zenoc
Which dies my lookes so livelesse as they are.	1Tamb	3.2.15	Zenoc
And might, if my extreams had full events,	1Tamb	3.2.16	Zenoc
And leave my body sencelesse as the earth.	1Tamb	3.2.22	Zenoc
So lookes my Lordly love, faire Tamburlaine.	1Tamb	3.2.49	Zenoc
And higher would I reare my estimate,	1Tamb	3.2.53	Zenoc
Thence rise the tears that so distain my cheeks,	1Tamb	3.2.64	Zenoc
Fearing his love through my unworthynesse.	1Tamb	3.2.65	Zenoc
late felt frownes/That sent a tempest to my daunted thoughtes,	1Tamb	3.2.86	Agidas
And makes my soule devine her overthrow.	1Tamb	3.2.87	Agidas
He needed not with words confirme my feare,	1Tamb	3.2.92	Agidas
working tooles present/The naked action of my threatned end.	1Tamb	3.2.94	Agidas
see how right the man/Hath hit the meaning of my Lord the King.	1Tamb	3.2.108	Techel
View well my Camp, and speake indifferently,	1Tamb	3.3.8	Tamb
Doo not my captaines and my souldiers looke/As if they meant to	1Tamb	3.3.9	Tamb
My Lord, the great Commander of the worlde,	1Tamb	3.3.13	Bassoe
Bassoes and Janisaries of my Guard,	1Tamb	3.3.61	Bajzth
those that lead my horse/Have to their names tytles of dignity,	1Tamb	3.3.69	Bajzth
And know thou Turke, that those which lead my horse,	1Tamb	3.3.72	Tamb
By Mahomet, my Kinsmans sepulcher,	1Tamb	3.3.75	Bajzth
And in my Sarell tend my Concubines:	1Tamb	3.3.78	Bajzth
Shall draw the chariot of my Emperesse,	1Tamb	3.3.80	Bajzth
By this my sword that conquer'd Persea,	1Tamb	3.3.82	Tamb
But every common souldier of my Camp/Shall smile to see thy	1Tamb	3.3.85	Tamb
Wel said my stout contributory kings,	1Tamb	3.3.93	Bajzth
Your threefold armie and my hugie hoste,	1Tamb	3.3.94	Bajzth
I speake it, and my words are oracles.	1Tamb	3.3.102	Tamb
And on thy head weare my Emperiall crowne,	1Tamb	3.3.113	Bajzth
adorned with my Crowne,/As if thou wert the Empresse of the	1Tamb	3.3.124	Tamb
untill thou see/Me martch victoriously with all my men,	1Tamb	3.3.127	Tamb
Til then take thou my crowne, vaunt of my worth,	1Tamb	3.3.130	Tamb
And may my love, the king of Persea,	1Tamb	3.3.132	Zenoc

MY (cont.)

And as the heads of Hydra, so my power/Subdued, shall stand as	1Tamb	3.3.140		Bajzth
My Campe is like to Julius Caesars Hoste,	1Tamb	3.3.152		Tamb
As these my followers willingly would have:	1Tamb	3.3.155		Tamb
Resting her selfe upon my milk-white Tent:	1Tamb	3.3.161		Tamb
But come my Lords, to weapons let us fall.	1Tamb	3.3.162		Tamb
Thou shalt be Landresse to my waiting maid.	1Tamb	3.3.177		Zabina
And how my slave, her mistresse menaceth.	1Tamb	3.3.183		Zenoc
send for them/To do the work my chamber maid disdaines.	1Tamb	3.3.188		Anippe
And made my lordly Love her worthy King:	1Tamb	3.3.190		Zenoc
As when my Emperour overthrew the Greeks:	1Tamb	3.3.204		Zabina
Prepare thy selfe to live and die my slave.	1Tamb	3.3.207		Zabina
My royall Lord is slaine or conquered,	1Tamb	3.3.209		Zenoc
Deliver them into my treasurie.	1Tamb	3.3.217		Tamb
Now let me offer to my gracious Lord,	1Tamb	3.3.218		Zenoc
How dare you thus abuse my Majesty?	1Tamb	3.3.226		Zabina
Are falne in clusters at my conquering feet.	1Tamb	3.3.230		Tamb
And making bonfires for my overthrow.	1Tamb	3.3.238		Bajzth
And write my selfe great Lord of Affrica:	1Tamb	3.3.245		Tamb
And dig for treasure to appease my wrath:	1Tamb	3.3.265		Tamb
The Turkesse let my Loves maid lead away.	1Tamb	3.3.267		Tamb
Ah villaines, dare ye touch my sacred armes?	1Tamb	3.3.268		Bajzth
Of my faire daughter, and his princely Love:	1Tamb	4.1.70		Souldn
Bring out my foot-stocle.	1Tamb	4.2.1		Tamb
Then it should so conspire my overthrow.	1Tamb	4.2.11		Tamb
That I may rise into my royall throne.	1Tamb	4.2.15		Tamb
First shalt thou rip my bowels with thy sword,	1Tamb	4.2.16		Bajzth
And sacrifice my heart to death and hell,	1Tamb	4.2.17		Bajzth
That beares the honor of my royall waight.	1Tamb	4.2.21		Tamb
Smile Stars that raign'd at my nativity,	1Tamb	4.2.33		Tamb
My sword stroke fire from his coat of steele,	1Tamb	4.2.41		Tamb
It shall be said, I made it red my selfe,	1Tamb	4.2.54		Tamb
Before thou met my husband in the field,	1Tamb	4.2.59		Zabina
You must devise some torment worsse, my Lord,	1Tamb	4.2.66		Techel
She is my Handmaids slave, and she shal looke/That these abuses	1Tamb	4.2.69		Zenoc
Let these be warnings for you then my slave,	1Tamb	4.2.72		Anippe
Great Tamburlaine, great in my overthrow,	1Tamb	4.2.75		Bajzth
with the scraps/My servitures shall bring the from my boord.	1Tamb	4.2.88		Tamb
This is my minde, and I will have it so.	1Tamb	4.2.91		Tamb
If they would lay their crownes before my feet,	1Tamb	4.2.93		Tamb
Techelles, and my loving followers,	1Tamb	4.2.101		Tamb
until the bloody flag/Be once advanc'd on my vermilion Tent,	1Tamb	4.2.117		Tamb
Yet would you have some pitie for my sake,	1Tamb	4.2.123		Zenoc
Because it is my countries, and my Fathers.	1Tamb	4.2.124		Zenoc
My Lord it is the bloody Tamburlaine,	1Tamb	4.3.11		Souldn
I long to breake my speare upon his crest,	1Tamb	4.3.46		Arabia
My mind presageth fortunate successe,	1Tamb	4.3.58		Arabia
my spirit doth foresee/The utter ruine of thy men and thee.	1Tamb	4.3.59		Arabia
Halfe dead for feare before they feele my wrath:	1Tamb	4.4.4		Tamb
My Lord, how can you suffer these outragious curses by these	1Tamb	4.4.26	P	Zenoc
them see (divine Zenocrate)/I glorie in the curses of my foes,	1Tamb	4.4.29		Tamb
take it from my swords point, or Ile thrust it to thy heart.	1Tamb	4.4.40	P	Tamb
He stamps it under his feet my Lord.	1Tamb	4.4.42	P	Therid
Here is my dagger, dispatch her while she is fat, for if she	1Tamb	4.4.48	P	Tamb
Yes, my Lord.	1Tamb	4.4.59	P	Zenoc
My lord, to see my fathers towne besieg'd,	1Tamb	4.4.65		Zenoc
The countrie wasted where my selfe was borne,	1Tamb	4.4.66		Zenoc
How can it but afflict my verie soule?	1Tamb	4.4.67		Zenoc
If any love remaine in you my Lord,	1Tamb	4.4.68		Zenoc
Or if my love unto your majesty/May merit favour at your	1Tamb	4.4.69		Zenoc
And with my father take a frindly truce.	1Tamb	4.4.72		Zenoc
Yet would I with my sword make Jove to stoope.	1Tamb	4.4.74		Tamb
Citties and townes/After my name and thine Zenocrate:	1Tamb	4.4.80		Tamb
Yet give me leave to plead for him my Lord.	1Tamb	4.4.86		Zenoc
thou maist thinke thy selfe happie to be fed from my trencher.	1Tamb	4.4.93	P	Tamb
My empty stomacke ful of idle heat,	1Tamb	4.4.94		Bajzth
Drawes bloody humours from my feeble partes,	1Tamb	4.4.95		Bajzth
My vaines are pale, my sinowes hard and drie,	1Tamb	4.4.97		Bajzth
My jointes benumb'd, unlesse I eat, I die.	1Tamb	4.4.98		Bajzth
So it would my lord, specially having so smal a walke, and so	1Tamb	4.4.105	P	Therid
I (my Lord) but none save kinges must feede with these.	1Tamb	4.4.109	P	Therid
these three crownes, and pledge me, my contributorie Kings.	1Tamb	4.4.115	P	Tamb
Leave us my Lord, and loving countrimen,	1Tamb	5.1.60		2Virgn
They know my custome:	1Tamb	5.1.67		Tamb
when first my milkwhite flags/Through which sweet mercie threw	1Tamb	5.1.68		Tamb
hate/Flings slaughtering terrour from my coleblack tents.	1Tamb	5.1.72		Tamb
Behold my sword, what see you at the point?	1Tamb	5.1.108		Tamb
Nothing but feare and fatall steele my Lord.	1Tamb	5.1.109		1Virgn
He now is seated on my horsmens speares,	1Tamb	5.1.114		Tamb
few of them/To chardge these Dames, and shew my servant death,	1Tamb	5.1.117		Tamb
Nor change my Martiall observations,	1Tamb	5.1.122		Tamb
And know my customes are as peremptory/As wrathfull Planets,	1Tamb	5.1.127		Tamb
They have my Lord, and on Damascus wals/Have hoisted up their	1Tamb	5.1.130		Techel
But goe my Lords, put the rest to the sword.	1Tamb	5.1.134		Tamb
armours fight/A doubtfull battell with my tempted thoughtes,	1Tamb	5.1.152		Tamb
Whose sorrowes lay more siege unto my soule,	1Tamb	5.1.155		Tamb
Than all my Army to Damascus walles.	1Tamb	5.1.156		Tamb
nor the Turk/Troubled my sences with conceit of foile,	1Tamb	5.1.158		Tamb
What is beauty, saith my sufferings then?	1Tamb	5.1.160		Tamb
But how unseemly is it for my Sex,	1Tamb	5.1.174		Tamb
My discipline of armes and Chivalrie,	1Tamb	5.1.175		Tamb
My nature and the terrour of my name,	1Tamb	5.1.176		Tamb
Shal give the world to note, for all my byrth,	1Tamb	5.1.188		Tamb

MY (cont.)

I, my Lord.	1Tamb	5.1.193	P Attend
The town is ours my Lord, and fresh supply/Of conquest, and of	1Tamb	5.1.196	Techel
We know the victorie is ours my Lord,	1Tamb	5.1.203	Therid
And now my footstoole, if I loose the field,	1Tamb	5.1.209	Tamb
Here let him stay my maysters from the tents,	1Tamb	5.1.211	Tamb
O life more loathsome to my vexed thoughts,	1Tamb	5.1.255	Bajzth
O dreary Engines of my loathed sight,	1Tamb	5.1.259	Bajzth
That sees my crowne, my honor and my name,	1Tamb	5.1.260	Bajzth
And sink not quite into my tortur'd soule.	1Tamb	5.1.263	Bajzth
You see my wife, my Queene and Emperesse,	1Tamb	5.1.264	Bajzth
From whence the issues of my thoughts doe breake:	1Tamb	5.1.274	Bajzth
O poore Zabina, O my Queen, my Queen,	1Tamb	5.1.275	Bajzth
Fetch me some water for my burning breast,	1Tamb	5.1.276	Bajzth
That in the shortned sequel of my life,	1Tamb	5.1.278	Bajzth
I may poure foorth my soule into thine armes,	1Tamb	5.1.279	Bajzth
sparke of breath/Can quench or coole the torments of my griefe.	1Tamb	5.1.285	Zabina
That may be ministers of my decay.	1Tamb	5.1.289	Bajzth
Accursed day infected with my griefs,	1Tamb	5.1.291	Bajzth
And my pin'd soule resolv'd in liquid [ayre] <ay>,	1Tamb	5.1.300	Bajzth
Pierce through the center of my withered heart,	1Tamb	5.1.303	Bajzth
And make a passage for my loathed life.	1Tamb	5.1.304	Bajzth
What do mine eies behold, my husband dead?	1Tamb	5.1.305	Zabina
The braines of Bajazeth, my Lord and Soveraigne?	1Tamb	5.1.307	Zabina
O Bajazeth, my husband and my Lord,	1Tamb	5.1.308	Zabina
and fire, and my blood I bring him againe, teare me in peeces,	1Tamb	5.1.310	P Zabina
Goe to, my child, away, away, away.	1Tamb	5.1.313	P Zabina
Make ready my Coch, my chaire, my jewels, I come, I come, I come	1Tamb	5.1.317	P Zabina
Ah wretched eies, the enemies of my hart,	1Tamb	5.1.340	Zenoc
And tell my soule mor tales of bleeding ruth?	1Tamb	5.1.342	Zenoc
Ah Tamburlaine, my love, sweet Tamburlaine,	1Tamb	5.1.355	Zenoc
Pardon my Love, oh pardon his contempt,	1Tamb	5.1.364	Zenoc
Ready for battaile gainst my Lord the King.	1Tamb	5.1.382	Philem
and feare presents/A thousand sorrowes to my martyred soule:	1Tamb	5.1.384	Zenoc
When my poore pleasures are devided thus,	1Tamb	5.1.386	Zenoc
And rackt by dutie from my cursed heart:	1Tamb	5.1.387	Zenoc
My father and my first betrothed love,	1Tamb	5.1.388	Zenoc
Must fight against my life and present love:	1Tamb	5.1.389	Zenoc
Wherin the change I use condemns my faith,	1Tamb	5.1.390	Zenoc
And makes my deeds infamous through the world.	1Tamb	5.1.391	Zenoc
So for a finall Issue to my griefes,	1Tamb	5.1.395	Zenoc
To pacifie my countrie and my love,	1Tamb	5.1.396	Zenoc
Conclude a league of honor to my hope.	1Tamb	5.1.399	Zenoc
With happy safty of my fathers life,	1Tamb	5.1.401	Zenoc
Too deare a witnesse for such love, my Lord.	1Tamb	5.1.412	Zenoc
Whose sight with joy would take away my life,	1Tamb	5.1.419	Arabia
As now it bringeth sweetnesse to my wound,	1Tamb	5.1.420	Arabia
Would lend an howers license to my tongue:	1Tamb	5.1.423	Arabia
To drive all sorrow from my fainting soule:	1Tamb	5.1.429	Arabia
Depriv'd of care, my heart with comfort dies,	1Tamb	5.1.431	Arabia
Though my right hand have thus enthralled thee,	1Tamb	5.1.435	Tamb
She that hath calmde the furie of my sword,	1Tamb	5.1.437	Tamb
O sight thrice welcome to my joiful soule,	1Tamb	5.1.440	Zenoc
To see the king my Father issue safe,	1Tamb	5.1.441	Zenoc
From dangerous battel of my conquering Love.	1Tamb	5.1.442	Zenoc
Wel met my only deare Zenocrate,	1Tamb	5.1.443	Souldn
Though with the losse of Egypt and my Crown.	1Tamb	5.1.444	Souldn
Twas I my lord that gat the victory,	1Tamb	5.1.445	Tamb
Fearing my power should pull him from his throne.	1Tamb	5.1.453	Tamb
To doo their ceassles homag to my sword:	1Tamb	5.1.456	Tamb
Since I arriv'd with my triumphant hoste,	1Tamb	5.1.458	Tamb
To spread my fame through hell and up to heaven:	1Tamb	5.1.467	Tamb
And see my Lord, a sight of strange import,	1Tamb	5.1.468	Tamb
Emperours and kings lie breathlesse at my feet.	1Tamb	5.1.469	Tamb
Al sights of power to grace my victory:	1Tamb	5.1.474	Tamb
And I am pleasde with this my overthrow,	1Tamb	5.1.482	Souldn
But here these kings that on my fortunes wait,	1Tamb	5.1.490	Tamb
Invest her here my Queene of Persea.	1Tamb	5.1.494	Tamb
Els should I much forget my self, my Lord.	1Tamb	5.1.500	Zenoc
My hand is ready to performe the deed,	1Tamb	5.1.503	Techel
And here's the crown my Lord, help set it on.	1Tamb	5.1.505	Usumc
So lookes my Love, shadowing in her browes/Triumphes and	1Tamb	5.1.512	Tamb
in her browes/Triumphes and Trophees for my victories:	1Tamb	5.1.513	Tamb
Adding more courage to my conquering mind.	1Tamb	5.1.515	Tamb
And now my Lords and loving followers,	1Tamb	5.1.522	Tamb
Gainst him my Lord must you addresse your power.	2Tamb	1.1.19	Gazell
My realme, the Center of our Empery/Once lost, All Turkie would	2Tamb	1.1.55	Orcan
If peace, restore it to my hands againe:	2Tamb	1.1.84	Sgsmnd
Forgetst thou, that to have me raise my siege,	2Tamb	1.1.98	Orcan
Wagons of gold were set before my tent:	2Tamb	1.1.99	Orcan
But now Orcanes, view my royall hoste,	2Tamb	1.1.106	Sgsmnd
Then here I sheath it, and give thee my hand,	2Tamb	1.1.127	Sgsmnd
By him that made the world and sav'd my soule,	2Tamb	1.1.133	Sgsmnd
Affrica, and Greece/Follow my Standard and my thundring Drums:	2Tamb	1.1.159	Orcan
I will dispatch chiefe of my army hence/To faire Natolia, and	2Tamb	1.1.161	Orcan
To stay my comming gainst proud Tamburlaine.	2Tamb	1.1.163	Orcan
My Lord I pitie it, and with my heart/Wish your release, but he	2Tamb	1.2.5	Almeda
My soveraigne Lord, renowmed Tamburlain,	2Tamb	1.2.7	Almeda
Yet heare me speake my gentle Almeda.	2Tamb	1.2.13	Callap
wherin at anchor lies/A Turkish Gally of my royall fleet,	2Tamb	1.2.21	Callap
Waiting my comming to the river side,	2Tamb	1.2.22	Callap
but tel me my Lord, if I should goe, would you bee as good as	2Tamb	1.2.61	P Almeda

MY (cont.)

Shall I be made a king for my labour?	2Tamb	1.2.63	P Almeda
Thou shalt be crown'd a king and be my mate.	2Tamb	1.2.66	Callap
When you will my Lord, I am ready.	2Tamb	1.2.76	Almeda
Now goe I to revenge my fathers death.	2Tamb	1.2.78	Callap
And when the ground wheron my souldiers march/Shal rise aloft	2Tamb	1.3.13	Tamb
And not before, my sweet Zenocrate:	2Tamb	1.3.15	Tamb
When these my sonnes, more precious in mine eies/Than all the	2Tamb	1.3.18	Tamb
Would make me thinke them Bastards, not my sons,	2Tamb	1.3.32	Tamb
My gratious Lord, they have their mothers looks,	2Tamb	1.3.35	Zenoc
Wel done my boy, thou shalt have shield and lance,	2Tamb	1.3.43	Tamb
These words assure me boy, thou art my sonne,	2Tamb	1.3.58	Tamb
Why may not I my Lord, as wel as he,	2Tamb	1.3.61	Amyras
But while my brothers follow armes my lord,	2Tamb	1.3.65	Calyph
Let me accompany my gratious mother,	2Tamb	1.3.66	Calyph
My royal chaire of state shall be advanc'd:	2Tamb	1.3.82	Tamb
My Lord, such speeches to our princely sonnes,	2Tamb	1.3.85	Zenoc
And cleave him to the channell with my sword.	2Tamb	1.3.103	Calyph
To make it parcel of my Empery.	2Tamb	1.3.110	Tamb
My Lord the great and mighty Tamburlain,	2Tamb	1.3.113	Therid
My crowne, my selfe, and all the power I have,	2Tamb	1.3.115	Therid
Under my collors march ten thousand Greeks,	2Tamb	1.3.118	Therid
Meet for your service on the sea, my Lord,	2Tamb	1.3.123	Therid
I and my neighbor King of Fesse have brought/To aide thee in	2Tamb	1.3.130	Usumc
Which with my crowne I gladly offer thee.	2Tamb	1.3.136	Usumc
Jove shall send his winged Messenger/To bid me sheath my sword,	2Tamb	1.3.167	Tamb
But now my friends, let me examine ye,	2Tamb	1.3.172	Tamb
My Lord, our men of Barbary have martcht/Foure hundred miles	2Tamb	1.3.174	Usumc
And therefore let them rest a while my Lord.	2Tamb	1.3.184	Usumc
And made him sweare obedience to my crowne.	2Tamb	1.3.190	Techel
And with my power did march to Zansibar,	2Tamb	1.3.194	Techel
Therfore I tooke my course to Manico:	2Tamb	1.3.198	Techel
where unresisted I remoov'd my campe.	2Tamb	1.3.199	Techel
Yet shall my souldiers make no period/Untill Natolia kneele	2Tamb	1.3.216	Therid
Now say my Lords of Buda and Bohemia,	2Tamb	2.1.1	Sgsmnd
Now then my Lord, advantage take hereof,	2Tamb	2.1.22	Fredrk
No whit my Lord:	2Tamb	2.1.33	Baldwn
Then arme my Lords, and issue sodainly,	2Tamb	2.1.60	Sgsmnd
Arme dread Soveraign and my noble Lords.	2Tamb	2.2.24	1Msngr
To armes my Lords, on Christ still let us crie,	2Tamb	2.2.63	Orcan
For my accurst and hatefull perjurie.	2Tamb	2.3.3	Sgsmnd
In this my mortall well deserved wound,	2Tamb	2.3.6	Sgsmnd
End all my penance in my sodaine death,	2Tamb	2.3.7	Sgsmnd
And Christ or Mahomet hath bene my friend.	2Tamb	2.3.11	Orcan
Tis but the fortune of the wars my Lord,	2Tamb	2.3.31	Gazell
Yet in my thoughts shall Christ be honoured,	2Tamb	2.3.33	Orcan
I will my Lord.	2Tamb	2.3.41	Uribas
Then let some holy trance convay my thoughts,	2Tamb	2.4.34	Tamb
That this my life may be as short to me/As are the daies of	2Tamb	2.4.36	Tamb
My Lord, your Majesty shall soone perceive:	2Tamb	2.4.39	1Phstn
Tell me, how fares my faire Zenocrate?	2Tamb	2.4.41	Tamb
I fare my Lord, as other Emperesses,	2Tamb	2.4.42	Zenoc
May never such a change transfourme my love/In whose sweet	2Tamb	2.4.47	Tamb
transfourme my love/In whose sweet being I repose my life,	2Tamb	2.4.48	Tamb
Live still my Love and so conserve my life,	2Tamb	2.4.55	Tamb
Or dieng, be the [author] <anchor> of my death.	2Tamb	2.4.56	Tamb
Live still my Lord, O let my soveraigne live,	2Tamb	2.4.57	Zenoc
The comfort of my future happinesse/And hope to meet your	2Tamb	2.4.62	Zenoc
Turn'd to dispaire, would break my wretched breast,	2Tamb	2.4.64	Zenoc
And furie would confound my present rest.	2Tamb	2.4.65	Zenoc
But let me die my Love, yet let me die,	2Tamb	2.4.66	Zenoc
Your griefe and furie hurtes my second life:	2Tamb	2.4.68	Zenoc
Yet let me kisse my Lord before I die,	2Tamb	2.4.69	Zenoc
And let me die with kissing of my Lord.	2Tamb	2.4.70	Zenoc
But since my life is lengthened yet a while,	2Tamb	2.4.71	Zenoc
Let me take leave of these my loving sonnes,	2Tamb	2.4.72	Zenoc
And of my Lords whose true nobilitie/Have merited my latest	2Tamb	2.4.73	Zenoc
my Lords whose true nobilitie/Have merited my latest memorie:	2Tamb	2.4.74	Zenoc
Some musicke, and my fit wil cease my Lord.	2Tamb	2.4.77	Zenoc
That dares torment the body of my Love,	2Tamb	2.4.79	Tamb
Whose darts do pierce the Center of my soule:	2Tamb	2.4.84	Tamb
For taking hence my faire Zenocrate.	2Tamb	2.4.101	Tamb
For amorous Jove hath snatcht my love from hence,	2Tamb	2.4.107	Tamb
Breaking my steeled lance, with which I burst/The rusty beames	2Tamb	2.4.113	Tamb
Ah good my Lord be patient, she is dead,	2Tamb	2.4.119	Therid
Nothing prevailes, for she is dead my Lord.	2Tamb	2.4.124	Therid
For she is dead? thy words doo pierce my soule.	2Tamb	2.4.125	Tamb
And feed my mind that dies for want of her:	2Tamb	2.4.128	Tamb
As I have conquered kingdomes with my sword.	2Tamb	2.4.136	Tamb
Because this place bereft me of my Love:	2Tamb	2.4.138	Tamb
stature <statue>/And martch about it with my mourning campe,	2Tamb	2.4.141	Tamb
your royall gratitudes/With all the benefits my Empire yeelds:	2Tamb	3.1.9	Callap
as when Bajazeth/My royall Lord and father fild the throne,	2Tamb	3.1.12	Callap
For so hath heaven provided my escape,	2Tamb	3.1.32	Callap
From al the crueltie my soule sustaind,	2Tamb	3.1.33	Callap
By this my friendly keepers happy meanes,	2Tamb	3.1.34	Callap
And so unto my citie of Damasco,	2Tamb	3.1.59	Soria
I march to meet and aide my neigbor kings,	2Tamb	3.1.60	Soria
Wel then my noble Lords, for this my friend,	2Tamb	3.1.68	Callap
That freed me from the bondage of my foe:	2Tamb	3.1.69	Callap
To keep my promise, and to make him king,	2Tamb	3.1.71	Callap
Then wil I shortly keep my promise Almeda.	2Tamb	3.1.78	P Callap
Over my Zenith hang a blazing star,	2Tamb	3.2.6	Tamb

MY (cont.)

Because my deare Zenocrate is dead.	2Tamb	3.2.14	Tamb
Thou shalt be set upon my royall tent.	2Tamb	3.2.37	Tamb
[Those] <whose> looks will shed such influence in my campe,/As	2Tamb	3.2.39	Tamb
And now my lords, advance your speares againe,	2Tamb	3.2.43	Tamb
Sorrow no more my sweet Casane now:	2Tamb	3.2.44	Tamb
As is that towne, so is my heart consum'd,	2Tamb	3.2.49	Amyras
With griefe and sorrow for my mothers death.	2Tamb	3.2.50	Amyras
My mothers death hath mortified my mind,	2Tamb	3.2.51	Celeb
And sorrow stops the passage of my speech.	2Tamb	3.2.52	Celeb
But now my boies, leave off, and list to me,	2Tamb	3.2.53	Tamb
My Lord, but this is dangerous to be done,	2Tamb	3.2.93	Calyph
Hast thou not seene my horsmen charge the foe,	2Tamb	3.2.103	Tamb
And yet at night carrouse within my tent,	2Tamb	3.2.106	Tamb
Come boyes and with your fingers search my wound,	2Tamb	3.2.126	Tamb
And in my blood wash all your hands at once,	2Tamb	3.2.127	Tamb
Now my boyes, what think you of a wound?	2Tamb	3.2.129	Tamb
And me another my Lord.	2Tamb	3.2.133	P Amyras
My boy, Thou shalt not loose a drop of blood,	2Tamb	3.2.137	Tamb
My speech of war, and this my wound you see,	2Tamb	3.2.142	Tamb
Teach you my boyes to beare couragious minds,	2Tamb	3.2.143	Tamb
I long to pierce his bowels with my sword,	2Tamb	3.2.152	Usumc
That hath betraied my gracious Soveraigne,	2Tamb	3.2.153	Usumc
Yes, my Lord, yes, come lets about it.	2Tamb	3.3.10	Soldrs
What requier you my maisters?	2Tamb	3.3.15	Capt
We will my Lord.	2Tamb	3.3.46	Pionrs
Come good my Lord, and let us haste from hence/Along the cave	2Tamb	3.4.1	Olymp
A deadly bullet gliding through my side,	2Tamb	3.4.4	Capt
Lies heavy on my heart, I cannot live.	2Tamb	3.4.5	Capt
I feele my liver pierc'd and all my vaines,	2Tamb	3.4.6	Capt
and all my entrals bath'd/In blood that straineth from their	2Tamb	3.4.8	Capt
Mother dispatch me, or Ile kil my selfe,	2Tamb	3.4.26	Sonne
Sweet mother strike, that I may meet my father.	2Tamb	3.4.30	Sonne
And purge my soule before it come to thee.	2Tamb	3.4.33	Olymp
Killing my selfe, as I have done my sonne,	2Tamb	3.4.35	Olymp
My Lord deceast, was dearer unto me,	2Tamb	3.4.42	Olymp
And for his sake here will I end my daies.	2Tamb	3.4.44	Olymp
And let the end of this my fatall journey,	2Tamb	3.4.81	Olymp
Be likewise end to my accursed life.	2Tamb	3.4.82	Olymp
My royal army is as great as his,	2Tamb	3.5.10	Callap
and stout Bythinians/Came to my bands full fifty thousand more,	2Tamb	3.5.42	Trebiz
My Lord, your presence makes them pale and wan.	2Tamb	3.5.60	Usumc
And fly my glove as from a Scorpion.	2Tamb	3.5.74	Tamb
I shall now revenge/My fathers vile abuses and mine owne.	2Tamb	3.5.91	Callap
And harnest like my horses, draw my coch,	2Tamb	3.5.104	Tamb
Seest thou not death within my wrathfull looks?	2Tamb	3.5.119	Tamb
T'appease my wrath, or els Ile torture thee,	2Tamb	3.5.122	Tamb
Good my Lord, let me take it.	2Tamb	3.5.133	P Almeda
in the stable, when you shall come sweating from my chariot.	2Tamb	3.5.142	P Tamb
Sirha, prepare whips, and bring my chariot to my Tent:	2Tamb	3.5.144	P Tamb
I, my Lord, he was Calapines keeper.	2Tamb	3.5.152	P Therid
But now my followers and my loving friends,	2Tamb	3.5.159	Tamb
My sterne aspect shall make faire Victory,	2Tamb	3.5.162	Tamb
For if my father misse him in the field,	2Tamb	4.1.8	Celeb
Away ye fools, my father needs not me,	2Tamb	4.1.15	Calyph
My father were enough to scar the foe:	2Tamb	4.1.19	Calyph
Knowing my father hates thy cowardise,	2Tamb	4.1.23	Amyras
Nor care for blood when wine wil quench my thirst.	2Tamb	4.1.30	Calyph
And take my other toward brother here,	2Tamb	4.1.34	Calyph
Twill please my mind as wel to heare both you/Have won a heape	2Tamb	4.1.36	Calyph
Turn'd into pearle and proffered for my stay,	2Tamb	4.1.44	Amyras
I would not bide the furie of my father:	2Tamb	4.1.45	Amyras
Take you the honor, I will take my ease,	2Tamb	4.1.49	Calyph
My wisedome shall excuse my cowardise:	2Tamb	4.1.50	Calyph
the good I have/Join'd with my fathers crowne would never cure.	2Tamb	4.1.58	Calyph
Here my Lord.	2Tamb	4.1.60	P Perdic
Content my Lord, but what shal we play for?	2Tamb	4.1.63	P Perdic
Turkes Concubines first, when my father hath conquered them.	2Tamb	4.1.65	P Calyph
Such a feare (my Lord) would never make yee retire.	2Tamb	4.1.71	P Perdic
my father would let me be put in the front of such a battaile	2Tamb	4.1.72	P Calyph
be put in the front of such a battaile once, to trie my valour.	2Tamb	4.1.73	P Calyph
my children stoops your pride/And leads your glories <bodies>	2Tamb	4.1.76	Tamb
Bring them my boyes, and tel me if the warres/Be not a life	2Tamb	4.1.78	Tamb
Shal we let goe these kings again my Lord/To gather greater	2Tamb	4.1.82	Amyras
But wher's this coward, villaine, not my sonne,	2Tamb	4.1.89	Tamb
But traitor to my name and majesty.	2Tamb	4.1.90	Tamb
The obloquie and skorne of my renowne,	2Tamb	4.1.92	Tamb
How may my hart, thus fired with mine eies,	2Tamb	4.1.93	Tamb
Shrowd any thought may holde my striving hands/From martiall	2Tamb	4.1.95	Tamb
Good my Lord, let him be forgiven for once,	2Tamb	4.1.101	Amyras
Stand up my boyes, and I wil teach ye arms,	2Tamb	4.1.103	Tamb
In sending to my issue such a soule,	2Tamb	4.1.122	Tamb
I must apply my selfe to fit those tearmes,	2Tamb	4.1.155	Tamb
Then bring those Turkish harlots to my tent,	2Tamb	4.1.165	Tamb
We will my Lord.	2Tamb	4.1.167	Soldrs
And with the paines my rigour shall inflict,	2Tamb	4.1.184	Tamb
or by speach I heare/Immortall Jove say, Cease my Tamburlaine,	2Tamb	4.1.199	Tamb
For honor of my woondrous victories.	2Tamb	4.1.205	Tamb
Wel met Olympia, I sought thee in my tent,	2Tamb	4.2.14	Therid
Tell me Olympia, wilt thou graunt my suit?	2Tamb	4.2.21	Therid
My Lord and husbandes death, with my sweete sons,	2Tamb	4.2.22	Olymp
Save griefe and sorrow which torment my heart,	2Tamb	4.2.24	Olymp
Forbids my mind to entertaine a thought/That tends to love, but	2Tamb	4.2.25	Olymp

MY (cont.)

For with thy view my joyes are at the full,	2Tamb	4.2.31	Therid
Ah, pity me my Lord, and draw your sword,	2Tamb	4.2.33	Olymp
Making a passage for my troubled soule,	2Tamb	4.2.34	Olymp
And meet my husband and my loving sonne.	2Tamb	4.2.36	Olymp
Leave this my Love, and listen more to me.	2Tamb	4.2.38	Therid
Upon the marble turrets of my Court/Sit like to Venus in her	2Tamb	4.2.41	Therid
Spending my life in sweet discourse of love.	2Tamb	4.2.45	Therid
Such is the sodaine fury of my love,	2Tamb	4.2.52	Therid
Stay good my Lord, and wil you save my honor,	2Tamb	4.2.55	Olymp
To proove it, I wil noint my naked throat,	2Tamb	4.2.68	Olymp
My purpose was (my Lord) to spend it so,	2Tamb	4.2.73	Olymp
Now stab my Lord, and mark your weapons point/That wil be	2Tamb	4.2.79	Olymp
Cut off this arme that murthered my Love:	2Tamb	4.2.83	Therid
Infernall Dis is courting of my Love,	2Tamb	4.2.93	Therid
with all the pompe/The treasure of my kingdome may affoord.	2Tamb	4.2.98	Therid
To make you fierce, and fit my appetite,	2Tamb	4.3.17	Tamb
live, and draw/My chariot swifter than the racking cloudes:	2Tamb	4.3.21	Tamb
And see the figure of my dignitie,	2Tamb	4.3.25	Tamb
By which I hold my name and majesty.	2Tamb	4.3.26	Tamb
Let me have coach my Lord, that I may ride,	2Tamb	4.3.27	Amyras
Thy youth forbids such ease my kingly boy,	2Tamb	4.3.29	Tamb
They shall tc morrow draw my chariot,	2Tamb	4.3.30	Tamb
them for the funerall/They have bestowed on my abortive sonne.	2Tamb	4.3.66	Tamb
Where are my common souldiers now that fought/So Lion-like upon	2Tamb	4.3.67	Tamb
Here my Lord.	2Tamb	4.3.69	Soldrs
O pity us my Lord, and save our honours.	2Tamb	4.3.83	Ladies
It seemes they meant to conquer us my Lord,	2Tamb	4.3.88	Therid
Let us not be idle then my Lord,	2Tamb	4.3.95	Techel
Adding their wealth and treasure to my store.	2Tamb	4.3.101	Tamb
Then shal my native city Samarcanda/And christall waves of	2Tamb	4.3.107	Tamb
For there my Pallace royal shal be plac'd:	2Tamb	4.3.111	Tamb
And in my helme a triple plume shal spring,	2Tamb	4.3.116	Tamb
Then in my coach like Saturnes royal son,	2Tamb	4.3.125	Tamb
Until my soule dissevered from this flesh,	2Tamb	4.3.131	Tamb
To Babylon my Lords, to Babylon.	2Tamb	4.3.133	Tamb
My Lord, the breach the enimie hath made/Gives such assurance	2Tamb	5.1.2	Maxim
Then hang out flagges (my Lord) of humble truce,	2Tamb	5.1.6	Maxim
Is not my life and state as deere to me,	2Tamb	5.1.12	Govnr
The citie and my native countries weale,	2Tamb	5.1.13	Govnr
My Lord, if ever you did deed of ruth,	2Tamb	5.1.24	1Citzn
How is my scule environed,	2Tamb	5.1.34	Govnr
My Lord, if ever you wil win our hearts,	2Tamb	5.1.38	2Citzn
For I wil cast my selfe from off these walles,	2Tamb	5.1.40	2Citzn
the towne will never yeeld/As long as any life is in my breast.	2Tamb	5.1.48	Govnr
Hath trode the Meisures, do my souldiers martch,	2Tamb	5.1.75	Tamb
My horsmen brandish their unruly blades.	2Tamb	5.1.79	Tamb
Who have ye there my Lordes?	2Tamb	5.1.80	Tamb
dcwn to the earth/Could not affright you, no, nor I my selfe,	2Tamb	5.1.91	Tamb
Nor if my body could have stopt the breach,	2Tamb	5.1.101	Govnr
My heart did never quake, or corrage faint.	2Tamb	5.1.106	Govnr
And let my souldiers shoot the slave to death.	2Tamb	5.1.109	Tamb
Torture or paine can daunt my dreadlesse minde.	2Tamb	5.1.113	Govnr
Save but my life and I wil give it thee.	2Tamb	5.1.118	Govnr
I will my Lord.	2Tamb	5.1.135	Therid
They will talk still my Lord, if you doe not bridle them.	2Tamb	5.1.146	P Amyras
Bridle them, and let me to my coach.	2Tamb	5.1.148	Tamb
See now my Lord how brave the Captaine hangs.	2Tamb	5.1.149	Amyras
Tis brave indeed my boy, wel done,	2Tamb	5.1.150	Tamb
Shoot first my Lord, and then the rest shall follow.	2Tamb	5.1.151	Tamb
Yet save my life, and let this wound appease/The mortall furie	2Tamb	5.1.153	Govnr
What shal be done with their wives and children my Lord.	2Tamb	5.1.168	P Techel
Here they are my Lord.	2Tamb	5.1.177	Usumc
My sword hath sent millions of Turks to hell,	2Tamb	5.1.180	Tamb
I have fulfil'd your highnes wil, my Lord,	2Tamb	5.1.203	Techel
Wel then my friendly Lordes, what now remaines/But that we	2Tamb	5.1.210	Tamb
I, good my Lord, let us in hast to Persea,	2Tamb	5.1.214	Therid
But stay, I feele my selfe distempered sudainly.	2Tamb	5.1.218	Tamb
Doubt not my lord, but we shal conquer him.	2Tamb	5.2.12	Amasia
When I record my Parents slavish life,	2Tamb	5.2.19	Callap
My Viceroies bondage under Tamburlaine,	2Tamb	5.2.21	Callap
Feare not my Lord, I see great Mahomet/Clothed in purple	2Tamb	5.2.31	Amasia
What daring God torments my body thus,	2Tamb	5.3.42	Tamb
And threaten him whose hand afflicts my soul,	2Tamb	5.3.47	Tamb
Ah good my Lord, leave these impatient words,	2Tamb	5.3.54	Therid
To cure me, or Ile fetch him downe my selfe.	2Tamb	5.3.63	Tamb
Sit stil my gratious Lord, this griefe wil cease,	2Tamb	5.3.64	Techel
See where my slave, the uglie monster death/Shaking and	2Tamb	5.3.67	Tamb
Tel me, what think you of my sicknes now?	2Tamb	5.3.81	Tamb
Besides my Lord, this day is Criticall,	2Tamb	5.3.91	Phsitn
Then will I comfort all my vital parts,	2Tamb	5.3.100	Tamb
My lord, yong Callapine that lately fled from your majesty,	2Tamb	5.3.102	P 3Msngr
See my Phisitions now, how Jove hath sent/A present medicine to	2Tamb	5.3.105	Tamb
now, how Jove hath sent/A present medicine to recure my paine:	2Tamb	5.3.106	Tamb
My looks shall make them flie, and might I follow,	2Tamb	5.3.107	Tamb
I joy my Lord, your highnesse is so strong,	2Tamb	5.3.110	Usumc
In spight of death I will goe show my face.	2Tamb	5.3.114	Tamb
That Callapine should be my slave againe.	2Tamb	5.3.118	Tamb
But I perceive my martial strength is spent,	2Tamb	5.3.119	Tamb
That these my boies may finish all my wantes.	2Tamb	5.3.125	Tamb
Graecia, and from thence/To Asia, where I stay against my will,	2Tamb	5.3.142	Tamb
Looke here my boies, see what a world of ground,	2Tamb	5.3.145	Tamb
Loe here my sonnes, are all the golden Mines,	2Tamb	5.3.151	Tamb

MY (cont.)

Here lovely boies, what death forbids my life,	2Tamb	5.3.159	Tamb
Alas my Lord, how shculd our bleeding harts/Wounded and broken	2Tamb	5.3.161	Amyras
My flesh devided in your precious shapes,	2Tamb	5.3.172	Tamb
Shal still retaine my spirit, though I die,	2Tamb	5.3.173	Tamb
me, that I may resigne/My place and proper tytle to my sonne:	2Tamb	5.3.176	Tamb
First take my Scourge and my imperiall Crowne,	2Tamb	5.3.177	Tamb
And mount my royall chariot of estate,	2Tamb	5.3.178	Tamb
Help me (my Lords) tc make my last remoove.	2Tamb	5.3.180	Tamb
A woful change my Lord, that daunts our thoughts,	2Tamb	5.3.181	Therid
Sit up my sonne, let me see how well/Thou wilt become thy	2Tamb	5.3.183	Tamb
The breath of life, and burthen of my soule,	2Tamb	5.3.186	Amyras
My bodies mortified lineaments/Should exercise the motions of	2Tamb	5.3.188	Amyras
mortified lineaments/Should exercise the motions of my heart,	2Tamb	5.3.189	Amyras
unrelenting eares/Of death and hell be shut against my praiers,	2Tamb	5.3.192	Amyras
Denie my soule fruition of her joy,	2Tamb	5.3.194	Amyras
How should I step or stir my hatefull feete,	2Tamb	5.3.195	Amyras
Against the inward powers of my heart,	2Tamb	5.3.196	Amyras
Sit up my boy, and with those silken raines,	2Tamb	5.3.202	Tamb
My Lord, you must obey his majesty,	2Tamb	5.3.204	Therid
And send my soule before my father die,	2Tamb	5.3.208	Amyras
Let it be plac'd by this my fatall chaire,	2Tamb	5.3.211	Tamb
And serve as parcell of my funerall.	2Tamb	5.3.212	Tamb
And eielesse Monster that torments my soule,	2Tamb	5.3.217	Tamb
And when my soule hath vertue of your sight,	2Tamb	5.3.225	Tamb
So, raigne my sonne, scourge and controlle those slaves,	2Tamb	5.3.228	Tamb
chariot wil not beare/A guide of baser temper than my selfe,	2Tamb	5.3.243	Tamb
Farewel my boies, my dearest friends, farewel,	2Tamb	5.3.245	Tamb
My body feeles, my soule dooth weepe to see/Your sweet desires	2Tamb	5.3.246	Tamb
my soule dooth weepe to see/Your sweet desires depriv'd my	2Tamb	5.3.246	Tamb
dooth weepe to see/Your sweet desires depriv'd my company,	2Tamb	5.3.247	Tamb
To some perhaps my name is odious,	Jew	Prol.5	Machvl
Though some speake openly against my bookes,	Jew	Prol.10	Machvl
Are poyson'd by my climing followers.	Jew	Prol.13	Machvl
which mony was not got without my meanes.	Jew	Prol.32	Machvl
That bought my Spanish Oyles, and Wines of Greece,	Jew	1.1.5	Barab
of judgement frame/This is the ware wherein consists my wealth:	Jew	1.1.33	Barab
Into what corner peeres my Halcions bill?	Jew	1.1.39	Barab
why then I hope my ships/I sent for Egypt and the bordering	Jew	1.1.41	Barab
And therefore farre exceeds my credit, Sir.	Jew	1.1.65	1Merch
Sirra, which of my ships art thou Master of?	Jew	1.1.70	Barab
And bid my Factor bring his loading in.	Jew	1.1.83	Barab
goe/And bid the Merchants and my men dispatch/And come ashore,	Jew	1.1.100	Barab
who hateth me but for my happinesse?	Jew	1.1.112	Barab
My selfe in Malta, some in Italy,	Jew	1.1.126	Barab
So they spare me, my daughter, and my wealth.	Jew	1.1.153	Barab
our state/Assure your selves I'le looke--unto my selfe.	Jew	1.1.173	Barab
Alas, my Lord, the summe is overgreat,	Jew	1.2.8	Govnr
grave [Governour], 'twere in my power/To favour you, but 'tis my	Jew	1.2.10	Calym
'twere in my power/To favour you, but 'tis my fathers cause,	Jew	1.2.11	Calym
They were, my Lord, and here they come.	Jew	1.2.36	Offcrs
Then good my Lord, to keepe your quiet still,	Jew	1.2.43	Barab
Alas, my Lord, we are no souldiers:	Jew	1.2.50	Barab
How, my Lord, my mony?	Jew	1.2.55	Barab
Alas, my Lord, the most of us are poore!	Jew	1.2.57	1Jew
Oh my Lord we will give halfe.	Jew	1.2.77	3Jews
Halfe of my substance is a Cities wealth.	Jew	1.2.85	Barab
Let me be us'd but as my brethren are.	Jew	1.2.91	Barab
Will you then steale my goods?	Jew	1.2.94	Barab
Preach me not out of my possessions.	Jew	1.2.111	Barab
I, my Lord, we have seiz'd upon the goods/And wares of Barabas,	Jew	1.2.132	Offcrs
Well then my Lord, say, are you satisfied?	Jew	1.2.137	Barab
You have my goods, my mony, and my wealth,	Jew	1.2.138	Barab
My ships, my store, and all that I enjoy'd;	Jew	1.2.139	Barab
And now shall move you to bereave my life.	Jew	1.2.143	Barab
You have my wealth, the labour of my life,	Jew	1.2.149	Barab
The comfort of mine age, my childrens hope,	Jew	1.2.150	Barab
And here upon my knees, striking the earth,	Jew	1.2.165	Barab
That thus have dealt with me in my distresse.	Jew	1.2.168	Barab
Why stand you thus unmov'd with my laments?	Jew	1.2.171	Barab
Why weepe you not to thinke upon my wrongs?	Jew	1.2.172	Barab
That clouds of darkenesse may inclose my flesh,	Jew	1.2.194	Barab
I, I,/Pray leave me in my patience.	Jew	1.2.200	Barab
'Tis in the trouble of my spirit I speake;	Jew	1.2.207	Barab
But whither wends my beauteous Abigall?	Jew	1.2.224	Barab
Oh what has made my lovely daughter sad?	Jew	1.2.225	Barab
Not for my selfe, but aged Barabas:	Jew	1.2.228	Abigal
And urg'd thereto with my afflictions,	Jew	1.2.231	Abigal
And rent their hearts with tearing of my haire,	Jew	1.2.234	Abigal
Till they reduce the wrongs done to my father.	Jew	1.2.235	Abigal
my girle, thinke me not all so fond/As negligently to forgoe so	Jew	1.2.241	Barab
In my house, my girle.	Jew	1.2.249	Barab
will give me leave once more, I trow,/To goe into my house.	Jew	1.2.253	Barab
My gold, my gold, and all my wealth is gone.	Jew	1.2.258	Barab
To make me desperate in my poverty?	Jew	1.2.261	Barab
in distresse/Thinke me so mad as I will hang my selfe,	Jew	1.2.263	Barab
No, I will live; nor loath I this my life:	Jew	1.2.266	Barab
me in the Ocean thus/To sinke or swim, and put me to my shifts,	Jew	1.2.268	Barab
I'le rouse my senses, and awake my selfe.	Jew	1.2.269	Barab
thus; thou toldst me they have turn'd my house/Into a Nunnery,	Jew	1.2.277	Barab
there must my girle/Intreat the Abbasse to be entertain'd.	Jew	1.2.279	Barab
Be close, my girle, for this must fetch my gold.	Jew	1.2.304	Barab
Fearing the afflictions which my father feeles,	Jew	1.2.322	Abigal

I'de passe away my life in penitence,	Jew	1.2.324	Abigal
To make attonement for my labouring soule.	Jew	1.2.326	Abigal
Novice learne to frame/My solitary life to your streight lawes,	Jew	1.2.332	Abigal
I charge thee on my blessing that thou leave/These divels, and	Jew	1.2.346	Barab
Wilt thou forsake mee too in my distresse,	Jew	1.2.358	Barab
Lodowicke, I have seene/The strangest sight, in my opinion,	Jew	1.2.376	Mthias
And of my former riches rests no more/But bare remembrance;	Jew	2.1.9	Barab
No sleepe can fasten on my watchfull eyes,	Jew	2.1.17	Barab
Nor quiet enter my distemper'd thoughts,	Jew	2.1.18	Barab
Till I have answer of my Abigail.	Jew	2.1.19	Barab
espy'd a time/To search the plancke my father did appoint;	Jew	2.1.21	Abigal
Who in my wealth wud tell me winters tales,	Jew	2.1.25	Barab
For whilst I live, here lives my soules sole hope,	Jew	2.1.29	Barab
And when I dye, here shall my spirit walke.	Jew	2.1.30	Barab
Now that my fathers fortune were so good/As but to be about	Jew	2.1.31	Abigal
The Loadstarre of my life, if Abigall.	Jew	2.1.42	Barab
Oh my girle,/my gold, my fortune, my felicity;	Jew	2.1.47	Barab
My gold, my fortune, my felicity;	Jew	2.1.48	Barab
Strength to my soule, death to mine enemy;	Jew	2.1.49	Barab
Welcome the first beginner of my blisse:	Jew	2.1.50	Barab
Then my desires were fully satisfied,	Jew	2.1.52	Barab
Oh girle, oh gold, oh beauty, oh my blisse!	Jew	2.1.54	Barab
Farewell my joy, and by my fingers take/A kisse from him that	Jew	2.1.58	Barab
and by my fingers take/A kisse from him that sends it from his	Jew	2.1.58	Barab
My Ship, the flying Dragon, is of Spaine,	Jew	2.2.5	Bosco
And so am I, Delbosco is my name;	Jew	2.2.6	Bosco
'Tis true, my Lord, therefore intreat him well.	Jew	2.2.8	1Knght
My Lord, Remember that to Europ's shame,	Jew	2.2.30	Bosco
My Lord and King hath title to this Isle,	Jew	2.2.37	Bosco
They hop'd my daughter would ha bin a Nun;	Jew	2.3.12	Barab
I learn'd in Florence how to kisse my hand,	Jew	2.3.23	Barab
Heave up my shoulders when they call me dogge,	Jew	2.3.24	Barab
Will I shew my selfe to have more of the Serpent then the Dove;	Jew	2.3.36	P Barab
Oh, Sir, your father had my Diamonds.	Jew	2.3.49	Barab
I meane my daughter:--	Jew	2.3.51	Barab
Oh my Lord we will not jarre about the price;	Jew	2.3.65	Barab
Come to my house and I will giv't your honour--	Jew	2.3.66	Barab
Your father has deserv'd it at my hands,	Jew	2.3.70	Barab
To make me mindfull of my mortall sinnes,	Jew	2.3.74	Barab
Against my will, and whether I would or no,	Jew	2.3.75	Barab
And made my house a place for Nuns most chast.	Jew	2.3.77	Barab
I, but my Lord, the harvest is farre off:	Jew	2.3.79	Barab
No more, my Lord.	Jew	2.3.108	1Offcr
and thou hast, breake my head with it, I'le forgive thee.	Jew	2.3.112	P Barab
be under colour of shaving, thou'lt cut my throat for my goods.	Jew	2.3.120	P Barab
So much the better, thou art for my turne.	Jew	2.3.129	Barab
That by my helpe shall doe much villanie.	Jew	2.3.133	Barab
My Lord farewell: Come Sirra you are mine.	Jew	2.3.134	Barab
I pray, Sir, be no stranger at my house,	Jew	2.3.136	Barab
He loves my daughter, and she holds him deare:	Jew	2.3.141	Barab
when you have brought her home, come to my house;	Jew	2.3.148	Barab
and my talke with him was [but]/About the borrowing of a booke	Jew	2.3.155	Mthias
Faith, Sir, my birth is but meane, my name's Ithimor,	Jew	2.3.165	Ithimr
My profession what you please.	Jew	2.3.166	Ithimr
then listen to my words,/And I will teach [thee] that shall	Jew	2.3.167	Barab
As for my selfe, I walke abroad a nights/And kill sicke people	Jew	2.3.174	Barab
I am content to lose some of my Crownes;	Jew	2.3.178	Barab
That I may, walking in my Gallery,	Jew	2.3.179	Barab
See 'em goe pinion'd along by my doore.	Jew	2.3.180	Barab
Slew friend and enemy with my stratagems.	Jew	2.3.189	Barab
Abigall, bid him welcome for my sake.	Jew	2.3.232	Barab
O father, Don Mathias is my love.	Jew	2.3.237	Abigal
Nay on my life it is my Factors hand,	Jew	2.3.240	Barab
My Factor sends me word a Merchant's fled/That owes me for a	Jew	2.3.243	Barab
his father was my chiefest enemie.	Jew	2.3.250	Barab
Whither but to my faire love Abigall?	Jew	2.3.252	Mthias
That I intend my daughter shall be thine.	Jew	2.3.254	Barab
If you love me, no quarrels in my house;	Jew	2.3.271	Barab
My death? what, is the base borne peasant mad?	Jew	2.3.281	Lodowk
My daughter here, a paltry silly girle.	Jew	2.3.284	Barab
He has my heart, I smile against my will.	Jew	2.3.287	Abigal
And now I can no longer hold my minde.	Jew	2.3.290	Lodowk
I cannot chuse, seeing my father bids:--	Jew	2.3.316	Abigal
Nothing but death shall part my love and me.	Jew	2.3.317	Abigal
Now have I that for which my soule hath long'd.	Jew	2.3.318	Lodowk
Then my faire Abigal should frowne on me.	Jew	2.3.332	Lodowk
My life is not so deare as Abigall.	Jew	2.3.348	Mthias
My heart misgives me, that to crosse your love,	Jew	2.3.349	Barab
what, is he gone unto my mother?	Jew	2.3.351	Mthias
I cannot stay; for if my mother come,	Jew	2.3.353	Mthias
I cannot take my leave of him for teares:	Jew	2.3.355	Abigal
I will have Don Mathias, he is my love.	Jew	2.3.361	Abigal
As I behave my selfe in this, imploy me hereafter.	Jew	2.3.379	Ithimr
Since this Towne was besieg'd, my gaine growes cold:	Jew	3.1.1	Curtzn
But now against my will I must be chast.	Jew	3.1.4	Curtzn
And yet I know my beauty doth not faile.	Jew	3.1.5	Curtzn
And he is very seldome from my house.	Jew	3.1.10	Curtzn
and in the night I clamber'd up with my hooks, and as I was	Jew	3.1.19	P Pilia
and as I was taking my choyce, I heard a rumbling in the house;	Jew	3.1.20	P Pilia
rumbling in the house; so I tooke onely this, and runne my way:	Jew	3.1.21	P Pilia
What sight is this? my [Lodovico] <Lodowicke> slaine!	Jew	3.2.10	Govnr
Who is this? my sonne Mathias slaine!	Jew	3.2.12	Mater

MY (cont.)

Oh that my sighs could turne to lively breath;	Jew	3.2.18	Govnr
And these my teares to blood, that he might live.	Jew	3.2.19	Govnr
My sonne lov'd thine.	Jew	3.2.22	Mater
Lend me that weapon that did kill my sonne,	Jew	3.2.23	Mater
Nay Madam stay, that weapon was my son's,	Jew	3.2.25	Govnr
Altar I will offer up/My daily sacrifice of sighes and teares,	Jew	3.2.32	Govnr
And with my prayers pierce [th']impartiall heavens,	Jew	3.2.33	Govnr
Oh my master.	Jew	3.3.7	P Ithimr
bottle-nos'd knave to my Master, that ever Gentleman had.	Jew	3.3.10	P Ithimr
Say, knave, why rail'st upon my father thus?	Jew	3.3.11	Abigal
Oh, my master has the bravest policy.	Jew	3.3.12	P Ithimr
devil invented a challenge, my master writ it, and I carried it,	Jew	3.3.18	P Ithimr
And was my father furtherer of their deaths?	Jew	3.3.22	Abigal
That by my favour they should both be slaine?	Jew	3.3.39	Abigal
Then were my thoughts so fraile and unconfirm'd,	Jew	3.3.59	Abigal
My sinfull soule, alas, hath pac'd too long/The fatall	Jew	3.3.63	Abigal
That was my father's fault.	Jew	3.3.72	Abigal
Though thou deservest hardly at my hands,	Jew	3.3.74	Abigal
My duty waits on you.	Jew	3.3.76	Abigal
I feare she knowes ('tis so) of my device/In Don Mathias and	Jew	3.4.7	Barab
Come neere, my love, come neere, thy masters life,	Jew	3.4.14	Barab
My trusty servant, nay, my second [selfe] <life>;	Jew	3.4.15	Barab
And on that hope my happinesse is built:	Jew	3.4.17	Barab
Be blest of me, nor come within my gates,	Jew	3.4.31	Barab
But perish underneath my bitter curse/Like Cain by Adam, for	Jew	3.4.32	Barab
And she is hatefull to my soule and me:	Jew	3.4.36	Barab
I cannot thinke but that thou hat'st my life.	Jew	3.4.38	Barab
run to some rocke and throw my selfe headlong into the sea;	Jew	3.4.40	P Ithimr
Oh trusty Ithimore; no servant, but my friend;	Jew	3.4.42	Barab
And whilst I live use halfe; spend as my selfe;	Jew	3.4.45	Barab
Here take my keyes, I'le give 'em thee anon:	Jew	3.4.46	Barab
I hold my head my master's hungry:	Jew	3.4.51	P Ithimr
That thou mayst freely live to be my heire.	Jew	3.4.63	Barab
My purse, my Coffer, and my selfe is thine.	Jew	3.4.93	Barab
Oh my sweet Ithimore go set it downe/And come againe so soone	Jew	3.4.108	Barab
Pay me my wages for my worke is done.	Jew	3.4.115	Ithimr
but seeing you are come/Be you my ghostly father; and first	Jew	3.6.12	Abigal
Chast, and devout, much sorrowing for my sinnes,	Jew	3.6.14	Abigal
As I am almost desperate for my sinnes:	Jew	3.6.18	Abigal
My father did contract me to 'em both:	Jew	3.6.22	Abigal
Both jealous of my love, envied each other:	Jew	3.6.27	Abigal
And by my father's practice, which is there/Set downe at large,	Jew	3.6.28	Abigal
To worke my peace, this I confesse to thee;	Jew	3.6.31	Abigal
Reveale it not, for then my father dyes.	Jew	3.6.32	Abigal
Death seizeth on my heart:	Jew	3.6.38	Abigal
Convert my father that he may be sav'd,	Jew	3.6.39	Abigal
For my part feare you not.	Jew	4.1.10	Ithimr
My bosome [inmate] <inmates> <intimates>, but I must dissemble.	Jew	4.1.47	Barab
Oh holy Fryars, the burthen of my sinnes/Lye heavy on my soule;	Jew	4.1.48	Barab
the burthen of my sinnes/Lye heavy on my soule; then pray you	Jew	4.1.49	Barab
That would for Lucars sake have sold my soule.	Jew	4.1.53	Barab
Would pennance serve for this my sinne,	Jew	4.1.58	Barab
I could afford to whip my selfe to death.	Jew	4.1.59	Barab
And on my knees creepe to Jerusalem.	Jew	4.1.62	Barab
much weight in Pearle/Orient and round, have I within my house;	Jew	4.1.67	Barab
You shall convert me, you shall have all my wealth.	Jew	4.1.81	Barab
and I am resolv'd/You shall confesse me, and have all my goods.	Jew	4.1.86	Barab
Come to my house at one a clocke this night.	Jew	4.1.91	Barab
You know my mind, let me alone with him.	Jew	4.1.100	Barab
Marry the Turke shall be one of my godfathers,	Jew	4.1.111	Barab
For he that shriv'd her is within my house.	Jew	4.1.115	Barab
One turn'd my daughter, therefore he shall dye;	Jew	4.1.119	Barab
The other knowes enough to have my life,	Jew	4.1.120	Barab
not both these wise men to suppose/That I will leave my house,	Jew	4.1.123	Barab
men to suppose/That I will leave my house, my goods, and all,	Jew	4.1.123	Barab
And after that, I and my trusty Turke--	Jew	4.1.127	Barab
What, will you [have] <save> my life?	Jew	4.1.148	2Fryar
Pull hard, I say, you would have had my goods.	Jew	4.1.149	Barab
And intercept my going to the Jew;	Jew	4.1.167	1Fryar
nay then I'le force my way;/And see, a staffe stands ready for	Jew	4.1.171	1Fryar
So might my man and I hang with you for company.	Jew	4.1.182	Barab
now I to keepe my word,/And give my goods and substance to your	Jew	4.1.189	Barab
And give my goods and substance to your house,	Jew	4.1.190	Barab
And didst thou deliver my letter?	Jew	4.2.3	P Curtzn
a non-plus at the critical aspect of my terrible countenance.	Jew	4.2.14	P Pilia
sort as if he had meant to make cleane my Boots with his lips;	Jew	4.2.31	P Ithimr
It may be she sees more in me than I can find in my selfe:	Jew	4.2.33	P Ithimr
this Gentlewoman, who as my selfe, and the rest of the family,	Jew	4.2.43	P Pilia
I'le goe steale some mony from my Master to make me hansome:	Jew	4.2.49	P Ithimr
Sweet Bellamira, would I had my Masters wealth for thy sake.	Jew	4.2.55	P Ithimr
Now, gentle Ithimore, lye in my lap.	Jew	4.2.82	Curtzn
Where are my Maids?	Jew	4.2.83	Curtzn
Shall Ithimore my love goe in such rags?	Jew	4.2.85	Curtzn
I'le be thy Jason, thou my golden Fleece;	Jew	4.2.90	Ithimr
Shalt live with me and be my love.	Jew	4.2.98	Ithimr
Take thou the mony, spend it for my sake.	Jew	4.2.123	Ithimr
That kisse againe; she runs division of my lips.	Jew	4.2.127	P Ithimr
Come my deare love, let's in and sleepe together.	Jew	4.2.129	Curtzn
Well, my hope is, he will not stay there still;	Jew	4.3.16	Barab
I cannot doe it, I have lost my keyes.	Jew	4.3.32	Barab
Or climbe up to my Counting-house window:	Jew	4.3.34	P Barab
you know my meaning.	Jew	4.3.35	P Barab

MY (cont.)

the gold, or know Jew it is in my power to hang thee.	Jew	4.3.37	P Pilia
That he who knowes I love him as my selfe/Should write in this	Jew	4.3.42	Barab
As I wud see thee hang'd; oh, love stops my breath:	Jew	4.3.53	Barab
Pray when, Sir, shall I see you at my house?	Jew	4.3.56	Barab
And how the villaine revels with my gold.	Jew	4.3.68	Barab
Come gentle Ithimore, lye in my lap.	Jew	4.4.27	Curtzn
Must tuna my Lute for sound, twang twang first.	Jew	4.4.31	Barab
Sirra, you must give my mistris your posey.	Jew	4.4.37	Pilia
How sweet, my Ithimore, the flowers smell.	Jew	4.4.39	Curtzn
So did you when you stole my gold.	Jew	4.4.50	Barab
You run swifter when you threw my gold out of my Window.	Jew	4.4.52	P Barab
Oh raskall! I change my selfe twice a day.	Jew	4.4.65	Barab
proofe, my Lord, his man's now at my lodging/That was his Agent,	Jew	5.1.16	Curtzn
my Lord, his man's now at my lodging/That was his Agent, he'll	Jew	5.1.16	Curtzn
Nor me neither, I cannot out-run you Constable, oh my belly.	Jew	5.1.21	P Ithimr
Nay stay, my Lord, 'tmay be he will confesse.	Jew	5.1.25	1Knght
Thou and thy Turk; 'twas you that slew my son.	Jew	5.1.27	Govnr
Gilty, my Lord, I confesse; your sonne and Mathias were both	Jew	5.1.28	P Ithimr
And he my bondman, let me have law,	Jew	5.1.38	Barab
For none of this can prejudice my life.	Jew	5.1.39	Barab
Was my Mathias murder'd by the Jew?	Jew	5.1.44	Mater
My Lord, the Curtezane and her man are dead;	Jew	5.1.50	1Offcr
Dead, my Lord, and here they bring his body.	Jew	5.1.53	1Offcr
For by my meanes Calymath shall enter in.	Jew	5.1.63	Barab
Take my goods too, and seize upon my lands:	Jew	5.1.66	Barab
Yes, my good Lord, one that can spy a place/Where you may enter,	Jew	5.1.70	Barab
My name is Barabas; I am a Jew.	Jew	5.1.72	Barab
The very same, my Lord:	Jew	5.1.74	Barab
And since that time they have hir'd a slave my man/To accuse me	Jew	5.1.75	Barab
Feare not, my Lord, for here, against the [sluice] <Truce>,/The	Jew	5.1.86	Barab
Thankes, my Lord.	Jew	5.2.11	Barab
and in hating me/My life's in danger, and what boots it thee	Jew	5.2.31	Barab
My Lord?	Jew	5.2.48	Govnr
Are at my Arbitrament; and Barabas/At his discretion may	Jew	5.2.53	Barab
said, within this Ile/In Malta here, that I have got my goods,	Jew	5.2.68	Barab
And by my letters privately procure/Great summes of mony for	Jew	5.2.87	Govnr
Here is my hand that I'le set Malta free:	Jew	5.2.95	Barab
Here is my hand, beleeve me, Barabas,	Jew	5.2.102	Govnr
Making a profit of my policie;	Jew	5.2.112	Barab
And he from whom my most advantage comes,	Jew	5.2.113	Barab
Shall be my friend.	Jew	5.2.114	Barab
My policie detests prevention:	Jew	5.2.121	Barab
To what event my secret purpose drives,	Jew	5.2.122	Barab
to feast my traine/Within a Towne of warre so lately pillag'd,	Jew	5.3.21	Calym
I cannot feast my men in Malta wals,	Jew	5.3.34	Calym
I shall, my Lord.	Jew	5.3.42	Msngr
In this, my Countrimen, be rul'd by me,	Jew	5.4.1	Govnr
Leave nothing loose, all leveld to my mind.	Jew	5.5.3	Barab
Downe to the Celler, taste of all my wines.	Jew	5.5.7	Barab
We shall, my Lord, and thanke you.	Jew	5.5.8	Crpntr
Then now are all things as my wish wud have 'em,	Jew	5.5.17	Barab
wel since it is no more/I'le satisfie my selfe with that; nay,	Jew	5.5.22	Barab
And Governour, now partake my policy:	Jew	5.5.24	Barab
my Companion-Bashawes, see I pray/How busie Barrabas is there	Jew	5.5.51	Calym
My men are all aboord,	Jew	5.5.103	Calym
And doe attend my comming there by this.	Jew	5.5.104	Calym
Prince of Navarre my honourable brother,	P 1	1.1	Charls
Prince Condy, and my good Lord Admirall,	P 2	1.2	Charls
And now my Lords the mariage rites perfourm'd,	P 18	1.18	Charls
I will my good Lord.	P 22	1.22	QnMarg
The rest that will not goe (my Lords) may stay:	P 23	1.23	Charls
Prince Condy and my good Lord Admiral,	P 27	1.27	Navrre
My Lord I mervaile that th'aspiring Guise/Dares once adventure	P 36	1.36	Admral
My Lord you need not mervaile at the Guise,	P 39	1.39	Condy
My Lord, but did you mark the Cardinall/The Guises brother, and	P 47	1.47	Admral
Come my Lords lets go to the Church and pray,	P 55	1.55	Navrre
My Lord.	P 67	2.10	Pothec
See where they be my good Lord, and he that smelles but to	P 73	2.16	P Pothec
I am my Lord, in what your grace commaundes till death.	P 76	2.19	P Pothec
Thankes my good freend, I will requite thy love.	P 78	2.21	Guise
Be gone my freend, present them to her straite.	P 82	2.25	Guise
My Lord.	P 84	2.27	P Souldr
I will my Lord.	P 90	2.33	P Souldr
That like I best that flyes beyond my reach.	P 99	2.42	Guise
Ile either rend it with my nayles to naught,	P 102	2.45	Guise
Or mount the top with my aspiring winges,	P 103	2.46	Guise
Although my downfall be the deepest hell.	P 104	2.47	Guise
For this, my quenchles thirst whereon I builde,	P 107	2.50	Guise
For this, this earth sustaines my bodies [waight],	P 114	2.57	Guise
My policye hath framde religion.	P 122	2.65	Guise
The Mother Queene workes wonders for my sake,	P 133	2.76	Guise
And in my love entombes the hope of Fraunce:	P 134	2.77	Guise
To supply my wants and necessitie.	P 136	2.79	Guise
of my knowledge in one cloyster keeps,/Five hundred fatte	P 141	2.84	Guise
Pale death may walke in furrowes of my face:	P 158	2.101	Guise
An eare, to heare what my detractors say,	P 160	2.103	Guise
Thanks my good freend, holde, take thou this reward.	P 168	3.3	OldQn
The sent whereof doth make my head to ake.	P 171	3.6	OldQn
Too late it is my Lord if that be true/To blame her highnes,	P 181	3.16	QnMarg
the fatall poyson/Workes within my head, my brain pan breakes,	P 185	3.20	OldQn
My heart doth faint, I dye.	P 186	3.21	OldQn
My Mother poysoned heere before my face:	P 187	3.22	Navrre

MY (cont.)

O graunt sweet God my daies may end with hers,	P 189	3.24	Navrre
Let not this heavy chaunce my dearest Lord,	P 191	3.26	QnMarg
(For whose effects my soule is massacred)/Infect thy gracious	P 192	3.27	QnMarg
Come my Lords let us beare her body hence,	P 195	3.30	Admral
What are you hurt my Lord high Admiral?	P 197	3.32	Condy
I my good Lord, shot through the arme.	P 198	3.33	Admral
betraide, come my Lords, and let us goe tell the King of this.	P 199	3.34	P Navrre
My noble sonne, and princely Duke of Guise,	P 203	4.1	QnMoth
Besides my heart relentes that noble men,	P 211	4.9	Charls
Me thinkes my Lord, Anjoy hath well advisde/Your highnes to	P 219	4.17	Guise
I hope these reasons may serve my princely Sonne,	P 223	4.21	QnMoth
And to my Nephew heere the Duke of Guise:	P 226	4.24	Charls
Thankes to my princely sonne, then tell me Guise,	P 228	4.26	QnMoth
How fares it with my Lord high Admiral,	P 253	4.51	Charls
Ah my good Lord, these are the Guisians,	P 260	4.58	Admral
Assure your selfe my good Lord Admirall,	P 262	4.60	Charls
And that I am not more secure my selfe,	P 264	4.62	Charls
Plac'd by my brother, will betray his Lord:	P 294	5.21	Anjoy
But look my Lord, ther's some in the Admirals house.	P 297	5.24	Retes
O God forgive my sins.	P 303	5.30	Admral
I my Lord.	P 305	5.32	Gonzag
See where my Souldier shot him through the arm.	P 310	5.37	Guise
I will my Lord.	P 331	5.58	Mntsrl
And now my Lords let us closely to our busines.	P 332	5.59	Guise
Stay my Lord, let me begin the psalme.	P 344	5.71	Anjoy
O let me pray before I take my death.	P 352	6.7	Seroun
O Christ my Saviour--	P 354	6.9	Seroun
[Sanctus] <Sancta> Jacobus hee was my Saint, pray to him.	P 358	6.13	Mntsrl
O let me pray unto my God.	P 359	6.14	Seroun
All that I have is but my stipend from the King,	P 378	7.18	Ramus
O good my Lord,/Wherein hath Ramus	P 383	7.23	Ramus
O good my Lord, let me but speak a word.	P 399	7.39	Ramus
Not for my life doe I desire this pause,	P 401	7.41	Ramus
But in my latter houre to purge my selfe,	P 402	7.42	Ramus
Because my places being but three, contains all his:	P 405	7.45	Ramus
My Lord of Anjoy, there are a hundred Protestants,	P 417	7.57	Guise
And in the mean time my Lord, could we devise,	P 425	7.65	Guise
How now my Lords, how fare you?	P 430	7.70	Anjoy
My Lord, they say/That all the protestants are massacred.	P 431	7.71	Navrre
But yet my Lord the report doth run,	P 435	7.75	Navrre
Come sirs, Ile whip you to death with my punniards point.	P 441	7.81	Guise
My Lords of Poland I must needs confesse,	P 451	8.1	Anjoy
of your Prince Electors, farre/Beyond the reach of my desertes:	P 453	8.3	Anjoy
Yet by my brother Charles our King of France,	P 464	8.14	Anjoy
prejudice their hope/Of my inheritance to the crowne of France:	P 468	8.18	Anjoy
For if th'almighty take my brother hence,	P 469	8.19	Anjoy
on me, then with your leaves/I may retire me to my native home.	P 474	8.24	Anjoy
Then come my Lords, lets goe.	P 481	8.31	Anjoy
No by my faith Madam.	P 498	9.17	Guise
My Lord of Loraine have you markt of late,/How Charles our	P 512	9.31	QnMoth
For the late nights worke which my Lord of Guise/Did make in	P 514	9.33	QnMoth
I, but my Lord let me alone for that,	P 519	9.38	QnMoth
Come my Lord [let] <lets> us goe.	P 527	9.46	QnMoth
To make the justice of my heart relent:	P 533	10.6	Guise
A griping paine hath ceasde upon my heart:	P 537	11.2	Charls
Comfort your selfe my Lord and have no doubt,	P 541	11.6	Navrre
O no, my loving brother of Navarre.	P 543	11.8	Charls
God graunt my neerest freends may prove no worse.	P 547	11.12	Charls
O holde me up, my sight begins to faile,	P 548	11.13	Charls
My sinnewes shrinke, my braines turne upside downe,	P 549	11.14	Charls
My heart doth break, I faint and dye.	P 550	11.15	Charls
My Lords, what resteth there now for to be done?	P 554	11.19	QnMoth
And now my Lords after these funerals be done,	P 561	11.26	QnMoth
My opportunity may serve me fit,	P 566	11.31	Navrre
To steale from France, and hye me to my home.	P 567	11.32	Navrre
It is my due by just succession:	P 570	11.35	Navrre
And so they shall, if fortune speed my will,	P 601	12.14	King
And yeeld your thoughts to height of my desertes.	P 602	12.15	King
Shall slacke my loves affection from his bent.	P 607	12.20	King
Come sir, give me my buttons and heers your eare.	P 620	12.33	Mugern
Lets goe my Lords, our dinner staies for us.	P 630	12.43	King
My Lord Cardinall of Loraine, tell me,	P 631	12.44	QnMoth
How likes your grace my sonnes pleasantnes?	P 632	12.45	QnMoth
My brother Guise hath gathered a power of men,	P 642	12.55	Cardnl
Tush, all shall dye unles I have my will:	P 653	12.66	QnMoth
Come my [Lord] <Lords>, let us goe seek the Guise,	P 655	12.68	QnMoth
That I may write unto my dearest Lord.	P 659	13.3	Duchss
Sweet Mugeroune, tis he that hath my heart,	P 660	13.4	Duchss
So, set it down and leave me to my selfe.	P 666	13.10	Duchss
What, all alone my love, and writing too:	P 670	13.14	Guise
To such a one my Lord, as when she reads my lines,	P 672	13.16	Duchss
O no my Lord, a woman only must/Partake the secrets of my	P 675	13.19	Duchss
no my Lord, a woman only must/Partake the secrets of my heart.	P 676	13.20	Duchss
O pardon me my Lord.	P 679	13.23	Duchss
Or hath my love been so obscurde in thee,	P 682	13.26	Guise
That others needs to comment on my text?	P 683	13.27	Guise
Is all my love forgot which helde thee deare?	P 684	13.28	Guise
And fly my presence if thou looke to live.	P 692	13.36	Guise
My Lords, sith in a quarrell just and right,	P 698	14.1	Navrre
Upon the hauty mountains of my brest:	P 718	14.21	Navrre
My Lord, as by our scoutes we understande,	P 724	14.27	1Msngr
Not yet my Lord, for thereon doe they stay:	P 732	14.35	1Msngr

MY (cont.)

But come my Lords, let us away with speed,	P 741	14.44	Navrre
My sweet Joyeux, I make thee Generall,	P 743	15.1	King
Of all my army now in readines,	P 744	15.2	King
Although my love to thee can hardly [suffer't] <suffer>,	P 747	15.5	King
Thanks to your Majestie, and so I take my leave.	P 749	15.7	Joyeux
Farwell to my Lord of Guise and Epernoune.	P 750	15.8	Joyeux
Health and harty farwell to my Lord Joyeux.	P 751	15.9	Guise
Which your wife writ to my deare Minion,	P 755	15.13	King
How now my Lord, faith this is more then need,	P 757	15.15	Guise
My Lord, twere good to make them frends,	P 772	15.30	Eprnon
Not I my Lord, what if I had?	P 775	15.33	Mugern
And with the Queene of England joyne my force,	P 801	16.15	Navrre
Come my Lords, now that this storme is overpast,	P 804	16.18	Navrre
My Lord of Guise, we understand that you/Have gathered a power	P 821	17.16	King
What should I doe but stand upon my guarde?	P 839	17.34	Guise
My Lord, to speak more plainely, thus it is:	P 847	17.42	Guise
And know my Lord, the Pope will sell his triple crowne,	P 851	17.46	Guise
My Lord, in token of my true humilitie,	P 866	17.61	Guise
I kisse your graces hand, and take my leave,	P 868	17.63	Guise
Intending to dislodge my campe with speed.	P 869	17.64	Guise
But trust him not my Lord,	P 871	17.66	Eprnon
Make a discharge of all my counsell straite,	P 882	17.77	King
And Ile subscribe my name and seale it straight.	P 883	17.78	King
My head shall be my counsell, they are false:	P 884	17.79	King
My Lord,/I think for safety of your royall person,	P 886	17.81	Eprnon
My Lord, I am advertised from France,	P 900	18.1	Navrre
I will my Lord.	P 913	18.14	Bartus
My Lord.	P 915	18.16	Pleshe
I goe my Lord.	P 920	18.21	Pleshe
O that his heart were leaping in my hand.	P 936	19.6	P 2Mur
Now Captain of my guarde, are these murtherers ready?	P 947	19.17	King
They be my good Lord.	P 948	19.18	Capt
I warrant ye my Lord.	P 951	19.21	Capt
Breath out that life wherein my death was hid,	P 954	19.24	King
Good morrow to my loving Cousin of Guise.	P 965	19.35	King
Twere hard with me if I should doubt my kinne,	P 971	19.41	King
Or be suspicious of my deerest freends:	P 972	19.42	King
And he shall follow my proud Chariots wheeles.	P 984	19.54	Guise
And all my former time was spent in vaine:	P 986	19.56	Guise
O pardon me my Lord of Guise.	P 990	19.60	P 3Mur
O my Lord, I am one of them that is set to murder you.	P 992	19.62	P 3Mur
I my Lord, the rest have taine their standings in the next	P 994	19.64	P 3Mur
in the next roome, therefore good my Lord goe not foorth.	P 995	19.65	P 3Mur
Oh I have my deaths wound, give me leave to speak.	P1003	19.73	Guise
Oh that I have not power to stay my life,	P1007	19.77	Guise
My Lord, see where the Guise is slaine.	P1019	19.89	Capt
Ah this sweet sight is phisick to my soule,	P1020	19.90	King
This is the traitor that hath spent my golde,	P1028	19.98	King
To spend the treasure that should strength my land,	P1037	19.107	King
My Lord heer is his sonne.	P1045	19.115	Eprnon
My father slaine, who hath done this deed?	P1047	19.117	YngGse
Ile clippe his winges/Or ere he passe my handes, away with him.	P1053	19.123	King
And will him in my name to kill the Duke.	P1058	19.128	King
My Lord, see where she comes, as if she droupt/To heare these	P1062	19.132	Eprnon
And let her droup, my heart is light enough.	P1064	19.134	King
But now I will be King and rule my selfe,	P1070	19.140	King
I would that I had murdered thee my sonne.	P1073	19.143	QnMoth
My sonne: thou art a changeling, not my sonne.	P1074	19.144	QnMoth
To whom shall I bewray my secrets now,	P1083	19.153	QnMoth
And all for thee my Guise: what may I doe?	P1088	19.158	QnMoth
But sorrow seaze upon my toyling soule,	P1089	19.159	QnMoth
Yet lives/My brother Duke Dumaine, and many moe:	P1099	20.9	Cardnl
Yours my Lord Cardinall, you should have saide.	P1103	20.13	1Mur
My noble brother murthered by the King,	P1107	21.1	Dumain
My Lord, I come to bring you newes, that your brother the	P1122	21.16	P Frier
My brother Cardenall slaine and I alive?	P1125	21.19	Dumain
My Lord, here me but speak.	P1129	21.23	P Frier
the Jacobyns, that for my conscience sake will kill the King.	P1130	21.24	P Frier
O my Lord, I have beene a great sinner in my dayes, and the	P1133	21.27	P Frier
I have beene a great sinner in my dayes, and the deed is	P1133	21.27	P Frier
Tush my Lord, let me alone for that.	P1136	21.30	P Frier
That ever I vouchsafte my dearest freends.	P1146	22.8	King
Thankes to my Kingly Brother of Navarre.	P1150	22.12	King
Twere not amisse my Lord, if he were searcht.	P1160	22.22	Eprnon
I my good Lord, and will dye therein.	P1165	22.27	Frier
My Lord,/The President of Paris greets your grace,	P1167	22.29	Frier
O my Lord, let him live a while.	P1173	22.35	Eprnon
Take hence that damned villaine from my sight.	P1182	22.44	King
Ile send my sister England newes of this,	P1189	22.51	King
The wound I warrant ye is deepe my Lord,	P1192	22.54	King
These words revive my thoughts and comforts me,	P1209	22.71	Navrre
Alas my Lord, the wound is dangerous,	P1212	22.74	Srgeon
O the fatall poyson workes within my brest,	P1221	22.83	King
Alas my Lord, your highnes cannot live.	P1223	22.85	Srgeon
My Lords,/Fight in the quarrell of this valiant Prince,	P1228	22.90	King
For he is your lawfull King and my next heire:	P1230	22.92	King
Valoyses lyne ends in my tragedie.	P1231	22.93	King
Weep not sweet Navarre, but revenge my death.	P1234	22.96	King
I dye Navarre, come beare me to my Sepulchre.	P1242	22.104	King
Salute the Queene of England in my name,	P1243	22.105	King
and that thow most reposest one my faythe	Paris	ms31,p391	Guise
thie folishe dreame/and lett thee see thie selfe my prysoner	Paris	ms33,p391	Guise

MY (cont.)

My father is deceast, come Gaveston,	Edw	1.1.1	Gavstn
The sight of London to my exiled eyes,	Edw	1.1.10	Gavstn
My knee shall bowe to none but to the king.	Edw	1.1.19	Gavstn
That glaunceth at my lips and flieth away:	Edw	1.1.23	Gavstn
thou wouldst do well/To waite at my trencher, and tell me lies	Edw	1.1.31	Gavstn
And dart her plumes, thinking to pierce my brest,	Edw	1.1.41	Gavstn
And yet I have not viewd my Lord the king,	Edw	1.1.45	Gavstn
I have some busines, leave me to my selfe.	Edw	1.1.48	Gavstn
Like Sylvian <Sylvan> Nimphes my pages shall be clad,	Edw	1.1.58	Gavstn
My men like Satyres grazing on the lawnes,	Edw	1.1.59	Gavstn
Such things as these best please his majestie,/My lord.	Edw	1.1.72	Gavstn
My Lorde.	Edw	1.1.75	Lncstr
Ile have my will, and these two Mortimers,	Edw	1.1.78	Edward
If you love us my lord, hate Gaveston.	Edw	1.1.80	MortSr
Mine unckle heere, this Earle, and I my selfe,	Edw	1.1.82	Mortmr
And know my lord, ere I will breake my oath,	Edw	1.1.85	Mortmr
My lord, why do you thus incense your peeres,	Edw	1.1.99	Lncstr
These will I sell to give my souldiers paye,	Edw	1.1.104	Lncstr
I do remember in my fathers dayes,	Edw	1.1.109	Kent
All Warwickshire will love him for my sake.	Edw	1.1.128	Warwck
Adew my Lord, and either change your minde,	Edw	1.1.130	Lncstr
Brother displaie my ensignes in the field,	Edw	1.1.136	Edward
I can no longer keepe me from my lord.	Edw	1.1.139	Gavstn
kis not my hand,/Embrace me Gaveston as I do thee:	Edw	1.1.140	Edward
I know it, brother welcome home my friend.	Edw	1.1.148	Edward
I have my wish, in that I joy thy sight,	Edw	1.1.151	Edward
And sooner shall the sea orewhelme my land,	Edw	1.1.152	Edward
My lord, these titles far exceed my worth.	Edw	1.1.157	Gavstn
Thy woorth sweet friend is far above my guifts,	Edw	1.1.161	Edward
Therefore to equall it receive my hart.	Edw	1.1.162	Edward
Wants thou gold? go to my treasurie:	Edw	1.1.167	Edward
receive my seale,/Save or condemne, and in our name commaund,	Edw	1.1.168	Edward
Which whiles I have, I thinke my selfe as great,	Edw	1.1.172	Gavstn
Whether goes my Lord of Coventrie so fast?	Edw	1.1.175	Edward
Ile be revengd on him for my exile.	Edw	1.1.192	Gavstn
Come follow me, and thou shalt have my guarde,	Edw	1.1.204	Edward
My lord of Cornewall now, at every worde,	Edw	1.2.17	Lncstr
Were all the Earles and Barons of my minde,	Edw	1.2.28	Mortmr
Here comes my lord of Canterburies grace.	Edw	1.2.33	Warwck
My lord, will you take armes against the king?	Edw	1.2.39	Lncstr
What els my lords, for it concernes me neere,	Edw	1.2.44	ArchBp
For now my lord the king regardes me not,	Edw	1.2.49	Queene
for rather then my lord/Shall be opprest by civill mutinies,	Edw	1.2.64	Queene
My lords, to eaze all this, but heare me speake.	Edw	1.2.68	ArchBp
But say my lord, where shall this meeting bee?	Edw	1.2.74	Warwck
Farewell sweet Mortimer, and for my sake,	Edw	1.2.81	Queene
Quick quick my lorde, I long to write my name.	Edw	1.4.4	Lncstr
No, threaten not my lord, but pay them home.	Edw	1.4.26	Gavstn
Were he a peasant, being my minion,	Edw	1.4.30	Edward
My lord, you may not thus disparage us,	Edw	1.4.32	Lncstr
Warwicke and Lancaster, weare you my crowne,	Edw	1.4.37	Edward
Anger and wrathfull furie stops my speech.	Edw	1.4.42	Edward
Why are you moov'd, be patient my lord,	Edw	1.4.43	ArchBp
My lords, now let us all be resolute,	Edw	1.4.45	Mortmr
Ere my sweete Gaveston shall part from me,	Edw	1.4.48	Edward
Then linger not my lord but do it straight.	Edw	1.4.58	Lncstr
My lord, you shalbe Chauncellor of the realme,	Edw	1.4.65	Edward
To frolike with my deerest Gaveston.	Edw	1.4.73	Edward
Would seeke the ruine of my Gaveston,	Edw	1.4.79	Edward
Urge him, my lord.	Edw	1.4.83	MortSr
In steede of inke, ile write it with my teares.	Edw	1.4.86	Edward
Now is my heart at ease.	Edw	1.4.91	ArchBp
My lord I heare it whispered every where,	Edw	1.4.106	Gavstn
Ile come to thee, my love shall neare decline.	Edw	1.4.115	Edward
Is all my hope turnd to this hell of greefe.	Edw	1.4.116	Gavstn
Rend not my hart with thy too piercing words,	Edw	1.4.117	Edward
Thou from this land, I from my selfe am banisht.	Edw	1.4.118	Edward
And onely this torments my wretched soule,	Edw	1.4.123	Edward
Be governour of Ireland in my stead,	Edw	1.4.125	Edward
Here take my picture, and let me weare thine,	Edw	1.4.127	Edward
For every looke, my lord, drops downe a teare,	Edw	1.4.136	Gavstn
Seeing I must go, do not renew my sorrow.	Edw	1.4.137	Gavstn
And therefore give me leave to looke my fill,	Edw	1.4.139	Edward
Whether goes my lord?	Edw	1.4.144	Queene
On whom but on my husband should I fawne?	Edw	1.4.146	Queene
I say no more, judge you the rest my lord.	Edw	1.4.148	Gavstn
Ist not enough, that thou corrupts my lord,	Edw	1.4.150	Queene
Your highnes knowes, it lies not in my power.	Edw	1.4.158	Queene
Villaine, tis thou that robst me of my lord.	Edw	1.4.160	Queene
Madam, tis you that rob me of my lord.	Edw	1.4.161	Gavstn
Wherein my lord, have I deservd these words?	Edw	1.4.163	Queene
How deare my lord is to poore Isabell.	Edw	1.4.166	Queene
There weepe, for till my Gaveston be repeald,	Edw	1.4.168	Edward
Assure thy selfe thou comst not in my sight.	Edw	1.4.169	Edward
Had chaungd my shape, or at the mariage day/The cup of Hymen	Edw	1.4.173	Queene
Or with those armes that twind about my neck,	Edw	1.4.175	Queene
The king my lord thus to abandon me:	Edw	1.4.177	Queene
With gastlie murmure of my sighes and cries,	Edw	1.4.179	Queene
This wils my lord, and this must I performe,	Edw	1.4.202	Queene
Be thou my advocate unto these peeres.	Edw	1.4.212	Queene
And so am I my lord, diswade the Queene.	Edw	1.4.215	Lncstr
For tis against my will he should returne.	Edw	1.4.217	Queene

MY (cont.)

Tis for my selfe I speake, and not for him.	Edw	1.4.219	Queene
My Lords, albeit the Queen winne Mortimer,	Edw	1.4.230	Lncstr
Not I against my nephew.	Edw	1.4.232	MortSr
She smiles, now for my life his mind is changd.	Edw	1.4.236	Warwck
My Lords, that I abhorre base Gaveston,	Edw	1.4.239	Mortmr
My Lord of Lancaster, marke the respect.	Edw	1.4.248	Mortmr
Yet good my lord, heare what he can alledge.	Edw	1.4.250	Queene
Why then my lord, give me but leave to speak.	Edw	1.4.254	Mortmr
Marke you but that my lord of Lancaster.	Edw	1.4.263	Warwck
Because my lords, it was not thought upon:	Edw	1.4.273	Mortmr
Such a one as my Lord of Cornewall is,	Edw	1.4.285	Mortmr
My lords, if to performe this I be slack,	Edw	1.4.290	Mortmr
But see in happie time, my lord the king,	Edw	1.4.299	Queene
Did never sorrow go so neere my heart,	Edw	1.4.306	Edward
As dooth the want of my sweete Gaveston,	Edw	1.4.307	Edward
And could my crownes revenew bring him back,	Edw	1.4.308	Edward
My heart is as an anvill unto sorrow,	Edw	1.4.312	Edward
And with the noise turnes up my giddie braine,	Edw	1.4.314	Edward
And makes me frantick for my Gaveston:	Edw	1.4.315	Edward
And with my kinglie scepter stroke me dead,	Edw	1.4.317	Edward
When I was forst to leave my Gaveston.	Edw	1.4.318	Edward
My gratious lord, I come to bring you newes.	Edw	1.4.320	Queene
That Gaveston, my Lord, shalbe repeald.	Edw	1.4.322	Queene
No other jewels hang about my neck/Then these my lord, nor let	Edw	1.4.330	Queene
No other jewels hang about my neck/Then these my lord, nor let	Edw	1.4.331	Queene
Once more receive my hand, and let this be,	Edw	1.4.334	Edward
My gentle lord, bespeake these nobles faire,	Edw	1.4.337	Queene
Live thou with me as my companion.	Edw	1.4.343	Edward
This salutation overjoyes my heart.	Edw	1.4.344	Lncstr
Warwick shalbe my chiefest counseller:	Edw	1.4.345	Edward
These silver haires will more adorne my court,	Edw	1.4.346	Edward
Slay me my lord, when I offend your grace.	Edw	1.4.349	Warwck
My lord, ile marshall so your enemies,	Edw	1.4.357	Mortmr
For with my nature warre doth best agree.	Edw	1.4.365	MortSr
I Isabell, nere was my heart so light.	Edw	1.4.368	Edward
It shalbe done my gratious Lord.	Edw	1.4.372	Beamnt
Such newes we heare my lord.	Edw	1.4.380	Lncstr
That day, if not for him, yet for my sake,	Edw	1.4.381	Edward
You know my minde, come unckle lets away.	Edw	1.4.424	Mortmr
My life for thine she will have Gaveston.	Edw	2.1.28	Spencr
That he would take exceptions at my buttons,	Edw	2.1.47	Baldck
Leave of this jesting, here my lady comes.	Edw	2.1.56	Baldck
This letter came from my sweete Gaveston,	Edw	2.1.59	Neece
This argues the entire love of my Lord.	Edw	2.1.63	Neece
When I forsake thee, death seaze on my heart,	Edw	2.1.64	Neece
Now to the letter of my Lord the King,	Edw	2.1.66	Neece
He wils me to repaire unto the court,/And meete my Gaveston:	Edw	2.1.68	Neece
Seeing that he talkes thus of my mariage day?	Edw	2.1.69	Neece
See that my coache be readie, I must hence.	Edw	2.1.71	Neece
My lord of Cornewall is a comming over,	Edw	2.1.76	Neece
My Lord.	Edw	2.2.5	Lncstr
A homely one my lord, not worth the telling.	Edw	2.2.13	Mortmr
And what is yours my lord of Lancaster?	Edw	2.2.21	Edward
My lord, mines more obscure then Mortimers.	Edw	2.2.22	Lncstr
this fish my lord I beare,/The motto this:	Edw	2.2.27	Lncstr
Against the Earle of Cornewall and my brother?	Edw	2.2.35	Edward
They love me not that hate my Gaveston.	Edw	2.2.37	Edward
My Gaveston,/Welcome to Tinmouth,	Edw	2.2.50	Edward
was thy parting hence/Bitter and irkesome to my sobbing heart.	Edw	2.2.58	Edward
Yet have I words left to expresse my joy:	Edw	2.2.60	Gavstn
Will none of you salute my Gaveston?	Edw	2.2.64	Edward
My Lord I cannot brooke these injuries.	Edw	2.2.71	Gavstn
Out of my presence, come not neere the court.	Edw	2.2.89	Edward
From Scotland my lord.	Edw	2.2.113	1Msngr
My unckles taken prisoner by the Scots.	Edw	2.2.115	Mortmr
Meane time my lord of Penbrooke and my selfe,	Edw	2.2.122	Warwck
Content, ile beare my part, holla whose there?	Edw	2.2.130	Lncstr
You may not in, my lord.	Edw	2.2.137	Guard
Nay, stay my lord, I come to bring you newes,	Edw	2.2.141	Mortmr
My lord, the familie of the Mortimers/Are not so poore, but	Edw	2.2.150	Mortmr
Nay, now you are heere alone, ile speake my minde.	Edw	2.2.155	Mortmr
And so will I, and then my lord farewell.	Edw	2.2.156	Lncstr
Wigmore shall flie, to set my unckle free.	Edw	2.2.196	Mortmr
My swelling hart for very anger breakes,	Edw	2.2.200	Edward
My lord, I see your love to Gaveston,	Edw	2.2.208	Kent
Art thou an enemie to my Gaveston?	Edw	2.2.212	Edward
Out of my sight, and trouble me no more.	Edw	2.2.216	Edward
My lord, tis thought, the Earles are up in armes.	Edw	2.2.225	Queene
My lord, dissemble with her, speake her faire.	Edw	2.2.229	Gavstn
Pardon me sweet, I forgot my selfe.	Edw	2.2.230	Edward
That to my face he threatens civill warres.	Edw	2.2.233	Edward
Two of my fathers servants whilst he liv'de,	Edw	2.2.240	Neece
My name is Baldock, and my gentrie/Is fetcht from Oxford, not	Edw	2.2.243	Baldck
The fitter art thou Baldock for my turne,	Edw	2.2.245	Edward
I my lord,/His name is Spencer, he is well alied,	Edw	2.2.248	Gavstn
For my sake let him waite upon your grace,	Edw	2.2.250	Gavstn
I know my lord, many will stomack me,	Edw	2.2.260	Gavstn
My lords, of love to this our native land,	Edw	2.3.1	Kent
Mine honor shalbe hostage of my truth,	Edw	2.3.9	Kent
If that will not suffice, farwell my lords.	Edw	2.3.10	Kent
now my lords know this,/That Gaveston is secretlie arrivde,	Edw	2.3.15	Lncstr
This tottered ensigne of my auncesters,	Edw	2.3.21	Mortmr

MY (cont.)

I feare me he is slaine my gratious lord.	Edw	2.4.2	Spencr
Flie, flie, my lords, the earles have got the holde,	Edw	2.4.4	Edward
O stay my lord, they will not injure you.	Edw	2.4.7	Gavstn
Farewell my Lord.	Edw	2.4.9	Gavstn
From my imbracements thus he breakes away,	Edw	2.4.16	Queene
These hands are tir'd, with haling of my lord/From Gaveston,	Edw	2.4.26	Queene
No Mortimer, ile to my lord the king.	Edw	2.4.51	Queene
If he be straunge and not regarde my wordes,	Edw	2.4.64	Queene
My sonne and I will over into France,	Edw	2.4.65	Queene
And to the king my brother there complaine,	Edw	2.4.66	Queene
But yet I hope my sorrowes will have end,	Edw	2.4.68	Queene
Upon my weapons point here shouldst thou fall,	Edw	2.5.13	Mortmr
Go souldiers take him hence, for by my sword,	Edw	2.5.20	Warwck
My Lord!	Edw	2.5.25	Gavstn
I thanke you all my lords, then I perceive,	Edw	2.5.29	Gavstn
How now my lord of Arundell?	Edw	2.5.32	Lncstr
My lords, king Edward greetes you all by me.	Edw	2.5.33	Arundl
Why my Lord of Warwicke,	Edw	2.5.46	Gavstn
Will not these delaies beget my hopes?	Edw	2.5.47	Gavstn
Not so my Lord, least he bestow more cost,	Edw	2.5.55	Lncstr
My lords, it is his majesties request,	Edw	2.5.57	Arundl
My lords, I will be pledge for his returne.	Edw	2.5.66	Arundl
My lord Mortimer, and you my lords each one,	Edw	2.5.74	Penbrk
Provided this, that you my lord of Arundell/Will joyne with me.	Edw	2.5.81	Penbrk
My lords, I will not over wooe your honors,	Edw	2.5.86	Penbrk
My lord of Lancaster, what say you in this?	Edw	2.5.89	Arundl
How say you my lord of Warwick?	Edw	2.5.92	Mortmr
My lord of Penbrooke, we deliver him you,	Edw	2.5.97	Mortmr
My Lord, you shall go with me,	Edw	2.5.99	Penbrk
My house is not farre hence, out of the way/A little, but our	Edw	2.5.100	Penbrk
Tis verie kindlie spoke my lord of Penbrooke,	Edw	2.5.104	Arundl
So my lord.	Edw	2.5.106	Penbrk
My lord, weele quicklie be at Cobham.	Edw	2.5.111	HrsBoy
O must this day be period of my life,	Edw	2.6.4	Gavstn
O must this day be period of my life,/Center of all my blisse!	Edw	2.6.5	Gavstn
My lord of Penbrookes men,	Edw	2.6.6	Warwck
No James, it is my countries cause I follow.	Edw	2.6.10	Warwck
commend me to your maister/My friend, and tell him that I	Edw	2.6.13	Warwck
I long to heare an answer from the Barons/Touching my friend,	Edw	3.1.2	Edward
answer from the Barons/Touching my friend, my deerest Gaveston.	Edw	3.1.2	Edward
Ah Spencer, not the riches of my realme/Can ransome him, ah he	Edw	3.1.3	Edward
Inexorable, and I shall never see/My lovely Pierce, my Gaveston	Edw	3.1.8	Edward
and I shall never see/My lovely Pierce, my Gaveston againe,	Edw	3.1.8	Edward
suffer uncontrowld/These Barons thus to beard me in my land,	Edw	3.1.14	Spencr
my lord pardon my speeche,/Did you retaine your fathers	Edw	3.1.15	Spencr
And if they send me not my Gaveston,	Edw	3.1.26	Edward
Long live my soveraigne the noble Edward,	Edw	3.1.32	SpncrP
His life, my lord, before your princely feete.	Edw	3.1.45	Spencr
My lord, here comes the Queene.	Edw	3.1.58	Spencr
But to my Gaveston:	Edw	3.1.68	Edward
Commit not to my youth things of more waight/Then fits a prince	Edw	3.1.74	Prince
Then shall your charge committed to my trust.	Edw	3.1.78	Prince
God end them once, my lord I take my leave,	Edw	3.1.87	Queene
To make my preparation for Fraunce.	Edw	3.1.88	Queene
Yea my good lord, for Gaveston is dead.	Edw	3.1.90	Arundl
Ah traitors, have they put my friend to death?	Edw	3.1.91	Edward
Or didst thou see my friend to take his death?	Edw	3.1.93	Edward
Neither my lord, for as he was surprizd,	Edw	3.1.94	Arundl
And said, upon the honour of my name,	Edw	3.1.98	Arundl
My lords, because our soveraigne sends for him,	Edw	3.1.109	Arundl
My lord, referre your vengeance to the sword,	Edw	3.1.123	Spencr
By this right hand, and by my fathers sword,	Edw	3.1.130	Edward
And all the honors longing to my crowne,	Edw	3.1.131	Edward
And staine my roiall standard with the same,	Edw	3.1.138	Edward
That so my bloudie colours may suggest/Remembrance of revenge	Edw	3.1.139	Edward
You villaines that have slaine my Gaveston:	Edw	3.1.142	Edward
My lord, [here] is <heres> a messenger from the Barons,/Desires	Edw	3.1.148	Spencr
My [lords] <lord>, perceive you how these rebels swell:	Edw	3.1.181	Edward
This day I shall powre vengeance with my sword/On those proud	Edw	3.1.186	Edward
I doubt it not my lord, right will prevaile.	Edw	3.1.189	Spencr
Tis not amisse my liege for eyther part,	Edw	3.1.190	SpncrP
And for the murther of my deerest friend,	Edw	3.1.226	Edward
Good Pierce of Gaveston my sweet favoret,	Edw	3.1.228	Edward
my lord of Winchester,/These lustie leaders Warwicke and	Edw	3.1.245	Edward
Sound drums and trumpets, marche with me my friends,	Edw	3.1.260	Edward
Have you no doubts my lords, ile [clap so] <claps> close,/Among	Edw	3.1.276	Levune
Nature, yeeld to my countries cause in this.	Edw	4.1.3	Kent
Holla, who walketh there, ist you my lord?	Edw	4.1.12	Mortmr
It hath my lord, the warders all a sleepe,	Edw	4.1.15	Mortmr
And please my father well, and then a Fig/For all my unckles	Edw	4.2.4	Prince
and then a Fig/For all my unckles frienship here in Fraunce.	Edw	4.2.5	Prince
How say you my Lord, will you go with your friends,	Edw	4.2.19	SrJohn
So pleaseth the Queene my mother, me it likes.	Edw	4.2.21	Prince
Shall have me from my gratious mothers side,	Edw	4.2.23	Prince
Well said my lord.	Edw	4.2.26	SrJohn
Oh my sweet hart, how do I mone thy wrongs,	Edw	4.2.27	Queene
Yet triumphe in the hope of thee my joye?	Edw	4.2.28	Queene
the newes was heere my lord,/That you were dead, or very neare	Edw	4.2.37	Queene
And lives t'advance your standard good my lord.	Edw	4.2.42	Mortmr
How meane you, and the king my father lives?	Edw	4.2.43	Prince
No my lord Mortimer, not I, I trow.	Edw	4.2.44	Prince
But by the sword, my lord, it must be deserv'd.	Edw	4.2.59	Mortmr

MY (cont.)

My Lords of England, sith the ungentle king/Of Fraunce refuseth	Edw	4.2.61	SrJohn
Madam along, and you my lord, with me,	Edw	4.2.81	SrJohn
My lord of Gloster, do you heare the newes?	Edw	4.3.4	Edward
What newes my lord?	Edw	4.3.5	Spencr
Done through the realme, my lord of Arundell/You have the note,	Edw	4.3.7	Edward
From the lieutenant of the tower my lord.	Edw	4.3.9	Arundl
Now on my life, theile neither barke nor bite.	Edw	4.3.13	Edward
What now remaines, have you proclaimed, my lord,	Edw	4.3.17	Edward
My lord, we have, and if he be in England,	Edw	4.3.19	Spencr
Letters my lord, and tidings foorth of Fraunce,	Edw	4.3.25	Post
To you my lord of Gloster from [Levune] <Lewne>.	Edw	4.3.26	Post
My dutie to your honor [premised] <promised>, &c. I have	Edw	4.3.28	P Spencr
Ah nothing greeves me but my little boye,	Edw	4.3.48	Edward
Sound trumpets my lord and forward let us martch,	Edw	4.4.28	SrJohn
Fly, fly, my Lord, the Queene is over strong,	Edw	4.5.1	Spencr
Give me my horse and lets r'enforce our troupes:	Edw	4.5.6	Edward
O no my lord, this princely resolution/Fits not the time, away,	Edw	4.5.8	Baldck
Edward, alas my hart relents for thee,	Edw	4.6.2	Kent
Raigne showers of vengeance on my cursed head/Thou God, to whom	Edw	4.6.7	Kent
Ere farther we proceede my noble lordes,	Edw	4.6.23	Queene
Deale you my lords in this, my loving lords,	Edw	4.6.28	Queene
My lord of Kent, what needes these questions?	Edw	4.6.34	Mortmr
My lord, the Maior of Bristow knows our mind.	Edw	4.6.40	Queene
A goodly chauncelor, is he not my lord?	Edw	4.6.43	Queene
Shall I not see the king my father yet?	Edw	4.6.61	Prince
I rue my lords ill fortune, but alas,	Edw	4.6.64	Queene
Care of my countrie cald me to this warre.	Edw	4.6.65	Queene
Have you no doubt my Lorde, have you no feare,	Edw	4.7.1	Abbot
a king, thy hart/Pierced deeply with sence of my distresse,	Edw	4.7.10	Edward
Could not but take compassion of my state.	Edw	4.7.11	Edward
But we alas are chaste, and you my friends,	Edw	4.7.22	Edward
Your lives and my dishonor they pursue,	Edw	4.7.23	Edward
A gave a long looke after us my lord,	Edw	4.7.30	Spencr
Looke up my lord.	Edw	4.7.44	Spencr
Upon my life, those be the men ye seeke.	Edw	4.7.46	Mower
my lord I pray be short,/A faire commission warrants what we	Edw	4.7.47	Rice
My lord, why droope you thus?	Edw	4.7.60	Leistr
the last of all my blisse on earth,/Center of all misfortune.	Edw	4.7.61	Edward
Center of all misfortune. O my starres!	Edw	4.7.62	Edward
To take my life, my companie from me?	Edw	4.7.65	Edward
And take my heart, in reskew of my friends.	Edw	4.7.67	Edward
My heart with pittie earnes to see this sight,	Edw	4.7.70	Abbot
We must my lord, so will the angry heavens.	Edw	4.7.74	Spencr
My lord, it is in vaine to greeve or storme,	Edw	4.7.77	Baldck
Let Plutos bels ring out my fatall knell,	Edw	4.7.89	Edward
And hags howle for my death at Charons shore,	Edw	4.7.90	Edward
My lord, be going, care not for these,	Edw	4.7.93	Rice
Hence fained weeds, unfained are my woes,	Edw	4.7.97	Edward
And go I must, life farewell with my friends.	Edw	4.7.99	Edward
Earth melt to ayre, gone is my soveraigne,	Edw	4.7.103	Spencr
Be patient good my lord, cease to lament,	Edw	5.1.1	Leistr
Thy speeches long agoe had easde my sorrowes,	Edw	5.1.6	Edward
For such outragious passions cloye my soule,	Edw	5.1.19	Edward
My nobles rule, I beare the name of king,	Edw	5.1.28	Edward
By Mortimer, and my unconstant Queene,	Edw	5.1.30	Edward
Who spots my nuptiall bed with infamie,	Edw	5.1.31	Edward
Where sorrow at my elbow still attends,	Edw	5.1.33	Edward
To companie my hart with sad laments,	Edw	5.1.34	Edward
But tell me, must I now resigne my crowne,	Edw	5.1.36	Edward
My lord, why waste you thus the time away,	Edw	5.1.49	Leistr
way how hardly I can brooke/To loose my crowne and kingdome,	Edw	5.1.52	Edward
To give ambitious Mortimer my right,	Edw	5.1.53	Edward
That like a mountaine overwhelmes my blisse,	Edw	5.1.54	Edward
In which extreame my minde here murthered is:	Edw	5.1.55	Edward
Here, take my crowne, the life of Edward too,	Edw	5.1.57	Edward
So shall my eyes receive their last content,	Edw	5.1.61	Edward
My head, the latest honor dew to it,	Edw	5.1.62	Edward
And needes I must resigne my wished crowne.	Edw	5.1.70	Edward
My diadem I meane, and guiltlesse life.	Edw	5.1.73	Edward
See monsters see, ile weare my crowne againe,	Edw	5.1.74	Edward
Which fils my mind with strange despairing thoughts,	Edw	5.1.79	Edward
But that I feele the crowne upon my head,	Edw	5.1.82	Edward
My lorde, the parlement must have present newes,	Edw	5.1.84	Trussl
Call them againe my lorde, and speake them faire,	Edw	5.1.91	Leistr
My lord, the king is willing to resigne.	Edw	5.1.94	Leistr
heere receive my crowne.	Edw	5.1.97	Edward
He of you all that most desires my bloud,	Edw	5.1.100	Edward
Come death, and with thy fingers close my eyes,	Edw	5.1.110	Edward
Or if I live, let me forget my selfe.	Edw	5.1.111	Edward
My lorde--	Edw	5.1.112	Bishop
Call me not lorde, away, out of my sight:	Edw	5.1.113	Edward
Let not that Mortimer protect my sonne,	Edw	5.1.115	Edward
Wet with my teares, and dried againe with sighes,	Edw	5.1.118	Edward
Returne it backe and dip it in my bloud.	Edw	5.1.120	Edward
Commend me to my sonne, and bid him rule/Better then I, yet how	Edw	5.1.121	Edward
Will be my death, and welcome shall it be,	Edw	5.1.126	Edward
And tell thy message to my naked brest.	Edw	5.1.130	Edward
My lord, thinke not a thought so villanous/Can harbor in a man	Edw	5.1.131	Bartly
My lorde, the counsell of the Queene commaunds,	Edw	5.1.135	Leistr
That I resigne my charge.	Edw	5.1.136	Leistr
And who must keepe mee now, must you my lorde?	Edw	5.1.137	Edward
I, my most gratious lord, so tis decreed.	Edw	5.1.138	Bartly

MY (cont.)

Well may I rent his name, that rends my hart.	Edw	5.1.140	Edward
This poore revenge hath something easd my minde,	Edw	5.1.141	Edward
Favor him my lord, as much as lieth in you.	Edw	5.1.147	Leistr
Even so betide my soule as I use him.	Edw	5.1.148	Bartly
Mine enemie hath pitied my estate,	Edw	5.1.149	Edward
Not yet my lorde, ile beare you on your waye.	Edw	5.1.155	Leistr
And therefore so the prince my sonne be safe,	Edw	5.2.17	Queene
And I my selfe will willinglie subscribe.	Edw	5.2.20	Queene
From Killingworth my lorde.	Edw	5.2.23	2Msngr
How fares my lord the king?	Edw	5.2.24	Queene
O happie newes, send for the prince my sonne.	Edw	5.2.29	Queene
long as he survives/What safetie rests for us, or for my sonne?	Edw	5.2.43	Queene
I would hee were, so it were not by my meanes.	Edw	5.2.45	Queene
It shall be done my lord.	Edw	5.2.51	Matrvs
My Lorde.	Edw	5.2.51	Gurney
I warrant you my lord.	Edw	5.2.56	Gurney
Feare not my Lord, weele do as you commaund.	Edw	5.2.66	Matrvs
Whither goes this letter, to my lord the king?	Edw	5.2.68	Queene
And beare him this, as witnesse of my love.	Edw	5.2.72	Queene
How fares my honorable lord of Kent?	Edw	5.2.80	Mortmr
Well, if my Lorde your brother were enlargde.	Edw	5.2.82	Queene
The more my greefe.	Edw	5.2.84	Queene
Not I my lord:	Edw	5.2.90	Kent
My lord, he hath betraied the king his brother,	Edw	5.2.106	Mortmr
Sister, Edward is my charge, redeeme him.	Edw	5.2.116	Kent
Edward is my sonne, and I will keepe him.	Edw	5.2.117	Queene
My lord, be not pensive, we are your friends.	Edw	5.3.1	Matrvs
And give my heart to Isabell and him,	Edw	5.3.11	Edward
Not so my liege, the Queene hath given this charge,	Edw	5.3.13	Gurney
This usage makes my miserie increase.	Edw	5.3.16	Edward
But can my ayre of life continue long,	Edw	5.3.17	Edward
When all my sences are anoyde with stenche?	Edw	5.3.18	Edward
My daily diet, is heart breaking sobs,	Edw	5.3.21	Edward
That almost rents the closet of my heart,	Edw	5.3.22	Edward
O water gentle friends to coole my thirst,	Edw	5.3.25	Edward
And cleare my bodie from foule excrements.	Edw	5.3.26	Edward
That waites upon my poore distressed soule,	Edw	5.3.38	Edward
I, lead me whether you will, even to my death,	Edw	5.3.66	Kent
Seeing that my brother cannot be releast.	Edw	5.3.67	Kent
What else my lord? and farre more resolute.	Edw	5.4.23	Ltborn
Nay, you shall pardon me, none shall knowe my trickes.	Edw	5.4.39	Ltborn
That will I quicklie do, farewell my lord.	Edw	5.4.47	Ltborn
Till being interrupted by my friends,	Edw	5.4.62	Mortmr
Mine enemies will I plague, my friends advance,	Edw	5.4.67	Mortmr
The trumpets sound, I must go take my place.	Edw	5.4.72	Mortmr
Strike of my head? base traitor I defie thee.	Edw	5.4.90	Kent
My lord, he is my unckle, and shall live.	Edw	5.4.91	King
My lord, he is your enemie, and shall die.	Edw	5.4.92	Mortmr
Intreate my lord Protector for his life.	Edw	5.4.95	King
My lord, if you will let my unckle live,	Edw	5.4.99	King
Either my brother or his sonne is king,	Edw	5.4.106	Kent
If that my Unckle shall be murthered thus?	Edw	5.4.110	King
And shall my Unckle Edmund ride with us?	Edw	5.4.114	King
My lord protector greetes you.	Edw	5.5.14	Ltborn
Doe as you are commaunded by my lord.	Edw	5.5.26	Matrvs
Foh, heeres a place in deed with all my hart.	Edw	5.5.41	Ltborn
To murther you my most gratious lorde?	Edw	5.5.46	Ltborn
Farre is it from my hart to do you harme,	Edw	5.5.47	Ltborn
Yet will it melt, ere I have done my tale.	Edw	5.5.55	Edward
My mindes distempered, and my bodies numde,	Edw	5.5.64	Edward
O would my bloud dropt out from every vaine,	Edw	5.5.66	Edward
As doth this water from my tattered robes:	Edw	5.5.67	Edward
O speake no more my lorde, this breakes my heart.	Edw	5.5.71	Ltborn
I see my tragedie written in thy browes,	Edw	5.5.74	Edward
That <and> even then when I shall lose my life,	Edw	5.5.77	Edward
My minde may be more stedfast on my God.	Edw	5.5.78	Edward
Forgive my thought, for having such a thought,	Edw	5.5.83	Edward
I feele a hell of greefe: where is my crowne?	Edw	5.5.90	Edward
Your overwatchde my lord, lie downe and rest.	Edw	5.5.92	Ltborn
If you mistrust me, ile be gon my lord.	Edw	5.5.97	Ltborn
How now my Lorde.	Edw	5.5.102	Ltborn
Assist me sweete God, and receive my soule.	Edw	5.5.109	Edward
I my good Lord, I would it were undone.	Edw	5.6.2	Matrvs
Gurney, my lord, is fled, and will I feare,	Edw	5.6.7	Matrvs
As for my selfe, I stand as Joves huge tree,	Edw	5.6.11	Mortmr
All tremble at my name, and I feare none,	Edw	5.6.13	Mortmr
A Mortimer, the king my sonne hath news,	Edw	5.6.15	Queene
Feare not my lord, know that you are a king.	Edw	5.6.24	1Lord
How now my lord?	Edw	5.6.26	Mortmr
My father's murdered through thy treacherie,	Edw	5.6.28	King
Forbid not me to weepe, he was my father,	Edw	5.6.34	King
Why speake you not unto my lord the king?	Edw	5.6.38	1Lord
Traitor, in me my loving father speakes,	Edw	5.6.41	King
Tis my hand, what gather you by this.	Edw	5.6.47	Mortmr
For my sake sweete sonne pittie Mortimer.	Edw	5.6.55	Queene
Why should I greeve at my declining fall?	Edw	5.6.63	Mortmr
This argues, that you spilt my fathers bloud,	Edw	5.6.70	King
My lord, I feare me it will proove too true.	Edw	5.6.77	2Lord
Nay, to my death, for too long have I lived,	Edw	5.6.83	Queene
When as my sonne thinkes to abridge my daies.	Edw	5.6.84	Queene
Shall I not moorne for my beloved lord,	Edw	5.6.87	Queene
My lord, here is the head of Mortimer.	Edw	5.6.93	1Lord

MY (cont.)

Goe fetche my fathers hearse, where it shall lie,	Edw	5.6.94	King
hearse, where it shall lie,/And bring my funerall robes:	Edw	5.6.95	King
Heere comes the hearse, helpe me to moorne, my lords:	Edw	5.6.98	King
Be witnesse of my greefe and innocencie.	Edw	5.6.102	King
that move betweene the quiet Poles/Shall be at my command:	F 84	1.1.56	Faust
god>,/Here <Faustus> tire my <trie thy> braines to get a Deity.	F 90	1.1.62	Faust
Then all my labours, plod I ne're so fast.	F 96	1.1.68	Faust
I'le make my servile spirits to invent.	F 124	1.1.96	Faust
no object, for my head]/[But ruminates on Negromantique skill].	F 131	1.1.103A	Faust
of Wittenberg <Wertenberge>/[Swarme] <Sworne> to my Problemes,	F 142	1.1.114	Faust
Nothing Cornelius; O this cheeres my soule:	F 176	1.1.148	Faust
<Aske my fellow if I be a thiefe>.	F 204	(HC258)A	P Wagner
I will set my countenance like a Precisian, and begin to speake	F 213	1.2.20	P Wagner
Truely my deere brethren, my Maister is within at dinner, with	F 214	1.2.21	P Wagner
my Maister is within at dinner, with Valdes and Cornelius,	F 215	1.2.22	P Wagner
you, and keepe you, my deere brethren <my deare brethren>.	F 217	1.2.24	P Wagner
you, and keepe you, my deere brethren <my deare brethren>.	F 218	1.2.25	P Wagner
I see there's vertue in my heavenly words.	F 255	1.3.27	Faust
Such is the force of Magicke, and my spels.	F 259	1.3.31	Faust
Did not my conjuring [speeches] raise thee? speake.	F 273	1.3.45	Faust
My <His> Ghost be with the old Phylosophers.	F 288	1.3.60	Faust
Which [strike] <strikes> a terror to my fainting soule.	F 310	1.3.82	Mephst
To slay mine enemies, and aid my friends,	F 324	1.3.96	Faust
And alwaies be obedient to my will.	F 325	1.3.97	Faust
And meet me in my Study, at Midnight,	F 327	1.3.99	Faust
And both contributary to my Crowne.	F 337	1.3.109	Faust
The Emperour shall not live, but by my leave,	F 338	1.3.110	Faust
O disgrace to my person:	F 344	1.4.2	P Robin
Sirra, wilt thou be my man and waite on me?	F 354	1.4.12	P Wagner
your right eye be alwaies Diametrally fixt upon my left heele,	F 387	1.4.45	P Wagner
So he will buy my service with his soule.	F 421	2.1.33	Mephst
And tell me, what good will my soule do thy Lord?	F 428	2.1.40	Faust
and with his <my> proper bloud/Assures his <assure my> soule to	F 443	2.1.55	Faust
bloud/Assures his <assure my> soule to be great Lucifers,	F 444	2.1.56	Faust
And let it be propitious for my wish.	F 447	2.1.59	Faust
My bloud congeales, and I can write no more.	F 451	2.1.63	Faust
What might the staying of my bloud portend?	F 453	2.1.65	Faust
My sences are deceiv'd, here's nothing writ:	F 468	2.1.80	Faust
This will I keepe, as chary as my life.	F 551	2.1.163	Faust
My heart is <hearts so> hardned, I cannot repent:	F 569	2.2.18	Faust
Are laid before me to dispatch my selfe:	F 574	2.2.23	Faust
long e're this, I should have done the deed <slaine my selfe>,	F 575	2.2.24	Faust
Made musicke with my Mephostophilis?	F 581	2.2.30	Faust
[Ah] <O> Christ my Saviour, my Saviour,	F 634	2.2.83	Faust
And this is my companion Prince in hell.	F 640	2.2.89	Lucifr
[And make my spirites pull his churches downe].	F 651	2.2.100A	Faust
And then turning my selfe to a wrought Smocke do what I list.	F 668	2.2.117	P Pride
bag; and might I now obtaine <have> my wish, this house,	F 675	2.2.124	P Covet
that I might locke you safe into <uppe in> my <goode> Chest:	F 676	2.2.125	P Covet
O my sweete Gold!	F 677	2.2.126	P Covet
my selfe when I could get none <had no body> to fight withall:	F 689	2.2.138	P Wrath
in hell, and look to it, for some of you shall be my father.	F 690	2.2.139	P Wrath
my parents are all dead, and the devill a peny they have left	F 693	2.2.142	P Glutny
my father <grandfather> was a Gammon of Bacon, and my mother	F 696	2.2.145	P Glutny
and my mother <grandmother> was a Hogshead of Claret Wine.	F 697	2.2.146	P Glutny
My godfathers were these:	F 697	2.2.146	P Glutny
<O> But my godmother, O she was an ancient Gentlewoman, her	F 699	2.2.148	P Glutny
Now Faustus thou hast heard all my progeny, wilt thou bid me to	F 701	2.2.150	P Glutny
<No, Ile see thee hanged, thou wilt eate up all my victualls>.	F 702	(HC264)A	P Faust
the first letter of my name begins with Letchery <leachery>.	F 709	2.2.161	P Ltchry
O how this sight doth delight <this feedes> my soule.	F 712	2.2.164	Faust
[This will I keepe as chary as my life].	F 719.1	2.2.172	Faust
your foolery, for an my Maister come, he'le conjure you 'faith.	F 735	2.3.14	P Dick
My Maister conjure me?	F 736	2.3.15	P Robin
an my Maister come here, I'le clap as faire a paire of hornes	F 736	2.3.15	P Robin
Thou needst not do that, for my Mistresse hath done it.	F 739	2.3.18	P Dick
Having now my good Mephostophilis,	F 779	3.1.1	Faust
I have my Faustus, and for proofe thereof,	F 803	3.1.25	Mephst
But <And> now my Faustus, that thou maist perceive,	F 809	3.1.31	Mephst
Nay stay my Faustus:	F 831	3.1.53	Mephst
My foure and twenty yeares of liberty/I'le spend in pleasure	F 839	3.1.61	Faust
Nay stay my gentle Mephostophilis,	F 845	3.1.67	Faust
And grant me my request, and then I go.	F 846	3.1.68	Faust
No bigger then my hand in quantity.	F 851	3.1.73	Faust
Let it be so my Faustus, but first stay,	F 856	3.1.78	Mephst
We go my Lord.	F 889	3.1.111	1Card
Behold my Lord, the Cardinals are return'd.	F 945	3.1.167	Raymnd
Make haste againe, my good Lord Cardinalls,	F 972	3.1.194	Pope
Whilst on thy head I lay my hand,	F 995	3.2.15	Mephst
My good Lord Archbishop, heres a most daintie dish,	F1046	3.2.66	Pope
My wine gone too?	F1055	3.2.75	Pope
I pray my Lords have patience at this troublesome banquet.	F1058	3.2.78	Pope
O I am slaine, help me my Lords:	F1068	3.2.88	Pope
O come and help to beare my body hence:	F1069	3.2.89	Pope
circle, and stand close at my backe, and stir not for thy life,	F1113	3.3.26	P Robin
I'le wing my selfe and forth-with flie amaine/Unto my Faustus	F1136	3.3.49	Mephst
flie amaine/Unto my Faustus to the great Turkes Court.	F1137	3.3.50	Mephst
I am content for this once to thrust my head out at a window:	F1200	4.1.46	P Benvol
I have a charme in my head, shall controule him as well as the	F1202	4.1.48	P Benvol
zounds I could eate my selfe for anger, to thinke I have beene	F1243	4.1.89	P Benvol
Il'e make you feele something anon, if my Art faile me not.	F1246	4.1.92	P Faust
My Lord, I must forewarne your Majesty,	F1248	4.1.94	Faust

MY (cont.)

That when my Spirits present the royall shapes/Of Alexander and	F1249	4.1.95		Faust
the Emperour, Il'e be Acteon, and turne my selfe to a Stagge.	F1256	4.1.102	P	Benvol
My gracious Lord, you doe forget your selfe,	F1258	4.1.104		Faust
my thoughts are ravished so/With sight of this renowned	F1260	4.1.106		Emper
To satisfie my longing thoughts at full,	F1264	4.1.110		Emper
see, my gracious Lord, what strange beast is yon, that thrusts	F1274	4.1.120	P	Faust
He sleeps my Lord, but dreames not of his hornes.	F1280	4.1.126		Faust
The Emperour? where? O zounds my head.	F1287	4.1.133		Benvol
And therefore my Lord, so please your Majesty,	F1300	4.1.146		Faust
good my Lord intreate for me:	F1306	4.1.152	P	Benvol
My gracious Lord, not so much for injury done to me, as to	F1311	4.1.157	P	Faust
When every servile groome jeasts at my wrongs,	F1329	4.2.5		Benvol
Till with my sword I have that Conjurer slaine.	F1333	4.2.9		Benvol
But Faustus death shall quit my infamie.	F1337	4.2.13		Benvol
My head is lighter then it was by th'hornes,	F1350	4.2.26		Benvol
But yet my [heart's] <heart> more ponderous then my head,	F1351	4.2.27		Benvol
Thou soone shouldst see me quit my foule disgrace.	F1356	4.2.32		Benvol
First, on his head, in quittance of my wrongs,	F1379	4.2.55		Benvol
That all the world may see my just revenge.	F1382	4.2.58		Benvol
And had you cut my body with your swords,	F1397	4.2.73		Faust
Yet in a minute had my spirit return'd,	F1399	4.2.75		Faust
But wherefore doe I dally my revenge?	F1401	4.2.77		Faust
Whilst with my gentle Mephostophilis,	F1412	4.2.88		Faust
Fly hence, dispatch my charge immediatly.	F1416	4.2.92		Faust
What's here? an ambush to betray my life:	F1424	4.2.100		Faust
For loe these Trees remove at my command,	F1426	4.2.102		Faust
My friends transformed thus:	F1441	4.3.11		Benvol
Despaire doth drive distrust into my thoughts.	F1480	4.4.24		Faust
I riding my horse into the water, thinking some hidden mystery	F1484	4.4.28	P	HrsCsr
go rouse him, and make him give me my forty Dollors againe.	F1488	4.4.32	P	HrsCsr
and give me my mony againe, for your horse is turned to a	F1489	4.4.33	P	HrsCsr
and one to whom I must be no niggard of my cunning; Come,	F1504	4.4.48	P	Faust
Come my Maisters, I'le bring you to the best beere in Europe,	F1505	4.5.1	P	Carter
What my old Guesse?	F1507	4.5.3	P	Hostss
what my old Guest?	F1514	4.5.10	P	Hostss
I hope my score stands still.	F1515	4.5.11	P	Robin
so he presently gave me my mony, and fell to eating;	F1529	4.5.25	P	Carter
he never left eating, till he had eate up all my loade of hay.	F1531	4.5.27	P	Carter
so when I had my horse, Doctor Fauster bad me ride him night	F1539	4.5.35	P	HrsCsr
and when I came just in the midst my horse vanisht away, and I	F1544	4.5.40	P	HrsCsr
I do thinke my selfe my good Lord, highly recompenced, in that	F1563	4.6.6	P	Faust
kind I will make knowne unto you what my heart desires to have,	F1571	4.6.14	P	Lady
Why, how now my [good] <goods> friends?	F1608	4.6.51		Faust
My Lord, beseech you give me leave a while,	F1621	4.6.64		Faust
I'le gage my credit, 'twill content your grace.	F1622	4.6.65		Faust
With all my heart kind Doctor, please thy selfe,	F1623	4.6.66		Duke
My woodden leg? what dost thou meane by that?	F1628	4.6.71		Faust
Do you remember sir, how you cosened me and eat up my load of--	F1660	4.6.103	P	Carter
now you have sent away my guesse, I pray who shall pay me for	F1667	4.6.110	P	Hostss
you have sent away my guesse, I pray who shall pay me for my A--	F1668	4.6.111	P	Hostss
My Lord,/We are much beholding to this learned man.	F1669	4.6.112		Lady
I think my Maister means to die shortly, he has made his will,	F1674	5.1.1	P	Wagner
Too simple is my wit to tell her worth <praise>,/Whom all the	F1697	5.1.24		2Schol
It may be this my exhortation/Seemes harsh, and all unpleasant;	F1717	5.1.44		OldMan
And so have hope, that this my kinde rebuke,	F1722	5.1.49		OldMan
[Ah] <O> [my sweete] friend,	F1734	5.1.61		Faust
I feele thy words to comfort my distressed soule,	F1735	5.1.62		Faust
Leave me a while, to ponder on my sinnes.	F1736	5.1.63		Faust
Hell strives with grace for conquest in my breast:	F1741	5.1.68		Faust
For disobedience to my soveraigne Lord,	F1744	5.1.71		Mephst
intreat thy Lord/To pardon my unjust presumption,	F1748	5.1.75		Faust
And with my bloud againe I will confirme/The <My> former vow I	F1749	5.1.76		Faust
againe I will confirme/The <My> former vow I made to Lucifer.	F1750	5.1.77		Faust
To glut the longing of my hearts desire,	F1760	5.1.87		Faust
That I may <might> have unto my paramour,	F1761	5.1.88		Faust
Those <These> thoughts that do disswade me from my vow,	F1764	5.1.91		Faust
And keepe [mine oath] <my vow> I made to Lucifer.	F1765	5.1.92		Faust
This, or what else my Faustus shall <thou shalt> desire,	F1766	5.1.93		Mephst
Her lips sucke <suckes> forth my soule, see where it flies.	F1771	5.1.98		Faust
Come Hellen, come, give me my soule againe,	F1772	5.1.99		Faust
And weare thy colours on my plumed crest.	F1778	5.1.105		Faust
And none but thou shalt be my Paramour.	F1787	5.1.114		Faust
[As in this furnace God shal try my faith],	F1792	5.1.119A		OldMan
[My faith, vile hel, shall triumph over thee],	F1793	5.1.120A		OldMan
[Hence hel, for hence I flie unto my God].	F1796	5.1.123A		OldMan
Say Wagner, thou hast perus'd my will,	F1816	5.2.20		Faust
dutie, I do yeeld/My life and lasting service for your love.	F1819	5.2.23		Wagner
Ah my sweet chamber-fellow, had I liv'd with thee, then had I	F1824	5.2.28	P	Faust
O my deere Faustus what imports this feare?	F1827	5.2.31		1Schol
heare [me] with patience, and tremble not at my speeches.	F1839	5.2.43	P	Faust
my heart pant <pants> and quiver <quivers> to remember that I	F1840	5.2.44	P	Faust
[Ah] <O> my God, I would weepe, but the Divell drawes in my	F1850	5.2.54	P	Faust
<O> my God, I would weepe, but the Divell drawes in my teares.	F1851	5.2.55	P	Faust
oh hee stayes my tongue:	F1852	5.2.56	P	Faust
I would lift up my hands, but see they hold 'em <them>, they	F1852	5.2.56	P	Faust
[Ah] <O> gentlemen, I gave them my soule for my cunning.	F1856	5.2.60		Faust
O I'le leape up to [my God] <heaven>: who puls me downe?	F1938	5.2.142		Faust
One drop [would save my soule, halfe a drop, ah] my Christ.	F1940	5.2.144		Faust
One drop <of bloud will save me; oh> my Christ.	F1940	(HC271)B		Faust
One drop [would save my soule, halfe a drop, ah] my Christ.	F1940	5.2.144		Faust
Rend <Ah rend> not my heart, for naming of my Christ,	F1941	5.2.145		Faust
You Starres that raign'd at my nativity,	F1950	5.2.154		Faust

My limbes may issue from your smoky mouthes, ...	F1955	5.2.159		Faust
[So that] my soule [may but] ascend to heaven. . . .	F1956	5.2.160		Faust
<But let my soule mount and> ascend to heaven. . . .	F1956	(HC271)B		Faust
<O, if my soule must suffer for my sinne>, . . .	F1958	(HC271)B		Faust
[O God, if thou wilt not have mercy on my soule], . .	F1958	5.2.162A		Faust
Impose some end to my incessant paine:	F1960	5.2.164		Faust
[My God, my God] <O mercy heaven>, looke not so fierce on me;	F1979	5.2.183		Faust
I'le burne my bookes; [ah] <oh> Mephostophilis. . .	F1982	5.2.186		Faust
my soule to the Divel for a shoulder of mutton though twere	F App	p.229 10	P	Clown
swowns they are as bolde with my flesh, as if they had payd for	F App	p.230 28	P	Clown
with my flesh, as if they had payd for my meate and drinke.	F App	p.230 29	P	Clown
and let thy left eye be diametarily fixt upon my right heele,	F App	p.231 70	P	Wagner
My Lord of Lorraine, wilt please you draw neare. . .	F App	p.231 1	P	Pope
My Lord, here is a daintie dish was sent me from the Bishop of	F App	p.231 5	P	Pope
My Lord, this dish was sent me from the Cardinall of Florence.	F App	p.231 9	P	Pope
my Lord Ile drinke to your grace	F App	p.231 12	P	Pope
My Lord, it may be some ghost newly crept out of Purgatory come	F App	p.232 14	P	Lorein
to lay the fury of this ghost, once again my Lord fall too.	F App	p.232 17	P	Pope
and ifaith I meane to search some circles for my owne use:	F App	p.233 3	P	Robin
in our parish dance at my pleasure starke naked before me,	F App	p.233 4	P	Robin
he keepes such a chafing with my mistris about it, and she has	F App	p.233 8	P	Rafe
my maister and mistris shal finde that I can reade, he for his	F App	p.233 15	P	Robin
study, shee's borne to beare with me, or else my Art failes.	F App	p.233 17	P	Robin
in Europe for nothing, thats one of my conjuring workes. .	F App	p.234 24	P	Robin
how that none in my Empire, nor in the whole world can compare	F App	p.236 2	P	Emper
this therefore is my request, that thou let me see some proofe	F App	p.236 5	P	Emper
My gratious Soveraigne, though I must confesse my selfe farre	F App	p.236 12	P	Faust
my selfe farre inferior to the report men have published,	F App	p.236 12	P	Faust
sometime solitary set, within my Closet, sundry thoughts arose,	F App	p.236 18	P	Emper
It grieves my soule I never saw the man:	F App	p.237 28		Emper
Thou shalt both satisfie my just desire, ...	F App	p.237 35		Emper
My gratious Lord, I am ready to accomplish your request, so	F App	p.237 37	P	Faust
forth as by art and power of my spirit I am able to performe.	F App	p.237 38	P	Faust
it is not in my abilitie to present before your eyes, the true	F App	p.237 41	P	Faust
heere they are my gratious Lord.	F App	p.238 59	P	Faust
how you crossed me in my conference with the emperour? .	F App	p.238 77	P	Faust
at my intreaty release him, he hath done penance sufficient.	F App	p.238 79	P	Emper
My Gratious Lord, not so much for the injury hee offred me	F App	p.238 81	P	Faust
Now my good Lord having done my duety, I humbly take my leave.	F App	p.238 86	P	Faust
Now my good Lord having done my duety, I humbly take my leave.	F App	p.238 87	P	Faust
Shortning my dayes and thred of vitall life, ...	F App	p.239 92		Faust
Calls for the payment of my latest yeares, ...	F App	p.239 93		Faust
Wel, come give me your money, my boy wil deliver him to you:	F App	p.239 107	P	Faust
Now am I made man for ever, Ile not leave my horse for fortie:	F App	p.239 115	P	HrsCsr
but hark ye sir, if my horse be sick, or ill at ease, if I bring	F App	p.240 118	P	HrsCsr
Dispaire doth drive distrust unto my thoughts, . . .	F App	p.240 123		Faust
my horse had had some rare qualitie that he would not have had	F App	p.240 131	P	HrsCsr
pond, but my horse vanisht away, and I sat upon a bottle of hey,	F App	p.240 134	P	HrsCsr
I sat upon a bottle of hey, never so neare drowning in my life:	F App	p.240 135	P	HrsCsr
but Ile seeke out my Doctor, and have my fortie dollers againe,	F App	p.240 136	P	HrsCsr
and have my fortie dollers againe, or Ile make it the dearest	F App	p.240 136	P	HrsCsr
O my legge, my legge, helpe Mephastophilis, call the Officers,	F App	p.241 155	P	Faust
helpe Mephastophilis, call the Officers, my legge, my legge.	F App	p.241 156	P	Faust
I have none about me, come to my Oastrie, and Ile give them you.	F App	p.241 161	P	HrsCsr
to whom I must be no niggard of my cunning, come . .	F App	p.241 171	P	Faust
My gratious Lord, I am glad it contents you so wel: . .	F App	p.242 3	P	Faust
I wil not hide from you the thing my heart desires, and were it	F App	p.242 9	P	Duchss
they be the best grapes that ere I tasted in my life before.	F App	p.242 26	P	Duchss
And so I wil my Lord, and whilst I live, Rest beholding for	F App	p.243 30	P	Duchss
I thinke my maister meanes to die shortly, ...	F App	p.243 1		Wagner
Thou Caesar at this instant art my God, ...	Lucan, First Booke			63
Whether goes my standarde?	Lucan, First Booke			193
My thoughts sole goddes, aide mine enterprise, ...	Lucan, First Booke			202
I hate thee not, to thee my conquests stoope, ...	Lucan, First Booke			203
Warre and the destinies shall trie my cause.	Lucan, First Booke			229
Because at his commaund I wound not up/My conquering Eagles?	Lucan, First Booke			340
Love over-rules my will, I must obay thee, ...	Lucan, First Booke			373
thou bid me/Intombe my sword within my brothers bowels; .	Lucan, First Booke			377
My feare transcends my words,/Yet more will happen then I can	Lucan, First Booke			633
[Love] <I> slackt my Muse, and made my [numbers] <number> soft.	Ovid's Elegies			1.1.22
Tooke out the shaft, ordaind my hart to shiver: . . .	Ovid's Elegies			1.1.26
I burne, love in my idle bosome sits.	Ovid's Elegies			1.1.30
Let my first verse be sixe, my last five feete, . . .	Ovid's Elegies			1.1.31
Girt my shine browe with sea banke mirtle praise <sprays>.	Ovid's Elegies			1.1.34
What makes my bed seem hard seeing it is soft? . . .	Ovid's Elegies			1.2.1
My sides are sore with tumbling to and fro.	Ovid's Elegies			1.2.4
Tis cruell love turmoyles my captive hart.	Ovid's Elegies			1.2.8
And hold my conquered hands for thee to tie.	Ovid's Elegies			1.2.20
I gladly graunt my parents given to save, ...	Ovid's Elegies			1.3.10
My spotlesse life, which but to Gods [gives] <give> place,	Ovid's Elegies			1.3.13
Be thou the happie subject of my Bookes, ...	Ovid's Elegies			1.3.19
And with my name shall thine be alwaies sung.	Ovid's Elegies			1.3.26
Yet scarse my hands from thee containe I well.	Ovid's Elegies			1.4.10
Nor let the windes away my warnings blowe.	Ovid's Elegies			1.4.12
his limbes he spread/Upon the bed, but on my foote first tread.	Ovid's Elegies			1.4.16
View me, my becks, and speaking countenance:	Ovid's Elegies			1.4.17
Words without voyce shall on my eye browes sit, . . .	Ovid's Elegies			1.4.19
Lines thou shalt read in wine by my hand writ. . . .	Ovid's Elegies			1.4.20
When I (my light) do or say ought that please thee, . .	Ovid's Elegies			1.4.25
Suspitious feare in all my veines will hover, ...	Ovid's Elegies			1.4.42
I and my wench oft under clothes did lurke, ...	Ovid's Elegies			1.4.47
not onely kisse/But force thee give him my stolne honey blisse.	Ovid's Elegies			1.4.64

MY (cont.)

To rest my limbes, uppon a bedde I lay,	Ovid's Elegies	1.5.2
The gate halfe ope my bent side in will take.	Ovid's Elegies	1.6.4
Long Love my body to such use [makes] <make> slender/And to get	Ovid's Elegies	1.6.5
And guides my feete least stumbling falles they catch.	Ovid's Elegies	1.6.8
Thy lightning can my life in pieces batter.	Ovid's Elegies	1.6.16
See how the gates with my teares wat'red are.	Ovid's Elegies	1.6.18
would, I cannot him cashiere/Before I be divided from my geere.	Ovid's Elegies	1.6.36
See Love with me, wine moderate in my braine,	Ovid's Elegies	1.6.37
And on my haires a crowne of flowers remaine.	Ovid's Elegies	1.6.38
Giving the windes my words running in thine eare?	Ovid's Elegies	1.6.42
Ah howe thy lot is above my lot blest:	Ovid's Elegies	1.6.46
Aie me now high that gale did lift my hope!	Ovid's Elegies	1.6.52
And with my brand these gorgeous houses burne.	Ovid's Elegies	1.6.58
But thou my crowne, from sad haires tane away,	Ovid's Elegies	1.6.67
That when my mistresse there beholds thee cast,	Ovid's Elegies	1.6.69
Carelesse, farewell, with my falt not distaind.	Ovid's Elegies	1.6.72
Binde fast my hands, they have deserved chaines,	Ovid's Elegies	1.7.1
For rage against my wench mov'd my rash arme,	Ovid's Elegies	1.7.3
My Mistresse weepes whom my mad hand did harme.	Ovid's Elegies	1.7.4
I might have then my parents deare misus'd,	Ovid's Elegies	1.7.5
Would of mine armes, my shoulders had beene scanted,	Ovid's Elegies	1.7.23
Better I could part of my selfe have wanted.	Ovid's Elegies	1.7.24
And to my selfe could I be so injurious?	Ovid's Elegies	1.7.26
Over my Mistris is my right more great?	Ovid's Elegies	1.7.30
My nayles to scratch her lovely cheekes I bent.	Ovid's Elegies	1.7.50
My bloud, the teares were that from her descended.	Ovid's Elegies	1.7.60
My feared hands thrice back she did repell.	Ovid's Elegies	1.7.62
griefe appease)/With thy sharpe nayles upon my face to seaze.	Ovid's Elegies	1.7.64
Bescratch mine eyes, spare not my lockes to breake,	Ovid's Elegies	1.7.65
And least the sad signes of my crime remaine,	Ovid's Elegies	1.7.67
Wert thou rich, poore should not be my state.	Ovid's Elegies	1.8.28
Nor let my words be with the windes hence blowne,	Ovid's Elegies	1.8.106
That my dead bones may in their grave lie soft.	Ovid's Elegies	1.8.108
As thus she spake, my shadow me betraide,	Ovid's Elegies	1.8.109
With much a do my hands I scarsely staide.	Ovid's Elegies	1.8.110
My selfe was dull, and faint, to sloth inclinde,	Ovid's Elegies	1.9.41
Pleasure, and ease had mollifide my minde.	Ovid's Elegies	1.9.42
And to her tentes wild me my selfe addresse.	Ovid's Elegies	1.9.44
Now all feare with my mindes hot love abates,	Ovid's Elegies	1.10.9
In verse to praise kinde Wenches tis my part,	Ovid's Elegies	1.10.59
Receive these lines, them to my Mistrisse carry,	Ovid's Elegies	1.11.7
The rest my hand doth in my letters write.	Ovid's Elegies	1.11.14
give her my writ/But see that forth-with shee peruseth it.	Ovid's Elegies	1.11.15
to her I consecrate/My faithfull tables being vile maple late.	Ovid's Elegies	1.11.28
Bewaile my chaunce, the sad booke is returned,	Ovid's Elegies	1.12.1
This day denyall hath my sport adjourned.	Ovid's Elegies	1.12.2
To these my love I foolishly committed/And then with sweete	Ovid's Elegies	1.12.21
committed/And then with sweete words to my Mistrisse fitted.	Ovid's Elegies	1.12.22
If ever, now well lies she by my side.	Ovid's Elegies	1.13.6
O thou oft wilt blush/And say he likes me for my borrowed bush,	Ovid's Elegies	1.14.48
But I remember when it was my fame.	Ovid's Elegies	1.14.50
Envie, why carpest thou my time is spent so ill,	Ovid's Elegies	1.15.1
And tearmes <termst> [my] <our> works fruits of an idle quill?	Ovid's Elegies	1.15.2
Nor set my voyce to sale in everie cause?	Ovid's Elegies	1.15.6
That all the world [may] <might> ever chaunt my name.	Ovid's Elegies	1.15.8
About my head be quivering Mirtle wound,	Ovid's Elegies	1.15.37
Then though death rackes <rakes> my bones in funerall fier,	Ovid's Elegies	1.15.41
I Ovid Poet of [my] <thy> wantonnesse,	Ovid's Elegies	2.1.1
You are unapt my looser lines to heare.	Ovid's Elegies	2.1.4
what meanes learnd/Hath this same Poet my sad chaunce discernd?	Ovid's Elegies	2.1.10
My wench her dore shut, Joves affares I left,	Ovid's Elegies	2.1.17
Even Jove himselfe out off my wit was reft.	Ovid's Elegies	2.1.18
Toyes, and light Elegies my darts I tooke,	Ovid's Elegies	2.1.21
famous names/Farewel, your favour nought my minde inflames.	Ovid's Elegies	2.1.36
Wenches apply your faire lookes to my verse/Which golden love	Ovid's Elegies	2.1.37
My hands an unsheath'd shyning weapon have not.	Ovid's Elegies	2.2.64
Aye me an Eunuch keepes my mistrisse chaste,	Ovid's Elegies	2.3.1
Or justifie my vices being many,	Ovid's Elegies	2.4.2
Heere I display my lewd and loose behaviour.	Ovid's Elegies	2.4.4
I cannot rule my selfe, but where love please/[Am] <And> driven	Ovid's Elegies	2.4.7
Seeing she likes my bookes, why should we jarre?	Ovid's Elegies	2.4.20
To leave my selfe, that am in love [with all] <withall>,	Ovid's Elegies	2.4.31
My love alludes to everie historie:	Ovid's Elegies	2.4.44
But my ambitious ranging mind approoves?	Ovid's Elegies	2.4.48
Cupid flie)/That my chiefe wish should be so oft to die.	Ovid's Elegies	2.5.2
O would my proofes as vaine might be withstood,	Ovid's Elegies	2.5.7
Aye me poore soule, why is my cause so good.	Ovid's Elegies	2.5.8
(Such with my tongue it likes me to purloyne).	Ovid's Elegies	2.5.24
What doest, I cryed, transportst thou my delight?	Ovid's Elegies	2.5.29
My lordly hands ile throwe upon my right.	Ovid's Elegies	2.5.30
With her owne armor was my wench defended.	Ovid's Elegies	2.5.48
Tis ill they pleas'd so much, for in my lips,	Ovid's Elegies	2.5.57
What helpes it thou wert given to please my wench,	Ovid's Elegies	2.6.19
My wenches vowes for thee what should I show,	Ovid's Elegies	2.6.43
This tombe approoves, I pleasde my mistresse well,	Ovid's Elegies	2.6.61
My mouth in speaking did all birds excell.	Ovid's Elegies	2.6.62
If blame, dissembling of my fault thou fearest.	Ovid's Elegies	2.7.8
Forbid thine anger to procure my griefe.	Ovid's Elegies	2.7.14
To take repulse, and cause her shew my lust?	Ovid's Elegies	2.7.26
My selfe unguilty of this crime I know.	Ovid's Elegies	2.7.28
Greater then these my selfe I not esteeme,	Ovid's Elegies	2.8.13
In both [thy] <my> cheekes she did perceive thee blush,	Ovid's Elegies	2.8.16

MY (cont.)

My [false] <selfe> oathes in Carpathian seas to cast.	Ovid's Elegies	2.8.20
For which good turne my sweete reward repay,	Ovid's Elegies	2.8.21
O Cupid that doest never cease my smart,	Ovid's Elegies	2.9.1
O boy that lyest so slothfull in my heart.	Ovid's Elegies	2.9.2
In naked bones? love hath my bones left naked.	Ovid's Elegies	2.9.14
For when my loathing it of heate deprives me,	Ovid's Elegies	2.9.27
I know not whether my mindes whirle-wind drives me.	Ovid's Elegies	2.9.28
Strike boy, I offer thee my naked brest,	Ovid's Elegies	2.9.35
Within my brest no desert empire beare.	Ovid's Elegies	2.9.52
So with this love and that, wavers my minde.	Ovid's Elegies	2.10.10
Venus, why doublest thou my endlesse smart?	Ovid's Elegies	2.10.11
Was not one wench inough to greeve my heart?	Ovid's Elegies	2.10.12
Yea, let my foes sleepe in an emptie bed,	Ovid's Elegies	2.10.17
But may soft love rowse up my drowsie eies,	Ovid's Elegies	2.10.19
And from my mistris bosome let me rise:	Ovid's Elegies	2.10.20
Pleasure addes fuell to my lustfull fire,	Ovid's Elegies	2.10.25
And in the midst thereof, set my soule going,	Ovid's Elegies	2.10.36
That at my funeralles some may weeping crie,	Ovid's Elegies	2.10.37
But if my words with winged stormes hence slip,	Ovid's Elegies	2.11.33
Mine owne desires why should my selfe not flatter?	Ovid's Elegies	2.11.54
About my temples go triumphant bayes,	Ovid's Elegies	2.12.1
Conquer'd Corinna in my bosome layes.	Ovid's Elegies	2.12.2
But to my share a captive damsell falles.	Ovid's Elegies	2.12.8
But I no partner of my glory brooke,	Ovid's Elegies	2.12.11
Nor in my act hath fortune mingled chance,	Ovid's Elegies	2.12.15
Nor is my warres cause new, but for a Queene/Europe, and Asia	Ovid's Elegies	2.12.17
Angry I was, but feare my wrath exempted.	Ovid's Elegies	2.13.4
Thou givest my mistris life, she mine againe.	Ovid's Elegies	2.13.16
My wench, Lucina, I intreat thee favour,	Ovid's Elegies	2.13.21
My selfe will bring vowed gifts before thy feete,	Ovid's Elegies	2.13.24
My selfe that better dye with loving may/Had seene, my mother	Ovid's Elegies	2.14.21
with loving may/Had seene, my mother killing me, [no] <to> day.	Ovid's Elegies	2.14.22
And my presages of no weight be thought.	Ovid's Elegies	2.14.42
Thou ring that shalt my faire girles finger binde,	Ovid's Elegies	2.15.1
Blest ring thou in my mistris hand shalt lye,	Ovid's Elegies	2.15.7
My selfe poore wretch mine owne gifts now envie.	Ovid's Elegies	2.15.8
O would that sodainly into my gift,	Ovid's Elegies	2.15.9
I could my selfe by secret Magicke shift.	Ovid's Elegies	2.15.10
Then would I wish thee touch my mistris pappe,	Ovid's Elegies	2.15.11
Would first my beautious wenches moist lips touch,	Ovid's Elegies	2.15.17
My life, that I will shame thee never feare,	Ovid's Elegies	2.15.21
But seeing thee, I thinke my thing will swell,	Ovid's Elegies	2.15.25
Let her my faith with thee given understand.	Ovid's Elegies	2.15.28
But absent is my fire, lyes ile tell none,	Ovid's Elegies	2.16.11
My heate is heere, what moves my heate is gone.	Ovid's Elegies	2.16.12
My hard way with my mistrisse would seeme soft.	Ovid's Elegies	2.16.20
With thy white armes upon my shoulders seaze,	Ovid's Elegies	2.16.29
Nor do I like the country of my birth.	Ovid's Elegies	2.16.38
Why doth my mistresse from me oft devide?	Ovid's Elegies	2.16.42
By me, and by my starres, thy radiant eyes.	Ovid's Elegies	2.16.44
(Their reines let loose) right soone my house approach.	Ovid's Elegies	2.16.50
Let me be slandered, while my fire she hides,	Ovid's Elegies	2.17.3
Would I had beene my mistresse gentle prey,	Ovid's Elegies	2.17.5
And thou my light accept me how so ever,	Ovid's Elegies	2.17.23
Lay in the mid bed, there be my law giver.	Ovid's Elegies	2.17.24
My stay no crime, my flight no joy shall breede,	Ovid's Elegies	2.17.25
Nor in my bookes shall one but thou be writ,	Ovid's Elegies	2.17.33
Thou doest alone give matter to my wit.	Ovid's Elegies	2.17.34
Often at length, my wench depart, I bid,	Ovid's Elegies	2.18.5
Shee in my lap sits still as earst she did.	Ovid's Elegies	2.18.6
Then wreathes about my necke her winding armes,	Ovid's Elegies	2.18.9
And thousand kisses gives, that worke my harmes:	Ovid's Elegies	2.18.10
I yeeld, and back my wit from battells bring,	Ovid's Elegies	2.18.11
Yet tragedies, and scepters fild my lines,	Ovid's Elegies	2.18.13
Love laughed at my cloak, and buskines painted,	Ovid's Elegies	2.18.15
My Mistris deity also drewe me fro it,	Ovid's Elegies	2.18.17
(Alas my precepts turne my selfe to smart)/We write, or what	Ovid's Elegies	2.18.20
Phedra, and Hipolite may read, my care is,	Ovid's Elegies	2.18.24
Keepe her for me, my more desire to breede.	Ovid's Elegies	2.19.2
So having vext she nourisht my warme fire,	Ovid's Elegies	2.19.15
And was againe most apt to my desire.	Ovid's Elegies	2.19.16
So shall my love continue many yeares,	Ovid's Elegies	2.19.23
This doth delight me, this my courage cheares.	Ovid's Elegies	2.19.24
Aye me, let not my warnings cause my paine.	Ovid's Elegies	2.19.34
But of my love it will an end procure.	Ovid's Elegies	2.19.52
In sleeping shall I fearelesse drawe my breath?	Ovid's Elegies	2.19.55
To finde, what worke my muse might move, I strove.	Ovid's Elegies	3.1.6
To fill my lawes thy wanton spirit frame.	Ovid's Elegies	3.1.30
Light am I, and with me, my care, light love,	Ovid's Elegies	3.1.41
My flatt'ring speeches soone wide open knocke.	Ovid's Elegies	3.1.46
Thou hast my gift, which she would from thee sue.	Ovid's Elegies	3.1.60
To empty aire may go my fearefull speech.	Ovid's Elegies	3.1.62
The other gives my love a conquering name,	Ovid's Elegies	3.1.65
And from my hands the reines will slip away.	Ovid's Elegies	3.2.14
But spare my wench thou at her right hand seated,	Ovid's Elegies	3.2.21
That from thy fanne, mov'd by my hand may blow?	Ovid's Elegies	3.2.38
Or is my heate, of minde, not of the skie?	Ovid's Elegies	3.2.39
Ist womens love my captive brest doth frie?	Ovid's Elegies	3.2.40
Goddesse come here, make my love conquering.	Ovid's Elegies	3.2.46
The sea I use not: me my earth must have.	Ovid's Elegies	3.2.48
We praise: great goddesse ayde my enterprize.	Ovid's Elegies	3.2.56
Let my new mistris graunt to be beloved:	Ovid's Elegies	3.2.57

MY (cont.)			
For evermore thou shalt my mistris be.	Ovid's Elegies	3.2.62	
To hide thee in my bosome straight repaire.	Ovid's Elegies	3.2.76	
My mistris wish confirme with my request.	Ovid's Elegies	3.2.80	
My mistris hath her wish, my wish remaine:	Ovid's Elegies	3.2.81	
He holdes the palme: my palme is yet to gaine.	Ovid's Elegies	3.2.82	
But by my paine to purge her perjuries,	Ovid's Elegies	3.3.21	
Mars girts his deadly sword on for my harme:	Ovid's Elegies	3.3.27	
With lying lips my God-head to deceave,	Ovid's Elegies	3.3.44	
My selfe would sweare, the wenches true did sweare,	Ovid's Elegies	3.3.45	
I to my mistris hast.	Ovid's Elegies	3.5.2	
When thy waves brim did scarse my anckles touch.	Ovid's Elegies	3.5.6	
What helpes my hast: what to have tane small rest?	Ovid's Elegies	3.5.9	
My foote upon the further banke to set.	Ovid's Elegies	3.5.12	
Nere was, nor shall be, what my verse mentions.	Ovid's Elegies	3.5.18	
Saying, why sadly treadst my banckes upon,	Ovid's Elegies	3.5.53	
much (I crave)/Gifts then my promise greater thou shalt have.	Ovid's Elegies	3.5.66	
O would in my fore-fathers tombe deepe layde,	Ovid's Elegies	3.5.73	
My bones had beene, while yet I was a maide.	Ovid's Elegies	3.5.74	
Clowne, from my journey why doest me deterre?	Ovid's Elegies	3.5.88	
She on my necke her Ivorie armes did throw,	Ovid's Elegies	3.6.7	
What will my age do, age I cannot shunne,	Ovid's Elegies	3.6.17	
Seeing <When> in my prime my force is spent and done?	Ovid's Elegies	3.6.18	
What, wast my limbs through some Thesalian charms,	Ovid's Elegies	3.6.27	
With virgin waxe hath some imbast my joynts,	Ovid's Elegies	3.6.29	
And pierst my liver with sharpe needle poynts <needles>?	Ovid's Elegies	3.6.30	
Why might not then my sinews be inchanted,	Ovid's Elegies	3.6.35	
My idle thoughts delighted her no more,	Ovid's Elegies	3.6.39	
When our bookes did my mistris faire content,	Ovid's Elegies	3.7.5	
I might not go, whether my papers went.	Ovid's Elegies	3.7.6	
At thy deafe dores in verse sing my abuses.	Ovid's Elegies	3.7.24	
Was I: thou liv'dst, while thou esteemdst my faith.	Ovid's Elegies	3.8.56	
Nemesis answeares, what's my losse to thee?	Ovid's Elegies	3.8.57	
In emptie bed alone my mistris lies.	Ovid's Elegies	3.9.2	
Dishonest love my wearied brest forsake,	Ovid's Elegies	3.10.2	
Now have I freed my selfe, and fled the chaine,	Ovid's Elegies	3.10.3	
Victorious wreathes at length my Temples greete.	Ovid's Elegies	3.10.6	
To lay my body on the hard moist floore.	Ovid's Elegies	3.10.10	
The people by my company she pleasd,	Ovid's Elegies	3.10.19	
My love was cause that more mens love she seazd.	Ovid's Elegies	3.10.20	
And to my losse God-wronging perjuries?	Ovid's Elegies	3.10.22	
But with my rivall sicke she was not than.	Ovid's Elegies	3.10.26	
Now my ship in the wished haven crownd,	Ovid's Elegies	3.10.29	
Now love, and hate my light brest each way move;	Ovid's Elegies	3.10.33	
Ile hate, if I can; if not, love gainst my will:	Ovid's Elegies	3.10.35	
That I may love yet, though against my minde.	Ovid's Elegies	3.10.52	
Or is I thinke my wish against the [starres] <starre>?	Ovid's Elegies	3.11.3	
Erre I? or by my [bookes] <lookes> is she so knowne?	Ovid's Elegies	3.11.7	
'Tis so: by my witte her abuse is growne.	Ovid's Elegies	3.11.8	
The wench by my fault is set forth to sell.	Ovid's Elegies	3.11.10	
Her gate by my hands is set open wide.	Ovid's Elegies	3.11.12	
Against my good they were an envious charme.	Ovid's Elegies	3.11.14	
Alone Corinna moves my wanton wit.	Ovid's Elegies	3.11.16	
With Muse oppos'd would I my lines had done,	Ovid's Elegies	3.11.17	
And Phoebus had forsooke my worke begun.	Ovid's Elegies	3.11.18	
Would I my words would any credit beare.	Ovid's Elegies	3.11.20	
And my wench ought to have seem'd falsely praisd,	Ovid's Elegies	3.11.43	
To know their rites, well recompenc'd my stay,	Ovid's Elegies	3.12.5	
There in your rosie lippes my tongue intombe,	Ovid's Elegies	3.13.23	
My soule fleetes when I thinke what you have done,	Ovid's Elegies	3.13.37	
This last end to my Elegies is set,	Ovid's Elegies	3.14.2	
Both loves to whom my heart long time did yeeld,	Ovid's Elegies	3.14.15	
Your golden ensignes [plucke] <pluckt> out of my field,	Ovid's Elegies	3.14.16	
A worke, that after my death, heere shall dwell	Ovid's Elegies	3.14.20	
That runs along his backe, but my rude pen,	Hero and Leander	1.69	
That my slacke muse, sings of Leanders eies,	Hero and Leander	1.72	
I would my rude words had the influence,	Hero and Leander	1.200	
My words shall be as spotlesse as my youth,	Hero and Leander	1.207	
My turret stands, and there God knowes I play/With Venus	Hero and Leander	1.351	
Descends upon my radiant Heroes tower.	Hero and Leander	2.204	
Come live with mee, and be my love,	Passionate Shepherd	1	
Come <Then> live with mee, and be my love.	Passionate Shepherd	20	
Then live with mee, and be my love.	Passionate Shepherd	24	
MYCENAE			
as did Thiestes towne/(Mycenae), Phoebus flying through the	Lucan, First Booke	542	
MYCETES			
Yet live, yea, live, Mycetes wils it so:	1Tamb	1.1.27	Mycet
The chiefest Captaine of Mycetes hoste,	1Tamb	1.1.58	Mycet
MYGHTY			
Ah myghty Jove and holy Mahomet,	1Tamb	5.1.363	Zenoc
MYNE			
I and myne armie come to lode thy barke/With soules of thousand	2Tamb	5.3.73	Tamb
MYNES			
Give me the Merchants of the Indian Mynes,	Jew	1.1.19	Barab
MYRACLE			
Beares figures of renowne and myracle:	1Tamb	2.1.4	Cosroe
Whose power is often proov'd a myracle.	2Tamb	2.3.32	Gazell
Come downe thy selfe and worke a myracle,	2Tamb	5.1.188	Tamb
MYRACLES			
Might find as many woondrous myracles,	2Tamb	4.2.85	Therid
MYRMIDON (See MIRMIDONS)			
MYRRE			
stay with me/Embalm'd with Cassia, Amber Greece and Myrre,	2Tamb	2.4.130	Tamb

MYRROUR				
Wherein as in a myrrour we perceive/The highest reaches of a	1Tamb	5.1.167		Tamb
MYRTLE (See also MIRTLE)				
Upon her head she ware a myrtle wreath,	Hero and Leander	1.17		
With Cupids myrtle was his bonet crownd,	Hero and Leander	2.105		
MYSCHIEFES				
By these he seeing what myschiefes must ensue,	Lucan, First Booke	629		
MY SELF				
Els should I much forget my self, my Lord.	1Tamb	5.1.500		Zenoc
MY SELFE				
My selfe will see they shall not trouble ye,	Dido	1.2.38		Iarbus
O if I speake/I shall betray my selfe:--	Dido	3.1.173		Dido
That have I not determinde with my selfe.	Dido	5.1.19		Aeneas
Iarbus, I am cleane besides my selfe,	Dido	5.1.63		Aeneas
I, I must be the murderer of my selfe:	Dido	5.1.270		Dido
Brother Cosroe, I find my selfe agreev'd,	1Tamb	1.1.1		Mycet
And then my selfe to faire Zenocrate.	1Tamb	1.2.105		Tamb
My selfe will bide the danger of the brunt.	1Tamb	1.2.151		Tamb
I yeeld my selfe, my men and horse to thee:	1Tamb	1.2.229		Therid
To get the Persean Kingdome to my selfe:	1Tamb	2.5.82		Tamb
And write my selfe great Lord of Affrica:	1Tamb	3.3.245		Tamb
It shall be said, I made it red my selfe,	1Tamb	4.2.54		Tamb
The countrie wasted where my selfe was borne,	1Tamb	4.4.66		Zenoc
My crowne, my selfe, and all the power I have,	2Tamb	1.3.115		Therid
Mother dispatch me, or Ile kil my selfe,	2Tamb	3.4.26		Sonne
Killing my selfe, as I have done my sonne,	2Tamb	3.4.35		Olymp
I must apply my selfe to fit those tearmes,	2Tamb	4.1.155		Tamb
For I wil cast my selfe from off these walles,	2Tamb	5.1.40		2Citzn
down to the earth/Could not affright you, no, nor I my selfe,	2Tamb	5.1.91		Tamb
But stay, I feele my selfe distempered sudainly.	2Tamb	5.1.218		Tamb
To cure me, or Ile fetch him downe my selfe.	2Tamb	5.3.63		Tamb
chariot wil not beare/A guide of baser temper than my selfe,	2Tamb	5.3.243		Tamb
My selfe in Malta, some in Italy,	Jew	1.1.126		Barab
our state/Assure your selves I'le looke--unto my selfe.	Jew	1.1.173		Barab
Not for my selfe, but aged Barabas:	Jew	1.2.228		Abigal
in distresse/Thinke me so mad as I will hang my selfe,	Jew	1.2.263		Barab
I'le rouse my senses, and awake my selfe.	Jew	1.2.269		Barab
will I shew my selfe to have more of the Serpent then the Dove;	Jew	2.3.36	P	Barab
As for my selfe, I walke abroad a nights/And kill sicke people	Jew	2.3.174		Barab
As I behave my selfe in this, imploy me hereafter.	Jew	2.3.379		Ithimr
run to some rocke and throw my selfe headlong into the sea;	Jew	3.4.40	P	Ithimr
And whilst I live use halfe; spend as my selfe;	Jew	3.4.45		Barab
My purse, my Coffer, and my selfe is thine.	Jew	3.4.93		Barab
I could afford to whip my selfe to death.	Jew	4.1.59		Barab
It may be she sees more in me than I can find in my selfe:	Jew	4.2.33	P	Ithimr
That he who knowes I love him as my selfe/Should write in this	Jew	4.3.42		Barab
Oh raskall! I change my selfe twice a day.	Jew	4.4.65		Barab
wel since it is no more/I'le satisfie my selfe with that; nay,	Jew	5.5.22		Barab
And that I am not more secure my selfe,	P 264	4.62		Charls
But in my latter houre to purge my selfe,	P 402	7.42		Ramus
So, set it down and leave me to my selfe.	P 666	13.10		Duchss
But now I will be King and rule my selfe,	P1070	19.140		King
I have some busines, leave me to my selfe.	Edw	1.1.48		Gavstn
Mine unckle heere, this Earle, and I my selfe,	Edw	1.1.82		Mortmr
Which whiles I have, I thinke my selfe as great,	Edw	1.1.172		Gavstn
Thou from this land, I from my selfe am banisht.	Edw	1.4.118		Edward
Tis for my selfe I speake, and not for him.	Edw	1.4.219		Queene
Meane time my lord of Penbrooke and my selfe,	Edw	2.2.122		Warwck
Pardon me sweet, I forgot my selfe.	Edw	2.2.230		Edward
Or if I live, let me forget my selfe.	Edw	5.1.111		Edward
And I my selfe will willinglie subscribe.	Edw	5.2.20		Queene
As for my selfe, I stand as Joves huge tree,	Edw	5.6.11		Mortmr
Are laid before me to dispatch my selfe:	F 574	2.2.23		Faust
long e're this, I should have done the deed <slaine my selfe>,	F 575	2.2.24		Faust
And then turning my selfe to a wrought Smocke do what I list.	F 668	2.2.117	P	Pride
my selfe when I could get none <had no body> to fight withall:	F 689	2.2.138	P	Wrath
I'le wing my selfe and forth-with flie amaine/Unto my Faustus	F1136	3.3.49		Mephst
zounds I could eate my selfe for anger, to thinke I have beene	F1243	4.1.89	P	Benvol
the Emperour, Il'e be Acteon, and turne my selfe to a Stagge.	F1256	4.1.102	P	Benvol
I do thinke my selfe my good Lord, highly recompenced, in that	F1563	4.6.6	P	Faust
my selfe farre inferior to the report men have published,	F App	p.236 12	P	Faust
Better I could part of my selfe have wanted.	Ovid's Elegies	1.7.24		
And to my selfe could I be so injurious?	Ovid's Elegies	1.7.26		
My selfe was dull, and faint, to sloth inclinde,	Ovid's Elegies	1.9.41		
And to her tentes wild me my selfe addresse.	Ovid's Elegies	1.9.44		
I cannot rule my selfe, but where love please/[Am] <And> driven	Ovid's Elegies	2.4.7		
To leave my selfe, that am in love [with all] <withall>,	Ovid's Elegies	2.4.31		
My selfe unguilty of this crime I know.	Ovid's Elegies	2.7.28		
Greater then these my selfe I not esteeme,	Ovid's Elegies	2.8.13		
Mine owne desires why should my selfe not flatter?	Ovid's Elegies	2.11.54		
My selfe will bring vowed gifts before thy feete,	Ovid's Elegies	2.13.24		
My selfe that better dye with loving may/Had seene, my mother	Ovid's Elegies	2.14.21		
My selfe poore wretch mine owne gifts now envie.	Ovid's Elegies	2.15.8		
I could my selfe by secret Magicke shift.	Ovid's Elegies	2.15.10		
(Alas my precepts turne my selfe to smart)/We write, or what	Ovid's Elegies	2.18.20		
My selfe would sweare, the wenches true did sweare,	Ovid's Elegies	3.3.45		
Now have I freed my selfe, and fled the chaine,	Ovid's Elegies	3.10.3		
MYSTERIE				
And more frequented for this mysterie,	F 169	1.1.141		Cornel
MYSTERIES				
But Figulus more seene in heavenly mysteries,	Lucan, First Booke	638		
Upon their heads the holy mysteries had.	Ovid's Elegies	3.12.28		
MYSTERY				
thinking some hidden mystery had beene in the horse, I had	F1481	4.4.29	P	Horse-

MYSTIE			
And night deepe drencht in mystie Acheron,	Hero and Leander	1.189	
MYSTY			
Now light had quite dissolv'd the mysty [night] <might>,	Lucan, First Booke	263	
MYTER			
Whose triple Myter I did take by force,	2Tamb	1.3.189	Techel
NAGGS			
And with swift Naggs drawing thy little Coach,	Ovid's Elegies	2.16.49	
NAILE (See also 'SNAYLES, NAYLES)			
Il'e naile huge forked hornes, and let them hang/Within the	F1380	4.2.56	Benvol
NAILES			
they have vilde long nailes, there was a hee divell and a shee	F App	p.230 52	P Clown
NAK'D			
Or els I sweare to have you whipt stark nak'd.	1Tamb	4.2.74	Anippe
NAKED			
working tooles present/The naked action of my threatned end.	1Tamb	3.2.94	Agidas
That naked rowe about the Terrene sea.	1Tamb	3.3.50	Tamb
for as the Romans usde/I here present thee with a naked sword.	2Tamb	1.1.82	Sgsmnd
With naked Negros shall thy coach be drawen,	2Tamb	1.2.40	Callap
of the war/Threw naked swords and sulphur bals of fire,	2Tamb	3.2.41	Tamb
With naked swords and scarlet liveries:	2Tamb	3.4.55	Therid
as I doe a naked Lady in a net of golde, and for feare I should	2Tamb	4.1.69	P Calyph
To proove it, I wil noint my naked throat,	2Tamb	4.2.68	Olymp
Crownets of pearle about his naked armes,	Edw	1.1.63	Gavstn
And henceforth parle with our naked swords.	Edw	1.1.126	Mortmr
Thy court is naked, being bereft of those,	Edw	2.2.174	Mortmr
And tell thy message to my naked brest.	Edw	5.1.130	Edward
If thou't dance naked, put off thy cloathes, and I'le conjure	F 746	2.3.25	P Robin
in our parish dance at my pleasure starke naked before me,	F App	p.233 4	P Robin
And armes all naked, who with broken sighes,	Lucan, First Booke	191	
And sentence given in rings of naked swords,	Lucan, First Booke	321	
Naked simplicitie, and modest grace.	Ovid's Elegies	1.3.14	
Starke naked as she stood before mine eie,	Ovid's Elegies	1.5.17	
I clinged her naked bodie, downe she fell,	Ovid's Elegies	1.5.24	
When thou stood'st naked ready to be beate,	Ovid's Elegies	1.6.19	
Love is a naked boy, his yeares saunce staine,	Ovid's Elegies	1.10.15	
painted stands/All naked holding in her wave-moist hands.	Ovid's Elegies	1.14.34	
In naked bones? love hath my bones left naked.	Ovid's Elegies	2.9.14	
Strike boy, I offer thee my naked brest,	Ovid's Elegies	2.9.35	
In skipping out her naked feete much grac'd her.	Ovid's Elegies	3.6.82	
Where Venus in her naked glory strove,	Hero and Leander	1.12	
About her naked necke his bare armes threw.	Hero and Leander	1.42	
Full of simplicitie and naked truth.	Hero and Leander	1.208	
Where seeing a naked man, she scriecht for feare,	Hero and Leander	2.237	
But as her naked feet were whipping out,	Hero and Leander	2.313	
And her all naked to his sight displayd.	Hero and Leander	2.324	
NAKEDNESSE			
see how poverty jests in his nakednesse, I know the Villaines	F 348	1.4.6	P Wagner
see how poverty jesteth in his nakednesse, the vilaine is bare,	F App	p.229 6	P Wagner
NAM'D			
Had not bene nam'd in Homers Iliads:	2Tamb	2.4.89	Tamb
Nor Lesbia, nor Corrinna had bene nam'd,	2Tamb	2.4.93	Tamb
but the Divel threatned to teare me in peeces if I nam'd God:	F1865	5.2.69	P Faust
I know not what expecting, I ere while/Nam'd Achelaus, Inachus,	Ovid's Elegies	3.5.104	
NAME			
Whose azured gates enchased with his name,	Dido	1.1.101	Jupitr
But what may I faire Virgin call your name?	Dido	1.1.188	Aeneas
Of Troy am I, Aeneas is my name,	Dido	1.1.216	Aeneas
A Gods name on and hast thee to the Court,	Dido	1.1.233	Venus
Which now we call Italia of his name,	Dido	1.2.23	Cloan
or whatsoever stile/Belongs unto your name, vouchsafe of ruth	Dido	2.1.40	Aeneas
O Hector who weepes not to heare thy name?	Dido	2.1.209	Dido
Name not Iarbus, but sweete Anna say,	Dido	3.1.67	Dido
Yet must I heare that lothsome name againe?	Dido	3.1.78	Dido
Let it be term'd Aenea by your name.	Dido	5.1.20	Cloan
Of my old fathers name.	Dido	5.1.23	Aeneas
And in his name rebukt me bitterly,	Dido	5.1.96	Aeneas
were woont to quake/And tremble at the Persean Monarkes name,	1Tamb	1.1.116	Cosroe
We in the name of other Persean states,	1Tamb	1.1.137	Ortyg
admyre me not)/And when my name and honor shall be spread,	1Tamb	1.2.205	Tamb
The slave usurps the glorious name of war.	1Tamb	4.1.67	Souldn
Confirming it with Ibis holy name,	1Tamb	4.3.37	Souldn
Citties and townes/After my name and thine Zenocrate:	1Tamb	4.4.80	Tamb
My nature and the terrour of my name,	1Tamb	5.1.176	Tamb
That sees my crowne, my honor and my name,	1Tamb	5.1.260	Bajzth
A title higher than thy Souldans name:	1Tamb	5.1.434	Tamb
From thence I crost the Gulfe, call'd by the name/Mare magiore,	2Tamb	1.3.214	Therid
If he be jealous of his name and honor,	2Tamb	2.2.43	Orcan
Her name had bene in every line he wrote:	2Tamb	2.4.90	Tamb
The name of mightie Tamburlain is spread:	2Tamb	3.4.66	Therid
But traitor to my name and majesty.	2Tamb	4.1.90	Tamb
But since I exercise a greater name,	2Tamb	4.1.153	Tamb
By which I hold my name and majesty.	2Tamb	4.3.26	Tamb
Than honor of thy countrie or thy name?	2Tamb	5.1.11	Govnr
Blush heaven to loose the honor of thy name,	2Tamb	5.3.28	Usumc
To some perhaps my name is odious,	Jew	Prol.5	Machvl
But take it to you i'th devils name.	Jew	1.2.154	Barab
And so am I, Delbosco is my name;	Jew	2.2.6	Bosco
Now let me know thy name, and therewithall/Thy birth,	Jew	2.3.163	Barab
My name is Barabas; I am a Jew.	Jew	5.1.72	Barab
So that for proofe, he barely beares the name:	P 131	2.74	Guise
In Gods name, let them come.	P 728	14.31	Navrre
And Ile subscribe my name and seale it straight.	P 883	17.78	King

NAME (cont.)			
And there salute his highnesse in our name,	P 908	18.9	Navrre
And will him in my name to kill the Duke.	P1058	19.128	King
Hee wild the Governour of Orleance in his name,	P1117	21.11	Dumain
Salute the Queene of England in my name,	P1243	22.105	King
Save or condemne, and in our name commaund,	Edw	1.1.169	Edward
May it please your lordship to subscribe your name.	Edw	1.4.2	Lncstr
Quick quick my lorde, I long to write my name.	Edw	1.4.4	Lncstr
The name of Mortimer shall fright the king,	Edw	1.4.6	Mortmr
And in the Chronicle, enrowle his name,	Edw	1.4.269	Mortmr
Cursing the name of thee and Gaveston.	Edw	2.2.181	Lncstr
My name is Baldock, and my gentrie/Is fetcht from Oxford, not	Edw	2.2.243	Baldck
His name is Spencer, he is well alied,	Edw	2.2.249	Gavstn
Whereof we got the name of Mortimer,	Edw	2.3.23	Mortmr
Shame and dishonour to a souldiers name,	Edw	2.5.12	Mortmr
Renowmed Edward, how thy name/Revives poore Gaveston.	Edw	2.5.41	Gavstn
And said, upon the honour of my name,	Edw	3.1.98	Arundl
Welcome a Gods name Madam and your sonne,	Edw	4.3.41	Edward
Who wounds me with the name of Mortimer/That bloudy man?	Edw	4.7.38	Edward
Tis in the name of Isabell the Queene:	Edw	4.7.59	Leistr
Comes Leister then in Isabellas name,	Edw	4.7.64	Edward
My nobles rule, I beare the name of king,	Edw	5.1.28	Edward
But Edwards name survives, though Edward dies.	Edw	5.1.48	Edward
By Mortimer, whose name is written here,	Edw	5.1.139	Edward
Well may I rent his name, that rends my hart.	Edw	5.1.140	Edward
the greater sway/When as a kings name shall be under writ.	Edw	5.2.14	Mortmr
And when tis done, we will subscribe our name.	Edw	5.2.50	Mortmr
Know that I am a king, oh at that name,	Edw	5.5.89	Edward
All tremble at my name, and I feare none,	Edw	5.6.13	Mortmr
That shortly he was grac'd with Doctors name,	F 17	Prol.17	1Chor
Within this circle is Jehova's Name,	F 236	1.3.8	Faust
For when we heare one racke the name of God,	F 275	1.3.47	Mephst
Ile fetch thee a wife in the divels name>.	F 531	(HC261)A	P Mephst
Scarce can I name salvation, faith, or heaven,	F 570	2.2.19	Faust
[Never to name God, or to pray to him],	F 649	2.2.98A	Faust
Gentlewoman, her name was <mistress> Margery March-beere:	F 699	2.2.148	P Glutny
the first letter of my name begins with Letchery <leachery>.	F 710	2.2.162	P Ltchry
That Faustus name, whilst this bright frame doth stand,	F 841	3.1.63	Faust
may adde more shame/To the blacke scandall of his hated name.	F1378	4.2.54	Fredrk
name of french crownes a man were as good have as many english	F App	p.230 33	P Clown
upon our handes, and then to our conjuring in the divels name.	F App	p.234 34	P Robin
stand aside you had best, I charge you in the name of Belzabub:	F App	p.235 19	P Robin
And thought his name sufficient to uphold him,	Lucan, First Booke	136	
And ere he sees the sea looseth his name;	Lucan, First Booke	402	
Thou Roome at name of warre runst from thy selfe,	Lucan, First Booke	517	
Let all Lawes yeeld, sinne beare the name of vertue,	Lucan, First Booke	666	
By verses horned Io got hir name,	Ovid's Elegies	1.3.21	
And with my name shall thine be alwaies sung.	Ovid's Elegies	1.3.26	
Her name comes from the thing:	Ovid's Elegies	1.8.3	
The vaine name of inferiour slaves despize.	Ovid's Elegies	1.8.64	
Your name approves you made for such like things,	Ovid's Elegies	1.12.27	
That all the world [may] <might> ever chaunt my name.	Ovid's Elegies	1.15.8	
What age of Varroes name shall not be tolde,	Ovid's Elegies	1.15.21	
What would not she give that faire name to winne?	Ovid's Elegies	2.17.30	
Now give the Roman Tragedie a name,	Ovid's Elegies	3.1.29	
The other gives my love a conquering name,	Ovid's Elegies	3.1.65	
God is a name, no substance, feard in vaine,	Ovid's Elegies	3.3.23	
What should I name Aesope, that Thebe lov'd,	Ovid's Elegies	3.5.33	
Thou hast no name, but com'st from snowy mountaines;	Ovid's Elegies	3.5.91	
Ah now a name too true thou hast, I finde.	Ovid's Elegies	3.8.4	
If ought remaines of us but name, and spirit,	Ovid's Elegies	3.8.59	
Nor on the earth was knowne the name of floore.	Ovid's Elegies	3.9.8	
Proteus what should I name? teeth, Thebes first seed?	Ovid's Elegies	3.11.35	
Will you make shipwracke of your honest name,	Ovid's Elegies	3.13.11	
And know that some have wrong'd Dianas name?	Hero and Leander	1.284	
Whose name is it, if she be false or not,	Hero and Leander	1.285	
hast sworne/To rob her name and honour, and thereby/Commit'st a	Hero and Leander	1.305	
As if her name and honour had beene wrong'd,	Hero and Leander	2.35	
Whose waight consists in nothing but her name,	Hero and Leander	2.114	
NAME'S			
Faith, Sir, my birth is but meane, my name's Ithimor,	Jew	2.3.165	Ithimr
NAMES			
He [names] <meanes> Aeneas, let us kisse his feete.	Dido	2.1.51	Illion
those that lead my horse/Have to their names tytles of dignity,	1Tamb	3.3.70	Bajzth
Thy names and tytles, and thy dignities,	1Tamb	4.2.79	Tamb
basely on their knees/In all your names desirde a truce of me?	2Tamb	1.1.97	Orcan
Spencer and Baldocke, by no other names,	Edw	4.7.56	Leistr
Th'abreviated <breviated> names of holy Saints,	F 238	1.3.10	Faust
Nor are the names of Saturne, Mars, or Jupiter,	F 594	2.2.43	Mephst
<examine> them of their <several> names and dispositions.	F 661	2.2.110	P Belzeb
Heroes, O <of> famous names/Farewel, your favour nought my minde	Ovid's Elegies	2.1.35	
I shame so great names to have usde so vainly:	Ovid's Elegies	3.5.102	
Such as confesse, have lost their good names by it.	Ovid's Elegies	3.13.6	
NAMING			
Rend <Ah rend> not my heart, for naming of my Christ,	F1941	5.2.145	Faust
NAN			
if thou hast any mind to Nan Spit our kitchin maide, then turn	F App	p.234 27	P Robin
O brave Robin, shal I have Nan Spit, and to mine owne use?	F App	p.234 29	P Rafe
NAPE			
Nape free-borne, whose cunning hath no border,	Ovid's Elegies	1.11.2	
when she departed/Nape by stumbling on the thre-shold started.	Ovid's Elegies	1.12.4	
NAPKIN			
Or holding of a napkin in your hand,	Edw	2.1.36	Spencr

NAPLES			
I learnde in Naples how to poison flowers,	Edw	5.4.31	Ltborn
Then up to Naples rich Campania,	F 787	3.1.9	Faust
NAR			
bands were spread/Along Nar floud that into Tiber fals,	Lucan, First Booke		472
NARROW			
We kept the narrow straight of Gibralter,	2Tamb	1.3.180	Usumc
the Counterscarps/Narrow and steepe, the wals made high and	2Tamb	3.2.69	Tamb
The hautie Dane commands the narrow seas,	Edw	2.2.168	Mortmr
And pray'd the narrow toyling Hellespont,	Hero and Leander		2.150
NASO			
Subscribing, Naso with Corinna sav'd:	Ovid's Elegies		2.13.25
NASTY			
A masty <nasty> slave he is.	Jew	4.4.69	Pilia
NATION			
They say we are a scatter'd Nation:	Jew	1.1.121	Barab
(Unchosen Nation, never circumciz'd;	Jew	2.3.8	Barab
having in their company divers of your nation, and others,	Edw	4.3.33	P Spencr
Of me Pelignis nation boasts alone,	Ovid's Elegies		3.14.8
NATIONS			
The Nations far remoov'd admyre me not)/And when my name and	1Tamb	1.2.204	Tamb
So am I fear'd among all Nations.	2Tamb	1.1.151	Orcan
Shall make all Nations to Canonize us:	F 147	1.1.119	Valdes
So use we women of strange nations stocke.	Ovid's Elegies		3.4.34
Thee, goddesse, bountifull all nations judge,	Ovid's Elegies		3.9.5
NATIVE			
Who driven by warre from forth my native world,	Dido	1.1.217	Aeneas
I never vow'd at Aulis gulfe/The desolation of his native Troy,	Dido	5.1.203	Dido
Then shal my native city Samarcanda/And christall waves of	2Tamb	4.3.107	Tamb
The citie and my native countries weale,	2Tamb	5.1.13	Govnr
And that the native sparkes of princely love,	P 6	1.6	Charls
on me, then with your leaves/I may retire me to my native home.	P 474	8.24	Anjoy
And beate proud Burbon to his native home,	P1114	21.8	Dumain
My lords, of love to this our native land,	Edw	2.3.1	Kent
And deem'd renowne to spoile their native towne,	Lucan, First Booke		176
And be heereafter seene with native haire.	Ovid's Elegies		1.14.56
NATIVITY			
Smile Stars that raign'd at my nativity,	1Tamb	4.2.33	Tamb
Fal starres that governe his nativity,	2Tamb	5.3.2	Therid
You Starres that raign'd at my nativity,	F1950	5.2.154	Faust
NATOLIA			
Now have we martcht from faire Natolia/Two hundred leagues, and	2Tamb	1.1.6	Orcan
King of Natolia, let us treat of peace,	2Tamb	1.1.13	Gazell
forces for the hot assaults/Proud Tamburlaine intends Natolia.	2Tamb	1.1.53	Gazell
Kings of Natolia and of Hungarie,	2Tamb	1.1.114	Gazell
Orcanes of Natolia/Confirm'd this league beyond Danubius	2Tamb	1.1.148	Orcan
If any heathen potentate or king/Invade Natolia, Sigismond will	2Tamb	1.1.153	Sgsmnd
I will dispatch chiefe of my army hence/To faire Natolia, and	2Tamb	1.1.162	Orcan
All which have sworne to sacke Natolia:	2Tamb	1.3.121	Therid
Will quickly ride before Natolia:	2Tamb	1.3.125	Therid
And proud Orcanes of Natolia,	2Tamb	1.3.161	Tamb
make no period/Untill Natolia kneele before your feet.	2Tamb	1.3.217	Therid
Natolia hath dismist the greatest part/Of all his armie, pitcht	2Tamb	2.1.16	Fredrk
Now will we march from proud Orminius mount/To faire Natolia,	2Tamb	2.2.3	Orcan
of God and his friend Mahomet, Emperour of Natolia, Jerusalem,	2Tamb	3.1.3	P Orcan
Thrice worthy kings of Natolia, and the rest,	2Tamb	3.1.7	Callap
Who by this time is at Natolia,	2Tamb	3.4.86	Therid
Where legions of devils (knowing he must die/Here in Natolia,	2Tamb	3.5.26	Orcan
And rich Natolia ours, our men shall sweat/With carrieng pearle	2Tamb	3.5.166	Techel
The Euxine sea North to Natolia,	2Tamb	4.3.102	Tamb
NATOLIAN			
Or treat of peace with the Natolian king?	2Tamb	1.1.113	Sgsmnd
And happily with full Natolian bowles/Of Greekish wine now let	2Tamb	2.3.45	Orcan
NATOLIANS			
Natolians, Sorians, blacke Egyptians,	2Tamb	1.1.63	Orcan
NATOLIAS			
Who meanes to gyrt Natolias walles with siege,	2Tamb	3.5.8	2Msngr
NATURALE			
For is he not Corpus naturale?	F 208	1.2.15	P Wagner
NATURALIZED			
Naturalized Turks and stout Bythinians/Came to my bands full	2Tamb	3.5.41	Trebiz
NATURALL			
but I hope it be/Only some naturall passion makes her sicke.	P 183	3.18	QnMarg
To hatch forth treason gainst their naturall Queene?	P1032	19.102	King
That the first is finisht in a naturall day?	F 603	2.2.52	Faust
this houre be but/A yeare, a month, a weeke, a naturall day,	F1933	5.2.137	Faust
NATURALLIE			
All women are ambitious naturallie:	Hero and Leander		1.428
NATURALLY			
That naturally would love and honour you,	Edw	1.1.100	Lncstr
NATURE			
Nature, why mad'st me not some poysonous beast,	Dido	4.1.21	Iarbus
Monster of Nature, shame unto thy stocke,	1Tamb	1.1.104	Mycet
Nature doth strive with Fortune and his stars,	1Tamb	2.1.33	Cosroe
If Nature had not given me wisedomes lore?	1Tamb	2.4.7	Mycet
Nature that fram'd us of foure Elements,	1Tamb	2.7.18	Tamb
The strangest men that ever nature made,	1Tamb	2.7.40	Cosroe
My nature and the terrour of my name,	1Tamb	5.1.176	Tamb
Invincible by nature of the place.	2Tamb	3.2.90	Tamb
In frame of which, Nature hath shewed more skill,	2Tamb	3.4.75	Techel
And shame of nature [which] <with> Jaertis streame,	2Tamb	4.1.108	Tamb
The nature of these proud rebelling Jades/Wil take occasion by	2Tamb	5.3.238	Tamb
The nature of thy chariot wil not beare/A guide of baser temper	2Tamb	5.3.242	Tamb

NATURE (cont.)			
For with my nature warre doth best agree.	Edw	1.4.365	MortSr
Thou seest by nature he is milde and calme,	Edw	1.4.388	MortSr
Nature, yeeld to my countries cause in this.	Edw	4.1.3	Kent
But that I am by nature flegmatique, slow to wrath, and prone	F 209	1.2.16	P Wagner
a small trifle to suffice nature.	F 695	2.2.144	P Glutny
If sin by custome grow not into nature:	F1713	5.1.40	OldMan
Nature, and every power shal give thee place,	Lucan, First Booke		51
birthes with more and ugly jointes/Then nature gives,	Lucan, First Booke		561
First he commands such monsters Nature hatcht/Against her kind	Lucan, First Booke		588
That Nature shall dissolve this earthly bowre.	Ovid's Elegies		1.15.24
Ah whether is [thy] <they> brests soft nature [fled] <sled>?	Ovid's Elegies		3.7.18
Against thy selfe, mans nature, thou wert cunning,	Ovid's Elegies		3.7.45
As nature wept, thinking she was undone;	Hero and Leander		1.46
By nature have a mutuall appetence,	Hero and Leander		2.56
NATURES			
That shaken thrise, makes Natures buildings quake,	Dido	1.1.11	Jupitr
so imbellished/With Natures pride, and richest furniture?	1Tamb	1.2.156	Therid
is compriz'd the Sum/Of natures Skill and heavenly majestie.	1Tamb	5.1.79	1Virgn
And Natures beauty choake with stifeling clouds,	Jew	2.3.331	Lodowk
Pay natures debt with cheerefull countenance,	Edw	4.7.109	Baldck
Art/Wherein all natures [treasury] <treasure> is contain'd:	F 102	1.1.74	BdAngl
Now <Since> we have seene the pride of Natures worke <workes>,	F1702	5.1.29	1Schol
Faire natures eye, rise, rise againe and make/Perpetuall day:	F1931	5.2.135	Faust
And quite confound natures sweet harmony.	Hero and Leander		1.252
NAUGHT (See also NOUGHT)			
Ile either rend it with my nayles to naught,	P 102	2.45	Guise
NAUGHTINESSE			
Wine-bibbing banquets tell thy naughtinesse,	Ovid's Elegies		3.1.17
The fainting seedes of naughtinesse doth kill.	Ovid's Elegies		3.4.10
NAVARRE			
Prince of Navarre my honourable brother,	P 1	1.1	Charls
Thanks sonne Navarre, you see we love you well,	P 13	1.13	QnMoth
Goe then, present them to the Queene Navarre:	P 79	2.22	Guise
I but, Navarre, Navarre.	P 149	2.92	Guise
Help sonne Navarre, I am poysoned.	P 176	3.11	OldQn
To get those pedantes from the King Navarre,	P 426	7.66	Guise
With the rebellious King of Navarre,	P 517	9.36	Cardnl
O no, my loving brother of Navarre.	P 543	11.8	Charls
And now Navarre whilste that these broiles doe last,	P 565	11.30	Navrre
To march against the rebellious King Navarre:	P 745	15.3	King
Navarre that cloakes them underneath his wings,	P 855	17.50	Guise
In civill broiles between Navarre and me?	P1038	19.108	King
Wicked Navarre will get the crowne of France,	P1086	19.156	QnMoth
Brother of Navarre, I sorrow much,	P1139	22.1	King
It is enough if that Navarre may be/Esteemed faithfull to the	P1147	22.9	Navrre
Thankes to my Kingly Brother of Navarre.	P1150	22.12	King
Yes Navarre, but not to death I hope.	P1177	22.39	King
Navarre, give me thy hand, I heere do sweare,	P1203	22.65	King
Oh no Navarre, thou must be King of France.	P1225	22.87	King
Weep not sweet Navarre, but revenge my death.	P1234	22.96	King
I dye Navarre, come beare me to my Sepulchre.	P1242	22.104	King
Shall curse the time that ere Navarre was King,	P1249	22.111	Navrre
NAVELL			
Then from the navell to the throat at once,	Dido	2.1.255	Aeneas
NAVIE			
Yea all my Navie split with Rockes and Shelfes:	Dido	3.1.108	Aeneas
NAY			
Nay leave not here, resolve me of the rest.	Dido	2.1.160	Dido
Nay, nothing, but Aeneas loves me not.	Dido	3.4.32	Dido
Nay, where is my warlike father, can you tell?	Dido	4.1.15	Cupid
Nay, no such waightie busines of import,	Dido	4.2.25	Anna
O how unwise was I to say him nay!	Dido	4.5.37	Nurse
Nay, I will have it calde Anchisaeon,	Dido	5.1.22	Aeneas
Nay, pray you let him stay, a greater [task]/Fits Menaphon,	1Tamb	1.1.87	Cosroe
Nay, though I praise it, I can live without it.	1Tamb	2.5.66	Therid
Nay quickly then, before his roome be hot.	1Tamb	2.5.89	Usumc
Nay take the Turkish Crown from her, Zenocrate,	1Tamb	3.3.220	Tamb
Nay (mightie Souldan) did your greatnes see/The frowning lookes	1Tamb	4.1.12	2Msngr
Nay could their numbers countervail the stars,	1Tamb	4.1.30	Souldn
Nay, thine owne is easier to come by, plucke out that, and twil	1Tamb	4.4.13	P Tamb
Nay, twere better he kild his wife, and then she shall be sure	1Tamb	4.4.45	P Usumc
Nay Captain, thou art weary of thy life,	2Tamb	3.3.18	Techel
Nay, when the battaile ends, al we wil meet,	2Tamb	3.5.97	Callap
O damned monster, nay a Feend of Hell,	2Tamb	4.1.168	Jrslem
Nay Lady, then if nothing wil prevaile,	2Tamb	4.2.50	Therid
Nay, we wil break the hedges of their mouths/And pul their	2Tamb	4.3.48	Techel
Nay let 'em combat, conquer, and kill all,	Jew	1.1.152	Barab
Wherein I may not, nay I dare not dally.	Jew	1.2.12	Calym
Nay backe, Abigall,	Jew	1.2.348	Barab
nay we dare not give consent/By reason of a Tributary league.	Jew	2.2.22	Govnr
Nay on my life it is my Factors hand,	Jew	2.3.240	Barab
Nay, if you will, stay till she comes her selfe.	Jew	2.3.352	Barab
Nay Madam stay, that weapon was my son's,	Jew	3.2.25	Govnr
Nay, you shall pardon me:	Jew	3.3.73	Abigal
My trusty servant, nay, my second [selfe] <life>;	Jew	3.4.15	Barab
Nay, master, be rul'd by me a little; so, let him leane upon	Jew	4.1.153	P Ithimr
nay then I'le force my way;/And see, a staffe stands ready for	Jew	4.1.171	1Fryar
Nay, I care not how much she loves me; Sweet Bellamira, would I	Jew	4.2.54	P Ithimr
Nay [to] thine owne cost, villaine, if thou com'st.	Jew	4.3.59	Barab
Nay, I'le have all or none.	Jew	4.4.5	Curtzn
Nay stay, my Lord, 'tmay be he will confesse.	Jew	5.1.25	1Knght
Nay more, doe this, and live thou Governor still.	Jew	5.2.89	Govnr

NAY (cont.)
Nay, doe thou this, Ferneze, and be free; Jew 5.2.90 Barab
no more/I'le satisfie my selfe with that; nay, keepe it still, Jew 5.5.22 Barab
Nay, Selim, stay, for since we have thee here, Jew 5.5.97 Govnr
Nay rather, Christians, let me goe to Turkey, Jew 5.5.115 Calym
Nay for the Popes sake, and thine owne benefite. P 827 17.22 Eprnon
Nay, they fear'd not to speak in the streetes, P 876 17.71 Eprnon
As pale as ashes, nay then tis time to look about. P1001 19.71 Guise
Nay he was King and countermanded me, P1069 19.139 King
Nay more, the guarde upon his lordship waites: Edw 1.2.21 Lncstr
Nay, then lay violent hands upon your king, Edw 1.4.35 Edward
Nay, for the realms behoofe and for the kings. Edw 1.4.243 Mortmr
Nay more, when he shall know it lies in us, Edw 1.4.274 Mortmr
Nay all of them conspire to crosse me thus, Edw 2.2.95 Edward
Nay, stay my lord, I come to bring you newes, Edw 2.2.141 Mortmr
Nay, now you are heere alone, ile speake my minde. Edw 2.2.155 Mortmr
Nay, rather saile with us to Scarborough. Edw 2.4.52 Mortmr
Nay, do your pleasures, I know how twill proove. Edw 2.5.93 Warwck
Nay sonne, not so, and you must not discourage/Your friends Edw 4.2.69 Queene
Nay madam, if you be a warriar, Edw 4.4.15 Mortmr
Nay so will hell, and cruell Mortimer, Edw 4.7.75 Edward
Nay, you shall pardon me, none shall knowe my trickes. Edw 5.4.39 Ltborn
Nay, to my death, for too long have I lived, Edw 5.6.83 Queene
O Faustus <Nay>,/Then I feare that which F 219 1.2.26 1Schol
Nay sir, you may save your selfe a labour, for they are as F 364 1.4.22 P Robin
Nay, and this be hell, I'le willingly be damn'd <damned here>. F 527 2.1.139 Faust
<Nay sweete Mephastophilis fetch me one, for I will have one>. F 530 (HC261)A P Faust
[Nay let me have one booke more, and then I have done, wherein F 551.8 2.1.171A P Faust
Nay stay my Faustus: F 831 3.1.53 Mephst
Nay stay my gentle Mephostophilis, F 845 3.1.67 Faust
Nay then take that. F1067 3.2.87 Faust
Nay there you lie, 'tis beyond us both. F1109 3.3.22 P Robin
Nay, and thy hornes hold, tis no matter for thy head, for F1288 4.1.134 P Emper
Nay sweet Benvolio, let us sway thy thoughts/From this attempt F1325 4.2.1 Mrtino
Nay, we will stay with thee, betide what may, F1338 4.2.14 Fredrk
Nay keepe it: F1393 4.2.69 Faust
Nay feare not man, we have no power to kill. F1440 4.3.10 Mrtino
Nay chafe not man, we all are sped. F1444 4.3.14 Mrtino
Nay sir, we will be wellcome for our mony, and we will pay for F1611 4.6.54 P Robin
Nay, hearke you, can you tell me where you are? F1614 4.6.57 Faust
Nay, thou must feele them, taste the smart of all: F1922 5.2.126 BdAngl
Nay I know not, we shalbe curst with bell, booke, and candle. F App p.232 23 P Mephst
nay Ile tickle you Vintner, looke to the goblet Rafe, F App p.235 23 P Robin
Nay, and you go to conjuring, Ile be gone. F App p.237 57 P Knight
Nay, til I am past this faire and pleasant greene, ile walke on F App p.239 96 P Faust
Nay what is she that any Romane loves, Ovid's Elegies 2.4.47
Oft couzen me, oft being wooed say nay. Ovid's Elegies 2.19.20
Nay more, the wench did not disdaine a whit, Ovid's Elegies 3.6.73
And hands so pure, so innocent, nay such, Hero and Leander 1.365

NAYLES
And in his eyelids hanging by the nayles, Dido 2.1.245 Aeneas
Ile either rend it with my nayles to naught, P 102 2.45 Guise
My nayles to scratch her lovely cheekes I bent. Ovid's Elegies 1.7.50
griefe appease)/With thy sharpe nayles upon my face to seaze. Ovid's Elegies 1.7.64

NEAERA
When nimph-Neaera rapt thy lookes Scamander. Ovid's Elegies 3.5.28

NEARE (See also NEER, NERE)
From Azamor to Tunys neare the sea, 2Tamb 1.3.133 Usumc
Yes, give me leave, and Hebrews now come neare. Jew 1.2.38 Govnr
Trouble me not, I neare offended him, P1005 19.75 Guise
Ile come to thee, my love shall neare decline. Edw 1.4.115 Edward
Sir, must not come so neare and balke their lips. Edw 2.5.103 Penbrk
our men with sweat and dust/All chockt well neare, begin to Edw 3.1.192 SpncrP
That you were dead, or very neare your death. Edw 4.2.38 Queene
Proud Mortimer pries neare into thy walkes. Edw 4.6.18 Kent
My Lord of Lorraine, wilt please you draw neare. F App p.231 1 P Pope
I sat upon a bottle of hey, never so neare drowning in my life: F App p.240 135 P HrsCsr
Wars radge draws neare; and to the swords strong hand, Lucan, First Booke 665

NEAREST
[I meane his friends and nearest companions], F1142 3.3.55A 3Chor

NEASTES
What, are the Turtles fraide out of their neastes? 1Tamb 5.1.64 Tamb

NEASTS
Why live we Bajazeth, and build up neasts, 1Tamb 5.1.249 Zabina

NEAT
But they that dayly tast neat wine, despise it. Hero and Leander 1.261

NEATLY
So neatly plotted, and so well perform'd? Jew 3.3.2 Ithimr
'Tis neatly done, Sir, here's no print at all. Jew 4.1.151 Ithimr

NECESSARY
faith which they prophanely plight/Is not by necessary pollycy, 2Tamb 2.1.38 Baldwn
Wanes with enforst and necessary change. 2Tamb 2.4.46 Zenoc
'Tis necessary that be look'd unto: Jew 1.2.157 1Knght
No, Abigall, in this/It is not necessary I be seene. Jew 1.2.302 Barab
That followes not <necessary> by force of argument, which F 202 1.2.9 P Wagner

NECESSITIE
See what strange arts necessitie findes out, Dido 1.1.169 Venus
To supply my wants and necessitie. P 136 2.79 Guise
Well of necessitie it must be so. Edw 1.4.238 Mortmr
Not of compulsion or necessitie. Edw 5.1.4 Leistr

NECESSITY
Be honored with your love, but for necessity. 1Tamb 3.2.30 Agidas
That nobly must admit necessity: 2Tamb 5.3.201 Tamb

NECESSITY (ccnt.)				
Since Fate commands, and proud necessity.	2Tamb	5.3.205		Therid
of necessity, for here's the scrowle/In which <Wherein> thou	F 519	2.1.131		Mephst
NECK				
conning his neck-verse I take it, looking of a Fryars	Jew	4.2.17	P	Pilia
He claps his cheekes, and hanges about his neck,	Edw	1.2.51		Queene
Or with those armes that twind about my neck,	Edw	1.4.175		Queene
Ile hang a golden tongue about thy neck,	Edw	1.4.328		Edward
No other jewels hang about my neck/Then these my lord, nor let	Edw	1.4.330		Queene
Trode on the neck of Germane Fredericke,	F 916	3.1.138		Pope
About thy neck shall he at pleasure skippe?	Ovid's Elegies			1.4.6
let him viewe/And thy neck with lascivious markes made blew.	Ovid's Elegies			1.8.98
And a rich neck-lace caus'd that punnishment.	Ovid's Elegies			1.10.52
NECKE				
Put thou about thy necke my owne sweet heart,	Dido	1.1.44		Jupitr
About whose withered necke hung Hecuba,	Dido	2.1.226		Aeneas
Will Dido let me hang about her necke?	Dido	3.1.30		Cupid
Then Thetis hangs abcut Apolloes necke,	Dido	3.1.132		Dido
Their armes to hang about a Ladies necke:	2Tamb	1.3.30		Tamb
That we may tread upon his captive necke,	2Tamb	3.2.157		Tamb
Ile hang a clogge about your necke for running away againe, you	2Tamb	3.5.100	P	Tamb
he was ready to leape off e're the halter was about his necke;	Jew	4.2.23	P	Ithimr
next, like a Neckelace I hang about her Necke:	F 667	2.2.116	P	Pride
Had on her necke a little wart, or mole;	F1267	4.1.113		Emper
this Lady while she liv'd had a wart or moale in her necke,	F App	p.238 61	P	Emper
Let not thy necke by his vile armes be prest,	Ovid's Elegies			1.4.35
Her white necke hid with tresses hanging downe,	Ovid's Elegies			1.5.10
lockes spred/On her white necke but for hurt cheekes be led.	Ovid's Elegies			1.7.40
with kissing/And on her necke a wantons marke not missing.	Ovid's Elegies			1.7.42
If her white necke be shadowde with blacke haire,	Ovid's Elegies			2.4.41
Then wreathes about my necke her winding armes,	Ovid's Elegies			2.18.9
She on my necke her Ivorie armes did throw,	Ovid's Elegies			3.6.7
The locks spred on his necke receive his teares,	Ovid's Elegies			3.8.11
And with a wantons tooth, your necke new raste?	Ovid's Elegies			3.13.34
About her necke hung chaines of peble stone,	Hero and Leander			1.25
Which lightned by her necke, like Diamonds shone.	Hero and Leander			1.26
About her naked necke his bare armes threw.	Hero and Leander			1.42
So was his necke in touching, and surpast/The white of Pelops	Hero and Leander			1.64
NECKELACE				
next, like a Neckelace I hang about her Necke:	F 666	2.2.115	P	Pride
NECKES				
and about their neckes/Hangs massie chaines of golde downe to	1Tamb	1.2.125		Souldr
Drawne by the strength of yoked <yoky> Dragons neckes;	F 759	2.3.38		2Chor
There sat the hang-man for mens neckes to angle.	Ovid's Elegies			1.12.18
On tell-tales neckes thou seest the linke-knitt chaines,	Ovid's Elegies			2.2.41
NECK-LACE				
And a rich neck-lace caus'd that punnishment.	Ovid's Elegies			1.10.52
NECKS				
If they should yeeld their necks unto the sword,	1Tamb	3.3.142		Bajzth
She first constraind bulles necks to beare the yoake,	Ovid's Elegies			3.9.13
NECKT				
I saw a horse against the bitte stiffe-neckt,	Ovid's Elegies			3.4.13
NECK-VERSE				
conning his neck-verse I take it, looking of a Fryars	Jew	4.2.17	P	Pilia
NECROMANCIE (See also NEGROMANTICK)				
He surfets upon cursed Necromancie:	F 25	Prol.25		1Chor
NECROMANTICK				
Then if by powerfull Necromantick spels,	F1209	4.1.55		Emper
NECTAR				
Giving thee Nectar and Ambrosia,	2Tamb	2.4.110		Tamb
Jove might have sipt out Nectar from his hand.	Hero and Leander			1.62
A draught of flowing Nectar, she requested,	Hero and Leander			1.431
Then drerie Mars, carowsing Nectar boules.	Hero and Leander			2.258
NED				
Well doone, Ned.	Edw	1.1.98		Gavstn
NEECE				
That I may swim to him like Tritons neece:	Dido	5.1.247		Dido
To wed thee to our neece, the onely heire/Unto the Earle of	Edw	2.2.258		Edward
Farewell sweete Gaveston, and farewell Neece.	Edw	2.4.12		Edward
NEED				
letters to command/Aide and assistance if we stand in need.	1Tamb	1.2.20		Magnet
But need we not be spied going aboord?	2Tamb	1.2.56		Almeda
We shall not need to nourish any doubt,	2Tamb	3.1.26		Callap
I goe into the field before I need?	2Tamb	4.1.51		Calyph
What need they treat of peace that are in league?	Jew	1.1.158		Barab
saies, he that eats with the devil had need of a long spoone.	Jew	3.4.59	P	Ithimr
You shall nct need trcuble your selves so farre,	Jew	3.5.22		Basso
Thou shalt nct need, for now the Nuns are dead,	Jew	4.1.15		Barab
My Lord you need not mervaile at the Guise,	P 39	1.39		Condy
Hcw now my Lord, faith this is more then need,	P 737	15.15		Guise
You shall nct need to give instructions,	Edw	5.4.29		Ltborn
Yet be not farre off, I shall need your helpe,	Edw	5.5.28		Ltborn
I had need to have it well rosted, and good sauce to it,	F 352	1.4.10	P	Robin
I have no great need to sell him, but if thou likest him for	F1460	4.4.4	P	Faust
Thee if I invocate, I shall not need/To crave Apolloes ayde, or	Lucan, First Booke			64
This need no forraine proofe, nor far fet story:	Lucan, First Booke			94
Nor of our love to be asham'd we need,	Ovid's Elegies			2.17.26
Wide open stood the doore, hee need not clime,	Hero and Leander			2.19
NEEDE				
For this so friendly ayde in time of neede.	Dido	1.1.138		Venus
What neede the artick people love star-light,	Edw	1.1.16		Gavstn
Shall sleepe within the scabberd at thy neede,	Edw	1.1.87		Mortmr
What neede I, God himselfe is up in armes,	Edw	1.2.40		ArchBp

NEEDE (cont.)			
Neede you any thing besides?	Edw	5.5.32	Gurney
burladie I had neede have it wel roasted, and good sawce to it,	F App	p.229 11 P	Clown
What neede she [tyre] <try> her hand to hold the quill, .	Ovid's Elegies		1.11.23
Foole if to keepe thy wife thou hast no neede, . . .	Ovid's Elegies		2.19.1
NEEDED			
He needed not with words confirme my feare, . . .	1Tamb	3.2.92	Agidas
NEEDES			
And more than needes to make an Emperour. . . .	1Tamb	2.3.65	Tamb
My lord of Kent, what needes these questions? . . .	Edw	4.6.34	Mortmr
And needes I must resigne my wished crowne. . . .	Edw	5.1.70	Edward
what needes thou warre, I sue to thee for grace, . .	Ovid's Elegies		1.2.21
what needes defence/When [un-protected] <un-protested> ther is	Ovid's Elegies		2.2.11
NEEDETH			
No, it needeth not.	Edw	2.5.42	Warwck
NEEDFULL			
And him that hew'd you out for needfull uses/Ile prove had	Ovid's Elegies		1.12.15
NEEDIE			
And all thy needie followers Noblemen?	Dido	5.1.164	Dido
NEEDLE			
Nor hath the needle, or the combes teeth reft them, . .	Ovid's Elegies		1.14.15
And pierst my liver with sharpe needle poynts <needles>? .	Ovid's Elegies		3.6.30
NEEDLE POYNTS			
And pierst my liver with sharpe needle poynts <needles>? .	Ovid's Elegies		3.6.30
NEEDLES			
To pierce the wind-pipe with a needles point, . . .	Edw	5.4.33	Ltborn
And pierst my liver with sharpe needle poynts <needles>? .	Ovid's Elegies		3.6.30
NEEDS			
Your Highnesse needs not doubt but in short time, . .	1Tamb	3.2.32	Agidas
Must needs have beauty beat on his conceites. . . .	1Tamb	5.1.182	Tamb
Away ye fools, my father needs not me, ...	2Tamb	4.1.15	Calyph
Thou needs must saile by Alexandria.	Jew	1.1.76	Barab
are such/That you will needs have ten yeares tribute past,	Jew	1.2.19	Govnr
What needs all this? I know I am a Jew.	Jew	4.1.33	Barab
I must needs say that I have beene a great usurer. . .	Jew	4.1.39	Barab
My Lords of Poland I must needs confesse, ...	P 451	8.1	Anjoy
That others needs to comment on my text?	P 683	13.27	Guise
Your highnes needs not feare mine armies force, . . .	P 857	17.52	Guise
and will needs enter by defaulte | whatt thoughe you were once	Paris	ms10,p390 P	Souldr
Now Faustus, must thou needs be damn'd, ...	F 389	2.1.1	Faust
What needs this question?	F1016	3.2.36	Pope
He must needs goe that the Divell drives.	F1419	4.2.95	Fredrk
(Whom from his youth he bribde) needs make him king? .	Lucan, First Booke		315
his parentage, would needs discover/The way to new Elisium:	Hero and Leander		1.410
NEEDST			
And they shall have what thing so ere thou needst. . .	Dido	5.1.74	Iarbus
What needst thou, love, thus to excuse thy selfe? . .	Edw	2.1.60	Neece
Thou needst not do that, for my Mistresse hath done it. .	F 739	2.3.18 P	Dick
NEEDY			
The needy groome that never fingred groat, ...	Jew	1.1.12	Barab
NEER			
That now is marching neer to Parthia:	1Tamb	2.1.65	Cosroe
He mist him neer, but we have strook him now. . . .	P 311	5.38	Guise
But slay as many as we can come neer.	P 326	5.53	Anjoy
Then come thou neer, and tell what newes thou bringst. .	P1166	22.28	King
And snatcht armes neer their houshold gods hung up/Such as	Lucan, First Booke		242
NEERE			
How neere my sweet Aeneas art thou driven?	Dido	1.1.170	Venus
shall have leaves and windfall bowes enow/Neere to these woods,	Dido	1.1.173	Aeneas
Forbids all hope to harbour neere our hearts. . . .	Dido	1.2.16	Illion
Intending your investion so neere/The residence of your .	1Tamb	1.1.180	Ortyg
Looke for orations when the foe is neere.	1Tamb	1.2.131	Techel
Neere Guyrons head doth set his conquering feet, . .	2Tamb	1.1.17	Gazell
Poore soules they looke as if their deaths were neere. .	2Tamb	3.5.61	Usumc
Bordering on Mare Roso neere to Meca.	2Tamb	3.5.131	Callap
From thence to Nubia neere Borno Lake, ...	2Tamb	5.3.136	Tamb
Oh Ithimore come neere;/Come neere, my love, come neere, thy	Jew	3.4.13	Barab
Come neere, my love, come neere, thy masters life, . .	Jew	3.4.14	Barab
Stand in some window opening neere the street, . . .	P 86	2.29	Guise
What els my lords, for it concernes me neere, . . .	Edw	1.2.44	ArchBp
Did never sorrow go so neere my heart, ...	Edw	1.4.306	Edward
Out of my presence, come not neere the court. . . .	Edw	2.2.89	Edward
Admit him neere.	Edw	3.1.150	Edward
By this (I know) the Conjurer is neere, ...	F1343	4.2.19	Benvol
I have a Castle joyning neere these woods, ...	F1452	4.3.22	Benvol
'Faith you are too outragious, but come neere, . . .	F1609	4.6.52	Faust
And yet me thinkes, if that death were neere, . . .	F App	p.243 3	Wagner
O wals unfortunate too neere to France, ...	Lucan, First Booke		250
rageth now in armes/As if the Carthage Hannibal were neere;	Lucan, First Booke		305
where swift Rhodanus/Drives Araris to sea; They neere the hils,	Lucan, First Booke		435
Or if Fate rule them, Rome thy Cittizens/Are neere some plague:	Lucan, First Booke		644
And with the waters sees death neere him thrusts, . .	Ovid's Elegies		2.11.26
They say Peneus neere Phthias towne did hide. . . .	Ovid's Elegies		3.5.32
Than she the hearts of those that neere her stood. . .	Hero and Leander		1.112
Thus neere the bed she blushing stood upright, . . .	Hero and Leander		2.317
NEERER			
Isabell is neerer then the earle of Kent.	Edw	5.2.115	Queene
The neerer that he came, the more she fled, . . .	Hero and Leander		2.243
NEEREST			
God graunt my neerest freends may prove no worse. . .	P 547	11.12	Charls
NEGAMUS			
Si peccasse negamus, fallimur, et nulla est in nobis veritas:	F 68	1.1.40 P	Faust
NEGLECT			
If we neglect this offered victory.	2Tamb	2.1.59	Fredrk

NEGLECTED			
yet he suspected/Some amorous rites or other were neglected.	Hero and Leander	2.64	
NEGLECTING			
For lingering here, neglecting Italy.	Dido	5.1.97	Aeneas
NEGLIGENTLY			
As negligently to forgoe so much/Without provision for	Jew	1.2.242	Barab
NEGO			
your nego argumentum/Cannot serve, sirra:	P 397	7.37	Guise
NEGROMANTICK			
And Negromantick bookes are heavenly.	F 77	1.1.49	Faust
NEGROMANTIQUE			
no object, for my head]/[But ruminates on Negromantique skill].	F 132	1.1.104A	Faust
NEGROS			
With naked Negros shall thy coach be drawen,	2Tamb	1.2.40	Callap
I came to Cubar, where the Negros dwell,	2Tamb	1.3.201	Techel
NEIGBOR			
I march to meet and aide my neigbor kings,	2Tamb	3.1.60	Soria
NEIGHBOR			
Now send Ambassage to thy neighbor Kings,	1Tamb	2.5.20	Cosroe
And dim the brightnesse of their neighbor Lamps:	1Tamb	4.2.34	Tamb
I and my neighbor King of Fesse have brought/To aide thee in	2Tamb	1.3.130	Usumc
That shew faire weather to the neighbor morne.	2Tamb	3.1.48	Jrslem
Halla is repair'd/And neighbor cities of your highnesse land,	2Tamb	3.5.47	Soria
NEIGHBOUR			
Hast thou forgot how many neighbour kings/Were up in armes, for	Dido	5.1.141	Dido
That holds us up, and foiles our neighbour foes.	1Tamb	1.1.61	Mycet
where our neighbour kings/Expect our power and our royall	2Tamb	2.2.3	Orcan
NEIGHBOURS			
To see our neighbours that were woont to quake/And tremble at	1Tamb	1.1.115	Cosroe
NEITHER			
I neither saw nor heard of any such:	Dido	1.1.187	Aeneas
And now am neither father, Lord, nor King:	Dido	2.1.239	Aeneas
And left me neither saile nor sterne abourd.	Dido	5.1.61	Aeneas
Which neither art nor reason may atchieve,	Dido	5.1.65	Aeneas
For neither rain can fall upon the earth,	1Tamb	3.1.51	Moroc
And neither Perseans Soveraign, nor the Turk/Troubled my sences	1Tamb	5.1.157	Tamb
But neither man nor child in al the land:	2Tamb	1.3.197	Techel
Wherein was neither corrage, strength or wit,	2Tamb	4.1.125	Tamb
Wherein he spareth neither man nor child,	2Tamb	5.1.30	1Citzn
I neither saw them, nor inquir'd of them.	Jew	1.1.77	1Merch
Happily for neither, but to passe along/Towards Venice by the	Jew	1.1.162	Barab
Where they must neither see the messenger,	Jew	3.4.80	Barab
Nor me neither, I cannot out-run you Constable, oh my belly.	Jew	5.1.20	P Ithimr
And neither gets him friends, nor fils his bags,	Jew	5.2.39	Barab
Thus loving neither, will I live with both,	Jew	5.2.111	Barab
and let due praise be given/Neither to Fate nor Fortune, but to	Jew	5.5.124	Govnr
She neither walkes abroad, nor comes in sight:	Edw	2.1.24	Baldck
But I respect neither their love nor hate.	Edw	2.2.261	Gavstn
But neither spare you Gaveston, nor his friends.	Edw	2.3.28	Lncstr
Neither my lord, for as he was surprizd,	Edw	3.1.94	Arundl
Now on my life, theile neither barke nor bite.	Edw	4.3.13	Edward
And neither give him kinde word, nor good looke.	Edw	5.2.55	Mortmr
Not so neither; I had need to have it well rosted, and good	F 352	1.4.10	P Robin
I had neither father nor mother, I leapt out of a Lyons mouth	F 686	2.2.135	P Wrath
felow, and he has a great charge, neither wife nor childe.	F App	p.239 106	P Mephst
Fierce Pirhus, neither thou nor Hanniball/Art cause, no forraine	Lucan, First Booke	30	
But neither chuse the north t'erect thy seat;	Lucan, First Booke	53	
Neither spoile, nor kingdom seeke we by these armes,	Lucan, First Booke	351	
Yet although [neither] <either>, mixt of eithers hue,	Ovid's Elegies	1.14.10	
And hasting to me, neither darkesome night,	Ovid's Elegies	2.11.51	
I prove neither youth nor man, but old and rustie.	Ovid's Elegies	3.6.20	
But neither was I man, nor lived then.	Ovid's Elegies	3.6.60	
She ware no gloves for neither sunne nor wind/Would burne or	Hero and Leander	1.27	
Neither themselves nor others, if not worne.	Hero and Leander	1.238	
Is neither essence subject to the eie,	Hero and Leander	1.270	
Though neither gods nor men may thee deserve,	Hero and Leander	1.315	
And neither would denie, nor graunt his sute.	Hero and Leander	1.424	
NEMEAN			
shouldst thou with thy rayes now sing/The fell Nemean beast,	Lucan, First Booke	655	
NEMES			
They came that dwell/By Nemes fields, and bankes of Satirus,	Lucan, First Booke	421	
NEMESIS			
So Nemesis, so Delia famous are,	Ovid's Elegies	3.8.31	
Nemesis and thy first wench joyne their kisses,	Ovid's Elegies	3.8.53	
Nemesis answeares, what's my losse to thee?	Ovid's Elegies	3.8.57	
NEOPTOLEMUS			
his entrailes, Neoptolemus/Setting his speare upon the ground,	Dido	2.1.183	Aeneas
O let me live, great Neoptolemus.	Dido	2.1.239	Aeneas
NEPHEW			
Sleepe my sweete nephew in these cooling shades,	Dido	2.1.334	Venus
And to my Nephew heere the Duke of Guise:	P 226	4.24	Charls
Not I against my nephew.	Edw	1.4.232	MortSr
But nephew, do not play the sophister.	Edw	1.4.255	MortSr
But how if he do not Nephew?	Edw	1.4.278	MortSr
But nephew, now you see the king is changd.	Edw	1.4.420	MortSr
Nephew, your father, I dare not call him king.	Edw	4.6.33	Kent
I, do sweete Nephew.	Edw	5.2.96	Kent
NEPHUE			
Nephue, I must to Scotland, thou staiest here.	Edw	1.4.386	MortSr
NEPOTES			
pugnent ipsique nepotes:	Dido	5.1.311	Dido
NEPTUNE			
Theile breake his ships, O Proteus, Neptune, Jove,	Dido	5.1.255	Dido

NEPTUNE (cont.)
Neptune and Dis gain'd each of them a Crowne, . . . 1Tamb 2.7.37 Usumc
Or when Minerva did with Neptune strive. . . . 1Tamb 3.2.52 Zenoc
Applaud you Neptune, that dare trust his wave, . . . Ovid's Elegies 3.2.47
Where kingly Neptune and his traine abode. . . . Hero and Leander 2.166
And looking backe, saw Neptune follow him. . . . Hero and Leander 2.176
Thereat smilde Neptune, and then told a tale, . . . Hero and Leander 2.193
Neptune was angrie that hee gave no eare, ... Hero and Leander 2.207
went and came, as if he rewd/The greefe which Neptune felt. Hero and Leander 2.215

NEPTUNES
And Neptunes waves be envious men of warre, . . . Dido 1.1.65 Venus
Hermes awake, and haste to Neptunes realme, . . . Dido 1.1.114 Jupitr
And hoyst aloft on Neptunes hideous hilles, . . . Dido 3.3.47 Iarbus
Till he hath furrowed Neptunes glassie fieldes, . . Dido 4.3.11 Aeneas
the world againe/I goe; o Phoebus shew me Neptunes shore, Lucan, First Booke 692
But if sterne Neptunes windie powre prevaile, . . . Ovid's Elegies 2.16.27
With joy heares Neptunes swelling waters sound. . . Ovid's Elegies 3.10.30
[Seabordereres] <Seaborders>, disjoin'd by Neptunes might: Hero and Leander 1.3

NE'R
The Diamond that I talke of, ne'r was foild: . . . . Jew 2.3.56 Barab

NE'RE
And therefore ne're distinguish of the wrong. . . . Jew 1.2.151 Barab
You that/Were ne're possest of wealth, are pleas'd with want. Jew 1.2.201 Barab
Then shall they ne're be seene of Barrabas: . . . Jew 1.2.250 Abigal
were ne're thought upon/Till Titus and Vespasian conquer'd us) Jew 2.3.9 Barab
stands in feare/Of that which you, I thinke, ne're dreame upon, Jew 2.3.283 Barab
Yet Don Mathias ne're offended thee: . . . . . Jew 3.3.41 Abigal
from hence/Ne're shall she grieve me more with her disgrace; Jew 3.4.29 Barab
Ne're shall she live to inherit ought of mine, . . . Jew 3.4.30 Barab
ambles after wealth/Although he ne're be richer then in hope: Jew 3.4.53 Barab
No, none can heare him, cry he ne're so loud. . . . Jew 4.1.136 Ithimr
Or Selim ne're returne to Ottoman. . . . . . Jew 5.5.114 Govnr
Then all my labours, plod I ne're so fast. . . . F 96 1.1.68 Faust
why thou canst not tell ne're a word on't. . . . F 731 2.3.10 P Dick
and two such Cardinals/Ne're serv'd a holy Pope, as we shall F 942 3.1.164 Faust
And fall into the Ocean, ne're be found. . . . . F1978 5.2.182 Faust
on the Altar/He laies a ne're-yoakt Bull, and powers downe Lucan, First Booke 608
Ne're king more sought to keepe his diademe, . . . Hero and Leander 2.77

NER'E
are live quarters broyling on the coles,/That ner'e can die: F1914 5.2.118 BdAngl

NERE (Homograph)
O had that ticing strumpet nere been borne: . . . Dido 2.1.300 Dido
But playd he nere so sweet, I let him goe: . . . Dido 3.1.160 Dido
But much I feare my sonne will nere consent, . . . Dido 3.2.82 Venus
Who nere will cease to soare till he be slaine. . . Dido 3.3.85 Iarbus
Ile follow thee with outcryes nere the lesse, . . . Dido 4.2.55 Anna
For we will scorne they should come nere our selves. . 1Tamb 3.3.186 Zenoc
A wound is nothing be it nere so deepe, ... 2Tamb 3.2.115 Tamb
Backeward and forwards nere five thousand leagues. . . 2Tamb 5.3.144 Tamb
that despiseth him, can nere/Be good in Logick or Philosophie. P 409 7.49 Ramus
Nere was there Colliars sonne so full of pride. . . P 416 7.56 Anjoy
I nere was King of France untill this houre: . . . P1027 19.97 King
Nere was there King of France so yoakt as I. . . . P1044 19.114 King
That he should nere returne into the realme: . . . Edw 1.1.84 Mortmr
Or thou shalt nere be reconcild to me. . . . . Edw 1.4.157 Edward
And yet I love in vaine, heele nere love me. . . . Edw 1.4.197 Queene
I Isabell, nere was my heart so light. . . . . Edw 1.4.368 Edward
And you the Eagles, sore ye nere so high, ... Edw 2.2.39 Edward
The king will nere forsake his flatterers. . . . . Edw 4.2.60 Mortmr
geare, nere was there any/So finely handled as this king shalbe. Edw 5.5.39 Ltborn
I am resolv'd, Faustus shall not <nere> repent. . . F 583 2.2.32 Faust
order, Il'e nere trust smooth faces, and small ruffes more. F1318 4.1.164 P Benvol
such belly-cheere, as Wagner in his life nere saw the like: F1679 5.1.6 P Wagner
But Faustus offence can nere be pardoned, the serpent that F1837 5.2.41 P Faust
As Wagner nere beheld in all his life. . . . . F App p.243 7 Wagner
And cruel field, nere burning Aetna fought: . . . Lucan, First Booke 43
(Anger will helpe thy hands though nere so weake). . . Ovid's Elegies 1.7.66
Pray him to lend what thou maist nere restore. . . . Ovid's Elegies 1.8.102
Verse is immortall, and shall nere decay. . . . . Ovid's Elegies 1.15.32
The [haven] <heaven> touching barcke now nere the lea, . Ovid's Elegies 2.9.32
What should I do with fortune that nere failes me? . . Ovid's Elegies 2.19.7
And see at home much, that thou nere broughtst thether. . Ovid's Elegies 3.4.48
Nere was, nor shall be, what my verse mentions. . . Ovid's Elegies 3.5.18
And as shee spake those words, came somewhat nere him. . Hero and Leander 1.180
By this Leander being nere the land, ... Hero and Leander 2.227

NERE THE LESSE
Ile follow thee with outcryes nere the lesse, . . . Dido 4.2.55 Anna

NERETHELESSE
And in the morne beene lively nerethelesse. . . . Ovid's Elegies 2.10.28

NEREUS
Let Nereus bend the waves unto this shore, . . . Ovid's Elegies 2.11.39

NE'RE-YOAKT
on the Altar/He laies a ne're-yoakt Bull, and powers downe Lucan, First Booke 608

NERO
But if for Nero (then unborne) the fates/Would find no other Lucan, First Booke 33

NEROS
not heavens, but gladly beare these evils/For Neros sake: Lucan, First Booke 38

NERVIANS
The stubborne Nervians staind with Cottas bloud; . . Lucan, First Booke 430

NEST (See NEAST, NEASTS)

NESTLED
Vultures and furies nestled in the boughes. . . . Ovid's Elegies 1.12.20

NET
Why, that was in a net, where we are loose, . . . Dido 3.4.5 Dido

NET (cont.)			
as I doe a naked Lady in a net of golde, and for feare I should	2Tamb	4.1.69	P Calyph
Mars in the deed the black-smithes net did stable,	Ovid's Elegies		1.9.39
Blood-quaffing Mars, heaving the yron net,	Hero and Leander		1.151
NETS			
Convaid me from their crooked nets and bands:	Dido	2.1.222	Aeneas
Make a small price, while thou thy nets doest lay,	Ovid's Elegies		1.8.69
NETWORKE			
And Flamins last, with networke wollen vailes.	Lucan, First Booke		603
NEVER (See also NE'R, NE'RE-YOAKT, NERE)			
O had it never entred, Troy had stood.	Dido	2.1.172	Aeneas
Which thousand battering Rams could never pierce,	Dido	2.1.175	Aeneas
No, but I charge thee never looke on me.	Dido	3.1.54	Dido
Dido, that till now/Didst never thinke Aeneas beautifull:	Dido	3.1.83	Dido
All these and others which I never sawe,	Dido	3.1.150	Dido
Then never say that thou art miserable,	Dido	3.1.169	Dido
And wish that I had never wrongd him so:	Dido	3.2.48	Juno
Never to leave these newe upreared walles,	Dido	3.4.49	Aeneas
Never to like or love any but her.	Dido	3.4.51	Aeneas
In all my life I never knew the like,	Dido	4.1.7	Anna
If he forsake me not, I never dye,	Dido	4.4.121	Dido
Then let me goe and never say farewell?	Dido	5.1.109	Aeneas
Then let me goe, and never say farewell?	Dido	5.1.124	Dido
I never vow'd at Aulis gulfe/The desolation of his native Troy,	Dido	5.1.202	Dido
Betwixt this land and that be never league,	Dido	5.1.309	Dido
And Jove may never let me longer live,	1Tamb	1.1.170	Cosroe
Will never prosper your intended driftes,	1Tamb	1.2.69	Zenoc
Thy selfe and them shall never part from me,	1Tamb	1.2.245	Tamb
And they will never leave thee till the death.	1Tamb	1.2.248	Tamb
For he was never sprong of humaine race,	1Tamb	2.6.11	Meandr
Wils us to weare our selves and never rest,	1Tamb	2.7.26	Tamb
That never fought but had the victorie:	1Tamb	3.3.153	Tamb
And never had the Turkish Emperour/So great a foile by any	1Tamb	3.3.234	Bajzth
Dar'st thou that never saw an Emperour,	1Tamb	4.2.58	Zabina
Fall to, and never may your meat digest.	1Tamb	4.4.16	Bajzth
And be renowm'd, as never Emperours were.	1Tamb	4.4.138	Tamb
Will never be dispenc'd with til our deaths.	1Tamb	5.1.17	Govnr
Had never bene erected as they bee,	1Tamb	5.1.32	1Virgn
To thinke thy puisant never staied arme/Will part their bodies,	1Tamb	5.1.88	1Virgn
That never nourisht thought against thy rule,	1Tamb	5.1.98	1Virgn
Go, never to returne with victorie:	1Tamb	5.1.214	Bajzth
Smother the earth with never fading mistes:	1Tamb	5.1.296	Bajzth
the cursed object/Whose Fortunes never mastered her griefs:	1Tamb	5.1.414	Zenoc
That never sea-man yet discovered:	2Tamb	1.1.71	Orcan
Never to draw it out, or manage armes/Against thy selfe or thy	2Tamb	1.1.128	Sgsmnd
That never look'd on man but Tamburlaine.	2Tamb	1.3.34	Tamb
Yet never did they recreate themselves,	2Tamb	1.3.182	Usumc
imperiall heaven/That he that sits on high and never sleeps,	2Tamb	2.2.49	Orcan
From paine to paine, whose change shal never end:	2Tamb	2.3.26	Orcan
May never such a change transfourme my love/In whose sweet	2Tamb	2.4.47	Tamb
Whose lovely faces never any viewed,	2Tamb	3.2.30	Tamb
And Moores, in whom was never pitie found,	2Tamb	3.4.20	Olymp
And never meant to make a Conquerour,	2Tamb	3.5.83	Tamb
And sooner far than he that never fights.	2Tamb	4.1.55	Calyph
the good I have/Join'd with my fathers crowne would never cure.	2Tamb	4.1.58	Calyph
Such a feare (my Lord) would never make yee retire.	2Tamb	4.1.71	P Perdic
Can never wash from thy distained browes.	2Tamb	4.1.110	Tamb
May never day give vertue to his eies,	2Tamb	4.1.174	Trebiz
May never spirit, vaine or Artier feed/The cursed substance of	2Tamb	4.1.177	Soria
I will with Engines, never exercisde,	2Tamb	4.1.191	Tamb
That like unruly never broken Jades,	2Tamb	4.3.45	Therid
nor the towne will never yeeld/As long as any life is in my	2Tamb	5.1.47	Govnr
Assault and spare not, we wil never yeeld.	2Tamb	5.1.62	Govnr
My heart did never quake, or corrage faint.	2Tamb	5.1.106	Govnr
Sicknes or death can never conquer me.	2Tamb	5.1.222	Tamb
for never sepulchre/Shall grace that base-borne Tyrant	2Tamb	5.2.17	Amasia
And never wil we sunder camps and armes,	2Tamb	5.2.52	Callap
Eastward behold/As much more land, which never was descried,	2Tamb	5.3.155	Tamb
H'had never bellowed in a brasen Bull/Of great ones envy; o'th	Jew	Prol.25	Machvl
The needy groome that never fingred groat,	Jew	1.1.12	Barab
by a Spanish Fleet/That never left us till within a league,	Jew	1.1.96	2Merch
But never could effect their Stratagem.	Jew	1.1.165	Barab
As good dissemble that thou never mean'st/As first meane truth,	Jew	1.2.290	Barab
(Unchosen Nation, never circumciz'd;	Jew	2.3.8	Barab
That never tasted of the Passeover,	Jew	2.3.302	Barab
Yet never shall these lips bewray thy life.	Jew	3.3.75	Abigal
First to Don Lodowicke, him I never lov'd;	Jew	3.6.23	Abigal
I never heard of any man but he/Malign'd the order of the	Jew	4.1.103	Barab
As never Jew nor Christian knew the like:	Jew	4.1.118	Barab
I never knew a man take his death so patiently as this Fryar;	Jew	4.2.21	P Ithimr
Never lov'd man servant as I doe Ithimore.	Jew	4.3.54	Barab
son; he and I kild 'em both, and yet never touch'd 'em.	Jew	4.4.18	P Ithimr
We two, and 'twas never knowne, nor never shall be for me.	Jew	4.4.23	P Ithimr
He never put on cleane shirt since he was circumcis'd.	Jew	4.4.64	P Ithimr
And dye he shall, for we will never yeeld.	Jew	5.1.6	1Knght
ingendred thoughts/To burst abroad, those never dying flames,	P 92	2.35	Guise
And never cease untill that bell shall cease,	P 240	4.38	Guise
With death delay'd and torments never usde,	P 257	4.55	Charls
And yet didst never sound any thing to the depth.	P 386	7.26	Guise
And either never mannage army more,	P 793	16.7	Bartus
And may it never end in bloud as mine hath done.	P1233	22.95	King
For never doted Jove on Ganimed,	Edw	1.4.180	Queene
O never Lancaster!	Edw	1.4.200	Queene

NEVER (cont.)

Did never sorrow go so neere my heart,	Edw	1.4.306	Edward
Whose mounting thoughts did never creepe so low,	Edw	2.2.77	Gavstn
As never subject did unto his King.	Edw	2.2.129	Mortmr
We never beg, but use such praiers as these.	Edw	2.2.153	Mortmr
Stay Edmund, never was Plantagenet/False of his word, and	Edw	2.3.11	Mortmr
That when I had him we might never part.	Edw	2.4.21	Queene
Lancaster/Inexorable, and I shall never see/My lovely Pierce,	Edw	3.1.7	Edward
shall I never see,/Never behold thee now?	Edw	3.1.68	Edward
shall I never see,/Never behold thee now?	Edw	3.1.69	Edward
A ranker route of rebels never was:	Edw	3.1.154	Edward
Never so cheereles, nor so farre distrest.	Edw	4.2.14	Queene
I would he never had bin flattered more.	Edw	4.4.30	Kent
O might I never open these eyes againe,	Edw	4.7.41	Edward
Never againe lift up this drooping head,	Edw	4.7.42	Edward
O never more lift up this dying hart!	Edw	4.7.43	Edward
In heaven wee may, in earth never shall wee meete,	Edw	4.7.80	Edward
Parted from hence, never to see us more!	Edw	4.7.101	Spencr
Gone, gone alas, never to make returne.	Edw	4.7.104	Spencr
Let never silent night possesse this clime,	Edw	5.1.65	Edward
Take this, away, and never see me more.	Edw	5.4.43	Mortmr
These handes were never stainde with innocent bloud,	Edw	5.5.81	Ltborn
And tels me, if I sleepe I never wake,	Edw	5.5.104	Edward
you were not dunces, you would never aske me such a question:	F 207	1.2.14	P Wagner
And scorne those Joyes thou never shalt possesse.	F 314	1.3.86	Faust
I, but Faustus never shall repent.	F 568	2.2.17	BdAngl
Never too late, if Faustus will <can> repent.	F 631	2.2.80	GdAngl
Repent and they shall never raise thy skin.	F 633	2.2.82	GdAngl
And Faustus vowes never to looke to heaven,	F 648	2.2.97	Faust
[Never to name God, or to pray to him],	F 649	2.2.98A	Faust
So, so, was never Divell thus blest before.	F 974	3.1.196	Mephst
The Pope had never such a frolicke guest.	F1036	3.2.56	Faust
him, as he was never conjur'd in his life, I warrant him:	F1092	3.3.5	P Robin
Now Robin, now or never shew thy cunning.	F1094	3.3.7	P Dick
Never deny't, for I know you have it, and I'le search you.	F1101	3.3.14	P Vintnr
Never out face me for the matter, for sure the cup is betweene	F1107	3.3.20	P Vintnr
As never yet was seene in Germany.	F1188	4.1.34	Mrtino
'sbloud I am never able to endure these torments.	F1306	4.1.152	P Benvol
O may these eye-lids never close againe,	F1332	4.2.8	Benvol
he never left eating, till he had eate up all my loade of hay.	F1530	4.5.26	P Carter
run over hedge and ditch, and never tyre, I gave him his money;	F1539	4.5.35	P HrsCsr
and never rested pulling, till I had pul'd me his leg quite	F1550	4.5.46	P HrsCsr
<to cure him, tis but a surffet, never feare man>.	F1831	(HC270)A	P 2Schol
O would I had never seene Wittenberg <Wertenberge>, never read	F1841	5.2.45	P Faust
I had never seene Wittenberg <Wertenberge>, never read book:	F1842	5.2.46	P Faust
That time may cease, and midnight never come.	F1930	5.2.134	Faust
For such a dreadfull night, was never seene,	F1984	5.3.2	1Schol
Such fearefull shrikes, and cries, were never heard,	F1986	5.3.4	1Schol
they were never so knocht since they were divels, say I should	F App	p.230 46	P Clown
good divel forgive me now, and Ile never rob thy Library more.	F App	p.235 31	P Robin
Ifaith thy head will never be out of the potage pot.	F App	p.236 48	P Robin
never attaine to that degree of high renowne and great	F App	p.236 22	P Emper
It grieves my soule I never saw the man:	F App	p.237 28	Emper
mas Doctor Lopus was never such a Doctor, has given me a	F App	p.240 128	P HrsCsr
has purg'd me of fortie Dollers, I shall never see them more:	F App	p.240 129	P HrsCsr
I sat upon a bottle of hey, never so neare drowning in my life:	F App	p.240 135	P HrsCsr
Shall never faith be found in fellow kings.	Lucan, First Booke	92	
Whose like Aegiptian Memphis never had/For skill in stars, and	Lucan, First Booke	639	
Oh woe is me, he never shootes but hits,	Ovid's Elegies	1.1.29	
Either love, or cause that I may never hate:	Ovid's Elegies	1.3.2	
I love but one, and hir I love change never,	Ovid's Elegies	1.3.15	
Strike, so againe hard chaines shall binde thee never,	Ovid's Elegies	1.6.25	
But never give a spatious time to ire,	Ovid's Elegies	1.8.81	
rise/And who thou never think'st should fall downe lies.	Ovid's Elegies	1.9.30	
In heaven was never more notorious fable.	Ovid's Elegies	1.9.40	
Ill gotten goods good end will never have.	Ovid's Elegies	1.10.48	
Never to harme me made thy faith evasion.	Ovid's Elegies	1.11.6	
Oft was she drest before mine eyes, yet never,	Ovid's Elegies	1.14.17	
What two determine never wants effect.	Ovid's Elegies	2.3.16	
To whom his wench can say, I never did it.	Ovid's Elegies	2.5.10	
By chaunce her beauty never shined fuller.	Ovid's Elegies	2.5.42	
O Cupid that doest never cease my smart,	Ovid's Elegies	2.9.1	
Armenian Tygers never did so ill,	Ovid's Elegies	2.14.35	
My life, that I will shame thee never feare,	Ovid's Elegies	2.15.21	
But sundry floods in one banke never go,	Ovid's Elegies	2.17.31	
Shall I poore soule be never interdicted?	Ovid's Elegies	2.19.53	
Nor never with nights sharpe revenge afflicted?	Ovid's Elegies	2.19.54	
Never can these by any meanes agree.	Ovid's Elegies	3.4.42	
His dangling tresses that were never shorne,	Hero and Leander	1.55	
For faithfull love will never turne to hate.	Hero and Leander	1.128	
Though never-singling Hymen couple thee.	Hero and Leander	1.258	
Things that are not at all, are never lost.	Hero and Leander	1.276	
Jewels being lost are found againe, this never,	Hero and Leander	2.85	
And swore he never should returne to Jove.	Hero and Leander	2.168	
And swore the sea should never doe him harme.	Hero and Leander	2.180	
And now she wisht this night were never done,	Hero and Leander	2.301	

NEVER-SINGLING

Though never-singling Hymen couple thee.	Hero and Leander	1.258	

NEVERTHELESS (See NERETHELESSE)

NEW (See also ANEW)

And rost our new found victuals on this shoare.	Dido	1.1.168	Aeneas
Welcome to Carthage new erected towne.	Dido	5.1.26	Aeneas
And raise a new foundation to old Troy,	Dido	5.1.79	Aeneas

Line	Work	Reference	Speaker
NEW (cont.)			
Why are thy ships new rigd?	Dido	5.1.88	Dido
We now are almost at the new made Nunnery.	Jew	1.2.306	1Fryar
And waters of this new made Nunnery/Will much delight you.	Jew	1.2.311	1Fryar
the slave looks like a hogs cheek new sindg'd.	Jew	2.3.42	P Barab
Belike he has some new tricke for a purse;	Jew	2.3.101	Barab
That maidens new betroth'd should weepe a while:	Jew	2.3.326	Barab
Goe to the new made Nunnery, and inquire/For any of the Fryars	Jew	3.3.27	Abigal
And caus'd the ruines to be new repair'd,	Jew	5.3.2	Calym
That we might torture him with some new found death.	P1217	22.79	Eprnon
Is as Elizium to a new come soule.	Edw	1.1.11	Gavstn
And in the channell christen him a new.	Edw	1.1.188	Edward
At the new temple.	Edw	1.2.75	ArchBp
For no where else the new earle is so safe.	Edw	1.4.11	Lncstr
Is new returnd, this newes will glad him much,	Edw	1.4.301	Queene
Edward this day hath crownd him king a new.	Edw	3.1.261	Edward
Make for a new life man, throw up thy eyes,	Edw	4.7.107	Baldck
But seekes to make a new elected king,	Edw	5.1.78	Edward
And search all corners of the new-found-world/For pleasant	F 111	1.1.83	Faust
The Hebrew Psalter, and new Testament;	F 182	1.1.154	Valdes
And offer luke-warme bloud, of new borne babes.	F 402	2.1.14	Faust
But new exploits do hale him out agen,	F 770	2.3.49	2Chor
New factions rise; now through the world againe/I goe; o	Lucan, First Booke		691
I lately cought, will have a new made wound,	Ovid's Elegies		1.2.29
Behold what gives the Poet but new verses?	Ovid's Elegies		1.8.57
Ascreus lives, while grapes with new wine swell,	Ovid's Elegies		1.15.11
And ever seemed as some new sweete befell.	Ovid's Elegies		2.5.56
Doost me of new crimes alwayes guilty frame?	Ovid's Elegies		2.7.1
Ungrate why feignest new feares?	Ovid's Elegies		2.8.23
Nor is my warres cause new, but for a Queene/Europe, and Asia	Ovid's Elegies		2.12.17
A woman forc'd the Troyanes new to enter/Warres, just Latinus,	Ovid's Elegies		2.12.21
And new sworne souldiours maiden armes retainst,	Ovid's Elegies		2.18.2
Let my new mistris graunt to be beloved:	Ovid's Elegies		3.2.57
Either th'art witcht with blood <bould> of frogs new dead,	Ovid's Elegies		3.6.79
The one his first love, th'other his new care.	Ovid's Elegies		3.8.32
And with a wantons tooth, your necke new raste?	Ovid's Elegies		3.13.34
Tender loves Mother a new Poet get,	Ovid's Elegies		3.14.1
his parentage, would needs discover/The way to new Elisium:	Hero and Leander		1.411
Thinking to quench the sparckles new begonne.	Hero and Leander		2.138
NEW BORNE			
And offer luke-warme bloud, of new borne babes.	F 402	2.1.14	Faust
NEWCASTELL			
Will to Newcastell heere, and gather head.	Edw	2.2.123	Warwck
NEW COME			
Is as Elizium to a new come soule.	Edw	1.1.11	Gavstn
NEWE			
And mould her minde unto newe fancies shapes:	Dido	3.3.79	Iarbus
Never to leave these newe upreared walles,	Dido	3.4.49	Aeneas
NEWES			
And Priam dead, yet how we heare no newes.	Dido	2.1.113	Dido
Newes, newes.	1Tamb	1.2.109	Souldr
Thats wel Techelles, what's the newes?	1Tamb	5.1.198	Tamb
not a man surviv'd/To bring the haplesse newes to Christendome.	Jew	2.2.51	Bosco
I bring thee newes by whom thy sonne was slaine:	Jew	5.1.10	Curtzn
How now fellow, what newes?	P 242	4.40	Charls
How now sirra, what newes?	P 723	14.26	Navrre
see where she comes, as if she droupt/To heare these newes.	P1063	19.133	Eprnon
I come to bring you newes, that your brother the Cardinall of	P1122	21.16	P Frier
Then come thou neer, and tell what newes thou bringst.	P1166	22.28	King
Ile send my sister England newes of this,	P1189	22.51	King
This will be good newes to the common sort.	Edw	1.4.92	Penbrk
Is new returnd, this newes will glad him much,	Edw	1.4.301	Queene
My gratious lord, I come to bring you newes.	Edw	1.4.320	Queene
Repeald, the newes is too sweet to be true.	Edw	1.4.323	Edward
Such newes we heare my lord.	Edw	1.4.380	Lncstr
For I have joyfull newes to tell thee of,	Edw	2.1.75	Neece
How now, what newes, is Gaveston arrivde?	Edw	2.2.6	Edward
Nay, stay my lord, I come to bring you newes,	Edw	2.2.141	Mortmr
Madam, what newes?	Edw	3.1.58	Edward
Newes of dishonor lord, and discontent,	Edw	3.1.59	Queene
the newes was heere my lord,/That you were dead, or very neare	Edw	4.2.37	Queene
Tould us at our arrivall all the newes,	Edw	4.2.48	Mortmr
My lord of Gloster, do you heare the newes?	Edw	4.3.4	Edward
What newes my lord?	Edw	4.3.5	Spencr
Now sirs, the newes from Fraunce.	Edw	4.3.14	Edward
How now, what newes with thee, from whence come these?	Edw	4.3.24	Edward
this is all the newes of import.	Edw	4.3.36	P Spencr
My lorde, the parlement must have present newes,	Edw	5.1.84	Trussl
Farewell, I know the next newes that they bring,	Edw	5.1.125	Edward
An other poast, what newes bringes he?	Edw	5.1.128	Leistr
Such newes as I expect, come Bartley, come,	Edw	5.1.129	Edward
First would I heare newes that hee were deposde,	Edw	5.2.21	Mortmr
O happie newes, send for the prince my sonne.	Edw	5.2.29	Queene
Unlesse thou bring me newes of Edwards death.	Edw	5.4.46	Mortmr
To comfort you, and bring you joyfull newes.	Edw	5.5.43	Ltborn
How now Wagner what newes with thee?	F1499	4.4.43	P Faust
How now Wagner, what's the newes with thee?	F App	p.241 167	P Faust
Slaughter to come, and swiftly bringing newes/Of present war,	Lucan, First Booke		467
NEW FOUND			
And rost our new found victuals on this shoare.	Dido	1.1.168	Aeneas
NEW-FOUND-WORLD			
And search all corners of the new-found-world/For pleasant	F 111	1.1.83	Faust
NEWLY			
When sleepe but newly had imbrast the night,	Dido	4.3.17	Aeneas

NEWLY (cont.)			
newly crept out of Purgatory come to begge a pardon of your	F App	p.232 14	P Lorein
Yong oxen newly yokt are beaten more,	Ovid's Elegies		1.2.13
NEWS (See also NEWES)			
What other heavie news now brings Philemus?	1Tamb	5.1.377	Zenoc
A Mortimer, the king my sonne hath news,	Edw	5.6.15	Queene
NEXT			
We meane to take his mornings next arise/For messenger, he will	1Tamb	3.1.38	Bajzth
Then next, the way to fortifie your men,	2Tamb	3.2.62	Tamb
Whether we next make expedition.	2Tamb	4.3.94	Tamb
more than if the region/Next underneath the Element of fire,	2Tamb	5.1.88	Tamb
Revenge it on him when you meet him next.	Jew	2.3.343	Barab
If that be all, the next time that I meet her,	P 781	15.39	Mugern
the rest have taine their standings in the next roome,	P 994	19.64	P 3Mur
For he is your lawfull King and my next heire:	P1230	22.92	King
laide they violent hands upon him, next/Himselfe imprisoned,	Edw	1.2.36	ArchBp
Looke next to see us with our ensignes spred.	Edw	2.2.199	Lncstr
Farewell, I know the next newes that they bring,	Edw	5.1.125	Edward
Thou being his unckle, and the next of bloud,	Edw	5.2.88	Mortmr
See that in the next roome I have a fier,	Edw	5.5.29	Ltborn
I do not doubt but to see you both hang'd the next Sessions.	F 212	1.2.19	P Wagner
next, like a Neckelace I hang about her Necke:	F 666	2.2.115	P Pride
From Paris next, costing the Realme of France,	F 784	3.1.6	Faust
but let us into the next roome, and [there] pray for him.	F1871	5.2.75	P 1Schol
Next, an inferiour troupe, in tuckt up vestures,	Lucan, First Booke		595
Next learned Augures follow;/Apolloes southsayers; and Joves	Lucan, First Booke		600
And on the next fault punishment inflict.	Ovid's Elegies		2.14.44
With snow thaw'd from the next hill now thou rushest,	Ovid's Elegies		3.5.7
NICE			
Faire fooles delight to be accounted nice.	Hero and Leander		1.326
NIE			
what he meanes, if death were nie, he would not frolick thus:	F1677	5.1.4	P Wagner
And crave the helpe of sheap-heards that were nie.	Hero and Leander		1.414
NIECE (See NEECE)			
NIGGARD			
and one to whom I must be no niggard of my cunning; Come,	F1504	4.4.48	P Faust
to whom I must be no niggard of my cunning, come	F App	p.241 171	P Faust
NIGH (See also NIE, NY, NYE)			
That nigh Larissa swaies a mighty hoste,	2Tamb	2.2.6	Orcan
That with one worde hath nigh himselfe undone,	Ovid's Elegies		1.13.20
The shout is nigh; the golden pompe comes heere.	Ovid's Elegies		3.2.44
And ever as he thought himselfe most nigh it,	Hero and Leander		2.74
NIGHT			
Have oft driven backe the horses of the night,	Dido	1.1.26	Jupitr
See how the night Ulysses-like comes forth,	Dido	1.1.70	Venus
Whose night and day descendeth from thy browes:	Dido	1.1.156	Achat
The day, the night, my Swannes, my sweetes are thine.	Dido	3.2.61	Venus
I thinke it was the divels revelling night,	Dido	4.1.9	Achat
Hermes this night descending in a dreame,	Dido	4.3.3	Aeneas
When sleepe but newly had imbrast the night,	Dido	4.3.17	Aeneas
me, for I forgot/That yong Ascanius lay with me this night:	Dido	4.4.32	Dido
he lay with me last night,/And in the morning he was stolne	Dido	5.1.213	Nurse
To shroud his shame in darknes of the night.	1Tamb	4.1.46	Souldn
Making the mantle of the richest night,	1Tamb	5.1.149	Tamb
Hide now thy stained face in endles night,	1Tamb	5.1.292	Bajzth
Sleep'st every night with conquest on thy browes,	1Tamb	5.1.359	Zenoc
Ready to darken earth with endlesse night:	2Tamb	2.4.7	Tamb
And yet at night carrouse within my tent,	2Tamb	3.2.106	Tamb
And henceforth wish for an eternall night,	Jew	1.2.193	Barab
And in the shadow of the silent night/Doth shake contagion from	Jew	2.1.3	Barab
and direct the hand/Of Abigall this night; or let the day/Turne	Jew	2.1.15	Barab
And speake of spirits and ghosts that glide by night/About the	Jew	2.1.26	Barab
How showes it by night?	Jew	2.3.62	Lodowk
And in the night time secretly would I steale/To travellers	Jew	2.3.206	Ithimr
that but for one bare night/A hundred Duckets have bin freely	Jew	3.1.2	Curtzn
and in the night I clamber'd up with my hooks, and as I was	Jew	3.1.19	P Pilia
I'le be with you to night.	Jew	4.1.90	2Fryar
Come to my house at one a clocke this night.	Jew	4.1.91	Barab
What time a night is't now, sweet Ithimore?	Jew	4.1.157	Barab
Should have been murdered the other night?	P 35	1.35	Navrre
If ever day were turnde to ugly night,	P 62	2.5	Guise
And night made semblance of the hue of hell,	P 63	2.6	Guise
This day, this houre, this fatall night,	P 64	2.7	Guise
And now sirs for this night let our fury stay.	P 443	7.83	Guise
To whom the sunne shines both by day and night.	Edw	1.1.17	Gavstn
Therefore ile have Italian maskes by night,	Edw	1.1.55	Gavstn
Such reasons make white blacke, and darke night day.	Edw	1.4.247	Lncstr
But cannot brooke a night growne mushrump,	Edw	1.4.284	Mortmr
Be thou this night his keeper, in the morning/We will discharge	Edw	2.5.108	Penbrk
Stand gratious gloomie night to his device.	Edw	4.1.11	Kent
And duskie night, in rustie iron carre:	Edw	4.3.44	Edward
But stay a while, let me be king till night,	Edw	5.1.59	Edward
Let never silent night possesse this clime,	Edw	5.1.65	Edward
Remoove him still from place to place by night,	Edw	5.2.59	Mortmr
This night I'le conjure tho I die therefore.	F 193	1.1.165	Faust
Now that the gloomy shadow of the night <earth>,	F 229	1.3.1	Faust
Chiefe Lord and Regent of perpetuall night.	F 445	2.1.57	Faust
if a man be drunke over night, the Divell cannot hurt him in	F1201	4.1.47	P Benvol
Doctor Fauster bad me ride him night and day, and spare him no	F1540	4.5.36	P HrsCsr
Be both your legs bedfellowes every night together?	F1645	4.6.88	P Carter
And this gloomy night,/Here in this roome will wretched Faustus	F1803	5.2.7	Mephst
For such a dreadfull night, was never seene,	F1984	5.3.2	1Schol
As far as Titan springs where night dims heaven,	Lucan, First Booke		15

NIGHT (cont.)		
At night in dreadful vision fearefull Roome,	Lucan, First Booke	188
Now light had quite dissolv'd the mysty [night] <might>,	Lucan, First Booke	263
With slender trench they escape night stratagems,	Lucan, First Booke	514
And wilt not trust thy Citty walls one night:	Lucan, First Booke	518
Which wont to run their course through empty night/At noone day	Lucan, First Booke	534
birds/Defil'd the day, and <at night> wilde beastes were seene,	Lucan, First Booke	557
such and more strange/Blacke night brought forth in secret:	Lucan, First Booke	579
But we must part, when heav'n with black night lowers.	Ovid's Elegies	1.4.60
At night thy husband clippes thee, I will weepe/And to the	Ovid's Elegies	1.4.61
But though this night thy fortune be to trie it,	Ovid's Elegies	1.4.69
Or night being past, and yet not day begunne.	Ovid's Elegies	1.5.6
But in times past I fear'd vaine shades, and night,	Ovid's Elegies	1.6.9
no darke night-flying spright/Nor hands prepar'd to slaughter,	Ovid's Elegies	1.6.13
Night goes away: the dores barre backeward strike.	Ovid's Elegies	1.6.24
Strike backe the barre, night fast away doth goe.	Ovid's Elegies	1.6.32
Night runnes away; with open entrance greete them.	Ovid's Elegies	1.6.40
Watching till after mid-night did not tire thee.	Ovid's Elegies	1.6.44
Night goes away: I pray thee ope the dore.	Ovid's Elegies	1.6.48
Night, Love, and wine to all extreames perswade:	Ovid's Elegies	1.6.59
Night shamelesse, wine and Love are fearelesse made.	Ovid's Elegies	1.6.60
Now frosty night her flight beginnes to take,	Ovid's Elegies	1.6.65
Who seekes, for being faire, a night to have,	Ovid's Elegies	1.8.67
Since maist thou see me watch and night warres move:	Ovid's Elegies	1.9.45
If, what I do, she askes, say hope for night,	Ovid's Elegies	1.11.13
How oft wisht I night would not give thee place,	Ovid's Elegies	1.13.27
Then wouldst thou cry, stay night and runne not thus.	Ovid's Elegies	1.13.40
Haples is he that all the night lies quiet/And slumbring,	Ovid's Elegies	2.9.39
If one can doote, if not, two everie night,	Ovid's Elegies	2.10.22
Oft have I spent the night in wantonnesse,	Ovid's Elegies	2.10.27
And hasting to me, neither darkesome night,	Ovid's Elegies	2.11.51
And slipt from bed cloth'd in a loose night-gowne,	Ovid's Elegies	3.1.51
What day and night to travaile in her quest?	Ovid's Elegies	3.5.10
Corinna cravde it in a summers night,	Ovid's Elegies	3.6.25
What madnesse ist to tell night <nights> prankes by day,	Ovid's Elegies	3.13.7
Nor that night-wandring pale and watrie starre,	Hero and Leander	1.107
And night deepe drencht in mystie Acheron,	Hero and Leander	1.189
Breath'd darkenesse forth (darke night is Cupids day).	Hero and Leander	1.191
In silence of the night to viste us),	Hero and Leander	1.350
And spends the night (that might be better spent)/In vaine	Hero and Leander	1.355
So that in silence of the cloudie night,	Hero and Leander	2.101
But what the secret trustie night conceal'd,	Hero and Leander	2.103
And now she wisht this night were never done,	Hero and Leander	2.301
Should know the pleasure of this blessed night,	Hero and Leander	2.304
And with his flaring beames mockt ougly night,	Hero and Leander	2.332
NIGHT-FLYING		
no darke night-flying spright/Nor hands prepar'd to slaughter,	Ovid's Elegies	1.6.13
NIGHT-GOWNE		
And slipt from bed cloth'd in a loose night-gowne,	Ovid's Elegies	3.1.51
NIGHTLY		
Must I be vexed like the nightly birde,	Edw 5.3.6	Edward
NIGHTS		
And painefull nights have bin appointed me.	Jew 1.2.198	Barab
You'le like it better farre a nights than dayes.	Jew 2.3.63	Barab
I walke abroad a nights/And kill sicke people groaning under	Jew 2.3.174	Barab
Oh that ten thousand nights were put in one,	Jew 4.2.130	Ithimr
For the late nights worke which my Lord of Guise/Did make in	P 514 9.33	QnMoth
Thorough a rocke of stone in one nights space:	F 793 3.1.15	Faust
I tell thee he has not slept this eight nights.	F App p.240 144 P	Mephst
Or Cynthia nights Queene waights upon the day;	Lucan, First Booke	91
Although the nights be long, I sleepe not tho,	Ovid's Elegies	1.2.3
nights deawie hoast/March fast away:	Ovid's Elegies	1.6.55
Her I suspect among nights spirits to fly,	Ovid's Elegies	1.8.13
is bould/To suffer storme mixt snowes with nights sharpe cold?	Ovid's Elegies	1.9.16
Farmes out her-self on nights for what she can.	Ovid's Elegies	1.10.30
Faire Dames for-beare rewards for nights to crave,	Ovid's Elegies	1.10.47
Thy service for nights scapes is knowne commodious/And to give	Ovid's Elegies	1.11.3
Made two nights one to finish up his pleasure.	Ovid's Elegies	1.13.46
Suffring much cold by hoary nights frost bred.	Ovid's Elegies	2.19.22
In nights deepe silence why the ban-dogges barke.	Ovid's Elegies	2.19.40
Nor never with nights sharpe revenge afflicted?	Ovid's Elegies	2.19.54
And that slowe webbe nights fals-hood did unframe.	Ovid's Elegies	3.8.30
What madnesse ist to tell night <nights> prankes by day,	Ovid's Elegies	3.13.7
NIGHT TIME		
And in the night time secretly would I steal /To travellers	Jew 2.3.206	Ithimr
NIGHT-WANDRING		
Nor that night-wandring pale and watrie starre,	Hero and Leander	1.107
NIGRA		
And Nigra Silva, where the Devils dance,	2Tamb 1.3.212	Therid
NILE		
Lie slumbering on the flowrie bankes of Nile,	1Tamb 4.1.9	Souldn
As vast and deep as Euphrates or Nile.	1Tamb 5.1.439	Tamb
And I have martch'd along the river Nile,	2Tamb 1.3.186	Techel
To drinke the river Nile or Euphrates,	2Tamb 3.1.42	Orcan
Where Nile augmenteth the Pelusian sea:	Lucan, First Booke	683
And where swift Nile in his large channell slipping <skipping>,	Ovid's Elegies	2.13.9
Rich Nile by seaven mouthes to the vast sea flowing,	Ovid's Elegies	3.5.39
I ere while/Nam'd Achelaus, Inachus, and [Nile] <Ile>,	Ovid's Elegies	3.5.104
NILUS (See also NYLUS)		
As looks the sun through Nilus flowing stream,	1Tamb 3.2.47	Zenoc
and the bordering Iles/Are gotten up by Nilus winding bankes:	Jew 1.1.43	Barab
Where Nilus payes his tribute to the maine,	Jew 1.1.75	Barab
And they of Nilus mouth (if there live any).	Lucan, First Booke	20

NIMBLE			
On whom the nimble windes may all day waight,	Dido	4.3.23	Aeneas
Me thinkes she should <would> be nimble when shees downe.	Ovid's Elegies		2.4.14
Did charme her nimble feet, and made her stay,	Hero and Leander		1.399
NIMBLER			
She would be nimbler, lying with a man.	Ovid's Elegies		2.4.24
NIMPH			
The water which our Poets terme a Nimph,	Dido	4.4.144	Dido
The water is an Element, no Nimph,	Dido	4.4.147	Dido
Whither gost thou hateful nimph?	Ovid's Elegies		1.13.31
When nimph-Neaera rapt thy lookes Scamander.	Ovid's Elegies		3.5.28
A heavenly Nimph, belov'd of humane swaines,	Hero and Leander		1.216
NIMPHES			
Like Sylvian <Sylvan> Nimphes my pages shall be clad,	Edw	1.1.58	Gavstn
Both to the Sea-nimphes, and the Sea-nimphes father.	Ovid's Elegies		2.11.36
A mortall nimphes refusing Lord to stay.	Ovid's Elegies		2.17.16
Thou ore a hundreth Nimphes, or more shalt raigne:	Ovid's Elegies		3.5.63
For five score Nimphes, or more our flouds conteine.	Ovid's Elegies		3.5.64
NIMPH-NEAERA			
When nimph-Neaera rapt thy lookes Scamander.	Ovid's Elegies		3.5.28
NIMPHS			
Or one of chast Dianas fellow Nimphs,	Dido	1.1.194	Aeneas
Daughter unto the Nimphs Hesperides,	Dido	5.1.276	Dido
For like Sea-nimphs inveigling harmony,	Hero and Leander		1.105
NINE			
And my nine Daughters sing when thou art sad,	Dido	1.1.33	Jupitr
Nine, the seven Planets, the Firmament, and the Emperiall	F 610	2.2.59	P Mephst
Whose life nine ages scarce bring out of date.	Ovid's Elegies		2.6.36
And nine sweete bouts had we before day light.	Ovid's Elegies		3.6.26
NINUS			
Where Belus, Ninus and great Alexander/Have rode in triumph,	2Tamb	5.1.69	Tamb
NIOBE			
O my Achates, Theban Niobe,	Dido	2.1.3	Aeneas
Niobe flint, Callist we make a Beare,	Ovid's Elegies		3.11.31
NIPT			
The sheepeherd nipt with biting winters rage,	Edw	2.2.61	Gavstn
NISI			
non potest pater, nisi--Such is the subject of the Institute,	F 58	1.1.30	P Faust
NO (See also NAY)			
Hermes no more shall shew the world his wings,	Dido	1.1.38	Jupitr
Since that religion hath no recompence.	Dido	1.1.81	Venus
No bounds but heaven shall bound his Emperie,	Dido	1.1.100	Jupitr
No steps of men imprinted in the earth.	Dido	1.1.181	Achat
Whose lookes set forth no mortall forme to view,	Dido	1.1.189	Aeneas
And when my grieved heart sighes and sayes no,	Dido	2.1.26	Aeneas
This is no seate for one thats comfortles,	Dido	2.1.86	Aeneas
And Priam dead, yet how we heare no newes.	Dido	2.1.113	Dido
O end Aeneas, I can heare no more.	Dido	2.1.243	Dido
Albeit the Gods doe know no wanton thought/Had ever residence	Dido	3.1.16	Dido
No Dido will not take me in her armes,	Dido	3.1.22	Cupid
No more my child, now talke another while,	Dido	3.1.26	Dido
Why staiest thou here? thou art no love of mine.	Dido	3.1.39	Dido
No, live Iarbus, what hast thou deserv'd,	Dido	3.1.41	Dido
That I should say thou art no love of mine?	Dido	3.1.42	Dido
No, but I charge thee never looke on me.	Dido	3.1.54	Dido
No, for thy sake Ile love thy father well.	Dido	3.1.81	Dido
No, but now thou art here, tell me in sooth/In what might Dido	Dido	3.1.101	Dido
As without blushing I can aske no more:	Dido	3.1.104	Aeneas
No Madame, but it seemes that these are Kings.	Dido	3.1.149	Aeneas
Troy shall no more call him her second hope,	Dido	3.2.8	Juno
O no God wot, I cannot watch my time,	Dido	3.2.14	Juno
And have no gall at all to grieve my foes:	Dido	3.2.17	Juno
Aeneas no, although his eyes doe pearce.	Dido	3.4.12	Dido
It was because I sawe no King like thee,	Dido	3.4.35	Dido
Nay, no such waightie busines of import,	Dido	4.2.25	Anna
Graunt she or no, Aeneas must away,	Dido	4.3.7	Aeneas
This is no life for men at armes to live,	Dido	4.3.33	Achat
No no, she cares not how we sinke or swimme,	Dido	4.3.41	Illion
Speake of no other land, this land is thine,	Dido	4.4.83	Dido
The water is an Element, no Nimph,	Dido	4.4.147	Dido
Ye shall no more offend the Carthage Queene.	Dido	4.4.158	Dido
No, thou shalt goe with me unto my house,	Dido	4.5.3	Nurse
Now speake Ascanius, will ye goe or no?	Dido	4.5.12	Nurse
Ile be no more a widowe, I am young,	Dido	4.5.22	Nurse
A husband and no teeth!	Dido	4.5.24	Cupid
Carthage shall vaunt her pettie walles no more,	Dido	5.1.4	Aeneas
No marvell Dido though thou be in love,	Dido	5.1.44	Aeneas
Who have no sailes nor tackling for my ships?	Dido	5.1.56	Aeneas
O no, the Gods wey not what Lovers doe,	Dido	5.1.131	Dido
Thy mother was no Goddesse perjurd man,	Dido	5.1.156	Dido
No but I am not, yet I will be straight.	Dido	5.1.271	Dido
And reape no guerdon for my truest love?	Dido	5.1.282	Iarbus
No, a foe,/Monster of Nature, shame unto thy stocke,	1Tamb	1.1.103	Mycet
No: cowards and faintharted runawaies,	1Tamb	1.2.130	Techel
No, but the trustie friend of Tamburlaine.	1Tamb	1.2.227	Tamb
No, I tooke it prisoner.	1Tamb	2.4.32	Tamb
No, I meane, I let you keep it.	1Tamb	2.4.35	Mycet
Thou art no match for mightie Tamburlaine.	1Tamb	2.4.40	Tamb
That no reliefe or succour come by Land.	1Tamb	3.1.62	Bajzth
And gives no more than common courtesies.	1Tamb	3.2.63	Agidas
That leave no ground for thee to martch upon.	1Tamb	3.3.147	Bajzth
No Tamburlain, though now thou gat the best,	1Tamb	3.3.222	Zabina
that the Souldan is/No more dismaide with tidings of his fall,	1Tamb	4.3.31	Souldn

NO (cont.)

Your byrthes shall be no blemish to your fame,	1Tamb	4.4.127		Tamb
Which into words no vertue can digest:	1Tamb	5.1.173		Tamb
As if there were no way but one with us.	1Tamb	5.1.201		Techel
No more there is not I warrant thee Techelles.	1Tamb	5.1.202		Tamb
And have no hope to end our extasies.	1Tamb	5.1.238		Bajzth
Then is there left no Mahomet, no God,	1Tamb	5.1.239		Zabina
No Feend, no Fortune, nor no hope of end/To our infamous	1Tamb	5.1.240		Zabina
no Fortune, nor no hope of end/To our infamous monstrous	1Tamb	5.1.240		Zabina
Fortune, nor no hope of end/To our infamous monstrous slaveries?	1Tamb	5.1.240		Zabina
See, se Anippe if they breathe or no.	1Tamb	5.1.343		Zenoc
No breath nor sence, nor motion in them both.	1Tamb	5.1.344		Anippe
That she shall stay and turne her wheele no more,	1Tamb	5.1.374		Anippe
That no escape may save their enemies:	1Tamb	5.1.405		Arabia
Her state and person wants no pomp you see,	1Tamb	5.1.485		Tamb
Then let me find no further time to grace/Her princely Temples	1Tamb	5.1.488		Tamb
No speach to that end, by your favour sir.	2Tamb	1.2.14		Almeda
No talke of running, I tell you sir.	2Tamb	1.2.16		Almeda
No Madam, these are speeches fit for us,	2Tamb	1.3.88		Celeb
Yet shall my souldiers make no period/Untill Natolia kneele	2Tamb	1.3.216		Therid
No whit my Lord:	2Tamb	2.1.33		Baldwn
In whom no faith nor true religion rests,	2Tamb	2.1.34		Baldwn
Whose jealousie admits no second Mate,	2Tamb	2.4.12		Tamb
Shine downwards now no more, but deck the heavens/To entertaine	2Tamb	2.4.20		Tamb
Phisitions, wil no phisicke do her good?	2Tamb	2.4.38		Tamb
Ah sweet Theridamas, say so no more,	2Tamb	2.4.126		Tamb
That's no matter sir, for being a king, for Tamburlain came up	2Tamb	3.1.73	P	Almeda
Sorrow no more my sweet Casane now:	2Tamb	3.2.44		Tamb
That no supply of victuall shall come in,	2Tamb	3.3.32		Techel
No hope is left to save this conquered hold.	2Tamb	3.4.3		Olymp
That you must goe with us, no remedy.	2Tamb	3.4.79		Therid
No Madam, but the beginning of your joy,	2Tamb	3.4.83		Techel
No, let him hang a bunch of keies on his standerd, to put him	2Tamb	3.5.139	P	Tamb
No Tamburlaine, hee shall not be put to that exigent, I warrant	2Tamb	3.5.156	P	Soria
No, we wil meet thee slavish Tamburlain.	2Tamb	3.5.170		Orcan
I take no pleasure to be murtherous,	2Tamb	4.1.29		Calyph
He comes and findes his sonnes have had no shares/In all the	2Tamb	4.1.47		Amyras
No, no Amyras, tempt not Fortune so,	2Tamb	4.1.86		Tamb
whose weeping eies/Since thy arrivall here beheld no Sun,	2Tamb	4.2.2		Olymp
Affoords no hearbs, whose taste may poison thee,	2Tamb	4.2.9		Olymp
No such discourse is pleasant in mine eares,	2Tamb	4.2.46		Olymp
And have no terrour but his threatning lookes?	2Tamb	5.1.23		Govnr
And that shal bide no more regard of parlie.	2Tamb	5.1.61		Techel
down to the earth/Could not affright you, no, nor I my selfe,	2Tamb	5.1.91		Tamb
Away with him hence, let him speake no more:	2Tamb	5.1.125		Tamb
No, though Asphaltis lake were liquid gold,	2Tamb	5.1.155		Tamb
And let no basenesse in thy haughty breast,	2Tamb	5.3.30		Usumc
No, strike the drums, and in revenge of this,	2Tamb	5.3.57		Tamb
Not last Techelles, no, for I shall die.	2Tamb	5.3.66		Tamb
No doubt, but you shal soone recover all.	2Tamb	5.3.99		Phsitn
Your paines do pierce our soules, no hope survives,	2Tamb	5.3.166		Celeb
Then feeles your majesty no sovereraigne ease,	2Tamb	5.3.213		Usumc
Casane no, the Monarke of the earth,	2Tamb	5.3.216		Tamb
For both their woorths wil equall him no more.	2Tamb	5.3.253		Amyras
And hold there is no sinne but Ignorance.	Jew	Prol.15		Machvl
For I can see no fruits in all their faith,	Jew	1.1.116		Barab
I have no charge, nor many children,	Jew	1.1.136		Barab
Alas, my Lord, we are no souldiers:	Jew	1.2.50		Barab
Tut, Jew, we know thou art no souldier;	Jew	1.2.52		1Knght
No, Jew, like infidels.	Jew	1.2.62		Govnr
Oh earth-mettall'd villaines, and no Hebrews born!	Jew	1.2.78		Barab
No, Governour, I will be no convertite.	Jew	1.2.82		Barab
No, Jew, thou hast denied the Articles,	Jew	1.2.92		Govnr
No, Jew, we take particularly thine/To save the ruine of a	Jew	1.2.96		Govnr
And having all, you can request no more;	Jew	1.2.140		Barab
No, Barabas, to staine our hands with blood/Is farre from us	Jew	1.2.144		Govnr
And knowes no meanes of his recoverie:	Jew	1.2.205		Barab
Who for the villaines have no wit themselves,	Jew	1.2.215		Barab
No, Barabas is borne to better chance,	Jew	1.2.218		Barab
No, Abigail, things past recovery/Are hardly cur'd with	Jew	1.2.236		Barab
And leave no memory that e're I was.	Jew	1.2.265		Barab
No, I will live; nor loath I this my life:	Jew	1.2.266		Barab
by me, for in extremitie/We ought to make barre of no policie.	Jew	1.2.273		Barab
No, Abigall, in this/It is not necessary I be seene.	Jew	1.2.301		Barab
No doubt, brother, but this proceedeth of the spirit.	Jew	1.2.327		1Fryar
Yet let thy daughter be no longer blinde.	Jew	1.2.354		1Fryar
No come not at me, if thou wilt be damn'd,	Jew	1.2.362		Barab
I must and will, Sir, there's no remedy.	Jew	1.2.391		Mthias
And of my former riches rests no more/But bare remembrance;	Jew	2.1.9		Barab
That has no further comfort for his maime.	Jew	2.1.11		Barab
No sleepe can fasten on my watchfull eyes,	Jew	2.1.17		Barab
Bien para todos mi ganado no es:	Jew	2.1.39		Barab
I, I, no doubt but shee's at your command.	Jew	2.3.39		Barab
No further:	Jew	2.3.44		Barab
No, Barabas, I will deserve it first.	Jew	2.3.68		Lodowk
Against my will, and whether I would or no,	Jew	2.3.75		Barab
No doubt your soule shall reape the fruit of it.	Jew	2.3.78		Lodowk
Are wondrous; and indeed doe no man good:	Jew	2.3.82		Barab
No, but I doe it through a burning zeale,	Jew	2.3.87		Barab
Come home and there's no price shall make us part,	Jew	2.3.92		Barab
No more, my Lord.	Jew	2.3.108		1Offcr
No Sir, I can cut and shave.	Jew	2.3.113	P	Slave
I pray, Sir, be no stranger at my house,	Jew	2.3.136		Barab

NO (cont.)

No, this is the better, mother, view this well.	Jew	2.3.145	Mthias
Hast thou no Trade?	Jew	2.3.167	Barab
Be true and secret, thou shalt want no gold.	Jew	2.3.216	Barab
the Governors sonne/Will, whether I will or no, have Abigall:	Jew	2.3.258	Barab
No, Mathias, no, but sends them backe,/And when he comes, she	Jew	2.3.261	Barab
If you love me, no quarrels in my house;	Jew	2.3.271	Barab
No, no, but happily he stands in feare/Of that which you, I	Jew	2.3.282	Barab
And now I can no longer hold my minde.	Jew	2.3.290	Lodowk
It's no sinne to deceive a Christian;	Jew	2.3.309	Barab
Here must no speeches passe, nor swords be drawne.	Jew	2.3.339	Barab
No; so shall I, if any hurt be done,	Jew	2.3.341	Barab
No, no, and yet it might be done that way:	Jew	2.3.373	Barab
now Abigall shall see/Whether Mathias holds her deare or no.	Jew	3.2.2	Mthias
Why, no.	Jew	3.3.15	Abigal
No, what was it?	Jew	3.3.17	Abigal
But I perceive there is no love on earth,	Jew	3.3.47	Abigal
Abigal I will, but see thou change no more,	Jew	3.3.70	1Fryar
For I have now no hope but even in thee;	Jew	3.4.16	Barab
That's no lye, for she sent me for him.	Jew	3.4.25	P Ithimr
Oh trusty Ithimore; no servant, but my friend;	Jew	3.4.42	Barab
In Malta are no golden Minerals.	Jew	3.5.6	Govnr
Bashaw, in briefe, shalt have no tribute here,	Jew	3.5.11	Govnr
No, but a worse thing:	Jew	3.6.50	2Fryar
There is no musicke to a Christians knell:	Jew	4.1.1	Barab
Or though it wrought, it would have done no good,	Jew	4.1.5	Barab
No, but I grieve because she liv'd so long.	Jew	4.1.18	Barab
Oh no, good Barabas come to our house.	Jew	4.1.78	2Fryar
They weare no shirts, and they goe bare-foot too.	Jew	4.1.84	1Fryar
No more but so: it must and shall be done.	Jew	4.1.128	Barab
No, 'tis an order which the Fryars use:	Jew	4.1.134	Barab
No, none can heare him, cry he ne're so loud.	Jew	4.1.136	Ithimr
'Tis neatly done, Sir, here's no print at all.	Jew	4.1.151	Ithimr
No, wilt thou not?	Jew	4.1.171	1Fryar
I have don't, but no body knowes it but you two, I may escape.	Jew	4.1.180	P 1Fryar
No, let us beare him to the Magistrates.	Jew	4.1.183	Ithimr
No, pardon me, the Law must have his course.	Jew	4.1.185	Barab
No, for this example I'le remaine a Jew:	Jew	4.1.195	Barab
Why, a Turke could ha done no more.	Jew	4.1.198	P Ithimr
I can with-hold no longer; welcome sweet love.	Jew	4.2.46	Curtzn
By no meanes possible.	Jew	4.2.61	P Ithimr
Goe to, no more, I'le make him send me half he has, and glad he	Jew	4.2.66	P Ithimr
and this shall be your warrant; if you doe not, no more but so.	Jew	4.2.76	P Ithimr
I have no husband, sweet, I'le marry thee.	Jew	4.2.87	Curtzn
No; but three hundred will not serve his turne.	Jew	4.3.20	P Pilia
No Sir; and therefore I must have five hundred more.	Jew	4.3.22	P Pilia
No god-a-mercy, shall I have these crownes?	Jew	4.3.31	Pilia
You know I have no childe, and unto whom/Should I leave all but	Jew	4.3.44	Barab
Here's many words but no crownes; the crownes.	Jew	4.3.46	P Pilia
Like thy breath, sweet-hart, no violet like 'em.	Jew	4.4.40	Ithimr
Pardona moy, be no in tune yet; so, now, now all be in.	Jew	4.4.45	P Barab
Very mush, Mounsier, you no be his man?	Jew	4.4.57	P Barab
Pardona moy, Mounsier, [me] <we> be no well.	Jew	4.4.71	Barab
No, I'le send by word of mouth now; Bid him deliver thee a	Jew	4.4.74	P Ithimr
No, no:/I dranke of Poppy and cold mandrake juyce;	Jew	5.1.79	Barab
Away, no more, let him not trouble me.	Jew	5.2.26	Barab
No simple place, no small authority,	Jew	5.2.28	Barab
No, Barabas, this must be look'd into;	Jew	5.2.34	Barab
I see no reason but of Malta's wracke,	Jew	5.2.58	Govnr
Wherein no danger shall betide thy life,	Jew	5.2.100	Barab
Have speciall care that no man sally forth/Till you shall heare	Jew	5.4.2	Govnr
wel since it is no more/I'le satisfie my selfe with that;	Jew	5.5.21	Barab
No, Governor, I'le satisfie thee first,	Jew	5.5.44	Barab
No, Selim, doe not flye;	Jew	5.5.68	Govnr
No, thus I'le see thy treachery repaid,	Jew	5.5.74	Govnr
No, villaine, no.	Jew	5.5.76	Govnr
Tush, Governor, take thou no care for that,	Jew	5.5.102	Calym
O no, sweet Margaret, the fatall poyson/Workes within my head,	P 184	3.19	OldQn
Which is no sooner receiv'd but it is spent.	P 379	7.19	Ramus
O no, his bodye will infect the fire, and the fire the aire,	P 484	9.3	P 1Atndt
No, no, to decide all doubts, be rulde by me, lets hang him	P 491	9.10	P 2Atndt
No by my faith Madam.	P 498	9.17	Guise
Doe so sweet Guise, let us delay no time,	P 505	9.24	QnMoth
Be gone, delay no time sweet Guise.	P 509	9.28	QnMoth
No villain, that toung of thine,	P 530	10.3	Guise
Shall drive no plaintes into the Guises eares,	P 532	10.5	Guise
Comfort your selfe my Lord and have no doubt,	P 541	11.6	Navrre
O no, my loving brother of Navarre.	P 543	11.8	Charls
God graunt my neerest freends may prove no worse.	P 547	11.12	Charls
O no, his soule is fled from out his breast,	P 552	11.17	QnMoth
For heers no saftie in the Realme for me,	P 568	11.33	Navrre
No person, place, or time, or circumstance,	P 606	12.19	King
goe sirra, worke no more,/Till this our Coronation day be past:	P 623	12.36	King
O no my Lord, a woman only must/Partake the secrets of my	P 675	13.19	Duchss
Are these your secrets that no man must know?	P 678	13.22	Guise
But for you know our quarrell is no more,	P 704	14.7	Navrre
Of King or Country, no not for them both.	P 740	14.43	Navrre
Whether he have dishonoured me or no.	P 769	15.27	Guise
Why I am no traitor to the crowne of France.	P 825	17.20	Guise
Heere is no staying for the King of France,	P 897	17.92	King
O Lord no: for we entend to strangle you.	P1095	20.5	2Mur
Then there is no remedye but I must dye?	P1096	20.6	Cardnl
No remedye, therefore prepare your selfe.	P1097	20.7	1Mur

NO (cont.)

Now thou art dead, heere is no stay for us:	P1111	21.5	Dumain
No, let the villaine dye, and feele in hell, . . .	P1174	22.36	King
Oh no Navarre, thou must be King of France. . . .	P1225	22.87	King
thats no answere	Paris	ms 7,p390	P Souldr
But I have no horses. What art thou?	Edw	1.1.28	Gavstn
I have no warre, and therefore sir be gone. . . .	Edw	1.1.36	Gavstn
But yet it is no paine to speake men faire, . . .	Edw	1.1.42	Gavstn
I can no longer keepe me from my lord.	Edw	1.1.139	Gavstn
no soule in hell/Hath felt more torment then poore Gaveston.	Edw	1.1.146	Gavstn
I did no more then I was bound to do, ...	Edw	1.1.182	BshpCv
No, spare his life, but seaze upon his goods, . . .	Edw	1.1.193	Edward
Doth no man take exceptions at the slave?	Edw	1.2.25	MortSr
No, but weele lift Gaveston from hence.	Edw	1.2.62	Lncstr
For no where else the new earle is so safe. . . .	Edw	1.4.11	Lncstr
We are no traitors, therefore threaten not. . . .	Edw	1.4.25	MortSr
No, threaten not my lord, but pay them home. . . .	Edw	1.4.26	Gavstn
Be it or no, he shall not linger here.	Edw	1.4.93	MortSr
For no where else seekes he felicitie.	Edw	1.4.122	Gavstn
That whether I will or no thou must depart: . . .	Edw	1.4.124	Edward
I say no more, judge you the rest my lord. . . .	Edw	1.4.148	Gavstn
No, rather will I die a thousand deaths, ...	Edw	1.4.196	Queene
No speaking will prevaile, and therefore cease. . .	Edw	1.4.220	Penbrk
No? doe but marke how earnestly she pleads. . . .	Edw	1.4.234	Warwck
I hope your honors make no question, ...	Edw	1.4.240	Mortmr
In no respect can contraries be true.	Edw	1.4.249	Lncstr
No other jewels hang about my neck/Then these my lord, nor let	Edw	1.4.330	Queene
Deserves no common place, nor meane reward: . . .	Edw	1.4.361	Edward
Spare for no cost, we will requite your love. . . .	Edw	1.4.383	Edward
No, his companion, for he loves me well, ...	Edw	2.1.13	Spencr
No sooner is it up, but thers a foule, ...	Edw	2.2.26	Lncstr
No more then I would answere were he slaine. . . .	Edw	2.2.86	Mortmr
Cosin it is no dealing with him now, ...	Edw	2.2.102	Lncstr
Out of my sight, and trouble me no more.	Edw	2.2.216	Edward
No marvell though thou scorne thy noble peeres, . .	Edw	2.2.217	Kent
Poore Gaveston, that hast no friend but me, . . .	Edw	2.2.220	Edward
No greater titles happen unto me, ...	Edw	2.2.254	Spencr
No, here he comes, now let them spoile and kill: . .	Edw	2.4.3	Edward
No farewell, to poore Isabell, thy Queene?	Edw	2.4.13	Queene
No madam, but that cursed Gaveston.	Edw	2.4.32	Lncstr
Forslowe no time, sweet Lancaster lets march. . . .	Edw	2.4.40	Warwck
No Mortimer, ile to my lord the king.	Edw	2.4.51	Queene
Looke for no other fortune wretch then death, . . .	Edw	2.5.17	Lncstr
No, it needeth not.	Edw	2.5.42	Warwck
Arundell no,/We wot, he that the care of realme remits, .	Edw	2.5.60	Warwck
Strive you no longer, I will have that Gaveston. . .	Edw	2.6.7	Warwck
No James, it is my countries cause I follow. . . .	Edw	2.6.10	Warwck
The king of heaven perhaps, no other king, ...	Edw	2.6.16	Warwck
No doubt, such lessons they will teach the rest, . .	Edw	3.1.21	Spencr
Away, tarrie no answer, but be gon.	Edw	3.1.173	Edward
No Edward, no, thy flatterers faint and flie. . . .	Edw	3.1.201	Mortmr
No Edward, Englands scourge, it may not be, ...	Edw	3.1.258	Mortmr
Have you no doubts my lords, ile [clap so] <claps> close,/Among	Edw	3.1.276	Levune
A brother, no, a butcher of thy friends, ...	Edw	4.1.4	Kent
that we can yet be tun'd together,/No, no, we jarre too farre.	Edw	4.2.10	Queene
No my lord Mortimer, not I, I trow.	Edw	4.2.44	Prince
I would it were no worse,/But gentle lords, friendles we are in	Edw	4.2.45	Queene
As Isabella <Isabell> gets no aide from thence. . . .	Edw	4.3.16	Edward
O no my lord, this princely resolution/Fits not the time, away,	Edw	4.5.8	Baldck
Have you no doubt my Lorde, have you no feare, . . .	Edw	4.7.1	Abbot
Father, thy face should harbor no deceit, ...	Edw	4.7.8	Edward
this drowsines/Betides no good, here even we are betraied.	Edw	4.7.45	Spencr
Spencer and Baldocke, by no other names, ...	Edw	4.7.56	Leistr
No, tis for Mortimer, not Edwards head, ...	Edw	5.1.40	Edward
And therefore say, will you resigne or no.	Edw	5.1.85	Trussl
Call thou them back, I have no power to speake. . .	Edw	5.1.93	Edward
no, these innocent hands of mine/Shall not be guiltie of so	Edw	5.1.98	Edward
To set his brother free, no more but so.	Edw	5.2.33	BshpWn
and in any case/Let no man comfort him, if he chaunce to weepe,	Edw	5.2.64	Mortmr
No, God forbid.	Edw	5.2.99	Queene
Will hatefull Mortimer appoint no rest?	Edw	5.3.5	Edward
No, but wash your face, and shave away your beard, . .	Edw	5.3.31	Gurney
Twixt theirs and yours, shall be no enmitie. . . .	Edw	5.3.46	Matrvs
No?	Edw	5.4.44	Ltborn
No,/Unlesse thou bring me newes of Edwards death. . .	Edw	5.4.45	Mortmr
And whether I have limmes or no, I know not. . . .	Edw	5.5.65	Edward
O speake no more my lorde, this breakes my heart. . .	Edw	5.5.71	Ltborn
No, no, for if thou meanst to murther me, ...	Edw	5.5.98	Edward
But hath your grace no other proofe then this? . . .	Edw	5.6.43	Mortmr
And seeing there was no place to mount up higher, . .	Edw	5.6.62	Mortmr
I spill his bloud? no.	Edw	5.6.72	Queene
Affoords this Art no greater miracle?	F 37	1.1.9	Faust
Then read no more, thou hast attain'd that <the> end; . .	F 38	1.1.10	Faust
If we say that we have no sinne we deceive our selves, and	F 69	1.1.41	P Faust
we deceive our selves, and there is <theres> no truth in us.	F 70	1.1.42	P Faust
[That will receive no object, for my head]/[But ruminates on	F 131	1.1.103A	Faust
[Now <No> Faustus, thou art Conjurer laureate]/[That canst	F 260	1.3.32A	Faust
No more then he commands, must we performe. . . .	F 270	1.3.42	Mephst
No, I came now hether of mine owne accord.	F 272	1.3.44	Mephst
There is no chiefe but onely Beelzebub:	F 284	1.3.56	Faust
Sirra, hast thou no commings in?	F 346	1.4.4	P Wagner
No slave, in beaten silke, and staves-aker.	F 357	1.4.15	P Wagner
Why so thou shalt be, whether thou dost it or no: . .	F 360	1.4.18	P Wagner

NO (cont.)

Now go not backward: no, Faustus, be resolute.	F 394	2.1.6		Faust
No Faustus, thinke of honour and of wealth.	F 410	2.1.22		BdAngl
Cast no more doubts; Mephostophilis come/And bring glad tydings	F 415	2.1.27		Faust
My bloud congeales, and I can write no more.	F 451	2.1.63		Faust
Hell hath no limits, nor is circumscrib'd,	F 510	2.1.122		Mephst
[Tush] <No>, these are trifles, and meere old wives Tales.	F 524	2.1.136		Faust
Here's a hot whore indeed; no, I'le no wife.	F 534	2.1.146		Faust
And if thou lovest me thinke no more of it.	F 536	2.1.148		Mephst
Hath Mephostophilis no greater skill?	F 601	2.2.50		Faust
No Faustus they be but Fables.	F 613	2.2.62	P	Mephst
my selfe when I could get none <had no body> to fight withall:	F 689	2.2.138	P	Wrath
<No, Ile see thee hanged, thou wilt eate up all my victualls>.	F 702	(HC264)A	P	Faust
And cause we are no common guests,	F 805	3.1.27		Mephst
<Tut, tis no matter man>, wee'l be bold with his <good cheare>.	F 808	(HC265)A	P	Mephst
No bigger then my hand in quantity.	F 851	3.1.73		Faust
That no eye may thy body see.	F1003	3.2.23		Mephst
Faustus no more: see where the Cardinals come.	F1008	3.2.28		Mephst
Your Grace mistakes, you gave us no such charge.	F1024	3.2.44		1Card
'Tis no matter, let him come; an he follow us, I'le so conjure	F1091	3.3.4	P	Robin
Your grace demand no questions of the King,	F1251	4.1.97		Faust
hold, tis no matter for thy head, for that's arm'd sufficiently.	F1288	4.1.134	P	Emper
the Doctor has no skill,/No Art, no cunning, to present these	F1294	4.1.140		Faust
No Art, no cunning, to present these Lords,	F1295	4.1.141		Faust
No words:	F1362	4.2.38		Benvol
Nay feare not man, we have no power to kill.	F1440	4.3.10		Mrtino
I have no great need to sell him, but if thou likest him for	F1460	4.4.4	P	Faust
and one to whom I must be no niggard of my cunning; Come,	F1504	4.4.48	P	Faust
No Robin, why is't?	F1510	4.5.6	P	Dick
I there's no doubt of that, for me thinkes you make no hast to	F1516	4.5.12	P	Hostss
doubt of that, for me thinkes you make no hast to wipe it out.	F1516	4.5.12	P	Hostss
and he would by no meanes sell him under forty Dollors; so sir,	F1537	4.5.33	P	HrsCsr
bad me ride him night and day, and spare him no time; but,	F1540	4.5.36	P	HrsCsr
that you have taken no pleasure in those sights; therefor I	F1566	4.6.9	P	Faust
I would request no better meate, then a dish of ripe grapes.	F1573	4.6.16	P	Lady
We have no reason for it, therefore a fig for him.	F1593	4.6.36	P	Dick
No faith, not much upon a woodden leg.	F1631	4.6.74		Faust
No in good sooth.	F1640	4.6.83	P	Faust
No truelie sir, I would make nothing of you, but I would faine	F1648	4.6.91	P	Carter
No [otherwaies] <otherwise> for pompe or <and> Majesty,	F1693	5.1.20		Faust
[No marvel tho the angry Greekes pursu'd]/[With tenne yeares	F1699	5.1.26A		3Schol
No mortall can expresse the paines of hell.	F1716	5.1.43		OldMan
I, Faustus, now thou hast no hope of heaven,	F1880	5.2.84		Mephst
Hell, or the Divell, had had no power on thee.	F1902	5.2.106		GdAngl
No, [no]?	F1947	5.2.151		Faust
Gape earth; O no, it will not harbour me.	F1949	5.2.153		Faust
<O> No end is limited to damned soules.	F1963	5.2.167		Faust
No Faustus, curse thy selfe, curse Lucifer,	F1973	5.2.177		Faust
No sirra, in beaten silke and staves acre.	F App	p.229 16	P	Wagner
So thou shalt, whether thou beest with me, or no:	F App	p.229 22	P	Wagner
No, no, here take your gridirons againe.	F App	p.230 38	P	Clown
no, no sir, if you turne me into any thing, let it be in the	F App	p.231 61	P	Clown
Heere's no body, if it like your Holynesse.	F App	p.231 4	P	Frier
will no man looke?	F App	p.231 9	P	Pope
Well use that tricke no more, I would advise you.	F App	p.232 19		Faust
No more sweete Rafe, letts goe and make cleane our bootes which	F App	p.234 32	P	Robin
our horses shal eate no hay as long as this lasts.	F App	p.234 3	P	Robin
thou hast no goblet.	F App	p.235 27	P	Vintnr
thou doest, thou shalt be no wayes prejudiced or indamaged.	F App	p.236 9	P	Emper
No sir, but when Acteon died, he left the hornes for you:	F App	p.237 55	P	Faust
or moale in her necke, how shal I know whether it be so or no?	F App	p.238 62	P	Emper
Sure these are no spirites, but the true substantiall bodies of	F App	p.238 64	P	Emper
theres no haste but good, are you remembred how you crossed me	F App	p.238 76	P	Faust
Alas sir, I have no more, I pray you speake for me.	F App	p.239 104	P	HrsCsr
by him, for he bade me I should ride him into no water; now,	F App	p.240 131	P	HrsCsr
I was no sooner in the middle of the pond, but my horse vanisht	F App	p.240 134	P	HrsCsr
No, will you not wake?	F App	p.241 153	P	HrsCsr
to whom I must be no niggard of my cunning, come	F App	p.241 171	P	Faust
you take no delight in this, I have heard that great bellied	F App	p.242 4	P	Faust
I would desire no better meate then a dish of ripe grapes.	F App	p.242 10	P	Duchss
As no commiseration may expel,	F App	p.243 43		OldMan
And where stiffe winter whom no spring resolves,	Lucan, First Booke	17		
nor Hanniball/Art cause, no forraine foe could so afflict us,	Lucan, First Booke	31		
for Nero (then unborne) the fates/Would find no other meanes,	Lucan, First Booke	34		
[There] <Their> Caesar may'st thou shine and no cloud dim thee;	Lucan, First Booke	59		
Affording it no shoare, and Phoebe's waine/Chace Phoebus and	Lucan, First Booke	77		
men so strong/By land, and sea, no forraine force could ruine:	Lucan, First Booke	83		
This need no forraine proofe, nor far fet story:	Lucan, First Booke	94		
alwaies scorn'd/A second place; Pompey could bide no equall,	Lucan, First Booke	125		
Nor Caesar no superior, which of both/Had justest cause	Lucan, First Booke	126		
Caesar; he whom I heare thy trumpets charge/I hould no Romaine;	Lucan, First Booke	375		
No vaine sprung out but from the yawning gash,	Lucan, First Booke	613		
Why grapples Rome, and makes war, having no foes?	Lucan, First Booke	681		
I have no mistris, nor no favorit,	Ovid's Elegies	1.1.23		
I am no halfe horse, nor in woods I dwell,	Ovid's Elegies	1.4.9		
To him I pray it no delight may bring,	Ovid's Elegies	1.4.67		
Or if it do, to thee no joy thence spring:	Ovid's Elegies	1.4.68		
no darke night-flying spright/Nor hands prepar'd to slaughter,	Ovid's Elegies	1.6.13		
no threats or prayers move thee,/O harder then the dores thou	Ovid's Elegies	1.6.61		
No pritty wenches keeper maist thou bee:	Ovid's Elegies	1.6.63		
Slaughter and mischiefs instruments, no better,	Ovid's Elegies	1.7.27		
Aye me, thy body hath no worthy weedes.	Ovid's Elegies	1.8.26		
When thou hast so much as he gives no more,	Ovid's Elegies	1.8.101		

NO (cont.)

The gods send thee no house, a poore old age,	Ovid's Elegies	1.8.113
No more this beauty mine eyes captivates.	Ovid's Elegies	1.10.10
And hath no cloathes, but open doth remaine.	Ovid's Elegies	1.10.16
He hath no bosome, where to hide base pelfe.	Ovid's Elegies	1.10.18
Yet thinke no scorne to aske a wealthy churle,	Ovid's Elegies	1.10.53
He wants no gifts into thy lap to hurle.	Ovid's Elegies	1.10.54
Nape free-borne, whose cunning hath no border,	Ovid's Elegies	1.11.2
Be sedulous, let no stay cause thee tarry.	Ovid's Elegies	1.11.8
The number two no good divining bringes.	Ovid's Elegies	1.12.28
I chid no more, she blusht, and therefore heard me,	Ovid's Elegies	1.13.47
Now hast thou left no haires at all to die.	Ovid's Elegies	1.14.2
And did to thee no cause of dolour raise.	Ovid's Elegies	1.14.14
Farre off be force, no fire to them may reach,	Ovid's Elegies	1.14.29
No charmed herbes of any harlot skathd thee,	Ovid's Elegies	1.14.39
No faithlesse witch in Thessale waters bath'd thee.	Ovid's Elegies	1.14.40
No sicknesse harm'd thee, farre be that a way,	Ovid's Elegies	1.14.41
No envious tongue wrought thy thicke lockes decay.	Ovid's Elegies	1.14.42
defence/When [un-protected] <un-protested> ther is no expence?	Ovid's Elegies	2.2.12
Condemne his eyes, and say there is no tryall.	Ovid's Elegies	2.2.58
No one face likes me best, all faces moove,	Ovid's Elegies	2.4.9
And she thats coy I like for being no clowne,	Ovid's Elegies	2.4.13
[And nut-browne girles in doing have no fellowe].	Ovid's Elegies	2.4.40
No love is so dere (quiverd Cupid flie)/That my chiefe wish	Ovid's Elegies	2.5.1
No intercepted lines thy deedes display,	Ovid's Elegies	2.5.5
No gifts given secretly thy crime bewray.	Ovid's Elegies	2.5.6
This grieves me not, no joyned kisses spent,	Ovid's Elegies	2.5.59
No where can they be taught but in the bed,	Ovid's Elegies	2.5.61
I know no maister of so great hire sped.	Ovid's Elegies	2.5.62
No such voice-feigning bird was on the ground,	Ovid's Elegies	2.6.23
Envy hath rapt thee, no fierce warres thou movedst,	Ovid's Elegies	2.6.25
Our pleasant scapes shew thee no clowne to be,	Ovid's Elegies	2.8.3
What graced Kings, in me no shame I deeme.	Ovid's Elegies	2.8.14
Within my brest no desert empire beare.	Ovid's Elegies	2.9.52
O would that no Oares might in seas have suncke,	Ovid's Elegies	2.11.5
Thou shalt admire no woods or Citties there,	Ovid's Elegies	2.11.11
The Ocean hath no painted stones or shelles,	Ovid's Elegies	2.11.13
what each one speakes/Beleeve, no tempest the beleever wreakes.	Ovid's Elegies	2.11.22
In all thy face will be no crimsen bloud.	Ovid's Elegies	2.11.28
No little ditched townes, no lowlie walles,	Ovid's Elegies	2.12.7
But I no partner of my glory brooke,	Ovid's Elegies	2.12.11
with loving may/Had seene, my mother killing me, [no] <to> day.	Ovid's Elegies	2.14.22
Life is no light price of a small surcease.	Ovid's Elegies	2.14.26
And my presages of no weight be thought.	Ovid's Elegies	2.14.42
No barking Dogs that Syllaes intrailes beare,	Ovid's Elegies	2.16.23
No flowing waves with drowned ships forth poured,	Ovid's Elegies	2.16.25
My stay no crime, my flight no joy shall breede,	Ovid's Elegies	2.17.25
Foole if to keepe thy wife thou hast no neede,	Ovid's Elegies	2.19.1
Thou doest beginne, she shall be mine no longer.	Ovid's Elegies	2.19.48
Thou suffrest what no husband can endure,	Ovid's Elegies	2.19.51
From no mans reading fearing to be sav'd.	Ovid's Elegies	3.1.54
no warres we move,/Peace pleaseth me, and in mid peace is love.	Ovid's Elegies	3.2.49
God is a name, no substance, feard in vaine,	Ovid's Elegies	3.3.23
Or in mine eyes good wench no paine transfuse.	Ovid's Elegies	3.3.48
Penelope, though no watch look'd unto her,	Ovid's Elegies	3.4.23
A free-borne wench, no right 'tis up to locke:	Ovid's Elegies	3.4.33
Thou hast no bridge, nor boate with ropes to throw,	Ovid's Elegies	3.5.3
If standing here I can by no meanes get,	Ovid's Elegies	3.5.11
(Trust me) land-streame thou shalt no envie lack,	Ovid's Elegies	3.5.21
Shame, that should make me blush, I have no more.	Ovid's Elegies	3.5.78
Thou hast no name, but com'st from snowy mountaines;	Ovid's Elegies	3.5.91
No certaine house thou hast, nor any fountaines.	Ovid's Elegies	3.5.92
And fruit from trees, when ther's no wind at al.	Ovid's Elegies	3.6.34
My idle thoughts delighted her no more,	Ovid's Elegies	3.6.39
Lie downe with shame, and see thou stirre no more,	Ovid's Elegies	3.6.69
But when she saw it would by no meanes stand,	Ovid's Elegies	3.6.75
In hell were harbourd, here was found no masse.	Ovid's Elegies	3.7.38
With strong plough shares no man the earth did cleave,	Ovid's Elegies	3.7.41
The ditcher no markes on the ground did leave.	Ovid's Elegies	3.7.42
A clowne, nor no love from her warme brest yeelds.	Ovid's Elegies	3.9.18
Ceres, I thinke, no knowne fault will deny.	Ovid's Elegies	3.9.24
And calves from whose feard front no threatning flyes,	Ovid's Elegies	3.12.15
Forbare no wanton words you there would speake,	Ovid's Elegies	3.13.25
She ware no gloves for neither sunne nor wind/Would burne or	Hero and Leander	1.27
The reason no man knowes, let it suffise,	Hero and Leander	1.173
Receives no blemish, but oft-times more grace,	Hero and Leander	1.217
One is no number, mayds are nothing then,	Hero and Leander	1.255
No, nor to any one exterior sence,	Hero and Leander	1.271
Of that which hath no being, doe not boast,	Hero and Leander	1.275
in being bold/To eie those parts, which no eie should behold.	Hero and Leander	1.408
vowd he love, she wanting no excuse/To feed him with delaies,	Hero and Leander	1.425
Then muse not, Cupids sute no better sped,	Hero and Leander	1.483
No marvell then, though Hero would not yeeld/So soone to part	Hero and Leander	2.83
But still the rising billowes answered no.	Hero and Leander	2.152
You are deceav'd, I am no woman I.	Hero and Leander	2.192
Neptune was angrie that hee gave no eare,	Hero and Leander	2.207
Which watchfull Hesperus no sooner heard,	Hero and Leander	2.329

NOBILITIE

Whereas Nobilitie abhors to stay,	Dido	4.3.19	Aeneas
and vallours be advaunst/To roomes of honour and Nobilitie.	1Tamb	2.3.41	Cosroe
Image of Honor and Nobilitie.	1Tamb	5.1.75	1Virgn
And of my Lords whose true nobilitie/Have merited my latest	2Tamb	2.4.73	Zenoc
Should beare us downe of the nobilitie,	Edw	1.4.286	Mortmr

Line	Work	Ref.		Speaker
NOBILITIE (cont.)				
not suffer thus your majestie/Be counterbuft of your nobilitie.	Edw	3.1.19		Spencr
To cherish vertue and nobilitie,	Edw	3.1.167		Herald
England, unkinde to thy nobilitie,	Edw	3.1.250		Mortmr
NOBILITY				
And fashions men with true nobility.	1Tamb	5.1.190		Tamb
For deeds of bounty or nobility:	2Tamb	4.1.152		Tamb
NOBIS				
Si peccasse negamus, fallimur, et nulla est in nobis veritas:	F 68	1.1.40	P	Faust
per vota nostra ipse nunc surgat nobis dicatus Mephostophilis.	F 250	1.3.22	P	Faust
Misericordia pro nobis, what shal I doe?	F App	p.235 30	P	Robin
NOBLE				
Like Illioneus speakes this Noble man,	Dido	2.1.47		Achat
But I refer me to my noble men,	1Tamb	1.1.21		Mycet
The plot is laid by Persean Noble men,	1Tamb	1.1.110		Cosroe
Noble and milde this Persean seemes to be,	1Tamb	1.2.162		Tamb
Are <To> <Ah> these resolved noble Scythians?	1Tamb	1.2.225		Therid
Nor thee, nor them, thrice noble Tamburlain,	1Tamb	1.2.249		Therid
And now faire Madam, and my noble Lords,	1Tamb	1.2.253		Tamb
In faire Persea noble Tamburlaine/Shall be my Regent, and	1Tamb	2.1.48		Cosroe
Then noble souldiors, to intrap these theeves,	1Tamb	2.2.59		Meandr
And cry me mercie, noble King.	1Tamb	2.4.22		Mycet
And might in noble minds be counted princely.	1Tamb	3.2.39		Zenoc
he persecutes/The noble Turke and his great Emperesse?	1Tamb	4.3.27		Arabia
But noble Lord of great Arabia,	1Tamb	4.3.29		Souldn
What saith the noble Souldane and Zenocrate?	1Tamb	5.1.495		Tamb
Environed with troopes of noble men,	1Tamb	5.1.526		Tamb
Arme dread Soveraign and my noble Lords.	2Tamb	2.2.24		1Msngr
Wel then my noble Lords, for this my friend,	2Tamb	3.1.68		Callap
Beleeve me, Noble Lodowicke, I have seene/The strangest sight,	Jew	1.2.375		Mthias
My noble sonne, and princely Duke of Guise,	P 203	4.1		QnMoth
Besides my heart relentes that noble men,	P 211	4.9		Charls
To hurt the noble man their soveraign loves.	P 259	4.57		Charls
see they keep/All trecherous violence from our noble freend,	P 268	4.66		Charls
We know that noble mindes change not their thoughts/For wearing	P 610	12.23		Mugern
How many noble men have lost their lives,	P 795	16.9		Navrre
My noble brother murthered by the King,	P1107	21.1		Dumain
That durst attempt to murder noble Guise.	P1121	21.15		Dumain
What man of noble birth can brooke this sight?	Edw	1.4.12		MortSr
You that be noble borne should pitie him.	Edw	1.4.80		Edward
And feare to offend the meanest noble man.	Edw	1.4.277		Mortmr
Or making lowe legs to a noble man,	Edw	2.1.38		Spencr
No marvell though thou scorne thy noble peeres,	Edw	2.2.217		Kent
But for we know thou art a noble gentleman,	Edw	2.5.68		Mortmr
Long live my soveraigne the noble Edward,	Edw	3.1.32		SpncrP
Argues thy noble minde and disposition:	Edw	3.1.48		Edward
A noble attempt, and honourable deed,	Edw	3.1.206		SpncrP
Unnaturall king, to slaughter noble men/And cherish flatterers:	Edw	4.1.8		Kent
But droope not madam, noble mindes contemne/Despaire:	Edw	4.2.16		SrJohn
The Marques is a noble Gentleman,	Edw	4.2.32		Queene
Mounsier le Grand, a noble friend of yours,	Edw	4.2.47		Mortmr
This noble gentleman, forward in armes,	Edw	4.2.76		Mortmr
Ere farther we proceede my noble lordes,	Edw	4.6.23		Queene
is noble Edward gone,/Parted from hence, never to see us more!	Edw	4.7.100		Spencr
not a thought so villanous/Can harbor in a man of noble birth.	Edw	5.1.132		Bartly
Make hast to help these noble Gentlemen,	F1421	4.2.97		1Soldr
Then wilt thou Laedas noble twinne-starres pray,	Ovid's Elegies			2.11.29
I sit not here the noble horse to see,	Ovid's Elegies			3.2.1
Now wish I those wings noble Perseus had,	Ovid's Elegies			3.5.13
How wouldst thou flowe wert thou a noble floud,	Ovid's Elegies			3.5.89
NOBLEMEN				
And all thy needie followers Noblemen?	Dido	5.1.164		Dido
at whose pallace now]/[Faustus is feasted mongst his noblemen].	F1152	3.3.65A		3Chor
NOBLES				
Heere comes the king and the nobles/From the parlament, ile	Edw	1.1.72		Gavstn
And when the commons and the nobles joyne,	Edw	1.4.287		Mortmr
My gentle lord, bespeake these nobles faire,	Edw	1.4.337		Queene
Which of the nobles dost thou meane to serve?	Edw	2.1.3		Baldck
For now the wrathfull nobles threaten warres,	Edw	2.2.210		Kent
And drives his nobles to these exigents/For Gaveston, will if	Edw	2.5.62		Warwck
Away base upstart, brav'st thou nobles thus?	Edw	3.1.205		Penbrk
How hard the nobles, how unkinde the king/Hath shewed himself:	Edw	4.2.49		Mortmr
That Englands Queene, and nobles in distresse,	Edw	4.2.79		Mortmr
My nobles rule, I beare the name of king,	Edw	5.1.28		Edward
and whose tongue/Could tune the people to the Nobles mind:	Lucan, First Booke			273
NOBLY				
Nobly resolv'd, sweet friends and followers.	1Tamb	1.2.60		Tamb
Nobly resolv'd, my good Ortygius.	1Tamb	2.6.24		Cosroe
That nobly must admit necessity:	2Tamb	5.3.201		Tamb
NO BODY				
I have don't, but no body knowes it but you two, I may escape.	Jew	4.1.180	P	1Fryar
my selfe when I could get none <had no body> to fight withall:	F 689	2.2.138	P	Wrath
Heere's no body, if it like your Holynesse.	F App	p.231 4	P	Frier
NOCERE				
Major sum quam cui possit fortuna nocere.	Edw	5.4.69		Mortmr
NOCTIS				
O lente lente currite noctis equi:	F1935	5.2.139		Faust
NOD				
Not a wise word, only gave me a nod, as who shold say, Is it	Jew	4.2.12	P	Pilia
Though every blast it nod, and seeme to fal,	Lucan, First Booke			142
NODDING				
Nodding and shaking of thy spangled crest,	Edw	2.2.186		Mortmr
I sawe your nodding eye-browes much to speake,	Ovid's Elegies			2.5.15

NODS
He nods, and scornes, and smiles at those that passe. . Edw 1.2.24 Warwck
NOINT
With which if you but noint your tender Skin, ... 2Tamb 4.2.65 Olymp
To proove it, I wil noint my naked throat, ... 2Tamb 4.2.68 Olymp
NOISE (See also NOYSE)
And with the noise turnes up my giddie braine, . . . Edw 1.4.314 Edward
How now, what noise is this? . . . . Edw 2.2.139 Edward
There spred the colours, with confused noise/Of trumpets clange, Lucan, First Booke 239
heard to sound; and with what noise/An armed battaile joines, Lucan, First Booke 577
To get the dore with little noise unbard. . . . . Ovid's Elegies 3.1.50
And knockt and cald, at which celestiall noise, . . Hero and Leander 2.231
NOISOME (See also NOYSOME)
Than noisome parbreak of the Stygian Snakes, ... 1Tamb 5.1.256 Bajzth
NOLITE
Edwardum occidere nolite timere bonum est. . . . . Edw 5.4.8 Mortmr
Edwardum occidere nolite timere bonum est. . . . . Edw 5.4.11 Mortmr
Edwardum occidere nolite timere, ... Edw 5.5.17 Matrvs
NOMINE
O nomine Domine, what meanst thou Robin? . . . . . F App p.235 26 P Vintnr
NON (Homograph)
Italiam non sponte sequor. . . . . Dido 5.1.140 Aeneas
a non-plus at the critical aspect of my terrible countenance. Jew 4.2.13 P Pilia
Exhereditare filium non potest pater, nisi--Such is the . F 58 1.1.30 P Faust
NONCE
And suite themselves in purple for the nonce, ... Dido 1.1.206 Venus
Gurney, it was left unpointed for the nonce, ... Edw 5.5.16 Matrvs
NONE
For none of these can be our Generall. . . . . . Dido 2.1.46 Illion
But tell them none shall gaze on him but I, ... Dido 3.1.73 Dido
But speake Aeneas, know you none of these? . . . . Dido 3.1.148 Dido
Yet none obtaind me, I am free from all.-- . . . . Dido 3.1.153 Dido
And none but base Aeneas will abide: . . . . . . Dido 4.3.20 Aeneas
None in the world shall have my love but thou: . . . . Dido 5.1.290 Dido
So, leave me now, let none approach this place. . . . Dido 5.1.291 Dido
And none shall keepe the crowne but Tamburlaine: . . . 1Tamb 2.5.7 Cosroe
That none can quence but blood and Emperie. . . . . 1Tamb 2.6.33 Cosroe
Here Madam, you are Empresse, she is none. . . . . 1Tamb 3.3.227 Therid
I (my Lord) but none save kinges must feede with these. . 1Tamb 4.4.109 P Therid
She lies so close that none can find her out. . . . . 2Tamb 1.2.60 Callap
And few or none shall perish by their shot. . . . . 2Tamb 3.3.45 Therid
For he is God alone, and none but he. . . . . . 2Tamb 5.1.202 Tamb
To make a Nunnery, where none but their owne sect/Must enter in; Jew 1.2.256 Abigal
And few or none scape but by being purg'd. . . . . Jew 2.3.106 Barab
Be mov'd at nothing, see thou pitty none, ... Jew 2.3.171 Barab
And now, save Pilia-borza, comes there none. . . . . Jew 3.1.9 Curtzn
To fast and be well whipt; I'le none of that. . . . . Jew 4.1.124 Barab
No, none can heare him, cry he ne're so loud. . . . . Jew 4.1.136 Ithimr
goe whither he will, I'le be none of his followers in haste: Jew 4.2.25 P Ithimr
Nay, I'le have all or none. . . . . Jew 4.4.5 Curtzn
What wudst thou doe if he should send thee none? . . . Jew 4.4.13 Pilia
For none of this can prejudice my life. . . . . . Jew 5.1.39 Barab
Whence none can possibly escape alive: . . . . . . Jew 5.5.31 Barab
Yet understoode by none. . . . . P 112 2.55 Guise
I am disguisde and none knows who I am, ... P 278 5.5 Anjoy
Let none escape, murder the Hugonets. . . . . . P 337 5.64 Guise
Tue, tue, tue, let none escape: . . . . P 534 10.7 Guise
Flourish in France, and none deny the same. . . . . P 640 12.53 QnMoth
I know none els but holdes them in disgrace: . . . . P 764 15.22 Guise
thoughe you take out none but your owne treasure . . . Paris ms 3,p390 P Souldr
My knee shall bowe to none but to the king. . . . . Edw 1.1.19 Gavstn
All stomack him, but none dare speake a word. . . . . Edw 1.2.26 Lncstr
Ah none but rude and savage minded men, ... Edw 1.4.78 Edward
Theres none here, but would run his horse to death. . . . Edw 1.4.207 Warwck
Then thus, but none shal heare it but our selves. . . . Edw 1.4.229 Queene
And none so much as blame the murtherer, ... Edw 1.4.267 Mortmr
I am none of these common [pedants] <pendants> I, ... Edw 2.1.52 Baldck
Will none of you salute my Gaveston? . . . . . . Edw 2.2.64 Edward
None be so hardie as to touche the King, ... Edw 2.3.27 Lncstr
Heavens can witnesse, I love none but you. . . . . Edw 2.4.15 Queene
Whose eyes are fixt on none but Gaveston: . . . . . Edw 2.4.62 Queene
grace may sit secure, if none but wee/Doe wot of your abode. Edw 4.7.26 Monk
For friends hath Edward none, but these, and these, . . . Edw 4.7.91 Edward
And in this torment, comfort finde I none, ... Edw 5.1.81 Edward
And none but we shall know where he lieth. . . . . . Edw 5.2.41 Mortmr
I, I, and none shall know which way he died. . . . . Edw 5.4.25 Ltborn
Nay, you shall pardon me, none shall knowe my trickes. . . Edw 5.4.39 Ltborn
and Mortimer/Shall rule the realme, the king, and none rule us, Edw 5.4.66 Mortmr
None comes, sound trumpets. . . . . Edw 5.4.79 Mortmr
And none of both [them] <then> thirst for Edmunds bloud. . . Edw 5.4.107 Kent
All tremble at my name, and I feare none, ... Edw 5.6.13 Mortmr
Here, take your Guilders [againe], I'le none of 'em. . . F 371 1.4.29 P Robin
There's none but I have interest in the same. . . . . F 637 2.2.86 Lucifr
my selfe when I could get none <had no body> to fight withall: F 689 2.2.138 P Wrath
And therefore none of his Decrees can stand. . . . . F 929 3.1.151 Pope
And none but thou shalt be my Paramour. . . . . . F1787 5.1.114 Faust
Truly Ile none of them. . . . . F App p.230 39 P Wagner
how that none in my Empire, nor in the whole world can compare F App p.236 2 P Emper
I have none about me, come to my Oastrie, and Ile give them F App p.241 161 P HrsCsr
whispered they, and none durst speake/And shew their feare, Lucan, First Booke 259
This spoke none answer'd, but a murmuring buz/Th'unstable Lucan, First Booke 353
Their houshould gods restrain them not, none lingered, . Lucan, First Booke 505
We are the Muses prophets, none of thine. . . . . . Ovid's Elegies 1.1.10

NONE (cont.)
Or lies he close, and shoots where none can spie him? . Ovid's Elegies 1.2.6
none thy face exceedes,/Aye me, thy body hath no worthy weedes. Ovid's Elegies 1.8.25
Faire women play, shee's chast whom none will have, . . Ovid's Elegies 1.8.43
Who can indure, save him with whom none lies? . . . Ovid's Elegies 1.13.26
None such the sister gives her brother grave, . . . Ovid's Elegies 2.5.25
The seventh day came, none following mightst thou see, . Ovid's Elegies 2.6.45
Worthy to keembe none but a Goddesse faire, . . . Ovid's Elegies 2.8.2
Let such as be mine enemies have none, ... Ovid's Elegies 2.10.16
But absent is my fire, lyes ile tell none, . . . Ovid's Elegies 2.16.11
Cruell is he, that loves whom none protect. . . . Ovid's Elegies 2.19.4
And I would be none of the Gods severe. . . . . Ovid's Elegies 3.3.46
Thee I have pass'd, and knew thy streame none such, . . Ovid's Elegies 3.5.5
To stay thy tresses white veyle hast thou none? . . Ovid's Elegies 3.5.56
Musaeus soong)/Dwelt at Abidus; since him, dwelt there none, Hero and Leander 1.53
To meet their loves; such as had none at all, . . . Hero and Leander 1.95
So faire a church as this, had Venus none, . . . Hero and Leander 1.135
When you fleet hence, can be bequeath'd to none. . . Hero and Leander 1.248
O none but gods have power their love to hide, . . Hero and Leander 2.131
Whose fruit none rightly can describe, but hee/That puls or Hero and Leander 2.299

NONES
Obed in Bairseth, Nones in Portugall, ... Jew 1.1.125 Barab

NONE SUCH
Thee I have pass'd, and knew thy streame none such, . . Ovid's Elegies 3.5.5

NON-PLUS
a non-plus at the critical aspect of my terrible countenance. Jew 4.2.13 P Pilia

NOOK
Tis but a nook of France,/Sufficient yet for such a pettie P 149 2.92 Guise

NOOKE
So I may have some nooke or corner left, ... Edw 1.4.72 Edward
They by Lemannus nooke forsooke their tents; . . . Lucan, First Booke 397

NOOKES
Which fils the nookes of Hell with standing aire, . . 1Tamb 5.1.257 Bajzth

NOONE
to run their course through empty night/At noone day mustered, Lucan, First Booke 535
And call the sunnes white horses [backe] <blacke> at noone. Ovid's Elegies 2.1.24

NOONE DAY
to run their course through empty night/At noone day mustered, Lucan, First Booke 535

NOOSE
Off with your girdle, make a hansom noose; . . . Jew 4.1.142 Barab

NOR
I neither saw nor heard of any such: . . . . . . Dido 1.1.187 Aeneas
Nor speech bewraies ought humaine in thy birth, . . . Dido 1.1.190 Aeneas
Nor armed to offend in any kind: . . . . . . Dido 1.2.13 Illion
And now am neither father, Lord, nor King: . . . . Dido 2.1.239 Aeneas
Nor Sterne nor Anchor have our maimed Fleete, . . . Dido 3.1.109 Aeneas
Nor Venus triumph in his tender youth: . . . . . Dido 3.2.9 Juno
Nor quit good turnes with double fee downe told: . . Dido 3.2.15 Juno
And cannot talke nor thinke of ought but him: . . . Dido 3.2.73 Juno
I may nor will list to such loathsome chaunge, . . . Dido 4.2.47 Iarbus
Nor blazing Commets threatens Didos death, ... Dido 4.4.119 Dido
Who have no sailes nor tackling for my ships? . . . Dido 5.1.56 Aeneas
And left me neither saile nor sterne abourd. . . . Dido 5.1.61 Aeneas
Which neither art nor reason may atchieve, ... Dido 5.1.65 Aeneas
Nor I devise by what meanes to contrive. . . . . Dido 5.1.66 Aeneas
Nor Dardanus the author of thy stocke: . . . . . Dido 5.1.157 Dido
Though thou nor he will pitie me a whit. . . . . Dido 5.1.178 Dido
Nor sent a thousand ships unto the walles, ... Dido 5.1.204 Dido
Nor ever violated faith to him: . . . . Dido 5.1.205 Dido
My teares nor plaints could mollifie a whit: . . . . Dido 5.1.235 Anna
Nor are Apollos Oracles more true, ... 1Tamb 1.2.212 Tamb
Nor thee, nor them, thrice noble Tamburlain, ... 1Tamb 1.2.249 Therid
nor by princely deeds/Doth meane to soare above the highest 1Tamb 2.7.32 Therid
Nor raise our siege before the Gretians yeeld, . . . 1Tamb 3.1.14 Bajzth
Nor Sun reflexe his vertuous beames thereon, ... 1Tamb 3.1.52 Moroc
Nor in Pharsalia was there such hot war, ... 1Tamb 3.3.154 Tamb
Nor shall they long be thine, I warrant them. . . . 1Tamb 4.4.119 Bajzth
Nor you depend on such weake helps as we. 1Tamb 5.1.33 1Virgn
Nor change my Martiall observations, ... 1Tamb 5.1.122 Tamb
nor the Turk/Troubled my sences with conceit of foile, . 1Tamb 5.1.157 Tamb
Fortune, nor no hope of end/To our infamous monstrous slaveries? 1Tamb 5.1.240 Zabina
No breath nor sence, nor motion in them both. . . . 1Tamb 5.1.344 Anippe
Nor fortune keep them selves from victory. . . . . 1Tamb 5.1.406 Arabia
Nor he but Fortune that hath made him great. . . . 2Tamb 1.1.60 Orcan
But neither man nor child in al the land: . . . . 2Tamb 1.3.197 Techel
In whom no faith nor true religion rests, ... 2Tamb 2.1.34 Baldwn
Nor in one place is circumscriptible, ... 2Tamb 2.2.50 Orcan
Nor Lesbia, nor Corrinna had bene nam'd, ... 2Tamb 2.4.93 Tamb
Nor [any] issue foorth, but they shall die: . . . . 2Tamb 3.3.33 Techel
Nor ere returne but with the victory, ... 2Tamb 3.5.44 Trebiz
Nor you in faith, but that you wil be thought/More childish 2Tamb 4.1.16 Calyph
Nor care for blood when wine wil quench my thirst. . . 2Tamb 4.1.30 Calyph
And should I goe and do nor harme nor good, ... 2Tamb 4.1.56 Calyph
Nor am I made Arch-monark of the world, ... 2Tamb 4.1.150 Tamb
Nor yet imposd, with such a bitter hate. . . . . . 2Tamb 4.1.170 Jrslem
Nor yet this aier, beat often with thy sighes, . . . 2Tamb 4.2.10 Olymp
Nor thy close Cave a sword to murther thee, ... 2Tamb 4.2.12 Olymp
Nor Pistol, Sword, nor Lance can pierce your flesh. . . 2Tamb 4.2.66 Olymp
Wherein he spareth neither man nor child, ... 2Tamb 5.1.30 1Citzn
nor the towne will never yeeld/As long as any life is in my 2Tamb 5.1.47 Govnr
down to the earth/Could not affright you, no, nor I my selfe, 2Tamb 5.1.91 Tamb
Nor if my body could have stopt the breach, ... 2Tamb 5.1.101 Govnr
Nor yet thy selfe, the anger of the highest, ... 2Tamb 5.1.104 Govnr

NOR (cont.)

Do all thy wurst, nor death, nor Tamburlaine,	2Tamb	5.1.112	Govnr
Nor plowman, Priest, nor Merchant staies at home,	2Tamb	5.2.50	Callap
Nor bar thy mind that magnanimitie,	2Tamb	5.3.200	Tamb
Nor may our hearts all drown'd in teares of blood,	2Tamb	5.3.214	Usumc
I neither saw them, nor inquir'd of them.	Jew	1.1.77	1Merch
I have no charge, nor many children,	Jew	1.1.136	Barab
Nor will I part so slightly therewithall.	Jew	1.2.87	Barab
No, I will live; nor loath I this my life:	Jew	1.2.266	Barab
Nor quiet enter my distemper'd thoughts,	Jew	2.1.18	Barab
Nor I the affection that I beare to you.	Jew	2.3.291	Barab
Nor e're shall see the land of Canaan,	Jew	2.3.303	Barab
Nor our Messias that is yet to come,	Jew	2.3.304	Barab
Here must no speeches passe, nor swords be drawne.	Jew	2.3.339	Barab
Nor on his sonne, but by Mathias meanes;	Jew	3.3.45	Abigal
Nor on Mathias, but by murdering me.	Jew	3.3.46	Abigal
Pitty in Jewes, nor piety in Turkes.	Jew	3.3.48	Abigal
Be blest of me, nor come within my gates,	Jew	3.4.31	Barab
Nor make enquiry who hath sent it them.	Jew	3.4.81	Barab
Nor shall the Heathens live upon our spoyle:	Jew	3.5.12	Govnr
As never Jew nor Christian knew the like:	Jew	4.1.118	Barab
Nor goe to bed, but sleepes in his owne clothes;	Jew	4.1.132	Ithimr
We two, and 'twas never knowne, nor never shall be for me.	Jew	4.4.23	P Ithimr
Nor me neither, I cannot out-run you Constable, oh my belly.	Jew	5.1.20	P Ithimr
And neither gets him friends, nor fils his bags,	Jew	5.2.39	Barab
Nor hope of thee but extreme cruelty,	Jew	5.2.59	Govnr
Nor feare I death, nor will I flatter thee.	Jew	5.2.60	Govnr
and let due praise be given/Neither to Fate nor Fortune, but to	Jew	5.5.124	Govnr
And he nor heares, nor sees us what we doe:	P 553	11.18	QnMoth
Nor will I aske forgivenes of the King.	P1006	19.76	Guise
Nor immortalitie to be reveng'd:	P1008	19.78	Guise
I cannot, nor I will not, I must speake.	Edw	1.1.122	Mortmr
We may not, nor we will not suffer this.	Edw	1.2.15	MortSr
about my neck/Then these my lord, nor let me have more wealth,	Edw	1.4.331	Queene
Deserves no common place, nor meane reward:	Edw	1.4.361	Edward
Not Mortimer, nor any of his side,	Edw	2.1.4	Spencr
She neither walkes abroad, nor comes in sight:	Edw	2.1.24	Baldck
Nor fowlest Harpie that shall swallow him.	Edw	2.2.46	Edward
But I respect neither their love nor hate.	Edw	2.2.261	Gavstn
But neither spare you Gaveston, nor his friends.	Edw	2.3.28	Lncstr
Never so cheereles, nor so farre distrest.	Edw	4.2.14	Queene
The king of England, nor the court of Fraunce,	Edw	4.2.22	Prince
Now on my life, theile neither barke nor bite.	Edw	4.3.13	Edward
Tis not in her controulment, nor in ours,	Edw	4.6.35	Mortmr
Yet gentle monkes, for treasure, golde nor fee,	Edw	4.7.24	Edward
And neither give him kinde word, nor good looke.	Edw	5.2.55	Mortmr
Nor I, and yet me thinkes I should commaund,	Edw	5.4.97	King
Nor shall they now be tainted with a kings.	Edw	5.5.82	Ltborn
Nor sporting in the dalliance of love/In Courts of Kings, where	F 3	Prol.3	1Chor
Nor in the pompe of proud audacious deeds,	F 5	Prol.5	1Chor
[Nor can they raise the winde, or rend the cloudes]:	F 86	1.1.58A	Faust
Nor will we come unlesse he use such meanes,	F 278	1.3.50	Mephst
Why this is hell: nor am I out of it.	F 304	1.3.76	Mephst
Nor any Potentate of Germany.	F 339	1.3.111	Faust
Hell hath no limits, nor is circumscrib'd,	F 510	2.1.122	Mephst
Nor are the names of Saturne, Mars, or Jupiter,	F 594	2.2.43	Mephst
Nor will [I] <Faustus> henceforth:	F 647	2.2.96	Faust
Talke not of Paradice or <nor> Creation, but marke the <this>	F 659	2.2.108	P Lucifr
I had neither father nor mother, I leapt out of a Lyons mouth	F 686	2.2.135	P Wrath
nor know I how sufficiently to recompence your great deserts	F1558	4.6.1	P Duke
nor in the whole world can compare with thee, for the rare	F App	p.236 3	P Emper
felow, and he has a great charge, neither wife nor childe.	F App	p.239 106	P Mephst
Fierce Pirhus, neither thou nor Hanniball/Art cause, no forraine	Lucan, First Booke	30	
nor Jove joide heaven/Untill the cruel Giants war was done)	Lucan, First Booke	35	
Nor yet the adverse reking southerne pole,	Lucan, First Booke	54	
This need no forraine proofe, nor far fet story:	Lucan, First Booke	94	
Nor then was land, or sea, to breed such hate,	Lucan, First Booke	96	
Nor Caesar no superior, which of both/Had justest cause	Lucan, First Booke	126	
Nor shalt thou triumph when thou comst to Roome;	Lucan, First Booke	287	
Nor capitall be adorn'd with sacred bayes:	Lucan, First Booke	288	
Neither spoile, nor kingdom seeke we by these armes,	Lucan, First Booke	351	
and where the north-west wind/Nor Zephir rules not, but the	Lucan, First Booke	408	
Which is nor sea, nor land, but oft times both,	Lucan, First Booke	411	
Nor were the Commons only strooke to heart/With this vaine	Lucan, First Booke	483	
in armes; nor could the bed-rid parents/Keep back their sons,	Lucan, First Booke	502	
I have no mistris, nor no favorit,	Ovid's Elegies	1.1.23	
I am no halfe horse, nor in woods I dwell,	Ovid's Elegies	1.4.9	
Nor let the windes away my warnings blowe.	Ovid's Elegies	1.4.12	
Nor [leane] <leave> thy soft head on his boistrous brest.	Ovid's Elegies	1.4.36	
Mingle not thighes, nor to his legge joyne thine,	Ovid's Elegies	1.4.43	
Nor thy soft foote with his hard foote combine.	Ovid's Elegies	1.4.44	
no darke night-flying spright/Nor hands prepar'd to slaughter,	Ovid's Elegies	1.6.14	
Nor servile water shalt thou drinke for ever.	Ovid's Elegies	1.6.26	
Nor thunder in rough threatings haughty pride?	Ovid's Elegies	1.7.46	
Nor shamefully her coate pull ore her crowne,	Ovid's Elegies	1.7.47	
Nor doth her tongue want harmefull eloquence.	Ovid's Elegies	1.8.20	
Nor one or two men are sufficient.	Ovid's Elegies	1.8.54	
Nor, so thou maist obtaine a wealthy prize,	Ovid's Elegies	1.8.63	
Nor let the armes of antient [lines] <lives> beguile thee,	Ovid's Elegies	1.8.65	
Nor, if thou couzenst one, dread to for-sweare,	Ovid's Elegies	1.8.85	
Nor let my words be with the windes hence blowne,	Ovid's Elegies	1.8.106	
he doth not chide/Nor to hoist saile attends fit time and tyde.	Ovid's Elegies	1.9.14	
Nor the milde Ewe gifts from the Ramme doth pull.	Ovid's Elegies	1.10.28	

NOR (cont.)			
Nor flint, nor iron, are in thy soft brest/But pure simplicity	Ovid's Elegies	1.11.9	
nor iron, are in thy soft brest/But pure simplicity in thee	Ovid's Elegies	1.11.9	
Nor morning starres shunne thy uprising face.	Ovid's Elegies	1.13.28	
Not black, nor golden were they to our viewe,	Ovid's Elegies	1.14.9	
Nor hath the needle, or the combes teeth reft them,	Ovid's Elegies	1.14.15	
Nor that I studie not the brawling lawes,	Ovid's Elegies	1.15.5	
Nor set my voyce to sale in everie cause?	Ovid's Elegies	1.15.6	
Nor is her husband wise, what needes defence/When	Ovid's Elegies	2.2.11	
Isis may be done/Nor feare least she to th'theater's runne.	Ovid's Elegies	2.2.26	
such faults are sad/Nor make they any man that heare them glad.	Ovid's Elegies	2.2.52	
Nor is it easily prov'd though manifest,	Ovid's Elegies	2.2.55	
Yet blusht I not, nor usde I any saying,	Ovid's Elegies	2.8.7	
Nor want I strength, but weight to presse her with:	Ovid's Elegies	2.10.24	
Nor violent South-windes did thee ought affright.	Ovid's Elegies	2.11.52	
Nor can an other say his helpe I tooke.	Ovid's Elegies	2.12.12	
Nor in my act hath fortune mingled chance,	Ovid's Elegies	2.12.15	
Nor is my warres cause new, but for a Queene/Europe, and Asia	Ovid's Elegies	2.12.17	
Nor being arm'd fierce troupes to follow farre?	Ovid's Elegies	2.14.2	
Nor dares the Lyonesse her young whelpes kill.	Ovid's Elegies	2.14.36	
Nor thy gulfes crooked Malea, would I feare.	Ovid's Elegies	2.16.24	
Nor do I like the country of my birth.	Ovid's Elegies	2.16.38	
Nor she her selfe but first trim'd up discernes.	Ovid's Elegies	2.17.10	
Nor of our love to be asham'd we need,	Ovid's Elegies	2.17.26	
Nor in my bookes shall one but thou be writ,	Ovid's Elegies	2.17.33	
Nor of thee Macer that resoundst forth armes,	Ovid's Elegies	2.18.35	
Nor never with nights sharpe revenge afflicted?	Ovid's Elegies	2.19.54	
Nor, least she will, can any be restrainde.	Ovid's Elegies	3.4.6	
Nor canst by watching keepe her minde from sinne.	Ovid's Elegies	3.4.7	
Nor doth her face please, but her husbands love;	Ovid's Elegies	3.4.27	
Thou hast no bridge, nor boate with ropes to throw,	Ovid's Elegies	3.5.3	
Nere was, nor shall be, what my verse mentions.	Ovid's Elegies	3.5.18	
Not Calydon, nor Aetolia did please:	Ovid's Elegies	3.5.37	
Nor passe I thee, who hollow rocks downe tumbling,	Ovid's Elegies	3.5.45	
Nor Romane stocke scorne me so much (I crave)/Gifts then my	Ovid's Elegies	3.5.65	
No certaine house thou hast, nor any fountaines.	Ovid's Elegies	3.5.92	
I prove neither youth nor man, but old and rustie.	Ovid's Elegies	3.6.20	
Nor usde the slight nor <and> cunning which she could,	Ovid's Elegies	3.6.56	
But neither was I man, nor lived then.	Ovid's Elegies	3.6.60	
Nor hanging oares the troubled seas did sweepe,	Ovid's Elegies	3.7.43	
Nor feared they thy body to annoy?	Ovid's Elegies	3.8.42	
Nor did thy ashes her last offrings lose.	Ovid's Elegies	3.8.50	
With thine, nor this last fire their presence misses.	Ovid's Elegies	3.8.54	
Nor lesse at mans prosperity any grudge.	Ovid's Elegies	3.9.6	
Nor on the earth was knowne the name of floore.	Ovid's Elegies	3.9.8	
Nor is she, though she loves the fertile fields,	Ovid's Elegies	3.9.17	
A clowne, nor no love from her warme brest yeelds.	Ovid's Elegies	3.9.18	
Be witnesse Crete (nor Crete doth all things feigne)/Crete	Ovid's Elegies	3.9.19	
Nor with thee, nor without thee can I live,	Ovid's Elegies	3.10.39	
Nor, as use will not Poets record heare,	Ovid's Elegies	3.11.19	
Nor have their words true histories pretence,	Ovid's Elegies	3.11.42	
Nor do I give thee counsaile to live chaste,	Ovid's Elegies	3.13.3	
(Nor am I by such wanton toyes defamde)/Heire of an antient	Ovid's Elegies	3.14.4	
She ware no gloves for neither sunne nor wind/Would burne or	Hero and Leander	1.27	
Nor that night-wandring pale and watrie starre,	Hero and Leander	1.107	
As thou in beautie doest exceed Loves mother/Nor heaven, nor	Hero and Leander	1.223	
Loves mother/Nor heaven, nor thou, were made to gaze upon,	Hero and Leander	1.223	
Neither themselves nor others, if not worne.	Hero and Leander	1.238	
No, nor to any one exterior sence,	Hero and Leander	1.271	
Nor hath it any place of residence,	Hero and Leander	1.272	
Nor is't of earth or mold celestiall,	Hero and Leander	1.273	
Then Hero hate me not, nor from me flie,	Hero and Leander	1.291	
Though neither gods nor men may thee deserve,	Hero and Leander	1.315	
Nor staine thy youthfull years with avarice,	Hero and Leander	1.325	
answered Love, nor would vouchsafe so much/As one poore word,	Hero and Leander	1.383	
And neither would denie, nor graunt his sute.	Hero and Leander	1.424	
As he ought not performe, nor yet she aske.	Hero and Leander	1.430	
Nor could the youth abstaine, but he must weare/The sacred ring	Hero and Leander	2.108	
NORMANDIE			
The King of Fraunce sets foote in Normandie.	Edw	2.2.9	Mortmr
Hath seazed Normandie into his hands.	Edw	3.1.64	Queene
NORTH			
The Euxine sea North to Natolia,	2Tamb	4.3.102	Tamb
The Terrene west, the Caspian north north-east,	2Tamb	4.3.103	Tamb
Lord Percie of the North being highly mov'd,	Edw	1.1.110	Kent
And you lord Warwick, president of the North,	Edw	1.4.68	Edward
But neither chuse the north t'erect thy seat;	Lucan, First Booke	53	
See how they quit our [bloud shed] <bloudshed> in the North;	Lucan, First Booke	302	
rocks, and where the north-west wind/Nor Zephir rules not,	Lucan, First Booke	407	
the north-west wind/Nor Zephir rules not, but the north alone,	Lucan, First Booke	408	
strange and unknown stars were seene/Wandering about the North,	Lucan, First Booke	525	
NORTH-EAST			
The Terrene west, the Caspian north north-east,	2Tamb	4.3.103	Tamb
NORTHERNE			
Then by the Northerne part of Affrica,	2Tamb	5.3.140	Tamb
NORTHREN			
Though from the shortest Northren Paralell,	2Tamb	1.1.25	Orcan
The Northren borderers seeing [their] <the> houses burnt,/Their	Edw	2.2.179	Lncstr
Doubtles these northren men/Whom death the greatest of all	Lucan, First Booke	454	
which he hath brought/From out their Northren parts, and that	Lucan, First Booke	479	
And from the northren climat snatching fier/Blasted the	Lucan, First Booke	532	
NORTHWARD			
Marching from Cairon northward with his camp,	2Tamb	1.1.47	Gazell

NORTHWARD (cont.)			
And Northward Gaveston hath many friends.	Edw	1.1.129	Lncstr
NORTHWARDE			
Thus have wee martcht Northwarde from Tamburlaine,	2Tamb	3.3.1	Therid
NORTH-WEST			
rocks, and where the north-west wind/Nor Zephir rules not,	Lucan, First Booke		407
NOS'D			
bottle-nos'd knave to my Master, that ever Gentleman had.	Jew	3.3.10	P Ithimr
NOSE			
Oh brave, master, I worship your nose for this.	Jew	2.3.173	Ithimr
God-a-mercy nose; come let's begone.	Jew	4.1.23	Ithimr
I, master, he's slain; look how his brains drop out on's nose.	Jew	4.1.179	P Ithimr
NOSEGAY			
And smelling to a Nosegay all the day,	Edw	2.1.35	Spencr
NOSTERILS			
And blow the morning from their nosterils,	2Tamb	4.3.8	Tamb
NOSTRA			
per vota nostra ipse nunc surgat nobis dicatus Mephostophilis.	F 250	1.3.22	P Faust
NOSTRAS			
upon my right heele, with quasi vestigias nostras insistere.	F App	p.231 70	P Wagner
NOSTRELS (See also NOSTERILS)			
And let her horses from their nostrels breathe/Rebellious winds	1Tamb	5.1.297	Bajzth
NOSTRIS			
left heele, that thou maist, Quasi vestigiis nostris insistere.	F 387	1.4.45	P Wagner
NOT			
That will not shield me from her shrewish blowes:	Dido	1.1.4	Ganimd
Why, are not all the Gods at thy commaund,	Dido	1.1.30	Jupitr
What? is not pietie exempt from woe?	Dido	1.1.79	Venus
Had not the heavens conceav'd with hel-borne clowdes,	Dido	1.1.125	Venus
Such honour, stranger, doe I not affect:	Dido	1.1.203	Venus
And have not any coverture but heaven.	Dido	1.1.230	Aeneas
Not one of them hath perisht in the storme,	Dido	1.1.236	Venus
But are arived safe not farre from hence:	Dido	1.1.237	Venus
Stay gentle Venus, flye not from thy sonne,	Dido	1.1.242	Aeneas
Why talke we not together hand in hand?	Dido	1.1.245	Aeneas
We come not we to wrong your Libian Gods,	Dido	1.2.10	Illion
Our hands are not prepar'd to lawles spoyle,	Dido	1.2.12	Illion
And will not let us lodge upon the sands:	Dido	1.2.35	Serg
My selfe will see they shall not trouble ye,	Dido	1.2.38	Iarbus
Had not such passions in her head as I.	Dido	2.1.6	Aeneas
And when I know it is not, then I dye.	Dido	2.1.9	Aeneas
O were I not at all so thou mightst be.	Dido	2.1.28	Aeneas
He is alive, Troy is not overcome.	Dido	2.1.30	Aeneas
Sweete father leave to weepe, this is not he:	Dido	2.1.35	Ascan
I heare Aeneas voyce, but see him not,	Dido	2.1.45	Illion
But Illioneus goes not in such robes.	Dido	2.1.48	Achat
passe through the hall/Bearing a banket, Dido is not farre.	Dido	2.1.71	Serg
Well may I view her, but she sees not me.	Dido	2.1.73	Aeneas
But Troy is not, what shall I say I am?	Dido	2.1.76	Aeneas
This place beseemes me not, O pardon me.	Dido	2.1.94	Aeneas
Then be assured thou art not miserable.	Dido	2.1.104	Dido
Nay leave not here, resolve me of the rest.	Dido	2.1.160	Dido
Through which it could not enter twas so huge.	Dido	2.1.171	Aeneas
O Hector who weepes not to heare thy name?	Dido	2.1.209	Dido
Not mov'd at all, but smiling at his teares,	Dido	2.1.240	Aeneas
Through which he could not passe for slaughtred men:	Dido	2.1.262	Aeneas
and had not we/Fought manfully, I had not told this tale:	Dido	2.1.270	Aeneas
and had not we/Fought manfully, I had not told this tale:	Dido	2.1.271	Aeneas
Yet manhood would not serve, of force we fled,	Dido	2.1.272	Aeneas
Tis not enough that thou doest graunt me love,	Dido	3.1.8	Iarbus
Feare not Iarbus, Dido may be thine.	Dido	3.1.19	Dido
No Dido will not take me in her armes,	Dido	3.1.22	Cupid
I shall not be her sonne, she loves me not.	Dido	3.1.23	Cupid
Weepe not sweet boy, thou shalt be Didos sonne,	Dido	3.1.24	Dido
Depart from Carthage, come not in my sight.	Dido	3.1.44	Dido
Am I not King of rich Getulia?	Dido	3.1.45	Iarbus
Am not I Queen of Libia? then depart.	Dido	3.1.49	Dido
Yet not from Carthage for a thousand worlds.	Dido	3.1.51	Iarbus
Is not Aeneas faire and beautifull?	Dido	3.1.63	Dido
Is he not eloquent in all his speech?	Dido	3.1.65	Dido
Name not Iarbus, but sweete Anna say,	Dido	3.1.67	Dido
Is not Aeneas worthie Didos love?	Dido	3.1.68	Dido
You shall not hurt my father when he comes.	Dido	3.1.80	Cupid
shall be wrought/The warres of Troy, but not Troyes overthrow:	Dido	3.1.125	Dido
Aeneas, thinke not Dido is in love:	Dido	3.1.136	Dido
And are not these as faire as faire may be?	Dido	3.1.140	Dido
But his fantastick humours pleasde not me:	Dido	3.1.158	Dido
But weapons gree not with my tender yeares:	Dido	3.1.164	Dido
Yet boast not of it, for I love thee not,	Dido	3.1.171	Dido
not of it, for I love thee not,/And yet I hate thee not:--	Dido	3.1.172	Dido
But not so much for thee, thou art but one,	Dido	3.1.175	Dido
Avaunt old witch and trouble not my wits.	Dido	3.2.25	Venus
Are not we both sprong of celestiall rase,	Dido	3.2.28	Juno
Had not my Doves discov'rd thy entent:	Dido	3.2.33	Venus
Why should not they then joyne in marriage,	Dido	3.2.74	Juno
Aeneas, thinke not but I honor thee,	Dido	3.3.1	Dido
And meddle not with any that I love:	Dido	3.3.22	Dido
Aeneas, be not movde at what he sayes,	Dido	3.3.23	Dido
Huntsmen, why pitch you not your toyles apace,	Dido	3.3.30	Dido
Who would not undergoe all kind of toyle,	Dido	3.3.58	Aeneas
So doth he now, though not with equall gaine,	Dido	3.3.83	Iarbus
And yet I am not free, oh would I were.	Dido	3.4.6	Dido
Why, what is it that Dido may desire/And not obtaine, be it in	Dido	3.4.8	Aeneas

NOT (cont.)

It is not ought Aeneas may atchieve?	Dido	3.4.11	Aeneas
Not angred me, except in angring thee.	Dido	3.4.15	Dido
Not sicke my love, but sicke:--	Dido	3.4.25	Dido
I must conceale/The torment, that it bootes me not reveale,/And	Dido	3.4.26	Dido
Nay, nothing, but Aeneas loves me not.	Dido	3.4.32	Dido
Aeneas thoughts dare not ascend so high/As Didos heart, which	Dido	3.4.33	Aeneas
ascend so high/As Didos heart, which Monarkes might not scale.	Dido	3.4.34	Aeneas
Sicheus, not Aeneas be thou calde:	Dido	3.4.59	Dido
The King of Carthage, not Anchises sonne:	Dido	3.4.60	Dido
Nature, why mad'st me not some poysonous beast,	Dido	4.1.21	Iarbus
Not with Aeneas in the ugly Cave.	Dido	4.1.32	Iarbus
I will not leave Iarbus whom I love,	Dido	4.2.43	Anna
Hard hearted, wilt not deigne to heare me speake?	Dido	4.2.54	Anna
And not stand lingering here for amorous lookes:	Dido	4.3.38	Illion
No no, she cares not how we sinke or swimme,	Dido	4.3.41	Illion
We will not stay a minute longer here.	Dido	4.3.44	Cloan
To leave her so and not once say farewell,	Dido	4.3.47	Aeneas
I may not dure this female drudgerie,	Dido	4.3.55	Aeneas
Stay not to answere me, runne Anna runne.	Dido	4.4.4	Dido
And not let Dido understand their drift:	Dido	4.4.6	Dido
How haps Achates bid me not farewell?	Dido	4.4.19	Dido
I charge thee put to sea and stay not here.	Dido	4.4.22	Dido
Hath not the Carthage Queene mine onely sonne?	Dido	4.4.29	Aeneas
A Burgonet cf steele, and not a Crowne,	Dido	4.4.42	Aeneas
A Sword, and not a Scepter fits Aeneas.	Dido	4.4.43	Aeneas
Not all the world can take thee from mine armes,	Dido	4.4.61	Dido
Speakes not Aeneas like a Conqueror?	Dido	4.4.93	Dido
I must prevent him, wishing will not serve:	Dido	4.4.104	Dido
Aeneas will not goe without his sonne:	Dido	4.4.107	Dido
I cannot see him frowne, it may not be:	Dido	4.4.112	Dido
Affright me not, onely Aeneas frowne/Is that which terrifies	Dido	4.4.115	Dido
Not bloudie speares appearing in the ayre,	Dido	4.4.117	Dido
If he forsake me not, I never dye,	Dido	4.4.121	Dido
And yet I blame thee not, thou art but wood.	Dido	4.4.143	Dido
And shrunke not backe, knowing my love was there?	Dido	4.4.146	Dido
O Dido, blame not him, but breake his oares,	Dido	4.4.149	Dido
Theres not so much as this base tackling too,	Dido	4.4.151	Dido
Was it not you that hoysed up these sailes?	Dido	4.4.153	Dido
Why burst you not, and they fell in the seas?	Dido	4.4.154	Dido
So youle love me, I care not if I doe.	Dido	4.5.17	Cupid
Say Dido what she will I am not old,	Dido	4.5.21	Nurse
A grave, and not a lover fits thy age:--	Dido	4.5.30	Nurse
Not past foure thousand paces at the most.	Dido	5.1.17	Aeneas
That have I not determinde with my selfe.	Dido	5.1.19	Aeneas
And givest not eare unto the charge I bring?	Dido	5.1.52	Hermes
Aeneas will not faine with his deare love,	Dido	5.1.92	Aeneas
But yet Aeneas will not leave his love?	Dido	5.1.98	Dido
These words proceed not from Aeneas heart.	Dido	5.1.102	Dido
Not from my heart, for I can hardly goe,	Dido	5.1.103	Aeneas
And yet I may not stay, Dido farewell.	Dido	5.1.104	Aeneas
Aeneas could not choose but hold thee deare,	Dido	5.1.126	Aeneas
Yet must he not gainsay the Gods behest.	Dido	5.1.127	Aeneas
O no, the Gods wey not what Lovers doe,	Dido	5.1.131	Dido
And wilt thcu not be mov'd with Didos words?	Dido	5.1.155	Dido
Wast thou nct wrackt upon this Libian shoare,	Dido	5.1.161	Dido
Repairde not I thy ships, made thee a King,	Dido	5.1.163	Dido
Goe goe and spare not, seeke out Italy,	Dido	5.1.169	Dido
If not, turne from me, and Ile turne from thee:	Dido	5.1.181	Dido
I have not power to stay thee: is he gone?	Dido	5.1.183	Dido
Yet he that in my sight would not relent,	Dido	5.1.186	Dido
Call him not wicked, sister, speake him faire,	Dido	5.1.200	Dido
Run Anna, run, stay not to answere me.	Dido	5.1.210	Dido
I know not what you meane by treason, I,	Dido	5.1.222	Nurse
Away with her, suffer her not to speake.	Dido	5.1.224	Dido
My sister ccmes, I like not her sad lookes.	Dido	5.1.225	Dido
Which seene to all, though he beheld me not,	Dido	5.1.237	Anna
No but I am not, yet I will be straight.	Dido	5.1.271	Dido
Not farre from hence/There is a woman famoused for arts,	Dido	5.1.274	Dido
Iarbus, talke not of Aeneas, let him goe,	Dido	5.1.283	Dido
I am not wise enough to be a kinge,	1Tamb	1.1.20	Mycet
Meander, might I not?	1Tamb	1.1.24	Mycet
Not for so small a fault my soveraigne Lord.	1Tamb	1.1.25	Meandr
I meane it not, but yet I know I might,	1Tamb	1.1.26	Mycet
Is it not a kingly resolution?	1Tamb	1.1.55	Mycet
Doubt not my Lord and gratious Soveraigne,	1Tamb	1.1.70	Therid
Ah Menaphon, I passe not for his threates,	1Tamb	1.1.109	Cosroe
I doubt not shortly but to raigne sole king,	1Tamb	1.1.175	Cosroe
The [Lords] <Lord> would not be too exasperate,	1Tamb	1.1.182	Ortyg
Come lady, let not this appal your thoughts.	1Tamb	1.2.1	Tamb
thou art so meane a man)/And seeke not to inrich thy followers,	1Tamb	1.2.9	Zenoc
Not all the Gold in Indias welthy armes,	1Tamb	1.2.85	Tamb
How say you Lordings, Is not this your hope?	1Tamb	1.2.116	Tamb
Keep all your standings, and not stir a foote,	1Tamb	1.2.150	Tamb
The Nations far remoov'd admyre me not)/And when my name and	1Tamb	1.2.204	Tamb
Not Hermes Prolocutor to the Gods,	1Tamb	1.2.210	Therid
Proud is his fortune if we pierce it not.	1Tamb	2.1.44	Cosroe
Would it not grieve a King to be so abusde,	1Tamb	2.2.5	Mycet
his Diadem/Sought for by such scalde knaves as love him not?	1Tamb	2.2.8	Mycet
Aurora shall not peepe out of her doores,	1Tamb	2.2.10	Mycet
Drums, why sound ye not when Meander speaks.	1Tamb	2.2.75	Mycet
And so mistake you not a whit my Lord.	1Tamb	2.3.6	Tamb
And doubt you not, but if you favour me,	1Tamb	2.3.10	Tamb

NOT (cont.)

With dutie [and] <not> with amitie we yeeld/Our utmost service	1Tamb	2.3.33		Techel
They knew not, ah, they knew not simple men,	1Tamb	2.4.2		Mycet
If Nature had not given me wisedomes lore?	1Tamb	2.4.7		Mycet
So shall not I be knowen, or if I bee,	1Tamb	2.4.13		Mycet
Away, I am the King: go, touch me not.	1Tamb	2.4.20		Mycet
You will not sell it, wil ye?	1Tamb	2.4.29		Tamb
I marveile much he stole it not away.	1Tamb	2.4.42		Mycet
From one that knew not what a King should do,	1Tamb	2.5.22		Cosroe
I will not thank thee (sweet Ortigius)/Better replies shall	1Tamb	2.5.36		Cosroe
Is it not brave to be a King, Techelles?	1Tamb	2.5.51		Tamb
Is it not passing brave to be a King,	1Tamb	2.5.53		Tamb
A God is not so glorious as a King:	1Tamb	2.5.57		Therid
enjoy in heaven/Can nct compare with kingly joyes in earth.	1Tamb	2.5.59		Therid
And so would you my maisters, would you not?	1Tamb	2.5.70		Tamb
Me thinks we should not, I am strongly moov'd,	1Tamb	2.5.75		Tamb
And would nct all our souldiers soone consent,	1Tamb	2.5.78		Tamb
Judge by thy selfe Theridamas, not me,	1Tamb	2.5.93		Tamb
We will not steale upon him cowardly,	1Tamb	2.5.102		Tamb
That mooves not upwards, nor by princely deeds/Doth meane to	1Tamb	2.7.32		Therid
I know not how to take their tyrannies.	1Tamb	2.7.41		Cosroe
Not all the curses which the furies breathe,	1Tamb	2.7.53		Tamb
Yet would we not be brav'd with forrain power,	1Tamb	3.1.13		Bajzth
Wils and commands (for say not I intreat)/Not once to set his	1Tamb	3.1.27		Bajzth
(for say not I intreat)/Not once to set his foot in Affrica,	1Tamb	3.1.28		Bajzth
have measured heaven/With triple circuit thou regreet us not,	1Tamb	3.1.37		Bajzth
mornings next arise/For messenger, he will not be reclaim'd,	1Tamb	3.1.39		Bajzth
Let not a man so vile and barbarous,	1Tamb	3.2.26		Agidas
Your Highnesse needs not doubt but in short time,	1Tamb	3.2.32		Agidas
Yet be not so inconstant in your love,	1Tamb	3.2.56		Agidas
He needed not with words confirme my feare,	1Tamb	3.2.92		Agidas
Doo not my captaines and my souldiers looke/As if they meant to	1Tamb	3.3.9		Tamb
I will not tell thee how Ile handle thee,	1Tamb	3.3.84		Tamb
What Coward wold not fight for such a prize?	1Tamb	3.3.100		Usumc
Stir not Zenocrate untill thou see/Me martch victoriously with	1Tamb	3.3.126		Tamb
Thy souldiers armes could not endure to strike/So many blowes	1Tamb	3.3.143		Bajzth
Thou knowest not (foolish hardy Tamburlaine)/What tis to meet	1Tamb	3.3.145		Bajzth
Yet should he not perswade me otherwise,	1Tamb	3.3.210		Zenoc
Thou shalt not yet be Lord of Affrica.	1Tamb	3.3.223		Zabina
Not now Theridamas, her time is past:	1Tamb	3.3.228		Tamb
Not all the world shall ransom Bajazeth.	1Tamb	3.3.232		Tamb
The Souldane would not start a foot from him.	1Tamb	4.1.19		Souldn
That not a man should live to rue their fall.	1Tamb	4.1.35		Souldn
Not sparing any that can manage armes.	1Tamb	4.1.57		2Msngr
But if these threats moove not submission,	1Tamb	4.1.58		2Msngr
and she shal looke/That these abuses flow not from her tongue:	1Tamb	4.2.70		Zenoc
Not all the Kings and Emperours of the Earth:	1Tamb	4.2.92		Tamb
Shall not defend it from our battering shot.	1Tamb	4.2.107		Tamb
I doubt not but the Governour will yeeld,	1Tamb	4.2.113		Therid
Not one should scape: but perish by our swords.	1Tamb	4.2.122		Tamb
Not for the world Zenocrate, if I have sworn:	1Tamb	4.2.125		Tamb
Sirra, why fall you not too, are you so daintily brought up, you	1Tamb	4.4.36	P	Tamb
and then she shall be sure not to be starv'd, and he be	1Tamb	4.4.46	P	Usumc
with freatting, and then she will not bee woorth the eating.	1Tamb	4.4.50	P	Tamb
what, not a bit?	1Tamb	4.4.54	P	Tamb
belike he hath not bene watered to day, give him some drinke.	1Tamb	4.4.55	P	Tamb
not the Turke and his wife make a goodly showe at a banquet?	1Tamb	4.4.57	P	Tamb
Casane, here are the cates you desire to finger, are they not?	1Tamb	4.4.108	P	Tamb
say you to this (Turke) these are not your contributorie kings.	1Tamb	4.4.118	P	Tamb
If we deserve them not with higher meeds/Then erst our states	1Tamb	4.4.131		Therid
Zenocrate, I will nct crowne thee yet,	1Tamb	4.4.139		Tamb
Would not with too much cowardize or feare,	1Tamb	5.1.37		Govnr
could they not as well/Have sent ye out, when first my	1Tamb	5.1.67		Tamb
But I am pleasde you shall not see him there:	1Tamb	5.1.113		Tamb
I will not spare these proud Egyptians,	1Tamb	5.1.121		Tamb
No more there is not I warrant thee Techelles.	1Tamb	5.1.202		Tamb
And sink not quite into my tortur'd soule.	1Tamb	5.1.263		Bajzth
Not I, bring milk and fire, and my blood I bring him againe,	1Tamb	5.1.310	P	Zabina
And let not conquest ruthlesly pursewde/Be equally against his	1Tamb	5.1.366		Zenoc
And pardon me that was not moov'd with ruthe,	1Tamb	5.1.369		Zenoc
If I had not bin wounded as I am.	1Tamb	5.1.421		Arabia
And therfore grieve not at your overthrow,	1Tamb	5.1.446		Tamb
Then doubt I not but faire Zenocrate/Will soone consent to	1Tamb	5.1.498		Tamb
and Danes/[Feares] <feare> not Orcanes, but great Tamburlaine:	2Tamb	1.1.59		Orcan
And not to dare ech other to the field:	2Tamb	1.1.116		Gazell
if Sigismond/Speake as a friend, and stand not upon tearmes,	2Tamb	1.1.123		Orcan
Not for all Affrike, therefore moove me not.	2Tamb	1.2.12		Almeda
But need we not be spied going aboord?	2Tamb	1.2.56		Almeda
And not before, my sweet Zenocrate:	2Tamb	1.3.15		Tamb
Not martiall as the sons of Tamburlaine.	2Tamb	1.3.22		Tamb
Would make me thinke them Bastards, not my sons,	2Tamb	1.3.32		Tamb
Not long agoe bestrid a Scythian Steed:	2Tamb	1.3.38		Zenoc
Why may not I my Lord, as wel as he,	2Tamb	1.3.61		Amyras
Or els you are not sons of Tamburlaine.	2Tamb	1.3.64		Tamb
And not the issue of great Tamburlaine:	2Tamb	1.3.70		Tamb
Of all the provinces I have subdued/Thou shalt not have a foot,	2Tamb	1.3.72		Tamb
It could not more delight me than your sight.	2Tamb	1.3.156		Tamb
They have not long since massacred our Camp.	2Tamb	2.1.10		Fredrk
But cals not then your Grace to memorie/The league we lately	2Tamb	2.1.27		Sgsmnd
We are not bound to those accomplishments,	2Tamb	2.1.35		Baldwn
faith which they prophanely plight/Is not by necessary pollycy,	2Tamb	2.1.38		Baldwn
So what we vow to them should not infringe/Our liberty of armes	2Tamb	2.1.40		Baldwn
Should not give us presumption to the like.	2Tamb	2.1.46		Sgsmnd

NOT (cont.)

That would not kill and curse at Gods command,	2Tamb	2.1.55		Fredrk
That could not but before be terrified:	2Tamb	2.2.22		Uribas
Have I not here the articles of peace,	2Tamb	2.2.30		Orcan
Not dooing Mahomet an injurie,	2Tamb	2.3.34		Orcan
Had not bene nam'd in Homers Iliads:	2Tamb	2.4.89		Tamb
Not lapt in lead but in a sheet of gold,	2Tamb	2.4.131		Tamb
And till I die thou shalt not be interr'd.	2Tamb	2.4.132		Tamb
And now I doubt not but your royall cares/Hath so provided for	2Tamb	3.1.20		Callap
We shall not need to nourish any doubt,	2Tamb	3.1.26		Callap
That have not past the Centers latitude,	2Tamb	3.2.31		Tamb
Thou shalt not beautifie Larissa plaines,	2Tamb	3.2.34		Tamb
It would not ease the sorrow I sustaine.	2Tamb	3.2.48		Calyph
Hast thou not seene my horsmen charge the foe,	2Tamb	3.2.103		Tamb
That by the warres lost not a dram of blood,	2Tamb	3.2.113		Tamb
I know not what I should think of it.	2Tamb	3.2.130	P	Calyph
My boy, Thou shalt not loose a drop of blood,	2Tamb	3.2.137		Tamb
How say ye Souldiers, Shal we not?	2Tamb	3.3.9		Techel
And when we enter in, not heaven it selfe/Shall ransome thee,	2Tamb	3.3.27		Therid
I would not yeeld it: therefore doo your worst.	2Tamb	3.3.37		Capt
death, why comm'st thou not?	2Tamb	3.4.14		Olymp
The Scythians shall not tyrannise on me.	2Tamb	3.4.29		Sonne
Then carie me I care not where you will,	2Tamb	3.4.80		Olymp
By Mahomet not one of them shal live.	2Tamb	3.5.17		Callap
That fighting, knowes not what retreat doth meane,	2Tamb	3.5.43		Trebiz
Raile not proud Scythian, I shall now revenge/My fathers vile	2Tamb	3.5.90		Callap
againe, you shall not trouble me thus to come and fetch you.	2Tamb	3.5.101	P	Tamb
Seest thou not death within my wrathfull looks?	2Tamb	3.5.119		Tamb
not any Element/Shal shrowde thee from the wrath of	2Tamb	3.5.126		Tamb
hee shall not be put to that exigent, I warrant thee.	2Tamb	3.5.156	P	Soria
You knowe not sir:	2Tamb	3.5.158		Tamb
Away ye fools, my father needs not me,	2Tamb	4.1.15		Calyph
You wil not goe then?	2Tamb	4.1.40		Amyras
I would not bide the furie of my father:	2Tamb	4.1.45		Amyras
tel me if the warres/Be not a life that may illustrate Gods,	2Tamb	4.1.79		Tamb
And tickle not your Spirits with desire/Stil to be train'd in	2Tamb	4.1.80		Tamb
That they may say, it is not chance doth this,	2Tamb	4.1.84		Amyras
No, no Amyras, tempt not Fortune so,	2Tamb	4.1.86		Tamb
And glut it not with stale and daunted foes.	2Tamb	4.1.88		Tamb
But wher's this coward, villaine, not my sonne,	2Tamb	4.1.89		Tamb
Know ye not yet the argument of Armes?	2Tamb	4.1.100		Tamb
A Forme not meet to give that subject essence,	2Tamb	4.1.112		Tamb
That will not see the strength of Tamburlaine,	2Tamb	4.1.133		Tamb
For not a common Souldier shall defile/His manly fingers with	2Tamb	4.1.163		Tamb
Whose cruelties are not so harsh as thine,	2Tamb	4.1.169		Jrslem
Why gave you not your husband some of it,	2Tamb	4.2.71		Therid
That I dissemble not, trie it on me.	2Tamb	4.2.76		Olymp
Are not so honoured in their Governour,	2Tamb	4.3.10		Tamb
Were not subdew'd with valour more divine,	2Tamb	4.3.15		Tamb
If not, then dy like beasts, and fit for nought/But perches for	2Tamb	4.3.22		Tamb
How like you that sir king? why speak you not?	2Tamb	4.3.53		Celeb
Brawle not (I warne you) for your lechery,	2Tamb	4.3.75		Tamb
Live [continent] <content> then (ye slaves) and meet not me	2Tamb	4.3.81		Tamb
Are ye not gone ye villaines with your spoiles?	2Tamb	4.3.84		Tamb
Let us not be idle then my Lord,	2Tamb	4.3.95		Techel
Is not my life and state as deere to me,	2Tamb	5.1.12		Govnr
Have we not hope, for all our battered walles,	2Tamb	5.1.15		Govnr
I care not, nor the towne will never yeeld/As long as any life	2Tamb	5.1.47		Govnr
Assault and spare not, we wil never yeeld.	2Tamb	5.1.62		Govnr
traines should reach down to the earth/Could not affright you,	2Tamb	5.1.91		Tamb
Could not perswade you to submission,	2Tamb	5.1.94		Tamb
Yet could not enter till the breach was made.	2Tamb	5.1.100		Tamb
Tis not thy bloody tents can make me yeeld,	2Tamb	5.1.103		Govnr
A thousand deathes could not torment our hearts/More than the	2Tamb	5.1.144		Jrslem
They will talk still my Lord, if you doe not bridle them.	2Tamb	5.1.146	P	Amyras
Leave not a Babylonian in the towne.	2Tamb	5.1.171		Tamb
Thou art not woorthy to be worshipped,	2Tamb	5.1.189		Tamb
Why send'st thou not a furious whyrlwind downe,	2Tamb	5.1.192		Tamb
Something Techelles, but I know not what,	2Tamb	5.1.220		Tamb
Doubt not my lord, but we shal conquer him.	2Tamb	5.2.12		Amasia
Feare not my Lord, I see great Mahomet/Clothed in purple	2Tamb	5.2.31		Amasia
Be not inconstant, carelesse of your fame,	2Tamb	5.3.21		Techel
Beare not the burthen of your enemies joyes,	2Tamb	5.3.22		Techel
Not last Techelles, no, for I shall die.	2Tamb	5.3.66		Tamb
and Calor, which some holde/Is not a parcell of the Elements,	2Tamb	5.3.87		Phsitn
Can not indure by argument of art.	2Tamb	5.3.97		Phsitn
There should not one of all the villaines power/Live to give	2Tamb	5.3.108		Tamb
And here not far from Alexandria,	2Tamb	5.3.131		Tamb
But sons, this subject not of force enough,	2Tamb	5.3.168		Tamb
If not resolv'd into resolved paines,	2Tamb	5.3.187		Amyras
Let not thy love exceed thyne honor sonne,	2Tamb	5.3.199		Tamb
For if thy body thrive not full of thoughtes/As pure and fiery	2Tamb	5.3.236		Tamb
The nature of thy chariot wil not beare/A guide of baser temper	2Tamb	5.3.242		Tamb
And weigh not men, and therefore not mens words.	Jew	Prol.8		Machvl
Let me be envy'd and not pittied!	Jew	Prol.27		Machvl
But whither am I bound, I come not, I,	Jew	Prol.28		Machvl
Which mony was not got without my meanes.	Jew	Prol.32		Machvl
And let him not be entertain'd the worse/Because he favours me.	Jew	Prol.34		Machvl
And is thy credit not enough for that?	Jew	1.1.62		Barab
Tush, who amongst 'em knowes not Barrabas?	Jew	1.1.67		Barab
And saw'st thou not/Mine Argosie at Alexandria?	Jew	1.1.71		Barab
Thou couldst not come from Egypt, or by Caire/But at the entry	Jew	1.1.73		Barab
How chance you came not with those other ships/That sail'd by	Jew	1.1.89		Barab

NOT (cont.)

Sir we saw 'em not.	Jew	1.1.90		2Merch
Which me thinkes fits not their profession.	Jew	1.1.118		Barab
I must confesse we come not to be Kings:	Jew	1.1.129		Barab
That's not our fault:	Jew	1.1.130		Barab
Tush, tell not me 'twas done of policie.	Jew	1.1.140		1Jew
Why let 'em come, so they come not to warre;	Jew	1.1.150		Barab
They would not come in warlike manner thus.	Jew	1.1.155		1Jew
Wherein I may not, nay I dare not dally.	Jew	1.2.12		Calym
For happily we shall not tarry here:	Jew	1.2.16		Calym
Let's know their time, perhaps it is not long;	Jew	1.2.24		Calym
Were they not summon'd to appeare to day?	Jew	1.2.35		Govnr
Governour, it was not got so easily;	Jew	1.2.86		Barab
Yet Barrabas we will not banish thee,	Jew	1.2.100		Govnr
'Tis not our fault, but thy inherent sinne.	Jew	1.2.109		1Knght
Preach me not out of my possessions.	Jew	1.2.111		Barab
Sham'st thou not thus to justifie thy selfe,	Jew	1.2.119		Govnr
As if we knew not thy profession?	Jew	1.2.120		Govnr
tush, take not from me then,/For that is theft; and if you rob	Jew	1.2.125		Barab
Grave [Governor], list not to his exclames:	Jew	1.2.128		1Knght
And not simplicity, as they suggest.	Jew	1.2.161		Barab
Why weepe you not to thinke upon my wrongs?	Jew	1.2.172		Barab
Why pine not I, and dye in this distresse?	Jew	1.2.173		Barab
So that not he, but I may curse the day,	Jew	1.2.191		Barab
Great injuries are not so soone forgot.	Jew	1.2.208		Barab
What, woman, moane not for a little losse:	Jew	1.2.226		Barab
Not for my selfe, but aged Barabas:	Jew	1.2.228		Abigal
thinke me not all so fond/As negligently to forgoe so much	Jew	1.2.241		Barab
That may they not:	Jew	1.2.253		Abigal
have so manifestly wronged us,/What will not Abigall attempt?	Jew	1.2.276		Abigal
No, Abigall, in this/It is not necessary I be seene.	Jew	1.2.302		Barab
The better; for we love not to be seene:	Jew	1.2.307		Abbass
I doe not doubt by your divine precepts/And mine owne industry,	Jew	1.2.334		Abigal
Hinder her not, thou man of little faith,	Jew	1.2.340		1Fryar
And wilt not see thine owne afflictions,	Jew	1.2.353		1Fryar
Blind, Fryer, I wrecke not thy perswasions.	Jew	1.2.355		Barab
Seduced Daughter, Goe, forget not.	Jew	1.2.359		Barab
No come not at me, if thou wilt be damn'd,	Jew	1.2.362		Barab
Forget me, see me not, and so be gone.	Jew	1.2.363		Barab
As but to be about this happy place;/'Tis not so happy:	Jew	2.1.33		Abigal
Because we vail'd not to the [Turkish] <Spanish> Fleet,/Their	Jew	2.2.11		Bosco
But to admit a sale of these thy Turkes/We may not, nay we dare	Jew	2.2.22		Govnr
nay we dare not give consent/By reason of a Tributary league.	Jew	2.2.22		Govnr
And not depart untill I see you free.	Jew	2.2.41		Bosco
and not a man surviv'd/To bring the haplesse newes to	Jew	2.2.50		Bosco
Honor is bought with bloud and not with gold.	Jew	2.2.56		Govnr
Feare not their sale, for they'll be quickly bought.	Jew	2.3.2		1Offcr
And so much must they yeeld or not be sold.	Jew	2.3.4		2Offcr
Here comes the Jew, had not his goods bin seiz'd,	Jew	2.3.5		1Offcr
I am not of the Tribe of Levy, I,	Jew	2.3.18		Barab
Pointed it is, good Sir,--but not for you.	Jew	2.3.60		Barab
Oh my Lord we will not jarre about the price;	Jew	2.3.65		Barab
And seeing they are not idle, but still doing,	Jew	2.3.83		Barab
Good Barabas glance not at our holy Nuns.	Jew	2.3.86		Lodowk
Let me see, sirra, are you not an old shaver?	Jew	2.3.114	P	Barab
not a stone of beef a day will maintaine you in these chops;	Jew	2.3.124	P	Barab
This Moore is comeliest, is he not? speake son.	Jew	2.3.144		Mater
Seeme not to know me here before your mother/Lest she mistrust	Jew	2.3.146		Barab
Tush man, we talk'd of Diamonds, not of Abigal.	Jew	2.3.151		Barab
Tell me, Mathias, is not that the Jew?	Jew	2.3.152		Mater
Converse not with him, he is cast off from heaven.	Jew	2.3.157		Mater
He is not of the seed of Abraham.	Jew	2.3.230		Barab
Not for all Malta, therefore sheath your sword;	Jew	2.3.270		Barab
But steale you in, and seeme to see him not;	Jew	2.3.272		Barab
Mathias, as thou lov'st me, not a word.	Jew	2.3.277		Barab
Barabas, is not that the widowes sonne?	Jew	2.3.279		Lodowk
Doth she not with her smiling answer you?	Jew	2.3.286		Barab
'Tis not thy wealth, but her that I esteeme,	Jew	2.3.298		Lodowk
Faith is not to be held with Heretickes;	Jew	2.3.311		Barab
But all are Hereticks that are not Jewes;	Jew	2.3.312		Barab
This followes well, and therefore daughter feare not.	Jew	2.3.313		Barab
So have not I, but yet I hope I shall.	Jew	2.3.319		Barab
I know not, but farewell, I must be gone.	Jew	2.3.322		Abigal
Stay her,--but let her not speake one word more.	Jew	2.3.323		Barab
Oh muse not at it, 'tis the Hebrewes guize,	Jew	2.3.325		Barab
Trouble her not, sweet Lodowicke depart:	Jew	2.3.327		Barab
went in at dores/You had bin stab'd, but not a word on't now;	Jew	2.3.338		Barab
My life is not so deare as Abigall.	Jew	2.3.348		Mthias
Are there not Jewes enow in Malta,	Jew	2.3.359		Barab
I thinke by this/You purchase both their lives; is it not so?	Jew	2.3.366		Ithimr
'Tis poyson'd, is it not?	Jew	2.3.372		Ithimr
Feare not, I'le so set his heart a fire,	Jew	2.3.375		Ithimr
And yet I know my beauty doth not faile.	Jew	3.1.5		Curtzn
Looke not towards him, let's away:	Jew	3.1.24		Pilia
Oh bravely fought, and yet they thrust not home.	Jew	3.2.5		Barab
I know not, and that grieves me most of all.	Jew	3.2.21		Govnr
why, know you not?	Jew	3.3.14	P	Ithimr
Know you not of Mathias and Don Lodowickes disaster?	Jew	3.3.16	P	Ithimr
one; have not the Nuns fine sport with the Fryars now and then?	Jew	3.3.32	P	Ithimr
Admit thou lov'dst not Lodowicke for his [sire] <sinne>,	Jew	3.3.40		Abigal
And couldst not venge it, but upon his sonne,	Jew	3.3.44		Abigal
Why Abigal it is not yet long since/That I did labour thy	Jew	3.3.56		1Fryar
And then thou didst not like that holy life.	Jew	3.3.58		1Fryar

NOT (cont.)

me in beleefe/Gives great presumption that she loves me not;	Jew	3.4.11	Barab
Ithimore, intreat not for her, I am mov'd,	Jew	3.4.35	Barab
Goe buy thee garments: but thou shalt not want:	Jew	3.4.47	Barab
yet not appeare/In forty houres after it is tane.	Jew	3.4.71	Barab
Talke not of racing downe your City wals,	Jew	3.5.21	Basso
You shall not need trouble your selves so farre,	Jew	3.5.22	Basso
And Physicke will not helpe them; they must dye.	Jew	3.6.2	1Fryar
Reveale it not, for then my father dyes.	Jew	3.6.32	Abigal
Know that Confession must not be reveal'd,	Jew	3.6.33	2Fryar
I was afraid the poyson had not wrought;	Jew	4.1.4	Barab
Now all are dead, not one remaines alive.	Jew	4.1.7	Barab
That's brave, master, but think you it wil not be known?	Jew	4.1.8	P Ithimr
For my part feare you not.	Jew	4.1.10	Ithimr
Thou shalt not need, for now the Nuns are dead,	Jew	4.1.15	Barab
Doe you not sorrow for your daughters death?	Jew	4.1.17	Ithimr
Oh speake not of her, then I dye with griefe.	Jew	4.1.36	Barab
I will not say that by a forged challenge they met.	Jew	4.1.45	P 2Fryar
Is't not too late now to turne Christian?	Jew	4.1.50	Barab
And so could I; but pennance will not serve.	Jew	4.1.60	Ithimr
Besides I know not how much weight in Pearle/Orient and round,	Jew	4.1.66	Barab
Frankeford, Lubecke, Mosco, and where not,	Jew	4.1.72	Barab
Then 'tis not for me; and I am resolv'd/You shall confesse me,	Jew	4.1.85	Barab
I will not goe for thee.	Jew	4.1.94	1Fryar
Not? then I'le make thee, [rogue] <goe>.	Jew	4.1.95	2Fryar
And so I will, oh Jacomo, faile not but come.	Jew	4.1.108	Barab
But not a word to any of your Covent.	Jew	4.1.112	Barab
Therefore 'tis not requisite he should live.	Jew	4.1.121	Barab
But are not both these wise men to suppose/That I will leave my	Jew	4.1.122	Barab
Yes; and I know not what the reason is:	Jew	4.1.130	Ithimr
Doe what I can he will not strip himselfe,	Jew	4.1.131	Ithimr
Blame not us but the proverb, Confes and be hang'd.	Jew	4.1.146	P Barab
Who would not thinke but that this Fryar liv'd?	Jew	4.1.156	Barab
Then will not Jacomo be long from hence.	Jew	4.1.159	Barab
But soft, is not this Bernardine?	Jew	4.1.164	1Fryar
Bernardine--/Wilt thou not speake?	Jew	4.1.169	1Fryar
thou think'st I see thee not;/Away, I'de wish thee, and let me	Jew	4.1.169	1Fryar
No, wilt thou not?	Jew	4.1.171	1Fryar
Villaines, I am a sacred person, touch me not.	Jew	4.1.201	1Fryar
Not a wise word, only gave me a nod, as who shold say, Is it	Jew	4.2.12	P Pilia
me ever since she saw me, and who would not requite such love?	Jew	4.2.34	P Ithimr
and now would I were gone, I am not worthy to looke upon her.	Jew	4.2.36	P Ithimr
Is't not a sweet fac'd youth, Pilia?	Jew	4.2.40	P Curtzn
sweet youth; did not you, Sir, bring the sweet youth a letter?	Jew	4.2.41	P Ithimr
Nay, I care not how much she loves me; Sweet Bellamira, would I	Jew	4.2.54	P Ithimr
And is't not possible to find it out?	Jew	4.2.60	Pilia
Write not so submissively, but threatning him.	Jew	4.2.72	P Pilia
and this shall be your warrant; if you doe not, no more but so.	Jew	4.2.76	P Ithimr
Whither will I not goe with gentle Ithimore?	Jew	4.2.99	Curtzn
Here's goodly 'parrell, is there not?	Jew	4.2.112	Ithimr
I'le not leave him worth a gray groat.	Jew	4.2.114	P Ithimr
'Tis not thy mony, but thy selfe I weigh:	Jew	4.2.124	Curtzn
He was not wont to call me Barabas.	Jew	4.3.3	Barab
Well, my hope is, he will not stay there still;	Jew	4.3.16	Barab
No; but three hundred will not serve his turne.	Jew	4.3.20	P Pilia
Not serve his turne, Sir?	Jew	4.3.21	P Barab
Might he not as well come as send; pray bid him come and fetch	Jew	4.3.26	P Barab
enough, and therfore talke not to me of your Counting-house:	Jew	4.3.36	P Pilia
'Tis not five hundred Crownes that I esteeme,	Jew	4.3.40	Barab
five hundred Crownes that I esteeme,/I am not mov'd at that:	Jew	4.3.41	Barab
There, if thou lov'st me doe not leave a drop.	Jew	4.4.6	P Ithimr
I had not thought he had been so brave a man.	Jew	4.4.16	Curtzn
Dost not know a Jew, one Barabas?	Jew	4.4.56	P Ithimr
The Governour feeds not as I doe.	Jew	4.4.63	P Barab
To undoe a Jew is charity, and not sinne.	Jew	4.4.81	Ithimr
Mathias did it not, it was the Jew.	Jew	5.1.11	Curtzn
Nuns, strangled a Fryar, and I know not what mischiefe beside.	Jew	5.1.14	P Pilia
I'le goe alone, dogs, do not hale me thus.	Jew	5.1.19	Barab
Wonder not at it, Sir, the heavens are just:	Jew	5.1.55	Govnr
Their deaths were like their lives, then think not of 'em;	Jew	5.1.56	Govnr
Feare not, my Lord, for here, against the [sluice] <Truce>,/The	Jew	5.1.86	Barab
And if it be not true, then let me dye.	Jew	5.1.96	Barab
had it not beene much better/To [have] kept thy promise then be	Jew	5.2.4	Calym
Away, no more, let him not trouble me.	Jew	5.2.26	Barab
At least unprofitably lose it not:	Jew	5.2.37	Barab
Slip not thine opportunity, for feare too late/Thou seek'st for	Jew	5.2.45	Barab
too late/Thou seek'st for much, but canst not compasse it.	Jew	5.2.46	Barab
Governor, good words, be not so furious;	Jew	5.2.61	Barab
'Tis not thy life which can availe me ought,	Jew	5.2.62	Barab
Malta's ruine, thinke you not/'Twere slender policy for Barabas	Jew	5.2.64	Barab
Your selves shall see it shall not be forgot:	Jew	5.2.71	Barab
For as a friend not knowne, but in distresse,	Jew	5.2.72	Barab
Tush, send not letters to 'em, goe thy selfe,	Jew	5.2.93	Barab
Doe so, but faile not; now farewell Ferneze:	Jew	5.2.109	Barab
intreat your Highnesse/Not to depart till he has feasted you.	Jew	5.3.33	Msngr
What will we not adventure?	Jew	5.4.9	1Knght
For if I keepe not promise, trust not me.	Jew	5.5.23	Barab
And fire the house; say, will not this be brave?	Jew	5.5.41	Barab
Thou shalt not live in doubt of any thing.	Jew	5.5.45	Barab
Why, is not this/A kingly kinde of trade	Jew	5.5.46	Barab
No, Selim, doe not flye;	Jew	5.5.68	Govnr
You will not helpe me then?	Jew	5.5.76	Barab
We will not let thee part so suddenly:	Jew	5.5.98	Govnr

NOT (cont.)

For with thy Gallyes couldst thou not get hence,	Jew	5.5.100	Govnr
Why, hardst thou not the trumpet sound a charge?	Jew	5.5.105	Govnr
The ruines done to Malta and to us,/Thou canst not part:	Jew	5.5.113	Govnr
May not desolve, till death desolve our lives,	P 5	1.5	Charls
The rest that will not goe (my Lords) may stay:	P 23	1.23	Charls
Have you not heard of late how he decreed,	P 32	1.32	Navrre
My Lord you need not mervaile at the Guise,	P 39	1.39	Condy
If I repaire not what he ruinates:	P 129	2.72	Guise
Doth not your grace know the man that gave them you?	P 172	3.7	Navrre
Not wel, but do remember such a man.	P 173	3.8	OldQn
Let not this heavy chaunce my dearest Lord,	P 191	3.26	QnMarg
And that I am not more secure my selfe,	P 264	4.62	Charls
them thither, and then/Beset his house that not a man may live.	P 289	5.16	Guise
There shall not a Hugonet breath in France.	P 324	5.51	Guise
I sweare by this crosse, wee'l not be partiall,	P 325	5.52	Anjoy
Was it not thou that scoftes the Organon,	P 387	7.27	Guise
Not for my life doe I desire this pause,	P 401	7.41	Ramus
Yet will we not that the Massacre shall end:	P 444	7.84	Guise
unto Roan, and spare not one/That you suspect of heresy.	P 446	7.86	Guise
But come lets walke aside, th'airs not very sweet.	P 497	9.16	QnMoth
O say not so, thou kill'st thy mothers heart.	P 539	11.4	QnMoth
they Henries heart/Will not both harbour love and Majestie?	P 604	12.17	King
We know that noble mindes change not their thoughts/For wearing	P 610	12.23	Mugern
As not a man may live without our leaves.	P 638	12.51	QnMoth
Mor du, wert <were> not the fruit within thy wombe,	P 688	13.32	Guise
Not yet my Lord, for thereon doe they stay:	P 732	14.35	1Msngr
It will not countervaile his paines I hope,	P 735	14.38	Navrre
So he be safe he cares not what becomes,	P 739	14.42	Navrre
Of King or Country, no not for them both.	P 740	14.43	Navrre
How now Mugeroun, metst thou not the Guise at the doore?	P 774	15.32	King
Not I my Lord, what if I had?	P 775	15.33	Mugern
I like not this, come Epernoune/Lets goe seek the Duke and make	P 785	15.43	King
his market, and set up your standing where you should not:	P 810	17.5	P Souldr
If it be not too free there's the question:	P 813	17.8	P Souldr
not to take possession (as I would I might) yet I meane to	P 813	17.8	P Souldr
But we presume it is not for our good.	P 824	17.19	King
Ah base Epernoune, were not his highnes heere,	P 831	17.26	Guise
Be patient Guise and threat not Epernoune,	P 833	17.28	King
Your highnes needs not feare mine armies force,	P 857	17.52	Guise
But trust him not my Lord,	P 871	17.66	Eprnon
Nay, they fear'd not to speak in the streetes,	P 876	17.71	Eprnon
For not effecting of his holines will.	P 878	17.73	Eprnon
Thinke not but I am tragicall within:	P 894	17.89	King
What, will you not feare when you see him come?	P 933	19.3	Capt
I, I, feare not: stand close, so, be resolute:	P 943	19.13	Capt
Not to suspect disloyaltye in thee,	P 975	19.45	King
in the next roome, therefore good my Lord goe not foorth.	P 995	19.65	P 3Mur
Trouble me not, I neare offended him,	P1005	19.75	Guise
Oh that I have not power to stay my life,	P1007	19.77	Guise
Did he not draw a sorte of English priestes/From Doway to the	P1030	19.100	King
Did he not cause the King of Spaines huge fleete,	P1033	19.103	King
Did he not injure Mounser thats deceast?	P1035	19.105	King
Hath he not made me in the Popes defence,	P1036	19.106	King
My sonne: thou art a changeling, not my sonne.	P1074	19.144	QnMoth
For since the Guise is dead, I will not live.	P1090	19.160	QnMoth
Murder me not, I am a Cardenall.	P1091	20.1	Cardnl
Wert thou the Pope thou mightst not scape from us.	P1092	20.2	1Mur
I like not this Friers look.	P1159	22.21	Eprnon
Twere not amisse my Lord, if he were searcht.	P1160	22.22	Eprnon
And will not offer violence to their King,	P1162	22.24	King
Yes Navarre, but not to death I hope.	P1177	22.39	King
Ah curse him not sith he is dead.	P1220	22.82	King
Tell me Surgeon and flatter not, may I live?	P1222	22.84	King
Weep not sweet Navarre, but revenge my death.	P1234	22.96	King
He loves me not that sheds most teares,	P1239	22.101	King
the markett and sett upe your standinge where you shold not:	Paris	ms 6,p390	P Souldr
yf it be not to free theres the questione | now ser where he is	Paris	ms 9,p390	P Souldr
And thoughe I come not to keep possessione as I wold I mighte	Paris	ms14,p390	P Souldr
exhalatione/which our great sonn of fraunce cold not effecte	Paris	ms20,p390	Guise
Not that I love the citie or the men,	Edw	1.1.12	Gavstn
And yet I have not viewd my Lord the king,	Edw	1.1.45	Gavstn
these are not men for me,/I must have wanton Poets, pleasant	Edw	1.1.50	Gavstn
Will you not graunt me this?--	Edw	1.1.77	Edward
For which, had not his highnes lov'd him well,	Edw	1.1.112	Kent
I cannot, nor I will not, I must speake.	Edw	1.1.122	Mortmr
kis not my hand,/Embrace me Gaveston as I do thee:	Edw	1.1.140	Edward
Why shouldst thou kneele, knowest thou not who I am?	Edw	1.1.142	Edward
Not Hilas was more mourned of Hercules,	Edw	1.1.144	Edward
Thou shouldst not plod one foote beyond this place.	Edw	1.1.181	Gavstn
Ah brother, lay not violent hands on him,	Edw	1.1.189	Kent
We may not, nor we will not suffer this.	Edw	1.2.15	MortSr
Why post we not from hence to levie men?	Edw	1.2.16	Mortmr
For now my lord the king regardes me not,	Edw	1.2.49	Queene
Is it not straunge, that he is thus bewitcht?	Edw	1.2.55	MortSr
But yet lift not your swords against the king.	Edw	1.2.61	ArchBp
I, if words will serve, if not, I must.	Edw	1.2.83	Mortmr
We will not thus be facst and overpeerd.	Edw	1.4.19	Mortmr
We are no traitors, therefore threaten not.	Edw	1.4.25	MortSr
No, threaten not my lord, but pay them home.	Edw	1.4.26	Gavstn
My lord, you may not thus disparage us,	Edw	1.4.32	Lncstr
I there it goes, but yet I will not yeeld,	Edw	1.4.56	Edward
Then linger not my lord but do it straight.	Edw	1.4.58	Lncstr

NOT (cont.)

It bootes me not to threat, I must speake faire,	Edw	1.4.63	Edward
if this content you not,/Make severall kingdomes of this	Edw	1.4.69	Edward
Be it or no, he shall not linger here.	Edw	1.4.93	MortSr
They would not stir, were it to do me good:	Edw	1.4.95	Edward
If I be king, not one of them shall live.	Edw	1.4.105	Edward
And long thou shalt not stay, or if thou doost,	Edw	1.4.114	Edward
Rend not my hart with thy too piercing words,	Edw	1.4.117	Edward
To go from hence, greeves not poore Gaveston,	Edw	1.4.119	Gavstn
Thou shalt not hence, ile hide thee Gaveston.	Edw	1.4.131	Edward
Seeing I must go, do not renew my sorrow.	Edw	1.4.137	Gavstn
I passe not for their anger, come lets go.	Edw	1.4.142	Edward
Fawne not on me French strumpet, get thee gone.	Edw	1.4.145	Edward
Ist not enough, that thou corrupts my lord,	Edw	1.4.150	Queene
I meane not so, your grace must pardon me.	Edw	1.4.153	Gavstn
Your highnes knowes, it lies not in my power.	Edw	1.4.158	Queene
Away then, touch me not, come Gaveston.	Edw	1.4.159	Edward
Speake not unto her, let her droope and pine.	Edw	1.4.162	Edward
Assure thy selfe thou comst not in my sight.	Edw	1.4.169	Edward
I had beene stifled, and not lived to see,	Edw	1.4.176	Queene
And he confesseth that he loves me not.	Edw	1.4.194	Queene
Crie quittance Madam then, and love not him.	Edw	1.4.195	Mortmr
Feare ye not Madam, now his minions gone,	Edw	1.4.198	Lncstr
he comes not back,/Unlesse the sea cast up his shipwrack body.	Edw	1.4.204	Lncstr
Then speake not for him, let the pesant go.	Edw	1.4.218	Warwck
Tis for my selfe I speake, and not for him.	Edw	1.4.219	Queene
Not I against my nephew.	Edw	1.4.232	MortSr
Feare not, the queens words cannot alter him.	Edw	1.4.233	Penbrk
Tis not for his sake, but for our availe:	Edw	1.4.242	Mortmr
Fie Mortimer, dishonor not thy selfe,	Edw	1.4.244	Lncstr
Do you not wish that Gaveston were dead?	Edw	1.4.252	Mortmr
But nephew, do not play the sophister.	Edw	1.4.255	MortSr
Know you not Gaveston hath store of golde,	Edw	1.4.258	Mortmr
I, but how chance this was not done before?	Edw	1.4.272	Lncstr
Because my lords, it was not thought upon:	Edw	1.4.273	Mortmr
But how if he do not Nephew?	Edw	1.4.278	MortSr
Tis not the king can buckler Gaveston,	Edw	1.4.288	Mortmr
returnd, this newes will glad him much,/Yet not so much as me.	Edw	1.4.302	Queene
If it be so, what will not Edward do?	Edw	1.4.325	Edward
For Gaveston, but not for Isabell.	Edw	1.4.326	Queene
Or if that loftie office like thee not,	Edw	1.4.355	Edward
For wot you not that I have made him sure,	Edw	1.4.378	Edward
That day, if not for him, yet for my sake,	Edw	1.4.381	Edward
And not kings onelie, but the wisest men,	Edw	1.4.395	MortSr
Unckle, his wanton humor greeves not me,	Edw	1.4.402	Mortmr
I have not seene a dapper jack so briske,	Edw	1.4.412	Mortmr
I will not yeeld to any such upstart.	Edw	1.4.423	Mortmr
Not Mortimer, nor any of his side,	Edw	2.1.4	Spencr
Our Ladies first love is not wavering,	Edw	2.1.27	Spencr
Tis not a black coate and a little band,	Edw	2.1.33	Spencr
The greefe for his exile was not so much,	Edw	2.1.57	Neece
I know thou couldst not come and visit me.	Edw	2.1.61	Neece
I will not long be from thee though I die:	Edw	2.1.62	Neece
A homely one my lord, not worth the telling.	Edw	2.2.13	Mortmr
They love me not that hate my Gaveston.	Edw	2.2.37	Edward
I am that Cedar, shake me not too much,	Edw	2.2.38	Edward
Tis not the hugest monster of the sea,	Edw	2.2.45	Edward
Frolicks not more to see the paynted springe,	Edw	2.2.62	Gavstn
And come not here to scoffe at Gaveston,	Edw	2.2.76	Gavstn
Yet I disdaine not to doe this for you.	Edw	2.2.79	Lncstr
Out of my presence, come not neere the court.	Edw	2.2.89	Edward
Ile not be barde the court for Gaveston.	Edw	2.2.90	Mortmr
By heaven, the abject villaine shall not live.	Edw	2.2.106	Mortmr
Cosin, and if he will not ransome him,	Edw	2.2.127	Mortmr
You may not in, my lord.	Edw	2.2.137	Guard
May we not?	Edw	2.2.138	Mortmr
What Mortimer, you will not threaten him?	Edw	2.2.146	Kent
the familie of the Mortimers/Are not so poore, but would they	Edw	2.2.151	Mortmr
With garish robes, not armor, and thy selfe/Bedaubd with golde,	Edw	2.2.184	Mortmr
And dare not be revengde, for their power is great:	Edw	2.2.202	Edward
Why do you not commit him to the tower?	Edw	2.2.234	Gavstn
I dare not, for the people love him well.	Edw	2.2.235	Edward
and my gentrie/Is fetcht from Oxford, not from Heraldrie.	Edw	2.2.244	Baldck
Waite on me, and ile see thou shalt not want.	Edw	2.2.246	Edward
The head-strong Barons shall not limit me.	Edw	2.2.262	Edward
If that will not suffice, farwell my lords.	Edw	2.3.10	Kent
O stay my lord, they will not injure you.	Edw	2.4.7	Gavstn
I will not trust them, Gaveston away.	Edw	2.4.8	Edward
If he be straunge and not regarde my wordes,	Edw	2.4.64	Queene
Base flatterer, yeeld, and were it not for shame,	Edw	2.5.11	Mortmr
[King] <Kind> Edward is not heere to buckler thee.	Edw	2.5.18	Lncstr
No, it needeth not.	Edw	2.5.42	Warwck
Will not these delaies beget my hopes?	Edw	2.5.47	Gavstn
Not so my Lord, least he bestow more cost,	Edw	2.5.55	Lncstr
Then if you will not trust his grace in keepe,	Edw	2.5.65	Arundl
We will not wrong thee so,	Edw	2.5.69	Mortmr
is it not enough/That we have taken him, but must we now	Edw	2.5.83	Warwck
My lords, I will not over wooe your honors,	Edw	2.5.86	Penbrk
Yet not perhaps,	Edw	2.5.95	Warwck
My house is not farre hence, out of the way/A little, but our	Edw	2.5.100	Penbrk
Sir, must not come so neare and balke their lips.	Edw	2.5.103	Penbrk
Treacherous earle, shall I not see the king?	Edw	2.6.15	Gavstn
Come fellowes, it booted not for us to strive,	Edw	2.6.18	James

NOT (cont.)

Ah Spencer, not the riches of my realme/Can ransome him, ah he	Edw	3.1.3	Edward
You would not suffer thus your majestie/Be counterbuft of your	Edw	3.1.17	Spencr
And if they send me not my Gaveston,	Edw	3.1.26	Edward
Not to be tied to their affection,	Edw	3.1.29	Baldck
And Spencer, spare them not, but lay it on.	Edw	3.1.56	Edward
Commit not to my youth things of more waight/Then fits a prince	Edw	3.1.74	Prince
And feare not lord and father, heavens great beames/On Atlas	Edw	3.1.76	Prince
great beames/On Atlas shoulder, shall not lie more safe,	Edw	3.1.77	Prince
thy mother feare/Thou art not markt to many daies on earth.	Edw	3.1.80	Queene
The earle of Warwick would not bide the hearing,	Edw	3.1.104	Arundl
Well, and how fortunes that he came not?	Edw	3.1.113	Edward
Let them not unrevengd murther your friends,	Edw	3.1.125	Spencr
So wish not they Iwis that sent thee hither,	Edw	3.1.152	Edward
I doubt it not my lord, right will prevaile.	Edw	3.1.189	Spencr
Tis not amisse my liege for eyther part,	Edw	3.1.190	SpncrP
Is it not, trowe ye, to assemble aide,	Edw	3.1.207	SpncrP
Now lustie lords, now not by chance of warre,	Edw	3.1.221	Edward
No Edward, Englands scourge, it may not be,	Edw	3.1.258	Mortmr
Feare it not.	Edw	4.1.18	Kent
But droope not madam, noble mindes contemne/Despaire:	Edw	4.2.16	SrJohn
No my lord Mortimer, not I, I trow.	Edw	4.2.44	Prince
Not sonne, why not?	Edw	4.2.45	Queene
doubt yee not,/We will finde comfort, money, men, and friends	Edw	4.2.64	SrJohn
not so, and you must not discourage/Your friends that are so	Edw	4.2.69	Queene
and you must not discourage/Your friends that are so forward in	Edw	4.2.69	Queene
realme, my lord of Arundell/You have the note, have you not?	Edw	4.3.8	Edward
A will be had ere long I doubt it not.	Edw	4.3.20	Spencr
our port-maisters/Are not so careles of their kings commaund.	Edw	4.3.23	Edward
Ye must not grow so passionate in speeches:	Edw	4.4.16	Mortmr
O no my lord, this princely resolution/Fits not the time, away,	Edw	4.5.9	Baldck
to Longshankes blood/Is false, be not found single for suspect:	Edw	4.6.17	Kent
Nephew, your father, I dare not call him king.	Edw	4.6.33	Kent
Tis not in her controulment, nor in ours,	Edw	4.6.35	Mortmr
I like not this relenting moode in Edmund,	Edw	4.6.38	Mortmr
Yea madam, and they scape not easilie,	Edw	4.6.41	Mortmr
A goodly chauncelor, is he not my lord?	Edw	4.6.43	Queene
They shalbe started thence I doubt it not.	Edw	4.6.60	Mortmr
Shall I not see the king my father yet?	Edw	4.6.61	Prince
So fought not they that fought in Edwards right.	Edw	4.6.72	SpncrP
Could not but take compassion of my state.	Edw	4.7.11	Edward
rule and emperie/Have not in life or death made miserable?	Edw	4.7.15	Edward
Not one alive, but shrewdly I suspect,	Edw	4.7.28	Spencr
Stand not on titles, but obay th'arrest,	Edw	4.7.58	Leistr
The gentle heavens have not to do in this.	Edw	4.7.76	Edward
My lord, be going, care not for these,	Edw	4.7.93	Rice
Not of compulsion or necessitie.	Edw	5.1.4	Leistr
The greefes of private men are soone allayde,/But not of kings:	Edw	5.1.9	Edward
No, tis for Mortimer, not Edwards head,	Edw	5.1.40	Edward
So shall not Englands [Vine] <Vines> be perished,	Edw	5.1.47	Edward
What, feare you not the furie of your king?	Edw	5.1.75	Edward
They passe not for thy frownes as late they did,	Edw	5.1.77	Edward
Ile not resigne, but whilst I live, [be king].	Edw	5.1.86	Edward
If he be not, let him choose.	Edw	5.1.95	BshpWn
hands of mine/Shall not be guiltie of so foule a crime.	Edw	5.1.99	Edward
Call me not lorde, away, out of my sight:	Edw	5.1.113	Edward
Let not that Mortimer protect my sonne,	Edw	5.1.115	Edward
If with the sight thereof she be not mooved,	Edw	5.1.119	Edward
thinke not a thought so villanous/Can harbor in a man of noble	Edw	5.1.131	Bartly
I know not, but of this am I assured,	Edw	5.1.152	Edward
Not yet my lorde, ile beare you on your waye.	Edw	5.1.155	Leistr
I would hee were, so it were not by my meanes.	Edw	5.2.45	Queene
Feare not my Lord, weele do as you commaund.	Edw	5.2.66	Matrvs
Not I my lord:	Edw	5.2.90	Kent
Mother, perswade me not to weare the crowne,	Edw	5.2.92	Prince
I tell thee tis not meet, that one so false/Should come about	Edw	5.2.104	Mortmr
And therefore trust him not.	Edw	5.2.107	Mortmr
With you I will, but not with Mortimer.	Edw	5.2.110	Prince
Brother Edmund, strive not, we are his friends,	Edw	5.2.114	Queene
My lord, be not pensive, we are your friends.	Edw	5.3.1	Matrvs
Not so my liege, the Queene hath given this charge,	Edw	5.3.13	Gurney
Thus lives old Edward not reliev'd by any,	Edw	5.3.23	Edward
Feare not to kill the king tis good he die.	Edw	5.4.9	Mortmr
Kill not the king tis good to feare the worst.	Edw	5.4.12	Mortmr
You shall not need to give instructions,	Edw	5.4.29	Ltborn
Tis not the first time I have killed a man.	Edw	5.4.30	Ltborn
I care not how it is, so it be not spide:	Edw	5.4.40	Mortmr
And not unlike a bashfull puretaine,	Edw	5.4.59	Mortmr
Dares but affirme, that Edwards not true king,	Edw	5.4.76	Champn
Sonne, be content, I dare not speake a worde.	Edw	5.4.96	Queene
Let me but stay and speake, I will not go,	Edw	5.4.105	Kent
Feare not sweete boye, ile garde thee from thy foes,	Edw	5.4.111	Queene
He is a traitor, thinke not on him, come.	Edw	5.4.115	Queene
Gurney, I wonder the king dies not,	Edw	5.5.1	Matrvs
Whats heere? I know not how to conster it.	Edw	5.5.15	Gurney
Yet be not farre off, I shall need your helpe,	Edw	5.5.28	Ltborn
Feare not you that.	Edw	5.5.36	Matrvs
And whether I have limmes or no, I know not.	Edw	5.5.65	Edward
Tell Isabell the Queene, I lookt not thus,	Edw	5.5.68	Edward
Still feare I, and I know not whats the cause,	Edw	5.5.85	Edward
For not these ten daies have these eyes lids closd.	Edw	5.5.94	Edward
O let me not die yet, stay, O stay a while.	Edw	5.5.101	Edward
But not too hard, least that you bruse his body.	Edw	5.5.113	Ltborn

NCT (cont.)

Tell me sirs, was it not bravelie done?	Edw		5.5.116		Ltborn
Feare not my lord, know that you are a king.	Edw		5.6.24		1Lord
Thinke not that I am frighted with thy words,	Edw		5.6.27		King
Weepe not sweete sonne.	Edw		5.6.33		Queene
Forbid not me to weepe, he was my father,	Edw		5.6.34		King
You could not beare his death thus patiently,	Edw		5.6.36		King
Why speake you not unto my lord the king?	Edw		5.6.38		1Lord
Madam, intreat not, I will rather die,	Edw		5.6.56		Mortmr
Farewell faire Queene, weepe not for Mortimer,	Edw		5.6.64		Mortmr
Spill not the bloud of gentle Mortimer.	Edw		5.6.69		Queene
Els would you not intreate for Mortimer.	Edw		5.6.71		King
I doe not thinke her so unnaturall.	Edw		5.6.76		King
Thinke not to finde me slack or pitifull.	Edw		5.6.82		King
Shall I not moorne for my beloved lord,	Edw		5.6.87		Queene
That bootes not, therefore gentle madam goe.	Edw		5.6.91		2Lord
Thou hadst not hatcht this monstrous treacherie!	Edw		5.6.97		King
Not marching <now> in the fields of Thrasimen,	F	1	Prol.1		1Chor
Why Faustus, hast thou not attain'd that end?	F	46	1.1.18		Faust
[Is not thy common talke sound Aphorismes]?	F	47	1.1.19A		Faust
Are not thy bils hung up as monuments,	F	48	1.1.20		Faust
And gaze not on it least it tempt thy soule,	F	98	1.1.70		GdAngl
[Yet not your words onely, but mine owne fantasie],	F	130	1.1.102A		Faust
As thou to live, therefore object it not.	F	162	1.1.134		Faust
Then doubt not Faustus but to be renowm'd,	F	168	1.1.140		Cornel
Why, dost not thou know then?	F	199	1.2.6	P	2Schol
Yes, I know, but that followes not.	F	200	1.2.7	P	Wagner
That followes not <necessary> by force of argument, which	F	202	1.2.9	P	Wagner
<Why, didst thou not say thou knewst>?	F	204	(HC258)A	P	2Schol
Then <Well> you will not tell us?	F	205	1.2.12	P	2Schol
yet if you were not dunces, you would never aske me such a	F	206	1.2.13	P	Wagner
For is he not Corpus naturale?	F	207	1.2.14	P	Wagner
and is not that Mobile?	F	208	1.2.15	P	Wagner
not for you to come within fortie foot of the place of	F	211	1.2.18	P	Wagner
I do not doubt but to see you both hang'd the next Sessions.	F	212	1.2.19	P	Wagner
Were he a stranger, <and> not allyed to me,	F	223	1.2.30		2Schol
Then feare not Faustus to <but> be resolute/And try the utmost	F	242	1.3.14		Faust
Who would not be proficient in this Art?	F	256	1.3.28		Faust
And may not follow thee without his leave;	F	269	1.3.41		Mephst
Did not he charge thee to appeare to me?	F	271	1.3.43		Faust
Did not my conjuring [speeches] raise thee? speake.	F	273	1.3.45		Faust
This word Damnation, terrifies not me <him>,	F	286	1.3.58		Faust
Was not that Lucifer an Angell once?	F	292	1.3.64		Faust
Am not tormented with ten thousand hels,	F	307	1.3.79		Mephst
The Emperour shall not live, but by my leave,	F	338	1.3.110		Faust
Not so neither; I had need to have it well rosted, and good	F	352	1.4.10	P	Robin
thou dost not presently bind thy selfe to me for seven yeares,	F	361	1.4.19	P	Wagner
Not I, thou art Prest, prepare thy selfe, for I will presently	F	372	1.4.30	P	Wagner
I am not afraid of a devill.	F	374	1.4.32	P	Robin
[And] canst <thou> not [now] be sav'd.	F	390	2.1.2		Faust
Now go not backward: no, Faustus, be resolute.	F	394	2.1.6		Faust
[To God]? <Why> he loves thee not:	F	398	2.1.10		Faust
Ist not midnight? come Mephostophilis <Mephastophilis>.	F	417	2.1.29		Faust
Why streames it not, that I may write a fresh?	F	455	2.1.67		Faust
Why shouldst thou not? is not thy soule thine owne?	F	457	2.1.69		Faust
What will not I do to obtaine his soule?	F	462	2.1.74		Mephst
yet shall not Faustus flye.	F	470	2.1.82		Faust
All places shall be hell that is not heaven.	F	515	2.1.127		Mephst
<How, a wife? I prithee Faustus talke not of a wife>.	F	530	(HC261)A	P	Mephst
I tell thee Faustus it is <tis> not halfe so faire/As thou, or	F	557	2.2.6		Mephst
Had not sweete pleasure conquer'd deepe despaire.	F	576	2.2.25		Faust
Have not I made blind Homer sing to me/Of Alexanders love, and	F	577	2.2.26		Faust
And hath not he that built the walles of Thebes/With ravishing	F	579	2.2.28		Faust
I am resolv'd, Faustus shall not <nere> repent.	F	583	2.2.32		Faust
Who knowes not the double motion of the Planets?	F	602	2.2.51		Faust
But is there not Coelum igneum, [and] <&> <et> Christalinum?	F	612	2.2.61	P	Faust
Why are <have wee> not Conjunctions, Oppositions, Aspects,	F	615	2.2.64	P	Faust
I will not.	F	619	2.2.68	P	Mephst
Move me not Faustus <for I will not tell thee>.	F	621	2.2.70	P	Mephst
Villaine, have I not bound thee to tell me any thing?	F	622	2.2.71	P	Faust
I, that is not against our Kingdome:	F	623	2.2.72	P	Mephst
Ist not too late?	F	629	2.2.78		Faust
Thou should'st not thinke on <of> God.	F	644	2.2.93		Belzeb
Talke not of Paradice or <nor> Creation, but marke the <this>	F	659	2.2.108	P	Lucifr
<indeede I doe, what doe I not>?	F	668	(HC263)A	P	Pride
not speake a word more for a Kings ransome <an other worde>,	F	669	2.2.118	P	Pride
Not I.	F	702	2.2.151	P	Faust
I'le not speake <an other word for a King's raunsome>.	F	706	(HC264)A	P	Sloth
I'le not speake <a word more for a kings ransome>.	F	706	(HC264)B	P	Sloth
I'le not speake [an other] word.	F	706	2.2.158	P	Sloth
why thou canst not tell ne're a word on't.	F	731	2.3.10	P	Dick
Thou needst not do that, for my Mistresse hath done it.	F	739	2.3.18	P	Dick
thought you did not sneake up and downe after her for nothing.	F	742	2.3.21	P	Dick
hold belly hold, and wee'le not pay one peny for it.	F	749	2.3.28	P	Robin
Not long he stayed within his quiet house,	F	768	2.3.47		2Chor
Not to be wonne by any conquering Prince:	F	783	3.1.5		Faust
<Faustus I have, and because we wil not be unprovided,	F	805	(HC265)A	P	Mephst
But thus I fall to Peter, not to thee.	F	872	3.1.94		Bruno
Is not all power on earth bestowed on us?	F	930	3.1.152		Pope
Now tell me Faustus, are we not fitted well?	F	940	3.1.162		Mephst
Do what thou wilt, thou shalt not be discern'd.	F	1005	3.2.25		Mephst
Did I not tell you,/To morrow we would sit i'th Consistory,	F	1016	3.2.36		Pope
Deny it not, we all are witnesses/That Bruno here was late	F	1025	3.2.45		Raymnd

NOT (cont.)

By holy Paul we saw them not.	F1029	3.2.49		BthCrd
Villaines why speake you not?	F1045	3.2.65		Pope
what you say, we looke not like cup-stealers I can tell you.	F1100	3.3.13	P	Robin
I and spare not:	F1102	3.3.15	P	Robin
I feare not your searching; we scorne to steale your cups I can	F1105	3.3.18	P	Dick
and stir not for thy life, Vintner you shall have your cup	F1113	3.3.26	P	Robin
Will not his grace consort the Emperour?	F1162	4.1.8		Fredrk
Has not the Pope enough of conjuring yet?	F1189	4.1.35	P	Benvol
Not I.	F1194	4.1.40	P	Benvol
I, and I fall not asleepe i'th meane time.	F1196	4.1.42		Benvol
I doe not greatly beleeve him, he lookes as like [a] conjurer	F1227	4.1.73	P	Benvol
an your Divels come not away quickly, you shall have me asleepe	F1241	4.1.87	P	Benvol
Il'e make you feele something anon, if my Art faile me not.	F1247	4.1.93	P	Faust
These are but shadowes, not substantiall.	F1259	4.1.105		Faust
But Faustus, since I may not speake to them,	F1263	4.1.109		Emper
He sleeps my Lord, but dreames not of his hornes.	F1280	4.1.126		Faust
I blame thee not to sleepe much, having such a head of thine	F1284	4.1.130	P	Emper
in your head for shame, let not all the world wonder at you.	F1291	4.1.137	P	Faust
O say not so sir:	F1294	4.1.140		Faust
not so much for injury done to me, as to delight your Majesty	F1311	4.1.157	P	Faust
But an I be not reveng'd for this, would I might be turn'd to a	F1319	4.1.165	P	Benvol
Away, you love me not, to urge me thus,	F1327	4.2.3		Benvol
If not, depart:	F1336	4.2.12		Benvol
Knew you not Traytors, I was limitted/For foure and twenty	F1395	4.2.71		Faust
Nay feare not man, we have no power to kill.	F1440	4.3.10		Mrtino
Nay chafe not man, we all are sped.	F1444	4.3.14		Mrtino
thou canst not buy so good a horse, for so small a price:	F1459	4.4.3	P	Faust
Well, I will not stand with thee, give me the money:	F1466	4.4.10	P	Faust
him o're hedge and ditch, and spare him not; but do you heare?	F1468	4.4.12	P	Faust
in any case, ride him not into the water.	F1469	4.4.13	P	Faust
How sir, not into the water?	F1470	4.4.14	P	HrsCsr
why will he not drink of all waters?	F1470	4.4.14	P	HrsCsr
waters, but ride him not into the water; o're hedge and ditch,	F1472	4.4.16	P	Faust
hedge and ditch, or where thou wilt, but not into the water:	F1473	4.4.17	P	Faust
Murder or not murder, now he has but one leg, I'le out-run him,	F1494	4.4.38	P	HrsCsr
time; but, quoth he, in any case ride him not into the water.	F1541	4.5.37	P	HrsCsr
had had some [rare] quality that he would not have me know of,	F1542	4.5.38	P	HrsCsr
and whooping in his eares, but all could not wake him:	F1549	4.5.45	P	HrsCsr
And trouble not the Duke.	F1598	4.6.41		Servnt
Be not so furious: come you shall have Beere.	F1620	4.6.63		Faust
I, I, he does not stand much upon that.	F1630	4.6.73	P	HrsCsr
No faith, not much upon a woodden leg.	F1631	4.6.74		Faust
do not you remember a Horse-courser you sold a horse to?	F1633	4.6.76	P	Carter
you remember you bid he should not ride [him] into the water?	F1636	4.6.79	P	Carter
'Tis not so much worth; I pray you tel me one thing.	F1643	4.6.86	P	Carter
sir, did not I pull off one of your legs when you were asleepe?	F1655	4.6.98	P	HrsCsr
what he meanes, if death were nie, he would not frolick thus:	F1677	5.1.4	P	Wagner
<It is not Faustus custome> to deny	F1690	(HC269)B		Faust
[And] Faustus custome is not to deny/The just [requests]	F1690	5.1.17		Faust
Doe not persever in it like a Divell;	F1711	5.1.38		OldMan
If sin by custome grow not into nature:	F1713	5.1.40		OldMan
my exhortation/Seemes harsh, and all unpleasant; let it not,	F1718	5.1.45		OldMan
For gentle sonne, I speake it not in wrath,	F1719	5.1.46		OldMan
And all is drosse that is not Helena.	F1774	5.1.101		Faust
Looke sirs, comes he not, comes he not?	F1826	5.2.30	P	Faust
He is not well with being over solitarie.	F1829	5.2.33		3Schol
the serpent that tempted Eve may be saved, but not Faustus.	F1838	5.2.42	P	Faust
heare [me] with patience, and tremble not at my speeches.	F1839	5.2.43	P	Faust
Why did not Faustus tell us of this before, that Divines might	F1862	5.2.66	P	1Schol
Talke not of me, but save your selves and depart.	F1869	5.2.73	P	Faust
Tempt not God sweet friend, but let us into the next roome, and	F1871	5.2.75	P	1Schol
you <yee> heare, come not unto me, for nothing can rescue me.	F1874	5.2.78	P	Faust
if not, Faustus is gone to hell.	F1878	5.2.82	P	Faust
Rend <Ah rend> not my heart, for naming of my Christ,	F1941	5.2.145		Faust
Gape earth; O no, it will not harbour me.	F1949	5.2.153		Faust
[O God, if thou wilt not have mercy on my soule],	F1958	5.2.162A		Faust
Why wert thou not a creature wanting soule?	F1964	5.2.168		Faust
[My God, my God] <O mercy heaven>, looke not so fierce on me;	F1979	5.2.183		Faust
Ugly hell gape not; come not Lucifer,	F1981	5.2.185		Faust
not so good friend, burladie I had neede have it wel roasted,	F App	p.229 11	P	Clown
Nay I know not, we shalbe curst with bell, booke, and candle.	F App	p.232 23	P	Mephst
what doest thou with that same booke thou canst not reade?	F App	p.233 14	P	Rafe
did not I tell thee, we were for ever made by this doctor	F App	p.234 1	P	Robin
it is not in my abilitie to present before your eyes, the true	F App	p.237 41	P	Faust
I doubt not shal sufficiently content your Imperiall majesty.	F App	p.237 48	P	Faust
that not only gives thee hornes, but makes thee weare them,	F App	p.238 70	P	Emper
O not so fast sir, theres no haste but good, are you remembred	F App	p.238 76	P	Faust
not so much for the injury hee offred me heere in your	F App	p.238 81	P	Faust
before you have him, ride him not into the water at any hand.	F App	p.239 109	P	Faust
why sir, wil he not drinke of all waters?	F App	p.239 110	P	HrsCsr
but ride him not into the water, ride him over hedge or ditch,	F App	p.239 111	P	Faust
hedge or ditch, or where thou wilt, but not into the water.	F App	p.239 113	P	Faust
Now am I made man for ever, Ile not leave my horse for fortie:	F App	p.239 114	P	HrsCsr
I would not be ruled by him, for he bade me I should ride him	F App	p.240 130	P	HrsCsr
had some rare qualitie that he would not have had me knowne of,	F App	p.240 132	P	HrsCsr
I tell thee he has not slept this eight nights.	F App	p.240 144	P	Mephst
And he have not slept this eight weekes Ile speake with him.	F App	p.240 145	P	HrsCsr
Why, thou seest he heares thee not.	F App	p.241 151	P	Mephst
No, will you not wake?	F App	p.241 153	P	HrsCsr
I wil not hide from you the thing my heart desires, and were it	F App	p.242 8	P	Duchss
He would not banquet, and carowse, and swill/Amongst the	F App	p.243 4		Wagner
Will ye wadge war, for which you shall not triumph?	Lucan, First Booke	12		

NOT (cont.)

as yet thou wants not foes.	Lucan, First Booke	23
other meanes, (and gods not sleightly/Purchase immortal thrones;	Lucan, First Booke	34
Untill the cruel Giants war was done)/We plaine not heavens,	Lucan, First Booke	37
Thee if I invocate, I shall not need/To crave Apolloes ayde, or	Lucan, First Booke	64
Roome was so great it could not beare it selfe:	Lucan, First Booke	72
Dire league of partners in a kingdome last not.	Lucan, First Booke	86
earth, the sea, the world it selfe,/Would not admit two Lords:	Lucan, First Booke	111
His body (not his boughs) send forth a shade;	Lucan, First Booke	141
shoots/Alongst the ayre and [nought] <not> resisting it/Falls,	Lucan, First Booke	157
Againe, this people could not brooke calme peace,	Lucan, First Booke	172
Them freedome without war might not suffice,	Lucan, First Booke	173
I hate thee not, to thee my conquests stoope,	Lucan, First Booke	203
or blustring south were cause/I know not, but the cloudy ayre	Lucan, First Booke	237
decrees/To expel the father; share the world thou canst not;	Lucan, First Booke	291
Who sees not warre sit by the quivering Judge;	Lucan, First Booke	320
me,/Because at his commaund I wound not up/My conquering Eagles?	Lucan, First Booke	339
Mild Atax glad it beares not Roman [boats] <bloats>;	Lucan, First Booke	404
and where the north-west wind/Nor Zephir rules not, but the	Lucan, First Booke	408
That soules passe not to silent Erebus/Or Plutoes bloodles	Lucan, First Booke	451
men/Whom death the greatest of all feares affright not,	Lucan, First Booke	455
and the rest/Marcht not intirely, and yet hide the ground,	Lucan, First Booke	474
They stai'd not either to pray or sacrifice,	Lucan, First Booke	504
Their houshould gods restrain them not, none lingered,	Lucan, First Booke	505
And wilt not trust thy Citty walls one night:	Lucan, First Booke	518
Which flamed not on high; but headlong pitcht/Her burning head	Lucan, First Booke	544
The heart stird not, and from the gaping liver/Squis'd matter;	Lucan, First Booke	623
But thy fiers hurt not; Mars, 'tis thou enflam'st/The	Lucan, First Booke	657
Although the nights be long, I sleepe not tho,	Ovid's Elegies	1.2.3
Which being not shakt <slackt>, I saw it die at length.	Ovid's Elegies	1.2.12
Marveile not though the faire Bride did incite/The drunken	Ovid's Elegies	1.4.7
Before thy husband come, though I not see/What may be done, yet	Ovid's Elegies	1.4.13
Let not thy necke by his vile armes be prest,	Ovid's Elegies	1.4.35
Thy bosomes Roseat buds let him not finger,	Ovid's Elegies	1.4.37
Chiefely on thy lips let not his lips linger.	Ovid's Elegies	1.4.38
Mingle not thighes, nor to his legge joyne thine,	Ovid's Elegies	1.4.43
Do not thou so, but throw thy mantle hence,	Ovid's Elegies	1.4.49
Entreat thy husband drinke, but do not kisse,	Ovid's Elegies	1.4.51
And while he drinkes, to adde more do not misse,	Ovid's Elegies	1.4.52
and not onely kisse/But force thee give him my stolne honey	Ovid's Elegies	1.4.63
Or night being past, and yet not day begunne.	Ovid's Elegies	1.5.6
Not one wen in her bodie could I spie,	Ovid's Elegies	1.5.18
Hard-hearted Porter doest and wilt not heare?	Ovid's Elegies	1.6.27
With armes or armed men I come not guarded,	Ovid's Elegies	1.6.33
Who feares these armes? who wil not go to meete them?	Ovid's Elegies	1.6.39
Watching till after mid-night did not tire thee.	Ovid's Elegies	1.6.44
Though it be so, shut me not out therefore,	Ovid's Elegies	1.6.47
Carelesse, farewell, with my falt not distaind.	Ovid's Elegies	1.6.72
with kissing/And on her necke a wantons marke not missing.	Ovid's Elegies	1.7.42
Wa'st not enough the fearefull Wench to chide?	Ovid's Elegies	1.7.45
But doubt thou not (revenge doth griefe appease)/With thy	Ovid's Elegies	1.7.63
Bescratch mine eyes, spare not my lockes to breake,	Ovid's Elegies	1.7.65
Sees not the morne on rosie horses rise.	Ovid's Elegies	1.8.4
And why shouldst not please?	Ovid's Elegies	1.8.25
Wert thou rich, poore should not be my state.	Ovid's Elegies	1.8.28
Would he not buy thee thou for him shouldst care.	Ovid's Elegies	1.8.34
Houses not dwelt in, are with filth forlorne.	Ovid's Elegies	1.8.52
Beauty not exercisde with age is spent,	Ovid's Elegies	1.8.53
And sister, Nurse, and mother spare him not,	Ovid's Elegies	1.8.91
Take strife away, love doth not well endure.	Ovid's Elegies	1.8.96
East windes he doth not chide/Nor to hoist saile attends fit	Ovid's Elegies	1.9.13
He that will not growe slothfull let him love.	Ovid's Elegies	1.9.46
To serve for pay beseemes not wanton gods.	Ovid's Elegies	1.10.20
The Mare askes not the Horse, the Cowe the Bull,	Ovid's Elegies	1.10.27
Presages are not vaine, when she departed/Nape by stumbling on	Ovid's Elegies	1.12.3
Whither runst thou, that men, and women, love not?	Ovid's Elegies	1.13.9
Hold in thy rosie horses that they move not.	Ovid's Elegies	1.13.10
How oft wisht I night would not give thee place,	Ovid's Elegies	1.13.27
Say that thy love with Caephalus were not knowne,	Ovid's Elegies	1.13.33
Then thinkest thou thy loose life is not showne?	Ovid's Elegies	1.13.34
Not one in heaven should be more base and vile.	Ovid's Elegies	1.13.36
Then wouldst thou cry, stay night and runne not thus.	Ovid's Elegies	1.13.40
I did not bid thee wed an aged swaine.	Ovid's Elegies	1.13.42
Jove that thou shouldst not hast but wait his leasure,	Ovid's Elegies	1.13.45
Yet lingered not the day, but morning scard me.	Ovid's Elegies	1.13.48
Not black, nor golden were they to our viewe,	Ovid's Elegies	1.14.9
Oft in the morne her haires not yet digested,	Ovid's Elegies	1.14.19
Bee not to see with wonted eyes inclinde,	Ovid's Elegies	1.14.37
Nor that I studie not the brawling lawes,	Ovid's Elegies	1.15.5
What age of Varroes name shall not be tolde,	Ovid's Elegies	1.15.21
The living, not the dead can envie bite,	Ovid's Elegies	1.15.39
Her trembling hand writ back she might not doo.	Ovid's Elegies	2.2.6
Let him goe see her though she doe not languish/And then report	Ovid's Elegies	2.2.21
Enquire not what with Isis may be done/Nor feare least she to	Ovid's Elegies	2.2.25
If he loves not, deafe eares thou doest importune,	Ovid's Elegies	2.2.53
To meete for poyson or vilde facts we crave not,	Ovid's Elegies	2.2.63
My hands an unsheath'd shyning weapon have not.	Ovid's Elegies	2.2.64
Thou wert not borne to ride, or armes to beare,	Ovid's Elegies	2.3.7
Thy hands agree not with the warlike speare.	Ovid's Elegies	2.3.8
I meane not to defend the scapes of any,	Ovid's Elegies	2.4.1
If not, because shees simple I would have her.	Ovid's Elegies	2.4.18
Who would not love those hands for their swift running?	Ovid's Elegies	2.4.28
Not drunke, your faults [in] <on> the spilt wine I numbred.	Ovid's Elegies	2.5.14

NOT (cont.)

Not silent were thine eyes, the boord with wine/Was scribled,	Ovid's Elegies	2.5.17
I knew your speech (what do not lovers see)?	Ovid's Elegies	2.5.19
Phoebus gave not Diana such tis thought,	Ovid's Elegies	2.5.27
This grieves me not, no joyned kisses spent,	Ovid's Elegies	2.5.59
All wasting years have that complaint [out] <not> worne.	Ovid's Elegies	2.6.8
Whose earth doth not perpetuall greene-grasse lacke,	Ovid's Elegies	2.6.50
If I looke well, thou thinkest thou doest not move,	Ovid's Elegies	2.7.9
Yet blusht I not, nor usde I any saying,	Ovid's Elegies	2.8.7
Greater then these my selfe I not esteeme,	Ovid's Elegies	2.8.13
Did not Pelides whom his Speare did grieve,	Ovid's Elegies	2.9.7
Rome if her strength the huge world had not fild,	Ovid's Elegies	2.9.17
I know not whether my mindes whirle-wind drives me.	Ovid's Elegies	2.9.28
Better then I their quiver knowes them not.	Ovid's Elegies	2.9.38
I could not be in love with twoo at once,	Ovid's Elegies	2.10.2
Was not one wench inough to greeve my heart?	Ovid's Elegies	2.10.12
If one can doote, if not, two everie night,	Ovid's Elegies	2.10.22
Mine owne desires why should my selfe not flatter?	Ovid's Elegies	2.11.54
He had not beene that conquering Rome did build.	Ovid's Elegies	2.14.16
I would not out, might I in one place hit,	Ovid's Elegies	2.15.19
In heaven without thee would I not be fixt.	Ovid's Elegies	2.16.14
Thou swearest, devision should not twixt us rise,	Ovid's Elegies	2.16.43
Not though thy face in all things make thee raigne,	Ovid's Elegies	2.17.11
This kinde of verse is not alike, yet fit,	Ovid's Elegies	2.17.21
What would not she give that faire name to winne?	Ovid's Elegies	2.17.30
In brazen tower had not Danae dwelt,	Ovid's Elegies	2.19.27
A mothers joy by Jove she had not felt.	Ovid's Elegies	2.19.28
Aye me, let not my warnings cause my paine.	Ovid's Elegies	2.19.34
Thy lofty stile with mine I not compare,	Ovid's Elegies	3.1.39
Not stronger am I, then the thing I move.	Ovid's Elegies	3.1.42
By suffring much not borne by thy severity.	Ovid's Elegies	3.1.48
But till the [keeper] <keepes> went forth, I forget not,	Ovid's Elegies	3.1.55
The maide to hide me in her bosome let not.	Ovid's Elegies	3.1.56
I sit not here the noble horse to see,	Ovid's Elegies	3.2.1
For shame presse not her backe with thy hard knee.	Ovid's Elegies	3.2.24
Or is my heate, of minde, not of the skie?	Ovid's Elegies	3.2.39
The sea I use not: me my earth must have.	Ovid's Elegies	3.2.48
Pay it not heere, but in an other place.	Ovid's Elegies	3.2.84
But did you not so envy Cepheus Daughter,	Ovid's Elegies	3.3.17
Tis not enough, she shakes your record off,	Ovid's Elegies	3.3.19
Tut, men should not their courage so consume.	Ovid's Elegies	3.3.34
Who, because meanes want, doeth not, she doth.	Ovid's Elegies	3.4.4
Was not defilde by any gallant wooer.	Ovid's Elegies	3.4.24
I know not, what men thinke should thee so move.	Ovid's Elegies	3.4.28
She is not chaste, that's kept, but a deare whore:	Ovid's Elegies	3.4.29
And this townes well knowne customes not beleeves,	Ovid's Elegies	3.4.38
Where Mars his sonnes not without fault did breed,	Ovid's Elegies	3.4.39
Cannot a faire one, if not chast, please thee?	Ovid's Elegies	3.4.41
Troy had not yet beene ten yeares siege out-stander,	Ovid's Elegies	3.5.27
not Alpheus in strange lands to runne,/Th'Arcadian Virgins	Ovid's Elegies	3.5.29
Not Calydon, nor Aetolia did please:	Ovid's Elegies	3.5.37
As his deepe whirle-pooles could not quench the same.	Ovid's Elegies	3.5.42
Feare not: to thee our Court stands open wide,	Ovid's Elegies	3.5.61
I know not what expecting, I ere while/Nam'd Achelaus, Inachus,	Ovid's Elegies	3.5.103
Or she was not the wench I wisht t'have had.	Ovid's Elegies	3.6.2
Idly I lay with her, as if I lovde <her> not,	Ovid's Elegies	3.6.3
And like a burthen greevde the bed that mooved not.	Ovid's Elegies	3.6.4
Yet could I not cast ancor where I meant,	Ovid's Elegies	3.6.6
Why might not then my sinews be inchanted,	Ovid's Elegies	3.6.35
Chuf-like had I not gold, and could not use it?	Ovid's Elegies	3.6.50
Well, I beleeve she kist not as she should,	Ovid's Elegies	3.6.55
Now when he should not jette, he boults upright,	Ovid's Elegies	3.6.67
Nay more, the wench did not disdaine a whit,	Ovid's Elegies	3.6.73
But still droupt downe, regarding not her hand,	Ovid's Elegies	3.6.76
I might not go, whether my papers went.	Ovid's Elegies	3.7.6
Knowest not this head a helme was wont to beare,	Ovid's Elegies	3.7.13
Not what we slouthfull [knowe] <knewe>, let wise men learne,	Ovid's Elegies	3.7.25
Men kept the shoare, and sailde not into deepe.	Ovid's Elegies	3.7.44
Why seek'st not heav'n the third realme to frequent?	Ovid's Elegies	3.7.50
Onely our loves let not such rich churles gaine,	Ovid's Elegies	3.7.59
Gallus that [car'dst] <carst> not bloud, and life to spend.	Ovid's Elegies	3.8.64
Rude husband-men bak'd not their corne before,	Ovid's Elegies	3.9.7
I know not whom thou lewdly didst imbrace,	Ovid's Elegies	3.10.11
When have not I fixt to thy side close layed?	Ovid's Elegies	3.10.17
But with my rivall sicke she was not than.	Ovid's Elegies	3.10.26
I am not as I was before, unwise.	Ovid's Elegies	3.10.32
Ile hate, if I can; if not, love gainst my will:	Ovid's Elegies	3.10.35
White birdes to lovers did not alwayes sing.	Ovid's Elegies	3.11.2
Nor, as use will not Poets record heare,	Ovid's Elegies	3.11.19
Seeing thou art faire, I barre not thy false playing,	Ovid's Elegies	3.13.1
But let not mee poore soule know of thy straying.	Ovid's Elegies	3.13.2
She hath not trode <tred> awrie that doth denie it,	Ovid's Elegies	3.13.5
The strumpet with the stranger will not do,	Ovid's Elegies	3.13.9
Be not ashamed to strippe you being there,	Ovid's Elegies	3.13.21
Graunt this, that what you do I may not see,	Ovid's Elegies	3.13.35
If you wey not ill speeches, yet wey mee:	Ovid's Elegies	3.13.36
Ile not sift much, but hold thee soone excusde,	Ovid's Elegies	3.13.41
Sweare I was blinde, yeeld not <deny>, if you be wise,	Ovid's Elegies	3.13.45
Teach but your tongue to say, I did it not,	Ovid's Elegies	3.13.48
two words, thinke/The cause acquits you not, but I that winke.	Ovid's Elegies	3.13.50
Not onely by warres rage made Gentleman.	Ovid's Elegies	3.14.6
Greefe makes her pale, because she mooves not there.	Hero and Leander	1.60
Why art thou not in love, and lov'd of all?	Hero and Leander	1.89

NOT (cont.)
Though thou be faire, yet be not thine owne thrall. Hero and Leander 1.90
It lies not in our power to love, or hate, Hero and Leander 1.167
Who ever lov'd, that lov'd not at first sight? Hero and Leander 1.176
Be not unkind and faire, mishapen stuffe/Are of behaviour Hero and Leander 1.203
O shun me not, but heare me ere you goe, Hero and Leander 1.205
for both not us'de,/Are of like worth. Hero and Leander 1.233
Neither themselves nor others, if not worne. Hero and Leander 1.238
Of that which hath no being, doe not boast, Hero and Leander 1.275
Things that are not at all, are never lost. Hero and Leander 1.276
Beleeve me Hero, honour is not wone, Hero and Leander 1.281
Whose name is it, if she be false or not, Hero and Leander 1.285
Then Hero hate me not, nor from me flie, Hero and Leander 1.291
Love Hero then, and be not tirannous, Hero and Leander 1.323
The richest corne dies, if it be not reapt, Hero and Leander 1.327
not to love at all, and everie part/Strove to resist the Hero and Leander 1.363
Maids are not woon by brutish force and might, Hero and Leander 1.419
As he ought not performe, nor yet she aske. Hero and Leander 1.430
These he regarded not, but did intreat, Hero and Leander 1.451
But long this blessed time continued not; Hero and Leander 1.459
Then muse not, Cupids sute no better sped, Hero and Leander 1.483
He being a novice, knew not what she meant, Hero and Leander 2.13
Wide open stood the doore, hee need not clime, Hero and Leander 2.19
And oft look't out, and mus'd he did not come. Hero and Leander 2.22
I, and shee wisht, albeit not from her hart, Hero and Leander 2.37
O what god would not therewith be appeas'd? Hero and Leander 2.50
But know you not that creatures wanting sence, Hero and Leander 2.55
though Hero would not yeeld/So soone to part from that she Hero and Leander 2.83
Home when he came, he seem'd not to be there, Hero and Leander 2.117
But when he knew it was not Ganimed, Hero and Leander 2.169
That of the cooling river durst not drinke, Hero and Leander 2.197
Breathlesse albeit he were, he rested not, Hero and Leander 2.229
She stayd not for her robes, but straight arose, Hero and Leander 2.235
If not for love, yet love for pittie sake, Hero and Leander 2.247
Love is not ful of pittie (as men say)/But deaffe and cruell, Hero and Leander 2.287
Seeming not woon, yet woon she was at length, Hero and Leander 2.295
Againe she knew not how to frame her looke, Hero and Leander 2.307
NOTE
Note the presumption of this Scythian slave: 1Tamb 3.3.68 Bajzth
Shal give the world to note, for all my byrth, 1Tamb 5.1.188 Tamb
To note me Emperour of the three fold world: 2Tamb 4.3.118 Tamb
Thy instrument and note of Majesty, 2Tamb 5.3.38 Usumc
Now Selim note the unhallowed deeds of Jewes: Jew 5.5.92 Govnr
Yet will the wisest note their proper greefes: P 216 4.14 Anjoy
the realme, my lord of Arundell/You have the note, have you not? Edw 4.3.8 Edward
NOTED
Madam, it wilbe noted through the world, P 207 4.5 Charls
NOTES
wood be flying/And thou the waxe stuft full with notes denying, Ovid's Elegies 1.12.8
And birdes send forth shrill notes from everie bow. Ovid's Elegies 1.13.8
For long shrild trumpets let your notes resound. Ovid's Elegies 2.6.6
Or voice that howe to change the wilde notes knew? Ovid's Elegies 2.6.18
NOTHING
but saving ayre/Is nothing here, and what is this but stone? Dido 2.1.14 Achat
Grecians, which rejoyce/That nothing now is left of Priamus: Dido 2.1.20 Aeneas
And nothing interrupt thy quiet sleepe, Dido 2.1.338 Venus
Nay, nothing, but Aeneas loves me not. Dido 3.4.32 Dido
Nothing can beare me to him but a ship, Dido 5.1.267 Dido
Famous for nothing but for theft and spoile, 1Tamb 4.3.66 Souldn
Nothing but feare and fatall steele my Lord. 1Tamb 5.1.109 1Virgn
Nothing prevailes, for she is dead my Lord. 2Tamb 2.4.124 Therid
sir, for being a king, for Tamburlain came up of nothing. 2Tamb 3.1.74 P Almeda
A wound is nothing be it nere so deepe, 2Tamb 3.2.115 Tamb
Tis nothing: give me a wound father. 2Tamb 3.2.132 P Celeb
Nothing, but stil thy husband and thy sonne? 2Tamb 4.2.37 Therid
Nay Lady, then if nothing wil prevaile, 2Tamb 4.2.50 Therid
either by succession/Or urg'd by force; and nothing violent, Jew 1.1.132 Barab
Of nought is nothing made. Jew 1.2.104 Barab
Be mov'd at nothing, see thou pitty none, Jew 2.3.171 Barab
Nothing but death shall part my love and me. Jew 2.3.317 Abigal
Doe? nothing; but I know what I know. Jew 4.4.14 P Ithimr
Leave nothing loose, all leveld to my mind. Jew 5.5.3 Barab
There wanteth nothing but the Governors pelfe, Jew 5.5.18 Barab
And seen in nothing but Epitomies: P 390 7.30 Guise
And although you take out nothing but your owne, yet you put in P 808 17.3 P Souldr
Nothing shall alter us, wee are resolv'd. Edw 1.4.74 ArchBp
All that he speakes, is nothing, we are resolv'd. Edw 1.4.251 Warwck
Nothing but Gaveston, what means your grace? Edw 2.2.7 Mortmr
Ah nothing greeves me but my little boye, Edw 4.3.48 Edward
Nothing so sweet as Magicke is to him, F 26 Prol.26 1Chor
Who aimes at nothing but externall trash, F 62 1.1.34 Faust
Will make thee vow to study nothing else. F 164 1.1.136 Cornel
Nothing Cornelius; O this cheeres my soule: F 176 1.1.148 Faust
<O but> I feare me, nothing will <can> reclaime him now. F 227 1.2.34 1Schol
My sences are deceiv'd, here's nothing writ: F 468 2.1.80 Faust
Nothing Faustus but to delight thy mind <withall>,/And let thee F 473 2.1.85 Mephst
<talke of the divel, and nothing else: come away>. F 660 (HC263)A P Lucifr
thought you did not sneake up and downe after her for nothing. F 743 2.3.22 P Dick
life, Vintner you shall have your cup anon, say nothing Dick: F1114 3.3.27 P Robin
to stand gaping after the divels Governor, and can see nothing. F1245 4.1.91 P Benvol
turn'd to a gaping Oyster, and drinke nothing but salt water. F1320 4.1.166 P Benvol
I had nothing under me but a little straw, and had much ado to F1486 4.4.30 P HrsCsr
on the score, but say nothing, see if she have forgotten me. F1511 4.5.7 P Robin

NOTHING (cont.)
so delighted me, as nothing in the world could please me more. F1561 4.6.4 P Duke
And do you remember nothing of your leg? . . . . . F1639 4.6.82 P Carter
sir, I would make nothing of you, but I would faine know that. F1648 4.6.91 P Carter
For nothing sir: . . . . F1653 4.6.96 P Carter
Tis but a surfet sir, feare nothing. F1832 5.2.36 3Schol
you <yee> heare, come not unto me, for nothing can rescue me. F1874 5.2.78 P Faust
Nothing but vexe thee more,/To want in hell, that had on earth F1897 5.2.101 BdAngl
But yet all these are nothing, thou shalt see/Ten thousand F1919 5.2.123 BdAngl
druncke with ipocrase at any taberne in Europe for nothing, F App p.234 23 P Robin
Our maister Parson sayes thats nothing. . . . . . F App p.234 25 P Rafe
and nothing answerable to the honor of your Imperial majesty, F App p.236 13 P Faust
Ifaith thats just nothing at all. . . . . F App p.237 40 P Knight
Alas Madame, thats nothing, Mephastophilis, be gone. . F App p.242 12 P Faust
gods and heavenly powers you know,/Or only know you nothing. Lucan, First Booke 450
She nothing said, pale feare her tongue had tyed. . . Ovid's Elegies 1.7.20
If he gives nothing, let him from thee wend. . . . Ovid's Elegies 1.8.100
Nothing I love, that at all times availes me. . . . Ovid's Elegies 2.19.8
Wilt nothing do, why I should wish thy death? . . . Ovid's Elegies 2.19.56
Homer without this shall be nothing worth. . . . Ovid's Elegies 3.7.28
One is no number, mayds are nothing then, ... Hero and Leander 1.255
He askt, she gave, and nothing was denied, ... Hero and Leander 2.25
Supposing nothing else was to be done, ... Hero and Leander 2.53
dallying with Hero, nothing saw/That might delight him more, Hero and Leander 2.62
Whose waight consists in nothing but her name, . . . Hero and Leander 2.114
And nothing more than counsaile, lovers hate. . . . Hero and Leander 2.140

NOTORIOUS
In heaven was never more notorious fable. . . . . Ovid's Elegies 1.9.40

NOTWITHSTANDING
Yet notwithstanding, like one dead it lay, . . . Ovid's Elegies 3.6.65

NOUGHT (See also NAUGHT)
To make me think of nought but blood and war. . . . 1Tamb 4.2.55 Tamb
Tis nought for your majesty to give a kingdome. . . 2Tamb 3.1.77 Jrslem
and fit for nought/But perches for the black and fatall Ravens. 2Tamb 4.3.22 Tamb
Of nought is nothing made. . . . . Jew 1.2.104 Barab
From nought at first thou camst to little welth, . . Jew 1.2.105 1Knght
Content thee, Barabas, thou hast nought but right. . . Jew 1.2.152 Govnr
That measure nought but by the present time. . . . Jew 1.2.220 Barab
And nought is to be look'd for now but warres, . . . Jew 3.5.35 Govnr
And nought to us more welcome is then wars. . . . Jew 3.5.36 Govnr
To keepe me here will nought advantage you. . . . Jew 5.5.117 Calym
These lookes of thine can harbor nought but death. . . Edw 5.5.73 Edward
shoots/Alongst the ayre and [nought] <not> resisting it/Falls, Lucan, First Booke 157
say I merit nought,/Yet for long service done, reward these Lucan, First Booke 340
And take heed least he gets that love for nought. . . Ovid's Elegies 1.8.72
For beds ill hyr'd we are indebted nought. . . . Ovid's Elegies 1.10.44
Pardon me Jove, thy weapons ayde me nought, . . . Ovid's Elegies 2.1.19
famous names/Farewel, your favour nought my minde inflames. Ovid's Elegies 2.1.36
But in the ayre let these words come to nought, . . Ovid's Elegies 2.14.41
Onely Ile signe nought, that may grieve me much. . . Ovid's Elegies 2.15.18
Healthfull Peligny I esteeme nought worth, . . . Ovid's Elegies 2.16.37
Thy springs are nought but raine and melted snowe: . . Ovid's Elegies 3.5.93
And may th'earths weight thy ashes nought molest. . . Ovid's Elegies 3.8.68
The barbarous Thratian soldier moov'd with nought, . . Hero and Leander 1.81

NOURCERY
things feigne)/Crete proud that Jove her nourcery maintaine. Ovid's Elegies 3.9.20

NOURISH
We shall not need to nourish any doubt, ... 2Tamb 3.1.26 Callap
That there begin and nourish every part, ... 2Tamb 3.4.7 Capt

NOURISHMENT
For want of nourishment to feed them both, ... 1Tamb 2.7.47 Cosroe

NOURISHT
That never nourisht thought against thy rule, ... 1Tamb 5.1.98 1Virgn
So having vext she nourisht my warme fire, ... Ovid's Elegies 2.19.15

NOVELL
And bid him battell for his novell Crowne? . . . . 1Tamb 2.5.88 Techel

NOVELTIE
we wish for ought/The world affoords in greatest noveltie, 1Tamb 2.5.73 Tamb

NOVICE
And be a Novice in your Nunnery, ... Jew 1.2.325 Abigal
First let me as a Novice learne to frame/My solitary life to Jew 1.2.331 Abigal
He being a novice, knew not what she meant, ... Hero and Leander 2.13

NOW
Poore Troy must now be sackt upon the Sea, ... Dido 1.1.64 Venus
Whereas the Wind-god warring now with Fate, ... Dido 1.1.115 Jupitr
What? doe I see my sonne now come on shoare: . . . . Dido 1.1.134 Venus
Though we be now in extreame miserie, ... Dido 1.1.157 Achat
Now is the time for me to play my part: . . . . . Dido 1.1.182 Venus
As to instruct us under what good heaven/We breathe as now, and Dido 1.1.198 Aeneas
Which now we call Italia of his name, ... Dido 1.2.23 Cloan
Where am I now? these should be Carthage walles. . . Dido 2.1.1 Aeneas
Grecians, which rejoyce/That nothing now is left of Priamus: Dido 2.1.20 Aeneas
And now she sees thee how will she rejoyce? . . . . Dido 2.1.69 Illion
And now am neither father, Lord, nor King: . . . . Dido 2.1.239 Aeneas
Now is he fast asleepe, and in this grove/Amongst greene brakes Dido 2.1.316 Venus
Now Cupid turne thee to Ascanius shape, ... Dido 2.1.323 Venus
Now Cupid cause the Carthaginian Queene, ... Dido 3.1.1 Cupid
No more my child, now talke another while, ... Dido 3.1.26 Dido
What will you give me now? Ile have this Fanne. . . Dido 3.1.32 Cupid
Dido, that till now/Didst never thinke Aeneas beautifull: Dido 3.1.82 Dido
But now for quittance of this oversight, ... Dido 3.1.84 Dido
but now thou art here, tell me in sooth/In what might Dido Dido 3.1.101 Dido
Yet how <here> <now> I sweare by heaven and him I love, . Dido 3.1.166 Dido

NOW (cont.)

But I will take another order now,	Dido	3.2.6	Juno
Say Paris, now shall Venus have the ball?	Dido	3.2.12	Juno
Say vengeance, now shall her Ascanius dye?	Dido	3.2.13	Juno
Yet now I doe repent me of his ruth,	Dido	3.2.47	Juno
Thy sonne thou knowest with Dido now remaines,	Dido	3.2.70	Juno
Unto the purpose which we now propound.	Dido	3.2.95	Juno
All fellowes now, disposde alike to sporte,	Dido	3.3.5	Dido
How now Getulian, are ye growne so brave,	Dido	3.3.19	Dido
Yea little sonne, are you so forward now?	Dido	3.3.34	Dido
O how these irksome labours now delight,	Dido	3.3.56	Aeneas
But Dido that now holdeth him so deare,	Dido	3.3.76	Iarbus
So doth he now, though not with equall gaine,	Dido	3.3.83	Iarbus
Something it was that now I have forgot.	Dido	3.4.30	Dido
But now that I have found what to effect,	Dido	3.4.37	Dido
Now if thou beest a pitying God of power,	Dido	4.2.19	Iarbus
him to his ships/That now afflicts me with his flattering eyes.	Dido	4.2.22	Iarbus
How now Iarbus, at your prayers so hard?	Dido	4.2.23	Anna
O false Aeneas, now the sea is rough,	Dido	4.4.26	Dido
Now lookes Aeneas like immortall Jove,	Dido	4.4.45	Dido
Lets see what tempests can anoy me now.	Dido	4.4.60	Aeneas
And now to make experience of my love,	Dido	4.4.64	Dido
Now serve to chastize shipboyes for their faults,	Dido	4.4.157	Dido
Now let him hang my favours on his masts,	Dido	4.4.159	Dido
Now speake Ascanius, will ye goe or no?	Dido	4.5.12	Nurse
Why doe I thinke of love now I should dye?	Dido	4.5.34	Nurse
How now Aeneas, sad, what meanes these dumpes?	Dido	5.1.62	Iarbus
Now will I haste unto Lavinian shoare,	Dido	5.1.78	Aeneas
But here he is, now Dido trie thy wit.	Dido	5.1.86	Dido
Now if thou goest, what canst thou leave behind,	Dido	5.1.151	Dido
Wilt thou now slay me with thy venomed sting,	Dido	5.1.167	Dido
But he shrinkes backe, and now remembring me,	Dido	5.1.190	Dido
Now bring him backe, and thou shalt be a Queene,	Dido	5.1.197	Dido
And now downe falles the keeles into the deepe:	Dido	5.1.253	Dido
Now is he come on shoare safe without hurt:	Dido	5.1.257	Dido
now have I found a meane/To rid me from these thoughts of	Dido	5.1.272	Dido
So, leave me now, let none approach this place.	Dido	5.1.291	Dido
Now Dido, with these reliques burne thy selfe,	Dido	5.1.292	Dido
And now ye gods that guide the starrie frame,	Dido	5.1.302	Dido
What can my teares or cryes prevaile me now?	Dido	5.1.319	Anna
But Anna now shall honor thee in death,	Dido	5.1.325	Anna
Now sweet Iarbus stay, I come to thee.	Dido	5.1.329	Anna
Now to be rulde and governed by a man,	1Tamb	1.1.12	Cosroe
Now Turkes and Tartars shake their swords at thee,	1Tamb	1.1.16	Cosroe
Then now my Lord, I humbly take my leave.	1Tamb	1.1.81	Therid
O where is dutie and allegeance now?	1Tamb	1.1.101	Mycet
How now my Lord, what, mated and amaz'd/To heare the king thus	1Tamb	1.1.107	Menaph
Now sits and laughs our regiment to scorne:	1Tamb	1.1.117	Cosroe
Now living idle in the walled townes,	1Tamb	1.1.146	Ceneus
But now you see these letters and commandes,	1Tamb	1.2.21	Tamb
What now? In love?	1Tamb	1.2.106	Techel
How now, what's the matter?	1Tamb	1.2.110	Tamb
How now my Lords of Egypt and Zenocrate?	1Tamb	1.2.113	Tamb
Now must your jewels be restor'd againe:	1Tamb	1.2.114	Tamb
As if he now devis'd some Stratageme:	1Tamb	1.2.159	Therid
Joine with me now in this my meane estate,	1Tamb	1.2.202	Tamb
And now faire Madam, and my noble Lords,	1Tamb	1.2.253	Tamb
That now is marching neer to Parthia:	1Tamb	2.1.65	Cosroe
Then having past Armenian desarts now,	1Tamb	2.2.14	Meandr
Now worthy Tamburlaine, have I reposde,	1Tamb	2.3.1	Cosroe
The King your Brother is now hard at hand,	1Tamb	2.3.45	Tamb
now whet thy winged sword/And lift thy lofty arme into the	1Tamb	2.3.51	Cosroe
Thinke thee invested now as royally,	1Tamb	2.5.2	Tamb
Now send Ambassage to thy neighbor Kings,	1Tamb	2.5.20	Cosroe
And now we will to faire Persepolis,	1Tamb	2.5.24	Cosroe
Now will i gratify your former good,	1Tamb	2.5.30	Cosroe
And now Lord Tamburlaine, my brothers Campe/I leave to thee,	1Tamb	2.5.38	Cosroe
Resolve my Lords and loving souldiers now,	1Tamb	2.6.34	Cosroe
and now dooth gastly death/With greedy tallents gripe my	1Tamb	2.7.48	Cosroe
Who thinke you now is king of Persea?	1Tamb	2.7.56	Tamb
So, now it is more surer on my head,	1Tamb	2.7.65	Tamb
So now the mighty Souldan heares of you,	1Tamb	3.2.31	Agidas
Now in his majesty he leaves those lookes,	1Tamb	3.2.61	Agidas
I prophecied before and now I proove,	1Tamb	3.2.90	Agidas
Let us afford him now the bearing hence.	1Tamb	3.2.111	Usumc
Hath now in armes ten thousand Janisaries,	1Tamb	3.3.15	Bassoe
Now shalt thou feel the force of Turkish arms,	1Tamb	3.3.134	Bajzth
Now strengthen him against the Turkish Bajazeth,	1Tamb	3.3.191	Zenoc
Now Mahomet, solicit God himselfe,	1Tamb	3.3.195	Zabina
Now king of Bassoes, who is Conqueror?	1Tamb	3.3.212	Tamb
Now let me offer to my gracious Lord,	1Tamb	3.3.218	Zenoc
No Tamburlain, though now thou gat the best,	1Tamb	3.3.222	Zabina
Not now Theridamas, her time is past:	1Tamb	3.3.228	Tamb
Now will the Christian miscreants be glad,	1Tamb	3.3.236	Bajzth
Now cleare the triple region of the aire,	1Tamb	4.2.30	Tamb
But fixed now in the Meridian line,	1Tamb	4.2.38	Tamb
To faire Damascus, where we now remaine,	1Tamb	4.2.99	Tamb
Now may we see Damascus lofty towers,	1Tamb	4.2.102	Tamb
Your tentes of white now pitch'd before the gates/And gentle	1Tamb	4.2.111	Therid
Now Tamburlaine, the mightie Souldane comes,	1Tamb	4.3.63	Souldn
Now hang our bloody collours by Damascus,	1Tamb	4.4.1	Tamb
And now Bajazeth, hast thou any stomacke?	1Tamb	4.4.10	Tamb
How now Zenocrate, dooth not the Turke and his wife make a	1Tamb	4.4.57	P Tamb

NOW (cont.)

Wel, here is now to the Souldane of Egypt, the King of Arabia,	1Tamb	4.4.113	P	Tamb
Now take these three crownes, and pledge me, my contributorie	1Tamb	4.4.114	P	Tamb
We see his tents have now bene altered,	1Tamb	5.1.7		Govnr
As now when furie and incensed hate/Flings slaughtering terrour	1Tamb	5.1.71		Tamb
Embraceth now with teares of ruth and blood,	1Tamb	5.1.85		1Virgn
Now waxe all pale and withered to the death,	1Tamb	5.1.91		1Virgn
He now is seated on my horsmens speares,	1Tamb	5.1.114		Tamb
And now my footstoole, if I loose the field,	1Tamb	5.1.209		Tamb
Now throwen to roomes of blacke abjection,	1Tamb	5.1.267		Bajzth
Now Bajazeth, abridge thy banefull daies,	1Tamb	5.1.286		Bajzth
Hide now thy stained face in endles night,	1Tamb	5.1.292		Bajzth
What other heavie news now brings Philemus?	1Tamb	5.1.377		Zenoc
Comes now as Turnus gainst Eneas did,	1Tamb	5.1.380		Philem
Now shame and duty, love and feare presents/A thousand sorrowes	1Tamb	5.1.383		Zenoc
As now it bringeth sweetnesse to my wound,	1Tamb	5.1.420		Arabia
Ah that the deadly panges I suffer now,	1Tamb	5.1.422		Arabia
But making now a vertue of thy sight,	1Tamb	5.1.428		Arabia
Shal now, adjoining al their hands with mine,	1Tamb	5.1.493		Tamb
For now her mariage time shall worke us rest.	1Tamb	5.1.504		Techel
And now my Lords and loving followers,	1Tamb	5.1.522		Tamb
Now have we martcht from faire Natolia/Two hundred leagues, and	2Tamb	1.1.6		Orcan
Proud Tamburlaine, that now in Asia,	2Tamb	1.1.16		Gazell
Then County-Pallatine, but now a king:	2Tamb	1.1.104		Sgsmnd
But now Orcanes, view my royall hoste,	2Tamb	1.1.106		Sgsmnd
Now Sigismond, if any Christian King/Encroche upon the confines	2Tamb	1.1.146		Orcan
Ah were I now but halfe so eloquent/To paint in woords, what	2Tamb	1.2.9		Callap
Now goe I to revenge my fathers death.	2Tamb	1.2.78		Callap
Now bright Zenocrate, the worlds faire eie,	2Tamb	1.3.1		Tamb
Now rest thee here on faire Larissa Plaines,	2Tamb	1.3.5		Tamb
So, now she sits in pompe and majestie:	2Tamb	1.3.17		Tamb
Now will we banquet on these plaines a while,	2Tamb	1.3.157		Tamb
But now my friends, let me examine ye,	2Tamb	1.3.172		Tamb
Now say my Lords of Buda and Bohemia,	2Tamb	2.1.1		Sgsmnd
It resteth now then that your Majesty/Take all advantages of	2Tamb	2.1.11		Fredrk
Now then my Lord, advantage take hereof,	2Tamb	2.1.22		Fredrk
Now will we march from proud Orminius mount/To faire Natolia,	2Tamb	2.2.2		Orcan
And now come we to make his sinowes shake,	2Tamb	2.2.9		Gazell
Be now reveng'd upon this Traitors soule,	2Tamb	2.2.58		Orcan
Now lie the Christians bathing in their bloods,	2Tamb	2.3.10		Orcan
Now shall his barbarous body be a pray/To beasts and foules,	2Tamb	2.3.14		Orcan
Now scaldes his soule in the Tartarian streames,	2Tamb	2.3.18		Orcan
And now Gazellus, let us haste and meete/Our Army and our	2Tamb	2.3.42		Orcan
Of Greekish wine now let us celebrate/Our happy conquest,	2Tamb	2.3.46		Orcan
Now wants the fewell that enflamde his beames:	2Tamb	2.4.4		Tamb
Now by the malice of the angry Skies,	2Tamb	2.4.11		Tamb
Now walk the angels on the walles of heaven,	2Tamb	2.4.15		Tamb
Shine downwards now no more, but deck the heavens/To entertaine	2Tamb	2.4.20		Tamb
Now are those Spheares where Cupid usde to sit,	2Tamb	2.4.81		Tamb
And now I doubt not but your royall cares/Hath so provided for	2Tamb	3.1.20		Callap
Will now retaine her olde inconstancie,	2Tamb	3.1.29		Callap
And now my Lords, advance your speares againe,	2Tamb	3.2.43		Tamb
Sorrow no more my sweet Casane now:	2Tamb	3.2.44		Tamb
But now my boies, leave off, and list to me,	2Tamb	3.2.53		Tamb
Now look I like a souldier, and this wound/As great a grace and	2Tamb	3.2.117		Tamb
Now my boyes, what think you of a wound?	2Tamb	3.2.129		Tamb
Usumcasane now come let us martch/Towards Techelles and	2Tamb	3.2.145		Tamb
Now ugly death stretch out thy Sable wings,	2Tamb	3.4.16		Olymp
Who gently now wil lance thy Ivory throat,	2Tamb	3.4.24		Olymp
How now Madam, what are you doing?	2Tamb	3.4.34		Therid
Souldiers now let us meet the Generall,	2Tamb	3.4.85		Therid
Now, he that cals himself the scourge of Jove,	2Tamb	3.5.21		Orcan
Who now with Jove opens the firmament,	2Tamb	3.5.56		Callap
How now Casane?	2Tamb	3.5.58		Tamb
Now thou art fearfull of thy armies strength,	2Tamb	3.5.75		Orcan
I shall now revenge/My fathers vile abuses and mine owne.	2Tamb	3.5.90		Callap
So sirha, now you are a king you must give armes.	2Tamb	3.5.137	P	Tamb
How now ye pety kings, loe, here are Bugges/Wil make the haire	2Tamb	3.5.147		Tamb
Wel, now you see hee is a king, looke to him Theridamas, when we	2Tamb	3.5.153	P	Tamb
But now my followers and my loving friends,	2Tamb	3.5.159		Tamb
Now in their glories shine the golden crownes/Of these proud	2Tamb	4.1.1		Amyras
Now brother, follow we our fathers sword,	2Tamb	4.1.4		Amyras
See now ye slaves, my children stoops your pride/And leads your	2Tamb	4.1.76		Tamb
And now ye cankred curres of Asia,	2Tamb	4.1.132		Tamb
Now you shal feele the strength of Tamburlain,	2Tamb	4.1.135		Tamb
But now I finde thee, and that feare is past.	2Tamb	4.2.20		Therid
Now stab my Lord, and mark your weapons point/That wil be	2Tamb	4.2.79		Olymp
Now Hell is fairer than Elisian,	2Tamb	4.2.87		Therid
And now the damned soules are free from paine,	2Tamb	4.2.91		Therid
Now fetch me out the Turkish Concubines,	2Tamb	4.3.64		Tamb
Where are my common souldiers now that fought/So Lion-like upon	2Tamb	4.3.67		Tamb
And now themselves shal make our Pageant,	2Tamb	4.3.90		Tamb
Now crowch ye kings of greatest Asia,	2Tamb	4.3.98		Tamb
And now will work a refuge to our lives,	2Tamb	5.1.25		1Citzn
Now fil the mouth of Limnasphaltes lake,	2Tamb	5.1.67		Tamb
Now in the place where faire Semiramis,	2Tamb	5.1.73		Tamb
Wel, now Ile make it quake, go draw him up,	2Tamb	5.1.107		Tamb
So, now their best is done to honour me,	2Tamb	5.1.131		Tamb
See now my Lord how brave the Captaine hangs.	2Tamb	5.1.149		Amyras
So now he hangs like Bagdets Governour,	2Tamb	5.1.158		Tamb
Goe now and bind the Burghers hand and foot,	2Tamb	5.1.161		Tamb
Now Casane, wher's the Turkish Alcaron,	2Tamb	5.1.173		Tamb
Now Mahomet, if thou have any power,	2Tamb	5.1.187		Tamb

NOW (cont.)

Lordes, what now remaines/But that we leave sufficient garrison	2Tamb	5.1.210	Tamb
King of Amasia, now our mighty hoste,	2Tamb	5.2.1	Callap
Now in defiance of that woonted love,	2Tamb	5.3.10	Therid
Shall sicknesse proove me now to be a man,	2Tamb	5.3.44	Tamb
Tel me, what think you of my sicknes now?	2Tamb	5.3.81	Tamb
See my Phisitions now, how Jove hath sent/A present medicine to	2Tamb	5.3.105	Tamb
Then now remoove me, that I may resigne/My place and proper	2Tamb	5.3.175	Tamb
Now fetch the hearse of faire Zenocrate,	2Tamb	5.3.210	Tamb
Now eies, injoy your latest benefite,	2Tamb	5.3.224	Tamb
And now the Guize is dead, is come from France/To view this	Jew	Prol.3	Machvl
But now how stands the wind?	Jew	1.1.38	Barab
Loaden with Spice and Silkes, now under saile,	Jew	1.1.45	Barab
But who comes heare? How now.	Jew	1.1.48	Barab
Or who is honour'd now but for his wealth?	Jew	1.1.113	Barab
Why, how now Countrymen?	Jew	1.1.143	Barab
And Barabas now search this secret out.	Jew	1.1.177	Barab
And now by that advantage thinkes, belike,	Jew	1.1.184	Barab
Now Bassoes, what demand you at our hands?	Jew	1.2.1	Govnr
Now [Governour], how are you resolv'd?	Jew	1.2.17	Calym
Now lanch our Gallies backe againe to Sea,	Jew	1.2.29	Calym
Yes, give me leave, and Hebrews now come neare.	Jew	1.2.38	Govnr
Now then here know that it concerneth us--	Jew	1.2.42	Govnr
And now it cannot be recall'd.	Jew	1.2.93	Govnr
It shall be so: now Officers have you done?	Jew	1.2.131	Govnr
And now shall move you to bereave my life.	Jew	1.2.143	Barab
We now are almost at the new made Nunnery.	Jew	1.2.306	1Fryar
Which they have now turn'd to a Nunnery.	Jew	1.2.320	Abigal
Why how now Abigall, what mak'st thou/Amongst these hateful	Jew	1.2.338	Barab
Why how now Don Mathias, in a dump?	Jew	1.2.374	Lodowk
Now have I happily espy'd a time/To search the plancke my	Jew	2.1.20	Abigal
Now I remember those old womens words,	Jew	2.1.24	Barab
And now me thinkes that I am one of those:	Jew	2.1.28	Barab
Now that my fathers fortune were so good/As but to be about	Jew	2.1.31	Abigal
Father, it draweth towards midnight now,	Jew	2.1.55	Abigal
Now Phoebus ope the eye-lids of the day,	Jew	2.1.60	Barab
Now Captaine tell us whither thou art bound?	Jew	2.2.1	Govnr
Now will I shew my selfe to have more of the Serpent then the	Jew	2.3.36	P Barab
Yond walks the Jew, now for faire Abigall.	Jew	2.3.38	Lodowk
But now I must be gone to buy a slave.	Jew	2.3.95	Barab
Now let me know thy name, and therewithall/Thy birth,	Jew	2.3.163	Barab
And now and then, to cherish Christian theeves,	Jew	2.3.177	Barab
And now and then one hang himselfe for griefe,	Jew	2.3.196	Barab
But tell me now, How hast thou spent thy time?	Jew	2.3.201	Barab
For now by this has he kist Abigall;	Jew	2.3.246	Barab
Even now as I came home, he slipt me in,	Jew	2.3.267	Barab
And now I can no longer hold my minde.	Jew	2.3.290	Lodowk
Now have I that for which my soule hath long'd.	Jew	2.3.318	Lodowk
There comes the villaine, now I'le be reveng'd.	Jew	2.3.333	Lodowk
went in at dores/You had bin stab'd, but not a word on't now;	Jew	2.3.338	Barab
Now tell me, Ithimore, how lik'st thou this?	Jew	2.3.364	Barab
So, now will I goe in to Lodowicke,	Jew	2.3.381	Barab
But now against my will I must be chast.	Jew	3.1.4	Curtzn
And now, save Pilia-borza, comes there none.	Jew	3.1.9	Curtzn
now would I give a hundred of the Jewes Crownes that I had such	Jew	3.1.27	P Ithimr
now Abigall shall see/Whether Mathias holds her deare or no.	Jew	3.2.1	Mthias
Now Lodowicke, now Mathias, so;	Jew	3.2.6	Barab
So, now they have shew'd themselves to be tall fellowes.	Jew	3.2.7	Barab
I, part 'em now they are dead: Farewell, farewell.	Jew	3.2.9	Barab
Why, how now Ithimore, why laugh'st thou so?	Jew	3.3.4	Abigal
one; have not the Nuns fine sport with the Fryars now and then?	Jew	3.3.33	P Ithimr
But now experience, purchased with griefe,	Jew	3.3.61	Abigal
Now here she writes, and wils me to repent.	Jew	3.4.5	Barab
For I have now no hope but even in thee;	Jew	3.4.16	Barab
Very well, Ithimore, then now be secret;	Jew	3.4.60	Barab
Now shalt thou see the death of Abigall,	Jew	3.4.62	Barab
Prethe doe: what saist thou now?	Jew	3.4.88	Barab
And now you men of Malta looke about,	Jew	3.5.29	Govnr
So now couragiously encounter them;	Jew	3.5.33	Govnr
And nought is to be look'd for now but warres,	Jew	3.5.35	Govnr
How sweet the Bels ring now the Nuns are dead/That sound at	Jew	4.1.2	Barab
Now all are dead, not one remaines alive.	Jew	4.1.7	Barab
Thou shalt not need, for now the Nuns are dead,	Jew	4.1.15	Barab
Is't not too late now to turne Christian?	Jew	4.1.50	Barab
And now for store of wealth may I compare/With all the Jewes in	Jew	4.1.55	Barab
So, now the feare is past, and I am safe:	Jew	4.1.114	Barab
Now I have such a plot for both their lives,	Jew	4.1.117	Barab
Now Fryar Bernardine I come to you,	Jew	4.1.125	Barab
What time a night is't now, sweet Ithimore?	Jew	4.1.157	Barab
Why, how now Jacomo, what hast thou done?	Jew	4.1.174	Barab
now out alas,/He is slaine.	Jew	4.1.176	Barab
now I to keepe my word,/And give my goods and substance to your	Jew	4.1.189	Barab
And now I thinke on't, going to the execution, a fellow met me	Jew	4.2.27	P Ithimr
and now would I were gone, I am not worthy to looke upon her.	Jew	4.2.35	P Ithimr
Now am I cleane, or rather fouly out of the way.	Jew	4.2.47	P Ithimr
Now, gentle Ithimore, lye in my lap.	Jew	4.2.82	Curtzn
How now?	Jew	4.2.100	P Ithimr
Now to the Jew.	Jew	4.4.11	Curtzn
So, now I am reveng'd upon 'em all.	Jew	4.4.42	Barab
Pardona moy, be no in tune yet; so, now, now all be in.	Jew	4.4.45	P Barab
Whether now, Fidler?	Jew	4.4.70	Pilia
I'le send by word of mouth now; Bid him deliver thee a thousand	Jew	4.4.74	P Ithimr
Let me alone to urge it now I know the meaning.	Jew	4.4.79	Pilia

NOW (cont.)

Now, Gentlemen, betake you to your Armes,	Jew	5.1.1	Govnr
my Lord, his man's now at my lodging/That was his Agent, he'll	Jew	5.1.16	Curtzn
So, now away and fortifie the Towne.	Jew	5.1.60	Govnr
Now whilst you give assault unto the wals,	Jew	5.1.90	Barab
Now vaile your pride you captive Christians,	Jew	5.2.1	Calym
Now where's the hope you had of haughty Spaine?	Jew	5.2.3	Calym
And now, brave Bashawes, come, wee'll walke about/The ruin'd	Jew	5.2.18	Calym
And now, as entrance to our safety,	Jew	5.2.22	Barab
I now am Governour of Malta; true,	Jew	5.2.29	Barab
Now Governor--stand by there, wait within.--	Jew	5.2.50	Barab
Now tell me, Governor, and plainely too,	Jew	5.2.55	Barab
And now at length am growne your Governor,	Jew	5.2.70	Barab
I'le reare up Malta now remedilesse.	Jew	5.2.73	Barab
Doe so, but faile not; now farewell Ferneze:	Jew	5.2.109	Barab
Well, now about effecting this device:	Jew	5.2.117	Barab
And now I see the Scituation,	Jew	5.3.5	Calym
And now, bold Bashawes, let us to our Tents,	Jew	5.3.43	Calym
Why now I see that you have Art indeed.	Jew	5.5.4	Barab
Now Selim-Calymath, returne me word/That thou wilt come, and I	Jew	5.5.11	Barab
Now sirra, what, will he come?	Jew	5.5.13	Barab
Then now are all things as my wish wud have 'em,	Jew	5.5.17	Barab
And see he brings it: Now, Governor, the summe?	Jew	5.5.19	Barab
And Governour, now partake my policy:	Jew	5.5.24	Barab
Now as for Calymath and his consorts,	Jew	5.5.32	Barab
Now tell me, worldlings, underneath the [sunne] <summe>,	Jew	5.5.49	Barab
How now, what means this?	Jew	5.5.64	Calym
And villaines, know you cannot helpe me now.	Jew	5.5.77	Barab
But now begins the extremity of heat/To pinch me with	Jew	5.5.87	Barab
Now Selim note the unhallowed deeds of Jewes:	Jew	5.5.92	Govnr
[all] <call> the world/To rescue thee, so will we guard us now,	Jew	5.5.120	Govnr
And now my Lords the mariage rites perfourm'd,	P 18	1.18	Charls
Now Guise may storme but doe us little hurt:	P 28	1.28	Navrre
Because the house of Burbon now comes in,	P 50	1.50	Admral
Now shall I prove and guerdon to the ful,	P 68	2.11	Guise
Now come thou forth and play thy tragick part,	P 85	2.28	Guise
Now Guise, begins those deepe ingendred thoughts/To burst	P 91	2.34	Guise
Now have we got the fatall stragling deere,	P 204	4.2	QnMoth
How now fellow, what newes?	P 242	4.40	Charls
What shall we doe now with the Admirall?	P 248	4.46	Charls
Now Guise shall catholiques flourish once againe,	P 295	5.22	Anjoy
Now cosin view him well,	P 307	5.34	Anjoy
He mist him neer, but we have strook him now.	P 311	5.38	Guise
And now my Lords let us closely to our busines.	P 332	5.59	Guise
How now my Lords, how fare you?	P 430	7.70	Anjoy
Who I? you are deceived, I rose but now.	P 437	7.77	Anjoy
And now sirs for this night let our fury stay.	P 443	7.83	Guise
And now stay/That bel that to the devils mattins rings.	P 447	7.87	Guise
Now every man put of his burgonet,	P 449	7.89	Guise
Now sirra, what shall we doe with the Admirall?	P 482	9.1	P 1Atndt
Now Madame, how like you our lusty Admirall?	P 494	9.13	Guise
And now Madam as I understand,	P 500	9.19	Guise
My Lords, what resteth there now for to be done?	P 554	11.19	QnMoth
And now my Lords after these funerals be done,	P 561	11.26	QnMoth
And now Navarre whilste that these broiles doe last,	P 565	11.30	Navrre
And now that Henry is cal'd from Polland;	P 569	11.34	Navrre
As now you are, so shall you still persist,	P 608	12.21	King
And now,/Our solemne rites of Coronation done,	P 625	12.38	King
What now remaines, but for a while to feast,	P 627	12.40	King
Thy brother Guise and we may now provide,	P 636	12.49	QnMoth
Now Madam must you insinuate with the King,	P 645	12.58	Cardnl
Now doe I see that from the very first,	P 694	13.38	Guise
And Guise for Spaine hath now incenst the King,	P 711	14.14	Navrre
The power of vengeance now incampes it selfe,	P 717	14.20	Navrre
How now sirra, what newes?	P 723	14.26	Navrre
Of all my army now in readines,	P 744	15.2	King
How now my Lord, faith this is more then need,	P 757	15.15	Guise
How now Mugeroun, metst thou not the Guise at the doore?	P 774	15.32	King
Come my Lords, now that this storme is overpast,	P 804	16.18	Navrre
For now that Paris takes the Guises parte,	P 896	17.91	King
Now fals the star whose influence governes France,	P 944	19.14	Capt
Now must he fall and perish in his height.	P 946	19.16	Capt
Now Captain of my guarde, are these murtherers ready?	P 947	19.17	King
Now sues the King for favour to the Guise,	P 978	19.48	Guise
Now by the holy sacrament I sweare,	P 981	19.51	Guise
Now doe I but begin to look about,	P 985	19.55	Guise
Pray God thou be a King now this is done.	P1068	19.138	QnMoth
But now I will be King and rule my selfe,	P1070	19.140	King
And now will I to armes, come Epernoune:	P1079	19.149	King
To whom shall I bewray my secrets now,	P1083	19.153	QnMoth
Now thou art dead, heere is no stay for us:	P1111	21.5	Dumain
Sancte [Jacobe] <Jacobus>, now have mercye upon me.	P1172	22.34	Frier
Now let the house of Bourbon weare the crowne,	P1232	22.94	King
Now ser to you that dares make a duke a cuckolde and use a	Paris	ms 1,p390	P Souldr
now ser where he is your landlorde you take upon you to be	Paris	ms 9,p390	P Souldr
the armye I have gathered now shall ayme/more at thie end then	Paris	ms28,p391	Guise
But how now, what are these?	Edw	1.1.24	Gavstn
And hew these knees that now are growne so stiffe.	Edw	1.1.95	Edward
But now ile speake, and to the proofe I hope:	Edw	1.1.108	Kent
Now let the treacherous Mortimers conspire,	Edw	1.1.149	Edward
So will I now, and thou shalt back to France.	Edw	1.1.185	BshpCv
How now, why droops the earle of Lancaster?	Edw	1.2.9	MortSr
My lord of Cornewall now, at every worde,	Edw	1.2.17	Lncstr

NOW (cont.)

For now my lord the king regardes me not,	Edw		1.2.49	Queene
My lords, now let us all be resolute,	Edw		1.4.45	Mortmr
Tis done, and now accursed hand fall off.	Edw		1.4.88	Edward
Now is my heart at ease.	Edw		1.4.91	ArchBp
Happie were I, but now most miserable.	Edw		1.4.129	Edward
now breaks the kings hate forth,/And he confesseth that he	Edw		1.4.193	Queene
Feare ye not Madam, now his minions gone,	Edw		1.4.198	Lncstr
That now I hope flotes on the Irish seas.	Edw		1.4.224	Mortmr
She smiles, now for my life his mind is changd.	Edw		1.4.236	Warwck
That now are readie to assaile the Scots.	Edw		1.4.363	Edward
Now is the king of England riche and strong,	Edw		1.4.366	Queene
Now let us in, and feast it roiallie:	Edw		1.4.374	Edward
Leave now to oppose thy selfe against the king,	Edw		1.4.387	MortSr
But nephew, now you see the king is changd.	Edw		1.4.420	MortSr
And even now, a poast came from the court,	Edw		2.1.19	Spencr
And now and then, stab as occasion serves.	Edw		2.1.43	Spencr
Now to the letter of my Lord the King,	Edw		2.1.66	Neece
How now, what newes, is Gaveston arrivde?	Edw		2.2.6	Edward
and now thy sight/Is sweeter farre, then was thy parting hence	Edw		2.2.56	Edward
Cosin it is no dealing with him now,	Edw		2.2.102	Lncstr
Now send our Heralds to defie the King,	Edw		2.2.110	Lncstr
Why how now cosin, how fares all our friends?	Edw		2.2.114	Lncstr
How now, what noise is this?	Edw		2.2.139	Edward
Nay, now you are heere alone, ile speake my minde.	Edw		2.2.155	Mortmr
Now let them thanke themselves, and rue too late.	Edw		2.2.207	Edward
For now the wrathfull nobles threaten warres,	Edw		2.2.210	Kent
Mait please your grace to entertaine them now.	Edw		2.2.241	Neece
But whats the reason you should leave him now?	Edw		2.3.13	Penbrk
now my lords know this,/That Gaveston is secretlie arrivde,	Edw		2.3.15	Lncstr
No, here he comes, now let them spoile and kill:	Edw		2.4.3	Edward
How now my lord of Arundell?	Edw		2.5.32	Lncstr
How now?	Edw		2.5.41	Warwck
That we have taken him, but must we now/Leave him on had-I-wist,	Edw		2.5.84	Warwck
Unhappie Gaveston, whether goest thou now.	Edw		2.5.110	Gavstn
Too kinde to them, but now have drawne our sword,	Edw		3.1.25	Edward
shall I never see,/Never behold thee now?	Edw		3.1.69	Edward
now get thee to thy lords,/And tell them I will come to	Edw		3.1.177	Edward
For now, even now, we marche to make them stoope,	Edw		3.1.183	Edward
Now lustie lords, now not by chance of warre,	Edw		3.1.221	Edward
traitors, now tis time/To be avengd on you for all your braves,	Edw		3.1.224	Edward
denied/To Isabell the Queene, that now in France/Makes friends,	Edw		3.1.269	Spencr
Now on my life, theile neither barke nor bite.	Edw		4.3.13	Edward
Now sirs, the newes from Fraunce.	Edw		4.3.14	Edward
What now remaines, have you proclaimed, my lord,	Edw		4.3.17	Edward
How now, what newes with thee, from whence come these?	Edw		4.3.24	Edward
Now lords, our loving friends and countrimen,	Edw		4.4.1	Queene
Make triall now of that philosophie,	Edw		4.7.17	Edward
But tell me, must I now resigne my crowne,	Edw		5.1.36	Edward
now sweete God of heaven,/Make me despise this transitorie	Edw		5.1.107	Edward
And who must keepe mee now, must you my lorde?	Edw		5.1.137	Edward
And thats the cause that I am now remoovde.	Edw		5.1.150	Edward
Faire Isabell, now have we our desire,	Edw		5.2.1	Mortmr
For now we hould an old Wolfe by the eares,	Edw		5.2.7	Mortmr
So that he now is gone from Killingworth,	Edw		5.2.31	BshpWn
Who now makes Fortunes wheele turne as he please,	Edw		5.2.53	Mortmr
So now away, post thither wards amaine.	Edw		5.2.67	Mortmr
The more cause have I now to make amends.	Edw		5.2.103	Kent
But hee repents, and sorrowes for it now.	Edw		5.2.108	Prince
Come, come, away, now put the torches out,	Edw		5.3.47	Matrvs
How now, who comes there?	Edw		5.3.49	Gurney
The commons now begin to pitie him,	Edw		5.4.2	Mortmr
And to conclude, I am Protector now,	Edw		5.4.64	Mortmr
Now is all sure, the Queene and Mortimer/Shall rule the realme,	Edw		5.4.65	Mortmr
Lord Mortimer, now take him to your charge.	Edw		5.4.81	Queene
More then we can enflict, and therefore now,	Edw		5.5.11	Matrvs
So,/Now must I about this geare, nere was there any/So finely	Edw		5.5.39	Ltborn
Nor shall they now be tainted with a kings.	Edw		5.5.82	Ltborn
Now as I speake they fall, and yet with feare/Open againe.	Edw		5.5.95	Edward
How now my Lorde.	Edw		5.5.102	Ltborn
if thou now growest penitent/Ile be thy ghostly father,	Edw		5.6.3	Mortmr
Now Mortimer begins our tragedie.	Edw		5.6.23	Queene
How now my lord?	Edw		5.6.26	Mortmr
Base fortune, now I see, that in thy wheele/There is a point, to	Edw		5.6.59	Mortmr
Could I have rulde thee then, as I do now,	Edw		5.6.96	King
Not marching <now> in the fields of Thrasimen,	F	1	Prol.1	1Chor
we must now performe/The forme of Faustus fortunes, good or	F	7	Prol.7	1Chor
And now <so> to patient judgements we appeale <our plaude>,	F	9	Prol.9	1Chor
Now is he borne, of parents base of stocke,	F	11	Prol.11	1Chor
And glutted now <more> with learnings golden gifts,	F	24	Prol.24	1Chor
How now sirra, where's thy Maister?	F	197	1.2.4	P 1Schol
<O but> I feare me, nothing will <can> reclaime him now.	F	227	1.2.34	1Schol
Now that the gloomy shadow of the night <earth>,	F	229	1.3.1	Faust
[Now <No> Faustus, thou art Conjurer laureate]/[That canst	F	260	1.3.32A	Faust
Now Faustus what wouldst thou have me do?	F	263	1.3.35	Mephst
No, I came now hether of mine owne accord.	F	272	1.3.44	Mephst
Now that I have obtain'd what I desir'd <desire>/I'le live in	F	340	1.3.112	Faust
So, now thou art to bee at an̄ howres warning, whensoever, and	F	369	1.4.27	P Wagner
How now sir, will you serve me now?	F	376	1.4.34	P Wagner
Now sirra follow me.	F	379	1.4.37	P Wagner
Now Faustus, must thou needs be damn'd,	F	389	2.1.1	Faust
[And] canst <thou> not [now] be sav'd.	F	390	2.1.2	Faust
Now go not backward: no, Faustus, be resolute.	F	394	2.1.6	Faust

NOW (cont.)

Now tell me what saith <sayes> Lucifer thy Lord.	F 419	2.1.31		Faust
But now <Faustus> thou must bequeath it solemnly,	F 423	2.1.35		Mephst
So, now the bloud begins to cleere againe:	F 460	2.1.72		Faust
Now will I make an end immediately.	F 461	2.1.73		Faust
So, now Faustus aske me what thou wilt.	F 503	2.1.115		Mephst
For I tell thee I am damn'd, and <am> now in hell.	F 526	2.1.138		Mephst
<How? now in hell?>	F 527	(HC261)A		Faust
Now Faustus wilt thou have a wife?	F 533	2.1.145		Mephst
[Now would I have a booke where I might see al characters of	F 551.4	2.1.167A	P	Faust
now tell me who made the world?	F 618	2.2.67	P	Faust
Now Faustus, question <examine> them of their <several> names	F 661	2.2.110	P	Belzeb
bag; and might I now obtaine <have> my wish, this house,	F 675	2.2.124	P	Covet
Now Faustus thou hast heard all my progeny, wilt thou bid me to	F 700	2.2.149	P	Glutny
<Now Faustus, how dost thou like this>?	F 711	(HC264)A		Lucifr
Now Faustus farewell.	F 720	2.2.172		Lucifr
conjuring bookes, and now we'le have such knavery, as't passes.	F 723	2.3.2	P	Robin
He now is gone to prove Cosmography,	F 773	2.3.52		2Chor
Having now my good Mephostophilis,	F 779	3.1.1		Faust
But tell me now, what resting place is this?	F 800	3.1.22		Faust
But <And> now my Faustus, that thou maist perceive,	F 809	3.1.31		Mephst
Now by the Kingdomes of Infernall Rule,	F 825	3.1.47		Faust
So shall our sleeping vengeance now arise,	F 879	3.1.101		Pope
Now tell me Faustus, are we not fitted well?	F 940	3.1.162		Mephst
Now Faustus, come prepare thy selfe for mirth,	F 981	3.2.1		Mephst
But now, that Faustus may delight his minde,	F 989	3.2.9		Faust
So Faustus, now for all their holinesse,	F1004	3.2.24		Mephst
now Friers take heed,/Lest Faustus make your shaven crownes to	F1006	3.2.26		Faust
You brought us word even now, it was decreed,	F1019	3.2.39		Pope
now Faustus to the feast,/The Pope had never such a frolicke	F1035	3.2.55		Faust
How now? who snatch't the meat from me!	F1044	3.2.64		Pope
Purgatory, and now is come unto your holinesse for his pardon.	F1060	3.2.80	P	Archbp
How now?	F1065	3.2.85		Faust
Now Faustus, what will you do now?	F1071	3.2.91	P	Mephst
Now Robin, now or never shew thy cunning.	F1094	3.3.7	P	Dick
Come on sirra, let me search you now.	F1104	3.3.17	P	Vintnr
Constantinople have they brought me now <am I hither brought>,	F1118	3.3.31		Mephst
Now with the flames of ever-burning fire,	F1135	3.3.48		Mephst
[Now is his fame spread forth in every land],	F1149	3.3.62A		3Chor
at whose pallace now]/[Faustus is feasted mongst his noblemen].	F1151	3.3.64A		3Chor
Why how now sir Knight, what, hang'd by the hornes?	F1290	4.1.136	P	Faust
He has done penance now sufficently.	F1310	4.1.156		Emper
now sword strike home,/For hornes he gave, Il'e have his head	F1360	4.2.36		Benvol
The Divel's dead, the Furies now may laugh.	F1369	4.2.45		Benvol
and now sirs, having divided him, what shall the body doe?	F1389	4.2.65	P	Mrtino
How now Benvolio?	F1438	4.3.8		Mrtino
now sirra I must tell you, that you may ride him o're hedge and	F1467	4.4.11	P	Faust
Now am I a made man for ever.	F1476	4.4.20	P	HrsCsr
Murder or not murder, now he has but one leg, I'le out-run him,	F1494	4.4.38	P	HrsCsr
How now Wagner what newes with thee?	F1499	4.4.43	P	Faust
How now, what lacke you?	F1507	4.5.3	P	Hostss
Come sirs, what shall we do now till mine Hostesse comes?	F1520	4.5.16	P	Dick
eate; now sir, I thinking that a little would serve his turne,	F1527	4.5.23	P	Carter
Now sirs, you shall heare how villanously he serv'd mee:	F1535	4.5.31	P	HrsCsr
Now sir, I thinking the horse had had some [rare] quality that	F1541	4.5.37	P	HrsCsr
me his leg quite off, and now 'tis at home in mine Hostry.	F1551	4.5.47	P	HrsCsr
heart desires to have, and were it now Summer, as it is January,	F1572	4.6.15	P	Lady
Here, now taste yee these, they should be good, for they come	F1576	4.6.19	P	Faust
Why how now Maisters, what a coyle is there?	F1591	4.6.34		Servnt
Why, how now my [good] <goods> friends?	F1608	4.6.51		Faust
But I have it againe now I am awake:	F1657	4.6.100	P	Faust
now you have sent away my guesse, I pray who shall pay me for	F1667	4.6.110	P	Hostss
hee's now at supper with the schollers, where ther's such	F1678	5.1.5	P	Wagner
Now <Since> we have seene the pride of Natures worke <workes>,	F1702	5.1.29		1Schol
Though thou hast now offended like a man,	F1710	5.1.37		OldMan
And Faustus now will come to do thee right.	F1728	5.1.55		Faust
Accursed Faustus, [where is mercy now]?	F1739	5.1.66		Faust
Fond worldling, now his heart bloud dries with griefe;	F1808	5.2.12		Mephst
Now worthy Faustus: me thinks your looks are chang'd.	F1821	5.2.25		1Schol
thee, then had I lived still, but now must <I> dye eternally.	F1825	5.2.29	P	Faust
and now ['tis] <'ts> too late.	F1866	5.2.70	P	Faust
I, Faustus, now thou hast no hope of heaven,	F1880	5.2.84		Mephst
And now must taste hels paines perpetually.	F1895	5.2.99		BdAngl
O what will all thy riches, pleasures, pompes,/Availe thee now?	F1897	5.2.101		GdAngl
And now poore soule must thy good Angell leave thee,	F1907	5.2.111		GdAngl
Now Faustus let thine eyes with horror stare/Into that vaste	F1909	5.2.113		BdAngl
Now hast thou but one bare houre to live,	F1927	5.2.131		Faust
Where is it now?	F1943	5.2.147		Faust
Now draw up Faustus like a foggy mist,	F1952	5.2.156		Faust
<O> It strikes, it strikes; now body turne to aire,	F1975	5.2.179		Faust
now sirra thou art at an houres warning whensoever or	F App	p.230 36	P	Wagner
How now, whose that which spake?	F App	p.231 3	P	Pope
How now, whose that which snatcht the meate from me?	F App	p.231 8	P	Pope
now wil I make al the maidens in our parish dance at my	F App	p.233 3	P	Robin
How say you now?	F App	p.234 12	P	Robin
now sir, you may be ashamed to burden honest men with a matter	F App	p.234 14	P	Rafe
good divel forgive me now, and Ile never rob thy Library more.	F App	p.235 31	P	Robin
now theres a signe of grace in you, when you will confesse the	F App	p.237 44	P	Knight
now to send for the knight that was so pleasent with me here of	F App	p.238 66	P	Faust
How now sir Knight?	F App	p.238 69	P	Emper
but now I see thou hast a wife, that not only gives thee	F App	p.238 70	P	Emper
Now my good Lord having done my duety, I humbly take my leave.	F App	p.238 86	P	Faust
Now Mephastophilis, the restlesse course that time doth runne	F App	p.239 90	P	Faust

NOW (cont.)

Now am I made man for ever, Ile not leave my horse for fortie:	F App	p.239 114 P HrsCsr
now, I thinking my horse had had some rare qualitie that he	F App	p.240 131 P HrsCsr
Ile speake with him now, or Ile breake his glasse-windowes	F App	p.240 142 P HrsCsr
How now Wagner, what's the newes with thee?	F App	p.241 167 P Faust
carowse, and swill/Amongst the Students, as even now he doth,	F App	p.243 5 Wagner
Now Babilon, (proud through our spoile) should stoop,	Lucan, First Booke	10
That now the walles of houses halfe [rear'd] <reaer'd> totter,	Lucan, First Booke	24
Now Caesar overpast the snowy Alpes,	Lucan, First Booke	185
But now the winters wrath and wat'ry moone,	Lucan, First Booke	219
Now light had quite dissolv'd the mysty [night] <might>,	Lucan, First Booke	263
That crost them; both which now approacht the camp,	Lucan, First Booke	270
Now while their part is weake, and feares, march hence,	Lucan, First Booke	281
Roome rageth now in armes/As if the Carthage Hannibal were	Lucan, First Booke	304
And now least age might waine his state, he casts/For civill	Lucan, First Booke	324
What, now Scicillian Pirats are supprest,	Lucan, First Booke	336
Whether now shal these olde bloudles soules repaire?	Lucan, First Booke	343
force, they that now thwart right/In wars wil yeeld to wrong:	Lucan, First Booke	349
And Druides you now in peace renew/Your barbarous customes, and	Lucan, First Booke	446
is by cowards/Left as a pray now Caesar doth approach:	Lucan, First Booke	512
Now evermore least some one hope might ease/The Commons	Lucan, First Booke	520
Now spearlike, long; now like a spreading torch:	Lucan, First Booke	530
to unfould/What you intend, great Jove is now displeas'd,	Lucan, First Booke	631
If cold noysome Saturne/Were now exalted, and with blew beames	Lucan, First Booke	651
O Phoebus shouldst thou with thy rayes now sing/The fell Nemean	Lucan, First Booke	654
Whither turne I now?	Lucan, First Booke	682
now throughout the aire I flie,/To doubtfull Sirtes and drie	Lucan, First Booke	685
New factions rise; now through the world againe/I goe; o Phoebus	Lucan, First Booke	691
We which were Ovids five books, now are three,	Ovid's Elegies	1.1.1
But how thou shouldst behave thy selfe now know;	Ovid's Elegies	1.4.11
(O mischiefe) now for me obtaine small grace.	Ovid's Elegies	1.6.22
But now perchaunce thy wench with thee doth rest,	Ovid's Elegies	1.6.45
Now frosty night her flight beginnes to take,	Ovid's Elegies	1.6.65
Go now thou Conqueror, glorious triumphs raise,	Ovid's Elegies	1.7.35
starre of Mars hath done thee harme,/Now Mars is gone:	Ovid's Elegies	1.8.30
Now Mars doth rage abroad without all pitty,	Ovid's Elegies	1.8.41
Deny him oft, feigne now thy head doth ake:	Ovid's Elegies	1.8.73
And Isis now will shew what scuse to make.	Ovid's Elegies	1.8.74
Now all feare with my mindes hot love abates,	Ovid's Elegies	1.10.9
Now inward faults thy outward forme disgrace.	Ovid's Elegies	1.10.14
Now on <ore> the sea from her old love comes shee,	Ovid's Elegies	1.13.1
Now in her tender armes I sweetly bide,	Ovid's Elegies	1.13.5
If ever, now well lies she by my side.	Ovid's Elegies	1.13.6
The aire is colde, and sleepe is sweetest now,	Ovid's Elegies	1.13.7
Now hast thou left no haires at all to die.	Ovid's Elegies	1.14.2
Now Germany shall captive haire-tyers send thee,	Ovid's Elegies	1.14.45
Now many guests were gone, the feast being done,	Ovid's Elegies	2.5.21
I that ere-while was fierce, now humbly sue,	Ovid's Elegies	2.5.49
Now rash accusing, and thy vaine beliefe,	Ovid's Elegies	2.7.13
With strawie cabins now her courts should build.	Ovid's Elegies	2.9.18
The [haven] <heaven> touching barcke now nere the lea,	Ovid's Elegies	2.9.32
Now let her flatter me, now chide me hard,	Ovid's Elegies	2.9.45
For now I love two women equallie:	Ovid's Elegies	2.10.4
The carefull ship-man now feares angry gusts,	Ovid's Elegies	2.11.25
My selfe poore wretch mine owne gifts now envie.	Ovid's Elegies	2.15.8
And Phillis hath to reade; if now she lives.	Ovid's Elegies	2.18.32
Now I forewarne, unlesse to keepe her stronger,	Ovid's Elegies	2.19.47
Now give the Roman Tragedie a name,	Ovid's Elegies	3.1.29
Now would I slacke the reines, now lash their hide,	Ovid's Elegies	3.2.11
With wheeles bent inward now the ring-turne ride.	Ovid's Elegies	3.2.12
In vaine why flyest backe? force conjoynes us now:	Ovid's Elegies	3.2.19
Now comes the pompe; themselves let all men cheere:	Ovid's Elegies	3.2.43
Now greatest spectacles the Praetor sends,	Ovid's Elegies	3.2.65
But now againe the barriers open lye;	Ovid's Elegies	3.2.77
At least now conquer, and out-runne the rest:	Ovid's Elegies	3.2.79
Now shine her lookes pure white and red betwixt.	Ovid's Elegies	3.3.6
Who now will care the Altars to perfume?	Ovid's Elegies	3.3.33
With snow thaw'd from the next hill now thou rushest,	Ovid's Elegies	3.5.7
Now wish I those wings noble Perseus had,	Ovid's Elegies	3.5.13
Now wish the chariot, whence corne [seedes] <fields> were	Ovid's Elegies	3.5.15
Now when he should not jette, he boults upright,	Ovid's Elegies	3.6.67
Seeing now thou wouldst deceive me as before:	Ovid's Elegies	3.6.70
What man will now take liberall arts in hand,	Ovid's Elegies	3.7.1
Now poverty great barbarisme we hold.	Ovid's Elegies	3.7.4
Romulus, temples brave/Bacchus, Alcides, and now Caesar have.	Ovid's Elegies	3.7.52
Now, Sabine-like, though chast she seemes to live,	Ovid's Elegies	3.7.61
Ah now a name too true thou hast, I finde.	Ovid's Elegies	3.8.4
Now have I freed my selfe, and fled the chaine,	Ovid's Elegies	3.10.3
Now my ship in the wished haven crownd,	Ovid's Elegies	3.10.29
Now love, and hate my light brest each way move;	Ovid's Elegies	3.10.33
I feare with me is common now to many.	Ovid's Elegies	3.11.6
The ships, whose God-head in the sea now glisters?	Ovid's Elegies	3.11.38
Now your credulity harme to me hath raisd.	Ovid's Elegies	3.11.44
Now is the goat brought through the boyes with darts,	Ovid's Elegies	3.12.21
And having wandred now through sea and land,	Ovid's Elegies	3.12.33
for the lovely boy/That now is turn'd into a Cypres tree,	Hero and Leander	1.155
And now begins Leander to display/Loves holy fire, with words,	Hero and Leander	1.192
Having striv'ne in vaine, was now about to crie,	Hero and Leander	1.413
Now waxt she jealous, least his love abated,	Hero and Leander	2.43
Now he her favour and good will had wone.	Hero and Leander	2.54
And now the same gan so to scorch and glow,	Hero and Leander	2.70
Now had the morne espy'de her lovers steeds,	Hero and Leander	2.87
her selfe the clouds among/And now Leander fearing to be mist,	Hero and Leander	2.91

NOW (cont.)			
And now the sunne that through th'orizon peepes, . .	Hero and Leander		2.99
What is it now, but mad Leander dares?	Hero and Leander		2.146
That now should shine on Thetis glassie bower, . . .	Hero and Leander		2.203
And now she lets him whisper in her eare, ...	Hero and Leander		2.267
Leander now like Theban Hercules, ...	Hero and Leander		2.297
And now she wisht this night were never done, . . .	Hero and Leander		2.301
NOWE			
hath nowe gathered a fresh Armie, and hearing your absence in	2Tamb	5.3.103	P 3Msngr
my heart desires, and were it nowe summer, as it is January,	F App	p.242 9	P Duchss
even nowe when youthfull bloud/Pricks forth our lively bodies,	Lucan, First Booke		363
NO WHERE			
For no where else the new earle is so safe.	Edw	1.4.11	Lncstr
For no where else seekes he felicitie.	Edw	1.4.122	Gavstn
No where can they be taught but in the bed, . . .	Ovid's Elegies		2.5.61
NOYSE			
Frighted with this confused noyse, I rose, . . .	Dido	2.1.191	Aeneas
And with a solemne noyse of trumpets sound, . . .	F1237	4.1.83	Faust
and what noyse soever you <yee> heare, come not unto me, for	F1873	5.2.77	P Faust
And opening dores with creaking noyse abound? . . .	Ovid's Elegies		1.6.50
NOYSOME			
If cold noysome Saturne/Were now exalted, and with blew beames	Lucan, First Booke		650
NUBIA			
And conquering that, made haste to Nubia, ...	2Tamb	1.3.202	Techel
From thence to Nubia neere Borno Lake, ...	2Tamb	5.3.136	Tamb
NULLA			
Si peccasse negamus, fallimur, et nulla est in nobis veritas:	F 68	1.1.40	P Faust
NUMA			
Egeria with just Numa had good sport, ...	Ovid's Elegies		2.17.18
NUMB (See NUMDE, NUMM'D)			
NUMBER			
Seeing the number of their men decreast, ...	Dido	2.1.132	Aeneas
Suppose they be in number infinit, ...	1Tamb	2.2.43	Meandr
Your men are valiant but their number few, ...	1Tamb	3.3.11	Bassoe
The number of your hostes united is, ...	1Tamb	4.3.52	Capol
In number more than are the drops that fall/When Boreas rents a	2Tamb	1.3.159	Tamb
Thinke them in number yet sufficient, ...	2Tamb	3.1.41	Orcan
In number more than are the quyvering leaves/Of Idas forrest,	2Tamb	3.5.5	2Msngr
Tell me Viceroies the number of your men, ...	2Tamb	3.5.30	Callap
Small though the number was that kept the Towne, . .	Jew	2.2.49	Bosco
Do [match] <watch> the number of the daies contain'd, .	F 821	3.1.43	Mephst
[Love] <I> slackt my Muse, and made my [numbers] <number> soft.	Ovid's Elegies		1.1.22
The number two no good divining bringes.	Ovid's Elegies		1.12.28
One is no number, mayds are nothing then, ...	Hero and Leander		1.255
NUMBER'S			
Alas, our number's few,/And Crownes come either by succession	Jew	1.1.130	Barab
NUMBERS			
That register the numbers of my ruth, ...	Dido	4.2.39	Iarbus
Nay could their numbers countervail the stars, . . .	1Tamb	4.1.30	Souldn
And numbers more than infinit of men, ...	2Tamb	2.2.18	Gazell
kings again my Lord/To gather greater numbers gainst our power,	2Tamb	4.1.83	Amyras
[Love] <I> slackt my Muse, and made my [numbers] <number> soft.	Ovid's Elegies		1.1.22
With shorter numbers the heroicke sit.	Ovid's Elegies		2.17.22
And by those numbers is thy first youth spent. . . .	Ovid's Elegies		3.1.28
NUMBRED			
Since last we numbred to your Majesty.	2Tamb	3.5.39	Orcan
Since last we numbred to your majesty.	2Tamb	3.5.45	Trebiz
Since last we numbred to your majestie:	2Tamb	3.5.49	Soria
Not drunke, your faults [in] <on> the spilt wine I numbred.	Ovid's Elegies		2.5.14
NUMDE			
My mindes distempered, and my bodies numde, ...	Edw	5.5.64	Edward
NUMEN			
Dei Acherontis propitii, valeat numen triplex Jehovae, Ignei,	F 244	1.3.16	P Faust
NUMM'D			
And faintnes numm'd his steps there on the brincke: . .	Lucan, First Booke		196
NUMMING			
Through numming cold, all feeble, faint and wan: . .	Hero and Leander		2.246
NUN			
Well, daughter, we admit you for a Nun.	Jew	1.2.330	Abbass
Faire Abigall the rich Jewes daughter/Become a Nun? . .	Jew	1.2.367	Mthias
And strangely metamorphis'd Nun.	Jew	1.2.381	Mthias
They hop'd my daughter would ha bin a Nun;	Jew	2.3.12	Barab
To get me be admitted for a Nun.	Jew	3.3.55	Abigal
Pure rose shee, like a Nun to sacrifice, ...	Ovid's Elegies		3.6.21
So lovely faire was Hero, Venus Nun, ...	Hero and Leander		1.45
Then shall you most resemble Venus Nun, ...	Hero and Leander		1.319
NUNC			
et consecratam aquam quam nunc spargo; signumque crucis quod	F 249	1.3.21	P Faust
signumque crucis quod nunc facio; et per vota nostra ipse nunc	F 249	1.3.21	P Faust
per vota nostra ipse nunc surgat nobis dicatus Mephostophilis.	F 250	1.3.22	P Faust
NUNNE			
How, as a Nunne?	Jew	1.2.281	Abigal
What, Abigall become a Nunne againe?	Jew	3.4.1	Barab
Why, made mine Abigall a Nunne.	Jew	3.4.24	Barab
And for his sake did I become a Nunne.	Jew	3.6.25	Abigal
too dearely wunne/That unto death did presse the holy Nunne.	Ovid's Elegies		1.10.50
To whom you offer, and whose Nunne you are.	Hero and Leander		1.212
NUNNERIES			
and then I say they use/To send their Almes unto the Nunneries:	Jew	3.4.77	Barab
NUNNERY			
Convert his mansion to a Nunnery, ...	Jew	1.2.129	1Knght
and of thy house they meane/To make a Nunnery, where none but	Jew	1.2.256	Abigal
thou toldst me they have turn'd my house/Into a Nunnery, and	Jew	1.2.278	Barab

NUNNERY (cont.)
We now are almost at the new made Nunnery. Jew 1.2.306 1Fryar
And waters of this new made Nunnery/Will much delight you. Jew 1.2.311 1Fryar
Which they have now turn'd to a Nunnery. Jew 1.2.320 Abigal
And be a Novice in your Nunnery, Jew 1.2.325 Abigal
I'le have a saying to that Nunnery. Jew 2.3.90 Barab
Goe to the new made Nunnery, and inquire/For any of the Fryars Jew 3.3.27 Abigal
Art thou againe got to the Nunnery? Jew 3.4.4 Barab

NUNNES
For there I left the Governour placing Nunnes, Jew 1.2.254 Abigal
then the Nunnes/And their vaild Matron, who alone might view Lucan, First Booke 596
As is the use, the Nunnes in white veyles clad, Ovid's Elegies 3.12.27

NUNS
His house will harbour many holy Nuns. Jew 1.2.130 1Knght
have turn'd my house/Into a Nunnery, and some Nuns are there. Jew 1.2.278 Barab
And 'bout this time the Nuns begin to wake; Jew 2.1.56 Abigal
And made my house a place for Nuns most chast. Jew 2.3.77 Barab
And yet I know the prayers of those Nuns/And holy Fryers, Jew 2.3.80 Barab
Good Barabas glance not at our holy Nuns. Jew 2.3.86 Lodowk
one; have not the Nuns fine sport with the Fryars now and then? Jew 3.3.32 P Ithimr
I'le carry't to the Nuns with a powder. Jew 3.4.112 P Ithimr
Oh brother, brother, all the Nuns are sicke, Jew 3.6.1 1Fryar
Oh he is gone to see the other Nuns. Jew 3.6.10 2Fryar
Oh brother, all the Nuns are dead, let's bury them. Jew 3.6.44 1Fryar
How sweet the Bels ring now the Nuns are dead/That sound at Jew 4.1.2 Barab
Thou shalt not need, for now the Nuns are dead, Jew 4.1.15 Barab
I carried the broth that poyson'd the Nuns, and he and I, Jew 4.4.20 P Ithimr
that the Nuns lov'd Rice, that Fryar Bernardine slept in his Jew 4.4.76 P Ithimr
poyson'd his owne daughter and the Nuns, strangled a Fryar, Jew 5.1.13 P Pilia
strangled Bernardine, poyson'd the Nuns, and his owne daughter. Jew 5.1.33 P Ithimr

NUPTIALL
Knit in these hands, thus joyn'd in nuptiall rites, P 4 1.4 Charls
How they did storme at these your nuptiall rites, P 49 1.49 Admral
Who spots my nuptiall bed with infamie, Edw 5.1.31 Edward

NURSE
Goe, bid my Nurse take yong Ascanius, Dido 4.4.105 Dido
Your Nurse is gone with yong Ascanius, Dido 4.4.124 Lord
Nurse I am wearie, will you carrie me? Dido 4.5.15 Cupid
Come Nurse. Dido 4.5.35 Cupid
And sister, Nurse, and mother spare him not, Ovid's Elegies 1.8.91

NURSERIES (See also NOURCERY)
That in our famous nurseries of artes/Thou suckedst from Plato, Edw 4.7.18 Edward

NURST
Inhumaine creatures, nurst with Tigers milke, Edw 5.1.71 Edward

NUT
[And nut-browne girles in doing have no fellowe]. Ovid's Elegies 2.4.40

NUT-BROWNE
[And nut-browne girles in doing have no fellowe]. Ovid's Elegies 2.4.40

NUTS
have fine sport with the boyes, Ile get nuts and apples enow. F App p.236 46 P Robin
Nuts were thy food, and Poppie causde thee sleepe, Ovid's Elegies 2.6.31

NY
So beautie, sweetly quickens when t'is ny, Hero and Leander 2.126

NYE
Or art thou grievde thy betters presse so nye? Dido 3.3.18 Iarbus

NYLUS
This headlesse trunke that lies on Nylus sande/I know: Lucan, First Booke 684

NYMPH (See also NIMPH)
To see how he this captive Nymph beguil'd. Hero and Leander 2.40

NYMPHES
As Seaborne Nymphes shall swarme about thy ships, Dido 3.1.129 Dido

NYMPHS
Even as, when gawdie Nymphs pursue the chace, Hero and Leander 1.113
And to those sterne nymphs humblie made request, Hero and Leander 1.379
Least water-nymphs should pull him from the brinke. Hero and Leander 2.198
heart of Hero much more joies/Then nymphs and sheapheards, Hero and Leander 2.233

O'
in a brasen Bull/Of great ones envy; o'th poore petty wites, Jew Prol.26 Machvl
to clap hornes of honest mens heades o'this order, F1317 4.1.163 P Benvol

O (Homograph; See also OH)
O how would I with Helens brother laugh, Dido 1.1.17 Ganimd
Tell us, O tell us that are ignorant, Dido 1.1.200 Aeneas
Save, save, O save our ships from cruell fire, Dido 1.2.7 Illion
O my Achates, Theban Niobe, Dido 2.1.3 Aeneas
And kisse his hand: O where is Hecuba? Dido 2.1.12 Achat
O yet this stone doth make Aeneas weepe, Dido 2.1.15 Aeneas
O Priamus is left and this is he, Dido 2.1.21 Aeneas
O were I not at all so thou mightst be. Dido 2.1.28 Aeneas
O Illioneus, art thou yet alive? Dido 2.1.55 Achat
O what destinies/Have brought my sweete companions in such Dido 2.1.59 Aeneas
O tell me, for I long to be resolv'd. Dido 2.1.61 Aeneas
This place beseemes me not, O pardon me. Dido 2.1.94 Aeneas
O Priamus, O Troy, oh Hecuba! Dido 2.1.105 Aeneas
And then--O Dido, pardon me. Dido 2.1.159 Aeneas
O th'inchaunting words of that base slave, Dido 2.1.161 Aeneas
O had it never entred, Troy had stood. Dido 2.1.172 Aeneas
O Hector who weepes not to heare thy name? Dido 2.1.209 Dido
O let me live, great Neoptolemus. Dido 2.1.239 Aeneas
O end Aeneas, I can heare no more. Dido 2.1.243 Dido
O there I lost my wife: Dido 2.1.270 Aeneas
O what became of aged Hecuba? Dido 2.1.290 Anna
O had that ticing strumpet nere been borne: Dido 2.1.300 Dido
O stay Iarbus, and Ile goe with thee. Dido 3.1.37 Dido

O (cont.)

O Anna, didst thou know how sweet love were,	Dido	3.1.59	Dido
O that Iarbus could but fancie me.	Dido	3.1.62	Anna
O sister, were you Empresse of the world,	Dido	3.1.69	Anna
O dull conceipted Dido, that till now/Didst never thinke Aeneas	Dido	3.1.82	Dido
O here he comes, love, love, give Dido leave/To be more modest	Dido	3.1.94	Dido
O happie shall he be whom Dido loves.	Dido	3.1.168	Aeneas
O if I speake/I shall betray my selfe:--	Dido	3.1.172	Dido
O no God wot, I cannot watch my time,	Dido	3.2.14	Juno
O how these irksome labours now delight,	Dido	3.3.56	Aeneas
O love, O hate, O cruell womens hearts,	Dido	3.3.66	Iarbus
O God of heaven, turne the hand of fate/Unto that happie day of	Dido	3.3.80	Iarbus
Aeneas, O Aeneas, quench these flames.	Dido	3.4.23	Dido
Heare, heare, O heare Iarbus plaining prayers,	Dido	4.2.8	Iarbus
O leave me, leave me to my silent thoughts,	Dido	4.2.38	Iarbus
O Anna, runne unto the water side,	Dido	4.4.1	Dido
O foolish Troians that would steale from hence,	Dido	4.4.5	Dido
O princely Dido, give me leave to speake,	Dido	4.4.17	Aeneas
O false Aeneas, now the sea is rough,	Dido	4.4.26	Dido
O how a Crowne becomes Aeneas head!	Dido	4.4.38	Dido
O keepe them still, and let me gaze my fill:	Dido	4.4.44	Dido
O where is Ganimed to hold his cup,	Dido	4.4.46	Dido
O that the Clowdes were here wherein thou [fledst] <fleest>,	Dido	4.4.50	Dido
O Dido, patronesse of all our lives,	Dido	4.4.55	Aeneas
O blessed tempests that did drive him in,	Dido	4.4.94	Dido
O happie sand that made him runne aground:	Dido	4.4.95	Dido
O that I had a charme to keepe the windes/Within the closure of	Dido	4.4.99	Dido
What if I sinke his ships? O heele frowne:	Dido	4.4.110	Dido
O cursed tree, hadst thou but wit or sense,	Dido	4.4.139	Dido
O Dido, blame not him, but breake his oares,	Dido	4.4.149	Dido
O what meane I to have such foolish thoughts!	Dido	4.5.25	Nurse
O sacred love,/If there be any heaven in earth, tis love:	Dido	4.5.26	Nurse
O how unwise was I to say him nay!	Dido	4.5.37	Nurse
O pardon me, if I resolve thee why:	Dido	5.1.91	Aeneas
O speake like my Aeneas, like my love:	Dido	5.1.112	Dido
O then Aeneas, tis for griefe of thee:	Dido	5.1.116	Dido
O thy lips have sworne/To stay with Dido:	Dido	5.1.120	Dido
O Queene of Carthage, wert thou ugly blacke,	Dido	5.1.125	Aeneas
O no, the Gods wey not what Lovers doe,	Dido	5.1.131	Dido
O Serpent that came creeping from the shoare,	Dido	5.1.165	Dido
O Anna, my Aeneas is abourd,	Dido	5.1.194	Dido
O Dido, your little sonne Ascanius/Is gone!	Dido	5.1.212	Nurse
O cursed hagge and false dissembling wretch!	Dido	5.1.216	Dido
O Anna, Anna, I will follow him.	Dido	5.1.241	Dido
O Anna, fetch [Arions] <Orions> Harpe,	Dido	5.1.248	Dido
O sister, sister, take away the Rockes,	Dido	5.1.254	Dido
Theile breake his ships, O Proteus, Neptune, Jove,	Dido	5.1.255	Dido
O helpe Iarbus, Dido in these flames/Hath burnt her selfe, aye	Dido	5.1.314	Anna
O sweet Iarbus, Annas sole delight,	Dido	5.1.322	Anna
O where is dutie and allegeance now?	1Tamb	1.1.101	Mycet
O Gods, is this Tamburlaine the thiefe,	1Tamb	2.4.41	Mycet
O my Lord, tis sweet and full of pompe.	1Tamb	2.5.55	Techel
O Mahomet, Oh sleepie Mahomet.	1Tamb	3.3.269	Bajzth
O cursed Mahomet that makest us thus/The slaves to Scythians	1Tamb	3.3.270	Zabina
O let him alone:	1Tamb	4.4.40	P Tamb
Pittie our plightes, O pitie poore Damascus:	1Tamb	5.1.80	1Virgn
O then for these, and such as we our selves,	1Tamb	5.1.96	1Virgn
O pitie, (sacred Emperour)/The prostrate service of this	1Tamb	5.1.99	1Virgn
O pitie us.	1Tamb	5.1.119	Omnes
Why should we live, O wretches, beggars, slaves,	1Tamb	5.1.248	Zabina
O life more loathsome to my vexed thoughts,	1Tamb	5.1.255	Bajzth
O dreary Engines of my loathed sight,	1Tamb	5.1.259	Bajzth
O poore Zabina, O my Queen, my Queen,	1Tamb	5.1.275	Bajzth
O highest Lamp of everliving Jove,	1Tamb	5.1.290	Bajzth
O Bajazeth, my husband and my Lord,	1Tamb	5.1.308	Zabina
O Bajazeth, O Turk, O Emperor.	1Tamb	5.1.309	Zabina
O sight thrice welcome to my joiful soule,	1Tamb	5.1.440	Zenoc
O just and dreadfull punisher of sinne,	2Tamb	2.3.4	Sgsmnd
Live still my Lord, O let my soveraigne live,	2Tamb	2.4.57	Zenoc
O cowardly boy, fie for shame, come foorth.	2Tamb	4.1.31	Celeb
O Samarcanda, where I breathed first,	2Tamb	4.1.105	Tamb
O damned monster, nay a Feend of Hell,	2Tamb	4.1.168	Jrslem
O thou that swaiest the region under earth,	2Tamb	4.3.32	Orcan
O pity us my Lord, and save our honours.	2Tamb	4.3.83	Ladies
O mercilesse infernall cruelty.	2Tamb	4.3.85	Jrslem
O then ye Powers that sway eternal seates,	2Tamb	5.3.17	Techel
O father, if the unrelenting eares/Of death and hell be shut	2Tamb	5.3.191	Amyras
O father, Don Mathias is my love.	Jew	2.3.237	Abigal
O the sweetest face that ever I beheld!	Jew	3.1.26	P Ithimr
Religion: O Diabole.	P 123	2.65	Guise
O no, sweet Margaret, the fatall poyson/Workes within my head,	P 184	3.19	OldQn
O gracious God, what times are these?	P 188	3.23	Navrre
O graunt sweet God my daies may end with hers,	P 189	3.24	Navrre
O let me pray before I dye.	P 301	5.28	Admral
O God forgive my sins.	P 303	5.30	Admral
O let me pray before I take my death.	P 352	6.7	Seroun
O Christ my Saviour--	P 354	6.9	Seroun
O let me pray unto my God.	P 359	6.14	Seroun
O let him goe, he is a catholick.	P 375	7.15	Retes
O good my Lord,/Wherein hath Ramus	P 383	7.23	Ramus
O good my Lord, let me but speak a word.	P 399	7.39	Ramus
O no, his bodye will infect the fire, and the fire the aire,	P 484	9.3	P 1Atndt
O Mounser de Guise, heare me but speake.	P 529	10.2	Prtsnt

O (cont.)

O let me stay and rest me heer a while,	P 536	11.1	Charls
O say not so, thou kill'st thy mothers heart.	P 539	11.4	QnMoth
O no, my loving brother of Navarre.	P 543	11.8	Charls
O holde me up, my sight begins to faile,	P 548	11.13	Charls
O no, his soule is fled from out his breast,	P 552	11.17	QnMoth
O Lord, mine eare.	P 619	12.32	Cutprs
O would to God this quill that heere doth write,	P 667	13.11	Duchss
O no my Lord, a woman only must/Partake the secrets of my	P 675	13.19	Duchss
O pardon me my Lord.	P 679	13.23	Duchss
O wicked sexe, perjured and unjust,	P 693	13.37	Guise
O that his heart were leaping in my hand.	P 936	19.6	P 2Mur
O pardon me my Lord of Guise.	P 990	19.60	P 3Mur
O my Lord, I am one of them that is set to murder you.	P 992	19.62	P 3Mur
O Lord no: for we entend to strangle you.	P1095	20.5	2Mur
O wordes of power to kill a thousand men.	P1126	21.20	Dumain
O my Lord, I have beene a great sinner in my dayes, and the	P1133	21.27	P Frier
O my Lord, let him live a while.	P1173	22.35	Eprnon
O that that damned villaine were alive againe,	P1216	22.78	Eprnon
O the fatall poyson workes within my brest,	P1221	22.83	King
O our heads?	Edw	1.1.119	Warwck
O might I keepe thee heere, as I doe this,	Edw	1.4.128	Edward
O that we might as well returne as goe.	Edw	1.4.143	Edward
O miserable and distressed Queene!	Edw	1.4.170	Queene
O never Lancaster!	Edw	1.4.200	Queene
O Lancaster, let him diswade the king,	Edw	1.4.216	Queene
O how a kisse revives poore Isabell.	Edw	1.4.333	Queene
O tell me Spencer, where is Gaveston?	Edw	2.4.1	Edward
O stay my lord, they will not injure you.	Edw	2.4.7	Gavstn
O that mine armes could close this Ile about,	Edw	2.4.17	Queene
O treacherous Warwicke thus to wrong thy friend!	Edw	2.6.1	Gavstn
O must this day be period of my life,	Edw	2.6.4	Gavstn
O shall I speake, or shall I sigh and die!	Edw	3.1.122	Edward
Whether, O whether doost thou bend thy steps?	Edw	4.2.12	Queene
O no my lord, this princely resolution/Fits not the time, away,	Edw	4.5.8	Baldck
O fly him then, but Edmund calme this rage,	Edw	4.6.11	Kent
O hadst thou ever beene a king, thy hart/Pierced deeply with	Edw	4.7.9	Edward
O that I might this life in quiet lead,	Edw	4.7.21	Edward
O might I never open these eyes againe,	Edw	4.7.41	Edward
O never more lift up this dying hart!	Edw	4.7.43	Edward
O day!	Edw	4.7.61	Edward
Center of all misfortune. O my starres!	Edw	4.7.62	Edward
O is he gone!	Edw	4.7.100	Spencr
O would I might, but heavens and earth conspire/To make me	Edw	5.1.96	Edward
O happie newes, send for the prince my sonne.	Edw	5.2.29	Queene
O water gentle friends to coole my thirst,	Edw	5.3.25	Edward
O levell all your lookes upon these daring men,	Edw	5.3.39	Edward
O Gaveston, it is for thee that I am wrongd,	Edw	5.3.41	Edward
O gentle brother, helpe to rescue me.	Edw	5.3.51	Edward
O miserable is that commonweale,	Edw	5.3.63	Kent
O villaines!	Edw	5.5.58	Ltborn
O would my bloud dropt out from every vaine,	Edw	5.5.66	Edward
O speake no more my lorde, this breakes my heart.	Edw	5.5.71	Ltborn
O if thou harborst murther in thy hart,	Edw	5.5.87	Edward
O wherefore sits thou heare?	Edw	5.5.96	Edward
O let me not die yet, stay, O stay a while.	Edw	5.5.101	Edward
O spare me, or dispatche me in a trice.	Edw	5.5.111	Edward
O what a world of profite and delight,	F 80	1.1.52	Faust
O Faustus, lay that damned booke aside,	F 97	1.1.69	GdAngl
Nothing Cornelius; O this cheeres my soule:	F 176	1.1.148	Faust
O Faustus <Nay>,/Then I feare that which	F 219	1.2.26	1Schol
<O but> I feare me, nothing will <can> reclaime him now.	F 227	1.2.34	1Schol
O: by aspiring pride and insolence,	F 295	1.3.67	Mephst
O Faustus leave these frivolous demandes,	F 309	1.3.81	Mephst
O disgrace to my person:	F 344	1.4.2	P Robin
O brave Wagner.	F 384	1.4.42	P Robin
O something soundeth in mine [eares] <eare>,/Abjure this	F 395	2.1.7	Faust
O they are meanes to bring thee unto heaven.	F 406	2.1.18	GdAngl
Faustus gives to thee his soule: [ah] <O> there it staid.	F 456	2.1.68	Faust
O yes, I see it plaine, even heere <in this place> is writ/Homo	F 469	2.1.81	Faust
[O thou art deceived].	F 551.12	2.1.175A	P Faust
[Ah] <O> Christ my Saviour, my Saviour,	F 634	2.2.83	Faust
O what art thou that look'st so [terrible] <terribly>.	F 638	2.2.87	Faust
O Faustus they are come to fetch <away> thy soule.	F 641	2.2.90	Faust
O my sweete Gold!	F 677	2.2.126	P Covet
O that there would come a famine over <through> all the world,	F 681	2.2.130	P Envy
I <O I> come of a Royall Pedigree <parentage>, my father	F 696	2.2.145	P Glutny
<O> But my godmother, O she was an ancient Gentlewoman, her	F 699	2.2.148	P Glutny
O she was an ancient Gentlewoman, her name was <mistress>	F 699	2.2.148	P Glutny
O how this sight doth delight <this feedes> my soule.	F 712	2.2.164	Faust
O might I see hell, and returne againe safe, how happy were I	F 714	2.2.166	P Faust
o per se, o, [demy] <deny> orgon, gorgon:	F 728	2.3.7	P Robin
keepe further from me O thou illiterate, and unlearned Hostler.	F 729	2.3.8	P Robin
O brave, prethee let's to it presently, for I am as dry as a	F 751	2.3.30	P Dick
O I am slaine, help me my Lords:	F1068	3.2.88	Pope
O come and help to beare my body hence:	F1069	3.2.89	Pope
O, are you here?	F1096	3.3.9	P Vintnr
O per se o, demogorgon, Belcher and Mephostophilis.	F1114	3.3.27	P Robin
O brave, an Ape?	F1128	3.3.41	P Robin
O yes,/And with him comes the Germane Conjurer,	F1163	4.1.9	Mrtino
O pardon me, my thoughts are ravished so/With sight of this	F1260	4.1.106	Emper
O wondrous sight:	F1276	4.1.122	Emper
The Emperour? where? O zounds my head.	F1287	4.1.133	Benvol

O (cont.)

O say not sc sir:	F1294	4.1.140		Faust
O may these eye-lids never close againe,	F1332	4.2.8		Benvol
O were that damned Hell-hound but in place,	F1355	4.2.31		Benvol
O help me gentle friend; where is Martino?	F1432	4.3.2		Fredrk
O misery.	F1437	4.3.7		Mrtino
O hellish spite,/Your heads are all set with hornes.	F1441	4.3.11		Benvol
I warrant you sir; O joyfull day:	F1476	4.4.20	P	HrsCsr
O what a cosening Doctor was this?	F1484	4.4.28	P	HrsCsr
O help, help, the villaine hath murder'd me.	F1493	4.4.37	P	Faust
O Hostisse how do you?	F1515	4.5.11	P	Robin
O monstrous, eate a whole load of Hay!	F1532	4.5.28	P	All
O brave Doctor.	F1546	4.5.42	P	All
O horrible, had the Doctor three legs?	F1658	4.6.101	P	All
O gentle Faustus leave this damned Art,	F1707	5.1.34		OldMan
[Ah] <O> stay good Faustus, stay thy desperate steps.	F1729	5.1.56		OldMan
[Ah] <O> [my sweete] friend,	F1734	5.1.61		Faust
O thou art fairer then the evenings <evening> aire,	F1781	5.1.108		Faust
O my deere Faustus what imports this feare?	F1827	5.2.31		1Schol
[Ah] <O> gentlemen, heare [me] with patience, and tremble not	F1838	5.2.42	P	Faust
O would I had never seene Wittenberg <Wertenberge>, never read	F1841	5.2.45	P	Faust
Hell, [ah] <O> hell for ever.	F1846	5.2.50	P	Faust
[Ah] <O> my God, I would weepe, but the Divell drawes in my	F1850	5.2.54	P	Faust
[Ah] <O> gentlemen, I gave them my soule for my cunning.	F1856	5.2.60		Faust
O God forbid.	F1857	5.2.61		AllSch
O what may <shal> we do to save Faustus?	F1868	5.2.72	P	2Schol
O thou bewitching fiend, 'twas thy temptation,	F1883	5.2.87		Faust
O what will all thy riches, pleasures, pompes,	F1896	5.2.100		GdAngl
O thou hast lost celestiall happinesse,	F1899	5.2.103		GdAngl
O, I have seene enough to torture me.	F1921	5.2.125		Faust
[Ah] <O> Faustus,	F1926	5.2.130		Faust
O lente lente currite noctis equi:	F1935	5.2.139		Faust
O I'le leape up to [my God] <heaven>: who puls me downe?	F1938	5.2.142		Faust
Yet will I call on him: O spare me Lucifer.	F1942	5.2.146		Faust
Gape earth; O no, it will not harbour me.	F1949	5.2.153		Faust
[Ah] <O> halfe the houre is past:	F1957	5.2.161		Faust
[O God, if thou wilt not have mercy on my soule],	F1958	5.2.162A		Faust
<O, if my soule must suffer for my sinne>,	F1958	(HC271)B		Faust
<O> No end is limited to damned soules.	F1963	5.2.167		Faust
<O> It strikes, it strikes; now body turne to aire,	F1975	5.2.179		Faust
O soule be chang'd into <to> [little] <small> water drops,	F1977	5.2.181		Faust
[My God, my God] <O mercy heaven>, looke not so fierce on me;	F1979	5.2.183		Faust
O help us heaven, see, here are Faustus limbs,	F1988	5.3.6		2Schol
O Ile tickle the pretie wenches plackets Ile be amongst them	F App	p.231 63	P	Clown
O Lord I pray sir, let Banio and Belcher go sleepe.	F App	p.231 68	P	Clown
O this is admirable!	F App	p.233 1	P	Robin
O brave Robin, shal I have Nan Spit, and to mine owne use?	F App	p.234 29	P	Rafe
O nomine Domine, what meanst thou Robin?	F App	p.235 26	P	Vintnr
O not so fast sir, theres no haste but good, are you remembred	F App	p.238 76	P	Faust
O yes, he wil drinke of al waters, but ride him not into the	F App	p.239 111	P	Faust
O yonder is his snipper snapper, do you heare?	F App	p.240 137	P	HrsCsr
O my legge, my legge, helpe Mephastophilis, call the Officers,	F App	p.241 155	P	Faust
O Lord sir, let me goe, and Ile give you fortie dollers more.	F App	p.241 158	P	HrsCsr
Ay me, O what a world of land and sea,	Lucan, First Booke	13		
O Roome thy selfe art cause of all these evils,	Lucan, First Booke	84		
O faintly joyn'd friends with ambition blind,	Lucan, First Booke	87		
rites and Latian Jove advanc'd/On Alba hill o Vestall flames,	Lucan, First Booke	201		
Latian Jove advanc'd/On Alba hill o Vestall flames, o Roome,	Lucan, First Booke	201		
O wals unfortunate too neere to France,	Lucan, First Booke	250		
O gods that easie grant men great estates,	Lucan, First Booke	508		
these he seeing what myschiefes must ensue,/Cride out, O gods!	Lucan, First Booke	630		
O Gods what death prepare ye?	Lucan, First Booke	648		
O Phoebus shouldst thou with thy rayes now sing/The fell Nemean	Lucan, First Booke	654		
onely gives us peace, o Rome continue/The course of mischiefe,	Lucan, First Booke	669		
the world againe/I goe; o Phoebus shew me Neptunes shore,	Lucan, First Booke	692		
(O mischiefe) now for me obtaine small grace.	Ovid's Elegies	1.6.22		
O harder then the dores thou gardest I prove thee.	Ovid's Elegies	1.6.62		
O thou oft wilt blush/And say he likes me for my borrowed bush,	Ovid's Elegies	1.14.47		
Heroes, O <of> famous names/Farewel, your favour nought my minde	Ovid's Elegies	2.1.35		
O would my proofes as vaine might be withstood,	Ovid's Elegies	2.5.7		
O Cupid that doest never cease my smart,	Ovid's Elegies	2.9.1		
O boy that lyest so slothfull in my heart.	Ovid's Elegies	2.9.2		
O would that no Oares might in seas have suncke,	Ovid's Elegies	2.11.5		
O care-got triumph hetherwards advance.	Ovid's Elegies	2.12.16		
O would that sodainly into my gift,	Ovid's Elegies	2.15.9		
(O face most cunning mine eyes to detaine)/Thou oughtst	Ovid's Elegies	2.17.12		
O Poet carelesse of thy argument?	Ovid's Elegies	3.1.16		
O would in my fore-fathers tombe deepe layde,	Ovid's Elegies	3.5.73		
O let him change goods so ill got to dust.	Ovid's Elegies	3.7.66		
O by our fellow bed, by all/The Gods who by thee to be perjurde	Ovid's Elegies	3.10.45		
On this feast day, O cursed day and hower,	Hero and Leander	1.131		
O shun me not, but heare me ere you goe,	Hero and Leander	1.205		
At last he came, O who can tell the greeting,	Hero and Leander	2.23		
O what god would not therewith be appeas'd?	Hero and Leander	2.50		
O none but gods have power their love to hide,	Hero and Leander	2.131		
O Hero, Hero, thus he cry'de full oft,	Hero and Leander	2.147		
O let mee viste Hero ere I die.	Hero and Leander	2.178		
O that these tardie armes of mine were wings,	Hero and Leander	2.205		

OAKE (See also OKES)

Like to a tall oake in a fruitfull field,	Lucan, First Booke	137
With stiffe oake propt the gate doth still appeare.	Ovid's Elegies	1.6.28
and lockes put in the poast/Although of oake, to yeeld to	Ovid's Elegies	2.1.28

OAKEN (See also OKEN)

then Laelius/The chiefe Centurion crown'd with Oaken leaves,	Lucan, First Booke	358

OAKES			
Apples, and hony in oakes hollow boughes.	Ovid's Elegies	3.7.40	
On mast of oakes, first oracles, men fed,	Ovid's Elegies	3.9.9	
OARES			
My Oares broken, and my Tackling lost,	Dido	3.1.107	Aeneas
Oares of massie Ivorie full of holes,	Dido	3.1.118	Dido
Bring me his oares, his tackling, and his sailes:	Dido	4.4.109	Dido
And heres Aeneas tackling, oares and sailes.	Dido	4.4.125	Lord
O Dido, blame not him, but breake his oares,	Dido	4.4.149	Dido
In steed of oares, let him use his hands,	Dido	4.4.163	Dido
Yet hath she tane away my oares and masts,	Dido	5.1.60	Aeneas
O would that no Oares might in seas have suncke,	Ovid's Elegies	2.11.5	
That may transport me without oares to rowe.	Ovid's Elegies	3.5.4	
Nor hanging oares the troubled seas did sweepe,	Ovid's Elegies	3.7.43	
OASTRIE			
I have none about me, come to my Oastrie, and Ile give them you.	F App	p.241 161 P	HrsCsr
OATH (See also OTH, OTHES)			
But (Sigismond) confirme it with an oath,	2Tamb	1.1.131	Orcan
And know my lord, ere I will breake my oath,	Edw	1.1.85	Mortmr
The like oath Penbrooke takes.	Edw	2.2.108	Penbrk
Upon mine oath I will returne him back.	Edw	2.5.88	Penbrk
And keepe [mine oath] <my vow> I made to Lucifer.	F1765	5.1.92	Faust
How long her lockes were, ere her oath she tooke:	Ovid's Elegies	3.3.3	
Tell me, to whom mad'st thou that heedlesse oath?	Hero and Leander	1.294	
OATHES			
My [false] <selfe> oathes in Carpathian seas to cast.	Ovid's Elegies	2.8.20	
OBAY			
Stand not on titles, but obay th'arrest,	Edw	4.7.58	Leistr
Love over-rules my will, I must obay thee,	Lucan, First Booke	373	
OBAYD			
The Legate of the Pope will be obayd:	Edw	1.4.64	Edward
OBAYE			
But what the heavens appoint, I must obaye,	Edw	5.1.56	Edward
OBDURAT			
And Fraunce shall be obdurat with her teares.	Edw	3.1.279	Levune
And who have hard hearts, and obdurat minds,	Hero and Leander	2.217	
OBDURATE			
Will, being absent, be obdurate still.	Dido	5.1.187	Dido
some your children)/Might have intreated your obdurate breasts,	1Tamb	5.1.28	1Virgn
OBED			
Obed in Bairseth, Nones in Portugall,	Jew	1.1.125	Barab
OBEDIENCE			
And made him sweare obedience to my crowne.	2Tamb	1.3.190	Techel
And learne obedience to their lawfull king.	Edw	3.1.23	Spencr
Full of obedience and humility,	F 258	1.3.30	Faust
Thou couldst command the worlds obedience:	F1210	4.1.56	Emper
OBEDIENT			
Aid thy obedient servant Callapine,	2Tamb	5.2.28	Callap
And alwaies be obedient to my will.	F 325	1.3.97	Faust
So shalt thou shew thy selfe an obedient servant <Do so>,/And	F 652	2.2.101	Lucifr
OBEIED			
To aske, and have: commaund, and be obeied.	1Tamb	2.5.62	Therid
OBEY (See also OBAY)			
Whose Scourge I am, and him will I obey.	2Tamb	5.1.185	Tamb
My Lord, you must obey his majesty,	2Tamb	5.3.204	Therid
As Indian Moores, obey their Spanish Lords,	F 148	1.1.120	Valdes
And try if devils will obey thy Hest,	F 234	1.3.6	Faust
Since some faire one I should of force obey.	Ovid's Elegies	2.17.6	
OBEY'D			
Are but obey'd in their severall Provinces:	F 85	1.1.57	Faust
OBJECT			
the cursed object/Whose Fortunes never mastered her griefs:	1Tamb	5.1.413	Zenoc
[That will receive no object, for my head]/[But ruminates on	F 131	1.1.103A	Faust
As thou to live, therefore object it not.	F 162	1.1.134	Faust
Object thou then what she may well excuse,	Ovid's Elegies	2.2.37	
OBJECTS			
How are ye glutted with these grievous objects,	1Tamb	5.1.341	Zenoc
And such are objects fit for Tamburlaine.	1Tamb	5.1.475	Tamb
Fit objects for thy princely eie to pierce.	2Tamb	1.2.45	Callap
Fires and inflames objects remooved farre,	Hero and Leander	2.124	
OBLATION			
For thy returne shall fall the vowd oblation,	Ovid's Elegies	2.11.46	
An Altar takes mens incense, and oblation,	Ovid's Elegies	3.12.9	
OBLIA			
Then crost the sea and came to Oblia,	2Tamb	1.3.211	Therid
OBLOQUIE			
The obloquie and skorne of my renowne,	2Tamb	4.1.92	Tamb
OBSCURDE			
Or hath my love been so obscurde in thee,	P 682	13.26	Guise
OBSCURE			
(I cal it meane, because being yet obscure,	1Tamb	1.2.203	Tamb
In this obscure infernall servitude?	1Tamb	5.1.254	Zabina
But when I saw the place obscure and darke,	2Tamb	4.2.15	Therid
<Hipostates>/Thick and obscure doth make your danger great,	2Tamb	5.3.83	Phsitn
But for that base and obscure Gaveston:	Edw	1.1.101	Lncstr
My lord, mines more obscure then Mortimers.	Edw	2.2.22	Lncstr
Philosophy is odious and obscure,	F 133	1.1.105	Faust
And thither wee'le repaire and live obscure,	F1453	4.3.23	Benvol
When she will, cloudes the darckned heav'n obscure,	Ovid's Elegies	1.8.9	
all holy things/And on all creatures obscure darcknesse brings.	Ovid's Elegies	3.8.20	
These hardned me, with what I keepe obscure,	Ovid's Elegies	3.10.27	
OBSCURITY			
To dim thy basenesse and obscurity,	1Tamb	4.3.65	Souldn

OBSERVATIONS			
Nor change my Martiall observations, ...	1Tamb	5.1.122	Tamb
OBSERV'D			
Which maxime had Phaleris observ'd, ...	Jew	Prol.24	Machvl
OBSERVES			
Which he observes as parcell of his fame, ...	1Tamb	5.1.14	Govnr
OBTAIN'D			
Now that I have obtain'd what I desir'd <desire>/I'le live in	F 340	1.3.112	Faust
OBTAIND			
Yet none obtaind me, I am free from all.--	Dido	3.1.153	Dido
OBTAINE			
Why, what is it that Dido may desire/And not obtaine, be it in	Dido	3.4.8	Aeneas
And 'tis more Kingly to obtaine by peace/Then to enforce .	Jew	1.2.25	Calym
What will not I do to obtaine his soule?	F 462	2.1.74	Mephst
bag; and might I now obtaine <have> my wish, this house, .	F 675	2.2.124	P Covet
(O mischiefe) now for me obtaine small grace. . . .	Ovid's Elegies		1.6.22
Nor, so thou maist obtaine a wealthy prize, ...	Ovid's Elegies		1.8.63
Stolne liberty she may by thee obtaine, ...	Ovid's Elegies		2.2.15
Till gentle parlie did the truce obtaine.	Hero and Leander		2.278
OCCASION			
you knowe I shall have occasion shortly to journey you. .	2Tamb	3.5.115	P Tamb
rebelling Jades/Wil take occasion by the slenderest haire,	2Tamb	5.3.239	Tamb
And time may yeeld us an occasion/Which on the sudden cannot	Jew	1.2.239	Barab
And now and then, stab as occasion serves. . . .	Edw	2.1.43	Spencr
OCCASION'S			
Begin betimes, Occasion's bald behind, ...	Jew	5.2.44	Barab
OCCIDERE			
Edwardum occidere nolite timere bonum est.	Edw	5.4.8	Mortmr
Edwardum occidere nolite timere bonum est.	Edw	5.4.11	Mortmr
Edwardum occidere nolite timere, ...	Edw	5.5.17	Matrvs
OCCUPATION			
you Maister, will you teach me this conjuring Occupation?	F 381	1.4.39	P Robin
OCCUPIE			
displeases him | And fill up his rome that he shold occupie.	Paris	ms 5,p390	P Souldr
OCCUPY			
and tyll the ground that he himself should occupy, which is his	P 812	17.7	P Souldr
OCEAN			
Then gan they drive into the Ocean, ...	Dido	5.1.231	Anna
Fled to the Caspean or the Ocean maine?	1Tamb	1.1.102	Mycet
As hath the Ocean or the Terrene sea/Small drops of water, when	1Tamb	3.1.10	Bajzth
The Ocean, Terrene, and the cole-blacke sea, ...	1Tamb	3.1.25	Bajzth
And all the Ocean by the British shore.	1Tamb	3.3.259	Tamb
Or as the Ocean to the Traveiler/That restes upon the snowy	2Tamb	1.1.110	Sgsmnd
And since you leave me in the Ocean thus/To sinke or swim, and	Jew	1.2.267	Barab
As sooner shall they drinke the Ocean dry, ...	Jew	5.5.121	Govnr
This Ile shall fleete upon the Ocean, ...	Edw	1.4.49	Edward
Ransacke the Ocean for Orient Pearle, ...	F 110	1.1.82	Faust
Or the Ocean to overwhelme the world.	F 267	1.3.39	Faust
To passe the Ocean with a band of men, ...	F 334	1.3.106	Faust
And fall into the Ocean, ne're be found.	F1978	5.2.182	Faust
Hath with thee past the swelling Ocean;	Lucan, First Booke		371
And changeth as the Ocean ebbes and flowes:	Lucan, First Booke		412
The Ocean swell'd, as high as Spanish Calpe, ...	Lucan, First Booke		553
The Ocean hath no painted stones or shelles, ...	Ovid's Elegies		2.11.13
The Ocean maketh more majesticall:	Hero and Leander		1.226
To the rich Ocean for gifts he flies.	Hero and Leander		2.224
To sound foorth musicke to the Ocean, ...	Hero and Leander		2.328
OCEANUS			
For my sake pitie him Oceanus, ...	Dido	1.1.127	Venus
O'CLOCK (See A CLOCKE)			
OCTAVIUS			
The Romaine Tullie loved Octavius, ...	Edw	1.4.396	MortSr
ODDES (See also ODS)			
A towne with one poore church set them at oddes. . .	Lucan, First Booke		97
Love and Loves sonne are with fierce armes to oddes; .	Ovid's Elegies		1.10.19
Why fightst gainst oddes?	Ovid's Elegies		2.2.61
ODIOUS			
To some perhaps my name is odious, ...	Jew	Prol.5	Machvl
Philosophy is odious and obscure, ...	F 133	1.1.105	Faust
commodious/And to give signes dull wit to thee is odious.	Ovid's Elegies		1.11.4
ODORIFEROUS			
Wound on the barkes of odoriferous trees, ...	Dido	3.1.117	Dido
ODORS			
The Sunne from Egypt shall rich odors bring, ...	Dido	5.1.11	Aeneas
ODOUR			
When t'was the odour which her breath foorth cast. . .	Hero and Leander		1.22
ODS			
An ods too great, for us to stand against:	1Tamb	1.2.122	Tamb
OENONS			
blind Homer sing to me/Of Alexanders love, and Oenons death?	F 578	2.2.27	Faust
O'ER (See also O'RE, ORE)			
To see a Phrigian far fet [on] <o'er> <forfeit to> the sea,	Dido	3.3.64	Iarbus
OFF (Homograph)			
Treading upon his breast, strooke off his hands. . .	Dido	2.1.242	Aeneas
But I had gold enough and cast him off:	Dido	3.1.162	Dido
Spurning their crownes from off their captive heads. .	1Tamb	1.2.57	Techel
Cast off your armor, put on scarlet roabes. . . .	1Tamb	5.1.524	Tamb
Wher death cuts off the progres of his pomp, ...	2Tamb	Prol.4	Prolog
Should breake out off the bowels of the clowdes/And fall as	2Tamb	2.2.14	Gazell
But now my boies, leave off, and list to me, ...	2Tamb	3.2.53	Tamb
Cut off the water, all convoies that can, ...	2Tamb	3.3.39	Capt
I should be affraid, would put it off and come to bed with me.	2Tamb	4.1.70	P Calyph

OFF (cont.)			
And I will cast off armes and sit with thee,	2Tamb	4.2.44	Therid
Cut off this arme that murthered my Love:	2Tamb	4.2.83	Therid
For I wil cast my selfe from off these walles,	2Tamb	5.1.40	2Citzn
And when they cast me off,/Are poyson'd by my climing	Jew	Prol.12	Machvl
Light Abrahams off-spring; and direct the hand/Of Abigall this	Jew	2.1.14	Barab
I, but my Lord, the harvest is farre off:	Jew	2.3.79	Barab
Converse not with him, he is cast off from heaven.	Jew	2.3.157	Mater
yet let me talke to her;/This off-spring of Cain, this Jebusite	Jew	2.3.301	Barab
Off with your girdle, make a hansom noose;	Jew	4.1.142	Barab
he was ready to leape off e're the halter was about his necke;	Jew	4.2.22	P Ithimr
His hands are hackt, some fingers cut quite off;	Jew	4.3.10	Barab
I'le pledge thee, love, and therefore drinke it off.	Jew	4.4.1	Curtzn
And leaves it off to snap on Thistle tops:	Jew	5.2.42	Barab
A warning-peece shall be shot off from the Tower,	Jew	5.5.39	Barab
Ile make her shake off love with her heeles.	P 782	15.40	Mugern
And strike off his that makes you threaten us.	Edw	1.1.124	Mortmr
You that are princely borne should shake him off,	Edw	1.4.81	Warwck
Tis done, and now accursed hand fall off.	Edw	1.4.88	Edward
But I had thought the match had beene broke off,	Edw	2.1.25	Baldck
Then Balduck, you must cast the scholler off,	Edw	2.1.31	Spencr
souldiers take him hence, for by my sword,/His head shall off:	Edw	2.5.21	Warwck
Strike off their heads, and let them preach on poles,	Edw	3.1.20	Spencr
and in a trenche/Strake off his head, and marcht unto the	Edw	3.1.120	Arundl
And shake off smooth dissembling flatterers:	Edw	3.1.169	Herald
I charge you roundly off with both their heads,	Edw	3.1.247	Edward
And shake off all our fortunes equallie?	Edw	4.2.20	SrJohn
Hath shaken off the thraldome of the tower,	Edw	4.2.41	Mortmr
Strike off his head, he shall have marshall lawe.	Edw	5.4.89	Mortmr
Yet be not farre off, I shall need your helpe,	Edw	5.5.28	Ltborn
But leaving <off> this, let me have a wife, the fairest Maid in	F 529	2.1.141	P Faust
put off thy cloathes, and I'le conjure thee about presently:	F 746	2.3.25	P Robin
Strike with a willing hand, his head is off.	F1368	4.2.44	Mrtino
I have puld off his leg.	F1492	4.4.36	P HrsCsr
till I had pul'd me his leg quite off, and now 'tis at home in	F1551	4.5.47	P HrsCsr
sir, did not I pull off one of your legs when you were asleepe?	F1655	4.6.98	P HrsCsr
And what made madding people shake off peace.	Lucan, First Booke	69	
The earth went off hir hinges; And the Alpes/Shooke the old	Lucan, First Booke	551	
the Alpes/Shooke the old snow from off their trembling laps.	Lucan, First Booke	552	
Shake off these wrinckles that thy front assault,	Ovid's Elegies	1.8.45	
Farre off be force, no fire to them may reach,	Ovid's Elegies	1.14.29	
Even Jove himselfe out off my wit was reft.	Ovid's Elegies	2.1.18	
Wilt thou thy wombe-inclosed off-spring wracke?	Ovid's Elegies	2.14.8	
I would get off though straight, and sticking fast,	Ovid's Elegies	2.15.13	
Tis not enough, she shakes your record off,	Ovid's Elegies	3.3.19	
And alwaies cut him off as he replide.	Hero and Leander	1.196	
As she to heare his tale, left off her running.	Hero and Leander	1.418	
OFFENCE			
Commaund my guard to slay for their offence:	Dido	4.4.72	Dido
And one offence torments me more then all.	Jew	3.6.19	Abigal
Hands of good fellow, I will be his baile/For this offence:	P 623	12.36	King
For this offence be thou accurst of God.	Edw	1.1.199	BshpCv
Madam, without offence if I may aske,	Edw	4.6.30	Kent
But Faustus offence can nere be pardoned, the serpent that	F1837	5.2.41	P Faust
Least I should thinke thee guilty of offence.	Ovid's Elegies	1.4.50	
Would I were culpable of some offence,	Ovid's Elegies	2.7.11	
Ah oft how much she might she feignd offence;	Ovid's Elegies	2.19.13	
Faire creature, let me speake without offence,	Hero and Leander	1.199	
OFFENCES			
Let Tamburlaine for his offences feele/Such plagues as heaven	1Tamb	4.3.44	Arabia
OFFENCIOUS			
Wherein hath Ramus been so offencious?	P 384	7.24	Ramus
OFFEND			
Nor armed to offend in any kind:	Dido	1.2.13	Illion
Why, man of Troy, doe I offend thine eyes?	Dido	3.3.17	Iarbus
Ye shall no more offend the Carthage Queene.	Dido	4.4.158	Dido
I did offend high heaven so grievously,	Jew	3.6.17	Abigal
This sword of mine that should offend your foes,	Edw	1.1.86	Mortmr
And feare to offend the meanest noble man.	Edw	1.4.277	Mortmr
Slay me my lord, when I offend your grace.	Edw	1.4.349	Warwck
What if a man with bond-women offend,	Ovid's Elegies	2.8.9	
The wronged Gods dread faire ones to offend,	Ovid's Elegies	3.3.31	
Who may offend, sinnes least; power to do ill,	Ovid's Elegies	3.4.9	
OFFENDED			
What though I was offended with thy sonne,	Dido	3.2.40	Juno
Wherein have I offended Jupiter,	Dido	5.1.129	Dido
For I will seeme offended with thee for't.	Jew	1.2.303	Barab
Yet Don Mathias ne're offended thee:	Jew	3.3.41	Abigal
Thou hast offended, therefore must be damn'd.	Jew	4.1.25	1Fryar
Trouble me not, I neare offended him,	P1005	19.75	Guise
T'appeaze the wrath of their offended king.	Edw	3.1.210	Edward
Though thou hast now offended like a man,	F1710	5.1.37	OldMan
I do repent I ere offended him,	F1746	5.1.73	Faust
Then first I did perceive I had offended,	Ovid's Elegies	1.7.59	
OFFENDS			
Because his lothsome sight offends mine eye,	Dido	3.1.57	Dido
For every man that so offends shall die.	2Tamb	4.3.76	Tamb
OFFENSIVE (See also OFFENCIOUS)			
When your offensive rape by Tamburlaine,	1Tamb	3.2.6	Agidas
OFFER			
altar, where Ile offer up/As many kisses as the Sea hath sands,	Dido	3.1.87	Dido
Shall all we offer to Zenocrate,	1Tamb	1.2.104	Tamb
But if they offer word or violence,	1Tamb	1.2.142	Tamb

OFFER (cont.)			
the Persean king/Should offer present Dukedomes to our state,	1Tamb	1.2.215	Techel
Now let me offer to my gracious Lord,	1Tamb	3.3.218	Zenoc
Offer their mines (to sew for peace) to me,	1Tamb	3.3.264	Tamb
Offer our safeties to his clemencie,	1Tamb	5.1.12	Govnr
They have refusde the offer of their lives,	1Tamb	5.1.126	Tamb
How canst thou think of this and offer war?	2Tamb	1.1.102	Orcan
Arch-Monarke of the world, I offer here,	2Tamb	1.3.114	Therid
Which with my crowne I gladly offer thee.	2Tamb	1.3.136	Usumc
Offer submission, hang up flags of truce,	2Tamb	5.1.26	1Citzn
we offer more/Than ever yet we did to such proud slaves,	2Tamb	5.1.57	Techel
of all the villaines power/Live to give offer of another fight.	2Tamb	5.3.109	Tamb
Upon which Altar I will offer up/My daily sacrifice of sighes	Jew	3.2.31	Govnr
The offer of your Prince Electors, farre/Beyond the reach of my	P 452	8.2	Anjoy
And will not offer violence to their King,	P1162	22.24	King
To offer violence to his soveraigne,	Edw	2.4.34	Lncstr
It is honourable in thee to offer this,	Edw	2.5.67	Mortmr
I offer up this wicked traitors head,	Edw	5.6.100	King
And offer luke-warme bloud, of new borne babes.	F 402	2.1.14	Faust
and fell Mercury <(Jove)>/They offer humane flesh, and where	Lucan, First Booke		441
Strike boy, I offer thee my naked brest,	Ovid's Elegies		2.9.35
To whom you offer, and whose Nunne you are.	Hero and Leander		1.212
OFFER'D			
And offer'd me as ransome for thy life,	2Tamb	5.1.156	Tamb
OFFERED			
That offered jewels to thy sacred shrine,	1Tamb	3.3.199	Zabina
and fresh supply/Of conquest, and of spoile is offered us.	1Tamb	5.1.197	Techel
If we neglect this offered victory.	2Tamb	2.1.59	Fredrk
When violence is offered to the church.	Edw	1.2.41	ArchBp
Even in his face his offered [Gobbets] <Goblets> cast.	Ovid's Elegies		1.4.34
OFFERING			
Offering Damascus to your Majesty.	1Tamb	4.2.114	Therid
That when the offering-Bason comes to me,	Jew	2.3.28	Barab
Offering him aide against his enemies,	P 905	18.6	Bartus
OFFERING-BASON			
That when the offering-Bason comes to me,	Jew	2.3.28	Barab
OFFERS			
your absence in the field, offers to set upon us presently.	2Tamb	5.3.104 P	3Msngr
Offers to poure the same into thy soule,	F1732	5.1.59	OldMan
She offers up her selfe a sacrifice,	Hero and Leander		2.48
OFFICE			
Or if that loftie office like thee not,	Edw	1.4.355	Edward
OFFICERS			
It shall be so: now Officers have you done?	Jew	1.2.131	Govnr
Goe Officers and set them straight in shew.	Jew	2.2.43	Govnr
What ho, Officers, Gentlemen,	F1155	4.1.1	Mrtino
helpe Mephastophilis, call the Officers, my legge, my legge.	F App	p.241 156 P	Faust
OFFICES			
Sale made of offices, and peoples voices/Bought by themselves	Lucan, First Booke		180
OFFRED			
so much for the injury hee offred me heere in your presence,	F App	p.238 81 P	Faust
And offred as a dower his burning throne,	Hero and Leander		1.7
They offred him the deadly fatall knife,	Hero and Leander		1.447
OFFRING			
In offring parlie, to be counted light.	Hero and Leander		2.9
OFFRINGS			
And the dull snake about thy offrings creepe,	Ovid's Elegies		2.13.13
Nor did thy ashes her last offrings lose.	Ovid's Elegies		3.8.50
OFF-SPRING			
Light Abrahams off-spring; and direct the hand/Of Abigall this	Jew	2.1.14	Barab
yet let me talke to her;/This off-spring of Cain, this Jebusite	Jew	2.3.301	Barab
Wilt thou thy wombe-inclosed off-spring wracke?	Ovid's Elegies		2.14.8
OFSPRING			
Besiege the ofspring of our kingly loynes,	Dido	1.1.116	Jupitr
OFT			
Have oft driven backe the horses of the night,	Dido	1.1.26	Jupitr
Or in these shades deceiv'st mine eye so oft?	Dido	1.1.244	Aeneas
Oft hath she askt us under whom we serv'd,	Dido	2.1.66	Illion
As oft as he attempts to hoyst up saile:	Dido	4.4.103	Dido
Oft have I heard your Majestie complain,	1Tamb	1.1.35	Meandr
Bene oft resolv'd in bloody purple showers,	1Tamb	5.1.460	Tamb
And oft hath warn'd thee to be stil in field,	2Tamb	4.1.24	Amyras
Oft have I heard tell, can be permanent.	Jew	1.1.133	Barab
Oft have I leveld, and at last have learnd,	P 94	2.37	Guise
How oft have I beene baited by these peeres?	Edw	2.2.201	Edward
Oft have I thought to have done so:	F1864	5.2.68 P	Faust
As oft as Roome was sackt, here gan the spoile:	Lucan, First Booke		258
Which is nor sea, nor land, but oft times both,	Lucan, First Booke		411
Or why slips downe the Coverlet so oft?	Ovid's Elegies		1.2.2
I and my wench oft under clothes did lurke,	Ovid's Elegies		1.4.47
Deny him oft, feigne now thy head doth ake:	Ovid's Elegies		1.8.73
Or least his love oft beaten backe should waine.	Ovid's Elegies		1.8.76
Anger delaide doth oft to hate retire.	Ovid's Elegies		1.8.82
Oft thou wilt say, live well, thou wilt pray oft,	Ovid's Elegies		1.8.107
Oft to invade the sleeping foe tis good/And arm'd to shed	Ovid's Elegies		1.9.21
Corinna clips me oft by thy perswasion,	Ovid's Elegies		1.11.5
How oft wisht I night would not give thee place,	Ovid's Elegies		1.13.27
How oft, that either wind would breake thy coche,	Ovid's Elegies		1.13.29
Oft was she drest before mine eyes, yet never,	Ovid's Elegies		1.14.17
Oft in the morne her haires not yet digested,	Ovid's Elegies		1.14.19
O thou oft wilt blush/And say he likes me for my borrowed bush,	Ovid's Elegies		1.14.47
a pretty wenches face/Shee in requitall doth me oft imbrace.	Ovid's Elegies		2.1.34
Cupid flie)/That my chiefe wish should be so oft to die.	Ovid's Elegies		2.5.2

OFT (cont.)			
To over-come, so oft to fight I shame.	Ovid's Elegies	2.7.2	
How oft, and by what meanes we did agree.	Ovid's Elegies	2.8.28	
That have so oft serv'd pretty wenches dyet.	Ovid's Elegies	2.9.24	
Let [me] <her> enjoy [her] <me> oft, oft be debard.	Ovid's Elegies	2.9.46	
Oft have I spent the night in wantonnesse,	Ovid's Elegies	2.10.27	
of me, or I am sure/I oft have done, what might as much procure.	Ovid's Elegies	2.13.6	
Shee oft hath serv'd thee upon certaine dayes,	Ovid's Elegies	2.13.17	
Oft dyes she that her paunch-wrapt child hath slaine.	Ovid's Elegies	2.14.38	
The youth oft swimming to his Hero kinde,	Ovid's Elegies	2.16.31	
Why doth my mistresse from me oft devide?	Ovid's Elegies	2.16.42	
Ah oft how much she might she feignd offence;	Ovid's Elegies	2.19.13	
Oft couzen me, oft being wooed say nay.	Ovid's Elegies	2.19.20	
Search at the dore who knocks oft in the darke,	Ovid's Elegies	2.19.39	
Why she alone in empty bed oft tarries.	Ovid's Elegies	2.19.42	
Oft some points at the prophet passing by,	Ovid's Elegies	3.1.19	
Ah howe oft on hard doores hung I engrav'd,	Ovid's Elegies	3.1.53	
By which she perjurd oft hath lyed [to] <by> me.	Ovid's Elegies	3.3.10	
Perhaps he'ele tell howe oft he slewe a man,	Ovid's Elegies	3.7.21	
Oft bitter juice brings to the sicke reliefe.	Ovid's Elegies	3.10.8	
I have sustainde so oft thrust from the dore,	Ovid's Elegies	3.10.9	
Why see I lines so oft receivde and given,	Ovid's Elegies	3.13.31	
Those with sweet water oft her handmaid fils,	Hero and Leander	1.35	
True love is mute, and oft amazed stands.	Hero and Leander	1.186	
Receives no blemish, but oft-times more grace,	Hero and Leander	1.217	
Vessels of Brasse oft handled, brightly shine,	Hero and Leander	1.231	
that dwels/In tow'red courts, is oft in sheapheards cels).	Hero and Leander	1.394	
And oft look't out, and mus'd he did not come.	Hero and Leander	2.22	
O Hero, Hero, thus he cry'de full oft,	Hero and Leander	2.147	
Foorth plungeth, and oft flutters with her wing,	Hero and Leander	2.290	
OFTEN			
Whose power is often proov'd a myracle.	2Tamb	2.3.32	Gazell
Nor yet this aier, beat often with thy sighes,	2Tamb	4.2.10	Olymp
Hath often pleaded kindred to the King.	P 108	2.51	Guise
Full often am I sowring up to heaven,	Edw	5.1.21	Edward
How often shall I bid you beare him hence?	Edw	5.4.102	Mortmr
hir to thy owne use, as often as thou wilt, and at midnight.	F App	p.234 28 P	Robin
The flattering skie gliter'd in often flames,	Lucan, First Booke	528	
But Venus often to her Mars such brought.	Ovid's Elegies	2.5.28	
Often at length, my wench depart, I bid,	Ovid's Elegies	2.18.5	
Ah often, that her [hale] <haole> head aked, she lying,	Ovid's Elegies	2.19.11	
Great flouds the force of it do often prove.	Ovid's Elegies	3.5.24	
in the grasse, he often strayd/Beyond the bounds of shame,	Hero and Leander	1.406	
Yet as she went, full often look'd behind,	Hero and Leander	2.5	
We often kisse it, often looke thereon,	Hero and Leander	2.81	
OFTENTIMES			
And oftentimes into her bosome flew,	Hero and Leander	1.41	
OFT-TIMES			
Receives no blemish, but oft-times more grace,	Hero and Leander	1.217	
OH (See also O)			
O Priamus, O Troy, oh Hecuba!	Dido	2.1.105	Aeneas
And yet I am not free, oh would I were.	Dido	3.4.6	Dido
O Mahomet, Oh sleepie Mahomet.	1Tamb	3.3.269	Bajzth
Pardon my Love, oh pardon his contempt,	1Tamb	5.1.364	Zenoc
Oh they were going up to Sicily:	Jew	1.1.98	Barab
Oh my Lord we will give halfe.	Jew	1.2.77	3Jews
Oh earth-mettall'd villaines, and no Hebrews born!	Jew	1.2.78	Barab
And covetousnesse, oh 'tis a monstrous sinne.	Jew	1.2.124	Govnr
Oh yet be patient, gentle Barabas.	Jew	1.2.169	1Jew
Oh silly brethren, borne to see this day!	Jew	1.2.170	Barab
Oh what has made my lovely daughter sad?	Jew	1.2.225	Barab
Oh thou that with a fiery piller led'st/The sonnes of Israel	Jew	2.1.12	Barab
Oh my girle,/My gold, my fortune, my felicity;	Jew	2.1.47	Barab
Oh Abigal, Abigal, that I had thee here too,	Jew	2.1.51	Barab
Oh girle, oh gold, oh beauty, oh my blisse!	Jew	2.1.54	Barab
Oh, Sir, your father had my Diamonds.	Jew	2.3.49	Barab
Oh my Lord we will not jarre about the price;	Jew	2.3.65	Barab
Oh brave, master, I worship your nose for this.	Jew	2.3.173	Ithimr
Oh Barabas well met;	Jew	2.3.218	Lodowk
Oh heaven forbid I should have such a thought.	Jew	2.3.256	Barab
Oh treacherous Lodowicke!	Jew	2.3.266	Mthias
Oh but I know your Lordship wud disdaine/To marry with the	Jew	2.3.294	Barab
Oh wretched Abigal, what hast [thou] <thee> done?	Jew	2.3.320	Abigal
Oh muse not at it, 'tis the Hebrewes guize,	Jew	2.3.325	Barab
Oh, is't the custome, then I am resolv'd:	Jew	2.3.329	Lodowk
Oh, master, that I might have a hand in this.	Jew	2.3.368	Ithimr
Oh bravely fought, and yet they thrust not home.	Jew	3.2.5	Barab
Oh Lodowicke!	Jew	3.2.13	Govnr
Oh leave to grieve me, I am griev'd enough.	Jew	3.2.17	Mater
Oh that my sighs could turne to lively breath;	Jew	3.2.18	Govnr
Oh, Mistresse, ha ha ha.	Jew	3.3.5	P Ithimr
Oh my master.	Jew	3.3.7	P Ithimr
Oh Mistris!	Jew	3.3.9	P Ithimr
Oh, my master has the bravest policy.	Jew	3.3.12	P Ithimr
Oh therefore, Jacomo, let me be one,	Jew	3.3.68	Abigal
oh Barabas,/Though thou deservest hardly	Jew	3.3.73	Abigal
Oh Ithimore come neere;/Come neere, my love, come neere, thy	Jew	3.4.13	Barab
Oh unhappy day,	Jew	3.4.26	Barab
Oh master.	Jew	3.4.34	P Ithimr
Oh trusty Ithimore; no servant, but my friend;	Jew	3.4.42	Barab
Oh my sweet Ithimore go set it downe/And come againe so soone	Jew	3.4.108	Barab
Oh brother, brother, all the Nuns are sicke,	Jew	3.6.1	1Fryar
Oh what a sad confession will there be?	Jew	3.6.4	2Fryar

OH (cont.)			
Oh he is gone to see the other Nuns.	Jew	3.6.10	2Fryar
Oh monstrous villany.	Jew	3.6.30	2Fryar
Oh brother, all the Nuns are dead, let's bury them.	Jew	3.6.44	1Fryar
Oh speake not of her, then I dye with griefe.	Jew	4.1.36	Barab
Oh holy Fryars, the burthen of my sinnes/Lye heavy on my soule;	Jew	4.1.48	Barab
Oh good Barabas come to our house.	Jew	4.1.77	1Fryar
Oh no, good Barabas come to our house.	Jew	4.1.78	2Fryar
Oh Barabas, their Lawes are strict.	Jew	4.1.82	1Fryar
And so I will, oh Jacomo, faile not but come.	Jew	4.1.108	Barab
Oh how I long to see him shake his heeles.	Jew	4.1.140	Ithimr
This is the houre/Wherein I shall proceed; Oh happy houre,	Jew	4.1.161	1Fryar
Oh that ten thousand nights were put in one,	Jew	4.2.130	Ithimr
Plaine Barabas: oh that wicked Curtezane!	Jew	4.3.2	Barab
And when he comes: Oh that he were but here!	Jew	4.3.17	Barab
Oh good words, Sir, and send it you, were best see; there's his	Jew	4.3.24	P Pilia
Oh, if that be all, I can picke ope your locks.	Jew	4.3.33	Pilia
Oh that I should part with so much gold!	Jew	4.3.51	Barab
As I wud see thee hang'd; oh, love stops my breath:	Jew	4.3.53	Barab
Oh bravely done.	Jew	4.4.19	Pilia
Oh raskall! I change my selfe twice a day.	Jew	4.4.65	Barab
Oh bring us to the Governor.	Jew	5.1.7	Curtzn
Nor me neither, I cannot out-run you Constable, oh my belly.	Jew	5.1.20	P Ithimr
Oh fatall day, to fall into the hands/Of such a Traitor and	Jew	5.2.12	Govnr
Oh villaine, Heaven will be reveng'd on thee.	Jew	5.2.25	Govnr
Oh excellent!	Jew	5.5.42	Govnr
Oh helpe me, Selim, helpe me, Christians.	Jew	5.5.70	Barab
Oh monstrous treason!	Jew	5.5.108	Calym
Oh fatall was this mariage to us all.	P 202	3.37	Admral
Oh twill corrupt the water, and the water the fish, and by the	P 488	9.7	P 2Atndt
Oh I have my deaths wound, give me leave to speak.	P1003	19.73	Guise
Oh that I have not power to stay my life,	P1007	19.77	Guise
Oh what may I doe, for to revenge thy death?	P1108	21.2	Dumain
Oh no Navarre, thou must be King of France.	P1225	22.87	King
Tis true sweete Gaveston, oh were it false.	Edw	1.4.108	Edward
Oh my sweet hart, how do I mone thy wrongs,	Edw	4.2.27	Queene
Know that I am a king, oh at that name,	Edw	5.5.89	Edward
Oh.	F1364	4.2.40	Faust
[Ah] <Oh> gentlemen.	F1822	5.2.26	Faust
oh hee stayes my tongue:	F1852	5.2.56	P Faust
Oh <Ah> Faustus, if thou hadst given eare to me,	F1892	5.2.96	GdAngl
One drop <of bloud will save me; oh> my Christ.	F1940	(HC271)B	Faust
[Ah] <Oh> Pythagoras Metemsycosis <metem su cossis>; were that	F1966	5.2.170	Faust
I'le burne my bookes; [ah] <oh> Mephostophilis.	F1982	5.2.186	Faust
Oh woe is me, he never shootes but hits,	Ovid's Elegies		1.1.29
Oh how the burthen irkes, that we should shun.	Ovid's Elegies		2.4.6
OHO			
Oho, oho, staves acre, why then belike, if I were your man,	F App	p.229 21	P Clown
OIL (See OYLES)			
OINTMENT			
An ointment which a cunning Alcumist/Distilled from the purest	2Tamb	4.2.59	Olymp
OKEN			
As every tide tilts twixt their oken sides:	Dido	1.1.224	Aeneas
OKES			
By charmes maste drops from okes, from vines grapes fall,	Ovid's Elegies		3.6.33
Huge okes, hard Adamantes might she have moved,	Ovid's Elegies		3.6.57
OLBIA (See OBLIA)			
OLD (See also ELD)			
As therewithall the old man overcome,	Dido	2.1.157	Aeneas
Old men with swords thrust through their aged sides,	Dido	2.1.197	Aeneas
Then from the navell to the throat at once,/He ript old Priam:	Dido	2.1.256	Aeneas
And dipt it in the old Kings chill cold bloud,	Dido	2.1.260	Aeneas
Avaunt old witch and trouble not my wits.	Dido	3.2.25	Venus
Will Dido raise old Priam forth his grave,	Dido	4.3.39	Illion
Say Dido what she will I am not old,	Dido	4.5.21	Nurse
Of my old fathers name.	Dido	5.1.23	Aeneas
And raise a new foundation to old Troy,	Dido	5.1.79	Aeneas
For as when Jove did thrust old Saturn down,	1Tamb	2.7.36	Usumc
When I am old and cannot mannage armes,	2Tamb	1.3.59	Tamb
And herein was old Abrams happinesse:	Jew	1.1.106	Barab
Now I remember those old womens words,	Jew	2.1.24	Barab
Let me see, sirra, are you not an old shaver?	Jew	2.3.114	P Barab
whom I saluted with an old hempen proverb, Hodie tibi,	Jew	4.2.18	P Pilia
Mine old lord whiles he livde, was so precise,	Edw	2.1.46	Baldck
Welcome old man, comst thou in Edwards aide?	Edw	3.1.34	Edward
Welcome ten thousand times, old man againe.	Edw	3.1.46	Edward
And have old servitors in high esteeme,	Edw	3.1.168	Herald
That waites your pleasure, and the day growes old.	Edw	4.7.85	Leistr
For now we hould an old Wolfe by the eares,	Edw	5.2.7	Mortmr
Thus lives old Edward not reliev'd by any,	Edw	5.3.23	Edward
That yearely [stuffes] <stuff'd> old Phillips treasury,	F 159	1.1.131	Valdes
Go and returne an old Franciscan Frier,	F 253	1.3.25	Faust
My <His> Ghost be with the old Phylosophers.	F 288	1.3.60	Faust
[Tush] <No>, these are trifles, and meere old wives Tales.	F 524	2.1.136	Faust
of an old Churle in a <an olde> leather <leatherne> bag;	F 674	2.2.123	P Covet
out of a Lyons mouth when I was scarce <half> an houre old,	F 687	2.2.136	P Wrath
What my old Guesse?	F1507	4.5.3	P Hostss
what my old Guest?	F1514	4.5.10	P Hostss
thee (seeing thou being old/Must shine a star) shal heaven	Lucan, First Booke		45
Time ends and to old Chaos all things turne;	Lucan, First Booke		74
Bearing old spoiles and conquerors monuments,	Lucan, First Booke		138
And scorn'd old sparing diet, and ware robes/Too light for	Lucan, First Booke		165
Being three daies old inforst the floud to swell,	Lucan, First Booke		220

OLD (cont.)			
the Alpes/Shooke the old snow from off their trembling laps.	Lucan, First Booke		552
To these ostents (as their old custome was)/They call	Lucan, First Booke		583
a bawde aright/Give eare, there is an old trot Dipsas hight.	Ovid's Elegies		1.8.2
And her old body in birdes plumes to lie.	Ovid's Elegies		1.8.14
The gods send thee no house, a poore old age,	Ovid's Elegies		1.8.113
Now on <ore> the sea from her old love comes shee,	Ovid's Elegies		1.13.1
foote drawes out/Fastning her light web some old beame about.	Ovid's Elegies		1.14.8
She holds, and viewes her old lockes in her lappe,	Ovid's Elegies		1.14.53
A yong wench pleaseth, and an old is good,	Ovid's Elegies		2.4.45
Which do perchance old age unto them give.	Ovid's Elegies		2.6.28
An old wood, stands uncut of long yeares space,	Ovid's Elegies		3.1.1
I speake old Poets wonderfull inventions,	Ovid's Elegies		3.5.17
I prove neither youth nor man, but old and rustie.	Ovid's Elegies		3.6.20
Yet when old Saturne heavens rule possest,	Ovid's Elegies		3.7.35
There stands an old wood with thick trees darke clouded,	Ovid's Elegies		3.12.7
OLDE			
breadth of shoulders as might mainely beare/Olde Atlas burthen.	1Tamb	2.1.11	Menaph
Pitie olde age, within whose silver haires/Honor and reverence	1Tamb	5.1.81	1Virgn
for whose byrth/Olde Rome was proud, but gasde a while on her,	2Tamb	2.4.92	Tamb
Will now retaine her olde inconstancie,	2Tamb	3.1.29	Callap
Am I growne olde, or is thy lust growne yong,	P 681	13.25	Guise
Especially with our olde mothers helpe.	P1061	19.131	King
of an old Churle in a <an olde> leather <leatherne> bag;	F 674	2.2.123 P	Covet
(great Pompey) that late deeds would dim/Olde triumphs,	Lucan, First Booke		122
darts, olde swords/With ugly teeth of blacke rust fouly scarr'd:	Lucan, First Booke		244
Whether now shal these olde bloudles soules repaire?	Lucan, First Booke		343
OLIMPUS			
Did mount him up <himselfe> to scale Olimpus top.	F 757	2.3.36	2Chor
With earthes revenge and how Olimpus toppe/High Ossa bore,	Ovid's Elegies		2.1.13
OLIVE			
And in his sportfull hands an Olive tree,	Edw	1.1.64	Gavstn
OLIVES			
And some few pastures Pallas Olives bore.	Ovid's Elegies		2.16.8
OLYMPIA			
Distrest Olympia, whose weeping eies/Since thy arrivall here	2Tamb	4.2.1	Olymp
Wel met Olympia, I sought thee in my tent,	2Tamb	4.2.14	Therid
Tell me Olympia, wilt thou graunt my suit?	2Tamb	4.2.21	Therid
Olympia, pitie him, in whom thy looks/Have greater operation	2Tamb	4.2.28	Therid
I wil Olympia, and will keep it for/The richest present of this	2Tamb	4.2.77	Therid
Here then Olympia.	2Tamb	4.2.81	Therid
OLYMPUS (See also OLIMPUS)			
This man and I were at Olympus games.	Dido	3.1.143	Illion
And aged Saturne in Olympus dwell.	Hero and Leander		1.454
OMENOUS			
And may this banquet proove as omenous,	1Tamb	4.4.23	Zabina
OMINOUS			
for Julia/Snatcht hence by cruel fates with ominous howles,	Lucan, First Booke		112
Crownes fell from holy statues, ominous birds/Defil'd the day,	Lucan, First Booke		556
OMNES			
[Et omnes sancti. Amen].	F1087	3.2.107A	1Frier
Et omnes sancti Amen.	F App	p.233 41	Frier
OMNIPOTENCE			
Of power, of honour, and <of> omnipotence,	F 81	1.1.53	Faust
OMNIPOTENT			
Thou Christ that art esteem'd omnipotent,	2Tamb	2.2.55	Orcan
ON (Homograph; See also ON'S, ON'T)			
I vow, if she but once frowne on thee more,	Dido	1.1.12	Jupitr
Sit on my knee, and call for thy content,	Dido	1.1.28	Jupitr
Whiles my Aeneas wanders on the Seas,	Dido	1.1.52	Venus
And Proteus raising hils of flouds on high,	Dido	1.1.76	Venus
And therefore will take pitie on his toyle,	Dido	1.1.131	Venus
What? doe I see my sonne now come on shoare:	Dido	1.1.134	Venus
And rost our new found victuals on this shoare.	Dido	1.1.168	Aeneas
To know what coast the winde hath driven us on,	Dido	1.1.176	Aeneas
On which by tempests furie we are cast.	Dido	1.1.199	Aeneas
Adjoyning on Agenors stately towne,	Dido	1.1.211	Venus
A Gods name on and hast thee to the Court,	Dido	1.1.233	Venus
and be revengde/On these hard harted Grecians, which rejoyce	Dido	2.1.19	Aeneas
For were it Priam he would smile on me.	Dido	2.1.36	Ascan
For we are strangers driven on this shore,	Dido	2.1.43	Aeneas
Who looking on the scarres we Troians gave,	Dido	2.1.131	Aeneas
Ulysses on the sand/Assayd with honey words to turne them	Dido	2.1.136	Aeneas
And with maine force flung on a ring of pikes,	Dido	2.1.196	Aeneas
and on his speare/The mangled head of Priams yongest sonne,	Dido	2.1.214	Aeneas
joyntly both/Beating their breasts and falling on the ground,	Dido	2.1.228	Aeneas
At which the franticke Queene leapt on his face,	Dido	2.1.244	Aeneas
So leaning on his sword he stood stone still,	Dido	2.1.263	Aeneas
By this I got my father on my backe,	Dido	2.1.265	Aeneas
Thinking to beare her on my backe abourd,	Dido	2.1.284	Aeneas
And as I swomme, she standing on the shoare,	Dido	2.1.286	Aeneas
in stead of him/Will set thee on her lap and play with thee:	Dido	2.1.325	Venus
And when she strokes thee softly on the head,	Dido	3.1.5	Cupid
No, but I charge thee never looke on me.	Dido	3.1.54	Dido
But tell them none shall gaze on him but I,	Dido	3.1.73	Dido
Wound on the barkes of odoriferous trees,	Dido	3.1.117	Dido
Shall finde it written on confusions front,	Dido	3.2.19	Juno
If thou but lay thy fingers on my boy.	Dido	3.2.36	Venus
And wrought him mickle woe on sea and land,	Dido	3.2.41	Juno
Whose armed soule alreadie on the sea,	Dido	3.2.83	Venus
But love and duetie led him on perhaps,	Dido	3.3.15	Aeneas
And hoyst aloft on Neptunes hideous hilles,	Dido	3.3.47	Iarbus
To see a Phrigian far fet [on] <o'er> <forfeit to> the sea,	Dido	3.3.64	Iarbus

ON (cont.)

Revenge me on Aeneas, or on her:	Dido	3.3.70	Iarbus
On her?	Dido	3.3.71	Iarbus
And will she be avenged on his life?	Dido	3.4.14	Aeneas
When as he buts his beames on Floras bed,	Dido	3.4.20	Dido
Prometheus hath put on Cupids shape,	Dido	3.4.21	Dido
On whom ruth and compassion ever waites,	Dido	4.2.20	Iarbus
On whom the nimble windes may all day waight,	Dido	4.3.23	Aeneas
As parting friends accustome on the shoare,	Dido	4.3.50	Aeneas
And seated on my Gennet, let him ride/As Didos husband through	Dido	4.4.66	Dido
That he might suffer shipwracke on my breast,	Dido	4.4.102	Dido
Now let him hang my favours on his masts,	Dido	4.4.159	Dido
Jove hath heapt on me such a desperate charge,	Dido	5.1.64	Aeneas
Achates and the rest shall waite on thee,	Dido	5.1.76	Aeneas
Now is he come on shoare safe without hurt:	Dido	5.1.257	Dido
When first he came on shoare, perish thou to:	Dido	5.1.299	Dido
the verie legges/Whereon our state doth leane, as on a staffe,	1Tamb	1.1.60	Mycet
Affrike and Europe bordering on your land,	1Tamb	1.1.127	Menaph
That in conceit bear Empires on our speares,	1Tamb	1.2.64	Tamb
Fairer than whitest snow on Scythian hils,	1Tamb	1.2.89	Tamb
A hundreth <hundred> Tartars shall attend on thee,	1Tamb	1.2.93	Tamb
Mounted on Steeds, swifter than Pegasus.	1Tamb	1.2.94	Tamb
Wun on the fiftie headed Vuolgas waves,	1Tamb	1.2.103	Tamb
And looke we friendly on them when they come:	1Tamb	1.2.141	Tamb
On which the breath of heaven delights to play,	1Tamb	2.1.25	Menaph
And such shall wait on worthy Tamburlaine.	1Tamb	2.1.60	Cosroe
To seeke revenge on me and Tamburlaine.	1Tamb	2.1.67	Cosroe
On this same theevish villaine Tamburlaine.	1Tamb	2.2.3	Mycet
Go on my Lord, and give your charge I say,	1Tamb	2.2.57	Mycet
And you march on their slaughtered carkasses:	1Tamb	2.2.69	Meandr
And set it safe on my victorious head.	1Tamb	2.3.54	Cosroe
On your submission we with thanks excuse,	1Tamb	2.5.13	Cosroe
A jest to chardge on twenty thousand men?	1Tamb	2.5.91	Therid
Goe on for me.	1Tamb	2.5.106	Therid
Let us put on our meet incountring mindes,	1Tamb	2.6.19	Ortyg
And like a Harpyr <Harpye> tires on my life.	1Tamb	2.7.50	Cosroe
So, now it is more surer on my head,	1Tamb	2.7.65	Tamb
But if presuming on his silly power,	1Tamb	3.1.33	Bajzth
And casts a pale complexion on his cheeks.	1Tamb	3.2.75	Agidas
Which thy prolonged Fates may draw on thee:	1Tamb	3.2.101	Agidas
Mounted on lusty Mauritanian Steeds,	1Tamb	3.3.16	Bassoe
We meane to seate our footmen on their Steeds,	1Tamb	3.3.25	Techel
This hand shal set them on your conquering heads:	1Tamb	3.3.31	Tamb
That they lie panting on the Gallies side,	1Tamb	3.3.53	Tamb
And on thy head weare my Emperiall crowne,	1Tamb	3.3.113	Bajzth
Brave horses, bred on the white Tartarian hils:	1Tamb	3.3.151	Tamb
Yet set a ransome on me Tamburlaine.	1Tamb	3.3.261	Bajzth
Lie slumbering on the flowrie bankes of Nile,	1Tamb	4.1.9	Souldn
While thundring Cannons rattle on their Skins.	1Tamb	4.1.11	Souldn
Steeds, disdainfully/With wanton paces trampling on the ground.	1Tamb	4.1.23	2Msngr
and on his silver crest/A snowy Feather spangled white he	1Tamb	4.1.50	2Msngr
Fall prostrate on the lowe disdainefull earth.	1Tamb	4.2.13	Tamb
Feends looke on me, and thou dread God of hell,	1Tamb	4.2.27	Bajzth
heaven beholde/Their Scourge and Terrour treade on Emperours.	1Tamb	4.2.32	Tamb
For treading on the back of Bajazeth,	1Tamb	4.2.77	Bajzth
That should be horsed on fower mightie kings.	1Tamb	4.2.78	Bajzth
Confusion light on him that helps thee thus.	1Tamb	4.2.84	Bajzth
until the bloody flag/Be once advanc'd on my vermilion Tent,	1Tamb	4.2.117	Tamb
Let griefe and furie hasten on revenge,	1Tamb	4.3.43	Arabia
offences feele/Such plagues as heaven and we can poure on him.	1Tamb	4.3.45	Arabia
While they walke quivering on their citie walles,	1Tamb	4.4.3	Tamb
Honor still waight on happy Tamburlaine:	1Tamb	4.4.85	Zenoc
Whose honors and whose lives relie on him:	1Tamb	5.1.19	Govnr
Nor you depend on such weake helps as we.	1Tamb	5.1.33	1Virgn
Farewell (sweet Virgins) on whose safe return/Depends our	1Tamb	5.1.62	Govnr
Reflexing them on your disdainfull eies:	1Tamb	5.1.70	Tamb
And on whose throne the holy Graces sit.	1Tamb	5.1.77	1Virgn
He now is seated on my horsmens speares,	1Tamb	5.1.114	Tamb
And on their points his fleshlesse bodie feedes.	1Tamb	5.1.115	Tamb
Sitting in scarlet on their armed speares.	1Tamb	5.1.118	Tamb
and on Damascus wals/Have hoisted up their slaughtered	1Tamb	5.1.130	Techel
Rain'st on the earth resolved pearle in showers,	1Tamb	5.1.142	Tamb
And sprinklest Saphyrs on thy shining face,	1Tamb	5.1.143	Tamb
Their minds, and muses on admyred theames:	1Tamb	5.1.164	Tamb
Must needs have beauty beat on his conceites.	1Tamb	5.1.182	Tamb
Arabian king together/Martch on us with such eager violence,	1Tamb	5.1.200	Techel
Why feed ye still on daies accursed beams,	1Tamb	5.1.262	Bajzth
On horsmens Lances to be hoisted up,	1Tamb	5.1.328	Zenoc
Stead/That stampt on others with their thundring hooves,	1Tamb	5.1.331	Zenoc
Sleep'st every night with conquest on thy browes,	1Tamb	5.1.359	Zenoc
Millions of soules sit on the bankes of Styx,	1Tamb	5.1.463	Tamb
But here these kings that on my fortunes wait,	1Tamb	5.1.490	Tamb
And here's the crown my Lord, help set it on.	1Tamb	5.1.505	Usumc
Cast off your armor, put on scarlet roabes.	1Tamb	5.1.524	Tamb
Hang up your weapons on Alcides poste,	1Tamb	5.1.528	Tamb
from faire Natolia/Two hundred leagues, and on Danubius banks,	2Tamb	1.1.7	Orcan
And make faire Europe mounted on her bull,	2Tamb	1.1.42	Orcan
Lantchidol/Beates on the regions with his boysterous blowes,	2Tamb	1.1.70	Orcan
which basely on their knees/In all your names desirde a truce	2Tamb	1.1.96	Orcan
Desart of Arabia/To those that stand on Badgeths lofty Tower,	2Tamb	1.1.109	Sgsmnd
let peace be ratified/On these conditions specified before,	2Tamb	1.1.125	Orcan
And hung on stately Mecas Temple roofe,	2Tamb	1.1.141	Orcan
The Grecian virgins shall attend on thee,	2Tamb	1.2.36	Callap

ON (cont.)

in crimson silk/Shall ride before the on Barbarian Steeds:	2Tamb	1.2.47	Callap
Now rest thee here on faire Larissa Plaines,	2Tamb	1.3.5	Tamb
When heaven shal cease to moove on both the poles/And when the	2Tamb	1.3.12	Tamb
Plac'd by her side, looke on their mothers face.	2Tamb	1.3.20	Tamb
Their fingers made to quaver on a Lute,	2Tamb	1.3.29	Tamb
That never look'd on man but Tamburlaine.	2Tamb	1.3.34	Tamb
Promist to meet me on Larissa plaines/With hostes apeece	2Tamb	1.3.107	Tamb
Meet for your service on the sea, my Lord,	2Tamb	1.3.123	Therid
And batter downe the castles on the shore.	2Tamb	1.3.126	Therid
Now will we banquet on these plaines a while,	2Tamb	1.3.157	Tamb
have martcht/Foure hundred miles with armour on their backes,	2Tamb	1.3.175	Usumc
Which in despight of them I set on fire:	2Tamb	1.3.213	Therid
tis superstition/To stand so strictly on dispensive faith:	2Tamb	2.1.50	Fredrk
his fearefull arme/Be pour'd with rigour on our sinfull heads,	2Tamb	2.1.58	Fredrk
Comes marching on us, and determines straight,	2Tamb	2.2.27	1Msngr
imperiall heaven/That he that sits on high and never sleeps,	2Tamb	2.2.49	Orcan
To armes my Lords, on Christ still let us crie,	2Tamb	2.2.63	Orcan
And God hath thundered vengeance from on high,	2Tamb	2.3.2	Sgsmnd
That danc'd with glorie on the silver waves,	2Tamb	2.4.3	Tamb
Now walk the angels on the walles of heaven,	2Tamb	2.4.15	Tamb
Their Spheares are mounted on the serpents head,	2Tamb	2.4.53	Tamb
for whose byrth/Olde Rome was proud, but gasde a while on her,	2Tamb	2.4.92	Tamb
Will poure it downe in showers on our heads:	2Tamb	3.1.36	Callap
That on mount Sinay with their ensignes spread,	2Tamb	3.1.46	Jrslem
All bordring on the Mare-major sea:	2Tamb	3.1.51	Trebiz
The cursed Scythian sets on all their townes,	2Tamb	3.1.55	Trebiz
When this is learn'd for service on the land,	2Tamb	3.2.83	Tamb
Lies heavy on my heart, I cannot live.	2Tamb	3.4.5	Capt
The Scythians shall not tyrannise on me.	2Tamb	3.4.29	Sonne
On whom death and the fatall sisters waite,	2Tamb	3.4.54	Therid
Before whom (mounted on a Lions backe)/Rhamnusia beares a	2Tamb	3.4.56	Therid
Ile have you learne to feed on provander,	2Tamb	3.5.106	Tamb
Bordering on Mare Roso neere to Meca.	2Tamb	3.5.131	Callap
let him hang a bunch of keies on his standerd, to put him in	2Tamb	3.5.139	P Tamb
here are Bugges/Wil make the haire stand upright on your heads,	2Tamb	3.5.148	Tamb
Hovering betwixt our armies, light on me,	2Tamb	3.5.163	Tamb
shall sweat/With carrieng pearle and treasure on their backes.	2Tamb	3.5.167	Techel
my striving hands/From martiall justice on thy wretched soule.	2Tamb	4.1.96	Tamb
Will poure down blood and fire on thy head:	2Tamb	4.1.143	Jrslem
And with our bloods, revenge our bloods on thee.	2Tamb	4.1.145	Jrslem
entertaine a thought/That tends to love, but meditate on death,	2Tamb	4.2.26	Olymp
Which when you stab, looke on your weapons point,	2Tamb	4.2.69	Olymp
That I dissemble not, trie it on me.	2Tamb	4.2.76	Olymp
For every Fury gazeth on her lookes:	2Tamb	4.2.92	Therid
them for the funerall/They have bestowed on my abortive sonne.	2Tamb	4.3.66	Tamb
And on the south Senus Arabicus,	2Tamb	4.3.104	Tamb
Drawen with these kings on heaps of carkasses.	2Tamb	5.1.72	Tamb
And sent from hell to tyrannise on earth,	2Tamb	5.1.111	Govnr
Or vengeance on the head of Tamburlain,	2Tamb	5.1.195	Tamb
clowdes, and on his head/A Chaplet brighter than Apollos crowne,	2Tamb	5.2.32	Amasia
And threaten conquest on our Soveraigne:	2Tamb	5.3.14	Therid
And when I look away, comes stealing on:	2Tamb	5.3.71	Tamb
And thus are wee on every side inrich'd:	Jew	1.1.104	Barab
And all good fortune wait on Calymath.	Jew	1.2.33	Govnr
Read on.	Jew	1.2.72	Govnr
Either pay that, or we will seize on all.	Jew	1.2.89	Govnr
If your first curse fall heavy on thy head,	Jew	1.2.107	1Knght
On then:	Jew	1.2.211	2Jew
us an occasion/Which on the sudden cannot serve the turne.	Jew	1.2.240	Barab
I charge thee on my blessing that thou leave/These divels, and	Jew	1.2.346	Barab
No sleepe can fasten on my watchfull eyes,	Jew	2.1.17	Barab
As good goe on, as sit so sadly thus.	Jew	2.1.40	Barab
On this condition shall thy Turkes be sold.	Jew	2.2.42	Govnr
Every ones price is written on his backe,	Jew	2.3.3	2Offcr
I'le sacrifice her on a pile of wood.	Jew	2.3.52	Barab
As for the Comment on the Machabees/I have it, Sir, and 'tis at	Jew	2.3.153	Barab
In setting Christian villages on fire,	Jew	2.3.203	Ithimr
I strowed powder on the Marble stones,	Jew	2.3.209	Ithimr
to see the cripples/Goe limping home to Christendome on stilts.	Jew	2.3.212	Ithimr
Nay on my life it is my Factors hand,	Jew	2.3.240	Barab
Why on the sudden is your colour chang'd?	Jew	2.3.321	Lodowk
Then my faire Abigal should frowne on me.	Jew	2.3.332	Lodowk
Revenge it on him when you meet him next.	Jew	2.3.343	Barab
And on that rather should Ferneze dye.	Jew	3.2.26	Govnr
Nor on his sonne, but by Mathias meanes;	Jew	3.3.45	Abigal
Nor on Mathias, but by murdering me.	Jew	3.3.46	Abigal
But I perceive there is no love on earth,	Jew	3.3.47	Abigal
My duty waits on you.	Jew	3.3.76	Abigal
And on that hope my happinesse is built:	Jew	3.4.17	Barab
Death seizeth on my heart:	Jew	3.6.38	Abigal
But I must to the Jew and exclaime on him,	Jew	3.6.42	2Fryar
the burthen of my sinnes/Lye heavy on my soule; then pray you	Jew	4.1.49	Barab
And on my knees creepe to Jerusalem.	Jew	4.1.62	Barab
Come on, sirra,	Jew	4.1.141	Barab
and when the Hangman had put on his hempen Tippet, he made such	Jew	4.2.23	P Ithimr
What an eye she casts on me?	Jew	4.2.128	P Ithimr
here's to thee with a--pox on this drunken hick-up.	Jew	4.4.32	P Ithimr
He never put on cleane shirt since he was circumcis'd.	Jew	4.4.64	P Ithimr
In prison till the Law has past on him.	Jew	5.1.49	Govnr
I'le be reveng'd on this accursed Towne;	Jew	5.1.62	Barab
Oh villaine, Heaven will be reveng'd on thee.	Jew	5.2.25	Govnr
And leaves it off to snap on Thistle tops:	Jew	5.2.42	Barab

ON (cont.)

On then, begone.	Jew	5.4.10	Govnr
That on the sudden shall dissever it,	Jew	5.5.29	Barab
I would have brought confusion on you all,	Jew	5.5.85	Barab
Having the King, Queene Mother on our sides,	P 29	1.29	Navrre
And made it look with terrour on the worlde:	P 61	2.4	Guise
Shall weare white crosses on their Burgonets,	P 232	4.30	Guise
The Duke of Guise stampes on thy liveles bulke.	P 315	5.42	Guise
Why, darst thou presume to call on Christ,	P 356	6.11	Mntsrl
Well, say on.	P 400	7.40	Anjoy
And on the other side against the Turke,	P 462	8.12	Anjoy
the diadem/Of France be cast on me, then with your leaves/I may	P 473	8.23	Anjoy
His minde you see runnes on his minions,	P 633	12.46	QnMoth
That others needs to comment on my text?	P 683	13.27	Guise
And makes his footstoole on securitie:	P 738	14.41	Navrre
dote on them your selfe,/I know none els but holdes them in	P 763	15.21	Guise
<make> a walk/On purpose from the Court to meet with him.	P 784	15.42	Mugern
And takes his vantage on Religion,	P 924	18.25	Navrre
Come on sirs, what, are you resolutely bent,	P 931	19.1	Capt
And bids thee whet thy sword on Sextus bones,	P1237	22.99	King
Ile [fawne] <fanne> first on the winde,/That glaunceth at my	Edw	1.1.22	Gavstn
My men like Satyres grazing on the lawnes,	Edw	1.1.59	Gavstn
I priest, and lives to be revengd on thee,	Edw	1.1.178	Edward
Ah brother, lay not violent hands on him,	Edw	1.1.189	Kent
Ile be revengd on him for my exile.	Edw	1.1.192	Gavstn
Thus leaning on the shoulder of the king,	Edw	1.2.23	Warwck
Can kinglie Lions fawne on creeping Ants?	Edw	1.4.15	Penbrk
Lay hands on that traitor Mortimer.	Edw	1.4.20	Edward
Lay hands on that traitor Gaveston.	Edw	1.4.21	MortSr
On your allegeance to the sea of Rome,	Edw	1.4.52	ArchBp
But come sweete friend, ile beare thee on thy way.	Edw	1.4.140	Edward
Fawne not on me French strumpet, get thee gone.	Edw	1.4.145	Edward
On whom but on my husband should I fawne?	Edw	1.4.146	Queene
On Mortimer, with whom ungentle Queene--	Edw	1.4.147	Gavstn
That charming Circes walking on the waves,	Edw	1.4.172	Queene
For never doted Jove on Ganimed,	Edw	1.4.180	Queene
So much as he on cursed Gaveston.	Edw	1.4.181	Queene
And yet heele ever dote on Gaveston,	Edw	1.4.185	Queene
That now I hope flotes on the Irish seas.	Edw	1.4.224	Mortmr
On that condition Lancaster will graunt.	Edw	1.4.292	Lncstr
Having brought the Earle of Cornewall on his way,	Edw	1.4.300	Queene
And on their knees salute your majestie.	Edw	1.4.339	Queene
And seeing his minde so dotes on Gaveston,	Edw	1.4.389	MortSr
He weares a lords revenewe on his back,	Edw	1.4.407	Mortmr
On whose good fortune Spencers hope depends.	Edw	2.1.11	Spencr
When I forsake thee, death seaze on my heart,	Edw	2.1.64	Neece
And still his minde runs on his minion.	Edw	2.2.4	Queene
On whose top-branches Kinglie Eagles pearch,	Edw	2.2.17	Mortmr
As to bestow a looke on such as you.	Edw	2.2.78	Gavstn
Lead on the way.	Edw	2.2.132	Lncstr
lascivious showes/And prodigall gifts bestowed on Gaveston,	Edw	2.2.158	Mortmr
Waite on me, and ile see thou shalt not want.	Edw	2.2.246	Edward
Whose eyes are fixt on none but Gaveston:	Edw	2.4.62	Queene
let him bestow/His teares on that, for that is all he gets/Of	Edw	2.5.53	Mortmr
him, but must we now/Leave him on had-I-wist, and let him go?	Edw	2.5.85	Warwck
Why I say, let him go on Penbrookes word.	Edw	2.5.90	Lncstr
Returne him on your honor. Sound, away.	Edw	2.5.98	Mortmr
Strike off their heads, and let them preach on poles,	Edw	3.1.20	Spencr
Weele steele it on their crest, and powle their tops.	Edw	3.1.27	Edward
And Spencer, spare them not, but lay it on.	Edw	3.1.56	Edward
heavens great beames/On Atlas shoulder, shall not lie more	Edw	3.1.77	Prince
thy mother feare/Thou art not markt to many daies on earth.	Edw	3.1.80	Queene
The earle of Warwick seazde him on his way,	Edw	3.1.115	Arundl
On your accursed traiterous progenie,	Edw	3.1.141	Edward
with my sword/On those proud rebels that are up in armes,	Edw	3.1.187	Edward
Traitor on thy face, rebellious Lancaster.	Edw	3.1.204	Spencr
traitors, now tis time/To be avengd on you for all your braves,	Edw	3.1.225	Edward
Do speedie execution on them all,	Edw	3.1.254	Edward
Bestowe that treasure on the lords of Fraunce,	Edw	3.1.265	Spencr
These Barons lay their heads on blocks together,	Edw	3.1.274	Baldck
Now on my life, theile neither barke nor bite.	Edw	4.3.13	Edward
Raigne showers of vengeance on my cursed head/Thou God, to whom	Edw	4.6.7	Kent
Fie on that love that hatcheth death and hate.	Edw	4.6.15	Kent
and sore tempests driven/To fall on shoare, and here to pine in	Edw	4.7.35	Baldck
good father on thy lap/Lay I this head, laden with mickle care,	Edw	4.7.39	Edward
Stand not on titles, but obay th'arrest,	Edw	4.7.58	Leistr
the last of all my blisse on earth,/Center of all misfortune.	Edw	4.7.61	Edward
Why do you lowre unkindly on a king?	Edw	4.7.63	Edward
Yet stay, for rather then I will looke on them,	Edw	5.1.106	Edward
Not yet my lorde, ile beare you on your waye.	Edw	5.1.155	Leistr
To be revengde on Mortimer and thee.	Edw	5.2.121	Kent
Wherefore stay we? on sirs to the court.	Edw	5.3.65	Souldr
He is a traitor, thinke not on him, come.	Edw	5.4.115	Queene
Lie on this bed, and rest your selfe a while.	Edw	5.5.72	Ltborn
My minde may be more stedfast on my God.	Edw	5.5.78	Edward
So, lay the table downe, and stampe on it,	Edw	5.5.112	Ltborn
And thou shalt die, and on his mournefull hearse,	Edw	5.6.29	King
Is this report raisde on poore Isabell.	Edw	5.6.75	Queene
Bid [on kai me on] <Oncaymaeon> farewell, <and> Galen come:	F 40	1.1.12	Faust
And gaze not on it least it tempt thy soule,	F 98	1.1.70	GdAngl
Be thou on earth as Jove is in the skye,	F 103	1.1.75	BdAngl
no object, for my head]/[But ruminates on Negromantique skill].	F 132	1.1.104A	Faust
as th'infernall spirits/On sweet Musaeus when he came to hell,	F 143	1.1.115	Faust

ON (cont.)

Thou art too ugly to attend on me:	F 252	1.3.24		Faust
Having thee ever to attend on me,	F 321	1.3.93		Faust
Sirra, wilt thou be my man and waite on me?	F 354	1.4.12	P	Wagner
What bootes it then to thinke on <of> God or Heaven?	F 391	2.1.3		Faust
That I shall waite on Faustus whilst he lives,	F 420	2.1.32		Mephst
And I will be thy slave and waite on thee,	F 435	2.1.47		Mephst
See <come> Faustus, here is <heres> fire, set it on.	F 459	2.1.71		Mephst
But what is this Inscription on mine Arme?	F 465	2.1.77		Faust
On these conditions following:	F 484	2.1.96	P	Faust
<A plague on her for a hote whore>.	F 534	(HC261)A	P	Faust
The framing of this circle on the ground/Brings Thunder,	F 545	2.1.157		Mephst
faire/As thou, or any man that [breathes] <breathe> on earth.	F 558	2.2.7		Mephst
<Thinke thou on hell Faustus, for thou art damnd>.	F 624	(HC262)A		Mephst
Thou calst on <talkst of> Christ contrary to thy promise.	F 643	2.2.92		Lucifr
Thou should'st not thinke on <of> God.	F 644	2.2.93		Belzeb
Thinke [of] <on> the devill.	F 645	2.2.94		Lucifr
I was begotten on a sunny bank:	F 705	2.2.154	P	Sloth
Away to hell, away: on piper.	F 711	2.2.163		Lucifr
<Farewel Faustus, and thinke on the divel>.	F 720	(HC264)A		Lucifr
Whilst I am here on earth let me be cloyd/With all things that	F 837	3.1.59		Faust
Whilst on thy backe his hollinesse ascends/Saint Peters Chaire	F 869	3.1.91		Raymnd
Thus, as the Gods creepe on with feete of wool,	F 877	3.1.99		Pope
Trode on the neck of Germane Fredericke,	F 916	3.1.138		Pope
That Peters heires should tread on Emperours,	F 918	3.1.140		Pope
Is not all power on earth bestowed on us?	F 930	3.1.152		Pope
And on a pile of Fagots burnt to death.	F 963	3.1.185		Faust
And on a proud pac'd Steed, as swift as thought,	F 984	3.2.4		Mephst
Whilst on thy head I lay my hand,	F 995	3.2.15		Mephst
Cursed be he that stroke his holinesse a blow [on] the face.	F1079	3.2.99		1Frier
be he that strucke <tooke> fryer Sandelo a blow on the pate.	F1081	3.2.101		1Frier
Come on sirra, let me search you now.	F1104	3.3.17	P	Vintnr
That on a furies back came post from Rome,	F1161	4.1.7		Fredrk
That this faire Lady, whilest she liv'd on earth,	F1266	4.1.112		Emper
Had on her necke a little wart, or mole;	F1267	4.1.113		Emper
First, on his head, in quittance of my wrongs,	F1379	4.2.55		Benvol
was limitted/For foure and twenty yeares, to breathe on earth?	F1396	4.2.72		Faust
Go horse these traytors on your fiery backes,	F1403	4.2.79		Faust
It is your owne you meane, feele on your head.	F1443	4.3.13		Fredrk
I am eighteene pence on the score, but say nothing, see if she	F1511	4.5.7	P	Robin
Leave me a while, to ponder on my sinnes.	F1736	5.1.63		Faust
And weare thy colours on my plumed crest.	F1778	5.1.105		Faust
Yet Faustus call on God.	F1848	5.2.52	P	2Schol
On God, whom Faustus hath abjur'd?	F1849	5.2.53	P	Faust
on God, whom Faustus hath blasphem'd?	F1849	5.2.53	P	Faust
Fooles that will laugh on earth, [must] <most> weepe in hell.	F1891	5.2.95		Mephst
To want in hell, that had on earth such store.	F1898	5.2.102		BdAngl
Hell, or the Divell, had had no power on thee.	F1902	5.2.106		GdAngl
Hadst thou kept on that way, Faustus behold,	F1903	5.2.107		GdAngl
On burning forkes: their bodies [boyle] <broyle> in lead.	F1912	5.2.116		BdAngl
There are live quarters broyling on the coles,	F1913	5.2.117		BdAngl
Yet will I call on him: O spare me Lucifer.	F1942	5.2.146		Faust
Mountaines and Hils, come, come, and fall on me,	F1945	5.2.149		Faust
[O God, if thou wilt not have mercy on my soule],	F1958	5.2.162A		Faust
[My God, my God] <O mercy heaven>, looke not so fierce on me;	F1979	5.2.183		Faust
At which selfe time the house seem'd all on fire,	F1993	5.3.11		3Schol
end be such/As every Christian heart laments to thinke on:	F1996	5.3.14		2Schol
a vengeance on them, they have vilde long nailes, there was a	F App	p.230 51	P	Clown
Come on Mephastophilis, what shall we do?	F App	p.232 22	P	Faust
Cursed be hee that strooke his holinesse a blowe on the face.	F App	p.232 33		Frier
Cursed be he that tooke Frier Sandelo a blow on the pate.	F App	p.232 35		Frier
On that condition Ile feede thy divel with horse-bread as long	F App	p.234 30	P	Rafe
thee hornes, but makes thee weare them, feele on thy head.	F App	p.238 71	P	Emper
what, wil you goe on horse backe, or on foote?	F App	p.239 95	P	Mephst
I am past this faire and pleasant greene, ile walke on foote.	F App	p.239 97	P	Faust
Ide make a brave living on him; hee has a buttocke as slicke as	F App	p.239 116	P	HrsCsr
here they be madam, wilt please you taste on them.	F App	p.242 15	P	Faust
Wars worse then civill on Thessalian playnes,	Lucan, First Booke	1		
Th'affrighted worlds force bent on publique spoile,	Lucan, First Booke	5		
celestiall fire/Fleete on the flouds, the earth shoulder the	Lucan, First Booke	76		
And on her Turret-bearing head disperst,	Lucan, First Booke	190		
And faintnes numm'd his steps there on the brincke:	Lucan, First Booke	196		
that guardst/Roomes mighty walles built on Tarpeian rocke,	Lucan, First Booke	198		
rites and Latian Jove advanc'd/On Alba hill o Vestall flames,	Lucan, First Booke	201		
Or darts which Parthians backward shoot) marcht on/And then	Lucan, First Booke	232		
Must Pompey as his last foe plume on me,	Lucan, First Booke	338		
If to incampe on Thuscan Tybers streames,	Lucan, First Booke	382		
Or flaming Titan (feeding on the deepe)/Puls them aloft, and	Lucan, First Booke	416		
this makes them/Run on the swords point and desire to die,	Lucan, First Booke	457		
and that Roome/He looking on by these men should be sackt.	Lucan, First Booke	480		
inconsiderate multitude/Thorough the City hurried headlong on,	Lucan, First Booke	493		
Which flamed not on high; but headlong pitcht/Her burning head	Lucan, First Booke	544		
high; but headlong pitcht/Her burning head on bending Hespery.	Lucan, First Booke	545		
on the Altar/He laies a ne're-yoakt Bull, and powers downe	Lucan, First Booke	607		
Then crams salt levin on his crooked knife;	Lucan, First Booke	609		
hornes/The quick priest pull'd him on his knees and slew him:	Lucan, First Booke	612		
As [Maenas] <Maenus> full of wine on Pindus raves,	Lucan, First Booke	674		
This headlesse trunke that lies on Nylus sande/I know:	Lucan, First Booke	684		
Yoke Venus Doves, put Mirtle on thy haire,	Ovid's Elegies	1.2.23		
Which troopes hath alwayes bin on Cupids side:	Ovid's Elegies	1.2.36		
And on their faces heapes of Roses strow.	Ovid's Elegies	1.2.40		
And she that on a faind Bull swamme to land,	Ovid's Elegies	1.3.23		
his limbes he spread/Upon the bed, but on my foote first tread.	Ovid's Elegies	1.4.16		

ON (cont.)

Words without voyce shall on my eye browes sit,	Ovid's Elegies	1.4.19
Strike on the boord like them that pray for evill,	Ovid's Elegies	1.4.27
And where thou drinkst, on that part I will sup.	Ovid's Elegies	1.4.32
Nor [leane] <leave> thy soft head on his boistrous brest.	Ovid's Elegies	1.4.36
Chiefely on thy lips let not his lips linger.	Ovid's Elegies	1.4.38
Say they are mine, and hands on thee impose.	Ovid's Elegies	1.4.40
On mooved hookes set ope the churlish dore.	Ovid's Elegies	1.6.2
And on my haires a crowne of flowers remaine.	Ovid's Elegies	1.6.38
On this hard threshold till the morning lay.	Ovid's Elegies	1.6.68
And he who on his mother veng'd his sire,	Ovid's Elegies	1.7.9
lockes spred/On her white necke but for hurt cheekes be led.	Ovid's Elegies	1.7.40
with kissing/And on her necke a wantons marke not missing.	Ovid's Elegies	1.7.42
Sees not the morne on rosie horses rise.	Ovid's Elegies	1.8.4
with thrids on wrong wheeles spun/And what with Mares ranck	Ovid's Elegies	1.8.7
He staide, and on thy lookes his gazes seaz'd.	Ovid's Elegies	1.8.24
a rich lover plants/His love on thee, and can supply thy wants.	Ovid's Elegies	1.8.32
When on thy lappe thine eyes thou dost deject,	Ovid's Elegies	1.8.37
On all the [bed mens] <beds men> tumbling let him viewe/And thy	Ovid's Elegies	1.8.97
Both of them watch: each on the hard earth sleepes:	Ovid's Elegies	1.9.7
And on Andromache his helmet laces.	Ovid's Elegies	1.9.36
On Priams loose-trest daughter when he gazed.	Ovid's Elegies	1.9.38
the drie fields strayed/When on her head a water pitcher laied.	Ovid's Elegies	1.10.6
Farmes out her-self on nights for what she can.	Ovid's Elegies	1.10.30
blotted letter/On the last edge to stay mine eyes the better.	Ovid's Elegies	1.11.22
when she departed/Nape by stumbling on the thre-shold started.	Ovid's Elegies	1.12.4
Poore wretches on the tree themselves did strangle,	Ovid's Elegies	1.12.17
Now on <ore> the sea from her old love comes shee,	Ovid's Elegies	1.13.1
Halfe sleeping on a purple bed she rested,	Ovid's Elegies	1.14.20
Bacchinall/That tyr'd doth rashly on the greene grasse fall.	Ovid's Elegies	1.14.22
I had in hand/Which for his heaven fell on the Gyants band.	Ovid's Elegies	2.1.16
On tell-tales neckes thou seest the linke-knitt chaines,	Ovid's Elegies	2.2.41
To quaver on her lippes even in her song,	Ovid's Elegies	2.4.26
[Amber] <Yellow> trest is shee, then on the morne thinke I,/My	Ovid's Elegies	2.4.43
Not drunke, your faults [in] <on> the spilt wine I numbred.	Ovid's Elegies	2.5.14
No such voice-feigning bird was on the ground,	Ovid's Elegies	2.6.23
A grave her bones hides, on her corps great <small> grave,	Ovid's Elegies	2.6.59
If on the Marble Theater I looke,	Ovid's Elegies	2.7.3
But when on thee her angry eyes did rush,	Ovid's Elegies	2.8.15
Maides on the shore, with marble white feete tread,	Ovid's Elegies	2.11.15
Shee looking on them did more courage give.	Ovid's Elegies	2.12.26
On labouring women thou doest pitty take,	Ovid's Elegies	2.13.19
[Or] <On> stones, our stockes originall, should be hurld,	Ovid's Elegies	2.14.11
And on the next fault punishment inflict.	Ovid's Elegies	2.14.44
And on the soft ground fertile greene grasse growe.	Ovid's Elegies	2.16.6
Then on the rough Alpes should I tread aloft,	Ovid's Elegies	2.16.19
And on thy thre-shold let me lie dispred,	Ovid's Elegies	2.19.21
Sterne was her front, her [cloake] <looke> on ground did lie.	Ovid's Elegies	3.1.12
Ah howe oft on hard doores hung I engrav'd,	Ovid's Elegies	3.1.53
What gift with me was on her birth day sent,	Ovid's Elegies	3.1.57
Some greater worke will urge me on at last.	Ovid's Elegies	3.1.70
Because on him thy care doth hap to rest.	Ovid's Elegies	3.2.8
On swift steedes mounted till the race were done.	Ovid's Elegies	3.2.10
But on the ground thy cloathes too loosely lie,	Ovid's Elegies	3.2.25
[A] <Or> while thy tiptoes on the foote-stoole rest.	Ovid's Elegies	3.2.64
And forth the gay troupes on swift horses flie.	Ovid's Elegies	3.2.78
Mars girts his deadly sword on for my harme:	Ovid's Elegies	3.3.27
And on his loose mane the loose bridle laide.	Ovid's Elegies	3.4.16
Strayd bare-foote through sole places on a time.	Ovid's Elegies	3.5.50
Which wealth, cold winter doth on thee bestowe.	Ovid's Elegies	3.5.94
Or full of dust doest on the drye earth slide.	Ovid's Elegies	3.5.96
She on my necke her Ivorie armes did throw,	Ovid's Elegies	3.6.7
With that her loose gowne on, from me she cast her,	Ovid's Elegies	3.6.81
To cover it, spilt water in <on> the place.	Ovid's Elegies	3.6.84
The ditcher no markes on the ground did leave.	Ovid's Elegies	3.7.42
The locks spred on his necke receive his teares,	Ovid's Elegies	3.8.11
all holy things/And on all creatures obscure darcknesse brings.	Ovid's Elegies	3.8.20
Nor on the earth was knowne the name of floore.	Ovid's Elegies	3.9.8
On mast of oakes, first oracles, men fed,	Ovid's Elegies	3.9.9
The goddesse sawe Iasion on Candyan Ide,	Ovid's Elegies	3.9.25
To lay my body on the hard moist floore.	Ovid's Elegies	3.10.10
The annuall pompe goes on the covered ground.	Ovid's Elegies	3.12.12
But with your robes, put on an honest face,	Ovid's Elegies	3.13.27
On Hellespont guiltie of True-loves blood,	Hero and Leander	1.1
And all that view'd her, were enamour'd on her.	Hero and Leander	1.118
Pyn'd as they went, and thinking on her died.	Hero and Leander	1.130
On this feast day, O cursed day and hower,	Hero and Leander	1.131
Who on Loves seas more glorious wouldst appeare?	Hero and Leander	1.228
Save that the sea playing on yellow sand,	Hero and Leander	1.347
And wound them on his arme, and for her mourn'd.	Hero and Leander	1.376
On her, this god/Enamoured was, and with his snakie rod,	Hero and Leander	1.397
And sweetly on his pipe began to play,	Hero and Leander	1.401
As sheap-heards do, her on the ground hee layd,	Hero and Leander	1.405
To be reveng'd on Jove, did undertake,	Hero and Leander	1.442
And those on whom heaven, earth, and hell relies,	Hero and Leander	1.443
To venge themselves on Hermes, have concluded/That Midas brood	Hero and Leander	1.474
So on she goes, and in her idle flight,	Hero and Leander	2.10
She, fearing on the rushes to be flung,	Hero and Leander	2.66
Whereat she starts, puts on her purple weeds,	Hero and Leander	2.88
Had left the heavens, therefore on him hee seaz'd.	Hero and Leander	2.158
sported with their loves/On heapes of heavie gold, and tooke	Hero and Leander	2.163
He heav'd him up, and looking on his face,	Hero and Leander	2.171
The god put Helles bracelet on his arme,	Hero and Leander	2.179

ON (cont.)			
That now should shine on Thetis glassie bower,	Hero and Leander	2.203	
Wherein Leander on her quivering brest,	Hero and Leander	2.279	
He on the suddaine cling'd her so about,	Hero and Leander	2.314	
Than Dis, on heapes of gold fixing his looke.	Hero and Leander	2.326	
ONCAYMAEON			
Bid [on kai me on] <Oncaymaeon> farewell, <and> Galen come:	F 40	1.1.12	Faust
ONCE			
I vow, if she but once frowne on thee more,	Dido	1.1.12	Jupitr
As once I did for harming Hercules.	Dido	1.1.15	Jupitr
Which once performd, poore Troy so long suppress,	Dido	1.1.93	Jupitr
And flourish once againe that erst was dead:	Dido	1.1.95	Jupitr
Might we but once more see Aeneas face,	Dido	1.2.45	Serg
He with his faulchions poynt raisde up at once,	Dido	2.1.229	Aeneas
Then from the navell to the throat at once,	Dido	2.1.255	Aeneas
Unlesse I be deceiv'd disputed once.	Dido	3.1.147	Cloan
Be it as you will have [it] for this once,	Dido	3.2.97	Venus
It haild, it snowde, it lightned all at once.	Dido	4.1.8	Anna
To leave her so and not once say farewell,	Dido	4.3.47	Aeneas
and once againe conspire/Against the life of me poore Carthage	Dido	4.4.131	Dido
Once didst thou goe, and he came backe againe,	Dido	5.1.196	Dido
Passe into Graecia, as did Cyrus once.	1Tamb	1.1.130	Menaph
(for say not I intreat)/Not once to set his foot in Affrica,	1Tamb	3.1.28	Bajzth
And make it swallow both of us at once.	1Tamb	4.2.29	Bajzth
until the bloody flag/Be once advanc'd on my vermilion Tent,	1Tamb	4.2.117	Tamb
the Center of our Empery/Once lost, All Turkie would be	2Tamb	1.1.56	Orcan
And in my blood wash all your hands at once,	2Tamb	3.2.127	Tamb
would let me be put in the front of such a battaile once,	2Tamb	4.1.73	P Calyph
Good my Lord, let him be forgiven for once,	2Tamb	4.1.101	Amyras
Come once in furie and survay his pride,	2Tamb	4.3.41	Orcan
Yet shouldst thou die, shoot at him all at once.	2Tamb	5.1.157	Tamb
But they will give me leave once more, I trow,	Jew	1.2.252	Barab
Once at Jerusalem, where the pilgrims kneel'd,	Jew	2.3.208	Ithimr
Because the Pryor <Governor> <Sire> dispossest thee once,/And	Jew	3.3.43	Abigal
a precious powder that I bought/Of an Italian in Ancona once,	Jew	3.4.69	Barab
Once more away with him; you shall have law.	Jew	5.1.40	Govnr
For sith, as once you said, within this Ile/In Malta here, that	Jew	5.2.67	Barab
Guise/Dares once adventure without the Kings consent,	P 37	1.37	Admral
Now Guise shall catholiques flourish once againe,	P 295	5.22	Anjoy
And meane once more to menace me.	P 364	7.4	Ramus
Welcome from Poland Henry once agayne,	P 589	12.2	QnMoth
Wounded and poysoned, both at once?	P1215	22.77	King
enter by defaulte | whatt thoughe you were once in possession	Paris	ms11,p390	P Souldr
yett comminge upon you once unawares he frayde you out againe.	Paris	ms12,p390	P Souldr
Once more receive my hand, and let this be,	Edw	1.4.334	Edward
And would have once preferd me to the king.	Edw	2.1.14	Spencr
But once, and then thy souldiers marcht like players,	Edw	2.2.183	Mortmr
Yet once more ile importune him with praiers,	Edw	2.4.63	Queene
against your king)/To see his royall soveraigne once againe.	Edw	2.5.7	Gavstn
For Gaveston, will if he [seaze] <zease> <sees> him once,	Edw	2.5.63	Warwck
God end them once, my lord I take my leave,	Edw	3.1.87	Queene
Two kings in England cannot raigne at once:	Edw	5.1.58	Edward
That death ends all, and I can die but once.	Edw	5.1.153	Edward
At our commaund, once more away with him.	Edw	5.4.104	Mortmr
Was not that Lucifer an Angell once?	F 292	1.3.64	Faust
I am content for this once to thrust my head out at a window:	F1200	4.1.46	P Benvol
me <both> body and soule, if I once gave eare to Divinitie:	F1866	5.2.70	P Faust
once admired/For wondrous knowledge in our Germane schooles,	F1997	5.3.15	2Schol
to lay the fury of this ghost, once again my Lord fall too.	F App	p.232 17	P Pope
Made all shake hands as once the Sabines did;	Lucan, First Booke	118	
And having once got head still shal he raigne?	Lucan, First Booke	317	
Graecinus (well I wot) thou touldst me once,	Ovid's Elegies	2.10.1	
I could not be in love with twoo at once,	Ovid's Elegies	2.10.2	
Leave thy once powerfull words, and flatteries,	Ovid's Elegies	3.10.31	
They granted what he crav'd, and once againe,	Hero and Leander	1.455	
To linger by the way, and once she stayd,	Hero and Leander	2.7	
T'is lost but once, and once lost, lost for ever.	Hero and Leander	2.86	
But love resisted once, growes passionate,	Hero and Leander	2.139	
ONE (Homograph; See also TONE)			
But as this one Ile teare them all from him,	Dido	1.1.40	Jupitr
Who with the Sunne devides one radiant shape,	Dido	1.1.97	Jupitr
Or one of chast Dianas fellow Nimphs,	Dido	1.1.194	Aeneas
And lighten our extreames with this one boone,	Dido	1.1.196	Aeneas
Not one of them hath perisht in the storme,	Dido	1.1.236	Venus
This is no seate for one thats comfortles,	Dido	2.1.86	Aeneas
And scarcely doe agree upon one poynt:	Dido	2.1.109	Dido
and both his eyes/Turnd up to heaven as one resolv'd to dye,	Dido	2.1.152	Aeneas
The rather for that one Laocoon/Breaking a speare upon his	Dido	2.1.164	Aeneas
And yet God knowes intangled unto one.--	Dido	3.1.154	Dido
But not so much for thee, thou art but one,	Dido	3.1.175	Dido
We two as friends one fortune will devide:	Dido	3.2.55	Venus
And both our Deities conjoynd in one,	Dido	3.2.79	Juno
Then in one Cave the Queene and he shall meete,	Dido	3.2.92	Juno
I mother, I shall one day be a man,	Dido	3.3.35	Cupid
And with one shaft provoke ten thousand darts:	Dido	3.3.72	Iarbus
I followe one that loveth fame for me,	Dido	3.4.38	Dido
We may as one saile into Italy.	Dido	4.3.30	Aeneas
I am as true as any one of yours.	Dido	5.1.223	Nurse
Weele fight five hundred men at armes to one,	1Tamb	1.2.143	Tamb
Would make one thrust and strive to be retain'd/In such a great	1Tamb	2.3.31	Therid
From one that knew not what a King should do,	1Tamb	2.5.22	Cosroe
To one that can commaund what longs thereto:	1Tamb	2.5.23	Cosroe
And since we all have suckt one wholsome aire,	1Tamb	2.6.25	Cosroe

ONE (cont.)

and the Easterne theeves/Under the conduct of one Tamburlaine,	1Tamb	3.1.3	Bajzth
when the Moon begins/To joine in one her semi-circled hornes:	1Tamb	3.1.12	Bajzth
How can you fancie one that lookes so fierce,	1Tamb	3.2.40	Agidas
mighty Turkish Emperor/To talk with one so base as Tamburlaine?	1Tamb	3.3.88	Fesse
Where they shall meete, and joine their force in one,	1Tamb	3.3.257	Tamb
Come bind them both and one lead in the Turke.	1Tamb	3.3.266	Tamb
Not one should scape: but perish by our swords.	1Tamb	4.2.122	Tamb
Let us unite our royall bandes in one,	1Tamb	4.3.17	Souldn
If these had made one Poems period/And all combin'd in Beauties	1Tamb	5.1.169	Tamb
One thought, one grace, one woonder at the least,	1Tamb	5.1.172	Tamb
As if there were no way but one with us.	1Tamb	5.1.201	Techel
And every one Commander of a world.	2Tamb	1.3.8	Tamb
Water and ayre being simbolisde in one,	2Tamb	1.3.23	Tamb
Or cease one day from war and hot alarms,	2Tamb	1.3.183	Usumc
Nor in one place is circumscriptible,	2Tamb	2.2.50	Orcan
the sun and Moone as darke/As when opposde in one Diamiter,	2Tamb	2.4.52	Tamb
We both will rest and have one Epitaph/Writ in as many severall	2Tamb	2.4.134	Tamb
One minute end our daies, and one sepulcher/Containe our bodies:	2Tamb	3.4.13	Olymp
By Mahomet not one of them shal live.	2Tamb	3.5.17	Callap
Whose tender blossoms tremble every one,	2Tamb	4.3.123	Tamb
And but one hoste is left to honor thee:	2Tamb	5.2.27	Callap
There should not one of all the villaines power/Live to give	2Tamb	5.3.108	Tamb
As one of them indifferently rated,	Jew	1.1.29	Barab
Many in France, and wealthy every one:	Jew	1.1.127	Barab
But one sole Daughter, whom I hold as deare/As Agamemnon did	Jew	1.1.137	Barab
How ere the world goe, I'le make sure for one,	Jew	1.1.186	Barab
Goe one and call those Jewes of Malta hither:	Jew	1.2.34	Govnr
the Jewes, and each of them to pay one halfe of his estate.	Jew	1.2.69	P Reader
And better one want for a common good,	Jew	1.2.98	Govnr
You were a multitude, and I but one,	Jew	1.2.178	Barab
but for every one of those,/Had they beene valued at	Jew	1.2.185	Barab
And now me thinkes that I am one of those:	Jew	2.1.28	Barab
But one amongst the rest became our prize:	Jew	2.2.16	Bosco
One that I love for his good fathers sake.	Jew	2.3.31	Barab
Yet I have one left that will serve your turne:	Jew	2.3.50	Barab
I must have one that's sickly, and be but for sparing vittles:	Jew	2.3.123	P Barab
you in these chops; let me see one that's somewhat leaner.	Jew	2.3.125	P Barab
And now and then one hang himselfe for griefe,	Jew	2.3.196	Barab
One time I was an Hostler in an Inne,	Jew	2.3.205	Ithimr
Stay her,--but let her not speake one word more.	Jew	2.3.323	Barab
that but for one bare night/A hundred Duckets have bin freely	Jew	3.1.2	Curtzn
and let them be interr'd/Within one sacred monument of stone;	Jew	3.2.30	Govnr
I pray, mistris, wil you answer me to one question?	Jew	3.3.30	P Ithimr
A very feeling one; have not the Nuns fine sport with the	Jew	3.3.32	P Ithimr
Oh therefore, Jacomo, let me be one,	Jew	3.3.68	Abigal
And one offence torments me more then all.	Jew	3.6.19	Abigal
Now all are dead, not one remaines alive.	Jew	4.1.7	Barab
Come to my house at one a clocke this night.	Jew	4.1.91	Barab
Marry the Turke shall be one of my godfathers,	Jew	4.1.111	Barab
One turn'd my daughter, therefore he shall dye;	Jew	4.1.119	Barab
Towards one.	Jew	4.1.158	P Ithimr
when holy Friars turne devils and murder one another.	Jew	4.1.194	P Ithimr
and he gave me a letter from one Madam Bellamira, saluting me	Jew	4.2.29	P Ithimr
send me five hundred crowns, and give the Bearer one hundred.	Jew	4.2.118	P Ithimr
Oh that ten thousand nights were put in one,	Jew	4.2.130	Ithimr
and looks/Like one that is imploy'd in Catzerie/And crosbiting,	Jew	4.3.12	Barab
Dost not know a Jew, one Barabas?	Jew	4.4.56	P Ithimr
Farewell Fidler: One letter more to the Jew.	Jew	4.4.72	Pilia
Prethe sweet love, one more, and write it sharp.	Jew	4.4.73	Curtzn
One dram of powder more had made all sure.	Jew	5.1.22	Barab
my good Lord, one that can spy a place/Where you may enter, and	Jew	5.1.70	Barab
onely to performe/One stratagem that I'le impart to thee,	Jew	5.2.99	Barab
That at one instant all things may be done,	Jew	5.2.120	Barab
Besides, if we should let thee goe, all's one,	Jew	5.5.99	Govnr
of my knowledge in one cloyster keeps,/Five hundred fatte	P 141	2.84	Guise
down, heer's one would speak with you from the Duke of Guise.	P 348	6.3	P SrnsWf
Which as I heare one [Shekius] <Shekins> takes it ill,	P 404	7.44	Ramus
That you were one that made this Massacre.	P 436	7.76	Navrre
unto Roan, and spare not one/That you suspect of heresy.	P 446	7.86	Guise
Where we may one injoy the others sight.	P 665	13.9	Duchss
To such a one my Lord, as when she reads my lines,	P 672	13.16	Duchss
O my Lord, I am one of them that is set to murder you.	P 992	19.62	P 3Mur
These two will make one entire Duke of Guise,	P1060	19.130	King
and that thow most reposest one my faythe	Paris	ms31,p391	Guise
One like Actaeon peeping through the grove,	Edw	1.1.67	Gavstn
these may well suffice/For one of greater birth then Gaveston.	Edw	1.1.159	Kent
Thou shouldst not plod one foote beyond this place.	Edw	1.1.181	Gavstn
whom he vouchsafes/For vailing of his bonnet one good looke.	Edw	1.2.19	Lncstr
If I be king, not one of them shall live.	Edw	1.4.105	Edward
Such a one as my Lord of Cornewall is,	Edw	1.4.285	Mortmr
But this I scorne, that one so baselie borne,	Edw	1.4.403	Mortmr
May with one word, advaunce us while we live:	Edw	2.1.9	Spencr
But one of those that saith quandoquidem,	Edw	2.1.54	Spencr
A homely one my lord, not worth the telling.	Edw	2.2.13	Mortmr
That heading is one, and hanging is the other,	Edw	2.5.30	Gavstn
My lord Mortimer, and you my lords each one,	Edw	2.5.74	Penbrk
And Edward thou art one among them all,	Edw	4.4.10	Queene
Not one alive, but shrewdly I suspect,	Edw	4.7.28	Spencr
that one so false/Should come about the person of a prince.	Edw	5.2.104	Mortmr
Souldiers, let me but talke to him one worde.	Edw	5.3.53	Kent
Or whilst one is a sleepe, to take a quill/And blowe a little	Edw	5.4.34	Ltborn

ONE (cont.)

One plaies continually upon a Drum,	Edw	5.5.61	Edward
One jewell have I left, receive thou this.	Edw	5.5.84	Edward
For when we heare one racke the name of God,	F 275	1.3.47	Mephst
Hell hath no limits, nor is circumscrib'd,/In one selfe place:	F 511	2.1.123	Mephst
<Nay sweete Mephastophilis fetch me one, for I will have one>.	F 530	(HC261) A	P Faust
<Well thou wilt have one, sit there till I come,	F 531	(HC261) A	P Mephst
[Nay let me have one booke more, and then I have done, wherein	F 551.8	2.1.171A	P Faust
Are all Celestiall bodies but one Globe,	F 587	2.2.36	Faust
And <Faustus all> jointly move upon one Axle-tree,	F 592	2.2.41	Mephst
But <tell me> have they all/One motion, both situ et tempore?	F 596	2.2.45	Faust
<Well>, Resolve me then in this one question:	F 614	2.2.63	P Faust
Eclipses, all at one time, but in some years we have more, in	F 616	2.2.65	P Faust
I am one that loves an inch of raw Mutton, better then an ell	F 708	2.2.160	P Ltchry
I have gotten one of Doctor Faustus conjuring bookes, and now	F 723	2.3.2	P Robin
hold belly hold, and wee'le not pay one peny for it.	F 750	2.3.29	P Robin
Thorough a rocke of stone in one nights space:	F 793	3.1.15	Faust
In [midst] <one> of which a sumptuous Temple stands,	F 795	3.1.17	Faust
All's one, for wee'l be bold with his Venison.	F 808	3.1.30	Mephst
<As match the dayes within one compleate yeare>,	F 821	(HC265) A	Mephst
Within the compasse of one compleat yeare:	F 822	3.1.44	Mephst
[Amongst the rest the Emperour is one],	F1150	3.3.63A	3Chor
Murder or not murder, now he has but one leg, I'le out-run him,	F1494	4.4.38	P HrsCsr
and one to whom I must be no niggard of my cunning; Come,	F1504	4.4.48	P Faust
be; for I have heard of one, that ha's eate a load of logges.	F1533	4.5.29	P Robin
And has the Doctor but one leg then?	F1553	4.5.49	P Dick
one of his devils turn'd me into the likenesse of an Apes face.	F1554	4.5.50	P Dick
Yes, I remember I sold one a horse.	F1635	4.6.78	Faust
'Tis not so much worth; I pray you tel me one thing.	F1643	4.6.86	P Carter
me thinkes you should have a wooden bedfellow of one of 'em.	F1654	4.6.97	P Carter
sir, did not I pull off one of your legs when you were asleepe?	F1655	4.6.98	P HrsCsr
One thing good servant let me crave of thee,	F1759	5.1.86	Faust
Now hast thou but one bare houre to live,	F1927	5.2.131	Faust
One drop [would save my soule, halfe a drop, ah] my Christ.	F1940	5.2.144	Faust
One drop <of bloud will save me; oh> my Christ.	F1940	(HC271) B	Faust
For twixt the houres of twelve and one, me thought/I heard him	F1991	5.3.9	3Schol
divels, say I should kill one of them, what would folkes say?	F App	p.230 47	P Clown
here I ha stolne one of doctor Faustus conjuring books, and	F App	p.233 1	P Robin
in Europe for nothing, thats one of my conjuring workes.	F App	p.234 24	P Robin
One of you call him foorth.	F App	p.238 68	P Emper
I have beene al this day seeking one maister Fustian:	F App	p.239 98	P HrsCsr
but I must tel you one thing before you have him, ride him not	F App	p.239 108	P Faust
If any one part of vast heaven thou swayest,	Lucan, First Booke	56	
A towne with one poore church set them at oddes.	Lucan, First Booke	97	
One that was feed for Caesar, and whose tongue/Could tune the	Lucan, First Booke	272	
One sweares his troupes of daring horsemen fought/Upon Mevanias	Lucan, First Booke	469	
And wilt not trust thy Citty walls one night:	Lucan, First Booke	518	
Now evermore least some one hope might ease/The Commons	Lucan, First Booke	520	
Well skild in Pyromancy; one that knew/The hearts of beasts, and	Lucan, First Booke	586	
appear'd/A knob of flesh, whereof one halfe did looke/Dead, and	Lucan, First Booke	627	
the death of many men/Meetes in one period.	Lucan, First Booke	650	
(men say)/Began to smile and [tooke] <take> one foote away.	Ovid's Elegies	1.1.8	
I love but one, and hir I love change never,	Ovid's Elegies	1.3.15	
One window shut, the other open stood,	Ovid's Elegies	1.5.3	
And striving thus as one that would be cast,	Ovid's Elegies	1.5.15	
Not one wen in her bodie could I spie,	Ovid's Elegies	1.5.18	
Each one according to his gifts respect.	Ovid's Elegies	1.8.38	
To yeeld their love to more then one disdainde.	Ovid's Elegies	1.8.40	
Nor one or two men are sufficient.	Ovid's Elegies	1.8.54	
Nor, if thou couzenst one, dread to for-sweare,	Ovid's Elegies	1.8.85	
One as a spy doth to his enemies goe,	Ovid's Elegies	1.9.17	
Why should one sell it, and the other buy it?	Ovid's Elegies	1.10.34	
That with one worde hath nigh himselfe undone,	Ovid's Elegies	1.13.20	
Not one in heaven should be more base and vile.	Ovid's Elegies	1.13.36	
Made two nights one to finish up his pleasure.	Ovid's Elegies	1.13.46	
No one face likes me best, all faces moove,	Ovid's Elegies	2.4.9	
Before Callimachus one preferres me farre,	Ovid's Elegies	2.4.19	
And when one sweetely sings, then straight I long,	Ovid's Elegies	2.4.25	
Or if one touch the lute with art and cunning,	Ovid's Elegies	2.4.27	
Some one of these might make the chastest fall.	Ovid's Elegies	2.4.32	
[I thinke what one undeckt would be, being drest];	Ovid's Elegies	2.4.37	
There lives the Phoenix one alone bird ever.	Ovid's Elegies	2.6.54	
One among many is to grieve thee tooke.	Ovid's Elegies	2.7.4	
Well maiest thou one thing for thy Mistresse use.	Ovid's Elegies	2.8.24	
Was not one wench inough to greeve my heart?	Ovid's Elegies	2.10.12	
Let one wench cloy me with sweete loves delight,	Ovid's Elegies	2.10.21	
If one can doote, if not, two everie night,	Ovid's Elegies	2.10.22	
Let others tell this, and what each one speakes/Beleeve, no	Ovid's Elegies	2.11.21	
Turne thy lookes hether, and in one spare twaine,	Ovid's Elegies	2.13.15	
Forgive her gratious Gods this one delict,	Ovid's Elegies	2.14.43	
I would not out, might I in one place hit,	Ovid's Elegies	2.15.19	
Since some faire one I should of force obey.	Ovid's Elegies	2.17.6	
But sundry floods in one banke never go,	Ovid's Elegies	2.17.31	
Nor in my bookes shall one but thou be writ,	Ovid's Elegies	2.17.33	
And one, I thinke, was longer, of her feete.	Ovid's Elegies	3.1.8	
With scepters, and high buskins th'one would dresse me,	Ovid's Elegies	3.1.63	
One slowe we favour, Romans him revoke:	Ovid's Elegies	3.2.73	
Cannot a faire one, if not chast, please thee?	Ovid's Elegies	3.4.41	
One Deianira was more worth then these.	Ovid's Elegies	3.5.38	
Or one that with her tender brother lies,	Ovid's Elegies	3.6.22	
And one gave place still as another came.	Ovid's Elegies	3.6.64	
Yet notwithstanding, like one dead it lay,	Ovid's Elegies	3.6.65	
Canst touch that hand wherewith some one lie dead?	Ovid's Elegies	3.7.17	

ONE (cont.)			
One [her] <she> commands, who many things can give.	Ovid's Elegies	3.7.62	
The one his first love, th'other his new care.	Ovid's Elegies	3.8.32	
Like one start up your haire tost and displast,	Ovid's Elegies	3.13.33	
The one Abydos, the other Sestos hight.	Hero and Leander	1.4	
But this is true, so like was one the other,	Hero and Leander	1.39	
There might you see one sigh, another rage,	Hero and Leander	1.125	
Where by one hand, light headed Bacchus hoong,	Hero and Leander	1.139	
We wish that one should loose, the other win.	Hero and Leander	1.170	
And one especiallie doe we affect,	Hero and Leander	1.171	
He started up, she blusht as one asham'd;	Hero and Leander	1.181	
As heaven preserves all things, so save thou one.	Hero and Leander	1.224	
In time it will returne us two for one.	Hero and Leander	1.236	
One is no number, mayds are nothing then,	Hero and Leander	1.255	
one shalt thou bee,/Though never-singling Hymen couple thee.	Hero and Leander	1.257	
No, nor to any one exterior sence,	Hero and Leander	1.271	
Some one or other keepes you as his owne.	Hero and Leander	1.290	
At one selfe instant, she poore soule assaies,	Hero and Leander	1.362	
nor would vouchsafe so much/As one poore word, their hate to	Hero and Leander	1.384	
Glist'red with deaw, as one that seem'd to skorne it:	Hero and Leander	1.390	
Wherewith as one displeas'd, away she trips.	Hero and Leander	2.4	
One halfe appear'd, the other halfe was hid.	Hero and Leander	2.316	
O'NEIL (See ONEYLE)			
ONELIE			
Onelie disposed to martiall Stratagems?	1Tamb	3.2.41	Agidas
And not kings onelie, but the wisest men,	Edw	1.4.395	MortSr
ONELY			
Brave Prince of Troy, thou onely art our God,	Dido	1.1.152	Achat
That onely Juno rules in Rhamnuse towne.	Dido	3.2.20	Juno
Hath not the Carthage Queene mine onely sonne?	Dido	4.4.29	Aeneas
onely Aeneas frowne/Is that which terrifies poore Didos heart:	Dido	4.4.115	Dido
That onely made him King to make us sport.	1Tamb	2.5.101	Tamb
The onely feare and terrour of the world,	1Tamb	3.3.45	Tamb
The onely Paragon of Tamburlaine,	1Tamb	3.3.119	Tamb
for us to see them, and for Tamburlaine onely to enjoy them.	1Tamb	4.4.112	P Techel
Save onely that in Beauties just applause,	1Tamb	5.1.178	Tamb
Onely to gaze upon Zenocrate.	2Tamb	3.2.33	Tamb
Whose drift is onely to dishonor thee.	2Tamb	4.2.7	Olymp
Which onely will dismay the enemy.	2Tamb	5.3.112	Usumc
Leading a life that onely strives to die,	2Tamb	5.3.197	Amyras
And of me onely have they taken all.	Jew	1.2.179	Barab
For onely I have toyl'd to inherit here/The months of vanity	Jew	1.2.196	Barab
rumbling in the house; so I tooke onely this, and runne my way:	Jew	3.1.21	P Pilia
I here adopt thee for mine onely heire,	Jew	3.4.43	Barab
Onely know this, that thus thou art to doe:	Jew	3.4.48	Barab
What, all dead save onely Abigall?	Jew	3.6.7	2Fryar
Where be thou present onely to performe/One stratagem that I'le	Jew	5.2.98	Barab
Onely corrupted in religion,	P 212	4.10	Charls
I did it onely in dispight of thee	Paris	ms24,p391	Guise
That wert the onely cause of his exile.	Edw	1.1.179	Edward
And onely this torments my wretched soule,	Edw	1.4.123	Edward
neece, the onely heire/Unto the Earle of Gloster late deceased.	Edw	2.2.258	Edward
<daunt> his heavenly verse;/Onely this, Gentles <Gentlemen>:	F 7	Prol.7	1Chor
[Yet not your words onely, but mine owne fantasie],	F 130	1.1.102A	Faust
There is no chiefe but onely Beelzebub:	F 284	1.3.56	Faust
Onely for pleasure of these damned slaves.	F1119	3.3.32	Mephst
Therefore despaire, thinke onely upon hell;	F1881	5.2.85	Mephst
may exhort the wise/Onely to wonder at unlawfull things,	F2007	5.3.25	4Chor
Onely for pleasure of these damned slaves.	F App	p.235 39	Mephst
is faint; swift Hermes retrograde;/Mars onely rules the heaven:	Lucan, First Booke	662	
War onely gives us peace, o Rome continue/The course of	Lucan, First Booke	669	
out the date/Of slaughter; onely civill broiles make peace.	Lucan, First Booke	671	
and not onely kisse/But force thee give him my stolne honey	Ovid's Elegies	1.4.63	
Such blisse is onely common to us two,	Ovid's Elegies	2.5.31	
Bewaile I onely, though I them lament.	Ovid's Elegies	2.5.60	
Onely Ile signe nought, that may grieve me much.	Ovid's Elegies	2.15.18	
Onely our loves let not such rich churles gaine,	Ovid's Elegies	3.7.59	
Onely was Crete fruitfull that plenteous yeare,	Ovid's Elegies	3.9.37	
Onely the Goddesse hated Goate did lack,	Ovid's Elegies	3.12.18	
Slippe still, onely denie it when tis done,	Ovid's Elegies	3.13.15	
Not onely by warres rage made Gentleman.	Ovid's Elegies	3.14.6	
ONES			
Bequeath her young ones to our scanted foode.	Dido	1.1.162	Achat
H'had never bellowed in a brasen Bull/Of great ones envy; o'th	Jew	Prol.26	Machvl
Every ones price is written on his backe,	Jew	2.3.3	2Offcr
I sawe ones legges with fetters blacke and blewe,	Ovid's Elegies	2.2.47	
The wronged Gods dread faire ones to offend,	Ovid's Elegies	3.3.31	
ONEYLE			
The wilde Oneyle, with swarmes of Irish Kernes,	Edw	2.2.164	Lncstr
ON KAI ME ON			
Bid [on kai me on] <Oncaymaeon> farewell, <and> Galen come:	F 40	1.1.12	Faust
ONLY (See also ONELIE)			
His lookes shall be my only Librarie,	Dido	3.1.90	Dido
Whiles only danger beat upon our walles,	1Tamb	5.1.30	1Virgn
Wel met my only deare Zenocrate,	1Tamb	5.1.443	Souldn
Not a wise word, only gave me a nod, as who shold say, Is it	Jew	4.2.12	P Pilia
but I hope it be/Only some naturall passion makes her sicke.	P 183	3.18	QnMarg
O no my Lord, a woman only must/Partake the secrets of my heart.	P 675	13.19	Duchss
I did it only in despite of thee.	P 820	17.15	Guise
[And only Paragon of excellence],	F1703	5.1.30A	1Schol
Were gluttons, and lov'd only delicates,	F1917	5.2.121	BdAngl
that not only gives thee hornes, but makes thee weare them,	F App	p.238 70	P Emper
And only gods and heavenly powers you know,	Lucan, First Booke	449	

ONLY (cont.)				
gods and heavenly powers you know,/Or only know you nothing.	Lucan, First Booke	450		
Nor were the Commons only strooke to heart/With this vaine	Lucan, First Booke	483		
the only hope (that did remaine/To their afflictions) were	Lucan, First Booke	494		
only thee I flatter,/Thy lightning can my life in pieces .	Ovid's Elegies	1.6.15		
Only a woman gets spoiles from a Man, ...	Ovid's Elegies	1.10.29		
Whose only dower was her chastitie, ...	Hero and Leander	1.412		
To which the Muses sonnes are only heire:	Hero and Leander	1.476		
ON'S				
I, master, he's slain; look how his brains drop out on's nose.	Jew	4.1.178	P	Ithimr
a paire of hornes on's head as e're thou sawest in thy life.	F 737	2.3.16	P	Robin
heere's some on's have cause to know him; did he conjure thee	F1523	4.5.19	P	HrsCsr
ONSET				
Ile give the onset.	Edw	2.3.20		Mortmr
ON'T				
went in at dores/You had bin stab'd, but not a word on't now;	Jew	2.3.338		Barab
And now I thinke on't, going to the execution, a fellow met me	Jew	4.2.27	P	Ithimr
<Have you any witnesse on't>?	F 204	(HC258)A	P	Wagner
I, take it, and the devill give thee good of it <on't>. .	F 502	2.1.114		Faust
why thou canst not tell ne're a word on't. . . .	F 731	2.3.10	P	Dick
Where having spy'de her tower, long star'd he on't, . .	Hero and Leander	2.149		
ONUS				
Saying it is, onus quam gravissimum, ...	Edw	5.4.61		Mortmr
OPALS				
Bags of fiery Opals, Saphires, Amatists, ...	Jew	1.1.25		Barab
OPE				
Then gan the windes breake ope their brazen doores, . .	Dido	1.1.62		Venus
Now Phoebus ope the eye-lids of the day, ...	Jew	2.1.60		Barab
Oh, if that be all, I can picke ope your locks. . .	Jew	4.3.33		Pilia
See, see his window's ope, we'l call to him. . . .	F1177	4.1.23		Fredrk
Go pacifie their fury, set it ope, ...	F1589	4.6.32		Duke
On mooved hookes set ope the churlish dore. . . .	Ovid's Elegies	1.6.2		
The gate halfe ope my bent side in will take. . . .	Ovid's Elegies	1.6.4		
Night goes away: I pray thee ope the dore. . . .	Ovid's Elegies	1.6.48		
We erre: a strong blast seem'd the gates to ope: . .	Ovid's Elegies	1.6.51		
To beggers shut, to bringers ope thy gate, . . .	Ovid's Elegies	1.8.77		
Verses ope dores, and lockes put in the poast/Although of oake,	Ovid's Elegies	2.1.27		
She held her lap ope to receive the same.	Ovid's Elegies	3.7.34		
And I see when you ope the two leavde booke: . . .	Ovid's Elegies	3.13.44		
OPEN				
Ile set the casement open that the windes/May enter in, and	Dido	4.4.130		Dido
Leape in mine armes, mine armes are open wide: . . .	Dido	5.1.180		Dido
Open the Males, yet guard the treasure sure, . . .	1Tamb	1.2.138		Tamb
hardy Tamburlaine)/What tis to meet me in the open field,	1Tamb	3.3.146		Bajzth
Open thou shining vaile of Cynthia/And make a passage from the	2Tamb	2.2.47		Orcan
With open crie pursues the wounded Stag:	2Tamb	3.5.7		2Msngr
What, ho, Abigall; open the doore I say.	Jew	2.3.221		Barab
Open an entrance for the wastfull sea, ...	Jew	3.5.16		Govnr
The other Chambers open towards the street. . . .	Jew	4.1.138		Barab
Open the gates for you to enter in, ...	Jew	5.1.93		Barab
And for the open wronges and injuries/Edward hath done to us,	Edw	4.4.21		Mortmr
O might I never open these eyes againe, ...	Edw	4.7.41		Edward
Or open his mouth, and powre quick silver downe, . .	Edw	5.4.36		Ltborn
Now as I speake they fall, and yet with feare/Open againe.	Edw	5.5.96		Edward
The jawes of hell are open to receive thee. . . .	F1908	5.2.112		GdAngl
With jawes wide open ghastly roaring out;	Lucan, First Booke	212		
And Vangions who like those of Sarmata,/Were open slops: .	Lucan, First Booke	432		
fierce men of Rhene/Leaving your countrey open to the spoile.	Lucan, First Booke	461		
Tav'ron peering/(His grave broke open) did affright the Boores.	Lucan, First Booke	582		
One window shut, the other open stood, ...	Ovid's Elegies	1.5.3		
Night runnes away; with open entrance greete them. . .	Ovid's Elegies	1.6.40		
And hath no cloathes, but open doth remaine. . . .	Ovid's Elegies	1.10.16		
Quickly soft words hard dores wide open strooke. . .	Ovid's Elegies	2.1.22		
My flatt'ring speeches soone wide open knocke. . .	Ovid's Elegies	3.1.46		
But now againe the barriers open lye;	Ovid's Elegies	3.2.77		
And fiercely knockst thy brest that open lyes? . . .	Ovid's Elegies	3.5.58		
to thee our Court stands open wide,/There shalt be lov'd:	Ovid's Elegies	3.5.61		
Her gate by my hands is set open wide.	Ovid's Elegies	3.11.12		
Wide open stood the doore, hee need not clime, . . .	Hero and Leander	2.19		
OPEND				
He watcht his armes, and as they opend wide, . . .	Hero and Leander	2.183		
OPENED				
all the christall gates of Joves high court/Were opened wide,	2Tamb	1.3.154		Tamb
yesternight/I opened but the doore to throw him meate,/And I	Edw	5.5.8		Gurney
And modestly they opened as she rose:	Hero and Leander	1.160		
OPENING				
Opening the doores of his rich treasurie, ...	2Tamb	4.2.95		Therid
Stand in some window opening neere the street, . . .	P 86	2.29		Guise
And opening dores with creaking noyse abound? . . .	Ovid's Elegies	1.6.50		
OPENLIE				
[And] <Or> hidden secrets openlie to bewray? . . .	Ovid's Elegies	3.13.8		
OPENLY				
And openly exclaime against the King.	1Tamb	1.1.149		Ceneus
Though some speake openly against my bookes, . . .	Jew	Prol.10		Machvl
OPENS				
Who now with Jove opens the firmament, ...	2Tamb	3.5.56		Callap
OPERATION				
Have greater operation and more force/Than Cynthias in the	2Tamb	4.2.29		Therid
Whose operation is to binde, infect, ...	Jew	3.4.70		Barab
OPINION				
Lodowicke, I have seene/The strangest sight, in my opinion,	Jew	1.2.376		Mthias
OPORTUNITIE				
Then hath your grace fit oportunitie, ...	P 903	18.4		Bartus

OPPORTUNITY			
Since Fortune gives you opportunity,	1Tamb	1.1.124	Menaph
And should we lose the opportunity/That God hath given to venge	2Tamb	2.1.51	Fredrk
Slip not thine opportunity, for feare too late/Thou seek'st for	Jew	5.2.45	Barab
My opportunity may serve me fit,	P 566	11.31	Navrre
OPPORTUNITYE			
But how wilt thou get opportunitye?	P1135	21.29	Dumain
OPPOS'D			
With Muse oppos'd would I my lines had done,	Ovid's Elegies		3.11.17
OPPOSDE			
the sun and Moone as darke/As when opposde in one Diamiter,	2Tamb	2.4.52	Tamb
OPPOSE			
Then let some God oppose his holy power,	2Tamb	5.3.220	Techel
What, will you thus oppose me, lucklesse Starres,	Jew	1.2.260	Barab
Leave now to oppose thy selfe against the king,	Edw	1.4.387	MortSr
OPPOSED			
Th'opposed starre of Mars hath done thee harme,	Ovid's Elegies		1.8.29
OPPOSETH			
That thus opposeth him against the Gods,	1Tamb	2.6.39	Cosroe
OPPOSIT			
In view and opposit two citties stood,	Hero and Leander		1.2
OPPOSITE			
And join'd those stars that shall be opposite,	2Tamb	3.5.81	Tamb
bank, right opposite/Against the Westerne gate of Babylon.	2Tamb	5.1.121	Govnr
OPPOSITIONS			
Why are <have wee> not Conjunctions, Oppositions, Aspects,	F 615	2.2.64	P Faust
OPPRESSE			
That thus oppresse poore friendles passengers.	1Tamb	1.2.70	Zenoc
OPPRESSED			
the plight/Wherein these Christians have oppressed me:	Jew	1.2.271	Barab
OPPRESSION			
By living long in this oppression,	1Tamb	5.1.251	Zabina
OPPREST			
for rather then my lord/Shall be opprest by civill mutinies,	Edw	1.2.65	Queene
If hee lyes downe with Wine and sleepe opprest,	Ovid's Elegies		1.4.53
OPPROBRIOUS			
men (Dido except)/Have taunted me in these opprobrious termes,	Dido	3.3.27	Iarbus
OPS			
That causde the eldest sonne of heavenly Ops,	1Tamb	2.7.13	Tamb
Saturne and Ops, began their golden raigne.	Hero and Leander		1.456
OR			
Or seemed faire walde in with Egles wings,	Dido	1.1.20	Ganimd
Or force her smile that hetherto hath frownd:	Dido	1.1.88	Jupitr
Or whether men or beasts inhabite it.	Dido	1.1.177	Aeneas
Or one of chast Dianas fellow Nimphs,	Dido	1.1.194	Aeneas
Whence may you come, or whither will you goe?	Dido	1.1.215	Venus
Or in these shades deceiv'st mine eye so oft?	Dido	1.1.244	Aeneas
Why, what are you, or wherefore doe you sewe?	Dido	1.2.3	Iarbus
Or steale your houshold lares from their shrines:	Dido	1.2.11	Illion
Lords of this towne, or whatsoever stile/Belongs unto your name,	Dido	2.1.39	Aeneas
You are Achates, or I [am] deciv'd.	Dido	2.1.49	Serg
Aeneas see, Sergestus or his ghost.	Dido	2.1.50	Achat
Or els in Carthage make his kingly throne.	Dido	2.1.331	Venus
Or whisking of these leaves, all shall be still,	Dido	2.1.337	Venus
Then pull out both mine eyes, or let me dye.	Dido	3.1.55	Iarbus
Runne for Aeneas, or Ile flye to him.	Dido	3.1.79	Dido
Or art thou grievde thy betters presse so nye?	Dido	3.3.18	Iarbus
Or els I would have given my life in gage.	Dido	3.3.29	Iarbus
Revenge me on Aeneas, or on her:	Dido	3.3.70	Iarbus
Never to like or love any but her.	Dido	3.4.51	Aeneas
Or day so cleere so suddenly orecast?	Dido	4.1.2	Achat
Or aged Atlas shoulder out of joynt,	Dido	4.1.12	Achat
Or drop out both mine eyes in drisling teares,	Dido	4.2.41	Iarbus
Graunt she or no, Aeneas must away,	Dido	4.3.7	Aeneas
Or banquet in bright honors burnisht hall,	Dido	4.3.10	Aeneas
What willes our Lord, or wherefore did he call?	Dido	4.3.15	Achat
No no, she cares not how we sinke or swimme,	Dido	4.3.41	Illion
Or that the Tyrrhen sea were in mine armes,	Dido	4.4.101	Dido
Or impious traitors vowde to have my life,	Dido	4.4.114	Dido
O cursed tree, hadst thou but wit or sense,	Dido	4.4.139	Dido
Now speake Ascanius, will ye goe or no?	Dido	4.5.12	Nurse
Ile have a husband, or els a lover.	Dido	4.5.23	Nurse
What length or bredth shal this brave towne containe?	Dido	5.1.16	Achat
Or with what thought sleepst thou in Libia shoare?	Dido	5.1.35	Hermes
Or els abide the wrath of frowning Jove.	Dido	5.1.54	Hermes
or to what end/Launcht from the haven, lye they in the Rhode?	Dido	5.1.88	Dido
I crave but this, he stay a tide or two,	Dido	5.1.207	Dido
Yet he whose [hearts] <heart> of adamant or flint,	Dido	5.1.234	Anna
Or els Ile make a prayer unto the waves,	Dido	5.1.246	Dido
What can my teares or cryes prevaile me now?	Dido	5.1.319	Anna
And rue our ends senceles of life or breath:	Dido	5.1.328	Anna
in Asia, or display/His vagrant Ensigne in the Persean fields,	1Tamb	1.1.44	Meandr
Or plead for mercie at your highnesse feet.	1Tamb	1.1.73	Therid
Fled to the Caspean or the Ocean maine?	1Tamb	1.1.102	Mycet
To injure or suppresse your woorthy tytle.	1Tamb	1.1.183	Ortyg
Or if they would, there are in readines/Ten thousand horse to	1Tamb	1.1.184	Ortyg
Or you my Lordes to be my followers?	1Tamb	1.2.83	Tamb
Or looke you, I should play the Orator?	1Tamb	1.2.129	Tamb
But if they offer word or violence,	1Tamb	1.2.142	Tamb
Or take him prisoner, and his chaine shall serve/For Manackles,	1Tamb	1.2.147	Tamb
Or meant to pierce Avernus darksome vaults,	1Tamb	1.2.160	Therid
Than Tamburlaine be slaine or overcome.	1Tamb	1.2.177	Tamb
Or faire Bootes sends his cheerefull light,	1Tamb	1.2.207	Tamb

OR (cont.)

To be partaker of thy good or ill,	1Tamb	1.2.230		Therid
Or els you shall be forc'd with slaverie.	1Tamb	1.2.256		Tamb
He that can take or slaughter Tamburlaine,	1Tamb	2.2.30		Meandr
If wealth or riches may prevaile with them,	1Tamb	2.2.61		Meandr
Your speech will stay, or so extol his worth,	1Tamb	2.3.27		Therid
As dooth the lightening, or the breath of heaven:	1Tamb	2.3.58		Tamb
So shall not I be knowen, or if I bee,	1Tamb	2.4.13		Mycet
or els infernall, mixt/Their angry seeds at his conception:	1Tamb	2.6.9		Meandr
What God or Feend, or spirit of the earth,	1Tamb	2.6.15		Ortyg
Or Monster turned to a manly shape,	1Tamb	2.6.16		Ortyg
Or of what mould or mettel he be made,	1Tamb	2.6.17		Ortyg
What star or state soever governe him,	1Tamb	2.6.18		Ortyg
Whether from earth, or hell, or heaven he grow.	1Tamb	2.6.23		Ortyg
As hath the Ocean or the Terrene sea/Small drops of water, when	1Tamb	3.1.10		Bajzth
Or breathles lie before the citie walles.	1Tamb	3.1.15		Bajzth
Or els to threaten death and deadly armes,	1Tamb	3.1.19		Fesse
Or spread his collours in Grecia,	1Tamb	3.1.29		Bajzth
That no reliefe or succour come by Land.	1Tamb	3.1.62		Bajzth
Or els unite you to his life and soule,	1Tamb	3.2.23		Zenoc
Is far from villanie or servitude.	1Tamb	3.2.38		Zenoc
Or when the morning holds him in her armes:	1Tamb	3.2.48		Zenoc
Or when Minerva did with Neptune strive.	1Tamb	3.2.52		Zenoc
Europe, and pursue/His scattered armie til they yeeld or die.	1Tamb	3.3.39		Therid
My royall Lord is slaine or conquered,	1Tamb	3.3.209		Zenoc
Or ever drisling drops of Aprill showers,	1Tamb	4.1.31		Souldn
Or withered leaves that Autume shaketh downe:	1Tamb	4.1.32		Souldn
Without respect of Sex, degree or age,	1Tamb	4.1.62		2Msngr
Of lawfull armes, or martiall discipline:	1Tamb	4.1.65		Souldn
Unworthy to imbrace or touch the ground,	1Tamb	4.2.20		Tamb
Or scattered like the lofty Cedar trees,	1Tamb	4.2.24		Tamb
Or leave Damascus and th'Egyptian fields,	1Tamb	4.2.48		Tamb
Or els I sweare to have you whipt stark nak'd.	1Tamb	4.2.74		Anippe
Shall ransome him, or take him from his cage.	1Tamb	4.2.94		Tamb
Or Cephalus with lustie Thebane youths,	1Tamb	4.3.4		Souldn
vagabond/Should brave a king, or weare a princely crowne.	1Tamb	4.3.22		Souldn
Or kept the faire Zenocrate so long,	1Tamb	4.3.41		Souldn
Or winged snakes of Lerna cast your stings,	1Tamb	4.4.21		Bajzth
take it from my swords point, or Ile thrust it to thy heart.	1Tamb	4.4.41	P	Tamb
or I will make thee slice the brawnes of thy armes into	1Tamb	4.4.43	P	Tamb
Or if my love unto your majesty/May merit favour at your	1Tamb	4.4.69		Zenoc
Or may be forc'd, to make me Emperour.	1Tamb	4.4.90		Tamb
Stil dooth this man or rather God of war,	1Tamb	5.1.1		Govnr
Or hope of rescue from the Souldans power,	1Tamb	5.1.4		Govnr
By any innovation or remorse,	1Tamb	5.1.16		Govnr
If humble suites or imprecations,	1Tamb	5.1.24		1Virgn
Would not with too much cowardize or feare,	1Tamb	5.1.37		Govnr
Or be the means the overweighing heavens/Have kept to qualifie	1Tamb	5.1.45		Govnr
and Furies dread)/As for their liberties, their loves or lives.	1Tamb	5.1.95		1Virgn
Or for the love of Venus, would she leave/The angrie God of	1Tamb	5.1.124		Tamb
are as peremptory/As wrathfull Planets, death, or destinie.	1Tamb	5.1.128		Tamb
to their soules I think/As are Thessalian drugs or Mithradate.	1Tamb	5.1.133		Tamb
Or roaring Cannons sever all thy joints,	1Tamb	5.1.223		Bajzth
More than Cymerian Stix or Distinie.	1Tamb	5.1.234		Bajzth
As long as any blood or sparke of breath/Can quench or coole	1Tamb	5.1.284		Zabina
sparke of breath/Can quench or coole the torments of my griefe.	1Tamb	5.1.285		Zabina
to Zenocrate/Than her owne life, or ought save thine owne love.	1Tamb	5.1.338		Zenoc
See, se Anippe if they breathe or no.	1Tamb	5.1.343		Zenoc
As vast and deep as Euphrates or Nile.	1Tamb	5.1.439		Tamb
Or as Latonas daughter bent to armes,	1Tamb	5.1.514		Tamb
Or crosse the streame, and meet him in the field?	2Tamb	1.1.12		Orcan
crost Danubius stream/To treat of friendly peace or deadly war:	2Tamb	1.1.80		Sgsmnd
Or as the Ocean to the Traveiler/That restes upon the snowy	2Tamb	1.1.110		Sgsmnd
Or treat of peace with the Natolian king?	2Tamb	1.1.113		Sgsmnd
Which if your General refuse or scorne,	2Tamb	1.1.119		Fredrk
it out, or manage armes/Against thy selfe or thy confederates:	2Tamb	1.1.128		Sgsmnd
it out, or manage armes/Against thy selfe or thy confederates:	2Tamb	1.1.129		Sgsmnd
If any heathen potentate or king/Invade Natolia, Sigismond will	2Tamb	1.1.152		Sgsmnd
Or lovely Io metamorphosed.	2Tamb	1.2.39		Callap
As blacke as Jeat, and hard as Iron or steel,	2Tamb	1.3.27		Tamb
Or els you are not sons of Tamburlaine.	2Tamb	1.3.64		Tamb
Or make a bridge of murthered Carcases,	2Tamb	1.3.93		Amyras
Hold him, and cleave him too, or Ile cleave thee,	2Tamb	1.3.104		Tamb
Or cease one day from war and hot alarms,	2Tamb	1.3.183		Usumc
Or treason in the fleshly heart of man,	2Tamb	2.2.37		Orcan
And Christ or Mahomet hath bene my friend.	2Tamb	2.3.11		Orcan
Or els discended to his winding traine:	2Tamb	2.4.54		Tamb
Or dieng, be the [author] <anchor> of my death.	2Tamb	2.4.56		Tamb
Or had those wanton Poets, for whose byrth/Olde Rome was proud,	2Tamb	2.4.91		Tamb
Zenocrate had bene the argument/Of every Epigram or Eligie.	2Tamb	2.4.95		Tamb
To drinke the river Nile or Euphrates,	2Tamb	3.1.42		Orcan
We may be slaine or wounded ere we learne.	2Tamb	3.2.94		Calyph
or with a Curtle-axe/To hew thy flesh and make a gaping wound?	2Tamb	3.2.96		Tamb
And few or none shall perish by their shot.	2Tamb	3.3.45		Therid
Or els invent some torture worse than that.	2Tamb	3.4.22		Olymp
Mother dispatch me, or Ile kil my selfe,	2Tamb	3.4.26		Sonne
Give me your knife (good mother) or strike home:	2Tamb	3.4.28		Sonne
Wil match thee with a viceroy or a king.	2Tamb	3.4.41		Techel
Than any Viceroy, King or Emperour.	2Tamb	3.4.43		Olymp
Or bind thee in eternall torments wrath.	2Tamb	3.5.113		Soria
Or rip thy bowels, and rend out thy heart,	2Tamb	3.5.121		Tamb
T'appease my wrath, or els Ile torture thee,	2Tamb	3.5.122		Tamb
Come fight ye Turks, or yeeld us victory.	2Tamb	3.5.169		Tamb

OR (cont.)

their swordes or their cannons, as I doe a naked Lady in a net	2Tamb	4.1.68	P Calyph
Wherein was neither corrage, strength or wit,	2Tamb	4.1.125	Tamb
For deeds of bounty or nobility:	2Tamb	4.1.152	Tamb
vaine or Artier feed/The cursed substance of that cruel heart,	2Tamb	4.1.177	Soria
And til by vision, or by speach I heare/Immortall Jove say,	2Tamb	4.1.198	Tamb
Or hold our citie from the Conquerours hands.	2Tamb	5.1.5	Maxim
Than honor of thy countrie or thy name?	2Tamb	5.1.11	Govnr
More strong than are the gates of death or hel?	2Tamb	5.1.20	Govnr
Or die some death of quickest violence,	2Tamb	5.1.41	2Citzn
Or els be sure thou shalt be forc'd with paines,	2Tamb	5.1.52	Therid
My heart did never quake, or corrage faint.	2Tamb	5.1.106	Govnr
Torture or paine can daunt my dreadlesse minde.	2Tamb	5.1.113	Govnr
Or vengeance on the head of Tamburlain,	2Tamb	5.1.195	Tamb
Sicknes or death can never conquer me.	2Tamb	5.1.222	Tamb
If God or Mahomet send any aide.	2Tamb	5.2.11	Callap
Before himselfe or his be conquered.	2Tamb	5.2.53	Callap
Or that it be rejoin'd again at full,	2Tamb	5.2.58	Callap
To cure me, or Ile fetch him downe my selfe.	2Tamb	5.3.63	Tamb
Retaine a thought of joy, or sparke of life?	2Tamb	5.3.163	Amyras
How should I step or stir my hatefull feete,	2Tamb	5.3.195	Amyras
from Egypt, or by Caire/But at the entry there into the sea,	Jew	1.1.73	Barab
round by Candie shoare/About their Oyles, or other businesses.	Jew	1.1.92	Barab
you to come so farre/Without the ayd or conduct of their ships.	Jew	1.1.94	Barab
Or who is honour'd now but for his wealth?	Jew	1.1.113	Barab
And Crownes come either by succession/Or urg'd by force; and	Jew	1.1.132	Barab
Or let 'em warre, so we be conquerors:	Jew	1.1.151	Barab
Why, Barabas, they come for peace or warre.	Jew	1.1.161	1Jew
What's Cyprus, Candy, and those other Iles/To us, or Malta?	Jew	1.2.6	Govnr
Either pay that, or we will seize on all.	Jew	1.2.89	Govnr
Christians; what, or how can I multiply?	Jew	1.2.103	Barab
And since you leave me in the Ocean thus/To sinke or swim, and	Jew	1.2.268	Barab
Proceed from sinne, or want of faith in us,	Jew	1.2.323	Abigal
Or at the least to pitty.	Jew	1.2.387	Mthias
And so will I too, or it shall goe hard.--	Jew	1.2.392	Lodowk
night; or let the day/Turne to eternall darkenesse after this:	Jew	2.1.15	Barab
And so much must they yeeld or not be sold.	Jew	2.3.4	2Offcr
I, and his sonnes too, or it shall goe hard.	Jew	2.3.17	Barab
Or else be gather'd for in our Synagogue;	Jew	2.3.27	Barab
Is it square or pointed, pray let me know.	Jew	2.3.59	Lodowk
Against my will, and whether I would or no,	Jew	2.3.75	Barab
And few or none scape but by being purg'd.	Jew	2.3.106	Barab
Some wicked trick or other.	Jew	2.3.119	P Barab
talke with him was [but]/About the borrowing of a booke or two.	Jew	2.3.156	Mthias
And every Mcone made some or other mad,	Jew	2.3.195	Barab
I, Barabas, or else thou wrong'st me much.	Jew	2.3.255	Mthias
the Governors sonne/Will, whether I will or no, have Abigall:	Jew	2.3.258	Barab
And I will have it or it shall goe hard.	Jew	3.1.15	Pilia
now Abigall shall see/Whether Mathias holds her deare or no.	Jew	3.2.2	Mthias
Or loving, doth dislike of something done.	Jew	3.4.12	Barab
Or though it wrought, it would have done no good,	Jew	4.1.5	Barab
and the rest of the family, stand or fall at your service.	Jew	4.2.44	P Pilia
Now am I cleane, or rather fouly out of the way.	Jew	4.2.47	P Ithimr
Or else I will confesse: I, there it goes:	Jew	4.3.4	Barab
And winds it twice or thrice about his eare;	Jew	4.3.8	Barab
I, and the rest too, or else--	Jew	4.3.28	P Pilia
Or climbe up to my Counting-house window:	Jew	4.3.34	P Barab
the gold, or know Jew it is in my power to hang thee.	Jew	4.3.37	P Pilia
Nay, I'le have all or none.	Jew	4.4.5	Curtzn
Play, Fidler, or I'le cut your cats guts into chitterlins.	Jew	4.4.44	P Ithimr
Will winne the Towne, or dye before the wals.	Jew	5.1.5	Govnr
so, or how else,/The Jew is here, and rests at your command.	Jew	5.1.82	Barab
Or you released of this servitude.	Jew	5.4.7	Govnr
Should I in pitty of thy plaints or thee,	Jew	5.5.72	Govnr
Or Selim ne're returne to Ottoman.	Jew	5.5.114	Govnr
Then conquer Malta, or endanger us.	Jew	5.5.122	Govnr
In what Queen Mother or your grace commands.	P 12	1.12	Navrre
To meddle or attempt such dangerous things.	P 38	1.38	Admral
In murder, mischeefe, or in tiranny.	P 41	1.41	Condy
Or mount the top with my aspiring winges,	P 103	2.46	Guise
Or with seditions weary all the worlde:	P 116	2.59	Guise
thou hast all the Cardes within thy hands/To shuffle or cut,	P 147	2.90	Guise
That right or wrong, thou deale thy selfe a King.	P 148	2.91	Guise
Then pittie or releeve these upstart hereticks.	P 222	4.20	Guise
Shall dye, be he King or Emperour.	P 235	4.33	Guise
Come Ramus, more golde, or thou shalt have the stabbe.	P 376	7.16	Gonzag
that despiseth him, can nere/Be good in Logick or Philosophie.	P 410	7.50	Ramus
And if he grudge or crosse his Mothers will,	P 523	9.42	QnMoth
No person, place, or time, or circumstance,	P 606	12.19	King
Am I growne olde, or is thy lust growne yong,	P 681	13.25	Guise
Or hath my love been so obscurde in thee,	P 682	13.26	Guise
Of King or Country, no not for them both.	P 740	14.43	Navrre
Tis more then kingly or Emperious.	P 759	15.17	Guise
Whether he have dishonoured me or no.	P 769	15.27	Guise
Or else employ them in some better cause.	P 794	16.8	Bartus
Revenge it Henry as thou list or dare,	P 819	17.14	Guise
And as Dictator make or warre or peace,	P 860	17.55	King
Dismisse thy campe or else by our Edict,	P 863	17.58	King
Or be suspicious of my deerest freends:	P 972	19.42	King
Or else to murder me, and so be King.	P1040	19.110	King
Ile clippe his winges/Or ere he passe my handes, away with him.	P1053	19.123	King
Or who will helpe to builde Religion?	P1084	19.154	QnMoth
Or else dye Epernoune.	P1227	22.89	Eprnon

OR (cont.)

revenge it henry yf thow liste or darst	Paris	ms23,p391	Guise
Not that I love the citie or the men,	Edw	1.1.12	Gavstn
Or looke to see the throne where you should sit,	Edw	1.1.131	Lncstr
And eyther die, or live with Gaveston.	Edw	1.1.138	Edward
Save or condemne, and in our name commaund,	Edw	1.1.169	Edward
What so thy minde affectes or fancie likes.	Edw	1.1.170	Edward
I, to the tower, the fleete, or where thou wilt.	Edw	1.1.198	Edward
Shall be their timeles sepulcher, or mine.	Edw	1.2.6	Lncstr
with us that be his peeres/To banish or behead that Gaveston?	Edw	1.2.43	Mortmr
That slie inveigling Frenchman weele exile,/Or lose our lives:	Edw	1.2.58	Mortmr
And war must be the meanes, or heele stay stil.	Edw	1.2.63	Warwck
Whether will you beare him, stay or ye shall die.	Edw	1.4.24	Edward
And either have our wils, or lose our lives.	Edw	1.4.46	Mortmr
Or I will presentlie discharge these lords,	Edw	1.4.61	ArchBp
So I may have some nooke or corner left,	Edw	1.4.72	Edward
Be it or no, he shall not linger here.	Edw	1.4.93	MortSr
And thou must hence, or I shall be deposd,	Edw	1.4.110	Edward
And long thou shalt not stay, or if thou doost,	Edw	1.4.114	Edward
That whether I will or no thou must depart:	Edw	1.4.124	Edward
Or thou shalt nere be reconcild to me.	Edw	1.4.157	Edward
or at the mariage day/The cup of Hymen had beene full of	Edw	1.4.173	Queene
Or with those armes that twind about my neck,	Edw	1.4.175	Queene
Or else be banisht from his highnesse presence.	Edw	1.4.203	Queene
Then gaudie silkes, or rich imbrotherie.	Edw	1.4.347	Edward
Or if that loftie office like thee not,	Edw	1.4.355	Edward
As fast as Iris, or Joves Mercurie.	Edw	1.4.371	Edward
In this, or ought, your highnes shall commaund us.	Edw	1.4.384	Warwck
Or holding of a napkin in your hand,	Edw	2.1.36	Spencr
Or saying a long grace at a tables end,	Edw	2.1.37	Spencr
Or making lowe legs to a noble man,	Edw	2.1.38	Spencr
Or looking downeward, with your eye lids close,	Edw	2.1.39	Spencr
And threatenest death whether he rise or fall,	Edw	2.2.44	Edward
Ile have his bloud, or die in seeking it.	Edw	2.2.107	Warwck
And you shall ransome him, or else--	Edw	2.2.145	Mortmr
Or that these teares that drissell from mine eyes,	Edw	2.4.19	Queene
that is all he gets/Of Gaveston, or else his sencelesse trunck.	Edw	2.5.54	Mortmr
Or didst thou see my friend to take his death?	Edw	3.1.93	Edward
Some treason, or some villanie was cause.	Edw	3.1.114	Spencr
O shall I speake, or shall I sigh and die!	Edw	3.1.122	Edward
And shall or Warwicks sword shal smite in vaine.	Edw	3.1.199	Warwck
even to the utmost verge/Of Europe, or the shore of Tanaise,	Edw	4.2.30	Queene
That you were dead, or very neare your death.	Edw	4.2.38	Queene
Dissemble or thou diest, for Mortimer/And Isabell doe kisse	Edw	4.6.12	Kent
Some whirle winde fetche them backe, or sincke them all:--	Edw	4.6.59	Mortmr
rule and emperie/Have not in life or death made miserable?	Edw	4.7.15	Edward
My lord, it is in vaine to greeve or storme,	Edw	4.7.77	Baldck
Not of compulsion or necessitie.	Edw	5.1.4	Leistr
Or like the snakie wreathe of Tisiphon,	Edw	5.1.45	Edward
And therefore say, will you resigne or no.	Edw	5.1.85	Trussl
Or if I live, let me forget my selfe.	Edw	5.1.111	Edward
Further, or this letter was sealed, Lord Bartley came,	Edw	5.2.30	BshpWn
long as he survives/What safetie rests for us, or for my sonne?	Edw	5.2.43	Queene
Or choake your soveraigne with puddle water?	Edw	5.3.30	Edward
Edmund, yeeld thou thy self, or thou shalt die.	Edw	5.3.56	Matrvs
The king must die, or Mortimer goes downe,	Edw	5.4.1	Mortmr
Or whilst one is a sleepe, to take a quill/And blowe a little	Edw	5.4.34	Ltborn
Or open his mouth, and powre quick silver downe,	Edw	5.4.36	Ltborn
If any Christian, Heathen, Turke, or Jew,	Edw	5.4.75	Champn
Either my brother or his sonne is king,	Edw	5.4.106	Kent
Or as Matrevis, hewne from the Caucasus,	Edw	5.5.54	Edward
And whether I have limmes or no, I know not.	Edw	5.5.65	Edward
O spare me, or dispatche me in a trice.	Edw	5.5.111	Edward
Or else die by the hand of Mortimer.	Edw	5.6.6	Mortmr
Thinke not to finde me slack or pitifull.	Edw	5.6.82	King
must now performe/The forme of Faustus fortunes, good or bad,	F 8	Prol.8	1Chor
Or being dead, raise them to life againe,	F 53	1.1.25	Faust
[Nor can they raise the winde, or rend the cloudes]:	F 86	1.1.58A	Faust
Or Lapland Giants trotting by our sides:	F 153	1.1.125	Valdes
Sometimes like women or unwedded Maides,	F 154	1.1.126	Valdes
Or the Ocean to overwhelme the world.	F 267	1.3.39	Faust
Why so thou shalt be, whether thou dost it or no:	F 360	1.4.18	P Wagner
teach thee to turne thy selfe to a Dog, or a Cat, or a Mouse,	F 382	1.4.40	P Wagner
thy selfe to a Dog, or a Cat, or a Mouse, or a Rat, or any thing	F 383	1.4.41	P Wagner
to a Dog, or a Cat, or a Mouse, or a Rat, or any thing.	F 383	1.4.41	P Wagner
A Dog, or a Cat, or a Mouse, or a Rat?	F 384	1.4.42	P Robin
What bootes it then to thinke on <of> God or Heaven?	F 391	2.1.3	Faust
Fourthly, that he shall be in his chamber or house invisible.	F 490	2.1.102	P Faust
at all times, in what shape [or] <and> forme soever he please.	F 492	2.1.104	P Faust
full power to fetch or carry the said John Faustus, body and	F 497	2.1.109	P Faust
[and] bloud, <or goods> into their habitation wheresoever.	F 498	2.1.110	P Faust
as Saba, or as beautifull/As was bright Lucifer before his fall.	F 541	2.1.153	Mephst
faire/As thou, or any man that [breathes] <breathe> on earth.	F 558	2.2.7	Mephst
Scarce can I name salvation, faith, or heaven,	F 570	2.2.19	Faust
Why should I die then, or basely despaire?	F 582	2.2.31	Faust
Nor are the names of Saturne, Mars, or Jupiter,	F 594	2.2.43	Mephst
hath every Spheare a Dominion, or Intelligentia <Inteligentij>?	F 607	2.2.56	P Faust
How many Heavens, or Spheares, are there?	F 609	2.2.58	P Faust
[Never to name God, or to pray to him],	F 649	2.2.98A	Faust
Talke not of Paradice or <nor> Creation, but marke the <this>	F 659	2.2.108	P Lucifr
Then <or>, like a Fan of Feathers, I kisse her [lippes]; And	F 667	2.2.116	P Pride
Or if thou't go but to the Taverne with me, I'le give thee	F 747	2.3.26	P Robin
Or dash the pride of this solemnity:	F 860	3.1.82	Mephst

OR (cont.)

Or clap huge hornes, upon the Cardinals heads:	F 864	3.1.86		Mephst
Or any villany thou canst devise,	F 865	3.1.87		Mephst
To binde or loose, lock fast, condemne, or judge,	F 935	3.1.157		Pope
Resigne, or seale, or what so pleaseth us.	F 936	3.1.158		Pope
Or be assured of our dreadfull curse,	F 938	3.1.160		Pope
We will determine of his life or death.	F 969	3.1.191		Pope
Or by our sanctitude you all shall die.	F1057	3.2.77		Pope
Now Robin, now or never shew thy cunning.	F1094	3.3.7	P	Dick
Had on her necke a little wart, or mole;	F1267	4.1.113		Emper
What, is he asleepe, or dead?	F1279	4.1.125		Saxony
Or bring before this royall Emperour/The mightie Monarch,	F1296	4.1.142		Faust
Or hew'd this flesh and bones as small as sand,	F1398	4.2.74		Faust
hedge and ditch, or where thou wilt, but not into the water:	F1473	4.4.17	P	Faust
Murder or not murder, now he has but one leg, I'le out-run him,	F1494	4.4.38	P	HrsCsr
I'le out-run him, and cast this leg into some ditch or other.	F1495	4.4.39	P	HrsCsr
or we'll breake all the barrels in the house, and dash out all	F1618	4.6.61	P	HrsCsr
No [otherwaies] <otherwise> for pompe or <and> Majesty,	F1693	5.1.20		Faust
Or envy of thee, but in tender love,	F1720	5.1.47		OldMan
Revolt, or I'le in peece-meale teare thy flesh.	F1745	5.1.72		Mephst
This, or what else my Faustus shall <thou shalt> desire,	F1766	5.1.93		Mephst
Hell, or the Divell, had had no power on thee.	F1902	5.2.106		GdAngl
or let this houre be but/A yeare, a month, a weeke, a naturall	F1932	5.2.136		Faust
Or why is this immortall that thou hast?	F1965	5.2.169		Faust
Or Lucifer will beare thee quicke to hell.	F1976	5.2.180		Faust
So thou shalt, whether thou beest with me, or no:	F App	p.229 22	P	Wagner
or Ile turne al the lice about thee into familiars, and they	F App	p.229 25	P	Wagner
warning whensoever or wheresoever the divell shall fetch thee.	F App	p.230 37	P	Wagner
to anything, to a dogge, or a catte, or a mouse, or a ratte,	F App	p.231 59	P	Wagner
to a dogge, or a catte, or a mouse, or a ratte, or any thing.	F App	p.231 59	P	Wagner
a Christian fellow to a dogge or a catte, a mouse or a ratte?	F App	p.231 60	P	Clown
so by that meanes I shal see more then ere I felt, or saw yet.	F App	p.233 5	P	Robin
keep out, or else you are blowne up, you are dismembred Rafe,	F App	p.233 10	P	Robin
study, shee's borne to beare with me, or else my Art failes.	F App	p.233 17	P	Robin
thou doest, thou shalt be no wayes prejudiced or indamaged.	F App	p.236 9	P	Emper
or they that shal hereafter possesse our throne, shal (I feare	F App	p.236 21	P	Emper
this Lady while she liv'd had a wart or moale in her necke,	F App	p.238 61	P	Emper
or moale in her necke, how shal I know whether it be so or no?	F App	p.238 62	P	Emper
what, wil you goe on horse backe, or on foote?	F App	p.239 95	P	Mephst
the water, ride him over hedge or ditch, or where thou wilt,	F App	p.239 112	P	Faust
over hedge or ditch, or where thou wilt, but not into the water.	F App	p.239 112	P	Faust
my horse be sick, or ill at ease, if I bring his water to you,	F App	p.240 118	P	HrsCsr
my fortie dollers againe, or Ile make it the dearest horse:	F App	p.240 137	P	HrsCsr
him now, or Ile breake his glasse-windowes about his eares.	F App	p.240 142	P	HrsCsr
that great bellied women do long for some dainties or other,	F App	p.242 5	P	Faust
Or mount the sunnes flame bearing <plume bearing> charriot,	Lucan, First Booke	48		
What God it please thee be, or where to sway:	Lucan, First Booke	52		
I shall not need/To crave Apolloes ayde, or Bacchus helpe;	Lucan, First Booke	65		
Or Cynthia nights Queene waights upon the day;	Lucan, First Booke	91		
Nor then was land, or sea, to breed such hate,	Lucan, First Booke	96		
When yre, or hope provokt, heady, and bould,	Lucan, First Booke	147		
(Albeit the Moores light Javelin or his speare/Sticks in his	Lucan, First Booke	213		
Or darts which Parthians backward shoot) marcht on/And then	Lucan, First Booke	232		
Whether the gods, or blustring south were cause/I know not, but	Lucan, First Booke	236		
Under the frosty beare, or parching East,	Lucan, First Booke	254		
Wagons or tents, then in this frontire towne.	Lucan, First Booke	255		
they, and none durst speake/And shew their feare, or griefe:	Lucan, First Booke	260		
Or sea far from the land, so all were whist.	Lucan, First Booke	262		
forraine wars ill thriv'd; or wrathful France/Pursu'd us hither,	Lucan, First Booke	308		
Or Scythia; or hot Libiaes thirsty sands.	Lucan, First Booke	369		
Or fathers throate; or womens groning wombe;	Lucan, First Booke	378		
Or rob the gods; or sacred temples fire;	Lucan, First Booke	380		
Beates Thracian Boreas; or when trees [bowe] <bowde> down,/And	Lucan, First Booke	391		
Or that the wandring maine follow the moone;	Lucan, First Booke	415		
Or flaming Titan (feeding on the deepe)/Puls them aloft, and	Lucan, First Booke	416		
gods and heavenly powers you know,/Or only know you nothing.	Lucan, First Booke	450		
soules passe not to silent Erebus/Or Plutoes bloodles kingdom,	Lucan, First Booke	452		
would have thought their houses had bin fierd/Or dropping-ripe,	Lucan, First Booke	491		
parents/Keep back their sons, or womens teares their husbands;	Lucan, First Booke	503		
They stai'd not either to pray or sacrifice,	Lucan, First Booke	504		
Or Atlas head; their saints and houshold gods/Sweate teares to	Lucan, First Booke	554		
Or fierce Agave mad; or like Megaera/That scar'd Alcides, when	Lucan, First Booke	574		
whom/The gravest, Aruns, dwelt in forsaken Leuca <or Luna>,	Lucan, First Booke	585		
Or if Fate rule them, Rome thy Cittizens/Are neere some plague:	Lucan, First Booke	643		
Or why slips downe the Coverlet so oft?	Ovid's Elegies	1.2.2		
Or lies he close, and shoots where none can spie him?	Ovid's Elegies	1.2.6		
Yeelding or striving <strugling> doe we give him might,	Ovid's Elegies	1.2.9		
Either love, or cause that I may never hate:	Ovid's Elegies	1.3.2		
live with thee, and die, or <ere> thou shalt <shall> grieve.	Ovid's Elegies	1.3.18		
When I (my light) do or say ought that please thee,	Ovid's Elegies	1.4.25		
There will I finde thee, or be found by thee,	Ovid's Elegies	1.4.57		
Or if it do, to thee no joy thence spring:	Ovid's Elegies	1.4.68		
Or night being past, and yet not day begunne.	Ovid's Elegies	1.5.6		
Or Layis of a thousand [wooers] <lovers> [sped] <spread>.	Ovid's Elegies	1.5.12		
With armes or armed men I come not guarded,	Ovid's Elegies	1.6.33		
or ist sleepe forbids thee heare,/Giving the windes my words	Ovid's Elegies	1.6.41		
or do the turned hinges sound,/And opening dores with creaking	Ovid's Elegies	1.6.49		
Or I more sterne then fire or sword will turne,	Ovid's Elegies	1.6.57		
no threats or prayers move thee,/O harder then the dores thou	Ovid's Elegies	1.6.61		
Or holy gods with cruell strokes abus'd.	Ovid's Elegies	1.7.6		
Or slender eares, with gentle Zephire shaken,	Ovid's Elegies	1.7.55		
Or waters tops with the warme south-winde taken.	Ovid's Elegies	1.7.56		
Or, but for bashfulnesse her selfe would crave.	Ovid's Elegies	1.8.44		

OR (cont.)

Nor one or two men are sufficient. — Ovid's Elegies 1.8.54
Or least his love oft beaten backe should waine. — Ovid's Elegies 1.8.76
That this, or that man may thy cheekes moist keepe. — Ovid's Elegies 1.8.84
Tis shame for eld in warre or love to be. — Ovid's Elegies 1.9.4
Who but a souldiour or a lover is bould/To suffer storme mixt — Ovid's Elegies 1.9.15
should defend/Or great wealth from a judgement seate ascend. — Ovid's Elegies 1.10.40
Or prostitute thy beauty for bad prize. — Ovid's Elegies 1.10.42
Or steeds might fal forcd with thick clouds approch. — Ovid's Elegies 1.13.30
Or thrids which spiders slender foote drawes out/Fastning her — Ovid's Elegies 1.14.7
Nor hath the needle, or the combes teeth reft them, — Ovid's Elegies 1.14.15
Or that unlike the line from whence I [sprong] <come>, — Ovid's Elegies 1.15.3
Or [into] <to the> sea swift Symois [doth] <shall> slide. — Ovid's Elegies 1.15.10
Or men with crooked sickles corne downe fell. — Ovid's Elegies 1.15.12
Or he who war'd and wand'red twenty yeare? — Ovid's Elegies 2.1.31
Or wofull Hector whom wilde jades did teare? — Ovid's Elegies 2.1.32
Or if he loves, thy tale breedes his misfortune. — Ovid's Elegies 2.2.54
To meete for poyson or vilde facts we crave not, — Ovid's Elegies 2.2.63
Thou wert not borne to ride, or armes to beare, — Ovid's Elegies 2.3.7
Or justifie my vices being many, — Ovid's Elegies 2.4.2
Or if one touch the lute with art and cunning, — Ovid's Elegies 2.4.27
Or maides that their betrothed husbands spie. — Ovid's Elegies 2.5.36
Or when the Moone travailes with charmed steedes. — Ovid's Elegies 2.5.38
Or such, as least long yeares should turne the die, — Ovid's Elegies 2.5.39
To these, or some of these like was her colour, — Ovid's Elegies 2.5.41
Or voice that howe to change the wilde notes knew? — Ovid's Elegies 2.6.18
Or any back made rough with stripes imbrace? — Ovid's Elegies 2.7.22
Or as a sodaine gale thrustes into sea, — Ovid's Elegies 2.9.31
Thou shalt admire no woods or Citties there, — Ovid's Elegies 2.11.11
The Ocean hath no painted stones or shelles, — Ovid's Elegies 2.11.13
But she conceiv'd of me, or I am sure/I oft have done, what — Ovid's Elegies 2.13.5
[Or] <On> stones, our stockes originall, should be hurld, — Ovid's Elegies 2.14.11
Or [be] a loade thou shouldst refuse to beare. — Ovid's Elegies 2.15.22
Or els will maidens, yong-mens mates, to go/If they determine — Ovid's Elegies 2.16.17
What lawfull is, or we professe Loves art, — Ovid's Elegies 2.18.19
my selfe to smart)/We write, or what Penelope sends Ulysses, — Ovid's Elegies 2.18.21
Or Phillis teares that her [Demophoon] <Domoophon> misses,/What — Ovid's Elegies 2.18.22
Erre I? or mirtle in her right hand lies. — Ovid's Elegies 3.1.34
Gather them up, or lift them loe will I. — Ovid's Elegies 3.2.26
Or is my heate, of minde, not of the skie? — Ovid's Elegies 3.2.39
[A] <Or> while thy tiptoes on the foote-stoole rest. — Ovid's Elegies 3.2.64
Or if there be a God, he loves fine wenches, — Ovid's Elegies 3.3.25
Or in mine eyes good wench no paine transfuse. — Ovid's Elegies 3.3.48
Thou ore a hundreth Nimphes, or more shalt raigne: — Ovid's Elegies 3.5.63
For five score Nimphes, or more our flouds conteine. — Ovid's Elegies 3.5.64
Or full of dust doest on the drye earth slide. — Ovid's Elegies 3.5.96
Either she was foule, or her attire was bad, — Ovid's Elegies 3.6.1
Or she was not the wench I wisht t'have had. — Ovid's Elegies 3.6.2
Like a dull Cipher, or rude blocke I lay, — Ovid's Elegies 3.6.15
Or shade, or body was [I] <Io>, who can say? — Ovid's Elegies 3.6.16
Or one that with her tender brother lies, — Ovid's Elegies 3.6.22
Then did the robe or garment which she wore <more>, — Ovid's Elegies 3.6.40
Or Thamiras in curious painted things? — Ovid's Elegies 3.6.62
Why mockst thou me she cried, or being ill, — Ovid's Elegies 3.6.77
Or jaded camst thou from some others bed. — Ovid's Elegies 3.6.80
Or thinke soft verse in any stead to stand? — Ovid's Elegies 3.7.2
Or songs amazing wilde beasts of the wood? — Ovid's Elegies 3.8.22
Or lesse faire, or lesse lewd would thou mightst bee, — Ovid's Elegies 3.10.41
Wilt have me willing, or to love by force? — Ovid's Elegies 3.10.50
Or is I thinke my wish against the [starres] <starre>? — Ovid's Elegies 3.11.3
Or shall I plaine some God against me warres? — Ovid's Elegies 3.11.4
Erre I? or by my [bookes] <lookes> is she so knowne? — Ovid's Elegies 3.11.7
'Tis doubtfull whether verse availe, or harme, — Ovid's Elegies 3.11.13
Jove turnes himselfe into a Swanne, or gold, — Ovid's Elegies 3.11.33
Or his Bulles hornes Europas hand doth hold. — Ovid's Elegies 3.11.34
[And] <Or> hidden secrets openlie to bewray? — Ovid's Elegies 3.13.8
for neither sunne nor wind/Would burne or parch her hands, — Hero and Leander 1.28
or parch her hands, but to her mind,/Or warme or coole them: — Hero and Leander 1.29
Their fellowes being slaine or put to flight, — Hero and Leander 1.120
It lies not in our power to love, or hate, — Hero and Leander 1.167
Or if it could, downe from th'enameld skie, — Hero and Leander 1.249
Nor is't of earth or mold celestiall, — Hero and Leander 1.273
Or capable of any forme at all. — Hero and Leander 1.274
Whose name is it, if she be false or not, — Hero and Leander 1.285
Some one or other keepes you as his owne. — Hero and Leander 1.290
Or thirsting after immortalitie, — Hero and Leander 1.427
yet he suspected/Some amorous rites or other were neglected. — Hero and Leander 2.64
Or crooked Dolphin when the sailer sings; — Hero and Leander 2.234
Unto her was he led, or rather drawne, — Hero and Leander 2.241
describe, but hee/That puls or shakes it from the golden tree: — Hero and Leander 2.300
Or speake to him who in a moment tooke, — Hero and Leander 2.308
Woods, or steepie mountaine yeeldes. — Passionate Shepherd 4

ORACLE

For even as from assured oracle, — 1Tamb 2.3.4 Cosroe
Then heeretofore the Delphian <Dolphian> Oracle. — F 170 1.1.142 Cornel

ORACLES

Nor are Apollos Oracles more true, — 1Tamb 1.2.212 Tamb
For Fates and Oracles [of] heaven have sworne, — 1Tamb 2.3.7 Tamb
I speake it, and my words are oracles. — 1Tamb 3.3.102 Tamb
Sylla's ghost/Was seene to walke, singing sad Oracles,/And — Lucan, First Booke 580
On mast of oakes, first oracles, men fed, — Ovid's Elegies 3.9.9

ORANGE (See ORENGES)

ORATIONS

Looke for orations when the foe is neere. — 1Tamb 1.2.131 Techel

ORATOR

This was an Orator, and thought by words/To compasse me, but — Dido 3.1.155 — Dido
Or looke you, I should play the Orator? — 1Tamb 1.2.129 — Tamb
And yet I like them for the Orator. — Hero and Leander 1.340

ORATORIE

When deepe perswading Oratorie failes. — Hero and Leander 2.226

ORATORS

Our swordes shall play the Orators for us. — 1Tamb 1.2.132 — Techel

ORBE

Of Joves vast pallace the imperiall Orbe, — 2Tamb 3.4.49 — Therid
Rent sphere of heaven, and fier forsake thy orbe, — Edw 4.7.102 — Spencr
Even from the Moone unto the Emperiall Orbe, — F 590 2.2.39 — Mephst
Mutually folded in each others Spheares <orbe>, — F 591 2.2.40 — Mephst

ORBES

By heaven, and all the mooving orbes thereof, — Edw 3.1.129 — Edward

ORCANES

Yet stout Orcanes, Prorex of the world, — 2Tamb 1.1.45 — Gazell
and Danes/[Feares] <feare> not Orcanes, but great Tamburlaine: — 2Tamb 1.1.59 — Orcan
Orcanes (as our Legates promist thee)/Wee with our Peeres have — 2Tamb 1.1.78 — Sgsmnd
But now Orcanes, view my royall hoste, — 2Tamb 1.1.106 — Sgsmnd
Orcanes of Natolia/Confirm'd this league beyond Danubius — 2Tamb 1.1.148 — Orcan
And proud Orcanes of Natolia, — 2Tamb 1.3.161 — Tamb
Grace to memorie/The league we lately made with king Orcanes, — 2Tamb 2.1.28 — Sgsmnd

ORCHARD

I have an Orchard that hath store of plums, — Dido 4.5.4 — Nurse
Entred the orchard of Th'esperides, — Hero and Leander 2.298

ORCHARDS

The Meads, the Orchards, and the Primrose lanes, — Jew 4.2.95 — Ithimr

ORCUS

And with their Cannons mouth'd like Orcus gulfe/Batter the — 1Tamb 3.1.65 — Bajzth
Shall lead his soule through Orcus burning gulfe: — 2Tamb 2.3.25 — Orcan

ORDAIN'D

the man, ordain'd by heaven/To further every action to the best. — 1Tamb 2.1.52 — Ortyg

ORDAIND

Men are ordaind to live in miserie, — Edw 5.3.2 — Matrvs
Tooke out the shaft, ordaind my hart to shiver: — Ovid's Elegies 1.1.26

ORDAINING

A watchfull Senate for ordaining lawes, — P 593 12.6 — QnMoth

ORDER

I will take order for that presently: — Dido 1.1.113 — Jupitr
But I will take another order now, — Dido 3.2.6 — Juno
And order all things at your high dispose, — Dido 5.1.303 — Dido
Your Grace hath taken order by Theridamas, — 1Tamb 1.1.46 — Meandr
(Staying to order all the scattered troopes)/Farewell Lord — 1Tamb 2.5.45 — Cosroe
Then wee'll take order for the residue. — Jew 1.2.136 — Govnr
heard of any man but he/Malign'd the order of the Jacobines: — Jew 4.1.104 — Barab
No, 'tis an order which the Fryars use: — Jew 4.1.134 — Barab
What order wil you set downe for the Massacre? — P 229 4.27 — QnMoth
And I will goe take order for his death. — P 252 4.50 — Guise
And place our selves in order for the fight. — P 742 14.45 — Navrre
I am a Frier of the order of the Jacobyns, that for my — P1130 21.24 — P Frier
your Majestie heere is a Frier of the order of the Jacobins, — P1156 22.18 — P 1Msngr
to clap hornes of honest mens heades o'this order, — F1318 4.1.164 — P Benvol
In [skilfull] <skilfuld> gathering ruffled haires in order, — Ovid's Elegies 1.11.1

ORDINANCE

And store of ordinance that from every flanke/May scoure the — 2Tamb 3.2.79 — Tamb
Hast thou beheld a peale of ordinance strike/A ring of pikes, — 2Tamb 3.2.98 — Tamb
of thy hold/Volleies of ordinance til the breach be made, — 2Tamb 3.3.25 — Therid
Then see the bringing of our ordinance/Along the trench into — 2Tamb 3.3.54 — Therid
Betwixt which, shall our ordinance thunder foorth, — 2Tamb 3.3.58 — Therid
Then Ile have a peale of ordinance shot from the tower, — P 236 4.34 — Guise
Mountsorrell, goe shoote the ordinance of, — P 327 5.54 — Guise
Where thou shalt see such store of Ordinance, — F 819 3.1.41 — Mephst

ORDNANCE

<Within whose walles such store of ordnance are>, — F 819 (HC265)A — Mephst

O'RE

Where painted Carpets o're the meads are hurl'd, — Jew 4.2.91 — Ithimr
For the Jewes body, throw that o're the wals, — Jew 5.1.58 — Govnr
belike they thought me dead,/And threw me o're the wals: — Jew 5.1.82 — Barab
that you may ride him o're hedge and ditch, and spare him not; — F1467 4.4.11 — P Faust
not into the water; o're hedge and ditch, or where thou wilt, — F1473 4.4.17 — P Faust

ORE

That they may trip more lightly ore the lawndes, — Dido 1.1.207 — Venus
And fire proude Lacedemon ore their heads. — Dido 4.4.92 — Aeneas
And ore his ships will soare unto the Sunne, — Dido 5.1.244 — Dido
That I may vanish ore the earth in ayre, — Jew 1.2.264 — Barab
Singing ore these, as she does ore her young. — Jew 2.1.63 — Barab
And Bacchus vineyards [over-spread] <ore-spread> the world: — Jew 4.2.92 — Ithimr
That as the sun-shine shall reflect ore thee: — Edw 3.1.51 — Edward
Flies ore the Alpes to fruitfull Germany, — F 985 3.2.5 — Mephst
I see an Angell hover <hovers> ore thy head, — F1730 5.1.57 — OldMan
Is for ore-tortur'd soules to rest them in. — F1915 5.2.119 — BdAngl
Nor shamefully her coate pull ore her crowne, — Ovid's Elegies 1.7.47
Take clustred grapes from an ore-laden vine, — Ovid's Elegies 1.10.55
Now on <ore> the sea from her old love comes shee, — Ovid's Elegies 1.13.1
[And] <The> banks ore which gold bearing Tagus flowes. — Ovid's Elegies 1.15.34
And Love triumpheth ore his buskind Poet. — Ovid's Elegies 2.18.18
Thou ore a hundreth Nimphes, or more shalt raigne: — Ovid's Elegies 3.5.63

O'RECAST

O'recast with dim and darksome coverture. — Hero and Leander 2.266

ORECAST

Or day so cleere so suddenly orecast? — Dido 4.1.2 — Achat

O'RECOME

Till she o'recome with anguish, shame, and rage, — Hero and Leander 2.333

OREGONE
and grim Ceranias seate/Have you oregone, and yet remaine — Dido 1.1.148 Aeneas

O'REHEAD
Wherein was Proteus carved, and o'rehead, ... — Hero and Leander 1.137

OREITHYIA (See ORITHYAS)

ORE-LADEN
Take clustred grapes from an ore-laden vine, ... — Ovid's Elegies 1.10.55

ORENGES
Dewberries, Apples, yellow Orenges, ... — Dido 4.5.6 Nurse

ORE-SPREAD
And Bacchus vineyards [over-spread] <ore-spread> the world: — Jew 4.2.92 Ithimr

ORESTES
And by the love of Pyllades and Orestes, ... — 1Tamb 1.2.243 Tamb
What Pylades did to Orestes prove, ... — Ovid's Elegies 2.6.15

ORE-TORTUR'D
is for ore-tortur'd soules to rest them in. . . . . — F1915 5.2.119 BdAngl

OREWHELME
And sooner shall the sea orewhelme my land, ... — Edw 1.1.152 Edward

ORGANE
And death arrests the organe of my voice, ... — 1Tamb 2.7.8 Cosroe

ORGANNONS
that the soule/Wanting those Organnons by which it mooves, — 2Tamb 5.3.96 Phsitn

ORGANON
Was it not thou that scoftes the Organon, ... — P 387 7.27 Guise
I knew the Organon to be confusde, ... — P 406 7.46 Ramus

ORGANS
And wanting organs to advaunce a step, ... — Hero and Leander 2.57

ORGON
o per se, o, [demy] <deny> orgon, gorgon: . . . . . — F 728 2.3.7 P Robin

ORIENT
Mingled with corrall and with [orient] <orientall> pearle: — 2Tamb 1.3.224 Tamb
exceeding store/Of Persian silkes, of gold, and Orient Perle. — Jew 1.1.88 2Merch
Besides I know not how much weight in Pearle/Orient and round, — Jew 4.1.67 Barab
So precious, and withall so orient, ... — Jew 5.3.28 Msngr
Ransacke the Ocean for Orient Pearle, ... — F 110 1.1.82 Faust
Those orient cheekes and lippes, exceeding his/That leapt into — Hero and Leander 1.73
As from an orient cloud, glymse <glimps'd> here and there. — Hero and Leander 2.320

ORIENTALL
Sailing along the Orientall sea, ... — 1Tamb 3.3.253 Tamb
From Scythia to the Orientall Plage/Of India, wher raging — 2Tamb 1.1.68 Orcan
Mingled with corrall and with [orient] <orientall> pearle: — 2Tamb 1.3.224 Tamb

ORIENTIS
Orientis Princeps [Lucifer], Belzebub inferni ardentis . — F 245 1.3.17 P Faust

ORIFEX
my entrals bath'd/In blood that straineth from their orifex. — 2Tamb 3.4.9 Capt

ORIGINALL
[Or] <On> stones, our stockes originall, should be hurld, — Ovid's Elegies 2.14.11

ORION
When suddenly gloomie Orion rose, ... — Dido 1.2.26 Cloan

ORIONS
O Anna, fetch [Arions] <Orions> Harpe, ... — Dido 5.1.248 Dido
Longing to view Orions drisling looke <looks>, . . . — F 230 1.3.2 Faust
Sword-girt Orions side glisters too bright. . . . — Lucan, First Booke 664

ORITHYAS
If Boreas beares Orithyas rape in minde, ... — Ovid's Elegies 1.6.53

ORIZON
And now the sunne that through th'orizon peepes, . . — Hero and Leander 2.99

ORIZONS
fitter for a tale of love/Then to be tired out with Orizons: — Jew 1.2.370 Mthias

ORLEANCE
Gonzago poste you to Orleance, Retes to Deep, ... — P 445 7.85 Guise
Goe to the Governour of Orleance, ... — P1057 19.127 King
Hee wild the Governour of Orleance in his name, . . — P1117 21.11 Dumain

ORMINIUS
pitcht against our power/Betwixt Cutheia and Orminius mount: — 2Tamb 2.1.18 Fredrk
Now will we march from proud Orminius mount/To faire Natolia, — 2Tamb 2.2.2 Orcan

ORMUS
here are letters come/From Ormus, and the Post stayes here — Jew 2.3.223 Abigal

ORO
et istam/Oro, si quis [adhuc] <ad haec> precibus locus, exue — Dido 5.1.138 Dido

ORPHANS
And with young Orphans planted Hospitals, ... — Jew 2.3.194 Barab

ORPHEUS
To Thracian Orpheus what did parents good? . . . — Ovid's Elegies 3.8.21

ORTIGIUS
Behold, my Lord, Ortigius and the rest, ... — 1Tamb 1.1.134 Menaph
Ortigius and Menaphon, my trustie friendes, . . . — 1Tamb 2.5.29 Cosroe
I will not thank thee (sweet Ortigius)/Better replies shall — 1Tamb 2.5.36 Cosroe

ORTYGIUS
Nobly resolv'd, my good Ortygius. . . . . . — 1Tamb 2.6.24 Cosroe

OSIRIS
So in thy Temples shall Osiris stay, ... — Ovid's Elegies 2.13.12

OSSA
With earthes revenge and how Olimpus toppe/High Ossa bore, — Ovid's Elegies 2.1.14

OSSA'S
As when against pine bearing Ossa's rocks, ... — Lucan, First Booke 390

OSTENTS
To these ostents (as their old custome was)/They call . — Lucan, First Booke 583

OSTLER (See HOSTLER)

OSTRY
I say, least I send you into the Ostry with a vengeance. . — F 733 2.3.12 P Robin

O'TH
in a brasen Bull/Of great ones envy; o'th poore petty wites, — Jew Prol.26 Machvl

OTH

Confirm'd by oth and Articles of peace, ...	2Tamb	2.1.29		Sgsmnd

OTHER

And better able unto other armes.	Dido	3.3.36		Cupid
Be rul'd by me, and seeke some other love, ...	Dido	4.2.35		Anna
Speake of no other land, this land is thine, . . .	Dido	4.4.83		Dido
When other men prease forward for renowne:	1Tamb	1.1.84		Mycet
We in the name of other Persean states, ...	1Tamb	1.1.137		Ortyg
What saies my other friends, wil you be kings? . . .	1Tamb	2.5.67		Tamb
The heat and moisture which did feed each other, . .	1Tamb	2.7.46		Cosroe
But I shall turne her into other weedes, ...	1Tamb	3.3.180		Ebea
For he that gives him other food than this: . . .	1Tamb	4.2.89		Tamb
Since other meanes are all forbidden me, ...	1Tamb	5.1.288		Bajzth
What other heavie news now brings Philemus? . . .	1Tamb	5.1.377		Zenoc
And not to dare ech other to the field:	2Tamb	1.1.116		Gazell
I fare my Lord, as other Emperesses, ...	2Tamb	2.4.42		Zenoc
And take my other toward brother here, ...	2Tamb	4.1.34		Calyph
Ile use some other means to make you yeeld, . . .	2Tamb	4.2.51		Therid
And all the Merchants with other Merchandize/Are safe arriv'd,	Jew	1.1.51		1Merch
How chance you came not with those other ships/That sail'd by	Jew	1.1.89		Barab
round by Candie shoare/About their Oyles, or other businesses.	Jew	1.1.92		Barab
Tut, tut, there is some other matter in't.	Jew	1.1.160		Barab
and those other Iles/That lye betwixt the Mediterranean seas.	Jew	1.2.3		Basso
What's Cyprus, Candy, and those other Iles/To us, or Malta?	Jew	1.2.5		Govnr
And of the other we have seized halfe.	Jew	1.2.135		Offcrs
and in mine Argosie/And other ships that came from Egypt last,	Jew	1.2.188		Barab
Some wicked trick or other.	Jew	2.3.119	P	Barab
And every Moone made some or other mad, ...	Jew	2.3.195		Barab
For I have other businesse for thee.	Jew	3.4.110		Barab
Oh he is gone to see the other Nuns.	Jew	3.6.10		2Fryar
Both jealous of my love, envied each other:	Jew	3.6.27		Abigal
the Nuns are dead/That sound at other times like Tinkers pans?	Jew	4.1.3		Barab
The other knowes enough to have my life, ...	Jew	4.1.120		Barab
The other Chambers open towards the street.	Jew	4.1.138		Barab
Strong contermin'd <countermur'd> with other petty Iles; .	Jew	5.3.8		Calym
Should have been murdered the other night?	P 35	1.35		Navrre
It may be it is some other, and he escapte. . . .	P 308	5.35		Anjoy
And on the other side against the Turke, ...	P 462	8.12		Anjoy
he refuse, and then may we/Depose him and elect an other king.	Edw	1.4.55		Mortmr
No other jewels hang about my neck/Then these my lord, nor let	Edw	1.4.330		Queene
Whiles other walke below, the king and he/From out a window,	Edw	1.4.416		Mortmr
Which all the other fishes deadly hate, ...	Edw	2.2.24		Lncstr
Looke for no other fortune wretch then death, . . .	Edw	2.5.17		Lncstr
That heading is one, and hanging is the other, . . .	Edw	2.5.30		Gavstn
Arundell, we will gratifie the king/In other matters, he must	Edw	2.5.44		Warwck
The king of heaven perhaps, no other king, ...	Edw	2.6.16		Warwck
But wheres the king and the other Spencer fled? . . .	Edw	4.6.55		Mortmr
Spencer and Baldocke, by no other names, ...	Edw	4.7.56		Leistr
An other poast, what newes bringes he?	Edw	5.1.128		Leistr
Then let some other be his guardian.	Edw	5.2.36		Queene
But read it thus, and thats an other sence: . . .	Edw	5.4.10		Mortmr
But hath your grace no other proofe then this? . . .	Edw	5.6.43		Mortmr
And then all other ceremonies learn'd, ...	F 186	1.1.158		Cornel
Why, have you any paine that torture other <tortures others>?	F 432	2.1.44		Faust
not speake a word more for a Kings ransome <an other worde>,	F 670	2.2.119	P	Pride
I'le not speake <an other word for a King's raunsome>.	F 706	(HC264)A	P	Sloth
I'le not speake [an other] word.	F 706	2.2.158	P	Sloth
I have other matters in hand, let the horses walk themselves	F 726	2.3.5	P	Robin
into matters, as other men, if they were disposed to talke.	F 741	2.3.20	P	Robin
Take thou this other, dragge him through the woods, . .	F1410	4.2.86		Faust
I'le out-run him, and cast this leg into some ditch or other.	F1495	4.4.39	P	HrsCsr
As I was going to Wittenberge t'other day, with a loade of Hay,	F1526	4.5.22	P	Carter
th'one like an Ape, an other like a Beare, the third an Asse,	F App	p.235 32	P	Mephst
Why hee's fast asleepe, come some other time. . . .	F App	p.240 141	P	Mephst
that great bellied women do long for some dainties or other,	F App	p.242 5	P	Faust
Trumpets and drums, like deadly threatning other, . .	Lucan, First Booke	6		
for Nero (then unborne) the fates/Would find no other meanes,	Lucan, First Booke	34		
Keepes each from other, but being worne away/They both burst	Lucan, First Booke	102		
being worne away/They both burst out, and each incounter other:	Lucan, First Booke	103		
The gods abetted; Cato likt the other;	Lucan, First Booke	129		
Other that Caesars barbarous bands were spread/Along Nar floud	Lucan, First Booke	471		
did looke/Dead, and discoulour'd; th'other leane and thinne.	Lucan, First Booke	628		
And other Regions, I have seene Philippi:	Lucan, First Booke	693		
One window shut, the other open stood, ...	Ovid's Elegies	1.5.3		
his tender mother/And smiling sayed, be thou as bold as other.	Ovid's Elegies	1.6.12		
He first a Goddesse strooke; an other I.	Ovid's Elegies	1.7.32		
The other eyes his rivall as his foe.	Ovid's Elegies	1.9.18		
Why should one sell it, and the other buy it? . . .	Ovid's Elegies	1.10.34		
Nor can an other say his helpe I tooke.	Ovid's Elegies	2.12.12		
Some other seeke that may in patience strive with thee,	Ovid's Elegies	2.19.59		
The other smilde, (I wot) with wanton eyes, ...	Ovid's Elegies	3.1.33		
The other gives my love a conquering name, ...	Ovid's Elegies	3.1.65		
Pay it not heere, but in an other place.	Ovid's Elegies	3.2.84		
The one his first love, th'other his new care. . . .	Ovid's Elegies	3.8.32		
Some other seeke, who will these things endure. . .	Ovid's Elegies	3.10.28		
The one Abydos, the other Sestos hight.	Hero and Leander	1.4		
But this is true, so like was one the other, . . .	Hero and Leander	1.39		
He whom she favours lives, the other dies.	Hero and Leander	1.124		
As after chaunc'd, they did each other spye. . . .	Hero and Leander	1.134		
And with the other, wine from grapes out wroong. . .	Hero and Leander	1.140		
We wish that one should loose, the other win. . . .	Hero and Leander	1.170		
And I in dutie will excell all other, ...	Hero and Leander	1.221		
Which after his disceasse, some other gains. . . .	Hero and Leander	1.246		

OTHER (cont.)			
Some one or other keepes you as his owne.	Hero and Leander	1.290	
Both might enjoy ech other, and be blest.	Hero and Leander	1.380	
Both to each other quickly were affied.	Hero and Leander	2.26	
Mov'd by Loves force, unto ech other lep?	Hero and Leander	2.58	
yet he suspected/Some amorous rites or other were neglected.	Hero and Leander	2.64	
One halfe appear'd, the other halfe was hid.	Hero and Leander	2.316	
OTHERS			
Others report twas Sinons perjurie:	Dido	2.1.111	Dido
Some surfetted, and others soundly slept.	Dido	2.1.179	Aeneas
All these and others which I never sawe,	Dido	3.1.150	Dido
Some came in person, others sent their Legats:	Dido	3.1.152	Dido
As others did, by running to the wood.	Dido	4.1.30	Anna
Stead/That stampt on others with their thundring hooves,	1Tamb	5.1.331	Zenoc
For this, I wake, when others think I sleepe,	P 105	2.48	Guise
Though gentle mindes should pittie others paines,	P 215	4.13	Anjoy
Where we may one injoy the others sight.	P 665	13.9	Duchss
That others needs to comment on my text?	P 683	13.27	Guise
A bowle of poison to each others health:	Edw	2.2.238	Edward
And others of our partie and faction,	Edw	4.2.53	Mortmr
divers of your nation, and others, and as constant report goeth,	Edw	4.3.34	P Spencr
Slaughter themselves in others and their sides/With their owne	Edw	4.4.7	Queene
And others are but shrubs compard to me,	Edw	5.6.12	Mortmr
Why, have you any paine that torture other <tortures others>?	F 432	2.1.44	Faust
Mutually folded in each others Spheares <orbe>,	F 591	2.2.40	Mephst
I am leane with seeing others eate:	F 681	2.2.130	P Envy
These Captaines emulous of each others glory.	Lucan, First Booke	120	
And others came from that uncertaine shore,	Lucan, First Booke	410	
While others touch the damsell I love best?	Ovid's Elegies	1.4.4	
Chiefely shew him the gifts, which others send:	Ovid's Elegies	1.8.99	
Please her, her hate makes others thee abhorre,	Ovid's Elegies	2.3.11	
I grieve least others should such good perceive,	Ovid's Elegies	2.5.53	
If ill, thou saiest I die for others love.	Ovid's Elegies	2.7.10	
Let others tell how winds fierce battailes wage,	Ovid's Elegies	2.11.17	
Let others tell this, and what each one speakes/Beleeve, no	Ovid's Elegies	2.11.21	
For others faults, why do I losse receive?	Ovid's Elegies	3.3.16	
Few love, what others have unguarded left.	Ovid's Elegies	3.4.26	
Perchance these, others, me mine owne losse mooves.	Ovid's Elegies	3.5.100	
Or jaded camst thou from some others bed.	Ovid's Elegies	3.6.80	
Rich robes, themselves and others do adorne,	Hero and Leander	1.237	
Neither themselves nor others, if not worne.	Hero and Leander	1.238	
Both in each others armes chaind as they layd.	Hero and Leander	2.306	
OTHERWAIES			
No [otherwaies] <otherwise> for pompe or <and> Majesty,	F1693	5.1.20	Faust
OTHERWHILE			
For otherwhile he will be out of joynt.	Dido	3.3.24	Dido
OTHERWISE			
Yet should he not perswade me otherwise,	1Tamb	3.3.210	Zenoc
otherwise Cybelius, son and successive heire to the late mighty	2Tamb	3.1.1	P Orcan
And which of you can charge me otherwise?	Jew	1.2.117	Barab
Otherwise I'le confesse all:--	Jew	4.2.78	P Ithimr
But wish thou hadst behav'd thee otherwise.	Jew	5.5.75	Govnr
No [otherwaies] <otherwise> for pompe or <and> Majesty,	F1693	5.1.20	Faust
OTHES			
whose conditions, and our solemne othes/Sign'd with our handes,	2Tamb	1.1.143	Orcan
Though I confesse the othes they undertake,	2Tamb	2.1.42	Sgsmnd
For his othes are seldome spent in vaine.	P 773	15.31	Eprnon
O'THIS			
to clap hornes of honest mens heades o'this order,	F1317	4.1.163	P Benvol
OTTOMAN			
Will take his leave and saile toward Ottoman.	Jew	5.2.106	Barab
To saile to Turkey, to great Ottoman,	Jew	5.3.16	Msngr
Or Selim ne're returne to Ottoman.	Jew	5.5.114	Govnr
OUGHT (Homograph)			
Nor speech bewraies ought humaine in thy birth,	Dido	1.1.190	Aeneas
And cannot talke nor thinke of ought but him:	Dido	3.2.73	Juno
It is not ought Aeneas may atchieve?	Dido	3.4.11	Aeneas
What, hath Iarbus angred her in ought?	Dido	3.4.13	Aeneas
I Anna, is there ought you would with me?	Dido	4.2.24	Iarbus
shall we wish for ought/The world affoords in greatest	1Tamb	2.5.72	Tamb
to Zenocrate/Than her owne life, or ought save thine owne love.	1Tamb	5.1.338	Zenoc
by me, for in extremitie/We ought to make barre of no policie.	Jew	1.2.273	Barab
Ne're shall she live to inherit ought of mine,	Jew	3.4.30	Barab
'Tis not thy life which can availe me ought,	Jew	5.2.62	Barab
In this, or ought, your highnes shall commaund us.	Edw	1.4.384	Warwck
If ought of me thou speak'st in inward thought,	Ovid's Elegies	1.4.23	
When I (my light) do or say ought that please thee,	Ovid's Elegies	1.4.25	
Yet this Ile see, but if thy gowne ought cover,	Ovid's Elegies	1.4.41	
With selfe same woundes he gave, he ought to smart.	Ovid's Elegies	2.3.4	
Nor violent South-windes did thee ought affright.	Ovid's Elegies	2.11.52	
Great floods ought to assist young men in love,	Ovid's Elegies	3.5.23	
If ought remaines of us but name, and spirit,	Ovid's Elegies	3.8.59	
And my wench ought to have seem'd falsely praisd,	Ovid's Elegies	3.11.43	
As he ought not performe, nor yet she aske.	Hero and Leander	1.430	
OUGHTST			
to detaine)/Thou oughtst therefore to scorne me for thy mate,	Ovid's Elegies	2.17.13	
OUGLY			
Which th'earth from ougly Chaos den up-wayd:	Hero and Leander	1.450	
And with his flaring beames mockt ougly night,	Hero and Leander	2.332	
OUR			
She humbly did beseech him for our bane,	Dido	1.1.60	Venus
When as the waves doe threat our Chrystall world,	Dido	1.1.75	Venus
Besiege the ofspring of our kingly loynes,	Dido	1.1.116	Jupitr

OUR (cont.)

That durst thus proudly wrong our kinsmans peace.	Dido	1.1.119	Jupitr
Venus farewell, thy sonne shall be our care:	Dido	1.1.120	Jupitr
Pluck up your hearts, since fate still rests our friend,	Dido	1.1.149	Aeneas
Brave Prince of Troy, thou onely art our God,	Dido	1.1.152	Achat
And makes our hopes survive to [coming] <cunning> joyes:	Dido	1.1.154	Achat
To make us live unto our former heate,	Dido	1.1.160	Achat
Bequeath her young ones to our scanted foode.	Dido	1.1.162	Achat
And rost our new found victuals on this shoare.	Dido	1.1.168	Aeneas
Thou art a Goddesse that delud'st our eyes,	Dido	1.1.191	Aeneas
And lighten our extreames with this one boone,	Dido	1.1.196	Aeneas
And tell our griefes in more familiar termes:	Dido	1.1.246	Aeneas
Save, save, O save our ships from cruell fire,	Dido	1.2.7	Illion
And spare our lives whom every spite pursues.	Dido	1.2.9	Illion
Our hands are not prepar'd to lawles spoyle,	Dido	1.2.12	Illion
Such force is farre from our unweaponed thoughts,	Dido	1.2.14	Illion
Forbids all hope to harbour neere our hearts.	Dido	1.2.16	Illion
And led our ships into the shallow sands,	Dido	1.2.27	Cloan
I but the barbarous sort doe threat our ships,	Dido	1.2.34	Serg
And from the first earth interdict our feete.	Dido	1.2.37	Serg
Your men and you shall banquet in our Court,	Dido	1.2.39	Iarbus
As shall surpasse the wonder of our speech.	Dido	1.2.47	Serg
Leave to lament lest they laugh at our feares.	Dido	2.1.38	Achat
For none of these can be our Generall.	Dido	2.1.46	Illion
It is our Captaine, see Ascanius.	Dido	2.1.52	Cloan
Renowmed Dido, tis our Generall:	Dido	2.1.77	Illion
Both happie that Aeneas is our guest:	Dido	2.1.82	Dido
Began to crye, let us unto our ships,	Dido	2.1.127	Aeneas
Ulysses sent to our unhappie towne:	Dido	2.1.149	Aeneas
Our Phrigian [shepherds] <shepherd> haled within the gates,/And	Dido	2.1.153	Aeneas
And as we went unto our ships, thou knowest/We sawe Cassandra	Dido	2.1.273	Aeneas
Whom I tooke up to beare unto our ships:	Dido	2.1.277	Aeneas
Then got we to our ships, and being abourd,	Dido	2.1.280	Aeneas
For all our ships were launcht into the deepe:	Dido	2.1.285	Aeneas
Nor Sterne nor Anchor have our maimed Fleete,	Dido	3.1.109	Aeneas
Our Masts the furious windes strooke over bourd:	Dido	3.1.110	Aeneas
We will account her author of our lives.	Dido	3.1.112	Aeneas
And both our Deities conjoynd in one,	Dido	3.2.79	Juno
Whose emptie Altars have enlarg'd our illes.	Dido	4.2.3	Iarbus
Where straying in our borders up and downe,	Dido	4.2.12	Iarbus
Scorning our loves and royall marriage rites,	Dido	4.2.16	Iarbus
What willes our Lord, or wherefore did he call?	Dido	4.3.15	Achat
Effeminate our mindes inur'd to warre.	Dido	4.3.36	Achat
Why, let us build a Citie of our owne,	Dido	4.3.37	Illion
That thou and I unseene might sport our selves:	Dido	4.4.51	Dido
Heavens envious of our joyes is waxen pale,	Dido	4.4.52	Dido
To be partakers of our honey talke.	Dido	4.4.54	Dido
O Dido, patronesse of all our lives,	Dido	4.4.55	Aeneas
Our kinsmens [lives] <loves>, and thousand guiltles soules,	Dido	4.4.90	Aeneas
Henceforth you shall be our Carthage Gods:	Dido	4.4.96	Dido
The water which our Poets terme a Nimph,	Dido	4.4.144	Dido
Especially in women of [our] <your> yeares.--	Dido	4.5.28	Nurse
Triumph, my mates, our travels are at end,	Dido	5.1.1	Aeneas
And plant our pleasant suburbes with her fumes.	Dido	5.1.15	Aeneas
Sergestus, beare him hence unto our ships,	Dido	5.1.49	Aeneas
By this right hand, and by our spousall rites,	Dido	5.1.134	Dido
And rue our ends senceles of life or breath:	Dido	5.1.328	Anna
and the verie legges/Whereon our state doth leane, as on a	1Tamb	1.1.60	Mycet
That holds us up, and foiles our neighbour foes.	1Tamb	1.1.61	Mycet
Our life is fraile, and we may die to day.	1Tamb	1.1.68	Mycet
Shall either perish by our warlike hands,	1Tamb	1.1.72	Therid
To see our neighbours that were woont to quake/And tremble at	1Tamb	1.1.115	Cosroe
Now sits and laughs our regiment to scorne:	1Tamb	1.1.117	Cosroe
And made their spoiles from all our provinces.	1Tamb	1.1.122	Cosroe
These Lords (perhaps) do scorne our estimates,	1Tamb	1.2.61	Tamb
But since they measure our deserts so meane,	1Tamb	1.2.63	Tamb
That in conceit bear Empires on our speares,	1Tamb	1.2.64	Tamb
They shall be kept our forced followers,	1Tamb	1.2.66	Tamb
I hope our Ladies treasure and our owne,	1Tamb	1.2.74	Agidas
May serve for ransome to our liberties:	1Tamb	1.2.75	Agidas
Returne our Mules and emptie Camels backe,	1Tamb	1.2.76	Agidas
And wheresoever we repose our selves,	1Tamb	1.2.80	Magnet
Our swordes shall play the Orators for us.	1Tamb	1.2.132	Techel
Lay out our golden wedges to the view,	1Tamb	1.2.139	Tamb
Before we part with our possession.	1Tamb	1.2.144	Tamb
And gainst the Generall we will lift our swords,	1Tamb	1.2.145	Tamb
And mightie kings shall be our Senators.	1Tamb	1.2.198	Tamb
the Persean king/Should offer present Dukedomes to our state,	1Tamb	1.2.215	Techel
exchange for that/We are assured of by our friends successe.	1Tamb	1.2.217	Techel
Where kings shall crouch unto our conquering swords,	1Tamb	1.2.220	Usumc
Untill our bodies turne to Elements:	1Tamb	1.2.236	Tamb
And both our soules aspire celestiall thrones.	1Tamb	1.2.237	Tamb
Then when our powers in points of swords are join'd,	1Tamb	2.1.40	Cosroe
set the Crowne/Upon your kingly head, that seeks our honor,	1Tamb	2.1.51	Ortyg
Our army will be forty thousand strong,	1Tamb	2.1.61	Cosroe
And [pitcht] <pitch> our tents under the Georgean hilles,	1Tamb	2.2.15	Meandr
But if Cosrce (as our Spials say,	1Tamb	2.2.35	Meandr
We have our Cammels laden all with gold:	1Tamb	2.2.62	Meandr
Fortune her selfe dooth sit upon our Crests.	1Tamb	2.2.73	Meandr
What thinkst thou man, shal come of our attemptes?	1Tamb	2.3.3	Cosroe
Our quivering Lances shaking in the aire,	1Tamb	2.3.18	Tamb
and with our Sun-bright armour as we march,	1Tamb	2.3.221	Tamb
and dim their eies/That stand and muse at our admyred armes.	1Tamb	2.3.24	Tamb

OUR (cont.)

with amitie we yeeld/Our utmost service to the faire Cosroe.	1Tamb	2.3.34	Techel
May triumph in our long expected Fate.	1Tamb	2.3.44	Tamb
Our Crowne the pin that thousands seeke to cleave.	1Tamb	2.4.9	Mycet
Meander, you that were our brothers Guide,	1Tamb	2.5.10	Cosroe
And give you equall place in our affaires.	1Tamb	2.5.14	Cosroe
So will we with our powers and our lives,	1Tamb	2.5.34	Ortyg
And would not all our souldiers soone consent,	1Tamb	2.5.78	Tamb
I know they would with our perswasions.	1Tamb	2.5.80	Therid
Let us put on our meet incountring mindes,	1Tamb	2.6.19	Ortyg
Vowing our loves to equall death and life.	1Tamb	2.6.28	Cosroe
Let's cheere our souldiers to incounter him,	1Tamb	2.6.29	Cosroe
Warring within our breasts for regiment,	1Tamb	2.7.19	Tamb
Our soules, whose faculties can comprehend/The wondrous	1Tamb	2.7.21	Tamb
Wils us to weare our selves and never rest,	1Tamb	2.7.26	Tamb
To lift our swords against the Persean King.	1Tamb	2.7.35	Techel
And thinks to rouse us from our dreadful siege/Of the famous	1Tamb	3.1.5	Bajzth
You know our Armie is invincible:	1Tamb	3.1.7	Bajzth
Nor raise our siege before the Gretians yeeld,	1Tamb	3.1.14	Bajzth
And all the trees are blasted with our breathes.	1Tamb	3.1.55	Bajzth
Then shall our footmen lie within the trench,	1Tamb	3.1.64	Bajzth
For when they perish by our warlike hands,	1Tamb	3.3.24	Techel
We meane to seate our footmen on their Steeds,	1Tamb	3.3.25	Techel
I long to see those crownes won by our swords,	1Tamb	3.3.98	Therid
Our conquering swords shall marshal us the way/We use to march	1Tamb	3.3.148	Tamb
Trampling their bowels with our horses hooffes:	1Tamb	3.3.150	Tamb
Direct our Bullets and our weapons pointes/And make our <your>	1Tamb	3.3.157	Tamb
make our <your> strokes to wound the sencelesse [aire] <lure>.	1Tamb	3.3.158	Tamb
And when she sees our bloody Collours spread,	1Tamb	3.3.159	Tamb
let us glut our swords/That thirst to drinke the feble Perseans	1Tamb	3.3.164	Bajzth
For we will scorne they should come nere our selves.	1Tamb	3.3.186	Zenoc
Hath spread his collours to our high disgrace:	1Tamb	4.1.7	Souldn
So shall our swords, our lances and our shot,	1Tamb	4.2.51	Tamb
Shall not defend it from our battering shot.	1Tamb	4.2.107	Tamb
Not one should scape: but perish by our swords.	1Tamb	4.2.122	Tamb
That dares controll us in our Territories.	1Tamb	4.3.14	Souldn
Let us unite our royall bandes in one,	1Tamb	4.3.17	Souldn
Capolin, hast thou survaid our powers?	1Tamb	4.3.50	Souldn
your sounding Drummes/Direct our Souldiers to Damascus walles.	1Tamb	4.3.62	Souldn
Now hang our bloody collours by Damascus,	1Tamb	4.4.1	Tamb
higher meeds/Then erst our states and actions have retain'd,	1Tamb	4.4.132	Therid
Conquering the people underneath our feet,	1Tamb	4.4.137	Tamb
Batter our walles, and beat our Turrets downe.	1Tamb	5.1.2	Govnr
Were but to bring our wilfull overthrow,	1Tamb	5.1.5	Govnr
And make us desperate of our threatned lives:	1Tamb	5.1.6	Govnr
Threaten our citie with a generall spoile:	1Tamb	5.1.10	Govnr
Offer our safeties to his clemencie,	1Tamb	5.1.12	Govnr
Will never be dispenc'd with til our deaths.	1Tamb	5.1.17	Govnr
Therefore, for these our harmlesse virgines sakes,	1Tamb	5.1.18	Govnr
Shead from the heads and hearts of all our Sex,	1Tamb	5.1.26	1Virgn
To entertaine some care of our securities,	1Tamb	5.1.29	1Virgn
Whiles only danger beat upon our walles,	1Tamb	5.1.30	1Virgn
These more than dangerous warrants of our death,	1Tamb	5.1.31	1Virgn
Wel, lovely Virgins, think our countries care,	1Tamb	5.1.34	Govnr
Our love of honor loth to be enthral'd/To forraine powers, and	1Tamb	5.1.35	Govnr
Therefore in that your safeties and our owne,	1Tamb	5.1.40	Govnr
lives were weigh'd/In equall care and ballance with our owne,	1Tamb	5.1.42	Govnr
Endure as we the malice of our stars,	1Tamb	5.1.43	Govnr
we intreate/Grace to our words and pitie to our lookes,	1Tamb	5.1.51	2Virgn
(sweet Virgins) on whose safe return/Depends our citie,	1Tamb	5.1.63	Govnr
Pittie our plightes, O pitie poore Damascus:	1Tamb	5.1.80	1Virgn
As well for griefe our ruthlesse Governour/Have thus refusde	1Tamb	5.1.92	1Virgn
O then for these, and such as we our selves,	1Tamb	5.1.96	1Virgn
For us, for infants, and for all our bloods,	1Tamb	5.1.97	1Virgn
with horror aie/Griping our bowels with retorqued thoughtes,	1Tamb	5.1.237	Bajzth
And have no hope to end our extasies.	1Tamb	5.1.238	Bajzth
nor no hope of end/To our infamous monstrous slaveries?	1Tamb	5.1.241	Zabina
The former triumphes of our mightines,	1Tamb	5.1.253	Zabina
And make our soules resolve in ceasles teares:	1Tamb	5.1.272	Bajzth
staid, with wrath and hate/Of our expreslesse band inflictions.	1Tamb	5.1.282	Bajzth
We wil our celebrated rites of mariage solemnize.	1Tamb	5.1.534	Tamb
When he arrived last upon our stage,	2Tamb	Prol.2	Prolog
Hath made our Poet pen his second part,	2Tamb	Prol.3	Prolog
Our warlike hoste in compleat armour rest,	2Tamb	1.1.8	Orcan
the king of Hungary/Should meet our person to conclude a truce.	2Tamb	1.1.10	Orcan
Our Turky blades shal glide through al their throats,	2Tamb	1.1.31	Orcan
As martiall presents to our friends at home,	2Tamb	1.1.35	Orcan
Meaning to make a conquest of our land:	2Tamb	1.1.49	Gazell
And save our forces for the hot assaults/Proud Tamburlaine	2Tamb	1.1.52	Gazell
My realme, the Center of our Empery/Once lost, All Turkie would	2Tamb	1.1.55	Orcan
Orcanes (as our Legates promist thee)/Wee with our Peeres have	2Tamb	1.1.78	Sgsmnd
Wee with our Peeres have crost Danubius stream/To treat of	2Tamb	1.1.79	Sgsmnd
Our Tents are pitcht, our men stand in array,	2Tamb	1.1.120	Fredrk
Drawen with advise of our Ambassadors.	2Tamb	1.1.126	Orcan
whose conditions, and our solemne othes/Sign'd with our handes,	2Tamb	1.1.143	Orcan
and our solemne othes/Sign'd with our handes, each shal retaine	2Tamb	1.1.144	Orcan
As memorable witnesse of our league.	2Tamb	1.1.145	Orcan
Come let us goe and banquet in our tents:	2Tamb	1.1.160	Orcan
And then depart we to our territories.	2Tamb	1.1.166	Orcan
My Lord, such speeches to our princely sonnes,	2Tamb	1.3.85	Zenoc
And mighty Tamburlaine, our earthly God,	2Tamb	1.3.138	Techel
And after martch to Turky with our Campe,	2Tamb	1.3.158	Tamb
our men of Barbary have martcht/Foure hundred miles with armour	2Tamb	1.3.174	Usumc

OUR (cont.)

I am sure/What cruell slaughter of our Christian bloods,	2Tamb	2.1.5	Fredrk
They have not long since massacred our Camp.	2Tamb	2.1.10	Fredrk
pitcht against our power/Betwixt Cutheia and Orminius mount:	2Tamb	2.1.17	Fredrk
And calling Christ for record of our trueths?	2Tamb	2.1.30	Sgsmnd
Against the grace of our profession.	2Tamb	2.1.32	Sgsmnd
To be esteem'd assurance for our selves,	2Tamb	2.1.39	Baldwn
to them should not infringe/Our liberty of armes and victory.	2Tamb	2.1.41	Baldwn
Breed litle strength to our securitie,	2Tamb	2.1.43	Sgsmnd
Our faiths are sound, and must be [consumate] <consinuate>,	2Tamb	2.1.47	Sgsmnd
That God hath given to venge our Christians death/And scourge	2Tamb	2.1.52	Fredrk
his fearefull arme/Be pour'd with rigour on our sinfull heads,	2Tamb	2.1.58	Fredrk
Giving commandement to our generall hoste,	2Tamb	2.1.61	Sgsmnd
And take the victorie our God hath given.	2Tamb	2.1.63	Sgsmnd
where our neighbour kings/Expect our power and our royall	2Tamb	2.2.3	Orcan
our neighbour kings/Expect our power and our royall presence,	2Tamb	2.2.4	Orcan
of the clowdes/And fall as thick as haile upon our heads,	2Tamb	2.2.15	Gazell
Yet should our courages and steeled crestes,	2Tamb	2.2.17	Gazell
With unacquainted power of our hoste.	2Tamb	2.2.23	Uribas
To bid us battaile for our dearest lives.	2Tamb	2.2.28	1Msngr
That with such treason seek our overthrow,	2Tamb	2.2.34	Gazell
As is our holy prophet Mahomet,	2Tamb	2.2.44	Orcan
Take here these papers as our sacrifice/And witnesse of thy	2Tamb	2.2.45	Orcan
(Too litle to defend our guiltlesse lives)/Sufficient to	2Tamb	2.2.60	Orcan
Whose power had share in this our victory:	2Tamb	2.3.35	Orcan
let us haste and meete/Our Army and our brother of Jerusalem,	2Tamb	2.3.43	Orcan
Of Greekish wine now let us celebrate/Our happy conquest, and	2Tamb	2.3.47	Orcan
The God that tunes this musicke to our soules,	2Tamb	2.4.31	Tamb
If woords might serve, our voice hath rent the aire,	2Tamb	2.4.121	Therid
If teares, our eies have watered all the earth:	2Tamb	2.4.122	Therid
If griefe, our murthered harts have straind forth blood.	2Tamb	2.4.123	Therid
Bearing the vengeance of our fathers wrongs,	2Tamb	3.1.17	Callap
As all the world should blot our dignities/Out of the booke of	2Tamb	3.1.18	Callap
And raise our honors to as high a pitch/In this our strong and	2Tamb	3.1.30	Callap
to as high a pitch/In this our strong and fortunate encounter.	2Tamb	3.1.31	Callap
That Jove surchardg'd with pity of our wrongs,	2Tamb	3.1.35	Callap
Will poure it downe in showers on our heads:	2Tamb	3.1.36	Callap
Our battaile then in martiall maner pitcht,	2Tamb	3.1.63	Orcan
According to our ancient use, shall beare/The figure of the	2Tamb	3.1.64	Orcan
As Pilgrimes traveile to our Hemi-spheare,	2Tamb	3.2.32	Tamb
Upon the heads of all our enemies.	2Tamb	3.2.42	Tamb
see if coward Calapine/Dare levie armes against our puissance,	2Tamb	3.2.156	Tamb
Then let us bring our light Artilery,	2Tamb	3.3.5	Techel
Both we (Theridamas) wil intrench our men,	2Tamb	3.3.49	Techel
That we may know if our artillery/Will carie full point blancke	2Tamb	3.3.52	Techel
Then see the bringing of our ordinance/Along the trench into	2Tamb	3.3.54	Therid
To save our Cannoniers from musket shot,	2Tamb	3.3.57	Therid
Betwixt which, shall our ordinance thunder foorth,	2Tamb	3.3.58	Therid
One minute end our daies, and one sepulcher/Containe our	2Tamb	3.4.13	Olymp
minute end our daies, and one sepulcher/Containe our bodies:	2Tamb	3.4.14	Olymp
And carie both our soules, where his remaines.	2Tamb	3.4.17	Olymp
Out of the coffers of our treasurie.	2Tamb	3.4.91	Therid
In memorie of this our victory.	2Tamb	3.5.20	Callap
And what our Army royall is esteem'd.	2Tamb	3.5.31	Callap
To see the slaughter of our enemies.	2Tamb	3.5.57	Callap
The common souldiers of our mighty hoste/Shal bring thee bound	2Tamb	3.5.110	Trebiz
Hovering betwixt our armies, light on me,	2Tamb	3.5.163	Tamb
our men shall sweat/With carrieng pearle and treasure on their	2Tamb	3.5.166	Techel
Now brother, follow we our fathers sword,	2Tamb	4.1.4	Amyras
That flies with fury swifter than our thoughts,	2Tamb	4.1.5	Amyras
Call foorth our laisie brother from the tent,	2Tamb	4.1.7	Celeb
when our enemies drums/And ratling cannons thunder in our eares	2Tamb	4.1.12	Amyras
And ratling cannons thunder in our eares/Our proper ruine,	2Tamb	4.1.13	Amyras
And ratling cannons thunder in our eares/Our proper ruine, and	2Tamb	4.1.14	Amyras
thunder in our eares/Our proper ruine, and our fathers foile?	2Tamb	4.1.14	Amyras
If halfe our campe should sit and sleepe with me,	2Tamb	4.1.18	Calyph
To think our helps will doe him any good.	2Tamb	4.1.21	Calyph
troopes/Beats downe our foes to flesh our taintlesse swords?	2Tamb	4.1.26	Amyras
kings again my Lord/To gather greater numbers gainst our power,	2Tamb	4.1.83	Amyras
Thou shewest the difference twixt our selves and thee/In this	2Tamb	4.1.138	Orcan
And with our bloods, revenge our bloods on thee.	2Tamb	4.1.145	Jrslem
Expell the hate wherewith he paines our soules.	2Tamb	4.1.173	Orcan
Come bring them in to our Pavilion.	2Tamb	4.1.206	Tamb
O pity us my Lord, and save our honours.	2Tamb	4.3.83	Ladies
And now themselves shal make our Pageant,	2Tamb	4.3.90	Tamb
Till we prepare our martch to Babylon,	2Tamb	4.3.93	Tamb
the enimie hath made/Gives such assurance of our overthrow,	2Tamb	5.1.3	Maxim
That little hope is left to save our lives,	2Tamb	5.1.4	Maxim
Or hold our citie from the Conquerours hands.	2Tamb	5.1.5	Maxim
intollorable wrath/May be suppresst by our submission.	2Tamb	5.1.9	Maxim
Have we not hope, for all our battered walles,	2Tamb	5.1.15	Govnr
When this our famous lake of Limnasphaltis/Makes walles a fresh	2Tamb	5.1.17	Govnr
What faintnesse should dismay our courages,	2Tamb	5.1.21	Govnr
When we are thus defenc'd against our Foe,	2Tamb	5.1.22	Govnr
And now will work a refuge to our lives,	2Tamb	5.1.25	1Citzn
That Tamburlaine may pitie our distresse,	2Tamb	5.1.27	1Citzn
My Lord, if ever you wil win our hearts,	2Tamb	5.1.38	2Citzn
Yeeld up the towne, save our wives and children:	2Tamb	5.1.39	2Citzn
Villaines, cowards, Traitors to our state,	2Tamb	5.1.43	Govnr
Yeeld speedily the citie to our hands,	2Tamb	5.1.51	Therid
As durst resist us till our third daies siege:	2Tamb	5.1.59	Techel
Sirha, the view of our vermillion tents,	2Tamb	5.1.86	Tamb
And make our greatest haste to Persea:	2Tamb	5.1.128	Tamb

OUR (cont.)

First let thy Scythyan horse teare both our limmes/Rather then	2Tamb	5.1.138	Orcan
And like base slaves abject our princely mindes/To vile and	2Tamb	5.1.140	Orcan
A thousand deathes could not torment our hearts/More than the	2Tamb	5.1.144	Jrslem
our hearts/More than the thought of this dooth vexe our soules.	2Tamb	5.1.145	Jrslem
To triumph after all our victories.	2Tamb	5.1.213	Tamb
King of Amasia, now our mighty hoste,	2Tamb	5.2.1	Callap
And so revenge our latest grievous losse,	2Tamb	5.2.10	Callap
Our Turkish swords shal headlong send to hell,	2Tamb	5.2.15	Amasia
Are greatest to discourage all our drifts,	2Tamb	5.2.45	Callap
And threaten conquest on our Soveraigne:	2Tamb	5.3.14	Therid
As your supreame estates instruct our thoughtes,	2Tamb	5.3.20	Techel
Come let us chardge our speares and pierce his breast,	2Tamb	5.3.58	Tamb
Whereas the Sun declining from our sight,	2Tamb	5.3.148	Tamb
Begins the day with our Antypodes:	2Tamb	5.3.149	Tamb
how should our bleeding harts/Wounded and broken with your	2Tamb	5.3.161	Amyras
Your soul gives essence to our wretched subjects,	2Tamb	5.3.164	Amyras
Your paines do pierce our soules, no hope survives,	2Tamb	5.3.166	Celeb
For by your life we entertaine our lives.	2Tamb	5.3.167	Celeb
A woful change my Lord, that daunts our thoughts,	2Tamb	5.3.181	Therid
More than the ruine of our proper soules.	2Tamb	5.3.182	Therid
Nor may our hearts all drown'd in teares of blood,	2Tamb	5.3.214	Usumc
downe by Candie shoare/To Malta, through our Mediterranean sea.	Jew	1.1.47	Barab
I hope our credit in the Custome-house/Will serve as well as I	Jew	1.1.57	Barab
But this we heard some of our sea-men say,	Jew	1.1.78	1Merch
Thus trowles our fortune in by land and Sea,	Jew	1.1.103	Barab
That's not our fault:	Jew	1.1.130	Barab
Alas, our number's few,/And Crownes come either by succession	Jew	1.1.130	Barab
Are come from Turkey, and lye in our Rhode:	Jew	1.1.147	1Jew
If any thing shall there concerne our state/Assure your selves	Jew	1.1.172	Barab
Let's take our leaves; Farewell good Barabas.	Jew	1.1.175	2Jew
Now Bassoes, what demand you at our hands?	Jew	1.2.1	Govnr
What at our hands demand ye?	Jew	1.2.6	Govnr
And send to keepe our Gallies under-saile,	Jew	1.2.15	Calym
That's more then is in our Commission.	Jew	1.2.22	Basso
Now lanch our Gallies backe againe to Sea,	Jew	1.2.29	Calym
And for the mony send our messenger.	Jew	1.2.31	Calym
compasse it/By reason of the warres, that robb'd our store;	Jew	1.2.48	Govnr
And what's our aid against so great a Prince?	Jew	1.2.51	Barab
For through our sufferance of your hatefull lives,	Jew	1.2.63	Govnr
Reade there the Articles of our decrees.	Jew	1.2.67	Govnr
Sir, halfe is the penalty of our decree,	Jew	1.2.88	Govnr
'Tis not our fault, but thy inherent sinne.	Jew	1.2.109	1Knght
to staine our hands with blood/Is farre from us and our	Jew	1.2.144	Govnr
our hands with blood/Is farre from us and our profession.	Jew	1.2.145	Govnr
For if we breake our day, we breake the league,	Jew	1.2.158	1Knght
hardly can we brooke/The cruell handling of our selves in this:	Jew	1.2.175	1Jew
Thou seest they have taken halfe our goods.	Jew	1.2.176	1Jew
Our words will but increase his extasie.	Jew	1.2.210	1Jew
Whence is thy ship that anchors in our Rhoad?	Jew	2.2.2	Govnr
And why thou cam'st ashore without our leave?	Jew	2.2.3	Govnr
Our fraught is Grecians, Turks, and Africk Moores.	Jew	2.2.9	Bosco
But one amongst the rest became our prize:	Jew	2.2.16	Bosco
The Captain's slaine, the rest remaine our slaves,	Jew	2.2.17	Bosco
Perswade our Governor against the Turke;	Jew	2.2.25	1Knght
Captaine we know it, but our force is small.	Jew	2.2.34	Govnr
We and our warlike Knights will follow thee/Against these	Jew	2.2.45	Govnr
bite, yet are our lookes/As innocent and harmelesse as a Lambes.	Jew	2.3.21	Barab
Or else be gather'd for in our Synagogue;	Jew	2.3.27	Barab
We turne into the Ayre to purge our selves:	Jew	2.3.46	Barab
Good Barabas glance not at our holy Nuns.	Jew	2.3.86	Lodowk
Nor our Messias that is yet to come,	Jew	2.3.304	Barab
Till they [reveal] the causers of our smarts,	Jew	3.2.34	Govnr
Come, Katherina, our losses equall are,	Jew	3.2.36	Govnr
me in the pot of Rice/That for our supper stands upon the fire.	Jew	3.4.50	Barab
Nor shall the Heathens live upon our spoyle:	Jew	3.5.12	Govnr
First will we race the City wals our selves,	Jew	3.5.13	Govnr
And shipping of our goods to Sicily,	Jew	3.5.15	Govnr
Oh good Barabas come to our house.	Jew	4.1.77	1Fryar
Oh no, good Barabas come to our house.	Jew	4.1.78	2Fryar
Yet if he knew our meanings, could he scape?	Jew	4.1.135	Barab
I, and our lives too, therfore pull amaine.	Jew	4.1.150	Ithimr
And bring his gold into our treasury.	Jew	4.1.163	1Fryar
under Turkish yokes/Shall groning beare the burthen of our ire;	Jew	5.2.8	Calym
'Tis our command:	Jew	5.2.15	Calym
and Barabas we give/To guard thy person, these our Janizaries:	Jew	5.2.16	Calym
And now, as entrance to our safety,	Jew	5.2.22	Barab
Which with our Bombards shot and Basiliske,	Jew	5.3.3	Calym
We rent in sunder at our entry:	Jew	5.3.4	Calym
And now, bold Bashawes, let us to our Tents,	Jew	5.3.43	Calym
we may grace us best/To solemnize our Governors great feast.	Jew	5.3.45	Calym
To ascend our homely stayres?	Jew	5.5.58	Barab
For he that did by treason worke our fall,	Jew	5.5.109	Govnr
May not desolve, till death desolve our lives,	P 5	1.5	Charls
That kindled first this motion in our hearts,	P 7	1.7	Charls
May still be feweld in our progenye.	P 8	1.8	Charls
That linke you in mariage with our daughter heer:	P 14	1.14	QnMoth
our difference in Religion/Might be a meanes to crosse you in	P 15	1.15	QnMoth
Having the King, Queene Mother on our sides,	P 29	1.29	Navrre
For she is that huge blemish in our eye,	P 80	2.23	Guise
To bring the will of our desires to end.	P 144	2.87	Guise
Blindes Europs eyes and troubleth our estate:	P 152	2.95	Guise
That hinder our possession to the crowne:	P 154	2.97	Guise

OUR (cont.)

To agravate our sodaine miserie.	P 194	3.29	QnMarg
These are the cursed Guisians that doe seeke our death.	P 201	3.36	Admral
Cheefely since under safetie of our word,	P 209	4.7	Charls
That seeke to massacre our guiltles lives.	P 261	4.59	Admral
[Cossin] <Cosin> <Cousin>, take twenty of our strongest guarde,	P 266	4.64	Charls
see they keep/All trecherous violence from our noble freend,	P 268	4.66	Charls
Upon the cursed breakers of our peace.	P 270	4.68	Charls
Then pray unto our Ladye, kisse this crosse.	P 302	5.29	Gonzag
And now my Lords let us closely to our busines.	P 332	5.59	Guise
And now sirs for this night let our fury stay.	P 443	7.83	Guise
The greatest warres within our Christian bounds,	P 460	8.10	Anjoy
I meane our warres against the Muscovites:	P 461	8.11	Anjoy
Yet by my brother Charles our King of France,	P 464	8.14	Anjoy
water the fish, and by the fish our selves when we eate them.	P 489	9.8	P 2Atndt
Now Madame, how like you our lusty Admirall?	P 494	9.13	Guise
How Charles our sonne begins for to lament/For the late nights	P 513	9.32	QnMoth
The vertues of our true Religion,	P 577	11.42	Pleshe
Graunt that our deeds may wel deserve your loves:	P 600	12.13	King
What saies our Minions, think they Henries heart/Will not both	P 603	12.16	King
Till this our Coronation day be past:	P 624	12.37	King
Our solemne rites of Coronation done,	P 626	12.39	King
Lets goe my Lords, our dinner staies for us.	P 630	12.43	King
To plant our selves with such authoritie,	P 637	12.50	QnMoth
As not a man may live without our leaves.	P 638	12.51	QnMoth
We undertake to mannage these our warres/Against the proud	P 699	14.2	Navrre
And rent our true religion from this land:	P 703	14.6	Navrre
But for you know our quarrell is no more,	P 704	14.7	Navrre
In honor of our God and countries good.	P 708	14.11	Navrre
My Lord, as by our scoutes we understande,	P 724	14.27	1Msngr
And place our selves in order for the fight.	P 742	14.45	Navrre
of Guise you and your wife/Doe both salute our lovely Minions.	P 753	15.11	King
To beat the papall Monarck from our lands,	P 802	16.16	Navrre
And keep those relicks from our countries coastes.	P 803	16.17	Navrre
Let us away with triumph to our tents.	P 805	16.19	Navrre
But we presume it is not for our good.	P 824	17.19	King
To countermaund our will and check our freends.	P 846	17.41	King
Guise, weare our crowne, and be thou King of France,	P 859	17.54	King
Dismisse thy campe or else by our Edict,	P 863	17.58	King
Then meanes he present treason to our state.	P 880	17.75	King
First let us set our hand and seale to this,	P 890	17.85	King
And there salute his highnesse in our name,	P 908	18.9	Navrre
Pleshe, goe muster up our men with speed,	P 916	18.17	Navrre
You will give us our money?	P 942	19.12	P AllMur
(As all the world shall know our Guise is dead)/Rest satisfied	P1042	19.112	King
Especially with our olde mothers helpe.	P1061	19.131	King
To revenge our deaths upon that cursed King,	P1100	20.10	Cardnl
Sweet Duke of Guise our prop to leane upon,	P1110	21.4	Dumain
Girting this strumpet Cittie with our siege,	P1152	22.14	King
Till surfeiting with our afflicting armes,	P1153	22.15	King
Sweete Epernoune, our Friers are holy men,	P1161	22.23	King
exhalatione/which our great sonn of fraunce cold not effecte	Paris	ms20,p390	Guise
O our heads?	Edw	1.1.119	Warwck
Cosin, our hands I hope shall fence our heads,	Edw	1.1.123	Mortmr
And henceforth parle with our naked swords.	Edw	1.1.126	Mortmr
Wilshire hath men enough to save our heads.	Edw	1.1.127	MortSr
Save or condemne, and in our name commaund,	Edw	1.1.169	Edward
That slie inveigling Frenchman weele exile,/Or lose our lives:	Edw	1.2.58	Mortmr
Confirme his banishment with our handes and seales.	Edw	1.2.71	ArchBp
It is our pleasure, we will have it so.	Edw	1.4.9	Edward
We know our duties, let him know his peeres.	Edw	1.4.23	Warwck
What we have done, our hart bloud shall maintaine.	Edw	1.4.40	Mortmr
And either have our wils, or lose our lives.	Edw	1.4.46	Mortmr
Thou Lancaster, high admirall of our fleete,	Edw	1.4.66	Edward
Kinde wordes, and mutuall talke, makes our greefe greater,	Edw	1.4.133	Edward
Then thus, but none shal heare it but our selves.	Edw	1.4.229	Queene
Tis not for his sake, but for our availe:	Edw	1.4.242	Mortmr
To mend the king, and do our countrie good:	Edw	1.4.257	Mortmr
So shall we have the people of our side,	Edw	1.4.282	Mortmr
Be thou commaunder of our royall fleete,	Edw	1.4.354	Edward
Whose great atchivements in our forrain warre,	Edw	1.4.360	Edward
Clarke of the crowne, direct our warrant forth,	Edw	1.4.369	Edward
Against our friend the earle of Cornewall comes,	Edw	1.4.375	Edward
Unto our cosin, the earle of Glosters heire.	Edw	1.4.379	Edward
And floute our traine, and jest at our attire:	Edw	1.4.418	Mortmr
Seeing that our Lord th'earle of Glosters dead,	Edw	2.1.2	Baldck
With letters to our ladie from the King,	Edw	2.1.20	Spencr
Our Ladies first love is not wavering,	Edw	2.1.27	Spencr
Lets to our castels, for the king is moovde.	Edw	2.2.100	Warwck
Now send our Heralds to defie the King,	Edw	2.2.110	Lncstr
Why how now cosin, how fares all our friends?	Edw	2.2.114	Lncstr
And when tis gone, our swordes shall purchase more.	Edw	2.2.197	Lncstr
Looke next to see us with our ensignes spred.	Edw	2.2.199	Lncstr
To wed thee to our neece, the onely heire/Unto the Earle of	Edw	2.2.258	Edward
My lords, of love to this our native land,	Edw	2.3.1	Kent
Let us with these our followers scale the walles,	Edw	2.3.18	Lncstr
The wind that bears him hence, wil fil our sailes,	Edw	2.4.48	Lncstr
it is our countries cause,/That here severelie we will execute	Edw	2.5.22	Warwck
Thou shalt have so much honor at our hands.	Edw	2.5.28	Warwck
hence, out of the way/A little, but our men shall go along.	Edw	2.5.101	Penbrk
We that have prettie wenches to our wives,	Edw	2.5.102	Penbrk
And wrong our lord, your honorable friend.	Edw	2.6.9	James
We will in hast go certifie our Lord.	Edw	2.6.19	James

OUR (cont.)

Too kinde to them, but now have drawne our sword,	Edw	3.1.25	Edward
And daily will enrich thee with our favour,	Edw	3.1.50	Edward
Beside, the more to manifest our love,	Edw	3.1.52	Edward
Our friend [Levune] <Lewne>, faithfull and full of trust,	Edw	3.1.60	Queene
That lord Valoyes our brother, king of Fraunce,	Edw	3.1.62	Queene
And this our sonne, [Levune] <Lewne> shall follow you,	Edw	3.1.82	Edward
Choose of our lords to beare you companie,	Edw	3.1.84	Edward
My lords, because our soveraigne sends for him,	Edw	3.1.109	Arundl
And meerely of our love we do create thee/Earle of Gloster, and	Edw	3.1.145	Edward
a while, our men with sweat and dust/All chockt well neare,	Edw	3.1.191	SpncrP
And plowes to go about our pallace gates.	Edw	3.1.216	Edward
To whome right well you knew our soule was knit,	Edw	3.1.227	Edward
So sir, you have spoke, away, avoid our presence.	Edw	3.1.232	Edward
when we had sent our messenger to request/He might be spared to	Edw	3.1.234	Edward
A boye, our friends do faile us all in Fraunce,	Edw	4.2.1	Queene
And shake off all our fortunes equallie?	Edw	4.2.20	SrJohn
Tould us at our arrivall all the newes,	Edw	4.2.48	Mortmr
And others of our partie and faction,	Edw	4.2.53	Mortmr
To see us there appointed for our foes.	Edw	4.2.56	Mortmr
These comforts that you give our wofull queene,	Edw	4.2.72	Kent
Was borne I see to be our anchor hold.	Edw	4.2.77	Mortmr
our port-maisters/Are not so careles of their kings commaund.	Edw	4.3.22	Edward
Now lords, our loving friends and countrimen,	Edw	4.4.1	Queene
Our kindest friends in Belgia have we left,	Edw	4.4.3	Queene
Heere for our countries cause sweare we to him/All homage,	Edw	4.4.19	Mortmr
Shape we our course to Ireland there to breath.	Edw	4.5.3	Spencr
Give me my horse and lets r'enforce our troupes:	Edw	4.5.6	Edward
We heere create our welbeloved sonne,	Edw	4.6.24	Queene
My lord, the Maior of Bristow knows our mind.	Edw	4.6.40	Queene
That in our famous nurseries of artes/Thou suckedst from Plato,	Edw	4.7.18	Edward
Do you betray us and our companie.	Edw	4.7.25	Edward
Armes that pursue our lives with deadly hate.	Edw	4.7.32	Spencr
To let us take our farewell of his grace.	Edw	4.7.69	Spencr
Here humblie of your grace we take our leaves,	Edw	4.7.78	Baldck
Our lots are cast, I feare me so is thine.	Edw	4.7.79	Baldck
Spencer, I see our soules are fleeted hence,	Edw	4.7.105	Baldck
We are deprivde the sun-shine of our life,	Edw	4.7.106	Baldck
Reduce we all our lessons unto this,	Edw	4.7.110	Baldck
And thus, most humbly do we take our leave.	Edw	5.1.124	Trussl
Faire Isabell, now have we our desire,	Edw	5.2.1	Mortmr
For our behoofe will beare the greater sway/When as a kings	Edw	5.2.13	Mortmr
a letter presently/Unto the Lord of Bartley from our selfe,	Edw	5.2.48	Mortmr
And when tis done, we will subscribe our name.	Edw	5.2.50	Mortmr
Our plots and stratagems will soone be dasht.	Edw	5.2.78	Mortmr
Therefore come, dalliance dangereth our lives.	Edw	5.3.3	Matrvs
Heeres channell water, as our charge is given.	Edw	5.3.27	Matrvs
Mortimer, I did, he is our king,	Edw	5.4.87	Kent
At our commaund, once more away with him.	Edw	5.4.104	Mortmr
And beare the kings to Mortimer our lord,	Edw	5.5.119	Gurney
Now Mortimer begins our tragedie.	Edw	5.6.23	Queene
Intends our Muse to vaunt <daunt> his heavenly verse;	F 6	Prol.6	1Chor
And now <so> to patient judgements we appeale <our plaude>,	F 9	Prol.9	1Chor
The end of Physicke is our bodies health:	F 45	1.1.17	Faust
If we say that we have no sinne we deceive our selves, and	F 69	1.1.41	P Faust
And chase the Prince of Parma from our Land,	F 120	1.1.92	Faust
And raigne sole King of all [our] Provinces.	F 121	1.1.93	Faust
Faustus, these bookes, thy wit, and our experience,	F 146	1.1.118	Valdes
Or Lapland Giants trotting by our sides:	F 153	1.1.125	Valdes
Yea <I> all the wealth that our fore-fathers hid,	F 173	1.1.145	Cornel
We will informe thee e're our conference cease.	F 184	1.1.156	Valdes
become of Faustus that/Was wont to make our schooles ring,	F 195	1.2.2	1Schol
Conspir'd against our God with Lucifer,	F 299	1.3.71	Mephst
I, that is not against our Kingdome:	F 623	2.2.72	P Mephst
I chuse his privy chamber for our use.	F 806	3.1.28	Mephst
I have taken up his holinesse privy chamber for our use>.	F 806	(HC265) A	P Mephst
So high our Dragons soar'd into the aire,	F 849	3.1.71	Faust
Cast downe our Foot-stoole.	F 868	3.1.90	Pope
So shall our sleeping vengeance now arise,	F 879	3.1.101	Pope
Go forth-with to our holy Consistory,	F 882	3.1.104	Pope
And as Pope Alexander our Progenitour,	F 915	3.1.137	Pope
Adding this golden sentence to our praise;	F 917	3.1.139	Pope
In token of our seven-fold power from heaven,	F 934	3.1.156	Pope
Or be assured of our dreadfull curse,	F 938	3.1.160	Pope
What have our holy Councell there decreed,	F 947	3.1.169	Pope
In quittance of their late conspiracie/Against our State, and	F 950	3.1.172	Pope
To morrow, sitting in our Consistory,	F 967	3.1.189	Pope
With all our Colledge of grave Cardinals,	F 968	3.1.190	Pope
And take our blessing Apostolicall.	F 973	3.1.195	Pope
Drinke to our late and happy victory.	F 980	3.1.202	Pope
What Lollards do attend our Hollinesse,	F1049	3.2.69	Pope
Or by our sanctitude you all shall die.	F1057	3.2.77	Pope
Go then command our Priests to sing a Dirge,	F1063	3.2.83	Pope
Come brethren, let's about our businesse with good devotion.	F1076	3.2.96	P 1Frier
Cursed be he that disturbeth our holy Dirge.	F1083	3.2.103	1Frier
But where is Bruno our elected Pope,	F1160	4.1.6	Fredrk
Thrice learned Faustus, welcome to our Court.	F1205	4.1.51	Emper
thine, in setting Bruno free/From his and our professed enemy,	F1207	4.1.53	Emper
And place our servants, and our followers/Close in an ambush	F1341	4.2.17	Benvol
and our followers/Close in an ambush there behinde the trees,	F1341	4.2.17	Benvol
Where shall we place our selves Benvolio?	F1353	4.2.29	Mrtino
Pitie us gentle Faustus, save our lives.	F1417	4.2.93	Fredrk
That spite of spite, our wrongs are doubled?	F1446	4.3.16	Benvol

OUR (cont.)

What may we do, that we may hide our shames?	F1447	4.3.17		Fredrk
Till time shall alter this our brutish shapes:	F1454	4.3.24		Benvol
Sith blacke disgrace hath thus eclipst our fame,	F1455	4.3.25		Benvol
we will be wellcome for our mony, and we will pay for what we	F1611	4.6.54	P	Robin
Our servants, and our Courts at thy command.	F1624	4.6.67		Duke
since our conference about faire Ladies, which was the	F1681	5.1.8	P	1Schol
we have determin'd with our selves, that Hellen of Greece was	F1683	5.1.10	P	1Schol
Majesty, we should thinke our selves much beholding unto you.	F1687	5.1.14	P	1Schol
<Wee'l take our leaves>, and for this blessed sight	F1704	(HC269)B		1Schol
With greatest [torments] <torment> that our hell affoords.	F1755	5.1.82		Faust
Dis do we ascend/To view the subjects of our Monarchy,	F1798	5.2.2		Lucifr
Is all our pleasure turn'd to melancholy?	F1828	5.2.32		2Schol
once admired/For wondrous knowledge in our Germane schooles,	F1998	5.3.16		2Schol
Come brethren, lets about our businesse with good devotion.	F App	p.232 29	P	Frier
Cursed be he that disturbeth our holy Dirge.	F App	p.232 37		Frier
in our parish dance at my pleasure starke naked before me,	F App	p.233 3	P	Robin
Our maister Parson sayes thats nothing.	F App	p.234 25	P	Rafe
if thou hast any mind to Nan Spit our kitchin maide, then turn	F App	p.234 27	P	Robin
goe and make cleane our bootes which lie foule upon our handes,	F App	p.234 32	P	Robin
goe and make cleane our bootes which lie foule upon our handes,	F App	p.234 33	P	Robin
upon our handes, and then to our conjuring in the divels name.	F App	p.234 33	P	Robin
our horses shal eate no hay as long as this lasts.	F App	p.234 3	P	Robin
or they that shal hereafter possesse our throne, shal (I feare	F App	p.236 22	P	Emper
Now Babilon, (proud through our spoile) should stoop,	Lucan, First Booke			10
huge heapes of stone/Lye in our townes, that houses are	Lucan, First Booke			26
And Carthage soules be glutted with our blouds;	Lucan, First Booke			39
Swords share our Empire, fortune that made Roome/Governe the	Lucan, First Booke			109
wars,/We from our houses driven, most willingly/Suffered exile:	Lucan, First Booke			279
See how they quit our [bloud shed] <bloudshed> in the North;	Lucan, First Booke			302
Our friends death; and our wounds; our wintering/Under the	Lucan, First Booke			303
friends death; and our wounds; our wintering/Under the Alpes;	Lucan, First Booke			303
and our wounds; our wintering/Under the Alpes; Roome rageth now	Lucan, First Booke			303
Lets use our tried force, they that now thwart right/In wars	Lucan, First Booke			349
even nowe when youthfull bloud/Pricks forth our lively bodies,	Lucan, First Booke			364
When our lascivious toyes come in thy minde,	Ovid's Elegies			1.4.21
When pleasure mov'd us to our sweetest worke.	Ovid's Elegies			1.4.48
Not black, nor golden were they to our viewe,	Ovid's Elegies			1.14.9
And tearmes <termst> [my] <our> works fruits of an idle quill?	Ovid's Elegies			1.15.2
Our prayers move thee to assist our drift,	Ovid's Elegies			2.3.17
And passe our scarlet of red saffrons marke.	Ovid's Elegies			2.6.22
Our pleasant scapes shew thee no clowne to be,	Ovid's Elegies			2.8.3
Who that our bodies were comprest bewrayde?	Ovid's Elegies			2.8.5
That might be urg'd to witnesse our false playing.	Ovid's Elegies			2.8.8
If thou deniest foole, Ile our deeds expresse,	Ovid's Elegies			2.8.25
[Or] <On> stones, our stockes originall, should be hurld,	Ovid's Elegies			2.14.11
Nor of our love to be asham'd we need,	Ovid's Elegies			2.17.26
And may repulse place for our wishes strike.	Ovid's Elegies			2.19.6
By thy default thou doest our joyes defraude.	Ovid's Elegies			2.19.58
Let us all conquer by our mistris favour.	Ovid's Elegies			3.2.18
to thee our Court stands open wide,/There shalt be lov'd:	Ovid's Elegies			3.5.61
For five score Nimphes, or more our floods conteine.	Ovid's Elegies			3.5.64
Mad streame, why doest our mutuall joyes deferre?	Ovid's Elegies			3.5.87
Though both of us performd our true intent,	Ovid's Elegies			3.6.5
When our bookes did my mistris faire content,	Ovid's Elegies			3.7.5
Onely our loves let not such rich churles gaine,	Ovid's Elegies			3.7.59
What profit to us hath our pure life bred?	Ovid's Elegies			3.8.33
Why are our pleasures by thy meanes forborne?	Ovid's Elegies			3.9.4
O by our fellow bed, by all/The Gods who by thee to be perjurde	Ovid's Elegies			3.10.45
Our verse great Tityus a huge space out-spreads,	Ovid's Elegies			3.11.25
It lies not in our power to love, or hate,	Hero and Leander			1.167
What we behold is censur'd by our eies.	Hero and Leander			1.174
By which alone, our reverend fathers say,	Hero and Leander			1.267
Above our life we love a stedfast friend,	Hero and Leander			2.79
Even as a bird, which in our hands we wring,	Hero and Leander			2.289
Which from our pretty Lambes we pull,	Passionate Shepherd			14

OURS

The field is ours, the Turk, his wife and all.	1Tamb	3.3.163		Tamb
The men, the treasure, and the towne is ours.	1Tamb	4.2.110		Tamb
The town is ours my Lord, and fresh supply/Of conquest, and of	1Tamb	5.1.196		Techel
We know the victorie is ours my Lord,	1Tamb	5.1.203		Therid
And rich Natolia ours, our men shall sweat/With carrieng pearle	2Tamb	3.5.166		Techel
Canst thou, as thou reportest, make Malta ours?	Jew	5.1.85		Calym
Tis not in her controulment, nor in ours,	Edw	4.6.35		Mortmr
This letter written by a friend of ours,	Edw	5.4.6		Mortmr

OUR SELFE

a letter presently/Unto the Lord of Bartley from our selfe,	Edw	5.2.48		Mortmr

OUR SELVES

That thou and I unseene might sport our selves:	Dido	4.4.51		Dido
And wheresoever we repose our selves,	1Tamb	1.2.80		Magnet
Wils us to weare our selves and never rest,	1Tamb	2.7.26		Tamb
For we will scorne they should come nere our selves.	1Tamb	3.3.186		Zenoc
O then for these, and such as we our selves,	1Tamb	5.1.96		1Virgn
To be esteem'd assurance for our selves,	2Tamb	2.1.39		Baldwn
Thou shewest the difference twixt our selves and thee/In this	2Tamb	4.1.138		Orcan
hardly can we brooke/The cruell handling of our selves in this:	Jew	1.2.175		1Jew
We turne into the Ayre to purge our selves:	Jew	2.3.46		Barab
First will we race the City wals our selves,	Jew	3.5.13		Govnr
water the fish, and by the fish our selves when we eate them.	P 489	9.8	P	2Atndt
To plant our selves with such authoritie,	P 637	12.50		QnMoth
And place our selves in order for the fight.	P 742	14.45		Navrre
Then thus, but none shal heare it but our selves.	Edw	1.4.229		Queene
If we say that we have no sinne we deceive our selves, and	F 69	1.1.41	P	Faust

OUR SELVES (cont.)				
Where shall we place our selves Benvolio?	F1353	4.2.29		Mrtino
we have determin'd with our selves, that Hellen of Greece was	F1683	5.1.10	P	1Schol
Majesty, we should thinke our selves much beholding unto you.	F1687	5.1.14	P	1Schol
OUT				
To sweeten out the slumbers of thy bed:	Dido	1.1.37		Jupitr
See what strange arts necessitie findes out, . . .	Dido	1.1.169		Venus
Put sailes to sea to seeke out Italy, ...	Dido	1.1.218		Aeneas
Who for her sonnes death wept out life and breath, . .	Dido	2.1.4		Aeneas
Then would it leape out to give Priam life: . . .	Dido	2.1.27		Aeneas
And the remainder weake and out of heart, ...	Dido	2.1.133		Aeneas
and suddenly/From out his entrailes, Neoptolemus/Setting his	Dido	2.1.183		Aeneas
Who with steele Pol-axes dasht out their braines. . .	Dido	2.1.199		Aeneas
Polixena cryed out, Aeneas stay, ...	Dido	2.1.281		Aeneas
Then pull out both mine eyes, or let me dye. . . .	Dido	3.1.55		Iarbus
And feede infection with his [let] <left> out life: . .	Dido	3.2.11		Juno
Out hatefull hag, thou wouldst have slaine my sonne, .	Dido	3.2.32		Venus
For otherwhile he will be out of joynt.	Dido	3.3.24		Dido
Tell me deare love, how found you out this Cave? . .	Dido	3.4.3		Dido
Or aged Atlas shoulder out of joynt, ...	Dido	4.1.12		Achat
Or drop out both mine eyes in drisling teares, . .	Dido	4.2.41		Iarbus
Yet Dido casts her eyes like anchors out, . . .	Dido	4.3.25		Aeneas
To sea Aeneas, finde out Italy.	Dido	4.3.56		Aeneas
Thou wouldst have leapt from out the Sailers hands, . .	Dido	4.4.141		Dido
While Italy is cleane out of thy minde?	Dido	5.1.29		Hermes
Goe goe and spare not, seeke out Italy, ...	Dido	5.1.169		Dido
But I cride out, Aeneas, false Aeneas stay. . . .	Dido	5.1.228		Anna
As any prizes out of my precinct.	1Tamb	1.2.28		Tamb
Lay out our golden wedges to the view, ...	1Tamb	1.2.139		Tamb
For you then Maddam, I am out of doubt.	1Tamb	1.2.258		Tamb
Aurora shall not peepe out of her doores, ...	1Tamb	2.2.10		Mycet
And prest out fire from their burning jawes:	1Tamb	2.6.6		Cosroe
Shall rouse him out of Europe, and pursue/His scattered armie	1Tamb	3.3.38		Therid
Bring out my foot-stoole.	1Tamb	4.2.1		Tamb
He dies, and those that kept us out so long. . . .	1Tamb	4.2.118		Tamb
to come by, plucke out that, and twil serve thee and thy wife:	1Tamb	4.4.13	P	Tamb
What, are the Turtles fraide out of their neastes? . .	1Tamb	5.1.64		Tamb
could they not as well/Have sent ye out, when first my .	1Tamb	5.1.68		Tamb
And beat thy braines out of thy conquer'd head: . .	1Tamb	5.1.287		Bajzth
His Skul al rivin in twain, his braines dasht out? . .	1Tamb	5.1.306		Zabina
Sent Herralds out, which basely on their knees/In all your	2Tamb	1.1.96		Orcan
Never to draw it out, or manage armes/Against thy selfe or thy	2Tamb	1.1.128		Sgsmnd
She lies so close that none can find her out. . . .	2Tamb	1.2.60		Callap
As I cried out for feare he should have falne. . . .	2Tamb	1.3.42		Zenoc
Should breake out off the bowels of the clowdes/And fall as	2Tamb	2.2.14		Gazell
Holds out his hand in highest majesty/To entertaine divine	2Tamb	2.4.32		Tamb
Letting out death and tyrannising war, ...	2Tamb	2.4.115		Tamb
blot our dignities/Out of the booke of base borne infamies.	2Tamb	3.1.19		Callap
Now ugly death stretch out thy Sable wings, . . .	2Tamb	3.4.16		Olymp
Out of the coffers of our treasurie.	2Tamb	3.4.91		Therid
Or rip thy bowels, and rend out thy heart, ...	2Tamb	3.5.121		Tamb
I may knocke out his braines with them, and lock you in the	2Tamb	3.5.141	P	Tamb
Which beates against this prison to get out, ...	2Tamb	4.2.35		Olymp
their mouths/And pul their kicking colts out of their pastures.	2Tamb	4.3.49		Techel
Now fetch me out the Turkish Concubines, ...	2Tamb	4.3.64		Tamb
Then hang out flagges (my Lord) of humble truce, . .	2Tamb	5.1.6		Maxim
To live secure, and keep his forces out, ...	2Tamb	5.1.16		Govnr
Seeke out another Godhead to adore, ...	2Tamb	5.1.200		Tamb
And though they think their painfull date is out, . .	2Tamb	5.3.34		Usumc
for earthly man/Then thus to powre out plenty in their laps,	Jew	1.1.108		Barab
And Barabas now search this secret out.	Jew	1.1.177		Barab
Preach me not out of my possessions.	Jew	1.2.111		Barab
Out wretched Barabas, ...	Jew	1.2.118		Govnr
Out, out thou wretch.	Jew	1.2.365		Barab
fitter for a tale of love/Then to be tired out with Orizons:	Jew	1.2.370		Mthias
They fought it out, and not a man surviv'd/To bring the .	Jew	2.2.50		Bosco
So will we fight it out; come, let's away: . . .	Jew	2.2.52		Govnr
I'le seeke him out, and so insinuate, ...	Jew	2.3.33		Lodowk
Seiz'd all I had, and thrust me out a doores, . . .	Jew	2.3.76		Barab
That ye be both made sure e're you come out. . . .	Jew	2.3.236		Barab
While she runs to the window looking out/When you should come	Jew	2.3.264		Barab
now out alas,/He is slaine.	Jew	4.1.176		Barab
I, master, he's slain; look how his brains drop out on's nose.	Jew	4.1.178	P	Ithimr
by this Bernardine/To be a Christian, I shut him out, .	Jew	4.1.188		Barab
Now am I cleane, or rather fouly out of the way. . .	Jew	4.2.47	P	Ithimr
And is't not possible to find it out?	Jew	4.2.60		Pilia
That when he speakes, drawes out his grisly beard, .	Jew	4.3.7		Barab
Give him a crowne, and fill me out more wine. . . .	Jew	4.4.46		Ithimr
You run swifter when you threw my gold out of my Window.	Jew	4.4.52	P	Barab
Nor me neither, I cannot out-run you Constable, oh my belly.	Jew	5.1.20	P	Ithimr
And in an out-house of the City shut/His souldiers, till I have	Jew	5.2.81		Barab
is a monastery/Which standeth as an out-house to the Towne;	Jew	5.3.37		Msngr
Then issue out and come to rescue me, ...	Jew	5.4.5		Govnr
At which they all shall issue out and set the streetes. .	P 237	4.35		Guise
And slay his servants that shall issue out. . . .	P 299	5.26		Anjoy
Harke, harke they come, Ile leap out at the window. . .	P 369	7.9		Taleus
O no, his soule is fled from out his breast, . . .	P 552	11.17		QnMoth
Had late been pluckt from out faire Cupids wing: . . .	P 668	13.12		Duchss
And although you take out nothing but your owne, yet you put in	P 808	17.3	P	Souldr
possession (as I would I might) yet I meane to keepe you out,	P 814	17.9	P	Souldr
Breath out that life wherein my death was hid, . . .	P 954	19.24		King
Cry out, exclaime, houle till thy throat be hoarce, . .	P1077	19.147		King
And let her greeve her heart out if she will. . . .	P1080	19.150		King

OUT (cont.)

thoughe you take out none but your owne treasure . .	Paris	ms 3,p390	P	Souldr
yett comminge upon you once unawares he frayde you out againe.	Paris	ms13,p390	P	Souldr
yet I come to keepe you out ser.	Paris	ms16,p390	P	Souldr
You know that I came lately out of France, . . .	Edw	1.1.44		Gavstn
For howsoever we have borne it out, ...	Edw	1.4.280		Mortmr
below, the king and he/From out a window, laugh at such as we,	Edw	1.4.417		Mortmr
If all things sort out, as I hope they will, ...	Edw	2.1.79		Neece
Out of my presence, come not neere the court. . . .	Edw	2.2.89		Edward
Thy garrisons are beaten out of Fraunce, ...	Edw	2.2.162		Lncstr
Out of my sight, and trouble me no more.	Edw	2.2.216		Edward
My house is not farre hence, out of the way/A little, but our	Edw	2.5.100		Penbrk
Thou shalt have crownes of us, t'out bid the Barons, .	Edw	3.1.55		Edward
As much as thou in rage out wentst the rest. . . .	Edw	3.1.240		Edward
I thinke king Edward will out-run us all.	Edw	4.2.68		Prince
Let Plutos bels ring out my fatall knell, ...	Edw	4.7.89		Edward
Call me not lorde, away, out of my sight:	Edw	5.1.113		Edward
Come, come, away, now put the torches out, ...	Edw	5.3.47		Matrvs
Send for him out thence, and I will anger him. . . .	Edw	5.5.13		Gurney
O would my bloud dropt out from every vaine, ...	Edw	5.5.66		Edward
How comes it then that thou art out of hell? . . .	F 303	1.3.75		Faust
Why this is hell: nor am I out of it.	F 304	1.3.76		Mephst
Yes, and goings out too, you may see sir.	F 347	1.4.5	P	Robin
nakednesse, I know the Villaines out of service, and so hungry,	F 349	1.4.7	P	Wagner
I'le cull thee out the fairest Curtezans, ...	F 537	2.1.149		Mephst
Out envious wretch <Away envious rascall>: . . .	F 685	2.2.134		Faust
out of a Lyons mouth when I was scarce <half> an houre old,	F 687	2.2.136	P	Wrath
keep out of the circle, I say, least I send you into the Ostry	F 732	2.3.11	P	Robin
But new exploits do hale him out agen, ...	F 770	2.3.49		2Chor
I thinke it be some Ghost crept out of Purgatory, and now is	F1060	3.2.80	P	Archbp
Never out face me for the matter, for sure the cup is betweene	F1107	3.3.20	P	Vintnr
I am content for this once to thrust my head out at a window:	F1200	4.1.46	P	Benvol
beast is yon, that thrusts his head out at [the] window. .	F1275	4.1.121	P	Faust
it will weare out ten birchin broomes I warrant you. .	F1384	4.2.60	P	Benvol
Wee'l put out his eyes, and they shall serve for buttons to his	F1387	4.2.63	P	Benvol
I'le out-run him, and cast this leg into some ditch or other.	F1495	4.4.39	P	HrsCsr
doubt of that, for me thinkes you make no hast to wipe it out.	F1517	4.5.13	P	Hostss
and drinke a while, and then we'le go seeke out the Doctor.	F1557	4.5.53	P	Robin
They all cry out to speake with Doctor Faustus. . .	F1600	4.6.43		Servnt
in the house, and dash out all your braines with your Bottles.	F1619	4.6.62	P	HrsCsr
And see [where God]/[Stretcheth out his Arme, and bends his	F1944	5.2.148A		Faust
I, and goings out too, you may see else.	F App	p.229 5	P	Clown
the vilaine is bare, and out of service, and so hungry, that I	F App	p.229 7	P	Wagner
out of Purgatory come to begge a pardon of your holinesse.	F App	p.232 14	P	Lorein
it, and she has sent me to looke thee out, prethee come away.	F App	p.233 9	P	Rafe
Keepe out, keep out, or else you are blowne up, you are .	F App	p.233 10	P	Robin
Rafe, keepe out, for I am about a roaring peece of worke.	F App	p.233 11	P	Robin
Ifaith thy head will never be out of the potage pot. .	F App	p.236 48	P	Robin
but Ile seeke out my Doctor, and have my fortie dollers againe,	F App	p.240 136	P	HrsCsr
Thy selfe thus shivered out to three mens shares: . .	Lucan, First Booke			85
but being worne away/They both burst out, and each incounter	Lucan, First Booke			103
Filling the world, leapes out and throwes forth fire, .	Lucan, First Booke			154
He thus cride out:	Lucan, First Booke			197
With jawes wide open ghastly roaring out;	Lucan, First Booke			212
Ile bouldly quarter out the fields of Rome;	Lucan, First Booke			383
which he hath brought/From out their Northren parts, and that	Lucan, First Booke			479
Fierce Mastives hould; the vestall fires went out, . .	Lucan, First Booke			547
While these thus in and out had circled Roome, . . .	Lucan, First Booke			604
No vaine sprung out but from the yawning gash, . . .	Lucan, First Booke			613
these he seeing what myschiefes must ensue,/Cride out, O gods!	Lucan, First Booke			630
The course of mischiefe, and stretch out the date/Of slaughter;	Lucan, First Booke			670
Tooke out the shaft, ordaind my hart to shiver: . .	Ovid's Elegies			1.1.26
<make> slender/And to get out doth like apt members render.	Ovid's Elegies			1.6.6
Though it be so, shut me not out therefore, . . .	Ovid's Elegies			1.6.47
Let him within heare bard out lovers prate. . . .	Ovid's Elegies			1.8.78
Farmes out her-self on nights for what she can. . .	Ovid's Elegies			1.10.30
Going out againe passe forth the dore more wisely/And som-what	Ovid's Elegies			1.12.5
And him that hew'd you out for needfull uses/Ile prove had	Ovid's Elegies			1.12.15
Or thrids which spiders slender foote drawes out/Fastning her	Ovid's Elegies			1.14.7
Snatching the combe, to beate the wench out drive <drave> her.	Ovid's Elegies			1.14.18
To please thy selfe, thy selfe put out of minde. . .	Ovid's Elegies			1.14.38
Even Jove himselfe out off my wit was reft. . . .	Ovid's Elegies			2.1.18
All wasting years have that complaint [out] <not> worne. .	Ovid's Elegies			2.6.8
Whose life nine ages scarce bring out of date. . .	Ovid's Elegies			2.6.36
While rashly her wombes burthen she casts out, . . .	Ovid's Elegies			2.13.1
I would not out, might I in one place hit, . . .	Ovid's Elegies			2.15.19
At least now conquer, and out-runne the rest: . . .	Ovid's Elegies			3.2.79
All being shut out, th'adulterer is within. . . .	Ovid's Elegies			3.4.8
Troy had not yet beene ten yeares siege out-stander, .	Ovid's Elegies			3.5.27
In skipping out her naked feete much grac'd her. . .	Ovid's Elegies			3.6.82
Courts shut the poore out; wealth gives estimation, . .	Ovid's Elegies			3.7.55
And by thine eyes whose radiance burnes out mine. . .	Ovid's Elegies			3.10.48
Our verse great Tityus a huge space out-spreads, . .	Ovid's Elegies			3.11.25
Your golden ensignes [plucke] <pluckt> out of my field, .	Ovid's Elegies			3.14.16
Jove might have sipt out Nectar from his hand. . . .	Hero and Leander			1.62
And with the other, wine from grapes out wroong. . .	Hero and Leander			1.140
And oft look't out, and mus'd he did not come. . .	Hero and Leander			2.22
As loath to see Leander going out.	Hero and Leander			2.98
And steale a kisse, and then run out and daunce, . .	Hero and Leander			2.185
Defend the fort, and keep the foe-man out. . . .	Hero and Leander			2.272
Breathlesse spoke some thing, and sigh'd out the rest; .	Hero and Leander			2.280
But as her naked feet were whipping out, ...	Hero and Leander			2.313

OUT A DOORES

Seiz'd all I had, and thrust me out a doores, . . .	Jew	2.3.76		Baraba

OUTCRYES			
With whose outcryes Atrides being apal'd, ...	Dido	2.1.129	Aeneas
Ile follow thee with outcryes nere the lesse, . . .	Dido	4.2.55	Anna
OUT FACE			
Never out face me for the matter, for sure the cup is betweene	F1107	3.3.20	P Vintnr
OUTFACE			
I, and outface him to, doe what he can.	Dido	3.3.40	Cupid
OUT-HOUSE			
And in an out-house of the City shut/His souldiers, till I have	Jew	5.2.81	Barab
is a monastery/Which standeth as an out-house to the Towne;	Jew	5.3.37	Msngr
OUTLANDISH			
With base outlandish cullions at his heeles, ...	Edw	1.4.409	Mortmr
OUTLAST (See LASTS)			
OUT OF DATE			
Whose life nine ages scarce bring out of date. . . .	Ovid's Elegies		2.6.36
OUTRAGE			
And outrage strangling law and people strong, . . .	Lucan, First Booke		2
OUTRAGEOUS			
Outrageous death profanes all holy things/And on all creatures	Ovid's Elegies		3.8.19
OUTRAGES			
Daily commits incivill outrages, ...	1Tamb	1.1.40	Meandr
His losse made way for Roman outrages.	Lucan, First Booke		106
OUTRAGIOUS			
This countrie swarmes with vile outragious men, . .	1Tamb	2.2.22	Meandr
you suffer these outragious curses by these slaves of yours?	1Tamb	4.4.26	P Zenoc
Desirde her more, and waxt outragious, ...	Edw	2.2.55	Edward
For such outragious passions cloye my soule, . . .	Edw	5.1.19	Edward
'Faith you are too outragious, but come neere, . . .	F1609	4.6.52	Faust
OUTREACHT			
Come Guise and see thy traiterous guile outreacht, . .	P 962	19.32	King
OUT-RUN			
Nor me neither, I cannot out-run you Constable, oh my belly.	Jew	5.1.20	P Ithimr
I thinke king Edward will out-run us all.	Edw	4.2.68	Prince
I'le out-run him, and cast this leg into some ditch or other.	F1495	4.4.39	P HrsCsr
OUT-RUNNE			
At least now conquer, and out-runne the rest: . . .	Ovid's Elegies		3.2.79
OUTSHINES			
Outshines Cinthia's rayes:	Jew	2.3.62	Barab
OUTSIDE			
The outside of her garments were of lawne, . . .	Hero and Leander		1.9
OUT-SPREADS			
Our verse great Tityus a huge space out-spreads, . .	Ovid's Elegies		3.11.25
OUT-STANDER			
Troy had not yet beene ten yeares siege out-stander, .	Ovid's Elegies		3.5.27
OUTSTRETCHED			
And hath the power of his outstretched arme, . . .	2Tamb	2.2.42	Orcan
OUTWAIES			
as outwaies the sands/And all the craggie rockes of Caspea.	1Tamb	2.3.47	Tamb
OUTWARD			
If outward habit judge the inward man.	1Tamb	1.2.163	Tamb
from every flanke/May scoure the outward curtaines of the Fort,	2Tamb	3.2.80	Tamb
Now inward faults thy outward forme disgrace. . . .	Ovid's Elegies		1.10.14
OUTWEARE			
That ugly impe that shall outweare my wrath, . . .	Dido	3.2.4	Juno
OVER (See also O'ER, O'RE, ORE)			
How many dangers have we over past?	Dido	1.1.145	Aeneas
Our Masts the furious windes strooke over bourd: . .	Dido	3.1.110	Aeneas
The motion was so over violent.	Dido	4.1.13	Achat
Have triumpht over Affrike, and the bounds/Of Europe wher the	1Tamb	1.1.9	Cosroe
To triumph over many Provinces.	1Tamb	1.1.173	Cosroe
do but joine with me/And we will triumph over all the world.	1Tamb	1.2.173	Tamb
Triumphing over him and these his kings, ...	1Tamb	3.3.128	Tamb
whose worthinesse/Deserves a conquest over every hart: .	1Tamb	5.1.208	Tamb
Over my Zenith hang a blazing star, ...	2Tamb	3.2.6	Tamb
And over thy Argins and covered waies/Shal play upon the .	2Tamb	3.3.23	Therid
Over whose Zenith cloth'd in windy aire, ...	2Tamb	3.4.61	Therid
Gods great lieftenant over all the world:	2Tamb	3.5.2	2Msngr
To triumph over cursed Tamburlaine.	2Tamb	5.2.30	Callap
And Bacchus vineyards [over-spread] <ore-spread> the world:	Jew	4.2.92	Ithimr
As ancient Romanes over their Captive Lords, . . .	P 982	19.52	Guise
So will I triumph over this wanton King, ...	P 983	19.53	Guise
Am I a king and must be over rulde?	Edw	1.1.135	Edward
Was ever king thus over rulde as I?	Edw	1.4.38	Edward
My lord of Cornewall is a comming over, ...	Edw	2.1.76	Neece
My sonne and I will over into France, ...	Edw	2.4.65	Queene
How meanst thou Mortimer? that is over base. . . .	Edw	2.5.71	Gavstn
My lords, I will not over wooe your honors, . . .	Edw	2.5.86	Penbrk
For which thy head shall over looke the rest, . . .	Edw	3.1.239	Edward
Fly, fly, my Lord, the Queene is over strong, . . .	Edw	4.5.1	Spencr
And that I be protector over him, ...	Edw	5.2.12	Mortmr
Doe looke to be protector over the prince?	Edw	5.2.89	Mortmr
of love/In Courts of Kings, where state is over-turn'd, .	F 4	Prol.4	1Chor
And melting, heavens conspir'd his over-throw: . . .	F 22	Prol.22	1Chor
Thus having triumpht over you, I will set my countenance like a	F 213	1.2.20	P Wagner
O that there would come a famine over <through> all the world,	F 682	2.2.131	P Envy
Over the which [foure] <two> stately Bridges leane, . .	F 815	3.1.37	Mephst
And like a Steeple over-peeres the Church.	F 913	3.1.135	Pope
if a man be drunke over night, the Divell cannot hurt him in	F1201	4.1.47	P Benvol
such a horse, as would run over hedge and ditch, and never tyre,	F1538	4.5.34	P HrsCsr
the yeare is divided into two circles over the whole world, so	F1582	4.6.25	P Faust
[My faith, vile hel, shall triumph over thee], . . .	F1793	5.1.120A	OldMan
To over-reach the Divell, but all in vaine;	F1811	5.2.15	Mephst
He is not well with being over solitarie.	F1829	5.2.33	3Schol

OVER (cont.)

<Belike he is growne into some sicknesse, by> being over — F1829 (HC270)A P 3Schol
like those bright shining Saints,/And triumpht over hell: — F1906 5.2.110 GdAngl
divell, so I should be cald kill divell all the parish over. — F App p.230 49 P Clown
the water, ride him over hedge or ditch, or where thou wilt, — F App p.239 112 P Faust
the yeere is divided into twoo circles over the whole worlde, — F App p.242 20 P Faust
Love over-rules my will, I must obay thee, — Lucan, First Booke 373
Great are thy kingdomes, over strong and large, — Ovid's Elegies 1.1.17
Over my Mistris is my right more great? — Ovid's Elegies 1.7.30
Mounts, and raine-doubled flouds he passeth over, — Ovid's Elegies 1.9.11
To over-come, so oft to fight I shame. — Ovid's Elegies 2.7.2
Had then swum over, but the way was blinde. — Ovid's Elegies 2.16.32
Rather thou large banke over-flowing river, — Ovid's Elegies 3.5.19
She proudly sits) more over-rules the flood, — Hero and Leander 1.111
For will in us is over-rul'd by fate. — Hero and Leander 1.168

OVERBEARE
The Barons overbeare me with their pride. — Edw 3.1.9 Edward

OVER BOURD
Our Masts the furious windes strooke over bourd: — Dido 3.1.110 Aeneas

OVERCLOY
That overcloy my soule with their content: — Dido 3.2.63 Juno

OVER-COME (See also O'RECOME)
To over-come, so oft to fight I shame. — Ovid's Elegies 2.7.2

OVERCOME
He is alive, Troy is not overcome. — Dido 2.1.30 Aeneas
And truely to, how Troy was overcome: — Dido 2.1.107 Dido
But all in this that Troy is overcome, — Dido 2.1.112 Dido
And prophecied Troy should be overcome: — Dido 2.1.142 Aeneas
As therewithall the old man overcome, — Dido 2.1.157 Aeneas
We banquetted till overcome with wine, — Dido 2.1.178 Aeneas
If words might move me I were overcome. — Dido 5.1.154 Aeneas
Sent from the King to overcome us all. — 1Tamb 1.2.112 Souldr
And I that triumpht so be overcome. — 1Tamb 1.2.115 Tamb
Than Tamburlaine be slaine or overcome. — 1Tamb 1.2.177 Tamb
Were turnde to men, he should be overcome: — 2Tamb 1.3.164 Tamb
She overcome with shame and sallow feare, — Hero and Leander 2.260

OVERDARE
To overdare the pride of Graecia, — 2Tamb 3.5.66 Tamb

OVERDARING
Meete you for this, proud overdaring peeres? — Edw 1.4.47 Edward

OVERFLOW
Shall overflow it with their refluence. — Jew 3.5.18 Govnr
And made the channels overflow with blood, — Edw 4.4.12 Queene

OVER-FLOWING
Rather thou large banke over-flowing river, — Ovid's Elegies 3.5.19

OVERGO (See CERGONE)

OVERGREAT
Alas, my Lord, the summe is overgreat, — Jew 1.2.8 Govnr

OVERGROWE
age you wrackes/And sluttish white-mould overgrowe the waxe. — Ovid's Elegies 1.12.30

OVERHEAD (See O'REHEAD)

OVERJOY
And overjoy my thoughts with their escape: — Dido 3.3.57 Aeneas

OVERJOYED
Achates, speake, for I am overjoyed. — Dido 2.1.54 Aeneas
At whose accursed feete as overjoyed, — Dido 2.1.177 Aeneas

OVERJOYES
This salutation overjoyes my heart. — Edw 1.4.344 Lncstr

OVER LOOKE
For which thy head shall over looke the rest, — Edw 3.1.239 Edward

OVERMATCH
Thou wouldst with overmatch of person fight, — 2Tamb 3.5.76 Orcan

OVERMATCHING
A thousand sworne and overmatching foes: — 1Tamb 2.1.39 Cosroe

OVER NIGHT
if a man be drunke over night, the Divell cannot hurt him in — F1201 4.1.47 P Benvol

OVER PAST
How many dangers have we over past? — Dido 1.1.145 Aeneas

OVERPAST
Come my Lords, now that this storme is overpast, — P 804 16.18 Navrre
Now Caesar overpast the snowy Alpes, — Lucan, First Booke 185

OVERPEERD
We will not thus be facst and overpeerd. — Edw 1.4.19 Mortmr

OVER-PEERES
And like a Steeple over-peeres the Church. — F 913 3.1.135 Pope

OVER-REACH
To over-reach the Divell, but all in vaine; — F1811 5.2.15 Mephst

OVERRUL'D
Hence came it that th'edicts were overrul'd, — Lucan, First Booke 178

OVER-RUL'D
For will in us is over-rul'd by fate. — Hero and Leander 1.168

OVER RULDE
Am I a king and must be over rulde? — Edw 1.1.135 Edward
Was ever king thus over rulde as I? — Edw 1.4.38 Edward

OVER-RULES
Love over-rules my will, I must obay thee, — Lucan, First Booke 373
She proudly sits) more over-rules the flood, — Hero and Leander 1.111

OVERRUN
Fire the towne and overrun the land. — 2Tamb 3.5.9 2Msngr

OVERSIGHT
But now for quittance of this oversight, — Dido 3.1.84 Dido
fleete, what shall I doe/But dye in furie of this oversight? — Dido 5.1.269 Dido

OVER-SPREAD
And Bacchus vineyards [over-spread] <ore-spread> the world: — Jew 4.2.92 Ithimr

OVERSTRETCHED			
The murmuring commons overstretched hath.	Edw	2.2.160	Mortmr
OVERTAKE			
And overtake the tusked Bore in chase.	Dido	1.1.208	Venus
And till thou overtake me Tamburlaine, ...	1Tamb	2.5.44	Cosroe
OVERTHREW			
Then that which grim Atrides overthrew:	Dido	5.1.3	Aeneas
As when my Emperour overthrew the Greeks:	1Tamb	3.3.204	Zabina
OVER-THROW			
And melting, heavens conspir'd his over-throw:	F 22	Prol.22	1Chor
OVERTHROW			
shall be wrought/The warres of Troy, but not Troyes overthrow:	Dido	3.1.125	Dido
their fellowes throats/And make us triumph in their overthrow.	1Tamb	2.2.50	Meandr
best to be atchiev'd/In pursuit of the Cities overthrow? .	1Tamb	3.1.57	Fesse
And makes my soule devine her overthrow.	1Tamb	3.2.87	Agidas
Whom I have brought to see their overthrow.	1Tamb	3.3.81	Bajzth
And making bonfires for my overthrow.	1Tamb	3.3.238	Bajzth
Then it should so conspire my overthrow.	1Tamb	4.2.11	Tamb
Great Tamburlaine, great in my overthrow, ...	1Tamb	4.2.75	Bajzth
have ye lately heard/The overthrow of mightie Bajazeth, .	1Tamb	4.3.24	Arabia
Were but to bring our wilfull overthrow, ...	1Tamb	5.1.5	Govnr
And therfore grieve not at your overthrow, ...	1Tamb	5.1.446	Tamb
And I am pleasde with this my overthrow, ...	1Tamb	5.1.482	Souldn
That in the fortune of their overthrow, ...	2Tamb	2.1.24	Fredrk
That with such treason seek our overthrow, ...	2Tamb	2.2.34	Gazell
the enimie hath made/Gives such assurance of our overthrow,	2Tamb	5.1.3	Maxim
Know, Calymath, I aym'd thy overthrow, ...	Jew	5.5.83	Barab
To overthrow those [sectious] <sexious> <factious> Puritans:	P 850	17.45	Guise
Whose murderous thoughts will be his overthrow. . .	P1116	21.10	Dumain
Tis hard for us to worke his overthrow.	Edw	1.4.262	Mortmr
Ballads and rimes, made of thy overthrow.	Edw	2.2.178	Mortmr
Why gape you for your soveraignes overthrow? . . .	Edw	5.1.72	Edward
OVERTHROWES			
And make him after all these overthrowes, ...	2Tamb	5.2.29	Callap
OVERTHROWNE			
of our Empery/Once lost, All Turkie would be overthrowne:	2Tamb	1.1.56	Orcan
OVERTHWART			
Shot through the armes, cut overthwart the hands, . .	2Tamb	3.2.104	Tamb
OVERTHWARTING			
and blasts their eyes/With overthwarting flames, and raging	Lucan, First Booke		156
OVER-TURN'D			
of love/In Courts of Kings, where state is over-turn'd, .	F 4	Prol.4	1Chor
OVERWATCHDE			
Your overwatchde my lord, lie downe and rest. . . .	Edw	5.5.92	Ltborn
OVERWAY			
Shall overway his wearie witlesse head, ...	1Tamb	2.1.46	Cosroe
OVERWEIGHING			
Or be the means the overweighing heavens/Have kept to qualifie	1Tamb	5.1.45	Govnr
OVERWHELME (See also OREWHELME)			
Or the Ocean to overwhelme the world.	F 267	1.3.39	Faust
OVERWHELMES			
That like a mountaine overwhelmes my blisse, ...	Edw	5.1.54	Edward
OVID			
I Ovid Poet of [my] <thy> wantonnesse, ...	Ovid's Elegies		2.1.1
And to the Gods for that death Ovid prayes.	Ovid's Elegies		2.10.30
OVIDS			
I am like to Ovids Flea, I can creepe into every corner of a	F 665	2.2.114	P Pride
We which were Ovids five books, now are three, ...	Ovid's Elegies		1.1.1
OWE			
Is this the dutie that you owe your king?	Edw	1.4.22	Kent
OWES			
word a Merchant's fled/That owes me for a hundred Tun of Wine:	Jew	2.3.244	Barab
OWING			
Have I debts owing; and in most of these, ...	Jew	4.1.73	Barab
OWLES			
To hoarse scrich-owles foule shadowes it allowes, . .	Ovid's Elegies		1.12.19
OWN			
Here father, cut it bravely as you did your own. . .	2Tamb	3.2.135	P Celeb
For your sake and his own he's welcome hither. . . .	Jew	2.3.233	Abigal
How liberally the villain gives me mine own gold. . .	Jew	4.4.48	P Barab
that he himself should occupy, which is his own free land.	P 812	17.7	P Souldr
blood,/Of thine own people patron shouldst thou be/But thou--	Edw	4.4.13	Queene
'Twas thine own seeking Faustus, thanke thy selfe. . .	F 555	2.2.4	Mephst
We sing, whose conquering swords their own breasts launcht,	Lucan, First Booke		3
OWNE			
Put thou about thy necke my owne sweet heart, ...	Dido	1.1.44	Jupitr
Why, let us build a Citie of our owne, ...	Dido	4.3.37	Illion
To too forgetfull of thine owne affayres, ...	Dido	5.1.30	Hermes
I hope our Ladies treasure and our owne, ...	1Tamb	1.2.74	Agidas
Enchast with precious juelles of mine owne:	1Tamb	1.2.96	Tamb
Nay, thine owne is easier to come by, plucke out that, and twil	1Tamb	4.4.13	P Tamb
are you so daintily brought up, you cannot eat your owne flesh?	1Tamb	4.4.37	P Tamb
Zenocrate, were Egypt Joves owne land, ...	1Tamb	4.4.73	Tamb
Therefore in that your safeties and our owne, ...	1Tamb	5.1.40	Govnr
lives were weigh'd/In equall care and ballance with our owne,	1Tamb	5.1.42	Govnr
Whose lives were dearer to Zenocrate/Than her owne life, or	1Tamb	5.1.338	Zenoc
to Zenocrate/Than her owne life, or ought save thine owne love.	1Tamb	5.1.338	Zenoc
I shall now revenge/My fathers vile abuses and mine owne.	2Tamb	3.5.91	Callap
Their cruel death, mine owne captivity, ...	2Tamb	5.2.20	Callap
To make a Nunnery, where none but their owne sect/Must enter in;	Jew	1.2.256	Abigal
I doe not doubt by your divine precepts/And mine owne industry,	Jew	1.2.335	Abigal
And wilt not see thine owne afflictions, ...	Jew	1.2.353	1Fryar
Nor goe to bed, but sleepes in his owne clothes; . .	Jew	4.1.132	Ithimr

OWNE (cont.)

Upon mine owne free-hold within fortie foot of the gallowes, Jew 4.2.16 P Pilia
Nay [to] thine owne cost, villaine, if thou com'st. . . Jew 4.3.59 Barab
lov'd Rice, that Fryar Bernardine slept in his owne clothes. Jew 4.4.76 P Ithimr
poyson'd his owne daughter and the Nuns, strangled a Fryar, Jew 5.1.13 P Pilia
strangled Bernardine, poyson'd the Nuns, and his owne daughter. Jew 5.1.34 P Ithimr
And by this meanes the City is your owne. . . . . . Jew 5.1.94 Barab
And although you take out nothing but your owne, yet you put in P 808 17.3 P Souldr
Nay for the Popes sake, and thine owne benefite. . . P 827 17.22 Eprnon
thoughe you take out none but your owne treasure . . Paris ms 3,p390 P Souldr
hes to have the choyce of his owne freeland | yf it be not to Paris ms 8,p390 P Souldr
Looke to your owne heads, his is sure enough. . . . Edw 2.2.92 Edward
Looke to your owne crowne, if you back him thus. . . Edw 2.2.93 Warwck
These Barons thus to beard me in my land,/In mine owne realme? Edw 3.1.15 Spencr
in others and their sides/With their owne weapons gorde, . Edw 4.4.8 Queene
[Yet not your words onely, but mine owne fantasie], . . F 130 1.1.102A Faust
No, I came now hether of mine owne accord. . . . F 272 1.3.44 Mephst
The god thou serv'st is thine owne appetite, . . . F 399 2.1.11 Faust
And wright a Deed of Gift with thine owne bloud; . . F 424 2.1.36 Mephst
at some certaine day/Great Lucifer may claime it as his owne, F 440 2.1.52 Mephst
Why shouldst thou not? is not thy soule thine owne? . . F 457 2.1.69 Faust
appeare to thee in their owne proper shapes and likenesse. F 656 2.2.105 P Belzeb
And if that Bruno by his owne assent, ... F 957 3.1.179 Faust
thee not to sleepe much, having such a head of thine owne. F1285 4.1.131 P Emper
It is your owne you meane, feele on your head. . . . F1443 4.3.13 Fredrk
I writ them a bill with mine owne bloud, the date is expired: F1860 5.2.64 P Faust
and ifaith I meane to search some circles for my owne use: F App p.233 3 P Robin
then turn her and wind hir to thy owne use, as often as thou F App p.234 28 P Robin
O brave Robin, shal I have Nan Spit, and to mine owne use? F App p.234 29 P Rafe
root be weake, and his owne waight/Keepe him within the ground, Lucan, First Booke 139
And that his owne ten ensignes, and the rest/Marcht not . Lucan, First Booke 473
To mine owne selfe have I had strength so furious? . . Ovid's Elegies 1.7.25
By thine owne hand and fault thy hurt doth growe, . . Ovid's Elegies 1.14.43
loves bowe/His owne flames best acquainted signes may knowe, Ovid's Elegies 2.1.8
With her owne armor was my wench defended. . . . Ovid's Elegies 2.5.48
And as a traitour mine owne fault confesse. . . . Ovid's Elegies 2.8.26
Mine owne desires why should my selfe not flatter? . . Ovid's Elegies 2.11.54
And their owne privie weapon'd hands destroy them. . . Ovid's Elegies 2.14.4
My selfe poore wretch mine owne gifts now envie. . . Ovid's Elegies 2.15.8
Domesticke acts, and mine owne warres to sing. . . . Ovid's Elegies 2.18.12
Thou fightst against me using mine owne verse. . . . Ovid's Elegies 3.1.38
Her owne request to her owne torment turnd. . . . Ovid's Elegies 3.3.38
Perchance these, others, me mine owne losse mooves. . . Ovid's Elegies 3.5.100
And to thine owne losse was thy wit swift running. . . Ovid's Elegies 3.7.46
That leapt into the water for a kis/Of his owne shadow, and Hero and Leander 1.75
Though thou be faire, yet be not thine owne thrall. . . Hero and Leander 1.90
Some one or other keepes you as his owne. . . . . Hero and Leander 1.290
Fearing her owne thoughts made her to be hated. . . Hero and Leander 2.44
The mace returning backe, his owne hand hit, . . . Hero and Leander 2.211
And in her owne mind thought her selfe secure, . . . Hero and Leander 2.265

OWNER

Sometimes the owner of a goodly house, ... Jew 1.2.319 Abigal

OXEN

and two hundred yoake/Of labouring Oxen, and five hundred/Shee Jew 1.2.184 Barab
Yong oxen newly yokt are beaten more, ... Ovid's Elegies 1.2.13
Then oxen which have drawne the plow before. . . . Ovid's Elegies 1.2.14
Slow oxen early in the yoake are pent. . . . . Ovid's Elegies 1.13.16
Oxen in whose mouthes burning flames did breede? . . Ovid's Elegies 3.11.36

OXFORD

and my gentrie/Is fetcht from Oxford, not from Heraldrie. Edw 2.2.244 Baldck

OYLES

That bought my Spanish Oyles, and Wines of Greece, . . Jew 1.1.5 Barab
Belike they coasted round by Candie shoare/About their Oyles, Jew 1.1.92 Barab

OYSTER

I am Envy, begotten of a Chimney-sweeper, and an Oyster-wife: F 680 2.2.129 P Envy
would I might be turn'd to a gaping Oyster, and drinke nothing F1320 4.1.166 P Benvol

OYSTER-WIFE

I am Envy, begotten of a Chimney-sweeper, and an Oyster-wife: F 680 2.2.129 P Envy

PAC'D

alas, hath pac'd too long/The fatall Labyrinth of misbeleefe, Jew 3.3.63 Abigal
And on a proud pac'd Steed, as swift as thought, . . F 984 3.2.4 Mephst

PACE (See also APACE)

Why so, they barkt a pace a month agoe, ... Edw 4.3.12 Edward
Gallop a pace bright Phoebus through the skie, . . . Edw 4.3.43 Edward
And then things found do ever further pace. . . . Ovid's Elegies 2.9.10

PACES

Not past foure thousand paces at the most. . . . Dido 5.1.17 Aeneas
Steeds, disdainfully/With wanton paces trampling on the ground. 1Tamb 4.1.23 2Msngr
The Lydian buskin [in] fit [paces] <places> kept her. . Ovid's Elegies 3.1.14

PACIENCE

Yet is [their] <there> pacience of another sort, . . . P 545 11.10 Charls

PACIENT

And so be pacient good Lord Admirall, ... P 271 4.69 Charls

PACIFIE

That I may pacifie that gloomie Jove, ... Dido 4.2.2 Iarbus
To pacifie my countrie and my love, ... 1Tamb 5.1.396 Zenoc
Go pacifie their fury, set it ope, ... F1589 4.6.32 Duke

PACIS

I will be Paris <Pacis>, and for love of thee, ... F1775 5.1.102 Faust

PACKE

Fill'd with a packe of faintheart Fugitives, ... 2Tamb 5.1.36 Govnr

PACKT

Packt with the windes to beare Aeneas hence? . . . . Dido 4.4.127 Dido

PACOSTIPHOS			
Belseborams framanto pacostiphos tostu Mephastophilis, .	F App	p.235 25 P	Robin
PADALIA			
by the river Tyros I subdew'd/Stoka, Padalia, and Codemia.	2Tamb	1.3.210	Therid
PADUA			
and from Padua/Were wont to come rare witted Gentlemen, .	Jew	3.1.6	Curtzn
From thence to Venice, Padua, and the [rest] <East>, .	F 794	3.1.16	Faust
Lord Cardinals of France and Padua, ...	F 881	3.1.103	Pope
PAEAN (See PEAN)			
PAGAN			
We may discourage all the pagan troope, ...	2Tamb	2.1.25	Fredrk
With expedition to assaile the Pagan, ...	2Tamb	2.1.62	Sgsmnd
PAGANISME			
Christians death/And scourge their foule blasphemous Paganisme?	2Tamb	2.1.53	Fredrk
PAGANS			
These heathnish Turks and Pagans lately made, . . .	2Tamb	2.1.6	Fredrk
What irreligeous Pagans partes be these, ...	P1180	22.42	King
PAGEANT			
And now themselves shal make our Pageant, ...	2Tamb	4.3.90	Tamb
PAGEANTS			
And make us jeasting Pageants for their Trulles. . .	2Tamb	4.3.89	Therid
With famous pageants, and their home-bred beasts. . .	Ovid's Elegies	3.12.4	
PAGES			
Like Sylvian <Sylvan> Nimphes my pages shall be clad, .	Edw	1.1.58	Gavstn
PAID (See PAYD)			
PAIE			
While souldiers mutinie for want of paie.	Edw	1.4.406	Mortmr
PAILES			
And drinke in pailes the strongest Muscadell: . . .	2Tamb	4.3.19	Tamb
PAIND			
What ere thou art, farewell, be like me paind, . . .	Ovid's Elegies	1.6.71	
PAINE (See also PAYNES)			
That resteth in the rivall of thy paine, ...	Dido	3.3.84	Iarbus
For her that so delighteth in thy paine:	Dido	4.2.34	Anna
An uncouth paine torments my grieved soule, . . .	1Tamb	2.7.7	Cosroe
More honor and lesse paine it may procure, . . .	1Tamb	3.2.97	Agidas
From paine to paine, whose change shal never end: . .	2Tamb	2.3.26	Orcan
And quickly rid thee both of paine and life. . . .	2Tamb	3.4.25	Olymp
And sit in councell to invent some paine, ...	2Tamb	3.5.98	Callap
And now the damned soules are free from paine, . . .	2Tamb	4.2.91	Therid
Torture or paine can daunt my dreadlesse minde. . .	2Tamb	5.1.113	Govnr
Why, shal I sit and languish in this paine? . . .	2Tamb	5.3.56	Tamb
now, how Jove hath sent/A present medicine to recure my paine:	2Tamb	5.3.106	Tamb
A griping paine hath ceasde upon my heart:	P 537	11.2	Charls
I must say so, paine forceth me complaine. . . .	P 540	11.5	Charls
But yet it is no paine to speake men faire, . . .	Edw	1.1.42	Gavstn
Why, have you any paine that torture other <tortures others>?	F 432	2.1.44	Faust
That after this life there is any paine?	F 523	2.1.135	Faust
His store of pleasures must be sauc'd with paine. . .	F1812	5.2.16	Mephst
Impose some end to my incessant paine:	F1960	5.2.164	Faust
They that deserve paine, beare't with patience. . .	Ovid's Elegies	2.7.12	
But tender Damsels do it, though with paine, . . .	Ovid's Elegies	2.14.37	
Aye me, let not my warnings cause my paine. . . .	Ovid's Elegies	2.19.34	
But by my paine to purge her perjuries, ...	Ovid's Elegies	3.3.21	
Or in mine eyes good wench no paine transfuse. . . .	Ovid's Elegies	3.3.48	
And worshipt by their paine, and lying apart? . . .	Ovid's Elegies	3.9.16	
PAINED			
And by mine eyes, and mine were pained sore. . . .	Ovid's Elegies	3.3.14	
PAINEFULL			
And painefull nights have bin appointed me. . . .	Jew	1.2.198	Barab
PAINES			
That lingring paines may massacre his heart. . . .	1Tamb	5.1.228	Zabina
Let the dishonor of the paines I feele, ...	2Tamb	2.3.5	Sgsmnd
And let your hates extended in his paines, ...	2Tamb	4.1.172	Orcan
Expell the hate wherewith he paines our soules. . .	2Tamb	4.1.173	Orcan
And with the paines my rigour shall inflict, . . .	2Tamb	4.1.184	Tamb
spirits may vex/Your slavish bosomes with continuall paines,	2Tamb	5.1.46	Govnr
Or els be sure thou shalt be forc'd with paines, . .	2Tamb	5.1.52	Therid
Your paines do pierce our soules, no hope survives, . .	2Tamb	5.3.166	Celeb
If not resolv'd into resolved paines, ...	2Tamb	5.3.187	Amyras
I banne their soules to everlasting paines/And extreme tortures	Jew	1.2.166	Barab
of those Nuns/And holy Fryers, having mony for their paines,	Jew	2.3.81	Barab
Though gentle mindes should pittie others paines, . .	P 215	4.13	Anjoy
It will not countervaile his paines I hope, . . .	P 735	14.38	Navrre
To light as heavy as the paines of hell.	F 939	3.1.161	Pope
No mortall can expresse the paines of hell. . . .	F1716	5.1.43	OldMan
And now must taste hels paines perpetually. . . .	F1895	5.2.99	BdAngl
Trust in good verse, Tibullus feeles deaths paines, . .	Ovid's Elegies	3.8.39	
PAINFULL			
And though they think their painfull date is out, . .	2Tamb	5.3.34	Usumc
Immortall powers, that knowes the painfull cares, . .	Edw	5.3.37	Edward
The painfull Hinde by thee to field is sent, . . .	Ovid's Elegies	1.13.15	
PAINT (See also PAYNTED)			
As these thy protestations doe paint forth, . . .	Dido	3.2.54	Venus
Ah were I now but halfe so eloquent/To paint in woords, what	2Tamb	1.2.10	Callap
PAINTED			
Where painted Carpets o're the meads are hurl'd, . .	Jew	4.2.91	Ithimr
They whom the Lingones foild with painted speares, . .	Lucan, First Booke	398	
Such were they as [Dione] <Diana> painted stands/All naked	Ovid's Elegies	1.14.33	
The Ocean hath no painted stones or shelles, . . .	Ovid's Elegies	2.11.13	
Love laughed at my cloak, and buskines painted, . .	Ovid's Elegies	2.18.15	
Coate-tuckt Dianas legges are painted like them, . .	Ovid's Elegies	3.2.31	
Or Thamiras in curious painted things?	Ovid's Elegies	3.6.62	

PAINTED (cont.)			
Her painted fanne of curled plumes let fall,	Hero and Leander		2.11
PAIRE			
a paire of hornes on's head as e're thou sawest in thy life.	F 737	2.3.16	P Robin
PAISANT			
His presence made the rudest paisant melt,	Hero and Leander		1.79
PAIS'D			
Where fancie is in equall ballance pais'd).	Hero and Leander		2.32
PALACE (See also PALLACE)			
This is the goodly Palace of the Pope:	F 804	3.1.26	Mephst
PALATE			
Yet words in thy benummed palate rung,	Ovid's Elegies		2.6.47
PALATINE (See PALLATINE)			
PALE (Homograph)			
Whose memorie like pale deaths stony mace,	Dido	2.1.115	Aeneas
Heavens envious of our joyes is waxen pale,	Dido	4.4.52	Dido
Pale of complexion:	1Tamb	2.1.19	Menaph
a heavenly face/Should by hearts sorrow wax so wan and pale,	1Tamb	3.2.5	Agidas
And casts a pale complexion on his cheeks.	1Tamb	3.2.75	Agidas
My vaines are pale, my sinowes hard and drie,	1Tamb	4.4.97	Bajzth
Now waxe all pale and withered to the death,	1Tamb	5.1.91	1Virgn
Jove viewing me in armes, lookes pale and wan,	1Tamb	5.1.452	Tamb
Sadly supplied with pale and ghastly death,	2Tamb	2.4.83	Tamb
My Lord, your presence makes them pale and wan.	2Tamb	3.5.60	Usumc
monster death/Shaking and quivering, pale and wan for feare,	2Tamb	5.3.68	Tamb
Pale death may walke in furrowes of my face:	P 158	2.101	Guise
As pale as ashes, nay then tis time to look about.	P1001	19.71	Guise
And meete me at the parke pale presentlie:	Edw	2.1.73	Neece
Lives uncontroulde within the English pale,	Edw	2.2.165	Lncstr
And when I frowne, make all the court looke pale,	Edw	5.4.53	Mortmr
Strooke with th'earths suddaine shadow waxed pale,	Lucan, First Booke		537
She nothing said, pale feare her tongue had tyed.	Ovid's Elegies		1.7.20
For thee the East and West winds make me pale,	Ovid's Elegies		2.11.9
Grew pale, and in cold foords hot lecherous.	Ovid's Elegies		3.5.26
Greefe makes her pale, because she mooves not there.	Hero and Leander		1.60
Nor that night-wandring pale and watrie starre,	Hero and Leander		1.107
PALESTINA			
From Palestina and Jerusalem,	2Tamb	3.5.32	Jrslem
PALLACE			
Who then ran to the pallace of the King,	Dido	2.1.224	Aeneas
That leads to Pallace of my brothers life,	1Tamb	2.1.43	Cosroe
Up to the pallace of th'imperiall heaven:	2Tamb	2.4.35	Tamb
Batter the shining pallace of the Sun,	2Tamb	2.4.105	Tamb
Of Joves vast pallace the imperiall Orbe,	2Tamb	3.4.49	Therid
For there my Pallace royal shal be plac'd:	2Tamb	4.3.111	Tamb
And plowes to go about our pallace gates.	Edw	3.1.216	Edward
at whose pallace now]/[Faustus is feasted mongst his noblemen].	F1151	3.3.64A	3Chor
Who builds a pallace and rams up the gate,	Hero and Leander		1.239
Then towards the pallace of the Destinies,	Hero and Leander		1.377
For here the stately azure pallace stood,	Hero and Leander		2.165
PALLACES			
That rooffes of golde, and sun-bright Pallaces,	1Tamb	4.2.62	Zabina
and utterly consume/Your cities and your golden pallaces,	2Tamb	4.1.193	Tamb
PALLAS			
Crowes <crow> [survive] <survives> armes-bearing Pallas hate,	Ovid's Elegies		2.6.35
And some few pastures Pallas Olives bore.	Ovid's Elegies		2.16.8
Pallas launce strikes me with unconquerd arme.	Ovid's Elegies		3.3.28
Flint-brested Pallas joies in single life,	Hero and Leander		1.321
But Pallas and your mistresse are at strife.	Hero and Leander		1.322
PALLATINE			
That thou thy self, then County-Pallatine,	2Tamb	1.1.94	Orcan
Then County-Pallatine, but now a king:	2Tamb	1.1.104	Sgsmnd
PALME			
He holdes the palme: my palme is yet to gaine.	Ovid's Elegies		3.2.82
And doubt to which desire the palme to give.	Ovid's Elegies		3.10.40
From him that yeelds the garland <palme> is quickly got,	Ovid's Elegies		3.13.47
PALPABLY			
Why Madam, thinke ye to mocke me thus palpably?	2Tamb	4.2.67	Therid
PALTRIE			
To apprehend that paltrie Scythian.	1Tamb	1.1.53	Mycet
Then sue for life unto a paltrie boye.	Edw	5.6.57	Mortmr
PALTRY			
Here have I purst their paltry [silverlings] <silverbings>.	Jew	1.1.6	Barab
My daughter here, a paltry silly girle.	Jew	2.3.284	Barab
Content, but we will leave this paltry land,	Jew	4.2.88	Ithimr
A petty <pretty> case of paltry Legacies:	F 57	1.1.29	Faust
PAMPELONIA			
And at the length in Pampelonia crowne,	P 580	11.45	Pleshe
PAMPERED			
Holla, ye pampered Jades of Asia:	2Tamb	4.3.1	Tamb
PAN			
and a Dagger with a hilt like a warming-pan, and he gave me a	Jew	4.2.29	P Ithimr
the fatall poyson/Workes within my head, my brain pan breakes,	P 185	3.20	OldQn
PANG (See also PANGUE)			
A sodaine pang, the messenger of death.	P 538	11.3	Charls
PANGES			
Ah that the deadly panges I suffer now,	1Tamb	5.1.422	Arabia
PANGEUS			
I see Pangeus hill,/With hoarie toppe, and under Hemus mount	Lucan, First Booke		678
PANGS			
the extremity of heat/To pinch me with intolerable pangs:	Jew	5.5.88	Barab
PANGUE			
Will every savour breed a pangue of death?	P 72	2.15	Guise

PANS			
the Nuns are dead/That sound at otner times like Tinkers pans?	Jew	4.1.3	Barab
PANT			
pant <pants> and quiver <quivers> to remember that I have beene	F1840	5.2.44	P Faust
PANTING			
That they lie panting on the Gallies side,	1Tamb	3.3.53	Tamb
Here man, rip up this panting brest of mine,	Edw	4.7.66	Edward
And with still panting rockt, there tooke his rest.	Hero and Leander		1.44
PANTS			
And pants untill I see that Conjurer dead.	F1352	4.2.28	Benvol
<pants> and quiver <quivers> to remember that I have beene a	F1840	5.2.44	P Faust
PAPALL			
To beat the papall Monarck from our lands,	P 802	16.16	Navrre
Which if I doe, the Papall Monarck goes/To wrack, and [his]	P1197	22.59	King
<incense>/The papall towers to kisse the [lowly] <holy> earth.	P1202	22.64	King
and enforce/The papall towers, to kisse the lowlie ground,	Edw	1.4.101	Edward
And crouch before the Papall dignity:	F 874	3.1.96	Pope
That doth assume the Papall government,	F 886	3.1.108	Pope
their late conspiracie/Against our State, and Papall dignitie?	F 950	3.1.172	Pope
PAPER			
Give me a Reame of paper, we'll have a kingdome of gold for't.	Jew	4.2.115	P Ithimr
Give me the paper.	Edw	1.4.3	ArchBp
So may his limmes be torne, as is this paper,	Edw	5.1.142	Edward
I hate faire Paper should writte matter lacke.	Ovid's Elegies		1.11.20
PAPERS			
These letters, lines, and perjurd papers all,	Dido	5.1.300	Dido
Take here these papers as our sacrifice/And witnesse of thy	2Tamb	2.2.45	Orcan
I might not go, whether my papers went.	Ovid's Elegies		3.7.6
PAPESTRY			
Whom God hath blest for hating Papestry.	P1208	22.70	King
PAPHOS			
By Paphos, Capys, and the purple Sea,	Dido	3.4.46	Aeneas
That Paphos, and the floud-beate Cithera guides.	Ovid's Elegies		2.17.4
PAPPE			
Then would I wish thee touch my mistris pappe,	Ovid's Elegies		2.15.11
PAR			
Par [le] <la> mor du, Il mora.	P 770	15.28	Guise
PARA			
Bien para todos mi ganado no es:	Jew	2.1.39	Barab
PARADICE			
Like tried silver runs through Paradice/To entertaine divine	2Tamb	2.4.24	Tamb
Talke not of Paradice or <nor> Creation, but marke the <this>	F 659	2.2.108	P Lucifr
PARADISE			
me, as Paradise was to Adam the first day of his creation.	F 657	2.2.106	P Faust
PARAGON			
The onely Paragon of Tamburlaine,	1Tamb	3.3.119	Tamb
[And only Paragon of excellence],	F1703	5.1.30A	1Schol
PARALELL			
Though from the shortest Northren Paralell,	2Tamb	1.1.25	Orcan
PARAMOUR			
and warlike semblances/Of Alexander and his beauteous Paramour.	F1171	4.1.17	Mrtino
Great Alexander, and his Paramour,	F1232	4.1.78	Emper
Great Alexander and his beauteous Paramour.	F1239	4.1.85	Faust
present the royall shapes/Of Alexander and his Paramour,	F1250	4.1.96	Faust
and thou bring Alexander and his Paramour before the Emperour,	F1255	4.1.101	P Benvol
That I may <might> have unto my paramour,	F1761	5.1.88	Faust
And none but thou shalt be my Paramour.	F1787	5.1.114	Faust
And bring with him his beauteous Paramour,	F App	p.237 32	Emper
spirites as can lively resemble Alexander and his Paramour,	F App	p.237 47	P Faust
you bring Alexander and his paramour before the emperor?	F App	p.237 52	P Knight
PARAPETS			
And Parapets to hide the Muscatters:	2Tamb	3.2.77	Tamb
PARBREAK			
Than noisome parbreak of the Stygian Snakes,	1Tamb	5.1.256	Bajzth
PARCEL			
To make it parcel of my Empery.	2Tamb	1.3.110	Tamb
PARCELL			
Which he observes as parcell of his fame,	1Tamb	5.1.14	Govnr
and Calor, which some holde/Is not a parcell of the Elements,	2Tamb	5.3.87	Phsitn
And serve as parcell of my funerall.	2Tamb	5.3.212	Tamb
PARCH (See also PARTCHT)			
for neither sunne nor wind/Would burne or parch her hands,	Hero and Leander		1.28
PARCHING			
Under the frosty beare, or parching East,	Lucan, First Booke		254
PARDON			
This place beseemes me not, O pardon me.	Dido	2.1.94	Aeneas
And then--O Dido, pardon me.	Dido	2.1.159	Aeneas
Iarbus pardon me, and stay a while.	Dido	3.1.46	Dido
Aeneas pardon me, for I forgot/That yong Ascanius lay with me	Dido	4.4.31	Dido
Pardon me though I aske, love makes me aske.	Dido	5.1.90	Dido
O pardon me, if I resolve thee why:	Dido	5.1.91	Aeneas
And bring us pardon in your chearfull lookes.	1Tamb	5.1.47	Govnr
Pardon my Love, oh pardon his contempt,	1Tamb	5.1.364	Zenoc
And pardon me that was not moov'd with ruthe,	1Tamb	5.1.369	Zenoc
Intreat a pardon of the God of heaven,	2Tamb	3.4.32	Olymp
thou shalt kneele to us/And humbly crave a pardon for thy life.	2Tamb	3.5.109	Orcan
Yet pardon him I pray your Majesty.	2Tamb	4.1.97	Therid
Let al of us intreat your highnesse pardon.	2Tamb	4.1.98	Tec&Us
Wil get his pardon if your grace would send.	2Tamb	5.1.33	1Citzn
I am a little busie, Sir, pray pardon me.	Jew	2.3.231	Barab
Pardon me though I weepe; the Governors sonne/Will, whether I	Jew	2.3.257	Barab
Nay, you shall pardon me:	Jew	3.3.73	Abigal
No, pardon me, the Law must have his course.	Jew	4.1.185	Barab

PARDON (cont.)

Pray pardon me, I must goe see a ship discharg'd. . . Jew 4.2.51 P Ithimr
O pardon me my Lord. . . . . P 679 13.23 Duchss
O pardon me my Lord of Guise. . . . . P 990 19.60 P 3Mur
Pardon thee, why what hast thou done? . . . . . P 991 19.61 Guise
Saving your reverence, you must pardon me. . . . . Edw 1.1.186 Gavstn
I meane not so, your grace must pardon me. . . . . Edw 1.4.153 Gavstn
Pardon me sweet, I forgot my selfe. . . . . . . Edw 2.2.230 Edward
Your pardon is quicklie got of Isabell. . . . . . Edw 2.2.231 Queene
gratifie the king/In other matters, he must pardon us in this, Edw 2.5.44 Warwck
my lord pardon my speeche,/Did you retaine your fathers . Edw 3.1.15 Spencr
Sir John of Henolt, pardon us I pray, ... Edw 4.2.71 Kent
Ah pardon me, greefe makes me lunatick. . . . . . Edw 5.1.114 Edward
Nay, you shall pardon me, none shall knowe my trickes. . Edw 5.4.39 Ltborn
Sweete mother, if I cannot pardon him, ... Edw 5.4.94 King
pardon [me] <him> for <in> this,/And Faustus vowes never to F 647 2.2.96 Faust
Purgatory, and now is come unto your holinesse for his pardon. F1061 3.2.81 P Archbp
O pardon me, my thoughts are ravished so/With sight of this F1260 4.1.106 Emper
intreat thy Lord/To pardon my unjust presumption, . . . F1748 5.1.75 Faust
out of Purgatory come to begge a pardon of your holinesse. F App p.232 15 P Lorein
Pardon me Jove, thy weapons ayde me nought, ... Ovid's Elegies 2.1.19

PARDONA

Pardona moy, be no in tune yet; so, now, now all be in. . Jew 4.4.45 P Barab
Pardona moy, Mounsier, [me] <we> be no well. . . . . Jew 4.4.71 Barab

PARDONED

But Faustus offence can nere be pardoned, the serpent that F1837 5.2.41 P Faust

PARDONS

I have procur'd your pardons: welcome all. . . . . F1610 4.6.53 Faust

PARENTAGE

Aeneas for his parentage deserves/As large a kingdome as is Dido 4.4.79 Achat
And yet a shepheard by my Parentage: . . . . . 1Tamb 1.2.35 Tamb
I <O I> come of a Royall Pedigree <parentage>, my father . F 696 2.2.145 P Glutny
Boasting his parentage, would needs discover/The way to new Hero and Leander 1.410

PARENTS

might behold/Young infants swimming in their parents bloud, Dido 2.1.193 Aeneas
When I record my Parents slavish life, ... 2Tamb 5.2.19 Callap
Now is he borne, of parents base of stocke, ... F 11 Prol.11 1Chor
I am Pride; I disdaine to have any parents: . . . . F 664 2.2.113 P Pride
my parents are all dead, and the devill a peny they have left F 693 2.2.142 P Glutny
Curst be the parents that ingendred me; . . . . . F1972 5.2.176 Faust
in armes; nor could the bed-rid parents/Keep back their sons, Lucan, First Booke 502
I gladly graunt my parents given to save, ... Ovid's Elegies 1.3.10
I might have then my parents deare misus'd, ... Ovid's Elegies 1.7.5
Both unkinde parents, but for causes sad, ... Ovid's Elegies 2.14.31
To Thracian Orpheus what did parents good? . . . . Ovid's Elegies 3.8.21

PARIAN

lookes shewed/Like marble from the Parian Mountaines hewed. Ovid's Elegies 1.7.52

PARIS (Homograph)

I this in Greece when Paris stole faire Helen. . . . . Dido 3.1.142 Aeneas
Say Paris, now shall Venus have the ball? . . . . . Dido 3.2.12 Juno
And Paris judgement of the heavenly ball, ... Dido 3.2.44 Juno
So thou wouldst prove as true as Paris did, ... Dido 5.1.146 Dido
As did Sir Paris with the Grecian Dame: . . . . . 1Tamb 1.1.66 Mycet
That all the protestants that are in Paris, ... P 34 1.34 Navrre
Paris hath full five hundred Colledges, ... P 137 2.80 Guise
which my Lord of Guise/Did make in Paris amongst the Hugonites? P 515 9.34 QnMoth
For had your highnesse seene with what a pompe/He entred Paris, P 873 17.68 Eprnon
Did they of Paris entertaine him so? . . . . . . P 879 17.74 King
For now that Paris takes the Guises parte, ... P 896 17.91 King
And that Paris is revolted from his grace. . . . . P 902 18.3 Navrre
sent from the President of Paris, that craves accesse unto your P1156 22.18 P 1Msngr
The President of Paris greetes your grace, ... P1168 22.30 Frier
Fire Paris where these trecherous rebels lurke. . . . P1241 22.103 King
From Paris next, costing the Realme of France, . . . F 784 3.1.6 Faust
Then when sir Paris crost the seas with <for> her, . . . F1694 5.1.21 Faust
I will be Paris <Pacis>, and for love of thee, ... F1775 5.1.102 Faust
What thanklesse Jason, Macareus, and Paris, ... Ovid's Elegies 2.18.23
There Paris is, and Helens crymes record, ... Ovid's Elegies 2.18.37

PARISH

divell, so I should be cald kill divell all the parish over. F App p.230 49 P Clown
in our parish dance at my pleasure starke naked before me, F App p.233 3 P Robin

PARKE

And meete me at the parke pale presentlie: . . . . Edw 2.1.73 Neece
Come sonne, weele ride a hunting in the parke. . . . Edw 5.4.113 Queene

PARLAMENT

Heere comes the king and the nobles/From the parlament, ile Edw 1.1.73 Gavstn

PARLE

Shall we parle with the Christian,/Or crosse the streame, and 2Tamb 1.1.11 Orcan
Tis requisit to parle for a peace/With Sigismond the king of 2Tamb 1.1.50 Gazell
A friendly parle might become ye both. . . . . . 2Tamb 1.1.117 Gazell
But stay a while, summon a parle, Drum, ... 2Tamb 3.3.11 Therid
And henceforth parle with our naked swords. . . . . Edw 1.1.126 Mortmr

PARLED

That you have parled with your Mortimer? . . . . . Edw 1.4.321 Edward
These lovers parled by the touch of hands, ... Hero and Leander 1.185

PARLEE

Stay Techelles, aske a parlee first. . . . . . . 1Tamb 1.2.137 Tamb

PARLEMENT

As then I did incense the parlement, ... Edw 1.1.184 BshpCv
But as the realme and parlement shall please, ... Edw 4.6.36 Mortmr
My lorde, the parlement must have present newes, . . . Edw 5.1.84 Trussl

PARLEY

Come, let thy shadow parley with king Edward. . . . Edw 2.6.14 Warwck

PARLEY (cont.)			
You shall gc parley with the king of Fraunce.	Edw	3.1.71	Edward
PARLIAMENT (See also PARLAMENT, PARLEMENT)			
Than if the Gods had held a Parliament:	1Tamb	2.7.66	Tamb
PARLIE			
And that shal bide no more regard of parlie.	2Tamb	5.1.61	Techel
In offring parlie, to be counted light.	Hero and Leander		2.9
Till gentle parlie did the truce obtaine.	Hero and Leander		2.278
PARLY (See also PARLEE)			
Thy selfe and I, may parly with this Pope:	F 896	3.1.118	Faust
I heard them parly with the Conjurer.	F1422	4.2.98	1Soldr
PARMA			
Philip and Parma, I am slaine for you:	P1011	19.81	Guise
And chase the Prince of Parma from our Land,	F 120	1.1.92	Faust
PARRAT			
The parrat from east India to me sent,	Ovid's Elegies		2.6.1
Such to the parrat was the turtle dove.	Ovid's Elegies		2.6.16
The Parrat given me, the farre [worlds] <words> best choice.	Ovid's Elegies		2.6.38
The Parrat into wood receiv'd with these,	Ovid's Elegies		2.6.57
'PARRELL			
Here's goodly 'parrell, is there not?	Jew	4.2.112	Ithimr
PARSON			
Our maister Parson sayes thats nothing.	F App	p.234 25 P	Rafe
PART			
Now is the time for me to play my part:	Dido	1.1.182	Venus
I will faire mother, and so play my part,	Dido	2.1.332	Cupid
In every part exceeding brave and rich.	1Tamb	1.2.127	Souldr
Before we part with our possession.	1Tamb	1.2.144	Tamb
Thy selfe and them shall never part from me,	1Tamb	1.2.245	Tamb
In every part proportioned like the man,	1Tamb	2.1.29	Menaph
To thinke thy puisant never staied arme/Will part their bodies,	1Tamb	5.1.89	1Virgn
Hath made our Poet pen his second part,	2Tamb	Prol.3	Prolog
The Westerne part of Affrike, where I view'd/The Ethiopian sea,	2Tamb	1.3.195	Techel
Natolia hath dismist the greatest part/Of all his armie, pitcht	2Tamb	2.1.16	Fredrk
Dismount the Cannon of the adverse part,	2Tamb	3.2.81	Tamb
That there begin and nourish every part,	2Tamb	3.4.7	Capt
Then by the Northerne part of Affrica,	2Tamb	5.3.140	Tamb
Must part, imparting his impressions,	2Tamb	5.3.170	Tamb
And of the third part of the Persian ships,	Jew	1.1.2	Barab
Nor will I part so slightly therewithall.	Jew	1.2.87	Barab
To shun suspition, therefore, let us part.	Jew	2.1.57	Abigal
Come home and there's no price shall make us part,	Jew	2.3.92	Barab
Nothing but death shall part my love and me.	Jew	2.3.317	Abigal
Part 'em, part 'em.	Jew	3.2.8	Within
I, part 'em now they are dead: Farewell, farewell.	Jew	3.2.9	Barab
For my part feare you not.	Jew	4.1.10	Ithimr
Part 'em, master, part 'em.	Jew	4.1.97	P Ithimr
Oh that I should part with so much gold!	Jew	4.3.51	Barab
We will not let thee part so suddenly:	Jew	5.5.98	Govnr
The ruines done to Malta and to us,/Thou canst not part:	Jew	5.5.113	Govnr
Now come thou forth and play thy tragick part,	P 85	2.28	Guise
Ere my sweete Gaveston shall part from me,	Edw	1.4.48	Edward
Therefore with dum imbracement let us part.	Edw	1.4.134	Edward
Content, ile beare my part, holla whose there?	Edw	2.2.130	Lncstr
That when I had him we might never part.	Edw	2.4.21	Queene
A bloudie part, flatly against law of armes.	Edw	3.1.121	Spencr
Tis not amisse my liege for eyther part,	Edw	3.1.190	SpncrP
A sweet Spencer, thus then must we part.	Edw	4.7.73	Edward
part we must,/Sweete Spencer, gentle Baldocke, part we must.	Edw	4.7.95	Edward
Sweete Spencer, gentle Baldocke, part we must.	Edw	4.7.96	Edward
That with his wings did part the subtle aire,	F 772	2.3.51	2Chor
And take some part of holy Peters feast,	F 777	2.3.56	2Chor
That make <makes> safe passage, to each part of Rome.	F 816	3.1.38	Mephst
<faine> see the Pope/And take some part of holy Peters feast,	F 832	3.1.54	Mephst
If any one part of vast heaven thou swayest,	Lucan, First Booke		56
Now while their part is weake, and feares, march hence,	Lucan, First Booke		281
And where thou drinkst, on that part I will sup.	Ovid's Elegies		1.4.32
But we must part, when heav'n with black night lowers.	Ovid's Elegies		1.4.60
Better I could part of my selfe have wanted.	Ovid's Elegies		1.7.24
In verse to praise kinde Wenches tis my part,	Ovid's Elegies		1.10.59
Who first depriv'd yong boyes of their best part,	Ovid's Elegies		2.3.3
And even the ring performe a mans part well.	Ovid's Elegies		2.15.26
Sulmo, Pelignies third part me containes,	Ovid's Elegies		2.16.1
Part of her sorrowe heere thy sister bearing,	Ovid's Elegies		3.8.51
And corne with least part of it selfe returnd.	Ovid's Elegies		3.9.30
all, and everie part/Strove to resist the motions of her hart.	Hero and Leander		1.363
would not yeeld/So soone to part from that she deerely held.	Hero and Leander		2.84
To part in twaine, that hee might come and go,	Hero and Leander		2.151
PARTAKE			
Yet if you would partake with me the cause/Of this devotion	Dido	4.2.27	Anna
And Governour, now partake my policy:	Jew	5.5.24	Barab
no my Lord, a woman only must/Partake the secrets of my heart.	P 676	13.20	Duchss
PARTAKER			
To be partaker of thy good or ill,	1Tamb	1.2.230	Therid
PARTAKERS			
To be partakers of our honey talke.	Dido	4.4.54	Dido
Each side had great partakers; Caesars cause,	Lucan, First Booke		128
PARTCHT			
which the heart ingenders/Are partcht and void of spirit,	2Tamb	5.3.95	Phsitn
PARTE			
For now that Paris takes the Guises parte,	P 896	17.91	King
Even from your cheekes parte of a voice did breake.	Ovid's Elegies		2.5.16
PARTED			
yet when we parted last,/He said he wud attend me in the morne.	Jew	2.1.33	Abigal

PARTED (cont.)
How comes it, that the king and he is parted? — Edw 2.4.41 Mortmr
Parted from hence, never to see us more! — Edw 4.7.101 Spencr
Parted in twaine, and with a double point/Rose like the Theban — Lucan, First Booke 549

PARTES
Drawes bloody humours from my feeble partes, — 1Tamb 4.4.95 Bajzth
What irreligeous Pagans partes be these, — P1180 22.42 King

PARTHIA
Mesopotamia and of Parthia, — 1Tamb 1.1.165 Ortyg
That now is marching neer to Parthia: — 1Tamb 2.1.65 Cosroe
Then thou for Parthia, they for Scythia and Medea. — 1Tamb 2.5.83 Tamb

PARTHIAN
which by fame is said/To drinke the mightie Parthian Araris, — 1Tamb 2.3.16 Tamb

PARTHIANS
Parthians y'afflict us more then ye suppose, — Lucan, First Booke 107
Or darts which Parthians backward shoot) marcht on/And then — Lucan, First Booke 232

PARTI
Looke like the parti-coloured cloudes of heaven, — 2Tamb 3.1.47 Jrslem

PARTIALL
In sounding through the world his partiall praise. — 1Tamb 4.3.49 Arabia
In partiall aid of that proud Scythian, — 2Tamb 2.2.16 Gazell
You partiall heavens, have I deserv'd this plague? — Jew 1.2.259 Barab
I sweare by this crosse, wee'l not be partiall, — P 325 5.52 Anjoy

PARTI-COLOURED
Looke like the parti-coloured cloudes of heaven, — 2Tamb 3.1.47 Jrslem

PARTICULAR
Law wils that each particular be knowne. — Jew 4.1.205 Barab

PARTICULARLY
we take particularly thine/To save the ruine of a multitude: — Jew 1.2.96 Govnr

PARTIE
And others of our partie and faction, — Edw 4.2.53 Mortmr

PARTING
As parting friends accustome on the shoare, — Dido 4.3.50 Aeneas
then was thy parting hence/Bitter and irkesome to my sobbing — Edw 2.2.57 Edward

PARTNER
But I no partner of my glory brooke, — Ovid's Elegies 2.12.11

PARTNERS
Dire league of partners in a kingdome last not. — Lucan, First Booke 86

PARTNERSHIP
Dominion cannot suffer partnership; — Lucan, First Booke 93

PARTRIDGES
but hee hides and buries it up as Partridges doe their egges, — Jew 4.2.58 P Ithimr

PARTS
Egregious Viceroyes of these Eastern parts/Plac'd by the issue — 2Tamb 1.1.1 Orcan
Where Egypt and the Turkish Empire parts, — 2Tamb 1.3.6 Tamb
Then will I comfort all my vital parts, — 2Tamb 5.3.100 Tamb
To hide those parts which men delight to see, — Edw 1.1.65 Gavstn
With winding bankes that cut it in two parts; — F 814 3.1.36 Mephst
which he hath brought/From out their Northren parts, and that — Lucan, First Booke 479
A small thin skinne contain'd the vital parts, — Lucan, First Booke 622
in being bold/To eie those parts, which no eie should behold. — Hero and Leander 1.408

PARTY (See PARTIE)

PASH
that in his infancie/Did pash the jawes of Serpents venomous: — 1Tamb 3.3.105 Bajzth
And through the gemme let thy lost waters pash. — Ovid's Elegies 2.15.24

PASSAGE
And cut a passage through his toples hilles: — Dido 4.3.12 Aeneas
Fighting for passage, tilt within the earth. — 1Tamb 1.2.51 Tamb
Though straight the passage and the port be made, — 1Tamb 2.1.42 Cosroe
And makes a passage for all prosperous Armes, — 1Tamb 2.3.38 Cosroe
That ere made passage thorow Persean Armes. — 1Tamb 2.3.56 Tamb
Fighting for passage, [makes] <make> the Welkin cracke, — 1Tamb 4.2.45 Tamb
To get a passage to Elisian. — 1Tamb 5.1.247 Zabina
And make a passage for my loathed life. — 1Tamb 5.1.304 Bajzth
And make a passage from the imperiall heaven/That he that sits — 2Tamb 2.2.48 Orcan
And sorrow stops the passage of my speech. — 2Tamb 3.2.52 Celeb
Making a passage for my troubled soule, — 2Tamb 4.2.34 Olymp
To make a passage for the running streames/And common channels — Jew 5.1.88 Barab
That make <makes> safe passage, to each part of Rome. — F 816 3.1.38 Mephst
Damb'd up thy passage; when thou took'st the booke, — F1887 5.2.91 Mephst
Which being broke the foot had easie passage. — Lucan, First Booke 224
Souse downe the wals, and make a passage forth: — Lucan, First Booke 296

PASS'D
Thee I have pass'd, and knew thy streame none such, — Ovid's Elegies 3.5.5

PASSE
See where her servitors passe through the hall/Bearing a — Dido 2.1.70 Serg
Through which he could not passe for slaughtred men: — Dido 2.1.262 Aeneas
To leave this towne and passe to Italy, — Dido 5.1.100 Aeneas
Ah Menaphon, I passe not for his threates, — 1Tamb 1.1.109 Cosroe
Passe into Graecia, as did Cyrus once. — 1Tamb 1.1.130 Menaph
To bid him battaile ere he passe too farre, — 1Tamb 2.5.95 Tamb
And if she passe this fit, the worst is past. — 2Tamb 2.4.40 1Phstn
And passe their fixed boundes exceedingly. — 2Tamb 4.3.47 Therid
neither, but to passe along/Towards Venice by the Adriatick Sea; — Jew 1.1.162 Barab
I'le passe away my life in penitence, — Jew 1.2.324 Abigal
Well, let it passe, another time shall serve. — Jew 2.3.278 Mthias
Here must no speeches passe, nor swords be drawne. — Jew 2.3.339 Barab
Doe but bring this to passe which thou pretendest, — Jew 5.2.84 Govnr
The plot is laide, and things shall come to passe, — P 164 2.107 Guise
To work the way to bring this thing to passe: — P 649 12.62 QnMoth
Ile clippe his winges/Or ere he passe my handes, away with him. — P1053 19.123 King
He nods, and scornes, and smiles at those that passe. — Edw 1.2.24 Warwck
I passe not for their anger, come lets go. — Edw 1.4.142 Edward

PASSE (cont.)

That suffered Jove to passe in showers of golde/To Danae, all — Edw 3.1.267 Spencr
I thanke them, gave me leave to passe in peace: — Edw 4.1.16 Mortmr
They passe not for thy frownes as late they did, — Edw 5.1.77 Edward
The proudest lords salute me as I passe, — Edw 5.4.50 Mortmr
To passe the Ocean with a band of men, — F 334 1.3.106 Faust
And view their triumphs, as they passe this way. — F 857 3.1.79 Mephst
you thinke to carry it away with your Hey-passe, and Re-passe: — F1665 4.6.108 P Robin
you, hey, passe, where's your maister? — F App p.240 138 P HrsCsr
That soules passe not to silent Erebus/Or Plutoes bloodles — Lucan, First Booke 451
He shewes me how unheard to passe the watch, — Ovid's Elegies 1.6.7
The keepers hands and corps-dugard to passe/The souldiours, and — Ovid's Elegies 1.9.27
Going out againe passe forth the dore more wisely/And som-what — Ovid's Elegies 1.12.5
And passe our scarlet of red saffrons marke. — Ovid's Elegies 2.6.22
Duld with much beating slowly forth doth passe. — Ovid's Elegies 2.7.16
Nor passe I thee, who hollow rocks downe tumbling, — Ovid's Elegies 3.5.45

PASSENGERS

Dooth pray uppon my flockes of Passengers, — 1Tamb 1.1.32 Mycet
That thus oppresse poore friendles passengers. — 1Tamb 1.2.70 Zenoc

PASSEOVER

That never tasted of the Passeover, — Jew 2.3.302 Barab

PASSEPORT

Raven that tolls/The sicke mans passeport in her hollow beake, — Jew 2.1.2 Barab

PASSES

conjuring bookes, and now we'le have such knavery, as't passes. — F 724 2.3.3 P Robin

PASSETH

Returne with speed, time passeth swift away, — 1Tamb 1.1.67 Mycet
[Whose heavenly beauty passeth all compare]. — F1701 5.1.28A 3Schol
Mounts, and raine-doubled flouds he passeth over, — Ovid's Elegies 1.9.11
Time passeth while I speake, give her my writ/But see that — Ovid's Elegies 1.11.15

PASSING

Is it not passing brave to be a King, — 1Tamb 2.5.53 Tamb
I, passing well. — Jew 2.3.122 P Slave
Erected is a Castle passing strong, — F 818 3.1.40 Mephst
To leave the rest, all likt me passing well, — Ovid's Elegies 1.5.23
Be broake with wheeles of chariots passing by. — Ovid's Elegies 1.12.14
Oft some points at the prophet passing by, — Ovid's Elegies 3.1.19

PASSION

wrought in him with passion,/Thirsting with soverainty, with — 1Tamb 2.1.19 Menaph
Yet since a farther passion feeds my thoughts, — 1Tamb 3.2.13 Zenoc
That in thy passion for thy countries love, — 1Tamb 5.1.137 Tamb
but I hope it be/Only some naturall passion makes her sicke. — P 183 3.18 QnMarg

PASSIONATE

His deep affections make him passionate. — 1Tamb 1.2.164 Techel
Looke Lancaster how passionate he is, — Edw 2.2.3 Queene
Ye must not grow so passionate in speeches: — Edw 4.4.16 Mortmr
But Leister leave to growe so passionate, — Edw 4.7.55 Leistr
is great Mephostophilis so passionate/For being deprived of the — F 311 1.3.83 Faust
But love resisted once, growes passionate, — Hero and Leander 2.139

PASSIONS

Had not such passions in her head as I. — Dido 2.1.6 Aeneas
Diablo, what passions call you these? — Edw 1.4.319 Lncstr
For such outragious passions cloye my soule, — Edw 5.1.19 Edward
Your passions make your dolours to increase. — Edw 5.3.15 Gurney
Confound these passions with a quiet sleepe: — F1481 4.4.25 Faust
Confound these passions with a quiet sleepe: — F App p.240 124 Faust
And some (their violent passions to asswage)/Compile sharpe — Hero and Leander 1.126

PASSPORT (See PASSEPORT)

PAST

How many dangers have we over past? — Dido 1.1.145 Aeneas
Not past foure thousand paces at the most. — Dido 5.1.17 Aeneas
Have past the armie of the mightie Turke: — 1Tamb 1.2.14 Zenoc
Then having past Armenian desarts now, — 1Tamb 2.2.14 Meandr
Not now Theridamas, her time is past: — 1Tamb 3.3.228 Tamb
Least time be past, and lingring let us both. — 2Tamb 1.2.75 Callap
And if she passe this fit, the worst is past. — 2Tamb 2.4.40 1Phstn
That have not past the Centers latitude, — 2Tamb 3.2.31 Tamb
But now I finde thee, and that feare is past. — 2Tamb 4.2.20 Therid
Birds of the Aire will tell of murders past; — Jew Prol.16 Machvl
are such/That you will needs have ten yeares tribute past, — Jew 1.2.19 Govnr
To levie of us ten yeares tribute past, — Jew 1.2.41 Govnr
things past recovery/Are hardly cur'd with exclamations. — Jew 1.2.236 Barab
For the performance of your promise past; — Jew 3.5.9 Basso
So, now the feare is past, and I am safe: — Jew 4.1.114 Barab
In prison till the Law has past on him. — Jew 5.1.49 Govnr
asunder; so that it doth sinke/Into a deepe pit past recovery. — Jew 5.5.36 Barab
I feare the Guisians have past the bridge, — P 363 7.3 Ramus
Till this our Coronation day be past: — P 624 12.37 King
Past with delight the stately Towne of Trier: — F 780 3.1.2 Faust
[Ah] <O> halfe the houre is past: — F1957 5.2.161 Faust
'twill all be past anone: — F1957 5.2.161 Faust
til I am past this faire and pleasant greene, ile walke on — F App p.239 96 P Faust
denies all, with thy bloud must thou/Abie thy conquest past: — Lucan, First Booke 290
Hath with thee past the swelling Ocean; — Lucan, First Booke 371
And Trevier; thou being glad that wars are past thee; — Lucan, First Booke 437
Or night being past, and yet not day begunne. — Ovid's Elegies 1.5.6
But in times past I fear'd vaine shades, and night, — Ovid's Elegies 1.6.9
<redde-growne> slime bankes, till I be past/Thy waters stay: — Ovid's Elegies 3.5.1
His side past service, and his courage spent. — Ovid's Elegies 3.10.14
Many would praise the sweet smell as she past, — Hero and Leander 1.21

PASTE

But that thou wouldst dissemble when tis paste. — Ovid's Elegies 3.13.4

PASTIME

we are come from hell in person to shew thee some pastime: — F 651 2.2.104 P Belzeb

PASTIME (cont.)			
And with your pastime let the bedsted creake, ...	Ovid's Elegies	3.13.26	
PASTIMES			
The youthfull sort to divers pastimes runne. . . .	Ovid's Elegies	2.5.22	
PASTORS			
<Consissylogismes>/Gravel'd the Pastors of the Germane Church,	F 140	1.1.112	Faust
PASTURES			
their mouths/And pul their kicking colts out of their pastures.	2Tamb	4.3.49	Techel
And some few pastures Pallas Olives bore.	Ovid's Elegies	2.16.8	
PATE			
<Where thou shalt see a troupe of bald-pate Friers>, .	F 833	(HC265)A	Mephst
be he that strucke <tooke> fryer Sandelo a blow on the pate.	F1081	3.2.101	1Frier
Cursed be he that tooke Frier Sandelo a blow on the pate.	F App	p.232 35	Frier
PATER			
Exhereditare filium non potest pater, nisi--Such is the .	F 58	1.1.30	P Faust
PATES			
To beate the beades about the Friers Pates, . . .	F 863	3.1.85	Mephst
PATH			
And drawen with princely Eagles through the path, . .	2Tamb	4.3.127	Tamb
By which sweete path thou maist attaine the gole/That shall	F App	p.243 36	OldMan
That heavenly path, with many a curious dint, . . .	Hero and Leander	1.68	
PATHETICALL			
Could use perswasions more patheticall.	1Tamb	1.2.211	Therid
PATHS			
which downe her face/Made milk-white paths, wheron the gods	Hero and Leander	1.298	
PATIENCE (See also PACIENCE)			
With love and patience let your true love die, . . .	2Tamb	2.4.67	Zenoc
I, I,/Pray leave me in my patience.	Jew	1.2.200	Barab
I pray my Lords have patience at this troublesome banquet.	F1058	3.2.78	Pope
heare [me] with patience, and tremble not at my speeches.	F1839	5.2.43	P Faust
We grieve at this thy patience and delay:	Lucan, First Booke	362	
They that deserve paine, beare't with patience. . .	Ovid's Elegies	2.7.12	
Some other seeke that may in patience strive with thee, .	Ovid's Elegies	2.19.59	
PATIENT			
Ah good my Lord be patient, she is dead, ...	2Tamb	2.4.119	Therid
Be patient and thy riches will increase.	Jew	1.2.122	Govnr
Oh yet be patient, gentle Barabas.	Jew	1.2.169	1Jew
Good Barabas be patient.	Jew	1.2.199	2Jew
Be patient, gentle Madam, it was he, ...	Jew	5.1.46	Govnr
Be patient Guise and threat not Epernoune, ...	P 833	17.28	King
Why are you moov'd, be patient my lord, ...	Edw	1.4.43	ArchBp
Be patient good my lord, cease to lament, ...	Edw	5.1.1	Leistr
And now <so> to patient judgements we appeale <our plaude>,	F 9	Prol.9	1Chor
Receive him soone, least patient use he gaine, . . .	Ovid's Elegies	1.8.75	
PATIENTLY			
That I may learne to beare it patiently, ...	Dido	5.1.208	Dido
I never knew a man take his death so patiently as this Fryar;	Jew	4.2.21	P Ithimr
And therefore sweete friend, take it patiently, . .	Edw	1.4.112	Edward
You could not beare his death thus patiently, . . .	Edw	5.6.36	King
How patiently hot irons they did take/In crooked [tramells]	Ovid's Elegies	1.14.25	
PATROCLUS			
And for Patroclus sterne Achillis droopt:	Edw	1.4.394	MortSr
PATRON			
blood,/Of thine own people patron shouldst thou be/But thou--	Edw	4.4.13	Queene
Most sacred Patron of the Church of Rome, ...	F 951	3.1.173	Faust
PATRONES			
And holy Patrones <Patrons> of Egyptia, ...	1Tamb	5.1.49	2Virgn
PATRONESSE			
O Dido, patronesse of all our lives, ...	Dido	4.4.55	Aeneas
PATRONS			
And holy Patrones <Patrons> of Egyptia, ...	1Tamb	5.1.49	2Virgn
PAUL			
By holy Paul we saw them not.	F1029	3.2.49	BthCrd
PAUNCH			
Oft dyes she that her paunch-wrapt child hath slaine. .	Ovid's Elegies	2.14.38	
PAUNCH-WRAPT			
Oft dyes she that her paunch-wrapt child hath slaine. .	Ovid's Elegies	2.14.38	
PAUS'D			
So having paus'd a while, at last shee said: . . .	Hero and Leander	1.337	
PAUSE			
Not for my life doe I desire this pause, ...	P 401	7.41	Ramus
PAUSETH			
Who seeing hunters pauseth till fell wrath/And kingly rage	Lucan, First Booke	209	
PAV'D			
Pav'd with bright Christall, and enchac'd with starres, .	2Tamb	4.3.128	Tamb
In midst thereof a stone-pav'd sacred spring, . . .	Ovid's Elegies	3.1.3	
PAVED			
<The> streetes straight forth, and paved with finest bricke,	F 789	3.1.11	Faust
Whose frame is paved with sundry coloured stones, . .	F 797	3.1.19	Faust
PAVEMENT			
The pavement underneath thy chariot wheels/With Turky Carpets	2Tamb	1.2.42	Callap
Of Christall shining faire, the pavement was, . . .	Hero and Leander	1.141	
PAVILION			
Black are his collours, blacke Pavilion, ...	1Tamb	4.1.59	2Msngr
Come bring them in to our Pavilion.	2Tamb	4.1.206	Tamb
PAVILIONS			
Ransacke the tents and the pavilions/Of these proud Turks, and	2Tamb	4.1.160	Tamb
PAWE			
He rends and teares it with his wrathfull pawe, . .	Edw	5.1.12	Edward
PAWES			
With balles of wilde fire in their murdering pawes, . .	Dido	2.1.217	Aeneas
Stretching their pawes, and threatning heardes of Beastes,	1Tamb	1.2.53	Techel
Streching their monstrous pawes, grin with their teeth, .	2Tamb	3.5.28	Orcan

PAWES (cont.)			
And with their pawes drench his black soule in hell.	P1102	20.12	Cardnl
Edward, untolde thy pawes,/And let their lives bloud slake thy	Edw	2.2.204	Edward
PAY (See also PAIE)			
And such conceits as clownage keepes in pay,	1Tamb	Prol.2	Prolog
Wanting both pay and martiall discipline,	1Tamb	1.1.147	Ceneus
As if he meant to give my Souldiers pay,	1Tamb	1.2.183	Tamb
Shall pay a yearly tribute to thy Syre.	1Tamb	5.1.519	Tamb
Shall pay me tribute for, in Babylon.	2Tamb	5.1.167	Tamb
who so richly pay/The things they traffique for with wedge of	Jew	1.1.8	Barab
As all the wealth of Malta cannot pay;	Jew	1.1.183	Barab
the Jewes, and each of them to pay one halfe of his estate.	Jew	1.2.69	P Reader
hee that denies to pay, shal straight become a Christian.	Jew	1.2.73	P Reader
Then pay thy halfe.	Jew	1.2.83	Govnr
Either pay that, or we will seize on all.	Jew	1.2.89	Govnr
Pay me my wages for my worke is done.	Jew	3.4.115	Ithimr
Ile pay thee with a vengeance Ithamore.	Jew	3.4.116	Barab
And being able, Ile keep an hoast in pay.	P 840	17.35	Guise
Thou able to maintaine an hoast in pay,	P 841	17.36	Eprnon
No, threaten not my lord, but pay them home.	Edw	1.4.26	Gavstn
Till hee pay deerely for their companie.	Edw	3.1.198	Lncstr
Pay natures debt with cheerefull countenance,	Edw	4.7.109	Baldck
Is sure to pay for it when his sonne is of age,	Edw	5.4.4	Mortmr
rosted, and good sauce to it, if I pay so deere, I can tell you.	F 353	1.4.11	P Robin
hold belly hold, and wee'le not pay one peny for it.	F 749	2.3.28	P Robin
be wellcome for our mony, and we will pay for what we take:	F1612	4.6.55	P Robin
have sent away my guesse, I pray who shall pay me for my A--	F1667	4.6.110	P Hostss
have it wel roasted, and good sawce to it, if I pay so deere.	F App	p.229 12	P Clown
wil you take sixe pence in your purse to pay for your supper,	F App	p.235 41	P Robin
Pay vowes to Jove, engirt thy hayres with baies,	Ovid's Elegies		1.7.36
To serve for pay beseemes not wanton gods.	Ovid's Elegies		1.10.20
dost betray them/To Pedants, that with cruell lashes pay them.	Ovid's Elegies		1.13.18
I pay them home with that they most desire:	Ovid's Elegies		2.10.26
Pay it not heere, but in an other place.	Ovid's Elegies		3.2.84
PAYD			
me, as if they payd for their meate and drinke, I can tell you.	F 365	1.4.23	P Robin
with my flesh, as if they had payd for my meate and drinke.	F App	p.230 29	P Clown
Drawer, I hope al is payd, God be with you, come Rafe.	F App	p.234 6	P Robin
PAYDE			
with you, I must yet have a goblet payde from you ere you goe.	F App	p.234 7	P Vintnr
PAYE			
These will I sell to give my souldiers paye,	Edw	1.1.104	Lncstr
PAYES			
Where Nilus payes his tribute to the maine,	Jew	1.1.75	Barab
Who payes for the Ale?	F1666	4.6.109	P Hostss
PAYETH			
The hirer payeth al, his rent discharg'd/From further duty he	Ovid's Elegies		1.10.45
PAYMENT			
Calls for the payment of my latest yeares,	F App	p.239 93	Faust
PAYNES			
While rage is absent, take some friend the paynes.	Ovid's Elegies		1.7.2
PAYNTED			
Frolicks not more to see the paynted springe,	Edw	2.2.62	Gavstn
PEACE			
That durst thus proudly wrong our kinsmans peace.	Dido	1.1.119	Jupitr
That in such peace long time did rule the same:	Dido	1.2.24	Cloan
And yet Ile speake, and yet Ile hold my peace,	Dido	3.4.27	Dido
That doe pursue my peace where ere it goes.	Dido	4.2.51	Iarbus
Offer their mines (to sew for peace) to me,	1Tamb	3.3.264	Tamb
King of Natolia, let us treat of peace,	2Tamb	1.1.13	Gazell
Tis requisit to parle for a peace/With Sigismond the king of	2Tamb	1.1.50	Gazell
And for that cause the Christians shall have peace.	2Tamb	1.1.57	Orcan
Therefore Viceroies the Christians must have peace.	2Tamb	1.1.77	Orcan
crost Danubius stream/To treat of friendly peace or deadly war:	2Tamb	1.1.80	Sgsmnd
If peace, restore it to my hands againe:	2Tamb	1.1.84	Sgsmnd
Or treat of peace with the Natolian king?	2Tamb	1.1.113	Sgsmnd
let peace be ratified/On these conditions specified before,	2Tamb	1.1.124	Orcan
And vow to keepe this peace inviolable.	2Tamb	1.1.136	Sgsmnd
Confirm'd by oth and Articles of peace,	2Tamb	2.1.29	Sgsmnd
Have I not here the articles of peace,	2Tamb	2.2.30	Orcan
What need they treat of peace that are in league?	Jew	1.1.158	Barab
Why, Barabas, they come for peace or warre.	Jew	1.1.161	1Jew
And 'tis more Kingly to obtaine by peace/Then to enforce	Jew	1.2.25	Calym
Peace, Abigal, 'tis I.	Jew	2.1.43	Barab
Peace, Ithimore, 'tis better so then spar'd.	Jew	3.4.91	Barab
To worke my peace, this I confesse to thee;	Jew	3.6.31	Abigal
In person there to [mediate] <meditate> your peace;	Jew	5.5.116	Calym
Upon the cursed breakers of our peace.	P 270	4.68	Charls
Spaine is the place where he makes peace and warre,	P 710	14.13	Navrre
And as Dictator make or warre or peace,	P 860	17.55	King
Thou proud disturber of thy countries peace,	Edw	2.5.9	Mortmr
In peace triumphant, fortunate in warres.	Edw	3.1.33	SpncrP
And go in peace, leave us in warres at home.	Edw	3.1.85	Edward
I thanke them, gave me leave to passe in peace:	Edw	4.1.16	Mortmr
For Englands honor, peace, and quietnes.	Edw	4.2.58	Kent
That Englands queene in peace may reposesse/Her dignities and	Edw	4.4.24	Mortmr
And proud disturbers of the Churches peace.	F 956	3.1.178	Faust
In peace possesse the triple Diadem,	F1213	4.1.59	Emper
Peace through the world from Janus Phane shal flie,	Lucan, First Booke		61
And what made madding people shake off peace.	Lucan, First Booke		69
T'was peace against their wils; betwixt them both/Stept Crassus	Lucan, First Booke		99
Bare downe to hell her sonne, the pledge of peace,	Lucan, First Booke		113
Againe, this people could not brooke calme peace,	Lucan, First Booke		172

PEACE (cont.)
here, here (saith he)/An end of peace; here end polluted lawes; Lucan, First Booke 227
armes neer their houshold gods hung up/Such as peace yeelds; Lucan, First Booke 243
all lands else/Have stable peace, here wars rage first begins, Lucan, First Booke 252
Let come their [leader] <leaders whom long peace hath quail'd; Lucan, First Booke 311
And Druides you now in peace renew/Your barbarous customes, and Lucan, First Booke 446
War onely gives us peace, o Rome continue/The course of Lucan, First Booke 669
out the date/Of slaughter; onely civill broiles make peace. Lucan, First Booke 671
In midst of peace why art of armes afraide? Ovid's Elegies 1.6.30
And what lesse labour then to hold thy peace? Ovid's Elegies 2.2.28
Vaine babling speech, and pleasant peace thou lovedst. Ovid's Elegies 2.6.26
but for a Queene/Europe, and Asia in firme peace had beene. Ovid's Elegies 2.12.18
Peace pleaseth me, and in mid peace is love. Ovid's Elegies 3.2.50
they manadge peace, and rawe warres bloudy jawes, Ovid's Elegies 3.7.58

PEACEFULL
Give us a peacefull rule, make Christians Kings, Jew 1.1.134 Barab

PEACOCKES
And thy faire peacockes by my pigeons pearch: Dido 3.2.59 Venus

PEALE
Hast thou beheld a peale of ordinance strike/A ring of pikes, 2Tamb 3.2.98 Tamb
Then Ile have a peale of ordinance shot from the tower, P 236 4.34 Guise
Ile thunder such a peale into his eares, Edw 2.2.128 Mortmr

PEAN
Whose amorous face like Pean sparkles fire, Dido 3.4.19 Dido
Pean whither am I halde? Lucan, First Booke 677

PEARCE
Aeneas no, although his eyes doe pearce. Dido 3.4.12 Dido

PEARCH
And thy faire peacockes by my pigeons pearch: Dido 3.2.59 Venus
On whose top-branches Kinglie Eagles pearch, Edw 2.2.17 Mortmr

PEARCHT
Where sparrowes pearcht, of hollow pearle and gold, Hero and Leander 1.33

PEARDE
liver/Squis'd matter; through the cal, the intralls pearde, Lucan, First Booke 624

PEARLE (See also PERLE)
And teares of pearle, crye stay, Aeneas, stay: Dido 4.3.52 Aeneas
A pearle more worth, then all the world is plaste: 1Tamb 2.1.12 Menaph
To weare a Crowne enchac'd with pearle and golde, 1Tamb 2.5.60 Therid
Fairer than rockes of pearle and pretious stone, 1Tamb 3.3.118 Tamb
Rain'st on the earth resolved pearle in showers, 1Tamb 5.1.142 Tamb
Mingled with corrall and with [orient] <orientall> pearle: 2Tamb 1.3.224 Tamb
And fairest pearle of welthie India/Were mounted here under a 2Tamb 3.2.121 Tamb
The gold, the silver, and the pearle ye got, 2Tamb 3.4.88 Therid
shall sweat/With carrieng pearle and treasure on their backes. 2Tamb 3.5.167 Techel
Turn'd into pearle and proffered for my stay, 2Tamb 4.1.44 Amyras
Wherein are rockes of Pearle, that shine as bright/As all the 2Tamb 5.3.156 Tamb
And in his house heape pearle like pibble-stones, Jew 1.1.23 Barab
Besides I know not how much weight in Pearle/Orient and round, Jew 4.1.66 Barab
That he hath in store a Pearle so big, Jew 5.3.27 Msngr
Crownets of pearle about his naked armes, Edw 1.1.63 Gavstn
Larded with pearle, and in his tuskan cap/A jewell of more Edw 1.4.414 Mortmr
Ransacke the Ocean for Orient Pearle, F 110 1.1.82 Faust
Where sparrowes pearcht, of hollow pearle and gold, Hero and Leander 1.33
A streame of liquid pearle, which downe her face/Made Hero and Leander 1.297
And as she wept, her teares to pearle he turn'd, Hero and Leander 1.375
Whose carelesse haire, in stead of pearle t'adorne it, Hero and Leander 1.389
where the ground/Was strewd with pearle, and in low corrall Hero and Leander 2.161

PEASANT (See also PAISANT, PESANT, PESSANT, PEZANT)
My death? what, is the base borne peasant mad? Jew 2.3.281 Lodowk
I scorne the Peasant, tell him so. Jew 4.4.59 P Ithimr
That hanges for every peasant to atchive? P 98 2.41 Guise
Why suffer you that peasant to declaime? P 414 7.54 Guise
Were he a peasant, being my minion, Edw 1.4.30 Edward
Be ready then, and strike the Peasant downe. F1359 4.2.35 Fredrk

PEBLE (See also PIBBLE)
About her necke hung chaines of peble stone, Hero and Leander 1.25

PEBLE STONE
About her necke hung chaines of peble stone, Hero and Leander 1.25

PECCASSE
Si peccasse negamus, fallimur, et nulla est in nobis veritas: F 68 1.1.40 P Faust

PECCATI
Stipendium peccati mors est: F 66 1.1.38 P Faust

PECCATORUM
Peccatum peccatorum, heeres thy goblet, good Vintner. F App p.235 28 P Rafe

PECCATUM
Peccatum peccatorum, heeres thy goblet, good Vintner. F App p.235 28 P Rafe

PEDANTES
To get those pedantes from the King Navarre, P 426 7.66 Guise
Murder the Hugonets, take those pedantes hence. P 438 7.78 Guise

PEDANTS
I am none of these common [pedants] <pendants> I, Edw 2.1.52 Baldck
and dost betray them/To Pedants, that with cruell lashes pay Ovid's Elegies 1.13.18

PEDIGREE
I <O I> come of a Royall Pedigree <parentage>, my father F 696 2.2.145 P Glutny

PEECE
A warning-peece shall be shot off from the Tower, Jew 5.5.39 Barab
Revolt, or I'le in peece-meale teare thy flesh. F1745 5.1.72 Mephst
Rafe, keepe out, for I am about a roaring peece of worke. F App p.233 11 P Robin

PEECE-MEALE
Revolt, or I'le in peece-meale teare thy flesh. F1745 5.1.72 Mephst

PEECEMEALE
That may command thee peecemeale to be torne, 1Tamb 4.2.23 Tamb
Will hew us peecemeale, put us to the wheele, 2Tamb 3.4.21 Olymp

PEECEMEALE (cont.)			
And draw thee peecemeale like Hyppolitus, ...	2Tamb	5.3.240	Tamb
PEECES			
First legions of devils shall teare thee in peeces. . .	1Tamb	4.4.38	P Bajzth
teare me in peeces, give me the sworde with a ball of wildefire	1Tamb	5.1.311	P Zabina
about thee into Familiars, and make them tare thee in peeces.	F 363	1.4.21	P Wagner
If thou repent, devils will <shall> teare thee in peeces.	F 632	2.2.81	BdAngl
but the Divel threatned to teare me in peeces if I nam'd God:	F1865	5.2.69	P Faust
about thee into familiars, and they shal teare thee in peeces.	F App	p.229 26	P Wagner
PEEPE			
Aurora shall not peepe out of her doores, ...	1Tamb	2.2.10	Mycet
PEEPES			
And now the sunne that through th'orizon peepes, . .	Hero and Leander		2.99
PEEPING			
One like Actaeon peeping through the grove, ...	Edw	1.1.67	Gavstn
PEER'D (See also PEARDE)			
Through which the wood peer'd, headles darts, olde swords/With	Lucan, First Booke		244
PEERE			
What Peere in France but thou (aspiring Guise)/Durst be in	P 828	17.23	Eprnon
Unto the proudest peere of Britanie:	Edw	2.2.42	Edward
PEERELESSE			
as to let us see that peerelesse dame of Greece, whom all the	F1685	5.1.12	P 1Schol
You shall behold that peerelesse dame of Greece, . .	F1692	5.1.19	Faust
PEERES			
And Dido and you Carthaginian Peeres/Heare me, but yet with	Dido	2.1.122	Aeneas
Wee with our Peeres have crost Danubius stream/To treat of	2Tamb	1.1.79	Sgsmnd
Freend Sigismond, and peeres of Hungary, ...	2Tamb	1.1.164	Orcan
Viceroies and Peeres of Turky play the men, ...	2Tamb	3.5.14	Callap
Courted by kings and peeres of Asia, ...	2Tamb	5.1.74	Tamb
Into what corner peeres my Halcions bill?	Jew	1.1.39	Barab
Farewell base stooping to the lordly peeres, ...	Edw	1.1.18	Gavstn
My lord, why do you thus incense your peeres, . . .	Edw	1.1.99	Lncstr
Then wil you joine with us that be his peeres/To banish or	Edw	1.2.42	Mortmr
We know our duties, let him know his peeres.	Edw	1.4.23	Warwck
Meete you for this, proud overdaring peeres?	Edw	1.4.47	Edward
As for the peeres that backe the cleargie thus, . . .	Edw	1.4.104	Edward
The peeres will frowne.	Edw	1.4.141	Gavstn
Be thou my advocate unto these peeres.	Edw	1.4.212	Queene
Having the love of his renowned peeres.	Edw	1.4.367	Queene
I meane the peeres, whom thou shouldst dearly love: . .	Edw	2.2.176	Mortmr
How oft have I beene baited by these peeres?	Edw	2.2.201	Edward
No marvell though thou scorne thy noble peeres, . . .	Edw	2.2.217	Kent
That Englands peeres may Henolts welcome see. . . .	Edw	4.2.82	SrJohn
To crave the aide and succour of his peeres.	Edw	5.6.21	Queene
And like a Steeple over-peeres the Church.	F 913	3.1.135	Pope
Without inforcement of the German Peeres, ...	F 958	3.1.180	Faust
PEERING			
And Marius head above cold Tav'ron peering/(His grave broke	Lucan, First Booke		581
PEERLESSE			
Magnificent and peerlesse Tamburlaine, ...	2Tamb	1.3.129	Usumc
PEEVISH			
Wel, let that peevish Frenchman guard him sure, . . .	Edw	1.2.7	Mortmr
PEGASUS			
Mounted on Steeds, swifter than Pegasus.	1Tamb	1.2.94	Tamb
PEISE (See PAIS'D)			
PELEUS (See PELIUS)			
PELFE			
There wanteth nothing but the Governors pelfe, ...	Jew	5.5.18	Barab
He hath no bosome, where to hide base pelfe.	Ovid's Elegies		1.10.18
In heaping up a masse of drossie pelfe, ...	Hero and Leander		1.244
PELIDES			
Did not Pelides whom his Speare did grieve, ...	Ovid's Elegies		2.9.7
PELIGNIAN			
Pelignian fields [with] <which> liqued rivers flowe, .	Ovid's Elegies		2.16.5
PELIGNIES			
Sulmo, Pelignies third part me containes, ...	Ovid's Elegies		2.16.1
PELIGNIS			
Which I Pelignis foster-child have framde, ...	Ovid's Elegies		3.14.3
Of me Pelignis nation boasts alone, ...	Ovid's Elegies		3.14.8
PELIGNY			
Borne at Peligny, to write more addresse.	Ovid's Elegies		2.1.2
Healthfull Peligny I esteeme nought worth, ...	Ovid's Elegies		2.16.37
PELION			
how Olimpus toppe/High Ossa bore, mount Pelion up to proppe.	Ovid's Elegies		2.1.14
The lofty Pine from high mount Pelion raught/Ill waies by rough	Ovid's Elegies		2.11.1
PELIUS			
Who doubts, with Pelius, Thetis did consort, ...	Ovid's Elegies		2.17.17
PELOPS			
Ah Pelops from his coach was almost feld, ...	Ovid's Elegies		3.2.15
necke in touching, and surpast/The white of Pelops shoulder.	Hero and Leander		1.65
PELTING			
How those were hit by pelting Cannon shot, ...	1Tamb	2.4.3	Mycet
PELUSIAN			
Where Nile augmenteth the Pelusian sea:	Lucan, First Booke		683
PEMBROKE (See PENBROOKE)			
PEN			
And with this pen reduce them to a Map, ...	1Tamb	4.4.78	Tamb
And comments vollumes with her Yvory pen, ...	1Tamb	5.1.145	Tamb
Hath made our Poet pen his second part, ...	2Tamb	Prol.3	Prolog
Pen and Inke:	Jew	4.2.68	P Ithimr
Goe fetch me pen and inke.	P 657	13.1	Duchss
Why grieve I? and of heaven reproches pen?	Ovid's Elegies		3.3.41
That runs along his backe, but my rude pen, ...	Hero and Leander		1.69

PENALTY				
Sir, halfe is the penalty of our decree,	Jew	1.2.88		Govnr
PENANCE (See also PENNANCE)				
End all my penance in my sodaine death,	2Tamb	2.3.7		Sgsmnd
He has done penance now sufficently.	F1310	4.1.156		Emper
at my intreaty release him, he hath done penance sufficient.	F App	p.238 80	P	Emper
PENBROOKE				
And so will Penbrooke and I.	Edw	1.4.293		Warwck
Penbrooke shall beare the sword before the king.	Edw	1.4.351		Edward
And with this sword, Penbrooke wil fight for you.	Edw	1.4.352		Penbrk
The like oath Penbrooke takes.	Edw	2.2.108		Penbrk
Meane time my lord of Penbrooke and my selfe,	Edw	2.2.122		Warwck
Penbrooke, what wilt thou do?	Edw	2.5.82		Warwck
But if you dare trust Penbrooke with the prisoner,	Edw	2.5.87		Penbrk
My lord of Penbrooke, we deliver him you,	Edw	2.5.97		Mortmr
Tis verie kindlie spoke my lord of Penbrooke,	Edw	2.5.104		Arundl
hearing,/Mortimer hardly, Penbrooke and Lancaster/Spake least:	Edw	3.1.105		Arundl
The earle of Penbrooke mildlie thus bespake.	Edw	3.1.108		Arundl
And Penbrooke undertooke for his returne,	Edw	3.1.236		Edward
PENBROOKES				
Why I say, let him go on Penbrookes word.	Edw	2.5.90		Lncstr
My lord of Penbrookes men,	Edw	2.6.6		Warwck
For being delivered unto Penbrookes men,	Edw	3.1.116		Arundl
PENCE				
he flouts me, what gentry can be in a poore Turke of ten pence?	Jew	4.2.39	P	Ithimr
I am eighteene pence on the score, but say nothing, see if she	F1511	4.5.7	P	Robin
wil you take sixe pence in your purse to pay for your supper,	F App	p.235 41	P	Robin
PENDANTS				
I am none of these common [pedants] <pendants> I,	Edw	2.1.52		Baldck
PENELOPE				
Were <Be> she as chaste as was Penelope,	F 540	2.1.152		Mephst
Penelope in bowes her youths strength tride,	Ovid's Elegies			1.8.47
my selfe to smart)/We write, or what Penelope sends Ulysses,	Ovid's Elegies			2.18.21
White-cheekt Penelope knewe Ulisses signe,	Ovid's Elegies			2.18.29
Penelope, though no watch look'd unto her,	Ovid's Elegies			3.4.23
PENEUS				
They say Peneus neere Phthias towne did hide.	Ovid's Elegies			3.5.32
PENITENCE				
I'de passe away my life in penitence,	Jew	1.2.324		Abigal
PENITENT				
if thou now growest penitent/Ile be thy ghostly father,	Edw	5.6.3		Mortmr
PENNANCE				
Would pennance serve for this my sinne,	Jew	4.1.58		Barab
And so could I; but pennance will not serve.	Jew	4.1.60		Ithimr
PENNY (See PENY)				
PENS				
If all the pens that ever poets held,	1Tamb	5.1.161		Tamb
whose immortal pens/Renowne the valiant soules slaine in your	Lucan, First Booke			443
PENSION (See also PENTION)				
A pension and a dispensation too:	P 120	2.63		Guise
PENSIONS				
Cookes shall have pensions to provide us cates,	2Tamb	1.3.219		Tamb
PENSIVE				
A fitter subject for a pensive soule.	2Tamb	4.2.27		Olymp
My lord, be not pensive, we are your friends.	Edw	5.3.1		Matrvs
Upon the cold earth pensive let them lay,	Ovid's Elegies			2.16.15
PENSIVENES				
In this delight of dying pensivenes:	Dido	4.2.44		Anna
In health madam, but full of pensivenes.	Edw	5.2.25		Msngr
PENT				
That thus hath pent and mu'd me in a prison,	Edw	5.1.18		Edward
Slow oxen early in the yoake are pent.	Ovid's Elegies			1.13.16
PENTION				
but a [bare] <small> pention, and that buyes me <is> thirty	F 694	2.2.143	P	Glutny
PENY				
and the devill a peny they have left me, but a [bare] <small>	F 694	2.2.143	P	Glutny
hold belly hold, and wee'le not pay one peny for it.	F 750	2.3.29	P	Robin
PEOPLE				
What kind of people, and who governes them:	Dido	2.1.42		Aeneas
The people swarme to gaze him in the face.	Dido	3.1.72		Anna
Conquering the people underneath our feet,	1Tamb	4.4.137		Tamb
He brings a world of people to the field,	2Tamb	1.1.67		Orcan
abroad a nights/And kill sicke people groaning under walls:	Jew	2.3.175		Barab
A martiall people, worthy such a King,	P 455	8.5		Anjoy
A warlike people to maintaine thy right,	P 592	12.5		QnMoth
What neede the artick people love star-light,	Edw	1.1.16		Gavstn
So shall we have the people of our side,	Edw	1.4.282		Mortmr
And make the people sweare to put him downe.	Edw	2.2.111		Lncstr
I dare not, for the people love him well.	Edw	2.2.235		Edward
blood,/Of thine own people patron shouldst thou be/But thou--	Edw	4.4.13		Queene
and all the people in it were turnd> to Gold,	F 676	(HC263)A	P	Covet
And curse the people that submit to him;	F 907	3.1.129		Pope
And outrage strangling law and people strong,	Lucan, First Booke			2
And what made madding people shake off peace.	Lucan, First Booke			69
Againe, this people could not brooke calme peace,	Lucan, First Booke			172
The people started; young men left their beds,	Lucan, First Booke			241
and whose tongue/Could tune the people to the Nobles mind:	Lucan, First Booke			273
none answer'd, but a murmuring buz/Th'unstable people made:	Lucan, First Booke			354
Th'irrevocable people flie in troupes.	Lucan, First Booke			507
The people thee applauding thou shalte stand,	Ovid's Elegies			1.2.25
Io, triumphing shall thy people sing.	Ovid's Elegies			1.2.34
And vanquisht people curious dressings lend thee,	Ovid's Elegies			1.14.46
We people wholy given thee, feele thine armes,	Ovid's Elegies			2.9.11

PEOPLE (cont.)			
So of both people shalt thou homage gaine.	Ovid's Elegies	2.9.54	
The people by my company she pleasd,	Ovid's Elegies	3.10.19	
White Heifers by glad people forth are led,	Ovid's Elegies	3.12.13	
When the chiefe pompe comes, lowd the people hollow,	Ovid's Elegies	3.12.29	
So ran the people foorth to gaze upon her,	Hero and Leander	1.117	
PEOPLES			
And satisfie the peoples generall praiers,	2Tamb	5.1.7	Maxim
of offices, and peoples voices/Bought by themselves and solde,	Lucan, First Booke	180	
and did invade/The peoples minds, and laide before their eies	Lucan, First Booke	466	
sleeping foe tis good/And arm'd to shed unarmed peoples bloud.	Ovid's Elegies	1.9.22	
PER			
[Quid tu moraris] <quod tumeraris>; per Jehovam, Gehennam, et	F 248	1.3.20	P Faust
nunc facio; et per vota nostra ipse nunc surgat nobis dicatus	F 249	1.3.21	P Faust
That was the cause, but yet per accidens:	F 274	1.3.46	Mephst
A per se, a, t. h. e. the:	F 727	2.3.6	P Robin
o per se, o, [demy] <deny> orgon, gorgon:	F 728	2.3.7	P Robin
O per se o, demogorgon, Belcher and Mephostophilis.	F1114	3.3.27	P Robin
PERAMIDES			
Set me to scale the high Peramides,	P 100	2.43	Guise
PERCEAV'D			
Her, from his swift waves, the bold floud perceav'd,	Ovid's Elegies	3.5.51	
PERCEIVD			
When he perceivd the reines let slacke, he stayde,	Ovid's Elegies	3.4.15	
PERCEIVE			
But that thou maist more easilie perceive,	Dido	3.2.66	Juno
And thorough your Planets I perceive you thinke,	1Tamb	1.1.19	Mycet
Wherein as in a myrrour we perceive/The highest reaches of a	1Tamb	5.1.167	Tamb
My Lord, your Majesty shall soone perceive:	2Tamb	2.4.39	1Phstn
But I perceive my martial strength is spent,	2Tamb	5.3.119	Tamb
But I perceive there is no love on earth,	Jew	3.3.47	Abigal
Thou shouldst perceive the Duke of Guise is mov'd.	P 832	17.27	Guise
Least thou perceive the King of France be mov'd.	P 834	17.29	King
I thanke you all my lords, then I perceive,	Edw	2.5.29	Gavstn
My [lords] <lord>, perceive you how these rebels swell:	Edw	3.1.181	Edward
But <And> now my Faustus, that thou maist perceive,	F 809	3.1.31	Mephst
She may perceive how we the time did wast:	Ovid's Elegies	1.6.70	
Then first I did perceive I had offended,	Ovid's Elegies	1.7.59	
I grieve least others should such good perceive,	Ovid's Elegies	2.5.53	
In both [thy] <my> cheekes she did perceive thee blush,	Ovid's Elegies	2.8.16	
PERCEIV'ST			
thou perceiv'st the plight/Wherein these Christians have	Jew	1.2.270	Barab
PERCHANCE			
Which do perchance old age unto them give.	Ovid's Elegies	2.6.28	
Perchance these, others, me mine owne losse mooves.	Ovid's Elegies	3.5.100	
PERCHAUNCE			
But now perchaunce thy wench with thee doth rest,	Ovid's Elegies	1.6.45	
PERCHES (See also PEARCH)			
and fit for nought/But perches for the black and fatall Ravens.	2Tamb	4.3.23	Tamb
PERCIE			
Lord Percie of the North being highly mov'd,	Edw	1.1.110	Kent
The undaunted spirit of Percie was appeasd,	Edw	1.1.114	Kent
PERDICAS			
Ile to cardes: Perdicas.	2Tamb	4.1.59	Calyph
(Perdicas) and I feare as litle their tara, tantaras, their	2Tamb	4.1.67	P Calyph
PERDITION			
Child of perdition, and thy fathers shame,	Jew	1.2.344	Barab
PEREAT			
See how he must be handled for his labour,/Pereat iste:	Edw	5.5.24	Matrvs
PEREMPTORY			
And know my customes are as peremptory/As wrathfull Planets,	1Tamb	5.1.127	Tamb
PERFECT			
That perfect blisse and sole felicitie,	1Tamb	2.7.28	Tamb
If thou wilt proove thy selfe a perfect God,	2Tamb	2.2.56	Orcan
That lift themselves against the perfect truth,	P 799	16.13	Navrre
But perfect shadowes in a sun-shine day?	Edw	5.1.27	Edward
PERFECTER			
And then wilt thou be perfecter then I.	F 189	1.1.161	Valdes
PERFECTION			
I meane in fulnesse of perfection.	Jew	2.3.85	Barab
Women receave perfection everie way.	Hero and Leander	1.268	
PERFECTIONS			
this table as a Register/Of all her vertues and perfections.	2Tamb	3.2.24	Celeb
PERFORCE			
I must be pleasde perforce, wretched Zenocrate.	1Tamb	1.2.259	Zenoc
A would have taken the king away perforce,	Edw	5.4.84	Souldr
PERFORMANCE			
For the performance of your promise past;	Jew	3.5.9	Basso
PERFORM'D			
to prevent/That which mine honor sweares shal be perform'd:	1Tamb	5.1.107	Tamb
True; and it shall be cunningly perform'd.	Jew	2.3.367	Barab
So neatly plotted, and so well perform'd?	Jew	3.3.2	Ithimr
Shall be perform'd in twinkling of an eye.	F1767	5.1.94	Mephst
When Venus sweet rites are perform'd and done.	Hero and Leander	1.320	
PERFORMD			
Which once performd, poore Troy so long supprest,	Dido	1.1.93	Jupitr
[I leave untold, your eyes shall see performd].	F1154	3.3.67A	3Chor
Though both of us performd our true intent,	Ovid's Elegies	3.6.5	
PERFORME			
The Rockes and Sea-gulfes will performe at large,	Dido	5.1.171	Dido
are ful of brags/And menace more than they can wel performe:	1Tamb	3.3.4	Tamb
My hand is ready to performe the deed,	1Tamb	5.1.503	Techel
Where be thou present onely to performe/One stratagem that I'le	Jew	5.2.98	Barab

PERFORME (cont.)

This wils my lord, and this must I performe,	Edw	1.4.202	Queene
My lords, if to performe this I be slack,	Edw	1.4.290	Mortmr
That shall conveie it, and performe the rest,	Edw	5.4.18	Mortmr
we must now performe/The forme of Faustus fortunes, good or	F 7	Prol.7	1Chor
Performe what desperate enterprise I will?	F 108	1.1.80	Faust
The miracles that magick will performe,	F 163	1.1.135	Cornel
resolute/And try the utmost <uttermost> Magicke can performe.	F 243	1.3.15	Faust
No more then he commands, must we performe.	F 270	1.3.42	Mephst
And let thee see <shewe thee> what Magicke can performe.	F 474	2.1.86	Mephst
But yet conditionally, that thou performe/All Covenants, and	F 479	2.1.91	Faust
And I'le performe it Faustus: heark they come:	F 866	3.1.88	Mephst
and thou shalt see/This Conjurer performe such rare exploits,	F1186	4.1.32	Mrtino
forth as by art and power of my spirit I am able to performe.	F App	p.237 39 P	Faust
This hand (albeit unwilling) should performe it;	Lucan, First Booke		379
And even the ring performe a mans part well.	Ovid's Elegies		2.15.26
To this ad shame, shame to performe it quaild mee,	Ovid's Elegies		3.6.37
As he ought not performe, nor yet she aske.	Hero and Leander		1.430
PERFORMED			
grace to thinke but well of that which Faustus hath performed.	F1565	4.6.8 P	Faust
PERFOURM'D			
And now my Lords the mariage rites perfourm'd,	P 18	1.18	Charls
PERFOURME			
so eloquent/To paint in woords, what Ile perfourme in deeds,	2Tamb	1.2.10	Callap
Discharge thy musket and perfourme his death:	P 88	2.31	Guise
And as we late decreed we may perfourme.	P 206	4.4	QnMoth
And therefore as speedily as I can perfourme,	P 571	11.36	Navrre
PERFOURMING			
Perfourming all your promise to the full:	2Tamb	3.1.76	Jrslem
PERFUM'D			
unlesse <except> the ground be <were> perfum'd, and cover'd	F 670	2.2.119 P	Pride
PERFUME			
Me thinkes the gloves have a very strong perfume,	P 170	3.5	OldQn
Who now will care the Altars to perfume?	Ovid's Elegies		3.3.33
This sacrifice (whose sweet perfume descending,	Hero and Leander		1.209
PERFUMED			
Where are those perfumed gloves which I sent/To be poysoned,	P 70	2.13	Guise
Elegia came with haires perfumed sweete,	Ovid's Elegies		3.1.7
PERGAMA			
Which Pergama did vaunt in all her pride.	Dido	1.1.151	Aeneas
PERHAPS			
But love and duetie led him on perhaps,	Dido	3.3.15	Aeneas
These Lords (perhaps) do scorne our estimates,	1Tamb	1.2.61	Tamb
Madame, she thinks perhaps she is too fine.	1Tamb	3.3.179	Ebea
To some perhaps my name is odious,	Jew	Prol.5	Machvl
Let's know their time, perhaps it is not long;	Jew	1.2.24	Calym
Yet not perhaps,	Edw	2.5.95	Warwck
The king of heaven perhaps, no other king,	Edw	2.6.16	Warwck
Perhaps the Sabines rude, when Tatius raignde,	Ovid's Elegies		1.8.39
Perhaps he'ele tell howe oft he slewe a man,	Ovid's Elegies		3.7.21
Perhaps, thy sacred Priesthood makes thee loath,	Hero and Leander		1.293
PERICRANION			
And cleave his Pericranion with thy sword.	2Tamb	1.3.101	Tamb
PERILL			
May serve in perill of calamity/To ransome great Kings from	Jew	1.1.31	Barab
That perill is the cheefest way to happines,	P 95	2.38	Guise
PERIOD			
If these had made one Poems period/And all combin'd in Beauties	1Tamb	5.1.169	Tamb
Yet shall my souldiers make no period/Untill Natolia kneele	2Tamb	1.3.216	Therid
But that where every period ends with death,	2Tamb	4.2.47	Olymp
O must this day be period of my life,	Edw	2.6.4	Gavstn
the death of many men/Meetes in one period.	Lucan, First Booke		650
PERIPHRASTICON			
Sanctobulorum Periphrasticon:	F App	p.235 23 P	Robin
PERISH			
And I must perish in his burning armes.	Dido	3.4.22	Dido
And thou shalt perish in the billowes waies,	Dido	5.1.172	Dido
When first he came on shoare, perish thou to:	Dido	5.1.299	Dido
Shall either perish by our warlike hands,	1Tamb	1.1.72	Therid
For when they perish by our warlike hands,	1Tamb	3.3.24	Techel
Not one should scape: but perish by our swords.	1Tamb	4.2.122	Tamb
For halfe the world shall perish in this fight:	2Tamb	1.3.171	Tamb
And few or none shall perish by their shot.	2Tamb	3.3.45	Therid
thou that hast seene/Millions of Turkes perish by Tamburlaine,	2Tamb	5.2.25	Callap
That if I perish, heaven and earth may fade.	2Tamb	5.3.60	Tamb
Then many perish for a private man:	Jew	1.2.99	Govnr
But perish underneath my bitter curse/Like Cain by Adam, for	Jew	3.4.32	Barab
For so I live, perish may all the world.	Jew	5.5.10	Barab
Now must he fall and perish in his height.	P 946	19.16	Capt
And perish in the pit thou mad'st for me.	P 963	19.33	King
Vive la messe, perish Hugonets,	P1014	19.84	Guise
Farewell, and perish by a souldiers hand,	Edw	1.1.37	3PrMan
And as grosse vapours perish by the sunne,	Edw	1.4.341	Edward
Moov'd may he be, and perish in his wrath.	Edw	2.2.101	Mortmr
Gentlemen away, least you perish with me.	F1867	5.2.71 P	Faust
The fates are envious, high seats quickly perish,	Lucan, First Booke		70
Beleeve me, whom we feare, we wish to perish.	Ovid's Elegies		2.2.10
Lone women like to emptie houses perish.	Hero and Leander		1.242
PERISH'D			
hadst thou perish'd by the Turke,/Wretched Ferneze might have	Jew	3.2.13	Govnr
PERISHED			
So shall not Englands [Vine] <Vines> be perished,	Edw	5.1.47	Edward
PERISHT			
Not one of them hath perisht in the storme,	Dido	1.1.236	Venus

PERISHT (cont.)			
All humaine kinde by their default had perisht.	Ovid's Elegies	2.14.10	
PERIWIG (See PERRIWIG)			
PERJUR'D			
See here the perjur'd traitor Hungary,	2Tamb	2.3.12	Gazell
Some, that in conquest of the perjur'd Christian,	2Tamb	3.1.39	Orcan
when she bewayles/Her perjur'd Theseus flying vowes and sayles,	Ovid's Elegies	1.7.16	
PERJURD			
Thy mother was no Goddesse perjurd man,	Dido	5.1.156	Dido
These letters, lines, and perjurd papers all,	Dido	5.1.300	Dido
By which she perjurd oft hath lyed [to] <by> me.	Ovid's Elegies	3.3.10	
But bids his darts from perjurd girles retire.	Ovid's Elegies	3.3.36	
PERJURDE			
fellow bed, by all/The Gods who by thee to be perjurde fall,	Ovid's Elegies	3.10.46	
PERJURED			
O wicked sexe, perjured and unjust,	P 693	13.37	Guise
Let marchants seeke wealth, [and] with perjured lips,	Ovid's Elegies	2.10.33	
PERJURIE			
Others report twas Sinons perjurie:	Dido	2.1.111	Dido
A man compact of craft and perjurie,	Dido	2.1.144	Aeneas
For perjurie and slaughter of a Queene:	Dido	5.1.294	Dido
For my accurst and hatefull perjurie.	2Tamb	2.3.3	Sgsmnd
honour, and thereby/Commit'st a sinne far worse than perjurie.	Hero and Leander	1.306	
PERJURIES			
Knights of the post of perjuries make saile,	Ovid's Elegies	1.10.37	
But by my paine to purge her perjuries,	Ovid's Elegies	3.3.21	
And to my losse God-wronging perjuries?	Ovid's Elegies	3.10.22	
PERJURY			
papers as our sacrifice/And witnesse of thy servants perjury.	2Tamb	2.2.46	Orcan
power and puritie/Behold and venge this Traitors perjury.	2Tamb	2.2.54	Orcan
Her eyes and lookes sow'd seeds of perjury,	P 695	13.39	Guise
PERLE			
exceeding store/Of Persian silkes, of gold, and Orient Perle.	Jew	1.1.88	2Merch
PERLES			
Ten thousand Portagues besides great Perles,	Jew	1.2.244	Barab
I have found/The gold, the perles, and Jewels which he hid.	Jew	2.1.23	Abigal
PERMANENT			
Oft have I heard tell, can be permanent.	Jew	1.1.133	Barab
PERMITS			
To practise more then heavenly power permits.	F2009	5.3.27	4Chor
PERNICIOUS			
Then banish that pernicious companie?	Edw	3.1.213	Mortmr
PERNITIOUS			
Whose brightnes such pernitious upstarts dim,	Edw	3.1.165	Herald
PERPENDICULAR			
will I make the Point/That shall begin the Perpendicular.	1Tamb	4.4.82	Tamb
PERPETUALL			
Chiefe Lord and Regent of perpetuall night.	F 445	2.1.57	Faust
with horror stare/Into that vaste perpetuall torture-house,	F1910	5.2.114	BdAngl
Faire natures eye, rise, rise againe and make/Perpetuall day:	F1932	5.2.136	Faust
Perpetuall thirst, and winters lasting rage.	Ovid's Elegies	1.8.114	
Alas a wench is a perpetuall evill.	Ovid's Elegies	2.5.4	
Whose earth doth not perpetuall greene-grasse lacke,	Ovid's Elegies	2.6.50	
Who sayd with gratefull voyce perpetuall bee?	Ovid's Elegies	3.5.98	
PERPETUALLY			
And now must taste hels paines perpetually.	F1895	5.2.99	BdAngl
And then thou must be damn'd perpetually.	F1928	5.2.132	Faust
PERPLEXT			
I have beene wanton, therefore am perplext,	Ovid's Elegies	1.4.45	
PERRIWIG			
Sometimes, like a Perriwig, I sit upon her Brow:	F 666	2.2.115	P Pride
PERSEA			
Unhappie Persea, that in former age/Hast bene the seat of	1Tamb	1.1.6	Cosroe
The hope of Persea, and the verie legges/Whereon our state doth	1Tamb	1.1.59	Mycet
Wel, since I see the state of Persea droope,	1Tamb	1.1.155	Cosroe
Emperour of Asia, and of Persea,	1Tamb	1.1.162	Ortyg
In thee (thou valiant man of Persea)	1Tamb	1.2.166	Tamb
Than dooth the King of Persea in his Crowne:	1Tamb	1.2.242	Tamb
In faire Persea noble Tamburlaine/Shall be my Regent, and	1Tamb	2.1.48	Cosroe
And live like Gentlemen in Persea.	1Tamb	2.2.71	Meandr
Are you the witty King of Persea?	1Tamb	2.4.23	Tamb
Thee doo I make my Regent of Persea,	1Tamb	2.5.8	Cosroe
then Cosroe raign/And governe Persea in her former pomp:	1Tamb	2.5.19	Cosroe
And scornes the Powers that governe Persea.	1Tamb	2.6.40	Cosroe
If Tamburlain be plac'd in Persea.	1Tamb	2.7.39	Usumc
Who thinke you now is king of Persea?	1Tamb	2.7.56	Tamb
And all pronounst me king of Persea.	1Tamb	2.7.67	Tamb
Hie thee my Bassoe fast to Persea,	1Tamb	3.1.21	Bajzth
They say he is the King of Persea.	1Tamb	3.1.45	Argier
You see though first the King of Persea/(Being a Shepheard)	1Tamb	3.2.59	Agidas
By this my sword that conquer'd Persea,	1Tamb	3.3.82	Tamb
And may my Love, the king of Persea,	1Tamb	3.3.132	Zenoc
Ye Gods and powers that governe Persea,	1Tamb	3.3.189	Zenoc
But ere I martch to wealthy Persea,	1Tamb	4.2.47	Tamb
Invest her here my Queene of Persea.	1Tamb	5.1.494	Tamb
And here we crowne thee Queene of Persea,	1Tamb	5.1.507	Tamb
For he shall weare the crowne of Persea,	2Tamb	1.3.74	Tamb
This proud usurping king of Persea,	2Tamb	3.1.15	Callap
with an hoste of men/Lies Tamburlaine, this king of Persea:	2Tamb	3.5.4	2Msngr
least hee hide his crowne as the foolish king of Persea did.	2Tamb	3.5.155	P Tamb
with the martiall spoiles/We will convay with us to Persea.	2Tamb	4.3.106	Tamb
And make our greatest haste to Persea:	2Tamb	5.1.128	Tamb
we leave sufficient garrison/And presently depart to Persea,	2Tamb	5.1.212	Tamb

PERSEA (cont.)

I, good my Lord, let us in hast to Persea,	2Tamb	5.1.214	Therid
Here I began to martch towards Persea,	2Tamb	5.3.126	Tamb

PERSEAN

in Asia, or display/His vagrant Ensigne in the Persean fields,	1Tamb	1.1.45	Meandr
Which will revolt from Persean government,	1Tamb	1.1.91	Cosroe
The plot is laid by Persean Noble men,	1Tamb	1.1.110	Cosroe
were woont to quake/And tremble at the Persean Monarkes name,	1Tamb	1.1.116	Cosroe
We in the name of other Persean states,	1Tamb	1.1.137	Ortyg
Than the possession of the Persean Crowne,	1Tamb	1.2.91	Tamb
A thousand Persean horsmen are at hand,	1Tamb	1.2.111	Souldr
Whom seekst thou Persean? I am Tamburlain.	1Tamb	1.2.153	Tamb
Noble and milde this Persean seemes to be,	1Tamb	1.2.162	Tamb
and if the Persean king/Should offer present Dukedomes to our	1Tamb	1.2.214	Techel
Welcome renowmed Persean to us all.	1Tamb	1.2.239	Techel
And when the princely Persean Diadem,	1Tamb	2.1.45	Cosroe
That ere made passage thorow Persean Armes.	1Tamb	2.3.56	Tamb
And let them know the Persean King is chang'd:	1Tamb	2.5.21	Cosroe
That if I should desire the Persean Crowne,	1Tamb	2.5.76	Tamb
To get the Persean Kingdome to my selfe:	1Tamb	2.5.82	Tamb
Make but a jest to win the Persean crowne.	1Tamb	2.5.98	Tamb
To lift our swords against the Persean King.	1Tamb	2.7.35	Techel
And show your pleasure to the Persean,	1Tamb	3.1.43	Bassoe
Untill the Persean Fleete and men of war,	1Tamb	3.3.252	Tamb
Unlawfully usurpest the Persean seat:	1Tamb	4.2.57	Zabina
By murder raised to the Persean Crowne,	1Tamb	4.3.13	Souldn
time to grace/Her princely Temples with the Persean crowne:	1Tamb	5.1.489	Tamb
shal be plac'd/Wrought with the Persean and Egyptian armes,	2Tamb	3.2.20	Amyras
<Affrica>/Which hath bene subject to the Persean king,	2Tamb	5.1.166	Tamb

PERSEANS

That their reflexions may amaze the Perseans.	1Tamb	1.2.140	Tamb
Shall swallow up these base borne Perseans.	1Tamb	3.3.95	Bajzth
glut our swords/That thirst to drinke the feble Perseans blood.	1Tamb	3.3.165	Bajzth
And neither Perseans Soveraign, nor the Turk/Troubled my sences	1Tamb	5.1.157	Tamb
For ever terme, the Perseans sepulchre,	2Tamb	3.5.19	Callap
(The Perseans Sepulchre) and sacrifice/Mountaines of	2Tamb	3.5.54	Callap
Tartars and Perseans shall inhabit there,	2Tamb	5.1.163	Tamb

PERSEAS

That it may reach the King of Perseas crowne,	1Tamb	2.3.53	Cosroe

PERSECUTES

The slaverie wherewith he persecutes/The noble Turke and his	1Tamb	4.3.26	Arabia

PERSEPOLIS

That robs your merchants of Persepolis,	1Tamb	1.1.37	Meandr
That heretofore have fild Persepolis/With Affrike Captaines,	1Tamb	1.1.141	Ceneus
And now we will to faire Persepolis,	1Tamb	2.5.24	Cosroe
To follow me to faire Persepolis.	1Tamb	2.5.40	Cosroe
And ride in triumph through Persepolis.	1Tamb	2.5.49	Menaph
And ride in triumph through Persepolis?	1Tamb	2.5.50	Tamb
And ride in triumph through Persepolis?	1Tamb	2.5.54	Tamb
Even from Persepolis to Mexico,	1Tamb	3.3.255	Tamb

PERSEUS

Now wish I those wings noble Perseus had,	Ovid's Elegies		3.5.13
Victorious Perseus a wingd steedes back takes.	Ovid's Elegies		3.11.24

PERSEVER

Doe not persever in it like a Divell;	F1711	5.1.38	OldMan
yong-mens mates, to go/If they determine to persever so.	Ovid's Elegies		2.16.18

PERSIA (See PERSEA)

PERSIAN (See also PERSEAN)

I know this face, he is a Persian borne,	Dido	3.1.144	Serg
And of the third part of the Persian ships,	Jew	1.1.2	Barab
with riches, and exceeding store/Of Persian silkes, of gold,	Jew	1.1.88	2Merch

PERSIANS

Of Scythians and slavish Persians.	1Tamb	4.3.68	Souldn

PERSIST

I will persist a terrour to the world,	2Tamb	4.1.200	Tamb
As now you are, so shall you still persist,	P 608	12.21	King

PERSON

Some came in person, others sent their Legats:	Dido	3.1.152	Dido
That thus in person goe with thee to hunt:	Dido	3.3.2	Dido
Expects th'arrivall of her highnesse person.	1Tamb	1.2.79	Agidas
Thy person is more woorth to Tamburlaine,	1Tamb	1.2.90	Tamb
Attend upon the person of your Lord,	1Tamb	3.3.62	Bajzth
How you abuse the person of the king:	1Tamb	4.2.73	Anippe
Unto the hallowed person of a prince,	1Tamb	4.3.40	Souldn
Content thy selfe, his person shall be safe,	1Tamb	4.4.87	Tamb
In whose sweete person is compriz'd the Sum/Of natures Skill	1Tamb	5.1.78	1Virgn
If as beseemes a person of thy state,	1Tamb	5.1.483	Souldn
Her state and person wants no pomp you see,	1Tamb	5.1.485	Tamb
the king of Hungary/Should meet our person to conclude a truce.	2Tamb	1.1.10	Orcan
leave these armes/And save thy sacred person free from scathe:	2Tamb	1.3.10	Zenoc
And set his warlike person to the view/Of fierce Achilles,	2Tamb	3.5.67	Tamb
Thou wouldst with overmatch of person fight,	2Tamb	3.5.76	Orcan
For person like to proove a second Mars.	2Tamb	4.1.35	Calyph
Should come in person to resist your power,	2Tamb	5.2.38	Amasia
Villaines, I am a sacred person, touch me not.	Jew	4.1.201	1Fryar
and Barabas we give/To guard thy person, these our Janizaries:	Jew	5.2.16	Calym
In person there to [mediate] <meditate> your peace;	Jew	5.5.116	Calym
No person, place, or time, or circumstance,	P 606	12.19	King
I think for safety of your royall person,	P 887	17.82	Eprnon
Fearst thou thy person? thou shalt have a guard:	Edw	1.1.166	Edward
That here severelie we will execute/Upon thy person:	Edw	2.5.24	Warwck
I come in person to your majestie,	Edw	3.1.39	SpncrP
That from your princely person you remoove/This Spencer, as a	Edw	3.1.161	Herald

PERSON (cont.)			
Of love and care unto his royall person,	Edw	4.6.25	Queene
To keepe your royall person safe with us,	Edw	4.7.3	Abbot
that one so false/Should come about the person of a prince.	Edw	5.2.105	Mortmr
O disgrace to my person:	F 344	1.4.2	P Robin
we are come from hell in person to shew thee some pastime:	F 654	2.2.103	P Belzeb
PERSONAGE			
What stature wields he, and what personage?	1Tamb	2.1.6	Cosroe
The face and personage of a woondrous man:	1Tamb	2.1.32	Cosroe
PERSWADE			
That could perswade at such a sodaine pinch,	1Tamb	2.1.37	Cosroe
Yet should he not perswade me otherwise,	1Tamb	3.3.210	Zenoc
What simple Virgins may perswade, we will.	1Tamb	5.1.61	2Virgn
Could not perswade you to submission,	2Tamb	5.1.94	Tamb
Perswade our Governor against the Turke;	Jew	2.2.25	1Knght
Mother, perswade me not to weare the crowne,	Edw	5.2.92	Prince
Night, Love, and wine to all extreames perswade:	Ovid's Elegies		1.6.59
PERSWADED			
Be so perswaded, that the Souldan is/No more dismaide with	1Tamb	4.3.30	Souldn
Be thou perswaded, that I love thee well,	Edw	5.2.16	Queene
PERSWADING			
When deepe perswading Oratorie failes.	Hero and Leander		2.226
PERSWASION			
Corinna clips me oft by thy perswasion,	Ovid's Elegies		1.11.5
PERSWASIONS			
Could use perswasions more patheticall.	1Tamb	1.2.211	Therid
I know they would with our perswasions.	1Tamb	2.5.80	Therid
Blind, Fryer, I wrecke not thy perswasions.	Jew	1.2.355	Barab
PERT			
Should by his soveraignes favour grow so pert,	Edw	1.4.404	Mortmr
PERUS'D			
Say Wagner, thou hast perus'd my will,	F1816	5.2.20	Faust
PERUSE			
<Here>, take this booke, <and> peruse it [thoroughly] <well>:	F 543	2.1.155	Mephst
Meane while peruse this booke, and view it throughly,	F 717	2.2.169	Lucifr
<in mean time take this booke, peruse it throwly>,	F 717	(HC264)A	Lucifr
PERUSETH			
give her my writ/But see that forth-with shee peruseth it.	Ovid's Elegies		1.11.16
PERUSIAN			
Adde, Caesar, to these illes Perusian famine;	Lucan, First Booke		41
PESANT			
Pesant, goe seeke companions like thy selfe,	Dido	3.3.21	Dido
Mercilesse villaine, Pesant ignorant,	1Tamb	4.1.64	Souldn
Unlesse he be declinde from that base pesant.	Edw	1.4.7	Mortmr
See what a scornfull looke the pesant casts.	Edw	1.4.14	MortSr
Then speake not for him, let the pesant go.	Edw	1.4.218	Warwck
PESANTES			
To dye by Pesantes, what a greefe is this?	P1009	19.79	Guise
PESANTS			
Shall vulgar pesants storme at what I doe?	Dido	4.4.73	Dido
And plague such Pesants as [resist in] <resisting> me/The power	2Tamb	4.1.157	Tamb
Tut they are pesants, I am Duke of Guise:	P 998	19.68	Guise
base pesants stand,/For loe these Trees remove at my command,	F1425	4.2.101	Faust
PESSANT			
And at the court gate hang the pessant up,	Edw	1.2.30	Mortmr
PESTILENCE			
And the horse pestilence to boot; away.	Jew	3.4.113	Barab
PETER			
Peter Pickeld-herring <Pickle-herring>, and Martin	F 698	2.2.147	P Glutny
But thus I fall to Peter, not to thee.	F 872	3.1.94	Bruno
To me and Peter, shalt thou groveling lie,	F 873	3.1.95	Pope
By Peter you shall dye,	F1030	3.2.50	Pope
PETERS			
Yet will they reade me, and thereby attaine/To Peters Chayre:	Jew	Prol.12	Machvl
And take some part of holy Peters feast,	F 777	2.3.56	2Chor
<faine> see the Pope/And take some part of holy Peters feast,	F 832	3.1.54	Mephst
hollinesse ascends/Saint Peters Chaire and State Pontificall.	F 870	3.1.92	Raymnd
Sound Trumpets then, for thus Saint Peters Heire,	F 875	3.1.97	Pope
From Bruno's backe, ascends Saint Peters Chaire.	F 876	3.1.98	Pope
That Peters heires should tread on Emperours,	F 918	3.1.140	Pope
And by your death to clime Saint Peters Chaire,	F 960	3.1.182	Faust
That we may solemnize Saint Peters feast,	F 978	3.1.200	Pope
And sit in Peters Chaire, despite of chance,	F1214	4.1.60	Emper
bleate, and an asse braye, because it is S. Peters holy day.	F App	p.232 28	P Faust
PETTIE			
Carthage shall vaunt her pettie walles no more,	Dido	5.1.4	Aeneas
Thou for some pettie guift hast let him goe,	Dido	5.1.218	Dido
Sufficient yet for such a pettie King:	P 150	2.93	Guise
PETTY			
Ye petty kings of Turkye I am come,	2Tamb	3.5.64	Tamb
in a brasen Bull/Of great ones envy; o'th poore petty wites,	Jew	Prol.26	Machvl
Strong contermin'd <countermur'd> with other petty Iles;	Jew	5.3.8	Calym
A petty <pretty> case of paltry Legacies:	F 57	1.1.29	Faust
Both Law and Physicke are for petty wits:	F 134	1.1.106	Faust
PETY			
How now ye pety kings, loe, here are Bugges/Wil make the haire	2Tamb	3.5.147	Tamb
PEZANT			
Constrain'd against thy will give it the pezant,	Ovid's Elegies		1.4.65
PHAEDRA (See PHEDRA)			
PHAEMIUS (See PHEMIUS)			
PHAETON			
More then heavens coach, the pride of Phaeton.	2Tamb	5.3.244	Tamb
Ignoble vassaile that like Phaeton,	Edw	1.4.16	Warwck

PHAETON (cont.)
As if another Phaeton had got/The guidance of the sunnes rich — Hero and Leander 1.101
PHALERIS
Which maxime had Phaleris observ'd, ... — Jew Prol.24 Machvl
PHANE
Peace through the world from Janus Phane shal flie, . . — Lucan, First Booke 61
PHANGS
To keepe his Carkasse from their bloudy phangs. . . — F1303 4.1.149 Faust
PHAROS
Memphis, and Pharos that sweete date trees yeelds, . . — Ovid's Elegies 2.13.8
PHARSALIA
Nor in Pharsalia was there such hot war, ... — 1Tamb 3.3.154 Tamb
Pharsalia grone with slaughter;/And Carthage soules be glutted — Lucan, First Booke 38
PHEDRA
Phedra, and Hipolite may read, my care is, ... — Ovid's Elegies 2.18.24
PHEMIUS
Can deafe [eares] <yeares> take delight when Phemius sings,/Or — Ovid's Elegies 3.6.61
PHENISSA
Let my Phenissa graunt, and then I goe: . . . . . — Dido 4.3.6 Aeneas
PHILEMUS
What other heavie news now brings Philemus? . . . — 1Tamb 5.1.377 Zenoc
PHILIP
I, and the catholick Philip King of Spaine, . . . — P 852 17.47 Guise
Philip and Parma, I am slaine for you: . . . . . — P1011 19.81 Guise
Pope excommunicate, Philip depose, ... — P1012 19.82 Guise
PHILIPPI
and under Hemus mount/Philippi plaines; Phoebus what radge is — Lucan, First Booke 680
And other Regions, I have seene Philippi: . . . . . — Lucan, First Booke 693
PHILISTINE
Use him as if he were a--Philistine. . . . . — Jew 2.3.228 Barab
PHILLIPS
That yearely [stuffes] <stuff'd> old Phillips treasury, . — F 159 1.1.131 Valdes
PHILLIS
Or Phillis teares that her [Demophoon] <Domoophon> misses,/What — Ovid's Elegies 2.18.22
And Phillis hath to reade; if now she lives. . . . . — Ovid's Elegies 2.18.32
PHILOMELE
Why Philomele doest Tereus leudnesse mourne? . . . — Ovid's Elegies 2.6.7
PHILOSOPHERS (See also PHYLOSOPHERS)
What, hast the Philosophers stone? . . . . . . — Jew 2.3.111 P Barab
Philosophers looke you, for unto me/Thou cause, what ere thou — Lucan, First Booke 418
PHILOSOPHIE
that despiseth him, can nere/Be good in Logick or Philosophie. — P 410 7.50 Ramus
Make triall now of that philosophie, ... — Edw 4.7.17 Edward
PHILOSOPHUS
[Seeing ubi desinit philosophus, ibi incipit medicus]. . — F 41 1.1.13A Faust
PHILOSOPHY
I'le have them read me strange Philosophy, ... — F 113 1.1.85 Faust
Philosophy is odious and obscure, ... — F 133 1.1.105 Faust
PHISICK
Ah this sweet sight is phisick to my soule, . . . — P1020 19.90 King
PHISICKE
Phisitions, wil no phisicke do her good? . . . . . — 2Tamb 2.4.38 Tamb
PHISITIAN
Be a Phisitian Faustus, heape up gold, ... — F 42 1.1.14 Faust
PHISITIONS
Phisitions, wil no phisicke do her good? . . . . . — 2Tamb 2.4.38 Tamb
See my Phisitions now, how Jove hath sent/A present medicine to — 2Tamb 5.3.105 Tamb
PHLEGETON
Compast with Lethe, Styx, and Phlegeton, ... — 2Tamb 3.2.13 Tamb
Of ever-burning Phlegeton, I sweare, ... — F 827 3.1.49 Faust
PHLEGMATIC (See FLEGMATIQUE)
PHOEBE
Phoebe having fild/Her meeting hornes to match her brothers — Lucan, First Booke 535
With Augures Phoebus, Phoebe with hunters standes, . . — Ovid's Elegies 3.2.51
PHOEBE'S
and Phoebe's waine/Chace Phoebus and inrag'd affect his place, — Lucan, First Booke 77
PHOEBES
And all that pierceth Phoebes silver eie, ... — 1Tamb 3.2.19 Agidas
When wandring Phoebes Ivory cheeks were scortcht/And all the — 2Tamb 5.3.232 Tamb
PHOEBUS
And Phoebus as in Stygian pooles, refraines/To taint his . — Dido 1.1.111 Venus
of his Emperie/By East and west, as Phoebus doth his course: — 1Tamb 1.2.40 Tamb
When Phoebus leaping from his Hemi-Spheare, ... — 2Tamb 1.2.51 Callap
Gives light to Phoebus and the fixed stars, ... — 2Tamb 2.4.50 Tamb
Now Phoebus ope the eye-lids of the day, ... — Jew 2.1.60 Barab
Gallop a pace bright Phoebus through the skie, ... — Edw 4.3.43 Edward
and Phoebe's waine/Chace Phoebus and inrag'd affect his place, — Lucan, First Booke 78
did Thiestes towne/(Mycenae), Phoebus flying through the East: — Lucan, First Booke 542
O Phoebus shouldst thou with thy rayes now sing/The fell Nemean — Lucan, First Booke 654
Disclosing Phoebus furie in this sort: . . . . . — Lucan, First Booke 676
under Hemus mount/Philippi plaines; Phoebus what radge is this? — Lucan, First Booke 680
the world againe/I goe; o Phoebus shew me Neptunes shore, — Lucan, First Booke 692
Then scarse can Phoebus say, this harpe is mine. . . . — Ovid's Elegies 1.1.20
from their crowne/Phoebus and Bacchus wisht were hanging downe. — Ovid's Elegies 1.14.32
Faire Phoebus leade me to the Muses springs. . . . . — Ovid's Elegies 1.15.36
Phoebus gave not Diana such tis thought, ... — Ovid's Elegies 2.5.27
Sappho her vowed harpe laies at Phoebus feete. . . . — Ovid's Elegies 2.18.34
With Augures Phoebus, Phoebe with hunters standes, . . — Ovid's Elegies 3.2.51
I the pure priest of Phoebus and the muses, ... — Ovid's Elegies 3.7.23
Where Linus by his father Phoebus layed/To sing with his . — Ovid's Elegies 3.8.23
And Phoebus had forsooke my worke begun. . . . . . — Ovid's Elegies 3.11.18
PHOENISSA (See PHENISSA)
PHOENIX
There lives the Phoenix one alone bird ever. . . . — Ovid's Elegies 2.6.54

PHRIGIA			
That from the bounds of Phrigia to the sea/Which washeth Cyprus	2Tamb	3.5.11	Callap
Ye gods of Phrigia and Iulus line,	Lucan, First Booke		199
PHRIGIAN			
With twise twelve Phrigian ships I plowed the deepe,	Dido	1.1.220	Aeneas
Our Phrigian [shepherds] <shepherd> haled within the gates,/And	Dido	2.1.153	Aeneas
To see a Phrigian far fet [on] <o'er> <forfeit to> the sea,	Dido	3.3.64	Iarbus
PHTHIAS			
They say Peneus neere Phthias towne did hide.	Ovid's Elegies		3.5.32
PHYLLIS (See PHILLIS)			
PHYLOSOPHERS			
My <His> Ghost be with the old Phylosophers.	F 288	1.3.60	Faust
PHYSICKE (See also PHISICKE)			
Being young I studied Physicke, and began/To practise first	Jew	2.3.181	Barab
And Physicke will not helpe them; they must dye.	Jew	3.6.2	1Fryar
The end of Physicke is our bodies health:	F 45	1.1.17	Faust
Physicke farewell: where is Justinian?	F 55	1.1.27	Faust
Both Law and Physicke are for petty wits:	F 134	1.1.106	Faust
PHYSITIANS (See also PHISITIAN, PHISITIONS)			
If it be so, wee'l have Physitians,	F1830	5.2.34	2Schol
PHYTEUS			
not full of thoughtes/As pure and fiery as Phyteus beames,	2Tamb	5.3.237	Tamb
PIBBLE			
And in his house heape pearle like pibble-stones,	Jew	1.1.23	Barab
PIBBLE-STONES			
And in his house heape pearle like pibble-stones,	Jew	1.1.23	Barab
PICKADEVAUNTS			
seene many boyes with [such pickadevaunts] <beards> I am sure.	F 345	1.4.3	P Robin
you have seene many boyes with such pickadevaunts as I have.	F App	p.229 3	P Clown
PICKE			
the Easterne rockes/Without controule can picke his riches up,	Jew	1.1.22	Barab
Oh, if that be all, I can picke ope your locks.	Jew	4.3.33	Pilia
PICKELD			
Peter Pickeld-herring <Pickle-herring>, and Martin	F 698	2.2.147	P Glutny
PICKELD-HERRING			
Peter Pickeld-herring <Pickle-herring>, and Martin	F 698	2.2.147	P Glutny
PICKLE			
Peter Pickeld-herring <Pickle-herring>, and Martin	F 698	2.2.147	P Glutny
PICKLED			
Jew, he lives upon pickled Grashoppers, and sauc'd Mushrumbs.	Jew	4.4.61	P Ithimr
PICKLE-HERRING			
Peter Pickeld-herring <Pickle-herring>, and Martin	F 698	2.2.147	P Glutny
PICTURE			
View but his picture in this tragicke glasse,	1Tamb	Prol.7	Prolog
And here the picture of Zenocrate,	2Tamb	3.2.25	Tamb
Sweet picture of divine Zenocrate,	2Tamb	3.2.27	Tamb
Image of sloth, and picture of a slave,	2Tamb	4.1.91	Tamb
Here take my picture, and let me weare thine,	Edw	1.4.127	Edward
PICTURES			
See where the pictures of my suiters hang,	Dido	3.1.139	Dido
PIECE (See also PECES, PEECE, PEECES)			
For wofull haires let piece-torne plumes abound,	Ovid's Elegies		2.6.5
PIECEMEAL (See PEECEMEALE)			
PIECES			
and underneath/In severall places are field-pieces pitch'd,	Jew	5.5.27	Barab
Thy lightning can my life in pieces batter.	Ovid's Elegies		1.6.16
hoary flieces/And riveld cheekes I would have puld a pieces.	Ovid's Elegies		1.8.112
PIECE-TORNE			
For wofull haires let piece-torne plumes abound,	Ovid's Elegies		2.6.5
PIERC'D			
Shal want my heart to be with gladnes pierc'd/To do you honor	1Tamb	1.2.250	Therid
I feele my liver pierc'd and all my vaines,	2Tamb	3.4.6	Capt
Pierc'd with the joy of any dignity?	2Tamb	5.3.190	Amyras
PIERCE (Homograph; See also PEARCE, PIERST)			
Which thousand battering Rams could never pierce,	Dido	2.1.175	Aeneas
Or meant to pierce Avernus darksome vaults,	1Tamb	1.2.160	Therid
Proud is his fortune if we pierce it not.	1Tamb	2.1.44	Cosroe
Volleyes of shot pierce through thy charmed Skin,	1Tamb	5.1.221	Bajzth
Pierce through the center of my withered heart,	1Tamb	5.1.303	Bajzth
Fit objects for thy princely eie to pierce.	2Tamb	1.2.45	Callap
Should pierce the blacke circumference of hell,	2Tamb	1.3.145	Techel
Whose darts do pierce the Center of my soule:	2Tamb	2.4.84	Tamb
For she is dead? thy words doo pierce my soule.	2Tamb	2.4.125	Tamb
I long to pierce his bowels with my sword,	2Tamb	3.2.152	Usumc
Whose scalding drops wil pierce thy seething braines,	2Tamb	4.1.144	Jrslem
Nor Pistol, Sword, nor Lance can pierce your flesh.	2Tamb	4.2.66	Olymp
Fall to the earth, and pierce the pit of Hel,	2Tamb	5.1.44	Govnr
Come let us chardge our speares and pierce his breast,	2Tamb	5.3.58	Tamb
Your paines do pierce our soules, no hope survives,	2Tamb	5.3.166	Celeb
Pierce through the coffin and the sheet of gold,	2Tamb	5.3.226	Tamb
And with my prayers pierce [th']impartiall heavens,	Jew	3.2.33	Govnr
And dart her plumes, thinking to pierce my brest,	Edw	1.1.41	Gavstn
Yet liveth Pierce of Gaveston unsurprizd,	Edw	2.5.4	Gavstn
Inexorable, and I shall never see/My lovely Pierce, my Gaveston	Edw	3.1.8	Edward
Good Pierce of Gaveston my sweet favoret,	Edw	3.1.228	Edward
Poore Pierce, and headed him against lawe of armes?	Edw	3.1.238	Edward
To pierce the wind-pipe with a needles point,	Edw	5.4.33	Ltborn
that shall pierce through/The Ebon gates of ever-burning hell,	F1223	4.1.69	Faust
PIERCED			
a king, thy hart/Pierced deeply with sence of my distresse,	Edw	4.7.10	Edward
PIERCETH			
And all that pierceth Phoebes silver eie,	1Tamb	3.2.19	Agidas
PIERCING			
And fixt his piercing instruments of sight:	1Tamb	2.1.14	Menaph

PIERCING (cont.)
Rend not my hart with thy too piercing words, ... Edw 1.4.117 Edward

PIERIAN
Pierian deawe to Poets is distild. . . . . . . Ovid's Elegies 3.8.26

PIERIDES
They sung for honor gainst Pierides, ... Ovid's Elegies 3.6.30

PIERST
And pierst my liver with sharpe needle poynts <needles>? . 1Tamb 3.2.51 Zenoc

PIETIE
What? is not pietie exempt from woe? . . . . . . Ovid's Elegies 3.6.30

PIETY
Pitty in Jewes, nor piety in Turkes. . . . . . . Dido 1.1.79 Venus
The gods care we are cald, and men of piety, ... Jew 3.3.48 Abigal

PIGEONS
And thy faire peacockes by my pigeons pearch: . . . . Ovid's Elegies 3.8.17
Guiding the harmelesse Pigeons with thy hand. . . . . Dido 3.2.59 Venus

PIGGS
And little Piggs, base Hog-sties sacrifice, ... Ovid's Elegies 1.2.26

PIGMALIONS
And would my prayers (as Pigmalions did)/Could give it life, Ovid's Elegies 3.12.16
As faire as was Pigmalions Ivory gyrle, ... Dido 2.1.16 Aeneas

PIGSTY (See HOG-STIES) 2Tamb 1.2.38 Callap

PIKES
And with maine force flung on a ring of pikes, ... Dido 2.1.196 Aeneas
Enforce thee run upon the banefull pikes. . . . . 1Tamb 5.1.220 Bajzth
And harmelesse run among the deadly pikes. . . . . 2Tamb 1.3.46 Tamb
Hast thou beheld a peale of ordinance strike/A ring of pikes, 2Tamb 3.2.99 Tamb
Loe, with a band of bowmen and of pikes, ... Edw 3.1.36 SpncrP
Those of Bituriges and light Axon pikes; . . . . . Lucan, First Booke 424

PILE
I'le sacrifice her on a pile of wood. . . . . . . Jew 2.3.52 Barab
And on a pile of Fagots burnt to death. . . . . . F 963 3.1.185 Faust

PILED
Headles carkasses piled up in heapes, ... Dido 2.1.194 Aeneas

PILGRIMES
As Pilgrimes traveile to our Hemi-spheare, ... 2Tamb 3.2.32 Tamb

PILGRIMS
Once at Jerusalem, where the pilgrims kneel'd, ... Jew 2.3.208 Ithimr

PILIA-BORZA
And now, save Pilia-borza, comes there none. . . . . Jew 3.1.9 Curtzn
Pilia-borza, didst thou meet with Ithimore? . . . . Jew 4.2.1 P Curtzn
Pilia-borza, bid the Fidler give me the posey in his hat there. Jew 4.4.35 P Curtzn

PILIUS
Yet might her touch make youthfull Pilius fire, . . . Ovid's Elegies 3.6.41

PILLAG'D
to feast my traine/Within a Towne of warre so lately pillag'd, Jew 5.3.22 Calym

PILLAGE (See also PILLING)
Pillage and murder are his usuall trades. . . . . . 1Tamb 4.1.66 Souldn

PILLER
This Piller plac'd in memorie of her, ... 2Tamb 3.2.15 Calyph
Oh thou that with a fiery piller led'st/The sonnes of Israel Jew 2.1.12 Barab

PILLERS
The pillers that have bolstered up those tearmes, . . . 1Tamb 3.3.229 Tamb
Whose lofty Pillers, higher than the cloudes, ... 2Tamb 5.1.64 Tamb

PILLING
The Galles and those pilling Briggandines, ... 1Tamb 3.3.248 Tamb

PILLOW
And therefore let it rest upon thy pillow. . . . . Hero and Leander 2.252

PILOT
Than in the haven when the Pilot stands/And viewes a strangers 1Tamb 4.3.32 Souldn
The Pilot from the helme leapes in the sea; . . . . Lucan, First Booke 499

PIN
Our Crowne the pin that thousands seeke to cleave. . . 1Tamb 2.4.9 Mycet

PINCH
That could perswade at such a sodaine pinch, ... 1Tamb 2.1.37 Cosroe
the extremity of heat/To pinch me with intolerable pangs: Jew 5.5.88 Barab

PIN'D
And my pin'd soule resolv'd in liquid [ayre] <ay>, . . . 1Tamb 5.1.300 Bajzth

PINDUS
As [Maenas] <Maenus> full of wine on Pindus raves, . . . Lucan, First Booke 674

PINE (Homograph; See also PINNING, PYN'D)
Made him to thinke Epeus pine-tree Horse/A sacrifize t'appease Dido 2.1.162 Aeneas
How long faire Dido shall I pine for thee? . . . . Dido 3.1.7 Iarbus
Why pine not I, and dye in this distresse? . . . . Jew 1.2.173 Barab
Speake not unto her, let her droope and pine. . . . Edw 1.4.162 Edward
Thy absence made me droope, and pine away, ... Edw 2.2.52 Edward
and here to pine in feare/Of Mortimer and his confederates. Edw 4.7.35 Baldck
As when against pine bearing Ossa's rocks, ... Lucan, First Booke 390
Shaking her snakie haire and crooked pine/With flaming toppe, Lucan, First Booke 571
from thence/To the pine bearing hils, hence to the mounts Lucan, First Booke 688
The lofty Pine from high mount Pelion raught/Ill waies by rough Ovid's Elegies 2.11.1
From steepe Pine-bearing mountains to the plaine: . . . Hero and Leander 1.116

PINE-BEARING
From steepe Pine-bearing mountains to the plaine: . . . Hero and Leander 1.116

PINEONS
All you whose pineons in the cleare aire sore, ... Ovid's Elegies 2.6.11

PINE-TREE
Made him to thinke Epeus pine-tree Horse/A sacrifize t'appease Dido 2.1.162 Aeneas

PINING
Drooping and pining for Zenocrate. . . . . . . 2Tamb 2.4.142 Tamb
Whose pining heart, her inward sighes have blasted, . . . Edw 2.4.24 Queene

PINION'D (See also PINEONS)
See 'em goe pinion'd along by my doore. . . . . . Jew 2.3.180 Barab

PINNING			
Pinning upon his breast a long great Scrowle/How I with	Jew	2.3.197	Barab
PINS			
And being like pins heads, blame me for the bignesse,	Edw	2.1.48	Baldck
PIONERS			
I wil the captive Pioners of Argier,	1Tamb	3.1.58	Bajzth
These Pioners of Argier in Affrica,	2Tamb	3.3.20	Therid
Pioners away, and where I stuck the stake,	2Tamb	3.3.41	Therid
PIPE			
Whose ticing tongue was made of Hermes pipe,	Dido	2.1.145	Aeneas
To pierce the wind-pipe with a needles point,	Edw	5.4.33	Ltborn
Here when the Pipe with solemne tunes doth sound,	Ovid's Elegies		3.12.11
And sweetly on his pipe began to play,	Hero and Leander		1.401
PIPER			
Away to hell, away: on piper.	F 711	2.2.163	Lucifr
PIPES			
that by leaden pipes/Runs to the citie from the mountain	1Tamb	3.1.59	Bajzth
Captaine, these Moores shall cut the leaden pipes,	2Tamb	3.3.29	Techel
PIRACY (See PYRACIE)			
PIRATES			
These are the cruell pirates of Argeire,	1Tamb	3.3.55	Tamb
PIRATS			
Would dash the wreath thou wearst for Pirats wracke.	Lucan, First Booke		123
What, now Scicillian Pirats are supprest,	Lucan, First Booke		336
say Pompey, are these worse/Then Pirats of Sycillia?	Lucan, First Booke		347
PIRENE			
hils, hence to the mounts/Pirene, and so backe to Rome againe.	Lucan, First Booke		689
PIRHUS			
Fierce Pirhus, neither thou nor Hanniball/Art cause, no	Lucan, First Booke		30
PIRRHUS			
At last came Pirrhus fell and full of ire,	Dido	2.1.213	Aeneas
So I escapt the furious Pirrhus wrath:	Dido	2.1.223	Aeneas
As lothing Pirrhus for this wicked act:	Dido	2.1.258	Aeneas
And after by that Pirrhus sacrifizde.	Dido	2.1.288	Aeneas
PISTOL			
Nor Pistol, Sword, nor Lance can pierce your flesh.	2Tamb	4.2.66	Olymp
PIT			
Fall to the earth, and pierce the pit of Hel,	2Tamb	5.1.44	Govnr
asunder; so that it doth sinke/Into a deepe pit past recovery.	Jew	5.5.36	Barab
And perish in the pit thou mad'st for me.	P 963	19.33	King
PITCH			
Huntsmen, why pitch you not your toyles apace,	Dido	3.3.30	Dido
Twixt his manly pitch,/A pearle more worth, then all the world	1Tamb	2.1.11	Menaph
And [pitcht] <pitch> our tents under the Georgean hilles,	1Tamb	2.2.15	Meandr
And raise our honors to as high a pitch/In this our strong and	2Tamb	3.1.30	Callap
For hell and darknesse pitch their pitchy tentes,	2Tamb	5.3.7	Therid
Thence pitch them headlong to the lowest hell:	F1405	4.2.81	Faust
PITCH'D			
Your tentes of white now pitch'd before the gates/And gentle	1Tamb	4.2.111	Therid
and underneath/In severall places are field-pieces pitch'd,	Jew	5.5.27	Barab
PITCHER			
the drie fields strayed/When on her head a water pitcher laied.	Ovid's Elegies		1.10.6
PITCHETH			
The first day when he pitcheth downe his tentes,	1Tamb	4.1.49	2Msngr
PITCHT			
And [pitcht] <pitch> our tents under the Georgean hilles,	1Tamb	2.2.15	Meandr
Our Tents are pitcht, our men stand in array,	2Tamb	1.1.120	Fredrk
pitcht against our power/Betwixt Cutheia and Orminius mount:	2Tamb	2.1.17	Fredrk
Our battaile then in martiall maner pitcht,	2Tamb	3.1.63	Orcan
Which he hath pitcht within his deadly toyle.	P 54	1.54	Navrre
high; but headlong pitcht/Her burning head on bending Hespery.	Lucan, First Booke		544
PITCHY			
her rusty coach/Engyrt with tempests wrapt in pitchy clouds,	1Tamb	5.1.295	Bajzth
Cloth'd with a pitchy cloud for being seene.	2Tamb	4.1.131	Tamb
For hell and darknesse pitch their pitchy tentes,	2Tamb	5.3.7	Therid
And dyms the Welkin, with her pitchy breathe:	F 232	1.3.4	Faust
PITEOUS			
Which piteous wants if Dido will supplie,	Dido	3.1.111	Aeneas
PITEOUSLY			
How piteously with drouping wings he stands,	Ovid's Elegies		3.8.9
PITH			
Though I am slender, I have store of pith,	Ovid's Elegies		2.10.23
PITHO			
And Libas, and the white cheek'de Pitho thrise,	Ovid's Elegies		3.6.24
PITIE			
For my sake pitie him Oceanus,	Dido	1.1.127	Venus
And therefore will take pitie on his toyle,	Dido	1.1.131	Venus
And I for pitie harbord in my bosome,	Dido	5.1.166	Dido
Though thou nor he will pitie me a whit.	Dido	5.1.178	Dido
That Gods and men may pitie this my death,	Dido	5.1.327	Anna
Yet would you have some pitie for my sake,	1Tamb	4.2.123	Zenoc
of them, looking some happie power will pitie and inlarge us.	1Tamb	4.4.100	P Zabina
we intreate/Grace to our words and pitie to our lookes,	1Tamb	5.1.51	2Virgn
Pittie our plightes, O pitie poore Damascus:	1Tamb	5.1.80	1Virgn
Pitie olde age, within whose silver haires/Honor and reverence	1Tamb	5.1.81	1Virgn
Pitie the mariage bed, where many a Lord/In prime and glorie of	1Tamb	5.1.83	1Virgn
Pitie, O pitie, (sacred Emperour)/The prostrate service of this	1Tamb	5.1.99	1Virgn
O pitie, (sacred Emperour)/The prostrate service of this	1Tamb	5.1.99	1Virgn
O pitie us.	1Tamb	5.1.119	Omnes
Of earthly fortune, and respect of pitie,	1Tamb	5.1.365	Zenoc
My Lord I pitie it, and with my heart/Wish your release, but he	2Tamb	1.2.5	Almeda
And Moores, in whom was never pitie found,	2Tamb	3.4.20	Olymp
Take pitie of a Ladies ruthfull teares,	2Tamb	3.4.69	Olymp

PITIE (cont.)
pitie him, in whom thy looks/Have greater operation and more 2Tamb 4.2.28 Therid
That Tamburlaine may pitie our distresse, 2Tamb 5.1.27 1Citzn
You that be noble borne should pitie him. Edw 1.4.80 Edward
Take it: what are you moovde, pitie you me? Edw 5.1.102 Edward
The commons now begin to pitie him, Edw 5.4.2 Mortmr
And I shall pitie her if she speake againe. Edw 5.6.86 King
Pitie us gentle Faustus, save our lives. F1417 4.2.93 Fredrk
PITIED
Whose state he ever pitied and reliev'd, 2Tamb 5.1.32 1Citzn
Tis something to be pitied of a king. Edw 1.4.130 Gavstn
Mine enemie hath pitied my estate, Edw 5.1.149 Edward
And so must die, though pitied by many. Edw 5.3.24 Edward
PITIEST
And if thou pitiest Tamburlain the great, 2Tamb 2.4.117 Tamb
PITIFULL
To whom he used action so pitifull, Dido 2.1.155 Aeneas
Me thinks tis a pitifull sight. 2Tamb 3.2.131 P Calyph
The lord of Bartley is so pitifull, Edw 5.2.34 BshpWn
Thinke not to finde me slack or pitifull. Edw 5.6.82 King
PITTIE
Pittie our plightes, O pitie poore Damascus: 1Tamb 5.1.80 1Virgn
Though gentle mindes should pittie others paines, P 215 4.13 Anjoy
Then pittie or releeve these upstart hereticks. P 222 4.20 Guise
My heart with pittie earnes to see this sight, Edw 4.7.70 Abbot
For my sake sweete sonne pittie Mortimer. Edw 5.6.55 Queene
Relenting thoughts, remorse and pittie rests. Hero and Leander 2.216
The god seeing him with pittie to be moved, Hero and Leander 2.219
If not for love, yet love for pittie sake, Hero and Leander 2.247
Love is not ful of pittie (as men say)/But deaffe and cruell, Hero and Leander 2.287
PITTIED
Let me be envy'd and not pittied! Jew Prol.27 Machvl
Then pittied in a Christian poverty: Jew 1.1.115 Barab
PITTILESSE
Governour, why stand you all so pittilesse? Jew 5.5.71 Barab
PITTIOUS
To see a king in this most pittious state? Edw 5.5.51 Ltborn
PITTY
Tis more then pitty such a heavenly face/Should by hearts 1Tamb 3.2.4 Agidas
flinty hearts/Suppresse all pitty in your stony breasts, Jew 1.2.142 Barab
Pitty the state of a distressed Maid. Jew 1.2.315 Abigal
Or at the least to pitty. Jew 1.2.387 Mthias
Be mov'd at nothing, see thou pitty none, Jew 2.3.171 Barab
Pitty in Jewes, nor piety in Turkes. Jew 3.3.48 Abigal
Should I in pitty of thy plaints or thee, Jew 5.5.72 Govnr
Faustus repent, yet God will pitty thee. F 563 2.2.12 GdAngl
Be I a devill yet God may pitty me, F 566 2.2.15 Faust
Yea <I>, God will pitty me if I repent. F 567 2.2.16 Faust
And pitty of thy future miserie. F1721 5.1.48 OldMan
Now Mars doth rage abroad without all pitty, Ovid's Elegies 1.8.41
On labouring women thou doest pitty take, Ovid's Elegies 2.13.19
PITTYING
As pittying these lovers, downeward creepes. Hero and Leander 2.100
PITY
Ah Shepheard, pity my distressed plight, 1Tamb 1.2.7 Zenoc
That would with pity chear Zabinas heart, 1Tamb 5.1.271 Bajzth
Sweet Almeda, pity the ruthfull plight/Of Callapine, the sonne 2Tamb 1.2.1 Callap
That Jove surchardg'd with pity of our wrongs, 2Tamb 3.1.35 Callap
Ah, pity me my Lord, and draw your sword, 2Tamb 4.2.33 Olymp
O pity us my Lord, and save our honours. 2Tamb 4.3.83 Ladies
Thou art a spirit, God cannot pity thee. F 564 2.2.13 BdAngl
PITYING
Now if thou beest a pitying God of power, Dido 4.2.19 Iarbus
PLAC'D
If Tamburlain be plac'd in Persea. 1Tamb 2.7.39 Usumc
must thou be plac'd by me/That am the Empresse of the mighty 1Tamb 3.3.166 Zabina
of these Eastern parts/Plac'd by the issue of great Bajazeth, 2Tamb 1.1.2 Orcan
Plac'd by her side, looke on their mothers face. 2Tamb 1.3.20 Tamb
This Piller plac'd in memorie of her, 2Tamb 3.2.15 Calyph
And here this mournful streamer shal be plac'd/Wrought with the 2Tamb 3.2.19 Amyras
For there my Pallace royal shal be plac'd: 2Tamb 4.3.111 Tamb
Earth droopes and saies, that hell in heaven is plac'd. 2Tamb 5.3.16 Therid
Earth droopes and saies that hel in heaven is plac'd. 2Tamb 5.3.41 Usumc
Let it be plac'd by this my fatall chaire, 2Tamb 5.3.211 Tamb
Plac'd by my brother, will betray his Lord: P 294 5.21 Anjoy
PLACE (See also PLASTE)
There is a place Hesperia term'd by us, Dido 1.2.20 Cloan
Sit downe Aeneas, sit in Didos place, Dido 2.1.91 Dido
This place beseemes me not, O pardon me. Dido 2.1.94 Aeneas
So, leave me now, let none approach this place. Dido 5.1.291 Dido
And give you equall place in our affaires. 1Tamb 2.5.14 Cosroe
And place himselfe in the Emperiall heaven, 1Tamb 2.7.15 Tamb
Is this a place for mighty Bajazeth? 1Tamb 4.2.83 Bajzth
As far as from the frozen [plage] <place> of heaven, 1Tamb 4.4.122 Tamb
And place their chiefest good in earthly pompe: 1Tamb 5.1.353 Zenoc
And he that meanes to place himselfe therin/Must armed wade up 2Tamb 1.3.83 Tamb
Nor in one place is circumscriptible, 2Tamb 2.2.50 Orcan
Because this place bereft me of my Love: 2Tamb 2.4.138 Tamb
Casemates to place the great Artillery, 2Tamb 3.2.78 Tamb
Invincible by nature of the place. 2Tamb 3.2.90 Tamb
But when I saw the place obscure and darke, 2Tamb 4.2.15 Therid
Now in the place where faire Semiramis, 2Tamb 5.1.73 Tamb
me, that I may resigne/My place and proper tytle to my sonne: 2Tamb 5.3.176 Tamb

PLACE (cont.)
glide by night/About the place where Treasure hath bin hid: Jew 2.1.27 Barab
fortune were so good/As but to be about this happy place; Jew 2.1.32 Abigal
This is the Market-place, here let 'em stand: Jew 2.3.1 1Offcr
And made my house a place for Nuns most chast. Jew 2.3.77 Barab
This is the place, now Abigall shall see/Whether Mathias holds Jew 3.2.1 Mthias
There Ithimore must thou goe place this [pot] <plot>: Jew 3.4.84 Barab
Why true, therefore did I place him there: Jew 4.1.137 Barab
my good Lord, one that can spy a place/Where you may enter, and Jew 5.1.70 Barab
No simple place, no small authority, Jew 5.2.28 Barab
policy for Barabas/To dispossesse himselfe of such a place? Jew 5.2.66 Barab
Except he place his Tables in the streets. Jew 5.3.35 Calym
Goe place some men upon the bridge, P 421 7.61 Dumain
Beleeve me Guise he becomes the place so well, P 495 9.14 QnMoth
No person, place, or time, or circumstance, P 606 12.19 King
That he may come and meet me in some place, P 664 13.8 Duchss
Spaine is the place where he makes peace and warre, P 710 14.13 Navrre
And place our selves in order for the fight. P 742 14.45 Navrre
Thou shouldst not plod one foote beyond this place. Edw 1.1.181 Gavstn
Your grace doth wel to place him by your side, Edw 1.4.10 Lncstr
Deserves no common place, nor meane reward: Edw 1.4.361 Edward
And in this place of honor and of trust, Edw 3.1.143 Edward
keepe these preachments till you come to the place appointed. Edw 4.7.114 P Rice
Remoove him still from place to place by night, Edw 5.2.59 Mortmr
The trumpets sound, I must go take my place. Edw 5.4.72 Mortmr
Foh, heeres a place in deed with all my hart. Edw 5.5.41 Ltborn
And seeing there was no place to mount up higher, Edw 5.6.62 Mortmr
for you to come within fortie foot of the place of execution, F 211 1.2.18 P Wagner
I see it plaine, even heere <in this place> is writ/Homo fuge: F 469 2.1.81 Faust
Tell me, where is the place that men call Hell? F 505 2.1.117 Faust
Hell hath no limits, nor is circumscrib'd,/In one selfe place: F 511 2.1.123 Mephst
But tell me now, what resting place is this? F 800 3.1.22 Faust
And place our servants, and our followers/Close in an ambush F1341 4.2.17 Benvol
Where shall we place our selves Benvolio? F1353 4.2.29 Mrtino
O were that damned Hell-hound but in place, F1355 4.2.31 Benvol
I but sir sauce box, know you in what place? F1616 4.6.59 Servnt
Nature, and every power shal give thee place, Lucan, First Booke 51
The midst is best; that place is pure, and bright, Lucan, First Booke 58
and Phoebe's waine/Chace Phoebus and inrag'd affect his place, Lucan, First Booke 78
and thoughts that alwaies scorn'd/A second place; Pompey could Lucan, First Booke 125
The soldiours having won the market place, Lucan, First Booke 238
it inters with murmurs dolorous,/And cals the place Bidentall: Lucan, First Booke 607
My spotlesse life, which but to Gods [gives] <give> place, Ovid's Elegies 1.3.13
The thing and place shall counsell us the rest. Ovid's Elegies 1.4.54
But what entreates for thee some-times tooke place, Ovid's Elegies 1.6.21
Put in their place thy keembed haires againe. Ovid's Elegies 1.7.68
will I grace them/And in the midst of Venus temple place them. Ovid's Elegies 1.11.26
How oft wisht I night would not give thee place, Ovid's Elegies 1.13.27
Let Kings give place to verse, and kingly showes, Ovid's Elegies 1.15.33
I would not out, might I in one place hit, Ovid's Elegies 2.15.19
And may repulse place for our wishes strike. Ovid's Elegies 2.19.6
Tis credible some [god-head] <good head> haunts the place. Ovid's Elegies 3.1.2
Pay it not heere, but in an other place. Ovid's Elegies 3.2.84
his [streame] <shame> chargd, the streame chargd, gave place. Ovid's Elegies 3.5.44
And one gave place still as another came. Ovid's Elegies 3.6.64
To cover it, spilt water in <on> the place. Ovid's Elegies 3.6.84
Where Ceres went each place was harvest there. Ovid's Elegies 3.9.38
When I to watch supplyed a servants place. Ovid's Elegies 3.10.12
Nor hath it any place of residence, Hero and Leander 1.272
And Jupiter unto his place restor'd. Hero and Leander 1.464
Set in a forren place, and straight from thence, Hero and Leander 2.119
And in her luke-warme place Leander lay. Hero and Leander 2.254

PLACER
Hermoso Placer de los Dineros. Jew 2.1.64 Barab

PLACES
Mount up your royall places of estate, 1Tamb 5.1.525 Tamb
and underneath/In severall places are field-pieces pitch'd, Jew 5.5.27 Barab
Because my places being but three, contains all his: P 405 7.45 Ramus
Whether you will, all places are alike, Edw 5.1.145 Edward
All places shall be hell that is not heaven. F 515 2.1.127 Mephst
Supplying their voide places with the worst. Ovid's Elegies 2.6.40
His sword layed by, safe, though rude places yeelds. Ovid's Elegies 2.9.20
And writings did from diverse places frame, Ovid's Elegies 2.18.28
The Lydian buskin [in] fit [paces] <places> kept her. Ovid's Elegies 3.1.14
The places lawes this benefit allowe. Ovid's Elegies 3.2.20
Strayd bare-foote through sole places on a time. Ovid's Elegies 3.5.50

PLACET
Whilste I cry placet like a Senator. P 861 17.56 King

PLACING
For there I left the Governour placing Nunnes, Jew 1.2.254 Abigal

PLACKETS
tickle the pretie wenches plackets Ile be amongst them ifaith. F App p.231 63 P Clown

PLAGE
As far as from the frozen [plage] <place> of heaven, 1Tamb 4.4.122 Tamb
From Scythia to the Orientall Plage/Of India, wher raging 2Tamb 1.1.68 Orcan

PLAGU'D
The Cardinals will be plagu'd for this anon. F 976 3.1.198 Faust
But mine must live still to be plagu'd in hell. F1971 5.2.175 Faust

PLAGUE (See also PLAUGDE)
Harkening when he shall bid them plague the world. 2Tamb 3.4.60 Therid
And plague such Pesants as [resist in] <resisting> me/The power 2Tamb 4.1.157 Tamb
You partiall heavens, have I deserv'd this plague? Jew 1.2.259 Barab
For purging of the realme of such a plague. Edw 1.4.270 Mortmr

PLAGUE (cont.)

Mine enemies will I plague, my friends advance,	Edw	5.4.67		Mortmr
Wherby whole Cities have escap't the plague,	F 49	1.1.21		Faust
<A plague on her for a hote whore>.	F 534	(HC261)A	P	Faust
A plague take you, I thought you did not sneake up and downe	F 742	2.3.21	P	Dick
A plague take you, I thought 'twas your knavery to take it	F1110	3.3.23	P	Vintnr
A plague upon you, let me sleepe a while.	F1283	4.1.129		Benvol
And hell shall after plague their treacherie.	F1407	4.2.83		Faust
I, a plague take him, heere's some on's have cause to know him;	F1523	4.5.19	P	HrsCsr
Or if Fate rule them, Rome thy Cittizens/Are neere some plague:	Lucan, First Booke			644
with what plague/Meane ye to radge?	Lucan, First Booke			648
To plague your bodies with such harmefull strokes?	Ovid's Elegies			2.14.34
PLAGUES				
Then haste Agydas, and prevent the plagues:	1Tamb	3.2.100		Agidas
offences feele/Such plagues as heaven and we can poure on him.	1Tamb	4.3.45		Arabia
The plagues of Egypt, and the curse of heaven,	Jew	1.2.162		Barab
These plagues arise from wreake of civill power.	Lucan, First Booke			32
PLAGUING				
But marke how I am blest for plaguing them,	Jew	2.3.199		Barab
PLAIED				
art thou aye gravely plaied?	Ovid's Elegies			3.1.36
I have thy husband, guard, and fellow plaied.	Ovid's Elegies			3.10.18
PLAIES				
Plaies with her goary coulours of revenge,	P 719	14.22		Navrre
One plaies continually upon a Drum,	Edw	5.5.61		Edward
Plaies, maskes, and all that stern age counteth evill.	Hero and Leander			1.302
PLAINE (Homograph; See also PLAYNES)				
And plaine to him the summe of your distresse.	Dido	1.2.2		Illion
By plaine and easie demonstration,	2Tamb	3.2.84		Tamb
Plaine Barabas: oh that wicked Curtezane!	Jew	4.3.2		Barab
To plaine me to the gods against them both:	Edw	5.1.22		Edward
I see it plaine, even heere <in this place> is writ/Homo fuge:	F 469	2.1.81		Faust
Faustus I see it plaine,	F1270	4.1.116		Emper
Untill the cruel Giants war was done)/We plaine not heavens,	Lucan, First Booke			37
his troupes of daring horsemen fought/Upon Mevanias plaine,	Lucan, First Booke			470
And quiver bearing Dian till the plaine:	Ovid's Elegies			1.1.14
While thou wert plaine, I lov'd thy minde and face:	Ovid's Elegies			1.10.13
Or shall I plaine some God against me warres?	Ovid's Elegies			3.11.4
From steepe Pine-bearing mountains to the plaine:	Hero and Leander			1.116
As in plaine termes (yet cunningly) he crav'd it,	Hero and Leander			2.71
PLAINELY				
Now tell me, Governor, and plainely too,	Jew	5.2.55		Barab
My Lord, to speak more plainely, thus it is:	P 847	17.42		Guise
And plainely saith, twas thou that murdredst him.	Edw	5.6.42		King
PLAINER				
And bid me say as plainer to your grace,	Edw	3.1.158		Herald
PLAINES				
Is this the wood that grew in Carthage plaines,	Dido	4.4.136		Dido
of my company/Scowting abroad upon these champion plaines,	1Tamb	2.2.40		Spy
That hides these plaines, and seems as vast and wide,	2Tamb	1.1.107		Sgsmnd
Now rest thee here on faire Larissa Plaines,	2Tamb	1.3.5		Tamb
Promist to meet me on Larissa plaines/With hostes apeece	2Tamb	1.3.107		Tamb
Now will we banquet on these plaines a while,	2Tamb	1.3.157		Tamb
watch and ward shall keepe his trunke/Amidst these plaines,	2Tamb	2.3.39		Orcan
Sindge these fair plaines, and make them seeme as black/As is	2Tamb	3.2.11		Tamb
Thou shalt not beautifie Larissa plaines,	2Tamb	3.2.34		Tamb
A hundred horse shall scout about the plaines/To spie what	2Tamb	3.3.47		Techel
Covers the hils, the valleies and the plaines.	2Tamb	3.5.13		Callap
souldiers now that fought/So Lion-like upon Asphaltis plaines?	2Tamb	4.3.68		Tamb
and under Hemus mount/Philippi plaines; Phoebus what radge is	Lucan, First Booke			680
Such as in hilly Idas watry plaines,	Ovid's Elegies			1.14.11
PLAINING				
Heare, heare, O heare Iarbus plaining prayers,	Dido	4.2.8		Iarbus
PLAINLY				
To this I fondly loves of flouds told plainly:	Ovid's Elegies			3.5.101
PLAINST				
If reading five thou plainst of tediousnesse,	Ovid's Elegies			1.1.3
PLAINTES				
Shall drive no plaintes into the Guises eares,	P 532	10.5		Guise
PLAINTS				
Whiles my Aeneas spends himselfe in plaints,	Dido	1.1.140		Venus
My teares nor plaints could mollifie a whit:	Dido	5.1.235		Anna
Should I in pitty of thy plaints or thee,	Jew	5.5.72		Govnr
That Isabell shall make her plaints in vaine,	Edw	3.1.278		Levune
PLANCKE				
There have I hid close underneath the plancke/That runs along	Jew	1.2.296		Barab
espy'd a time/To search the plancke my father did appoint;	Jew	2.1.21		Abigal
PLANE				
The sworde shall plane the furrowes of thy browes,	Edw	1.1.94		Edward
PLANET				
And like a planet, mooving severall waies,	Hero and Leander			1.361
PLANETING				
Memphis never had/For skill in stars, and tune-full planeting,	Lucan, First Booke			640
PLANETS				
And like the Planets ever love to raunge:	Dido	3.3.68		Iarbus
And thorough your Planets I perceive you thinke,	1Tamb	1.1.19		Mycet
And know my customes are as peremptory/As wrathfull Planets,	1Tamb	5.1.128		Tamb
The Moone, the Planets, and the Meteors light.	1Tamb	5.1.150		Tamb
I might see al characters of <and> planets of the heavens,	F 551.5	2.1.168A	P	Faust
Who knowes not the double motion of the Planets?	F 602	2.2.51		Faust
Nine, the seven Planets, the Firmament, and the Emperiall	F 610	2.2.59	P	Mephst
He viewes the cloudes, the Planets, and the Starres,	F 760	2.3.39		2Chor
The Planets seven, the gloomy aire,	F 999	3.2.19		Mephst

PLANETS (cont.)
why doe the Planets/Alter their course; and vainly dim their — Lucan, First Booke 662

PLANKS
And in a stable lie upon the planks. — 2Tamb 3.5.107 Tamb

PLANNETS
And measure every wandring plannets course: — 1Tamb 2.7.23 Tamb

PLANT
And plant our pleasant suburbes with her fumes. — Dido 5.1.15 Aeneas
To plant our selves with such authoritie, — P 637 12.50 QnMoth
To plant the true succession of the faith, — P 715 14.18 Bartus
To plant the Pope and popelings in the Realme, — P 925 18.26 Navrre

PLANTAGENET
Stay Edmund, never was Plantagenet/False of his word, and — Edw 2.3.11 Mortmr

PLANTED
And planted love where envie erst had sprong. — Dido 3.2.52 Juno
I shall be planted in as rich a land. — Dido 4.4.82 Aeneas
And with young Orphans planted Hospitals, — Jew 2.3.194 Barab
But without thee, although vine-planted ground/Conteines me, — Ovid's Elegies 2.16.33

PLANTS
wherein I might see al plants, hearbes and trees that grow upon — F 551.9 2.1.172A P Faust
And brings good fortune, a rich lover plants/His love on thee, — Ovid's Elegies 1.8.31

PLASTE
A pearle more worth, then all the world is plaste: — 1Tamb 2.1.12 Menaph

PLATE (See also PLATS)
Hollow Pyramides of silver plate: — Dido 3.1.123 Dido
and store of golden plate; besides two thousand duckets ready — F1676 5.1.3 P Wagner
Men tooke delight in Jewels, houses, plate, — Lucan, First Booke 164

PLATFORME
swift Mercury/When I was laying a platforme for these walles, — Dido 5.1.94 Aeneas

PLATO
That in our famous nurseries of artes/Thou suckedst from Plato, — Edw 4.7.19 Edward

PLATOES
Even from this day to Platoes wondrous yeare, — 1Tamb 4.2.96 Tamb

PLATS
And if he has, he is worth three hundred plats. — Jew 2.3.102 Barab
Ratest thou this Moore but at two hundred plats? — Jew 2.3.107 Lodowk

PLAUDE
And now <so> to patient judgements we appeale <our plaude>, — F 9 Prol.9 1Chor

PLAUGDE
Being conquered, we are plaugde with civil war. — Lucan, First Booke 108

PLAUTUS
Rude Ennius, and Plautus full of wit, — Ovid's Elegies 1.15.19

PLAY (See also PLAIES)
Come gentle Ganimed and play with me, — Dido 1.1.1 Jupitr
Now is the time for me to play my part: — Dido 1.1.182 Venus
in stead of him/Will set thee on her lap and play with thee: — Dido 2.1.325 Venus
I will faire mother, and so play my part, — Dido 2.1.332 Cupid
Through which the water shall delight to play: — Dido 3.1.119 Dido
Or looke you, I should play the Orator? — 1Tamb 1.2.129 Tamb
Our swordes shall play the Orators for us. — 1Tamb 1.2.132 Techel
On which the breath of heaven delights to play, — 1Tamb 2.1.25 Menaph
and holy Seraphins/That sing and play before the king of kings, — 2Tamb 2.4.27 Tamb
Shal play upon the bulwarks of thy hold/Volleies of ordinance — 2Tamb 3.3.24 Therid
And souldiers play the men, the [hold] <holds> is yours. — 2Tamb 3.3.63 Techel
Viceroies and Peeres of Turky play the men, — 2Tamb 3.5.14 Callap
Content my Lord, but what shal we play for? — 2Tamb 4.1.63 P Perdic
Play, Fidler, or I'le cut your cats guts into chitterlins. — Jew 4.4.44 P Ithimr
There's two crownes for thee, play. — Jew 4.4.47 Pilia
Now come thou forth and play thy tragick part, — P 85 2.28 Guise
As if a Goose should play the Porpintine, — Edw 1.1.40 Gavstn
But nephew, do not play the sophister. — Edw 1.4.255 MortSr
And Il'e play Diana, and send you the hornes presently. — F1257 4.1.103 P Faust
While Mars doth take the Aonian harpe to play? — Ovid's Elegies 1.1.16
Faire women play, shee's chast whom none will have, — Ovid's Elegies 1.8.43
Least they should fly, being tane, the tirant play. — Ovid's Elegies 1.8.70
Thou art as faire as shee, then kisse and play. — Ovid's Elegies 1.13.44
Good forme there is, yeares apt to play togither, — Ovid's Elegies 2.3.13
Although thou chafe, stolne pleasure is sweet play, — Ovid's Elegies 3.4.31
To take it in her hand and play with it. — Ovid's Elegies 3.6.74
The bawde I play, lovers to her I guide: — Ovid's Elegies 3.11.11
for they tooke delite/To play upon those hands, they were so — Hero and Leander 1.30
Leander, thou art made for amorous play: — Hero and Leander 1.88
and there God knowes I play/With Venus swannes and sparrowes — Hero and Leander 1.351
And sweetly on his pipe began to play, — Hero and Leander 1.401

PLAYD
But playd he nere so sweet, I let him goe: — Dido 3.1.160 Dido
He clapt his plumpe cheekes, with his tresses playd, — Hero and Leander 2.181
Playd with a boy so faire and [so] kind, — Hero and Leander 2.195
greedily assayd/To touch those dainties, she the Harpey playd, — Hero and Leander 2.270

PLAYDE
Whence knowes Corinna that with thee I playde? — Ovid's Elegies 2.8.6

PLAYED
Thy muse hath played what may milde girles content, — Ovid's Elegies 3.1.27

PLAYERS
But once, and then thy souldiers marcht like players, — Edw 2.2.183 Mortmr

PLAYES
little sonne/Playes with your garments and imbraceth you. — Dido 3.1.21 Anna

PLAYFELLOW
And this yong Prince shall be thy playfellow. — Dido 2.1.307 Venus

PLAYING
And playing with that female wanton boy, — Dido 1.1.51 Venus
That might be urg'd to witnesse our false playing. — Ovid's Elegies 2.8.8
Seeing thou art faire, I barre not thy false playing, — Ovid's Elegies 3.13.1

PLAYING (cont.)
Save that the sea playing on yellow sand, — Hero and Leander 1.347
PLAYNES
Wars worse then civill on Thessalian playnes, — Lucan, First Booke 1
PLEACE
Champions pleace <please> Pollux, Castor [love] <loves> — Ovid's Elegies 3.2.54
PLEAD
Or plead for mercie at your highnesse feet. — 1Tamb 1.1.73 Therid
Must plead for mercie at his kingly feet, — 1Tamb 3.3.174 Zenoc
Yet give me leave to plead for him my Lord. — 1Tamb 4.4.86 Zenoc
And plead in vaine, unpleasing soverainty. — 2Tamb 5.3.198 Amyras
What, would ye have me plead for Gaveston? — Edw 1.4.213 Mortmr
Plead for him he that will, I am resolvde. — Edw 1.4.214 MortSr
PLEADE
As poore distressed miserie may pleade: — Dido 1.2.6 Illion
And therefore though I pleade for his repeall, — Edw 1.4.241 Mortmr
And I might pleade, and draw the Commons minds/To favour thee, — Lucan, First Booke 275
PLEADED
Hath often pleaded kindred to the King. — P 108 2.51 Guise
Seeing thou hast pleaded with so good successe. — Edw 1.4.329 Edward
PLEADS
No? doe but marke how earnestly she pleads. — Edw 1.4.234 Warwck
PLEASANCE
And held the cloath of pleasance whiles you dranke, — Dido 1.1.6 Ganimd
PLEASANT (See also PLEASENT)
The ayre is pleasant, and the soyle most fit/For Cities, and — Dido 1.1.178 Achat
And plant our pleasant suburbes with her fumes. — Dido 5.1.15 Aeneas
And speech more pleasant than sweet harmony: — 1Tamb 3.3.121 Tamb
No such discourse is pleasant in mine eares, — 2Tamb 4.2.46 Olymp
I must have wanton Poets, pleasant wits, — Edw 1.1.51 Gavstn
You must be proud, bold, pleasant, resolute, — Edw 2.1.42 Spencr
search all corners of the new-found-world/For pleasant fruites, — F 112 1.1.84 Faust
That sight will be as pleasant to <pleasing unto> me, as — F 657 2.2.106 P Faust
for these pleasant sights, nor know I how sufficiently to — F1558 4.6.1 P Duke
til I am past this faire and pleasant greene, ile walke on — F App p.239 96 P Faust
Vaine babling speech, and pleasant peace thou lovedst. — Ovid's Elegies 2.6.26
Our pleasant scapes shew thee no clowne to be, — Ovid's Elegies 2.8.3
Thou that frequents Canopus pleasant fields, — Ovid's Elegies 2.13.7
A pleasant smiling cheeke, a speaking eye, — Hero and Leander 1.85
PLEASANTNES
How likes your grace my sonnes pleasantnes? — P 632 12.45 QnMoth
PLEAS'D
You that/Were ne're possest of wealth, are pleas'd with want. — Jew 1.2.201 Barab
For proofe whereof, if so your Grace be pleas'd, — F1221 4.1.67 Faust
Mistris thou knowest, thou hast a blest youth pleas'd, — Ovid's Elegies 1.8.23
Shee pleas'd me, soone I sent, and did her woo, — Ovid's Elegies 2.2.5
Tis ill they pleas'd so much, for in my lips, — Ovid's Elegies 2.5.57
PLEASD
Whom Ilia pleasd, though in her lookes griefe reveld, — Ovid's Elegies 3.5.47
The people by my company she pleasd, — Ovid's Elegies 3.10.19
PLEASDE
Sweet Jupiter, if ere I pleasde thine eye, — Dido 1.1.19 Ganimd
But his fantastick humours pleasde not me: — Dido 3.1.158 Dido
I must be pleasde perforce, wretched Zenocrate. — 1Tamb 1.2.259 Zenoc
If with their lives they will be pleasde to yeeld, — 1Tamb 4.4.89 Tamb
But I am pleasde you shall not see him there: — 1Tamb 5.1.113 Tamb
And I am pleasde with this my overthrow, — 1Tamb 5.1.482 Souldn
I must and wil be pleasde, and you shall yeeld: — 2Tamb 4.2.53 Therid
I heard your Majestie was scarsely pleasde, — P 967 19.37 Guise
This tombe approoves, I pleasde my mistresse well, — Ovid's Elegies 2.6.61
PLEASE (See also PLEAZD)
May it please your grace to let Aeneas waite: — Dido 2.1.87 Aeneas
Achates, how doth Carthage please your Lord? — Dido 3.1.97 Dido
That can call them forth when as she please, — Dido 4.1.4 Iarbus
And then applaud his fortunes if you please. — 1Tamb Prol.8 Prolog
Such as his Highnesse please, but some must stay/To rule the — 1Tamb 3.3.28 Bassoe
Twill please my mind as wel to heare both you/Have won a heape — 2Tamb 4.1.36 Calyph
We Jewes can fawne like Spaniels when we please; — Jew 2.3.20 Barab
My profession what you please. — Jew 2.3.166 Ithimr
I have it for you, Sir; please you walke in with me: — Jew 2.3.220 Barab
And you can have it, Sir, and if you please. — Jew 4.2.56 Pilia
please you dine with me, Sir, and you shal be most hartily — Jew 4.3.29 P Barab
Will't please thee, mighty Selim-Calymath, — Jew 5.5.57 Barab
And it please your grace the Lord high Admirall, — P 243 4.41 Man
To please himselfe with mannage of the warres, — P 459 8.9 Anjoy
Then may it please your Majestie to give me leave, — P 616 12.29 Mugern
And please your grace the Duke of Guise doth crave/Accesse unto — P 959 19.29 Eprnon
please your Majestie heere is a Frier of the order of the — P1155 22.17 P 1Msngr
of a string/May draw the pliant king which way I please: — Edw 1.1.53 Gavstn
Such things as these best please his majestie, — Edw 1.1.71 Gavstn
May it please your lordship to subscribe your name. — Edw 1.4.2 Lncstr
And saying, trulie ant may please your honor, — Edw 2.1.40 Spencr
A trifle, weele expell him when we please: — Edw 2.2.10 Edward
Mait please your grace to entertaine them now. — Edw 2.2.241 Neece
And please my father well, and then a Fig/For all my unckles — Edw 4.2.4 Prince
But as the realme and parlement shall please, — Edw 4.6.36 Mortmr
Who now makes Fortunes wheele turne as he please, — Edw 5.2.53 Mortmr
Shall I make spirits fetch me what I please? — F 106 1.1.78 Faust
Like Lyons shall they guard us when we please, — F 151 1.1.123 Valdes
But may I raise such <up> spirits when I please? — F 475 2.1.87 Faust
at all times, in what shape [or] <and> forme soever he please. — F 492 2.1.104 P Faust
and incantations, that I might raise up spirits when I please]. — F 551.2 2.1.165A P Faust
And what might please mine eye, I there beheld. — F 853 3.1.75 Faust

PLEASE (cont.)

And doe what ere I please, unseene of any.	F 993	3.2.13		Faust
<to do what I please unseene of any whilst I stay in Rome>.	F 993	(HC266)A	P	Faust
First, may it please your sacred Holinesse,	F1013	3.2.33		1Card
Please it your holinesse, I thinke it be some Ghost crept out	F1059	3.2.79	P	Archbp
will it please you to take a shoulder of Mutton to supper, and	F1121	3.3.34	P	Robin
To accomplish what soever the Doctor please.	F1183	4.1.29		Mrtino
Be it as Faustus please, we are content.	F1253	4.1.99		Emper
And therefore my Lord, so please your Majesty,	F1300	4.1.146		Faust
If it please you, the Duke of Vanholt doth earnestly entreate	F1500	4.4.44	P	Wagner
so delighted me, as nothing in the world could please me more.	F1561	4.6.4	P	Duke
Please it your grace, the yeare is divided into two circles	F1581	4.6.24	P	Faust
With all my heart kind Doctor, please thy selfe,	F1623	4.6.66		Duke
My Lord of Lorraine, wilt please you draw neare.	F App	p.231 1	P	Pope
please your highnes now to send for the knight that was so	F App	p.238 66	P	Faust
here they be madam, wilt please you taste on them.	F App	p.242 15	P	Faust
What God it please thee be, or where to sway:	Lucan, First Booke	52		
Caesar is thine, so please it thee, thy soldier;	Lucan, First Booke	204		
held up, all joyntly cryde/They'ill follow where he please:	Lucan, First Booke	389		
When I (my light) do or say ought that please thee,	Ovid's Elegies	1.4.25		
And why shouldst not please?	Ovid's Elegies	1.8.25		
To please thy selfe, thy selfe put out of minde.	Ovid's Elegies	1.14.38		
Let him please, haunt the house, be kindly usd,	Ovid's Elegies	2.2.29		
Please her, her hate makes others thee abhorre,	Ovid's Elegies	2.3.11		
but where love please/[Am] <And> driven like a ship upon rough	Ovid's Elegies	2.4.7		
Both short and long please me, for I love both:	Ovid's Elegies	2.4.36		
What helpes it thou wert given to please my wench,	Ovid's Elegies	2.6.19		
Turnes all the goodly <godly> birdes to what she please.	Ovid's Elegies	2.6.58		
[And] this doth please me most, and so doth she.	Ovid's Elegies	2.10.8		
To please me, what faire termes and sweet words ha's shee,	Ovid's Elegies	2.19.17		
let either heed/What please them, and their eyes let either	Ovid's Elegies	3.2.6		
Champions pleace <please> Pollux, Castor [love] <loves>	Ovid's Elegies	3.2.54		
Nor doth her face please, but her husbands love;	Ovid's Elegies	3.4.27		
Cannot a faire one, if not chast, please thee?	Ovid's Elegies	3.4.41		
Not Calydon, nor Aetolia did please:	Ovid's Elegies	3.5.37		
These gifts are meete to please the powers divine.	Ovid's Elegies	3.9.48		
To please the carelesse and disdainfull eies,	Hero and Leander	1.13		
And [throw] <threw> him gawdie toies to please his eie,	Hero and Leander	2.187		

PLEASED

Beleeve me maister Doctor, this merriment hath much pleased me.	F App	p.242 2	P	Duke

PLEASENT

send for the knight that was so pleasent with me here of late?	F App	p.238 67	P	Faust

PLEASEST

Sweete Mephostophilis, thou pleasest me:	F 836	3.1.58		Faust
And in this sight thou better pleasest me,	F1271	4.1.117		Emper

PLEASETH

Doe thou but say their colour pleaseth me.	Dido	1.1.41		Jupitr
Pleaseth your mightinesse to understand,	1Tamb	4.1.47		2Msngr
Pleaseth your Majesty to drink this potion,	2Tamb	5.3.78		Phsitn
Pleaseth your grace to let the Surgeon search your wound.	P1191	22.53		Navrre
So pleaseth the Queene my mother, me it likes.	Edw	4.2.21		Prince
It pleaseth me, and Isabell the Queene.	Edw	5.4.71		Mortmr
Resigne, or seale, or what so pleaseth us.	F 936	3.1.158		Pope
pleaseth your grace to thinke but well of that which Faustus	F1564	4.6.7	P	Faust
A yong wench pleaseth, and an old is good,	Ovid's Elegies	2.4.45		
Peace pleaseth me, and in mid peace is love.	Ovid's Elegies	3.2.50		
She pleaseth best, I feare, if any say.	Ovid's Elegies	3.4.32		

PLEASING

Come let us thinke upon some pleasing sport,	Dido	2.1.302		Dido
Sweete speeches, comedies, and pleasing showes,	Edw	1.1.56		Gavstn
That sight will be as pleasant to <pleasing unto> me, as	F 657	2.2.106	P	Faust
This cause hath thee from pleasing me debard.	Ovid's Elegies	1.10.12		
The more a gentle pleasing heat revived,	Hero and Leander	2.68		

PLEASURE

Whose face reflects such pleasure to mine eyes,	Dido	1.1.24		Jupitr
here, tell me in sooth/In what might Dido highly pleasure thee.	Dido	3.1.102		Dido
His Highnesse pleasure is that he should live,	1Tamb	2.2.37		Meandr
I thinke the pleasure they enjoy in heaven/Can not compare with	1Tamb	2.5.58		Therid
And show your pleasure to the Persean,	1Tamb	3.1.43		Bassoe
I take no pleasure to be murtherous,	2Tamb	4.1.29		Calyph
Let them take pleasure soundly in their spoiles,	2Tamb	4.3.92		Tamb
The gentle King whose pleasure uncontrolde,	P 127	2.70		Guise
It is our pleasure, we will have it so.	Edw	1.4.9		Edward
That waites your pleasure, and the day growes old.	Edw	4.7.85		Leistr
And that you lay for pleasure here a space,	Edw	5.1.3		Leistr
But bee content, seeing it his highnesse pleasure.	Edw	5.2.94		Queene
Had not sweete pleasure conquer'd deepe despaire.	F 576	2.2.25		Faust
yeares of liberty/I'le spend in pleasure and in daliance,	F 840	3.1.62		Faust
Onely for pleasure of these damned slaves.	F1119	3.3.32		Mephst
[When Faustus had with pleasure tane the view]/[Of rarest	F1138	3.3.51A		3Chor
that you have taken no pleasure in those sights; therefor I	F1566	4.6.9	P	Faust
Is all our pleasure turn'd to melancholy?	F1828	5.2.32		2Schol
pleasure of foure and twenty yeares hath Faustus lost eternall	F1859	5.2.63	P	Faust
He that loves pleasure, must for pleasure fall.	F1923	5.2.127		BdAngl
in our parish dance at my pleasure starke naked before me,	F App	p.233 4	P	Robin
Onely for pleasure of these damned slaves.	F App	p.235 39		Mephst
And for I see your curteous intent to pleasure me, I wil not	F App	p.242 8	P	Duchss
About thy neck shall he at pleasure skippe?	Ovid's Elegies	1.4.6		
When pleasure mov'd us to our sweetest worke.	Ovid's Elegies	1.4.48		
Pleasure, and ease had mollifide my minde.	Ovid's Elegies	1.9.42		
and thou gaine by the pleasure/Which man and woman reape in	Ovid's Elegies	1.10.35		
Made two nights one to finish up his pleasure.	Ovid's Elegies	1.13.46		
That cannot Venus mutuall pleasure taste.	Ovid's Elegies	2.3.2		

PLEASURE (cont.)
Pleasure addes fuell to my lustfull fire, ... Ovid's Elegies 2.10.25
To pleasure me, for-bid me to corive with thee. . . Ovid's Elegies 2.19.60
Although thou chafe, stolne pleasure is sweet play, . . Ovid's Elegies 3.4.31
But speeches full of pleasure and delight. . . . Hero and Leander 1.420
The mirthfull God of amorous pleasure smil'd, . . . Hero and Leander 2.39
their loves/On heapes of heavie gold, and tooke great pleasure, Hero and Leander 2.163
Should know the pleasure of this blessed night, . . Hero and Leander 2.304
Whence his admiring eyes more pleasure tooke, . . . Hero and Leander 2.325
PLEASURES
When my poore pleasures are devided thus, ... 1Tamb 5.1.386 Zenoc
Cropt from the pleasures of the fruitfull earth, . . Jew 1.2.380 Mthias
The incertaine pleasures of swift-footed time/Have tane their Jew 2.1.7 Barab
Nay, do your pleasures, I know how twill proove. . . Edw 2.5.93 Warwck
their soveraigne/His sports, his pleasures, and his companie: Edw 3.1.175 Edward
His store of pleasures must be sauc'd with paine. . . F1812 5.2.16 Mephst
O what will all thy riches, pleasures, pompes, . . . F1896 5.2.100 GdAngl
Pleasures unspeakeable, blisse without end. . . . F1900 5.2.104 GdAngl
Why are our pleasures by thy meanes forborne? . . . Ovid's Elegies 3.9.4
And we will all the pleasures prove, ... Passionate Shepherd 2
And if these pleasures may thee <things thy minde may> move, Passionate Shepherd 19
PLEAZD
Is Edward pleazd with kinglie regiment. . . . . Edw 1.1.165 Edward
PLEDGE
Lest Dido spying him keepe him for a pledge. . . . Dido 5.1.50 Aeneas
take these three crownes, and pledge me, my contributorie Kings. 1Tamb 4.4.115 P Tamb
I'le pledge thee, love, and therefore drinke it off. . Jew 4.4.1 Curtzn
Three and fifty dozen, I'le pledge thee. . . . . . Jew 4.4.8 P Ithimr
My lords, I will be pledge for his returne. . . . Edw 2.5.66 Arundl
Refusing to receive me pledge for him, ... Edw 3.1.107 Arundl
I pledge your grace. . . . . F1054 3.2.74 Faust
Ile pledge your grace. . . . . F App p.232 13 P Faust
Bare downe to hell her sonne, the pledge of peace, . . Lucan, First Booke 113
PLEDGES
Their wedlocks pledges veng'd their husbands bad. . . Ovid's Elegies 2.14.32
PLENTEOUS
Onely was Crete fruitfull that plenteous yeare, . . Ovid's Elegies 3.9.37
PLENTIE
And all the fruites that plentie els sends forth, . . Dido 4.2.15 Iarbus
PLENTY
for earthly man/Then thus to powre out plenty in their laps, Jew 1.1.108 Barab
PLESHE
Truth Pleshe, and God so prosper me in all, ... P 584 11.49 Navrre
Come Pleshe, lets away whilste time doth serve. . . P 587 11.52 Navrre
Pleshe. . . . . P 914 18.15 Navrre
Pleshe, goe muster up our men with speed, ... P 916 18.17 Navrre
PLIANT
of a string/May draw the pliant king which way I please: . Edw 1.1.53 Gavstn
How pliant is this Mephostophilis? . . . . . . F 257 1.3.29 Faust
At me Apollo bends his pliant bowe: . . . . . . Ovid's Elegies 3.3.29
PLIGHT (Homograph)
destinies/Have brought my sweete companions in such plight? Dido 2.1.60 Aeneas
Ah Shepheard, pity my distressed plight, ... 1Tamb 1.2.7 Zenoc
Sweet Almeda, pity the ruthfull plight/Of Callapine, the sonne 2Tamb 1.2.1 Callap
But as the faith which they prophanely plight/Is not by . 2Tamb 2.1.37 Baldwn
thou perceiv'st the plight/Wherein these Christians have . Jew 1.2.270 Barab
Then gentle Abigal plight thy faith to me. . . . . Jew 2.3.315 Lodowk
PLIGHTED
Thy hand and mine have plighted mutuall faith, ... Dido 5.1.122 Dido
PLIGHTES
Pittie our plightes, O pitie poore Damascus: 1Tamb 5.1.80 1Virgn
PLINIE
Plinie reports, there is a flying Fish, ... Edw 2.2.23 Lncstr
PLOD
Thou shouldst not plod one foote beyond this place. . . Edw 1.1.181 Gavstn
Then all my labours, plod I ne're so fast. . . . F 96 1.1.68 Faust
PLODS
Trips she, it likes me well, plods she, what than? . . Ovid's Elegies 2.4.23
PLOT
The plot is laid by Persean Noble men, ... 1Tamb 1.1.110 Cosroe
Joying the fruit of Ceres garden plot, ... 2Tamb 4.3.37 Orcan
There Ithimore must thou goe place this [pot] <plot>: . Jew 3.4.84 Barab
Now I have such a plot for both their lives, . . . Jew 4.1.117 Barab
The plot is laide, and things shall come to passe, . . P 164 2.107 Guise
And we have heard that Edmund laid a plot, . . . Edw 5.2.32 BshpWn
[The fruitfull plot of Scholerisme grac'd], . . . F 16 Prol.16 1Chor
PLOTS
Our plots and stratagems will soone be dasht. . . . Edw 5.2.78 Mortmr
PLOTTED
So neatly plotted, and so well perform'd? . . . . Jew 3.3.2 Ithimr
PLOUGH
And raging Seas in boistrous South-winds plough. . . Ovid's Elegies 2.16.22
With strong plough shares no man the earth did cleave, . Ovid's Elegies 3.7.41
And untild ground with crooked plough-shares broake. . Ovid's Elegies 3.9.14
The plough-mans hopes were frustrate at the last. . . Ovid's Elegies 3.9.34
PLOUGHES
But better things it gave, corne without ploughes, . . Ovid's Elegies 3.7.39
PLOUGH-MANS
The plough-mans hopes were frustrate at the last. . . Ovid's Elegies 3.9.34
PLOUGH-SHARES
And untild ground with crooked plough-shares broake. . Ovid's Elegies 3.9.14
PLOW
with Russian stems/Plow up huge furrowes in the Caspian sea, 1Tamb 1.2.195 Tamb

PLOW (cont.)			
Then oxen which have drawne the plow before.	Ovid's Elegies	1.2.14	
Soone may you plow the little lands <land> I have,	Ovid's Elegies	1.3.9	
PLOWED			
With twise twelve Phrigian ships I plowed the deepe,	Dido	1.1.220	Aeneas
PLOWES			
And plowes to go about our pallace gates.	Edw	3.1.216	Edward
PLOWING			
By plowing up his Countries with the Sword:	Dido	5.1.308	Dido
PLOWMAN			
Nor plowman, Priest, nor Merchant staies at home,	2Tamb	5.2.50	Callap
PLUCK			
From Junos bird Ile pluck her spotted pride,	Dido	1.1.34	Jupitr
Pluck up your hearts, since fate still rests our friend,	Dido	1.1.149	Aeneas
So, pluck amaine,	P1104	20.14	1Mur
Gold from the earth in steade of fruits we pluck,	Ovid's Elegies	3.7.53	
PLUCKE			
to come by, plucke out that, and twil serve thee and thy wife:	1Tamb	4.4.13	P Tamb
Your golden ensignes [plucke] <pluckt> out of my field,	Ovid's Elegies	3.14.16	
PLUCKT			
Had late been pluckt from out faire Cupids wing:	P 668	13.12	Duchss
Your golden ensignes [plucke] <pluckt> out of my field,	Ovid's Elegies	3.14.16	
PLUME			
And in my helme a triple plume shal spring,	2Tamb	4.3.116	Tamb
Or mount the sunnes flame bearing <plume bearing> charriot,	Lucan, First Booke	48	
Must Pompey as his last foe plume on me,	Lucan, First Booke	338	
PLUME BEARING			
Or mount the sunnes flame bearing <plume bearing> charriot,	Lucan, First Booke	48	
PLUMED			
Their plumed helmes are wrought with beaten golde.	1Tamb	1.2.124	Souldr
And weare thy colours on my plumed crest.	F1778	5.1.105	Faust
PLUMES			
And as I heare, doth meane to pull my plumes.	1Tamb	1.1.33	Mycet
His speare, his shield, his horse, his armour, plumes,	1Tamb	4.1.60	2Msngr
And dart her plumes, thinking to pierce my brest,	Edw	1.1.41	Gavstn
And her old body in birdes plumes to lie.	Ovid's Elegies	1.8.14	
God deluded/In snowe-white plumes of a false swanne included.	Ovid's Elegies	1.10.4	
For wofull haires let piece-torne plumes abound,	Ovid's Elegies	2.6.5	
Her painted fanne of curled plumes let fall,	Hero and Leander	2.11	
Is swifter than the wind, whose tardie plumes,	Hero and Leander	2.115	
PLUMP			
make her round and plump, and batten more then you are aware.	Jew	3.4.65	P Ithimr
PLUMPE			
He clapt his plumpe cheekes, with his tresses playd,	Hero and Leander	2.181	
PLUMS			
I have an Orchard that hath store of plums,	Dido	4.5.4	Nurse
PLUNG'D			
His burning chariot plung'd in sable cloudes,	Lucan, First Booke	539	
PLUNGETH			
Foorth plungeth, and oft flutters with her wing,	Hero and Leander	2.290	
PLUS			
a non-plus at the critical aspect of my terrible countenance.	Jew	4.2.13	P Pilia
PLUTO			
when by Junoes taske/He had before lookt Pluto in the face.	Lucan, First Booke	576	
PLUTOES			
soules passe not to silent Erebus/Or Plutoes bloodles kingdom,	Lucan, First Booke	452	
PLUTO'S			
Pluto's blew fire, and Hecat's tree,	F1001	3.2.21	Mephst
PLUTOS			
Let Plutos bels ring out my fatall knell,	Edw	4.7.89	Edward
PO			
Eurotas cold, and poplar-bearing Po.	Ovid's Elegies	2.17.32	
POAST (Homograph)			
Bartus, it shall be so, poast then to Fraunce,	P 907	18.8	Navrre
And even now, a poast came from the court,	Edw	2.1.19	Spencr
An other poast, what newes bringes he?	Edw	5.1.128	Leistr
the barre strike from the poast.	Ovid's Elegies	1.6.56	
Verses ope dores, and lockes put in the poast/Although of oake,	Ovid's Elegies	2.1.27	
PODOLIA (See PADALIA)			
POEMS			
If these had made one Poems period/And all combin'd in Beauties	1Tamb	5.1.169	Tamb
POESIE			
Sit safe at home and chaunt sweet Poesie.	Lucan, First Booke	445	
POESIES			
And a thousand fragrant [posies] <poesies>,	Passionate Shepherd	10	
POESY			
Quintessence they still/From their immortall flowers of Poesy,	1Tamb	5.1.166	Tamb
POET			
And tis a prety toy to be a Poet.	1Tamb	2.2.54	Mycet
Hath made our Poet pen his second part,	2Tamb	Prol.3	Prolog
You'd make a rich Poet, Sir.	Jew	4.2.122	P Pilia
Saying, Poet heers a worke beseeming thee.	Ovid's Elegies	1.1.28	
Behold what gives the Poet but new verses?	Ovid's Elegies	1.8.57	
I Ovid Poet of [my] <thy> wantonnesse,	Ovid's Elegies	2.1.1	
what meanes learnd/Hath this same Poet my sad chaunce discernd?	Ovid's Elegies	2.1.10	
And Love triumpheth ore his buskind Poet.	Ovid's Elegies	2.18.18	
O Poet carelesse of thy argument?	Ovid's Elegies	3.1.16	
Graunt Tragedie thy Poet times least tittle,	Ovid's Elegies	3.1.67	
Tibullus, thy workes Poet, and thy fame,	Ovid's Elegies	3.8.5	
Thee sacred Poet could sad flames destroy?	Ovid's Elegies	3.8.41	
Tender loves Mother a new Poet get,	Ovid's Elegies	3.14.1	
How such a Poet could you bring forth, sayes,	Ovid's Elegies	3.14.13	
POETRIE			
Musicke and poetrie is his delight,	Edw	1.1.54	Gavstn

POETS			
The water which our Poets terme a Nimph,	Dido	4.4.144	Dido
So Poets say, my Lord.	1Tamb	2.2.53	Meandr
If all the pens that ever poets held,	1Tamb	5.1.161	Tamb
Or had those wanton Poets, for whose byrth/Olde Rome was proud,	2Tamb	2.4.91	Tamb
I must have wanton Poets, pleasant wits,	Edw	1.1.51	Gavstn
Fare well sterne warre, for blunter Poets meete.	Ovid's Elegies		1.1.32
The Poets God arayed in robes of gold,	Ovid's Elegies		1.8.59
I speake old Poets wonderfull inventions,	Ovid's Elegies		3.5.17
Pierian deawe to Poets is distild.	Ovid's Elegies		3.8.26
The worke of Poets lasts Troyes labours fame,	Ovid's Elegies		3.8.29
Nor, as use will not Poets record heare,	Ovid's Elegies		3.11.19
Poets large power is boundlesse, and immense,	Ovid's Elegies		3.11.41
POINT (See also POYNT)			
And kill proud Tamburlaine with point of sword.	1Tamb	2.2.12	Mycet
take it from my swords point, or Ile thrust it to thy heart.	1Tamb	4.4.41	P Tamb
Here at Damascus will I make the Point/That shall begin the	1Tamb	4.4.81	Tamb
Behold my sword, what see you at the point?	1Tamb	5.1.108	Tamb
Unto the frontier point of Soria:	2Tamb	3.3.2	Therid
if our artillery/Will carie full point blancke unto their wals.	2Tamb	3.3.53	Techel
Which when you stab, looke on your weapons point,	2Tamb	4.2.69	Olymp
and mark your weapons point/That wil be blunted if the blow be	2Tamb	4.2.79	Olymp
Come sirs, Ile whip you to death with my punniards point.	P 441	7.81	Guise
Upon my weapons point here shouldst thou fall,	Edw	2.5.13	Mortmr
To pierce the wind-pipe with a needles point,	Edw	5.4.33	Ltborn
that in thy wheele/There is a point, to which when men aspire,	Edw	5.6.60	Mortmr
that point I touchte,/And seeing there was no place to mount up	Edw	5.6.61	Mortmr
And point like Antiques at his triple Crowne:	F 862	3.1.84	Mephst
Whether the sea roul'd alwaies from that point,	Lucan, First Booke		413
this makes them/Run on the swords point and desire to die,	Lucan, First Booke		457
and with a double point/Rose like the Theban brothers funerall	Lucan, First Booke		549
men point at me for a whore,/Shame, that should make me blush,	Ovid's Elegies		3.5.77
POINTED			
Standard round, that stood/As bristle-pointed as a thorny wood.	1Tamb	4.1.27	2Msngr
Your Majesty may choose some pointed time,	2Tamb	3.1.75	Jrslem
Is it square or pointed, pray let me know.	Jew	2.3.59	Lodowk
Pointed it is, good Sir,--but not for you.	Jew	2.3.60	Barab
And she her selfe before the pointed time,	Hero and Leander		2.20
POINTES			
Leave words and let them feele your lances pointes,	1Tamb	3.3.91	Argier
Direct our Bullets and our weapons pointes/And make our <your>	1Tamb	3.3.157	Tamb
POINTS			
Then when our powers in points of swords are join'd,	1Tamb	2.1.40	Cosroe
And on their points his fleshlesse bodie feedes.	1Tamb	5.1.115	Tamb
Oft some points at the prophet passing by,	Ovid's Elegies		3.1.19
POISE (See PAIS'D)			
POISON (See also POYSON)			
every fixed starre/To sucke up poison from the moorish Fens,	1Tamb	4.2.6	Bajzth
And in your hands bring hellish poison up,	1Tamb	4.4.19	Bajzth
Affoords no hearbs, whose taste may poison thee,	2Tamb	4.2.9	Olymp
master, wil you poison her with a messe of rice [porredge]?	Jew	3.4.64	P Ithimr
A bowle of poison to each others health:	Edw	2.2.238	Edward
I learnde in Naples how to poison flowers,	Edw	5.4.31	Ltborn
That were enough to poison any man,	Edw	5.5.5	Matrvs
Under sweete hony deadly poison lurkes.	Ovid's Elegies		1.8.104
And why dire poison give you babes unborne?	Ovid's Elegies		2.14.28
POISONED			
And every bullet dipt in poisoned drugs.	1Tamb	5.1.222	Bajzth
The poisoned braines of this proud Scythian.	2Tamb	3.1.67	Orcan
And jaded king of Pontus poisoned slaine,	Lucan, First Booke		337
POL			
Who with steele Pol-axes dasht out their braines.	Dido	2.1.199	Aeneas
POLAND (See also POLLAND, POLONIE)			
My Lords of Poland I must needs confesse,	P 451	8.1	Anjoy
For Poland is as I have been enformde,	P 454	8.4	Anjoy
That if I undertake to weare the crowne/Of Poland, it may	P 467	8.17	Anjoy
With Poland therfore must I covenant thus,	P 471	8.21	Anjoy
But that we presently despatch Embassadours/To Poland, to call	P 556	11.21	QnMoth
Welcome from Poland Henry once agayne,	P 589	12.2	QnMoth
Hath worne the Poland diadem, before/You were invested in the	P 612	12.25	Mugern
POLANDS			
For Polands crowne and kingly diadem.	P 480	8.30	Lord
POL-AXES			
Who with steele Pol-axes dasht out their braines.	Dido	2.1.199	Aeneas
POLE (See also POL)			
We meane to traveile to th'Antartique Pole,	1Tamb	4.4.136	Tamb
And from th'Antartique Pole, Eastward behold/As much more land,	2Tamb	5.3.154	Tamb
Whose termine <terminine>, is tearmed the worlds wide Pole.	F 593	2.2.42	Mephst
Within the concave compasse of the Pole,	F 765	2.3.44	2Chor
Nor yet the adverse reking southerne pole,	Lucan, First Booke		54
POLES (Homograph)			
When heaven shal cease to moove on both the poles/And when the	2Tamb	1.3.12	Tamb
That to the adverse poles of that straight line,	2Tamb	3.4.64	Therid
Preach upon poles for trespasse of their tongues.	Edw	1.1.118	Kent
Strike off their heads, and let them preach on poles,	Edw	3.1.20	Spencr
All things that move betweene the quiet Poles/Shall be at my	F 83	1.1.55	Faust
upon the poles of the world, but differ in their motions	F 598	2.2.47	P Mephst
in their motions <motion> upon the poles of the Zodiacke.	F 599	2.2.48	P Mephst
POLICIE			
Tush, tell not me 'twas done of policie.	Jew	1.1.140	1Jew
Which Tribute all in policie, I feare,	Jew	1.1.181	Barab
And that will prove but simple policie.	Jew	1.2.159	1Knght
I, policie?	Jew	1.2.160	Barab

POLICIE (cont.)			
by me, for in extremitie/We ought to make barre of no policie.	Jew	1.2.273	Barab
Was this the pursuit of thy policie?	Jew	3.3.37	Abigal
Thus hast thou gotten, by thy policie,	Jew	5.2.27	Barab
Making a profit of my policie;	Jew	5.2.112	Barab
My policie detests prevention:	Jew	5.2.121	Barab
If Warwickes wit and policie prevaile.	Edw	2.5.96	Warwck
An excellent policie:	F1389	4.2.65	P Mrtino
POLICY			
Oh, my master has the bravest policy.	Jew	3.3.12	P Ithimr
Maintaine it bravely by firme policy,	Jew	5.2.36	Barab
'Twere slender policy for Barabas/To dispossesse himselfe of	Jew	5.2.65	Barab
And Governour, now partake my policy:	Jew	5.5.24	Barab
POLICYE			
My policye hath framde religion.	P 122	2.65	Guise
POLIXENA			
Polixena cryed out, Aeneas stay,	Dido	2.1.281	Aeneas
POLL (See POWLE)			
POLLAND			
And now that Henry is cal'd from Polland,	P 569	11.34	Navrre
POLLICIE			
Therefore in pollicie I thinke it good/To hide it close:	1Tamb	2.4.10	Mycet
I feare me you are sent of pollicie,	Edw	2.3.5	Lncstr
POLLICIES			
That in their prowesse and their pollicies,	1Tamb	1.1.8	Cosroe
POLLUTED			
here, here (saith he)/An end of peace; here end polluted lawes;	Lucan, First Booke		227
POLLUX			
Pollux and Castor, might I stand betwixt,	Ovid's Elegies		2.16.13
Champions pleace <please> Pollux, Castor [love] <loves>	Ovid's Elegies		3.2.54
POLLYCY			
faith which they prophanely plight/Is not by necessary pollycy,	2Tamb	2.1.38	Baldwn
POLONIE			
the speed we can, provide/For Henries coronation from Polonie:	P 563	11.28	QnMoth
POLYPHEME			
Gyants as big as hugie Polypheme:	2Tamb	1.1.28	Orcan
POLYPRAGMOS			
Polypragmos Belseborams framanto pacostiphos tostu	F App	p.235 24	P Robin
POLYXENA (See POLIXENA)			
POMP			
then Cosroe raign/And governe Persea in her former pomp:	1Tamb	2.5.19	Cosroe
Her state and person wants no pomp you see,	1Tamb	5.1.485	Tamb
Wher death cuts off the progres of his pomp,	2Tamb	Prol.4	Prolog
When all the Gods stand gazing at his pomp:	2Tamb	4.3.129	Tamb
POMPE			
Juno, false Juno in her Chariots pompe,	Dido	1.1.54	Venus
Whose glittering pompe Dianas shrowdes supplies,	Dido	3.3.4	Dido
Sister, see see Ascanius in his pompe,	Dido	3.3.32	Anna
With greatest pompe had crown'd thee Emperour.	1Tamb	2.5.5	Tamb
O my Lord, tis sweet and full of pompe.	1Tamb	2.5.55	Techel
And place their chiefest good in earthly pompe:	1Tamb	5.1.353	Zenoc
So, now she sits in pompe and majestie:	2Tamb	1.3.17	Tamb
Whose body shall be tomb'd with all the pompe/The treasure of	2Tamb	4.2.97	Therid
That must (advaunst in higher pompe than this)/Rifle the	2Tamb	4.3.58	Tamb
brave Assirian Dames/Have rid in pompe like rich Saturnia,	2Tamb	5.1.77	Tamb
For had your highnesse seene with what a pompe/He entred Paris,	P 872	17.67	Eprnon
Whilom I was, powerfull and full of pompe,	Edw	4.7.13	Edward
Make me despise this transitorie pompe,	Edw	5.1.108	Edward
Nor in the pompe of proud audacious deeds,	F 5	Prol.5	1Chor
No [otherwaies] <otherwise> for pompe or <and> Majesty,	F1693	5.1.20	Faust
And in thy pompe hornd Apis with thee keepe,	Ovid's Elegies		2.13.14
Now comes the pompe; themselves let all men cheere:	Ovid's Elegies		3.2.43
The shout is nigh; the golden pompe comes heere.	Ovid's Elegies		3.2.44
The Gods, and their rich pompe witnesse with me,	Ovid's Elegies		3.2.61
The annuall pompe goes on the covered ground.	Ovid's Elegies		3.12.12
When the chiefe pompe comes, lowd the people hollow,	Ovid's Elegies		3.12.29
Such was the Greeke pompe, Agamemnon dead,	Ovid's Elegies		3.12.31
POMPEIS			
Must Pompeis followers with strangers ayde,	Lucan, First Booke		314
POMPES			
O what will all thy riches, pleasures, pompes,	F1896	5.2.100	GdAngl
POMPEY			
Thou feard'st (great Pompey) that late deeds would dim/Olde	Lucan, First Booke		121
alwaies scorn'd/A second place; Pompey could bide no equall,	Lucan, First Booke		125
Both differ'd much, Pompey was strooke in yeares,	Lucan, First Booke		130
so Pompey thou having lickt/Warme goare from Syllas sword art	Lucan, First Booke		330
Must Pompey as his last foe plume on me,	Lucan, First Booke		338
say Pompey, are these worse/Then Pirats of Sycillia?	Lucan, First Booke		346
Wel might these feare, when Pompey fear'd and fled.	Lucan, First Booke		519
POMPEYS			
Caesars, and Pompeys jarring love soone ended,	Lucan, First Booke		98
POMPOUS			
Thee Pompous birds and him two tygres drew.	Ovid's Elegies		1.2.48
POND			
rid him into the deepe pond at the townes ende, I was no sooner	F App	p.240 133	P HrsCsr
I was no sooner in the middle of the pond, but my horse vanisht	F App	p.240 134	P HrsCsr
PONDER			
Leave me a while, to ponder on my sinnes.	F1736	5.1.63	Faust
PONDEROUS			
But yet my [heart's] <heart> more ponderous then my head,	F1351	4.2.27	Benvol
PONIARD (See also PUNNIARDS)			
To greet his lordship with a poniard,	Edw	1.4.266	Mortmr
PONTE			
Upon the Bridge, call'd Ponte Angelo,	F 813	3.1.39	Mephst

PONTE (cont.)			
And beare him streight to Ponte Angelo,	F 965	3.1.187	Pope
PONTIFICALL			
hollinesse ascends/Saint Peters Chaire and State Pontificall.	F 870	3.1.92	Raymnd
PONTUS			
And jaded king of Pontus poisoned slaine,	Lucan, First Booke		337
POOLE			
Dive to the bottome of Avernus poole,	1Tamb	4.4.18	Bajzth
And all the poysons of the Stygian poole/Breake from the fiery	Jew	3.4.102	Barab
POOLES			
And Phoebus as in Stygian pooles, refraines/To taint his	Dido	1.1.111	Venus
Thou shalt be drawen amidst the frosen Pooles,	1Tamb	1.2.99	Tamb
And I would strive to swim through pooles of blood,	2Tamb	1.3.92	Amyras
That you may dryfoot martch through lakes and pooles,	2Tamb	3.2.86	Tamb
And Angels dive into the pooles of hell.	2Tamb	5.3.33	Usumc
As his deepe whirle-pooles could not quench the same.	Ovid's Elegies		3.5.42
POOR			
Else all France knowes how poor a Duke thou art.	P 844	17.39	Eprnon
POORE			
Poore Troy must now be sackt upon the Sea,	Dido	1.1.64	Venus
Which once performd, poore Troy so long suppress,	Dido	1.1.93	Jupitr
But haples I, God wot, poore and unknowne,	Dido	1.1.227	Aeneas
As poore distressed miserie may pleade:	Dido	1.2.6	Illion
Ah, how could poore Aeneas scape their hands?	Dido	2.1.220	Dido
Poore soule I know too well the sower of love,	Dido	3.1.61	Anna
Alas poore King that labours so in vaine,	Dido	4.2.33	Anna
onely Aeneas frowne/Is that which terrifies poore Didos heart:	Dido	4.4.116	Dido
againe conspire/Against the life of me poore Carthage Queene:	Dido	4.4.132	Dido
These words are poyson to poore Didos soule,	Dido	5.1.111	Dido
To whom poore Dido doth bequeath revenge.	Dido	5.1.173	Dido
That thus oppresse poore friendles passengers.	1Tamb	1.2.70	Zenoc
and excusde/For turning my poore charge to his direction.	1Tamb	2.3.29	Therid
Alas (poore Turke) his fortune is to weake,	1Tamb	3.3.6	Tamb
Alas poore fooles, must you be first shal feele/The sworne	1Tamb	5.1.65	Tamb
Pittie our plightes, O pitie poore Damascus:	1Tamb	5.1.80	1Virgn
O poore Zabina, O my Queen, my Queen,	1Tamb	5.1.275	Bajzth
When my poore pleasures are devided thus,	1Tamb	5.1.386	Zenoc
Poore soules they looke as if their deaths were neere.	2Tamb	3.5.61	Usumc
in a brasen Bull/Of great ones envy; o'th poore petty wites,	Jew	Prol.26	Machvl
Alas, my Lord, the most of us are poore!	Jew	1.2.57	1Jew
And make thee poore and scorn'd of all the world,	Jew	1.2.108	1Knght
Vex'd and tormented runnes poore Barabas/With fatall curses	Jew	2.1.5	Barab
poore villaines, were ne're thought upon/Till Titus and	Jew	2.3.9	Barab
What greater gift can poore Mathias have?	Jew	2.3.346	Mthias
Hard harted to the poore, a covetous wretch,	Jew	4.1.52	Barab
he flouts me, what gentry can be in a poore Turke of ten pence?	Jew	4.2.39	P Ithimr
and what boots it thee/Poore Barabas, to be the Governour,	Jew	5.2.32	Barab
That frightes poore Ramus sitting at his book?	P 362	7.2	Ramus
no soule in hell/Hath felt more torment then poore Gaveston.	Edw	1.1.147	Gavstn
To go from hence, greeves not poore Gaveston,	Edw	1.4.119	Gavstn
How deare my lord is to poore Isabell.	Edw	1.4.166	Queene
O how a kisse revives poore Isabell.	Edw	1.4.333	Queene
Aye me poore soule when these begin to jarre.	Edw	2.2.72	Queene
the familie of the Mortimers/Are not so poore, but would they	Edw	2.2.151	Mortmr
And lame and poore, lie groning at the gates,	Edw	2.2.163	Lncstr
Poore Gaveston, that hast no friend but me,	Edw	2.2.220	Edward
No farewell, to poore Isabell, thy Queene?	Edw	2.4.13	Queene
Renowmed Edward, how thy name/Revives poore Gaveston.	Edw	2.5.42	Gavstn
Poore Pierce, and headed him against lawe of armes?	Edw	3.1.238	Edward
This poore revenge hath something easd my minde,	Edw	5.1.141	Edward
Alas poore soule, would I could ease his greefe.	Edw	5.2.26	Queene
That waites upon my poore distressed soule,	Edw	5.3.38	Edward
Small comfort findes poore Edward in thy lookes,	Edw	5.5.44	Edward
Is this report raisde on poore Isabell.	Edw	5.6.75	Queene
Alas poore slave, see how poverty jests in his nakednesse, I	F 348	1.4.6	P Wagner
Shall make poore Faustus to his utmost power,	F1218	4.1.64	Faust
I am a very poore man, and have lost very much of late by horse	F1463	4.4.7	P HrsCsr
worth>/<Made Greece with ten yeares warres afflict poore Troy>?	F1696	(HC269)B	2Schol
And now poore soule must thy good Angell leave thee,	F1907	5.2.111	GdAngl
And laught to see the poore starve at their gates:	F1918	5.2.122	BdAngl
Alas poore slave, see how poverty jesteth in his nakednesse,	F App	p.229 6	P Wagner
A towne with one poore church set them at oddes.	Lucan, First Booke		97
Affrights poore fearefull men, and blasts their eyes/With	Lucan, First Booke		155
Quarrels were rife, greedy desire stil poore/Did vild deeds,	Lucan, First Booke		174
And crowing Cocks poore soules to worke awake.	Ovid's Elegies		1.6.66
Wert thou rich, poore should not be my state.	Ovid's Elegies		1.8.28
Poore lover with thy gransires I exile thee.	Ovid's Elegies		1.8.66
The gods send thee no house, a poore old age,	Ovid's Elegies		1.8.113
to passe/The souldiours, and poore lovers worke ere was.	Ovid's Elegies		1.9.28
Let poore men show their service, faith, and care;	Ovid's Elegies		1.10.57
Poore wretches on the tree themselves did strangle,	Ovid's Elegies		1.12.17
Poore travailers though tiard, rise at thy sight,	Ovid's Elegies		1.13.13
Aye me poore soule, why is my cause so good.	Ovid's Elegies		2.5.8
Poore [wretch] <wench> I sawe when thou didst thinke I	Ovid's Elegies		2.5.13
If I praise any, thy poore haires thou tearest,	Ovid's Elegies		2.7.7
My selfe poore wretch mine owne gifts now envie.	Ovid's Elegies		2.15.8
And what poore Dido with her drawne sword sharpe,	Ovid's Elegies		2.18.25
Shall I poore soule be never interdicted?	Ovid's Elegies		2.19.53
Poore Semele, among so many burn'd;	Ovid's Elegies		3.3.37
Courts shut the poore out; wealth gives estimation,	Ovid's Elegies		3.7.55
Tis well, if some wench for the poore remaine.	Ovid's Elegies		3.7.60
But let not mee poore soule know of thy straying.	Ovid's Elegies		3.13.2
Poore soldiers stand with fear of death dead strooken,	Hero and Leander		1.121

POORE (cont.)
Lesse sinnes the poore rich man that starves himselfe, . Hero and Leander 1.243
At one selfe instant, she poore soule assaies, . . . Hero and Leander 1.362
nor would vouchsafe so much/As one poore word, their hate to Hero and Leander 1.384
And to this day is everie scholler poore, ... Hero and Leander 1.471
And many poore excuses did she find, ... Hero and Leander 2.6
And love that is conceal'd, betraies poore lovers. . . Hero and Leander 2.134
Whereat agast, the poore soule gan to crie, . . . Hero and Leander 2.177
(Poore sillie maiden) at his mercie was. . . . Hero and Leander 2.286

POPE
As if the Turke, the Pope, Affrike and Greece, . . . 1Tamb 2.5.85 Tamb
Whereof his sire, the Pope, was poysoned. . . . Jew 3.4.99 Barab
For what he doth the Pope will ratifie: . . . . P 40 1.40 Condy
For this have I a largesse from the Pope, ... P 119 2.62 Guise
And send them for a present to the Pope: . . . . P 317 5.44 Anjoy
I meane the Guise, the Pope, and King of Spaine, . . . P 701 14.4 Navrre
Spaine is the counsell chamber of the pope, . . . P 709 14.12 Navrre
The Pope and King of Spaine are thy good frends, . . P 843 17.38 Eprnon
And know my Lord, the Pope will sell his triple crowne, . P 851 17.46 Guise
To plant the Pope and popelings in the Realme, . . . P 925 18.26 Navrre
Pope excommunicate, Philip depose, ... P1012 19.82 Guise
Wert thou the Pope thou mightst not scape from us. . . P1092 20.2 1Mur
This certifie the Pope, away, take horsse. . . . Edw 1.2.38 ArchBp
You know that I am legate to the Pope, ... Edw 1.4.51 ArchBp
The Legate of the Pope will be obayd: . . . . Edw 1.4.64 Edward
The Legate of the Pope will have it so, ... Edw 1.4.109 Edward
To see the Pope and manner of his Court, ... F 776 2.3.55 2Chor
This is the goodly Palace of the Pope: . . . . F 804 3.1.26 Mephst
I know you'd <faine> see the Pope/And take some part of holy F 831 3.1.53 Mephst
be,/That this proud Pope may Faustus [cunning] <comming> see. F 855 3.1.77 Faust
By [cunning] <comming> in <of> thine Art to crosse the Pope,/Or F 859 3.1.81 Mephst
Thy selfe and I, may parly with this Pope: . . . . F 896 3.1.118 Faust
The Pope shall curse that Faustus came to Rome. . . . F 903 3.1.125 Faust
Pope Adrian let me have some right of Law, ... F 904 3.1.126 Bruno
And as Pope Alexander our Progenitour, ... F 915 3.1.137 Pope
Pope Julius swore to Princely Sigismond, ... F 925 3.1.147 Bruno
Pope Julius did abuse the Churches Rites, ... F 928 3.1.150 Pope
and two such Cardinals/Ne're serv'd a holy Pope, as we shall F 942 3.1.164 Faust
The Pope will curse them for their sloth to day, . . F 987 3.2.7 Faust
The Pope had never such a frolicke guest. . . . . F1036 3.2.56 Faust
But where is Bruno our elected Pope, ... F1160 4.1.6 Fredrk
Before the Pope and royall Emperour, ... F1187 4.1.33 Mrtino
Has not the Pope enough of conjuring yet? . . . . F1189 4.1.35 P Benvol
he lookes as like [a] conjurer as the Pope to a Coster-monger. F1228 4.1.74 P Benvol

POPEDOME
The Popedome cannot stand, all goes to wrack, . . . P1087 19.157 QnMoth

POPELINGS
To plant the Pope and popelings in the Realme, . . . P 925 18.26 Navrre

POPES
Nay for the Popes sake, and thine owne benefite. . . P 827 17.22 Eprnon
Hath he not made me in the Popes defence, ... P1036 19.106 King
In honour of the Popes triumphant victory. . . . F 835 3.1.57 Mephst
For him, and the succeeding Popes of Rome, . . . F 926 3.1.148 Bruno

POPISH
In spite of Spaine and all the popish power, . . . P 581 11.46 Pleshe
As Rome and all those popish Prelates there, . . . P1248 22.110 Navrre

POPLAR
Eurotas cold, and poplar-bearing Po. . . . . . Ovid's Elegies 2.17.32

POPLAR-BEARING
Eurotas cold, and poplar-bearing Po. . . . . . Ovid's Elegies 2.17.32

POPLER
Like Popler leaves blowne with a stormy flawe, . . . Ovid's Elegies 1.7.54

POPPIE
Nuts were thy food, and Poppie causde thee sleepe, . . Ovid's Elegies 2.6.31

POPPY
I dranke of Poppy and cold mandrake juyce; . . . . Jew 5.1.80 Barab

POPULAR
And being popular sought by liberal gifts, ... Lucan, First Booke 132

PORCH
yesterday/There where the porch doth Danaus fact display. Ovid's Elegies 2.2.4

PORCUPINES (See also PORPINTINE)
Which should be like the quilles of Porcupines, . . 2Tamb 1.3.26 Tamb

PORE
At every pore let blood comme dropping foorth, . . . 1Tamb 5.1.227 Zabina

PORPINTINE
As if a Goose should play the Porpintine, ... Edw 1.1.40 Gavstn

PORREDGE
master, wil you poison her with a messe of rice [porredge]? Jew 3.4.65 P Ithimr
was ever pot of rice porredge so sauc't? . . . . Jew 3.4.107 P Ithimr

PORRIDGE
let the Maids looke well to their porridge-pots, for I'le into F1134 3.3.47 P Robin

PORRIDGE-POTS
let the Maids looke well to their porridge-pots, for I'le into F1134 3.3.47 P Robin

PORT (Homograph)
Though straight the passage and the port be made, . . 1Tamb 2.1.42 Cosroe
Close your Port-cullise, charge your Basiliskes, . . Jew 3.5.31 Govnr
our port-maisters/Are not so careles of their kings commaund. Edw 4.3.22 Edward
Sent aide; so did Alcides port, whose seas/Eate hollow rocks, Lucan, First Booke 406
heady rout/That in chain'd troupes breake forth at every port; Lucan, First Booke 489

PORTAGUES
Ten thousand Portagues besides great Perles, . . . Jew 1.2.244 Barab

PORT-CULLISE
Close your Port-cullise, charge your Basiliskes, . . Jew 3.5.31 Govnr

PORTEND
Tell me, you Christians, what doth this portend? Jew 5.5.90 Calym
What might the staying of my bloud portend? F 453 2.1.65 Faust
PORTER
Unworthy porter, bound in chaines full sore, Ovid's Elegies 1.6.1
Hard-hearted Porter doest and wilt not heare? Ovid's Elegies 1.6.27
PORTINGALE
Keeping in aw the Bay of Portingale: 1Tamb 3.3.258 Tamb
PORTION
Which I esteeme as portion of my crown. 1Tamb 2.3.35 Cosroe
PORTIONS
By equall portions into both your breasts: 2Tamb 5.3.171 Tamb
Then let the rich increase your portions. Jew 1.2.58 Govnr
PORTLY
To be my Queen and portly Emperesse. 1Tamb 1.2.187 Tamb
Great Kings of Barbary, and my portly Bassoes, 1Tamb 3.1.1 Bajzth
PORT-MAISTERS
our port-maisters/Are not so careles of their kings commaund. Edw 4.3.22 Edward
PORTRAY (See POURTRAID)
PORTS
not perswade you to submission,/But stil the ports were shut: 2Tamb 5.1.95 Tamb
PORTUGALL (See also PORTINGALE)
Obed in Bairseth, Nones in Portugall, Jew 1.1.125 Barab
POSEY
Pilia-borza, bid the Fidler give me the posey in his hat there. Jew 4.4.35 P Curtzn
Sirra, you must give my mistris your posey. Jew 4.4.37 Pilia
POSIES
a golden crosse/With Christian posies round about the ring. Jew 2.3.297 Barab
And a thousand fragrant [posies] <poesies>, Passionate Shepherd 10
POSSESSE
Violate any promise to possesse him. Edw 2.5.64 Warwck
Let never silent night possesse this clime, Edw 5.1.65 Edward
And scorne those Joyes thou never shalt possesse. F 314 1.3.86 Faust
In peace possesse the triple Diadem, F1213 4.1.59 Emper
or they that shal hereafter possesse our throne, shal (I feare F App p.236 21 P Emper
All, they possesse: Ovid's Elegies 3.7.57
POSSESSION
Than the possession of the Persean Crowne, 1Tamb 1.2.91 Tamb
Before we part with our possession. 1Tamb 1.2.144 Tamb
That hinder our possession to the crowne: P 154 2.97 Guise
possession (as I would I might) yet I meane to keepe you out, P 814 17.9 P Souldr
enter by defaulte | whatt thoughe you were once in possession Paris ms11,p390 P Souldr
And take possession of his house and goods: Edw 1.1.203 Edward
And have these joies in full possession. F 179 1.1.151 Faust
POSSESSIONE
And thoughe I come not to keep possessione as I wold I mighte Paris ms15,p390 P Souldr
POSSESSIONS
Preach me not out of my possessions. Jew 1.2.111 Barab
POSSEST
You that/Were ne're possest of wealth, are pleas'd with want. Jew 1.2.201 Barab
Yet when old Saturne heavens rule possest, Ovid's Elegies 3.7.35
By being possest of him for whom she long'd: Hero and Leander 2.36
POSSIBLE
And is't not possible to find it out? Jew 4.2.60 Pilia
By no meanes possible. Jew 4.2.61 P Ithimr
POSSIBLY
Whence none can possibly escape alive: Jew 5.5.31 Barab
POSSIT
Major sum quam cui possit fortuna nocere. Edw 5.4.69 Mortmr
POST (Homograph; See also POAST)
are letters come/From Ormus, and the Post stayes here within. Jew 2.3.223 Abigal
Why post we not from hence to levie men? Edw 1.2.16 Mortmr
Spencer and I will post away by land. Edw 2.4.6 Edward
So now away, post thither wards amaine. Edw 5.2.67 Mortmr
That on a furies back came post from Rome, F1161 4.1.7 Fredrk
love with him, I would he would post with him to Rome againe. F1191 4.1.37 P Benvol
Knights of the post of perjuries make saile, Ovid's Elegies 1.10.37
POSTE (Homograph)
Hang up your weapons on Alcides poste, 1Tamb 5.1.528 Tamb
Gonzago poste you to Orleance, Retes to Deep, P 445 7.85 Guise
POSTED
To censure Bruno, that is posted hence, F 983 3.2.3 Mephst
POSTS
And farewell cruell posts, rough thresholds block, Ovid's Elegies 1.6.73
The posts of brasse, the walles of iron were. Ovid's Elegies 3.7.32
POT
But first goe fetch me in the pot of Rice/That for our supper Jew 3.4.49 Barab
There Ithimore must thou goe place this [pot] <plot>: Jew 3.4.84 Barab
Troth master, I'm loth such a pot of pottage should be spoyld. Jew 3.4.89 P Ithimr
was ever pot of rice porredge so sauc't? Jew 3.4.106 P Ithimr
Ifaith thy head will never be out of the potage pot. F App p.236 48 P Robin
POTAGE
Ifaith thy head will never be out of the potage pot. F App p.236 48 P Robin
POTENTATE
The greatest Potentate of Affrica. 1Tamb 3.3.63 Bajzth
If any heathen potentate or king/Invade Natolia, Sigismond will 2Tamb 1.1.152 Sgsmnd
That late adorn'd the Affrike Potentate, 2Tamb 3.2.124 Tamb
Nor any Potentate of Germany. F 339 1.3.111 Faust
POTENTATES
And all the earthly Potentates conspire, 1Tamb 2.7.59 Tamb
blacke survey/Great Potentates do kneele with awful feare, F App p.235 35 Mephst
POTEST
Exhereditare filium non potest pater, nisi--Such is the F 58 1.1.30 P Faust

POTION
Pleaseth your Majesty to drink this potion, 2Tamb 5.3.78 Phsitn
But hath thy potion wrought so happilie? Edw 4.1.14 Kent
POTS
let the Maids looke well to their porridge-pots, for I'le into F1134 3.3.47 P Robin
POTTAGE
Troth master, I'm loth such a pot of pottage should be spoyld. Jew 3.4.89 P Ithimr
POUND
And for a pound to sweat himselfe to death: Jew 1.1.18 Barab
They rate his ransome at five thousand pound. Edw 2.2.117 Mortmr
POUNDS
With free consent a hundred thousand pounds. Jew 5.5.20 Govnr
Pounds saist thou, Governor, wel since it is no more/I'le Jew 5.5.21 Barab
POUR'D
his fearefull arme/Be pour'd with rigour on our sinfull heads, 2Tamb 2.1.58 Fredrk
Your sacred vertues pour'd upon his throne, 2Tamb 5.3.11 Therid
POURE (See also POWREST)
And poure it in this glorious Tyrants throat. 1Tamb 4.2.7 Bajzth
offences feele/Such plagues as heaven and we can poure on him. 1Tamb 4.3.45 Arabia
I may poure foorth my soule into thine armes, 1Tamb 5.1.279 Bajzth
Will poure it downe in showers on our heads: 2Tamb 3.1.36 Callap
Will poure down blood and fire on thy head: 2Tamb 4.1.143 Jrslem
Offers to poure the same into thy soule, F1732 5.1.59 OldMan
POURED
No flowing waves with drowned ships forth poured, Ovid's Elegies 2.16.25
POURTRAID
Wel hast thou pourtraid in thy tearms of life, 1Tamb 2.1.31 Cosroe
Upon his browes was pourtraid ugly death, 1Tamb 3.2.72 Agidas
POVERTIE
Rakt up in embers of their povertie, Edw 1.1.21 Gavstn
That he and Povertie should alwaies kis. Hero and Leander 1.470
POVERTY
Then pittied in a Christian poverty: Jew 1.1.115 Barab
To make me desperate in my poverty? Jew 1.2.261 Barab
see how poverty jests in his nakednesse, I know the Villaines F 348 1.4.6 P Wagner
see how poverty jesteth in his nakednesse, the vilaine is bare, F App p.229 6 P Wagner
women; Poverty (who hatcht/Roomes greatest wittes) was loath'd, Lucan, First Booke 166
Now poverty great barbarisme we hold. Ovid's Elegies 3.7.4
POWDER
I strowed powder on the Marble stones, Jew 2.3.209 Ithimr
It is a precious powder that I bought/Of an Italian in Ancona Jew 3.4.68 Barab
I'le carry't to the Nuns with a powder. Jew 3.4.112 P Ithimr
One dram of powder more had made all sure. Jew 5.1.22 Barab
sleepe, to take a quill/And blowe a little powder in his eares, Edw 5.4.35 Ltborn
POWDERED
Mingled with powdered shot and fethered steele/So thick upon 2Tamb 1.1.92 Orcan
POWER (See also POWRE)
that Dido may desire/And not obtaine, be it in humaine power? Dido 3.4.8 Aeneas
Now if thou beest a pitying God of power, Dido 4.2.19 Iarbus
I have not power to stay thee: is he gone? Dido 5.1.183 Dido
They gather strength by power of fresh supplies. 1Tamb 2.2.21 Meandr
Such power attractive shines in princes eies. 1Tamb 2.5.64 Therid
Yet would we not be brav'd with forrain power, 1Tamb 3.1.13 Bajzth
But if presuming on his silly power, 1Tamb 3.1.33 Bajzth
And as the heads of Hydra, so my power/Subdued, shall stand as 1Tamb 3.3.140 Bajzth
But speake, what power hath he? 1Tamb 4.1.20 Souldn
Yet would the Souldane by his conquering power, 1Tamb 4.1.33 Souldn
Joine your Arabians with the Souldans power: 1Tamb 4.3.16 Souldn
Having the power from the Emperiall heaven, 1Tamb 4.4.30 Tamb
of them, looking some happie power will pitie and inlarge us. 1Tamb 4.4.100 P Zabina
Or hope of rescue from the Souldans power, 1Tamb 5.1.4 Govnr
The wrath of Tamburlain, and power of warres. 1Tamb 5.1.44 Govnr
Ah faire Zabina, we may curse his power, 1Tamb 5.1.230 Bajzth
What cursed power guides the murthering hands, 1Tamb 5.1.403 Arabia
Fearing my power should pull him from his throne. 1Tamb 5.1.453 Tamb
Al sights of power to grace my victory: 1Tamb 5.1.474 Tamb
and dominions/That late the power of Tamburlaine subdewed: 1Tamb 5.1.509 Tamb
Gainst him my Lord must you addresse your power. 2Tamb 1.1.19 Gazell
My crowne, my selfe, and all the power I have, 2Tamb 1.3.115 Therid
And with my power did march to Zansibar, 2Tamb 1.3.194 Techel
then that your Majesty/Take all advantages of time and power, 2Tamb 2.1.12 Fredrk
pitcht against our power/Betwixt Cutheia and Orminius mount: 2Tamb 2.1.17 Fredrk
our neighbour kings/Expect our power and our royall presence, 2Tamb 2.2.4 Orcan
With greater power than erst his pride hath felt, 2Tamb 2.2.10 Gazell
With unacquainted power of our hoste. 2Tamb 2.2.23 Uribas
Taking advantage of your slender power, 2Tamb 2.2.26 1Msngr
And hath the power of his outstretched arme, 2Tamb 2.2.42 Orcan
May in his endlesse power and puritie/Behold and venge this 2Tamb 2.2.53 Orcan
And make the power I have left behind/(Too litle to defend our 2Tamb 2.2.59 Orcan
And to his power, which here appeares as full/As raies of 2Tamb 2.3.29 Orcan
Whose power is often proov'd a myracle. 2Tamb 2.3.32 Gazell
Whose power had share in this our victory: 2Tamb 2.3.35 Orcan
And for their power, ynow to win the world. 2Tamb 3.1.43 Orcan
Stand at the walles, with such a mighty power. 2Tamb 3.3.14 Therid
kings again my Lord/To gather greater numbers gainst our power, 2Tamb 4.1.83 Amyras
Ready to levie power against thy throne, 2Tamb 4.1.117 Tamb
in] <resisting> me/The power of heavens eternall majesty. 2Tamb 4.1.158 Tamb
and to subdew/This proud contemner of thy dreadfull power, 2Tamb 4.3.40 Orcan
Now Mahomet, if thou have any power, 2Tamb 5.1.187 Tamb
Should come in person to resist your power, 2Tamb 5.2.38 Amasia
And that their power is puissant as Joves, 2Tamb 5.3.35 Usumc
There should not one of all the villaines power/Live to give 2Tamb 5.3.108 Tamb
Then let some God oppose his holy power, 2Tamb 5.3.220 Techel

POWER (cont.)
grave [Governour], 'twere in my power/To favour you, but 'tis my   Jew 1.2.10   Calym
the gold, or know Jew it is in my power to hang thee.   Jew 4.3.37   P Pilia
This, Barabas; since things are in thy power,   Jew 5.2.57   Govnr
In spite of Spaine and all the popish power,   P 581 11.46   Pleshe
My brother Guise hath gathered a power of men,   P 642 12.55   Cardnl
To send his power to meet us in the field.   P 712 14.15   Navrre
The power of vengeance now incampes it selfe,   P 717 14.20   Navrre
The Duke is slaine and all his power dispearst,   P 787 16.1   Navrre
of Guise, we understand that you/Have gathered a power of men.   P 822 17.17   King
I meane to muster all the power I can,   P 849 17.44   Guise
Oh that I have not power to stay my life,   P1007 19.77   Guise
O wordes of power to kill a thousand men.   P1126 21.20   Dumain
The king shall lose his crowne, for we have power,   Edw 1.2.59   Mortmr
Your highnes knowes, it lies not in my power.   Edw 1.4.158   Queene
And dare not be revengde, for their power is great: Edw 2.2.202   Edward
Had power to mollifie his stonie hart,   Edw 2.4.20   Queene
force, and with the power/That he intendeth presentlie to raise,   Edw 2.4.43   Queene
Your honor hath an adamant, of power/To drawe a prince.   Edw 2.5.105   Arundl
Call thou them back, I have no power to speake.   Edw 5.1.93   Edward
Of power, of honour, and <of> omnipotence,   F 81 1.1.53   Faust
shall stand by me,/What [god] <power> can hurt me <thee>?   F 414 2.1.26   Faust
full power to fetch or carry the said John Faustus, body and   F 497 2.1.109   P Faust
Is not all power on earth bestowed on us?   F 930 3.1.152   Pope
In token of our seven-fold power from heaven,   F 934 3.1.156   Pope
Shall make poore Faustus to his utmost power,   F1218 4.1.64   Faust
The Doctor stands prepar'd, by power of Art,   F1222 4.1.68   Faust
Nay feare not man, we have no power to kill.   F1440 4.3.10   Mrtino
Hell, or the Divell, had had no power on thee.   F1902 5.2.106   GdAngl
To practise more then heavenly power permits.   F2009 5.3.27   4Chor
forth as by art and power of my spirit I am able to performe.   F App p.237 38   P Faust
These plagues arise from wreake of civill power.   Lucan, First Booke   32
Nature, and every power shal give thee place,   Lucan, First Booke   51
Thy power inspires the Muze that sings this war.   Lucan, First Booke   66
Speake, when shall this thy long usurpt power end?   Lucan, First Booke   333
come, their huge power made him bould/To mannage greater deeds;   Lucan, First Booke   462
Rash boy, who gave thee power to change a line?   Ovid's Elegies   1.1.9
cold hemlocks flower/Wherein bad hony Corsicke Bees did power.   Ovid's Elegies   1.12.10
And all things too much in their sole power drenches.   Ovid's Elegies   3.3.26
Who may offend, sinnes least; power to do ill,   Ovid's Elegies   3.4.9
Jove being admonisht gold had soveraigne power,   Ovid's Elegies   3.7.29
Poets large power is boundlesse, and immense,   Ovid's Elegies   3.11.41
It lies not in our power to love, or hate,   Hero and Leander   1.167
O none but gods have power their love to hide,   Hero and Leander   2.131

POWERFULL
Whilom I was, powerfull and full of pompe,   Edw 4.7.13   Edward
Then if by powerfull Necromantick spels,   F1209 4.1.55   Emper
Leave thy once powerfull words, and flatteries,   Ovid's Elegies   3.10.31
blazon foorth the loves of men,/Much lesse of powerfull gods.   Hero and Leander   1.71

POWERS
Charge him from me to turne his stormie powers,   Dido 1.1.117   Jupitr
Then when our powers in points of swords are join'd,   1Tamb 2.1.40   Cosroe
So will we with our powers and our lives,   1Tamb 2.5.34   Ortyg
Some powers divine, or els infernall, mixt/Their angry seeds at   1Tamb 2.6.9   Meandr
And scornes the Powers that governe Persea.   1Tamb 2.6.40   Cosroe
Ye Gods and powers that governe Persea,   1Tamb 3.3.189   Zenoc
Capolin, hast thou survaid our powers?   1Tamb 4.3.50   Souldn
Our love of honor loth to be enthral'd/To forraine powers, and   1Tamb 5.1.36   Govnr
For whome the Powers divine have made the world,   1Tamb 5.1.76   1Virgn
Must Tamburlaine by their resistlesse powers,   1Tamb 5.1.397   Zenoc
Then as the powers devine have preordainde,   1Tamb 5.1.400   Zenoc
O then ye Powers that sway eternal seates,   2Tamb 5.3.17   Techel
Come let us march against the powers of heaven,   2Tamb 5.3.48   Tamb
In vaine I strive and raile against those powers,   2Tamb 5.3.120   Tamb
Against the inward powers of my heart,   2Tamb 5.3.196   Amyras
Immortall powers, that knowes the painfull cares,   Edw 5.3.37   Edward
And only gods and heavenly powers you know,   Lucan, First Booke   449
the Altar/He laies a ne're-yoakt Bull, and powers downe wine,   Lucan, First Booke   608
the brest of this slaine Bull are crept,/Th'infernall powers.   Lucan, First Booke   633
Insooth th'eternall powers graunt maides society/Falsely to   Ovid's Elegies   3.3.11
These gifts are meete to please the powers divine.   Ovid's Elegies   3.9.48

POWLE
Weele steele it on their crest, and powle their tops.   Edw 3.1.27   Edward

POWRE
for earthly man/Then thus to powre out plenty in their laps,   Jew 1.1.108   Barab
This day I shall powre vengeance with my sword/On those proud   Edw 3.1.186   Edward
Or open his mouth, and powre quick silver downe,   Edw 5.4.36   Ltborn
But if sterne Neptunes windie powre prevaile,   Ovid's Elegies   2.16.27
And by thy face to me a powre divine,   Ovid's Elegies   3.10.47

POWRES
That powres in lieu of all your goodnes showne,   Edw 3.1.44   Spencr

POWREST
Flames into flame, flouds thou powrest seas into.   Ovid's Elegies   3.2.34

POX
here's to thee with a--pox on this drunken hick-up.   Jew 4.4.32   P Ithimr

POYNT
And scarcely doe agree upon one poynt: Dido 2.1.109   Dido
He with his faulchions poynt raisde up at once,   Dido 2.1.229   Aeneas

POYNTS
And pierst my liver with sharpe needle poynts <needles>?   Ovid's Elegies   3.6.30

POYSON
These words are poyson to poore Didos soule,   Dido 5.1.111   Dido
I ha the poyson of the City for him,   Jew 2.3.53   Barab

POYSON (cont.)			
Sometimes I goe about and poyson wells;	Jew	2.3.176	Barab
Whose operation is to binde, infect,/And poyson deeply:	Jew	3.4.71	Barab
Here's a drench to poyson a whole stable of Flanders mares:	Jew	3.4.111	P Ithimr
I was afraid the poyson had not wrought;	Jew	4.1.4	Barab
Good master let me poyson all the Monks.	Jew	4.1.14	Ithimr
sweet Margaret, the fatall poyson/Workes within my head, my	P 184	3.19	OldQn
O the fatall poyson workes within my brest,	P1221	22.83	King
at the mariage day/The cup of Hymen had beene full of poyson,	Edw	1.4.174	Queene
[Gunnes] <Swords>, poyson, halters, and invenomb'd steele,	F 573	2.2.22	Faust
Thou mad'st thy head with compound poyson flow.	Ovid's Elegies		1.14.44
To meete for poyson or vilde facts we crave not,	Ovid's Elegies		2.2.63
POYSON'D			
Are poyson'd by my climing followers.	Jew	Prol.13	Machvl
'Tis poyson'd, is it not?	Jew	2.3.372	Ithimr
I feare they know we sent the poyson'd broth.	Jew	4.1.26	Barab
you dine with me, Sir, and you shal be most hartily poyson'd.	Jew	4.3.30	P Barab
I carried the broth that poyson'd the Nuns, and he and I,	Jew	4.4.20	P Ithimr
The scent thereof was death, I poyson'd it.	Jew	4.4.43	Barab
poyson'd his owne daughter and the Nuns, strangled a Fryar,	Jew	5.1.13	P Pilia
strangled Bernardine, poyson'd the Nuns, and his owne daughter.	Jew	5.1.33	P Ithimr
I hope the poyson'd flowers will worke anon.	Jew	5.1.43	Barab
POYSONED			
Whereof his sire, the Pope, was poysoned.	Jew	3.4.99	Barab
Where are those perfumed gloves which I sent/To be poysoned,	P 71	2.14	Guise
Help sonne Navarre, I am poysoned.	P 176	3.11	OldQn
My Mother poysoned heere before my face:	P 187	3.22	Navrre
and the fire the aire, and so we shall be poysoned with him.	P 485	9.4	P 1Atndt
For you are stricken with a poysoned knife.	P1213	22.75	Srgeon
A poysoned knife?	P1214	22.76	King
Wounded and poysoned, both at once?	P1215	22.77	King
POYSONOUS			
Nature, why mad'st me not some poysonous beast,	Dido	4.1.21	Iarbus
POYSONS			
And all the poysons of the Stygian poole/Breake from the fiery	Jew	3.4.102	Barab
PRACTICE			
And by my father's practice, which is there/Set downe at large,	Jew	3.6.28	Abigal
PRACTISE			
But I will practise thy enlargement thence:	Jew	2.1.53	Barab
studied Physicke, and began/To practise first upon the Italian;	Jew	2.3.182	Barab
And such a King whom practise long hath taught,	P 458	8.8	Anjoy
To practise Magicke and concealed Arts.	F 129	1.1.101	Faust
To practise more then heavenly power permits.	F2009	5.3.27	4Chor
Practise a thousand sports when there you come,	Ovid's Elegies		3.13.24
PRACTISES			
That hatcheth up such bloudy practises.	P1205	22.67	King
PRACTIZE			
To practize tauntes and bitter tyrannies?	2Tamb	4.3.56	Jrslem
PRAETOR			
Now greatest spectacles the Praetor sends,	Ovid's Elegies		3.2.65
PRAID			
He kneel'd, but unto her devoutly praid;	Hero and Leander		1.177
PRAIDE			
As she might straight have gone to church and praide:	Ovid's Elegies		3.6.54
PRAIERS			
Let us have hope that their unspotted praiers,	1Tamb	5.1.20	Govnr
And satisfie the peoples generall praiers,	2Tamb	5.1.7	Maxim
unrelenting eares/Of death and hell be shut against my praiers,	2Tamb	5.3.192	Amyras
Doth heare and see the praiers of the just:	P 43	1.43	Navrre
We never beg, but use such praiers as these.	Edw	2.2.153	Mortmr
Yet once more ile importune him with praiers,	Edw	2.4.63	Queene
Love <Jove> knowes with such like praiers, I dayly move hir:	Ovid's Elegies		1.3.4
Cupid beats downe her praiers with his wings,	Hero and Leander		1.369
PRAIS'D			
She prais'd me, yet the gate shutt fast upon her,	Ovid's Elegies		3.7.7
PRAISD			
And my wench ought to have seem'd falsely praisd,	Ovid's Elegies		3.11.43
PRAISE (See also PRAYSING)			
As my despised worths, that shun all praise,	Dido	3.4.42	Aeneas
And thou despise the praise of such attempts:	Dido	5.1.37	Hermes
Nay, though I praise it, I can live without it.	1Tamb	2.5.66	Therid
In sounding through the world his partiall praise.	1Tamb	4.3.49	Arabia
away, and let due praise be given/Neither to Fate nor Fortune,	Jew	5.5.123	Govnr
But rather praise him for that brave attempt,	Edw	1.4.268	Mortmr
Adding this golden sentence to our praise;	F 917	3.1.139	Pope
Too simple is my wit to tell her worth <praise>,/Whom all the	F1697	5.1.24	2Schol
And give me cause to praise thee whilst I live.	F App	p.237 36	Emper
Girt my shine browe with sea banke mirtle praise <sprays>.	Ovid's Elegies		1.1.34
In verse to praise kinde Wenches tis my part,	Ovid's Elegies		1.10.59
But when I praise a pretty wenches face/Shee in requitall doth	Ovid's Elegies		2.1.33
If I praise any, thy poore haires thou tearest,	Ovid's Elegies		2.7.7
We praise: great goddesse ayde my enterprize.	Ovid's Elegies		3.2.56
Faith to the witnesse Joves praise doth apply,	Ovid's Elegies		3.9.23
And justly: for her praise why did I tell?	Ovid's Elegies		3.11.9
How small sc ere, Ile you for greatest praise.	Ovid's Elegies		3.14.14
Many would praise the sweet smell as she past,	Hero and Leander		1.21
PRANKES			
What madnesse ist to tell night <nights> prankes by day,	Ovid's Elegies		3.13.7
PRANSING			
Upon their pransing Steeds, disdainfully/With wanton paces	1Tamb	4.1.22	2Msngr
PRATE			
Let him within heare bard out lovers prate.	Ovid's Elegies		1.8.78
PRATES			
Take him away, he prates. You Rice ap Howell,	Edw	4.6.73	Mortmr

PRATTLE				
And thinke we prattle with distempered spirits:	1Tamb	1.2.62		Tamb
PRAY (Homograph; See also PRAIDE, PRETHE, PRETHEE)				
And rests a pray to every billowes pride.	Dido	1.1.53		Venus
Anna, against this Troian doe I pray,	Dido	4.2.30		Iarbus
As how I pray, may I entreate you tell.	Dido	5.1.67		Iarbus
Dooth pray uppon my flockes of Passengers,	1Tamb	1.1.32		Mycet
Nay, pray you let him stay, a greater [task]/Fits Menaphon, than	1Tamb	1.1.87		Cosroe
That lie in ambush, waiting for a pray:	1Tamb	2.2.17		Meandr
I pray you give them leave Madam, this speech is a goodly	1Tamb	4.4.32	P	Techel
pray thee tel, why art thou so sad?	1Tamb	4.4.63	P	Tamb
Pray for us Bajazeth, we are going.	1Tamb	5.1.213		Tamb
Now shall his barbarous body be a pray/To beasts and foules,	2Tamb	2.3.14		Orcan
keepe his trunke/Amidst these plaines, for Foules to pray upon.	2Tamb	2.3.39		Orcan
Yet pardon him I pray your Majesty.	2Tamb	4.1.97		Therid
I, I,/Pray leave me in my patience.	Jew	1.2.200		Barab
Is it square or pointed, pray let me know.	Jew	2.3.59		Lodowk
I pray, Sir, be no stranger at my house,	Jew	2.3.136		Barab
I am a little busie, Sir, pray pardon me.	Jew	2.3.231		Barab
And say, I pray them come and speake with me.	Jew	3.3.29		Abigal
I pray, mistris, wil you answer me to one question?	Jew	3.3.30	P	Ithimr
Pray doe, and let me help you, master.	Jew	3.4.86	P	Ithimr
Pray let me taste first.	Jew	3.4.86	P	Ithimr
So I have heard; pray therefore keepe it close.	Jew	3.6.37		Abigal
of my sinnes/Lye heavy on my soule; then pray you tell me,	Jew	4.1.49		Barab
To fast, to pray, and weare a shirt of haire,	Jew	4.1.61		Barab
Pray pardon me, I must goe see a ship discharg'd.	Jew	4.2.51	P	Ithimr
he not as well come as send; pray bid him come and fetch it:	Jew	4.3.26	P	Barab
Pray when, Sir, shall I see you at my house?	Jew	4.3.56		Barab
Companion-Bashawes, see I pray/How busie Barrabas is there above	Jew	5.5.51		Calym
Come my Lords lets go to the Church and pray,	P 55	1.55		Navrre
O let me pray before I dye.	P 301	5.28		Admral
Then pray unto our Ladye, kisse this crosse.	P 302	5.29		Gonzag
O let me pray before I take my death.	P 352	6.7		Seroun
[Sanctus] <Sancta> Jacobus hee was my Saint, pray to him.	P 358	6.13		Mntsrl
O let me pray unto my God.	P 359	6.14		Seroun
I pray thee let me see.	P 674	13.18		Guise
Then pray to God, and aske forgivenes of the King.	P1004	19.74	P	2Mur
Pray God thou be a King now this is done.	P1068	19.138		QnMoth
Sir John of Henolt, pardon us I pray,	Edw	4.2.71		Kent
I pray let us see it, what have we there?	Edw	4.3.10		Edward
Betweene you both, shorten the time I pray,	Edw	4.3.45		Edward
my lord I pray be short,/A faire commission warrants what we	Edw	4.7.47		Rice
And pray devoutely to the Prince of hell.	F 282	1.3.54		Mephst
[Never to name God, or to pray to him],	F 649	2.2.98A		Faust
Lord Raymond pray fall too, I am beholding/To the Bishop of	F1041	3.2.61		Pope
I, pray do, for Faustus is a dry.	F1052	3.2.72		Faust
I pray my Lords have patience at this troublesome banquet.	F1058	3.2.78		Pope
pray where's the cup you stole from the Taverne?	F1097	3.3.10	P	Vintnr
I pray you heartily sir; for wee cal'd you but in jeast I	F1123	3.3.36	P	Dick
I pray sir, let me have the carrying of him about to shew some	F1128	3.3.41	P	Robin
therefor I pray you tell me, what is the thing you most desire	F1566	4.6.9	P	Faust
It appeares so, pray be bold else-where,	F1597	4.6.40		Servnt
Then I pray remember your curtesie.	F1641	4.6.84	P	Carter
'Tis not so much worth; I pray you tel me one thing.	F1643	4.6.86	P	Carter
have sent away my guesse, I pray who shall pay me for my A--	F1667	4.6.110	P	Hostss
but let us into the next roome, and [there] pray for him.	F1872	5.2.76	P	1Schol
I, pray for me, pray for me:	F1873	5.2.77	P	Faust
Pray thou, and we will pray, that God may have mercie upon thee.	F1875	5.2.79	P	2Schol
Pray heaven the Doctor have escapt the danger.	F1987	5.3.5		1Schol
O Lord I pray sir, let Banio and Belcher go sleepe.	F App	p.231 68	P	Clown
Alas sir, I have no more, I pray you speake for me.	F App	p.239 104	P	HrsCsr
I pray you let him have him, he is an honest felow, and he has	F App	p.239 105	P	Mephst
The soldiours pray, and rapine brought in ryot,	Lucan, First Booke	163		
They kennel'd in Hircania, evermore/Wil rage and pray:	Lucan, First Booke	330		
They stai'd not either to pray or sacrifice,	Lucan, First Booke	504		
is by cowards/Left as a pray now Caesar doth approach:	Lucan, First Booke	512		
And Cupide who hath markt me for thy pray,	Ovid's Elegies	1.3.12		
Pray God it may his latest supper be,	Ovid's Elegies	1.4.2		
Strike on the boord like them that pray for evill,	Ovid's Elegies	1.4.27		
To him I pray it no delight may bring,	Ovid's Elegies	1.4.67		
Night goes away: I pray thee ope the dore.	Ovid's Elegies	1.6.48		
And as a pray unto blinde anger given,	Ovid's Elegies	1.7.44		
Pray him to lend what thou maist nere restore.	Ovid's Elegies	1.8.102		
Oft thou wilt say, live well, thou wilt pray oft,	Ovid's Elegies	1.8.107		
I pray that rotten age you wrackes/And sluttish white-mould	Ovid's Elegies	1.12.29		
What can be easier then the thing we pray?	Ovid's Elegies	2.2.66		
Then wilt thou Laedas noble twinne-starres pray,	Ovid's Elegies	2.11.29		
Which without bloud-shed doth the pray inherit.	Ovid's Elegies	2.12.6		
By fear'd Anubis visage I thee pray,	Ovid's Elegies	2.13.11		
Love-snarde Calypso is supposde to pray,	Ovid's Elegies	2.17.15		
Yet whom thou favourst, pray may conquerour be.	Ovid's Elegies	3.2.2		
What Venus promisd, promise thou we pray,	Ovid's Elegies	3.2.59		
Thy bones I pray may in the urne safe rest,	Ovid's Elegies	3.8.67		
(as men say)/But deaffe and cruell, where he meanes to pray.	Hero and Leander	2.288		
PRAY'D				
Seeing thou hast pray'd and sacrific'd to them.	F 235	1.3.7		Faust
And pray'd the narrow toyling Hellespont,	Hero and Leander	2.150		
PRAYD				
tell us of this before, that Divines might have prayd for thee?	F1863	5.2.67	P	1Schol
PRAYER (See also PRAIERS)				
Or els Ile make a prayer unto the waves,	Dido	5.1.246		Dido

PRAYER (cont.)			
Contrition, Prayer, Repentance?	F 405	2.1.17	Faust
PRAYERS			
And would my prayers (as Pigmalions did)/Could give it life,	Dido	2.1.16	Aeneas
Heare, heare, O heare Iarbus plaining prayers,	Dido	4.2.8	Iarbus
How now Iarbus, at your prayers so hard?	Dido	4.2.23	Anna
Lifting his prayers to the heavens for aid,	1Tamb	3.2.83	Agidas
And yet I know the prayers of those Nuns/And holy Fryers,	Jew	2.3.80	Barab
And with my prayers pierce [th']impartiall heavens,	Jew	3.2.33	Govnr
he made such haste to his prayers, as if hee had had another	Jew	4.2.24	P Ithimr
no threats or prayers move thee,/O harder then the dores thou	Ovid's Elegies		1.6.61
Our prayers move thee to assist our drift,	Ovid's Elegies		2.3.17
PRAYES			
And to the Gods for that death Ovid prayes.	Ovid's Elegies		2.10.30
PRAYSING			
Praysing for me some unknowne Guelder dame,	Ovid's Elegies		1.14.49
PREACH			
Preach me not out of my possessions.	Jew	1.2.111	Barab
And he forsooth must goe and preach in Germany:	P 392	7.32	Guise
Preach upon poles for trespasse of their tongues.	Edw	1.1.118	Kent
Strike off their heads, and let them preach on poles,	Edw	3.1.20	Spencr
PREACHER			
Are you a preacher of these heresies?	P 340	5.67	Guise
I am a preacher of the word of God,	P 341	5.68	Lorein
PREACHMENTS			
As by their preachments they will profit much,	Edw	3.1.22	Spencr
keepe these preachments till you come to the place appointed.	Edw	4.7.113	P Rice
PREASE			
When other men prease forward for renowne:	1Tamb	1.1.84	Mycet
PRECEDENT (See PRESIDENT)			
PRECEPTS			
I doe not doubt by your divine precepts/And mine owne industry,	Jew	1.2.334	Abigal
(Alas my precepts turne my selfe to smart)/We write, or what	Ovid's Elegies		2.18.20
PRECIBUS			
Oro, si quis [adhuc] <ad haec> precibus locus, exue mentem.	Dido	5.1.138	Dido
PRECINCT			
As any prizes out of my precinct.	1Tamb	1.2.28	Tamb
PRECIOUS (See also PRETIOUS)			
Enchast with precious juelles of mine owne:	1Tamb	1.2.96	Tamb
more precious in mine eies/Than all the wealthy kingdomes I	2Tamb	1.3.18	Tamb
If you loved him, and it so precious?	2Tamb	4.2.72	Therid
Inestimable drugs and precious stones,	2Tamb	5.3.152	Tamb
My flesh devided in your precious shapes,	2Tamb	5.3.172	Tamb
As precious is the charge thou undertak'st/As that which	2Tamb	5.3.230	Tamb
It is a precious powder that I bought/Of an Italian in Ancona	Jew	3.4.68	Barab
So precious, and withall so orient,	Jew	5.3.28	Msngr
PRECISE			
but be thou so precise/As they may thinke it done of Holinesse.	Jew	1.2.284	Barab
Mine old lord whiles he livde, was so precise,	Edw	2.1.46	Baldck
PRECISELY			
dore more wisely/And som-what higher beare thy foote precisely.	Ovid's Elegies		1.12.6
PRECISIAN			
I will set my countenance like a Precisian, and begin to speake	F 214	1.2.21	P Wagner
PREDESTINATE			
Predestinate to ruine; all lands else/Have stable peace, here	Lucan, First Booke		251
PRE-EMINENCE (See PREHEMINENCE)			
PREFER			
I will prefer them for the funerall/They have bestowed on my	2Tamb	4.3.65	Tamb
PREFERD			
Preferd before a man of majestie:	Dido	3.3.65	Iarbus
And would have once preferd me to the king.	Edw	2.1.14	Spencr
Then hope I by her meanes to be preferd,	Edw	2.1.29	Baldck
PREFERR'D			
For bloudshed knighted, before me preferr'd.	Ovid's Elegies		3.7.10
PREFERRES			
Which he preferres before his chiefest blisse;	F 27	Prol.27	1Chor
Before Callimachus one preferres me farre,	Ovid's Elegies		2.4.19
PREFERRETH			
For these before the rest preferreth he:	Ovid's Elegies		1.1.2
PREHEMINENCE			
chiefe spectacle of the worldes preheminence, The bright	F App	p.237 24	P Emper
PREJUDICE			
For none of this can prejudice my life.	Jew	5.1.39	Barab
it may prejudice their hope/Of my inheritance to the crowne of	P 467	8.17	Anjoy
PREJUDICED			
thou doest, thou shalt be no wayes prejudiced or indamaged.	F App	p.236 9	P Emper
PRELATES			
As Rome and all those popish Prelates there,	P1248	22.110	Navrre
of all the [reverend] <holy> Synod/Of Priests and Prelates,	F 953	3.1.175	Faust
False Prelates, for this hatefull treachery,	F1033	3.2.53	Pope
PREMISED			
My dutie to your honor [premised] <promised>, &c. I have	Edw	4.3.28	P Spencr
PREORDAINDE			
Then as the powers devine have preordainde,	1Tamb	5.1.400	Zenoc
PREPARATION			
To make my preparation for Fraunce.	Edw	3.1.88	Queene
PREPAR'D			
Our hands are not prepar'd to lawles spoyle,	Dido	1.2.12	Illion
Should have prepar'd to entertaine his Grace?	1Tamb	4.2.63	Zabina
Was this the banquet he prepar'd for us?	Jew	5.5.95	Calym
The Doctor stands prepar'd, by power of Art,	F1222	4.1.68	Faust
Muse upreard <prepar'd> I [meant] <meane> to sing of armes,	Ovid's Elegies		1.1.5
no darke night-flying spright/Nor hands prepar'd to slaughter,	Ovid's Elegies		1.6.14

PREPAR'D (cont.)
Thrice she prepar'd to flie, thrice she did stay, . . Ovid's Elegies 3.5.69
But he the [days] <day> bright-bearing Car prepar'd. . Hero and Leander 2.330

PREPARE
Therefore cheere up your mindes, prepare to fight, . . 1Tamb 2.2.29 Meandr
Techelles, and the rest prepare your swordes, . . . 1Tamb 3.3.64 Tamb
Prepare thy selfe to live and die my slave. . . . 1Tamb 3.3.207 Zabina
I would prepare a ship and saile to it, ... 2Tamb 1.3.90 Celeb
Sirha, prepare whips, and bring my chariot to my Tent: . 2Tamb 3.5.144 P Tamb
Till we prepare our martch to Babylon, ... 2Tamb 4.3.93 Tamb
No remedye, therefore prepare your selfe. P1097 20.7 1Mur
prepare thy selfe, for I will presently raise up two devils to F 372 1.4.30 P Wagner
Now Faustus, come prepare thy selfe for mirth, . . . F 981 3.2.1 Mephst
Come sirs, prepare your selves in readinesse, . . . F1420 4.2.96 1Soldr
Friers prepare a dirge to lay the fury of this ghost, once F App p.232 16 P Pope
O Gods what death prepare ye? . . . . Lucan, First Booke 648
All for their Mistrisse, what they have, prepare. . . Ovid's Elegies 1.10.58
When well-toss'd mattocks did the ground prepare, . . Ovid's Elegies 3.9.31
The Priests to Juno did prepare chaste feasts, . . . Ovid's Elegies 3.12.3

PREPARED
Prepared stands to wracke their woodden walles, . . Dido 1.1.67 Venus

PRESAGE
Presage the downfall of my Emperie, ... Dido 4.4.118 Dido
That being fiery meteors, may presage, ... 2Tamb 3.2.4 Tamb
And Commets that presage the fal of kingdoms. . . . Lucan, First Booke 527

PRESAGES
These sad presages were enough to scarre/The quivering Romans, Lucan, First Booke 672
Presages are not vaine, when she departed/Nape by stumbling on Ovid's Elegies 1.12.3
And my presages of no weight be thought. . . . . Ovid's Elegies 2.14.42

PRESAGETH
My mind presageth fortunate successe, ... 1Tamb 4.3.58 Arabia

PRESAGING
Thus like the sad presaging Raven that tolls/The sicke mans Jew 2.1.1 Barab
And all bands of that death presaging aliance. . . . Lucan, First Booke 114

PRESCRIB'D
All <articles prescrib'd> <covenant-articles> betweene us both. F 480 (HC260) Faust

PRESCRIBED
Intrench with those dimensions I prescribed: . . . 2Tamb 3.3.42 Therid

PRESENCE
Himselfe in presence shal unfold at large. . . . . 2Tamb Prol.9 Prolog
Your presence (loving friends and fellow kings)/Makes me to 2Tamb 1.3.151 Tamb
our neighbour kings/Expect our power and our royall presence, 2Tamb 2.2.4 Orcan
Whose heavenly presence beautified with health, . . 2Tamb 2.4.49 Tamb
My Lord, your presence makes them pale and wan. . . 2Tamb 3.5.60 Usumc
That can endure so well your royall presence, . . . 2Tamb 5.3.111 Usumc
And fly my presence if thou looke to live. . . . P 692 13.36 Guise
And heere in presence of you all I sweare, . . . P1026 19.96 King
Brav'd Mowberie in presence of the king, ... Edw 1.1.111 Kent
Or else be banisht from his highnesse presence. . . . Edw 1.4.203 Queene
Out of my presence, come not neere the court. . . . Edw 2.2.89 Edward
So sir, you have spoke, away, avoid our presence. . . Edw 3.1.232 Edward
Proud Edward, doost thou banish me thy presence? . . Edw 4.1.5 Kent
In signe of love and dutie to this presence, . . . Edw 4.6.48 Rice
Hye to the presence to attend the Emperour. . . . F1156 4.1.2 Mrtino
And bring in presence of his Majesty, ... F1169 4.1.15 Mrtino
so much for the injury hee offred me heere in your presence, F App p.238 82 P Faust
With thine, nor this last fire their presence misses. . Ovid's Elegies 3.8.54
His presence made the rudest paisant melt, . . . Hero and Leander 1.79
So at her presence all surpris'd and tooken, . . . Hero and Leander 1.122

PRESENT
For I have honey to present thee with: . . . . . Dido 4.2.53 Anna
Present thee with th'Emperiall Diadem. . . . . 1Tamb 1.1.139 Ortyg
the Persean king/Should offer present Dukedomes to our state, 1Tamb 1.2.215 Techel
from the camp/When Kings themselves are present in the field? 1Tamb 2.4.17 Tamb
For words are vaine where working tooles present/The naked 1Tamb 3.2.93 Agidas
Must fight against my life and present love: . . . 1Tamb 5.1.389 Zenoc
for as the Romans usde/I here present thee with a naked sword. 2Tamb 1.1.82 Sgsmnd
I here present thee with the crowne of Fesse, . . . 2Tamb 1.3.140 Techel
And furie would confound my present rest. . . . . 2Tamb 2.4.65 Zenoc
Ile give your Grace a present of such price, . . . 2Tamb 4.2.56 Olymp
And for a present easie proofe hereof, ... 2Tamb 4.2.75 Olymp
will keep it for/The richest present of this Easterne world. 2Tamb 4.2.78 Therid
now, how Jove hath sent/A present medicine to recure my paine: 2Tamb 5.3.106 Tamb
But to present the Tragedy of a Jew, ... Jew Prol.30 Machvl
the Custome-house/Will serve as well as I were present there. Jew 1.1.58 Barab
That measure nought but by the present time. . . . Jew 1.2.220 Barab
He'de give us present mony for them all. . . . . Jew 2.3.6 1Offcr
'Twas sent me for a present from the great Cham. . . Jew 4.4.68 Barab
Where be thou present onely to performe/One stratagem that I'le Jew 5.2.98 Barab
Goe then, present them to the Queene Navarre: . . . P 79 2.22 Guise
Be gone my freend, present them to her straite. . . P 82 2.25 Guise
Repaying all attempts with present death, ... P 269 4.67 Charls
And send them for a present to the Pope: . . . . P 317 5.44 Anjoy
Then meanes he present treason to our state. . . . P 880 17.75 King
What will he do when as he shall be present? . . . Edw 2.2.48 Mortmr
Present by me this traitor to the state, ... Edw 4.6.49 Rice
My lorde, the parlement must have present newes, . . Edw 5.1.84 Trussl
To the Bishop of Millaine, for this so rare a present. . F1042 3.2.62 Pope
Present before this royall Emperour, ... F1238 4.1.84 Faust
That when my Spirits present the royall shapes/Of Alexander and F1249 4.1.95 Faust
No Art, no cunning, to present these Lords, ... F1295 4.1.141 Faust
it is not in my abilitie to present before your eyes, the true F App p.237 41 P Faust
and swiftly bringing newes/Of present war, made many lies and Lucan, First Booke 468

PRESENT (cont.)
But being present, might that worke the best, ... Ovid's Elegies 2.8.17

PRESENTLIE
Or I will presentlie discharge these lords, ... Edw 1.4.61 ArchBp
And meete me at the parke pale presentlie: . . . . Edw 2.1.73 Neece
and with the power/That he intendeth presentlie to raise, Edw 2.4.44 Queene

PRESENTLY
I will take order for that presently: . . . . . Dido 1.1.113 Jupitr
Away with her to prison presently, ... Dido 5.1.220 Dido
Whether we presently will flie (my Lords)/To rest secure . 1Tamb 1.1.177 Cosroe
For presently Techelles here shal haste, ... 1Tamb 2.5.94 Tamb
For we will martch against them presently. . . . . 2Tamb 1.3.105 Tamb
Trumpets and drums, alarum presently, ... 2Tamb 3.3.62 Techel
But presently be prest to conquer it. . . . . . 2Tamb 4.3.96 Techel
Take them, and hang them both up presently. . . . 2Tamb 5.1.132 Tamb
Wel said, let there be a fire presently. . . . . 2Tamb 5.1.178 Tamb
we leave sufficient garrison/And presently depart to Persea, 2Tamb 5.1.212 Tamb
your absence in the field, offers to set upon us presently. 2Tamb 5.3.104 P 3Msngr
For presently you shall be shriv'd. . . . . . . Jew 4.1.110 1Fryar
Well, I must seeke a meanes to rid 'em all,/And presently: Jew 4.3.64 Barab
Thou'st doom'd thy selfe, assault it presently. . . . Jew 5.1.97 Calym
Governor, presently. . . . . Jew 5.2.104 Barab
But that we presently despatch Embassadours/To Poland, to call P 555 11.20 QnMoth
Epernoune, goe see it presently be done, ... P 558 11.23 QnMoth
Ile dispatch him with his brother presently, ... P 651 12.64 QnMoth
So, convey this to the counsell presently. . . . . P 892 17.87 King
tush, were he heere, we would kill him presently. . . P 935 19.5 P 1Mur
Ile see him presently dispatched away. . . . . . Edw 1.4.90 Mortmr
Speake, shall he presently be dispatch'd and die? . . . Edw 5.2.44 Mortmr
write a letter presently/Unto the Lord of Bartley from . Edw 5.2.47 Mortmr
But bring his head back presently to me. . . . . Edw 5.6.54 King
That shall we presently know, <for see> here comes his boy. F 196 1.2.3 2Schol
thou dost not presently bind thy selfe to me for seven yeares, F 361 1.4.19 P Wagner
for I will presently raise up two devils to carry thee away: F 373 1.4.31 P Wagner
That thou shalt see presently: . . . . F 732 2.3.11 P Robin
put off thy cloathes, and I'le conjure thee about presently: F 747 2.3.26 P Robin
brave, prethee let's to it presently, for I am as dry as a dog. F 751 2.3.30 P Dick
Welcome grave Fathers, answere presently, ... F 946 3.1.168 Pope
Go presently, and bring a banket forth, ... F 977 3.1.199 Pope
Faustus thou shalt, then kneele downe presently, . . . F 994 3.2.14 Mephst
to their porridge-pots, for I'le into the Kitchin presently: F1134 3.3.47 P Robin
Your Majesty shall see them presently. . . . . . F1235 4.1.81 Faust
come not away quickly, you shall have me asleepe presently: F1242 4.1.88 P Benvol
And Il'e play Diana, and send you the hornes presently. . F1257 4.1.103 P Faust
You shall presently: . . . . F1519 4.5.15 P Hostss
so he presently gave me my mony, and fell to eating; . F1529 4.5.25 P Carter
and binde your selfe presently unto me for seaven yeeres, or F App p.229 24 P Wagner
two divels presently to fetch thee away Baliol and Belcher. F App p.230 43 P Wagner
Go to maister Doctor, let me see them presently. . . F App p.237 50 P Emper
Might presently be banisht into hell, ... Hero and Leander 1.453

PRESENTS
Besides rich presents from the puisant Cham, ... 1Tamb 1.2.18 Magnet
love and feare presents/A thousand sorrowes to my martyred 1Tamb 5.1.383 Zenoc
As martiall presents to our friends at home, ... 2Tamb 1.1.35 Orcan
by these presents doe give both body and soule to Lucifer, F 493 2.1.105 P Faust
Let Homer yeeld to such as presents bring, ... Ovid's Elegies 1.8.61

PRESERVE
Indevor to preserve and prosper it. . . . . . . 1Tamb 2.5.35 Ortyg
that wil preserve life, make her round and plump, and batten Jew 3.4.65 P Ithimr
That swim about and so preserve their lives: . . . . P 419 7.59 Guise
Will shew his mercy and preserve us still. . . . . P 576 11.41 Navrre
A loving mother to preserve thy state, ... P 594 12.7 QnMoth
and so the Lord blesse you, preserve you, and keepe you, my F 217 1.2.24 P Wagner

PRESERVED
Then I am carefull you should be preserved. . . . . P 265 4.63 Charls

PRESERVES
As heaven preserves all things, so save thou one. . . . Hero and Leander 1.224

PRESERVETH
And say it brings her that preserveth me; . . . . Ovid's Elegies 2.11.44

PRESERVING
And hisse at Dido for preserving thee? . . . . . Dido 5.1.168 Dido
Preserving life, by hasting cruell death. . . . . 1Tamb 4.4.96 Bajzth

PRESIDENT (Homograph)
What better president than mightie Jove? . . . . . 1Tamb 2.7.17 Tamb
sent from the President of Paris, that craves accesse unto your P1156 22.18 P 1Msngr
The President of Paris greetes your grace, ... P1168 22.30 Frier
And you lord Warwick, president of the North, ... Edw 1.4.68 Edward
Take from irrationall beasts a president, ... Ovid's Elegies 1.10.25

PRESSE (See also PREASE)
To presse beyond acceptance to your sight. . . . . Dido 3.3.16 Aeneas
Or art thou grievde thy betters presse so nye? . . . . Dido 3.3.18 Iarbus
too dearely wunne/That unto death did presse the holy Nunne. Ovid's Elegies 1.10.50
Nor want I strength, but weight to presse her with: . . . Ovid's Elegies 2.10.24
For shame presse not her backe with thy hard knee. . . . Ovid's Elegies 3.2.24

PREST (Homograph)
Who warne me of such daunger prest at hand, ... Dido 3.2.22 Venus
And prest out fire from their burning jawes: . . . . 1Tamb 2.6.6 Cosroe
So prest are we, but yet if Sigismond/Speake as a friend, and 2Tamb 1.1.122 Orcan
But presently be prest to conquer it. . . . . . 2Tamb 4.3.96 Techel
Thou seest us prest to give the last assault, ... 2Tamb 5.1.60 Techel
Not I, thou art Prest, prepare thy selfe, for I will presently F 372 1.4.30 P Wagner
Raw soldiours lately prest; and troupes of gownes; . . Lucan, First Booke 312
Let not thy necke by his vile armes be prest, ... Ovid's Elegies 1.4.35

PREST (cont.)
How apt her breasts were to be prest by me, — Ovid's Elegies — 1.5.20

PRESUME
That dar'st presume thy Soveraigne for to mocke. — 1Tamb 1.1.105 — Mycet
Presume a bickering with your Emperour: — 1Tamb 3.1.4 — Bajzth
may I presume/To know the cause of these unquiet fits: — 1Tamb 3.2.1 — Agidas
When men presume to manage armes with him. — 1Tamb 5.1.478 — Tamb
That durst presume for hope of any gaine, — P 258 4.56 — Charls
Why, darst thou presume to call on Christ, — P 356 6.11 — Mntsrl
But we presume it is not for our good. — P 824 17.19 — King
His grace I dare presume will welcome me, — Edw 4.2.33 — Queene

PRESUMING
But if presuming on his silly power, — 1Tamb 3.1.33 — Bajzth

PRESUMPTION
divelish shepheard to aspire/With such a Giantly presumption, — 1Tamb 2.6.2 — Cosroe
Note the presumption of this Scythian slave: — 1Tamb 3.3.68 — Bajzth
Should not give us presumption to the like. — 2Tamb 2.1.46 — Sgsmnd
me in beleefe/Gives great presumption that she loves me not; — Jew 3.4.11 — Barab
intreat thy Lord/To pardon my unjust presumption, — F1748 5.1.75 — Faust
villaines, for your presumption, I transforme thee into an Ape, — F App p.235 43 — P Mephst

PRESUMPTUOUS
To tame the pride of this presumptuous Beast, — 1Tamb 4.3.15 — Souldn

PRETENCE
Under pretence of helping Charles the fifth, — Jew 2.3.188 — Barab
Nor have their words true histories pretence, — Ovid's Elegies — 3.11.42

PRETENDED
Let's hence, lest further mischiefe be pretended. — Jew 5.5.96 — Calym

PRETENDEST
Doe but bring this to passe which thou pretendest, — Jew 5.2.84 — Govnr

PRETENDETH
Repentance? Spurca: what pretendeth this? — Jew 3.4.6 — Barab
And which (aie me) ever pretendeth ill, — Lucan, First Booke — 625

PRETHE
What wast I prethe? — Jew 1.2.377 — Lodowk
Prethe doe: what saist thou now? — Jew 3.4.88 — Barab
Prethe, Pilia-borza, bid the Fidler give me the posey in his — Jew 4.4.35 — P Curtzn
Prethe sweet love, one more, and write it sharp. — Jew 4.4.73 — Curtzn

PRETHEE
I prethee say to whome thou writes? — P 671 13.15 — Guise
I prethee tell him that the Guise is heere. — P 958 19.28 — Guise
Prethee let me know it. — Edw 2.2.14 — Edward
But I prethee tell me, in good sadnesse Robin, is that a — F 743 2.3.22 — P Dick
brave, prethee let's to it presently, for I am as dry as a dog. — F 751 2.3.30 — P Dick
prethee come away, theres a Gentleman tarries to have his — F App p.233 6 — P Rafe
it, and she has sent me to looke thee out, prethee come away. — F App p.233 9 — P Rafe

PRETIE
Might I but see that pretie sport a foote, — Dido 1.1.16 — Ganimd
And tell me where [learndst] <learnst> thou this pretie song? — Dido 3.1.27 — Dido
Twil proove a pretie jest (in faith) my friends. — 1Tamb 2.5.90 — Tamb
let it be in the likenesse of a little pretie frisking flea, — F App p.231 62 — P Clown
tickle the pretie wenches plackets Ile be amongst them ifaith. — F App p.231 63 — P Clown

PRETILIE
How pretilie he laughs, goe ye wagge, — Dido 4.5.19 — Nurse

PRETIOUS
Shall burne to cinders in this pretious flame. — Dido 5.1.301 — Dido
Lading their shippes with golde and pretious stones: — 1Tamb 1.1.121 — Cosroe
Fairer than rockes of pearle and pretious stone, — 1Tamb 3.3.118 — Tamb
a golden Canapie/Enchac'd with pretious stones, which shine as — 2Tamb 1.2.49 — Callap
And with a vyoll full of pretious grace, — F1731 5.1.58 — OldMan
Wit was some-times more pretious then gold, — Ovid's Elegies — 3.7.3

PRETTIE
We that have prettie wenches to our wives, — Edw 2.5.102 — Penbrk

PRETTY (See also PRITTY)
A petty <pretty> case of paltry Legacies: — F 57 1.1.29 — Faust
Those in their lovers, pretty maydes desire. — Ovid's Elegies — 1.9.6
But when I praise a pretty wenches face/Shee in requitall doth — Ovid's Elegies — 2.1.33
That have so oft serv'd pretty wenches dyet. — Ovid's Elegies — 2.9.24
Where Juno comes, each youth, and pretty maide, — Ovid's Elegies — 3.12.23
Which from our pretty Lambes we pull, — Passionate Shepherd — 14

PRETY
And tis a prety toy to be a Poet. — 1Tamb 2.2.54 — Mycet

PREVAIL'D
Caesar (said he) while eloquence prevail'd, — Lucan, First Booke — 274
Which so prevail'd, as he with small ado, — Hero and Leander — 2.281

PREVAILE
What can my teares or cryes prevaile me now? — Dido 5.1.319 — Anna
If wealth or riches may prevaile with them, — 1Tamb 2.2.61 — Meandr
Nay Lady, then if nothing wil prevaile, — 2Tamb 4.2.50 — Therid
No speaking will prevaile, and therefore cease. — Edw 1.4.220 — Penbrk
If Warwickes wit and policie prevaile. — Edw 2.5.96 — Warwck
I doubt it not my lord, right will prevaile. — Edw 3.1.189 — Spencr
As all his footmanship shall scarce prevaile, — F1302 4.1.148 — Faust
Ah Doctor Faustus, that I might prevaile, — F App p.243 34 — OldMan
But if sterne Neptunes windie powre prevaile, — Ovid's Elegies — 2.16.27

PREVAILES
Nothing prevailes, for she is dead my Lord. — 2Tamb 2.4.124 — Therid
'Tis wisedome to give much, a gift prevailes, — Hero and Leander — 2.225

PREVAYLED
Since then succesfully we have prevayled, — Edw 4.6.21 — Queene

PREVENT
I must prevent him, wishing will not serve: — Dido 4.4.104 — Dido
Then haste Agydas, and prevent the plagues: — 1Tamb 3.2.100 — Agidas
their bodies, and prevent their soules/From heavens of comfort, — 1Tamb 5.1.89 — 1Virgn

PREVENT (cont.)			
in vaine ye labour to prevent/That which mine honor sweares	1Tamb	5.1.106	Tamb
PREVENTED			
Prevented Turnus of Lavinia, ...	1Tamb	5.1.393	Zenoc
But was prevented by his sodaine end.	2Tamb	4.2.74	Olymp
But thats prevented, for to end his life, ...	P1119	21.13	Dumain
PREVENTETH			
Sweet Lord and King, your speech preventeth mine, . .	Edw	2.2.59	Gavstn
PREVENTION			
My policie detests prevention:	Jew	5.2.121	Barab
PREY (See also PRAY)			
To be a prey for Vultures and wild beasts.	Jew	5.1.59	Govnr
Would I had beene my mistresse gentle prey, . . .	Ovid's Elegies		2.17.5
PREYS			
From dog-kept flocks come preys to woolves most gratefull.	Ovid's Elegies		1.8.56
PRIAM			
Then would it leape out to give Priam life:	Dido	2.1.27	Aeneas
Achates, see King Priam wags his hand, ...	Dido	2.1.29	Aeneas
For were it Priam he would smile on me.	Dido	2.1.36	Ascan
And Priam dead, yet how we heare no newes. . . .	Dido	2.1.113	Dido
Then from the navell to the throat at once,/He ript old Priam:	Dido	2.1.256	Aeneas
Will Dido raise old Priam forth his grave, ...	Dido	4.3.39	Illion
For Troy, for Priam, for his fiftie sonnes, ...	Dido	4.4.89	Aeneas
PRIAMS			
Priams misfortune followes us by sea, ...	Dido	1.1.143	Aeneas
and on his speare/The mangled head of Priams yongest sonne,	Dido	2.1.215	Aeneas
Then here in me shall flourish Priams race, ...	Dido	4.4.87	Aeneas
On Priams loose-trest daughter when he gazed. . . .	Ovid's Elegies		1.9.38
Who should have Priams wealthy substance wonne, . .	Ovid's Elegies		2.14.13
PRIAMUS			
There Zanthus streame, because here's Priamus, . . .	Dido	2.1.8	Aeneas
Grecians, which rejoyce/That nothing now is left of Priamus:	Dido	2.1.20	Aeneas
O Priamus is left and this is he, ...	Dido	2.1.21	Aeneas
Yet thinkes my minde that this is Priamus:	Dido	2.1.25	Aeneas
that would have it so/Deludes thy eye sight, Priamus is dead.	Dido	2.1.32	Achat
O Priamus, O Troy, oh Hecuba!	Dido	2.1.105	Aeneas
And brought unto the Court of Priamus:	Dido	2.1.154	Aeneas
But Priamus impatient of delay, ...	Dido	2.1.173	Aeneas
And at Joves Altar finding Priamus, ...	Dido	2.1.225	Aeneas
PRICE			
Ile give your Grace a present of such price, ...	2Tamb	4.2.56	Olymp
As any thing of price with thy conceit?	2Tamb	5.1.14	Govnr
And seildsene costly stones of so great price, . . .	Jew	1.1.28	Barab
Every ones price is written on his backe, ...	Jew	2.3.3	2Offcr
And what's the price?	Jew	2.3.64	Lodowk
Oh my Lord we will not jarre about the price; . . .	Jew	2.3.65	Barab
Come home and there's no price shall make us part, . .	Jew	2.3.92	Barab
marketplace; whats the price of this slave, two hundred Crowns?	Jew	2.3.97 P	Barab
Sir, that's his price.	Jew	2.3.99	1Offcr
The price thereof will serve to entertaine/Selim and all his	Jew	5.3.30	Msngr
thou canst not buy so good a horse, for so small a price:	F1460	4.4.4 P	Faust
stil poore/Did vild deeds, then t'was worth the price of bloud,	Lucan, First Booke		175
Make a small price, while thou thy nets doest lay, . .	Ovid's Elegies		1.8.69
Life is no light price of a small surcease.	Ovid's Elegies		2.14.26
PRICKE			
That to deceits it may me forward pricke.	Ovid's Elegies		2.19.44
PRICKING			
Amongst the pricking thornes, and sharpest briers, . .	F1411	4.2.87	Faust
PRICKS			
even nowe when youthfull bloud/Pricks forth our lively bodies,	Lucan, First Booke		364
PRICKT			
But gods and fortune prickt him to this war, ...	Lucan, First Booke		265
PRIDE			
From Junos bird Ile pluck her spotted pride, ...	Dido	1.1.34	Jupitr
And rests a pray to every billowes pride.	Dido	1.1.53	Venus
Which Pergama did vaunt in all her pride.	Dido	1.1.151	Aeneas
That after burnt the pride of Asia.	Dido	2.1.187	Aeneas
Least you subdue the pride of Christendome?	1Tamb	1.1.132	Menaph
so imbellished/With Natures pride, and richest furniture?	1Tamb	1.2.156	Therid
Since with the spirit of his fearefull pride, . . .	1Tamb	2.6.12	Meandr
Straight will I use thee as thy pride deserves: . .	1Tamb	3.3.206	Zabina
Ambitious pride shall make thee fall as low, . . .	1Tamb	4.2.76	Bajzth
To tame the pride of this presumptuous Beast, . . .	1Tamb	4.3.15	Souldn
And like to Flora in her mornings pride, ...	1Tamb	5.1.140	Tamb
With greater power than erst his pride hath felt, . .	2Tamb	2.2.10	Gazell
Yet flourisheth as Flora in her pride, ...	2Tamb	2.3.22	Orcan
Scourging the pride of cursed Tamburlain.	2Tamb	3.1.37	Callap
To overdare the pride of Graecia, ...	2Tamb	3.5.66	Tamb
my children stoops your pride/And leads your glories <bodies>	2Tamb	4.1.76	Tamb
To scourge the pride of such as heaven abhors: . . .	2Tamb	4.1.149	Tamb
teares of Mahomet/For hot consumption of his countries pride:	2Tamb	4.1.197	Tamb
Come once in furie and survay his pride, ...	2Tamb	4.3.41	Orcan
The pride and beautie of her princely seat, ...	2Tamb	4.3.109	Tamb
Yet when the pride of Cynthia is at full, ...	2Tamb	5.2.46	Callap
More then heavens coach, the pride of Phaeton. . . .	2Tamb	5.3.244	Tamb
For earth hath spent the pride of all her fruit, . .	2Tamb	5.3.250	Amyras
But malice, falshood, and excessive pride, ...	Jew	1.1.117	Barab
Now vaile your pride you captive Christians, ...	Jew	5.2.1	Calym
Nere was there Colliars sonne so full of pride. . .	P 416	7.56	Anjoy
Tis warre that must asswage this tyrantes pride. . .	P1128	21.22	Dumain
Barons and Earls, your pride hath made me mute, . .	Edw	1.1.107	Kent
Who swolne with venome of ambitious pride, ...	Edw	1.2.31	Mortmr
Think you that we can brooke this upstart pride? . .	Edw	1.4.41	Warwck

PRIDE (cont.)			
Twill make him vaile the topflag of his pride, ...	Edw	1.4.276	Mortmr
Tis warre that must abate these Barons pride. . . .	Edw	2.2.99	Edward
The Barons overbeare me with their pride.	Edw	3.1.9	Edward
A traitors, will they still display their pride? . .	Edw	3.1.172	Spencr
But justice of the quarrell and the cause,/Vaild is your pride:	Edw	3.1.223	Edward
And made the flowring pride of Wittenberg <Wertenberge> .	F 141	1.1.113	Faust
by aspiring pride and insolence,/For which God threw him from	F 295	1.3.67	Mephst
I am Pride; I disdaine to have any parents: . . .	F 664	2.2.113 P	Pride
Or dash the pride of this solemnity;	F 860	3.1.82	Mephst
Now <Since> we have seene the pride of Natures worke <workes>,	F1702	5.1.29	1Schol
[Sathan begins to sift me with his pride]: . . .	F1791	5.1.118A	OldMan
Nor thunder in rough threatings haughty pride? . . .	Ovid's Elegies		1.7.46
But by her glasse disdainefull pride she learnes, . .	Ovid's Elegies		2.17.9
prowd she was, (for loftie pride that dwels/In tow'red courts,	Hero and Leander		1.393
PRIE			
And dive into the water, and there prie/Upon his brest, his	Hero and Leander		2.188
PRIES			
Proud Mortimer pries neare into thy walkes. . . .	Edw	4.6.18	Kent
PRIEST			
Till that a Princesse priest conceav'd by Mars, . .	Dido	1.1.106	Jupitr
Machda, where the mighty Christian Priest/Cal'd John the great,	2Tamb	1.3.187	Techel
Nor plowman, Priest, nor Merchant staies at home, . .	2Tamb	5.2.50	Callap
The Canon Law forbids it, and the Priest/That makes it knowne,	Jew	3.6.34	2Fryar
I priest, and lives to be revengd on thee, . . .	Edw	1.1.178	Edward
Whose there? conveie this priest to the tower. . . .	Edw	1.1.200	Edward
What should a priest do with so faire a house? . . .	Edw	1.1.206	Gavstn
Why should a king be subject to a priest?	Edw	1.4.96	Edward
hornes/The quick priest pull'd him on his knees and slew him:	Lucan, First Booke		612
I the pure priest of Phoebus and the muses, . . .	Ovid's Elegies		3.7.23
PRIESTES			
Five hundred fatte Franciscan Fryers and priestes. . .	P 142	2.85	Guise
Did he not draw a sorte of English priestes/From Doway to the	P1030	19.100	King
PRIESTHOOD			
Perhaps, thy sacred Priesthood makes thee loath, . .	Hero and Leander		1.293
PRIESTS			
Ye holy Priests of heavenly Mahomet, ...	1Tamb	4.2.2	Bajzth
Slew all his Priests, his kinsmen, and his friends, . .	2Tamb	5.1.181	Tamb
There I enrich'd the Priests with burials, . . .	Jew	2.3.183	Barab
With slaughtered priests [make] <may> Tibers channell swell,	Edw	1.4.102	Edward
of all the [reverend] <holy> Synod/Of Priests and Prelates,	F 953	3.1.175	Faust
Go then command our Priests to sing a Dirge, . . .	F1063	3.2.83	Pope
moves/To wound their armes, sing vengeance, Sibils priests,	Lucan, First Booke		564
then the sacred priests/That with divine lustration purg'd the	Lucan, First Booke		592
Apolloes southsayers; and Joves feasting priests; . .	Lucan, First Booke		601
The Priests to Juno did prepare chaste feasts, . . .	Ovid's Elegies		3.12.3
And she her vestall virgin Priests doth follow. . .	Ovid's Elegies		3.12.30
PRIME			
bed, where many a Lord/In prime and glorie of his loving joy,	1Tamb	5.1.84	1Virgn
Seeing <When> in my prime my force is spent and done? .	Ovid's Elegies		3.6.18
PRIMROSE			
The Meads, the Orchards, and the Primrose lanes, . .	Jew	4.2.95	Ithimr
PRIMUM			
Even to the height of Primum Mobile:	F 763	2.3.42	2Chor
PRIMUS			
and all mens hatred/Inflict upon them, thou great Primus Motor.	Jew	1.2.164	Barab
PRINCE			
Brave Prince of Troy, thou onely art our God, . . .	Dido	1.1.152	Achat
Brave Prince, welcome to Carthage and to me, . . .	Dido	2.1.81	Dido
And this yong Prince shall be thy playfellow. . . .	Dido	2.1.307	Venus
This Meleagers sonne, a warlike Prince, ...	Dido	3.1.163	Dido
Magnificent and mightie Prince Cosroe, ...	1Tamb	1.1.136	Ortyg
were that Tamburlaine/As monsterous as Gorgon, prince of Hell,	1Tamb	4.1.18	Souldn
Unto the hallowed person of a prince, ...	1Tamb	4.3.40	Souldn
And what's our aid against so great a Prince? . . .	Jew	1.2.51	Barab
Prince of Navarre my honourable brother, ...	P 1	1.1	Charls
Prince Condy, and my good Lord Admirall, ...	P 2	1.2	Charls
Prince Condy and my good Lord Admiral, ...	P 27	1.27	Navrre
That are tutors to him and the prince of Condy-- . .	P 427	7.67	Guise
The offer of your Prince Electors, farre/Beyond the reach of my	P 452	8.2	Anjoy
I am a Prince of the Valoyses line,/Therfore an enemy to the	P 835	17.30	Guise
Fight in the quarrell of this valiant Prince, . . .	P1229	22.91	King
Sweete prince I come, these these thy amorous lines, .	Edw	1.1.6	Gavstn
the mightie prince of Lancaster/That hath more earldomes then	Edw	1.3.1	Gavstn
What forraine prince sends thee embassadors? . . .	Edw	2.2.170	Lncstr
Your honor hath an adamant, of power/To drawe a prince. .	Edw	2.5.106	Arundl
Then tell thy prince, of whence, and what thou art. . .	Edw	3.1.35	Edward
things of more waight/Then fits a prince so yong as I to beare,	Edw	3.1.75	Prince
How say yong Prince, what thinke you of the match? . .	Edw	4.2.67	SrJohn
Rebell is he that fights against his prince, . . .	Edw	4.6.71	SpncrP
For if they goe, the prince shall lose his right. . .	Edw	5.1.92	Leistr
And therefore so the prince my sonne be safe, . . .	Edw	5.2.17	Queene
O happie newes, send for the prince my sonne. . . .	Edw	5.2.29	Queene
Heere comes the yong prince, with the Earle of Kent. .	Edw	5.2.75	Mortmr
If he have such accesse unto the prince, ...	Edw	5.2.77	Mortmr
Doe looke to be protector over the prince?	Edw	5.2.89	Mortmr
that one so false/Should come about the person of a prince.	Edw	5.2.105	Mortmr
The prince I rule, the queene do I commaund, . . .	Edw	5.4.48	Mortmr
I view the prince with Aristarchus eyes, ...	Edw	5.4.54	Mortmr
And thou compelst this prince to weare the crowne. . .	Edw	5.4.88	Kent
And chase the Prince of Parma from our Land, . . .	F 120	1.1.92	Faust
And pray devoutely to the Prince of hell.	F 282	1.3.54	Mephst
How comes it then that he is Prince of Devils? . . .	F 294	1.3.66	Faust

PRINCE (cont.)
to Lucifer, Prince of the East, and his Minister Mephostophilis, F 494 2.1.106 P Faust
And this is my companion Prince in hell. F 640 2.2.89 Lucifr
Not to be wonne by any conquering Prince: F 783 3.1.5 Faust

PRINCELIE
whose golden leaves/Empale your princelie head, your diadem, Edw 3.1.164 Herald
Deserveth princelie favors and rewardes, Edw 4.6.54 Mortmr

PRINCELY
Summoned the Captaines to his princely tent, Dido 2.1.130 Aeneas
My princely robes thou seest are layd aside, Dido 3.3.3 Dido
O princely Dido, give me leave to speake, Dido 4.4.17 Aeneas
As princely Lions when they rouse themselves, 1Tamb 1.2.52 Techel
And when the princely Persean Diadem, 1Tamb 2.1.45 Cosroe
And be reclaim'd with princely lenitie. 1Tamb 2.2.38 Meandr
nor by princely deeds/Doth meane to soare above the highest 1Tamb 2.7.32 Therid
And might in noble minds be counted princely. 1Tamb 3.2.39 Zenoc
Of my faire daughter, and his princely Love: 1Tamb 4.1.70 Souldn
vagabond/Should brave a king, or weare a princely crowne. 1Tamb 4.3.22 Souldn
Thy princely daughter here shall set thee free. 1Tamb 5.1.436 Tamb
time to grace/Her princely Temples with the Persean crowne: 1Tamb 5.1.489 Tamb
Stampt with the princely Foule that in her wings/Caries the 2Tamb 1.1.100 Orcan
Fit objects for thy princely eie to pierce. 2Tamb 1.2.45 Callap
My Lord, such speeches to our princely sonnes, 2Tamb 1.3.85 Zenoc
Commanding all thy princely eie desires, 2Tamb 4.2.43 Therid
The pride and beautie of her princely seat, 2Tamb 4.3.109 Tamb
And drawen with princely Eagles through the path, 2Tamb 4.3.127 Tamb
And like base slaves abject our princely mindes/To vile and 2Tamb 5.1.140 Orcan
And that the native sparkes of princely love, P 6 1.6 Charls
My noble sonne, and princely Duke of Guise, P 203 4.1 QnMoth
I hope these reasons may serve my princely Sonne, P 223 4.21 QnMoth
Thankes to my princely sonne, then tell me Guise, P 228 4.26 QnMoth
The sole endevour of your princely care, P 714 14.17 Bartus
And that the sweet and princely minde you beare, P1141 22.3 King
You that are princely borne should shake him off, Edw 1.4.81 Warwck
His life, my lord, before your princely feete. Edw 3.1.45 Spencr
That from your princely person you remoove/This Spencer, as a Edw 3.1.161 Herald
O no my lord, this princely resolution/Fits not the time, away, Edw 4.5.8 Baldck
God save Queene Isabell, and her princely sonne. Edw 4.6.46 Rice
And princely Edwards right we crave the crowne. Edw 5.1.39 BshpWn
new-found-world/For pleasant fruites, and Princely delicates. F 112 1.1.84 Faust
Pope Julius swore to Princely Sigismond, F 925 3.1.147 Bruno
You Princely Legions of infernall Rule, F1116 3.3.29 Mephst

PRINCEPS
Orientis Princeps [Lucifer], Belzebub inferni ardentis F 245 1.3.17 P Faust

PRINCES
And loade his speare with Grecian Princes heads, Dido 3.3.43 Aeneas
Such power attractive shines in princes eies. 1Tamb 2.5.64 Therid
You shall be princes all immediatly: 2Tamb 3.5.168 Tamb
Rich Princes both, and mighty Emperours: P 463 8.13 Anjoy
And princes with their lookes ingender feare. P 999 19.69 Guise
Let Christian princes that shall heare of this, P1041 19.111 King
Arrivde and armed in this princes right, Edw 4.4.18 Mortmr
two deceased princes which long since are consumed to dust. F App p.237 43 P Faust
but the true substantiall bodies of those two deceased princes. F App p.238 65 P Emper
And many seeing great princes were denied, Hero and Leander 1.129

PRINCESSE
Till that a Princesse priest conceav'd by Mars, Dido 1.1.106 Jupitr
To signifie she was a princesse borne, 2Tamb 3.2.21 Amyras

PRINCESSE PRIEST
Till that a Princesse priest conceav'd by Mars, Dido 1.1.106 Jupitr

PRINCIPALITY
That thirst so much for Principality. Jew 1.1.135 Barab

PRINCIPLE
For they themselves hold it a principle, Jew 2.3.310 Barab
hath <I have> already done, and holds <hold> this principle, F 283 1.3.55 Faust

PRINCIPLES
Hath all the Principles Magick doth require: F 167 1.1.139 Cornel

PRINT
'Tis neatly done, Sir, here's no print at all. Jew 4.1.151 Ithimr
That it might print these lines within his heart. P 669 13.13 Duchss

PRIOR (See PRYOR)

PRIORIES
As Monestaries, Priories, Abbyes and halles, P 138 2.81 Guise

PRISE
Besides thy share of this Egyptian prise, 1Tamb 1.2.190 Tamb
Virginitie, albeit some highly prise it, Hero and Leander 1.262

PRISES
My martiall prises with five hundred men, 1Tamb 1.2.102 Tamb

PRISON
Away with her to prison presently, Dido 5.1.220 Dido
Which beates against this prison to get out, 2Tamb 4.2.35 Olymp
In prison till the Law has past on him. Jew 5.1.49 Govnr
Didst breake prison? Jew 5.1.78 Calym
To prison with the Governour and these/Captaines, his consorts Jew 5.2.23 Barab
Away to prison with him, Ile clippe his winges/Or ere he passe P1052 19.122 King
He shall to prison, and there die in boults. Edw 1.1.197 Gavstn
A prison may beseeme his holinesse. Edw 1.1.207 Gavstn
That thus hath pent and mu'd me in a prison, Edw 5.1.18 Edward
Where lords keepe courts, and kings are lockt in prison! Edw 5.3.64 Kent
Hale them to prison, lade their limbes with gyves: F1032 3.2.52 Pope
The carefull prison is more meete for thee. Ovid's Elegies 1.6.64
The filthy prison faithlesse breasts restraines. Ovid's Elegies 2.2.42

PRISONER (See also PRYSONER)
Or take him prisoner, and his chaine shall serve/For Manackles, 1Tamb 1.2.147 Tamb

PRISONER (cont.)
No, I tooke it prisoner. 1Tamb 2.4.32 Tamb
Though he be prisoner, he may be ransomed. 1Tamb 3.3.231 Zabina
Who lives in Egypt, prisoner to that slave, 2Tamb 1.1.4 Orcan
And live in Malta prisoner; for come [all] <call> the world/To Jew 5.5.119 Govnr
My unckles taken prisoner by the Scots. Edw 2.2.115 Mortmr
Seeing he is taken prisoner in his warres? Edw 2.2.119 Mortmr
Mine unckles taken prisoner by the Scots. Edw 2.2.142 Mortmr
But if you dare trust Penbrooke with the prisoner, Edw 2.5.87 Penbrk
Their lord rode home, thinking his prisoner safe, Edw 3.1.117 Arundl
That thou proud Warwicke watcht the prisoner, Edw 3.1.237 Edward
Then shouldst thou bee his prisoner who is thine. Hero and Leander 1.202

PRISONERS
where I tooke/The Turke and his great Empresse prisoners, 2Tamb 5.3.129 Tamb

PRITHEE (See also PRETHE, PRETHEE)
<How, a wife? I prithee Faustus talke not of a wife>. F 530 (HC261)A P Mephst

PRITTY
No pritty wenches keeper maist thou bee: Ovid's Elegies 1.6.63

PRIVATE
And I will live a private life with him. Dido 5.1.198 Dido
For I entend a private Sacrifize, Dido 5.1.286 Dido
Then many perish for a private man: Jew 1.2.99 Govnr
What makes the Jew and Lodowicke so private? Jew 2.3.138 Mthias
What call you this but private libelling, Edw 2.2.34 Edward
The greefes of private men are soone allayde, Edw 5.1.8 Edward
she for her private study, shee's borne to beare with me, F App p.233 16 P Robin
And rule so soone with private hands acquainted. Ovid's Elegies 2.18.16

PRIVATELY
And by my letters privately procure/Great summes of mony for Jew 5.2.87 Govnr

PRIVIE
Bearing his privie signet and his hand: 1Tamb 1.2.15 Zenoc
and use a counterfeite key to his privie Chamber doore: P 807 17.2 P Souldr
Let me alone, here is the privie seale, Edw 5.2.37 Mortmr
And their owne privie weapon'd hands destroy them. Ovid's Elegies 2.14.4

PRIVILEDGE
Women may wrong by priviledge of love: Dido 3.3.25 Iarbus
And by that priviledge to worke upon, P 121 2.64 Guise
Your lordship cannot priviledge your head. Edw 4.6.70 Mortmr
And interdict from Churches priviledge, F 909 3.1.131 Pope

PRIVILIE
Why then weele have him privilie made away. Edw 2.2.236 Gavstn

PRIVY
And that I might be privy to the state, 1Tamb 5.1.426 Arabia
It must have privy ditches, countermines, 2Tamb 3.2.73 Tamb
duke a cuckolde and use a counterfeyt key to his privy chamber Paris ms 2,p390 P Souldr
I chuse his privy chamber for our use. F 806 3.1.28 Mephst
I have taken up his holinesse privy chamber for our use>. F 806 (HC265)A P Mephst
Then I, that I may seale her privy leaves, Ovid's Elegies 2.15.15
With privy signes, and talke dissembling truths? Ovid's Elegies 3.10.24

PRIVY CHAMBER
duke a cuckolde and use a counterfeyt key to his privy chamber Paris ms 2,p390 P Souldr
I chuse his privy chamber for our use. F 806 3.1.28 Mephst
I have taken up his holinesse privy chamber for our use>. F 806 (HC265)A P Mephst

PRIZE (See also PRISE)
How highly I doe prize this amitie, Dido 3.2.67 Juno
To measure how I prize Aeneas love, Dido 4.4.140 Dido
When looks breed love, with lookes to gaine the prize. 1Tamb 2.5.63 Therid
Shall make me leave so rich a prize as this: 1Tamb 2.7.54 Tamb
What Coward wold not fight for such a prize? 1Tamb 3.3.100 Usumc
But one amongst the rest became our prize: Jew 2.2.16 Bosco
Nor, so thou maist obtaine a wealthy prize, Ovid's Elegies 1.8.63
Or prostitute thy beauty for bad prize. Ovid's Elegies 1.10.42

PRIZES
As any prizes out of my precinct. 1Tamb 1.2.28 Tamb

PRO
Misericordia pro nobis, what shal I doe? F App p.235 30 P Robin

PROANE
When Caesar saw his army proane to war, Lucan, First Booke 393

PROBLEMES
of Wittenberg <Wertenberge>/[Swarme] <Sworne> to my Problemes, F 142 1.1.114 Faust

PROBO
that/Was wont to make our schooles ring, with sic probo. F 195 1.2.2 1Schol

PROCEED
These words proceed not from Aeneas heart. Dido 5.1.102 Dido
Proceed from sinne, or want of faith in us, Jew 1.2.323 Abigal
This is the houre/Wherein I shall proceed; Oh happy houre, Jew 4.1.161 1Fryar

PROCEEDE
Ere farther we proceede my noble lordes, Edw 4.6.23 Queene

PROCEEDED
I would those wordes proceeded from your heart. Edw 5.2.100 Kent

PROCEEDETH
No doubt, brother, but this proceedeth of the spirit. Jew 1.2.327 1Fryar

PROCLAIMDE
Be thou proclaimde a traitor throughout France. P 864 17.59 King

PROCLAIME
Proclaime king Edwards warres and victories. Edw 3.1.281 Spencr

PROCLAIMED
What now remaines, have you proclaimed, my lord, Edw 4.3.17 Edward

PROCNE (See PROGNE)

PROCUR'D
Thou hast procur'd a greater enemie, 2Tamb 4.1.127 Tamb
I have procur'd your pardons: welcome all. F1610 4.6.53 Faust

PROCURE
More honor and lesse paine it may procure, 1Tamb 3.2.97 Agidas

PROCURE (cont.)
give me, Governor, to procure/A dissolution of the slavish Bands — Jew 5.2.76 Barab
And by my letters privately procure/Great summes of mony for — Jew 5.2.87 Govnr
Forbid thine anger to procure my griefe. — Ovid's Elegies 2.7.14
me, or I am sure/I oft have done, what might as much procure. — Ovid's Elegies 2.13.6
But of my love it will an end procure. — Ovid's Elegies 2.19.52
Dutifull service may thy love procure, — Hero and Leander 1.220

PROCURETH
What will you give him that procureth this? — Jew 5.2.83 Barab

PRODEGIES
threatning gods/Fill'd both the earth and seas with prodegies; — Lucan, First Booke 523

PRODIGALL
For Fame I feare hath bene too prodigall, — 1Tamb 4.3.48 Arabia
lascivious showes/And prodigall gifts bestowed on Gaveston, — Edw 2.2.158 Mortmr

PRODIGIOUS
Prodigious birthes with more and ugly jointes/Then nature — Lucan, First Booke 560

PROFANES
Outrageous death profanes all holy things/And on all creatures — Ovid's Elegies 3.8.19

PROFESS'D
Yet he harm'd lesse, whom I profess'd to love, — Ovid's Elegies 1.7.33

PROFESSE
and begin/To sound the depth of that thou wilt professe, — F 30 1.1.2 Faust
What lawfull is, or we professe Loves art, — Ovid's Elegies 2.18.19

PROFESSED
thine, in setting Bruno free/From his and our professed enemy, — F1207 4.1.53 Emper

PROFESSION
And by profession be ambitious. — 1Tamb 2.6.14 Meandr
Against the grace of our profession. — 2Tamb 2.1.32 Sgsmnd
Which me thinkes fits not their profession. — Jew 1.1.118 Barab
As if we knew not thy profession? — Jew 1.2.120 Govnr
our hands with blood/Is farre from us and our profession. — Jew 1.2.145 Govnr
that's their profession,/And not simplicity, as they suggest. — Jew 1.2.160 Barab
it,/A counterfet profession is better/Then unseene hypocrisie. — Jew 1.2.292 Barab
name, and therewithall/Thy birth, condition, and profession. — Jew 2.3.164 Barab
My profession what you please. — Jew 2.3.166 Ithimr
And true profession of his holy word: — P 586 11.51 Navrre
Then this profession were to be esteem'd. — F 54 1.1.26 Faust

PROFESSOR
Tis Ramus, the Kings professor of Logick. — P 381 7.21 Retes

PROFFERED
Turn'd into pearle and proffered for my stay, — 2Tamb 4.1.44 Amyras

PROFICIENT
Who would not be proficient in this Art? — F 256 1.3.28 Faust

PROFIT
divine precepts/And mine owne industry, but to profit much. — Jew 1.2.335 Abigal
Making a profit of my policie; — Jew 5.2.112 Barab
And common profit of Religion. — P 647 12.60 Cardnl
As by their preachments they will profit much, — Edw 3.1.22 Spencr
What profit to us hath our pure life bred? — Ovid's Elegies 3.8.33

PROFITABLY
And as you profitably take up Armes, — Jew 3.5.32 Govnr

PROFITE
O what a world of profite and delight, — F 80 1.1.52 Faust

PROFITS
So much <soone> he profits in Divinitie, — F 15 Prol.15 1Chor
Aye me I warne what profits some few howers, — Ovid's Elegies 1.4.59

PROGENIE
On your accursed traiterous progenie, — Edw 3.1.141 Edward

PROGENITORS
The race of all his stout progenitors; — F1168 4.1.14 Mrtino

PROGENITOUR
And as Pope Alexander our Progenitour, — F 915 3.1.137 Pope

PROGENY (See also PROGENIE)
Now Faustus thou hast heard all my progeny, wilt thou bid me to — F 701 2.2.150 P Glutny

PROGENYE
May still be feweld in our progenye. — P 8 1.8 Charls

PROGNE
Bird-changed Progne doth her Itys teare. — Ovid's Elegies 3.11.32

PROGNES
As Prognes to th'adulterous Thracian King, — 1Tamb 4.4.24 Zabina

PROGRES
When death cuts off the progres of his pomp, — 2Tamb Prol.4 Prolog

PROGRESSE
Shal end the warlike progresse he intends, — 2Tamb 3.5.23 Orcan

PROHIBITION
Forbeare to kindle vice by prohibition, — Ovid's Elegies 3.4.11

PROLOCUTOR
Not Hermes Prolocutor to the Gods, — 1Tamb 1.2.210 Therid

PROLONG
Sweet Bajazeth, I will prolong thy life, — 1Tamb 5.1.283 Zabina

PROLONG'D
A little while prolong'd her husbands life: — Dido 2.1.246 Aeneas

PROLONGED
Which thy prolonged Fates may draw on thee: — 1Tamb 3.2.101 Agidas

PROLONGING
Why stay we thus prolonging all their lives? — 1Tamb 3.3.97 Techel

PROMETHEUS
Prometheus hath put on Cupids shape, — Dido 3.4.21 Dido
And rockes dyed crimson with Prometheus bloud. — Ovid's Elegies 2.16.40
Than for the fire filcht by Prometheus; — Hero and Leander 1.438

PROMIS'D
These are the Blessings promis'd to the Jewes, — Jew 1.1.105 Barab
hast broke the league/By flat denyall of the promis'd Tribute, — Jew 3.5.20 Basso

PROMIS'D (cont.)			
And Barabas, as erst we promis'd thee,	Jew	5.2.9	Calym
I trust thy word, take what I promis'd thee.	Jew	5.5.43	Govnr
PROMISD			
What Venus promisd, promise thou we pray,	Ovid's Elegies		3.2.59
PROMISE			
To keep my promise, and to make him king,	2Tamb	3.1.71	Callap
Perfourming all your promise to the full:	2Tamb	3.1.76	Jrslem
Then wil I shortly keep my promise Almeda.	2Tamb	3.1.78	P Callap
We grant a month, but see you keep your promise.	Jew	1.2.28	Calym
For unto us the Promise doth belong.	Jew	2.3.47	Barab
For the performance of your promise past;	Jew	3.5.9	Basso
much better/To [have] kept thy promise then be thus surpriz'd?	Jew	5.2.5	Calym
For if I keepe not promise, trust not me.	Jew	5.5.23	Barab
Violate any promise to possesse him.	Edw	2.5.64	Warwck
Thou calst on <talkst of> Christ contrary to thy promise.	F 643	2.2.92	Lucifr
you heartily sir; for wee cal'd you but in jeast I promise you.	F1124	3.3.37	P Dick
Then Faustus as thou late didst promise us,	F1230	4.1.76	Emper
What Venus promisd, promise thou we pray,	Ovid's Elegies		3.2.59
much (I crave)/Gifts then my promise greater thou shalt have.	Ovid's Elegies		3.5.66
He recklesse of his promise, did despise/The love of	Hero and Leander		1.461
Flatter, intreat, promise, protest and sweare,	Hero and Leander		2.268
PROMISED			
shewes did entertaine him/And promised to be at his commaund:	P 875	17.70	Eprnon
My dutie to your honor [premised] <promised>, &c. I have	Edw	4.3.28	P Spencr
Is promised to the Studious Artizan?	F 82	1.1.54	Faust
PROMISES			
And he that could with giftes and promises/Inveigle him that	1Tamb	2.2.25	Meandr
To effect all promises betweene us [made] <both>.	F 482	2.1.94	Mephst
Adde deeds unto thy promises at last.	Ovid's Elegies		2.16.48
Saying, let your vowes and promises be kept.	Hero and Leander		2.96
PROMISETH			
And promiseth as much as we can wish,	Edw	1.4.399	MortSr
And promiseth he shall be safe returnd,	Edw	3.1.110	Arundl
PROMIST			
In those faire walles I promist him of yore:	Dido	1.1.85	Jupitr
Which gratious starres have promist at my birth.	1Tamb	1.2.92	Tamb
Orcanes (as our Legates promist thee)/Wee with our Peeres have	2Tamb	1.1.78	Sgsmnd
Promist to meet me on Larissa plaines/With hostes apeece	2Tamb	1.3.107	Tamb
PRONE (See also PROANE)			
prone to letcherie (to love I would say) it were not for you to	F 210	1.2.17	P Wagner
And therewith Caesar prone ennough to warre,	Lucan, First Booke		293
steeld their harts/And minds were prone) restrain'd them:	Lucan, First Booke		356
PRONOUNCE			
Pronounce this thrice devoutly to thy selfe,	F 547	2.1.159	Mephst
Her teares, she silent, guilty did pronounce me.	Ovid's Elegies		1.7.22
PRONOUNST			
And all pronounst me king of Persea.	1Tamb	2.7.67	Tamb
PROOFE			
Armour of proofe, horse, helme, and Curtle-axe,	2Tamb	1.3.44	Tamb
And for a present easie proofe hereof,	2Tamb	4.2.75	Olymp
Had we but proofe of this--	Jew	5.1.15	Govnr
Strong proofe, my Lord, his man's now at my lodging/That was	Jew	5.1.16	Curtzn
So that for proofe, he barely beares the name:	P 131	2.74	Guise
But now ile speake, and to the proofe I hope:	Edw	1.1.108	Kent
Unlesse his brest be sword proofe he shall die.	Edw	1.2.8	Mortmr
But hath your grace no other proofe then this?	Edw	5.6.43	Mortmr
I have my Faustus, and for proofe thereof,	F 803	3.1.25	Mephst
For proofe whereof, if so your Grace be pleas'd,	F1221	4.1.67	Faust
that thou let me see some proofe of thy skil, that mine eies	F App	p.236 6	P Emper
This need no forraine proofe, nor far fet story:	Lucan, First Booke		94
PROOFES			
O would my proofes as vaine might be withstood,	Ovid's Elegies		2.5.7
PROOV'D			
Whose power is often proov'd a myracle.	2Tamb	2.3.32	Gazell
PROOVE			
I am a Lord, for so my deeds shall proove,	1Tamb	1.2.34	Tamb
But shall I proove a Traitor to my King?	1Tamb	1.2.226	Therid
thee (sweet Ortigius)/Better replies shall proove my purposes.	1Tamb	2.5.37	Cosroe
Twil proove a pretie jest (in faith) my friends.	1Tamb	2.5.90	Tamb
I prophecied before and now I proove,	1Tamb	3.2.90	Agidas
And proove the waight of his victorious arme:	1Tamb	4.3.47	Arabia
And may this banquet proove as omenous,	1Tamb	4.4.23	Zabina
That this devise may proove propitious,	1Tamb	5.1.52	2Virgn
Dismaies their mindes before they come to proove/The wounding	2Tamb	1.3.86	Zenoc
If thou wilt proove thy selfe a perfect God,	2Tamb	2.2.56	Orcan
For person like to proove a second Mars.	2Tamb	4.1.35	Calyph
To proove it, I wil noint my naked throat,	2Tamb	4.2.68	Olymp
Shall sicknesse proove me now to be a man,	2Tamb	5.3.44	Tamb
And may it proove more happie then the first.	Edw	1.4.336	Queene
Nay, do your pleasures, I know how twill proove.	Edw	2.5.93	Warwck
My lord, I feare me it will proove too true.	Edw	5.6.77	2Lord
PROOVED			
And have bene crown'd for prooved worthynesse:	1Tamb	5.1.491	Tamb
PROP (See also PROPPE)			
Sweet Duke of Guise our prop to leane upon,	P1110	21.4	Dumain
PROPER			
To turne them al upon their proper heades.	1Tamb	4.4.31	Tamb
I feare the custome proper to his sword,	1Tamb	5.1.13	Govnr
Stick in his breast, as in their proper roomes.	1Tamb	5.1.226	Zabina
And ratling cannons thunder in our eares/Our proper ruine, and	2Tamb	4.1.14	Amyras
me, that I may resigne/My place and proper tytle to my sonne:	2Tamb	5.3.176	Tamb
More than the ruine of our proper soules.	2Tamb	5.3.182	Therid

PROPER (cont.)			
Yet will the wisest note their proper greefes: . . .	P 216	4.14	Anjoy
and with his <my> proper bloud/Assures his <assure my> soule to	F 443	2.1.55	Faust
appeare to thee in their owne proper shapes and likenesse.	F 656	2.2.105	P Belzeb
PROPHANE			
To punish those that doe prophane this holy feast. . .	P 617	12.30	Mugern
PROPHANELY			
But as the faith which they prophanely plight/Is not by .	2Tamb	2.1.37	Baldwn
PROPHECIED			
And prophecied Troy should be overcome:	Dido	2.1.142	Aeneas
I prophecied before and now I proove, ...	1Tamb	3.2.90	Agidas
PROPHESIE			
Yet thinke upon Ascanius prophesie, ...	Dido	5.1.38	Hermes
He bids you prophesie what it imports.	1Tamb	3.2.89	Techel
PROPHESIES			
Hoping (misled by dreaming prophesies)/To raigne in Asia, and	1Tamb	1.1.41	Meandr
And dismall Prophesies were spread abroad:	Lucan, First Booke		562
PROPHET			
And cares so litle for their prophet Christ.	2Tamb	2.2.35	Gazell
As is our holy prophet Mahomet, ...	2Tamb	2.2.44	Orcan
Oft some points at the prophet passing by, ...	Ovid's Elegies		3.1.19
PROPHETS			
We are the Muses prophets, none of thine.	Ovid's Elegies		1.1.10
PROPITIAMUS			
et Demogorgon, propitiamus vos, ut appareat, et surgat .	F 246	1.3.18	P Faust
PROPITII			
Sint mihi Dei Acherontis propitii, valeat numen triplex .	F 244	1.3.16	P Faust
PROPITIOUS			
That this devise may proove propitious, ...	1Tamb	5.1.52	2Virgn
And let it be propitious for my wish.	F 447	2.1.59	Faust
PROPORTION			
And with the same proportion of Elements/Resolve, I hope we are	1Tamb	2.6.26	Cosroe
PROPORTIONED			
In every part proportioned like the man, ...	1Tamb	2.1.29	Menaph
PROPOSDE			
sonnes have had no shares/In all the honors he proposde for us.	2Tamb	4.1.48	Amyras
PROPOUND			
Unto the purpose which we now propound.	Dido	3.2.95	Juno
PROPPE			
how Olimpus toppe/High Ossa bore, mount Pelion up to proppe.	Ovid's Elegies		2.1.14
PROPPED			
Brought up and propped by the hand of fame, ...	1Tamb	5.1.265	Bajzth
PROPT			
With stiffe oake propt the gate doth still appeare. . .	Ovid's Elegies		1.6.28
PROPTEREA			
That cannot speake without propterea quod.	Edw	2.1.53	Baldck
PROREX			
Create him Prorex of [Assiria] <Affrica>, ...	1Tamb	1.1.89	Cosroe
Yet stout Orcanes, Prorex of the world, ...	2Tamb	1.1.45	Gazell
PROSECUTE			
To prosecute that Gaveston to the death.	Edw	2.2.105	Lncstr
PROSECUTION			
In prosecution of these cruell armes, ...	P 796	16.10	Navrre
PROSERPINA			
And as thou took'st the faire Proserpina, ...	2Tamb	4.3.36	Orcan
PROSERPINE			
Why am I sad, when Proserpine is found, ...	Ovid's Elegies		3.9.45
PROSPER			
Will never prosper your intended driftes, ...	1Tamb	1.2.69	Zenoc
Indevor to preserve and prosper it.	1Tamb	2.5.35	Ortyg
And if I prosper, all shall be as sure, ...	1Tamb	2.5.84	Tamb
Truth Pleshe, and God so prosper me in all, ...	P 584	11.49	Navrre
But if that God doe prosper mine attempts, ...	P 927	18.28	Navrre
Prosper your happie motion good sir John.	Edw	4.2.75	Queene
PROSPERITY			
Nor lesse at mans prosperity any grudge.	Ovid's Elegies		3.9.6
PROSPEROUS			
And makes a passage for all prosperous Armes, ...	1Tamb	2.3.38	Cosroe
Welcome to England all with prosperous windes, . . .	Edw	4.4.2	Queene
Few battailes fought with prosperous successe/May bring her	Lucan, First Booke		285
Beholde thy kinsmans Caesars prosperous bandes, . . .	Ovid's Elegies		1.2.51
Go, minding to returne with prosperous winde, . . .	Ovid's Elegies		2.11.37
She beckt, and prosperous signes gave as she moved. . .	Ovid's Elegies		3.2.58
Built walles high towred with a prosperous hand. . .	Ovid's Elegies		3.12.34
PROSTITUTE			
Or prostitute thy beauty for bad prize.	Ovid's Elegies		1.10.42
PROSTRATE			
Fall prostrate on the lowe disdainefull earth. . . .	1Tamb	4.2.13	Tamb
(sacred Emperour)/The prostrate service of this wretched towne.	1Tamb	5.1.100	1Virgn
Before her feete thrice prostrate downe I fell, . . .	Ovid's Elegies		1.7.61
PROTECT			
Let not that Mortimer protect my sonne, ...	Edw	5.1.115	Edward
who should protect the sonne,/But she that gave him life, I	Edw	5.2.90	Kent
Shee may deceive thee, though thou her protect, . . .	Ovid's Elegies		2.3.15
Cruell is he, that loves whom none protect. . . .	Ovid's Elegies		2.19.4
PROTECTED			
defence/When [un-protected] <un-protested> ther is no expence?	Ovid's Elegies		2.2.12
PROTECTION			
They justly challenge their protection:	P 210	4.8	Charls
PROTECTOR			
And that I be protector over him, ...	Edw	5.2.12	Mortmr
Doe looke to be protector over the prince?	Edw	5.2.89	Mortmr
And to conclude, I am Protector now, ...	Edw	5.4.64	Mortmr

Line	Work	Ref	Speaker
PROTECTOR (cont.)			
Intreate my lord Protector for his life.	Edw	5.4.95	King
My lord protector greetes you.	Edw	5.5.14	Ltborn
PROTECTORSHIP			
They thrust upon me the Protectorship,	Edw	5.4.56	Mortmr
PROTESILAUS			
Thersites did Protesilaus survive,	Ovid's Elegies	2.6.41	
PROTEST			
Sweet Jesus Christ, I sollemnly protest,	2Tamb	1.1.135	Sgsmnd
Dissemble, sweare, protest, vow to love him,	Jew	2.3.229	Barab
And heere protest eternall love to thee,	P1206	22.68	King
And therefore let us jointlie here protest,	Edw	2.2.104	Lncstr
By Venus Deity how did I protest.	Ovid's Elegies	2.8.18	
Flatter, intreat, promise, protest and sweare,	Hero and Leander	2.268	
PROTESTANTS			
That seekes to murder all the Protestants:	P 31	1.31	Navrre
That all the protestants that are in Paris,	P 34	1.34	Navrre
My Lord of Anjoy, there are a hundred Protestants,	P 417	7.57	Guise
My Lord, they say/That all the protestants are massacred.	P 432	7.72	Navrre
And therfore hated of the Protestants.	P 838	17.33	Guise
Whose light was deadly to the Protestants:	P 945	19.15	Capt
The Protestants will glory and insulte,	P1085	19.155	QnMoth
PROTESTATIONS			
As these thy protestations doe paint forth,	Dido	3.2.54	Venus
I yeeld with thanks and protestations/Of endlesse honor to thee	1Tamb	5.1.496	Souldn
PROTESTED			
defence/When [un-protected] <un-protested> ther is no expence?	Ovid's Elegies	2.2.12	
PROTEUS			
And Proteus raising hils of floods on high,	Dido	1.1.76	Venus
Theile breake his ships, O Proteus, Neptune, Jove,	Dido	5.1.255	Dido
As if that Proteus god of shapes appearde.	Edw	1.4.411	Mortmr
Proteus what should I name? teeth, Thebes first seed?	Ovid's Elegies	3.11.35	
Wherein was Proteus carved, and o'rehead,	Hero and Leander	1.137	
PROUD (See also PROWD)			
Controule proud Fate, and cut the thred of time.	Dido	1.1.29	Jupitr
Proud is his fortune if we pierce it not.	1Tamb	2.1.44	Cosroe
And kill proud Tamburlaine with point of sword.	1Tamb	2.2.12	Mycet
I will not spare these proud Egyptians,	1Tamb	5.1.121	Tamb
Those that are proud of fickle Empery,	1Tamb	5.1.352	Zenoc
Proud Tamburlaine, that now in Asia,	2Tamb	1.1.16	Gazell
The wandring Sailers of proud Italy,	2Tamb	1.1.39	Orcan
forces for the hot assaults/Proud Tamburlaine intends Natolia.	2Tamb	1.1.53	Gazell
To stay my comming gainst proud Tamburlaine.	2Tamb	1.1.163	Orcan
And proud Orcanes of Natolia,	2Tamb	1.3.161	Tamb
Now will we march from proud Orminius mount/To faire Natolia,	2Tamb	2.2.2	Orcan
In partiall aid of that proud Scythian,	2Tamb	2.2.16	Gazell
Proud furie and intollorable fit,	2Tamb	2.4.78	Tamb
for whose byrth/Olde Rome was proud, but gasde a while on her,	2Tamb	2.4.92	Tamb
This proud usurping king of Persea,	2Tamb	3.1.15	Callap
But that proud Fortune, who hath followed long/The martiall	2Tamb	3.1.27	Callap
The poisoned braines of this proud Scythian.	2Tamb	3.1.67	Orcan
By whose proud side the ugly furies run,	2Tamb	3.4.59	Therid
Raile not proud Scythian, I shall now revenge/My fathers vile	2Tamb	3.5.90	Callap
in their glories shine the golden crownes/Of these proud Turks,	2Tamb	4.1.2	Amyras
Which makes me valiant, proud, ambitious,	2Tamb	4.1.116	Tamb
Ransacke the tents and the pavilions/Of these proud Turks, and	2Tamb	4.1.161	Tamb
And have so proud a chariot at your heeles,	2Tamb	4.3.3	Tamb
and to subdew/This proud contemner of thy dreadfull power,	2Tamb	4.3.40	Orcan
we offer more/Than ever yet we did to such proud slaves,	2Tamb	5.1.58	Techel
And pull prcud Tamburlaine upon his knees,	2Tamb	5.2.40	Amasia
Since Fate commands, and proud necessity.	2Tamb	5.3.205	Therid
The nature of these proud rebelling Jades/Wil take occasion by	2Tamb	5.3.238	Tamb
Proud-daring Calymath, instead of gold,	Jew	2.2.53	Govnr
And turne proud Malta to a wildernesse/For these intolerable	Jew	3.5.25	Basso
these our warres/Against the proud disturbers of the faith,	P 700	14.3	Navrre
Then come proud Guise and heere disgordge thy brest,	P 952	19.22	King
And he shall follow my proud Chariots wheeles.	P 984	19.54	Guise
And that young Cardinall that is growne so proud?	P1056	19.126	King
And beate proud Burbon to his native home,	P1114	21.8	Dumain
Meete you for this, proud overdaring peeres?	Edw	1.4.47	Edward
Proud Rome, that hatchest such imperiall groomes,	Edw	1.4.97	Edward
Whose proud fantastick liveries make such show,	Edw	1.4.410	Mortmr
You must be proud, bold, pleasant, resolute,	Edw	2.1.42	Spencr
Proud Mortimer, ungentle Lancaster,	Edw	2.2.29	Edward
Thou proud disturber of thy countries peace,	Edw	2.5.9	Mortmr
Proud recreants.	Edw	3.1.102	Spencr
with my sword/On those proud rebels that are up in armes,	Edw	3.1.187	Edward
That thou proud Warwicke watcht the prisoner,	Edw	3.1.237	Edward
Proud Edward, doost thou banish me thy presence?	Edw	4.1.5	Kent
Proud traytor Mortimer why doost thou chase/Thy lawfull king	Edw	4.6.3	Kent
Proud Mortimer pries neare into thy walkes.	Edw	4.6.18	Kent
Stately and proud, in riches and in traine,	Edw	4.7.12	Edward
A king to beare these words and proud commaunds.	Edw	4.7.71	Abbot
But if proud Mortimer do weare this crowne,	Edw	5.1.43	Edward
The proud corrupters of the light-brainde king,	Edw	5.2.2	Mortmr
Nor in the pompe of proud audacious deeds,	F 5	Prol.5	1Chor
Thou art a proud knave indeed:	F 672	2.2.121	P Faust
be,/That this proud Pope may Faustus [cunning] <comming> see.	F 855	3.1.77	Faust
Proud Lucifer, that State belongs to me:	F 871	3.1.93	Bruno
This proud confronter of the Emperour,	F 897	3.1.119	Faust
And proud disturbers of the Churches peace.	F 956	3.1.178	Faust
And on a prcud pac'd Steed, as swift as thought,	F 984	3.2.4	Mephst
Now Babilon, (proud through our spoile) should stoop,	Lucan, First Booke	10	

PROUD (cont.)			
Destroying what withstood his proud desires,	Lucan, First Booke	150	
For ever lasts high Sophocles proud vaine,	Ovid's Elegies	1.15.15	
things feigne)/Crete proud that Jove her nourcery maintaine.	Ovid's Elegies	3.9.20	
Of proud Adonis that before her lies.	Hero and Leander	1.14	
PROUD-DARING			
Proud-daring Calymath, instead of gold,	Jew	2.2.53	Govnr
PROUDE			
Whose beautious burden well might make you proude,	Dido	1.1.124	Venus
And fire proude Lacedemon ore their heads.	Dido	4.4.92	Aeneas
PROUDEST			
And sure if all the proudest Kings/In Christendome, should	P 760	15.18	Guise
Unto the proudest peere of Britanie:	Edw	2.2.42	Edward
And then have at the proudest Spencers head.	Edw	4.2.25	Prince
The proudest lords salute me as I passe,	Edw	5.4.50	Mortmr
PROUDLY			
That durst thus proudly wrong our kinsmans peace.	Dido	1.1.119	Jupitr
And in their rusticke gambals proudly say,	F1330	4.2.6	Benvol
She proudly sits) more over-rules the flood,	Hero and Leander	1.111	
PROVANDER			
Ile have you learne to feed on provander,	2Tamb	3.5.106	Tamb
PROV'D			
That ever I was prov'd your enemy,	P1140	22.2	King
Nor is it easily prov'd though manifest,	Ovid's Elegies	2.2.55	
Thebe who Mother of five Daughters prov'd?	Ovid's Elegies	3.5.34	
PROVE (See also PROV'ST)			
So thou wouldst prove as true as Paris did,	Dido	5.1.146	Dido
And that will prove but simple policie.	Jew	1.2.159	1Knght
Now shall I prove and guerdon to the ful,	P 68	2.11	Guise
God graunt my neerest freends may prove no worse.	P 547	11.12	Charls
him, and will slay/Thee too, and thou prove such a traitor.	P1049	19.119	King
But <Faustus> I am an instance to prove the contrary:	F 525	2.1.137	Mephst
He now is gone to prove Cosmography,	F 773	2.3.52	2Chor
How may I prove that saying to be true?	F1268	4.1.114	Emper
long struggled, as being like to prove/An aukward sacrifice,	Lucan, First Booke	610	
O harder then the dores thou gardest I prove thee.	Ovid's Elegies	1.6.62	
for needfull uses/Ile prove had hands impure with all abuses.	Ovid's Elegies	1.12.16	
To kinde requests thou wouldst more gentle prove,	Ovid's Elegies	2.3.5	
What Pylades did to Orestes prove,	Ovid's Elegies	2.6.15	
To prove him foolish did I ere contend?	Ovid's Elegies	2.8.10	
Great flouds the force of it do often prove.	Ovid's Elegies	3.5.24	
I prove neither youth nor man, but old and rustie.	Ovid's Elegies	3.6.20	
Ah, she doth more worth then her vices prove.	Ovid's Elegies	3.10.44	
And we will all the pleasures prove,	Passionate Shepherd	2	
PROVENDER (See PROVANDER)			
PROVERB			
the proverb saies, he that eats with the devil had need of a	Jew	3.4.58	P Ithimr
Blame not us but the proverb, Confes and be hang'd.	Jew	4.1.146	P Barab
whom I saluted with an old hempen proverb, Hodie tibi,	Jew	4.2.18	P Pilia
PROVES			
Harmefull to beasts, and to the fields thou proves:	Ovid's Elegies	3.5.99	
PROVIDE			
Cookes shall have pensions to provide us cates,	2Tamb	1.3.219	Tamb
why then let every man/Provide him, and be there for	Jew	1.1.171	Barab
And let's provide to welcome Calymath:	Jew	3.5.30	Govnr
provide a running Banquet;/Send to the Merchant, bid him bring	Jew	4.2.83	Curtzn
the speed we can, provide/For Henries coronation from Polonie:	P 562	11.27	QnMoth
Thy brother Guise and we may now provide,	P 636	12.49	QnMoth
Assure him all the aide we can provide,	P 909	18.10	Navrre
PROVIDED			
starv'd, and he be provided for a moneths victuall before hand.	1Tamb	4.4.46	P Usumc
not but your royall cares/Hath so provided for this cursed foe,	2Tamb	3.1.21	Callap
For so hath heaven provided my escape,	2Tamb	3.1.32	Callap
Provided, that you keepe your Maiden-head.	Jew	2.3.227	Barab
Provided this, that you my lord of Arundell/Will joyne with me.	Edw	2.5.81	Penbrk
PROVINCE			
Shall rule the Province of Albania.	1Tamb	2.2.31	Meandr
PROVINCES			
Meaning to mangle all thy Provinces.	1Tamb	1.1.17	Cosroe
And made their spoiles from all our provinces.	1Tamb	1.1.122	Cosroe
To triumph over many Provinces.	1Tamb	1.1.173	Cosroe
And through my provinces you must expect/Letters of conduct	1Tamb	1.2.23	Tamb
but some must stay/To rule the provinces he late subdude.	1Tamb	3.3.29	Bassoe
Calling the Provinces, Citties and townes/After my name and	1Tamb	4.4.79	Tamb
And there make lawes to rule your provinces:	1Tamb	5.1.527	Tamb
Of all the provinces I have subdued/Thou shalt not have a foot,	2Tamb	1.3.71	Tamb
Are but obey'd in their severall Provinces:	F 85	1.1.57	Faust
And raigne sole King of all [our] Provinces.	F 121	1.1.93	Faust
PROVINCIAM			
Suscepi that provinciam as they terme it,	Edw	5.4.63	Mortmr
PROVISION			
to forgoe so much/Without provision for thy selfe and me.	Jew	1.2.243	Barab
And then to make provision for the feast,	Jew	5.2.119	Barab
of his men to attend you with provision fit for your journey.	F1502	4.4.46	P Wagner
PROVOKE			
And with one shaft provoke ten thousand darts:	Dido	3.3.72	Iarbus
And usde all speech that might provoke and stirre.	Ovid's Elegies	3.6.12	
such lovelinesse and beautie had/As could provoke his liking,	Hero and Leander	1.423	
PROVOKES			
What Tereus, what Jason you provokes,	Ovid's Elegies	2.14.33	
PROVOKT			
When yre, or hope provokt, heady, and bould,	Lucan, First Booke	147	
PROV'ST			
How prov'st thou that?	F 555	2.2.8	Faust

PROWD
He growes to prowd in his authority, F 911 3.1.133 Pope
Yet prowd she was, (for loftie pride that dwels/In tow'red Hero and Leander 1.393
For as a hote prowd horse highly disdaines, Hero and Leander 2.141
Whereat the saphir visag'd god grew prowd, Hero and Leander 2.155
PROWDEST
Ile make the prowdest of you stoope to him. Edw 1.4.31 Edward
PROWESSE
That in their prowesse and their pollicies, 1Tamb 1.1.8 Cosroe
how they had wonne by prowesse such exploits, gote such riches, F App p.236 20 P Emper
When carefull Rome in doubt their prowesse held. Ovid's Elegies 3.14.10
PROXIMUS
Ego mihimet sum semper proximus. Jew 1.1.189 Barab
PRY (See PRIE)
PRYOR
Because the Pryor <Governor> <Sire> dispossest thee once,/And Jew 3.3.43 Abigal
PRYSONER
thie folishe dreame/and lett thee see thie selfe my prysoner Paris ms33,p391 Guise
PSALME
Stay my Lord, let me begin the psalme. P 344 5.71 Anjoy
PSALTER
The Hebrew Psalter, and new Testament; F 182 1.1.154 Valdes
PUBLIKE
In sollemne triumphes, and in publike showes, Edw 1.4.350 Edward
PUBLIQUE
I'le have them fill the publique Schooles with [siike] <skill>, F 117 1.1.89 Faust
Th'affrighted worlds force bent on publique spoile, Lucan, First Booke 5
PUBLISHED
Give it me, ile have it published in the streetes. Edw 1.4.89 Lncstr
my selfe farre inferior to the report men have published, F App p.236 13 P Faust
PUDDLE
Or choake your soveraigne with puddle water? Edw 5.3.30 Edward
And there in mire and puddle have I stood, Edw 5.5.59 Edward
PUGNENT
pugnent ipsique nepotes: Dido 5.1.311 Dido
PUISANT
Besides rich presents from the puisant Cham, 1Tamb 1.2.18 Magnet
Most great and puisant Monarke of the earth, 1Tamb 3.1.41 Bassoe
Shall Tamburlain extend his puisant arme. 1Tamb 3.3.247 Tamb
To thinke thy puisant never staied arme/Will part their bodies, 1Tamb 5.1.88 1Virgn
PUISSANCE
see if coward Calapine/Dare levie armes against our puissance, 2Tamb 3.2.156 Tamb
PUISSANT
Puissant, renowmed and mighty Tamburlain, 1Tamb 3.3.96 Techel
Come puissant Viceroies, let us to the field, 2Tamb 3.5.53 Callap
And that their power is puissant as Joves, 2Tamb 5.3.35 Usumc
PUL
their mouths/And pul their kicking colts out of their pastures. 2Tamb 4.3.49 Techel
But wee'le pul downe his haughty insolence: F 914 3.1.136 Pope
PUL'D
till I had pul'd me his leg quite off, and now 'tis at home in F1551 4.5.47 P HrsCsr
PULD
At last the souldiers puld her by the heeles, Dido 2.1.247 Aeneas
By yelping hounds puld downe, and seeme to die. Edw 1.1.70 Gavstn
I have puld off his leg. F1492 4.4.36 P HrsCsr
hoary flieces/And riveld cheekes I would have puld a pieces. Ovid's Elegies 1.8.112
Drouping more then a Rose puld yesterday: Ovid's Elegies 3.6.66
And puld him to the bottome, where the ground/Was strewd with Hero and Leander 2.160
PULL
Then pull out both mine eyes, or let me dye. Dido 3.1.55 Iarbus
And as I heare, doth meane to pull my plumes. 1Tamb 1.1.33 Mycet
[and] <To> pull the triple headed dog from hell. 1Tamb 1.2.161 Therid
Then shalt thou see me pull it from thy head: 1Tamb 2.4.39 Tamb
Fearing my power should pull him from his throne. 1Tamb 5.1.453 Tamb
And pull proud Tamburlaine upon his knees, 2Tamb 5.2.40 Amasia
Pull hard. Jew 4.1.147 P Barab
Pull hard, I say, you would have had my goods. Jew 4.1.149 Barab
I, and our lives too, therfore pull amaine. Jew 4.1.150 Ithimr
To fire the Churches, pull their houses downe, Jew 5.1.65 Barab
And if they storme, I then may pull them downe. P 526 9.45 QnMoth
He is hard hearted, therfore pull with violence. P1105 20.15 1Mur
Weele pull him from the strongest hould he hath. Edw 1.4.289 Mortmr
I have the [gesses] <gresses> that will pull you downe, Edw 2.2.40 Edward
That I might pull him to me where I would, Edw 2.4.18 Queene
[And make my spirites pull his churches downe]. F 651 2.2.100A Faust
pull in your head for shame, let not all the world wonder at F1291 4.1.137 P Faust
sir, did not I pull off one of your legs when you were asleepe? F1655 4.6.98 P HrsCsr
These troupes should soone pull down the church of Jove. Lucan, First Booke 381
Nor shamefully her coate pull ore her crowne, Ovid's Elegies 1.7.47
Nor the milde Ewe gifts from the Ramme doth pull. Ovid's Elegies 1.10.28
With cruell hand why doest greene Apples pull? Ovid's Elegies 2.14.24
Least water-nymphs should pull him from the brinke. Hero and Leander 2.198
Which from our pretty Lambes we pull, Passionate Shepherd 14
PULL'D
hornes/The quick priest pull'd him on his knees and slew him: Lucan, First Booke 612
PULLEYES
Are all the Cranes and Pulleyes sure? Jew 5.5.2 Barab
PULLING
and never rested pulling, till I had pul'd me his leg quite F1550 4.5.46 P HrsCsr
PULS
O I'le leape up to [my God] <heaven>: who puls me downe? F1938 5.2.142 Faust
Or flaming Titan (feeding on the deepe)/Puls them aloft, and Lucan, First Booke 417
Ile live, and as he puls me downe, mount higher. Ovid's Elegies 1.15.42

PULS (cont.)			
describe, but hee/That puls or shakes it from the golden tree:	Hero and Leander		2.300
PUNICK			
It is the Punick kingdome rich and strong,	Dido	1.1.210	Venus
PUNICKE			
let him ride/As Didos husband through the Punicke streetes,	Dido	4.4.67	Dido
PUNIKE			
Sway thou the Punike Scepter in my steede,	Dido	4.4.35	Dido
PUNISH			
And punish me Aeneas for this crime.	Dido	4.4.36	Dido
To punish those that doe prophane this holy feast.	P 617	12.30	Mugern
to whom in justice it belongs/To punish this unnaturall revolt:	Edw	4.6.9	Kent
Long ere with Iron hands they punish men,	F 878	3.1.100	Pope
[Doest] punish <ye >me, because yeares make him waine?	Ovid's Elegies		1.13.41
PUNISHER			
O just and dreadfull punisher of sinne,	2Tamb	2.3.4	Sgsmnd
PUNISHMENT			
This kisse shall be faire Didos punishment.	Dido	4.4.37	Aeneas
When I leave thee, death be my punishment,	Dido	4.4.56	Aeneas
Shall take example by [his] <their> punishment,	P1186	22.48	King
And there determine of his punishment?	F1018	3.2.38	Pope
And on the next fault punishment inflict.	Ovid's Elegies		2.14.44
Yet as a punishment they added this,	Hero and Leander		1.469
PUNISHT			
Are punisht with Bastones so grievously,	1Tamb	3.3.52	Tamb
Whose cheekes and hearts so punisht with conceit,	1Tamb	5.1.87	1Virgn
We might have punisht him to his deserts.	P1184	22.46	Eprnon
Punisht I am, if I a Romaine beat,	Ovid's Elegies		1.7.29
PUNNIARDS			
Come sirs, Ile whip you to death with my punniards point.	P 441	7.81	Guise
PUNNISHMENT			
And a rich neck-lace caus'd that punnishment.	Ovid's Elegies		1.10.52
he will lament/And say this blabbe shall suffer punnishment.	Ovid's Elegies		2.2.60
PURCHAC'D			
That purchac'd kingdomes by your martiall deeds,	1Tamb	5.1.523	Tamb
Honour is purchac'd by the deedes wee do.	Hero and Leander		1.280
PURCHASE			
I judge the purchase more important far.	1Tamb	2.5.92	Therid
I thinke by this/You purchase both their lives; is it not so?	Jew	2.3.366	Ithimr
A kingly kinde of trade to purchase Townes/By treachery, and	Jew	5.5.47	Barab
Which may in Ireland purchase him such friends,	Edw	1.4.259	Mortmr
And when tis gone, our swordes shall purchase more.	Edw	2.2.197	Lncstr
heeres a simple purchase for horse-keepers, our horses shal	F App	p.234 2 P	Robin
(and gods not sleightly/Purchase immortal thrones; nor Jove	Lucan, First Booke		35
PURCHASED			
But now experience, purchased with griefe,	Jew	3.3.61	Abigal
PURE			
But of a substance more divine and pure,	2Tamb	5.3.88	Phsitn
not full of thoughtes/As pure and fiery as Phyteus beames,	2Tamb	5.3.237	Tamb
The midst is best; that place is pure, and bright,	Lucan, First Booke		58
When she will, day shines every where most pure.	Ovid's Elegies		1.8.10
are in thy soft brest/But pure simplicity in thee doth rest.	Ovid's Elegies		1.11.10
Pure waters moisture thirst away did keepe.	Ovid's Elegies		2.6.32
Now shine her lookes pure white and red betwixt.	Ovid's Elegies		3.3.6
Pure rose shee, like a Nun to sacrifice,	Ovid's Elegies		3.6.21
I the pure priest of Phoebus and the muses,	Ovid's Elegies		3.7.23
What profit to us hath our pure life bred?	Ovid's Elegies		3.8.33
Base in respect of thee, divine and pure,	Hero and Leander		1.219
And hands so pure, so innocent, nay such,	Hero and Leander		1.365
Her mind pure, and her toong untaught to glose.	Hero and Leander		1.392
PUREST			
which a cunning Alcumist/Distilled from the purest Balsamum,	2Tamb	4.2.60	Olymp
That trade in mettall of the purest mould;	Jew	1.1.20	Barab
With buckles of the purest gold.	Passionate Shepherd		16
PURETAINE			
And not unlike a bashfull puretaine,	Edw	5.4.59	Mortmr
PURGATION			
has given me a purgation, has purg'd me of fortie Dollers,	F App	p.240 128 P	HrsCsr
PURGATORY			
I thinke it be some Ghost crept out of Purgatory, and now is	F1060	3.2.80 P	Archbp
out of Purgatory come to begge a pardon of your holinesse.	F App	p.232 15 P	Lorein
PURG'D			
And few or none scape but by being purg'd.	Jew	2.3.106	Barab
has purg'd me of fortie Dollers, I shall never see them more:	F App	p.240 128 P	HrsCsr
the sacred priests/That with divine lustration purg'd the wals,	Lucan, First Booke		593
PURGE			
And purge my soule before it come to thee.	2Tamb	3.4.33	Olymp
We turne into the Ayre to purge our selves:	Jew	2.3.46	Barab
But in my latter houre to purge my selfe,	P 402	7.42	Ramus
To purge the rashnesse of this cursed deed,	F1125	3.3.38	Mephst
But by my paine to purge her perjuries,	Ovid's Elegies		3.3.21
PURGING			
For purging of the realme of such a plague.	Edw	1.4.270	Mortmr
PURIFI'D			
And every creature shall be purifi'd,	F 514	2.1.126	Mephst
PURITANE (See also PURETAINE)			
Be more advisde, walke as a puritane,	Ovid's Elegies		3.13.13
PURITANS			
Which [are] <as> he saith, to kill the Puritans,	P 643	12.56	Cardnl
To overthrow those [sectious] <sexious> <factious> Puritans:	P 850	17.45	Guise
PURITIE			
May in his endlesse power and puritie/Behold and venge this	2Tamb	2.2.53	Orcan
Through regular and formall puritie.	Hero and Leander		1.308

PURITY
To bring me to religious purity, ... Jew 2.3.72 Barab
PURLOYNE
(Such with my tongue it likes me to purloyne). . . . Ovid's Elegies 2.5.24
PURPLE
And suite themselves in purple for the nonce, ... Dido 1.1.206 Venus
Blushing Roses, purple Hyacinthe: . . . . . Dido 2.1.319 Venus
And couch him in Adonis purple downe. . . . . Dido 3.2.100 Venus
By Paphos, Capys, and the purple Sea, ... Dido 3.4.46 Aeneas
Staining his Altars with your purple blood: . . . 1Tamb 4.2.4 Bajzth
Bene oft resolv'd in bloody purple showers, . . . 1Tamb 5.1.460 Tamb
<superfluities>/Is covered with a liquid purple veile, . 2Tamb 1.3.80 Tamb
I see great Mahomet/Clothed in purple clowdes, and on his head 2Tamb 5.2.32 Amasia
In summer time the purple Rubicon, ... Lucan, First Booke 215
mainly throw the dart; wilt thou indure/These purple groomes? Lucan, First Booke 366
The purple moone with sanguine visage stood. . . . Ovid's Elegies 1.8.12
Halfe sleeping on a purple bed she rested, . . . Ovid's Elegies 1.14.20
And purple Love resumes his dartes againe. . . . Ovid's Elegies 2.9.34
The lining, purple silke, with guilt starres drawne, . Hero and Leander 1.10
Whereat she starts, puts on her purple weeds, . . . Hero and Leander 2.88
About his armes the purple riband wound, ... Hero and Leander 2.106
PURPOSE
Unto the purpose which we now propound. . . . . Dido 3.2.95 Juno
My purpose was (my Lord) to spend it so, ... 2Tamb 4.2.73 Olymp
Stands here a purpose, meaning me some wrong, . . . Jew 4.1.166 1Fryar
And see, a staffe stands ready for the purpose: . . . Jew 4.1.172 1Fryar
The rocke is hollow, and of purpose digg'd, . . . Jew 5.1.87 Barab
To what event my secret purpose drives, ... Jew 5.2.122 Barab
<make> a walk/On purpose from the Court to meet with him. P 784 15.42 Mugern
The causes first I purpose to unfould/Of these garboiles, Lucan, First Booke 67
And by him kept of purpose for a dearth? . . . . Lucan, First Booke 319
(his vassals)/And that he lags behind with them of purpose, Lucan, First Booke 477
Servants fit for thy purpose thou must hire/To teach thy lover, Ovid's Elegies 1.8.87
As soone as he his wished purpose got, ... Hero and Leander 1.460
PURPOSES
thee (sweet Ortigius)/Better replies shall proove my purposes. 1Tamb 2.5.37 Cosroe
PURSE
A silver girdle, and a golden purse, ... Dido 2.1.306 Venus
Belike he has some new tricke for a purse; . . . . Jew 2.3.101 Barab
My purse, my Coffer, and my selfe is thine. . . . . Jew 3.4.93 Barab
to supper, and a Tester in your purse, and go backe againe. F1122 3.3.35 P Robin
wil you take sixe pence in your purse to pay for your supper, F App p.235 41 P Robin
PURSEWDE
And let not conquest ruthlesly pursewde/Be equally against his 1Tamb 5.1.366 Zenoc
PURST
Here have I purst their paltry [silverlings] <silverbings>. Jew 1.1.6 Barab
PURSU'D
princely resolution/Fits not the time, away, we are pursu'd. Edw 4.5.9 Baldck
[No marvel tho the angry Greekes pursu'd]/[With tenne yeares F1699 5.1.26A 3Schol
or wrathful France/Pursu'd us hither, how were we bestead/When Lucan, First Booke 309
PURSUDE
Pursude by hunters, flie his angrie lookes, ... 1Tamb 3.3.193 Zenoc
PURSUE
Come, come abourd, pursue the hatefull Greekes. . . . Dido 2.1.22 Aeneas
The Greekes pursue me, stay and take me in. . . . Dido 2.1.282 Aeneas
That doe pursue my peace where ere it goes. . . . Dido 4.2.51 Iarbus
of Europe, and pursue/His scattered armie til they yeeld or die. 1Tamb 3.3.38 Therid
And could I but a while pursue the field, ... 2Tamb 5.3.117 Tamb
Pursue him quicklie, and he cannot scape, ... Edw 2.4.38 Queene
I see it is your life these armes pursue. . . . . Edw 2.6.2 James
Your lives and my dishonor they pursue, ... Edw 4.7.23 Edward
Armes that pursue our lives with deadly hate. . . . Edw 4.7.32 Spencr
Hunters leave taken beasts, pursue the chase, . . . Ovid's Elegies 2.9.9
Even as, when gawdie Nymphs pursue the chace, . . . Hero and Leander 1.113
PURSUED
And dead to scorne that hath pursued me so. . . . Dido 3.3.49 Iarbus
And therefore being pursued, it takes the aire: . . Edw 2.2.25 Lncstr
PURSUES
And spare our lives whom every spite pursues. . . . Dido 1.2.9 Illion
With open crie pursues the wounded Stag: 2Tamb 3.5.7 2Msngr
PURSUIT
best to be atchiev'd/In pursuit of the Cities overthrow? . 1Tamb 3.1.57 Fesse
Was this the pursuit of thy policie? . . . . . Jew 3.3.37 Abigal
PURSUTES
Your threats, your larums, and your hote pursutes, . . Edw 2.5.2 Gavstn
PUT (See also PUTT)
Put thou about thy necke my owne sweet heart, . . . Dido 1.1.44 Jupitr
And a fine brouch to put in my hat, ... Dido 1.1.47 Ganimd
Put sailes to sea to seeke out Italy, ... Dido 1.1.218 Aeneas
Prometheus hath put on Cupids shape, ... Dido 3.4.21 Dido
But I will soone put by that stumbling blocke, . . . Dido 4.1.34 Dido
I charge thee put to sea and stay not here. . . . Dido 4.4.22 Dido
How should I put into the raging deepe, ... Dido 5.1.55 Aeneas
But see, Achates wils him put to sea, ... Dido 5.1.258 Dido
Let us put on our meet incountring mindes, ... 1Tamb 2.6.19 Ortyg
Put him in againe. . . . . 1Tamb 4.2.82 Tamb
But goe my Lords, put the rest to the sword. . . . 1Tamb 5.1.134 Tamb
Cast off your armor, put on scarlet roabes. . . . . 1Tamb 5.1.524 Tamb
And soon put foorth into the Terrene sea: . . . . 2Tamb 1.2.25 Callap
Will hew us peecemeale, put us to the wheele, . . . 2Tamb 3.4.21 Olymp
to put him in remembrance he was a Jailor, that when I take 2Tamb 3.5.140 P Tamb
hee shall not be put to that exigent, I warrant thee. . 2Tamb 3.5.156 P Soria
I should be affraid, would put it off and come to bed with me. 2Tamb 4.1.70 P Calyph

PUT (cont.)			
would let me be put in the front of such a battaile once,	2Tamb	4.1.72	P Calyph
me in the Ocean thus/To sinke or swim, and put me to my shifts,	Jew	1.2.268	Barab
Yes, you shall have him: Goe put her in.	Jew	2.3.362	Barab
I, I'le put her in.	Jew	2.3.363	Ithimr
and when the Hangman had put on his hempen Tippet, he made such	Jew	4.2.23	P Ithimr
Put in two hundred at least.	Jew	4.2.74	P Pilia
Oh that ten thousand nights were put in one,	Jew	4.2.130	Ithimr
He never put on cleane shirt since he was circumcis'd.	Jew	4.4.64	P Ithimr
Now every man put of his burgonet,	P 449	7.89	Guise
And thither will I to put them to the sword.	P 504	9.23	Guise
Put of that feare, they are already joynde,	P 605	12.18	King
Which they will put us to with sword and fire:	P 706	14.9	Navrre
But God we know will alwaies put them downe,	P 798	16.12	Navrre
yet you put in that which displeaseth him, and so forestall his	P 808	17.3	P Souldr
That I with speed should have beene put to death.	P1118	21.12	Dumain
And make the people sweare to put him downe.	Edw	2.2.111	Lncstr
Ah traitors, have they put my friend to death?	Edw	3.1.91	Edward
Come, come, away, now put the torches out,	Edw	5.3.47	Matrvs
put off thy cloathes, and I'le conjure thee about presently:	F 746	2.3.25	P Robin
And put into the Churches treasury.	F1028	3.2.48	Raymnd
[They put forth questions of Astrologie],	F1146	3.3.59A	3Chor
What use shall we put his beard to?	F1383	4.2.59	P Mrtino
Wee'l put out his eyes, and they shall serve for buttons to his	F1387	4.2.63	P Benvol
But law being put to silence by the wars,	Lucan, First Booke		278
Yoke Venus Doves, put Mirtle on thy haire,	Ovid's Elegies		1.2.23
Put in their place thy keembed haires againe.	Ovid's Elegies		1.7.68
To please thy selfe, thy selfe put out of minde.	Ovid's Elegies		1.14.38
Verses ope dores, and lockes put in the poast/Although of oake,	Ovid's Elegies		2.1.27
Came forth a mother, though a maide there put.	Ovid's Elegies		3.4.22
And blabbing Tantalus in mid-waters put.	Ovid's Elegies		3.11.30
Before the roome be cleere, and doore put too.	Ovid's Elegies		3.13.10
But with your robes, put on an honest face,	Ovid's Elegies		3.13.27
Their fellowes being slaine or put to flight,	Hero and Leander		1.120
When misers keepe it; being put to lone,	Hero and Leander		1.235
As put thereby, yet might he hope for mo.	Hero and Leander		1.312
Shee, with a kind of graunting, put him by it,	Hero and Leander		2.73
The god put Helles bracelet on his arme,	Hero and Leander		2.179
PUTRIFYING			
person you remoove/This Spencer, as a putrifying branche,	Edw	3.1.162	Herald
PUTS			
Whereat she starts, puts on her purple weeds,	Hero and Leander		2.88
PUTT			
yett you putt in that displeases him | And fill up his rome	Paris	ms 4,p390	P Souldr
PUTTOCK			
The ravenous vulture lives, the Puttock hovers/Around the aire,	Ovid's Elegies		2.6.33
PYGMALION (See PIGMALIONS)			
PYLADES			
What Pylades did to Orestes prove,	Ovid's Elegies		2.6.15
PYLIUS (See PILIUS)			
PYLLADES			
And by the love of Pyllades and Orestes,	1Tamb	1.2.243	Tamb
PYN'D			
Some say, for her the fairest Cupid pyn'd,	Hero and Leander		1.37
Pyn'd as they went, and thinking on her died.	Hero and Leander		1.130
As for his love, both earth and heaven pyn'd;	Hero and Leander		2.196
PYRACIE			
Compact of Rapine, Pyracie, and spoile,	1Tamb	4.3.8	Souldn
PYRAMIDES (See also PERAMIDES)			
Hollow Pyramides of silver plate:	Dido	3.1.123	Dido
Like to the shadowes of Pyramides,	1Tamb	4.2.103	Tamb
PYRAMYDES			
Beside <Besides> the gates, and high Pyramydes,	F 823	3.1.45	Mephst
PYRENE (See PIRENE)			
PYROMANCY			
Well skild in Pyromancy; one that knew/The hearts of beasts,	Lucan, First Booke		586
PYRRHUS (See PIRHUS, PIRRHUS)			
PYTHAGORAS			
[Ah] <Oh> Pythagoras Metemsycosis <metem su cossis>; were that	F1966	5.2.170	Faust
QUAFFE			
That you may drinke your fill, and quaffe in bloud,	Edw	3.1.137	Edward
QUAFFING			
wines/Shall common Souldiers drink in quaffing boules,	2Tamb	1.3.222	Tamb
Blood-quaffing Mars, heaving the yron net,	Hero and Leander		1.151
QUAIL'D			
That with his sword hath quail'd all earthly kings,	2Tamb	5.1.93	Tamb
Let come their [leader] <leaders whom long peace hath quail'd;	Lucan, First Booke		311
This [band] <hand> that all behind us might be quail'd,	Lucan, First Booke		370
QUAILD			
To this ad shame, shame to performe it quaild mee,	Ovid's Elegies		3.6.37
QUAILE			
I think I make your courage something quaile.	2Tamb	5.1.126	Tamb
QUAILES			
Behould how quailes among their battailes live,	Ovid's Elegies		2.6.27
QUAINT (See QUEINTLY)			
QUAKE			
That shaken thrise, makes Natures buildings quake,	Dido	1.1.11	Jupitr
To see our neighbours that were woont to quake/And tremble at	1Tamb	1.1.115	Cosroe
As with their waight shall make the mountains quake,	1Tamb	1.2.49	Tamb
Which lately made all Europe quake for feare:	1Tamb	3.3.135	Bajzth
The heavens may frowne, the earth for anger quake,	1Tamb	5.1.231	Bajzth
And make it quake at every drop it drinks:	1Tamb	5.1.462	Tamb
Whose lookes make this inferiour world to quake,	2Tamb	1.3.139	Techel

QUAKE (cont.)			
And quake for feare, as if infernall Jove/Meaning to aid [thee]	2Tamb	1.3.143	Techel
My heart did never quake, or corrage faint.	2Tamb	5.1.106	Govnr
Wel, now Ile make it quake, go draw him up,	2Tamb	5.1.107	Tamb
Tremble and quake at his commanding charmes?	F1372	4.2.48	Fredrk
QUAKES			
For all flesh quakes at your magnificence.	1Tamb	3.1.48	Argier
QUALIFIE			
overweighing heavens/Have kept to qualifie these hot extreames,	1Tamb	5.1.46	Govnr
QUALITIE			
if he had but the qualitie of hey ding, ding, hey, ding, ding,	F App	p.239 115	P HrsCsr
had some rare qualitie that he would not have had me knowne of,	F App	p.240 132	P HrsCsr
QUALITIES			
Because he is young and has more qualities.	Jew	2.3.110	1Offcr
QUALITY			
had had some [rare] quality that he would not have me know of,	F1542	4.5.38	P HrsCsr
QUAM			
Quam male conveniunt:	Edw	1.4.13	MortSr
Saying it is, onus quam gravissimum,	Edw	5.4.61	Mortmr
Major sum quam cui possit fortuna nocere.	Edw	5.4.69	Mortmr
et consecratam aquam quam nunc spargo; signumque crucis quod	F 249	1.3.21	P Faust
QUANDOQUIDEM			
But one of those that saith quandoquidem,	Edw	2.1.54	Spencr
QUANTITY			
And of a Carrect of this quantity,	Jew	1.1.30	Barab
No bigger then my hand in quantity.	F 851	3.1.73	Faust
QUARRELL			
My Lords, sith in a quarrell just and right,	P 698	14.1	Navrre
But for you know our quarrell is no more,	P 704	14.7	Navrre
Fight in the quarrell of this valiant Prince,	P1229	22.91	King
And in your quarrell and the realmes behoofe,	Edw	2.3.3	Kent
But justice of the quarrell and the cause,	Edw	3.1.222	Edward
And laboring to approve his quarrell good.	Lucan, First Booke		267
QUARRELS			
If you love me, no quarrels in my house;	Jew	2.3.271	Barab
Quarrels were rife, greedy desire stil poore/Did vild deeds,	Lucan, First Booke		174
QUARTER			
[Quarter <Quarters> the towne in foure equivolence].	F 790	3.1.12A	Faust
Ile bouldly quarter out the fields of Rome;	Lucan, First Booke		383
QUARTERS			
Unto what fruitfull quarters were ye bound,	Dido	1.2.18	Iarbus
Hang him I say, and set his quarters up,	Edw	5.6.53	King
The [Tropicks] <Tropick>, Zones, and quarters of the skye,/From	F 761	2.3.40	2Chor
[Quarter <Quarters> the towne in foure equivolence].	F 790	3.1.12A	Faust
There are live quarters broyling on the coles,	F1913	5.2.117	BdAngl
And in all quarters musters men for Roome.	Lucan, First Booke		396
QUASI			
left heele, that thou maist, Quasi vestigiis nostris insistere.	F 387	1.4.45	P Wagner
upon my right heele, with quasi vestigias nostras insistere.	F App	p.231 70	P Wagner
QUAVER			
Their fingers made to quaver on a Lute,	2Tamb	1.3.29	Tamb
To quaver on her lippes even in her song,	Ovid's Elegies		2.4.26
QUEEN			
Am not I Queen of Libia? then depart.	Dido	3.1.49	Dido
To be my Queen and portly Emperesse.	1Tamb	1.2.187	Tamb
Queen of fifteene contributory Queens,	1Tamb	5.1.266	Bajzth
O poore Zabina, O my Queen, my Queen,	1Tamb	5.1.275	Bajzth
In what Queen Mother or your grace commands.	P 12	1.12	Navrre
My Lords, albeit the Queen winne Mortimer,	Edw	1.4.230	Lncstr
QUEENE			
Whereas Sidonian Dido rules as Queene.	Dido	1.1.213	Venus
Come in with me, Ile bring you to my Queene,	Dido	1.2.42	Iarbus
And here Queene Dido weares th'imperiall Crowne,	Dido	2.1.63	Illion
Sometime I was a Troian, mightie Queene:	Dido	2.1.75	Aeneas
Sit in this chaire and banquet with a Queene,	Dido	2.1.83	Dido
Too meane to be companion to a Queene.	Dido	2.1.89	Aeneas
At which the franticke Queene leapt on his face,	Dido	2.1.244	Aeneas
What happened to the Queene we cannot shewe,	Dido	2.1.294	Achat
Are you Queene Didos sonne?	Dido	2.1.308	Ascan
As every touch shall wound Queene Didos heart.	Dido	2.1.333	Cupid
Now Cupid cause the Carthaginian Queene,	Dido	3.1.1	Cupid
Ungentle Queene, is this thy love to me?	Dido	3.1.36	Iarbus
Yet Queene of Affricke, are my ships unrigd,	Dido	3.1.105	Aeneas
Faire Queene of love, I will devorce these doubts,	Dido	3.2.85	Juno
Then in one Cave the Queene and he shall meete,	Dido	3.2.92	Juno
By chance sweete Queene, as Mars and Venus met.	Dido	3.4.4	Aeneas
What ailes my Queene, is she falne sicke of late?	Dido	3.4.24	Aeneas
Then to the Carthage Queene that dyes for him.	Dido	3.4.40	Dido
In all this coyle, where have ye left the Queene?	Dido	4.1.14	Iarbus
Hath not the Carthage Queene mine onely sonne?	Dido	4.4.29	Aeneas
againe conspire/Against the life of me poore Carthage Queene:	Dido	4.4.132	Dido
Ye shall no more offend the Carthage Queene.	Dido	4.4.158	Dido
And beautifying the Empire of this Queene,	Dido	5.1.28	Hermes
This was my mother that beguild the Queene,	Dido	5.1.42	Aeneas
Eating sweet Comfites with Queene Didos maide,	Dido	5.1.47	Ascan
Say thou wilt stay in Carthage with [thy] <my> Queene,	Dido	5.1.117	Dido
O Queene of Carthage, wert thou ugly blacke,	Dido	5.1.125	Aeneas
Now bring him backe, and thou shalt be a Queene,	Dido	5.1.197	Dido
For perjurie and slaughter of a Queene:	Dido	5.1.294	Dido
That may revenge this treason to a Queene,	Dido	5.1.307	Dido
And might content the Queene of heaven as well,	1Tamb	3.2.11	Zenoc
And keeps you from the honors of a Queene,	1Tamb	3.2.28	Agidas
You see my wife, my Queene and Emperesse,	1Tamb	5.1.264	Bajzth

QUIET (cont.)			
Nor quiet enter my distemper'd thoughts, ...	Jew	2.1.18	Barab
Be quiet Lodowicke, it is enough/That I have made thee sure to	Jew	2.3.334	Barab
As England shall be quiet, and you safe.	Edw	1.4.358	Mortmr
Quiet your self, you shall have the broad seale, . .	Edw	2.2.147	Edward
Begets the quiet of king Edwards land, ...	Edw	3.1.263	Spencr
O that I might this life in quiet lead, ...	Edw	4.7.21	Edward
All things that move betweene the quiet Poles/Shall be at my	F 83	1.1.55	Faust
Not long he stayed within his quiet house, ...	F 768	2.3.47	2Chor
Confound these passions with a quiet sleepe:	F1481	4.4.25	Faust
Then rest thee Faustus quiet in conceit.	F1483	4.4.27	Faust
Confound these passions with a quiet sleepe:	F App	p.240 124	Faust
Then rest thee Faustus quiet in conceit.	F App	p.240 126	Faust
Soules quiet and appeas'd [sigh'd] <sight> from their graves,	Lucan, First Booke		566
And time it was for me to live in quiet, ...	Ovid's Elegies		2.9.23
Haples is he that all the night lies quiet/And slumbring,	Ovid's Elegies		2.9.39
QUIETLY			
It may be they will yeeld it quietly, ...	2Tamb	3.3.12	Therid
And therefore Captaine, yeeld it quietly.	2Tamb	3.3.34	Techel
QUIETNES			
For Englands honor, peace, and quietnes.	Edw	4.2.58	Kent
QUIGHT			
And lose more labor than the gaine will quight. . .	1Tamb	2.5.96	Tamb
QUILL			
O would to God this quill that heere doth write, . .	P 667	13.11	Duchss
sleepe, to take a quill/And blowe a little powder in his eares,	Edw	5.4.34	Ltborn
What neede she [tyre] <try> her hand to hold the quill, .	Ovid's Elegies		1.11.23
And tearmes <termst> [my] <our> works fruits of an idle quill?	Ovid's Elegies		1.15.2
QUILLES			
Which should be like the quilles of Porcupines, . .	2Tamb	1.3.26	Tamb
Thou with thy quilles mightst make greene Emeralds darke,	Ovid's Elegies		2.6.21
QUIN			
[Quin redis <regis> Mephostophilis fratris imagine]. .	F 262	1.3.34A	Faust
QUINQUE			
For [which] <with> the quinque-angle fourme is meet: .	2Tamb	3.2.64	Tamb
QUINQUE-ANGLE			
For [which] <with> the quinque-angle fourme is meet: .	2Tamb	3.2.64	Tamb
QUINTESSENCE			
If all the heavenly Quintessence they still/From their .	1Tamb	5.1.165	Tamb
QUIRINUS			
Quirinus rites and Latian Jove advanc'd/On Alba hill o Vestall	Lucan, First Booke		200
QUIS			
Oro, si quis [adhuc] <ad haec> precibus locus, exue mentem.	Dido	5.1.138	Dido
QUIT (Homograph; See also QUITE)			
Nor quit good turnes with double fee downe told: . .	Dido	3.2.15	Juno
Doe Troians use to quit their Lovers thus? . . .	Dido	5.1.106	Dido
And we be quit that causde it to be done:	Edw	5.4.16	Mortmr
But Faustus death shall quit my infamie.	F1337	4.2.13	Benvol
Thou soone shouldst see me quit my foule disgrace. . .	F1356	4.2.32	Benvol
See how they quit our [bloud shed] <bloudshed> in the North;	Lucan, First Booke		302
QUITE (Homograph)			
Then would we hope to quite such friendly turnes, . .	Dido	1.2.46	Serg
Achates speake, sorrow hath tired me quite. . . .	Dido	2.1.293	Aeneas
And sink not quite into my tortur'd soule. . . .	1Tamb	5.1.263	Bajzth
Quite voide of skars, and cleare from any wound, . .	2Tamb	3.2.112	Tamb
His hands are hackt, some fingers cut quite off; . .	Jew	4.3.10	Barab
And so to quite your grace of all suspect. . . .	P 889	17.84	Eprnon
till I had pul'd me his leg quite off, and now 'tis at home in	F1551	4.5.47	P HrsCsr
And quite bereave thee of salvation.	F1709	5.1.36	OldMan
Now light had quite dissolv'd the mysty [night] <might>, .	Lucan, First Booke		263
Loe Cupid brings his quiver spoyled quite, . . .	Ovid's Elegies		3.8.7
And quite confound natures sweet harmony.	Hero and Leander		1.252
QUITTANCE			
But now for quittance of this oversight, ...	Dido	3.1.84	Dido
Which I will make in quittance of thy love:	Dido	3.2.69	Juno
Crie quittance Madam then, and love not him. . . .	Edw	1.4.195	Mortmr
In quittance of their late conspiracie/Against our State, and	F 949	3.1.171	Pope
First, on his head, in quittance of my wrongs, . . .	F1379	4.2.55	Benvol
QUIVER (See also QUYVERING)			
Having a quiver girded to her side, ...	Dido	1.1.185	Venus
maides to weare/Their bowe and quiver in this modest sort,	Dido	1.1.205	Venus
Shall I have such a quiver and a bow?	Dido	2.1.310	Ascan
Such bow, such quiver, and such golden shafts, . . .	Dido	2.1.311	Venus
Untill I gird my quiver to my side:	Dido	3.3.8	Dido
Bearing her bowe and quiver at her backe.	Dido	3.3.55	Achat
Quiver about the Axeltree of heaven.	2Tamb	1.1.90	Orcan
quiver <quivers> to remember that I have beene a student here	F1840	5.2.44	P Faust
And quiver bearing Dian till the plaine:	Ovid's Elegies		1.1.14
Thus I complaind, but Love unlockt his quiver, . . .	Ovid's Elegies		1.1.25
Better then I their quiver knowes them not. . . .	Ovid's Elegies		2.9.38
Loe Cupid brings his quiver spoyled quite, . . .	Ovid's Elegies		3.8.7
QUIVERD			
No love is so dere (quiverd Cupid flie)/That my chiefe wish	Ovid's Elegies		2.5.1
QUIVERING			
Our quivering Lances shaking in the aire, ...	1Tamb	2.3.18	Tamb
Stand staggering like a quivering Aspen leafe, . . .	1Tamb	2.4.4	Mycet
While they walke quivering on their citie walles, . .	1Tamb	4.4.3	Tamb
When al their riders chardg'd their quivering speares/Began to	1Tamb	5.1.332	Zenoc
the uglie monster death/Shaking and quivering, pale and wan for	2Tamb	5.3.68	Tamb
Who sees not warre sit by the quivering Judge;	Lucan, First Booke		320
These sad presages were enough to scarre/The quivering Romans,	Lucan, First Booke		673
About my head be quivering Mirtle wound, ...	Ovid's Elegies		1.15.37
Wherein Leander on her quivering brest, ...	Hero and Leander		2.279

QUIVERS
<quivers> to remember that I have beene a student here these F1840 5.2.44 P Faust
QUOD
That cannot speake without propterea quod. Edw 2.1.53 Baldck
[Quid tu moraris] <quod tumeraris>; per Jehovam, Gehennam, et F 248 1.3.20 P Faust
signumque crucis quod nunc facio; et per vota nostra ipse nunc F 249 1.3.21 P Faust
QUOTH
no time; but, quoth he, in any case ride him not into the water. F1541 4.5.37 P HrsCsr
Doctor Fustian quoth a, mas Doctor Lopus was never such a F App p.240 127 P HrsCsr
QUOTH A
Doctor Fustian quoth a, mas Doctor Lopus was never such a F App p.240 127 P HrsCsr
QUOTHA
Boy quotha? F App p.229 3 P Clown
QUYVERING
In number more than are the quyvering leaves/Of Idas forrest, 2Tamb 3.5.5 2Msngr
RABBI (See RABIES)
RABIES
In whom the learned Rabies of this age, 2Tamb 4.2.84 Therid
RABLEMENT
That with a rablement of his hereticks, P 151 2.94 Guise
RACE (Homograph; See also RASE)
Thus in stoute Hectors race three hundred yeares, Dido 1.1.104 Jupitr
And race th'eternall Register of time: Dido 3.2.7 Juno
Then here in me shall flourish Priams race, Dido 4.4.87 Aeneas
For he was never sprong of humaine race, 1Tamb 2.6.11 Meandr
To race and scatter thy inglorious crue, 1Tamb 4.3.67 Souldn
First will we race the City wals our selves, Jew 3.5.13 Govnr
The race of all his stout progenitors; F1168 4.1.14 Mrtino
faine themselves/The Romanes brethren, sprung of Ilian race; Lucan, First Booke 429
On swift steedes mounted till the race were done. Ovid's Elegies 3.2.10
Wretched Ixions shaggie footed race, Hero and Leander 1.114
RACETH
He raceth all his foes with fire and sword. 1Tamb 4.1.63 2Msngr
RACING
Talke not of racing downe your City wals, Jew 3.5.21 Basso
RACKE (Homograph)
Make fires, heat irons, let the racke be fetch'd. Jew 5.1.24 Govnr
For when we heare one racke the name of God, F 275 1.3.47 Mephst
RACKES
Then though death rackes <rakes> my bones in funerall fier, Ovid's Elegies 1.15.41
RACKING
live, and draw/My chariot swifter than the racking cloudes: 2Tamb 4.3.21 Tamb
RACKT
And rackt by dutie from my cursed heart: 1Tamb 5.1.387 Zenoc
while all thy joints/Be rackt and beat asunder with the wheele, 2Tamb 3.5.125 Tamb
RADAMANTH
Revenge it Radamanth and Eacus, 2Tamb 4.1.171 Orcan
RADGE
lawlesse/And casuall; all the starres at randome radge <range>: Lucan, First Booke 642
with what plague/Meane ye to radge? Lucan, First Booke 649
Wars radge draws neare; and to the swords strong hand, Lucan, First Booke 665
under Hemus mount/Philippi plaines; Phoebus what radge is this? Lucan, First Booke 680
RADIANCE
And by thine eyes whose radiance burnes out mine. Ovid's Elegies 3.10.48
RADIANT
Who with the Sunne devides one radiant shape, Dido 1.1.97 Jupitr
From whence my radiant mother did descend, Dido 3.4.47 Aeneas
By me, and by my starres, thy radiant eyes. Ovid's Elegies 2.16.44
radiant like starres they be,/By which she perjurd oft hath Ovid's Elegies 3.3.9
For know, that underneath this radiant floure, Hero and Leander 1.145
Descends upon my radiant Heroes tower. Hero and Leander 2.204
RAFE
or else you are blowne up, you are dismembred Rafe, keepe out, F App p.233 11 P Robin
True Rafe, and more Rafe, if thou hast any mind to Nan Spit our F App p.234 26 P Robin
and more Rafe, if thou hast any mind to Nan Spit our kitchin F App p.234 26 P Robin
No more sweete Rafe, letts goe and make cleane our bootes which F App p.234 32 P Robin
Come Rafe, did not I tell thee, we were for ever made by this F App p.234 1 P Robin
Drawer, I hope al is payd, God be with you, come Rafe. F App p.234 6 P Robin
I a goblet Rafe, I a goblet? F App p.234 9 P Robin
looke to the goblet Rafe. F App p.235 20 P Robin
looke to the goblet Rafe, Polypragmos Belseborams framanto F App p.235 24 P Robin
RAG
To have a shag-rag knave to come [demand]/Three hundred Jew 4.3.61 Barab
RAGE (See also RADGE)
Whose foming galle with rage and high disdaine, 1Tamb 1.1.63 Mycet
Go wander free from feare of Tyrants rage, 1Tamb 3.2.102 Agidas
And calme the rage of thundring Jupiter: 1Tamb 3.3.123 Tamb
So scatter and consume them in his rage, 1Tamb 4.1.34 Souldn
I goe as whirl-windes rage before a storme. P 511 9.30 Guise
The sheepeherd nipt with biting winters rage, Edw 2.2.61 Gavstn
this rage, and suffer uncontrowld/These Barons thus to beard me Edw 3.1.13 Spencr
As much as thou in rage out wentst the rest. Edw 3.1.240 Edward
O fly him then, but Edmund calme this rage, Edw 4.6.11 Kent
longer life/Thou hadst restrainde thy headstrong husbands rage, Lucan, First Booke 116
hunters pauseth till fell wrath/And kingly rage increase, Lucan, First Booke 210
all lands else/Have stable peace, here wars rage first begins, Lucan, First Booke 252
but as the fields/When birds are silent thorough winters rage; Lucan, First Booke 261
They kennel'd in Hircania, evermore/Wil rage and pray: Lucan, First Booke 330
Smooth speeches, feare and rage shall by thee ride, Ovid's Elegies 1.2.35
While rage is absent, take some friend the paynes. Ovid's Elegies 1.7.2
For rage against my wench mov'd my rash arme, Ovid's Elegies 1.7.3
Now Mars doth rage abroad without all pitty, Ovid's Elegies 1.8.41
Perpetuall thirst, and winters lasting rage. Ovid's Elegies 1.8.114

RAGE (cont.)			
How Scyllaes and Caribdis waters rage.	Ovid's Elegies	2.11.18	
Not onely by warres rage made Gentleman.	Ovid's Elegies	3.14.6	
There might you see one sigh, another rage, . . .	Hero and Leander	1.125	
Till she o'recome with anguish, shame, and rage, . .	Hero and Leander	2.333	
RAGETH			
Roome rageth now in armes/As if the Carthage Hannibal were	Lucan, First Booke	304	
RAGGED			
can ragged stonie walles/Immure thy vertue that aspires to	Edw	3.1.256	Mortmr
RAGING			
Swell raging seas, frowne wayward destinies, ...	Dido	4.4.57	Aeneas
How should I put into the raging deepe, ...	Dido	5.1.55	Aeneas
And of the ever raging Caspian Lake:	1Tamb	1.1.168	Ortyg
wher raging Lantchidol/Beates on the regions with his .	2Tamb	1.1.69	Orcan
And all this raging cannot make her live, ...	2Tamb	2.4.120	Therid
And make a Fortresse in the raging waves, ...	2Tamb	3.2.88	Tamb
and raging shoots/Alongst the ayre and [nought] <not> resisting	Lucan, First Booke	156	
And raging Seas in boistrous South-winds plough. . .	Ovid's Elegies	2.16.22	
And Scyllaes wombe mad raging dogs conceales. . . .	Ovid's Elegies	3.11.22	
RAGS			
Shall Ithimore my love goe in such rags?	Jew	4.2.85	Curtzn
RAIES			
appeares as full/As raies of Cynthia to the clearest sight?	2Tamb	2.3.30	Orcan
RAIGN			
then Cosroe raign/And governe Persea in her former pomp: .	1Tamb	2.5.18	Cosroe
So do we hope to raign in Asia, ...	1Tamb	2.7.38	Usumc
RAIGN'D			
Smile Stars that raign'd at my nativity, ...	1Tamb	4.2.33	Tamb
whose silver haires/Honor and reverence evermore have raign'd,	1Tamb	5.1.82	1Virgn
He raign'd him straight and made him so curvet, . .	2Tamb	1.3.41	Zenoc
You Starres that raign'd at my nativity, ...	F1950	5.2.154	Faust
RAIGNDE			
Perhaps the Sabines rude, when Tatius raignde, . . .	Ovid's Elegies	1.8.39	
RAIGNE			
Hoping (misled by dreaming prophesies)/To raigne in Asia, and	1Tamb	1.1.42	Meandr
I doubt not shortly but to raigne sole king, . . .	1Tamb	1.1.175	Cosroe
Both we will raigne as Consuls of the earth, . . .	1Tamb	1.2.197	Tamb
The thirst of raigne and sweetnes of a crown, . . .	1Tamb	2.7.12	Tamb
If you but say that Tamburlaine shall raigne. . . .	1Tamb	2.7.63	Tamb
Long live Tamburlaine, and raigne in Asia. . . .	1Tamb	2.7.64	All
That we may raigne as kings of Affrica.	1Tamb	3.3.99	Therid
Thou shalt be made a King and raigne with me, . . .	2Tamb	1.3.48	Tamb
So, raigne my sonne, scourge and controlle those slaves, .	2Tamb	5.3.228	Tamb
But I will raigne to be reveng'd of them, ...	Edw	1.4.111	Edward
Raigne showers of vengeance on my cursed head/Thou God, to whom	Edw	4.6.7	Kent
Two kings in England cannot raigne at once:	Edw	5.1.58	Edward
Let him be king, I am too yong to raigne.	Edw	5.2.93	Prince
And raigne sole King of all [our] Provinces. . . .	F 121	1.1.93	Faust
Receive with shouts; where thou wilt raigne as King, .	Lucan, First Booke	47	
And having once got head still shal he raigne? . . .	Lucan, First Booke	317	
In wooddie groves ist meete that Ceres Raigne, . . .	Ovid's Elegies	1.1.13	
Subdue the wandring wenches to thy raigne, . . .	Ovid's Elegies	2.9.53	
Not though thy face in all things make thee raigne, . .	Ovid's Elegies	2.17.11	
Her lover let her mocke, that long will raigne, . . .	Ovid's Elegies	2.19.33	
Thou ore a hundreth Nimphes, or more shalt raigne: . .	Ovid's Elegies	3.5.63	
Saturne and Ops, began their golden raigne. . . .	Hero and Leander	1.456	
RAIGNES			
And Juno like with Dis raignes under ground?	Ovid's Elegies	3.9.46	
RAILE			
Raile not proud Scythian, I shall now revenge/My fathers vile	2Tamb	3.5.90	Callap
In vaine I strive and raile against those powers, . .	2Tamb	5.3.120	Tamb
At Colchis stain'd with childrens bloud men raile, . .	Ovid's Elegies	2.14.29	
RAILES			
Another railes at me, and that I write, ...	Ovid's Elegies	2.4.21	
RAIL'ST			
Say, knave, why rail'st upon my father thus?	Jew	3.3.11	Abigal
RAIN (Homograph)			
For neither rain can fall upon the earth, ...	1Tamb	3.1.51	Moroc
speares/Began to checke the ground, and rain themselves: .	1Tamb	5.1.333	Zenoc
RAINBOW			
And tumbling with the Rainbow in a cloud:	Hero and Leander	1.150	
RAIN'D			
As sure as heaven rain'd Manna for the Jewes, ...	Jew	2.3.248	Barab
RAINE			
And make him raine down murthering shot from heaven/To dash the	1Tamb	3.3.196	Zabina
Mounts, and raine-doubled flouds he passeth over, . .	Ovid's Elegies	1.9.11	
Puttock hovers/Around the aire, the Cadesse raine discovers,	Ovid's Elegies	2.6.34	
Thy springs are nought but raine and melted snowe: . .	Ovid's Elegies	3.5.93	
RAINE-DOUBLED			
Mounts, and raine-doubled flouds he passeth over, . .	Ovid's Elegies	1.9.11	
RAINES (Homograph)			
See how he raines down heaps of gold in showers, . . .	1Tamb	1.2.182	Tamb
And here in Affrick where it seldom raines, ...	1Tamb	5.1.457	Tamb
Sit up my boy, and with those silken raines, ...	2Tamb	5.3.202	Tamb
To have his head control'd, but breakes the raines, . .	Hero and Leander	2.142	
RAIN'ST			
Rain'st on the earth resolved pearle in showers, . .	1Tamb	5.1.142	Tamb
RAIS'D			
For from the earth to heaven, is Cupid rais'd, . . .	Hero and Leander	2.31	
RAISD			
And bankes raisd higher with their sepulchers: . . .	Edw	1.4.103	Edward
Now your credulity harme to me hath raisd. . . .	Ovid's Elegies	3.11.44	
RAISDE			
He with his faulchions poynt raisde up at once, . .	Dido	2.1.229	Aeneas

RAISDE (cont.)
Is this report raisde on poore Isabell. . . . . . Edw 5.6.75 Queene
And suddaine rampire raisde of turfe snatcht up/Would make them Lucan, First Booke 515
RAISE (Homograph)
Will Dido raise old Priam forth his grave, ... Dido 4.3.39 Illion
And raise a new foundation to old Troy, ... Dido 5.1.79 Aeneas
Nor raise our siege before the Gretians yeeld, ... 1Tamb 3.1.14 Bajzth
time to sort/Your fighting men, and raise your royall hoste. 1Tamb 4.1.37 Capol
Then raise your seige from faire Damascus walles, . . . 1Tamb 4.4.71 Zenoc
Forgetst thou, that to have me raise my siege, . . . 2Tamb 1.1.98 Orcan
Raise Cavalieros higher than the cloudes, ... 2Tamb 2.4.103 Tamb
And raise our honors to as high a pitch/In this our strong and 2Tamb 3.1.30 Callap
Even in the cannons face shall raise a hill/Of earth and fagots 2Tamb 3.3.21 Therid
Raise mounts, batter, intrench, and undermine, . . . 2Tamb 3.3.38 Capt
Raise me to match the faire Aldeboran, ... 2Tamb 4.3.61 Tamb
Drums strike alarum, raise them from their sport, . . Edw 2.3.25 Mortmr
and with the power/That he intendeth presentlie to raise, Edw 2.4.44 Queene
I feare mee that this crie will raise the towne, . . Edw 5.5.114 Matrvs
Or being dead, raise them to life againe, ... F 53 1.1.25 Faust
[Nor can they raise the winde, or rend the cloudes]: . F 86 1.1.58A Faust
Did not my conjuring [speeches] raise thee? speake. . . F 273 1.3.45 Faust
for I will presently raise up two devils to carry thee away: F 373 1.4.31 P Wagner
But may I raise such <up> spirits when I please? . . F 475 2.1.87 Faust
and incantations, that I might raise up spirits when I please]. F 551.2 2.1.165A P Faust
Repent and they shall never raise thy skin. . . . . F 633 2.2.82 GdAngl
Il'e raise a kennell of Hounds shall hunt him so, . . F1301 4.1.147 Faust
zounds hee'l raise up a kennell of Divels I thinke anon: . F1305 4.1.151 P Benvol
serve you, would you teach me to raise up Banios and Belcheos? F App p.230 57 P Clown
Canst raise this man from hollow vaults below, ... F App p.237 30 Emper
Go now thou Conqueror, glorious triumphs raise, . . Ovid's Elegies 1.7.35
And did to thee no cause of dolour raise. . . . . . Ovid's Elegies 1.14.14
RAISED
By murder raised to the Persean Crowne, ... 1Tamb 4.3.13 Souldn
RAISEST
Both whom thou raisest up to toyle anew. . . . . . Ovid's Elegies 1.13.22
RAISING
And Proteus raising hils of floods on high, ... Dido 1.1.76 Venus
RAKES
Then though death rackes <rakes> my bones in funerall fier, Ovid's Elegies 1.15.41
RAKT
Rakt up in embers of their povertie, ... Edw 1.1.21 Gavstn
RAM
These hands shall thrust the ram, and make them flie, . Lucan, First Booke 385
RAMME
Nor the milde Ewe gifts from the Ramme doth pull. . . Ovid's Elegies 1.10.28
RAMPIERD
Inforst a wide breach in that rampierd wall, ... Dido 2.1.174 Aeneas
Such rampierd gates beseiged Cittyes ayde, ... Ovid's Elegies 1.6.29
RAMPIERS
The Bulwarks and the rampiers large and strong, . . . 2Tamb 3.2.70 Tamb
That rampiers fallen down, huge heapes of stone/Lye in our Lucan, First Booke 25
RAMPIRE
And suddaine rampire raisde of turfe snatcht up/Would make them Lucan, First Booke 515
RAMS
Which thousand battering Rams could never pierce, . . . Dido 2.1.175 Aeneas
And Rams with hornes their hard heads wreathed back. . Ovid's Elegies 3.12.17
Who builds a pallace and rams up the gate, ... Hero and Leander 1.239
RAMUS
That frightes poore Ramus sitting at his book? . . . . P 362 7.2 Ramus
Flye Ramus flye, if thou wilt save thy life. . . . . P 365 7.5 Taleus
Tis Taleus, Ramus bedfellow. . . . . P 372 7.12 Retes
I am as Ramus is, a Christian. . . . . P 374 7.14 Taleus
Come Ramus, more golde, or thou shalt have the stabbe. . P 376 7.16 Gonzag
Tis Ramus, the Kings professor of Logick. . . . . . P 381 7.21 Retes
Wherein hath Ramus been so offencious? . . . . . P 384 7.24 Ramus
To contradict which, I say Ramus shall dye: . . . . P 396 7.36 Guise
RAN (See also RANNE)
Ran in the thickest throngs, and with this sword/Sent many of Dido 2.1.211 Aeneas
Who then ran to the pallace of the King, ... Dido 2.1.224 Aeneas
And then in triumph ran into the streetes, ... Dido 2.1.261 Aeneas
Enrag'd I ran about the fields for thee, ... 2Tamb 4.2.17 Therid
When for her sake I ran at tilt in Fraunce, ... Edw 5.5.69 Edward
So ran the people foorth to gaze upon her, ... Hero and Leander 1.117
away she ran,/After went Mercurie, who us'd such cunning, Hero and Leander 1.416
And ran into the darke her selfe to hide, ... Hero and Leander 2.239
And ran before, as Harbenger of light, ... Hero and Leander 2.331
RANCK
wheeles spun/And what with Mares ranck humour may be done. Ovid's Elegies 1.8.8
RANCKLE
And therewithall their knees would ranckle, so/That I have Jew 2.3.210 Ithimr
RANCOR
As with the wings of rancor and disdaine, ... Edw 5.1.20 Edward
RANCOROUS
And in your shields display your rancorous minds? . . . Edw 2.2.33 Edward
RANDOM
The bullets fly at random where they list. . . . . 2Tamb 4.1.52 Calyph
RANDOME
lawlesse/And casuall; all the starres at randome radge <range>: Lucan, First Booke 642
RANG'D
And here and there her eies through anger rang'd. . . Hero and Leander 1.360
RANGE (See also RAUNGE)
lawlesse/And casuall; all the starres at randome radge <range>: Lucan, First Booke 642
Horse freed from service range abroad the woods. . . Ovid's Elegies 2.9.22

RANGING			
But my ambitious ranging mind approoves?	Ovid's Elegies	2.4.48	
RANK (See RANCK)			
RANKER			
A ranker route of rebels never was:	Edw	3.1.154	Edward
RANNE			
a dead blacknesse/Ranne through the bloud, that turn'd it all	Lucan, First Booke	618	
Hearing her to be sicke, I thether ranne,	Ovid's Elegies	3.10.25	
RANSACKE			
Ransacke the tents and the pavilions/Of these proud Turks, and	2Tamb	4.1.160	Tamb
Ransacke the Ocean for Orient Pearle,	F 110	1.1.82	Faust
RANSACKT			
Bring him forth, and let us know if the towne be ransackt.	1Tamb	5.1.195 P	Tamb
and al the world/Ransackt for golde, which breeds the world	Lucan, First Booke	168	
RANSOM			
Not all the world shall ransom Bajazeth.	1Tamb	3.3.232	Tamb
RANSOM'D			
his chaine shall serve/For Manackles, till he be ransom'd home.	1Tamb	1.2.148	Tamb
[Yet for Christs sake, whose bloud hath ransom'd me],	F1959	5.2.163A	Faust
RANSOMD			
Weel have him ransomd man, be of good cheere.	Edw	2.2.116	Lncstr
RANSOME			
Whose ransome made them martch in coates of gold,	1Tamb	1.1.143	Ceneus
May serve for ransome to our liberties:	1Tamb	1.2.75	Agidas
And ransome them with fame and usurie.	1Tamb	2.5.43	Cosroe
Yet set a ransome on me Tamburlaine.	1Tamb	3.3.261	Bajzth
Shall ransome him, or take him from his cage.	1Tamb	4.2.94	Tamb
in, not heaven it selfe/Shall ransome thee, thy wife and family.	2Tamb	3.3.28	Therid
And offer'd me as ransome for thy life,	2Tamb	5.1.156	Tamb
in peril of calamity/To ransome great Kings from captivity.	Jew	1.1.32	Barab
They rate his ransome at five thousand pound.	Edw	2.2.117	Mortmr
Cosin, and if he will not ransome him,	Edw	2.2.127	Mortmr
Then ransome him.	Edw	2.2.143	Edward
Twas in your wars, you should ransome him.	Edw	2.2.144	Lncstr
And you shall ransome him, or else--	Edw	2.2.145	Mortmr
not the riches of my realme/Can ransome him, ah he is markt to	Edw	3.1.4	Edward
not speake a word more for a Kings ransome <an other worde>,	F 670	2.2.119 P	Pride
I'le not speake <a word more for a kings ransome>.	F 706	(HC264)B P	Sloth
RANSOMED			
Though he be prisoner, he may be ransomed.	1Tamb	3.3.231	Zabina
RAP			
She reacht me such a rap for that I spilde,	Dido	1.1.7	Ganimd
RAPE			
And Helens rape doth haunt [ye] <thee> at the heeles.	Dido	1.1.144	Aeneas
When your offensive rape by Tamburlaine,	1Tamb	3.2.6	Agidas
pursu'd]/[With tenne yeares warre the rape of such a queene],	F1700	5.1.27A	3Schol
If Boreas beares Orithyas rape in minde,	Ovid's Elegies	1.6.53	
Murder, rape, warre, lust and trecherie,	Hero and Leander	1.457	
RAPES			
Committing headdie ryots, incest, rapes:	Hero and Leander	1.144	
RAPIERS			
run up and downe the world with these <this> case of Rapiers,	F 689	2.2.138 P	Wrath
RAPINE			
By lawlesse rapine from a silly maide.	1Tamb	1.2.10	Zenoc
That live by rapine and by lawlesse spoile,	1Tamb	2.2.23	Meandr
Compact of Rapine, Pyracie, and spoile,	1Tamb	4.3.8	Souldn
The soildiours pray, and rapine brought in ryot,	Lucan, First Booke	163	
RAPT			
And every warriour that is rapt with love/Of fame, of valour,	1Tamb	5.1.180	Tamb
Envy hath rapt thee, no fierce warres thou movedst,	Ovid's Elegies	2.6.25	
When nimph-Neaera rapt thy lookes Scamander.	Ovid's Elegies	3.5.28	
RARE			
and from Padua/Were wont to come rare witted Gentlemen,	Jew	3.1.7	Curtzn
To the Bishop of Millaine, for this so rare a present.	F1042	3.2.62	Pope
and thou shalt see/This Conjurer performe such rare exploits,	F1186	4.1.32	Mrtino
had had some [rare] quality that he would not have me know of,	F1542	4.5.38 P	HrsCsr
great bellyed women, do long for things, are rare and dainty.	F1569	4.6.12 P	Faust
world can compare with thee, for the rare effects of Magicke:	F App	p.236 3 P	Emper
had some rare qualitie that he would not have had me knowne of,	F App	p.240 132 P	HrsCsr
Aye me rare gifts unworthy such a happe.	Ovid's Elegies	1.14.54	
Thy tunes let this rare birdes sad funerall borrowe,	Ovid's Elegies	2.6.9	
Such sights as this, to tender maids are rare.	Hero and Leander	2.238	
RAREST			
Faustus had with pleasure tane the view]/[Of rarest things,	F1139	3.3.52A	3Chor
But what availde this faith? her rarest hue?	Ovid's Elegies	2.6.17	
RARE WITTED			
and from Padua/Were wont to come rare witted Gentlemen,	Jew	3.1.7	Curtzn
RASCALL (See also RASKALL)			
Out envious wretch <Away envious rascall>:	F 685	2.2.134	Faust
RASCALS			
Will you sir? Commit the Rascals.	F1602	4.6.45	Duke
RASE (Homograph; See also RAISE)			
Are not we both sprong of celestiall rase,	Dido	3.2.28	Juno
Intending but to rase my charmed skin:	1Tamb	1.2.179	Tamb
RASH			
Rash boy, who gave thee power to change a line?	Ovid's Elegies	1.1.9	
For rage against my wench mov'd my rash arme,	Ovid's Elegies	1.7.3	
Now rash accusing, and thy vaine beliefe,	Ovid's Elegies	2.7.13	
RASHLY			
Bacchinall/That tyr'd doth rashly on the greene grasse fall.	Ovid's Elegies	1.14.22	
Which rashly twixt the sharpe rocks in the deepe,	Ovid's Elegies	2.11.3	
While rashly her wombes burthen she casts out,	Ovid's Elegies	2.13.1	
RASHNESSE			
To purge the rashnesse of this cursed deed,	F1121	3.3.38	Mephst

RASHNESSE (cont.)			
Yet she this rashnesse sodainly repented,	Hero and Leander	2.33	
RASKALL			
Oh raskall! I change my selfe twice a day.	Jew	4.4.65	Barab
RA'ST			
Albeit the Citty thou wouldst have so ra'st/Be Roome it selfe.	Lucan, First Booke	386	
RASTE			
And with a wantons tooth, your necke new raste?	Ovid's Elegies	3.13.34	
RAT (See alsc RATTE)			
to a Dog, or a Cat, or a Mouse, or a Rat, or any thing.	F 383	1.4.41	P Wagner
A Dog, or a Cat, or a Mouse, or a Rat?	F 384	1.4.42	P Robin
RATE			
Had they beene valued at indifferent rate,	Jew	1.2.186	Barab
They rate his ransome at five thousand pound.	Edw	2.2.117	Mortmr
RATED			
As one of them indifferently rated,	Jew	1.1.29	Barab
RATEST			
Ratest thou this Moore but at two hundred plats?	Jew	2.3.107	Lodowk
RATHER			
The rather for that one Laocoon/Breaking a speare upon his	Dido	2.1.164	Aeneas
And rather had seeme faire [to] Sirens eyes,	Dido	3.4.39	Dido
Rather Ascania by your little sonne.	Dido	5.1.21	Serg
But rather will augment then ease my woe?	Dido	5.1.152	Dido
Stil dooth this man or rather God of war,	1Tamb	5.1.1	Govnr
Rather than yeeld to his detested suit,	2Tamb	4.2.6	Olymp
teare both cur limmes/Rather then we should draw thy chariot,	2Tamb	5.1.139	Orcan
Rather lend me thy weapon Tamburlain,	2Tamb	5.1.142	Jrslem
Rather had I a Jew be hated thus,	Jew	1.1.114	Barab
For I had rather dye, then see her thus.	Jew	1.2.357	Barab
But rather let the brightsome heavens be dim,	Jew	2.3.330	Lodowk
And on that rather should Ferneze dye.	Jew	3.2.26	Govnr
Now am I cleane, or rather fouly out of the way.	Jew	4.2.47	P Ithimr
Rather for feare then love.	Jew	4.2.107	P Ithimr
I'le rather--	Jew	4.3.23	P Barab
Rather then thus to live as Turkish thrals,	Jew	5.4.8	1Knght
But I have rather chose to save thy life.	Jew	5.5.94	Govnr
Nay rather, Christians, let me goe to Turkey,	Jew	5.5.115	Calym
And rather seeke to scourge their enemies,	P 217	4.15	Anjoy
And rather chuse to seek your countries good,	P 221	4.19	Guise
for rather then my lord/Shall be opprest by civill mutinies,	Edw	1.2.64	Queene
No, rather will I die a thousand deaths,	Edw	1.4.196	Queene
Ile rather loose his friendship I, then graunt.	Edw	1.4.237	Lncstr
But rather praise him for that brave attempt,	Edw	1.4.268	Mortmr
So will I, rather then with Gaveston.	Edw	2.2.215	Kent
Nay, rather saile with us to Scarborough.	Edw	2.4.52	Mortmr
Demanding him of them, entreating rather,	Edw	3.1.97	Arundl
And rather bathe thy sword in subjects bloud,	Edw	3.1.212	Mortmr
I traitors all, rather then thus be bravde,	Edw	3.1.214	Edward
Yet stay, for rather then I will looke on them,	Edw	5.1.106	Edward
Madam, intreat not, I will rather die,	Edw	5.6.56	Mortmr
Rather illusions, fruits of lunacy,	F 407	2.1.19	BdAngl
We'le rather die with griefe, then live with shame.	F1456	4.3.26	Benvol
Rather thou large banke over-flowing river,	Ovid's Elegies	3.5.19	
Rather Ile hoist up saile, and use the winde,	Ovid's Elegies	3.10.51	
Unto her was he led, or rather drawne,	Hero and Leander	2.241	
RATIFIDE			
And what she likes, let both hold ratifide.	Ovid's Elegies	2.2.32	
RATIFIE			
For what he doth the Pope will ratifie:	P 40	1.40	Condy
What you determine, I will ratifie.	P 227	4.25	Charls
RATIFIED			
let peace be ratified/On these conditions specified before,	2Tamb	1.1.124	Orcan
RATLING			
The crye of beasts, the ratling of the windes,	Dido	2.1.336	Venus
And ratling cannons thunder in our eares/Our proper ruine,	2Tamb	4.1.13	Amyras
Sends foorth a ratling murmure to the land,	Hero and Leander	1.348	
RATTE			
to a dogge, or a catte, or a mouse, or a ratte, or any thing.	F App	p.231 59	P Wagner
a Christian fellow to a dogge or a catte, a mouse or a ratte?	F App	p.231 61	P Clown
RATTLE			
Will rattle foorth his facts of war and blood.	1Tamb	3.2.45	Agidas
While thundring Cannons rattle on their Skins.	1Tamb	4.1.11	Souldn
RAUGHT			
The lofty Pine from high mount Pelion raught/Ill waies by rough	Ovid's Elegies	2.11.1	
RAUNGE			
And like the Planets ever love to raunge:	Dido	3.3.68	Iarbus
RAUNSOME			
I'le not speake <an other word for a King's raunsome>.	F 706	(HC264)A	P Sloth
RAVE			
What meanes my sister thus to rave and crye?	Dido	5.1.193	Anna
And must I rave thus for a runnagate?	Dido	5.1.265	Dido
RAVEN			
Thus like the sad presaging Raven that tolls/The sicke mans	Jew	2.1.1	Barab
And for the Raven wake the morning Larke,	Jew	2.1.61	Barab
RAVENOUS			
The ravenous vulture lives, the Puttock hovers/Around the aire,	Ovid's Elegies	2.6.33	
RAVENS			
and fit for nought/But perches for the black and fatall Ravens.	2Tamb	4.3.23	Tamb
a fellow met me with a muschatoes like a Ravens wing, and a	Jew	4.2.28	P Ithimr
RAVES			
Raves in Egyptia, and annoyeth us.	1Tamb	4.3.10	Souldn
As [Maenas] <Maenus> full of wine on Pindus raves,	Lucan, First Booke	674	
RAVING			
Raving, impatient, desperate and mad,	2Tamb	2.4.112	Tamb

RAVISHED
my thoughts are ravished so/With sight of this renowned . F1260 4.1.106 Emper
RAVISHING
walles of Thebes/With ravishing sound of his melodious Harpe, F 580 2.2.29 Faust
RAVISHT
Whom Ajax ravisht in Dianas [Fane] <Fawne>, . . . Dido 2.1.275 Aeneas
Sweet Analitikes <Anulatikes>, tis thou hast ravisht me, . F 34 1.1.6 Faust
'Tis magick, magick, that hath ravisht me. . . . F 137 1.1.109 Faust
RAW
Tamburlane) as I could willingly feed upon thy blood-raw hart. 1Tamb 4.4.12 P Bajzth
You shal be fed with flesh as raw as blood, . . . 2Tamb 4.3.18 Tamb
to the devill, for a shoulder of Mutton, tho it were bloud raw. F 351 1.4.9 P Wagner
I am one that loves an inch of raw Mutton, better then an ell F 708 2.2.160 P Ltchry
Raw soldiours lately prest; and troupes of gownes; . . Lucan, First Booke 312
Albeit Leander rude in love, and raw, ... Hero and Leander 2.61
RAWE
the Divel for a shoulder of mutton, though it were blood rawe. F App p.229 9 P Wagner
to the Divel for a shoulder of mutton though twere blood rawe? F App p.229 11 P Clown
they manadge peace, and rawe warres bloudy jawes, . . Ovid's Elegies 3.7.58
RAY (See also RAIES)
Who'le set the faire treste [sunne] <sonne> in battell ray, Ovid's Elegies 1.1.15
While thus I speake, blacke dust her white robes ray: . Ovid's Elegies 3.2.41
RAYES
Outshines Cinthia's rayes: . . . . Jew 2.3.62 Barab
O Phoebus shouldst thou with thy rayes now sing/The fell Nemean Lucan, First Booke 654
RAYMOND
Lord Raymond-- . . . . F 890 3.1.112 Pope
And with Lord Raymond, King of Hungary, ... F 979 3.1.201 Pope
Lord Raymond, take your seate, Friers attend, . . . F1010 3.2.30 Pope
Lord Raymond pray fall too, I am beholding/To the Bishop of F1041 3.2.61 Pope
Lord Raymond, I drink unto your grace. . . . . F1053 3.2.73 Pope
RAZE (See RA'ST, RAISE, RASE)
RE
you thinke to carry it away with your Hey-passe, and Re-passe: F1665 4.6.108 P Robin
Which makes him quickly re-enforce his speech, . . . Hero and Leander 1.313
REACH
Gentle Achates, reach the Tinder boxe, ... Dido 1.1.166 Aeneas
That it may reach the King of Perseas crowne, . . . 1Tamb 2.3.53 Cosroe
Untill we reach the ripest fruit of all, ... 1Tamb 2.7.27 Tamb
Whose flaming traines should reach down to the earth/Could not 2Tamb 5.1.90 Tamb
That like I best that flyes beyond my reach. . . . P 99 2.42 Guise
of your Prince Electors, farre/Beyond the reach of my desertes: P 453 8.3 Anjoy
His waxen wings did mount above his reach, . . . F 21 Prol.21 1Chor
To over-reach the Divell, but all in vaine; . . . F1811 5.2.15 Mephst
Farre off be force, no fire to them may reach, . . . Ovid's Elegies 1.14.29
REACHES
in a myrrour we perceive/The highest reaches of a humaine wit: 1Tamb 5.1.168 Tamb
REACHING
A reaching thought will search his deepest wits, . . Jew 1.2.221 Barab
REACHT
She reacht me such a rap for that I spilde, . . . Dido 1.1.7 Ganimd
From whence her vaile reacht to the ground beneath. . . Hero and Leander 1.18
READ (See also RED)
Wel, wel (Meander) thou art deeply read: . . . . . 1Tamb 2.2.55 Mycet
Read on. . . . . Jew 1.2.72 Govnr
Ile read them Frier, and then Ile answere thee. . . . P1171 22.33 King
Having read unto her since she was a childe. . . . . Edw 2.1.30 Baldck
Read it Spencer. . . . . Edw 4.3.11 Edward
But read it thus, and thats an other sence: . . . Edw 5.4.10 Mortmr
Then read no more, thou hast attain'd that <the> end; . F 38 1.1.10 Faust
I'le have them read me strange Philosophy, ... F 113 1.1.85 Faust
Then heare me read it Mephostophilis <them>. . . . F 483 2.1.95 Faust
I cannot read, and therefore wish all books burn'd <were . F 680 2.2.129 P Envy
And read amongst the Statutes Decretall, ... F 883 3.1.105 Pope
I had never seene Wittenberg <Wertenberge>, never read book: F1842 5.2.46 P Faust
they that keepe, and read/Sybillas secret works, and [wash] Lucan, First Booke 598
Lines thou shalt read in wine by my hand writ. . . . Ovid's Elegies 1.4.20
Straight being read, will her to write much backe, . . Ovid's Elegies 1.11.19
Aeneas warre, and Titerus shall be read, ... Ovid's Elegies 1.15.25
It is more safe to sleepe, to read a booke, . . . Ovid's Elegies 2.11.31
Phedra, and Hipolite may read, my care is, . . . Ovid's Elegies 2.18.24
The stepdame read Hyppolitus lustlesse line. . . . Ovid's Elegies 2.18.30
READE
Yet will they reade me, and thereby attaine/To Peters Chayre: Jew Prol.11 Machvl
To reade a lecture here in [Britanie] <Britaine>, . . Jew Prol.29 Machvl
Reade there the Articles of our decrees. . . . . Jew 1.2.67 Govnr
Reade. . . . . Edw 4.3.27 Edward
Reade, reade the Scriptures: that is blasphemy. . . . F 100 1.1.72 GdAngl
what doest thou with that same booke thou canst not reade? F App p.233 14 P Rafe
my maister and mistris shal finde that I can reade, he for his F App p.233 15 P Robin
And rude boyes toucht with unknowne love me reade, . . Ovid's Elegies 2.1.6
And Phillis hath to reade; if now she lives. . . . Ovid's Elegies 2.18.32
READES
Thinke when she reades, her mother letters sent her, . Ovid's Elegies 2.2.19
READIE
That now are readie to assaile the Scots. . . . . Edw 1.4.363 Edward
See that my coache be readie, I must hence. . . . Edw 2.1.71 Neece
Here is a Litter readie for your grace, ... Edw 4.7.84 Leistr
He readie to accomplish what she wil'd, ... Hero and Leander 1.433
READINES
there are in readines/Ten thousand horse to carie you from 1Tamb 1.1.184 Ortyg
Of all my army now in readines, ... P 744 15.2 King
READINESSE
I cannot choose but like thy readinesse: . . . . . Jew 2.3.377 Baraba

READINESSE (cont.)			
And see that all things be in readinesse,	F1011	3.2.31	Pope
Go backe, and see the State in readinesse.	F1159	4.1.5	Mrtino
Come sirs, prepare your selves in readinesse,	F1420	4.2.96	1Soldr
READING			
for at the reading of the letter, he look'd like a man of	Jew	4.2.6	P Pilia
At reading of the letter, he star'd and stamp'd, and turnd	Jew	4.2.104	P Pilia
If reading five thou plainst of tediousnesse,	Ovid's Elegies		1.1.3
I charge thee marke her eyes and front in reading,	Ovid's Elegies		1.11.17
From no mans reading fearing to be sav'd.	Ovid's Elegies		3.1.54
READS			
To such a one my Lord, as when she reads my lines,	P 672	13.16	Duchss
READY			
discovered the enemie/Ready to chardge you with a mighty armie.	1Tamb	2.3.50	1Msngr
Till we have made us ready for the field.	1Tamb	5.1.212	Tamb
Make ready my Coch, my chaire, my jewels, I come, I come, I	1Tamb	5.1.317	P Zabina
Ready for battaile gainst my Lord the King.	1Tamb	5.1.382	Philem
My hand is ready to performe the deed,	1Tamb	5.1.503	Techel
Ready to charge you ere you stir your feet.	2Tamb	1.1.121	Fredrk
When you will my Lord, I am ready.	2Tamb	1.2.76	Almeda
Ready to darken earth with endlesse night:	2Tamb	2.4.7	Tamb
Ready to charge the army of the Turke.	2Tamb	3.4.87	Therid
Ready to levie power against thy throne,	2Tamb	4.1.117	Tamb
Wee may lie ready to encounter him,	2Tamb	5.2.8	Callap
And see, a staffe stands ready for the purpose:	Jew	4.1.172	1Fryar
he was ready to leape off e're the halter was about his necke;	Jew	4.2.22	P Ithimr
Now Captain of my guarde, are these murtherers ready?	P 947	19.17	King
Ready to execute what thou commandst <desirst>.	F 549	2.1.161	Mephst
Be ready then, and strike the Peasant downe.	F1359	4.2.35	Fredrk
of golden plate; besides two thousand duckets ready coin'd:	F1676	5.1.3	P Wagner
I am ready to accomplish your request, so farre forth as by art	F App	p.237 37	P Faust
Where men are ready, lingering ever hurts:	Lucan, First Booke		282
had bin fierd/Or dropping-ripe, ready to fall with Ruine,	Lucan, First Booke		491
When thou stood'st naked ready to be beate,	Ovid's Elegies		1.6.19
And souldiours make them ready to the fight,	Ovid's Elegies		1.13.14
REAER'D			
That now the walles of houses halfe [rear'd] <reaer'd> totter,	Lucan, First Booke		24
REALME (See also REAMES)			
Hermes awake, and haste to Neptunes realme,	Dido	1.1.114	Jupitr
My realme, the Center of our Empery/Once lost, All Turkie would	2Tamb	1.1.55	Orcan
if any Christian King/Encroche upon the confines of thy realme,	2Tamb	1.1.147	Orcan
Weakneth his body, and will waste his Realme,	P 128	2.71	Guise
And disperse themselves throughout the Realme of France,	P 507	9.26	QnMoth
For heers no saftie in the Realme for me,	P 568	11.33	Navrre.
The ruine of that famous Realme of France:	P 922	18.23	Navrre
To plant the Pope and popelings in the Realme,	P 925	18.26	Navrre
That basely seekes the ruine of his Realme.	P 930	18.31	Navrre
Traitor to God, and to the realme of France.	P1076	19.146	QnMoth
That he should nere returne into the realme:	Edw	1.1.84	Mortmr
Ere Gaveston shall stay within the realme.	Edw	1.1.105	Lncstr
I, and besides, lord Chamberlaine of the realme,	Edw	1.2.13	Warwck
Will be the ruine of the realme and us.	Edw	1.2.32	Mortmr
Learne then to rule us better and the realme.	Edw	1.4.39	Lncstr
My lord, you shalbe Chauncellor of the realme,	Edw	1.4.65	Edward
Are you content to banish him the realme?	Edw	1.4.84	ArchBp
For purging of the realme of such a plague.	Edw	1.4.270	Mortmr
I make thee heere lord Marshall of the realme.	Edw	1.4.356	Edward
And riote it with the treasure of the realme,	Edw	1.4.405	Mortmr
To gather for him thoroughout the realme.	Edw	2.2.148	Edward
Will be the ruine of the realme and you,	Edw	2.2.209	Kent
We would but rid the realme of Gaveston,	Edw	2.4.35	Lncstr
We wot, he that the care of realme remits,	Edw	2.5.61	Warwck
Ah Spencer, not the riches of my realme/Can ransome him, ah he	Edw	3.1.3	Edward
These Barons thus to beard me in my land,/In mine owne realme?	Edw	3.1.15	Spencr
they say there is great execution/Done through the realme, my	Edw	4.3.7	Edward
Lord warden of the realme, and sith the fates/Have made his	Edw	4.6.26	Queene
But as the realme and parlement shall please,	Edw	4.6.36	Mortmr
This, Edward, is the ruine of the realme.	Edw	4.6.45	Kent
Be rulde by me, and we will rule the realme,	Edw	5.2.5	Mortmr
sure, the Queene and Mortimer/Shall rule the realme, the king,	Edw	5.4.66	Mortmr
From Paris next, costing the Realme of France,	F 784	3.1.6	Faust
Why seek'st not heav'n the third realme to frequent?	Ovid's Elegies		3.7.50
REALMES			
And in your quarrell and the realmes behoofe,	Edw	2.3.3	Kent
Tis for your highnesse good, and for the realmes.	Edw	5.4.101	Mortmr
REALMS			
Nay, for the realms behoofe and for the kings.	Edw	1.4.243	Mortmr
REAME			
Give me a Reame of paper, we'll have a kingdome of gold for't.	Jew	4.2.115	P Ithimr
REAMES (Homograph)			
Commaunds me leave these unrenowmed [reames] <beames>,	Dido	4.3.18	Aeneas
Lord Archbishop of Reames, sit downe with us.	F1037	3.2.57	Pope
REAPE			
And reape no guerdon for my truest love?	Dido	5.1.282	Iarbus
No doubt your soule shall reape the fruit of it.	Jew	2.3.78	Lodowk
'Tis likely they in time may reape some fruit,	Jew	2.3.84	Barab
by the pleasure/Which man and woman reape in equall measure?	Ovid's Elegies		1.10.36
Do this and soone thou shalt thy freedome reape.	Ovid's Elegies		2.2.40
REAPT			
What should I talke of mens corne reapt by force,	Lucan, First Booke		318
The richest corne dies, if it be not reapt,	Hero and Leander		1.327
REAR'D			
That now the walles of houses halfe [rear'd] <reaer'd> totter,	Lucan, First Booke		24

REARE			
And higher would I reare my estimate, ...	1Tamb	3.2.53	Zenoc
Then reare your standardes, let your sounding Drummes/Direct	1Tamb	4.3.61	Souldn
I'le reare up Malta now remedilesse.	Jew	5.2.73	Barab
REARS			
With what a majesty he rears his looks:--	1Tamb	1.2.165	Tamb
REASON			
Which neither art nor reason may atchieve, ...	Dido	5.1.65	Aeneas
but cannot compasse it/By reason of the warres, that robb'd our	Jew	1.2.48	Govnr
nay we dare not give consent/By reason of a Tributary league.	Jew	2.2.23	Govnr
And reason too;	Jew	4.1.12	Ithimr
Yes; and I know not what the reason is:	Jew	4.1.130	Ithimr
I wonder what the reason is.	Jew	4.2.32	P Ithimr
This is the reason that I sent for thee;	Jew	5.2.51	Barab
I see no reason but of Malta's wracke, ...	Jew	5.2.58	Govnr
And reason too, for Christians doe the like:	Jew	5.2.116	Barab
But whats the reason you should leave him now? . . .	Edw	2.3.13	Penbrk
Is that the reason why he tempts us thus?	F 430	2.1.42	Faust
And reason <argue> of divine Astrology.	F 585	2.2.34	Faust
What is the reason you disturbe the Duke?	F1592	4.6.35	Servnt
We have no reason for it, therefore a fig for him. . .	F1593	4.6.36	P Dick
The reason no man knowes, let it suffise, ...	Hero and Leander		1.173
REASONABLE			
Come, I have made a reasonable market, ...	Jew	2.3.161	1Offcr
REASONS			
With reasons of his valour and his life, ...	1Tamb	2.1.38	Cosroe
I hope these reasons may serve my princely Sonne, . . .	P 223	4.21	QnMoth
And I will tell thee reasons of such waighte, ...	Edw	1.4.226	Queene
Such reasons make white blacke, and darke night day. .	Edw	1.4.247	Lncstr
A hundred reasons makes <make> me ever love. . . .	Ovid's Elegies		2.4.10
REAVE (See also RAUGHT)			
T'escape their hands that seeke to reave his life: . . .	Edw	4.7.52	Leistr
REBATED			
And you shall se't rebated with the blow.	2Tamb	4.2.70	Olymp
REBELL			
How Carthage did rebell, Iarbus storme, ...	Dido	5.1.143	Dido
Meane while, have hence this rebell to the blocke, . .	Edw	4.6.69	Mortmr
Rebell is he that fights against his prince, ...	Edw	4.6.71	SpncrP
REBELLING			
The nature of these proud rebelling Jades/Wil take occasion by	2Tamb	5.3.238	Tamb
REBELLION			
Looke for rebellion, looke to be deposde, ...	Edw	2.2.161	Lncstr
REBELLIOUS			
nostreis breathe/Rebellious winds and dreadfull thunderclaps:	1Tamb	5.1.298	Bajzth
With the rebellious King of Navarre, ...	P 517	9.36	Cardnl
To march against the rebellious King Navarre:	P 745	15.3	King
Traitor on thy face, rebellious Lancaster.	Edw	3.1.204	Spencr
To follow these rebellious runnagates.	Edw	4.6.76	Mortmr
REBELS			
Sweet Epernoune all Rebels under heaven, ...	P1185	22.47	King
Fire Paris where these trecherous rebels lurke. . . .	P1241	22.103	King
Have at the rebels, and their complices.	Edw	2.2.265	Edward
That muster rebels thus against your king)/To see his royall	Edw	2.5.6	Gavstn
And tell me, would the rebels denie me that?	Edw	3.1.101	Edward
A ranker route of rebels never was:	Edw	3.1.154	Edward
Rebels, will they appoint their soveraigne/His sports, his	Edw	3.1.174	Edward
My [lords] <lord>, perceive you how these rebels swell: .	Edw	3.1.181	Edward
with my sword/On those proud rebels that are up in armes,	Edw	3.1.187	Edward
Heere come the rebels.	Edw	3.1.194	Spencr
What rebels, do you shrinke, and sound retreat? . . .	Edw	3.1.200	Edward
A rebels, recreants, you made him away.	Edw	3.1.229	Edward
REBUKE			
And so have hope, that this my kinde rebuke, ...	F1722	5.1.49	OldMan
REBUK'T			
And for the same mildly rebuk't his sonne, ...	Hero and Leander		2.137
REBUKT			
And in his name rebukt me bitterly, ...	Dido	5.1.96	Aeneas
RECALL'D			
And now it cannot be recall'd.	Jew	1.2.93	Govnr
RECEAVE			
Women receave perfection everie way.	Hero and Leander		1.268
RECEIV'D			
So much have I receiv'd at Didos hands, ...	Dido	3.1.103	Aeneas
The generall welcomes Tamburlain receiv'd, ...	2Tamb	Prol.1	Prolog
Which is no sooner receiv'd but it is spent. . . .	P 379	7.19	Ramus
Which cannot but be thankfully receiv'd.	P 906	18.7	Bartus
The Parrat into wood receiv'd with these, ...	Ovid's Elègies		2.6.57
RECEIVDE			
Why see I lines so oft receivde and given, ...	Ovid's Elegies		3.13.31
RECEIVE			
Where Dido will receive ye with her smiles:	Dido	1.1.234	Venus
I willingly receive th'emperiall crowne, ...	1Tamb	1.1.157	Cosroe
Wel said Argier, receive thy crowne againe.	2Tamb	1.3.127	Tamb
Come Almeda, receive this crowne of me, ...	2Tamb	3.5.129	Callap
Here Jove, receive his fainting soule againe, ...	2Tamb	4.1.111	Tamb
Receive them free, and sell them by the weight; . . .	Jew	1.1.24	Barab
Come and receive the Treasure I have found.	Jew	2.1.38	Abigal
Then father here receive thy happinesse.	Jew	2.1.44	Abigal
Does she receive them?	Jew	2.3.260	Mthias
Therefore to equall it receive my hart.	Edw	1.1.162	Edward
receive my seale,/Save or condemne, and in our name commaund,	Edw	1.1.168	Edward
Be thou lord bishop, and receive his rents, ...	Edw	1.1.194	Edward
Once more receive my hand, and let this be, ...	Edw	1.4.334	Edward

RECEIVE (cont.)

Refusing to receive me pledge for him, ... Edw 3.1.107 Arundl
So shall my eyes receive their last content, ... Edw 5.1.61 Edward
heere receive my crowne. . . . . Edw 5.1.97 Edward
Receive it? . . . . Edw 5.1.98 Edward
One jewell have I left, receive thou this. . . . . Edw 5.1.98 Edward
Assist me sweete God, and receive my soule. . . . . Edw 5.5.84 Edward
[That will receive no object, for my head]/[But ruminates on F 131 1.1.103A Faust
Then Mephostophilis receive this scrole, ... Edw 5.5.109 Edward
Then Mephostophilis receive this scrole, ... F 477 2.1.89 Faust
<Here Mephastophilis> receive this scrole, ... F 477 (HC260)A Faust
That we receive such great indignity? . . . . . F1050 3.2.70 Pope
The jawes of hell are open to receive thee. . . . . F1908 5.2.112 GdAngl
Come, maister Doctor follow us, and receive your reward. . F App p.243 33 P Duke
Receive with shouts; where thou wilt raigne as King, . Lucan, First Booke 47
Take, and receive each secret amorous glaunce. . . . Ovid's Elegies 1.4.18
Receive him soone, least patient use he gaine, . . . Ovid's Elegies 1.8.75
Receive these lines, them to my Mistrisse carry, . . . Ovid's Elegies 1.11.7
For after death all men receive their right: . . . . Ovid's Elegies 1.15.40
For others faults, why do I losse receive? . . . . Ovid's Elegies 3.3.16
She held her lap ope to receive the same. . . . . Ovid's Elegies 3.7.34
The locks spred on his necke receive his teares, . . . Ovid's Elegies 3.8.11

RECEIVED

Memnon the elfe/Received his cole-blacke colour from thy selfe. Ovid's Elegies 1.13.32
I wisht to be received in, <and> in I [get] <got> me, . Ovid's Elegies 3.6.47

RECEIVEDST

As thou receivedst thy life from me, ... Edw 5.6.68 Queene

RECEIVES

Receives no blemish, but oft-times more grace, ... Hero and Leander 1.217

RECKLESSE

He recklesse of his promise, did despise/The love of . Hero and Leander 1.461

RECKNING

And usde such slender reckning of [your] <you> majesty. . 2Tamb 5.1.83 Therid

RECLAIM'D

And be reclaim'd with princely lenitie. . . . . . 1Tamb 2.2.38 Meandr
mornings next arise/For messenger, he will not be reclaim'd, 1Tamb 3.1.39 Bajzth

RECLAIMD

And Gaveston unlesse thou be reclaimd, ... Edw 1.1.183 BshpCv
Would all were well, and Edward well reclaimd, ... Edw 4.2.57 Kent

RECLAIME

<and see if hee by> his grave counsell may <can> reclaime him. F 226 1.2.33 2Schol
<O but> I feare me, nothing will <can> reclaime him now. . F 227 1.2.34 1Schol

RECOMPENC'D

To know their rites, well recompenc'd my stay, ... Ovid's Elegies 3.12.5

RECOMPENCE

Since that religion hath no recompence. . . . . . Dido 1.1.81 Venus
privately procure/Great summes of mony for thy recompence: Jew 5.2.88 Govnr
To recompence your reconciled love, ... P1144 22.6 King
In recompence of this thy high desert, ... F1322 4.1.168 Emper
I, [all] <I call> your hearts to recompence this deed. . F1394 4.2.70 Faust
recompence your great deserts in erecting that inchanted Castle F1559 4.6.2 P Duke
which we will recompence/With all the love and kindnesse that F1671 4.6.114 Duke

RECOMPENCED

highly recompenced, in that it pleaseth your grace to thinke F1563 4.6.6 P Faust

RECONCIL'D

And so was reconcil'd to Menelaus. . . . . Dido 2.1.299 Achat

RECONCILD

And Mowberie and he were reconcild: . . . . Edw 1.1.115 Kent
Or thou shalt nere be reconcild to me. . . . . . . Edw 1.4.157 Edward

RECONCILE

Whose bloud will reconcile thee to content, ... Dido 3.3.74 Iarbus
But I would wish thee reconcile the lords, ... Edw 1.4.156 Edward

RECONCILED

To recompence your reconciled love, ... P1144 22.6 King

RECONCILEMENT

Is this the fruite your reconcilement beares? . . . . Edw 2.2.31 Edward

RECONCILEMENTS

Well could I like this reconcilements meanes, ... Dido 3.2.81 Venus

RECORD

I record heaven, her heavenly selfe is cleare: . . . . 1Tamb 5.1.487 Tamb
And calling Christ for record of our trueths? . . . . 2Tamb 2.1.30 Sgsmnd
When I record my Parents slavish life, ... 2Tamb 5.2.19 Callap
There Paris is, and Helens crymes record, ... Ovid's Elegies 2.18.37
Tis not enough, she shakes your record off, ... Ovid's Elegies 3.3.19
Nor, as use will not Poets record heare, ... Ovid's Elegies 3.11.19

RECOVER

No doubt, but you shal soone recover all. . . . . . 2Tamb 5.3.99 Phsitn
Will Barabas recover Malta's losse? . . . . Jew 5.2.74 Govnr

RECOVERIE

And knowes no meanes of his recoverie: . . . . . . Jew 1.2.205 Barab

RECOVERY

Joy any hope of your recovery? . . . . 2Tamb 5.3.215 Usumc
things past recovery/Are hardly cur'd with exclamations. . Jew 1.2.236 Barab
asunder; so that it doth sinke/Into a deepe pit past recovery. Jew 5.5.36 Barab

RECREANTS

Proud recreants. . . . . Edw 3.1.102 Spencr
A rebels, recreants, you made him away. . . . . . . Edw 3.1.229 Edward

RECREATE

Yet never did they recreate themselves, ... 2Tamb 1.3.182 Usumc

RECTOR

But come, let us go, and informe the Rector: . . . . F 225 1.2.32 2Schol

RECURE

now, how Jove hath sent/A present medicine to recure my paine: 2Tamb 5.3.106 Tamb

RED (Homograph)

Where thou shalt see the red gild fishes leape, . . . Dido 4.5.10 Nurse

RED (cont.)
As red as scarlet is his furniture, — 1Tamb 4.1.55 — 2Msngr
Then when the Sky shal waxe as red as blood, — 1Tamb 4.2.53 — Tamb
It shall be said, I made it red my selfe, — 1Tamb 4.2.54 — Tamb
Streamers white, Red, Blacke. — 1Tamb 5.1.315 — P Zabina
Whereas the Terren and the red sea meet, — 2Tamb 5.3.132 — Tamb
And as she red, she smild, which makes me thinke, — Edw 2.1.21 — Spencr
And get me a spit, and let it be red hote. — Edw 5.5.30 — Ltborn
with me, I'le give thee white wine, red wine, claret wine, Sacke — F 748 2.3.27 — P Robin
In steed of red bloud wallowed venemous gore. — Lucan, First Booke 614
red shame becomes white cheekes, but this/If feigned, doth — Ovid's Elegies 1.8.35
Yet as if mixt with red leade thou wert ruddy, — Ovid's Elegies 1.12.11
Died red with shame, to hide from shame she seekes. — Ovid's Elegies 1.14.52
And passe our scarlet of red saffrons marke. — Ovid's Elegies 2.6.22
Faire white with rose red was before commixt: — Ovid's Elegies 3.3.5
Now shine her lookes pure white and red betwixt. — Ovid's Elegies 3.3.6
And red for anger that he stayd so long, — Hero and Leander 2.89

REDDE
Floud with [reede-growne] <redde-growne> slime bankes, till I — Ovid's Elegies 3.5.1

REDDE-GROWNE
Floud with [reede-growne] <redde-growne> slime bankes, till I — Ovid's Elegies 3.5.1

REDEEM'D
And if this Bruno thou hast late redeem'd, — F1212 4.1.58 — Emper

REDEEME
destruction/Redeeme you from this deadly servitude. — 1Tamb 3.2.34 — Agidas
Sister, Edward is my charge, redeeme him. — Edw 5.2.116 — Kent

REDELIVERED
And see him redelivered to your hands. — Edw 3.1.112 — Arundl

REDIS
[Quin redis <regis> Mephostophilis fratris imagine]. — F 262 1.3.34A — Faust

REDOUBLED
And asking why, this answeare she redoubled, — Ovid's Elegies 2.2.7
on the rushes to be flung,/Striv'd with redoubled strength: — Hero and Leander 2.67

REDOUBTED
With Guie of Warwick that redoubted knight, — Edw 1.3.4 — Gavstn

REDRESSE
Redresse these wrongs, and warne him to his ships/That now — Dido 4.2.21 — Iarbus
They gan to move him to redresse my ruth, — Dido 5.1.238 — Anna

REDUC'D
And I reduc'd it into better forme. — P 407 7.47 — Ramus

REDUCE
And with this pen reduce them to a Map, — 1Tamb 4.4.78 — Tamb
Till they reduce the wrongs done to my father. — Jew 1.2.235 — Abigal
Reduce we all our lessons unto this, — Edw 4.7.110 — Baldck
Verses [deduce] <reduce> the horned bloudy moone/And call the — Ovid's Elegies 2.1.23

REED (See also REDDE)
Instead of Sedge and Reed, beare Sugar Canes: — Jew 4.2.96 — Ithimr

REEDE
Floud with [reede-growne] <redde-growne> slime bankes, till I — Ovid's Elegies 3.5.1

REEDE-GROWNE
Floud with [reede-growne] <redde-growne> slime bankes, till I — Ovid's Elegies 3.5.1

REEDIFIED
land, whose brave Metropolis/Reedified the faire Semyramis, — 2Tamb 3.5.37 — Orcan

REEKING (See also REKING)
Are reeking water, and dull earthlie fumes. — Hero and Leander 2.116

RE-ENFORCE (See also R'ENFORCE)
Which makes him quickly re-enforce his speech, — Hero and Leander 1.313

REFER
But I refer me to my noble men, — 1Tamb 1.1.21 — Mycet

REFERD
Which we referd to justice of his Christ, — 2Tamb 2.3.28 — Orcan

REFERRE
Well Madam, I referre it to your Majestie, — P 225 4.23 — Charls
My lord, referre your vengeance to the sword, — Edw 3.1.123 — Spencr

REFINED
whose taste illuminates/Refined eies with an eternall sight, — 2Tamb 2.4.23 — Tamb

REFLECT
That as the sun-shine shall reflect ore thee: — Edw 3.1.51 — Edward

REFLECTING
glorious actes/Lightens the world with his reflecting beames, — F App p.237 26 — Emper

REFLECTS
Whose face reflects such pleasure to mine eyes, — Dido 1.1.24 — Jupitr

REFLEXE
Nor Sun reflexe his vertuous beames thereon, — 1Tamb 3.1.52 — Moroc

REFLEXING
Reflexing hewes of blood upon their heads, — 1Tamb 4.4.2 — Tamb
Reflexing them on your disdainfull eies: — 1Tamb 5.1.70 — Tamb

REFLEXIONS
That their reflexions may amaze the Perseans. — 1Tamb 1.2.140 — Tamb

REFLUENCE
Shall overflow it with their refluence. — Jew 3.5.18 — Govnr

REFRAIN'D
And some, that she refrain'd teares, have deni'd. — Ovid's Elegies 3.8.46

REFRAINE
And what eyes can refraine from shedding teares, — Edw 5.5.50 — Ltborn
Leave asking, and Ile give what I refraine. — Ovid's Elegies 1.10.64

REFRAINES
pooles, refraines/To taint his tresses in the Tyrrhen maine? — Dido 1.1.111 — Venus

REFRESHETH
And this retire refresheth horse and man. — Edw 3.1.193 — SpncrP

REFRESHING
them leave Madam, this speech is a goodly refreshing to them. — 1Tamb 4.4.33 — P Techel

REFRESHT
While these their fellow kings may be refresht. — 2Tamb 4.3.31 — Tamb

REFT
Nor hath the needle, or the combes teeth reft them, Ovid's Elegies 1.14.15
Even Jove himselfe out off my wit was reft. Ovid's Elegies 2.1.18
REFUGE
And now will work a refuge to our lives, 2Tamb 5.1.25 1Citzn
And seeking refuge, slipt into her bed. Hero and Leander 2.244
REFUSD
Enjoy the wench, let all else be refusd. Ovid's Elegies 2.2.30
REFUSDE
ruthlesse Governour/Have thus refusde the mercie of thy hand, 1Tamb 5.1.93 1Virgn
They have refusde the offer of their lives, 1Tamb 5.1.126 Tamb
why made king [to refuse] <and refusde> it? Ovid's Elegies 3.6.49
REFUSE
Which if your General refuse or scorne, 2Tamb 1.1.119 Fredrk
I see how fearfully ye would refuse, 2Tamb 3.5.73 Tamb
if he refuse, and then may we/Depose him and elect an other Edw 1.4.54 Mortmr
and doest refuse;/Well maiest thou one thing for thy Mistresse Ovid's Elegies 2.8.23
Or [be] a loade thou shouldst refuse to beare. Ovid's Elegies 2.15.22
why made king [to refuse] <and refusde> it? Ovid's Elegies 3.6.49
REFUSED
Wars dustie <rustie> honors are refused being yong, Ovid's Elegies 1.15.4
REFUSETH
That satiate with spoile refuseth blood. 1Tamb 4.1.53 2Msngr
the ungentle king/Of Fraunce refuseth to give aide of armes, Edw 4.2.62 SrJohn
REFUSING
Refusing to receive me pledge for him, Edw 3.1.107 Arundl
A mortall nimphes refusing Lord to stay. Ovid's Elegies 2.17.16
REGAL
Her left hand held abroad a regal scepter, Ovid's Elegies 3.1.13
REGALL
By due discent the Regall seat is mine. P 470 8.20 Anjoy
authority Apostolicall/Depose him from his Regall Government. F 924 3.1.146 Pope
REGARD
And that shal bide no more regard of parlie. 2Tamb 5.1.61 Techel
Brother, in regard of thee and of thy land, Edw 3.1.230 Kent
Accursed wretches, wast in regard of us, Edw 3.1.233 Edward
Faustus is gone, regard his hellish fall, F2005 5.3.23 4Chor
REGARDE
If he be straunge and not regarde my wordes, Edw 2.4.64 Queene
REGARDED
These he regarded not, but did intreat, Hero and Leander 1.451
REGARDES
For now my lord the king regardes me not, Edw 1.2.49 Queene
REGARDING
And more regarding gaine than victory: 1Tamb 2.2.46 Meandr
Regarding still the danger of thy life. P 748 15.6 King
But still droupt downe, regarding not her hand, Ovid's Elegies 3.6.76
REGENT
In faire Persea noble Tamburlaine/Shall be my Regent, and 1Tamb 2.1.49 Cosroe
Thee doo I make my Regent of Persea, 1Tamb 2.5.8 Cosroe
to order all the scattered troopes)/Farewell Lord Regent, 1Tamb 2.5.46 Cosroe
Arch-regent and Commander of all Spirits. F 291 1.3.63 Mephst
Chiefe Lord and Regent of perpetuall night. F 445 2.1.57 Faust
REGIMENT
Now sits and laughs our regiment to scorne: 1Tamb 1.1.117 Cosroe
Warring within our breasts for regiment, 1Tamb 2.7.19 Tamb
Is Edward pleazd with kinglie regiment. Edw 1.1.165 Edward
And step into his fathers regiment. Edw 3.1.271 Spencr
But what are kings, when regiment is gone, Edw 5.1.26 Edward
REGION
Now cleare the triple region of the aire, 1Tamb 4.2.30 Tamb
those blind Geographers/That make a triple region in the world, 1Tamb 4.4.76 Tamb
So high within the region of the aire, 1Tamb 5.1.250 Zabina
Flame to the highest region of the aire: 2Tamb 3.2.2 Tamb
For earth and al this aery region/Cannot containe the state of 2Tamb 4.1.119 Tamb
O thou that swaiest the region under earth, 2Tamb 4.3.32 Orcan
Which threatned more than if the region/Next underneath the 2Tamb 5.1.87 Tamb
If thy great fame in every region stood? Ovid's Elegies 3.5.90
REGIONS
Excluding Regions which I meane to trace, 1Tamb 4.4.77 Tamb
Lantchidol/Beates on the regions with his boysterous blowes, 2Tamb 1.1.70 Orcan
And other Regions, I have seene Philippi: Lucan, First Booke 693
Shall discontent run into regions farre; Hero and Leander 1.478
By which love sailes to regions full of blis), Hero and Leander 2.276
REGIS
[Quin redis <regis> Mephostophilis fratris imagine]. F 262 1.3.34A Faust
REGISTER
And race th'eternall Register of time: Dido 3.2.7 Juno
That register the numbers of my ruth, Dido 4.2.39 Iarbus
And here this table as a Register/Of all her vertues and 2Tamb 3.2.23 Celeb
REGREET
have measured heaven/With triple circuit thou regreet us not, 1Tamb 3.1.37 Bajzth
REGULAR
Through regular and formall puritie. Hero and Leander 1.308
REHEARSE
lookes to my verse/Which golden love doth unto me rehearse. Ovid's Elegies 2.1.38
Thou deignst unequall lines should thee rehearse, Ovid's Elegies 3.1.37
REHEARSES
And therof many thousand he rehearses. Ovid's Elegies 1.8.58
REI
eademque res legatur duobus, alter rem, alter valorem rei, &c. F 56 1.1.28 P Faust
REIGN'D (See also RAIGN, RAIGNE)
[Where] <When> Siracusian Dionisius reign'd, Jew 5.3.10 Calym

REINE (See also RAIN, RAINES)			
To make these captives reine their lavish tongues.	1Tamb	4.2.67	Techel
Let with strong hand the reine to bend be made.	Ovid's Elegies	3.2.72	
REINES			
(Their reines let loose) right soone my house approach.	Ovid's Elegies	2.16.50	
Now would I slacke the reines, now lash their hide,	Ovid's Elegies	3.2.11	
And from my hands the reines will slip away.	Ovid's Elegies	3.2.14	
When he perceivd the reines let slacke, he stayde,	Ovid's Elegies	3.4.15	
REJECTED			
When I thy brother am rejected thus.	Edw	2.2.218	Kent
REJECTS			
Unhappie Isabell, when Fraunce rejects,	Edw	4.2.11	Queene
REJOICE			
This should intreat your highnesse to rejoice,	1Tamb	1.1.123	Menaph
These are my friends in whom I more rejoice,	1Tamb	1.2.241	Tamb
REJOIN'D			
Or that it be rejoin'd again at full,	2Tamb	5.2.58	Callap
REJOYCE			
Grecians, which rejoyce/That nothing now is left of Priamus:	Dido	2.1.19	Aeneas
And now she sees thee how will she rejoyce?	Dido	2.1.69	Illion
The Guise is slaine, and I rejoyce therefore:	P1078	19.148	King
I doe confesse it Faustus, and rejoyce:	F1885	5.2.89	Mephst
The Santons that rejoyce in Caesars love,	Lucan, First Booke	423	
REKING			
Nor yet the adverse reking southerne pole,	Lucan, First Booke	54	
RELEASE			
and with my heart/Wish your release, but he whose wrath is	2Tamb	1.2.6	Almeda
at my intreaty release him, he hath done penance sufficient.	F App	p.238 79 P	Emper
being all I desire, I am content to release him of his hornes:	F App	p.238 84 P	Faust
With these thy soule walkes, soules if death release,	Ovid's Elegies	3.8.65	
RELEASED			
Or you released of this servitude.	Jew	5.4.7	Govnr
RELEAST			
Hoping by some means I shall be releast,	2Tamb	1.2.23	Callap
Seeing that my brother cannot be releast.	Edw	5.3.67	Kent
RELEEVE			
Then pittie or releeve these upstart hereticks.	P 222	4.20	Guise
RELENT			
Yet he that in my sight would not relent,	Dido	5.1.186	Dido
Accursed Barabas, base Jew, relent?	Jew	5.5.73	Govnr
To make the justice of my heart relent:	P 533	10.6	Guise
But at his lookes Lightborne thou wilt relent.	Edw	5.4.26	Mortmr
Relent, ha, ha, I use much to relent.	Edw	5.4.27	Ltborn
RELENTES			
Besides my heart relentes that noble men,	P 211	4.9	Charls
RELENTING			
I like not this relenting moode in Edmund,	Edw	4.6.38	Mortmr
Relenting Heroes gentle heart was strooke,	Hero and Leander	1.165	
Relenting thoughts, remorse and pittie rests.	Hero and Leander	2.216	
RELENTS			
Edward, alas my hart relents for thee,	Edw	4.6.2	Kent
For she relents at this your miserie.	Edw	5.5.49	Ltborn
RELICKS (See also RELIQUES)			
And keep those relicks from our countries coastes.	P 803	16.17	Navrre
RELIE			
Whose honors and whose lives relie on him:	1Tamb	5.1.19	Govnr
RELIEFE			
Whose yeelding heart may yeeld thee more reliefe.	Dido	4.2.36	Anna
That no reliefe or succour come by Land.	1Tamb	3.1.62	Bajzth
Oft bitter juice brings to the sicke reliefe.	Ovid's Elegies	3.10.8	
RELIES			
And those on whom heaven, earth, and hell relies,	Hero and Leander	1.443	
RELIEV'D			
Whose state he ever pitied and reliev'd,	2Tamb	5.1.32	1Citzn
Thus lives old Edward not reliev'd by any,	Edw	5.3.23	Edward
RELIEVE (See also RELEEVE)			
the plaines/To spie what force comes to relieve the holde.	2Tamb	3.3.48	Techel
Being requirde, with speedy helpe relieve?	Ovid's Elegies	2.9.8	
RELIGION			
Since that religion hath no recompence.	Dido	1.1.81	Venus
In whom no faith nor true religion rests,	2Tamb	2.1.34	Baldwn
thus defame/Their faiths, their honors, and their religion,	2Tamb	2.1.45	Sgsmnd
fire to burne the writ/Wherein the sum of thy religion rests.	2Tamb	5.1.191	Tamb
I count Religion but a childish Toy,	Jew	Prol.14	Machvl
Is theft the ground of your Religion?	Jew	1.2.95	Barab
I, Daughter, for Religion/Hides many mischiefes from suspition.	Jew	1.2.281	Barab
our difference in Religion/Might be a meanes to crosse you in	P 15	1.15	QnMoth
My policye hath framde religion.	P 122	2.65	Guise
Religion: O Diabole.	P 123	2.66	Guise
Onely corrupted in religion,	P 212	4.10	Charls
Thus in despite of thy Religion,	P 314	5.41	Guise
The vertues of our true Religion,	P 577	11.42	Pleshe
And common profit of Religion.	P 647	12.60	Cardnl
And rent our true religion from this land:	P 703	14.6	Navrre
And takes his vantage on Religion,	P 924	18.25	Navrre
Or who will helpe to builde Religion?	P1084	19.154	QnMoth
RELIGIOUS			
Religious, righteous, and inviolate.	2Tamb	2.1.48	Sgsmnd
To bring me to religious purity,	Jew	2.3.72	Barab
Look, look, master, here come two religious Caterpillers.	Jew	4.1.21	P Ithimr
All this I'le give to some religious house/So I may be baptiz'd	Jew	4.1.75	Barab
I wishe this union and religious league,	P 3	1.3	Charls
Being animated by Religious zeale,	P 848	17.43	Guise

RELIGIOUS (cont.)			
When first religious chastitie she vow'd:	Hero and Leander		2.110
RELIGIOUSLY			
That in this house I liv'd religiously,	Jew	3.6.13	Abigal
RELIQUES			
Now Dido, with these reliques burne thy selfe,	Dido	5.1.292	Dido
RELLIQUES			
Who wild me sacrifize his ticing relliques:	Dido	5.1.277	Dido
RELY (See also RELIE)			
If thou rely upon thy righteousnesse,	Jew	1.2.121	Govnr
REM			
una eademque res legatur duobus, alter rem, alter valorem rei,	F 56	1.1.28	P Faust
REMAINDER			
And the remainder weake and out of heart,	Dido	2.1.133	Aeneas
REMAINE			
The Romane Scepter royall shall remaine,	Dido	1.1.105	Jupitr
grim Ceranias seate/Have you oregone, and yet remaine alive?	Dido	1.1.148	Aeneas
Desires Aeneas to remaine with her:	Dido	5.1.135	Dido
Long may Theridamas remaine with us.	1Tamb	1.2.240	Usumc
If you will willingly remaine with me,	1Tamb	1.2.254	Tamb
noble Tamburlaine/Shall be my Regent, and remaine as King.	1Tamb	2.1.49	Cosroe
To charge him to remaine in Asia.	1Tamb	3.1.18	Fesse
Are fled from Bajazeth, and remaine with me,	1Tamb	4.2.80	Tamb
To faire Damascus, where we now remaine,	1Tamb	4.2.99	Tamb
If any love remaine in you my Lord,	1Tamb	4.4.68	Zenoc
The Captain's slaine, the rest remaine our slaves,	Jew	2.2.17	Bosco
No, for this example I'le remaine a Jew:	Jew	4.1.195	Barab
Are gone towards Lambeth, there let them remaine.	Edw	1.3.5	Gavstn
The Spencers ghostes, where ever they remaine,	Edw	5.3.44	Edward
Gone, gone, and doe I remaine alive?	Edw	5.5.91	Edward
Where we are tortur'd, and remaine for ever.	F 509	2.1.121	Mephst
the Kingdome of Joy, and must remaine in hell for ever.	F1845	5.2.49	P Faust
the only hope (that did remaine/To their afflictions) were	Lucan, First Booke		494
And on my haires a crowne of flowers remaine.	Ovid's Elegies		1.6.38
And least the sad signes of my crime remaine,	Ovid's Elegies		1.7.67
And hath no cloathes, but open doth remaine.	Ovid's Elegies		1.10.16
With sunne and moone Aratus shall remaine.	Ovid's Elegies		1.15.16
My mistris hath her wish, my wish remaine:	Ovid's Elegies		3.2.81
Tis well, if some wench for the poore remaine.	Ovid's Elegies		3.7.60
And would be dead, but dying <dead> with thee remaine.	Ovid's Elegies		3.13.40
REMAINES			
Thy sonne thou knowest with Dido now remaines,	Dido	3.2.70	Juno
And as we know) remaines with Tamburlaine,	1Tamb	2.2.36	Meandr
Whose holy Alcaron remaines with us,	2Tamb	1.1.138	Orcan
And carie both our soules, where his remaines.	2Tamb	3.4.17	Olymp
Wel souldiers, Mahomet remaines in hell,	2Tamb	5.1.198	Tamb
Lordes, what now remaines/But that we leave sufficient garrison	2Tamb	5.1.210	Tamb
The ten yeares tribute that remaines unpaid.	Jew	1.2.7	Calym
Now all are dead, not one remaines alive.	Jew	4.1.7	Barab
What now remaines, but for a while to feast,	P 627	12.40	King
in whose gratious lookes/The blessednes of Gaveston remaines,	Edw	1.4.121	Gavstn
Tell us where he remaines, and he shall die.	Edw	2.4.36	Lncstr
What now remaines, have you proclaimed, my lord,	Edw	4.3.17	Edward
The court is where lord Mortimer remaines,	Edw	5.3.61	Matrvs
And yet remaines the face she had before.	Ovid's Elegies		3.3.2
If ought remaines of us but name, and spirit,	Ovid's Elegies		3.8.59
REMAINEST			
Then thou remainest resolute.	P 75	2.18	Guise
REMAINS			
his golden earth remains,/Which after his disceasse, some other	Hero and Leander		1.245
REMEDIE			
You will this greefe have ease and remedie,	Edw	3.1.160	Herald
REMEDILESSE			
I'le reare up Malta now remedilesse.	Jew	5.2.73	Barab
REMEDY			
That you must goe with us, no remedy.	2Tamb	3.4.79	Therid
I must and will, Sir, there's no remedy.	Jew	1.2.391	Mthias
I, so they are, but yet what remedy:	P 433	7.73	Anjoy
REMEDYE			
Then there is no remedye but I must dye?	P1096	20.6	Cardnl
No remedye, therefore prepare your selfe.	P1097	20.7	1Mur
REMEMBER			
Remember who thou art, speake like thy selfe,	Dido	2.1.100	Dido
What, faints Aeneas to remember Troy?	Dido	2.1.118	Dido
Achilles sonne, remember what I was,	Dido	2.1.233	Aeneas
As I remember, here you shot the Deere,	Dido	3.3.51	Achat
Sweet sister cease, remember who you are.	Dido	5.1.263	Anna
Yet brother Barabas remember Job.	Jew	1.2.180	1Jew
Farewell, Remember to morrow morning.	Jew	1.2.364	Barab
Now I remember those old womens words,	Jew	2.1.24	Barab
My Lord, Remember that to Europ's shame,	Jew	2.2.30	Bosco
Sirra, Jew, remember the booke.	Jew	2.3.159	Mthias
Remember that--	Jew	4.1.37	2Fryar
I, remember that--	Jew	4.1.38	1Fryar
I, but Barabas, remember Mathias and Don Lodowick.	Jew	4.1.43	P 2Fryar
Not wel, but do remember such a man.	P 173	3.8	OldQn
Remember you the letter gentle sir,	P 754	15.12	King
I do remember in my fathers dayes,	Edw	1.1.109	Kent
Remember how the Bishop was abusde,	Edw	1.4.59	ArchBp
Your worship I trust will remember me?	Edw	4.7.117	Mower
Remember thee fellow? what else?	Edw	4.7.118	Rice
Remember this.--	F 626	2.2.75	P Mephst
bid the Hostler deliver him unto you, and remember what I say.	F1474	4.4.18	P Faust

REMEMBER (cont.)
do not you remember a Horse-courser you sold a horse to? F1633 4.6.76 P Carter
Yes, I remember I sold one a horse. F1635 4.6.78 Faust
you remember you bid he should not ride [him] into the water? F1636 4.6.79 P Carter
Yes, I do verie well remember that. F1638 4.6.81 P Faust
And do you remember nothing of your leg? F1639 4.6.82 P Carter
Then I pray remember your curtesie. F1641 4.6.84 P Carter
Do you remember sir, how you cosened me and eat up my load of-- F1659 4.6.102 P Carter
Do you remember how you made me weare an Apes-- F1661 4.6.104 P Dick
scab, do you remember how you cosened me with <of> a ho-- F1662 4.6.105 P HrsCsr
do you remember the dogs fa-- F1665 4.6.108 P Robin
to heaven, and remember [Gods] mercy is <mercies are> infinite. F1835 5.2.39 P 2Schol
remember that I have beene a student here these thirty yeares, F1840 5.2.44 P Faust
Well I remember when I first did hire thee, Ovid's Elegies 1.6.43
But I remember when it was my fame. Ovid's Elegies 1.14.50
By her eyes I remember late she swore, Ovid's Elegies 3.3.13

REMEMBERS
Your Majesty remembers I am sure/What cruell slaughter of our 2Tamb 2.1.4 Fredrk

REMEMBRANCE
to put him in remembrance he was a Jailor, that when I take 2Tamb 3.5.140 P Tamb
And of my former riches rests no more/But bare remembrance; Jew 2.1.10 Barab
And in remembrance of those bloudy broyles, P1024 19.94 King
bloudie colours may suggest/Remembrance of revenge immortallie, Edw 3.1.140 Edward

REMEMBRED
remembred how you crossed me in my conference with the F App p.238 76 P Faust

REMEMBRING
But he shrinkes backe, and now remembring me, Dido 5.1.190 Dido
But he remembring me shrinkes backe againe: Dido 5.1.260 Dido

REMES
sorte of English priestes/From Doway to the Seminary at Remes, P1031 19.101 King

REMITS
We wot, he that the care of realme remits, Edw 2.5.61 Warwck

REMOOV'D
The Nations far remoov'd admyre me not)/And when my name and 1Tamb 1.2.204 Tamb
Where unresisted I remoov'd my campe. 2Tamb 1.3.199 Techel
And let this Captaine be remoov'd the walles, 2Tamb 5.1.215 Therid

REMOOVDE
And thats the cause that I am now remoovde. Edw 5.1.150 Edward
Bartley shall be dischargd, the king remoovde, Edw 5.2.40 Mortmr

REMOOVE
And hasten to remoove Damascus siege. 1Tamb 4.3.18 Souldn
Then now remoove me, that I may resigne/My place and proper 2Tamb 5.3.175 Tamb
Help me (my Lords) to make my last remoove. 2Tamb 5.3.180 Tamb
That from your princely person you remoove/This Spencer, as a Edw 3.1.161 Herald
Did they remoove that flatterer from thy throne. Edw 3.1.231 Kent
and withall/We may remoove these flatterers from the king, Edw 4.4.26 Mortmr
Remoove him still from place to place by night, Edw 5.2.59 Mortmr

REMOOVED
Remooved from the Torments and the hell: 1Tamb 3.2.103 Agidas
Fires and inflames objects remooved farre, Hero and Leander 2.124
But being separated and remooved, Hero and Leander 2.127

REMOOVELES
Remooveles from the favours of your King. P 609 12.22 King

REMORCEFULL
Lookes so remorcefull, vowes so forcible, Dido 2.1.156 Aeneas

REMORSE
By any innovation or remorse, 1Tamb 5.1.16 Govnr
and hartie humble mones/Will melt his furie into some remorse: 1Tamb 5.1.22 Govnr
It works remorse of conscience in me, 2Tamb 4.1.28 Calyph
Relenting thoughts, remorse and pittie rests. Hero and Leander 2.216

REMORSEFULL
But (wanting moisture and remorsefull blood)/Drie up with 2Tamb 4.1.179 Soria

REMOVE (See also REMOOVE)
Let me intreate you to remove his hornes, F1309 4.1.155 Emper
which being all I desire, I am content to remove his hornes. F1314 4.1.160 P Faust
For loe these Trees remove at my command, F1426 4.2.102 Faust

REMUS
Remus and Romulus, Ilias twinne-borne seed. Ovid's Elegies 3.4.40

REND
Or rip thy bowels, and rend out thy heart, 2Tamb 3.5.121 Tamb
Ile either rend it with my nayles to naught, P 102 2.45 Guise
Throwe of his golden miter, rend his stole, Edw 1.1.187 Edward
Rend not my hart with thy too piercing words, Edw 1.4.117 Edward
[Nor can they raise the winde, or rend the cloudes]: F 86 1.1.58A Faust
Rend <Ah rend> not my heart, for naming of my Christ, F1941 5.2.145 Faust
Even kembed as they were, her lockes to rend, Ovid's Elegies 2.5.45

RENDER
Since I shall render all into your hands. 1Tamb 5.1.447 Tamb
What will you give me if I render you/The life of Calymath, Jew 5.2.79 Barab
<make> slender/And to get out doth like apt members render. Ovid's Elegies 1.6.6

RENDING
Yet rending with enraged thumbe her tresses, Ovid's Elegies 3.5.71

RENDS
He rends and teares it with his wrathfull pawe, Edw 5.1.12 Edward
Well may I rent his name, that rends my hart. Edw 5.1.140 Edward

RENE
What fearfull cries comes from the river [Sene] <Rene>,/That P 361 7.1 Ramus
Which we have chaste into the river [Sene] <Rene>, P 418 7.58 Guise

RENEGADE (See RUNNAGATE)

RENEW
Before the Moone renew her borrowed light, 1Tamb 1.1.69 Therid
Seeing I must go, do not renew my sorrow. Edw 1.4.137 Gavstn
And Druides you now in peace renew/Your barbarous customes, and Lucan, First Booke 446

RENEW (cont.)
Then Gaynimede would renew Deucalions flood, ... Lucan, First Booke 652
R'ENFORCE
Give me my horse and lets r'enforce our troupes: . . Edw 4.5.6 Edward
RENIED
And warlike bands of Christians renied, ... 1Tamb 3.1.9 Bajzth
RENOUNCE
I will renounce this Magicke and repent. . . . . . F 562 2.2.11 Faust
RENOWM'D
And be renowm'd, as never Emperours were. . . . . 1Tamb 4.4.138 Tamb
Then doubt not Faustus but to be renowm'd, . . . F 168 1.1.140 Cornel
RENOWME
Away base groome, robber of kings renowme, . . . Edw 2.5.72 Mortmr
RENOWMED
Renowmed Dido, tis our Generall: . . . . . . Dido 2.1.77 Illion
If thou wilt stay with me, renowmed man, ... 1Tamb 1.2.188 Tamb
Welcome renowmed Persean to us all. . . . . . 1Tamb 1.2.239 Techel
And these his two renowmed friends my Lord, . . . 1Tamb 2.3.30 Therid
So do I thrice renowmed man at armes, ... 1Tamb 2.5.6 Cosroe
Renowmed Emperour, and mighty Generall, ... 1Tamb 3.1.16 Fesse
Puissant, renowmed and mighty Tamburlain, ... 1Tamb 3.3.96 Techel
Renowmed Souldane, have ye lately heard/The overthrow of . 1Tamb 4.3.23 Arabia
(Renowmed Tamburlain) to whom all kings/Of force must yeeld 1Tamb 5.1.480 Souldn
My soveraigne Lord, renowmed Tamburlain, ... 2Tamb 1.2.7 Almeda
Renowmed Emperour, mighty Callepine, ... 2Tamb 3.5.1 2Msngr
Renowmed Generall mighty Callapine, ... 2Tamb 5.2.36 Amasia
Renowmed Edward, how thy name/Revives poore Gaveston. . Edw 2.5.41 Gavstn
RENOWN
So through the world shold bright renown expresse me. . Ovid's Elegies 3.1.64
RENOWN'D
Wonder of men, renown'd Magitian, ... F1204 4.1.50 Emper
RENOWNE
When other men prease forward for renowne: . . . 1Tamb 1.1.84 Mycet
Beares figures of renowne and myracle: . . . . 1Tamb 2.1.4 Cosroe
The obloquie and skorne of my renowne, ... 2Tamb 4.1.92 Tamb
Sir John of Henolt, be it thy renowne, ... Edw 4.2.78 Mortmr
attaine to that degree of high renowne and great authoritie, F App p.237 23 P Emper
Caesars renowne for war was lesse, he restles, . . . Lucan, First Booke 145
And deem'd renowne to spoile their native towne, . . Lucan, First Booke 176
immortal pens/Renowne the valiant soules slaine in your wars, Lucan, First Booke 444
With the Atrides many gainde renowne. . . . . . Ovid's Elegies 2.12.10
RENOWNED
Having the love of his renowned peeres. . . . . Edw 1.4.367 Queene
thoughts are ravished so/With sight of this renowned Emperour, F1261 4.1.107 Emper
RENT (Homograph)
Her cheekes swolne with sighes, her haire all rent, . . . Dido 2.1.276 Aeneas
My Sailes all rent in sunder with the winde, . . . Dido 3.1.106 Aeneas
Then carelesly I rent my haire for griefe, ... Dido 5.1.236 Anna
the Pilot stands/And viewes a strangers ship rent in the winds, 1Tamb 4.3.33 Souldn
If woords might serve, our voice hath rent the aire, . 2Tamb 2.4.121 Therid
And rent their hearts with tearing of my haire, . . . Jew 1.2.234 Abigal
We rent in sunder at our entry: . . . . Jew 5.3.4 Calym
And rent our true religion from this land: . . . . P 703 14.6 Navrre
First were his sacred garments rent and torne, . . . Edw 1.2.35 ArchBp
Rent sphere of heaven, and fier forsake thy orbe, . . Edw 4.7.102 Spencr
Well may I rent his name, that rends my hart. . . . Edw 5.1.140 Edward
the showts rent heaven,/As when against pine bearing Ossa's Lucan, First Booke 389
But cruelly her tresses having rent, ... Ovid's Elegies 1.7.49
his rent discharg'd/From further duty he rests then inlarg'd. Ovid's Elegies 1.10.45
But cruelly by her was drown'd and rent. . . . . Ovid's Elegies 3.1.58
As when the wilde boare Adons groine had rent. . . . Ovid's Elegies 3.8.16
RENTS (Homograph)
drops that fall/When Boreas rents a thousand swelling cloudes, 2Tamb 1.3.160 Tamb
Be thou lord bishop, and receive his rents, ... Edw 1.1.194 Edward
That almost rents the closet of my heart, ... Edw 5.3.22 Edward
REPAID
No, thus I'le see thy treachery repaid, ... Jew 5.5.74 Govnr
REPAIR'D (Homograph)
Of Sorians from Halla is repair'd/And neighbor cities of your 2Tamb 3.5.46 Soria
And caus'd the ruines to be new repair'd, ... Jew 5.3.2 Calym
REPAIRDE
Though she repairde my fleete and gave me ships, . . Dido 5.1.59 Aeneas
Repairde not I thy ships, made thee a King, . . . Dido 5.1.163 Dido
REPAIRE (Homograph)
And by that meanes repaire his broken ships, . . . Dido 2.1.328 Venus
Aeneas, Ile repaire thy Troian ships, ... Dido 3.1.113 Dido
Your Highnesse knowes for Tamburlaines repaire, . . . 2Tamb 2.1.14 Fredrk
If I repaire not what he ruinates: . . . . . . P 129 2.72 Guise
He wils me to repaire unto the court, ... Edw 2.1.67 Neece
And thither wee'le repaire and live obscure, . . . F1453 4.3.23 Benvol
Whether now shal these olde bloudles soules repaire? . Lucan, First Booke 343
Cheere up thy selfe, thy losse thou maiest repaire, . . Ovid's Elegies 1.14.55
To hide thee in my bosome straight repaire. . . . Ovid's Elegies 3.2.76
RE-PASSE
you thinke to carry it away with your Hey-passe, and Re-passe: F1665 4.6.108 P Robin
REPAY
To finde and to repay the man with death: . . . . P 256 4.54 Charls
For which good turne my sweete reward repay, . . . Ovid's Elegies 2.8.21
REPAYING
Repaying all attempts with present death, ... P 269 4.67 Charls
REPEALD
There weepe, for till my Gaveston be repeald, . . . Edw 1.4.168 Edward
That Gaveston, my Lord, shalbe repeald. . . . . . Edw 1.4.322 Queene

REPEALD (cont.)			
Repeald, the newes is too sweet to be true.	Edw	1.4.323	Edward
That hees repeald, and sent for back againe,	Edw	2.1.18	Spencr
REPEALE			
To sue unto you all for his repeale:	Edw	1.4.201	Queene
For his repeale, Madam!	Edw	1.4.204	Lncstr
As thou wilt soone subscribe to his repeale.	Edw	1.4.227	Queene
REPEALL			
And therefore though I pleade for his repeall,	Edw	1.4.241	Mortmr
REPELL			
My feared hands thrice back she did repell.	Ovid's Elegies		1.7.62
REPENT			
Yet now I doe repent me of his ruth,	Dido	3.2.47	Juno
Thou wilt repent these lavish words of thine,	1Tamb	3.3.172	Zenoc
Now here she writes, and wils me to repent.	Jew	3.4.5	Barab
Stay wicked Jew, repent, I say, and stay.	Jew	4.1.24	2Fryar
When I behold the heavens then I repent/And curse thee wicked	F 552	2.2.1	Faust
I will renounce this Magicke and repent.	F 562	2.2.11	Faust
Faustus repent, yet God will pitty thee.	F 563	2.2.12	GdAngl
Yea <I>, God will pitty me if I repent.	F 567	2.2.16	Faust
I, but Faustus never shall repent.	F 568	2.2.17	BdAngl
My heart is <hearts so> hardned, I cannot repent:	F 569	2.2.18	Faust
I am resolv'd, Faustus shall not <nere> repent.	F 583	2.2.32	Faust
Never too late, if Faustus will <can> repent.	F 631	2.2.80	GdAngl
If thou repent, devils will <shall> teare thee in peeces.	F 632	2.2.81	BdAngl
Repent and they shall never raise thy skin.	F 633	2.2.82	GdAngl
I do repent, and yet I doe despaire,	F1740	5.1.67	Faust
I do repent I ere offended him,	F1746	5.1.73	Faust
That Faustus may repent, and save his soule.	F1934	5.2.138	Faust
He cald it in, for love made him repent.	Hero and Leander		2.210
REPENTANCE			
Repentance? Spurca: what pretendeth this?	Jew	3.4.6	Barab
Contrition, Prayer, Repentance?	F 405	2.1.17	Faust
Then Faustus, will repentance come too late,	F1714	5.1.41	OldMan
REPENTANT			
Teares falling from repentant heavinesse/Of thy most vilde and	F App	p.243 39	OldMan
REPENTED			
Yet she this rashnesse sodainly repented,	Hero and Leander		2.33
REPENTS			
But hee repents, and sorrowes for it now.	Edw	5.2.108	Prince
REPINE			
What if the Citizens repine thereat?	Dido	4.4.70	Anna
REPLIDE			
And alwaies cut him off as he replide.	Hero and Leander		1.196
Hee thus replide:	Hero and Leander		1.299
REPLIE			
Leander made replie,/You are deceav'd, I am no woman I.	Hero and Leander		2.191
REPLIES			
thee (sweet Ortigius)/Better replies shall proove my purposes.	1Tamb	2.5.37	Cosroe
REPLY			
Humblye craving your gracious reply.	P1170	22.32	Frier
REPORT			
Others report twas Sinons perjurie:	Dido	2.1.111	Dido
We will report but well of Tamburlaine.	1Tamb	1.2.81	Magnet
Where men report, thou sitt'st by God himselfe,	2Tamb	5.1.194	Tamb
And if she be so faire as you report,	Jew	1.2.388	Lodowk
But yet my Lord the report doth run,	P 435	7.75	Navrre
But as report doth goe, the Duke of Joyeux/Hath made great sute	P 733	14.36	1Msngr
and as constant report goeth, they intend to give king Edward	Edw	4.3.34	P Spencr
Is this report raisde on poore Isabell.	Edw	5.6.75	Queene
have heard strange report of thy knowledge in the blacke Arte,	F App	p.236 1	P Emper
my selfe farre inferior to the report men have published,	F App	p.236 13	P Faust
doe not languish/And then report her sicke and full of anguish.	Ovid's Elegies		2.2.22
So at Aeneas buriall men report,	Ovid's Elegies		3.8.13
REPORTED			
be witnesses to confirme what mine eares have heard reported,	F App	p.236 7	P Emper
REPORTEST			
Canst thou, as thou reportest, make Malta ours?	Jew	5.1.85	Calym
REPORTS			
Which make reports it far exceeds the Kings.	1Tamb	2.2.42	Spy
Plinie reports, there is a flying Fish,	Edw	2.2.23	Lncstr
I know a wench reports her selfe Corinne,	Ovid's Elegies		2.17.29
REPOSDE			
Now worthy Tamburlaine, have I reposde,	1Tamb	2.3.1	Cosroe
REPOSE			
Whose wearie lims shall shortly make repose,	Dido	1.1.84	Jupitr
And wheresoever we repose our selves,	1Tamb	1.2.80	Magnet
transfourme my love/In whose sweet being I repose my life,	2Tamb	2.4.48	Tamb
[Levune] <Lewne>, the trust that we repose in thee,/Begets the	Edw	3.1.262	Spencr
REPOSESSE			
That Englands queene in peace may reposesse/Her dignities and	Edw	4.4.24	Mortmr
REPOSEST			
and that thow most reposest one my faythe	Paris	ms31,p391	Guise
REPREHEND			
And in the Senate reprehend them all,	Jew	1.2.233	Abigal
REPROCHES			
Why grieve I? and of heaven reproches pen?	Ovid's Elegies		3.3.41
REPULS'D			
•Thy fault with his fault so repuls'd will vanish.	Ovid's Elegies		1.8.80
REPULSE			
see how the heavens smiles]/[At your repulse, and laughs your	F1795	5.1.122A	OldMan
To take repulse, and cause her shew my lust?	Ovid's Elegies		2.7.26
And may repulse place for our wishes strike.	Ovid's Elegies		2.19.6

REPULST				
You likewise that repulst the Caicke foe,	Lucan, First Booke			459
REPUTATION				
Thence growes the Judge, and knight of reputation.	Ovid's Elegies			3.7.56
REPUTE				
tyrannies/(If tyrannies wars justice ye repute)/I execute,	2Tamb	4.1.147		Tamb
REQUEST				
But Dido is the favour I request.	Dido	3.1.18		Iarbus
Request him gently (Anna) to returne,	Dido	5.1.206		Dido
And therefore are we to request your ayd.	Jew	1.2.49		Govnr
And having all, you can request no more;	Jew	1.2.140		Barab
Well, Ithimore, let me request thee this,	Jew	3.3.26		Abigal
At thy request I am content thou goe,	P 746	15.4		King
My lords, it is his majesties request,	Edw	2.5.57		Arundl
To gratifie the kings request therein,	Edw	2.5.75		Penbrk
When we had sent our messenger to request/He might be spared to	Edw	3.1.234		Edward
Request them earnestly to visit me.	F 93	1.1.65		Faust
And grant me my request, and then I go.	F 846	3.1.68		Faust
I would request no better meate, then a dish of ripe grapes.	F1573	4.6.16	P	Lady
deny/The just [requests] <request> of those that wish him well,	F1691	5.1.18		Faust
this therefore is my request, that thou let me see some proofe	F App	p.236 5	P	Emper
I am ready to accomplish your request, so farre forth as by art	F App	p.237 38	P	Faust
Request milde Zephires helpe for thy availe,	Ovid's Elegies			2.11.41
My mistris wish confirme with my request.	Ovid's Elegies			3.2.80
Her owne request to her owne torment turnd.	Ovid's Elegies			3.3.38
And to those sterne nymphs humblie made request,	Hero and Leander			1.379
REQUESTED				
A draught of flowing Nectar, she requested,	Hero and Leander			1.431
REQUESTS				
deny/The just [requests] <request> of those that wish him well,	F1691	5.1.18		Faust
To kinde requests thou wouldst more gentle prove,	Ovid's Elegies			2.3.5
REQUIER				
What requier you my maisters?	2Tamb	3.3.15		Capt
REQUIRDE				
Being requirde, with speedy helpe relieve?	Ovid's Elegies			2.9.8
REQUIRE				
Hath all the Principles Magick doth require:	F 167	1.1.139		Cornel
Against the destinies durst sharpe darts require.	Ovid's Elegies			1.7.10
When causes fale thee to require a gift,	Ovid's Elegies			1.8.93
What yeares in souldiours Captaines do require,	Ovid's Elegies			1.9.5
And Tithon livelier then his yeeres require.	Ovid's Elegies			3.6.42
REQUIRES				
For it requires a great and thundring speech:	1Tamb	1.1.3		Mycet
What is the summe that Calymath requires?	Jew	2.2.35		Bosco
As daunger of this stormie time requires.	Edw	4.7.7		Abbot
REQUISIT				
Tis requisit to parle for a peace/With Sigismond the king of	2Tamb	1.1.50		Gazell
REQUISITE				
Twere requisite he should be ten times more,	1Tamb	3.1.47		Argier
I thinke it requisite and honorable,	2Tamb	3.1.70		Callap
Doe, it is requisite it should be so.	Jew	2.3.239		Barab
Therefore 'tis not requisite he should live.	Jew	4.1.121		Barab
And whatsoever else is requisite,	F 183	1.1.155		Valdes
REQUITALL				
a pretty wenches face/Shee in requitall doth me oft imbrace.	Ovid's Elegies			2.1.34
REQUITE (See also QUIGHT, QUIT, QUITE)				
I will requite your royall gratitudes/With all the benefits my	2Tamb	3.1.8		Callap
And I am bound in charitie to requite it,	Jew	4.1.107		Barab
me ever since she saw me, and who would not requite such love?	Jew	4.2.35	P	Ithimr
Thankes my good freend, I will requite thy love.	P 78	2.21		Guise
Spare for no cost, we will requite your love.	Edw	1.4.383		Edward
I will requite it when I come to age.	Edw	5.4.100		King
REQUITED				
hath Faustus justly requited this injurious knight, which being	F1313	4.1.159	P	Faust
hath Faustus worthily requited this injurious knight, which	F App	p.238 83	P	Faust
And what he did, she willingly requited.	Hero and Leander			2.28
RES				
Si una eademque res legatur duobus, alter rem, alter valorem	F 56	1.1.28	P	Faust
RESCUE (See also RESKEW)				
After your rescue to enjoy his choise.	1Tamb	3.2.58		Agidas
Or hope of rescue from the Souldans power,	1Tamb	5.1.4		Govnr
Before all hope of rescue were denied,	1Tamb	5.1.38		Govnr
Then issue out and come to rescue me,	Jew	5.4.5		Govnr
for come [all] <call> the world/To rescue thee, so will we	Jew	5.5.120		Govnr
And rescue aged Edward from his foes,	Edw	5.2.120		Kent
O gentle brother, helpe to rescue me.	Edw	5.3.51		Edward
Did you attempt his rescue, Edmund speake?	Edw	5.4.86		Mortmr
you <yee> heare, come not unto me, for nothing can rescue me.	F1874	5.2.78	P	Faust
RESCUED				
Least you be knowne, and so be rescued.	Edw	5.3.32		Gurney
RESEMBLE				
Sweet sons farewell, in death resemble me,	2Tamb	2.4.75		Zenoc
spirites as can lively resemble Alexander and his Paramour,	F App	p.237 46	P	Faust
Though her sowre looks a Sabines browe resemble,	Ovid's Elegies			2.4.15
Then shall you most resemble Venus Nun,	Hero and Leander			1.319
RESEMBLED				
same proportion of Elements/Resolve, I hope we are resembled,	1Tamb	2.6.27		Cosroe
So fayre she was, Atalanta she resembled,	Ovid's Elegies			1.7.13
RESEMBLING				
Resembling faire Semiramis going to bed,	Ovid's Elegies			1.5.11
RESERV'D				
The jewels and the treasure we have tane/Shall be reserv'd, and	1Tamb	1.2.3		Tamb
With his rich triple crowne to be reserv'd,	F1027	3.2.47		Raymnd

RESERVDE			
But Mortimer reservde for better hap,	Edw	4.2.40	Mortmr
RESIDENCE			
doe know no wanton thought/Had ever residence in Didos breast.	Dido	3.1.17	Dido
your investion so neere/The residence of your dispised brother,	1Tamb	1.1.181	Ortyg
Nor hath it any place of residence,	Hero and Leander		1.272
RESIDUE			
Then wee'll take order for the residue.	Jew	1.2.136	Govnr
RESIGNDE			
The king hath willingly resignde his crowne.	Edw	5.2.28	BshpWn
RESIGNE			
me, that I may resigne/My place and proper tytle to my sonne:	2Tamb	5.3.175	Tamb
But tell me, must I now resigne my crowne,	Edw	5.1.36	Edward
And needes I must resigne my wished crowne.	Edw	5.1.70	Edward
And therefore say, will you resigne or no.	Edw	5.1.85	Trussl
Ile not resigne, but whilst I live, [be king].	Edw	5.1.86	Edward
My lord, the king is willing to resigne.	Edw	5.1.94	Leistr
That I resigne my charge.	Edw	5.1.136	Leistr
That he resigne the king to thee and Gurney,	Edw	5.2.49	Mortmr
Resigne, or seale, or what so pleaseth us.	F 936	3.1.158	Pope
[May] <Many> bounteous [lome] <love> Alcinous fruite resigne.	Ovid's Elegies		1.10.56
Men handle those, all manly hopes resigne,	Ovid's Elegies		2.3.9
RESIGNES			
The God of war resignes his roume to me,	1Tamb	5.1.450	Tamb
RESIST			
And to resist with longer stubbornesse,	1Tamb	5.1.3	Govnr
And plague such Pesants as [resist in] <resisting> me/The power	2Tamb	4.1.157	Tamb
As durst resist us till our third daies siege:	2Tamb	5.1.59	Techel
Should come in person to resist your power,	2Tamb	5.2.38	Amasia
I am too weake and feeble to resist,	Edw	5.5.108	Edward
all, and everie part/Strove to resist the motions of her hart.	Hero and Leander		1.364
RESISTED			
But love resisted once, growes passionate,	Hero and Leander		2.139
RESISTING			
And plague such Pesants as [resist in] <resisting> me/The power	2Tamb	4.1.157	Tamb
shoots/Alongst the ayre and [nought] <not> resisting it/Falls,	Lucan, First Booke		157
RESISTLESSE			
Must Tamburlaine by their resistlesse powers,	1Tamb	5.1.397	Zenoc
Whose billowes beating the resistlesse bankes,	Jew	3.5.17	Govnr
RESKEW			
And take my heart, in reskew of my friends.	Edw	4.7.67	Edward
RESOLUTE			
Yet I am resolute, and so farewell.	2Tamb	3.3.40	Capt
Who when he heares how resolute thou wert,	2Tamb	3.4.40	Techel
And it behoves you to be resolute;	Jew	5.1.3	Govnr
Then thou remainest resolute.	P 75	2.18	Guise
Will be as resolute as I and Dumaine:	P 323	5.50	Guise
We must with resolute mindes resolve to fight,	P 707	14.10	Navrre
Well then, I see you are resolute.	P 938	19.8	Capt
I, I, feare not: stand close, so, be resolute:	P 943	19.13	Capt
But are they resolute and armde to kill,	P 949	19.19	King
Cousin, assure you I am resolute,	P 973	19.43	King
My lords, now let us all be resolute,	Edw	1.4.45	Mortmr
Will you be resolute and hold with me?	Edw	1.4.231	Lncstr
You must be proud, bold, pleasant, resolute,	Edw	2.1.42	Spencr
Be resolute, and full of secrecie.	Edw	2.2.125	Lncstr
Come forth. Art thou as resolute as thou wast?	Edw	5.4.22	Mortmr
What else my lord? and farre more resolute.	Edw	5.4.23	Ltborn
If learned Faustus will be resolute.	F 160	1.1.132	Valdes
Valdes, as resolute am I in this,	F 161	1.1.133	Faust
Then feare not Faustus to <but> be resolute/And try the utmost	F 242	1.3.14	Faust
Now go not backward: no, Faustus, be resolute.	F 394	2.1.6	Faust
Then draw your weapons, and be resolute:	F1335	4.2.11	Benvol
RESOLUTELY			
Come on sirs, what, are you resolutely bent,	P 931	19.1	Capt
RESOLUTION			
Is it not a kingly resolution?	1Tamb	1.1.55	Mycet
His resolution far exceedeth all:	1Tamb	4.1.48	2Msngr
fury of thy torments, strive/To end thy life with resolution:	Jew	5.5.80	Barab
And resolution honors fairest aime.	P 96	2.39	Guise
Where resolution strives for victory.	P 165	2.108	Guise
A desperate and unnaturall resolution,	Edw	3.1.217	Warwck
O no my lord, this princely resolution/Fits not the time, away,	Edw	4.5.8	Baldck
RESOLV'D			
O tell me, for I long to be resolv'd.	Dido	2.1.61	Aeneas
and both his eyes/Turnd up to heaven as one resolv'd to dye,	Dido	2.1.152	Aeneas
Armies of foes resolv'd to winne this towne,	Dido	4.4.113	Dido
Nobly resolv'd, sweet friends and followers.	1Tamb	1.2.60	Tamb
Which with thy beautie will be soone resolv'd.	1Tamb	1.2.101	Tamb
Nobly resolv'd, my good Ortygius.	1Tamb	2.6.24	Cosroe
And my pin'd soule resolv'd in liquid [ayre] <ay>,	1Tamb	5.1.300	Bajzth
Madam content your self and be resolv'd,	1Tamb	5.1.372	Anippe
Bene oft resolv'd in bloody purple showers,	1Tamb	5.1.460	Tamb
If not resolv'd into resolved paines,	2Tamb	5.3.187	Amyras
Now [Governour], how are you resolv'd?	Jew	1.2.17	Calym
Claime tribute where thou wilt, we are resolv'd,	Jew	2.2.55	Govnr
Oh, is't the custome, then I am resolv'd:	Jew	2.3.329	Lodowk
Then 'tis not for me; and I am resolv'd/You shall confesse me,	Jew	4.1.85	Barab
Nothing shall alter us, wee are resolv'd.	Edw	1.4.74	ArchBp
All that he speakes, is nothing, we are resolv'd.	Edw	1.4.251	Warwck
I am resolv'd, Faustus shall not <nere> repent.	F 583	2.2.32	Faust
If Faustus do it, you are streight resolv'd,	F1298	4.1.144	Faust
RESOLVDE			
Plead for him he that will, I am resolvde.	Edw	1.4.214	Mortmr

RESOLVE				
Nay leave not here, resolve me of the rest.	Dido	2.1.160		Dido
O pardon me, if I resolve thee why:	Dido	5.1.91		Aeneas
And that which might resolve me into teares,	1Tamb	1.1.118		Cosroe
He dares so doubtlesly resolve of rule,	1Tamb	2.6.13		Meandr
And with the same proportion of Elements/Resolve, I hope we are	1Tamb	2.6.27		Cosroe
Resolve my Lords and loving souldiers now,	1Tamb	2.6.34		Cosroe
And make our soules resolve in ceasles teares:	1Tamb	5.1.272		Bajzth
We must with resolute mindes resolve to fight,	P 707	14.10		Navrre
Search Surgeon and resolve me what thou seest.	P1193	22.55		King
This haught resolve becomes your majestie,	Edw	3.1.28		Baldck
Resolve me of all ambiguities?	F 107	1.1.79		Faust
And then resolve me of thy Maisters mind.	F 328	1.3.100		Faust
<Well>, Resolve me then in this one question:	F 614	2.2.63	P	Faust
RESOLVED				
Are <To> <Ah> these resolved noble Scythians?	1Tamb	1.2.225		Therid
To dy by this resolved hand of thine,	1Tamb	3.2.98		Agidas
Rain'st on the earth resolved pearle in showers,	1Tamb	5.1.142		Tamb
If not resolv'd into resolved paines,	2Tamb	5.3.187		Amyras
RESOLVES				
And where stiffe winter whom no spring resolves,	Lucan, First Booke			17
RESOLVING				
And frozen Alpes thaw'd with resolving winds.	Lucan, First Booke			221
RESORTED				
Thither resorted many a wandring guest,	Hero and Leander			1.94
RESOUND				
And all the woods Eliza to resound:	Dido	4.2.10		Iarbus
For long shrild trumpets let your notes resound.	Ovid's Elegies			2.6.6
The subject hides thy wit, mens acts resound,	Ovid's Elegies			3.1.25
RESOUNDING				
earth may eccho foorth/The far resounding torments ye sustaine,	2Tamb	4.1.186		Tamb
RESOUNDST				
Nor of thee Macer that resoundst forth armes,	Ovid's Elegies			2.18.35
RESPECT				
Without respect of Sex, degree or age,	1Tamb	4.1.62		2Msngr
Of earthly fortune, and respect of pitie,	1Tamb	5.1.365		Zenoc
Whom I respect as leaves of boasting greene,	P 720	14.23		Navrre
My Lord of Lancaster, marke the respect.	Edw	1.4.248		Mortmr
In no respect can contraries be true.	Edw	1.4.249		Lncstr
But I respect neither their love nor hate.	Edw	2.2.261		Gavstn
Each one according to his gifts respect.	Ovid's Elegies			1.8.38
Of two gold Ingots like in each respect.	Hero and Leander			1.172
Base in respect of thee, divine and pure,	Hero and Leander			1.219
RESPECTS				
Villaine, respects thou more thy slavish life,	2Tamb	5.1.10		Govnr
RESPIT				
What respit aske you [Governour]?	Jew	1.2.27		Calym
Where wee'll attend the respit you have tane,	Jew	1.2.30		Calym
RESPITE				
The time you tooke for respite, is at hand,	Jew	3.5.8		Basso
RESPLENDANT				
Vaild his resplendant glorie from your view.	Dido	1.1.126		Venus
In what resplendant glory thou hadst set/In yonder throne, like	F1904	5.2.108		GdAngl
REST (Homograph)				
And rest the map of weatherbeaten woe:	Dido	1.1.158		Achat
The rest we feare are foulded in the flouds.	Dido	1.2.31		Cloan
Sergestus, Illioneus and the rest,	Dido	2.1.58		Aeneas
Nay leave not here, resolve me of the rest.	Dido	2.1.160		Dido
Where meeting with the rest, kill kill they cryed.	Dido	2.1.190		Aeneas
The rest are such as all the world well knowes,	Dido	3.1.165		Dido
What makes Iarbus here of all the rest?	Dido	3.3.13		Dido
Achates and the rest shall waite on thee,	Dido	5.1.76		Aeneas
Whil'st I rest thankfull for this curtesie.	Dido	5.1.77		Aeneas
Behold, my Lord, Ortigius and the rest,	1Tamb	1.1.134		Menaph
will flie (my Lords)/To rest secure against my brothers force.	1Tamb	1.1.178		Cosroe
Tell you the rest (Meander) I have said.	1Tamb	2.2.13		Mycet
And rest attemplesse, faint and destitute?	1Tamb	2.5.74		Tamb
Wils us to weare our selves and never rest,	1Tamb	2.7.26		Tamb
Theridamas, Techelles, and the rest,	1Tamb	2.7.55		Tamb
That worke such trouble to your woonted rest:	1Tamb	3.2.3		Agidas
And when they chance to breath and rest a space,	1Tamb	3.3.51		Tamb
Techelles, and the rest prepare your swordes,	1Tamb	3.3.64		Tamb
Carkasses/Shall serve for walles and bulwarkes to the rest:	1Tamb	3.3.139		Bajzth
As Crocodiles that unaffrighted rest,	1Tamb	4.1.10		Souldn
So shall he have his life, and all the rest.	1Tamb	4.2.115		Tamb
Wel Zenocrate, Techelles, and the rest, fall to your victuals.	1Tamb	4.4.15	P	Tamb
But goe my Lords, put the rest to the sword.	1Tamb	5.1.134		Tamb
For now her mariage time shall worke us rest.	1Tamb	5.1.504		Techel
Our warlike hoste in compleat armour rest,	2Tamb	1.1.8		Orcan
Now rest thee here on faire Larissa Plaines,	2Tamb	1.3.5		Tamb
Sit up and rest thee like a lovely Queene.	2Tamb	1.3.16		Tamb
And therefore let them rest a while my Lord.	2Tamb	1.3.184		Usumc
And issue sodainly upon the rest:	2Tamb	2.1.23		Fredrk
As fell to Saule, to Balaam and the rest,	2Tamb	2.1.54		Fredrk
Gazellus, Uribassa, and the rest,	2Tamb	2.2.1		Orcan
And furie would confound my present rest.	2Tamb	2.4.65		Zenoc
We both will rest and have one Epitaph/Writ in as many severall	2Tamb	2.4.134		Tamb
Thrice worthy kings of Natolia, and the rest,	2Tamb	3.1.7		Callap
The rest forward with execution,	2Tamb	5.1.124		Tamb
Shoot first my Lord, and then the rest shall follow.	2Tamb	5.1.151		Tamb
Techelles and the rest, come take your swords,	2Tamb	5.3.46		Tamb
Thine and the rest.	Jew	1.2.55		Govnr
But one amongst the rest became our prize:	Jew	2.2.16		Bosco

REST (cont.)

Line	Work	Ref		Speaker
The Captain's slaine, the rest remaine our slaves,	Jew	2.2.17		Bosco
Among the rest beare this, and set it there;	Jew	3.4.78		Barab
and the rest of the family, stand or fall at your service.	Jew	4.2.44	P	Pilia
I, and the rest too, or else--	Jew	4.3.28	P	Pilia
Well Madam, let that rest:	P 17	1.17		Charls
We think it good to goe and consumate/The rest, with hearing of	P 20	1.20		Charls
The rest that will not goe (my Lords) may stay:	P 23	1.23		Charls
Ile disinherite him and all the rest:	P 524	9.43		QnMoth
O let me stay and rest me heer a while,	P 536	11.1		Charls
the rest have taine their standings in the next roome,	P 994	19.64	P	3Mur
our Guise is dead)/Rest satisfied with this that heer I sweare,	P1043	19.113		King
But what doth move thee above the rest to doe the deed?	P1132	21.26	P	Dumain
We and the rest that are his counsellers,	Edw	1.2.69		ArchBp
I say no more, judge you the rest my lord.	Edw	1.4.148		Gavstn
And Mortimer will rest at your commaund.	Edw	1.4.296		Mortmr
But rest thee here where Gaveston shall sleepe.	Edw	2.1.65		Neece
and thy selfe/Bedaubd with golde, rode laughing at the rest,	Edw	2.2.185		Mortmr
No doubt, such lessons they will teach the rest,	Edw	3.1.21		Spencr
For which thy head shall over looke the rest,	Edw	3.1.239		Edward
As much as thou in rage out wentst the rest.	Edw	3.1.240		Edward
There see him safe bestowed, and for the rest,	Edw	3.1.253		Edward
All times and seasons rest you at a stay,	Edw	5.1.67		Edward
And this above the rest, because we heare/That Edmund casts to	Edw	5.2.57		Mortmr
Will hatefull Mortimer appoint no rest?	Edw	5.3.5		Edward
Matrevis and the rest may beare the blame,	Edw	5.4.15		Mortmr
That shall conveie it, and performe the rest,	Edw	5.4.18		Mortmr
Lie on this bed, and rest your selfe a while.	Edw	5.5.72		Ltborn
Your overwatchde my lord, lie downe and rest.	Edw	5.5.92		Ltborn
And with the rest accompanie him to his grave?	Edw	5.6.88		Queene
To rest his bones after his weary toyle,	F 769	2.3.48		2Chor
From thence to Venice, Padua, and the [rest] <East>,	F 794	3.1.16		Faust
[Amongst the rest the Emperour is one],	F1150	3.3.63A		3Chor
Then rest thee Faustus quiet in conceit.	F1483	4.4.27		Faust
This makes me wonder more then all the rest, that at this time	F1578	4.6.21	P	Duke
Is for ore-tortur'd soules to rest them in.	F1915	5.2.119		BdAngl
Then rest thee Faustus quiet in conceit.	F App	p.240 126		Faust
this makes me wonder above the rest, that being in the dead	F App	p.242 17	P	Duke
my Lord, and whilst I live, Rest beholding for this curtesie.	F App	p.243 31	P	Duchss
attaine the gole/That shall conduct thee to celestial rest.	F App	p.243 37		OldMan
And by long rest forgot to manage armes,	Lucan, First Booke	131		
what Colonies/To rest their bones?	Lucan, First Booke	346		
were wont/In large spread heire to exceed the rest of France;	Lucan, First Booke	439		
that his owne ten ensignes, and the rest/Marcht not intirely,	Lucan, First Booke	473		
For these before the rest preferreth he:	Ovid's Elegies	1.1.2		
The thing and place shall counsell us the rest.	Ovid's Elegies	1.4.54		
To rest my limbes, uppon a bedde I lay,	Ovid's Elegies	1.5.2		
To leave the rest, all likt me passing well,	Ovid's Elegies	1.5.23		
Judge you the rest, being tyrde <tride> she bad me kisse.	Ovid's Elegies	1.5.25		
But now perchaunce thy wench with thee doth rest,	Ovid's Elegies	1.6.45		
are in thy soft brest/But pure simplicity in thee doth rest.	Ovid's Elegies	1.11.10		
The rest my hand doth in my letters write.	Ovid's Elegies	1.11.14		
By thy meanes women of their rest are bard,	Ovid's Elegies	1.13.23		
She safe by favour of her judge doth rest.	Ovid's Elegies	2.2.56		
There good birds rest (if we beleeve things hidden)/Whence	Ovid's Elegies	2.6.51		
Heere thou hast strength, here thy right hand doth rest.	Ovid's Elegies	2.9.36		
Long shalt thou rest when Fates expire thy breath.	Ovid's Elegies	2.9.42		
Because on him thy care doth hap to rest.	Ovid's Elegies	3.2.8		
By these I judge, delight me may the rest,	Ovid's Elegies	3.2.35		
[A] <Or> while thy tiptoes on the foote-stoole rest.	Ovid's Elegies	3.2.64		
At least now conquer, and out-runne the rest:	Ovid's Elegies	3.2.79		
What helpes my hast: what to have tane small rest?	Ovid's Elegies	3.5.9		
Thy bones I pray may in the urne safe rest,	Ovid's Elegies	3.8.67		
And with still panting rockt, there tooke his rest.	Hero and Leander	1.44		
And therefore let it rest upon thy pillow.	Hero and Leander	2.252		
Breathlesse spoke some thing, and sigh'd out the rest;	Hero and Leander	2.280		

RESTED

Line	Work	Ref		Speaker
and never rested pulling, till I had pul'd me his leg quite	F1550	4.5.46	P	HrsCsr
Halfe sleeping on a purple bed she rested,	Ovid's Elegies	1.14.20		
Breathlesse albeit he were, he rested not,	Hero and Leander	2.229		

RESTES

Line	Work	Ref		Speaker
Ocean to the Traveiler/That restes upon the snowy Appenines:	2Tamb	1.1.111		Sgsmnd

RESTETH (Homograph)

Line	Work	Ref		Speaker
That resteth in the rivall of thy paine,	Dido	3.3.84		Iarbus
It resteth now then that your Majesty/Take all advantages of	2Tamb	2.1.11		Fredrk
My Lords, what resteth there now for to be done?	P 554	11.19		QnMoth
Madam, what resteth, why stand ye in a muse?	Edw	4.6.63		SrJohn

RESTING

Line	Work	Ref		Speaker
Resting her selfe upon my milk-white Tent:	1Tamb	3.3.161		Tamb
But tell me now, what resting place is this?	F 800	3.1.22		Faust

RESTITUTION

Line	Work	Ref		Speaker
You hope of libertie and restitution:	1Tamb	5.1.210		Tamb

RESTLES

Line	Work	Ref		Speaker
And alwaies mooving as the restles Spheares,	1Tamb	2.7.25		Tamb
And with bright restles fire compasse the earth,	Lucan, First Booke	49		
Caesars renowne for war was lesse, he restles,	Lucan, First Booke	145		
the restles generall through the darke/(Swifter then bullets	Lucan, First Booke	230		

RESTLESSE

Line	Work	Ref		Speaker
Yet should ther hover in their restlesse heads,	1Tamb	5.1.171		Tamb
restlesse course that time doth runne with calme and silent	F App	p.239 90	P	Faust

RESTOR'D

Line	Work	Ref		Speaker
Now must your jewels be restor'd againe:	1Tamb	1.2.114		Tamb
And Jupiter unto his place restor'd.	Hero and Leander	1.464		

RESTORDE
I Mortimer, for till he be restorde, Edw 1.4.209 Queene
RESTORE
We hope your selfe wil willingly restore them. 1Tamb 1.2.117 Agidas
If peace, restore it to my hands againe: 2Tamb 1.1.84 Sgsmnd
But God will sure restore you to your health. P 542 11.7 Navrre
despite of all his Holinesse/Restore this Bruno to his liberty, F 899 3.1.121 Faust
Pray him to lend what thou maist nere restore. Ovid's Elegies 1.8.102
RESTORED
Have beene by thee restored and comforted. Edw 4.2.80 Mortmr
RESTRAIN
Their houshould gods restrain them not, none lingered, Lucan, First Booke 505
RESTRAIN'D
steeld their harts/And minds were prone) restrain'd them; Lucan, First Booke 356
The more he is restrain'd, the woorse he fares, Hero and Leander 2.145
RESTRAINDE
longer life/Thou hadst restrainde thy headstrong husbands rage, Lucan, First Booke 116
Nor, least she will, can any be restrainde. Ovid's Elegies 3.4.6
RESTRAINE
as fit as may be to restraine/These coltish coach-horse tongues 2Tamb 4.3.51 Usumc
RESTRAINES
The filthy prison faithlesse breasts restraines. Ovid's Elegies 2.2.42
RESTS (Homograph)
And rests a pray to every billowes pride. Dido 1.1.53 Venus
Pluck up your hearts, since fate still rests our friend, Dido 1.1.149 Aeneas
Whose Crowne and kingdome rests at thy commande: Dido 3.4.58 Dido
In whom no faith nor true religion rests, 2Tamb 2.1.34 Baldwn
fire to burne the writ/Wherein the sum of thy religion rests. 2Tamb 5.1.191 Tamb
And of my former riches rests no more/But bare remembrance; Jew 2.1.9 Barab
Then, gentle sleepe, where e're his bodie rests, Jew 2.1.35 Abigal
The Jew is here, and rests at your command. Jew 5.1.83 Barab
as long as he survives/What safetie rests for us, or for my Edw 5.2.43 Queene
his rent discharg'd/From further duty he rests then inlarg'd. Ovid's Elegies 1.10.46
Scarse rests of all what a small urne conteines. Ovid's Elegies 3.8.40
Relenting thoughts, remorse and pittie rests. Hero and Leander 2.216
RESUME
Or Plutoes bloodles kingdom, but else where/Resume a body: Lucan, First Booke 453
RESUMES
And purple Love resumes his dartes againe. Ovid's Elegies 2.9.34
RETAIN'D
Would make one thrust and strive to be retain'd/In such a great 1Tamb 2.3.31 Therid
higher meeds/Then erst our states and actions have retain'd, 1Tamb 4.4.132 Therid
RETAINE
othes/Sign'd with our handes, each shal retaine a scrowle: 2Tamb 1.1.144 Orcan
Will now retaine her olde inconstancie, 2Tamb 3.1.29 Callap
If you retaine desert of holinesse, 2Tamb 5.3.19 Techel
Retaine a thought of joy, or sparke of life? 2Tamb 5.3.163 Amyras
Shal still retaine my spirit, though I die, 2Tamb 5.3.173 Tamb
Did you retaine your fathers magnanimitie, Edw 3.1.16 Spencr
RETAINES
The Cedar tall spoyld of his barke retaines. Ovid's Elegies 1.14.12
A Diamond set in lead his worth retaines, Hero and Leander 1.215
RETAINST
And new sworne souldiours maiden armes retainst, Ovid's Elegies 2.18.2
RETES
Gonzago, Retes, sweare by/The argent crosses in your burgonets, P 274 5.1 Guise
Anjoy, Gonzago, Retes, if that you three, P 322 5.49 Guise
Gonzago poste you to Orleance, Retes to Deep, P 445 7.85 Guise
RETIRE
Whose coleblacke faces make their foes retire, 2Tamb 1.3.142 Techel
Such a feare (my Lord) would never make yee retire. 2Tamb 4.1.71 P Perdic
on me, then with your leaves/I may retire me to my native home. P 474 8.24 Anjoy
And this retire refresheth horse and man. Edw 3.1.193 SpncrP
Anger delaide doth oft to hate retire. Ovid's Elegies 1.8.82
But bids his darts from perjurd girles retire. Ovid's Elegies 3.3.36
RETORQUED
with horror aie/Griping our bowels with retorqued thoughtes, 1Tamb 5.1.237 Bajzth
RETREAT
And they will (trembling) sound a quicke retreat, 2Tamb 1.1.150 Orcan
That fighting, knowes not what retreat doth meane, 2Tamb 3.5.43 Trebiz
Why do we sound retreat? Edw 3.1.185 Edward
What rebels, do you shrinke, and sound retreat? Edw 3.1.200 Edward
RETROGRADE
Venus is faint; swift Hermes retrograde; Lucan, First Booke 661
RETURN
Farewell (sweet Virgins) on whose safe return/Depends our 1Tamb 5.1.62 Govnr
RETURN'D
Behold my Lord, the Cardinals are return'd. P 945 3.1.167 Raymnd
Yet in a minute had my spirit return'd, F1399 4.2.75 Faust
RETURND
my Doves are back returnd,/Who warne me of such daunger prest Dido 3.2.21 Venus
But is that wicked Gaveston returnd? Edw 1.1.177 BshpCv
Is new returnd, this newes will glad him much, Edw 1.4.301 Queene
And promiseth he shall be safe returnd, Edw 3.1.110 Arundl
And corne with least part of it selfe returnd. Ovid's Elegies 3.9.30
RETURNE
And chaunging heavens may those good daies returne, Dido 1.1.150 Aeneas
Till I returne and take thee hence againe. Dido 2.1.339 Venus
And Didos beautie will returne againe: Dido 5.1.118 Dido
Request him gently (Anna) to returne, Dido 5.1.206 Dido
Returne with speed, time passeth swift away, 1Tamb 1.1.67 Mycet
I long to see thee backe returne from thence, 1Tamb 1.1.76 Mycet
Returne our Mules and emptie Camels backe, 1Tamb 1.2.76 Agidas

RETURNE (cont.)
Returne with victorie, and free from wound. 1Tamb 3.3.133 Zenoc
Go, never to returne with victorie: 1Tamb 5.1.214 Bajzth
Waiting the back returne of Charons boat, 1Tamb 5.1.464 Tamb
Nor ere returne but with the victory, 2Tamb 3.5.44 Trebiz
So that of thus much that returne was made: Jew 1.1.1 Barab
Vanish and returne in a twinckle. Jew 4.2.79 P Ithimr
Now Selim-Calymath, returne me word/That thou wilt come, and I Jew 5.5.11 Barab
Or Selim ne're returne to Ottoman. Jew 5.5.114 Govnr
That he should nere returne into the realme: Edw 1.1.84 Mortmr
Madam, returne unto the court againe: Edw 1.2.56 Mortmr
O that we might as well returne as goe. Edw 1.4.143 Edward
For tis against my will he should returne. Edw 1.4.217 Queene
Returne it to their throtes, ile be thy warrant. Edw 2.2.73 Edward
My lords, I will be pledge for his returne. Edw 2.5.66 Arundl
Upon mine oath I will returne him back. Edw 2.5.88 Penbrk
Returne him on your honor. Sound, away. Edw 2.5.98 Mortmr
And Penbrooke undertooke for his returne, Edw 3.1.236 Edward
Madam, returne to England,/And please my father well, and then Edw 4.2.3 Prince
Gone, gone alas, never to make returne. Edw 4.7.104 Spencr
This answer weele returne, and so farewell. Edw 5.1.90 BshpWn
Returne it backe and dip it in my bloud. Edw 5.1.120 Edward
Thou wilt returne againe, and therefore stay. Edw 5.5.99 Edward
I charge thee to returne, and change thy shape, F 251 1.3.23 Faust
Go and returne an old Franciscan Frier, F 253 1.3.25 Faust
Go, and returne to mighty Lucifer, F 326 1.3.98 Faust
in speculation of this Art/Till Mephostophilis returne againe. F 342 1.3.114 Faust
I see hell, and returne againe safe, how happy were I then. F 714 2.2.166 P Faust
And then returne to Hellen for a kisse. F1780 5.1.107 Faust
Go, minding to returne with prosperous winde, Ovid's Elegies 2.11.37
For thy returne shall fall the vowd oblation, Ovid's Elegies 2.11.46
In time it will returne us two for one. Hero and Leander 1.236
And swore he never should returne to Jove. Hero and Leander 2.168

RETURNED
[Hee stayde his course, and so returned home], F1140 3.3.53A 3Chor
Bewaile my chaunce, the sad booke is returned, Ovid's Elegies 1.12.1

RETURNES
Returnes amaine: welcome, welcome my love: Dido 5.1.191 Dido
resisting it/Falls, and returnes, and shivers where it lights. Lucan, First Booke 158

RETURNING
As is the joy of his returning home. Edw 2.1.58 Neece
The mace returning backe, his owne hand hit, Hero and Leander 2.211

REVEAL
Till they [reveal] the causers of our smarts, Jew 3.2.34 Govnr

REVEAL'D
Know that Confession must not be reveal'd, Jew 3.6.33 2Fryar
Thou know'st 'tis death and if it be reveal'd. Jew 3.6.51 2Fryar
Which if they were reveal'd, would doe him harme. Jew 4.2.65 Pilia
Leanders amorous habit soone reveal'd. Hero and Leander 2.104

REVEALE
I must conceale/The torment, that it bootes me not reveale,/And Dido 3.4.26 Dido
Reveale it not, for then my father dyes. Jew 3.6.32 Abigal

REVELD (Homograph)
Reveld in Englands wealth and treasurie. Edw 4.6.52 Rice
Whom Ilia pleasd, though in her lookes griefe reveld, Ovid's Elegies 3.5.47

REVELL
Thankes gentle Warwick, come lets in and revell. Edw 1.4.385 Edward
Are banquets, Dorick musicke, midnight-revell, Hero and Leander 1.301

REVELLING
I thinke it was the divels revelling night, Dido 4.1.9 Achat

REVELS
And how the villaine revels with my gold. Jew 4.3.68 Barab

REVENEW
And could my crownes revenew bring him back, Edw 1.4.308 Edward

REVENEWE
He weares a lords revenewe on his back, Edw 1.4.407 Mortmr

REVENEWS
For great revenews I good verses have, Ovid's Elegies 2.17.27

REVENG'D
To be reveng'd for these contemptuous words. 1Tamb 1.1.100 Mycet
And be reveng'd for her disparadgement. 1Tamb 4.1.72 Souldn
Be now reveng'd upon this Traitors soule, 2Tamb 2.2.58 Orcan
To be reveng'd of all his Villanie. 2Tamb 5.2.23 Callap
And be reveng'd upon the--Governor. Jew 2.3.143 Barab
There comes the villaine, now I'le be reveng'd. Jew 2.3.333 Lodowk
So, now I am reveng'd upon 'em all. Jew 4.4.42 Barab
I'le be reveng'd on this accursed Towne; Jew 5.1.62 Barab
Oh villaine, Heaven will be reveng'd on thee. Jew 5.2.25 Govnr
Nor immortalitie to be reveng'd: P1008 19.78 Guise
Ah Sextus, be reveng'd upon the King, P1010 19.80 Guise
But I will raigne to be reveng'd of them, Edw 1.4.111 Edward
But an I be not reveng'd for this, would I might be turn'd to a F1319 4.1.165 P Benvol
To be reveng'd on Jove, did undertake, Hero and Leander 1.442

REVENGD
I priest, and lives to be revengd on thee, Edw 1.1.178 Edward
Ile be revengd on him for my exile. Edw 1.1.192 Gavstn
And vowes to be revengd upon us both, Edw 5.6.19 Queene

REVENGDE
backe to Troy, and be revengde/On these hard harted Grecians, Dido 2.1.18 Aeneas
Ile be revengde. P1051 19.121 YngGse
And courage to, to be revengde at full. Edw 1.2.60 Mortmr
And dare not be revengde, for their power is great: Edw 2.2.202 Edward
To be revengde on Mortimer and thee. Edw 5.2.121 Kent

REVENGE (See also VENGE)			
Revenge me on Aeneas, or on her:	Dido	3.3.70	Iarbus
And thou and I Achates, for revenge,	Dido	4.4.88	Aeneas
To whom poore Dido doth bequeath revenge.	Dido	5.1.173	Dido
That may revenge this treason to a Queene,	Dido	5.1.307	Dido
To seeke revenge on me and Tamburlaine.	1Tamb	2.1.67	Cosroe
Surpriz'd with feare of hideous revenge,	1Tamb	3.2.68	Agidas
That shine as Comets, menacing revenge,	1Tamb	3.2.74	Agidas
Yet in revenge of faire Zenocrate,	1Tamb	4.1.43	Souldn
Let griefe and furie hasten on revenge,	1Tamb	4.3.43	Arabia
Now goe I to revenge my fathers death.	2Tamb	1.2.78	Callap
Harbors revenge, war, death and cruelty:	2Tamb	1.3.78	Tamb
And worke revenge upon these Infidels:	2Tamb	2.1.13	Fredrk
I shall now revenge/My fathers vile abuses and mine owne.	2Tamb	3.5.90	Callap
And with our bloods, revenge our bloods on thee.	2Tamb	4.1.145	Jrslem
Revenge it Radamanth and Eacus,	2Tamb	4.1.171	Orcan
And so revenge our latest grievous losse,	2Tamb	5.2.10	Callap
No, strike the drums, and in revenge of this,	2Tamb	5.3.57	Tamb
Revenge it on him when you meet him next.	Jew	2.3.343	Barab
I did it, and revenge it if thou dar'st.	Jew	3.2.4	Mthias
Thy sonne slew mine, and I'le revenge his death.	Jew	3.2.15	Mater
But thou wert set upon extreme revenge,	Jew	3.3.42	Abigal
And will revenge the bloud of innocents,	P 44	1.44	Navrre
And when this just revenge is finished,	P 318	5.45	Anjoy
For to revenge their deaths upon us all.	P 518	9.37	Cardnl
Plaies with her goary coulours of revenge,	P 719	14.22	Navrre
When I shall vaunt as victor in revenge.	P 722	14.25	Navrre
Revenge it Henry as thou list or dare,	P 819	17.14	Guise
To revenge our deaths upon that cursed King,	P1100	20.10	Cardnl
Oh what may I doe, for to revenge thy death?	P1108	21.2	Dumain
I am thy brother, and ile revenge thy death,	P1112	21.6	Dumain
Weep not sweet Navarre, but revenge my death.	P1234	22.96	King
And then I vow for to revenge his death,	P1247	22.109	Navrre
revenge it henry yf thow liste or darst	Paris	ms23,p391	Guise
Brother revenge it, and let these their heads,	Edw	1.1.117	Kent
If ye be moov'de, revenge it as you can,	Edw	2.2.198	Lncstr
bloudie colours may suggest/Remembrance of revenge immortallie,	Edw	3.1.140	Edward
Me thinkes I should revenge me of the wronges,	Edw	5.1.24	Edward
This poore revenge hath something easd my minde,	Edw	5.1.141	Edward
That all the world may see my just revenge.	F1382	4.2.58	Benvol
But wherefore doe I dally my revenge?	F1401	4.2.77	Faust
If we should follow him to worke revenge,	F1448	4.3.18	Benvol
But doubt thou not (revenge doth griefe appease)/With thy	Ovid's Elegies		1.7.63
With earthes revenge and how Olimpus toppe/High Ossa bore,	Ovid's Elegies		2.1.13
Nor never with nights sharpe revenge afflicted?	Ovid's Elegies		2.19.54
REVENGING			
There is a God full of revenging wrath,	2Tamb	5.1.183	Tamb
And in his heart revenging malice bare:	Hero and Leander		2.208
REVENUE (See REVENEW)			
REVERBERATE			
May be upon himselfe reverberate.	2Tamb	5.3.223	Techel
REVERENCE			
we were commanded straight/With reverence to draw it into Troy.	Dido	2.1.168	Aeneas
whose silver haires/Honor and reverence evermore have raign'd,	1Tamb	5.1.82	1Virgn
Tis true, and but for reverence of these robes,	Edw	1.1.180	Gavstn
Saving your reverence, you must pardon me.	Edw	1.1.186	Gavstn
Yet he alone is held in reverence.	Lucan, First Booke		144
Brabbling Marcellus; Cato whom fooles reverence;	Lucan, First Booke		313
REVEREND			
But let us save the reverend Souldans life,	1Tamb	5.1.204	Therid
Let us salute his reverend Father-hood.	F 944	3.1.166	Faust
By full consent of all the [reverend] <holy> Synod/Of Priests	F 952	3.1.174	Faust
To view the sentence of the reverend Synod,	F1014	3.2.34	1Card
By which alone, our reverend fathers say,	Hero and Leander		1.267
REVILL			
Minding thy fault, with death I wish to revill,	Ovid's Elegies		2.5.3
REVIVE			
These words revive my thoughts and comforts me,	P1209	22.71	Navrre
REVIVED			
The more a gentle pleasing heat revived,	Hero and Leander		2.68
REVIVES			
for his vertues)/Revives the spirits of true Turkish heartes,	2Tamb	3.1.24	Callap
O how a kisse revives poore Isabell.	Edw	1.4.333	Queene
Renowmed Edward, how thy name/Revives poore Gaveston.	Edw	2.5.42	Gavstn
REVOKE			
One slowe we favour, Romans him revoke:	Ovid's Elegies		3.2.73
REVOLT			
Which will revolt from Persean government,	1Tamb	1.1.91	Cosroe
Then may we lawfully revolt from him.	Edw	1.2.73	Mortmr
have we cause/To cast the worst, and doubt of your revolt.	Edw	2.3.8	Warwck
to whom in justice it belongs/To punish this unnaturall revolt:	Edw	4.6.9	Kent
Revolt, or I'le in peece-meale teare thy flesh.	F1745	5.1.72	Mephst
REVOLTED			
We have revolted Grecians, Albanees,	2Tamb	1.1.61	Orcan
And that Paris is revolted from his grace.	P 902	18.3	Navrre
REWARD			
Unworthie are they of a Queenes reward:	Dido	4.4.12	Dido
Thanks my good freend, holde, take thou this reward.	P 168	3.3	OldQn
That wouldst reward them with an hospitall.	Edw	1.1.38	3PrMan
Deserves no common place, nor meane reward:	Edw	1.4.361	Edward
Reward for them can bring in Mortimer?	Edw	4.3.18	Edward
The reward of sin is death? that's hard:	F 67	1.1.39	Faust
Doctor, yet ere you goe, expect from me a bounteous reward.	F App	p.239 89 P	Emper

REWARD (cont.)			
reward this learned man for the great kindnes he hath shewd to	F App	p.243 28 P	Duke
Come, maister Doctor follow us, and receive your reward. .	F App	p.243 34 P	Duke
Yet for long service done, reward these men, . . .	Lucan, First Booke		341
Ask'st why I chaunge? because thou crav'st reward: . .	Ovid's Elegies		1.10.11
A great reward:	Ovid's Elegies		2.1.35
For which good turne my sweete reward repay, . . .	Ovid's Elegies		2.8.21
REWARDE			
Excellent well, take this for thy rewarde. . . .	Edw	5.5.117	Gurney
REWARDED			
I were as soone rewarded with a shot, ...	2Tamb	4.1.54	Calyph
Justly rewarded for his villanies.	F1376	4.2.52	Benvol
REWARDES			
Deserveth princelie favors and rewardes, ...	Edw	4.6.54	Mortmr
REWARDS			
And take his leave, laden with rich rewards. . . .	F1345	4.2.21	Benvol
Faire Dames for-beare rewards for nights to crave, . .	Ovid's Elegies		1.10.47
REWARDST			
False Jupiter, rewardst thou vertue so?	Dido	1.1.78	Venus
REWD			
went and came, as if he rewd/The greefe which Neptune felt.	Hero and Leander		2.214
RHADAMANTHUS (See RADAMANTH)			
RHAMNIS			
When she that rules in Rhamnis golden gates, ...	1Tamb	2.3.37	Cosroe
RHAMNUSE			
That onely Juno rules in Rhamnuse towne.	Dido	3.2.20	Juno
RHAMNUSIA			
on a Lions backe)/Rhamnusia beares a helmet ful of blood,	2Tamb	3.4.57	Therid
RHEIMS (See REAMES, REMES)			
RHENE (Homograph)			
Ocean;/And swept the foming brest of [Artick] <Articks> Rhene.	Lucan, First Booke		372
And they of Rhene and Leuca, cunning darters, ...	Lucan, First Booke		425
and you fierce men of Rhene/Leaving your countrey open to the	Lucan, First Booke		460
Borne twixt the Alpes and Rhene, which he hath brought/From out	Lucan, First Booke		478
RHENNISH			
He took his rouse with stopes of Rhennish wine, . .	F1174	4.1.20	Mrtino
RHESUS			
the Starres supprisde like Rhesus Steedes,/Are drawne by .	Dido	1.1.72	Venus
So the fierce troupes of Thracian Rhesus fell/And Captive	Ovid's Elegies		1.9.23
RHETHORICKE			
Who taught thee Rhethoricke to deceive a maid?	Hero and Leander		1.338
RHINE (See also RHENE)			
And make swift Rhine, circle faire Wittenberge <Wertenberge>:	F 116	1.1.88	Faust
We saw the River Maine, fall into Rhine <Rhines>, . .	F 785	3.1.7	Faust
RHINES			
We saw the River Maine, fall into Rhine <Rhines>, . .	F 785	3.1.7	Faust
RHOAD			
Whence is thy ship that anchors in our Rhoad?	Jew	2.2.2	Govnr
RHODANUS			
Cyngas streame, and where swift Rhodanus/Drives Araris to sea;	Lucan, First Booke		434
RHODE (Homograph)			
or to what end/Launcht from the haven, lye they in the Rhode?	Dido	5.1.89	Dido
Thy ships are safe, riding in Malta Rhode:	Jew	1.1.50	1Merch
Know Barabas, doth ride in Malta Rhode, ...	Jew	1.1.86	2Merch
Are come from Turkey, and lye in our Rhode:	Jew	1.1.147	1Jew
fares Callymath, What wind drives you thus into Malta rhode?	Jew	3.5.2 P	Govnr
In Germany, within a Towne cal'd [Rhode] <Rhodes>: . .	F 12	Prol.12	1Chor
RHODES			
Know Knights of Malta, that we came from Rhodes, . .	Jew	1.2.2	Basso
The Christian Ile of Rhodes, from whence you came, . .	Jew	2.2.31	Bosco
For when their hideous force inviron'd Rhodes, . . .	Jew	2.2.48	Bosco
In Germany, within a Towne cal'd [Rhode] <Rhodes>: . .	F 12	Prol.12	1Chor
RHODOLFE			
Brighter than is the silver [Rhodope] <Rhodolfe>, . .	1Tamb	1.2.88	Tamb
RHODOPE			
Brighter than is the silver [Rhodope] <Rhodolfe>, . .	1Tamb	1.2.88	Tamb
RIBAND			
About his armes the purple riband wound, ...	Hero and Leander		2.106
RICE (Homograph)			
But first goe fetch me in the pot of Rice/That for our supper	Jew	3.4.49	Barab
master, wil you poison her with a messe of rice [porredge]?	Jew	3.4.64	P Ithimr
was ever pot of rice porredge so sauc't?	Jew	3.4.107	P Ithimr
that the Nuns lov'd Rice, that Fryar Bernardine slept in his	Jew	4.4.76	P Ithimr
Take him away, he prates. You Rice ap Howell, ...	Edw	4.6.73	Mortmr
RICE AP HOWELL			
Take him away, he prates. You Rice ap Howell, ...	Edw	4.6.73	Mortmr
RICH (See also RITCH)			
It is the Punick kingdome rich and strong, ...	Dido	1.1.210	Venus
Viewing the fire wherewith rich Ilion burnt. . . .	Dido	2.1.264	Aeneas
Am I not King of rich Getulia?	Dido	3.1.45	Iarbus
What telst thou me of rich Getulia?	Dido	3.1.48	Dido
And mought I live to see him sacke rich Thebes, . . .	Dido	3.3.42	Aeneas
The common souldiers rich imbrodered coates, . . .	Dido	4.4.9	Dido
I shall be planted in as rich a land.	Dido	4.4.82	Aeneas
And let rich Carthage fleete upon the seas, . . .	Dido	4.4.134	Dido
The Sunne from Egypt shall rich odors bring, . . .	Dido	5.1.11	Aeneas
Besides rich presents from the puisant Cham, . . .	1Tamb	1.2.18	Magnet
More rich and valurous than Zenocrates.	1Tamb	1.2.97	Tamb
But are they rich? And is their armour good? . . .	1Tamb	1.2.123	Tamb
In every part exceeding brave and rich.	1Tamb	1.2.127	Souldr
He sends this Souldans daughter rich and brave, . . .	1Tamb	1.2.186	Tamb
Shall make me leave so rich a prize as this: . . .	1Tamb	2.7.54	Tamb
And make Damascus spoiles as rich to you, ...	1Tamb	4.4.8	Tamb

RICH (cont.)			
Fraughted with golde of rich America:	2Tamb	1.2.35	Callap
Then in as rich a tombe as Mausolus,	2Tamb	2.4.133	Tamb
Blood is the God of Wars rich livery.	2Tamb	3.2.116	Tamb
And rich Natolia ours, our men shall sweat/With carrieng pearle	2Tamb	3.5.166	Techel
Opening the doores of his rich treasurie,	2Tamb	4.2.95	Therid
brave Assirian Dames/Have rid in pompe like rich Saturnia,	2Tamb	5.1.77	Tamb
Then let the rich increase your portions.	Jew	1.2.58	Govnr
Rich costly Jewels, and Stones infinite,	Jew	1.2.245	Barab
Faire Abigall the rich Jewes daughter/Become a Nun?	Jew	1.2.366	Mthias
Why, the rich Jewes daughter.	Jew	1.2.382	Mthias
You'd make a rich Poet, Sir.	Jew	4.2.122	P Pilia
Rich Princes both, and mighty Emperours:	P 463	8.13	Anjoy
Then gaudie silkes, or rich imbrotherie.	Edw	1.4.347	Edward
Then up to Naples rich Campania,	F 787	3.1.9	Faust
With his rich triple crowne to be reserv'd,	F1027	3.2.47	Raymnd
And take his leave, laden with rich rewards.	F1345	4.2.21	Benvol
And brought the spoyles to rich Dardania:	F1695	5.1.22	Faust
Vulcan will give thee Chariots rich and faire.	Ovid's Elegies		1.2.24
Wert thou rich, poore should not be my state.	Ovid's Elegies		1.8.28
And brings good fortune, a rich lover plants/His love on thee,	Ovid's Elegies		1.8.31
Tis shame to grow rich by bed merchandize,	Ovid's Elegies		1.10.41
And a rich neck-lace caus'd that punnishment.	Ovid's Elegies		1.10.52
Both are wel favoured, both rich in array,	Ovid's Elegies		2.10.5
The Gods, and their rich pompe witnesse with me,	Ovid's Elegies		3.2.61
Rich Nile by seaven mouthes to the vast sea flowing,	Ovid's Elegies		3.5.39
See a rich chuffe whose wounds great wealth inferr'd,	Ovid's Elegies		3.7.9
Onely our loves let not such rich churles gaine,	Ovid's Elegies		3.7.59
The graine-rich goddesse in high woods did stray,	Ovid's Elegies		3.9.35
Scylla by us her fathers rich haire steales,	Ovid's Elegies		3.11.21
Phaeton had got/The guidance of the sunnes rich chariot.	Hero and Leander		1.102
Rich robes, themselves and others do adorne,	Hero and Leander		1.237
Lesse sinnes the poore rich man that starves himselfe,	Hero and Leander		1.243
To the rich Ocean for gifts he flies.	Hero and Leander		2.224
Rich jewels in the darke are soonest spide.	Hero and Leander		2.240
RICHE			
Now is the king of England riche and strong,	Edw	1.4.366	Queene
And unresisted, drave away riche spoiles.	Edw	2.2.167	Lncstr
RICHER			
ambles after wealth/Although he ne're be richer then in hope:	Jew	3.4.53	Barab
RICHES			
If wealth or riches may prevaile with them,	1Tamb	2.2.61	Meandr
Trapt with the wealth and riches of the world,	2Tamb	1.1.43	Orcan
the Easterne rockes/Without controule can picke his riches up,	Jew	1.1.22	Barab
increaseth, so inclose/Infinite riches in a little roome.	Jew	1.1.37	Barab
Laden with riches, and exceeding store/Of Persian silkes, of	Jew	1.1.87	2Merch
Be patient and thy riches will increase.	Jew	1.2.122	Govnr
And of my former riches rests no more/But bare remembrance;	Jew	2.1.9	Barab
Ah Spencer, not the riches of my realme/Can ransome him, ah he	Edw	3.1.3	Edward
Stately and proud, in riches and in traine,	Edw	4.7.12	Edward
O what will all thy riches, pleasures, pompes,	F1896	5.2.100	GdAngl
such exploits, gote such riches, subdued so many kingdomes,	F App	p.236 20	P Emper
RICHEST			
so imbellished/With Natures pride, and richest furniture?	1Tamb	1.2.156	Therid
Making the mantle of the richest night,	1Tamb	5.1.149	Tamb
will keep it for/The richest present of this Easterne world.	2Tamb	4.2.78	Therid
What difference betwixt the richest mine/And basest mold, but	Hero and Leander		1.232
The richest corne dies, if it be not reapt,	Hero and Leander		1.327
RICHLY			
who so richly pay/The things they traffique for with wedge of	Jew	1.1.8	Barab
The ships are safe thou saist, and richly fraught.	Jew	1.1.54	Barab
Ride golden Love in Chariots richly builded.	Ovid's Elegies		1.2.42
RID (Homograph)			
To rid me from these melancholly thoughts.	Dido	2.1.303	Dido
To rid thee of that doubt, abourd againe,	Dido	4.4.21	Dido
have I found a meane/To rid me from these thoughts of Lunacie:	Dido	5.1.273	Dido
And rid the world of those detested troopes?	1Tamb	2.2.19	Meandr
with the foole, and rid your royall shoulders/Of such a burthen,	1Tamb	2.3.46	Tamb
And quickly rid thee both of paine and life.	2Tamb	3.4.25	Olymp
Devise some meanes to rid thee of thy life,	2Tamb	4.2.5	Olymp
brave Assirian Dames/Have rid in pompe like rich Saturnia,	2Tamb	5.1.77	Tamb
Rid him away, and goe you home with me.	Jew	4.1.89	Barab
Well, I must seeke a meanes to rid 'em all,	Jew	4.3.63	Barab
We would but rid the realme of Gaveston,	Edw	2.4.35	Lncstr
To rid thee of thy life. Matrevis come.	Edw	5.5.107	Ltborn
Then come sweete death, and rid me of this greefe.	Edw	5.6.92	Queene
what did I but rid him into a great river, and when I came just	F1543	4.5.39	P HrsCsr
rid him into the deepe pond at the townes ende, I was no sooner	F App	p.240 133	P HrsCsr
But Roome at thraldoms feet to rid from tyrants.	Lucan, First Booke		352
in armes; nor could the bed-rid parents/Keep back their sons,	Lucan, First Booke		502
The Gods from this sinne rid me of suspition,	Ovid's Elegies		2.7.19
RIDDEN (See RODE)			
RIDDLE (See RIDLES)			
RIDE			
This day they both a hunting forth will ride/Into these woods,	Dido	3.2.87	Juno
let him ride/As Didos husband through the Punicke streetes,	Dido	4.4.66	Dido
of all these, commaund/Aeneas ride as Carthaginian King.	Dido	4.4.78	Dido
And ride upon his backe unto my love:	Dido	5.1.250	Dido
And ride in triumph through Persepolis.	1Tamb	2.5.49	Menaph
And ride in triumph through Persepolis?	1Tamb	2.5.50	Tamb
And ride in triumph through Persepolis?	1Tamb	2.5.54	Tamb
in crimson silk/Shall ride before the on Barbarian Steeds:	2Tamb	1.2.47	Callap
Will quickly ride before Natolia:	2Tamb	1.3.125	Therid

RIDE (cont.)
as the battaile is done, Ile ride in triumph through the Camp. 2Tamb 3.5.145 P Tamb
Let me have coach my Lord, that I may ride, ... 2Tamb 4.3.27 Amyras
Ile ride in golden armour like the Sun, ... 2Tamb 4.3.115 Tamb
So will I ride through Samarcanda streets, ... 2Tamb 4.3.130 Tamb
Know Barabas, doth ride in Malta Rhode, ... Jew 1.1.86 2Merch
And when thou seest the Admirall ride by, ... P 87 2.30 Guise
I can ride. . . . . Edw 1.1.27 1PrMan
While in the harbor ride thy ships unrigd. . . . . Edw 2.2.169 Mortmr
Come sonne, weele ride a hunting in the parke. . . . Edw 5.4.113 Queene
And shall my Unckle Edmund ride with us? . . . . Edw 5.4.114 King
that you may ride him o're hedge and ditch, and spare him not; F1467 4.4.11 P Faust
in any case, ride him not into the water. . . . . . F1468 4.4.12 P Faust
waters, but ride him not into the water; o're hedge and ditch, F1472 4.4.16 P Faust
Doctor Fauster bad me ride him night and day, and spare him no F1540 4.5.36 P HrsCsr
time; but, quoth he, in any case ride him not into the water. F1541 4.5.37 P HrsCsr
you remember you bid he should not ride [him] into the water? F1636 4.6.79 P Carter
before you have him, ride him not into the water at any hand. F App p.239 109 P Faust
but ride him not into the water, ride him over hedge or ditch, F App p.239 111 P Faust
the water, ride him over hedge or ditch, or where thou wilt, F App p.239 112 P Faust
by him, for he bade me I should ride him into no water; now, F App p.240 131 P HrsCsr
Smooth speeches, feare and rage shall by thee ride, . . . Ovid's Elegies 1.2.35
Ride golden Love in Chariots richly builded. . . . . Ovid's Elegies 1.2.42
Thou wert not borne to ride, or armes to beare, . . . Ovid's Elegies 2.3.7
With wheeles bent inward now the ring-turne ride. . . Ovid's Elegies 3.2.12

RIDER
His rider vainely striving him to stay, ... Ovid's Elegies 2.9.30

RIDERS
When al their riders chardg'd their quivering speares/Began to 1Tamb 5.1.332 Zenoc

RIDES
Heere in the river rides a Flemish hoie, ... Edw 2.4.46 Mortmr

RIDING
Thy ships are safe, riding in Malta Rhode: . . . . Jew 1.1.50 1Merch
Riding the streetes was traiterously shot, ... P 244 4.42 Man
As Caesar riding in the Romaine streete, ... Edw 1.1.173 Gavstn
I riding my horse into the water, thinking some hidden mystery F1484 4.4.28 P HrsCsr

RIDLES
Sitting as if they were a telling ridles. . . . . . 2Tamb 3.5.59 Tamb

RID'ST
And as thou rid'st in triumph through the streets, . . 2Tamb 1.2.41 Callap

RIFE
Quarrels were rife, greedy desire stil poore/Did vild deeds, Lucan, First Booke 174

RIFLE
And rifle all those stately Janisars. . . . . . 1Tamb 3.3.26 Techel
pompe than this)/Rifle the kingdomes I shall leave unsackt, 2Tamb 4.3.59 Tamb

RIFLING
Rifling this Fort, devide in equall shares: . . . . 2Tamb 3.4.89 Therid
Rifling the bowels of her treasurie, ... P 135 2.78 Guise

RIG'D
A stately builded ship, well rig'd and tall, ... Hero and Leander 1.225

RIGD
Why are thy ships new rigd? . . . . Dido 5.1.88 Dido

RIGGE
Without fresh men to rigge and furnish them. . . . . Jew 5.5.101 Govnr

RIGGING
When as I want both rigging for my fleete, ... Dido 5.1.69 Aeneas

RIGHT
And this right hand shall make thy Altars crack/With mountaine Dido 1.1.201 Aeneas
By this right hand, and by our spousall rites, ... Dido 5.1.134 Dido
In love of honor and defence of right, ... 1Tamb 2.6.21 Ortyg
see how right the man/Hath hit the meaning of my Lord the King. 1Tamb 3.2.107 Techel
Though my right hand have thus enthralled thee, . . . 1Tamb 5.1.435 Tamb
Hunger and [thirst] <cold>, right adjuncts of the war. . 2Tamb 3.2.58 Tamb
Thus am I right the Scourge of highest Jove, ... 2Tamb 4.3.24 Tamb
bank, right opposite/Against the Westerne gate of Babylon. 2Tamb 5.1.121 Govnr
What right had Caesar to the [Empery] <Empire>? . . . Jew Prol.19 Machvl
Content thee, Barabas, thou hast nought but right. . . Jew 1.2.152 Govnr
Your extreme right does me exceeding wrong: . . . . Jew 1.2.153 Barab
That God may still defend the right of France: . . . P 56 1.56 Navrre
That right or wrong, thou deale thy selfe a King. . . P 148 2.91 Guise
maintaine/The wealth and safety of your kingdomes right. . P 478 8.28 Anjoy
But God that alwaies doth defend the right, ... P 575 11.40 Navrre
A warlike people to maintaine thy right, ... P 592 12.5 QnMoth
My Lords, sith in a quarrell just and right, ... P 698 14.1 Navrre
Thus God we see doth ever guide the right, ... P 789 16.3 Navrre
Sworne to defend king Edwards royall right, ... Edw 3.1.38 SpncrP
By this right hand, and by my fathers sword, ... Edw 3.1.130 Edward
Souldiers, good harts, defend your soveraignes right, . . Edw 3.1.182 Edward
I doubt it not my lord, right will prevaile. . . . . Edw 3.1.189 Spencr
Saint George for England, and the Barons right. . . . Edw 3.1.219 Warwck
Saint George for England, and king Edwards right. . . Edw 3.1.220 Edward
To whome right well you knew our soule was knit, . . . Edw 3.1.227 Edward
but madam, right makes roome,/Where weapons want, and though a Edw 4.2.50 Mortmr
Arrivde and armed in this princes right, ... Edw 4.4.18 Mortmr
To them that fight in right and feare his wrath: . . . Edw 4.6.20 Queene
And we must seeke to right it as we may, ... Edw 4.6.68 Mortmr
So fought not they that fought in Edwards right. . . . Edw 4.6.72 SpncrP
And princely Edwards right we crave the crowne. . . . Edw 5.1.39 BshpWn
To give ambitious Mortimer my right, ... Edw 5.1.53 Edward
And joyntly both yeeld up their wished right. . . . . Edw 5.1.63 Edward
For if they goe, the prince shall lose his right. . . . Edw 5.1.92 Leistr
your right eye be alwaies Diametrally fixt upon my left heele, F 386 1.4.44 P Wagner
Pope Adrian let me have some right of Law, ... F 904 3.1.126 Bruno

RIGHT (cont.)

You hit it right,/It is your owne you meane, feele on your — F1442 4.3.12 Fredrk
Hell claimes his <calls for> right, and with a roaring voyce, — F1726 5.1.53 Faust
And Faustus now will come to do thee right. — F1728 5.1.55 Faust
and let thy left eye be diametarily fixt upon my right heele, — F App p.231 70 P Wagner
Both in their right shapes, gesture, and attire/They usde to — F App p.237 33 Emper
When all the woods about stand bolt up-right, — Lucan, First Booke 143
Force mastered right, the strongest govern'd all. — Lucan, First Booke 177
appeasd/The wrastling tumult, and right hand made silence: — Lucan, First Booke 299
force, they that now thwart right/In wars wil yeeld to wrong: — Lucan, First Booke 349
I aske but right: — Ovid's Elegies 1.3.1
Over my Mistris is my right more great? — Ovid's Elegies 1.7.30
For after death all men receive their right: — Ovid's Elegies 1.15.40
My lordly hands ile throwe upon my right. — Ovid's Elegies 2.5.30
Heere thou hast strength, here thy right hand doth rest. — Ovid's Elegies 2.9.36
(Their reines let loose) right soone my house approach. — Ovid's Elegies 2.16.50
Erre I? or mirtle in her right hand lies. — Ovid's Elegies 3.1.34
But spare my wench thou at her right hand seated, — Ovid's Elegies 3.2.21
At me Joves right-hand lightning hath to throwe. — Ovid's Elegies 3.3.30
A free-borne wench, no right 'tis up to locke: — Ovid's Elegies 3.4.33
A target bore: bloud sprinckled was his right. — Ovid's Elegies 3.7.16
Beauty with lewdnesse doth right ill agree. — Ovid's Elegies 3.10.42
Deceive all, let me erre, and thinke I am right, — Ovid's Elegies 3.13.29

RIGHTEOUS

Religious, righteous, and inviolate. — 2Tamb 2.1.48 Sgsmnd

RIGHTEOUSLY

The man that dealeth righteously shall live: — Jew 1.2.116 Barab

RIGHTEOUSNESSE

If thou rely upon thy righteousnesse, — Jew 1.2.121 Govnr

RIGHTFULL

Your Majestie her rightfull Lord and Soveraigne. — P 583 11.48 Pleshe

RIGHT-HAND

At me Joves right-hand lightning hath to throwe. — Ovid's Elegies 3.3.30

RIGHTLY

That colour rightly did appeare so bloudy. — Ovid's Elegies 1.12.12
Whose fruit none rightly can describe, but hee/That puls or — Hero and Leander 2.299

RIGOUR

his fearefull arme/Be pour'd with rigour on our sinfull heads, — 2Tamb 2.1.58 Fredrk
And with the paines my rigour shall inflict, — 2Tamb 4.1.184 Tamb

RIMES

Ballads and rimes, made of thy overthrow. — Edw 2.2.178 Mortmr

RIMING

From jygging vaines of riming mother wits, — 1Tamb Prol.1 Prolog

RING (Homograph)

And with maine force flung on a ring of pikes, — Dido 2.1.196 Aeneas
These golden bracelets, and this wedding ring, — Dido 3.4.62 Dido
Trotting the ring, and tilting at a glove: — 2Tamb 1.3.39 Zenoc
Hast thou beheld a peale of ordinance strike/A ring of pikes, — 2Tamb 3.2.99 Tamb
a golden crosse/With Christian posies round about the ring. — Jew 2.3.297 Barab
How sweet the Bels ring now the Nuns are dead/That sound at — Jew 4.1.2 Barab
And then the watchword being given, a bell shall ring, — P 238 4.36 Guise
And ring alcude the knell of Gaveston. — Edw 2.3.26 Mortmr
Let Plutos bels ring out my fatall knell, — Edw 4.7.89 Edward
become of Faustus that/Was wont to make our schooles ring, — F 195 1.2.2 1Schol
Turne round thy gold-ring, as it were to ease thee. — Ovid's Elegies 1.4.26
Thou ring that shalt my faire girles finger binde, — Ovid's Elegies 2.15.1
Blest ring thou in my mistris hand shalt lye, — Ovid's Elegies 2.15.7
And even the ring performe a mans part well. — Ovid's Elegies 2.15.26
With wheeles bent inward now the ring-turne ride. — Ovid's Elegies 3.2.12
Alas he runnes too farre about the ring, — Ovid's Elegies 3.2.69
but he must weare/The sacred ring wherewith she was endow'd, — Hero and Leander 2.109

RINGING

Ringing with joy their superstitious belles: — 1Tamb 3.3.237 Bajzth
armes in ure/With digging graves and ringing dead mens knels: — Jew 2.3.185 Barab

RINGLED

Spits foorth the ringled bit, and with his hoves, — Hero and Leander 2.143

RINGS (Homograph)

He sends her letters, bracelets, jewels, rings. — Jew 2.3.259 Barab
And now stay/That bel that to the devils mattins rings. — P 448 7.88 Guise
And sentence given in rings of naked swords, — Lucan, First Booke 321
Wandering about the North, and rings of fire/Flie in the ayre, — Lucan, First Booke 525
joies/Then nymphs and sheapheards, when the timbrell rings, — Hero and Leander 2.233

RING-TURNE

With wheeles bent inward now the ring-turne ride. — Ovid's Elegies 3.2.12

RIOTE (See also RYOT)

And riote it with the treasure of the realme, — Edw 1.4.405 Mortmr

RIOTOUS

Deare shall you both abie this riotous deede: — Edw 2.2.88 Edward

RIP

First shalt thou rip my bowels with thy sword, — 1Tamb 4.2.16 Bajzth
Or rip thy bowels, and rend out thy heart, — 2Tamb 3.5.121 Tamb
To rip the golden bowels of America. — P 854 17.49 Guise
Here man, rip up this panting brest of mine, — Edw 4.7.66 Edward

RIPE

Browne Almonds, Servises, ripe Figs and Dates, — Dido 4.5.5 Nurse
I would request no better meate, then a dish of ripe grapes. — F1573 4.6.16 P Lady
is barren of his fruite, from whence you had these ripe grapes. — F1580 4.6.23 P Duke
I would desire no better meate then a dish of ripe grapes. — F App p.242 11 P Duchss
would have thought their houses had bin fierd/Or dropping-ripe, — Lucan, First Booke 491
Fruites ripe will fall, let springing things increase, — Ovid's Elegies 2.14.25
And ripe-earde corne with sharpe-edg'd sithes to fell. — Ovid's Elegies 3.9.12

RIPE-EARDE

And ripe-earde corne with sharpe-edg'd sithes to fell. — Ovid's Elegies 3.9.12

RIPER			
For riper yeares will weane him from such toyes.	Edw	1.4.401	MortSr
At <of> riper yeares to Wittenberg <Wertenberg> he went,	F 13	Prol.13	1Chor
RIPEST			
Untill we reach the ripest fruit of all,	1Tamb	2.7.27	Tamb
RIPPING			
Ripping the bowels of the earth for them,	Jew	1.1.109	Barab
RIPT			
Then from the navell to the throat at once,/He ript old Priam:	Dido	2.1.256	Aeneas
RISE			
And from mine ashes let a Conquerour rise,	Dido	5.1.306	Dido
Thence rise the tears that so distain my cheeks,	1Tamb	3.2.64	Zenoc
That I may rise into my royall throne.	1Tamb	4.2.15	Tamb
my souldiers march/Shal rise aloft and touch the horned Moon,	2Tamb	1.3.14	Tamb
Then rise at midnight to a solemne masse.	Jew	1.2.373	Mthias
But suddenly the wind began to rise,	Jew	2.2.13	Bosco
And rise with them i'th middle of the Towne,	Jew	5.1.92	Barab
Then may we with some colour rise in armes,	Edw	1.4.279	Mortmr
And threatenest death whether he rise or fall,	Edw	2.2.44	Edward
Spencer, all live to die, and rise to fall.	Edw	4.7.112	Baldck
As thou intendest to rise by Mortimer,	Edw	5.2.52	Mortmr
By which the spirits are inforc'd to rise:	F 241	1.3.13	Faust
Maister Doctor awake, and rise, and give me my mony againe, for	F1489	4.4.33	P HrsCsr
Faire natures eye, rise, rise againe and make/Perpetuall day:	F1931	5.2.135	Faust
All rise in armes; nor could the bed-rid parents/Keep back	Lucan, First Booke		502
New factions rise; now through the world againe/I goe; o	Lucan, First Booke		691
When to go homewards we rise all along,	Ovid's Elegies		1.4.55
Sees not the morne on rosie horses rise.	Ovid's Elegies		1.8.4
Who slumbring, they rise up in swelling armes.	Ovid's Elegies		1.9.26
the vanquisht rise/And who thou never think'st should fall	Ovid's Elegies		1.9.29
Ere thou rise starres teach seamen where to saile,	Ovid's Elegies		1.13.11
Poore travailers though tierd, rise at thy sight,	Ovid's Elegies		1.13.13
[All] <This> could I beare, but that the wench should rise,/Who	Ovid's Elegies		1.13.25
And from my mistris bosome let me rise:	Ovid's Elegies		2.10.20
Thou swearest, devision should not twixt us rise,	Ovid's Elegies		2.16.43
he stayd his furie, and began/To give her leave to rise:	Hero and Leander		1.416
RISING			
First rising in the East with milde aspect,	1Tamb	4.2.37	Tamb
Unto the rising of this earthly globe,	2Tamb	5.3.147	Tamb
And by the rising herbes, where cleare springs slide,	Ovid's Elegies		2.16.9
But still the rising billowes answered no.	Hero and Leander		2.152
For though the rising yv'rie mount he scal'd,	Hero and Leander		2.273
RISO			
Riso, Sancina, and the bordering townes,	2Tamb	3.1.52	Trebiz
RITCH			
Then I may fetch from this ritch treasurie:	Edw	1.4.332	Queene
RITES			
Scorning our loves and royall marriage rites,	Dido	4.2.16	Iarbus
By this right hand, and by our spousall rites,	Dido	5.1.134	Dido
And if we should with common rites of Armes,	1Tamb	5.1.11	Govnr
We wil our celebrated rites of mariage solemnize.	1Tamb	5.1.534	Tamb
Knit in these hands, thus joyn'd in nuptiall rites,	P 4	1.4	Charls
And now my Lords the mariage rites perfourm'd,	P 18	1.18	Charls
How they did storme at these your nuptiall rites,	P 49	1.49	Admral
If ever Hymen lowr'd at marriage rites,	P 58	2.1	Guise
Our solemne rites of Coronation done,	P 626	12.39	King
Pope Julius did abuse the Churches Rites,	F 928	3.1.150	Pope
Quirinus rites and Latian Jove advanc'd/On Alba hill o Vestall	Lucan, First Booke		200
now in peace renew/Your barbarous customes, and sinister rites,	Lucan, First Booke		447
To know their rites, well recompenc'd my stay,	Ovid's Elegies		3.12.5
The rites/In which Loves beauteous Empresse most delites,	Hero and Leander		1.299
When Venus sweet rites are perform'd and done.	Hero and Leander		1.320
yet he suspected/Some amorous rites or other were neglected.	Hero and Leander		2.64
RIVALL			
That resteth in the rivall of thy paine,	Dido	3.3.84	Iarbus
person to the view/Of fierce Achilles, rivall of his fame.	2Tamb	3.5.68	Tamb
The other eyes his rivall as his foe.	Ovid's Elegies		1.9.18
But with my rivall sicke she was not than.	Ovid's Elegies		3.10.26
RIVE			
Although the sunne to rive the earth incline,	Ovid's Elegies		2.16.3
RIVELD			
Ile give thee tackling made of riveld gold,	Dido	3.1.116	Dido
hoary flieces/And riveld cheekes I would have puld a pieces.	Ovid's Elegies		1.8.112
RIVEN (See also RIVIN)			
With cracke of riven ayre and hideous sound,	Lucan, First Booke		153
RIVER			
and brave Theridamas/Have met us by the river Araris:	1Tamb	2.1.63	Cosroe
Waiting my comming to the river side,	2Tamb	1.2.22	Callap
And I have martch'd along the river Nile,	2Tamb	1.3.186	Techel
Where by the river Tyros I subdew'd/Stoka, Padalia, and	2Tamb	1.3.209	Therid
To drinke the river Nile or Euphrates,	2Tamb	3.1.42	Orcan
What fearfull cries comes from the river [Sene] <Rene>,/That	P 361	7.1	Ramus
Which we have chaste into the river [Sene] <Rene>,	P 418	7.58	Guise
And sinke them in the river as they swim.	P 423	7.63	Dumain
Lets throw him into the river.	P 487	9.6	P 1Atndt
Heere in the river rides a Flemish hoie,	Edw	2.4.46	Mortmr
We saw the River Maine, fall into Rhine <Rhines>,	F 785	3.1.7	Faust
what did I but rid him into a great river, and when I came just	F1543	4.5.39	P HrsCsr
There harmelesse Swans feed all abroad the river,	Ovid's Elegies		2.6.53
Rather thou large banke over-flowing river,	Ovid's Elegies		3.5.19
That of the cooling river durst not drinke,	Hero and Leander		2.197
RIVERS			
of Affrike, where I view'd/The Ethiopian sea, rivers and lakes:	2Tamb	1.3.196	Techel

RIVERS (cont.)			
Deep rivers, havens, creekes, and litle seas,	2Tamb	3.2.87	Tamb
Pelignian fields [with] <which> liqued rivers flowe,	Ovid's Elegies		2.16.5
By shallow Rivers, to whose falls,	Passionate Shepherd		7
RIVER SIDE			
Waiting my comming to the river side,	2Tamb	1.2.22	Callap
RIVIN			
His Skul al rivin in twain, his braines dasht out?	1Tamb	5.1.306	Zabina
RIVO			
Hey Rivo Castiliano, a man's a man.	Jew	4.4.10	P Ithimr
ROABES			
Cast off your armor, put on scarlet roabes.	1Tamb	5.1.524	Tamb
ROAD (See RHOAD, RHODE, RODE)			
ROAN			
Mountsorrell unto Roan, and spare not one/That you suspect of	P 446	7.86	Guise
ROARE (See also RORE)			
Ile make ye roare, that earth may eccho foorth/The far	2Tamb	4.1.185	Tamb
ROARING			
That roaring, shake Damascus turrets downe.	1Tamb	4.1.3	Souldn
Or roaring Cannons sever all thy joints,	1Tamb	5.1.223	Bajzth
Hell claimes his <calls for> right, and with a roaring voyce,	F1726	5.1.53	Faust
Rafe, keepe out, for I am about a roaring peece of worke.	F App	p.233 11 P	Robin
With jawes wide open ghastly roaring out;	Lucan, First Booke		212
ROASTED (See also ROST)			
burladie I had neede have it wel roasted, and good sawce to it,	F App	p.229 12 P	Clown
ROAVE			
Whiles I with my Achates roave abroad,	Dido	1.1.175	Aeneas
ROB			
Who seekes to rob me of thy Sisters love,	Dido	4.2.31	Iarbus
To rob their mistresse of her Troian guest?	Dido	4.4.138	Dido
About the Grecian Isles to rob and spoile:	2Tamb	3.5.94	Jrslem
For that is theft; and if you rob me thus,	Jew	1.2.126	Barab
Shall Lodowicke rob me of so faire a love?	Jew	2.3.347	Mthias
Madam, tis you that rob me of my lord.	Edw	1.4.161	Gavstn
good divel forgive me now, and Ile never rob thy Library more.	F App	p.235 31 P	Robin
Or rob the gods; or sacred temples fire;	Lucan, First Booke		380
Many to rob is more sure, and lesse hatefull,	Ovid's Elegies		1.8.55
hast sworne/To rob her name and honour, and thereby/Commit'st a	Hero and Leander		1.305
ROBB'D			
compasse it/By reason of the warres, that robb'd our store;	Jew	1.2.48	Govnr
ROBBE			
Doe yee heare, I would be sorie to robbe you of your living.	F App	p.229 18 P	Clown
ROBBER			
Away base groome, robber of kings renowme,	Edw	2.5.72	Mortmr
ROB'D			
Hath rob'd me of eternall happinesse.	F1884	5.2.88	Faust
ROBD			
How Gaveston hath robd me of his love:	Edw	2.4.67	Queene
ROBE (See also ROABES)			
Priest/Cal'd John the great, sits in a milk-white robe,	2Tamb	1.3.188	Techel
And I sat downe, cloth'd with the massie robe,	2Tamb	3.2.123	Tamb
Like lovely Thetis in a Christall robe:	2Tamb	3.4.51	Therid
A decent forme, thinne robe, a lovers looke,	Ovid's Elegies		3.1.9
Then did the robe or garment which she wore <more>,	Ovid's Elegies		3.6.40
ROBES			
But Illioneus goes not in such robes.	Dido	2.1.48	Achat
And clad us in these wealthie robes we weare.	Dido	2.1.65	Illion
Warlike Aeneas, and in these base robes?	Dido	2.1.79	Dido
My princely robes thou seest are layd aside,	Dido	3.3.3	Dido
Tis true, and but for reverence of these robes,	Edw	1.1.180	Gavstn
With garish robes, not armor, and thy selfe/Bedaubd with golde,	Edw	2.2.184	Mortmr
As doth this water from my tattered robes:	Edw	5.5.67	Edward
hearse, where it shall lie,/And bring my funerall robes:	Edw	5.6.95	King
scorn'd old sparing diet, and ware robes/Too light for women;	Lucan, First Booke		165
The Poets God arayed in robes of gold,	Ovid's Elegies		1.8.59
Beyond thy robes thy dangling [lockes] <lackes> had sweept.	Ovid's Elegies		1.14.4
While thus I speake, blacke dust her white robes ray:	Ovid's Elegies		3.2.41
And stately robes to their gilt feete hang downe.	Ovid's Elegies		3.12.26
But with your robes, put on an honest face,	Ovid's Elegies		3.13.27
Rich robes, themselves and others do adorne,	Hero and Leander		1.237
She stayd not for her robes, but straight arose,	Hero and Leander		2.235
ROBIN			
What Robin, you must come away and walk the horses.	F 725	2.3.4 P	Dick
tell me, in good sadnesse Robin, is that a conjuring booke?	F 744	2.3.23 P	Dick
Sirra Robin, we were best looke that your devill can answere	F1088	3.3.1 P	Dick
Now Robin, now or never shew thy cunning.	F1094	3.3.7 P	Dick
do, hold the cup Robin, I feare not your searching; we scorne to	F1105	3.3.18 P	Dick
No Robin, why is't?	F1510	4.5.6 P	Dick
Robin, prethee come away, theres a Gentleman tarries to have	F App	p.233 6 P	Rafe
Why Robin what booke is that?	F App	p.233 18 P	Rafe
O brave Robin, shal I have Nan Spit, and to mine owne use?	F App	p.234 29 P	Rafe
But Robin, here comes the vintner.	F App	p.234 4 P	Rafe
O nomine Domine, what meanst thou Robin?	F App	p.235 26 P	Vintnr
ROBS			
That robs your merchants of Persepolis,	1Tamb	1.1.37	Meandr
ROBST			
Villaine, tis thou that robst me of my lord.	Edw	1.4.160	Queene
ROCK			
hollow hanging of a hill/And crooked bending of a craggy rock,	2Tamb	1.2.58	Callap
Goe villaine, cast thee headlong from a rock,	2Tamb	3.5.120	Tamb
ROCKE			
And shivered against a craggie rocke.	1Tamb	4.3.34	Souldn
Fenc'd with the concave of a monstrous rocke,	2Tamb	3.2.89	Tamb

Context	Work	Reference	Speaker
ROCKE (cont.)			
run to some rocke and throw my selfe headlong into the sea;	Jew	3.4.39	P Ithimr
The rocke is hollow, and of purpose digg'd,	Jew	5.1.87	Barab
Thorough a rocke of stone in one nights space:	F 793	3.1.15	Faust
This Traytor flies unto some steepie rocke,	F1413	4.2.89	Faust
Bred in the concave of some monstrous rocke:	F App	p.238 73	Knight
that guardst/Roomes mighty walles built on Tarpeian rocke,	Lucan, First Booke		198
what [rockes] <rocke> the feard Ceránnia <Ceraunia> threat,	Ovid's Elegies		2.11.19
Upon a rocke, and underneath a hill,	Hero and Leander		1.345
And then he got him to a rocke aloft.	Hero and Leander		2.148
ROCKES			
Disperst them all amongst the wrackfull Rockes:	Dido	1.2.29	Cloan
Yea all my Navie split with Rockes and Shelfes:	Dido	3.1.108	Aeneas
Thy Anchors shall be hewed from Christall Rockes,	Dido	3.1.120	Dido
Blow windes, threaten ye Rockes and sandie shelfes,	Dido	4.4.58	Aeneas
The Rockes and Sea-gulfes will performe at large,	Dido	5.1.171	Dido
O sister, sister, take away the Rockes,	Dido	5.1.254	Dido
as outwaies the sands/And all the craggie rockes of Caspea.	1Tamb	2.3.48	Tamb
Fairer than rockes of pearle and pretious stone,	1Tamb	3.3.118	Tamb
Wherein are rockes of Pearle, that shine as bright/As all the	2Tamb	5.3.156	Tamb
that in the Easterne rockes/Without controule can picke his	Jew	1.1.21	Barab
Under the rockes by crooked Vogesus;	Lucan, First Booke		399
what [rockes] <rocke> the feard Ceránnia <Ceraunia> threat,	Ovid's Elegies		2.11.19
And rockes dyed crimson with Prometheus bloud.	Ovid's Elegies		2.16.40
And with sweete words cause deafe rockes to have loved <moned>,	Ovid's Elegies		3.6.58
ROCKS			
Both barking Scilla, and the sounding Rocks,	Dido	1.1.146	Aeneas
Through rocks more steepe and sharp than Caspian cliftes.	2Tamb	5.3.241	Tamb
As when against pine bearing Ossa's rocks,	Lucan, First Booke		390
whose seas/Eate hollow rocks, and where the north-west wind/Nor	Lucan, First Booke		407
Under whose hoary rocks Gebenna hangs;	Lucan, First Booke		436
Which rashly twixt the sharpe rocks in the deepe,	Ovid's Elegies		2.11.3
Nor passe I thee, who hollow rocks downe tumbling,	Ovid's Elegies		3.5.45
And wee will sit upon the Rocks,	Passionate Shepherd		5
ROCKT			
And with still panting rockt, there tooke his rest.	Hero and Leander		1.44
ROD			
Which when he tainted with his slender rod,	2Tamb	1.3.40	Zenoc
On her, this god/Enamoured was, and with his snakie rod,/Did	Hero and Leander		1.398
RODE (Homograph)			
Ninus and great Alexander/Have rode in triumph, triumphs	2Tamb	5.1.70	Tamb
Unto the walles of Yorke the Scots made rode,	Edw	2.2.166	Lncstr
and thy selfe/Bedaubd with golde, rode laughing at the rest,	Edw	2.2.185	Mortmr
Their lord rode home, thinking his prisoner safe,	Edw	3.1.117	Arundl
ROES			
And let his foes like flockes of fearfull Roes,	1Tamb	3.3.192	Zenoc
ROGUE			
The rogue of Volga holds Zenocrate,	1Tamb	4.1.4	Souldn
Not? then I'le make thee, [rogue] <goe>.	Jew	4.1.95	2Fryar
How, dost call me rogue?	Jew	4.1.96	1Fryar
crosbiting, such a Rogue/As is the husband to a hundred whores:	Jew	4.3.13	Barab
ROGUISH			
That like a roguish runnaway, suborn'd/That villaine there,	2Tamb	3.5.86	Tamb
ROIALISE			
To roialise the deedes of Tamburlaine:	1Tamb	2.3.8	Tamb
ROIALL			
And staine my roiall standard with the same,	Edw	3.1.138	Edward
ROIALLIE			
Now let us in, and feast it roiallie:	Edw	1.4.374	Edward
ROIALLYE			
A brow for Love to banquet roiallye,	Hero and Leander		1.86
ROLL (See ROUL'D, ROULES, ROWLING)			
ROMAINE			
As Caesar riding in the Romaine streete,	Edw	1.1.173	Gavstn
The Romaine Tullie loved Octavius,	Edw	1.4.396	MortSr
For saving of a Romaine Citizen,	Lucan, First Booke		359
Caesar; he whom I heare thy trumpets charge/I hould no Romaine;	Lucan, First Booke		375
Punisht I am, if I a Romaine beat,	Ovid's Elegies		1.7.29
ROMAN			
His losse made way for Roman outrages.	Lucan, First Booke		106
Mild Atax glad it beares not Roman [boats] <bloats>;	Lucan, First Booke		404
Now give the Roman Tragedie a name,	Ovid's Elegies		3.1.29
ROMANE			
The Romane Scepter royall shall remaine,	Dido	1.1.105	Jupitr
Nay what is she that any Romane loves,	Ovid's Elegies		2.4.47
Nor Romane stocke scorne me so much (I crave)/Gifts then my	Ovid's Elegies		3.5.65
ROMANES			
As ancient Romanes over their Captive Lords,	P 982	19.52	Guise
which bouldly faine themselves/The Romanes brethren, sprung of	Lucan, First Booke		429
ROMANS			
for as the Romans usde/I here present thee with a naked sword.	2Tamb	1.1.81	Sgsmnd
Romans, what madnes, what huge lust of warre/Hath made	Lucan, First Booke		8
Romans if ye be,/And beare true harts, stay heare:	Lucan, First Booke		193
When Romans are besieg'd by forraine foes,	Lucan, First Booke		513
These sad presages were enough to scarre/The quivering Romans,	Lucan, First Booke		673
One slowe we favour, Romans him revoke:	Ovid's Elegies		3.2.73
ROMBELOW			
With a rombelow.	Edw	2.2.195	Lncstr
ROME (Homograph; See also ROOM, ROOME, ROOMES, ROOMS)			
of Verna and Bulgaria/And almost to the very walles of Rome,	2Tamb	2.1.9	Fredrk
for whose byrth/Olde Rome was proud, but gasde a while on her,	2Tamb	2.4.92	Tamb
That hath blasphemde the holy Church of Rome,	P 531	10.4	Guise
Then shall the Catholick faith of Rome,	P 639	12.52	QnMoth

ROME (cont.)			
And binde it wholy to the Sea of Rome:	P 926	18.27	Navrre
And all those traitors to the Church of Rome,	P1120	21.14	Dumain
And fire accursed Rome about his eares.	P1200	22.62	King
To ruinate that wicked Church of Rome,	P1204	22.66	King
As Rome and all those popish Prelates there,	P1248	22.110	Navrre
displeases him | And fill up his rome that he shold occupie.	Paris	ms 4,p390	P Souldr
But you will saye you leave him rome enoughe besides:	Paris	ms 7,p390	P Souldr
For heele complaine unto the sea of Rome.	Edw	1.1.190	Kent
On your allegeance to the sea of Rome,	Edw	1.4.52	ArchBp
Proud Rome, that hatchest such imperiall groomes,	Edw	1.4.97	Edward
That like the lawles Catiline of Rome,	Edw	4.6.51	Rice
And as I guesse will first arrive at Rome,	F 775	2.3.54	2Chor
Conducted me within the walles of Rome?	F 802	3.1.24	Faust
Rome containes <containeth> for to delight thine eyes <thee	F 810	3.1.32	Mephst
That make <makes> safe passage, to each part of Rome.	F 816	3.1.38	Mephst
to see the Monuments/And situation of bright splendent Rome,	F 829	3.1.51	Faust
This day is held through Rome and Italy,	F 834	3.1.56	Mephst
This day shall make thee be admir'd in Rome.	F 867	3.1.89	Mephst
The Pope shall curse that Faustus came to Rome.	F 903	3.1.125	Faust
For him, and the succeeding Popes of Rome,	F 926	3.1.148	Bruno
Most sacred Patron of the Church of Rome,	F 951	3.1.173	Faust
<to do what I please unseene of any whilst I stay in Rome>.	F 993	(HC266)A	P Faust
That on a furies back came post from Rome,	F1161	4.1.7	Fredrk
love with him, I would he would post with him to Rome againe.	F1191	4.1.37	P Benvol
Ile bouldly quarter out the fields of Rome;	Lucan, First Booke	383	
Leaving the woods, lodge in the streetes of Rome.	Lucan, First Booke	558	
Or if Fate rule them, Rome thy Cittizens/Are neere some plague:	Lucan, First Booke	643	
onely gives us peace, o Rome continue/The course of mischiefe,	Lucan, First Booke	669	
Why grapples Rome, and makes war, having no foes?	Lucan, First Booke	681	
hils, hence to the mounts/Pirene, and so backe to Rome againe.	Lucan, First Booke	689	
While Rome of all the [conquered] <conquering> world is head.	Ovid's Elegies	1.15.26	
Rome if her strength the huge world had not fild,	Ovid's Elegies	2.9.17	
A woman against late-built Rome did send/The Sabine Fathers,	Ovid's Elegies	2.12.23	
He had not beene that conquering Rome did build.	Ovid's Elegies	2.14.16	
When carefull Rome in doubt their prowesse held.	Ovid's Elegies	3.14.10	
ROMULUS			
Remus and Romulus, Ilias twinne-borne seed.	Ovid's Elegies	3.4.40	
Heaven thou affects, with Romulus, temples brave/Bacchus,	Ovid's Elegies	3.7.51	
ROOFE			
And hung on stately Mecas Temple roofe,	2Tamb	1.1.141	Orcan
ROOFFES			
That rooffes of golde, and sun-bright Pallaces,	1Tamb	4.2.62	Zabina
ROOF'T			
And roof't aloft with curious worke in gold.	F 798	3.1.20	Faust
ROOM			
Yet Room is much bound to these civil armes,	Lucan, First Booke	44	
And love to Room (thogh slaughter steeld their harts/And minds	Lucan, First Booke	355	
ROOME (Homograph; See also ROUME)			
Nay quickly then, before his roome be hot.	1Tamb	2.5.89	Usumc
And roome within to lodge sixe thousand men.	2Tamb	3.2.72	Tamb
increaseth, so inclose/Infinite riches in a little roome.	Jew	1.1.37	Barab
the rest have taine their standings in the next roome,	P 995	19.65	P 3Mur
but madam, right makes roome,/Where weapons want, and though a	Edw	4.2.50	Mortmr
Within this roome is lockt the messenger,	Edw	5.4.17	Mortmr
See that in the next roome I have a fier,	Edw	5.5.29	Ltborn
we'le into another roome and drinke a while, and then we'le go	F1556	4.5.52	P Robin
Here in this roome will wretched Faustus be.	F1804	5.2.8	Mephst
but let us into the next roome, and [there] pray for him.	F1872	5.2.76	P 1Schol
Roome, if thou take delight in impious warre,	Lucan, First Booke	21	
Whence thou shouldst view thy Roome with squinting beams.	Lucan, First Booke	55	
Roome was so great it could not beare it selfe:	Lucan, First Booke	72	
O Roome thy selfe art cause of all these evils,	Lucan, First Booke	84	
share our Empire, fortune that made Roome/Governe the earth,	Lucan, First Booke	109	
At night in dreadful vision fearefull Roome,	Lucan, First Booke	188	
Latian Jove advanc'd/On Alba hill o Vestall flames, o Roome,	Lucan, First Booke	201	
He, he afflicts Roome that made me Roomes foe.	Lucan, First Booke	205	
As oft as Roome was sackt, here gan the spoile:	Lucan, First Booke	258	
From doubtfull Roome wrongly expel'd the Tribunes,	Lucan, First Booke	269	
wonst thou France; Roome may be won/With farre lesse toile,	Lucan, First Booke	283	
Nor shalt thou triumph when thou comst to Roome;	Lucan, First Booke	287	
Roome rageth now in armes/As if the Carthage Hannibal were	Lucan, First Booke	304	
were we bestead/When comming conqueror, Roome afflicts me thus?	Lucan, First Booke	310	
But Roome at thraldoms feet to rid from tyrants.	Lucan, First Booke	352	
Albeit the Citty thou wouldst have so ra'st/Be Roome it selfe.	Lucan, First Booke	387	
And in all quarters musters men for Roome.	Lucan, First Booke	396	
March towards Roome; and you fierce men of Rhene/Leaving your	Lucan, First Booke	460	
and that Roome/He looking on by these men should be sackt.	Lucan, First Booke	479	
(that did remaine/To their afflictions) were t'abandon Roome.	Lucan, First Booke	495	
As loath to leave Roome whom they held so deere,	Lucan, First Booke	506	
Roome that flowes/With Citizens and [Captives] <Captaines>, and	Lucan, First Booke	509	
Thou Roome at name of warre runst from thy selfe,	Lucan, First Booke	517	
While these thus in and out had circled Roome,	Lucan, First Booke	604	
Before the roome be cleere, and doore put too.	Ovid's Elegies	3.13.10	
Had spread the boord, with roses strowed the roome,	Hero and Leander	2.21	
At least vouchsafe these armes some little roome,	Hero and Leander	2.249	
ROOMES (Homograph)			
and vallours be advaunst/To roomes of honour and Nobilitie.	1Tamb	2.3.41	Cosroe
Stick in his breast, as in their proper roomes.	1Tamb	5.1.226	Zabina
Now throwen to roomes of blacke abjection,	1Tamb	5.1.267	Bajzth
Good Fredericke see the roomes be voyded straight,	F1157	4.1.3	Mrtino
Roomes infant walles were steept in brothers bloud;	Lucan, First Booke	95	
Poverty (who hatcht/Roomes greatest wittes) was loath'd, and al	Lucan, First Booke	167	

ROOMES (cont.)			
that guardst/Roomes mighty walles built on Tarpeian rocke,	Lucan, First Booke	198	
He, he afflicts Roome that made me Roomes foe.	Lucan, First Booke	205	
But seeing white Eagles, and Roomes flags wel known,	Lucan, First Booke	246	
ROOMS			
chiefe leader of Rooms force,/So be I may be bold to speake a	Lucan, First Booke	360	
ROOT			
Sharp hunger bites upon and gripes the root,	1Tamb	5.1.273	Bajzth
Who though his root be weake, and his owne waight/Keepe him	Lucan, First Booke	139	
ROOTE			
And roote Valoys his line from forth of France,	P1113	21.7	Dumain
ROPES			
Thou hast no bridge, nor boate with ropes to throw,	Ovid's Elegies	3.5.3	
RORE			
Hether the windes blowe, here the spring-tide rore.	Ovid's Elegies	2.11.40	
ROSE (Homograph)			
When suddenly gloomie Orion rose,	Dido	1.2.26	Cloan
Frighted with this confused noyse, I rose,	Dido	2.1.191	Aeneas
Who I? you are deceived, I rose but now.	P 437	7.77	Anjoy
Ah had some bloudlesse furie rose from hell,	Edw	1.4.316	Edward
Day rose and viewde these tumultes of the war;	Lucan, First Booke	235	
a double point/Rose like the Theban brothers funerall fire;	Lucan, First Booke	550	
Such as a rose mixt with a lilly breedes,	Ovid's Elegies	2.5.37	
Faire white with rose red was before commixt:	Ovid's Elegies	3.3.5	
Pure rose shee, like a Nun to sacrifice,	Ovid's Elegies	3.6.21	
Hath any rose so from a fresh yong maide,	Ovid's Elegies	3.6.53	
Drouping more then a Rose puld yesterday:	Ovid's Elegies	3.6.66	
Rose-cheekt Adonis) kept a solemne feast.	Hero and Leander	1.93	
And modestly they opened as she rose:	Hero and Leander	1.160	
Her breath as fragrant as the morning rose,	Hero and Leander	1.391	
ROSEAT			
Thy bosomes Roseat buds let him not finger,	Ovid's Elegies	1.4.37	
ROSE-CHEEKT			
Rose-cheekt Adonis) kept a solemne feast.	Hero and Leander	1.93	
ROSES			
Blushing Roses, purple Hyacinthe:	Dido	2.1.319	Venus
Musk-roses, and a thousand sort of flowers,	Dido	4.5.8	Nurse
And on their faces heapes of Roses strow.	Ovid's Elegies	1.2.40	
Had spread the boord, with roses strowed the roome,	Hero and Leander	2.21	
And I will make thee beds of Roses,	Passionate Shepherd	9	
ROSIE			
Thy Rosie cheekes be to thy thombe inclinde.	Ovid's Elegies	1.4.22	
Sees not the morne on rosie horses rise.	Ovid's Elegies	1.8.4	
Hold in thy rosie horses that they move not.	Ovid's Elegies	1.13.10	
There in your rosie lippes my tongue intombe,	Ovid's Elegies	3.13.23	
ROSO			
Bordering on Mare Roso neere to Meca.	2Tamb	3.5.131	Callap
ROST			
And rost our new found victuals on this shoare.	Dido	1.1.168	Aeneas
bowes enow/Neere to these woods, to rost your meate withall:	Dido	1.1.173	Aeneas
ROSTED			
I had need to have it well rosted, and good sauce to it,	F 352	1.4.10	P Robin
ROTTEN			
I pray that rotten age you wrackes/And sluttish white-mould	Ovid's Elegies	1.12.29	
ROUGH (See also RUFFE)			
The sea is rough, the windes blow to the shoare.	Dido	4.4.25	Aeneas
O false Aeneas, now the sea is rough,	Dido	4.4.26	Dido
to be enthral'd/To forraine powers, and rough imperious yokes:	1Tamb	5.1.36	Govnr
And rough jades mouths with stubburn bits are torne,	Ovid's Elegies	1.2.15	
And farewell cruell posts, rough thresholds block,	Ovid's Elegies	1.6.73	
Nor thunder in rough threatings haughty pride?	Ovid's Elegies	1.7.46	
love please/[Am] <And> driven like a ship upon rough seas,	Ovid's Elegies	2.4.8	
And with rough clawes your tender cheekes assaile.	Ovid's Elegies	2.6.4	
Or any back made rough with stripes imbrace?	Ovid's Elegies	2.7.22	
raught/Ill waies by rough seas wondring waves first taught,	Ovid's Elegies	2.11.2	
Because thy belly should rough wrinckles lacke,	Ovid's Elegies	2.14.7	
Then on the rough Alpes should I tread aloft,	Ovid's Elegies	2.16.19	
Looke gently, and rough husbands lawes despise.	Ovid's Elegies	3.4.44	
Till then, rough was her father, she severe,	Ovid's Elegies	3.7.31	
Though thether leades a rough steepe hilly way.	Ovid's Elegies	3.12.6	
ROUGHE			
Warwick I know is roughe, and Lancaster/Inexorable, and I shall	Edw	3.1.6	Edward
ROUL'D			
Whether the sea roul'd alwaies from that point,	Lucan, First Booke	413	
ROULES			
from the breach/Of Libian Syrtes roules a monstrous wave,	Lucan, First Booke	497	
ROUME			
The God of war resignes his roume to me,	1Tamb	5.1.450	Tamb
ROUND			
And we were round inviron'd with the Greekes:	Dido	2.1.269	Aeneas
Her silver armes will coll me round about,	Dido	4.3.51	Aeneas
And triple wise intrench her round about:	Dido	5.1.10	Aeneas
Environing their Standard round, that stood/As bristle-pointed	1Tamb	4.1.26	2Msngr
And with his hoste [martcht] <martch> round about the earth,	2Tamb	3.2.111	Tamb
Run mourning round about the Femals misse,	2Tamb	4.1.188	Tamb
Run tilting round about the firmament,	2Tamb	4.1.203	Tamb
Belike they coasted round by Candie shoare/About their Oyles,	Jew	1.1.91	Barab
a golden crosse/With Christian posies round about the ring.	Jew	2.3.297	Barab
make her round and plump, and batten more then you are aware.	Jew	3.4.65	P Ithimr
Besides I know not how much weight in Pearle/Orient and round,	Jew	4.1.67	Barab
What care I though the Earles begirt us round?	Edw	2.2.223	Edward
Begirt with weapons, and with enemies round,	Edw	3.1.95	Arundl
And will sir John of Henolt lead the round?	Edw	4.3.40	Edward

ROUND (cont.)
And whirling round with this circumference, ... F 764 2.3.43 2Chor
Invironed round with airy mountaine tops, ... F 781 3.1.3 Faust
do ye see yonder tall fellow in the round slop, hee has kild F App p.230 48 P Clown
And went the round, in, and without the towne. . . . Lucan, First Booke 594
Turne round thy gold-ring, as it were to ease thee. . . Ovid's Elegies 1.4.26
And her small joynts incircling round hoope make thee. . Ovid's Elegies 2.15.4
Where round about small birdes most sweetely sing. . . Ovid's Elegies 3.1.4
And round about the chamber this false morne, ... Hero and Leander 2.321

ROUND ABOUT
Run mourning round about the Femals misse, ... 2Tamb 4.1.188 Tamb
Run tilting round about the firmament, ... 2Tamb 4.1.203 Tamb

ROUNDER
If short, she lies the rounder: . . . . . Ovid's Elegies 2.4.35
And sit thou rounder, that behind us see, ... Ovid's Elegies 3.2.23

ROUNDLY
And thus farre roundly goes the businesse: . . . Jew 5.2.110 Barab
I charge you roundly off with both their heads, . . Edw 3.1.247 Edward

ROUSE (Homograph; See also ROUZE, ROWSE)
As princely Lions when they rouse themselves, ... 1Tamb 1.2.52 Techel
And thinks to rouse us from our dreadful siege/Of the famous 1Tamb 3.1.5 Bajzth
Shall rouse him out of Europe, and pursue/His scattered armie 1Tamb 3.3.38 Therid
I'le rouse my senses, and awake my selfe. . . . . . Jew 1.2.269 Barab
He took his rouse with stopes of Rhennish wine, . . . F1174 4.1.20 Mrtino
Well I'le go rouse him, and make him give me my forty Dollors F1487 4.4.31 P HrsCsr

ROUT (Homograph)
But Tamburlaine, and that Tartarian rout, ... 1Tamb 1.1.71 Therid
See ye this rout, and know ye this same king? . . . . 2Tamb 3.5.151 Tamb
Their sway of fleight carries the heady rout/That in chain'd Lucan, First Booke 488
Where the French rout engirt themselves with Bayes. . . Ovid's Elegies 2.13.18

ROUTE
A ranker route of rebels never was: . . . . . . Edw 3.1.154 Edward
England shall welcome you, and all your route. . . . Edw 4.3.42 Edward

ROUZE
I'le rouze him thence. . . . . Jew 2.3.269 Mthias

ROVE (See ROAVE)

ROWE
That naked rowe about the Terrene sea. . . . . . 1Tamb 3.3.50 Tamb
That may transport me without oares to rowe. . . . Ovid's Elegies 3.5.4

ROWING
Rowing with Christians in a Brigandine, ... 2Tamb 3.5.93 Jrslem
And, rowing in a Gally, whipt to death. . . . . Jew 5.1.68 Barab

ROWLING
That rowling downe, may breake the villaines bones, . . F1414 4.2.90 Faust

ROWSE
And rowse the light foote Deere from forth their laire? . Dido 3.3.31 Dido
But may soft love rowse up my drowsie eies, ... Ovid's Elegies 2.10.19

ROY
Vive [le] <la> Roy, vive [le] <la> Roy. . . . . . P 588 12.1 All
Vive [le] <la> Roy, vive [le] <la> Roy. . . . . . P 598 12.11 All

ROYAL (See also ROIALL)
Well here I sweare by this my royal seat-- . . . . 1Tamb 1.1.97 Mycet
Sit here upon this royal chaire of state, ... 1Tamb 3.3.112 Bajzth
My royal chaire of state shall be advanc'd: . . . . 2Tamb 1.3.82 Tamb
My royal army is as great as his, ... 2Tamb 3.5.10 Callap
For there my Pallace royal shal be plac'd: . . . . 2Tamb 4.3.111 Tamb
Then in my coach like Saturnes royal son, ... 2Tamb 4.3.125 Tamb
tane the view]/[Of rarest things, and royal courts of kings], F1139 3.3.52A 3Chor

ROYALL
The Romane Scepter royall shall remaine, ... Dido 1.1.105 Jupitr
Scorning our loves and royall marriage rites, ... Dido 4.2.16 Iarbus
With the foole, and rid your royall shoulders/Of such a burthen, 1Tamb 2.3.46 Tamb
Scarce being seated in my royall throne, ... 1Tamb 2.7.5 Cosroe
My royall Lord is slaine or conquered, ... 1Tamb 3.3.209 Zenoc
His royall Crowne againe, so highly won. . . . . . 1Tamb 3.3.219 Zenoc
It might amaze your royall majesty. 1Tamb 4.1.16 2Msngr
time to sort/Your fighting men, and raise your royall hoste. 1Tamb 4.1.37 Capol
That I may rise into my royall throne. . . . . . 1Tamb 4.2.15 Tamb
That beares the honor of my royall waight. . . . . 1Tamb 4.2.21 Tamb
Let us unite our royall bandes in one, ... 1Tamb 4.3.17 Souldn
To be investers of thy royall browes, ... 1Tamb 5.1.104 1Virgn
Mount up your royall places of estate, ... 1Tamb 5.1.525 Tamb
But now Orcanes, view my royall hoste, ... 2Tamb 1.1.106 Sgsmnd
wherein at anchor lies/A Turkish Gally of my royall fleet, 2Tamb 1.2.21 Callap
our neighbour kings/Expect our power and our royall presence, 2Tamb 2.2.4 Orcan
I will requite your royall gratitudes/With all the benefits my 2Tamb 3.1.8 Callap
as when Bajazeth/My royall Lord and father fild the throne, 2Tamb 3.1.12 Callap
And now I doubt not but your royall cares/Hath so provided for 2Tamb 3.1.20 Callap
Thou shalt be set upon my royall tent. . . . . . 2Tamb 3.2.37 Tamb
And what our Army royall is esteem'd. . . . . . 2Tamb 3.5.31 Callap
So that the Army royall is esteem'd/Six hundred thousand . 2Tamb 3.5.50 Soria
That can endure so well your royall presence, ... 2Tamb 5.3.111 Usumc
And mount my royall chariot of estate, ... 2Tamb 5.3.178 Tamb
But here's a royall Monastry hard by, ... Jew 4.1.13 Ithimr
A royall seate, a scepter and a crowne: . . . . . P 161 2.104 Guise
I humbly thank your royall Majestie. . . . . . P 273 4.71 Admral
Welcome to France thy fathers royall seate, ... P 590 12.3 QnMoth
I think for safety of your royall person, ... P 887 17.82 Eprnon
Mounted his royall Cabonet. . . . . P 957 19.27 Eprnon
Be thou commaunder of our royall fleete, ... Edw 1.4.354 Edward
against your king)/To see his royall soveraigne once againe. Edw 2.5.7 Gavstn
Sworne to defend king Edwards royall right, ... Edw 3.1.38 SpncrP
That deads the royall vine, whose golden leaves/Empale your Edw 3.1.163 Herald

ROYALL (cont.)
Of love and care unto his royall person, Edw 4.6.25 Queene
To keepe your royall person safe with us, Edw 4.7.3 Abbot
I <O I> come of a Royall Pedigree <parentage>, my father F 696 2.2.145 P Glutny
The royall shapes and warlike semblances/Of Alexander and his F1170 4.1.16 Mrtino
Before the Pope and royall Emperour, F1187 4.1.33 Mrtino
These gracious words, most royall Carolus, F1217 4.1.63 Faust
Present before this royall Emperour, F1238 4.1.84 Faust
That when my Spirits present the royall shapes/Of Alexander and F1249 4.1.95 Faust
Or bring before this royall Emperour/The mightie Monarch, F1296 4.1.142 Faust

ROYALLY
Where honor sits invested royally: 1Tamb 2.1.18 Menaph
Thinke thee invested now as royally, 1Tamb 2.5.2 Tamb

RUBD
his horse, and he would have his things rubd and made cleane: F App p.233 7 P Rafe

RUBICON
And comming to the foord of Rubicon, Lucan, First Booke 187
In summer time the purple Rubicon, Lucan, First Booke 215

RUBIES
Diamondes, Saphyres, Rubies/And fairest pearle of welthie India 2Tamb 3.2.120 Tamb

RUBYES
Beauteous Rubyes, sparkling Diamonds, Jew 1.1.27 Barab

RUDDIE
So Heroes ruddie cheeke, Hero betrayd, Hero and Leander 2.323

RUDDY
Unto the watry mornings ruddy [bower] <hower>, 1Tamb 4.4.123 Tamb
Yet as if mixt with red leade thou wert ruddy, Ovid's Elegies 1.12.11

RUDE (See also REWD)
Yes, and Iarbus rude and rusticall. Dido 3.1.66 Anna
that makest us thus/The slaves to Scythians rude and barbarous. 1Tamb 3.3.271 Zabina
Ah none but rude and savage minded men, Edw 1.4.78 Edward
What rude disturbers have we at the gate? F1588 4.6.31 Duke
And then we grew licencious and rude, Lucan, First Booke 162
Perhaps the Sabines rude, when Tatius raignde, Ovid's Elegies 1.8.39
Rude Ennius, and Plautus full of wit, Ovid's Elegies 1.15.19
And rude boyes toucht with unknowne love me reade, Ovid's Elegies 2.1.6
His sword layed by, safe, though rude places yeelds. Ovid's Elegies 2.9.20
Rude man, 'tis vaine, thy damsell to commend/To keepers trust: Ovid's Elegies 3.4.1
Like a dull Cipher, or rude blocke I lay, Ovid's Elegies 3.6.15
Rude husband-men bak'd not their corne before, Ovid's Elegies 3.9.7
That runs along his backe, but my rude pen, Hero and Leander 1.69
I would my rude words had the influence, Hero and Leander 1.200
Albeit Leander rude in love, and raw, Hero and Leander 2.61

RUDEST
His presence made the rudest paisant melt, Hero and Leander 1.79

RUDIMENTS
That meane to teach you rudiments of war: 2Tamb 3.2.54 Tamb
First I'le instruct thee in the rudiments, F 188 1.1.160 Valdes

RUE
And rue our ends senceles of life or breath: Dido 5.1.328 Anna
That not a man should live to rue their fall. 1Tamb 4.1.35 Souldn
That Tamburlaine shall rue the day, the hower, 1Tamb 4.3.38 Souldn
Well Mortimer, ile make thee rue these words, Edw 1.1.91 Edward
Now let them thanke themselves, and rue too late. Edw 2.2.207 Edward
I rue my lords ill fortune, but alas, Edw 4.6.64 Queene

RUFFE
faire, mishapen stuffe/Are of behaviour boisterous and ruffe. Hero and Leander 1.204

RUFFES
order, Il'e nere trust smooth faces, and small ruffes more. F1318 4.1.164 P Benvol

RUFFLED
Yet was she graced with her ruffled hayre. Ovid's Elegies 1.7.12
In [skilfull] <skilfuld> gathering ruffled haires in order, Ovid's Elegies 1.11.1

RUINATE
To ruinate that wicked Church of Rome, P1204 22.66 King

RUINATES
If I repaire not what he ruinates: P 129 2.72 Guise

RUIN'D
wee'll walke about/The ruin'd Towne, and see the wracke we Jew 5.2.19 Calym

RUINE
my spirit doth foresee/The utter ruine of thy men and thee. 1Tamb 4.3.60 Arabia
That with his ruine fils up all the trench. 2Tamb 3.3.26 Therid
And ratling cannons thunder in our eares/Our proper ruine, and 2Tamb 4.1.14 Amyras
More than the ruine of our proper soules. 2Tamb 5.3.182 Therid
we take particularly thine/To save the ruine of a multitude: Jew 1.2.97 Govnr
And as for Malta's ruine, thinke you not/'Twere slender policy Jew 5.2.64 Barab
The ruine of that famous Realme of France: P 922 18.23 Navrre
That basely seekes the ruine of his Realme. P 930 18.31 Navrre
Will be the ruine of the realme and us. Edw 1.2.32 Mortmr
Would seeke the ruine of my Gaveston, Edw 1.4.79 Edward
Will be the ruine of the realme and you, Edw 2.2.209 Kent
This, Edward, is the ruine of the realme. Edw 4.6.45 Kent
Fearing the enemy <ruine> of thy haplesse <hopelesse> soule. F1738 5.1.65 OldMan
men so strong/By land, and sea, no forreine force could ruine: Lucan, First Booke 83
And glad when bloud, and ruine made him way: Lucan, First Booke 151
Predestinate to ruine; all lands else/Have stable peace, here Lucan, First Booke 251
had bin fierd/Or dropping-ripe, ready to fall with Ruine, Lucan, First Booke 491

RUINES
Upon the ruines of this conquered towne. 2Tamb 5.1.85 Tamb
And caus'd the ruines to be new repair'd, Jew 5.3.2 Calym
thy father hath made good/The ruines done to Malta and to us, Jew 5.5.112 Govnr

RUINOUS
Shall see it ruinous and desolate. Hero and Leander 1.240

RUL'D
Be rul'd by me, and seeke some other love, Dido 4.2.35 Anna

RUL'D (cont.)
Be rul'd by me, for in extremitie/We ought to make barre of no — Jew 1.2.272 Barab
Therefore be rul'd by me, and keepe the gold: — Jew 2.2.39 Bosco
master, be rul'd by me a little; so, let him leane upon his — Jew 4.1.153 P Ithimr
In this, my Countrimen, be rul'd by me, — Jew 5.4.1 Govnr
For will in us is over-rul'd by fate. — Hero and Leander 1.168

RULDE
Now to be rulde and governed by a man, — 1Tamb 1.1.12 Cosroe
all doubts, be rulde by me, lets hang him heere upon this tree. — P 491 9.10 P 2Atndt
And Epernoune I will be rulde by thee. — P 885 17.80 King
And rulde in France by Henries fatall death. — P1250 22.112 Navrre
Am I a king and must be over rulde? — Edw 1.1.135 Edward
Was ever king thus over rulde as I? — Edw 1.4.38 Edward
Be rulde by me, and we will rule the realme, — Edw 5.2.5 Mortmr
Could I have rulde thee then, as I do now, — Edw 5.6.96 King

RULE
That in such peace long time did rule the same: — Dido 1.2.24 Cloan
Shall rule the Province of Albania. — 1Tamb 2.2.31 Meandr
And gladly yeeld them to my gracious rule: — 1Tamb 2.5.28 Cosroe
He dares so doubtlesly resolve of rule, — 1Tamb 2.6.13 Meandr
but some must stay/To rule the provinces he late subdude. — 1Tamb 3.3.29 Bassoe
That never nourisht thought against thy rule, — 1Tamb 5.1.98 1Virgn
Whereto ech man of rule hath given his hand, — 1Tamb 5.1.102 1Virgn
And there make lawes to rule your provinces: — 1Tamb 5.1.527 Tamb
Give us a peacefull rule, make Christians Kings, — Jew 1.1.134 Barab
For Ile rule France, but they shall weare the crowne: — P 525 9.44 QnMoth
But now I will be King and rule my selfe, — P1070 19.140 King
Learne then to rule us better and the realme. — Edw 1.4.39 Lncstr
whome rule and emperie/Have not in life or death made — Edw 4.7.14 Edward
My nobles rule, I beare the name of king, — Edw 5.1.28 Edward
Commend me to my sonne, and bid him rule/Better then I, yet how — Edw 5.1.121 Edward
Be rulde by me, and we will rule the realme, — Edw 5.2.5 Mortmr
The prince I rule, the queene do I commaund, — Edw 5.4.48 Mortmr
sure, the Queene and Mortimer/Shall rule the realme, the king, — Edw 5.4.66 Mortmr
and Mortimer/Shall rule the realme, the king, and none rule us, — Edw 5.4.66 Mortmr
Now by the Kingdomes of Infernall Rule, — F 825 3.1.47 Faust
You Princely Legions of infernall Rule, — F1116 3.3.29 Mephst
Or if Fate rule them, Rome thy Cittizens/Are neere some plague: — Lucan, First Booke 643
I cannot rule my selfe, but where love please/[Am] <And> driven — Ovid's Elegies 2.4.7
And rule so soone with private hands acquainted. — Ovid's Elegies 2.18.16
Yet when old Saturne heavens rule possest, — Ovid's Elegies 3.7.35

RULED
I would not be ruled by him, for he bade me I should ride him — F App p.240 130 P HrsCsr

RULES
Whereas Sidonian Dido rules as Queene. — Dido 1.1.213 Venus
That onely Juno rules in Rhamnuse towne. — Dido 3.2.20 Juno
Whiles Dido lives and rules in Junos towne, — Dido 3.4.50 Aeneas
When she that rules in Rhamnis golden gates, — 1Tamb 2.3.37 Cosroe
As rules the Skies, and countermands the Gods: — 1Tamb 5.1.233 Bajzth
But he that sits and rules above the clowdes, — P 42 1.42 Navrre
Love over-rules my will, I must obay thee, — Lucan, First Booke 373
and where the north-west wind/Nor Zephir rules not, but the — Lucan, First Booke 408
is faint; swift Hermes retrograde;/Mars onely rules the heaven: — Lucan, First Booke 662
And Venus rules in her Aeneas Citty. — Ovid's Elegies 1.8.42
There, he who rules the worlds starre-spangled towers, — Ovid's Elegies 3.9.21
She proudly sits) more over-rules the flood, — Hero and Leander 1.111

RUMBLE
Love me little, love me long, let musicke rumble, — Jew 4.4.28 Ithimr

RUMBLING
choyce, I heard a rumbling in the house; so I tooke onely this, — Jew 3.1.20 P Pilia
In Tiburs field with watry fome art rumbling, — Ovid's Elegies 3.5.46

RUMINATES
no object, for my head]/[But ruminates on Negromantique skill]. — F 132 1.1.104A Faust

RUMOR
I, madam, you, for so the rumor runnes. — Edw 5.6.73 King
That rumor is untrue, for loving thee, — Edw 5.6.74 Queene

RUN
As made the bloud run downe about mine eares. — Dido 1.1.8 Ganimd
And in the midst doth run a silver streame, — Dido 4.5.9 Nurse
Run Anna, run, stay not to answere me. — Dido 5.1.210 Dido
Enforce thee run upon the banefull pikes. — 1Tamb 5.1.220 Bajzth
And harmelesse run among the deadly pikes. — 2Tamb 1.3.46 Tamb
But then run desperate through the thickest throngs, — 2Tamb 3.2.139 Tamb
By whose proud side the ugly furies run, — 2Tamb 3.4.59 Therid
Run mourning round about the Femals misse, — 2Tamb 4.1.188 Tamb
Run tilting round about the firmament, — 2Tamb 4.1.203 Tamb
With fierce exclaimes run to the Senate-house, — Jew 1.2.232 Abigal
run to some rocke and throw my selfe headlong into the sea; — Jew 3.4.39 P Ithimr
You run swifter when you threw my gold out of my Window. — Jew 4.4.52 P Barab
Nor me neither, I cannot out-run you Constable, oh my belly. — Jew 5.1.20 P Ithimr
But yet my Lord the report doth run, — P 435 7.75 Navrre
How fast they run to banish him I love, — Edw 1.4.94 Edward
Theres none here, but would run his horse to death. — Edw 1.4.207 Warwck
Their wives and children slaine, run up and downe, — Edw 2.2.180 Lncstr
I thinke king Edward will out-run us all. — Edw 4.2.68 Prince
run up and downe the world with these <this> case of Rapiers, — F 688 2.2.137 P Wrath
I'le out-run him, and cast this leg into some ditch or other. — F1495 4.4.39 P HrsCsr
such a horse, as would run over hedge and ditch, and never tyre, — F1538 4.5.34 P HrsCsr
Then will I headlong run into the earth: — F1948 5.2.152 Faust
this makes them/Run on the swords point and desire to die, — Lucan, First Booke 457
Which wont to run their course through empty night/At noone day — Lucan, First Booke 534
And turned streames run back-ward to their fountaines. — Ovid's Elegies 2.1.26
Shall discontent run into regions farre; — Hero and Leander 1.478

RUN (cont.)			
And steale a kisse, and then run out and daunce,	Hero and Leander	2.185	
RUNAWAIES			
cowards and fainthearted runawaies,/Looke for orations when the	1Tamb	1.2.130	Techel
RUNAWAY			
And hunt that Coward, faintheart runaway,	2Tamb	3.2.149	Tamb
RUNG			
So likewise we will through the world be rung,	Ovid's Elegies	1.3.25	
Yet words in thy benummed palate rung,	Ovid's Elegies	2.6.47	
RUNNAGATE			
And must I rave thus for a runnagate?	Dido	5.1.265	Dido
RUNNAGATES			
Inhabited with stragling Runnagates,	1Tamb	3.3.57	Tamb
Injurious villaines, thieves, runnagates,	1Tamb	3.3.225	Zabina
To follow these rebellious runnagates.	Edw	4.6.76	Mortmr
RUNNAWAY			
That like a roguish runnaway, suborn'd/That villaine there,	2Tamb	3.5.86	Tamb
RUNNE			
Runne for Aeneas, or Ile flye to him.	Dido	3.1.79	Dido
O Anna, runne unto the water side,	Dido	4.4.1	Dido
Stay not to answere me, runne Anna runne.	Dido	4.4.4	Dido
Twas time to runne, Aeneas had been gone,	Dido	4.4.14	Anna
O happie sand that made him runne aground:	Dido	4.4.95	Dido
rumbling in the house; so I tooke onely this, and runne my way:	Jew	3.1.21	P Pilia
What, was I borne to flye and runne away,	Edw	4.5.4	Edward
To which the channels of the castell runne,	Edw	5.5.3	Matrvs
Runne for the table.	Edw	5.5.110	Ltborn
course that time doth runne with calme and silent foote,	F App	p.239 91	P Faust
Thou makste the suretie to the lawyer runne,	Ovid's Elegies	1.13.19	
Then wouldst thou cry, stay night and runne not thus.	Ovid's Elegies	1.13.40	
Isis may be done/Nor feare least she to th'theater's runne.	Ovid's Elegies	2.2.26	
I loathe, yet after that I loathe, I runne:	Ovid's Elegies	2.4.5	
The youthfull sort to divers pastimes runne.	Ovid's Elegies	2.5.22	
I would bravely runne,/On swift steedes mounted till the race	Ovid's Elegies	3.2.9	
At least now conquer, and out-runne the rest:	Ovid's Elegies	3.2.79	
Slide in thy bounds, so shalt thou runne for ever.	Ovid's Elegies	3.5.20	
not Alpheus in strange lands to runne,/Th'Arcadian Virgins	Ovid's Elegies	3.5.29	
By feare depriv'd of strength to runne away.	Ovid's Elegies	3.5.70	
And thorough everie vaine doth cold bloud runne,	Ovid's Elegies	3.13.38	
RUNNES			
Vex'd and tormented runnes poore Barabas/With fatall curses	Jew	2.1.5	Barab
How swift he runnes.	Jew	4.4.51	Pilia
His minde you see runnes on his minions,	P 633	12.46	QnMoth
being strucke/Runnes to an herbe that closeth up the wounds,	Edw	5.1.10	Edward
I, madam, you, for so the rumor runnes.	Edw	5.6.73	King
Just through the midst runnes flowing Tybers streame,	F 813	3.1.35	Mephst
So runnes a Matron through th'amazed streetes,	Lucan, First Booke	675	
Night runnes away; with open entrance greete them.	Ovid's Elegies	1.6.40	
Alas he runnes too farre about the ring,	Ovid's Elegies	3.2.69	
RUNNING			
Free from the murmure of these running streames,	Dido	2.1.335	Venus
As others did, by running to the wood.	Dido	4.1.30	Anna
All running headlong after greedy spoiles:	1Tamb	2.2.45	Meandr
And griesly death, by running to and fro,	1Tamb	5.1.455	Tamb
No talke of running, I tell you sir.	2Tamb	1.2.16	Almeda
Ile hang a clogge about your necke for running away againe, you	2Tamb	3.5.101	P Tamb
provide a running Banquet;/Send to the Merchant, bid him bring	Jew	4.2.83	Curtzn
To make a passage for the running streames/And common channels	Jew	5.1.88	Barab
And running in the likenes of an Hart,	Edw	1.1.69	Gavstn
Who running long, fals in a greater floud,	Lucan, First Booke	401	
Giving the windes my words running in thine eare?	Ovid's Elegies	1.6.42	
Who would not love those hands for their swift running?	Ovid's Elegies	2.4.28	
Though Hindes in brookes the running waters bring,	Ovid's Elegies	2.16.35	
In running if I see thee, I shall stay,	Ovid's Elegies	3.2.13	
By charmes are running springs and fountaines drie,	Ovid's Elegies	3.6.32	
And to thine owne losse was thy wit swift running.	Ovid's Elegies	3.7.46	
Wild savages, that drinke of running springs,	Hero and Leander	1.259	
As she to heare his tale, left off her running.	Hero and Leander	1.418	
RUNS			
by leaden pipes/Runs to the citie from the mountain Carnon.	1Tamb	3.1.60	Bajzth
Danubius stream that runs to Trebizon,	2Tamb	1.1.33	Orcan
By [Cairo] <Cario> runs--	2Tamb	1.2.15	Callap
By [Cairo] <Cario> runs to Alexandria Bay,	2Tamb	1.2.19	Callap
Like tried silver runs through Paradice/To entertaine divine	2Tamb	2.4.24	Tamb
Of Euphrates and Tigris swiftly runs,	2Tamb	5.2.3	Callap
the plancke/That runs along the upper chamber floore,	Jew	1.2.297	Barab
While she runs to the window looking out/When you should come	Jew	2.3.264	Barab
That kisse againe; she runs division of my lips.	Jew	4.2.127	P Ithimr
And still his minde runs on his minion.	Edw	2.2.4	Queene
The Stars move still, Time runs, the Clocke will strike,	F1936	5.2.140	Faust
or his speare/Sticks in his side) yet runs upon the hunter.	Lucan, First Booke	214	
That runs along his backe, but my rude pen,	Hero and Leander	1.69	
Grosse gold, from them runs headlong to the boore.	Hero and Leander	1.472	
RUNST			
Thou Roome at name of warre runst from thy selfe,	Lucan, First Booke	517	
Whither runst thou, that men, and women, love not?	Ovid's Elegies	1.13.9	
RUSH			
But when on thee her angry eyes did rush,	Ovid's Elegies	2.8.15	
RUSHES			
She, fearing on the rushes to be flung,	Hero and Leander	2.66	
RUSHEST			
With snow thaw'd from the next hill now thou rushest,	Ovid's Elegies	3.5.7	
And in thy foule deepe waters thicke thou [gushest] <rushest>.	Ovid's Elegies	3.5.8	

RUSHT
So rusht the inconsiderate multitude/Thorough the City hurried — Lucan, First Booke 492
RUSSIAN
And Christian Merchants that with Russian stems/Plow up huge — 1Tamb 1.2.194 Tamb
RUST
olde swords/With ugly teeth of blacke rust fouly scarr'd: — Lucan, First Booke 245
RUSTICALL
Yes, and Iarbus rude and rusticall. — Dido 3.1.66 Anna
Venus without me should be rusticall, — Ovid's Elegies 3.1.43
RUSTICKE
And in their rusticke gambals proudly say, — F1330 4.2.6 Benvol
RUSTIE
And duskie night, in rustie iron carre: — Edw 4.3.44 Edward
Wars dustie <rustie> honors are refused being yong, — Ovid's Elegies 1.15.4
I prove neither youth nor man, but old and rustie. — Ovid's Elegies 3.6.20
RUSTIKE
And gave it to his simple rustike love, — Hero and Leander 1.435
RUSTLING
And rustling swing up as the wind fets breath. — Lucan, First Booke 392
RUSTY
Let ugly darknesse with her rusty coach/Engyrt with tempests — 1Tamb 5.1.294 Bajzth
with which I burst/The rusty beames of Janus Temple doores, — 2Tamb 2.4.114 Tamb
Should I but touch the rusty gates of hell, — 2Tamb 5.1.96 Tamb
RUTH
vouchsafe of ruth/To tell us who inhabits this faire towne, — Dido 2.1.40 Aeneas
I dye with melting ruth, Aeneas leave. — Dido 2.1.289 Dido
Yet now I doe repent me of his ruth, — Dido 3.2.47 Juno
On whom ruth and compassion ever waites, — Dido 4.2.20 Iarbus
That register the numbers of my ruth, — Dido 4.2.39 Iarbus
They gan to move him to redresse my ruth, — Dido 5.1.238 Anna
Embraceth now with teares of ruth and blood, — 1Tamb 5.1.85 1Virgn
Accursed Bajazeth, whose words of ruth, — 1Tamb 5.1.270 Bajzth
And tell my soule mor tales of bleeding ruth? — 1Tamb 5.1.342 Zenoc
My Lord, if ever you did deed of ruth, — 2Tamb 5.1.24 1Citzn
Who of meere charity and Christian ruth, — Jew 2.3.71 Barab
Is ruth and almost death to call to minde: — P 797 16.11 Navrre
RUTHE
With happy looks of ruthe and lenity. — 1Tamb 5.1.59 2Virgn
And pardon me that was not moov'd with ruthe, — 1Tamb 5.1.369 Zenoc
RUTHELES
Should for their conscience taste such rutheles ends. — P 214 4.12 Charls
RUTHENS
The yellow Ruthens left their garrisons; — Lucan, First Booke 403
RUTHFULL
Troian, thy ruthfull tale hath made me sad: — Dido 2.1.301 Dido
Sweet Almeda, pity the ruthfull plight/Of Callapine, the sonne — 2Tamb 1.2.1 Callap
Take pitie of a Ladies ruthfull teares, — 2Tamb 3.4.69 Olymp
RUTHLESLY
And let not conquest ruthlesly pursewde/Be equally against his — 1Tamb 5.1.366 Zenoc
RUTHLESSE
As well for griefe our ruthlesse Governour/Have thus refusde — 1Tamb 5.1.92 1Virgn
And ruthlesse cruelty of Tamburlaine. — 1Tamb 5.1.346 Anippe
RUTILES
Three winters shall he with the Rutiles warre, — Dido 1.1.89 Jupitr
RUTTERS
Sclavonians, [Almain Rutters] <Almains, Rutters>, Muffes, and — 2Tamb 1.1.22 Uribas
[Almain Rutters] <Almains, Rutters>, Muffes, and Danes/That — 2Tamb 1.1.22 Uribas
Slavonians, [Almain Rutters] <Almains, Rutters>, Muffes, and — 2Tamb 1.1.58 Orcan
[Almain Rutters] <Almains, Rutters>, Muffes, and Danes/[Feares] — 2Tamb 1.1.58 Orcan
Like Almaine Rutters with their horsemens staves, — F 152 1.1.124 Valdes
RYOT
The soldiours pray, and rapine brought in ryot, — Lucan, First Booke 163
RYOTS
Committing headdie ryots, incest, rapes: — Hero and Leander 1.144
S.
bleate, and an asse braye, because it is S. Peters holy day. — F App p.232 28 P Faust
SABA
As wise as Saba, or as beautifull/As was bright Lucifer before — F 541 2.1.153 Mephst
as in India, Saba, and such Countries that lye farre East, — F1583 4.6.26 P Faust
as in India, Saba, and farther countries in the East, and by — F App p.242 21 P Faust
SABINE
The Sabine gauntlets were too dearely wunne/That unto death did — Ovid's Elegies 1.10.49
A woman against late-built Rome did send/The Sabine Fathers, — Ovid's Elegies 2.12.24
Now, Sabine-like, though chast she seemes to live, — Ovid's Elegies 3.7.61
SABINE-LIKE
Now, Sabine-like, though chast she seemes to live, — Ovid's Elegies 3.7.61
SABINES
Made all shake hands as once the Sabines did; — Lucan, First Booke 118
Perhaps the Sabines rude, when Tatius raignde, — Ovid's Elegies 1.8.39
Though her sowre looks a Sabines browe resemble, — Ovid's Elegies 2.4.15
SABINUS
As soone as from strange lands Sabinus came, — Ovid's Elegies 2.18.27
SABLE
And slice the Sea with sable coloured ships, — Dido 4.3.22 Aeneas
Now ugly death stretch out thy Sable wings, — 2Tamb 3.4.16 Olymp
of the silent night/Doth shake contagion from her sable wings; — Jew 2.1.4 Barab
His burning chariot plung'd in sable cloudes, — Lucan, First Booke 539
SACKE (Homograph)
And mought I live to see him sacke rich Thebes, — Dido 3.3.42 Aeneas
All which have sworne to sacke Natolia: — 2Tamb 1.3.121 Therid
sacke, and utterly consume/Your cities and your golden — 2Tamb 4.1.192 Tamb
Thus have we view'd the City, seene the sacke, — Jew 5.3.1 Calym
Goe swill in bowles of Sacke and Muscadine: — Jew 5.5.6 Barab

SACKE (cont.)				
wine, claret wine, Sacke, Muskadine, Malmesey and Whippincrust,	F 748	2.3.27	P	Robin
SACKES				
Sackes every vaine and artier of my heart.	1Tamb	2.7.10		Cosroe
SACK'T				
In stead of Troy shall Wittenberg <Wertenberge> be sack't,/And	F1776	5.1.103		Faust
SACKT				
Poore Troy must now be sackt upon the Sea,	Dido	1.1.64		Venus
I saw this man at Troy ere Troy was sackt.	Dido	3.1.141		Achat
Would, as faire Troy was, Carthage might be sackt,	Dido	5.1.147		Dido
martiall spoile/Of conquered kingdomes, and of Cities sackt.	1Tamb	1.2.192		Tamb
There having sackt Borno the Kingly seat,	2Tamb	1.3.203		Techel
Kingdomes made waste, brave cities sackt and burnt,	2Tamb	5.2.26		Callap
As oft as Roome was sackt, here gan the spoile:	Lucan, First Booke			258
and that Roome/He looking on by these men should be sackt.	Lucan, First Booke			480
SACRAMENT				
Now by the holy sacrament I sweare,	P 981	19.51		Guise
SACRED				
O sacred love,/If there be any heaven in earth, tis love:	Dido	4.5.26		Nurse
That offered jewels to thy sacred shrine,	1Tamb	3.3.199		Zabina
Ah villaines, dare ye touch my sacred armes?	1Tamb	3.3.268		Bajzth
A sacred vow to heaven and him I make,	1Tamb	4.3.36		Souldn
(sacred Emperour)/The prostrate service of this wretched towne.	1Tamb	5.1.99		1Virgn
And sacred Lord, the mighty Calapine:	2Tamb	1.1.3		Orcan
By sacred Mahomet, the friend of God,	2Tamb	1.1.137		Orcan
leave these armes/And save thy sacred person free from scathe:	2Tamb	1.3.10		Zenoc
For I have sworne by sacred Mahomet,	2Tamb	1.3.109		Tamb
With strange infusion of his sacred vigor,	2Tamb	2.2.52		Orcan
Her sacred beauty hath enchaunted heaven,	2Tamb	2.4.85		Tamb
Ah sacred Mahomet, if this be sin,	2Tamb	3.4.31		Olymp
Ah sacred Mahomet, thou that hast seene/Millions of Turkes	2Tamb	5.2.24		Callap
Your sacred vertues pour'd upon his throne,	2Tamb	5.3.11		Therid
and let them be interr'd/Within one sacred monument of stone;	Jew	3.2.30		Govnr
Villaines, I am a sacred person, touch me not.	Jew	4.1.201		1Fryar
First were his sacred garments rent and torne,	Edw	1.2.35		ArchBp
The sacred Sinod hath decreed for him,	F 885	3.1.107		Pope
Most sacred Patron of the Church of Rome,	F 951	3.1.173		Faust
First, may it please your sacred Holinesse,	F1013	3.2.33		1Card
Nor capitall be adorn'd with sacred bayes:	Lucan, First Booke			288
Or rob the gods; or sacred temples fire;	Lucan, First Booke			380
In unfeld woods, and sacred groves you dwell,	Lucan, First Booke			448
then the sacred priests/That with divine lustration purg'd the	Lucan, First Booke			592
In midst thereof a stone-pav'd sacred spring,	Ovid's Elegies			3.1.3
Thee sacred Poet could sad flames destroy?	Ovid's Elegies			3.8.41
Perhaps, thy sacred Priesthood makes thee loath,	Hero and Leander			1.293
youth forbeare/To touch the sacred garments which I weare.	Hero and Leander			1.344
but he must weare/The sacred ring wherewith she was endow'd,	Hero and Leander			2.109
SACRIFIC'D				
Seeing thou hast pray'd and sacrific'd to them.	F 235	1.3.7		Faust
SACRIFICE				
And sacrifice my heart to death and hell,	1Tamb	4.2.17		Bajzth
And with how manie cities sacrifice/He celebrated her [sad]	2Tamb	Prol.7		Prolog
Take here these papers as our sacrifice/And witnesse of thy	2Tamb	2.2.45		Orcan
(The Perseans Sepulchre) and sacrifice/Mountaines of	2Tamb	3.5.54		Callap
I'le sacrifice her on a pile of wood.	Jew	2.3.52		Barab
Altar I will offer up/My daily sacrifice of sighes and teares,	Jew	3.2.32		Govnr
They stai'd not either to pray or sacrifice,	Lucan, First Booke			504
as being like to prove/An aukward sacrifice, but by the hornes	Lucan, First Booke			611
Couzend, I am the couzeners sacrifice.	Ovid's Elegies			3.3.22
Pure rose shee, like a Nun to sacrifice,	Ovid's Elegies			3.6.21
And little Piggs, base Hog-sties sacrifice,	Ovid's Elegies			3.12.16
This sacrifice (whose sweet perfume descending,	Hero and Leander			1.209
Such sacrifice as this, Venus demands.	Hero and Leander			1.310
She offers up her selfe a sacrifice,	Hero and Leander			2.48
SACRIFICING				
With sacrificing wreathes upon his head,	Dido	2.1.148		Aeneas
That sacrificing slice and cut your flesh,	1Tamb	4.2.3		Bajzth
There Hero sacrificing turtles blood,	Hero and Leander			1.158
SACRIFIZDE				
And after by that Pirrhus sacrifizde.	Dido	2.1.288		Aeneas
SACRIFIZE				
Altars crack/With mountaine heapes of milke white Sacrifize.	Dido	1.1.202		Aeneas
Epeus pine-tree Horse/A sacrifize t'appease Minervas wrath:	Dido	2.1.163		Aeneas
Come servants, come bring forth the Sacrifize,	Dido	4.2.1		Iarbus
Who wild me sacrifize his ticing relliques:	Dido	5.1.277		Dido
For I entend a private Sacrifize,	Dido	5.1.286		Dido
Come were the times of Ceres sacrifize,	Ovid's Elegies			3.9.1
As in thy sacrifize we them forbeare?	Ovid's Elegies			3.9.44
SACRILEGE				
Even sacrilege against her Deitie,	Hero and Leander			1.307
SAD				
And my nine Daughters sing when thou art sad,	Dido	1.1.33		Jupitr
Lest you be mov'd too much with my sad tale.	Dido	2.1.125		Aeneas
Troian, thy ruthfull tale hath made me sad:	Dido	2.1.301		Dido
How now Aeneas, sad, what meanes these dumpes?	Dido	5.1.62		Iarbus
My sister comes, I like not her sad lookes.	Dido	5.1.225		Dido
pray thee tel, why art thou so sad?	1Tamb	4.4.63	P	Tamb
manie cities sacrifice/He celebrated her [sad] <said> funerall,	2Tamb	Prol.8		Prolog
Oh what has made my lovely daughter sad?	Jew	1.2.225		Barab
Thus like the sad presaging Raven that tolls/The sicke mans	Jew	2.1.1		Barab
Oh what a sad confession will there be?	Jew	3.6.4		2Fryar
Madam, have done with care and sad complaint,	Edw	4.6.66		Mortmr
To companie my hart with sad laments,	Edw	5.1.34		Edward

SAD (cont.)

His Artfull sport, drives all sad thoughts away.	F1673	4.6.116		Duke
Sylla's ghost/Was seene to walke, singing sad Oracles,/And	Lucan, First Booke	580		
These sad presages were enough to scarre/The quivering Romans,	Lucan, First Booke	672		
But thou my crowne, from sad haires tane away,	Ovid's Elegies	1.6.67		
Let the sad captive formost with lockes spred/On her white	Ovid's Elegies	1.7.39		
And least the sad signes of my crime remaine,	Ovid's Elegies	1.7.67		
Bewaile my chaunce, the sad booke is returned,	Ovid's Elegies	1.12.1		
And in sad lovers heads let me be found.	Ovid's Elegies	1.15.38		
what meanes learnd/Hath this same Poet my sad chaunce discernd?	Ovid's Elegies	2.1.10		
Trust me all husbands for such faults are sad/Nor make they any	Ovid's Elegies	2.2.51		
She looked sad: sad, comely I esteem'd her.	Ovid's Elegies	2.5.44		
Thy tunes let this rare birdes sad funerall borrowe,	Ovid's Elegies	2.6.9		
Both unkinde parents, but for causes sad,	Ovid's Elegies	2.14.31		
Jasons sad letter doth Hipsipile greete,	Ovid's Elegies	2.18.33		
Sad Elegia thy wofull haires unbinde:	Ovid's Elegies	3.8.3		
Thee sacred Poet could sad flames destroy?	Ovid's Elegies	3.8.41		
Why am I sad, when Proserpine is found,	Ovid's Elegies	3.9.45		
What day was that, which all sad haps to bring,	Ovid's Elegies	3.11.1		
tearmes, with sad and heavie cheare/Complaind to Cupid:	Hero and Leander	1.440		
By this, sad Hero, with love unacquainted,	Hero and Leander	2.1		
Sad Hero wroong him by the hand, and wept,	Hero and Leander	2.95		

SADLY

Sadly supplied with pale and ghastly death,	2Tamb	2.4.83		Tamb
As good goe on, as sit so sadly thus.	Jew	2.1.40		Barab
Saying, why sadly treadst my banckes upon,	Ovid's Elegies	3.5.53		

SADNESSE

tell me, in good sadnesse Robin, is that a conjuring booke?	F 743	2.3.22	P	Dick

SAFE

But of them all scarce seven doe anchor safe,	Dido	1.1.222		Aeneas
But are arived safe not farre from hence:	Dido	1.1.237		Venus
Now is he come on shoare safe without hurt:	Dido	5.1.257		Dido
To safe conduct us thorow Affrica.	1Tamb	1.2.16		Zenoc
If you intend to keep your treasure safe.	1Tamb	1.2.25		Tamb
To ward the blow, and shield me safe from harme.	1Tamb	1.2.181		Tamb
And set it safe on my victorious head.	1Tamb	2.3.54		Cosroe
Content thy selfe, his person shall be safe,	1Tamb	4.4.87		Tamb
Farewell (sweet Virgins) on whose safe return/Depends our	1Tamb	5.1.62		Govnr
To see the king my Father issue safe,	1Tamb	5.1.441		Zenoc
Thy ships are safe, riding in Malta Rhode:	Jew	1.1.50		1Merch
And all the Merchants with other Merchandize/Are safe arriv'd,	Jew	1.1.52		1Merch
The ships are safe thou saist, and richly fraught.	Jew	1.1.54		Barab
So, now the feare is past, and I am safe:	Jew	4.1.114		Barab
So he be safe he cares not what becomes,	P 739	14.42		Navrre
To see it done, and bring thee safe againe.	Edw	1.1.205		Edward
For no where else the new earle is so safe.	Edw	1.4.11		Lncstr
As England shall be quiet, and you safe.	Edw	1.4.358		Mortmr
great beames/On Atlas shoulder, shall not lie more safe,	Edw	3.1.77		Prince
And promiseth he shall be safe returnd,	Edw	3.1.110		Arundl
Their lord rode home, thinking his prisoner safe,	Edw	3.1.117		Arundl
There see him safe bestowed, and for the rest,	Edw	3.1.253		Edward
To keepe your royall person safe with us,	Edw	4.7.3		Abbot
And therefore so the prince my sonne be safe,	Edw	5.2.17		Queene
Faustus thou art safe.	F 414	2.1.26		Faust
that I might locke you safe into <uppe in> my <goode> Chest:	F 676	2.2.125	P	Covet
I see hell, and returne againe safe, how happy were I then.	F 714	2.2.166	P	Faust
That make <makes> safe passage, to each part of Rome.	F 816	3.1.38		Mephst
So, they are safe:	F1035	3.2.55		Faust
Sit safe at home and chaunt sweet Poesie.	Lucan, First Booke	445		
She safe by favour of her judge doth rest.	Ovid's Elegies	2.2.56		
His sword layed by, safe, though rude places yeelds.	Ovid's Elegies	2.9.20		
So farre 'tis safe, but to go farther dread.	Ovid's Elegies	2.11.16		
It is more safe to sleepe, to read a booke,	Ovid's Elegies	2.11.31		
Thy bones I pray may in the urne safe rest,	Ovid's Elegies	3.8.67		

SAFELY

And send us safely to arrive in France:	P 928	18.29		Navrre
The maide that kembd them ever safely left them.	Ovid's Elegies	1.14.16		
Wee seeke that through thee safely love we may,	Ovid's Elegies	2.2.65		

SAFER

We bide the first brunt, safer might we dwel,	Lucan, First Booke	253		

SAFETIE

Cheefely since under safetie of our word,	P 209	4.7		Charls
Tis for your safetie and your enemies wrack.	P 858	17.53		Guise
More safetie is there in a Tigers jawes,	Edw	5.1.116		Edward
as long as he survives/What safetie rests for us, or for my	Edw	5.2.43		Queene
To keepe your grace in safetie,	Edw	5.3.14		Gurney
What safetie may I looke for at his hands,	Edw	5.4.109		King
[Did gratulate his safetie with kinde words],	F1143	3.3.56A		3Chor

SAFETIES

Offer our safeties to his clemencie,	1Tamb	5.1.12		Govnr
Therefore in that your safeties and our owne,	1Tamb	5.1.40		Govnr

SAFETY

And now, as entrance to our safety,	Jew	5.2.22		Barab
maintaine/The wealth and safety of your kingdomes right.	P 478	8.28		Anjoy
I think for safety of your royall person,	P 887	17.82		Eprnon

SAFFRONS

And passe our scarlet of red saffrons marke.	Ovid's Elegies	2.6.22		

SAFTIE

For heers no saftie in the Realme for me,	P 568	11.33		Navrre

SAFTY

With happy safty of my fathers life,	1Tamb	5.1.401		Zenoc

SAGE

And make me blest with your sage conference.	F 126	1.1.98		Faust

SAGE (cont.)			
When you are up and drest, be sage and grave,	Ovid's Elegies	3.13.19	
SAID			
Tell you the rest (Meander) I have said.	1Tamb	2.2.13	Mycet
which by fame is said/To drinke the mightie Parthian Araris,	1Tamb	2.3.15	Tamb
Why, that's wel said Techelles, so would I,	1Tamb	2.5.69	Tamb
Wel said Theridamas, speake in that mood,	1Tamb	3.3.40	Tamb
Wel said my stout contributory kings,	1Tamb	3.3.93	Bajzth
It shall be said, I made it red my selfe,	1Tamb	4.2.54	Tamb
Wel said Theridamas, when holy Fates/Shall stablish me in	1Tamb	4.4.134	Tamb
manie cities sacrifice/He celebrated her [sad] <said> funerall,	2Tamb	Prol.8	Prolog
Viceroy of Byron, wisely hast thou said:	2Tamb	1.1.54	Orcan
Wel said Argier, receive thy crowne againe.	2Tamb	1.3.127	Tamb
Wel said, let there be a fire presently.	2Tamb	5.1.178	Tamb
He said he wud attend me in the morne.	Jew	2.1.34	Abigal
Well said, Ithimore;	Jew	3.4.56	Barab
And what said he?	Jew	4.2.11	P Curtzn
for your sake, and said what a faithfull servant you had bin.	Jew	4.2.109	P Pilia
For sith, as once you said, within this Ile/In Malta here, that	Jew	5.2.67	Barab
And said it was a heape of vanities?	P 388	7.28	Guise
Feare him said you?	P 934	19.4	P 1Mur
They were to blame that said I was displeasde,	P 969	19.39	King
And said, upon the honour of my name,	Edw	3.1.98	Arundl
Well said my lord.	Edw	4.2.26	SrJohn
that hee shall appeare to the said John Faustus, at all times,	F 491	2.1.103	P Faust
full power to fetch or carry the said John Faustus, body and	F 497	2.1.109	P Faust
'Tis well said Faustus, come then stand by me/And thou shalt	F 843	3.1.65	Mephst
I have heard it said,/That this faire Lady, whilest she liv'd	F1265	4.1.111	Emper
This said, he laying aside all lets of war,	Lucan, First Booke	206	
This said, the restles generall through the darke/(Swifter then	Lucan, First Booke	230	
Caesar (said he) while eloquence prevail'd,	Lucan, First Booke	274	
This said, being tir'd with fury she sunke downe.	Lucan, First Booke	694	
She nothing said, pale feare her tongue had tyed.	Ovid's Elegies	1.7.20	
things hidden)/Whence uncleane fowles are said to be forbidden.	Ovid's Elegies	2.6.52	
Yet should I curse a God, if he but said,	Ovid's Elegies	2.9.25	
In mid Bithynia 'tis said Inachus,	Ovid's Elegies	3.5.25	
This said he: shee her modest eyes held downe,	Ovid's Elegies	3.5.67	
This said: her coite hood-winckt her fearefull eyes,	Ovid's Elegies	3.5.79	
Tis said the slippery streame held up her brest,	Ovid's Elegies	3.5.81	
Is said to have attempted flight forsooke.	Ovid's Elegies	3.12.20	
Chast Hero to her selfe thus softly said:	Hero and Leander	1.178	
So having paus'd a while, at last shee said:	Hero and Leander	1.337	
SAIDE			
Yours my Lord Cardinall, you should have saide.	P1103	20.13	1Mur
SAIED			
This saied, she mov'd her buskins gaily varnisht,	Ovid's Elegies	3.1.31	
SAIES			
What saies my other friends, wil you be kings?	1Tamb	2.5.67	Tamb
It saies, Agydas, thou shalt surely die,	1Tamb	3.2.95	Agidas
Earth droopes and saies, that hell in heaven is plac'd.	2Tamb	5.3.16	Therid
Earth droopes and saies that hel in heaven is plac'd.	2Tamb	5.3.41	Usumc
the proverb saies, he that eats with the devil had need of a	Jew	3.4.58	P Ithimr
What saies our Minions, think they Henries heart/Will not both	P 603	12.16	King
by me, yet but he may/See him before he dies, for why he saies,	Edw	2.5.37	Arundl
Saies Faustus come, thine houre is almost come,	F1727	5.1.54	Faust
SAIEST			
What saiest thou yet Gazellus to his foile:	2Tamb	2.3.27	Orcan
If ill, thou saiest I die for others love.	Ovid's Elegies	2.7.10	
Thou saiest broke with Alcides angry hand.	Ovid's Elegies	3.5.36	
SAIL'D			
you came not with those other ships/That sail'd by Egypt?	Jew	1.1.90	Barab
SAILD			
But he clapt under hatches saild away.	Dido	5.1.240	Anna
SAILDE			
Men kept the shoare, and sailde not into deepe.	Ovid's Elegies	3.7.44	
SAILE (See also SAYLES)			
that under his conduct/We might saile backe to Troy, and be	Dido	2.1.18	Aeneas
And let Achates saile to Italy:	Dido	3.1.115	Dido
We may as one saile into Italy.	Dido	4.3.30	Aeneas
Thou and Achates ment to saile away.	Dido	4.4.28	Dido
As oft as he attempts to hoyst up saile:	Dido	4.4.103	Dido
And left me neither saile nor sterne abourd.	Dido	5.1.61	Aeneas
With speede he bids me saile to Italy,	Dido	5.1.68	Aeneas
And leaving me will saile to Italy.	Dido	5.1.195	Dido
Must I make ships for him to saile away?	Dido	5.1.266	Dido
That yeerely saile to the Venetian gulfe,	1Tamb	3.3.249	Tamb
Which when I come aboord will hoist up saile,	2Tamb	1.2.24	Callap
I would prepare a ship and saile to it,	2Tamb	1.3.90	Celeb
Five hundred Briggandines are under saile,	2Tamb	1.3.122	Therid
That men might quickly saile to India.	2Tamb	5.3.135	Tamb
Loaden with Spice and Silkes, now under saile,	Jew	1.1.45	Barab
Thou needs must saile by Alexandria.	Jew	1.1.76	Barab
And send to keepe our Gallies under-saile,	Jew	1.2.15	Calym
And saile from hence to Greece, to lovely Greece,	Jew	4.2.89	Ithimr
Will take his leave and saile toward Ottoman.	Jew	5.2.106	Barab
To saile to Turkey, to great Ottoman,	Jew	5.3.16	Msngr
Nay, rather saile with us to Scarborough.	Edw	2.4.52	Mortmr
Which makes the maine saile fal with hideous sound;	Lucan, First Booke	498	
he doth not chide/Nor to hoist saile attends fit time and tyde.	Ovid's Elegies	1.9.14	
Knights of the post of perjuries make saile,	Ovid's Elegies	1.10.37	
Ere thou rise starres teach seamen where to saile,	Ovid's Elegies	1.13.11	
And with thy hand assist [the] <thy> swelling saile.	Ovid's Elegies	2.11.42	
Rather Ile hoist up saile, and use the winde,	Ovid's Elegies	3.10.51	

SAILE (cont.)			
Than he could saile, for incorporeal Fame,	Hero and Leander	2.113	
SAILER			
Or crooked Dolphin when the sailer sings;	Hero and Leander	2.234	
SAILERS			
Thou wouldst have leapt from out the Sailers hands,	Dido	4.4.141	Dido
And, see the Sailers take him by the hand,	Dido	5.1.189	Dido
And all the Sailers merrie make for joy,	Dido	5.1.259	Dido
The wandring Sailers of proud Italy,	2Tamb	1.1.39	Orcan
SAILES			
Put sailes to sea to seeke out Italy,	Dido	1.1.218	Aeneas
Before that Boreas buckled with your sailes?	Dido	1.2.19	Iarbus
My Sailes all rent in sunder with the winde,	Dido	3.1.106	Aeneas
The Masts whereon thy swelling sailes shall hang,	Dido	3.1.122	Dido
The sailes of foulded Lawne, where shall be wrought/The warres	Dido	3.1.124	Dido
The sailes were hoysing up, and he abourd.	Dido	4.4.15	Anna
Bring me his oares, his tackling, and his sailes:	Dido	4.4.109	Dido
And heres Aeneas tackling, oares and sailes.	Dido	4.4.125	Lord
Are these the sailes that in despight of me,	Dido	4.4.126	Dido
Was it not you that hoysed up these sailes?	Dido	4.4.153	Dido
And see if those will serve in steed of sailes:	Dido	4.4.160	Dido
Who have no sailes nor tackling for my ships?	Dido	5.1.56	Aeneas
And spying me, hoyst up the sailes amaine:	Dido	5.1.227	Anna
strike flames of lightening)/All fearefull foldes his sailes,	1Tamb	3.2.82	Agidas
The sailes wrapt up, the mast and tacklings downe,	2Tamb	1.2.59	Callap
The wind that bears him hence, wil fil our sailes,	Edw	2.4.48	Lncstr
The crooked Barque hath her swift sailes displayd.	Ovid's Elegies	2.11.24	
By which love sailes to regions full of blis),	Hero and Leander	2.276	
SAILING			
Sailing along the Orientall sea,	1Tamb	3.3.253	Tamb
Come, come aboord, tis but an houres sailing.	Edw	2.4.49	Lncstr
SAINT (See also S., SANCTA, SANCTUS)			
and inquire/For any of the Fryars of Saint [Jaques] <Jaynes>,	Jew	3.3.28	Abigal
Saint Jaques Even) and then I say they use/To send their Almes	Jew	3.4.76	Barab
Without the intercession of some Saint?	P 357	6.12	Mntsrl
[Sanctus] <Sancta> Jacobus hee was my Saint, pray to him.	P 358	6.13	Mntsrl
Hard is the hart, that injures such a saint.	Edw	1.4.190	Penbrk
Saint George for England, and the Barons right.	Edw	3.1.219	Warwck
Saint George for England, and king Edwards right.	Edw	3.1.220	Edward
hollinesse ascends/Saint Peters Chaire and State Pontificall.	F 870	3.1.92	Raymnd
Sound Trumpets then, for thus Saint Peters Heire,	F 875	3.1.97	Pope
From Bruno's backe, ascends Saint Peters Chaire.	F 876	3.1.98	Pope
And by your death to clime Saint Peters Chaire,	F 960	3.1.182	Faust
That we may solemnize Saint Peters feast,	F 978	3.1.200	Pope
secret works, and [wash] <washt> their saint/In Almo's floud:	Lucan, First Booke	599	
Were I the saint hee worships, I would heare him,	Hero and Leander	1.179	
SAINTS			
And heer by all the Saints in heaven I sweare,	P 765	15.23	Guise
Th'abreviated <breviated> names of holy Saints,	F 238	1.3.10	Faust
hadst set/In yonder throne, like those bright shining Saints,	F1905	5.2.109	GdAngl
their saints and houshold gods/Sweate teares to shew the	Lucan, First Booke	554	
SAIST			
The ships are safe thou saist, and richly fraught.	Jew	1.1.54	Barab
Prethe doe: what saist thou now?	Jew	3.4.88	Barab
Saist thou me so?	Jew	4.4.2	P Ithimr
Pounds saist thou, Governor, wel since it is no more/I'le	Jew	5.5.21	Barab
Surgeon, why saist thou so? the King may live.	P1224	22.86	Navrre
SAITH			
What saith Theridamas?	1Tamb	2.5.105	Tamb
What is beauty, saith my sufferings then?	1Tamb	5.1.160	Tamb
What saith the noble Souldane and Zenocrate?	1Tamb	5.1.495	Tamb
Well done Techelles: what saith Theridamas?	2Tamb	1.3.206	Tamb
What saith Maximus?	2Tamb	5.1.1	Govnr
To you of Malta thus saith Calymath:	Jew	3.5.7	Basso
Selim, for that, thus saith the Governor,	Jew	5.3.26	Msngr
Which [are] <as> he saith, to kill the Puritans,	P 643	12.56	Cardnl
He saith true.	Edw	1.4.271	Penbrk
But one of those that saith quandoquidem,	Edw	2.1.54	Spencr
And plainely saith, twas thou that murdredst him.	Edw	5.6.42	King
Now tell me what saith <sayes> Lucifer thy Lord.	F 419	2.1.31	Faust
here, here (saith he)/An end of peace; here end polluted lawes;	Lucan, First Booke	226	
Fame saith as I suspect, and in her eyes/Two eye-balles shine,	Ovid's Elegies	1.8.15	
Delia departing, happier lov'd, she saith,	Ovid's Elegies	3.8.55	
SAKARS			
Minions, Fauknets, and Sakars to the trench,	2Tamb	3.3.6	Techel
SAKE			
For my sake pitie him Oceanus,	Dido	1.1.127	Venus
Who for Troyes sake hath entertaind us all,	Dido	2.1.64	Illion
For Didos sake I take thee in my armes,	Dido	2.1.313	Venus
Take it Ascanius, for thy fathers sake.	Dido	3.1.33	Dido
No, for thy sake Ile love thy father well.	Dido	3.1.81	Dido
Yet would you have some pitie for my sake,	1Tamb	4.2.123	Zenoc
Is Barbary unpeopled for thy sake,	2Tamb	1.3.134	Usumc
All Barbary is unpeopled for thy sake.	2Tamb	1.3.149	Techel
And for his sake here will I end my daies.	2Tamb	3.4.44	Olymp
then let every man/Provide him, and be there for fashion-sake.	Jew	1.1.171	Barab
One that I love for his good fathers sake.	Jew	2.3.31	Barab
Even for your Honourable fathers sake.	Jew	2.3.93	Barab
Abigall, bid him welcome for my sake.	Jew	2.3.232	Barab
For your sake and his own he's welcome hither.	Jew	2.3.233	Abigal
into the sea; why I'le doe any thing for your sweet sake.	Jew	3.4.41	P Ithimr
And for thy sake, whom I so dearely love,	Jew	3.4.61	Barab
And for his sake did I become a Nunne.	Jew	3.6.25	Abigal

SAKE (cont.)			
That would for Lucars sake have sold my soule.	Jew	4.1.53	Barab
Sweet Bellamira, would I had my Masters wealth for thy sake.	Jew	4.2.55	P Ithimr
and told me he lov'd me for your sake, and said what a	Jew	4.2.109	P Pilia
Take thou the mony, spend it for my sake.	Jew	4.2.123	Ithimr
The Mother Queene workes wonders for my sake,	P 133	2.76	Guise
What I have done tis for the Gospell sake.	P 826	17.21	Guise
Nay for the Popes sake, and thine owne benefite.	P 827	17.22	Eprnon
the Jacobyns, that for my conscience sake will kill the King.	P1131	21.25	P Frier
All Warwickshire will love him for my sake.	Edw	1.1.128	Warwck
Farewell sweet Mortimer, and for my sake,	Edw	1.2.81	Queene
Tis not for his sake, but for our availe:	Edw	1.4.242	Mortmr
Which for his fathers sake leane to the king,	Edw	1.4.283	Mortmr
That day, if not for him, yet for my sake,	Edw	1.4.381	Edward
For my sake let him waite upon your grace,	Edw	2.2.250	Gavstn
me, for his sake/Ile grace thee with a higher stile ere long.	Edw	2.2.252	Edward
Yes, yes, for Mortimer your lovers sake.	Edw	2.4.14	Edward
When for her sake I ran at tilt in Fraunce,	Edw	5.5.69	Edward
For my sake sweete sonne pittie Mortimer.	Edw	5.6.55	Queene
Give him his head for Gods sake.	F1392	4.2.68	P Fredrk
[Yet for Christs sake, whose bloud hath ransom'd me],	F1959	5.2.163A	Faust
not heavens, but gladly beare these evils/For Neros sake:	Lucan, First Booke		38
(For his sake whom their goddesse held so deare,	Hero and Leander		1.92
Base boullion for the stampes sake we allow,	Hero and Leander		1.265
Yet for her sake whom you have vow'd to serve,	Hero and Leander		1.316
sad and heavie cheare/Complaind to Cupid; Cupid for his sake,	Hero and Leander		1.441
If not for love, yet love for pittie sake,	Hero and Leander		2.247
SAKERS (See SAKARS)			
SAKES			
Therefore, for these our harmlesse virgines sakes,	1Tamb	5.1.18	Govnr
And for your sakes, a thousand wronges ile take,	Edw	5.3.43	Edward
SALE			
Of whom we would make sale in Malta here.	Jew	2.2.18	Bosco
But to admit a sale of these thy Turkes/We may not, nay we dare	Jew	2.2.21	Govnr
Feare not their sale, for they'll be quickly bought.	Jew	2.3.2	1Offcr
Sale made of offices, and peoples voices/Bought by themselves	Lucan, First Booke		180
Nor set my voyce to sale in everie cause?	Ovid's Elegies		1.15.6
SALII			
The skipping Salii with shields like wedges;	Lucan, First Booke		602
SALLOW			
She overcome with shame and sallow feare,	Hero and Leander		2.260
SALLY			
Have speciall care that no man sally forth/Till you shall heare	Jew	5.4.2	Govnr
SALMACIS			
And like light Salmacis, her body throes/Upon his bosome, where	Hero and Leander		2.46
SALSBURIE			
Darbie, Salsburie, Lincolne, Leicester,	Edw	1.1.103	Lncstr
SALT			
turn'd to a gaping Oyster, and drinke nothing but salt water.	F1320	4.1.166	P Benvol
Then crams salt levin on his crooked knife;	Lucan, First Booke		609
SALUTATION			
This salutation overjoyes my heart.	Edw	1.4.344	Lncstr
SALUTE			
Let us salute him. Save thee, Barabas.	Jew	5.5.54	Calym
of Guise you and your wife/Doe both salute our lovely Minions.	P 753	15.11	King
And there salute his highnesse in our name,	P 908	18.9	Navrre
Salute the Queene of England in my name,	P1243	22.105	King
And on their knees salute your majestie.	Edw	1.4.339	Queene
Will none of you salute my Gaveston?	Edw	2.2.64	Edward
Salute him? yes: welcome Lord Chamberlaine.	Edw	2.2.65	Lncstr
The Barons up in armes, by me salute/Your highnes, with long	Edw	3.1.156	Herald
The proudest lords salute me as I passe,	Edw	5.4.50	Mortmr
Let us salute his reverend Father-hood.	F 944	3.1.166	Faust
There to salute the wofull Emperour.	F 986	3.2.6	Mephst
SALUTED			
base slave as he should be saluted by such a tall man as I am,	Jew	4.2.9	P Pilia
whom I saluted with an old hempen proverb, Hodie tibi,	Jew	4.2.18	P Pilia
SALUTES			
See you Agidas how the King salutes you.	1Tamb	3.2.88	Techel
SALUTING			
saluting me in such sort as if he had meant to make cleane my	Jew	4.2.30	P Ithimr
SALVATION			
Scarce can I name salvation, faith, or heaven,	F 570	2.2.19	Faust
And quite bereave thee of salvation.	F1709	5.1.36	OldMan
SALVE (Homograph)			
Virgo, salve.	Jew	3.3.50	1Fryar
The life of thee shall salve this foule disgrace.	Edw	2.2.83	Gavstn
SALVETE			
Aerii, [Aquatici] <Aquatani>, [Terreni], spiritus salvete:	F 245	1.3.17	P Faust
SAMARCANDA			
O Samarcanda, where I breathed first,	2Tamb	4.1.105	Tamb
Then shal my native city Samarcanda/And christall waves of	2Tamb	4.3.107	Tamb
So will I ride through Samarcanda streets,	2Tamb	4.3.130	Tamb
SAME			
That in such peace long time did rule the same:	Dido	1.2.24	Cloan
Yet insufficient to expresse the same:	1Tamb	1.1.2	Mycet
On this same theevish villaine Tamburlaine.	1Tamb	2.2.3	Mycet
And with the same proportion of Elements/Resolve, I hope we are	1Tamb	2.6.26	Cosroe
And I wil sheath it to confirme the same.	2Tamb	1.1.85	Sgsmnd
And we from Europe to the same intent,	2Tamb	1.1.118	Fredrk
See ye this rout, and know ye this same king?	2Tamb	3.5.151	Tamb
I Turke, I tel thee, this same Boy is he,	2Tamb	4.3.57	Tamb
a thousand Crownes, by the same token, that the Nuns lov'd Rice,	Jew	4.4.75	P Ithimr

SAME (cont.)			
The very same, my Lord:	Jew	5.1.74	Barab
Flourish in France, and none deny the same.	P 640	12.53	QnMoth
And staine my roiall standard with the same,	Edw	3.1.138	Edward
There's none but I have interest in the same.	F 637	2.2.86	Lucifr
That underprop <underprops> the ground-worke of the same:	F 812	3.1.34	Mephst
To lay the fury of this same troublesome ghost.	F1064	3.2.84	Pope
that your devill can answere the stealing of this same cup,	F1089	3.3.2 P	Dick
Gentlemen farewell: the same wish I to you.	F1706	5.1.33	Faust
Offers to poure the same into thy soule,	F1732	5.1.59	OldMan
what doest thou with that same booke thou canst not reade?	F App	p.233 13 P	Rafe
even the same that wrack's all great [dominions] <dominion>.	Lucan, First Booke		160
what meanes learnd/Hath this same Poet my sad chaunce discernd?	Ovid's Elegies		2.1.10
With selfe same woundes he gave, he ought to smart.	Ovid's Elegies		2.3.4
As his deepe whirle-pooles could not quench the same.	Ovid's Elegies		3.5.42
What sweete thought is there but I had the same?	Ovid's Elegies		3.6.63
She held her lap ope to receive the same.	Ovid's Elegies		3.7.34
And let the world be witnesse of the same?	Ovid's Elegies		3.13.12
The self-same day that he asleepe had layd/Inchaunted Argus,	Hero and Leander		1.387
And now the same gan so to scorch and glow,	Hero and Leander		2.70
And for the same mildly rebuk't his sonne,	Hero and Leander		2.137
SAMINTES			
As for those [Samnites] <Samintes>, and the men of Uzz,/That	Jew	1.1.4	Barab
SAMNITES			
As for those [Samnites] <Samintes>, and the men of Uzz,/That	Jew	1.1.4	Barab
SANCINA			
Riso, Sancina, and the bordering townes,	2Tamb	3.1.52	Trebiz
SANCTA			
[Sanctus] <Sancta> Jacobus hee was my Saint, pray to him.	P 358	6.13	Mntsrl
SANCTE			
Sancte [Jacobe] <Jacobus>, now have mercye upon me.	P1172	22.34	Frier
SANCTI			
[Et omnes sancti. Amen].	F1087	3.2.107A	1Frier
Et omnes sancti Amen.	F App	p.233 41	Frier
SANCTITUDE			
Or by our sanctitude you all shall die.	F1057	3.2.77	Pope
SANCTOBULORUM			
Sanctobulorum Periphrasticon:	F App	p.235 23 P	Robin
SANCTUS			
[Sanctus] <Sancta> Jacobus hee was my Saint, pray to him.	P 358	6.13	Mntsrl
SAND			
Ulysses on the sand/Assayd with honey words to turne them	Dido	2.1.136	Aeneas
O happie sand that made him runne aground:	Dido	4.4.95	Dido
Or hew'd this flesh and bones as small as sand,	F1398	4.2.74	Faust
And in the forme of beds weele strowe soft sand,	Ovid's Elegies		2.11.47
Save that the sea playing on yellow sand,	Hero and Leander		1.347
Cast downe his wearie feet, and felt the sand.	Hero and Leander		2.228
SANDE			
And like Leander gaspt upon the sande,	Edw	1.1.8	Gavstn
This headlesse trunke that lies on Nylus sande/I know:	Lucan, First Booke		684
SANDELO			
be he that strucke <tooke> fryer Sandelo a blow on the pate.	F1081	3.2.101	1Frier
Cursed be he that tooke Frier Sandelo a blow on the pate.	F App	p.232 35	Frier
SANDIE			
Blow windes, threaten ye Rockes and sandie shelfes,	Dido	4.4.58	Aeneas
SANDS			
When yet both sea and sands beset their ships,	Dido	1.1.110	Venus
And led our ships into the shallow sands,	Dido	1.2.27	Cloan
And will not let us lodge upon the sands:	Dido	1.2.35	Serg
altar, where Ile offer up/As many kisses as the Sea hath sands,	Dido	3.1.88	Dido
as outwaies the sands/And all the craggie rockes of Caspea.	1Tamb	2.3.47	Tamb
Or Scythia; or hot Libiaes thirsty sands.	Lucan, First Booke		369
To steale sands from the shore he loves alife,	Ovid's Elegies		2.19.45
SANGUINE			
The purple moone with sanguine visage stood.	Ovid's Elegies		1.8.12
SANITAS			
Summum bonum medicinae sanitas,	F 44	1.1.16	Faust
SANS (See SAUNCE)			
SANTONS			
The Santons that rejoyce in Caesars love,	Lucan, First Booke		423
SAPHIR			
Whereat the saphir visag'd god grew prowd,	Hero and Leander		2.155
SAPHIRES			
Bags of fiery Opals, Saphires, Amatists,	Jew	1.1.25	Barab
SAPHYRES			
Diamondes, Saphyres, Rubies/And fairest pearle of welthie India	2Tamb	3.2.120	Tamb
SAPHYRS			
And sprinklest Saphyrs on thy shining face,	1Tamb	5.1.143	Tamb
SAPPHO			
Sappho her vowed harpe laies at Phoebus feete.	Ovid's Elegies		2.18.34
SARELL			
And in my Sarell tend my Concubines:	1Tamb	3.3.78	Bajzth
SARMATA			
And Vangions who like those of Sarmata,	Lucan, First Booke		431
SAT			
And I sat downe, cloth'd with the massie robe,	2Tamb	3.2.123	Tamb
and I sat upon a bottle of hey, never so neare drowning in my	F App	p.240 135 P	HrsCsr
There sat the hang-man for mens neckes to angle.	Ovid's Elegies		1.12.18
SATAN (See SATHAN)			
SATE			
To be a Christian, I shut him out,/And there he sate:	Jew	4.1.189	Barab
horse vanisht away, and I sate straddling upon a bottle of Hay.	F1545	4.5.41 P	HrsCsr
SATHAN			
[Sathan begins to sift me with his pride]:	F1787	5.1.118A	OldMan

SATIATE
That satiate with spoile refuseth blood. 1Tamb 4.1.53 2Msngr
SATIRUS
They came that dwell/By Nemes fields, and bankes of Satirus, Lucan, First Booke 421
SATISFACTION
I take thy doome for satisfaction. 1Tamb 2.3.5 Cosroe
SATISFIE
And satisfie the peoples generall praiers, 2Tamb 5.1.7 Maxim
wel since it is no more/I'le satisfie my selfe with that; nay, Jew 5.5.22 Barab
No, Governor, I'le satisfie thee first, Jew 5.5.44 Barab
The Kings alone, it cannot satisfie. P1109 21.3 Dumain
For which ere long, their heads shall satisfie, Edw 3.1.209 Edward
To satisfie my longing thoughts at full, F1264 4.1.110 Emper
Thou shalt both satisfie my just desire, F App p.237 35 Emper
SATISFIED
There was the venture summ'd and satisfied. Jew 1.1.3 Barab
Well then my Lord, say, are you satisfied? Jew 1.2.137 Barab
Then my desires were fully satisfied, Jew 2.1.52 Barab
returne me word/That thou wilt come, and I am satisfied. Jew 5.5.12 Barab
our Guise is dead)/Rest satisfied with this that heer I sweare, P1043 19.113 King
When will his hart be satisfied with bloud? Edw 5.3.9 Edward
I thanke you, I am fully satisfied. F1651 4.6.94 P Carter
SATISFY
not but faire Zenocrate/Will soone consent to satisfy us both. 1Tamb 5.1.499 Tamb
SATURN
For as when Jove did thrust old Saturn down, 1Tamb 2.7.36 Usumc
SATURNE
At whose byrth-day Cynthia with Saturne joinde, 1Tamb 1.1.13 Cosroe
Nor are the names of Saturne, Mars, or Jupiter, F 594 2.2.43 Mephst
<as> Saturne in thirty yeares, Jupiter in twelve, Mars in four, F 604 2.2.53 P Faust
If cold noysome Saturne/Were now exalted, and with blew beames Lucan, First Booke 650
Yet when old Saturne heavens rule possest, Ovid's Elegies 3.7.35
And aged Saturne in Olympus dwell. Hero and Leander 1.454
Saturne and Ops, began their golden raigne. Hero and Leander 1.456
SATURNES
By Saturnes soule, and this earth threatning [haire] <aire>, Dido 1.1.10 Jupitr
Then in my coach like Saturnes royal son, 2Tamb 4.3.125 Tamb
SATURNIA
brave Assirian Dames/Have rid in pompe like rich Saturnia, 2Tamb 5.1.77 Tamb
SATYRES
My men like Satyres grazing on the lawnes, Edw 1.1.59 Gavstn
SATYRS
some (their violent passions to asswage)/Compile sharpe satyrs, Hero and Leander 1.127
Gote-footed Satyrs, and up-staring <upstarting> Fawnes, Hero and Leander 2.200
SAUC'D
Jew, he lives upon pickled Grashoppers, and sauc'd Mushrumbs. Jew 4.4.62 P Ithimr
His store of pleasures must be sauc'd with paine. F1812 5.2.16 Mephst
SAUCE (See also SAWCE)
Go to, sirra sauce, is this your question? Jew 3.3.34 P Abigal
to have it well rosted, and good sauce to it, if I pay so deere, F 353 1.4.11 P Robin
I but sir sauce box, know you in what place? F1616 4.6.59 Servnt
SAUC'T
was ever pot of rice porredge so sauc't? Jew 3.4.107 P Ithimr
SAUCY
Why saucy varlets, dare you be so bold. F1594 4.6.37 Servnt
SAULE
As fell to Saule, to Balaam and the rest, 2Tamb 2.1.54 Fredrk
SAUNCE
Love is a naked boy, his yeares saunce staine, Ovid's Elegies 1.10.15
SAUSINESSE
Both for their sausinesse shall be employed, 1Tamb 3.3.184 Zenoc
SAVADGE
and with this sword/Sent many of their savadge ghosts to hell. Dido 2.1.212 Aeneas
SAVAGE
To chace the savage [Calidonian] <Caldonian> Boare: 1Tamb 4.3.3 Souldn
hunters in the chace/Of savage beastes amid the desart woods. 1Tamb 4.3.57 Capol
Ah none but rude and savage minded men, Edw 1.4.78 Edward
Incenst with savage heat, gallop amaine, Hero and Leander 1.115
SAVAGES
Flie to the Savages. Edw 5.6.9 Mortmr
Wild savages, that drinke of running springs, Hero and Leander 1.259
SAV'D
That sav'd your famisht souldiers lives from death, Dido 3.3.52 Achat
By him that made the world and sav'd my soule, 2Tamb 1.1.133 Sgsmnd
Convert my father that he may be sav'd, Jew 3.6.39 Abigal
[And] canst <thou> not [now] be sav'd. F 390 2.1.2 Faust
A hundred thousand, and at last be sav'd. F1962 5.2.166 Faust
Subscribing, Naso with Corinna sav'd: Ovid's Elegies 2.13.25
From no mans reading fearing to be sav'd. Ovid's Elegies 3.1.54
SAV'DE
And seeming lavish, sav'de her maydenhead. Hero and Leander 2.76
SAVE (Homograph)
What shall I doe to save thee my sweet boy? Dido 1.1.74 Venus
Save, save, O save our ships from cruell fire, Dido 1.2.7 Illion
Save, save Aeneas, Didos leefest love! Dido 5.1.256 Dido
Sound up the trumpets then, God save the King. 1Tamb 1.1.188 Ortyg
To save your King and country from decay: 1Tamb 2.6.35 Cosroe
I (my Lord) but none save kinges must feede with these. 1Tamb 4.4.109 P Therid
Save onely that in Beauties just applause, 1Tamb 5.1.178 Tamb
But let us save the reverend Souldans life, 1Tamb 5.1.204 Therid
Ah, save that Infant, save him, save him. 1Tamb 5.1.313 P Zabina
Ah, save that Infant, save him, save him. 1Tamb 5.1.314 P Zabina
to Zenocrate/Than her owne life, or ought save thine owne love. 1Tamb 5.1.338 Zenoc

SAVE (cont.)

That no escape may save their enemies: 1Tamb 5.1.405 Arabia
And save our forces for the hot assaults/Proud Tamburlaine 2Tamb 1.1.52 Gazell
leave these armes/And save thy sacred person free from scathe: 2Tamb 1.3.10 Zenoc
Murther the Foe and save [the] <their> walles from breach. 2Tamb 3.2.82 Tamb
To save our Cannoniers from musket shot, 2Tamb 3.3.57 Therid
No hope is left to save this conquered hold. 2Tamb 3.4.3 Olymp
But yet Ile save their lives and make them slaves. 2Tamb 3.5.63 Tamb
Save griefe and sorrow which torment my heart, 2Tamb 4.2.24 Olymp
Stay good my Lord, and wil you save my honor, 2Tamb 4.2.55 Olymp
O pity us my Lord, and save our honours. 2Tamb 4.3.83 Ladies
Save your honours? 2Tamb 4.3.86 Tamb
That litle hope is left to save our lives, 2Tamb 5.1.4 Maxim
Yeeld up the towne, save our wives and children: 2Tamb 5.1.39 2Citzn
To save thy life, and us a litle labour, 2Tamb 5.1.50 Therid
Save but my life and I wil give it thee. 2Tamb 5.1.118 Govnr
Then for all your valour, you would save your life. 2Tamb 5.1.119 Tamb
Yet save my life, and let this wound appease/The mortall furie 2Tamb 5.1.153 Govnr
we take particularly thine/To save the ruine of a multitude: Jew 1.2.97 Govnr
And now, save Pilia-borza, comes there none. Jew 3.1.9 Curtzn
What, all dead save onely Abigall? Jew 3.6.7 2Fryar
What, will you [have] <save> my life? Jew 4.1.148 2Fryar
Let us salute him. Save thee, Barabas. Jew 5.5.54 Calym
But I have rather chose to save thy life. Jew 5.5.94 Govnr
Flye Ramus flye, if thou wilt save thy life. P 365 7.5 Taleus
Wilshire hath men enough to save our heads. Edw 1.1.127 MortSr
Save or condemne, and in our name commaund, Edw 1.1.169 Edward
God save Queene Isabell, and her princely sonne. Edw 4.6.46 Rice
And save you from your foes, Bartley would die. Edw 5.1.134 Bartly
Containes his death, yet bids them save his life. Edw 5.4.7 Mortmr
Let this gift change thy minde, and save thy soule, Edw 5.5.88 Edward
you may save your selfe a labour, for they are as familiar with F 364 1.4.22 P Robin
Helpe <seeke> to save distressed Faustus soule. F 635 2.2.84 Faust
Christ cannot save thy soule, for he is just, F 636 2.2.85 Lucifr
Pitie us gentle Faustus, save our lives. F1417 4.2.93 Fredrk
O what may <shal> we do to save Faustus? F1868 5.2.72 P 2Schol
Talke not of me, but save your selves and depart. F1869 5.2.73 P Faust
That Faustus may repent, and save his soule. F1934 5.2.138 Faust
One drop [would save my soule, halfe a drop, ah] my Christ. F1940 5.2.144 Faust
One drop <of bloud will save me; oh> my Christ. F1940 (HC271)B Faust
you may save that labour, they are too familiar with me F App p.229 27 P Clown
masse see where he is, God save you maister doctor. F App p.239 99 P HrsCsr
this is he, God save ye maister doctor, maister doctor, maister F App p.241 148 P HrsCsr
I gladly graunt my parents given to save, Ovid's Elegies 1.3.10
Who can indure, save him with whom none lies? Ovid's Elegies 1.13.26
Worthy she is, thou shouldst in mercy save her. Ovid's Elegies 2.13.22
As heaven preserves all things, so save thou one. Hero and Leander 1.224
Save that the sea playing on yellow sand, Hero and Leander 1.347

SAVED

And by this Sword that saved me from the Greekes, Dido 3.4.48 Aeneas
the serpent that tempted Eve may be saved, but not Faustus. F1838 5.2.42 P Faust

SAVING (Homograph)

Here she was wont to sit, but saving ayre/Is nothing here, and Dido 2.1.13 Achat
For saving him from Snakes and Serpents stings, Dido 3.2.38 Juno
Saving your reverence, you must pardon me. Edw 1.1.186 Gavstn
For saving of a Romaine Citizen, Lucan, First Booke 359

SAVIOUR

O Christ my Saviour-- P 354 6.9 Seroun
Abjure the Scriptures, and his Saviour Christ; F 276 1.3.48 Mephst
[Ah] <O> Christ my Saviour, my Saviour, F 634 2.2.83 Faust
But mercie Faustus of thy Saviour sweete, F App p.243 44 OldMan

SAVOR

And I was almost stifeled with the savor. Edw 5.5.9 Gurney

SAVOUR

Sister, I see you savour of my wiles, Dido 3.2.96 Venus
Will every savour breed a pangue of death? P 72 2.15 Guise

SAW

men, saw you as you came/Any of all my Sisters wandring here? Dido 1.1.183 Venus
I neither saw nor heard of any such: Dido 1.1.187 Aeneas
I saw this man at Troy ere Troy was sackt. Dido 3.1.141 Achat
Dar'st thou that never saw an Emperour, 1Tamb 4.2.58 Zabina
But when I saw the place obscure and darke, 2Tamb 4.2.15 Therid
I neither saw them, nor inquir'd of them. Jew 1.1.77 1Merch
Sir we saw 'em not. Jew 1.1.90 2Merch
up to the Jewes counting-house where I saw some bags of mony, Jew 3.1.19 P Pilia
that she loves me ever since she saw me, and who would not Jew 4.2.34 P Ithimr
Think'st thou that I [who] saw the face of God, F 305 1.3.77 Mephst
We saw the River Maine, fall into Rhine <Rhines>, F 785 3.1.7 Faust
There saw we learned Maroes golden tombe: F 791 3.1.13 Faust
By holy Paul we saw them not. F1029 3.2.49 BthCrd
I saw him kneele, and kisse the Emperours hand, F1344 4.2.20 Benvol
such belly-cheere, as Wagner in his life nere saw the like: F1679 5.1.6 P Wagner
That heavenly Hellen, which I saw of late, F1762 5.1.89 Faust
so by that meanes I shal see more then ere I felt, or saw yet. F App p.233 5 P Robin
It grieves my soule I never saw the man: F App p.237 28 Emper
When Caesar saw his army proane to war, Lucan, First Booke 393
I saw a brandisht fire increase in strength, Ovid's Elegies 1.2.11
Which being not shakt <slackt>, I saw it die at length. Ovid's Elegies 1.2.12
I saw how Bulls for a white Heifer strive, Ovid's Elegies 2.12.25
I saw a horse against the bitte stiffe-neckt, Ovid's Elegies 3.4.13
But when she saw it would by no meanes stand, Ovid's Elegies 3.6.75
I saw when forth a tyred lover went, Ovid's Elegies 3.10.13
dallying with Hero, nothing saw/That might delight him more, Hero and Leander 2.62

Line	Work	Reference	P	Speaker
SAW (cont.)				
And looking backe, saw Neptune follow him.	Hero and Leander	2.176		
SAWCE				
have it wel roasted, and good sawce to it, if I pay so deere.	F App	p.229 12	P	Clown
SAWE				
thou knowest/We sawe Cassandra sprauling in the streetes,	Dido	2.1.274		Aeneas
All these and others which I never sawe,	Dido	3.1.150		Dido
Bootles I sawe it was to warre with fate,	Dido	3.2.49		Juno
It was because I sawe no King like thee,	Dido	3.4.35		Dido
I feare I sawe Aeneas little sonne,	Dido	5.1.83		Dido
How smoothe a bellie, under her waste sawe I,	Ovid's Elegies	1.5.21		
Her halfe dead joynts, and trembling limmes I sawe,	Ovid's Elegies	1.7.53		
(If I have faith) I sawe the starres drop bloud,	Ovid's Elegies	1.8.11		
I sawe the damsell walking yesterday/There where the porch doth	Ovid's Elegies	2.2.3		
I sawe ones legges with fetters blacke and blewe,	Ovid's Elegies	2.2.47		
[wretch] <wench> I sawe when thou didst thinke I slumbred,	Ovid's Elegies	2.5.13		
I sawe your nodding eye-browes much to speake,	Ovid's Elegies	2.5.15		
I sawe you then unlawfull kisses joyne,	Ovid's Elegies	2.5.23		
Wily Corinna sawe this blemish in me,	Ovid's Elegies	2.19.9		
The goddesse sawe Iasion on Candyan Ide,	Ovid's Elegies	3.9.25		
She sawe, and as her marrowe tooke the flame,	Ovid's Elegies	3.9.27		
SAWEST				
Am I lesse faire then when thou sawest me first?	Dido	5.1.115		Dido
a paire of hornes on's head as e're thou sawest in thy life.	F 738	2.3.17	P	Robin
SAW'ST				
And saw'st thou not/Mine Argosie at Alexandria?	Jew	1.1.71		Barab
When saw'st thou Abigall?	Jew	3.4.18		Barab
SAXON				
Saxon Bruno stoope,/Whilst on thy backe his hollinesse ascends	F 868	3.1.90		Raymnd
SAXONY				
see Duke of Saxony,/Two spreading hornes most strangely	F1276	4.1.122		Emper
SAY (See also SAIES, SAIST, SAYD)				
I love thee well, say Juno what she will.	Dido	1.1.2		Jupitr
Doe thou but say their colour pleaseth me.	Dido	1.1.41		Jupitr
Achates though mine eyes say this is stone,	Dido	2.1.24		Aeneas
But Troy is not, what shall I say I am?	Dido	2.1.76		Aeneas
Some say Antenor did betray the towne,	Dido	2.1.110		Dido
That I should say thou art no love of mine?	Dido	3.1.42		Dido
Away I say,/Depart from Carthage, come not in my sight.	Dido	3.1.43		Dido
Name not Iarbus, but sweete Anna say,	Dido	3.1.67		Dido
Then never say that thou art miserable,	Dido	3.1.169		Dido
Say Paris, now shall Venus have the ball?	Dido	3.2.12		Juno
Say vengeance, now shall her Ascanius dye?	Dido	3.2.13		Juno
Aeneas, thou art he, what did I say?	Dido	3.4.29		Dido
To leave her so and not once say farewell,	Dido	4.3.47		Aeneas
They say Aeneas men are going abourd,	Dido	4.4.2		Dido
Say Dido what she will I am not old,	Dido	4.5.21		Nurse
O how unwise was I to say him nay!	Dido	4.5.37		Nurse
I dye, if my Aeneas say farewell.	Dido	5.1.108		Dido
Then let me goe and never say farewell?	Dido	5.1.109		Aeneas
Say thou wilt stay in Carthage with [thy] <my> Queene,	Dido	5.1.117		Dido
Aeneas, say, how canst thou take thy leave?	Dido	5.1.119		Dido
Therefore unkind Aeneas, must thou say,	Dido	5.1.123		Dido
Then let me goe, and never say farewell?	Dido	5.1.124		Dido
For though thou hast the heart to say farewell,	Dido	5.1.182		Dido
And stay a while to heare what I could say,	Dido	5.1.239		Anna
How say you Lordings, Is not this your hope?	1Tamb	1.2.116		Tamb
But if Cosroe (as our Spials say,	1Tamb	2.2.35		Meandr
Was there such brethren, sweet Meander, say,	1Tamb	2.2.51		Mycet
So Poets say, my Lord.	1Tamb	2.2.53		Meandr
Go on my Lord, and give your charge I say,	1Tamb	2.2.57		Mycet
Why say Theridamas, wilt thou be a king?	1Tamb	2.5.65		Tamb
If you but say that Tamburlaine shall raigne.	1Tamb	2.7.63		Tamb
Wils and commands (for say not I intreat)/Not once to set his	1Tamb	3.1.27		Bajzth
Then stay thou with him, say I bid thee so.	1Tamb	3.1.35		Bajzth
They say he is the King of Persea.	1Tamb	3.1.45		Argier
say you to this (Turke) these are not your contributorie kings.	1Tamb	4.4.117	P	Tamb
Away with them I say and shew them death.	1Tamb	5.1.120		Tamb
How far hence lies the Galley, say you?	2Tamb	1.2.54		Almeda
Now say my Lords of Buda and Bohemia,	2Tamb	2.1.1		Sgsmnd
Then if there be a Christ, as Christians say,	2Tamb	2.2.39		Orcan
Ah sweet Theridamas, say so no more,	2Tamb	2.4.126		Tamb
How say ye Souldiers, Shal we not?	2Tamb	3.3.9		Techel
You say true.	2Tamb	4.1.41		Calyph
They say I am a coward, (Perdicas) and I feare as litle their	2Tamb	4.1.67	P	Calyph
That they may say, it is not chance doth this,	2Tamb	4.1.84		Amyras
or by speach I heare/Immortall Jove say, Cease my Tamburlaine,	2Tamb	4.1.199		Tamb
villaine I say,/Should I but touch the rusty gates of hell,	2Tamb	5.1.95		Tamb
But this we heard some of our sea-men say,	Jew	1.1.78		1Merch
They say we are a scatter'd Nation:	Jew	1.1.121		Barab
Have you determin'd what to say to them?	Jew	1.2.37		1Knght
But say the Tribe that I descended of/Were all in generall cast	Jew	1.2.113		Barab
Well then my Lord, say, are you satisfied?	Jew	1.2.137		Barab
Well father, say I be entertain'd,	Jew	1.2.294		Abigal
Well, daughter, say, what is thy suit with us?	Jew	1.2.321		Abbass
But say, What was she?	Jew	1.2.382		Lodowk
How say you, shall we?	Jew	1.2.390		Lodowk
What, ho, Abigall; open the doore I say.	Jew	2.3.221		Barab
yet I say make love to him;/Doe, it is requisite it should be	Jew	2.3.238		Barab
Say, knave, why rail'st upon my father thus?	Jew	3.3.11		Abigal
And say, I pray them come and speake with me.	Jew	3.3.29		Abigal
Saint Jaques Even) and then I say they use/To send their Almes	Jew	3.4.76		Barab
So, say how was their end?	Jew	3.6.26		2Fryar

SAY (cont.)

Stay wicked Jew, repent, I say, and stay.	Jew	4.1.24	2Fryar
I must needs say that I have beene a great usurer. . . .	Jew	4.1.39	Barab
I will not say that by a forged challenge they met. . .	Jew	4.1.45	P 2Fryar
Pull hard, I say, you would have had my goods. . . .	Jew	4.1.149	Barab
only gave me a nod, as who shold say, Is it even so; and so I	Jew	4.2.13	P Pilia
What should I say? we are captives and must yeeld. . .	Jew	5.2.6	Govnr
And fire the house; say, will not this be brave? . .	Jew	5.5.41	Barab
As Caesar to his souldiers, so say I:	P 155	2.98	Guise
An eare, to heare what my detractors say, ...	P 160	2.103	Guise
To contradict which, I say Ramus shall dye: . . .	P 396	7.36	Guise
Well, say on.	P 400	7.40	Anjoy
And this for Aristotle will I say, ...	P 408	7.48	Ramus
Stab him I say and send him to his freends in hell. . .	P 415	7.55	Guise
My Lord, they say/That all the protestants are massacred.	P 431	7.71	Navrre
O say not so, thou kill'st thy mothers heart. . . .	P 539	11.4	QnMoth
I must say so, paine forceth me complaine. . . .	P 540	11.5	Charls
And if he doe deny what I doe say, ...	P 650	12.63	QnMoth
I prethee say to whome thou writes?	P 671	13.15	Guise
Be gone I say, tis time that we were there. . . .	P 919	18.20	Navrre
And when I come, he frownes, as who should say, . .	Edw	1.2.53	Queene
But say my lord, where shall this meeting bee? . . .	Edw	1.2.74	Warwck
Away I say with hatefull Gaveston.	Edw	1.4.33	Lncstr
I say no more, judge you the rest my lord. . . .	Edw	1.4.148	Gavstn
Arundell, say your message.	Edw	2.5.34	Warwck
My lord of Lancaster, what say you in this? . . .	Edw	2.5.89	Arundl
Why I say, let him go on Penbrookes word. . . .	Edw	2.5.90	Lncstr
How say you my lord of Warwick?	Edw	2.5.92	Mortmr
Well, say thy message.	Edw	3.1.155	Edward
And bid me say as plainer to your grace, ...	Edw	3.1.158	Herald
Say they, and lovinglie advise your grace, . . .	Edw	3.1.166	Herald
How say you my Lord, will you go with your friends, . .	Edw	4.2.19	SrJohn
How say yong Prince, what thinke you of the match? . .	Edw	4.2.67	SrJohn
man, they say there is great execution/Done through the realme,	Edw	4.3.6	Edward
If, doost thou say?	Edw	4.3.21	Edward
And Leister say, what shall become of us?	Edw	4.7.81	Edward
And therefore say, will you resigne or no. . . .	Edw	5.1.85	Trussl
Who is the man dare say I murdered him?	Edw	5.6.40	Mortmr
Hang him I say, and set his quarters up, ...	Edw	5.6.53	King
If we say that we have no sinne we deceive our selves, and	F 69	1.1.41	P Faust
<Why, didst thou not say thou knewst>?	F 204	(HC258) A	P 2Schol
say) it were not for you to come within fortie foot of the	F 210	1.2.17	P Wagner
Say he surrenders up to him his soule, ...	F 318	1.3.90	Faust
circle, I say, least I send you into the Ostry with a vengeance.	F 732	2.3.11	P Robin
take heed what you say, we looke not like cup-stealers I can	F1099	3.3.12	P Robin
life, Vintner you shall have your cup anon, say nothing Dick:	F1114	3.3.27	P Robin
for they say, if a man be drunke over night, the Divell cannot	F1200	4.1.46	P Benvol
O say not so sir:	F1294	4.1.140	Faust
And in their rusticke gambals proudly say, ...	F1330	4.2.6	Benvol
bid the Hostler deliver him unto you, and remember what I say.	F1475	4.4.19	P Faust
on the score, but say nothing, see if she have forgotten me.	F1511	4.5.7	P Robin
Why Hostesse, I say, fetch us some Beere.	F1518	4.5.14	P Dick
Say Wagner, thou hast perus'd my will, ...	F1816	5.2.20	Faust
Sirra, I say in staves acre.	F App	p.229 20	P Wagner
divels, say I should kill one of them, what would folkes say?	F App	p.230 46	P Clown
divels, say I should kill one of them, what would folkes say?	F App	p.230 47	P Clown
You say true, Ile hate.	F App	p.231 11	P Faust
How say you now?	F App	p.234 12	P Robin
I must say somewhat to your felow, you sir. . . .	F App	p.234 13	P Vintnr
they say thou hast a familiar spirit, by whome thou canst	F App	p.236 4	P Emper
Faustus, marke what I shall say, As I was sometime solitary set,	F App	p.236 17	P Emper
Vilaine I say, undo what thou hast done.	F App	p.238 75	Knight
say I merit nought,/Yet for long service done, reward these	Lucan, First Booke		340
say Pompey, are these worse/Then Pirats of Sycillia? .	Lucan, First Booke		346
Both verses were alike till Love (men say)/Began to smile and	Ovid's Elegies		1.1.7
Then scarse can Phoebus say, this harpe is mine. . .	Ovid's Elegies		1.1.20
When I (my light) do or say ought that please thee, . .	Ovid's Elegies		1.4.25
Say they are mine, and hands on thee impose. . . .	Ovid's Elegies		1.4.40
Oft thou wilt say, live well, thou wilt pray oft, . .	Ovid's Elegies		1.8.107
Great Agamemnon was, men say, amazed, ...	Ovid's Elegies		1.9.37
If, what I do, she askes, say hope for night, . . .	Ovid's Elegies		1.11.13
Say that thy love with Caephalus were not knowne, . .	Ovid's Elegies		1.13.33
O thou oft wilt blush/And say he likes me for my borrowed bush,	Ovid's Elegies		1.14.48
And long admiring say by what meanes learnd/Hath this same Poet	Ovid's Elegies		2.1.9
Condemne his eyes, and say there is no tryall. . . .	Ovid's Elegies		2.2.58
he will lament/And say this blabbe shall suffer punnishment.	Ovid's Elegies		2.2.60
to speake <say> troth,/Both short and long please me, for I	Ovid's Elegies		2.4.35
To whom his wench can say, I never did it. . . .	Ovid's Elegies		2.5.10
This, and what grife inforc'd me say I say'd, . . .	Ovid's Elegies		2.5.33
Which is the loveliest it is hard to say:	Ovid's Elegies		2.10.6
And he is happy whom the earth holds, say. . . .	Ovid's Elegies		2.11.30
And say it brings her that preserveth me;	Ovid's Elegies		2.11.44
Nor can an other say his helpe I tooke.	Ovid's Elegies		2.12.12
Doth say, with her that lov'd the Aonian harpe. . .	Ovid's Elegies		2.18.26
Oft couzen me, oft being wooed say nay.	Ovid's Elegies		2.19.20
This thou wilt say to be a worthy ground. . . .	Ovid's Elegies		3.1.26
Greater then her, by her leave th'art, Ile say. . .	Ovid's Elegies		3.2.60
Say gods: if she unpunisht you deceive, ...	Ovid's Elegies		3.3.15
She pleaseth best, I feare, if any say.	Ovid's Elegies		3.4.32
Because the keeper may come say, I did it, . . .	Ovid's Elegies		3.4.35
They say Peneus neere Phthias towne did hide. . . .	Ovid's Elegies		3.5.32
Or shade, or body was [I] <Io>, who can say? . . .	Ovid's Elegies		3.6.16
Say but thou wert injurously accusde.	Ovid's Elegies		3.13.42

SAY (cont.)
Teach but your tongue to say, I did it not, — Ovid's Elegies 3.13.48
Some say, for her the fairest Cupid pyn'd, — Hero and Leander 1.37
And such as knew he was a man would say, — Hero and Leander 1.87
By which alone, our reverend fathers say, — Hero and Leander 1.267
Love is not ful of pittie (as men say)/But deaffe and cruell, — Hero and Leander 2.287

SAY'D
This, and what grife inforc'd me say I say'd, — Ovid's Elegies 2.5.33
She left; I say'd, you both I must beseech, — Ovid's Elegies 3.1.61

SAYD
And very wisely sayd, it may be so. — Jew 1.1.166 3Jew
these words she sayd/While closely hid betwixt two dores I — Ovid's Elegies 1.8.21
I sayd it irkes me: — Ovid's Elegies 2.18.7
And first [she] <he> sayd, when will thy love be spent, — Ovid's Elegies 3.1.15
With lofty wordes stout Tragedie (she sayd)/Why treadst me — Ovid's Elegies 3.1.35
Who sayd with gratefull voyce perpetuall bee? — Ovid's Elegies 3.5.98

SAYE
But you will saye you leave him rome enoughe besides: — Paris ms 7,p390 P Souldr

SAYED
hearing it laugh'd with his tender mother/And smiling sayed, — Ovid's Elegies 1.6.12
father Phoebus layed/To sing with his unequald harpe is sayed. — Ovid's Elegies 3.8.24

SAYES
And when my grieved heart sighes and sayes no, — Dido 2.1.26 Aeneas
Aeneas, be not movde at what he sayes, — Dido 3.3.23 Dido
Each word she sayes will then containe a Crowne, — Dido 4.3.53 Aeneas
And then they met, [and] as the story sayes, — Jew 3.3.20 Ithimr
Now tell me what saith <sayes> Lucifer thy Lord. — F 419 2.1.31 Faust
Our maister Parson sayes thats nothing. — F App p.234 25 P Rafe
How such a Poet could you bring forth, sayes, — Ovid's Elegies 3.14.13

SAYING
I'le have a saying to that Nunnery. — Jew 2.3.90 Barab
In saying this, thou wrongst me Gaveston, — Edw 1.4.149 Queene
Or saying a long grace at a tables end, — Edw 2.1.37 Spencr
And saying, trulie ant may please your honor, — Edw 2.1.40 Spencr
Saying it is, onus quam gravissimum, — Edw 5.4.61 Mortmr
And will avouche his saying with the sworde, — Edw 5.4.77 Champn
How may I prove that saying to be true? — F1268 4.1.114 Emper
Saying, Poet heers a worke beseeming thee. — Ovid's Elegies 1.1.28
Yet blusht I not, nor usde I any saying, — Ovid's Elegies 2.8.7
Saying, why sadly treadst my banckes upon, — Ovid's Elegies 3.5.53
Saying, let your vowes and promises be kept. — Hero and Leander 2.96

SAYLES
when she bewayles/Her perjur'd Theseus flying vowes and sayles, — Ovid's Elegies 1.7.16

'SBLOUD
'sbloud I am never able to endure these torments. — F1306 4.1.152 P Benvol
'sbloud and Schollers be such Cuckold-makers to clap hornes of — F1316 4.1.162 P Benvol

SCAB
Ho sirra Doctor, you cosoning scab; Maister Doctor awake, and — F1489 4.4.33 P HrsCsr
You whoreson conjuring scab, do you remember how you cosened me — F1662 4.6.105 P HrsCsr

SCABBERD
Shall sleepe within the scabberd at thy neede, — Edw 1.1.87 Mortmr

SCAL'D
And by those steps that he hath scal'd the heavens, — 1Tamb 1.2.200 Tamb
For though the rising yv'rie mount he scal'd, — Hero and Leander 2.273

SCALDE
his Diadem/Sought for by such scalde knaves as love him not? — 1Tamb 2.2.8 Mycet

SCALDES
Now scaldes his soule in the Tartarian streames, — 2Tamb 2.3.18 Orcan

SCALDING
And drops of scalding lead, while all thy joints/Be rackt and — 2Tamb 3.5.124 Tamb
Whose scalding drops wil pierce thy seething braines, — 2Tamb 4.1.144 Jrslem

SCALE
ascend so high/As Didos heart, which Monarkes might not scale. — Dido 3.4.34 Aeneas
And scale the ysie mountaines lofty tops: — 1Tamb 1.2.100 Tamb
And after this, to scale a castle wal, — 2Tamb 3.2.59 Tamb
Set me to scale the high Peramides, — P 100 2.43 Guise
Let us with these our followers scale the walles, — Edw 2.3.18 Lncstr
Did mount him up <himselfe> to scale Olimpus top. — F 757 2.3.36 2Chor
As he had hope to scale the beauteous fort, — Hero and Leander 2.16

SCALONIANS
Judaea, Gaza, and Scalonians bounds, — 2Tamb 3.1.45 Jrslem

SCALPES
balde scalpes [thin] <thine> hoary flieces/And riveld cheekes I — Ovid's Elegies 1.8.111

SCAMANDER
When nimph-Neaera rapt thy lookes Scamander. — Ovid's Elegies 3.5.28

SCAMBLED
but we have scambled up/More wealth by farre then those that — Jew 1.1.122 Barab

SCANDALL
may adde more shame/To the blacke scandall of his hated name. — F1378 4.2.54 Fredrk

SCANTED
Bequeath her young ones to our scanted foode. — Dido 1.1.162 Achat
Would of mine armes, my shoulders had beene scanted, — Ovid's Elegies 1.7.23

SCAPE
Ah, how could poore Aeneas scape their hands? — Dido 2.1.220 Dido
Not one should scape: but perish by our swords. — 1Tamb 4.2.122 Tamb
And few or none scape but by being purg'd. — Jew 2.3.106 Barab
Yet if he knew our meanings, could he scape? — Jew 4.1.135 Barab
Wert thou the Pope thou mightst not scape from us. — P1092 20.2 1Mur
Pursue him quicklie, and he cannot scape, — Edw 2.4.38 Queene
Yea madam, and they scape not easilie, — Edw 4.6.41 Mortmr
To scape the violence of the streame first waded, — Lucan, First Booke 223

SCAPES
I'le make him send me half he has, and glad he scapes so too. — Jew 4.2.67 P Ithimr

SCAPES (cont.)				
Thy service for nights scapes is knowne commodious/And to give	Ovid's Elegies	1.11.3		
Knowing her scapes thine honour shall encrease,	Ovid's Elegies	2.2.27		
I meane not to defend the scapes of any,	Ovid's Elegies	2.4.1		
Our pleasant scapes shew thee no clowne to be,	Ovid's Elegies	2.8.3		
SCAPT				
But how scapt Helen, she that causde this warre?	Dido	2.1.292		Dido
I wonder how he scapt.	Edw	2.4.22		Lncstr
SCAR (See also SKARRE)				
My father were enough to scar the foe:	2Tamb	4.1.19		Calyph
SCARBOROUGH				
Take shipping and away to Scarborough,	Edw	2.4.5		Edward
Hees gone by water unto Scarborough,	Edw	2.4.37		Queene
Nay, rather saile with us to Scarborough.	Edw	2.4.52		Mortmr
SCARCE (See also SCARSE)				
But of them all scarce seven doe anchor safe,	Dido	1.1.222		Aeneas
and the bounds/Of Europe wher the Sun dares scarce appeare,	1Tamb	1.1.10		Cosroe
Scarce being seated in my royall throne,	1Tamb	2.7.5		Cosroe
A faire young maid scarce fourteene yeares of age,	Jew	1.2.378		Mthias
Scarce shall you finde a man of more desart.	Edw	2.2.251		Gavstn
Scarce can I name salvation, faith, or heaven,	F 570	2.2.19		Faust
out of a Lyons mouth when I was scarce <half> an houre old,	F 687	2.2.136	P	Wrath
As all his footmanship shall scarce prevaile,	F1302	4.1.148		Faust
Whose life nine ages scarce bring out of date.	Ovid's Elegies	2.6.36		
SCARCELY				
And scarcely know within what Clime we are.	Dido	2.1.44		Aeneas
And scarcely doe agree upon one poynt:	Dido	2.1.109		Dido
SCAR'D				
or like Megaera/That scar'd Alcides, when by Junoes taske/He	Lucan, First Booke	575		
SCARD (Homograph)				
Up with him then, his body shalbe scard.	2Tamb	5.1.114		Tamb
The very cullor scard him; a dead blacknesse/Ranne through the	Lucan, First Booke	617		
Yet lingered not the day, but morning scard me.	Ovid's Elegies	1.13.48		
SCARFES				
And tye white linnen scarfes about their armes.	P 233	4.31		Guise
SCARLET				
As red as scarlet is his furniture,	1Tamb	4.1.55		2Msngr
Sitting in scarlet on their armed speares.	1Tamb	5.1.118		Tamb
Cast off your armor, put on scarlet roabes.	1Tamb	5.1.524		Tamb
Shall carie wrapt within his scarlet waves,	2Tamb	1.1.34		Orcan
With naked swords and scarlet liveries:	2Tamb	3.4.55		Therid
A scarlet blush her guilty face arayed.	Ovid's Elegies	2.5.34		
And passe our scarlet of red saffrons marke.	Ovid's Elegies	2.6.22		
SCARR'D				
olde swords/With ugly teeth of blacke rust fouly scarr'd:	Lucan, First Booke	245		
SCARRE (See also SCARD)				
We are enough to scarre the enemy,	1Tamb	2.3.64		Tamb
These sad presages were enough to scarre/The quivering Romans,	Lucan, First Booke	672		
SCARRES				
Who looking on the scarres we Troians gave,	Dido	2.1.131		Aeneas
Whose head hath deepest scarres, whose breast most woundes,	2Tamb	1.3.75		Tamb
SCARSE				
Yet scarse enough t'encounter Tamburlaine.	2Tamb	1.1.66		Orcan
Sweet Almeda, scarse halfe a league from hence.	2Tamb	1.2.55		Callap
Then scarse can Phoebus say, this harpe is mine.	Ovid's Elegies	1.1.20		
Yet scarse my hands from thee containe I well.	Ovid's Elegies	1.4.10		
When thy waves brim did scarse my anckles touch.	Ovid's Elegies	3.5.6		
Scarse rests of all what a small urne conteines.	Ovid's Elegies	3.8.40		
SCARSELY				
I heard your Majestie was scarsely pleasde,	P 967	19.37		Guise
With much a do my hands I scarsely staide.	Ovid's Elegies	1.8.110		
SCARVES (See SCARFES)				
SCATHE (See also SKATHD)				
leave these armes/And save thy sacred person free from scathe:	2Tamb	1.3.10		Zenoc
SCATTER				
So scatter and consume them in his rage,	1Tamb	4.1.34		Souldn
To race and scatter thy inglorious crue,	1Tamb	4.3.67		Souldn
SCATTER'D				
They say we are a scatter'd Nation:	Jew	1.1.121		Barab
SCATTERED				
And when their scattered armie is subdu'd,	1Tamb	2.2.68		Meandr
(Staying to order all the scattered troopes)/Farewell Lord	1Tamb	2.5.45		Cosroe
Europe, and pursue/His scattered armie til they yeeld or die.	1Tamb	3.3.39		Therid
Or scattered like the lofty Cedar trees,	1Tamb	4.2.24		Tamb
SCENT (See also SENT)				
The scent thereof was death, I poyson'd it.	Jew	4.4.43		Barab
But fye, what a smell <scent> is heere?	F 669	2.2.118	P	Pride
SCEPTER				
The Romane Scepter royall shall remaine,	Dido	1.1.105		Jupitr
And to a Scepter chaunge his golden shafts,	Dido	3.2.57		Venus
Sway thou the Punike Scepter in my steede,	Dido	4.4.35		Dido
And beare this golden Scepter in my hand?	Dido	4.4.41		Aeneas
A Sword, and not a Scepter fits Aeneas.	Dido	4.4.43		Aeneas
With Eban Scepter strike this hatefull earth,	1Tamb	4.2.28		Bajzth
(Whose scepter Angels kisse, and Furies dread)/As for their	1Tamb	5.1.94		1Virgn
A royall seate, a scepter and a crowne:	P 161	2.104		Guise
And with my kinglie scepter stroke me dead,	Edw	1.4.317		Edward
Her left hand held abroad a regal scepter,	Ovid's Elegies	3.1.13		
SCEPTERS				
That fights for Scepters and for slippery crownes,	1Tamb	5.1.356		Zenoc
Yet tragedies, and scepters fild my lines,	Ovid's Elegies	2.18.13		
With scepters, and high buskins th'one would dresse me,	Ovid's Elegies	3.1.63		
SCEPTRED				
And my divine descent from sceptred Jove:	Dido	1.1.219		Aeneas

SCHECKIUS (See SHEKIUS)				
SCHISMATIQUE				
So will we quell that haughty Schismatique;	F 922	3.1.144		Pope
SCHISMATIQUES				
Germane Emperour/Be held as Lollords, and bold Schismatiques,	F 955	3.1.177		Faust
both condemn'd/For lothed Lollords, and base Schismatiques:	F1022	3.2.42		Pope
SCHOLERISME				
[The fruitfull plot of Scholerisme grac'd], . . .	F 16	Prol.16		1Chor
SCHOLERS				
and sir knight, hereafter speake well of Scholers: . .	F App	p.238 85	P	Faust
SCHOLLER				
Alas I am a scholler, how should I have golde? . . .	P 377	7.17		Ramus
Then Balduck, you must cast the scholler off, . . .	Edw	2.1.31		Spencr
Is with that smoothe toongd scholler Baldock gone, . .	Edw	4.6.57		Rice
Yet for he was a Scholler, once admired/For wondrous knowledge	F1997	5.3.15		2Schol
And to this day is everie scholler poore, ...	Hero and Leander			1.471
SCHOLLERS				
Schollers I meane, learned and liberall;	Jew	3.1.8		Curtzn
him; and hereafter sir, looke you speake well of Schollers.	F1315	4.1.161	P	Faust
Schollers be such Cuckold-makers to clap hornes of honest mens	F1316	4.1.162	P	Benvol
hee's now at supper with the schollers, where ther's such	F1678	5.1.5	P	Wagner
SCHOOLE				
As though your highnes were a schoole boy still, . .	Edw	3.1.30		Baldck
SCHOOLE BOY				
As though your highnes were a schoole boy still, . .	Edw	3.1.30		Baldck
SCHOOLES				
I'le have them fill the publique Schooles with [silke] <skill>,	F 117	1.1.89		Faust
become of Faustus that/Was wont to make our schooles ring,	F 195	1.2.2		1Schol
once admired/For wondrous knowledge in our Germane schooles,	F1998	5.3.16		2Schol
SCHRIGHT				
in untrod woods/Shrill voices schright, and ghoasts incounter	Lucan, First Booke			568
SCICILIE				
Come as thou didst in fruitfull Scicilie, ...	2Tamb	4.3.34		Orcan
SCICILLIAN				
What, now Scicillian Pirats are supprest, ...	Lucan, First Booke			336
SCIENCE				
Tempered by science metaphisicall, ...	2Tamb	4.2.63		Olymp
SCILLA				
Both barking Scilla, and the sounding Rocks, ...	Dido	1.1.146		Aeneas
SCITHEAN				
white as is <Her armes farre whiter, then> the Scithean snow,	Ovid's Elegies			3.6.8
SCITUATION				
And now I see the Scituation, ...	Jew	5.3.5		Calym
SCLAVONIANS				
of stout Hungarians,/Sclavonians, [Almain Rutters] <Almains,	2Tamb	1.1.22		Uribas
SCOFFE				
And come not here to scoffe at Gaveston, ...	Edw	2.2.76		Gavstn
And unrevengd mockt Gods with me doth scoffe. . . .	Ovid's Elegies			3.3.20
SCOFTES				
Was it not thou that scoftes the Organon, ...	P 387	7.27		Guise
SCOPE				
Thy scope is mortall, mine eternall fame, ...	Ovid's Elegies			1.15.7
SCORCH (See also SCORTCH)				
And now the same gan so to scorch and glow, ...	Hero and Leander			2.70
SCORCHING				
A scorching flame burnes all the standers by.	Ovid's Elegies			1.2.46
SCORE				
And hundred thousands subjects to each score:	2Tamb	2.2.12		Gazell
three score thousand fighting men/Are come since last we shewed	2Tamb	3.5.33		Jrslem
I am eighteene pence on the score, but say nothing, see if she	F1511	4.5.7	P	Robin
I hope my score stands still.	F1515	4.5.11	P	Robin
For five score Nimphes, or more our flouds conteine. .	Ovid's Elegies			3.5.64
SCORES				
An hundred kings by scores wil bid him armes, ...	2Tamb	2.2.11		Gazell
SCORN'D				
And make thee poore and scorn'd of all the world, . .	Jew	1.2.108		1Knght
use stirde, and thoughts that alwaies scorn'd/A second place;	Lucan, First Booke			124
And scorn'd old sparing diet, and ware robes/Too light for	Lucan, First Booke			165
SCORND				
If of scornd lovers god be venger just, ...	Ovid's Elegies			3.7.65
SCORNDE				
Am I thus to be jested at and scornde?	P 758	15.16		Guise
They should know how I scornde them and their mockes. .	P 762	15.20		Guise
SCORNE (See also SKORNE)				
And dead to scorne that hath pursued me so.	Dido	3.3.49		Iarbus
Now sits and laughs our regiment to scorne:	1Tamb	1.1.117		Cosroe
These Lords (perhaps) do scorne our estimates, . . .	1Tamb	1.2.61		Tamb
For we will scorne they should come nere our selves. .	1Tamb	3.3.186		Zenoc
That all the world will see and laugh to scorne, . . .	1Tamb	5.1.252		Zabina
Which if your General refuse or scorne, ...	2Tamb	1.1.119		Fredrk
tell him, I scorne to write a line under a hundred crownes.	Jew	4.2.121	P	Ithimr
I scorne the Peasant, tell him so.	Jew	4.4.59	P	Ithimr
Lye there the Kings delight, and Guises scorne. . . .	P 818	17.13		Guise
lye there the kinges delyght and guises scorne . . .	Paris	ms22,p390		Guise
But this I scorne, that one so baselie borne, ...	Edw	1.4.403		Mortmr
No marvell though thou scorne thy noble peeres, . . .	Edw	2.2.217		Kent
Tyrant, I scorne thy threats and menaces, ...	Edw	3.1.241		Warwck
Because I thinke scorne to be accusde, ...	Edw	5.6.39		Mortmr
And scorne those Joyes thou never shalt possesse. . . .	F 314	1.3.86		Faust
your searching; we scorne to steale your cups I can tell you.	F1106	3.3.19	P	Dick
smiles]/[At your repulse, and laughs your state to scorne],	F1795	5.1.122A		OldMan
I scorne you:	F App	p.234 9	P	Robin
Yet thinke no scorne to aske a wealthy churle, ...	Ovid's Elegies			1.10.53

SCORNE (cont.)
to detaine)/Thou oughtst therefore to scorne me for thy mate,		Ovid's Elegies	2.17.13
Nor Romane stocke scorne me so much (I crave)/Gifts then my		Ovid's Elegies	3.5.65
Thee as a holy Idiot doth she scorne,	• • •	Hero and Leander	1.303

SCORNEFULL
Await the sentence of her scornefull eies:	• •	Hero and Leander	1.123

SCORNES
And scornes the Powers that governe Persea.	• •	1Tamb 2.6.40	Cosroe
For this, I waite, that scornes attendance else:	•	P 106 2.49	Guise
He nods, and scornes, and smiles at those that passe.	•	Edw 1.2.24	Warwck
That scornes the world, and as a traveller,	• •	Edw 5.6.65	Mortmr

SCORNFULL
See what a scornfull looke the pesant casts.	• •	Edw 1.4.14	MortSr

SCORNING
Scorning our loves and royall marriage rites,	• • •	Dido 4.2.16	Iarbus
[And] highly scorning, that the lowly earth/Should drinke his		Edw 5.1.13	Edward

SCORN'T
the horses, I scorn't 'faith, I have other matters in hand,		F 726 2.3.5	P Robin

SCORPION
And fly my glove as from a Scorpion.	• • •	2Tamb 3.5.74	Tamb
The threatning Scorpion with the burning taile/And fier'st his		Lucan, First Booke	658

SCORTCH
Then scortch a face so beautiful as this,	• • •	2Tamb 3.4.74	Techel

SCORTCHING
Sustaine the scortching heat and freezing cold,	• •	2Tamb 3.2.57	Tamb

SCORTCHT
When wandring Phoebes Ivory cheeks were scortcht/And all the		2Tamb 5.3.232	Tamb
Like to a Lyon of scortcht desart Affricke,	• • •	Lucan, First Booke	208

SCOT
A souldier, that hath serv'd against the Scot.	• • •	Edw 1.1.34	3PrMan

SCOTLAND
Nephue, I must to Scotland, thou staiest here.		Edw 1.4.386	MortSr
From Scotland my lord.	• • • • •	Edw 2.2.113	1Msngr
So soone to have woone Scotland,	• • •	Edw 2.2.194	Lncstr

SCOTS
That now are readie to assaile the Scots.	•	Edw 1.4.363	Edward
My unckles taken prisoner by the Scots.	• •	Edw 2.2.115	Mortmr
Mine unckles taken prisoner by the Scots.	•	Edw 2.2.142	Mortmr
Unto the walles of Yorke the Scots made rode,	•	Edw 2.2.166	Lncstr
And thereof came it, that the fleering Scots,	• •	Edw 2.2.188	Lncstr

SCOURE (See also SCOWRE)
from every flanke/May scoure the outward curtaines of the Fort,		2Tamb 3.2.80	Tamb

SCOURGE
I that am tearm'd the Scourge and Wrath of God,		1Tamb 3.3.44	Tamb
heaven beholde/Their Scourge and Terrour treade on Emperours.	•	1Tamb 4.2.32	Tamb
The Scum of men, the hate and Scourge of God,	•	1Tamb 4.3.9	Souldn
Be thou the scourge and terrour of the world.	•	2Tamb 1.3.60	Tamb
Be tearm'd the scourge and terrour of the world?	•	2Tamb 1.3.62	Amyras
Be al a scourge and terror to the world,	•	2Tamb 1.3.63	Tamb
Christians death/And scourge their foule blasphemous Paganisme?		2Tamb 2.1.53	Fredrk
And scourge the Scourge of the immortall God:	• •	2Tamb 2.4.80	Tamb
Now, he that cals himself the scourge of Jove,	• •	2Tamb 3.5.21	Orcan
To scourge the pride of such as heaven abhors:	• •	2Tamb 4.1.149	Tamb
The Scourge of God and terrour of the world,	• •	2Tamb 4.1.154	Tamb
Thus am I right the Scourge of highest Jove,	• •	2Tamb 4.3.24	Tamb
And tremble when ye heare this Scourge wil come,	•	2Tamb 4.3.99	Tamb
Whose Scourge I am, and him will I obey.	• •	2Tamb 5.1.185	Tamb
First take my Scourge and my imperiall Crowne,	• •	2Tamb 5.3.177	Tamb
So, raigne my sonne, scourge and controlle those slaves,	•	2Tamb 5.3.228	Tamb
For Tamburlaine, the Scourge of God must die.	• •	2Tamb 5.3.248	Tamb
And rather seeke to scourge their enemies.	• •	P 217 4.15	Anjoy
I have deserv'd a scourge I must confesse,	• •	P 544 11.9	Charls
No Edward, Englands scourge, it may not be,	• •	Edw 3.1.258	Mortmr

SCOURGING
tearms/And scourging kingdoms with his conquering sword.	•	1Tamb Prol.6	Prolog
Scourging the pride of cursed Tamburlain.	• •	2Tamb 3.1.37	Callap

SCOUT (See also SCOWTING)
A hundred horse shall scout about the plaines/To spie what		2Tamb 3.3.47	Techel

SCOUTES
My Lord, as by our scoutes we understande,	• • •	P 724 14.27	1Msngr

SCOWRE
stand by, Ile scowre you for a goblet, stand aside you had best,		F App p.235 18	P Robin

SCOWTING
of my company/Scowting abroad upon these champion plaines,		1Tamb 2.2.40	Spy

SCRAPS
And thou his wife shalt feed him with the scraps/My servitures		1Tamb 4.2.87	Tamb

SCRATCH
My nayles to scratch her lovely cheekes I bent.	• •	Ovid's Elegies	1.7.50
And scratch her faire soft cheekes I did intend.	• •	Ovid's Elegies	2.5.46

SCRATCHT
Her cheekes were scratcht, her goodly haires discheveld.	•	Ovid's Elegies	3.5.48

SCREECH (See SCRICH-OWL, SCRIECHT)

SCRIBLED
the boord with wine/Was scribled, and thy fingers writ a line.		Ovid's Elegies	2.5.18

SCRICH
To hoarse scrich-owles foule shadowes it allowes,	•	Ovid's Elegies	1.12.19

SCRICH-OWLES
To hoarse scrich-owles foule shadowes it allowes,	•	Ovid's Elegies	1.12.19

SCRIECHT
Where seeing a naked man, she scriecht for feare,	• •	Hero and Leander	2.237

SCRIPTURE
What? bring you Scripture to confirm your wrongs?	• •	Jew 1.2.110	Barab

SCRIPTURES
Reade, reade the Scriptures: that is blasphemy.	• •	F 96 1.1.72	GdAngl

SCRIPTURES (cont.)
Abjure the Scriptures, and his Saviour Christ; — F 276 1.3.48 Mephst
[To burne his Scriptures, slay his Ministers], — F 650 2.2.99A Faust
To view the Scriptures, then I turn'd the leaves/And led thine — F1888 5.2.92 Mephst

SCROLE
Then Mephostophilis receive this scrole, — F 477 2.1.89 Faust
<Here Mephastophilis> receive this scrole, — F 477 (HC260)A Faust

SCROWLE
othes/Sign'd with our handes, each shal retaine a scrowle: — 2Tamb 1.1.144 Orcan
Pinning upon his breast a long great Scrowle/How I with — Jew 2.3.197 Barab
for here's the scrowle/In which <Wherein> thou hast given thy — F 519 2.1.131 Mephst

SCUM
That damned traine, the scum of Affrica, — 1Tamb 3.3.56 Tamb
The Scum of men, the hate and Scourge of God, — 1Tamb 4.3.9 Souldn
The scum and tartar of the Elements, — 2Tamb 4.1.124 Tamb

SCUSE
And Isis now will shew what scuse to make. — Ovid's Elegies 1.8.74

SCUTCHION
So he shal, and weare thy head in his Scutchion. — 2Tamb 3.5.138 P Orcan

SCYLLA (See also SCILLA, SYLLAES)
Scylla by us her fathers rich haire steales, — Ovid's Elegies 3.11.21

SCYLLAES
How Scyllaes and Caribdis waters rage. — Ovid's Elegies 2.11.18
And Scyllaes wombe mad raging dogs conceales. — Ovid's Elegies 3.11.22

SCYTHE (See SITHES)

SCYTHIA (See also SCITHEAN, SYTHIA)
Go Menaphon, go into Scythia, — 1Tamb 1.1.85 Mycet
And since we have arriv'd in Scythia, — 1Tamb 1.2.17 Magnet
Whose [statues] <statutes> we adore in Scythia, — 1Tamb 1.2.244 Tamb
Then thou for Parthia, they for Scythia and Medea. — 1Tamb 2.5.83 Tamb
From Scythia to the Orientall Plage/Of India, wher raging — 2Tamb 1.1.68 Orcan
Then should you see this Thiefe of Scythia, — 2Tamb 3.1.14 Callap
Which is from Scythia, where I first began, — 2Tamb 5.3.143 Tamb
Scythia and wilde Armenia had bin yoakt, — Lucan, First Booke 19
Or Scythia; or hot Libiaes thirsty sands. — Lucan, First Booke 369

SCYTHIAN
But thou art sprung from Scythian Caucasus, — Dido 5.1.158 Dido
Where you shall heare the Scythian Tamburlaine, — 1Tamb Prol.4 Prolog
Of Tamburlaine, that sturdie Scythian thiefe, — 1Tamb 1.1.36 Meandr
To apprehend that paltrie Scythian. — 1Tamb 1.1.53 Mycet
Fairer than whitest snow on Scythian hils, — 1Tamb 1.2.89 Tamb
Where is this Scythian Tamburlaine? — 1Tamb 1.2.152 Therid
A Scythian Shepheard, so imbellished/With Natures pride, and — 1Tamb 1.2.155 Therid
Then shalt thou see the Scythian Tamburlaine, — 1Tamb 2.5.97 Tamb
Note the presumption of this Scythian slave: — 1Tamb 3.3.68 Bajzth
heare the clange/Of Scythian trumpets, heare the Basiliskes, — 1Tamb 4.1.2 Souldn
Not long agoe bestrid a Scythian Steed: — 2Tamb 1.3.38 Zenoc
In partiall aid of that proud Scythian, — 2Tamb 2.2.16 Gazell
The cursed Scythian sets on all their townes, — 2Tamb 3.1.55 Trebiz
The poisoned braines of this proud Scythian. — 2Tamb 3.1.67 Orcan
Raile not proud Scythian, I shall now revenge/My fathers vile — 2Tamb 3.5.90 Callap

SCYTHIANS
Are <To> <Ah> these resolved noble Scythians? — 1Tamb 1.2.225 Therid
Have view'd the army of the Scythians, — 1Tamb 2.2.41 Spy
down murthering shot from heaven/To dash the Scythians braines, — 1Tamb 3.3.197 Zabina
that makest us thus/The slaves to Scythians rude and barbarous. — 1Tamb 3.3.271 Zabina
Of Scythians and slavish Persians. — 1Tamb 4.3.68 Souldn
These barbarous Scythians full of cruelty, — 2Tamb 3.4.19 Olymp
The Scythians shall not tyrannise on me. — 2Tamb 3.4.29 Sonne
Least cruell Scythians should dismember him. — 2Tamb 3.4.37 Olymp
[Jove] <it> seemes/Bloudy like Dian, whom the Scythians serve; — Lucan, First Booke 442

SCYTHYAN
First let thy Scythyan horse teare both our limmes/Rather then — 2Tamb 5.1.138 Orcan

S'DAINST
Why yongling, s'dainst thou so of Mortimer. — Edw 5.2.111 Mortmr

SE'
And you shall se't rebated with the blow. — 2Tamb 4.2.70 Olymp

SE (Homograph)
See, se Anippe if they breathe or no. — 1Tamb 5.1.343 Zenoc
A per se, a, t. h. e. the: — F 727 2.3.6 P Robin
o per se, o, [demy] <deny> orgon, gorgon: — F 728 2.3.7 P Robin
O per se o, demogorgon, Belcher and Mephostophilis. — F1114 3.3.27 P Robin
Se impious warre defiles the Senat house, — Lucan, First Booke 690

SEA (Homograph)
Poore Troy must now be sackt upon the Sea, — Dido 1.1.64 Venus
When yet both sea and sands beset their ships, — Dido 1.1.110 Venus
Priams misfortune followes us by sea, — Dido 1.1.143 Aeneas
Put sailes to sea to seeke out Italy, — Dido 1.1.218 Aeneas
Thinking the sea had swallowed up thy ships, — Dido 2.1.68 Illion
Moved with her voyce, I lept into the sea, — Dido 2.1.283 Aeneas
altar, where Ile offer up/As many kisses as the Sea hath sands, — Dido 3.1.88 Dido
And wrought him mickle woe on sea and land, — Dido 3.2.41 Juno
Whom casualtie of sea hath made such friends? — Dido 3.2.76 Juno
Whose armed soule alreadie on the sea, — Dido 3.2.83 Venus
To see a Phrigian far fet [on] <o'er> <forfeit to> the sea, — Dido 3.3.64 Iarbus
By Paphos, Capys, and the purple Sea, — Dido 3.4.46 Aeneas
And slice the Sea with sable coloured ships, — Dido 4.3.22 Aeneas
To sea Aeneas, finde out Italy. — Dido 4.3.56 Aeneas
I charge thee put to sea and stay not here. — Dido 4.4.22 Dido
The sea is rough, the windes blow to the shoare. — Dido 4.4.25 Aeneas
O false Aeneas, now the sea is rough, — Dido 4.4.26 Dido
As in the Sea are little water drops: — Dido 4.4.63 Dido
Or that the Tyrrhen sea were in mine armes, — Dido 4.4.101 Dido

SEA (cont.)

Why look'st thou toward the sea?	Dido	5.1.113	Dido
The Rockes and Sea-gulfes will performe at large,	Dido	5.1.171	Dido
But see, Achates wils him put to sea,	Dido	5.1.258	Dido
Chiefe Lord of all the wide vast Euxine sea,	1Tamb	1.1.167	Ortyg
with Russian stems/Plow up huge furrowes in the Caspian sea,	1Tamb	1.2.195	Tamb
As hath the Ocean or the Terrene sea/Small drops of water, when	1Tamb	3.1.10	Bajzth
The Ocean, Terrene, and the cole-blacke sea,	1Tamb	3.1.25	Bajzth
And all the sea my Gallies countermaund.	1Tamb	3.1.63	Bajzth
As when the Sea-man sees the Hyades/Gather an armye of Cemerian	1Tamb	3.2.76	Agidas
That naked rowe about the Terrene sea.	1Tamb	3.3.50	Tamb
Sailing along the Orientall sea,	1Tamb	3.3.253	Tamb
Vast Gruntland compast with the frozen sea,	2Tamb	1.1.26	Orcan
Shall by this battell be the bloody Sea.	2Tamb	1.1.38	Orcan
That never sea-man yet discovered:	2Tamb	1.1.71	Orcan
And soon put foorth into the Terrene sea:	2Tamb	1.2.25	Callap
For if his chaire were in a sea of blood,	2Tamb	1.3.89	Celeb
Meet for your service on the sea, my Lord,	2Tamb	1.3.123	Therid
From Azamor to Tunys neare the sea,	2Tamb	1.3.133	Usumc
of Affrike, where I view'd/The Ethiopian sea, rivers and lakes:	2Tamb	1.3.196	Techel
Then crost the sea and came to Oblia,	2Tamb	1.3.211	Therid
All bordring on the Mare-major sea:	2Tamb	3.1.51	Trebiz
If I had wept a sea of teares for her,	2Tamb	3.2.47	Calyph
That from the bounds of Phrigia to the sea/Which washeth Cyprus	2Tamb	3.5.11	Callap
The Euxine sea North to Natolia,	2Tamb	4.3.102	Tamb
The Monster that hath drunke a sea of blood,	2Tamb	5.2.13	Amasia
Along Armenia and the Caspian sea,	2Tamb	5.3.127	Tamb
Whereas the Terren and the red sea meet,	2Tamb	5.3.132	Tamb
And so along the Ethiopian sea,	2Tamb	5.3.137	Tamb
downe by Candie shoare/To Malta, through our Mediterranean sea.	Jew	1.1.47	Barab
from Egypt, or by Caire/But at the entry there into the sea,	Jew	1.1.74	Barab
But this we heard some of our sea-men say,	Jew	1.1.78	1Merch
Thus trowles our fortune in by land and Sea,	Jew	1.1.103	Barab
Making the Sea their [servant] <servants>, and the winds/To	Jew	1.1.110	Barab
but to passe along/Towards Venice by the Adriatick Sea;	Jew	1.1.163	Barab
Now lanch our Gallies backe againe to Sea,	Jew	1.2.29	Calym
run to some rocke and throw my selfe headlong into the sea;	Jew	3.4.40	P Ithimr
Open an entrance for the wastfull sea,	Jew	3.5.16	Govnr
conquer'd Iland stands/Inviron'd with the mediterranean Sea,	Jew	5.3.7	Calym
Hearing his Soveraigne was bound for Sea,	Jew	5.3.15	Msngr
And binde it wholy to the Sea of Rome:	P 926	18.27	Navrre
And sooner shall the sea orewhelme my land,	Edw	1.1.152	Edward
For heele complaine unto the sea of Rome.	Edw	1.1.190	Kent
Let him complaine unto the sea of hell,	Edw	1.1.191	Gavstn
On your allegeance to the sea of Rome,	Edw	1.4.52	ArchBp
Unlesse the sea cast up his shipwrack body.	Edw	1.4.205	Lncstr
I feare me he is wrackt upon the sea.	Edw	2.2.2	Edward
Tis not the hugest monster of the sea,	Edw	2.2.45	Edward
Which swept the desart shore of that dead sea,	Edw	2.3.22	Mortmr
The spirits tell me they can dry the sea,	F 171	1.1.143	Cornel
Ay me, O what a world of land and sea,	Lucan, First Booke	13	
Fetters the Euxin sea, with chaines of yce:	Lucan, First Booke	18	
fire/Fleete on the floods, the earth shoulder the sea,	Lucan, First Booke	76	
men so strong/By land, and sea, no forreine force could ruine:	Lucan, First Booke	83	
While th'earth the sea, and ayre the earth sustaines;	Lucan, First Booke	89	
Nor then was land, or sea, to breed such hate,	Lucan, First Booke	96	
Betwixt the Aegean and the Ionian sea,	Lucan, First Booke	101	
that made Roome/Governe the earth, the sea, the world it selfe,	Lucan, First Booke	110	
Or sea far from the land, so all were whist.	Lucan, First Booke	262	
Woods turn'd to ships; both land and sea against us:	Lucan, First Booke	307	
And ere he sees the sea looseth his name;	Lucan, First Booke	402	
Which is nor sea, nor land, but oft times both,	Lucan, First Booke	411	
Whether the sea roul'd alwaies from that point,	Lucan, First Booke	413	
Where Tarbels winding shoares imbrace the sea,	Lucan, First Booke	422	
and where swift Rhodanus/Drives Araris to sea; They neere the	Lucan, First Booke	435	
The Pilot from the helme leapes in the sea;	Lucan, First Booke	499	
Cole-blacke Charibdis whirl'd a sea of bloud;	Lucan, First Booke	546	
And in the fleeting sea the earth be drencht.	Lucan, First Booke	653	
Where Nile augmenteth the Pelusian sea:	Lucan, First Booke	683	
Girt my shine browe with sea banke mirtle praise <sprays>.	Ovid's Elegies	1.1.34	
Going to sea, East windes he doth not chide/Nor to hoist saile	Ovid's Elegies	1.9.13	
Now on <ore> the sea from her old love comes shee,	Ovid's Elegies	1.13.1	
Or [into] <to the> sea swift Symois [doth] <shall> slide.	Ovid's Elegies	1.15.10	
Which stormie South-windes into sea did blowe?	Ovid's Elegies	2.6.44	
Or as a sodaine gale thrustes into sea,	Ovid's Elegies	2.9.31	
And to the vast deep sea fresh water flouds?	Ovid's Elegies	2.10.14	
Being wrackt, carowse the sea tir'd by their ships:	Ovid's Elegies	2.10.34	
Both to the Sea-nimphes, and the Sea-nimphes father.	Ovid's Elegies	2.11.36	
By seaven huge mouthes into the sea is [skipping] <slipping>,	Ovid's Elegies	2.13.10	
Which as it seemes, hence winde and sea bereaves.	Ovid's Elegies	2.16.46	
The sea I use not: me my earth must have.	Ovid's Elegies	3.2.48	
Rich Nile by seaven mouthes to the vast sea flowing,	Ovid's Elegies	3.5.39	
The ships, whose God-head in the sea now glisters?	Ovid's Elegies	3.11.38	
And having wandred now through sea and land,	Ovid's Elegies	3.12.33	
For like Sea-nimphs inveigling harmony,	Hero and Leander	1.105	
A livelie vine of greene sea agget spread;	Hero and Leander	1.138	
Save that the sea playing on yellow sand,	Hero and Leander	1.347	
And swore the sea should never doe him harme.	Hero and Leander	2.180	

SEA BANKE

Girt my shine browe with sea banke mirtle praise <sprays>.	Ovid's Elegies	1.1.34	

SEABORDERERS

stood,/[Seaborderers] <Seaborders>, disjoin'd by Neptunes might:	Hero and Leander	1.3	

SEABORDERS

stood,/[Seaborderers] <Seaborders>, disjoin'd by Neptunes might:	Hero and Leander	1.3	

SEABORNE
As Seaborne Nymphes shall swarme about thy ships, Dido 3.1.129 Dido
SEA-GULFES
The Rockes and Sea-gulfes will performe at large, Dido 5.1.171 Dido
SEALE
Whose short conclusion will seale up their hearts, Dido 3.2.94 Juno
the Towne-seale might be got/To keepe him for his life time Jew 2.3.103 Barab
And Ile subscribe my name and seale it straight. P 883 17.78 King
First let us set our hand and seale to this, P 890 17.85 King
receive my seale,/Save or condemne, and in our name commaund, Edw 1.1.168 Edward
Quiet your self, you shall have the broad seale, Edw 2.2.147 Edward
Their bloud and yours shall seale these treacheries. Edw 5.1.89 Edward
Let me alone, here is the privie seale, Edw 5.2.37 Mortmr
I seale, I cancell, I do what I will, Edw 5.4.51 Mortmr
Resigne, or seale, or what so pleaseth us. F 936 3.1.158 Pope
Then I, that I may seale her privy leaves, Ovid's Elegies 2.15.15
SEALED
Further, or this letter was sealed, Lord Bartley came, Edw 5.2.30 BshpWn
Seven golden [keys] <seales> fast sealed with seven seales, F 933 3.1.155 Pope
SEALES
Confirme his banishment with our handes and seales. Edw 1.2.71 ArchBp
Seven golden [keys] <seales> fast sealed with seven seales, F 933 3.1.155 Pope
Those soules which sinne seales the blacke sonnes of hell, F1799 5.2.3 Lucifr
SEA-MAN
As when the Sea-man sees the Hyades/Gather an armye of Cemerian 1Tamb 3.2.76 Agidas
That never sea-man yet discovered: 2Tamb 1.1.71 Orcan
SEAMAN
Were woont to guide the seaman in the deepe, 2Tamb 5.1.65 Tamb
SEA-MEN
But this we heard some of our sea-men say, Jew 1.1.78 1Merch
SEAMEN
Ere thou rise starres teach seamen where to saile, Ovid's Elegies 1.13.11
SEA-NIMPHES
Both to the Sea-nimphes, and the Sea-nimphes father. Ovid's Elegies 2.11.36
SEA-NIMPHS
For like Sea-nimphs inveigling harmony, Hero and Leander 1.105
SEARCH
Come boyes and with your fingers search my wound, 2Tamb 3.2.126 Tamb
And Barabas now search this secret out. Jew 1.1.177 Barab
A reaching thought will search his deepest wits, Jew 1.2.221 Barab
espy'd a time/To search the plancke my father did appoint; Jew 2.1.21 Abigal
Pleaseth your grace to let the Surgeon search your wound. P1191 22.53 Navrre
Search Surgeon and resolve me what thou seest. P1193 22.55 King
And search all corners of the new-found-world/For pleasant F 111 1.1.83 Faust
Never deny't, for I know you have it, and I'le search you. F1101 3.3.14 P Vintnr
Search me? F1102 3.3.15 P Robin
hold the cup Dick, come, come, search me, search me. F1103 3.3.16 P Robin
Come on sirra, let me search you now. F1104 3.3.17 P Vintnr
and ifaith I meane to search some circles for my owne use: F App p.233 2 P Robin
search me. F App p.234 10 P Robin
me sir, me sir, search your fill: F App p.234 14 P Rafe
Search at the dore who knocks oft in the darke, Ovid's Elegies 2.19.39
SEARCHING
I feare not your searching; we scorne to steale your cups I can F1105 3.3.18 P Dick
And searching farther for the gods displeasure, Lucan, First Booke 616
SEARCHT
Twere not amisse my Lord, if he were searcht. P1160 22.22 Eprnon
SEARING
Searing thy hatefull flesh with burning yrons, 2Tamb 3.5.123 Tamb
SEAS
Whiles my Aeneas wanders on the Seas, Dido 1.1.52 Venus
Disquiet Seas lay downe your swelling lookes, Dido 1.1.122 Venus
Swell raging seas, frowne wayward destinies, Dido 4.4.57 Aeneas
And let rich Carthage fleete upon the seas, Dido 4.4.134 Dido
Why burst you not, and they fell in the seas? Dido 4.4.154 Dido
We quickly may in Turkish seas arrive. 2Tamb 1.2.27 Callap
Deep rivers, havens, creekes, and litle seas, 2Tamb 3.2.87 Tamb
and those other Iles/That lye betwixt the Mediterranean seas. Jew 1.2.4 Basso
That now I hope flotes on the Irish seas. Edw 1.4.224 Mortmr
The hautie Dane commands the narrow seas, Edw 2.2.168 Mortmr
France/Makes friends, to crosse the seas with her yong sonne, Edw 3.1.270 Spencr
Then when sir Paris crost the seas with <for> her, F1694 5.1.21 Faust
so did Alcides port, whose seas/Eate hollow rocks, and where the Lucan, First Booke 406
threatning gods/Fill'd both the earth and seas with prodegies; Lucan, First Booke 523
love please/[Am] <And> driven like a ship upon rough seas, Ovid's Elegies 2.4.8
My [false] <selfe> oathes in Carpathian seas to cast. Ovid's Elegies 2.8.20
raught/Ill waies by rough seas wondring waves first taught, Ovid's Elegies 2.11.2
O would that no Oares might in seas have suncke, Ovid's Elegies 2.11.5
The unjust seas all blewish do appeare. Ovid's Elegies 2.11.12
How almost wrackt thy ship in maine seas fell. Ovid's Elegies 2.11.50
And raging Seas in boistrous South-winds plough. Ovid's Elegies 2.16.22
Flames into flame, flouds thou powrest seas into. Ovid's Elegies 3.2.34
Nor hanging oares the troubled seas did sweepe, Ovid's Elegies 3.7.43
What doest with seas? Ovid's Elegies 3.7.49
Who on Loves seas more glorious wouldst appeare? Hero and Leander 1.228
SEASETH
No sooner is it up, but thers a foule,/That seaseth it: Edw 2.2.27 Lncstr
SEASONS
All times and seasons rest you at a stay, Edw 5.1.67 Edward
SEAT
that in former age/Hast bene the seat of mightie Conquerors, 1Tamb 1.1.7 Cosroe
Well here I sweare by this my royal seat-- 1Tamb 1.1.97 Mycet
Unlawfully usurpest the Persean seat: 1Tamb 4.2.57 Zabina

SEAT (cont.)
That long hath lingred for so high a seat. 1Tamb 5.1.502 Therid
The strength and sinewes of the imperiall seat. 2Tamb 1.1.156 Sgsmnd
There having sackt Borno the Kingly seat, 2Tamb 1.3.203 Techel
And were the sinowes of th'imperiall seat/So knit and 2Tamb 3.1.10 Callap
The pride and beautie of her princely seat, 2Tamb 4.3.109 Tamb
With what a broken hart/And damned spirit I ascend this seat, 2Tamb 5.3.207 Amyras
By due discent the Regall seat is mine. P 470 8.20 Anjoy
But neither chuse the north t'erect thy seat; Lucan, First Booke 53
That Jove, usurper of his fathers seat, Hero and Leander 1.452
And to the seat of Jove it selfe advaunce, Hero and Leander 1.467

SEATE
The Cyclops shelves, and grim Ceranias seate/Have you oregone, Dido 1.1.147 Aeneas
The kingly seate of Southerne Libia, Dido 1.1.212 Venus
This is no seate for one thats comfortles, Dido 2.1.86 Aeneas
That calles my soule from forth his living seate, Dido 3.4.53 Dido
We meane to seate our footmen on their Steeds, 1Tamb 3.3.25 Techel
A royall seate, a scepter and a crowne: P 161 2.104 Guise
Welcome to France thy fathers royall seate, P 590 12.3 QnMoth
Lord Raymond, take your seate, Friers attend, F1010 3.2.30 Pope
[And fliest the throne of his tribunall seate], F1790 5.1.117A OldMan
heaven the seate of God, the Throne of the Blessed, the F1844 5.2.48 P Faust
should defend/Or great wealth from a judgement seate ascend. Ovid's Elegies 1.10.40
In what gulfe either Syrtes have their seate. Ovid's Elegies 2.11.20
Ida the seate of groves did sing with corne, Ovid's Elegies 3.9.39

SEATED
And seated on my Gennet, let him ride/As Didos husband through Dido 4.4.66 Dido
Scarce being seated in my royall throne, 1Tamb 2.7.5 Cosroe
He now is seated on my horsmens speares, 1Tamb 5.1.114 Tamb
Where sitting <Being seated> in a Chariot burning bright, F 758 2.3.37 2Chor
But spare my wench thou at her right hand seated, Ovid's Elegies 3.2.21

SEATES
O then ye Powers that sway eternal seates, 2Tamb 5.3.17 Techel
What seates for their deserts? Lucan, First Booke 344

SEATS
And few live that behold their ancient seats; Lucan, First Booke 27
The fates are envious, high seats quickly perish, Lucan, First Booke 70
The fathers selves leapt from their seats; and flying/Left Lucan, First Booke 485

SEAVEN
and binde your selfe presently unto me for seaven yeeres, or F App p.229 25 P Wagner
By seaven huge mouthes into the sea is [skipping] <slipping>, Ovid's Elegies 2.13.10
And seaven [times] <time> shooke her head with thicke locks Ovid's Elegies 3.1.32
Rich Nile by seaven mouthes to the vast sea flowing, Ovid's Elegies 3.5.39

SEAZ'D
He staide, and on thy lookes his gazes seaz'd. Ovid's Elegies 1.8.24
Had left the heavens, therefore on him hee seaz'd. Hero and Leander 2.158

SEAZD
My love was cause that more mens love she seazd. Ovid's Elegies 3.10.20

SEAZDE
The earle of Warwick seazde him on his way, Edw 3.1.115 Arundl

SEAZE
And enter in, to seaze upon the gold: 2Tamb 3.3.8 Techel
But sorrow seaze upon my toyling soule, P1089 19.159 QnMoth
No, spare his life, but seaze upon his goods, Edw 1.1.193 Edward
When I forsake thee, death seaze on my heart, Edw 2.1.64 Neece
For Gaveston, will if he [seaze] <zease> <sees> him once, Edw 2.5.63 Warwck
That if he slip will seaze upon us both, Edw 5.2.8 Mortmr
griefe appease)/With thy sharpe nayles upon my face to seaze. Ovid's Elegies 1.7.64
With thy white armes upon my shoulders seaze, Ovid's Elegies 2.16.29

SEAZED
Hath seazed Normandie into his hands. Edw 3.1.64 Queene

SECOND
Troy shall no more call him her second hope, Dido 3.2.8 Juno
And all the world calles me a second Helen, Dido 5.1.144 Dido
And I be calde a second Helena. Dido 5.1.148 Dido
But when Aurora mounts the second time, 1Tamb 4.1.54 2Msngr
Hath made our Poet pen his second part, 2Tamb Prol.3 Prolog
Conceive a second life in endlesse mercie. 2Tamb 2.3.9 Sgsmnd
Whose jealousie admits no second Mate, 2Tamb 2.4.12 Tamb
Your griefe and furie hurtes my second life: 2Tamb 2.4.68 Zenoc
For person like to proove a second Mars. 2Tamb 4.1.35 Calyph
My trusty servant, nay, my second [selfe] <life>; Jew 3.4.15 Barab
A second mariage twixt thy selfe and me. Edw 1.4.335 Edward
The second thus: F 604 2.2.53 P Faust
What art thou the second? F 673 2.2.122 P Faust
Well, theres the second time, aware the third, I give you faire F App p.232 20 P Faust
and thoughts that alwaies scorn'd/A second place; Pompey could Lucan, First Booke 125
And was the second cause why vigor failde mee: Ovid's Elegies 3.6.38

SECONDLY
Secondly, hee that denies to pay, shal straight become a Jew 1.2.73 P Reader
Secondly, that Mephostophilis shall be his servant, and be by F 486 2.1.98 P Faust

SECREAT
By secreat thoughts to thinke there is a god. Ovid's Elegies 3.8.36

SECRECIE
A friend of mine told me in secrecie, Edw 2.1.17 Spencr
Be resolute, and full of secrecie. Edw 2.2.125 Lncstr

SECRECY
Madam, as in secrecy I was tolde, P 641 12.54 Cardnl

SECRET
And secret issuings to defend the ditch. 2Tamb 3.2.74 Tamb
And Barabas now search this secret out. Jew 1.1.177 Barab
Be true and secret, thou shalt want no gold. Jew 2.3.216 Barab
gravest, secret, subtil, bottle-nos'd knave to my Master, Jew 3.3.9 P Ithimr

SECRET (cont.)

Very well, Ithimore, then now be secret;	Jew	3.4.60	Barab
How can it if we two be secret.	Jew	4.1.9	Barab
To what event my secret purpose drives,	Jew	5.2.122	Barab
And by a secret token that he beares,	Edw	5.4.19	Mortmr
Well, do it bravely, and be secret.	Edw	5.4.28	Mortmr
Whether thou wilt be secret in this,	Edw	5.6.5	Mortmr
such and more strange/Blacke night brought forth in secret:	Lucan, First Booke		579
and read/Sybillas secret works, and [wash] <washt> their saint	Lucan, First Booke		599
Take, and receive each secret amorous glaunce.	Ovid's Elegies		1.4.18
Thou arguest she doth secret markes unfold.	Ovid's Elegies		2.7.6
I could my selfe by secret Magicke shift.	Ovid's Elegies		2.15.10
What secret becks in banquets with her youths,	Ovid's Elegies		3.10.23
But what the secret trustie night conceal'd,	Hero and Leander		2.103
His secret flame apparantly was seene,	Hero and Leander		2.135

SECRETARIE

Cheefe Secretarie to the state and me,	Edw	1.1.155	Edward
Welcome maister secretarie.	Edw	2.2.68	Penbrk

SECRETARY

And secretary to, and lord of Man.	Edw	1.2.14	Warwck

SECRETE

but most astonied/To see his choller shut in secrete thoughtes,	1Tamb	3.2.70	Agidas

SECRETLIE

That Gaveston is secretlie arrivde,	Edw	2.3.16	Lncstr
But secretlie her lookes with checks did trounce mee,	Ovid's Elegies		1.7.21

SECRETLY

And in the night time secretly would I steale/To travellers	Jew	2.3.206	Ithimr
Ile muster up an army secretly,	P 572	11.37	Navrre
Ile secretly convay me unto Bloyse,	P 895	17.90	King
No gifts given secretly thy crime bewray.	Ovid's Elegies		2.5.6
If some faire wench me secretly behold,	Ovid's Elegies		2.7.5
She secretly with me such harme attempted,	Ovid's Elegies		2.13.3
And to some corner secretly have gone,	Hero and Leander		2.311

SECRETS

But you know some secrets of the Jew,	Jew	4.2.64	Pilia
no my Lord, a woman only must/Partake the secrets of my heart.	P 676	13.20	Duchss
Are these your secrets that no man must know?	P 678	13.22	Guise
To whom shall I bewray my secrets now,	P1083	19.153	QnMoth
And tell the secrets of all forraine Kings:	F 114	1.1.86	Faust
Learned Faustus/To find <know> the secrets of Astronomy,/Graven	F 755	2.3.34	2Chor
[And] <Or> hidden secrets openlie to bewray?	Ovid's Elegies		3.13.8

SECT

To make a Nunnery, where none but their owne sect/Must enter in;	Jew	1.2.256	Abigal

SECTIOUS

To overthrow those [sectious] <sexious> <factious> Puritans:	P 850	17.45	Guise

SECURE

will flie (my Lords)/To rest secure against my brothers force.	1Tamb	1.1.178	Cosroe
To live secure, and keep his forces out,	2Tamb	5.1.16	Govnr
And how secure this conquer'd Iland stands/Inviron'd with the	Jew	5.3.6	Calym
And that I am not more secure my selfe,	P 264	4.62	Charls
Your grace may sit secure, if none but wee/Doe wot of your	Edw	4.7.26	Monk
He liv'd secure boasting his former deeds,	Lucan, First Booke		135
Beware least he unrival'd loves secure,	Ovid's Elegies		1.8.95
But thou of thy faire damsell too secure,	Ovid's Elegies		2.19.37
And in her owne mind thought her selfe secure,	Hero and Leander		2.265

SECURELY

And whilste he sleepes securely thus in ease,	P 635	12.48	QnMoth
snatcht up/Would make them sleepe securely in their tents.	Lucan, First Booke		516

SECURITIE

heart to be with gladnes pierc'd/To do you honor and securitie.	1Tamb	1.2.251	Therid
Breed litle strength to our securitie,	2Tamb	2.1.43	Sgsmnd
And makes his footstoole on securitie:	P 738	14.41	Navrre

SECURITIES

To entertaine some care of our securities,	1Tamb	5.1.29	1Virgn

SECURITY

For that security craves <great> Lucifer.	F 425	2.1.37	Mephst

SEDGE

Instead of Sedge and Reed, beare Sugar Canes:	Jew	4.2.96	Ithimr

SEDITIONS

Or with seditions weary all the worlde:	P 116	2.59	Guise

SEDUCED

Seduced Daughter, Goe, forget not.	Jew	1.2.359	Barab

SEDULOUS

Be sedulous, let no stay cause thee tarry.	Ovid's Elegies		1.11.8

SEE (See also SE, SE'T, SEA)

Might I but see that pretie sport a foote,	Dido	1.1.16	Ganimd
See how the night Ulysses-like comes forth,	Dido	1.1.70	Venus
What? doe I see my sonne now come on shoare:	Dido	1.1.134	Venus
See what strange arts necessitie findes out,	Dido	1.1.169	Venus
My selfe will see they shall not trouble ye,	Dido	1.2.38	Iarbus
Might we but once more see Aeneas face,	Dido	1.2.45	Serg
Achates, see King Priam wags his hand,	Dido	2.1.29	Aeneas
Aeneas see, here come the Citizens,	Dido	2.1.37	Achat
I heare Aeneas voyce, but see him not,	Dido	2.1.45	Illion
Aeneas see, Sergestus or his ghost.	Dido	2.1.50	Achat
It is our Captaine, see Ascanius.	Dido	2.1.52	Cloan
Blest be the time I see Achates face.	Dido	2.1.56	Illion
See where her servitors passe through the hall/Bearing a	Dido	2.1.70	Serg
See where the pictures of my suiters hang,	Dido	3.1.139	Dido
Sister, I see you savour of my wiles,	Dido	3.2.96	Venus
Sister, see see Ascanius in his pompe,	Dido	3.3.32	Anna
And mought I live to see him sacke rich Thebes,	Dido	3.3.42	Aeneas
And might I live to see thee shipt away,	Dido	3.3.46	Iarbus

SEE (cont.)

To see a Phrigian far fet [on] <o'er> <forfeit to> the sea,	Dido	3.3.64	Iarbus
Did ever men see such a sudden storme?	Dido	4.1.1	Achat
I see Aeneas sticketh in your minde,	Dido	4.1.33	Dido
See where they come, how might I doe to chide?	Dido	4.4.13	Dido
Lets see what tempests can anoy me now.	Dido	4.4.60	Aeneas
I cannot see him frowne, it may not be:	Dido	4.4.112	Dido
For in his lookes I see eternitie,	Dido	4.4.122	Dido
And see if those will serve in steed of sailes:	Dido	4.4.160	Dido
Where thou shalt see the red gild fishes leape,	Dido	4.5.10	Nurse
That I might live to see this boy a man,	Dido	4.5.18	Nurse
Whom doe I see, Joves winged messenger?	Dido	5.1.25	Aeneas
That I might see Aeneas in his face:	Dido	5.1.150	Dido
And, see the Sailers take him by the hand,	Dido	5.1.189	Dido
See see, the billowes heave him up to heaven,	Dido	5.1.252	Dido
But see, Achates wils him put to sea,	Dido	5.1.258	Dido
See where he comes, welcome, welcome my love.	Dido	5.1.261	Dido
To see my sweet Iarbus slay himselfe?	Dido	5.1.324	Anna
Brother, I see your meaning well enough.	1Tamb	1.1.18	Mycet
I long to see thee backe returne from thence,	1Tamb	1.1.76	Mycet
to them, that all Asia/Lament to see the follie of their King.	1Tamb	1.1.96	Cosroe
To see our neighbours that were woont to quake/And tremble at	1Tamb	1.1.115	Cosroe
Wel, since I see the state of Persea droope,	1Tamb	1.1.155	Cosroe
But now you see these letters and commandes,	1Tamb	1.2.21	Tamb
Me thinks I see kings kneeling at his feet,	1Tamb	1.2.55	Techel
I see the folly of thy Emperour:	1Tamb	1.2.167	Tamb
See how he raines down heaps of gold in showers,	1Tamb	1.2.182	Tamb
You see my Lord, what woorking woordes he hath.	1Tamb	2.3.25	Therid
But when you see his actions [top] <stop> his speech,	1Tamb	2.3.26	Therid
See where it is, the keenest Cutle-axe <curtle-axe>,/That ere	1Tamb	2.3.55	Tamb
So I can when I see my time.	1Tamb	2.4.26	Mycet
I, Didst thou ever see a fairer?	1Tamb	2.4.28	Mycet
Till I may see thee hem'd with armed men.	1Tamb	2.4.38	Tamb
Then shalt thou see me pull it from thy head:	1Tamb	2.4.39	Tamb
Then shalt thou see the Scythian Tamburlaine,	1Tamb	2.5.97	Tamb
You see though first the King of Persea/(Being a Shepheard)	1Tamb	3.2.59	Agidas
but most astonied/To see his choller shut in secrete thoughtes,	1Tamb	3.2.70	Agidas
See you Agidas how the King salutes you.	1Tamb	3.2.88	Techel
see how right the man/Hath hit the meaning of my Lord the King.	1Tamb	3.2.107	Techel
See how he comes?	1Tamb	3.3.3	Tamb
Whom I have brought to see their overthrow.	1Tamb	3.3.81	Bajzth
souldier of my Camp/Shall smile to see thy miserable state.	1Tamb	3.3.86	Tamb
I long to see those crownes won by our swords,	1Tamb	3.3.98	Therid
Stir not Zenocrate untill thou see/Me martch victoriously with	1Tamb	3.3.126	Tamb
That I may see him issue Conquerour.	1Tamb	3.3.194	Zenoc
Nay (mightie Souldan) did your greatnes see/The frowning lookes	1Tamb	4.1.12	2Msngr
See Capolin, the faire Arabian king/That hath bene disapointed	1Tamb	4.1.68	Souldn
Now may we see Damascus lofty towers,	1Tamb	4.2.102	Tamb
And when they see me march in black aray.	1Tamb	4.2.119	Tamb
To let them see (divine Zenocrate)/I glorie in the curses of my	1Tamb	4.4.28	Tamb
My lord, to see my fathers towne besieg'd,	1Tamb	4.4.65	Zenoc
Tis enough for us to see them, and for Tamburlaine onely to	1Tamb	4.4.111	P Techel
We see his tents have now bene altered,	1Tamb	5.1.7	Govnr
Behold my sword, what see you at the point?	1Tamb	5.1.108	Tamb
But I am pleasde you shall not see him there:	1Tamb	5.1.113	Tamb
And feare to see thy kingly Fathers harme,	1Tamb	5.1.138	Tamb
That will we chiefly see unto, Theridamas,	1Tamb	5.1.206	Tamb
That all the world will see and laugh to scorne,	1Tamb	5.1.252	Zabina
You see my wife, my Queene and Emperesse,	1Tamb	5.1.264	Bajzth
Wretched Zenocrate, that livest to see,	1Tamb	5.1.319	Zenoc
to see the Sun-bright troope/Of heavenly vyrgins and unspotted	1Tamb	5.1.324	Zenoc
But see another bloody spectacle.	1Tamb	5.1.339	Zenoc
See, se Anippe if they breathe or no.	1Tamb	5.1.343	Zenoc
To see them live so long in misery:	1Tamb	5.1.370	Zenoc
To see the king my Father issue safe,	1Tamb	5.1.441	Zenoc
And see my Lord, a sight of strange import,	1Tamb	5.1.468	Tamb
Her state and person wants no pomp you see,	1Tamb	5.1.485	Tamb
Then shalt thou see a hundred kings and more/Upon their knees,	2Tamb	1.2.28	Callap
Yes father, you shal see me if I live,	2Tamb	1.3.54	Celeb
and I might enter in/To see the state and majesty of heaven,	2Tamb	1.3.155	Tamb
Me thinks I see how glad the christian King/Is made, for joy of	2Tamb	2.2.20	Uribas
See here the perjur'd traitor Hungary,	2Tamb	2.3.12	Gazell
Then should you see this Thiefe of Scythia,	2Tamb	3.1.14	Callap
And see him lance his flesh to teach you all.	2Tamb	3.2.114	Tamb
My speech of war, and this my wound you see,	2Tamb	3.2.142	Tamb
Then let us see if coward Calapine/Dare levie armes against our	2Tamb	3.2.155	Tamb
Then see the bringing of our ordinance/Along the trench into	2Tamb	3.3.54	Therid
For think ye I can live, and see him dead?	2Tamb	3.4.27	Sonne
And thou shalt see a man greater than Mahomet,	2Tamb	3.4.46	Therid
To see the slaughter of our enemies.	2Tamb	3.5.57	Callap
See a knot of kings,/Sitting as if they were a telling ridles.	2Tamb	3.5.58	Tamb
I see how fearfully ye would refuse,	2Tamb	3.5.73	Tamb
See father, how Almeda the Jaylor lookes upon us.	2Tamb	3.5.116	Celeb
See ye this rout, and know ye this same king?	2Tamb	3.5.151	Tamb
Wel, now you see hee is a king, looke to him Theridamas, when we	2Tamb	3.5.153	P Tamb
See now ye slaves, my children stoops your pride/And leads your	2Tamb	4.1.76	Tamb
That will not see the strength of Tamburlaine,	2Tamb	4.1.133	Tamb
And see the figure of my dignitie,	2Tamb	4.3.25	Tamb
Take them away Theridamas, see them dispatcht.	2Tamb	5.1.134	Tamb
See now my Lord how brave the Captaine hangs.	2Tamb	5.1.149	Amyras
In vaine I see men worship Mahomet,	2Tamb	5.1.179	Tamb
not my Lord, I see great Mahomet/Clothed in purple clowdes,	2Tamb	5.2.31	Amasia
To see thy foot-stoole set upon thy head,	2Tamb	5.3.29	Usumc

SEE (cont.)

To see the devils mount in Angels throanes,	2Tamb	5.3.32	Usumc
See where my slave, the uglie monster death/Shaking and	2Tamb	5.3.67	Tamb
Looke where he goes, but see, he comes againe/Because I stay:	2Tamb	5.3.75	Tamb
See my Phisitions now, how Jove hath sent/A present medicine to	2Tamb	5.3.105	Tamb
then let me see how much/Is left for me to conquer all the	2Tamb	5.3.123	Tamb
Looke here my boies, see what a world of ground,	2Tamb	5.3.145	Tamb
That I may see thee crown'd before I die.	2Tamb	5.3.179	Tamb
let me see how well/Thou wilt become thy fathers majestie.	2Tamb	5.3.183	Tamb
my soule dooth weepe to see/Your sweet desires depriv'd my	2Tamb	5.3.246	Tamb
Who smiles to see how full his bags are cramb'd,	Jew	Prol.31	Machvl
Ha, to the East? yes: See how stands the Vanes?	Jew	1.1.40	Barab
men dispatch/And come ashore, and see the fraught discharg'd.	Jew	1.1.101	Barab
For I can see no fruits in all their faith,	Jew	1.1.116	Barab
We grant a month, but see you keep your promise.	Jew	1.2.28	Calym
Oh silly brethren, borne to see this day!	Jew	1.2.170	Barab
Doth see his souldiers slaine, himselfe disarm'd,	Jew	1.2.204	Barab
but trust me 'tis a misery/To see a man in such affliction:	Jew	1.2.212	2Jew
See the simplicitie of these base slaves,	Jew	1.2.214	Barab
And wilt not see thine owne afflictions,	Jew	1.2.353	1Fryar
For I had rather dye, then see her thus.	Jew	1.2.357	Barab
Forget me, see me not, and so be gone.	Jew	1.2.363	Barab
And not depart untill I see you free.	Jew	2.2.41	Bosco
Hoping to see them starve upon a stall,	Jew	2.3.26	Barab
It shall goe hard but I will see your death.	Jew	2.3.94	Barab
Let me see, sirra, are you not an old shaver?	Jew	2.3.114	P Barab
you in these chops; let me see one that's somewhat leaner.	Jew	2.3.125	P Barab
Be mov'd at nothing, see thou pitty none,	Jew	2.3.171	Barab
See 'em goe pinion'd along by my doore.	Jew	2.3.180	Barab
That I have laugh'd agood to see the cripples/Goe limping home	Jew	2.3.211	Ithimr
But steale you in, and seeme to see him not;	Jew	2.3.272	Barab
Nor e're shall see the land of Canaan,	Jew	2.3.303	Barab
now Abigall shall see/Whether Mathias holds her deare or no.	Jew	3.2.1	Mthias
Has made me see the difference of things.	Jew	3.3.62	Abigal
Abigal I will, but see thou change no more,	Jew	3.3.70	1Fryar
Now shalt thou see the death of Abigall,	Jew	3.4.62	Barab
Where they must neither see the messenger,	Jew	3.4.80	Barab
Oh he is gone to see the other Nuns.	Jew	3.6.10	2Fryar
You see I answer him, and yet he stayes;	Jew	4.1.88	Barab
Oh how I long to see him shake his heeles.	Jew	4.1.140	Ithimr
thou think'st I see thee not;/Away, I'de wish thee, and let me	Jew	4.1.169	1Fryar
And see, a staffe stands ready for the purpose:	Jew	4.1.172	1Fryar
When shall you see a Jew commit the like?	Jew	4.1.197	Barab
but the Exercise being done, see where he comes.	Jew	4.2.20	P Pilia
Pray pardon me, I must goe see a ship discharg'd.	Jew	4.2.51	P Ithimr
words, Sir, and send it you, were best see; there's his letter.	Jew	4.3.24	P Pilia
As I wud see thee hang'd; oh, love stops my breath:	Jew	4.3.53	Barab
Pray when, Sir, shall I see you at my house?	Jew	4.3.56	Barab
I will in some disguize goe see the slave,	Jew	4.3.67	Barab
And see that Malta be well fortifi'd;	Jew	5.1.2	Govnr
I hope to see the Governour a slave,	Jew	5.1.67	Barab
walke about/The ruin'd Towne, and see the wracke we made:	Jew	5.2.19	Calym
I see no reason but of Malta's wracke,	Jew	5.2.58	Govnr
Your selves shall see it shall not be forgot:	Jew	5.2.71	Barab
Goe walke about the City, see thy friends:	Jew	5.2.92	Barab
And let me see what mony thou canst make;	Jew	5.2.94	Barab
And now I see the Scituation,	Jew	5.3.5	Calym
would intreat your Majesty/To come and see his homely Citadell,	Jew	5.3.18	Msngr
Why now I see that you have Art indeed.	Jew	5.5.4	Barab
And see he brings it: Now, Governor, the summe?	Jew	5.5.19	Barab
Companion-Bashawes, see I pray/How busie Barrabas is there above	Jew	5.5.51	Calym
See Calymath, this was devis'd for thee.	Jew	5.5.66	Govnr
See his end first, and flye then if thou canst.	Jew	5.5.69	Govnr
No, thus I'le see thy treachery repaid,	Jew	5.5.74	Govnr
Thanks sonne Navarre, you see we love you well,	P 13	1.13	QnMoth
Doth heare and see the praiers of the just:	P 43	1.43	Navrre
See where they be my good Lord, and he that smelles but to	P 73	2.16	P Pothec
And see it honoured with just solemnitie.	P 196	3.31	Admral
Messenger, tell him I will see him straite.	P 247	4.45	Charls
And under your direction see they keep/All trecherous violence	P 267	4.65	Charls
See where my Souldier shot him through the arm.	P 310	5.37	Guise
With bowes and dartes to shoot at them they see,	P 422	7.62	Dumain
Tis well advisde Dumain, goe see it strait be done.	P 424	7.64	Guise
And when you see me in, then follow hard.	P 429	7.69	Anjoy
Epernoune, goe see it presently be done,	P 558	11.23	QnMoth
His minde you see runnes on his minions,	P 633	12.46	QnMoth
I pray thee let me see.	P 674	13.18	Guise
But Madam I must see.	P 677	13.21	Guise
Now doe I see that from the very first,	P 694	13.38	Guise
Thus God we see doth ever guide the right,	P 789	16.3	Navrre
What, will you not feare when you see him come?	P 933	19.3	Capt
Well then, I see you are resolute.	P 938	19.8	Capt
Come Guise and see thy traiterous guile outreacht,	P 962	19.32	King
But see where he comes.	P1018	19.88	Capt
My Lord, see where the Guise is slaine.	P1019	19.89	Capt
see where she comes, as if she droupt/To heare these newes.	P1062	19.132	Eprnon
To see your highnes in this vertuous minde.	P1210	22.72	Navrre
That we may see it honourably interde:	P1246	22.108	Navrre
thie folishe dreame/and lett thee see thie selfe my prysoner	Paris	ms33,p391	Guise
Let me see, thou wouldst do well/To waite at my trencher, and	Edw	1.1.30	Gavstn
To hide those parts which men delight to see,	Edw	1.1.65	Gavstn
Or looke to see the throne where you should sit,	Edw	1.1.131	Lncstr
To see it done, and bring thee safe againe.	Edw	1.1.205	Edward

SEE (cont.)

But I long more to see him banisht hence.	Edw	1.4.5		Warwck
See what a scornfull looke the pesant casts.	Edw	1.4.14		MortSr
And see what we your councellers have done.	Edw	1.4.44		ArchBp
I see I must, and therefore am content.	Edw	1.4.85		Edward
Ile see him presently dispatched away.	Edw	1.4.90		Mortmr
I had beene stifled, and not lived to see,	Edw	1.4.176		Queene
And see how coldly his lookes make deniall.	Edw	1.4.235		Lncstr
But see in happie time, my lord the king,	Edw	1.4.299		Queene
But nephew, now you see the king is changd.	Edw	1.4.420		MortSr
See that my coache be readie, I must hence.	Edw	2.1.71		Neece
That shall wee see, looke where his lordship comes.	Edw	2.2.49		Lncstr
Frolicks not more to see the paynted springe,	Edw	2.2.62		Gavstn
Looke next to see us with our ensignes spred.	Edw	2.2.199		Lncstr
My lord, I see your love to Gaveston,	Edw	2.2.208		Kent
Waite on me, and ile see thou shalt not want.	Edw	2.2.246		Edward
against your king)/To see his royall soveraigne once againe.	Edw	2.5.7		Gavstn
by me, yet but he may/See him before he dies, for why he saies,	Edw	2.5.37		Arundl
majestie so earnestlie/Desires to see the man before his death,	Edw	2.5.78		Penbrk
Sweete soveraigne, yet I come/To see thee ere I die.	Edw	2.5.95		Gavstn
I see it is your life these armes pursue.	Edw	2.6.2		James
Treacherous earle, shall I not see the king?	Edw	2.6.15		Gavstn
Lancaster/Inexorable, and I shall never see/My lovely Pierce,	Edw	3.1.7		Edward
shall I never see,/Never behold thee now?	Edw	3.1.68		Edward
Boye, see you beare you bravelie to the king,	Edw	3.1.72		Edward
Or didst thou see my friend to take his death?	Edw	3.1.93		Edward
And see him redelivered to your hands.	Edw	3.1.112		Arundl
Yet ere thou go, see how I do devorce	Edw	3.1.176		Edward
There see him safe bestowed, and for the rest,	Edw	3.1.253		Edward
To see us there appointed for our foes.	Edw	4.2.56		Mortmr
Was borne I see to be our anchor hold.	Edw	4.2.77		Mortmr
That Englands peeres may Henolts welcome see.	Edw	4.2.82		SrJohn
I pray let us see it, what have we there?	Edw	4.3.10		Edward
That I may see that most desired day,	Edw	4.3.46		Edward
Shall I not see the king my father yet?	Edw	4.6.61		Prince
Alas, see where he sits, and hopes unseene,	Edw	4.7.51		Leistr
My heart with pittie earnes to see this sight,	Edw	4.7.70		Abbot
For we shall see them shorter by the heads.	Edw	4.7.94		Rice
Parted from hence, never to see us more!	Edw	4.7.101		Spencr
Spencer, I see our soules are fleeted hence,	Edw	4.7.105		Baldck
See monsters see, ile weare my crowne againe,	Edw	5.1.74		Edward
Let me but see him first, and then I will.	Edw	5.2.95		Prince
Take this, away, and never see me more.	Edw	5.4.43		Mortmr
See how he must be handled for his labour,	Edw	5.5.23		Matrvs
See that in the next roome I have a fier,	Edw	5.5.29		Ltborn
The Queene sent me, to see how you were used,	Edw	5.5.48		Ltborn
To see a king in this most pittious state?	Edw	5.5.51		Ltborn
I see my tragedie written in thy browes,	Edw	5.5.74		Edward
And let me see the stroke before it comes,	Edw	5.5.76		Edward
Lets see who dare impeache me for his death?	Edw	5.6.14		Mortmr
Aye me, see where he comes, and they with him,	Edw	5.6.22		Queene
Base fortune, now I see, that in thy wheele/There is a point, to	Edw	5.6.59		Mortmr
That shall we presently know, <for see> here comes his boy.	F 196	1.2.3		2Schol
I do not doubt but to see you both hang'd the next Sessions.	F 212	1.2.19	P	Wagner
<and see if hee by> his grave counsell may <can> reclaime him.	F 226	1.2.33		2Schol
Yet let us see <trie> what we can do.	F 228	1.2.35		2Schol
I see there's vertue in my heavenly words.	F 255	1.3.27		Faust
Yes, and goings out too, you may see sir.	F 347	1.4.5	P	Robin
see how poverty jests in his nakednesse, I know the Villaines	F 348	1.4.6	P	Wagner
and see that you walke attentively, and let your right eye be	F 385	1.4.43	P	Wagner
See <come> Faustus, here is <heres> fire, set it on.	F 459	2.1.71		Mephst
I see it plaine, even heere <in this place> is writ/Homo fuge:	F 469	2.1.81		Faust
And let thee see <shewe thee> what Magicke can performe.	F 474	2.1.86		Mephst
I might see al characters of <and> planets of the heavens,	F 551.4	2.1.167A	P	Faust
wherein I might see al plants, hearbes and trees that grow upon	F 551.9	2.1.172A	P	Faust
<see al> the seven deadly sinnes appeare to thee in their owne	F 655	2.2.104	P	Belzeb
live along, then thou should'st see how fat I'de <I would> be.	F 683	2.2.132	P	Envy
<No, Ile see thee hanged, thou wilt eate up all my victualls>.	F 702	(HC264)A	P	Faust
O might I see hell, and returne againe safe, how happy were I	F 714	2.2.166	P	Faust
That thou shalt see presently:	F 732	2.3.11	P	Robin
To see the Pope and manner of his Court,	F 776	2.3.55		2Chor
Where thou shalt see such store of Ordinance,	F 819	3.1.41		Mephst
That I do long to see the Monuments/And situation of bright	F 828	3.1.50		Faust
I know you'd <faine> see the Pope/And take some part of holy	F 831	3.1.53		Mephst
<Where thou shalt see a troupe of bald-pate Friers>,	F 833	(HC265)A		Mephst
come then stand by me/And thou shalt see them come immediately.	F 844	3.1.66		Mephst
be,/That this proud Pope may Faustus [cunning] <comming> see.	F 855	3.1.77		Faust
That no eye may thy body see.	F1003	3.2.23		Mephst
Faustus no more: see where the Cardinals come.	F1008	3.2.28		Mephst
And see that all things be in readinesse,	F1011	3.2.31		Pope
let me see the cup.	F1093	3.3.6	P	Robin
[I leave untold, your eyes shall see performd].	F1154	3.3.67A		3Chor
Good Fredericke see the roomes be voyded straight,	F1157	4.1.3		Mrtino
Go backe, and see the State in readinesse.	F1159	4.1.5		Mrtino
See, see his window's ope, we'l call to him.	F1177	4.1.23		Fredrk
and thou shalt see/This Conjurer performe such rare exploits,	F1185	4.1.31		Mrtino
Speake, wilt thou come and see this sport?	F1193	4.1.39		Fredrk
Wilt thou stand in thy Window, and see it then?	F1195	4.1.41		Mrtino
who comes to see/What wonders by blacke spels may compast be.	F1197	4.1.43		Mrtino
Your Majesty shall see them presently.	F1235	4.1.81		Faust
to stand gaping after the divels Governor, and can see nothing.	F1244	4.1.90	P	Benvol
Your Majesty may boldly goe and see.	F1269	4.1.115		Faust
Faustus I see it plaine,	F1270	4.1.116		Emper

Word / Context	Work	Reference	P	Speaker
SEE (cont.)				
See, see, my gracious Lord, what strange beast is yon, that	F1274	4.1.120	P	Faust
see Duke of Saxony,/Two spreading hornes most strangely	F1276	4.1.122		Emper
And pants untill I see that Conjurer dead.	F1352	4.2.28		Benvol
Thou soone shouldst see me quit my foule disgrace.	F1356	4.2.32		Benvol
See, see, he comes.	F1362	4.2.38		Mrtino
Breake may his heart with grones: deere Frederik see,	F1366	4.2.42		Benvol
That all the world may see my just revenge.	F1382	4.2.58		Benvol
Yet stay, the world shall see their miserie,	F1406	4.2.82		Faust
See where he comes, dispatch, and kill the slave.	F1423	4.2.99		2Soldr
Martino see,/Benvolio's hornes againe.	F1436	4.3.6		Fredrk
more, take him, because I see thou hast a good minde to him.	F1461	4.4.5	P	Faust
on the score, but say nothing, see if she have forgotten me.	F1511	4.5.7	P	Robin
spirit that I have, I had these grapes brought as you see.	F1586	4.6.29	P	Faust
and see where they come, belike the feast is done.	F1679	5.1.6	P	Wagner
as to let us see that peerelesse dame of Greece, whom all the	F1685	5.1.12	P	1Schol
I see an Angell hover <hovers> ore thy head,	F1730	5.1.57		OldMan
Her lips sucke <suckes> forth my soule, see where it flies.	F1771	5.1.98		Faust
[Ambitious fiends, see how the heavens smiles]/[At your repulse,	F1794	5.1.121A		OldMan
See where they come.	F1815	5.2.19		Mephst
up my hands, but see they hold 'em <them>, they hold 'em <them>.	F1853	5.2.57	P	Faust
And laught to see the poore starve at their gates:	F1918	5.2.122		BdAngl
thou shalt see/Ten thousand tortures that more horrid be.	F1919	5.2.123		BdAngl
[See see where Christs bloud streames in the firmament],	F1939	5.2.143A		Faust
And see [where God]/[Stretcheth out his Arme, and bends his	F1943	5.2.147		Faust
O help us heaven, see, here are Faustus limbs,	F1988	5.3.6		2Schol
I, and goings out too, you may see else.	F App	p.229 5	P	Clown
see how poverty jesteth in his nakednesse, the vilaine is bare,	F App	p.229 6	P	Wagner
do ye see yonder tall fellow in the round slop, hee has kild	F App	p.230 47	P	Clown
and so by that meanes I shal see more then ere I felt, or saw	F App	p.233 5	P	Robin
that thou let me see some proofe of thy skil, that mine eies	F App	p.236 6	P	Emper
Go to maister Doctor, let me see them presently.	F App	p.237 50	P	Emper
Your highnes may boldly go and see.	F App	p.238 63	P	Faust
but now I see thou hast a wife, that not only gives thee	F App	p.238 70	P	Emper
masse see where he is, God save you maister doctor.	F App	p.239 99	P	HrsCsr
has purg'd me of fortie Dollers, I shall never see them more:	F App	p.240 129	P	HrsCsr
See where he is fast asleepe.	F App	p.241 147	P	Mephst
And for I see your curteous intent to pleasure me, I wil not	F App	p.242 8	P	Duchss
had them brought hither, as ye see, how do you like them Madame,	F App	p.242 23	P	Faust
See where they come: belike the feast is ended.	F App	p.243 8		Wagner
See how they quit our [bloud shed] <bloudshed> in the North;	Lucan, First Booke	302		
I see Pangeus hill,/With hoarie toppe, and under Hemus mount	Lucan, First Booke	678		
Before thy husband come, though I not see/What may be done, yet	Ovid's Elegies	1.4.13		
Yet this Ile see, but if thy gowne ought cover,	Ovid's Elegies	1.4.41		
What armes and shoulders did I touch and see,	Ovid's Elegies	1.5.19		
See how the gates with my teares wat'red are.	Ovid's Elegies	1.6.18		
See Love with me, wine moderate in my braine,	Ovid's Elegies	1.6.37		
Since maist thou see me watch and night warres move:	Ovid's Elegies	1.9.45		
give her my writ/But see that forth-with shee peruseth it.	Ovid's Elegies	1.11.16		
Bee not to see with wonted eyes inclinde,	Ovid's Elegies	1.14.37		
Let him goe see her though she doe not languish/And then report	Ovid's Elegies	2.2.21		
Though himselfe see; heele credit her denyall,	Ovid's Elegies	2.2.57		
I knew your speech (what do not lovers see)?	Ovid's Elegies	2.5.19		
The seventh day came, none following mightst thou see,	Ovid's Elegies	2.6.45		
I from the shore thy knowne ship first will see,	Ovid's Elegies	2.11.43		
And who ere see her, worthily lament.	Ovid's Elegies	2.14.40		
I sit not here the noble horse to see,	Ovid's Elegies	3.2.1		
In running if I see thee, I shall stay,	Ovid's Elegies	3.2.13		
And sit thou rounder, that behind us see,	Ovid's Elegies	3.2.23		
I see whom thou affectest:	Ovid's Elegies	3.2.67		
And see at home much, that thou nere broughtst thether.	Ovid's Elegies	3.4.48		
Lie downe with shame, and see thou stirre no more,	Ovid's Elegies	3.6.69		
See a rich chuffe whose wounds great wealth inferr'd,	Ovid's Elegies	3.7.9		
See Homer from whose fountaine ever fild,	Ovid's Elegies	3.8.25		
Why see I lines so oft receivde and given,	Ovid's Elegies	3.13.31		
Graunt this, that what you do I may not see,	Ovid's Elegies	3.13.35		
And I see when you ope the two leavde booke:	Ovid's Elegies	3.13.44		
There might you see one sigh, another rage,	Hero and Leander	1.125		
There might you see the gods in sundrie shapes,	Hero and Leander	1.143		
Shall see it ruinous and desolate.	Hero and Leander	1.240		
As made Love sigh, to see his tirannie.	Hero and Leander	1.374		
To see how he this captive Nymph beguil'd.	Hero and Leander	2.40		
As loath to see Leander going out.	Hero and Leander	2.98		
SEED				
them, and thy seed/Shall issue crowned from their mothers wombe.	2Tamb	1.3.52		Tamb
He is not of the seed of Abraham.	Jew	2.3.230		Barab
Such humors stirde them up; but this warrs seed,	Lucan, First Booke	159		
Remus and Romulus, Ilias twinne-borne seed.	Ovid's Elegies	3.4.40		
Proteus what should I name? teeth, Thebes first seed?	Ovid's Elegies	3.11.35		
SEEDE				
First Ceres taught the seede in fields to swell,	Ovid's Elegies	3.9.11		
SEEDES				
And live in all your seedes immortally:	2Tamb	5.3.174		Tamb
First of thy minde the happy seedes I knewe,	Ovid's Elegies	3.1.59		
The fainting seedes of naughtinesse doth kill.	Ovid's Elegies	3.4.10		
wish the chariot, whence corne [seedes] <fields> were found,	Ovid's Elegies	3.5.15		
And seedes were equally in large fields cast,	Ovid's Elegies	3.9.33		
SEEDS				
or els infernall, mixt/Their angry seeds at his conception:	1Tamb	2.6.10		Meandr
Her eyes and lookes sow'd seeds of perjury,	P 695	13.39		Guise
SEEING				
Seeing the number of their men decreast,	Dido	2.1.132		Aeneas
Iarbus dye, seeing she abandons thee.	Dido	3.1.40		Iarbus

SEEING (cont.)

And seeing they are not idle, but still doing,	Jew	2.3.83	Barab
I cannot chuse, seeing my father bids:--	Jew	2.3.316	Abigal
sent for him, but seeing you are come/Be you my ghostly father;	Jew	3.6.11	Abigal
Go whether thou wilt seeing I have Gaveston.	Edw	1.2.54	Queene
Seeing I must go, do not renew my sorrow.	Edw	1.4.137	Gavstn
Seeing thou hast pleaded with so good successe.	Edw	1.4.329	Edward
And seeing his minde so dotes on Gaveston,	Edw	1.4.389	MortSr
Seeing that our Lord th'earle of Glosters dead,	Edw	2.1.2	Baldck
Seeing that he talkes thus of my mariage day?	Edw	2.1.69	Neece
But seeing you are so desirous, thus it is:	Edw	2.2.15	Mortmr
Seeing he is taken prisoner in his warres?	Edw	2.2.119	Mortmr
The Northren borderers seeing [their] <the> houses burnt,/Their	Edw	2.2.179	Lncstr
But bee content, seeing it his highnesse pleasure.	Edw	5.2.94	Queene
Seeing that my brother cannot be releast.	Edw	5.3.67	Kent
But seeing I cannot, ile entreate for him:	Edw	5.4.98	King
And seeing there was no place to mount up higher,	Edw	5.6.62	Mortmr
[Seeing ubi desinit philosophuŝ, ibi incipit medicus].	F 41	1.1.13A	Faust
Seeing thou hast pray'd and sacrific'd to them.	F 235	1.3.7	Faust
Seeing Faustus hath incur'd eternall death,	F 316	1.3.88	Faust
I am leane with seeing others eate:	F 681	2.2.130 P	Envy
I seeing that, tooke him by the leg, and never rested pulling,	F1550	4.5.46 P	HrsCsr
thee (seeing thou being old/Must shine a star) shal heaven	Lucan, First Booke		45
Who seeing hunters pauseth till fell wrath/And kingly rage	Lucan, First Booke		209
But seeing white Eagles, and Roomes flags wel known,	Lucan, First Booke		246
By these he seeing what myschiefes must ensue,	Lucan, First Booke		629
What makes my bed seem hard seeing it is soft?	Ovid's Elegies		1.2.1
Then seeing I grace thy show in following thee,	Ovid's Elegies		1.2.49
Seeing she likes my bookes, why should we jarre?	Ovid's Elegies		2.4.20
Seeing her face, mine upreard armes discended,	Ovid's Elegies		2.5.47
But seeing thee, I thinke my thing will swell,	Ovid's Elegies		2.15.25
That seeing thy teares can any joy then feele.	Ovid's Elegies		3.5.60
Seeing <When> in my prime my force is spent and done?	Ovid's Elegies		3.6.18
Seeing now thou wouldst deceive me as before:	Ovid's Elegies		3.6.70
Seeing thou art faire, I barre not thy false playing,	Ovid's Elegies		3.13.1
And many seeing great princes were denied,	Hero and Leander		1.129
They seeing it, both Love and him abhor'd,	Hero and Leander		1.463
Seeing in their loves, the Fates were injured.	Hero and Leander		1.484
The god seeing him with pittie to be moved,	Hero and Leander		2.219
Where seeing a naked man, she scriecht for feare,	Hero and Leander		2.237
Seeing the Sheepheards feede theyr flocks,	Passionate Shepherd		6

SEEK

That with such treason seek our overthrow,	2Tamb	2.2.34	Gazell
And rather chuse to seek your countries good,	P 221	4.19	Guise
Might seeme <seek> to crosse me in mine enterprise.	P 574	11.39	Navrre
Come my [Lord] <Lords>, let us goe seek the Guise,	P 655	12.68	QnMoth
come Epernoune/Lets goe seek the Duke and make them freends.	P 786	15.44	King
What would you with the king, ist him you seek?	Edw	2.4.31	Queene

SEEKE

Put sailes to sea to seeke out Italy,	Dido	1.1.218	Aeneas
Who if that any seeke to doe him hurt,	Dido	2.1.321	Venus
Pesant, goe seeke companions like thy selfe,	Dido	3.3.21	Dido
Be rul'd by me, and seeke some other love,	Dido	4.2.35	Anna
And seeke a forraine land calde Italy:	Dido	4.4.98	Dido
The Gods, what Gods be those that seeke my death?	Dido	5.1.128	Dido
Goe goe and spare not, seeke out Italy,	Dido	5.1.169	Dido
Then I may seeke to gratifie your love,	1Tamb	1.1.171	Cosroe
thou art so meane a man)/And seeke not to inrich thy followers,	1Tamb	1.2.9	Zenoc
To seeke revenge on me and Tamburlaine.	1Tamb	2.1.67	Cosroe
Our Crowne the pin that thousands seeke to cleave.	1Tamb	2.4.9	Mycet
Seeke out another Godhead to adore,	2Tamb	5.1.200	Tamb
And seeke in time to intercept the worst,	Jew	1.1.187	Barab
And 'tis thy mony, Barabas, we seeke.	Jew	1.2.54	1Knght
I'le seeke him out, and so insinuate,	Jew	2.3.33	Lodowk
Well, I must seeke a meanes to rid 'em all,	Jew	4.3.63	Barab
These are the cursed Guisians that doe seeke our death.	P 201	3.36	Admral
And rather seeke to scourge their enemies,	P 217	4.15	Anjoy
That seeke to massacre our guiltles lives.	P 261	4.59	Admral
Would seeke the ruine of my Gaveston,	Edw	1.4.79	Edward
And we must seeke to right it as we may,	Edw	4.6.68	Mortmr
Upon my life, those be the men ye seeke.	Edw	4.7.46	Mower
T'escape their hands that seeke to reave his life:	Edw	4.7.52	Leistr
dauntlesse minde/The ambitious Mortimer would seeke to curbe,	Edw	5.1.16	Edward
Seeke all the meanes thou canst to make him droope,	Edw	5.2.54	Mortmr
To seeke for mercie at a tyrants hand.	Edw	5.3.36	Edward
Helpe <seeke> to save distressed Faustus soule.	F 635	2.2.84	Faust
Did seeke to weare the triple Dyadem,	F 959	3.1.181	Faust
and drinke a while, and then we'le go seeke out the Doctor.	F1557	4.5.53 P	Robin
but Ile seeke out my Doctor, and have my fortie dollers againe,	F App	p.240 136 P	HrsCsr
Neither spoile, nor kingdom seeke we by these armes,	Lucan, First Booke		351
shame, and such as seeke loves wrack/Shall follow thee, their	Ovid's Elegies		1.2.31
Wee seeke that through thee safely love we may,	Ovid's Elegies		2.2.65
Let marchants seeke wealth, [and] with perjured lips,	Ovid's Elegies		2.10.33
Some other seeke that may in patience strive with thee,	Ovid's Elegies		2.19.59
Some other seeke, who will these things endure.	Ovid's Elegies		3.10.28
Seeke you for chastitie, immortall fame,	Hero and Leander		1.283

SEEKES

Who seekes to rob me of thy Sisters love,	Dido	4.2.31	Iarbus
This is the harbour that Aeneas seekes,	Dido	4.4.59	Aeneas
To seize upon the Towne: I, that he seekes.	Jew	1.1.185	Barab
That seekes to murder all the Protestants:	P 31	1.31	Navrre
That basely seekes the ruine of his Realme.	P 930	18.31	Navrre
That basely seekes to joyne with such a King,	P1115	21.9	Dumain

SEEKES (cont.)
For no where else seekes he felicitie. — Edw 1.4.122 Gavstn
But seekes to make a new elected king, — Edw 5.1.78 Edward
Who seekes, for being faire, a night to have, — Ovid's Elegies 1.8.67
each mans mony/And seekes vild wealth by selling of her Cony, — Ovid's Elegies 1.10.22
Died red with shame, to hide from shame she seekes. — Ovid's Elegies 1.14.52
and fruite flying touch/Tantalus seekes, his long tongues gaine — Ovid's Elegies 2.2.44
doth favour/That seekes the conquest by her loose behaviour. — Ovid's Elegies 2.5.12
And craves his taske, and seekes to be at fight. — Ovid's Elegies 3.6.68

SEEKING
Ile have his bloud, or die in seeking it. — Edw 2.2.107 Warwck
'Twas thine own seeking Faustus, thanke thy selfe. — F 555 2.2.4 Mephst
I have beene al this day seeking one maister Fustian: — F App p.239 98 P HrsCsr
And seeking refuge, slipt into her bed. — Hero and Leander 2.244

SEEKS
set the Crowne/Upon your kingly head, that seeks our honor, — 1Tamb 2.1.51 Ortyg
And seeks to conquer mighty Tamburlaine, — 2Tamb 5.3.43 Tamb

SEEK'ST
for feare too late/Thou seek'st for much, but canst not — Jew 5.2.46 Barab
Why seek'st not heav'n the third realme to frequent? — Ovid's Elegies 3.7.50

SEEKST
Whom seekst thou Persean? I am Tamburlain. — 1Tamb 1.2.153 Tamb
Ambitious Imp, why seekst thou further charge? — Ovid's Elegies 1.1.18

SEEM
What makes my bed seem hard seeing it is soft? — Ovid's Elegies 1.2.1

SEEM'D
should be most)/Hath seem'd to be digested long agoe. — 1Tamb 3.2.8 Agidas
the King of Persea/(Being a Shepheard) seem'd to love you much, — 1Tamb 3.2.60 Agidas
At which selfe time the house seem'd all on fire, — F1993 5.3.11 3Schol
We erre: a strong blast seem'd the gates to ope: — Ovid's Elegies 1.6.51
And words that seem'd for certaine markes to be. — Ovid's Elegies 2.5.20
And my wench ought to have seem'd falsely praisd, — Ovid's Elegies 3.11.43
Eternall heaven to burne, for so it seem'd, — Hero and Leander 1.100
Glist'red with deaw, as one that seem'd to skorne it: — Hero and Leander 1.390
Home when he came, he seem'd not to be there, — Hero and Leander 2.117

SEEME
And rather had seeme faire [to] Sirens eyes, — Dido 3.4.39 Dido
And these that seeme but silly country Swaines, — 1Tamb 1.2.47 Tamb
and make them seeme as black/As is the Island where the Furies — 2Tamb 3.2.11 Tamb
And seeme to them as if thy sinnes were great, — Jew 1.2.287 Barab
For I will seeme offended with thee for't. — Jew 1.2.303 Barab
Seeme not to know me here before your mother/Lest she mistrust — Jew 2.3.146 Barab
But steale you in, and seeme to see him not; — Jew 2.3.272 Barab
Fye, I am ashamde, how ever that I seeme, — P 124 2.67 Guise
Might seeme <seek> to crosse me in mine enterprise. — P 574 11.39 Navrre
And Epernoune though I seeme milde and calme, — P 893 17.88 King
By yelping hounds puld downe, and seeme to die. — Edw 1.1.70 Gavstn
That makes a king seeme glorious to the world, — Edw 2.2.175 Mortmr
Though every blast it nod, and seeme to fal, — Lucan, First Booke 142
So will thy [triumph] <triumphs> seeme magnificall. — Ovid's Elegies 1.2.28
Where they may sport, and seeme to be unknowne. — Ovid's Elegies 1.5.8
My hard way with my mistrisse would seeme soft. — Ovid's Elegies 2.16.20
The horses seeme, as [thy] <they> desire they knewe. — Ovid's Elegies 3.2.68
And blush, and seeme as you were full of grace. — Ovid's Elegies 3.13.28

SEEMED
Or seemed faire walde in with Egles wings, — Dido 1.1.20 Ganimd
And ever seemed as some new sweete befell. — Ovid's Elegies 2.5.56

SEEMELY
Yet seemely like a Thracian Bacchinall/That tyr'd doth rashly — Ovid's Elegies 1.14.21

SEEMES
No Madame, but it seemes that these are Kings. — Dido 3.1.149 Aeneas
Noble and milde this Persean seemes to be, — 1Tamb 1.2.162 Tamb
It seemes they meant to conquer us my Lord, — 2Tamb 4.3.88 Therid
As to your wisdomes fittest seemes in all. — Edw 4.6.29 Queene
It may be this my exhortation/Seemes harsh, and all unpleasant; — F1718 5.1.45 OldMan
humane flesh, and where [Jove] <it> seemes/Bloudy like Dian, — Lucan, First Booke 441
This seemes the fairest, so doth that to mee, — Ovid's Elegies 2.10.7
Which as it seemes, hence winde and sea bereaves. — Ovid's Elegies 2.16.46
Now, Sabine-like, though chast she seemes to live, — Ovid's Elegies 3.7.61

SEEMING
And seeming lavish, sav'de her maydenhead. — Hero and Leander 2.76
Seeming not woon, yet woon she was at length, — Hero and Leander 2.295

SEEMS
The Turk and his great Emperesse as it seems, — 1Tamb 5.1.470 Tamb
That hides these plaines, and seems as vast and wide, — 2Tamb 1.1.107 Sgsmnd

SEEM'ST
(If as thou seem'st, thou art so meane a man)/And seeke not to — 1Tamb 1.2.8 Zenoc

SEEN (See also SEILDSENE)
And seen in nothing but Epitomies: — P 390 7.30 Guise

SEENE
Which seene to all, though he beheld me not, — Dido 5.1.237 Anna
But tell me, that hast seene him, Menaphon, — 1Tamb 2.1.5 Cosroe
Wherein as in a mirrour may be seene, — 1Tamb 5.1.476 Tamb
Hast thou not seene my horsmen charge the foe, — 2Tamb 3.2.103 Tamb
Cloth'd with a pitchy cloud for being seene. — 2Tamb 4.1.131 Tamb
like armed men/Are seene to march upon the towers of heaven, — 2Tamb 4.1.202 Tamb
thou that hast seene/Millions of Turkes perish by Tamburlaine, — 2Tamb 5.2.24 Callap
Then shall they ne're be seene of Barrabas: — Jew 1.2.250 Abigal
No, Abigall, in this/It is not necessary I be seene. — Jew 1.2.302 Barab
The better; for we love not to be seene: — Jew 1.2.307 Abbass
Noble Lodowicke, I have seene/The strangest sight, in my — Jew 1.2.375 Mthias
As had you seene her 'twould have mov'd your heart, — Jew 1.2.385 Mthias
Why, was there ever seene such villany, — Jew 3.3.1 Ithimr

SEENE (cont.)			
If so, 'tis time that it be seene into:	Jew	3.4.9	Barab
Thus have we view'd the City, seene the sacke,	Jew	5.3.1	Calym
For had your highnesse seene with what a pompe/He entred Paris,	P 872	17.67	Eprnon
I have not seene a dapper jack so briske,	Edw	1.4.412	Mortmr
Inricht with tongues, well seene in Minerals,	F 166	1.1.138	Cornel
seene many boyes with [such pickadevaunts] <beards> I am sure.	F 345	1.4.3	P Robin
As never yet was seene in Germany.	F1188	4.1.34	Mrtino
Now <Since> we have seene the pride of Natures worke <workes>,	F1702	5.1.29	1Schol
O would I had never seene Wittenberg <Wertenberge>, never read	F1841	5.2.45	P Faust
O, I have seene enough to torture me.	F1921	5.2.125	Faust
For such a dreadfull night, was never seene,	F1984	5.3.2	1Schol
you have seene many boyes with such pickadevaunts as I have.	F App	p.229 2	P Clown
Great store of strange and unknown stars were seene/Wandering	Lucan, First Booke	524	
birds/Defil'd the day, and <at night> wilde beastes were seene,	Lucan, First Booke	557	
Cattell were seene that muttered humane speech:	Lucan, First Booke	559	
Sylla's ghost/Was seene to walke, singing sad Oracles,/And	Lucan, First Booke	580	
But Figulus more seene in heavenly mysteries,	Lucan, First Booke	638	
And other Regions, I have seene Philippi:	Lucan, First Booke	693	
And be heereafter seene with native haire.	Ovid's Elegies	1.14.56	
My selfe that better dye with loving may/Had seene, my mother	Ovid's Elegies	2.14.22	
Wherein is seene the givers loving minde:	Ovid's Elegies	2.15.2	
Ere these were seene, I burnt: what will these do?	Ovid's Elegies	3.2.33	
Yet this is lesse, then if he had seene me,	Ovid's Elegies	3.10.15	
Had wilde Hippolitus, Leander seene,	Hero and Leander	1.77	
His secret flame apparantly was seene,	Hero and Leander	2.135	
SEES			
And now she sees thee how will she rejoyce?	Dido	2.1.69	Illion
Well may I view her, but she sees not me.	Dido	2.1.73	Aeneas
As when the Sea-man sees the Hyades/Gather an armye of Cemerian	1Tamb	3.2.76	Agidas
And when she sees our bloody Collours spread,	1Tamb	3.3.159	Tamb
That sees my crowne, my honor and my name,	1Tamb	5.1.260	Bajzth
It may be she sees more in me than I can find in my selfe:	Jew	4.2.33	P Ithimr
And he nor heares, nor sees us what we doe:	P 553	11.18	QnMoth
For Gaveston, will if he [seaze] <zease> <sees> him once,	Edw	2.5.63	Warwck
Who sees not warre sit by the quivering Judge;	Lucan, First Booke	320	
And ere he sees the sea looseth his name;	Lucan, First Booke	402	
Sees not the morne on rosie horses rise.	Ovid's Elegies	1.8.4	
And with the waters sees death neere him thrusts,	Ovid's Elegies	2.11.26	
Who sees it, graunts some deity there is shrowded.	Ovid's Elegies	3.12.8	
SEEST			
My princely robes thou seest are layd aside,	Dido	3.3.3	Dido
Seest thou not death within my wrathfull looks?	2Tamb	3.5.119	Tamb
Thou seest us prest to give the last assault,	2Tamb	5.1.60	Techel
Thou seest they have taken halfe our goods.	Jew	1.2.176	1Jew
I but Ithimore seest thou this?	Jew	3.4.67	Barab
Thou seest thy life, and Malta's happinesse,	Jew	5.2.52	Barab
Here, hold that knife, and when thou seest he comes,	Jew	5.5.37	Barab
And when thou seest the Admirall ride by,	P 87	2.30	Guise
Search Surgeon and resolve me what thou seest.	P1193	22.55	King
Thou seest by nature he is milde and calme,	Edw	1.4.388	MortSr
Yea, but [Levune] <Lewne> thou seest,/These Barons lay their	Edw	3.1.273	Baldck
Why, thou seest he heares thee not.	F App	p.241 151	P Mephst
On tell-tales neckes thou seest the linke-knitt chaines,	Ovid's Elegies	2.2.41	
SEETHING			
Whose scalding drops wil pierce thy seething braines,	2Tamb	4.1.144	Jrslem
SEIGE			
Then raise your seige from faire Damascus walles,	1Tamb	4.4.71	Zenoc
SEILDSENE			
And seildsene costly stones of so great price,	Jew	1.1.28	Barab
SEINE (See SENE)			
SEIZ'D			
my Lord, we have seiz'd upon the goods/And wares of Barabas,	Jew	1.2.132	Offcrs
For they have seiz'd upon thy house and wares.	Jew	1.2.251	Abigal
What, Barabas, whose goods were lately seiz'd?	Jew	1.2.383	Lodowk
Here comes the Jew, had not his goods bin seiz'd,	Jew	2.3.5	1Offcr
Seiz'd all I had, and thrust me out a doores,	Jew	2.3.76	Barab
SEIZE (See also ASCEASED, CEASDE, SEASETH, SEAZE)			
To seize upon the Towne: I, that he seekes.	Jew	1.1.185	Barab
Either pay that, or we will seize on all.	Jew	1.2.89	Govnr
Take my goods too, and seize upon my lands:	Jew	5.1.66	Barab
SEIZED			
And of the other we have seized halfe.	Jew	1.2.135	Offcrs
SEIZETH			
Death seizeth on my heart:	Jew	3.6.38	Abigal
SEL			
I cannot sel him so:	F App	p.239 103	P Faust
SELDOM (See also SEILDSENE)			
And here in Affrick where it seldom raines,	1Tamb	5.1.457	Tamb
SELDOME			
And he is very seldome from my house;	Jew	3.1.10	Curtzn
For his othes are seldome spent in vaine.	P 773	15.31	Eprnon
SELDSEEN (See SEILDSENE)			
SELECTED			
For we have here the chiefe selected men/Of twenty severall	2Tamb	5.2.48	Callap
SELF			
Madam content your self and be resolv'd,	1Tamb	5.1.372	Anippe
Els should I much forget my self, my Lord.	1Tamb	5.1.500	Zenoc
That thou thy self, then County-Pallatine,	2Tamb	1.1.94	Orcan
that of it self was hote enoughe to worke/thy Just degestione	Paris	ms26,p391	Guise
Quiet your self, you shall have the broad seale,	Edw	2.2.147	Edward
Edmund, yeeld thou thy self, or thou shalt die.	Edw	5.3.56	Matrvs
Farmes out her-self on nights for what she can.	Ovid's Elegies	1.10.30	

SELF (cont.)

The self-same day that he asleepe had layd/Inchaunted Argus,	Hero and Leander	1.387	

SELFE

My selfe will see they shall not trouble ye,	Dido	1.2.38	Iarbus
Remember who thou art, speake like thy selfe,	Dido	2.1.100	Dido
O if I speake/I shall betray my selfe:--	Dido	3.1.173	Dido
Pesant, goe seeke companions like thy selfe,	Dido	3.3.21	Dido
That have I not determinde with my selfe.	Dido	5.1.19	Aeneas
Iarbus, I am cleane besides my selfe,	Dido	5.1.63	Aeneas
I, I must be the murderer of my selfe:	Dido	5.1.270	Dido
Now Dido, with these reliques burne thy selfe,	Dido	5.1.292	Dido
helpe Iarbus, Dido in these flames/Hath burnt her selfe, aye me,	Dido	5.1.315	Anna
Brother Cosroe, I find my selfe agreev'd,	1Tamb	1.1.1	Mycet
Ful true thou speakst, and like thy selfe my lord,	1Tamb	1.1.49	Mycet
And then my selfe to faire Zenocrate.	1Tamb	1.2.105	Tamb
We hope your selfe wil willingly restore them.	1Tamb	1.2.117	Agidas
My selfe will bide the danger of the brunt.	1Tamb	1.2.151	Tamb
I yeeld my selfe, my men and horse to thee:	1Tamb	1.2.229	Therid
Thy selfe and them shall never part from me,	1Tamb	1.2.245	Tamb
Fortune her selfe dooth sit upon our Crests.	1Tamb	2.2.73	Meandr
To get the Persean Kingdome to my selfe:	1Tamb	2.5.82	Tamb
Judge by thy selfe Theridamas, not me,	1Tamb	2.5.93	Tamb
Resting her selfe upon my milk-white Tent:	1Tamb	3.3.161	Tamb
When thy great Bassoe-maister and thy selfe,	1Tamb	3.3.173	Zenoc
Prepare thy selfe to live and die my slave.	1Tamb	3.3.207	Zabina
And write my selfe great Lord of Affrica:	1Tamb	3.3.245	Tamb
It shall be said, I made it red my selfe,	1Tamb	4.2.54	Tamb
The countrie wasted where my selfe was borne,	1Tamb	4.4.66	Zenoc
Content thy selfe, his person shall be safe,	1Tamb	4.4.87	Tamb
thou maist thinke thy selfe happie to be fed from my trencher.	1Tamb	4.4.92	P Tamb
I record heaven, her heavenly selfe is cleare:	1Tamb	5.1.487	Tamb
it out, or manage armes/Against thy selfe or thy confederates:	2Tamb	1.1.129	Sgsmnd
My crowne, my selfe, and all the power I have,	2Tamb	1.3.115	Therid
If thou wilt proove thy selfe a perfect God,	2Tamb	2.2.56	Orcan
And when we enter in, not heaven it selfe/Shall ransome thee,	2Tamb	3.3.27	Therid
Mother dispatch me, or Ile kil my selfe,	2Tamb	3.4.26	Sonne
Killing my selfe, as I have done my sonne,	2Tamb	3.4.35	Olymp
Made of the mould whereof thy selfe consists,	2Tamb	4.1.115	Tamb
I must apply my selfe to fit those tearmes,	2Tamb	4.1.155	Tamb
What, have I slaine her? Villaine, stab thy selfe:	2Tamb	4.2.82	Therid
For I wil cast my selfe from off these walles,	2Tamb	5.1.40	2Citzn
down to the earth/Could not affright you, no, nor I my selfe,	2Tamb	5.1.91	Tamb
Nor yet thy selfe, the anger of the highest,	2Tamb	5.1.104	Govnr
Come downe thy selfe and worke a myracle,	2Tamb	5.1.188	Tamb
But stay, I feele my selfe distempered sudainly.	2Tamb	5.1.218	Tamb
To cure me, or Ile fetch him downe my selfe.	2Tamb	5.3.63	Tamb
chariot wil not beare/A guide of baser temper than my selfe,	2Tamb	5.3.243	Tamb
sent me to know/Whether your selfe will come and custome them.	Jew	1.1.53	1Merch
My selfe in Malta, some in Italy,	Jew	1.1.126	Barab
our state/Assure your selves I'le looke--unto my selfe.	Jew	1.1.173	Barab
Sham'st thou not thus to justifie thy selfe,	Jew	1.2.119	Govnr
Not for my selfe, but aged Barabas:	Jew	1.2.228	Abigal
to forgoe so much/Without provision for thy selfe and me.	Jew	1.2.243	Barab
in distresse/Thinke me so mad as I will hang my selfe,	Jew	1.2.263	Barab
I'le rouse my senses, and awake my selfe.	Jew	1.2.269	Barab
For she has mortified her selfe.	Jew	1.2.341	1Fryar
will I shew my selfe to have more of the Serpent then the Dove;	Jew	2.3.36	P Barab
But to thy selfe smile when the Christians moane.	Jew	2.3.172	Barab
As for my selfe, I walke abroad a nights/And kill sicke people	Jew	2.3.174	Barab
And when he comes, she lockes her selfe up fast;	Jew	2.3.262	Barab
Nay, if you will, stay till she comes her selfe.	Jew	2.3.352	Barab
As I behave my selfe in this, imploy me hereafter.	Jew	2.3.379	Ithimr
My trusty servant, nay, my second [selfe] <life>;	Jew	3.4.15	Barab
run to some rocke and throw my selfe headlong into the sea;	Jew	3.4.40	P Ithimr
And whilst I live use halfe; spend as my selfe;	Jew	3.4.45	Barab
Assure thy selfe thou shalt have broth by the eye.	Jew	3.4.92	Barab
My purse, my Coffer, and my selfe is thine.	Jew	3.4.93	Barab
I could afford to whip my selfe to death.	Jew	4.1.59	Barab
It may be she sees more in me than I can find in my selfe:	Jew	4.2.33	P Ithimr
this Gentlewoman, who as my selfe, and the rest of the family,	Jew	4.2.44	P Pilia
'Tis not thy mony, but thy selfe I weigh:	Jew	4.2.124	Curtzn
That he who knowes I love him as my selfe/Should write in this	Jew	4.3.42	Barab
Oh raskall! I change my selfe twice a day.	Jew	4.4.65	Barab
Thou'st doom'd thy selfe, assault it presently.	Jew	5.1.97	Calym
Tush, send not letters to 'em, goe thy selfe,	Jew	5.2.93	Barab
wel since it is no more/I'le satisfie my selfe with that; nay,	Jew	5.5.22	Barab
Sister, I think your selfe will beare us company.	P 21	1.21	Charls
That right or wrong, thou deale thy selfe a King.	P 148	2.91	Guise
Assure your selfe my good Lord Admirall,	P 262	4.60	Charls
And that I am not more secure my selfe,	P 264	4.62	Charls
But in my latter houre to purge my selfe,	P 402	7.42	Ramus
Comfort your selfe my Lord and have no doubt,	P 541	11.6	Navrre
So, set it down and leave me to my selfe.	P 666	13.10	Duchss
The power of vengeance now incampes it selfe,	P 717	14.20	Navrre
dote on them your selfe,/I know none els but holdes them in	P 763	15.21	Guise
But now I will be King and rule my selfe,	P1070	19.140	King
No remedye, therefore prepare your selfe.	P1097	20.7	1Mur
thie folishe dreame/and lett thee see thie selfe my prysoner	Paris	ms33,p391	Guise
I have some busines, leave me to my selfe.	Edw	1.1.48	Gavstn
Mine unckle heere, this Earle, and I my selfe,	Edw	1.1.82	Mortmr
Thy friend, thy selfe, another Gaveston.	Edw	1.1.143	Edward
Which whiles I have, I thinke my selfe as great,	Edw	1.1.172	Gavstn
Thou from this land, I from my selfe am banisht.	Edw	1.4.118	Edward

SELFE (cont.)

Assure thy selfe thou comst not in my sight.	Edw	1.4.169	Edward
Tis for my selfe I speake, and not for him.	Edw	1.4.219	Queene
Fie Mortimer, dishonor not thy selfe,	Edw	1.4.244	Lncstr
A second mariage twixt thy selfe and me.	Edw	1.4.335	Edward
Leave now to oppose thy selfe against the king,	Edw	1.4.387	MortSr
What needst thou, love, thus to excuse thy selfe?	Edw	2.1.60	Neece
Meane time my lord of Penbrooke and my selfe,	Edw	2.2.122	Warwck
not armor, and thy selfe/Bedaubd with golde, rode laughing at	Edw	2.2.184	Mortmr
Pardon me sweet, I forgot my selfe.	Edw	2.2.230	Edward
Your lordship doth dishonor to your selfe,	Edw	2.6.8	James
Your selfe, and those your chosen companie,	Edw	4.7.6	Abbot
Or if I live, let me forget my selfe.	Edw	5.1.111	Edward
And I my selfe will willinglie subscribe.	Edw	5.2.20	Queene
a letter presently/Unto the Lord of Bartley from our selfe,	Edw	5.2.48	Mortmr
Lie on this bed, and rest your selfe a while.	Edw	5.5.72	Ltborn
As for my selfe, I stand as Joves huge tree,	Edw	5.6.11	Mortmr
Till swolne with cunning of a selfe conceit,	F 20	Prol.20	1Chor
thou dost not presently bind thy selfe to me for seven yeares,	F 361	1.4.19	P Wagner
you may save your selfe a labour, for they are as familiar with	F 364	1.4.22	P Robin
prepare thy selfe, for I will presently raise up two devils to	F 372	1.4.30	P Wagner
I sirra, I'le teach thee to turne thy selfe to a Dog, or a Cat,	F 382	1.4.40	P Wagner
Hell hath no limits, nor is circumscrib'd,/In one selfe place:	F 511	2.1.123	Mephst
Pronounce this thrice devoutly to thy selfe,	F 547	2.1.159	Mephst
'Twas thine own seeking Faustus, thanke thy selfe.	F 555	2.2.4	Mephst
Are laid before me to dispatch my selfe:	F 574	2.2.23	Faust
long e're this, I should have done the deed <slaine my selfe>,	F 575	2.2.24	Faust
So shalt thou shew thy selfe an obedient servant <Do so>,/And	F 652	2.2.101	Lucifr
And then turning my selfe to a wrought Smocke do what I list.	F 668	2.2.117	P Pride
my selfe when I could get none <had no body> to fight withall:	F 689	2.2.138	P Wrath
Choke thy selfe Glutton: What are thou the sixt?	F 704	2.2.153	Faust
And thou shalt turne thy selfe into what shape thou wilt.	F 718	2.2.170	Lucifr
Thy selfe and I, may parly with this Pope:	F 896	3.1.118	Faust
Now Faustus, come prepare thy selfe for mirth,	F 981	3.2.1	Mephst
I'le wing my selfe and forth-with flie amaine/Unto my Faustus	F1136	3.3.49	Mephst
zounds I could eate my selfe for anger, to thinke I have beene	F1243	4.1.89	P Benvol
the Emperour, Il'e be Acteon, and turne my selfe to a Stagge.	F1256	4.1.102	P Benvol
My gracious Lord, you doe forget your selfe,	F1258	4.1.104	Faust
I do thinke my selfe my good Lord, highly recompenced, in that	F1563	4.6.6	P Faust
With all my heart kind Doctor, please thy selfe,	F1623	4.6.66	Duke
hath lost both Germany and the world, yea heaven it selfe:	F1844	5.2.48	P Faust
No Faustus, curse thy selfe, curse Lucifer,	F1973	5.2.177	Faust
At which selfe time the house seem'd all on fire,	F1993	5.3.11	3Schol
and binde your selfe presently unto me for seaven yeeres, or	F App	p.229 24	P Wagner
I will teach thee to turne thy selfe to anything, to a dogge,	F App	p.231 58	P Wagner
What, are you crossing of your selfe?	F App	p.232 18	Faust
my selfe farre inferior to the report men have published,	F App	p.236 12	P Faust
conquer all the earth, then turne thy force/Against thy selfe:	Lucan, First Booke		23
Roome was so great it could not beare it selfe:	Lucan, First Booke		72
O Roome thy selfe art cause of all these evils,	Lucan, First Booke		84
Thy selfe thus shivered out to three mens shares:	Lucan, First Booke		85
that made Rcome/Governe the earth, the sea, the world it selfe,	Lucan, First Booke		110
Albeit the Citty thou wouldst have so ra'st/Be Roome it selfe.	Lucan, First Booke		387
Thou Roome at name of warre runst from thy selfe,	Lucan, First Booke		517
Forbeare to hurt thy selfe in spoyling mee.	Ovid's Elegies		1.2.50
But how thou shouldst behave thy selfe now know;	Ovid's Elegies		1.4.11
I will weepe/And to the dores sight of thy selfe [will] keepe:	Ovid's Elegies		1.4.62
Betrayde her selfe, and yeelded at the last.	Ovid's Elegies		1.5.16
Better I could part of my selfe have wanted.	Ovid's Elegies		1.7.24
To mine owne selfe have I had strength so furious?	Ovid's Elegies		1.7.25
And to my selfe could I be so injurious?	Ovid's Elegies		1.7.26
Or, but for bashfulnesse her selfe would crave.	Ovid's Elegies		1.8.44
My selfe was dull, and faint, to sloth inclinde,	Ovid's Elegies		1.9.41
And to her tentes wild me my selfe addresse.	Ovid's Elegies		1.9.44
Memnon the elfe/Received his cole-blacke colour from thy selfe.	Ovid's Elegies		1.13.32
To please thy selfe, thy selfe put out of minde.	Ovid's Elegies		1.14.38
Cheere up thy selfe, thy losse thou maiest repaire,	Ovid's Elegies		1.14.55
With selfe same woundes he gave, he ought to smart.	Ovid's Elegies		2.3.4
I cannot rule my selfe, but where love please/[Am] <And> driven	Ovid's Elegies		2.4.7
To leave my selfe, that am in love [with all] <withall>,	Ovid's Elegies		2.4.31
My selfe unguilty of this crime I know.	Ovid's Elegies		2.7.28
Greater then these my selfe I not esteeme,	Ovid's Elegies		2.8.13
My [false] <selfe> oathes in Carpathian seas to cast.	Ovid's Elegies		2.8.20
Mine owne desires why should my selfe not flatter?	Ovid's Elegies		2.11.54
My selfe will bring vowed gifts before thy feete,	Ovid's Elegies		2.13.24
If without battell selfe-wrought wounds annoy them,	Ovid's Elegies		2.14.3
My selfe that better dye with loving may/Had seene, my mother	Ovid's Elegies		2.14.21
My selfe poore wretch mine owne gifts now envie.	Ovid's Elegies		2.15.8
I could my selfe by secret Magicke shift.	Ovid's Elegies		2.15.10
Nor she her selfe but first trim'd up discernes.	Ovid's Elegies		2.17.10
I know a wench reports her selfe Corinne,	Ovid's Elegies		2.17.29
(Alas my precepts turne my selfe to smart)/We write, or what	Ovid's Elegies		2.18.20
her selfe she hath forswore,/And yet remaines the face she had	Ovid's Elegies		3.3.1
My selfe would sweare, the wenches true did sweare,	Ovid's Elegies		3.3.45
Against thy selfe, mans nature, thou wert cunning,	Ovid's Elegies		3.7.45
And knocks his bare brest with selfe-angry hands.	Ovid's Elegies		3.8.10
And corne with least part of it selfe returnd.	Ovid's Elegies		3.9.30
Now have I freed my selfe, and fled the chaine,	Ovid's Elegies		3.10.3
Chast Hero to her selfe thus softly said:	Hero and Leander		1.178
Ah simple Hero, learne thy selfe to cherish,	Hero and Leander		1.241
At one selfe instant, she poore soule assaies,	Hero and Leander		1.362
And to the seat of Jove it selfe advaunce,	Hero and Leander		1.467
And she her selfe before the pointed time,	Hero and Leander		2.20

SELFE (cont.)			
And turn'd aside, and to her selfe lamented.	Hero and Leander		2.34
She offers up her selfe a sacrifice,	Hero and Leander		2.48
All headlong throwes her selfe the clouds among/And now Leander	Hero and Leander		2.90
The light of hidden fire it selfe discovers,	Hero and Leander		2.133
And ran into the darke her selfe to hide,	Hero and Leander		2.239
And in her owne mind thought her selfe secure,	Hero and Leander		2.265
And cunningly to yeeld her selfe she sought.	Hero and Leander		2.294
SELFE-ANGRY			
And knocks his bare brest with selfe-angry hands.	Ovid's Elegies		3.8.10
SELFE CONCEIT			
Till swolne with cunning of a selfe conceit,	F 20	Prol.20	1Chor
SELFE SAME			
With selfe same woundes he gave, he ought to smart.	Ovid's Elegies		2.3.4
SELFE-WROUGHT			
If without battell selfe-wrought wounds annoy them,	Ovid's Elegies		2.14.3
SELF-SAME			
The self-same day that he asleepe had layd/Inchaunted Argus,	Hero and Leander		1.387
SELIM			
Then give us leave, great Selim-Calymath.	Jew	1.2.13	Govnr
From the Emperour of Turkey is arriv'd/Great Selim-Calymath,	Jew	1.2.40	Govnr
For Selim-Calymath shall come himselfe,	Jew	3.5.23	Basso
To a solemne feast/I will invite young Selim-Calymath,/Where be	Jew	5.2.97	Barab
Selim, for that, thus saith the Governor,	Jew	5.3.26	Msngr
serve to entertaine/Selim and all his souldiers for a month;	Jew	5.3.31	Msngr
Selim, that there is a monastery/Which standeth as an out-house	Jew	5.3.36	Msngr
Now Selim-Calymath, returne me word/That thou wilt come, and I	Jew	5.5.11	Barab
Will't please thee, mighty Selim-Calymath,	Jew	5.5.57	Barab
No, Selim, doe not flye;	Jew	5.5.68	Govnr
Oh helpe me, Selim, helpe me, Christians.	Jew	5.5.70	Barab
Now Selim note the unhallowed deeds of Jewes:	Jew	5.5.92	Govnr
Nay, Selim, stay, for since we have thee here,	Jew	5.5.97	Govnr
Or Selim ne're returne to Ottoman.	Jew	5.5.114	Govnr
SELIM-CALYMATH			
Then give us leave, great Selim-Calymath.	Jew	1.2.13	Govnr
From the Emperour of Turkey is arriv'd/Great Selim-Calymath,	Jew	1.2.40	Govnr
For Selim-Calymath shall come himselfe,	Jew	3.5.23	Basso
To a solemne feast/I will invite young Selim-Calymath,/Where be	Jew	5.2.97	Barab
Now Selim-Calymath, returne me word/That thou wilt come, and I	Jew	5.5.11	Barab
Will't please thee, mighty Selim-Calymath,	Jew	5.5.57	Barab
SELIMS			
First to surprize great Selims souldiers,	Jew	5.2.118	Barab
SELINUS			
Of [ever] <every> greene Selinus queintly dect/With bloomes	2Tamb	4.3.121	Tamb
SELL (See also SEL, SOULD)			
You will not sell it, wil ye?	1Tamb	2.4.29	Tamb
Receive them free, and sell them by the weight;	Jew	1.1.24	Barab
trade to purchase Townes/By treachery, and sell 'em by deceit?	Jew	5.5.48	Barab
And know my Lord, the Pope will sell his triple crowne,	P 851	17.46	Guise
These will I sell to give my souldiers paye,	Edw	1.1.104	Lncstr
the Mortimers/Are not so poore, but would they sell their land,	Edw	2.2.151	Mortmr
Because we heare Lord Bruse dooth sell his land,	Edw	3.1.53	Edward
Wee'l sell it to a Chimny-sweeper:	F1384	4.2.60	P Benvol
I have no great need to sell him, but if thou likest him for	F1460	4.4.4	P Faust
and he would by no meanes sell him under forty Dollors; so sir,	F1537	4.5.33	P HrsCsr
Will you for gaine have Cupid sell himselfe?	Ovid's Elegies		1.10.17
Why should one sell it, and the other buy it?	Ovid's Elegies		1.10.34
The wench by my fault is set forth to sell.	Ovid's Elegies		3.11.10
SELLING			
each mans mony/And seekes vild wealth by selling of her Cony,	Ovid's Elegies		1.10.22
SELVES			
That thou and I unseene might sport our selves:	Dido	4.4.51	Dido
And wheresoever we repose our selves,	1Tamb	1.2.80	Magnet
Wils us to weare our selves and never rest,	1Tamb	2.7.26	Tamb
For we will scorne they should come nere our selves.	1Tamb	3.3.186	Zenoc
Submit your selves and us to servitude.	1Tamb	5.1.39	Govnr
O then for these, and such as we our selves,	1Tamb	5.1.96	1Virgn
Nor fortune keep them selves from victory.	1Tamb	5.1.406	Arabia
To be esteem'd assurance for our selves,	2Tamb	2.1.39	Baldwn
diet your selves, you knowe I shall have occasion shortly to	2Tamb	3.5.114	P Tamb
Thou shewest the difference twixt our selves and thee/In this	2Tamb	4.1.138	Orcan
shall there concerne our state/Assure your selves I'le looke--	Jew	1.1.173	Barab
And will you basely thus submit your selves/To leave your goods	Jew	1.2.79	Barab
hardly can we brooke/The cruell handling of our selves in this:	Jew	1.2.175	1Jew
We turne into the Ayre to purge our selves:	Jew	2.3.46	Barab
First will we race the City wals our selves,	Jew	3.5.13	Govnr
You shall not need trouble your selves so farre,	Jew	3.5.22	Basso
Your selves shall see it shall not be forgot:	Jew	5.2.71	Barab
water the fish, and by the fish our selves when we eate them.	P 489	9.8	P 2Atndt
To plant our selves with such authoritie,	P 637	12.50	QnMoth
And place our selves in order for the fight.	P 742	14.45	Navrre
Then thus, but none shal heare it but our selves.	Edw	1.4.229	Queene
If we say that we have no sinne we deceive our selves, and	F 69	1.1.41	P Faust
Where shall we place our selves Benvolio?	F1353	4.2.29	Mrtino
Come sirs, prepare your selves in readinesse,	F1420	4.2.96	1Soldr
And stand as Bulwarkes twixt your selves and me,	F1427	4.2.103	Faust
we have determin'd with our selves, that Hellen of Greece was	F1683	5.1.10	P 1Schol
Majesty, we should thinke our selves much beholding unto you.	F1687	5.1.14	P 1Schol
Talke not of me, but save your selves and depart.	F1869	5.2.73	P Faust
The fathers selves leapt from their seats; and flying/Left	Lucan, First Booke		485
To cruell armes their drunken selves did summon.	Ovid's Elegies		2.12.20
SEMBLANCE			
And night made semblance of the hue of hell,	P 63	2.6	Guise

SEMBLANCES			
The royall shapes and warlike semblances/Of Alexander and his	F1170	4.1.16	Mrtino
SEMELE			
When he appear'd to haplesse Semele:	F1784	5.1.111	Faust
Poore Semele, among so many burn'd;	Ovid's Elegies		3.3.37
SEMI			
when the Moon begins/To joine in one her semi-circled hornes:	1Tamb	3.1.12	Bajzth
ancient use, shall beare/The figure of the semi-circled Moone:	2Tamb	3.1.65	Orcan
SEMI-CIRCLED			
when the Moon begins/To joine in one her semi-circled hornes:	1Tamb	3.1.12	Bajzth
ancient use, shall beare/The figure of the semi-circled Moone:	2Tamb	3.1.65	Orcan
SEMINARY			
sorte of English priestes/From Doway to the Seminary at Remes,	P1031	19.101	King
SEMIRAMIS			
Now in the place where faire Semiramis, ...	2Tamb	5.1.73	Tamb
Resembling faire Semiramis going to bed, ...	Ovid's Elegies		1.5.11
SEMPER			
Ego mihimet sum semper proximus.	Jew	1.1.189	Barab
SEMYRAMIS			
land, whose brave Metropolis/Reedified the faire Semyramis,	2Tamb	3.5.37	Orcan
SENAT			
Se impious warre defiles the Senat house, ...	Lucan, First Booke		690
SENATE			
But there's a meeting in the Senate-house, ...	Jew	1.1.167	2Jew
With fierce exclaimes run to the Senate-house, ...	Jew	1.2.232	Abigal
And in the Senate reprehend them all, ...	Jew	1.2.233	Abigal
A watchfull Senate for ordaining lawes, ...	P 593	12.6	QnMoth
The angry Senate urging Grachus deeds, ...	Lucan, First Booke		268
And lawes assailde, and arm'd men in the Senate? . .	Lucan, First Booke		322
to heart/With this vaine terror; but the Court, the Senate;	Lucan, First Booke		484
SENATE-HOUSE			
But there's a meeting in the Senate-house, ...	Jew	1.1.167	2Jew
With fierce exclaimes run to the Senate-house, ...	Jew	1.2.232	Abigal
SENATES			
that Senates tyranny?	Lucan, First Booke		366
SENATOR			
Whilste I cry placet like a Senator.	P 861	17.56	King
SENATORS			
And mightie kings shall be our Senators.	1Tamb	1.2.198	Tamb
SENATS			
draw the Commons minds/To favour thee, against the Senats will,	Lucan, First Booke		276
SENCE			
No breath nor sence, nor motion in them both.	1Tamb	5.1.344	Anippe
a king, thy hart/Pierced deeply with sence of my distresse,	Edw	4.7.10	Edward
But read it thus, and thats an other sence:	Edw	5.4.10	Mortmr
No, nor to any one exterior sence, ...	Hero and Leander		1.271
But know you not that creatures wanting sence, ...	Hero and Leander		2.55
SENCELES			
And rue our ends senceles of life or breath:	Dido	5.1.328	Anna
SENCELESSE			
And leave my body sencelesse as the earth.	1Tamb	3.2.22	Zenoc
make our <your> strokes to wound the sencelesse [aire] <lure>.	1Tamb	3.3.158	Tamb
Then let the stony dart of sencelesse colde, ...	1Tamb	5.1.302	Bajzth
shall breath/Through shady leaves of every sencelesse tree,	2Tamb	2.3.16	Orcan
that is all he gets/Of Gaveston, or else his sencelesse trunck.	Edw	2.5.54	Mortmr
Venus to mockt men lendes a sencelesse eare.	Ovid's Elegies		1.8.86
SENCES			
And sommons all my sences to depart.	1Tamb	2.7.45	Cosroe
nor the Turk/Troubled my sences with conceit of foile, .	1Tamb	5.1.158	Tamb
Summon thy sences, call thy wits together:	Jew	1.1.178	Barab
When all my sences are anoyde with stenche?	Edw	5.3.18	Edward
My sences are deceiv'd, here's nothing writ:	F 468	2.1.80	Faust
SEND			
And every beast the forrest doth send forth, ...	Dido	1.1.161	Achat
To send my thousand horse incontinent, ...	1Tamb	1.1.52	Mycet
Now send Ambassage to thy neighbor Kings, ...	1Tamb	2.5.20	Cosroe
Then shall we send to this triumphing King, ...	1Tamb	2.5.87	Techel
So will I send this monstrous slave to hell, ...	1Tamb	2.6.7	Cosroe
Yet somtimes let your highnesse send for them/To do the work my	1Tamb	3.3.187	Anippe
This arme should send him downe to Erebus, ...	1Tamb	4.1.45	Souldn
Will send up fire to your turning Spheares, ...	1Tamb	4.2.39	Tamb
And madnesse send his damned soule to hell.	1Tamb	5.1.229	Zabina
Send like defence of faire Arabia.	1Tamb	5.1.402	Zenoc
Send woord, Orcanes of Natolia/Confirm'd this league beyond	2Tamb	1.1.148	Orcan
Sigismond will send/A hundred thousand horse train'd to the	2Tamb	1.1.153	Sgsmnd
That Jove shall send his winged Messenger/To bid me sheath my	2Tamb	1.3.166	Tamb
Wil send a deadly lightening to his heart.	2Tamb	4.1.10	Celeb
and of fire/Doth send such sterne affections to his heart.	2Tamb	4.1.176	Trebiz
Wil get his pardon if your grace would send. . . .	2Tamb	5.1.33	1Citzn
If God or Mahomet send any aide.	2Tamb	5.2.11	Callap
Our Turkish swords shal headlong send to hell, ...	2Tamb	5.2.15	Amasia
Will him to send Apollo hether straight, ...	2Tamb	5.3.62	Tamb
And send my soule before my father die, ...	2Tamb	5.3.208	Amyras
Goe send 'um threescore Camels, thirty Mules, ...	Jew	1.1.59	Barab
And send to keepe our Gallies under-saile, ...	Jew	1.2.15	Calym
And for the mony send our messenger.	Jew	1.2.31	Calym
Wee'll send [thee] <the> bullets wrapt in smoake and fire:	Jew	2.2.54	Govnr
and then I say they use/To send their Almes unto the Nunneries:	Jew	3.4.77	Barab
And so did faire Maria send for me:	Jew	3.6.5	1Fryar
I'le make him send me half he has, and glad he scapes so too.	Jew	4.2.67	P Ithimr
Send for a hundred Crownes at least.	Jew	4.2.70	P Pilia
Sirra Barabas, send me a hundred crownes.	Jew	4.2.73	P Ithimr
I charge thee send me three hundred by this bearer, and this	Jew	4.2.75	P Ithimr

SEND (cont.)
Send to the Merchant, bid him bring me silkes, — Jew 4.2.84 Curtzn
told him he were best to send it; then he hug'd and imbrac'd — Jew 4.2.106 P Pilia
as you love your life send me five hundred crowns, and give the — Jew 4.2.117 P Ithimr
Barabas send me three hundred Crownes. — Jew 4.3.1 Barab
And I by him must send three hundred crownes. — Jew 4.3.15 Barab
words, Sir, and send it you, were best see; there's his letter. — Jew 4.3.24 P Pilia
Might he not as well come as send; pray bid him come and fetch — Jew 4.3.26 P Barab
Ha, to the Jew, and send me mony you were best. — Jew 4.4.12 P Ithimr
What wudst thou doe if he should send thee none? — Jew 4.4.13 Pilia
I'le send by word of mouth now; Bid him deliver thee a thousand — Jew 4.4.74 P Ithimr
And I will send amongst the Citizens/And by my letters — Jew 5.2.86 Govnr
Tush, send not letters to 'em, goe thy selfe, — Jew 5.2.93 Barab
And send them for a present to the Pope: — P 317 5.44 Anjoy
Stab him I say and send him to his freends in hell. — P 415 7.55 Guise
To send his power to meet us in the field. — P 712 14.15 Navrre
And send us safely to arrive in France: — P 928 18.29 Navrre
And sends <send> his dutie by these speedye lines, — P1169 22.31 Frier
Ile send my sister England newes of this, — P1189 22.51 King
Agent for England, send thy mistres word, — P1194 22.56 King
Live where thou wilt, ile send thee gould enough, — Edw 1.4.113 Edward
Now send our Heralds to defie the King, — Edw 2.2.110 Lncstr
Weele send his head by thee, let him bestow/His teares on that, — Edw 2.5.52 Mortmr
He will but talke with him and send him backe. — Edw 2.5.59 Arundl
And if they send me not my Gaveston, — Edw 3.1.26 Edward
Then send for unrelenting Mortimer/And Isabell, whose eyes — Edw 5.1.103 Edward
O happie newes, send for the prince my sonne. — Edw 5.2.29 Queene
Send for him out thence, and I will anger him. — Edw 5.5.13 Gurney
That thither thou didst send a murtherer. — Edw 5.6.48 King
Faustus, thou shalt, at midnight I will send for thee; — F 716 2.2.168 Lucifr
I say, least I send you into the Ostry with a vengeance. — F 733 2.3.12 P Robin
And Il'e play Diana, and send you the hornes presently. — F1257 4.1.103 P Faust
send for the knight that was so pleasent with me here of late? — F App p.238 66 P Faust
His body (not his boughs) send forth a shade; — Lucan, First Booke 141
Jove send me more such afternoones as this. — Ovid's Elegies 1.5.26
Chiefely shew him the gifts, which others send: — Ovid's Elegies 1.8.99
The gods send thee no house, a poore old age, — Ovid's Elegies 1.8.113
the wench forth send,/Her valiant lover followes without end. — Ovid's Elegies 1.9.9
And birdes send forth shrill notes from everie bow. — Ovid's Elegies 1.13.8
Now Germany shall captive haire-tyers send thee, — Ovid's Elegies 1.14.45
A woman against late-built Rome did send/The Sabine Fathers, — Ovid's Elegies 2.12.23
Yet when a token of great worth we send, — Hero and Leander 2.80

SENDING
In sending thee unto this curteous Coast: — Dido 1.1.232 Venus
In sending to my issue such a soule, — 2Tamb 4.1.122 Tamb
Touching the sending of this Gaveston, — Edw 2.5.76 Penbrk

SENDS
And all the fruites that plentie els sends forth, — Dido 4.2.15 Iarbus
He sends this Souldans daughter rich and brave, — 1Tamb 1.2.186 Tamb
Or faire Bootes sends his cheerefull light, — 1Tamb 1.2.207 Tamb
Which being wroth, sends lightning from his eies, — 2Tamb 1.3.76 Tamb
my fingers take/A kisse from him that sends it from his soule. — Jew 2.1.59 Barab
My Factor sends me word a Merchant's fled/That owes me for a — Jew 2.3.243 Barab
He sends her letters, bracelets, jewels, rings. — Jew 2.3.259 Barab
No, Mathias, no, but sends them backe,/And when he comes, she — Jew 2.3.261 Barab
Catholickes/Sends Indian golde to coyne me French ecues: — P 118 2.61 Guise
And sends <send> his dutie by these speedye lines, — P1169 22.31 Frier
What forraine prince sends thee embassadors? — Edw 2.2.170 Lncstr
And sends you word, he knowes that die he shall, — Edw 2.5.38 Arundl
My lords, because our soveraigne sends for him, — Edw 3.1.109 Arundl
my selfe to smart)/We write, or what Penelope sends Ulysses, — Ovid's Elegies 2.18.21
Now greatest spectacles the Praetor sends, — Ovid's Elegies 3.2.65
Sends foorth a ratling murmure to the land, — Hero and Leander 1.348

SEND'ST
Why send'st thou not a furious whyrlwind downe, — 2Tamb 5.1.192 Tamb

SENE
What fearfull cries comes from the river [Sene] <Rene>,/That — P 361 7.1 Ramus
Which we have chaste into the river [Sene] <Rene>, — P 418 7.58 Guise

SENSE (See also SENCE)
O cursed tree, hadst thou but wit or sense, — Dido 4.4.139 Dido

SENSELESS (See SENCELESSE)

SENSELESSE
Thinke me to be a senselesse lumpe of clay/That will with every — Jew 1.2.216 Barab

SENSES
Beates forth my senses from this troubled soule, — Dido 2.1.116 Aeneas
I'le rouse my senses, and awake my selfe. — Jew 1.2.269 Barab

SENT (Homograph)
Ulysses sent to our unhappie towne: — Dido 2.1.149 Aeneas
and with this sword/Sent many of their savadge ghosts to hell. — Dido 2.1.212 Aeneas
Which sent an eccho to the wounded King: — Dido 2.1.249 Aeneas
I understand your highnesse sent for me. — Dido 3.1.100 Aeneas
Some came in person, others sent their Legats: — Dido 3.1.152 Dido
Kind clowdes that sent forth such a curteous storme, — Dido 3.4.55 Dido
Which Circes sent Sicheus when he lived: — Dido 4.4.11 Dido
The king of Gods sent me from highest heaven, — Dido 5.1.32 Hermes
Sent from his father Jove, appeard to me, — Dido 5.1.95 Aeneas
Nor sent a thousand ships unto the walles, — Dido 5.1.204 Dido
Sent from the King to overcome us all. — 1Tamb 1.2.112 Souldr
What if you sent the Bassoes of your guard, — 1Tamb 3.1.17 Fesse
late felt frownes/That sent a tempest to my daunted thoughtes, — 1Tamb 3.2.86 Agidas
Against the Woolfe that angrie Themis sent, — 1Tamb 4.3.5 Souldn
could they not as well/Have sent ye out, when first my — 1Tamb 5.1.68 Tamb
That I have sent from sundry foughten fields, — 1Tamb 5.1.466 Tamb

SENT (cont.)			
Forgetst thou that I sent a shower of dartes/Mingled with	2Tamb	1.1.91	Orcan
Sent Herralds out, which basely on their knees/In all your	2Tamb	1.1.96	Orcan
Although he sent a thousand armed men/To intercept this haughty	2Tamb	1.2.70	Almeda
And sent them marching up to Belgasar,	2Tamb	2.1.19	Fredrk
That we have sent before to fire the townes,	2Tamb	3.2.147	Tamb
Supposing amorous Jove had sent his sonne,	2Tamb	4.2.18	Therid
But I have sent volleies of shot to you,	2Tamb	5.1.99	Tamb
And sent from hell to tyrannise on earth,	2Tamb	5.1.111	Govnr
My sword hath sent millions of Turks to hell,	2Tamb	5.1.180	Tamb
now, how Jove hath sent/A present medicine to recure my paine:	2Tamb	5.3.105	Tamb
I sent for Egypt and the bordering Iles/Are gotten up by Nilus	Jew	1.1.42	Barab
and have sent me to know/Whether your selfe will come and	Jew	1.1.52	1Merch
Goe tell 'em the Jew of Malta sent thee, man:	Jew	1.1.66	Barab
That's no lye, for she sent me for him.	Jew	3.4.25	P Ithimr
Nor make enquiry who hath sent it them.	Jew	3.4.81	Barab
And for the Tribute-mony I am sent.	Jew	3.5.10	Basso
The Abbasse sent for me to be confest:	Jew	3.6.3	2Fryar
I sent for him, but seeing you are come/Be you my ghostly	Jew	3.6.11	Abigal
Shall be condemn'd, and then sent to the fire.	Jew	3.6.36	2Fryar
I feare they know we sent the poyson'd broth.	Jew	4.1.26	Barab
He sent a shaggy totter'd staring slave,	Jew	4.3.6	Barab
'Twas sent me for a present from the great Cham.	Jew	4.4.68	Barab
This is the reason that I sent for thee;	Jew	5.2.51	Barab
First, for his Army, they are sent before,	Jew	5.5.25	Barab
Where are those perfumed gloves which I sent/To be poysoned,	P 70	2.13	Guise
The sent whereof doth make my head to ake.	P 171	3.6	OldQn
sent from the President of Paris, that craves accesse unto your	P1156	22.18	P 1Msngr
That hees repeald, and sent for back againe,	Edw	2.1.18	Spencr
I feare me you are sent of pollicie,	Edw	2.3.5	Lncstr
So wish not they Iwis that sent thee hither,	Edw	3.1.152	Edward
When we had sent our messenger to request/He might be spared to	Edw	3.1.234	Edward
This villain's sent to make away the king.	Edw	5.5.21	Matrvs
The Queene sent me, to see how you were used,	Edw	5.5.48	Ltborn
What murtherer? bring foorth the man I sent.	Edw	5.6.49	Mortmr
Was sent me from a Cardinall in France.	F1047	3.2.67	Pope
sent some of his men to attend you with provision fit for your	F1501	4.4.45	P Wagner
now you have sent away my guesse, I pray who shall pay me for	F1667	4.6.110	P Hostss
here is a daintie dish was sent me from the Bishop of Millaine.	F App	p.231 5	P Pope
My Lord, this dish was sent me from the Cardinall of Florence.	F App	p.231 9	P Pope
it, and she has sent me to looke thee out, prethee come away.	F App	p.233 8	P Rafe
Sent aide; so did Alcides port, whose seas/Eate hollow rocks,	Lucan, First Booke		406
Atticke, all lovers are to warre farre sent.	Ovid's Elegies		1.9.2
The painfull Hinde by thee to field is sent,	Ovid's Elegies		1.13.15
Shee pleas'd me, soone I sent, and did her woo,	Ovid's Elegies		2.2.5
Thinke when she reades, her mother letters sent her,	Ovid's Elegies		2.2.19
The parrat from east India to me sent,	Ovid's Elegies		2.6.1
Shee dyes, and with loose haires to grave is sent,	Ovid's Elegies		2.14.39
What gift with me was on her birth day sent,	Ovid's Elegies		3.1.57
But stayd, and after her a letter sent.	Hero and Leander		2.14
SENTENCE			
Adding this golden sentence to our praise;	F 917	3.1.139	Pope
To view the sentence of the reverend Synod,	F1014	3.2.34	1Card
And sentence given in rings of naked swords,	Lucan, First Booke		321
Await the sentence of her scornefull eies:	Hero and Leander		1.123
SENTINEL (See CENTINELS)			
SENUS			
And on the south Senus Arabicus,	2Tamb	4.3.104	Tamb
SEPARATED			
But being separated and remooved,	Hero and Leander		2.127
SEPULCHER			
By Mahomet, my Kinsmans sepulcher,	1Tamb	3.3.75	Bajzth
One minute end our daies, and one sepulcher/Containe our bodies:	2Tamb	3.4.13	Olymp
Shall be their timeles sepulcher, or mine.	Edw	1.2.6	Lncstr
SEPULCHERS			
And bankes raisd higher with their sepulchers:	Edw	1.4.103	Edward
SEPULCHRE			
For ever terme, the Perseans sepulchre,	2Tamb	3.5.19	Callap
(The Perseans Sepulchre) and sacrifice/Mountaines of	2Tamb	3.5.54	Callap
for never sepulchre/Shall grace that base-borne Tyrant	2Tamb	5.2.17	Amasia
These armes of mine shall be thy Sepulchre.	Jew	3.2.11	Govnr
I dye Navarre, come beare me to my Sepulchre.	P1242	22.104	King
SEQUANA			
And Sequana that well could manage steeds;	Lucan, First Booke		426
SEQUEL			
That in the shortned sequel of my life,	1Tamb	5.1.278	Bajzth
SEQUOR			
Italiam non sponte sequor.	Dido	5.1.140	Aeneas
SER			
ser to you that dares make a duke a cuckolde and use a	Paris	ms 1,p390	P Souldr
ser you forestalle the markett and sett upe your standinge	Paris	ms 5,p390	P Souldr
ser where he is your landlorde you take upon you to be his	Paris	ms 9,p390	P Souldr
this is againste the lawe ser:	Paris	ms14,p390	P Souldr
yet I come to keepe you out ser.	Paris	ms16,p390	P Souldr
yow are wellcome ser have at you	Paris	ms16,p390	P Souldr
SERA			
What doctrine call you this? Che sera, sera:	F 74	1.1.46	Faust
SERAPHINS			
The Cherubins and holy Seraphins/That sing and play before the	2Tamb	2.4.26	Tamb
SERES			
fine and thinne/Like to the silke the curious Seres spinne,	Ovid's Elegies		1.14.6
SERGE			
A Velvet cap'de cloake, fac'st before with Serge,	Edw	2.1.34	Spencr

SERGESTUS
Aeneas see, Sergestus or his ghost. Dido 2.1.50 Achat
Sergestus, Illioneus and the rest, Dido 2.1.58 Aeneas
Achates come forth, Sergestus, Illioneus, Dido 4.3.13 Aeneas
Sergestus, beare him hence unto our ships, Dido 5.1.49 Aeneas
SEROUNE
I, I, for this Seroune, and thou shalt [ha't] <hate>. P 351 6.6 Mntsrl
SERPENT
O Serpent that came creeping from the shoare, Dido 5.1.165 Dido
will I shew my selfe to have more of the Serpent then the Dove; Jew 2.3.36 P Barab
the serpent that tempted Eve may be saved, but not Faustus. F1837 5.2.41 P Faust
SERPENTS
Was with two winged Serpents stung to death. Dido 2.1.166 Aeneas
For saving him from Snakes and Serpents stings, Dido 3.2.38 Juno
that in his infancie/Did pash the jawes of Serpents venomous: 1Tamb 3.3.105 Bajzth
Their Spheares are mounted on the serpents head, 2Tamb 2.4.53 Tamb
Adders and serpents, let me breathe a while: F1980 5.2.184 Faust
SERVANT
few of them/To chardge these Dames, and shew my servant death, 1Tamb 5.1.117 Tamb
Aid thy obedient servant Callapine, 2Tamb 5.2.28 Callap
Making the Sea their [servant] <servants>, and the winds/To Jew 1.1.110 Barab
My trusty servant, nay, my second [selfe] <life>; Jew 3.4.15 Barab
Oh trusty Ithimore; no servant, but my friend; Jew 3.4.42 Barab
for your sake, and said what a faithfull servant you had bin. Jew 4.2.109 P Pilia
Never lov'd man servant as I doe Ithimore. Jew 4.3.54 Barab
I am a servant to great Lucifer, F 268 1.3.40 Mephst
that Mephostophilis shall be his servant, and be by him F 486 2.1.98 P Faust
So shalt thou shew thy selfe an obedient servant <Do so>,/And F 652 2.2.101 Lucifr
One thing good servant let me crave of thee, F1759 5.1.86 Faust
He and his servant Wagner are at hand, F1813 5.2.17 Mephst
With Venus game who will a servant grace? Ovid's Elegies 2.7.21
Great Agamemnon lov'd his servant Chriseis. Ovid's Elegies 2.8.12
SERVANTS
Come servants, come bring forth the Sacrifize, Dido 4.2.1 Iarbus
Servants, come fetch these emptie vessels here, Dido 4.2.49 Iarbus
Goe Anna, bid my servants bring me fire. Dido 5.1.278 Dido
papers as our sacrifice/And witnesse of thy servants perjury. 2Tamb 2.2.46 Orcan
Making the Sea their [servant] <servants>, and the winds/To Jew 1.1.110 Barab
And slay his servants that shall issue out. P 299 5.26 Anjoy
Two of my fathers servants whilst he liv'de, Edw 2.2.240 Neece
And place our servants, and our followers/Close in an ambush F1341 4.2.17 Benvol
Our servants, and our Courts at thy command. F1624 4.6.67 Duke
Servants fit for thy purpose thou must hire/To teach thy lover, Ovid's Elegies 1.8.87
She must be honest to thy servants credit. Ovid's Elegies 3.4.36
When I to watch supplyed a servants place. Ovid's Elegies 3.10.12
SERV'D
Oft hath she askt us under whom we serv'd, Dido 2.1.66 Illion
Two hundred thousand footmen that have serv'd/In two set 1Tamb 3.3.18 Bassoe
A souldier, that hath serv'd against the Scot. Edw 1.1.34 3PrMan
and two such Cardinals/Ne're serv'd a holy Pope, as we shall F 942 3.1.164 Faust
I'le tell you the bravest tale how a Conjurer serv'd me; you F1522 4.5.18 P Carter
I'le tell you how he serv'd me: F1525 4.5.21 P Carter
Now sirs, you shall heare how villanously he serv'd mee: F1535 4.5.31 P HrsCsr
But you shall heare how bravely I serv'd him for it; I went me F1547 4.5.43 P HrsCsr
The devils whom Faustus serv'd have torne him thus: F1990 5.3.8 3Schol
That have so oft serv'd pretty wenches dyet. Ovid's Elegies 2.9.24
Shee oft hath serv'd thee upon certaine dayes, Ovid's Elegies 2.13.17
SERVE
Yet manhood would not serve, of force we fled, Dido 2.1.272 Aeneas
Meane time these wanton weapons serve my warre, Dido 3.3.37 Cupid
I must prevent him, wishing will not serve: Dido 4.4.104 Dido
Now serve to chastize shipboyes for their faults, Dido 4.4.157 Dido
And see if those will serve in steed of sailes: Dido 4.4.160 Dido
He loves me to too well to serve me so: Dido 5.1.185 Dido
May serve for ransome to our liberties: 1Tamb 1.2.75 Agidas
Or take him prisoner, and his chaine shall serve/For Manackles, 1Tamb 1.2.147 Tamb
Carkasses/Shall serve for walles and bulwarkes to the rest: 1Tamb 3.3.139 Bajzth
How lik'st thou her Ebea, will she serve? 1Tamb 3.3.178 Zabina
to come by, plucke out that, and twil serve thee and thy wife: 1Tamb 4.4.14 P Tamb
If woords might serve, our voice hath rent the aire, 2Tamb 2.4.121 Therid
And let them equally serve all your turnes. 2Tamb 4.3.73 Tamb
And serve as parcell of my funerall. 2Tamb 5.3.212 Tamb
May serve in perill of calamity/To ransome great Kings from Jew 1.1.31 Barab
the Custome-house/Will serve as well as I were present there. Jew 1.1.58 Barab
us an occasion/Which on the sudden cannot serve the turne. Jew 1.2.240 Barab
Yet I have one left that will serve your turne: Jew 2.3.50 Barab
I will serve you, Sir. Jew 2.3.118 P Slave
Well, let it passe, another time shall serve. Jew 2.3.278 Mthias
Would pennance serve for this my sinne, Jew 4.1.58 Barab
And so could I; but pennance will not serve. Jew 4.1.60 Ithimr
to his prayers, as if hee had had another Cure to serve; well, Jew 4.2.25 P Ithimr
No; but three hundred will not serve his turne. Jew 4.3.20 P Pilia
Not serve his turne, Sir? Jew 4.3.21 P Barab
The price thereof will serve to entertaine/Selim and all his Jew 5.3.30 Msngr
I hope these reasons may serve my princely Sonne, P 223 4.21 QnMoth
your nego argumentum/Cannot serve, sirra: P 398 7.38 Guise
If your commission serve to warrant this, P 475 8.25 Anjoy
My opportunity may serve me fit, P 566 11.31 Navrre
Come Pleshe, lets away whilste time doth serve. P 587 11.52 Navrre
And make him serve thee as thy chaplaine, Edw 1.1.195 Edward
I, if words will serve, if not, I must. Edw 1.2.83 Mortmr
Which of the nobles dost thou meane to serve? Edw 2.1.3 Baldck
Gaveston, short warning/Shall serve thy turne: Edw 2.5.22 Warwck

SERVE (cont.)
If mine will serve, unbowell straight this brest, — Edw 5.3.10 Edward
then belike if I serve you, I shall be lousy. — F 359 1.4.17 P Robin
How now sir, will you serve me now? — F 376 1.4.34 P Wagner
Both love and serve the Germane Emperour, — F1219 4.1.65 Faust
and they shall serve for buttons to his lips, to keepe his — F1387 4.2.63 P Benvol
I thinking that a little would serve his turne, bad him take as — F1528 4.5.24 P Carter
wilt thou serve me, and Ile make thee go like Qui mihi — F App p.229 13 P Wagner
if I should serve you, would you teach me to raise up Banios — F App p.230 56 P Clown
well, Ile folow him, Ile serve him, thats flat. — F App p.231 73 P Clown
[Jove] <it> seemes/Bloudy like Dian, whom the Scythians serve; — Lucan, First Booke 442
Accept him that will serve thee all his youth, — Ovid's Elegies 1.3.5
To serve for pay beseemes not wanton gods. — Ovid's Elegies 1.10.20
To serve a wench if any thinke it shame, — Ovid's Elegies 2.17.1
Yet for her sake whom you have vow'd to serve, — Hero and Leander 1.316

SERVES
In champion grounds, what figure serves you best, — 2Tamb 3.2.63 Tamb
And now and then, stab as occasion serves. — Edw 2.1.43 Spencr
This side that serves thee, a sharpe sword did weare. — Ovid's Elegies 3.7.14

SERVEST
If she discardes thee, what use servest thou for? — Ovid's Elegies 2.3.12

SERVICE (See also SERVISES)
with amitie we yeeld/Our utmost service to the faire Cosroe. — 1Tamb 2.3.34 Techel
Emperour in humblest tearms/I vow my service to your Majestie, — 1Tamb 2.5.16 Meandr
(sacred Emperour)/The prostrate service of this wretched towne. — 1Tamb 5.1.100 1Virgn
Meet for your service on the sea, my Lord, — 2Tamb 1.3.123 Therid
When this is learn'd for service on the land, — 2Tamb 3.2.83 Tamb
To false his service to his Soveraigne, — 2Tamb 3.5.88 Tamb
and the rest of the family, stand or fall at your service. — Jew 4.2.44 P Pilia
As to the service of the eternall God. — P 413 7.53 Ramus
Whose service he may still commaund till death. — P1149 22.11 Navrre
Such as desire your worships service. — Edw 1.1.25 Poorem
Then so am I, and live to do him service, — Edw 1.4.421 Mortmr
Thy service Spencer shalbe thought upon. — Edw 2.1.80 Neece
Your honors in all service, [Levune] <Lewne>. — Edw 4.3.37 P Spencr
Shall do good service to her Majestie, — Edw 4.6.74 Mortmr
To do your highnes service and devoire, — Edw 5.1.133 Bartly
nakednesse, I know the Villaines out of service, and so hungry, — F 349 1.4.7 P Wagner
So he will buy my service with his soule. — F 421 2.1.33 Mephst
dutie, I do yeeld/My life and lasting service for your love. — F1819 5.2.23 Wagner
the vilaine is bare, and out of service, and so hungry, that I — F App p.229 7 P Wagner
Yet for long service done, reward these men, — Lucan, First Booke 341
Let poore men show their service, faith, and care; — Ovid's Elegies 1.10.57
Thy service for nights scapes is knowne commodious/And to give — Ovid's Elegies 1.11.3
Horse freed from service range abroad the woods. — Ovid's Elegies 2.9.22
His side past service, and his courage spent. — Ovid's Elegies 3.10.14
Dutifull service may thy love procure, — Hero and Leander 1.220

SERVICEABLE
Be alwaies serviceable to us three: — F 150 1.1.122 Valdes

SERVILE
Too servile <The devill> and illiberall for mee. — F 63 1.1.35 Faust
I'le make my servile spirits to invent. — F 124 1.1.96 Faust
When every servile groome jeasts at my wrongs, — F1329 4.2.5 Benvol
Nor servile water shalt thou drinke for ever. — Ovid's Elegies 1.6.26
And still inrich the loftie servile clowne, — Hero and Leander 1.481

SERVISES
Browne Almonds, Servises, ripe Figs and Dates, — Dido 4.5.5 Nurse

SERVITORS (See also SERVITURES)
See where her servitors passe through the hall/Bearing a — Dido 2.1.70 Serg
And have old servitors in high esteeme, — Edw 3.1.168 Herald
what store of ground/For servitors to till? — Lucan, First Booke 345

SERVITUDE
And must maintaine my life exempt from servitude. — 1Tamb 1.2.31 Tamb
destruction/Redeeme you from this deadly servitude. — 1Tamb 3.2.34 Agidas
Is far from villanie or servitude. — 1Tamb 3.2.38 Zenoc
Submit your selves and us to servitude. — 1Tamb 5.1.39 Govnr
In this obscure infernall servitude? — 1Tamb 5.1.254 Zabina
That thus intreat their shame and servitude? — 2Tamb 5.1.37 Govnr
abject our princely mindes/To vile and ignominious servitude. — 2Tamb 5.1.141 Orcan
Or you released of this servitude. — Jew 5.4.7 Govnr

SERVITURES
with the scraps/My servitures shall bring the from my boord. — 1Tamb 4.2.88 Tamb

SERV'ST
The god thou serv'st is thine owne appetite, — F 399 2.1.11 Faust

SESSIONS
The Sessions day is criticall to theeves, — Jew 2.3.105 Barab
To morrow is the Sessions; you shall to it. — Jew 4.1.199 Barab
I do not doubt but to see you both hang'd the next Sessions. — F 213 1.2.20 P Wagner

SESTOS
The one Abydos, the other Sestos hight. — Hero and Leander 1.4
At Sestos, Hero dwelt; Hero the faire, — Hero and Leander 1.5
The men of wealthie Sestos, everie yeare, — Hero and Leander 1.91
Went Hero thorow Sestos, from her tower/To Venus temple, — Hero and Leander 1.132
The towne of Sestos cal'd it Venus glasse. — Hero and Leander 1.142
Why vowest thou then to live in Sestos here, — Hero and Leander 1.227
Which made his love through Sestos to bee knowne, — Hero and Leander 2.111

SE'T
And you shall se't rebated with the blow. — 2Tamb 4.2.70 Olymp

SET
Whose lookes set forth no mortall forme to view, — Dido 1.1.189 Aeneas
in stead of him/Will set thee on her lap and play with thee: — Dido 2.1.325 Venus
When first you set your foote upon the shoare, — Dido 3.3.53 Achat
Ile set the casement open that the windes/May enter in, and — Dido 4.4.130 Dido

SET (cont.)			
Where thou and false Achates first set foote:	Dido	5.1.175	Dido
These are his words, Meander set them downe.	1Tamb	1.1.94	Mycet
In happy hower we have set the Crowne/Upon your kingly head,	1Tamb	2.1.50	Ortyg
And set it safe on my victorious head.	1Tamb	2.3.54	Cosroe
(for say not I intreat)/Not once to set his foot in Affrica,	1Tamb	3.1.28	Bajzth
footmen that have serv'd/In two set battels fought in Grecia:	1Tamb	3.3.19	Bassoe
This hand shal set them on your conquering heads:	1Tamb	3.3.31	Tamb
shall curse the time/That Tamburlaine set foot in Affrica.	1Tamb	3.3.60	Tamb
Yet set a ransome on me Tamburlaine.	1Tamb	3.3.261	Bajzth
Thy princely daughter here shall set thee free.	1Tamb	5.1.436	Tamb
Then let us set the crowne upon her head,	1Tamb	5.1.501	Therid
And here's the crown my Lord, help set it on.	1Tamb	5.1.505	Usumc
Neere Guyrons head doth set his conquering feet,	2Tamb	1.1.17	Gazell
Wagons of gold were set before my tent:	2Tamb	1.1.99	Orcan
Which in despight of them I set on fire:	2Tamb	1.3.213	Therid
And here will I set up her stature <statue>/And martch about it	2Tamb	2.4.140	Tamb
Thou shalt be set upon my royall tent.	2Tamb	3.2.37	Tamb
And set his warlike person to the view/Of fierce Achilles,	2Tamb	3.5.67	Tamb
To see thy foot-stoole set upon thy head,	2Tamb	5.3.29	Usumc
And set blacke streamers in the firmament,	2Tamb	5.3.49	Tamb
your absence in the field, offers to set upon us presently.	2Tamb	5.3.104	P 3Msngr
Goe Officers and set them straight in shew.	Jew	2.2.43	Govnr
Hoping ere long to set the house a fire;	Jew	2.3.88	Barab
Feare not, I'le so set his heart a fire,	Jew	2.3.375	Ithimr
Till I have set 'em both at enmitie.	Jew	2.3.383	Barab
But thou wert set upon extreme revenge,	Jew	3.3.42	Abigal
Among the rest beare this, and set it there;	Jew	3.4.78	Barab
Oh my sweet Ithimore go set it downe/And come againe so soone	Jew	3.4.108	Barab
which is there/Set downe at large, the Gallants were both	Jew	3.6.29	Abigal
Here is my hand that I'le set Malta free:	Jew	5.2.95	Barab
And with his Bashawes shall be blithely set,	Jew	5.5.38	Barab
Set me to scale the high Peramides,	P 100	2.43	Guise
And thereon set the Diadem of Fraunce,	P 101	2.44	Guise
What order wil you set downe for the Massacre?	P 229	4.27	QnMoth
At which they all shall issue out and set the streetes.	P 237	4.35	Guise
That they which have already set the street/May know their	P 328	5.55	Guise
So, set it down and leave me to my selfe.	P 666	13.10	Duchss
Of whose encrease I set some longing hope,	P 689	13.33	Guise
Who set themselves to tread us under foot,	P 702	14.5	Navrre
his market, and set up your standing where you should not:	P 809	17.4	P Souldr
First let us set our hand and seale to this,	P 890	17.85	King
O my Lord, I am one of them that is set to murder you.	P 992	19.62	P 3Mur
Wigmore shall flie, to set my unckle free.	Edw	2.2.196	Mortmr
To set his brother free, no more but so.	Edw	5.2.33	BshpWn
Hang him I say, and set his quarters up,	Edw	5.6.53	King
I will set my countenance like a Precisian, and begin to speake	F 213	1.2.20	P Wagner
See <come> Faustus, here is <heres> fire, set it on.	F 459	2.1.71	Mephst
Whose bankes are set with Groves of fruitfull Vines.	F 786	3.1.8	Faust
O hellish spite,/Your heads are all set with hornes.	F1442	4.3.12	Benvol
late by horse flesh, and this bargaine will set me up againe.	F1465	4.4.9	P HrsCsr
Go pacifie their fury, set it ope,	F1589	4.6.32	Duke
In what resplendant glory thou hadst set/In yonder throne, like	F1904	5.2.108	GdAngl
I shall say, As I was sometime solitary set, within my Closet,	F App	p.236 18	P Emper
A towne with one poore church set them at oddes.	Lucan, First Booke		97
Who'le set the faire treste [sunne] <sonne> in battell ray,	Ovid's Elegies		1.1.15
On mooved hookes set ope the churlish dore.	Ovid's Elegies		1.6.2
Nor set my voyce to sale in everie cause?	Ovid's Elegies		1.15.6
And in the midst thereof, set my soule going,	Ovid's Elegies		2.10.36
My foote upon the further banke to set.	Ovid's Elegies		3.5.12
The wench by my fault is set forth to sell.	Ovid's Elegies		3.11.10
Her gate by my hands is set open wide.	Ovid's Elegies		3.11.12
This last end to my Elegies is set,	Ovid's Elegies		3.14.2
Which limping Vulcan and his Cyclops set:	Hero and Leander		1.152
A Diamond set in lead his worth retaines,	Hero and Leander		1.215
Set in a forren place, and straight from thence,	Hero and Leander		2.119
and higher set/The drooping thoughts of base declining soules,	Hero and Leander		2.256
SETS			
The cursed Scythian sets on all their townes,	2Tamb	3.1.55	Trebiz
The King of Fraunce sets foote in Normandie.	Edw	2.2.9	Mortmr
SETST			
Thou setst their labouring hands to spin and card.	Ovid's Elegies		1.13.24
SETT			
the markett and sett upe your standinge where you shold not:	Paris	ms 6,p390	P Souldr
SETTING			
Neoptolemus/Setting his speare upon the ground, leapt forth,	Dido	2.1.184	Aeneas
In setting Christian villages on fire,	Jew	2.3.203	Ithimr
thine, in setting Bruno free/From his and our professed enemy,	F1206	4.1.52	Emper
Like twilight glimps at setting of the sunne,	Ovid's Elegies		1.5.5
To move her feete unheard in [setting] <sitting> downe.	Ovid's Elegies		3.1.52
SETTLE			
Settle thy studies Faustus, and begin/To sound the depth of	F 29	1.1.1	Faust
SEVEN			
But of them all scarce seven doe anchor safe,	Dido	1.1.222	Aeneas
he had seven thousand sheepe,/Three thousand Camels, and two	Jew	1.2.182	Barab
That wee might sleepe seven yeeres together afore we wake.	Jew	4.2.131	Ithimr
thou dost not presently bind thy selfe to me for seven yeares,	F 361	1.4.19	P Wagner
Nine, the seven Planets, the Firmament, and the Emperiall	F 610	2.2.59	P Mephst
seven deadly sinnes appeare to thee in their owne proper shapes	F 655	2.2.104	P Belzeb
Know that this City stands upon seven hils,	F 811	3.1.33	Mephst
Seven golden [keys] <seales> fast sealed with seven seales,	F 933	3.1.155	Pope
In token of our seven-fold power from heaven,	F 934	3.1.156	Pope
The Planets seven, the gloomy aire,	F 999	3.2.19	Mephst

SEVEN (cont.)
Ajax, maister of the seven-fould shield,/Butcherd the flocks he   Ovid's Elegies   1.7.7
SEVEN-FOLD
In token of our seven-fold power from heaven,   F 934   3.1.156   Pope
SEVEN-FOULD
Ajax, maister of the seven-fould shield,/Butcherd the flocks he   Ovid's Elegies   1.7.7
SEVENTH
And what are you Mistris Minkes, the seventh and last?   F 707   2.2.159   Faust
The seventh day came, none following mightst thou see,   Ovid's Elegies   2.6.45
SEVENTY
From Soria with seventy thousand strong,   2Tamb   3.1.57   Soria
SEVER
Or roaring Cannons sever all thy joints,   1Tamb   5.1.223   Bajzth
SEVERAL
<examine> them of their <several> names and dispositions.   F 661   2.2.110   P Belzeb
by these ten blest ensignes/And all thy several triumphs,   Lucan, First Booke   376
SEVERALL
rest and have one Epitaph/Writ in as many severall languages,   2Tamb   2.4.135   Tamb
chiefe selected men/Of twenty severall kingdomes at the least: 2Tamb   5.2.49   Callap
and underneath/In severall places are field-pieces pitch'd,   Jew   5.5.27   Barab
Make severall kingdomes of this monarchie,   Edw   1.4.70   Edward
That this your armie going severall waies,   Edw   2.4.42   Queene
Are but obey'd in their severall Provinces: F 85   1.1.57   Faust
Straight summon'd he his severall companies/Unto the standard: Lucan, First Booke   297
And like a planet, mooving severall waies,   Hero and Leander   1.361
SEVERALLY
To make me shew them favour severally,   Jew   3.3.38   Abigal
SEVERE
So Cupid wills, farre hence be the severe,   Ovid's Elegies   2.1.3
And I would be none of the Gods severe.   Ovid's Elegies   3.3.46
Till then, rough was her father, she severe,   Ovid's Elegies   3.7.31
SEVERELIE
cause,/That here severelie we will execute/Upon thy person: Edw   2.5.23   Warwck
SEVERITY
By suffring much not borne by thy severity.   Ovid's Elegies   3.1.48
SEW
Offer their mines (to sew for peace) to me,   1Tamb   3.3.264   Tamb
SEWE
Why, what are you, or wherefore doe you sewe?   Dido   1.2.3   Iarbus
SEX
Without respect of Sex, degree or age,   1Tamb   4.1.62   2Msngr
Shead from the heads and hearts of all our Sex,   1Tamb   5.1.26   1Virgn
But how unseemly is it for my Sex,   1Tamb   5.1.174   Tamb
SEXE
O wicked sexe, perjured and unjust,   P 693   13.37   Guise
SEXIOUS
To overthrow those [sectious] <sexious> <factious> Puritans: P 850   17.45   Guise
SEXTON'S
And alwayes kept the Sexton's armes in ure/With digging graves   Jew   2.3.184   Barab
SEXTUS
Ah Sextus, be reveng'd upon the King,   P1010   19.80   Guise
And bids thee whet thy sword on Sextus bones,   P1237   22.99   King
SHADE
His body (not his boughs) send forth a shade;   Lucan, First Booke   141
Wee Macer sit in Venus slothfull shade,   Ovid's Elegies   2.18.3
Or shade, or body was [I] <Io>, who can say?   Ovid's Elegies   3.6.16
Under whose shade the Wood-gods love to bee.   Hero and Leander   1.156
SHADES
Or in these shades deceiv'st mine eye so oft?   Dido   1.1.244   Aeneas
Sleepe my sweete nephew in these cooling shades,   Dido   2.1.334   Venus
piller led'st/The sonnes of Israel through the dismall shades,   Jew   2.1.13   Barab
But in times past I fear'd vaine shades, and night,   Ovid's Elegies   1.6.9
SHADIE
Heere while I walke hid close in shadie grove,   Ovid's Elegies   3.1.5
SHADOW
And shadow his displeased countenance,   1Tamb   5.1.58   2Virgn
And in the shadow of the silent night/Doth shake contagion from   Jew   2.1.3   Barab
Come, let thy shadow parley with king Edward.   Edw   2.6.14   Warwck
Now that the gloomy shadow of the night <earth>,   F 229   1.3.1   Faust
Strooke with th'earths suddaine shadow waxed pale,   Lucan, First Booke   537
As thus she spake, my shadow me betraide,   Ovid's Elegies   1.8.109
That leapt into the water for a kis/Of his owne shadow, and   Hero and Leander   1.75
SHADOWDE
If her white necke be shadowde with blacke haire,   Ovid's Elegies   2.4.41
SHADOWES
Like to the shadowes of Pyramides,   1Tamb   4.2.103   Tamb
But perfect shadowes in a sun-shine day?   Edw   5.1.27   Edward
These are but shadowes, not substantiall.   F1259   4.1.105   Faust
To hoarse scrich-owles foule shadowes it allowes,   Ovid's Elegies   1.12.19
SHADOWING
shadowing in her browes/Triumphes and Trophees for my   1Tamb   5.1.512   Tamb
Shadowing more beauty in their Airie browes,   F 155   1.1.127   Valdes
SHADOWS
Whose [shadows] made all Europe honour him.   F 145   1.1.117   Faust
SHADY (See also SHADIE)
shall breath/Through shady leaves of every sencelesse tree,   2Tamb   2.3.16   Orcan
SHAFT
And with one shaft provoke ten thousand darts: Dido   3.3.72   Iarbus
Tooke out the shaft, ordaind my hart to shiver: Ovid's Elegies   1.1.26
And shot a shaft that burning from him went,   Hero and Leander   1.372
SHAFTS
Such bow, such quiver, and such golden shafts,   Dido   2.1.311   Venus
And to a Scepter chaunge his golden shafts,   Dido   3.2.57   Venus

SHAFTS (cont.)
Till Cupids bow, and fierie shafts be broken, — Ovid's Elegies 1.15.27
Here of themselves thy shafts come, as if shot, — Ovid's Elegies 2.9.37

SHAG
To have a shag-rag knave to come [demand]/Three hundred — Jew 4.3.61 Barab

SHAGGIE
Wretched Ixions shaggie footed race, — Hero and Leander 1.114

SHAGGY
He sent a shaggy totter'd staring slave, — Jew 4.3.6 Barab

SHAG-RAG
To have a shag-rag knave to come [demand]/Three hundred — Jew 4.3.61 Barab

SHAKE
Now Turkes and Tartars shake their swords at thee, — 1Tamb 1.1.16 Cosroe
That roaring, shake Damascus turrets downe. — 1Tamb 4.1.3 Souldn
Shake with their waight in signe of feare and griefe: — 1Tamb 5.1.349 Zenoc
Wilt thou have war, then shake this blade at me, — 2Tamb 1.1.83 Sgsmnd
And now come we to make his sinowes shake, — 2Tamb 2.2.9 Gazell
of the silent night/Doth shake contagion from her sable wings; — Jew 2.1.4 Barab
Oh how I long to see him shake his heeles. — Jew 4.1.140 Ithimr
Ile make her shake off love with her heeles. — P 782 15.40 Mugern
You that are princely borne should shake him off, — Edw 1.4.81 Warwck
I am that Cedar, shake me not too much, — Edw 2.2.38 Edward
And shake off smooth dissembling flatterers: — Edw 3.1.169 Herald
And shake off all our fortunes equallie? — Edw 4.2.20 SrJohn
And what made madding people shake off peace. — Lucan, First Booke 69
Made all shake hands as once the Sabines did; — Lucan, First Booke 118
Shake off these wrinckles that thy front assault, — Ovid's Elegies 1.8.45
as might make/Wrath-kindled Jove away his thunder shake. — Ovid's Elegies 2.5.52
And coole gales shake the tall trees leavy spring, — Ovid's Elegies 2.16.36
To expiat which sinne, kisse and shake hands, — Hero and Leander 1.309

SHAKED
Doest joy to have thy hooked Arrowes shaked, — Ovid's Elegies 2.9.13

SHAKEN
That shaken thrise, makes Natures buildings quake, — Dido 1.1.11 Jupitr
Hath shaken off the thraldome of the tower, — Edw 4.2.41 Mortmr
Or slender eares, with gentle Zephire shaken, — Ovid's Elegies 1.7.55

SHAKES
And fall like mellowed fruit, with shakes of death, — 1Tamb 2.1.47 Cosroe
That shakes his sword against thy majesty, — 2Tamb 5.1.196 Tamb
But everie jointe shakes as I give it thee: — Edw 5.5.86 Edward
Tis not enough, she shakes your record off, — Ovid's Elegies 3.3.19
describe, but hee/That puls or shakes it from the golden.tree: — Hero and Leander 2.300

SHAKETH
Or withered leaves that Autume shaketh downe: — 1Tamb 4.1.32 Souldn

SHAKING
Our quivering Lances shaking in the aire, — 1Tamb 2.3.18 Tamb
Shaking their swords, their speares and yron bils, — 1Tamb 4.1.25 2Msngr
Shaking her silver tresses in the aire, — 1Tamb 5.1.141 Tamb
Where shaking ghosts with ever howling grones, — 1Tamb 5.1.245 Zabina
Shaking the burthen mighty Atlas beares: — 2Tamb 4.1.129 Tamb
the uglie monster death/Shaking and quivering, pale and wan for — 2Tamb 5.3.68 Tamb
Nodding and shaking of thy spangled crest, — Edw 2.2.186 Mortmr
Shaking her snakie haire and crooked pine/With flaming toppe, — Lucan, First Booke 571
And shaking sobbes his mouth for speeches beares. — Ovid's Elegies 3.8.12

SHAKT
Which being not shakt <slackt>, I saw it die at length. — Ovid's Elegies 1.2.12

SHAL
What length or bredth shal this brave towne containe? — Dido 5.1.16 Achat
I heare them come, shal we encounter them? — 1Tamb 1.2.149 Techel
Shal want my heart to be with gladnes pierc'd/To do you honor — 1Tamb 1.2.250 Therid
Shal have a government in Medea: — 1Tamb 2.2.33 Meandr
Their carelesse swords shal lanch their fellowes throats/And — 1Tamb 2.2.49 Meandr
What thinkst thou man, shal come of our attemptes? — 1Tamb 2.3.3 Cosroe
For presently Techelles here shal haste, — 1Tamb 2.5.94 Tamb
This hand shal set them on your conquering heads: — 1Tamb 3.3.31 Tamb
Then when the Sky shal waxe as red as blood, — 1Tamb 4.2.53 Tamb
and she shal looke/That these abuses flow not from her tongue: — 1Tamb 4.2.69 Zenoc
There whiles he lives, shal Bajazeth be kept, — 1Tamb 4.2.85 Tamb
must you be first shal feele/The sworne destruction of — 1Tamb 5.1.65 Tamb
to prevent/That which mine honor sweares shal be perform'd: — 1Tamb 5.1.107 Tamb
Shal give the world to note, for all my byrth, — 1Tamb 5.1.188 Tamb
Then shal I die with full contented heart, — 1Tamb 5.1.417 Arabia
Shal now, adjoining al their hands with mine, — 1Tamb 5.1.493 Tamb
Himselfe in presence shal unfold at large. — 2Tamb Prol.9 Prolog
Our Turky blades shal glide through al their throats, — 2Tamb 1.1.31 Orcan
othes/Sign'd with our handes, each shal retaine a scrowle: — 2Tamb 1.1.144 Orcan
When heaven shal cease to moove on both the poles/And when the — 2Tamb 1.3.12 Tamb
my souldiers march/Shal rise aloft and touch the horned Moon, — 2Tamb 1.3.14 Tamb
Yes father, you shal see me if I live, — 2Tamb 1.3.54 Celeb
Wel lovely boies, you shal be Emperours both, — 2Tamb 1.3.96 Tamb
They shal Casane, and tis time yfaith. — 2Tamb 1.3.185 Tamb
From paine to paine, whose change shal never end: — 2Tamb 2.3.26 Orcan
And here this mournful streamer shal be plac'd/Wrought with the — 2Tamb 3.2.19 Amyras
How say ye Souldiers, Shal we not? — 2Tamb 3.3.9 Techel
Shal play upon the bulwarks of thy hold/Volleies of ordinance — 2Tamb 3.3.24 Therid
By Mahomet not one of them shal live. — 2Tamb 3.5.17 Callap
Shal end the warlike progresse he intends, — 2Tamb 3.5.23 Orcan
As ye shal curse the byrth of Tamburlaine. — 2Tamb 3.5.89 Tamb
By Mahomet he shal be tied in chaines, — 2Tamb 3.5.92 Jrslem
But as for you (Viceroy) you shal have bits, — 2Tamb 3.5.103 Tamb
our mighty hoste/Shal bring thee bound unto the Generals tent. — 2Tamb 3.5.111 Trebiz
any Element/Shal shrowde thee from the wrath of Tamburlaine. — 2Tamb 3.5.127 Tamb
So he shal, and weare thy head in his Scutchion. — 2Tamb 3.5.138 P Orcan

SHAL (cont.)

Content my Lord, but what shal we play for?	2Tamb	4.1.63	P Perdic
Who shal kisse the fairest of the Turkes Concubines first, when	2Tamb	4.1.64	P Calyph
Shal we let goe these kings again my Lord/To gather greater	2Tamb	4.1.82	Amyras
Now you shal feele the strength of Tamburlain,	2Tamb	4.1.135	Tamb
You shal be fed with flesh as raw as blood,	2Tamb	4.3.18	Tamb
And now themselves shal make our Pageant,	2Tamb	4.3.90	Tamb
Shal al be loden with the martiall spoiles/We will convay with	2Tamb	4.3.105	Tamb
Then shal my native city Samarcanda/And christall waves of	2Tamb	4.3.107	Tamb
For there my Pallace royal shal be plac'd:	2Tamb	4.3.111	Tamb
Whose shyning Turrets shal dismay the heavens,	2Tamb	4.3.112	Tamb
And in my helme a triple plume shal spring,	2Tamb	4.3.116	Tamb
And that shal bide no more regard of parlie.	2Tamb	5.1.61	Techel
What shal be done with their wives and children my Lord.	2Tamb	5.1.168	P Techel
Whom I have thought a God? they shal be burnt.	2Tamb	5.1.176	Tamb
Doubt not my lord, but we shal conquer him.	2Tamb	5.2.12	Amasia
Our Turkish swords shal headlong send to hell,	2Tamb	5.2.15	Amasia
Ah friends, what shal I doe, I cannot stand,	2Tamb	5.3.51	Tamb
Why, shal I sit and languish in this paine?	2Tamb	5.3.56	Tamb
No doubt, but you shal soone recover all.	2Tamb	5.3.99	Phsitn
And shal I die, and this unconquered?	2Tamb	5.3.158	Tamb
Shal still retaine my spirit, though I die,	2Tamb	5.3.173	Tamb
hee that denies to pay, shal straight become a Christian.	Jew	1.2.73	P Reader
you dine with me, Sir, and you shal be most hartily poyson'd.	Jew	4.3.30	P Barab
I shal be found, and then twil greeve me more.	Edw	1.4.132	Gavstn
Then thus, but none shal heare it but our selves.	Edw	1.4.229	Queene
And shall or Warwicks sword shal smite in vaine.	Edw	3.1.199	Warwck
[As in this furnace God shal try my faith],	F1792	5.1.119A	OldMan
O what may <shal> we do to save Faustus?	F1868	5.2.72	P 2Schol
about thee into familiars, and they shal teare thee in peeces.	F App	p.229 26	P Wagner
Anon you shal heare a hogge grunt, a calfe bleate, and an asse	F App	p.232 27	P Faust
and so by that meanes I shal see more then ere I felt, or saw	F App	p.233 4	P Robin
my maister and mistris shal finde that I can reade, he for his	F App	p.233 15	P Robin
O brave Robin, shal I have Nan Spit, and to mine owne use?	F App	p.234 29	P Rafe
our horses shal eate no hay as long as this lasts.	F App	p.234 3	P Robin
Misericordia pro nobis, what shal I doe?	F App	p.235 30	P Robin
or they that shal hereafter possesse our throne, shal (I feare	F App	p.236 21	P Emper
shal (I feare me) never attaine to that degree of high renowne	F App	p.236 22	P Emper
shal appeare before your Grace, in that manner that they best	F App	p.237 47	P Faust
I doubt not shal sufficiently content your Imperiall majesty.	F App	p.237 49	P Faust
or moale in her necke, how shal I know whether it be so or no?	F App	p.238 61	P Emper
his labour; wel, this tricke shal cost him fortie dollers more.	F App	p.241 166	P Faust
tell me, and you shal have it.	F App	p.242 6	P Faust
being old/Must shine a star) shal heaven (whom thou lovest),	Lucan, First Booke	46	
Nature, and every power shal give thee place,	Lucan, First Booke	51	
Then men from war shal bide in league, and ease,	Lucan, First Booke	60	
Peace through the world from Janus Phane shal flie,	Lucan, First Booke	61	
Confused stars shal meete, celestiall fire/Fleete on the	Lucan, First Booke	75	
And shal he triumph long before his time,	Lucan, First Booke	316	
And having once got head still shal he raigne?	Lucan, First Booke	317	
Whether now shal these olde bloudles soules repaire?	Lucan, First Booke	343	

SHALBE

Up with him then, his body shalbe scard.	2Tamb	5.1.114	Tamb
They that shalbe actors in this Massacre,	P 231	4.29	Guise
My lord, you shalbe Chauncellor of the realme,	Edw	1.4.65	Edward
Yong Mortimer and his unckle shalbe earles,	Edw	1.4.67	Edward
That Gaveston, my Lord, shalbe repeald.	Edw	1.4.322	Queene
Warwick shalbe my chiefest counseller:	Edw	1.4.345	Edward
It shalbe done my gratious Lord.	Edw	1.4.372	Beamnt
And then his mariage shalbe solemnized,	Edw	1.4.377	Edward
Thy service Spencer shalbe thought upon.	Edw	2.1.80	Neece
Cosin, this day shalbe your mariage feast,	Edw	2.2.256	Edward
Mine honor shalbe hostage of my truth,	Edw	2.3.9	Kent
They shalbe started thence I doubt it not.	Edw	4.6.60	Mortmr
Well, that shalbe, shalbe:	Edw	4.7.95	Edward
nere was there any/So finely handled as this king shalbe.	Edw	5.5.40	Ltborn
Nay I know not, we shalbe curst with bell, booke, and candle.	F App	p.232 23	P Mephst

SHALL

Vulcan shall daunce to make thee laughing sport,	Dido	1.1.32	Jupitr
And Venus Swannes shall shed their silver downe,	Dido	1.1.36	Jupitr
Hermes no more shall shew the world his wings,	Dido	1.1.38	Jupitr
And shall have Ganimed, if thou wilt be my love.	Dido	1.1.49	Jupitr
What shall I doe to save thee my sweet boy?	Dido	1.1.74	Venus
Whose wearie lims shall shortly make repose,	Dido	1.1.84	Jupitr
Three winters shall he with the Rutiles warre,	Dido	1.1.89	Jupitr
And full three Sommers likewise shall he waste,	Dido	1.1.91	Jupitr
From forth her ashes shall advance her head,	Dido	1.1.94	Jupitr
Shall build his throne amidst those starrie towers,	Dido	1.1.98	Jupitr
No bounds but heaven shall bound his Emperie,	Dido	1.1.100	Jupitr
Shall make the morning hast her gray uprise,	Dido	1.1.102	Jupitr
The Romane Scepter royall shall remaine,	Dido	1.1.105	Jupitr
Shall yeeld to dignitie a dubble birth,	Dido	1.1.107	Jupitr
Venus farewell, thy sonne shall be our care:	Dido	1.1.120	Jupitr
Yet shall the aged Sunne shed forth his [haire] <aire>,	Dido	1.1.159	Achat
You shall have leaves and windfall bowes enow/Neere to these	Dido	1.1.172	Aeneas
And this right hand shall make thy Altars crack/With mountaine	Dido	1.1.201	Aeneas
My selfe will see they shall not trouble ye,	Dido	1.2.38	Iarbus
Your men and you shall banquet in our Court,	Dido	1.2.39	Iarbus
Who shall confirme my words with further deedes.	Dido	1.2.43	Iarbus
As shall surpasse the wonder of our speech.	Dido	1.2.47	Serg
But Troy is not, what shall I say I am?	Dido	2.1.76	Aeneas
Madame, you shall be my mother.	Dido	2.1.96	Ascan
And this yong Prince shall be thy playfellow.	Dido	2.1.307	Venus

SHALL (cont.)

Shall I have such a quiver and a bow?	Dido	2.1.310	Ascan
These milke white Doves shall be his Centronels:	Dido	2.1.320	Venus
As every touch shall wound Queene Didos heart.	Dido	2.1.333	Cupid
Or whisking of these leaves, all shall be still,	Dido	2.1.337	Venus
Then shall I touch her breast and conquer her.	Dido	3.1.6	Cupid
How long faire Dido shall I pine for thee?	Dido	3.1.7	Iarbus
I shall not be her sonne, she loves me not.	Dido	3.1.23	Cupid
Goe thou away, Ascanius shall stay.	Dido	3.1.35	Dido
But tell them none shall gaze on him but I,	Dido	3.1.73	Dido
You shall not hurt my father when he comes.	Dido	3.1.80	Cupid
His glistering eyes shall be my looking glasse,	Dido	3.1.86	Dido
His lookes shall be my only Librarie,	Dido	3.1.90	Dido
Through which the water shall delight to play:	Dido	3.1.119	Dido
Thy Anchors shall be hewed from Christall Rockes,	Dido	3.1.120	Dido
Which if thou lose shall shine above the waves:	Dido	3.1.121	Dido
The Masts whereon thy swelling sailes shall hang,	Dido	3.1.122	Dido
of foulded Lawne, where shall be wrought/The warres of Troy,	Dido	3.1.124	Dido
As Seaborne Nymphes shall swarme about thy ships,	Dido	3.1.129	Dido
O happie shall he be whom Dido loves.	Dido	3.1.168	Aeneas
O if I speake/I shall betray my selfe:--	Dido	3.1.173	Dido
That ugly impe that shall outweare my wrath,	Dido	3.2.4	Juno
Troy shall no more call him her second hope,	Dido	3.2.8	Juno
Say Paris, now shall Venus have the ball?	Dido	3.2.12	Juno
Say vengeance, now shall her Ascanius dye?	Dido	3.2.13	Juno
Shall finde it written on confusions front,	Dido	3.2.19	Juno
Is this then all the thankes that I shall have,	Dido	3.2.37	Juno
Cupid shall lay his arrowes in thy lap,	Dido	3.2.56	Venus
Fancie and modestie shall live as mates,	Dido	3.2.58	Venus
Shall chaine felicitie unto their throne.	Dido	3.2.80	Juno
Then in one Cave the Queene and he shall meete,	Dido	3.2.92	Juno
Meane time, Ascanius shall be my charge,	Dido	3.2.98	Venus
I mother, I shall one day be a man,	Dido	3.3.35	Cupid
What shall I doe thus wronged with disdaine?	Dido	3.3.69	Iarbus
And then, what then? Iarbus shall but love:	Dido	3.3.82	Iarbus
This kisse shall be faire Didos punishment.	Dido	4.4.37	Aeneas
Shall vulgar pesants storme at what I doe?	Dido	4.4.73	Dido
I shall be planted in as rich a land.	Dido	4.4.82	Aeneas
Then here in me shall flourish Priams race,	Dido	4.4.87	Aeneas
Henceforth you shall be our Carthage Gods:	Dido	4.4.96	Dido
Ye shall no more offend the Carthage Queene.	Dido	4.4.158	Dido
But hereby child, we shall get thither straight.	Dido	4.5.14	Nurse
Well, if he come a wooing he shall speede,	Dido	4.5.36	Nurse
Carthage shall vaunt her pettie walles no more,	Dido	5.1.4	Aeneas
The Sunne from Egypt shall rich odors bring,	Dido	5.1.11	Aeneas
Shall here unburden their exhaled sweetes,	Dido	5.1.14	Aeneas
But what shall it be calde, Troy as before?	Dido	5.1.18	Illion
And they shall have what thing so ere thou needst.	Dido	5.1.74	Iarbus
Achates and the rest shall waite on thee,	Dido	5.1.76	Aeneas
I traytor, and the waves shall cast thee up,	Dido	5.1.174	Dido
fleete, what shall I doe/But dye in furie of this oversight?	Dido	5.1.268	Dido
How long shall I with griefe consume my daies,	Dido	5.1.281	Iarbus
That shall consume all that this stranger left,	Dido	5.1.285	Dido
None in the world shall have my love but thou:	Dido	5.1.290	Dido
Shall burne to cinders in this pretious flame.	Dido	5.1.301	Dido
But Anna now shall honor thee in death,	Dido	5.1.325	Anna
And mixe her bloud with thine, this shall I doe,	Dido	5.1.326	Anna
Where you shall heare the Scythian Tamburlaine,	1Tamb	Prol.4	Prolog
Shall either perish by our warlike hands,	1Tamb	1.1.72	Therid
What, shall I call thee brother?	1Tamb	1.1.103	Mycet
In spight of them shall malice my estate.	1Tamb	1.1.159	Cosroe
The jewels and the treasure we have tane/Shall be reserv'd, and	1Tamb	1.2.3	Tamb
I am a Lord, for so my deeds shall proove,	1Tamb	1.2.34	Tamb
As with their waight shall make the mountains quake,	1Tamb	1.2.49	Tamb
They shall be kept our forced followers,	1Tamb	1.2.66	Tamb
Shall buy the meanest souldier in my traine.	1Tamb	1.2.86	Tamb
A hundreth <hundred> Tartars shall attend on thee,	1Tamb	1.2.93	Tamb
Thy Garments shall be made of Medean silke,	1Tamb	1.2.95	Tamb
Shall all we offer to Zenocrate,	1Tamb	1.2.104	Tamb
Then shall we fight couragiously with them.	1Tamb	1.2.128	Tamb
Our swordes shall play the Orators for us.	1Tamb	1.2.132	Techel
Or take him prisoner, and his chaine shall serve/For Manackles,	1Tamb	1.2.147	Tamb
And sooner shall the Sun fall from his Spheare,	1Tamb	1.2.176	Tamb
That I shall be the Monark of the East,	1Tamb	1.2.185	Tamb
Those thousand horse shall sweat with martiall spoile/Of	1Tamb	1.2.191	Tamb
Shall vaile to us, as Lords of all the Lake.	1Tamb	1.2.196	Tamb
And mightie kings shall be our Senators.	1Tamb	1.2.198	Tamb
admyre me not)/And when my name and honor shall be spread,	1Tamb	1.2.205	Tamb
Where kings shall crouch unto our conquering swords,	1Tamb	1.2.220	Usumc
When with their fearfull tongues they shall confesse/Theise are	1Tamb	1.2.222	Usumc
But shall I proove a Traitor to my King?	1Tamb	1.2.226	Therid
Thus shall my heart be still combinde with thine,	1Tamb	1.2.235	Tamb
Thy selfe and them shall never part from me,	1Tamb	1.2.245	Tamb
You shall have honors, as your merits be:	1Tamb	1.2.255	Tamb
Or els you shall be forc'd with slaverie.	1Tamb	1.2.256	Tamb
Shall overway his wearie witlesse head,	1Tamb	2.1.46	Cosroe
In faire Persea noble Tamburlaine/Shall be my Regent, and	1Tamb	2.1.49	Cosroe
And such shall wait on worthy Tamburlaine.	1Tamb	2.1.60	Cosroe
Aurora shall not peepe out of her doores,	1Tamb	2.2.10	Mycet
Shall rule the Province of Albania.	1Tamb	2.2.31	Meandr
Shall fling in every corner of the field:	1Tamb	2.2.64	Meandr
Shall massacre those greedy minded slaves.	1Tamb	2.2.67	Meandr
Shall threat the Gods more than Cyclopian warres,	1Tamb	2.3.21	Tamb

SHALL (cont.)

As I shall be commended and excusde/For turning my poore charge	1Tamb	2.3.28	Therid
Shall make me solely Emperour of Asia:	1Tamb	2.3.39	Cosroe
Then shall your meeds and vallours be advaunst/To roomes of	1Tamb	2.3.40	Cosroe
These are the wings shall make it flie as swift,	1Tamb	2.3.57	Tamb
So shall not I be knowen, or if I bee,	1Tamb	2.4.13	Mycet
Wel, I meane you shall have it againe.	1Tamb	2.4.36	Tamb
And none shall keepe the crowne but Tamburlaine:	1Tamb	2.5.7	Cosroe
thee (sweet Ortigius)/Better replies shall proove my purposes.	1Tamb	2.5.37	Cosroe
Your Majestie shall shortly have your wish,	1Tamb	2.5.48	Menaph
shall we wish for ought/The world affoords in greatest	1Tamb	2.5.72	Tamb
And if I prosper, all shall be as sure,	1Tamb	2.5.84	Tamb
Then shall we send to this triumphing King,	1Tamb	2.5.87	Techel
Where flames shall ever feed upon his soule.	1Tamb	2.6.8	Cosroe
Shall make me leave so rich a prize as this:	1Tamb	2.7.54	Tamb
If you but say that Tamburlaine shall raigne.	1Tamb	2.7.63	Tamb
Two thousand horse shall forrage up and downe,	1Tamb	3.1.61	Bajzth
Then shall our footmen lie within the trench,	1Tamb	3.1.64	Bajzth
And thus the Grecians shall be conquered.	1Tamb	3.1.67	Bajzth
Who when he shall embrace you in his armes,	1Tamb	3.2.42	Agidas
Shall rouse him out of Europe, and pursue/His scattered armie	1Tamb	3.3.38	Therid
For Wil and Shall best fitteth Tamburlain,	1Tamb	3.3.41	Tamb
But as I live that towne shall curse the time/That Tamburlaine	1Tamb	3.3.59	Tamb
Shall lead thee Captive thorow Affrica.	1Tamb	3.3.73	Tamb
He shall be made a chast and lustlesse Eunuke,	1Tamb	3.3.77	Bajzth
Shall draw the chariot of my Emperesse,	1Tamb	3.3.80	Bajzth
Thy fall shall make me famous through the world:	1Tamb	3.3.83	Tamb
souldier of my Camp/Shall smile to see thy miserable state.	1Tamb	3.3.86	Tamb
Shall swallow up these base borne Perseans.	1Tamb	3.3.95	Bajzth
Carkasses/Shall serve for walles and bulwarkes to the rest:	1Tamb	3.3.139	Bajzth
of Hydra, so my power/Subdued, shall stand as mighty as before:	1Tamb	3.3.141	Bajzth
Our conquering swords shall marshal us the way/We use to march	1Tamb	3.3.148	Tamb
But I shall turne her into other weedes,	1Tamb	3.3.180	Ebea
Both for their sausinesse shall be employed,	1Tamb	3.3.184	Zenoc
Not all the world shall ransom Bajazeth.	1Tamb	3.3.232	Tamb
foule Idolaters/Shall make me bonfires with their filthy bones,	1Tamb	3.3.240	Bajzth
Shall Tamburlain extend his puisant arme.	1Tamb	3.3.247	Tamb
Shall lie at anchor in the Isle Asant,	1Tamb	3.3.251	Tamb
Where they shall meete, and joine their force in one,	1Tamb	3.3.257	Tamb
So shall our swords, our lances and our shot,	1Tamb	4.2.51	Tamb
It shall be said, I made it red my selfe,	1Tamb	4.2.54	Tamb
Ambitious pride shall make thee fall as low,	1Tamb	4.2.76	Bajzth
with the scraps/My servitures shall bring the from my boord.	1Tamb	4.2.88	Tamb
Shall sit by him and starve to death himselfe.	1Tamb	4.2.90	Tamb
Shall ransome him, or take him from his cage.	1Tamb	4.2.94	Tamb
The ages that shall talk of Tamburlain,	1Tamb	4.2.95	Tamb
Shall talke how I have handled Bajazeth.	1Tamb	4.2.97	Tamb
Shall lead him with us wheresoere we goe.	1Tamb	4.2.100	Tamb
Shall not defend it from our battering shot.	1Tamb	4.2.107	Tamb
So shall he have his life, and all the rest.	1Tamb	4.2.115	Tamb
That Tamburlaine shall rue the day, the hower,	1Tamb	4.3.38	Souldn
First legions of devils shall teare thee in peeces.	1Tamb	4.4.38	P Bajzth
and then she shall be sure not to be starv'd, and he be	1Tamb	4.4.46	P Usumc
If thou wilt have a song, the Turke shall straine his voice:	1Tamb	4.4.64	P Tamb
will I make the Point/That shall begin the Perpendicular.	1Tamb	4.4.82	Tamb
Content thy selfe, his person shall be safe,	1Tamb	4.4.87	Tamb
Nor shall they long be thine, I warrant them.	1Tamb	4.4.119	Bajzth
Your byrthes shall be no blemish to your fame,	1Tamb	4.4.127	Tamb
when holy Fates/Shall stablish me in strong Egyptia,	1Tamb	4.4.135	Tamb
But I am pleasde you shall not see him there:	1Tamb	5.1.113	Tamb
And then shall we in this detested guyse,	1Tamb	5.1.235	Bajzth
That she shall stay and turne her wheele no more,	1Tamb	5.1.374	Anippe
Since thy desired hand shall close mine eies.	1Tamb	5.1.432	Arabia
Thy princely daughter here shall set thee free.	1Tamb	5.1.436	Tamb
Since I shall render all into your hands.	1Tamb	5.1.447	Tamb
Even by this hand that shall establish them,	1Tamb	5.1.492	Tamb
For now her mariage time shall worke us rest.	1Tamb	5.1.504	Techel
Shall pay a yearly tribute to thy Syre.	1Tamb	5.1.519	Tamb
Affrick to the banks/Of Ganges, shall his mighty arme extend.	1Tamb	5.1.521	Tamb
Shall we with honor (as beseemes) entombe,	1Tamb	5.1.531	Tamb
Shall we parle with the Christian,/Or crosse the streame, and	2Tamb	1.1.11	Orcan
Shall carie wrapt within his scarlet waves,	2Tamb	1.1.34	Orcan
Shall by this battell be the bloody Sea.	2Tamb	1.1.38	Orcan
Shall meet those Christians fleeting with the tyde,	2Tamb	1.1.40	Orcan
And for that cause the Christians shall have peace.	2Tamb	1.1.57	Orcan
Hoping by some means I shall be releast,	2Tamb	1.2.23	Callap
slaves/I freely give thee, which shall cut the straights,	2Tamb	1.2.33	Callap
The Grecian virgins shall attend on thee,	2Tamb	1.2.36	Callap
With naked Negros shall thy coach be drawen,	2Tamb	1.2.40	Callap
thy chariot wheels/With Turky Carpets shall be covered:	2Tamb	1.2.43	Callap
in crimson silk/Shall ride before the on Barbarian Steeds:	2Tamb	1.2.47	Callap
Shall I be made a king for my labour?	2Tamb	1.2.62	P Almeda
Betweene thy sons that shall be Emperours,	2Tamb	1.3.7	Tamb
and thy seed/Shall issue crowned from their mothers wombe.	2Tamb	1.3.53	Tamb
As all the world shall tremble at their view.	2Tamb	1.3.57	Celeb
For he shall weare the crowne of Persea,	2Tamb	1.3.74	Tamb
My royal chaire of state shall be advanc'd:	2Tamb	1.3.82	Tamb
When we shall meet the Turkish Deputie/And all his Viceroies,	2Tamb	1.3.99	Tamb
With all his viceroies shall be so affraide,	2Tamb	1.3.162	Tamb
That Jove shall send his winged Messenger/To bid me sheath my	2Tamb	1.3.166	Tamb
Shall hide his head in Thetis watery lap,	2Tamb	1.3.169	Tamb
For halfe the world shall perish in this fight:	2Tamb	1.3.171	Tamb
Yet shall my souldiers make no period/Untill Natolia kneele	2Tamb	1.3.216	Therid

SHALL (cont.)

Cookes shall have pensions to provide us cates,	2Tamb	1.3.219		Tamb
wines/Shall common Souldiers drink in quaffing boules,	2Tamb	1.3.222		Tamb
If there be Christ, we shall have victorie.	2Tamb	2.2.64		Orcan
Now shall his barbarous body be a pray/To beasts and foules,	2Tamb	2.3.14		Orcan
and al the winds shall breath/Through shady leaves of every	2Tamb	2.3.15		Orcan
Shall lead his soule through Orcus burning gulfe:	2Tamb	2.3.25		Orcan
Yet in my thoughts shall Christ be honoured,	2Tamb	2.3.33		Orcan
We wil both watch and ward shall keepe his trunke/Amidst these	2Tamb	2.3.38		Orcan
My Lord, your Majesty shall soone perceive:	2Tamb	2.4.39		1Phstn
We shall not need to nourish any doubt,	2Tamb	3.1.26		Callap
ancient use, shall beare/The figure of the semi-circled Moone:	2Tamb	3.1.64		Orcan
Whose hornes shall sprinkle through the tainted aire,	2Tamb	3.1.66		Orcan
Boyes leave to mourne, this towne shall ever mourne,	2Tamb	3.2.45		Tamb
It shall suffice thou darst abide a wound.	2Tamb	3.2.136		Tamb
Even in the cannons face shall raise a hill/Of earth and fagots	2Tamb	3.3.21		Therid
in, not heaven it selfe/Shall ransome thee, thy wife and family.	2Tamb	3.3.28		Therid
Captaine, these Moores shall cut the leaden pipes,	2Tamb	3.3.29		Techel
That no supply of victuall shall come in,	2Tamb	3.3.32		Techel
Nor [any] issue foorth, but they shall die:	2Tamb	3.3.33		Techel
And few or none shall perish by their shot.	2Tamb	3.3.45		Therid
A hundred horse shall scout about the plaines/To spie what	2Tamb	3.3.47		Techel
Betwixt which, shall our ordinance thunder foorth,	2Tamb	3.3.58		Therid
The Scythians shall not tyrannise on me.	2Tamb	3.4.29		Sonne
Harkening when he shall bid them plague the world.	2Tamb	3.4.60		Therid
And him faire Lady shall thy eies behold.	2Tamb	3.4.67		Therid
Madam, sooner shall fire consume us both,	2Tamb	3.4.73		Techel
This Lady shall have twice so much againe,	2Tamb	3.4.90		Therid
The field wherin this battaile shall be fought,	2Tamb	3.5.18		Callap
Thinke of thy end, this sword shall lance thy throat.	2Tamb	3.5.78		Orcan
And join'd those stars that shall be opposite,	2Tamb	3.5.81		Tamb
Shall so torment thee and that Callapine,	2Tamb	3.5.85		Tamb
I shall now revenge/My fathers vile abuses and mine owne.	2Tamb	3.5.90		Callap
againe, you shall not trouble me thus to come and fetch you.	2Tamb	3.5.101	P	Tamb
you knowe I shall have occasion shortly to journey you.	2Tamb	3.5.114	P	Tamb
Wel, in despight of thee he shall be king:	2Tamb	3.5.128		Callap
in the stable, when you shall come sweating from my chariot.	2Tamb	3.5.142	P	Tamb
hee shall not be put to that exigent, I warrant thee.	2Tamb	3.5.156	P	Soria
My sterne aspect shall make faire Victory,	2Tamb	3.5.162		Tamb
our men shall sweat/With carrieng pearle and treasure on their	2Tamb	3.5.166		Techel
You shall be princes all immediatly:	2Tamb	3.5.168		Tamb
My wisedome shall excuse my cowardise:	2Tamb	4.1.50		Calyph
For not a common Souldier shall defile/His manly fingers with	2Tamb	4.1.163		Tamb
And with the paines my rigour shall inflict,	2Tamb	4.1.184		Tamb
I must and wil be pleasde, and you shall yeeld:	2Tamb	4.2.53		Therid
And you shall se't rebated with the blow.	2Tamb	4.2.70		Olymp
Whose body shall be tomb'd with all the pompe/The treasure of	2Tamb	4.2.97		Therid
They shall to morrow draw my chariot,	2Tamb	4.3.30		Tamb
pompe than this)/Rifle the kingdomes I shall leave unsackt,	2Tamb	4.3.59		Tamb
For every man that so offends shall die.	2Tamb	4.3.76		Tamb
Shall mount the milk-white way and meet him there.	2Tamb	4.3.132		Tamb
Go bind the villaine, he shall hang in chaines,	2Tamb	5.1.84		Tamb
Shoot first my Lord, and then the rest shall follow.	2Tamb	5.1.151		Tamb
Tartars and Perseans shall inhabit there,	2Tamb	5.1.163		Tamb
Shall pay me tribute for, in Babylon.	2Tamb	5.1.167		Tamb
The Foules shall eate, for never sepulchre/Shall grace that	2Tamb	5.2.17		Amasia
never sepulchre/Shall grace that base-borne Tyrant Tamburlaine.	2Tamb	5.2.18		Amasia
She waines againe, and so shall his I hope,	2Tamb	5.2.47		Callap
Shall sicknesse proove me now to be a man,	2Tamb	5.3.44		Tamb
Not last Techelles, no, for I shall die.	2Tamb	5.3.66		Tamb
My looks shall make them flie, and might I follow,	2Tamb	5.3.107		Tamb
And shall I die, and this unconquered?	2Tamb	5.3.150		Tamb
If any thing shall there concerne our state/Assure your selves	Jew	1.1.172		Barab
For happily we shall not tarry here:	Jew	1.2.16		Calym
Your Lordship shall doe well to let them have it.	Jew	1.2.44		Barab
mony of the Turkes shall all be levyed amongst the Jewes,	Jew	1.2.68	P	Reader
Lastly, he that denies this, shall absolutely lose al he has.	Jew	1.2.76	P	Reader
Corpo di dio stay, you shall have halfe,	Jew	1.2.90		Barab
Shall I be tryed by their transgression?	Jew	1.2.115		Barab
The man that dealeth righteously shall live:	Jew	1.2.116		Barab
It shall be so: now Officers have you done?	Jew	1.2.131		Govnr
And now shall move you to bereave my life.	Jew	1.2.143		Barab
Then shall they ne're be seene of Barrabas:	Jew	1.2.250		Abigal
Thus father shall I much dissemble.	Jew	1.2.289		Abigal
Well father, say I be entertain'd,/What then shall follow?	Jew	1.2.295		Abigal
This shall follow then;/There have I hid close underneath the	Jew	1.2.295		Barab
How say you, shall we?	Jew	1.2.390		Lodowk
And so will I too, or it shall goe hard.--	Jew	1.2.392		Lodowk
And when I dye, here shall my spirit walke.	Jew	2.1.30		Barab
On this condition shall thy Turkes be sold.	Jew	2.2.42		Govnr
So shall you imitate those you succeed:	Jew	2.2.47		Bosco
I, and his sonnes too, or it shall goe hard.	Jew	2.3.17		Barab
but e're he shall have her	Jew	2.3.51		Barab
No doubt your soule shall reape the fruit of it.	Jew	2.3.78		Lodowk
Come home and there's no price shall make us part,	Jew	2.3.92		Barab
It shall goe hard but I will see your death.	Jew	2.3.94		Barab
That by my helpe shall doe much villanie.	Jew	2.3.133		Barab
As for the Diamond it shall be yours;	Jew	2.3.135		Barab
All that I have shall be at your command.	Jew	2.3.137		Barab
And I will teach [thee] that shall sticke by thee:	Jew	2.3.168		Barab
So sure shall he and Don Mathias dye:	Jew	2.3.249		Barab
That I intend my daughter shall be thine.	Jew	2.3.254		Barab
a warning e're he goes/As he shall have small hopes of Abigall.	Jew	2.3.274		Barab

SHALL (cont.)

Well, let it passe, another time shall serve.	Jew	2.3.278	Mthias
This is thy Diamond, tell me, shall I have it?	Jew	2.3.292	Lodowk
Nor e're shall see the land of Canaan,	Jew	2.3.303	Barab
What, shall I be betroth'd to Lodowicke?	Jew	2.3.308	Abigal
Nothing but death shall part my love and me.	Jew	2.3.317	Abigal
So have not I, but yet I hope I shall.	Jew	2.3.319	Barab
No; so shall I, if any hurt be done,	Jew	2.3.341	Barab
Shall Lodowicke rob me of so faire a love?	Jew	2.3.347	Mthias
Yes, you shall have him: Goe put her in.	Jew	2.3.362	Barab
True; and it shall be cunningly perform'd.	Jew	2.3.367	Barab
That he shall verily thinke it comes from him.	Jew	2.3.376	Ithimr
And I will have it or it shall goe hard.	Jew	3.1.15	Pilia
now Abigall shall see/Whether Mathias holds her deare or no.	Jew	3.2.1	Mthias
These armes of mine shall be thy Sepulchre.	Jew	3.2.11	Govnr
And it shall murder me.	Jew	3.2.24	Mater
Nay, you shall pardon me:	Jew	3.3.73	Abigal
Yet never shall these lips bewray thy life.	Jew	3.3.75	Abigal
Come, shall we goe?	Jew	3.3.76	1Fryar
from hence/Ne're shall she grieve me more with her disgrace;	Jew	3.4.29	Barab
Ne're shall she live to inherit ought of mine,	Jew	3.4.30	Barab
what shall I doe with it?	Jew	3.4.107	P Ithimr
Nor shall the Heathens live upon our spoyle:	Jew	3.5.12	Govnr
Shall overflow it with their refluence.	Jew	3.5.18	Govnr
You shall not need trouble your selves so farre,	Jew	3.5.22	Basso
For Selim-Calymath shall come himselfe,	Jew	3.5.23	Basso
And I shall dye too, for I feele death comming.	Jew	3.6.8	Abigal
Shall be condemn'd, and then sent to the fire.	Jew	3.6.36	2Fryar
You shall convert me, you shall have all my wealth.	Jew	4.1.81	Barab
and I am resolv'd/You shall confesse me, and have all my goods.	Jew	4.1.86	Barab
But Barabas, who shall be your godfathers,	Jew	4.1.109	1Fryar
For presently you shall be shriv'd.	Jew	4.1.110	1Fryar
Marry the Turke shall be one of my godfathers,	Jew	4.1.111	Barab
One turn'd my daughter, therefore he shall dye;	Jew	4.1.119	Barab
No more but so: it must and shall be done.	Jew	4.1.128	Barab
This is the houre/Wherein I shall proceed; Oh happy houre,	Jew	4.1.161	1Fryar
Wherein I shall convert an Infidell,	Jew	4.1.162	1Fryar
When shall you see a Jew commit the like?	Jew	4.1.197	Barab
To morrow is the Sessions; you shall to it.	Jew	4.1.199	Barab
The Law shall touch you, we'll but lead you, we:	Jew	4.1.202	Barab
What shall we doe with this base villaine then?	Jew	4.2.62	Curtzn
by this bearer, and this shall be your warrant; if you doe not,	Jew	4.2.76	P Ithimr
Shall Ithimore my love goe in such rags?	Jew	4.2.85	Curtzn
I warrant your worship shall hav't.	Jew	4.2.119	P Pilia
what hee writes for you, ye shall have streight.	Jew	4.3.27	P Barab
No god-a-mercy, shall I have these crownes?	Jew	4.3.31	Pilia
Speake, shall I have 'um, Sir?	Jew	4.3.49	Pilia
Pray when, Sir, shall I see you at my house?	Jew	4.3.56	Barab
his villany/He will tell all he knowes and I shall dye for't.	Jew	4.3.65	Barab
Goe to, it shall be so.	Jew	4.4.3	Curtzn
We two, and 'twas never knowne, nor never shall be for me.	Jew	4.4.23	P Ithimr
This shall with me unto the Governor.	Jew	4.4.25	Pilia
And dye he shall, for we will never yeeld.	Jew	5.1.6	1Knght
Once more away with him; you shall have law.	Jew	5.1.40	Govnr
For by my meanes Calymath shall enter in.	Jew	5.1.63	Barab
under Turkish yokes/Shall groning beare the burthen of our ire;	Jew	5.2.8	Calym
When as thy life shall be at their command?	Jew	5.2.33	Barab
What thinkst thou shall become of it and thee?	Jew	5.2.56	Barab
Yet you doe live, and live for me you shall:	Jew	5.2.63	Barab
Your selves shall see it shall not be forgot:	Jew	5.2.71	Barab
Wherein no danger shall betide thy life,	Jew	5.2.100	Barab
Shall be my friend.	Jew	5.2.114	Barab
I know; and they shall witnesse with their lives.	Jew	5.2.123	Barab
I shall, my Lord.	Jew	5.3.42	Msngr
Till you shall heare a Culverin discharg'd/By him that beares	Jew	5.4.3	Govnr
For happily I shall be in distresse,	Jew	5.4.6	Govnr
We shall, my Lord, and thanke you.	Jew	5.5.8	Crpntr
That on the sudden shall dissever it,	Jew	5.5.29	Barab
And with his Bashawes shall be blithely set,	Jew	5.5.38	Barab
A warning-peece shall be shot off from the Tower,	Jew	5.5.39	Barab
for Malta shall be freed,/Or Selim ne're returne to Ottoman.	Jew	5.5.113	Govnr
As sooner shall they drinke the Ocean dry,	Jew	5.5.121	Govnr
Shall binde me ever to your highnes will,	P 11	1.11	Navrre
Shall fully shew the fury of them all.	P 65	2.8	Guise
Now shall I prove and guerdon to the ful,	P 68	2.11	Guise
The plot is laide, and things shall come to passe,	P 164	2.107	Guise
Shall weare white crosses on their Burgonets,	P 232	4.30	Guise
Shall dye, be he King or Emperour.	P 235	4.33	Guise
At which they all shall issue out and set the streetes.	P 237	4.35	Guise
And then the watchword being given, a bell shall ring,	P 238	4.36	Guise
Which when they heare, they shall begin to kill:	P 239	4.37	Guise
And never cease untill that bell shall cease,	P 240	4.38	Guise
What shall we doe now with the Admirall?	P 248	4.46	Charls
Shall in the entrance of this Massacre,	P 286	5.13	Guise
And at ech corner shall the Kings garde stand.	P 291	5.18	Anjoy
Now Guise shall catholiques flourish once againe,	P 295	5.22	Anjoy
And slay his servants that shall issue out.	P 299	5.26	Anjoy
Shall being dead, be hangd thereon in chaines.	P 321	5.48	Anjoy
There shall not a Hugonet breath in France.	P 324	5.51	Guise
To contradict which, I say Ramus shall dye:	P 396	7.36	Guise
Yet will we not that the Massacre shall end:	P 444	7.84	Guise
I thankfully shall undertake the charge/Of you and yours, and	P 476	8.26	Anjoy
All this and more your highnes shall commaund,	P 479	8.29	Lord

SHALL (cont.)

Now sirra, what shall we doe with the Admirall?	P 482	9.1	P 1Atndt
and the fire the aire, and so we shall be poysoned with him.	P 485	9.4	P 1Atndt
What shall we doe then?	P 486	9.5	P 2Atndt
As I doe live, so surely shall he dye,	P 521	9.40	QnMoth
And Henry then shall weare the diadem.	P 522	9.41	QnMoth
For Ile rule France, but they shall weare the crowne:	P 525	9.44	QnMoth
Shall drive no plaintes into the Guises eares,	P 532	10.5	Guise
Whose army shall discomfort all your foes,	P 579	11.44	Pleshe
And so they shall, if fortune speed my will,	P 601	12.14	King
Shall slacke my loves affection from his bent.	P 607	12.20	King
As now you are, so shall you still persist,	P 608	12.21	King
Then shall the Catholick faith of Rome,	P 639	12.52	QnMoth
And then shall Mounser weare the diadem.	P 652	12.65	QnMoth
Tush, all shall dye unles I have my will:	P 653	12.66	QnMoth
Shall buy her love even with his dearest bloud.	P 697	13.41	Guise
When I shall vaunt as victor in revenge.	P 722	14.25	Navrre
Shall buy that strumpets favour with his blood,	P 768	15.26	Guise
Ere I shall want, will cause his Indians,	P 853	17.48	Guise
Shall feele the house of Lorayne is his foe:	P 856	17.51	Guise
My head shall be my counsell, they are false:	P 884	17.79	King
But as I live, so sure the Guise shall dye.	P 899	17.94	King
Bartus, it shall be so, poast then to Fraunce,	P 907	18.8	Navrre
And he shall follow my proud Chariots wheeles.	P 984	19.54	Guise
Yet Caesar shall goe forth.	P 996	19.66	Guise
Let Christian princes that shall heare of this,	P1041	19.111	King
(As all the world shall know our Guise is dead)/Rest satisfied	P1042	19.112	King
To whom shall I bewray my secrets now,	P1083	19.153	QnMoth
Shall take example by [his] <their> punishment,	P1186	22.48	King
These bloudy hands shall teare his triple Crowne,	P1199	22.61	King
Tell me Surgeon, shall I live?	P1211	22.73	King
what, shall the French king dye,/Wounded and poysoned, both at	P1214	22.76	King
Shall curse the time that ere Navarre was King,	P1249	22.111	Navrre
the armye I have gathered now shall ayme/more at thie end then	Paris	ms28,p391	Guise
My knee shall bowe to none but to the king.	Edw	1.1.19	Gavstn
And in the day when he shall walke abroad,	Edw	1.1.57	Gavstn
Like Sylvian <Sylvan> Nimphes my pages shall be clad,	Edw	1.1.58	Gavstn
Shall with their Goate feete daunce an antick hay.	Edw	1.1.60	Gavstn
Shall bathe him in a spring, and there hard by,	Edw	1.1.66	Gavstn
Shall by the angrie goddesse be transformde,	Edw	1.1.68	Gavstn
That crosse me thus, shall know I am displeasd.	Edw	1.1.79	Edward
Shall sleepe within the scabberd at thy neede,	Edw	1.1.87	Mortmr
The sworde shall plane the furrowes of thy browes,	Edw	1.1.94	Edward
I will have Gaveston, and you shall know,	Edw	1.1.96	Edward
Ere Gaveston shall stay within the realme.	Edw	1.1.105	Lncstr
Cosin, our hands I hope shall fence our heads,	Edw	1.1.123	Mortmr
And sooner shall the sea orewhelme my land,	Edw	1.1.152	Edward
Then beare the ship that shall transport thee hence:	Edw	1.1.153	Edward
It shall suffice me to enjoy your love,	Edw	1.1.171	Gavstn
He shall to prison, and there die in boults.	Edw	1.1.197	Gavstn
Shall be their timeles sepulcher, or mine.	Edw	1.2.6	Lncstr
Unlesse his brest be sword proofe he shall die.	Edw	1.2.8	Mortmr
The king shall lose his crowne, for we have power,	Edw	1.2.59	Mortmr
for rather then my lord/Shall be opprest by civill mutinies,	Edw	1.2.65	Queene
But say my lord, where shall this meeting bee?	Edw	1.2.74	Warwck
The name of Mortimer shall fright the king,	Edw	1.4.6	Mortmr
Whether will you beare him, stay or ye shall die.	Edw	1.4.24	Edward
What we have done, our hart bloud shall maintaine.	Edw	1.4.40	Mortmr
Ere my sweete Gaveston shall part from me,	Edw	1.4.48	Edward
This Ile shall fleete upon the Ocean,	Edw	1.4.49	Edward
Nothing shall alter us, wee are resolv'd.	Edw	1.4.74	ArchBp
Be it or no, he shall not linger here.	Edw	1.4.93	MortSr
If I be king, not one of them shall live.	Edw	1.4.105	Edward
And thou must hence, or I shall be deposd,	Edw	1.4.110	Edward
Ile come to thee, my love shall neare decline.	Edw	1.4.115	Edward
And whereas he shall live and be belovde,	Edw	1.4.261	Mortmr
Nay more, when he shall know it lies in us,	Edw	1.4.274	Mortmr
So shall we have the people of our side,	Edw	1.4.282	Mortmr
Penbrooke shall beare the sword before the king.	Edw	1.4.351	Edward
As England shall be quiet, and you safe.	Edw	1.4.358	Mortmr
In this, or ought, your highnes shall commaund us.	Edw	1.4.384	Warwck
a factious lord/Shall hardly do himselfe good, much lesse us,	Edw	2.1.7	Spencr
But rest thee here where Gaveston shall sleepe.	Edw	2.1.65	Neece
It shall be done madam.	Edw	2.1.72	Baldck
And Aeque tandem shall that canker crie,	Edw	2.2.41	Edward
Nor fowlest Harpie that shall swallow him.	Edw	2.2.46	Edward
What will he do when as he shall be present?	Edw	2.2.48	Mortmr
That shall wee see, looke where his lordship comes.	Edw	2.2.49	Lncstr
The life of thee shall salve this foule disgrace.	Edw	2.2.83	Gavstn
Deare shall you both abie this riotous deede:	Edw	2.2.88	Edward
By heaven, the abject villaine shall not live.	Edw	2.2.106	Mortmr
And you shall ransome him, or else--	Edw	2.2.145	Mortmr
Quiet your self, you shall have the broad seale,	Edw	2.2.147	Edward
Shall I still be haunted thus?	Edw	2.2.154	Edward
Wigmore shall flie, to set my unckle free.	Edw	2.2.196	Mortmr
And when tis gone, our swordes shall purchase more.	Edw	2.2.197	Lncstr
Yet, shall the crowing of these cockerels,	Edw	2.2.203	Edward
Scarce shall you finde a man of more desart.	Edw	2.2.251	Gavstn
The head-strong Barons shall not limit me.	Edw	2.2.262	Edward
He that I list to favour shall be great:	Edw	2.2.263	Edward
Will be the first that shall adventure life.	Edw	2.3.4	Kent
Tell us where he remaines, and he shall die.	Edw	2.4.36	Lncstr
souldiers take him hence, for by my sword,/His head shall off:	Edw	2.5.21	Warwck

SHALL (cont.)

Gaveston, short warning/Shall serve thy turne:	Edw	2.5.22	Warwck
And sends you word, he knowes that die he shall,	Edw	2.5.38	Arundl
Shalt thou appoint/What we shall graunt?	Edw	2.5.50	Mortmr
My Lord, you shall go with me,	Edw	2.5.99	Penbrk
hence, out of the way/A little, but our men shall go along.	Edw	2.5.101	Penbrk
Treacherous earle, shall I not see the king?	Edw	2.6.15	Gavstn
Lancaster/Inexorable, and I shall never see/My lovely Pierce,	Edw	3.1.7	Edward
That as the sun-shine shall reflect ore thee:	Edw	3.1.51	Edward
shall I never see,/Never behold thee now?	Edw	3.1.68	Edward
You shall go parley with the king of Fraunce.	Edw	3.1.71	Edward
great beames/On Atlas shoulder, shall not lie more safe,	Edw	3.1.77	Prince
Then shall your charge committed to my trust.	Edw	3.1.78	Prince
And this our sonne, [Levune] <Lewne> shall follow you,	Edw	3.1.82	Edward
And promiseth he shall be safe returnd,	Edw	3.1.110	Arundl
O shall I speake, or shall I sigh and die!	Edw	3.1.122	Edward
This day I shall powre vengeance with my sword/On those proud	Edw	3.1.186	Edward
And shall or Warwicks sword shal smite in vaine.	Edw	3.1.199	Warwck
For which ere long, their heads shall satisfie,	Edw	3.1.209	Edward
For which thy head shall over looke the rest,	Edw	3.1.239	Edward
That Isabell shall make her plaints in vaine,	Edw	3.1.278	Levune
And Fraunce shall be obdurat with her teares.	Edw	3.1.279	Levune
The lords are cruell, and the king unkinde,/What shall we doe?	Edw	4.2.3	Queene
Shall have me from my gratious mothers side,	Edw	4.2.23	Prince
England shall welcome you, and all your route.	Edw	4.3.42	Edward
But as the realme and parlement shall please,	Edw	4.6.36	Mortmr
So shall your brother be disposed of.	Edw	4.6.37	Mortmr
Shall I not see the king my father yet?	Edw	4.6.61	Prince
Shall do good service to her Majestie,	Edw	4.6.74	Mortmr
In heaven wee may, in earth never shall wee meete,	Edw	4.7.80	Edward
And Leister say, what shall become of us?	Edw	4.7.81	Edward
For we shall see them shorter by the heads.	Edw	4.7.94	Rice
So shall not Englands [Vine] <Vines> be perished,	Edw	5.1.47	Edward
So shall my eyes receive their last content,	Edw	5.1.61	Edward
Their bloud and yours shall seale these treacheries.	Edw	5.1.89	Edward
For if they goe, the prince shall lose his right.	Edw	5.1.92	Leistr
hands of mine/Shall not be guiltie of so foule a crime.	Edw	5.1.99	Edward
Will be my death, and welcome shall it be,	Edw	5.1.126	Edward
the greater sway/When as a kings name shall be under writ.	Edw	5.2.14	Mortmr
Bartley shall be dischargd, the king remoovde,	Edw	5.2.40	Mortmr
And none but we shall know where he lieth.	Edw	5.2.41	Mortmr
Speake, shall he presently be dispatch'd and die?	Edw	5.2.44	Mortmr
It shall be done my lord.	Edw	5.2.51	Matrvs
Mortimer shall know that he hath wrongde mee.	Edw	5.2.118	Kent
Twixt theirs and yours, shall be no enmitie.	Edw	5.3.46	Matrvs
Thither shall your honour go, and so farewell.	Edw	5.3.62	Matrvs
Unpointed as it is, thus shall it goe,	Edw	5.4.13	Mortmr
That shall conveie it, and performe the rest,	Edw	5.4.18	Mortmr
Shall he be murdered when the deed is done.	Edw	5.4.20	Mortmr
I, I, and none shall know which way he died.	Edw	5.4.25	Ltborn
You shall not need to give instructions,	Edw	5.4.29	Ltborn
Nay, you shall pardon me, none shall knowe my trickes.	Edw	5.4.39	Ltborn
sure, the Queene and Mortimer/Shall rule the realme, the king,	Edw	5.4.66	Mortmr
Strike off his head, he shall have marshall lawe.	Edw	5.4.89	Mortmr
My lord, he is my unckle, and shall live.	Edw	5.4.91	King
My lord, he is your enemie, and shall die.	Edw	5.4.92	Mortmr
How often shall I bid you beare him hence?	Edw	5.4.102	Mortmr
If that my Unckle shall be murthered thus?	Edw	5.4.110	King
And shall my Unckle Edmund ride with us?	Edw	5.4.114	King
Yet be not farre off, I shall need your helpe,	Edw	5.5.28	Ltborn
That <and> even then when I shall lose my life,	Edw	5.5.77	Edward
Nor shall they now be tainted with a kings.	Edw	5.5.82	Ltborn
Thy hatefull and accursed head shall lie,	Edw	5.6.30	King
And I shall pitie her if she speake againe.	Edw	5.6.86	King
Shall I not moorne for my beloved lord,	Edw	5.6.87	Queene
Thus madam, tis the kings will you shall hence.	Edw	5.6.89	2Lord
Goe fetche my fathers hearse, where it shall lie,	Edw	5.6.94	King
What will be, shall be; Divinitie adeiw.	F 75	1.1.47	Faust
that move betweene the quiet Poles/Shall be at my command:	F 84	1.1.56	Faust
Shall I make spirits fetch me what I please?	F 106	1.1.78	Faust
Wherewith the Students shall be bravely clad.	F 118	1.1.90	Faust
Shall make all Nations to Canonize us:	F 147	1.1.119	Valdes
So shall the spirits <subjects> of every element,	F 149	1.1.121	Valdes
Like Lyons shall they guard us when we please,	F 151	1.1.123	Valdes
From <For> Venice shall they drag <dregge> huge Argosies,/And	F 157	1.1.129	Valdes
Then tell me Faustus what shall we three want?	F 175	1.1.147	Cornel
That shall we presently know, <for see> here comes his boy.	F 196	1.2.3	2Schol
upon me whilst I live/To do what ever Faustus shall command:	F 265	1.3.37	Faust
To give me whatsoever I shall aske;	F 322	1.3.94	Faust
The Emperour shall not live, but by my leave,	F 338	1.3.110	Faust
then belike if I serve you, I shall be lousy.	F 359	1.4.17	P Robin
whensoever, and wheresoever the devill shall fetch thee.	F 370	1.4.28	P Wagner
Why, the Signory of Embden shall be mine:	F 412	2.1.24	Faust
When Mephostophilis shall stand by me,	F 413	2.1.25	Faust
That I shall waite on Faustus whilst he lives,	F 420	2.1.32	Mephst
But tell me Faustus, shall I have thy soule?	F 434	2.1.46	Mephst
yet shall not Faustus flye.	F 470	2.1.82	Faust
that Mephostophilis shall be his servant, and be by him	F 486	2.1.98	P Faust
that Mephostophilis shall doe for him, and bring him	F 488	2.1.100	P Faust
Fourthly, that he shall be in his chamber or house invisible.	F 490	2.1.102	P Faust
that hee shall appeare to the said John Faustus, at all times,	F 491	2.1.103	P Faust
And every creature shall be purifi'd,	F 514	2.1.126	Mephst
All places shall be hell that is not heaven.	F 515	2.1.127	Mephst

SHALL (cont.)

Why, dost thou think <think'st thou then> that Faustus shall be	F 518	2.1.130		Faust
She whom thine eye shall like, thy heart shall have,	F 539	2.1.151		Mephst
And men in harnesse <armour> shall appeare to thee,	F 548	2.1.160		Mephst
I, but Faustus never shall repent.	F 568	2.2.17		BdAngl
I am resolv'd, Faustus shall not <nere> repent.	F 583	2.2.32		Faust
If thou repent, devils will <shall> teare thee in peeces.	F 632	2.2.81		BdAngl
Repent and they shall never raise thy skin.	F 633	2.2.82		GdAngl
That shall I soone: What art thou the first?	F 663	2.2.112		Faust
in hell, and look to it, for some of you shall be my father.	F 690	2.2.139	P	Wrath
This day shall make thee be admir'd in Rome.	F 867	3.1.89		Mephst
So shall our sleeping vengeance now arise,	F 879	3.1.101		Pope
The Pope shall curse that Faustus came to Rome.	F 903	3.1.125		Faust
Then he and thou, and all the world shall stoope,	F 937	3.1.159		Pope
two such Cardinals/Ne're serv'd a holy Pope, as we shall do.	F 942	3.1.164		Faust
He shall be streight condemn'd of heresie,	F 962	3.1.184		Faust
By Peter you shall dye,	F1030	3.2.50		Pope
Or by our sanctitude you all shall die.	F1057	3.2.77		Pope
life, Vintner you shall have your cup anon, say nothing Dick:	F1114	3.3.27	P	Robin
[I leave untold, your eyes shall see performd].	F1154	3.3.67A		3Chor
shall controule him as well as the Conjurer, I warrant you.	F1202	4.1.48	P	Benvol
Shall adde more excellence unto thine Art,	F1208	4.1.54		Emper
Shall make poore Faustus to his utmost power,	F1218	4.1.64		Faust
that shall pierce through/The Ebon gates of ever-burning hell,	F1223	4.1.69		Faust
Your Majesty shall see them presently.	F1235	4.1.81		Faust
come not away quickly, you shall have me asleepe presently:	F1242	4.1.88	P	Benvol
Il'e raise a kennell of Hounds shall hunt him so,	F1301	4.1.147		Faust
As all his footmanship shall scarce prevaile,	F1302	4.1.148		Faust
Shall I let slip so great an injury,	F1328	4.2.4		Benvol
But Faustus death shall quit my infamie.	F1337	4.2.13		Benvol
Who kils him shall have gold, and endlesse love.	F1349	4.2.25		Fredrk
Where shall we place our selves Benvolio?	F1353	4.2.29		Mrtino
What use shall we put his beard to?	F1383	4.2.59	P	Mrtino
What shall [his] eyes doe?	F1386	4.2.62	P	Fredrk
and they shall serve for buttons to his lips, to keepe his	F1387	4.2.63	P	Benvol
and now sirs, having divided him, what shall the body doe?	F1390	4.2.66	P	Mrtino
Yet stay, the world shall see their miserie,	F1406	4.2.82		Faust
And hell shall after plague their treacherie.	F1407	4.2.83		Faust
Defend me heaven, shall I be haunted still?	F1439	4.3.9		Benvol
What shall we then do deere Benvolio?	F1451	4.3.21		Mrtino
Till time shall alter this our brutish shapes:	F1454	4.3.24		Benvol
Alas I am undone, what shall I do?	F1492	4.4.36	P	HrsCsr
You shall presently:	F1519	4.5.15	P	Hostss
Come sirs, what shall we do now till mine Hostesse comes?	F1520	4.5.16	P	Dick
Now sirs, you shall heare how villanously he serv'd mee:	F1535	4.5.31	P	HrsCsr
But you shall heare how bravely I serv'd him for it; I went me	F1547	4.5.43	P	HrsCsr
be it in the world, it shall be yours:	F1568	4.6.11	P	Faust
Be not so furious: come you shall have Beere.	F1620	4.6.63		Faust
have sent away my guesse, I pray who shall pay me for my A--	F1667	4.6.110	P	Hostss
You shall behold that peerelesse dame of Greece,	F1692	5.1.19		Faust
What shall I doe to shun the snares of death?	F1742	5.1.69		Faust
This, or what else my Faustus shall <thou shalt> desire,	F1766	5.1.93		Mephst
Shall be perform'd in twinkling of an eye.	F1767	5.1.94		Mephst
In stead of Troy shall Wittenberg <Wertenberge> be sack't,/And	F1776	5.1.103		Faust
[My faith, vile hel, shall triumph over thee],	F1793	5.1.120A		OldMan
And Faustus shall bee cur'd.	F1831	5.2.35		2Schol
friends, what shall become of Faustus being in hell for ever?	F1846	5.2.50	P	Faust
Shall waite upon his heavy funerall.	F2001	5.3.19		2Schol
warning whensoever or wheresoever the divell shall fetch thee.	F App	p.230 37	P	Wagner
Truly but you shall.	F App	p.230 40	P	Clown
Ile tell you how you shall know them, all hee divels has	F App	p.230 53	P	Clown
Come on Mephastophilis, what shall we do?	F App	p.232 22	P	Faust
I am content to do whatsoever your majesty shall command me.	F App	p.236 16	P	Faust
Faustus, marke what I shall say, As I was sometime solitary set,	F App	p.236 17	P	Emper
has purg'd me of fortie Dollers, I shall never see them more:	F App	p.240 129	P	HrsCsr
Alas, I am undone, what shall I do:	F App	p.241 154	P	HrsCsr
attaine the gole/That shall conduct thee to celestial rest.	F App	p.243 37		OldMan
Will ye wadge war, for which you shall not triumph?	Lucan, First Booke	12		
Thee if I invocate, I shall not need/To crave Apolloes ayde, or	Lucan, First Booke	64		
Shall never faith be found in fellow kings.	Lucan, First Booke	92		
Warre and the destinies shall trie my cause.	Lucan, First Booke	229		
Speake, when shall this thy long usurpt power end?	Lucan, First Booke	333		
These hands shall thrust the ram, and make them flie,	Lucan, First Booke	385		
what mischiefe shall insue?	Lucan, First Booke	644		
Shall townes be swallowed?	Lucan, First Booke	645		
shall the thickned aire,/Become intemperate?	Lucan, First Booke	645		
Become intemperate? shall the earth be barraine?	Lucan, First Booke	646		
Shall water be conjeal'd and turn'd to ice?	Lucan, First Booke	647		
where shall I fall,/Thus borne aloft?	Lucan, First Booke	677		
Shall Dian fanne when love begins to glowe?	Ovid's Elegies	1.1.12		
and such as seeke loves wrack/Shall follow thee, their hands	Ovid's Elegies	1.2.32		
Thee all shall feare and worship as a King,	Ovid's Elegies	1.2.33		
Io, triumphing shall thy people sing.	Ovid's Elegies	1.2.34		
Smooth speeches, feare and rage shall by thee ride,	Ovid's Elegies	1.2.35		
Thy mother shall from heaven applaud this show,	Ovid's Elegies	1.2.39		
The yeares that fatall destenie shall give,	Ovid's Elegies	1.3.17		
live with thee, and die, or <ere> thou shalt <shall> grieve.	Ovid's Elegies	1.3.18		
And with my name shall thine be alwaies sung.	Ovid's Elegies	1.3.26		
Shall I sit gazing as a bashfull guest,	Ovid's Elegies	1.4.3		
About thy neck shall he at pleasure skippe?	Ovid's Elegies	1.4.6		
Words without voyce shall on my eye browes sit,	Ovid's Elegies	1.4.19		
If thou givest kisses, I shall all disclose,	Ovid's Elegies	1.4.39		
The thing and place shall counsell us the rest.	Ovid's Elegies	1.4.54		

SHALL (cont.)

Strike, so againe hard chaines shall binde thee never, Ovid's Elegies 1.6.25
Deserved chaines these cursed hands shall fetter, Ovid's Elegies 1.7.28
And let the troupes which shall thy Chariot follow, Ovid's Elegies 1.7.37
And birds for <from> Memnon yearly shall be slaine. Ovid's Elegies 1.13.4
Now Germany shall captive haire-tyers send thee, Ovid's Elegies 1.14.45
Homer shall live while Tenedos stands and Ide, Ovid's Elegies 1.15.9
Or [into] <to the> sea swift Symois [doth] <shall> slide. Ovid's Elegies 1.15.10
[The world shall of Callimachus ever speake], Ovid's Elegies 1.15.13
With sunne and moone Aratus shall remaine. Ovid's Elegies 1.15.16
And strumpets flatter, shall Menander flourish. Ovid's Elegies 1.15.18
What age of Varroes name shall not be tolde, Ovid's Elegies 1.15.21
Loftie Lucretius shall live that houre, Ovid's Elegies 1.15.23
That Nature shall dissolve this earthly bowre. Ovid's Elegies 1.15.24
Aeneas warre, and Titerus shall be read, Ovid's Elegies 1.15.25
Thy verses sweet Tibullus shall be spoken. Ovid's Elegies 1.15.28
And Gallus shall be knowne from East to West, Ovid's Elegies 1.15.29
So shall Licoris whom he loved best: Ovid's Elegies 1.15.30
Verse is immortall, and shall nere decay. Ovid's Elegies 1.15.32
Knowing her scapes thine honour shall encrease, Ovid's Elegies 2.2.27
Of wealth and honour so shall grow thy heape, Ovid's Elegies 2.2.39
he will lament/And say this blabbe shall suffer punnishment. Ovid's Elegies 2.2.60
Great joyes by hope I inly shall conceive. Ovid's Elegies 2.9.44
For thy returne shall fall the vowd oblation, Ovid's Elegies 2.11.46
Each little hill shall for a table stand: Ovid's Elegies 2.11.48
So in thy Temples shall Osiris stay, Ovid's Elegies 2.13.12
My stay no crime, my flight no joy shall breede, Ovid's Elegies 2.17.25
Nor in my bookes shall one but thou be writ, Ovid's Elegies 2.17.33
So shall my love continue many yeares, Ovid's Elegies 2.19.23
Thou doest beginne, she shall be mine no longer. Ovid's Elegies 2.19.48
Shall I poore soule be never interdicted? Ovid's Elegies 2.19.53
In sleeping shall I fearelesse drawe my breath? Ovid's Elegies 2.19.55
In running if I see thee, I shall stay, Ovid's Elegies 3.2.13
he shall subdue,/The horses seeme, as [thy] <they> desire they Ovid's Elegies 3.2.67
Sooner shall kindnesse gaine thy wills fruition. Ovid's Elegies 3.4.12
Least labour so shall winne great grace of any. Ovid's Elegies 3.4.46
Nere was, nor shall be, what my verse mentions. Ovid's Elegies 3.5.18
Homer without this shall be nothing worth. Ovid's Elegies 3.7.28
Yet shall thy life be forcibly bereaven. Ovid's Elegies 3.8.38
Or shall I plaine some God against me warres? Ovid's Elegies 3.11.4
And I shall thinke you chaste, do what you can. Ovid's Elegies 3.13.14
A worke, that after my death, heere shall dwell Ovid's Elegies 3.14.20
My words shall be as spotlesse as my youth, Hero and Leander 1.207
Shall see it ruinous and desolate. Hero and Leander 1.240
Then shall you most resemble Venus Nun, Hero and Leander 1.319
have concluded/That Midas brood shall sit in Honors chaire, Hero and Leander 1.475
Shall discontent run into regions farre; Hero and Leander 1.478
And few great lords in vertuous deeds shall joy, Hero and Leander 1.479
The Sheepheards Swaines shall daunce and sing, Passionate Shepherd 21

SHALLOW

And led our ships into the shallow sands, Dido 1.2.27 Cloan
Which issues from a small spring, is but shallow, Lucan, First Booke 216
And many came from shallow Isara, Lucan, First Booke 400
By shallow Rivers, to whose falls, Passionate Shepherd 7

SHALT (See also THOU'LT)

Weepe not sweet boy, thou shalt be Didos sonne, Dido 3.1.24 Dido
Achates, thou shalt be so [manly] <meanly> clad, Dido 3.1.128 Dido
Because it may be thou shalt be my love: Dido 3.1.170 Dido
No, thou shalt goe with me unto my house, Dido 4.5.3 Nurse
Where thou shalt see the red gild fishes leape, Dido 4.5.10 Nurse
And thou shalt perish in the billowes waies, Dido 5.1.172 Dido
Now bring him backe, and thou shalt be a Queene, Dido 5.1.197 Dido
Thou shalt burne first, thy crime is worse then his: Dido 5.1.297 Dido
Thou shalt be leader of this thousand horse, 1Tamb 1.1.62 Mycet
Thou shalt be drawen amidst the frosen Pooles, 1Tamb 1.2.99 Tamb
Then shalt thou be Competitor with me, 1Tamb 1.2.208 Tamb
Then thou shalt find my vaunts substantiall. 1Tamb 1.2.213 Tamb
Then shalt thou see me pull it from thy head: 1Tamb 2.4.39 Tamb
Then shalt thou see the Scythian Tamburlaine, 1Tamb 2.5.97 Tamb
It saies, Agydas, thou shalt surely die, 1Tamb 3.2.95 Agidas
Now shalt thou feel the force of Turkish arms, 1Tamb 3.3.134 Bajzth
Thou shalt be Landresse to my waiting maid. 1Tamb 3.3.177 Zabina
Thou shalt not yet be Lord of Affrica. 1Tamb 3.3.223 Zabina
First shalt thou rip my bowels with thy sword, 1Tamb 4.2.16 Bajzth
And thou his wife shalt feed him with the scraps/My servitures 1Tamb 4.2.87 Tamb
Then shalt thou see a hundred kings and more/Upon their knees, 2Tamb 1.2.28 Callap
Thou shalt be crown'd a king and be my mate. 2Tamb 1.2.66 Callap
Wel done my boy, thou shalt have shield and lance, 2Tamb 1.3.43 Tamb
Thou shalt be made a King and raigne with me, 2Tamb 1.3.48 Tamb
Thou shalt be king before them, and thy seed/Shall issue 2Tamb 1.3.52 Tamb
Of all the provinces I have subdued/Thou shalt not have a foot, 2Tamb 1.3.72 Tamb
her soule be, thou shalt stay with me/Embalm'd with Cassia, 2Tamb 2.4.129 Tamb
And till I die thou shalt not be interr'd. 2Tamb 2.4.132 Tamb
Thou shalt not beautifie Larissa plaines, 2Tamb 3.2.34 Tamb
Thou shalt be set upon my royall tent. 2Tamb 3.2.37 Tamb
My boy, Thou shalt not loose a drop of blood, 2Tamb 3.2.137 Tamb
Thou shalt with us to Tamburlaine the great, 2Tamb 3.4.39 Techel
And thou shalt see a man greater than Mahomet, 2Tamb 3.4.46 Therid
first thou shalt kneele to us/And humbly crave a pardon for thy 2Tamb 3.5.108 Orcan
Thou shalt be stately Queene of faire Argier, 2Tamb 4.2.39 Therid
Or els be sure thou shalt be forc'd with paines, 2Tamb 5.1.52 Therid
Bosco, thou shalt be Malta's Generall; Jew 2.2.44 Govnr
Be true and secret, thou shalt want no gold. Jew 2.3.216 Barab

SHALT (cont.)

Shee is thy wife, and thou shalt be mine heire.	Jew	2.3.328	Barab
I, so thou shalt, 'tis thou must doe the deed:	Jew	2.3.369	Barab
Goe buy thee garments: but thou shalt not want:	Jew	3.4.47	Barab
Now shalt thou see the death of Abigall,	Jew	3.4.62	Barab
Assure thy selfe thou shalt have broth by the eye.	Jew	3.4.92	Barab
Bashaw, in briefe, shalt have no tribute here,	Jew	3.5.11	Govnr
Thou shalt not need, for now the Nuns are dead,	Jew	4.1.15	Barab
I'le be Adonis, thou shalt be Loves Queene.	Jew	4.2.94	Ithimr
Shalt live with me and be my love.	Jew	4.2.98	Ithimr
Thou shalt not live in doubt of any thing.	Jew	5.5.45	Barab
I, I, for this Seroune, and thou shalt [ha't] <hate>.	P 351	6.6	Mntsrl
Come Ramus, more golde, or thou shalt have the stabbe.	P 376	7.16	Gonzag
Fearst thou thy person? thou shalt have a guard:	Edw	1.1.166	Edward
So will I now, and thou shalt back to France.	Edw	1.1.185	BshpCv
Come follow me, and thou shalt have my guarde,	Edw	1.1.204	Edward
And long thou shalt not stay, or if thou doost,	Edw	1.4.114	Edward
Thou shalt not hence, ile hide thee Gaveston.	Edw	1.4.131	Edward
Or thou shalt nere be reconcild to me.	Edw	1.4.157	Edward
Waite on me, and ile see thou shalt not want.	Edw	2.2.246	Edward
Thou shalt have so much honor at our hands.	Edw	2.5.28	Warwck
Shalt thou appoint/What we shall graunt?	Edw	2.5.49	Mortmr
Thou shalt have crownes of us, t'out bid the Barons,	Edw	3.1.55	Edward
Edmund, yeeld thou thy self, or thou shalt die.	Edw	5.3.56	Matrvs
I, stay a while, thou shalt have answer straight.	Edw	5.5.20	Matrvs
And thou shalt die, and on his mournefull hearse,	Edw	5.6.29	King
And so shalt thou be too: why staies he heere?	Edw	5.6.51	King
And scorne those Joyes thou never shalt possesse.	F 314	1.3.86	Faust
Why so thou shalt be, whether thou dost it or no:	F 360	1.4.18	P Wagner
Well Faustus, thou shalt have a wife.	F 531	2.1.143	Mephst
So shalt thou shew thy selfe an obedient servant <Do so>,/And	F 652	2.2.101	Lucifr
shalt behold <see al> the seven deadly sinnes appeare to thee	F 655	2.2.104	P Belzeb
Faustus, thou shalt, at midnight I will send for thee;	F 716	2.2.168	Lucifr
And thou shalt turne thy selfe into what shape thou wilt.	F 718	2.2.170	Lucifr
That thou shalt see presently:	F 732	2.3.11	P Robin
Where thou shalt see such store of Ordinance,	F 819	3.1.41	Mephst
<Where thou shalt see a troupe of bald-pate Friers>,	F 833	(HC265) A	Mephst
come then stand by me/And thou shalt see them come immediately.	F 844	3.1.66	Mephst
To me and Peter, shalt thou groveling lie,	F 873	3.1.95	Pope
Both he and thou shalt stand excommunicate,	F 908	3.1.130	Pope
Faustus thou shalt, then kneele downe presently,	F 994	3.2.14	Mephst
Do what thou wilt, thou shalt not be discern'd.	F1005	3.2.25	Mephst
And so thou shalt:	F1130	3.3.43	Mephst
and thou shalt see/This Conjurer performe such rare exploits,	F1185	4.1.31	Mrtino
Thou shalt be famous through all Italy,	F1215	4.1.61	Emper
Thou shalt command the state of Germany,	F1323	4.1.169	Emper
This, or what else my Faustus shall <thou shalt> desire,	F1766	5.1.93	Mephst
And none but thou shalt be my Paramour.	F1787	5.1.114	Faust
thou shalt see/Ten thousand tortures that more horrid be.	F1919	5.2.123	BdAngl
So thou shalt, whether thou beest with me, or no:	F App	p.229 22	P Wagner
thou doest, thou shalt be no wayes prejudiced or indamaged.	F App	p.236 9	P Emper
Thou shalt both satisfie my just desire,	F App	p.237 35	Emper
Nor shalt thou triumph when thou comst to Roome;	Lucan, First Booke		287
Yong men and women, shalt thou lead as thrall,	Ovid's Elegies		1.2.27
Unlesse I erre, full many shalt thou burne,	Ovid's Elegies		1.2.43
live with thee, and die, or <ere> thou shalt <shall> grieve.	Ovid's Elegies		1.3.18
Lines thou shalt read in wine by my hand writ.	Ovid's Elegies		1.4.20
Nor servile water shalt thou drinke for ever.	Ovid's Elegies		1.6.26
Do this and soone thou shalt thy freedome reape.	Ovid's Elegies		2.2.40
Long shalt thou rest when Fates expire thy breath.	Ovid's Elegies		2.9.42
So of both people shalt thou homage gaine.	Ovid's Elegies		2.9.54
Thou shalt admire no woods or Citties there,	Ovid's Elegies		2.11.11
There wine being fild, thou many things shalt tell,	Ovid's Elegies		2.11.49
Thou ring that shalt my faire girles finger binde,	Ovid's Elegies		2.15.1
Blest ring thou in my mistris hand shalt lye,	Ovid's Elegies		2.15.7
For evermore thou shalt my mistris be.	Ovid's Elegies		3.2.62
So shalt thou go with youths to feasts together,	Ovid's Elegies		3.4.47
Slide in thy bounds, so shalt thou runne for ever.	Ovid's Elegies		3.5.20
(Trust me) land-streame thou shalt no envie lack,	Ovid's Elegies		3.5.21
There shalt be lov'd: Ilia lay feare aside.	Ovid's Elegies		3.5.62
Thou ore a hundreth Nimphes, or more shalt raigne:	Ovid's Elegies		3.5.63
much (I crave)/Gifts then my promise greater thou shalt have.	Ovid's Elegies		3.5.66
Live godly, thou shalt die, though honour heaven,	Ovid's Elegies		3.8.37
one shalt thou bee,/Though never-singling Hymen couple thee.	Hero and Leander		1.257

SHALTE

The people thee applauding thou shalte stand,	Ovid's Elegies		1.2.25

SHAME

That was advanced by my Hebes shame,	Dido	3.2.43	Juno
Doe shame her worst, I will disclose my griefe:--	Dido	3.4.28	Dido
Who having wrought her shame, is straight way fled:	Dido	4.2.18	Iarbus
Blush blush for shame, why shouldst thou thinke of love?	Dido	4.5.29	Nurse
Monster of Nature, shame unto thy stocke,	1Tamb	1.1.104	Mycet
To shroud his shame in darknes of the night.	1Tamb	4.1.46	Souldn
With shame, with hungar, and with horror aie/Griping our bowels	1Tamb	5.1.236	Bajzth
And Villanesse to shame, disdaine, and misery:	1Tamb	5.1.269	Bajzth
Now shame and duty, love and feare presents/A thousand sorrowes	1Tamb	5.1.383	Zenoc
In grievous memorie of his fathers shame,	2Tamb	3.1.25	Callap
O cowardly boy, fie for shame, come foorth.	2Tamb	4.1.31	Celeb
Wounded with shame, and kill'd with discontent,	2Tamb	4.1.94	Tamb
And shame of nature [which] <with> Jaertis streame,	2Tamb	4.1.108	Tamb
for shame, and to subdew/This proud contemner of thy dreadfull	2Tamb	4.3.39	Orcan
That thus intreat their shame and servitude?	2Tamb	5.1.37	Govnr
Sustaine a shame of such inexcellence:	2Tamb	5.3.31	Usumc

SHAME (cont.)

Child of perdition, and thy fathers shame, ... Jew 1.2.344 Barab
My Lord, Remember that to Europ's shame, ... Jew 2.2.30 Bosco
Hence strumpet, hide thy head for shame, ... P 691 13.35 Guise
enoughe to worke/thy Just degestione with extreamest shame Paris ms27,p391 Guise
For shame subscribe, and let the lowne depart. . . . Edw 1.4.82 Warwck
Base flatterer, yeeld, and were it not for shame, . . Edw 2.5.11 Mortmr
Shame and dishonour to a souldiers name, ... Edw 2.5.12 Mortmr
pull in your head for shame, let not all the world wonder at F1291 4.1.137 P Faust
heart <art> conspir'd/Benvolio's shame before the Emperour? F1374 4.2.50 Mrtino
let's devise how we may adde more shame/To the blacke scandall F1377 4.2.53 Fredrk
We'le rather die with griefe, then live with shame. . . F1456 4.3.26 Benvol
Infringing all excuse of modest shame, ... Lucan, First Booke 266
And shame to spare life which being lost is wonne. . . Lucan, First Booke 458
shame, and such as seeke loves wrack/Shall follow thee, . Ovid's Elegies 1.2.31
red shame becomes white cheekes, but this/If feigned, doth Ovid's Elegies 1.8.35
Tis shame for eld in warre or love to be. . . . . Ovid's Elegies 1.9.4
Tis shame their wits should be more excelent. . . . Ovid's Elegies 1.10.26
Tis shame sould tongues the guilty should defend/Or great Ovid's Elegies 1.10.39
Tis shame to grow rich by bed merchandize, . . . Ovid's Elegies 1.10.41
Died red with shame, to hide from shame she seekes. . . Ovid's Elegies 1.14.52
To over-come, so oft to fight I shame. . . . . Ovid's Elegies 2.7.2
What graced Kings, in me no shame I deeme. . . . Ovid's Elegies 2.8.14
My life, that I will shame thee never feare, . . . Ovid's Elegies 2.15.21
To serve a wench if any thinke it shame, ... Ovid's Elegies 2.17.1
While without shame thou singst thy lewdnesse ditty. . . Ovid's Elegies 3.1.22
For shame presse not her backe with thy hard knee. . . Ovid's Elegies 3.2.24
Flye backe his [streame] <shame> chargd, the streame chargd, Ovid's Elegies 3.5.44
Shame, that should make me blush, I have no more. . . Ovid's Elegies 3.5.78
I shame so great names to have usde so vainly: . . . Ovid's Elegies 3.5.102
To this ad shame, shame to performe it quaild mee, . . Ovid's Elegies 3.6.37
Lie downe with shame, and see thou stirre no more, . . Ovid's Elegies 3.6.69
Was divers waies distract with love, and shame. . . Ovid's Elegies 3.9.28
Love conquer'd shame, the furrowes dry were burnd, . . Ovid's Elegies 3.9.29
And what I have borne, shame to beare againe. . . Ovid's Elegies 3.10.4
May that shame fall mine enemies chance to be. . . . Ovid's Elegies 3.10.16
There use all tricks, and tread shame under feete. . . Ovid's Elegies 3.13.18
he often strayd/Beyond the bounds of shame, in being bold/To Hero and Leander 1.407
She overcome with shame and sallow feare, ... Hero and Leander 2.260
Till she o'recome with anguish, shame, and rage, . . Hero and Leander 2.333

SHAMED

Aye me she cries, to love, why art a shamed? . . . Ovid's Elegies 2.18.8

SHAMEFASTE

Such light to shamefaste maidens must be showne, . . Ovid's Elegies 1.5.7

SHAMEFULLY

Nor shamefully her coate pull ore her crowne, . . . Ovid's Elegies 1.7.47

SHAMELESSE

I tell thee shamelesse girle,/Thou shalt be Landresse to my 1Tamb 3.3.176 Zabina
Night shamelesse, wine and Love are fearelesse made. . Ovid's Elegies 1.6.60

SHAMES

What may we do, that we may hide our shames? . . . F1447 4.3.17 Fredrk

SHAMING

Shaming to strive but where he did subdue, . . . Lucan, First Booke 146

SHAM'ST

Sham'st thou not thus to justifie thy selfe, . . . Jew 1.2.119 Govnr

SHAPE

Who with the Sunne devides one radiant shape, . . . Dido 1.1.97 Jupitr
And shrowdes thy beautie in this borrowd shape: . . Dido 1.1.192 Aeneas
Now Cupid turne thee to Ascanius shape, ... Dido 2.1.323 Venus
Prometheus hath put on Cupids shape, ... Dido 3.4.21 Dido
Or Monster turned to a manly shape, ... 1Tamb 2.6.16 Ortyg
Whose shape is figure of the highest God? . . . . 2Tamb 2.2.38 Orcan
Sometime a lovelie boye in Dians shape, ... Edw 1.1.61 Gavstn
Had chaungd my shape, or at the mariage day/The cup of Hymen Edw 1.4.173 Queene
Shape we our course to Ireland there to breath. . . Edw 4.5.3 Spencr
I charge thee to returne, and change thy shape, . . F 251 1.3.23 Faust
That holy shape becomes a devill best. . . . . F 254 1.3.26 Faust
at all times, in what shape [or] <and> forme soever he please. F 492 2.1.104 P Faust
And thou shalt turne thy selfe into what shape thou wilt. F 718 2.2.170 Lucifr
First, be thou turned to this ugly shape, ... F1126 3.3.39 Mephst
In bold Acteons shape to turne a Stagge. . . . . F1299 4.1.145 Faust
And she to whom in shape of [Swanne] <Bull> Jove came. . Ovid's Elegies 1.3.22

SHAPES

And mould her minde unto newe fancies shapes: . . . Dido 3.3.79 Iarbus
My flesh devided in your precious shapes, ... 2Tamb 5.3.172 Tamb
As if that Proteus god of shapes appearde. . . . Edw 1.4.411 Mortmr
appeare to thee in their owne proper shapes and likenesse. F 656 2.2.105 P Belzeb
And make them sleepe so sound, that in their shapes, . F 895 3.1.117 Faust
The royall shapes and warlike semblances/Of Alexander and his F1170 4.1.16 Mrtino
In their true shapes, and state Majesticall, . . . F1233 4.1.79 Emper
That when my Spirits present the royall shapes/Of Alexander and F1249 4.1.95 Faust
Till time shall alter this our brutish shapes: . . . F1454 4.3.24 Benvol
Both in their right shapes, gesture, and attire/They usde to F App p.237 33 Emper
There might you see the gods in sundrie shapes, . . Hero and Leander 1.143

SHARE

Besides thy share of this Egyptian prise, ... 1Tamb 1.2.190 Tamb
Share equally the gold that bought their lives, . . 1Tamb 2.2.70 Meandr
And make them blest that share in his attemptes. . . 1Tamb 2.3.9 Tamb
Whose power had share in this our victory: . . . 2Tamb 2.3.35 Orcan
Then of true griefe let us take equall share. . . . Jew 3.2.37 Govnr
And share the kingdom with thy deerest friend. . . Edw 1.1.2 Gavstn
And share it equally amongst you all, ... Edw 1.4.71 Edward
Why joine you force to share the world betwixt you? . . Lucan, First Booke 88

SHARE (cont.)			
Swords share our Empire, fortune that made Roome/Governe the	Lucan, First Booke	109	
decrees/To expel the father; share the world thou canst not;	Lucan, First Booke	291	
But to my share a captive damsell falles.	Ovid's Elegies	2.12.8	
Being fit broken with the crooked share,	Ovid's Elegies	3.9.32	
SHARES			
Rifling this Fort, devide in equall shares:	2Tamb	3.4.89	Therid
He comes and findes his sonnes have had no shares/In all the	2Tamb	4.1.47	Amyras
Thy selfe thus shivered out to three mens shares:	Lucan, First Booke	85	
With strong plough shares no man the earth did cleave,	Ovid's Elegies	3.7.41	
And untild ground with crooked plough-shares broake.	Ovid's Elegies	3.9.14	
SHARP			
Sharp hunger bites upon and gripes the root,	1Tamb	5.1.273	Bajzth
Through rocks more steepe and sharp than Caspian cliftes.	2Tamb	5.3.241	Tamb
Prethe sweet love, one more, and write it sharp.	Jew	4.4.73	Curtzn
SHARPE			
Sharpe forked arrowes light upon thy horse:	1Tamb	5.1.217	Bajzth
Against the destinies durst sharpe darts require.	Ovid's Elegies	1.7.10	
griefe appease)/With thy sharpe nayles upon my face to seaze.	Ovid's Elegies	1.7.64	
is bould/To suffer storme mixt snowes with nights sharpe cold?	Ovid's Elegies	1.9.16	
to thee being cast do happe/Sharpe stripes, she sitteth in the	Ovid's Elegies	2.2.62	
Which rashly twixt the sharpe rocks in the deepe,	Ovid's Elegies	2.11.3	
Rome did send/The Sabine Fathers, who sharpe warres intend.	Ovid's Elegies	2.12.24	
And what poore Dido with her drawne sword sharpe,	Ovid's Elegies	2.18.25	
Nor never with nights sharpe revenge afflicted?	Ovid's Elegies	2.19.54	
Sharpe eyes she had:	Ovid's Elegies	3.3.9	
And pierst my liver with sharpe needle poynts <needles>?	Ovid's Elegies	3.6.30	
This side that serves thee, a sharpe sword did weare.	Ovid's Elegies	3.7.14	
And ripe-earde corne with sharpe-edg'd sithes to fell.	Ovid's Elegies	3.9.12	
some (their violent passions to asswage)/Compile sharpe satyrs,	Hero and Leander	1.127	
At last, like to a bold sharpe Sophister,	Hero and Leander	1.197	
SHARPE-EDG'D			
And ripe-earde corne with sharpe-edg'd sithes to fell.	Ovid's Elegies	3.9.12	
SHARPEST			
And sharpest where th'assault is desperate.	2Tamb	3.2.67	Tamb
Amongst the pricking thornes, and sharpest briers,	F1411	4.2.87	Faust
SHARPNES			
That with the sharpnes of my edged sting,	Dido	4.1.22	Iarbus
SHATILLIAN			
Ah base Shatillian and degenerate,	P 312	5.39	Guise
SHATTERED			
Whose shattered lims, being tost as high as heaven,	2Tamb	3.2.100	Tamb
SHAVE			
No Sir, I can cut and shave.	Jew	2.3.113	P Slave
No, but wash your face, and shave away your beard,	Edw	5.3.31	Gurney
SHAVEN			
Lest Faustus make your shaven crownes to bleed.	F1007	3.2.27	Faust
SHAVER			
Let me see, sirra, are you not an old shaver?	Jew	2.3.114	P Barab
SHAVING			
It may be under colour of shaving, thou'lt cut my throat for my	Jew	2.3.120	P Barab
SHE (See also SHE'S, SHEE, SHEELE, SHEES)			
I love thee well, say Juno what she will.	Dido	1.1.2	Jupitr
She reacht me such a rap for that I spilde,	Dido	1.1.7	Ganimd
What? dares she strike the darling of my thoughts?	Dido	1.1.9	Jupitr
I vow, if she but once frowne on thee more,	Dido	1.1.12	Jupitr
She humbly did beseech him for our bane,	Dido	1.1.60	Venus
Here she was wont to sit, but saving ayre/Is nothing here, and	Dido	2.1.13	Achat
Oft hath she askt us under whom we serv'd,	Dido	2.1.66	Illion
And when we told her she would weepe for griefe,	Dido	2.1.67	Illion
And now she sees thee how will she rejoyce?	Dido	2.1.69	Illion
Looke where she comes: Aeneas [view] <viewd> her well.	Dido	2.1.72	Illion
Well may I view her, but she sees not me.	Dido	2.1.73	Aeneas
And as I swomme, she standing on the shoare,	Dido	2.1.286	Aeneas
But how scapt Helen, she that causde this warre?	Dido	2.1.292	Dido
That she may dote upon Aeneas love:	Dido	2.1.327	Venus
Lest she imagine thou art Venus sonne:	Dido	3.1.4	Cupid
And when she strokes thee softly on the head,	Dido	3.1.5	Cupid
I shall not be her sonne, she loves me not.	Dido	3.1.23	Cupid
Iarbus dye, seeing she abandons thee.	Dido	3.1.40	Iarbus
She likewise in admyring spends her time,	Dido	3.2.72	Juno
Ungentle, can she wrong Iarbus so?	Dido	3.3.10	Iarbus
And will she be avenged on his life?	Dido	3.4.14	Aeneas
What ailes my Queene, is she falne sicke of late?	Dido	3.4.24	Aeneas
That can call them forth when as she please,	Dido	4.1.4	Iarbus
When as she meanes to maske the world with clowdes.	Dido	4.1.6	Iarbus
She crav'd a hide of ground to build a towne,	Dido	4.2.13	Iarbus
Graunt she or no, Aeneas must away,	Dido	4.3.7	Aeneas
No no, she cares not how we sinke or swimme,	Dido	4.3.41	Illion
So she may have Aeneas in her armes.	Dido	4.3.42	Illion
Each word she sayes will then containe a Crowne,	Dido	4.3.53	Aeneas
Say Dido what she will I am not old,	Dido	4.5.21	Nurse
Though she repairde my fleete and gave me ships,	Dido	5.1.59	Aeneas
Yet hath she tane away my oares and masts,	Dido	5.1.60	Aeneas
But this is she with whom I am in love.	1Tamb	1.2.108	Tamb
When she that rules in Rhamnis golden gates,	1Tamb	2.3.37	Cosroe
And when she sees our bloody Collours spread,	1Tamb	3.3.159	Tamb
How lik'st thou her Ebea, will she serve?	1Tamb	3.3.178	Zabina
Madame, she thinks perhaps she is too fine.	1Tamb	3.3.179	Ebea
Here Madam, you are Empresse, she is none.	1Tamb	3.3.227	Therid
She is my Handmaids slave, and she shal looke/That these abuses	1Tamb	4.2.69	Zenoc
and she shal looke/That these abuses flow not from her tongue:	1Tamb	4.2.69	Zenoc
and then she shall be sure not to be starv'd, and he be	1Tamb	4.4.45	P Usumc

SHE (cont.)

dispatch her while she is fat, for if she live but a while	1Tamb	4.4.48	P	Tamb
for if she live but a while longer, shee will fall into a	1Tamb	4.4.49	P	Tamb
with freatting, and then she will not bee woorth the eating.	1Tamb	4.4.50	P	Tamb
And they are worthy she investeth kings.	1Tamb	4.4.129		Tamb
for the love of Venus, would she leave/The angrie God of Armes,	1Tamb	5.1.124		Tamb
That she shall stay and turne her wheele no more,	1Tamb	5.1.374		Anippe
She that hath calmde the furie of my sword,	1Tamb	5.1.437		Tamb
She lies so close that none can find her out.	2Tamb	1.2.60		Callap
So, now she sits in pompe and majestie:	2Tamb	1.3.17		Tamb
And if she passe this fit, the worst is past.	2Tamb	2.4.40		1Phstn
And had she liv'd before the siege of Troy,	2Tamb	2.4.86		Tamb
What, is she dead?	2Tamb	2.4.96		Tamb
Ah good my Lord be patient, she is dead,	2Tamb	2.4.119		Therid
Nothing prevailes, for she is dead my Lord.	2Tamb	2.4.124		Therid
For she is dead? thy words doo pierce my soule.	2Tamb	2.4.125		Tamb
Though she be dead, yet let me think she lives,	2Tamb	2.4.127		Tamb
To signifie she was a princesse borne,	2Tamb	3.2.21		Amyras
Than when she gave eternall Chaos forme,	2Tamb	3.4.76		Techel
She waines againe, and so shall his I hope,	2Tamb	5.2.47		Callap
Let us intreat she may be entertain'd.	Jew	1.2.329		2Fryar
For she has mortified her selfe.	Jew	1.2.341		1Fryar
she were fitter for a tale of love/Then to be tired out with	Jew	1.2.369		Mthias
And better would she farre become a bed/Embraced in a friendly	Jew	1.2.371		Mthias
But say, What was she?	Jew	1.2.382		Lodowk
Is she so faire?	Jew	1.2.384		Lodowk
And if she be so faire as you report,	Jew	1.2.388		Lodowk
Singing ore these, as she does ore her young.	Jew	2.1.63		Barab
For Don Mathias tels me she is faire.	Jew	2.3.35		Lodowk
He loves my daughter, and she holds him deare:	Jew	2.3.141		Barab
before your mother/Lest she mistrust the match that is in hand:	Jew	2.3.147		Barab
And she vowes love to him, and hee to her.	Jew	2.3.247		Barab
Does she receive them?	Jew	2.3.260		Mthias
And when he comes, she lockes her selfe up fast;	Jew	2.3.262		Barab
While she runs to the window looking out/When you should come	Jew	2.3.264		Barab
Why, loves she Don Mathias?	Jew	2.3.285		Lodowk
Doth she not with her smiling answer you?	Jew	2.3.286		Barab
And so has she done you, even from a child.	Jew	2.3.289		Barab
I have intreated her, and she will grant.	Jew	2.3.314		Barab
Nay, if you will, stay till she comes her selfe.	Jew	2.3.352		Barab
I know she is a Curtezane by her attire:	Jew	3.1.26	P	Ithimr
Now here she writes, and wils me to repent.	Jew	3.4.5		Barab
I feare she knowes ('tis so) of my device/In Don Mathias and	Jew	3.4.7		Barab
For she that varies from me in beleefe/Gives great presumption	Jew	3.4.10		Barab
me in beleefe/Gives great presumption that she loves me not;	Jew	3.4.11		Barab
That's no lye, for she sent me for him.	Jew	3.4.25	P	Ithimr
from hence/Ne're shall she grieve me more with her disgrace;	Jew	3.4.29		Barab
Ne're shall she live to inherit ought of mine,	Jew	3.4.30		Barab
And she is hatefull to my soule and me:	Jew	3.4.36		Barab
I'le to her lodging; hereabouts she lyes.	Jew	3.6.6		1Fryar
No, but I grieve because she liv'd so long.	Jew	4.1.18		Barab
She has confest, and we are both undone,	Jew	4.1.46		Barab
It may be she sees more in me than I can find in my selfe:	Jew	4.2.32	P	Ithimr
for she writes further, that she loves me ever since she saw	Jew	4.2.33	P	Ithimr
that she loves me ever since she saw me, and who would not	Jew	4.2.34	P	Ithimr
here's her house, and here she comes, and now would I were gone,	Jew	4.2.35	P	Ithimr
And ye did but know how she loves you, Sir.	Jew	4.2.53		Pilia
Nay, I care not how much she loves me; Sweet Bellamira, would I	Jew	4.2.54	P	Ithimr
That kisse againe; she runs division of my lips.	Jew	4.2.127	P	Ithimr
What an eye she casts on me?	Jew	4.2.128	P	Ithimr
Away with her, she is a Curtezane.	Jew	5.1.8		Govnr
For she is that huge blemish in our eye,	P 80	2.23		Guise
For while she lives Katherine will be Queene.	P 654	12.67		QnMoth
To such a one my Lord, as when she reads my lines,	P 672	13.16		Duchss
see where she comes, as if she droupt/To heare these newes.	P1062	19.132		Eprnon
And let her greeve her heart out if she will.	P1080	19.150		King
She cast her hatefull stomack to the earth.	P1154	22.16		King
I know tis long of Gaveston she weepes.	Edw	1.4.191		Mortmr
No? doe but marke how earnestly she pleads.	Edw	1.4.234		Warwck
She smiles, now for my life his mind is changd.	Edw	1.4.236		Warwck
And as she red, she smild, which makes me thinke,	Edw	2.1.21		Spencr
She neither walkes abroad, nor comes in sight:	Edw	2.1.24		Baldck
My life for thine she will have Gaveston.	Edw	2.1.28		Spencr
Having read unto her since she was a childe.	Edw	2.1.30		Baldck
When she was lockt up in a brasen tower,	Edw	2.2.54		Edward
Heere comes she thats cause of all these jarres.	Edw	2.2.224		Edward
And yet she beares a face of love forsooth:	Edw	4.6.14		Kent
If with the sight thereof she be not mooved,	Edw	5.1.119		Edward
But she that gave him life, I meane the Queene?	Edw	5.2.91		Kent
For she relents at this your miserie.	Edw	5.5.49		Ltborn
And I shall pitie her if she speake againe.	Edw	5.6.86		King
She whom thine eye shall like, thy heart shall have,	F 539	2.1.151		Mephst
Were <Be> she as chaste as was Penelope,	F 540	2.1.152		Mephst
O she was an ancient Gentlewoman, her name was <mistress>	F 699	2.2.148	P	Glutny
That this faire Lady, whilest she liv'd on earth,	F1266	4.1.112		Emper
on the score, but say nothing, see if she have forgotten me.	F1512	4.5.8	P	Robin
it, and she has sent me to looke thee out, prethee come away.	F App	p.233 8	P	Rafe
she for her private study, shee's borne to beare with me,	F App	p.233 16	P	Robin
this Lady while she liv'd had a wart or moale in her necke,	F App	p.238 60	P	Emper
This said, being tir'd with fury she sunke downe.	Lucan, First Booke			694
I aske too much, would she but let me love hir,	Ovid's Elegies			1.3.3
And she to whom in shape of [Swanne] <Bull> Jove came.	Ovid's Elegies			1.3.22
And she that on a faind Bull swamme to land,	Ovid's Elegies			1.3.23

SHE (cont.)

Yet strivde she to be covered therewithall,	Ovid's Elegies	1.5.14
Starke naked as she stood before mine eie,	Ovid's Elegies	1.5.17
I clinged her naked bodie, downe she fell,	Ovid's Elegies	1.5.24
Judge you the rest, being tyrde <tride> she bad me kisse.	Ovid's Elegies	1.5.25
She may perceive how we the time did wast:	Ovid's Elegies	1.6.70
Yet was she graced with her ruffled hayre.	Ovid's Elegies	1.7.12
So fayre she was, Atalanta she resembled,	Ovid's Elegies	1.7.13
when she bewayles/Her perjur'd Theseus flying vowes and sayles,	Ovid's Elegies	1.7.15
She nothing said, pale feare her tongue had tyed.	Ovid's Elegies	1.7.20
Her teares, she silent, guilty did pronounce me.	Ovid's Elegies	1.7.22
Sighing she stood, her bloodlesse white lookes shewed/Like	Ovid's Elegies	1.7.51
My feared hands thrice back she did repell.	Ovid's Elegies	1.7.62
she being wise,/Sees not the morne on rosie horses rise.	Ovid's Elegies	1.8.3
She magick arts and Thessale charmes doth know,	Ovid's Elegies	1.8.5
She knows with gras, with thrids on wrong wheeles spun/And what	Ovid's Elegies	1.8.7
When she will, cloudes the darckned heav'n obscure,	Ovid's Elegies	1.8.9
When she will, day shines every where most pure.	Ovid's Elegies	1.8.10
Great grand-sires from their antient graves she chides/And with	Ovid's Elegies	1.8.17
She drawes chast women to incontinence,	Ovid's Elegies	1.8.19
these words she sayd/While closely hid betwixt two dores I	Ovid's Elegies	1.8.21
She blusht:	Ovid's Elegies	1.8.35
As thus she spake, my shadow me betraide,	Ovid's Elegies	1.8.109
Yet greedy Bauds command she curseth still,	Ovid's Elegies	1.10.23
Farmes out her-self on nights for what she can.	Ovid's Elegies	1.10.30
If, what I do, she askes, say hope for night,	Ovid's Elegies	1.11.13
What neede she [tyre] <try> her hand to hold the quill,	Ovid's Elegies	1.11.23
when she departed/Nape by stumbling on the thre-shold started.	Ovid's Elegies	1.12.3
If ever, now well lies she by my side.	Ovid's Elegies	1.13.6
I chid no more, she blusht, and therefore heard me,	Ovid's Elegies	1.13.47
Oft was she drest before mine eyes, yet never,	Ovid's Elegies	1.14.17
Halfe sleeping on a purple bed she rested,	Ovid's Elegies	1.14.20
Alas she almost weepes, and her white cheekes,	Ovid's Elegies	1.14.51
Died red with shame, to hide from shame she seekes.	Ovid's Elegies	1.14.52
She holds, and viewes her old lockes in her lappe,	Ovid's Elegies	1.14.53
Her trembling hand writ back she might not doo.	Ovid's Elegies	2.2.6
And asking why, this answeare she redoubled,	Ovid's Elegies	2.2.7
Stolne liberty she may by thee obtaine,	Ovid's Elegies	2.2.15
Which giving her, she may give thee againe.	Ovid's Elegies	2.2.16
Wilt thou her fault learne, she may make thee tremble,	Ovid's Elegies	2.2.17
Thinke when she reades, her mother letters sent her,	Ovid's Elegies	2.2.19
Let him goe see her though she doe not languish/And then report	Ovid's Elegies	2.2.21
If long she stayes, to thinke the time more short/Lay downe thy	Ovid's Elegies	2.2.23
Isis may be done/Nor feare least she to th'theater's runne.	Ovid's Elegies	2.2.26
And what she likes, let both hold ratifide.	Ovid's Elegies	2.2.32
Object thou then what she may well excuse,	Ovid's Elegies	2.2.37
Him timelesse death tooke, she was deifide.	Ovid's Elegies	2.2.46
She safe by favour of her judge doth rest.	Ovid's Elegies	2.2.56
cast do happe/Sharpe stripes, she sitteth in the judges lappe.	Ovid's Elegies	2.2.62
If she discardes thee, what use servest thou for?	Ovid's Elegies	2.3.12
And she thats coy I like for being no clowne,	Ovid's Elegies	2.4.13
Me thinkes she should <would> be nimble when shees downe.	Ovid's Elegies	2.4.14
If she be learned, then for her skill I crave her,	Ovid's Elegies	2.4.17
Seeing she likes my bookes, why should we jarre?	Ovid's Elegies	2.4.20
Trips she, it likes me well, plods she, what than?	Ovid's Elegies	2.4.23
She would be nimbler, lying with a man.	Ovid's Elegies	2.4.24
And she <her> I like that with a majestie,	Ovid's Elegies	2.4.29
If she be tall, shees like an Amazon,	Ovid's Elegies	2.4.33
And therefore filles the bed she lies uppon:	Ovid's Elegies	2.4.34
If short, she lies the rounder:	Ovid's Elegies	2.4.35
[Is she attired, then shew her graces best].	Ovid's Elegies	2.4.38
Nay what is she that any Romane loves,	Ovid's Elegies	2.4.47
She viewed the earth: the earth to viewe, beseem'd her.	Ovid's Elegies	2.5.43
She looked sad: sad, comely I esteem'd her.	Ovid's Elegies	2.5.44
Least with worse kisses she should me indue.	Ovid's Elegies	2.5.50
She laught, and kissed so sweetely as might make/Wrath-kindled	Ovid's Elegies	2.5.51
Lay her whole tongue hid, mine in hers she dips.	Ovid's Elegies	2.5.58
Turnes all the goodly <godly> birdes to what she please.	Ovid's Elegies	2.6.58
Thou arguest she doth secret markes unfold.	Ovid's Elegies	2.7.6
Adde she was diligent thy locks to braide,	Ovid's Elegies	2.7.23
In both [thy] <my> cheekes she did perceive thee blush,	Ovid's Elegies	2.8.16
[And] this doth please me most, and so doth she.	Ovid's Elegies	2.10.8
She whom her husband, guard, and gate as foes,	Ovid's Elegies	2.12.3
While rashly her wombes burthen she casts out,	Ovid's Elegies	2.13.1
She secretly with me such harme attempted,	Ovid's Elegies	2.13.3
But she conceiv'd of me, or I am sure/I oft have done, what	Ovid's Elegies	2.13.5
Thou givest my mistris life, she mine againe.	Ovid's Elegies	2.13.16
Worthy she is, thou shouldst in mercy save her.	Ovid's Elegies	2.13.22
Oft dyes she that her paunch-wrapt child hath slaine.	Ovid's Elegies	2.14.38
Fit her so well, as she is fit for me:	Ovid's Elegies	2.15.5
But when she comes, [you] <your> swelling mounts sinck downe,	Ovid's Elegies	2.16.51
Let me be slandered, while my fire she hides,	Ovid's Elegies	2.17.3
But by her glasse disdainefull pride she learnes,	Ovid's Elegies	2.17.9
Nor she her selfe but first trim'd up discernes.	Ovid's Elegies	2.17.10
What would not she give that faire name to winne?	Ovid's Elegies	2.17.30
Shee in my lap sits still as earst she did.	Ovid's Elegies	2.18.6
Aye me she cries, to love, why art a shamed?	Ovid's Elegies	2.18.8
And Phillis hath to reade; if now she lives.	Ovid's Elegies	2.18.32
Ah often, that her [hale] <haole> head aked, she lying,	Ovid's Elegies	2.19.11
Ah oft how much she might she feignd offence;	Ovid's Elegies	2.19.13
So having vext she nourisht my warme fire,	Ovid's Elegies	2.19.15
Great gods what kisses, and how many gave she?	Ovid's Elegies	2.19.18
A mothers joy by Jove she had not felt.	Ovid's Elegies	2.19.28

SHE (cont.)

While Juno Io keepes when hornes she wore,	Ovid's Elegies	2.19.29
Why she alone in empty bed oft tarries.	Ovid's Elegies	2.19.42
Thou doest beginne, she shall be mine no longer.	Ovid's Elegies	2.19.48
By her footes blemish greater grace she tooke.	Ovid's Elegies	3.1.10
And first [she] <he> sayd, when will thy love be spent,	Ovid's Elegies	3.1.15
This saied, she mov'd her buskins gaily varnisht,	Ovid's Elegies	3.1.31
With lofty wordes stout Tragedie (she sayd)/Why treadst me	Ovid's Elegies	3.1.35
Thou hast my gift, which she would from thee sue.	Ovid's Elegies	3.1.60
She left; I say'd, you both I must beseech,	Ovid's Elegies	3.1.61
Thy labour ever lasts, she askes but little.	Ovid's Elegies	3.1.68
She gave me leave, soft loves in time make hast,	Ovid's Elegies	3.1.69
By thy sides touching ill she is entreated.	Ovid's Elegies	3.2.22
When strong wilde beasts, she stronger hunts to strike them.	Ovid's Elegies	3.2.32
She beckt, and prosperous signes gave as she moved.	Ovid's Elegies	3.2.58
She smilde, and with quicke eyes behight some grace:	Ovid's Elegies	3.2.83
her selfe she hath forswore,/And yet remaines the face she had	Ovid's Elegies	3.3.1
And yet remaines the face she had before.	Ovid's Elegies	3.3.2
How long her lockes were, ere her oath she tooke:	Ovid's Elegies	3.3.3
So long they be, since she her faith forsooke.	Ovid's Elegies	3.3.4
Comely tall was she, comely tall shee's yet.	Ovid's Elegies	3.3.8
Sharpe eyes she had:	Ovid's Elegies	3.3.9
By which she perjurd oft hath lyed [to] <by> me.	Ovid's Elegies	3.3.10
By her eyes I remember late she swore,	Ovid's Elegies	3.3.13
if she unpunisht you deceive,/For others faults, why do I losse	Ovid's Elegies	3.3.15
Tis not enough, she shakes your record off,	Ovid's Elegies	3.3.19
But when her lover came, had she drawne backe,	Ovid's Elegies	3.3.39
Who, because meanes want, doeth not, she doth.	Ovid's Elegies	3.4.4
Nor, least she will, can any be restrainde.	Ovid's Elegies	3.4.6
She is not chaste, that's kept, but a deare whore:	Ovid's Elegies	3.4.29
She pleaseth best, I feare, if any say.	Ovid's Elegies	3.4.32
She must be honest to thy servants credit.	Ovid's Elegies	3.4.36
She wailing Mars sinne, and her uncles crime,	Ovid's Elegies	3.5.49
Thrice she prepar'd to flie, thrice she did stay,	Ovid's Elegies	3.5.69
And into water desperately she flies.	Ovid's Elegies	3.5.80
And kindly gave her, what she liked best.	Ovid's Elegies	3.5.82
Either she was foule, or her attire was bad,	Ovid's Elegies	3.6.1
Or she was not the wench I wisht t'have had.	Ovid's Elegies	3.6.2
She on my necke her Ivorie armes did throw,	Ovid's Elegies	3.6.7
And eagerlie she kist me with her tongue,	Ovid's Elegies	3.6.9
And under mine her wanton thigh she flong,	Ovid's Elegies	3.6.10
Yea, and she soothde me up, and calde me sir <sire>,	Ovid's Elegies	3.6.11
Then did the robe or garment which she wore <more>,	Ovid's Elegies	3.6.40
Even her I had, and she had me in vaine,	Ovid's Elegies	3.6.43
As she might straight have gone to church and praide:	Ovid's Elegies	3.6.54
Well, I beleeve she kist not as she should,	Ovid's Elegies	3.6.55
Nor usde the slight nor <and> cunning which she could,	Ovid's Elegies	3.6.56
Huge okes, hard Adamantes might she have moved,	Ovid's Elegies	3.6.57
Worthy she was to move both Gods and men,	Ovid's Elegies	3.6.59
But when she saw it would by no meanes stand,	Ovid's Elegies	3.6.75
Why mockst thou me she cried, or being ill,	Ovid's Elegies	3.6.77
With that her loose gowne on, from me she cast her,	Ovid's Elegies	3.6.81
She prais'd me, yet the gate shutt fast upon her,	Ovid's Elegies	3.7.7
Till then, rough was her father, she severe,	Ovid's Elegies	3.7.31
She held her lap ope to receive the same.	Ovid's Elegies	3.7.34
Now, Sabine-like, though chast she seemes to live,	Ovid's Elegies	3.7.61
One [her] <she> commands, who many things can give.	Ovid's Elegies	3.7.62
For me, she doth keeper, and husband feare,	Ovid's Elegies	3.7.63
And some, that she refrain'd teares, have deni'd.	Ovid's Elegies	3.8.46
Delia departing, happier lov'd, she saith,	Ovid's Elegies	3.8.55
She first constraind bulles necks to beare the yoake,	Ovid's Elegies	3.9.13
Nor is she, though she loves the fertile fields,	Ovid's Elegies	3.9.17
She sawe, and as her marrowe tooke the flame,	Ovid's Elegies	3.9.27
The people by my company she pleasd,	Ovid's Elegies	3.10.19
My love was cause that more mens love she seazd.	Ovid's Elegies	3.10.20
But with my rivall sicke she was not than.	Ovid's Elegies	3.10.26
Ah, she doth more worth then her vices prove.	Ovid's Elegies	3.10.44
Erre I? or by my [bookes] <lookes> is she so knowne?	Ovid's Elegies	3.11.7
By whom disclosd, she in the high woods tooke,	Ovid's Elegies	3.12.19
And she her vestall virgin Priests doth follow.	Ovid's Elegies	3.12.30
She hath not trode <tred> awrie that doth denie it,	Ovid's Elegies	3.13.5
Where she should sit for men to gaze upon.	Hero and Leander	1.8
Upon her head she ware a myrtle wreath,	Hero and Leander	1.17
Many would praise the sweet smell as she past,	Hero and Leander	1.21
She ware no gloves for neither sunne nor wind/Would burne or	Hero and Leander	1.27
Buskins of shels all silvered, used she,	Hero and Leander	1.31
As nature wept, thinking she was undone;	Hero and Leander	1.46
Because she tooke more from her than she left,	Hero and Leander	1.47
Greefe makes her pale, because she mooves not there.	Hero and Leander	1.60
She proudly sits) more over-rules the flood,	Hero and Leander	1.111
Than she the hearts of those that neere her stood.	Hero and Leander	1.112
He whom she favours lives, the other dies.	Hero and Leander	1.124
And modestly they opened as she rose:	Hero and Leander	1.160
He started up, she blusht as one asham'd;	Hero and Leander	1.181
He toucht her hand, in touching it she trembled,	Hero and Leander	1.183
Whose name is it, if she be false or not,	Hero and Leander	1.285
So she be faire, but some vile toongs will blot?	Hero and Leander	1.286
Thee as a holy Idiot doth she scorne,	Hero and Leander	1.303
Thereat she smild, and did denie him so,	Hero and Leander	1.311
Wherewith she yeelded, that was woon before.	Hero and Leander	1.330
The more she striv'd, the deeper was she strooke.	Hero and Leander	1.334
Yet evilly faining anger, strove she still,	Hero and Leander	1.335
But from his spreading armes away she cast her,	Hero and Leander	1.342

SHE (cont.)

Come thither; As she spake this, her toong tript,	Hero and Leander	1.357
At one selfe instant, she poore soule assaies,	Hero and Leander	1.362
Did she uphold to Venus, and againe,	Hero and Leander	1.367
Wherewith she strooken, look'd so dolefully,	Hero and Leander	1.373
And as she wept, her teares to pearle he turn'd,	Hero and Leander	1.375
Yet prowd she was, (for loftie pride that dwels/In tow'red	Hero and Leander	1.393
but she,/Whose only dower was her chastitie,	Hero and Leander	1.411
away she ran,/After went Mercurie, who us'd such cunning,	Hero and Leander	1.416
As she to heare his tale, left off her running.	Hero and Leander	1.418
That she such lovelinesse and beautie had/As could provoke his	Hero and Leander	1.422
vowd he love, she wanting no excuse/To feed him with delaies,	Hero and Leander	1.425
As he ought not performe, nor yet she aske.	Hero and Leander	1.430
A draught of flowing Nectar, she requested,	Hero and Leander	1.431
He readie to accomplish what she wil'd,	Hero and Leander	1.433
Wherewith as one displeas'd, away she trips.	Hero and Leander	2.4
Yet as she went, full often look'd behind,	Hero and Leander	2.5
And many poore excuses did she find,	Hero and Leander	2.6
To linger by the way, and once she stayd,	Hero and Leander	2.7
So on she goes, and in her idle flight,	Hero and Leander	2.10
He being a novice, knew not what she meant,	Hero and Leander	2.13
And she her selfe before the pointed time,	Hero and Leander	2.20
He askt, she gave, and nothing was denied,	Hero and Leander	2.25
And what he did, she willingly requited.	Hero and Leander	2.28
Yet she this rashnesse sodainly repented,	Hero and Leander	2.33
By being possest of him for whom she long'd:	Hero and Leander	2.36
Now waxt she jealous, least his love abated,	Hero and Leander	2.43
Therefore unto him hastily she goes,	Hero and Leander	2.45
She offers up her selfe a sacrifice,	Hero and Leander	2.48
She, fearing on the rushes to be flung,	Hero and Leander	2.66
the more she strived,/The more a gentle pleasing heat revived,	Hero and Leander	2.67
Like to the tree of Tantalus she fled,	Hero and Leander	2.75
would not yeeld/So soone to part from that she deerely held.	Hero and Leander	2.84
Whereat she starts, puts on her purple weeds,	Hero and Leander	2.88
Then standing at the doore, she turnd about,	Hero and Leander	2.97
Wherewith she wreath'd her largely spreading heare,	Hero and Leander	2.107
but he must weare/The sacred ring wherewith she was endow'd,	Hero and Leander	2.109
When first religious chastitie she vow'd:	Hero and Leander	2.110
She stayd not for her robes, but straight arose,	Hero and Leander	2.235
And drunke with gladnesse, to the dore she goes.	Hero and Leander	2.236
Where seeing a naked man, she scriecht for feare,	Hero and Leander	2.237
The neerer that he came, the more she fled,	Hero and Leander	2.243
She overcome with shame and sallow feare,	Hero and Leander	2.260
With both her hands she made the bed a tent,	Hero and Leander	2.264
And now she lets him whisper in her eare,	Hero and Leander	2.267
greedily assayd/To touch those dainties, she the Harpey playd,	Hero and Leander	2.270
So that the truce was broke, and she alas,	Hero and Leander	2.285
She trembling strove, this strife of hers (like that/Which made	Hero and Leander	2.291
And cunningly to yeeld her selfe she sought.	Hero and Leander	2.294
Seeming not woon, yet woon she was at length,	Hero and Leander	2.295
And now she wisht this night were never done,	Hero and Leander	2.301
Againe she knew not how to frame her looke,	Hero and Leander	2.307
That which so long so charily she kept,	Hero and Leander	2.309
And faine by stealth away she would have crept,	Hero and Leander	2.310
That Meremaid-like unto the floore she slid,	Hero and Leander	2.315
Thus neere the bed she blushing stood upright,	Hero and Leander	2.317
Till she o'recome with anguish, shame, and rage,	Hero and Leander	2.333

SHEAD

Shead from the heads and hearts of all our Sex,	1Tamb	5.1.26	1Virgn

SHEADING

His honor, that consists in sheading blood,	1Tamb	5.1.477	Tamb

SHEAP

As sheap-heards do, her on the ground hee layd,	Hero and Leander	1.405
And crave the helpe of sheap-heards that were nie.	Hero and Leander	1.414

SHEAPHEARD

How that a sheapheard sitting in a vale,	Hero and Leander	2.194

SHEAP-HEARDS

As sheap-heards do, her on the ground hee layd,	Hero and Leander	1.405
And crave the helpe of sheap-heards that were nie.	Hero and Leander	1.414

SHEAPHEARDS

that dwels/In tow'red courts, is oft in sheapheards cels).	Hero and Leander	1.394
heart of Hero much more joies/Then nymphs and sheapheards,	Hero and Leander	2.233

SHEARES (See also SHEERE)

That sheares the slender threads of humane life,	Hero and Leander	1.448

SHEATH

And I wil sheath it to confirme the same.	2Tamb	1.1.85	Sgsmnd
Then here I sheath it, and give thee my hand,	2Tamb	1.1.127	Sgsmnd
Jove shall send his winged Messenger/To bid me sheath my sword,	2Tamb	1.3.167	Tamb
That I may sheath it in this breast of mine,	2Tamb	5.1.143	Jrslem
Not for all Malta, therefore sheath your sword;	Jew	2.3.270	Barab

SHEBA (See SABA)

SHED (See also SHEAD)

And Venus Swannes shall shed their silver downe,	Dido	1.1.36	Jupitr
Yet shall the aged Sunne shed forth his [haire] <aire>,	Dido	1.1.159	Achat
denied/To shed [their] <his> influence in his fickle braine,	1Tamb	1.1.15	Cosroe
[Those] <Whose> looks will shed such influence in my campe,/As	2Tamb	3.2.39	Tamb
And shed their feble influence in the aire.	2Tamb	5.3.5	Therid
Cannot behold the teares ye shed for me,	2Tamb	5.3.218	Tamb
Shed your bloud?	P1094	20.4	2Mur
Will sooner sparkle fire then shed a teare:	Edw	5.1.105	Edward
See how they quit our [bloud shed] <bloudshed> in the North;	Lucan, First Booke		302
sleeping foe tis good/And arm'd to shed unarmed peoples bloud.	Ovid's Elegies		1.9.22
Which without bloud-shed doth the pray inherit.	Ovid's Elegies		2.12.6

SHEDDING
And what eyes can refraine from shedding teares, . . . Edw 5.5.50 Ltborn
SHEDS
He loves me not that sheds most teares, ... P1239 22.101 King
Witnesse the teares that Isabella sheds, ... Edw 1.4.164 Queene
SHEE
shee will fall into a consumption with freatting, and then she 1Tamb 4.4.49 P Tamb
Of labouring Oxen, and five hundred/Shee Asses: . . Jew 1.2.185 Barab
Shee? No, Mathias, no, but sends them backe, . . . Jew 2.3.261 Barab
Shee is thy wife, and thou shalt be mine heire. . . Jew 2.3.328 Barab
Shee is a Curtezane and he a theefe, ... Jew 5.1.37 Barab
there was a hee divell and a shee divell, Ile tell you how you F App p.230 52 P Clown
has hornes, and all shee divels has clifts and cloven feete. F App p.230 53 P Clown
give her my writ/But see that forth-with shee peruseth it. Ovid's Elegies 1.11.16
Now on <ore> the sea from her old love comes shee, . . Ovid's Elegies 1.13.1
Thou art as faire as shee, then kisse and play. . . Ovid's Elegies 1.13.44
a pretty wenches face/Shee in requitall doth me oft imbrace. Ovid's Elegies 2.1.34
Shee pleas'd me, soone I sent, and did her woo, . . Ovid's Elegies 2.2.5
Shee may deceive thee, though thou her protect, . . Ovid's Elegies 2.3.15
[Amber] <Yellow> trest is shee, then on the morne thinke I,/My Ovid's Elegies 2.4.43
Shee looking on them did more courage give. . . . Ovid's Elegies 2.12.26
Shee oft hath serv'd thee upon certaine dayes, . . . Ovid's Elegies 2.13.17
Shee dyes, and with loose haires to grave is sent, . . Ovid's Elegies 2.14.39
Shee in my lap sits still as earst she did. . . . Ovid's Elegies 2.18.6
To please me, what faire termes and sweet words ha's shee, Ovid's Elegies 2.19.17
shee her modest eyes held downe,/Her wofull bosome a warme Ovid's Elegies 3.5.67
Pure rose shee, like a Nun to sacrifice, ... Ovid's Elegies 3.6.21
To kisse, I kisse, to lie with her shee let me. . . Ovid's Elegies 3.6.48
Which as shee went would cherupe through the bils. . . Hero and Leander 1.36
And as shee spake those words, came somewhat nere him. . Hero and Leander 1.180
And yet at everie word shee turn'd aside, ... Hero and Leander 1.195
To Venus, answered shee, and as shee spake, ... Hero and Leander 1.295
So having paus'd a while, at last shee said: . . . Hero and Leander 1.337
I, and shee wisht, albeit not from her hart, . . . Hero and Leander 2.37
Shee, with a kind of graunting, put him by it, . . . Hero and Leander 2.73
SHEELE
I thinke sheele doe, but deepely can dissemble. . . Ovid's Elegies 2.4.16
Honour what friends thy wife gives, sheele give many: . Ovid's Elegies 3.4.45
SHEE'LL
Shee'll dye with griefe. . . . . Jew 2.3.354 Mthias
SHEEP (See also SHEAP)
pride/And leads your glories <bodies> sheep-like to the sword. 2Tamb 4.1.77 Tamb
SHEEPE
he had seven thousand sheepe,/Three thousand Camels, and two Jew 1.2.182 Barab
Caried the famous golden-fleeced sheepe. . . . . . Ovid's Elegies 2.11.4
SHEEPEHERD
The sheepeherd nipt with biting winters rage, ... Edw 2.2.61 Gavstn
SHEEPHEARDS
Seeing the Sheepheards feede theyr flocks, . . . Passionate Shepherd 6
The Sheepheards Swaines shall daunce and sing, . . . Passionate Shepherd 21
SHEEP-LIKE
pride/And leads your glories <bodies> sheep-like to the sword. 2Tamb 4.1.77 Tamb
SHEERE
And sheere ye all asunder with her hands: . . . . Dido 4.4.156 Dido
SHEE'S
I, I, no doubt but shee's at your command. . . . . Jew 2.3.39 Barab
study, shee's borne to beare with me, or else my Art failes. F App p.233 16 P Robin
Faire women play, shee's chast whom none will have, . . Ovid's Elegies 1.8.43
Comely tall was she, comely tall shee's yet. . . . . Ovid's Elegies 3.3.8
SHEES
Me thinkes she should <would> be nimble when shees downe. Ovid's Elegies 2.4.14
If not, because shees simple I would have her. . . . Ovid's Elegies 2.4.18
If she be tall, shees like an Amazon, ... Ovid's Elegies 2.4.33
SHEET
Not lapt in lead but in a sheet of gold, ... 2Tamb 2.4.131 Tamb
Pierce through the coffin and the sheet of gold, . . 2Tamb 5.3.226 Tamb
SHEILD
To sheild me from your hated treachery: . . . . . F1428 4.2.104 Faust
SHEKINS
Which as I heare one [Shekius] <Shekins> takes it ill, . P 404 7.44 Ramus
SHEKIUS
Which as I heare one [Shekius] <Shekins> takes it ill, . P 404 7.44 Ramus
SHELFES
Yea all my Navie split with Rockes and Shelfes: . . Dido 3.1.108 Aeneas
Blow windes, threaten ye Rockes and sandie shelfes, . . Dido 4.4.58 Aeneas
SHELLES
The Ocean hath no painted stones or shelles, ... Ovid's Elegies 2.11.13
SHELS
Buskins of shels all silvered, used she, ... Hero and Leander 1.31
SHELVES
The Cyclops shelves, and grim Ceranias seate/Have you oregone, Dido 1.1.147 Aeneas
SHEPHEARD
Ah Shepheard, pity my distressed plight, ... 1Tamb 1.2.7 Zenoc
And yet a shepheard by my Parentage: . . . . . . 1Tamb 1.2.35 Tamb
A Scythian Shepheard, so imbellished/With Natures pride, and 1Tamb 1.2.155 Therid
What means this divelish shepheard to aspire/With such a . 1Tamb 2.6.1 Cosroe
the King of Persea/(Being a Shepheard) seem'd to love you much, 1Tamb 3.2.60 Agidas
SHEPHEARDS
Jove sometime masked in a Shepheards weed, ... 1Tamb 1.2.199 Tamb
He that with Shepheards and a litle spoile, ... 1Tamb 2.1.54 Ceneus
To feele the lovely warmth of shepheards flames, . . . 1Tamb 5.1.186 Tamb
But Shepheards issue, base borne Tamburlaine, ... 2Tamb 3.5.77 Orcan
the shepheards issue, at whose byrth/Heaven did affoord a 2Tamb 3.5.79 Tamb

SHEPHERD (See also SHEAPHEARD, SHEEPEHERD)			
Our Phrigian [shepherds] <shepherd> haled within the gates,/And	Dido	2.1.153	Aeneas
SHEPHERDS			
Our Phrigian [shepherds] <shepherd> haled within the gates,/And	Dido	2.1.153	Aeneas
SHE'S			
But she's at home, and I have bought a house/As great and faire	Jew	2.3.13	Barab
SHEW			
Hermes no more shall shew the world his wings,	Dido	1.1.38	Jupitr
few of them/To chardge these Dames, and shew my servant death,	1Tamb	5.1.117	Tamb
Away with them I say and shew them death.	1Tamb	5.1.120	Tamb
That shew faire weather to the neighbor morne.	2Tamb	3.1.48	Jrslem
To shew her beautie, which the world admyr'd,	2Tamb	3.2.26	Tamb
Goe Officers and set them straight in shew.	Jew	2.2.43	Govnr
will I shew my selfe to have more of the Serpent then the Dove;	Jew	2.3.36	P Barab
To make me shew them favour severally,	Jew	3.3.38	Abigal
For I will shew thee greater curtesie/Then Barabas would have	Jew	5.5.61	Govnr
Shall fully shew the fury of them all.	P 65	2.8	Guise
And make a shew as if all were well.	P 250	4.48	QnMoth
Will shew his mercy and preserve us still.	P 576	11.41	Navrre
To shew your love unto the King of France:	P 904	18.5	Bartus
Having commenc'd, be a Divine in shew,	F 31	1.1.3	Faust
Come, shew me some demonstrations Magicall,	F 177	1.1.149	Faust
What meanes this shew? speake Mephostophilis.	F 472	2.1.84	Faust
So shalt thou shew thy selfe an obedient servant <Do so>,/And	F 652	2.2.101	Lucifr
we are come from hell in person to shew thee some pastime:	F 654	2.2.103	P Belzeb
not of Paradice or <nor> Creation, but marke the <this> shew.	F 659	2.2.108	P Lucifr
Then in this shew let me an Actor be,	F 854	3.1.76	Faust
Now Robin, now or never shew thy cunning.	F1095	3.3.8	P Dick
let me have the carrying of him about to shew some trickes.	F1129	3.3.42	P Robin
And he intends to shew great Carolus,	F1167	4.1.13	Mrtino
they, and none durst speake/And shew their feare, or griefe:	Lucan, First Booke		260
gods/Sweate teares to shew the travailes of their citty.	Lucan, First Booke		555
the world againe/I goe; o Phoebus shew me Neptunes shore,	Lucan, First Booke		692
And Isis now will shew what scuse to make.	Ovid's Elegies		1.8.74
Chiefely shew him the gifts, which others send:	Ovid's Elegies		1.8.99
[Is she attired, then shew her graces best].	Ovid's Elegies		2.4.38
To take repulse, and cause her shew my lust?	Ovid's Elegies		2.7.26
Our pleasant scapes shew thee no clowne to be,	Ovid's Elegies		2.8.3
And doing wrong made shew of innocence.	Ovid's Elegies		2.19.14
Shew large wayes with their garments there displayed.	Ovid's Elegies		3.12.24
SHEW'D			
So, now they have shew'd themselves to be tall fellowes.	Jew	3.2.7	Barab
SHEWD			
this learned man for the great kindnes he hath shewd to you.	F App	p.243 29	P Duke
SHEWE			
What happened to the Queene we cannot shewe,	Dido	2.1.294	Achat
That will Aeneas shewe your majestie.	Dido	3.1.98	Achat
And let thee see <shewe thee> what Magicke can performe.	F 474	2.1.86	Mephst
SHEWED			
In frame of which, Nature hath shewed more skill,	2Tamb	3.4.75	Techel
fighting men/Are come since last we shewed your majesty.	2Tamb	3.5.34	Jrslem
How hard the nobles, how unkinde the king/Hath shewed himself:	Edw	4.2.50	Mortmr
her bloodlesse white lookes shewed/Like marble from the Parian	Ovid's Elegies		1.7.51
SHEWEN			
What, have your horsmen shewen the virgins Death?	1Tamb	5.1.129	Tamb
SHEWER			
To winne the maide came in a golden shewer.	Ovid's Elegies		3.7.30
SHEWERS			
And drench Silvanus dwellings with their shewers,	Dido	3.2.91	Juno
SHEWES			
With gifts and shewes did entertaine him/And promised to be at	P 874	17.69	Eprnon
He shewes me how unheard to passe the watch,	Ovid's Elegies		1.6.7
SHEWEST			
Thou shewest the difference twixt our selves and thee/In this	2Tamb	4.1.138	Orcan
SHIELD (See also SHEILD)			
That will not shield me from her shrewish blowes:	Dido	1.1.4	Ganimd
To ward the blow, and shield me safe from harme.	1Tamb	1.2.181	Tamb
His speare, his shield, his horse, his armour, plumes,	1Tamb	4.1.60	2Msngr
Wel done my boy, thou shalt have shield and lance,	2Tamb	1.3.43	Tamb
God shield your grace from such a sodaine death:	P1178	22.40	Navrre
Ajax, maister of the seven-fould shield,/Butcherd the flocks he	Ovid's Elegies		1.7.7
SHIELDES			
And from their shieldes strike flames of lightening)/All	1Tamb	3.2.81	Agidas
SHIELDS			
And in your shields display your rancorous minds?	Edw	2.2.33	Edward
The skipping Salii with shields like wedges;	Lucan, First Booke		602
SHIFT			
By keeping of thy birth make but a shift.	Ovid's Elegies		1.8.94
I could my selfe by secret Magicke shift.	Ovid's Elegies		2.15.10
SHIFTS			
me in the Ocean thus/To sinke or swim, and put me to my shifts,	Jew	1.2.268	Barab
SHIN'D			
In whose sterne faces shin'd the quenchles fire,	Dido	2.1.186	Aeneas
But far above the loveliest, Hero shin'd,	Hero and Leander		1.103
SHINDE			
noysome Saturne/Were now exalted, and with blew beames shinde,	Lucan, First Booke		651
SHINE (See also SHYNING)			
Which if thou lose shall shine above the waves:	Dido	3.1.121	Dido
That shine as Comets, menacing revenge,	1Tamb	3.2.74	Agidas
which shine as bright/As that faire vail that covers all the	2Tamb	1.2.49	Callap
And shine in compleat vertue more than they,	2Tamb	1.3.51	Tamb
Shine downwards now no more, but deck the heavens/To entertaine	2Tamb	2.4.20	Tamb
Now in their glories shine the golden crownes/Of these proud	2Tamb	4.1.1	Amyras

SHINE (cont.)			
Although it shine as brightly as the Sun.	2Tamb	4.1.134	Tamb
that shine as bright/As all the Lamps that beautifie the Sky,	2Tamb	5.3.156	Tamb
That as the sun-shine shall reflect ore thee:	Edw	3.1.51	Edward
We are deprivde the sun-shine of our life,	Edw	4.7.106	Baldck
But perfect shadowes in a sun-shine day?	Edw	5.1.27	Edward
being old/Must shine a star) shal heaven (whom thou lovest),	Lucan, First Booke		46
[There] <Their> Caesar may'st thou shine and no cloud dim thee;	Lucan, First Booke		59
And strive to shine by day, and ful of strife/Disolve the	Lucan, First Booke		79
shoot) marcht on/And then (when Lucifer did shine alone,	Lucan, First Booke		233
Girt my shine browe with sea banke mirtle praise <sprays>.	Ovid's Elegies		1.1.34
and in her eyes/Two eye-balles shine, and double light thence	Ovid's Elegies		1.8.16
And the Icarian froward Dog-starre shine,	Ovid's Elegies		2.16.4
Now shine her lookes pure white and red betwixt.	Ovid's Elegies		3.3.6
Vessels of Brasse oft handled, brightly shine,	Hero and Leander		1.231
That now should shine on Thetis·glassie bower,	Hero and Leander		2.203
SHINED			
By chaunce her beauty never shined fuller.	Ovid's Elegies		2.5.42
SHINES			
Such power attractive shines in princes eies.	1Tamb	2.5.64	Therid
But stay, what starre shines yonder in the East?	Jew	2.1.41	Barab
To whom the sunne shines both by day and night.	Edw	1.1.17	Gavstn
When she will, day shines every where most pure.	Ovid's Elegies		1.8.10
Brasse shines with use; good garments would be worne,	Ovid's Elegies		1.8.51
SHINING			
And shining stones upon their loftie Crestes:	1Tamb	1.1.145	Ceneus
of that Spheare/Enchac'd with thousands ever shining lamps,	1Tamb	4.2.9	Tamb
And sprinklest Saphyrs on thy shining face,	1Tamb	5.1.143	Tamb
Open thou shining vaile of Cynthia/And make a passage from the	2Tamb	2.2.47	Orcan
Batter the shining pallace of the Sun,	2Tamb	2.4.105	Tamb
Unto the shining bower where Cynthia sits,	2Tamb	3.4.50	Therid
Drawing from it the shining Lamps of heaven.	2Tamb	3.4.77	Techel
Mounted his shining [chariot] <chariots>, gilt with fire,	2Tamb	4.3.126	Tamb
And sommon al the shining lamps of heaven/To cast their	2Tamb	5.3.3	Therid
hadst set/In yonder throne, like those bright shining Saints,	F1905	5.2.109	GdAngl
The bright shining of whose glorious actes/Lightens the world	F App	p.237 25	Emper
Of Christall shining faire, the pavement was,	Hero and Leander		1.141
And heateth kindly, shining lat'rally;	Hero and Leander		2.125
SHIP			
Nothing can beare me to him but a ship,	Dido	5.1.267	Dido
the Pilot stands/And viewes a strangers ship rent in the winds,	1Tamb	4.3.33	Souldn
I would prepare a ship and saile to it,	2Tamb	1.3.90	Celeb
But art thou master in a ship of mine,	Jew	1.1.61	Barab
[But] <by> goe, goe thou thy wayes, discharge thy Ship,	Jew	1.1.82	Barab
Whence is thy ship that anchors in our Rhoad?	Jew	2.2.2	Govnr
My Ship, the flying Dragon, is of Spaine,	Jew	2.2.5	Bosco
Pray pardon me, I must goe see a ship discharg'd.	Jew	4.2.51	P Ithimr
Then beare the ship that shall transport thee hence:	Edw	1.1.153	Edward
love please/[Am] <And> driven like a ship upon rough seas,	Ovid's Elegies		2.4.8
The carefull ship-man now feares angry gusts,	Ovid's Elegies		2.11.25
Yet Galatea favour thou her ship.	Ovid's Elegies		2.11.34
I from the shore thy knowne ship first will see,	Ovid's Elegies		2.11.43
How almost wrackt thy ship in maine seas fell.	Ovid's Elegies		2.11.50
Now my ship in the wished haven crownd,	Ovid's Elegies		3.10.29
A stately builded ship, well rig'd and tall,	Hero and Leander		1.225
SHIPBOYES			
Now serve to chastize shipboyes for their faults,	Dido	4.4.157	Dido
SHIP-MAN			
The carefull ship-man now feares angry gusts,	Ovid's Elegies		2.11.25
SHIPPES			
Lading their shippes with golde and pretious stones:	1Tamb	1.1.121	Cosroe
SHIPPING			
And shipping of our goods to Sicily,	Jew	3.5.15	Govnr
Take shipping and away to Scarborough,	Edw	2.4.5	Edward
But hath your grace got shipping unto Fraunce?	Edw	4.1.17	Mortmr
SHIPS			
When yet both sea and sands beset their ships,	Dido	1.1.110	Venus
With twise twelve Phrigian ships I plowed the deepe,	Dido	1.1.220	Aeneas
And for thy ships which thou supposest lost,	Dido	1.1.235	Venus
Save, save, O save our ships from cruell fire,	Dido	1.2.7	Illion
And led our ships into the shallow sands,	Dido	1.2.27	Cloan
I but the barbarous sort doe threat our ships,	Dido	1.2.34	Serg
Thinking the sea had swallowed up thy ships,	Dido	2.1.68	Illion
Began to crye, let us unto our ships,	Dido	2.1.127	Aeneas
And as we went unto our ships, thou knowest/We sawe Cassandra	Dido	2.1.273	Aeneas
Whom I tooke up to beare unto our ships:	Dido	2.1.277	Aeneas
Then got we to our ships, and being abourd,	Dido	2.1.280	Aeneas
For all our ships were launcht into the deepe:	Dido	2.1.285	Aeneas
And by that meanes repaire his broken ships,	Dido	2.1.328	Venus
Yet Queene of Affricke, are my ships unrigd,	Dido	3.1.105	Aeneas
Aeneas, Ile repaire thy Troian ships,	Dido	3.1.113	Dido
As Seaborne Nymphes shall swarme about thy ships,	Dido	3.1.129	Dido
and warne him to his ships/That now afflicts me with his	Dido	4.2.21	Iarbus
And slice the Sea with sable coloured ships,	Dido	4.3.22	Aeneas
What if I sinke his ships? O heele frowne:	Dido	4.4.110	Dido
Sergestus, beare him hence unto our ships,	Dido	5.1.49	Aeneas
Who have no sailes nor tackling for my ships?	Dido	5.1.56	Aeneas
Though she repairde my fleete and gave me ships,	Dido	5.1.59	Aeneas
Why are thy ships new rigd?	Dido	5.1.88	Dido
Repairde not I thy ships, made thee a King,	Dido	5.1.163	Dido
Nor sent a thousand ships unto the walles,	Dido	5.1.204	Dido
And ore his ships will soare unto the Sunne,	Dido	5.1.244	Dido
Looke sister, looke lovely Aeneas ships,	Dido	5.1.251	Dido

SHIPS (cont.)			
Theile breake his ships, O Proteus, Neptune, Jove,	Dido	5.1.255	Dido
Must I make ships for him to saile away?	Dido	5.1.266	Dido
And drew a thousand ships to Tenedos,	2Tamb	2.4.88	Tamb
And of the third part of the Persian ships,	Jew	1.1.2	Barab
why then I hope my ships/I sent for Egypt and the bordering	Jew	1.1.41	Barab
Thy ships are safe, riding in Malta Rhode:	Jew	1.1.50	1Merch
The ships are safe thou saist, and richly fraught.	Jew	1.1.54	Barab
Sirra, which of my ships art thou Master of?	Jew	1.1.70	Barab
How chance you came not with those other ships/That sail'd by	Jew	1.1.89	Barab
you to come so farre/Without the ayd or conduct of their ships.	Jew	1.1.94	Barab
My ships, my store, and all that I enjoy'd;	Jew	1.2.139	Barab
and in mine Argosie/And other ships that came from Egypt last,	Jew	1.2.188	Barab
But yesterday two ships went from this Towne,	Jew	4.1.69	Barab
While in the harbor ride thy ships unrigd.	Edw	2.2.169	Mortmr
Was this the face that Launcht a thousand ships,	F1768	5.1.95	Faust
Woods turn'd to ships; both land and sea against us:	Lucan, First Booke		307
Whom Troiane ships fecht from Europa farre.	Ovid's Elegies		1.10.2
The Docke in harbours ships drawne from the flouds,	Ovid's Elegies		2.9.21
Being wrackt, carowse the sea tir'd by their ships:	Ovid's Elegies		2.10.34
No flowing waves with drowned ships forth poured,	Ovid's Elegies		2.16.25
The ships, whose God-head in the sea now glisters?	Ovid's Elegies		3.11.38
SHIPT			
And might I live to see thee shipt away,	Dido	3.3.46	Iarbus
Madam, we will that you with speed be shipt,	Edw	3.1.81	Edward
And shipt but late for Ireland with the king.	Edw	4.6.58	Rice
SHIPWRACK			
Unlesse the sea cast up his shipwrack body.	Edw	1.4.205	Lncstr
SHIPWRACKE			
That he might suffer shipwracke on my breast,	Dido	4.4.102	Dido
Marriners, albeit the keele be sound,/Shipwracke themselves:	Lucan, First Booke		501
Will you make shipwracke of your honest name,	Ovid's Elegies		3.13.11
To spurne in carelesse sort, the shipwracke treasure.	Hero and Leander		2.164
SHIRT			
To fast, to pray, and weare a shirt of haire,	Jew	4.1.61	Barab
He never put on cleane shirt since he was circumcis'd.	Jew	4.4.64	P Ithimr
SHIRTS			
They weare no shirts, and they goe bare-foot too.	Jew	4.1.84	1Fryar
SHIVER			
And shiver all the starry firmament:	2Tamb	2.4.106	Tamb
Tooke out the shaft, ordaind my hart to shiver:	Ovid's Elegies		1.1.26
SHIVERED			
And shivered against a craggie rocke.	1Tamb	4.3.34	Souldn
Thy selfe thus shivered out to three mens shares:	Lucan, First Booke		85
SHIVERING			
With shivering speares enforcing thunderclaps,	1Tamb	3.2.80	Agidas
SHIVERS			
resisting it/Falls, and returnes, and shivers where it lights.	Lucan, First Booke		158
SHOARE			
What? doe I see my sonne now come on shoare:	Dido	1.1.134	Venus
And rost our new found victuals on this shoare.	Dido	1.1.168	Aeneas
In multitudes they swarme unto the shoare,	Dido	1.2.36	Serg
his entent/The windes did drive huge billowes to the shoare,	Dido	2.1.139	Aeneas
And as I swomme, she standing on the shoare,	Dido	2.1.286	Aeneas
Darts forth her light to Lavinias shoare.	Dido	3.2.84	Venus
When first you set your foote upon the shoare,	Dido	3.3.53	Achat
Since destinie doth call me from [thy] <the> shoare:	Dido	4.3.2	Aeneas
As parting friends accustome on the shoare,	Dido	4.3.50	Aeneas
The sea is rough, the windes blow to the shoare.	Dido	4.4.25	Aeneas
Or with what thought sleepst thou in Libia shoare?	Dido	5.1.35	Hermes
Now will I haste unto Lavinian shoare,	Dido	5.1.78	Aeneas
Wast thou not wrackt upon this Libian shoare,	Dido	5.1.161	Dido
O Serpent that came creeping from the shoare,	Dido	5.1.165	Dido
That I may tice a Dolphin to the shoare,	Dido	5.1.249	Dido
Now is he come on shoare safe without hurt:	Dido	5.1.257	Dido
When first he came on shoare, perish thou to:	Dido	5.1.299	Dido
Are smoothly gliding downe by Candie shoare/To Malta, through	Jew	1.1.46	Barab
Belike they coasted round by Candie shoare/About their Oyles,	Jew	1.1.91	Barab
and sore tempests driven/To fall on shoare, and here to pine in	Edw	4.7.35	Baldck
Affording it no shoare, and Phoebe's waine/Chace Phoebus and	Lucan, First Booke		77
Well, leade us then to Syrtes desart shoare;	Lucan, First Booke		368
Men kept the shoare, and sailde not into deepe.	Ovid's Elegies		3.7.44
SHOARES			
Where Tarbels winding shoares imbrace the sea,	Lucan, First Booke		422
SHOLD (Homograph)			
only gave me a nod, as who shold say, Is it even so; and so I	Jew	4.2.12	P Pilia
displeases him | And fill up his rome that he shold occupie.	Paris	ms 5,p390	P Souldr
the markett and sett upe your standinge where you shold not:	Paris	ms 6,p390	P Souldr
when she departed/Nape by stumbling on the thre-shold started.	Ovid's Elegies		1.12.4
And on thy thre-shold let me lie dispred,	Ovid's Elegies		2.19.21
So through the world shold bright renown expresse me.	Ovid's Elegies		3.1.64
SHONE			
Which lightned by her necke, like Diamonds shone.	Hero and Leander		1.26
SHOOKE			
thou I am he/That with the Cannon shooke Vienna walles,	2Tamb	1.1.87	Orcan
For though thy cannon shooke the citie walles,	2Tamb	5.1.105	Govnr
They shooke for feare, and cold benumm'd their lims,	Lucan, First Booke		248
the Alpes/Shooke the old snow from off their trembling laps.	Lucan, First Booke		552
And seaven [times] <time> shooke her head with thicke locks	Ovid's Elegies		3.1.32
SHOOT			
And let my souldiers shoot the slave to death.	2Tamb	5.1.109	Tamb
Shoot first my Lord, and then the rest shall follow.	2Tamb	5.1.151	Tamb
Yet shouldst thou die, shoot at him all at once.	2Tamb	5.1.157	Tamb

SHOOT (cont.)

With bowes and dartes to shoot at them they see, — P 422 7.62 Dumain
Or darts which Parthians backward shoot) marcht on/And then — Lucan, First Booke 232

SHOOTE

Mountsorrell, goe shoote the ordinance of, — P 327 5.54 Guise

SHOOTES

Oh woe is me, he never shootes but hits, — Ovid's Elegies 1.1.29

SHOOTS

For Kings are clouts that every man shoots at, — 1Tamb 2.4.8 Mycet
and raging shoots/Alongst the ayre and [nought] <not> resisting — Lucan, First Booke 156
Or lies he close, and shoots where none can spie him? — Ovid's Elegies 1.2.6

SHORE (See also SHOARE)

For we are strangers driven on this shore, — Dido 2.1.43 Aeneas
And all the Ocean by the British shore. — 1Tamb 3.3.259 Tamb
And batter downe the castles on the shore. — 2Tamb 1.3.126 Therid
Which swept the desart shore of that dead sea, — Edw 2.3.22 Mortmr
even to the utmost verge/Of Europe, or the shore of Tanaise, — Edw 4.2.30 Queene
And hags howle for my death at Charons shore, — Edw 4.7.90 Edward
I'le joyne the Hils that bind the Affrick shore, — F 335 1.3.107 Faust
And others came from that uncertaine shore, — Lucan, First Booke 410
the world againe/I goe; o Phoebus shew me Neptunes shore, — Lucan, First Booke 692
The sucking shore with their aboundance swels. — Ovid's Elegies 2.11.14
Maides on the shore, with marble white feete tread, — Ovid's Elegies 2.11.15
Let Nereus bend the waves unto this shore, — Ovid's Elegies 2.11.39
I from the shore thy knowne ship first will see, — Ovid's Elegies 2.11.43
To steale sands from the shore he loves alife, — Ovid's Elegies 2.19.45

SHORNE

And you late shorne Ligurians, who were wont/In large spread — Lucan, First Booke 438
Which by the wild boare in the woods was shorne. — Ovid's Elegies 3.9.40
His dangling tresses that were never shorne, — Hero and Leander 1.55

SHORT

Whose short conclusion will seale up their hearts, — Dido 3.2.94 Juno
Your Highnesse needs not doubt but in short time, — 1Tamb 3.2.32 Agidas
That this my life may be as short to me/As are the daies of — 2Tamb 2.4.36 Tamb
For to be short, amongst you 'tmust be had. — Jew 1.2.56 Govnr
Tush, to be short, he meant to make me Munke, — P1039 19.109 King
He weares a short Italian hooded cloake, — Edw 1.4.413 Mortmr
Gaveston, short warning/Shall serve thy turne: — Edw 2.5.21 Warwck
my lord I pray be short,/A faire commission warrants what we — Edw 4.7.47 Rice
And to be short <conclude>, when all the world dissolves, — F 513 2.1.125 Mephst
to thinke the time more short/Lay downe thy forehead in thy lap — Ovid's Elegies 2.2.23
If short, she lies the rounder: — Ovid's Elegies 2.4.35
Both short and long please me, for I love both: — Ovid's Elegies 2.4.36

SHORTEN

Betweene you both, shorten the time I pray, — Edw 4.3.45 Edward

SHORTER

For we shall see them shorter by the heads. — Edw 4.7.94 Rice
With shorter numbers the heroicke sit. — Ovid's Elegies 2.17.22
Come therefore, and to long verse shorter frame. — Ovid's Elegies 3.1.66

SHORTEST

Though from the shortest Northren Paralell, — 2Tamb 1.1.25 Orcan
Therefore the shortest cut for conjuring/Is stoutly to abjure — F 280 1.3.52 Mephst

SHORTLY

Whose wearie lims shall shortly make repose, — Dido 1.1.84 Jupitr
I doubt not shortly but to raigne sole king, — 1Tamb 1.1.175 Cosroe
Your Majestie shall shortly have your wish, — 1Tamb 2.5.48 Menaph
Then wil I shortly keep my promise Almeda. — 2Tamb 3.1.78 P Callap
you knowe I shall have occasion shortly to journey you. — 2Tamb 3.5.115 P Tamb
That shortly heaven, fild with the meteors/Of blood and fire — 2Tamb 4.1.141 Jrslem
That shortly he was grac'd with Doctors name, — F 17 Prol.17 1Chor
I think my Maister means to die shortly, he has made his will, — F1674 5.1.1 P Wagner
I thinke my maister meanes to die shortly, — F App p.243 1 Wagner

SHORTNED

That in the shortned sequel of my life, — 1Tamb 5.1.278 Bajzth

SHORTNING

Shortning my dayes and thred of vitall life, — F App p.239 92 Faust

SHOT

As I remember, here you shot the Deere, — Dido 3.3.51 Achat
How those were hit by pelting Cannon shot, — 1Tamb 2.4.3 Mycet
And make him raine down murthering shot from heaven/To dash the — 1Tamb 3.3.196 Zabina
Five hundred thousand footmen threatning shot, — 1Tamb 4.1.24 2Msngr
So shall our swords, our lances and our shot, — 1Tamb 4.2.51 Tamb
Shall not defend it from our battering shot. — 1Tamb 4.2.107 Tamb
Volleyes of shot pierce through thy charmed Skin, — 1Tamb 5.1.221 Bajzth
Mingled with powdered shot and fethered steele/So thick upon — 2Tamb 1.1.92 Orcan
Whose eies shot fire from their Ivory bowers, — 2Tamb 2.4.9 Tamb
ordinance strike/A ring of pikes, mingled with shot and horse, — 2Tamb 3.2.99 Tamb
Shot through the armes, cut overthwart the hands, — 2Tamb 3.2.104 Tamb
And few or none shall perish by their shot. — 2Tamb 3.3.45 Therid
To save our Cannoniers from musket shot, — 2Tamb 3.3.57 Therid
I were as soone rewarded with a shot, — 2Tamb 4.1.54 Calyph
But I have sent volleies of shot to you, — 2Tamb 5.1.99 Tamb
Which with our Bombards shot and Basiliske, — Jew 5.3.3 Calym
A warning-peece shall be shot off from the Tower, — Jew 5.5.39 Barab
I my good Lord, shot through the arme. — P 198 3.33 Admral
Then Ile have a peale of ordinance shot from the tower, — P 236 4.34 Guise
Riding the streetes was traiterously shot, — P 244 4.42 Man
See where my Souldier shot him through the arm. — P 310 5.37 Guise
Here of themselves thy shafts come, as if shot, — Ovid's Elegies 2.9.37
And shot a shaft that burning from him went, — Hero and Leander 1.372

SHOTTEN

And feast the birds with their bloud-shotten balles, — Dido 3.2.35 Venus

SHOULD (See also SHOLD, SHULD)

What ist sweet wagge I should deny thy youth? — Dido 1.1.23 Jupitr

SHOULD (cont.)

Where am I now? these should be Carthage walles.	Dido	2.1.1	Aeneas
Me thinkes that towne there should be Troy, yon Idas hill,	Dido	2.1.7	Aeneas
And prophecied Troy should be overcome:	Dido	2.1.142	Aeneas
That I should say thou art no love of mine?	Dido	3.1.42	Dido
What should this meane?	Dido	3.2.21	Venus
Should ere defile so faire a mouth as thine:	Dido	3.2.27	Juno
Why is it then displeasure should disjoyne,	Dido	3.2.30	Juno
Why should not they then joyne in marriage,	Dido	3.2.74	Juno
But should that man of men (Dido except)/Have taunted me in	Dido	3.3.26	Iarbus
That should detaine thy eye in his defects?	Dido	3.4.17	Aeneas
Yet lest he should, for I am full of feare,	Dido	4.4.108	Dido
Better he frowne, then I should dye for griefe:	Dido	4.4.111	Dido
Why should I blame Aeneas for his flight?	Dido	4.4.148	Dido
Why doe I thinke of love now I should dye?	Dido	4.5.34	Nurse
How should I put into the raging deepe,	Dido	5.1.55	Aeneas
That he should take Aeneas from mine armes?	Dido	5.1.130	Dido
This should intreat your highnesse to rejoice,	1Tamb	1.1.123	Menaph
Or looke you, I should play the Orator?	1Tamb	1.2.129	Tamb
the Persean king/Should offer present Dukedomes to our state,	1Tamb	1.2.215	Techel
Should make the world subdued to Tamburlaine.	1Tamb	2.1.30	Menaph
What should we doe but bid them battaile straight,	1Tamb	2.2.18	Meandr
His Highnesse pleasure is that he should live,	1Tamb	2.2.37	Meandr
From one that knew not what a King should do,	1Tamb	2.5.22	Cosroe
Me thinks we should not, I am strongly moov'd,	1Tamb	2.5.75	Tamb
That if I should desire the Persean Crowne,	1Tamb	2.5.76	Tamb
If we should aime at such a dignitie?	1Tamb	2.5.79	Tamb
Twere requisite he should be ten times more,	1Tamb	3.1.47	Argier
a heavenly face/Should by hearts sorrow wax so wan and pale,	1Tamb	3.2.5	Agidas
(Which of your whole displeasures should be most)/Hath seem'd	1Tamb	3.2.7	Agidas
If they should yeeld their necks unto the sword,	1Tamb	3.3.142	Bajzth
For we will scorne they should come nere our selves.	1Tamb	3.3.186	Zenoc
If Mahomet should come from heaven and sweare,	1Tamb	3.3.208	Zenoc
Yet should he not perswade me otherwise,	1Tamb	3.3.210	Zenoc
That not a man should live to rue their fall.	1Tamb	4.1.35	Souldn
This arme should send him downe to Erebus,	1Tamb	4.1.45	Souldn
Then it should so conspire my overthrow.	1Tamb	4.2.11	Tamb
Should have prepar'd to entertaine his Grace?	1Tamb	4.2.63	Zabina
That should be horsed on fower mightie kings.	1Tamb	4.2.78	Bajzth
Not one should scape: but perish by our swords.	1Tamb	4.2.122	Tamb
That such a base usurping vagabond/Should brave a king, or	1Tamb	4.3.22	Souldn
And if we should with common rites of Armes,	1Tamb	5.1.11	Govnr
Yet should ther hover in their restlesse heads,	1Tamb	5.1.171	Tamb
Why should we live, O wretches, beggars, slaves,	1Tamb	5.1.248	Zabina
Whom should I wish the fatall victory,	1Tamb	5.1.385	Zenoc
Fearing my power should pull him from his throne.	1Tamb	5.1.453	Tamb
Els should I much forget my self, my Lord.	1Tamb	5.1.500	Zenoc
the king of Hungary/Should meet our person to conclude a truce.	2Tamb	1.1.10	Orcan
And tell me whether I should stoope so low,	2Tamb	1.1.112	Sgsmnd
me my Lord, if I should goe, would you bee as good as your word?	2Tamb	1.2.61	P Almeda
Which should be like the quilles of Porcupines,	2Tamb	1.3.26	Tamb
As I cried out for feare he should have falne.	2Tamb	1.3.42	Zenoc
Whose arches should be fram'd with bones of Turks,	2Tamb	1.3.94	Amyras
Should pierce the blacke circumference of hell,	2Tamb	1.3.145	Techel
Were turnde to men, he should be overcome:	2Tamb	1.3.164	Tamb
This should be treacherie and violence,	2Tamb	2.1.31	Sgsmnd
So what we vow to them should not infringe/Our liberty of armes	2Tamb	2.1.40	Baldwn
Should not give us presumption to the like.	2Tamb	2.1.46	Sgsmnd
And should we lose the opportunity/That God hath given to venge	2Tamb	2.1.51	Fredrk
Should breake out off the bowels of the clowdes/And fall as	2Tamb	2.2.14	Gazell
Yet should our courages and steeled crestes,	2Tamb	2.2.17	Gazell
Than this base earth should shroud your majesty:	2Tamb	2.4.60	Zenoc
For should I but suspect your death by mine,	2Tamb	2.4.61	Zenoc
Then should you see this Thiefe of Scythia,	2Tamb	3.1.14	Callap
As all the world should blot our dignities/Out of the booke of	2Tamb	3.1.18	Callap
I know not what I should think of it.	2Tamb	3.2.130	P Calyph
Least cruell Scythians should dismember him.	2Tamb	3.4.37	Olymp
For if I should as Hector did Achilles,	2Tamb	3.5.70	Tamb
Me thinks the slave should make a lusty theefe.	2Tamb	3.5.96	Jrslem
If halfe our campe should sit and sleepe with me,	2Tamb	4.1.18	Calyph
And should I goe and kill a thousand men,	2Tamb	4.1.53	Calyph
And should I goe and do nor harme nor good,	2Tamb	4.1.56	Calyph
and for feare I should be affraid, would put it off and come to	2Tamb	4.1.69	P Calyph
What faintnesse should dismay our courages,	2Tamb	5.1.21	Govnr
Whose flaming traines should reach down to the earth/Could not	2Tamb	5.1.90	Tamb
Should I but touch the rusty gates of hell,	2Tamb	5.1.96	Tamb
teare both our limmes/Rather then we should draw thy chariot,	2Tamb	5.1.139	Orcan
Should come in person to resist your power,	2Tamb	5.2.38	Amasia
There should not one of all the villaines power/Live to give	2Tamb	5.3.108	Tamb
That Callapine should be my slave againe.	2Tamb	5.3.118	Tamb
how should our bleeding harts/Wounded and broken with your	2Tamb	5.3.161	Amyras
With what a flinty bosome should I joy,	2Tamb	5.3.185	Amyras
mortified lineaments/Should exercise the motions of my heart,	2Tamb	5.3.189	Amyras
How should I step or stir my hatefull feete,	2Tamb	5.3.195	Amyras
And thus me thinkes should men of judgement frame/This is the	Jew	1.1.34	Barab
Why should this Turke be dearer then that Moore?	Jew	2.3.109	Barab
Doe, it is requisite it should be so.	Jew	2.3.239	Barab
Oh heaven forbid I should have such a thought.	Jew	2.3.256	Barab
looking out/When you should come and hale him from the doore.	Jew	2.3.265	Barab
That maidens new betroth'd should weepe a while:	Jew	2.3.326	Barab
Then my faire Abigal should frowne on me.	Jew	2.3.332	Lodowk
And on that rather should Ferneze dye.	Jew	3.2.26	Govnr
That by my favour they should both be slaine?	Jew	3.3.39	Abigal

SHOULD (cont.)

Troth master, I'm loth such a pot of pottage should be spoyld.	Jew	3.4.89	P Ithimr
Therefore 'tis not requisite he should live.	Jew	4.1.121	Barab
Then is it as it should be, take him up.	Jew	4.1.152	Barab
And understanding I should come this way,	Jew	4.1.165	1Fryar
base slave as he should be saluted by such a tall man as I am,	Jew	4.2.9	P Pilia
with his lips; the effect was, that I should come to her house.	Jew	4.2.31	P Ithimr
Though womans modesty should hale me backe,	Jew	4.2.45	Curtzn
I love him as my selfe/Should write in this imperious vaine!	Jew	4.3.43	Barab
no childe, and unto whom/Should I leave all but unto Ithimore?	Jew	4.3.45	Barab
Oh that I should part with so much gold!	Jew	4.3.51	Barab
What wudst thou doe if he should send thee none?	Jew	4.4.13	Pilia
And fit it should: but first let's ha more gold.	Jew	4.4.26	Curtzn
Confesse; what meane you, Lords, who should confesse?	Jew	5.1.26	Barab
What should I say? we are captives and must yeeld.	Jew	5.2.6	Govnr
Should I in pitty of thy plaints or thee,	Jew	5.5.72	Govnr
Besides, if we should let thee goe, all's one,	Jew	5.5.99	Govnr
Should have been murdered the other night?	P 35	1.35	Navrre
Of so great matter should be made the ground.	P 126	2.69	Guise
Should for their conscience taste such rutheles ends.	P 214	4.12	Charls
Though gentle mindes should pittie others paines,	P 215	4.13	Anjoy
Then I am carefull you should be preserved.	P 265	4.63	Charls
Tell me Taleus, wherfore should I flye?	P 366	7.6	Ramus
Alas I am a scholler, how should I have golde?	P 377	7.17	Ramus
This wrathfull hand should strike thee to the hart.	P 690	13.34	Guise
But villaine he to whom these lines should goe,	P 696	13.40	Guise
proudest Kings/In Christendome, should beare me such derision,	P 761	15.19	Guise
They should know how I scornde them and their mockes.	P 762	15.20	Guise
his market, and set up your standing where you should not:	P 810	17.5	P Souldr
and tyll the ground that he himself should occupy, which is his	P 812	17.7	P Souldr
What should I doe but stand upon my guarde?	P 839	17.34	Guise
Twere hard with me if I should doubt my kinne,	P 971	19.41	King
To spend the treasure that should strength my land,	P1037	19.107	King
Yours my Lord Cardinall, you should have saide.	P1103	20.13	1Mur
That I with speed should have beene put to death.	P1118	21.12	Dumain
As if a Goose should play the Porpintine,	Edw	1.1.40	Gavstn
That he should nere returne into the realme:	Edw	1.1.84	Mortmr
This sword of mine that should offend your foes,	Edw	1.1.86	Mortmr
He should have lost his head, but with his looke,	Edw	1.1.113	Kent
Or looke to see the throne where you should sit,	Edw	1.1.131	Lncstr
What should a priest do with so faire a house?	Edw	1.1.206	Gavstn
And when I come, he frownes, as who should say,	Edw	1.2.53	Queene
Why should you love him, whome the world hates so?	Edw	1.4.76	Mortmr
You that be noble borne should pitie him.	Edw	1.4.80	Edward
You that are princely borne should shake him off,	Edw	1.4.81	Warwck
Why should a king be subject to a priest?	Edw	1.4.96	Edward
On whom but on my husband should I fawne?	Edw	1.4.146	Queene
For tis against my will he should returne.	Edw	1.4.217	Queene
Should beare us downe of the nobilitie,	Edw	1.4.286	Mortmr
Should by his soveraignes favour grow so pert,	Edw	1.4.404	Mortmr
Who should defray the money, but the King,	Edw	2.2.118	Mortmr
Twas in your wars, you should ransome him.	Edw	2.2.144	Lncstr
But whats the reason you should leave him now?	Edw	2.3.13	Penbrk
Father, thy face should harbor no deceit,	Edw	4.7.8	Edward
that the lowly earth/Should drinke his bloud, mounts up into	Edw	5.1.14	Edward
Me thinkes I should revenge me of the wronges,	Edw	5.1.24	Edward
who should protect the sonne,/But she that gave him life, I	Edw	5.2.90	Kent
that one so false/Should come about the person of a prince.	Edw	5.2.105	Mortmr
Nor I, and yet me thinkes I should command,	Edw	5.4.97	King
This ten dayes space, and least that I should sleepe,	Edw	5.5.60	Edward
Why should I greeve at my declining fall?	Edw	5.6.63	Mortmr
should stand upon; therefore acknowledge your errour,	F 203	1.2.10	P Wagner
Then wherefore should you aske me such a question?	F 208	1.2.15	P Wagner
<yet should I grieve for him>:	F 224	(HC258) A	2Schol
Is it unwilling I should write this byll?	F 454	2.1.66	Faust
Homo fuge: whether should I flye?	F 466	2.1.78	Faust
long e're this, I should have done the deed <slaine my selfe>,	F 575	2.2.24	Faust
Why should I die then, or basely despaire?	F 582	2.2.31	Faust
should turne to Gold, that I might locke you safe into <uppe	F 676	2.2.125	P Covet
That Peters heires should tread on Emperours,	F 918	3.1.140	Pope
If we should follow him to worke revenge,	F1448	4.3.18	Benvol
me what he should give me for as much Hay as he could eate;	F1527	4.5.23	P Carter
they should be good, for they come from a farre Country I can	F1576	4.6.19	P Faust
that flesh and bloud should be so fraile with your Worship:	F1632	4.6.75	P Carter
you remember you bid he should not ride [him] into the water?	F1636	4.6.79	P Carter
me thinkes you should have a wooden bedfellow of one of 'em.	F1653	4.6.96	P Carter
Majesty, we should thinke our selves much beholding unto you.	F1686	5.1.13	P 1Schol
How should he, but in <with> desperate lunacie.	F1807	5.2.11	Mephst
This soule should flie from me, and I be chang'd/[Unto] <Into>	F1967	5.2.171	Faust
then belike, if I were your man, I should be ful of vermine.	F App	p.229 22	P Clown
have as many english counters, and what should I do with these?	F App	p.230 34	P Clown
divels, say I should kill one of them, what would folkes say?	F App	p.230 46	P Clown
divell, so I should be cald kill divell all the parish over.	F App	p.230 48	P Clown
if I should serve you, would you teach me to raise up Banios	F App	p.230 56	P Clown
by him, for he bade me I should ride him into no water; now,	F App	p.240 131	P HrsCsr
thing then this, so it would content you, you should have it	F App	p.242 14	P Faust
Now Babilon, (proud through our spoile) should stoop,	Lucan, First Booke		10
What should I talke of mens corne reapt by force,	Lucan, First Booke		318
This hand (albeit unwilling) should performe it;	Lucan, First Booke		379
These troupes should soone pull down the church of Jove.	Lucan, First Booke		381
and that Roome/He looking on by these men should be sackt.	Lucan, First Booke		480
Then, that the trembling Citizens should walke/About the City;	Lucan, First Booke		591
Why should we wish the gods should ever end them?	Lucan, First Booke		668

SHOULD (cont.)

Least I should thinke thee guilty of offence. Ovid's Elegies 1.4.50
Wert thou rich, poore should not be my state. Ovid's Elegies 1.8.28
Least they should fly, being tane, the tirant play. Ovid's Elegies 1.8.70
Or least his love oft beaten backe should waine. Ovid's Elegies 1.8.76
rise/And who thou never think'st should fall downe lies. Ovid's Elegies 1.9.30
Bull and Eagle/And what ere love made Jove should thee invegle. Ovid's Elegies 1.10.8
Tis shame their wits should be more excelent. Ovid's Elegies 1.10.26
Why should one sell it, and the other buy it? Ovid's Elegies 1.10.34
Why should I loose, and thou gaine by the pleasure/Which man Ovid's Elegies 1.10.35
Tis shame sould tongues the guilty should defend/Or great Ovid's Elegies 1.10.39
I hate faire Paper should writte matter lacke. Ovid's Elegies 1.11.20
[All] <This> could I beare, but that the wench should rise,/Who Ovid's Elegies 1.13.25
Not one in heaven should be more base and vile. Ovid's Elegies 1.13.36
Oh how the burthen irkes, that we should shun. Ovid's Elegies 2.4.6
Me thinkes she should <would> be nimble when shees downe. Ovid's Elegies 2.4.14
Seeing she likes my bookes, why should we jarre? Ovid's Elegies 2.4.20
Cupid flie)/That my chiefe wish should be so oft to die. Ovid's Elegies 2.5.2
Or such, as least long yeares should turne the die, Ovid's Elegies 2.5.39
Least with worse kisses she should me indue. Ovid's Elegies 2.5.50
I grieve least others should such good perceive, Ovid's Elegies 2.5.53
My wenches vowes for thee what should I show, Ovid's Elegies 2.6.43
Should I sollicit her that is so just: Ovid's Elegies 2.7.25
With strawie cabins now her courts should build. Ovid's Elegies 2.9.18
Yet should I curse a God, if he but said, Ovid's Elegies 2.9.25
Mine owne desires why should my selfe not flatter? Ovid's Elegies 2.11.54
Least Arte should winne her, firmely did inclose. Ovid's Elegies 2.12.4
Because thy belly should rough wrinckles lacke, Ovid's Elegies 2.14.7
[Or] <On> stones, our stockes originall, should be hurld, Ovid's Elegies 2.14.11
Who should have Priams wealthy substance wonne, Ovid's Elegies 2.14.13
Then on the rough Alpes should I tread aloft, Ovid's Elegies 2.16.19
Thou swearest, devision should not twixt us rise, Ovid's Elegies 2.16.43
Since some faire one I should of force obey. Ovid's Elegies 2.17.6
What should I do with fortune that nere failes me? Ovid's Elegies 2.19.7
Wilt nothing do, why I should wish thy death? Ovid's Elegies 2.19.56
Thou deignst unequall lines should thee rehearse, Ovid's Elegies 3.1.37
Venus without me should be rusticall, Ovid's Elegies 3.1.43
Tut, men should not their courage so consume. Ovid's Elegies 3.3.34
The fathers thigh should unborne Bacchus lacke. Ovid's Elegies 3.3.40
Were I a God, I should give women leave, Ovid's Elegies 3.3.43
their wits should them defend. Ovid's Elegies 3.4.2
I know not, what men thinke should thee so move. Ovid's Elegies 3.4.28
What should I name Aesope, that Thebe lov'd, Ovid's Elegies 3.5.33
Shame, that should make me blush, I have no more. Ovid's Elegies 3.5.78
Well, I beleeve she kist not as she should, Ovid's Elegies 3.6.55
Now when he should not jette, he boults upright, Ovid's Elegies 3.6.67
And least her maide should know of this disgrace, Ovid's Elegies 3.6.83
If I should give, both would the house forbeare. Ovid's Elegies 3.7.64
What should I tell her vaine tongues filthy lyes, Ovid's Elegies 3.10.21
When Thebes, when Troy, when Caesar should be writ, Ovid's Elegies 3.11.15
Proteus what should I name? teeth, Thebes first seed? Ovid's Elegies 3.11.35
When fruite fild Tuscia should a wife give me, Ovid's Elegies 3.12.1
Where she should sit for men to gaze upon. Hero and Leander 1.8
We wish that one should loose, the other win. Hero and Leander 1.170
Why should you worship her? Hero and Leander 1.213
We humane creatures should enjoy that blisse. Hero and Leander 1.254
Aye me, such words as these should I abhor, Hero and Leander 1.339
in being bold/To eie those parts, which no eie should behold. Hero and Leander 1.408
That he and Povertie should alwaies kis. Hero and Leander 1.470
And swore he never should returne to Jove. Hero and Leander 2.168
And swore the sea should never doe him harme. Hero and Leander 2.180
Least water-nymphs should pull him from the brinke. Hero and Leander 2.198
That now should shine on Thetis glassie bower, Hero and Leander 2.203
Should know the pleasure of this blessed night, Hero and Leander 2.304

SHOULDE

But that greefe keepes me waking, I shoulde sleepe, Edw 5.5.93 Edward
Were Love the cause, it's like I shoulde descry him, Ovid's Elegies 1.2.5

SHOULDER

Or aged Atlas shoulder out of joynt, Dido 4.1.12 Achat
Thus leaning on the shoulder of the king, Edw 1.2.23 Warwck
heavens great beames/On Atlas shoulder, shall not lie more Edw 3.1.77 Prince
to the devill, for a shoulder of Mutton, tho it were bloud raw. F 350 1.4.8 P Wagner
will it please you to take a shoulder of Mutton to supper, and F1121 3.3.34 P Robin
he would give his soule to the Divel for a shoulder of mutton, F App p.229 8 P Wagner
to the Divel for a shoulder of mutton though twere blood rawe? F App p.229 10 P Clown
fire/Fleete on the flouds, the earth shoulder the sea, Lucan, First Booke 76
necke in touching, and surpast/The white of Pelops shoulder. Hero and Leander 1.65

SHOULDERS

And tricke thy armes and shoulders with my theft. Dido 1.1.45 Jupitr
His armes torne from his shoulders, and his breast/Furrowd with Dido 2.1.203 Aeneas
Such breadth of shoulders as might mainely beare/Olde Atlas 1Tamb 2.1.10 Menaph
with the foole, and rid your royall shoulders/Of such a burthen, 1Tamb 2.3.46 Tamb
Their shoulders broad, for complet armour fit, 1Tamb 3.3.107 Bajzth
Whose shoulders beare the Axis of the world, 2Tamb 5.3.59 Tamb
Heave up my shoulders when they call me dogge, Jew 2.3.24 Barab
What armes and shoulders did I touch and see, Ovid's Elegies 1.5.19
Would of mine armes, my shoulders had beene scanted, Ovid's Elegies 1.7.23
With thy white armes upon my shoulders seaze, Ovid's Elegies 2.16.29

SHOULD'ST

Thou should'st not thinke on <of> God. F 644 2.2.93 Belzeb
live along, then thou should'st see how fat I'de <I would> be. F 683 2.2.132 P Envy

SHOULDST

Blush blush for shame, why shouldst thou thinke of love? Dido 4.5.29 Nurse

SHOULDST (cont.)

Shouldst thou have entred, cruel Tamburlaine: 2Tamb 5.1.102 Govnr
Yet shouldst thou die, shoot at him all at once. 2Tamb 5.1.157 Tamb
Thou shouldst perceive the Duke of Guise is mov'd. P 832 17.27 Guise
Why shouldst thou kneele, knowest thou not who I am? Edw 1.1.142 Edward
Thou shouldst not plod one foote beyond this place. Edw 1.1.181 Gavstn
I meane the peeres, whom thou shouldst dearly love: Edw 2.2.176 Mortmr
Upon my weapons point here shouldst thou fall, Edw 2.5.13 Mortmr
blood,/Of thine own people patron shouldst thou be/But thou-- Edw 4.4.13 Queene
Why shouldst thou not? is not thy soule thine owne? F 457 2.1.69 Faust
Thou soone shouldst see me quit my foule disgrace. F1356 4.2.32 Benvol
Whence thou shouldst view thy Roome with squinting beams. Lucan, First Booke 55
shouldst thou bid me/Intombe my sword within my brothers Lucan, First Booke 376
O Phoebus shouldst thou with thy rayes now sing/The fell Nemean Lucan, First Booke 654
But how thou shouldst behave thy selfe now know; Ovid's Elegies 1.4.11
And why shouldst not please? Ovid's Elegies 1.8.25
Would he not buy thee thou for him shouldst care. Ovid's Elegies 1.8.34
Jove that thou shouldst not hast but wait his leasure, Ovid's Elegies 1.13.45
Worthy she is, thou shouldst in mercy save her. Ovid's Elegies 2.13.22
Or [be] a loade thou shouldst refuse to beare. Ovid's Elegies 2.15.22
Then shouldst thou bee his prisoner who is thine. Hero and Leander 1.202

SHOUT (See also SHOWTS)

The shout is nigh; the golden pompe comes heere. Ovid's Elegies 3.2.44

SHOUTS

Receive with shouts; where thou wilt raigne as King, Lucan, First Booke 47

SHOW (See also SHEW)

Besmer'd with blood, that makes a dainty show. 1Tamb 1.1.80 Mycet
And well his merits show him to be made/His Fortunes maister, 1Tamb 2.1.35 Cosroe
And show your pleasure to the Persean, 1Tamb 3.1.43 Bassoe
In spight of death I will goe show my face. 2Tamb 5.3.114 Tamb
Whose proud fantastick liveries make such show, Edw 1.4.410 Mortmr
Thy mother shall from heaven applaud this show, Ovid's Elegies 1.2.39
Then seeing I grace thy show in following thee, Ovid's Elegies 1.2.49
Let poore men show their service, faith, and care; Ovid's Elegies 1.10.57
My wenches vowes for thee what should I show, Ovid's Elegies 2.6.43

SHOWE

not the Turke and his wife make a goodly showe at a banquet? 1Tamb 4.4.58 P Tamb
Can you in words make showe of amitie, Edw 2.2.32 Edward
To undermine us with a showe of love. Edw 2.3.6 Lncstr

SHOWER (See also SHEWER)

Faire Anna, how escapt you from the shower? Dido 4.1.29 Aeneas
Forgetst thou that I sent a shower of dartes/Mingled with 2Tamb 1.1.91 Orcan
Which if a shower of wounding thunderbolts/Should breake out 2Tamb 2.2.13 Gazell
Her wofull bosome a warme shower did drowne. Ovid's Elegies 3.5.68

SHOWERS

See how he raines down heaps of gold in showers, 1Tamb 1.2.182 Tamb
Or ever drisling drops of Aprill showers, 1Tamb 4.1.31 Souldn
Rain'st on the earth resolved pearle in showers, 1Tamb 5.1.142 Tamb
Bene oft resolv'd in bloody purple showers, 1Tamb 5.1.460 Tamb
Will poure it downe in showers on our heads: 2Tamb 3.1.36 Callap
That suffered Jove to passe in showers of golde/To Danae, all Edw 3.1.267 Spencr
Raigne showers of vengeance on my cursed head/Thou God, to whom Edw 4.6.7 Kent
Weare me, when warmest showers thy members wash, Ovid's Elegies 2.15.23
A little boy druncke teate-distilling showers. Ovid's Elegies 3.9.22

SHOWES

Inventing maskes and stately showes for her, 2Tamb 4.2.94 Therid
How showes it by night? Jew 2.3.62 Lodowk
Sweete speeches, comedies, and pleasing showes, Edw 1.1.56 Gavstn
In sollemne triumphes, and in publike showes, Edw 1.4.350 Edward
lascivious showes/And prodigall gifts bestowed on Gaveston, Edw 2.2.157 Mortmr
Let Kings give place to verse, and kingly showes, Ovid's Elegies 1.15.33

SHOWNE

Take in the staffe too, for that must be showne: Jew 4.1.204 Barab
The many favours which your grace hath showne, P 9 1.9 Navrre
That powres in lieu of all your goodnes showne, Edw 3.1.44 Spencr
Such light to shamefaste maidens must be showne, Ovid's Elegies 1.5.7
Then thinkest thou thy loose life is not showne? Ovid's Elegies 1.13.34

SHOWTS

the showts rent heaven,/As when against pine bearing Ossa's Lucan, First Booke 389

SHREEKE

one, me thought/I heard him shreeke and call aloud for helpe: F1992 5.3.10 3Schol

SHREWDLY

Not one alive, but shrewdly I suspect, Edw 4.7.28 Spencr

SHREWISH

That will not shield me from her shrewish blowes: Dido 1.1.4 Ganimd

SHRIEK (See SCHRIGHT, SHREEKE)

SHRIFT

'twas told me in shrift,/Thou know'st 'tis death and if it be Jew 3.6.50 2Fryar

SHRIKES

Such fearefull shrikes, and cries, were never heard, F1986 5.3.4 1Schol

SHRIL

noise/Of trumpets clange, shril cornets, whistling fifes; Lucan, First Booke 240

SHRILD

For long shrild trumpets let your notes resound. Ovid's Elegies 2.6.6

SHRILL

in untrod woods/Shrill voices schright, and ghoasts incounter Lucan, First Booke 568
And birdes send forth shrill notes from everie bow. Ovid's Elegies 1.13.8

SHRIN'D

And in my thoughts is shrin'd another [love] <Iove>: Dido 3.1.58 Dido

SHRINE

That offered jewels to thy sacred shrine, 1Tamb 3.3.199 Zabina

SHRINES

Or steale your houshold lares from their shrines: Dido 1.2.11 Illion

SHRINKE			
My sinnewes shrinke, my braines turne upside downe,	P 549	11.14	Charls
What rebels, do you shrinke, and sound retreat?	Edw	3.1.200	Edward
SHRINKES			
But he shrinkes backe, and now remembring me,	Dido	5.1.190	Dido
But he remembring me shrinkes backe againe:	Dido	5.1.260	Dido
SHRIV'D (See also SHRIFT)			
For presently you shall be shriv'd.	Jew	4.1.110	1Fryar
For he that shriv'd her is within my house.	Jew	4.1.115	Barab
SHROUD			
To shroud his shame in darknes of the night.	1Tamb	4.1.46	Souldn
Than this base earth should shroud your majesty:	2Tamb	2.4.60	Zenoc
you have had a shroud journey of it, will it please you to take	F1120	3.3.33	P Robin
SHROWD			
Shrowd any thought may holde my striving hands/From martiall	2Tamb	4.1.95	Tamb
SHROWDE			
any Element/Shal shrowde thee from the wrath of Tamburlaine.	2Tamb	3.5.127	Tamb
SHROWDED			
Who sees it, graunts some deity there is shrowded.	Ovid's Elegies		3.12.8
SHROWDES			
And shrowdes thy beautie in this borrowd shape:	Dido	1.1.192	Aeneas
Whose glittering pompe Dianas shrowdes supplies,	Dido	3.3.4	Dido
SHRUBS			
And others are but shrubs compard to me,	Edw	5.6.12	Mortmr
SHRUNKE			
And shrunke not backe, knowing my love was there?	Dido	4.4.146	Dido
Herewith afrighted Hero shrunke away,	Hero and Leander		2.253
SHUFFLE			
thou hast all the Cardes within thy hands/To shuffle or cut,	P 147	2.90	Guise
SHULD			
in the month of January, how you shuld come by these grapes.	F App	p.242 18	P Duke
SHUN			
As my despised worths, that shun all praise,	Dido	3.4.42	Aeneas
And yet wouldst shun the wavering turnes of war,	1Tamb	5.1.360	Zenoc
And wilt thou shun the field for feare of woundes?	2Tamb	3.2.109	Tamb
To shun suspition, therefore, let us part.	Jew	2.1.57	Abigal
What shall I doe to shun the snares of death?	F1742	5.1.69	Faust
Oh how the burthen irkes, that we should shun.	Ovid's Elegies		2.4.6
O shun me not, but heare me ere you goe,	Hero and Leander		1.205
SHUNNE			
Nor morning starres shunne thy uprising face.	Ovid's Elegies		1.13.28
What flies, I followe, what followes me I shunne.	Ovid's Elegies		2.19.36
What will my age do, age I cannot shunne,	Ovid's Elegies		3.6.17
And before folke immodest speeches shunne,	Ovid's Elegies		3.13.16
SHUT			
but most astonied/To see his choller shut in secrete thoughtes,	1Tamb	3.2.70	Agidas
And shut the windowes of the lightsome heavens.	1Tamb	5.1.293	Bajzth
not perswade you to submission,/But stil the ports were shut:	2Tamb	5.1.95	Tamb
unrelenting eares/Of death and hell be shut against my praiers,	2Tamb	5.3.192	Amyras
by this Bernardine/To be a Christian, I shut him out,	Jew	4.1.188	Barab
And in an out-house of the City shut/His souldiers, till I have	Jew	5.2.81	Barab
One window shut, the other open stood,	Ovid's Elegies		1.5.3
Though it be so, shut me not out therefore,	Ovid's Elegies		1.6.47
To beggers shut, to bringers ope thy gate,	Ovid's Elegies		1.8.77
My wench her dore shut, Joves affares I left,	Ovid's Elegies		2.1.17
Her shut gates greater lightning then thyne brought.	Ovid's Elegies		2.1.20
Beginne to shut thy house at evening sure.	Ovid's Elegies		2.19.38
All being shut out, th'adulterer is within.	Ovid's Elegies		3.4.8
In stone, and Yron walles Danae shut,	Ovid's Elegies		3.4.21
Courts shut the poore out; wealth gives estimation,	Ovid's Elegies		3.7.55
The East winds in Ulisses baggs we shut,	Ovid's Elegies		3.11.29
SHUTT			
She prais'd me, yet the gate shutt fast upon her,	Ovid's Elegies		3.7.7
SHYNING			
Whose shyning Turrets shal dismay the heavens,	2Tamb	4.3.112	Tamb
My hands an unsheath'd shyning weapon have not.	Ovid's Elegies		2.2.64
SI			
Si bene quid de te merui, fuit aut tibi quidquam/Dulce meum,	Dido	5.1.136	Dido
Oro, si quis [adhuc] <ad haec> precibus locus, exue mentem.	Dido	5.1.138	Dido
Si una eademque res legatur duobus, alter rem, alter valorem	F 56	1.1.28	P Faust
Si peccasse negamus, fallimur, et nulla est in nobis veritas:	F 68	1.1.40	P Faust
SIB			
tush Sib, if this be all/Valoys and I will soone be friends	Edw	3.1.66	Edward
SIBILS			
moves/To wound their armes, sing vengeance, Sibils priests,	Lucan, First Booke		564
SIBYLLA (See SYBILLAS)			
SIC			
Sic sic juvat ire sub umbras.	Dido	5.1.313	Dido
that/Was wont to make our schooles ring, with sic probo.	F 195	1.2.2	1Schol
SICHEUS			
Goe fetch the garment which Sicheus ware:	Dido	2.1.80	Dido
Sicheus, not Aeneas be thou calde:	Dido	3.4.59	Dido
Which Circes sent Sicheus when he lived:	Dido	4.4.11	Dido
SICILY (See also SCICILIE, SYCILLIA, CICILIANS)			
Oh they were going up to Sicily:	Jew	1.1.98	Barab
And shipping of our goods to Sicily,	Jew	3.5.15	Govnr
And toward Calabria, back'd by Sicily,	Jew	5.3.9	Calym
SICK			
<humble> intreates your Majestie/To visite him sick in his bed.	P 246	4.44	Man
The king is love-sick for his minion.	Edw	1.4.87	Mortmr
but hark ye sir, if my horse be sick, or ill at ease, if I bring	F App	p.240 118	P HrsCsr
SICKE			
What ailes my Queene, is she falne sicke of late?	Dido	3.4.24	Aeneas

SICKE (cont.)

Not sicke my love, but sicke:-- Dido 3.4.25 Dido
As was the fame of [Clymens] <Clymeus> brain-sicke sonne,/That 1Tamb 4.2.49 Tamb
Raven that tolls/The sicke mans passeport in her hollow beake, Jew 2.1.2 Barab
abroad a nights/And kill sicke people groaning under walls: Jew 2.3.175 Barab
Oh brother, brother, all the Nuns are sicke, Jew 3.6.1 1Fryar
but I hope it be/Only some naturall passion makes her sicke. P 183 3.18 QnMarg
doe not languish/And then report her sicke and full of anguish. Ovid's Elegies 2.2.22
Even as the sicke desire forbidden drinke. Ovid's Elegies 3.4.18
Oft bitter juice brings to the sicke reliefe. Ovid's Elegies 3.10.8
Hearing her to be sicke, I thether ranne, Ovid's Elegies 3.10.25
But with my rivall sicke she was not than. Ovid's Elegies 3.10.26

SICKLES

Or men with crooked sickles corne downe fell. Ovid's Elegies 1.15.12

SICKLY

I must have one that's sickly, and be but for sparing vittles: Jew 2.3.123 P Barab

SICKNES

Sicknes or death can never conquer me. 2Tamb 5.1.222 Tamb
Tel me, what think you of my sicknes now? 2Tamb 5.3.81 Tamb

SICKNESSE

Shall sicknesse proove me now to be a man, 2Tamb 5.3.44 Tamb
<Belike he is growne into some sicknesse, by> being over F1829 (HC270)A P 3Schol
No sicknesse harm'd thee, farre be that a way, Ovid's Elegies 1.14.41

SIDE

Having a quiver girded to her side, Dido 1.1.185 Venus
Untill I gird my quiver to my side: Dido 3.3.8 Dido
O Anna, runne unto the water side, Dido 4.4.1 Dido
By this is he got to the water side, Dido 5.1.188 Dido
That they lie panting on the Gallies side, 1Tamb 3.3.53 Tamb
Waiting my comming to the river side, 2Tamb 1.2.22 Callap
Plac'd by her side, looke on their mothers face. 2Tamb 1.3.20 Tamb
A deadly bullet gliding through my side, 2Tamb 3.4.4 Capt
By whose proud side the ugly furies run, 2Tamb 3.4.59 Therid
And thus are wee on every side inrich'd: Jew 1.1.104 Barab
And on the other side against the Turke, P 462 8.12 Anjoy
Your grace doth wel to place him by your side, Edw 1.4.10 Lncstr
So shall we have the people of our side, Edw 1.4.282 Mortmr
Not Mortimer, nor any of his side, Edw 2.1.4 Spencr
Shall have me from my gratious mothers side, Edw 4.2.23 Prince
Each side had great partakers; Caesars cause, Lucan, First Booke 128
or his speare/Sticks in his side) yet runs upon the hunter. Lucan, First Booke 214
Sword-girt Orions side glisters too bright. Lucan, First Booke 664
Which troopes hath alwayes bin on Cupids side: Ovid's Elegies 1.2.36
The gate halfe ope my bent side in will take. Ovid's Elegies 1.6.4
Venus thy side doth warme,/And brings good fortune, a rich Ovid's Elegies 1.8.30
Of horne the bowe was that approv'd their side. Ovid's Elegies 1.8.48
If ever, now well lies she by my side. Ovid's Elegies 1.13.6
This side that serves thee, a sharpe sword did weare. Ovid's Elegies 3.7.14
His side past service, and his courage spent. Ovid's Elegies 3.10.14
When have not I fixt to thy side close layed? Ovid's Elegies 3.10.17

SIDES

As every tide tilts twixt their oken sides: Dido 1.1.224 Aeneas
Old men with swords thrust through their aged sides, Dido 2.1.197 Aeneas
Having the King, Queene Mother on our sides, P 29 1.29 Navrre
Slaughter themselves in others and their sides/With their owne Edw 4.4.7 Queene
Or Lapland Giants trotting by our sides: F 153 1.1.125 Valdes
My sides are sore with tumbling to and fro. Ovid's Elegies 1.2.4
By thy sides touching ill she is entreated. Ovid's Elegies 3.2.22

SIDONIAN

Whereas Sidonian Dido rules as Queene. Dido 1.1.213 Venus

SIEGE

And thinks to rouse us from our dreadful siege/Of the famous 1Tamb 3.1.5 Bajzth
Nor raise our siege before the Gretians yeeld, 1Tamb 3.1.14 Bajzth
But if he dare attempt to stir your siege, 1Tamb 3.1.46 Argier
And hasten to remoove Damascus siege. 1Tamb 4.3.18 Souldn
Whose sorrowes lay more siege unto my soule, 1Tamb 5.1.155 Tamb
Forgetst thou, that to have me raise my siege, 2Tamb 1.1.98 Orcan
And had she liv'd before the siege of Troy, 2Tamb 2.4.86 Tamb
Who meanes to gyrt Natolias walles with siege, 2Tamb 3.5.8 2Msngr
Though this be held his last daies dreadfull siege, 2Tamb 5.1.29 1Citzn
As durst resist us till our third daies siege: 2Tamb 5.1.59 Techel
Which being faint and weary with the siege, 2Tamb 5.2.7 Callap
Girting this strumpet Cittie with our siege, P1152 22.14 King
Troy had not yet beene ten yeares siege out-stander, Ovid's Elegies 3.5.27

SIFT

[Sathan begins to sift me with his pride]: F1791 5.1.118A OldMan
Ile not sift much, but hold thee soone excusde, Ovid's Elegies 3.13.41

SIGH

O shall I speake, or shall I sigh and die! Edw 3.1.122 Edward
There might you see one sigh, another rage, Hero and Leander 1.125
As made Love sigh, to see his tirannie. Hero and Leander 1.374

SIGH'D

Soules quiet and appeas'd [sigh'd] <sight> from their graves, Lucan, First Booke 566
Breathlesse spoke some thing, and sigh'd out the rest; Hero and Leander 2.280
And sigh'd to thinke upon th'approching sunne, Hero and Leander 2.302

SIGHES

And when my grieved heart sighes and sayes no, Dido 2.1.26 Aeneas
Her cheekes swolne with sighes, her haire all rent, Dido 2.1.276 Aeneas
Nor yet this aier, beat often with thy sighes, 2Tamb 4.2.10 Olymp
Altar I will offer up/My daily sacrifice of sighes and teares, Jew 3.2.32 Govnr
With gastlie murmure of my sighes and cries, Edw 1.4.179 Queene
Whose pining heart, her inward sighes have blasted, Edw 2.4.24 Queene
Wet with my teares, and dried againe with sighes, Edw 5.1.118 Edward

SIGHES (cont.)			
And armes all naked, who with broken sighes,	Lucan, First Booke		191
SIGHING			
Witnesse this hart, that sighing for thee breakes,	Edw	1.4.165	Queene
Thus sighing whispered they, and none durst speake/And shew	Lucan, First Booke		259
Sighing she stood, her bloodlesse white lookes shewed/Like	Ovid's Elegies		1.7.51
SIGHS			
Oh that my sighs could turne to lively breath;	Jew	3.2.18	Govnr
to display/Loves holy fire, with words, with sighs and teares,	Hero and Leander		1.193
SIGHT (Homograph)			
When as they would have hal'd thee from my sight:	Dido	1.1.27	Jupitr
Thy mind Aeneas that would have it so/Deludes thy eye sight,	Dido	2.1.32	Achat
Your sight amazde me, O what destinies/Have brought my sweete	Dido	2.1.59	Aeneas
Depart from Carthage, come not in my sight.	Dido	3.1.44	Dido
Because his lothsome sight offends mine eye,	Dido	3.1.57	Dido
To presse beyond acceptance to your sight.	Dido	3.3.16	Aeneas
Come forth the Cave: can heaven endure this sight?	Dido	4.1.17	Iarbus
Yet he that in my sight would not relent,	Dido	5.1.186	Dido
Are fixt his piercing instruments of sight:	1Tamb	2.1.14	Menaph
A sight as banefull to their soules I think/As are Thessalian	1Tamb	5.1.132	Tamb
O dreary Engines of my loathed sight,	1Tamb	5.1.259	Bajzth
Whose sight with joy would take away my life,	1Tamb	5.1.419	Arabia
But making now a vertue of thy sight,	1Tamb	5.1.428	Arabia
O sight thrice welcome to my joiful soule,	1Tamb	5.1.440	Zenoc
And see my Lord, a sight of strange import,	1Tamb	5.1.468	Tamb
And sweare in sight of heaven and by thy Christ.	2Tamb	1.1.132	Orcan
It could not more delight me than your sight.	2Tamb	1.3.156	Tamb
The Sun unable to sustaine the sight,	2Tamb	1.3.168	Tamb
appeares as full/As raies of Cynthia to the clearest sight?	2Tamb	2.3.30	Orcan
whose taste illuminates/Refined eies with an eternall sight,	2Tamb	2.4.23	Tamb
While I sit smiling to behold the sight.	2Tamb	3.2.128	Tamb
Me thinks tis a pitifull sight.	2Tamb	3.2.131	P Calyph
Whose sight composde of furie and of fire/Doth send such sterne	2Tamb	4.1.175	Trebiz
Whereas the Sun declining from our sight,	2Tamb	5.3.148	Tamb
And when my soule hath vertue of your sight,	2Tamb	5.3.225	Tamb
Who stand accursed in the sight of heaven,	Jew	1.2.64	Govnr
Away accursed from thy fathers sight.	Jew	1.2.351	Barab
Lodowicke, I have seene/The strangest sight, in my opinion,	Jew	1.2.376	Mthias
That I may have a sight of Abigall;	Jew	2.3.34	Lodowk
What sight is this? my [Lodovico] <Lodowicke> slaine!	Jew	3.2.10	Govnr
Away with him, his sight is death to me.	Jew	5.1.35	Govnr
O holde me up, my sight begins to faile,	P 548	11.13	Charls
Where we may one injoy the others sight.	P 665	13.9	Duchss
In sight and judgement of thy lustfull eye?	P 687	13.31	Guise
Ah this sweet sight is phisick to my soule,	P1020	19.90	King
Take hence that damned villaine from my sight.	P1182	22.44	King
The sight of London to my exiled eyes,	Edw	1.1.10	Gavstn
I have my wish, in that I joy thy sight,	Edw	1.1.151	Edward
What man of noble birth can brooke this sight?	Edw	1.4.12	MortSr
Assure thy selfe thou comst not in my sight.	Edw	1.4.169	Edward
And to behold so sweete a sight as that,	Edw	1.4.206	Warwck
She neither walkes abroad, nor comes in sight:	Edw	2.1.24	Baldck
and now thy sight/Is sweeter farre, then was thy parting hence	Edw	2.2.56	Edward
Out of my sight, and trouble me no more.	Edw	2.2.216	Edward
My heart with pittie earnes to see this sight,	Edw	4.7.70	Abbot
Call me not lorde, away, out of my sight:	Edw	5.1.113	Edward
If with the sight thereof she be not mooved,	Edw	5.1.119	Edward
Whose sight is loathsome to all winged fowles?	Edw	5.3.7	Edward
What sight is this?	F 532	2.1.144	Faust
That sight will be as pleasant to <pleasing unto> me, as	F 657	2.2.106	P Faust
O how this sight doth delight <this feedes> my soule.	F 712	2.2.164	Faust
thoughts are ravished so/With sight of this renowned Emperour,	F1261	4.1.107	Emper
And in this sight thou better pleasest me,	F1271	4.1.117	Emper
O wondrous sight:	F1276	4.1.122	Emper
the sight whereof so delighted me, as nothing in the world	F1560	4.6.3	P Duke
and for this blessed sight <glorious deed>/Happy and blest be	F1704	5.1.31	1Schol
<Wee'l take our leaves>, and for this blessed sight	F1704	(HC269)B	1Schol
Then thou art banisht from the sight of heaven;	F1715	5.1.42	OldMan
ugly jointes/Then nature gives, whose sight appauls the mother,	Lucan, First Booke		561
Soules quiet and appeas'd [sigh'd] <sight> from their graves,	Lucan, First Booke		566
I will weepe/And to the dores sight of thy selfe [will] keepe:	Ovid's Elegies		1.4.62
Poore travailers though tierd, rise at thy sight,	Ovid's Elegies		1.13.13
Who ever lov'd, that lov'd not at first sight?	Hero and Leander		1.176
And her all naked to his sight displayd.	Hero and Leander		2.324
SIGHTS			
Al sights of power to grace my victory:	1Tamb	5.1.474	Tamb
for these pleasant sights, nor know I how sufficiently to	F1558	4.6.1	P Duke
that you have taken no pleasure in those sights; therefor I	F1566	4.6.9	P Faust
Strange sights appear'd, the angry threatning gods/Fill'd both	Lucan, First Booke		522
Such sights as this, to tender maids are rare.	Hero and Leander		2.238
SIGISMOND			
Where Sigismond the king of Hungary/Should meet our person to	2Tamb	1.1.9	Orcan
Besides, king Sigismond hath brought from Christendome,	2Tamb	1.1.20	Uribas
to parle for a peace/With Sigismond the king of Hungary:	2Tamb	1.1.51	Gazell
Enough to swallow forcelesse Sigismond,	2Tamb	1.1.65	Orcan
Stay Sigismond, forgetst thou I am he/That with the Cannon	2Tamb	1.1.86	Orcan
So prest are we, but yet if Sigismond/Speake as a friend, and	2Tamb	1.1.122	Orcan
But (Sigismond) confirme it with an oath,	2Tamb	1.1.131	Orcan
Now Sigismond, if any Christian King/Encroche upon the confines	2Tamb	1.1.146	Orcan
Sigismond will send/A hundred thousand horse train'd to the	2Tamb	1.1.153	Sgsmnd
I thank thee Sigismond, but when I war/All Asia Minor, Affrica,	2Tamb	1.1.157	Orcan
Freend Sigismond, and peeres of Hungary,	2Tamb	1.1.164	Orcan
Pope Julius swore to Princely Sigismond,	F 925	3.1.147	Bruno

Line	Work	Reference	Speaker
SIGN'D			
and our solemne othes/Sign'd with our handes, each shal retaine	2Tamb	1.1.144	Orcan
SIGNE			
And take in signe thereof this gilded wreath,	1Tamb	5.1.101	1Virgn
Shake with their waight in signe of feare and griefe:	1Tamb	5.1.349	Zenoc
In signe of love and dutie to this presence,	Edw	4.6.48	Rice
now theres a signe of grace in you, when you will confesse the	F App	p.237 44	P Knight
Onely Ile signe nought, that may grieve me much.	Ovid's Elegies		2.15.18
White-cheekt Penelope knewe Ulisses signe,	Ovid's Elegies		2.18.29
Therefore in signe her treasure suffred wracke,	Hero and Leander		1.49
SIGNES			
Graunt that these signes of victorie we yeeld/May bind the	1Tamb	5.1.55	2Virgn
Lines, Circles, [Signes], Letters, [and] Characters,	F 78	1.1.50	Faust
And Characters of Signes, and [erring] <evening> Starres,	F 240	1.3.12	Faust
might ease/The Commons jangling minds, apparant signes arose,	Lucan, First Booke		521
These direful signes made Aruns stand amaz'd,	Lucan, First Booke		615
Tydides left worst signes of villanie,	Ovid's Elegies		1.7.31
And least the sad signes of my crime remaine,	Ovid's Elegies		1.7.67
commodious/And to give signes dull wit to thee is odious.	Ovid's Elegies		1.11.4
loves bowe/His owne flames best acquainted signes may knowe,	Ovid's Elegies		2.1.8
She beckt, and prosperous signes gave as she moved.	Ovid's Elegies		3.2.58
And each give signes by casting up his cloake.	Ovid's Elegies		3.2.74
Behold the signes of antient fight, his skarres,	Ovid's Elegies		3.7.19
With privy signes, and talke dissembling truths?	Ovid's Elegies		3.10.24
SIGNET			
Bearing his privie signet and his hand:	1Tamb	1.2.15	Zenoc
SIGNIFIE			
To signifie she was a princesse borne,	2Tamb	3.2.21	Amyras
To signifie the slaughter of the Gods.	2Tamb	5.3.50	Tamb
SIGNIFY			
To signify the mildnesse of his minde:	1Tamb	4.1.52	2Msngr
SIGNORY			
Why, the Signory of Embden shall be mine:	F 412	2.1.24	Faust
SIGNS			
Thus while dum signs their yeelding harts entangled,	Hero and Leander		1.187
SIGNUM			
ecce signum, heeres a simple purchase for horse-keepers, our	F App	p.234 2	P Robin
SIGNUMQUE			
signumque crucis quod nunc facio; et per vota nostra ipse nunc	F 249	1.3.21	P Faust
SILENCE			
And wrapt in silence of his angry soule.	1Tamb	3.2.71	Agidas
In silence of thy solemn Evenings walk,	1Tamb	5.1.148	Tamb
But in dumbe silence let them come and goe.	F1252	4.1.98	Faust
But law being put to silence by the wars,	Lucan, First Booke		278
appeasd/The wrastling tumult, and right hand made silence:	Lucan, First Booke		299
Lightning in silence, stole forth without clouds,	Lucan, First Booke		531
In nights deepe silence why the ban-dogges barke.	Ovid's Elegies		2.19.40
In silence of the night to viste us),	Hero and Leander		1.350
So that in silence of the cloudie night,	Hero and Leander		2.101
SILENT			
O leave me, leave me to my silent thoughts,	Dido	4.2.38	Iarbus
Be silent, Daughter, sufferance breeds ease,	Jew	1.2.238	Barab
And in the shadow of the silent night/Doth shake contagion from	Jew	2.1.3	Barab
As silent and as carefull will we be,	Edw	4.7.2	Abbot
Let never silent night possesse this clime,	Edw	5.1.65	Edward
Be silent then, for danger is in words.	F1696	5.1.23	Faust
course that time doth runne with calme and silent foote,	F App	p.239 91	P Faust
but as the fields/When birds are silent thorough winters rage;	Lucan, First Booke		261
That soules passe not to silent Erebus/Or Plutoes bloodles	Lucan, First Booke		451
Silent the Cittie is:	Ovid's Elegies		1.6.55
Her teares, she silent, guilty did pronounce me.	Ovid's Elegies		1.7.22
Not silent were thine eyes, the boord with wine/Was scribled,	Ovid's Elegies		2.5.17
SILK			
A hundred Bassoes cloath'd in crimson silk/Shall ride before	2Tamb	1.2.46	Callap
SILKE			
Embost with silke as best beseemes my state,	1Tamb	1.1.99	Mycet
Thy Garments shall be made of Medean silke,	1Tamb	1.2.95	Tamb
The townes-men maske in silke and cloath of gold,	1Tamb	4.2.108	Tamb
I'le have them fill the publique Schooles with [silke] <skill>,	F 117	1.1.89	Faust
No slave, in beaten silke, and staves-aker.	F 357	1.4.15	P Wagner
No sirra, in beaten silke and staves acre.	F App	p.229 16	P Wagner
fine and thinne/Like to the silke the curious Seres spinne,	Ovid's Elegies		1.14.6
The lining, purple silke, with guilt starres drawne,	Hero and Leander		1.10
SILKEN			
Sit up my boy, and with those silken raines,	2Tamb	5.3.202	Tamb
SILKES			
Loaden with Spice and Silkes, now under saile,	Jew	1.1.45	Barab
with riches, and exceeding store/Of Persian silkes, of gold,	Jew	1.1.88	2Merch
Send to the Merchant, bid him bring me silkes,	Jew	4.2.84	Curtzn
Then gaudie silkes, or rich imbrotherie.	Edw	1.4.347	Edward
SILLIE			
As Jupiter to sillie [Baucis] <Vausis> house:	Dido	1.2.41	Iarbus
May spelles and droughs <drugges> do sillie soules such harmes?	Ovid's Elegies		3.6.28
(Poore sillie maiden) at his mercie was.	Hero and Leander		2.286
SILLOGISMES			
have with [concise] <subtle> Sillogismes <Consissylogismes>	F 139	1.1.111	Faust
SILLY			
By lawlesse rapine from a silly maide.	1Tamb	1.2.10	Zenoc
And these that seeme but silly country Swaines,	1Tamb	1.2.47	Tamb
But if presuming on his silly power,	1Tamb	3.1.33	Bajzth
These silly men mistake the matter cleane.	Jew	1.1.179	Barab
Oh silly brethren, borne to see this day!	Jew	1.2.170	Barab
My daughter here, a paltry silly girle.	Jew	2.3.284	Barab

SILVA			
And Nigra Silva, where the Devils dance,	2Tamb	1.3.212	Therid
SILVANUS			
And drench Silvanus dwellings with their shewers,	Dido	3.2.91	Juno
SILVER			
And Venus Swannes shall shed their silver downe,	Dido	1.1.36	Jupitr
A silver girdle, and a golden purse,	Dido	2.1.306	Venus
Hollow Pyramides of silver plate:	Dido	3.1.123	Dido
Her silver armes will coll me round about,	Dido	4.3.51	Aeneas
And silver whistles to controule the windes,	Dido	4.4.10	Dido
And in the midst doth run a silver streame,	Dido	4.5.9	Nurse
Brighter than is the silver [Rhodope] <Rhodolfe>,	1Tamb	1.2.88	Tamb
And all that pierceth Phoebes silver eie,	1Tamb	3.2.19	Agidas
and on his silver crest/A snowy Feather spangled white he	1Tamb	4.1.50	2Msngr
within whose silver haires/Honor and reverence evermore have	1Tamb	5.1.81	1Virgn
Shaking her silver tresses in the aire,	1Tamb	5.1.141	Tamb
That danc'd with glorie on the silver waves,	2Tamb	2.4.3	Tamb
Like tried silver runs through Paradice/To entertaine divine	2Tamb	2.4.24	Tamb
The gold, the silver, and the pearle ye got,	2Tamb	3.4.88	Therid
'Tis silver, I disdaine it.	Jew	3.1.13	Curtzn
These silver haires will more adorne my court,	Edw	1.4.346	Edward
Or open his mouth, and powre quick silver downe,	Edw	5.4.36	Ltborn
Behold this Silver Belt whereto is fixt/Seven golden [keys]	F 932	3.1.154	Pope
Gold, silver, irons heavy weight, and brasse,	Ovid's Elegies		3.7.37
And in the midst a silver altar stood,	Hero and Leander		1.157
And silver tincture of her cheekes, that drew/The love of	Hero and Leander		1.396
And as her silver body downeward went,	Hero and Leander		2.263
SILVERBINGS			
Here have I purst their paltry [silverlings] <silverbings>.	Jew	1.1.6	Barab
SILVERED			
Buskins of shels all silvered, used she,	Hero and Leander		1.31
SILVERLINGS			
Here have I purst their paltry [silverlings] <silverbings>.	Jew	1.1.6	Barab
SIMBOLISDE			
Water and ayre being simbolisde in one,	2Tamb	1.3.23	Tamb
SIMILE			
I doe you honor in the simile,	2Tamb	3.5.69	Tamb
SIMOIS (See SYMOIS)			
SIMPLE			
Tut, I am simple, without [minde] <made> to hurt,	Dido	3.2.16	Juno
They knew not, ah, they knew not simple men,	1Tamb	2.4.2	Mycet
Here will I hide it in this simple hole.	1Tamb	2.4.15	Mycet
What simple Virgins may perswade, we will.	1Tamb	5.1.61	2Virgn
And that will prove but simple policie.	Jew	1.2.159	1Knght
No simple place, no small authority,	Jew	5.2.28	Barab
To think a word of such a simple sound,	P 125	2.68	Guise
Maddame, I beseech your grace to except this simple gift.	P 166	3.1	P Pothec
And simple meaning to your Majestie,	P 867	17.62	Guise
Too simple is my wit to tell her worth <praise>,/Whom all the	F1697	5.1.24	2Schol
heeres a simple purchase for horse-keepers, our horses shal	F App	p.234 2	P Robin
If not, because shees simple I would have her.	Ovid's Elegies		2.4.18
Ah simple Hero, learne thy selfe to cherish,	Hero and Leander		1.241
And gave it to his simple rustike love,	Hero and Leander		1.435
SIMPLEST			
And simplest extracts of all Minerals,	2Tamb	4.2.61	Olymp
SIMPLICITIE			
See the simplicitie of these base slaves,	Jew	1.2.214	Barab
Naked simplicitie, and modest grace.	Ovid's Elegies		1.3.14
Full of simplicitie and naked truth.	Hero and Leander		1.208
SIMPLICITY			
And not simplicity, as they suggest.	Jew	1.2.161	Barab
are in thy soft brest/But pure simplicity in thee doth rest.	Ovid's Elegies		1.11.10
SIN (See also SINNE)			
Murmures and hisses for his hainous sin.	2Tamb	2.3.17	Orcan
Ah sacred Mahomet, if this be sin,	2Tamb	3.4.31	Olymp
The reward of sin is death? that's hard:	F 67	1.1.39	Faust
If sin by custome grow not into nature:	F1713	5.1.40	OldMan
A surfet of deadly sin, that hath damn'd both body and soule.	F1833	5.2.37	P Faust
SINAY			
That on mount Sinay with their ensignes spread,	2Tamb	3.1.46	Jrslem
SINCE (See also SITH)			
Since that religion hath no recompence.	Dido	1.1.81	Venus
Since thy Aeneas wandring fate is firme,	Dido	1.1.83	Jupitr
Pluck up your hearts, since fate still rests our friend,	Dido	1.1.149	Aeneas
Since Carthage knowes to entertaine distresse.	Dido	1.2.33	Iarbus
Since gloomie Aeolus doth cease to frowne.	Dido	4.1.27	Aeneas
Since destinie doth call me from [thy] <the> shoare:	Dido	4.3.2	Aeneas
Abourd, abourd, since Fates doe bid abourd,	Dido	4.3.21	Aeneas
Who ever since hath luld me in her armes.	Dido	5.1.48	Ascan
Since Fortune gives you opportunity,	1Tamb	1.1.124	Menaph
Wel, since I see the state of Persea droope,	1Tamb	1.1.155	Cosroe
And since we have arriv'd in Scythia,	1Tamb	1.2.17	Magnet
But since I love to live at liberty,	1Tamb	1.2.26	Tamb
But since they measure our deserts so meane,	1Tamb	1.2.63	Tamb
Since he is yeelded to the stroke of War,	1Tamb	2.5.12	Cosroe
Since with the spirit of his fearefull pride,	1Tamb	2.6.12	Meandr
And since we all have suckt one wholsome aire,	1Tamb	2.6.25	Cosroe
Yet since a farther passion feeds my thoughts,	1Tamb	3.2.13	Zenoc
And since he was so wise and honorable,	1Tamb	3.2.110	Usumc
And since your highnesse hath so well vouchsaft,	1Tamb	4.4.130	Therid
Since other meanes are all forbidden me,	1Tamb	5.1.288	Bajzth
Since Death denies me further cause of joy,	1Tamb	5.1.430	Arabia
Since thy desired hand shall close mine eies.	1Tamb	5.1.432	Arabia

SINCE (cont.)			
Since I shall render all into your hands.	1Tamb	5.1.447	Tamb
Since I arriv'd with my triumphant hoste, ...	1Tamb	5.1.458	Tamb
Since Tamburlaine hath mustred all his men, ...	2Tamb	1.1.46	Gazell
For since we left you at the Souldans court, ...	2Tamb	1.3.177	Usumc
They have not long since massacred our Camp.	2Tamb	2.1.10	Fredrk
And since this miscreant hath disgrac'd his faith, . .	2Tamb	2.3.36	Orcan
But since my life is lengthened yet a while, . . .	2Tamb	2.4.71	Zenoc
That since the heire of mighty Bajazeth/(An Emperour so .	2Tamb	3.1.22	Callap
fighting men/Are come since last we shewed your majesty. .	2Tamb	3.5.34	Jrslem
Since last we numbred to your Majesty.	2Tamb	3.5.39	Orcan
Since last we numbred to your majesty.	2Tamb	3.5.45	Trebiz
Since last we numbred to your majestie:	2Tamb	3.5.49	Soria
But since I exercise a greater name, ...	2Tamb	4.1.153	Tamb
whose weeping eies/Since thy arrivall here beheld no Sun,	2Tamb	4.2.2	Olymp
And since this earth, dew'd with thy brinish teares, .	2Tamb	4.2.8	Olymp
Since Fate commands, and proud necessity.	2Tamb	5.3.205	Therid
Since your hard conditions are such/That you will needs have	Jew	1.2.18	Govnr
And since you leave me in the Ocean thus/To sinke or swim, and	Jew	1.2.267	Barab
'Tis thirtie winters long since some of us/Did stray so farre	Jew	1.2.308	Abbass
Since this Towne was besieg'd, my gaine growes cold: .	Jew	3.1.1	Curtzn
Why Abigal it is not yet long since/That I did labour thy	Jew	3.3.56	1Fryar
since thou hast broke the league/By flat denyall of the .	Jew	3.5.19	Basso
that she loves me ever since she saw me, and who would not	Jew	4.2.34	P Ithimr
He never put on cleane shirt since he was circumcis'd.	Jew	4.4.64	P Ithimr
Since they are dead, let them be buried.	Jew	5.1.57	Govnr
And since that time they have hir'd a slave my man/To accuse me	Jew	5.1.75	Barab
And since by wrong thou got'st Authority, ...	Jew	5.2.35	Barab
This, Barabas; since things are in thy power, . . .	Jew	5.2.57	Govnr
wel since it is no more/I'le satisfie my selfe with that;	Jew	5.5.21	Barab
Nay, Selim, stay, for since we have thee here, . . .	Jew	5.5.97	Govnr
Since thou hast all the Cardes within thy hands/To shuffle or	P 146	2.89	Guise
Cheefely since under safetie of our word, ...	P 209	4.7	Charls
For since the Guise is dead, I will not live. . . .	P1090	19.160	QnMoth
Then thou hast beene of me since thy exile. . . .	Edw	1.1.145	Edward
And since I went from hence, no soule in hell/Hath felt more	Edw	1.1.146	Gavstn
Tis like enough, for since he was exild, ...	Edw	2.1.23	Baldck
Having read unto her since she was a childe. . . .	Edw	2.1.30	Baldck
Since then succesfully we have prevayled, ...	Edw	4.6.21	Queene
since <I> have run up and downe the world with these <this>	F 688	2.2.137	P Wrath
[where I have laine ever since, and you have done me great	F 705.1	2.2.155A	P Sloth
But Faustus, since I may not speake to them, . . .	F1263	4.1.109	Emper
since I finde you so kind I will make knowne unto you what my	F1570	4.6.13	P Lady
since our conference about faire Ladies, which was the .	F1681	5.1.8	P 1Schol
Now <Since> we have seene the pride of Natures worke <workes>,	F1702	5.1.29	1Schol
Since first the worlds creation did begin. . . .	F1985	5.3.3	1Schol
they were never so knocht since they were divels, say I should	F App	p.230 46	P Clown
two deceased princes which long since are consumed to dust.	F App	p.237 43	P Faust
Since maist thou see me watch and night warres move: .	Ovid's Elegies		1.9.45
Since some faire one I should of force obey. . . .	Ovid's Elegies		2.17.6
So long they be, since she her faith forsooke. . . .	Ovid's Elegies		3.3.4
Since Heroes time, hath halfe the world beene blacke.	Hero and Leander		1.50
Musaeus soong)/Dwelt at Abidus; since him, dwelt there none,	Hero and Leander		1.53
SINCK			
But when she comes, [you] <your> swelling mounts sinck downe,	Ovid's Elegies		2.16.51
SINCKE			
Some whirle winde fetche them backe, or sincke them all:--	Edw	4.6.59	Mortmr
This dungeon where they keepe me, is the sincke, . .	Edw	5.5.56	Edward
SINDG'D			
the slave looks like a hogs cheek new sindg'd. . . .	Jew	2.3.42	P Barab
SINDGE (See also SING)			
Sindge these fair plaines, and make them seeme as black/As is	2Tamb	3.2.11	Tamb
SINEWES			
My vaines are withered, and my sinewes drie, . . .	Dido	4.5.33	Nurse
The strength and sinewes of the imperiall seat. . .	2Tamb	1.1.156	Sgsmnd
SINEWS (See also SINNEWES, SINOWES)			
Why might not then my sinews be inchanted, . . .	Ovid's Elegies		3.6.35
SINEWY (See also SINOWIE, SINOWY)			
And bent his sinewy bow upon his knee, ...	Ovid's Elegies		1.1.27
SINFULL			
his fearefull arme/Be pour'd with rigour on our sinfull heads,	2Tamb	2.1.58	Fredrk
My sinfull soule, alas, hath pac'd too long/The fatall .	Jew	3.3.63	Abigal
SING (Homograph)			
And my nine Daughters sing when thou art sad, . . .	Dido	1.1.33	Jupitr
Eate Comfites in mine armes, and I will sing. . . .	Dido	2.1.315	Venus
Sit in my lap and let me heare thee sing.	Dido	3.1.25	Dido
and holy Seraphins/That sing and play before the king of kings,	2Tamb	2.4.27	Tamb
Have not I made blind Homer sing to me/Of Alexanders love, and	F 577	2.2.26	Faust
Go then command our Priests to sing a Dirge, . . .	F1063	3.2.83	Pope
We sing, whose conquering swords their own breasts launcht,	Lucan, First Booke		3
so (if truth you sing)/Death brings long life. . . .	Lucan, First Booke		453
fury moves/To wound their armes, sing vengeance, Sibils priests,	Lucan, First Booke		564
Involving all, did Aruns darkly sing.	Lucan, First Booke		637
O Phoebus shouldst thou with thy rayes now sing/The fell Nemean	Lucan, First Booke		654
Muse upreard <prepar'd> I [meant] <meane> to sing of armes,	Ovid's Elegies		1.1.5
Io, triumphing shall thy people sing.	Ovid's Elegies		1.2.34
What helpes it me of fierce Achill to sing? . . .	Ovid's Elegies		2.1.29
Domesticke acts, and mine owne warres to sing. . .	Ovid's Elegies		2.18.12
Where round about small birdes most sweetely sing. . .	Ovid's Elegies		3.1.4
At thy deafe dores in verse sing my abuses. . . .	Ovid's Elegies		3.7.24
father Phoebus layed/To sing with his unequald harpe is sayed.	Ovid's Elegies		3.8.24
Ida the seate of groves did sing with corne, . . .	Ovid's Elegies		3.9.39
White birdes to lovers did not alwayes sing. . . .	Ovid's Elegies		3.11.2

SING (cont.)
Melodious byrds [sing] <sings> Madrigalls. | Passionate Shepherd | 8
The Sheepheards Swaines shall daunce and sing, | Passionate Shepherd | 21

SINGING
Singing ore these, as she does ore her young. | Jew 2.1.63 | Barab
Sylla's ghost/Was seene to walke, singing sad Oracles,/And | Lucan, First Booke | 580
And men inthralld by Mermaids singing charmes. | Ovid's Elegies | 3.11.28
Sweet singing Meremaids, sported with their loves/On heapes of | Hero and Leander | 2.162

SINGLE
Full soone wouldst thou abjure this single life. | Dido 3.1.60 | Dido
to Longshankes blood/Is false, be not found single for suspect: | Edw 4.6.17 | Kent
Wilt thou live single still? | Hero and Leander | 1.257
Flint-brested Pallas joies in single life, | Hero and Leander | 1.321

SINGLING
Though never-singling Hymen couple thee. | Hero and Leander | 1.258

SINGS
Thy power inspires the Muze that sings this war. | Lucan, First Booke | 66
And when one sweetely sings, then straight I long, | Ovid's Elegies | 2.4.25
Can deafe [eares] <yeares> take delight when Phemius sings,/Or | Ovid's Elegies | 3.6.61
That my slacke muse, sings of Leanders eies, | Hero and Leander | 1.72
Or crooked Dolphin when the sailer sings; | Hero and Leander | 2.234
Melodious byrds [sing] <sings> Madrigalls. | Passionate Shepherd | 8

SINGST
While without shame thou singst thy lewdnesse ditty. | Ovid's Elegies | 3.1.22

SINISTER
now in peace renew/Your barbarous customes, and sinister rites, | Lucan, First Booke | 447

SINK (See also SINCK)
And sink not quite into my tortur'd soule. | 1Tamb 5.1.263 | Bajzth

SINKE
And makes Aeneas sinke at Didos feete. | Dido 2.1.117 | Aeneas
No no, she cares not how we sinke or swimme, | Dido 4.3.41 | Illion
What if I sinke his ships? O heele frowne: | Dido 4.4.110 | Dido
And since you leave me in the Ocean thus/To sinke or swim, and | Jew 1.2.268 | Barab
asunder; so that it doth sinke/Into a deepe pit past recovery. | Jew 5.5.35 | Barab
And sinke them in the river as they swim. | P 423 7.63 | Dumain
Mounser of Loraine sinke away to hell, | P1023 19.93 | King

SINN'D
I know that I have highly sinn'd, | Jew 4.1.80 | Barab

SINNE
Whiles these adulterors surfetted with sinne: | Dido 4.1.20 | Iarbus
O just and dreadfull punisher of sinne, | 2Tamb 2.3.4 | Sgsmnd
And let this death wherein to sinne I die, | 2Tamb 2.3.8 | Sgsmnd
And hold there is no sinne but Ignorance. | Jew Prol.15 | Machvl
'Tis not our fault, but thy inherent sinne. | Jew 1.2.109 | 1Knght
that I descended of/Were all in generall cast away for sinne, | Jew 1.2.114 | Barab
And covetousnesse, oh 'tis a monstrous sinne. | Jew 1.2.124 | Govnr
Proceed from sinne, or want of faith in us, | Jew 1.2.323 | Abigal
It's no sinne to deceive a Christian; | Jew 2.3.309 | Barab
Admit thou lov'dst not Lodowicke for his [sire] <sinne>, | Jew 3.3.40 | Abigal
Would pennance serve for this my sinne, | Jew 4.1.58 | Barab
To undoe a Jew is charity, and not sinne. | Jew 4.4.81 | Ithimr
If we say that we have no sinne we deceive our selves, and | F 69 1.1.41 | P Faust
Why then belike/We must sinne, and so consequently die,/I, we | F 72 1.1.44 | Faust
Those soules which sinne seales the blacke sonnes of hell, | F1799 5.2.3 | Lucifr
<O, if my scule must suffer for my sinne>, | F1958 (HC271)B | Faust
Let all Lawes yeeld, sinne beare the name of vertue, | Lucan, First Booke | 666
I cryed, tis sinne, tis sinne, these haires to burne, | Ovid's Elegies | 1.14.27
The Gods from this sinne rid me of suspition, | Ovid's Elegies | 2.7.19
Nor canst by watching keepe her minde from sinne. | Ovid's Elegies | 3.4.7
She wailing Mars sinne, and her uncles crime, | Ovid's Elegies | 3.5.49
honour, and thereby/Commit'st a sinne far worse than perjurie. | Hero and Leander | 1.306
To expiat which sinne, kisse and shake hands, | Hero and Leander | 1.309

SINNER
I have beene a great sinner in my dayes, and the deed is | P1133 21.27 | P Frier

SINNES
And seeme to them as if thy sinnes were great, | Jew 1.2.287 | Barab
To make me mindfull of my mortall sinnes, | Jew 2.3.74 | Barab
Chast, and devout, much sorrowing for my sinnes, | Jew 3.6.14 | Abigal
As I am almost desperate for my sinnes: | Jew 3.6.18 | Abigal
Oh holy Fryars, the burthen of my sinnes/Lye heavy on my soule; | Jew 4.1.48 | Barab
sinnes appeare to thee in their owne proper shapes and | F 656 2.2.105 | P Belzeb
Leave me a while, to ponder on my sinnes. | F1736 5.1.63 | Faust
the inward soule/With such flagitious crimes of hainous sinnes, | F App p.243 42 | OldMan
Who may offend, sinnes least; power to do ill, | Ovid's Elegies | 3.4.9
Lesse sinnes the poore rich man that starves himselfe, | Hero and Leander | 1.243

SINNEWES
My sinnewes shrinke, my braines turne upside downe, | P 549 11.14 | Charls

SINOD
The sacred Sinod hath decreed for him, | F 885 3.1.107 | Pope

SINON
And therewithall he calde false Sinon forth, | Dido 2.1.143 | Aeneas
Which Sinon viewing, causde the Greekish spyes/To hast to | Dido 2.1.180 | Aeneas

SINONS
Others report twas Sinons perjurie: | Dido 2.1.111 | Dido

SINOWES
My vaines are pale, my sinowes hard and drie, | 1Tamb 4.4.97 | Bajzth
And now come we to make his sinowes shake, | 2Tamb 2.2.9 | Gazell
And were the sinowes of th'imperiall seat/So knit and | 2Tamb 3.1.10 | Callap

SINOWIE
All deepe enrag'd, his sinowie bow he bent, | Hero and Leander | 1.371

SINOWY
His armes and fingers long and [sinowy] <snowy>, | 1Tamb 2.1.27 | Menaph

SINS
O God forgive my sins. | P 303 5.30 | Admral

Line	Work	Ref		Speaker
SINT				
Sint mihi Dei Acherontis propitii, valeat numen triplex	F 244	1.3.16	P	Faust
SINUS (See SENUS)				
SIPT				
Jove might have sipt out Nectar from his hand.	Hero and Leander			1.62
SIR (See also SER, SIRRE)				
As did Sir Paris with the Grecian Dame:	1Tamb	1.1.66		Mycet
here, eat sir, take it from my swords point, or Ile thrust it to	1Tamb	4.4.40	P	Tamb
Paste and welcome sir, while hunger make you eat.	1Tamb	4.4.56	P	Tamb
Soft sir, you must be dieted, too much eating will make you	1Tamb	4.4.103	P	Tamb
No speach to that end, by your favour sir.	2Tamb	1.2.14		Almeda
No talke of running, I tell you sir.	2Tamb	1.2.16		Almeda
Wel sir, what of this?	2Tamb	1.2.18		Almeda
That's no matter sir, for being a king, for Tamburlain came up	2Tamb	3.1.73	P	Almeda
You knowe not sir:	2Tamb	3.5.158		Tamb
I know sir, what it is to kil a man,	2Tamb	4.1.27		Calyph
How like you that sir king? why speak you not?	2Tamb	4.3.53		Celeb
And therefore farre exceeds my credit, Sir.	Jew	1.1.65		1Merch
Of the Speranza, Sir.	Jew	1.1.71		1Merch
Sir we saw 'em not.	Jew	1.1.90		2Merch
Sir, we were wafted by a Spanish Fleet/That never left us till	Jew	1.1.95		2Merch
Sir, halfe is the penalty of our decree,	Jew	1.2.88		Govnr
I must and will, Sir, there's no remedy.	Jew	1.2.391		Mthias
you were his father too, Sir, that's al the harm I wish you:	Jew	2.3.41	P	Barab
Oh, Sir, your father had my Diamonds.	Jew	2.3.49		Barab
Pointed it is, good Sir,--but not for you.	Jew	2.3.60		Barab
Good Sir,/Your father has deserv'd it at my hands,	Jew	2.3.69		Barab
As for the Diamond, Sir, I told you of,	Jew	2.3.91		Barab
Sir, that's his price.	Jew	2.3.99		1Offcr
No Sir, I can cut and shave.	Jew	2.3.113	P	Slave
Alas, Sir, I am a very youth.	Jew	2.3.115	P	Slave
I will serve you, Sir.	Jew	2.3.118	P	Slave
Then marke him, Sir, and take him hence.	Jew	2.3.131		1Offcr
I pray, Sir, be no stranger at my house,	Jew	2.3.136		Barab
on the Machabees/I have it, Sir, and 'tis at your command.	Jew	2.3.154		Barab
Marry will I, Sir.	Jew	2.3.160		Barab
Faith, Sir, my birth is but meane, my name's Ithimor,	Jew	2.3.165		Ithimr
I have it for you, Sir; please you walke in with me:	Jew	2.3.220		Barab
I am a little busie, Sir, pray pardon me.	Jew	2.3.231		Barab
Know, holy Sir, I am bold to sollicite thee.	Jew	3.3.53		Abigal
How, Sir?	Jew	3.4.23	P	Ithimr
I goe Sir.	Jew	3.4.51	P	Ithimr
Yes, Sir, the proverb saies, he that eats with the devil had	Jew	3.4.58	P	Ithimr
Desire of gold, great Sir?	Jew	3.5.4		Govnr
'Tis neatly done, Sir, here's no print at all.	Jew	4.1.151		Ithimr
sweet youth; did not you, Sir, bring the sweet youth a letter?	Jew	4.2.41	P	Ithimr
I did Sir, and from this Gentlewoman, who as my selfe, and the	Jew	4.2.43	P	Pilia
And ye did but know how she loves you, Sir.	Jew	4.2.53		Pilia
And you can have it, Sir, and if you please.	Jew	4.2.56		Pilia
You'd make a rich Poet, Sir.	Jew	4.2.122	P	Pilia
Not serve his turne, Sir?	Jew	4.3.21	P	Barab
No Sir; and therefore I must have five hundred more.	Jew	4.3.22	P	Pilia
Oh good words, Sir, and send it you, were best see; there's his	Jew	4.3.24	P	Pilia
you dine with me, Sir, and you shal be most hartily poyson'd.	Jew	4.3.30	P	Barab
why Sir,/You know I have no childe, and unto whom	Jew	4.3.43		Barab
Commend me to him, Sir, most humbly,	Jew	4.3.47		Barab
Speake, shall I have 'um, Sir?	Jew	4.3.49		Pilia
Sir, here they are.	Jew	4.3.50		Barab
I know it, Sir.	Jew	4.3.55		Pilia
Pray when, Sir, shall I see you at my house?	Jew	4.3.56		Barab
Soone enough to your cost, Sir:	Jew	4.3.57		Pilia
Wonder not at it, Sir, the heavens are just:	Jew	5.1.55		Govnr
Marry sir, in having a smack in all,	P 385	7.25		Guise
Come sir, give me my buttons and heers your eare.	P 620	12.33		Mugern
Remember you the letter gentle sir,	P 754	15.12		King
Sir, to you sir, that dares make the Duke a cuckolde, and use a	P 806	17.1	P	Souldr
have at ye sir.	P 816	17.11	P	Souldr
I have no warre, and therefore sir be gone.	Edw	1.1.36		Gavstn
Sir, must not come so neare and balke their lips.	Edw	2.5.103		Penbrk
So sir, you have spoke, away, avoid our presence.	Edw	3.1.232		Edward
A good sir John of Henolt,/Never so cheereles, nor so farre	Edw	4.2.13		Queene
Ah sweete sir John, even to the utmost verge/Of Europe, or the	Edw	4.2.29		Queene
Sir John of Henolt, pardon us I pray,	Edw	4.2.71		Kent
Prosper your happie motion good sir John.	Edw	4.2.75		Queene
Sir John of Henolt, be it thy renowne,	Edw	4.2.78		Mortmr
if you aske, with sir John of Henolt, brother to the Marquesse,	Edw	4.3.31	P	Spencr
And will sir John of Henolt lead the round?	Edw	4.3.40		Edward
I will sir.	F 94	1.1.66		Wagner
You are deceiv'd, for <Yes sir>, I will tell you:	F 206	1.2.13	P	Wagner
Yes, and goings out too, you may see sir.	F 347	1.4.5	P	Robin
Nay sir, you may save your selfe a labour, for they are as	F 364	1.4.22	P	Robin
Yes marry sir, and I thanke you to.	F 368	1.4.26	P	Robin
How now sir, will you serve me now?	F 376	1.4.34	P	Wagner
I will sir; but hearke you Maister, will you teach me this	F 380	1.4.38	P	Robin
Well sir, I warrant you.	F 388	1.4.46	P	Robin
I <who I sir, I> am Gluttony; my parents are all dead, and the	F 693	2.2.142	P	Glutny
Who I <I I> sir?	F 708	2.2.160	P	Ltchry
I thanke you sir.	F1043	3.2.63		Faust
By Lady sir, you have had a shroud journey of it, will it	F1120	3.3.33	P	Robin
I pray you heartily sir; for wee cal'd you but in jeast I	F1123	3.3.36	P	Dick
I pray sir, let me have the carrying of him about to shew some	F1128	3.3.41	P	Robin
Speak softly sir, least the devil heare you:	F1180	4.1.26		Mrtino
Why how now sir Knight, what, hang'd by the hornes?	F1290	4.1.136	P	Faust

SIR (cont.)				
O say not sc sir:	F1294	4.1.140		Faust
him; and hereafter sir, looke you speake well of Schollers.	F1315	4.1.161	P	Faust
I beseech you sir accept of this; I am a very poore man, and	F1463	4.4.7	P	HrsCsr
How sir, not into the water?	F1470	4.4.14	P	HrsCsr
I warrant you sir; O joyfull day:	F1476	4.4.20	P	HrsCsr
Marry sir, I'le tell you the bravest tale how a Conjurer serv'd	F1521	4.5.17	P	Carter
eate; now sir, I thinking that a little would serve his turne,	F1528	4.5.24	P	Carter
forty Dollors; so sir, because I knew him to be such a horse,	F1537	4.5.33	P	HrsCsr
Now sir, I thinking the horse had had some [rare] quality that	F1542	4.5.38	P	HrsCsr
I hope sir, we have wit enough to be more bold then welcome.	F1595	4.6.38	P	HrsCsr
Will you sir? Commit the Rascals.	F1602	4.6.45		Duke
Nay sir, we will be wellcome for our mony, and we will pay for	F1611	4.6.54	P	Robin
I but sir sauce box, know you in what place?	F1616	4.6.59		Servnt
I thank you sir.	F1642	4.6.85	P	Faust
No truelie sir, I would make nothing of you, but I would faine	F1648	4.6.91	P	Carter
For nothing sir:	F1653	4.6.96	P	Carter
do you heare sir, did not I pull off one of your legs when you	F1655	4.6.98	P	HrsCsr
looke you heere sir.	F1657	4.6.100	P	Faust
Do you remember sir, how you cosened me and eat up my load of--	F1659	4.6.102	P	Carter
Then when sir Paris crost the seas with <for> her,	F1694	5.1.21		Faust
Sir, so wondrous well,/As in all humble dutie, I do yeeld	F1817	5.2.21		Wagner
Tis but a surfet sir, feare nothing.	F1832	5.2.36		3Schol
Doe you heare sir?	F App	p.229 27	P	Clown
no, no sir, if you turne me into any thing, let it be in the	F App	p.231 61	P	Clown
O Lord I pray sir, let Banio and Belcher go sleepe.	F App	p.231 68	P	Clown
I thanke you sir.	F App	p.231 7	P	Faust
Soft sir, a word with you, I must yet have a goblet payde from	F App	p.234 7	P	Vintnr
I meane so sir with your favor.	F App	p.234 11	P	Vintnr
I must say somewhat to your felow, you sir.	F App	p.234 13	P	Vintnr
me sir, me sir, search your fill:	F App	p.234 14	P	Rafe
now sir, you may be ashamed to burden honest men with a matter	F App	p.234 14	P	Rafe
How then sir?	F App	p.237 53	P	Faust
No sir, but when Acteon died, he left the hornes for you:	F App	p.237 55	P	Faust
How now sir Knight?	F App	p.238 69	P	Emper
O not so fast sir, theres no haste but good, are you remembred	F App	p.238 76	P	Faust
and sir knight, hereafter speake well of Scholers:	F App	p.238 84	P	Faust
Do you heare sir?	F App	p.239 101	P	HrsCsr
Alas sir, I have no more, I pray you speake for me.	F App	p.239 104	P	HrsCsr
why sir, wil he not drinke of all waters?	F App	p.239 110	P	HrsCsr
Wel sir, Now am I made man for ever, Ile not leave my horse for	F App	p.239 114	P	HrsCsr
slicke as an Ele; wel god buy sir, your boy wil deliver him me:	F App	p.240 117	P	HrsCsr
but hark ye sir, if my horse be sick, or ill at ease, if I	F App	p.240 118	P	HrsCsr
why sir, what would you?	F App	p.240 139	P	Mephst
O Lord sir, let me goe, and Ile give you fortie dollers more.	F App	p.241 158	P	HrsCsr
Sir, the Duke of Vanholt doth earnestly entreate your company.	F App	p.241 168	P	Wagner
Yea, and she soothde me up, and calde me sir <sire>,	Ovid's Elegies			3.6.11
SIRACUSIAN				
[Where] <When> Siracusian Dionisius reign'd,	Jew	5.3.10		Calym
SIRE (See also SYRE)				
Admit thou lov'dst not Lodowicke for his [sire] <sinne>,	Jew	3.3.40		Abigal
Because the Pryor <Governor> <Sire> dispossest thee once,/And	Jew	3.3.43		Abigal
Whereof his sire, the Pope, was poysoned.	Jew	3.4.99		Barab
And he who on his mother veng'd his sire,	Ovid's Elegies			1.7.9
Yea, and she soothde me up, and calde me sir <sire>,	Ovid's Elegies			3.6.11
SIRENS				
And rather had seeme faire [to] Sirens eyes,	Dido	3.4.39		Dido
SIRES				
Great grand-sires from their antient graves she chides/And with	Ovid's Elegies			1.8.17
SIRHA				
And sirha, if you meane to weare a crowne,	2Tamb	1.3.98		Tamb
Sirha, Callapine, Ile hang a clogge about your necke for	2Tamb	3.5.100	P	Tamb
Go too sirha, take your crown, and make up the halfe dozen.	2Tamb	3.5.135	P	Tamb
So sirha, now you are a king you must give armes.	2Tamb	3.5.137	P	Tamb
Sirha, prepare whips, and bring my chariot to my Tent:	2Tamb	3.5.144	P	Tamb
Sirha, the view of our vermillion tents,	2Tamb	5.1.86		Tamb
SIRIA				
Than if you were arriv'd in Siria,	1Tamb	1.2.4		Tamb
That we may traveile into Siria,	1Tamb	1.2.77		Agidas
SIRRA				
Sirra, why fall you not too, are you so daintily brought up,	1Tamb	4.4.36	P	Tamb
Come sirra, give me your arme.	2Tamb	3.2.134	P	Tamb
Sirra, which of my ships art thou Master of?	Jew	1.1.70		Barab
Let me see, sirra, are you not an old shaver?	Jew	2.3.114	P	Barab
My Lord farewell: Come Sirra you are mine.	Jew	2.3.134		Barab
Sirra, Jew, remember the booke.	Jew	2.3.159		Mthias
Well, sirra, what is't?	Jew	3.3.31		Abigal
Go to, sirra sauce, is this your question?	Jew	3.3.34	P	Abigal
Come on, sirra,/Off with your girdle,	Jew	4.1.141		Barab
Sirra Barabas, send me a hundred crownes.	Jew	4.2.73	P	Ithimr
Sirra Jew, as you love your life send me five hundred crowns,	Jew	4.2.117	P	Ithimr
Sirra, you must give my mistris your posey.	Jew	4.4.37		Pilia
Now sirra, what, will he come?	Jew	5.5.13		Barab
Sirra,/Are you a preacher of these heresies?	P 339	5.66		Guise
your nego argumentum/Cannot serve, sirra:	P 398	7.38		Guise
Now sirra, what shall we doe with the Admirall?	P 482	9.1	P	1Atndt
Sirra, take him away.	P 621	12.34		Guise
goe sirra, worke no more,/Till this our Coronation day be past:	P 623	12.36		King
How now sirra, what newes?	P 723	14.26		Navrre
Sirra twas I that slew him, and will slay/Thee too, and thou	P1048	19.118		King
Thankes gentle Winchester: sirra, be gon.	Edw	5.2.27		Queene
How now sirra, where's thy Maister?	F 197	1.2.4	P	1Schol
Go to sirra, leave your jesting, and tell us where he is.	F 201	1.2.8	P	1Schol

SIRRA (cont.)

Come hither sirra boy.	F 343	1.4.1	P Wagner
Sirra, hast thou no commings in?	F 346	1.4.4	P Wagner
Sirra, wilt thou be my man and waite on me?	F 354	1.4.12	P Wagner
for sirra, if thou dost not presently bind thy selfe to me for	F 361	1.4.19	P Wagner
Well sirra, leave your jesting, and take these Guilders.	F 367	1.4.25	P Wagner
Now sirra follow me.	F 379	1.4.37	P Wagner
I sirra, I'le teach thee to turne thy selfe to a Dog, or a Cat,	F 382	1.4.40	P Wagner
Sirra Robin, we were best looke that your devill can answere	F1088	3.3.1	P Dick
Come on sirra, let me search you now.	F1104	3.3.17	P Vintnr
now sirra I must tell you, that you may ride him o're hedge and	F1467	4.4.11	P Faust
Ho sirra Doctor, you cosoning scab; Maister Doctor awake, and	F1488	4.4.32	P HrsCsr
Sirra Dick, dost thou know why I stand so mute?	F1509	4.5.5	P Robin
Sirra boy, come hither.	F App	p.229 1	P Wagner
Tel me sirra, hast thou any commings in?	F App	p.229 4	P Wagner
No sirra, in beaten silke and staves acre.	F App	p.229 16	P Wagner
Sirra, I say in staves acre.	F App	p.229 20	P Wagner
but sirra, leave your jesting, and binde your selfe presently	F App	p.229 24	P Wagner
wel, do you heare sirra?	F App	p.230 30	P Wagner
sirra thou art at an houres warning whensoever or wheresoever	F App	p.230 36	P Wagner
Well sirra follow me.	F App	p.230 55	P Wagner
Wel sirra, come.	F App	p.231 65	P Wagner
sirra you, Ile teach ye to impeach honest men:	F App	p.235 17	P Robin
what meane you sirra?	F App	p.235 21	P Vintnr

SIRRE

<Yes sirre, I heard you>.	F 204	(HC258)A	P 1Schol

SIRS

Wel sirs, diet your selves, you knowe I shall have occasion	2Tamb	3.5.114	P Tamb
Good sirs I have don't, but no body knowes it but you two, I	Jew	4.1.180	P 1Fryar
Come sirs follow me.	P 292	5.19	Gonzag
Come sirs, Ile whip you to death with my punniards point.	P 441	7.81	Guise
And now sirs for this night let our fury stay.	P 443	7.83	Guise
Sirs, take him away and throw him in some ditch.	P 499	9.18	Guise
Come on sirs, what, are you resolutely bent,	P 931	19.1	Capt
Then sirs take your standings within this Chamber,	P 940	19.10	Capt
Now sirs, the newes from Fraunce.	Edw	4.3.14	Edward
Wherefore stay we? on sirs to the court.	Edw	5.3.65	Souldr
Tell me sirs, was it not bravelie done?	Edw	5.5.116	Ltborn
and now sirs, having divided him, what shall the body doe?	F1389	4.2.65	P Mrtino
Come sirs, prepare your selves in readinesse,	F1420	4.2.96	1Soldr
Come sirs, what shall we do now till mine Hostesse comes?	F1520	4.5.16	P Dick
Now sirs, you shall heare how villanously he serv'd mee:	F1535	4.5.31	P HrsCsr
Looke sirs, comes he not, comes he not?	F1826	5.2.30	P Faust

SIRTES

To doubtfull Sirtes and drie Affricke, where/A fury leades the	Lucan, First Booke	686

SISTER

But whether thou the Sunnes bright Sister be,	Dido	1.1.193	Aeneas
Looke sister how Aeneas little sonne/Playes with your garments	Dido	3.1.20	Anna
O sister, were you Empresse of the world,	Dido	3.1.69	Anna
Anna, good sister Anna goe for him,	Dido	3.1.75	Dido
Then sister youle abjure Iarbus love?	Dido	3.1.77	Anna
Sister of Jove, if that thy love be such,	Dido	3.2.53	Venus
Sister, I see you savour of my wiles,	Dido	3.2.96	Venus
Sister, see see Ascanius in his pompe,	Dido	3.3.32	Anna
Faire sister Anna leade my lover forth,	Dido	4.4.65	Dido
Doe as I bid thee sister, leade the way,	Dido	4.4.85	Dido
What meanes my sister thus to rave and crye?	Dido	5.1.193	Anna
Call him not wicked, sister, speake him faire,	Dido	5.1.200	Dido
I goe faire sister, heavens graunt good successe.	Dido	5.1.211	Anna
My sister comes, I like not her sad lookes.	Dido	5.1.225	Dido
Looke sister, looke lovely Aeneas ships,	Dido	5.1.251	Dido
O sister, sister, take away the Rockes,	Dido	5.1.254	Dido
Ah sister, leave these idle fantasies,	Dido	5.1.262	Anna
Sweet sister cease, remember who you are.	Dido	5.1.263	Anna
Than Juno sister to the highest God,	1Tamb	3.2.54	Zenoc
And is admitted to the Sister-hood.	Jew	1.2.343	1Fryar
Although unworthy of that Sister-hood.	Jew	3.3.69	Abigal
Sister, I think your selfe will beare us company.	P 21	1.21	Charls
Ile send my sister England newes of this,	P1189	22.51	King
Looke where the sister of the king of Fraunce,	Edw	1.4.187	Lncstr
Thy gentle Queene, sole sister to Valoys,	Edw	2.2.172	Lncstr
To this distressed Queene his sister heere,	Edw	4.2.63	SrJohn
Sister, Edward is my charge, redeeme him.	Edw	5.2.116	Kent
And sister, Nurse, and mother spare him not,	Ovid's Elegies		1.8.91
None such the sister gives her brother grave,	Ovid's Elegies		2.5.25
Part of her sorrowe heere thy sister bearing,	Ovid's Elegies		3.8.51
And as a brother with his sister toyed,	Hero and Leander		2.52

SISTER-HOOD

And is admitted to the Sister-hood.	Jew	1.2.343	1Fryar
Although unworthy of that Sister-hood.	Jew	3.3.69	Abigal

SISTERS

men, saw you as you came/Any of all my Sisters wandring here?	Dido	1.1.184	Venus
And banquet as two Sisters with the Gods?	Dido	3.2.29	Juno
Who seekes to rob me of thy Sisters love,	Dido	4.2.31	Iarbus
Where ere I come the fatall sisters sweat,	1Tamb	5.1.454	Tamb
To haile the fatall Sisters by the haire,	2Tamb	2.4.99	Tamb
On whom death and the fatall sisters waite,	2Tamb	3.4.54	Therid
Sisters,	Jew	1.2.305	1Fryar
Heav'n starre Electra that bewaild her sisters?	Ovid's Elegies		3.11.37
Jove, slylie stealing from his sisters bed,	Hero and Leander		1.147
Likewise the angrie sisters thus deluded,	Hero and Leander		1.473

SISYPHUS (See SYSIPHUS)

SIT (See also SITT'ST)

Sit on my knee, and call for thy content,	Dido	1.1.28	Jupitr

SIT (cont.)			
I, this is it, you can sit toying there,	Dido	1.1.50	Venus
Here she was wont to sit, but saving ayre/Is nothing here, and	Dido	2.1.13	Achat
Sit in this chaire and banquet with a Queene,	Dido	2.1.83	Dido
Sit downe Aeneas, sit in Didos place,	Dido	2.1.91	Dido
Here let him sit, be merrie lovely child.	Dido	2.1.93	Dido
Sit in my lap and let me heare thee sing.	Dido	3.1.25	Dido
And sit with Tamburlaine in all his majestie.	1Tamb	1.2.209	Tamb
Fortune her selfe dooth sit upon our Crests.	1Tamb	2.2.73	Meandr
I long to sit upon my brothers throne.	1Tamb	2.5.47	Cosroe
Sit here upon this royal chaire of state,	1Tamb	3.3.112	Bajzth
Sit downe by her:	1Tamb	3.3.124	Tamb
Shall sit by him and starve to death himselfe.	1Tamb	4.2.90	Tamb
And on whose throne the holy Graces sit.	1Tamb	5.1.77	1Virgn
Millions of soules sit on the bankes of Styx,	1Tamb	5.1.463	Tamb
Then sit thou downe divine Zenocrate,	1Tamb	5.1.506	Tamb
Sit up and rest thee like a lovely Queene.	2Tamb	1.3.16	Tamb
Now are those Spheares where Cupid usde to sit,	2Tamb	2.4.81	Tamb
While I sit smiling to behold the sight.	2Tamb	3.2.128	Tamb
And sit in councell to invent some paine,	2Tamb	3.5.98	Callap
If halfe our campe should sit and sleepe with me,	2Tamb	4.1.18	Calyph
turrets of my Court/Sit like to Venus in her chaire of state,	2Tamb	4.2.42	Therid
And I will cast off armes and sit with thee,	2Tamb	4.2.44	Therid
Why, shal I sit and languish in this paine?	2Tamb	5.3.56	Tamb
Sit stil my gratious Lord, this griefe wil cease,	2Tamb	5.3.64	Techel
Sit up my sonne, let me see how well/Thou wilt become thy	2Tamb	5.3.183	Tamb
Sit up my boy, and with those silken raines,	2Tamb	5.3.202	Tamb
And they this day sit in the Counsell-house/To entertaine them	Jew	1.1.148	1Jew
As good goe on, as sit so sadly thus.	Jew	2.1.40	Barab
Or looke to see the throne where you should sit,	Edw	1.1.131	Lncstr
Here Mortimer, sit thou in Edwards throne,	Edw	1.4.36	Edward
Sweete Mortimer, sit downe by me a while,	Edw	1.4.225	Queene
Goe sit at home and eate your tenants beefe:	Edw	2.2.75	Gavstn
Come Spencer, come Baldocke, come sit downe by me,	Edw	4.7.16	Edward
Your grace may sit secure, if none but wee/Doe wot of your	Edw	4.7.26	Monk
And sit for aye inthronized in heaven,	Edw	5.1.109	Edward
Sit downe, for weele be Barbars to your grace.	Edw	5.3.28	Matrvs
<Well thou wilt have one, sit there till I come,	F 531	(HC261)A P	Mephst
sit downe and thou shalt behold <see al> the seven deadly	F 655	2.2.104 P	Belzeb
Sometimes, like a Perriwig, I sit upon her Brow:	F 666	2.2.115 P	Pride
but must thou sit, and I stand?	F 683	2.2.132 P	Envy
Welcome Lord Cardinals: come sit downe.	F1009	3.2.29	Pope
To morrow we would sit i'th Consistory,	F1017	3.2.37	Pope
Lord Archbishop of Reames, sit downe with us.	F1037	3.2.57	Pope
And sit in Peters Chaire, despite of chance,	F1214	4.1.60	Emper
Who sees not warre sit by the quivering Judge;	Lucan, First Booke		320
Sit safe at home and chaunt sweet Poesie.	Lucan, First Booke		445
Shall I sit gazing as a bashfull guest,	Ovid's Elegies		1.4.3
Words without voyce shall on my eye browes sit,	Ovid's Elegies		1.4.19
With shorter numbers the heroicke sit.	Ovid's Elegies		2.17.22
Wee Macer sit in Venus slothfull shade,	Ovid's Elegies		2.18.3
I sit not here the noble horse to see,	Ovid's Elegies		3.2.1
To sit, and talke with thee I hether came,	Ovid's Elegies		3.2.3
And sit thou rounder, that behind us see,	Ovid's Elegies		3.2.23
Where she should sit for men to gaze upon.	Hero and Leander		1.8
have concluded/That Midas brood shall sit in Honors chaire,	Hero and Leander		1.475
And wee will sit upon the Rocks,	Passionate Shepherd		5
SITH			
For sith, as once you said, within this Ile/In Malta here, that	Jew	5.2.67	Barab
My Lords, sith in a quarrell just and right,	P 698	14.1	Navrre
Ah curse him not sith he is dead.	P1220	22.82	King
sith the ungentle king/Of Fraunce refuseth to give aide of	Edw	4.2.61	SrJohn
Lords, sith that we are by sufferance of heaven,	Edw	4.4.17	Mortmr
realme, and sith the fates/Have made his father so infortunate,	Edw	4.6.26	Queene
Sith blacke disgrace hath thus eclipst our fame,	F1455	4.3.25	Benvol
SITHES			
And ripe-earde corne with sharpe-edg'd sithes to fell.	Ovid's Elegies		3.9.12
SITS			
Now sits and laughs our regiment to scorne:	1Tamb	1.1.117	Cosroe
Where honor sits invested royally:	1Tamb	2.1.18	Menaph
For there sits Death, there sits imperious Death,	1Tamb	5.1.111	Tamb
Wher Beauty, mother to the Muses sits,	1Tamb	5.1.144	Tamb
So, now she sits in pompe and majestie:	2Tamb	1.3.17	Tamb
Priest/Cal'd John the great, sits in a milk-white robe,	2Tamb	1.3.188	Techel
imperiall heaven/That he that sits on high and never sleeps,	2Tamb	2.2.49	Orcan
Unto the shining bower where Cynthia sits,	2Tamb	3.4.50	Therid
The God that sits in heaven, if any God,	2Tamb	5.1.201	Tamb
But he that sits and rules above the clowdes,	P 42	1.42	Navrre
What? are you mov'd that Gaveston sits heere?	Edw	1.4.8	Edward
Sits wringing of her hands, and beats her brest.	Edw	1.4.188	Lncstr
Alas, see where he sits, and hopes unseene,	Edw	4.7.51	Leistr
O wherefore sits thou heare?	Edw	5.5.96	Edward
And this the man that in his study sits.	F 28	Prol.28	1Chor
I burne, love in my idle bosome sits.	Ovid's Elegies		1.1.30
Shee in my lap sits still as earst she did.	Ovid's Elegies		2.18.6
She proudly sits) more over-rules the flood,	Hero and Leander		1.111
SITTETH			
cast do happe/Sharpe stripes, she sitteth in the judges lappe.	Ovid's Elegies		2.2.62
SITTING			
Sitting in scarlet on their armed speares.	1Tamb	5.1.118	Tamb
Sitting as if they were a telling ridles.	2Tamb	3.5.59	Tamb
That frightes poore Ramus sitting at his book?	P 362	7.2	Ramus
Where sitting <Being seated> in a Chariot burning bright,	F 758	2.3.37	2Chor

SITTING (cont.)
To morrow, sitting in our Consistory, F 967 3.1.189 Pope
To move her feete unheard in [setting] <sitting> downe. Ovid's Elegies 3.1.52
How that a sheapheard sitting in a vale, Hero and Leander 2.194
Whereon Leander sitting, thus began, Hero and Leander 2.245
SITT'ST
Where men report, thou sitt'st by God himselfe, 2Tamb 5.1.194 Tamb
SITU
But <tell me> have they all/One motion, both situ et tempore? F 596 2.2.45 Faust
SITUATION (See also SCITUATION)
to see the Monuments/And situation of bright splendent Rcme, F 829 3.1.51 Faust
SIX
royall is esteem'd/Six hundred thousand valiant fighting men. 2Tamb 3.5.51 Soria
SIXE
And roome within to lodge sixe thousand men. 2Tamb 3.2.72 Tamb
Where we will have [Gabions] <Galions> of sixe foot broad,/To 2Tamb 3.3.56 Therid
wil you take sixe pence in your purse to pay for your supper, F App p.235 41 P Robin
Let my first verse be sixe, my last five feete, Ovid's Elegies 1.1.31
SIXT
Choke thy selfe Glutton: What are thou the sixt? F 704 2.2.153 Faust
SIZE
Their lims more large and of a bigger size/Than all the brats 1Tamb 3.3.108 Bajzth
SKARRE
rests no more/But bare remembrance; like a souldiers skarre, Jew 2.1.10 Barab
SKARRES
Behold the signes of antient fight, his skarres, Ovid's Elegies 3.7.19
SKARS
Quite voide of skars, and cleare from any wound, 2Tamb 3.2.112 Tamb
SKATHD
No charmed herbes of any harlot skathd thee, Ovid's Elegies 1.14.39
SKIE
Entends ere long to sport him in the skie. Dido 1.1.77 Venus
Gallop a pace bright Phoebus through the skie, Edw 4.3.43 Edward
Leapes from th'Antarticke world unto the skie, F 231 1.3.3 Faust
The flattering skie gliter'd in often flames, Lucan, First Booke 528
Even such as by Aurora hath the skie, Ovid's Elegies 2.5.35
Or is my heate, of minde, not of the skie? Ovid's Elegies 3.2.39
From Latmus mount up to the glomie skie, Hero and Leander 1.109
Or if it could, downe from th'enameld skie, Hero and Leander 1.249
SKIES
As rules the Skies, and countermands the Gods: 1Tamb 5.1.233 Bajzth
Now by the malice of the angry Skies, 2Tamb 2.4.11 Tamb
SKIL
that thou let me see some proofe of thy skil, that mine eies F App p.236 6 P Emper
SKILD
Well skild in Pyromancy; one that knew/The hearts of beasts, Lucan, First Booke 586
SKILFUL
Skilful in musicke and in amorous laies: 2Tamb 1.2.37 Callap
SKILFULD
In [skilfull] <skilfuld> gathering ruffled haires in order, Ovid's Elegies 1.11.1
SKILFULL
In [skilfull] <skilfuld> gathering ruffled haires in order, Ovid's Elegies 1.11.1
SKILL
is compriz'd the Sum/Of natures Skill and heavenly majestie. 1Tamb 5.1.79 1Virgn
In frame of which, Nature hath shewed more skill, 2Tamb 3.4.75 Techel
A French Musician, come let's heare your skill? Jew 4.4.30 Curtzn
I'le have them fill the publique Schooles with [silke] <skill>, F 117 1.1.89 Faust
no object, for my head]/[But ruminates on Negromantique skill]. F 132 1.1.104A Faust
Hath Mephostophilis no greater skill? F 601 2.2.50 Faust
[Which Faustus answered with such learned skill], F1147 3.3.60A 3Chor
the Doctor has no skill,/No Art, no cunning, to present these F1294 4.1.140 Faust
Then Faustus try thy skill: F1425 4.2.101 Faust
Whose like Aegiptian Memphis never had/For skill in stars, and Lucan, First Booke 640
If she be learned, then for her skill I crave her, Ovid's Elegies 2.4.17
And for her skill to thee a gratefull maide. Ovid's Elegies 2.7.24
SKIN
And cloathed in a spotted Leopards skin. Dido 1.1.186 Venus
Intending but to rase my charmed skin: 1Tamb 1.2.179 Tamb
Volleyes of shot pierce through thy charmed Skin, 1Tamb 5.1.221 Bajzth
With which if you but noint your tender Skin, 2Tamb 4.2.65 Olymp
Repent and they shall never raise thy skin. F 633 2.2.82 GdAngl
With that hee stript him to the yv'rie skin, Hero and Leander 2.153
SKINNE
A small thin skinne contain'd the vital parts, Lucan, First Booke 622
SKINS
While thundring Cannons rattle on their Skins. 1Tamb 4.1.11 Souldn
SKIPPE
About thy neck shall he at pleasure skippe? Ovid's Elegies 1.4.6
SKIPPING
The skipping Salii with shields like wedges; Lucan, First Booke 602
And where swift Nile in his large channell slipping <skipping>, Ovid's Elegies 2.13.9
By seaven huge mouthes into the sea is [skipping] <slipping>, Ovid's Elegies 2.13.10
In skipping out her naked feete much grac'd her. Ovid's Elegies 3.6.82
SKIRMISH
Hees happie who loves mutuall skirmish slayes <layes>, Ovid's Elegies 2.10.29
To have this skirmish fought, let it suffice thee. Ovid's Elegies 2.13.28
SKORNE
The obloquie and skorne of my renowne, 2Tamb 4.1.92 Tamb
Wee skorne things lawfull, stolne sweetes we affect, Ovid's Elegies 2.19.3
Glist'red with deaw, as one that seem'd to skorne it: Hero and Leander 1.390
SKUL
His Skul al rivin in twain, his braines dasht out? 1Tamb 5.1.306 Zabina
SKY (See also SKIE)
That with thy lookes canst cleare the darkened Sky: 1Tamb 3.3.122 Tamb

SKY (cont.)			
Then when the Sky shal waxe as red as blood,	1Tamb	4.2.53	Tamb
the fiery Element/Dissolve, and make your kingdome in the Sky,	2Tamb	2.4.59	Zenoc
souldiers crie/Make deafe the aire, and dim the Christall Sky.	2Tamb	3.3.61	Therid
that shine as bright/As all the Lamps that beautifie the Sky,	2Tamb	5.3.157	Tamb
More lovely then the Monarch of the sky,	F1785	5.1.112	Faust
SKYE			
Be thou on earth as Jove is in the skye,	F 103	1.1.75	BdAngl
The [Tropicks] <Tropick>, Zones, and quarters of the skye,/From	F 761	2.3.40	2Chor
SLACK			
My lords, if to performe this I be slack,	Edw	1.4.290	Mortmr
Because your highnesse hath beene slack in homage,	Edw	3.1.63	Queene
Thinke not to finde me slack or pitifull.	Edw	5.6.82	King
SLACKE			
Shall slacke my loves affection from his bent.	P 607	12.20	King
Now would I slacke the reines, now lash their hide,	Ovid's Elegies		3.2.11
when he perceivd the reines let slacke, he stayde,	Ovid's Elegies		3.4.15
That my slacke muse, sings of Leanders eies,	Hero and Leander		1.72
SLACKT			
But may be slackt untill another time:	Dido	4.2.26	Anna
[Love] <I> slackt my Muse, and made my [numbers] <number> soft.	Ovid's Elegies		1.1.22
Which being not shakt <slackt>, I saw it die at length.	Ovid's Elegies		1.2.12
SLAIN			
I, master, he's slain; look how his brains drop out on's nose.	Jew	4.1.178	P Ithimr
SLAINE			
Father of fiftie sonnes, but they are slaine,	Dido	2.1.234	Aeneas
Out hatefull hag, thou wouldst have slaine my sonne,	Dido	3.2.32	Venus
Who nere will cease to soare till he be slaine.	Dido	3.3.85	Iarbus
Iarbus slaine, Iarbus my deare love,	Dido	5.1.321	Anna
I might command you to be slaine for this,	1Tamb	1.1.23	Mycet
Than Tamburlaine be slaine or overcome.	1Tamb	1.2.177	Tamb
My royall Lord is slaine or conquered,	1Tamb	3.3.209	Zenoc
We may be slaine or wounded ere we learne.	2Tamb	3.2.94	Calyph
Away, let us to the field, that the villaine may be slaine.	2Tamb	3.5.143	P Trebiz
What, have I slaine her? Villaine, stab thy selfe:	2Tamb	4.2.82	Therid
Doth see his souldiers slaine, himselfe disarm'd,	Jew	1.2.204	Barab
The Captain's slaine, the rest remaine our slaves,	Jew	2.2.17	Bosco
What sight is this? my [Lodovico] <Lodowicke> slaine!	Jew	3.2.10	Govnr
Who is this? my sonne Mathias slaine!	Jew	3.2.12	Mater
That by my favour they should both be slaine?	Jew	3.3.39	Abigal
is there/Set downe at large, the Gallants were both slaine.	Jew	3.6.29	Abigal
He is slaine.	Jew	4.1.177	Barab
I bring thee newes by whom thy sonne was slaine:	Jew	5.1.10	Curtzn
That Guise hath slaine by treason of his heart,	P 45	1.45	Navrre
The Duke is slaine and all his power dispearst,	P 787	16.1	Navrre
Philip and Parma, I am slaine for you:	P1011	19.81	Guise
My Lord, see where the Guise is slaine.	P1019	19.89	Capt
My father slaine, who hath done this deed?	P1047	19.117	YngGse
The Guise is slaine, and I rejoyce therefore:	P1078	19.148	King
My brother Cardenall slaine and I alive?	P1125	21.19	Dumain
No more then I would answere were he slaine.	Edw	2.2.86	Mortmr
Their wives and children slaine, run up and downe,	Edw	2.2.180	Lncstr
I feare me he is slaine my gratious lord.	Edw	2.4.2	Spencr
And Gaveston this blessed day be slaine.	Edw	2.4.69	Queene
You villaines that have slaine my Gaveston:	Edw	3.1.142	Edward
A Mortimer, thou knowest that he is slaine,	Edw	5.6.50	King
long e're this, I should have done the deed <slaine my selfe>,	F 575	2.2.24	Faust
O I am slaine, help me my Lords:	F1068	3.2.88	Pope
Till with my sword I have that Conjurer slaine.	F1333	4.2.9	Benvol
Might they have won whom civil broiles have slaine,	Lucan, First Booke		14
And jaded king of Pontus poisoned slaine,	Lucan, First Booke		337
immortal pens/Renowne the valiant soules slaine in your wars,	Lucan, First Booke		444
And in the brest of this slaine Bull are crept,	Lucan, First Booke		632
And birds for <from> Memnon yearly shall be slaine.	Ovid's Elegies		1.13.4
Oft dyes she that her paunch-wrapt child hath slaine.	Ovid's Elegies		2.14.38
Made with the blood of wretched Lovers slaine.	Hero and Leander		1.16
Their fellowes being slaine or put to flight,	Hero and Leander		1.120
SLAKE			
And let their lives bloud slake thy furies hunger:	Edw	2.2.205	Edward
To slake his anger, if he were displeas'd,	Hero and Leander		2.49
SLANDERED			
Let me be slandered, while my fire she hides,	Ovid's Elegies		2.17.3
SLAUGHTER			
For perjurie and slaughter of a Queene:	Dido	5.1.294	Dido
He that can take or slaughter Tamburlaine,	1Tamb	2.2.30	Meandr
With litle slaughter take Meanders course,	1Tamb	2.5.27	Cosroe
I am sure/What cruell slaughter of our Christian bloods,	2Tamb	2.1.5	Fredrk
To see the slaughter of our enemies.	2Tamb	3.5.57	Callap
To signifie the slaughter of the Gods.	2Tamb	5.3.50	Tamb
besides the slaughter of these Gentlemen, poyson'd his owne	Jew	5.1.12	P Pilia
Unnaturall king, to slaughter noble men/And cherish flatterers:	Edw	4.1.8	Kent
Slaughter themselves in others and their sides/With their owne	Edw	4.4.7	Queene
Pharsalia grone with slaughter;/And Carthage soules be glutted	Lucan, First Booke		38
And love to Room (thogh slaughter steeld their harts/And minds	Lucan, First Booke		355
and laide before their eies/Slaughter to come, and swiftly	Lucan, First Booke		467
and stretch out the date/Of slaughter; onely civill broiles	Lucan, First Booke		671
no darke night-flying spright/Nor hands prepar'd to slaughter,	Ovid's Elegies		1.6.14
Slaughter and mischiefs instruments, no better,	Ovid's Elegies		1.7.27
For her ill-beautious Mother judgd to slaughter?	Ovid's Elegies		3.3.18
SLAUGHTERED			
And you march on their slaughtered carkasses:	1Tamb	2.2.69	Meandr
their slaughtered Carkasses/Shall serve for walles and	1Tamb	3.3.138	Bajzth
marshal us the way/We use to march upon the slaughtered foe:	1Tamb	3.3.149	Tamb

SLAUGHTERED (cont.)

on Damascus wals/Have hoisted up their slaughtered carcases. 1Tamb 5.1.131 Techel
The slaughtered bodies of these Christians. 2Tamb 1.1.36 Orcan
And sprinkled with the braines of slaughtered men, 2Tamb 1.3.81 Tamb
And strowes the way with braines of slaughtered men: 2Tamb 3.4.58 Therid
With slaughtered priests [make] <may> Tibers channell swell, Edw 1.4.102 Edward

SLAUGHTERING

hate/Flings slaughtering terrour from my coleblack tents. 1Tamb 5.1.72 Tamb

SLAUGHTRED

Through which he could not passe for slaughtred men: Dido 2.1.262 Aeneas
While slaughtred Crassus ghost walks unreveng'd, Lucan, First Booke 11

SLAVE

O th'inchaunting words of that base slave, Dido 2.1.161 Aeneas
So will I send this monstrous slave to hell, 1Tamb 2.6.7 Cosroe
Note the presumption of this Scythian slave: 1Tamb 3.3.68 Bajzth
And how my slave, her mistresse menaceth. 1Tamb 3.3.183 Zenoc
Prepare thy selfe to live and die my slave. 1Tamb 3.3.207 Zabina
The slave usurps the glorious name of war. 1Tamb 4.1.67 Souldn
faire Arabian king/That hath bene disapointed by this slave, 1Tamb 4.1.69 Souldn
Base villain, vassall, slave to Tamburlaine: 1Tamb 4.2.19 Tamb
Zenocrate, looke better to your slave. 1Tamb 4.2.68 Tamb
She is my Handmaids slave, and she shal looke/That these abuses 1Tamb 4.2.69 Zenoc
Let these be warnings for you then my slave, 1Tamb 4.2.72 Anippe
Feede you slave, thou maist thinke thy selfe happie to be fed 1Tamb 4.4.92 P Tamb
Who lives in Egypt, prisoner to that slave, 2Tamb 1.1.4 Orcan
And makes the mighty God of armes his slave: 2Tamb 3.4.53 Therid
suborn'd/That villaine there, that slave, that Turkish dog, 2Tamb 3.5.87 Tamb
Me thinks the slave should make a lusty theefe. 2Tamb 3.5.96 Jrslem
Image of sloth, and picture of a slave, 2Tamb 4.1.91 Tamb
And let my souldiers shoot the slave to death. 2Tamb 5.1.109 Tamb
See where my slave, the uglie monster death/Shaking and 2Tamb 5.3.67 Tamb
That Callapine should be my slave againe. 2Tamb 5.3.118 Tamb
the slave looks like a hogs cheek new sindg'd. Jew 2.3.42 P Barab
But now I must be gone to buy a slave. Jew 2.3.95 Barab
marketplace; whats the price of this slave, two hundred Crowns? Jew 2.3.98 P Barab
base slave as he should be saluted by such a tall man as I am, Jew 4.2.9 P Pilia
He sent a shaggy totter'd staring slave, Jew 4.3.6 Barab
I will in some disguize goe see the slave, Jew 4.3.67 Barab
A masty <nasty> slave he is. Jew 4.4.69 Pilia
What a damn'd slave was I? Jew 5.1.23 Barab
I hope to see the Governour a slave, Jew 5.1.67 Barab
And since that time they have hir'd a slave my man/To accuse me Jew 5.1.75 Barab
How the slave jeeres at him? Jew 5.5.56 Govnr
Doth no man take exceptions at the slave? Edw 1.2.25 MortSr
How easilie might some base slave be subbornd, Edw 1.4.265 Mortmr
Lancaster, why talkst thou to the slave? Edw 2.5.19 Warwck
Alas poore slave, see how poverty jests in his nakednesse, I F 348 1.4.6 P Wagner
No slave, in beaten silke, and staves-aker. F 357 1.4.15 P Wagner
And I will be thy slave and waite on thee, F 435 2.1.47 Mephst
See where he comes, dispatch, and kill the slave. F1423 4.2.99 2Soldr
Alas poore slave, see how poverty jesteth in his nakednesse, F App p.229 6 P Wagner

SLAVERIE

Or els you shall be forc'd with slaverie. 1Tamb 1.2.256 Tamb
The slaverie wherewith he persecutes/The noble Turke and his 1Tamb 4.3.26 Arabia

SLAVERIES

nor no hope of end/To our infamous monstrous slaveries? 1Tamb 5.1.241 Zabina
And treble all his fathers slaveries. 2Tamb 3.2.158 Tamb

SLAVERY

Before I yeeld to such a slavery. 1Tamb 4.2.18 Bajzth
Ah Madam, this their slavery hath Enforc'd, 1Tamb 5.1.345 Anippe
And cast your crownes in slavery at their feet. 2Tamb 3.5.149 Tamb

SLAVE'S

What a slave's this? Jew 4.4.63 P Barab

SLAVES

Shall massacre those greedy minded slaves. 1Tamb 2.2.67 Meandr
inlarge/Those Christian Captives, which you keep as slaves, 1Tamb 3.3.47 Tamb
that makest us thus/The slaves to Scythians rude and barbarous. 1Tamb 3.3.271 Zabina
you suffer these outragious curses by these slaves of yours? 1Tamb 4.4.27 P Zenoc
Take them away againe and make us slaves. 1Tamb 4.4.133 Therid
Why should we live, O wretches, beggars, slaves, 1Tamb 5.1.248 Zabina
A thousand Gallies mann'd with Christian slaves/I freely give 2Tamb 1.2.32 Callap
But yet Ile save their lives and make them slaves. 2Tamb 3.5.63 Tamb
See now ye slaves, my children stoops your pride/And leads your 2Tamb 4.1.76 Tamb
As you (ye slaves) in mighty Tamburlain. 2Tamb 4.3.11 Tamb
Live [continent] <content> then (ye slaves) and meet not me 2Tamb 4.3.81 Tamb
we offer more/Than ever yet we did to such proud slaves, 2Tamb 5.1.58 Techel
And like base slaves abject our princely mindes/To vile and 2Tamb 5.1.140 Orcan
draw you slaves,/In spight of death I will goe show my face. 2Tamb 5.3.113 Tamb
So, raigne my sonne, scourge and controlle those slaves, 2Tamb 5.3.228 Tamb
See the simplicitie of these base slaves, Jew 1.2.214 Barab
The Captain's slaine, the rest remaine our slaves, Jew 2.2.17 Bosco
Chaining of Eunuches, binding gally-slaves. Jew 2.3.204 Ithimr
I, Lord, thus slaves will learne. Jew 5.2.49 Barab
Onely for pleasure of these damned slaves. F1119 3.3.32 Mephst
Onely for pleasure of these damned slaves. F App p.235 39 Mephst
The vaine name of inferiour slaves despize. Ovid's Elegies 1.8.64

SLAVISH

Of Scythians and slavish Persians. 1Tamb 4.3.68 Souldn
Have desperatly dispatcht their slavish lives: 1Tamb 5.1.472 Tamb
No, we wil meet thee slavish Tamburlain. 2Tamb 3.5.170 Orcan
Villaine, respects thou more thy slavish life, 2Tamb 5.1.10 Govnr
spirits may vex/Your slavish bosomes with continuall paines, 2Tamb 5.1.46 Govnr
When I record my Parents slavish life, 2Tamb 5.2.19 Callap

SLAVISH (cont.)			
A dissolution of the slavish Bands/Wherein the Turke hath	Jew	5.2.77	Barab
SLAVONIANS (See also SCLAVONIANS)			
Slavonians, [Almain Rutters] <Almains, Rutters>, Muffes, and	2Tamb	1.1.58	Orcan
SLAY			
Commaund my guard to slay for their offence:	Dido	4.4.72	Dido
Wilt thou now slay me with thy venomed sting,	Dido	5.1.167	Dido
To see my sweet Iarbus slay himselfe?	Dido	5.1.324	Anna
I'le helpe to slay their children and their wives,	Jew	5.1.64	Barab
And slay his servants that shall issue out.	P 299	5.26	Anjoy
But slay as many as we can come neer.	P 326	5.53	Anjoy
Sirra twas I that slew him, and will slay/Thee too, and thou	P1048	19.118	King
Slay me my lord, when I offend your grace.	Edw	1.4.349	Warwck
To slay mine enemies, and aid my friends,	F 324	1.3.96	Faust
[To burne his Scriptures, slay his Ministers],	F 650	2.2.99A	Faust
Who unborne infants first to slay invented,	Ovid's Elegies		2.14.5
SLAYES			
Hees happie who loves mutuall skirmish slayes <layes>,	Ovid's Elegies		2.10.29
SLAYEST			
That slayest me with thy harsh and hellish tale,	Dido	5.1.217	Dido
SLED			
With milke-white Hartes upon an Ivorie sled,	1Tamb	1.2.98	Tamb
Ah whether is [thy] <they> brests soft nature [fled] <sled>?	Ovid's Elegies		3.7.18
SLEEP			
what, given so much to sleep/You cannot leave it, when our	2Tamb	4.1.11	Amyras
Come Amorous wag, first banquet and then sleep.	Jew	4.2.132	Curtzn
For e're I sleep, I'le try what I can do:	F 192	1.1.164	Faust
SLEEPE			
To force an hundred watchfull eyes to sleepe:	Dido	2.1.146	Aeneas
Sleepe my sweete nephew in these cooling shades,	Dido	2.1.334	Venus
And nothing interrupt thy quiet sleepe,	Dido	2.1.338	Venus
When sleepe but newly had imbrast the night,	Dido	4.3.17	Aeneas
Ile have you learne to sleepe upon the ground,	2Tamb	3.2.55	Tamb
If halfe our campe should sit and sleepe with me,	2Tamb	4.1.18	Calyph
No sleepe can fasten on my watchfull eyes,	Jew	2.1.17	Barab
Then, gentle sleepe, where e're his bodie rests,	Jew	2.1.35	Abigal
Come my deare love, let's in and sleepe together.	Jew	4.2.129	Curtzn
That wee might sleepe seven yeeres together afore we wake.	Jew	4.2.131	Ithimr
For this, I wake, when others think I sleepe,	P 105	2.48	Guise
Shall sleepe within the scabberd at thy neede,	Edw	1.1.87	Mortmr
But rest thee here where Gaveston shall sleepe.	Edw	2.1.65	Neece
It hath my lord, the warders all a sleepe,	Edw	4.1.15	Mortmr
Or whilst one is a sleepe, to take a quill/And blowe a little	Edw	5.4.34	Ltborn
This ten dayes space, and least that I should sleepe,	Edw	5.5.60	Edward
So that for want of sleepe and sustenance,	Edw	5.5.63	Edward
But that greefe keepes me waking, I shoulde sleepe,	Edw	5.5.93	Edward
And tels me, if I sleepe I never wake,	Edw	5.5.104	Edward
And make them sleepe so sound, that in their shapes,	F 895	3.1.117	Faust
But whilst they sleepe within the Consistory,	F 943	3.1.165	Faust
Fast a sleepe I warrant you,	F1173	4.1.19	Mrtino
A plague upon you, let me sleepe a while.	F1283	4.1.129	Benvol
I blame thee not to sleepe much, having such a head of thine	F1284	4.1.130	P Emper
Confound these passions with a quiet sleepe:	F1481	4.4.25	Faust
O Lord I pray sir, let Banio and Belcher go sleepe.	F App	p.231 68	P Clown
Confound these passions with a quiet sleepe:	F App	p.240 124	Faust
snatcht up/Would make them sleepe securely in their tents.	Lucan, First Booke		516
Although the nights be long, I sleepe not tho,	Ovid's Elegies		1.2.3
If hee lyes downe with Wine and sleepe opprest,	Ovid's Elegies		1.4.53
or ist sleepe forbids thee heare,/Giving the windes my words	Ovid's Elegies		1.6.41
Sooth Lovers watch till sleepe the hus-band charmes,	Ovid's Elegies		1.9.25
The aire is colde, and sleepe is sweetest now,	Ovid's Elegies		1.13.7
Thou coosnest boyes of sleepe, and dost betray them/To Pedants,	Ovid's Elegies		1.13.17
Nuts were thy food, and Poppie causde thee sleepe,	Ovid's Elegies		2.6.31
Foole, what is sleepe but image of cold death,	Ovid's Elegies		2.9.41
Yea, let my foes sleepe in an emptie bed,	Ovid's Elegies		2.10.17
It is more safe to sleepe, to read a booke,	Ovid's Elegies		2.11.31
SLEEPES			
Nor goe to bed, but sleepes in his owne clothes;	Jew	4.1.132	Ithimr
And whilste he sleepes securely thus in ease,	P 635	12.48	QnMoth
He sleepes.	Edw	5.5.100	Ltborn
Both of them watch: each on the hard earth sleepes:	Ovid's Elegies		1.9.7
The Moone sleepes with Endemion everie day,	Ovid's Elegies		1.13.43
SLEEPIE			
O Mahomet, Oh sleepie Mahomet.	1Tamb	3.3.269	Bajzth
SLEEPING			
That would have kild him sleeping as he lay?	Dido	3.2.39	Juno
What, sleeping, eating, walking and disputing?	F 528	2.1.140	Faust
So shall our sleeping vengeance now arise,	F 879	3.1.101	Pope
Oft to invade the sleeping foe tis good/And arm'd to shed	Ovid's Elegies		1.9.21
Halfe sleeping on a purple bed she rested,	Ovid's Elegies		1.14.20
In sleeping shall I fearelesse drawe my breath?	Ovid's Elegies		2.19.55
SLEEPS			
imperiall heaven/That he that sits on high and never sleeps,	2Tamb	2.2.49	Orcan
He sleeps my Lord, but dreames not of his hornes.	F1280	4.1.126	Faust
SLEEP'ST			
Sleep'st every night with conquest on thy browes,	1Tamb	5.1.359	Zenoc
SLEEPST			
Or with what thought sleepst thou in Libia shoare?	Dido	5.1.35	Hermes
SLEEPY			
What, all alone? well fare sleepy drinke.	Jew	5.1.61	Barab
The sleepy Cardinals are hard at hand,	F 982	3.2.2	Mephst
SLEEVE			
Convey this golden arrowe in thy sleeve,	Dido	3.1.3	Cupid

SLEEVES
Her wide sleeves greene, and bordered with a grove, . . | Hero and Leander 1.11
SLEIGHT (See SLIGHT)
SLEIGHTLY
other meanes, (and gods not sleightly/Purchase immortal thrones; | Lucan, First Booke 34
SLENDER
And feeding them with thin and slender fare, ... | 1Tamb 3.3.49 Tamb
Which when he tainted with his slender rod, ... | 2Tamb 1.3.40 Zenoc
Taking advantage of your slender power, ... | 2Tamb 2.2.26 1Msngr
And left your slender carkasses behind, ... | 2Tamb 4.1.38 Calyph
And usde such slender reckning of [your] <you> majesty. . | 2Tamb 5.1.83 Therid
'Twere slender policy for Barabas/To dispossesse himselfe of | Jew 5.2.65 Barab
<Tush>, These slender questions <trifles> Wagner can decide: | F 600 2.2.49 Faust
even as the slender Isthmos,/Betwixt the Aegean and the Ionian | Lucan, First Booke 100
With slender trench they escape night stratagems, . . | Lucan, First Booke 514
T'was so, he stroke me with a slender dart, ... | Ovid's Elegies 1.2.7
Long Love my body to such use [makes] <make> slender/And to get | Ovid's Elegies 1.6.5
Or slender eares, with gentle Zephire shaken, . . . | Ovid's Elegies 1.7.55
Or thrids which spiders slender foote drawes out/Fastning her | Ovid's Elegies 1.14.7
When they were slender, and like downy mosse, . . . | Ovid's Elegies 1.14.23
Though I am slender, I have store of pith, . . . | Ovid's Elegies 2.10.23
That sheares the slender threads of humane life, . . | Hero and Leander 1.448
SLENDEREST
rebelling Jades/Wil take occasion by the slenderest haire, | 2Tamb 5.3.239 Tamb
SLEPT
Some surfetted, and others soundly slept. . . . . . | Dido 2.1.179 Aeneas
Whose flintie darts slept in Tipheus den, ... | Dido 4.1.19 Iarbus
Whom I have brought from Ida where he slept, . . . | Dido 5.1.40 Hermes
lov'd Rice, that Fryar Bernardine slept in his owne clothes. | Jew 4.4.76 P Ithimr
That slept both Bruno and his crowne away. . . . . | F 988 3.2.8 Faust
I tell thee he has not slept this eight nights. . . | F App p.240 144 P Mephst
And he have not slept this eight weekes Ile speake with him. | F App p.240 145 P HrsCsr
Hermes had slept in hell with ignoraunce. . . . . | Hero and Leander 1.468
SLEW
Will tell how many thousand men he slew. . . . . | 1Tamb 3.2.43 Agidas
Slew all his Priests, his kinsmen, and his friends, . . | 2Tamb 5.1.181 Tamb
Slew friend and enemy with my stratagems. . . . . | Jew 2.3.189 Barab
Thy sonne slew mine, and I'le revenge his death. . . | Jew 3.2.15 Mater
Thou and thy Turk; 'twas you that slew my son. . . . | Jew 5.1.27 Govnr
Know, Governor, 'twas I that slew thy sonne; . . . | Jew 5.5.81 Barab
Sirra twas I that slew him, and will slay/Thee too, and thou | P1048 19.118 King
I slew the Guise, because I would be King. . . . . | P1066 19.136 King
hornes/The quick priest pull'd him on his knees and slew him: | Lucan, First Booke 612
The sonne slew her, that forth to meete him went, . . | Ovid's Elegies 1.10.51
SLEWE
Perhaps he'ele tell howe oft he slewe a man, ... | Ovid's Elegies 3.7.21
SLICE
And slice the Sea with sable coloured ships, ... | Dido 4.3.22 Aeneas
That sacrificing slice and cut your flesh, ... | 1Tamb 4.2.3 Bajzth
will make thee slice the brawnes of thy armes into carbonadoes, | 1Tamb 4.4.44 P Tamb
That it may keenly slice the Catholicks. . . . . | P1238 22.100 King
SLICING
Keeping his circuit by the slicing edge. . . . . | 1Tamb 5.1.112 Tamb
SLICKE
on him; hee has a buttocke as slicke as an Ele; wel god buy sir, | F App p.240 117 P HrsCsr
SLID
That Meremaid-like unto the floore she slid, ... | Hero and Leander 2.315
SLIDE
Or [into] <to the> sea swift Symois [doth] <shall> slide. | Ovid's Elegies 1.15.10
And by the rising herbes, where cleare springs slide, . | Ovid's Elegies 2.16.9
Slide in thy bounds, so shalt thou runne for ever. . . | Ovid's Elegies 3.5.20
Or full of dust doest on the drye earth slide. . . . | Ovid's Elegies 3.5.96
At every stroke, betwixt them would he slide, . . . | Hero and Leander 2.184
SLIDES
And with my blood my life slides through my wound, . . | 1Tamb 2.7.43 Cosroe
Time flying slides hence closely, and deceaves us, . . | Ovid's Elegies 1.8.49
SLIDEST
Aurora whither slidest thou? . . . . | Ovid's Elegies 1.13.3
SLIE
That slie inveigling Frenchman weele exile, ... | Edw 1.2.57 Mortmr
SLIGHT (Homograph)
Nor usde the slight nor <and> cunning which she could, . | Ovid's Elegies 3.6.56
And like a wittall thinke thee voyde of slight. . . | Ovid's Elegies 3.13.30
Where both deliberat, the love is slight, ... | Hero and Leander 1.175
SLIGHTLY (See also SLEIGHTLY)
Nor will I part so slightly therewithall. . . . . | Jew 1.2.87 Barab
SLIME
Floud with [reede-growne] <redde-growne> slime bankes, till I | Ovid's Elegies 3.5.1
SLINGES
the darke/(Swifter then bullets throwne from Spanish slinges, | Lucan, First Booke 231
SLIP
Slip not thine opportunity, for feare too late/Thou seek'st for | Jew 5.2.45 Barab
That if he slip will seaze upon us both, ... | Edw 5.2.8 Mortmr
Shall I let slip so great an injury, ... | F1328 4.2.4 Benvol
But if my words with winged stormes hence slip, . . | Ovid's Elegies 2.11.33
And from my hands the reines will slip away. . . . | Ovid's Elegies 3.2.14
SLIPPE
Slippe still, onely denie it when tis done, ... | Ovid's Elegies 3.13.15
SLIPPERS
Fayre lined slippers for the cold: . . . . . . | Passionate Shepherd 15
SLIPPERY
That fights for Scepters and for slippery crownes, . . | 1Tamb 5.1.356 Zenoc
Tis said the slippery streame held up her brest, . . | Ovid's Elegies 3.5.81

SLIPPING
And where swift Nile in his large channell slipping <skipping>, Ovid's Elegies 2.13.9
By seaven huge mouthes into the sea is [skipping] <slipping>, Ovid's Elegies 2.13.10
SLIPS
Or why slips downe the Coverlet so oft? . . . . . Ovid's Elegies 1.2.2
SLIPT
Even now as I came home, he slipt me in, ... Jew 2.3.267 Barab
And slipt from bed cloth'd in a loose night-gowne, . . Ovid's Elegies 3.1.51
For unawares (Come thither) from her slipt, . . . Hero and Leander 1.358
And seeking refuge, slipt into her bed. . . . . Hero and Leander 2.244
SLOATHFULNESSE
Therefore who ere love sloathfulnesse doth call, . . Ovid's Elegies 1.9.31
SLOOTHFUL
meet not me/With troopes of harlots at your sloothful heeles. 2Tamb 4.3.82 Tamb
SLOP
do ye see yonder tall fellow in the round slop, hee has kild F App p.230 48 P Clown
SLOPS
And Vangions who like those of Sarmata,/Were open slops: . Lucan, First Booke 432
SLOTH
Image of sloth, and picture of a slave, ... 2Tamb 4.1.91 Tamb
But follie, sloth, and damned idlenesse: . . . . 2Tamb 4.1.126 Tamb
Hey ho; I am Sloth: . . . . F 705 2.2.154 P Sloth
Strike them with sloth, and drowsy idlenesse; . . . F 894 3.1.116 Faust
The Pope will curse them for their sloth to day, . . F 987 3.2.7 Faust
And fates so bent, least sloth and long delay/Might crosse him, Lucan, First Booke 394
My selfe was dull, and faint, to sloth inclinde, . . Ovid's Elegies 1.9.41
SLOTHFULL
He that will not growe slothfull let him love. . . . Ovid's Elegies 1.9.46
O boy that lyest so slothfull in my heart. . . . Ovid's Elegies 2.9.2
Wee Macer sit in Venus slothfull shade, ... Ovid's Elegies 2.18.3
SLOUTHFULL
Not what we slouthfull [knowe] <knewe>, let wise men learne, Ovid's Elegies 3.7.25
SLOW (See also FORSLOWE)
slow to wrath, and prone to letcherie (to love I would say) it F 210 1.2.17 P Wagner
Slow oxen early in the yoake are pent. . . . . Ovid's Elegies 1.13.16
SLOWE
Wild me, whose slowe feete sought delay, be flying. . . Ovid's Elegies 2.19.12
One slowe we favour, Romans him revoke: . . . . Ovid's Elegies 3.2.73
And that slowe webbe nights fals-hood did unframe. . . Ovid's Elegies 3.8.30
SLOWLY
Duld with much beating slowly forth doth passe. . . Ovid's Elegies 2.7.16
SLUGGARD
That all this day the sluggard keepes his bed. . . . F1176 4.1.22 Mrtino
SLUGGISHNESSE
A faire maides care expeld this sluggishnesse, . . . Ovid's Elegies 1.9.43
SLUICE
Feare not, my Lord, for here, against the [sluice] <Truce>,/The Jew 5.1.86 Barab
SLUMBER
And with this stab slumber eternally. . . . . 1Tamb 3.2.106 Agidas
SLUMBERING
Lie slumbering on the flowrie bankes of Nile, . . . 1Tamb 4.1.9 Souldn
SLUMBERS
To sweeten out the slumbers of thy bed: . . . . Dido 1.1.37 Jupitr
SLUMBRED
[wretch] <wench> I sawe when thou didst thinke I slumbred, Ovid's Elegies 2.5.13
SLUMBRING
Who slumbring, they rise up in swelling armes. . . . Ovid's Elegies 1.9.26
Haples is he that all the night lies quiet/And slumbring, Ovid's Elegies 2.9.40
SLUTTISH
age you wrackes/And sluttish white-mould overgrowe the waxe. Ovid's Elegies 1.12.30
SLYLIE (See also SLIE)
Jove, slylie stealing from his sisters bed, . . . Hero and Leander 1.147
SMACK
Marry sir, in having a smack in all, ... P 385 7.25 Guise
SMAL
lord, specially having so smal a walke, and so litle exercise. 1Tamb 4.4.105 P Therid
SMALL
Not for so small a fault my soveraigne Lord. . . . 1Tamb 1.1.25 Meandr
As hath the Ocean or the Terrene sea/Small drops of water, when 1Tamb 3.1.11 Bajzth
Captaine we know it, but our force is small. . . . Jew 2.2.34 Govnr
Small though the number was that kept the Towne, . . Jew 2.2.49 Bosco
a warning e're he goes/As he shall have small hopes of Abigall. Jew 2.3.274 Barab
No simple place, no small authority, ... Jew 5.2.28 Barab
But he is banisht, theres small hope of him. . . . Edw 2.1.15 Baldck
The king hath left him, and his traine is small. . . Edw 2.4.39 Queene
Small comfort findes poore Edward in thy lookes, . . Edw 5.5.44 Edward
but a [bare] <small> pention, and that buyes me <is> thirty F 694 2.2.143 P Glutny
a small trifle to suffice nature. . . . . . . F 695 2.2.144 P Glutny
order, Il'e nere trust smooth faces, and small ruffes more. F1318 4.1.164 P Benvol
Or hew'd this flesh and bones as small as sand, . . F1398 4.2.74 Faust
thou canst not buy so good a horse, for so small a price: F1459 4.4.3 P Faust
This is but a small matter: . . . . F1574 4.6.17 P Faust
O soule be chang'd into <to> [little] <small> water drops, F1977 5.2.181 Faust
Which issues from a small spring, is but shallow, . . Lucan, First Booke 216
A small thin skinne contain'd the vital parts, . . . Lucan, First Booke 622
being thin, the harme was small,/Yet strivde she to be covered Ovid's Elegies 1.5.13
(O mischiefe) now for me obtaine small grace. . . . Ovid's Elegies 1.6.22
Make a small price, while thou thy nets doest lay, . . Ovid's Elegies 1.8.69
A grave her bones hides, on her corps great <small> grave, Ovid's Elegies 2.6.59
Life is no light price of a small surcease. . . . Ovid's Elegies 2.14.26
And her small joynts incircling round hoope make thee. . Ovid's Elegies 2.15.4
But in lesse compasse her small fingers knit. . . . Ovid's Elegies 2.15.20
go small gift from hand,/Let her my faith with thee given Ovid's Elegies 2.15.27

Line	Work	Reference	Speaker
SMALL (cont.)			
A small, but wholesome soyle with watrie veynes.	Ovid's Elegies	2.16.2	
Small things with greater may be copulate.	Ovid's Elegies	2.17.14	
Where round about small birdes most sweetely sing.	Ovid's Elegies	3.1.4	
Small doores unfitting for large houses are.	Ovid's Elegies	3.1.40	
Yet in the meane time wilt small windes bestowe,	Ovid's Elegies	3.2.37	
Her foote was small: her footes forme is most fit:	Ovid's Elegies	3.3.7	
What helpes my hast: what to have tane small rest?	Ovid's Elegies	3.5.9	
Scarse rests of all what a small urne conteines.	Ovid's Elegies	3.8.40	
How small so ere, Ile you for greatest praise.	Ovid's Elegies	3.14.14	
Which so prevail'd, as he with small ado,	Hero and Leander	2.281	
SMART			
Nay, thou must feele them, taste the smart of all:	F1922	5.2.126	BdAngl
With selfe same woundes he gave, he ought to smart.	Ovid's Elegies	2.3.4	
O Cupid that doest never cease my smart,	Ovid's Elegies	2.9.1	
Venus, why doublest thou my endlesse smart?	Ovid's Elegies	2.10.11	
(Alas my precepts turne my selfe to smart)/We write, or what	Ovid's Elegies	2.18.20	
Who thinkes her to be glad at lovers smart,	Ovid's Elegies	3.9.15	
SMARTS			
Till they [reveal] the causers of our smarts,	Jew	3.2.34	Govnr
SMEAR'D			
Smear'd with blots of basest drudgery:	1Tamb	5.1.268	Bajzth
SMELL			
How sweet, my Ithimore, the flowers smell.	Jew	4.4.39	Curtzn
But fye, what a smell <scent> is heere?	F 669	2.2.118	P Pride
Many would praise the sweet smell as she past,	Hero and Leander	1.21	
SMELLES			
they be my good Lord, and he that smelles but to them, dyes.	P 73	2.16	P Pothec
SMELLING			
And strewe him with sweete smelling Violets,	Dido	2.1.318	Venus
And smelling to a Nosegay all the day,	Edw	2.1.35	Spencr
SMELS			
Contagious smels, and vapors to infect thee,	2Tamb	4.2.11	Olymp
SMELT			
I smelt 'em e're they came.	Jew	4.1.22	Barab
SMIL'D			
The mirthfull God of amorous pleasure smil'd,	Hero and Leander	2.39	
SMILD			
And as she red, she smild, which makes me thinke,	Edw	2.1.21	Spencr
Thereat she smild, and did denie him so,	Hero and Leander	1.311	
SMILDE			
The other smilde, (I wot) with wanton eyes,	Ovid's Elegies	3.1.33	
She smilde, and with quicke eyes behight some grace:	Ovid's Elegies	3.2.83	
Thereat smilde Neptune, and then told a tale,	Hero and Leander	2.193	
SMILE (See also SMYLING)			
Or force her smile that hetherto hath frownd:	Dido	1.1.88	Jupitr
Doe thou but smile, and clowdie heaven will cleare,	Dido	1.1.155	Achat
For were it Priam he would smile on me.	Dido	2.1.36	Ascan
souldier of my Camp/Shall smile to see thy miserable state.	1Tamb	3.3.86	Tamb
Smile Stars that raign'd at my nativity,	1Tamb	4.2.33	Tamb
I smile to think, how when this field is fought,	2Tamb	3.5.165	Techel
But to thy selfe smile when the Christians moane.	Jew	2.3.172	Barab
He has my heart, I smile against my will.	Jew	2.3.287	Abigal
So thou wouldst smile and take me in thy <thine> armes.	Edw	1.1.9	Gavstn
Even so let hatred with thy [soveraignes] <soveraigne> smile.	Edw	1.4.342	Edward
(men say)/Began to smile and [tooke] <take> one foote away.	Ovid's Elegies	1.1.8	
SMILES			
Where Dido will receive ye with her smiles:	Dido	1.1.234	Venus
How lovely is Ascanius when he smiles?	Dido	3.1.29	Dido
Who smiles to see how full his bags are cramb'd,	Jew	Prol.31	Machvl
He nods, and scornes, and smiles at those that passe.	Edw	1.2.24	Warwck
Smiles in his face, and whispers in his eares,	Edw	1.2.52	Queene
She smiles, now for my life his mind is changd.	Edw	1.4.236	Warwck
He turnes away, and smiles upon his minion.	Edw	2.4.29	Queene
[Ambitious fiends, see how the heavens smiles]/[At your repulse,	F1794	5.1.121A	OldMan
SMILING			
Not mov'd at all, but smiling at his teares,	Dido	2.1.240	Aeneas
Whose smiling stars gives him assured hope/Of martiall triumph,	1Tamb	3.3.42	Tamb
While I sit smiling to behold the sight.	2Tamb	3.2.128	Tamb
Doth she not with her smiling answer you?	Jew	2.3.286	Barab
hearing it laugh'd with his tender mother/And smiling sayed,	Ovid's Elegies	1.6.12	
A pleasant smiling cheeke, a speaking eye,	Hero and Leander	1.85	
And smiling wantonly, his love bewrayd.	Hero and Leander	2.182	
SMITE			
And shall or Warwicks sword shal smite in vaine.	Edw	3.1.199	Warwck
And smite with death thy hated enterprise.	F 880	3.1.102	Pope
SMITHES			
Mars in the deed the black-smithes net did stable,	Ovid's Elegies	1.9.39	
SMITHS			
Venus with Vulcan, though smiths tooles laide by,	Ovid's Elegies	2.17.19	
SMOAKE			
And with the breaches fall, smoake, fire, and dust,	2Tamb	3.3.59	Therid
Wee'll send [thee] <the> bullets wrapt in smoake and fire:	Jew	2.2.54	Govnr
SMOCKE			
And then turning my selfe to a wrought Smocke do what I list.	F 668	2.2.117	P Pride
SMOKY			
My limbes may issue from your smoky mouthes,	F1955	5.2.159	Faust
SMOLDERING			
Enrolde in flames and fiery smoldering mistes,	1Tamb	2.3.20	Tamb
SMOOTH			
And shake off smooth dissembling flatterers:	Edw	3.1.169	Herald
order, Il'e nere trust smooth faces, and small ruffes more.	F1318	4.1.164	P Benvol
Smooth speeches, feare and rage shall by thee ride,	Ovid's Elegies	1.2.35	

SMOOTH (cont.)
And falling vallies be the smooth-wayes crowne. . . Ovid's Elegies 2.16.52
How smooth his brest was, and how white his bellie, . . Hero and Leander 1.66
And with smooth speech, her fancie to assay, . . . Hero and Leander 1.402

SMOOTHE
Is with that smoothe toongd scholler Baldock gone, . . Edw 4.6.57 Rice
How smoothe a bellie, under her waste sawe I, . . . Ovid's Elegies 1.5.21

SMOOTHERING
The spring is hindred by your smoothering host, . . 1Tamb 3.1.50 Moroc

SMOOTHE TOONGD
Is with that smoothe toongd scholler Baldock gone, . . Edw 4.6.57 Rice

SMOOTHLY
Are smoothly gliding downe by Candie shoare/To Malta, through Jew 1.1.46 Barab

SMOOTHNESSE
And in their smoothnesse, amitie and life: . . . 1Tamb 2.1.22 Menaph

SMOOTH-WAYES
And falling vallies be the smooth-wayes crowne. . . Ovid's Elegies 2.16.52

SMOTHER (See also SMOOTHERING)
Smother the earth with never fading mistes: . . . . 1Tamb 5.1.296 Bajzth

SMOTHER'D
Halfe smother'd in a Lake of mud and durt, . . . F1434 4.3.4 Mrtino

SMYLING
Go frowning foorth, but come thou smyling home, . . 1Tamb 1.1.65 Mycet

SNAKE
And the dull snake about thy offrings creepe, . . . Ovid's Elegies 2.13.13

SNAKES
For saving him from Snakes and Serpents stings, . . Dido 3.2.38 Juno
Or winged snakes of Lerna cast your stings, . . . 1Tamb 4.4.21 Bajzth
Than noisome parbreak of the Stygian Snakes, . . . 1Tamb 5.1.256 Bajzth
Snakes leape by verse from caves of broken mountaines/And Ovid's Elegies 2.1.25
Wee cause feete flie, wee mingle haires with snakes, . Ovid's Elegies 3.11.23

SNAKIE
Or like the snakie wreathe of Tisiphon, ... Edw 5.1.45 Edward
Shaking her snakie haire and crooked pine/With flaming toppe, Lucan, First Booke 571
On her, this god/Enamoured was, and with his snakie rod,/Did Hero and Leander 1.398

SNAP
And leaves it off to snap on Thistle tops: . . . . Jew 5.2.42 Barab

SNAPPER
O yonder is his snipper snapper, do you heare? . . . F App p.240 137 P HrsCsr

SNARDE
Love-snarde Calypso is supposde to pray, ... Ovid's Elegies 2.17.15

SNARE
His hands he cast upon her like a snare, ... Hero and Leander 2.259

SNARES
What shall I doe to shun the snares of death? . . . F1742 5.1.69 Faust

SNATCH
Turkish Deputie/And all his Viceroies, snatch it from his head, 2Tamb 1.3.100 Tamb

SNATCHING
And from the northren climat snatching fier/Blasted the . Lucan, First Booke 532
Snatching the combe, to beate the wench out drive <drave> her. Ovid's Elegies 1.14.18

SNATCH'T
How now? who snatch't the meat from me! . . . . . F1044 3.2.64 Pope

SNATCHT
For amorous Jove hath snatcht my love from hence, . . 2Tamb 2.4.107 Tamb
How now, whose that which snatcht the meate from me? . F App p.231 8 P Pope
for Julia/Snatcht hence by cruel fates with ominous howles, Lucan, First Booke 112
And snatcht armes neer their houshold gods hung up/Such as Lucan, First Booke 242
And suddaine rampire raisde of turfe snatcht up/Would make them Lucan, First Booke 515
I snatcht her gowne: . . . . Ovid's Elegies 1.5.13

'SNAYLES
'Snayles, what hast thou got there, a book? . . . . F 730 2.3.9 P Dick

SNEAKE
thought you did not sneake up and downe after her for nothing. F 742 2.3.21 P Dick

SNICLE
the Nuns, and he and I, snicle hand too fast, strangled a Fryar. Jew 4.4.21 P Ithimr

SNIPPER
O yonder is his snipper snapper, do you heare? . . . F App p.240 137 P HrsCsr

SNIPPER SNAPPER
O yonder is his snipper snapper, do you heare? . . . F App p.240 137 P HrsCsr

SNORT
the time more short/Lay downe thy forehead in thy lap to snort. Ovid's Elegies 2.2.24

SNOW
Fairer than whitest snow on Scythian hils, ... 1Tamb 1.2.89 Tamb
the Alpes/Shooke the old snow from off their trembling laps. Lucan, First Booke 552
With snow thaw'd from the next hill now thou rushest, . Ovid's Elegies 3.5.7
white as is <Her armes farre whiter, then> the Scithean snow, Ovid's Elegies 3.6.8

SNOWDE
It haild, it snowde, it lightned all at once. . . . Dido 4.1.8 Anna

SNOWE
Like water gushing from consuming snowe. . . . . . Ovid's Elegies 1.7.58
God deluded/In snowe-white plumes of a false swanne included. Ovid's Elegies 1.10.4
Thy springs are nought but raine and melted snowe: . . Ovid's Elegies 3.5.93

SNOWES
is bould/To suffer storme mixt snowes with nights sharpe cold? Ovid's Elegies 1.9.16

SNOWE-WHITE
God deluded/In snowe-white plumes of a false swanne included. Ovid's Elegies 1.10.4

SNOWY
His armes and fingers long and [sinowy] <snowy>, . . . 1Tamb 2.1.27 Menaph
on his silver crest/A snowy Feather spangled white he beares, 1Tamb 4.1.51 2Msngr
Ocean to the Traveiler/That restes upon the snowy Appenines: 2Tamb 1.1.111 Sgsmnd
Now Caesar overpast the snowy Alpes, ... Lucan, First Booke 185
And treades the deserts snowy heapes [do] <to> cover. . Ovid's Elegies 1.9.12
Thou hast no name, but com'st from snowy mountaines; . Ovid's Elegies 3.5.91

SO

False Jupiter, rewardst thou vertue so?	Dido	1.1.78	Venus
Which once performd, poore Troy so long suppresst,	Dido	1.1.93	Jupitr
For this so friendly ayde in time of neede.	Dido	1.1.138	Venus
And they so wrackt and weltred by the waves,	Dido	1.1.223	Aeneas
And so I leave thee to thy fortunes lot,	Dido	1.1.238	Venus
Or in these shades deceiv'st mine eye so oft?	Dido	1.1.244	Aeneas
O were I not at all so thou mightst be.	Dido	2.1.28	Aeneas
Thy mind Aeneas that would have it so/Deludes thy eye sight,	Dido	2.1.31	Achat
Ile have it so, Aeneas be content.	Dido	2.1.95	Dido
And so I will sweete child:	Dido	2.1.97	Dido
And who so miserable as Aeneas is?	Dido	2.1.102	Aeneas
In whose defence he fought so valiantly:	Dido	2.1.119	Dido
And so in troopes all marcht to Tenedos:	Dido	2.1.135	Aeneas
To whom he used action so pitifull,	Dido	2.1.155	Aeneas
Lookes so remorcefull, vowes so forcible,	Dido	2.1.156	Aeneas
Through which it could not enter twas so huge.	Dido	2.1.171	Aeneas
And so came in this fatall instrument:	Dido	2.1.176	Aeneas
So I escapt the furious Pirrhus wrath:	Dido	2.1.223	Aeneas
Yet who so wretched but desires to live?	Dido	2.1.238	Aeneas
So leaning on his sword he stood stone still,	Dido	2.1.263	Aeneas
And so was reconcil'd to Menelaus.	Dido	2.1.299	Achat
I will faire mother, and so play my part,	Dido	2.1.332	Cupid
So lovely is he that where ere he goes,	Dido	3.1.71	Anna
So much have I receiv'd at Didos hands,	Dido	3.1.103	Aeneas
Achates, thou shalt be so [manly] <meanly> clad,	Dido	3.1.128	Dido
So that Aeneas may but stay with me.	Dido	3.1.133	Dido
But playd he nere so sweet, I let him goe:	Dido	3.1.160	Dido
But not so much for thee, thou art but one,	Dido	3.1.175	Dido
Should ere defile so faire a mouth as thine:	Dido	3.2.27	Juno
And wish that I had never wrongd him so:	Dido	3.2.48	Juno
That hath so many unresisted friends:	Dido	3.2.50	Juno
a match confirmd/Betwixt these two, whose loves are so alike,	Dido	3.2.78	Juno
Ungentle, can she wrong Iarbus so?	Dido	3.3.10	Iarbus
Or art thou grievde thy betters presse so nye?	Dido	3.3.18	Iarbus
How now Getulian, are ye growne so brave,	Dido	3.3.19	Dido
Yea little sonne, are you so forward now?	Dido	3.3.34	Dido
And dead to scorne that hath pursued me so.	Dido	3.3.49	Iarbus
But Dido that now holdeth him so deare,	Dido	3.3.76	Iarbus
So doth he now, though not with equall gaine,	Dido	3.3.83	Iarbus
Who then of all so cruell may he be,	Dido	3.4.16	Aeneas
Aeneas thoughts dare not ascend so high/As Didos heart, which	Dido	3.4.33	Aeneas
If that your majestie can looke so lowe,	Dido	3.4.41	Aeneas
Or day so cleere so suddenly orecast?	Dido	4.1.2	Achat
The motion was so over violent.	Dido	4.1.13	Achat
How now Iarbus, at your prayers so hard?	Dido	4.2.23	Anna
Alas poore King that labours so in vaine,	Dido	4.2.33	Anna
For her that so delighteth in thy paine:	Dido	4.2.34	Anna
Jove wils it so, my mother wils it so:	Dido	4.3.5	Aeneas
So she may have Aeneas in her armes.	Dido	4.3.42	Illion
To leave her so and not once say farewell,	Dido	4.3.47	Aeneas
So I may have Aeneas in mine armes.	Dido	4.4.135	Dido
Theres not so much as this base tackling too,	Dido	4.4.151	Dido
I, so youle dwell with me and call me mother.	Dido	4.5.16	Nurse
So youle love me, I care not if I doe.	Dido	4.5.17	Cupid
Why wilt thou so betray thy sonnes good hap?	Dido	5.1.31	Hermes
And they shall have what thing so ere thou needst.	Dido	5.1.74	Iarbus
If it be so, his father meanes to flye:	Dido	5.1.85	Dido
Fare well may Dido, so Aeneas stay,	Dido	5.1.107	Dido
So thou wouldst prove as true as Paris did,	Dido	5.1.146	Dido
He loves me to too well to serve me so:	Dido	5.1.185	Dido
So, leave me now, let none approach this place.	Dido	5.1.291	Dido
Not for so small a fault my soveraigne Lord.	1Tamb	1.1.25	Meandr
Yet live, yea, live, Mycetes wils it so:	1Tamb	1.1.27	Mycet
Therefore tis best, if so it lik you all,	1Tamb	1.1.51	Mycet
Intending your investion so neere/The residence of your	1Tamb	1.1.180	Ortyg
thou art so meane a man)/And seeke not to inrich thy followers,	1Tamb	1.2.8	Zenoc
I am (my Lord), for so you do import.	1Tamb	1.2.33	Zenoc
I am a Lord, for so my deeds shall proove,	1Tamb	1.2.34	Tamb
May have the leading of so great an host,	1Tamb	1.2.48	Tamb
So in his Armour looketh Tamburlaine:	1Tamb	1.2.54	Techel
But since they measure our deserts so meane,	1Tamb	1.2.63	Tamb
And I that triumpht so be overcome.	1Tamb	1.2.115	Tamb
A Scythian Shepheard, so imbellished/With Natures pride, and	1Tamb	1.2.155	Therid
So large of lims, his joints so strongly knit,	1Tamb	2.1.9	Menaph
Would it not grieve a King to be so abusde,	1Tamb	2.2.5	Mycet
So Poets say, my Lord.	1Tamb	2.2.53	Meandr
He tells you true, my maisters, so he does.	1Tamb	2.2.74	Mycet
And so mistake you not a whit my Lord.	1Tamb	2.3.6	Tamb
Your speech will stay, or so extol his worth,	1Tamb	2.3.27	Therid
So shall not I be knowen, or if I bee,	1Tamb	2.4.13	Mycet
So I can when I see my time.	1Tamb	2.4.26	Mycet
So do I thrice renowmed man at armes,	1Tamb	2.5.6	Cosroe
So will we with our powers and our lives,	1Tamb	2.5.34	Ortyg
A God is not so glorious as a King:	1Tamb	2.5.57	Therid
Why, that's wel said Techelles, so would I,	1Tamb	2.5.69	Tamb
And so would you my maisters, would you not?	1Tamb	2.5.70	Tamb
So will I send this monstrous slave to hell,	1Tamb	2.6.7	Cosroe
He dares so doubtlesly resolve of rule,	1Tamb	2.6.13	Meandr
So do we hope to raign in Asia,	1Tamb	2.7.38	Usumc
Shall make me leave so rich a prize as this:	1Tamb	2.7.54	Tamb
So, now it is more surer on my head,	1Tamb	2.7.65	Tamb
He be so mad to manage Armes with me,	1Tamb	3.1.34	Bajzth

SO (cont.)

Then stay thou with him, say I bid thee so.	1Tamb	3.1.35		Bajzth
a heavenly face/Should by hearts sorrow wax so wan and pale,	1Tamb	3.2.5		Agidas
Which dies my lookes so livelesse as they are.	1Tamb	3.2.15		Zenoc
Let not a man so vile and barbarous,	1Tamb	3.2.26		Agidas
So now the mighty Souldan heares of you,	1Tamb	3.2.31		Agidas
How can you fancie one that lookes so fierce,	1Tamb	3.2.40		Agidas
So lookes my Lordly love, faire Tamburlaine.	1Tamb	3.2.49		Zenoc
Yet be not so inconstant in your love,	1Tamb	3.2.56		Agidas
Thence rise the tears that so distain my cheeks,	1Tamb	3.2.64		Zenoc
So fares Agydas for the late felt frownes/That sent a tempest	1Tamb	3.2.85		Agidas
And since he was so wise and honorable,	1Tamb	3.2.110		Usumc
Are punisht with Bastones so grievously,	1Tamb	3.3.52		Tamb
mighty Turkish Emperor/To talk with one so base as Tamburlaine?	1Tamb	3.3.88		Fesse
And as the heads of Hydra, so my power/Subdued, shall stand as	1Tamb	3.3.140		Bajzth
not endure to strike/So many blowes as I have heads for thee.	1Tamb	3.3.144		Bajzth
His royall Crowne againe, so highly won.	1Tamb	3.3.219		Zenoc
had the Turkish Emperour/So great a foile by any forraine foe.	1Tamb	3.3.235		Bajzth
So from the East unto the furthest West,	1Tamb	3.3.246		Tamb
So scatter and consume them in his rage,	1Tamb	4.1.34		Souldn
So might your highnesse, had you time to sort/Your fighting	1Tamb	4.1.36		Capol
Then it should so conspire my overthrow.	1Tamb	4.2.11		Tamb
Stoop villaine, stoope, stoope for so he bids,	1Tamb	4.2.22		Tamb
So shall our swords, our lances and our shot,	1Tamb	4.2.51		Tamb
This is my minde, and I will have it so.	1Tamb	4.2.91		Tamb
So shall he have his life, and all the rest.	1Tamb	4.2.115		Tamb
He dies, and those that kept us out so long.	1Tamb	4.2.118		Tamb
Be so perswaded, that the Souldan is/No more dismaide with	1Tamb	4.3.30		Souldn
Or kept the faire Zenocrate so long,	1Tamb	4.3.41		Souldn
are you so daintily brought up, you cannot eat your owne flesh?	1Tamb	4.4.36	P	Tamb
pray thee tel, why art thou so sad?	1Tamb	4.4.63	P	Tamb
So it would my lord, specially having so smal a walke, and so	1Tamb	4.4.105	P	Therid
lord, specially having so smal a walke, and so litle exercise.	1Tamb	4.4.105	P	Therid
lord, specially having so smal a walke, and so litle exercise.	1Tamb	4.4.106	P	Therid
And since your highnesse hath so well vouchsaft,	1Tamb	4.4.130		Therid
Intending so to terrifie the world:	1Tamb	5.1.15		Govnr
Whose cheekes and hearts so punisht with conceit,	1Tamb	5.1.87		1Virgn
His life that so consumes Zenocrate,	1Tamb	5.1.154		Tamb
So much by much, as dooth Zenocrate.	1Tamb	5.1.159		Tamb
For faire Zenocrate, that so laments his state.	1Tamb	5.1.205		Therid
So high within the region of the aire,	1Tamb	5.1.250		Zabina
And let them die a death so barbarous.	1Tamb	5.1.351		Zenoc
To see them live so long in misery:	1Tamb	5.1.370		Zenoc
Your love hath fortune so at his command,	1Tamb	5.1.373		Anippe
So for a finall Issue to my griefes,	1Tamb	5.1.395		Zenoc
Even so for her thou diest in these armes:	1Tamb	5.1.410		Arabia
That long hath lingred for so high a seat.	1Tamb	5.1.502		Therid
So lookes my Love, shadowing in her browes/Triumphes and	1Tamb	5.1.512		Tamb
fethered steele/So thick upon the blink-ei'd Burghers heads,	2Tamb	1.1.93		Orcan
And tell me whether I should stoope so low,	2Tamb	1.1.112		Sgsmnd
So prest are we, but yet if Sigismond/Speake as a friend, and	2Tamb	1.1.122		Orcan
So am I fear'd among all Nations.	2Tamb	1.1.151		Orcan
Ah were I now but halfe so eloquent/To paint in woords, what	2Tamb	1.2.9		Callap
Amongst so many crownes of burnisht gold,	2Tamb	1.2.30		Callap
She lies so close that none can find her out.	2Tamb	1.2.60		Callap
So, now she sits in pompe and majestie:	2Tamb	1.3.17		Tamb
He raign'd him straight and made him so curvet,	2Tamb	1.3.41		Zenoc
With all his viceroies shall be so affraide,	2Tamb	1.3.162		Tamb
So what we vow to them should not infringe/Our liberty of armes	2Tamb	2.1.40		Baldwn
tis superstition/To stand so strictly on dispensive faith:	2Tamb	2.1.50		Fredrk
So surely will the vengeance of the highest/And jealous anger	2Tamb	2.1.56		Fredrk
And cares so litle for their prophet Christ.	2Tamb	2.2.35		Gazell
Live still my Love and so conserve my life,	2Tamb	2.4.55		Tamb
What God so ever holds thee in his armes,	2Tamb	2.4.109		Tamb
Ah sweet Theridamas, say so no more,	2Tamb	2.4.126		Tamb
were the sinowes of th'imperiall seat/So knit and strengthned,	2Tamb	3.1.11		Callap
Whose cursed fate hath so dismembred it,	2Tamb	3.1.13		Callap
not but your royall cares/Hath so provided for this cursed foe,	2Tamb	3.1.21		Callap
(An Emperour so honoured for his vertues)/Revives the spirits	2Tamb	3.1.23		Callap
For so hath heaven provided my escape,	2Tamb	3.1.32		Callap
And so unto my citie of Damasco,	2Tamb	3.1.59		Soria
So, burne the turrets of this cursed towne,	2Tamb	3.2.1		Tamb
As is that towne, so is my heart consum'd,	2Tamb	3.2.49		Amyras
A wound is nothing be it nere so deepe,	2Tamb	3.2.115		Tamb
Yet I am resolute, and so farewell.	2Tamb	3.3.40		Capt
Then scortch a face so beautiful as this,	2Tamb	3.4.74		Techel
Madam, I am so far in love with you,	2Tamb	3.4.78		Therid
This Lady shall have twice so much againe,	2Tamb	3.4.90		Therid
So from Arabia desart, and the bounds/Of that sweet land, whose	2Tamb	3.5.35		Orcan
So that the Army royall is esteem'd/Six hundred thousand	2Tamb	3.5.50		Soria
Why, so he is Casane, I am here,	2Tamb	3.5.62		Tamb
So famous as is mighty Tamburlain:	2Tamb	3.5.84		Tamb
Shall so torment thee and that Callapine,	2Tamb	3.5.85		Tamb
So sirha, now you are a king you must give armes.	2Tamb	3.5.137	P	Tamb
So he shal, and weare thy head in his Scutchion.	2Tamb	3.5.138	P	Orcan
much like so many suns/That halfe dismay the majesty of heaven:	2Tamb	4.1.2		Amyras
what, given so much to sleep/You cannot leave it, when our	2Tamb	4.1.11		Amyras
No, no Amyras, tempt not Fortune so,	2Tamb	4.1.86		Tamb
Thy victories are growne so violent,	2Tamb	4.1.140		Jrslem
Souldier shall defile/His manly fingers with so faint a boy.	2Tamb	4.1.164		Tamb
Whose cruelties are not so harsh as thine,	2Tamb	4.1.169		Jrslem
If you loved him, and it so precious?	2Tamb	4.2.72		Therid
My purpose was (my Lord) to spend it so,	2Tamb	4.2.73		Olymp

SO (cont.)

And have so proud a chariot at your heeles,	2Tamb	4.3.3		Tamb
Are not so honoured in their Governour,	2Tamb	4.3.10		Tamb
And made so wanton that they knew their strengths,	2Tamb	4.3.14		Tamb
So for just hate, for shame, and to subdew/This proud contemner	2Tamb	4.3.39		Orcan
souldiers now that fought/So Lion-like upon Asphaltis plaines?	2Tamb	4.3.68		Tamb
For every man that so offends shall die.	2Tamb	4.3.76		Tamb
wilt thou so defame/The hatefull fortunes of thy victory,	2Tamb	4.3.77		Orcan
So will I ride through Samarcanda streets,	2Tamb	4.3.130		Tamb
So, now their best is done to honour me,	2Tamb	5.1.131		Tamb
So now he hangs like Bagdets Governour,	2Tamb	5.1.158		Tamb
So Casane, fling them in the fire.	2Tamb	5.1.186		Tamb
Let it be so, about it souldiers:	2Tamb	5.1.217		Tamb
But foorth ye vassals, what so ere it be,	2Tamb	5.1.221		Tamb
And so revenge our latest grievous losse,	2Tamb	5.2.10		Callap
and the victories/Wherewith he hath so sore dismaide the world,	2Tamb	5.2.44		Callap
She waines againe, and so shall his I hope,	2Tamb	5.2.47		Callap
So honour heaven til heaven dissolved be,	2Tamb	5.3.26		Techel
And cannot last, it is so violent.	2Tamb	5.3.65		Techel
I joy my Lord, your highnesse is so strong,	2Tamb	5.3.110		Usumc
That can endure so well your royall presence,	2Tamb	5.3.111		Usumc
And so along the Ethiopian sea,	2Tamb	5.3.137		Tamb
So, raigne my sonne, scourge and controlle those slaves,	2Tamb	5.3.228		Tamb
So that of thus much that returne was made:	Jew	1.1.1		Barab
who so richly pay/The things they traffique for with wedge of	Jew	1.1.8		Barab
Would in his age be loath to labour so,	Jew	1.1.17		Barab
And seildsene costly stones of so great price,	Jew	1.1.28		Barab
wealth increaseth, so inclose/Infinite riches in a little roome.	Jew	1.1.36		Barab
So then, there's somewhat come.	Jew	1.1.69		Barab
They wondred how you durst with so much wealth/Trust such a	Jew	1.1.79		1Merch
with so much wealth/Trust such a crazed Vessell, and so farre.	Jew	1.1.80		1Merch
But 'twas ill done of you to come so farre/Without the ayd or	Jew	1.1.93		Barab
That thirst so much for Principality.	Jew	1.1.135		Barab
Why let 'em come, so they come not to warre;	Jew	1.1.150		Barab
Or let 'em warre, so we be conquerors:	Jew	1.1.151		Barab
So they spare me, my daughter, and my wealth.	Jew	1.1.153		Barab
And very wisely sayd, it may be so.	Jew	1.1.166		3Jew
Doe so; Farewell Zaareth, farewell Temainte.	Jew	1.1.176		Barab
Soft Barabas, there's more longs too't than so.	Jew	1.2.45		Govnr
And what's our aid against so great a Prince?	Jew	1.2.51		Barab
Governour, it was not got so easily;	Jew	1.2.86		Barab
Nor will I part so slightly therewithall.	Jew	1.2.87		Barab
It shall be so: now Officers have you done?	Jew	1.2.131		Govnr
So that not he, but I may curse the day,	Jew	1.2.191		Barab
Great injuries are not so soone forgot.	Jew	1.2.208		Barab
thinke me not all so fond/As negligently to forgoe so much	Jew	1.2.241		Barab
As negligently to forgoe so much/Without provision for	Jew	1.2.242		Barab
in distresse/Thinke me so mad as I will hang my selfe,	Jew	1.2.263		Barab
it be to injure them/That have so manifestly wronged us,	Jew	1.2.275		Abigal
Why so,/Then thus; thou toldst me they have turn'd my house	Jew	1.2.276		Barab
but be thou so precise/As they may thinke it done of Holinesse.	Jew	1.2.284		Barab
long since some of us/Did stray so farre amongst the multitude.	Jew	1.2.309		Abbass
It may be so: but who comes here?	Jew	1.2.313		Abbass
Becomes it Jewes to be so credulous,	Jew	1.2.360		Barab
Forget me, see me not, and so be gone.	Jew	1.2.363		Barab
Is she so faire?	Jew	1.2.384		Lodowk
And if she be so faire as you report,	Jew	1.2.388		Lodowk
And so will I too, or it shall goe hard.--	Jew	1.2.392		Lodowk
Now that my fathers fortune were so good/As but to be about	Jew	2.1.31		Abigal
As but to be about this happy place;/'Tis not so happy:	Jew	2.1.33		Abigal
As good goe on, as sit so sadly thus.	Jew	2.1.40		Barab
And so am I, Delbosco is my name;	Jew	2.2.6		Bosco
So shall you imitate those you succeed:	Jew	2.2.47		Bosco
So will we fight it out; come, let's away:	Jew	2.2.52		Govnr
And so much must they yeeld or not be sold.	Jew	2.3.4		2Offcr
That can so soone forget an injury.	Jew	2.3.19		Barab
I'le seeke him out, and so insinuate,	Jew	2.3.33		Lodowk
So doe I too.	Jew	2.3.61		Barab
Do the [Turkes] <Turke> weigh so much?	Jew	2.3.98	P	Barab
What, can he steale that you demand so much?	Jew	2.3.100		Barab
So that, being bought, the Towne-seale might be got/To keepe	Jew	2.3.103		Barab
So much the worse; I must have one that's sickly, and be but	Jew	2.3.123	P	Barab
So much the better, thou art for my turne.	Jew	2.3.129		Barab
What makes the Jew and Lodowicke so private?	Jew	2.3.138		Mthias
would rankle, so/That I have laugh'd agood to see the cripples	Jew	2.3.210		Ithimr
And like a cunning Jew so cast about,	Jew	2.3.235		Barab
Doe, it is requisite it should be so.	Jew	2.3.239		Barab
So sure shall he and Don Mathias dye:	Jew	2.3.249		Barab
And so has she done you, even from a child.	Jew	2.3.289		Barab
So have not I, but yet I hope I shall.	Jew	2.3.319		Barab
No; so shall I, if any hurt be done,	Jew	2.3.341		Barab
Doe so; loe here I give thee Abigall.	Jew	2.3.345		Barab
Shall Lodowicke rob me of so faire a love?	Jew	2.3.347		Mthias
My life is not so deare as Abigall.	Jew	2.3.348		Mthias
I thinke by this/You purchase both their lives; is it not so?	Jew	2.3.366		Ithimr
I, so thou shalt, 'tis thou must doe the deed:	Jew	2.3.369		Barab
Feare not, I'le so set his heart a fire,	Jew	2.3.375		Ithimr
So, now will I goe in to Lodowicke,	Jew	2.3.381		Barab
rumbling in the house; so I tooke onely this, and runne my way:	Jew	3.1.21	P	Pilia
Now Lodowicke, now Mathias, so;	Jew	3.2.6		Barab
So, now they have shew'd themselves to be tall fellowes.	Jew	3.2.7		Barab
And so did Lodowicke him.	Jew	3.2.22		Govnr
So neatly plotted, and so well perform'd?	Jew	3.3.2		Ithimr

SO (cont.)

Why, how now Ithimore, why laugh'st thou so?	Jew	3.3.4	Abigal
So sure did your father write, and I cary the chalenge.	Jew	3.3.25	P Ithimr
Then were my thoughts so fraile and unconfirm'd,	Jew	3.3.59	Abigal
I feare she knowes ('tis so) of my device/In Don Mathias and	Jew	3.4.7	Barab
If so, 'tis time that it be seene into:	Jew	3.4.9	Barab
And for thy sake, whom I so dearely love,	Jew	3.4.61	Barab
How so?	Jew	3.4.82	P Ithimr
Peace, Ithimore, 'tis better so then spar'd.	Jew	3.4.91	Barab
was ever pot of rice porredge so sauc't?	Jew	3.4.107	P Ithimr
go set it downe/And come againe so soone as thou hast done,	Jew	3.4.109	Barab
You shall not need trouble your selves so farre,	Jew	3.5.22	Basso
And so farewell.	Jew	3.5.27	Basso
So now couragiously encounter them;	Jew	3.5.33	Govnr
And so did faire Maria send for me:	Jew	3.6.5	1Fryar
I did offend high heaven so grievously,	Jew	3.6.17	Abigal
So, say how was their end?	Jew	3.6.26	2Fryar
So I have heard; pray therefore keepe it close.	Jew	3.6.37	Abigal
No, but I grieve because she liv'd so long.	Jew	4.1.18	Barab
And so doe I, master, therfore speake 'em faire.	Jew	4.1.27	Ithimr
And so could I; but pennance will not serve.	Jew	4.1.60	Ithimr
to some religious house/So I may be baptiz'd and live therein.	Jew	4.1.76	Barab
I'le give him something and so stop his mouth.	Jew	4.1.102	Barab
And so I will, oh Jacomo, faile not but come.	Jew	4.1.108	Barab
So, now the feare is past, and I am safe:	Jew	4.1.114	Barab
No more but so: it must and shall be done.	Jew	4.1.128	Barab
No, none can heare him, cry he ne're so loud.	Jew	4.1.136	Ithimr
be rul'd by me a little; so, let him leane upon his staffe;	Jew	4.1.153	P Ithimr
So might my man and I hang with you for company.	Jew	4.1.182	Barab
I think so, and yet I cannot tell, for at the reading of the	Jew	4.2.6	P Pilia
Why so?	Jew	4.2.8	P Curtzn
as who shold say, Is it even so; and so I left him, being driven	Jew	4.2.13	P Pilia
and so I left him, being driven to a non-plus at the critical	Jew	4.2.13	P Pilia
tibi, cras mihi, and so I left him to the mercy of the Hangman:	Jew	4.2.19	P Pilia
I never knew a man take his death so patiently as this Fryar;	Jew	4.2.21	P Ithimr
Whither so soone?	Jew	4.2.48	Curtzn
Canst thou be so unkind to leave me thus?	Jew	4.2.52	Curtzn
I'le make him send me half he has, and glad he scapes so too.	Jew	4.2.67	P Ithimr
Write not so submissively, but threatning him.	Jew	4.2.72	P Pilia
and this shall be your warrant; if you doe not, no more but so.	Jew	4.2.76	P Ithimr
And if he aske why I demand so much, tell him, I scorne to	Jew	4.2.120	P Ithimr
Oh that I should part with so much gold!	Jew	4.3.51	Barab
Saist thou me so?	Jew	4.4.2	P Ithimr
Goe to, it shall be so.	Jew	4.4.3	Curtzn
I had not thought he had been so brave a man.	Jew	4.4.16	Curtzn
So, now I am reveng'd upon 'em all.	Jew	4.4.42	Barab
Pardona moy, be no in tune yet; so, now, now all be in.	Jew	4.4.45	P Barab
So did you when you stole my gold.	Jew	4.4.50	Barab
I scorne the Peasant, tell him so.	Jew	4.4.59	P Ithimr
For Calymath having hover'd here so long,	Jew	5.1.4	Govnr
As these have spoke so be it to their soules:--	Jew	5.1.42	Barab
So is the Turke, and Barabas the Jew.	Jew	5.1.51	1Offcr
So, now away and fortifie the Towne.	Jew	5.1.60	Govnr
so, or how else,/The Jew is here, and rests at your command.	Jew	5.1.82	Barab
Governor, good words, be not so furious;	Jew	5.2.61	Barab
Doe so, but faile not; now farewell Ferneze:	Jew	5.2.109	Barab
to feast my traine/Within a Towne of warre so lately pillag'd,	Jew	5.3.22	Calym
That he hath in store a Pearle so big,	Jew	5.3.27	Msngr
So precious, and withall so orient,	Jew	5.3.28	Msngr
For so I live, perish may all the world.	Jew	5.5.10	Barab
asunder; so that it doth sinke/Into a deepe pit past recovery.	Jew	5.5.35	Barab
Governour, why stand you all so pittilesse?	Jew	5.5.71	Barab
We will not let thee part so suddenly:	Jew	5.5.98	Govnr
[all] <call> the world/To rescue thee, so will we guard us now,	Jew	5.5.120	Govnr
So march away, and let due praise be given/Neither to Fate nor	Jew	5.5.123	Govnr
And thats the cause that Guise so frowns at us,	P 52	1.52	Navrre
Of so great matter should be made the ground.	P 126	2.69	Guise
So that for proofe, he barely beares the name:	P 131	2.74	Guise
As Caesar to his souldiers, so say I:	P 155	2.98	Guise
And so be pacient good Lord Admirall,	P 271	4.69	Charls
And so will I.	P 280	5.7	Gonzag
And he that living hated so the crosse,	P 320	5.47	Anjoy
And so lets forward to the Massacre.	P 330	5.57	Guise
And so will Dumaine.	P 334	5.61	Dumain
Wherein hath Ramus been so offencious?	P 384	7.24	Ramus
Nere was there Colliars sonne so full of pride.	P 416	7.56	Anjoy
That swim about and so preserve their lives:	P 419	7.59	Guise
I, so they are, but yet what remedy:	P 433	7.73	Anjoy
And so convey him closely to his bed.	P 450	7.90	Guise
and the fire the aire, and so we shall be poysoned with him.	P 485	9.4	P 1Atndt
Beleeve me Guise he becomes the place so well,	P 495	9.14	QnMoth
Doe so sweet Guise, let us delay no time,	P 505	9.24	QnMoth
As I doe live, so surely shall he dye,	P 521	9.40	QnMoth
So, dragge them away.	P 535	10.8	Guise
O say not so, thou kill'st thy mothers heart.	P 539	11.4	QnMoth
I must say so, paine forceth me complaine.	P 540	11.5	Charls
Truth Pleshe, and God so prosper me in all,	P 584	11.49	Navrre
And so they shall, if fortune speed my will,	P 601	12.14	King
As now you are, so shall you still persist,	P 608	12.21	King
So, set it down and leave me to my selfe.	P 666	13.10	Duchss
Or hath my love been so obscurde in thee,	P 682	13.26	Guise
So he be safe he cares not what becomes,	P 739	14.42	Navrre
Thanks to your Majestie, and so I take my leave.	P 749	15.7	Joyeux

SO (cont.)

So kindely Cosin of Guise you and your wife/Doe both salute our	P 752	15.10	King
Even for your words that have incenst me so,	P 767	15.25	Guise
Which Ile maintaine so long as life doth last:	P 800	16.14	Navrre
and so forestall his market, and set up your standing where you	P 809	17.4	P Souldr
what are ye come so soone?	P 815	17.10	P Souldr
Did they of Paris entertaine him so?	P 879	17.74	King
And so to quite your grace of all suspect.	P 889	17.84	Eprnon
So, convey this to the counsell presently.	P 892	17.87	King
But as I live, so sure the Guise shall dye.	P 899	17.94	King
Bartus, it shall be so, poast then to Fraunce,	P 907	18.8	Navrre
I, I, feare not: stand close, so, be resolute:	P 943	19.13	Capt
That in the Court I bare so great a traine.	P 968	19.38	Guise
And so sweet Cuz farwell.	P 976	19.46	King
So,/Now sues the King for favour to the Guise,	P 977	19.47	Guise
So will I triumph over this wanton King,	P 983	19.53	Guise
Villaine, why dost thou look so gastly? speake.	P 989	19.59	Guise
Or else to murder me, and so be King.	P1040	19.110	King
Nere was there King of France so yoakt as I.	P1044	19.114	King
And that young Cardinall that is growne so proud?	P1056	19.126	King
King, why so thou wert before.	P1067	19.137	QnMoth
Sweet Guise, would he had died so thou wert heere:	P1082	19.152	QnMoth
So, pluck amaine,	P1104	20.14	1Mur
Surgeon, why saist thou so? the King may live.	P1224	22.86	Navrre
So thou wouldst smile and take me in thy <thine> armes.	Edw	1.1.9	Gavstn
But that it harbors him I hold so deare,	Edw	1.1.13	Gavstn
And hew these knees that now are growne so stiffe.	Edw	1.1.95	Edward
What so thy minde affectes or fancie likes.	Edw	1.1.170	Edward
Whether goes my Lord of Coventrie so fast?	Edw	1.1.175	Edward
So will I now, and thou shalt back to France.	Edw	1.1.185	BshpCv
What should a priest do with so faire a house?	Edw	1.1.206	Gavstn
Madam, whether walks your majestie so fast?	Edw	1.2.46	Mortmr
It is our pleasure, we will have it so.	Edw	1.4.9	Edward
For no where else the new earle is so safe.	Edw	1.4.11	Lncstr
So I may have some nooke or corner left,	Edw	1.4.72	Edward
Why should you love him, whome the world hates so?	Edw	1.4.76	Mortmr
And so is mine.	Edw	1.4.91	Warwck
The Legate of the Pope will have it so,	Edw	1.4.109	Edward
I meane not so, your grace must pardon me.	Edw	1.4.153	Gavstn
So much as he on cursed Gaveston.	Edw	1.4.181	Queene
And so am I for ever miserable.	Edw	1.4.186	Queene
And to behold so sweete a sight as that,	Edw	1.4.206	Warwck
And so am I my lord, diswade the Queene.	Edw	1.4.215	Lncstr
Well of necessitie it must be so.	Edw	1.4.238	Mortmr
And none so much as blame the murtherer,	Edw	1.4.267	Mortmr
So shall we have the people of our side,	Edw	1.4.282	Mortmr
And so will Penbrooke and I.	Edw	1.4.293	Warwck
returnd, this newes will glad him much,/Yet not so much as me.	Edw	1.4.302	Queene
would he lov'd me/But halfe so much, then were I treble blest.	Edw	1.4.304	Queene
Did never sorrow go so neere my heart,	Edw	1.4.306	Edward
And thinke I gaind, having bought so deare a friend.	Edw	1.4.310	Edward
But will you love me, if you finde it so?	Edw	1.4.324	Queene
If it be so, what will not Edward do?	Edw	1.4.325	Edward
Seeing thou hast pleaded with so good successe.	Edw	1.4.329	Edward
Even so let hatred with thy [soveraignes] <soveraigne> smile.	Edw	1.4.342	Edward
My lord, ile marshall so your enemies,	Edw	1.4.357	Mortmr
I Isabell, nere was my heart so light.	Edw	1.4.368	Edward
And seeing his minde so dotes on Gaveston,	Edw	1.4.389	MortSr
But this I scorne, that one so baselie borne,	Edw	1.4.403	Mortmr
Should by his soveraignes favour grow so pert,	Edw	1.4.404	Mortmr
I have not seene a dapper jack so briske,	Edw	1.4.412	Mortmr
Then so am I, and live to do him service,	Edw	1.4.421	Mortmr
Mine old lord whiles he livde, was so precise,	Edw	2.1.46	Baldck
The greefe for his exile was not so much,	Edw	2.1.57	Neece
But seeing you are so desirous, thus it is:	Edw	2.2.15	Mortmr
And you the Eagles, sore ye nere so high,	Edw	2.2.39	Edward
Desirde her more, and waxt outragious,/So did it sure with me:	Edw	2.2.56	Edward
Whose mounting thoughts did never creepe so low,	Edw	2.2.77	Gavstn
And so doth Lancaster:	Edw	2.2.109	Lncstr
Why, so he may, but we will speake to him.	Edw	2.2.136	Lncstr
the familie of the Mortimers/Are not so poore, but would they	Edw	2.2.151	Mortmr
And so will I, and then my lord farewell.	Edw	2.2.156	Lncstr
So soone to have woone Scotland,	Edw	2.2.194	Lncstr
So will I, rather then with Gaveston.	Edw	2.2.215	Kent
And so I walke with him about the walles,	Edw	2.2.222	Edward
The yonger Mortimer is growne so brave,	Edw	2.2.232	Edward
None be so hardie as to touche the King,	Edw	2.3.27	Lncstr
You know the king is so suspitious,	Edw	2.4.53	Queene
So well hast thou deserv'de sweete Mortimer.	Edw	2.4.59	Queene
traind to armes/And bloudie warres, so many valiant knights,	Edw	2.5.16	Lncstr
Thou shalt have so much honor at our hands.	Edw	2.5.28	Warwck
And if you gratifie his grace so farre,	Edw	2.5.39	Arundl
Not so my Lord, least he bestow more cost,	Edw	2.5.55	Lncstr
We will not wrong thee so,	Edw	2.5.69	Mortmr
Because his majestie so earnestlie/Desires to see the man	Edw	2.5.77	Penbrk
Sir, must not come so neare and balke their lips.	Edw	2.5.103	Penbrk
So my lord.	Edw	2.5.106	Penbrk
things of more waight/Then fits a prince so yong as I to beare,	Edw	3.1.75	Prince
That so my bloudie colours may suggest/Remembrance of revenge	Edw	3.1.139	Edward
So wish not they Iwis that sent thee hither,	Edw	3.1.152	Edward
So sir, you have spoke, away, avoid our presence.	Edw	3.1.232	Edward
Have you no doubts my lords, ile [clap so] <claps> close,/Among	Edw	3.1.276	Levune
But hath thy potion wrought so happilie?	Edw	4.1.14	Kent

SO (cont.)

Never so cheereles, nor so farre distrest.	Edw		4.2.14	Queene
So pleaseth the Queene my mother, me it likes.	Edw		4.2.21	Prince
Will we with thee to Henolt, so we will.	Edw		4.2.31	Queene
not so, and you must not discourage/Your friends that are so	Edw		4.2.69	Queene
not discourage/Your friends that are so forward in your aide.	Edw		4.2.70	Queene
Why so, they barkt a pace a month agoe,	Edw		4.3.12	Edward
I trowe/The lords of Fraunce love Englands gold so well,	Edw		4.3.15	Edward
our port-maisters/Are not so careles of their kings commaund.	Edw		4.3.23	Edward
Ye must not grow so passionate in speeches:	Edw		4.4.16	Mortmr
realme, and sith the fates/Have made his father so infortunate,	Edw		4.6.27	Queene
So shall your brother be disposed of.	Edw		4.6.37	Mortmr
So are the Spencers, the father and the sonne.	Edw		4.6.44	SrJohn
So fought not they that fought in Edwards right.	Edw		4.6.72	SpncrP
But Leister leave to growe so passionate,	Edw		4.7.55	Leistr
We must my lord, so will the angry heavens.	Edw		4.7.74	Spencr
Nay so will hell, and cruell Mortimer,	Edw		4.7.75	Edward
Our lots are cast, I feare me so is thine.	Edw		4.7.79	Baldck
And so it fares with me, whose dauntlesse minde/The ambitious	Edw		5.1.15	Edward
So shall not Englands [Vine] <Vines> be perished,	Edw		5.1.47	Edward
So shall my eyes receive their last content,	Edw		5.1.61	Edward
This answer weele returne, and so farewell.	Edw		5.1.90	BshpWn
hands of mine/Shall not be guiltie of so foule a crime.	Edw		5.1.99	Edward
thinke not a thought so villanous/Can harbor in a man of noble	Edw		5.1.131	Bartly
I, my most gratious lord, so tis decreed.	Edw		5.1.138	Bartly
So may his limmes be torne, as is this paper,	Edw		5.1.142	Edward
Even so betide my soule as I use him.	Edw		5.1.148	Bartly
And therefore so the prince my sonne be safe,	Edw		5.2.17	Queene
So that he now is gone from Killingworth,	Edw		5.2.31	BshpWn
To set his brother free, no more but so.	Edw		5.2.33	BshpWn
The lord of Bartley is so pitifull,	Edw		5.2.34	BshpWn
I would hee were, so it were not by my meanes.	Edw		5.2.45	Queene
So now away, post thither wards amaine.	Edw		5.2.67	Mortmr
Finely dissembled, do so still sweet Queene.	Edw		5.2.74	Mortmr
that one so false/Should come about the person of a prince.	Edw		5.2.104	Mortmr
Why yongling, s'dainst thou so of Mortimer.	Edw		5.2.111	Mortmr
Not so my liege, the Queene hath given this charge,	Edw		5.3.13	Gurney
And so must die, though pitied by many.	Edw		5.3.24	Edward
Least you be knowne, and so be rescued.	Edw		5.3.32	Gurney
But all in vaine, so vainely do I strive,	Edw		5.3.35	Edward
Binde him, and so convey him to the court.	Edw		5.3.58	Gurney
Thither shall your honour go, and so farewell.	Edw		5.3.62	Matrvs
I care not how it is, so it be not spide:	Edw		5.4.40	Mortmr
Much more a king brought up so tenderlie.	Edw		5.5.6	Matrvs
And so do I, Matrevis:	Edw		5.5.7	Gurney
I, I, so: when I call you, bring it in.	Edw		5.5.35	Ltborn
So,/Now must I about this geare,	Edw		5.5.38	Ltborn
nere was there any/So finely handled as this king shalbe.	Edw		5.5.40	Ltborn
So that for want of sleepe and sustenance,	Edw		5.5.63	Edward
So, lay the table downe, and stampe on it,	Edw		5.5.112	Ltborn
And had you lov'de him halfe so well as I,	Edw		5.6.35	King
And so shalt thou be too: why staies he heere?	Edw		5.6.51	King
I, madam, you, for so the rumor runnes.	Edw		5.6.73	King
I doe not thinke her so unnaturall.	Edw		5.6.76	King
And now <so> to patient judgements we appeale <our plaude>,	F	9	Prol.9	1Chor
So much <soone> he profits in Divinitie,	F	15	Prol.15	1Chor
Nothing so sweet as Magicke is to him,	F	26	Prol.26	1Chor
Why then belike/We must sinne, and so consequently die,/I, we	F	72	1.1.44	Faust
Then all my labours, plod I ne're so fast.	F	96	1.1.68	Faust
So shall the spirits <subjects> of every element,	F	149	1.1.121	Valdes
and so the Lord blesse you, preserve you, and keepe you, my	F	217	1.2.24	P Wagner
So Faustus hath <I have> already done, and holds <hold> this	F	283	1.3.55	Faust
is great Mephostophilis so passionate/For being deprived of the	F	311	1.3.83	Faust
So he will spare him foure and twenty yeares,	F	319	1.3.91	Faust
and so hungry, that <I know> he would give his soule to the	F	349	1.4.7	P Wagner
Not so neither; I had need to have it well rosted, and good	F	352	1.4.10	P Robin
rosted, and good sauce to it, if I pay so deere, I can tell you.	F	353	1.4.11	P Robin
Why so thou shalt be, whether thou dost it or no:	F	360	1.4.18	P Wagner
So, now thou art to bee at an howres warning, whensoever, and	F	369	1.4.27	P Wagner
So he will buy my service with his soule.	F	421	2.1.33	Mephst
I so I do <will>; but Mephostophilis,	F	450	2.1.62	Faust
So, now the bloud begins to cleere againe:	F	460	2.1.72	Faust
So, now Faustus aske me what thou wilt.	F	503	2.1.115	Mephst
I, so are all things else; but whereabouts <where about>?	F	507	2.1.119	Faust
I, thinke so still, till experience change thy mind.	F	517	2.1.129	Mephst
Think'st thou that Faustus, is so fond to imagine,	F	522	2.1.134	Faust
I tell thee Faustus it is <tis> not halfe so faire/As thou, or	F	557	2.2.6	Mephst
My heart is <hearts so> hardned, I cannot repent:	F	569	2.2.18	Faust
O what art thou that look'st so [terrible] <terribly>.	F	638	2.2.87	Faust
So shalt thou shew thy selfe an obedient servant <Do so>,/And	F	652	2.2.101	Lucifr
So high our Dragons soar'd into the aire,	F	849	3.1.71	Faust
Let it be so my Faustus, but first stay,	F	856	3.1.78	Mephst
So shall our sleeping vengeance now arise,	F	879	3.1.101	Pope
And make them sleepe so sound, that in their shapes,	F	895	3.1.117	Faust
So will we quell that haughty Schismatique;	F	922	3.1.144	Pope
Resigne, or seale, or what so pleaseth us.	F	936	3.1.158	Pope
So, so, was never Divell thus blest before.	F	974	3.1.196	Mephst
Sweet Mephostophilis so charme me here,	F	991	3.2.11	Faust
With Magicke spels so compasse thee,	F	1002	3.2.22	Mephst
So Faustus, now for all their holinesse,	F	1004	3.2.24	Mephst
So, they are safe:	F	1035	3.2.55	Faust
To the Bishop of Millaine, for this so rare a present.	F	1042	3.2.62	Pope
It may be so:	F	1062	3.2.82	Pope

SO (cont.)

us, I'le so conjure him, as he was never conjur'd in his life,	F1091	3.3.4	P	Robin
And so thou shalt:	F1130	3.3.43		Mephst
[Hee stayde his course, and so returned home],	F1140	3.3.53A		3Chor
So kindly yesternight to Bruno's health,	F1175	4.1.21		Mrtino
and if he be so farre in love with him, I would he would post	F1190	4.1.36	P	Benvol
For proofe whereof, if so your Grace be pleas'd,	F1221	4.1.67		Faust
my thoughts are ravished so/With sight of this renowned	F1260	4.1.106		Emper
O say not so sir:	F1294	4.1.140		Faust
And therefore my Lord, so please your Majesty,	F1300	4.1.146		Faust
Il'e raise a kennell of Hounds shall hunt him so,	F1301	4.1.147		Faust
not so much for injury done to me, as to delight your Majesty	F1311	4.1.157	P	Faust
Shall I let slip so great an injury,	F1328	4.2.4		Benvol
thou canst not buy so good a horse, for so small a price:	F1459	4.4.3	P	Faust
Sirra Dick, dost thou know why I stand so mute?	F1509	4.5.5	P	Robin
Who's this, that stands so solemnly by himselfe:	F1513	4.5.9	P	Hostss
so he presently gave me my mony, and fell to eating;	F1529	4.5.25	P	Carter
forty Dollors; so sir, because I knew him to be such a horse,	F1537	4.5.33	P	HrsCsr
so when I had my horse, Doctor Fauster bad me ride him night	F1539	4.5.35	P	HrsCsr
the sight whereof so delighted me, as nothing in the world	F1561	4.6.4	P	Duke
so kind I will make knowne unto you what my heart desires to	F1570	4.6.13	P	Lady
so that when it is Winter with us, in the contrary circle it is	F1582	4.6.25	P	Faust
Why saucy varlets, dare you be so bold.	F1594	4.6.37		Servnt
It appeares so, pray be bold else-where,	F1597	4.6.40		Servnt
Be not so furious: come you shall have Beere.	F1620	4.6.63		Faust
that flesh and bloud should be so fraile with your Worship:	F1632	4.6.75	P	Carter
'Tis not so much worth; I pray you tel me one thing.	F1643	4.6.86	P	Carter
So are we Madam, which we will recompence/With all the love and	F1671	4.6.114		Duke
if you will doe us so much <that> favour, as to let us see that	F1685	5.1.12	P	1Schol
And so have hope, that this my kinde rebuke,	F1722	5.1.49		OldMan
Sir, so wondrous well,/As in all humble dutie, I do yeeld	F1817	5.2.21		Wagner
If it be so, wee'l have Physitians,	F1830	5.2.34		2Schol
Oft have I thought to have done so:	F1864	5.2.68	P	Faust
And so I leave thee Faustus till anon,	F1924	5.2.128		BdAngl
[So that] my soule [may but] ascend to heaven.	F1956	5.2.160		Faust
[My God, my God] <O mercy heaven>, looke not so fierce on me;	F1979	5.2.183		Faust
and so hungry, that I know he would give his soule to the Divel	F App	p.229 7	P	Wagner
not so good friend, burladie I had neede have it wel roasted,	F App	p.229 11	P	Clown
have it wel roasted, and good sawce to it, if I pay so deere.	F App	p.229 12	P	Clown
So thou shalt, whether thou beest with me, or no:	F App	p.229 22	P	Wagner
they were never so knocht since they were divels, say I should	F App	p.230 46	P	Clown
divell, so I should be cald kill divell all the parish over.	F App	p.230 48	P	Clown
It may be so, Friers prepare a dirge to lay the fury of this	F App	p.232 16	P	Pope
and so by that meanes I shal see more then ere I felt, or saw	F App	p.233 4	P	Robin
I meane so sir with your favor.	F App	p.234 11	P	Vintnr
thee into an Ape, and thee into a Dog, and so be gone.	F App	p.235 44	P	Mephst
such riches, subdued so many kingdomes, as we that do succeede,	F App	p.236 20	P	Emper
so farre forth as by art and power of my spirit I am able to	F App	p.237 38	P	Faust
Ile meete with you anone for interrupting me so:	F App	p.238 58	P	Faust
or moale in her necke, how shal I know whether it be so or no?	F App	p.238 61	P	Emper
send for the knight that was so pleasent with me here of late?	F App	p.238 67	P	Faust
O not so fast sir, theres no haste but good, are you remembred	F App	p.238 76	P	Faust
so much for the injury hee offred me heere in your presence,	F App	p.238 81	P	Faust
I cannot sel him so:	F App	p.239 103	P	Faust
I sat upon a bottle of hey, never so neare drowning in my life:	F App	p.240 135	P	HrsCsr
So, ho, ho:	F App	p.241 152	P	HrsCsr
so, ho, ho.	F App	p.241 152	P	HrsCsr
My gratious Lord, I am glad it contents you so wel:	F App	p.242 3	P	Faust
thing then this, so it would content you, you should have it	F App	p.242 13	P	Faust
I am glad they content you so Madam.	F App	p.242 27	P	Faust
And so I wil my Lord, and whilst I live, Rest beholding for	F App	p.243 30	P	Duchss
nor Hanniball/Art cause, no forraine foe could so afflict us,	Lucan, First Booke	31		
Roome was so great it could not beare it selfe:	Lucan, First Booke	72		
So when this worlds compounded union breakes,	Lucan, First Booke	73		
end the gods/Allot the height of honor, men so strong/By land,	Lucan, First Booke	82		
So when as Crassus wretched death who stayd them,	Lucan, First Booke	104		
So thunder which the wind teares from the cloudes,	Lucan, First Booke	152		
Caesar is thine, so please it thee, thy soldier;	Lucan, First Booke	204		
Or sea far from the land, so all were whist.	Lucan, First Booke	262		
to warre,/Was so incenst as are Eleius steedes/With clamors:	Lucan, First Booke	294		
so Pompey thou having lickt/Warme goare from Syllas sword art	Lucan, First Booke	330		
And so they triumph, be't with whom ye wil.	Lucan, First Booke	342		
So be I may be bold to speake a truth,	Lucan, First Booke	361		
Is conquest got by civill war so hainous?	Lucan, First Booke	367		
Albeit the Citty thou wouldst have so ra'st/Be Roome it selfe.	Lucan, First Booke	386		
And fates so bent, least sloth and long delay/Might crosse him,	Lucan, First Booke	394		
Sent aide; so did Alcides port, whose seas/Eate hollow rocks,	Lucan, First Booke	406		
so (if truth you sing)/Death brings long life.	Lucan, First Booke	453		
So rusht the inconsiderate multitude/Thorough the Citty hurried	Lucan, First Booke	492		
even so the Citty left,/All rise in armes; nor could the	Lucan, First Booke	501		
As loath to leave Roome whom they held so deere,	Lucan, First Booke	506		
So runnes a Matron through th'amazed streetes,	Lucan, First Booke	675		
hils, hence to the mounts/Pirene, and so backe to Rome againe.	Lucan, First Booke	689		
Or why slips downe the Coverlet so oft?	Ovid's Elegies	1.2.2		
T'was so, he stroke me with a slender dart,	Ovid's Elegies	1.2.7		
So will thy [triumph] <triumphs> seeme magnificall.	Ovid's Elegies	1.2.28		
So having conquerd Inde, was Bacchus hew,	Ovid's Elegies	1.2.47		
So likewise we will through the world be rung,	Ovid's Elegies	1.3.25		
Do not thou so, but throw thy mantle hence,	Ovid's Elegies	1.4.49		
Strike, so againe hard chaines shall binde thee never,	Ovid's Elegies	1.6.25		
Though it be so, shut me not out therefore,	Ovid's Elegies	1.6.47		
So fayre she was, Atalanta she resembled,	Ovid's Elegies	1.7.13		
So chast Minerva did Cassandra fall,	Ovid's Elegies	1.7.17		

SO (cont.)

To mine owne selfe have I had strength so furious?	Ovid's Elegies	1.7.25
And to my selfe could I be so injurious?	Ovid's Elegies	1.7.26
(Anger will helpe thy hands though nere so weake).	Ovid's Elegies	1.7.66
Nor, so thou maist obtaine a wealthy prize,	Ovid's Elegies	1.8.63
Dissemble so, as lov'd he may be thought,	Ovid's Elegies	1.8.71
Thy fault with his fault so repuls'd will vanish.	Ovid's Elegies	1.8.80
When thou hast so much as he gives no more,	Ovid's Elegies	1.8.101
So the fierce troupes of Thracian Rhesus fell/And Captive	Ovid's Elegies	1.9.23
That colour rightly did appeare so bloudy.	Ovid's Elegies	1.12.12
Envie, why carpest thou my time is spent so ill,	Ovid's Elegies	1.15.1
So shall Licoris whom he loved best:	Ovid's Elegies	1.15.30
So Cupid wills, farre hence be the severe,	Ovid's Elegies	2.1.3
Of wealth and honour so shall grow thy heape,	Ovid's Elegies	2.2.39
[A white wench thralles me, so doth golden yellowe],	Ovid's Elegies	2.4.39
Why so was Ledas, yet was Leda faire.	Ovid's Elegies	2.4.42
No love is so dere (quiverd Cupid flie)/That my chiefe wish	Ovid's Elegies	2.5.1
Cupid flie)/That my chiefe wish should be so oft to die.	Ovid's Elegies	2.5.2
Aye me poore soule, why is my cause so good.	Ovid's Elegies	2.5.8
and kissed so sweetely as might make/Wrath-kindled Jove away	Ovid's Elegies	2.5.51
Tis ill they pleas'd so much, for in my lips,	Ovid's Elegies	2.5.57
I know no maister of so great hire sped.	Ovid's Elegies	2.5.62
Thou spokest thy words so well with stammering sound.	Ovid's Elegies	2.6.24
To over-come, so oft to fight I shame.	Ovid's Elegies	2.7.2
Should I sollicit her that is so just:	Ovid's Elegies	2.7.25
O boy that lyest so slothfull in my heart.	Ovid's Elegies	2.9.2
So many men and maidens without love,	Ovid's Elegies	2.9.15
That have so oft serv'd pretty wenches dyet.	Ovid's Elegies	2.9.24
Live without love, so sweete ill is a maide.	Ovid's Elegies	2.9.26
So wavering Cupid bringes me backe amaine,	Ovid's Elegies	2.9.33
So of both people shalt thou homage gaine.	Ovid's Elegies	2.9.54
This seemes the fairest, so doth that to mee,	Ovid's Elegies	2.10.7
[And] this doth please me most, and so doth she.	Ovid's Elegies	2.10.8
So with this love and that, wavers my minde.	Ovid's Elegies	2.10.10
Even as he led his life, so did he die.	Ovid's Elegies	2.10.38
So farre 'tis safe, but to go farther dread.	Ovid's Elegies	2.11.16
To bring that happy time so soone as may be.	Ovid's Elegies	2.11.56
So in thy Temples shall Osiris stay,	Ovid's Elegies	2.13.12
But if in so great feare I may advize thee,	Ovid's Elegies	2.13.27
Armenian Tygers never did so ill,	Ovid's Elegies	2.14.35
Fit her so well, as she is fit for me:	Ovid's Elegies	2.15.5
yong-mens mates, to go/If they determine to persever so.	Ovid's Elegies	2.16.18
So sweete a burthen I will beare with eaze.	Ovid's Elegies	2.16.30
Aye me why is it knowne to her so well?	Ovid's Elegies	2.17.8
And thou my light accept me how so ever,	Ovid's Elegies	2.17.23
And rule so soone with private hands acquainted.	Ovid's Elegies	2.18.16
So having vext she nourisht my warme fire,	Ovid's Elegies	2.19.15
So shall my love continue many yeares,	Ovid's Elegies	2.19.23
So through the world shold bright renown expresse me.	Ovid's Elegies	3.1.64
Envious garments so good legges to hide,	Ovid's Elegies	3.2.27
So long they be, since she her faith forsooke.	Ovid's Elegies	3.3.4
But did you not so envy Cepheus Daughter,	Ovid's Elegies	3.3.17
Tut, men should not their courage so consume.	Ovid's Elegies	3.3.34
Poore Semele, among so many burn'd;	Ovid's Elegies	3.3.37
I know not, what men thinke should thee so move.	Ovid's Elegies	3.4.28
So use we women of strange nations stocke.	Ovid's Elegies	3.4.34
Least labour so shall winne great grace of any.	Ovid's Elegies	3.4.46
So shalt thou go with youths to feasts together,	Ovid's Elegies	3.4.47
Slide in thy bounds, so shalt thou runne for ever.	Ovid's Elegies	3.5.20
Who so well keepes his waters head from knowing,	Ovid's Elegies	3.5.40
Nor Romane stocke scorne me so much (I crave)/Gifts then my	Ovid's Elegies	3.5.65
I shame so great names to have usde so vainly:	Ovid's Elegies	3.5.102
So in a spring thrives he that told so much,	Ovid's Elegies	3.6.51
Hath any rose so from a fresh yong maide,	Ovid's Elegies	3.6.53
O let him change goods so ill got to dust,	Ovid's Elegies	3.7.66
So at Aeneas buriall men report,	Ovid's Elegies	3.8.13
So Nemesis, so Delia famous are,	Ovid's Elegies	3.8.31
That durst to so great wickednesse aspire.	Ovid's Elegies	3.8.44
Ceres what sports to thee so grievous were,	Ovid's Elegies	3.9.43
I have sustainde so oft thrust from the dore,	Ovid's Elegies	3.10.9
Erre I? or by my [bookes] <lookes> is she so knowne?	Ovid's Elegies	3.11.7
'Tis so: by my witte her abuse is growne.	Ovid's Elegies	3.11.8
Why see I lines so oft receivde and given,	Ovid's Elegies	3.13.31
How small so ere, Ile you for greatest praise.	Ovid's Elegies	3.14.14
they tooke delite/To play upon those hands, they were so white.	Hero and Leander	1.30
But this is true, so like was one the other,	Hero and Leander	1.39
So lovely faire was Hero, Venus Nun,	Hero and Leander	1.45
So was his necke in touching, and surpast/The white of Pelops	Hero and Leander	1.64
(For his sake whom their goddesse held so deare,	Hero and Leander	1.92
Eternall heaven to burne, for so it seem'd,	Hero and Leander	1.100
So was her beautie to the standers by.	Hero and Leander	1.106
So ran the people foorth to gaze upon her,	Hero and Leander	1.117
So at her presence all surpris'd and tooken,	Hero and Leander	1.122
So faire a church as this, had Venus none,	Hero and Leander	1.135
As heaven preserves all things, so save thou one.	Hero and Leander	1.224
Even so for mens impression do we you.	Hero and Leander	1.266
So she be faire, but some vile toongs will blot?	Hero and Leander	1.286
But you are faire (aye me) so wondrous faire,	Hero and Leander	1.287
So yoong, so gentle, and so debonaire,	Hero and Leander	1.288
Thereat she smild, and did denie him so,	Hero and Leander	1.311
So having paus'd a while, at last shee said:	Hero and Leander	1.337
And hands so pure, so innocent, nay such,	Hero and Leander	1.365
Wherewith she strooken, look'd so dolefully,	Hero and Leander	1.373

SO (cont.)

answered Love, nor would vouchsafe so much/As one poore word, Hero and Leander 1.383
So on she goes, and in her idle flight, Hero and Leander 2.10
Looke how their hands, so were their hearts united, Hero and Leander 2.27
And now the same gan so to scorch and glow, Hero and Leander 2.70
would not yeeld/So soone to part from that she deerely held. Hero and Leander 2.84
And red for anger that he stayd so long, Hero and Leander 2.89
So that in silence of the cloudie night, Hero and Leander 2.101
So beautie, sweetly quickens when t'is ny, Hero and Leander 2.126
So to his mind was yoong Leanders looke. Hero and Leander 2.130
so hee that loves,/The more he is restrain'd, the woorse he Hero and Leander 2.144
Playd with a boy so faire and [so] kind, Hero and Leander 2.195
Which so prevail'd, as he with small ado, Hero and Leander 2.281
So that the truce was broke, and she alas, Hero and Leander 2.285
That which so long so charily she kept, Hero and Leander 2.309
He on the suddaine cling'd her so about, Hero and Leander 2.314
So Heroes ruddie cheeke, Hero betrayd, Hero and Leander 2.323.

SOAR'D

So high our Dragons soar'd into the aire, F 849 3.1.71 Faust

SOARE (See also SOWRING)

Who nere will cease to soare till he be slaine. Dido 3.3.85 Iarbus
And ore his ships will soare unto the Sunne, Dido 5.1.244 Dido
by princely deeds/Doth meane to soare above the highest sort. 1Tamb 2.7.33 Therid
Making thee mount as high as Eagles soare. 1Tamb 5.1.224 Bajzth

SOBBES

And shaking sobbes his mouth for speeches beares. Ovid's Elegies 3.8.12

SOBBING

was thy parting hence/Bitter and irkesome to my sobbing heart. Edw 2.2.58 Edward

SOBS

My daily diet, is heart breaking sobs, Edw 5.3.21 Edward

SOCIETIE

Without the sweet societie of men. Hero and Leander 1.256

SOCIETIES

and the soyle most fit/For Cities, and societies supports: Dido 1.1.179 Achat

SOCIETY

And all society of holy men: F 910 3.1.132 Pope
Insooth th'eternall powers graunt maides society/Falsely to Ovid's Elegies 3.3.11

SOCIOS

Solamen miseris socios habuisse doloris. F 431 2.1.43 Mephst

SOCRATES

Grave Socrates, wilde Alcibiades: Edw 1.4.397 MortSr

SODAINE

Therefore to stay all sodaine mutinies, 1Tamb 1.1.150 Ceneus
And with a sodaine and an hot alarme/Drive all their horses 1Tamb 1.2.134 Usumc
That could perswade at such a sodaine pinch, 1Tamb 2.1.37 Cosroe
End all my penance in my sodaine death, 2Tamb 2.3.7 Sgsmnd
Such is the sodaine fury of my love, 2Tamb 4.2.52 Therid
But was prevented by his sodaine end. 2Tamb 4.2.74 Olymp
To agravate our sodaine miserie. P 194 3.29 QnMarg
A sodaine pang, the messenger of death. P 538 11.3 Charls
God shield your grace from such a sodaine death: P1178 22.40 Navrre
Bride did incite/The drunken Centaures to a sodaine fight. Ovid's Elegies 1.4.8
Or as a sodaine gale thrustes into sea, Ovid's Elegies 2.9.31

SODAINLY

And issue sodainly upon the rest: 2Tamb 2.1.23 Fredrk
Then arme my Lords, and issue sodainly, 2Tamb 2.1.60 Sgsmnd
O would that sodainly into my gift, Ovid's Elegies 2.15.9
And sodainly her former colour chang'd, Hero and Leander 1.359
Yet she this rashnesse sodainly repented, Hero and Leander 2.33
Imbrast her sodainly, tooke leave, and kist, Hero and Leander 2.92
Being sodainly betraide, dyv'd downe to hide her. Hero and Leander 2.262

SODDAINE

And stirs your valures to such soddaine armes? 2Tamb 2.1.3 Sgsmnd

SODENLY

And sodenly surprize them unawares. Edw 2.3.19 Lncstr

SO ERE

And they shall have what thing so ere thou needst. Dido 5.1.74 Iarbus
How small sc ere, Ile you for greatest praise. Ovid's Elegies 3.14.14

SO EVER

What God so ever holds thee in his armes, 2Tamb 2.4.109 Tamb

SOEVER

What star or state soever governe him, 1Tamb 2.6.18 Ortyg
at all times, in what shape [or] <and> forme soever he please. F 492 2.1.104 P Faust
To accomplish what soever the Doctor please. F1183 4.1.29 Mrtino
and what noyse soever you <yee> heare, come not unto me, for F1873 5.2.77 P Faust

SOFT

Soft ye my Lords and sweet Zenocrate. 1Tamb 1.2.119 Tamb
Soft sir, you must be dieted, too much eating will make you 1Tamb 4.4.103 P Tamb
Their haire as white as milke and soft as Downe, 2Tamb 1.3.25 Tamb
Soft Barabas, there's more longs too't than so. Jew 1.2.45 Govnr
But soft, is not this Bernardine? Jew 4.1.164 1Fryar
Soft sir, a word with you, I must yet have a goblet payde from F App p.234 7 P Vintnr
[Love] <I> slackt my Muse, and made my [numbers] <number> soft. Ovid's Elegies 1.1.22
What makes my bed seem hard seeing it is soft? Ovid's Elegies 1.2.1
Let thy soft finger to thy eare be brought. Ovid's Elegies 1.4.24
Nor [leane] <leave> thy soft head on his boistrous brest. Ovid's Elegies 1.4.36
Nor thy soft foote with his hard foote combine. Ovid's Elegies 1.4.44
That my dead bones may in their grave lie soft. Ovid's Elegies 1.8.108
are in thy soft brest/But pure simplicity in thee doth rest. Ovid's Elegies 1.11.9
Quickly soft words hard dores wide open strooke. Ovid's Elegies 2.1.22
And scratch her faire soft cheekes I did intend. Ovid's Elegies 2.5.46
But may soft love rowse up my drowsie eies, Ovid's Elegies 2.10.19
And in the forme of beds weele strowe soft sand, Ovid's Elegies 2.11.47

SOFT (cont.)
And on the soft ground fertile greene grasse growe. — Ovid's Elegies 2.16.6
My hard way with my mistrisse would seeme soft. — Ovid's Elegies 2.16.20
She gave me leave, soft loves in time make hast, — Ovid's Elegies 3.1.69
Or thinke soft verse in any stead to stand? — Ovid's Elegies 3.7.2
Ah whether is [thy] <they> brests soft nature [fled] <sled>? — Ovid's Elegies 3.7.18
This was [their] <there> meate, the soft grasse was their bed. — Ovid's Elegies 3.9.10

SOFTLY
And when she strokes thee softly on the head, — Dido 3.1.5 Cupid
Speak softly sir, least the devil heare you: — F1180 4.1.26 Mrtino
Chast Hero to her selfe thus softly said: — Hero and Leander 1.178

SOIL (See SOYLE)

SOILE
Thou, by the fortune of this damned [foile] <soile>. — 1Tamb 3.3.213 Bajzth

SOLAMEN
Solamen miseris socios habuisse doloris. — F 431 2.1.43 Mephst

SOLD
On this condition shall thy Turkes be sold. — Jew 2.2.42 Govnr
And so much must they yeeld or not be sold. — Jew 2.3.4 2Offcr
That would for Lucars sake have sold my soule. — Jew 4.1.53 Barab
Art thou that Jew whose goods we heard were sold/For — Jew 5.1.73 Calym
do not you remember a Horse-courser you sold a horse to? — F1633 4.6.76 P Carter
Yes, I remember I sold one a horse. — F1635 4.6.78 Faust

SOLDE
and peoples voices/Bought by themselves and solde, and every — Lucan, First Booke 181

SOLDIER (See also SOULDIER, SOULDIOUR, SOULDYER)
Hold thee tale soldier take the this and flye — Paris ms18,p390 Guise
Caesar is thine, so please it thee, thy soldier; — Lucan, First Booke 204
The barbarous Thratian soldier moov'd with nought, — Hero and Leander 1.81
And every lim did as a soldier stout, — Hero and Leander 2.271

SOLDIERS
Goe, take the villaine, soldiers come away, — Edw 2.6.11 Warwck
And therefore soldiers whether will you hale me? — Edw 5.4.108 Kent
Poore soldiers stand with fear of death dead strooken, — Hero and Leander 1.121

SOLDINO
Tane from Aleppo, Soldino, Tripoly, — 2Tamb 3.1.58 Soria

SOLDIOURS
The soldiours pray, and rapine brought in ryot, — Lucan, First Booke 163
The soldiours having won the market place, — Lucan, First Booke 238
Raw soldiours lately prest; and troupes of gownes; — Lucan, First Booke 312
townes/He garrison'd; and Italy he fild with soldiours. — Lucan, First Booke 464

SOLE
O sweet Iarbus, Annas sole delight, — Dido 5.1.322 Anna
I doubt not shortly but to raigne sole king, — 1Tamb 1.1.175 Cosroe
That perfect blisse and sole felicitie, — 1Tamb 2.7.28 Tamb
But one sole Daughter, whom I hold as deare/As Agamemnon did — Jew 1.1.137 Barab
For whilst I live, here lives my soules sole hope, — Jew 2.1.29 Barab
The sole endevour of your princely care, — P 714 14.17 Bartus
Thy gentle Queene, sole sister to Valoys, — Edw 2.2.172 Lncstr
And raigne sole King of all [our] Provinces. — F 121 1.1.93 Faust
My thoughts sole goddes, aide mine enterprise, — Lucan, First Booke 202
And all things too much in their sole power drenches. — Ovid's Elegies 3.3.26
Strayd bare-foote through sole places on a time. — Ovid's Elegies 3.5.50
The gentle queene of Loves sole enemie. — Hero and Leander 1.318

SOLELY
Shall make me solely Emperour of Asia: — 1Tamb 2.3.39 Cosroe
That Vertue solely is the sum of glorie, — 1Tamb 5.1.189 Tamb

SOLEMN (See also SOLLEMNE)
In silence of thy solemn Evenings walk, — 1Tamb 5.1.148 Tamb

SOLEMNE
Then after all these solemne Exequies, — 1Tamb 5.1.533 Tamb
whose conditions, and our solemne othes/Sign'd with our handes, — 2Tamb 1.1.143 Orcan
And solemne covenants we have both confirm'd, — 2Tamb 2.2.31 Orcan
Then rise at midnight to a solemne masse. — Jew 1.2.373 Mthias
To a solemne feast/I will invite young Selim-Calymath, — Jew 5.2.96 Barab
Our solemne rites of Coronation done, — P 626 12.39 King
As best beseemes this solemne festivall. — F1012 3.2.32 Pope
And with a solemne noyse of trumpets sound, — F1237 4.1.83 Faust
Here when the Pipe with solemne tunes doth sound, — Ovid's Elegies 3.12.11
Rose-cheekt Adonis) kept a solemne feast. — Hero and Leander 1.93

SOLEMNELY
For he hath solemnely sworne thy death. — P 777 15.35 King

SOLEMNITIE
Let us goe to honor this solemnitie. — P 25 1.25 Charls
And see it honoured with just solemnitie. — P 196 3.31 Admral

SOLEMNITY
The which this day with high solemnity, — F 833 3.1.55 Mephst
Or dash the pride of this solemnity; — F 860 3.1.82 Mephst

SOLEMNIZE
this happy conquest/Triumph, and solemnize a martiall feast. — 1Tamb 3.3.273 Tamb
We wil our celebrated rites of mariage solemnize. — 1Tamb 5.1.534 Tamb
we may grace us best/To solemnize our Governors great feast. — Jew 5.3.45 Calym
That we may solemnize Saint Peters feast, — F 978 3.1.200 Pope

SOLEMNIZED
And then his mariage shalbe solemnized, — Edw 1.4.377 Edward
The which <That to> this day is highly solemnized. — F 778 2.3.57 2Chor

SOLEMNLY
Madam, I have heard him solemnly vow, — P 516 9.35 Cardnl
But now <Faustus> thou must bequeath it solemnly, — F 423 2.1.35 Mephst
Who's this, that stands so solemnly by himselfe: — F1513 4.5.9 P Hostss

SOLICIT (See also SOLLICIT)
Now Mahomet, solicit God himselfe, — 1Tamb 3.3.195 Zabina

SOLIDE
she chides/And with long charmes the solide earth divides. — Ovid's Elegies 1.8.18

SOLITARIE				
He is not well with being over solitarie.	F1829	5.2.33		3Schol
he is growne into some sicknesse, by> being over solitarie.	F1829	(HC270)A	P	3Schol
Till to the solitarie tower he got.	Hero and Leander			2.230
SOLITARY				
Novice learne to frame/My solitary life to your streight lawes,	Jew	1.2.332		Abigal
Then hast thee to some solitary Grove,	F 180	1.1.152		Valdes
I shall say, As I was sometime solitary set, within my Closet,	F App	p.236 18	P	Emper
SOLLARS (See SOLLERS)				
SOLLEMNE				
In sollemne triumphes, and in publike showes,	Edw	1.4.350		Edward
SOLLEMNLY				
Sweet Jesus Christ, I sollemnly protest,	2Tamb	1.1.135		Sgsmnd
SOLLERS				
Cellers of Wine, and Sollers full of Wheat,	Jew	4.1.63		Barab
SOLLICIT				
Should I sollicit her that is so just:	Ovid's Elegies			2.7.25
SOLLICITE				
Know, holy Sir, I am bold to sollicite thee.	Jew	3.3.53		Abigal
SOM				
dore more wisely/And som-what higher beare thy foote precisely.	Ovid's Elegies			1.12.6
SOME				
Some say Antenor did betray the towne,	Dido	2.1.110		Dido
Some surfetted, and others soundly slept.	Dido	2.1.179		Aeneas
Come let us thinke upon some pleasing sport,	Dido	2.1.302		Dido
Some came in person, others sent their Legats:	Dido	3.1.152		Dido
Some to the mountaines, some unto the soyle,	Dido	3.3.61		Dido
I thinke some fell Inchantresse dwelleth here,	Dido	4.1.3		Iarbus
Nature, why mad'st me not some poysonous beast,	Dido	4.1.21		Iarbus
Be rul'd by me, and seeke some other love,	Dido	4.2.35		Anna
Let some of those thy followers goe with me,	Dido	5.1.73		Iarbus
I thinke some Fairies have beguiled me.	Dido	5.1.215		Nurse
Thou for some pettie guift hast let him goe,	Dido	5.1.218		Dido
As if he now devis'd some Stratageme:	1Tamb	1.2.159		Therid
To some direction in your martiall deeds,	1Tamb	2.3.12		Tamb
Some powers divine, or els infernall, mixt/Their angry seeds at	1Tamb	2.6.9		Meandr
but some must stay/To rule the provinces he late subdude.	1Tamb	3.3.28		Bassoe
You must devise some torment worsse, my Lord,	1Tamb	4.2.66		Techel
Yet would you have some pitie for my sake,	1Tamb	4.2.123		Zenoc
belike he hath not bene watered to day, give him some drinke.	1Tamb	4.4.55	P	Tamb
of them, looking some happie power will pitie and inlarge us.	1Tamb	4.4.99	P	Zabina
and hartie humble mones/Will melt his furie into some remorse:	1Tamb	5.1.22		Govnr
Some made your wives, and some your children)/Might have	1Tamb	5.1.27		1Virgn
and some your children)/Might have intreated your obdurate	1Tamb	5.1.27		1Virgn
To entertaine some care of our securities,	1Tamb	5.1.29		1Virgn
Fetch me some water for my burning breast,	1Tamb	5.1.276		Bajzth
To make discourse of some sweet accidents/Have chanc'd thy	1Tamb	5.1.424		Arabia
Hoping by some means I shall be releast,	2Tamb	1.2.23		Callap
Bastardly boy, sprong from some cowards loins,	2Tamb	1.3.69		Tamb
Then let some holy trance convay my thoughts,	2Tamb	2.4.34		Tamb
Some musicke, and my fit wil cease my Lord.	2Tamb	2.4.77		Zenoc
Some, that in conquest of the perjur'd Christian,	2Tamb	3.1.39		Orcan
Your Majesty may choose some pointed time,	2Tamb	3.1.75		Jrslem
Or els invent some torture worse than that.	2Tamb	3.4.22		Olymp
And sit in councell to invent some paine,	2Tamb	3.5.98		Callap
I beleeve there will be some hurt done anon amongst them.	2Tamb	4.1.74	P	Calyph
Devise some meanes to rid thee of thy life,	2Tamb	4.2.5		Olymp
Ile use some other means to make you yeeld,	2Tamb	4.2.51		Therid
Why gave you not your husband some of it,	2Tamb	4.2.71		Therid
Your Majesty must get some byts for these,	2Tamb	4.3.43		Therid
Or die some death of quickest violence,	2Tamb	5.1.41		2Citzn
Vile monster, borne of some infernal hag,	2Tamb	5.1.110		Govnr
Go thither some of you and take his gold,	2Tamb	5.1.123		Tamb
To some high hill about <above> the citie here.	2Tamb	5.1.216		Therid
And cause some milder spirits governe you.	2Tamb	5.3.80		Phsitn
and Calor, which some holde/Is not a parcell of the Elements,	2Tamb	5.3.86		Phsitn
Then let some God oppose his holy power,	2Tamb	5.3.220		Techel
To some perhaps my name is odious,	Jew	Prol.5		Machvl
Though some speake openly against my bookes,	Jew	Prol.10		Machvl
But this we heard some of our sea-men say,	Jew	1.1.78		1Merch
Happily some haplesse man hath conscience,	Jew	1.1.119		Barab
My selfe in Malta, some in Italy,	Jew	1.1.126		Barab
Tut, tut, there is some other matter in't.	Jew	1.1.160		Barab
Some Jewes are wicked, as all Christians are:	Jew	1.2.112		Barab
have turn'd my house/Into a Nunnery, and some Nuns are there.	Jew	1.2.278		Barab
'Tis thirtie winters long since some of us/Did stray so farre	Jew	1.2.308		Abbass
Some have we fir'd, and many have we sunke;	Jew	2.2.15		Bosco
'Tis likely they in time may reape some fruit,	Jew	2.3.84		Barab
Belike he has some new tricke for a purse;	Jew	2.3.101		Barab
Some wicked trick or other.	Jew	2.3.119	P	Barab
I am content to lose some of my Crownes;	Jew	2.3.178		Barab
And every Moone made some or other mad,	Jew	2.3.195		Barab
And like a cunning spirit feigne some lye,	Jew	2.3.382		Barab
up to the Jewes counting-house where I saw some bags of mony,	Jew	3.1.19	P	Pilia
run to some rocke and throw my selfe headlong into the sea;	Jew	3.4.39	P	Ithimr
Belike there is some Ceremony in't.	Jew	3.4.83		Barab
All this I'le give to some religious house/So I may be baptiz'd	Jew	4.1.75		Barab
Stands here a purpose, meaning me some wrong,	Jew	4.1.166		1Fryar
I'le goe steale some mony from my Master to make me hansome:	Jew	4.2.49	P	Ithimr
But you know some secrets of the Jew,	Jew	4.2.64		Pilia
His hands are hackt, some fingers cut quite off;	Jew	4.3.10		Barab
I will in some disguize goe see the slave,	Jew	4.3.67		Barab
Stand in some window opening neere the street,	P 86	2.29		Guise

SOME (cont.)

but I hope it be/Only some naturall passion makes her sicke.	P 183	3.18		QnMarg
To have some care for feare of enemies.	P 224	4.22		QnMoth
But look my Lord, ther's some in the Admirals house.	P 297	5.24		Retes
It may be it is some other, and he escapte.	P 308	5.35		Anjoy
Without the intercession of some Saint?	P 357	6.12		Mntsrl
Goe place some men upon the bridge,	P 421	7.61		Dumain
Sirs, take him away and throw him in some ditch.	P 499	9.18		Guise
And spend some daies in barriers, tourny, tylte,	P 628	12.41		King
Faine would I finde some means to speak with him/But cannot,	P 662	13.6		Duchss
That he may come and meet me in some place,	P 664	13.8		Duchss
Of whose encrease I set some longing hope,	P 689	13.33		Guise
Or else employ them in some better cause.	P 794	16.8		Bartus
That we might torture him with some new found death.	P1217	22.79		Eprnon
I have some busines, leave me to my selfe.	Edw	1.1.48		Gavstn
So I may have some nooke or corner left,	Edw	1.4.72		Edward
How easilie might some base slave be subbornd,	Edw	1.4.265		Mortmr
Then may we with some colour rise in armes,	Edw	1.4.279		Mortmr
Ah had some bloudlesse furie rose from hell,	Edw	1.4.316		Edward
Some treason, or some villanie was cause.	Edw	3.1.114		Spencr
Some whirle winde fetche them backe, or sincke them all:--	Edw	4.6.59		Mortmr
Then let some other be his guardian.	Edw	5.2.36		Queene
Some thing he whispers in his childish eares.	Edw	5.2.76		Queene
And be eterniz'd for some wondrous cure:	F 43	1.1.15		Faust
Come, shew me some demonstrations Magicall,	F 177	1.1.149		Faust
That I may conjure in some bushy <lustie> Grove,	F 178	1.1.150		Faust
Then hast thee to some solitary Grove,	F 180	1.1.152		Valdes
that at some certaine day/Great Lucifer may claime it as his	F 439	2.1.51		Mephst
all at one time, but in some years we have more, in some lesse?	F 616	2.2.65	P	Faust
we are come from hell in person to shew thee some pastime:	F 655	2.2.104	P	Belzeb
in hell, and look to it, for some of you shall be my father.	F 690	2.2.139	P	Wrath
And take some part of holy Peters feast,	F 777	2.3.56		2Chor
<faine> see the Pope/And take some part of holy Peters feast,	F 832	3.1.54		Mephst
Pope Adrian let me have some right of Law,	F 904	3.1.126		Bruno
<Well, I am content, to compasse then some sport>,	F 989	(HC266)A		Faust
And by their folly make some <us> merriment,	F 990	3.2.10		Faust
Fetch me some wine.	F1051	3.2.71		Pope
I thinke it be some Ghost crept out of Purgatory, and now is	F1059	3.2.79	P	Archbp
let me have the carrying of him about to shew some trickes.	F1129	3.3.42	P	Robin
as to delight your Majesty with some mirth, hath Faustus justly	F1312	4.1.158	P	Faust
And hurle him in some lake of mud and durt:	F1409	4.2.85		Faust
This Traytor flies unto some steepie rocke,	F1413	4.2.89		Faust
thinking some hidden mystery had beene in the horse, I had	F1485	4.4.29	P	HrsCsr
I'le out-run him, and cast this leg into some ditch or other.	F1495	4.4.39	P	HrsCsr
some of his men to attend you with provision fit for your	F1501	4.4.45	P	Wagner
Why Hostesse, I say, fetch us some Beere.	F1518	4.5.14	P	Dick
heere's some on's have cause to know him; did he conjure thee	F1523	4.5.19	P	HrsCsr
had had some [rare] quality that he would not have me know of,	F1542	4.5.38	P	HrsCsr
Some more drinke Hostesse.	F1555	4.5.51	P	Carter
Zons fill us some Beere, or we'll breake all the barrels in the	F1618	4.6.61	P	HrsCsr
I humbly thanke your grace: then fetch some Beere.	F1625	4.6.68		Faust
<Belike he is growne into some sicknesse, by> being over	F1829	(HC270)A	P	3Schol
Impose some end to my incessant paine:	F1960	5.2.164		Faust
from me, and I be chang'd/[Unto] <Into> some brutish beast.	F1968	5.2.172		Faust
some ghost newly crept out of Purgatory come to begge a pardon	F App	p.232 14	P	Lorein
and ifaith I meane to search some circles for my owne use:	F App	p.233 2	P	Robin
that thou let me see some proofe of thy skil, that mine eies	F App	p.236 6	P	Emper
Bred in the concave of some monstrous rocke:	F App	p.238 73		Knight
as to delight you with some mirth, hath Faustus worthily	F App	p.238 82	P	Faust
had some rare qualitie that he would not have had me knowne of,	F App	p.240 132	P	HrsCsr
Why hee's fast asleepe, come some other time.	F App	p.240 141	P	Mephst
that great bellied women do long for some dainties or other,	F App	p.242 5	P	Faust
And some dim stars) he Arriminum enter'd:	Lucan, First Booke	234		
Now evermore least some one hope might ease/The Commons	Lucan, First Booke	520		
Or if Fate rule them, Rome thy Cittizens/Are neere some plague:	Lucan, First Booke	644		
Aye me I warne what profits some few howers,	Ovid's Elegies	1.4.59		
But what entreates for thee some-times tooke place,	Ovid's Elegies	1.6.21		
While rage is absent, take some friend the paynes.	Ovid's Elegies	1.7.2		
And as first wrongd the wronged some-times banish,	Ovid's Elegies	1.8.79		
Let them aske some-what, many asking little,	Ovid's Elegies	1.8.89		
and some blotted letter/On the last edge to stay mine eyes the	Ovid's Elegies	1.11.21		
bondes contained/From barbarous lips of some Atturney strained.	Ovid's Elegies	1.12.24		
But [heldst] <hadst> thou in thine armes some Caephalus,	Ovid's Elegies	1.13.39		
foote drawes out/Fastning her light web some old beame about.	Ovid's Elegies	1.14.8		
Which some admiring, O thou oft wilt blush/And say he likes me	Ovid's Elegies	1.14.47		
Praysing for me some unknowne Guelder dame,	Ovid's Elegies	1.14.49		
That some youth hurt as I am with loves bowe/His owne flames	Ovid's Elegies	2.1.7		
While I speake some fewe, yet fit words be idle.	Ovid's Elegies	2.2.2		
Some one of these might make the chastest fall.	Ovid's Elegies	2.4.32		
To these, or some of these like was her colour,	Ovid's Elegies	2.5.41		
And ever seemed as some new sweete befell.	Ovid's Elegies	2.5.56		
If some faire wench me secretly behold,	Ovid's Elegies	2.7.5		
Would I were culpable of some offence,	Ovid's Elegies	2.7.11		
That at my funeralles some may weeping crie,	Ovid's Elegies	2.10.37		
Againe by some in this unpeopled world.	Ovid's Elegies	2.14.12		
And some few pastures Pallas Olives bore.	Ovid's Elegies	2.16.8		
That meane to travaile some long irkesome way.	Ovid's Elegies	2.16.16		
Since some faire one I should of force obey.	Ovid's Elegies	2.17.6		
Let this care some-times bite thee to the quick,	Ovid's Elegies	2.19.43		
Some other seeke that may in patience strive with thee,	Ovid's Elegies	2.19.59		
Tis credible some [god-head] <good head> haunts the place.	Ovid's Elegies	3.1.2		
Oft some points at the prophet passing by,	Ovid's Elegies	3.1.19		
Some greater worke will urge me on at last.	Ovid's Elegies	3.1.70		

SOME (cont.)			
She smilde, and with quicke eyes behight some grace:	Ovid's Elegies	3.2.83	
maides society/Falsely to sweare, their beauty hath some deity.	Ovid's Elegies	3.3.12	
And I beleeve some wench thou hast affected:	Ovid's Elegies	3.5.83	
What, wast my limbs through some Thesalian charms,	Ovid's Elegies	3.6.27	
With virgin waxe hath some imbast my joynts,	Ovid's Elegies	3.6.29	
And I grow faint, as with some spirit haunted?	Ovid's Elegies	3.6.36	
Or jaded camst thou from some others bed.	Ovid's Elegies	3.6.80	
Wit was some-times more pretious then gold,	Ovid's Elegies	3.7.3	
Canst touch that hand wherewith some one lie dead?	Ovid's Elegies	3.7.17	
Tis well, if some wench for the poore remaine.	Ovid's Elegies	3.7.60	
And some there be that thinke we have a deity.	Ovid's Elegies	3.8.18	
And some, that she refrain'd teares, have deni'd.	Ovid's Elegies	3.8.46	
Some other seeke, who will these things endure.	Ovid's Elegies	3.10.28	
Or shall I plaine some God against me warres?	Ovid's Elegies	3.11.4	
Who sees it, graunts some deity there is shrowded.	Ovid's Elegies	3.12.8	
And some guest viewing watry Sulmoes walles,	Ovid's Elegies	3.14.11	
Some say, for her the fairest Cupid pyn'd,	Hero and Leander	1.37	
Some swore he was a maid in mans attire,	Hero and Leander	1.83	
And some (their violent passions to asswage)/Compile sharpe	Hero and Leander	1.126	
Which after his disceasse, some other gains.	Hero and Leander	1.246	
Virginitie, albeit some highly prise it,	Hero and Leander	1.262	
Untill some honourable deed be done.	Hero and Leander	1.282	
And know that some have wrong'd Dianas name?	Hero and Leander	1.284	
So she be faire, but some vile toongs will blot?	Hero and Leander	1.286	
Some one or other keepes you as his owne.	Hero and Leander	1.290	
Stole some from Hebe (Hebe, Joves cup fil'd),	Hero and Leander	1.434	
Some hidden influence breeds like effect.	Hero and Leander	2.60	
yet he suspected/Some amorous rites or other were neglected.	Hero and Leander	2.64	
At least vouchsafe these armes some little roome,	Hero and Leander	2.249	
Breathlesse spoke some thing, and sigh'd out the rest;	Hero and Leander	2.280	
And to some corner secretly have gone,	Hero and Leander	2.311	
SOME ONE			
Canst touch that hand wherewith some one lie dead?	Ovid's Elegies	3.7.17	
Some one or other keepes you as his owne.	Hero and Leander	1.290	
SOME THING			
Some thing he whispers in his childish eares.	Edw	5.2.76	Queene
Breathlesse spoke some thing, and sigh'd out the rest;	Hero and Leander	2.280	
SOMETHING (See also SOMEWHAT)			
Something thou hast deserv'd.--	Dido	3.1.43	Dido
Something it was that now I have forgot.	Dido	3.4.30	Dido
I think I make your courage something quaile.	2Tamb	5.1.126	Tamb
Something Techelles, but I know not what,	2Tamb	5.1.220	Tamb
Why this is something:	Jew	2.3.213	Barab
Hold thee, wench, there's something for thee to spend.	Jew	3.1.12	Pilia
Or loving, doth dislike of something done.	Jew	3.4.12	Barab
I'le give him something and so stop his mouth.	Jew	4.1.102	Barab
Tis something to be pitied of a king.	Edw	1.4.130	Gavstn
This poore revenge hath something easd my minde,	Edw	5.1.141	Edward
Something still busseth in mine eares,	Edw	5.5.103	Edward
O something soundeth in mine [eares] <eare>,/Abjure this	F 395	2.1.7	Faust
Il'e make you feele something anon, if my Art faile me not.	F1246	4.1.92	P Faust
SOMETIME			
Sometime I was a Troian, mightie Queene:	Dido	2.1.75	Aeneas
Jove sometime masked in a Shepheards weed,	1Tamb	1.2.199	Tamb
Sometime a lovelie boye in Dians shape,	Edw	1.1.61	Gavstn
That sometime grew within this learned man:	F2004	5.3.22	4Chor
I shall say, As I was sometime solitary set, within my Closet,	F App	p.236 18	P Emper
And with them Curio, sometime Tribune too,	Lucan, First Booke	271	
SOME-TIMES			
But what entreates for thee some-times tooke place,	Ovid's Elegies	1.6.21	
And as first wrongd the wronged some-times banish,	Ovid's Elegies	1.8.79	
Let this care some-times bite thee to the quick,	Ovid's Elegies	2.19.43	
Wit was some-times more pretious then gold,	Ovid's Elegies	3.7.3	
SOMETIMES (See also SOMTIMES)			
Sometimes the owner of a goodly house,	Jew	1.2.319	Abigal
Sometimes I goe about and poyson wells;	Jew	2.3.176	Barab
Sometimes like women or unwedded Maides,	F 154	1.1.126	Valdes
Sometimes, like a Perriwig, I sit upon her Brow:	F 665	2.2.114	P Pride
But yet sometimes to chide thee let her fall/Counterfet teares:	Ovid's Elegies	2.2.35	
SOME-WHAT			
Let them aske some-what, many asking little,	Ovid's Elegies	1.8.89	
SOMEWHAT (See also SOMWHAT)			
So then, there's somewhat come.	Jew	1.1.69	Barab
you in these chops; let me see one that's somewhat leaner.	Jew	2.3.125	P Barab
I'le fetch him somewhat to delight his minde.	F 471	2.1.83	Mephst
I must say somewhat to your felow, you sir.	F App	p.234 13	P Vintnr
And as shee spake those words, came somewhat nere him.	Hero and Leander	1.180	
SOMMERS			
And full three Sommers likewise shall he waste,	Dido	1.1.91	Jupitr
SOMMON			
And sommon al the shining lamps of heaven/To cast their	2Tamb	5.3.3	Therid
SOMMOND			
Hellen, whose beauty sommond Greece to armes,	2Tamb	2.4.87	Tamb
SOMMONS			
And sommons all my sences to depart.	1Tamb	2.7.45	Cosroe
SOMTIMES			
Yet somtimes let your highnesse send for them/To do the work my	1Tamb	3.3.187	Anippe
SOM-WHAT			
dore more wisely/And som-what higher beare thy foote precisely.	Ovid's Elegies	1.12.6	
SOMWHAT			
Must! tis somwhat hard, when kings must go.	Edw	4.7.83	Edward
SON (See also SONN, SONNE)			
If he be son to everliving Jove,	2Tamb	2.2.41	Orcan

SON (cont.)			
son and successive heire to the late mighty Emperour Bajazeth,	2Tamb	3.1.1	P Orcan
Farewell sweet wife, sweet son farewell, I die.	2Tamb	3.4.10	Capt
Then in my coach like Saturnes royal son,	2Tamb	4.3.125	Tamb
This Moore is comeliest, is he not? speake son.	Jew	2.3.144	Mater
You knew Mathias and the Governors son; he and I kild 'em both,	Jew	4.4.17	P Ithimr
Thou and thy Turk; 'twas you that slew my son.	Jew	5.1.27	Govnr
SONG			
And tell me where [learndst] <learnst> thou this pretie song?	Dido	3.1.27	Dido
Away with Dido, Anna be thy song,	Dido	4.2.45	Anna
His talke much sweeter than the Muses song,	1Tamb	3.2.50	Zenoc
If thou wilt have a song, the Turke shall straine his voice:	1Tamb	4.4.63	P Tamb
To quaver on her lippes even in her song,	Ovid's Elegies		2.4.26
SONGS			
And wanton Mermaides court thee with sweete songs,	Dido	3.1.130	Dido
Or songs amazing wilde beasts of the wood?	Ovid's Elegies		3.8.22
Festivall dayes aske Venus, songs, and wine,	Ovid's Elegies		3.9.47
SONN			
exhalatione/which our great sonn of fraunce cold not effecte	Paris	ms20,p390	Guise
SONNE (Homograph)			
And charg'd him drowne my sonne with all his traine.	Dido	1.1.61	Venus
Venus farewell, thy sonne shall be our care:	Dido	1.1.120	Jupitr
What? doe I see my sonne now come on shoare:	Dido	1.1.134	Venus
Stay gentle Venus, flye not from thy sonne,	Dido	1.1.242	Aeneas
And if this be thy sonne as I suppose,	Dido	2.1.92	Dido
and on his speare/The mangled head of Priams yongest sonne,	Dido	2.1.215	Aeneas
Achilles sonne, remember what I was,	Dido	2.1.233	Aeneas
And would have grappeld with Achilles sonne,	Dido	2.1.251	Aeneas
Are you Queene Didos sonne?	Dido	2.1.308	Ascan
Lest she imagine thou art Venus sonne:	Dido	3.1.4	Cupid
Looke sister how Aeneas little sonne/Playes with your garments	Dido	3.1.20	Anna
I shall not be her sonne, she loves me not.	Dido	3.1.23	Cupid
Weepe not sweet boy, thou shalt be Didos sonne,	Dido	3.1.24	Dido
This Meleagers sonne, a warlike Prince,	Dido	3.1.163	Dido
Out hatefull hag, thou wouldst have slaine my sonne,	Dido	3.2.32	Venus
What though I was offended with thy sonne,	Dido	3.2.40	Juno
Thy sonne thou knowest with Dido now remaines,	Dido	3.2.70	Juno
But much I feare my sonne will nere consent,	Dido	3.2.82	Venus
Yea little sonne, are you so forward now?	Dido	3.3.34	Dido
The King of Carthage, not Anchises sonne:	Dido	3.4.60	Dido
Hath not the Carthage Queene mine onely sonne?	Dido	4.4.29	Aeneas
Aeneas will not goe without his sonne:	Dido	4.4.107	Dido
Rather Ascania by your little sonne.	Dido	5.1.21	Serg
And made me take my brother for my sonne:	Dido	5.1.43	Aeneas
I feare I sawe Aeneas little sonne,	Dido	5.1.83	Dido
Had I a sonne by thee, the griefe were lesse,	Dido	5.1.149	Dido
O Dido, your little sonne Ascanius/Is gone!	Dido	5.1.212	Nurse
That causde the eldest sonne of heavenly Ops,	1Tamb	2.7.13	Tamb
As was the fame of [Clymens] <Clymeus> brain-sicke sonne,/That	1Tamb	4.2.49	Tamb
The sonne of God and issue of a Mayd,	2Tamb	1.1.134	Sgsmnd
pity the ruthfull plight/Of Callapine, the sonne of Bajazeth,	2Tamb	1.2.2	Callap
These words assure me boy, thou art my sonne,	2Tamb	1.3.58	Tamb
Villain, art thou the sonne of Tamburlaine,	2Tamb	3.2.95	Tamb
Killing my selfe, as I have done my sonne,	2Tamb	3.4.35	Olymp
But wher's this coward, villaine, not my sonne,	2Tamb	4.1.89	Tamb
Supposing amorous Jove had sent his sonne,	2Tamb	4.2.18	Therid
And meet my husband and my loving sonne.	2Tamb	4.2.36	Olymp
Nothing, but stil thy husband and thy sonne?	2Tamb	4.2.37	Therid
them for the funerall/They have bestowed on my abortive sonne.	2Tamb	4.3.66	Tamb
me, that I may resigne/My place and proper tytle to my sonne:	2Tamb	5.3.176	Tamb
Sit up my sonne, let me see how well/Thou wilt become thy	2Tamb	5.3.183	Tamb
Let not thy love exceed thyne honor sonne,	2Tamb	5.3.199	Tamb
So, raigne my sonne, scourge and controlle those slaves,	2Tamb	5.3.228	Tamb
As that which [Clymens] <Clymeus> brainsicke sonne did guide,	2Tamb	5.3.231	Tamb
of Turkey is arriv'd/Great Selim-Calymath, his Highnesse sonne,	Jew	1.2.40	Govnr
Here comes Don Lodowicke the Governor's sonne,	Jew	2.3.30	Barab
Barabas, thou know'st I am the Governors sonne.	Jew	2.3.40	Lodowk
Thinke of me as thy father; Sonne farewell.	Jew	2.3.149	Barab
Entertaine Lodowicke the Governors sonne/With all the curtesie	Jew	2.3.225	Barab
Pardon me though I weepe; the Governors sonne/Will, whether I	Jew	2.3.257	Barab
Barabas, is not that the widowes sonne?	Jew	2.3.279	Lodowk
Who is this? my sonne Mathias slaine!	Jew	3.2.12	Mater
Thy sonne slew mine, and I'le revenge his death.	Jew	3.2.15	Mater
Looke, Katherin, looke, thy sonne gave mine these wounds.	Jew	3.2.16	Govnr
My sonne lov'd thine.	Jew	3.2.22	Mater
Lend me that weapon that did kill my sonne,	Jew	3.2.23	Mater
And couldst not venge it, but upon his sonne,	Jew	3.3.44	Abigal
Nor on his sonne, but by Mathias meanes;	Jew	3.3.45	Abigal
Farre from the Sonne that gives eternall life.	Jew	3.3.65	Abigal
I bring thee newes by whom thy sonne was slaine:	Jew	5.1.10	Curtzn
your sonne and Mathias were both contracted unto Abigall; [he]	Jew	5.1.28	P Ithimr
Ferneze, 'twas thy sonne that murder'd him.	Jew	5.1.45	Mater
Know, Governor, 'twas I that slew thy sonne;	Jew	5.5.81	Barab
Thanks sonne Navarre, you see we love you well,	P 13	1.13	QnMoth
Help sonne Navarre, I am poysoned.	P 176	3.11	OldQn
My noble sonne, and princely Duke of Guise,	P 203	4.1	QnMoth
I hope these reasons may serve my princely Sonne,	P 223	4.21	QnMoth
Thankes to my princely sonne, then tell me Guise,	P 228	4.26	QnMoth
Nere was there Colliars sonne so full of pride.	P 416	7.56	Anjoy
How Charles our sonne begins for to lament/For the late nights	P 513	9.32	QnMoth
What art thou dead, sweet sonne speak to thy Mother.	P 551	11.16	QnMoth
Goe fetch his sonne for to beholde his death:	P1021	19.91	King
My Lord heer is his sonne.	P1045	19.115	Eprnon

SONNE (cont.)			
I would that I had murdered thee my sonne.	P1073	19.143	QnMoth
My sonne: thou art a changeling, not my sonne.	P1074	19.144	QnMoth
My sonne and I will over into France,	Edw	2.4.65	Queene
Sonne to the lovelie Elenor of Spaine,	Edw	3.1.11	Spencr
Madam in this matter/We will employ you and your little sonne,	Edw	3.1.70	Edward
And this our sonne, [Levune] <Lewne> shall follow you,	Edw	3.1.82	Edward
France/Makes friends, to crosse the seas with her yong sonne,	Edw	3.1.270	Spencr
And there stay times advantage with your sonne?	Edw	4.2.18	SrJohn
Not sonne, why not?	Edw	4.2.45	Queene
Nay sonne, not so, and you must not discourage/Your friends	Edw	4.2.69	Queene
Welcome a Gods name Madam and your sonne,	Edw	4.3.41	Edward
We heere create our welbeloved sonne,	Edw	4.6.24	Queene
So are the Spencers, the father and the sonne.	Edw	4.6.44	SrJohn
God save Queene Isabell, and her princely sonne.	Edw	4.6.46	Rice
Spencer the sonne, created earle of Gloster,	Edw	4.6.56	Rice
Let not that Mortimer protect my sonne,	Edw	5.1.115	Edward
Commend me to my sonne, and bid him rule/Better then I, yet how	Edw	5.1.121	Edward
To erect your sonne with all the speed we may,	Edw	5.2.11	Mortmr
And therefore so the prince my sonne be safe,	Edw	5.2.17	Queene
O happie newes, send for the prince my sonne.	Edw	5.2.29	Queene
long as he survives/What safetie rests for us, or for my sonne?	Edw	5.2.43	Queene
Sweete sonne come hither, I must talke with thee.	Edw	5.2.87	Queene
who should protect the sonne,/But she that gave him life, I	Edw	5.2.90	Kent
Come sonne, and go with this gentle Lorde and me.	Edw	5.2.109	Queene
Edward is my sonne, and I will keepe him.	Edw	5.2.117	Queene
Is sure to pay for it when his sonne is of age,	Edw	5.4.4	Mortmr
Sonne, be content, I dare not speake a worde.	Edw	5.4.96	Queene
Either my brother or his sonne is king,	Edw	5.4.106	Kent
Come sonne, weele ride a hunting in the parke.	Edw	5.4.113	Queene
A Mortimer, the king my sonne hath news,	Edw	5.6.15	Queene
Weepe not sweete sonne.	Edw	5.6.33	Queene
For my sake sweete sonne pittie Mortimer.	Edw	5.6.55	Queene
If you be guiltie, though I be your sonne,	Edw	5.6.81	King
When as my sonne thinkes to abridge my daies.	Edw	5.6.84	Queene
For gentle sonne, I speake it not in wrath,	F1719	5.1.46	OldMan
Bare downe to hell her sonne, the pledge of peace,	Lucan, First Booke		113
the sonne decrees/To expel the father; share the world thou	Lucan, First Booke		290
Who'le set the faire treste [sunne] <sonne> in battell ray,	Ovid's Elegies		1.1.15
Love and Loves sonne are with fierce armes to oddes;	Ovid's Elegies		1.10.19
The sonne slew her, that forth to meete him went,	Ovid's Elegies		1.10.51
And for the same mildly rebuk't his sonne,	Hero and Leander		2.137
SONNES			
You sonnes of care, companions of my course,	Dido	1.1.142	Aeneas
Who for her sonnes death wept out life and breath,	Dido	2.1.4	Aeneas
Father of fiftie sonnes, but they are slaine,	Dido	2.1.234	Aeneas
For Troy, for Priam, for his fiftie sonnes,	Dido	4.4.89	Aeneas
Why wilt thou so betray thy sonnes good hap?	Dido	5.1.31	Hermes
When these my sonnes, more precious in mine eies/Than all the	2Tamb	1.3.18	Tamb
My Lord, such speeches to our princely sonnes,	2Tamb	1.3.85	Zenoc
Let me take leave of these my loving sonnes,	2Tamb	2.4.72	Zenoc
And worthy sonnes of Tamburlain the great.	2Tamb	3.2.92	Tamb
That feeds upon her sonnes and husbands flesh.	2Tamb	3.4.72	Olymp
His sonnes, his Captaines and his followers,	2Tamb	3.5.16	Callap
He comes and findes his sonnes have had no shares/In all the	2Tamb	4.1.47	Amyras
Loe here my sonnes, are all the golden Mines,	2Tamb	5.3.151	Tamb
piller led'st/The sonnes of Israel through the dismall shades,	Jew	2.1.13	Barab
I, and his sonnes too, or it shall goe hard.	Jew	2.3.17	Barab
How likes your grace my sonnes pleasantnes?	P 632	12.45	QnMoth
Those soules which sinne seales the blacke sonnes of hell,	F1799	5.2.3	Lucifr
Where Mars his sonnes not without fault did breed,	Ovid's Elegies		3.4.39
If Thetis, and the morne their sonnes did waile,	Ovid's Elegies		3.8.1
To which the Muses sonnes are only heire:	Hero and Leander		1.476
SON'S			
Nay Madam stay, that weapon was my son's,	Jew	3.2.25	Govnr
SONS			
Betweene thy sons that shall be Emperours,	2Tamb	1.3.7	Tamb
Not martiall as the sons of Tamburlaine.	2Tamb	1.3.22	Tamb
Would make me thinke them Bastards, not my sons,	2Tamb	1.3.32	Tamb
Or els you are not sons of Tamburlaine.	2Tamb	1.3.64	Tamb
Sweet sons farewell, in death resemble me,	2Tamb	2.4.75	Zenoc
My Lord and husbandes death, with my sweete sons,	2Tamb	4.2.22	Olymp
But sons, this subject not of force enough,	2Tamb	5.3.168	Tamb
nor could the bed-rid parents/Keep back their sons, or womens	Lucan, First Booke		503
SOON			
And soon put foorth into the Terrene sea:	2Tamb	1.2.25	Callap
SOONE			
Full soone wouldst thou abjure this single life.	Dido	3.1.60	Dido
But I will soone put by that stumbling blocke,	Dido	4.1.34	Dido
Which with thy beautie will be soone resolv'd.	1Tamb	1.2.101	Tamb
And would not all our souldiers soone consent,	1Tamb	2.5.78	Tamb
not but faire Zenocrate/Will soone consent to satisfy us both.	1Tamb	5.1.499	Tamb
My Lord, your Majesty shall soone perceive:	2Tamb	2.4.39	1Phstn
For as soone as the battaile is done, Ile ride in triumph	2Tamb	3.5.145	P Tamb
I were as soone rewarded with a shot,	2Tamb	4.1.54	Calyph
No doubt, but you shal soone recover all.	2Tamb	5.3.99	Phsitn
Great injuries are not so soone forgot.	Jew	1.2.208	Barab
That can so soone forget an injury.	Jew	2.3.19	Barab
go set it downe/And come againe so soone as thou hast done,	Jew	3.4.109	Barab
Whither so soone?	Jew	4.2.48	Curtzn
Soone enough to your cost, Sir:	Jew	4.3.57	Pilia
what are ye come so soone?	P 815	17.10	P Souldr
As thou wilt soone subscribe to his repeale.	Edw	1.4.227	Queene

Line	Work	Reference	Speaker
SOONE (cont.)			
And will be at the court as soone as we.	Edw	2.1.77	Neece
So soone to have woone Scotland,	Edw	2.2.194	Lncstr
Sib, if this be all/Valoys and I will soone be friends againe.	Edw	3.1.67	Edward
The greefes of private men are soone allayde,	Edw	5.1.8	Edward
Our plots and stratagems will soone be dasht.	Edw	5.2.78	Mortmr
His kingly body was too soone interrde.	Edw	5.6.32	King
So much <soone> he profits in Divinitie,	F 15	Prol.15	1Chor
That shall I soone: What art thou the first?	F 663	2.2.112	Faust
Dispatch it soone,	F 902	3.1.124	Faust
Thou soone shouldst see me quit my foule disgrace.	F1356	4.2.32	Benvol
Their soules are soone dissolv'd in elements,	F1970	5.2.174	Faust
Caesars, and Pompeys jarring love soone ended,	Lucan, First Booke	98	
As soone as Caesar got unto the banke/And bounds of Italy;	Lucan, First Booke	225	
These troupes should soone pull down the church of Jove.	Lucan, First Booke	381	
Soone may you plow the little lands <land> I have,	Ovid's Elegies	1.3.9	
And with swift horses the swift yeare soone leaves us.	Ovid's Elegies	1.8.50	
Receive him soone, least patient use he gaine,	Ovid's Elegies	1.8.75	
Shee pleas'd me, soone I sent, and did her woo,	Ovid's Elegies	2.2.5	
Do this and soone thou shalt thy freedome reape.	Ovid's Elegies	2.2.40	
To bring that happy time so soone as may be.	Ovid's Elegies	2.11.56	
(Their reines let loose) right soone my house approach.	Ovid's Elegies	2.16.50	
And rule so soone with private hands acquainted.	Ovid's Elegies	2.18.16	
As soone as from strange lands Sabinus came,	Ovid's Elegies	2.18.27	
My flatt'ring speeches soone wide open knocke.	Ovid's Elegies	3.1.46	
Ile not sift much, but hold thee soone excusde,	Ovid's Elegies	3.13.41	
As soone as he his wished purpose got,	Hero and Leander	1.460	
would not yeeld/So soone to part from that she deerely held.	Hero and Leander	2.84	
Leanders amcrous habit soone reveal'd.	Hero and Leander	2.104	
SOONER			
And sooner shall the Sun fall from his Spheare,	1Tamb	1.2.176	Tamb
Eternall heaven sooner be dissolv'd,	1Tamb	3.2.18	Agidas
Will sooner burne the glorious frame of Heaven,	1Tamb	4.2.10	Tamb
And sooner let the fiery Element/Dissolve, and make your	2Tamb	2.4.58	Zenoc
Madam, sooner shall fire consume us both,	2Tamb	3.4.73	Techel
And sooner far than he that never fights.	2Tamb	4.1.55	Calyph
As sooner shall they drinke the Ocean dry,	Jew	5.5.121	Govnr
Which is no sooner receiv'd but it is spent.	P 379	7.19	Ramus
And sooner shall the sea orewhelme my land,	Edw	1.1.152	Edward
No sooner is it up, but thers a foule,	Edw	2.2.26	Lncstr
Edward battell in England, sooner then he can looke for them:	Edw	4.3.35	P Spencr
Will sooner sparkle fire then shed a teare:	Edw	5.1.105	Edward
I was no sooner in the middle of the pond, but my horse vanisht	F App	p.240 134	P HrsCsr
Sooner shall kindnesse gaine thy wills fruition.	Ovid's Elegies	3.4.12	
And thence unto Abydus sooner blowne,	Hero and Leander	2.112	
Which watchfull Hesperus no sooner heard,	Hero and Leander	2.329	
SOONEST			
Rich jewels in the darke are soonest spide.	Hero and Leander	2.240	
SOONG			
(Whose tragedie divine Musaeus soong)/Dwelt at Abidus; since	Hero and Leander	1.52	
SOOTH			
here, tell me in sooth/In what might Dido highly pleasure thee.	Dido	3.1.101	Dido
No in good sooth.	F1640	4.6.83	P Faust
Sooth Lovers watch till sleepe the hus-band charmes,	Ovid's Elegies	1.9.25	
Who, without feare, is chaste, is chast in sooth:	Ovid's Elegies	3.4.3	
SOOTHDE			
Yea, and she soothde me up, and calde me sir <sire>,	Ovid's Elegies	3.6.11	
SOOTHSAYER (See SOUTHSAYERS)			
SOPHISTER			
But nephew, do not play the sophister.	Edw	1.4.255	MortSr
At last, like to a bold sharpe Sophister,	Hero and Leander	1.197	
SOPHOCLES			
For ever lasts high Sophocles proud vaine,	Ovid's Elegies	1.15.15	
SOPPES			
These, that are fed with soppes of flaming fire,	F1916	5.2.120	BdAngl
SORBONESTS			
And thats because the blockish [Sorbonests] <thorbonest>	P 411	7.51	Ramus
SORCERESSE			
Traytoresse too [keene] <keend> <kind> and cursed Sorceresse.	Dido	5.1.221	Dido
SORE			
and the victories/Wherewith he hath so sore dismaide the world,	2Tamb	5.2.44	Callap
Beleeve me this jest bites sore.	P 771	15.29	King
And you the Eagles, sore ye nere so high,	Edw	2.2.39	Edward
Maids of England, sore may you moorne,	Edw	2.2.190	Lncstr
With awkward windes, and sore tempests driven/To fall on shoare,	Edw	4.7.34	Baldck
My sides are sore with tumbling to and fro.	Ovid's Elegies	1.2.4	
Unworthy porter, bound in chaines full sore,	Ovid's Elegies	1.6.1	
All you whose pineons in the cleare aire sore,	Ovid's Elegies	2.6.11	
And by mine eyes, and mine were pained sore.	Ovid's Elegies	3.3.14	
And bide sore losse, with endlesse infamie.	Ovid's Elegies	3.6.72	
SORER			
And gripe the sorer being gript himselfe.	Edw	5.2.9	Mortmr
SORIA			
To aid the kings of Soria and Jerusalem.	2Tamb	2.1.21	Fredrk
Of Soria, Trebizon and Amasia,	2Tamb	2.3.44	Orcan
Natolia, Jerusalem, Trebizon, Soria, Amasia, Thracia, Illyria,	2Tamb	3.1.4	P Orcan
From Soria with seventy thousand strong,	2Tamb	3.1.57	Soria
Unto the frontier point of Soria:	2Tamb	3.3.2	Therid
SORIANS			
Natolians, Sorians, blacke Egyptians,	2Tamb	1.1.63	Orcan
Of Sorians from Halla is repair'd/And neighbor cities of your	2Tamb	3.5.46	Soria
SORIE			
Doe yee heare, I would be sorie to robbe you of your living.	F App	p.229 18	P Clown

SORROW
Achates speake, sorrow hath tired me quite. Dido 2.1.293 Aeneas
a heavenly face/Should by hearts sorrow wax so wan and pale, 1Tamb 3.2.5 Agidas
I have, and sorrow for his bad successe: 1Tamb 4.3.28 Souldn
To drive all sorrow from my fainting soule: 1Tamb 5.1.429 Arabia
Sorrow no more my sweet Casane now: 2Tamb 3.2.44 Tamb
It would not ease the sorrow I sustaine. 2Tamb 3.2.48 Calyph
With griefe and sorrow for my mothers death. 2Tamb 3.2.50 Amyras
And sorrow stops the passage of my speech. 2Tamb 3.2.52 Celeb
Save griefe and sorrow which torment my heart, 2Tamb 4.2.24 Olymp
I, let me sorrow for this sudden chance, Jew 1.2.206 Barab
Doe you not sorrow for your daughters death? Jew 4.1.17 Ithimr
I deepely sorrow for your trecherous wrong: P 263 4.61 Charls
But sorrow seaze upon my toyling soule, P1089 19.159 QnMoth
Brother of Navarre, I sorrow much, P1139 22.1 King
Seeing I must go, do not renew my sorrow. Edw 1.4.137 Gavstn
Did never sorrow go so neere my heart, Edw 1.4.306 Edward
My heart is as an anvill unto sorrow, Edw 1.4.312 Edward
Where sorrow at my elbow still attends, Edw 5.1.33 Edward
SORROWE
But dares to heape up sorrowe to my heart: Dido 4.4.152 Dido
[Itis is] <It is as> great, but auntient cause of sorrowe. Ovid's Elegies 2.6.10
Part of her sorrowe heere thy sister bearing, Ovid's Elegies 3.8.51
SORROWES
Before my sorrowes tide have any stint. Dido 4.2.42 Iarbus
Whose sorrowes lay more siege unto my soule, 1Tamb 5.1.155 Tamb
and feare presents/A thousand sorrowes to my martyred soule: 1Tamb 5.1.384 Zenoc
And hide these extreme sorrowes from mine eyes: Jew 1.2.195 Barab
But yet I hope my sorrowes will have end, Edw 2.4.68 Queene
Thy speeches long agoe had easde my sorrowes, Edw 5.1.6 Edward
But hee repents, and sorrowes for it now. Edw 5.2.108 Prince
SORROWING
Chast, and devout, much sorrowing for my sinnes, Jew 3.6.14 Abigal
SORRY (See SORIE)
SORT
maides to weare/Their bowe and quiver in this modest sort, Dido 1.1.205 Venus
I but the barbarous sort doe threat our ships, Dido 1.2.34 Serg
Musk-roses, and a thousand sort of flowers, Dido 4.5.8 Nurse
by princely deeds/Doth meane to soare above the highest sort. 1Tamb 2.7.33 Therid
So might your highnesse, had you time to sort/Your fighting men, 1Tamb 4.1.36 Capol
And as it were in Catechising sort, Jew 2.3.73 Barab
Well, I have deliver'd the challenge in such sort, Jew 3.1.29 Ithimr
sort as if he had meant to make cleane my Boots with his lips; Jew 4.2.30 P Ithimr
Yet is [their] <there> pacience of another sort, P 545 11.10 Charls
This will be good newes to the common sort. Edw 1.4.92 Penbrk
If all things sort out, as I hope they will, Edw 2.1.79 Neece
Who loves thee? but a sort of flatterers. Edw 2.2.171 Mortmr
skill in stars, and tune-full planeting,/In this sort spake. Lucan, First Booke 641
Disclosing Phoebus furie in this sort: Lucan, First Booke 676
The youthfull sort to divers pastimes runne. Ovid's Elegies 2.5.22
Which joyfull Hero answered in such sort, Hero and Leander 2.15
To spurne in carelesse sort, the shipwracke treasure. Hero and Leander 2.164
SORTE
Did he not draw a sorte of English priestes/From Doway to the P1030 19.100 King
SOUGHT
The while thine eyes attract their sought for joyes: Dido 1.1.136 Venus
his Diadem/Sought for by such scalde knaves as love him not? 1Tamb 2.2.8 Mycet
And sought your state all honor it deserv'd, 1Tamb 2.5.33 Ortyg
Wel met Olympia, I sought thee in my tent, 2Tamb 4.2.14 Therid
Had Edmund liv'de, he would have sought thy death. Edw 5.4.112 Queene
And being popular sought by liberal gifts, Lucan, First Booke 132
Wild me, whose slowe feete sought delay, be flying. Ovid's Elegies 2.19.12
And there for honie, bees have sought in vaine, Hero and Leander 1.23
Was moov'd with him, and for his favour sought. Hero and Leander 1.82
Ne're king more sought to keepe his diademe, Hero and Leander 2.77
And cunningly to yeeld her selfe she sought. Hero and Leander 2.294
SOUL (See also SOULE, SOWLE)
And threaten him whose hand afflicts my soul, 2Tamb 5.3.47 Tamb
Your soul gives essence to our wretched subjects, 2Tamb 5.3.164 Amyras
SOULD
Tis shame sould tongues the guilty should defend/Or great Ovid's Elegies 1.10.39
SOULDAN
The mightie Souldan of Egyptia. 1Tamb 1.2.6 Tamb
So now the mighty Souldan heares of you, 1Tamb 3.2.31 Agidas
Nay (mightie Souldan) did your greatnes see/The frowning lookes 1Tamb 4.1.12 2Msngr
that the Souldan is/No more dismaide with tidings of his fall, 1Tamb 4.3.30 Souldn
The Souldan and the Arabian king together/Martch on us with 1Tamb 5.1.199 Techel
SOULDANE
The Souldane would not start a foot from him. 1Tamb 4.1.19 Souldn
Yet would the Souldane by his conquering power, 1Tamb 4.1.33 Souldn
Renowmed Souldane, have ye lately heard/The overthrow of 1Tamb 4.3.23 Arabia
Now Tamburlaine, the mightie Souldane comes, 1Tamb 4.3.63 Souldn
Wel, here is now to the Souldane of Egypt, the King of Arabia, 1Tamb 4.4.113 P Tamb
What saith the noble Souldane and Zenocrate? 1Tamb 5.1.495 Tamb
SOULDANS
As easely may you get the Souldans crowne, 1Tamb 1.2.27 Tamb
He sends this Souldans daughter rich and brave, 1Tamb 1.2.186 Tamb
The Souldans daughter for his Concubine, 1Tamb 4.1.5 Souldn
Joine your Arabians with the Souldans power: 1Tamb 4.3.16 Souldn
Or hope of rescue from the Souldans power, 1Tamb 5.1.4 Govnr
For Egypts freedom and the Souldans life: 1Tamb 5.1.153 Tamb
But let us save the reverend Souldans life, 1Tamb 5.1.204 Therid
A title higher than thy Souldans name: 1Tamb 5.1.434 Tamb

SOULDANS (cont.)			
For since we left you at the Souldans court,	2Tamb	1.3.177	Usumc
SOULDIER			
Shall buy the meanest souldier in my traine.	1Tamb	1.2.86	Tamb
Go valiant Souldier, go before and charge/The fainting army of	1Tamb	2.3.61	Cosroe
But every common souldier of my Camp/Shall smile to see thy	1Tamb	3.3.85	Tamb
Now look I like a souldier, and this wound/As great a grace and	2Tamb	3.2.117	Tamb
For not a common Souldier shall defile/His manly fingers with	2Tamb	4.1.163	Tamb
Tut, Jew, we know thou art no souldier;	Jew	1.2.52	1Knght
See where my Souldier shot him through the arm.	P 310	5.37	Guise
Holde thee tall Souldier, take thee this and flye.	P 817	17.12	Guise
A souldier, that hath serv'd against the Scot.	Edw	1.1.34	3PrMan
SOULDIERS			
sounds/The surges, his fierce souldiers, to the spoyle:	Dido	1.1.69	Venus
The Grecian souldiers tired with ten yeares warre,	Dido	2.1.126	Aeneas
At last the souldiers puld her by the heeles,	Dido	2.1.247	Aeneas
Victuall his Souldiers, give him wealthie gifts,	Dido	2.1.329	Venus
That sav'd your famisht souldiers lives from death,	Dido	3.3.52	Achat
Where daliance doth consume a Souldiers strength,	Dido	4.3.34	Achat
The common souldiers rich imbrodered coates,	Dido	4.4.9	Dido
The warlike Souldiers, and the Gentlemen,	1Tamb	1.1.140	Ceneus
Whereat the Souldiers will conceive more joy,	1Tamb	1.1.152	Ceneus
And cause the souldiers that thus honour me,	1Tamb	1.1.172	Cosroe
As if he meant to give my Souldiers pay,	1Tamb	1.2.183	Tamb
And hostes of souldiers stand amaz'd at us,	1Tamb	1.2.221	Usumc
And with unwilling souldiers faintly arm'd,	1Tamb	2.1.66	Cosroe
Fit Souldiers for the wicked Tamburlaine.	1Tamb	2.2.24	Meandr
Which you that be but common souldiers,	1Tamb	2.2.63	Meandr
With twenty thousand expert souldiers.	1Tamb	2.5.25	Cosroe
And would not all our souldiers soone consent,	1Tamb	2.5.78	Tamb
Let's cheere our souldiers to incounter him,	1Tamb	2.6.29	Cosroe
Resolve my Lords and loving souldiers now,	1Tamb	2.6.34	Cosroe
Doo not my captaines and my souldiers looke/As if they meant to	1Tamb	3.3.9	Tamb
Thy souldiers armes could not endure to strike/So many blowes	1Tamb	3.3.143	Bajzth
To dresse the common souldiers meat and drink.	1Tamb	3.3.185	Zenoc
your sounding Drummes/Direct our Souldiers to Damascus walles.	1Tamb	4.3.62	Souldn
Let the souldiers be buried.	1Tamb	5.1.316	P Zabina
Of this infamous Tyrants souldiers,	1Tamb	5.1.404	Arabia
Millions of Souldiers cut the Artick line,	2Tamb	1.1.29	Orcan
And when the ground wheron my souldiers march/Shal rise aloft	2Tamb	1.3.13	Tamb
A hundred thousand expert souldiers:	2Tamb	1.3.132	Usumc
Yet shall my souldiers make no period/Untill Natolia kneele	2Tamb	1.3.216	Therid
wines/Shall common Souldiers drink in quaffing boules,	2Tamb	1.3.222	Tamb
When this is done, then are ye souldiers,	2Tamb	3.2.91	Tamb
How say ye Souldiers, Shal we not?	2Tamb	3.3.9	Techel
cracke, the Ecchoe and the souldiers crie/Make deafe the aire,	2Tamb	3.3.60	Therid
And souldiers play the men, the [hold] <holds> is yours.	2Tamb	3.3.63	Techel
Twas bravely done, and like a souldiers wife.	2Tamb	3.4.38	Techel
Souldiers now let us meet the Generall,	2Tamb	3.4.85	Therid
The common souldiers of our mighty hoste/Shal bring thee bound	2Tamb	3.5.110	Trebiz
Stand up, ye base unworthy souldiers,	2Tamb	4.1.99	Tamb
Where are my common souldiers now that fought/So Lion-like upon	2Tamb	4.3.67	Tamb
Hold ye tal souldiers, take ye Queens apeece/(I meane such	2Tamb	4.3.70	Tamb
And common souldiers jest with all their Truls.	2Tamb	4.3.91	Tamb
Call up the souldiers to defend these wals.	2Tamb	5.1.56	Govnr
Hath trode the Meisures, do my souldiers martch,	2Tamb	5.1.75	Tamb
And let my souldiers shoot the slave to death.	2Tamb	5.1.109	Tamb
I will about it straight, come Souldiers.	2Tamb	5.1.172	Techel
Wel souldiers, Mahomet remaines in hell,	2Tamb	5.1.198	Tamb
Let it be so, about it souldiers:	2Tamb	5.1.217	Tamb
Come Souldiers, let us lie in wait for him/And if we find him	2Tamb	5.2.56	Callap
Alas, my Lord, we are no souldiers:	Jew	1.2.50	Barab
Doth see his souldiers slaine, himselfe disarm'd,	Jew	1.2.204	Barab
rests no more/But bare remembrance; like a souldiers skarre,	Jew	2.1.10	Barab
I'le lead five hundred souldiers through the Vault,	Jew	5.1.91	Barab
And in an out-house of the City shut/His souldiers, till I have	Jew	5.2.82	Barab
First to surprize great Selims souldiers,	Jew	5.2.118	Barab
serve to entertaine/Selim and all his souldiers for a month;	Jew	5.3.31	Msngr
Blowne up, and all thy souldiers massacred.	Jew	5.5.107	Govnr
As Caesar to his souldiers, so say I:	P 155	2.98	Guise
Farewell, and perish by a souldiers hand,	Edw	1.1.37	3PrMan
These will I sell to give my souldiers paye,	Edw	1.1.104	Lncstr
While souldiers mutinie for want of paie.	Edw	1.4.406	Mortmr
But once, and then thy souldiers marcht like players,	Edw	2.2.183	Mortmr
Upon him souldiers, take away his weapons.	Edw	2.5.8	Warwck
Shame and dishonour to a souldiers name,	Edw	2.5.12	Mortmr
Go souldiers take him hence, for by my sword,	Edw	2.5.20	Warwck
Souldiers, have him away:	Edw	2.5.26	Warwck
Souldiers away with him.	Edw	2.5.45	Warwck
Souldiers away with him:	Edw	2.5.50	Mortmr
Souldiers a largis, and thrice welcome all.	Edw	3.1.57	Edward
Souldiers, good harts, defend your soveraignes right,	Edw	3.1.182	Edward
Souldiers, let me but talke to him one worde.	Edw	5.3.53	Kent
I'le leavy souldiers with the coyne they bring,	F 119	1.1.91	Faust
• Then Souldiers boldly fight; if Faustus die,	F1346	4.2.22	Benvol
Come souldiers, follow me unto the grove,	F1348	4.2.24	Fredrk
Thou with these souldiers conquerest gods and men,	Ovid's Elegies		1.2.37
Souldiers must travaile farre:	Ovid's Elegies		1.9.9
SOULDIORS			
Then noble souldiors, to intrap these theeves,	1Tamb	2.2.59	Meandr
SOULDIOUR			
Who but a souldiour or a lover is bould/To suffer storme mixt	Ovid's Elegies		1.9.15
Why me that alwayes was thy souldiour found,	Ovid's Elegies		2.9.3

SOULDIOUR (cont.)			
The weary souldiour hath the conquerd fields,	Ovid's Elegies	2.9.19	
Let souldiour <souldiours> chase his <their> enemies amaine,	Ovid's Elegies	2.10.31	
I guide and souldiour wunne the field and weare her,	Ovid's Elegies	2.12.13	
Souldiour applaud thy Mars:	Ovid's Elegies	3.2.49	
SOULDIOURS			
The violence of thy common Souldiours lust?	2Tamb	4.3.80	Orcan
What yeares in souldiours Captaines do require,	Ovid's Elegies	1.9.5	
The keepers hands and corps-dugard to passe/The souldiours, and	Ovid's Elegies	1.9.28	
And souldiours make them ready to the fight,	Ovid's Elegies	1.13.14	
Let souldiour <souldiours> chase his <their> enemies amaine,	Ovid's Elegies	2.10.31	
And new sworne souldiours maiden armes retainst,	Ovid's Elegies	2.18.2	
Souldiours by bloud to be inricht have lucke.	Ovid's Elegies	3.7.54	
SOULDYER			
Souldyer.--	P 83	2.26	Guise
SOULE			
By Saturnes soule, and this earth threatning [haire] <aire>,	Dido	1.1.10	Jupitr
Beates forth my senses from this troubled soule,	Dido	2.1.116	Aeneas
Poore soule I know too well the sower of love,	Dido	3.1.61	Anna
That overcloy my soule with their content:	Dido	3.2.63	Juno
Whose armed soule alreadie on the sea,	Dido	3.2.83	Venus
That calles my soule from forth his living seate,	Dido	3.4.53	Dido
These words are poyson to poore Didos soule,	Dido	5.1.111	Dido
dye to expiate/The griefe that tires upon thine inward soule.	Dido	5.1.317	Iarbus
is that doth excruciate/The verie substance of my vexed soule:	1Tamb	1.1.114	Cosroe
What stronge enchantments tice my yeelding soule?	1Tamb	1.2.224	Therid
Where flames shall ever feed upon his soule.	1Tamb	2.6.8	Cosroe
An uncouth paine torments my grieved soule,	1Tamb	2.7.7	Cosroe
My soule begins to take her flight to hell:	1Tamb	2.7.44	Cosroe
Ah, life and soule still hover in his Breast,	1Tamb	3.2.21	Zenoc
Or els unite you to his life and soule,	1Tamb	3.2.23	Zenoc
And wrapt in silence of his angry soule.	1Tamb	3.2.71	Agidas
And makes my soule devine her overthrow.	1Tamb	3.2.87	Agidas
Wherewith he may excruciate thy soule.	1Tamb	3.2.104	Agidas
How can it but afflict my verie soule?	1Tamb	4.4.67	Zenoc
Whose sorrowes lay more siege unto my soule,	1Tamb	5.1.155	Tamb
With whose instinct the soule of man is toucht,	1Tamb	5.1.179	Tamb
And madnesse send his damned soule to hell.	1Tamb	5.1.229	Zabina
And sink not quite into my tortur'd soule.	1Tamb	5.1.263	Bajzth
I may poure foorth my soule into thine armes,	1Tamb	5.1.279	Bajzth
And my pin'd soule resolv'd in liquid [ayre] <ay>,	1Tamb	5.1.300	Bajzth
And tell my soule mor tales of bleeding ruth?	1Tamb	5.1.342	Zenoc
and feare presents/A thousand sorrowes to my martyred soule:	1Tamb	5.1.384	Zenoc
To drive all sorrow from my fainting soule:	1Tamb	5.1.429	Arabia
O sight thrice welcome to my joiful soule,	1Tamb	5.1.440	Zenoc
By him that made the world and sav'd my soule,	2Tamb	1.1.133	Sgsmnd
Be now reveng'd upon this Traitors soule,	2Tamb	2.2.58	Orcan
Now scaldes his soule in the Tartarian streames,	2Tamb	2.3.18	Orcan
Shall lead his soule through Orcus burning gulfe:	2Tamb	2.3.25	Orcan
And tempered every soule with lively heat,	2Tamb	2.4.10	Tamb
Whose darts do pierce the Center of my soule:	2Tamb	2.4.84	Tamb
For she is dead? thy words doo pierce my soule.	2Tamb	2.4.125	Tamb
Where ere her soule be, thou shalt stay with me/Embalm'd with	2Tamb	2.4.129	Tamb
From al the crueltie my soule sustaind,	2Tamb	3.1.33	Callap
And purge my soule before it come to thee.	2Tamb	3.4.33	Olymp
And guard the gates to entertaine his soule.	2Tamb	3.5.29	Orcan
That most may vex his body and his soule.	2Tamb	3.5.99	Callap
my striving hands/From martiall justice on thy wretched soule.	2Tamb	4.1.96	Tamb
Here Jove, receive his fainting soule againe,	2Tamb	4.1.111	Tamb
In sending to my issue such a soule,	2Tamb	4.1.122	Tamb
A fitter subject for a pensive soule.	2Tamb	4.2.27	Olymp
Making a passage for my troubled soule,	2Tamb	4.2.34	Olymp
Until my soule dissevered from this flesh,	2Tamb	4.3.131	Tamb
How is my scule environed,	2Tamb	5.1.34	Govnr
These cowards invisiblie assaile hys soule,	2Tamb	5.3.13	Therid
that the soule/Wanting those Organnons by which it mooves,	2Tamb	5.3.95	Phsitn
The breath cf life, and burthen of my soule,	2Tamb	5.3.186	Amyras
Denie my soule fruition of her joy,	2Tamb	5.3.194	Amyras
And send my soule before my father die,	2Tamb	5.3.208	Amyras
And eielesse Monster that torments my soule,	2Tamb	5.3.217	Tamb
And when my soule hath vertue of your sight,	2Tamb	5.3.225	Tamb
my soule dooth weepe to see/Your sweet desires depriv'd my	2Tamb	5.3.246	Tamb
Yet was his soule but flowne beyond the Alpes,	Jew	Prol.2	Machvl
To make attonement for my labouring soule.	Jew	1.2.326	Abigal
Strength to my soule, death to mine enemy;	Jew	2.1.49	Barab
my fingers take/A kisse from him that sends it from his soule.	Jew	2.1.59	Barab
No doubt your soule shall reape the fruit of it.	Jew	2.3.78	Lodowk
Now have I that for which my soule hath long'd.	Jew	2.3.318	Lodowk
My sinfull soule, alas, hath pac'd too long/The fatall	Jew	3.3.63	Abigal
For that will be most heavy to thy soule.	Jew	3.3.71	1Fryar
And she is hatefull to my soule and me:	Jew	3.4.36	Barab
the burthen of my sinnes/Lye heavy on my soule; then pray you	Jew	4.1.49	Barab
That would for Lucars sake have sold my soule.	Jew	4.1.53	Barab
Dye life, flye soule, tongue curse thy fill and dye.	Jew	5.5.89	Barab
(For whose effects my soule is massacred)/Infect thy gracious	P 192	3.27	QnMarg
And thou a traitor to thy soule and him.	P 342	5.69	Lorein
O no, his soule is fled from out his breast,	P 552	11.17	QnMoth
Ah this sweet sight is phisick to my soule,	P1020	19.90	King
But sorrow seaze upon my toyling soule,	P1089	19.159	QnMoth
And with their pawes drench his black soule in hell.	P1102	20.12	Cardnl
a death too good, the devill of hell/Torture his wicked soule.	P1219	22.81	Bartus
Is as Elizium to a new come soule.	Edw	1.1.11	Gavstn
no soule in hell/Hath felt more torment then poore Gaveston.	Edw	1.1.146	Gavstn

SOULE (cont.)			
And onely this torments my wretched soule,	Edw	1.4.123	Edward
Aye me poore soule when these begin to jarre.	Edw	2.2.72	Queene
To whome right well you knew our soule was knit,	Edw	3.1.227	Edward
For such outragious passions cloye my soule,	Edw	5.1.19	Edward
Even so betide my soule as I use him.	Edw	5.1.148	Bartly
Alas poore soule, would I could ease his greefe.	Edw	5.2.26	Queene
That waites upon my poore distressed soule,	Edw	5.3.38	Edward
Let this gift change thy minde, and save thy soule,	Edw	5.5.88	Edward
Assist me sweete God, and receive my soule.	Edw	5.5.109	Edward
And gaze not on it least it tempt thy soule,	F 98	1.1.70	GdAngl
Nothing Cornelius; O this cheeres my soule:	F 176	1.1.148	Faust
The danger of his soule would make me mourne:	F 224	1.2.31	2Schol
We flye in hope to get his glorious soule:	F 277	1.3.49	Mephst
Which [strike] <strikes> a terror to my fainting soule.	F 310	1.3.82	Mephst
Say he surrenders up to him his soule,	F 318	1.3.90	Faust
that <I know> he would give his soule to the devill, for a	F 350	1.4.8	P Wagner
So he will buy my service with his soule.	F 421	2.1.33	Mephst
And tell me, what good will my soule do thy Lord?	F 428	2.1.40	Faust
But tell me Faustus, shall I have thy soule?	F 434	2.1.46	Mephst
And bind thy soule, that at some certaine day/Great Lucifer may	F 439	2.1.51	Mephst
bloud/Assures his <assure my> soule to be great Lucifers,	F 444	2.1.56	Faust
Faustus gives to thee his soule: [ah] <O> there it staid.	F 456	2.1.68	Faust
Why shouldst thou not? is not thy soule thine owne?	F 457	2.1.69	Faust
Then write againe: Faustus gives to thee his soule.	F 458	2.1.70	Faust
What will not I do to obtaine his soule?	F 462	2.1.74	Mephst
And Faustus hath bequeath'd his soule to Lucifer.	F 464	2.1.76	Faust
A Deed of Gift, of body and of soule:	F 478	2.1.90	Faust
by these presents doe give both body and soule to Lucifer,	F 494	2.1.106	P Faust
carry the said John Faustus, body and soule, flesh [and] bloud,	F 498	2.1.110	P Faust
In which <Wherein> thou hast given thy soule to Lucifer.	F 520	2.1.132	Mephst
'Tis thou hast damn'd distressed Faustus soule.	F 628	2.2.77	Faust
Helpe <seeke> to save distressed Faustus soule.	F 635	2.2.84	Faust
Christ cannot save thy soule, for he is just,	F 636	2.2.85	Lucifr
O Faustus they are come to fetch <away> thy soule.	F 641	2.2.90	Faust
O how this sight doth delight <this feedes> my soule.	F 712	2.2.164	Faust
Damb'd be this soule for ever, for this deed.	F1070	3.2.90	Pope
Hell take his soule, his body thus must fall.	F1363	4.2.39	Benvol
This Magicke, that will charme thy soule to hell,	F1708	5.1.35	OldMan
Yet, yet, thou hast an amiable soule,	F1712	5.1.39	OldMan
Checking thy body, may amend thy soule.	F1723	5.1.50	OldMan
Offers to poure the same into thy soule,	F1732	5.1.59	OldMan
I feele thy words to comfort my distressed soule,	F1735	5.1.62	Faust
Fearing the enemy <ruine> of thy haplesse <hopelesse> soule.	F1738	5.1.65	OldMan
Thou traytor Faustus, I arrest thy soule,	F1743	5.1.70	Mephst
His faith is great, I cannot touch his soule;	F1756	5.1.83	Mephst
Her lips sucke <suckes> forth my soule, see where it flies.	F1771	5.1.98	Faust
Come Hellen, come, give me my soule againe,	F1772	5.1.99	Faust
[That from thy soule exclud'st the grace of heaven],	F1789	5.1.116A	OldMan
To wait upon thy soule; the time is come/Which makes it	F1802	5.2.6	Lucifr
A surfet of deadly sin, that hath damn'd both body and soule.	F1834	5.2.38	P Faust
Gush forth bloud in stead of teares, yea life and soule:	F1852	5.2.56	P Faust
[Ah] <O> gentlemen, I gave them my soule for my cunning.	F1856	5.2.60	Faust
to fetch me <both> body and soule, if I once gave eare to	F1866	5.2.70	P Faust
And now poore soule must thy good Angell leave thee,	F1907	5.2.111	GdAngl
That Faustus may repent, and save his soule.	F1934	5.2.138	Faust
One drop [would save my soule, halfe a drop, ah] my Christ.	F1940	5.2.144	Faust
[So that] my soule [may but] ascend to heaven.	F1956	5.2.160	Faust
<But let my soule mount and> ascend to heaven.	F1956	(HC271)B	Faust
<O, if my soule must suffer for my sinne>,	F1958	(HC271)B	Faust
[O God, if thou wilt not have mercy on my soule],	F1958	5.2.162A	Faust
Why wert thou not a creature wanting soule?	F1964	5.2.168	Faust
This soule should flie from me, and I be chang'd/[Unto] <Into>	F1967	5.2.171	Faust
O soule be chang'd into <to> [little] <small> water drops,	F1977	5.2.181	Faust
he would give his soule to the Divel for a shoulder of mutton,	F App	p.229 8	P Wagner
soule to the Divel for a shoulder of mutton though twere blood	F App	p.229 10	P Clown
It grieves my soule I never saw the man:	F App	p.237 28	Emper
The stench whereof corrupts the inward soule/With such	F App	p.243 41	OldMan
Aye me poore soule, why is my cause so good.	Ovid's Elegies		2.5.8
And in the midst thereof, set my soule going,	Ovid's Elegies		2.10.36
Shall I poore soule be never interdicted?	Ovid's Elegies		2.19.53
With these thy soule walkes, soules if death release,	Ovid's Elegies		3.8.65
But let not mee poore soule know of thy straying.	Ovid's Elegies		3.13.2
My soule fleetes when I thinke what you have done,	Ovid's Elegies		3.13.37
At one selfe instant, she poore soule assaies,	Hero and Leander		1.362
Whereat agast, the poore soule gan to crie,	Hero and Leander		2.177
SOULES			
Our kinsmens [lives] <loves>, and thousand guiltles soules,	Dido	4.4.90	Aeneas
And both our soules aspire celestiall thrones.	1Tamb	1.2.237	Tamb
Our soules, whose faculties can comprehend/The wondrous	1Tamb	2.7.21	Tamb
their bodies, and prevent their soules/From heavens of comfort,	1Tamb	5.1.89	1Virgn
A sight as banefull to their soules I think/As are Thessalian	1Tamb	5.1.132	Tamb
And make our soules resolve in ceasles teares:	1Tamb	5.1.272	Bajzth
Millions of soules sit on the bankes of Styx,	1Tamb	5.1.463	Tamb
As Centinels to warne th'immortall soules,	2Tamb	2.4.16	Tamb
The God that tunes this musicke to our soules,	2Tamb	2.4.31	Tamb
And carie both our soules, where his remaines.	2Tamb	3.4.17	Olymp
Poore soules they looke as if their deaths were neere.	2Tamb	3.5.61	Usumc
Expell the hate wherewith he paines our soules.	2Tamb	4.1.173	Orcan
And now the damned soules are free from paine,	2Tamb	4.2.91	Therid
our hearts/More than the thought of this dooth vexe our soules.	2Tamb	5.1.145	Jrslem
to lode thy barke/With soules of thousand mangled carkasses.	2Tamb	5.3.74	Tamb
And weary Death with bearing soules to hell.	2Tamb	5.3.77	Tamb

SOULES (cont.)

Your paines do pierce our soules, no hope survives,	2Tamb	5.3.166	Celeb
More than the ruine of our proper soules.	2Tamb	5.3.182	Therid
I banne their soules to everlasting paines/And extreme tortures	Jew	1.2.166	Barab
For whilst I live, here lives my soules sole hope,	Jew	2.1.29	Barab
As these have spoke so be it to their soules:--	Jew	5.1.42	Barab
Spencer, I see our soules are fleeted hence,	Edw	4.7.105	Baldck
But leaving these vaine trifles of mens soules,	F 289	1.3.61	Faust
Had I as many soules, as there be Starres,	F 330	1.3.102	Faust
As great as have the humane soules of men.	F 433	2.1.45	Mephst
<Then theres inough for a thousand soules>,	F 477	(HC260)A	Faust
Curst be your soules to hellish misery.	F1034	3.2.54	Pope
Those soules which sinne seales the blacke sonnes of hell,	F1799	5.2.3	Lucifr
There are the Furies tossing damned soules,	F1911	5.2.115	BdAngl
Is for ore-tortur'd soules to rest them in.	F1915	5.2.119	BdAngl
<O> No end is limited to damned soules.	F1963	5.2.167	Faust
Their soules are soone dissolv'd in elements,	F1970	5.2.174	Faust
Upon whose altars thousand soules do lie,	F App	p.235 36	Mephst
And Carthage soules be glutted with our blouds;	Lucan, First Booke		39
Whether now shal these olde bloudles soules repaire?	Lucan, First Booke		343
immortal pens/Renowne the valiant soules slaine in your wars,	Lucan, First Booke		444
That soules passe not to silent Erebus/Or Plutoes bloodles	Lucan, First Booke		451
Soules quiet and appeas'd [sigh'd] <sight> from their graves,	Lucan, First Booke		566
And crowing Cocks poore soules to worke awake.	Ovid's Elegies		1.6.66
May spelles and droughs <drugges> do sillie soules such harmes?	Ovid's Elegies		3.6.28
With these thy soule walkes, soules if death release,	Ovid's Elegies		3.8.65
and higher set/The drooping thoughts of base declining soules,	Hero and Leander		2.257

SOUND (Homograph)

To sound this angrie message in thine eares.	Dido	5.1.33	Hermes
But Menaphon, what means this trumpets sound?	1Tamb	1.1.133	Cosroe
Sound up the trumpets then, God save the King.	1Tamb	1.1.188	Ortyg
Drums, why sound ye not when Meander speaks.	1Tamb	2.2.75	Mycet
Thou art deceiv'd, I heard the Trumpets sound,	1Tamb	3.3.203	Zabina
And they will (trembling) sound a quicke retreat,	2Tamb	1.1.150	Orcan
The trumpets sound, Zenocrate, they come.	2Tamb	1.3.111	Tamb
Our faiths are sound, and must be [consumate] <consinuate>,	2Tamb	2.1.47	Sgsmnd
the Nuns are dead/That sound at other times like Tinkers pans?	Jew	4.1.3	Barab
Must tuna my Lute for sound, twang twang first.	Jew	4.4.31	Barab
Sound a charge there.	Jew	5.5.63	1Knght
Why, hardst thou not the trumpet sound a charge?	Jew	5.5.105	Govnr
To think a word of such a simple sound,	P 125	2.68	Guise
And yet didst never sound any thing to the depth.	P 386	7.26	Guise
Returne him on your honor. Sound, away.	Edw	2.5.98	Mortmr
Why do we sound retreat?	Edw	3.1.185	Edward
What rebels, do you shrinke, and sound retreat?	Edw	3.1.200	Edward
Sound drums and trumpets, marche with me my friends,	Edw	3.1.260	Edward
Sound trumpets my lord and forward let us martch,	Edw	4.4.28	SrJohn
The trumpets sound, I must go take my place.	Edw	5.4.72	Mortmr
None comes, sound trumpets.	Edw	5.4.79	Mortmr
and begin/To sound the depth of that thou wilt professe,	F 30	1.1.2	Faust
[Is not thy common talke sound Aphorismes]?	F 47	1.1.19A	Faust
A sound Magitian is a Demi-god <mighty god>,	F 89	1.1.61	Faust
walles of Thebes/With ravishing sound of his melodious Harpe,	F 580	2.2.29	Faust
Sound Trumpets then, for thus Saint Peters Heire,	F 875	3.1.97	Pope
And make them sleepe so sound, that in their shapes,	F 895	3.1.117	Faust
And with a solemne noyse of trumpets sound,	F1237	4.1.83	Faust
With cracke of riven ayre and hideous sound,	Lucan, First Booke		153
Which makes the maine saile fal with hideous sound;	Lucan, First Booke		498
And Marriners, albeit the keele be sound,	Lucan, First Booke		500
Trumpets were heard to sound; and with what noise/An armed	Lucan, First Booke		577
or do the turned hinges sound,/And opening dores with creaking	Ovid's Elegies		1.6.49
Thou spokest thy words so well with stammering sound.	Ovid's Elegies		2.6.24
With joy heares Neptunes swelling waters sound.	Ovid's Elegies		3.10.30
Here when the Pipe with solemne tunes doth sound,	Ovid's Elegies		3.12.11
Whose sound allures the golden Morpheus,	Hero and Leander		1.349
And made his capring Triton sound alowd,	Hero and Leander		2.156
To sound foorth musicke to the Ocean,	Hero and Leander		2.328

SOUNDETH

O something soundeth in mine [eares] <eare>,/Abjure this	F 395	2.1.7	Faust

SOUNDING

Both barking Scilla, and the sounding Rocks,	Dido	1.1.146	Aeneas
In sounding through the world his partiall praise.	1Tamb	4.3.49	Arabia
let your sounding Drummes/Direct our Souldiers to Damascus	1Tamb	4.3.61	Souldn
Fame hovereth, sounding of her golden Trumpe:	2Tamb	3.4.63	Therid

SOUNDLY

Some surfetted, and others soundly slept.	Dido	2.1.179	Aeneas
Let them take pleasure soundly in their spoiles,	2Tamb	4.3.92	Tamb

SOUNDS

And Aeolus like Agamemnon sounds/The surges, his fierce	Dido	1.1.68	Venus
All fearefull foldes his sailes, and sounds the maine,	1Tamb	3.2.82	Agidas
Her trembling mouth these unmeete sounds expresses.	Ovid's Elegies		3.5.72

SOUR (See SOWRE)

SOUSE

Souse downe the wals, and make a passage forth:	Lucan, First Booke		296

SOUTH

And on the south Senus Arabicus,	2Tamb	4.3.104	Tamb
East and by-South:	Jew	1.1.41	Barab
Whether the gods, or blustring south were cause/I know not, but	Lucan, First Booke		236
Or waters tops with the warme south-winde taken.	Ovid's Elegies		1.7.56
Which stormie South-windes into sea did blowe?	Ovid's Elegies		2.6.44
Thou Goddesse doest command a warme South-blast,	Ovid's Elegies		2.8.19
Nor violent South-windes did thee ought affright.	Ovid's Elegies		2.11.52
And raging Seas in boistrous South-winds plough.	Ovid's Elegies		2.16.22

Line	Work	Ref.	Speaker
SOUTH-BLAST			
Thou Goddesse doest command a warme South-blast,	Ovid's Elegies		2.8.19
SOUTHERN			
And cause the stars fixt in the Southern arke,	2Tamb	3.2.29	Tamb
SOUTHERNE			
The kingly seate of Southerne Libia,	Dido	1.1.212	Venus
Whereas the Southerne winde with brackish breath,	Dido	1.2.28	Cloan
The ayre is cleere, and Southerne windes are whist,	Dido	4.1.25	Aeneas
We have subdude the Southerne Guallatia,	2Tamb	1.3.178	Usumc
Nor yet the adverse reking southerne pole,	Lucan, First Booke		54
With Icy Boreas, and the Southerne gale:	Ovid's Elegies		2.11.10
SOUTHSAYERS			
Apolloes southsayers; and Joves feasting priests;	Lucan, First Booke		601
SOUTH-WINDE			
Or waters tops with the warme south-winde taken.	Ovid's Elegies		1.7.56
SOUTH-WINDES			
Which stormie South-windes into sea did blowe?	Ovid's Elegies		2.6.44
Nor violent South-windes did thee ought affright.	Ovid's Elegies		2.11.52
SOUTH-WINDS			
And raging Seas in boistrous South-winds plough.	Ovid's Elegies		2.16.22
SOVERAIGN			
And neither Perseans Soveraign, nor the Turk/Troubled my sences	1Tamb	5.1.157	Tamb
Arme dread Soveraign and my noble Lords.	2Tamb	2.2.24	1Msngr
To hurt the noble man their soveraign loves.	P 259	4.57	Charls
SOVERAIGNE			
Flinging in favours of more soveraigne worth,	Dido	3.1.131	Dido
To waite upon him as their soveraigne Lord.	Dido	4.4.69	Dido
Not for so small a fault my soveraigne Lord.	1Tamb	1.1.25	Meandr
Doubt not my Lord and gratious Soveraigne,	1Tamb	1.1.70	Therid
That dar'st presume thy Soveraigne for to mocke.	1Tamb	1.1.105	Mycet
garrisons enough/To make me Soveraigne of the earth againe.	1Tamb	3.3.243	Bajzth
The braines of Bajazeth, my Lord and Soveraigne?	1Tamb	5.1.307	Zabina
My soveraigne Lord, renowmed Tamburlain,	2Tamb	1.2.7	Almeda
Live still my Lord, O let my soveraigne live,	2Tamb	2.4.57	Zenoc
That hath betraied my gracious Soveraigne,	2Tamb	3.2.153	Usumc
To false his service to his Soveraigne,	2Tamb	3.5.88	Tamb
And threaten conquest on our Soveraigne:	2Tamb	5.3.14	Therid
Hearing his Soveraigne was bound for Sea,	Jew	5.3.15	Msngr
Your Majestie her rightfull Lord and Soveraigne.	P 583	11.48	Pleshe
How they beare armes against their soveraigne.	P1187	22.49	King
Even so let hatred with thy [soveraignes] <soveraigne> smile.	Edw	1.4.342	Edward
Is this the love you beare your soveraigne?	Edw	2.2.30	Edward
To offer violence to his soveraigne,	Edw	2.4.34	Lncstr
against your king)/To see his royall soveraigne once againe.	Edw	2.5.7	Gavstn
Sweete soveraigne, yet I come/To see thee ere I die.	Edw	2.5.94	Gavstn
Were I king Edward, Englands soveraigne,	Edw	3.1.10	Spencr
Long live my soveraigne the noble Edward,	Edw	3.1.32	SpncrP
My lords, because our soveraigne sends for him,	Edw	3.1.109	Arundl
Rebels, will they appoint their soveraigne/His sports, his	Edw	3.1.174	Edward
thou chase/Thy lawfull king thy soveraigne with thy sword?	Edw	4.6.4	Kent
Earth melt to ayre, gone is my soveraigne,	Edw	4.7.103	Spencr
Or choake your soveraigne with puddle water?	Edw	5.3.30	Edward
That wronges their liege and soveraigne, Englands king.	Edw	5.3.40	Edward
For disobedience to my soveraigne Lord,	F1744	5.1.71	Mephst
My gratious Soveraigne, though I must confesse my selfe farre	F App	p.236 12	P Faust
Jove being admonisht gold had soveraigne power,	Ovid's Elegies		3.7.29
SOVERAIGNES			
Even so let hatred with thy [soveraignes] <soveraigne> smile.	Edw	1.4.342	Edward
Should by his soveraignes favour grow so pert,	Edw	1.4.404	Mortmr
Souldiers, good harts, defend your soveraignes right,	Edw	3.1.182	Edward
Why gape you for your soveraignes overthrow?	Edw	5.1.72	Edward
SOVERAIGNTIE			
That fiery thirster after Soveraigntie:	1Tamb	2.6.31	Cosroe
SOVERAINTIE			
Wherein by curious soveraintie of Art,	1Tamb	2.1.13	Menaph
SOVERAINTY			
Thirsting with soverainty, with love of armes:	1Tamb	2.1.20	Menaph
And plead in vaine, unpleasing soverainty.	2Tamb	5.3.198	Amyras
SOVERERAIGNE			
Then feeles your majesty no sovereraigne ease,	2Tamb	5.3.213	Usumc
SOW'D			
Her eyes and lookes sow'd seeds of perjury,	P 695	13.39	Guise
SOWER			
Poore soule I know too well the sower of love,	Dido	3.1.61	Anna
SOWLE			
fondlie hast thow in censte the guises sowle	Paris	ms25,p391	Guise
SOWRE			
Though her sowre looks a Sabines browe resemble,	Ovid's Elegies		2.4.15
SOWRING			
Full often am I sowring up to heaven,	Edw	5.1.21	Edward
SOYLE			
The ayre is pleasant, and the soyle most fit/For Cities, and	Dido	1.1.178	Achat
Some to the mountaines, some unto the soyle,	Dido	3.3.61	Dido
A small, but wholesome soyle with watrie veynes.	Ovid's Elegies		2.16.2
SPACE			
And when they chance to breath and rest a space,	1Tamb	3.3.51	Tamb
And that you lay for pleasure here a space,	Edw	5.1.3	Leistr
This ten dayes space, and least that I should sleepe,	Edw	5.5.60	Edward
Thorough a rocke of stone in one nights space:	F 793	3.1.15	Faust
spread these flags that ten years space have conquer'd,	Lucan, First Booke		348
An old wood, stands uncut of long yeares space,	Ovid's Elegies		3.1.1
Foole canst thou lie in his enfolding space?	Ovid's Elegies		3.7.12
Our verse great Tityus a huge space out-spreads,	Ovid's Elegies		3.11.25

SPACIOUS (See SPATIOUS)

SPAINE

And bring Armados from the coasts of Spaine, 2Tamb 1.2.34 Callap
And all the land unto the coast of Spaine. 2Tamb 1.3.179 Usumc
My Ship, the flying Dragon, is of Spaine, Jew 2.2.5 Bosco
Now where's the hope you had of haughty Spaine? Jew 5.2.3 Calym
from Spaine the stately Catholickes/Sends Indian golde to coyne P 117 2.60 Guise
For feare that Guise joyn'd with the King of Spaine, P 573 11.38 Navrre
In spite of Spaine and all the popish power, P 581 11.46 Pleshe
I meane the Guise, the Pope, and King of Spaine, P 701 14.4 Navrre
Spaine is the counsell chamber of the pope, P 709 14.12 Navrre
Spaine is the place where he makes peace and warre, P 710 14.13 Navrre
And Guise for Spaine hath now incenst the King, P 711 14.14 Navrre
In spite of Spaine and all his heresies. P 716 14.19 Bartus
The Pope and King of Spaine are thy good frends, P 843 17.38 Eprnon
I, and the catholick Philip King of Spaine, P 852 17.47 Guise
Sonne to the lovelie Elenor of Spaine, Edw 3.1.11 Spencr
And make that Country <land>, continent to Spaine, F 336 1.3.108 Faust

SPAINES

Did he not cause the King of Spaines huge fleete, P1033 19.103 King

SPAKE

Mortimer hardly, Penbrooke and Lancaster/Spake least: Edw 3.1.106 Arundl
there spake a Doctor indeed, and 'faith Ile drinke a health to F1626 4.6.69 P HrsCsr
How now, whose that which spake? F App p.231 3 P Pope
thus Curio spake,/And therewith Caesar prone ennough to warre, Lucan, First Booke 292
And thus he spake: Lucan, First Booke 300
skill in stars, and tune-full planeting,/In this sort spake. Lucan, First Booke 641
As thus she spake, my shadow me betraide, Ovid's Elegies 1.8.109
And as shee spake those words, came somewhat nere him. Hero and Leander 1.180
To Venus, answered shee, and as shee spake, Hero and Leander 1.295
Come thither; As she spake this, her toong tript, Hero and Leander 1.357
And as he spake, upon the waves he springs. Hero and Leander 2.206

SPANGLED

And sticke these spangled feathers in thy hat, Dido 2.1.314 Venus
on his silver crest/A snowy Feather spangled white he beares, 1Tamb 4.1.51 2Msngr
Even from the fiery spangled vaile of heaven, 1Tamb 5.1.185 Tamb
Spangled with Diamonds dancing in the aire, 2Tamb 4.3.117 Tamb
Nodding and shaking of thy spangled crest, Edw 2.2.186 Mortmr
There, he who rules the worlds starre-spangled towers, Ovid's Elegies 3.9.21
The aire with sparkes of living fire was spangled, Hero and Leander 1.188

SPANIELS

We Jewes can fawne like Spaniels when we please; Jew 2.3.20 Barab

SPANISH

That bought my Spanish Oyles, and Wines of Greece, Jew 1.1.5 Barab
we were wafted by a Spanish Fleet/That never left us till Jew 1.1.95 2Merch
Because we vail'd not to the [Turkish] <Spanish> Fleet,/Their Jew 2.2.11 Bosco
As Indian Moores, obey their Spanish Lords, F 148 1.1.120 Valdes
the darke/(Swifter then bullets throwne from Spanish slinges, Lucan, First Booke 231
The Ocean swell'd, as high as Spanish Calpe, Lucan, First Booke 553

SPARCKLED

By those white limmes, which sparckled through the lawne. Hero and Leander 2.242

SPARCKLES

Thinking to quench the sparckles new begonne. Hero and Leander 2.138

SPAR'D

Peace, Ithimore, 'tis better so then spar'd. Jew 3.4.91 Barab

SPARE

And spare our lives whom every spite pursues. Dido 1.2.9 Illion
Goe goe and spare not, seeke out Italy, Dido 5.1.169 Dido
I will not spare these proud Egyptians, 1Tamb 5.1.121 Tamb
Assault and spare not, we wil never yeeld. 2Tamb 5.1.62 Govnr
So they spare me, my daughter, and my wealth. Jew 1.1.153 Barab
unto Roan, and spare not one/That you suspect of heresy. P 446 7.86 Guise
No, spare his life, but seaze upon his goods, Edw 1.1.193 Edward
Spare for no cost, we will requite your love, Edw 1.4.383 Edward
But neither spare you Gaveston, nor his friends. Edw 2.3.28 Lncstr
And Spencer, spare them not, but lay it on. Edw 3.1.56 Edward
O spare me, or dispatche me in a trice. Edw 5.5.111 Edward
So he will spare him foure and twenty yeares, F 319 1.3.91 Faust
Fall to, the Divell choke you an you spare. F1039 3.2.59 Faust
I and spare not: F1102 3.3.15 P Robin
him o're hedge and ditch, and spare him not; but do you heare? F1468 4.4.12 P Faust
bad me ride him night and day, and spare him no time; but, F1540 4.5.36 P HrsCsr
Yet will I call on him: O spare me Lucifer. F1942 5.2.146 Faust
Fall too, and the divel choake you and you spare. F App p.231 2 P Faust
And shame to spare life which being lost is wonne. Lucan, First Booke 458
Bescratch mine eyes, spare not my lockes to breake, Ovid's Elegies 1.7.65
And sister, Nurse, and mother spare him not, Ovid's Elegies 1.8.91
They well become thee, then to spare them turne. Ovid's Elegies 1.14.28
Turne thy lookes hether, and in one spare twaine, Ovid's Elegies 2.13.15
But spare my wench thou at her right hand seated, Ovid's Elegies 3.2.21
Spare me, O by our fellow bed, by all/The Gods who by thee to Ovid's Elegies 3.10.45

SPARED

to request/He might be spared to come to speake with us, Edw 3.1.235 Edward

SPARETH

Wherein he spareth neither man nor child, 2Tamb 5.1.30 1Citzn

SPARGO

et consecratam aquam quam nunc spargo; signumque crucis quod F 249 1.3.21 P Faust

SPARING

Not sparing any that can manage armes. 1Tamb 4.1.57 2Msngr
I must have one that's sickly, and be but for sparing vittles: Jew 2.3.124 P Barab
And scorn'd old sparing diet, and ware robes/Too light for Lucan, First Booke 165

SPARKE

As long as any blood or sparke of breath/Can quench or coole 1Tamb 5.1.284 Zabina

SPARKE (cont.)			
Retaine a thought of joy, or sparke of life? . . .	2Tamb	5.3.163	Amyras
SPARKES			
And that the native sparkes of princely love, . . .	P 6	1.6	Charls
As for the multitude that are but sparkes, . . .	Edw	1.1.20	Gavstn
The aire with sparkes of living fire was spangled, . .	Hero and Leander		1.188
SPARKLE			
What sparkle does it give without a foile? . . .	Jew	2.3.55	Lodowk
Will sooner sparkle fire then shed a teare: . . .	Edw	5.1.105	Edward
SPARKLES (See also SPARCKLES)			
Whose amorous face like Pean sparkles fire, . . .	Dido	3.4.19	Dido
Lord Lodowicke, it sparkles bright and faire. . . .	Jew	2.3.58	Barab
SPARKLING			
Beauteous Rubyes, sparkling Diamonds, ...	Jew	1.1.27	Barab
As much as sparkling Diamonds flaring glasse. . . .	Hero and Leander		1.214
SPARROWES			
Where sparrowes pearcht, of hollow pearle and gold, . .	Hero and Leander		1.33
God knowes I play/With Venus swannes and sparrowes all the day.	Hero and Leander		1.352
SPARTAN			
And this a Spartan Courtier vaine and wilde, . . .	Dido	3.1.157	Dido
SPATIOUS			
Butcherd the flocks he found in spatious field, . .	Ovid's Elegies		1.7.8
But never give a spatious time to ire, ...	Ovid's Elegies		1.8.81
SPEACH			
No speach to that end, by your favour sir. . . .	2Tamb	1.2.14	Almeda
And til by vision, or by speach I heare/Immortall Jove say,	2Tamb	4.1.198	Tamb
SPEAD			
[Spread] <Spead>, spread these flags that ten years space have	Lucan, First Booke		348
SPEAK (See also SPAKE, SPEEK)			
I would intreat you to speak but three wise wordes. . .	1Tamb	2.4.25	Tamb
How like you that sir king? why speak you not? . . .	2Tamb	4.3.53	Celeb
down, heer's one would speak with you from the Duke of Guise.	P 348	6.3	P SrnsWf
O good my Lord, let me but speak a word.	P 399	7.39	Ramus
What art thou dead, sweet sonne speak to thy Mother.	P 551	11.16	QnMoth
Faine would I finde some means to speak with him/But cannot,	P 662	13.6	Duchss
My Lord, to speak more plainely, thus it is: . . .	P 847	17.42	Guise
Nay, they fear'd not to speak in the streetes, . . .	P 876	17.71	Eprnon
Oh I have my deaths wound, give me leave to speak. . .	P1003	19.73	Guise
I cannot speak for greefe: when thou wast borne, . .	P1072	19.142	QnMoth
My Lord, here me but speak.	P1129	21.23	P Frier
Why then my lord, give me but leave to speak. . . .	Edw	1.4.254	Mortmr
Speak softly sir, least the devil heare you: . . .	F1180	4.1.26	Mrtino
SPEAKE			
Achates, speake, for I am overjoyed.	Dido	2.1.54	Aeneas
Remember who thou art, speake like thy selfe, . . .	Dido	2.1.100	Dido
Looke up and speake.	Dido	2.1.120	Dido
Then speake Aeneas with Achilles tongue, ...	Dido	2.1.121	Aeneas
Achates speake, sorrow hath tired me quite. . . .	Dido	2.1.293	Aeneas
In stead of musicke I will heare him speake, . . .	Dido	3.1.89	Dido
But speake Aeneas, know you none of these? . . .	Dido	3.1.148	Dido
O if I speake/I shall betray my selfe:--	Dido	3.1.172	Dido
Aeneas speake,/We two will goe a hunting in the woods,	Dido	3.1.173	Dido
And yet Ile speake, and yet Ile hold my peace, . . .	Dido	3.4.27	Dido
Hard hearted, wilt not deigne to heare me speake? . .	Dido	4.2.54	Anna
O princely Dido, give me leave to speake, ...	Dido	4.4.17	Aeneas
Speake of no other land, this land is thine, . . .	Dido	4.4.83	Dido
Now speake Ascanius, will ye goe or no?	Dido	4.5.12	Nurse
O speake like my Aeneas, like my love:	Dido	5.1.112	Dido
Call him not wicked, sister, speake him faire, . . .	Dido	5.1.200	Dido
Away with her, suffer her not to speake.	Dido	5.1.224	Dido
Made me suppose he would have heard me speake: . . .	Dido	5.1.230	Anna
And speake of Tamburlaine as he deserves.	1Tamb	3.2.36	Zenoc
View well my Camp, and speake indifferently, . . .	1Tamb	3.3.8	Tamb
Wel said Theridamas, speake in that mood, ...	1Tamb	3.3.40	Tamb
I speake it, and my words are oracles.	1Tamb	3.3.102	Tamb
But speake, what power hath he?	1Tamb	4.1.20	Souldn
I, even I speake to her.	1Tamb	5.1.314	P Zabina
but yet if Sigismond/Speake as a friend, and stand not upon	2Tamb	1.1.123	Orcan
Yet heare me speake my gentle Almeda.	2Tamb	1.2.13	Callap
Away with him hence, let him speake no more: . . .	2Tamb	5.1.125	Tamb
Though some speake openly against my bookes, . . .	Jew	Prol.10	Machvl
'Tis in the trouble of my spirit I speake;	Jew	1.2.207	Barab
And speake of spirits and ghosts that glide by night/About the	Jew	2.1.26	Barab
That when we speake with Gentiles like to you, . . .	Jew	2.3.45	Barab
This Moore is comeliest, is he not? speake son. . .	Jew	2.3.144	Mater
Daughter, a word more; kisse him, speake him faire, . .	Jew	2.3.234	Barab
Stay her,--but let her not speake one word more. . .	Jew	2.3.323	Barab
And say, I pray them come and speake with me. . . .	Jew	3.3.29	Abigal
And so doe I, master, therfore speake 'em faire. . .	Jew	4.1.27	Ithimr
Oh speake not of her, then I dye with griefe. . . .	Jew	4.1.36	Barab
Bernardine--/Wilt thou not speake?	Jew	4.1.169	1Fryar
Let me alone, doe but you speake him faire: . . .	Jew	4.2.63	Pilia
Speake, shall I have 'um, Sir?	Jew	4.3.49	Pilia
What e're I am, yet Governor heare me speake; . . .	Jew	5.1.9	Curtzn
you men of Malta, heare me speake;/Shee is a Curtezane and he a	Jew	5.1.36	Barab
speake, had it not beene much better/To [have] kept thy promise	Jew	5.2.4	Calym
speake,/Will every savour breed a pangue of death? . .	P 71	2.14	Guise
O Mounser de Guise, heare me but speake.	P 529	10.2	Prtsnt
Villaine, why dost thou look so gastly? speake. . .	P 989	19.59	Guise
But yet it is no paine to speake men faire, . . .	Edw	1.1.42	Gavstn
But now ile speake, and to the proofe I hope: . . .	Edw	1.1.108	Kent
I cannot, nor I will not, I must speake.	Edw	1.1.122	Mortmr
All stomack him, but none dare speake a word. . . .	Edw	1.2.26	Lncstr

SPEAKE (cont.)

My lords, to eaze all this, but heare me speake.	Edw	1.2.68	ArchBp
It bootes me not to threat, I must speake faire,	Edw	1.4.63	Edward
Speake not unto her, let her droope and pine.	Edw	1.4.162	Edward
I must entreat him, I must speake him faire,	Edw	1.4.183	Queene
Then speake not for him, let the pesant go.	Edw	1.4.218	Warwck
Tis for my selfe I speake, and not for him.	Edw	1.4.219	Queene
It is impossible, but speake your minde.	Edw	1.4.228	Mortmr
That cannot speake without propterea quod.	Edw	2.1.53	Baldck
Why, so he may, but we will speake to him.	Edw	2.2.136	Lncstr
Nay, now you are heere alone, ile speake my minde.	Edw	2.2.155	Mortmr
Sweet unckle speake more kindly to the queene.	Edw	2.2.228	Neece
My lord, dissemble with her, speake her faire.	Edw	2.2.229	Gavstn
And all in vaine, for when I speake him faire,	Edw	2.4.28	Queene
O shall I speake, or shall I sigh and die!	Edw	3.1.122	Edward
to request/He might be spared to come to speake with us,	Edw	3.1.235	Edward
Call them againe my lorde, and speake them faire,	Edw	5.1.91	Leistr
Call thou them back, I have no power to speake.	Edw	5.1.93	Edward
Speake, shall he presently be dispatch'd and die?	Edw	5.2.44	Mortmr
Speake curstlie to him, and in any case/Let no man comfort him,	Edw	5.2.63	Mortmr
Did you attempt his rescue, Edmund speake?	Edw	5.4.86	Mortmr
Sonne, be content, I dare not speake a worde.	Edw	5.4.96	Queene
Let me but stay and speake, I will not go,	Edw	5.4.105	Kent
O speake no more my lorde, this breakes my heart.	Edw	5.5.71	Ltborn
Now as I speake they fall, and yet with feare/Open againe.	Edw	5.5.95	Edward
Why speake you not unto my lord the king?	Edw	5.6.38	1Lord
And I shall pitie her if she speake againe.	Edw	5.6.86	King
And speake for Faustus in his infancie.	F 10	Prol.10	1Chor
set my countenance like a Precisian, and begin to speake thus:	F 214	1.2.21	P Wagner
this wine, if it could speake, <it> would informe your Worships:	F 216	1.2.23	P Wagner
Did not my conjuring [speeches] raise thee? speake.	F 273	1.3.45	Faust
What meanes this shew? speake Mephostophilis.	F 472	2.1.84	Faust
Speake Faustus, do you deliver this as your Deed?	F 501	2.1.113	Mephst
Speake <Tel me>, are there many Spheares <heavens> above the	F 586	2.2.35	Faust
not speake a word more for a Kings ransome <an other worde>,	F 669	2.2.118	P Pride
I'le not speake <an other word for a King's raunsome>.	F 706	(HC264)A	P Sloth
I'le not speake <a word more for a kings ransome>.	F 706	(HC264)B	P Sloth
I'le not speake [an other] word.	F 706	2.2.158	P Sloth
Do but speake what thou't have me to do, and I'le do't:	F 745	2.3.24	P Robin
Villaines why speake you not?	F1045	3.2.65	Pope
Speake, wilt thou come and see this sport?	F1193	4.1.39	Fredrk
But Faustus, since I may not speake to them,	F1263	4.1.109	Emper
him; and hereafter sir, looke you speake well of Schollers.	F1315	4.1.161	P Faust
Speake well of yee?	F1316	4.1.162	P Benvol
They all cry out to speake with Doctor Faustus.	F1600	4.6.43	Servnt
I, and we will speake with him.	F1601	4.6.44	Carter
For gentle sonne, I speake it not in wrath,	F1719	5.1.46	OldMan
and sir knight, hereafter speake well of Scholers:	F App	p.238 85	P Faust
Alas sir, I have no more, I pray you speake for me.	F App	p.239 104	P HrsCsr
you cannot speake with him.	F App	p.240 139	P Mephst
But I wil speake with him.	F App	p.240 140	P HrsCsr
Ile speake with him now, or Ile breake his glasse-windowes	F App	p.240 142	P HrsCsr
And he have not slept this eight weekes Ile speake with him.	F App	p.240 145	P HrsCsr
whispered they, and none durst speake/And shew their feare,	Lucan, First Booke		259
Speake, when shall this thy long usurpt power end?	Lucan, First Booke		333
So be I may be bold to speake a truth,	Lucan, First Booke		361
Time passeth while I speake, give her my writ/But see that	Ovid's Elegies		1.11.15
[The world shall of Callimachus ever speake],	Ovid's Elegies		1.15.13
While I speake some fewe, yet fit words be idle.	Ovid's Elegies		2.2.2
to speake <say> troth,/Both short and long please me, for I	Ovid's Elegies		2.4.35
I sawe your nodding eye-browes much to speake,	Ovid's Elegies		2.5.15
While thus I speake, blacke dust her white robes ray:	Ovid's Elegies		3.2.41
I speake old Poets wonderfull inventions,	Ovid's Elegies		3.5.17
While thus I speake, the waters more abounded:	Ovid's Elegies		3.5.85
Forbare no wanton words you there would speake,	Ovid's Elegies		3.13.25
Faire creature, let me speake without offence,	Hero and Leander		1.199
Or speake to him who in a moment tooke,	Hero and Leander		2.308

SPEAKES

Like Illioneus speakes this Noble man,	Dido	2.1.47	Achat
Speakes not Aeneas like a Conqueror?	Dido	4.4.93	Dido
That when he speakes, drawes out his grisly beard,	Jew	4.3.7	Barab
Who when he speakes, grunts like a hog, and looks/Like one that	Jew	4.3.11	Barab
All that he speakes, is nothing, we are resolv'd.	Edw	1.4.251	Warwck
Traitor, in me my loving father speakes,	Edw	5.6.41	King
Bloud, he speakes terribly:	F1227	4.1.73	P Benvol
God forgive me, he speakes Dutch fustian:	F App	p.231 72	P Clown
Let others tell this, and what each one speakes/Beleeve, no	Ovid's Elegies		2.11.21

SPEAKEST

Villain, knowest thou to whom thou speakest?	1Tamb	4.4.39	P Usumc

SPEAKETH

How like his father speaketh he in all?	Dido	3.3.41	Anna
Lives like the Asse that Aesope speaketh of,	Jew	5.2.40	Barab

SPEAKING

No speaking will prevaile, and therefore cease.	Edw	1.4.220	Penbrk
View me, my becks, and speaking countenance:	Ovid's Elegies		1.4.17
Dead is that speaking image of mans voice,	Ovid's Elegies		2.6.37
My mouth in speaking did all birds excell.	Ovid's Elegies		2.6.62
A pleasant smiling cheeke, a speaking eye,	Hero and Leander		1.85

SPEAKS

Drums, why sound ye not when Meander speaks.	1Tamb	2.2.75	Mycet

SPEAK'ST

If ought of me thou speak'st in inward thought,	Ovid's Elegies		1.4.23

SPEAKST

Ful true thou speakst, and like thy selfe my lord,	1Tamb	1.1.49	Mycete

Text	Work	Ref	Speaker
SPEARE			
for that one Laocoon/Breaking a speare upon his hollow breast,	Dido	2.1.165	Aeneas
Neoptolemus/Setting his speare upon the ground, leapt forth,	Dido	2.1.184	Aeneas
and on his speare/The mangled head of Priams yongest sonne,	Dido	2.1.214	Aeneas
And loade his speare with Grecian Princes heads,	Dido	3.3.43	Aeneas
His speare, his shield, his horse, his armour, plumes,	1Tamb	4.1.60	2Msngr
I long to breake my speare upon his crest,	1Tamb	4.3.46	Arabia
(Albeit the Moores light Javelin or his speare/Sticks in his	Lucan, First Booke		213
Thy hands agree not with the warlike speare.	Ovid's Elegies		2.3.8
Did not Pelides whom his Speare did grieve,	Ovid's Elegies		2.9.7
SPEARES			
Not bloudie speares appearing in the ayre,	Dido	4.4.117	Dido
That in conceit bear Empires on our speares,	1Tamb	1.2.64	Tamb
With shivering speares enforcing thunderclaps,	1Tamb	3.2.80	Agidas
Shaking their swords, their speares and yron bils,	1Tamb	4.1.25	2Msngr
He now is seated on my horsmens speares,	1Tamb	5.1.114	Tamb
Sitting in scarlet on their armed speares.	1Tamb	5.1.118	Tamb
When al their riders chardg'd their quivering speares/Began to	1Tamb	5.1.332	Zenoc
And now my Lords, advance your speares againe,	2Tamb	3.2.43	Tamb
Come let us chardge our speares and pierce his breast,	2Tamb	5.3.58	Tamb
They whom the Lingones foild with painted speares,	Lucan, First Booke		398
SPEARLIKE			
Now spearlike, long; now like a spreading torch:	Lucan, First Booke		530
SPECIALL			
Have speciall care that no man sally forth/Till you shall heare	Jew	5.4.2	Govnr
And hath a speciall gift to forme a verbe.	Edw	2.1.55	Spencr
SPECIALLY			
lord, specially having so smal a walke, and so litle exercise.	1Tamb	4.4.105	P Therid
From time to time, but specially in this,	P 10	1.10	Navrre
And to the Queene of England specially,	P1207	22.69	King
SPECIFIED			
let peace be ratified/On these conditions specified before,	2Tamb	1.1.125	Orcan
SPECTACLE			
But see another bloody spectacle.	1Tamb	5.1.339	Zenoc
chiefe spectacle of the worldes preheminence, The bright	F App	p.237 24	P Emper
this spectacle/Stroake Caesars hart with feare, his hayre	Lucan, First Booke		194
SPECTACLES			
Now greatest spectacles the Praetor sends,	Ovid's Elegies		3.2.65
SPECULATION			
I'le live in speculation of this Art/Till Mephostophilis	F 341	1.3.113	Faust
SPED			
Nay chafe not man, we all are sped.	F1444	4.3.14	Mrtino
Or Layis of a thousand [wooers] <lovers> [sped] <spread>.	Ovid's Elegies		1.5.12
I know no maister of so great hire sped.	Ovid's Elegies		2.5.62
Then muse not, Cupids sute no better sped,	Hero and Leander		1.483
SPEECH (See also SPEACH)			
Nor speech bewraies ought humaine in thy birth,	Dido	1.1.190	Aeneas
As shall surpasse the wonder of our speech.	Dido	1.2.47	Serg
Is he not eloquent in all his speech?	Dido	3.1.65	Dido
What meanes faire Dido by this doubtfull speech?	Dido	3.4.31	Aeneas
And every speech be ended with a kisse:	Dido	4.3.54	Aeneas
For it requires a great and thundring speech:	1Tamb	1.1.3	Mycet
But when you see his actions [top] <stop> his speech,	1Tamb	2.3.26	Therid
Your speech will stay, or so extol his worth,	1Tamb	2.3.27	Therid
And speech more pleasant than sweet harmony:	1Tamb	3.3.121	Tamb
them leave Madam, this speech is a goodly refreshing to them.	1Tamb	4.4.32	P Techel
And sorrow stops the passage of my speech.	2Tamb	3.2.52	Celeb
My speech of war, and this my wound you see,	2Tamb	3.2.142	Tamb
Intreat 'em faire, and give them friendly speech,	Jew	1.2.286	Barab
Anger and wrathfull furie stops my speech.	Edw	1.4.42	Edward
Sweet Lord and King, your speech preventeth mine,	Edw	2.2.59	Gavstn
Cattell were seene that muttered humane speech:	Lucan, First Booke		559
I knew your speech (what do not lovers see)?	Ovid's Elegies		2.5.19
Vaine babling speech, and pleasant peace thou lovedst.	Ovid's Elegies		2.6.26
To empty aire may go my fearefull speech.	Ovid's Elegies		3.1.62
And usde all speech that might provoke and stirre.	Ovid's Elegies		3.6.12
Which makes him quickly re-enforce his speech,	Hero and Leander		1.313
And with smooth speech, her fancie to assay,	Hero and Leander		1.402
SPEECHE			
my lord pardon my speeche,/Did you retaine your fathers	Edw	3.1.15	Spencr
SPEECHES			
My Lord, such speeches to our princely sonnes,	2Tamb	1.3.85	Zenoc
No Madam, these are speeches fit for us,	2Tamb	1.3.88	Celeb
Here must no speeches passe, nor swords be drawne.	Jew	2.3.339	Barab
Sweete speeches, comedies, and pleasing showes,	Edw	1.1.56	Gavstn
Ye must not grow so passionate in speeches:	Edw	4.4.16	Mortmr
Thy speeches long agoe had easde my sorrowes,	Edw	5.1.6	Edward
Did not my conjuring [speeches] raise thee? speake.	F 273	1.3.45	Faust
heare [me] with patience, and tremble not at my speeches.	F1839	5.2.43	P Faust
Smooth speeches, feare and rage shall by thee ride,	Ovid's Elegies		1.2.35
My flatt'ring speeches soone wide open knocke.	Ovid's Elegies		3.1.46
And shaking sobbes his mouth for speeches beares.	Ovid's Elegies		3.8.12
And before folke immodest speeches shunne,	Ovid's Elegies		3.13.16
If you wey not ill speeches, yet wey mee:	Ovid's Elegies		3.13.36
But speeches full of pleasure and delight.	Hero and Leander		1.420
SPEECHLESSE			
By speechlesse lookes we guesse at things succeeding.	Ovid's Elegies		1.11.18
SPEED			
Returne with speed, time passeth swift away,	1Tamb	1.1.67	Mycet
We will with all the speed we can, provide/For Henries	P 562	11.27	QnMoth
And so they shall, if fortune speed my will,	P 601	12.14	King
A mighty army comes from France with speed:	P 725	14.28	1Msngr
But come my Lords, let us away with speed,	P 741	14.44	Navrre

SPEED (cont.)
Intending to dislodge my campe with speed. P 869 17.64 Guise
Pleshe, goe muster up our men with speed, P 916 18.17 Navrre
That I with speed should have beene put to death. P1118 21.12 Dumain
If I speed well, ile entertaine you all. Edw 1.1.46 Gavstn
Madam, we will that you with speed be shipt, Edw 3.1.81 Edward
To erect your sonne with all the speed we may, Edw 5.2.11 Mortmr
Away and bring us word <again> with speed. F 888 3.1.110 Pope
SPEEDE
Well, if he come a wooing he shall speede, Dido 4.5.36 Nurse
With speede he bids me saile to Italy, Dido 5.1.68 Aeneas
And yee be men,/Speede to the king. Edw 2.6.6 Gavstn
SPEEDIE
Do speedie execution on them all, Edw 3.1.254 Edward
SPEEDILY
Yeeld speedily the citie to our hands, 2Tamb 5.1.51 Therid
And therefore as speedily as I can perfourme, P 571 11.36 Navrre
SPEEDY
Being requirde, with speedy helpe relieve? Ovid's Elegies 2.9.8
SPEEDYE
And sends <send> his dutie by these speedye lines, P1169 22.31 Frier
SPEEK
To speek with me from such a man as he? P 350 6.5 Seroun
SPELLES
May spelles and droughs <drugges> do sillie soules such harmes? Ovid's Elegies 3.6.28
SPELS
And Spels of magicke from the mouthes of spirits, 2Tamb 4.2.64 Olymp
Such is the force of Magicke, and my spels. F 259 1.3.31 Faust
have a booke wherein I might beholde al spels and incantations, F 551.1 2.1.164A P Faust
With Magicke spels so compasse thee, F1002 3.2.22 Mephst
who comes to see/What wonders by blacke spels may compast be. F1198 4.1.44 Mrtino
Then if by powerfull Necromantick spels, F1209 4.1.55 Emper
SPENCER
Spencer,/Seeing that our Lord th'earle of Glosters Edw 2.1.1 Baldck
Spencer, thou knowest I hate such formall toies, Edw 2.1.44 Baldck
Spencer, stay you and beare me companie, Edw 2.1.74 Neece
Thy service Spencer shalbe thought upon. Edw 2.1.80 Neece
His name is Spencer, he is well alied, Edw 2.2.249 Gavstn
Then Spencer waite upon me, for his sake/Ile grace thee with a Edw 2.2.252 Edward
O tell me Spencer, where is Gaveston? Edw 2.4.1 Edward
Spencer and I will post away by land. Edw 2.4.6 Edward
Ah Spencer, not the riches of my realme/Can ransome him, ah he Edw 3.1.3 Edward
Yea gentle Spencer, we have beene too milde, Edw 3.1.24 Edward
Spencer, the father of Hugh Spencer there, Edw 3.1.40 SpncrP
Thy father Spencer? Edw 3.1.43 Edward
Spencer, this love, this kindnes to thy King, Edw 3.1.47 Edward
Spencer, I heere create thee earle of Wilshire, Edw 3.1.49 Edward
And Spencer, spare them not, but lay it on. Edw 3.1.56 Edward
Yea Spencer, traitors all. Edw 3.1.102 Edward
Spencer, sweet Spencer, I adopt thee heere, Edw 3.1.144 Edward
That from your princely person you remoove/This Spencer, as a Edw 3.1.162 Herald
see how I do devorce/Spencer from me: Edw 3.1.177 Edward
Read it Spencer. Edw 4.3.11 Edward
Spencer, as true as death,/He is in Englands ground, our Edw 4.3.21 Edward
Spencer, the father to that wanton Spencer, Edw 4.6.50 Rice
But wheres the king and the other Spencer fled? Edw 4.6.55 Mortmr
Spencer the sonne, created earle of Gloster, Edw 4.6.56 Rice
How Baldocke, Spencer, and their complices, Edw 4.6.78 Mortmr
Come Spencer, come Baldocke, come sit downe by me, Edw 4.7.16 Edward
Spencer and Baldocke, by no other names, Edw 4.7.56 Leistr
Spencer,/A sweet Spencer, thus then must we part Edw 4.7.72 Edward
A sweet Spencer, thus then must we part. Edw 4.7.73 Edward
Sweete Spencer, gentle Baldocke, part we must. Edw 4.7.96 Edward
Spencer, I see our soules are fleeted hence, Edw 4.7.105 Baldck
To die sweet Spencer, therefore live wee all, Edw 4.7.111 Baldck
Spencer, all live to die, and rise to fall. Edw 4.7.112 Baldck
SPENCERS
On whose good fortune Spencers hope depends. Edw 2.1.11 Spencr
A loves me better than a thousand Spencers. Edw 4.2.7 Prince
And then have at the proudest Spencers head. Edw 4.2.25 Prince
So are the Spencers, the father and the sonne. Edw 4.6.44 SrJohn
For me, both thou, and both the Spencers died, Edw 5.3.42 Edward
The Spencers ghostes, where ever they remaine, Edw 5.3.44 Edward
SPEND
And I will spend my time in thy bright armes. Dido 1.1.22 Ganimd
My purpose was (my Lord) to spend it so, 2Tamb 4.2.73 Olymp
Hold thee, wench, there's something for thee to spend. Jew 3.1.12 Pilia
And whilst I live use halfe; spend as my selfe; Jew 3.4.45 Barab
Take thou the mony, spend it for my sake. Jew 4.2.123 Ithimr
And spend some daies in barriers, tourny, tylte, P 628 12.41 King
To spend the treasure that should strength my land, P1037 19.107 King
yeares of liberty/I'le spend in pleasure and in daliance, F 840 3.1.62 Faust
Gallus that [car'dst] <carst> not bloud, and life to spend. Ovid's Elegies 3.8.64
SPENDING
Spending my life in sweet discourse of love. 2Tamb 4.2.45 Therid
SPENDS
Whiles my Aeneas spends himselfe in plaints, Dido 1.1.140 Venus
She likewise in admyring spends her time, Dido 3.2.72 Juno
And spends the night (that might be better spent)/In vaine Hero and Leander 1.355
SPENDST
Spendst thou thy time about this little boy, Dido 5.1.51 Hermes
In vaine my love thou spendst thy fainting breath, Dido 5.1.153 Aeneas
SPENT
How have ye spent your absent time from me? 2Tamb 1.3.173 Tamb

SPENT (cont.)			
Is almost cleane extinguished and spent,	2Tamb	5.3.89	Phsitn
But I perceive my martial strength is spent,	2Tamb	5.3.119	Tamb
For earth hath spent the pride of all her fruit,	2Tamb	5.3.250	Amyras
'Twere time well spent to goe and visit her:	Jew	1.2.389	Lodowk
But tell me now, How hast thou spent thy time?	Jew	2.3.201	Barab
Which is no sooner receiv'd but it is spent.	P 379	7.19	Ramus
For his othes are seldome spent in vaine.	P 773	15.31	Eprnon
And all my former time was spent in vaine:	P 986	19.56	Guise
This is the traitor that hath spent my golde,	P1028	19.98	King
Thus hitherto hath Faustus spent his time.	F 799	3.1.21	Faust
All have I spent:	Ovid's Elegies	1.6.61	
Beauty not exercisde with age is spent,	Ovid's Elegies	1.8.53	
Envie, why carpest thou my time is spent so ill,	Ovid's Elegies	1.15.1	
This grieves me not, no joyned kisses spent,	Ovid's Elegies	2.5.59	
Oft have I spent the night in wantonnesse,	Ovid's Elegies	2.10.27	
And first [she] <he> sayd, when will thy love be spent,	Ovid's Elegies	3.1.15	
And by those numbers is thy first youth spent.	Ovid's Elegies	3.1.28	
Seeing <When> in my prime my force is spent and done?	Ovid's Elegies	3.6.18	
And Venus grieves, Tibullus life being spent,	Ovid's Elegies	3.8.15	
His side past service, and his courage spent.	Ovid's Elegies	3.10.14	
And spends the night (that might be better spent)/In vaine	Hero and Leander	1.355	
SPERANZA			
Of the Speranza, Sir.	Jew	1.1.71	1Merch
SPHEARE			
And sooner shall the Sun fall from his Spheare,	1Tamb	1.2.176	Tamb
first moover of that Spheare/Enchac'd with thousands ever	1Tamb	4.2.8	Tamb
When Phoebus leaping from his Hemi-Spheare,	2Tamb	1.2.51	Callap
As Pilgrimes traveile to our Hemi-spheare,	2Tamb	3.2.32	Tamb
hath every Spheare a Dominion, or Intelligentia <Inteligentij>?	F 607	2.2.56	P Faust
Faire Cinthia wisht, his armes might be her spheare,	Hero and Leander	1.59	
SPHEARES			
A heaven of heavenly bodies in their Spheares/That guides his	1Tamb	2.1.16	Menaph
And alwaies mooving as the restles Spheares,	1Tamb	2.7.25	Tamb
Will send up fire to your turning Spheares,	1Tamb	4.2.39	Tamb
Their Spheares are mounted on the serpents head,	2Tamb	2.4.53	Tamb
Now are those Spheares where Cupid usde to sit,	2Tamb	2.4.81	Tamb
That I might moove the turning Spheares of heaven,	2Tamb	4.1.118	Tamb
<Tel me>, are there many Spheares <heavens> above the Moone?	F 586	2.2.35	Faust
As are the elements, such are the heavens <spheares>,/Even from	F 589	2.2.38	Mephst
Mutually folded in each others Spheares <orbe>,	F 591	2.2.40	Mephst
How many Heavens, or Spheares, are there?	F 609	2.2.58	P Faust
Stand still you ever moving Spheares of heaven,	F1929	5.2.133	Faust
SPHERE			
Rent sphere of heaven, and fier forsake thy orbe,	Edw	4.7.102	Spencr
Be it to make the Moone drop from her Sphere,	F 266	1.3.38	Faust
But like exiled aire thrust from his sphere,	Hero and Leander	2.118	
SPIALS			
But if Cosroe (as our Spials say,	1Tamb	2.2.35	Meandr
SPICE			
And Illioneus gum and Libian spice,	Dido	4.4.8	Dido
Loaden with Spice and Silkes, now under saile,	Jew	1.1.45	Barab
Stay, let me spice it first.	Jew	3.4.85	Barab
SPICED			
Must every bit be spiced with a Crosse?	F1066	3.2.86	Faust
SPICES			
Ware-houses stuft with spices and with drugs,	Jew	4.1.64	Barab
SPIDE			
I care not how it is, so it be not spide:	Edw	5.4.40	Mortmr
Rich jewels in the darke are soonest spide.	Hero and Leander	2.240	
SPIDERS			
Or thrids which spiders slender foote drawes out/Fastning her	Ovid's Elegies	1.14.7	
SPIE			
the plaines/To spie what force comes to relieve the holde.	2Tamb	3.3.48	Techel
Or lies he close, and shoots where none can spie him?	Ovid's Elegies	1.2.6	
Not one wen in her bodie could I spie,	Ovid's Elegies	1.5.18	
Or maides that their betrothed husbands spie.	Ovid's Elegies	2.5.36	
SPIED (See also SPYDE)			
But need we not be spied going aboord?	2Tamb	1.2.56	Almeda
he asleepe had layd/Inchaunted Argus, spied a countrie mayd,	Hero and Leander	1.388	
SPIGHT			
For here in spight of heaven Ile murder him,	Dido	3.2.10	Juno
In spight of them shall malice my estate.	1Tamb	1.1.159	Cosroe
And live in spight of death above a day.	2Tamb	5.3.101	Tamb
In spight of death I will goe show my face.	2Tamb	5.3.114	Tamb
That let your lives commaund in spight of death.	2Tamb	5.3.160	Tamb
In spight of them	Edw	1.1.77	Edward
SPIGHTFULL			
And that the spightfull influence of heaven,	2Tamb	5.3.193	Amyras
SPILDE			
She reacht me such a rap for that I spilde,	Dido	1.1.7	Ganimd
SPILL			
Spill not the bloud of gentle Mortimer.	Edw	5.6.69	Queene
I spill his bloud? no.	Edw	5.6.72	Queene
SPILT			
This argues, that you spilt my fathers bloud,	Edw	5.6.70	King
Not drunke, your faults [in] <on> the spilt wine I numbred.	Ovid's Elegies	2.5.14	
To cover it, spilt water in <on> the place.	Ovid's Elegies	3.6.84	
SPIN			
Thou setst their labouring hands to spin and card.	Ovid's Elegies	1.13.24	
SPINNE			
fine and thinne/Like to the silke the curious Seres spinne,	Ovid's Elegies	1.14.6	

SPIRIT (See also SPRIGHT)				
What God or Feend, or spirit of the earth,	1Tamb	2.6.15		Ortyg
my spirit doth foresee/The utter ruine of thy men and thee.	1Tamb	4.3.59		Arabia
Wherein an incorporeall spirit mooves,	2Tamb	4.1.114		Tamb
May never spirit, vaine or Artier feed/The cursed substance of	2Tamb	4.1.177		Soria
which the heart ingenders/Are partcht and void of spirit,	2Tamb	5.3.95		Phsitn
To hold the fiery spirit it containes,	2Tamb	5.3.169		Tamb
Shal still retaine my spirit, though I die,	2Tamb	5.3.173		Tamb
with what a broken hart/And damned spirit I ascend this seat,	2Tamb	5.3.207		Amyras
'Tis in the trouble of my spirit I speake;	Jew	1.2.207		Barab
No doubt, brother, but this proceedeth of the spirit.	Jew	1.2.327		1Fryar
I, and of a moving spirit too, brother; but come,	Jew	1.2.328		2Fryar
And when I dye, here shall my spirit walke.	Jew	2.1.30		Barab
And like a cunning spirit feigne some lye,	Jew	2.3.382		Barab
The undaunted spirit of Percie was appeasd,	Edw	1.1.114		Kent
First, that Faustus may be a spirit in forme and substance.	F 485	2.1.97	P	Faust
Thou art a spirit, God cannot pity thee.	F 564	2.2.13		BdAngl
Who buzzeth in mine eares I am a spirit?	F 565	2.2.14		Faust
I, go accursed spirit to ugly hell:	F 627	2.2.76		Faust
Yet in a minute had my spirit return'd,	F1399	4.2.75		Faust
by meanes of a swift spirit that I have, I had these grapes	F1585	4.6.28	P	Faust
they say thou hast a familiar spirit, by whome thou canst	F App	p.236 4	P	Emper
forth as by art and power of my spirit I am able to performe.	F App	p.237 38	P	Faust
and by means of a swift spirit that I have, I had them brought	F App	p.242 22	P	Faust
To fill my lawes thy wanton spirit frame.	Ovid's Elegies			3.1.30
And I grow faint, as with some spirit haunted?	Ovid's Elegies			3.6.36
If ought remaines of us but name, and spirit,	Ovid's Elegies			3.8.59
SPIRITES				
[And make my spirites pull his churches downe].	F 651	2.2.100A		Faust
spirites as can lively resemble Alexander and his Paramour,	F App	p.237 46	P	Faust
Sure these are no spirites, but the true substantiall bodies of	F App	p.238 64	P	Emper
SPIRITS				
And thinke we prattle with distempered spirits:	1Tamb	1.2.62		Tamb
Legions of Spirits fleeting in the [aire],	1Tamb	3.3.156		Tamb
And millions of his strong tormenting spirits:	2Tamb	1.3.147		Techel
for his vertues)/Revives the spirits of true Turkish heartes,	2Tamb	3.1.24		Callap
And tickle not your Spirits with desire/Stil to be train'd in	2Tamb	4.1.80		Tamb
And Spels of magicke from the mouthes of spirits,	2Tamb	4.2.64		Olymp
That legions of tormenting spirits may vex/Your slavish bosomes	2Tamb	5.1.45		Govnr
And Death with armies of Cymerian spirits/Gives battile gainst	2Tamb	5.3.8		Therid
And cause some milder spirits governe you.	2Tamb	5.3.80		Phsitn
The lively spirits which the heart ingenders/Are partcht and	2Tamb	5.3.94		Phsitn
And speake of spirits and ghosts that glide by night/About the	Jew	2.1.26		Barab
Shall I make spirits fetch me what I please?	F 106	1.1.78		Faust
I'le make my servile spirits to invent.	F 124	1.1.96		Faust
as th'infernall spirits/On sweet Musaeus when he came to hell,	F 142	1.1.114		Faust
So shall the spirits <subjects> of every element,	F 149	1.1.121		Valdes
The spirits tell me they can dry the sea,	F 171	1.1.143		Cornel
By which the spirits are inforc'd to rise:	F 241	1.3.13		Faust
Arch-regent and Commander of all Spirits.	F 291	1.3.63		Mephst
Unhappy spirits that [fell] <live> with Lucifer,	F 298	1.3.70		Mephst
Spirits away.	F 378	1.4.36	P	Wagner
But may I raise such <up> spirits when I please?	F 475	2.1.87		Faust
and incantations, that I might raise up spirits when I please].	F 551.2	2.1.165A	P	Faust
That when my Spirits present the royall shapes/Of Alexander and	F1249	4.1.95		Faust
Made the grim monarch of infernall spirits,	F1371	4.2.47		Fredrk
Balioll and Belcher, spirits away.	F App	p.230 50	P	Wagner
Her I suspect among nights spirits to fly,	Ovid's Elegies			1.8.13
The greedy spirits take the best things first,	Ovid's Elegies			2.6.39
SPIRITUS				
Aerii, [Aquatici] <Aquatani>, [Terreni], spiritus salvete:	F 245	1.3.17	P	Faust
SPIT (Homograph)				
Even for charity I may spit intoo't.	Jew	2.3.29		Barab
And get me a spit, and let it be red hote.	Edw	5.5.30		Ltborn
if thou hast any mind to Nan Spit our kitchin maide, then turn	F App	p.234 27	P	Robin
O brave Robin, shal I have Nan Spit, and to mine owne use?	F App	p.234 29	P	Rafe
SPITE (See also SPIGHT)				
And spare our lives whom every spite pursues.	Dido	1.2.9		Illion
In spite of all suspected enemies.	1Tamb	1.1.186		Ortyg
Let us live in spite of them, looking some happie power will	1Tamb	4.4.99	P	Zabina
In spite of these swine-eating Christians,	Jew	2.3.7		Barab
And there in spite of Malta will I dwell:	Jew	2.3.15		Barab
Devils doe your worst, [I'le] <I> live in spite of you.	Jew	5.1.41		Barab
In spite of Spaine and all the popish power,	P 581	11.46		Pleshe
In spite of Spaine and all his heresies.	P 716	14.19		Bartus
O hellish spite,/Your heads are all set with hornes.	F1441	4.3.11		Benvol
That spite of spite, our wrongs are doubled?	F1446	4.3.16		Benvol
In spite of thee, forth will thy <thine> arrowes flie,	Ovid's Elegies			1.2.45
SPITS				
Spits foorth the ringled bit, and with his hoves,	Hero and Leander			2.143
SPLENDENT				
to see the Monuments/And situation of bright splendent Rome,	F 829	3.1.51		Faust
SPLIT				
Yea all my Navie split with Rockes and Shelfes:	Dido	3.1.108		Aeneas
SPOILDE				
Had Venus spoilde her bellies Troyane fruite,	Ovid's Elegies			2.14.17
SPOILE (See also SPOYLD)				
Then did the Macedonians at the spoile/Of great Darius and his	1Tamb	1.1.153		Ceneus
Those thousand horse shall sweat with martiall spoile/Of	1Tamb	1.2.191		Tamb
He that with Shepheards and a litle spoile,	1Tamb	2.1.54		Ceneus
That live by rapine and by lawlesse spoile,	1Tamb	2.2.23		Meandr
Beside the spoile of him and all his traine:	1Tamb	2.2.34		Meandr
The more he brings, the greater is the spoile,	1Tamb	3.3.23		Techel

SPOILE (cont.)			
That satiate with spoile refuseth blood.	1Tamb	4.1.53	2Msngr
To waste and spoile the sweet Aonian fieldes.	1Tamb	4.3.6	Souldn
Compact of Rapine, Pyracie, and spoile,	1Tamb	4.3.8	Souldn
Famous for nothing but for theft and spoile,	1Tamb	4.3.66	Souldn
Threaten our citie with a generall spoile:	1Tamb	5.1.10	Govnr
and fresh supply/Of conquest, and of spoile is offered us.	1Tamb	5.1.197	Techel
About the Grecian Isles to rob and spoile:	2Tamb	3.5.94	Jrslem
No, here he comes, now let them spoile and kill:	Edw	2.4.3	Edward
Th'affrighted worlds force bent on publique spoile,	Lucan, First Booke		5
Now Babilon, (proud through our spoile) should stoop,	Lucan, First Booke		10
And deem'd renowne to spoile their native towne,	Lucan, First Booke		176
As oft as Rome was sackt, here gan the spoile:	Lucan, First Booke		258
Neither spoile, nor kingdom seeke we by these armes,	Lucan, First Booke		351
fierce men of Rhene/Leaving your countrey open to the spoile.	Lucan, First Booke		461
SPOILES			
And made their spoiles from all our provinces.	1Tamb	1.1.122	Cosroe
All running headlong after greedy spoiles:	1Tamb	2.2.45	Meandr
And make Damascus spoiles as rich to you,	1Tamb	4.4.8	Tamb
Are ye not gone ye villaines with your spoiles?	2Tamb	4.3.84	Tamb
Let them take pleasure soundly in their spoiles,	2Tamb	4.3.92	Tamb
Shal al be loden with the martiall spoiles/We will convay with	2Tamb	4.3.105	Tamb
And unresisted, drave away riche spoiles.	Edw	2.2.167	Lncstr
Bearing old spoiles and conquerors monuments,	Lucan, First Booke		138
Only a Woman gets spoiles from a Man,	Ovid's Elegies		1.10.29
SPOILST			
Why weepst? and spoilst with teares thy watry eyes?	Ovid's Elegies		3.5.57
SPOKE			
And as he spoke, to further his entent/The windes did drive	Dido	2.1.138	Aeneas
To whom the aged King thus trembling spoke:	Dido	2.1.232	Aeneas
Knavely spoke, and like a Knight at Armes.	Jew	4.4.9	Pilia
As these have spoke so be it to their soules:--	Jew	5.1.42	Barab
Tis verie kindlie spoke my lord of Penbrooke,	Edw	2.5.104	Arundl
So sir, you have spoke, away, avoid our presence.	Edw	3.1.232	Edward
Who's that spoke? Friers looke about.	F1040	3.2.60	Pope
This spoke none answer'd, but a murmuring buz/Th'unstable	Lucan, First Booke		353
Breathlesse spoke some thing, and sigh'd out the rest;	Hero and Leander		2.280
SPOKEN			
Thy verses sweet Tibullus shall be spoken.	Ovid's Elegies		1.15.28
SPOKEST			
Thou spokest thy words so well with stammering sound.	Ovid's Elegies		2.6.24
SPONTE			
Italiam non sponte sequor.	Dido	5.1.140	Aeneas
SPOONE			
saies, he that eats with the devil had need of a long spoone.	Jew	3.4.59	P Ithimr
SPORT			
Might I but see that pretie sport a foote,	Dido	1.1.16	Ganimd
Vulcan shall daunce to make thee laughing sport,	Dido	1.1.32	Jupitr
Entends ere long to sport him in the skie.	Dido	1.1.77	Venus
Come let us thinke upon some pleasing sport,	Dido	2.1.302	Dido
That thou and I unseene might sport our selves:	Dido	4.4.51	Dido
That onely made him King to make us sport.	1Tamb	2.5.101	Tamb
As meet they will, and fighting dye; brave sport.	Jew	3.1.30	Ithimr
one; have not the Nuns fine sport with the Fryars now and then?	Jew	3.3.32	P Ithimr
Drums strike alarum, raise them from their sport,	Edw	2.3.25	Mortmr
<Well, I am content, to compasse then some sport>,	F 989	(HC266)A	Faust
Speake, wilt thou come and see this sport?	F1193	4.1.39	Fredrk
This sport is excellent: wee'l call and wake him.	F1281	4.1.127	Emper
His Artfull sport, drives all sad thoughts away.	F1673	4.6.116	Duke
Ile have fine sport with the boyes, Ile get nuts and apples	F App	p.236 45	P Robin
Forbeare sweet wordes, and be your sport unpleasant.	Ovid's Elegies		1.4.66
Where they may sport, and seeme to be unknowne.	Ovid's Elegies		1.5.8
The sport being such, as both alike sweete try it,	Ovid's Elegies		1.10.33
This day denyall hath my sport adjourned.	Ovid's Elegies		1.12.2
Egeria with just Numa had good sport,	Ovid's Elegies		2.17.18
SPORTE			
All fellowes now, disposde alike to sporte,	Dido	3.3.5	Dido
SPORTED			
Meremaids, sported with their loves/On heapes of heavie gold,	Hero and Leander		2.162
And when hee sported in the fragrant lawnes,	Hero and Leander		2.199
SPORTFULL			
And in his sportfull hands an Olive tree,	Edw	1.1.64	Gavstn
SPORTING			
Whil'st they were sporting in this darksome Cave?	Dido	4.1.24	Iarbus
Nor sporting in the dalliance of love/In Courts of Kings, where	F 3	Prol.3	1Chor
SPORTS			
When in the midst of all their gamesome sports,	Dido	3.2.89	Juno
Rebels, will they appoint their soveraigne/His sports, his	Edw	3.1.175	Edward
Ceres what sports to thee so grievous were,	Ovid's Elegies		3.9.43
Practise a thousand sports when there you come,	Ovid's Elegies		3.13.24
SPOTLESSE			
Accept him that will love with spotlesse truth:	Ovid's Elegies		1.3.6
My spotlesse life, which but to Gods [gives] <give> place,	Ovid's Elegies		1.3.13
My words shall be as spotlesse as my youth,	Hero and Leander		1.207
Vow'd spotlesse chastitie, but all in vaine.	Hero and Leander		1.368
SPOTS			
Who spots my nuptiall bed with infamie,	Edw	5.1.31	Edward
And stain'd the bowels with darke lothsome spots:	Lucan, First Booke		619
SPOTTED			
From Junos bird Ile pluck her spotted pride,	Dido	1.1.34	Jupitr
And cloathed in a spotted Leopards skin.	Dido	1.1.186	Venus
SPOUSALL			
By this right hand, and by our spousall rites,	Dido	5.1.134	Dido

SPOYLD
Troth master, I'm loth such a pot of pottage should be spoyld. Jew 3.4.90 P Ithimr
The Cedar tall spoyld of his barke retaines. Ovid's Elegies 1.14.12
SPOYLE
sounds/The surges, his fierce souldiers, to the spoyle: Dido 1.1.69 Venus
Our hands are not prepar'd to lawles spoyle, Dido 1.2.12 Illion
Nor shall the Heathens live upon our spoyle: Jew 3.5.12 Govnr
Whose loosnes hath betrayed thy land to spoyle, Edw 4.4.11 Queene
SPOYLED
Loe Cupid brings his quiver spoyled quite, Ovid's Elegies 3.8.7
SPOYLES
That loade their thighes with Hyblas honeys spoyles, Dido 5.1.13 Aeneas
And brought the spoyles to rich Dardania: F1695 5.1.22 Faust
SPOYLING
Forbeare to hurt thy selfe in spoyling mee. Ovid's Elegies 1.2.50
SPRANG
Hence interest and devouring usury sprang, Lucan, First Booke 183
SPRAULING
thou knowest/We sawe Cassandra sprauling in the streetes, Dido 2.1.274 Aeneas
SPRAYS
Girt my shine browe with sea banke mirtle praise <sprays>. Ovid's Elegies 1.1.34
SPREAD
admyre me not)/And when my name and honor shall be spread, 1Tamb 1.2.205 Tamb
Or spread his collours in Grecia, 1Tamb 3.1.29 Bajzth
And when she sees our bloody Collours spread, 1Tamb 3.3.159 Tamb
Hath spread his collours to our high disgrace: 1Tamb 4.1.7 Souldn
To spread my fame through hell and up to heaven: 1Tamb 5.1.467 Tamb
That on mount Sinay with their ensignes spread, 2Tamb 3.1.46 Jrslem
The name of mightie Tamburlain is spread: 2Tamb 3.4.66 Therid
And Bacchus vineyards [over-spread] <ore-spread> the world: Jew 4.2.92 Ithimr
[Now is his fame spread forth in every land], F1149 3.3.62A 3Chor
[Spread] <Spead>, spread these flags that ten years space have Lucan, First Booke 348
spread these flags that ten years space have conquer'd, Lucan, First Booke 348
were wont/In large spread heire to exceed the rest of France; Lucan, First Booke 439
Other that Caesars barbarous bands were spread/Along Nar floud Lucan, First Booke 471
And dismall Prophesies were spread abroad: Lucan, First Booke 562
Lie with him gently, when his limbes he spread/Upon the bed, but Ovid's Elegies 1.4.15
Or Layis of a thousand [wooers] <lovers> [sped] <spread>. Ovid's Elegies 1.5.12
And in the midst their bodies largely spread: Ovid's Elegies 2.10.18
A livelie vine of greene sea agget spread; Hero and Leander 1.138
Had spread the boord, with roses strowed the roome, Hero and Leander 2.21
SPREADING
Two spreading hornes most strangely fastened/Upon the head of F1277 4.1.123 Emper
Now spearlike, long; now like a spreading torch: Lucan, First Booke 530
But from his spreading armes away she cast her, Hero and Leander 1.342
Wherewith she wreath'd her largely spreading heare, Hero and Leander 2.107
SPREADS
feathered bird/That spreads her wings upon the citie wals, 1Tamb 4.2.106 Tamb
Our verse great Tityus a huge space out-spreads, Ovid's Elegies 3.11.25
SPRED
When wert thou in the field with banner spred? Edw 2.2.182 Mortmr
Looke next to see us with our ensignes spred. Edw 2.2.199 Lncstr
There spred the colours, with confused noise/Of trumpets Lucan, First Booke 239
Let the sad captive formost with lockes spred/On her white Ovid's Elegies 1.7.39
First Victory is brought with large spred wing, Ovid's Elegies 3.2.45
The locks spred on his necke receive his teares, Ovid's Elegies 3.8.11
SPRIGHT
no darke night-flying spright/Nor hands prepar'd to slaughter, Ovid's Elegies 1.6.13
SPRINCKLED
A target bore: bloud sprinckled was his right. Ovid's Elegies 3.7.16
SPRING (See also YSPRONG)
The spring is hindred by your smoothering host, 1Tamb 3.1.50 Moroc
And in my helme a triple plume shal spring, 2Tamb 4.3.116 Tamb
Light Abrahams off-spring; and direct the hand/Of Abigall this Jew 2.1.14 Barab
yet let me talke to her;/This off-spring of Cain, this Jebusite Jew 2.3.301 Barab
Shall bathe him in a spring, and there hard by, Edw 1.1.66 Gavstn
And where stiffe winter whom no spring resolves, Lucan, First Booke 17
Which issues from a small spring, is but shallow, Lucan, First Booke 216
Or if it do, to thee no joy thence spring: Ovid's Elegies 1.4.68
Hether the windes blowe, here the spring-tide rore. Ovid's Elegies 2.11.40
Wilt thou thy wombe-inclosed off-spring wracke? Ovid's Elegies 2.14.8
And coole gales shake the tall trees leavy spring, Ovid's Elegies 2.16.36
In midst thereof a stone-pav'd sacred spring, Ovid's Elegies 3.1.3
So in a spring thrives he that told so much, Ovid's Elegies 3.6.51
SPRINGE
Frolicks not more to see the paynted springe, Edw 2.2.62 Gavstn
SPRINGING
Fruites ripe will fall, let springing things increase, Ovid's Elegies 2.14.25
SPRINGS
For vertue is the fount whence honor springs. 1Tamb 4.4.128 Tamb
The christall springs whose taste illuminates/Refined eies with 2Tamb 2.4.22 Tamb
As far as Titan springs where night dims heaven, Lucan, First Booke 15
Of these garboiles, whence springs [a long] <along> discourse, Lucan, First Booke 68
Faire Phoebus leade me to the Muses springs. Ovid's Elegies 1.15.36
And by the rising herbes, where cleare springs slide, Ovid's Elegies 2.16.9
Thy springs are nought but raine and melted snowe: Ovid's Elegies 3.5.93
By charmes are running springs and fountaines drie, Ovid's Elegies 3.6.32
Wild savages, that drinke of running springs, Hero and Leander 1.259
And as he spake, upon the waves he springs. Hero and Leander 2.206
SPRING-TIDE
Hether the windes blowe, here the spring-tide rore. Ovid's Elegies 2.11.40
SPRINKLE (See also SPRINCKLED)
Whose hornes shall sprinkle through the tainted aire, 2Tamb 3.1.66 Orcan

SPRINKLED			
And sprinkled with the braines of slaughtered men,	2Tamb	1.3.81	Tamb
SPRINKLEST			
And sprinklest Saphyrs on thy shining face,	1Tamb	5.1.143	Tamb
SPRITE (See SPRIGHT)			
SPRONG			
Are not we both sprong of celestiall rase,	Dido	3.2.28	Juno
And planted love where envie erst had sprong.	Dido	3.2.52	Juno
Sprong of the teeth of Dragons venomous,	1Tamb	2.2.48	Meandr
That sprong of teeth of Dragons venomous?	1Tamb	2.2.52	Mycet
For he was never sprong of humaine race,	1Tamb	2.6.11	Meandr
Bastardly boy, sprong from some cowards loins,	2Tamb	1.3.69	Tamb
Or that unlike the line from whence I [sprong] <come>,	Ovid's Elegies		1.15.3
SPRUNG			
But thou art sprung from Scythian Caucasus,	Dido	5.1.158	Dido
Ah cruel Brat, sprung from a tyrants loines,	2Tamb	4.3.54	Jrslem
faine themselves/The Romanes brethren, sprung of Ilian race;	Lucan, First Booke		429
No vaine sprung out but from the yawning gash,	Lucan, First Booke		613
Ilia, sprung from Idaean Laomedon?	Ovid's Elegies		3.5.54
SPUN			
with thrids on wrong wheeles spun/And what with Mares ranck	Ovid's Elegies		1.8.7
SPURCA			
Repentance? Spurca: what pretendeth this?	Jew	3.4.6	Barab
SPURNE			
And fearelesse spurne the killing Basiliske:	F 921	3.1.143	Pope
To spurne in carelesse sort, the shipwracke treasure.	Hero and Leander		2.164
SPURNING			
Spurning their crownes from off their captive heads.	1Tamb	1.2.57	Techel
SPURNS			
And spurns the Abstracts of thy foolish lawes.	2Tamb	5.1.197	Tamb
SPY (See also SPIE)			
Whom have we there, a spy?	Jew	5.1.69	Calym
my good Lord, one that can spy a place/Where you may enter, and	Jew	5.1.70	Barab
One as a spy doth to his enemies goe,	Ovid's Elegies		1.9.17
SPY'DE			
Where having spy'de her tower, long star'd he on't,	Hero and Leander		2.149
SPYDE			
Like chast Diana, when Acteon spyde her,	Hero and Leander		2.261
SPYE			
As after chaunc'd, they did each other spye.	Hero and Leander		1.134
SPYES			
causde the Greekish spyes/To hast to Tenedos and tell the	Dido	2.1.180	Aeneas
SPYING			
Lest Dido spying him keepe him for a pledge.	Dido	5.1.50	Aeneas
And spying me, hoyst up the sailes amaine:	Dido	5.1.227	Anna
Spying his mistrisse teares, he will lament/And say this blabbe	Ovid's Elegies		2.2.59
SQUARE			
Is it square or pointed, pray let me know.	Jew	2.3.59	Lodowk
SQUEASE			
And squease it in the cup of Tamburlain.	1Tamb	4.4.20	Bajzth
SQUINTING			
Whence thou shouldst view thy Roome with squinting beams.	Lucan, First Booke		55
SQUIS'D			
not, and from the gaping liver/Squis'd matter; through the cal,	Lucan, First Booke		624
STAB			
And with this stab slumber eternally.	1Tamb	3.2.106	Agidas
Which when you stab, looke on your weapons point,	2Tamb	4.2.69	Olymp
Now stab my Lord, and mark your weapons point/That wil be	2Tamb	4.2.79	Olymp
What, have I slaine her? Villaine, stab thy selfe:	2Tamb	4.2.82	Therid
Stab him.	P 382	7.22	Guise
Stab him I say and send him to his freends in hell.	P 415	7.55	Guise
Marry if thou hadst, thou mightst have had the stab,	P 776	15.34	King
And now and then, stab as occasion serves.	Edw	2.1.43	Spencr
Then Faustus stab thy <thine> Arme couragiously,	F 438	2.1.50	Mephst
STABBE			
Come Ramus, more golde, or thou shalt have the stabbe.	P 376	7.16	Gonzag
STAB'D			
as you went in at dores/You had bin stab'd, but not a word on't	Jew	2.3.338	Barab
STABD			
I may be stabd, and live till he be dead,	P 778	15.36	Mugern
STABLE (Homograph)			
And in a stable lie upon the planks.	2Tamb	3.5.107	Tamb
and lock you in the stable, when you shall come sweating from	2Tamb	3.5.141	P Tamb
Here's a drench to poyson a whole stable of Flanders mares:	Jew	3.4.111	P Ithimr
all lands else/Have stable peace, here wars rage first begins,	Lucan, First Booke		252
Mars in the deed the black-smithes net did stable,	Ovid's Elegies		1.9.39
STABLISH			
when holy Fates/Shall stablish me in strong Egyptia,	1Tamb	4.4.135	Tamb
STAFFE			
the verie legges/Whereon our state doth leane, as on a staffe,	1Tamb	1.1.60	Mycet
And with the Jacobs staffe measure the height/And distance of	2Tamb	3.3.50	Techel
so, let him leane upon his staffe; excellent, he stands as if he	Jew	4.1.154	P Ithimr
And see, a staffe stands ready for the purpose:	Jew	4.1.172	1Fryar
Take in the staffe too, for that must be showne:	Jew	4.1.204	Barab
Till I be strong enough to breake a staffe,	Edw	4.2.24	Prince
STAG			
With open crie pursues the wounded Stag:	2Tamb	3.5.7	2Msngr
Ifaith thats as true as Diana turned me to a stag.	F App	p.237 54	P Knight
STAGE			
When he arrived last upon our stage,	2Tamb	Prol.2	Prolog
STAGGE			
the Emperour, Il'e be Acteon, and turne my selfe to a Stagge.	F1256	4.1.102	P Benvol
In bold Acteons shape to turne a Stagge.	F1299	4.1.145	Faust

STAGGERING
Stand staggering like a quivering Aspen leafe, ... 1Tamb 2.4.4 Mycet
STAI'D
They stai'd not either to pray or sacrifice, ... Lucan, First Booke 504
STAID
whose moaning entercourse/Hath hetherto bin staid, with wrath 1Tamb 5.1.281 Bajzth
lead him bound in chaines/Unto Damasco, where I staid before. 2Tamb 1.3.205 Techel
early; with intent to goe/Unto your Friery, because you staid. Jew 4.1.192 Barab
Faustus gives to thee his soule: [ah] <O> there it staid. F 456 2.1.68 Faust
STAIDE
He staide, and on thy lookes his gazes seaz'd. . . . . Ovid's Elegies 1.8.24
With much a do my hands I scarsely staide. . . . . Ovid's Elegies 1.8.110
STAIE
Staie villaines. . . . . Edw 5.4.93 Kent
STAIED
To thinke thy puisant never staied arme/Will part their bodies, 1Tamb 5.1.88 1Virgn
STAIES
Nor plowman, Priest, nor Merchant staies at home, . . . 2Tamb 5.2.50 Callap
Lets goe my Lords, our dinner staies for us. . . . . P 630 12.43 King
And so shalt thou be too: why staies he heere? . . . . Edw 5.6.51 King
STAIEST
Why staiest thou here? thou art no love of mine. . . . Dido 3.1.39 Dido
Ah, Menaphon, why staiest thou thus behind, ... 1Tamb 1.1.83 Mycet
Nephue, I must to Scotland, thou staiest here. . . . . Edw 1.4.386 MortSr
STAIN'D
Hath stain'd thy cheekes, and made thee look like death, . 2Tamb 4.2.4 Olymp
And stain'd the bowels with darke lothsome spots: . . Lucan, First Booke 619
At Colchis stain'd with childrens bloud men raile, . . Ovid's Elegies 2.14.29
STAIND
The stubborne Nervians staind with Cottas bloud; . . Lucan, First Booke 430
Though thou her body guard, her minde is staind: . . Ovid's Elegies 3.4.5
STAINDE
If ever sunne stainde heaven with bloudy clowdes, . . P 60 2.3 Guise
These handes were never stainde with innocent bloud, . Edw 5.5.81 Ltborn
STAINE (See also STAYNES)
to staine our hands with blood/Is farre from us and our . Jew 1.2.144 Govnr
And staine my roiall standard with the same, ... Edw 3.1.138 Edward
Love is a naked boy, his yeares saunce staine, . . . Ovid's Elegies 1.10.15
To staine all faith in truth, by false crimes use. . . Ovid's Elegies 2.2.38
Her kirtle blew, whereon was many a staine, ... Hero and Leander 1.15
Nor staine thy youthfull years with avarice, ... Hero and Leander 1.325
STAINED
Hide now thy stained face in endles night, ... 1Tamb 5.1.292 Bajzth
Deflowr'd and stained in unlawfull bed? . . . . Ovid's Elegies 3.5.76
STAINING
Staining his Altars with your purple blood: . . . . 1Tamb 4.2.4 Bajzth
STAIR (See STAYRES)
STAIST
Leister, thou staist for me,/And go I must, life farewell with Edw 4.7.98 Edward
STAKE
Pioners away, and where I stuck the stake, ... 2Tamb 3.3.41 Therid
STAKTE
I might have stakte them both unto the earth, ... Dido 4.1.23 Iarbus
STALE (Homograph)
And glut it not with stale and daunted foes. . . . . 2Tamb 4.1.88 Tamb
The unjust Judge for bribes becomes a stale. . . . . Ovid's Elegies 1.10.38
STALKT
the suburbe fieldes/Fled, fowle Erinnis stalkt about the wals, Lucan, First Booke 570
STALL
Hoping to see them starve upon a stall, ... Jew 2.3.26 Barab
STALLS
who though lockt and chaind in stalls,/Souse downe the wals, Lucan, First Booke 295
STAMMERING
Thou spokest thy words so well with stammering sound. . Ovid's Elegies 2.6.24
STAMP'D
reading of the letter, he star'd and stamp'd, and turnd aside. Jew 4.2.104 P Pilia
STAMPE
So, lay the table downe, and stampe on it, ... Edw 5.5.112 Ltborn
STAMPES
The Duke of Guise stampes on thy liveles bulke. . . . P 315 5.42 Guise
Base boullion for the stampes sake we allow, ... Hero and Leander 1.265
STAMPS
He stamps it under his feet my Lord. . . . . . . 1Tamb 4.4.42 P Therid
STAMPT
Stead/That stampt on others with their thundring hooves, . 1Tamb 5.1.331 Zenoc
Stampt with the princely Foule that in her wings/Caries the 2Tamb 1.1.100 Orcan
STAND
Here in this bush disguised will I stand, ... Dido 1.1.139 Venus
And not stand lingering here for amorous lookes: . . . Dido 4.3.38 Illion
Why cosin, stand you building Cities here, ... Dido 5.1.27 Hermes
letters to command/Aide and assistance if we stand in need. 1Tamb 1.2.20 Magnet
An ods too great, for us to stand against: . . . . 1Tamb 1.2.122 Tamb
And hostes of souldiers stand amaz'd at us, ... 1Tamb 1.2.221 Usumc
and dim their eies/That stand and muse at our admyred armes. 1Tamb 2.3.24 Tamb
Stand staggering like a quivering Aspen leafe, ... 1Tamb 2.4.4 Mycet
Surpriz'd with feare of hideous revenge,/I stand agast: . 1Tamb 3.2.69 Agidas
And all his Captaines that thus stoutly stand, . . . 1Tamb 3.3.79 Bajzth
of Hydra, so my power/Subdued, shall stand as mighty as before: 1Tamb 3.3.141 Bajzth
Desart of Arabia/To those that stand on Badgeths lofty Tower, 2Tamb 1.1.109 Sgsmnd
Our Tents are pitcht, our men stand in array, ... 2Tamb 1.1.120 Fredrk
if Sigismond/Speake as a friend, and stand not upon tearmes, 2Tamb 1.1.123 Orcan
tis superstition/To stand so strictly on dispensive faith: 2Tamb 2.1.50 Fredrk
And canst thou Coward stand in feare of death? . . . . 2Tamb 3.2.102 Tamb

STAND (cont.)			
Stand at the walles, with such a mighty power.	2Tamb	3.3.14	Therid
here are Bugges/Wil make the haire stand upright on your heads,	2Tamb	3.5.148	Tamb
Stand up, ye base unworthy souldiers,	2Tamb	4.1.99	Tamb
Stand up my boyes, and I wil teach ye arms,	2Tamb	4.1.103	Tamb
When all the Gods stand gazing at his pomp:	2Tamb	4.3.129	Tamb
Ah friends, what shal I doe, I cannot stand,	2Tamb	5.3.51	Tamb
Stand all aside, and let the Knights determine,	Jew	1.2.14	Calym
Who stand accursed in the sight of heaven,	Jew	1.2.64	Govnr
Why stand you thus unmov'd with my laments?	Jew	1.2.171	Barab
This is the Market-place, here let 'em stand:	Jew	2.3.1	1Offcr
But stand aside, here comes Don Lodowicke.	Jew	2.3.217	Barab
And make him stand in feare of me.	Jew	3.6.43	2Fryar
and the rest of the family, stand or fall at your service.	Jew	4.2.44	P Pilia
Now Governor--stand by there, wait within.--	Jew	5.2.50	Barab
How stand the cords? How hang these hinges, fast?	Jew	5.5.1	Barab
Stand close, for here they come:	Jew	5.5.46	Barab
Governour, why stand you all so pittilesse?	Jew	5.5.71	Barab
Stand in some window opening neere the street,	P 86	2.29	Guise
they may become/As men that stand and gase against the Sunne.	P 163	2.106	Guise
And at ech corner shall the Kings garde stand.	P 291	5.18	Anjoy
The head being of, the members cannot stand.	P 296	5.23	Anjoy
What should I doe but stand upon my guarde?	P 839	17.34	Guise
That the Guise durst stand in armes against the King,	P 877	17.72	Eprnon
I, I, feare not: stand close, so, be resolute:	P 943	19.13	Capt
Stand close, he is comming, I know him by his voice.	P1000	19.70	P 1Mur
The Popedome cannot stand, all goes to wrack,	P1087	19.157	QnMoth
the king and the nobles/From the parlament, ile stand aside.	Edw	1.1.73	Gavstn
What danger tis to stand against your king.	Edw	1.1.97	Edward
Stand graticus gloomie night to his device.	Edw	4.1.11	Kent
Madam, what resteth, why stand ye in a muse?	Edw	4.6.63	SrJohn
Stand not on titles, but obay th'arrest,	Edw	4.7.58	Leistr
Stand still you watches of the element,	Edw	5.1.66	Edward
As for my selfe, I stand as Joves huge tree,	Edw	5.6.11	Mortmr
should stand upon; therefore acknowledge your errour,	F 203	1.2.10	P Wagner
When Mephostophilis shall stand by me,	F 413	2.1.25	Faust
but must thou sit, and I stand?	F 683	2.2.132	P Envy
That Faustus name, whilst this bright frame doth stand,	F 841	3.1.63	Faust
come then stand by me/And thou shalt see them come immediately.	F 843	3.1.65	Mephst
To make his Monkes and Abbots stand like Apes,	F 861	3.1.83	Mephst
Both he and thou shalt stand excommunicate,	F 908	3.1.130	Pope
And therefore none of his Decrees can stand.	F 929	3.1.151	Pope
circle, and stand close at my backe, and stir not for thy life,	F1113	3.3.26	P Robin
Wilt thou stand in thy Window, and see it then?	F1195	4.1.41	Mrtino
to stand gaping after the divels Governor, and can see nothing.	F1244	4.1.90	P Benvol
base pesants stand,/For loe these Trees remove at my command,	F1425	4.2.101	Faust
And stand as Bulwarkes twixt your selves and me,	F1427	4.2.103	Faust
Well, I will not stand with thee, give me the money:	F1466	4.4.10	P Faust
Sirra Dick, dost thou know why I stand so mute?	F1509	4.5.5	P Robin
I, I, he does not stand much upon that.	F1630	4.6.73	P HrsCsr
Stand still you ever moving Spheares of heaven,	F1929	5.2.133	Faust
stand by, Ile scowre you for a goblet, stand aside you had	F App	p.235 18	P Robin
stand aside you had best, I charge you in the name of Belzabub:	F App	p.235 18	P Robin
When all the woods about stand bolt up-right,	Lucan, First Booke	143	
These direful signes made Aruns stand amaz'd,	Lucan, First Booke	615	
The people thee applauding thou shalte stand,	Ovid's Elegies	1.2.25	
Each little hill shall for a table stand:	Ovid's Elegies	2.11.48	
Pollux and Castor, might I stand betwixt,	Ovid's Elegies	2.16.13	
If Achelous, I aske where thy hornes stand,	Ovid's Elegies	3.5.35	
But when she saw it would by no meanes stand,	Ovid's Elegies	3.6.75	
Or thinke soft verse in any stead to stand?	Ovid's Elegies	3.7.2	
Poore soldiers stand with fear of death dead strooken,	Hero and Leander	1.121	
STANDARD			
Environing their Standard round, that stood/As bristle-pointed	1Tamb	4.1.26	2Msngr
Affrica, and Greece/Follow my Standard and my thundring Drums:	2Tamb	1.1.159	Orcan
Cheefe standard bearer to the Lutheranes,	P 285	5.12	Guise
Cheef standard bearer to the Lutheranes,	P 313	5.40	Guise
Advaunce your standard Edward in the field,	Edw	3.1.126	Spencr
And staine my roiall standard with the same,	Edw	3.1.138	Edward
And lives t'advance your standard good my lord.	Edw	4.2.42	Mortmr
Straight summon'd he his severall companies/Unto the standard:	Lucan, First Booke	298	
I was both horse-man, foote-man, standard bearer.	Ovid's Elegies	2.12.14	
STANDARD BEARER			
Cheefe standard bearer to the Lutheranes,	P 285	5.12	Guise
Cheef standard bearer to the Lutheranes,	P 313	5.40	Guise
I was both horse-man, foote-man, standard bearer.	Ovid's Elegies	2.12.14	
STANDARDE			
Whether goes my standarde?	Lucan, First Booke	193	
STANDARDES			
Then reare your standardes, let your sounding Drummes/Direct	1Tamb	4.3.61	Souldn
STANDER			
Troy had not yet beene ten yeares siege out-stander,	Ovid's Elegies	3.5.27	
STANDERD			
let him hang a bunch of keies on his standerd, to put him in	2Tamb	3.5.139	P Tamb
STANDERS			
A scorching flame burnes all the standers by.	Ovid's Elegies	1.2.46	
So was her beautie to the standers by.	Hero and Leander	1.106	
STANDERS BY			
So was her beautie to the standers by.	Hero and Leander	1.106	
STANDES			
With Augures Phoebus, Phoebe with hunters standes,	Ovid's Elegies	3.2.51	
STANDETH			
is a monastery/Which standeth as an out-house to the Towne;	Jew	5.3.37	Msngr

STANDING			
And as I swomme, she standing on the shoare,	Dido	2.1.286	Aeneas
Which fils the nookes of Hell with standing aire,	1Tamb	5.1.257	Bajzth
his market, and set up your standing where you should not:	P 810	17.5	P Souldr
If standing here I can by no meanes get,	Ovid's Elegies		3.5.11
Then standing at the doore, she turnd about,	Hero and Leander		2.97
STANDINGE			
the markett and sett upe your standinge where you shold not:	Paris	ms 6,p390	P Souldr
STANDINGS			
Keep all your standings, and not stir a foote,	1Tamb	1.2.150	Tamb
Then sirs take your standings within this Chamber,	P 940	19.10	Capt
the rest have taine their standings in the next roome,	P 994	19.64	P 3Mur
STANDS			
Prepared stands to wracke their woodden walles,	Dido	1.1.67	Venus
Why stands my sweete Aeneas thus amazde?	Dido	2.1.2	Achat
Than in the haven when the Pilot stands/And viewes a strangers	1Tamb	4.3.32	Souldn
Stands aiming at me with his murthering dart,	2Tamb	5.3.69	Tamb
But now how stands the wind?	Jew	1.1.38	Barab
Ha, to the East? yes: See how stands the Vanes?	Jew	1.1.40	Barab
no, but happily he stands in feare/Of that which you, I thinke,	Jew	2.3.282	Barab
me in the pot of Rice/That for our supper stands upon the fire.	Jew	3.4.50	Barab
staffe; excellent, he stands as if he were begging of Bacon.	Jew	4.1.154	P Ithimr
Stands here a purpose, meaning me some wrong,	Jew	4.1.166	1Fryar
And see, a staffe stands ready for the purpose:	Jew	4.1.172	1Fryar
And how secure this conquer'd Iland stands/Inviron'd with the	Jew	5.3.6	Calym
In [midst] <one> of which a sumptuous Temple stands,	F 795	3.1.17	Faust
Know that this City stands upon seven hils,	F 811	3.1.33	Mephst
The Doctor stands prepar'd, by power of Art,	F1222	4.1.68	Faust
Who's this, that stands so solemnly by himselfe:	F1513	4.5.9	P Hostss
I hope my score stands still.	F1515	4.5.11	P Robin
The whore stands to be bought for each mans mony/And seekes	Ovid's Elegies		1.10.21
Such were they as [Dione] <Diana> painted stands/All naked	Ovid's Elegies		1.14.33
Homer shall live while Tenedos stands and Ide,	Ovid's Elegies		1.15.9
An old wood, stands uncut of long yeares space,	Ovid's Elegies		3.1.1
to thee our Court stands open wide,/There shalt be lov'd:	Ovid's Elegies		3.5.61
How piteously with drouping wings he stands,	Ovid's Elegies		3.8.9
There stands an old wood with thick trees darke clouded,	Ovid's Elegies		3.12.7
True love is mute, and oft amazed stands.	Hero and Leander		1.186
My turret stands, and there God knowes I play/With Venus	Hero and Leander		1.351
STAR			
What star or state soever governe him,	1Tamb	2.6.18	Ortyg
But such a Star hath influence in his sword,	1Tamb	5.1.232	Bajzth
Over my Zenith hang a blazing star,	2Tamb	3.2.6	Tamb
Now fals the star whose influence governes France,	P 944	19.14	Capt
What neede the artick people love star-light,	Edw	1.1.16	Gavstn
being old/Must shine a star) shal heaven (whom thou lovest),	Lucan, First Booke		46
STAR'D			
reading of the letter, he star'd and stamp'd, and turnd aside.	Jew	4.2.104	P Pilia
Where having spy'de her tower, long star'd he on't,	Hero and Leander		2.149
STARE (See also STAR'ST)			
Now Faustus let thine eyes with horror stare/Into that vaste	F1909	5.2.113	BdAngl
STARED			
And with Megeras eyes stared in their face,	Dido	2.1.230	Aeneas
STARING			
He sent a shaggy totter'd staring slave,	Jew	4.3.6	Barab
And staring, thus bespoke: what mean'st thou Caesar?	Lucan, First Booke		192
Gote-footed Satyrs, and up-staring <upstarting> Fawnes,	Hero and Leander		2.200
STARK			
Or els I sweare to have you whipt stark nak'd.	1Tamb	4.2.74	Anippe
STARKE			
in our parish dance at my pleasure starke naked before me,	F App	p.233 4	P Robin
Starke naked as she stood before mine eie,	Ovid's Elegies		1.5.17
STAR-LIGHT			
What neede the artick people love star-light,	Edw	1.1.16	Gavstn
STARRE			
Make heaven to frowne and every fixed starre/To sucke up poison	1Tamb	4.2.5	Bajzth
But stay, what starre shines yonder in the East?	Jew	2.1.41	Barab
It twinckles like a Starre.	Jew	4.2.128	P Ithimr
Th'opposed starre of Mars hath done thee harme,	Ovid's Elegies		1.8.29
Let the bright day-starre cause in heaven this day be,	Ovid's Elegies		2.11.55
And the Icarian froward Dog-starre shine,	Ovid's Elegies		2.16.4
There, he who rules the worlds starre-spangled towers,	Ovid's Elegies		3.9.21
Or is I thinke my wish against the [starres] <starre>?	Ovid's Elegies		3.11.3
Heav'n starre Electra that bewaild her sisters?	Ovid's Elegies		3.11.37
Nor that night-wandring pale and watrie starre,	Hero and Leander		1.107
STARRES			
the Starres supprisde like Rhesus Steedes,/Are drawne by	Dido	1.1.72	Venus
Heres to thy better fortune and good starres.	Dido	2.1.98	Dido
And follow your foreseeing starres in all;	Dido	4.3.32	Achat
And when we whisper, then the starres fall downe,	Dido	4.4.53	Dido
Which gratious starres have promist at my birth.	1Tamb	1.2.92	Tamb
and all the Starres that make/The loathsome Circle of my dated	1Tamb	2.6.36	Cosroe
the clowdes/Incense the heavens, and make the starres to melt,	2Tamb	4.1.195	Tamb
From whence the starres doo borrow all their light,	2Tamb	4.2.89	Therid
Pav'd with bright Christall, and enchac'd with starres,	2Tamb	4.3.128	Tamb
Fal starres that governe his nativity,	2Tamb	5.3.2	Therid
What, will you thus oppose me, lucklesse Starres,	Jew	1.2.260	Barab
Center of all misfortune. O my starres!	Edw	4.7.62	Edward
And Characters of Signes, and [erring] <evening> Starres,/By	F 240	1.3.12	Faust
Had I as many soules, as there be Starres,	F 330	1.3.102	Faust
Mars, or Jupiter,/Fain'd, but are [erring] <evening> Starres.	F 595	2.2.44	Mephst
He viewes the cloudes, the Planets, and the Starres,	F 760	2.3.39	2Chor
That threates the starres with her aspiring top,	F 796	3.1.18	Faust

STARRES (cont.)			
Clad in the beauty of a thousand starres:	F1782	5.1.109	Faust
You Starres that raign'd at my nativity,	F1950	5.2.154	Faust
lawlesse/And casuall; all the starres at randome radge <range>:	Lucan, First Booke		642
(If I have faith) I sawe the starres drop bloud,	Ovid's Elegies		1.8.11
Ere thou rise starres teach seamen where to saile,	Ovid's Elegies		1.13.11
Nor morning starres shunne thy uprising face.	Ovid's Elegies		1.13.28
Why addst thou starres to heaven, leaves to greene woods	Ovid's Elegies		2.10.13
Then wilt thou Laedas noble twinne-starres pray,	Ovid's Elegies		2.11.29
By me, and by my starres, thy radiant eyes.	Ovid's Elegies		2.16.44
radiant like starres they be,/By which she perjurd oft hath	Ovid's Elegies		3.3.9
Or is I thinke my wish against the [starres] <starre>?	Ovid's Elegies		3.11.3
The lining, purple silke, with guilt starres drawne,	Hero and Leander		1.10
STARRE-SPANGLED			
There, he who rules the worlds starre-spangled towers,	Ovid's Elegies		3.9.21
STARRIE			
Shall build his throne amidst those starrie towers,	Dido	1.1.98	Jupitr
And now ye gods that guide the starrie frame,	Dido	5.1.302	Dido
STARRY			
And shiver all the starry firmament:	2Tamb	2.4.106	Tamb
STARS			
Nature doth strive with Fortune and his stars,	1Tamb	2.1.33	Cosroe
Weel chase the Stars from heaven, and dim their eies/That stand	1Tamb	2.3.23	Tamb
Whose smiling stars gives him assured hope/Of martiall triumph,	1Tamb	3.3.42	Tamb
Nay could their numbers countervail the stars,	1Tamb	4.1.30	Souldn
Smile Stars that raign'd at my nativity,	1Tamb	4.2.33	Tamb
Endure as we the malice of our stars,	1Tamb	5.1.43	Govnr
Thou that in conduct of thy happy stars,	1Tamb	5.1.358	Zenoc
Gives light to Phoebus and the fixed stars,	2Tamb	2.4.50	Tamb
And cause the stars fixt in the Southern arke,	2Tamb	3.2.29	Tamb
And join'd those stars that shall be opposite,	2Tamb	3.5.81	Tamb
Were full of Commets and of blazing stars,	2Tamb	5.1.89	Tamb
The Stars move still, Time runs, the Clocke will strike,	F1936	5.2.140	Faust
Confused stars shal meete, celestiall fire/Fleete on the	Lucan, First Booke		75
And some dim stars) he Arriminum enter'd:	Lucan, First Booke		234
Great store of strange and unknown stars were seene/Wandering	Lucan, First Booke		524
rings of fire/Flie in the ayre, and dreadfull bearded stars,	Lucan, First Booke		526
The lesser stars/Which wont to run their course through empty	Lucan, First Booke		533
Whose like Aegiptian Memphis never had/For skill in stars, and	Lucan, First Booke		640
street like to a Firmament/Glistered with breathing stars,	Hero and Leander		1.98
STAR'ST			
Why star'st thou in my face?	Dido	5.1.179	Dido
START			
Mine eye is fixt where fancie cannot start,	Dido	4.2.37	Iarbus
The Souldane would not start a foot from him.	1Tamb	4.1.19	Souldn
Like one start up your haire tost and displast,	Ovid's Elegies		3.13.33
STARTED			
They shalbe started thence I doubt it not.	Edw	4.6.60	Mortmr
The people started; young men left their beds,	Lucan, First Booke		241
when she departed/Nape by stumbling on the thre-shold started.	Ovid's Elegies		1.12.4
He started up, she blusht as one asham'd;	Hero and Leander		1.181
STARTING			
And marche to fire them from their starting holes.	Edw	3.1.127	Spencr
STARTS			
Whereat she starts, puts on her purple weeds,	Hero and Leander		2.88
STARV'D			
and then she shall be sure not to be starv'd, and he be	1Tamb	4.4.46	P Usumc
STARVE (See also STERV'D)			
Shall sit by him and starve to death himselfe.	1Tamb	4.2.90	Tamb
Hoping to see them starve upon a stall,	Jew	2.3.26	Barab
And laught to see the poore starve at their gates:	F1918	5.2.122	BdAngl
STARVES			
Lesse sinnes the poore rich man that starves himselfe,	Hero and Leander		1.243
STATE			
and the verie legges/Whereon our state doth leane, as on a	1Tamb	1.1.60	Mycet
Embost with silke as best beseemes my state,	1Tamb	1.1.99	Mycet
Wel, since I see the state of Persea droope,	1Tamb	1.1.155	Cosroe
we have tane/Shall be reserv'd, and you in better state,	1Tamb	1.2.3	Tamb
For they are friends that help to weane my state,	1Tamb	1.2.29	Tamb
the Persean king/Should offer present Dukedomes to our state,	1Tamb	1.2.215	Techel
And sought your state all honor it deserv'd,	1Tamb	2.5.33	Ortyg
What star or state soever governe him,	1Tamb	2.6.18	Ortyg
Even at the morning of my happy state,	1Tamb	2.7.4	Cosroe
Moov'd me to manage armes against thy state.	1Tamb	2.7.16	Tamb
souldier of my Camp/Shall smile to see thy miserable state.	1Tamb	3.3.86	Tamb
Sit here upon this royal chaire of state,	1Tamb	3.3.112	Bajzth
Being thy Captive, thus abuse his state,	1Tamb	4.2.60	Zabina
Yet in compassion of his wretched state,	1Tamb	4.3.35	Souldn
For faire Zenocrate, that so laments his state.	1Tamb	5.1.205	Therid
And that I might be privy to the state,	1Tamb	5.1.426	Arabia
If as beseemes a person of thy state,	1Tamb	5.1.483	Souldn
Her state and person wants no pomp you see,	1Tamb	5.1.485	Tamb
My royal chaire of state shall be advanc'd:	2Tamb	1.3.82	Tamb
and I might enter in/To see the state and majesty of heaven,	2Tamb	1.3.155	Tamb
al this aery region/Cannot containe the state of Tamburlaine.	2Tamb	4.1.120	Tamb
And by the state of his supremacie,	2Tamb	4.1.136	Tamb
turrets of my Court/Sit like to Venus in her chaire of state,	2Tamb	4.2.42	Therid
Is not my life and state as deere to me,	2Tamb	5.1.12	Govnr
Whose state he ever pitied and reliev'd,	2Tamb	5.1.32	1Citzn
Villaines, cowards, Traitors to our state,	2Tamb	5.1.43	Govnr
And made his state an honor to the heavens,	2Tamb	5.3.12	Therid
Which makes them manage armes against thy state,	2Tamb	5.3.36	Usumc
If any thing shall there concerne our state/Assure your selves	Jew	1.1.172	Barab

STATE (cont.)			
Pitty the state of a distressed Maid.	Jew	1.2.315	Abigal
A loving mother to preserve thy state,	P 594	12.7	QnMoth
Then meanes he present treason to our state.	P 880	17.75	King
Cheefe Secretarie to the state and me,	Edw	1.1.155	Edward
Present by me this traitor to the state,	Edw	4.6.49	Rice
Could not but take compassion of my state.	Edw	4.7.11	Edward
To see a king in this most pittious state?	Edw	5.5.51	Ltborn
of love/In Courts of Kings, where state is over-turn'd,	F 4	Prol.4	1Chor
hollinesse ascends/Saint Peters Chaire and State Pontificall.	F 870	3.1.92	Raymnd
Proud Lucifer, that State belongs to me:	F 871	3.1.93	Bruno
In quittance of their late conspiracie/Against our State, and	F 950	3.1.172	Pope
Go backe, and see the State in readinesse.	F1159	4.1.5	Mrtino
In their true shapes, and state Majesticall,	F1233	4.1.79	Emper
Thou shalt command the state of Germany,	F1323	4.1.169	Emper
smiles]/[At your repulse, and laughs your state to scorne],	F1795	5.1.122A	OldMan
And now least age might waine his state, he casts/For civill	Lucan, First Booke		324
Wert thou rich, poore should not be my state.	Ovid's Elegies		1.8.28
STATED			
and you were stated here/To be at deadly enmity with Turkes.	Jew	2.2.32	Bosco
STATELIER			
Here will Aeneas build a statelier Troy,	Dido	5.1.2	Aeneas
STATELY			
Adjoyning on Agenors stately towne,	Dido	1.1.211	Venus
Weele leade you to the stately tent of War:	1Tamb	Prol.3	Prolog
As fits the Legate of the stately Turk.	1Tamb	3.1.44	Bassoe
And rifle all those stately Janisars.	1Tamb	3.3.26	Techel
And hung on stately Mecas Temple roofe,	2Tamb	1.1.141	Orcan
Meaning to make her stately Queene of heaven.	2Tamb	2.4.108	Tamb
Thou shalt be stately Queene of faire Argier,	2Tamb	4.2.39	Therid
Inventing maskes and stately showes for her,	2Tamb	4.2.94	Therid
The stately buildings of faire Babylon,	2Tamb	5.1.63	Tamb
from Spaine the stately Catholickes/Sends Indian golde to coyne	P 117	2.60	Guise
Against the stately triumph we decreed?	Edw	2.2.12	Edward
Stately and proud, in riches and in traine,	Edw	4.7.12	Edward
Past with delight the stately Towne of Trier:	F 780	3.1.2	Faust
Over the which [foure] <two> stately Bridges leane,	F 815	3.1.37	Mephst
What gate thy stately words cannot unlocke,	Ovid's Elegies		3.1.45
And stately robes to their gilt feete hang downe.	Ovid's Elegies		3.12.26
A stately builded ship, well rig'd and tall,	Hero and Leander		1.225
For here the stately azure pallace stood,	Hero and Leander		2.165
STATES			
We in the name of other Persean states,	1Tamb	1.1.137	Ortyg
higher meeds/Then erst our states and actions have retain'd,	1Tamb	4.4.132	Therid
And beare him to the States of Germany.	F 900	3.1.122	Faust
STATUE (See also STATURE, STATUTES)			
at whose latter gaspe/Joves marble statue gan to bend the brow,	Dido	2.1.257	Aeneas
And here will I set up her stature <statue>/And martch about it	2Tamb	2.4.140	Tamb
their vaild Matron, who alone might view/Minervas statue; then,	Lucan, First Booke		598
Was Danaes statue in a brazen tower,	Hero and Leander		1.146
STATUES			
Whose [statues] <statutes> we adore in Scythia,	1Tamb	1.2.244	Tamb
Crownes fell from holy statues, ominous birds/Defil'd the day,	Lucan, First Booke		556
STATURE (Homograph)			
What stature wields he, and what personage?	1Tamb	2.1.6	Cosroe
Of stature tall, and straightly fashioned,	1Tamb	2.1.7	Menaph
The golden stature of their feathered bird/That spreads her	1Tamb	4.2.105	Tamb
And here will I set up her stature <statue>/And martch about it	2Tamb	2.4.140	Tamb
STATUTES (Homograph)			
Whose [statues] <statutes> we adore in Scythia,	1Tamb	1.2.244	Tamb
And read amongst the Statutes Decretall,	F 883	3.1.105	Pope
The Statutes Decretall have thus decreed,	F 961	3.1.183	Faust
STAVES (Homograph)			
Like Almaine Rutters with their horsemens staves,	F 152	1.1.124	Valdes
No slave, in beaten silke, and staves-aker.	F 357	1.4.15	P Wagner
Staves-aker?	F 358	1.4.16	P Robin
No sirra, in beaten silke and staves acre.	F App	p.229 16	P Wagner
Sirra, I say in staves acre.	F App	p.229 20	P Wagner
Oho, oho, staves acre, why then belike, if I were your man,	F App	p.229 21	P Clown
STAVES ACRE			
No sirra, in beaten silke and staves acre.	F App	p.229 16	P Wagner
Sirra, I say in staves acre.	F App	p.229 20	P Wagner
Oho, oho, staves acre, why then belike, if I were your man,	F App	p.229 21	P Clown
STAVES-AKER			
No slave, in beaten silke, and staves-aker.	F 357	1.4.15	P Wagner
Staves-aker?	F 358	1.4.16	P Robin
STAY (See also STAIE)			
Stay gentle Venus, flye not from thy sonne,	Dido	1.1.242	Aeneas
Troy is invincible, why stay we here?	Dido	2.1.128	Aeneas
Then he alleag'd the Gods would have them stay,	Dido	2.1.141	Aeneas
Polixena cryed out, Aeneas stay,	Dido	2.1.281	Aeneas
The Greekes pursue me, stay and take me in.	Dido	2.1.282	Aeneas
Faire child stay thou with Didos waiting maide,	Dido	2.1.304	Venus
Goe thou away, Ascanius shall stay.	Dido	3.1.35	Dido
O stay Iarbus, and Ile goe with thee.	Dido	3.1.37	Dido
Iarbus pardon me, and stay a while.	Dido	3.1.46	Dido
Conditionally that thou wilt stay with me,	Dido	3.1.114	Dido
So that Aeneas may but stay with me.	Dido	3.1.133	Dido
Wherefore would Dido have Aeneas stay?	Dido	3.1.134	Aeneas
Iarbus stay, loving Iarbus stay,	Dido	4.2.52	Anna
Whereas Nobilitie abhors to stay,	Dido	4.3.19	Aeneas
To stay my Fleete from loosing forth the Bay:	Dido	4.3.26	Aeneas
We will not stay a minute longer here.	Dido	4.3.44	Cloan

STAY (cont.)

And teares of pearle, crye stay, Aeneas, stay:	Dido	4.3.52	Aeneas
Stay not to answere me, runne Anna runne.	Dido	4.4.4	Dido
I charge thee put to sea and stay not here.	Dido	4.4.22	Dido
Get you abourd, Aeneas meanes to stay.	Dido	4.4.24	Dido
Stay here Aeneas, and commaund as King.	Dido	4.4.39	Dido
Whither must I goe? Ile stay with my mother.	Dido	4.5.2	Cupid
Aeneas stay, Joves Herald bids thee stay.	Dido	5.1.24	Hermes
And yet I may not stay, Dido farewell.	Dido	5.1.104	Aeneas
Fare well may Dido, so Aeneas stay,	Dido	5.1.107	Dido
Say thou wilt stay in Carthage with [thy] <my> Queene,	Dido	5.1.117	Dido
O thy lips have sworne/To stay with Dido:	Dido	5.1.121	Dido
if thou wilt stay,/Leape in mine armes, mine armes are open	Dido	5.1.179	Dido
I have not power to stay thee: is he gone?	Dido	5.1.183	Dido
I crave but this, he stay a tide or two,	Dido	5.1.207	Dido
Run Anna, run, stay not to answere me.	Dido	5.1.210	Dido
But I cride out, Aeneas, false Aeneas stay.	Dido	5.1.228	Anna
Which when I viewd, I cride, Aeneas stay,	Dido	5.1.232	Anna
Dido, faire Dido wils Aeneas stay:	Dido	5.1.233	Anna
And stay a while to heare what I could say,	Dido	5.1.239	Anna
Now sweet Iarbus stay, I come to thee.	Dido	5.1.329	Anna
Nay, pray you let him stay, a greater [task]/Fits Menaphon, than	1Tamb	1.1.87	Cosroe
Therefore to stay all sodaine mutinies,	1Tamb	1.1.150	Ceneus
Stay Techelles, aske a parlee first.	1Tamb	1.2.137	Tamb
If thou wilt stay with me, renowmed man,	1Tamb	1.2.188	Tamb
Your speech will stay, or so extol his worth,	1Tamb	2.3.27	Therid
Then stay thou with him, say I bid thee so.	1Tamb	3.1.35	Bajzth
Than stay the torments he and heaven have sworne.	1Tamb	3.2.99	Agidas
but some must stay/To rule the provinces he late subdude.	1Tamb	3.3.28	Bassoe
Why stay we thus prolonging all their lives?	1Tamb	3.3.97	Techel
But if he stay until the bloody flag/Be once advanc'd on my	1Tamb	4.2.116	Tamb
Here let him stay my maysters from the tents,	1Tamb	5.1.211	Tamb
That she shall stay and turne her wheele no more,	1Tamb	5.1.374	Anippe
Stay Sigismond, forgetst thou I am he/That with the Cannon	2Tamb	1.1.86	Orcan
To stay my comming gainst proud Tamburlaine.	2Tamb	1.1.163	Orcan
her soule be, thou shalt stay with me/Embalm'd with Cassia,	2Tamb	2.4.129	Tamb
But stay a while, summon a parle, Drum,	2Tamb	3.3.11	Therid
That humbly craves upon her knees to stay,	2Tamb	3.4.70	Olymp
And when ye stay, be lasht with whips of wier:	2Tamb	3.5.105	Tamb
Turn'd into pearle and proffered for my stay,	2Tamb	4.1.44	Amyras
Stay good my Lord, and wil you save my honor,	2Tamb	4.2.55	Olymp
But stay, I feele my selfe distempered sudainly.	2Tamb	5.1.218	Tamb
Looke where he goes, but see, he comes againe/Because I stay:	2Tamb	5.3.76	Tamb
Graecia, and from thence/To Asia, where I stay against my will,	2Tamb	5.3.142	Tamb
Corpo di dic stay, you shall have halfe,	Jew	1.2.90	Barab
But stay, what starre shines yonder in the East?	Jew	2.1.41	Barab
Yonder comes Don Mathias, let us stay;	Jew	2.3.140	Barab
Whither goes Don Mathias? stay a while.	Jew	2.3.251	Barab
Stay her,--but let her not speake one word more.	Jew	2.3.323	Barab
Nay, if you will, stay till she comes her selfe.	Jew	2.3.352	Barab
I cannot stay; for if my mother come,	Jew	2.3.353	Mthias
Nay Madam stay, that weapon was my son's,	Jew	3.2.25	Govnr
Stay, let me spice it first.	Jew	3.4.85	Barab
Stay, first let me stirre it Ithimore.	Jew	3.4.95	Barab
Stay wicked Jew, repent, I say, and stay.	Jew	4.1.24	2Fryar
You loyter, master, wherefore stay [we] <me> thus?	Jew	4.1.139	Ithimr
Well, my hope is, he will not stay there still;	Jew	4.3.16	Barab
Nay stay, my Lord, 'tmay be he will confesse.	Jew	5.1.25	1Knght
Stay, Calymath;	Jew	5.5.60	Govnr
Nay, Selim, stay, for since we have thee here,	Jew	5.5.97	Govnr
Content thee, Calymath, here thou must stay,	Jew	5.5.118	Govnr
The rest that will not goe (my Lords) may stay:	P 23	1.23	Charls
Stay my Lord, let me begin the psalme.	P 344	5.71	Anjoy
Sweet Taleus stay.	P 370	7.10	Ramus
For that let me alone, Cousin stay you heer,	P 428	7.68	Anjoy
I have done what I could to stay this broile.	P 434	7.74	Anjoy
And now sirs for this night let our fury stay.	P 443	7.83	Guise
And now stay/That bel that to the devils mattins rings.	P 447	7.87	Guise
O let me stay and rest me heer a while,	P 536	11.1	Charls
Not yet my Lord, for thereon doe they stay:	P 732	14.35	1Msngr
Oh that I have not power to stay my life,	P1007	19.77	Guise
Then stay a while and Ile goe call the King,	P1017	19.87	Capt
Now thou art dead, heere is no stay for us:	P1111	21.5	Dumain
Ere Gaveston shall stay within the realme.	Edw	1.1.105	Lncstr
And war must be the meanes, or heele stay stil.	Edw	1.2.63	Warwck
Then let him stay, for rather then my lord/Shall be oppresst by	Edw	1.2.64	Queene
To crosse to Lambeth, and there stay with me.	Edw	1.2.78	ArchBp
Whether will you beare him, stay or ye shall die.	Edw	1.4.24	Edward
And long thou shalt not stay, or if thou doost,	Edw	1.4.114	Edward
Stay Gaveston, I cannot leave thee thus.	Edw	1.4.135	Edward
The time is little that thou hast to stay,	Edw	1.4.138	Edward
why do I stay,/Seeing that he talkes thus of my mariage day?	Edw	2.1.68	Neece
Spencer, stay you and beare me companie,	Edw	2.1.74	Neece
Nay, stay my lord, I come to bring you newes,	Edw	2.2.141	Mortmr
Stay Edmund, never was Plantagenet/False of his word, and	Edw	2.3.11	Mortmr
O stay my lord, they will not injure you.	Edw	2.4.7	Gavstn
Madam, stay you within this castell here.	Edw	2.4.50	Mortmr
Madam, I cannot stay to answer you,	Edw	2.4.57	Mortmr
Mortimer I stay thy sweet escape,	Edw	4.1.10	Kent
And there stay times advantage with your sonne?	Edw	4.2.18	SrJohn
As good be gon, as stay and be benighted.	Edw	4.7.86	Rice
They stay your answer, will you yeeld your crowne?	Edw	5.1.50	Leistr
But stay a while, let me be king till night,	Edw	5.1.59	Edward

STAY (cont.)			
All times and seasons rest you at a stay,	Edw	5.1.67	Edward
Yet stay, for rather then I will looke on them,	Edw	5.1.106	Edward
And I will visit him, why stay you me?	Edw	5.3.60	Kent
Wherefore stay we? on sirs to the court.	Edw	5.3.65	Souldr
Let me but stay and speake, I will not go,	Edw	5.4.105	Kent
But stay, whose this?	Edw	5.5.14	Matrvs
I, stay a while, thou shalt have answer straight.	Edw	5.5.20	Matrvs
Yet stay a while, forbeare thy bloudie hande,	Edw	5.5.75	Edward
Thou wilt returne againe, and therefore stay.	Edw	5.5.99	Edward
O let me not die yet, stay, O stay a while.	Edw	5.5.101	Edward
He hath forgotten me, stay, I am his mother.	Edw	5.6.90	Queene
Stay Mephostophilis/And tell me, what good will my soule do thy	F 427	2.1.39	Faust
Nay stay my Faustus:	F 831	3.1.53	Mephst
Nay stay my gentle Mephostophilis,	F 845	3.1.67	Faust
Let it be so my Faustus, but first stay,	F 856	3.1.78	Mephst
<to do what I please unseene of any whilst I stay in Rome>.	F 993	(HC266)A	P Faust
Nay, we will stay with thee, betide what may,	F1338	4.2.14	Fredrk
Here will we stay to bide the first assault,	F1354	4.2.30	Benvol
Yet stay, the world shall see their miserie,	F1406	4.2.82	Faust
[Ah] <O> stay good Faustus, stay thy desperate steps.	F1729	5.1.56	OldMan
And here wee'l stay,	F1805	5.2.9	Belzeb
God will strengthen me, I will stay with Faustus.	F1870	5.2.74	P 3Schol
Romans if ye be,/And beare true harts, stay heare:	Lucan, First Booke	194	
Be sedulous, let no stay cause thee tarry.	Ovid's Elegies	1.11.8	
blotted letter/On the last edge to stay mine eyes the better.	Ovid's Elegies	1.11.22	
Then wouldst thou cry, stay night and runne not thus.	Ovid's Elegies	1.13.40	
His rider vainely striving him to stay,	Ovid's Elegies	2.9.30	
So in thy Temples shall Osiris stay,	Ovid's Elegies	2.13.12	
A mortall nimphes refusing Lord to stay.	Ovid's Elegies	2.17.16	
My stay no crime, my flight no joy shall breede,	Ovid's Elegies	2.17.25	
In running if I see thee, I shall stay,	Ovid's Elegies	3.2.13	
<redde-growne> slime bankes, till I be past/Thy waters stay:	Ovid's Elegies	3.5.2	
To stay thy tresses white veyle hast thou none?	Ovid's Elegies	3.5.56	
Thrice she prepar'd to flie, thrice she did stay,	Ovid's Elegies	3.5.69	
Why stay I?	Ovid's Elegies	3.5.77	
To know their rites, well recompenc'd my stay,	Ovid's Elegies	3.12.5	
Did charme her nimble feet, and made her stay,	Hero and Leander	1.399	
And stay the messenger that would be gon:	Hero and Leander	2.82	
STAYD			
So when as Crassus wretched death who stayd them,	Lucan, First Booke	104	
Herewith he stayd his furie, and began/To give her leave to	Hero and Leander	1.415	
To linger by the way, and once she stayd,	Hero and Leander	2.7	
But stayd, and after her a letter sent.	Hero and Leander	2.14	
And red for anger that he stayd so long,	Hero and Leander	2.89	
She stayd not for her robes, but straight arose,	Hero and Leander	2.235	
STAYDE			
[Hee stayde his course, and so returned home],	F1140	3.3.53A	3Chor
When he perceivd the reines let slacke, he stayde,	Ovid's Elegies	3.4.15	
STAYED			
Not long he stayed within his quiet house,	F 768	2.3.47	2Chor
STAYES			
But though he goe, he stayes in Carthage still,	Dido	4.4.133	Dido
are letters come/From Ormus, and the Post stayes here within.	Jew	2.3.223	Abigal
You see I answer him, and yet he stayes;	Jew	4.1.88	Barab
The winde is good, I wonder why he stayes,	Edw	2.2.1	Edward
oh hee stayes my tongue:	F1852	5.2.56	P Faust
If long she stayes, to thinke the time more short/Lay downe thy	Ovid's Elegies	2.2.23	
Thy dull hand stayes thy striving enemies harmes.	Ovid's Elegies	2.9.12	
STAYING			
(Staying to order all the scattered troopes)/Farewell Lord	1Tamb	2.5.45	Cosroe
Heere is no staying for the King of France,	P 897	17.92	King
What might the staying of my bloud portend?	F 453	2.1.65	Faust
STAYNES			
Arachne staynes Assyrian ivory.	Ovid's Elegies	2.5.40	
STAYRES			
To ascend our homely stayres?	Jew	5.5.58	Barab
STEAD (Homograph; See also STEED)			
who in stead of him/Will set thee on her lap and play with	Dido	2.1.324	Venus
In stead of musicke I will heare him speake,	Dido	3.1.89	Dido
For every fell and stout Tartarian Stead/That stampt on others	1Tamb	5.1.330	Zenoc
Be governour of Ireland in my stead,	Edw	1.4.125	Edward
In stead of Troy shall Wittenberg <Wertenberge> be sack't,/And	F1776	5.1.103	Faust
Gush forth bloud in stead of teares, yea life and soule:	F1851	5.2.55	P Faust
Or thinke soft verse in any stead to stand?	Ovid's Elegies	3.7.2	
Whose carelesse haire, in stead of pearle t'adorne it,	Hero and Leander	1.389	
STEADE			
Gold from the earth in steade of fruits we pluck,	Ovid's Elegies	3.7.53	
STEADFAST (See STEDFAST)			
STEADS			
(Auster and Aquilon with winged Steads/All sweating, tilt about	1Tamb	3.2.78	Agidas
STEALE			
Or steale your houshold lares from their shrines:	Dido	1.2.11	Illion
It may be he will steale away with them:	Dido	4.4.3	Dido
O foolish Troians that would steale from hence,	Dido	4.4.5	Dido
We will not steale upon him cowardly,	1Tamb	2.5.102	Tamb
Will you then steale my goods?	Jew	1.2.94	Barab
I must be forc'd to steale and compasse more.	Jew	1.2.127	Barab
What, can he steale that you demand so much?	Jew	2.3.100	Barab
And in the night time secretly would I steale/To travellers	Jew	2.3.206	Ithimr
But steale you in, and seeme to see him not;	Jew	2.3.272	Barab
I'le goe steale some mony from my Master to make me hansome:	Jew	4.2.49	P Ithimr
To steale from France, and hye me to my home.	P 567	11.32	Navrre

STEALE (cont.)
we steale a cup? F1099 3.3.12 P Robin
your searching; we scorne to steale your cups I can tell you. F1106 3.3.19 P Dick
To steale sands from the shore he loves alife, Ovid's Elegies 2.19.45
And steale a kisse, and then run out and daunce, Hero and Leander 2.185
and up-staring <upstarting> Fawnes,/Would steale him thence. Hero and Leander 2.201

STEALERS
what you say, we looke not like cup-stealers I can tell you. F1100 3.3.13 P Robin

STEALES
Scylla by us her fathers rich haire steales, Ovid's Elegies 3.11.21

STEALING
And when I look away, comes stealing on: 2Tamb 5.3.71 Tamb
that your devill can answere the stealing of this same cup, F1089 3.3.2 P Dick
Jove, slylie stealing from his sisters bed, Hero and Leander 1.147

STEALTH
And therefore to her tower he got by stealth. Hero and Leander 2.18
And faine by stealth away she would have crept, Hero and Leander 2.310

STEDFAST
My minde may be more stedfast on my God. Edw 5.5.78 Edward
Above our life we love a stedfast friend, Hero and Leander 2.79

STEED (Homograph; See also STEAD, STEADS)
And see if those will serve in steed of sailes: Dido 4.4.160 Dido
In steed of oares, let him use his hands, Dido 4.4.163 Dido
Not long agoe bestrid a Scythian Steed: 2Tamb 1.3.38 Zenoc
I would the Guise in his steed might have come, P 736 14.39 Navrre
And on a proud pac'd Steed, as swift as thought, F 984 3.2.4 Mephst
In steed of red bloud wallowed venemous gore. Lucan, First Booke 614

STEEDE
Sway thou the Punike Scepter in my steede, Dido 4.4.35 Dido
In steede of inke, ile write it with my teares. Edw 1.4.86 Edward

STEEDES
Drawne through the heavens by Steedes of Boreas brood, Dido 1.1.55 Venus
the Starres supprisde like Rhesus Steedes,/Are drawne by Dido 1.1.72 Venus
to warre,/Was so incenst as are Eleius steedes/With clamors: Lucan, First Booke 294
Or when the Moone travailes with charmed steedes. Ovid's Elegies 2.5.38
On swift steedes mounted till the race were done. Ovid's Elegies 3.2.10
Victorious Perseus a wingd steedes back takes. Ovid's Elegies 3.11.24

STEEDS
That I may view these milk-white steeds of mine, 1Tamb 1.1.77 Mycet
Mounted on Steeds, swifter than Pegasus. 1Tamb 1.2.94 Tamb
Mounted on lusty Mauritanian Steeds, 1Tamb 3.3.16 Bassoe
We meane to seate our footmen on their Steeds, 1Tamb 3.3.25 Techel
Upon their pransing Steeds, disdainfully/With wanton paces 1Tamb 4.1.22 2Msngr
in crimson silk/Shall ride before the on Barbarian Steeds: 2Tamb 1.2.47 Callap
And leave his steeds to faire Boetes charge: 2Tamb 1.3.170 Tamb
And Sequana that well could manage steeds; Lucan, First Booke 426
Or steeds might fal forcd with thick clouds approch. Ovid's Elegies 1.13.30
Now had the morne espy'de her lovers steeds, Hero and Leander 2.87

STEEL
As blacke as Jeat, and hard as Iron or steel, 2Tamb 1.3.27 Tamb

STEELD
And love to Room (thogh slaughter steeld their harts/And minds Lucan, First Booke 355

STEELE
Who with steele Pol-axes dasht out their braines. Dido 2.1.199 Aeneas
A Burgonet of steele, and not a Crowne, Dido 4.4.42 Aeneas
My sword stroke fire from his coat of steele, 1Tamb 4.2.41 Tamb
Nothing but feare and fatall steele my Lord. 1Tamb 5.1.109 1Virgn
Mingled with powdered shot and fethered steele/So thick upon 2Tamb 1.1.92 Orcan
your tongues/And bind them close with bits of burnisht steele, 2Tamb 4.1.182 Tamb
But he whose steele-bard coffers are cramb'd full, Jew 1.1.14 Barab
Weele steele it on their crest, and powle their tops. Edw 3.1.27 Edward
And Isabell, whose eyes [being] <beene> turnd to steele, Edw 5.1.104 Edward
[Gunnes] <Swords>, poyson, halters, and invenomb'd steele, F 573 2.2.22 Faust
His heart consists of flint, and hardest steele, Ovid's Elegies 3.5.59

STEELE-BARD
But he whose steele-bard coffers are cramb'd full, Jew 1.1.14 Barab

STEELED
Yet should our courages and steeled crestes, 2Tamb 2.2.17 Gazell
Breaking my steeled lance, with which I burst/The rusty beames 2Tamb 2.4.113 Tamb
Bridle the steeled stomackes of those Jades. 2Tamb 5.3.203 Tamb

STEEPE
the Counterscarps/Narrow and steepe, the wals made high and 2Tamb 3.2.69 Tamb
Through rocks more steepe and sharp than Caspian cliftes. 2Tamb 5.3.241 Tamb
Though thether leades a rough steepe hilly way. Ovid's Elegies 3.12.6
From steepe Pine-bearing mountains to the plaine: Hero and Leander 1.116

STEEPIE
This Traytor flies unto some steepie rocke, F1413 4.2.89 Faust
Woods, or steepie mountaine yeeldes. Passionate Shepherd 4

STEEPLE
And like a Steeple over-peeres the Church. F 913 3.1.135 Pope

STEEPT
Roomes infant walles were steept in brothers bloud; Lucan, First Booke 95

STEMS
And Christian Merchants that with Russian stems/Plow up huge 1Tamb 1.2.194 Tamb

STENCH
The stench whereof corrupts the inward soule/With such F App p.243 41 OldMan

STENCHE
When all my sences are anoyde with stenche? Edw 5.3.18 Edward

STEP
How should I step or stir my hatefull feete, 2Tamb 5.3.195 Amyras
And step into his fathers regiment. Edw 3.1.271 Spencr
And thy step-father fights by thy example. Ovid's Elegies 2.9.48
And wanting organs to advaunce a step, Hero and Leander 2.57

STEPDAME
The stepdame read Hyppolitus lustlesse line. Ovid's Elegies 2.18.30
STEP-FATHER
And thy step-father fights by thy example. Ovid's Elegies 2.9.48
STEPS
No steps of men imprinted in the earth. Dido 1.1.181 Achat
Wishing good lucke unto thy wandring steps. Dido 1.1.239 Venus
And by those steps that he hath scal'd the heavens, 1Tamb 1.2.200 Tamb
their Spheares/That guides his steps and actions to the throne, 1Tamb 2.1.17 Menaph
Eies when that Ebena steps to heaven, 1Tamb 5.1.147 Tamb
This ground which is corrupted with their steps, Edw 1.2.5 Lncstr
Whether, O whether doost thou bend thy steps? Edw 4.2.12 Queene
[Ah] <O> stay good Faustus, stay thy desperate steps. F1729 5.1.56 OldMan
To guide thy steps unto the way of life, F App p.243 35 OldMan
And faintnes numm'd his steps there on the brincke: Lucan, First Booke 196
Then with huge steps came violent Tragedie, Ovid's Elegies 3.1.11
STEPT
peace against their wils; betwixt them both/Stept Crassus in: Lucan, First Booke 100
For saving of a Romaine Citizen,/Stept forth, and cryde: Lucan, First Booke 360
STERD
I tooke him by the [beard] <sterd>, and look'd upon him thus; Jew 4.2.105 P Pilia
STERN
Plaies, maskes, and all that stern age counteth evill. Hero and Leander 1.302
STERNE (Homograph)
In whose sterne faces shin'd the quenchles fire, Dido 2.1.186 Aeneas
Nor Sterne nor Anchor have our maimed Fleete, Dido 3.1.109 Aeneas
And left me neither saile nor sterne abourd. Dido 5.1.61 Aeneas
My sterne aspect shall make faire Victory, 2Tamb 3.5.162 Tamb
and of fire/Doth send such sterne affections to his heart. 2Tamb 4.1.176 Trebiz
And for Patroclus sterne Achillis droopt: Edw 1.4.394 MortSr
Was this that sterne aspect, that awfull frowne, F1370 4.2.46 Fredrk
hellish fiend/Which made the sterne Lycurgus wound his thigh, Lucan, First Booke 573
Fare well sterne warre, for blunter Poets meete. Ovid's Elegies 1.1.32
Or I more sterne then fire or sword will turne, Ovid's Elegies 1.6.57
But if sterne Neptunes windie powre prevaile, Ovid's Elegies 2.16.27
Sterne was her front, her [cloake] <looke> on ground did lie. Ovid's Elegies 3.1.12
But follow trembling campes, and battailes sterne, Ovid's Elegies 3.7.26
And to those sterne nymphs humblie made request, Hero and Leander 1.379
STERV'D
Where I am sterv'd for want of sustenance, Edw 5.3.20 Edward
STICK
Stick in his breast, as in their proper roomes. 1Tamb 5.1.226 Zabina
STICKE
And sticke these spangled feathers in thy hat, Dido 2.1.314 Venus
And I will teach [thee] that shall sticke by thee: Jew 2.3.168 Barab
STICKETH
I see Aeneas sticketh in your minde, Dido 4.1.33 Dido
STICKING
I would get off though straight, and sticking fast, Ovid's Elegies 2.15.13
STICKS
or his speare/Sticks in his side) yet runs upon the hunter. Lucan, First Booke 214
STIES
And little Piggs, base Hog-sties sacrifice, Ovid's Elegies 3.12.16
STIFELED
And I was almost stifeled with the savor. Edw 5.5.9 Gurney
STIFELING
And Natures beauty choake with stifeling clouds, Jew 2.3.331 Lodowk
STIFFE
And hew these knees that now are growne so stiffe. Edw 1.1.95 Edward
And where stiffe winter whom no spring resolves, Lucan, First Booke 17
With stiffe oake propt the gate doth still appeare. Ovid's Elegies 1.6.28
I saw a horse against the bitte stiffe-neckt, Ovid's Elegies 3.4.13
STIFFE-NECKT
I saw a horse against the bitte stiffe-neckt, Ovid's Elegies 3.4.13
STIFLED
I had beene stifled, and not lived to see, Edw 1.4.176 Queene
STIGIAN
Were with Jove clos'd in Stigian Emperie. Hero and Leander 1.458
STIL
Stil dooth this man or rather God of war, 1Tamb 5.1.1 Govnr
And oft hath warn'd thee to be stil in field, 2Tamb 4.1.24 Amyras
Spirits with desire/Stil to be train'd in armes and chivalry? 2Tamb 4.1.81 Tamb
Cherish thy valour stil with fresh supplies: 2Tamb 4.1.87 Tamb
Nothing, but stil thy husband and thy sonne? 2Tamb 4.2.37 Therid
not perswade you to submission,/But stil the ports were shut: 2Tamb 5.1.95 Tamb
And yet gapes stil for more to quench his thirst, 2Tamb 5.2.14 Amasia
Sit stil my gratious Lord, this griefe wil cease, 2Tamb 5.3.64 Techel
And therefore stil augments his cruelty. 2Tamb 5.3.219 Tamb
And war must be the meanes, or heele stay stil. Edw 1.2.63 Warwck
Stil wil these Earles and Barrons use me thus? Edw 2.2.70 Edward
Quarrels were rife, greedy desire stil poore/Did vild deeds, Lucan, First Booke 174
Whence the wind blowes stil forced to and fro; Lucan, First Booke 414
STILE
Lords of this towne, or whatsoever stile/Belongs unto your name, Dido 2.1.39 Aeneas
me, for his sake/Ile grace thee with a higher stile ere long. Edw 2.2.253 Edward
Tis time to move grave things in lofty stile, Ovid's Elegies 3.1.23
Thy lofty stile with mine I not compare, Ovid's Elegies 3.1.39
STILL (See also STYL)
Great Jupiter, still honourd maist thou be, Dido 1.1.137 Venus
Pluck up your hearts, since fate still rests our friend, Dido 1.1.149 Aeneas
Alas sweet boy, thou must be still a while, Dido 1.1.164 Aeneas
So leaning on his sword he stood stone still, Dido 2.1.263 Aeneas
Or whisking of these leaves, all shall be still, Dido 2.1.337 Venus

STILL (cont.)			
O keepe them still, and let me gaze my fill:	Dido	4.4.44	Dido
But though he goe, he stayes in Carthage still,	Dido	4.4.133	Dido
Will, being absent, be obdurate still.	Dido	5.1.187	Dido
They may be still tormented with unrest,	Dido	5.1.305	Dido
Thus shall my heart be still combinde with thine,	1Tamb	1.2.235	Tamb
Still climing after knowledge infinite,	1Tamb	2.7.24	Tamb
Ah, life and soule still hover in his Breast,	1Tamb	3.2.21	Zenoc
Honor still waight on happy Tamburlaine:	1Tamb	4.4.85	Zenoc
If all the heavenly Quintessence they still/From their	1Tamb	5.1.165	Tamb
Why feed ye still on daies accursed beams,	1Tamb	5.1.262	Bajzth
To armes my Lords, on Christ still let us crie,	2Tamb	2.2.63	Orcan
Live still my Love and so conserve my life,	2Tamb	2.4.55	Tamb
Live still my Lord, O let my soveraigne live,	2Tamb	2.4.57	Zenoc
They will talk still my Lord, if you doe not bridle them.	2Tamb	5.1.146	P Amyras
Shal still retaine my spirit, though I die,	2Tamb	5.3.173	Tamb
Then good my Lord, to keepe your quiet still,	Jew	1.2.43	Barab
Live still; and if thou canst, get more.	Jew	1.2.102	Govnr
And seeing they are not idle, but still doing,	Jew	2.3.83	Barab
Well, my hope is, he will not stay there still;	Jew	4.3.16	Barab
And in this City still have had successe,	Jew	5.2.69	Barab
Nay more, doe this, and live thou Governor still.	Jew	5.2.89	Govnr
no more/I'le satisfie my selfe with that; nay, keepe it still,	Jew	5.5.22	Barab
May still be feweld in our progenye.	P 8	1.8	Charls
That God may still defend the right of France:	P 56	1.56	Navrre
Will shew his mercy and preserve us still.	P 576	11.41	Navrre
As now you are, so shall you still persist,	P 608	12.21	King
Regarding still the danger of thy life.	P 748	15.6	King
Whose service he may still commaund till death.	P1149	22.11	Navrre
Long may you live, and still be King of France.	P1226	22.88	Navrre
And with the world be still at enmitie:	Edw	1.1.15	Gavstn
And still his minde runs on his minion.	Edw	2.2.4	Queene
Shall I still be haunted thus?	Edw	2.2.154	Edward
Thus do you still suspect me without cause.	Edw	2.2.227	Queene
As though your highnes were a schoole boy still,	Edw	3.1.30	Baldck
A traitors, will they still display their pride?	Edw	3.1.172	Spencr
Where sorrow at my elbow still attends,	Edw	5.1.33	Edward
Stand still you watches of the element,	Edw	5.1.66	Edward
That Edward may be still faire Englands king:	Edw	5.1.68	Edward
Remoove him still from place to place by night,	Edw	5.2.59	Mortmr
Finely dissembled, do so still sweet Queene.	Edw	5.2.74	Mortmr
Still feare I, and I know not whats the cause,	Edw	5.5.85	Edward
Something still busseth in mine eares,	Edw	5.5.103	Edward
Yet art thou still but Faustus, and a man.	F 51	1.1.23	Faust
I, thinke so still, till experience change thy mind.	F 517	2.1.129	Mephst
Defend me heaven, shall I be haunted still?	F1439	4.3.9	Benvol
I hope my score stands still.	F1515	4.5.11	P Robin
thee, then had I lived still, but now must <I> dye eternally.	F1825	5.2.29	P Faust
Stand still you ever moving Spheares of heaven,	F1929	5.2.133	Faust
The Stars move still, Time runs, the Clocke will strike,	F1936	5.2.140	Faust
But mine must live still to be plagu'd in hell.	F1971	5.2.175	Faust
And having once got head still shal he raigne?	Lucan, First Booke		317
With stiffe oake propt the gate doth still appeare.	Ovid's Elegies		1.6.28
Which to her wast her girdle still kept downe.	Ovid's Elegies		1.7.48
Yet greedy Bauds command she curseth still,	Ovid's Elegies		1.10.23
Shee in my lap sits still as earst she did.	Ovid's Elegies		2.18.6
And one gave place still as another came.	Ovid's Elegies		3.6.64
But still droupt downe, regarding not her hand,	Ovid's Elegies		3.6.76
Bulles hate the yoake, yet what they hate have still.	Ovid's Elegies		3.10.36
Slippe still, onely denie it when tis done,	Ovid's Elegies		3.13.15
And with still panting rockt, there tooke his rest.	Hero and Leander		1.44
Stone still he stood, and evermore he gazed,	Hero and Leander		1.163
Wilt thou live single still?	Hero and Leander		1.257
Yet evilly faining anger, strove she still,	Hero and Leander		1.335
Far from the towne (where all is whist and still,	Hero and Leander		1.346
Still vowd he love, she wanting no excuse/To feed him with	Hero and Leander		1.425
And still inrich the loftie servile clowne,	Hero and Leander		1.481
But still the rising billowes answered no.	Hero and Leander		2.152
STILTS			
to see the cripples/Goe limping home to Christendome on stilts.	Jew	2.3.212	Ithimr
STING			
That with the sharpnes of my edged sting,	Dido	4.1.22	Iarbus
Wilt thou now slay me with thy venomed sting,	Dido	5.1.167	Dido
STINGS			
For saving him from Snakes and Serpents stings,	Dido	3.2.38	Juno
Or winged snakes of Lerna cast your stings,	1Tamb	4.4.21	Bajzth
STINKE			
Foh, me thinkes they stinke like a Holly-Hoke.	Jew	4.4.41	Pilia
STINT			
Before my sorrowes tide have any stint.	Dido	4.2.42	Iarbus
STIPEND			
All that I have is but my stipend from the King,	P 378	7.18	Ramus
STIPENDIUM			
Stipendium peccati mors est:	F 66	1.1.38	P Faust
ha, Stipendium, &c.	F 66	1.1.38	P Faust
STIR			
Keep all your standings, and not stir a foote,	1Tamb	1.2.150	Tamb
But if he dare attempt to stir your siege,	1Tamb	3.1.46	Argier
Stir not Zenocrate untill thou see/Me martch victoriously with	1Tamb	3.3.126	Tamb
Ready to charge you ere you stir your feet.	2Tamb	1.1.121	Fredrk
How should I step or stir my hatefull feete,	2Tamb	5.3.195	Amyras
They would not stir, were it to do me good:	Edw	1.4.95	Edward
and stir not for thy life, Vintner you shall have your cup	F1113	3.3.26	P Robin

STIRD			
The heart stird not, and from the gaping liver/Squis'd matter;	Lucan, First Booke		623
STIRDE			
Thee wars use stirde, and thoughts that alwaies scorn'd/A	Lucan, First Booke		124
Such humors stirde them up; but this warrs seed, . .	Lucan, First Booke		159
STIRRE			
Stay, first let me stirre it Ithimore.	Jew	3.4.95	Barab
And usde all speech that might provoke and stirre. . .	Ovid's Elegies		3.6.12
Lie downe with shame, and see thou stirre no more, . .	Ovid's Elegies		3.6.69
STIRS			
And stirs your valures to such soddaine armes?	2Tamb	2.1.3	Sgsmnd
STIX			
More than Cymerian Stix or Distinie.	1Tamb	5.1.234	Bajzth
Of Stix, of Acheron, and the fiery Lake, ...	F 826	3.1.48	Faust
STOCKE			
Nor Dardanus the author of thy stocke:	Dido	5.1.157	Dido
Monster of Nature, shame unto thy stocke, ...	1Tamb	1.1.104	Mycet
Now is he borne, of parents base of stocke, ...	F 11	Prol.11	1Chor
A laughing stocke thou art to all the citty, . . .	Ovid's Elegies		3.1.21
So use we women of strange nations stocke. . . .	Ovid's Elegies		3.4.34
Nor Romane stocke scorne me so much (I crave)/Gifts then my	Ovid's Elegies		3.5.65
STOCKES			
And make us laughing stockes to all the world. . . .	F1450	4.3.20	Benvol
[Or] <On> stones, our stockes originall, should be hurld,	Ovid's Elegies		2.14.11
STOCKFISH			
an inch of raw Mutton, better then an ell of fryde Stockfish:	F 709	2.2.161	P Ltchry
STOKA			
Where by the river Tyros I subdew'd/Stoka, Padalia, and .	2Tamb	1.3.210	Therid
STOLE (Homograph)			
I this in Greece when Paris stole faire Helen.	Dido	3.1.142	Aeneas
I marveile much he stole it not away.	1Tamb	2.4.42	Mycet
So did you when you stole my gold.	Jew	4.4.50	Barab
Throwe of his golden miter, rend his stole, ...	Edw	1.1.187	Edward
be he that stole [away] his holinesse meate from the Table.	F1077	3.2.97	1Frier
pray where's the cup you stole from the Taverne? . .	F1097	3.3.10	P Vintnr
Cursed be hee that stole away his holinesse meate from/the	F App	p.232 31	Frier
Lightning in silence, stole forth without clouds, . .	Lucan, First Booke		531
And stole away th'inchaunted gazers mind, ...	Hero and Leander		1.104
Stole some from Hebe (Hebe, Joves cup fil'd), . . .	Hero and Leander		1.434
STOLNE			
And in the morning he was stolne from me, ...	Dido	5.1.214	Nurse
here I ha stolne one of doctor Faustus conjuring books, and	F App	p.233 1	P Robin
not onely kisse/But force thee give him my stolne honey blisse.	Ovid's Elegies		1.4.64
Stolne liberty she may by thee obtaine, ...	Ovid's Elegies		2.2.15
Wee skorne things lawfull, stolne sweetes we affect, .	Ovid's Elegies		2.19.3
And drinkes stolne waters in surrownding floudes. . .	Ovid's Elegies		2.19.32
Although thou chafe, stolne pleasure is sweet play, . .	Ovid's Elegies		3.4.31
STOMACK			
She cast her hatefull stomack to the earth. . . .	P1154	22.16	King
All stomack him, but none dare speake a word. . . .	Edw	1.2.26	Lncstr
I know my lord, many will stomack me, ...	Edw	2.2.260	Gavstn
STOMACKE			
And now Bajazeth, hast thou any stomacke?	1Tamb	4.4.10	Tamb
stomacke (cruel Tamburlane) as I could willingly feed upon thy	1Tamb	4.4.11	P Bajzth
My empty stomacke ful of idle heat, ...	1Tamb	4.4.94	Bajzth
Even as sweete meate a glutted stomacke cloyes. . .	Ovid's Elegies		2.19.26
STOMACKES			
Bridle the steeled stomackes of those Jades.	2Tamb	5.3.203	Tamb
STONE			
And drie with griefe was turnd into a stone, ...	Dido	2.1.5	Aeneas
but saving ayre/Is nothing here, and what is this but stone?	Dido	2.1.14	Achat
O yet this stone doth make Aeneas weepe, ...	Dido	2.1.15	Aeneas
Achates though mine eyes say this is stone, ...	Dido	2.1.24	Aeneas
So leaning on his sword he stood stone still, ...	Dido	2.1.263	Aeneas
Fairer than rockes of pearle and pretious stone, . . .	1Tamb	3.3.118	Tamb
In which the essentiall fourme of Marble stone, . . .	2Tamb	4.2.62	Olymp
What, hast the Philosophers stone?	Jew	2.3.111	P Barab
not a stone of beef a day will maintaine you in these chops;	Jew	2.3.124	P Barab
and let them be interr'd/Within one sacred monument of stone;	Jew	3.2.30	Govnr
Whose face has bin a grind-stone for mens swords, . . .	Jew	4.3.9	Barab
Thorough a rocke of stone in one nights space:	F 793	3.1.15	Faust
rampiers fallen down, huge heapes of stone/Lye in our townes,	Lucan, First Booke		25
In midst thereof a stone-pav'd sacred spring, ...	Ovid's Elegies		3.1.3
In stone, and Yron walles Danae shut, ...	Ovid's Elegies		3.4.21
About her necke hung chaines of peble stone, ...	Hero and Leander		1.25
The wals were of discoloured Jasper stone, ...	Hero and Leander		1.136
Stone still he stood, and evermore he gazed, ...	Hero and Leander		1.163
STONE-PAV'D			
In midst thereof a stone-pav'd sacred spring, ...	Ovid's Elegies		3.1.3
STONES			
Lading their shippes with golde and pretious stones: .	1Tamb	1.1.121	Cosroe
And shining stones upon their loftie Crestes: . . .	1Tamb	1.1.145	Ceneus
a golden Canapie/Enchac'd with pretious stones, which shine as	2Tamb	1.2.49	Callap
That though the stones, as at Deucalions flood, . . .	2Tamb	1.3.163	Tamb
Inestimable drugs and precious stones, ...	2Tamb	5.3.152	Tamb
And in his house heape pearle like pibble-stones, . . .	Jew	1.1.23	Barab
And seildsene costly stones of so great price, ...	Jew	1.1.28	Barab
Rich costly Jewels, and Stones infinite, ...	Jew	1.2.245	Barab
I strowed powder on the Marble stones, ...	Jew	2.3.209	Ithimr
And batter all the stones about their eares, ...	Jew	5.5.30	Barab
Make Englands civill townes huge heapes of stones, . . .	Edw	3.1.215	Edward
Whose frame is paved with sundry coloured stones, . . .	F 797	3.1.19	Faust
The little stones these little verses have.	Ovid's Elegies		2.6.60

STONES (cont.)			
The Ocean hath no painted stones or shelles,	Ovid's Elegies	2.11.13	
[Or] <On> stones, our stockes originall, should be hurld,	Ovid's Elegies	2.14.11	
And sweet toucht harpe that to move stones was able?	Ovid's Elegies	3.11.40	
STONE STILL			
Stone still he stood, and evermore he gazed,	Hero and Leander	1.163	
STONIE			
Had power to mollifie his stonie hart,	Edw	2.4.20	Queene
can ragged stonie walles/Immure thy vertue that aspires to	Edw	3.1.256	Mortmr
STONY			
Whose memorie like pale deaths stony mace,	Dido	2.1.115	Aeneas
Then let the stony dart of sencelesse colde,	1Tamb	5.1.302	Bajzth
flinty hearts/Suppresse all pitty in your stony breasts,	Jew	1.2.142	Barab
STOOD			
O had it never entred, Troy had stood.	Dido	2.1.172	Aeneas
So leaning on his sword he stood stone still,	Dido	2.1.263	Aeneas
Standard round, that stood/As bristle-pointed as a thorny wood.	1Tamb	4.1.26	2Msngr
And there in mire and puddle have I stood,	Edw	5.5.59	Edward
And Caesars mind unsetled musing stood;	Lucan, First Booke	264	
One window shut, the other open stood,	Ovid's Elegies	1.5.3	
Starke naked as she stood before mine eie,	Ovid's Elegies	1.5.17	
Sighing she stood, her bloodlesse white lookes shewed/Like	Ovid's Elegies	1.7.51	
The purple moone with sanguine visage stood.	Ovid's Elegies	1.8.12	
And to the end your constant faith stood fixt.	Ovid's Elegies	2.6.14	
And the fates distaffe emptie stood to thee,	Ovid's Elegies	2.6.46	
If thy great fame in every region stood?	Ovid's Elegies	3.5.90	
In view and opposit two citties stood,	Hero and Leander	1.2	
Than she the hearts of those that neere her stood.	Hero and Leander	1.112	
And in the midst a silver altar stood,	Hero and Leander	1.157	
Stone still he stood, and evermore he gazed,	Hero and Leander	1.163	
Wide open stood the doore, hee need not clime,	Hero and Leander	2.19	
For here the stately azure pallace stood,	Hero and Leander	2.165	
Thus neere the bed she blushing stood upright,	Hero and Leander	2.317	
STOODE			
spectacle/Stroake Caesars hart with feare, his hayre stoode up,	Lucan, First Booke	195	
STOOD'ST			
When thou stood'st naked ready to be beate,	Ovid's Elegies	1.6.19	
STOOLE			
Bring out my foot-stoole.	1Tamb	4.2.1	Tamb
And be the foot-stoole of great Tamburlain,	1Tamb	4.2.14	Tamb
To see thy foot-stoole set upon thy head,	2Tamb	5.3.29	Usumc
Cast downe our Foot-stoole.	F 868	3.1.90	Pope
[A] <Or> while thy tiptoes on the foote-stoole rest.	Ovid's Elegies	3.2.64	
STOOP (See also STOUP)			
Stoop villaine, stoope, stoope for so he bids,	1Tamb	4.2.22	Tamb
Now Babilon, (proud through our spoile) should stoop,	Lucan, First Booke	10	
STOOPE			
Stoop villaine, stoope, stoope for so he bids,	1Tamb	4.2.22	Tamb
Yet would I with my sword make Jove to stoope.	1Tamb	4.4.74	Tamb
And tell me whether I should stoope so low,	2Tamb	1.1.112	Sgsmnd
Ile make the prowdest of you stoope to him.	Edw	1.4.31	Edward
He meanes to make us stoope by force of armes,	Edw	2.2.103	Lncstr
For now, even now, we marche to make them stoope,	Edw	3.1.183	Edward
Saxon Bruno stoope,/Whilst on thy backe his hollinesse ascends	F 868	3.1.90	Raymnd
Then he and thou, and all the world shall stoope,	F 937	3.1.159	Pope
I hate thee not, to thee my conquests stoope,	Lucan, First Booke	203	
As might have made heaven stoope to have a touch,	Hero and Leander	1.366	
STOOPING			
Farewell base stooping to the lordly peeres,	Edw	1.1.18	Gavstn
STOOPS			
my children stoops your pride/And leads your glories <bodies>	2Tamb	4.1.76	Tamb
STOOPT			
That which hath [stoopt] <stopt> the tempest of the Gods,	1Tamb	5.1.184	Tamb
With that Leander stoopt, to have imbrac'd her,	Hero and Leander	1.341	
STOP			
But when you see his actions [top] <stop> his speech,	1Tamb	2.3.26	Therid
I'le give him something and so stop his mouth.	Jew	4.1.102	Barab
As thou lik'st that, stop me another time.	Jew	4.1.173	1Fryar
To stop the mallice of his envious heart,	P 30	1.30	Navrre
Stop him, stop him, stop him--ha, ha, ha, Faustus hath his leg	F1496	4.4.40	P Faust
STOPES			
He took his rouse with stopes of Rhennish wine,	F1174	4.1.20	Mrtino
STOPS			
And sorrow stops the passage of my speech.	2Tamb	3.2.52	Celeb
As I wud see thee hang'd; oh, love stops my breath:	Jew	4.3.53	Barab
Anger and wrathfull furie stops my speech.	Edw	1.4.42	Edward
STOPT			
That which hath [stoopt] <stopt> the tempest of the Gods,	1Tamb	5.1.184	Tamb
Nor if my body could have stopt the breach,	2Tamb	5.1.101	Govnr
STOR'D			
To be well stor'd with such a winters tale?	Dido	3.3.59	Aeneas
STORE			
The woods are wide, and we have store of game:	Dido	3.3.6	Dido
I would have given Achates store of gold,	Dido	4.4.7	Dido
I have an Orchard that hath store of plums,	Dido	4.5.4	Nurse
And store of ordinance that from every flanke/May scoure the	2Tamb	3.2.79	Tamb
Adding their wealth and treasure to my store.	2Tamb	4.3.101	Tamb
Laden with riches, and exceeding store/Of Persian silkes, of	Jew	1.1.87	2Merch
compasse it/By reason of the warres, that robb'd our store;	Jew	1.2.48	Govnr
My ships, my store, and all that I enjoy'd;	Jew	1.2.139	Barab
Thy father has enough in store for thee.	Jew	1.2.227	Barab
And now for store of wealth may I compare/With all the Jewes in	Jew	4.1.55	Barab
That he hath in store a Pearle so big,	Jew	5.3.27	Msngr

STORE (cont.)			
And then Ile guerdon thee with store of crownes.	P 89	2.32	Guise
Know you not Gaveston hath store of golde,	Edw	1.4.258	Mortmr
<Within whose walles such store of ordnance are>,	F 819	(HC265)A	Mephst
Where thou shalt see such store of Ordinance,	F 819	3.1.41	Mephst
and store of golden plate; besides two thousand duckets ready	F1675	5.1.2	P Wagner
His store of pleasures must be sauc'd with paine.	F1812	5.2.16	Mephst
To want in hell, that had on earth such store.	F1898	5.2.102	BdAngl
what store of ground/For servitors to till?	Lucan, First Booke		344
Great store of strange and unknown stars were seene/Wandering	Lucan, First Booke		524
Though I am slender, I have store of pith,	Ovid's Elegies		2.10.23
STORM'D			
He inly storm'd, and waxt more furious,	Hero and Leander		1.437
STORME			
Not one of them hath perisht in the storme,	Dido	1.1.236	Venus
Kind clowdes that sent forth such a curteous storme,	Dido	3.4.55	Dido
Did ever men see such a sudden storme?	Dido	4.1.1	Achat
Shall vulgar pesants storme at what I doe?	Dido	4.4.73	Dido
How Carthage did rebell, Iarbus storme,	Dido	5.1.143	Dido
Now Guise may storme but doe us little hurt:	P 28	1.28	Navrre
How they did storme at these your nuptiall rites,	P 49	1.49	Admral
I goe as whirl-windes rage before a storme.	P 511	9.30	Guise
And if they storme, I then may pull them downe.	P 526	9.45	QnMoth
Come my Lords, now that this storme is overpast,	P 804	16.18	Navrre
My lord, it is in vaine to greeve or storme,	Edw	4.7.77	Baldck
Brings Thunder, Whirle-winds, Storme <tempests> and Lightning:	F 546	2.1.158	Mephst
is bould/To suffer storme mixt snowes with nights sharpe cold?	Ovid's Elegies		1.9.16
STORMES			
Where finding Aeolus intrencht with stormes,	Dido	1.1.58	Venus
And fellowes to, what ever stormes arise.	P 615	12.28	King
But if my words with winged stormes hence slip,	Ovid's Elegies		2.11.33
STORMIE			
Charge him from me to turne his stormie powers,	Dido	1.1.117	Jupitr
As daunger of this stormie time requires.	Edw	4.7.7	Abbot
Which stormie South-windes into sea did blowe?	Ovid's Elegies		2.6.44
STORMY			
Looke how when stormy Auster from the breach/Of Libian Syrtes	Lucan, First Booke		496
Like Popler leaves blowne with a stormy flawe,	Ovid's Elegies		1.7.54
STORY			
And then they met, [and] as the story sayes,	Jew	3.3.20	Ithimr
This need no forraine proofe, nor far fet story:	Lucan, First Booke		94
STOUP (See also STOPES)			
And all his Minions stoup when I commaund:	P 979	19.49	Guise
And make the Guisians stoup that are alive.	P1071	19.141	King
STOUT			
Go, stout Theridamas, thy words are swords,	1Tamb	1.1.74	Mycet
And by thy martiall face and stout aspect,	1Tamb	1.2.170	Tamb
Wel said my stout contributory kings,	1Tamb	3.3.93	Bajzth
Where are your stout contributorie kings?	1Tamb	3.3.214	Tamb
For every fell and stout Tartarian Stead/That stampt on others	1Tamb	5.1.330	Zenoc
More then his Camp of stout Hungarians,	2Tamb	1.1.21	Uribas
Yet stout Orcanes, Prorex of the world,	2Tamb	1.1.45	Gazell
And backt by stout Lanceres of Germany,	2Tamb	1.1.155	Sgsmnd
Naturalized Turks and stout Bythinians/Came to my bands full	2Tamb	3.5.41	Trebiz
The race of all his stout progenitors;	F1168	4.1.14	Mrtino
With lofty wordes stout Tragedie (she sayd)/Why treadst me	Ovid's Elegies		3.1.35
And every lim did as a soldier stout,	Hero and Leander		2.271
STOUTE			
Thus in stoute Hectors race three hundred yeares,	Dido	1.1.104	Jupitr
Stoute friend Achates, doest thou know this wood?	Dido	3.3.50	Aeneas
Stoute love in mine armes make thy Italy,	Dido	3.4.57	Dido
STOUTLY			
And all his Captaines that thus stoutly stand,	1Tamb	3.3.79	Bajzth
conjuring/Is stoutly to abjure [the Trinity] <all godlinesse>,	F 281	1.3.53	Mephst
STRADDLING			
horse vanisht away, and I sate straddling upon a bottle of Hay.	F1545	4.5.41	P HrsCsr
STRAGLERS			
For if these straglers gather head againe,	P 506	9.25	QnMoth
STRAGLING			
stragling from the camp/When Kings themselves are present in	1Tamb	2.4.16	Tamb
Inhabited with stragling Runnagates,	1Tamb	3.3.57	Tamb
Now have we got the fatall stragling deere,	P 204	4.2	QnMoth
STRAIGHT (Homograph; See also STRAIT, STREIGHT)			
we were commanded straight/With reverence to draw it into Troy.	Dido	2.1.167	Aeneas
Who having wrought her shame, is straight way fled:	Dido	4.2.18	Iarbus
But hereby child, we shall get thither straight.	Dido	4.5.14	Nurse
I tell thee thou must straight to Italy,	Dido	5.1.53	Hermes
No but I am not, yet I will be straight.	Dido	5.1.271	Dido
Though straight the passage and the port be made,	1Tamb	2.1.42	Cosroe
To whom sweet Menaphon, direct me straight.	1Tamb	2.1.68	Cosroe
What should we doe but bid them battaile straight,	1Tamb	2.2.18	Meandr
Straight will I use thee as thy pride deserves:	1Tamb	3.3.206	Zabina
straight goe charge a few of them/To chardge these Dames,	1Tamb	5.1.116	Tamb
Even straight: and farewell cursed Tamburlaine.	2Tamb	1.2.77	Callap
He raign'd him straight and made him so curvet,	2Tamb	1.3.41	Zenoc
We kept the narrow straight of Gibralter,	2Tamb	1.3.180	Usumc
Comes marching on us, and determines straight,	2Tamb	2.2.27	1Msngr
Go Uribassa, give it straight in charge.	2Tamb	2.3.40	Orcan
That to the adverse poles of that straight line,	2Tamb	3.4.64	Therid
I will about it straight, come Souldiers.	2Tamb	5.1.172	Techel
Will him to send Apollo hether straight,	2Tamb	5.3.62	Tamb
hee that denies to pay, shal straight become a Christian.	Jew	1.2.73	P Reader
Goe Officers and set them straight in shew.	Jew	2.2.43	Govnr

STRAIGHT (cont.)
Goe fetch him straight. I alwayes fear'd that Jew. Jew 5.1.18 Govnr
And Ile subscribe my name and seale it straight. P 883 17.78 King
Therefore if he be come, expell him straight. Edw 1.1.106 Lncstr
Then linger not my lord but do it straight. Edw 1.4.58 Lncstr
Your grace must hence with mee to Bartley straight. Edw 5.1.144 Bartly
If mine will serve, unbowell straight this brest, Edw 5.3.10 Edward
I, stay a while, thou shalt have answer straight. Edw 5.5.20 Matrvs
[Whose] <The> streetes straight forth, and paved with finest F 789 3.1.11 Faust
Good Fredericke see the roomes be voyded straight, F1157 4.1.3 Mrtino
Cut is the branch that might have growne full straight, F2002 5.3.20 4Chor
Straight summon'd he his severall companies/Unto the standard: Lucan, First Booke 297
Straight being read, will her to write much backe, Ovid's Elegies 1.11.19
And when one sweetely sings, then straight I long, Ovid's Elegies 2.4.25
I would get off though straight, and sticking fast, Ovid's Elegies 2.15.13
To hide thee in my bosome straight repaire. Ovid's Elegies 3.2.76
As she might straight have gone to church and praide: Ovid's Elegies 3.6.54
His bodie was as straight as Circes wand, Hero and Leander 1.61
Set in a forren place, and straight from thence, Hero and Leander 2.119
She stayd not for her robes, but straight arose, Hero and Leander 2.235

STRAIGHTES
And hover in the straightes for Christians wracke, 1Tamb 3.3.250 Tamb
And thence unto the straightes of Jubalter: 1Tamb 3.3.256 Tamb

STRAIGHTLY
Of stature tall, and straightly fashioned, 1Tamb 2.1.7 Menaph

STRAIGHTS
slaves/I freely give thee, which shall cut the straights, 2Tamb 1.2.33 Callap

STRAIND
If griefe, our murthered harts have straind forth blood. 2Tamb 2.4.123 Therid

STRAINE
If thou wilt have a song, the Turke shall straine his voice: 1Tamb 4.4.64 P Tamb

STRAINED
bondes contained/From barbarous lips of some Atturney strained. Ovid's Elegies 1.12.24

STRAINETH
my entrals bath'd/In blood that straineth from their orifex. 2Tamb 3.4.9 Capt

STRAIT (Homograph; See also STRAIGHT, STREIGHT)
I'le write unto him, we'le have mony strait. Jew 4.2.69 P Ithimr
Tis well advisde Dumain, goe see it strait be done. P 424 7.64 Guise
Goe call a surgeon hether strait. P1179 22.41 Navrre
Goe call the English Agent hether strait, P1188 22.50 King
Mephastophilis, transforme him strait. F App p.238 86 P Faust

STRAITE
Be gone my freend, present them to her straite. P 82 2.25 Guise
Messenger, tell him I will see him straite. P 247 4.45 Charls
Make a discharge of all my counsell straite, P 882 17.77 King

STRAKE
and in a trenche/Strake off his head, and marcht unto the Edw 3.1.120 Arundl

STRANGE (See also STRAUNGE)
See what strange arts necessitie findes out, Dido 1.1.169 Venus
And see my Lord, a sight of strange import, 1Tamb 5.1.468 Tamb
With strange infusion of his sacred vigor, 2Tamb 2.2.52 Orcan
'Tis a strange thing of that Jew, he lives upon pickled Jew 4.4.61 P Ithimr
This sudden death of his is very strange. Jew 5.1.54 Bosco
But to defend their strange inventions, P 705 14.8 Navrre
That bleedes within me for this strange exchange. Edw 5.1.35 Edward
Which fils my mind with strange despairing thoughts, Edw 5.1.79 Edward
I'le have them read me strange Philosophy, F 113 1.1.85 Faust
what strange beast is yon, that thrusts his head out at [the] F1274 4.1.120 P Faust
have heard strange report of thy knowledge in the blacke Arte, F App p.236 1 P Emper
Strange sights appear'd, the angry threatning gods/Fill'd both Lucan, First Booke 522
Great store of strange and unknown stars were seene/Wandering Lucan, First Booke 524
such and more strange/Blacke night brought forth in secret: Lucan, First Booke 578
As soone as from strange lands Sabinus came, Ovid's Elegies 2.18.27
So use we women of strange nations stocke. Ovid's Elegies 3.4.34
not Alpheus in strange lands to runne,/Th'Arcadian Virgins Ovid's Elegies 3.5.29

STRANGELY
health and majesty/Were strangely blest and governed by heaven, 2Tamb 5.3.25 Techel
And strangely metamorphis'd Nun. Jew 1.2.381 Mthias
Two spreading hornes most strangely fastened/Upon the head of F1277 4.1.123 Emper
And in her bosome strangely fall at last. Ovid's Elegies 2.15.14

STRANGER
Such honour, stranger, doe I not affect: Dido 1.1.203 Venus
What stranger art thou that doest eye me thus? Dido 2.1.74 Dido
Ile dye before a stranger have that grace: Dido 3.3.11 Iarbus
That shall consume all that this stranger left, Dido 5.1.285 Dido
I pray, Sir, be no stranger at my house, Jew 2.3.136 Barab
Yea stranger engines for the brunt of warre, F 122 1.1.94 Faust
Were he a stranger, <and> not allyed to me, F 223 1.2.30 2Schol
The strumpet with the stranger will not do, Ovid's Elegies 3.13.9

STRANGERS
For we are strangers driven on this shore, Dido 2.1.43 Aeneas
Yeelds up her beautie to a strangers bed, Dido 4.2.17 Iarbus
For being intangled by a strangers lookes: Dido 5.1.145 Dido
How long will Dido mourne a strangers flight, Dido 5.1.279 Iarbus
the Pilot stands/And viewes a strangers ship rent in the winds, 1Tamb 4.3.33 Souldn
Are strangers with your tribute to be tax'd? Jew 1.2.59 Barab
Have strangers leave with us to get their wealth? Jew 1.2.60 2Knght
Must Pompeis followers with strangers ayde, Lucan, First Booke 314

STRANGEST
The strangest men that ever nature made, 1Tamb 2.7.40 Cosroe
Lodowicke, I have seene/The strangest sight, in my opinion, Jew 1.2.376 Mthias

STRANGLE
What, doe you meane to strangle me? Jew 4.1.144 2Fryar

STRANGLE (cont.)
Get you away and strangle the Cardinall. . . . . . P1059 19.129 King
O Lord no: for we entend to strangle you. P1095 20.5 2Mur
To strangle with a lawne thrust through the throte, . . Edw 5.4.32 Ltborn
Poore wretches on the tree themselves did strangle, . . Ovid's Elegies 1.12.17

STRANGLED
Nuns, and he and I, snicle hand too fast, strangled a Fryar. Jew 4.4.21 P Ithimr
Nuns, strangled a Fryar, and I know not what mischiefe beside. Jew 5.1.13 P Pilia
Marry, even he that strangled Bernardine, poyson'd the Nuns, and Jew 5.1.33 P Ithimr
of Loraine by the Kings consent is lately strangled unto death. P1123 21.17 P Frier

STRANGLING
And outrage strangling law and people strong, ... Lucan, First Booke 2

STRATAGEM
a goodly Stratagem,/And far from any man that is a foole. 1Tamb 2.4.11 Mycet
But never could effect their Stratagem. . . . . . Jew 1.1.165 Barab
onely to performe/One stratagem that I'le impart to thee, Jew 5.2.99 Barab
And had I but escap'd this stratagem, ... Jew 5.5.84 Barab

STRATAGEME
As if he now devis'd some Stratageme: . . . . . 1Tamb 1.2.159 Therid

STRATAGEMS
Onelie disposed to martiall Stratagems? . . . . . 1Tamb 3.2.41 Agidas
Slew friend and enemy with my stratagems. . . . . . Jew 2.3.189 Barab
Our plots and stratagems will soone be dasht. . . . Edw 5.2.78 Mortmr
With slender trench they escape night stratagems, . . Lucan, First Booke 514

STRAUNGE
Is it not straunge, that he is thus bewitcht? . . . . Edw 1.2.55 MortSr
If he be straunge and not regarde my wordes, ... Edw 2.4.64 Queene

STRAW
I had nothing under me but a little straw, and had much ado to F1486 4.4.30 P HrsCsr
A belt of straw, and Ivie buds, ... Passionate Shepherd 17

STRAWIE
With strawie cabins now her courts should build. . . . Ovid's Elegies 2.9.18

STRAY
long since some of us/Did stray so farre amongst the multitude. Jew 1.2.309 Abbass
The graine-rich goddesse in high woods did stray, . . Ovid's Elegies 3.9.35

STRAYD
Strayd bare-foote through sole places on a time. . . Ovid's Elegies 3.5.50
in the grasse, he often strayd/Beyond the bounds of shame, Hero and Leander 1.406

STRAYED
Such as Amimone through the drie fields strayed/When on her Ovid's Elegies 1.10.5

STRAYING
Where straying in our borders up and downe, ... Dido 4.2.12 Iarbus
But let not mee poore soule know of thy straying. . . . Ovid's Elegies 3.13.2

STREAM
As looks the sun through Nilus flowing stream, ... 1Tamb 3.2.47 Zenoc
Danubius stream that runs to Trebizon, ... 2Tamb 1.1.33 Orcan
Wee with our Peeres have crost Danubius stream/To treat of 2Tamb 1.1.79 Sgsmnd

STREAME
There Zanthus streame, because here's Priamus, ... Dido 2.1.8 Aeneas
And in the midst doth run a silver streame, ... Dido 4.5.9 Nurse
Or crosse the streame, and meet him in the field? . . . 2Tamb 1.1.12 Orcan
of Natolia/Confirm'd this league beyond Danubius streame, 2Tamb 1.1.149 Orcan
And shame of nature [which] <with> Jaertis streame, . . 2Tamb 4.1.108 Tamb
city Samarcanda/And christall waves of fresh Jaertis streame, 2Tamb 4.3.108 Tamb
that falles/Into the liquid substance of his streame, . 2Tamb 5.1.19 Govnr
Just through the midst runnes flowing Tybers streame, . F 813 3.1.35 Mephst
Approcht the swelling streame with drum and ensigne, . Lucan, First Booke 207
To scape the violence of the streame first waded, . . Lucan, First Booke 223
and those that dwel/By Cyngas streame, and where swift Rhodanus Lucan, First Booke 434
Thee I have pass'd, and knew thy streame none such, . . Ovid's Elegies 3.5.5
(Trust me) land-streame thou shalt no envie lack, . . Ovid's Elegies 3.5.21
Flye backe his [streame] <shame> chargd, the streame chargd, . Ovid's Elegies 3.5.44
his [streame] <shame> chargd, the streame chargd, gave place. Ovid's Elegies 3.5.44
Tis said the slippery streame held up her brest, . . Ovid's Elegies 3.5.81
Mad streame, why doest our mutuall joyes deferre? . . Ovid's Elegies 3.5.87
But for thy merits I wish thee, white streame, . . . Ovid's Elegies 3.5.105
A streame of liquid pearle, which downe her face/Made . Hero and Leander 1.297

STREAMER
And here this mournful streamer shal be plac'd/Wrought with the 2Tamb 3.2.19 Amyras

STREAMERS
With mournfull streamers hanging down their heads, . . 1Tamb 4.2.120 Tamb
Streamers white, Red, Blacke. . . . . 1Tamb 5.1.314 P Zabina
And set blacke streamers in the firmament, ... 2Tamb 5.3.49 Tamb

STREAMES
Free from the murmure of these running streames, . . Dido 2.1.335 Venus
Whose wealthie streames may waite upon her towers, . . Dido 5.1.9 Aeneas
Which had ere this bin bathde in streames of blood, . . 1Tamb 5.1.438 Tamb
Darotes streames, wherin at anchor lies/A Turkish Gally of my 2Tamb 1.2.20 Callap
Now scaldes his soule in the Tartarian streames, . . 2Tamb 2.3.18 Orcan
Marcheth in Asia major, where the streames, ... 2Tamb 5.2.2 Callap
To make a passage for the running streames/And common channels Jew 5.1.88 Barab
Why streames it not, that I may write a fresh? . . . F 455 2.1.67 Faust
[See see where Christs bloud streames in the firmament], . F1939 5.2.143A Faust
If to incampe on Thuscan Tybers streames, ... Lucan, First Booke 382
And turned streames run back-ward to their fountaines. . Ovid's Elegies 2.1.26
ground/Conteines me, though the streames in fields surround, Ovid's Elegies 2.16.34

STREAMING
Dieng their lances with their streaming blood, ... 2Tamb 3.2.105 Tamb

STREAMS
And makes large streams back to their fountaines flow, . Ovid's Elegies 1.8.6

STRECHING
Streching their monstrous pawes, grin with their teeth, . 2Tamb 3.5.28 Orcan

STREET
The other Chambers open towards the street. . . . . Jew 4.1.138 Barab

STREET (cont.)			
Stand in some window opening neere the street, . . .	P 86	2.29	Guise
Hath he been hurt with villaines in the street? . .	P 254	4.52	Charls
That they which have already set the street/May know their	P 328	5.55	Guise
For everie street like to a Firmament/Glistered with breathing	Hero and Leander		1.97
STREETE			
As Caesar riding in the Romaine streete, ...	Edw	1.1.173	Gavstn
Libels are cast againe thee in the streete, . . .	Edw	2.2.177	Mortmr
STREETES			
And through the breach did march into the streetes, . .	Dido	2.1.189	Aeneas
And then in triumph ran into the streetes, . . .	Dido	2.1.261	Aeneas
thou knowest/We sawe Cassandra sprauling in the streetes,	Dido	2.1.274	Aeneas
let him ride/As Didos husband through the Punicke streetes,	Dido	4.4.67	Dido
Thy streetes strowed with dissevered jointes of men, .	1Tamb	5.1.322	Zenoc
At which they all shall issue out and set the streetes. .	P 237	4.35	Guise
Riding the streetes was traiterously shot, ...	P 244	4.42	Man
Swizers keepe you the streetes,/And at ech corner shall the	P 290	5.17	Anjoy
Nay, they fear'd not to speak in the streetes, . . .	P 876	17.71	Eprnon
Give it me, ile have it published in the streetes. . .	Edw	1.4.89	Lncstr
[Whose] <The> streetes straight forth, and paved with finest	F 789	3.1.11	Faust
Leaving the woods, lodge in the streetes of Rome. . .	Lucan, First Booke		558
So runnes a Matron through th'amazed streetes, . . .	Lucan, First Booke		675
STREETS			
And as thou rid'st in triumph through the streets, . .	2Tamb	1.2.41	Callap
Thorow the streets with troops of conquered kings, . .	2Tamb	4.3.114	Tamb
So will I ride through Samarcanda streets, ...	2Tamb	4.3.130	Tamb
And in the streets, where brave Assirian Dames/Have rid in	2Tamb	5.1.76	Tamb
Except he place his Tables in the streets. . . .	Jew	5.3.35	Calym
all his men/To come ashore, and march through Malta streets,	Jew	5.5.15	Msngr
STREIGHT (Homograph)			
Novice learne to frame/My solitary life to your streight lawes,	Jew	1.2.332	Abigal
Take this and beare it to Mathias streight, ...	Jew	2.3.370	Barab
what hee writes for you, ye shall have streight. . .	Jew	4.3.27	P Barab
I'le fetch thee fire to dissolve it streight. . . .	F 452	2.1.64	Mephst
He shall be streight condemn'd of heresie, . . .	F 962	3.1.184	Faust
And beare him streight to Ponte Angelo, ...	F 965	3.1.187	Pope
If Faustus do it, you are streight resolv'd, . . .	F1298	4.1.144	Faust
STRENGTH			
Forgetting both his want of strength and hands, . .	Dido	2.1.252	Aeneas
Where daliance doth consume a Souldiers strength, . .	Dido	4.3.34	Achat
Betokening valour and excesse of strength: . . .	1Tamb	2.1.28	Menaph
They gather strength by power of fresh supplies. . .	1Tamb	2.2.21	Meandr
T'incounter with the strength of Tamburlaine. . . .	1Tamb	3.3.7	Tamb
And ad more strength to your dominions/Than ever yet confirm'd	1Tamb	5.1.448	Tamb
Bringing the strength of Europe to these Armes: . .	2Tamb	1.1.30	Orcan
The strength and sinewes of the imperiall seat. . .	2Tamb	1.1.156	Sgsmnd
Breed litle strength to our securitie, ...	2Tamb	2.1.43	Sgsmnd
Now thou art fearfull of thy armies strength, . . .	2Tamb	3.5.75	Orcan
But matchlesse strength and magnanimity?	2Tamb	4.1.85	Amyras
Wherein was neither corrage, strength or wit, . . .	2Tamb	4.1.125	Tamb
That will not see the strength of Tamburlaine, . . .	2Tamb	4.1.133	Tamb
Now you shal feele the strength of Tamburlain, . . .	2Tamb	4.1.135	Tamb
Yet make them feele the strength of Tamburlain, . . .	2Tamb	5.3.37	Usumc
But I perceive my martial strength is spent, . . .	2Tamb	5.3.119	Tamb
Tush, they are wise; I know her and her strength: . .	Jew	1.1.81	Barab
Strength to my soule, death to mine enemy; . . .	Jew	2.1.49	Barab
To spend the treasure that should strength my land, . .	P1037	19.107	King
The Wrenne may strive against the Lions strength, . .	Edw	5.3.34	Edward
Drawne by the strength of yoked <yoky> Dragons neckes; .	F 759	2.3.38	2Chor
I saw a brandisht fire increase in strength, . . .	Ovid's Elegies		1.2.11
To mine owne selfe have I had strength so furious? . .	Ovid's Elegies		1.7.25
Penelope in bowes her youths strength tride, . . .	Ovid's Elegies		1.8.47
Rome if her strength the huge world had not fild, . .	Ovid's Elegies		2.9.17
Heere thou hast strength, here thy right hand doth rest. .	Ovid's Elegies		2.9.36
Nor want I strength, but weight to presse her with: . .	Ovid's Elegies		2.10.24
By feare depriv'd of strength to runne away. . . .	Ovid's Elegies		3.5.70
on the rushes to be flung,/Striv'd with redoubled strength:	Hero and Leander		2.67
In such warres women use but halfe their strength. . .	Hero and Leander		2.296
STRENGTHEN			
Till men and kingdomes help to strengthen it: . . .	1Tamb	1.2.30	Tamb
Now strengthen him against the Turkish Bajazeth, . .	1Tamb	3.3.191	Zenoc
God will strengthen me, I will stay with Faustus. . .	F1870	5.2.74	P 3Schol
Thus in his fright did each man strengthen Fame, . .	Lucan, First Booke		481
STRENGTHNED			
were the sinowes of th'imperiall seat/So knit and strengthned,	2Tamb	3.1.11	Callap
STRENGTHS			
And made so wanton that they knew their strengths, . .	2Tamb	4.3.14	Tamb
STRETCH (See also STRECHING)			
And Jove himselfe will stretch his hand from heaven, .	1Tamb	1.2.180	Tamb
Now ugly death stretch out thy Sable wings, . . .	2Tamb	3.4.16	Olymp
The course of mischiefe, and stretch out the date/Of slaughter;	Lucan, First Booke		670
STRETCHETH			
Stretcheth as farre as doth the mind of man:	F 88	1.1.60	Faust
And see [where God]/[Stretcheth out his Arme, and bends his	F1944	5.2.148A	Faust
STRETCHING			
Stretching their pawes, and threatning heardes of Beastes,	1Tamb	1.2.53	Techel
Stretching your conquering armes from east to west: . .	2Tamb	1.3.97	Tamb
STRETCHT			
Was stretcht unto the fields of hinds unknowne; . .	Lucan, First Booke		171
STREW (See STROW)			
STREWD			
where the ground/Was strewd with pearle, and in low corrall	Hero and Leander		2.161
STREWE			
And strewe him with sweete smelling Violets, . . .	Dido	2.1.318	Venus

STREWE (cont.)
And strewe thy walkes with my discheveld haire. Dido 4.2.56 Anna
STRICKEN
Why, stricken him that would have stroke at me. Jew 4.1.175 1Fryar
For you are stricken with a poysoned knife. P1213 22.75 Srgeon
STRICT (See also STREIGHT)
Oh Barabas, their Lawes are strict. Jew 4.1.82 1Fryar
STRICTLY
tis superstition/To stand so strictly on dispensive faith: 2Tamb 2.1.50 Fredrk
STRIFE
day, and ful of strife/Disolve the engins of the broken world. Lucan, First Booke 79
Take strife away, love doth not well endure. Ovid's Elegies 1.8.96
But Pallas and your mistresse are at strife. Hero and Leander 1.322
this strife of hers (like that/Which made the world) another Hero and Leander 2.291
STRIKE (See also STRAKE, STROAKE, STROOK)
What? dares she strike the darling of my thoughts? Dido 1.1.9 Jupitr
Strike up the Drum and martch corragiously, 1Tamb 2.2.72 Meandr
Then strike up Drum, and all the Starres that make/The 1Tamb 2.6.36 Cosroe
And from their shieldes strike flames of lightening)/All 1Tamb 3.2.81 Agidas
Thy souldiers armes could not endure to strike/So many blowes 1Tamb 3.3.143 Bajzth
heaven/To dash the Scythians braines, and strike them dead, 1Tamb 3.3.197 Zabina
With Eban Scepter strike this hatefull earth, 1Tamb 4.2.28 Bajzth
If any man will hold him, I will strike, 2Tamb 1.3.102 Calyph
Hast thou beheld a peale of ordinance strike/A ring of pikes, 2Tamb 3.2.98 Tamb
Come back again (sweet death) and strike us both: 2Tamb 3.4.12 Olymp
Give me your knife (good mother) or strike home: 2Tamb 3.4.28 Sonne
Sweet mother strike, that I may meet my father. 2Tamb 3.4.30 Sonne
No, strike the drums, and in revenge of this, 2Tamb 5.3.57 Tamb
This wrathfull hand should strike thee to the hart. P 690 13.34 Guise
And strike off his that makes you threaten us. Edw 1.1.124 Mortmr
Drums strike alarum, raise them from their sport, Edw 2.3.25 Mortmr
Strike off their heads, and let them preach on poles, Edw 3.1.20 Spencr
Strike off his head, he shall have marshall lawe. Edw 5.4.89 Mortmr
Strike of my head? base traitor I defie thee. Edw 5.4.90 Kent
Which [strike] <strikes> a terror to my fainting soule. F 310 1.3.82 Mephst
Strike them with sloth, and drowsy idlenesse; F 894 3.1.116 Faust
Be ready then, and strike the Peasant downe. F1359 4.2.35 Fredrk
now sword strike home,/For hornes he gave, Il'e have his head F1360 4.2.36 Benvol
Strike with a willing hand, his head is off. F1368 4.2.44 Mrtino
The Stars move still, Time runs, the Clocke will strike, F1936 5.2.140 Faust
Strike on the boord like them that pray for evill, Ovid's Elegies 1.4.27
Night goes away: the dores barre backeward strike. Ovid's Elegies 1.6.24
Strike, so againe hard chaines shall binde thee never, Ovid's Elegies 1.6.25
Strike backe the barre, night fast away doth goe. Ovid's Elegies 1.6.32
the barre strike from the poast. Ovid's Elegies 1.6.56
Strike boy, I offer thee my naked brest, Ovid's Elegies 2.9.35
And may repulse place for our wishes strike. Ovid's Elegies 2.19.6
When strong wilde beasts, she stronger hunts to strike them. Ovid's Elegies 3.2.32
STRIKES
That strikes a terrour to all Turkish hearts, 2Tamb 2.1.15 Fredrk
Which being caught, strikes him that takes it dead, Edw 1.4.222 Mortmr
Which [strike] <strikes> a terror to my fainting soule. F 310 1.3.82 Mephst
<O> It strikes, it strikes; now body turne to aire, F1975 5.2.179 Faust
Why burnes thy brand, why strikes thy bow thy friends? Ovid's Elegies 2.9.5
Pallas launce strikes me with unconquerd arme. Ovid's Elegies 3.3.28
STRIKING
And here upon my knees, striking the earth, Jew 1.2.165 Barab
Go goodly <godly> birdes, striking your breasts bewaile, Ovid's Elegies 2.6.3
With strong hand striking wild-beasts brist'led hyde. Ovid's Elegies 3.9.26
STRING
that with touching of a string/May draw the pliant king which Edw 1.1.52 Gavstn
STRINGS
Of his gilt Harpe the well tun'd strings doth hold. Ovid's Elegies 1.8.60
Like untun'd golden strings all women are, Hero and Leander 1.229
STRIP
Doe what I can he will not strip himselfe, Jew 4.1.131 Ithimr
STRIPES
to thee being cast do happe/Sharpe stripes, she sitteth in the Ovid's Elegies 2.2.62
Or any back made rough with stripes imbrace? Ovid's Elegies 2.7.22
STRIPLING
Goe, goe tall stripling, fight you for us both, 2Tamb 4.1.33 Calyph
STRIPPE
Be not ashamed to strippe you being there, Ovid's Elegies 3.13.21
STRIPT
When two are stript, long ere the course begin, Hero and Leander 1.169
With that hee stript him to the yv'rie skin, Hero and Leander 2.153
STRIV'D
The more she striv'd, the deeper was she strooke. Hero and Leander 1.334
on the rushes to be flung,/Striv'd with redoubled strength: Hero and Leander 2.67
Leander striv'd, the waves about him wound, Hero and Leander 2.159
STRIVDE
Yet strivde she to be covered therewithall, Ovid's Elegies 1.5.14
STRIVE
Nature doth strive with Fortune and his stars, 1Tamb 2.1.33 Cosroe
The world will strive with hostes of men at armes, 1Tamb 2.3.13 Tamb
Would make one thrust and strive to be retain'd/In such a great 1Tamb 2.3.31 Therid
Or when Minerva did with Neptune strive. 1Tamb 3.2.52 Zenoc
And strive for life at every stroke they give. 1Tamb 3.3.54 Tamb
And I would strive to swim through pooles of blood, 2Tamb 1.3.92 Amyras
In vaine I strive and raile against those powers, 2Tamb 5.3.120 Tamb
fury of thy torments, strive/To end thy life with resolution: Jew 5.5.79 Barab
Strive you no longer, I will have that Gaveston. Edw 2.6.7 Warwck
Come fellowes, it booted not for us to strive, Edw 2.6.18 James

STRIVE (cont.)			
Brother Edmund, strive not, we are his friends,	Edw	5.2.114	Queene
Why strive you thus? your labour is in vaine.	Edw	5.3.33	Matrvs
The Wrenne may strive against the Lions strength,	Edw	5.3.34	Edward
But all in vaine, so vainely do I strive,	Edw	5.3.35	Edward
And strive to shine by day, and ful of strife/Disolve the	Lucan, First Booke		79
Shaming to strive but where he did subdue,	Lucan, First Booke		146
I saw how Bulls for a white Heifer strive,	Ovid's Elegies		2.12.25
Some other seeke that may in patience strive with thee,	Ovid's Elegies		2.19.59
STRIVED			
the more she strived,/The more a gentle pleasing heat revived,	Hero and Leander		2.67
STRIVES			
Leading a life that onely strives to die,	2Tamb	5.3.197	Amyras
Where resolution strives for victory.	P 165	2.108	Guise
Hell strives with grace for conquest in my breast:	F1741	5.1.68	Faust
While Titan strives against the worlds swift course;	Lucan, First Booke		90
STRIVING			
That tyed together by the striving tongues,	Dido	4.3.29	Aeneas
Shrowd any thought may holde my striving hands/From martiall	2Tamb	4.1.95	Tamb
Yeelding or striving <strugling> doe we give him might,	Ovid's Elegies		1.2.9
And striving thus as one that would be cast,	Ovid's Elegies		1.5.15
Thy dull hand stayes thy striving enemies harmes.	Ovid's Elegies		2.9.12
His rider vainely striving him to stay,	Ovid's Elegies		2.9.30
STRIV'NE			
Having striv'ne in vaine, was now about to crie,	Hero and Leander		1.413
STROAKE			
this spectacle/Stroake Caesars hart with feare, his hayre	Lucan, First Booke		195
STROKE (Homograph)			
Since he is yeelded to the stroke of War,	1Tamb	2.5.12	Cosroe
And strive for life at every stroke they give.	1Tamb	3.3.54	Tamb
My sword stroke fire from his coat of steele,	1Tamb	4.2.41	Tamb
Why, stricken him that would have stroke at me.	Jew	4.1.175	1Fryar
And with my kinglie scepter stroke me dead,	Edw	1.4.317	Edward
And let me see the stroke before it comes,	Edw	5.5.76	Edward
Cursed be he that stroke his holinesse a blow [on] the face.	F1079	3.2.99	1Frier
T'was so, he stroke me with a slender dart,	Ovid's Elegies		1.2.7
At every stroke, betwixt them would he slide,	Hero and Leander		2.184
STROKES (Homograph)			
And when she strokes thee softly on the head,	Dido	3.1.5	Cupid
make our <your> strokes to wound the sencelesse [aire] <lure>.	1Tamb	3.3.158	Tamb
Or holy gods with cruell strokes abus'd.	Ovid's Elegies		1.7.6
To plague your bodies with such harmefull strokes?	Ovid's Elegies		2.14.34
STRONG			
It is the Punick kingdome rich and strong,	Dido	1.1.210	Venus
Our army will be forty thousand strong,	1Tamb	2.1.61	Cosroe
when holy Fates/Shall stablish me in strong Egyptia,	1Tamb	4.4.135	Tamb
And millions of his strong tormenting spirits:	2Tamb	1.3.147	Techel
From strong Tesella unto Biledull,	2Tamb	1.3.148	Techel
to as high a pitch/In this our strong and fortunate encounter.	2Tamb	3.1.31	Callap
From Soria with seventy thousand strong,	2Tamb	3.1.57	Soria
The Bulwarks and the rampiers large and strong,	2Tamb	3.2.70	Tamb
More strong than are the gates of death or hel?	2Tamb	5.1.20	Govnr
I joy my Lord, your highnesse is so strong,	2Tamb	5.3.110	Usumc
that a strong built Citadell/Commands much more then letters	Jew	Prol.22	Machvl
Strong proofe, my Lord, his man's now at my lodging/That was	Jew	5.1.16	Curtzn
Strong contermin'd <countermur'd> with other petty Iles;	Jew	5.3.8	Calym
Me thinkes the gloves have a very strong perfume,	P 170	3.5	OldQn
Now is the king of England riche and strong,	Edw	1.4.366	Queene
The head-strong Barons shall not limit me.	Edw	2.2.262	Edward
Browne bils, and targetiers, foure hundred strong,	Edw	3.1.37	SpncrP
Till I be strong enough to breake a staffe,	Edw	4.2.24	Prince
Come friends to Bristow, there to make us strong,	Edw	4.3.50	Edward
Fly, fly, my Lord, the Queene is over strong,	Edw	4.5.1	Spencr
Erected is a Castle passing strong,	F 818	3.1.40	Mephst
And outrage strangling law and people strong,	Lucan, First Booke		2
end the gods/Allot the height of honor, men so strong/By land,	Lucan, First Booke		82
our lively bodies, and strong armes/Can mainly throw the dart;	Lucan, First Booke		364
Wars radge draws neare; and to the swords strong hand,	Lucan, First Booke		665
Great are thy kingdomes, over strong and large,	Ovid's Elegies		1.1.17
We erre: a strong blast seem'd the gates to ope:	Ovid's Elegies		1.6.51
Io, a strong man conquerd this Wench, hollow.	Ovid's Elegies		1.7.38
Even as a head-strong courser beares away,	Ovid's Elegies		2.9.29
When strong wilde beasts, she stronger hunts to strike them.	Ovid's Elegies		3.2.32
Let with strong hand the reine to bend be made.	Ovid's Elegies		3.2.72
With strong plough shares no man the earth did cleave,	Ovid's Elegies		3.7.41
With strong hand striking wild-beasts brist'led hyde.	Ovid's Elegies		3.9.26
STRONGE			
What stronge enchantments tice my yeelding soule?	1Tamb	1.2.224	Therid
STRONGER			
Now I forewarne, unlesse to keepe her stronger,	Ovid's Elegies		2.19.47
Not stronger am I, then the thing I move.	Ovid's Elegies		3.1.42
When strong wilde beasts, she stronger hunts to strike them.	Ovid's Elegies		3.2.32
STRONGEST			
And drinke in pailes the strongest Muscadell:	2Tamb	4.3.19	Tamb
[Cossin] <Cosin> <Cousin>, take twenty of our strongest guarde,	P 266	4.64	Charls
Weele pull him from the strongest hould he hath.	Edw	1.4.289	Mortmr
And in the strongest Tower inclose him fast.	F 966	3.1.188	Pope
Force mastered right, the strongest govern'd all.	Lucan, First Booke		177
STRONGLY			
So large of lims, his joints so strongly knit,	1Tamb	2.1.9	Menaph
Me thinks we should not, I am strongly moov'd,	1Tamb	2.5.75	Tamb
Whose blast may hether strongly be inclinde,	Ovid's Elegies		2.11.38
STROOK			
He mist him neer, but we have strook him now.	P 311	5.38	Guise

STROOKE			
Treading upon his breast, strooke off his hands.	Dido	2.1.242	Aeneas
Our Masts the furious windes strooke over bourd:	Dido	3.1.110	Aeneas
Strooke with the voice of thundring Jupiter.	1Tamb	4.2.25	Tamb
Cursed be hee that strooke his holinesse a blowe on the face.	F App	p.232 33	Frier
Both differ'd much, Pompey was strooke in yeares,	Lucan, First Booke		130
Nor were the Commons only strooke to heart/With this vaine	Lucan, First Booke		483
Strooke with th'earths suddaine shadow waxed pale,	Lucan, First Booke		537
He first a Goddesse strooke; an other I.	Ovid's Elegies		1.7.32
Quickly soft words hard dores wide open strooke.	Ovid's Elegies		2.1.22
The Thracian Harpe with cunning to have strooke,	Ovid's Elegies		2.11.32
Relenting Heroes gentle heart was strooke,	Hero and Leander		1.165
The more she striv'd, the deeper was she strooke.	Hero and Leander		1.334
STROOKEN			
And looking in her face, was strooken blind.	Hero and Leander		1.38
Poore soldiers stand with fear of death dead strooken,	Hero and Leander		1.121
Wherewith she strooken, look'd so dolefully,	Hero and Leander		1.373
STROVE			
That lawes were broake, Tribunes with Consuls strove,	Lucan, First Booke		179
To finde, what worke my muse might move, I strove.	Ovid's Elegies		3.1.6
Where Venus in her naked glory strove,	Hero and Leander		1.12
Yet evilly faining anger, strove she still,	Hero and Leander		1.335
all, and everie part/Strove to resist the motions of her hart.	Hero and Leander		1.364
She trembling strove, this strife of hers (like that/Which made	Hero and Leander		2.291
STROW			
And on their faces heapes of Roses strow.	Ovid's Elegies		1.2.40
STROWE			
We have their crownes, their bodies strowe the fielde.	1Tamb	3.3.215	Techel
And in the forme of beds weele strowe soft sand,	Ovid's Elegies		2.11.47
STROWED			
And martch in cottages of strowed weeds:	1Tamb	5.1.187	Tamb
Thy streetes strowed with dissevered jointes of men,	1Tamb	5.1.322	Zenoc
I strowed powder on the Marble stones,	Jew	2.3.209	Ithimr
Had spread the boord, with roses strowed the roome,	Hero and Leander		2.21
STROWES			
And strowes the way with braines of slaughtered men:	2Tamb	3.4.58	Therid
STRUCKE			
the forrest Deare being strucke/Runnes to an herbe that closeth	Edw	5.1.9	Edward
be he that strucke <tooke> fryer Sandelo a blow on the pate.	F1081	3.2.101	1Frier
STRUGGLED			
The beast long struggled, as being like to prove/An aukward	Lucan, First Booke		610
STRUGLING			
Yeelding or striving <strugling> doe we give him might,	Ovid's Elegies		1.2.9
Like lightning go, his strugling mouth being checkt.	Ovid's Elegies		3.4.14
STRUMPET			
O had that ticing strumpet nere been borne:	Dido	2.1.300	Dido
Hence strumpet, hide thy head for shame,	P 691	13.35	Guise
Girting this strumpet Cittie with our siege,	P1152	22.14	King
Fawne not on me French strumpet, get thee gone.	Edw	1.4.145	Edward
That like the Greekish strumpet traind to armes/And bloudie	Edw	2.5.15	Lncstr
The strumpet with the stranger will not do,	Ovid's Elegies		3.13.9
STRUMPETS			
Shall buy that strumpets favour with his blood,	P 768	15.26	Guise
And strumpets flatter, shall Menander flourish.	Ovid's Elegies		1.15.18
STUBBORNE			
And hale the stubborne Furies from their caves,	F1225	4.1.71	Faust
The stubborne Nervians staind with Cottas bloud;	Lucan, First Booke		430
STUBBORNESSE			
And to resist with longer stubbornesse,	1Tamb	5.1.3	Govnr
STUBBURN			
And rough jades mouths with stubburn bits are torne,	Ovid's Elegies		1.2.15
STUCK			
Pioners away, and where I stuck the stake,	2Tamb	3.3.41	Therid
STUDENT			
Besides a thousand sturdy student Catholicks,	P 140	2.83	Guise
remember that I have beene a student here these thirty yeares,	F1840	5.2.44 P	Faust
STUDENTS			
Wherewith the Students shall be bravely clad.	F 118	1.1.90	Faust
And all the Students clothed in mourning blacke,	F2000	5.3.18	2Schol
carowse, and swill/Amongst the Students, as even now he doth,	F App	p.243 5	Wagner
STUDIE			
Nor that I studie not the brawling lawes,	Ovid's Elegies		1.15.5
STUDIED			
Being young I studied Physicke, and began/To practise first	Jew	2.3.181	Barab
STUDIES			
Settle thy studies Faustus, and begin/To sound the depth of	F 29	1.1.1	Faust
STUDIOUS			
Is promised to the Studious Artizan?	F 82	1.1.54	Faust
STUDS			
With Corall clasps and Amber studs,	Passionate Shepherd		18
STUDY			
And this the man that in his study sits.	F 28	Prol.28	1Chor
This <His> study fits a Mercenarie drudge,	F 61	1.1.33	Faust
Will make thee vow to study nothing else.	F 164	1.1.136	Cornel
And meet me in my Study, at Midnight,	F 327	1.3.99	Faust
she for her private study, shee's borne to beare with me,	F App	p.233 16 P	Robin
STUFF'D			
That yearely [stuffes] <stuff'd> old Phillips treasury,	F 159	1.1.131	Valdes
STUFFE			
faire, mishapen stuffe/Are of behaviour boisterous and ruffe.	Hero and Leander		1.203
STUFFES			
That yearely [stuffes] <stuff'd> old Phillips treasury,	F 159	1.1.131	Valdes
STUFT			
And stuft with treasure for his highest thoughts?	1Tamb	2.1.59	Ceneus

STUFT (cont.)
Ware-houses stuft with spices and with drugs, ... Jew 4.1.64 Barab
wood be flying/And thou the waxe stuft full with notes denying, Ovid's Elegies 1.12.8
STUMBLING
But I will soone put by that stumbling blocke, . . . Dido 4.1.34 Dido
And guides my feete least stumbling falles they catch. . Ovid's Elegies 1.6.8
when she departed/Nape by stumbling on the thre-shold started. Ovid's Elegies 1.12.4
STUMPE
With his stumpe-foote he halts ill-favouredly. . . . Ovid's Elegies 2.17.20
STUMPE-FOOTE
With his stumpe-foote he halts ill-favouredly. . . . Ovid's Elegies 2.17.20
STUNG
Was with two winged Serpents stung to death. . . . Dido 2.1.166 Aeneas
And stung with furie of their following, ... 2Tamb 4.1.189 Tamb
STURDIE
And fetter them in Vulcans sturdie brasse, . . . Dido 1.1.118 Jupitr
Of Tamburlaine, that sturdie Scythian thiefe, . . . 1Tamb 1.1.36 Meandr
STURDY
Untill I bring this sturdy Tamburlain, ... 1Tamb 3.3.114 Bajzth
A sturdy Felon and a base-bred Thiefe, ... 1Tamb 4.3.12 Souldn
Inhabited with tall and sturdy men, ... 2Tamb 1.1.27 Orcan
The sturdy Governour of Babylon, ... 2Tamb 5.1.81 Therid
Besides a thousand sturdy student Catholicks, . . . P 140 2.83 Guise
STYGIAN (See also STIGIAN)
And Phoebus as in Stygian pooles, refraines/To taint his . Dido 1.1.111 Venus
Than noisome parbreak of the Stygian Snakes, . . . 1Tamb 5.1.256 Bajzth
And all the poysons of the Stygian poole/Breake from the fiery Jew 3.4.102 Barab
STYL
May styl excruciat his tormented thoughts. . . . 1Tamb 5.1.301 Bajzth
STYLE (See also STILE)
(For that's the style and tytle I have yet)/Although he sent a 2Tamb 1.2.69 Almeda
STYX (See also STIX)
Millions of soules sit on the bankes of Styx, . . . 1Tamb 5.1.463 Tamb
Compast with Lethe, Styx, and Phlegeton, ... 2Tamb 3.2.13 Tamb
SUB
Sic sic juvat ire sub umbras. . . . . . . Dido 5.1.313 Dido
SUBBORND
How easilie might some base slave be subbornd, . . . Edw 1.4.265 Mortmr
SUBDEW
and to subdew/This proud contemner of thy dreadfull power, 2Tamb 4.3.39 Orcan
SUBDEW'D
Where by the river Tyros I subdew'd/Stoka, Padalia, and . 2Tamb 1.3.209 Therid
Were not subdew'd with valour more divine, . . . 2Tamb 4.3.15 Tamb
SUBDEWED
and dominions/That late the power of Tamburlaine subdewed: 1Tamb 5.1.509 Tamb
in mine eies/Than all the wealthy kingdomes I subdewed: . 2Tamb 1.3.19 Tamb
SUBDU'D
And when their scattered armie is subdu'd, . . . 1Tamb 2.2.68 Meandr
SUBDUDE
but some must stay/To rule the provinces he late subdude. 1Tamb 3.3.29 Bassoe
We have subdude the Southerne Guallatia, ... 2Tamb 1.3.178 Usumc
SUBDUE
And in the end subdue them with his sword, . . . Dido 1.1.90 Jupitr
Least you subdue the pride of Christendome? . . . 1Tamb 1.1.132 Menaph
Wil first subdue the Turke, and then inlarge/Those Christian 1Tamb 3.3.46 Tamb
Those walled garrisons wil I subdue, ... 1Tamb 3.3.244 Tamb
Is greater far, than they can thus subdue. . . . 2Tamb 5.3.39 Usumc
Shaming to strive but where he did subdue, . . . Lucan, First Booke 146
Subdue the wandring wenches to thy raigne, . . . Ovid's Elegies 2.9.53
he shall subdue,/The horses seeme, as [thy] <they> desire they Ovid's Elegies 3.2.67
SUBDUED
Should make the world subdued to Tamburlaine. . . . 1Tamb 2.1.30 Menaph
of Hydra, so my power/Subdued, shall stand as mighty as before: 1Tamb 3.3.141 Bajzth
Of all the provinces I have subdued/Thou shalt not have a foot, 2Tamb 1.3.71 Tamb
such riches, subdued so many kingdomes, as we that do succeede, F App p.236 20 P Emper
SUBDUING
I thus conceiving and subduing both: . . . . . 1Tamb 5.1.183 Tamb
SUBJECT
Too harsh a subject for your dainty eares. . . . 1Tamb 3.2.46 Agidas
A Forme not meet to give that subject essence, . . . 2Tamb 4.1.112 Tamb
A fitter subject for a pensive soule. . . . . 2Tamb 4.2.27 Olymp
<Affrica>/Which hath bene subject to the Persean king, . 2Tamb 5.1.166 Tamb
But sons, this subject not of force enough, . . . 2Tamb 5.3.168 Tamb
Why should a king be subject to a priest? . . . Edw 1.4.96 Edward
As never subject did unto his King. . . . . . Edw 2.2.129 Mortmr
A greater subject fitteth Faustus wit: . . . . F 39 1.1.11 Faust
Such is the subject of the Institute, ... F 59 1.1.31 Faust
They are good subject for a merriment. . . . . F1606 4.6.49 Faust
Choosing a subject fit for feirse alarmes: . . . . Ovid's Elegies 1.1.6
Be thou the happie subject of my Bookes, ... Ovid's Elegies 1.3.19
The subject hides thy wit, mens acts resound, . . . Ovid's Elegies 3.1.25
Is neither essence subject to the eie, ... Hero and Leander 1.270
SUBJECTS
And wisht as worthy subjects happy meanes, . . . 1Tamb 5.1.103 1Virgn
Thy Fathers subjects and thy countrimen. . . . . 1Tamb 5.1.321 Zenoc
And hundred thousands subjects to each score: . . . 2Tamb 2.2.12 Gazell
Your soul gives essence to our wretched subjects, . . 2Tamb 5.3.164 Amyras
Then be themselves base subjects to the whip. . . . P 218 4.16 Anjoy
Unnatural wars, where subjects brave their king, . . . Edw 3.1.86 Queene
And rather bathe thy sword in subjects bloud, . . . Edw 3.1.212 Mortmr
So shall the spirits <subjects> of every element, . . F 149 1.1.121 Valdes
Dis do we ascend/To view the subjects of our Monarchy, . F1798 5.2.2 Lucifr
Much more in subjects having intellect, ... Hero and Leander 2.59

SUBMISSION
On your submission we with thanks excuse, ... 1Tamb 2.5.13 Cosroe
But if these threats moove not submission, . . . 1Tamb 4.1.58 2Msngr
intollorable wrath/May be suppresst by our submission. . 2Tamb 5.1.9 Maxim
Offer submission, hang up flags of truce, ... 2Tamb 5.1.26 1Citzn
Could not perswade you to submission, ... 2Tamb 5.1.94 Tamb
SUBMISSIONS
And tels for trueth, submissions comes too late. . . 1Tamb 5.1.73 Tamb
SUBMISSIVE
With knees and hearts submissive we intreate/Grace to our words 1Tamb 5.1.50 2Virgn
ringled bit, and with his hoves,/Checkes the submissive ground: Hero and Leander 2.144
SUBMISSIVELY
Write not so submissively, but threatning him. . . . . Jew 4.2.72 P Pilia
SUBMIT
Submit your selves and us to servitude. . . . . . 1Tamb 5.1.39 Govnr
And will you basely thus submit your selves/To leave your goods Jew 1.2.79 Barab
And curse the people that submit to him; . . . . . F 907 3.1.129 Pope
SUBORN'D (See also SUBBORND)
That like a roguish runnaway, suborn'd/That villaine there, that 2Tamb 3.5.86 Tamb
SUBSCRIBE
And Ile subscribe my name and seale it straight. . . P 883 17.78 King
May it please your lordship to subscribe your name. . . Edw 1.4.2 Lncstr
Subscribe as we have done to his exile. . . . . . Edw 1.4.53 ArchBp
Come, come, subscribe. . . . . Edw 1.4.75 Lncstr
For shame subscribe, and let the lowne depart. . . . Edw 1.4.82 Warwck
As thou wilt soone subscribe to his repeale. . . . . Edw 1.4.227 Queene
And I my selfe will willinglie subscribe. . . . . . Edw 5.2.20 Queene
And when tis done, we will subscribe our name. . . . Edw 5.2.50 Mortmr
SUBSCRIBING
Subscribing that to her I consecrate/My faithfull tables being Ovid's Elegies 1.11.27
Subscribing, Naso with Corinna sav'd: . . . . . Ovid's Elegies 2.13.25
SUBSTANCE
is that doth excruciate/The verie substance of my vexed soule: 1Tamb 1.1.114 Cosroe
That fed upon the substance of his child. . . . . . 1Tamb 4.4.25 Zabina
As when the massy substance of the earth, ... 2Tamb 1.1.89 Orcan
vaine or Artier feed/The cursed substance of that cruel heart, 2Tamb 4.1.178 Soria
that falles/Into the liquid substance of his streame, . 2Tamb 5.1.19 Govnr
And guide this massy substance of the earthe, ... 2Tamb 5.3.18 Techel
But of a substance more divine and pure, ... 2Tamb 5.3.88 Phsitn
the winds/To drive their substance with successefull blasts? Jew 1.1.111 Barab
Halfe of my substance is a Cities wealth. . . . . . Jew 1.2.85 Barab
And give my goods and substance to your house, ... Jew 4.1.190 Barab
First, that Faustus may be a spirit in forme and substance. F 485 2.1.97 P Faust
As is the substance of this centricke earth? . . . . F 588 2.2.37 Faust
Who should have Priams wealthy substance wonne, . . Ovid's Elegies 2.14.13
God is a name, no substance, feard in vaine, . . . Ovid's Elegies 3.3.23
SUBSTANTIALL
Then thou shalt find my vaunts substantiall. . . . . 1Tamb 1.2.213 Tamb
These are but shadowes, not substantiall. . . . . . F1259 4.1.105 Faust
substantiall bodies of those two deceased princes which long F App p.237 42 P Faust
but the true substantiall bodies of those two deceased princes. F App p.238 64 P Emper
SUBTIL
secret, subtil, bottle-nos'd knave to my Master, that ever Jew 3.3.9 P Ithimr
SUBTILE
To lighten doubts and frustrate subtile foes. . . . . P 457 8.7 Anjoy
Whether the subtile maide lines bringes and carries, . Ovid's Elegies 2.19.41
SUBTILL
Thats it these Barons and the subtill Queene, ... Edw 3.1.272 Levune
SUBTLE
have with [concise] <subtle> Sillogismes <Consissylogismes> F 139 1.1.111 Faust
That with his wings did part the subtle aire, ... F 772 2.3.51 2Chor
SUBURBE
Those that inhabited the suburbe fieldes/Fled, fowle Erinnis Lucan, First Booke 569
SUBURBES
And plant our pleasant suburbes with her fumes. . . . Dido 5.1.15 Aeneas
SUCCEED
So shall you imitate those you succeed: . . . . . . Jew 2.2.47 Bosco
SUCCEEDE
as we that do succeede, or they that shal hereafter possesse F App p.236 21 P Emper
SUCCEEDING
For him, and the succeeding Popes of Rome, ... F 926 3.1.148 Bruno
By speechlesse lookes we guesse at things succeeding. . Ovid's Elegies 1.11.18
For whom succeeding times make greater mone. . . . . Hero and Leander 1.54
SUCCESFULL
Succesfull battells gives the God of kings, ... Edw 4.6.19 Queene
SUCCESFULLY
Since then succesfully we have prevayled, ... Edw 4.6.21 Queene
SUCCESSE
I goe faire sister, heavens graunt good successe. . . Dido 5.1.211 Anna
And in assurance of desir'd successe, ... 1Tamb 1.1.160 Ortyg
whatsoever you esteeme/Of this successe, and losse unvallued, 1Tamb 1.2.45 Tamb
exchange for that/We are assured of by our friends successe. 1Tamb 1.2.217 Techel
Thy words assure me of kind successe: . . . . . . 1Tamb 2.3.60 Cosroe
Such good successe happen to Bajazeth. . . . . . 1Tamb 3.3.116 Zabina
I have, and sorrow for his bad successe: . . . . . 1Tamb 4.3.28 Souldn
My mind presageth fortunate successe, ... 1Tamb 4.3.58 Arabia
And in this City still have had successe, ... Jew 5.2.69 Barab
Seeing thou hast pleaded with so good successe. . . . Edw 1.4.329 Edward
Few battailes fought with prosperous successe/May bring her Lucan, First Booke 285
SUCCESSEFULL
the winds/To drive their substance with successefull blasts? Jew 1.1.111 Barab
SUCCESSION
And Crownes come either by succession/Or urg'd by force; and Jew 1.1.131 Barab

SUCCESSION (cont.)			
It is my due by just succession:	P 570	11.35	Navrre
To plant the true succession of the faith,	P 715	14.18	Bartus
SUCCESSIVE			
son and successive heire to the late mighty Emperour Bajazeth,	2Tamb	3.1.2	P Orcan
SUCCOUR			
To succour him in this extremitie.	Dido	1.1.133	Venus
That no reliefe or succour come by Land.	1Tamb	3.1.62	Bajzth
To crave the aide and succour of his peeres.	Edw	5.6.21	Queene
SUCH			
She reacht me such a rap for that I spilde,	Dido	1.1.7	Ganimd
Whose face reflects such pleasure to mine eyes,	Dido	1.1.24	Jupitr
I neither saw nor heard of any such:	Dido	1.1.187	Aeneas
Such honour, stranger, doe I not affect:	Dido	1.1.203	Venus
That crave such favour at your honors feete,	Dido	1.2.5	Illion
Such force is farre from our unweaponed thoughts,	Dido	1.2.14	Illion
That in such peace long time did rule the same:	Dido	1.2.24	Cloan
Thankes gentle Lord for such unlookt for grace.	Dido	1.2.44	Serg
Then would we hope to quite such friendly turnes,	Dido	1.2.46	Serg
Had not such passions in her head as I.	Dido	2.1.6	Aeneas
But Illioneus goes not in such robes.	Dido	2.1.48	Achat
destinies/Have brought my sweete companions in such plight?	Dido	2.1.60	Aeneas
Shall I have such a quiver and a bow?	Dido	2.1.310	Ascan
Such bow, such quiver, and such golden shafts,	Dido	2.1.311	Venus
The rest are such as all the world well knowes,	Dido	3.1.165	Dido
Who warne me of such daunger prest at hand,	Dido	3.2.22	Venus
Fie Venus, that such causeles words of wrath,	Dido	3.2.26	Juno
Sister of Jove, if that thy love be such,	Dido	3.2.53	Venus
how may I deserve/Such amourous favours at thy beautious hand?	Dido	3.2.65	Juno
Whom casualtie of sea hath made such friends?	Dido	3.2.76	Juno
And finde the way to wearie such fond thoughts:	Dido	3.2.86	Juno
To be well stor'd with such a winters tale?	Dido	3.3.59	Aeneas
Kind clowdes that sent forth such a curteous storme,	Dido	3.4.55	Dido
Did ever men see such a sudden storme?	Dido	4.1.1	Achat
There was such hurly burly in the heavens:	Dido	4.1.10	Achat
Nay, no such waightie busines of import,	Dido	4.2.25	Anna
I would be thankfull for such curtesie.	Dido	4.2.29	Anna
I may nor will list to such loathsome chaunge,	Dido	4.2.47	Iarbus
But if I use such ceremonious thankes,	Dido	4.3.49	Aeneas
O what meane I to have such foolish thoughts!	Dido	4.5.25	Nurse
And thou despise the praise of such attempts:	Dido	5.1.37	Hermes
Jove hath heapt on me such a desperate charge,	Dido	5.1.64	Aeneas
For I will furnish thee with such supplies:	Dido	5.1.72	Iarbus
And such conceits as clownage keepes in pay,	1Tamb	Prol.2	Prolog
Such hope, such fortune have the thousand horse.	1Tamb	1.2.118	Tamb
Such breadth of shoulders as might mainely beare/Olde Atlas	1Tamb	2.1.10	Menaph
That could perswade at such a sodaine pinch,	1Tamb	2.1.37	Cosroe
And such shall wait on worthy Tamburlaine.	1Tamb	2.1.60	Cosroe
his Diadem/Sought for by such scalde knaves as love him not?	1Tamb	2.2.8	Mycet
Will quickly win such as are like himselfe.	1Tamb	2.2.28	Meandr
Was there such brethren, sweet Meander, say,	1Tamb	2.2.51	Mycet
and strive to be retain'd/In such a great degree of amitie.	1Tamb	2.3.32	Therid
and rid your royall shoulders/Of such a burthen, as outwaies	1Tamb	2.3.47	Tamb
Such another word, and I will have thee executed.	1Tamb	2.4.30	Mycet
Such power attractive shines in princes eies.	1Tamb	2.5.64	Therid
If we should aime at such a dignitie?	1Tamb	2.5.79	Tamb
divelish shepheard to aspire/With such a Giantly presumption,	1Tamb	2.6.2	Cosroe
And in detesting such a divelish Thiefe,	1Tamb	2.6.20	Ortyg
Be arm'd against the hate of such a foe,	1Tamb	2.6.22	Ortyg
The ground is mantled with such multitudes.	1Tamb	3.1.53	Moroc
That worke such trouble to your woonted rest:	1Tamb	3.2.3	Agidas
Tis more then pitty such a heavenly face/Should by hearts	1Tamb	3.2.4	Agidas
Before such hap fall to Zenocrate.	1Tamb	3.2.20	Agidas
Such as his Highnesse please, but some must stay/To rule the	1Tamb	3.3.28	Bassoe
What Coward wold not fight for such a prize?	1Tamb	3.3.100	Usumc
Such good successe happen to Bajazeth.	1Tamb	3.3.116	Zabina
Nor in Pharsalia was there such hot war,	1Tamb	3.3.154	Tamb
Before I yeeld to such a slavery.	1Tamb	4.2.18	Bajzth
That such a base usurping vagabond/Should brave a king, or	1Tamb	4.3.21	Souldn
Wherein he wrought such ignominious wrong,	1Tamb	4.3.39	Souldn
offences feele/Such plagues as heaven and we can poure on him.	1Tamb	4.3.45	Arabia
such a stomacke (cruel Tamburlane) as I could willingly feed	1Tamb	4.4.11	P Bajzth
wouldst thou have me buy thy Fathers love/With such a losse?	1Tamb	4.4.84	Tamb
Nor you depend on such weake helps as we.	1Tamb	5.1.33	1Virgn
O then for these, and such as we our selves,	1Tamb	5.1.96	1Virgn
Arabian king together/Martch on us with such eager violence,	1Tamb	5.1.200	Techel
But such a Star hath influence in his sword,	1Tamb	5.1.232	Bajzth
Too deare a witnesse for such love my Lord.	1Tamb	5.1.412	Zenoc
And such are objects fit for Tamburlaine.	1Tamb	5.1.475	Tamb
And martch with such a multitude of men,	2Tamb	1.3.56	Celeb
My Lord, such speeches to our princely sonnes,	2Tamb	1.3.85	Zenoc
Such lavish will I make of Turkish blood,	2Tamb	1.3.165	Tamb
And stirs your valures to such soddaine armes?	2Tamb	2.1.3	Sgsmnd
for with such Infidels,/In whom no faith nor true religion	2Tamb	2.1.33	Baldwn
That with such treason seek our overthrow,	2Tamb	2.2.34	Gazell
Can there be such deceit in Christians,	2Tamb	2.2.36	Orcan
May never such a change transfourme my love/In whose sweet	2Tamb	2.4.47	Tamb
Do us such honor and supremacie,	2Tamb	3.1.16	Callap
[Those] <Whose> looks will shed such influence in my campe,/As	2Tamb	3.2.39	Tamb
Stand at the walles, with such a mighty power.	2Tamb	3.3.14	Therid
Such a feare (my Lord) would never make yee retire.	2Tamb	4.1.71	P Perdic
would let me be put in the front of such a battaile once,	2Tamb	4.1.73	P Calyph
In sending to my issue such a soule,	2Tamb	4.1.122	Tamb

SUCH (cont.)

To scourge the pride of such as heaven abhors:	2Tamb	4.1.149	Tamb
And plague such Pesants as [resist in] <resisting> me/The power	2Tamb	4.1.157	Tamb
Nor yet imposd, with such a bitter hate.	2Tamb	4.1.170	Jrslem
and of fire/Doth send such sterne affections to his heart.	2Tamb	4.1.176	Trebiz
No such discourse is pleasant in mine eares,	2Tamb	4.2.46	Olymp
Such is the sodaine fury of my love,	2Tamb	4.2.52	Therid
Ile give your Grace a present of such price,	2Tamb	4.2.56	Olymp
And such a Coachman as great Tamburlaine?	2Tamb	4.3.4	Tamb
Thy youth forbids such ease my kingly boy,	2Tamb	4.3.29	Tamb
(I meane such Queens as were kings Concubines)/Take them,	2Tamb	4.3.71	Tamb
To exercise upon such guiltlesse Dames,	2Tamb	4.3.79	Orcan
the enimie hath made/Gives such assurance of our overthrow,	2Tamb	5.1.3	Maxim
we offer more/Than ever yet we did to such proud slaves,	2Tamb	5.1.58	Techel
And usde such slender reckning of [your] <you> majesty.	2Tamb	5.1.83	Therid
taskes a while/And take such fortune as your fellowes felt.	2Tamb	5.1.137	Tamb
Sustaine a shame of such inexcellence:	2Tamb	5.3.31	Usumc
But such as love me, gard me from their tongues,	Jew	Prol.6	Machvl
I am asham'd to heare such fooleries.	Jew	Prol.17	Machvl
how you durst with so much wealth/Trust such a crazed Vessell,	Jew	1.1.80	1Merch
The Turkes have let increase to such a summe,	Jew	1.1.182	Barab
Since your hard conditions are such/That you will needs have	Jew	1.2.18	Govnr
but trust me 'tis a misery/To see a man in such affliction:	Jew	1.2.212	2Jew
Such as, poore villaines, were ne're thought upon/Till Titus	Jew	2.3.9	Barab
Oh heaven forbid I should have such a thought.	Jew	2.3.256	Barab
I'le give him such a warning e're he goes/As he shall have	Jew	2.3.273	Barab
a hundred of the Jewes Crownes that I had such a Concubine.	Jew	3.1.28	P Ithimr
Well, I have deliver'd the challenge in such sort,	Jew	3.1.29	Ithimr
What, dares the villain write in such base terms?	Jew	3.2.3	Lodowk
Why, was there ever seene such villany,	Jew	3.3.1	Ithimr
Troth master, I'm loth such a pot of pottage should be spoyld.	Jew	3.4.89	P Ithimr
Now I have such a plot for both their lives,	Jew	4.1.117	Barab
such a base slave as he should be saluted by such a tall man as	Jew	4.2.9	P Pilia
base slave as he should be saluted by such a tall man as I am,	Jew	4.2.10	P Pilia
by such a tall man as I am, from such a beautifull dame as you.	Jew	4.2.10	P Pilia
he made such haste to his prayers, as if hee had had another	Jew	4.2.24	P Ithimr
such sort as if he had meant to make cleane my Boots with his	Jew	4.2.30	P Ithimr
me ever since she saw me, and who would not requite such love?	Jew	4.2.35	P Ithimr
I, and such as--Goe to, no more, I'le make him send me half he	Jew	4.2.66	P Ithimr
Shall Ithimcre my love goe in such rags?	Jew	4.2.85	Curtzn
crosbiting, such a Rogue/As is the husband to a hundred whores:	Jew	4.3.13	Barab
to fall into the hands/Of such a Traitor and unhallowed Jew!	Jew	5.2.13	Govnr
policy for Barabas/To dispossesse himselfe of such a place?	Jew	5.2.66	Barab
To meddle or attempt such dangerous things.	P 38	1.38	Admral
To think a word of such a simple sound,	P 125	2.68	Guise
Sufficient yet for such a pettie King:	P 150	2.93	Guise
Not wel, but do remember such a man.	P 173	3.8	OldQn
The heavens forbid your highnes such mishap.	P 177	3.12	QnMarg
to beware/How you did meddle with such dangerous giftes.	P 180	3.15	Navrre
Should for their conscience taste such rutheles ends.	P 214	4.12	Charls
To speek with me from such a man as he?	P 350	6.5	Seroun
A martiall people, worthy such a King,	P 455	8.5	Anjoy
And such a King whom practise long hath taught,	P 458	8.8	Anjoy
And like disportes, such as doe fit the Court?	P 629	12.42	King
To plant our selves with such authoritie,	P 637	12.50	QnMoth
To such a one my Lord, as when she reads my lines,	P 672	13.16	Duchss
proudest Kings/In Christendome, should beare me such derision,	P 761	15.19	Guise
But wherfore beares he me such deadly hate?	P 779	15.37	Mugern
Because his wife beares thee such kindely love.	P 780	15.38	King
him, and will slay/Thee too, and thou prove such a traitor.	P1049	19.119	King
That basely seekes to joyne with such a King,	P1115	21.9	Dumain
God shield your grace from such a sodaine death:	P1178	22.40	Navrre
Of such as holde them of the holy church?	P1181	22.43	King
That hatcheth up such bloudy practises.	P1205	22.67	King
Such as desire your worships service.	Edw	1.1.25	Poorem
Why there are hospitals for such as you,	Edw	1.1.35	Gavstn
Such things as these best please his majestie,	Edw	1.1.71	Gavstn
Proud Rome, that hatchest such imperiall groomes,	Edw	1.4.97	Edward
Hard is the hart, that injures such a saint.	Edw	1.4.190	Penbrk
And I will tell thee reasons of such waighte,	Edw	1.4.226	Queene
Such reasons make white blacke, and darke night day.	Edw	1.4.247	Lncstr
Which may in Ireland purchase him such friends,	Edw	1.4.259	Mortmr
For purging of the realme of such a plague.	Edw	1.4.270	Mortmr
Such a one as my Lord of Cornewall is,	Edw	1.4.285	Mortmr
Such newes we heare my lord.	Edw	1.4.380	Lncstr
For riper yeares will weane him from such toyes.	Edw	1.4.401	MortSr
Whose proud fantastick liveries make such show,	Edw	1.4.410	Mortmr
below, the king and he/From out a window, laugh at such as we,	Edw	1.4.417	Mortmr
I will not yeeld to any such upstart.	Edw	1.4.423	Mortmr
Spencer, thou knowest I hate such formall toies,	Edw	2.1.44	Baldck
As to bestow a looke on such as you.	Edw	2.2.78	Gavstn
Ile thunder such a peale into his eares,	Edw	2.2.128	Mortmr
I marry, such a garde as this dooth well.	Edw	2.2.131	Mortmr
We never beg, but use such praiers as these.	Edw	2.2.153	Mortmr
No doubt, such lessons they will teach the rest,	Edw	3.1.21	Spencr
Whose brightnes such pernitious upstarts dim,	Edw	3.1.165	Herald
Then live in infamie under such a king.	Edw	3.1.244	Lncstr
and fell invasion/Of such as have your majestie in chase,	Edw	4.7.5	Abbot
You, and such as you are, have made wise worke in England.	Edw	4.7.114	P Rice
For such outragious passions cloye my soule,	Edw	5.1.19	Edward
Such newes as I expect, come Bartley, come,	Edw	5.1.129	Edward
If he have such accesse unto the prince,	Edw	5.2.77	Mortmr
Forgive my thought, for having such a thought,	Edw	5.5.83	Edward

SUCH (cont.)

Such is the subject of the Institute,	F 59	1.1.31	Faust
you were not dunces, you would never aske me such a question:	F 207	1.2.14	P Wagner
Then wherefore should you aske me such a question?	F 209	1.2.16	P Wagner
Such is the force of Magicke, and my spels.	F 259	1.3.31	Faust
Nor will we come unlesse he use such meanes,	F 278	1.3.50	Mephst
seene many boyes with [such pickadevaunts] <beards> I am sure.	F 345	1.4.3	P Robin
Away with such vaine fancies, and despaire,	F 392	2.1.4	Faust
But may I raise such <up> spirits when I please?	F 475	2.1.87	Faust
<why Faustus> think'st thou heaven is such a glorious thing?	F 556	2.2.5	Mephst
As are the elements, such are the heavens <spheares>,/Even from	F 589	2.2.38	Mephst
conjuring bookes, and now we'le have such knavery, as't passes.	F 724	2.3.3	P Robin
<Within whose walles such store of ordnance are>,	F 819	(HC265)A	Mephst
Where thou shalt see such store of Ordinance,	F 819	3.1.41	Mephst
Mephostophilis, and two such Cardinals/Ne're serv'd a holy Pope,	F 941	3.1.163	Faust
Your Grace mistakes, you gave us no such charge.	F1024	3.2.44	1Card
The Pope had never such a frolicke guest.	F1036	3.2.56	Faust
That we receive such great indignity?	F1050	3.2.70	Pope
[Where such as beare <bare> his absence but with griefe],	F1141	3.3.54A	3Chor
[Which Faustus answered with such learned skill],	F1147	3.3.60A	3Chor
and thou shalt see/This Conjurer performe such rare exploits,	F1186	4.1.32	Mrtino
to thinke I have beene such an Asse all this while, to stand	F1243	4.1.89	P Benvol
thee not to sleepe much, having such a head of thine owne.	F1284	4.1.130	P Emper
such Cuckold-makers to clap hornes of honest mens heades o'this	F1316	4.1.162	P Benvol
because I knew him to be such a horse, as would run over hedge	F1538	4.5.34	P HrsCsr
and such Countries that lye farre East, where they have fruit	F1584	4.6.27	P Faust
thou make a Colossus of me, that thou askest me such questions?	F1647	4.6.90	P Faust
where ther's such belly-cheere, as Wagner in his life nere saw	F1678	5.1.5	P Wagner
pursu'd]/[With tenne yeares warre the rape of such a queene],	F1700	5.1.27A	3Schol
To want in hell, that had on earth such store.	F1898	5.2.102	BdAngl
For such a dreadfull night, was never seene,	F1984	5.3.2	1Schol
Such fearefull shrikes, and cries, were never heard,	F1986	5.3.4	1Schol
tho Faustus end be such/As every Christian heart laments to	F1995	5.3.13	2Schol
Whose deepnesse doth intice such forward wits,	F2008	5.3.26	4Chor
you have seene many boyes with such pickadevaunts as I have.	F App	p.229 3	P Clown
he keepes such a chafing with my mistris about it, and she has	F App	p.233 8	P Rafe
how they had wonne by prowesse such exploits, gote such riches,	F App	p.236 20	P Emper
such exploits, gote such riches, subdued so many kingdomes,	F App	p.236 20	P Emper
such spirites as can lively resemble Alexander and his	F App	p.237 46	P Faust
mas Doctor Lopus was never such a Doctor, has given me a	F App	p.240 128	P HrsCsr
who are at supper with such belly-cheere,	F App	p.243 6	Wagner
the inward soule/With such flagitious crimes of hainous sinnes,	F App	p.243 42	OldMan
crush themselves, such end the gods/Allot the height of honor,	Lucan, First Booke	81	
Nor then was land, or sea, to breed such hate,	Lucan, First Booke	96	
Such humors stirde them up; but this warrs seed,	Lucan, First Booke	159	
armes neer their houshold gods hung up/Such as peace yeelds;	Lucan, First Booke	243	
Are blest by such sweet error, this makes them/Run on the	Lucan, First Booke	456	
such and more strange/Blacke night brought forth in secret:	Lucan, First Booke	578	
First he commands such monsters Nature hatcht/Against her kind	Lucan, First Booke	588	
Then such as in their bondage feele content.	Ovid's Elegies	1.2.18	
shame, and such as seeke loves wrack/Shall follow thee, their	Ovid's Elegies	1.2.31	
Love <Jove> knowes with such like praiers, I dayly move hir:	Ovid's Elegies	1.3.4	
Which gave such light, as twincles in a wood,	Ovid's Elegies	1.5.4	
Such light to shamefaste maidens must be showne,	Ovid's Elegies	1.5.7	
Jove send me more such afternoones as this.	Ovid's Elegies	1.5.26	
Long Love my body to such use [makes] <make> slender/And to get	Ovid's Elegies	1.6.5	
Such rampierd gates beseiged Cittyes ayde,	Ovid's Elegies	1.6.29	
Such Ariadne was, when she bewayles/Her perjur'd Theseus flying	Ovid's Elegies	1.7.15	
Such is his forme as may with thine compare,	Ovid's Elegies	1.8.33	
Let Homer yeeld to such as presents bring,	Ovid's Elegies	1.8.61	
Such as the cause was of two husbands warre,	Ovid's Elegies	1.10.1	
Such as was Leda, whom the God deluded/In snowe-white plumes of	Ovid's Elegies	1.10.3	
Such as Amimone through the drie fields strayed/When on her	Ovid's Elegies	1.10.5	
Such wert thou, and I fear'd the Bull and Eagle/And what ere	Ovid's Elegies	1.10.7	
The sport being such, as both alike sweete try it,	Ovid's Elegies	1.10.33	
Your name approves you made for such like things,	Ovid's Elegies	1.12.27	
Such as in hilly Idas watry plaines,	Ovid's Elegies	1.14.11	
Such were they as [Dione] <Diana> painted stands/All naked	Ovid's Elegies	1.14.33	
Aye me rare gifts unworthy such a happe.	Ovid's Elegies	1.14.54	
flying touch/Tantalus seekes, his long tongues gaine is such.	Ovid's Elegies	2.2.44	
Trust me all husbands for such faults are sad/Nor make they any	Ovid's Elegies	2.2.51	
(Such with my tongue it likes me to purloyne).	Ovid's Elegies	2.5.24	
None such the sister gives her brother grave,	Ovid's Elegies	2.5.25	
But such kinde wenches let their lovers have.	Ovid's Elegies	2.5.26	
Phoebus gave not Diana such tis thought,	Ovid's Elegies	2.5.27	
But Venus often to her Mars such brought.	Ovid's Elegies	2.5.28	
Such blisse is onely common to us two,	Ovid's Elegies	2.5.31	
Even such as by Aurora hath the skie,	Ovid's Elegies	2.5.35	
Such as a rose mixt with a lilly breedes,	Ovid's Elegies	2.5.37	
Or such, as least long yeares should turne the die,	Ovid's Elegies	2.5.39	
I grieve least others should such good perceive,	Ovid's Elegies	2.5.53	
Such to the parrat was the turtle dove.	Ovid's Elegies	2.6.16	
No such voice-feigning bird was on the ground,	Ovid's Elegies	2.6.23	
Let such as be mine enemies have none,	Ovid's Elegies	2.10.16	
The losse of such a wench much blame will gather,	Ovid's Elegies	2.11.35	
She secretly with me such harme attempted,	Ovid's Elegies	2.13.3	
If such a worke thy mother had assayed.	Ovid's Elegies	2.14.20	
To plague your bodies with such harmefull strokes?	Ovid's Elegies	2.14.34	
But though I apt were for such high deseignes,	Ovid's Elegies	2.18.14	
Such chaunce let me have:	Ovid's Elegies	3.2.9	
Thee I have pass'd, and knew thy streame none such,	Ovid's Elegies	3.5.5	
Is by Evadne thought to take such flame,	Ovid's Elegies	3.5.41	
May spelles and droughs <drugges> do sillie soules such harmes?	Ovid's Elegies	3.6.28	

SUCH (cont.)
Onely our loves let not such rich churles gaine, — Ovid's Elegies 3.7.59
Law-giving Minos did such yeares desire; — Ovid's Elegies 3.9.41
Such was the Greeke pompe, Agamemnon dead, — Ovid's Elegies 3.12.31
Such as confesse, have lost their good names by it. — Ovid's Elegies 3.13.6
(Nor am I by such wanton toyes defamde)/Heire of an antient — Ovid's Elegies 3.14.4
How such a Poet could you bring forth, sayes, — Ovid's Elegies 3.14.13
Such as the world would woonder to behold: — Hero and Leander 1.34
And of such wondrous beautie her bereft: — Hero and Leander 1.48
And such as knew he was a man would say, — Hero and Leander 1.87
To meet their loves; such as had none at all, — Hero and Leander 1.95
Love kindling fire, to burne such townes as Troy, — Hero and Leander 1.153
Such force and vertue hath an amorous looke. — Hero and Leander 1.166
In heaping up a masse of drossie pelfe,/Than such as you: — Hero and Leander 1.245
Such sacrifice as this, Venus demands. — Hero and Leander 1.310
Aye me, such words as these should I abhor, — Hero and Leander 1.339
And hands so pure, so innocent, nay such, — Hero and Leander 1.365
so much/As one poore word, their hate to him was such. — Hero and Leander 1.384
After went Mercurie, who us'd such cunning, — Hero and Leander 1.417
That she such lovelinesse and beautie had/As could provoke his — Hero and Leander 1.422
Impos'd upon her lover such a taske, — Hero and Leander 1.429
Which joyfull Hero answered in such sort, — Hero and Leander 2.15
Such sights as this, to tender maids are rare. — Hero and Leander 2.238
In such warres women use but halfe their strength. — Hero and Leander 2.296

SUCKE
And Tygers of Hircania gave thee sucke: — Dido 5.1.159 Dido
every fixed starre/To sucke up poison from the moorish Fens, — 1Tamb 4.2.6 Bajzth
Her lips sucke <suckes> forth my soule, see where it flies. — F1771 5.1.98 Faust

SUCKEDST
That in our famous nurseries of artes/Thou suckedst from Plato, — Edw 4.7.19 Edward

SUCKES
Her lips sucke <suckes> forth my soule, see where it flies. — F1771 5.1.98 Faust

SUCKING
The sucking shore with their aboundance swels. — Ovid's Elegies 2.11.14

SUCKT
And since we all have suckt one wholsome aire, — 1Tamb 2.6.25 Cosroe
Hath suckt the measure of that vitall aire/That feeds the body — 2Tamb 2.4.44 Zenoc

SUDAINLY
But stay, I feele my selfe distempered sudainly. — 2Tamb 5.1.218 Tamb

SUDDAINE
And suddaine rampire raisde of turfe snatcht up/Would make them — Lucan, First Booke 515
Strooke with th'earths suddaine shadow waxed pale, — Lucan, First Booke 537
He on the suddaine cling'd her so about, — Hero and Leander 2.314

SUDDEN (See also SODAINE, SODENLY)
Did ever men see such a sudden storme? — Dido 4.1.1 Achat
I, let me sorrow for this sudden chance, — Jew 1.2.206 Barab
us an occasion/Which on the sudden cannot serve the turne. — Jew 1.2.240 Barab
her fathers sudden fall/Has humbled her and brought her downe — Jew 1.2.367 Mthias
may dreame/A golden dreame, and of the sudden [wake] <walke>, — Jew 2.1.37 Abigal
Why on the sudden is your colour chang'd? — Jew 2.3.321 Lodowk
Mute a the sudden; here's a sudden change. — Jew 2.3.324 Lodowk
This sudden death of his is very strange. — Jew 5.1.54 Bosco
That on the sudden shall dissever it, — Jew 5.5.29 Barab

SUDDENLY
When suddenly gloomie Orion rose, — Dido 1.2.26 Cloan
Then he unlockt the Horse, and suddenly/From out his entrailes, — Dido 2.1.182 Aeneas
But suddenly the Grecians followed us, — Dido 2.1.278 Aeneas
Or day so cleere so suddenly orecast? — Dido 4.1.2 Achat
If he depart thus suddenly, I dye: — Dido 5.1.209 Dido
But suddenly the wind began to rise, — Jew 2.2.13 Bosco
We will not let thee part so suddenly: — Jew 5.5.98 Govnr

SUE (See also SEW, SEWE)
And sue to me to be your Advocates. — 1Tamb 3.3.175 Zenoc
And sue to thee? — 1Tamb 3.3.176 Zabina
To sue for mercie at your highnesse feete. — 2Tamb 5.2.41 Amasia
To sue unto you all for his repeale: — Edw 1.4.201 Queene
And sue to me for that that I desire, — Edw 5.4.57 Mortmr
Then sue for life unto a paltrie boye. — Edw 5.6.57 Mortmr
What needes thou warre, I sue to thee for grace, — Ovid's Elegies 1.2.21
I that ere-while was fierce, now humbly sue, — Ovid's Elegies 2.5.49
Thou hast my gift, which she would from thee sue. — Ovid's Elegies 3.1.60

SUES
Now sues the King for favour to the Guise, — P 978 19.48 Guise

SUFFER (See also SUFFREST)
That he might suffer shipwracke on my breast, — Dido 4.4.102 Dido
Why did it suffer thee to touch her breast, — Dido 4.4.145 Dido
Away with her, suffer her not to speake. — Dido 5.1.224 Dido
How can ye suffer these indignities? — 1Tamb 3.3.90 Moroc
you suffer these outragious curses by these slaves of yours? — 1Tamb 4.4.26 P Zenoc
Doost thou think that Mahomet wil suffer this? — 1Tamb 4.4.52 P Therid
Ah that the deadly panges I suffer now, — 1Tamb 5.1.422 Arabia
What, hand in hand, I cannot suffer this. — Jew 2.3.276 Mthias
Suffer me, Barabas, but to follow him. — Jew 2.3.340 Mthias
Why suffer you that peasant to declaime? — P 414 7.54 Guise
Although my love to thee can hardly [suffer't] <suffer>, — P 747 15.5 King
We may not, nor we will not suffer this. — Edw 1.2.15 MortSr
and suffer uncontrowld/These Barons thus to beard me in my — Edw 3.1.13 Spencr
You would not suffer thus your majestie/Be counterbuft of your — Edw 3.1.17 Spencr
What, suffer you the traitor to delay? — Edw 5.6.67 King
<O, if my soule must suffer for my sinne>, — F1958 (HC271)B Faust
Dominion cannot suffer partnership; — Lucan, First Booke 93
is bould/To suffer storme mixt snowes with nights sharpe cold? — Ovid's Elegies 1.9.16
he will lament/And say this blabbe shall suffer punnishment. — Ovid's Elegies 2.2.60

SUFFER (cont.)
Suffer, and harden: — Ovid's Elegies 3.10.7

SUFFERANCE (See also SUFFRANCE)
For through our sufferance of your hatefull lives, — Jew 1.2.63 Govnr
Be silent, Daughter, sufferance breeds ease, — Jew 1.2.238 Barab
Lords, sith that we are by sufferance of heaven, — Edw 4.4.17 Mortmr

SUFFERED
That suffered Jove to passe in showers of golde/To Danae, all — Edw 3.1.267 Spencr
We from our houses driven, most willingly/Suffered exile: — Lucan, First Booke 280

SUFFERINGS
What is beauty, saith my sufferings then? — 1Tamb 5.1.160 Tamb

SUFFERS
That suffers flames of fire to burne the writ/Wherein the sum — 2Tamb 5.1.190 Tamb

SUFFER'T
Although my love to thee can hardly [suffer't] <suffer>, — P 747 15.5 King

SUFFICE (See also SUFFISE)
It shall suffice thou darst abide a wound. — 2Tamb 3.2.136 Tamb
the least of these may well suffice/For one of greater birth — Edw 1.1.158 Kent
It shall suffice me to enjoy your love, — Edw 1.1.171 Gavstn
If that will not suffice, farwell my lords. — Edw 2.3.10 Kent
a small trifle to suffice nature. — F 695 2.2.144 P Glutny
Them freedome without war might not suffice, — Lucan, First Booke 173
To have this skirmish fought, let it suffice thee. — Ovid's Elegies 2.13.28

SUFFICENTLY
He has done penance now sufficently. — F1310 4.1.156 Emper

SUFFICETH
And it sufficeth: — Edw 2.3.15 Lncstr

SUFFICIENT
Sufficient to discomfort and confound/The trustlesse force of — 2Tamb 2.2.61 Orcan
Thinke them in number yet sufficient, — 2Tamb 3.1.41 Orcan
But that we leave sufficient garrison/And presently depart to — 2Tamb 5.1.211 Tamb
Sufficient yet for such a pettie King: — P 150 2.93 Guise
As hath sufficient counsaile in himselfe, — P 456 8.6 Anjoy
at my intreaty release him, he hath done penance sufficient. — F App p.238 80 P Emper
And thought his name sufficient to uphold him, — Lucan, First Booke 136
Nor one or two men are sufficient. — Ovid's Elegies 1.8.54

SUFFICIENTLY
tis no matter for thy head, for that's arm'd sufficiently. — F1289 4.1.135 P Emper
sufficiently to recompence your great deserts in erecting that — F1559 4.6.2 P Duke
I doubt not shal sufficiently content your Imperiall majesty. — F App p.237 49 P Faust

SUFFISE
Let it suffise,/That my slacke muse, sings of Leanders eies, — Hero and Leander 1.71
The reason no man knowes, let it suffise, — Hero and Leander 1.173

SUFFRANCE
What ever haps, by suffrance harme is done, — Ovid's Elegies 2.19.35

SUFFRED
Therefore in signe her treasure suffred wracke, — Hero and Leander 1.49

SUFFREST
Thou suffrest what no husband can endure, — Ovid's Elegies 2.19.51

SUFFRING
Suffring much cold by hoary nights frost bred. — Ovid's Elegies 2.19.22
By suffring much not borne by thy severity. — Ovid's Elegies 3.1.48

SUGAR
Ile give thee Sugar-almonds, sweete Conserves, — Dido 2.1.305 Venus
Instead of Sedge and Reed, beare Sugar Canes: — Jew 4.2.96 Ithimr

SUGAR-ALMONDS
Ile give thee Sugar-almonds, sweete Conserves, — Dido 2.1.305 Venus

SUGGEST
And not simplicity, as they suggest. — Jew 1.2.161 Barab
That so my bloudie colours may suggest/Remembrance of revenge — Edw 3.1.139 Edward

SUIT (See also SUTE)
Rather than yeeld to his detested suit, — 2Tamb 4.2.6 Olymp
Tell me Olympia, wilt thou graunt my suit? — 2Tamb 4.2.21 Therid
Well, daughter, say, what is thy suit with us? — Jew 1.2.321 Abbass
Well, tell the Governor we grant his suit, — Jew 5.3.40 Calym

SUITE
And suite themselves in purple for the nonce, — Dido 1.1.206 Venus
I marie am I: have you any suite to me? — 1Tamb 2.4.24 Mycet

SUITERS
See where the pictures of my suiters hang, — Dido 3.1.139 Dido
Have been most urgent suiters for my love, — Dido 3.1.151 Dido

SUITES
If humble suites or imprecations, — 1Tamb 5.1.24 1Virgn

SULLA (See SYLLA, SYLLAS)

SULMO
Sulmo, Pelignies third part me containes, — Ovid's Elegies 2.16.1

SULMOES
And some guest viewing watry Sulmoes walles, — Ovid's Elegies 3.14.11

SULPHUR
of the war/Threw naked swords and sulphur bals of fire, — 2Tamb 3.2.41 Tamb

SULPHURE
came Hectors ghost/With ashie visage, blewish sulphure eyes, — Dido 2.1.202 Aeneas

SULTAN (See SOULDAN)

SUM (Homograph)
In whose sweete person is compriz'd the Sum/Of natures Skill — 1Tamb 5.1.78 1Virgn
That Vertue solely is the sum of glorie, — 1Tamb 5.1.189 Tamb
fire to burne the writ/Wherein the sum of thy religion rests. — 2Tamb 5.1.191 Tamb
Ego mihimet sum semper proximus. — Jew 1.1.189 Barab
Major sum quam cui possit fortuna nocere. — Edw 5.4.69 Mortmr

SUMM'D
There was the venture summ'd and satisfied. — Jew 1.1.3 Barab

SUMME
And plaine to him the summe of your distresse. — Dido 1.2.2 Illion

SUMME (cont.)
The Turkes have let increase to such a summe, ... Jew 1.1.182 Barab
Alas, my Lord, the summe is overgreat, ... Jew 1.2.8 Govnr
And with that summe he craves might we wage warre. . . Jew 2.2.27 1Knght
What is the summe that Calymath requires? . . . . Jew 2.2.35 Bosco
And see he brings it: Now, Governor, the summe? . . Jew 5.5.19 Barab
Now tell me, worldlings, underneath the [sunne] <summe>, . Jew 5.5.49 Barab
SUMMER (See also SOMMERS)
Wee'll in this Summer Evening feast with him. . . . Jew 5.3.41 Calym
heart desires to have, and were it now Summer, as it is January, F1572 4.6.15 P Lady
in the contrary circle it is likewise Summer with them, as in F1583 4.6.26 P Faust
my heart desires, and were it nowe summer, as it is January, F App p.242 9 P Duchss
us, in the contrary circle it is summer with them, as in India, F App p.242 21 P Faust
In summer time the purple Rubicon, ... Lucan, First Booke 215
SUMMERS
Like Summers vapours, vanisht by the Sun. . . . . 2Tamb 5.3.116 Tamb
In summers heate, and midtime of the day, ... Ovid's Elegies 1.5.1
Corinna cravde it in a summers night, ... Ovid's Elegies 3.6.25
SUMMES
And buy it basely too for summes of gold? . . . . Jew 2.2.29 Bosco
Great summes of mony lying in the bancho; . . . . Jew 4.1.74 Barab
privately procure/Great summes of mony for thy recompence: Jew 5.2.88 Govnr
SUMMON (See also SOMMON)
But stay a while, summon a parle, Drum, ... 2Tamb 3.3.11 Therid
Summon thy sences, call thy wits together: . . . Jew 1.1.178 Barab
To cruell armes their drunken selves did summon. . . Ovid's Elegies 2.12.20
SUMMON'D
Were they not summon'd to appeare to day? . . . . Jew 1.2.35 Govnr
Straight summon'd he his severall companies/Unto the standard: Lucan, First Booke 297
SUMMOND
Hath summond me to fruitfull Italy: . . . . . . Dido 4.3.4 Aeneas
SUMMONED
Summoned the Captaines to his princely tent, . . . Dido 2.1.130 Aeneas
SUMMUM
Summum bonum medicinae sanitas, ... F 44 1.1.16 Faust
<Whose summum bonum is in belly-cheare>. . . . . F 834 (HC265)A Mephst
SUMPTUOUS
In [midst] <one> of which a sumptuous Temple stands, . F 795 3.1.17 Faust
SUN (See also SONNE)
and the bounds/Of Europe wher the Sun dares scarce appeare, 1Tamb 1.1.10 Cosroe
the Sun and Mercurie denied/To shed [their] <his> influence in 1Tamb 1.1.14 Cosroe
And sooner shall the Sun fall from his Spheare, . . . 1Tamb 1.2.176 Tamb
and with our Sun-bright armour as we march, . . . 1Tamb 2.3.221 Tamb
And if before the Sun have measured heaven/With triple circuit 1Tamb 3.1.36 Bajzth
Nor Sun reflexe his vertuous beames thereon, . . . 1Tamb 3.1.52 Moroc
As looks the sun through Nilus flowing stream, . . . 1Tamb 3.2.47 Zenoc
And cause the Sun to borrowe light of you. . . . 1Tamb 4.2.40 Tamb
That rooffes of golde, and sun-bright Pallaces, . . . 1Tamb 4.2.62 Zabina
The Sun was downe. . . . . 1Tamb 5.1.314 P Zabina
to see the Sun-bright troope/Of heavenly vyrgins and unspotted 1Tamb 5.1.324 Zenoc
The Sun unable to sustaine the sight, ... 2Tamb 1.3.168 Tamb
Whose absence make the sun and Moone as darke/As when opposde 2Tamb 2.4.51 Tamb
Batter the shining pallace of the Sun, ... 2Tamb 2.4.105 Tamb
Although it shine as brightly as the Sun. . . . . 2Tamb 4.1.134 Tamb
whose weeping eies/Since thy arrivall here beheld no Sun, 2Tamb 4.2.2 Olymp
Ile ride in golden armour like the Sun, ... 2Tamb 4.3.115 Tamb
Like Summers vapours, vanisht by the Sun. . . . . 2Tamb 5.3.116 Tamb
Whereas the Sun declining from our sight, ... 2Tamb 5.3.148 Tamb
That as the sun-shine shall reflect ore thee: . . . Edw 3.1.51 Edward
We are deprivde the sun-shine of our life, ... Edw 4.7.106 Baldck
But perfect shadowes in a sun-shine day? . . . . Edw 5.1.27 Edward
in twelve, Mars in four, the Sun, Venus, and Mercury in a yeare; F 605 2.2.54 P Faust
SUN-BRIGHT
and with our Sun-bright armour as we march, . . . 1Tamb 2.3.221 Tamb
That rooffes of golde, and sun-bright Pallaces, . . . 1Tamb 4.2.62 Zabina
to see the Sun-bright troope/Of heavenly vyrgins and unspotted 1Tamb 5.1.324 Zenoc
SUNCKE
The Mutin toyles; the fleet at Leuca suncke; . . . Lucan, First Booke 42
O would that no Oares might in seas have suncke, . . Ovid's Elegies 2.11.5
It mocked me, hung down the head and suncke, . . . Ovid's Elegies 3.6.14
SUNDER
My Sailes all rent in sunder with the winde, . . . Dido 3.1.106 Aeneas
And never wil we sunder camps and armes, ... 2Tamb 5.2.52 Callap
We rent in sunder at our entry: . . . . Jew 5.3.4 Calym
Keepe them a sunder, thrust in the king. . . . . Edw 5.3.52 Matrvs
Comes forth her [unkeembd] <unkeembe> locks a sunder tearing. Ovid's Elegies 3.8.52
SUNDRIE
There might you see the gods in sundrie shapes, . . Hero and Leander 1.143
SUNDRY
That I have sent from sundry foughten fields, . . . 1Tamb 5.1.466 Tamb
Whose frame is paved with sundry coloured stones, . . F 797 3.1.19 Faust
sundry thoughts arose, about the honour of mine auncestors, F App p.236 18 P Emper
And sundry fiery meteors blaz'd in heaven; . . . . Lucan, First Booke 529
But sundry flouds in one banke never go, ... Ovid's Elegies 2.17.31
SUNG (See also SOONG)
They sung for honor gainst Pierides, ... 1Tamb 3.2.51 Zenoc
And with my name shall thine be alwaies sung. . . . Ovid's Elegies 1.3.26
SUNKE
Some have we fir'd, and many have we sunke; . . . Jew 2.2.15 Bosco
This said, being tir'd with fury she sunke downe. . . Lucan, First Booke 694
SUNNE
Who with the Sunne devides one radiant shape, . . . Dido 1.1.97 Jupitr
Yet shall the aged Sunne shed forth his [haire] <aire>, . Dido 1.1.159 Achat

SUNNE (cont.)			
The Sunne from Egypt shall rich odors bring,	Dido	5.1.11	Aeneas
And ore his ships will soare unto the Sunne,	Dido	5.1.244	Dido
Now tell me, worldlings, underneath the [sunne] <summe>,	Jew	5.5.49	Barab
If ever sunne stainde heaven with bloudy clowdes,	P 60	2.3	Guise
they may become/As men that stand and gase against the Sunne.	P 163	2.106	Guise
To whom the sunne shines both by day and night.	Edw	1.1.17	Gavstn
Aspir'st unto the guidance of the sunne.	Edw	1.4.17	Warwck
And as grosse vapours perish by the sunne,	Edw	1.4.341	Edward
Continue ever thou celestiall sunne,	Edw	5.1.64	Edward
Who'le set the faire treste [sunne] <sonne> in battell ray,	Ovid's Elegies		1.1.15
Like twilight glimps at setting of the sunne,	Ovid's Elegies		1.5.5
With sunne and moone Aratus shall remaine.	Ovid's Elegies		1.15.16
Although the sunne to rive the earth incline,	Ovid's Elegies		2.16.3
The Sunne turnd backe from Atreus cursed table?	Ovid's Elegies		3.11.39
She ware no gloves for neither sunne nor wind/Would burne or	Hero and Leander		1.27
And now the sunne that through th'orizon peepes,	Hero and Leander		2.99
Like as the sunne in a Dyameter,	Hero and Leander		2.123
Aye me, Leander cryde, th'enamoured sunne,	Hero and Leander		2.202
And sigh'd to thinke upon th'approching sunne,	Hero and Leander		2.302
SUNNES			
But whether thou the Sunnes bright Sister be,	Dido	1.1.193	Aeneas
Or mount the sunnes flame bearing <plume bearing> charriot,	Lucan, First Booke		48
And call the sunnes white horses [backe] <blacke> at noone.	Ovid's Elegies		2.1.24
Drye winters aye, and sunnes in heate extreame.	Ovid's Elegies		3.5.106
Phaeton had got/The guidance of the sunnes rich chariot.	Hero and Leander		1.102
SUNNY			
Hang in the aire as thicke as sunny motes,	2Tamb	3.2.101	Tamb
I was begotten on a sunny bank:	F 705	2.2.154	P Sloth
SUNS			
much like so many suns/That halfe dismay the majesty of heaven:	2Tamb	4.1.2	Amyras
SUN-SHINE			
That as the sun-shine shall reflect ore thee:	Edw	3.1.51	Edward
We are deprivde the sun-shine of our life,	Edw	4.7.106	Baldck
But perfect shadowes in a sun-shine day?	Edw	5.1.27	Edward
SUP			
And where thou drinkst, on that part I will sup.	Ovid's Elegies		1.4.32
SUPERBUM			
Too true it is, quem dies vidit veniens superbum,	Edw	4.7.53	Leistr
SUPERFICIES			
For in a field whose [superficies] <superfluities>/Is covered	2Tamb	1.3.79	Tamb
lookes is much more majesty/Than from the Concave superficies,	2Tamb	3.4.48	Therid
SUPERFLUITIES			
For in a field whose [superficies] <superfluities>/Is covered	2Tamb	1.3.79	Tamb
SUPERIOR			
Nor Caesar no superior, which of both/Had justest cause	Lucan, First Booke		126
SUPERNATURALLY			
Hush, Ile gul him supernaturally:	F App	p.234 5	P Robin
SUPERSTICIOUS			
And all the heapes of supersticious bookes,	2Tamb	5.1.174	Tamb
SUPERSTITION			
Assure your Grace tis superstition/To stand so strictly on	2Tamb	2.1.49	Fredrk
SUPERSTITIOUS			
Ringing with joy their superstitious belles:	1Tamb	3.3.237	Bajzth
For these thy superstitious taperlights,	Edw	1.4.98	Edward
And as they turne their superstitious Bookes,	F 893	3.1.115	Faust
SUPPER			
me in the pot of Rice/That for our supper stands upon the fire.	Jew	3.4.50	Barab
thou hast heard all my progeny, wilt thou bid me to supper?	F 701	2.2.150	P Glutny
will it please you to take a shoulder of Mutton to supper, and	F1121	3.3.34	P Robin
hee's now at supper with the schollers, where ther's such	F1678	5.1.5	P Wagner
wil you take sixe pence in your purse to pay for your supper,	F App	p.235 42	P Robin
who are at supper with such belly-cheere,	F App	p.243 6	Wagner
Pray God it may his latest supper be,	Ovid's Elegies		1.4.2
SUPPLIE			
Which piteous wants if Dido will supplie,	Dido	3.1.111	Aeneas
SUPPLIED			
Sadly supplied with pale and ghastly death,	2Tamb	2.4.83	Tamb
SUPPLIES			
Whose glittering pompe Dianas shrowdes supplies,	Dido	3.3.4	Dido
For I will furnish thee with such supplies:	Dido	5.1.72	Iarbus
They gather strength by power of fresh supplies.	1Tamb	2.2.21	Meandr
Cherish thy valour stil with fresh supplies:	2Tamb	4.1.87	Tamb
SUPPLY			
The town is ours my Lord, and fresh supply/Of conquest, and of	1Tamb	5.1.196	Techel
Fed with the fresh supply of earthly dregs,	2Tamb	3.2.8	Tamb
That no supply of victuall shall come in,	2Tamb	3.3.32	Techel
To supply my wants and necessitie.	P 136	2.79	Guise
is massacred)/Infect thy gracious brest with fresh supply,	P 193	3.28	QnMarg
a rich lover plants/His love on thee, and can supply thy wants.	Ovid's Elegies		1.8.32
SUPPLYED			
When I to watch supplyed a servants place.	Ovid's Elegies		3.10.12
SUPPLYING			
Supplying their voide places with the worst.	Ovid's Elegies		2.6.40
SUPPORT			
To swarme unto the Ensigne I support.	1Tamb	2.3.14	Tamb
Yet he attain'd by her support to have her,	Ovid's Elegies		3.2.17
SUPPORTED			
What will he doe supported by a king?	1Tamb	2.1.57	Ceneus
SUPPORTS			
and the soyle most fit/For Cities, and societies supports:	Dido	1.1.179	Achat
SUPPOS'D			
And tis suppos'd Loves bowe hath wounded thee,	Ovid's Elegies		1.11.11

SUPPOSDE
Being supposde his worthlesse Concubine, 1Tamb 3.2.29 Agidas
Love-snarde Calypso is supposde to pray, Ovid's Elegies 2.17.15
SUPPOSE
And if this be thy sonne as I suppose, Dido 2.1.92 Dido
Made me suppose he would have heard me speake: Dido 5.1.230 Anna
Suppose they be in number infinit, 1Tamb 2.2.43 Meandr
But are not both these wise men to suppose/That I will leave my Jew 4.1.122 Barab
Parthians y'afflict us more then ye suppose, Lucan, First Booke 107
SUPPOSEST
And for thy ships which thou supposest lost, Dido 1.1.235 Venus
SUPPOSING
Supposing amorous Jove had sent his sonne, 2Tamb 4.2.18 Therid
Supposing nothing else was to be done, Hero and Leander 2.53
SUPPOSITIONS
[Tush], these are fresh mens [suppositions] <questions>: F 606 2.2.55 P Faust
SUPPRESSE
To injure or suppresse your woorthy tytle. 1Tamb 1.1.183 Ortyg
flinty hearts/Suppresse all pitty in your stony breasts, Jew 1.2.142 Barab
SUPPRESST
intollorable wrath/May be suppresst by our submission. 2Tamb 5.1.9 Maxim
SUPPREST
Which once performd, poore Troy so long supprest, Dido 1.1.93 Jupitr
As Juno, when the Giants were supprest, 1Tamb 5.1.510 Tamb
Be easilie supprest: and therefore be gone. Edw 2.4.45 Queene
What, now Scicillian Pirats are supprest, Lucan, First Booke 336
Which lie hid under her thinne veile supprest. Ovid's Elegies 3.2.36
All gaine in darknesse the deepe earth supprest. Ovid's Elegies 3.7.36
SUPPRISDE
the Starres supprisde like Rhesus Steedes,/Are drawne by Dido 1.1.72 Venus
SUPREAME
As your supreame estates instruct our thoughtes, 2Tamb 5.3.20 Techel
SUPREMACIE
Do us such honor and supremacie, 2Tamb 3.1.16 Callap
And by the state of his supremacie, 2Tamb 4.1.136 Tamb
SURCEASE
I hope will make the King surcease his hate: P 792 16.6 Bartus
Let him surcease: love tries wit best of all. Ovid's Elegies 1.9.32
Life is no light price of a small surcease. Ovid's Elegies 2.14.26
SURCHARDG'D
That Jove surchardg'd with pity of our wrongs, 2Tamb 3.1.35 Callap
SURCHARGDE
Surchargde with surfet of ambitious thoughts: P 953 19.23 King
Surchargde with guilt of thousand massacres, P1022 19.92 King
SURE
And swim to Italy, Ile keepe these sure: Dido 4.4.164 Dido
Open the Males, yet guard the treasure sure, 1Tamb 1.2.138 Tamb
And as a sure and grounded argument, 1Tamb 1.2.184 Tamb
And having thee, I have a jewell sure: 1Tamb 2.2.56 Mycet
And kill as sure as it swiftly flies. 1Tamb 2.3.59 Tamb
And if I prosper, all shall be as sure, 1Tamb 2.5.84 Tamb
and then she shall be sure not to be starv'd, and he be 1Tamb 4.4.46 P Usumc
Your Majesty remembers I am sure/What cruell slaughter of our 2Tamb 2.1.4 Fredrk
Or els be sure thou shalt be forc'd with paines, 2Tamb 5.1.52 Therid
Assaile it and be sure of victorie. 2Tamb 5.2.59 Callap
and Lawes were then most sure/When like the [Dracos] <Drancus> Jew Prol.20 Machvl
How ere the world goe, I'le make sure for one, Jew 1.1.186 Barab
That ye be both made sure e're you come out. Jew 2.3.236 Barab
As sure as heaven rain'd Manna for the Jewes, Jew 2.3.248 Barab
So sure shall he and Don Mathias dye: Jew 2.3.249 Barab
And I am sure he is with Abigall. Jew 2.3.268 Barab
Lodowicke, it is enough/That I have made thee sure to Abigal. Jew 2.3.335 Barab
So sure did your father write, and I cary the chalenge. Jew 3.3.25 P Ithimr
One dram of powder more had made all sure. Jew 5.1.22 Barab
Are all the Cranes and Pulleyes sure? Jew 5.5.2 Barab
But God will sure restore you to your health. P 542 11.7 Navrre
And sure if all the proudest Kings/In Christendome, should P 760 15.18 Guise
But as I live, so sure the Guise shall dye. P 899 17.94 King
Wel, let that peevish Frenchman guard him sure, Edw 1.2.7 Mortmr
For wot you not that I have made him sure, Edw 1.4.378 Edward
Desirde her more, and waxt outragious,/So did it sure with me: Edw 2.2.56 Edward
Looke to your owne heads, his is sure enough. Edw 2.2.92 Edward
Guarde the king sure, it is the earle of Kent. Edw 5.3.50 Matrvs
Is sure to pay for it when his sonne is of age, Edw 5.4.4 Mortmr
Now is all sure, the Queene and Mortimer/Shall rule the realme, Edw 5.4.65 Mortmr
seene many boyes with [such pickadevaunts] <beards> I am sure. F 345 1.4.3 P Robin
me for the matter, for sure the cup is betweene you two. F1107 3.3.20 P Vintnr
Sure these are no spirites, but the true substantiall bodies of F App p.238 64 P Emper
Many to rob is more sure, and lesse hatefull, Ovid's Elegies 1.8.55
But she conceiv'd of me, or I am sure/I oft have done, what Ovid's Elegies 2.13.5
Beginne to shut thy house at evening sure. Ovid's Elegies 2.19.38
SURELY
It saies, Agydas, thou shalt surely die, 1Tamb 3.2.95 Agidas
So surely will the vengeance of the highest/And jealous anger 2Tamb 2.1.56 Fredrk
As I doe live, so surely shall he dye, P 521 9.40 QnMoth
SURER
So, now it is more surer on my head, 1Tamb 2.7.65 Tamb
SUREST
within thy hands/To shuffle or cut, take this as surest thing: P 147 2.90 Guise
SURETIE
Thou makste the suretie to the lawyer runne, Ovid's Elegies 1.13.19
SURETY
Will hazard that we might with surety hold. 2Tamb 1.1.24 Uribas

SURFEIT				
sir, you must be dieted, too much eating will make you surfeit.	1Tamb	4.4.104	P	Tamb
SURFEITING				
Till surfeiting with our afflicting armes,	P1153	22.15		King
SURFET				
friends and fellow kings)/Makes me to surfet in conceiving joy.	2Tamb	1.3.152		Tamb
Surchargde with surfet of ambitious thoughts:	P 953	19.23		King
Ah words that make me surfet with delight:	Edw	1.1.3		Gavstn
Tis but a surfet sir, feare nothing.	F1832	5.2.36		3Schol
A surfet of deadly sin, that hath damn'd both body and soule.	F1833	5.2.37	P	Faust
SURFETS				
He surfets upon cursed Necromancie:	F 25	Prol.25		1Chor
SURFETTED				
Some surfetted, and others soundly slept.	Dido	2.1.179		Aeneas
Whiles these adulterors surfetted with sinne:	Dido	4.1.20		Iarbus
SURFFET				
<to cure him, tis but a surffet, never feare man>.	F1831	(HC270)A	P	2Schol
SURGAT				
propitiamus vos, ut appareat, et surgat Mephostophilis.	F 247	1.3.19	P	Faust
per vota nostra ipse nunc surgat nobis dicatus Mephostophilis.	F 250	1.3.22	P	Faust
SURGE				
the deepe)/Puls them aloft, and makes the surge kisse heaven,	Lucan, First Booke			417
SURGEON				
Goe call a surgeon hether strait.	P1179	22.41		Navrre
Pleaseth your grace to let the Surgeon search your wound.	P1191	22.53		Navrre
Search Surgeon and resolve me what thou seest.	P1193	22.55		King
Tell me Surgeon, shall I live?	P1211	22.73		King
Tell me Surgeon and flatter not, may I live?	P1222	22.84		King
Surgeon, why saist thou so? the King may live.	P1224	22.86		Navrre
SURGES				
And Aeolus like Agamemnon sounds/The surges, his fierce	Dido	1.1.69		Venus
SURMOUNTS				
Mortimers hope surmounts his fortune farre.	Edw	3.1.259		Mortmr
SURPASSE				
As shall surpasse the wonder of our speech.	Dido	1.2.47		Serg
her you surpasse,/As much as sparkling Diamonds flaring glasse.	Hero and Leander			1.213
SURPAST				
his necke in touching, and surpast/The white of Pelops shoulder.	Hero and Leander			1.64
SURPRIS'D				
So at her presence all surpris'd and tooken,	Hero and Leander			1.122
But be surpris'd with every garish toy.	-Hero and Leander			1.480
SURPRISDE				
By thee deceived, by thee surprisde am I,	Ovid's Elegies			2.10.3
SURPRIZ'D				
Surpriz'd with feare of hideous revenge,	1Tamb	3.2.68		Agidas
much better/To [have] kept thy promise then be thus surpriz'd?	Jew	5.2.5		Calym
SURPRIZD				
Was by the cruell Mirmidons surprizd,	Dido	2.1.287		Aeneas
Neither my lord, for as he was surprizd,	Edw	3.1.94		Arundl
SURPRIZDE				
Thou [cousenst] <cousendst> mee, by thee surprizde am I,	Ovid's Elegies			3.6.71
SURPRIZE (See also SUPPRISDE)				
can spy a place/Where you may enter, and surprize the Towne:	Jew	5.1.71		Barab
give me if I render you/The life of Calymath, surprize his men,	Jew	5.2.80		Barab
First to surprize great Selims souldiers,	Jew	5.2.118		Barab
And sodenly surprize them unawares.	Edw	2.3.19		Lncstr
Yet by deceit Love did them all surprize.	Ovid's Elegies			3.4.20
Wherefore Leanders fancie to surprize,	Hero and Leander			2.223
SURRENDERS				
Say he surrenders up to him his soule,	F 318	1.3.90		Faust
SURROUND				
ground/Conteines me, though the streames in fields surround,	Ovid's Elegies			2.16.34
SURROUNDED				
And from the channell all abroad surrounded.	Ovid's Elegies			3.5.86
SURROWNDING				
And drinkes stolne waters in surrownding floudes.	Ovid's Elegies			2.19.32
SURVAID				
Capolin, hast thou survaid our powers?	1Tamb	4.3.50		Souldn
SURVAIENG				
Survaieng all the glories of the land:	2Tamb	4.3.35		Orcan
SURVAY				
Come once in furie and survay his pride,	2Tamb	4.3.41		Orcan
SURVEY				
under whose blacke survey/Great Potentates do kneele with awful	F App	p.235 34		Mephst
SURVIV'D				
and not a man surviv'd/To bring the haplesse newes to	Jew	2.2.50		Bosco
SURVIVE				
And makes our hopes survive to [coming] <cunning> joyes:	Dido	1.1.154		Achat
Crowes <crow> [survive] <survives> armes-bearing Pallas hate,	Ovid's Elegies			2.6.35
Thersites did Protesilaus survive,	Ovid's Elegies			2.6.41
SURVIVES				
Your paines do pierce our soules, no hope survives,	2Tamb	5.3.166		Celeb
But Edwards name survives, though Edward dies.	Edw	5.1.48		Edward
But Mortimer, as long as he survives/What safetie rests for us,	Edw	5.2.42		Queene
Crowes <crow> [survive] <survives> armes-bearing Pallas hate,	Ovid's Elegies			2.6.35
SUSCEPI				
Suscepi that provinciam as they terme it,	Edw	5.4.63		Mortmr
SUSPECT				
For should I but suspect your death by mine,	2Tamb	2.4.61		Zenoc
I, but father they will suspect me there.	Jew	1.2.283		Abigal
Let 'em suspect, but be thou so precise/As they may thinke it	Jew	1.2.284		Barab
To kill all that you suspect of heresie.	P 276	5.3		Guise
unto Roan, and spare not one/That you suspect of heresy.	P 447	7.87		Guise

SUSPECT (cont.)
And so to quite your grace of all suspect. P 889 17.84 Eprnon
Not to suspect disloyaltye in thee, P 975 19.45 King
Thus do you still suspect me without cause. Edw 2.2.227 Queene
to Longshankes blood/Is false, be not found single for suspect: Edw 4.6.17 Kent
Free from suspect, and fell invasion/Of such as have your Edw 4.7.4 Abbot
Not one alive, but shrewdly I suspect, Edw 4.7.28 Spencr
Her I suspect among nights spirits to fly, Ovid's Elegies 1.8.13
Fame saith as I suspect, and in her eyes/Two eye-balles shine, Ovid's Elegies 1.8.15

SUSPECTED
In spite of all suspected enemies. 1Tamb 1.1.186 Ortyg
He that wantes these, and is suspected of heresie, P 234 4.32 Guise
Mother, you are suspected for his death, Edw 5.6.78 King
Then I feare that which I have long suspected: F 220 1.2.27 1Schol
yet he suspected/Some amorous rites or other were neglected. Hero and Leander 2.63

SUSPICIOUS
Or be suspicious of my deerest freends: P 972 19.42 King

SUSPITION
I, Daughter, for Religion/Hides many mischiefes from suspition. Jew 1.2.282 Barab
To shun suspition, therefore, let us part. Jew 2.1.57 Abigal
The late suspition of the Duke of Guise, P 178 3.13 Navrre
The Gods from this sinne rid me of suspition, Ovid's Elegies 2.7.19

SUSPITIOUS
Betraide by fortune and suspitious love, 1Tamb 3.2.66 Agidas
You know the king is so suspitious, Edw 2.4.53 Queene
Suspitious feare in all my veines will hover, Ovid's Elegies 1.4.42

SUSTAIN'D
We first sustain'd the uproares of the Gaules, Lucan, First Booke 256

SUSTAIND
From al the crueltie my soule sustaind, 2Tamb 3.1.33 Callap

SUSTAINDE
I have sustainde so oft thrust from the dore, Ovid's Elegies 3.10.9

SUSTAINE
The Sun unable to sustaine the sight, 2Tamb 1.3.168 Tamb
It would not ease the sorrow I sustaine. 2Tamb 3.2.48 Calyph
Sustaine the scortching heat and freezing cold, 2Tamb 3.2.57 Tamb
earth may eccho foorth/The far resounding torments ye sustaine, 2Tamb 4.1.186 Tamb
Me thinks I could sustaine a thousand deaths, 2Tamb 5.2.22 Callap
Sustaine a shame of such inexcellence: 2Tamb 5.3.31 Usumc

SUSTAINES
For this, this earth sustaines my bodies [waight], P 114 2.57 Guise
I execute, and he sustaines the blame. P 132 2.75 Guise
While th'earth the sea, and ayre the earth sustaines; Lucan, First Booke 89

SUSTENANCE
The ground is mine that gives them sustenance, Dido 4.4.74 Dido
Where I am sterv'd for want of sustenance, Edw 5.3.20 Edward
So that for want of sleepe and sustenance, Edw 5.5.63 Edward

SUTE
the Duke of Joyeux/Hath made great sute unto the King therfore. P 734 14.37 1Msngr
And neither would denie, nor graunt his sute. Hero and Leander 1.424
Then muse not, Cupids sute no better sped, Hero and Leander 1.483

SWAIES
That nigh Larissa swaies a mighty hoste, 2Tamb 2.2.6 Orcan

SWAIEST
O thou that swaiest the region under earth, 2Tamb 4.3.32 Orcan

SWAINE
And cam'st to Dido like a Fisher swaine? Dido 5.1.162 Dido
I did not bid thee wed an aged swaine. Ovid's Elegies 1.13.42
tincture of her cheekes, that drew/The love of everie swaine: Hero and Leander 1.397

SWAINES
And these that seeme but silly country Swaines, 1Tamb 1.2.47 Tamb
A heavenly Nimph, belov'd of humane swaines, Hero and Leander 1.216
The Sheepheards Swaines shall daunce and sing, Passionate Shepherd 21

SWALLOW
Shall swallow up these base borne Perseans. 1Tamb 3.3.95 Bajzth
And make it swallow both of us at once. 1Tamb 4.2.29 Bajzth
Enough to swallow forcelesse Sigismond, 2Tamb 1.1.65 Orcan
As when they swallow Assafitida, 2Tamb 5.1.208 Techel
Nor fowlest Harpie that shall swallow him. Edw 2.2.46 Edward

SWALLOW'D
Thus having swallow'd Cupids golden hooke, Hero and Leander 1.333

SWALLOWED
Thinking the sea had swallowed up thy ships, Dido 2.1.68 Illion
Ile make thee wish the earth had swallowed thee: 2Tamb 3.5.118 Tamb
Shall townes be swallowed? Lucan, First Booke 645

SWAMME
And she that on a faind Bull swamme to land, Ovid's Elegies 1.3.23

SWANNE
And she to whom in shape of [Swanne] <Bull> Jove came. Ovid's Elegies 1.3.22
God deluded/In snowe-white plumes of a false swanne included. Ovid's Elegies 1.10.4
Jove turnes himselfe into a Swanne, or gold, Ovid's Elegies 3.11.33

SWANNES
And Venus Swannes shall shed their silver downe, Dido 1.1.36 Jupitr
The day, the night, my Swannes, my sweetes are thine. Dido 3.2.61 Venus
White Swannes, and many lovely water fowles: Dido 4.5.11 Nurse
God knowes I play/With Venus swannes and sparrowes all the day. Hero and Leander 1.352

SWANS
There harmelesse Swans feed all abroad the river, Ovid's Elegies 2.6.53

SWARM'D
Have swarm'd in troopes into the Easterne India: 1Tamb 1.1.120 Cosroe

SWARME
In multitudes they swarme unto the shoare, Dido 1.2.36 Serg
The people swarme to gaze him in the face. Dido 3.1.72 Anna

SWARME (cont.)
As Seaborne Nymphes shall swarme about thy ships, . . . Dido 3.1.129 Dido
To swarme unto the Ensigne I support. . . . . 1Tamb 2.3.14 Tamb
Hell and Elisian swarme with ghosts of men, . . . 1Tamb 5.1.465 Tamb
of Wittenberg <Wertenberge>/[Swarme] <Sworne> to my Problemes, F 142 1.1.114 Faust
SWARMES
This countrie swarmes with vile outragious men, . . 1Tamb 2.2.22 Meandr
The wilde Oneyle, with swarmes of Irish Kernes, . . Edw 2.2.164 Lncstr
SWAY (See also SWAIES)
Sway thou the Punike Scepter in my steede, . . . Dido 4.4.35 Dido
And let my Fortunes and my valour sway, ... 1Tamb 2.3.11 Tamb
And grace your calling with a greater sway. . . . 1Tamb 2.5.31 Cosroe
O then ye Powers that sway eternal seates, . . . 2Tamb 5.3.17 Techel
learne with awfull eie/To sway a throane as dangerous as his: 2Tamb 5.3.235 Tamb
For our behoofe will beare the greater sway/When as a kings Edw 5.2.13 Mortmr
let us sway thy thoughts/From this attempt against the . F1325 4.2.1 Mrtino
What God it please thee be, or where to sway: . . Lucan, First Booke 52
Their sway of fleight carries the heady rout/That in chain'd Lucan, First Booke 488
SWAYEST
If any one part of vast heaven thou swayest, . . . Lucan, First Booke 56
SWEARE
Yet how <here> <now> I sweare by heaven and him I love, . Dido 3.1.166 Dido
Well here I sweare by this my royal seat-- . . . 1Tamb 1.1.97 Mycet
wel then, by heavens I sweare,/Aurora shall not peepe out of 1Tamb 2.2.9 Mycet
And by the holy Alcaron I sweare, ... 1Tamb 3.3.76 Bajzth
If Mahomet should come from heaven and sweare, . . . 1Tamb 3.3.208 Zenoc
Or els I sweare to have you whipt stark nak'd. . . . 1Tamb 4.2.74 Anippe
And sweare in sight of heaven and by thy Christ. . . 2Tamb 1.1.132 Orcan
I sweare to keepe this truce inviolable: . . . . 2Tamb 1.1.142 Orcan
And by the hand of Mahomet I sweare, ... 2Tamb 1.2.65 Callap
Then here I sweare, as I am Almeda, ... 2Tamb 1.2.67 Almeda
And made him sweare obedience to my crowne. . . . 2Tamb 1.3.190 Techel
By Mahomet, thy mighty friend I sweare, ... 2Tamb 4.1.121 Tamb
Dissemble, sweare, protest, vow to love him, . . . Jew 2.3.229 Barab
I vow and sweare as I am King of France, ... P 255 4.53 Charls
Gonzago, Retes, sweare by/The argent crosses in your burgonets, P 274 5.1 Guise
I sweare by this to be unmercifull. . . . . . P 277 5.4 Dumain
I sweare by this crosse, wee'l not be partiall, . . . P 325 5.52 Anjoy
And heer by all the Saints in heaven I sweare, . . . P 765 15.23 Guise
Now by the holy sacrament I sweare, ... P 981 19.51 Guise
And heere in presence of you all I sweare, ... P1026 19.96 King
our Guise is dead)/Rest satisfied with this that heer I sweare, P1043 19.113 King
Navarre, give me thy hand, I heere do sweare, . . . P1203 22.65 King
And make the people sweare to put him downe. . . . Edw 2.2.111 Lncstr
Heere for our countries cause sweare we to him/All homage, Edw 4.4.19 Mortmr
Faustus, I sweare by Hell and Lucifer, ... F 481 2.1.93 Mephst
Of ever-burning Phlegeton, I sweare, ... F 827 3.1.49 Faust
and here I sweare to thee, by the honor of mine Imperial . F App p.236 8 P Emper
Nor, if thou couzenst one, dread to for-sweare, . . . Ovid's Elegies 1.8.85
I sweare by Venus, and the wingd boyes bowe, . . . Ovid's Elegies 2.7.27
th'eternall powers graunt maides society/Falsely to sweare, Ovid's Elegies 3.3.12
My selfe would sweare, the wenches true did sweare, . . Ovid's Elegies 3.3.45
Sweare I was blinde, yeeld not <deny>, if you be wise, . Ovid's Elegies 3.13.45
Flatter, intreat, promise, protest and sweare, . . . Hero and Leander 2.268
SWEARES
to prevent/That which mine honor sweares shal be perform'd: 1Tamb 5.1.107 Tamb
And in the honor of a king he sweares, ... Edw 2.5.58 Arundl
One sweares his troupes of daring horsemen fought/Upon Mevanias Lucan, First Booke 469
SWEAREST
Thou swearest, devision should not twixt us rise, . . Ovid's Elegies 2.16.43
SWEAT
Those thousand horse shall sweat with martiall spoile/Of . 1Tamb 1.2.191 Tamb
Where ere I come the fatall sisters sweat, ... 1Tamb 5.1.454 Tamb
our men shall sweat/With carrieng pearle and treasure on their 2Tamb 3.5.166 Techel
And for a pound to sweat himselfe to death: . . . Jew 1.1.18 Barab
a while, our men with sweat and dust/All chockt well neare, Edw 3.1.191 SpncrP
SWEATE
gods/Sweate teares to shew the travailes of their citty. . Lucan, First Booke 555
SWEATING
(Auster and Aquilon with winged Steads/All sweating, tilt about 1Tamb 3.2.79 Agidas
in the stable, when you shall come sweating from my chariot. 2Tamb 3.5.142 P Tamb
SWEEPE
Nor hanging oares the troubled seas did sweepe, . . Ovid's Elegies 3.7.43
SWEEPER
I am Envy, begotten of a Chimney-sweeper, and an Oyster-wife: F 679 2.2.128 P Envy
Wee'l sell it to a Chimny-sweeper: . . . . . . F1384 4.2.60 P Benvol
SWEEPT
Beyond thy robes thy dangling [lockes] <lackes> had sweept. Ovid's Elegies 1.14.4
SWEET
Sweet Jupiter, if ere I pleasde thine eye, ... Dido 1.1.19 Ganimd
What ist sweet wagge I should deny thy youth? . . . Dido 1.1.23 Jupitr
Put thou about thy necke my owne sweet heart, . . . Dido 1.1.44 Jupitr
What shall I doe to save thee my sweet boy? . . . Dido 1.1.74 Venus
Alas sweet boy, thou must be still a while, . . . Dido 1.1.164 Aeneas
How neere my sweet Aeneas art thou driven? . . . Dido 1.1.170 Venus
Weepe not sweet boy, thou shalt be Didos sonne, . . . Dido 3.1.24 Dido
O Anna, didst thou know how sweet love were, . . . Dido 3.1.59 Dido
But playd he nere so sweet, I let him goe: . . . Dido 3.1.160 Dido
Welcome sweet child, where hast thou been this long? . . Dido 5.1.46 Aeneas
Eating sweet Comfites with Queene Didos maide, . . . Dido 5.1.47 Ascan
Sweet sister cease, remember who you are. . . . . Dido 5.1.263 Anna
O sweet Iarbus, Annas sole delight, ... Dido 5.1.322 Anna
To see my sweet Iarbus slay himselfe? . . . . . Dido 5.1.324 Anna

SWEET (cont.)

Now sweet Iarbus stay, I come to thee.	Dido	5.1.329	Anna
Nobly resolv'd, sweet friends and followers.	1Tamb	1.2.60	Tamb
Soft ye my Lords and sweet Zenocrate.	1Tamb	1.2.119	Tamb
To whom sweet Menaphon, direct me straight.	1Tamb	2.1.68	Cosroe
Was there such brethren, sweet Meander, say,	1Tamb	2.2.51	Mycet
I will not thank thee (sweet Ortigius)/Better replies shall	1Tamb	2.5.36	Cosroe
O my Lord, tis sweet and full of pompe.	1Tamb	2.5.55	Techel
The sweet fruition of an earthly crowne.	1Tamb	2.7.29	Tamb
And speech more pleasant than sweet harmony:	1Tamb	3.3.121	Tamb
To waste and spoile the sweet Aonian fieldes.	1Tamb	4.3.6	Souldn
Farewell (sweet Virgins) on whose safe return/Depends our	1Tamb	5.1.62	Govnr
flags/Through which sweet mercie threw her gentle beams,	1Tamb	5.1.69	Tamb
For sweet Zenocrate, whose worthinesse/Deserves a conquest over	1Tamb	5.1.207	Tamb
Sweet Bajazeth, I will prolong thy life,	1Tamb	5.1.283	Zabina
Ah Tamburlaine, my love, sweet Tamburlaine,	1Tamb	5.1.355	Zenoc
To make discourse of some sweet accidents/Have chanc'd thy	1Tamb	5.1.424	Arabia
To gratify the <thee> sweet Zenocrate,	1Tamb	5.1.516	Tamb
Sweet Jesus Christ, I sollemnly protest,	2Tamb	1.1.135	Sgsmnd
Sweet Almeda, pity the ruthfull plight/Of Callapine, the sonne	2Tamb	1.2.1	Callap
Sweet Almeda, scarse halfe a league from hence.	2Tamb	1.2.55	Callap
Sweet Tamburlain, when wilt thou leave these armes/And save thy	2Tamb	1.3.9	Zenoc
And not before, my sweet Zenocrate:	2Tamb	1.3.15	Tamb
And in this sweet and currious harmony,	2Tamb	2.4.30	Tamb
life may be as short to me/As are the daies of sweet Zenocrate:	2Tamb	2.4.37	Tamb
transfourme my love/In whose sweet being I repose my life,	2Tamb	2.4.48	Tamb
Sweet sons farewell, in death resemble me,	2Tamb	2.4.75	Zenoc
Ah sweet Theridamas, say so no more,	2Tamb	2.4.126	Tamb
Sweet picture of divine Zenocrate,	2Tamb	3.2.27	Tamb
Sorrow no more my sweet Casane now:	2Tamb	3.2.44	Tamb
Farewell sweet wife, sweet son farewell, I die.	2Tamb	3.4.10	Capt
Come back again (sweet death) and strike us both:	2Tamb	3.4.12	Olymp
Tell me sweet boie, art thou content to die?	2Tamb	3.4.18	Olymp
Sweet mother strike, that I may meet my father.	2Tamb	3.4.30	Sonne
and the bounds/Of that sweet land, whose brave Metropolis	2Tamb	3.5.36	Orcan
Spending my life in sweet discourse of love.	2Tamb	4.2.45	Therid
dooth weepe to see/Your sweet desires depriv'd my company,	2Tamb	5.3.247	Tamb
Trouble her not, sweet Lodowicke depart:	Jew	2.3.327	Barab
into the sea; why I'le doe any thing for your sweet sake.	Jew	3.4.41	P Ithimr
Oh my sweet Ithimore go set it downe/And come againe so soone	Jew	3.4.108	Barab
How sweet the Bels ring now the Nuns are dead/That sound at	Jew	4.1.2	Barab
What time a night is't now, sweet Ithimore?	Jew	4.1.157	Barab
Is't not a sweet fac'd youth, Pilia?	Jew	4.2.40	P Curtzn
Agen, sweet youth; did not you, Sir, bring the sweet youth a	Jew	4.2.41	P Ithimr
sweet youth; did not you, Sir, bring the sweet youth a letter?	Jew	4.2.41	P Ithimr
I can with-hold no longer; welcome sweet love.	Jew	4.2.46	Curtzn
me; Sweet Bellamira, would I had my Masters wealth for thy sake.	Jew	4.2.55	P Ithimr
I have no husband, sweet, I'le marry thee.	Jew	4.2.87	Curtzn
How sweet, my Ithimore, the flowers smell.	Jew	4.4.39	Curtzn
Like thy breath, sweet-hart, no violet like 'em.	Jew	4.4.40	Ithimr
Prethe sweet love, one more, and write it sharp.	Jew	4.4.73	Curtzn
O no, sweet Margaret, the fatall poyson/Workes within my head,	P 184	3.19	OldQn
O graunt sweet God my daies may end with hers,	P 189	3.24	Navrre
Sweet Taleus stay.	P 370	7.10	Ramus
But come lets walke aside, th'airs not very sweet.	P 497	9.16	QnMoth
Doe so sweet Guise, let us delay no time,	P 505	9.24	QnMoth
Be gone, delay no time sweet Guise.	P 509	9.28	QnMoth
What art thou dead, sweet sonne speak to thy Mother.	P 551	11.16	QnMoth
Sweet Mugeroune, tis he that hath my heart,	P 660	13.4	Duchss
My sweet Joyeux, I make thee Generall,	P 743	15.1	King
And so sweet Cuz farwell.	P 976	19.46	King
Ah this sweet sight is phisick to my soule,	P1020	19.90	King
Sweet Guise, would he had died so thou wert heere:	P1082	19.152	QnMoth
Sweet Duke of Guise our prop to leane upon,	P1110	21.4	Dumain
And that the sweet and princely minde you beare,	P1141	22.3	King
Sweet Epernoune all Rebels under heaven,	P1185	22.47	King
Sweet Epernoune thy King must dye.	P1228	22.90	King
Weep not sweet Navarre, but revenge my death.	P1234	22.96	King
Thy woorth sweet friend is far above my guifts,	Edw	1.1.161	Edward
Farewell sweet Mortimer, and for my sake,	Edw	1.2.81	Queene
Would when I left sweet France and was imbarkt,	Edw	1.4.171	Queene
Repeald, the newes is too sweet to be true.	Edw	1.4.323	Edward
Sweet Lord and King, your speech preventeth mine,	Edw	2.2.59	Gavstn
Sweet unckle speake more kindly to the queene.	Edw	2.2.228	Neece
Pardon me sweet, I forgot my selfe.	Edw	2.2.230	Edward
Forslowe no time, sweet Lancaster lets march.	Edw	2.4.40	Warwck
Spencer, sweet Spencer, I adopt thee heere,	Edw	3.1.144	Edward
Good Pierce of Gaveston my sweet favoret,	Edw	3.1.228	Edward
Mortimer I stay thy sweet escape,	Edw	4.1.10	Kent
Oh my sweet hart, how do I mone thy wrongs,	Edw	4.2.27	Queene
A sweet Spencer, thus then must we part.	Edw	4.7.73	Edward
To die sweet Spencer, therefore live wee all,	Edw	4.7.111	Baldck
Sweet Mortimer, the life of Isabell,	Edw	5.2.15	Queene
Finely dissembled, do so still sweet Queene.	Edw	5.2.74	Mortmr
Nothing so sweet as Magicke is to him,	F 26	Prol.26	1Chor
Sweet Analitikes <Anulatikes>, tis thou hast ravisht me,	F 34	1.1.6	Faust
as th'infernall spirits/On sweet Musaeus when he came to hell,	F 143	1.1.115	Faust
Sweet Faustus think of heaven, and heavenly things.	F 409	2.1.21	GdAngl
Sweet Mephostophilis tell me.	F 620	2.2.69	P Faust
Away sweet Mephostophilis be gone,	F 975	3.1.197	Faust
Sweet Mephostophilis so charme me here,	F 991	3.2.11	Faust
Nay sweet Benvolio, let us sway thy thoughts/From this attempt	F1325	4.2.1	Mrtino
Sweet Mephostophilis, intreat thy Lord/To pardon my unjust	F1747	5.1.74	Faust

SWEET (cont.)

Torment sweet friend, that base and [crooked age] <aged man>,	F1753	5.1.80		Faust
sweet embraces <imbracings> may extinguish cleare <cleane>,	F1763	5.1.90		Faust
Sweet Hellen make me immortall with a kisse:	F1770	5.1.97		Faust
Ah my sweet chamber-fellow, had I liv'd with thee, then had I	F1824	5.2.28	P	Faust
Sweet friends, what shall become of Faustus being in hell	F1846	5.2.50	P	Faust
Tempt not God sweet friend, but let us into the next roome, and	F1871	5.2.75	P	1Schol
Hadst thou affected sweet divinitie,	F1901	5.2.105		GdAngl
Therefore sweet Mephastophilis, let us make haste to Wertenberge	F App	p.239 94		Faust
Sit safe at home and chaunt sweet Poesie.	Lucan, First Booke			445
Are blest by such sweet error, this makes them/Run on the	Lucan, First Booke			456
Forbeare sweet wordes, and be your sport unpleasant.	Ovid's Elegies			1.4.66
Thy verses sweet Tibullus shall be spoken.	Ovid's Elegies			1.15.28
To please me, what faire termes and sweet words ha's shee,	Ovid's Elegies			2.19.17
Although thou chafe, stolne pleasure is sweet play,	Ovid's Elegies			3.4.31
And sweet toucht harpe that to move stones was able?	Ovid's Elegies			3.11.40
Many would praise the sweet smell as she past,	Hero and Leander			1.21
Those with sweet water oft her handmaid fils,	Hero and Leander			1.35
Which like sweet musicke entred Heroes eares,	Hero and Leander			1.194
This sacrifice (whose sweet perfume descending,	Hero and Leander			1.209
But this faire jem, sweet in the losse alone,	Hero and Leander			1.247
And quite confound natures sweet harmony.	Hero and Leander			1.252
Without the sweet societie of men.	Hero and Leander			1.256
When Venus sweet rites are perform'd and done.	Hero and Leander			1.320
(Sweet are the kisses, the imbracements sweet,	Hero and Leander			2.29
Sweet singing Meremaids, sported with their loves/On heapes of	Hero and Leander			2.162

SWEETE

Why stands my sweete Aeneas thus amazde?	Dido	2.1.2		Achat
Sweete father leave to weepe, this is not he:	Dido	2.1.35		Ascan
destinies/Have brought my sweete companions in such plight?	Dido	2.1.60		Aeneas
And so I will sweete child:	Dido	2.1.97		Dido
Ile give thee Sugar-almonds, sweete Conserves,	Dido	2.1.305		Venus
Will Dido give to sweete Ascanius:	Dido	2.1.312		Venus
And strewe him with sweete smelling Violets,	Dido	2.1.318		Venus
Sleepe my sweete nephew in these cooling shades,	Dido	2.1.334		Venus
Name not Iarbus, but sweete Anna say,	Dido	3.1.67		Dido
Lest with these sweete thoughts I melt cleane away.	Dido	3.1.76		Dido
And wanton Mermaides court thee with sweete songs,	Dido	3.1.130		Dido
To harme my sweete Ascanius lovely life.	Dido	3.2.23		Venus
sweete Venus, how may I deserve/Such amourous favours at thy	Dido	3.2.64		Juno
And make love drunken with thy sweete desire:	Dido	3.3.75		Iarbus
By chance sweete Queene, as Mars and Venus met.	Dido	3.4.4		Aeneas
To Italy, sweete friends to Italy,	Dido	4.3.43		Cloan
Fourescore is but a girles age, love is sweete:--	Dido	4.5.32		Nurse
In whose sweete person is compriz'd the Sum/Of natures Skill	1Tamb	5.1.78		1Virgn
My Lord and husbandes death, with my sweete sons,	2Tamb	4.2.22		Olymp
Sweete Epernoune, our Friers are holy men,	P1161	22.23		King
Sweete prince I come, these these thy amorous lines,	Edw	1.1.6		Gavstn
Sweete speeches, comedies, and pleasing showes,	Edw	1.1.56		Gavstn
Ere my sweete Gaveston shall part from me,	Edw	1.4.48		Edward
Tis true sweete Gaveston, oh were it false.	Edw	1.4.108		Edward
And therefore sweete friend, take it patiently,	Edw	1.4.112		Edward
But come sweete friend, ile beare thee on thy way.	Edw	1.4.140		Edward
And to behold so sweete a sight as that,	Edw	1.4.206		Warwck
Sweete Mortimer, sit downe by me a while,	Edw	1.4.225		Queene
As dooth the want of my sweete Gaveston,	Edw	1.4.307		Edward
Chide me sweete Warwick, if I go astray.	Edw	1.4.348		Edward
This letter came from my sweete Gaveston,	Edw	2.1.59		Neece
Sweete husband be content, they all love you.	Edw	2.2.36		Queene
Farewell sweete unckle till we meete againe.	Edw	2.4.11		Neece
Farewell sweete Gaveston, and farewell Neece.	Edw	2.4.12		Edward
So well hast thou deserv'de sweete Mortimer.	Edw	2.4.59		Queene
Sweete soveraigne, yet I come/To see thee ere I die.	Edw	2.5.94		Gavstn
Sweete Mortimer farewell.	Edw	3.1.249		Lncstr
I heare sweete lady of the kings unkindenes,	Edw	4.2.15		SrJohn
Ah sweete sir John, even to the utmost verge/Of Europe, or the	Edw	4.2.29		Queene
Sweete Spencer, gentle Baldocke, part we must.	Edw	4.7.96		Edward
now sweete God of heaven,/Make me despise this transitorie	Edw	5.1.107		Edward
In health sweete Mortimer, how fares your grace?	Edw	5.2.81		Kent
Sweete sonne come hither, I must talke with thee.	Edw	5.2.87		Queene
I, do sweete Nephew.	Edw	5.2.96		Kent
Sweete mother, if I cannot pardon him,	Edw	5.4.94		King
Feare not sweete boye, ile garde thee from thy foes,	Edw	5.4.111		Queene
Assist me sweete God, and receive my soule.	Edw	5.5.109		Edward
Weepe not sweete sonne.	Edw	5.6.33		Queene
For my sake sweete sonne pittie Mortimer.	Edw	5.6.55		Queene
Then come sweete death, and rid me of this greefe.	Edw	5.6.92		Queene
Sweete father heere, unto thy murdered ghost,	Edw	5.6.99		King
[whose sweete delight's] dispute/In th'heavenly matters of	F 18	Prol.18		1Chor
Excelling all, <whose sweete delight disputes>	F 18	(HC256) A		1Chor
Valdes, sweete Valdes, and Cornelius,	F 127	1.1.99		Faust
Sweete Faustus leave that execrable Art.	F 404	2.1.16		GdAngl
<Nay sweete Mephastophilis fetch me one, for I will have one>.	F 530	(HC261) A	P	Faust
Thankes Mephostophilis for this sweete booke.	F 550	2.1.162		Faust
Had not sweete pleasure conquer'd deepe despaire.	F 576	2.2.25		Faust
O my sweete Gold!	F 677	2.2.126	P	Covet
Sweete Mephostophilis, thou pleasest me:	F 836	3.1.58		Faust
[Ah] <O> [my sweete] friend,	F1734	5.1.61		Faust
<I goe sweete Faustus, but with heavy cheare>,	F1737	(HC269) A		OldMan
No more sweete Rafe, letts goe and make cleane our bootes which	F App	p.234 32	P	Robin
By which sweete path thou maist attaine the gole/That shall	F App	p.243 36		OldMan
But mercie Faustus of thy Saviour sweete,	F App	p.243 44		OldMan
Under sweete hony deadly poison lurkes.	Ovid's Elegies			1.8.104

SWEETE (cont.)

The sport being such, as both alike sweete try it, . . . Ovid's Elegies 1.10.33
committed/And then with sweete words to my Mistrisse fitted. Ovid's Elegies 1.12.22
In this sweete good, why hath a third to do? . . . . Ovid's Elegies 2.5.32
And ever seemed as some new sweete befell. . . . . Ovid's Elegies 2.5.56
For which good turne my sweete reward repay, . . . Ovid's Elegies 2.8.21
Live without love, so sweete ill is a maide. . . . Ovid's Elegies 2.9.26
Let one wench cloy me with sweete loves delight, . . Ovid's Elegies 2.10.21
Memphis, and Pharos that sweete date trees yeelds, . . Ovid's Elegies 2.13.8
So sweete a burthen I will beare with eaze. . . . Ovid's Elegies 2.16.30
Even as sweete meate a glutted stomacke cloyes. . . Ovid's Elegies 2.19.26
Elegia came with haires perfumed sweete, ... Ovid's Elegies 3.1.7
And nine sweete bouts had we before day light. . . . Ovid's Elegies 3.6.26
And with sweete words cause deafe rockes to have loved <moned>, Ovid's Elegies 3.6.58
What sweete thought is there but I had the same? . . Ovid's Elegies 3.6.63
The godly, sweete Tibullus doth increase. . . . . Ovid's Elegies 3.8.66

SWEETELY

And when one sweetely sings, then straight I long, . . Ovid's Elegies 2.4.25
and kissed so sweetely as might make/Wrath-kindled Jove away Ovid's Elegies 2.5.51
Where round about small birdes most sweetely sing. . . Ovid's Elegies 3.1.4

SWEETEN

To sweeten out the slumbers of thy bed: . . . . Dido 1.1.37 Jupitr

SWEETER

His talke much sweeter than the Muses song, ... 1Tamb 3.2.50 Zenoc
and now thy sight/Is sweeter farre, then was thy parting hence Edw 2.2.57 Edward

SWEETES

The day, the night, my Swannes, my sweetes are thine. . Dido 3.2.61 Venus
Shall here unburden their exhaled sweetes, ... Dido 5.1.14 Aeneas
Wee skorne things lawfull, stolne sweetes we affect, . Ovid's Elegies 2.19.3

SWEETEST

The sweetest flower in Citherea's field, ... Jew 1.2.379 Mthias
O the sweetest face that ever I beheld! . . . . . Jew 3.1.26 P Ithimr
And trust me, they are the sweetest grapes that e're I tasted. F1587 4.6.30 P Lady
When pleasure mov'd us to our sweetest worke. . . . Ovid's Elegies 1.4.48
The aire is colde, and sleepe is sweetest now, . . . Ovid's Elegies 1.13.7

SWEET-HART

Like thy breath, sweet-hart, no violet like 'em. . . Jew 4.4.40 Ithimr

SWEET HART

Oh my sweet hart, how do I mone thy wrongs, . . . Edw 4.2.27 Queene

SWEET HEART

Put thou about thy necke my owne sweet heart, . . . Dido 1.1.44 Jupitr

SWEETLY

Excelling all, <and sweetly can dispute> . . . . F 18 (HC256) B 1Chor
Now in her tender armes I sweetly bide, ... Ovid's Elegies 1.13.5
And sweetly on his pipe began to play, ... Hero and Leander 1.401
So beautie, sweetly quickens when t'is ny, ... Hero and Leander 2.126

SWEETNES

The thirst of raigne and sweetnes of a crown, . . . 1Tamb 2.7.12 Tamb
And every sweetnes that inspir'd their harts, . . . 1Tamb 5.1.163 Tamb

SWEETNESSE

As now it bringeth sweetnesse to my wound, ... 1Tamb 5.1.420 Arabia

SWELL

Swell raging seas, frowne wayward destinies, . . . Dido 4.4.57 Aeneas
Have made the water swell above the bankes, . . . 2Tamb 5.1.205 Techel
For every yeare they swell, and yet they live; . . . Jew 4.1.6 Barab
With slaughtered priests [make] <may> Tibers channell swell, Edw 1.4.102 Edward
My [lords] <lord>, perceive you how these rebels swell: . Edw 3.1.181 Edward
Being three daies old inforst the floud to swell, . . Lucan, First Booke 220
Ascreus lives, while grapes with new wine swell, . . Ovid's Elegies 1.15.11
But seeing thee, I thinke my thing will swell, . . . Ovid's Elegies 2.15.25
First Ceres taught the seede in fields to swell, . . . Ovid's Elegies 3.9.11

SWELL'D

The Ocean swell'd, as high as Spanish Calpe, ... Lucan, First Booke 553
The liver swell'd with filth, and every vaine/Did threaten Lucan, First Booke 620

SWELLING

Disquiet Seas lay downe your swelling lookes, . . . Dido 1.1.122 Venus
The Masts whereon thy swelling sailes shall hang, . . Dido 3.1.122 Dido
Have swelling cloudes drawen from wide gasping woundes, . 1Tamb 5.1.459 Tamb
drops that fall/When Boreas rents a thousand swelling cloudes, 2Tamb 1.3.160 Tamb
My swelling hart for very anger breakes, ... Edw 2.2.200 Edward
Approcht the swelling streame with drum and ensigne, . Lucan, First Booke 207
Hath with thee past the swelling Ocean; . . . . Lucan, First Booke 371
But though I like a swelling floud was driven, . . . Ovid's Elegies 1.7.43
Who slumbring, they rise up in swelling armes. . . . Ovid's Elegies 1.9.26
And with thy hand assist [the] <thy> swelling saile. . . Ovid's Elegies 2.11.42
In swelling wombe her twinnes had Ilia kilde? . . . Ovid's Elegies 2.14.15
But when she comes, [you] <your> swelling mounts sinck downe, Ovid's Elegies 2.16.51
With joy heares Neptunes swelling waters sound. . . . Ovid's Elegies 3.10.30
He would have chac'd away the swelling maine, . . . Hero and Leander 2.121

SWELS

The sucking shore with their aboundance swels. . . . Ovid's Elegies 2.11.14

SWEPT (See also SWEEPT)

Which swept the desart shore of that dead sea, . . . Edw 2.3.22 Mortmr
Ocean;/And swept the foming brest of [Artick] <Articks> Rhene. Lucan, First Booke 372

SWIFT

this day swift Mercury/When I was laying a platforme for these Dido 5.1.93 Aeneas
Returne with speed, time passeth swift away, . . . 1Tamb 1.1.67 Mycet
These are the wings shall make it flie as swift, . . 1Tamb 2.3.57 Tamb
The incertaine pleasures of swift-footed time/Have tane their Jew 2.1.7 Barab
How swift he runnes. . . . . Jew 4.4.51 Pilia
And make swift Rhine, circle faire Wittenberge <Wertenberge>: F 116 1.1.88 Faust
And on a proud pac'd Steed, as swift as thought, . . F 984 3.2.4 Mephst
by meanes of a swift spirit that I have, I had these grapes F1585 4.6.28 P Faust

SWIFT (cont.)			
and by means of a swift spirit that I have, I had them brought	F App	p.242 22 P	Faust
While Titan strives against the worlds swift course;	Lucan, First Booke		90
Cyngas streame, and where swift Rhodanus/Drives Araris to sea;	Lucan, First Booke		434
The worlds swift course is lawlesse/And casuall; all the	Lucan, First Booke		641
Venus is faint; swift Hermes retrograde;	Lucan, First Booke		661
And with swift horses the swift yeare soone leaves us.	Ovid's Elegies		1.8.50
Or [into] <to the> sea swift Symois [doth] <shall> slide.	Ovid's Elegies		1.15.10
Who would not love those hands for their swift running?	Ovid's Elegies		2.4.28
The crooked Barque hath her swift sailes displayd.	Ovid's Elegies		2.11.24
And where swift Nile in his large channell slipping <skipping>,	Ovid's Elegies		2.13.9
And with swift Naggs drawing thy little Coach,	Ovid's Elegies		2.16.49
On swift steedes mounted till the race were done.	Ovid's Elegies		3.2.10
Swift Atalantas flying legges like these,	Ovid's Elegies		3.2.29
And forth the gay troupes on swift horses flie.	Ovid's Elegies		3.2.78
Her, from his swift waves, the bold floud perceav'd,	Ovid's Elegies		3.5.51
And to thine owne losse was thy wit swift running.	Ovid's Elegies		3.7.46
SWIFTER			
Mounted on Steeds, swifter than Pegasus.	1Tamb	1.2.94	Tamb
That flies with fury swifter than our thoughts,	2Tamb	4.1.5	Amyras
live, and draw/My chariot swifter than the racking cloudes:	2Tamb	4.3.21	Tamb
You run swifter when you threw my gold out of my Window.	Jew	4.4.52 P	Barab
the darke/(Swifter then bullets throwne from Spanish slinges,	Lucan, First Booke		231
Is swifter than the wind, whose tardie plumes,	Hero and Leander		2.115
SWIFT-FOOTED			
The incertaine pleasures of swift-footed time/Have tane their	Jew	2.1.7	Barab
SWIFTLY			
And kill as sure as it swiftly flies.	1Tamb	2.3.59	Tamb
Of Euphrates and Tigris swiftly runs,	2Tamb	5.2.3	Callap
From East to West his Dragons swiftly glide,	F 766	2.3.45	2Chor
Slaughter to come, and swiftly bringing newes/Of present war,	Lucan, First Booke		467
To follow swiftly blasting infamie.	Hero and Leander		1.292
SWILL			
Goe swill in bowles of Sacke and Muscadine:	Jew	5.5.6	Barab
and carowse, and swill/Amongst the Students, as even now he	F App	p.243 4	Wagner
SWIM (See also SWOMME)			
And swim to Italy, Ile keepe these sure:	Dido	4.4.164	Dido
That I may swim to him like Tritons neece:	Dido	5.1.247	Dido
And I would strive to swim through pooles of blood,	2Tamb	1.3.92	Amyras
Amasde, swim up and downe upon the waves,	2Tamb	5.1.207	Techel
And since you leave me in the Ocean thus/To sinke or swim, and	Jew	1.2.268	Barab
That swim about and so preserve their lives:	P 419	7.59	Guise
And sinke them in the river as they swim.	P 423	7.63	Dumain
Leander being up, began to swim,	Hero and Leander		2.175
And up againe, and close beside him swim,	Hero and Leander		2.190
SWIMME			
No no, she cares not how we sinke or swimme,	Dido	4.3.41	Illion
SWIMMING			
might behold/Young infants swimming in their parents bloud,	Dido	2.1.193	Aeneas
The youth oft swimming to his Hero kinde,	Ovid's Elegies		2.16.31
SWINE			
In spite of these swine-eating Christians,	Jew	2.3.7	Barab
SWINE-EATING			
In spite of these swine-eating Christians,	Jew	2.3.7	Barab
SWING (See also SWONG)			
And rustling swing up as the wind fets breath.	Lucan, First Booke		392
SWISS (See MUFFES)			
SWIZERS			
Swizers keepe you the streetes,/And at ech corner shall the	P 290	5.17	Anjoy
SWOLNE			
Her cheekes swolne with sighes, her haire all rent,	Dido	2.1.276	Aeneas
I tel you true my heart is swolne with wrath,	1Tamb	2.2.2	Mycet
Who swolne with venome of ambitious pride,	Edw	1.2.31	Mortmr
Till swolne with cunning of a selfe conceit,	F 20	Prol.20	1Chor
SWOME			
Who hoping to imbrace thee, cherely swome.	Hero and Leander		2.250
SWOMME			
And as I swomme, she standing on the shoare,	Dido	2.1.286	Aeneas
As for Aeneas he swomme quickly backe,	Dido	2.1.296	Achat
SWONG			
And swong her howling in the emptie ayre,	Dido	2.1.248	Aeneas
SWORD			
And in the end subdue them with his sword,	Dido	1.1.90	Jupitr
Then buckled I mine armour, drew my sword,	Dido	2.1.200	Aeneas
and with this sword/Sent many of their savadge ghosts to hell.	Dido	2.1.211	Aeneas
Which he disdaining whiskt his sword about,	Dido	2.1.253	Aeneas
So leaning on his sword he stood stone still,	Dido	2.1.263	Aeneas
When thou Achates with thy sword mad'st way,	Dido	2.1.268	Aeneas
And by this Sword that saved me from the Greekes,	Dido	3.4.48	Aeneas
A Sword, and not a Scepter fits Aeneas.	Dido	4.4.43	Aeneas
Here lye the Sword that in the darksome Cave/He drew, and swore	Dido	5.1.295	Dido
By plowing up his Countries with the Sword:	Dido	5.1.308	Dido
tearms/And scourging kingdoms with his conquering sword.	1Tamb	Prol.6	Prolog
Draw foorth thy sword, thou mighty man at Armes,	1Tamb	1.2.178	Tamb
And kill proud Tamburlaine with point of sword.	1Tamb	2.2.12	Mycet
now whet thy winged sword/And lift thy lofty arme into the	1Tamb	2.3.51	Cosroe
Who entring at the breach thy sword hath made,	1Tamb	2.7.9	Cosroe
By this my sword that conquer'd Persea,	1Tamb	3.3.82	Tamb
If they should yeeld their necks unto the sword,	1Tamb	3.3.142	Bajzth
He raceth all his foes with fire and sword.	1Tamb	4.1.63	2Msngr
First shalt thou rip my bowels with thy sword,	1Tamb	4.2.16	Bajzth
My sword stroke fire from his coat of steele,	1Tamb	4.2.41	Tamb
Yet would I with my sword make Jove to stoope.	1Tamb	4.4.74	Tamb

SWORD (cont.)			
I feare the custome proper to his sword,	1Tamb	5.1.13	Govnr
Behold my sword, what see you at the point?	1Tamb	5.1.108	Tamb
But goe my Lords, put the rest to the sword.	1Tamb	5.1.134	Tamb
But such a Star hath influence in his sword,	1Tamb	5.1.232	Bajzth
To breake his sword, and mildly treat of love,	1Tamb	5.1.327	Zenoc
She that hath calmde the furie of my sword,	1Tamb	5.1.437	Tamb
To doo their ceassles homag to my sword:	1Tamb	5.1.456	Tamb
for as the Romans usde/I here present thee with a naked sword.	2Tamb	1.1.82	Sgsmnd
Here is his sword, let peace be ratified/On these conditions	2Tamb	1.1.124	Orcan
And cleave his Pericranion with thy sword.	2Tamb	1.3.101	Tamb
And cleave him to the channell with my sword.	2Tamb	1.3.103	Calyph
Jove shall send his winged Messenger/To bid me sheath my sword,	2Tamb	1.3.167	Tamb
Techelles, draw thy sword,/And wound the earth, that it may	2Tamb	2.4.96	Tamb
As I have conquered kingdomes with my sword.	2Tamb	2.4.136	Tamb
hath followed long/The martiall sword of mighty Tamburlaine,	2Tamb	3.1.28	Callap
Til fire and sword have found them at a bay.	2Tamb	3.2.151	Tamb
I long to pierce his bowels with my sword,	2Tamb	3.2.152	Usumc
(The worthiest knight that ever brandisht sword)/Challenge in	2Tamb	3.5.71	Tamb
Thinke of thy end, this sword shall lance thy throat.	2Tamb	3.5.78	Orcan
Now brother, follow we our fathers sword,	2Tamb	4.1.4	Amyras
pride/And leads your glories <bodies> sheep-like to the sword.	2Tamb	4.1.77	Tamb
Nor thy close Cave a sword to murther thee,	2Tamb	4.2.12	Olymp
Ah, pity me my Lord, and draw your sword,	2Tamb	4.2.33	Olymp
Nor Pistol, Sword, nor Lance can pierce your flesh.	2Tamb	4.2.66	Olymp
That with his sword hath quail'd all earthly kings,	2Tamb	5.1.93	Tamb
My sword hath sent millions of Turks to hell,	2Tamb	5.1.180	Tamb
That shakes his sword against thy majesty,	2Tamb	5.1.196	Tamb
Not for all Malta, therefore sheath your sword;	Jew	2.3.270	Barab
And thither will I to put them to the sword.	P 504	9.23	Guise
Which they will put us to with sword and fire:	P 706	14.9	Navrre
And bids thee whet thy sword on Sextus bones,	P1237	22.99	King
This sword of mine that should offend your foes,	Edw	1.1.86	Mortmr
Unlesse his brest be sword proofe he shall die.	Edw	1.2.8	Mortmr
Penbrooke shall beare the sword before the king.	Edw	1.4.351	Edward
And with this sword, Penbrooke wil fight for you.	Edw	1.4.352	Penbrk
But whiles I have a sword, a hand, a hart,	Edw	1.4.422	Mortmr
Go souldiers take him hence, for by my sword,	Edw	2.5.20	Warwck
Too kinde to them, but now have drawne our sword,	Edw	3.1.25	Edward
My lord, referre your vengeance to the sword,	Edw	3.1.123	Spencr
By this right hand, and by my fathers sword,	Edw	3.1.130	Edward
Edward with fire and sword, followes at thy heeles.	Edw	3.1.180	Edward
This day I shall powre vengeance with my sword/On those proud	Edw	3.1.186	Edward
And shall or Warwicks sword shal smite in vaine.	Edw	3.1.199	Warwck
And rather bathe thy sword in subjects bloud,	Edw	3.1.212	Mortmr
But by the sword, my lord, it must be deserv'd.	Edw	4.2.59	Mortmr
and sword and gleave/In civill broiles makes kin and country	Edw	4.4.5	Queene
We come in armes to wrecke it with the [sword] <swords>:	Edw	4.4.23	Mortmr
thou chase/Thy lawfull king thy soveraigne with thy sword?	Edw	4.6.4	Kent
And these must die under a tyrants sword.	Edw	4.7.92	Edward
Till with my sword I have that Conjurer slaine.	F1333	4.2.9	Benvol
now sword strike home,/For hornes he gave, Il'e have his head	F1360	4.2.36	Benvol
let thy sword bring us home.	Lucan, First Booke		280
having lickt/Warme goare from Syllas sword art yet athirst,	Lucan, First Booke		331
thou bid me/Intombe my sword within my brothers bowels;	Lucan, First Booke		377
Sword-girt Orions side glisters too bright.	Lucan, First Booke		664
Or I more sterne then fire or sword will turne,	Ovid's Elegies		1.6.57
His sword layed by, safe, though rude places yeelds.	Ovid's Elegies		2.9.20
And what poore Dido with her drawne sword sharpe,	Ovid's Elegies		2.18.25
Mars girts his deadly sword on for my harme:	Ovid's Elegies		3.3.27
This side that serves thee, a sharpe sword did weare.	Ovid's Elegies		3.7.14
SWORDE			
in peeces, give me the sworde with a ball of wildefire upon it.	1Tamb	5.1.311	P Zabina
For this, this head, this heart, this hand and sworde,	P 109	2.52	Guise
Holde Sworde,	P 987	19.57	Guise
The sworde shall plane the furrowes of thy browes,	Edw	1.1.94	Edward
And will avcuche his saying with the sworde,	Edw	5.4.77	Champn
SWORDES			
Our swordes shall play the Orators for us.	1Tamb	1.2.132	Techel
Techelles, and the rest prepare your swordes,	1Tamb	3.3.64	Tamb
their swordes or their cannons, as I doe a naked Lady in a net	2Tamb	4.1.68	P Calyph
And when tis gone, our swordes shall purchase more.	Edw	2.2.197	Lncstr
SWORD-GIRT			
Sword-girt Orions side glisters too bright.	Lucan, First Booke		664
SWORDS			
Old men with swords thrust through their aged sides,	Dido	2.1.197	Aeneas
Now Turkes and Tartars shake their swords at thee,	1Tamb	1.1.16	Cosroe
Go, stout Theridamas, thy words are swords,	1Tamb	1.1.74	Mycet
Their swords enameld, and about their neckes/Hangs massie	1Tamb	1.2.125	Souldr
And gainst the Generall we will lift our swords,	1Tamb	1.2.145	Tamb
Where kings shall crouch unto our conquering swords,	1Tamb	1.2.220	Usumc
Then when our powers in points of swords are join'd,	1Tamb	2.1.40	Cosroe
Their carelesse swords shal lanch their fellowes throats/And	1Tamb	2.2.49	Meandr
To lift our swords against the Persean King.	1Tamb	2.7.35	Techel
I long to see those crownes won by our swords,	1Tamb	3.3.98	Therid
Our conquering swords shall marshal us the way/We use to march	1Tamb	3.3.148	Tamb
let us glut our swords/That thirst to drinke the feble Perseans	1Tamb	3.3.164	Bajzth
Shaking their swords, their speares and yron bils,	1Tamb	4.1.25	2Msngr
So shall our swords, our lances and our shot,	1Tamb	4.2.51	Tamb
Not one should scape: but perish by our swords.	1Tamb	4.2.122	Tamb
take it from my swords point, or Ile thrust it to thy heart.	1Tamb	4.4.41	P Tamb
Let all the swords and Lances in the field,	1Tamb	5.1.225	Zabina
of the war/Threw naked swords and sulphur bals of fire,	2Tamb	3.2.41	Tamb

SWORDS (cont.)
With naked swords and scarlet liveries: 2Tamb 3.4.55 Therid
Whet all your swords to mangle Tamburlain, 2Tamb 3.5.15 Callap
troopes/Beats downe our foes to flesh our taintlesse swords? 2Tamb 4.1.26 Amyras
Our Turkish swords shal headlong send to hell, 2Tamb 5.2.15 Amasia
Techelles and the rest, come take your swords, 2Tamb 5.3.46 Tamb
Here must no speeches passe, nor swords be drawne. Jew 2.3.339 Barab
Whose face has bin a grind-stone for mens swords, Jew 4.3.9 Barab
And henceforth parle with our naked swords. Edw 1.1.126 Mortmr
But yet lift not your swords against the king. Edw 1.2.61 ArchBp
We come in armes to wrecke it with the [sword] <swords>: Edw 4.4.23 Mortmr
[Faustus, thou art damn'd, then swords <guns> and knives], F 572 2.2.21A Faust
[Gunnes] <Swords>, poyson, halters, and invenomb'd steele, F 573 2.2.22 Faust
And had you cut my body with your swords, F1397 4.2.73 Faust
We sing, whose conquering swords their own breasts launcht, Lucan, First Booke 3
Swords share our Empire, fortune that made Roome/Governe the Lucan, First Booke 109
Yea and thy father to, and swords thrown down, Lucan, First Booke 117
darts, olde swords/With ugly teeth of blacke rust fouly scarr'd: Lucan, First Booke 244
And sentence given in rings of naked swords, Lucan, First Booke 321
this makes them/Run on the swords point and desire to die, Lucan, First Booke 457
Wars radge draws neare; and to the swords strong hand, Lucan, First Booke 665

SWORE
in the darksome Cave/He drew, and swore by to be true to me, Dido 5.1.296 Dido
Which is as much as if I swore by heaven, 1Tamb 1.2.233 Tamb
Pope Julius swore to Princely Sigismond, F 925 3.1.147 Bruno
By her eyes I remember late she swore, Ovid's Elegies 3.3.13
Some swore he was a maid in mans attire, Hero and Leander 1.83
And swore he never should returne to Jove. Hero and Leander 2.168
And swore the sea should never doe him harme. Hero and Leander 2.180

SWORN
Not for the world Zenocrate, if I have sworn: 1Tamb 4.2.125 Tamb

SWORNE
O thy lips have sworne/To stay with Dido: Dido 5.1.120 Dido
Have sworne the death of wicked Tamburlaine. 1Tamb 1.1.64 Mycet
A thousand sworne and overmatching foes: 1Tamb 2.1.39 Cosroe
For Fates and Oracles [of] heaven have sworne, 1Tamb 2.3.7 Tamb
Than stay the torments he and heaven have sworne. 1Tamb 3.2.99 Agidas
you be first shal feele/The sworne destruction of Damascus. 1Tamb 5.1.66 Tamb
For I have sworne by sacred Mahomet, 2Tamb 1.3.109 Tamb
All which have sworne to sacke Natolia: 2Tamb 1.3.121 Therid
And all have jointly sworne thy cruell death, 2Tamb 3.5.112 Soria
But I have sworne to frustrate both their hopes, Jew 2.3.142 Barab
I, and take heed, for he hath sworne your death. Jew 2.3.280 Barab
For he hath solemnely sworne thy death. P 777 15.35 King
Were sworne to your father at his death, Edw 1.1.83 Mortmr
Sworne to defend king Edwards royall right, Edw 3.1.38 SpncrP
of Wittenberg <Wertenberge>/[Swarme] <Sworne> to my Problemes, F 142 1.1.114 Faust
And new sworne souldiours maiden armes retainst, Ovid's Elegies 2.18.2
in vowing chastitie, hast sworne/To rob her name and honour, Hero and Leander 1.304

SWOWNS
swowns boy, I hope you have seene many boyes with such F App p.229 2 P Clown
swowns they are as bolde with my flesh, as if they had payd for F App p.230 28 P Clown

SWUM
Might have enforst me to have swum from France, Edw 1.1.7 Gavstn
Had then swum over, but the way was blinde. Ovid's Elegies 2.16.32

SYBILLAS
and read/Sybillas secret works, and [wash] <washt> their saint Lucan, First Booke 599

SYCILLIA
say Pompey, are these worse/Then Pirats of Sycillia? Lucan, First Booke 347

SYLLA
use he's known/To exceed his maister, that arch-traitor Sylla. Lucan, First Booke 326
Sylla teaching thee,/At last learne wretch to leave thy Lucan, First Booke 334

SYLLAES
No barking Dogs that Syllaes intrailes beare, Ovid's Elegies 2.16.23

SYLLA'S
Sylla's ghost/Was seene to walke, singing sad Oracles, Lucan, First Booke 579

SYLLAS
having lickt/Warme goare from Syllas sword art yet athirst, Lucan, First Booke 331

SYLLOGISM (See SILLOGISMES)

SYLVAN
Like Sylvian <Sylvan> Nimphes my pages shall be clad, Edw 1.1.58 Gavstn

SYLVANUS
Sylvanus weeping for the lovely boy/That now is turn'd into a Hero and Leander 1.154

SYLVIAN
Like Sylvian <Sylvan> Nimphes my pages shall be clad, Edw 1.1.58 Gavstn

SYMBOLIZE (See SIMBOLISDE)

SYMOIS
Or [into] <to the> sea swift Symois [doth] <shall> slide. Ovid's Elegies 1.15.10

SYNAGOGUE
Or else be gather'd for in our Synagogue; Jew 2.3.27 Barab
Which in the woods doe holde their synagogue: P 502 9.21 Guise

SYNOD (See also SINOD)
By full consent of all the [reverend] <holy> Synod/Of Priests F 952 3.1.174 Faust
To view the sentence of the reverend Synod, F1014 3.2.34 1Card

SYRACUSE (See SIRACUSIAN)

SYRE
Shall pay a yearly tribute to thy Syre. 1Tamb 5.1.519 Tamb

SYRIA (See SIRIA)

SYRTES (See also SIRTES)
Well, leade us then to Syrtes desart shoare; Lucan, First Booke 368
from the breach/Of Libian Syrtes roules a monstrous wave, Lucan, First Booke 497
In what gulfe either Syrtes have their seate. Ovid's Elegies 2.11.20
With her I durst the Lybian Syrtes breake through, Ovid's Elegies 2.16.21

Line	Work	Reference	Speaker
SYSIPHUS			
Yet there with Sysiphus he toyld in vaine,	Hero and Leander	2.277	
SYTHIA			
Sythia, Cilicia, Brittaine are as good,	Ovid's Elegies	2.16.39	
T' (Homograph)			
Epeus pine-tree Horse/A sacrifize t'appease Minervas wrath:	Dido	2.1.163	Aeneas
T'incounter with the strength of Tamburlaine.	1Tamb	3.3.7	Tamb
I meane t'incounter with that Bajazeth.	1Tamb	3.3.65	Tamb
Yet scarse enough t'encounter Tamburlaine.	2Tamb	1.1.66	Orcan
T'incounter with the cruell Tamburlain,	2Tamb	2.2.5	Orcan
T'appease my wrath, or els Ile torture thee,	2Tamb	3.5.122	Tamb
That meane t'invest me in a higher throane,	2Tamb	5.3.121	Tamb
Thou shalt have crownes of us, t'out bid the Barons,	Edw	3.1.55	Edward
T'appeaze the wrath of their offended king.	Edw	3.1.210	Edward
And lives t'advance your standard good my lord.	Edw	4.2.42	Mortmr
T'escape their hands that seeke to reave his life:	Edw	4.7.52	Leistr
As I was going to Wittenberge t'other day, with a loade of Hay,	F1526	4.5.22	P Carter
But neither chuse the north t'erect thy seat;	Lucan, First Booke	53	
T'was peace against their wils; betwixt them both/Stept Crassus	Lucan, First Booke	99	
stil poore/Did vild deeds, then t'was worth the price of bloud,	Lucan, First Booke	175	
(that did remaine/To their afflictions) were t'abandon Roome.	Lucan, First Booke	495	
T'was so, he stroke me with a slender dart,	Ovid's Elegies	1.2.7	
Or she was not the wench I wisht t'have had.	Ovid's Elegies	3.6.2	
Whose carelesse haire, in stead of pearle t'adorne it,	Hero and Leander	1.389	
T.			
A per se, a, t. h. e. the:	F 728	2.3.7	P Robin
T'ABANDON			
(that did remaine/To their afflictions) were t'abandon Roome.	Lucan, First Booke	495	
TABERNE			
druncke with ipocrase at any taberne in Europe for nothing,	F App	p.234 23	P Robin
TABLE			
And here this table as a Register/Of all her vertues and	2Tamb	3.2.23	Celeb
While at the councell table, grave enough,	Edw	5.4.58	Mortmr
What else, a table and a fetherbed.	Edw	5.5.33	Ltborn
Runne for the table.	Edw	5.5.110	Ltborn
So, lay the table downe, and stampe on it,	Edw	5.5.112	Ltborn
be he that stole [away] his holinesse meate from the Table.	F1077	3.2.97	1Frier
be hee that stole away his holinesse meate from/the table.	F App	p.232 32	Frier
Each little hill shall for a table stand:	Ovid's Elegies	2.11.48	
The Sunne turnd backe from Atreus cursed table?	Ovid's Elegies	3.11.39	
TABLES			
Except he place his Tables in the streets.	Jew	5.3.35	Calym
Or saying a long grace at a tables end,	Edw	2.1.37	Spencr
Let this word, come, alone the tables fill.	Ovid's Elegies	1.11.24	
to her I consecrate/My faithfull tables being vile maple late.	Ovid's Elegies	1.11.28	
Hence luck-lesse tables, funerall wood be flying/And thou the	Ovid's Elegies	1.12.7	
TACKLING			
My Oares broken, and my Tackling lost,	Dido	3.1.107	Aeneas
Ile give thee tackling made of riveld gold,	Dido	3.1.116	Dido
Bring me his oares, his tackling, and his sailes:	Dido	4.4.109	Dido
And heres Aeneas tackling, oares and sailes.	Dido	4.4.125	Lord
Theres not so much as this base tackling too,	Dido	4.4.151	Dido
For tackling, let him take the chaines of gold,	Dido	4.4.161	Dido
Who have no sailes nor tackling for my ships?	Dido	5.1.56	Aeneas
TACKLINGS			
The sailes wrapt up, the mast and tacklings downe,	2Tamb	1.2.59	Callap
TACKT			
then we [luft] <left>, and [tackt] <tooke>, and fought at ease:	Jew	2.2.14	Bosco
T'ADORNE			
Whose carelesse haire, in stead of pearle t'adorne it,	Hero and Leander	1.389	
T'ADVANCE			
And lives t'advance your standard good my lord.	Edw	4.2.42	Mortmr
TAGES			
all to good, be Augury vaine, and Tages/Th'arts master falce.	Lucan, First Booke	635	
TAGUS			
[And] <The> banks ore which gold bearing Tagus flowes.	Ovid's Elegies	1.15.34	
TAILE			
then having whiskt/His taile athwart his backe, and crest	Lucan, First Booke	211	
The threatning Scorpion with the burning taile/And fier'st his	Lucan, First Booke	658	
TAINE (See also TANE)			
the rest have taine their standings in the next roome,	P 994	19.64	P 3Mur
TAINT			
pooles, refraines/To taint his tresses in the Tyrrhen maine?	Dido	1.1.112	Venus
Lest their grosse eye-beames taint my lovers cheekes:	Dido	3.1.74	Dido
TAINTED			
Which when he tainted with his slender rod,	2Tamb	1.3.40	Zenoc
Whose hornes shall sprinkle through the tainted aire,	2Tamb	3.1.66	Orcan
Nor shall they now be tainted with a kings.	Edw	5.5.82	Ltborn
TAINTLESSE			
troopes/Beats downe our foes to flesh our taintlesse swords?	2Tamb	4.1.26	Amyras
TAKE (See also TAINE, TANE)			
I will take order for that presently:	Dido	1.1.113	Jupitr
And therefore will take pitie on his toyle,	Dido	1.1.131	Venus
Hold, take this candle and goe light a fire,	Dido	1.1.171	Aeneas
The Greekes pursue me, stay and take me in.	Dido	2.1.282	Aeneas
For Didos sake I take thee in my armes,	Dido	2.1.313	Venus
Till I returne and take thee hence againe.	Dido	2.1.339	Venus
No Dido will not take me in her armes,	Dido	3.1.22	Cupid
Take it Ascanius, for thy fathers sake.	Dido	3.1.33	Dido
Take what ye will, but leave Aeneas here.	Dido	3.1.127	Dido
But I will take another order now,	Dido	3.2.6	Juno
Hold, take these Jewels at thy Lovers hand,	Dido	3.4.61	Dido

TAKE (cont.)

I went to take my farewell of Achates.	Dido	4.4.18		Aeneas
Not all the world can take thee from mine armes,	Dido	4.4.61		Dido
Goe, bid my Nurse take yong Ascanius,	Dido	4.4.105		Dido
For tackling, let him take the chaines of gold,	Dido	4.4.161		Dido
And made me take my brother for my sonne:	Dido	5.1.43		Aeneas
Aeneas, say, how canst thou take thy leave?	Dido	5.1.119		Dido
canst thou take her hand?	Dido	5.1.121		Dido
That he should take Aeneas from mine armes?	Dido	5.1.130		Dido
And, see the Sailers take him by the hand,	Dido	5.1.189		Dido
O sister, sister, take away the Rockes,	Dido	5.1.254		Dido
Then now my Lord, I humbly take my leave.	1Tamb	1.1.81		Therid
Or take him prisoner, and his chaine shall serve/For Manackles,	1Tamb	1.2.147		Tamb
Theridamas my friend, take here my hand,	1Tamb	1.2.232		Tamb
He that can take or slaughter Tamburlaine,	1Tamb	2.2.30		Meandr
And while the base borne Tartars take it up,	1Tamb	2.2.65		Meandr
I take thy doome for satisfaction.	1Tamb	2.3.5		Cosroe
They cannot take away my crowne from me.	1Tamb	2.4.14		Mycet
Here take it for a while, I lend it thee,	1Tamb	2.4.37		Tamb
With litle slaughter take Meanders course,	1Tamb	2.5.27		Cosroe
Techelles, take a thousand horse with thee,	1Tamb	2.5.99		Tamb
I know not how to take their tyrannies.	1Tamb	2.7.41		Cosroe
My soule begins to take her flight to hell:	1Tamb	2.7.44		Cosroe
Tell him, I am content to take a truce,	1Tamb	3.1.31		Bajzth
We meane to take his mornings next arise/For messenger, he will	1Tamb	3.1.38		Bajzth
Til then take thou my crowne, vaunt of my worth,	1Tamb	3.3.130		Tamb
Then Victorie begins to take her flight,	1Tamb	3.3.160		Tamb
Nay take the Turkish Crown from her, Zenocrate,	1Tamb	3.3.220		Tamb
Let him take all th'advantages he can,	1Tamb	4.1.40		Souldn
Shall ransome him, or take him from his cage.	1Tamb	4.2.94		Tamb
take it from my swords point, or Ile thrust it to thy heart.	1Tamb	4.4.40	P	Tamb
Take it up Villaine, and eat it, or I will make thee slice the	1Tamb	4.4.43	P	Tamb
And with my father take a frindly truce.	1Tamb	4.4.72		Zenoc
Now take these three crownes, and pledge me, my contributorie	1Tamb	4.4.114	P	Tamb
Take them away againe and make us slaves.	1Tamb	4.4.133		Therid
And take in signe thereof this gilded wreath,	1Tamb	5.1.101		1Virgn
Whose sight with joy would take away my life,	1Tamb	5.1.419		Arabia
Take which thou wilt, for as the Romans usde/I here present	2Tamb	1.1.81		Sgsmnd
Thanks king of Morocus, take your crown again.	2Tamb	1.3.137		Tamb
Thanks king of Fesse, take here thy crowne again.	2Tamb	1.3.150		Tamb
Whose triple Myter I did take by force,	2Tamb	1.3.189		Techel
then that your Majesty/Take all advantages of time and power,	2Tamb	2.1.12		Fredrk
Now then my Lord, advantage take hereof,	2Tamb	2.1.22		Fredrk
And take the victorie our God hath given.	2Tamb	2.1.63		Sgsmnd
Take here these papers as our sacrifice/And witnesse of thy	2Tamb	2.2.45		Orcan
Let me take leave of these my loving sonnes,	2Tamb	2.4.72		Zenoc
Take pitie of a Ladies ruthfull teares,	2Tamb	3.4.69		Olymp
What, take it man.	2Tamb	3.5.132	P	Orcan
Good my Lord, let me take it.	2Tamb	3.5.133	P	Almeda
Here, take it.	2Tamb	3.5.134	P	Callap
Go too sirha, take your crown, and make up the halfe dozen.	2Tamb	3.5.135	P	Tamb
that when I take him, I may knocke out his braines with them,	2Tamb	3.5.140	P	Tamb
I take no pleasure to be murtherous,	2Tamb	4.1.29		Calyph
And take my other toward brother here,	2Tamb	4.1.34		Calyph
Take you the honor, I will take my ease,	2Tamb	4.1.49		Calyph
the pavilions/Of these proud Turks, and take their Concubines,	2Tamb	4.1.161		Tamb
Ile dispose them as it likes me best,/Meane while take him in.	2Tamb	4.1.167		Tamb
take ye Queens apeece/(I meane such Queens as were kings	2Tamb	4.3.70		Tamb
(I meane such Queens as were kings Concubines)/Take them,	2Tamb	4.3.72		Tamb
Let them take pleasure soundly in their spoiles,	2Tamb	4.3.92		Tamb
Go thither some of you and take his gold,	2Tamb	5.1.123		Tamb
Take them, and hang them both up presently.	2Tamb	5.1.132		Tamb
Take them away Theridamas, see them dispatcht.	2Tamb	5.1.134		Tamb
taskes a while/And take such fortune as your fellowes felt.	2Tamb	5.1.137		Tamb
Techelles and the rest, come take your swords,	2Tamb	5.3.46		Tamb
First take my Scourge and my imperiall Crowne,	2Tamb	5.3.177		Tamb
rebelling Jades/Wil take occasion by the slenderest haire,	2Tamb	5.3.239		Tamb
Let's take our leaves; Farewell good Barabas.	Jew	1.1.175		2Jew
Why let 'em enter, let 'em take the Towne.	Jew	1.1.190		Barab
we take particularly thine/To save the ruine of a multitude:	Jew	1.2.96		Govnr
tush, take not from me then,/For that is theft; and if you rob	Jew	1.2.125		Barab
Then wee'll take order for the residue.	Jew	1.2.136		Govnr
To take the lives of miserable men,	Jew	1.2.147		Barab
But take it to you i'th devils name.	Jew	1.2.154		Barab
and by my fingers take/A kisse from him that sends it from his	Jew	2.1.58		Barab
Then marke him, Sir, and take him hence.	Jew	2.3.131		1Offcr
I, and take heed, for he hath sworne your death.	Jew	2.3.280		Barab
I cannot take my leave of him for teares:	Jew	2.3.355		Abigal
Take this and beare it to Mathias streight,	Jew	2.3.370		Barab
Then take them up, and let them be interr'd/Within one sacred	Jew	3.2.29		Govnr
Then of true griefe let us take equall share.	Jew	3.2.37		Govnr
Here take my keyes, I'le give 'em thee anon:	Jew	3.4.46		Barab
There's a darke entry where they take it in,	Jew	3.4.79		Barab
And as you profitably take up Armes,	Jew	3.5.32		Govnr
Then is it as it should be, take him up.	Jew	4.1.152		Barab
Come Ithimore, let's helpe to take him hence.	Jew	4.1.200		Barab
Take in the staffe too, for that must be showne:	Jew	4.1.204		Barab
conning his neck-verse I take it, looking of a Fryars	Jew	4.2.17	P	Pilia
I never knew a man take his death so patiently as this Fryar;	Jew	4.2.21	P	Ithimr
Take thou the mony, spend it for my sake.	Jew	4.2.123		Ithimr
Here take 'em, fellow, with as good a will--	Jew	4.3.52		Barab
Take my goods too, and seize upon my lands:	Jew	5.1.66		Barab

Will take his leave and saile toward Ottoman.	Jew	5.2.106	Barab
I trust thy word, take what I promis'd thee.	Jew	5.5.43	Govnr
Tush, Governor, take thou no care for that,	Jew	5.5.102	Calym
within thy hands/To shuffle or cut, take this as surest thing:	P 147	2.90	Guise
Thanks my good freend, holde, take thou this reward.	P 168	3.3	OldQn
Your grace was ill advisde to take them then,	P 174	3.9	Admral
And I will goe take order for his death.	P 252	4.50	Guise
[Cossin] <Cosin> <Cousin>, take twenty of our strongest guarde,	P 266	4.64	Charls
O let me pray before I take my death.	P 352	6.7	Seroun
Then take this with you.	P 360	6.15	Mntsrl
Murder the Hugonets, take those pedantes hence.	P 438	7.78	Guise
For if th'almighty take my brother hence,	P 469	8.19	Anjoy
Sirs, take him away and throw him in some ditch.	P 499	9.18	Guise
Come let us take his body hence.	P 564	11.29	QnMoth
Sirra, take him away.	P 621	12.34	Guise
Thanks to your Majestie, and so I take my leave.	P 749	15.7	Joyeux
Ile goe [take] <make> a walk/On purpose from the Court to meet	P 783	15.41	Mugern
And although you take out nothing but your owne, yet you put in	P 808	17.3	P Souldr
you will take upon you to be his, and tyll the ground that he	P 811	17.6	P Souldr
take possession (as I would I might) yet I meane to keepe you	P 813	17.8	P Souldr
Holde thee tall Souldier, take thee this and flye.	P 817	17.12	Guise
I kisse your graces hand, and take my leave,	P 868	17.63	Guise
Then sirs take your standings within this Chamber,	P 940	19.10	Capt
Come take him away.	P1106	20.16	1Mur
Take hence that damned villaine from my sight.	P1182	22.44	King
Shall take example by [his] <their> punishment,	P1186	22.48	King
Come Lords, take up the body of the King,	P1245	22.107	Navrre
thoughe you take out none but your owne treasure	Paris	ms 3,p390	P Souldr
ser where he is your landlorde you take upon you to be his |	Paris	ms10,p390	P Souldr
Hold thee tale soldier take the this and flye	Paris	ms18,p390	Guise
So thou wouldst smile and take me in thy <thine> armes.	Edw	1.1.9	Gavstn
And take possession of his house and goods:	Edw	1.1.203	Edward
Doth no man take exceptions at the slave?	Edw	1.2.25	MortSr
This certifie the Pope, away, take horsse.	Edw	1.2.38	ArchBp
My lord, will you take armes against the king?	Edw	1.2.39	Lncstr
And therefore sweete friend, take it patiently,	Edw	1.4.112	Edward
Here take my picture, and let me weare thine,	Edw	1.4.127	Edward
That he would take exceptions at my buttons,	Edw	2.1.47	Baldck
Take shipping and away to Scarborough,	Edw	2.4.5	Edward
Upon him souldiers, take away his weapons.	Edw	2.5.8	Warwck
Go souldiers take him hence, for by my sword,	Edw	2.5.20	Warwck
Goe, take the villaine, soldiers come away,	Edw	2.6.11	Warwck
God end them once, my lord I take my leave,	Edw	3.1.87	Queene
Or didst thou see my friend to take his death?	Edw	3.1.93	Edward
Go take that haughtie Mortimer to the tower,	Edw	3.1.252	Edward
Take him away, he prates. You Rice ap Howell,	Edw	4.6.73	Mortmr
We in meane while madam, must take advise,	Edw	4.6.77	Mortmr
Could not but take compassion of my state.	Edw	4.7.11	Edward
To take my life, my companie from me?	Edw	4.7.65	Edward
And take my heart, in reskew of my friends.	Edw	4.7.67	Edward
To let us take our farewell of his grace.	Edw	4.7.69	Spencr
Here humblie of your grace we take our leaves,	Edw	4.7.78	Baldck
Here, take my crowne, the life of Edward too,	Edw	5.1.57	Edward
Take it: what are you moovde, pitie you me?	Edw	5.1.102	Edward
And thus, most humbly do we take our leave.	Edw	5.1.124	Trussl
In any case, take heed of childish feare,	Edw	5.2.6	Mortmr
And for your sakes, a thousand wronges ile take,	Edw	5.3.43	Edward
sleepe, to take a quill/And blowe a little powder in his eares,	Edw	5.4.34	Ltborn
Take this, away, and never see me more.	Edw	5.4.43	Mortmr
The trumpets sound, I must go take my place.	Edw	5.4.72	Mortmr
Lord Mortimer, now take him to your charge.	Edw	5.4.81	Queene
And therefore let us take horse and away.	Edw	5.5.115	Matrvs
Excellent well, take this for thy rewarde.	Edw	5.5.117	Gurney
Well sirra, leave your jesting, and take these Guilders.	F 367	1.4.25	P Wagner
Here, take your Guilders [againe], I'le none of 'em.	F 371	1.4.29	P Robin
I good Wagner, take away the devill then.	F 377	1.4.35	P Robin
I, take it, and the devill give thee good of it <on't>.	F 502	2.1.114	Faust
<Here>, take this booke, <and> peruse it [thoroughly] <well>:	F 543	2.1.155	Mephst
<in mean time take this booke, peruse it throwly>,	F 717	(HC264)A	Lucifr
A plague take you, I thought you did not sneake up and downe	F 742	2.3.21	P Dick
And take some part of holy Peters feast,	F 777	2.3.56	2Chor
<faine> see the Pope/And take some part of holy Peters feast,	F 832	3.1.54	Mephst
here, take him to your charge,/And beare him streight to Ponte	F 964	3.1.186	Pope
Here, take his triple Crowne along with you,	F 970	3.1.192	Pope
And take our blessing Apostolicall.	F 973	3.1.195	Pope
now Friers take heed,/Lest Faustus make your shaven crownes to	F1006	3.2.26	Faust
Lord Raymond, take your seate, Friers attend,	F1010	3.2.30	Pope
Nay then take that.	F1067	3.2.87	Faust
take heed what you say, we looke not like cup-stealers I can	F1099	3.3.12	P Robin
A plague take you, I thought 'twas your knavery to take it	F1110	3.3.23	P Vintnr
plague take you, I thought 'twas your knavery to take it away:	F1111	3.3.24	P Vintnr
will it please you to take a shoulder of Mutton to supper, and	F1121	3.3.34	P Robin
And take his leave, laden with rich rewards.	F1345	4.2.21	Benvol
Take you the wealth, leave us the victorie.	F1347	4.2.23	Benvol
Hell take his soule, his body thus must fall.	F1363	4.2.39	Benvol
Go Belimothe, and take this caitife hence,	F1408	4.2.84	Faust
Take thou this other, dragge him through the woods,	F1410	4.2.86	Faust
more, take him, because I see thou hast a good minde to him.	F1461	4.4.5	P Faust
I, a plague take him, heere's some on's have cause to know him;	F1523	4.5.19	P HrsCsr
bad him take as much as he would for three-farthings; so he	F1528	4.5.24	P Carter
be wellcome for our mony, and we will pay for what we take:	F1612	4.6.55	P Robin

TAKE (cont.)
<Wee'l take our leaves>, and for this blessed sight . . F1704 (HC269)B 1Schol
holde, take these gilders. . . . . F App p.230 30 P Wagner
No, no, here take your gridirons againe. . . . . F App p.230 38 P Clown
wil you take sixe pence in your purse to pay for your supper, F App p.235 41 P Robin
Now my good Lord having done my duety, I humbly take my leave. F App p.238 86 P Faust
if thou likst him for fifty, take him. . . . . F App p.239 103 P Faust
and the Horsecourser I take it, a bottle of hey for his labour; F App p.241 165 P Faust
you take no delight in this, I have heard that great bellied F App p.242 4 P Faust
Roome, if thou take delight in impious warre, . . . Lucan, First Booke 21
(men say)/Began to smile and [tooke] <take> one foote away. Ovid's Elegies 1.1.8
[What] <That> if thy Mother take Dianas bowe, . . . Ovid's Elegies 1.1.11
While Mars doth take the Aonian harpe to play? . . . Ovid's Elegies 1.1.16
Take these away, where is thy <thine> honor then? . . Ovid's Elegies 1.2.38
Take, and receive each secret amorous glaunce. . . . Ovid's Elegies 1.4.18
When thou hast tasted, I will take the cup, . . . Ovid's Elegies 1.4.31
The gate halfe ope my bent side in will take. . . . Ovid's Elegies 1.6.4
Now frosty night her flight beginnes to take, . . . Ovid's Elegies 1.6.65
While rage is absent, take some friend the paynes. . . Ovid's Elegies 1.7.2
And take heed least he gets that love for nought. . . Ovid's Elegies 1.8.72
Take strife away, love doth not well endure. . . . Ovid's Elegies 1.8.96
Take from irrationall beasts a president, ... Ovid's Elegies 1.10.25
Take clustred grapes from an ore-laden vine, . . . Ovid's Elegies 1.10.55
How patiently hot irons they did take/In crooked [tramells] Ovid's Elegies 1.14.25
The greedy spirits take the best things first, . . . Ovid's Elegies 2.6.39
To take repulse, and cause her shew my lust? . . . Ovid's Elegies 2.7.26
Corinna meanes, and dangerous wayes to take. . . . Ovid's Elegies 2.11.8
On labouring women thou doest pitty take, ... Ovid's Elegies 2.13.19
Be welcome to her, gladly let her take thee, . . . Ovid's Elegies 2.15.3
Is by Evadne thought to take such flame, ... Ovid's Elegies 3.5.41
Can deafe [eares] <yeares> take delight when Phemius sings,/Or Ovid's Elegies 3.6.61
To take it in her hand and play with it. . . . . Ovid's Elegies 3.6.74
What man will now take liberall arts in hand, . . . Ovid's Elegies 3.7.1
When bad fates take good men, I am forbod, ... Ovid's Elegies 3.8.35
Though it was morning, did he take his flight. . . . Hero and Leander 2.102
Me in thy bed and maiden bosome take, ... Hero and Leander 2.248

TAKEN
Your Grace hath taken order by Theridamas, ... 1Tamb 1.1.46 Meandr
fill Persepolis/With Affrike Captaines, taken in the field: 1Tamb 1.1.142 Ceneus
Thou seest they have taken halfe our goods. . . . Jew 1.2.176 1Jew
And of me onely have they taken all. . . . . . Jew 1.2.179 Barab
That the Guise hath taken armes against the King, . . P 901 18.2 Navrre
My unckles taken prisoner by the Scots. . . . . Edw 2.2.115 Mortmr
Seeing he is taken prisoner in his warres? . . . . Edw 2.2.119 Mortmr
Mine unckles taken prisoner by the Scots. . . . . Edw 2.2.142 Mortmr
Hearing that you had taken Gaveston, ... Edw 2.5.35 Arundl
is it not enough/That we have taken him, but must we now/Leave Edw 2.5.84 Warwck
A would have taken the king away perforce, ... Edw 5.4.84 Souldr
I have taken up his holinesse privy chamber for our use>. F 806 (HC265)A P Mephst
that you have taken no pleasure in those sights; therefor I F1566 4.6.9 P Faust
Or waters tops with the warme south-winde taken. . . Ovid's Elegies 1.7.56
Hunters leave taken beasts, pursue the chase, . . . Ovid's Elegies 2.9.9

TAKES
by expedition/Advantage takes of your unreadinesse. . . 1Tamb 4.1.39 Capol
For Tamburlaine takes truce with al the world. . . . 1Tamb 5.1.529 Tamb
Which as I heare one [Shekius] <Shekins> takes it ill, . P 404 7.44 Ramus
For now that Paris takes the Guises parte, ... P 896 17.91 King
And takes his vantage on Religion, ... P 924 18.25 Navrre
Which being caught, strikes him that takes it dead, . . Edw 1.4.222 Mortmr
And therefore being pursued, it takes the aire: . . . Edw 2.2.25 Lncstr
The like oath Penbrooke takes. . . . . Edw 2.2.108 Penbrk
blasted, Aruns takes/And it inters with murmurs dolorous, Lucan, First Booke 605
Who covets lawfull things takes leaves from woods, . . Ovid's Elegies 2.19.31
Victorious Perseus a wingd steedes back takes. . . . Ovid's Elegies 3.11.24
An Altar takes mens incense, and oblation, ... Ovid's Elegies 3.12.9

TAKEST
Joyes with uncertaine faith thou takest and brings. . . Ovid's Elegies 2.9.50
Why takest increasing grapes from Vine-trees full? . . Ovid's Elegies 2.14.23

TAKING
Taking instructions from thy flowing eies: . . . . 1Tamb 5.1.146 Tamb
Taking advantage of your slender power, ... 2Tamb 2.2.26 1Msngr
For taking hence my faire Zenocrate. . . . . . . 2Tamb 2.4.101 Tamb
and as I was taking my choyce, I heard a rumbling in the house; Jew 3.1.20 P Pilia
Long was he taking leave, and loath to go, ... Hero and Leander 2.93

TAL
Hold ye tal souldiers, take ye Queens apeece/(I meane such 2Tamb 4.3.70 Tamb

TALE (Homograph)
A wofull tale bids Dido to unfould, ... Dido 2.1.114 Aeneas
Lest you be mov'd too much with my sad tale. . . . Dido 2.1.125 Aeneas
and had not we/Fought manfully, I had not told this tale: Dido 2.1.271 Aeneas
Troian, thy ruthfull tale hath made me sad: . . . . Dido 2.1.301 Dido
To be well stor'd with such a winters tale? . . . . Dido 3.3.59 Aeneas
That slayest me with thy harsh and hellish tale, . . . Dido 5.1.217 Dido
she were fitter for a tale of love/Then to be tired out with Jew 1.2.369 Mthias
Why, wantst thou any of thy tale? . . . . Jew 4.3.19 P Barab
Hold thee tale soldier take the this and flye . . . Paris ms18,p390 Guise
Yet will it melt, ere I have done my tale. . . . . Edw 5.5.55 Edward
I'le tell you the bravest tale how a Conjurer serv'd me; you F1521 4.5.17 P Carter
Or if he loves, thy tale breedes his misfortune. . . Ovid's Elegies 2.2.54
As she to heare his tale, left off her running. . . . Hero and Leander 1.418
Thereat smilde Neptune, and then told a tale, . . . Hero and Leander 2.193
Ere halfe this tale was done,/Aye me, Leander cryde, . . Hero and Leander 2.201

TALENT (See TALLENTS)

TALES

For many tales goe of that Cities fall, Dido 2.1.108 Dido
And tell my soule mor tales of bleeding ruth? 1Tamb 5.1.342 Zenoc
Who in my wealth wud tell me winters tales, Jew 2.1.25 Barab
[Tush] <No>, these are trifles, and meere old wives Tales. F 524 2.1.136 Faust
bringing newes/Of present war, made many lies and tales. Lucan, First Booke 468
On tell-tales neckes thou seest the linke-knitt chaines, Ovid's Elegies 2.2.41

TALEUS

Tell me Taleus, wherfore should I flye? P 366 7.6 Ramus
Sweet Taleus stay. P 370 7.10 Ramus
Tis Taleus, Ramus bedfellow. P 372 7.12 Retes

TALK

mighty Turkish Emperor/To talk with one so base as Tamburlaine? 1Tamb 3.3.88 Fesse
Hearst thou Anippe, how thy drudge doth talk, 1Tamb 3.3.182 Zenoc
The ages that shall talk of Tamburlain, 1Tamb 4.2.95 Tamb
They will talk still my Lord, if you doe not bridle them. 2Tamb 5.1.146 P Amyras

TALK'D

But wherefore talk'd Don Lodowick with you? Jew 2.3.150 Mthias
Tush man, we talk'd of Diamonds, not of Abigal. Jew 2.3.151 Barab

TALKE

Why talke we not together hand in hand? Dido 1.1.245 Aeneas
No more my child, now talke another while, Dido 3.1.26 Dido
And cannot talke nor thinke of ought but him: Dido 3.2.73 Juno
Lords goe before, we two must talke alone. Dido 3.3.9 Dido
We two will talke alone, what words be these? Dido 3.3.12 Iarbus
To be partakers of our honey talke. Dido 4.4.54 Dido
Iarbus, talke not of Aeneas, let him goe, Dido 5.1.283 Dido
His talke much sweeter than the Muses song, 1Tamb 3.2.50 Zenoc
Shall talke how I have handled Bajazeth. 1Tamb 4.2.97 Tamb
No talke of running, I tell you sir. 2Tamb 1.2.16 Almeda
Many will talke of Title to a Crowne: Jew Prol.18 Machvl
The Diamond that I talke of, ne'r was foild: Jew 2.3.56 Barab
and my talke with him was [but]/About the borrowing of a booke Jew 2.3.155 Mthias
Yet through the key-hole will he talke to her, Jew 2.3.263 Barab
And mine you have, yet let me talke to her; Jew 2.3.300 Barab
Talke not of racing downe your City wals, Jew 3.5.21 Basso
enough, and therfore talke not to me of your Counting-house: Jew 4.3.36 P Pilia
We will goe talke more of this within. P1138 21.32 Dumain
Kinde wordes, and mutuall talke, makes our greefe greater, Edw 1.4.133 Edward
He will but talke with him and send him backe. Edw 2.5.59 Arundl
Sweete sonne come hither, I must talke with thee. Edw 5.2.87 Queene
Souldiers, let me but talke to him one worde. Edw 5.3.53 Kent
[Is not thy common talke sound Aphorismes]? F 47 1.1.19A Faust
<How, a wife? I prithee Faustus talke not of a wife>. F 530 (HC261)A P Mephst
Talke not of Paradice or <nor> Creation, but marke the <this> F 659 2.2.108 P Lucifr
<talke of the divel, and nothing else: come away>. F 660 (HC263)A P Lucifr
into matters, as other men, if they were disposed to talke. F 741 2.3.20 P Robin
Talke not of me, but save your selves and depart. F1869 5.2.73 P Faust
What should I talke of mens corne reapt by force, Lucan, First Booke 318
By chaunce I heard her talke, these words she sayd/While Ovid's Elegies 1.8.21
Would Tithon might but talke of thee a while, Ovid's Elegies 1.13.35
A little fild thee, and for love of talke, Ovid's Elegies 2.6.29
To sit, and talke with thee I hether came, Ovid's Elegies 3.2.3
With privy signes, and talke dissembling truths? Ovid's Elegies 3.10.24
And up againe, and close beside him swim,/And talke of love: Hero and Leander 2.191

TALKES

Thou villaine, wherfore talkes thou of a king, Edw 1.4.28 Mortmr
Seeing that he talkes thus of my mariage day? Edw 2.1.69 Neece
Mortimer, who talkes of Mortimer, Edw 4.7.37 Edward

TALKST

Lancaster, why talkst thou to the slave? Edw 2.5.19 Warwck
Thou calst on <talkst of> Christ contrary to thy promise. F 643 2.2.92 Lucifr

TALKT

As if he heare I have but talkt with you, Edw 2.4.54 Queene

TALL (See also TAL, TALE)

Of stature tall, and straightly fashioned, 1Tamb 2.1.7 Menaph
Inhabited with tall and sturdy men, 2Tamb 1.1.27 Orcan
Goe, goe tall stripling, fight you for us both, 2Tamb 4.1.33 Calyph
So, now they have shew'd themselves to be tall fellowes. Jew 3.2.7 Barab
base slave as he should be saluted by such a tall man as I am, Jew 4.2.10 P Pilia
Holde thee tall Souldier, take thee this and flye. P 817 17.12 Guise
do ye see yonder tall fellow in the round slop, hee has kild F App p.230 47 P Clown
Like to a tall oake in a fruitfull field, Lucan, First Booke 137
The Cedar tall spoyld of his barke retaines. Ovid's Elegies 1.14.12
If she be tall, shees like an Amazon, Ovid's Elegies 2.4.33
And coole gales shake the tall trees leavy spring, Ovid's Elegies 2.16.36
Comely tall was she, comely tall shee's yet. Ovid's Elegies 3.3.8
A stately builded ship, well rig'd and tall, Hero and Leander 1.225

TALLENTS

dooth gastly death/With greedy tallents gripe my bleeding hart, 1Tamb 2.7.49 Cosroe

TAMBURLAIN

Whom seekst thou Persean? I am Tamburlain. 1Tamb 1.2.153 Tamb
Nor thee, nor them, thrice noble Tamburlain, 1Tamb 1.2.249 Therid
When Tamburlain and brave Theridamas/Have met us by the river 1Tamb 2.1.62 Cosroe
Tamburlain, now whet thy winged sword/And lift thy lofty arme 1Tamb 2.3.51 Cosroe
Bloody and insatiate Tamburlain. 1Tamb 2.7.11 Cosroe
And that made me to joine with Tamburlain, 1Tamb 2.7.30 Therid
If Tamburlain be plac'd in Persea. 1Tamb 2.7.39 Usumc
For wil and shall best fitteth Tamburlain, 1Tamb 3.3.41 Tamb
Puissant, renowmed and mighty Tamburlain, 1Tamb 3.3.96 Techel
Untill I bring this sturdy Tamburlain, 1Tamb 3.3.114 Bajzth

TAMBURLAIN (cont.)			
No Tamburlain, though now thou gat the best,	1Tamb	3.3.222	Zabina
Shall Tamburlain extend his puisant arme.	1Tamb	3.3.247	Tamb
What, thinkst thou Tamburlain esteems thy gold?	1Tamb	3.3.262	Tamb
And be the foot-stoole of great Tamburlain,	1Tamb	4.2.14	Tamb
The ages that shall talk of Tamburlain,	1Tamb	4.2.95	Tamb
And squease it in the cup of Tamburlain.	1Tamb	4.4.20	Bajzth
The wrath of Tamburlain, and power of warres.	1Tamb	5.1.44	Govnr
Hel, death, Tamburlain, Hell.	1Tamb	5.1.317	P Zabina
(Renowmed Tamburlain) to whom all kings/Of force must yeeld	1Tamb	5.1.480	Souldn
The generall welcomes Tamburlain receiv'd,	2Tamb	Prol.1	Prolog
My soveraigne Lord, renowmed Tamburlain,	2Tamb	1.2.7	Almeda
Sweet Tamburlain, when wilt thou leave these armes/And save thy	2Tamb	1.3.9	Zenoc
My Lord the great and mighty Tamburlain,	2Tamb	1.3.113	Therid
T'incounter with the cruell Tamburlain,	2Tamb	2.2.5	Orcan
And if thou pitiest Tamburlain the great,	2Tamb	2.4.117	Tamb
Scourging the pride of cursed Tamburlain.	2Tamb	3.1.37	Callap
All which will joine against this Tamburlain,	2Tamb	3.1.61	Soria
sir, for being a king, for Tamburlain came up of nothing.	2Tamb	3.1.73	P Almeda
And worthy sonnes of Tamburlain the great.	2Tamb	3.2.92	Tamb
Knowing two kings, the [friends] <friend> to Tamburlain,	2Tamb	3.3.13	Therid
If thou withstand the friends of Tamburlain.	2Tamb	3.3.19	Techel
Were you that are the friends of Tamburlain,	2Tamb	3.3.35	Capt
The name of mightie Tamburlain is spread:	2Tamb	3.4.66	Therid
Whet all your swords to mangle Tamburlain,	2Tamb	3.5.15	Callap
So famous as is mighty Tamburlain:	2Tamb	3.5.84	Tamb
No, we wil meet thee slavish Tamburlain.	2Tamb	3.5.170	Orcan
Whose matter is the flesh of Tamburlain,	2Tamb	4.1.113	Tamb
Now you shal feele the strength of Tamburlain,	2Tamb	4.1.135	Tamb
As you (ye slaves) in mighty Tamburlain.	2Tamb	4.3.11	Tamb
But Tamburlain, in Lymnasphaltis lake,	2Tamb	5.1.115	Govnr
Vild Tyrant, barbarous bloody Tamburlain.	2Tamb	5.1.133	Trebiz
Rather lend me thy weapon Tamburlain,	2Tamb	5.1.142	Jrslem
let this wound appease/The mortall furie of great Tamburlain.	2Tamb	5.1.154	Govnr
Or vengeance on the head of Tamburlain,	2Tamb	5.1.195	Tamb
He cannot heare the voice of Tamburlain,	2Tamb	5.1.199	Tamb
What is it dares distemper Tamburlain?	2Tamb	5.1.219	Techel
Yet make them feele the strength of Tamburlain,	2Tamb	5.3.37	Usumc
TAMBURLAINE			
Where you shall heare the Scythian Tamburlaine,	1Tamb	Prol.4	Prolog
Which is (God knowes) about that Tamburlaine,	1Tamb	1.1.30	Mycet
Of Tamburlaine, that sturdie Scythian thiefe,	1Tamb	1.1.36	Meandr
Have sworne the death of wicked Tamburlaine.	1Tamb	1.1.64	Mycet
But Tamburlaine, and that Tartarian rout,	1Tamb	1.1.71	Therid
and this curtle-axe/Are adjuncts more beseeming Tamburlaine.	1Tamb	1.2.43	Tamb
So in his Armour looketh Tamburlaine:	1Tamb	1.2.54	Techel
That even to death will follow Tamburlaine.	1Tamb	1.2.59	Usumc
We will report but well of Tamburlaine.	1Tamb	1.2.81	Magnet
Thy person is more woorth to Tamburlaine,	1Tamb	1.2.90	Tamb
Where is this Scythian Tamburlaine?	1Tamb	1.2.152	Therid
Tamburlaine?	1Tamb	1.2.154	Therid
Than Tamburlaine be slaine or overcome.	1Tamb	1.2.177	Tamb
And sit with Tamburlaine in all his majestie.	1Tamb	1.2.209	Tamb
No, but the trustie friend of Tamburlaine.	1Tamb	1.2.227	Tamb
We yeeld unto thee happie Tamburlaine.	1Tamb	1.2.257	Agidas
And valiant Tamburlaine, the man of fame,	1Tamb	2.1.2	Cosroe
Should make the world subdued to Tamburlaine.	1Tamb	2.1.30	Menaph
In faire Persea noble Tamburlaine/Shall be my Regent, and	1Tamb	2.1.48	Cosroe
And such shall wait on worthy Tamburlaine.	1Tamb	2.1.60	Cosroe
To seeke revenge on me and Tamburlaine.	1Tamb	2.1.67	Cosroe
On this same theevish villaine Tamburlaine.	1Tamb	2.2.3	Mycet
And kill proud Tamburlaine with point of sword.	1Tamb	2.2.12	Mycet
Fit Souldiers for the wicked Tamburlaine.	1Tamb	2.2.24	Meandr
He that can take or slaughter Tamburlaine,	1Tamb	2.2.30	Meandr
And as we know) remaines with Tamburlaine,	1Tamb	2.2.36	Meandr
Now worthy Tamburlaine, have I reposde,	1Tamb	2.3.1	Cosroe
To roialise the deedes of Tamburlaine:	1Tamb	2.3.8	Tamb
Thou art no match for mightie Tamburlaine.	1Tamb	2.4.40	Tamb
O Gods, is this Tamburlaine the thiefe,	1Tamb	2.4.41	Mycet
Even by the mighty hand of Tamburlaine,	1Tamb	2.5.3	Tamb
And none shall keepe the crowne but Tamburlaine:	1Tamb	2.5.7	Cosroe
And now Lord Tamburlaine, my brothers Campe/I leave to thee,	1Tamb	2.5.38	Cosroe
And till thou overtake me Tamburlaine,	1Tamb	2.5.44	Cosroe
Then shalt thou see the Scythian Tamburlaine,	1Tamb	2.5.97	Tamb
Barbarous and bloody Tamburlaine,	1Tamb	2.7.1	Cosroe
And that made us, the friends of Tamburlaine,	1Tamb	2.7.34	Techel
Theridamas and Tamburlaine, I die,	1Tamb	2.7.51	Cosroe
Tamburlaine, Tamburlaine.	1Tamb	2.7.57	All
If you but say that Tamburlaine shall raigne.	1Tamb	2.7.63	Tamb
Long live Tamburlaine, and raigne in Asia.	1Tamb	2.7.64	All
and the Easterne theeves/Under the conduct of one Tamburlaine,	1Tamb	3.1.3	Bajzth
When your offensive rape by Tamburlaine,	1Tamb	3.2.6	Agidas
That I may live and die with Tamburlaine.	1Tamb	3.2.24	Zenoc
With Tamburlaine?	1Tamb	3.2.25	Agidas
And speake of Tamburlaine as he deserves.	1Tamb	3.2.36	Zenoc
So lookes my Lordly love, faire Tamburlaine.	1Tamb	3.2.49	Zenoc
If I were matcht with mightie Tamburlaine.	1Tamb	3.2.55	Zenoc
T'incounter with the strength of Tamburlaine.	1Tamb	3.3.7	Tamb
shall curse the time/That Tamburlaine set foot in Affrica.	1Tamb	3.3.60	Tamb
And dar'st thou bluntly call me Tamburlaine?	1Tamb	3.3.74	Tamb
mighty Turkish Emperor/To talk with one so base as Tamburlaine?	1Tamb	3.3.88	Fesse
The onely Paragon of Tamburlaine,	1Tamb	3.3.119	Tamb

TAMBURLAINE (cont.)			
Thou knowest not (foolish hardy Tamburlaine)/What tis to meet	1Tamb	3.3.145	Bajzth
that am betroath'd/Unto the great and mighty Tamburlaine?	1Tamb	3.3.170	Zenoc
To Tamburlaine the great Tartarian thiefe?	1Tamb	3.3.171	Zabina
lie weltring in their blood/And Tamburlaine is Lord of Affrica.	1Tamb	3.3.202	Zenoc
Yet set a ransome on me Tamburlaine.	1Tamb	3.3.261	Bajzth
did your greatnes see/The frowning lookes of fiery Tamburlaine,	1Tamb	4.1.13	2Msngr
I tell thee, were that Tamburlaine/As monsterous as Gorgon,	1Tamb	4.1.17	Souldn
But Tamburlaine, by expedition/Advantage takes of your	1Tamb	4.1.38	Capol
Base villain, vassall, slave to Tamburlaine:	1Tamb	4.2.19	Tamb
Great Tamburlaine, great in my overthrow,	1Tamb	4.2.75	Bajzth
My Lord it is the bloody Tamburlaine,	1Tamb	4.3.11	Souldn
That Tamburlaine shall rue the day, the hower,	1Tamb	4.3.38	Souldn
Let Tamburlaine for his offences feele/Such plagues as heaven	1Tamb	4.3.44	Arabia
And Tamburlaine, my spirit doth foresee/The utter ruine of thy	1Tamb	4.3.59	Arabia
Now Tamburlaine, the mightie Souldane comes,	1Tamb	4.3.63	Souldn
Honor still waight on happy Tamburlaine:	1Tamb	4.4.85	Zenoc
for us to see them, and for Tamburlaine onely to enjoy them.	1Tamb	4.4.111	P Techel
You that have martcht with happy Tamburlaine,	1Tamb	4.4.121	Tamb
And through the eies and eares of Tamburlaine,	1Tamb	5.1.53	2Virgn
That in this terrour Tamburlaine may live.	1Tamb	5.1.299	Bajzth
Tamburlaine, Tamburlaine.	1Tamb	5.1.316	P Zabina
Ah Tamburlaine, wert thou the cause of this/That tearm'st	1Tamb	5.1.335	Zenoc
And ruthlesse cruelty of Tamburlaine.	1Tamb	5.1.346	Anippe
Ah Tamburlaine, my love, sweet Tamburlaine,	1Tamb	5.1.355	Zenoc
Must Tamburlaine by their resistlesse powers,	1Tamb	5.1.397	Zenoc
And such are objects fit for Tamburlaine.	1Tamb	5.1.475	Tamb
and dominions/That late the power of Tamburlaine subdewed:	1Tamb	5.1.509	Tamb
For Tamburlaine takes truce with al the world.	1Tamb	5.1.529	Tamb
Proud Tamburlaine, that now in Asia,	2Tamb	1.1.16	Gazell
Since Tamburlaine hath mustred all his men,	2Tamb	1.1.46	Gazell
forces for the hot assaults/Proud Tamburlaine intends Natolia.	2Tamb	1.1.53	Gazell
and Danes/[Feares] <feare> not Orcanes, but great Tamburlaine:	2Tamb	1.1.59	Orcan
Yet scarse enough t'encounter Tamburlaine.	2Tamb	1.1.66	Orcan
All Asia is in Armes with Tamburlaine.	2Tamb	1.1.72	Orcan
All Affrike is in Armes with Tamburlaine.	2Tamb	1.1.76	Orcan
To stay my comming gainst proud Tamburlaine.	2Tamb	1.1.163	Orcan
Yet here detain'd by cruell Tamburlaine.	2Tamb	1.2.4	Callap
Your Keeper under Tamburlaine the great,	2Tamb	1.2.68	Almeda
Even straight: and farewell cursed Tamburlaine.	2Tamb	1.2.77	Callap
Not martiall as the sons of Tamburlaine.	2Tamb	1.3.22	Tamb
That never look'd on man but Tamburlaine.	2Tamb	1.3.34	Tamb
Or els you are not sons of Tamburlaine.	2Tamb	1.3.64	Tamb
And not the issue of great Tamburlaine:	2Tamb	1.3.70	Tamb
Magnificent and peerlesse Tamburlaine,	2Tamb	1.3.129	Usumc
And mighty Tamburlaine, our earthly God,	2Tamb	1.3.138	Techel
hath followed long/The martiall sword of mighty Tamburlaine,	2Tamb	3.1.28	Callap
Greek, is writ/This towne being burnt by Tamburlaine the great,	2Tamb	3.2.17	Calyph
Villain, art thou the sonne of Tamburlaine,	2Tamb	3.2.95	Tamb
Fit for the followers of great Tamburlaine.	2Tamb	3.2.144	Tamb
Thus have wee martcht Northwarde from Tamburlaine,	2Tamb	3.3.1	Therid
Thou shalt with us to Tamburlaine the great,	2Tamb	3.4.39	Techel
But Lady goe with us to Tamburlaine,	2Tamb	3.4.45	Therid
Here at Alepo with an hoste of men/Lies Tamburlaine, this king	2Tamb	3.5.4	2Msngr
Then welcome Tamburlaine unto thy death.	2Tamb	3.5.52	Callap
But Shepheards issue, base borne Tamburlaine,	2Tamb	3.5.77	Orcan
As ye shal curse the byrth of Tamburlaine.	2Tamb	3.5.89	Tamb
But Tamburlaine, first thou shalt kneele to us/And humbly crave	2Tamb	3.5.108	Orcan
any Element/Shal shrowde thee from the wrath of Tamburlaine.	2Tamb	3.5.127	Tamb
No Tamburlaine, hee shall not be put to that exigent, I warrant	2Tamb	3.5.156	P Soria
al this aery region/Cannot containe the state of Tamburlaine.	2Tamb	4.1.120	Tamb
That will not see the strength of Tamburlaine,	2Tamb	4.1.133	Tamb
or by speach I heare/Immortall Jove say, Cease my Tamburlaine,	2Tamb	4.1.199	Tamb
And such a Coachman as great Tamburlaine?	2Tamb	4.3.4	Tamb
That Tamburlaine may pitie our distresse,	2Tamb	5.1.27	1Citzn
Before I bide the wrath of Tamburlaine.	2Tamb	5.1.42	2Citzn
and great Alexander/Have rode in triumph, triumphs Tamburlaine,	2Tamb	5.1.70	Tamb
Shouldst thou have entred, cruel Tamburlaine:	2Tamb	5.1.102	Govnr
Do all thy wurst, nor death, nor Tamburlaine,	2Tamb	5.1.112	Govnr
Where Tamburlaine with all his armie lies,	2Tamb	5.2.6	Callap
never sepulchre/Shall grace that base-borne Tyrant Tamburlaine.	2Tamb	5.2.18	Amasia
My Viceroies bondage under Tamburlaine,	2Tamb	5.2.21	Callap
thou that hast seene/Millions of Turkes perish by Tamburlaine,	2Tamb	5.2.25	Callap
To triumph over cursed Tamburlaine.	2Tamb	5.2.30	Callap
To joine with you against this Tamburlaine.	2Tamb	5.2.35	Amasia
And pull proud Tamburlaine upon his knees,	2Tamb	5.2.40	Amasia
Captaine, the force of Tamburlaine is great,	2Tamb	5.2.42	Callap
Cymerian spirits/Gives battile gainst the heart of Tamburlaine.	2Tamb	5.3.9	Therid
And seeks to conquer mighty Tamburlaine,	2Tamb	5.3.43	Tamb
That thus invie the health of Tamburlaine.	2Tamb	5.3.53	Tamb
For Tamburlaine, the Scourge of God must die.	2Tamb	5.3.248	Tamb
TAMBURLAINES			
He will with Tamburlaines destruction/Redeeme you from this	1Tamb	3.2.33	Agidas
Your Highnesse knowes for Tamburlaines repaire,	2Tamb	2.1.14	Fredrk
TAMBURLAINS			
That Tamburlains intollorable wrath/May be suppresst by our	2Tamb	5.1.8	Maxim
TAMBURLANE			
Tamburlane) as I could willingly feed upon thy blood-raw hart.	1Tamb	4.4.11	P Bajzth
TAM'D			
The headstrong Jades of Thrace, Alcides tam'd,	2Tamb	4.3.12	Tamb
We vanquish, and tread tam'd love under feete,	Ovid's Elegies		3.10.5
TAME			
To tame the pride of this presumptuous Beast,	1Tamb	4.3.15	Souldn

TANAISE			
even to the utmost verge/Of Europe, or the shore of Tanaise,	Edw	4.2.30	Queene
TANDEM			
The motto: Aeque tandem.	Edw	2.2.20	Mortmr
And Aeque tandem shall that canker crie, ...	Edw	2.2.41	Edward
TANE (See also TAINE)			
Yet hath she tane away my oares and masts, . . .	Dido	5.1.60	Aeneas
The jewels and the treasure we have tane/Shall be reserv'd, and	1Tamb	1.2.2	Tamb
And have a thousand horsmen tane away?	1Tamb	2.2.6	Mycet
Tane from Aleppo, Soldino, Tripoly, ...	2Tamb	3.1.58	Soria
Where wee'll attend the respit you have tane, . . .	Jew	1.2.30	Calym
pleasures of swift-footed time/Have tane their flight, .	Jew	2.1.8	Barab
yet not appeare/In forty houres after it is tane. . .	Jew	3.4.72	Barab
A hundred for a hundred I have tane;	Jew	4.1.54	Barab
[When Faustus had with pleasure tane the view]/[Of rarest	F1138	3.3.51A	3Chor
Two tane away, thy labor will be lesse:	Ovid's Elegies		1.1.4
But thou my crowne, from sad haires tane away, . . .	Ovid's Elegies		1.6.67
Least they should fly, being tane, the tirant play. . .	Ovid's Elegies		1.8.70
Achilles burnd Briseis being tane away:	Ovid's Elegies		1.9.33
What helpes my hast: what to have tane small rest? . .	Ovid's Elegies		3.5.9
TANTALUS			
and fruite flying touch/Tantalus seekes, his long tongues gaine	Ovid's Elegies		2.2.44
And blabbing Tantalus in mid-waters put.	Ovid's Elegies		3.11.30
Like to the tree of Tantalus she fled, ...	Hero and Leander		2.75
TANTARAS			
(Perdicas) and I feare as litle their tara, tantaras, their	2Tamb	4.1.68	P Calyph
TANTI			
Rakt up in embers of their povertie,/Tanti:	Edw	1.1.22	Gavstn
TAPERLIGHTS			
For these thy superstitious taperlights, ...	Edw	1.4.98	Edward
T'APPEASE			
Epeus pine-tree Horse/A sacrifize t'appease Minervas wrath:	Dido	2.1.163	Aeneas
T'appease my wrath, or els Ile torture thee, ...	2Tamb	3.5.122	Tamb
T'APPEAZE			
T'appeaze the wrath of their offended king. . . .	Edw	3.1.210	Edward
TARA			
(Perdicas) and I feare as litle their tara, tantaras, their	2Tamb	4.1.68	P Calyph
TARA TANTARAS			
(Perdicas) and I feare as litle their tara, tantaras, their	2Tamb	4.1.68	P Calyph
TARBELS			
Where Tarbels winding shoares imbrace the sea, ...	Lucan, First Booke		422
TARDIE			
Is swifter than the wind, whose tardie plumes, ...	Hero and Leander		2.115
O that these tardie armes of mine were wings, ...	Hero and Leander		2.205
TARE			
about thee into Familiars, and make them tare thee in peeces.	F 363	1.4.21	P Wagner
TARGET			
A target bore: bloud sprinckled was his right. . . .	Ovid's Elegies		3.7.16
TARGETIERS			
Browne bils, and targetiers, foure hundred strong, . .	Edw	3.1.37	SpncrP
TARGETS			
gods hung up/Such as peace yeelds; wormeaten leatherne targets,	Lucan, First Booke		243
TARPEIAN			
that guardst/Roomes mighty walles built on Tarpeian rocke,	Lucan, First Booke		198
TARRIE			
Away, tarrie no answer, but be gon.	Edw	3.1.173	Edward
TARRIES			
theres a Gentleman tarries to have his horse, and he would have	F App	p.233 6	P Rafe
Why she alone in empty bed oft tarries.	Ovid's Elegies		2.19.42
TARRY			
For happily we shall not tarry here:	Jew	1.2.16	Calym
Be sedulous, let no stay cause thee tarry.	Ovid's Elegies		1.11.8
TARTAR			
The scum and tartar of the Elements, ...	2Tamb	4.1.124	Tamb
TARTARIAN			
But Tamburlaine, and that Tartarian rout, ...	1Tamb	1.1.71	Therid
Whose tops are covered with Tartarian thieves, ...	1Tamb	2.2.16	Meandr
Brave horses, bred on the white Tartarian hils: . . .	1Tamb	3.3.151	Tamb
To Tamburlaine the great Tartarian thiefe?	1Tamb	3.3.171	Zabina
For every fell and stout Tartarian Stead/That stampt on others	1Tamb	5.1.330	Zenoc
Now scaldes his soule in the Tartarian streames, . . .	2Tamb	2.3.18	Orcan
TARTARS			
Now Turkes and Tartars shake their swords at thee, . . .	1Tamb	1.1.16	Cosroe
A hundreth <hundred> Tartars shall attend on thee, . . .	1Tamb	1.2.93	Tamb
And while the base borne Tartars take it up, ...	1Tamb	2.2.65	Meandr
the Tartars and the Easterne theeves/Under the conduct of one	1Tamb	3.1.2	Bajzth
Tartars and Perseans shall inhabit there, ...	2Tamb	5.1.163	Tamb
TARTARY			
That fill the midst of farthest Tartary, ...	2Tamb	4.1.43	Amyras
TASK			
pray you let him stay, a greater [task]/Fits Menaphon, than	1Tamb	1.1.87	Cosroe
TASKE			
when by Junoes taske/He had before lookt Pluto in the face.	Lucan, First Booke		575
And craves his taske, and seekes to be at fight. . .	Ovid's Elegies		3.6.68
Impos'd upon her lover such a taske, ...	Hero and Leander		1.429
TASKES			
to your taskes a while/And take such fortune as your fellowes	2Tamb	5.1.136	Tamb
TAST			
If hee gives thee what first himselfe did tast, . . .	Ovid's Elegies		1.4.33
Even as delicious meat is to the tast, ...	Hero and Leander		1.63
But they that dayly tast neat wine, despise it. . . .	Hero and Leander		1.261
TASTE			
The christall springs whose taste illuminates/Refined eies with	2Tamb	2.4.22	Tamb

TASTE (cont.)			
Affoords no hearbs, whose taste may poison thee,	2Tamb	4.2.9	Olymp
Pray let me taste first.	Jew	3.4.87	P Ithimr
Downe to the Celler, taste of all my wines.	Jew	5.5.7	Barab
Should for their conscience taste such rutheles ends.	P 214	4.12	Charls
Here, now taste yee these, they should be good, for they come	F1576	4.6.19	P Faust
And now must taste hels paines perpetually.	F1895	5.2.99	BdAngl
Nay, thou must feele them, taste the smart of all:	F1922	5.2.126	BdAngl
here they be madam, wilt please you taste on them.	F App	p.242 15	P Faust
That cannot Venus mutuall pleasure taste.	Ovid's Elegies		2.3.2
Thy mouth to taste of many meates did balke.	Ovid's Elegies		2.6.30
TASTED			
That never tasted of the Passeover,	Jew	2.3.302	Barab
And tasted the eternall Joyes of heaven,	F 306	1.3.78	Mephst
And trust me, they are the sweetest grapes that e're I tasted.	F1587	4.6.30	P Lady
they be the best grapes that ere I tasted in my life before.	F App	p.242 26	P Duchss
When thou hast tasted, I will take the cup,	Ovid's Elegies		1.4.31
TATIUS			
Perhaps the Sabines rude, when Tatius raignde,	Ovid's Elegies		1.8.39
TATTERED (See also TOTTER'D)			
As doth this water from my tattered robes:	Edw	5.5.67	Edward
TAUGHT			
My cosin Helen taught it me in Troy.	Dido	3.1.28	Cupid
Who taught thee this?	Jew	3.3.66	1Fryar
And such a King whom practise long hath taught,	P 458	8.8	Anjoy
Your minion Gaveston hath taught you this.	Edw	2.2.149	Lncstr
No where can they be taught but in the bed,	Ovid's Elegies		2.5.61
raught/Ill waies by rough seas wondring waves first taught,	Ovid's Elegies		2.11.2
First Ceres taught the seede in fields to swell,	Ovid's Elegies		3.9.11
Who taught thee Rhethoricke to deceive a maid?	Hero and Leander		1.338
Which taught him all that elder lovers know,	Hero and Leander		2.69
TAUNTED			
men (Dido except)/Have taunted me in these opprobrious termes,	Dido	3.3.27	Iarbus
TAUNTES			
To practize tauntes and bitter tyrannies?	2Tamb	4.3.56	Jrslem
TAVERNE (See also TABERNE)			
Or if thou't go but to the Taverne with me, I'le give thee	F 747	2.3.26	P Robin
pray where's the cup you stole from the Taverne?	F1098	3.3.11	P Vintnr
TAV'RON			
And Marius head above cold Tav'ron peering/(His grave broke	Lucan, First Booke		581
TAX'D			
Are strangers with your tribute to be tax'd?	Jew	1.2.59	Barab
TAXES			
These taxes and afflictions are befal'ne,	Jew	1.2.65	Govnr
TE			
Si bene quid de te merui, fuit aut tibi quidquam/Dulce meum,	Dido	5.1.136	Dido
TEACH			
Doth teach us all to have aspyring minds:	1Tamb	2.7.20	Tamb
And I will teach thee how to charge thy foe,	2Tamb	1.3.45	Tamb
That meane to teach you rudiments of war:	2Tamb	3.2.54	Tamb
Ile teach you how to make the water mount,	2Tamb	3.2.85	Tamb
And see him lance his flesh to teach you all.	2Tamb	3.2.114	Tamb
Teach you my boyes to beare couragious minds,	2Tamb	3.2.143	Tamb
Stand up my boyes, and I wil teach ye arms,	2Tamb	4.1.103	Tamb
And I will teach [thee] that shall sticke by thee:	Jew	2.3.168	Barab
No doubt, such lessons they will teach the rest,	Edw	3.1.21	Spencr
you Maister, will you teach me this conjuring Occupation?	F 380	1.4.38	P Robin
I sirra, I'le teach thee to turne thy selfe to a Dog, or a Cat,	F 382	1.4.40	P Wagner
serve you, would you teach me to raise up Banios and Belcheos?	F App	p.230 56	P Clown
I will teach thee to turne thy selfe to anything, to a dogge,	F App	p.231 58	P Wagner
sirra you, Ile teach ye to impeach honest men:	F App	p.235 17	P Robin
Servants fit for thy purpose thou must hire/To teach thy lover,	Ovid's Elegies		1.8.88
Ere thou rise starres teach seamen where to saile,	Ovid's Elegies		1.13.11
Thy very haires will the hot bodkin teach.	Ovid's Elegies		1.14.30
Teach but your tongue to say, I did it not,	Ovid's Elegies		3.13.48
TEACHING			
Sylla teaching thee,/At last learne wretch to leave thy	Lucan, First Booke		334
TEARE (Homograph; See also TARE)			
But as this one Ile teare them all from him,	Dido	1.1.40	Jupitr
But I will teare thy eyes fro forth thy head,	Dido	3.2.34	Venus
First legions of devils shall teare thee in peeces.	1Tamb	4.4.38	P Bajzth
teare me in peeces, give me the sworde with a ball of wildefire	1Tamb	5.1.311	P Zabina
First let thy Scythyan horse teare both our limmes/Rather then	2Tamb	5.1.138	Orcan
That his teare-thyrsty and unquenched hate,	2Tamb	5.3.222	Techel
These bloudy hands shall teare his triple Crowne,	P1199	22.61	King
For every looke, my lord, drops downe a teare,	Edw	1.4.136	Gavstn
Will sooner sparkle fire then shed a teare:	Edw	5.1.105	Edward
If thou repent, devils will <shall> teare thee in peeces.	F 632	2.2.81	BdAngl
Revolt, or I'le in peece-meale teare thy flesh.	F1745	5.1.72	Mephst
but the Divel threatned to teare me in peeces if I nam'd God:	F1865	5.2.69	P Faust
about thee into familiars, and they shal teare thee in peeces.	F App	p.229 26	P Wagner
Could I therefore her comely tresses teare?	Ovid's Elegies		1.7.11
Or wofull Hector whom wilde jades did teare?	Ovid's Elegies		2.1.32
Bird-changed Progne doth her Itys teare.	Ovid's Elegies		3.11.32
TEARES (Homograph)			
Not mov'd at all, but smiling at his teares,	Dido	2.1.240	Aeneas
Or drop out both mine eyes in drisling teares,	Dido	4.2.41	Iarbus
And teares of pearle, crye stay, Aeneas, stay:	Dido	4.3.52	Aeneas
My teares nor plaints could mollifie a whit:	Dido	5.1.235	Anna
What can my teares or cryes prevaile me now?	Dido	5.1.319	Anna
And that which might resolve me into teares,	1Tamb	1.1.118	Cosroe
(Uttered with teares of wretchednesse and blood,	1Tamb	5.1.25	1Virgn
Embraceth now with teares of ruth and blood,	1Tamb	5.1.85	1Virgn

TEARES (cont.)

And make our soules resolve in ceasles teares: 1Tamb 5.1.272 Bajzth
If teares, our eies have watered all the earth: 2Tamb 2.4.122 Therid
If I had wept a sea of teares for her, 2Tamb 3.2.47 Calyph
Take pitie of a Ladies ruthfull teares, 2Tamb 3.4.69 Olymp
As if they were the teares of Mahomet/For hot consumption of 2Tamb 4.1.196 Tamb
And since this earth, dew'd with thy brinish teares, 2Tamb 4.2.8 Olymp
Weepe heavens, and vanish into liquid teares, 2Tamb 5.3.1 Therid
Nor may our hearts all drown'd in teares of blood, 2Tamb 5.3.214 Usumc
Cannot behold the teares ye shed for me, 2Tamb 5.3.218 Tamb
But I will learne to leave these fruitlesse teares, Jew 1.2.230 Abigal
I cannot take my leave of him for teares: Jew 2.3.355 Abigal
And these my teares to blood, that he might live. Jew 3.2.19 Govnr
Altar I will offer up/My daily sacrifice of sighes and teares, Jew 3.2.32 Govnr
Henry thy King wipes of these childish teares, P1236 22.98 King
He loves me not that sheds most teares, P1239 22.101 King
In steede of inke, ile write it with my teares. Edw 1.4.86 Edward
Witnesse the teares that Isabella sheds, Edw 1.4.164 Queene
Or that these teares that drissell from mine eyes, Edw 2.4.19 Queene
let him bestow/His teares on that, for that is all he gets/Of Edw 2.5.53 Mortmr
And Fraunce shall be obdurat with her teares. Edw 3.1.279 Levune
He rends and teares it with his wrathfull pawe, Edw 5.1.12 Edward
Wet with my teares, and dried againe with sighes, Edw 5.1.118 Edward
And what eyes can refraine from shedding teares, Edw 5.5.50 Ltborn
I, I, but he teares his haire, and wrings his handes, Edw 5.6.18 Queene
Awaye with her, her wordes inforce these teares, Edw 5.6.85 King
And let these teares distilling from mine eyes, Edw 5.6.101 King
<O> my God, I would weepe, but the Divell drawes in my teares. F1851 5.2.55 P Faust
Gush forth bloud in stead of teares, yea life and soule: F1851 5.2.55 P Faust
Breake heart, drop bloud, and mingle it with teares, F App p.243 38 OldMan
Teares falling from repentant heavinesse/Of thy most vilde and F App p.243 39 OldMan
So thunder which the wind teares from the cloudes, Lucan, First Booke 152
parents/Keep back their sons, or womens teares their husbands; Lucan, First Booke 503
gods/Sweate teares to shew the travailes of their citty. Lucan, First Booke 555
See how the gates with my teares wat'red are. Ovid's Elegies 1.6.18
Her teares, she silent, guilty did pronounce me. Ovid's Elegies 1.7.22
And downe her cheekes, the trickling teares did flow, Ovid's Elegies 1.7.57
My bloud, the teares were that from her descended. Ovid's Elegies 1.7.60
But yet sometimes to chide thee let her fall/Counterfet teares: Ovid's Elegies 2.2.36
Spying his mistrisse teares, he will lament/And say this blabbe Ovid's Elegies 2.2.59
Or Phillis teares that her [Demophoon] <Domoophon> misses,/What Ovid's Elegies 2.18.22
Why weepst? and spoilst with teares thy watry eyes? Ovid's Elegies 3.5.57
That seeing thy teares can any joy then feele. Ovid's Elegies 3.5.60
The locks spred on his necke receive his teares, Ovid's Elegies 3.8.11
And some, that she refrain'd teares, have deni'd. Ovid's Elegies 3.8.46
to display/Loves holy fire, with words, with sighs and teares, Hero and Leander 1.193
And as she wept, her teares to pearle he turn'd, Hero and Leander 1.375
And fell in drops like teares, because they mist him. Hero and Leander 2.174

TEAREST

If I praise any, thy poore haires thou tearest, Ovid's Elegies 2.7.7

TEARE-THYRSTY

That his teare-thyrsty and unquenched hate, 2Tamb 5.3.222 Techel

TEARING

And rent their hearts with tearing of my haire, Jew 1.2.234 Abigal
Comes forth her [unkeembd] <unkeembe> locks a sunder tearing. Ovid's Elegies 3.8.52

TEARM'D

I that am tearm'd the Scourge and Wrath of God, 1Tamb 3.3.44 Tamb
Be tearm'd the scourge and terrour of the world? 2Tamb 1.3.62 Amyras
That have bene tearm'd the terrour of the world? 2Tamb 5.3.45 Tamb

TEARME

Whom I may tearme a Damon for thy love. 1Tamb 1.1.50 Mycet
Much like a globe, (a globe may I tearme this, Hero and Leander 2.275

TEARMED

Whose termine <terminine>, is tearmed the worlds wide Pole. F 593 2.2.42 Mephst

TEARMES

The pillers that have bolstered up those tearmes, 1Tamb 3.3.229 Tamb
if Sigismond/Speake as a friend, and stand not upon tearmes, 2Tamb 1.1.123 Orcan
I must apply my selfe to fit those tearmes, 2Tamb 4.1.155 Tamb
Thus in ambiguous tearmes,/Involving all, did Aruns darkly Lucan, First Booke 636
And tearmes <termst> [my] <our> works fruits of an idle quill? Ovid's Elegies 1.15.2
In mournfull tearmes, with sad and heavie cheare/Complaind to Hero and Leander 1.440

TEARMS

Threatning the world with high astounding tearms/And scourging 1Tamb Prol.5 Prolog
Wel hast thou pourtraid in thy tearms of life, 1Tamb 2.1.31 Cosroe
Most happy Emperour in humblest tearms/I vow my service to your 1Tamb 2.5.15 Meandr

TEARM'ST

the cause of this/That tearm'st Zenocrate thy dearest love? 1Tamb 5.1.336 Zenoc

TEARS

Thence rise the tears that so distain my cheeks, 1Tamb 3.2.64 Zenoc

TEATE

A little boy druncke teate-distilling showers. Ovid's Elegies 3.9.22

TEATE-DISTILLING

A little boy druncke teate-distilling showers. Ovid's Elegies 3.9.22

TECHELLES

And making thee and me Techelles, kinges, 1Tamb 1.2.58 Usumc
Techelles, women must be flatered. 1Tamb 1.2.107 Tamb
Stay Techelles, aske a parlee first. 1Tamb 1.2.137 Tamb
Techelles, and Casane, welcome him. 1Tamb 1.2.238 Tamb
Usumcasane and Techelles both, 1Tamb 2.3.36 Cosroe
Usumcasane and Techelles come, 1Tamb 2.3.63 Tamb
Is it not brave to be a King, Techelles? 1Tamb 2.5.51 Tamb
Why, that's wel said Techelles, so would I, 1Tamb 2.5.69 Tamb
For presently Techelles here shal haste, 1Tamb 2.5.94 Tamb

TECHELLES (cont.)				
Techelles, take a thousand horse with thee,	1Tamb	2.5.99		Tamb
Haste thee Techelles, we will follow thee.	1Tamb	2.5.104		Tamb
Theridamas, Techelles, and the rest,	1Tamb	2.7.55		Tamb
Faith, and Techelles, it was manly done:	1Tamb	3.2.109		Usumc
Techelles, and the rest prepare your swordes,	1Tamb	3.3.64		Tamb
Techelles, and my loving followers,	1Tamb	4.2.101		Tamb
Wel Zenocrate, Techelles, and the rest, fall to your victuals.	1Tamb	4.4.15	P	Tamb
Techelles and Casane, here are the cates you desire to finger,	1Tamb	4.4.107	P	Tamb
Techelles King of Fesse, and Usumcasane King of Morocus.	1Tamb	4.4.116	P	Tamb
Techelles, straight goe charge a few of them/To chardge these	1Tamb	5.1.116		Tamb
Thats wel Techelles, what's the newes?	1Tamb	5.1.198		Tamb
No more there is not I warrant thee Techelles.	1Tamb	5.1.202		Tamb
Techelles, and Casane/Promist to meet me on Larissa plaines	2Tamb	1.3.106		Tamb
Well done Techelles: what saith Theridamas?	2Tamb	1.3.206		Tamb
Techelles, draw thy sword,/And wound the earth, that it may	2Tamb	2.4.96		Tamb
now come let us martch/Towards Techelles and Theridamas,	2Tamb	3.2.146		Tamb
Welcome Theridamas and Techelles both,	2Tamb	3.5.150		Tamb
Theridamas, Techelles, and Casane,	2Tamb	4.1.159		Tamb
We wil Techelles, forward then ye Jades:	2Tamb	4.3.97		Tamb
Techelles, Drowne them all, man, woman, and child,	2Tamb	5.1.170		Tamb
Something Techelles, but I know not what,	2Tamb	5.1.220		Tamb
Techelles and the rest, come take your swords,	2Tamb	5.3.46		Tamb
Not last Techelles, no, for I shall die.	2Tamb	5.3.66		Tamb
Techelles let us march,/And weary Death with bearing soules to	2Tamb	5.3.76		Tamb
TEDIOUSNESSE				
If reading five thou plainst of tediousnesse,	Ovid's Elegies			1.1.3
TEETH				
A husband and no teeth!	Dido	4.5.24		Cupid
Sprong of the teeth of Dragons venomous,	1Tamb	2.2.48		Meandr
That sprong of teeth of Dragons venomous?	1Tamb	2.2.52		Mycet
Streching their monstrous pawes, grin with their teeth,	2Tamb	3.5.28		Orcan
olde swords/With ugly teeth of blacke rust fouly scarr'd:	Lucan, First Booke			245
Nor hath the needle, or the combes teeth reft them,	Ovid's Elegies			1.14.15
Proteus what should I name? teeth, Thebes first seed?	Ovid's Elegies			3.11.35
TEL				
I tel you true my heart is swolne with wrath,	1Tamb	2.2.2		Mycet
pray thee tel, why art thou so sad?	1Tamb	4.4.63	P	Tamb
but tel me my Lord, if I should goe, would you bee as good as	2Tamb	1.2.61	P	Almeda
and tel me if the warres/Be not a life that may illustrate	2Tamb	4.1.78		Tamb
I Turke, I tel thee, this same Boy is he,	2Tamb	4.3.57		Tamb
Tel me, what think you of my sicknes now?	2Tamb	5.3.81		Tamb
<Tel Faustus, how dost thou like thy wife>?	F 533	(HC261)A	P	Mephst
Speake <Tel me>, are there many Spheares <heavens> above the	F 586	2.2.35		Faust
'Tis not so much worth; I pray you tel me one thing.	F1643	4.6.86	P	Carter
Tel me sirra, hast thou any commings in?	F App	p.229 4	P	Wagner
Ile tel you what I meane.	F App	p.235 22	P	Robin
but I must tel you one thing before you have him, ride him not	F App	p.239 108	P	Faust
at ease, if I bring his water to you, youle tel me what it is?	F App	p.240 119	P	HrsCsr
TELL (See also TOULD)				
Tell us, O tell us that are ignorant,	Dido	1.1.200		Aeneas
And tell our griefes in more familiar termes:	Dido	1.1.246		Aeneas
But tell me Troians, Troians if you be,	Dido	1.2.17		Iarbus
vouchsafe of ruth/To tell us who inhabits this faire towne,	Dido	2.1.41		Aeneas
O tell me, for I long to be resolv'd.	Dido	2.1.61		Aeneas
the Greekish spyes/To hast to Tenedos and tell the Campe:	Dido	2.1.181		Aeneas
And tell me where [learndst] <learnst> thou this pretie song?	Dido	3.1.27		Dido
But tell them none shall gaze on him but I,	Dido	3.1.73		Dido
here, tell me in sooth/In what might Dido highly pleasure thee.	Dido	3.1.101		Dido
Tell me deare love, how found you out this Cave?	Dido	3.4.3		Dido
Nay, where is my warlike father, can you tell?	Dido	4.1.15		Cupid
I tell thee thou must straight to Italy,	Dido	5.1.53		Hermes
As how I pray, may I entreate you tell.	Dido	5.1.67		Iarbus
Tell him, I never vow'd at Aulis gulfe/The desolation of his	Dido	5.1.202		Dido
Good brother tell the cause unto my Lords,	1Tamb	1.1.4		Mycet
But tell me Maddam, is your grace betroth'd?	1Tamb	1.2.32		Tamb
But tell me, that hast seene him, Menaphon,	1Tamb	2.1.5		Cosroe
Tell you the rest (Meander) I have said.	1Tamb	2.2.13		Mycet
Tell him thy Lord the Turkish Emperour,	1Tamb	3.1.22		Bajzth
Tell him, I am content to take a truce,	1Tamb	3.1.31		Bajzth
Will tell how many thousand men he slew.	1Tamb	3.2.43		Agidas
I tell thee villaine, those that lead my horse/Have to their	1Tamb	3.3.69		Bajzth
I will not tell thee how Ile handle thee,	1Tamb	3.3.84		Tamb
I tell thee shamelesse girle,/Thou shalt be Landresse to my	1Tamb	3.3.176		Zabina
I tell thee, were that Tamburlaine/As monsterous as Gorgon,	1Tamb	4.1.17		Souldn
Tell me Zenocrate?	1Tamb	4.4.84		Tamb
And tell my soule mor tales of bleeding ruth?	1Tamb	5.1.342		Zenoc
And tell me whether I should stoope so low,	2Tamb	1.1.112		Sgsmnd
No talke of running, I tell you sir.	2Tamb	1.2.16		Almeda
And more than this, for all I cannot tell.	2Tamb	1.2.53		Callap
Tell me, how fares my faire Zenocrate?	2Tamb	2.4.41		Tamb
Tell me sweet boie, art thou content to die?	2Tamb	3.4.18		Olymp
Tell me Viceroies the number of your men,	2Tamb	3.5.30		Callap
Tell me Olympia, wilt thou graunt my suit?	2Tamb	4.2.21		Therid
Birds of the Aire will tell of murders past;	Jew	Prol.16		Machvl
easily in a day/Tell that which may maintaine him all his life.	Jew	1.1.11		Barab
Goe tell 'em the Jew of Malta sent thee, man:	Jew	1.1.66		Barab
I cannot tell, but we have scambled up/More wealth by farre	Jew	1.1.122		Barab
Oft have I heard tell, can be permanent.	Jew	1.1.133		Barab
Tush, tell not me 'twas done of policie.	Jew	1.1.140		1Jew
What tell you me of Job?	Jew	1.2.181		Barab
Who in my wealth wud tell me winters tales,	Jew	2.1.25		Barab
Now Captaine tell us whither thou art bound?	Jew	2.2.1		Govnr

TELL (cont.)

Tell me, hast thou thy health well?	Jew	2.3.121	P	Barab
Tell me, Mathias, is not that the Jew?	Jew	2.3.152		Mater
But tell me now, How hast thou spent thy time? . . .	Jew	2.3.201		Barab
This is thy Diamond, tell me, shall I have it? . . .	Jew	2.3.292		Lodowk
Now tell me, Ithimore, how lik'st thou this? . . .	Jew	2.3.364		Barab
And tell him that it comes from Lodowicke. . . .	Jew	2.3.371		Barab
Tell me, how cam'st thou by this?	Jew	3.1.16		Curtzn
of my sinnes/Lye heavy on my soule; then pray you tell me,	Jew	4.1.49		Barab
Ithimore, tell me, is the Fryar asleepe?	Jew	4.1.129		Barab
so, and yet I cannot tell, for at the reading of the letter,	Jew	4.2.6	P	Pilia
Tell him you will confesse.	Jew	4.2.77	P	Pilia
Tell him I must hav't.	Jew	4.2.118	P	Ithimr
tell him, I scorne to write a line under a hundred crownes.	Jew	4.2.120	P	Ithimr
his villany/He will tell all he knowes and I shall dye for't.	Jew	4.3.65		Barab
I scorne the Peasant, tell him so.	Jew	4.4.59	P	Ithimr
but tell me, Barabas,/Canst thou, as thou reportest, make Malta	Jew	5.1.84		Calym
Now tell me, Governor, and plainely too, ...	Jew	5.2.55		Barab
Well, tell the Governor we grant his suit, ...	Jew	5.3.40		Calym
Now tell me, worldlings, underneath the [sunne] <summe>, .	Jew	5.5.49		Barab
Tell me, you Christians, what doth this portend? . . .	Jew	5.5.90		Calym
betraide, come my Lords, and let us goe tell the King of this.	P 199	3.34	P	Navrre
Thankes to my princely sonne, then tell me Guise, . .	P 228	4.26		QnMoth
Messenger, tell him I will see him straite. . . .	P 247	4.45		Charls
Tell me Taleus, wherfore should I flye?	P 366	7.6		Ramus
Come let us goe tell the King.	P 440	7.80		Condy
I tell thee Mugeroun we will be freends, ...	P 614	12.27		King
My Lord Cardinall of Loraine, tell me, ...	P 631	12.44		QnMoth
And tell him that tis for his Countries good, . . .	P 646	12.59		Cardnl
But canst thou tell who is their generall?	P 731	14.34		Navrre
And then Ile tell thee what I meane to doe. . . .	P 891	17.86		King
And tell him ere it be long, Ile visite him. . . .	P 912	18.13		Navrre
I prethee tell him that the Guise is heere. . . .	P 958	19.28		Guise
Then come thou neer, and tell what newes thou bringst. .	P1166	22.28		King
Tell her for all this that I hope to live, ...	P1196	22.58		King
Tell me Surgeon, shall I live?	P1211	22.73		King
Tell me Surgeon and flatter not, may I live? . . .	P1222	22.84		King
And tell her Henry dyes her faithfull freend. . . .	P1244	22.106		King
well/To waite at my trencher, and tell me lies at dinner time,	Edw	1.1.31		Gavstn
And I will tell thee reasons of such waighte, . . .	Edw	1.4.226		Queene
For I have joyfull newes to tell thee of, ...	Edw	2.1.75		Neece
But tell me Mortimer, whats thy devise, ...	Edw	2.2.11		Edward
But let them go, and tell me what are these. . . .	Edw	2.2.239		Edward
Tell me, where wast thou borne? What is thine armes? .	Edw	2.2.242		Edward
O tell me Spencer, where is Gaveston?	Edw	2.4.1		Edward
Cease to lament, and tell us wheres the king? . . .	Edw	2.4.30		Mortmr
Tell us where he remaines, and he shall die. . . .	Edw	2.4.36		Lncstr
When, can you tell?	Edw	2.5.60		Warwck
to your maister/My friend, and tell him that I watcht it well.	Edw	2.6.13		Warwck
Then tell thy prince, of whence, and what thou art. . .	Edw	3.1.35		Edward
Tell me [Arundell] <Matre>, died he ere thou camst, . .	Edw	3.1.92		Edward
And tell me, would the rebels denie me that? . . .	Edw	3.1.101		Edward
And tell them I will come to chastise them, . . .	Edw	3.1.178		Edward
Tell me good unckle, what Edward doe you meane? . .	Edw	4.6.32		Prince
But tell me, must I now resigne my crowne, . . .	Edw	5.1.36		Edward
And tell thy message to my naked brest.	Edw	5.1.130		Edward
And tell him, that I labour all in vaine, ...	Edw	5.2.70		Queene
I tell thee tis not meet, that one so false/Should come about	Edw	5.2.104		Mortmr
Tell Isabell the Queene, I lookt not thus, ...	Edw	5.5.68		Edward
And therefore tell me, wherefore art thou come? . . .	Edw	5.5.106		Edward
Tell me sirs, was it not bravelie done?	Edw	5.5.116		Ltborn
And tell the secrets of all forraine Kings:	F 114	1.1.86		Faust
The spirits tell me they can dry the sea, ...	F 171	1.1.143		Cornel
Then tell me Faustus what shall we three want? . . .	F 175	1.1.147		Cornel
Go to sirra, leave your jesting, and tell us where he is.	F 201	1.2.8	P	1Schol
Then <Well> you will not tell us?	F 205	1.2.12	P	2Schol
You are deceiv'd, for <Yes sir>, I will tell you: . .	F 206	1.2.13	P	Wagner
Tell me, what is that Lucifer, thy Lord?	F 290	1.3.62		Faust
To tell me whatsoever I demand:	F 323	1.3.95		Faust
and good sauce to it, if I pay so deere, I can tell you. .	F 353	1.4.11	P	Robin
me, as if they payd for their meate and drinke, I can tell you.	F 366	1.4.24	P	Robin
Now tell me what saith <sayes> Lucifer thy Lord. . .	F 419	2.1.31		Faust
Stay Mephostophilis/And tell me, what good will my soule do thy	F 428	2.1.40		Faust
But tell me Faustus, shall I have thy soule? . . .	F 434	2.1.46		Mephst
Tell me, where is the place that men call Hell? . . .	F 505	2.1.117		Faust
For I tell thee I am damn'd, and <am> now in hell. . .	F 526	2.1.138		Mephst
I tell thee Faustus it is <tis> not halfe so faire/As thou, or	F 557	2.2.6		Mephst
But <tell me> have they all/One motion, both situ et tempore?	F 595	2.2.44		Faust
But tell me, hath every Spheare a Dominion, or Intelligentia	F 607	2.2.56	P	Faust
now tell me who made the world?	F 618	2.2.67	P	Faust
Sweet Mephostophilis tell me.	F 620	2.2.69	P	Faust
Move me not Faustus <for I will not tell thee>. . .	F 621	2.2.70	P	Mephst
Villaine, have I not bound thee to tell me any thing? .	F 622	2.2.71	P	Faust
We are come to tell thee thou dost injure us. . . .	F 642	2.2.91		Belzeb
why thou canst not tell ne're a word on't.	F 731	2.3.10	P	Dick
I'le tell thee what, an my Maister come here, I'le clap as	F 736	2.3.15	P	Robin
But I prethee tell me, in good sadnesse Robin, is that a .	F 743	2.3.22	P	Dick
But tell me now, what resting place is this?	F 800	3.1.22		Faust
Now tell me Faustus, are we not fitted well?	F 940	3.1.162		Mephst
Did I not tell you,/To morrow we would sit i'th Consistory,	F1016	3.2.36		Pope
for I can tell you, you'le be curst with Bell, Booke, and	F1072	3.2.92	P	Mephst
what you say, we looke not like cup-stealers I can tell you.	F1100	3.3.13	P	Robin
your searching; we scorne to steale your cups I can tell you.	F1106	3.3.19	P	Dick

Context	Work	Reference	Speaker
TELL (cont.)			
when, can you tell?	F1112	3.3.25	P Robin
To satisfie my longing thoughts at full,/Let me this tell thee:	F1265	4.1.111	Emper
now sirra I must tell you, that you may ride him o're hedge and	F1467	4.4.11	P Faust
I'le tell you the bravest tale how a Conjurer serv'd me; you	F1521	4.5.17	P Carter
I'le tell you how he serv'd me:	F1525	4.5.21	P Carter
therefor I pray you tell me, what is the thing you most desire	F1566	4.6.9	P Faust
be good, for they come from a farre Country I can tell you.	F1577	4.6.20	P Faust
Nay, hearke you, can you tell me where you are?	F1614	4.6.57	Faust
Too simple is my wit to tell her worth <praise>,/Whom all the	F1697	5.1.24	2Schol
Why did not Faustus tell us of this before, that Divines might	F1862	5.2.66	P 1Schol
Ile tell you how you shall know them, all hee divels has	F App	p.230 52	P Clown
did not I tell thee, we were for ever made by this doctor	F App	p.234 1	P Robin
I tell thee he has not slept this eight nights.	F App	p.240 144	P Mephst
tell me, and you shal have it.	F App	p.242 6	P Faust
I durst the great celestiall battells tell,	Ovid's Elegies	2.1.11	
On tell-tales neckes thou seest the linke-knitt chaines,	Ovid's Elegies	2.2.41	
Also much better were they then I tell,	Ovid's Elegies	2.5.55	
Let others tell how winds fierce battailes wage,	Ovid's Elegies	2.11.17	
Let others tell this, and what each one speakes/Beleeve, no	Ovid's Elegies	2.11.21	
There wine being fild, thou many things shalt tell,	Ovid's Elegies	2.11.49	
But absent is my fire, lyes ile tell none,	Ovid's Elegies	2.16.11	
Wine-bibbing banquets tell thy naughtinesse,	Ovid's Elegies	3.1.17	
Perhaps he'ele tell howe oft he slewe a man,	Ovid's Elegies	3.7.21	
What should I tell her vaine tongues filthy lyes,	Ovid's Elegies	3.10.21	
And justly: for her praise why did I tell?	Ovid's Elegies	3.11.9	
What madnesse ist to tell night <nights> prankes by day,	Ovid's Elegies	3.13.7	
I could tell ye,/How smooth his brest was, and how white his	Hero and Leander	1.65	
Tell me, to whom mad'st thou that heedlesse oath?	Hero and Leander	1.294	
Harken a while, and I will tell you why:	Hero and Leander	1.385	
At last he came, O who can tell the greeting,	Hero and Leander	2.23	
TELLING			
Sitting as if they were a telling ridles.	2Tamb	3.5.59	Tamb
Wearying his fingers ends with telling it,	Jew	1.1.16	Barab
A homely one my lord, not worth the telling.	Edw	2.2.13	Mortmr
Telling thy mistresse, where I was with thee,	Ovid's Elegies	2.8.27	
TELLS			
He tells you true, my maisters, so he does.	1Tamb	2.2.74	Mycet
TELL-TALES			
On tell-tales neckes thou seest the linke-knitt chaines,	Ovid's Elegies	2.2.41	
TELS			
And tels for trueth, submissions comes too late.	1Tamb	5.1.73	Tamb
For Don Mathias tels me she is faire.	Jew	2.3.35	Lodowk
And tels me, if I sleepe I never wake,	Edw	5.5.104	Edward
TELST			
What telst thou me of rich Getulia?	Dido	3.1.48	Dido
TEMAINTE			
Doe so; Farewell Zaareth, farewell Temainte.	Jew	1.1.176	Barab
TEMPE			
Are all things thine? the Muses Tempe <Temple> thine?	Ovid's Elegies	1.1.19	
TEMPER			
chariot wil not beare/A guide of baser temper than my selfe,	2Tamb	5.3.243	Tamb
TEMPERED			
And tempered every soule with lively heat,	2Tamb	2.4.10	Tamb
Tempered by science metaphisicall,	2Tamb	4.2.63	Olymp
TEMPEST			
late felt frownes/That sent a tempest to my daunted thoughtes,	1Tamb	3.2.86	Agidas
That which hath [stoopt] <stopt> the tempest of the Gods,	1Tamb	5.1.184	Tamb
what each one speakes/Beleeve, no tempest the beleever wreakes.	Ovid's Elegies	2.11.22	
TEMPESTS			
On which by tempests furie we are cast.	Dido	1.1.199	Aeneas
And dive into blacke tempests treasurie,	Dido	4.1.5	Iarbus
Lets see what tempests can anoy me now.	Dido	4.4.60	Aeneas
O blessed tempests that did drive him in,	Dido	4.4.94	Dido
her rusty coach/Engyrt with tempests wrapt in pitchy clouds,	1Tamb	5.1.295	Bajzth
With awkward windes, and sore tempests driven/To fall on shoare,	Edw	4.7.34	Baldck
Brings Thunder, Whirle-winds, Storme <tempests> and Lightning:	F 546	2.1.158	Mephst
TEMPESTUOUS			
And heaven was darkned with tempestuous clowdes:	Dido	2.1.140	Aeneas
TEMPLE			
And hung on stately Mecas Temple roofe,	2Tamb	1.1.141	Orcan
with which I burst/The rusty beames of Janus Temple doores,	2Tamb	2.4.114	Tamb
At the new temple.	Edw	1.2.75	ArchBp
In [midst] <one> of which a sumptuous Temple stands,	F 795	3.1.17	Faust
Are all things thine? the Muses Tempe <Temple> thine?	Ovid's Elegies	1.1.19	
Deflowr'd except, within thy Temple wall.	Ovid's Elegies	1.7.18	
will I grace them/And in the midst of Venus temple place them.	Ovid's Elegies	1.11.26	
from her tower/To Venus temple, [where] <were> unhappilye,	Hero and Leander	1.133	
TEMPLES (Homograph)			
victorie we yeeld/May bind the temples of his conquering head,	1Tamb	5.1.56	2Virgn
time to grace/Her princely Temples with the Persean crowne:	1Tamb	5.1.489	Tamb
He bindes his temples with a frowning cloude,	2Tamb	2.4.6	Tamb
Found in the Temples of that Mahomet,	2Tamb	5.1.175	Tamb
Lay waste the Iland, hew the Temples downe,	Jew	3.5.14	Govnr
Engirt the temples of his hatefull head,	Edw	5.1.46	Edward
Or rob the gods; or sacred temples fire;	Lucan, First Booke	380	
About my temples go triumphant bayes,	Ovid's Elegies	2.12.1	
So in thy Temples shall Osiris stay,	Ovid's Elegies	2.13.12	
thou affects, with Romulus, temples brave/Bacchus, Alcides,	Ovid's Elegies	3.7.51	
The holy gods gilt temples they might fire,	Ovid's Elegies	3.8.43	
Victorious wreathes at length my Temples greete.	Ovid's Elegies	3.10.6	
TEMPORALL			
Tis but temporall that thou canst inflict.	Edw	3.1.242	Warwck

TEMPORE

But <tell me> have they all/One motion, both situ et tempore? F 596 2.2.45 Faust

TEMPT

No, no Amyras, tempt not Fortune so, 2Tamb 4.1.86 Tamb
And gaze not on it least it tempt thy soule, F 98 1.1.70 GdAngl
Tempt not God sweet friend, but let us into the next roome, and F1871 5.2.75 P 1Schol

TEMPTATION

O thou bewitching fiend, 'twas thy temptation, F1883 5.2.87 Faust

TEMPTED

armours fight/A doubtfull battell with my tempted thoughtes, 1Tamb 5.1.152 Tamb
the serpent that tempted Eve may be saved, but not Faustus. F1838 5.2.42 P Faust

TEMPTS

Is that the reason why he tempts us thus? F 430 2.1.42 Faust

TEN (See also TENNE)

The Grecian souldiers tired with ten yeares warre, Dido 2.1.126 Aeneas
And with one shaft provoke ten thousand darts: Dido 3.3.72 Iarbus
Ten thousand Cupids hover in the ayre, Dido 4.4.48 Dido
Theridamas, farewel ten thousand times. 1Tamb 1.1.82 Mycet
are in readines/Ten thousand horse to carie you from hence, 1Tamb 1.1.185 Ortyg
Twere requisite he should be ten times more, 1Tamb 3.1.47 Argier
Hath now in armes ten thousand Janisaries, 1Tamb 3.3.15 Bassoe
Under my collors march ten thousand Greeks, 2Tamb 1.3.118 Therid
Ten thousand horse, and thirty thousand foot, 2Tamb 3.5.48 Soria
The ten yeares tribute that remaines unpaid. Jew 1.2.7 Calym
are such/That you will needs have ten yeares tribute past, Jew 1.2.19 Govnr
To levie of us ten yeares tribute past, Jew 1.2.41 Govnr
To what this ten yeares tribute will amount/That we have cast, Jew 1.2.46 Govnr
Ten thousand Portagues besides great Perles, Jew 1.2.244 Barab
Their voyage will be worth ten thousand Crownes. Jew 4.1.70 Barab
he flouts me, what gentry can be in a poore Turke of ten pence? Jew 4.2.39 P Ithimr
Ten hundred thousand crownes,--Master Barabas. Jew 4.2.71 P Ithimr
To conclude, he gave me ten crownes. Jew 4.2.113 P Pilia
But ten? Jew 4.2.114 P Ithimr
Oh that ten thousand nights were put in one, Jew 4.2.130 Ithimr
Welcome ten thousand times, old man againe. Edw 3.1.46 Edward
At every ten miles end thou hast a horse. Edw 5.4.42 Mortmr
This ten dayes space, and least that I should sleepe, Edw 5.5.60 Edward
For not these ten daies have these eyes lids closd. Edw 5.5.94 Edward
Am not tormented with ten thousand hels, F 307 1.3.79 Mephst
and that buyes me <is> thirty meales a day, and ten Beavers: F 695 2.2.144 P Glutny
it will weare out ten birchin broomes I warrant you. F1385 4.2.61 P Benvol
sell him, but if thou likest him for ten Dollors more, take him, F1461 4.4.5 P Faust
worth>/<Made Greece with ten yeares warres afflict poore Troy>? F1696 (HC269)B 2Schol
thou shalt see/Ten thousand tortures that more horrid be. F1920 5.2.124 BdAngl
In ten yeares wonst thou France; Roome may be won/With farre Lucan, First Booke 283
me have borne/A thousand brunts, and tride me ful ten yeeres, Lucan, First Booke 301
spread these flags that ten years space have conquer'd, Lucan, First Booke 348
by these ten blest ensignes/And all thy several triumphs, Lucan, First Booke 375
And that his owne ten ensignes, and the rest/Marcht not Lucan, First Booke 473
When Troy by ten yeares battle tumbled downe, Ovid's Elegies 2.12.9
Troy had not yet beene ten yeares siege out-stander, Ovid's Elegies 3.5.27

TENANTS

Goe sit at home and eate your tenants beefe: Edw 2.2.75 Gavstn

T'ENCOUNTER

Yet scarse enough t'encounter Tamburlaine. 2Tamb 1.1.66 Orcan

TEND

And in my Sarell tend my Concubines: 1Tamb 3.3.78 Bajzth

TENDER

But weapons gree not with my tender yeares: Dido 3.1.164 Dido
Nor Venus triumph in his tender youth: Dido 3.2.9 Juno
With which if you but noint your tender Skin, 2Tamb 4.2.65 Olymp
Whose tender blossoms tremble every one, 2Tamb 4.3.123 Tamb
Or envy of thee, but in tender love, F1720 5.1.47 OldMan
Love hearing it laugh'd with his tender mother/And smiling Ovid's Elegies 1.6.11
Now in her tender armes I sweetly bide, Ovid's Elegies 1.13.5
And with rough clawes your tender cheekes assaile. Ovid's Elegies 2.6.4
But tender Damsels do it, though with paine, Ovid's Elegies 2.14.37
And tender love hath great things hatefull made. Ovid's Elegies 2.18.4
Or one that with her tender brother lies, Ovid's Elegies 3.6.22
Tender loves Mother a new Poet get, Ovid's Elegies 3.14.1
Such sights as this, to tender maids are rare. Hero and Leander 2.238

TENDERLIE

Much more a king brought up so tenderlie. Edw 5.5.6 Matrvs

TENDREST

And therefore as thou lovest and tendrest me, Edw 1.4.211 Queene

TENDS

Forbids my mind to entertaine a thought/That tends to love, but 2Tamb 4.2.26 Olymp

TENEDOS

And so in troopes all marcht to Tenedos: Dido 2.1.135 Aeneas
the Greekish spyes/To hast to Tenedos and tell the Campe: Dido 2.1.181 Aeneas
And drew a thousand ships to Tenedos, 2Tamb 2.4.88 Tamb
Homer shall live while Tenedos stands and Ide, Ovid's Elegies 1.15.9

TENNE

pursu'd]/[With tenne yeares warre the rape of such a queene], F1700 5.1.27A 3Schol

TENT

Summoned the Captaines to his princely tent, Dido 2.1.130 Aeneas
Weele leade you to the stately tent of War: 1Tamb Prol.3 Prolog
Resting her selfe upon my milk-white Tent: 1Tamb 3.3.161 Tamb
until the bloody flag/Be once advanc'd on my vermilion Tent, 1Tamb 4.2.117 Tamb
Wagons of gold were set before my tent: 2Tamb 1.1.99 Orcan
Thou shalt be set upon my royall tent. 2Tamb 3.2.37 Tamb
And yet at night carrouse within my tent, 2Tamb 3.2.106 Tamb
our mighty hoste/Shal bring thee bound unto the Generals tent. 2Tamb 3.5.111 Trebiz

TENT (cont.)

Sirha, prepare whips, and bring my chariot to my Tent: 2Tamb 3.5.145 P Tamb
Call foorth our laisie brother from the tent, 2Tamb 4.1.7 Celeb
Then bring those Turkish harlots to my tent, 2Tamb 4.1.165 Tamb
But closde within the compasse of a tent, 2Tamb 4.2.3 Olymp
Wel met Olympia, I sought thee in my tent, 2Tamb 4.2.14 Therid
Come to the tent againe. 2Tamb 4.2.54 Therid
All Lovers warre, and Cupid hath his tent, Ovid's Elegies 1.9.1
With both her hands she made the bed a tent, Hero and Leander 2.264

TENTES

The first day when he pitcheth downe his tentes, 1Tamb 4.1.49 2Msngr
Your tentes of white now pitch'd before the gates/And gentle 1Tamb 4.2.111 Therid
For hell and darknesse pitch their pitchy tentes, 2Tamb 5.3.7 Therid
And to her tentes wild me my selfe addresse. Ovid's Elegies 1.9.44

TENTS

Are drawne by darknes forth Astraeus tents. Dido 1.1.73 Venus
And [pitcht] <pitch> our tents under the Georgean hilles, 1Tamb 2.2.15 Meandr
We see his tents have now bene altered, 1Tamb 5.1.7 Govnr
hate/Flings slaughtering terrour from my coleblack tents. 1Tamb 5.1.72 Tamb
Here let him stay my maysters from the tents, 1Tamb 5.1.211 Tamb
Our Tents are pitcht, our men stand in array, 2Tamb 1.1.120 Fredrk
Come let us goe and banquet in our tents: 2Tamb 1.1.160 Orcan
Ransacke the tents and the pavilions/Of these proud Turks, and 2Tamb 4.1.160 Tamb
Sirha, the view of our vermillion tents, 2Tamb 5.1.86 Tamb
Tis not thy bloody tents can make me yeeld, 2Tamb 5.1.103 Govnr
And now, bold Bashawes, let us to our Tents, Jew 5.3.43 Calym
Let us away with triumph to our tents. P 805 16.19 Navrre
Wagons or tents, then in this frontire towne. Lucan, First Booke 255
They by Lemannus nooke forsooke their tents; Lucan, First Booke 397
snatcht up/Would make them sleepe securely in their tents. Lucan, First Booke 516
Doest harme, and in thy tents why doest me wound? Ovid's Elegies 2.9.4
Then warres, and from thy tents wilt come to mine. Ovid's Elegies 2.18.40

TEQUE

Desine meque tuis incendere teque querelis, Dido 5.1.139 Aeneas

T'ERECT

But neither chuse the north t'erect thy seat; Lucan, First Booke 53

TEREUS

Why Philomele doest Tereus leudnesse mourne? Ovid's Elegies 2.6.7
What Tereus, what Jason you provokes, Ovid's Elegies 2.14.33

TERM'D

There is a place Hesperia term'd by us, Dido 1.2.20 Cloan
Let it be term'd Aenea by your name. Dido 5.1.20 Cloan

TERME (See also TEARME)

The water which our Poets terme a Nimph, Dido 4.4.144 Dido
For ever terme, the Perseans sepulchre, 2Tamb 3.5.19 Callap
Suscepi that provinciam as they terme it, Edw 5.4.63 Mortmr
This idoll which you terme Virginitie, Hero and Leander 1.269

TERMES

How may I credite these thy flattering termes, Dido 1.1.109 Venus
And tell our griefes in more familiar termes: Dido 1.1.246 Aeneas
men (Dido except)/Have taunted me in these opprobrious termes, Dido 3.3.27 Iarbus
To please me, what faire termes and sweet words ha's shee, Ovid's Elegies 2.19.17
As in plaine termes (yet cunningly) he crav'd it, Hero and Leander 2.71

TERMINE

Whose termine <terminine>, is tearmed the worlds wide Pole. F 593 2.2.42 Mephst

TERMININE

Whose termine <terminine>, is tearmed the worlds wide Pole. F 593 2.2.42 Mephst

TERMS

What, dares the villain write in such base terms? Jew 3.2.3 Lodowk

TERMST

And tearmes <termst> [my] <our> works fruits of an idle quill? Ovid's Elegies 1.15.2

TERREFIE

And cannot terrefie his mightie hoste. 1Tamb 3.3.12 Bassoe

TERREN

Whereas the Terren and the red sea meet, 2Tamb 5.3.132 Tamb

TERRENE

As hath the Ocean or the Terrene sea/Small drops of water, when 1Tamb 3.1.10 Bajzth
The Ocean, Terrene, and the cole-blacke sea, 1Tamb 3.1.25 Bajzth
That naked rowe about the Terrene sea. 1Tamb 3.3.50 Tamb
The Terrene main wherin Danubius fals, 2Tamb 1.1.37 Orcan
And soon put foorth into the Terrene sea: 2Tamb 1.2.25 Callap
The Terrene west, the Caspian north north-east, 2Tamb 4.3.103 Tamb

TERRENI

Aerii, [Aquatici] <Aquatani>, [Terreni], spiritus salvete: F 245 1.3.17 P Faust

TERRIBLE

a non-plus at the critical aspect of my terrible countenance. Jew 4.2.14 P Pilia
O what art thou that look'st so [terrible] <terribly>. F 638 2.2.87 Faust

TERRIBLY

O what art thou that look'st so [terrible] <terribly>. F 638 2.2.87 Faust
Bloud, he speakes terribly: F1227 4.1.73 P Benvol

TERRIFIE

Intending so to terrifie the world: 1Tamb 5.1.15 Govnr

TERRIFIED

That could not but before be terrified: 2Tamb 2.2.22 Uribas

TERRIFIES

onely Aeneas frowne/Is that which terrifies poore Didos heart: Dido 4.4.116 Dido
This word Damnation, terrifies not me <him>, F 286 1.3.58 Faust

TERRIFY (See also TERREFIE, TERRIFIE)

A meteor that might terrify the earth, 1Tamb 5.1.461 Tamb

TERRITORIES

That dares controll us in our Territories. 1Tamb 4.3.14 Souldn
And then depart we to our territories. 2Tamb 1.1.166 Orcan

TERROR

Be al a scourge and terror to the world, 2Tamb 1.3.63 Tamb

TERROR (cont.)			
Which [strike] <strikes> a terror to my fainting soule.	F 310	1.3.82	Mephst
were the Commons only strooke to heart/With this vaine terror;	Lucan, First Booke		484
TERROUR			
And meanes to be a terrour to the world,	1Tamb	1.2.38	Tamb
Against the terrour of the winds and waves.	1Tamb	3.2.84	Agidas
The onely feare and terrour of the world,	1Tamb	3.3.45	Tamb
That with his terrour and imperious eies,	1Tamb	4.1.14	2Msngr
heaven beholde/Their Scourge and Terrour treade on Emperours.	1Tamb	4.2.32	Tamb
hate/Flings slaughtering terrour from my coleblack tents.	1Tamb	5.1.72	Tamb
My nature and the terrour of my name,	1Tamb	5.1.176	Tamb
That in this terrour Tamburlaine may live.	1Tamb	5.1.299	Bajzth
Be thou the scourge and terrour of the world.	2Tamb	1.3.60	Tamb
Be tearm'd the scourge and terrour of the world?	2Tamb	1.3.62	Amyras
That strikes a terrour to all Turkish hearts,	2Tamb	2.1.15	Fredrk
The Scourge of God and terrour of the world,	2Tamb	4.1.154	Tamb
I will persist a terrour to the world,	2Tamb	4.1.200	Tamb
And have no terrour but his threatning lookes?	2Tamb	5.1.23	Govnr
That have bene tearm'd the terrour of the world?	2Tamb	5.3.45	Tamb
And made it look with terrour on the worlde:	P 61	2.4	Guise
The terrour of this happy victory,	P 791	16.5	Bartus
TERROURS			
With terrours to the last and cruelst hew:	1Tamb	5.1.8	Govnr
these terrours and these tyrannies/(If tyrannies wars justice	2Tamb	4.1.146	Tamb
T'ESCAPE			
T'escape their hands that seeke to reave his life:	Edw	4.7.52	Leistr
TESELLA			
From strong Tesella unto Biledull,	2Tamb	1.3.148	Techel
TESTAMENT			
The Hebrew Psalter, and new Testament;	F 182	1.1.154	Valdes
TESTER			
to supper, and a Tester in your purse, and go backe againe.	F1121	3.3.34	P Robin
TESTIFIE			
footsteps bending)/Doth testifie that you exceed her farre,	Hero and Leander		1.211
TESTIMONII			
[testimonii] <testimonis> est [inartificiale] <in arte	P 395	7.35	Guise
TESTIMONIS			
<testimonis> est [inartificiale] <in arte fetiales>.	P 395	7.35	Guise
TEXT			
That others needs to comment on my text?	P 683	13.27	Guise
TH' (Homograph)			
And here Queene Dido weares th'imperiall Crowne,	Dido	2.1.63	Illion
O th'inchaunting words of that base slave,	Dido	2.1.161	Aeneas
And race th'eternall Register of time:	Dido	3.2.7	Juno
Present thee with th'Emperiall Diadem.	1Tamb	1.1.139	Ortyg
I willingly receive th'emperiall crowne,	1Tamb	1.1.157	Cosroe
Expects th'arrivall of her highnesse person.	1Tamb	1.2.79	Agidas
Let him take all th'advantages he can,	1Tamb	4.1.40	Souldn
Or leave Damascus and th'Egyptian fields,	1Tamb	4.2.48	Tamb
As Prognes to th'adulterous Thracian King,	1Tamb	4.4.24	Zabina
We meane to traveile to th'Antartique Pole,	1Tamb	4.4.136	Tamb
Madam, your father and th'Arabian king,	1Tamb	5.1.378	Philem
to your dominions/Than ever yet confirm'd th'Egyptian Crown.	1Tamb	5.1.449	Tamb
Discendeth downward to th'Antipodes.	2Tamb	1.2.52	Callap
the Gulfe, call'd by the name/Mare magiore, of th'inhabitantes:	2Tamb	1.3.215	Therid
As Centinels to warne th'immortall soules,	2Tamb	2.4.16	Tamb
Up to the pallace of th'imperiall heaven:	2Tamb	2.4.35	Tamb
And we discend into th'infernall vaults,	2Tamb	2.4.98	Tamb
And were the sinowes of th'imperiall seat/So knit and	2Tamb	3.1.10	Callap
Death and destruction to th'inhabitants.	2Tamb	3.2.5	Tamb
And sharpest where th'assault is desperate.	2Tamb	3.2.67	Tamb
Whose chariot wheeles have burst th'Assirians bones,	2Tamb	5.1.71	Tamb
And from th'Antartique Pole, Eastward behold/As much more land,	2Tamb	5.3.154	Tamb
And with my prayers pierce [th']impartiall heavens,	Jew	3.2.33	Govnr
My Lord I mervaile that th'aspiring Guise/Dares once adventure	P 36	1.36	Admral
For if th'almighty take my brother hence,	P 469	8.19	Anjoy
But come lets walke aside, th'airs not very sweet.	P 497	9.16	QnMoth
Seeing that our Lord th'earle of Glosters dead,	Edw	2.1.2	Baldck
Th'ad best betimes forsake [them] <thee> and their trains,	Edw	3.1.202	Lncstr
Stand not on titles, but obay th'arrest,	Edw	4.7.58	Leistr
sweete delight's] dispute/In th'heavenly matters of Theologie,	F 19	Prol.19	1Chor
as th'infernall spirits/On sweet Musaeus when he came to hell,	F 142	1.1.114	Faust
Leapes from th'Antarticke world unto the skie,	F 231	1.3.3	Faust
Th'abreviated <breviated> names of holy Saints,	F 238	1.3.10	Faust
My head is lighter then it was by th'hornes,	F1350	4.2.26	Benvol
looke up into th'hall there ho.	F1519	4.5.15	P Hostss
Th'affrighted worlds force bent on publique spoile,	Lucan, First Booke		5
While th'earth the sea, and ayre the earth sustaines;	Lucan, First Booke		89
Hence came it that th'edicts were overrul'd,	Lucan, First Booke		178
none answer'd, but a murmuring buz/Th'unstable people made:	Lucan, First Booke		354
Th'Averni too, which bouldly faine themselves/The Romanes	Lucan, First Booke		428
Th'irrevocable people flie in troupes.	Lucan, First Booke		507
Strooke with th'earths suddaine shadow waxed pale,	Lucan, First Booke		537
(as their old custome was)/They call th'Etrurian Augures,	Lucan, First Booke		584
did looke/Dead, and discoulour'd; th'other leane and thinne.	Lucan, First Booke		628
the brest of this slaine Bull are crept,/Th'infernall powers.	Lucan, First Booke		633
all to good, be Augury vaine, and Tages/Th'arts master falce.	Lucan, First Booke		636
rayes now sing/The fell Nemean beast, th'earth would be fired,	Lucan, First Booke		655
So runnes a Matron through th'amazed streetes,	Lucan, First Booke		675
thou lead'st me toward th'east,/Where Nile augmenteth the	Lucan, First Booke		682
Before whose bow th'Arcadian wild beasts trembled.	Ovid's Elegies		1.7.14
Th'opposed starre of Mars hath done thee harme,	Ovid's Elegies		1.8.29
Isis may be done/Nor feare least she to th'theater's runne.	Ovid's Elegies		2.2.26

TH' (cont.)			
With scepters, and high buskins th'one would dresse me,	Ovid's Elegies	3.1.63	
Greater then her, by her leave th'art, Ile say.	Ovid's Elegies	3.2.60	
Insooth th'eternall powers graunt maides society/Falsely to	Ovid's Elegies	3.3.11	
All being shut out, th'adulterer is within.	Ovid's Elegies	3.4.8	
Th'Arcadian Virgins constant love hath wunne?	Ovid's Elegies	3.5.30	
Either th'art muddy in mid winter tide:	Ovid's Elegies	3.5.95	
Either th'art witcht with blood <bould> of frogs new dead,	Ovid's Elegies	3.6.79	
With th'earth thou wert content,/Why seek'st not heav'n the	Ovid's Elegies	3.7.49	
The one his first love, th'other his new care.	Ovid's Elegies	3.8.32	
And may th'earths weight thy ashes nought molest.	Ovid's Elegies	3.8.68	
He to th'Hetrurians Junoes feast commended,	Ovid's Elegies	3.12.35	
And stole away th'inchaunted gazers mind,	Hero and Leander	1.104	
Or if it could, downe from th'enameld skie,	Hero and Leander	1.249	
Which th'earth from ougly Chaos den up-wayd:	Hero and Leander	1.450	
his promise, did despise/The love of th'everlasting Destinies.	Hero and Leander	1.462	
And now the sunne that through th'orizon peepes,	Hero and Leander	2.99	
Aye me, Leander cryde, th'enamoured sunne,	Hero and Leander	2.202	
Entred the orchard of Th'esperides,	Hero and Leander	2.298	
And sigh'd to thinke upon th'approching sunne,	Hero and Leander	2.302	
TH			
in a brasen Bull/Of great ones envy; o'th poore petty wites,	Jew	Prol.26	Machvl
But take it to you i'th devils name.	Jew	1.2.154	Barab
And rise with them i'th middle of the Towne,	Jew	5.1.92	Barab
To morrow we would sit i'th Consistory,	F1017	3.2.37	Pope
I, and I fall not asleepe i'th meane time.	F1196	4.1.42	Benvol
TH'ABREVIATED			
Th'abreviated <breviated> names of holy Saints,	F 238	1.3.10	Faust
TH'AD			
Th'ad best betimes forsake [them] <thee> and their trains,	Edw	3.1.202	Lncstr
TH'ADULTERER			
All being shut out, th'adulterer is within.	Ovid's Elegies	3.4.8	
TH'ADULTEROUS			
As Prognes to th'adulterous Thracian King,	1Tamb	4.4.24	Zabina
TH'ADVANTAGES			
Let him take all th'advantages he can,	1Tamb	4.1.40	Souldn
TH'AFFRIGHTED			
Th'affrighted worlds force bent on publique spoile,	Lucan, First Booke	5	
THAILE			
Convey hence Gaveston, thaile murder him.	Edw	2.2.82	Edward
TH'AIRS			
But come lets walke aside, th'airs not very sweet.	P 497	9.16	QnMoth
TH'ALMIGHTY			
For if th'almighty take my brother hence,	P 469	8.19	Anjoy
TH'AMAZED			
So runnes a Matron through th'amazed streetes,	Lucan, First Booke	675	
THAMIRAS			
Or Thamiras in curious painted things?	Ovid's Elegies	3.6.62	
THAN (Homograph; See also THEN)			
I know you have a better wit than I.	1Tamb	1.1.5	Mycet
a greater [task]/Fits Menaphon, than warring with a Thiefe:	1Tamb	1.1.88	Cosroe
Unlesse they have a wiser king than you.	1Tamb	1.1.92	Cosroe
Unlesse they have a wiser king than you?	1Tamb	1.1.93	Mycet
Than if you were arriv'd in Siria,	1Tamb	1.2.4	Tamb
Thinke you I way this treasure more than you?	1Tamb	1.2.84	Tamb
Zenocrate, lovelier than the Love of Jove,	1Tamb	1.2.87	Tamb
Brighter than is the silver [Rhodope] <Rhodolfe>,	1Tamb	1.2.88	Tamb
Fairer than whitest snow on Scythian hils,	1Tamb	1.2.89	Tamb
Than the possession of the Persean Crowne,	1Tamb	1.2.91	Tamb
Mounted on Steeds, swifter than Pegasus.	1Tamb	1.2.94	Tamb
More rich and valurous than Zenocrates.	1Tamb	1.2.97	Tamb
Than Tamburlaine be slaine or overcome.	1Tamb	1.2.177	Tamb
Than dooth the King of Persea in his Crowne:	1Tamb	1.2.242	Tamb
And more regarding gaine than victory:	1Tamb	2.2.46	Meandr
You fighting more for honor than for gold,	1Tamb	2.2.66	Meandr
Shall threat the Gods more than Cyclopian warres,	1Tamb	2.3.21	Tamb
And more than needes to make an Emperour.	1Tamb	2.3.65	Tamb
And lose more labor than the gaine will quight.	1Tamb	2.5.96	Tamb
What better president than mightie Jove?	1Tamb	2.7.17	Tamb
Than if the Gods had held a Parliament:	1Tamb	2.7.66	Tamb
His talke much sweeter than the Muses song,	1Tamb	3.2.50	Zenoc
Than Juno sister to the highest God,	1Tamb	3.2.54	Zenoc
And gives no more than common courtesies.	1Tamb	3.2.63	Agidas
Than stay the torments he and heaven have sworne.	1Tamb	3.2.99	Agidas
are ful of brags/And menace more than they can wel performe:	1Tamb	3.3.4	Tamb
More mighty than the Turkish Emperour:	1Tamb	3.3.37	Therid
Than Hercules, that in his infancie/Did pash the jawes of	1Tamb	3.3.104	Bajzth
of a bigger size/Than all the brats ysprong from Typhons loins:	1Tamb	3.3.109	Bajzth
Fairer than rockes of pearle and pretious stone,	1Tamb	3.3.118	Tamb
Whose eies are brighter than the Lamps of heaven,	1Tamb	3.3.120	Tamb
And speech more pleasant than sweet harmony:	1Tamb	3.3.121	Tamb
For he that gives him other food than this:	1Tamb	4.2.89	Tamb
Than in the haven when the Pilot stands/And viewes a strangers	1Tamb	4.3.32	Souldn
Me thinks, tis a great deale better than a consort of musicke.	1Tamb	4.4.60	P Therid
These more than dangerous warrants of our death,	1Tamb	5.1.31	1Virgn
Than all my Army to Damascus walles.	1Tamb	5.1.156	Tamb
More than Cymerian Stix or Distinie.	1Tamb	5.1.234	Bajzth
Than noisome parbreak of the Stygian Snakes,	1Tamb	5.1.256	Bajzth
Whose lives were dearer to Zenocrate/Than her owne life, or	1Tamb	5.1.338	Zenoc
A title higher than thy Souldans name:	1Tamb	5.1.434	Tamb
to your dominions/Than ever yet confirm'd th'Egyptian Crown.	1Tamb	5.1.449	Tamb
Forbids you further liberty than this.	2Tamb	1.2.8	Almeda
And more than this, for all I cannot tell.	2Tamb	1.2.53	Callap

THAN (cont.)			
in mine eies/Than all the wealthy kingdomes I subdewed:	2Tamb	1.3.19	Tamb
And shine in compleat vertue more than they,	2Tamb	1.3.51	Tamb
It could not more delight me than your sight.	2Tamb	1.3.156	Tamb
In number more than are the drops that fall/When Boreas rents a	2Tamb	1.3.159	Tamb
With greater power than erst his pride hath felt,	2Tamb	2.2.10	Gazell
And numbers more than infinit of men,	2Tamb	2.2.18	Gazell
Than this base earth should shroud your majesty:	2Tamb	2.4.60	Zenoc
Raise Cavalieros higher than the cloudes,	2Tamb	2.4.103	Tamb
shall raise a hill/Of earth and fagots higher than thy Fort,	2Tamb	3.3.22	Therid
Or els invent some torture worse than that.	2Tamb	3.4.22	Olymp
Than any Viceroy, King or Emperour.	2Tamb	3.4.43	Olymp
And thou shalt see a man greater than Mahomet,	2Tamb	3.4.46	Therid
lookes is much more majesty/Than from the Concave superficies,	2Tamb	3.4.48	Therid
Than when she gave eternall Chaos forme,	2Tamb	3.4.76	Techel
In number more than are the quyvering leaves/Of Idas forrest,	2Tamb	3.5.5	2Msngr
That flies with fury swifter than our thoughts,	2Tamb	4.1.5	Amyras
you wil be thought/More childish valourous than manly wise:	2Tamb	4.1.17	Calyph
And sooner far than he that never fights.	2Tamb	4.1.55	Calyph
Than he that darted mountaines at thy head,	2Tamb	4.1.128	Tamb
Rather than yeeld to his detested suit,	2Tamb	4.2.6	Olymp
operation and more force/Than Cynthias in the watery wildernes,	2Tamb	4.2.30	Therid
Now Hell is fairer than Elisian,	2Tamb	4.2.87	Therid
A greater Lamp than that bright eie of heaven,	2Tamb	4.2.88	Therid
Than you by this unconquered arme of mine.	2Tamb	4.3.16	Tamb
live, and draw/My chariot swifter than the racking cloudes:	2Tamb	4.3.21	Tamb
That must (advaunst in higher pompe than this)/Rifle the	2Tamb	4.3.58	Tamb
queintly dect/With bloomes more white than Hericinas browes,	2Tamb	4.3.122	Tamb
Than honor of thy countrie or thy name?	2Tamb	5.1.11	Govnr
More strong than are the gates of death or hel?	2Tamb	5.1.20	Govnr
More exquisite than ever Traitor felt.	2Tamb	5.1.53	Therid
we offer more/Than ever yet we did to such proud slaves,	2Tamb	5.1.58	Techel
Whose lofty Pillers, higher than the cloudes,	2Tamb	5.1.64	Tamb
Which threatned more than if the region/Next underneath the	2Tamb	5.1.87	Tamb
There lies more gold than Babylon is worth,	2Tamb	5.1.116	Govnr
our hearts/More than the thought of this dooth vexe our soules.	2Tamb	5.1.145	Jrslem
and on his head/A Chaplet brighter than Apollos crowne,	2Tamb	5.2.33	Amasia
Is greater far, than they can thus subdue.	2Tamb	5.3.39	Usumc
Being distant lesse than ful a hundred leagues,	2Tamb	5.3.133	Tamb
More worth than Asia, and the world beside,	2Tamb	5.3.153	Tamb
More than the ruine of our proper soules.	2Tamb	5.3.182	Therid
Through rocks more steepe and sharp than Caspian cliftes.	2Tamb	5.3.241	Tamb
chariot wil not beare/A guide of baser temper than my selfe,	2Tamb	5.3.243	Tamb
Soft Barabas, there's more longs too't than so.	Jew	1.2.45	Govnr
of the Serpent then the Dove; that is, more knave than foole.	Jew	2.3.37	P Barab
You'le like it better farre a nights than dayes.	Jew	2.3.63	Barab
It may be she sees more in me than I can find in my selfe:	Jew	4.2.33	P Ithimr
A loves me better than a thousand Spencers.	Edw	4.2.7	Prince
Trips she, it likes me well, plods she, what than?	Ovid's Elegies	2.4.23	
Confessing this, why doest thou touch him than?	Ovid's Elegies	3.7.22	
But with my rivall sicke she was not than.	Ovid's Elegies	3.10.26	
Because she tooke more from her than she left,	Hero and Leander	1.47	
To hazard more, than for the golden Fleece.	Hero and Leander	1.58	
Than she the hearts of those that neere her stood.	Hero and Leander	1.112	
In heaping up a masse of drossie pelfe,/Than such as you:	Hero and Leander	1.245	
honour, and thereby/Commit'st a sinne far worse than perjurie.	Hero and Leander	1.306	
Than for the fire filcht by Prometheus;	Hero and Leander	1.438	
Than Hero this inestimable gemme.	Hero and Leander	2.78	
Than he could saile, for incorporeal Fame,	Hero and Leander	2.113	
Is swifter than the wind, whose tardie plumes,	Hero and Leander	2.115	
And nothing more than counsaile, lovers hate.	Hero and Leander	2.140	
Than Dis, on heapes of gold fixing his looke.	Hero and Leander	2.326	
THANK			
I will not thank thee (sweet Ortigius)/Better replies shall	1Tamb	2.5.36	Cosroe
I thank thee Sigismond, but when I war/All Asia Minor, Affrica,	2Tamb	1.1.157	Orcan
Why, I thank your Majesty.	2Tamb	3.1.79	P Almeda
We thank your majesty.	2Tamb	4.3.74	Soldrs
I humbly thank your Majestie.	P 169	3.4	P Pothec
I humbly thank your royall Majestie.	P 273	4.71	Admral
I thank you sir.	F1642	4.6.85	P Faust
THANKE			
In all humilitie I thanke your grace.	Dido	2.1.99	Aeneas
I know it wel my Lord, and thanke you all.	1Tamb	1.1.187	Cosroe
We shall, my Lord, and thanke you.	Jew	5.5.8	Crpntr
We thanke your worship.	Edw	1.1.47	Omnes
I humbly thanke your Ladieship.	Edw	2.1.81	Spencr
Now let them thanke themselves, and rue too late.	Edw	2.2.207	Edward
I humblie thanke your majestie.	Edw	2.2.247	Baldck
I thanke you all my lords, then I perceive,	Edw	2.5.29	Gavstn
I thanke them, gave me leave to passe in peace:	Edw	4.1.16	Mortmr
We thanke you all.	Edw	4.6.53	Queene
I humblie thanke your honour.	Edw	5.6.10	Matrvs
Yes marry sir, and I thanke you to.	F 368	1.4.26	P Robin
'Twas thine own seeking Faustus, thanke thy selfe.	F 555	2.2.4	Mephst
I thanke your Holinesse.	F1038	3.2.58	Archbp
I thanke you sir.	F1043	3.2.63	Faust
I thanke your grace.	F1608	4.6.51	Faust
I humbly thanke your grace: then fetch some Beere.	F1625	4.6.68	Faust
I thanke you, I am fully satisfied.	F1651	4.6.94	P Carter
I thanke you sir.	F App	p.231 7	P Faust
I humbly thanke your Grace.	F App	p.243 32	P Faust
THANKES			
Thankes gentle Lord for such unlookt for grace.	Dido	1.2.44	Serg

THANKES (cont.)			
Is this then all the thankes that I shall have,	Dido	3.2.37	Juno
But if I use such ceremonious thankes,	Dido	4.3.49	Aeneas
Thankes good Iarbus for thy friendly ayde,	Dido	5.1.75	Aeneas
A thousand thankes worthy Theridamas:	1Tamb	1.2.252	Tamb
Thankes, my Lord.	Jew	5.2.11	Barab
Thankes my good freend, I will requite thy love.	P 78	2.21	Guise
Thankes to my princely sonne, then tell me Guise,	P 228	4.26	QnMoth
Thankes to my Kingly Brother of Navarre.	P1150	22.12	King
Thankes gentle Warwick, come lets in and revell.	Edw	1.4.385	Edward
Thankes be heavens great architect and you.	Edw	4.6.22	Queene
Thankes gentle Winchester: sirra, be gon.	Edw	5.2.27	Queene
Thankes Mephostophilis for this sweete booke.	F 550	2.1.162	Faust
<Great> Thankes mighty Lucifer:	F 719	2.2.171	Faust
Thankes Mephostophilis:	F1006	3.2.26	Faust
Thankes Maister Doctor, for these pleasant sights, nor know I	F1558	4.6.1	P Duke
Thankes, good maister doctor.	F App	p.242 7	P Duchss
Thankes worthely are due for things unbought,	Ovid's Elegies		1.10.43
THANKFULL			
I would be thankfull for such curtesie.	Dido	4.2.29	Anna
Whil'st I rest thankfull for this curtesie.	Dido	5.1.77	Aeneas
THANKFULLY			
I thankfully shall undertake the charge/Of you and yours, and	P 476	8.26	Anjoy
Which cannot but be thankfully receiv'd.	P 906	18.7	Bartus
THANKLESSE			
What thanklesse Jason, Macareus, and Paris,	Ovid's Elegies		2.18.23
THANKS			
On your submission we with thanks excuse,	1Tamb	2.5.13	Cosroe
Thanks good Meander, then Cosroe raign/And governe Persea in	1Tamb	2.5.18	Cosroe
I yeeld with thanks and protestations/Of endlesse honor to thee	1Tamb	5.1.496	Souldn
Thanks gentle Almeda, then let us haste,	2Tamb	1.2.74	Callap
Thanks good Theridamas.	2Tamb	1.3.117	Tamb
Thanks king of Morocus, take your crown again.	2Tamb	1.3.137	Tamb
Thanks king of Fesse, take here thy crowne again.	2Tamb	1.3.150	Tamb
Thanks sonne Navarre, you see we love you well,	P 13	1.13	QnMoth
Thanks my good freend, holde, take thou this reward.	P 168	3.3	OldQn
Thanks to you al.	P 599	12.12	King
Thanks to your Majestie, and so I take my leave.	P 749	15.7	Joyeux
TH'ANTARTICKE			
Leapes from th'Antarticke world unto the skie,	F 231	1.3.3	Faust
TH'ANTARTIQUE			
We meane to traveile to th'Antartique Pole,	1Tamb	4.4.136	Tamb
And from th'Antartique Pole, Eastward behold/As much more land,	2Tamb	5.3.154	Tamb
TH'ANTIPODES			
Discendeth downward to th'Antipodes.	2Tamb	1.2.52	Callap
TH'APPROCHING			
And sigh'd to thinke upon th'approching sunne,	Hero and Leander		2.302
TH'ARABIAN			
Madam, your father and th'Arabian king,	1Tamb	5.1.378	Philem
TH'ARCADIAN			
Before whose bow th'Arcadian wild beasts trembled.	Ovid's Elegies		1.7.14
Th'Arcadian Virgins constant love hath wunne?	Ovid's Elegies		3.5.30
TH'ARREST			
Stand not on titles, but obay th'arrest,	Edw	4.7.58	Leistr
TH'ARRIVALL			
Expects th'arrivall of her highnesse person.	1Tamb	1.2.79	Agidas
TH'ART			
Greater then her, by her leave th'art, Ile say.	Ovid's Elegies		3.2.60
Either th'art muddy in mid winter tide:	Ovid's Elegies		3.5.95
Either th'art witcht with blood <bould> of frogs new dead,	Ovid's Elegies		3.6.79
TH'ARTS			
all to good, be Augury vaine, and Tages/Th'arts master falce.	Lucan, First Booke		636
TH'ASPIRING			
My Lord I mervaile that th'aspiring Guise/Dares once adventure	P 36	1.36	Admral
TH'ASSAULT			
And sharpest where th'assault is desperate.	2Tamb	3.2.67	Tamb
TH'ASSIRIANS			
Whose chariot wheeles have burst th'Assirians bones,	2Tamb	5.1.71	Tamb
THAT			
That will not shield me from her shrewish blowes:	Dido	1.1.4	Ganimd
She reacht me such a rap for that I spilde,	Dido	1.1.7	Ganimd
That shaken thrise, makes Natures buildings quake,	Dido	1.1.11	Jupitr
Might I but see that pretie sport a foote,	Dido	1.1.16	Ganimd
If that thy fancie in his feathers dwell,	Dido	1.1.39	Jupitr
And playing with that female wanton boy,	Dido	1.1.51	Venus
Since that religion hath no recompence.	Dido	1.1.81	Venus
Or force her smile that hetherto hath frownd:	Dido	1.1.88	Jupitr
And flourish once againe that erst was dead:	Dido	1.1.95	Jupitr
That earth-borne Atlas groning underprops:	Dido	1.1.99	Jupitr
Till that a Princesse priest conceav'd by Mars,	Dido	1.1.106	Jupitr
I will take order for that presently:	Dido	1.1.113	Jupitr
That durst thus proudly wrong our kinsmans peace.	Dido	1.1.119	Jupitr
That erst-while issued from thy watrie loynes,	Dido	1.1.128	Venus
That by thy vertues freest us from annoy,	Dido	1.1.153	Achat
That we may make a fire to warme us with,	Dido	1.1.167	Aeneas
Yet much I marvell that I cannot finde,	Dido	1.1.180	Achat
Thou art a Goddesse that delud'st our eyes,	Dido	1.1.191	Aeneas
Tell us, O tell us that are ignorant,	Dido	1.1.200	Aeneas
That they may trip more lightly ore the lawndes,	Dido	1.1.207	Venus
But what are you that aske of me these things?	Dido	1.1.214	Venus
And made that way my mother Venus led:	Dido	1.1.221	Aeneas
Achates, tis my mother that is fled,	Dido	1.1.240	Aeneas
That crave such favour at your honors feete,	Dido	1.2.5	Illion

THAT (cont.)

That doe complaine the wounds of thousand waves,	Dido	1.2.8	Illion
Before that Boreas buckled with your sailes?	Dido	1.2.19	Iarbus
That in such peace long time did rule the same:	Dido	1.2.24	Cloan
Me thinkes that towne there should be Troy, yon Idas hill,	Dido	2.1.7	Aeneas
it life, that under his conduct/We might saile backe to Troy,	Dido	2.1.17	Aeneas
Grecians, which rejoyce/That nothing now is left of Priamus:	Dido	2.1.20	Aeneas
Yet thinkes my minde that this is Priamus:	Dido	2.1.25	Aeneas
Thy mind Aeneas that would have it so/Deludes thy eye sight,	Dido	2.1.31	Achat
What stranger art thou that doest eye me thus?	Dido	2.1.74	Dido
Both happie that Aeneas is our guest:	Dido	2.1.82	Dido
For many tales goe of that Cities fall,	Dido	2.1.108	Dido
But all in this that Troy is overcome,	Dido	2.1.112	Dido
O th'inchaunting words of that base slave,	Dido	2.1.161	Aeneas
The rather for that one Laocoon/Breaking a speare upon his	Dido	2.1.164	Aeneas
Inforst a wide breach in that rampierd wall,	Dido	2.1.174	Aeneas
That after burnt the pride of Asia.	Dido	2.1.187	Aeneas
his breast/Furrowd with wounds, and that which made me weepe,	Dido	2.1.204	Aeneas
Which made the funerall flame that burnt faire Troy:	Dido	2.1.218	Aeneas
And after by that Pirrhus sacrifizde.	Dido	2.1.288	Aeneas
But how scapt Helen, she that causde this warre?	Dido	2.1.292	Dido
O had that ticing strumpet nere been borne:	Dido	2.1.300	Dido
Who if that any seeke to doe him hurt,	Dido	2.1.321	Venus
That she may dote upon Aeneas love:	Dido	2.1.327	Venus
And by that meanes repaire his broken ships,	Dido	2.1.328	Venus
Tis not enough that thou doest graunt me love,	Dido	3.1.8	Iarbus
But that I may enjoy what I desire:	Dido	3.1.9	Iarbus
That love is childish which consists in words.	Dido	3.1.10	Iarbus
know that thou of all my wooers/(And yet have I had many	Dido	3.1.11	Dido
That I should say thou art no love of mine?	Dido	3.1.42	Dido
O that Iarbus could but fancie me.	Dido	3.1.62	Anna
So lovely is he that where ere he goes,	Dido	3.1.71	Anna
Yet must I heare that lothsome name againe?	Dido	3.1.78	Dido
Dido, that till now/Didst never thinke Aeneas beautifull:	Dido	3.1.82	Dido
That will Aeneas shewe your majestie.	Dido	3.1.98	Achat
Conditionally that thou wilt stay with me,	Dido	3.1.114	Dido
So that Aeneas may but stay with me.	Dido	3.1.133	Dido
For if that any man could conquer me,	Dido	3.1.137	Dido
No Madame, but it seemes that these are Kings.	Dido	3.1.149	Aeneas
Then never say that thou art miserable,	Dido	3.1.169	Dido
That ugly impe that shall outweare my wrath,	Dido	3.2.4	Juno
That onely Juno rules in Rhamnuse towne.	Dido	3.2.20	Juno
Fie Venus, that such causeles words of wrath,	Dido	3.2.26	Juno
Is this then all the thankes that I shall have,	Dido	3.2.37	Juno
That would have kild him sleeping as he lay?	Dido	3.2.39	Juno
That was advanced by my Hebes shame,	Dido	3.2.43	Juno
And wish that I had never wrongd him so:	Dido	3.2.48	Juno
That hath so many unresisted friends:	Dido	3.2.50	Juno
Sister of Jove, if that thy love be such,	Dido	3.2.53	Venus
That overcloy my soule with their content:	Dido	3.2.63	Juno
But that thou maist more easilie perceive,	Dido	3.2.66	Juno
That thus in person goe with thee to hunt:	Dido	3.3.2	Dido
Ile dye before a stranger have that grace:	Dido	3.3.11	Iarbus
And meddle not with any that I love:	Dido	3.3.22	Dido
But should that man of men (Dido except)/Have taunted me in	Dido	3.3.26	Iarbus
And dead to honour that hath brought me up.	Dido	3.3.45	Aeneas
And dead to scorne that hath pursued me so.	Dido	3.3.49	Iarbus
That sav'd your famisht souldiers lives from death,	Dido	3.3.52	Achat
That imitate the Moone in every chaunge,	Dido	3.3.67	Iarbus
fond man, that were to warre gainst heaven,/And with one shaft	Dido	3.3.71	Iarbus
But Dido that now holdeth him so deare,	Dido	3.3.76	Iarbus
turne the hand of fate/Unto that happie day of my delight,	Dido	3.3.81	Iarbus
That resteth in the rivall of thy paine,	Dido	3.3.84	Iarbus
Why, that was in a net, where we are loose,	Dido	3.4.5	Dido
Why, what is it that Dido may desire/And not obtaine, be it in	Dido	3.4.7	Aeneas
The thing that I will dye before I aske,	Dido	3.4.9	Dido
That should detaine thy eye in his defects?	Dido	3.4.17	Aeneas
The man that I doe eye where ere I am,	Dido	3.4.18	Dido
I must conceale/The torment, that it bootes me not reveale,/And	Dido	3.4.26	Dido
Something it was that now I have forgot.	Dido	3.4.30	Dido
But now that I have found what to effect,	Dido	3.4.37	Dido
I followe one that loveth fame for me,	Dido	3.4.38	Dido
Then to the Carthage Queene that dyes for him.	Dido	3.4.40	Dido
If that your majestie can looke so lowe,	Dido	3.4.41	Aeneas
As my despised worths, that shun all praise,	Dido	3.4.42	Aeneas
And by this Sword that saved me from the Greekes,	Dido	3.4.48	Aeneas
That calles my soule from forth his living seate,	Dido	3.4.53	Dido
Kind clowdes that sent forth such a curteous storme,	Dido	3.4.55	Dido
That can call them forth when as she please,	Dido	4.1.4	Iarbus
Iarbus, curse that unrevenging Jove,	Dido	4.1.18	Iarbus
That with the sharpnes of my edged sting,	Dido	4.1.22	Iarbus
But I will soone put by that stumbling blocke,	Dido	4.1.34	Dido
And quell those hopes that thus employ your [cares] <eares>.	Dido	4.1.35	Dido
That I may pacifie that gloomie Jove,	Dido	4.2.2	Iarbus
That with thy gloomie hand corrects the heaven,	Dido	4.2.6	Iarbus
The woman that thou wild us entertaine,	Dido	4.2.11	Iarbus
And all the fruites that plentie els sends forth,	Dido	4.2.15	Iarbus
him to his ships/That now afflicts me with his flattering eyes.	Dido	4.2.22	Iarbus
partake with me the cause/Of this devotion that detaineth you,	Dido	4.2.28	Anna
Alas poore King that labours so in vaine,	Dido	4.2.33	Anna
For her that so delighteth in thy paine:	Dido	4.2.34	Anna
That register the numbers of my ruth,	Dido	4.2.39	Iarbus
Anna that doth admire thee more then heaven.	Dido	4.2.46	Anna

THAT (cont.)

That intercepts the course of my desire:	Dido	4.2.48	Iarbus
That doe pursue my peace where ere it goes.	Dido	4.2.51	Iarbus
The dreames (brave mates) that did beset my bed,	Dido	4.3.16	Aeneas
That tyed together by the striving tongues,	Dido	4.3.29	Aeneas
Banish that ticing dame from forth your mouth,	Dido	4.3.31	Achat
O foolish Troians that would steale from hence,	Dido	4.4.5	Dido
To rid thee of that doubt, abourd againe,	Dido	4.4.21	Dido
me, for I forgot/That yong Ascanius lay with me this night:	Dido	4.4.32	Dido
O that the Clowdes were here wherein thou [fledst] <fleest>,	Dido	4.4.50	Dido
That thou and I unseene might sport our selves:	Dido	4.4.51	Dido
This is the harbour that Aeneas seekes,	Dido	4.4.59	Aeneas
Those that dislike what Dido gives in charge,	Dido	4.4.71	Dido
The ground is mine that gives them sustenance,	Dido	4.4.74	Dido
All that they have, their lands, their goods, their lives,	Dido	4.4.76	Dido
O blessed tempests that did drive him in,	Dido	4.4.94	Dido
O happie sand that made him runne aground:	Dido	4.4.95	Dido
O that I had a charme to keepe the windes/Within the closure of	Dido	4.4.99	Dido
Or that the Tyrrhen sea were in mine armes,	Dido	4.4.101	Dido
That he might suffer shipwracke on my breast,	Dido	4.4.102	Dido
onely Aeneas frowne/Is that which terrifies poore Didos heart:	Dido	4.4.116	Dido
It is Aeneas frowne that ends my daies:	Dido	4.4.120	Dido
Are these the sailes that in despight of me,	Dido	4.4.126	Dido
Ile set the casement open that the windes/May enter in, and	Dido	4.4.130	Dido
Is this the wood that grew in Carthage plaines,	Dido	4.4.136	Dido
And told me that Aeneas ment to goe:	Dido	4.4.142	Dido
These were the instruments that launcht him forth,	Dido	4.4.150	Dido
Was it not you that hoysed up these sailes?	Dido	4.4.153	Dido
I have an Orchard that hath store of plums,	Dido	4.5.4	Nurse
That I might live to see this boy a man,	Dido	4.5.18	Nurse
Then that which grim Atrides overthrew:	Dido	5.1.3	Aeneas
That loade their thighes with Hyblas honeys spoyles,	Dido	5.1.13	Aeneas
That have I not determinde with my selfe.	Dido	5.1.19	Aeneas
If that all glorie hath forsaken thee,	Dido	5.1.36	Hermes
This was my mother that beguild the Queene,	Dido	5.1.42	Aeneas
That daylie dandlest Cupid in thy armes:	Dido	5.1.45	Aeneas
If that be all, then cheare thy drooping lookes,	Dido	5.1.71	Iarbus
But that eternall Jupiter commands.	Dido	5.1.82	Aeneas
The Gods, what Gods be those that seeke my death?	Dido	5.1.128	Dido
That he should take Aeneas from mine armes?	Dido	5.1.130	Dido
That I might see Aeneas in his face:	Dido	5.1.150	Dido
O Serpent that came creeping from the shoare,	Dido	5.1.165	Dido
I hope that that which love forbids me doe,	Dido	5.1.170	Dido
Yet he that in my sight would not relent,	Dido	5.1.186	Dido
That I may learne to beare it patiently,	Dido	5.1.208	Dido
That slayest me with thy harsh and hellish tale,	Dido	5.1.217	Dido
That they may melt and I fall in his armes:	Dido	5.1.245	Dido
That I may swim to him like Tritons neece:	Dido	5.1.247	Dido
That I may tice a Dolphin to the shoare,	Dido	5.1.249	Dido
That hath dishonord her and Carthage both?	Dido	5.1.280	Iarbus
That shall consume all that this stranger left,	Dido	5.1.285	Dido
To cure my minde that melts for unkind love.	Dido	5.1.287	Dido
Here lye the Sword that in the darksome Cave/He drew, and swore	Dido	5.1.295	Dido
And now ye gods that guide the starrie frame,	Dido	5.1.302	Dido
That may revenge this treason to a Queene,	Dido	5.1.307	Dido
Betwixt this land and that be never league,	Dido	5.1.309	Dido
dye to expiate/The griefe that tires upon thine inward soule.	Dido	5.1.317	Iarbus
That Gods and men may pitie this my death,	Dido	5.1.327	Anna
that in former age/Hast bene the seat of mightie Conquerors,	1Tamb	1.1.6	Cosroe
That in their prowesse and their pollicies,	1Tamb	1.1.8	Cosroe
That knowe my wit, and can be witnesses:	1Tamb	1.1.22	Mycet
Which is (God knowes) about that Tamburlaine,	1Tamb	1.1.30	Mycet
That like a Foxe in midst of harvest time,	1Tamb	1.1.31	Mycet
Of Tamburlaine, that sturdie Scythian thiefe,	1Tamb	1.1.36	Meandr
That robs your merchants of Persepolis,	1Tamb	1.1.37	Meandr
To apprehend that paltrie Scythian.	1Tamb	1.1.53	Mycet
That holds us up, and foiles our neighbour foes.	1Tamb	1.1.61	Mycet
But Tamburlaine, and that Tartarian rout,	1Tamb	1.1.71	Therid
That I may view these milk-white steeds of mine,	1Tamb	1.1.77	Mycet
Besmer'd with blood, that makes a dainty show.	1Tamb	1.1.80	Mycet
That he may win the Babylonians hearts,	1Tamb	1.1.90	Cosroe
to them, that all Asia/Lament to see the follie of their King.	1Tamb	1.1.95	Cosroe
That dar'st presume thy Soveraigne for to mocke.	1Tamb	1.1.105	Mycet
But this it is that doth excruciate/The verie substance of my	1Tamb	1.1.113	Cosroe
To see our neighbours that were woont to quake/And tremble at	1Tamb	1.1.115	Cosroe
And that which might resolve me into teares,	1Tamb	1.1.118	Cosroe
That heretofore have fild Persepolis/With Affrike Captaines,	1Tamb	1.1.141	Ceneus
And cause the souldiers that thus honour me,	1Tamb	1.1.172	Cosroe
For they are friends that help to weane my state,	1Tamb	1.2.29	Tamb
Must grace his bed that conquers Asia:	1Tamb	1.2.37	Tamb
Lie here ye weedes that I disdaine to weare,	1Tamb	1.2.41	Tamb
And these that seeme but silly country Swaines,	1Tamb	1.2.47	Tamb
That even to death will follow Tamburlaine.	1Tamb	1.2.59	Usumc
That in conceit bear Empires on our speares,	1Tamb	1.2.64	Tamb
That thus oppresse poore friendles passengers.	1Tamb	1.2.70	Zenoc
That we may traveile into Siria,	1Tamb	1.2.77	Agidas
And I that triumpht so be overcome.	1Tamb	1.2.115	Tamb
That their reflexions may amaze the Perseans.	1Tamb	1.2.140	Tamb
That by Characters graven in thy browes,	1Tamb	1.2.169	Tamb
That I shall be the Monark of the East,	1Tamb	1.2.185	Tamb
And Christian Merchants that with Russian stems/Plow up huge	1Tamb	1.2.194	Tamb
And by those steps that he hath scal'd the heavens,	1Tamb	1.2.200	Tamb
We thinke it losse to make exchange for that/We are assured of	1Tamb	1.2.216	Techel

THAT (cont.)

shall confesse/Theise are the men that all the world admires.	1Tamb	1.2.223	Usumc
The man that in the forhead of his fortune,	1Tamb	2.1.3	Cosroe
But tell me, that hast seene him, Menaphon,	1Tamb	2.1.5	Cosroe
their Spheares/That guides his steps and actions to the throne,	1Tamb	2.1.17	Menaph
That could perswade at such a sodaine pinch,	1Tamb	2.1.37	Cosroe
That leads to Pallace of my brothers life,	1Tamb	2.1.43	Cosroe
set the Crowne/Upon your kingly head, that seeks our honor,	1Tamb	2.1.51	Ortyg
He that with Shepheards and a litle spoile,	1Tamb	2.1.54	Ceneus
That now is marching neer to Parthia:	1Tamb	2.1.65	Cosroe
And of that false Cosroe, my traiterous brother.	1Tamb	2.2.4	Mycet
That lie in ambush, waiting for a pray:	1Tamb	2.2.17	Meandr
That live by rapine and by lawlesse spoile,	1Tamb	2.2.23	Meandr
And he that could with giftes and promises/Inveigle him that	1Tamb	2.2.25	Meandr
giftes and promises/Inveigle him that lead a thousand horse,	1Tamb	2.2.26	Meandr
He that can take or slaughter Tamburlaine,	1Tamb	2.2.30	Meandr
Who brings that Traitors head Theridamas,	1Tamb	2.2.32	Meandr
His Highnesse pleasure is that he should live,	1Tamb	2.2.37	Meandr
That sprong of teeth of Dragons venomous?	1Tamb	2.2.52	Mycet
That live confounded in disordered troopes,	1Tamb	2.2.60	Meandr
Which you that be but common souldiers,	1Tamb	2.2.63	Meandr
Share equally the gold that bought their lives,	1Tamb	2.2.70	Meandr
And make them blest that share in his attemptes.	1Tamb	2.3.9	Tamb
Was but a handful to that we will have.	1Tamb	2.3.17	Tamb
and dim their eies/That stand and muse at our admyred armes.	1Tamb	2.3.24	Tamb
When she that rules in Rhamnis golden gates,	1Tamb	2.3.37	Cosroe
That I with these my friends and all my men,	1Tamb	2.3.43	Tamb
That it may reach the King of Perseas crowne,	1Tamb	2.3.53	Cosroe
That ere made passage thorow Persean Armes.	1Tamb	2.3.56	Tamb
go before and charge/The fainting army of that foolish King.	1Tamb	2.3.62	Cosroe
Accurst be he that first invented war,	1Tamb	2.4.1	Mycet
For Kings are clouts that every man shoots at,	1Tamb	2.4.8	Mycet
Our Crowne the pin that thousands seeke to cleave.	1Tamb	2.4.9	Mycet
And far from any man that is a foole.	1Tamb	2.4.12	Mycet
Meander, you that were our brothers Guide,	1Tamb	2.5.10	Cosroe
From one that knew not what a King should do,	1Tamb	2.5.22	Cosroe
To one that can commaund what longs thereto:	1Tamb	2.5.23	Cosroe
That if I should desire the Persean Crowne,	1Tamb	2.5.76	Tamb
That onely made him King to make us sport.	1Tamb	2.5.101	Tamb
That grievous image of ingratitude:	1Tamb	2.6.30	Cosroe
That fiery thirster after Soveraigntie:	1Tamb	2.6.31	Cosroe
And burne him in the fury of that flame,	1Tamb	2.6.32	Cosroe
That none can quence but blood and Emperie.	1Tamb	2.6.33	Cosroe
and all the Starres that make/The loathsome Circle of my dated	1Tamb	2.6.36	Cosroe
That thus opposeth him against the Gods,	1Tamb	2.6.39	Cosroe
And scornes the Powers that governe Persea.	1Tamb	2.6.40	Cosroe
That causde the eldest sonne of heavenly Ops,	1Tamb	2.7.13	Tamb
Nature that fram'd us of foure Elements,	1Tamb	2.7.18	Tamb
That perfect blisse and sole felicitie,	1Tamb	2.7.28	Tamb
And that made me to joine with Tamburlain,	1Tamb	2.7.30	Therid
That mooves not upwards, nor by princely deeds/Doth meane to	1Tamb	2.7.32	Therid
And that made us, the friends of Tamburlaine,	1Tamb	2.7.34	Techel
The strangest men that ever nature made,	1Tamb	2.7.40	Cosroe
If you but say that Tamburlaine shall raigne.	1Tamb	2.7.63	Tamb
that by leaden pipes/Runs to the citie from the mountain	1Tamb	3.1.59	Bajzth
That no reliefe or succour come by Land.	1Tamb	3.1.62	Bajzth
That worke such trouble to your woonted rest:	1Tamb	3.2.3	Agidas
And all that pierceth Phoebes silver eie,	1Tamb	3.2.19	Agidas
That I may live and die with Tamburlaine.	1Tamb	3.2.24	Zenoc
That holds you from your father in despight,	1Tamb	3.2.27	Agidas
How can you fancie one that lookes so fierce,	1Tamb	3.2.40	Agidas
Thence rise the tears that so distain my cheeks,	1Tamb	3.2.64	Zenoc
That shine as Comets, menacing revenge,	1Tamb	3.2.74	Agidas
late felt frownes/That sent a tempest to my daunted thoughtes,	1Tamb	3.2.86	Agidas
Two hundred thousand footmen that have serv'd/In two set	1Tamb	3.3.18	Bassoe
That made me Emperour of Asia.	1Tamb	3.3.32	Tamb
Even he that in a trice vanquisht two kings,	1Tamb	3.3.36	Therid
Wel said Theridamas, speake in that mood,	1Tamb	3.3.40	Tamb
I that am tearm'd the Scourge and Wrath of God,	1Tamb	3.3.44	Tamb
That naked rowe about the Terrene sea.	1Tamb	3.3.50	Tamb
That they lie panting on the Gallies side,	1Tamb	3.3.53	Tamb
That damned traine, the scum of Affrica,	1Tamb	3.3.56	Tamb
That make quick havock of the Christian blood.	1Tamb	3.3.58	Tamb
But as I live that towne shall curse the time/That Tamburlaine	1Tamb	3.3.59	Tamb
shall curse the time/That Tamburlaine set foot in Affrica.	1Tamb	3.3.60	Tamb
I meane t'incounter with that Bajazeth.	1Tamb	3.3.65	Tamb
those that lead my horse/Have to their names tytles of dignity,	1Tamb	3.3.69	Bajzth
And know thou Turke, that those which lead my horse,	1Tamb	3.3.72	Tamb
And all his Captaines that thus stoutly stand,	1Tamb	3.3.79	Bajzth
By this my sword that conquer'd Persea,	1Tamb	3.3.82	Tamb
That we may raigne as kings of Affrica.	1Tamb	3.3.99	Therid
that in his infancie/Did pash the jawes of Serpents venomous:	1Tamb	3.3.104	Bajzth
That with thy lookes canst cleare the darkened Sky:	1Tamb	3.3.122	Tamb
That leave no ground for thee to martch upon.	1Tamb	3.3.147	Bajzth
That never fought but had the victorie:	1Tamb	3.3.153	Tamb
glut our swords/That thirst to drinke the feble Perseans blood.	1Tamb	3.3.165	Bajzth
thou be plac'd by me/That am the Empresse of the mighty Turke?	1Tamb	3.3.167	Zabina
Cal'st thou me Concubine that am betroath'd/Unto the great and	1Tamb	3.3.169	Zenoc
Ye Gods and powers that governe Persea,	1Tamb	3.3.189	Zenoc
That I may see him issue Conquerour.	1Tamb	3.3.194	Zenoc
That dare to manage armes with him,	1Tamb	3.3.198	Zabina
That offered jewels to thy sacred shrine,	1Tamb	3.3.199	Zabina
But that he lives and will be Conquerour.	1Tamb	3.3.211	Zenoc

THAT (cont.)

The pillers that have bolstered up those tearmes,	1Tamb	3.3.229	Tamb
That yeerely saile to the Venetian gulfe,	1Tamb	3.3.249	Tamb
O cursed Mahomet that makest us thus/The slaves to Scythians	1Tamb	3.3.270	Zabina
That roaring, shake Damascus turrets downe.	1Tamb	4.1.3	Souldn
As Crocodiles that unaffrighted rest,	1Tamb	4.1.10	Souldn
That with his terrour and imperious eies,	1Tamb	4.1.14	2Msngr
I tell thee, were that Tamburlaine/As monsterous as Gorgon,	1Tamb	4.1.17	Souldn
Standard round, that stood/As bristle-pointed as a thorny wood.	1Tamb	4.1.26	2Msngr
Or withered leaves that Autume shaketh downe:	1Tamb	4.1.32	Souldn
That not a man should live to rue their fall.	1Tamb	4.1.35	Souldn
That satiate with spoile refuseth blood.	1Tamb	4.1.53	2Msngr
Not sparing any that can manage armes.	1Tamb	4.1.57	2Msngr
faire Arabian king/That hath bene disapointed by this slave,	1Tamb	4.1.69	Souldn
That sacrificing slice and cut your flesh,	1Tamb	4.2.3	Bajzth
first moover of that Spheare/Enchac'd with thousands ever	1Tamb	4.2.8	Tamb
But Villaine, thou that wishest this to me,	1Tamb	4.2.12	Tamb
That I may rise into my royall throne.	1Tamb	4.2.15	Tamb
That beares the honor of my royall waight.	1Tamb	4.2.21	Tamb
That may command thee peecemeale to be torne,	1Tamb	4.2.23	Tamb
Smile Stars that raign'd at my nativity,	1Tamb	4.2.33	Tamb
That almost brent the Axeltree of heaven,	1Tamb	4.2.50	Tamb
Unworthy king, that by thy crueltie,	1Tamb	4.2.56	Zabina
Dar'st thou that never saw an Emperour,	1Tamb	4.2.58	Zabina
That rooffes of golde, and sun-bright Pallaces,	1Tamb	4.2.62	Zabina
and she shal looke/That these abuses flow not from her tongue:	1Tamb	4.2.70	Zenoc
That should be horsed on fower mightie kings.	1Tamb	4.2.78	Bajzth
That will maintaine it against a world of Kings.	1Tamb	4.2.81	Tamb
Confusion light on him that helps thee thus.	1Tamb	4.2.84	Bajzth
For he that gives him other food than this:	1Tamb	4.2.89	Tamb
The ages that shall talk of Tamburlain,	1Tamb	4.2.95	Tamb
These Mores that drew him from Bythinia,	1Tamb	4.2.98	Tamb
That with their beauties grac'd the Memphion fields:	1Tamb	4.2.104	Tamb
feathered bird/That spreads her wings upon the citie wals,	1Tamb	4.2.106	Tamb
He dies, and those that kept us out so long.	1Tamb	4.2.118	Tamb
Were in that citie all the world contain'd,	1Tamb	4.2.121	Tamb
Against the Woolfe that angrie Themis sent,	1Tamb	4.3.5	Souldn
That dares controll us in our Territories.	1Tamb	4.3.14	Souldn
That such a base usurping vagabond/Should brave a king, or	1Tamb	4.3.21	Souldn
that the Souldan is/No more dismaide with tidings of his fall,	1Tamb	4.3.30	Souldn
That Tamburlaine shall rue the day, the hower,	1Tamb	4.3.38	Souldn
That meanes to fill your helmets full of golde:	1Tamb	4.4.7	Tamb
to come by, plucke out that, and twil serve thee and thy wife:	1Tamb	4.4.14	P Tamb
Ye Furies that can maske invisible,	1Tamb	4.4.17	Bajzth
That fed upon the substance of his child.	1Tamb	4.4.25	Zabina
Doost thou think that Mahomet wil suffer this?	1Tamb	4.4.52	P Therid
those blind Geographers/That make a triple region in the world,	1Tamb	4.4.76	Tamb
will I make the Point/That shall begin the Perpendicular.	1Tamb	4.4.82	Tamb
You that have martcht with happy Tamburlaine,	1Tamb	4.4.121	Tamb
Let us have hope that their unspotted praiers,	1Tamb	5.1.20	Govnr
Therefore in that your safeties and our owne,	1Tamb	5.1.40	Govnr
That this devise may proove propitious,	1Tamb	5.1.52	2Virgn
Graunt that these signes of victorie we yeeld/May bind the	1Tamb	5.1.55	2Virgn
That never nourisht thought against thy rule,	1Tamb	5.1.98	1Virgn
to prevent/That which mine honor sweares shal be perform'd:	1Tamb	5.1.107	Tamb
That in thy passion for thy countries love,	1Tamb	5.1.137	Tamb
Eies when that Ebena steps to heaven,	1Tamb	5.1.147	Tamb
His life that so consumes Zenocrate,	1Tamb	5.1.154	Tamb
If all the pens that ever poets held,	1Tamb	5.1.161	Tamb
And every sweetnes that inspir'd their harts,	1Tamb	5.1.163	Tamb
Save onely that in Beauties just applause,	1Tamb	5.1.178	Tamb
And every warriour that is rapt with love/Of fame, of valour,	1Tamb	5.1.180	Tamb
That which hath [stoopt] <stopt> the tempest of the Gods,	1Tamb	5.1.184	Tamb
That Vertue solely is the sum of glorie,	1Tamb	5.1.189	Tamb
For faire Zenocrate, that so laments his state.	1Tamb	5.1.205	Therid
That will we chiefly see unto, Theridamas,	1Tamb	5.1.206	Tamb
That lingring paines may massacre his heart.	1Tamb	5.1.228	Zabina
That all the world will see and laugh to scorne,	1Tamb	5.1.252	Zabina
That sees my crowne, my honor and my name,	1Tamb	5.1.260	Bajzth
That would with pity chear Zabinas heart,	1Tamb	5.1.271	Bajzth
That in the shortned sequel of my life,	1Tamb	5.1.278	Bajzth
That may be ministers of my decay.	1Tamb	5.1.289	Bajzth
That in this terrour Tamburlaine may live.	1Tamb	5.1.299	Bajzth
Ah, save that Infant, save him, save him.	1Tamb	5.1.313	P Zabina
Wretched Zenocrate, that livest to see,	1Tamb	5.1.319	Zenoc
Stead/That stampt on others with their thundring hooves,	1Tamb	5.1.331	Zenoc
the cause of this/That tearm'st Zenocrate thy dearest love?	1Tamb	5.1.336	Zenoc
Blush heaven, that gave them honor at their birth,	1Tamb	5.1.350	Zenoc
Those that are proud of fickle Empery,	1Tamb	5.1.352	Zenoc
That fights for Scepters and for slippery crownes,	1Tamb	5.1.356	Zenoc
Thou that in conduct of thy happy stars,	1Tamb	5.1.358	Zenoc
And pardon me that was not moov'd with ruthe,	1Tamb	5.1.369	Zenoc
That she shall stay and turne her wheele no more,	1Tamb	5.1.374	Anippe
That fights for honor to adorne your head.	1Tamb	5.1.376	Anippe
That no escape may save their enemies:	1Tamb	5.1.405	Arabia
eies beholde/That as for her thou bearst these wretched armes,	1Tamb	5.1.409	Arabia
Ah that the deadly panges I suffer now,	1Tamb	5.1.422	Arabia
And that I might be privy to the state,	1Tamb	5.1.426	Arabia
She that hath calmde the furie of my sword,	1Tamb	5.1.437	Tamb
Twas I my lord that gat the victory,	1Tamb	5.1.445	Tamb
A meteor that might terrify the earth,	1Tamb	5.1.461	Tamb
That I have sent from sundry foughten fields,	1Tamb	5.1.466	Tamb
His honor, that consists in sheading blood,	1Tamb	5.1.477	Tamb

THAT (cont.)

But here these kings that on my fortunes wait,	1Tamb	5.1.490	Tamb
Even by this hand that shall establish them,	1Tamb	5.1.492	Tamb
That long hath lingred for so high a seat.	1Tamb	5.1.502	Therid
and dominions/That late the power of Tamburlaine subdewed:	1Tamb	5.1.509	Tamb
That darted mountaines at her brother Jove:	1Tamb	5.1.511	Tamb
That purchac'd kingdomes by your martiall deeds,	1Tamb	5.1.523	Tamb
Who lives in Egypt, prisoner to that slave,	2Tamb	1.1.4	Orcan
Proud Tamburlaine, that now in Asia,	2Tamb	1.1.16	Gazell
Muffes, and Danes/That with the Holbard, Lance, and murthering	2Tamb	1.1.23	Uribas
Will hazard that we might with surety hold.	2Tamb	1.1.24	Uribas
Danubius stream that runs to Trebizon,	2Tamb	1.1.33	Orcan
And for that cause the Christians shall have peace.	2Tamb	1.1.57	Orcan
Nor he but Fortune that hath made him great.	2Tamb	1.1.60	Orcan
That never sea-man yet discovered:	2Tamb	1.1.71	Orcan
thou I am he/That with the Cannon shooke Vienna walles,	2Tamb	1.1.87	Orcan
Forgetst thou that I sent a shower of dartes/Mingled with	2Tamb	1.1.91	Orcan
That thou thy self, then County-Pallatine,	2Tamb	1.1.94	Orcan
Forgetst thou, that to have me raise my siege,	2Tamb	1.1.98	Orcan
Stampt with the princely Foule that in her wings/Caries the	2Tamb	1.1.100	Orcan
That hides these plaines, and seems as vast and wide,	2Tamb	1.1.107	Sgsmnd
Desart of Arabia/To those that stand on Badgeths lofty Tower,	2Tamb	1.1.109	Sgsmnd
Ocean to the Traveiler/That restes upon the snowy Appenines:	2Tamb	1.1.111	Sgsmnd
By him that made the world and sav'd my soule,	2Tamb	1.1.133	Sgsmnd
No speach to that end, by your favour sir.	2Tamb	1.2.14	Almeda
shine as bright/As that faire vail that covers all the world:	2Tamb	1.2.50	Callap
She lies so close that none can find her out.	2Tamb	1.2.60	Callap
I like that well:	2Tamb	1.2.61	P Almeda
Betweene thy sons that shall be Emperours,	2Tamb	1.3.7	Tamb
But that I know they issued from thy wombe,	2Tamb	1.3.33	Tamb
That never look'd on man but Tamburlaine.	2Tamb	1.3.34	Tamb
And he that meanes to place himselfe therin/Must armed wade up	2Tamb	1.3.83	Tamb
That lanching from Argier to Tripoly,	2Tamb	1.3.124	Therid
In number more than are the drops that fall/When Boreas rents a	2Tamb	1.3.159	Tamb
That though the stones, as at Deucalions flood,	2Tamb	1.3.163	Tamb
That Jove shall send his winged Messenger/To bid me sheath my	2Tamb	1.3.166	Tamb
And conquering that, made haste to Nubia,	2Tamb	1.3.202	Techel
What motion is it that inflames your thoughts,	2Tamb	2.1.2	Sgsmnd
It resteth now then that your Majesty/Take all advantages of	2Tamb	2.1.11	Fredrk
That strikes a terrour to all Turkish hearts,	2Tamb	2.1.15	Fredrk
That in the fortune of their overthrow,	2Tamb	2.1.24	Fredrk
That dare attempt to war with Christians.	2Tamb	2.1.26	Fredrk
Yet those infirmities that thus defame/Their faiths, their	2Tamb	2.1.44	Sgsmnd
That God hath given to venge our Christians death/And scourge	2Tamb	2.1.52	Fredrk
That would not kill and curse at Gods command,	2Tamb	2.1.55	Fredrk
That nigh Larissa swaies a mighty hoste,	2Tamb	2.2.6	Orcan
In partiall aid of that proud Scythian,	2Tamb	2.2.16	Gazell
That could not but before be terrified:	2Tamb	2.2.22	Uribas
That with such treason seek our overthrow,	2Tamb	2.2.34	Gazell
imperiall heaven/That he that sits on high and never sleeps,	2Tamb	2.2.49	Orcan
Thou Christ that art esteem'd omnipotent,	2Tamb	2.2.55	Orcan
That Zoacum, that fruit of bytternesse,	2Tamb	2.3.20	Orcan
That in the midst of fire is ingraft,	2Tamb	2.3.21	Orcan
That danc'd with glorie on the silver waves,	2Tamb	2.4.3	Tamb
Now wants the fewell that enflamde his beames:	2Tamb	2.4.4	Tamb
Zenocrate that gave him light and life,	2Tamb	2.4.8	Tamb
ceaslesse lamps/That gently look'd upon this loathsome earth,	2Tamb	2.4.19	Tamb
and holy Seraphins/That sing and play before the king of kings,	2Tamb	2.4.27	Tamb
The God that tunes this musicke to our soules,	2Tamb	2.4.31	Tamb
That this my life may be as short to me/As are the daies of	2Tamb	2.4.36	Tamb
That when this fraile and transitory flesh/Hath suckt the	2Tamb	2.4.43	Zenoc
Hath suckt the measure of that vitall aire/That feeds the body	2Tamb	2.4.44	Zenoc
of that vitall aire/That feeds the body with his dated health,	2Tamb	2.4.45	Zenoc
That dares torment the body of my Love,	2Tamb	2.4.79	Tamb
And wound the earth, that it may cleave in twaine,	2Tamb	2.4.97	Tamb
And feed my mind that dies for want of her:	2Tamb	2.4.128	Tamb
That since the heire of mighty Bajazeth/(An Emperour so	2Tamb	3.1.22	Callap
But that proud Fortune, who hath followed long/The martiall	2Tamb	3.1.27	Callap
That Jove surchardg'd with pity of our wrongs,	2Tamb	3.1.35	Callap
Some, that in conquest of the perjur'd Christian,	2Tamb	3.1.39	Orcan
That on mount Sinay with their ensignes spread,	2Tamb	3.1.46	Jrslem
That shew faire weather to the neighbor morne.	2Tamb	3.1.48	Jrslem
That touch the end of famous Euphrates.	2Tamb	3.1.53	Trebiz
That freed me from the bondage of my foe:	2Tamb	3.1.69	Callap
That is a Gentleman (I know) at least.	2Tamb	3.1.72	Callap
That being fiery meteors, may presage,	2Tamb	3.2.4	Tamb
That may endure till heaven be dissolv'd,	2Tamb	3.2.7	Tamb
That hanging here, wil draw the Gods from heaven:	2Tamb	3.2.28	Tamb
That have not past the Centers latitude,	2Tamb	3.2.31	Tamb
As is that towne, so is my heart consum'd,	2Tamb	3.2.49	Amyras
That meane to teach you rudiments of war:	2Tamb	3.2.54	Tamb
And store of ordinance that from every flanke/May scoure the	2Tamb	3.2.79	Tamb
That you may dryfoot martch through lakes and pooles,	2Tamb	3.2.86	Tamb
That being concocted, turnes to crimson blood,	2Tamb	3.2.108	Tamb
View me thy father that hath conquered kings,	2Tamb	3.2.110	Tamb
That by the warres lost not a dram of blood,	2Tamb	3.2.113	Tamb
That late adorn'd the Affrike Potentate,	2Tamb	3.2.124	Tamb
That we have sent before to fire the townes,	2Tamb	3.2.147	Tamb
And hunt that Coward, faintheart runaway,	2Tamb	3.2.149	Tamb
With that accursed traitor Almeda,	2Tamb	3.2.150	Tamb
That hath betraied my gracious Soveraigne,	2Tamb	3.2.153	Usumc
That curst and damned Traitor Almeda.	2Tamb	3.2.154	Usumc
That we may tread upon his captive necke,	2Tamb	3.2.157	Tamb

THAT (cont.)

Captaine, that thou yeeld up thy hold to us.	2Tamb	3.3.16		Therid
That with his ruine fils up all the trench.	2Tamb	3.3.26		Therid
That bring fresh water to thy men and thee:	2Tamb	3.3.30		Techel
That no supply of victuall shall come in,	2Tamb	3.3.32		Techel
Were you that are the friends of Tamburlain,	2Tamb	3.3.35		Capt
Cut off the water, all convoies that can,	2Tamb	3.3.39		Capt
That we may know if our artillery/Will carie full point blancke	2Tamb	3.3.52		Techel
us haste from hence/Along the cave that leads beyond the foe,	2Tamb	3.4.2		Olymp
That there begin and nourish every part,	2Tamb	3.4.7		Capt
my entrals bath'd/In blood that straineth from their orifex.	2Tamb	3.4.9		Capt
Death, whether art thou gone that both we live?	2Tamb	3.4.11		Olymp
Or els invent some torture worse than that.	2Tamb	3.4.22		Olymp
Sweet mother strike, that I may meet my father.	2Tamb	3.4.30		Sonne
That treadeth Fortune underneath his feete,	2Tamb	3.4.52		Therid
That to the adverse poles of that straight line,	2Tamb	3.4.64		Therid
That humbly craves upon her knees to stay,	2Tamb	3.4.70		Olymp
That feeds upon her sonnes and husbands flesh.	2Tamb	3.4.72		Olymp
That you must goe with us, no remedy.	2Tamb	3.4.79		Therid
That from the bounds of Phrigia to the sea/Which washeth Cyprus	2Tamb	3.5.11		Callap
Now, he that cals himself the scourge of Jove,	2Tamb	3.5.21		Orcan
and the bounds/Of that sweet land, whose brave Metropolis	2Tamb	3.5.36		Orcan
That fighting, knowes not what retreat doth meane,	2Tamb	3.5.43		Trebiz
So that the Army royall is esteem'd/Six hundred thousand	2Tamb	3.5.50		Soria
(The worthiest knight that ever brandisht sword)/Challenge in	2Tamb	3.5.71		Tamb
And join'd those stars that shall be opposite,	2Tamb	3.5.81		Tamb
Shall so torment thee and that Callapine,	2Tamb	3.5.85		Tamb
That like a roguish runnaway, suborn'd/That villaine there,	2Tamb	3.5.86		Tamb
a roguish runnaway, suborn'd/That villaine there, that slave,	2Tamb	3.5.87		Tamb
suborn'd/That villaine there, that slave, that Turkish dog,	2Tamb	3.5.87		Tamb
That most may vex his body and his soule.	2Tamb	3.5.99		Tamb
that when I take him, I may knocke out his braines with them,	2Tamb	3.5.140	P	Callap
Away, let us to the field, that the villaine may be slaine.	2Tamb	3.5.143	P	Tamb
hee shall not be put to that exigent, I warrant thee.	2Tamb	3.5.156	P	Trebiz
much like so many suns/That halfe dismay the majesty of heaven:	2Tamb	4.1.3		Soria
That flies with fury swifter than our thoughts,	2Tamb	4.1.5		Amyras
but that you wil be thought/More childish valourous than manly	2Tamb	4.1.16		Amyras
That fill the midst of farthest Tartary,	2Tamb	4.1.43		Calyph
And sooner far than he that never fights.	2Tamb	4.1.55		Amyras
tel me if the warres/Be not a life that may illustrate Gods,	2Tamb	4.1.79		Calyph
That they may say, it is not chance doth this,	2Tamb	4.1.84		Tamb
A Forme not meet to give that subject essence,	2Tamb	4.1.112		Amyras
That I might moove the turning Spheares of heaven,	2Tamb	4.1.118		Tamb
Than he that darted mountaines at thy head,	2Tamb	4.1.128		Tamb
That will not see the strength of Tamburlaine,	2Tamb	4.1.133		Tamb
That shortly heaven, fild with the meteors/Of blood and fire	2Tamb	4.1.141		Tamb
vaine or Artier feed/The cursed substance of that cruel heart,	2Tamb	4.1.178		Jrslem
that earth may eccho foorth/The far resounding torments ye	2Tamb	4.1.185		Soria
And with the flames that beat against the clowdes/Incense the	2Tamb	4.1.194		Tamb
that like armed men/Are seene to march upon the towers of	2Tamb	4.1.201		Tamb
But now I finde thee, and that feare is past.	2Tamb	4.2.20		Tamb
Forbids my mind to entertaine a thought/That tends to love, but	2Tamb	4.2.26		Therid
But that where every period ends with death,	2Tamb	4.2.47		Olymp
That I dissemble not, trie it on me.	2Tamb	4.2.76		Olymp
your weapons point/That wil be blunted if the blow be great.	2Tamb	4.2.80		Olymp
Cut off this arme that murthered my Love:	2Tamb	4.2.83		Olymp
A greater Lamp than that bright eie of heaven,	2Tamb	4.2.88		Therid
The horse that guide the golden eie of heaven,	2Tamb	4.3.7		Therid
That King Egeus fed with humaine flesh,	2Tamb	4.3.13		Tamb
And made so wanton that they knew their strengths,	2Tamb	4.3.14		Tamb
Let me have coach my Lord, that I may ride,	2Tamb	4.3.27		Tamb
O thou that swaiest the region under earth,	2Tamb	4.3.32		Amyras
That like unruly never broken Jades,	2Tamb	4.3.45		Orcan
How like you that sir king? why speak you not?	2Tamb	4.3.53		Therid
That must (advaunst in higher pompe than this)/Rifle the	2Tamb	4.3.58		Celeb
Where are my common souldiers now that fought/So Lion-like upon	2Tamb	4.3.67		Tamb
For every man that so offends shall die.	2Tamb	4.3.76		Tamb
That whips downe cities, and controwleth crownes,	2Tamb	4.3.100		Tamb
At every little breath that thorow heaven is blowen:	2Tamb	4.3.124		Tamb
That litle hope is left to save our lives,	2Tamb	5.1.4		Tamb
That Tamburlains intollorable wrath/May be suppresst by our	2Tamb	5.1.8		Maxim
Makes walles a fresh with every thing that falles/Into the	2Tamb	5.1.18		Maxim
That Tamburlaine may pitie our distresse,	2Tamb	5.1.27		Govnr
That thus intreat their shame and servitude?	2Tamb	5.1.37		1Citzn
That legions of tormenting spirits may vex/Your slavish bosomes	2Tamb	5.1.45		Govnr
And that shal bide no more regard of parlie.	2Tamb	5.1.61		Govnr
That made us all the labour for the towne,	2Tamb	5.1.82		Techel
That with his sword hath quail'd all earthly kings,	2Tamb	5.1.93		Therid
That I may sheath it in this breast of mine,	2Tamb	5.1.143		Tamb
that all [Assiria] <Affrica>/Which hath bene subject to the	2Tamb	5.1.165		Jrslem
Found in the Temples of that Mahomet,	2Tamb	5.1.175		Tamb
That suffers flames of fire to burne the writ/Wherein the sum	2Tamb	5.1.190		Tamb
That shakes his sword against thy majesty,	2Tamb	5.1.196		Tamb
The God that sits in heaven, if any God,	2Tamb	5.1.201		Tamb
But that we leave sufficient garrison/And presently depart to	2Tamb	5.1.211		Tamb
The Monster that hath drunke a sea of blood,	2Tamb	5.2.13		Tamb
And that vile Carkasse drawne by warlike kings,	2Tamb	5.2.16		Amasia
never sepulchre/Shall grace that base-borne Tyrant Tamburlaine.	2Tamb	5.2.18		Amasia
thou that hast seene/Millions of Turkes perish by Tamburlaine,	2Tamb	5.2.24		Amasia
This is the time that must eternize me,	2Tamb	5.2.54		Callap
Or that it be rejoin'd again at full,	2Tamb	5.2.58		Callap
Fal starres that governe his nativity,	2Tamb	5.3.2		Callap
Now in defiance of that woonted love,	2Tamb	5.3.10		Therid

THAT (cont.)

Earth droopes and saies, that hell in heaven is plac'd.	2Tamb	5.3.16	Therid
O then ye Powers that sway eternal seates,	2Tamb	5.3.17	Techel
And that their power is puissant as Joves,	2Tamb	5.3.35	Usumc
Earth droopes and saies that hel in heaven is plac'd.	2Tamb	5.3.41	Usumc
That have bene tearm'd the terrour of the world?	2Tamb	5.3.45	Tamb
That thus invie the health of Tamburlaine.	2Tamb	5.3.53	Tamb
That if I perish, heaven and earth may fade.	2Tamb	5.3.60	Tamb
that the soule/Wanting those Organnons by which it mooves,	2Tamb	5.3.95	Phsitn
yong Callapine that lately fled from your majesty, hath nowe	2Tamb	5.3.102	P 3Msngr
That can endure so well your royall presence,	2Tamb	5.3.111	Usumc
That Callapine should be my slave againe.	2Tamb	5.3.118	Tamb
That meane t'invest me in a higher throane,	2Tamb	5.3.121	Tamb
That these my boies may finish all my wantes.	2Tamb	5.3.125	Tamb
That men might quickly saile to India.	2Tamb	5.3.135	Tamb
that shine as bright/As all the Lamps that beautifie the Sky,	2Tamb	5.3.156	Tamb
that shine as bright/As all the Lamps that beautifie the Sky,	2Tamb	5.3.157	Tamb
That let your lives command in spight of death.	2Tamb	5.3.160	Tamb
me, that I may resigne/My place and proper tytle to my sonne:	2Tamb	5.3.175	Tamb
That I may see thee crown'd before I die.	2Tamb	5.3.179	Tamb
A woful change my Lord, that daunts our thoughts,	2Tamb	5.3.181	Therid
And that the spightfull influence of heaven,	2Tamb	5.3.193	Amyras
Leading a life that onely strives to die,	2Tamb	5.3.197	Amyras
Nor bar thy mind that magnanimitie,	2Tamb	5.3.200	Tamb
That nobly must admit necessity:	2Tamb	5.3.201	Tamb
And eielesse Monster that torments my soule,	2Tamb	5.3.217	Tamb
That his teare-thyrsty and unquenched hate,	2Tamb	5.3.222	Techel
As that which [Clymens] <Clymeus> brainsicke sonne did guide,	2Tamb	5.3.231	Tamb
And let them know that I am Machevill,	Jew	Prol.7	Machvl
Admir'd I am of those that hate me most:	Jew	Prol.9	Machvl
that a strong built Citadell/Commands much more then letters	Jew	Prol.22	Machvl
So that of thus much that returne was made:	Jew	1.1.1	Barab
That bought my Spanish Oyles, and Wines of Greece,	Jew	1.1.5	Barab
easily in a day/Tell that which may maintaine him all his life.	Jew	1.1.11	Barab
The needy groome that never fingred groat,	Jew	1.1.12	Barab
That trade in mettall of the purest mould;	Jew	1.1.20	Barab
that in the Easterne rockes/Without controule can picke his	Jew	1.1.21	Barab
And is thy credit not enough for that?	Jew	1.1.62	Barab
you came not with those other ships/That sail'd by Egypt?	Jew	1.1.90	Barab
by a Spanish Fleet/That never left us till within a league,	Jew	1.1.96	2Merch
That had the Gallies of the Turke in chase.	Jew	1.1.97	2Merch
scambled up/More wealth by farre then those that brag of faith.	Jew	1.1.123	Barab
That thirst so much for Principality.	Jew	1.1.135	Barab
What need they treat of peace that are in league?	Jew	1.1.158	Barab
And now by that advantage thinkes, belike,	Jew	1.1.184	Barab
To seize upon the Towne: I, that he seekes.	Jew	1.1.185	Barab
Warily garding that which I ha got.	Jew	1.1.188	Barab
Know Knights of Malta, that we came from Rhodes,	Jew	1.2.2	Basso
and those other Iles/That lye betwixt the Mediterranean seas.	Jew	1.2.4	Basso
The ten yeares tribute that remaines unpaid.	Jew	1.2.7	Calym
are such/That you will needs have ten yeares tribute past,	Jew	1.2.19	Govnr
Now then here know that it concerneth us--	Jew	1.2.42	Govnr
To what this ten yeares tribute will amount/That we have cast,	Jew	1.2.47	Govnr
compasse it/By reason of the warres, that robb'd our store;	Jew	1.2.48	Govnr
hee that denies to pay, shal straight become a Christian.	Jew	1.2.73	P Reader
Lastly, he that denies this, shall absolutely lose al he has.	Jew	1.2.76	P Reader
Either pay that, or we will seize on all.	Jew	1.2.89	Govnr
But say the Tribe that I descended of/Were all in generall cast	Jew	1.2.113	Barab
The man that dealeth righteously shall live:	Jew	1.2.116	Barab
For that is theft; and if you rob me thus,	Jew	1.2.126	Barab
My ships, my store, and all that I enjoy'd;	Jew	1.2.139	Barab
'Tis necessary that be look'd unto:	Jew	1.2.157	1Knght
And that will prove but simple policie.	Jew	1.2.159	1Knght
That thus have dealt with me in my distresse.	Jew	1.2.168	Barab
and in mine Argosie/And other ships that came from Egypt last,	Jew	1.2.188	Barab
So that not he, but I may curse the day,	Jew	1.2.191	Barab
That clouds of darkenesse may inclose my flesh,	Jew	1.2.194	Barab
You that/Were ne're possest of wealth, are pleas'd with want.	Jew	1.2.200	Barab
That in a field amidst his enemies,	Jew	1.2.203	Barab
lumpe of clay/That will with every water wash to dirt:	Jew	1.2.217	Barab
That measure nought but by the present time.	Jew	1.2.220	Barab
That may they not:	Jew	1.2.253	Abigal
That I may vanish ore the earth in ayre,	Jew	1.2.264	Barab
And leave no memory that e're I was.	Jew	1.2.265	Barab
it be to injure them/That have so manifestly wronged us,	Jew	1.2.275	Abigal
As good dissemble that thou never mean'st/As first meane truth,	Jew	1.2.290	Barab
the plancke/That runs along the upper chamber floore,	Jew	1.2.297	Barab
I charge thee on my blessing that thou leave/These divels, and	Jew	1.2.346	Barab
The boord is marked thus that covers it.	Jew	1.2.350	Barab
The strangest sight, in my opinion,/That ever I beheld.	Jew	1.2.377	Mthias
Thus like the sad presaging Raven that tolls/The sicke mans	Jew	2.1.1	Barab
That has no further comfort for his maime.	Jew	2.1.11	Barab
Oh thou that with a fiery piller led'st/The sonnes of Israel	Jew	2.1.12	Barab
And speake of spirits and ghosts that glide by night/About the	Jew	2.1.26	Barab
And now me thinkes that I am one of those:	Jew	2.1.28	Barab
Now that my fathers fortune were so good/As but to be about	Jew	2.1.31	Abigal
Give charge to Morpheus that he may dreame/A golden dreame, and	Jew	2.1.36	Abigal
Who's that?	Jew	2.1.43	Abigal
Oh Abigal, Abigal, that I had thee here too,	Jew	2.1.51	Barab
my fingers take/A kisse from him that sends it from his soule.	Jew	2.1.59	Barab
That I may hover with her in the Ayre,	Jew	2.1.62	Barab
Whence is thy ship that anchors in our Rhoad?	Jew	2.2.2	Govnr
And with that summe he craves might we wage warre.	Jew	2.2.27	1Knght

THAT (cont.)

My Lord, Remember that to Europ's shame,	Jew	2.2.30	Bosco
What is the summe that Calymath requires?	Jew	2.2.35	Bosco
Small though the number was that kept the Towne,	Jew	2.2.49	Bosco
That can so soone forget an injury.	Jew	2.3.19	Barab
That when the offering-Bason comes to me,	Jew	2.3.28	Barab
One that I love for his good fathers sake.	Jew	2.3.31	Barab
That I may have a sight of Abigall;	Jew	2.3.34	Lodowk
of the Serpent then the Dove; that is, more knave than foole.	Jew	2.3.37	P Barab
That when we speake with Gentiles like to you,	Jew	2.3.45	Barab
Yet I have one left that will serve your turne:	Jew	2.3.50	Barab
The Diamond that I talke of, ne'r was foild:	Jew	2.3.56	Barab
I'le have a saying to that Nunnery.	Jew	2.3.90	Barab
What, can he steale that you demand so much?	Jew	2.3.100	Barab
So that, being bought, the Towne-seale might be got/To keepe	Jew	2.3.103	Barab
Why should this Turke be dearer then that Moore?	Jew	2.3.109	Barab
That by my helpe shall doe much villanie.	Jew	2.3.133	Barab
All that I have shall be at your command.	Jew	2.3.137	Barab
before your mother/Lest she mistrust the match that is in hand:	Jew	2.3.147	Barab
Tell me, Mathias, is not that the Jew?	Jew	2.3.152	Mater
And I will teach [thee] that shall sticke by thee:	Jew	2.3.168	Barab
That I may, walking in my Gallery,	Jew	2.3.179	Barab
And after that I was an Engineere,	Jew	2.3.186	Barab
Then after that was I an Usurer,	Jew	2.3.190	Barab
That I have laugh'd agood to see the cripples/Goe limping home	Jew	2.3.211	Ithimr
Provided, that you keepe your Maiden-head.	Jew	2.3.227	Barab
That ye be both made sure e're you come out.	Jew	2.3.236	Barab
word a Merchant's fled/That owes me for a hundred Tun of Wine:	Jew	2.3.244	Barab
That I intend my daughter shall be thine.	Jew	2.3.254	Barab
Barabas, is not that the widowes sonne?	Jew	2.3.279	Lodowk
no, but happily he stands in feare/Of that which you, I thinke,	Jew	2.3.283	Barab
Nor I the affection that I beare to you.	Jew	2.3.291	Barab
'Tis not thy wealth, but her that I esteeme,	Jew	2.3.298	Lodowk
That never tasted of the Passeover,	Jew	2.3.302	Barab
Nor our Messias that is yet to come,	Jew	2.3.304	Barab
But all are Hereticks that are not Jewes;	Jew	2.3.312	Barab
Now have I that for which my soule hath long'd.	Jew	2.3.318	Lodowk
That maidens new betroth'd should weepe a while:	Jew	2.3.326	Barab
Lodowicke, it is enough/That I have made thee sure to Abigal.	Jew	2.3.335	Barab
My heart misgives me, that to crosse your love,	Jew	2.3.349	Barab
What's that to thee?	Jew	2.3.357	Barab
Oh, master, that I might have a hand in this.	Jew	2.3.368	Ithimr
And tell him that it comes from Lodowicke.	Jew	2.3.371	Barab
No, no, and yet it might be done that way:	Jew	2.3.373	Barab
That he shall verily thinke it comes from him.	Jew	2.3.376	Ithimr
that but for one bare night/A hundred Duckets have bin freely	Jew	3.1.2	Curtzn
O the sweetest face that ever I beheld!	Jew	3.1.26	P Ithimr
a hundred of the Jewes Crownes that I had such a Concubine.	Jew	3.1.28	P Ithimr
Oh that my sighs could turne to lively breath;	Jew	3.2.18	Govnr
And these my teares to blood, that he might live.	Jew	3.2.19	Govnr
I know not, and that grieves me most of all.	Jew	3.2.21	Govnr
Lend me that weapon that did kill my sonne,	Jew	3.2.23	Mater
Nay Madam stay, that weapon was my son's,	Jew	3.2.25	Govnr
And on that rather should Ferneze dye.	Jew	3.2.26	Govnr
That we may venge their blood upon their heads.	Jew	3.2.28	Mater
bottle-nos'd knave to my Master, that ever Gentleman had.	Jew	3.3.10	P Ithimr
That by my favour they should both be slaine?	Jew	3.3.39	Abigal
Abigal it is not yet long since/That I did labour thy admition,	Jew	3.3.57	1Fryar
And then thou didst not like that holy life.	Jew	3.3.58	1Fryar
Farre from the Sonne that gives eternall life.	Jew	3.3.65	Abigal
Although unworthy of that Sister-hood.	Jew	3.3.69	Abigal
For that will be most heavy to thy soule.	Jew	3.3.71	1Fryar
That was my father's fault.	Jew	3.3.72	Abigal
If so, 'tis time that it be seene into:	Jew	3.4.9	Barab
For she that varies from me in beleefe/Gives great presumption	Jew	3.4.10	Barab
me in beleefe/Gives great presumption that she loves me not;	Jew	3.4.11	Barab
And on that hope my happinesse is built:	Jew	3.4.17	Barab
And [less] <least> thou yeeld to this that I intreat,	Jew	3.4.37	Barab
I cannot thinke but that thou hat'st my life.	Jew	3.4.38	Barab
All that I have is thine when I am dead,	Jew	3.4.44	Barab
Onely know this, that thus thou art to doe:	Jew	3.4.48	Barab
me in the pot of Rice/That for our supper stands upon the fire.	Jew	3.4.50	Barab
saies, he that eats with the devil had need of a long spoone.	Jew	3.4.58	P Ithimr
That thou mayst freely live to be my heire.	Jew	3.4.63	Barab
that wil preserve life, make her round and plump, and batten	Jew	3.4.65	P Ithimr
It is a precious powder that I bought/Of an Italian in Ancona	Jew	3.4.68	Barab
and invenome her/That like a fiend hath left her father thus.	Jew	3.4.105	Barab
The wind that bloweth all the world besides,	Jew	3.5.3	Basso
Where is the Fryar that converst with me?	Jew	3.6.9	Abigal
That in this house I liv'd religiously,	Jew	3.6.13	Abigal
Mathias was the man that I held deare,	Jew	3.6.24	Abigal
Know that Confession must not be reveal'd,	Jew	3.6.33	2Fryar
it, and the Priest/That makes it knowne, being degraded first,	Jew	3.6.35	2Fryar
Convert my father that he may be sav'd,	Jew	3.6.39	Abigal
And witnesse that I dye a Christian.	Jew	3.6.40	Abigal
I, and a Virgin too, that grieves me most:	Jew	3.6.41	2Fryar
A thing that makes me tremble to unfold.	Jew	3.6.48	2Fryar
the Nuns are dead/That sound at other times like Tinkers pans?	Jew	4.1.3	Barab
I, that thou hast--	Jew	4.1.29	1Fryar
I, that thou art a--	Jew	4.1.32	1Fryar
Remember that--	Jew	4.1.37	2Fryar
I, remember that--	Jew	4.1.38	1Fryar
I must needs say that I have beene a great usurer.	Jew	4.1.39	Barab

THAT (cont.)

Fornication? but that was in another Country:	Jew	4.1.41	Barab
I will not say that by a forged challenge they met.	Jew	4.1.45	P 2Fryar
That would for Lucars sake have sold my soule.	Jew	4.1.53	Barab
I know that I have highly sinn'd,	Jew	4.1.80	Barab
But doe you thinke that I beleeve his words?	Jew	4.1.105	Barab
For he that shriv'd her is within my house.	Jew	4.1.115	Barab
not both these wise men to suppose/That I will leave my house,	Jew	4.1.123	Barab
To fast and be well whipt; I'le none of that.	Jew	4.1.124	Barab
And after that, I and my trusty Turke--	Jew	4.1.127	Barab
Who would not thinke but that this Fryar liv'd?	Jew	4.1.156	Barab
As thou lik'st that, stop me another time.	Jew	4.1.173	1Fryar
Why, stricken him that would have stroke at me.	Jew	4.1.175	1Fryar
That being importun'd by this Bernardine/To be a Christian, I	Jew	4.1.187	Barab
Take in the staffe too, for that must be showne:	Jew	4.1.204	Barab
Law wils that each particular be knowne.	Jew	4.1.205	Barab
That such a base slave as he should be saluted by such a tall	Jew	4.2.9	P Pilia
with his lips; the effect was, that I should come to her house.	Jew	4.2.31	P Ithimr
that she loves me ever since she saw me, and who would not	Jew	4.2.34	P Ithimr
That kisse againe; she runs division of my lips.	Jew	4.2.127	P Ithimr
Oh that ten thousand nights were put in one,	Jew	4.2.130	Ithimr
That wee might sleepe seven yeeres together afore we wake.	Jew	4.2.131	Ithimr
Plaine Barabas: oh that wicked Curtezane!	Jew	4.3.2	Barab
But if I get him, Coupe de Gorge for that.	Jew	4.3.5	Barab
That when he speakes, drawes out his grisly beard,	Jew	4.3.7	Barab
and looks/Like one that is imploy'd in Catzerie/And crosbiting,	Jew	4.3.12	Barab
And when he comes: Oh that he were but here!	Jew	4.3.17	Barab
Oh, if that be all, I can picke ope your locks.	Jew	4.3.33	Pilia
'Tis not five hundred Crownes that I esteeme,	Jew	4.3.40	Barab
five hundred Crownes that I esteeme,/I am not mov'd at that:	Jew	4.3.41	Barab
That he who knowes I love him as my selfe/Should write in this	Jew	4.3.42	Barab
Oh that I should part with so much gold!	Jew	4.3.51	Barab
Of that condition I wil drink it up; here's to thee.	Jew	4.4.4	P Ithimr
I carried the broth that poyson'd the Nuns, and he and I,	Jew	4.4.20	P Ithimr
'Tis a strange thing of that Jew, he lives upon pickled	Jew	4.4.61	P Ithimr
that the Nuns lov'd Rice, that Fryar Bernardine slept in his	Jew	4.4.75	P Ithimr
lov'd Rice, that Fryar Bernardine slept in his owne clothes.	Jew	4.4.76	P Ithimr
And see that Malta be well fortifi'd;	Jew	5.1.2	Govnr
his man's now at my lodging/That was his Agent, he'll confesse	Jew	5.1.17	Curtzn
Goe fetch him straight. I alwayes fear'd that Jew.	Jew	5.1.18	Govnr
Thou and thy Turk; 'twas you that slew my son.	Jew	5.1.27	Govnr
Who carried that challenge?	Jew	5.1.31	Barab
Marry, even he that strangled Bernardine, poyson'd the Nuns, and	Jew	5.1.33	P Ithimr
Ferneze, 'twas thy sonne that murder'd him.	Jew	5.1.45	Mater
Where is the Jew, where is that murderer?	Jew	5.1.48	Mater
For the Jewes body, throw that o're the wals,	Jew	5.1.58	Govnr
my good Lord, one that can spy a place/Where you may enter, and	Jew	5.1.70	Barab
Art thou that Jew whose goods we heard were sold/For	Jew	5.1.73	Calym
And since that time they have hir'd a slave my man/To accuse me	Jew	5.1.75	Barab
For he that liveth in Authority,	Jew	5.2.38	Barab
Lives like the Asse that Aesope speaketh of,	Jew	5.2.40	Barab
That labours with a load of bread and wine,	Jew	5.2.41	Barab
This is the reason that I sent for thee;	Jew	5.2.51	Barab
said, within this Ile/In Malta here, that I have got my goods,	Jew	5.2.68	Barab
What will you give him that procureth this?	Jew	5.2.83	Barab
Here is my hand that I'le set Malta free:	Jew	5.2.95	Barab
onely to performe/One stratagem that I'le impart to thee,	Jew	5.2.99	Barab
That at one instant all things may be done,	Jew	5.2.120	Barab
Two lofty Turrets that command the Towne.	Jew	5.3.11	Calym
Selim, for that, thus saith the Governor,	Jew	5.3.26	Msngr
That he hath in store a Pearle so big,	Jew	5.3.27	Msngr
that there is a monastery/Which standeth as an out-house to the	Jew	5.3.36	Msngr
Have speciall care that no man sally forth/Till you shall heare	Jew	5.4.2	Govnr
heare a Culverin discharg'd/By him that beares the Linstocke,	Jew	5.4.4	Govnr
Why now I see that you have Art indeed.	Jew	5.5.4	Barab
There, Carpenters, divide that gold amongst you:	Jew	5.5.5	Barab
returne me word/That thou wilt come, and I am satisfied.	Jew	5.5.12	Barab
That thou maist feast them in thy Citadell.	Jew	5.5.16	Msngr
wel since it is no more/I'le satisfie my selfe with that; nay,	Jew	5.5.22	Barab
That on the sudden shall dissever it,	Jew	5.5.29	Barab
asunder; so that it doth sinke/Into a deepe pit past recovery.	Jew	5.5.35	Barab
Here, hold that knife, and when thou seest he comes,	Jew	5.5.37	Barab
Know, Governor, 'twas I that slew thy sonne;	Jew	5.5.81	Barab
I fram'd the challenge that did make them meet:	Jew	5.5.82	Barab
Tush, Governor, take thou no care for that,	Jew	5.5.102	Calym
Yes, what of that?	Jew	5.5.106	Calym
For he that did by treason worke our fall,	Jew	5.5.109	Govnr
And that the native sparkes of princely love,	P 6	1.6	Charls
That kindled first this motion in our hearts,	P 7	1.7	Charls
That linke you in mariage with our daughter heer:	P 14	1.14	QnMoth
Well Madam, let that rest:	P 17	1.17	Charls
The rest that will not goe (my Lords) may stay:	P 23	1.23	Charls
That seekes to murder all the Protestants:	P 31	1.31	Navrre
If that the King had given consent thereto,	P 33	1.33	Navrre
That all the protestants that are in Paris,	P 34	1.34	Navrre
My Lord I mervaile that th'aspiring Guise/Dares once adventure	P 36	1.36	Admral
But he that sits and rules above the clowdes,	P 42	1.42	Navrre
That Guise hath slaine by treason of his heart,	P 45	1.45	Navrre
And thats the cause that Guise so frowns at us,	P 52	1.52	Navrre
That God may still defend the right of France:	P 56	1.56	Navrre
they be my good Lord, and he that smelles but to them, dyes.	P 73	2.16	P Pothec
For she is that huge blemish in our eye,	P 80	2.23	Guise
That makes these upstart heresies in Fraunce:	P 81	2.24	Guise

THAT (cont.)

That perill is the cheefest way to happines,	P	95	2.38	Guise
That hanges for every peasant to atchive?	P	98	2.41	Guise
That like I best that flyes beyond my reach.	P	99	2.42	Guise
For this, I waite, that scornes attendance else:	P	106	2.49	Guise
And by that priviledge to worke upon,	P	121	2.64	Guise
Fye, I am ashamde, how ever that I seeme,	P	124	2.67	Guise
So that for proofe, he barely beares the name:	P	131	2.74	Guise
That right or wrong, thou deale thy selfe a King.	P	148	2.91	Guise
That with a rablement of his hereticks,	P	151	2.94	Guise
That hinder our possession to the crowne:	P	154	2.97	Guise
Those that hate me, will I learn to loath.	P	156	2.99	Guise
Give me a look, that when I bend the browes,	P	157	2.100	Guise
A hand, that with a graspe may gripe the world,	P	159	2.102	Guise
That those which doe beholde, they may become/As men that stand	P	162	2.105	Guise
they may become/As men that stand and gase against the Sunne.	P	163	2.106	Guise
Doth not your grace know the man that gave them you?	P	172	3.7	Navrre
Too late it is my Lord if that be true/To blame her highnes,	P	181	3.16	QnMarg
That I with her may dye and live againe.	P	190	3.25	Navrre
These are the cursed Guisians that doe seeke our death.	P	201	3.36	Admral
Besides my heart relentes that noble men,	P	211	4.9	Charls
They that shalbe actors in this Massacre,	P	231	4.29	Guise
He that wantes these, and is suspected of heresie,	P	234	4.32	Guise
And never cease untill that bell shall cease,	P	240	4.38	Guise
That durst presume for hope of any gaine,	P	258	4.56	Charls
That seeke to massacre our guiltles lives.	P	261	4.59	Admral
And that I am not more secure my selfe,	P	264	4.62	Charls
To kill all that you suspect of heresie.	P	276	5.3	Guise
them thither, and then/Beset his house that not a man may live.	P	289	5.16	Guise
That charge is mine.	P	290	5.17	Anjoy
And slay his servants that shall issue out.	P	299	5.26	Anjoy
And he that living hated so the crosse,	P	320	5.47	Anjoy
Anjoy, Gonzago, Retes, if that you three,	P	322	5.49	Guise
That they which have already set the street/May know their	P	328	5.55	Guise
Who is that which knocks there?	P	346	6.1	P SrnsWf
That frightes poore Ramus sitting at his book?	P	362	7.2	Ramus
All that I have is but my stipend from the King,	P	378	7.18	Ramus
Was it not thou that scoftes the Organon,	P	387	7.27	Guise
He that will be a flat decotamest,	P	389	7.29	Guise
How answere you that?	P	397	7.37	Guise
In that I know the things that I have wrote,	P	403	7.43	Ramus
That he that despiseth him, can nere/Be good in Logick or	P	409	7.49	Ramus
Why suffer you that peasant to declaime?	P	414	7.54	Guise
That swim about and so preserve their lives:	P	419	7.59	Guise
That are tutors to him and the prince of Condy--	P	427	7.67	Guise
For that let me alone, Cousin stay you heer,	P	428	7.68	Anjoy
My Lord, they say/That all the protestants are massacred.	P	432	7.72	Navrre
That you were one that made this Massacre.	P	436	7.76	Navrre
Yet will we not that the Massacre shall end:	P	444	7.84	Guise
unto Roan, and spare not one/That you suspect of heresy.	P	447	7.87	Guise
And now stay/That bel that to the devils mattins rings.	P	448	7.88	Guise
That if I undertake to weare the crowne/Of Poland, it may	P	466	8.16	Anjoy
That if by death of Charles, the diadem/Of France be cast on	P	472	8.22	Anjoy
I, but my Lord let me alone for that,	P	519	9.38	QnMoth
No villain, that toung of thine,	P	530	10.3	Guise
That hath blasphemde the holy Church of Rome,	P	531	10.4	Guise
But that we presently despatch Embassadours/To Poland, to call	P	555	11.20	QnMoth
And now Navarre whilste that these broiles doe last,	P	565	11.30	Navrre
And now that Henry is cal'd from Polland,	P	569	11.34	Navrre
For feare that Guise joyn'd with the King of Spaine,	P	573	11.38	Navrre
But God that alwaies doth defend the right,	P	575	11.40	Navrre
That holdes it from your highnesse wrongfully:	P	582	11.47	Pleshe
And all things that a King may wish besides:	P	595	12.8	QnMoth
Graunt that our deeds may wel deserve your loves:	P	600	12.13	King
Put of that feare, they are already joynde,	P	605	12.18	King
We know that noble mindes change not their thoughts/For wearing	P	610	12.23	Mugern
in that your grace,/Hath worne the Poland diadem, before	P	611	12.24	Mugern
To punish those that doe prophane this holy feast.	P	617	12.30	Mugern
How meanst thou that?	P	618	12.31	King
But tis the house of Burbon that he meanes.	P	644	12.57	Cardnl
And tell him that tis for his Countries good,	P	646	12.59	Cardnl
That I may write unto my dearest Lord.	P	659	13.3	Duchss
Sweet Mugeroune, tis he that hath my heart,	P	660	13.4	Duchss
That he may come and meet me in some place,	P	664	13.8	Duchss
O would to God this quill that heere doth write,	P	667	13.11	Duchss
That it might print these lines within his heart.	P	669	13.13	Duchss
Are these your secrets that no man must know?	P	678	13.22	Guise
That others needs to comment on my text?	P	683	13.27	Guise
Now doe I see that from the very first,	P	694	13.38	Guise
That change their coulour when the winter comes,	P	721	14.24	Navrre
This is the Guise that hath incenst the King,	P	729	14.32	Navrre
That villain for whom I beare this deep disgrace,	P	766	15.24	Guise
Even for your words that have incenst me so,	P	767	15.25	Guise
Shall buy that strumpets favour with his blood,	P	768	15.26	Guise
If that be all, the next time that I meet her,	P	781	15.39	Mugern
That lift themselves against the perfect truth,	P	799	16.13	Navrre
Come my Lords, now that this storme is overpast,	P	804	16.18	Navrre
that dares make the Duke a cuckolde, and use a counterfeite key	P	806	17.1	P Souldr
yet you put in that which displeaseth him, and so forestall his	P	809	17.4	P Souldr
and tyll the ground that he himself should occupy, which is his	P	812	17.7	P Souldr
of Guise, we understand that you/Have gathered a power of men.	P	821	17.16	King
That livest by forraine exhibition?	P	842	17.37	Eprnon
I, those are they that feed him with their golde,	P	845	17.40	King

THAT (cont.)

Navarre that cloakes them underneath his wings,	P 855	17.50		Guise
That the Guise durst stand in armes against the King,	P 877	17.72		Eprnon
For now that Paris takes the Guises parte,	P 896	17.91		King
That the Guise hath taken armes against the King,	P 901	18.2		Navrre
And that Paris is revolted from his grace.	P 902	18.3		Navrre
Be gone I say, tis time that we were there.	P 919	18.20		Navrre
That wicked Guise I feare me much will be,	P 921	18.22		Navrre
The ruine of that famous Realme of France:	P 922	18.23		Navrre
But if that God doe prosper mine attempts,	P 927	18.28		Navrre
That basely seekes the ruine of his Realme.	P 930	18.31		Navrre
O that his heart were leaping in my hand.	P 936	19.6	P	2Mur
But when will he come that we may murther him?	P 937	19.7	P	3Mur
Breath out that life wherein my death was hid,	P 954	19.24		King
I prethee tell him that the Guise is heere.	P 958	19.28		Guise
That in the Court I bare so great a traine.	P 968	19.38		Guise
They were to blame that said I was displeasde,	P 969	19.39		King
O my Lord, I am one of them that is set to murder you.	P 992	19.62	P	3Mur
Oh that I have not power to stay my life,	P1007	19.77		Guise
This is the traitor that hath spent my golde,	P1028	19.98		King
To spend the treasure that should strength my land,	P1037	19.107		King
Let Christian princes that shall heare of this,	P1041	19.111		King
our Guise is dead)/Rest satisfied with this that heer I sweare,	P1043	19.113		King
Sirra twas I that slew him, and will slay/Thee too, and thou	P1048	19.118		King
But what availeth that this traitors dead,	P1054	19.124		King
And that young Cardinall that is growne so proud?	P1056	19.126		King
And make the Guisians stoup that are alive.	P1071	19.141		King
I would that I had murdered thee my sonne.	P1073	19.143		QnMoth
To revenge our deaths upon that cursed King,	P1100	20.10		Cardnl
That basely seekes to joyne with such a King,	P1115	21.9		Dumain
That I with speed should have beene put to death.	P1118	21.12		Dumain
That durst attempt to murder noble Guise.	P1121	21.15		Dumain
that your brother the Cardinall of Loraine by the Kings consent	P1122	21.16	P	Frier
Tis warre that must asswage this tyrantes pride.	P1128	21.22		Dumain
the Jacobyns, that for my conscience sake will kill the King.	P1130	21.24	P	Frier
Tush my Lord, let me alone for that.	P1136	21.30	P	Frier
That ever I was prov'd your enemy,	P1140	22.2		King
And that the sweet and princely minde you beare,	P1141	22.3		King
That ever I vouchsafte my dearest freends.	P1146	22.8		King
It is enough if that Navarre may be/Esteemed faithfull to the	P1147	22.9		Navrre
the President of Paris, that craves accesse unto your grace.	P1156	22.18	P	1Msngr
Take hence that damned villaine from my sight.	P1182	22.44		King
Tell her for all this that I hope to live,	P1196	22.58		King
To ruinate that wicked Church of Rome,	P1204	22.66		King
That hatcheth up such bloudy practises.	P1205	22.67		King
O that that damned villaine were alive againe,	P1216	22.78		Eprnon
That we might torture him with some new found death.	P1217	22.79		Eprnon
That it may keenly slice the Catholicks.	P1238	22.100		King
He loves me not that sheds most teares,	P1239	22.101		King
But he that makes most lavish of his bloud.	P1240	22.102		King
That we may see it honourably interde:	P1246	22.108		Navrre
Shall curse the time that ere Navarre was King,	P1249	22.111		Navrre
that dares make a duke a cuckolde and use a counterfeyt key to	Paris	ms 1,p390	P	Souldr
yett you putt in that displeases him | And fill up his rome	Paris	ms 4,p390	P	Souldr
displeases him | And fill up his rome that he shold occupie.	Paris	ms 4,p390	P	Souldr
that of it self was hote enoughe to worke/thy Just degestione	Paris	ms26,p391		Guise
and that thow most reposest one my faythe	Paris	ms31,p391		Guise
Ah words that make me surfet with delight:	Edw	1.1.3		Gavstn
Not that I love the citie or the men,	Edw	1.1.12		Gavstn
But that it harbors him I hold so deare,	Edw	1.1.13		Gavstn
As for the multitude that are but sparkes,	Edw	1.1.20		Gavstn
That glaunceth at my lips and flieth away:	Edw	1.1.23		Gavstn
A souldier, that hath serv'd against the Scot.	Edw	1.1.34		3PrMan
That wouldst reward them with an hospitall.	Edw	1.1.38		3PrMan
You know that I came lately out of France,	Edw	1.1.44		Gavstn
that with touching of a string/May draw the pliant king which	Edw	1.1.52		Gavstn
With haire that gilds the water as it glides,	Edw	1.1.62		Gavstn
That Earle of Lancaster do I abhorre.	Edw	1.1.76		Gavstn
That crosse me thus, shall know I am displeasd.	Edw	1.1.79		Edward
That villaine Mortimer, ile be his death.	Edw	1.1.81		Gavstn
That he should nere returne into the realme:	Edw	1.1.84		Mortmr
This sword of mine that should offend your foes,	Edw	1.1.86		Mortmr
And hew these knees that now are growne so stiffe.	Edw	1.1.95		Edward
That naturally would love and honour you,	Edw	1.1.100		Lncstr
But for that base and obscure Gaveston:	Edw	1.1.101		Lncstr
And strike off his that makes you threaten us.	Edw	1.1.124		Mortmr
And that high minded earle of Lancaster,	Edw	1.1.150		Edward
I have my wish, in that I joy thy sight,	Edw	1.1.151		Edward
Then beare the ship that shall transport thee hence:	Edw	1.1.153		Edward
But is that wicked Gaveston returnd?	Edw	1.1.177		BshpCv
That wert the onely cause of his exile.	Edw	1.1.179		Edward
Wel, let that peevish Frenchman guard him sure,	Edw	1.2.7		Mortmr
That villaine Gaveston is made an Earle.	Edw	1.2.11		Lncstr
He nods, and scornes, and smiles at those that passe.	Edw	1.2.24		Warwck
Ah that bewraies their basenes Lancaster,	Edw	1.2.27		Mortmr
Then wil you joine with us that be his peeres/To banish or	Edw	1.2.42		Mortmr
with us that be his peeres/To banish or behead that Gaveston?	Edw	1.2.43		Mortmr
Is it not straunge, that he is thus bewitcht?	Edw	1.2.55		MortSr
That slie inveigling Frenchman weele exile,	Edw	1.2.57		Mortmr
and yet ere that day come,/The king shall lose his crowne, for	Edw	1.2.58		Mortmr
We and the rest that are his counsellers,	Edw	1.2.69		ArchBp
of Lancaster/That hath more earldomes then an asse can beare,	Edw	1.3.2		Gavstn
With Guie of Warwick that redoubted knight,	Edw	1.3.4		Gavstn

THAT (cont.)

Unlesse he be declinde from that base pesant.	Edw	1.4.7	Mortmr
What? are you mov'd that Gaveston sits heere?	Edw	1.4.8	Edward
Ignoble vassaile that like Phaeton,	Edw	1.4.16	Warwck
Lay hands on that traitor Mortimer.	Edw	1.4.20	Edward
Lay hands on that traitor Gaveston.	Edw	1.4.21	MortSr
Is this the dutie that you owe your king?	Edw	1.4.22	Kent
That hardly art a gentleman by birth?	Edw	1.4.29	Mortmr
And with the earle of Kent that favors him.	Edw	1.4.34	MortSr
Think you that we can brooke this upstart pride?	Edw	1.4.41	Warwck
You know that I am legate to the Pope,	Edw	1.4.51	ArchBp
Either banish him that was the cause thereof,	Edw	1.4.60	ArchBp
You that be noble borne should pitie him.	Edw	1.4.80	Edward
You that are princely borne should shake him off,	Edw	1.4.81	Warwck
Proud Rome, that hatchest such imperiall groomes,	Edw	1.4.97	Edward
As for the peeres that backe the cleargie thus,	Edw	1.4.104	Edward
That I am banishd, and must flie the land.	Edw	1.4.107	Gavstn
That whether I will or no thou must depart:	Edw	1.4.124	Edward
The time is little that thou hast to stay,	Edw	1.4.138	Edward
O that we might as well returne as goe.	Edw	1.4.143	Edward
Ist not enough, that thou corrupts my lord,	Edw	1.4.150	Queene
Thou art too familiar with that Mortimer,	Edw	1.4.154	Edward
Villaine, tis thou that robst me of my lord.	Edw	1.4.160	Queene
Madam, tis you that rob me of my lord.	Edw	1.4.161	Gavstn
Witnesse the teares that Isabella sheds,	Edw	1.4.164	Queene
Witnesse this hart, that sighing for thee breakes,	Edw	1.4.165	Queene
That charming Circes walking on the waves,	Edw	1.4.172	Queene
Or with those armes that twind about my neck,	Edw	1.4.175	Queene
But that will more exasperate his wrath,	Edw	1.4.182	Queene
Hard is the hart, that injures such a saint.	Edw	1.4.190	Penbrk
And he confesseth that he loves me not.	Edw	1.4.194	Queene
And to behold so sweete a sight as that,	Edw	1.4.206	Warwck
Plead for him he that will, I am resolvde.	Edw	1.4.214	MortSr
Which being caught, strikes him that takes it dead,	Edw	1.4.222	Mortmr
I meane that vile Torpedo, Gaveston,	Edw	1.4.223	Mortmr
That now I hope flotes on the Irish seas.	Edw	1.4.224	Mortmr
My Lords, that I abhorre base Gaveston,	Edw	1.4.239	Mortmr
All that he speakes, is nothing, we are resolv'd.	Edw	1.4.251	Warwck
Do you not wish that Gaveston were dead?	Edw	1.4.252	Mortmr
Marke you but that my lord of Lancaster.	Edw	1.4.263	Warwck
But rather praise him for that brave attempt,	Edw	1.4.268	Mortmr
On that condition Lancaster will graunt.	Edw	1.4.292	Lncstr
That you have parled with your Mortimer?	Edw	1.4.321	Edward
That Gaveston, my Lord, shalbe repeald.	Edw	1.4.322	Queene
That waite attendance for a gratious looke,	Edw	1.4.338	Queene
Or if that loftie office like thee not,	Edw	1.4.355	Edward
That now are readie to assaile the Scots.	Edw	1.4.363	Edward
For wot you not that I have made him sure,	Edw	1.4.378	Edward
That day, if not for him, yet for my sake,	Edw	1.4.381	Edward
Freely enjoy that vaine light-headed earle,	Edw	1.4.400	MortSr
But this I scorne, that one so baselie borne,	Edw	1.4.403	Mortmr
As if that Proteus god of shapes appearde.	Edw	1.4.411	Mortmr
Unckle, tis this that makes me impatient.	Edw	1.4.419	Mortmr
Seeing that our Lord th'earle of Glosters dead,	Edw	2.1.2	Baldck
But he that hath the favour of a king,	Edw	2.1.8	Spencr
That hees repeald, and sent for back againe,	Edw	2.1.18	Spencr
And that his banishment had changd her minde.	Edw	2.1.26	Baldck
That he would take exceptions at my buttons,	Edw	2.1.47	Baldck
That cannot speake without propterea quod.	Edw	2.1.53	Baldck
But one of those that saith quandoquidem,	Edw	2.1.54	Spencr
Seeing that he talkes thus of my mariage day?	Edw	2.1.69	Neece
See that my coache be readie, I must hence.	Edw	2.1.71	Neece
No sooner is it up, but thers a foule,/That seaseth it:	Edw	2.2.27	Lncstr
They love me not that hate my Gaveston.	Edw	2.2.37	Edward
I am that Cedar, shake me not too much,	Edw	2.2.38	Edward
I have the [gesses] <gresses> that will pull you downe,	Edw	2.2.40	Edward
And Aeque tandem shall that canker crie,	Edw	2.2.41	Edward
Nor fowlest Harpie that shall swallow him.	Edw	2.2.46	Edward
That shall wee see, looke where his lordship comes.	Edw	2.2.49	Lncstr
Base leaden Earles that glorie in your birth,	Edw	2.2.74	Gavstn
That thinke with high lookes thus to tread me down.	Edw	2.2.97	Edward
Tis warre that must abate these Barons pride.	Edw	2.2.99	Edward
To prosecute that Gaveston to the death.	Edw	2.2.105	Lncstr
Complaines, that thou hast left her all forlorne.	Edw	2.2.173	Lncstr
That makes a king seeme glorious to the world,	Edw	2.2.175	Mortmr
And thereof came it, that the fleering Scots,	Edw	2.2.188	Lncstr
I, and it greeves me that I favoured him.	Edw	2.2.213	Kent
Poore Gaveston, that hast no friend but me,	Edw	2.2.220	Edward
That to my face he threatens civill warres.	Edw	2.2.233	Edward
And Gaveston, thinke that I love thee well,	Edw	2.2.257	Edward
He that I list to favour shall be great:	Edw	2.2.263	Edward
Will be the first that shall adventure life.	Edw	2.3.4	Kent
If that will not suffice, farwell my lords.	Edw	2.3.10	Kent
That Gaveston is secretlie arrivde,	Edw	2.3.16	Lncstr
Which swept the desart shore of that dead sea,	Edw	2.3.22	Mortmr
O that mine armes could close this Ile about,	Edw	2.4.17	Queene
That I might pull him to me where I would,	Edw	2.4.18	Queene
Or that these teares that drissell from mine eyes,	Edw	2.4.19	Queene
That when I had him we might never part.	Edw	2.4.21	Queene
No madam, but that cursed Gaveston.	Edw	2.4.32	Lncstr
How comes it, that the king and he is parted?	Edw	2.4.41	Mortmr
That this your armie going severall waies,	Edw	2.4.42	Queene
and with the power/That he intendeth presentlie to raise,	Edw	2.4.44	Queene

THAT (cont.)

The wind that bears him hence, wil fil our sailes,	Edw	2.4.48	Lncstr
That muster rebels thus against your king)/To see his royall	Edw	2.5.6	Gavstn
That like the Greekish strumpet traind to armes/And bloudie	Edw	2.5.15	Lncstr
cause,/That here severelie we will execute/Upon thy person:	Edw	2.5.23	Warwck
That heading is one, and hanging is the other,	Edw	2.5.30	Gavstn
Hearing that you had taken Gaveston,	Edw	2.5.35	Arundl
And sends you word, he knowes that die he shall,	Edw	2.5.38	Arundl
let him bestow/His teares on that, for that is all he gets/Of	Edw	2.5.53	Mortmr
bestow/His teares on that, for that is all he gets/Of Gaveston,	Edw	2.5.53	Mortmr
We wot, he that the care of realme remits,	Edw	2.5.61	Warwck
How meanst thou Mortimer? that is over base.	Edw	2.5.71	Gavstn
Provided this, that you my lord of Arundell/Will joyne with me.	Edw	2.5.81	Penbrk
is it not enough/That we have taken him, but must we now/Leave	Edw	2.5.84	Warwck
We that have prettie wenches to our wives,	Edw	2.5.102	Penbrk
Strive you no longer, I will have that Gaveston.	Edw	2.6.7	Warwck
to your maister/My friend, and tell him that I watcht it well.	Edw	2.6.13	Warwck
That powres in lieu of all your goodnes showne,	Edw	3.1.44	Spencr
That as the sun-shine shall reflect ore thee:	Edw	3.1.51	Edward
And that the Mortimers are in hand withall,	Edw	3.1.54	Edward
That lord Valoyes our brother, king of Fraunce,	Edw	3.1.62	Queene
Madam, we will that you with speed be shipt,	Edw	3.1.81	Edward
That I would undertake to carrie him/Unto your highnes, and to	Edw	3.1.99	Arundl
And tell me, would the rebels denie me that?	Edw	3.1.101	Edward
Well, and how fortunes that he came not?	Edw	3.1.113	Edward
That you may drinke your fill, and quaffe in bloud,	Edw	3.1.137	Edward
That so my bloudie colours may suggest/Remembrance of revenge	Edw	3.1.139	Edward
You villaines that have slaine my Gaveston:	Edw	3.1.142	Edward
So wish not they Iwis that sent thee hither,	Edw	3.1.152	Edward
That if without effusion of bloud,	Edw	3.1.159	Herald
That from your princely person you remoove/This Spencer, as a	Edw	3.1.161	Herald
That deads the royall vine, whose golden leaves/Empale your	Edw	3.1.163	Herald
with my sword/On those proud rebels that are up in armes,	Edw	3.1.187	Edward
Then banish that pernicious companie?	Edw	3.1.213	Mortmr
Did they remoove that flatterer from thy throne.	Edw	3.1.231	Kent
That thou proud Warwicke watcht the prisoner,	Edw	3.1.237	Edward
Tis but temporall that thou canst inflict.	Edw	3.1.242	Warwck
Go take that haughtie Mortimer to the tower,	Edw	3.1.252	Edward
ragged stonie walles/Immure thy vertue that aspires to heaven?	Edw	3.1.257	Mortmr
[Levune] <Lewne>, the trust that we repose in thee,/Begets the	Edw	3.1.262	Spencr
Bestowe that treasure on the lords of Fraunce,	Edw	3.1.265	Spencr
That therewith all enchaunted like the guarde,	Edw	3.1.266	Spencr
That suffered Jove to passe in showers of golde/To Danae, all	Edw	3.1.267	Spencr
denied/To Isabell the Queene, that now in France/Makes friends,	Edw	3.1.269	Spencr
That Isabell shall make her plaints in vaine,	Edw	3.1.278	Levune
To thinke that we can yet be tun'd together,	Edw	4.2.9	Queene
That you were dead, or very neare your death.	Edw	4.2.38	Queene
not discourage/Your friends that are so forward in your aide.	Edw	4.2.70	Queene
These comforts that you give our wofull queene,	Edw	4.2.72	Kent
That Englands Queene, and nobles in distresse,	Edw	4.2.79	Mortmr
That Englands peeres may Henolts welcome see.	Edw	4.2.82	SrJohn
I have according to instructions in that behalfe,	Edw	4.3.29	P Spencr
that the Queene all discontented and discomforted, is gone,	Edw	4.3.30	P Spencr
A villaines, hath that Mortimer escapt?	Edw	4.3.38	Edward
That I may see that most desired day,	Edw	4.3.46	Edward
Lords, sith that we are by sufferance of heaven,	Edw	4.4.17	Mortmr
That Englands queene in peace may reposesse/Her dignities and	Edw	4.4.24	Mortmr
That havocks Englands wealth and treasurie.	Edw	4.4.27	Mortmr
Fie on that love that hatcheth death and hate.	Edw	4.6.15	Kent
To them that fight in right and feare his wrath:	Edw	4.6.20	Queene
Yea madam, and they scape not easilie,/That fled the feeld.	Edw	4.6.42	Mortmr
Spencer, the father to that wanton Spencer,	Edw	4.6.50	Rice
That like the lawles Catiline of Rome,	Edw	4.6.51	Rice
Is with that smoothe toongd scholler Baldock gone,	Edw	4.6.57	Rice
Rebell is he that fights against his prince,	Edw	4.6.71	SpncrP
So fought not they that fought in Edwards right.	Edw	4.6.72	SpncrP
Make triall now of that philosophie,	Edw	4.7.17	Edward
That in our famous nurseries of artes/Thou suckedst from Plato,	Edw	4.7.18	Edward
O that I might this life in quiet lead,	Edw	4.7.21	Edward
Armes that pursue our lives with deadly hate.	Edw	4.7.32	Spencr
Who wounds me with the name of Mortimer/That bloudy man?	Edw	4.7.39	Edward
T'escape their hands that seeke to reave his life:	Edw	4.7.52	Leistr
That waites your pleasure, and the day growes old.	Edw	4.7.85	Leistr
Well, that shalbe, shalbe:	Edw	4.7.95	Edward
And that you lay for pleasure here a space,	Edw	5.1.3	Leistr
being strucke/Runnes to an herbe that closeth up the wounds,	Edw	5.1.10	Edward
highly scorning, that the lowly earth/Should drinke his bloud,	Edw	5.1.13	Edward
And that unnaturall Queene false Isabell,	Edw	5.1.17	Edward
That thus hath pent and mu'd me in a prison,	Edw	5.1.18	Edward
That Mortimer and Isabell have done.	Edw	5.1.25	Edward
That bleedes within me for this strange exchange.	Edw	5.1.35	Edward
That like a mountaine overwhelmes my blisse,	Edw	5.1.54	Edward
That I may gaze upon this glittering crowne,	Edw	5.1.60	Edward
That Edward may be still faire Englands king:	Edw	5.1.68	Edward
But that I feele the crowne upon my head,	Edw	5.1.82	Edward
He of you all that most desires my bloud,	Edw	5.1.100	Edward
Let not that Mortimer protect my sonne,	Edw	5.1.115	Edward
Farewell, I know the next newes that they bring,	Edw	5.1.125	Edward
That I resigne my charge.	Edw	5.1.136	Leistr
Well may I rent his name, that rends my hart.	Edw	5.1.140	Edward
And thats the cause that I am now remoovde.	Edw	5.1.150	Edward
And thinkes your grace that Bartley will bee cruell?	Edw	5.1.151	Bartly
That death ends all, and I can die but once.	Edw	5.1.153	Edward

THAT (cont.)

That if he slip will seaze upon us both,	Edw	5.2.8	Mortmr
Thinke therefore madam that imports [us] <as> much,	Edw	5.2.10	Mortmr
And that I be protector over him,	Edw	5.2.12	Mortmr
Be thou perswaded, that I love thee well,	Edw	5.2.16	Queene
First would I heare newes that hee were deposde,	Edw	5.2.21	Mortmr
So that he now is gone from Killingworth,	Edw	5.2.31	BshpWn
And we have heard that Edmund laid a plot,	Edw	5.2.32	BshpWn
As Leicester that had charge of him before.	Edw	5.2.35	BshpWn
That he resigne the king to thee and Gurney,	Edw	5.2.49	Mortmr
rest, because we heare/That Edmund casts to worke his libertie,	Edw	5.2.58	Mortmr
And tell him, that I labour all in vaine,	Edw	5.2.70	Queene
But she that gave him life, I meane the Queene?	Edw	5.2.91	Kent
That wast a cause of his imprisonment?	Edw	5.2.102	Mortmr
that one so false/Should come about the person of a prince.	Edw	5.2.104	Mortmr
Mortimer shall know that he hath wrongde mee.	Edw	5.2.118	Kent
That almost rents the closet of my heart,	Edw	5.3.22	Edward
Immortall powers, that knowes the painfull cares,	Edw	5.3.37	Edward
That waites upon my poore distressed soule,	Edw	5.3.38	Edward
That wronges their liege and soveraigne, Englands king.	Edw	5.3.40	Edward
O Gaveston, it is for thee that I am wrongd,	Edw	5.3.41	Edward
O miserable is that commonweale,	Edw	5.3.63	Kent
Seeing that my brother cannot be releast.	Edw	5.3.67	Kent
Yet he that is the cause of Edwards death,	Edw	5.4.3	Mortmr
That being dead, if it chaunce to be found,	Edw	5.4.14	Mortmr
And we be quit that causde it to be done:	Edw	5.4.16	Mortmr
That shall conveie it, and performe the rest,	Edw	5.4.18	Mortmr
And by a secret token that he beares,	Edw	5.4.19	Mortmr
Whats that?	Edw	5.4.38	Mortmr
That will I quicklie do, farewell my lord.	Edw	5.4.47	Ltborn
And sue to me for that that I desire,	Edw	5.4.57	Mortmr
Suscepi that provinciam as they terme it,	Edw	5.4.63	Mortmr
And that this be the coronation day,	Edw	5.4.70	Mortmr
Dares but affirme, that Edwards not true king,	Edw	5.4.76	Champn
I am the Champion that will combate him!	Edw	5.4.78	Champn
If that my Unckle shall be murthered thus?	Edw	5.4.110	King
That were enough to poison any man,	Edw	5.5.5	Matrvs
See that in the next roome I have a fier,	Edw	5.5.29	Ltborn
Feare not you that.	Edw	5.5.36	Matrvs
Whose there, what light is that, wherefore comes thou?	Edw	5.5.42	Edward
This ten dayes space, and least that I should sleepe,	Edw	5.5.60	Edward
So that for want of sleepe and sustenance,	Edw	5.5.63	Edward
That <and> even then when I shall lose my life,	Edw	5.5.77	Edward
Know that I am a king, oh at that name,	Edw	5.5.89	Edward
But that greefe keepes me waking, I shoulde sleepe,	Edw	5.5.93	Edward
This feare is that which makes me tremble thus,	Edw	5.5.105	Edward
But not too hard, least that you bruse his body.	Edw	5.5.113	Ltborn
I feare mee that this crie will raise the towne,	Edw	5.5.114	Matrvs
Feare not my lord, know that you are a king.	Edw	5.6.24	1Lord
Thinke not that I am frighted with thy words,	Edw	5.6.27	King
To witnesse to the world, that by thy meanes,	Edw	5.6.31	King
And plainely saith, twas thou that murdredst him.	Edw	5.6.42	King
That thither thou didst send a murtherer.	Edw	5.6.48	King
A Mortimer, thou knowest that he is slaine,	Edw	5.6.50	King
now I see, that in thy wheele/There is a point, to which when	Edw	5.6.59	Mortmr
that point I touchte,/And seeing there was no place to mount up	Edw	5.6.61	Mortmr
That scornes the world, and as a traveller,	Edw	5.6.65	Mortmr
This argues, that you spilt my fathers bloud,	Edw	5.6.70	King
That rumor is untrue, for loving thee,	Edw	5.6.74	Queene
That bootes not, therefore gentle madam goe.	Edw	5.6.91	2Lord
That shortly he was grac'd with Doctors name,	F 17	Prol.17	1Chor
And this the man that in his study sits.	F 28	Prol.28	1Chor
and begin/To sound the depth of that thou wilt professe,	F 30	1.1.2	Faust
Then read no more, thou hast attain'd that <the> end:	F 38	1.1.10	Faust
Why Faustus, hast thou not attain'd that end?	F 46	1.1.18	Faust
If we say that we have no sinne we deceive our selves, and	F 69	1.1.41	P Faust
I these are those that Faustus most desires.	F 79	1.1.51	Faust
All things that move betweene the quiet Poles/Shall be at my	F 83	1.1.55	Faust
But his dominion that exceeds <excells> in this,	F 87	1.1.59	Faust
O Faustus, lay that damned booke aside,	F 97	1.1.69	GdAngl
Reade, reade the Scriptures: that is blasphemy.	F 100	1.1.72	GdAngl
Go forward Faustus in that famous Art/Wherein all natures	F 101	1.1.73	BdAngl
Know that your words have won me at the last,	F 128	1.1.100	Faust
[That will receive no object, for my head]/[But ruminates on	F 131	1.1.103A	Faust
'Tis magick, magick, that hath ravisht me.	F 137	1.1.109	Faust
that have with [concise] <subtle> Sillogismes	F 139	1.1.111	Faust
That yearely [stuffes] <stuff'd> old Phillips treasury,	F 159	1.1.131	Valdes
The miracles that magick will performe,	F 163	1.1.135	Cornel
He that is grounded in Astrology,	F 165	1.1.137	Cornel
Yea <I> all the wealth that our fore-fathers hid,	F 173	1.1.145	Cornel
That I may conjure in some bushy <lustie> Grove,	F 178	1.1.150	Faust
I wonder what's become of Faustus that/Was wont to make our	F 194	1.2.1	1Schol
That shall we presently know, <for see> here comes his boy.	F 196	1.2.3	2Schol
Yes, I know, but that followes not.	F 200	1.2.7	P Wagner
That followes not <necessary> by force of argument, which	F 202	1.2.9	P Wagner
of argument, which <that> you, being Licentiats <licentiate>,	F 202	1.2.9	P Wagner
and is not that Mobile?	F 208	1.2.15	P Wagner
But that I am by nature flegmatique, slow to wrath, and prone	F 209	1.2.16	P Wagner
Then I feare that which I have long suspected:	F 220	1.2.27	1Schol
That thou art <he is> falne into that damned Art/For which they	F 221	1.2.28	1Schol
Now that the gloomy shadow of the night <earth>,	F 229	1.3.1	Faust
That holy shape becomes a devill best.	F 254	1.3.26	Faust
Conjurer laureate]/[That canst commaund great Mephostophilis],	F 261	1.3.33A	Faust

THAT (cont.)

That was the cause, but yet per accidens:	F 274	1.3.46		Mephst
Tell me, what is that Lucifer, thy Lord?	F 290	1.3.62		Faust
Was not that Lucifer an Angell once?	F 292	1.3.64		Faust
How comes it then that he is Prince of Devils?	F 294	1.3.66		Faust
And what are you that live with Lucifer?	F 297	1.3.69		Faust
Unhappy spirits that [fell] <live> with Lucifer,	F 298	1.3.70		Mephst
How comes it then that thou art out of hell?	F 303	1.3.75		Faust
Think'st thou that I [who] saw the face of God,	F 305	1.3.77		Mephst
I'le joyne the Hils that bind the Affrick shore,	F 335	1.3.107		Faust
And make that Country <land>, continent to Spaine,	F 336	1.3.108		Faust
Now that I have obtain'd what I desir'd <desire>/I'le live in	F 340	1.3.112		Faust
that <I know> he would give his soule to the devill, for a	F 349	1.4.7	P	Wagner
and see that you walke attentively, and let your right eye be	F 385	1.4.43	P	Wagner
left heele, that thou maist, Quasi vestigiis nostris insistere.	F 387	1.4.45	P	Wagner
Go forward Faustus in that famous Art.	F 403	2.1.15		BdAngl
Sweete Faustus leave that execrable Art.	F 404	2.1.16		GdAngl
That [makes men] <make them> foolish that do use <trust> them	F 408	2.1.20		BdAngl
[makes men] <make them> foolish that do use <trust> them most.	F 408	2.1.20		BdAngl
That I shall waite on Faustus whilst he lives,	F 420	2.1.32		Mephst
Already Faustus hath hazarded that for thee.	F 422	2.1.34		Faust
For that security craves <great> Lucifer.	F 425	2.1.37		Mephst
Is that the reason why he tempts us thus?	F 430	2.1.42		Faust
Why, have you any paine that torture other <tortures others>?	F 432	2.1.44		Faust
that at some certaine day/Great Lucifer may claime it as his	F 439	2.1.51		Mephst
Veiw here this <the> bloud that trickles from mine arme,	F 446	2.1.58		Faust
Why streames it not, that I may write a fresh?	F 455	2.1.67		Faust
But yet conditionally, that thou performe/All Covenants, and	F 479	2.1.91		Faust
First, that Faustus may be a spirit in forme and substance.	F 485	2.1.97	P	Faust
that Mephostophilis shall be his servant, and be by him	F 486	2.1.98	P	Faust
that Mephostophilis shall doe for him, and bring him	F 488	2.1.100	P	Faust
Fourthly, that he shall be in his chamber or house invisible.	F 490	2.1.102	P	Faust
that hee shall appeare to the said John Faustus, at all times,	F 491	2.1.103	P	Faust
grant unto them that foure and twentie yeares being expired,	F 495	2.1.107	P	Faust
Tell me, where is the place that men call Hell?	F 505	2.1.117		Faust
All places shall be hell that is not heaven.	F 515	2.1.127		Mephst
Why, dost thou think <think'st thou then> that Faustus shall be	F 518	2.1.130		Faust
I, and body too, but what of that:	F 521	2.1.133		Faust
Think'st thou that Faustus, is so fond to imagine,	F 522	2.1.134		Faust
That after this life there is any paine?	F 523	2.1.135		Faust
and incantations, that I might raise up spirits when I please].	F 551.2	2.1.165A	P	Faust
heavens, that I might knowe their motions and dispositions].	F 551.5	2.1.168A	P	Faust
see al plants, hearbes and trees that grow upon the earth].	F 551.9	2.1.172A	P	Faust
faire/As thou, or any man that [breathes] <breathe> on earth.	F 558	2.2.7		Mephst
How prov'st thou that?	F 559	2.2.8		Faust
And hath not he that built the walles of Thebes/With ravishing	F 579	2.2.28		Faust
That the first is finisht in a naturall day?	F 603	2.2.52		Faust
I, that is not against our Kingdome:	F 623	2.2.72	P	Mephst
Thinke Faustus upon God, that made the world.	F 625	2.2.74	P	Faust
O what art thou that look'st so [terrible] <terribly>.	F 638	2.2.87		Faust
That sight will be as pleasant to <pleasing unto> me, as	F 657	2.2.106	P	Faust
That shall I soone: What art thou the first?	F 663	2.2.112		Faust
<I would desire, that this house,	F 675	(HC263)A	P	Covet
that I might locke you safe into <uppe in> my <goode> Chest:	F 676	2.2.125	P	Covet
O that there would come a famine over <through> all the world,	F 681	2.2.130	P	Envy
<through> all the world, that all might die, and I live along,	F 682	2.2.131	P	Envy
and that buyes me <is> thirty meales a day, and ten Beavers:	F 694	2.2.143	P	Glutny
I am one that loves an inch of raw Mutton, better then an ell	F 708	2.2.160	P	Ltchry
That thou shalt see presently:	F 732	2.3.11	P	Robin
Thou needst not do that, for my Mistresse hath done it.	F 739	2.3.18	P	Dick
of us here, that have waded as deepe into matters, as other men,	F 740	2.3.19	P	Robin
tell me, in good sadnesse Robin, is that a conjuring booke?	F 744	2.3.23	P	Dick
That with his wings did part the subtle aire,	F 772	2.3.51		2Chor
That measures costs, and kingdomes of the earth:	F 774	2.3.53		2Chor
The which <That to> this day is highly solemnized.	F 778	2.3.57		2Chor
That threates the starres with her aspiring top,	F 796	3.1.18		Faust
But <And> now my Faustus, that thou maist perceive,	F 809	3.1.31		Mephst
Know that this City stands upon seven hils,	F 811	3.1.33		Mephst
That underprop <underprops> the ground-worke of the same:	F 812	3.1.34		Mephst
With winding bankes that cut it in two parts;	F 814	3.1.36		Mephst
That make <makes> safe passage, to each part of Rome.	F 816	3.1.38		Mephst
As that the double Cannons forg'd of brasse,	F 820	3.1.42		Mephst
That <which> Julius caesar brought from Affrica.	F 824	3.1.46		Mephst
That I do long to see the Monuments/And situation of bright	F 828	3.1.50		Faust
let me be cloyd/With all things that delight the heart of man.	F 838	3.1.60		Faust
That Faustus name, whilst this bright frame doth stand,	F 841	3.1.63		Faust
That looking downe the earth appear'd to me,	F 850	3.1.72		Faust
be,/That this proud Pope may Faustus [cunning] <comming> see.	F 855	3.1.77		Faust
Proud Lucifer, that State belongs to me:	F 871	3.1.93		Bruno
That doth assume the Papall government,	F 886	3.1.108		Pope
And make them sleepe so sound, that in their shapes,	F 895	3.1.117		Faust
The Pope shall curse that Faustus came to Rome.	F 903	3.1.125		Faust
We will depose the Emperour for that deed,	F 906	3.1.128		Pope
And curse the people that submit to him;	F 907	3.1.129		Pope
That Peters heires should tread on Emperours,	F 918	3.1.140		Pope
So will we quell that haughty Schismatique;	F 922	3.1.144		Pope
That Bruno, and the Germane Emperour/Be held as Lollords, and	F 954	3.1.176		Faust
And if that Bruno by his owne assent,	F 957	3.1.179		Faust
That we may solemnize Saint Peters feast,	F 978	3.1.200		Pope
To censure Bruno, that is posted hence,	F 983	3.2.3		Mephst
That slept both Bruno and his crowne away.	F 988	3.2.8		Faust
But now, that Faustus may delight his minde,	F 989	3.2.9		Faust
<Then charme me that I may be invisible>,	F 991	(HC266)A		Faust

THAT (cont.)

That I may walke invisible to all,	F 992	3.2.12		Faust
That no eye may thy body see.	F1003	3.2.23		Mephst
And see that all things be in readinesse,	F1011	3.2.31		Pope
That Bruno and the cursed Emperour/Were by the holy Councell	F1020	3.2.40		Pope
Then wherefore would you have me view that booke?	F1023	3.2.43		Pope
we all are witnesses/That Bruno here was late delivered you,	F1026	3.2.46		Raymnd
Who's that spoke? Friers looke about.	F1040	3.2.60		Pope
I'le have that too.	F1048	3.2.68		Faust
That we receive such great indignity?	F1050	3.2.70		Pope
yee Lubbers look about/And find the man that doth this villany,	F1056	3.2.76		Pope
Nay then take that.	F1067	3.2.87		Faust
be he that stole [away] his holinesse meate from the Table.	F1077	3.2.97		1Frier
Cursed be he that stroke his holinesse a blow [on] the face.	F1079	3.2.99		1Frier
be he that strucke <tooke> fryer Sandelo a blow on the pate.	F1081	3.2.101		1Frier
Cursed be he that disturbeth our holy Dirge.	F1083	3.2.103		1Frier
Cursed be he that tooke away his holinesse wine.	F1085	3.2.105		1Frier
that your devill can answere the stealing of this same cup,	F1088	3.3.1	P	Dick
That on a furies back came post from Rome,	F1161	4.1.7		Fredrk
That all this day the sluggard keepes his bed.	F1176	4.1.22		Mrtino
if that bee true, I have a charme in my head, shall controule	F1202	4.1.48	P	Benvol
that shall pierce through/The Ebon gates of ever-burning hell,	F1223	4.1.69		Faust
but for all that, I doe not greatly beleeve him, he lookes as	F1227	4.1.73	P	Benvol
We would behold that famous Conquerour,	F1231	4.1.77		Emper
That we may wonder at their excellence.	F1234	4.1.80		Emper
That when my Spirits present the royall shapes/Of Alexander and	F1249	4.1.95		Faust
That in mine armes I would have compast him.	F1262	4.1.108		Emper
That this faire Lady, whilest she liv'd on earth,	F1266	4.1.112		Emper
How may I prove that saying to be true?	F1268	4.1.114		Emper
beast is yon, that thrusts his head out at [the] window.	F1274	4.1.120	P	Faust
Till with my sword I have that Conjurer slaine.	F1333	4.2.9		Benvol
And kill that Doctor if he come this way.	F1339	4.2.15		Fredrk
And pants untill I see that Conjurer dead.	F1352	4.2.28		Benvol
O were that damned Hell-hound but in place,	F1355	4.2.31		Benvol
Mine be that honour then:	F1360	4.2.36		Benvol
Was this that sterne aspect, that awfull frowne,	F1370	4.2.46		Fredrk
Was this that damned head, whose heart <art> conspir'd	F1373	4.2.49		Mrtino
That all the world may see my just revenge.	F1382	4.2.58		Benvol
That rowling downe, may breake the villaines bones,	F1414	4.2.90		Faust
He must needs goe that the Divell drives.	F1419	4.2.95		Fredrk
That spite of spite, our wrongs are doubled?	F1446	4.3.16		Benvol
What may we do, that we may hide our shames?	F1447	4.3.17		Fredrk
that you may ride him o're hedge and ditch, and spare him not;	F1467	4.4.11	P	Faust
Who's this, that stands so solemnly by himselfe:	F1513	4.5.9	P	Hostss
I there's no doubt of that, for me thinkes you make no hast to	F1516	4.5.12	P	Hostss
I thinking that a little would serve his turne, bad him take as	F1528	4.5.24	P	Carter
yes, that may be; for I have heard of one, that ha's eate a load	F1533	4.5.29	P	Robin
be; for I have heard of one, that ha's eate a load of logges.	F1533	4.5.29	P	Robin
had had some [rare] quality that he would not have me know of,	F1542	4.5.38	P	HrsCsr
I seeing that, tooke him by the leg, and never rested pulling,	F1550	4.5.46	P	HrsCsr
great deserts in erecting that inchanted Castle in the Aire:	F1560	4.6.3	P	Duke
that it pleaseth your grace to thinke but well of that which	F1564	4.6.7	P	Faust
grace to thinke but well of that which Faustus hath performed.	F1564	4.6.7	P	Faust
that you have taken no pleasure in those sights; therefor I	F1565	4.6.8	P	Faust
I have heard that great bellyed women, do long for things, are	F1568	4.6.11	P	Faust
that at this time of the yeare, when every Tree is barren of	F1578	4.6.21	P	Duke
so that when it is Winter with us, in the contrary circle it is	F1582	4.6.25	P	Faust
and such Countries that lye farre East, where they have fruit	F1584	4.6.27	P	Faust
by meanes of a swift spirit that I have, I had these grapes	F1585	4.6.28	P	Faust
And trust me, they are the sweetest grapes that e're I tasted.	F1587	4.6.30	P	Lady
'faith Ile drinke a health to thy wooden leg for that word.	F1627	4.6.70	P	HrsCsr
My wooden leg? what dost thou meane by that?	F1628	4.6.71		Faust
I, I, he does not stand much upon that.	F1630	4.6.73	P	HrsCsr
that flesh and bloud should be so fraile with your Worship:	F1632	4.6.75	P	Carter
Yes, I do verie well remember that.	F1638	4.6.81	P	Faust
What's that?	F1644	4.6.87	P	Faust
thou make a Colossus of me, that thou askest me such questions?	F1646	4.6.89	P	Faust
sir, I would make nothing of you, but I would faine know that.	F1649	4.6.92	P	Carter
we will recompence/With all the love and kindnesse that we may.	F1672	4.6.115		Duke
that Hellen of Greece was the admirablest Lady that ever liv'd:	F1683	5.1.10	P	1Schol
that Hellen of Greece was the admirablest Lady that ever liv'd:	F1684	5.1.11	P	1Schol
if you will doe us so much <that> favour, as to let us see that	F1685	5.1.12	P	1Schol
as to let us see that peerelesse dame of Greece, whom all the	F1685	5.1.12	P	1Schol
For that I know your friendship is unfain'd,	F1689	5.1.16		Faust
deny/The just [requests] <request> of those that wish him well,	F1691	5.1.18		Faust
You shall behold that peerelesse dame of Greece,	F1692	5.1.19		Faust
This Magicke, that will charme thy soule to hell,	F1708	5.1.35		OldMan
And so have hope, that this my kinde rebuke,	F1722	5.1.49		OldMan
Torment sweet friend, that base and [crooked age] <aged man>,	F1753	5.1.80		Faust
That durst disswade me from thy Lucifer,	F1754	5.1.81		Faust
With greatest [torments] <torment> that our hell affoords.	F1755	5.1.82		Faust
That I may <might> have unto my paramour,	F1761	5.1.88		Faust
That heavenly Hellen, which I saw of late,	F1762	5.1.89		Faust
Those <These> thoughts that do disswade me from my vow,	F1764	5.1.91		Faust
Was this the face that Launcht a thousand ships,	F1768	5.1.95		Faust
And all is drosse that is not Helena.	F1774	5.1.101		Faust
[That from thy soule exclud'st the grace of heaven],	F1789	5.1.116A		OldMan
A surfet of deadly sin, that hath damn'd both body and soule.	F1833	5.2.37	P	Faust
the serpent that tempted Eve may be saved, but not Faustus.	F1838	5.2.42	P	Faust
remember that I have beene a student here these thirty yeares,	F1840	5.2.44	P	Faust
tell us of this before, that Divines might have prayd for thee?	F1862	5.2.66	P	1Schol
thou, and we will pray, that God may have mercie upon thee.	F1875	5.2.79	P	2Schol
For that must be thy mansion, there to dwell.	F1882	5.2.86		Mephst

THAT (cont.)

'Twas I, that when thou wer't i'the way to heaven,	F1886	5.2.90	Mephst
Fooles that will laugh on earth, [must] <most> weepe in hell.	F1891	5.2.95	Mephst
To want in hell, that had on earth such store.	F1898	5.2.102	BdAngl
Hadst thou kept on that way, Faustus behold,	F1903	5.2.107	GdAngl
that hast thou lost,/And now poore soule must thy good Angell	F1906	5.2.110	GdAngl
with horror stare/Into that vaste perpetuall torture-house,	F1910	5.2.114	BdAngl
are live quarters broyling on the coles,/That ner'e can die:	F1914	5.2.118	BdAngl
These, that are fed with soppes of flaming fire,	F1916	5.2.120	BdAngl
thou shalt see/Ten thousand tortures that more horrid be.	F1920	5.2.124	BdAngl
He that loves pleasure, must for pleasure fall.	F1923	5.2.127	BdAngl
That time may cease, and midnight never come.	F1930	5.2.134	Faust
That Faustus may repent, and save his soule.	F1934	5.2.138	Faust
You Starres that raign'd at my nativity,	F1950	5.2.154	Faust
That when you vomite forth into the aire,	F1954	5.2.158	Faust
[So that] my soule [may but] ascend to heaven.	F1956	5.2.160	Faust
Or why is this immortall that thou hast?	F1965	5.2.169	Faust
<Oh> Pythagcras Metemsycosis <metem su cossis>; were that true,	F1966	5.2.170	Faust
Curst be the parents that ingendred me;	F1972	5.2.176	Faust
That hath depriv'd thee of the joies of heaven.	F1974	5.2.178	Faust
Cut is the branch that might have growne full straight,	F2002	5.3.20	4Chor
That sometime grew within this learned man:	F2004	5.3.22	4Chor
that I know he would give his soule to the Divel for a shoulder	F App	p.229 7 P	Wagner
I, I thought that was al the land his father left him:	F App	p.229 17 P	Clown
you may save that labour, they are too familiar with me	F App	p.229 27 P	Clown
that I may be here and there and every where, O Ile tickle the	F App	p.231 62 P	Clown
How now, whose that which spake?	F App	p.231 3 P	Pope
How now, whose that which snatcht the meate from me?	F App	p.231 8 P	Pope
Well use that tricke no more, I would advise you.	F App	p.232 19	Faust
Cursed be hee that stole away his holinesse meate from/the	F App	p.232 31	Frier
Cursed be hee that strooke his holinesse a blowe on the face.	F App	p.232 33	Frier
Cursed be he that tooke Frier Sandelo a blow on the pate.	F App	p.232 35	Frier
Cursed be he that disturbeth our holy Dirge.	F App	p.232 37	Frier
Cursed be he that tooke away his holinesse wine.	F App	p.233 39	Frier
and so by that meanes I shal see more then ere I felt, or saw	F App	p.233 4 P	Robin
what doest thou with that same booke thou canst not reade?	F App	p.233 13 P	Rafe
my maister and mistris shal finde that I can reade, he for his	F App	p.233 15 P	Robin
Why Robin what booke is that?	F App	p.233 18 P	Rafe
for conjuring that ere was invented by any brimstone divel.	F App	p.233 20 P	Robin
that condition Ile feede thy divel with horse-bread as long as	F App	p.234 30 P	Rafe
how that none in my Empire, nor in the whole world can compare	F App	p.236 2 P	Emper
that thou let me see some proofe of thy skil, that mine eies	F App	p.236 6 P	Emper
that mine eies may be witnesses to confirme what mine eares	F App	p.236 6 P	Emper
that what ever thou doest, thou shalt be no wayes prejudiced or	F App	p.236 9 P	Emper
yet for that love and duety bindes me thereunto, I am content	F App	p.236 14 P	Faust
as we that do succeede, or they that shal hereafter possesse	F App	p.236 21 P	Emper
or they that shal hereafter possesse our throne, shal (I feare	F App	p.236 21 P	Emper
attaine to that degree of high renowne and great authoritie,	F App	p.236 22 P	Emper
in that manner that they best liv'd in, in their most	F App	p.237 47 P	Faust
send for the knight that was so pleasent with me here of late?	F App	p.238 66 P	Faust
that not only gives thee hornes, but makes thee weare them,	F App	p.238 70 P	Emper
course that time doth runne with calme and silent foote,	F App	p.239 90 P	Faust
had some rare qualitie that he would not have had me knowne of,	F App	p.240 132 P	HrsCsr
that great bellied women do long for some dainties or other,	F App	p.242 4 P	Faust
that being in the dead time of winter, and in the month of	F App	p.242 17 P	Duke
that when it is heere winter with us, in the contrary circle it	F App	p.242 20 P	Faust
and by means of a swift spirit that I have, I had them brought	F App	p.242 22 P	Faust
they be the best grapes that ere I tasted in my life before.	F App	p.242 25 P	Duchss
And yet me thinkes, if that death were neere,	F App	p.243 3	Wagner
Ah Doctor Faustus, that I might prevaile,	F App	p.243 34	OldMan
attaine the gole/That shall conduct thee to celestial rest.	F App	p.243 37	OldMan
That now the walles of houses halfe [rear'd] <reaer'd> totter,	Lucan, First Booke	24	
That rampiers fallen down, huge heapes of stone/Lye in our	Lucan, First Booke	25	
heapes of stone/Lye in our townes, that houses are abandon'd,	Lucan, First Booke	26	
And few live that behold their ancient seats;	Lucan, First Booke	27	
And choakt with thorns, that greedy earth wants hinds,	Lucan, First Booke	29	
The midst is best; that place is pure, and bright,	Lucan, First Booke	58	
Thy power inspires the Muze that sings this war.	Lucan, First Booke	66	
share our Empire, fortune that made Roome/Governe the earth,	Lucan, First Booke	109	
And all bands of that death presaging aliance.	Lucan, First Booke	114	
Thou feard'st (great Pompey) that late deeds would dim/Olde	Lucan, First Booke	121	
would dim/Olde triumphs, and that Caesars conquering France,	Lucan, First Booke	122	
use stirde, and thoughts that alwaies scorn'd/A second place;	Lucan, First Booke	124	
even the same that wrack's all great [dominions] <dominion>.	Lucan, First Booke	160	
Hence came it that th'edicts were overrul'd,	Lucan, First Booke	178	
That lawes were broake, Tribunes with Consuls strove,	Lucan, First Booke	179	
Thou thunderer that guardst/Roomes mighty walles built on	Lucan, First Booke	197	
He, he afflicts Roome that made me Roomes foe.	Lucan, First Booke	205	
That crost them; both which now approacht the camp,	Lucan, First Booke	270	
One that was feed for Caesar, and whose tongue/Could tune the	Lucan, First Booke	272	
you that with me have borne/A thousand brunts, and tride me ful	Lucan, First Booke	300	
use he's known/To exceed his maister, that arch-traitor Sylla.	Lucan, First Booke	326	
spread these flags that ten years space have conquer'd,	Lucan, First Booke	348	
force, they that now thwart right/In wars wil yeeld to wrong:	Lucan, First Booke	349	
that Senates tyranny?	Lucan, First Booke	366	
This [band] <hand> that all behind us might be quail'd,	Lucan, First Booke	370	
And frontier Varus that the campe is farre,	Lucan, First Booke	405	
And others came from that uncertaine shore,	Lucan, First Booke	410	
Whether the sea roul'd alwaies from that point,	Lucan, First Booke	413	
Or that the wandring maine follow the moone;	Lucan, First Booke	415	
They came that dwell/By Nemes fields, and bankes of Satirus,	Lucan, First Booke	420	
The Santons that rejoyce in Caesars love,	Lucan, First Booke	423	
And Sequana that well could manage steeds;	Lucan, First Booke	426	

THAT (cont.)

trumpets clang incites, and those that dwel/By Cyngas streame,	Lucan, First Booke	433
And Trevier; thou being glad that wars are past thee;	Lucan, First Booke	437
That soules passe not to silent Erebus/Or Plutoes bloodles	Lucan, First Booke	451
You likewise that repulst the Caicke foe,	Lucan, First Booke	459
Other that Caesars barbarous bands were spread/Along Nar floud	Lucan, First Booke	471
bands were spread/Along Nar floud that into Tiber fals,	Lucan, First Booke	472
And that his owne ten ensignes, and the rest/Marcht not	Lucan, First Booke	473
And that he's much chang'd, looking wild and big,	Lucan, First Booke	475
(his vassals)/And that he lags behind with them of purpose,	Lucan, First Booke	477
and that Roome/He looking on by these men should be sackt.	Lucan, First Booke	479
heady rout/That in chain'd troupes breake forth at every port;	Lucan, First Booke	489
the only hope (that did remaine/To their afflictions) were	Lucan, First Booke	494
O gods that easie grant men great estates,	Lucan, First Booke	508
Roome that flowes/With Citizens and [Captives] <Captaines>, and	Lucan, First Booke	509
And Commets that presage the fal of kingdoms.	Lucan, First Booke	527
Cattell were seene that muttered humane speech:	Lucan, First Booke	559
Those that inhabited the suburbe fieldes/Fled, fowle Erinnis	Lucan, First Booke	569
much like that hellish fiend/Which made the sterne Lycurgus	Lucan, First Booke	572
or like Megaera/That scar'd Alcides, when by Junoes taske/He	Lucan, First Booke	575
Well skild in Pyromancy; one that knew/The hearts of beasts, and	Lucan, First Booke	586
Then, that the trembling Citizens should walke/About the City;	Lucan, First Booke	591
the sacred priests/That with divine lustration purg'd the wals,	Lucan, First Booke	593
then, they that keepe, and read/Sybillas secret works, and	Lucan, First Booke	598
Ranne through the bloud, that turn'd it all to gelly,	Lucan, First Booke	618
At that bunch where the liver is, appear'd/A knob of flesh,	Lucan, First Booke	626
This headlesse trunke that lies on Nylus sande/I know:	Lucan, First Booke	684
[What] <That> if thy Mother take Dianas bowe,	Ovid's Elegies	1.1.11
In wooddie groves ist meete that Ceres Raigne,	Ovid's Elegies	1.1.13
Elegian Muse, that warblest amorous laies,	Ovid's Elegies	1.1.33
let hir <he> that cought me late,/Either love, or cause that I	Ovid's Elegies	1.3.1
Either love, or cause that I may never hate:	Ovid's Elegies	1.3.2
Accept him that will serve thee all his youth,	Ovid's Elegies	1.3.5
Accept him that will love with spotlesse truth:	Ovid's Elegies	1.3.6
That am descended but of knightly line,	Ovid's Elegies	1.3.8
The yeares that fatall destenie shall give,	Ovid's Elegies	1.3.17
That I may write things worthy thy faire lookes:	Ovid's Elegies	1.3.20
And she that on a faind Bull swamme to land,	Ovid's Elegies	1.3.23
When I (my light) do or say ought that please thee,	Ovid's Elegies	1.4.25
Strike on the boord like them that pray for evill,	Ovid's Elegies	1.4.27
And where thou drinkst, on that part I will sup.	Ovid's Elegies	1.4.32
And striving thus as one that would be cast,	Ovid's Elegies	1.5.15
Aie me how high that gale did lift my hope!	Ovid's Elegies	1.6.52
That when my mistresse there beholds thee cast,	Ovid's Elegies	1.6.69
That I was mad, and barbarous all men cried,	Ovid's Elegies	1.7.19
My bloud, the teares were that from her descended.	Ovid's Elegies	1.7.60
Shake off these wrinckles that thy front assault,	Ovid's Elegies	1.8.45
Of horne the bowe was that approv'd their side.	Ovid's Elegies	1.8.48
And take heed least he gets that love for nought.	Ovid's Elegies	1.8.72
That this, or that man may thy cheekes moist keepe.	Ovid's Elegies	1.8.84
That my dead bones may in their grave lie soft.	Ovid's Elegies	1.8.108
His Mistris dores this: that his Captaines keepes.	Ovid's Elegies	1.9.8
He that will not growe slothfull let him love.	Ovid's Elegies	1.9.46
too dearely wunne/That unto death did presse the holy Nunne.	Ovid's Elegies	1.10.50
The sonne slew her, that forth to meete him went,	Ovid's Elegies	1.10.51
And a rich neck-lace caus'd that punnishment.	Ovid's Elegies	1.10.52
The fame that verse gives doth for ever last.	Ovid's Elegies	1.10.62
give her my writ/But see that forth-with shee peruseth it.	Ovid's Elegies	1.11.16
Subscribing that to her I consecrate/My faithfull tables being	Ovid's Elegies	1.11.27
That colour rightly did appeare so bloudy.	Ovid's Elegies	1.12.12
And him that hew'd you out for needfull uses/Ile prove had	Ovid's Elegies	1.12.15
I pray that rotten age you wrackes/And sluttish white-mould	Ovid's Elegies	1.12.29
That drawes the day from heavens cold axletree.	Ovid's Elegies	1.13.2
Whither runst thou, that men, and women, love not?	Ovid's Elegies	1.13.9
Hold in thy rosie horses that they move not.	Ovid's Elegies	1.13.10
dost betray them/To Pedants, that with cruell lashes pay them.	Ovid's Elegies	1.13.18
That with one worde hath nigh himselfe undone,	Ovid's Elegies	1.13.20
[All] <This> could I beare, but that the wench should rise,/Who	Ovid's Elegies	1.13.25
How oft, that either wind would breake thy coche,	Ovid's Elegies	1.13.29
Say that thy love with Caephalus were not knowne,	Ovid's Elegies	1.13.33
Jove that thou shouldst not hast but wait his leasure,	Ovid's Elegies	1.13.45
The maide that kembd them ever safely left them.	Ovid's Elegies	1.14.16
Bacchinall/That tyr'd doth rashly on the greene grasse fall.	Ovid's Elegies	1.14.22
No sicknesse harm'd thee, farre be that a way,	Ovid's Elegies	1.14.41
Or that unlike the line from whence I [sprong] <come>,	Ovid's Elegies	1.15.3
Nor that I studie not the brawling lawes,	Ovid's Elegies	1.15.5
That all the world [may] <might> ever chaunt my name.	Ovid's Elegies	1.15.8
Loftie Lucretius shall live that houre,	Ovid's Elegies	1.15.23
That Nature shall dissolve this earthly bowre.	Ovid's Elegies	1.15.24
That some youth hurt as I am with loves bowe/His owne flames	Ovid's Elegies	2.1.7
Let him goe forth knowne, that unknowne did enter,	Ovid's Elegies	2.2.20
such faults are sad/Nor make they any man that heare them glad.	Ovid's Elegies	2.2.52
Wee seeke that through thee safely love we may,	Ovid's Elegies	2.2.65
That cannot Venus mutuall pleasure taste.	Ovid's Elegies	2.3.2
While thou hast time yet to bestowe that gift.	Ovid's Elegies	2.3.18
For I confesse, if that might merite favour,	Ovid's Elegies	2.4.3
I loathe, yet after that I loathe, I runne:	Ovid's Elegies	2.4.5
Oh how the burthen irkes, that we should shun.	Ovid's Elegies	2.4.6
<blushe>, and by that blushfull [glance] <glasse> am tooke:	Ovid's Elegies	2.4.12
Another railes at me, and that I write,	Ovid's Elegies	2.4.21
Yet would I lie with her if that I might.	Ovid's Elegies	2.4.22
And she <her> I like that with a majestie,	Ovid's Elegies	2.4.29
To leave my selfe, that am in love [with all] <withall>,	Ovid's Elegies	2.4.31

THAT (cont.)

This for her looks, that for her woman-hood:	Ovid's Elegies	2.4.46
Nay what is she that any Romane loves,	Ovid's Elegies	2.4.47
Cupid flie)/That my chiefe wish should be so oft to die.	Ovid's Elegies	2.5.2
He's happy, that his love dares boldly credit,	Ovid's Elegies	2.5.9
doth favour/That seekes the conquest by her loose behaviour.	Ovid's Elegies	2.5.12
And words that seem'd for certaine markes to be.	Ovid's Elegies	2.5.20
Or maides that their betrothed husbands spie.	Ovid's Elegies	2.5.36
I that ere-while was fierce, now humbly sue,	Ovid's Elegies	2.5.49
All wasting years have that complaint [out] <not> worne.	Ovid's Elegies	2.6.8
Or voice that howe to change the wilde notes knew?	Ovid's Elegies	2.6.18
Dead is that speaking image of mans voice,	Ovid's Elegies	2.6.37
They that deserve paine, beare't with patience.	Ovid's Elegies	2.7.12
Should I sollicit her that is so just:	Ovid's Elegies	2.7.25
Cypassis that a thousand wayes trimst haire,	Ovid's Elegies	2.8.1
Who that our bodies were comprest bewrayde?	Ovid's Elegies	2.8.5
Whence knowes Corinna that with thee I playde?	Ovid's Elegies	2.8.6
That might be urg'd to witnesse our false playing.	Ovid's Elegies	2.8.8
But being present, might that worke the best,	Ovid's Elegies	2.8.17
O Cupid that doest never cease my smart,	Ovid's Elegies	2.9.1
O boy that lyest so slothfull in my heart.	Ovid's Elegies	2.9.2
Why me that alwayes was thy souldiour found,	Ovid's Elegies	2.9.3
That have so oft serv'd pretty wenches dyet.	Ovid's Elegies	2.9.24
Haples is he that all the night lies quiet/And slumbring,	Ovid's Elegies	2.9.39
This seemes the fairest, so doth that to mee,	Ovid's Elegies	2.10.7
So with this love and that, wavers my minde.	Ovid's Elegies	2.10.10
I pay them home with that they most desire:	Ovid's Elegies	2.10.26
And to the Gods for that death Ovid prayes.	Ovid's Elegies	2.10.30
That at my funeralles some may weeping crie,	Ovid's Elegies	2.10.37
O would that no Oares might in seas have suncke,	Ovid's Elegies	2.11.5
But if that Triton tosse the troubled floud,	Ovid's Elegies	2.11.27
And say it brings her that preserveth me;	Ovid's Elegies	2.11.44
To bring that happy time so soone as may be.	Ovid's Elegies	2.11.56
That victory doth chiefely triumph merit,	Ovid's Elegies	2.12.5
Thou that frequents Canopus pleasant fields,	Ovid's Elegies	2.13.7
Memphis, and Pharos that sweete date trees yeelds,	Ovid's Elegies	2.13.8
He had not beene that conquering Rome did build.	Ovid's Elegies	2.14.16
Thou also, that wert borne faire, hadst decayed,	Ovid's Elegies	2.14.19
My selfe that better dye with loving may/Had seene, my mother	Ovid's Elegies	2.14.21
Oft dyes she that her paunch-wrapt child hath slaine.	Ovid's Elegies	2.14.38
Thou ring that shalt my faire girles finger binde,	Ovid's Elegies	2.15.1
O would that sodainly into my gift,	Ovid's Elegies	2.15.9
Then I, that I may seale her privy leaves,	Ovid's Elegies	2.15.15
Onely Ile signe nought, that may grieve me much.	Ovid's Elegies	2.15.18
My life, that I will shame thee never feare,	Ovid's Elegies	2.15.21
That meane to travaile some long irkesome way.	Ovid's Elegies	2.16.16
No barking Dogs that Syllaes intrailes beare,	Ovid's Elegies	2.16.23
That Paphos, and the floud-beate Cithera guides.	Ovid's Elegies	2.17.4
What would not she give that faire name to winne?	Ovid's Elegies	2.17.30
And thousand kisses gives, that worke my harmes:	Ovid's Elegies	2.18.10
Or Phillis teares that her [Demophoon] <Domoophon> misses,/What	Ovid's Elegies	2.18.22
Doth say, with her that lov'd the Aonian harpe.	Ovid's Elegies	2.18.26
Nor of thee Macer that resoundst forth armes,	Ovid's Elegies	2.18.35
Cruell is he, that loves whom none protect.	Ovid's Elegies	2.19.4
What should I do with fortune that nere failes me?	Ovid's Elegies	2.19.7
Nothing I love, that at all times availes me.	Ovid's Elegies	2.19.8
Ah often, that her [hale] <haole> head aked, she lying,	Ovid's Elegies	2.19.11
Thou also that late tookest mine eyes away,	Ovid's Elegies	2.19.19
Her lover let her mocke, that long will raigne,	Ovid's Elegies	2.19.33
That to deceits it may me forward pricke.	Ovid's Elegies	2.19.44
That can effect <affect> a foolish wittalls wife.	Ovid's Elegies	2.19.46
beate thee/To guard her well, that well I might entreate thee.	Ovid's Elegies	2.19.50
Some other seeke that may in patience strive with thee,	Ovid's Elegies	2.19.59
That thou maiest know with love thou mak'st me flame.	Ovid's Elegies	3.2.4
And sit thou rounder, that behind us see,	Ovid's Elegies	3.2.23
That from thy fanne, mov'd by my hand may blow?	Ovid's Elegies	3.2.38
Applaud you Neptune, that dare trust his wave,	Ovid's Elegies	3.2.47
Thee gentle Venus, and the boy that flies,	Ovid's Elegies	3.2.55
thou maiest, if that be best,/[A] <Or> while thy tiptoes on the	Ovid's Elegies	3.2.63
And feare those, that to feare them least intend.	Ovid's Elegies	3.3.32
And see at home much, that thou nere broughtst thether.	Ovid's Elegies	3.4.48
That may transport me without oares to rowe.	Ovid's Elegies	3.5.4
What should I name Aesope, that Thebe lov'd,	Ovid's Elegies	3.5.33
And fiercely knockst thy brest that open lyes?	Ovid's Elegies	3.5.58
That seeing thy teares can any joy then feele.	Ovid's Elegies	3.5.60
Shame, that should make me blush, I have no more.	Ovid's Elegies	3.5.78
And like a burthen greevde the bed that mooved not.	Ovid's Elegies	3.6.4
That were as white as is <Her armes farre whiter, then> the	Ovid's Elegies	3.6.8
And usde all speech that might provoke and stirre.	Ovid's Elegies	3.6.12
I blush, [that] <and> being youthfull, hot, and lustie,	Ovid's Elegies	3.6.19
Or one that with her tender brother lies,	Ovid's Elegies	3.6.22
So in a spring thrives he that told so much,	Ovid's Elegies	3.6.51
With that her loose gowne on, from me she cast her,	Ovid's Elegies	3.6.81
This side that serves thee, a sharpe sword did weare.	Ovid's Elegies	3.7.14
Canst touch that hand wherewith some one lie dead?	Ovid's Elegies	3.7.17
And some there be that thinke we have a deity.	Ovid's Elegies	3.8.18
And that slowe webbe nights fals-hood did unframe.	Ovid's Elegies	3.8.30
That durst to so great wickednesse aspire.	Ovid's Elegies	3.8.44
And some, that she refrain'd teares, have deni'd.	Ovid's Elegies	3.8.46
Gallus that [car'dst] <carst> not bloud, and life to spend.	Ovid's Elegies	3.8.64
things feigne)/Crete proud that Jove her nourcery maintaine.	Ovid's Elegies	3.9.20
Onely was Crete fruitfull that plenteous yeare,	Ovid's Elegies	3.9.37
May that shame fall mine enemies chance to be.	Ovid's Elegies	3.10.16

THAT (cont.)

My love was cause that more mens love she seazd.	Ovid's Elegies	3.10.20
That I may love yet, though against my minde.	Ovid's Elegies	3.10.52
What day was that, which all sad haps to bring,	Ovid's Elegies	3.11.1
Heav'n starre Electra that bewaild her sisters?	Ovid's Elegies	3.11.37
And sweet toucht harpe that to move stones was able?	Ovid's Elegies	3.11.40
And give to him that the first wound imparts.	Ovid's Elegies	3.12.22
But that thou wouldst dissemble when tis paste.	Ovid's Elegies	3.13.4
She hath not trode <tred> awrie that doth denie it,	Ovid's Elegies	3.13.5
This bed, and that by tumbling made uneven,	Ovid's Elegies	3.13.32
Graunt this, that what you do I may not see,	Ovid's Elegies	3.13.35
From him that yeelds the garland <palme> is quickly got,	Ovid's Elegies	3.13.47
two words, thinke/The cause acquits you not, but I that winke.	Ovid's Elegies	3.13.50
toyes defamde)/Heire of an antient house, if helpe that can,	Ovid's Elegies	3.14.5
A worke, that after my death, heere shall dwell	Ovid's Elegies	3.14.20
Of proud Adonis that before her lies.	Hero and Leander	1.14
His dangling tresses that were never shorne,	Hero and Leander	1.55
That heavenly path, with many a curious dint,	Hero and Leander	1.68
That runs along his backe, but my rude pen,	Hero and Leander	1.69
That my slacke muse, sings of Leanders eies,	Hero and Leander	1.72
his/That leapt into the water for a kis/Of his owne shadow,	Hero and Leander	1.74
That in the vast uplandish countrie dwelt,	Hero and Leander	1.80
For in his lookes were all that men desire,	Hero and Leander	1.84
Nor that night-wandring pale and watrie starre,	Hero and Leander	1.107
Than she the hearts of those that neere her stood.	Hero and Leander	1.112
And all that view'd her, were enamour'd on her.	Hero and Leander	1.118
For know, that underneath this radiant floure,	Hero and Leander	1.145
for the lovely boy/That now is turn'd into a Cypres tree,	Hero and Leander	1.155
Till with the fire that from his count'nance blazed,	Hero and Leander	1.164
We wish that one should loose, the other win.	Hero and Leander	1.170
Who ever lov'd, that lov'd not at first sight?	Hero and Leander	1.176
footsteps bending)/Doth testifie that you exceed her farre,	Hero and Leander	1.211
Lesse sinnes the poore rich man that starves himselfe,	Hero and Leander	1.243
We humane creatures should enjoy that blisse.	Hero and Leander	1.254
Wild savages, that drinke of running springs,	Hero and Leander	1.259
But they that dayly tast neat wine, despise it.	Hero and Leander	1.261
Of that which hath no being, doe not boast,	Hero and Leander	1.275
Things that are not at all, are never lost.	Hero and Leander	1.276
What vertue is it that is borne with us?	Hero and Leander	1.278
And know that some have wrong'd Dianas name?	Hero and Leander	1.284
Tell me, to whom mad'st thou that heedlesse oath?	Hero and Leander	1.294
Plaies, maskes, and all that stern age counteth evill.	Hero and Leander	1.302
But heale the heart, that thou hast wounded thus,	Hero and Leander	1.324
Wherewith she yeelded, that was woon before.	Hero and Leander	1.330
With that Leander stoopt, to have imbrac'd her,	Hero and Leander	1.341
Save that the sea playing on yellow sand,	Hero and Leander	1.347
That hops about the chamber where I lie,	Hero and Leander	1.354
And spends the night (that might be better spent)/In vaine	Hero and Leander	1.355
And shot a shaft that burning from him went,	Hero and Leander	1.372
The self-same day that he asleepe had layd/Inchaunted Argus,	Hero and Leander	1.387
Glist'red with deaw, as one that seem'd to skorne it:	Hero and Leander	1.390
prowd she was, (for loftie pride that dwels/In tow'red courts,	Hero and Leander	1.393
tincture of her cheekes, that drew/The love of everie swaine:	Hero and Leander	1.396
And crave the helpe of sheap-heards that were nie.	Hero and Leander	1.414
That she such lovelinesse and beautie had/As could provoke his	Hero and Leander	1.422
That sheares the slender threads of humane life,	Hero and Leander	1.448
That Jove, usurper of his fathers seat,	Hero and Leander	1.452
And but that Learning, in despight of Fate,	Hero and Leander	1.465
That he and Povertie should alwaies kis.	Hero and Leander	1.470
have concluded/That Midas brood shall sit in Honors chaire,	Hero and Leander	1.475
And fruitfull wits that in aspiring <inaspiring> are,	Hero and Leander	1.477
That he would leave her turret and depart.	Hero and Leander	2.38
And kept it downe that it might mount the hier.	Hero and Leander	2.42
But know you not that creatures wanting sence,	Hero and Leander	2.55
nothing saw/That might delight him more, yet he suspected/Some	Hero and Leander	2.63
Which taught him all that elder lovers know,	Hero and Leander	2.69
Love alwaies makes those eloquent that have it.	Hero and Leander	2.72
And stay the messenger that would be gon:	Hero and Leander	2.82
would not yeeld/So soone to part from that she deerely held.	Hero and Leander	2.84
And red for anger that he stayd so long,	Hero and Leander	2.89
And now the sunne that through th'orizon peepes,	Hero and Leander	2.99
So that in silence of the cloudie night,	Hero and Leander	2.101
That him from her unjustly did detaine.	Hero and Leander	2.122
And love that is conceal'd, betraies poore lovers.	Hero and Leander	2.134
so hee that loves,/The more he is restrain'd, the woorse he	Hero and Leander	2.144
To part in twaine, that hee might come and go,	Hero and Leander	2.151
With that hee stript him to the yv'rie skin,	Hero and Leander	2.153
Imagining, that Ganimed displeas'd,	Hero and Leander	2.157
How that a sheapheard sitting in a vale,	Hero and Leander	2.194
That of the cooling river durst not drinke,	Hero and Leander	2.197
That now should shine on Thetis glassie bower,	Hero and Leander	2.203
O that these tardie armes of mine were wings,	Hero and Leander	2.205
Neptune was angrie that hee gave no eare,	Hero and Leander	2.207
Thereon concluded that he was beloved.	Hero and Leander	2.220
The neerer that he came, the more she fled,	Hero and Leander	2.243
So that the truce was broke, and she alas,	Hero and Leander	2.285
this strife of hers (like that/Which made the world) another	Hero and Leander	2.291
describe, but hee/That puls or shakes it from the golden tree:	Hero and Leander	2.300
For much it greev'd her that the bright day-light,	Hero and Leander	2.303
That which so long so charily she kept,	Hero and Leander	2.309
That Meremaid-like unto the floore she slid,	Hero and Leander	2.315
That Vallies, groves, hills and fieldes,	Passionate Shepherd	3

THAT'S

Why, that's wel said Techelles, so would I,	1Tamb 2.5.69	Tamb

Text	Work	Ref		Speaker
THAT'S (cont.)				
(For that's the style and tytle I have yet)/Although he sent a	2Tamb	1.2.69		Almeda
That's no matter sir, for being a king, for Tamburlain came up	2Tamb	3.1.73	P	Almeda
That's not our fault:	Jew	1.1.130		Barab
That's more then is in our Commission.	Jew	1.2.22		Basso
that's their profession,/And not simplicity, as they suggest.	Jew	1.2.160		Barab
you were his father too, Sir, that's al the harm I wish you:	Jew	2.3.41	P	Barab
Sir, that's his price.	Jew	2.3.99		1Offcr
I must have one that's sickly, and be but for sparing vittles:	Jew	2.3.123	P	Barab
you in these chops; let me see one that's somewhat leaner.	Jew	2.3.125	P	Barab
That's no lye, for she sent me for him.	Jew	3.4.25	P	Ithimr
That's to be gotten in the Westerne Inde:	Jew	3.5.5		Govnr
That's brave, master, but think you it wil not be known?	Jew	4.1.8	P	Ithimr
The reward of sin is death? that's hard:	F 67	1.1.39		Faust
that's good to kill Vermine:	F 358	1.4.16	P	Robin
That's like, 'faith:	F 734	2.3.13	P	Dick
that's excellent:	F1133	3.3.46	P	Robin
tis no matter for thy head, for that's arm'd sufficiently.	F1289	4.1.135	P	Emper
I, that's the head, and here the body lies,	F1375	4.2.51		Benvol
that's excellent, for one of his devils turn'd me into the	F1553	4.5.49	P	Dick
She is not chaste, that's kept, but a deare whore:	Ovid's Elegies	3.4.29		
THATS				
This is no seate for one thats comfortles,	Dido	2.1.86		Aeneas
Thats wel Techelles, what's the newes?	1Tamb	5.1.198		Tamb
And thats the cause that Guise so frowns at us,	P 52	1.52		Navrre
And thats because the blockish [Sorbonests] <thorbonest>	P 411	7.51		Ramus
Did he not injure Mounser thats deceast?	P1035	19.105		King
But thats prevented, for to end his life,	P1119	21.13		Dumain
thats no answere	Paris	ms 7,p390	P	Souldr
Heere comes she thats cause of all these jarres.	Edw	2.2.224		Edward
Thats it these Barons and the subtill Queene,	Edw	3.1.272		Levune
And thats the cause that I am now remoovde.	Edw	5.1.150		Edward
But read it thus, and thats an other sence:	Edw	5.4.10		Mortmr
Thats his meaning.	Edw	5.5.18		Matrvs
Thats all?	Edw	5.5.34		Gurney
well, Ile folow him, Ile serve him, thats flat.	F App	p.231 73	P	Clown
in Europe for nothing, thats one of my conjuring workes.	F App	p.234 24	P	Robin
Our maister Parson sayes thats nothing.	F App	p.234 25	P	Rafe
thats brave, Ile have fine sport with the boyes, Ile get nuts	F App	p.236 45	P	Robin
Ifaith thats just nothing at all.	F App	p.237 40	P	Knight
Ifaith thats as true as Diana turned me to a stag.	F App	p.237 54	P	Knight
Alas Madame, thats nothing, Mephastophilis, be gone.	F App	p.242 12	P	Faust
And she thats coy I like for being no clowne,	Ovid's Elegies	2.4.13		
T'HAVE				
Or she was not the wench I wisht t'have had.	Ovid's Elegies	3.6.2		
TH'AVERNI				
Th'Averni too, which bouldly faine themselves/The Romanes	Lucan, First Booke	428		
THAW'D				
And frozen Alpes thaw'd with resolving winds.	Lucan, First Booke	221		
With snow thaw'd from the next hill now thou rushest,	Ovid's Elegies	3.5.7		
THEAMES				
Their minds, and muses on admyred theames:	1Tamb	5.1.164		Tamb
TH'EARLE				
Seeing that our Lord th'earle of Glosters dead,	Edw	2.1.2		Baldck
TH'EARTH				
While th'earth the sea, and ayre the earth sustaines;	Lucan, First Booke	89		
rayes now sing/The fell Nemean beast, th'earth would be fired,	Lucan, First Booke	655		
with th'earth thou wert content,/Why seek'st not heav'n the	Ovid's Elegies	3.7.49		
Which th'earth from ougly Chaos den up-wayd:	Hero and Leander	1.450		
TH'EARTHS				
Strooke with th'earths suddaine shadow waxed pale,	Lucan, First Booke	537		
And may th'earths weight thy ashes nought molest.	Ovid's Elegies	3.8.68		
TH'EAST				
thou lead'st me toward th'east,/Where Nile augmenteth the	Lucan, First Booke	682		
THEATER				
If on the Marble Theater I looke,	Ovid's Elegies	2.7.3		
THEATER'S				
Isis may be done/Nor feare least she to th'theater's runne.	Ovid's Elegies	2.2.26		
THEATERS				
And joyed to heare his Theaters applause;	Lucan, First Booke	134		
THEBAN				
O my Achates, Theban Niobe,	Dido	2.1.3		Aeneas
a double point/Rose like the Theban brothers funerall fire;	Lucan, First Booke	550		
Leander now like Theban Hercules,	Hero and Leander	2.297		
THEBANE				
Or Cephalus with lustie Thebane youths,	1Tamb	4.3.4		Souldn
THEBE				
What should I name Aesope, that Thebe lov'd,	Ovid's Elegies	3.5.33		
Thebe who Mother of five Daughters prov'd?	Ovid's Elegies	3.5.34		
THEBES				
And mought I live to see him sacke rich Thebes,	Dido	3.3.42		Aeneas
And hath not he that built the walles of Thebes/With ravishing	F 579	2.2.28		Faust
When Thebes, when Troy, when Caesar should be writ,	Ovid's Elegies	3.11.15		
Proteus what should I name? teeth, Thebes first seed?	Ovid's Elegies	3.11.35		
TH'EDICTS				
Hence came it that th'edicts were overrul'd,	Lucan, First Booke	178		
THEE (See also PRETHE, PRETHEE)				
I love thee well, say Juno what she will.	Dido	1.1.2		Jupitr
I vow, if she but once frowne on thee more,	Dido	1.1.12		Jupitr
When as they would have hal'd thee from my sight:	Dido	1.1.27		Jupitr
Vulcan shall daunce to make thee laughing sport,	Dido	1.1.32		Jupitr
To make thee fannes wherewith to coole thy face,	Dido	1.1.35		Jupitr
What shall I doe to save thee my sweet boy?	Dido	1.1.74		Venus

THEE (cont.)

Content thee Cytherea in thy care,	Dido	1.1.82	Jupitr
And Helens rape doth haunt [ye] <thee> at the heeles.	Dido	1.1.144	Aeneas
Fortune hath favord thee what ere thou be,	Dido	1.1.231	Venus
In sending thee unto this curteous Coast:	Dido	1.1.232	Venus
A Gods name on and hast thee to the Court,	Dido	1.1.233	Venus
And so I leave thee to thy fortunes lot,	Dido	1.1.238	Venus
And now she sees thee how will she rejoyce?	Dido	2.1.69	Ilion
Lyes it in Didos hands to make thee blest,	Dido	2.1.103	Dido
May I entreat thee to discourse at large,	Dido	2.1.106	Dido
Ile give thee Sugar-almonds, sweete Conserves,	Dido	2.1.305	Venus
For Didos sake I take thee in my armes,	Dido	2.1.313	Venus
Now Cupid turne thee to Ascanius shape,	Dido	2.1.323	Venus
in stead of him/Will set thee on her lap and play with thee:	Dido	2.1.325	Venus
Till I returne and take thee hence againe.	Dido	2.1.339	Venus
And when she strokes thee softly on the head,	Dido	3.1.5	Cupid
How long faire Dido shall I pine for thee?	Dido	3.1.7	Iarbus
Sit in my lap and let me heare thee sing.	Dido	3.1.25	Dido
I wagge, and give thee leave to kisse her to.	Dido	3.1.31	Dido
O stay Iarbus, and Ile goe with thee.	Dido	3.1.37	Dido
Iarbus dye, seeing she abandons thee.	Dido	3.1.40	Iarbus
No, but I charge thee never looke on me.	Dido	3.1.54	Dido
here, tell me in sooth/In what might Dido highly pleasure thee.	Dido	3.1.102	Dido
Ile give thee tackling made of riveld gold,	Dido	3.1.116	Dido
And wanton Mermaides court thee with sweete songs,	Dido	3.1.130	Dido
Yet boast not of it, for I love thee not,	Dido	3.1.171	Dido
not of it, for I love thee not,/And yet I hate thee not:--	Dido	3.1.172	Dido
But not so much for thee, thou art but one,	Dido	3.1.175	Dido
Aeneas, thinke not but I honor thee,	Dido	3.3.1	Dido
That thus in person goe with thee to hunt:	Dido	3.3.2	Dido
And might I live to see thee shipt away,	Dido	3.3.46	Iarbus
Whose bloud will reconcile thee to content,	Dido	3.3.74	Iarbus
Not angred me, except in angring thee.	Dido	3.4.15	Dido
It was because I sawe no King like thee,	Dido	3.4.35	Dido
Whose yeelding heart may yeeld thee more reliefe.	Dido	4.2.36	Anna
Anna that doth admire thee more then heaven.	Dido	4.2.46	Anna
For I have honey to present thee with:	Dido	4.2.53	Anna
Ile follow thee with outcryes nere the lesse,	Dido	4.2.55	Anna
To rid thee of that doubt, abourd againe,	Dido	4.4.21	Dido
I charge thee put to sea and stay not here.	Dido	4.4.22	Dido
When I leave thee, death be my punishment,	Dido	4.4.56	Aeneas
Not all the world can take thee from mine armes,	Dido	4.4.61	Dido
Dido is thine, henceforth Ile call thee Lord:	Dido	4.4.84	Dido
Doe as I bid thee sister, leade the way,	Dido	4.4.85	Dido
And yet I blame thee not, thou art but wood.	Dido	4.4.143	Dido
Why did it suffer thee to touch her breast,	Dido	4.4.145	Dido
Aeneas stay, Joves Herald bids thee stay.	Dido	5.1.24	Hermes
If that all glorie hath forsaken thee,	Dido	5.1.36	Hermes
I tell thee thou must straight to Italy,	Dido	5.1.53	Hermes
For I will furnish thee with such supplies:	Dido	5.1.72	Iarbus
Achates and the rest shall waite on thee,	Dido	5.1.76	Aeneas
O pardon me, if I resolve thee why:	Dido	5.1.91	Aeneas
O then Aeneas, tis for griefe of thee:	Dido	5.1.116	Dido
Aeneas could not choose but hold thee deare,	Dido	5.1.126	Aeneas
many neighbour kings/Were up in armes, for making thee my love?	Dido	5.1.142	Dido
Had I a sonne by thee, the griefe were lesse,	Dido	5.1.149	Dido
And Tygers of Hircania gave thee sucke:	Dido	5.1.159	Dido
Repairde not I thy ships, made thee a King,	Dido	5.1.163	Dido
And hisse at Dido for preserving thee?	Dido	5.1.168	Dido
I traytor, and the waves shall cast thee up,	Dido	5.1.174	Dido
If not, turne from me, and Ile turne from thee:	Dido	5.1.181	Dido
I have not power to stay thee: is he gone?	Dido	5.1.183	Dido
Dido I come to thee, aye me Aeneas.	Dido	5.1.318	Iarbus
But Anna now shall honor thee in death,	Dido	5.1.325	Anna
Now sweet Iarbus stay, I come to thee.	Dido	5.1.329	Anna
Now Turkes and Tartars shake their swords at thee,	1Tamb	1.1.16	Cosroe
I long to see thee backe returne from thence,	1Tamb	1.1.76	Mycet
What, shall I call thee brother?	1Tamb	1.1.103	Mycet
Present thee with th'Emperiall Diadem.	1Tamb	1.1.139	Ortyg
We here doo crowne thee Monarch of the East,	1Tamb	1.1.161	Ortyg
And making thee and me Techelles, kinges,	1Tamb	1.2.58	Usumc
Till with their eies [they] <thee> view us Emperours.	1Tamb	1.2.67	Tamb
A hundreth <hundred> Tartars shall attend on thee,	1Tamb	1.2.93	Tamb
In thee (thou valiant man of Persea)	1Tamb	1.2.166	Tamb
I yeeld my selfe, my men and horse to thee:	1Tamb	1.2.229	Therid
And they will never leave thee till the death.	1Tamb	1.2.248	Tamb
Nor thee, nor them, thrice noble Tamburlain,	1Tamb	1.2.249	Therid
We yeeld unto thee happie Tamburlaine.	1Tamb	1.2.257	Agidas
And having thee, I have a jewell sure:	1Tamb	2.2.56	Mycet
Such another word, and I will have thee executed.	1Tamb	2.4.30	Mycet
Here take it for a while, I lend it thee,	1Tamb	2.4.37	Tamb
Till I may see thee hem'd with armed men.	1Tamb	2.4.38	Tamb
Holde thee Cosroe, weare two imperiall Crownes.	1Tamb	2.5.1	Tamb
Thinke thee invested now as royally,	1Tamb	2.5.2	Tamb
As if as many kinges as could encompasse thee,	1Tamb	2.5.4	Tamb
With greatest pompe had crown'd thee Emperour.	1Tamb	2.5.5	Tamb
Thee doo I make my Regent of Persea,	1Tamb	2.5.8	Cosroe
I will not thank thee (sweet Ortigius)/Better replies shall	1Tamb	2.5.36	Cosroe
my brothers Campe/I leave to thee, and to Theridamas,	1Tamb	2.5.39	Cosroe
Techelles, take a thousand horse with thee,	1Tamb	2.5.99	Tamb
Haste thee Techelles, we will follow thee.	1Tamb	2.5.104	Tamb
Hie thee my Bassoe fast to Persea,	1Tamb	3.1.21	Bajzth
Then stay thou with him, say I bid thee so.	1Tamb	3.1.35	Bajzth

THEE (cont.)

And meane to fetch thee in despight of him.	1Tamb	3.1.40		Bajzth
Which thy prolonged Fates may draw on thee:	1Tamb	3.2.101		Agidas
He meet me in the field and fetch thee hence?	1Tamb	3.3.5		Tamb
I tell thee villaine, those that lead my horse/Have to their	1Tamb	3.3.69		Bajzth
Shall lead thee Captive thorow Affrica.	1Tamb	3.3.73		Tamb
I will not tell thee how Ile handle thee,	1Tamb	3.3.84		Tamb
not endure to strike/So many blowes as I have heads for thee.	1Tamb	3.3.144		Bajzth
That leave no ground for thee to martch upon.	1Tamb	3.3.147		Bajzth
And sue to thee?	1Tamb	3.3.176		Zabina
I tell thee shamelesse girle,/Thou shalt be Landresse to my	1Tamb	3.3.176		Zabina
Straight will I use thee as thy pride deserves:	1Tamb	3.3.206		Zabina
I tell thee, were that Tamburlaine/As monsterous as Gorgon,	1Tamb	4.1.17		Souldn
That may command thee peecemeale to be torne,	1Tamb	4.2.23		Tamb
Ambitious pride shall make thee fall as low,	1Tamb	4.2.76		Bajzth
Confusion light on him that helps thee thus.	1Tamb	4.2.84		Bajzth
my spirit doth foresee/The utter ruine of thy men and thee.	1Tamb	4.3.60		Arabia
to come by, plucke out that, and twil serve thee and thy wife:	1Tamb	4.4.14	P	Tamb
First legions of devils shall teare thee in peeces.	1Tamb	4.4.38	P	Bajzth
will make thee slice the brawnes of thy armes into carbonadoes,	1Tamb	4.4.43	P	Tamb
pray thee tel, why art thou so sad?	1Tamb	4.4.63	P	Tamb
Zenocrate, I will not crowne thee yet,	1Tamb	4.4.139		Tamb
Faire is too foule an Epithite for thee,	1Tamb	5.1.136		Tamb
No more there is not I warrant thee Techelles.	1Tamb	5.1.202		Tamb
Millions of men encompasse thee about,	1Tamb	5.1.215		Bajzth
Enforce thee run upon the banefull pikes.	1Tamb	5.1.220		Bajzth
Making thee mount as high as Eagles soare.	1Tamb	5.1.224		Bajzth
Ah what may chance to thee Zenocrate?	1Tamb	5.1.371		Zenoc
Behold her wounded in conceit for thee,	1Tamb	5.1.415		Zenoc
Though my right hand have thus enthralled thee,	1Tamb	5.1.435		Tamb
Thy princely daughter here shall set thee free.	1Tamb	5.1.436		Tamb
and protestations/Of endlesse honor to thee for her love.	1Tamb	5.1.497		Souldn
And here we crowne thee Queene of Persea,	1Tamb	5.1.507		Tamb
To gratify the <thee> sweet Zenocrate,	1Tamb	5.1.516		Tamb
Orcanes (as our Legates promist thee)/Wee with our Peeres have	2Tamb	1.1.78		Sgsmnd
for as the Romans usde/I here present thee with a naked sword.	2Tamb	1.1.82		Sgsmnd
Then here I sheath it, and give thee my hand,	2Tamb	1.1.127		Sgsmnd
But whilst I live will be at truce with thee.	2Tamb	1.1.130		Sgsmnd
I thank thee Sigismond, but when I war/All Asia Minor, Affrica,	2Tamb	1.1.157		Orcan
Gallies mann'd with Christian slaves/I freely give thee,	2Tamb	1.2.33		Callap
The Grecian virgins shall attend on thee,	2Tamb	1.2.36		Callap
Now rest thee here on faire Larissa Plaines,	2Tamb	1.3.5		Tamb
Sit up and rest thee like a lovely Queene.	2Tamb	1.3.16		Tamb
And I will teach thee how to charge thy foe,	2Tamb	1.3.45		Tamb
Hold him, and cleave him too, or Ile cleave thee,	2Tamb	1.3.104		Tamb
of Fesse have brought/To aide thee in this Turkish expedition,	2Tamb	1.3.131		Usumc
Which with my crowne I gladly offer thee.	2Tamb	1.3.136		Usumc
I here present thee with the crowne of Fesse,	2Tamb	1.3.140		Techel
Meaning to aid [thee] <them> in this <these> Turkish armes,	2Tamb	1.3.144		Techel
What God so ever holds thee in his armes,	2Tamb	2.4.109		Tamb
Giving thee Nectar and Ambrosia,	2Tamb	2.4.110		Tamb
in, not heaven it selfe/Shall ransome thee, thy wife and family.	2Tamb	3.3.28		Therid
That bring fresh water to thy men and thee:	2Tamb	3.3.30		Techel
Wel, this must be the messenger for thee.	2Tamb	3.4.15		Olymp
And quickly rid thee both of paine and life.	2Tamb	3.4.25		Olymp
And purge my soule before it come to thee.	2Tamb	3.4.33		Olymp
Wil match thee with a viceroy or a king.	2Tamb	3.4.41		Techel
Shall so torment thee and that Callapine,	2Tamb	3.5.85		Tamb
our mighty hoste/Shal bring thee bound unto the Generals tent.	2Tamb	3.5.111		Trebiz
Or bind thee in eternall torments wrath.	2Tamb	3.5.113		Soria
Ile make thee wish the earth had swallowed thee:	2Tamb	3.5.118		Tamb
Goe villaine, cast thee headlong from a rock,	2Tamb	3.5.120		Tamb
T'appease my wrath, or els Ile torture thee,	2Tamb	3.5.122		Tamb
any Element/Shal shrowde thee from the wrath of Tamburlaine.	2Tamb	3.5.127		Tamb
Wel, in despight of thee he shall be king:	2Tamb	3.5.128		Callap
I here invest thee king of Ariadan,	2Tamb	3.5.130		Callap
hee shall not be put to that exigent, I warrant thee.	2Tamb	3.5.157	P	Soria
No, we wil meet thee slavish Tamburlain.	2Tamb	3.5.170		Orcan
And oft hath warn'd thee to be stil in field,	2Tamb	4.1.24		Amyras
Embracing thee with deepest of his love,	2Tamb	4.1.109		Tamb
Whereat thou trembling hid'st thee in the aire,	2Tamb	4.1.130		Tamb
Thou shewest the difference twixt our selves and thee/In this	2Tamb	4.1.138		Orcan
And with our bloods, revenge our bloods on thee.	2Tamb	4.1.145		Jrslem
Hath stain'd thy cheekes, and made thee look like death,	2Tamb	4.2.4		Olymp
Devise some meanes to rid thee of thy life,	2Tamb	4.2.5		Olymp
Whose drift is onely to dishonor thee.	2Tamb	4.2.7		Olymp
Affoords no hearbs, whose taste may poison thee,	2Tamb	4.2.9		Olymp
Contagious smels, and vapors to infect thee,	2Tamb	4.2.11		Olymp
Nor thy close Cave a sword to murther thee,	2Tamb	4.2.12		Olymp
Wel met Olympia, I sought thee in my tent,	2Tamb	4.2.14		Therid
Enrag'd I ran about the fields for thee,	2Tamb	4.2.17		Therid
The winged Hermes, to convay thee hence:	2Tamb	4.2.19		Therid
But now I finde thee, and that feare is past.	2Tamb	4.2.20		Therid
And I will cast off armes and sit with thee,	2Tamb	4.2.44		Therid
I Turke, I tel thee, this same Boy is he,	2Tamb	4.3.57		Tamb
And wil defend it in despight of thee.	2Tamb	5.1.55		Govnr
Save but my life and I wil give it thee.	2Tamb	5.1.118		Govnr
And but one hoste is left to honor thee:	2Tamb	5.2.27		Callap
Villaine away, and hie thee to the field,	2Tamb	5.3.72		Tamb
That I may see thee crown'd before I die.	2Tamb	5.3.179		Tamb
And draw thee peecemeale like Hyppolitus,	2Tamb	5.3.240		Tamb
Goe tell 'em the Jew of Malta sent thee, man:	Jew	1.1.66		Barab
Yet Barrabas we will not banish thee,	Jew	1.2.100		Govnr

THEE (cont.)

And make thee poore and scorn'd of all the world,	Jew	1.2.108	1Knght
Content thee, Barabas, thou hast nought but right.	Jew	1.2.152	Govnr
Thy father has enough in store for thee.	Jew	1.2.227	Barab
Father, for thee lamenteth Abigaile:	Jew	1.2.229	Abigal
The gold and Jewels which I kept for thee.	Jew	1.2.298	Barab
For I will seeme offended with thee for't.	Jew	1.2.303	Barab
I charge thee on my blessing that thou leave/These divels, and	Jew	1.2.346	Barab
Oh Abigal, Abigal, that I had thee here too,	Jew	2.1.51	Barab
Martin del Bosco, I have heard of thee;	Jew	2.2.19	Govnr
We and our warlike Knights will follow thee/Against these	Jew	2.2.45	Govnr
Wee'll send [thee] <the> bullets wrapt in smoake and fire:	Jew	2.2.54	Govnr
And, Barabas, I'le beare thee company.	Jew	2.3.96	Lodowk
and thou hast, breake my head with it, I'le forgive thee.	Jew	2.3.112	P Barab
And I will teach [thee] that shall sticke by thee:	Jew	2.3.168	Barab
Oh wretched Abigal, what hast [thou] <thee> done?	Jew	2.3.320	Abigal
Lodowicke, it is enough/That I have made thee sure to Abigal.	Jew	2.3.335	Barab
Doe so; loe here I give thee Abigall.	Jew	2.3.345	Barab
What's that to thee?	Jew	2.3.357	Barab
Hold thee, wench, there's something for thee to spend.	Jew	3.1.12	Pilia
Well, Ithimore, let me request thee this,	Jew	3.3.26	Abigal
Yet Don Mathias ne're offended thee:	Jew	3.3.41	Abigal
Because the Pryor <Governor> <Sire> dispossest thee once,/And	Jew	3.3.43	Abigal
Know, holy Sir, I am bold to sollicite thee.	Jew	3.3.53	Abigal
Who taught thee this?	Jew	3.3.66	1Fryar
For I have now no hope but even in thee;	Jew	3.4.16	Barab
I here adopt thee for mine onely heire,	Jew	3.4.43	Barab
Here take my keyes, I'le give 'em thee anon:	Jew	3.4.46	Barab
Goe buy thee garments: but thou shalt not want:	Jew	3.4.47	Barab
What, hast thou brought the Ladle with thee too?	Jew	3.4.57	Barab
For I have other businesse for thee.	Jew	3.4.110	Barab
Ile pay thee with a vengeance Ithamore.	Jew	3.4.116	Barab
To worke my peace, this I confesse to thee;	Jew	3.6.31	Abigal
I will not goe for thee.	Jew	4.1.94	1Fryar
Not? then I'le make thee, [rogue] <goe>.	Jew	4.1.95	2Fryar
I warrant thee, Barabas.	Jew	4.1.113	1Fryar
thou think'st I see thee not;/Away, I'de wish thee, and let me	Jew	4.1.169	1Fryar
Away, I'de wish thee, and let me goe by:	Jew	4.1.170	1Fryar
I charge thee send me three hundred by this bearer, and this	Jew	4.2.75	P Ithimr
I have no husband, sweet, I'le marry thee.	Jew	4.2.87	Curtzn
But thus of thee.--	Jew	4.2.126	Curtzn
the gold, or know Jew it is in my power to hang thee.	Jew	4.3.38	P Pilia
As I wud see thee hang'd; oh, love stops my breath:	Jew	4.3.53	Barab
I'le pledge thee, love, and therefore drinke it off.	Jew	4.4.1	Curtzn
Of that condition I wil drink it up; here's to thee.	Jew	4.4.4	P Ithimr
Love thee, fill me three glasses.	Jew	4.4.7	Curtzn
Three and fifty dozen, I'le pledge thee.	Jew	4.4.8	P Ithimr
What wudst thou doe if he should send thee none?	Jew	4.4.13	Pilia
French-man, here's to thee with a--pox on this drunken hick-up.	Jew	4.4.32	P Ithimr
There's two crownes for thee, play.	Jew	4.4.47	Pilia
now; Bid him deliver thee a thousand Crownes, by the same token,	Jew	4.4.75	P Ithimr
I bring thee newes by whom thy sonne was slaine:	Jew	5.1.10	Curtzn
If this be true, I'le make thee Governor.	Jew	5.1.95	Calym
And Barabas, as erst we promis'd thee,	Jew	5.2.9	Calym
For thy desert we make thee Governor,	Jew	5.2.10	Calym
Intreat them well, as we have used thee.	Jew	5.2.17	Calym
Oh villaine, Heaven will be reveng'd on thee.	Jew	5.2.25	Govnr
me/My life's in danger, and what boots it thee/Poore Barabas,	Jew	5.2.31	Barab
This is the reason that I sent for thee;	Jew	5.2.51	Barab
What thinkst thou shall become of it and thee?	Jew	5.2.56	Barab
Nor hope of thee but extreme cruelty,	Jew	5.2.59	Govnr
Nor feare I death, nor will I flatter thee.	Jew	5.2.60	Govnr
Governor, I enlarge thee, live with me,	Jew	5.2.91	Barab
onely to performe/One stratagem that I'le impart to thee,	Jew	5.2.99	Barab
And bring it with me to thee in the evening.	Jew	5.2.108	Govnr
There will he banquet them, but thee at home,	Jew	5.3.38	Msngr
To give thee knowledge when to cut the cord,	Jew	5.5.40	Barab
here, hold thee, Barabas,/I trust thy word, take what I promis'd	Jew	5.5.42	Govnr
I trust thy word, take what I promis'd thee.	Jew	5.5.43	Govnr
No, Governor, I'le satisfie thee first,	Jew	5.5.44	Barab
Let us salute him. Save thee, Barabas.	Jew	5.5.54	Calym
Will't please thee, mighty Selim-Calymath,	Jew	5.5.57	Barab
For I will shew thee greater curtesie/Then Barabas would have	Jew	5.5.61	Govnr
thee greater curtesie/Then Barabas would have affoorded thee.	Jew	5.5.62	Govnr
See Calymath, this was devis'd for thee.	Jew	5.5.66	Govnr
Should I in pitty of thy plaints or thee,	Jew	5.5.72	Govnr
But wish thou hadst behav'd thee otherwise.	Jew	5.5.75	Govnr
Thus he determin'd to have handled thee,	Jew	5.5.93	Govnr
Nay, Selim, stay, for since we have thee here,	Jew	5.5.97	Govnr
We will not let thee part so suddenly:	Jew	5.5.98	Govnr
Besides, if we should let thee goe, all's one,	Jew	5.5.99	Govnr
By treason hath delivered thee to us:	Jew	5.5.110	Govnr
Content thee, Calymath, here thou must stay,	Jew	5.5.118	Govnr
for come [all] <call> the world/To rescue thee, so will we	Jew	5.5.120	Govnr
And then Ile guerdon thee with store of crownes.	P 89	2.32	Guise
Anjoy will follow thee.	P 333	5.60	Anjoy
I tell thee Mugeroun we will be freends,	P 614	12.27	King
I pray thee let me see.	P 674	13.18	Guise
Or hath my love been so obscurde in thee,	P 682	13.26	Guise
Is all my love forgot which helde thee deare?	P 684	13.28	Guise
This wrathfull hand should strike thee to the hart.	P 690	13.34	Guise
My sweet Joyeux, I make thee Generall,	P 743	15.1	King
Although my love to thee can hardly [suffer't] <suffer>,	P 747	15.5	King

THEE (cont.)

Because his wife beares thee such kindely love.	P 780	15.38	King
Holde thee tall Souldier, take thee this and flye.	P 817	17.12	Guise
I did it only in despite of thee.	P 820	17.15	Guise
I challenge thee for treason in the cause.	P 830	17.25	Eprnon
And Epernoune I will be rulde by thee.	P 885	17.80	King
And then Ile tell thee what I meane to doe.	P 891	17.86	King
Not to suspect disloyaltye in thee,	P 975	19.45	King
For in thee is the Duke of Guises hope.	P 988	19.58	Guise
Pardon thee, why what hast thou done?	P 991	19.61	Guise
slew him, and will slay/Thee too, and thou prove such a traitor.	P1049	19.119	King
I would that I had murdered thee my sonne.	P1073	19.143	QnMoth
I curse thee and exclaime thee miscreant,	P1075	19.145	QnMoth
And all for thee my Guise: what may I doe?	P1088	19.158	QnMoth
But what doth move thee above the rest to doe the deed?	P1132	21.26	P Dumain
Ile read them Frier, and then Ile answere thee.	P1171	22.33	King
And heere protest eternall love to thee,	P1206	22.68	King
And bids thee whet thy sword on Sextus bones,	P1237	22.99	King
Hold thee tale soldier take the this and flye	Paris	ms18,p390	Guise
I did it onely in dispight of thee	Paris	ms24,p391	Guise
then will I wake thee from thie folishe dreame/and lett thee	Paris	ms32,p391	Guise
thie folishe dreame/and lett thee see thie selfe my prysoner	Paris	ms33,p391	Guise
Well Mortimer, ile make thee rue these words,	Edw	1.1.91	Edward
Beseemes it thee to contradict thy king?	Edw	1.1.92	Edward
Embrace me Gaveston as I do thee:	Edw	1.1.141	Edward
Then beare the ship that shall transport thee hence:	Edw	1.1.153	Edward
I heere create thee Lord high Chamberlaine,	Edw	1.1.154	Edward
Ile give thee more, for but to honour thee,	Edw	1.1.164	Edward
I priest, and lives to be revengd on thee,	Edw	1.1.178	Edward
And make him serve thee as thy chaplaine,	Edw	1.1.195	Edward
I give him thee, here use him as thou wilt.	Edw	1.1.196	Edward
To see it done, and bring thee safe againe.	Edw	1.1.205	Edward
Of dutie and allegeance due to thee.	Edw	1.4.62	ArchBp
Live where thou wilt, ile send thee gould enough,	Edw	1.4.113	Edward
Ile come to thee, my love shall neare decline.	Edw	1.4.115	Edward
And there abide till fortune call thee home.	Edw	1.4.126	Edward
O might I keepe thee heere, as I doe this,	Edw	1.4.128	Edward
Thou shalt not hence, ile hide thee Gaveston.	Edw	1.4.131	Edward
Stay Gaveston, I cannot leave thee thus.	Edw	1.4.135	Edward
But come sweete friend, ile beare thee on thy way.	Edw	1.4.140	Edward
Fawne not on me French strumpet, get thee gone.	Edw	1.4.145	Edward
But I would wish thee reconcile the lords,	Edw	1.4.156	Edward
Witnesse this hart, that sighing for thee breakes,	Edw	1.4.165	Queene
And I will tell thee reasons of such waighte,	Edw	1.4.226	Queene
For thee faire Queene, if thou lovest Gaveston,	Edw	1.4.327	Edward
Or if that loftie office like thee not,	Edw	1.4.355	Edward
I make thee heere lord Marshall of the realme.	Edw	1.4.356	Edward
I will not long be from thee though I die:	Edw	2.1.62	Neece
When I forsake thee, death seaze on my heart,	Edw	2.1.64	Neece
But rest thee here where Gaveston shall sleepe.	Edw	2.1.65	Neece
For I have joyfull newes to tell thee of,	Edw	2.1.75	Neece
The life of thee shall salve this foule disgrace.	Edw	2.2.83	Gavstn
Do cosin, and ile beare thee companie.	Edw	2.2.121	Lncstr
Have drawne thy treasure drie, and made thee weake,	Edw	2.2.159	Mortmr
What forraine prince sends thee embassadors?	Edw	2.2.170	Lncstr
Who loves thee? but a sort of flatterers.	Edw	2.2.171	Mortmr
Libels are cast againe thee in the streete,	Edw	2.2.177	Mortmr
Cursing the name of thee and Gaveston.	Edw	2.2.181	Lncstr
me, for his sake/Ile grace thee with a higher stile ere long.	Edw	2.2.253	Edward
And Gaveston, thinke that I love thee well,	Edw	2.2.257	Edward
To wed thee to our neece, the onely heire/Unto the Earle of	Edw	2.2.258	Edward
was Plantagenet/False of his word, and therefore trust we thee.	Edw	2.3.12	Mortmr
And ile follow thee.	Edw	2.3.20	Warwck
As Isabell could live with thee for ever.	Edw	2.4.60	Queene
[King] <Kind> Edward is not heere to buckler thee.	Edw	2.5.18	Lncstr
Weele send his head by thee, let him bestow/His teares on that,	Edw	2.5.52	Mortmr
It is honourable in thee to offer this,	Edw	2.5.67	Mortmr
We will not wrong thee so,	Edw	2.5.69	Mortmr
Sweete soveraigne, yet I come/To see thee ere I die.	Edw	2.5.95	Gavstn
I do commit this Gaveston to thee,	Edw	2.5.107	Penbrk
in the morning/We will discharge thee of thy charge, be gon.	Edw	2.5.109	Penbrk
Spencer, I heere create thee earle of Wilshire,	Edw	3.1.49	Edward
And daily will enrich thee with our favour,	Edw	3.1.50	Edward
That as the sun-shine shall reflect ore thee:	Edw	3.1.51	Edward
shall I never see,/Never behold thee now?	Edw	3.1.69	Edward
Spencer, sweet Spencer, I adopt thee heere,	Edw	3.1.144	Edward
And meerely of our love we do create thee/Earle of Gloster, and	Edw	3.1.145	Edward
So wish not they Iwis that sent thee hither,	Edw	3.1.152	Edward
now get thee to thy lords,/And tell them I will come to	Edw	3.1.177	Edward
hie thee, get thee gone,/Edward with fire and sword, followes	Edw	3.1.179	Edward
Th'ad best betimes forsake [them] <thee> and their trains,	Edw	3.1.202	Lncstr
For theile betray thee, traitors as they are.	Edw	3.1.203	Lncstr
Brother, in regard of thee and of thy land,	Edw	3.1.230	Kent
[Levune] <Lewne>, the trust that we repose in thee,/Begets the	Edw	3.1.262	Spencr
Yet triumphe in the hope of thee my joye?	Edw	4.2.28	Queene
Will we with thee to Henolt, so we will.	Edw	4.2.31	Queene
Have beene by thee restored and comforted.	Edw	4.2.80	Mortmr
How now, what newes with thee, from whence come these?	Edw	4.3.24	Edward
Edward, alas my hart relents for thee,	Edw	4.6.2	Kent
It may become thee yet,/To let us take our farewell of his	Edw	4.7.68	Spencr
Remember thee fellow? what else?	Edw	4.7.118	Rice
Be thou perswaded, that I love thee well,	Edw	5.2.16	Queene
That he resigne the king to thee and Gurney,	Edw	5.2.49	Mortmr

THEE (cont.)

Sweete sonne come hither, I must talke with thee.	Edw	5.2.87		Queene
I tell thee tis not meet, that one so false/Should come about	Edw	5.2.104		Mortmr
Then I will carrie thee by force away.	Edw	5.2.112		Mortmr
To be revengde on Mortimer and thee.	Edw	5.2.121		Kent
O Gaveston, it is for thee that I am wrongd,	Edw	5.3.41		Edward
Champion, heeres to thee.	Edw	5.4.80		King
Strike of my head? base traitor I defie thee.	Edw	5.4.90		Kent
Feare not sweete boye, ile garde thee from thy foes,	Edw	5.4.111		Queene
But everie jointe shakes as I give it thee:	Edw	5.5.86		Edward
To rid thee of thy life. Matrevis come.	Edw	5.5.107		Ltborn
That rumor is untrue, for loving thee,	Edw	5.6.74		Queene
Could I have rulde thee then, as I do now,	Edw	5.6.96		King
Will make thee vow to study nothing else.	F 164	1.1.136		Cornel
Then hast thee to some solitary Grove,	F 180	1.1.152		Valdes
We will informe thee e're our conference cease.	F 184	1.1.156		Valdes
First I'le instruct thee in the rudiments,	F 188	1.1.160		Valdes
I charge thee to returne, and change thy shape,	F 251	1.3.23		Faust
I charge thee waite upon me whilst I live/To do what ever	F 264	1.3.36		Faust
And may not follow thee without his leave;	F 269	1.3.41		Mephst
Did not he charge thee to appeare to me?	F 271	1.3.43		Faust
Did not my conjuring [speeches] raise thee? speake.	F 273	1.3.45		Faust
Having thee ever to attend on me,	F 321	1.3.93		Faust
and I will make thee go, like Qui mihi discipulus.	F 355	1.4.13	P	Wagner
I'le turne all the lice about thee into Familiars, and make	F 362	1.4.20	P	Wagner
about thee into Familiars, and make them tare thee in peeces.	F 363	1.4.21	P	Wagner
whensoever, and wheresoever the devill shall fetch thee.	F 370	1.4.28	P	Wagner
for I will presently raise up two devils to carry thee away:	F 373	1.4.31	P	Wagner
I sirra, I'le teach thee to turne thy selfe to a Dog, or a Cat,	F 382	1.4.40	P	Wagner
[To God]? <Why> he loves thee not:	F 398	2.1.10		Faust
O they are meanes to bring thee unto heaven.	F 406	2.1.18		GdAngl
shall stand by me,/What [god] <power> can hurt me <thee>?	F 414	2.1.26		Faust
Already Faustus hath hazarded that for thee.	F 422	2.1.34		Faust
And I will be thy slave and waite on thee,	F 435	2.1.47		Mephst
And give thee more then thou hast wit to aske.	F 436	2.1.48		Mephst
I Mephostophilis, I'le <I> give it him <thee>.	F 437	2.1.49		Faust
for love of thee/Faustus hath <I> cut his <mine> arme,	F 442	2.1.54		Faust
I'le fetch thee fire to dissolve it streight.	F 452	2.1.64		Mephst
Faustus gives to thee his soule: [ah] <O> there it staid.	F 456	2.1.68		Faust
Then write againe: Faustus gives to thee his soule.	F 458	2.1.70		Faust
If unto [God] <heaven>, hee'le throw me <thee> downe to hell.	F 467	2.1.79		Faust
And let thee see <shewe thee> what Magicke can performe.	F 474	2.1.86		Mephst
I, take it, and the devill give thee good of it <on't>.	F 502	2.1.114		Faust
First, I will question [with] thee about hell:	F 504	2.1.116		Faust
For I tell thee I am damn'd, and <am> now in hell.	F 526	2.1.138		Mephst
Ile fetch thee a wife in the divels name>.	F 531	(HC261) A	P	Mephst
I'le cull thee out the fairest Curtezans,	F 537	2.1.149		Mephst
And men in harnesse <armour> shall appeare to thee,	F 548	2.1.160		Mephst
[Tut I warrant thee].	F 551.13	2.1.176A	P	Mephst
the heavens then I repent/And curse thee wicked Mephostophilis,	F 553	2.2.2		Faust
I tell thee Faustus it is <tis> not halfe so faire/As thou, or	F 557	2.2.6		Mephst
Faustus repent, yet God will pitty thee.	F 563	2.2.12		GdAngl
Thou art a spirit, God cannot pity thee.	F 564	2.2.13		BdAngl
Move me not Faustus <for I will not tell thee>.	F 621	2.2.70	P	Mephst
Villaine, have I not bound thee to tell me any thing?	F 622	2.2.71	P	Faust
If thou repent, devils will <shall> teare thee in peeces.	F 632	2.2.81		BdAngl
We are come to tell thee thou dost injure us.	F 642	2.2.91		Belzeb
And we will highly gratify thee for it.	F 653	2.2.102		Lucifr
we are come from hell in person to shew thee some pastime:	F 654	2.2.103	P	Belzeb
appeare to thee in their owne proper shapes and likenesse.	F 656	2.2.105	P	Belzeb
<No, Ile see thee hanged, thou wilt eate up all my victualls>.	F 702	(HC264) A	P	Faust
Then the devill choke thee.	F 703	2.2.152	P	Glutny
Faustus, thou shalt, at midnight I will send for thee;	F 716	2.2.168		Lucifr
I'le tell thee what, an my Maister come here, I'le clap as	F 736	2.3.15	P	Robin
put off thy cloathes, and I'le conjure thee about presently:	F 746	2.3.25	P	Robin
but to the Taverne with me, I'le give thee white wine, red wine,	F 748	2.3.27	P	Robin
containes <containeth> for to delight thine eyes <thee with>,	F 810	3.1.32		Mephst
This day shall make thee be admir'd in Rome.	F 867	3.1.89		Mephst
But thus I fall to Peter, not to thee.	F 872	3.1.94		Bruno
Go hast thee gentle Mephostophilis,	F 891	3.1.113		Faust
And charme thee with this Magicke wand,	F 996	3.2.16		Mephst
With Magicke spels so compasse thee,	F1002	3.2.22		Mephst
To satisfie my longing thoughts at full,/Let me this tell thee:	F1265	4.1.111		Emper
I blame thee not to sleepe much, having such a head of thine	F1284	4.1.130	P	Emper
Nay, we will stay with thee, betide what may,	F1338	4.2.14		Fredrk
Then gentle Fredericke hie thee to the grove,	F1340	4.2.16		Benvol
Well, I will not stand with thee, give me the money:	F1466	4.4.10	P	Faust
Then rest thee Faustus quiet in conceit.	F1483	4.4.27		Faust
How now Wagner what newes with thee?	F1499	4.4.43	P	Faust
some on's have cause to know him; did he conjure thee too?	F1524	4.5.20	P	HrsCsr
Do as thou wilt Faustus, I give thee leave.	F1607	4.6.50		Duke
Then I assure thee certainelie they are.	F1650	4.6.93		Faust
And quite bereave thee of salvation.	F1709	5.1.36		OldMan
Or envy of thee, but in tender love,	F1720	5.1.47		OldMan
And Faustus now will come to do thee right.	F1728	5.1.55		Faust
Faustus I leave thee, but with griefe of heart,	F1737	5.1.64		OldMan
One thing good servant let me crave of thee,	F1759	5.1.86		Faust
I will be Paris <Pacis>, and for love of thee,	F1775	5.1.102		Faust
[My faith, vile hel, shall triumph over thee],	F1793	5.1.120A		OldMan
'Mong which as chiefe, Faustus we come to thee,	F1800	5.2.4		Lucifr
chamber-fellow, had I liv'd with thee, then had I lived still,	F1824	5.2.28	P	Faust
tell us of this before, that Divines might have prayd for thee?	F1863	5.2.67	P	1Schol
thou, and we will pray, that God may have mercie upon thee.	F1876	5.2.80	P	2Schol

THEE (cont.)

Innumerable joyes had followed thee.	F1893	5.2.97		GdAngl
O what will all thy riches, pleasures, pompes,/Availe thee now?	F1897	5.2.101		GdAngl
Nothing but vexe thee more,/To want in hell, that had on earth	F1897	5.2.101		BdAngl
Hell, or the Divell, had had no power on thee.	F1902	5.2.106		GdAngl
And now poore soule must thy good Angell leave thee,	F1907	5.2.111		GdAngl
The jawes of hell are open to receive thee.	F1908	5.2.112		GdAngl
And so I leave thee Faustus till anon,	F1924	5.2.128		BdAngl
That hath depriv'd thee of the joies of heaven.	F1974	5.2.178		Faust
Or Lucifer will beare thee quicke to hell.	F1976	5.2.180		Faust
thou serve me, and Ile make thee go like Qui mihi discipulus?	F App	p.229 13	P	Wagner
or Ile turne al the lice about thee into familiars, and they	F App	p.229 25	P	Wagner
about thee into familiars, and they shal teare thee in peeces.	F App	p.229 26	P	Wagner
warning whensoever or wheresoever the divell shall fetch thee.	F App	p.230 37	P	Wagner
two divels presently to fetch thee away Baliol and Belcher.	F App	p.230 43	P	Wagner
I will teach thee to turne thy selfe to anything, to a dogge,	F App	p.231 58	P	Wagner
it, and she has sent me to looke thee out, prethee come away.	F App	p.233 9	P	Rafe
thee druncke with ipocrase at any taberne in Europe for	F App	p.234 23	P	Robin
did not I tell thee, we were for ever made by this doctor	F App	p.234 1	P	Robin
presumption, I transforme thee into an Ape, and thee into a Dog,	F App	p.235 43	P	Mephst
thee into an Ape, and thee into a Dog, and so be gone.	F App	p.235 44	P	Mephst
nor in the whole world can compare with thee, for the rare	F App	p.236 3	P	Emper
and here I sweare to thee, by the honor of mine Imperial	F App	p.236 8	P	Emper
And give me cause to praise thee whilst I live.	F App	p.237 36		Emper
that not only gives thee hornes, but makes thee weare them,	F App	p.238 71	P	Emper
gives thee hornes, but makes thee weare them, feele on thy head.	F App	p.238 71	P	Emper
Then rest thee Faustus quiet in conceit.	F App	p.240 126		Faust
I tell thee he has not slept this eight nights.	F App	p.240 144	P	Mephst
Why, thou seest he heares thee not.	F App	p.241 151	P	Mephst
How now Wagner, what's the newes with thee?	F App	p.241 167	P	Faust
attaine the gole/That shall conduct thee to celestial rest.	F App	p.243 37		OldMan
Which made thee Emperor; thee (seeing thou being old/Must shine	Lucan, First Booke	45		
thee (seeing thou being old/Must shine a star) shal heaven	Lucan, First Booke	45		
Nature, and every power shal give thee place,	Lucan, First Booke	51		
What God it please thee be, or where to sway:	Lucan, First Booke	52		
[There] <Their> Caesar may'st thou shine and no cloud dim thee;	Lucan, First Booke	59		
Thee if I invocate, I shall not need/To crave Apolloes ayde, or	Lucan, First Booke	64		
had heaven given thee longer life/Thou hadst restrainde thy	Lucan, First Booke	115		
Thee wars use stirde, and thoughts that alwaies scorn'd/A	Lucan, First Booke	124		
I hate thee not, to thee my conquests stoope,	Lucan, First Booke	203		
Caesar is thine, so please it thee, thy soldier;	Lucan, First Booke	204		
Hence leagues, and covenants; Fortune thee I follow,	Lucan, First Booke	228		
and draw the Commons minds/To favour thee, against the Senats	Lucan, First Booke	276		
Sylla teaching thee,/At last learne wretch to leave thy	Lucan, First Booke	334		
Hath with thee past the swelling Ocean;	Lucan, First Booke	371		
Love over-rules my will, I must obay thee,	Lucan, First Booke	373		
And Trevier; thou being glad that wars are past thee;	Lucan, First Booke	437		
Rash boy, who gave thee power to change a line?	Ovid's Elegies	1.1.9		
Saying, Poet heers a worke beseeming thee.	Ovid's Elegies	1.1.28		
And hold my conquered hands for thee to tie.	Ovid's Elegies	1.2.20		
What needes thou warre, I sue to thee for grace,	Ovid's Elegies	1.2.21		
Vulcan will give thee Chariots rich and faire.	Ovid's Elegies	1.2.24		
The people thee applauding thou shalte stand,	Ovid's Elegies	1.2.25		
and such as seeke loves wrack/Shall follow thee, their hands	Ovid's Elegies	1.2.32		
Thee all shall feare and worship as a King,	Ovid's Elegies	1.2.33		
Smooth speeches, feare and rage shall by thee ride,	Ovid's Elegies	1.2.35		
In spite of thee, forth will thy <thine> arrowes flie,	Ovid's Elegies	1.2.45		
Thee Pompous birds and him two tygres drew.	Ovid's Elegies	1.2.48		
Then seeing I grace thy show in following thee,	Ovid's Elegies	1.2.49		
Who gardes [the] <thee> conquered with his conquering hands.	Ovid's Elegies	1.2.52		
Accept him that will serve thee all his youth,	Ovid's Elegies	1.3.5		
If men have Faith, Ile live with thee for ever.	Ovid's Elegies	1.3.16		
Ile live with thee, and die, or <ere> thou shalt <shall>	Ovid's Elegies	1.3.18		
Yet scarse my hands from thee containe I well.	Ovid's Elegies	1.4.10		
When I (my light) do or say ought that please thee,	Ovid's Elegies	1.4.25		
Turne round thy gold-ring, as it were to ease thee.	Ovid's Elegies	1.4.26		
What wine he fills thee, wisely will him drinke,	Ovid's Elegies	1.4.29		
If hee gives thee what first himselfe did tast,	Ovid's Elegies	1.4.33		
Say they are mine, and hands on thee impose.	Ovid's Elegies	1.4.40		
Least I should thinke thee guilty of offence.	Ovid's Elegies	1.4.50		
There will I finde thee, or be found by thee,	Ovid's Elegies	1.4.57		
At night thy husband clippes thee, I will weepe/And to the	Ovid's Elegies	1.4.61		
Then will he kisse thee, and not onely kisse/But force thee	Ovid's Elegies	1.4.63		
not onely kisse/But force thee give him my stolne honey blisse.	Ovid's Elegies	1.4.64		
Or if it do, to thee no joy thence spring:	Ovid's Elegies	1.4.68		
Thee feare I too much:	Ovid's Elegies	1.6.15		
only thee I flatter,/Thy lightning can my life in pieces	Ovid's Elegies	1.6.15		
For thee I did thy mistris faire entreate.	Ovid's Elegies	1.6.20		
But what entreates for thee some-times tooke place,	Ovid's Elegies	1.6.21		
Strike, so againe hard chaines shall binde thee never,	Ovid's Elegies	1.6.25		
or ist sleepe forbids thee heare,/Giving the windes my words	Ovid's Elegies	1.6.41		
Well I remember when I first did hire thee,	Ovid's Elegies	1.6.43		
Watching till after mid-night did not tire thee.	Ovid's Elegies	1.6.44		
But now perchaunce thy wench with thee doth rest,	Ovid's Elegies	1.6.45		
Night goes away: I pray thee ope the dore.	Ovid's Elegies	1.6.48		
no threats or prayers move thee,/O harder then the dores thou	Ovid's Elegies	1.6.61		
O harder then the dores thou gardest I prove thee.	Ovid's Elegies	1.6.62		
The carefull prison is more meete for thee.	Ovid's Elegies	1.6.64		
That when my mistresse there beholds thee cast,	Ovid's Elegies	1.6.69		
Th'opposed starre of Mars hath done thee harme,	Ovid's Elegies	1.8.29		
a rich lover plants/His love on thee, and can supply thy wants.	Ovid's Elegies	1.8.32		
Would he not buy thee thou for him shouldst care.	Ovid's Elegies	1.8.34		
Nor let the armes of antient [lines] <lives> beguile thee,	Ovid's Elegies	1.8.65		

THEE (cont.)

Poore lover with thy gransires I exile thee.	Ovid's Elegies	1.8.66
When causes fale thee to require a gift,	Ovid's Elegies	1.8.93
If he gives nothing, let him from thee wend.	Ovid's Elegies	1.8.100
The gods send thee no house, a poore old age,	Ovid's Elegies	1.8.113
Bull and Eagle/And what ere love made Jove should thee invegle.	Ovid's Elegies	1.10.8
This cause hath thee from pleasing me debard.	Ovid's Elegies	1.10.12
commodious/And to give signes dull wit to thee is odious.	Ovid's Elegies	1.11.4
Be sedulous, let no stay cause thee tarry.	Ovid's Elegies	1.11.8
are in thy soft brest/But pure simplicity in thee doth rest.	Ovid's Elegies	1.11.10
And tis suppos'd Loves bowe hath wounded thee,	Ovid's Elegies	1.11.11
I charge thee marke her eyes and front in reading,	Ovid's Elegies	1.11.17
The painfull Hinde by thee to field is sent,	Ovid's Elegies	1.13.15
How oft wisht I night would not give thee place,	Ovid's Elegies	1.13.27
Would Tithon might but talke of thee a while,	Ovid's Elegies	1.13.35
I did not bid thee wed an aged swaine.	Ovid's Elegies	1.13.42
And did to thee no cause of dolour raise.	Ovid's Elegies	1.14.14
They well become thee, then to spare them turne.	Ovid's Elegies	1.14.28
No charmed herbes of any harlot skathd thee,	Ovid's Elegies	1.14.39
No faithlesse witch in Thessale waters bath'd thee.	Ovid's Elegies	1.14.40
No sicknesse harm'd thee, farre be that a way,	Ovid's Elegies	1.14.41
Now Germany shall captive haire-tyers send thee,	Ovid's Elegies	1.14.45
And vanquisht people curious dressings lend thee,	Ovid's Elegies	1.14.46
Stolne liberty she may by thee obtaine,	Ovid's Elegies	2.2.15
Which giving her, she may give thee againe.	Ovid's Elegies	2.2.16
Wilt thou her fault learne, she may make thee tremble,	Ovid's Elegies	2.2.17
But yet sometimes to chide thee let her fall/Counterfet teares:	Ovid's Elegies	2.2.35
and thee lewd hangman call.	Ovid's Elegies	2.2.36
to thee being cast do happe/Sharpe stripes, she sitteth in the	Ovid's Elegies	2.2.61
Wee seeke that through thee safely love we may,	Ovid's Elegies	2.2.65
Please her, her hate makes others thee abhorre,	Ovid's Elegies	2.3.11
If she discardes thee, what use servest thou for?	Ovid's Elegies	2.3.12
Shee may deceive thee, though thou her protect,	Ovid's Elegies	2.3.15
Our prayers move thee to assist our drift,	Ovid's Elegies	2.3.17
Envy hath rapt thee, no fierce warres thou movedst,	Ovid's Elegies	2.6.25
A little fild thee, and for love of talke,	Ovid's Elegies	2.6.29
Nuts were thy food, and Poppie causde thee sleepe,	Ovid's Elegies	2.6.31
My wenches vowes for thee what should I show,	Ovid's Elegies	2.6.43
And the fates distaffe emptie stood to thee,	Ovid's Elegies	2.6.46
One among many is to grieve thee tooke.	Ovid's Elegies	2.7.4
And for her skill to thee a gratefull maide.	Ovid's Elegies	2.7.24
Our pleasant scapes shew thee no clowne to be,	Ovid's Elegies	2.8.3
Whence knowes Corinna that with thee I playde?	Ovid's Elegies	2.8.6
But when on thee her angry eyes did rush,	Ovid's Elegies	2.8.15
In both [thy] <my> cheekes she did perceive thee blush,	Ovid's Elegies	2.8.16
Let me lie with thee browne Cypasse to day.	Ovid's Elegies	2.8.22
Telling thy mistresse, where I was with thee,	Ovid's Elegies	2.8.27
We people wholy given thee, feele thine armes,	Ovid's Elegies	2.9.11
Strike boy, I offer thee my naked brest,	Ovid's Elegies	2.9.35
Cupid by thee, Mars in great doubt doth trample,	Ovid's Elegies	2.9.47
By thee deceived, by thee surprisde am I,	Ovid's Elegies	2.10.3
For thee the East and West winds make me pale,	Ovid's Elegies	2.11.9
Ile clip and kisse thee with all contentation,	Ovid's Elegies	2.11.45
Nor violent South-windes did thee ought affright.	Ovid's Elegies	2.11.52
By fear'd Anubis visage I thee pray,	Ovid's Elegies	2.13.11
And in thy pompe hornd Apis with thee keepe,	Ovid's Elegies	2.13.14
Shee oft hath serv'd thee upon certaine dayes,	Ovid's Elegies	2.13.17
My wench, Lucina, I intreat thee favour,	Ovid's Elegies	2.13.21
But if in so great feare I may advize thee,	Ovid's Elegies	2.13.27
To have this skirmish fought, let it suffice thee.	Ovid's Elegies	2.13.28
And mother-murtherd Itis [they] <thee> bewaile,	Ovid's Elegies	2.14.30
Be welcome to her, gladly let her take thee,	Ovid's Elegies	2.15.3
And her small joynts incircling round hoope make thee.	Ovid's Elegies	2.15.4
Then would I wish thee touch my mistris pappe,	Ovid's Elegies	2.15.11
My life, that I will shame thee never feare,	Ovid's Elegies	2.15.21
But seeing thee, I thinke my thing will swell,	Ovid's Elegies	2.15.25
Let her my faith with thee given understand.	Ovid's Elegies	2.15.28
In heaven without thee would I not be fixt.	Ovid's Elegies	2.16.14
But without thee, although vine-planted ground/Conteines me,	Ovid's Elegies	2.16.33
Not though thy face in all things make thee raigne,	Ovid's Elegies	2.17.11
Nor of thee Macer that resoundst forth armes,	Ovid's Elegies	2.18.35
Let this care some-times bite thee to the quick,	Ovid's Elegies	2.19.43
I borne much, hoping time would beate thee/To guard her well,	Ovid's Elegies	2.19.49
beate thee/To guard her well, that well I might entreate thee.	Ovid's Elegies	2.19.50
Some other seeke that may in patience strive with thee,	Ovid's Elegies	2.19.59
To pleasure me, for-bid me to corive with thee.	Ovid's Elegies	2.19.60
Thou deignst unequall lines should thee rehearse,	Ovid's Elegies	3.1.37
Thou hast my gift, which she would from thee sue.	Ovid's Elegies	3.1.60
To sit, and talke with thee I hether came,	Ovid's Elegies	3.2.3
Thou viewst the course, I thee:	Ovid's Elegies	3.2.5
In running if I see thee, I shall stay,	Ovid's Elegies	3.2.13
To thee Minerva turne the craftes-mens hands.	Ovid's Elegies	3.2.52
Thee gentle Venus, and the boy that flies,	Ovid's Elegies	3.2.55
To hide thee in my bosome straight repaire.	Ovid's Elegies	3.2.76
I know not, what men thinke should thee so move.	Ovid's Elegies	3.4.28
Cannot a faire one, if not chast, please thee?	Ovid's Elegies	3.4.41
Thee I have pass'd, and knew thy streame none such,	Ovid's Elegies	3.5.5
If I a lover bee by thee held back.	Ovid's Elegies	3.5.22
Nor passe I thee, who hollow rocks downe tumbling,	Ovid's Elegies	3.5.45
to thee our Court stands open wide,/There shalt be lov'd:	Ovid's Elegies	3.5.61
Which wealth, cold winter doth on thee bestowe.	Ovid's Elegies	3.5.94
What thirstie traveller ever drunke of thee?	Ovid's Elegies	3.5.97
But for thy merits I wish thee, white streame,	Ovid's Elegies	3.5.105

THEE (cont.)			
Thou [cousenst] <cousendst> mee, by thee surprizde am I,	Ovid's Elegies	3.6.71	
Who bad thee lie downe here against thy will?	Ovid's Elegies	3.6.78	
This side that serves thee, a sharpe sword did weare.	Ovid's Elegies	3.7.14	
Thee sacred Poet could sad flames destroy?	Ovid's Elegies	3.8.41	
if Corcyras Ile/Had thee unknowne interr'd in ground most vile.	Ovid's Elegies	3.8.48	
Nemesis answeares, what's my losse to thee?	Ovid's Elegies	3.8.57	
Thee, goddesse, bountifull all nations judge,	Ovid's Elegies	3.9.5	
Ceres what sports to thee so grievous were,	Ovid's Elegies	3.9.43	
Nor with thee, nor without thee can I live,	Ovid's Elegies	3.10.39	
fellow bed, by all/The Gods who by thee to be perjurde fall,	Ovid's Elegies	3.10.46	
We toucht the walles, Camillus wonne by thee.	Ovid's Elegies	3.12.2	
Nor do I give thee counsaile to live chaste,	Ovid's Elegies	3.13.3	
And like a wittall thinke thee voyde of slight.	Ovid's Elegies	3.13.30	
Then thee whom I must love I hate in vaine,	Ovid's Elegies	3.13.39	
And would be dead, but dying <dead> with thee remaine.	Ovid's Elegies	3.13.40	
Ile not sift much, but hold thee soone excusde,	Ovid's Elegies	3.13.41	
Base in respect of thee, divine and pure,	Hero and Leander	1.219	
Though never-singling Hymen couple thee.	Hero and Leander	1.258	
Perhaps, thy sacred Priesthood makes thee loath,	Hero and Leander	1.293	
Thee as a holy Idiot doth she scorne,	Hero and Leander	1.303	
Though neither gods nor men may thee deserve,	Hero and Leander	1.315	
Who taught thee Rhethoricke to deceive a maid?	Hero and Leander	1.338	
Who hoping to imbrace thee, cherely swome.	Hero and Leander	2.250	
And I will make thee beds of Roses,	Passionate Shepherd	9	
And if these pleasures may thee <things thy minde may> move,	Passionate Shepherd	19	
THEEFE			
Me thinks the slave should make a lusty theefe.	2Tamb	3.5.96	Jrslem
Shee is a Curtezane and he a theefe,	Jew	5.1.37	Barab
To make away a true man for a theefe.	Edw	2.5.70	Mortmr
Tush, Christ did call the Theefe upon the Crosse,	F1482	4.4.26	Faust
THEEVES			
Then noble souldiors, to intrap these theeves,	1Tamb	2.2.59	Meandr
the Tartars and the Easterne theeves/Under the conduct of one	1Tamb	3.1.2	Bajzth
And with a troope of theeves and vagabondes,	1Tamb	4.1.6	Souldn
The Sessions day is criticall to theeves,	Jew	2.3.105	Barab
And now and then, to cherish Christian theeves,	Jew	2.3.177	Barab
THEEVISH			
On this same theevish villaine Tamburlaine.	1Tamb	2.2.3	Mycet
THEFT			
And tricke thy armes and shoulders with my theft.	Dido	1.1.45	Jupitr
Famous for nothing but for theft and spoile,	1Tamb	4.3.66	Souldn
Is theft the ground of your Religion?	Jew	1.2.95	Barab
I, but theft is worse:	Jew	1.2.125	Barab
For that is theft; and if you rob me thus,	Jew	1.2.126	Barab
What's kept, we covet more: the care makes theft:	Ovid's Elegies	3.4.25	
TH'EGYPTIAN			
Or leave Damascus and th'Egyptian fields,	1Tamb	4.2.48	Tamb
to your dominions/Than ever yet confirm'd th'Egyptian Crown.	1Tamb	5.1.449	Tamb
THEILE			
Theile breake his ships, O Proteus, Neptune, Jove,	Dido	5.1.255	Dido
For theile betray thee, traitors as they are.	Edw	3.1.203	Lncstr
Now on my life, theile neither barke nor bite.	Edw	4.3.13	Edward
THEIR (See also THEYR)			
And Venus Swannes shall shed their silver downe,	Dido	1.1.36	Jupitr
Doe thou but say their colour pleaseth me.	Dido	1.1.41	Jupitr
Then gan the windes breake ope their brazen doores,	Dido	1.1.62	Venus
Prepared stands to wracke their woodden walles,	Dido	1.1.67	Venus
Who will eternish Troy in their attempts.	Dido	1.1.108	Jupitr
When yet both sea and sands beset their ships,	Dido	1.1.110	Venus
The while thine eyes attract their sought for joyes:	Dido	1.1.136	Venus
maides to weare/Their bowe and quiver in this modest sort,	Dido	1.1.205	Venus
As every tide tilts twixt their oken sides:	Dido	1.1.224	Aeneas
And all of them unburdened of their loade,	Dido	1.1.225	Aeneas
Or steale your houshold lares from their shrines:	Dido	1.2.11	Illion
Seeing the number of their men decreast,	Dido	2.1.132	Aeneas
Gave up their voyces to dislodge the Campe,	Dido	2.1.134	Aeneas
might behold/Young infants swimming in their parents bloud,	Dido	2.1.193	Aeneas
Virgins halfe dead dragged by their golden haire,	Dido	2.1.195	Aeneas
Old men with swords thrust through their aged sides,	Dido	2.1.197	Aeneas
Who with steele Pol-axes dasht out their braines.	Dido	2.1.199	Aeneas
and with this sword/Sent many of their savadge ghosts to hell.	Dido	2.1.212	Aeneas
With balles of wilde fire in their murdering pawes,	Dido	2.1.217	Aeneas
Ah, how could poore Aeneas scape their hands?	Dido	2.1.220	Dido
Convaid me from their crooked nets and bands:	Dido	2.1.222	Aeneas
joyntly both/Beating their breasts and falling on the ground,	Dido	2.1.228	Aeneas
And with Megeras eyes stared in their face,	Dido	2.1.230	Aeneas
Lest their grosse eye-beames taint my lovers cheekes:	Dido	3.1.74	Dido
Some came in person, others sent their Legats:	Dido	3.1.152	Dido
And feast the birds with their bloud-shotten balles,	Dido	3.2.35	Venus
That overcloy my soule with their content:	Dido	3.2.63	Juno
Shall chaine felicitie unto their throne.	Dido	3.2.80	Juno
When in the midst of all their gamesome sports,	Dido	3.2.89	Juno
Ile make the Clowdes dissolve their watrie workes,	Dido	3.2.90	Juno
And drench Silvanus dwellings with their shewers,	Dido	3.2.91	Juno
And interchangeably discourse their thoughts,	Dido	3.2.93	Juno
Whose short conclusion will seale up their hearts,	Dido	3.2.94	Juno
And rowse the light foote Deere from forth their laire?	Dido	3.3.31	Dido
And overjoy my thoughts with their escape:	Dido	3.3.57	Aeneas
And not let Dido understand their drift:	Dido	4.4.6	Dido
To waite upon him as their soveraigne Lord.	Dido	4.4.69	Dido
Commaund my guard to slay for their offence:	Dido	4.4.72	Dido
All that they have, their lands, their goods, their lives,	Dido	4.4.76	Dido

THEIR (cont.)

And fire proude Lacedemon ore their heads.	Dido	4.4.92	Aeneas
To rob their mistresse of her Troian guest?	Dido	4.4.138	Dido
Now serve to chastize shipboyes for their faults,	Dido	4.4.157	Dido
That loade their thighes with Hyblas honeys spoyles,	Dido	5.1.13	Aeneas
Shall here unburden their exhaled sweetes,	Dido	5.1.14	Aeneas
Doe Troians use to quit their Lovers thus?	Dido	5.1.106	Dido
That in their prowesse and their pollicies,	1Tamb	1.1.8	Cosroe
denied/To shed [their] <his> influence in his fickle braine,	1Tamb	1.1.15	Cosroe
Now Turkes and Tartars shake their swords at thee,	1Tamb	1.1.16	Cosroe
And from their knees, even to their hoofes below,	1Tamb	1.1.79	Mycet
to them, that all Asia/Lament to see the follie of their King.	1Tamb	1.1.96	Cosroe
Lading their shippes with golde and pretious stones:	1Tamb	1.1.121	Cosroe
And made their spoiles from all our provinces.	1Tamb	1.1.122	Cosroe
And cause them to withdraw their forces home,	1Tamb	1.1.131	Menaph
With costlie jewels hanging at their eares,	1Tamb	1.1.144	Ceneus
And shining stones upon their loftie Crestes:	1Tamb	1.1.145	Ceneus
As with their waight shall make the mountains quake,	1Tamb	1.2.49	Tamb
Stretching their pawes, and threatning heardes of Beastes,	1Tamb	1.2.53	Techel
Spurning their crownes from off their captive heads.	1Tamb	1.2.57	Techel
Till with their eies [they] <thee> view us Emperours.	1Tamb	1.2.67	Tamb
But are they rich? And is their armour good?	1Tamb	1.2.123	Tamb
Their plumed helmes are wrought with beaten golde.	1Tamb	1.2.124	Souldr
Their swords enameld, and about their neckes/Hangs massie	1Tamb	1.2.125	Souldr
and about their neckes/Hangs massie chaines of golde downe to	1Tamb	1.2.125	Souldr
an hot alarme/Drive all their horses headlong down the hill.	1Tamb	1.2.135	Usumc
That their reflexions may amaze the Perseans.	1Tamb	1.2.140	Tamb
When with their fearfull tongues they shall confesse/Theise are	1Tamb	1.2.222	Usumc
A heaven of heavenly bodies in their Spheares/That guides his	1Tamb	2.1.16	Menaph
And in their smoothnesse, amitie and life:	1Tamb	2.1.22	Menaph
Their carelesse swords shal lanch their fellowes throats/And	1Tamb	2.2.49	Meandr
their fellowes throats/And make us triumph in their overthrow.	1Tamb	2.2.50	Meandr
And when their scattered armie is subdu'd,	1Tamb	2.2.68	Meandr
And you march on their slaughtered carkasses:	1Tamb	2.2.69	Meandr
Share equally the gold that bought their lives,	1Tamb	2.2.70	Meandr
and dim their eies/That stand and muse at our admyred armes.	1Tamb	2.3.23	Tamb
Came creeping to us with their crownes apace.	1Tamb	2.5.86	Tamb
And prest out fire from their burning jawes:	1Tamb	2.6.6	Cosroe
or els infernall, mixt/Their angry seeds at his conception:	1Tamb	2.6.10	Meandr
I know not how to take their tyrannies.	1Tamb	2.7.41	Cosroe
And with their Cannons mouth'd like Orcus gulfe/Batter the	1Tamb	3.1.65	Bajzth
And from their shieldes strike flames of lightening)/All	1Tamb	3.2.81	Agidas
Your men are valiant but their number few,	1Tamb	3.3.11	Bassoe
We meane to seate our footmen on their Steeds,	1Tamb	3.3.25	Techel
Then fight couragiously, their crowns are yours.	1Tamb	3.3.30	Tamb
Burdening their bodies with your heavie chaines,	1Tamb	3.3.48	Tamb
those that lead my horse/Have to their names tytles of dignity,	1Tamb	3.3.70	Bajzth
Whom I have brought to see their overthrow.	1Tamb	3.3.81	Bajzth
Why stay we thus prolonging all their lives?	1Tamb	3.3.97	Techel
Their shoulders broad, for complet armour fit,	1Tamb	3.3.107	Bajzth
Their lims more large and of a bigger size/Than all the brats	1Tamb	3.3.108	Bajzth
Who, when they come unto their fathers age,	1Tamb	3.3.110	Bajzth
Will batter Turrets with their manly fists.	1Tamb	3.3.111	Bajzth
their slaughtered Carkasses/Shall serve for walles and	1Tamb	3.3.138	Bajzth
If they should yeeld their necks unto the sword,	1Tamb	3.3.142	Bajzth
Trampling their bowels with our horses hooffes:	1Tamb	3.3.150	Tamb
Both for their sausinesse shall be employed,	1Tamb	3.3.184	Zenoc
By this the Turks lie weltring in their blood/And Tamburlaine	1Tamb	3.3.201	Zenoc
We have their crownes, their bodies strowe the fielde.	1Tamb	3.3.215	Techel
Ringing with joy their superstitious belles:	1Tamb	3.3.237	Bajzth
foule Idolaters/Shall make me bonfires with their filthy bones,	1Tamb	3.3.240	Bajzth
Where they shall meete, and joine their force in one,	1Tamb	3.3.257	Tamb
Offer their mines (to sew for peace) to me,	1Tamb	3.3.264	Tamb
While thundring Cannons rattle on their Skins.	1Tamb	4.1.11	Souldn
Upon their pransing Steeds, disdainfully/With wanton paces	1Tamb	4.1.22	2Msngr
Shaking their swords, their speares and yron bils,	1Tamb	4.1.25	2Msngr
Environing their Standard round, that stood/As bristle-pointed	1Tamb	4.1.26	2Msngr
Their warlike Engins and munition/Exceed the forces of their	1Tamb	4.1.28	2Msngr
Engins and munition/Exceed the forces of their martial men.	1Tamb	4.1.29	2Msngr
Nay could their numbers countervail the stars,	1Tamb	4.1.30	Souldn
That not a man should live to rue their fall.	1Tamb	4.1.35	Souldn
White is their hew, and on his silver crest/A snowy Feather	1Tamb	4.1.50	2Msngr
heaven beholde/Their Scourge and Terrour treade on Emperours.	1Tamb	4.2.32	Tamb
And dim the brightnesse of their neighbor Lamps:	1Tamb	4.2.34	Tamb
To make these captives reine their lavish tongues.	1Tamb	4.2.67	Techel
If they would lay their crownes before my feet,	1Tamb	4.2.93	Tamb
That with their beauties grac'd the Memphion fields:	1Tamb	4.2.104	Tamb
The golden stature of their feathered bird/That spreads her	1Tamb	4.2.105	Tamb
With mournfull streamers hanging down their heads,	1Tamb	4.2.120	Tamb
Reflexing hewes of blood upon their heads,	1Tamb	4.4.2	Tamb
While they walke quivering on their citie walles,	1Tamb	4.4.3	Tamb
To turne them al upon their proper heades.	1Tamb	4.4.31	Tamb
If with their lives they will be pleasde to yeeld,	1Tamb	4.4.89	Tamb
Let us have hope that their unspotted praiers,	1Tamb	5.1.20	Govnr
Their blubbered cheekes and hartie humble mones/Will melt his	1Tamb	5.1.21	Govnr
What, are the Turtles fraide out of their neastes?	1Tamb	5.1.64	Tamb
To thinke thy puisant never staied arme/Will part their bodies,	1Tamb	5.1.89	1Virgn
their bodies, and prevent their soules/From heavens of comfort,	1Tamb	5.1.89	1Virgn
soules/From heavens of comfort, yet their age might beare,	1Tamb	5.1.90	1Virgn
and Furies dread)/As for their liberties, their loves or lives.	1Tamb	5.1.95	1Virgn
And on their points his fleshlesse bodie feedes.	1Tamb	5.1.115	Tamb
Sitting in scarlet on their armed speares.	1Tamb	5.1.118	Tamb
They have refusde the offer of their lives,	1Tamb	5.1.126	Tamb

THEIR (cont.)

on Damascus wals/Have hoisted up their slaughtered carcases.	1Tamb	5.1.131	Techel
A sight as banefull to their soules I think/As are Thessalian	1Tamb	5.1.132	Tamb
There Angels in their christal armours fight/A doubtfull	1Tamb	5.1.151	Tamb
Had fed the feeling of their maisters thoughts,	1Tamb	5.1.162	Tamb
And every sweetnes that inspir'd their harts,	1Tamb	5.1.163	Tamb
Their minds, and muses on admyred theames:	1Tamb	5.1.164	Tamb
Quintessence they still/From their immortall flowers of Poesy,	1Tamb	5.1.166	Tamb
Yet should ther hover in their restlesse heads,	1Tamb	5.1.171	Tamb
Breake up the earth, and with their firebrands,	1Tamb	5.1.219	Bajzth
Stick in his breast, as in their proper roomes.	1Tamb	5.1.226	Zabina
And let her horses from their nostrels breathe/Rebellious winds	1Tamb	5.1.297	Bajzth
Stead/That stampt on others with their thundring hooves,	1Tamb	5.1.331	Zenoc
When al their riders chardg'd their quivering speares/Began to	1Tamb	5.1.332	Zenoc
Gazing upon the beautie of their lookes:	1Tamb	5.1.334	Zenoc
Ah Madam, this their slavery hath Enforc'd,	1Tamb	5.1.345	Anippe
And wet thy cheeks for their untimely deathes:	1Tamb	5.1.348	Zenoc
Shake with their waight in signe of feare and griefe:	1Tamb	5.1.349	Zenoc
Blush heaven, that gave them honor at their birth,	1Tamb	5.1.350	Zenoc
And place their chiefest good in earthly pompe:	1Tamb	5.1.353	Zenoc
Must Tamburlaine by their resistlesse powers,	1Tamb	5.1.397	Zenoc
That no escape may save their enemies:	1Tamb	5.1.405	Arabia
To doo their ceassles homag to my sword:	1Tamb	5.1.456	Tamb
Have desperatly dispatcht their slavish lives:	1Tamb	5.1.472	Tamb
whom all kings/Of force must yeeld their crownes and Emperies:	1Tamb	5.1.481	Souldn
Shal now, adjoining al their hands with mine,	1Tamb	5.1.493	Tamb
Our Turky blades shal glide through al their throats,	2Tamb	1.1.31	Orcan
Beating in heaps against their Argoses,	2Tamb	1.1.41	Orcan
which basely on their knees/In all your names desirde a truce	2Tamb	1.1.96	Orcan
Then shalt thou see a hundred kings and more/Upon their knees,	2Tamb	1.2.29	Callap
Plac'd by her side, looke on their mothers face.	2Tamb	1.3.20	Tamb
But yet me thinks their looks are amorous,	2Tamb	1.3.21	Tamb
Argue their want of courage and of wit:	2Tamb	1.3.24	Tamb
Their haire as white as milke and soft as Downe,	2Tamb	1.3.25	Tamb
Their fingers made to quaver on a Lute,	2Tamb	1.3.29	Tamb
Their armes to hang about a Ladies necke:	2Tamb	1.3.30	Tamb
Their legs to dance and caper in the aire:	2Tamb	1.3.31	Tamb
My gratious Lord, they have their mothers looks,	2Tamb	1.3.35	Zenoc
But when they list, their conquering fathers hart:	2Tamb	1.3.36	Zenoc
and thy seed/Shall issue crowned from their mothers wombe.	2Tamb	1.3.53	Tamb
As all the world shall tremble at their view.	2Tamb	1.3.57	Celeb
Dismaies their mindes before they come to proove/The wounding	2Tamb	1.3.86	Zenoc
Whose coleblacke faces make their foes retire,	2Tamb	1.3.142	Techel
have martcht/Foure hundred miles with armour on their backes,	2Tamb	1.3.175	Usumc
That in the fortune of their overthrow,	2Tamb	2.1.24	Fredrk
Yet those infirmities that thus defame/Their faiths, their	2Tamb	2.1.45	Sgsmnd
that thus defame/Their faiths, their honors, and their religion,	2Tamb	2.1.45	Sgsmnd
thus defame/Their faiths, their honors, and their religion,	2Tamb	2.1.45	Sgsmnd
Christians death/And scourge their foule blasphemous Paganisme?	2Tamb	2.1.53	Fredrk
Hel and confusion light upon their heads,	2Tamb	2.2.33	Gazell
And cares so litle for their prophet Christ.	2Tamb	2.2.35	Gazell
But in their deeds deny him for their Christ:	2Tamb	2.2.40	Orcan
Now lie the Christians bathing in their bloods,	2Tamb	2.3.10	Orcan
Whose eies shot fire from their Ivory bowers,	2Tamb	2.4.9	Tamb
Use all their voices and their instruments/To entertaine divine	2Tamb	2.4.28	Tamb
Their Spheares are mounted on the serpents head,	2Tamb	2.4.53	Tamb
And for their power, ynow to win the world.	2Tamb	3.1.43	Orcan
That on mount Sinay with their ensignes spread,	2Tamb	3.1.46	Jrslem
The cursed Scythian sets on all their townes,	2Tamb	3.1.55	Trebiz
Murther the Foe and save [the] <their> walles from breach.	2Tamb	3.2.82	Tamb
Dieng their lances with their streaming blood,	2Tamb	3.2.105	Tamb
Filling their empty vaines with aiery wine,	2Tamb	3.2.107	Tamb
And this is Balsera their chiefest hold,	2Tamb	3.3.3	Therid
And few or none shall perish by their shot.	2Tamb	3.3.45	Therid
if our artillery/Will carie full point blancke unto their wals.	2Tamb	3.3.53	Techel
my entrals bath'd/In blood that straineth from their orifex.	2Tamb	3.4.9	Capt
hands)/All brandishing their brands of quenchlesse fire,	2Tamb	3.5.27	Orcan
Streching their monstrous pawes, grin with their teeth,	2Tamb	3.5.28	Orcan
Poore soules they looke as if their deaths were neere.	2Tamb	3.5.61	Usumc
But yet Ile save their lives and make them slaves.	2Tamb	3.5.63	Tamb
And cast your crownes in slavery at their feet.	2Tamb	3.5.149	Tamb
shall sweat/With carrieng pearle and treasure on their backes.	2Tamb	3.5.167	Techel
Now in their glories shine the golden crownes/Of these proud	2Tamb	4.1.1	Amyras
(Perdicas) and I feare as litle their tara, tantaras, their	2Tamb	4.1.68	P Calyph
their swordes or their cannons, as I doe a naked Lady in a net	2Tamb	4.1.68	P Calyph
the pavilions/Of these proud Turks, and take their Concubines,	2Tamb	4.1.161	Tamb
And stung with furie of their following,	2Tamb	4.1.189	Tamb
And breake their burning Lances in the aire,	2Tamb	4.1.204	Tamb
From whence the starres doo borrow all their light,	2Tamb	4.2.89	Therid
And blow the morning from their nosterils,	2Tamb	4.3.8	Tamb
Making their fiery gate above the cloudes,	2Tamb	4.3.9	Tamb
Are not so honoured in their Governour,	2Tamb	4.3.10	Tamb
And made so wanton that they knew their strengths,	2Tamb	4.3.14	Tamb
While these their fellow kings may be refresht.	2Tamb	4.3.31	Tamb
To bridle their contemptuous cursing tongues,	2Tamb	4.3.44	Therid
Breake through the hedges of their hateful mouthes,	2Tamb	4.3.46	Therid
And passe their fixed boundes exceedingly.	2Tamb	4.3.47	Therid
we wil break the hedges of their mouths/And pul their kicking	2Tamb	4.3.48	Techel
their mouths/And pul their kicking colts out of their pastures.	2Tamb	4.3.49	Techel
kings Concubines)/Take them, devide them and their jewels too,	2Tamb	4.3.72	Tamb
And make us jeasting Pageants for their Trulles.	2Tamb	4.3.89	Therid
And common souldiers jest with all their Truls.	2Tamb	4.3.91	Tamb
Let them take pleasure soundly in their spoiles,	2Tamb	4.3.92	Tamb

THEIR (cont.)

Adding their wealth and treasure to my store.	2Tamb	4.3.101	Tamb
That thus intreat their shame and servitude?	2Tamb	5.1.37	Govnr
My horsmen brandish their unruly blades.	2Tamb	5.1.79	Tamb
So, now their best is done to honour me,	2Tamb	5.1.131	Tamb
What shal be done with their wives and children my Lord.	2Tamb	5.1.168	P Techel
Their cruel death, mine owne captivity,	2Tamb	5.2.20	Callap
lamps of heaven/To cast their bootlesse fires to the earth,	2Tamb	5.3.4	Therid
And shed their feble influence in the aire.	2Tamb	5.3.5	Therid
For hell and darknesse pitch their pitchy tentes,	2Tamb	5.3.7	Therid
And though they think their painfull date is out,	2Tamb	5.3.34	Usumc
And that their power is puissant as Joves,	2Tamb	5.3.35	Usumc
For both their woorths wil equall him no more.	2Tamb	5.3.253	Amyras
But such as love me, gard me from their tongues,	Jew	Prol.6	Machvl
Here have I purst their paltry [silverlings] <silverbings>.	Jew	1.1.6	Barab
Their meanes of traffique from the vulgar trade,	Jew	1.1.35	Barab
And as their wealth increaseth, so inclose/Infinite riches in a	Jew	1.1.36	Barab
And bring with them their bils of entry:	Jew	1.1.56	Barab
Belike they coasted round by Candie shoare/About their Oyles,	Jew	1.1.92	Barab
you to come so farre/Without the ayd or conduct of their ships.	Jew	1.1.94	Barab
for earthly man/Then thus to powre out plenty in their laps,	Jew	1.1.108	Barab
Making the Sea their [servant] <servants>, and the winds/To	Jew	1.1.110	Barab
the winds/To drive their substance with successefull blasts?	Jew	1.1.111	Barab
For I can see no fruits in all their faith,	Jew	1.1.116	Barab
Which me thinkes fits not their profession.	Jew	1.1.118	Barab
in the Counsell-house/To entertaine them and their Embassie.	Jew	1.1.149	1Jew
I feare their comming will afflict us all.	Jew	1.1.156	2Jew
Fond men, what dreame you of their multitudes?	Jew	1.1.157	Barab
But never could effect their Stratagem.	Jew	1.1.165	Barab
Let's know their time, perhaps it is not long;	Jew	1.2.24	Calym
Have strangers leave with us to get their wealth?	Jew	1.2.60	2Knght
submit your selves/To leave your goods to their arbitrament?	Jew	1.2.80	Barab
Shall I be tryed by their transgression?	Jew	1.2.115	Barab
Then be the causers of their misery.	Jew	1.2.148	Barab
that's their profession,/And not simplicity, as they suggest.	Jew	1.2.160	Barab
I banne their soules to everlasting paines/And extreme tortures	Jew	1.2.166	Barab
Why did you yeeld to their extortion?	Jew	1.2.177	Barab
And rent their hearts with tearing of my haire,	Jew	1.2.234	Abigal
To make a Nunnery, where none but their owne sect/Must enter in;	Jew	1.2.256	Abigal
that thou leave/These divels, and their damned heresie.	Jew	1.2.347	Barab
pleasures of swift-footed time/Have tane their flight,	Jew	2.1.8	Barab
Their creeping Gallyes had us in the chase:	Jew	2.2.12	Bosco
For when their hideous force inviron'd Rhodes,	Jew	2.2.48	Bosco
Feare not their sale, for they'll be quickly bought.	Jew	2.3.2	1Offcr
of those Nuns/And holy Fryers, having mony for their paines,	Jew	2.3.81	Barab
But I have sworne to frustrate both their hopes,	Jew	2.3.142	Barab
I steale/To travellers Chambers, and there cut their throats:	Jew	2.3.207	Ithimr
And therewithall their knees would rranckle, so/That I have	Jew	2.3.210	Ithimr
I thinke by this/You purchase both their lives; is it not so?	Jew	2.3.366	Ithimr
Hold, let's inquire the causers of their deaths,	Jew	3.2.27	Mater
That we may venge their blood upon their heads.	Jew	3.2.28	Mater
Which forc'd their hands divide united hearts:	Jew	3.2.35	Govnr
In dolefull wise they ended both their dayes.	Jew	3.3.21	Ithimr
And was my father furtherer of their deaths?	Jew	3.3.22	Abigal
and then I say they use/To send their Almes unto the Nunneries:	Jew	3.4.77	Barab
Shall overflow it with their refluence.	Jew	3.5.18	Govnr
So, say how was their end?	Jew	3.6.26	2Fryar
Their voyage will be worth ten thousand Crownes.	Jew	4.1.70	Barab
Oh Barabas, their Lawes are strict.	Jew	4.1.82	1Fryar
Now I have such a plot for both their lives,	Jew	4.1.117	Barab
but hee hides and buries it up as Partridges doe their egges,	Jew	4.2.58	P Ithimr
As these have spoke so be it to their soules:--	Jew	5.1.42	Barab
Their deaths were like their lives, then think not of 'em;	Jew	5.1.56	Govnr
I'le helpe to slay their children and their wives,	Jew	5.1.64	Barab
To fire the Churches, pull their houses downe,	Jew	5.1.65	Barab
I was imprison'd, but escap'd their hands.	Jew	5.1.77	Barab
When as thy life shall be at their command?	Jew	5.2.33	Barab
I know; and they shall witnesse with their lives.	Jew	5.2.123	Barab
And batter all the stones about their eares,	Jew	5.5.30	Barab
And brought by murder to their timeles ends.	P 46	1.46	Navrre
They justly challenge their protection:	P 210	4.8	Charls
Should for their conscience taste such rutheles ends.	P 214	4.12	Charls
Yet will the wisest note their proper greefes:	P 216	4.14	Anjoy
And rather seeke to scourge their enemies,	P 217	4.15	Anjoy
Shall weare white crosses on their Burgonets,	P 232	4.30	Guise
And tye white linnen scarfes about their armes.	P 233	4.31	Guise
To hurt the noble man their soveraign loves.	P 259	4.57	Charls
which have already set the street/May know their watchword,	P 329	5.56	Guise
[Sorbonests] <thorbonest>/Attribute as much unto their workes,	P 412	7.52	Ramus
That swim about and so preserve their lives:	P 419	7.59	Guise
it may prejudice their hope/Of my inheritance to the crowne of	P 467	8.17	Anjoy
Which in the woods doe holde their synagogue:	P 502	9.21	Guise
It will be hard for us to worke their deaths.	P 508	9.27	QnMoth
For to revenge their deaths upon us all.	P 518	9.37	Cardnl
Yet is [their] <there> pacience of another sort,	P 545	11.10	Charls
Then to misdoe the welfare of their King:	P 546	11.11	Charls
We know that noble mindes change not their thoughts/For wearing	P 610	12.23	Mugern
Will laugh I feare me at their good aray.	P 673	13.17	Duchss
But to defend their strange inventions,	P 705	14.8	Navrre
That change their coulour when the winter comes,	P 721	14.24	Navrre
But canst thou tell who is their generall?	P 731	14.34	Navrre
They should know how I scornde them and their mockes.	P 762	15.20	Guise
How many noble men have lost their lives,	P 795	16.9	Navrre

THEIR (cont.)

I, those are they that feed him with their golde,	P 845	17.40	King
Against the Guisians and their complices.	P 910	18.11	Navrre
As ancient Romanes over their Captive Lords,	P 982	19.52	Guise
the rest have taine their standings in the next roome,	P 994	19.64	P 3Mur
And princes with their lookes ingender feare.	P 999	19.69	Guise
To hatch forth treason gainst their naturall Queene?	P1032	19.102	King
And with their pawes drench his black soule in hell.	P1102	20.12	Cardnl
And will not offer violence to their King,	P1162	22.24	King
Shall take example by [his] <their> punishment,	P1186	22.48	King
How they beare armes against their soveraigne.	P1187	22.49	King
Rakt up in embers of their povertie,	Edw	1.1.21	Gavstn
Shall with their Goate feete daunce an antick hay.	Edw	1.1.60	Gavstn
Brother revenge it, and let these their heads,	Edw	1.1.117	Kent
Preach upon poles for trespasse of their tongues.	Edw	1.1.118	Kent
This ground which is corrupted with their steps,	Edw	1.2.5	Lncstr
Shall be their timeles sepulcher, or mine.	Edw	1.2.6	Lncstr
Ah that bewraies their basenes Lancaster,	Edw	1.2.27	Mortmr
Their downfall is at hand, their forces downe,	Edw	1.4.18	Mortmr
And bankes raisd higher with their sepulchers:	Edw	1.4.103	Edward
I passe not for their anger, come lets go.	Edw	1.4.142	Edward
And on their knees salute your majestie.	Edw	1.4.339	Queene
The mightiest kings have had their minions,	Edw	1.4.391	MortSr
Returne it to their throtes, ile be thy warrant.	Edw	2.2.73	Edward
But if I live, ile tread upon their heads,	Edw	2.2.96	Edward
the Mortimers/Are not so poore, but would they sell their land,	Edw	2.2.151	Mortmr
The Northren borderers seeing [their] <the> houses burnt,/Their	Edw	2.2.179	Lncstr
Their wives and children slaine, run up and downe,	Edw	2.2.180	Lncstr
And dare not be revengde, for their power is great:	Edw	2.2.202	Edward
And let their lives bloud slake thy furies hunger:	Edw	2.2.205	Edward
But I respect neither their love nor hate.	Edw	2.2.261	Gavstn
Have at the rebels, and their complices.	Edw	2.2.265	Edward
Drums strike alarum, raise them from their sport,	Edw	2.3.25	Mortmr
Sir, must not come so neare and balke their lips.	Edw	2.5.103	Penbrk
The Barons overbeare me with their pride.	Edw	3.1.9	Edward
Strike off their heads, and let them preach on poles,	Edw	3.1.20	Spencr
As by their preachments they will profit much,	Edw	3.1.22	Spencr
And learne obedience to their lawfull king.	Edw	3.1.23	Spencr
Weele steele it on their crest, and powle their tops.	Edw	3.1.27	Edward
Not to be tied to their affection,	Edw	3.1.29	Baldck
Unnatural wars, where subjects brave their king,	Edw	3.1.86	Queene
Their lord rode home, thinking his prisoner safe,	Edw	3.1.117	Arundl
And marche to fire them from their starting holes.	Edw	3.1.127	Spencr
This graunted, they, their honors, and their lives,	Edw	3.1.170	Herald
A traitors, will they still display their pride?	Edw	3.1.172	Spencr
Rebels, will they appoint their soveraigne/His sports, his	Edw	3.1.174	Edward
And do confront and countermaund their king.	Edw	3.1.188	Edward
Till hee pay deerely for their companie.	Edw	3.1.198	Lncstr
Th'ad best betimes forsake [them] <thee> and their trains,	Edw	3.1.202	Lncstr
For which ere long, their heads shall satisfie,	Edw	3.1.209	Edward
T'appeaze the wrath of their offended king.	Edw	3.1.210	Edward
I charge you roundly off with both their heads,	Edw	3.1.247	Edward
These Barons lay their heads on blocks together,	Edw	3.1.274	Baldck
in England/Would cast up cappes, and clap their hands for joy,	Edw	4.2.55	Mortmr
our port-maisters/Are not so careles of their kings command.	Edw	4.3.23	Edward
having in their company divers of your nation, and others,	Edw	4.3.33	P Spencr
Is thus misled to countenance their ils.	Edw	4.3.49	Edward
Slaughter themselves in others and their sides/With their owne	Edw	4.4.7	Queene
in others and their sides/With their owne weapons gorde,	Edw	4.4.8	Queene
How Baldocke, Spencer, and their complices,	Edw	4.6.78	Mortmr
May in their fall be followed to their end.	Edw	4.6.79	Mortmr
T'escape their hands that seeke to reave his life:	Edw	4.7.52	Leistr
So shall my eyes receive their last content,	Edw	5.1.61	Edward
And joyntly both yeeld up their wished right.	Edw	5.1.63	Edward
Their bloud and yours shall seale these treacheries.	Edw	5.1.89	Edward
Have done their homage to the loftie gallowes,	Edw	5.2.3	Mortmr
That wronges their liege and soveraigne, Englands king.	Edw	5.3.40	Edward
Are but obey'd in their severall Provinces:	F 85	1.1.57	Faust
Their conference will be a greater helpe to me,	F 95	1.1.67	Faust
As Indian Moores, obey their Spanish Lords,	F 148	1.1.120	Valdes
Like Almaine Rutters with their horsemens staves,	F 152	1.1.124	Valdes
Shadowing more beauty in their Airie browes,	F 155	1.1.127	Valdes
me, as if they payd for their meate and drinke, I can tell you.	F 365	1.4.23	P Robin
[and] bloud, <or goods> into their habitation wheresoever.	F 498	2.1.110	P Faust
heavens, that I might knowe their motions and dispositions].	F 551.5	2.1.168A	P Faust
in their motions <motion> upon the poles of the Zodiacke.	F 598	2.2.47	P Mephst
appeare to thee in their owne proper shapes and likenesse.	F 656	2.2.105	P Belzeb
<examine> them of their <several> names and dispositions.	F 661	2.2.110	P Belzeb
And view their triumphs, as they passe this way.	F 857	3.1.79	Mephst
And as they turne their superstitious Bookes,	F 893	3.1.115	Faust
And make them sleepe so sound, that in their shapes,	F 895	3.1.117	Faust
To hold the Emperours their lawfull Lords.	F 927	3.1.149	Bruno
In quittance of their late conspiracie/Against our State, and	F 949	3.1.171	Pope
The Pope will curse them for their sloth to day,	F 987	3.2.7	Faust
And by their folly make some <us> merriment,	F 990	3.2.10	Faust
So Faustus, now for all their holinesse,	F1004	3.2.24	Mephst
Hale them to prison, lade their limbes with gyves:	F1032	3.2.52	Pope
let the Maids looke well to their porridge-pots, for I'le into	F1133	3.3.46	P Robin
[And in their conference of what befell],	F1144	3.3.57A	3Chor
And hale the stubborne Furies from their caves,	F1225	4.1.71	Faust
In their true shapes, and state Majesticall,	F1233	4.1.79	Emper
That we may wonder at their excellence.	F1234	4.1.80	Emper
To keepe his Carkasse from their bloudy phangs.	F1303	4.1.149	Faust

THEIR (cont.)

And in their rusticke gambals proudly say,	F1330	4.2.6	Benvol
Yet stay, the world shall see their miserie,	F1406	4.2.82	Faust
And hell shall after plague their treacherie.	F1407	4.2.83	Faust
Go pacifie their fury, set it ope,	F1589	4.6.32	Duke
On burning forkes: their bodies [boyle] <broyle> in lead.	F1912	5.2.116	BdAngl
And laught to see the poore starve at their gates:	F1918	5.2.122	BdAngl
Their soules are soone dissolv'd in elements,	F1970	5.2.174	Faust
Both in their right shapes, gesture, and attire/They usde to	F App	p.237 33	Emper
and attire/They usde to weare during their time of life,	F App	p.237 34	Emper
in their most florishing estate, which I doubt not shal	F App	p.237 48 P	Faust
We sing, whose conquering swords their own breasts launcht,	Lucan, First Booke	3	
And few live that behold their ancient seats;	Lucan, First Booke	27	
[There] <Their> Caesar may'st thou shine and no cloud dim thee;	Lucan, First Booke	59	
T'was peace against their wils; betwixt them both/Stept Crassus	Lucan, First Booke	99	
feareful men, and blasts their eyes/With overthwarting flames,	Lucan, First Booke	155	
And then large limits had their butting lands,	Lucan, First Booke	169	
And deem'd renowne to spoile their native towne,	Lucan, First Booke	176	
The people started; young men left their beds,	Lucan, First Booke	241	
And snatcht armes neer their houshold gods hung up/Such as	Lucan, First Booke	242	
They shooke for feare, and cold benumm'd their lims,	Lucan, First Booke	248	
they, and none durst speake/And shew their feare, or griefe:	Lucan, First Booke	260	
Now while their part is weake, and feares, march hence,	Lucan, First Booke	281	
Let come their [leader] <leaders whom long peace hath quail'd;	Lucan, First Booke	311	
many a heard, whilst with their dams/They kennel'd in Hircania,	Lucan, First Booke	328	
What seates for their deserts?	Lucan, First Booke	344	
what Colonies/To rest their bones?	Lucan, First Booke	346	
their houshold gods/And love to Room (thogh slaughter steeld	Lucan, First Booke	354	
And love to Room (thogh slaughter steeld their harts/And minds	Lucan, First Booke	355	
And with their hands held up, all joyntly cryde/They'ill follow	Lucan, First Booke	388	
They by Lemannus nooke forsooke their tents;	Lucan, First Booke	397	
The yellow Ruthens left their garrisons;	Lucan, First Booke	403	
come, their huge power made him bould/To mannage greater deeds;	Lucan, First Booke	462	
peoples minds, and laide before their eies/Slaughter to come,	Lucan, First Booke	466	
which he hath brought/From out their Northren parts, and that	Lucan, First Booke	479	
The fathers selves leapt from their seats; and flying/Left	Lucan, First Booke	485	
Then with their feare, and danger al distract,	Lucan, First Booke	487	
Their sway of fleight carries the heady rout/That in chain'd	Lucan, First Booke	488	
You would have thought their houses had bin fierd/Or	Lucan, First Booke	490	
(that did remaine/To their afflictions) were t'abandon Roome.	Lucan, First Booke	495	
nor could the bed-rid parents/Keep back their sons, or womens	Lucan, First Booke	503	
parents/Keep back their sons, or womens teares their husbands;	Lucan, First Booke	503	
Their houshould gods restrain them not, none lingered,	Lucan, First Booke	505	
snatcht up/Would make them sleepe securely in their tents.	Lucan, First Booke	516	
Which wont to run their course through empty night/At noone day	Lucan, First Booke	534	
the Alpes/Shooke the old snow from off their trembling laps.	Lucan, First Booke	552	
their saints and houshold gods/Sweate teares to shew the	Lucan, First Booke	554	
gods/Sweate teares to shew the travailes of their citty.	Lucan, First Booke	555	
And they whom fierce Bellonaes fury moves/To wound their armes,	Lucan, First Booke	564	
Curling their bloudy lockes, howle dreadfull things,	Lucan, First Booke	565	
Soules quiet and appeas'd [sigh'd] <sight> from their graves,	Lucan, First Booke	566	
To these ostents (as their old custome was)/They call	Lucan, First Booke	583	
then the Nunnes/And their vaild Matron, who alone might view	Lucan, First Booke	597	
secret works, and [wash] <washt> their saint/In Almo's floud:	Lucan, First Booke	599	
why doe the Planets/Alter their course; and vainly dim their	Lucan, First Booke	663	
the Planets/Alter their course; and vainly dim their vertue?	Lucan, First Booke	663	
Then such as in their bondage feele content.	Ovid's Elegies	1.2.18	
loves wrack/Shall follow thee, their hands tied at their backe.	Ovid's Elegies	1.2.32	
And on their faces heapes of Roses strow.	Ovid's Elegies	1.2.40	
Put in their place thy keembed haires againe.	Ovid's Elegies	1.7.68	
And makes large streams back to their fountaines flow,	Ovid's Elegies	1.8.6	
Great grand-sires from their antient graves she chides/And with	Ovid's Elegies	1.8.17	
To yeeld their love to more then one disdainde.	Ovid's Elegies	1.8.40	
Of horne the bowe was that approv'd their side.	Ovid's Elegies	1.8.48	
That my dead bones may in their grave lie soft.	Ovid's Elegies	1.8.108	
Those in their lovers, pretty maydes desire.	Ovid's Elegies	1.9.6	
Rhesus fell/And Captive horses bad their Lord fare-well.	Ovid's Elegies	1.9.24	
Tis shame their wits should be more excelent.	Ovid's Elegies	1.10.26	
Let poore men show their service, faith, and care;	Ovid's Elegies	1.10.57	
All for their Mistrisse, what they have, prepare.	Ovid's Elegies	1.10.58	
But when thou comest they of their courses faile.	Ovid's Elegies	1.13.12	
By thy meanes women of their rest are bard,	Ovid's Elegies	1.13.23	
Thou setst their labouring hands to spin and card.	Ovid's Elegies	1.13.24	
which from their crowne/Phoebus and Bacchus wisht were hanging	Ovid's Elegies	1.14.31	
For after death all men receive their right:	Ovid's Elegies	1.15.40	
And turned streames run back-ward to their fountaines.	Ovid's Elegies	2.1.26	
Who first depriv'd yong boyes of their best part,	Ovid's Elegies	2.3.3	
Who would not love those hands for their swift running?	Ovid's Elegies	2.4.28	
But such kinde wenches let their lovers have.	Ovid's Elegies	2.5.26	
Or maides that their betrothed husbands spie.	Ovid's Elegies	2.5.36	
Behould how quailes among their battailes live,	Ovid's Elegies	2.6.27	
Supplying their voide places with the worst.	Ovid's Elegies	2.6.40	
Better then I their quiver knowes them not.	Ovid's Elegies	2.9.38	
And in the midst their bodies largely spread:	Ovid's Elegies	2.10.18	
Let souldiour <souldiours> chase his <their> enemies amaine,	Ovid's Elegies	2.10.31	
And with his <their> bloud eternall honour gaine,	Ovid's Elegies	2.10.32	
Being wrackt, carowse the sea tir'd by their ships:	Ovid's Elegies	2.10.34	
The sucking shore with their aboundance swels.	Ovid's Elegies	2.11.14	
In what gulfe either Syrtes have their seate.	Ovid's Elegies	2.11.20	
To cruell armes their drunken selves did summon.	Ovid's Elegies	2.12.20	
Whose bodies with their heavy burthens ake.	Ovid's Elegies	2.13.20	
And their owne privie weapon'd hands destroy them.	Ovid's Elegies	2.14.4	
All humaine kinde by their default had perish.	Ovid's Elegies	2.14.10	

THEIR (cont.)			
Their wedlocks pledges veng'd their husbands bad.	Ovid's Elegies	2.14.32	
(Their reines let loose) right soone my house approach.	Ovid's Elegies	2.16.50	
either heed/What please them, and their eyes let either feede.	Ovid's Elegies	3.2.6	
Now would I slacke the reines, now lash their hide,	Ovid's Elegies	3.2.11	
The Gods, and their rich pompe witnesse with me,	Ovid's Elegies	3.2.61	
least their gownes tosse thy haire,/To hide thee in my bosome	Ovid's Elegies	3.2.75	
maides society/Falsely to sweare, their beauty hath some deity.	Ovid's Elegies	3.3.12	
And all things too much in their sole power drenches.	Ovid's Elegies	3.3.26	
Tut, men should not their courage so consume.	Ovid's Elegies	3.3.34	
But yet their gift more moderately use,	Ovid's Elegies	3.3.47	
their wits should them defend.	Ovid's Elegies	3.4.2	
If Thetis, and the morne their sonnes did waile,	Ovid's Elegies	3.8.1	
Nemesis and thy first wench joyne their kisses,	Ovid's Elegies	3.8.53	
With thine, nor this last fire their presence misses.	Ovid's Elegies	3.8.54	
Their <Your> youthfull browes with Ivie girt to meete him,/With	Ovid's Elegies	3.8.61	
Rude husband-men bak'd not their corne before,	Ovid's Elegies	3.9.7	
This was [their] <there> meate, the soft grasse was their bed.	Ovid's Elegies	3.9.10	
And worshipt by their paine, and lying apart?	Ovid's Elegies	3.9.16	
Nor have their words true histories pretence,	Ovid's Elegies	3.11.42	
With famous pageants, and their home-bred beasts.	Ovid's Elegies	3.12.4	
To know their rites, well recompenc'd my stay,	Ovid's Elegies	3.12.5	
And Rams with hornes their hard heads wreathed back.	Ovid's Elegies	3.12.17	
Shew large wayes with their garments there displayed.	Ovid's Elegies	3.12.24	
Jewels, and gold their Virgin tresses crowne,	Ovid's Elegies	3.12.25	
And stately robes to their gilt feete hang downe.	Ovid's Elegies	3.12.26	
Upon their heads the holy mysteries had.	Ovid's Elegies	3.12.28	
Such as confesse, have lost their good names by it.	Ovid's Elegies	3.13.6	
When carefull Rome in doubt their prowesse held.	Ovid's Elegies	3.14.10	
(For his sake whom their goddesse held so deare,	Hero and Leander	1.92	
To meet their loves; such as had none at all,	Hero and Leander	1.95	
Their fellowes being slaine or put to flight,	Hero and Leander	1.120	
And some (their violent passions to asswage)/Compile sharpe	Hero and Leander	1.126	
Thus while dum signs their yeelding harts entangled,	Hero and Leander	1.187	
so much/As one poore word, their hate to him was such.	Hero and Leander	1.384	
Saturne and Ops, began their golden raigne.	Hero and Leander	1.456	
Seeing in their loves, the Fates were injured.	Hero and Leander	1.484	
Wherein the liberall graces lock'd their wealth,	Hero and Leander	2.17	
These greedie lovers had, at their first meeting.	Hero and Leander	2.24	
Looke how their hands, so were their hearts united,	Hero and Leander	2.27	
O none but gods have power their love to hide,	Hero and Leander	2.131	
Meremaids, sported with their loves/On heapes of heavie gold,	Hero and Leander	2.162	
In such warres women use but halfe their strength.	Hero and Leander	2.296	
THEIRS			
Twixt theirs and yours, shall be no enmitie.	Edw	5.3.46	Matrvs
THEISE			
shall confesse/Theise are the men that all the world admires.	1Tamb	1.2.223	Usumc
THEM (See also 'EM, 'UM)			
But as this one Ile teare them all from him,	Dido	1.1.40	Jupitr
And in the end subdue them with his sword,	Dido	1.1.90	Jupitr
And fetter them in Vulcans sturdie brasse,	Dido	1.1.118	Jupitr
But of them all scarce seven doe anchor safe,	Dido	1.1.222	Aeneas
And all of them unburdened of their loade,	Dido	1.1.225	Aeneas
Not one of them hath perisht in the storme,	Dido	1.1.236	Venus
Disperst them all amongst the wrackfull Rockes:	Dido	1.2.29	Cloan
What kind of people, and who governes them:	Dido	2.1.42	Aeneas
on the sand/Assayd with honey words to turne them backe:	Dido	2.1.137	Aeneas
Then he alleag'd the Gods would have them stay,	Dido	2.1.141	Aeneas
But tell them none shall gaze on him but I,	Dido	3.1.73	Dido
That can call them forth when as she please,	Dido	4.1.4	Iarbus
Behold where both of them come forth the Cave.	Dido	4.1.16	Anna
I might have stakte them both unto the earth,	Dido	4.1.23	Iarbus
And follow them as footemen through the deepe:	Dido	4.3.24	Aeneas
It may be he will steale away with them:	Dido	4.4.3	Dido
O keepe them still, and let me gaze my fill:	Dido	4.4.44	Dido
The ground is mine that gives them sustenance,	Dido	4.4.74	Dido
Come beare them in.	Dido	4.4.165	Dido
For I will grace them with a fairer frame,	Dido	5.1.5	Aeneas
These are his words, Meander set them downe.	1Tamb	1.1.94	Mycet
And ad this to them, that all Asia/Lament to see the follie of	1Tamb	1.1.95	Cosroe
And cause them to withdraw their forces home,	1Tamb	1.1.131	Menaph
Whose ransome made them martch in coates of gold,	1Tamb	1.1.143	Ceneus
In spight of them shall malice my estate.	1Tamb	1.1.159	Cosroe
We hope your selfe wil willingly restore them.	1Tamb	1.2.117	Agidas
Then shall we fight couragiously with them.	1Tamb	1.2.128	Tamb
Come let us meet them at the mountain foot,	1Tamb	1.2.133	Usumc
And looke we friendly on them when they come:	1Tamb	1.2.141	Tamb
I heare them come, shal we encounter them?	1Tamb	1.2.149	Techel
Thy selfe and them shall never part from me,	1Tamb	1.2.245	Tamb
Make much of them gentle Theridamas,	1Tamb	1.2.247	Tamb
Nor thee, nor them, thrice noble Tamburlain,	1Tamb	1.2.249	Therid
About them hangs a knot of Amber heire,	1Tamb	2.1.23	Menaph
What should we doe but bid them battaile straight,	1Tamb	2.2.18	Meandr
Least if we let them lynger here a while,	1Tamb	2.2.20	Meandr
If wealth or riches may prevaile with them,	1Tamb	2.2.61	Meandr
And make them blest that share in his attemptes.	1Tamb	2.3.9	Tamb
And let them know the Persean King is chang'd:	1Tamb	2.5.21	Cosroe
And gladly yeeld them to my gracious rule:	1Tamb	2.5.28	Cosroe
And ransome them with fame and usurie.	1Tamb	2.5.43	Cosroe
But as he thrust them underneath the hils,	1Tamb	2.6.5	Cosroe
Neptune and Dis gain'd each of them a Crowne,	1Tamb	2.7.37	Usumc
For want of nourishment to feed them both,	1Tamb	2.7.47	Cosroe
Yet will I weare it in despight of them,	1Tamb	2.7.61	Tamb

THEM (cont.)

This hand shal set them on your conquering heads:	1Tamb	3.3.31	Tamb
And feeding them with thin and slender fare,	1Tamb	3.3.49	Tamb
Leave words and let them feele your lances pointes,	1Tamb	3.3.91	Argier
Yet somtimes let your highnesse send for them/To do the work my	1Tamb	3.3.187	Anippe
heaven/To dash the Scythians braines, and strike them dead,	1Tamb	3.3.197	Zabina
And led them Captive into Affrica.	1Tamb	3.3.205	Zabina
Deliver them into my treasurie.	1Tamb	3.3.217	Tamb
Come bind them both and one lead in the Turke.	1Tamb	3.3.266	Tamb
Come bring them in, and for this happy conquest/Triumph, and	1Tamb	3.3.272	Tamb
So scatter and consume them in his rage,	1Tamb	4.1.34	Souldn
To let them see (divine Zenocrate)/I glorie in the curses of my	1Tamb	4.4.28	Tamb
To turne them al upon their proper heades.	1Tamb	4.4.31	Tamb
I pray you give them leave Madam, this speech is a goodly	1Tamb	4.4.32	P Techel
them leave Madam, this speech is a goodly refreshing to them.	1Tamb	4.4.33	P Techel
But if his highnesse would let them be fed, it would doe them	1Tamb	4.4.34	P Therid
highnesse would let them be fed, it would doe them more good.	1Tamb	4.4.35	P Therid
slice the brawnes of thy armes into carbonadoes, and eat them.	1Tamb	4.4.44	P Tamb
And with this pen reduce them to a Map,	1Tamb	4.4.78	Tamb
Let us live in spite of them, looking some happie power will	1Tamb	4.4.99	P Zabina
Tis enough for us to see them, and for Tamburlaine onely to	1Tamb	4.4.111	P Techel
for us to see them, and for Tamburlaine onely to enjoy them.	1Tamb	4.4.112	P Techel
Nor shall they long be thine, I warrant them.	1Tamb	4.4.119	Bajzth
If we deserve them not with higher meeds/Then erst our states	1Tamb	4.4.131	Therid
Take them away againe and make us slaves.	1Tamb	4.4.133	Therid
Reflexing them on your disdainfull eies:	1Tamb	5.1.70	Tamb
straight goe charge a few of them/To chardge these Dames,	1Tamb	5.1.116	Tamb
Away with them I say and shew them death.	1Tamb	5.1.120	Tamb
No breath nor sence, nor motion in them both.	1Tamb	5.1.344	Anippe
Blush heaven, that gave them honor at their birth,	1Tamb	5.1.350	Zenoc
And let them die a death so barbarous.	1Tamb	5.1.351	Zenoc
To see them live so long in misery:	1Tamb	5.1.370	Zenoc
Nor fortune keep them selves from victory.	1Tamb	5.1.406	Arabia
With them Arabia too hath left his life,	1Tamb	5.1.473	Tamb
Even by this hand that shall establish them,	1Tamb	5.1.492	Tamb
Would make me thinke them Bastards, not my sons,	2Tamb	1.3.32	Tamb
Thou shalt be king before them, and thy seed/Shall issue	2Tamb	1.3.52	Tamb
For we will martch against them presently.	2Tamb	1.3.105	Tamb
Meaning to aid [thee] <them> in this <these> Turkish armes,	2Tamb	1.3.144	Techel
And therefore let them rest a while my Lord.	2Tamb	1.3.184	Usumc
Which in despight of them I set on fire:	2Tamb	1.3.213	Therid
And sent them marching up to Belgasar,	2Tamb	2.1.19	Fredrk
So what we vow to them should not infringe/Our liberty of armes	2Tamb	2.1.40	Baldwn
And throw them in the triple mote of Hell,	2Tamb	2.4.100	Tamb
Thinke them in number yet sufficient,	2Tamb	3.1.41	Orcan
and make them seeme as black/As is the Island where the Furies	2Tamb	3.2.11	Tamb
Til fire and sword have found them at a bay.	2Tamb	3.2.151	Tamb
Harkening when he shall bid them plague the world.	2Tamb	3.4.60	Therid
By Mahomet not one of them shal live.	2Tamb	3.5.17	Callap
My Lord, your presence makes them pale and wan.	2Tamb	3.5.60	Usumc
But yet Ile save their lives and make them slaves.	2Tamb	3.5.63	Tamb
I may knocke out his braines with them, and lock you in the	2Tamb	3.5.141	P Tamb
Turkes Concubines first, when my father hath conquered them.	2Tamb	4.1.65	P Calyph
I beleeve there will be some hurt done anon amongst them.	2Tamb	4.1.75	P Calyph
Bring them my boyes, and tel me if the warres/Be not a life	2Tamb	4.1.78	Tamb
Making them burie this effeminate brat,	2Tamb	4.1.162	Tamb
And Ile dispose them as it likes me best,	2Tamb	4.1.166	Tamb
your tongues/And bind them close with bits of burnisht steele,	2Tamb	4.1.182	Tamb
Come bring them in to our Pavilion.	2Tamb	4.1.206	Tamb
I will prefer them for the funerall/They have bestowed on my	2Tamb	4.3.65	Tamb
(I meane such Queens as were kings Concubines)/Take them,	2Tamb	4.3.72	Tamb
kings Concubines)/Take them, devide them and their jewels too,	2Tamb	4.3.72	Tamb
And let them equally serve all your turnes.	2Tamb	4.3.73	Tamb
Let them take pleasure soundly in their spoiles,	2Tamb	4.3.92	Tamb
Unharnesse them, and let me have fresh horse:	2Tamb	5.1.130	Tamb
Take them, and hang them both up presently.	2Tamb	5.1.132	Tamb
Take them away Theridamas, see them dispatcht.	2Tamb	5.1.134	Tamb
They will talk still my Lord, if you doe not bridle them.	2Tamb	5.1.147	P Amyras
Bridle them, and let me to my coach.	2Tamb	5.1.148	Tamb
And cast them headlong in the cities lake:	2Tamb	5.1.162	Tamb
Techelles, Drowne them all, man, woman, and child,	2Tamb	5.1.170	Tamb
So Casane, fling them in the fire.	2Tamb	5.1.186	Tamb
Which makes them fleet aloft and gaspe for aire.	2Tamb	5.1.209	Techel
Which makes them manage armes against thy state,	2Tamb	5.3.36	Usumc
Yet make them feele the strength of Tamburlain,	2Tamb	5.3.37	Usumc
My looks shall make them flie, and might I follow,	2Tamb	5.3.107	Tamb
I meant to cut a channell to them both,	2Tamb	5.3.134	Tamb
And let them know that I am Machevill,	Jew	Prol.7	Machvl
Receive them free, and sell them by the weight;	Jew	1.1.24	Barab
As one of them indifferently rated,	Jew	1.1.29	Barab
sent me to know/Whether your selfe will come and custome them.	Jew	1.1.53	1Merch
Why then goe bid them come ashore,/And bring with them their	Jew	1.1.55	Barab
And bring with them their bils of entry:	Jew	1.1.56	Barab
I neither saw them, nor inquir'd of them.	Jew	1.1.77	1Merch
Ripping the bowels of the earth for them,	Jew	1.1.109	Barab
in the Counsell-house/To entertaine them and their Embassie.	Jew	1.1.149	1Jew
Have you determin'd what to say to them?	Jew	1.2.37	1Knght
Your Lordship shall doe well to let them have it.	Jew	1.2.44	Barab
Then let them with us contribute.	Jew	1.2.61	2Knght
the Jewes, and each of them to pay one halfe of his estate.	Jew	1.2.69	P Reader
and all mens hatred/Inflict upon them, thou great Primus Motor.	Jew	1.2.164	Barab
And in the Senate reprehend them all,	Jew	1.2.233	Abigal
what e're it be to injure them/That have so manifestly wronged	Jew	1.2.274	Abigal

THEM (cont.)

Intreat 'em faire, and give them friendly speech,	Jew	1.2.286	Barab
And seeme to them as if thy sinnes were great,	Jew	1.2.287	Barab
Goe Officers and set them straight in shew.	Jew	2.2.43	Govnr
He'de give us present mony for them all.	Jew	2.3.6	1Offcr
Hoping to see them starve upon a stall,	Jew	2.3.26	Barab
But marke how I am blest for plaguing them,	Jew	2.3.199	Barab
Does she receive them?	Jew	2.3.260	Mthias
No, Mathias, no, but sends them backe,/And when he comes, she	Jew	2.3.261	Barab
Father, why have you thus incenst them both?	Jew	2.3.356	Abigal
Who made them enemies?	Jew	3.2.20	Mater
Then take them up, and let them be interr'd/Within one sacred	Jew	3.2.29	Govnr
and let them be interr'd/Within one sacred monument of stone;	Jew	3.2.29	Govnr
And say, I pray them come and speake with me.	Jew	3.3.29	Abigal
To make me shew them favour severally,	Jew	3.3.38	Abigal
Nor make enquiry who hath sent it them.	Jew	3.4.81	Barab
So now couragiously encounter them;	Jew	3.5.33	Govnr
And Physicke will not helpe them; they must dye.	Jew	3.6.2	1Fryar
Yes, what of them?	Jew	3.6.21	2Fryar
Oh brother, all the Nuns are dead, let's bury them.	Jew	3.6.44	1Fryar
Why, what of them?	Jew	4.1.44	P Barab
He forged the daring challenge made them fight.	Jew	5.1.47	Govnr
Since they are dead, let them be buried.	Jew	5.1.57	Govnr
And rise with them i'th middle of the Towne,	Jew	5.1.92	Barab
thy desert we make thee Governor,/Use them at thy discretion.	Jew	5.2.11	Calym
Intreat them well, as we have used thee.	Jew	5.2.17	Calym
There will he banquet them, but thee at home,	Jew	5.3.38	Msngr
And if you like them, drinke your fill and dye:	Jew	5.5.9	Barab
That thou maist feast them in thy Citadell.	Jew	5.5.16	Msngr
I fram'd the challenge that did make them meet:	Jew	5.5.82	Barab
Without fresh men to rigge and furnish them.	Jew	5.5.101	Govnr
Shall fully shew the fury of them all.	P 65	2.8	Guise
gloves which I sent/To be poysoned, hast thou done them?	P 71	2.14	Guise
they be my good Lord, and he that smelles but to them, dyes.	P 74	2.17	P Pothec
Goe then, present them to the Queene Navarre:	P 79	2.22	Guise
Be gone my freend, present them to her straite.	P 82	2.25	Guise
Doth not your grace know the man that gave them you?	P 172	3.7	Navrre
Your grace was ill advisde to take them then,	P 174	3.9	Admral
Gonzago conduct them thither, and then/Beset his house that not	P 288	5.15	Guise
And send them for a present to the Pope:	P 317	5.44	Anjoy
Kill them, kill them.	P 338	5.65	Anjoy
With bowes and dartes to shoot at them they see,	P 422	7.62	Dumain
And sinke them in the river as they swim.	P 423	7.63	Dumain
Away with them both.	P 442	7.82	Anjoy
water the fish, and by the fish our selves when we eate them.	P 489	9.8	P 2Atndt
And thither will I to put them to the sword.	P 504	9.23	Guise
And if they storme, I then may pull them downe.	P 526	9.45	QnMoth
Downe with the Hugonites, murder them.	P 528	10.1	Guise
So, dragge them away.	P 535	10.8	Guise
In Gods name, let them come.	P 728	14.31	Navrre
Of King or Country, no not for them both.	P 740	14.43	Navrre
They should know how I scornde them and their mockes.	P 762	15.20	Guise
dote on them your selfe,/I know none els but holdes them in	P 763	15.21	Guise
I know none els but holdes them in disgrace:	P 764	15.22	Guise
My Lord, twere good to make them frends,	P 772	15.30	Eprnon
come Epernoune/Lets goe seek the Duke and make them freends.	P 786	15.44	King
Or else employ them in some better cause.	P 794	16.8	Bartus
But God we know will alwaies put them downe,	P 798	16.12	Navrre
Navarre that cloakes them underneath his wings,	P 855	17.50	Guise
And let them march away to France amaine:	P 917	18.18	Navrre
O my Lord, I am one of them that is set to murder you.	P 992	19.62	P 3Mur
Ile read them Frier, and then Ile answere thee.	P1171	22.33	King
Of such as holde them of the holy church?	P1181	22.43	King
That wouldst reward them with an hospitall.	Edw	1.1.38	3PrMan
Ile flatter these, and make them live in hope:	Edw	1.1.43	Gavstn
In spight of them	Edw	1.1.77	Edward
Are gone towards Lambeth, there let them remaine.	Edw	1.3.5	Gavstn
No, threaten not my lord, but pay them home.	Edw	1.4.26	Gavstn
If I be king, not one of them shall live.	Edw	1.4.105	Edward
But I will raigne to be reveng'd of them,	Edw	1.4.111	Edward
And use them but of meere hypocrisie.	Edw	2.1.45	Baldck
Brother, doe you heare them?	Edw	2.2.69	Kent
Nay all of them conspire to crosse me thus,	Edw	2.2.95	Edward
Now let them thanke themselves, and rue too late.	Edw	2.2.207	Edward
I, and tis likewise thought you favour him <them> <'em> <hem>.	Edw	2.2.226	Edward
But let them go, and tell me what are these.	Edw	2.2.239	Edward
Mait please your grace to entertaine them now.	Edw	2.2.241	Neece
And sodenly surprize them unawares.	Edw	2.3.19	Lncstr
Drums strike alarum, raise them from their sport,	Edw	2.3.25	Mortmr
No, here he comes, now let them spoile and kill:	Edw	2.4.3	Edward
I will not trust them, Gaveston away.	Edw	2.4.8	Edward
Strike off their heads, and let them preach on poles,	Edw	3.1.20	Spencr
Too kinde to them, but now have drawne our sword,	Edw	3.1.25	Edward
And Spencer, spare them not, but lay it on.	Edw	3.1.56	Edward
God end them once, my lord I take my leave,	Edw	3.1.87	Queene
I did your highnes message to them all,	Edw	3.1.96	Arundl
Demanding him of them, entreating rather,	Edw	3.1.97	Arundl
I found them at the first inexorable,	Edw	3.1.103	Arundl
Let them not unrevengd murther your friends,	Edw	3.1.125	Spencr
And marche to fire them from their starting holes.	Edw	3.1.127	Spencr
And tell them I will come to chastise them,	Edw	3.1.178	Edward
For now, even now, we marche to make them stoope,	Edw	3.1.183	Edward
upon them lords,/This day I shall powre vengeance with my sword	Edw	3.1.185	Edward

THEM (cont.)

Th'ad best betimes forsake [them] <thee> and their trains,	Edw	3.1.202		Lncstr
But weele advance them traitors, now tis time/To be avengd on	Edw	3.1.224		Edward
Away with them:	Edw	3.1.245		Edward
Do speedie execution on them all,	Edw	3.1.254		Edward
I thanke them, gave me leave to passe in peace:	Edw	4.1.16		Mortmr
Reward for them can bring in Mortimer?	Edw	4.3.18		Edward
with them are gone lord Edmund, and the lord Mortimer, having	Edw	4.3.32	P	Spencr
Edward battell in England, sooner then he can looke for them:	Edw	4.3.35	P	Spencr
And windes as equall be to bring them in,	Edw	4.3.51		Edward
As you injurious were to beare them foorth.	Edw	4.3.52		Edward
And Edward thou art one among them all,	Edw	4.4.10		Queene
To them that fight in right and feare his wrath:	Edw	4.6.20		Queene
Some whirle winde fetche them backe, or sincke them all:--	Edw	4.6.59		Mortmr
Away with them.	Edw	4.7.68		Rice
For we shall see them shorter by the heads.	Edw	4.7.94		Rice
To plaine me to the gods against them both:	Edw	5.1.22		Edward
I weare the crowne, but am contrould by them,	Edw	5.1.29		Edward
Call them againe my lorde, and speake them faire,	Edw	5.1.91		Leistr
Call thou them back, I have no power to speake.	Edw	5.1.93		Edward
Yet stay, for rather then I will looke on them,	Edw	5.1.106		Edward
Wish well to mine, then tush, for them ile die.	Edw	5.3.45		Edward
Keepe them a sunder, thrust in the king.	Edw	5.3.52		Matrvs
Containes his death, yet bids them save his life.	Edw	5.4.7		Mortmr
And none of both [them] <then> thirst for Edmunds bloud.	Edw	5.4.107		Kent
Or being dead, raise them to life againe,	F 53	1.1.25		Faust
Request them earnestly to visit me.	F 93	1.1.65		Faust
I'le have them flie to [India] <Indian> for gold;	F 109	1.1.81		Faust
I'le have them read me strange Philosophy,	F 113	1.1.85		Faust
I'le have them wall all Germany with Brasse,	F 115	1.1.87		Faust
I'le have them fill the publique Schooles with [silke] <skill>,	F 117	1.1.89		Faust
Seeing thou hast pray'd and sacrific'd to them.	F 235	1.3.7		Faust
I'de give them all for Mephostophilis.	F 331	1.3.103		Faust
about thee into Familiars, and make them tare thee in peeces.	F 363	1.4.21	P	Wagner
what of these <them>?	F 405	2.1.17		Faust
[makes men] <make them> foolish that do use <trust> them most.	F 408	2.1.20		BdAngl
Then heare me read it Mephostophilis <them>.	F 483	2.1.95		Faust
grant unto them that foure and twentie yeares being expired,	F 495	2.1.107	P	Faust
And bring them every morning to thy bed:	F 538	2.1.150		Mephst
Go Mephostophilis, fetch them in.	F 660	2.2.109	P	Lucifr
<examine> them of their <several> names and dispositions.	F 661	2.2.110	P	Belzeb
come then stand by me/And thou shalt see them come immediately.	F 844	3.1.66		Mephst
Strike them with sloth, and drowsy idlenesse;	F 894	3.1.116		Faust
And make them sleepe so sound, that in their shapes,	F 895	3.1.117		Faust
The Pope will curse them for their sloth to day,	F 987	3.2.7		Faust
By holy Paul we saw them not.	F1029	3.2.49		BthCrd
Unlesse you bring them forth immediatly:	F1031	3.2.51		Pope
Hale them to prison, lade their limbes with gyves:	F1032	3.2.52		Pope
Your Majesty shall see them presently.	F1235	4.1.81		Faust
But in dumbe silence let them come and goe.	F1252	4.1.98		Faust
But Faustus, since I may not speake to them,	F1263	4.1.109		Emper
and let them hang/Within the window where he yoak'd me first,	F1380	4.2.56		Benvol
And mount aloft with them as high as heaven,	F1404	4.2.80		Faust
Thence pitch them headlong to the lowest hell:	F1405	4.2.81		Faust
I heard them parly with the Conjurer.	F1422	4.2.98		1Soldr
in the contrary circle it is likewise Summer with them, as in	F1583	4.6.26	P	Faust
And then demand of them, what they would have.	F1590	4.6.33		Duke
I do beseech your grace let them come in,	F1605	4.6.48		Faust
up my hands, but see they hold 'em <them>, they hold 'em <them>.	F1853	5.2.57	P	Faust
my hands, but see they hold 'em <them>, they hold 'em <them>.	F1853	5.2.57	P	Faust
[Ah] <O> gentlemen, I gave them my soule for my cunning.	F1856	5.2.60		Faust
I writ them a bill with mine owne bloud, the date is expired:	F1860	5.2.64	P	Faust
Is for ore-tortur'd soules to rest them in.	F1915	5.2.119		BdAngl
Nay, thou must feele them, taste the smart of all:	F1922	5.2.126		BdAngl
Truly Ile none of them.	F App	p.230 39	P	Wagner
Beare witnesse I gave them him.	F App	p.230 41	P	Wagner
Beare witnesse I give them you againe.	F App	p.230 42	P	Clown
and Ile knocke them, they were never so knocht since they were	F App	p.230 46	P	Clown
divels, say I should kill one of them, what would folkes say?	F App	p.230 47	P	Clown
a vengeance on them, they have vilde long nailes, there was a	F App	p.230 51	P	Clown
Ile tell you how you shall know them, all hee divels has	F App	p.230 53	P	Clown
tickle the pretie wenches plackets Ile be amongst them ifaith.	F App	p.231 64	P	Clown
Go to maister Doctor, let me see them presently.	F App	p.237 50	P	Emper
gives thee hornes, but makes thee weare them, feele on thy head.	F App	p.238 71	P	Emper
has purg'd me of fortie Dollers, I shall never see them more:	F App	p.240 129	P	HrsCsr
have none about me, come to my Oastrie, and Ile give them you.	F App	p.241 162	P	HrsCsr
here they be madam, wilt please you taste on them.	F App	p.242 15	P	Faust
us, in the contrary circle it is summer with them, as in India,	F App	p.242 21	P	Faust
swift spirit that I have, I had them brought hither, as ye see,	F App	p.242 23	P	Faust
hither, as ye see, how do you like them Madame, be they good?	F App	p.242 23	P	Faust
A towne with one poore church set them at oddes.	Lucan, First Booke			97
peace against their wils; betwixt them both/Stept Crassus in:	Lucan, First Booke			99
So when as Crassus wretched death who stayd them,	Lucan, First Booke			104
Such humors stirde them up; but this warrs seed,	Lucan, First Booke			159
Them freedome without war might not suffice,	Lucan, First Booke			173
That crost them; both which now approacht the camp,	Lucan, First Booke			270
And with them Curio, sometime Tribune too,	Lucan, First Booke			271
steeld their harts/And minds were prone) restrain'd them;	Lucan, First Booke			356
These hands shall thrust the ram, and make them flie,	Lucan, First Booke			385
Or flaming Titan (feeding on the deepe)/Puls them aloft, and	Lucan, First Booke			417
this makes them/Run on the swords point and desire to die,	Lucan, First Booke			456
(his vassals)/And that he lags behind with them of purpose,	Lucan, First Booke			477
Their houshould gods restrain them not, none lingered,	Lucan, First Booke			505

THEM (cont.)			
easie grant men great estates,/But hardly grace to keepe them:	Lucan, First Booke	509	
snatcht up/Would make them sleepe securely in their tents.	Lucan, First Booke	516	
Or if Fate rule them, Rome thy Cittizens/Are neere some plague:	Lucan, First Booke	643	
Why should we wish the gods should ever end them?	Lucan, First Booke	668	
to scarre/The quivering Romans, but worse things affright them.	Lucan, First Booke	673	
Strike on the boord like them that pray for evill,	Ovid's Elegies	1.4.27	
Who feares these armes? who wil not go to meete them?	Ovid's Elegies	1.6.39	
Night runnes away; with open entrance greete them.	Ovid's Elegies	1.6.40	
Let them aske some-what, many asking little,	Ovid's Elegies	1.8.89	
Both of them watch: each on the hard earth sleepes:	Ovid's Elegies	1.9.7	
Receive these lines, them to my Mistrisse carry,	Ovid's Elegies	1.11.7	
Then with triumphant laurell will I grace them/And in the midst	Ovid's Elegies	1.11.25	
will I grace them/And in the midst of Venus temple place them.	Ovid's Elegies	1.11.26	
And souldiours make them ready to the fight,	Ovid's Elegies	1.13.14	
Thou coosnest boyes of sleepe, and dost betray them/To Pedants,	Ovid's Elegies	1.13.17	
dost betray them/To Pedants, that with cruell lashes pay them.	Ovid's Elegies	1.13.18	
Feardst thou to dresse them?	Ovid's Elegies	1.14.5	
Nor hath the needle, or the combes teeth reft them,	Ovid's Elegies	1.14.15	
The maide that kembd them ever safely left them.	Ovid's Elegies	1.14.16	
They well become thee, then to spare them turne.	Ovid's Elegies	1.14.28	
Farre off be force, no fire to them may reach,	Ovid's Elegies	1.14.29	
such faults are sad/Nor make they any man that heare them glad.	Ovid's Elegies	2.2.52	
And wish hereby them all unknowne to leave.	Ovid's Elegies	2.5.54	
Bewaile I onely, though I them lament.	Ovid's Elegies	2.5.60	
Which do perchance old age unto them give.	Ovid's Elegies	2.6.28	
Better then I their quiver knowes them not.	Ovid's Elegies	2.9.38	
I pay them home with that they most desire:	Ovid's Elegies	2.10.26	
Shee looking on them did more courage give.	Ovid's Elegies	2.12.26	
If without battell selfe-wrought wounds annoy them,	Ovid's Elegies	2.14.3	
And their owne privie weapon'd hands destroy them.	Ovid's Elegies	2.14.4	
Upon the cold earth pensive let them lay,	Ovid's Elegies	2.16.15	
let either heed/What please them, and their eyes let either	Ovid's Elegies	3.2.6	
Gather them up, or lift them loe will I.	Ovid's Elegies	3.2.26	
Coate-tuckt Dianas legges are painted like them,	Ovid's Elegies	3.2.31	
When strong wilde beasts, she stronger hunts to strike them.	Ovid's Elegies	3.2.32	
And feare those, that to feare them least intend.	Ovid's Elegies	3.3.32	
their wits should them defend.	Ovid's Elegies	3.4.2	
Yet by deceit Love did them all surprize.	Ovid's Elegies	3.4.20	
As in thy sacrifize we them forbeare?	Ovid's Elegies	3.9.44	
Let me, and them by it be aye be-friended.	Ovid's Elegies	3.12.36	
or parch her hands, but to her mind,/Or warme or coole them:	Hero and Leander	1.29	
Compar'd with marriage, had you tried them both,	Hero and Leander	1.263	
And yet I like them for the Orator.	Hero and Leander	1.340	
And wound them on his arme, and for her mourn'd.	Hero and Leander	1.376	
He wounds with love, and forst them equallie,	Hero and Leander	1.445	
Grosse gold, from them runs headlong to the boore.	Hero and Leander	1.472	
At every stroke, betwixt them would he slide,	Hero and Leander	2.184	
And [them] <then> like Mars and Ericine displayd,	Hero and Leander	2.305	
THEME (See THEAMES)			
THEMIS			
Against the Woolfe that angrie Themis sent,	1Tamb	4.3.5	Souldn
TH'EMPERIALL			
Present thee with th'Emperiall Diadem.	1Tamb	1.1.139	Ortyg
I willingly receive th'emperiall crowne,	1Tamb	1.1.157	Cosroe
THEM SELVES			
Nor fortune keep them selves from victory.	1Tamb	5.1.406	Arabia
THEMSELVES			
And suite themselves in purple for the nonce,	Dido	1.1.206	Venus
When ayrie creatures warre amongst themselves:	Dido	4.2.7	Iarbus
As princely Lions when they rouse themselves,	1Tamb	1.2.52	Techel
from the camp/When Kings themselves are present in the field?	1Tamb	2.4.17	Tamb
speares/Began to checke the ground, and rain themselves:	1Tamb	5.1.333	Zenoc
Left to themselves while we were at the fight,	1Tamb	5.1.471	Tamb
Yet never did they recreate themselves,	2Tamb	1.3.182	Usumc
And now themselves shal make our Pageant,	2Tamb	4.3.90	Tamb
Who for the villaines have no wit themselves,	Jew	1.2.215	Barab
For they themselves hold it a principle,	Jew	2.3.310	Barab
So, now they have shew'd themselves to be tall fellowes.	Jew	3.2.7	Barab
Then be themselves base subjects to the whip.	P 218	4.16	Anjoy
And disperse themselves throughout the Realme of France,	P 507	9.26	QnMoth
Who set themselves to tread us under foot,	P 702	14.5	Navrre
That lift themselves against the perfect truth,	P 799	16.13	Navrre
Now let them thanke themselves, and rue too late.	Edw	2.2.207	Edward
Slaughter themselves in others and their sides/With their owne	Edw	4.4.7	Queene
matters in hand, let the horses walk themselves and they will.	F 727	2.3.6	P Robin
All great things crush themselves, such end the gods/Allot the	Lucan, First Booke	81	
and peoples voices/Bought by themselves and solde, and every	Lucan, First Booke	181	
And muttering much, thus to themselves complain'd:	Lucan, First Booke	249	
too, which bouldly faine themselves/The Romanes brethren,	Lucan, First Booke	428	
And without ground, fear'd, what themselves had faind:	Lucan, First Booke	482	
Marriners, albeit the keele be sound,/Shipwracke themselves:	Lucan, First Booke	501	
Poore wretches on the tree themselves did strangle,	Ovid's Elegies	1.12.17	
Here of themselves thy shafts come, as if shot,	Ovid's Elegies	2.9.37	
Where the French rout engirt themselves with Bayes.	Ovid's Elegies	2.13.18	
Now comes the pompe; themselves let all men cheere:	Ovid's Elegies	3.2.43	
Rich robes, themselves and others do adorne,	Hero and Leander	1.237	
Neither themselves nor others, if not worne.	Hero and Leander	1.238	
To venge themselves on Hermes, have concluded/That Midas brood	Hero and Leander	1.474	
THEN (Homograph; See also THAN)			
And then Ile hugge with you an hundred times.	Dido	1.1.48	Ganimd
Then gan the windes breake ope their brazen doores,	Dido	1.1.62	Venus
Then dye Aeneas in thine innocence,	Dido	1.1.80	Venus

THEN (cont.)

Then would we hope to quite such friendly turnes,	Dido	1.2.46	Serg
And when I know it is not, then I dye.	Dido	2.1.9	Aeneas
Then would it leape out to give Priam life:	Dido	2.1.27	Aeneas
Thy fortune may be greater then thy birth,	Dido	2.1.90	Dido
Then be assured thou art not miserable.	Dido	2.1.104	Dido
Then speake Aeneas with Achilles tongue,	Dido	2.1.121	Aeneas
Then he alleag'd the Gods would have them stay,	Dido	2.1.141	Aeneas
And then--O Dido, pardon me.	Dido	2.1.159	Aeneas
Then he unlockt the Horse, and suddenly/From out his entrailes,	Dido	2.1.182	Aeneas
Then buckled I mine armour, drew my sword,	Dido	2.1.200	Aeneas
Who then ran to the pallace of the King,	Dido	2.1.224	Aeneas
Then from the navell to the throat at once,	Dido	2.1.255	Aeneas
And then in triumph ran into the streetes,	Dido	2.1.261	Aeneas
Then got we to our ships, and being abourd,	Dido	2.1.280	Aeneas
Then touch her white breast with this arrow head,	Dido	2.1.326	Venus
Then shall I touch her breast and conquer her.	Dido	3.1.6	Cupid
Am not I Queen of Libia? then depart.	Dido	3.1.49	Dido
Then pull out both mine eyes, or let me dye.	Dido	3.1.55	Iarbus
Then sister youle abjure Iarbus love?	Dido	3.1.77	Anna
Then twentie thousand Indiaes can affoord:	Dido	3.1.93	Dido
give Dido leave/To be more modest then her thoughts admit,	Dido	3.1.95	Dido
Then Thetis hangs about Apolloes necke,	Dido	3.1.132	Dido
Then never say that thou art miserable,	Dido	3.1.169	Dido
Why is it then displeasure should disjoyne,	Dido	3.2.30	Juno
Is this then all the thankes that I shall have,	Dido	3.2.37	Juno
More then melodious are these words to me,	Dido	3.2.62	Juno
Why should not they then joyne in marriage,	Dido	3.2.74	Juno
Then in one Cave the Queene and he shall meete,	Dido	3.2.92	Juno
Then would I wish me with Anchises Tombe,	Dido	3.3.44	Aeneas
Then would I wish me in faire Didos armes,	Dido	3.3.48	Iarbus
And then, what then? Iarbus shall but love:	Dido	3.3.82	Iarbus
Who then of all so cruell may he be,	Dido	3.4.16	Aeneas
Then to the Carthage Queene that dyes for him.	Dido	3.4.40	Dido
What more then Delian musicke doe I heare,	Dido	3.4.52	Dido
Anna that doth admire thee more then heaven.	Dido	4.2.46	Anna
Let my Phenissa graunt, and then I goe:	Dido	4.3.6	Aeneas
Each word she sayes will then containe a Crowne,	Dido	4.3.53	Aeneas
Then let Aeneas goe abourd with us.	Dido	4.4.23	Achat
And when we whisper, then the starres fall downe,	Dido	4.4.53	Dido
Then here in me shall flourish Priams race,	Dido	4.4.87	Aeneas
Better he frowne, then I should dye for griefe:	Dido	4.4.111	Dido
Then that which grim Atrides overthrew:	Dido	5.1.3	Aeneas
And yong Iulus more then thousand yeares,	Dido	5.1.39	Hermes
If that be all, then cheare thy drooping lookes,	Dido	5.1.71	Iarbus
Then let me goe and never say farewell?	Dido	5.1.109	Aeneas
Am I lesse faire then when thou sawest me first?	Dido	5.1.115	Dido
O then Aeneas, tis for griefe of thee:	Dido	5.1.116	Dido
Then let me goe, and never say farewell?	Dido	5.1.124	Dido
But rather will augment then ease my woe?	Dido	5.1.152	Dido
Then gan he wagge his hand, which yet held up,	Dido	5.1.229	Anna
Then gan they drive into the Ocean,	Dido	5.1.231	Anna
Then carelesly I rent my haire for griefe,	Dido	5.1.236	Anna
Thou shalt burne first, thy crime is worse then his:	Dido	5.1.297	Dido
And then applaud his fortunes if you please.	1Tamb	Prol.8	Prolog
Then heare thy charge, valiant Theridamas,	1Tamb	1.1.57	Mycet
Then now my Lord, I humbly take my leave.	1Tamb	1.1.81	Therid
You may doe well to kisse it then.	1Tamb	1.1.98	Cosroe
Then did the Macedonians at the spoile/Of great Darius and his	1Tamb	1.1.153	Ceneus
Then I may seeke to gratifie your love,	1Tamb	1.1.171	Cosroe
Sound up the trumpets then, God save the King.	1Tamb	1.1.188	Ortyg
And then my selfe to faire Zenocrate.	1Tamb	1.2.105	Tamb
Then shall we fight couragiously with them.	1Tamb	1.2.128	Tamb
Then shalt thou be Competitor with me,	1Tamb	1.2.208	Tamb
Then thou shalt find my vaunts substantiall.	1Tamb	1.2.213	Tamb
For you then Maddam, I am out of doubt.	1Tamb	1.2.258	Tamb
A pearle more worth, then all the world is plaste:	1Tamb	2.1.12	Menaph
Then when our powers in points of swords are join'd,	1Tamb	2.1.40	Cosroe
wel then, by heavens I sweare,/Aurora shall not peepe out of	1Tamb	2.2.9	Mycet
Then having past Armenian desarts now,	1Tamb	2.2.14	Meandr
Then noble souldiors, to intrap these theeves,	1Tamb	2.2.59	Meandr
Then shall your meeds and vallours be advaunst/To roomes of	1Tamb	2.3.40	Cosroe
Then haste Cosroe to be king alone,	1Tamb	2.3.42	Tamb
Then tis mine.	1Tamb	2.4.34	Tamb
Then shalt thou see me pull it from thy head:	1Tamb	2.4.39	Tamb
then Cosroe raign/And governe Persea in her former pomp:	1Tamb	2.5.18	Cosroe
Then will we march to all those Indian Mines,	1Tamb	2.5.41	Cosroe
What then my Lord?	1Tamb	2.5.71	Usumc
Why then Casane, shall we wish for ought/The world affoords in	1Tamb	2.5.72	Tamb
Why then Theridamas, Ile first assay,	1Tamb	2.5.81	Tamb
Then thou for Parthia, they for Scythia and Medea.	1Tamb	2.5.83	Tamb
Then shall we send to this triumphing King,	1Tamb	2.5.87	Techel
Nay quickly then, before his roome be hot.	1Tamb	2.5.89	Usumc
Then shalt thou see the Scythian Tamburlaine,	1Tamb	2.5.97	Tamb
Then strike up Drum, and all the Starres that make/The	1Tamb	2.6.36	Cosroe
Then stay thou with him, say I bid thee so.	1Tamb	3.1.35	Bajzth
Then shall our footmen lie within the trench,	1Tamb	3.1.64	Bajzth
Tis more then pitty such a heavenly face/Should by hearts	1Tamb	3.2.4	Agidas
Then haste Agydas, and prevent the plagues:	1Tamb	3.2.100	Agidas
Then fight couragiously, their crowns are yours.	1Tamb	3.3.30	Tamb
subdue the Turke, and then inlarge/Those Christian Captives,	1Tamb	3.3.46	Tamb
Til then take thou my crowne, vaunt of my worth,	1Tamb	3.3.130	Tamb
Then Victorie begins to take her flight,	1Tamb	3.3.160	Tamb

THEN (cont.)

Then must his kindled wrath bee quencht with blood: . . .	1Tamb	4.1.56		2Msngr
Then it should so conspire my overthrow.	1Tamb	4.2.11		Tamb
Then as I look downe to the damned Feends, . . .	1Tamb	4.2.26		Bajzth
Then when the Sky shal waxe as red as blood, . . .	1Tamb	4.2.53		Tamb
Let these be warnings for you then my slave, . . .	1Tamb	4.2.72		Anippe
Then reare your standardes, let your sounding Drummes/Direct	1Tamb	4.3.61		Souldn
Then let us freely banquet and carouse/Full bowles of wine unto	1Tamb	4.4.5		Tamb
and then she shall be sure not to be starv'd, and he be .	1Tamb	4.4.45	P	Usumc
with freatting, and then she will not bee woorth the eating.	1Tamb	4.4.50	P	Tamb
Then raise your seige from faire Damascus walles, . . .	1Tamb	4.4.71		Zenoc
higher meeds/Then erst our states and actions have retain'd,	1Tamb	4.4.132		Therid
Then here before the majesty of heaven, ...	1Tamb	5.1.48		2Virgn
O then for these, and such as we our selves, . . .	1Tamb	5.1.96		1Virgn
Your fearfull minds are thicke and mistie then, . . .	1Tamb	5.1.110		Tamb
What is beauty, saith my sufferings then?	1Tamb	5.1.160		Tamb
And then shall we in this detested guyse, ...	1Tamb	5.1.235		Bajzth
Then is there left no Mahomet, no God, ...	1Tamb	5.1.239		Zabina
Then let the stony dart of sencelesse colde, ...	1Tamb	5.1.302		Bajzth
Then as the powers devine have preordainde, ...	1Tamb	5.1.400		Zenoc
Then shal I die with full contented heart, ...	1Tamb	5.1.417		Arabia
Then let me find no further time to grace/Her princely Temples	1Tamb	5.1.488		Tamb
Then doubt I not but faire Zenocrate/Will soone consent to	1Tamb	5.1.498		Tamb
Then let us set the crowne upon her head, ...	1Tamb	5.1.501		Therid
Then sit thou downe divine Zenocrate, ...	1Tamb	5.1.506		Tamb
Then after all these solemne Exequies, ...	1Tamb	5.1.533		Tamb
More then his Camp of stout Hungarians, ...	2Tamb	1.1.21		Uribas
Wilt thou have war, then shake this blade at me, . . .	2Tamb	1.1.83		Sgsmnd
That thou thy self, then County-Pallatine, ...	2Tamb	1.1.94		Orcan
Then County-Pallatine, but now a king:	2Tamb	1.1.104		Sgsmnd
Then here I sheath it, and give thee my hand, ...	2Tamb	1.1.127		Sgsmnd
And then depart we to our territories.	2Tamb	1.1.166		Orcan
Then shalt thou see a hundred kings and more/Upon their knees,	2Tamb	1.2.28		Callap
Then here I sweare, as I am Almeda, ...	2Tamb	1.2.67		Almeda
Thanks gentle Almeda, then let us haste, ...	2Tamb	1.2.74		Callap
Then crost the sea and came to Oblia, ...	2Tamb	1.3.211		Therid
Then wil we triumph, banquet and carouse, ...	2Tamb	1.3.218		Tamb
It resteth now then that your Majesty/Take all advantages of	2Tamb	2.1.11		Fredrk
Now then my Lord, advantage take hereof, ...	2Tamb	2.1.22		Fredrk
But cals not then your Grace to memorie/The league we lately	2Tamb	2.1.27		Sgsmnd
Then arme my Lords, and issue sodainly, ...	2Tamb	2.1.60		Sgsmnd
Then if there be a Christ, as Christians say, ...	2Tamb	2.2.39		Orcan
Then let some holy trance convay my thoughts, ...	2Tamb	2.4.34		Tamb
Then in as rich a tombe as Mausolus, ...	2Tamb	2.4.133		Tamb
Then should you see this Thiefe of Scythia, ...	2Tamb	3.1.14		Callap
Our battaile then in martiall maner pitcht, ...	2Tamb	3.1.63		Orcan
Wel then my noble Lords, for this my friend, ...	2Tamb	3.1.68		Callap
Then wil I shortly keep my promise Almeda.	2Tamb	3.1.78	P	Callap
Then next, the way to fortifie your men, ...	2Tamb	3.2.62		Tamb
When this is done, then are ye souldiers, ...	2Tamb	3.2.91		Tamb
But then run desperate through the thickest throngs, . .	2Tamb	3.2.139		Tamb
Then let us see if coward Calapine/Dare levie armes against our	2Tamb	3.2.155		Tamb
Then let us bring our light Artilery, ...	2Tamb	3.3.5		Techel
Then see the bringing of our ordinance/Along the trench into	2Tamb	3.3.54		Therid
Then scortch a face so beautiful as this, ...	2Tamb	3.4.74		Techel
Then carie me I care not where you will, ...	2Tamb	3.4.80		Olymp
Then welcome Tamburlaine unto thy death.	2Tamb	3.5.52		Callap
What, dar'st thou then be absent from the fight, . . .	2Tamb	4.1.22		Amyras
You wil not goe then?	2Tamb	4.1.40		Amyras
Then bring those Turkish harlots to my tent, ...	2Tamb	4.1.165		Tamb
Nay Lady, then if nothing wil prevaile, ...	2Tamb	4.2.50		Therid
Here then Olympia.	2Tamb	4.2.81		Therid
then live, and draw/My chariot swifter than the racking .	2Tamb	4.3.20		Tamb
then dy like beasts, and fit for nought/But perches for the	2Tamb	4.3.22		Tamb
Live [continent] <content> then (ye slaves) and meet not me	2Tamb	4.3.81		Tamb
Let us not be idle then my Lord, ...	2Tamb	4.3.95		Techel
We wil Techelles, forward then ye Jades:	2Tamb	4.3.97		Tamb
Then shal my native city Samarcanda/And christall waves of	2Tamb	4.3.107		Tamb
Then in my coach like Saturnes royal son, ...	2Tamb	4.3.125		Tamb
Then hang out flagges (my Lord) of humble truce, . . .	2Tamb	5.1.6		Maxim
Up with him then, his body shalbe scard.	2Tamb	5.1.114		Tamb
Then for all your valour, you would save your life. . .	2Tamb	5.1.119		Tamb
teare both our limmes/Rather then we should draw thy chariot,	2Tamb	5.1.139		Orcan
Shoot first my Lord, and then the rest shall follow. . .	2Tamb	5.1.151		Tamb
Then have at him to begin withall.	2Tamb	5.1.152		Therid
Wel then my friendly Lordes, what now remaines/But that we	2Tamb	5.1.210		Tamb
O then ye Powers that sway eternal seates, ...	2Tamb	5.3.17		Techel
Then will I comfort all my vital parts, ...	2Tamb	5.3.100		Tamb
then let me see how much/Is left for me to conquer all the	2Tamb	5.3.123		Tamb
Then martcht I into Egypt and Arabia, ...	2Tamb	5.3.130		Tamb
Then by the Northerne part of Affrica, ...	2Tamb	5.3.140		Tamb
Then now remoove me, that I may resigne/My place and proper	2Tamb	5.3.175		Tamb
Then feeles your majesty no sovereraigne ease, ...	2Tamb	5.3.213		Usumc
Then let some God oppose his holy power, ...	2Tamb	5.3.220		Techel
Be warn'd by him then, learne with awfull eie/To sway a throane	2Tamb	5.3.234		Tamb
More then heavens coach, the pride of Phaeton. . . .	2Tamb	5.3.244		Tamb
and Lawes were then most sure/When like the [Dracos] <Drancus>	Jew	Prol.20		Machvl
built Citadell/Commands much more then letters can import:	Jew	Prol.23		Machvl
why then I hope my ships/I sent for Egypt and the bordering	Jew	1.1.41		Barab
Why then goe bid them come ashore,/And bring with them their	Jew	1.1.55		Barab
comes to more/Then many Merchants of the Towne are worth,	Jew	1.1.64		1Merch
So then, there's somewhat come.	Jew	1.1.69		Barab
for earthly man/Then thus to powre out plenty in their laps,	Jew	1.1.108		Barab

THEN (cont.)

Then pittied in a Christian poverty:	Jew	1.1.115		Barab
scambled up/More wealth by farre then those that brag of faith.	Jew	1.1.123		Barab
I, wealthier farre then any Christian.	Jew	1.1.128		Barab
like enough, why then let every man/Provide him, and be there	Jew	1.1.170		Barab
Then give us leave, great Selim-Calymath.	Jew	1.2.13		Govnr
That's more then is in our Commission.	Jew	1.2.22		Basso
to obtaine by peace/Then to enforce conditions by constraint.	Jew	1.2.26		Calym
Now then here know that it concerneth us--	Jew	1.2.42		Govnr
Then good my Lord, to keepe your quiet still,	Jew	1.2.43		Barab
Then let the rich increase your portions.	Jew	1.2.58		Govnr
Then let them with us contribute.	Jew	1.2.61		2Knght
Then pay thy halfe.	Jew	1.2.83		Govnr
Will you then steale my goods?	Jew	1.2.94		Barab
Then many perish for a private man:	Jew	1.2.99		Govnr
tush, take not from me then,/For that is theft; and if you rob	Jew	1.2.125		Barab
which being valued/Amount to more then all the wealth in Malta.	Jew	1.2.134		Offcrs
Then wee'll take order for the residue.	Jew	1.2.136		Govnr
Well then my Lord, say, are you satisfied?	Jew	1.2.137		Barab
Then be the causers of their misery.	Jew	1.2.148		Barab
On then:	Jew	1.2.211		2Jew
And fram'd of finer mold then common men,	Jew	1.2.219		Barab
Then shall they ne're be seene of Barrabas:	Jew	1.2.250		Abigal
Then thus; thou toldst me they have turn'd my house/Into a	Jew	1.2.277		Barab
Then Abigall, there must my girle/Intreat the Abbasse to be	Jew	1.2.279		Barab
thou never mean'st/As first meane truth, and then dissemble it,	Jew	1.2.291		Barab
A counterfet profession is better/Then unseene hypocrisie.	Jew	1.2.293		Barab
Well father, say I be entertain'd,/What then shall follow?	Jew	1.2.295		Abigal
This shall follow then;/There have I hid close underneath the	Jew	1.2.295		Barab
Then father, goe with me.	Jew	1.2.300		Abigal
For I had rather dye, then see her thus.	Jew	1.2.357		Barab
fitter for a tale of love/Then to be tired out with Orizons:	Jew	1.2.370		Mthias
Then rise at midnight to a solemne masse.	Jew	1.2.373		Mthias
Then, gentle sleepe, where e're his bodie rests,	Jew	2.1.35		Abigal
Then father here receive thy happinesse.	Jew	2.1.44		Abigal
Then my desires were fully satisfied,	Jew	2.1.52		Barab
And then we [luft] <left>, and [tackt] <tooke>, and fought at	Jew	2.2.14		Bosco
will I shew my selfe to have more of the Serpent then the Dove;	Jew	2.3.37	P	Barab
Come then, here's the marketplace; whats the price of this	Jew	2.3.97	P	Barab
Why should this Turke be dearer then that Moore?	Jew	2.3.109		Barab
Then marke him, Sir, and take him hence.	Jew	2.3.131		1Offcr
then listen to my words,/And I will teach [thee] that shall	Jew	2.3.167		Barab
And now and then, to cherish Christian theeves,	Jew	2.3.177		Barab
Then after that was I an Usurer,	Jew	2.3.190		Barab
And now and then one hang himselfe for griefe,	Jew	2.3.196		Barab
Then gentle Abigal plight thy faith to me.	Jew	2.3.315		Lodowk
Oh, is't the custome, then I am resolv'd:	Jew	2.3.329		Lodowk
Then my faire Abigal should frowne on me.	Jew	2.3.332		Lodowk
Away then.	Jew	2.3.380		Barab
Then take them up, and let them be interr'd/Within one sacred	Jew	3.2.29		Govnr
Then of true griefe let us take equall share.	Jew	3.2.37		Govnr
And then they met, [and] as the story sayes,	Jew	3.3.20		Ithimr
one; have not the Nuns fine sport with the Fryars now and then?	Jew	3.3.33	P	Ithimr
And then thou didst not like that holy life.	Jew	3.3.58		1Fryar
Then were my thoughts so fraile and unconfirm'd,	Jew	3.3.59		Abigal
ambles after wealth/Although he ne're be richer then in hope:	Jew	3.4.53		Barab
Very well, Ithimore, then now be secret;	Jew	3.4.60		Barab
make her round and plump, and batten more then you are aware.	Jew	3.4.66	P	Ithimr
Saint Jaques Even) and then I say they use/To send their Almes	Jew	3.4.76		Barab
Peace, Ithimore, 'tis better so then spar'd.	Jew	3.4.91		Barab
And nought to us more welcome is then wars.	Jew	3.5.36		Govnr
What then?	Jew	3.6.16		2Fryar
And one offence torments me more then all.	Jew	3.6.19		Abigal
Reveale it not, for then my father dyes.	Jew	3.6.32		Abigal
Shall be condemn'd, and then sent to the fire.	Jew	3.6.36		2Fryar
this, then goe with me/And helpe me to exclaime against the Jew.	Jew	3.6.45		2Fryar
Oh speake not of her, then I dye with griefe.	Jew	4.1.36		Barab
of my sinnes/Lye heavy on my soule; then pray you tell me,	Jew	4.1.49		Barab
Then 'tis not for me; and I am resolv'd/You shall confesse me,	Jew	4.1.85		Barab
Not? then I'le make thee, [rogue] <goe>.	Jew	4.1.95		2Fryar
Then is it as it should be, take him up.	Jew	4.1.152		Barab
Then will not Jacomo be long from hence.	Jew	4.1.159		Barab
nay then I'le force my way;/And see, a staffe stands ready for	Jew	4.1.171		1Fryar
What shall we doe with this base villaine then?	Jew	4.2.62		Curtzn
him he were best to send it; then he hug'd and imbrac'd me.	Jew	4.2.106	P	Pilia
Rather for feare then love.	Jew	4.2.107	P	Ithimr
Then like a Jew he laugh'd and jeer'd, and told me he lov'd me	Jew	4.2.108	P	Pilia
Come Amorous wag, first banquet and then sleep.	Jew	4.2.132		Curtzn
[demand]/Three hundred Crownes, and then five hundred Crownes?	Jew	4.3.62		Barab
Their deaths were like their lives, then think not of 'em;	Jew	5.1.56		Govnr
And if it be not true, then let me dye.	Jew	5.1.96		Barab
much better/To [have] kept thy promise then be thus surpriz'd?	Jew	5.2.5		Calym
Then will I, Barabas, about this coyne,	Jew	5.2.107		Govnr
And then to make provision for the feast,	Jew	5.2.119		Barab
Then issue out and come to rescue me,	Jew	5.4.5		Govnr
Rather then thus to live as Turkish thrals,	Jew	5.4.8		1Knght
On then, begone.	Jew	5.4.10		Govnr
Then now are all things as my wish wud have 'em,	Jew	5.5.17		Barab
thee greater curtesie/Then Barabas would have affoorded thee.	Jew	5.5.62		Govnr
See his end first, and flye then if thou canst.	Jew	5.5.69		Govnr
You will not helpe me then?	Jew	5.5.76		Barab
Then Barabas breath forth thy latest fate,	Jew	5.5.78		Barab
Why, then the house was fir'd,/Blowne up, and all thy souldiers	Jew	5.5.106		Govnr

THEN (cont.)

Then conquer Malta, or endanger us.	Jew	5.5.122	Govnr
Then thou remainest resolute.	P 75	2.18	Guise
Goe then, present them to the Queene Navarre:	P 79	2.22	Guise
And then Ile guerdon thee with store of crownes.	P 89	2.32	Guise
Then Guise,/Since thou hast all the Cardes	P 145	2.88	Guise
Your grace was ill advisde to take them then,	P 174	3.9	Admral
Then be themselves base subjects to the whip.	P 218	4.16	Anjoy
Then pittie or releeve these upstart hereticks.	P 222	4.20	Guise
Thankes to my princely sonne, then tell me Guise,	P 228	4.26	QnMoth
Then Ile have a peale of ordinance shot from the tower,	P 236	4.34	Guise
And then the watchword being given, a bell shall ring,	P 238	4.36	Guise
Then breath a while.	P 241	4.39	Guise
Then I am carefull you should be preserved.	P 265	4.63	Charls
Away then, break into the Admirals house.	P 282	5.9	Guise
them thither, and then/Beset his house that not a man may live.	P 288	5.15	Guise
Then pray unto our Ladye, kisse this crosse.	P 302	5.29	Gonzag
Then throw him down.	P 306	5.33	Guise
set the street/May know their watchword, then tole the bell,	P 329	5.56	Guise
Come then, lets away.	P 335	5.62	Guise
Despatch then quickly.	P 353	6.8	Mntsrl
Then take this with you.	P 360	6.15	Mntsrl
And when you see me in, then follow hard.	P 429	7.69	Anjoy
on me, then with your leaves/I may retire me to my native home.	P 473	8.23	Anjoy
Then come my Lords, lets goe.	P 481	8.31	Anjoy
What shall we doe then?	P 486	9.5	P 2Atndt
Then throw him into the ditch.	P 490	9.9	P 1Atndt
And Henry then shall weare the diadem.	P 522	9.41	QnMoth
And if they storme, I then may pull them downe.	P 526	9.45	QnMoth
Then to misdoe the welfare of their King:	P 546	11.11	Charls
Then may it please your Majestie to give me leave,	P 616	12.29	Mugern
Then shall the Catholick faith of Rome,	P 639	12.52	QnMoth
And then shall Mounser weare the diadem.	P 652	12.65	QnMoth
And then determine of this enterprise.	P 656	12.69	QnMoth
I, dearer then the apple of mine eye?	P 685	13.29	Guise
Then in this bloudy brunt they may beholde,	P 713	14.16	Bartus
How now my Lord, faith this is more then need,	P 757	15.15	Guise
Tis more then kingly or Emperious.	P 759	15.17	Guise
Then farwell Guise, the King and thou are freends.	P 870	17.65	King
Then meanes he present treason to our state.	P 880	17.75	King
And then Ile tell thee what I meane to doe.	P 891	17.86	King
Then hath your grace fit oportunitie,	P 903	18.4	Bartus
Bartus, it shall be so, poast then to Fraunce,	P 907	18.8	Navrre
Well then, I see you are resolute.	P 938	19.8	Capt
Then sirs take your standings within this Chamber,	P 940	19.10	Capt
Then come proud Guise and heere disgordge thy brest,	P 952	19.22	King
As pale as ashes, nay then tis time to look about.	P1001	19.71	Guise
Then pray to God, and aske forgivenes of the King.	P1004	19.74	P 2Mur
Then stay a while and Ile goe call the King,	P1017	19.87	Capt
Then there is no remedye but I must dye?	P1096	20.6	Cardnl
Then heere wee'l lye before [Lutetia] <Lucrecia> walles,	P1151	22.13	King
Then come thou neer, and tell what newes thou bringst.	P1166	22.28	King
Ile read them Frier, and then Ile answere thee.	P1171	22.33	King
And then I vow for to revenge his death,	P1247	22.109	Navrre
gathered now shall ayme/more at thie end then exterpatione	Paris	ms29,p391	Guise
then will I wake thee from thie folishe dreame/and lett thee	Paris	ms32,p391	Guise
Then live and be the favorit of a king?	Edw	1.1.5	Gavstn
Then thou hast beene of me since thy exile.	Edw	1.1.145	Edward
no soule in hell/Hath felt more torment then poore Gaveston.	Edw	1.1.147	Gavstn
Then beare the ship that shall transport thee hence:	Edw	1.1.153	Edward
these may well suffice/For one of greater birth then Gaveston.	Edw	1.1.159	Kent
I did no more then I was bound to do,	Edw	1.1.182	BshpCv
As then I did incense the parlement,	Edw	1.1.184	BshpCv
Then laide they violent hands upon him, next/Himselfe	Edw	1.2.36	ArchBp
Then wil you joine with us that be his peeres/To banish or	Edw	1.2.42	Mortmr
Then let him stay, for rather then my lord/Shall be opprest by	Edw	1.2.64	Queene
for rather then my lord/Shall be opprest by civill mutinies,	Edw	1.2.64	Queene
Then may we lawfully revolt from him.	Edw	1.2.73	Mortmr
Come then lets away.	Edw	1.2.79	Lncstr
of Lancaster/That hath more earldomes then an asse can beare,	Edw	1.3.2	Gavstn
Nay, then lay violent hands upon your king,	Edw	1.4.35	Edward
Learne then to rule us better and the realme.	Edw	1.4.39	Lncstr
he refuse, and then may we/Depose him and elect an other king.	Edw	1.4.54	Mortmr
Then linger not my lord but do it straight.	Edw	1.4.58	Lncstr
Because he loves me more then all the world:	Edw	1.4.77	Edward
I shal be found, and then twil greeve me more.	Edw	1.4.132	Gavstn
Away then, touch me not, come Gaveston.	Edw	1.4.159	Edward
Crie quittance Madam then, and love not him.	Edw	1.4.195	Mortmr
Then speake not for him, let the pesant go.	Edw	1.4.218	Warwck
Then thus, but none shal heare it but our selves.	Edw	1.4.229	Queene
Ile rather loose his friendship I, then graunt.	Edw	1.4.237	Lncstr
Why then my lord, give me but leave to speak.	Edw	1.4.254	Mortmr
To banish him, and then to call him home,	Edw	1.4.275	Mortmr
Then may we with some colour rise in armes,	Edw	1.4.279	Mortmr
Then let her live abandond and forlorne.	Edw	1.4.298	Queene
I love him more/Then he can Gaveston, would he lov'd me/But	Edw	1.4.303	Queene
would he lov'd me/But halfe so much, then were I treble blest.	Edw	1.4.304	Queene
No other jewels hang about my neck/Then these my lord, nor let	Edw	1.4.331	Queene
Then I may fetch from this ritch treasurie:	Edw	1.4.332	Queene
And may it proove more happie then the first.	Edw	1.4.336	Queene
Then gaudie silkes, or rich imbrotherie.	Edw	1.4.347	Edward
And then his mariage shalbe solemnized,	Edw	1.4.377	Edward
Then let his grace, whose youth is flexible,	Edw	1.4.398	MortSr

THEN (cont.)

and in his tuskan cap/A jewell of more value then the crowne.	Edw		1.4.415	Mortmr
Then so am I, and live to do him service,	Edw		1.4.421	Mortmr
What, meane you then to be his follower?	Edw		2.1.12	Baldck
Then hope I by her meanes to be preferd,	Edw		2.1.29	Baldck
Then Balduck, you must cast the scholler off,	Edw		2.1.31	Spencr
And now and then, stab as occasion serves.	Edw		2.1.43	Spencr
My lord, mines more obscure then Mortimers.	Edw		2.2.22	Lncstr
then was thy parting hence/Bitter and irkesome to my sobbing	Edw		2.2.57	Edward
Then I doe to behold your Majestie.	Edw		2.2.63	Gavstn
No more then I would answere were he slaine.	Edw		2.2.86	Mortmr
Yes more then thou canst answer though he live,	Edw		2.2.87	Edward
About it then, and we will follow you.	Edw		2.2.124	Mortmr
Then ransome him.	Edw		2.2.143	Edward
And so will I, and then my lord farewell.	Edw		2.2.156	Lncstr
But once, and then thy souldiers marcht like players,	Edw		2.2.183	Mortmr
So will I, rather then with Gaveston.	Edw		2.2.215	Kent
Why then weele have him privilie made away.	Edw		2.2.236	Gavstn
Then Spencer waite upon me, for his sake/Ile grace thee with a	Edw		2.2.252	Edward
Then to be favoured of your majestie.	Edw		2.2.255	Spencr
Looke for no other fortune wretch then death,	Edw		2.5.17	Lncstr
I thanke you all my lords, then I perceive,	Edw		2.5.29	Gavstn
In burying him, then he hath ever earned.	Edw		2.5.56	Lncstr
Then if you will not trust his grace in keepe,	Edw		2.5.65	Arundl
Then give him me.	Edw		2.5.94	Penbrk
Then tell thy prince, of whence, and what thou art.	Edw		3.1.35	Edward
things of more waight/Then fits a prince so yong as I to beare,	Edw		3.1.75	Prince
Then shall your charge committed to my trust.	Edw		3.1.78	Prince
Then Edward, thou wilt fight it to the last,	Edw		3.1.211	Mortmr
Then banish that pernicious companie?	Edw		3.1.213	Mortmr
I traitors all, rather then thus be bravde,	Edw		3.1.214	Edward
Then live in infamie under such a king.	Edw		3.1.244	Lncstr
Then make for Fraunce amaine, [Levune] <Lewne> away,/Proclaime	Edw		3.1.280	Spencr
and then a Fig/For all my unckles frienship here in Fraunce.	Edw		4.2.4	Prince
And then have at the proudest Spencers head.	Edw		4.2.25	Prince
Much happier then your friends in England do.	Edw		4.2.35	Kent
Edward battell in England, sooner then he can looke for them:	Edw		4.3.35	P Spencr
O fly him then, but Edmund calme this rage,	Edw		4.6.11	Kent
Since then succesfully we have prevayled,	Edw		4.6.21	Queene
Comes Leister then in Isabellas name,	Edw		4.7.64	Edward
A sweet Spencer, thus then must we part.	Edw		4.7.73	Edward
Then send for unrelenting Mortimer/And Isabell, whose eyes	Edw		5.1.103	Edward
Will sooner sparkle fire then shed a teare:	Edw		5.1.105	Edward
Yet stay, for rather then I will looke on them,	Edw		5.1.106	Edward
is there in a Tigers jawes,/[Then] <This> his imbrasements:	Edw		5.1.117	Edward
and bid him rule/Better then I, yet how have I transgrest,	Edw		5.1.122	Edward
And then let me alone to handle him.	Edw		5.2.22	Mortmr
Then let some other be his guardian.	Edw		5.2.36	Queene
And then from thence to Bartley back againe:	Edw		5.2.61	Mortmr
Let me but see him first, and then I will.	Edw		5.2.95	Prince
Then I will carrie thee by force away.	Edw		5.2.112	Mortmr
Isabell is neerer then the earle of Kent.	Edw		5.2.115	Queene
Wish well to mine, then tush, for them ile die.	Edw		5.3.45	Edward
But yet I have a braver way then these.	Edw		5.4.37	Ltborn
Feard am I more then lov'd, let me be feard,	Edw		5.4.52	Mortmr
And none of both [them] <then> thirst for Edmunds bloud.	Edw		5.4.107	Kent
More then we can enflict, and therefore now,	Edw		5.5.11	Matrvs
And then thy heart, were it as Gurneys is,	Edw		5.5.53	Edward
That <and> even then when I shall lose my life,	Edw		5.5.77	Edward
But hath your grace no other proofe then this?	Edw		5.6.43	Mortmr
Then sue for life unto a paltrie boye.	Edw		5.6.57	Mortmr
Then come sweete death, and rid me of this greefe.	Edw		5.6.92	Queene
Could I have rulde thee then, as I do now,	Edw		5.6.96	King
Then read no more, thou hast attain'd that <the> end;	F	38	1.1.10	Faust
Then this profession were to be esteem'd.	F	54	1.1.26	Faust
Why then belike/We must sinne, and so consequently die,	F	71	1.1.43	Faust
Then all my labours, plod I ne're so fast.	F	96	1.1.68	Faust
Then was the fiery keele at [Antwerpe] <Anwerpe> <Antwarpes>	F	123	1.1.95	Faust
Then gentle friends aid me in this attempt,	F	138	1.1.110	Faust
Then has <in> the white breasts of the Queene of love.	F	156	1.1.128	Valdes
Then doubt not Faustus but to be renowm'd,	F	168	1.1.140	Cornel
Then heeretofore the Delphian <Dolphian> Oracle.	F	170	1.1.142	Cornel
Then tell me Faustus what shall we three want?	F	175	1.1.147	Cornel
Then hast thee to some solitary Grove,	F	180	1.1.152	Valdes
And then all other ceremonies learn'd,	F	186	1.1.158	Cornel
And then wilt thou be perfecter then I.	F	189	1.1.161	Valdes
Then come and dine with me, and after meate/We'le canvase every	F	190	1.1.162	Faust
Why, dost not thou know then?	F	199	1.2.6	P 2Schol
Then <Well> you will not tell us?	F	205	1.2.12	P 2Schol
Then wherefore should you aske me such a question?	F	208	1.2.15	P Wagner
Then I feare that which I have long suspected:	F	220	1.2.27	1Schol
Then feare not Faustus to <but> be resolute/And try the utmost	F	242	1.3.14	Faust
No more then he commands, must we performe.	F	270	1.3.42	Mephst
How comes it then that he is Prince of Devils?	F	294	1.3.66	Faust
How comes it then that thou art out of hell?	F	303	1.3.75	Faust
And then resolve me of thy Maisters mind.	F	328	1.3.100	Faust
then belike if I serve you, I shall be lousy.	F	358	1.4.16	P Robin
I good Wagner, take away the devill then.	F	377	1.4.35	P Robin
What bootes it then to thinke on <of> God or Heaven?	F	391	2.1.3	Faust
And give thee more then thou hast wit to aske.	F	436	2.1.48	Mephst
Then Faustus stab thy <thine> Arme couragiously,	F	438	2.1.50	Mephst
And then be thou as great as Lucifer.	F	441	2.1.53	Mephst
Then write againe: Faustus gives to thee his soule.	F	458	2.1.70	Faust

THEN (cont.)

I Faustus, and do greater things then these.	F 476	2.1.88		Mephst
Then Mephostophilis receive this scrole,	F 477	2.1.89		Faust
<Then theres inough for a thousand soules>,	F 477	(HC260)A		Faust
Then heare me read it Mephostophilis <them>.	F 483	2.1.95		Faust
Why, dost thou think <think'st thou then> that Faustus shall be	F 518	2.1.130		Faust
booke more, and then I have done, wherein I might see al plants,	F 551.8	2.1.171A	P	Faust
When I behold the heavens then I repent/And curse thee wicked	F 552	2.2.1		Faust
was> made for man; then he's <therefore is man> more excellent.	F 560	2.2.9		Mephst
[Faustus, thou art damn'd, then swords <guns> and knives],	F 572	2.2.21A		Faust
Why should I die then, or basely despaire?	F 582	2.2.31		Faust
<Well>, Resolve me then in this one question:	F 614	2.2.63	P	Faust
Then <or>, like a Fan of Feathers, I kisse her [lippes]; And	F 667	2.2.116	P	Pride
And then turning my selfe to a wrought Smocke do what I list.	F 668	2.2.117	P	Pride
live along, then thou should'st see how fat I'de <I would> be.	F 682	2.2.131	P	Envy
Then the devill choke thee.	F 703	2.2.152	P	Glutny
an inch of raw Mutton, better then an ell of fryde Stockfish:	F 709	2.2.161	P	Ltchry
I see hell, and returne againe safe, how happy were I then.	F 715	2.2.167	P	Faust
Come then let's away.	F 753	2.3.32	P	Robin
And mounted then upon a Dragons backe,	F 771	2.3.50		2Chor
Then up to Naples rich Campania,	F 787	3.1.9		Faust
come then stand by me/And thou shalt see them come immediately.	F 843	3.1.65		Mephst
And grant me my request, and then I go.	F 846	3.1.68		Faust
No bigger then my hand in quantity.	F 851	3.1.73		Faust
Then in this shew let me an Actor be,	F 854	3.1.76		Faust
And then devise what best contents thy minde,	F 858	3.1.80		Mephst
Sound Trumpets then, for thus Saint Peters Heire,	F 875	3.1.97		Pope
Then he and thou, and all the world shall stoope,	F 937	3.1.159		Pope
<Well, I am content, to compasse then some sport>,	F 989	(HC266)A		Faust
<Then charme me that I may be invisible>,	F 991	(HC266)A		Faust
Faustus thou shalt, then kneele downe presently,	F 994	3.2.14		Mephst
First weare this girdle, then appeare/Invisible to all are here:	F 997	3.2.17		Mephst
Then wherefore would you have me view that booke?	F1023	3.2.43		Pope
Go then command our Priests to sing a Dirge,	F1063	3.2.83		Pope
Nay then take that.	F1067	3.2.87		Faust
Wilt thou stand in thy Window, and see it then?	F1195	4.1.41		Mrtino
Then if by powerfull Necromantick spels,	F1209	4.1.55		Emper
Then Faustus as thou late didst promise us,	F1230	4.1.76		Emper
Then if I gain'd another Monarchie.	F1272	4.1.118		Emper
Then good Master Doctor,	F1308	4.1.154		Emper
Then draw your weapons, and be resolute:	F1335	4.2.11		Benvol
Then gentle Fredericke hie thee to the grove,	F1340	4.2.16		Benvol
Then Souldiers boldly fight; if Faustus die,	F1346	4.2.22		Benvol
My head is lighter then it was by th'hornes,	F1350	4.2.26		Benvol
But yet my [heart's] <heart> more ponderous then my head,	F1351	4.2.27		Benvol
Be ready then, and strike the Peasant downe.	F1359	4.2.35		Fredrk
Mine be that honour then:	F1360	4.2.36		Benvol
Then Faustus try thy skill:	F1425	4.2.101		Faust
What shall we then do deere Benvolio?	F1451	4.3.21		Mrtino
We'le rather die with griefe, then live with shame.	F1456	4.3.26		Benvol
Then rest thee Faustus quiet in conceit.	F1483	4.4.27		Faust
And has the Doctor but one leg then?	F1553	4.5.49	P	Dick
and drinke a while, and then we'le go seeke out the Doctor.	F1557	4.5.53	P	Robin
I would request no better meate, then a dish of ripe grapes.	F1573	4.6.16	P	Lady
Madam, I will do more then this for your content.	F1575	4.6.18	P	Faust
This makes me wonder more then all the rest, that at this time	F1578	4.6.21	P	Duke
And then demand of them, what they would have.	F1590	4.6.33		Duke
I hope sir, we have wit enough to be more bold then welcome.	F1596	4.6.39	P	HrsCsr
I humbly thanke your grace: then fetch some Beere.	F1625	4.6.68		Faust
Then I pray remember your curtesie.	F1641	4.6.84	P	Carter
Then I assure thee certainelie they are.	F1650	4.6.93		Faust
Then when sir Paris crost the seas with <for> her,	F1694	5.1.21		Faust
Be silent then, for danger is in words.	F1696	5.1.23		Faust
Then Faustus, will repentance come too late,	F1714	5.1.41		OldMan
Then thou art banisht from the sight of heaven;	F1715	5.1.42		OldMan
Then call for mercy, and avoyd despaire.	F1733	5.1.60		OldMan
Do it then Faustus <quickly>, with unfained heart,	F1751	5.1.78		Mephst
And then returne to Hellen for a kisse.	F1780	5.1.107		Faust
O thou art fairer then the evenings <evening> aire,	F1781	5.1.108		Faust
Brighter art thou then flaming Jupiter,	F1783	5.1.110		Faust
More lovely then the Monarch of the sky,	F1785	5.1.112		Faust
thee, then had I lived still, but now must <I> dye eternally.	F1824	5.2.28	P	Faust
view the Scriptures, then I turn'd the leaves/And led thine eye.	F1888	5.2.92		Mephst
Then wilt thou tumble in confusion.	F1925	5.2.129		BdAngl
And then thou must be damn'd perpetually.	F1928	5.2.132		Faust
Then will I headlong run into the earth:	F1948	5.2.152		Faust
To practise more then heavenly power permits.	F2009	5.3.27		4Chor
staves acre, why then belike, if I were your man, I should be	F App	p.229 21	P	Clown
and so by that meanes I shal see more then ere I felt, or saw	F App	p.233 5	P	Robin
then turn her and wind hir to thy owne use, as often as thou	F App	p.234 27	P	Robin
upon our handes, and then to our conjuring in the divels name.	F App	p.234 33	P	Robin
Then doctor Faustus, marke what I shall say, As I was sometime	F App	p.236 17	P	Emper
How then sir?	F App	p.237 53	P	Faust
Then rest thee Faustus quiet in conceit.	F App	p.240 126		Faust
I would desire no better meate then a dish of ripe grapes.	F App	p.242 11	P	Duchss
were it a greater thing then this, so it would content you, you	F App	p.242 13	P	Faust
Wars worse then civill on Thessalian playnes,	Lucan, First Booke	1		
conquer all the earth, then turne thy force/Against thy selfe:	Lucan, First Booke	22		
But if for Nero (then unborne) the fates/Would find no other	Lucan, First Booke	33		
Then men from war shal bide in league, and ease,	Lucan, First Booke	60		
Nor then was land, or sea, to breed such hate,	Lucan, First Booke	96		
Parthians y'afflict us more then ye suppose,	Lucan, First Booke	107		
And then we grew licencious and rude,	Lucan, First Booke	162		

THEN (cont.)

And then large limits had their butting lands,	Lucan, First Booke	169
stil poore/Did vild deeds, then t'was worth the price of bloud,	Lucan, First Booke	175
rage increase, then having whiskt/His taile athwart his backe,	Lucan, First Booke	210
the darke/(Swifter then bullets throwne from Spanish slinges,	Lucan, First Booke	231
shoot) marcht on/And then (when Lucifer did shine alone,	Lucan, First Booke	233
Wagons or tents, then in this frontire towne.	Lucan, First Booke	255
say Pompey, are these worse/Then Pirats of Sycillia?	Lucan, First Booke	347
then Laelius/The chiefe Centurion crown'd with Oaken leaves,	Lucan, First Booke	357
Well, leade us then to Syrtes desart shoare;	Lucan, First Booke	368
And far more barbarous then the French (his vassals)/And that	Lucan, First Booke	476
Then with their feare, and danger al distract,	Lucan, First Booke	487
birthes with more and ugly jointes/Then nature gives,	Lucan, First Booke	561
Then, that the trembling Citizens should walke/About the City;	Lucan, First Booke	591
then the sacred priests/That with divine lustration purg'd the	Lucan, First Booke	592
then the Nunnes/And their vaild Matron, who alone might view	Lucan, First Booke	596
who alone might view/Minervas statue; then, they that keepe,	Lucan, First Booke	598
Then crams salt levin on his crooked knife;	Lucan, First Booke	609
Yet more will happen then I can unfold;	Lucan, First Booke	634
Then Gaynimede would renew Deucalions flood,	Lucan, First Booke	652
Then scarse can Phoebus say, this harpe is mine.	Ovid's Elegies	1.1.20
Then oxen which have drawne the plow before.	Ovid's Elegies	1.2.14
Then such as in their bondage feele content.	Ovid's Elegies	1.2.18
Take these away, where is thy <thine> honor then?	Ovid's Elegies	1.2.38
Then seeing I grace thy show in following thee,	Ovid's Elegies	1.2.49
Then will he kisse thee, and not onely kisse/But force thee	Ovid's Elegies	1.4.63
Then came Corinna in a long loose gowne,	Ovid's Elegies	1.5.9
Or I more sterne then fire or sword will turne,	Ovid's Elegies	1.6.57
O harder then the dores thou gardest I prove thee.	Ovid's Elegies	1.6.62
I might have then my parents deare misus'd,	Ovid's Elegies	1.7.5
Then first I did perceive I had offended,	Ovid's Elegies	1.7.59
To yeeld their love to more then one disdainde.	Ovid's Elegies	1.8.40
his rent discharg'd/From further duty he rests then inlarg'd.	Ovid's Elegies	1.10.46
Then with triumphant laurell will I grace them/And in the midst	Ovid's Elegies	1.11.25
committed/And then with sweete words to my Mistrisse fitted.	Ovid's Elegies	1.12.22
Then thinkest thou thy loose life is not showne?	Ovid's Elegies	1.13.34
Then wouldst thou cry, stay night and runne not thus.	Ovid's Elegies	1.13.40
Thou art as faire as shee, then kisse and play.	Ovid's Elegies	1.13.44
They well become thee, then to spare them turne.	Ovid's Elegies	1.14.28
Then though death rackes <rakes> my bones in funerall fier,	Ovid's Elegies	1.15.41
Her shut gates greater lightning then thyne brought.	Ovid's Elegies	2.1.20
Feare to be guilty, then thou maiest desemble.	Ovid's Elegies	2.2.18
doe not languish/And then report her sicke and full of anguish.	Ovid's Elegies	2.2.22
And what lesse labour then to hold thy peace?	Ovid's Elegies	2.2.28
Object thou then what she may well excuse,	Ovid's Elegies	2.2.37
What can be easier then the thing we pray?	Ovid's Elegies	2.2.66
If she be learned, then for her skill I crave her,	Ovid's Elegies	2.4.17
And when one sweetely sings, then straight I long,	Ovid's Elegies	2.4.25
[Is she attired, then shew her graces best].	Ovid's Elegies	2.4.38
[Amber] <Yellow> trest is shee, then on the morne thinke I,/My	Ovid's Elegies	2.4.43
I sawe you then unlawfull kisses joyne,	Ovid's Elegies	2.5.23
Also much better were they then I tell,	Ovid's Elegies	2.5.55
Greater then these my selfe I not esteeme,	Ovid's Elegies	2.8.13
And then things found do ever further pace.	Ovid's Elegies	2.9.10
Better then I their quiver knowes them not.	Ovid's Elegies	2.9.38
Light art thou, and more windie then thy winges,	Ovid's Elegies	2.9.49
Yet this is better farre then lie alone,	Ovid's Elegies	2.10.15
Then wilt thou Laedas noble twinne-starres pray,	Ovid's Elegies	2.11.29
Then would I wish thee touch my mistris pappe,	Ovid's Elegies	2.15.11
Then I, that I may seale her privy leaves,	Ovid's Elegies	2.15.15
Then on the rough Alpes should I tread aloft,	Ovid's Elegies	2.16.19
Had then swum over, but the way was blinde.	Ovid's Elegies	2.16.32
Maides words more vaine and light then falling leaves,	Ovid's Elegies	2.16.45
Then wreathes about my necke her winding armes,	Ovid's Elegies	2.18.9
Then warres, and from thy tents wilt come to mine.	Ovid's Elegies	2.18.40
Jove liked her better then he did before.	Ovid's Elegies	2.19.30
Then with huge steps came violent Tragedie,	Ovid's Elegies	3.1.11
Not stronger am I, then the thing I move.	Ovid's Elegies	3.1.42
And I deserve more then thou canst in verity,	Ovid's Elegies	3.1.47
Greater then her, by her leave th'art, Ile say.	Ovid's Elegies	3.2.60
Thy feare is, then her body, valued more.	Ovid's Elegies	3.4.30
One Deianira was more worth then these.	Ovid's Elegies	3.5.38
That seeing thy teares can any joy then feele.	Ovid's Elegies	3.5.60
much (I crave)/Gifts then my promise greater thou shalt have.	Ovid's Elegies	3.5.66
white as is <Her armes farre whiter, then> the Scithean snow,	Ovid's Elegies	3.6.8
Why might not then my sinews be inchanted,	Ovid's Elegies	3.6.35
Then did the robe or garment which she wore <more>,	Ovid's Elegies	3.6.40
And Tithon livelier then his yeeres require.	Ovid's Elegies	3.6.42
But neither was I man, nor lived then.	Ovid's Elegies	3.6.60
Drouping more then a Rose puld yesterday:	Ovid's Elegies	3.6.66
Wit was some-times more pretious then gold,	Ovid's Elegies	3.7.3
Till then, rough was her father, she severe,	Ovid's Elegies	3.7.31
then if Corcyras Ile/Had thee unknowne interr'd in ground most	Ovid's Elegies	3.8.47
Yet this is lesse, then if he had seene me,	Ovid's Elegies	3.10.15
Ah, she doth more worth then her vices prove.	Ovid's Elegies	3.10.44
Who mine was cald, whom I lov'd more then any,	Ovid's Elegies	3.11.5
Then thee whom I must love I hate in vaine,	Ovid's Elegies	3.13.39
And I will trust your words more then mine eies.	Ovid's Elegies	3.13.46
Then shouldst thou bee his prisoner who is thine.	Hero and Leander	1.202
Why vowest thou then to live in Sestos here,	Hero and Leander	1.227
Then treasure is abus'de,/When misers keepe it; being put to	Hero and Leander	1.234
One is no number, mayds are nothing then,	Hero and Leander	1.255
Then Hero hate me not, nor from me flie,	Hero and Leander	1.291

THEN (cont.)

Line	Work	Ref	Speaker
Then shall you most resemble Venus Nun,	Hero and Leander	1.319	
Love Hero then, and be not tirannous,	Hero and Leander	1.323	
Then towards the pallace of the Destinies,	Hero and Leander	1.377	
And then he woo'd with kisses, and at last,	Hero and Leander	1.404	
Then muse not, Cupids sute no better sped,	Hero and Leander	1.483	
No marvell then, though Hero would not yeeld/So soone to part	Hero and Leander	2.83	
Then standing at the doore, she turnd about,	Hero and Leander	2.97	
And then he got him to a rocke aloft.	Hero and Leander	2.148	
And steale a kisse, and then run out and daunce,	Hero and Leander	2.185	
Thereat smilde Neptune, and then told a tale,	Hero and Leander	2.193	
heart of Hero much more joies/Then nymphs and sheapheards,	Hero and Leander	2.233	
Then drerie Mars, carowsing Nectar boules.	Hero and Leander	2.258	
And [them] <then> like Mars and Ericine displayd,	Hero and Leander	2.305	
Come <Then> live with mee, and be my love.	Passionate Shepherd	20	
Then live with mee, and be my love.	Passionate Shepherd	24	

TH'ENAMELD

Line	Work	Ref	Speaker
Or if it could, downe from th'enameld skie,	Hero and Leander	1.249	

TH'ENAMOURED

Line	Work	Ref	Speaker
Aye me, Leander cryde, th'enamoured sunne,	Hero and Leander	2.202	

THENCE

Line	Work	Ref	Speaker
From thence a fewe of us escapt to land,	Dido	1.2.30	Cloan
I long to see thee backe returne from thence,	1Tamb	1.1.76	Mycet
Thence rise the tears that so distain my cheeks,	1Tamb	3.2.64	Zenoc
And thence unto the straightes of Jubalter:	1Tamb	3.3.256	Tamb
And thence by land unto the Torrid Zone,	1Tamb	4.4.124	Tamb
And thence as far as Archipellago:	2Tamb	1.1.75	Orcan
From thence unto Cazates did I martch,	2Tamb	1.3.191	Techel
From thence I crost the Gulfe, call'd by the name/Mare magiore,	2Tamb	1.3.214	Therid
And thence unto Bythinia, where I tooke/The Turke and his great	2Tamb	5.3.128	Tamb
From thence to Nubia neere Borno Lake,	2Tamb	5.3.136	Tamb
I came at last to Graecia, and from thence/To Asia, where I stay	2Tamb	5.3.141	Tamb
But I will practise thy enlargement thence:	Jew	2.1.53	Barab
I'le rouze him thence.	Jew	2.3.269	Mthias
As Isabella <Isabell> gets no aide from thence.	Edw	4.3.16	Edward
They shalbe started thence I doubt it not.	Edw	4.6.60	Mortmr
And then from thence to Bartley back againe:	Edw	5.2.61	Mortmr
Send for him out thence, and I will anger him.	Edw	5.5.13	Gurney
and you have done me great injury to bring me from thence, let	F 705.2	2.2.156A	P Sloth
From thence to Venice, Padua, and the [rest] <East>,	F 794	3.1.16	Faust
Thence pitch them headlong to the lowest hell:	F1405	4.2.81	Faust
the Emathian bandes, from thence/To the pine bearing hils,	Lucan, First Booke	687	
Or if it do, to thee no joy thence spring:	Ovid's Elegies	1.4.68	
her eyes/Two eye-balles shine, and double light thence flies.	Ovid's Elegies	1.8.16	
Thence growes the Judge, and knight of reputation.	Ovid's Elegies	3.7.56	
And beat from thence, have lighted there againe.	Hero and Leander	1.24	
Thence flew Loves arrow with the golden head,	Hero and Leander	1.161	
And thence unto Abydus sooner blowne,	Hero and Leander	2.112	
Set in a forren place, and straight from thence,	Hero and Leander	2.119	
and up-staring <upstarting> Fawnes,/Would steale him thence.	Hero and Leander	2.201	

THEOLOGIE

Line	Work	Ref	Speaker
sweete delight's] dispute/In th'heavenly matters of Theologie,	F 19	Prol.19	1Chor

THEORIA

Line	Work	Ref	Speaker
As in the Theoria of the world.	2Tamb	4.2.86	Therid

THER

Line	Work	Ref	Speaker
Yet should ther hover in their restlesse heads,	1Tamb	5.1.171	Tamb
defence/When [un-protected] <un-protested> ther is no expence?	Ovid's Elegies	2.2.12	

THERE (See also THERES, THERS)

Line	Work	Ref	Speaker
I, this is it, you can sit toying there,	Dido	1.1.50	Venus
There is a place Hesperia term'd by us,	Dido	1.2.20	Cloan
Me thinkes that towne there should be Troy, yon Idas hill,	Dido	2.1.7	Aeneas
There Zanthus streame, because here's Priamus,	Dido	2.1.8	Aeneas
O there I lost my wife:	Dido	2.1.270	Aeneas
Aeneas, art thou there?	Dido	3.1.99	Dido
And Venus, let there be a match confirmd/Betwixt these two,	Dido	3.2.77	Juno
There was such hurly burly in the heavens:	Dido	4.1.10	Achat
I Anna, is there ought you would with me?	Dido	4.2.24	Iarbus
And shrunke not backe, knowing my love was there?	Dido	4.4.146	Dido
If there be any heaven in earth, tis love:	Dido	4.5.27	Nurse
Not farre from hence/There is a woman famoused for arts,	Dido	5.1.275	Dido
there are in readines/Ten thousand horse to carie you from	1Tamb	1.1.184	Ortyg
Was there such brethren, sweet Meander, say,	1Tamb	2.2.51	Mycet
Nor in Pharsalia was there such hot war,	1Tamb	3.3.154	Tamb
There whiles he lives, shal Bajazeth be kept,	1Tamb	4.2.85	Tamb
For there sits Death, there sits imperious Death,	1Tamb	5.1.111	Tamb
But I am pleasde you shall not see him there:	1Tamb	5.1.113	Tamb
There Angels in their christal armours fight/A doubtfull	1Tamb	5.1.151	Tamb
Who's within there?	1Tamb	5.1.191	Tamb
As if there were no way but one with us.	1Tamb	5.1.201	Techel
No more there is not I warrant thee Techelles.	1Tamb	5.1.202	Tamb
Then is there left no Mahomet, no God,	1Tamb	5.1.239	Zabina
And there make lawes to rule your provinces:	1Tamb	5.1.527	Tamb
Vienna was besieg'd, and I was there,	2Tamb	1.1.103	Sgsmnd
There having sackt Borno the Kingly seat,	2Tamb	1.3.203	Techel
Can there be such deceit in Christians,	2Tamb	2.2.36	Orcan
Then if there be a Christ, as Christians say,	2Tamb	2.2.39	Orcan
If there be Christ, we shall have victorie.	2Tamb	2.2.64	Orcan
The Dyvils there in chaines of quencelesse flame,	2Tamb	2.3.24	Orcan
Because the corners there may fall more flat,	2Tamb	3.2.65	Tamb
That there begin and nourish every part,	2Tamb	3.4.7	Capt
a roguish runnaway, suborn'd/That villaine there, that slave,	2Tamb	3.5.87	Tamb
I beleeve there will be some hurt done anon amongst them.	2Tamb	4.1.74	P Calyph
For there my Pallace royal shal be plac'd:	2Tamb	4.3.111	Tamb

THERE (cont.)

Shall mount the milk-white way and meet him there.	2Tamb	4.3.132	Tamb
Yet are there Christians of Georgia here,	2Tamb	5.1.31	1Citzn
Who have ye there my Lordes?	2Tamb	5.1.80	Tamb
There lies more gold than Babylon is worth,	2Tamb	5.1.116	Govnr
As there be breaches in her battered wall.	2Tamb	5.1.160	Tamb
Tartars and Perseans shall inhabit there,	2Tamb	5.1.163	Tamb
Wel said, let there be a fire presently.	2Tamb	5.1.178	Tamb
There is a God full of revenging wrath,	2Tamb	5.1.183	Tamb
There should not one of all the villaines power/Live to give	2Tamb	5.3.108	Tamb
And hold there is no sinne but Ignorance.	Jew	Prol.15	Machvl
There was the venture summ'd and satisfied.	Jew	1.1.3	Barab
the Custome-house/Will serve as well as I were present there.	Jew	1.1.58	Barab
from Egypt, or by Caire/But at the entry there into the sea,	Jew	1.1.74	Barab
Tut, tut, there is some other matter in't.	Jew	1.1.160	Barab
And all the Jewes in Malta must be there.	Jew	1.1.168	2Jew
Umh; All the Jewes in Malta must be there?	Jew	1.1.169	Barab
then let every man/Provide him, and be there for fashion-sake.	Jew	1.1.171	Barab
If any thing shall there concerne our state/Assure your selves	Jew	1.1.172	Barab
Reade there the Articles of our decrees.	Jew	1.2.67	Govnr
For there I left the Governour placing Nunnes,	Jew	1.2.254	Abigal
have turn'd my house/Into a Nunnery, and some Nuns are there.	Jew	1.2.278	Barab
there must my girle/Intreat the Abbasse to be entertain'd.	Jew	1.2.279	Barab
I, but father they will suspect me there.	Jew	1.2.283	Abigal
There have I hid close underneath the plancke/That runs along	Jew	1.2.296	Barab
Who's there?	Jew	2.1.43	Barab
And there in spite of Malta will I dwell:	Jew	2.3.15	Barab
There I enrich'd the Priests with burials,	Jew	2.3.183	Barab
I steale/To travellers Chambers, and there cut their throats:	Jew	2.3.207	Ithimr
There comes the villaine, now I'le be reveng'd.	Jew	2.3.333	Lodowk
Are there not Jewes enow in Malta,	Jew	2.3.359	Barab
And now, save Pilia-borza, comes there none.	Jew	3.1.9	Curtzn
Why, was there ever seene such villany,	Jew	3.3.1	Ithimr
But I perceive there is no love on earth,	Jew	3.3.47	Abigal
Among the rest beare this, and set it there;	Jew	3.4.78	Barab
Belike there is some Ceremony in't.	Jew	3.4.83	Barab
There Ithimore must thou goe place this [pot] <plot>:	Jew	3.4.84	Barab
Oh what a sad confession will there be?	Jew	3.6.4	2Fryar
And by my father's practice, which is there/Set downe at large,	Jew	3.6.28	Abigal
There is no musicke to a Christians knell:	Jew	4.1.1	Barab
Why true, therefore did I place him there:	Jew	4.1.137	Barab
To be a Christian, I shut him out,/And there he sate:	Jew	4.1.189	Barab
Here's goodly 'parrell, is there not?	Jew	4.2.112	Ithimr
Or else I will confesse: I, there it goes:	Jew	4.3.4	Barab
Well, my hope is, he will not stay there still;	Jew	4.3.16	Barab
There, if thou lov'st me doe not leave a drop.	Jew	4.4.6	P Ithimr
Pilia-borza, bid the Fidler give me the posey in his hat there.	Jew	4.4.36	P Curtzn
Whom have we there, a spy?	Jew	5.1.69	Calym
Within [there] <here>.	Jew	5.2.47	Barab
Now Governor--stand by there, wait within.--	Jew	5.2.50	Barab
I will be there, and doe as thou desirest;	Jew	5.2.103	Govnr
that there is a monastery/Which standeth as an out-house to the	Jew	5.3.36	Msngr
There will he banquet them, but thee at home,	Jew	5.3.38	Msngr
There, Carpenters, divide that gold amongst you:	Jew	5.5.5	Barab
There wanteth nothing but the Governors pelfe,	Jew	5.5.18	Barab
How busie Barrabas is there above/To entertaine us in his	Jew	5.5.52	Calym
Sound a charge there.	Jew	5.5.63	1Knght
And doe attend my comming there by this.	Jew	5.5.104	Calym
In person there to [mediate] <meditate> your peace;	Jew	5.5.116	Calym
What glory is there in a common good,	P 97	2.40	Guise
There shall not a Hugonet breath in France.	P 324	5.51	Guise
Who is that which knocks there?	P 346	6.1	P SrnsWf
Who goes there?	P 371	7.11	Gonzag
Who have you there?	P 380	7.20	Anjoy
Nere was there Colliars sonne so full of pride.	P 416	7.56	Anjoy
My Lord of Anjoy, there are a hundred Protestants,	P 417	7.57	Guise
As I could long ere this have wisht him there.	P 496	9.15	QnMoth
There are a hundred Hugonets and more,	P 501	9.20	Guise
Yet is [their] <there> pacience of another sort,	P 545	11.10	Charls
My Lords, what resteth there now for to be done?	P 554	11.19	QnMoth
Lye there the Kings delight, and Guises scorne.	P 818	17.13	Guise
Well, let me alone, whose within there?	P 881	17.76	King
And there salute his highnesse in our name,	P 908	18.9	Navrre
Be gone I say, tis time that we were there.	P 919	18.20	Navrre
Nere was there King of France so yoakt as I.	P1044	19.114	King
Then there is no remedye but I must dye?	P1096	20.6	Cardnl
As Rome and all those popish Prelates there,	P1248	22.110	Navrre
lye there the kinges delyght and guises scorne	Paris	ms22,p390	Guise
Why there are hospitals for such as you,	Edw	1.1.35	Gavstn
Shall bathe him in a spring, and there hard by,	Edw	1.1.66	Gavstn
He shall to prison, and there die in boults.	Edw	1.1.197	Gavstn
Whose there? conveie this priest to the tower.	Edw	1.1.200	Edward
To crosse to Lambeth, and there stay with me.	Edw	1.2.78	ArchBp
Are gone towards Lambeth, there let them remaine.	Edw	1.3.5	Gavstn
I there it goes, but yet I will not yeeld,	Edw	1.4.56	Edward
And there abide till fortune call thee home.	Edw	1.4.126	Edward
There weepe, for till my Gaveston be repeald,	Edw	1.4.168	Edward
Whose there, Balduck?	Edw	2.1.70	Neece
Come lead the way, I long till I am there.	Edw	2.1.82	Neece
Plinie reports, there is a flying Fish,	Edw	2.2.23	Lncstr
Content, ile beare my part, holla whose there?	Edw	2.2.130	Lncstr
Who have we there, ist you?	Edw	2.2.140	Edward
And to the king my brother there complaine,	Edw	2.4.66	Queene

THERE (cont.)

Spencer, the father of Hugh Spencer there,	Edw	3.1.40		SpncrP
And there let him bee,	Edw	3.1.197		Lncstr
There see him safe bestowed, and for the rest,	Edw	3.1.253		Edward
Holla, who walketh there, ist you my lord?	Edw	4.1.12		Mortmr
And there stay times advantage with your sonne?	Edw	4.2.18		SrJohn
To see us there appointed for our foes.	Edw	4.2.56		Mortmr
man, they say there is great execution/Done through the realme,	Edw	4.3.6		Edward
I pray let us see it, what have we there?	Edw	4.3.10		Edward
Come friends to Bristow, there to make us strong,	Edw	4.3.50		Edward
Shape we our course to Ireland there to breath.	Edw	4.5.3		Spencr
More safetie is there in a Tigers jawes,	Edw	5.1.116		Edward
Whose there? call hither Gurney and Matrevis.	Edw	5.2.38		Mortmr
How now, who comes there?	Edw	5.3.49		Gurney
What traitor have wee there with blades and billes?	Edw	5.4.82		Mortmr
geare, nere was there any/So finely handled as this king shalbe.	Edw	5.5.39		Ltborn
Whose there, what light is that, wherefore comes thou?	Edw	5.5.42		Edward
And there in mire and puddle have I stood,	Edw	5.5.59		Edward
And there unhorste the duke of Cleremont.	Edw	5.5.70		Edward
that in thy wheele/There is a point, to which when men aspire,	Edw	5.6.60		Mortmr
And seeing there was no place to mount up higher,	Edw	5.6.62		Mortmr
we deceive our selves, and there is <theres> no truth in us.	F 69	1.1.41	P	Faust
There is no chiefe but onely Beelzebub:	F 284	1.3.56		Faust
Had I as many soules, as there be Starres,	F 330	1.3.102		Faust
Faustus gives to thee his soule: [ah] <O> there it staid.	F 456	2.1.68		Faust
And where hell is there must we ever be.	F 512	2.1.124		Mephst
That after this life there is any paine?	F 523	2.1.135		Faust
<Well thou wilt have one, sit there till I come,	F 531	(HC261)A	P	Mephst
<Tel me>, are there many Spheares <heavens> above the Moone?	F 586	2.2.35		Faust
How many Heavens, or Spheares, are there?	F 609	2.2.58	P	Faust
But is there not Coelum igneum, [and] <&> <et> Christalinum?	F 612	2.2.61	P	Faust
O that there would come a famine over <through> all the world,	F 681	2.2.130	P	Envy
What Dick, looke to the horses there till I come againe.	F 722	2.3.1	P	Robin
'Snayles, what hast thou got there, a book?	F 730	2.3.9	P	Dick
I, there be of us here, that have waded as deepe into matters,	F 740	2.3.19	P	Robin
There saw we learned Maroes golden tombe:	F 791	3.1.13		Faust
There did we view the Kingdomes of the world,	F 852	3.1.74		Faust
And what might please mine eye, I there beheld.	F 853	3.1.75		Faust
What have our holy Councell there decreed,	F 947	3.1.169		Pope
There to salute the wofull Emperour.	F 986	3.2.6		Mephst
And there determine of his punishment?	F1018	3.2.38		Pope
Nay there you lie, 'tis beyond us both.	F1109	3.3.22	P	Robin
[What there he did in triall of his art],	F1153	3.3.66A		3Chor
and our followers/Close in an ambush there behinde the trees,	F1342	4.2.18		Benvol
looke up into th'hall there ho.	F1519	4.5.15	P	Hostss
and there I found him asleepe; I kept a hallowing and whooping	F1548	4.5.44	P	HrsCsr
Why how now Maisters, what a coyle is there?	F1591	4.6.34		Servnt
there spake a Doctor indeed, and 'faith Ile drinke a health to	F1626	4.6.69	P	HrsCsr
but let us into the next roome, and [there] pray for him.	F1872	5.2.76	P	1Schol
For that must be thy mansion, there to dwell.	F1882	5.2.86		Mephst
There are the Furies tossing damned soules,	F1911	5.2.115		BdAngl
There are live quarters broyling on the coles,	F1913	5.2.117		BdAngl
there was a hee divell and a shee divell, Ile tell you how you	F App	p.230 52	P	Clown
that I may be here and there and every where, O Ile tickle the	F App	p.231 62	P	Clown
And they of Nilus mouth (if there live any).	Lucan, First Booke	20		
[There] <Their> Caesar may'st thou shine and no cloud dim thee;	Lucan, First Booke	59		
And faintnes numm'd his steps there on the brincke:	Lucan, First Booke	196		
There spred the colours, with confused noise/Of trumpets	Lucan, First Booke	239		
though I not see/What may be done, yet there before him bee.	Ovid's Elegies	1.4.14		
There will I finde thee, or be found by thee,	Ovid's Elegies	1.4.57		
There touch what ever thou canst touch of mee.	Ovid's Elegies	1.4.58		
That when my mistresse there beholds thee cast,	Ovid's Elegies	1.6.69		
There is, who ere will knowe a bawde aright/Give eare, there is	Ovid's Elegies	1.8.1		
a bawde aright/Give eare, there is an old trot Dipsas hight.	Ovid's Elegies	1.8.2		
There sat the hang-man for mens neckes to angle.	Ovid's Elegies	1.12.18		
yesterday/There where the porch doth Danaus fact display.	Ovid's Elegies	2.2.4		
Condemne his eyes, and say there is no tryall.	Ovid's Elegies	2.2.58		
Good forme there is, yeares apt to play togither,	Ovid's Elegies	2.3.13		
There good birds rest (if we beleeve things hidden)/Whence	Ovid's Elegies	2.6.51		
There harmelesse Swans feed all abroad the river,	Ovid's Elegies	2.6.53		
There lives the Phoenix one alone bird ever.	Ovid's Elegies	2.6.54		
There Junoes bird displayes his gorgious feather,	Ovid's Elegies	2.6.55		
Thou shalt admire no woods or Citties there,	Ovid's Elegies	2.11.11		
There wine being fild, thou many things shalt tell,	Ovid's Elegies	2.11.49		
Lay in the mid bed, there be my law giver.	Ovid's Elegies	2.17.24		
There Paris is, and Helens crymes record,	Ovid's Elegies	2.18.37		
What, are there Gods?	Ovid's Elegies	3.3.1		
Or if there be a God, he loves fine wenches,	Ovid's Elegies	3.3.25		
Came forth a mother, though a maide there put.	Ovid's Elegies	3.4.22		
There shalt be lov'd: Ilia lay feare aside.	Ovid's Elegies	3.5.62		
What sweete thought is there but I had the same?	Ovid's Elegies	3.6.63		
I heere and there go witty with dishonour.	Ovid's Elegies	3.7.8		
And some there be that thinke we have a deity.	Ovid's Elegies	3.8.18		
By secreat thoughts to thinke there is a god.	Ovid's Elegies	3.8.36		
This was [their] <there> meate, the soft grasse was their bed.	Ovid's Elegies	3.9.10		
There, he who rules the worlds starre-spangled towers,	Ovid's Elegies	3.9.21		
Where Ceres went each place was harvest there.	Ovid's Elegies	3.9.38		
There stands an old wood with thick trees darke clouded,	Ovid's Elegies	3.12.7		
Who sees it, graunts some deity there is shrowded.	Ovid's Elegies	3.12.8		
Shew large wayes with their garments there displayed.	Ovid's Elegies	3.12.24		
There use all tricks, and tread shame under feete.	Ovid's Elegies	3.13.18		
Be not ashamed to strippe you being there,	Ovid's Elegies	3.13.21		
There in your rosie lippes my tongue intombe,	Ovid's Elegies	3.13.23		

THERE (cont.)			
Practise a thousand sports when there you come,	Ovid's Elegies	3.13.24	
Forbare no wanton words you there would speake,	Ovid's Elegies	3.13.25	
And there for honie, bees have sought in vaine,	Hero and Leander	1.23	
And beat from thence, have lighted there againe.	Hero and Leander	1.24	
And with still panting rockt, there tooke his rest.	Hero and Leander	1.44	
Musaeus soong)/Dwelt at Abidus; since him, dwelt there none,	Hero and Leander	1.53	
Greefe makes her pale, because she mooves not there.	Hero and Leander	1.60	
There might you see one sigh, another rage,	Hero and Leander	1.125	
There might you see the gods in sundrie shapes,	Hero and Leander	1.143	
There Hero sacrificing turtles blood,	Hero and Leander	1.158	
and there God knowes I play/With Venus swannes and sparrowes	Hero and Leander	1.351	
And here and there her eies through anger rang'd.	Hero and Leander	1.360	
Home when he came, he seem'd not to be there,	Hero and Leander	2.117	
And dive into the water, and there prie/Upon his brest, his	Hero and Leander	2.188	
Yet there with Sysiphus he toyld in vaine,	Hero and Leander	2.277	
As from an orient cloud, glymse <glimps'd> here and there.	Hero and Leander	2.320	
THEREAT			
What if the Citizens repine thereat?	Dido	4.4.70	Anna
Frownst thou thereat, aspiring Lancaster,	Edw	1.1.93	Edward
Thereat she smild, and did denie him so,	Hero and Leander	1.311	
Thereat smilde Neptune, and then told a tale,	Hero and Leander	2.193	
THEREBY			
Yet will they reade me, and thereby attaine/To Peters Chayre:	Jew	Prol.11	Machvl
Deserv'd thereby with death to be tormented.	Ovid's Elegies	2.14.6	
honour, and thereby/Commit'st a sinne far worse than perjurie.	Hero and Leander	1.305	
As put thereby, yet might he hope for mo.	Hero and Leander	1.312	
THEREFOR			
therefor I pray you tell me, what is the thing you most desire	F1566	4.6.9	P Faust
THEREFORE (See also THERFORE)			
And therefore will take pitie on his toyle,	Dido	1.1.131	Venus
And therefore must of force.	Dido	5.1.101	Aeneas
Therefore unkind Aeneas, must thou say,	Dido	5.1.123	Dido
Therefore tis good and meete for to be wise.	1Tamb	1.1.34	Mycet
Therefore tis best, if so it lik you all,	1Tamb	1.1.51	Mycet
Therefore to stay all sodaine mutinies,	1Tamb	1.1.150	Ceneus
Therefore at least admit us libertie,	1Tamb	1.2.71	Zenoc
Therefore cheere up your mindes, prepare to fight,	1Tamb	2.2.29	Meandr
Therefore in pollicie I thinke it good/To hide it close:	1Tamb	2.4.10	Mycet
Therefore, for these our harmlesse virgines sakes,	1Tamb	5.1.18	Govnr
Therefore in that your safeties and our owne,	1Tamb	5.1.40	Govnr
Therefore Viceroies the Christians must have peace.	2Tamb	1.1.77	Orcan
Not for all Affrike, therefore moove me not.	2Tamb	1.2.12	Almeda
And therefore let them rest a while my Lord.	2Tamb	1.3.184	Usumc
And therefore Captaine, yeeld it quietly.	2Tamb	3.3.34	Techel
I would not yeeld it: therefore doo your worst.	2Tamb	3.3.37	Capt
Therefore die by thy loving mothers hand,	2Tamb	3.4.23	Olymp
And therefore stil augments his cruelty.	2Tamb	5.3.219	Tamb
And weigh not men, and therefore not mens words.	Jew	Prol.8	Machvl
And therefore farre exceeds my credit, Sir.	Jew	1.1.65	1Merch
Come therefore let us goe to Barrabas;	Jew	1.1.141	2Jew
And therefore are we to request your ayd.	Jew	1.2.49	Govnr
And therefore thus we are determined;	Jew	1.2.66	Govnr
And therefore ne're distinguish of the wrong.	Jew	1.2.151	Barab
To shun suspition, therefore, let us part.	Jew	2.1.57	Abigal
'Tis true, my Lord, therefore intreat him well.	Jew	2.2.8	1Knght
Therefore be rul'd by me, and keepe the gold:	Jew	2.2.39	Bosco
Not for all Malta, therefore sheath your sword;	Jew	2.3.270	Barab
This followes well, and therefore daughter feare not.	Jew	2.3.313	Barab
Hee's with your mother, therefore after him.	Jew	2.3.350	Barab
Oh therefore, Jacomo, let me be one,	Jew	3.3.68	Abigal
So I have heard; pray therefore keepe it close.	Jew	3.6.37	Abigal
Thou hast offended, therefore must be damn'd.	Jew	4.1.25	1Fryar
I am a Jew, and therefore am I lost.	Jew	4.1.57	Barab
One turn'd my daughter, therefore he shall dye;	Jew	4.1.119	Barab
Therefore 'tis not requisite he should live.	Jew	4.1.121	Barab
Why true, therefore did I place him there:	Jew	4.1.137	Barab
No Sir; and therefore I must have five hundred more.	Jew	4.3.22	P Pilia
I'le pledge thee, love, and therefore drinke it off.	Jew	4.4.1	Curtzn
Therefore he humbly would intreat your Highnesse/Not to depart	Jew	5.3.32	Msngr
Know therefore, till thy father hath made good/The ruines done	Jew	5.5.111	Govnr
And therefore as speedily as I can perfourme,	P 571	11.36	Navrre
in the next roome, therefore good my Lord goe not foorth.	P 995	19.65	P 3Mur
The Guise is slaine, and I rejoyce therefore:	P1078	19.148	King
No remedye, therefore prepare your selfe.	P1097	20.7	1Mur
therefore your entrye is mere Intrusione	Paris	ms13,p390	P Souldr
I have no warre, and therefore sir be gone.	Edw	1.1.36	Gavstn
Therefore ile have Italian maskes by night,	Edw	1.1.55	Gavstn
Therefore if he be come, expell him straight.	Edw	1.1.106	Lncstr
I yours, and therefore I would wish you graunt.	Edw	1.1.120	Edward
Therefore to equall it receive my hart.	Edw	1.1.162	Edward
We are no traitors, therefore threaten not.	Edw	1.4.25	MortSr
I see I must, and therefore am content.	Edw	1.4.85	Edward
And therefore sweete friend, take it patiently,	Edw	1.4.112	Edward
Therefore with dum imbracement let us part.	Edw	1.4.134	Edward
And therefore give me leave to looke my fill,	Edw	1.4.139	Edward
And therefore as thou lovest and tendrest me,	Edw	1.4.211	Queene
No speaking will prevaile, and therefore cease.	Edw	1.4.220	Penbrk
And therefore though I pleade for his repeall,	Edw	1.4.241	Mortmr
And therefore being pursued, it takes the aire:	Edw	2.2.25	Lncstr
And therefore let us jointlie here protest,	Edw	2.2.104	Lncstr
And therefore brother banish him for ever.	Edw	2.2.211	Kent
He is your brother, therefore have we cause/To cast the worst,	Edw	2.3.7	Warwck

THEREFORE (cont.)

was Plantagenet/False of his word, and therefore trust we thee.	Edw	2.3.12	Mortmr
Be easilie supprest: and therefore be gone.	Edw	2.4.45	Queene
And therefore gentle Mortimer be gone.	Edw	2.4.56	Queene
Therefore be gon in hast, and with advice,	Edw	3.1.264	Spencr
To die sweet Spencer, therefore live wee all,	Edw	4.7.111	Baldck
And therefore let me weare it yet a while.	Edw	5.1.83	Edward
And therefore say, will you resigne or no.	Edw	5.1.85	Trussl
Thinke therefore madam that imports [us] <as> much,	Edw	5.2.10	Mortmr
And therefore so the prince my sonne be safe,	Edw	5.2.17	Queene
And therefore trust him not.	Edw	5.2.107	Mortmr
Therefore come, dalliance dangereth our lives.	Edw	5.3.3	Matrvs
And therefore will I do it cunninglie.	Edw	5.4.5	Mortmr
And therefore soldiers whether will you hale me?	Edw	5.4.108	Kent
More then we can enflict, and therefore now,	Edw	5.5.11	Matrvs
Thou wilt returne againe, and therefore stay.	Edw	5.5.99	Edward
And therefore tell me, wherefore art thou come?	Edw	5.5.106	Edward
And therefore let us take horse and away.	Edw	5.5.115	Matrvs
growest penitent/Ile be thy ghostly father, therefore choose,	Edw	5.6.4	Mortmr
Betray us both, therefore let me flie.	Edw	5.6.8	Matrvs
And therefore we commit you to the Tower,	Edw	5.6.79	King
That bootes not, therefore gentle madam goe.	Edw	5.6.91	2Lord
As thou to live, therefore object it not.	F 162	1.1.134	Faust
This night I'le conjure tho I die therefore.	F 193	1.1.165	Faust
stand upon; therefore acknowledge your errour, and be attentive.	F 203	1.2.10	P Wagner
Therefore the shortest cut for conjuring/Is stoutly to abjure	F 280	1.3.52	Mephst
was> made for man; then he's <therefore is man> more excellent.	F 560	2.2.9	Mephst
cannot read, and therefore wish all books burn'd <were burnt>.	F 680	2.2.129	P Envy
Come therefore, let's away.	F 830	3.1.52	Faust
And therefore none of his Decrees can stand.	F 929	3.1.151	Pope
And therefore tho we would we cannot erre.	F 931	3.1.153	Pope
And therefore my Lord, so please your Majesty,	F1300	4.1.146	Faust
We have no reason for it, therefore a fig for him.	F1593	4.6.36	P Dick
therefore Master Doctor, if you will doe us so much <that>	F1684	5.1.11	P 1Schol
Therefore despaire, thinke onely upon hell;	F1881	5.2.85	Mephst
this therefore is my request, that thou let me see some proofe	F App	p.236 5	P Emper
If therefore thou, by cunning of thine Art,	F App	p.237 29	Emper
Therefore sweet Mephastophilis, let us make haste to Wertenberge	F App	p.239 94	Faust
I have beene wanton, therefore am perplext,	Ovid's Elegies	1.4.45	
Though it be so, shut me not out therefore,	Ovid's Elegies	1.6.47	
Could I therefore her comely tresses teare?	Ovid's Elegies	1.7.11	
Therefore who ere love sloathfulnesse doth call,	Ovid's Elegies	1.9.31	
I chid no more, she blusht, and therefore heard me,	Ovid's Elegies	1.13.47	
Therefore when flint and yron weare away,	Ovid's Elegies	1.15.31	
And therefore filles the bed she lies uppon:	Ovid's Elegies	2.4.34	
to detaine)/Thou oughtst therefore to scorne me for thy mate,	Ovid's Elegies	2.17.13	
Come therefore, and to long verse shorter frame.	Ovid's Elegies	3.1.66	
Therefore in signe her treasure suffred wracke,	Hero and Leander	1.49	
Well therefore by the gods decreed it is,	Hero and Leander	1.253	
And therefore to her tower he got by stealth.	Hero and Leander	2.18	
Therefore unto him hastily she goes,	Hero and Leander	2.45	
Therefore unto his bodie, hirs he clung,	Hero and Leander	2.65	
Therefore even as an Index to a booke,	Hero and Leander	2.129	
Had left the heavens, therefore on him hee seaz'd.	Hero and Leander	2.158	
And therefore let it rest upon thy pillow.	Hero and Leander	2.252	

THEREIN (See also THERIN)

to some religious house/So I may be baptiz'd and live therein.	Jew	4.1.76	Barab
I my good Lord, and will dye therein.	P1165	22.27	Frier
To gratifie the kings request therein,	Edw	2.5.75	Penbrk

THEREOF (See also THEROF)

And with the [wind] <wound> thereof the King fell downe:	Dido	2.1.254	Aeneas
And take in signe thereof this gilded wreath,	1Tamb	5.1.101	1Virgn
The scent thereof was death, I poyson'd it.	Jew	4.4.43	Barab
The price thereof will serve to entertaine/Selim and all his	Jew	5.3.30	Msngr
Either banish him that was the cause thereof,	Edw	1.4.60	ArchBp
And thereof came it, that the fleering Scots,	Edw	2.2.188	Lncstr
By heaven, and all the mooving orbes thereof,	Edw	3.1.129	Edward
If with the sight thereof she be not mooved,	Edw	5.1.119	Edward
Till further triall may be made thereof.	Edw	5.6.80	King
with me, and after meate/We'le canvase every quidditie thereof:	F 191	1.1.163	Faust
I have my Faustus, and for proofe thereof,	F 803	3.1.25	Mephst
And in the midst thereof, set my soule going,	Ovid's Elegies	2.10.36	
In midst thereof a stone-pav'd sacred spring,	Ovid's Elegies	3.1.3	

THEREON

Nor Sun reflexe his vertuous beames thereon,	1Tamb	3.1.52	Moroc
And thereon set the Diadem of Fraunce,	P 101	2.44	Guise
Shall being dead, be hangd thereon in chaines.	P 321	5.48	Anjoy
Not yet my Lord, for thereon doe they stay:	P 732	14.35	1Msngr
We often kisse it, often looke thereon,	Hero and Leander	2.81	
Thereon concluded that he was beloved.	Hero and Leander	2.220	

THERE'S

So then, there's somewhat come.	Jew	1.1.69	Barab
There's Kirriah Jairim, the great Jew of Greece,	Jew	1.1.124	Barab
But there's a meeting in the Senate-house,	Jew	1.1.167	2Jew
Soft Barabas, there's more longs too't than so.	Jew	1.2.45	Govnr
I must and will, Sir, there's no remedy.	Jew	1.2.391	Mthias
There's more, and more, and	Jew	2.1.46	P Abigal
Come home and there's no price shall make us part,	Jew	2.3.92	Barab
An hundred Crownes, I'le have him; there's the coyne.	Jew	2.3.130	Barab
Hold thee, wench, there's something for thee to spend.	Jew	3.1.12	Pilia
There's a darke entry where they take it in,	Jew	3.4.79	Barab
words, Sir, and send it you, were best see; there's his letter.	Jew	4.3.25	P Pilia
There's two crownes for thee, play.	Jew	4.4.47	Pilia

THERE'S (cont.)				
If it be not too free there's the question: . . .	P 813	17.8	P	Souldr
I see there's vertue in my heavenly words. . . .	F 255	1.3.27		Faust
There's none but I have interest in the same. . . .	F 637	2.2.86		Lucifr
I there's nc doubt of that, for me thinkes you make no hast to	F1516	4.5.12	P	Hostss
THERES (See also THERS)				
Theres not so much as this base tackling too, . . .	Dido	4.4.151		Dido
yf it be not to free theres the questione | now ser where he is	Paris	ms 9,p390	P	Souldr
Theres none here, but would run his horse to death. . .	Edw	1.4.207		Warwck
But he is banisht, theres small hope of him. . . .	Edw	2.1.15		Baldck
we deceive our selves, and there is <theres> no truth in us.	F 70	1.1.42	P	Faust
<Then theres inough for a thousand soules>, . . .	F 477	(HC260)A		Faust
Well, theres the second time, aware the third, I give you faire	F App	p.232 20	P	Faust
theres a Gentleman tarries to have his horse, and he would have	F App	p.233 6	P	Rafe
now theres a signe of grace in you, when you will confesse the	F App	p.237 44	P	Knight
theres no haste but good, are you remembred how you crossed me	F App	p.238 76	P	Faust
THERETO				
To one that can commaund what longs thereto: . . .	1Tamb	2.5.23		Cosroe
And urg'd thereto with my afflictions, ...	Jew	1.2.231		Abigal
If that the King had given consent thereto, . . .	P 33	1.33		Navrre
Much lesse can honour bee ascrib'd thereto, . . .	Hero and Leander			1.279
THEREUNTO				
yet for that love and duety bindes me thereunto, I am content	F App	p.236 15	P	Faust
THEREWITH				
That therewith all enchaunted like the guarde, . . .	Edw	3.1.266		Spencr
And therewith Caesar prone ennough to warre, . . .	Lucan, First Booke			293
O what god would not therewith be appeas'd? . . .	Hero and Leander			2.50
THEREWITH ALL				
That therewith all enchaunted like the guarde, . . .	Edw	3.1.266		Spencr
THEREWITHALL				
And therewithall he calde false Sinon forth, . . .	Dido	2.1.143		Aeneas
As therewithall the old man overcome, ...	Dido	2.1.157		Aeneas
Nor will I part so slightly therewithall.	Jew	1.2.87		Barab
Now let me know thy name, and therewithall/Thy birth, condition,	Jew	2.3.163		Barab
And therewithall their knees would rankle, so/That I have	Jew	2.3.210		Ithimr
Yet strivde she to be covered therewithall, . . .	Ovid's Elegies			1.5.14
Thinking to traine Leander therewithall.	Hero and Leander			2.12
THERFORE				
And therfore grieve not at your overthrow, . . .	1Tamb	5.1.446		Tamb
Therfore I tooke my course to Manico:	2Tamb	1.3.198		Techel
Come willinglie, therfore.	2Tamb	3.4.84		Techel
And so doe I, master, therfore speake 'em faire. . .	Jew	4.1.27		Ithimr
I, and our lives too, therfore pull amaine. . . .	Jew	4.1.150		Ithimr
enough, and therfore talke not to me of your Counting-house:	Jew	4.3.36	P	Pilia
And therfore meane to murder all I meet.	P 279	5.6		Anjoy
With Poland therfore must I covenant thus, ...	P 471	8.21		Anjoy
to speak with him/But cannot, and therfore am enforst to write,	P 663	13.7		Duchss
the Duke of Joyeux/Hath made great sute unto the King therfore.	P 734	14.37		1Msngr
Therfore an enemy to the Burbonites.	P 836	17.31		Guise
And therfore hated of the Protestants.	P 838	17.33		Guise
He is hard hearted, therfore pull with violence. . .	P1105	20.15		1Mur
THERIDAMAS				
Your Grace hath taken order by Theridamas, ...	1Tamb	1.1.46		Meandr
Then heare thy charge, valiant Theridamas, ...	1Tamb	1.1.57		Mycet
Go, stout Theridamas, thy words are swords, . . .	1Tamb	1.1.74		Mycet
Theridamas, farewel ten thousand times.	1Tamb	1.1.82		Mycet
And foot by foot follow Theridamas.	1Tamb	1.1.86		Mycet
And with the Armie of Theridamas, ...	1Tamb	1.1.176		Cosroe
As long as life maintaines Theridamas.	1Tamb	1.2.231		Therid
Theridamas my friend, take here my hand, ...	1Tamb	1.2.232		Tamb
Long may Theridamas remaine with us.	1Tamb	1.2.240		Usumc
Make much of them gentle Theridamas, ...	1Tamb	1.2.247		Tamb
A thousand thankes worthy Theridamas:	1Tamb	1.2.252		Tamb
Thus farre are we towards Theridamas, ...	1Tamb	2.1.1		Cosroe
When Tamburlain and brave Theridamas/Have met us by the river	1Tamb	2.1.62		Cosroe
Who brings that Traitors head Theridamas, ...	1Tamb	2.2.32		Meandr
my brothers Campe/I leave to thee, and to Theridamas, .	1Tamb	2.5.39		Cosroe
Usumcasane and Theridamas, ...	1Tamb	2.5.52		Tamb
Why say Theridamas, wilt thou be a king?	1Tamb	2.5.65		Tamb
Why then Theridamas, Ile first assay, ...	1Tamb	2.5.81		Tamb
Judge by thy selfe Theridamas, not me, ...	1Tamb	2.5.93		Tamb
What saith Theridamas?	1Tamb	2.5.105		Tamb
Treacherous and false Theridamas, ...	1Tamb	2.7.3		Cosroe
Theridamas and Tamburlaine, I die, ...	1Tamb	2.7.51		Cosroe
Theridamas, Techelles, and the rest, ...	1Tamb	2.7.55		Tamb
Wel said Theridamas, speake in that mood, ...	1Tamb	3.3.40		Tamb'
Not now Theridamas, her time is past:	1Tamb	3.3.228		Tamb
Theridamas, Techelles and Casane, here are the cates you desire	1Tamb	4.4.107	P	Tamb
I crowne you here (Theridamas) King of Argier: . . .	1Tamb	4.4.116	P	Tamb
Wel said Theridamas, when holy Fates/Shall stablish me in	1Tamb	4.4.134		Tamb
That will we chiefly see unto, Theridamas, ...	1Tamb	5.1.206		Tamb
Theridamas, Techelles, and Casane/Promist to meet me on Larissa	2Tamb	1.3.106		Tamb
Welcome Theridamas, king of Argier.	2Tamb	1.3.112		Tamb
Thanks good Theridamas.	2Tamb	1.3.117		Tamb
Well done Techelles: what saith Theridamas? . . .	2Tamb	1.3.206		Tamb
Casane and Theridamas to armes:	2Tamb	2.4.102		Tamb
Ah sweet Theridamas, say so no more, ...	2Tamb	2.4.126		Tamb
now come let us martch/Towards Techelles and Theridamas, .	2Tamb	3.2.146		Tamb
Both we (Theridamas) wil intrench our men, ...	2Tamb	3.3.49		Techel
Welcome Theridamas and Techelles both, ...	2Tamb	3.5.150		Tamb
hee is a king, looke to him Theridamas, when we are fighting,	2Tamb	3.5.154	P	Tamb
Theridamas, Techelles, and Casane, ...	2Tamb	4.1.159		Tamb
Take them away Theridamas, see them dispatcht. . . .	2Tamb	5.1.134		Tamb

THERIDAMAS (cont.)			
Theridamas, haste to the court of Jove, ...	2Tamb	5.3.61	Tamb
THERIN			
And he that meanes to place himselfe therin/Must armed wade up	2Tamb	1.3.83	Tamb
THEROF			
And therof many thousand he rehearses.	Ovid's Elegies		1.8.58
THER'S			
But look my Lord, ther's some in the Admirals house. .	P 297	5.24	Retes
where ther's such belly-cheere, as Wagner in his life nere saw	F1678	5.1.5	P Wagner
And fruit from trees, when ther's no wind at al. . .	Ovid's Elegies		3.6.34
THERS			
No sooner is it up, but thers a foule, ...	Edw	2.2.26	Lncstr
THERSITES			
Thersites did Protesilaus survive, ...	Ovid's Elegies		2.6.41
THESALIAN			
What, wast my limbs through some Thesalian charms, . .	Ovid's Elegies		3.6.27
THESE (See also THEISE)			
these linked gems,/My Juno ware	Dido	1.1.42	Jupitr
How may I credite these thy flattering termes, ...	Dido	1.1.109	Venus
shall have leaves and windfall bowes enow/Neere to these woods,	Dido	1.1.173	Aeneas
But what are you that aske of me these things? . . .	Dido	1.1.214	Venus
Doe trace these Libian deserts all despisde, ...	Dido	1.1.228	Aeneas
Or in these shades deceiv'st mine eye so oft? . . .	Dido	1.1.244	Aeneas
Where am I now? these should be Carthage walles. . .	Dido	2.1.1	Aeneas
and be revengde/On these hard harted Grecians, which rejoyce	Dido	2.1.19	Aeneas
For none of these can be our Generall.	Dido	2.1.46	Illion
Lovely Aeneas, these are Carthage walles, ...	Dido	2.1.62	Illion
And clad us in these wealthie robes we weare. . . .	Dido	2.1.65	Illion
Warlike Aeneas, and in these base robes?	Dido	2.1.79	Dido
These hands did helpe to hale it to the gates, . . .	Dido	2.1.170	Aeneas
To rid me from these melancholly thoughts.	Dido	2.1.303	Dido
And sticke these spangled feathers in thy hat, . . .	Dido	2.1.314	Venus
These milke white Doves shall be his Centronels: . . .	Dido	2.1.320	Venus
Sleepe my sweete nephew in these cooling shades, . . .	Dido	2.1.334	Venus
Free from the murmure of these running streames, . . .	Dido	2.1.335	Venus
Or whisking of these leaves, all shall be still, . . .	Dido	2.1.337	Venus
Lest with these sweete thoughts I melt cleane away. . .	Dido	3.1.76	Dido
And are not these as faire as faire may be?	Dido	3.1.140	Dido
But speake Aeneas, know you none of these?	Dido	3.1.148	Dido
No Madame, but it seemes that these are Kings. . . .	Dido	3.1.149	Aeneas
All these and others which I never sawe, ...	Dido	3.1.150	Dido
As these thy protestations doe paint forth, ...	Dido	3.2.54	Venus
More then melodious are these words to me, ...	Dido	3.2.62	Juno
let there be a match confirmd/Betwixt these two, whose loves	Dido	3.2.78	Juno
Faire Queene of love, I will devorce these doubts, . .	Dido	3.2.85	Juno
This day they both a hunting forth will ride/Into these woods,	Dido	3.2.88	Juno
forth will ride/Into these woods, adjoyning to these walles,	Dido	3.2.88	Juno
We two will talke alone, what words be these? . . .	Dido	3.3.12	Iarbus
men (Dido except)/Have taunted me in these opprobrious termes,	Dido	3.3.27	Iarbus
Meane time these wanton weapons serve my warre, . . .	Dido	3.3.37	Cupid
O how these irksome labours now delight, ...	Dido	3.3.56	Aeneas
Aeneas, leave these dumpes and lets away, ...	Dido	3.3.60	Dido
Aeneas, O Aeneas, quench these flames.	Dido	3.4.23	Dido
Never to leave these newe upreared walles, ...	Dido	3.4.49	Aeneas
Hold, take these Jewels at thy Lovers hand, ...	Dido	3.4.61	Dido
These golden bracelets, and this wedding ring, ...	Dido	3.4.62	Dido
Whiles these adulterors surfetted with sinne:	Dido	4.1.20	Iarbus
Redresse these wrongs, and warne him to his ships/That now	Dido	4.2.21	Iarbus
Servants, come fetch these emptie vessels here, . . .	Dido	4.2.49	Iarbus
For I will flye from these alluring eyes, ...	Dido	4.2.50	Iarbus
Commaunds me leave these unrenowmed [reames] <beames>, .	Dido	4.3.18	Aeneas
And I the Goddesse of all these, commaund/Aeneas ride as .	Dido	4.4.77	Dido
Are these the sailes that in despight of me, ...	Dido	4.4.126	Dido
These were the instruments that launcht him forth, . .	Dido	4.4.150	Dido
Was it not you that hoysed up these sailes?	Dido	4.4.153	Dido
And swim to Italy, Ile keepe these sure:	Dido	4.4.164	Dido
How now Aeneas, sad, what meanes these dumpes? . . .	Dido	5.1.62	Iarbus
And also furniture for these my men.	Dido	5.1.70	Aeneas
How loth I am to leave these Libian bounds, ...	Dido	5.1.81	Aeneas
swift Mercury/When I was laying a platforme for these walles,	Dido	5.1.94	Aeneas
These words proceed not from Aeneas heart.	Dido	5.1.102	Dido
These words are poyson to poore Didos soule, ...	Dido	5.1.111	Dido
And wofull Dido by these blubbred cheekes, ...	Dido	5.1.133	Dido
Ah sister, leave these idle fantasies, ...	Dido	5.1.262	Anna
have I found a meane/To rid me from these thoughts of Lunacie:	Dido	5.1.273	Dido
Now Dido, with these reliques burne thy selfe, ...	Dido	5.1.292	Dido
These letters, lines, and perjurd papers all, ...	Dido	5.1.300	Dido
O helpe Iarbus, Dido in these flames/Hath burnt her selfe, aye	Dido	5.1.314	Anna
That I may view these milk-white steeds of mine, . . .	1Tamb	1.1.77	Mycet
These are his words, Meander set them downe.	1Tamb	1.1.94	Mycet
To be reveng'd for these contemptuous words.	1Tamb	1.1.100	Mycet
Who traveiling with these Medean Lords/To Memphis, from my	1Tamb	1.2.11	Zenoc
But now you see these letters and commandes, ...	1Tamb	1.2.21	Tamb
And these that seeme but silly country Swaines, . . .	1Tamb	1.2.47	Tamb
These Lords (perhaps) do scorne our estimates, ...	1Tamb	1.2.61	Tamb
Are <To> <Ah> these resolved noble Scythians?	1Tamb	1.2.225	Therid
These are my friends in whom I more rejoice, ...	1Tamb	1.2.241	Tamb
of my company/Scowting abroad upon these champion plaines,	1Tamb	2.2.40	Spy
Then noble souldiors, to intrap these theeves, ...	1Tamb	2.2.59	Meandr
And these his two renowmed friends my Lord, ...	1Tamb	2.3.30	Therid
That I with these my friends and all my men, ...	1Tamb	2.3.43	Tamb
These are the wings shall make it flie as swift, . . .	1Tamb	2.3.57	Tamb
may I presume/To know the cause of these unquiet fits: .	1Tamb	3.2.2	Agidas

THESE (cont.)

[Agidas], leave to wound me with these words:	1Tamb	3.2.35		Zenoc
These are the cruell pirates of Argeire,	1Tamb	3.3.55		Tamb
How can ye suffer these indignities?	1Tamb	3.3.90		Moroc
Shall swallow up these base borne Perseans.	1Tamb	3.3.95		Bajzth
Triumphing over him and these his kings,	1Tamb	3.3.128		Tamb
As these my followers willingly would have:	1Tamb	3.3.155		Tamb
Thou wilt repent these lavish words of thine,	1Tamb	3.3.172		Zenoc
But if these threats moove not submission,	1Tamb	4.1.58		2Msngr
To make these captives reine their lavish tongues.	1Tamb	4.2.67		Techel
and she shal looke/That these abuses flow not from her tongue:	1Tamb	4.2.70		Zenoc
Let these be warnings for you then my slave,	1Tamb	4.2.72		Anippe
These Mores that drew him from Bythinia,	1Tamb	4.2.98		Tamb
you suffer these outragious curses by these slaves of yours?	1Tamb	4.4.26	P	Zenoc
you suffer these outragious curses by these slaves of yours?	1Tamb	4.4.27	P	Zenoc
I (my Lord) but none save kinges must feede with these.	1Tamb	4.4.110	P	Therid
Now take these three crownes, and pledge me, my contributorie	1Tamb	4.4.115	P	Tamb
say you to this (Turke) these are not your contributorie kings.	1Tamb	4.4.118	P	Tamb
Deserve these tytles I endow you with,	1Tamb	4.4.125		Tamb
Therefore, for these our harmlesse virgines sakes,	1Tamb	5.1.18		Govnr
These more than dangerous warrants of our death,	1Tamb	5.1.31		1Virgn
overweighing heavens/Have kept to qualifie these hot extreames,	1Tamb	5.1.46		Govnr
Graunt that these signes of victorie we yeeld/May bind the	1Tamb	5.1.55		2Virgn
O then for these, and such as we our selves,	1Tamb	5.1.96		1Virgn
straight goe charge a few of them/To chardge these Dames,	1Tamb	5.1.117		Tamb
I will not spare these proud Egyptians,	1Tamb	5.1.121		Tamb
If these had made one Poems period/And all combin'd in Beauties	1Tamb	5.1.169		Tamb
How are ye glutted with these grievous objects,	1Tamb	5.1.341		Zenoc
eies beholde/That as for her thou bearst these wretched armes,	1Tamb	5.1.409		Arabia
Even so for her thou diest in these armes:	1Tamb	5.1.410		Arabia
But here these kings that on my fortunes wait,	1Tamb	5.1.490		Tamb
Then after all these solemne Exequies,	1Tamb	5.1.533		Tamb
Egregious Viceroyes of these Eastern parts/Plac'd by the issue	2Tamb	1.1.1		Orcan
Bringing the strength of Europe to these Armes:	2Tamb	1.1.30		Orcan
The slaughtered bodies of these Christians.	2Tamb	1.1.36		Orcan
That hides these plaines, and seems as vast and wide,	2Tamb	1.1.107		Sgsmnd
let peace be ratified/On these conditions specified before,	2Tamb	1.1.125		Orcan
when wilt thou leave these armes/And save thy sacred person	2Tamb	1.3.9		Zenoc
When these my sonnes, more precious in mine eies/Than all the	2Tamb	1.3.18		Tamb
These words assure me boy, thou art my sonne,	2Tamb	1.3.58		Tamb
No Madam, these are speeches fit for us,	2Tamb	1.3.88		Celeb
Meaning to aid [thee] <them> in this <these> Turkish armes,	2Tamb	1.3.144		Techel
Now will we banquet on these plaines a while,	2Tamb	1.3.157		Tamb
These heathnish Turks and Pagans lately made,	2Tamb	2.1.6		Fredrk
And worke revenge upon these Infidels:	2Tamb	2.1.13		Fredrk
Take here these papers as our sacrifice/And witnesse of thy	2Tamb	2.2.45		Orcan
watch and ward shall keepe his trunke/Amidst these plaines,	2Tamb	2.3.39		Orcan
Let me take leave of these my loving sonnes,	2Tamb	2.4.72		Zenoc
Sindge these fair plaines, and make them seeme as black/As is	2Tamb	3.2.11		Tamb
The towers and cities of these hatefull Turks,	2Tamb	3.2.148		Tamb
These Pioners of Argier in Affrica,	2Tamb	3.3.20		Therid
Captaine, these Moores shall cut the leaden pipes,	2Tamb	3.3.29		Techel
These barbarous Scythians full of cruelty,	2Tamb	3.4.19		Olymp
in their glories shine the golden crownes/Of these proud Turks,	2Tamb	4.1.2		Amyras
When made a victor in these hautie arms,	2Tamb	4.1.46		Amyras
Shal we let goe these kings again my Lord/To gather greater	2Tamb	4.1.82		Amyras
these terrours and these tyrannies/(If tyrannies wars justice	2Tamb	4.1.146		Tamb
Ransacke the tents and the pavilions/Of these proud Turks, and	2Tamb	4.1.161		Tamb
And thus be drawen with these two idle kings.	2Tamb	4.3.28		Amyras
While these their fellow kings may be refresht.	2Tamb	4.3.31		Tamb
Your Majesty must get some byts for these,	2Tamb	4.3.43		Therid
to restraine/These coltish coach-horse tongues from blasphemy.	2Tamb	4.3.52		Usumc
For I wil cast my selfe from off these walles,	2Tamb	5.1.40		2Citzn
Call up the souldiers to defend these wals.	2Tamb	5.1.56		Govnr
Drawen with these kings on heaps of carkasses.	2Tamb	5.1.72		Tamb
These Jades are broken winded, and halfe tyr'd,	2Tamb	5.1.129		Tamb
And make him after all these overthrowes,	2Tamb	5.2.29		Callap
These cowards invisiblie assaile hys soule,	2Tamb	5.3.13		Therid
Ah good my Lord, leave these impatient words,	2Tamb	5.3.54		Therid
That these my boies may finish all my wantes.	2Tamb	5.3.125		Tamb
The nature of these proud rebelling Jades/Wil take occasion by	2Tamb	5.3.238		Tamb
These are the Blessings promis'd to the Jewes,	Jew	1.1.105		Barab
For he can counsell best in these affaires;	Jew	1.1.142		2Jew
These silly men mistake the matter cleane.	Jew	1.1.179		Barab
These taxes and afflictions are befal'ne,	Jew	1.2.65		Govnr
and gather of these goods/The mony for this tribute of the	Jew	1.2.155		Govnr
And hide these extreme sorrowes from mine eyes:	Jew	1.2.195		Barab
See the simplicitie of these base slaves,	Jew	1.2.214		Barab
But I will learne to leave these fruitlesse teares,	Jew	1.2.230		Abigal
the plight/Wherein these Christians have oppressed me:	Jew	1.2.271		Barab
now Abigall, what mak'st thou/Amongst these hateful Christians?	Jew	1.2.339		Barab
What wilt thou doe among these hatefull fiends?	Jew	1.2.345		Barab
I charge thee on my blessing that thou leave/These divels, and	Jew	1.2.347		Barab
poore Barabas/With fatall curses towards these Christians.	Jew	2.1.6		Barab
Singing ore these, as she does ore her young.	Jew	2.1.63		Barab
But to admit a sale of these thy Turkes/We may not, nay we dare	Jew	2.2.21		Govnr
will follow thee/Against these barbarous mis-beleeving Turkes.	Jew	2.2.46		Govnr
In spite of these swine-eating Christians,	Jew	2.3.7		Barab
not a stone of beef a day will maintaine you in these chops;	Jew	2.3.125	P	Barab
First be thou voyd of these affections,	Jew	2.3.169		Barab
These armes of mine shall be thy Sepulchre.	Jew	3.2.11		Govnr
Looke, Katherin, looke, thy sonne gave mine these wounds.	Jew	3.2.16		Govnr
And these my teares to blood, that he might live.	Jew	3.2.19		Govnr

THESE (cont.)

Yet never shall these lips bewray thy life.	Jew	3.3.75	Abigal
Malta to a wildernesse/For these intolerable wrongs of yours;	Jew	3.5.26	Basso
Have I debts owing; and in most of these,	Jew	4.1.73	Barab
But are not both these wise men to suppose/That I will leave my	Jew	4.1.122	Barab
No god-a-mercy, shall I have these crownes?	Jew	4.3.31	Pilia
besides the slaughter of these Gentlemen, poyson'd his owne	Jew	5.1.12	P Pilia
As these have spoke so be it to their soules:--	Jew	5.1.42	Barab
and Barabas we give/To guard thy person, these our Janizaries:	Jew	5.2.16	Calym
To prison with the Governour and these/Captaines, his consorts	Jew	5.2.23	Barab
How stand the cords? How hang these hinges, fast?	Jew	5.5.1	Barab
Knit in these hands, thus joyn'd in nuptiall rites,	P 4	1.4	Charls
How they did storme at these your nuptiall rites,	P 49	1.49	Admral
That makes these upstart heresies in Fraunce:	P 81	2.24	Guise
Considering of these dangerous times.	P 175	3.10	Admral
O gracious God, what times are these?	P 188	3.23	Navrre
These are the cursed Guisians that doe seeke our death.	P 201	3.36	Admral
Then pittie or releeve these upstart hereticks.	P 222	4.20	Guise
I hope these reasons may serve my princely Sonne,	P 223	4.21	QnMoth
He that wantes these, and is suspected of heresie,	P 234	4.32	Guise
Ah my good Lord, these are the Guisians,	P 260	4.58	Admral
Are you a preacher of these heresies?	P 340	5.67	Guise
For if these straglers gather head againe,	P 506	9.25	QnMoth
And now my Lords after these funerals be done,	P 561	11.26	QnMoth
And now Navarre whilste that these broiles doe last,	P 565	11.30	Navrre
That it might print these lines within his heart.	P 669	13.13	Duchss
Are these your secrets that no man must know?	P 678	13.22	Guise
Thou trothles and unjust, what lines are these?	P 680	13.24	Guise
But villaine he to whom these lines should goe,	P 696	13.40	Guise
We undertake to mannage these our warres/Against the proud	P 699	14.2	Navrre
To leavy armes and make these civill broyles:	P 730	14.33	Navrre
In prosecution of these cruell armes,	P 796	16.10	Navrre
Now Captain of my guarde, are these murtherers ready?	P 947	19.17	King
These two will make one entire Duke of Guise,	P1060	19.130	King
see where she comes, as if she droupt/To heare these newes.	P1063	19.133	Eprnon
And sends <send> his dutie by these speedye lines,	P1169	22.31	Frier
What irreligeous Pagans partes be these,	P1180	22.42	King
These bloudy hands shall teare his triple Crowne,	P1199	22.61	King
These words revive my thoughts and comforts me,	P1209	22.71	Navrre
Henry thy King wipes of these childish teares,	P1236	22.98	King
Fire Paris where these trecherous rebels lurke.	P1241	22.103	King
Sweete prince I come, these these thy amorous lines,	Edw	1.1.6	Gavstn
But how now, what are these?	Edw	1.1.24	Gavstn
I, I, these wordes of his move me as much,	Edw	1.1.39	Gavstn
Ile flatter these, and make them live in hope:	Edw	1.1.43	Gavstn
these are not men for me,/I must have wanton Poets, pleasant	Edw	1.1.50	Gavstn
Such things as these best please his majestie,	Edw	1.1.71	Gavstn
Ile have my will, and these two Mortimers,	Edw	1.1.78	Edward
Well Mortimer, ile make thee rue these words,	Edw	1.1.91	Edward
And hew these knees that now are growne so stiffe.	Edw	1.1.95	Edward
These will I sell to give my souldiers paye,	Edw	1.1.104	Lncstr
Brother revenge it, and let these their heads,	Edw	1.1.117	Kent
I cannot brooke these hautie menaces:	Edw	1.1.134	Edward
My lord, these titles far exceed my worth.	Edw	1.1.157	Gavstn
the least of these may well suffice/For one of greater birth	Edw	1.1.158	Kent
Cease brother, for I cannot brooke these words:	Edw	1.1.160	Edward
If for these dignities thou be envied,	Edw	1.1.163	Edward
Tis true, and but for reverence of these robes,	Edw	1.1.180	Gavstn
Or I will presentlie discharge these lords,	Edw	1.4.61	ArchBp
For these thy superstitious taperlights,	Edw	1.4.98	Edward
Wherein my lord, have I deservd these words?	Edw	1.4.163	Queene
Be thou my advocate unto these peeres.	Edw	1.4.212	Queene
Diablo, what passions call you these?	Edw	1.4.319	Lncstr
No other jewels hang about my neck/Then these my lord, nor let	Edw	1.4.331	Queene
My gentle lord, bespeake these nobles faire,	Edw	1.4.337	Queene
These silver haires will more adorne my court,	Edw	1.4.346	Edward
I am none of these common [pedants] <pendants> I,	Edw	2.1.52	Baldck
Stil wil these Earles and Barrons use me thus?	Edw	2.2.70	Edward
My Lord I cannot brooke these injuries.	Edw	2.2.71	Gavstn
Aye me poore soule when these begin to jarre.	Edw	2.2.72	Queene
Warwicke, these words do ill beseeme thy years.	Edw	2.2.94	Kent
Tis warre that must abate these Barons pride.	Edw	2.2.99	Edward
We never beg, but use such praiers as these.	Edw	2.2.153	Mortmr
How oft have I beene baited by these peeres?	Edw	2.2.201	Edward
Yet, shall the crowing of these cockerels,	Edw	2.2.203	Edward
Heere comes she thats cause of all these jarres.	Edw	2.2.224	Edward
But let them go, and tell me what are these.	Edw	2.2.239	Edward
Let us with these our followers scale the walles,	Edw	2.3.18	Lncstr
Or that these teares that drissell from mine eyes,	Edw	2.4.19	Queene
These hands are tir'd, with haling of my lord/From Gaveston,	Edw	2.4.26	Queene
Corrupter of thy king, cause of these broiles,	Edw	2.5.10	Mortmr
Will not these delaies beget my hopes?	Edw	2.5.47	Gavstn
And drives his nobles to these exigents/For Gaveston, will if	Edw	2.5.62	Warwck
I see it is your life these armes pursue.	Edw	2.6.2	James
would I beare/These braves, this rage, and suffer uncontrowld	Edw	3.1.13	Spencr
suffer uncontrowld/These Barons thus to beard me in my land,	Edw	3.1.14	Spencr
These be the letters, this the messenger.	Edw	3.1.65	Queene
Upon these Barons, harten up your men,	Edw	3.1.124	Spencr
My [lords] <lord>, perceive you how these rebels swell:	Edw	3.1.181	Edward
These lustie leaders Warwicke and Lancaster,	Edw	3.1.246	Edward
Thats it these Barons and the subtill Queene,	Edw	3.1.272	Levune
These Barons lay their heads on blocks together,	Edw	3.1.274	Baldck
His grace I dare presume will welcome me,/But who are these?	Edw	4.2.34	Queene

THESE (cont.)

These comforts that you give our wofull queene,	Edw	4.2.72		Kent
How now, what newes with thee, from whence come these?	Edw	4.3.24		Edward
When we may meet these traitors in the field.	Edw	4.3.47		Edward
and withall/We may remoove these flatterers from the king,	Edw	4.4.26		Mortmr
My lord of Kent, what needes these questions?	Edw	4.6.34		Mortmr
To follow these rebellious runnagates.	Edw	4.6.76		Mortmr
O might I never open these eyes againe,	Edw	4.7.41		Edward
A king to beare these words and proud commaunds.	Edw	4.7.71		Abbot
For friends hath Edward none, but these, and these,	Edw	4.7.91		Edward
And these must die under a tyrants sword.	Edw	4.7.92		Edward
My lord, be going, care not for these,	Edw	4.7.93		Rice
keepe these preachments till you come to the place appointed.	Edw	4.7.113	P	Rice
Their bloud and yours shall seale these treacheries.	Edw	5.1.89		Edward
these innocent hands of mine/Shall not be guiltie of so foule a	Edw	5.1.98		Edward
Whome I esteeme as deare as these mine eyes,	Edw	5.2.18		Queene
O levell all your lookes upon these daring men,	Edw	5.3.39		Edward
But yet I have a braver way then these.	Edw	5.4.37		Ltborn
These lookes of thine can harbor nought but death.	Edw	5.5.73		Edward
These handes were never stainde with innocent bloud,	Edw	5.5.81		Ltborn
For not these ten daies have these eyes lids closd.	Edw	5.5.94		Edward
Awaye with her, her wordes inforce these teares,	Edw	5.6.85		King
And let these teares distilling from mine eyes,	Edw	5.6.101		King
These Metaphisicks of Magitians,	F 76	1.1.48		Faust
I these are those that Faustus most desires.	F 79	1.1.51		Faust
Lord and Commander of these elements.	F 104	1.1.76		BdAngl
Faustus, these bookes, thy wit, and our experience,	F 146	1.1.118		Valdes
And have these joies in full possession.	F 179	1.1.151		Faust
But leaving these vaine trifles of mens soules,	F 289	1.3.61		Faust
O Faustus leave these frivolous demandes,	F 309	1.3.81		Mephst
Go beare these <those> tydings to great Lucifer,	F 315	1.3.87		Faust
Well sirra, leave your jesting, and take these Guilders.	F 367	1.4.25	P	Wagner
what of these <them>?	F 405	2.1.17		Faust
I Faustus, and do greater things then these.	F 476	2.1.88		Mephst
On these conditions following:	F 484	2.1.96	P	Faust
by these presents doe give both body and soule to Lucifer,	F 493	2.1.105	P	Faust
and twentie yeares being expired, and these <the> Articles.	F 496	2.1.108	P	Faust
Within the bowels of these Elements,	F 508	2.1.120		Mephst
[Tush] <No>, these are trifles, and meere old wives Tales.	F 524	2.1.136		Faust
The iterating of these lines brings gold;	F 544	2.1.156		Mephst
<Tush>, These slender questions <trifles> Wagner can decide:	F 600	2.2.49		Faust
[Tush], these are fresh mens [suppositions] <questions>:	F 606	2.2.55	P	Faust
run up and downe the world with these <this> case of Rapiers,	F 688	2.2.137	P	Wrath
My godfathers were these:	F 698	2.2.147	P	Glutny
How am I vexed by these villaines Charmes?	F1117	3.3.30		Mephst
Onely for pleasure of these damned slaves.	F1119	3.3.32		Mephst
These gracious words, most royall Carolus,	F1217	4.1.63		Faust
These are but shadowes, not substantiall.	F1259	4.1.105		Faust
No Art, no cunning, to present these Lords,	F1295	4.1.141		Faust
'sbloud I am never able to endure these torments.	F1307	4.1.153	P	Benvol
O may these eye-lids never close againe,	F1332	4.2.8		Benvol
Go horse these traytors on your fiery backes,	F1403	4.2.79		Faust
Make hast to help these noble Gentlemen,	F1421	4.2.97		1Soldr
For loe these Trees remove at my command,	F1426	4.2.102		Faust
He'd joyne long Asses eares to these huge hornes,	F1449	4.3.19		Benvol
I have a Castle joyning neere these woods,	F1452	4.3.22		Benvol
I beseech your Worship accept of these forty Dollors.	F1457	4.4.1	P	HrsCsr
Confound these passions with a quiet sleepe:	F1481	4.4.25		Faust
best beere in Europe, what ho, Hostis; where be these Whores?	F1506	4.5.2	P	Carter
for these pleasant sights, nor know I how sufficiently to	F1558	4.6.1	P	Duke
Here, now taste yee these, they should be good, for they come	F1576	4.6.19	P	Faust
is barren of his fruite, from whence you had these ripe grapes.	F1580	4.6.23	P	Duke
spirit that I have, I had these grapes brought as you see.	F1586	4.6.29	P	Faust
Those <These> thoughts that do disswade me from my vow,	F1764	5.1.91		Faust
Here will I dwell, for heaven is <be> in these lippes,	F1773	5.1.100		Faust
remember that I have beene a student here these thirty yeares,	F1841	5.2.45	P	Faust
These, that are fed with soppes of flaming fire,	F1916	5.2.120		BdAngl
But yet all these are nothing, thou shalt see/Ten thousand	F1919	5.2.123		BdAngl
With dreadfull horror of these damned fiends.	F1994	5.3.12		3Schol
holde, take these gilders.	F App	p.230 30	P	Wagner
have as many english counters, and what should I do with these?	F App	p.230 35	P	Clown
I can do al these things easily with it:	F App	p.234 22	P	Robin
How am I vexed with these vilaines charmes?	F App	p.235 37		Mephst
Onely for pleasure of these damned slaves.	F App	p.235 39		Mephst
Sure these are no spirites, but the true substantiall bodies of	F App	p.238 64	P	Emper
Confound these passions with a quiet sleepe:	F App	p.240 124		Faust
in the month of January, how you shuld come by these grapes.	F App	p.242 18	P	Duke
These plagues arise from wreake of civill power.	Lucan, First Booke	32		
plaine not heavens, but gladly beare these evils/For Neros sake:	Lucan, First Booke	37		
Adde, Caesar, to these illes Perusian famine;	Lucan, First Booke	41		
Yet Room is much bound to these civil armes,	Lucan, First Booke	44		
The causes first I purpose to unfould/Of these garboiles,	Lucan, First Booke	68		
O Roome thy selfe art cause of all these evils,	Lucan, First Booke	84		
These Captaines emulous of each others glory.	Lucan, First Booke	120		
Day rose and viewde these tumultes of the war;	Lucan, First Booke	235		
Yet for long service done, reward these men,	Lucan, First Booke	341		
Whether now shal these olde bloudles soules repaire?	Lucan, First Booke	343		
say Pompey, are these worse/Then Pirats of Sycillia?	Lucan, First Booke	346		
spread these flags that ten years space have conquer'd,	Lucan, First Booke	348		
Neither spoile, nor kingdom seeke we by these armes,	Lucan, First Booke	351		
mainly throw the dart; wilt thou indure/These purple groomes?	Lucan, First Booke	366		
by these ten blest ensignes/And all thy several triumphs,	Lucan, First Booke	375		
These troupes should soone pull down the church of Jove.	Lucan, First Booke	381		

THESE (cont.)
These hands shall thrust the ram, and make them flie, — Lucan, First Booke 385
Doubtles these northren men/Whom death the greatest of all — Lucan, First Booke 454
These being come, their huge power made him bould/To mannage — Lucan, First Booke 462
and that Roome/He looking on by these men should be sackt. — Lucan, First Booke 480
Wel might these feare, when Pompey fear'd and fled. — Lucan, First Booke 519
To these ostents (as their old custome was)/They call — Lucan, First Booke 583
While these thus in and out had circled Roome, — Lucan, First Booke 604
These direful signes made Aruns stand amaz'd, — Lucan, First Booke 615
By these he seeing what myschiefes must ensue, — Lucan, First Booke 629
Many a yeare these [furious] <firious> broiles let last, — Lucan, First Booke 667
These sad presages were enough to scarre/The quivering Romans, — Lucan, First Booke 672
For these before the rest preferreth he: — Ovid's Elegies 1.1.2
Thou with these souldiers conquerest gods and men, — Ovid's Elegies 1.2.37
Take these away, where is thy <thine> honor then? — Ovid's Elegies 1.2.38
Who feares these armes? who wil not go to meete them? — Ovid's Elegies 1.6.39
Come breake these deafe dores with thy boysterous wind. — Ovid's Elegies 1.6.54
And with my brand these gorgeous houses burne. — Ovid's Elegies 1.6.58
Deserved chaines these cursed hands shall fetter, — Ovid's Elegies 1.7.28
these words she sayd/While closely hid betwixt two dores I — Ovid's Elegies 1.8.21
Shake off these wrinckles that thy front assault, — Ovid's Elegies 1.8.45
Receive these lines, them to my Mistrisse carry, — Ovid's Elegies 1.11.7
To these my love I foolishly committed/And then with sweete — Ovid's Elegies 1.12.21
I cryed, tis sinne, tis sinne, these haires to burne, — Ovid's Elegies 1.14.27
Some one of these might make the chastest fall. — Ovid's Elegies 2.4.32
To these, or some of these like was her colour, — Ovid's Elegies 2.5.41
The Parrat into wood receiv'd with these, — Ovid's Elegies 2.6.57
The little stones these little verses have. — Ovid's Elegies 2.6.60
Greater then these my selfe I not esteeme, — Ovid's Elegies 2.8.13
But in the ayre let these words come to nought, — Ovid's Elegies 2.14.41
Unlesse I erre to these thou more incline, — Ovid's Elegies 2.18.39
Swift Atalantas flying legges like these, — Ovid's Elegies 3.2.29
Ere these were seene, I burnt: what will these do? — Ovid's Elegies 3.2.33
By these I judge, delight me may the rest, — Ovid's Elegies 3.2.35
Never can these by any meanes agree. — Ovid's Elegies 3.4.42
One Deianira was more worth then these. — Ovid's Elegies 3.5.38
Her trembling mouth these unmeete sounds expresses. — Ovid's Elegies 3.5.72
Perchance these, others, me mine owne losse mooves. — Ovid's Elegies 3.5.100
With these thy soule walkes, soules if death release, — Ovid's Elegies 3.8.65
These gifts are meete to please the powers divine. — Ovid's Elegies 3.9.48
These hardned me, with what I keepe obscure, — Ovid's Elegies 3.10.27
Some other seeke, who will these things endure. — Ovid's Elegies 3.10.28
These lovers parled by the touch of hands, — Hero and Leander 1.185
These arguments he us'de, and many more, — Hero and Leander 1.329
Aye me, such words as these should I abhor, — Hero and Leander 1.339
These he regarded not, but did intreat, — Hero and Leander 1.451
These greedie lovers had, at their first meeting. — Hero and Leander 2.24
As pittying these lovers, downeward creepes. — Hero and Leander 2.100
O that these tardie armes of mine were wings, — Hero and Leander 2.205
At least vouchsafe these armes some little roome, — Hero and Leander 2.249
And if these pleasures may thee <things thy minde may> move, — Passionate Shepherd 19
If these delights thy minde may move; — Passionate Shepherd 23

THESEUS
when she bewayles/Her perjur'd Theseus flying vowes and sayles, — Ovid's Elegies 1.7.16

TH'ESPERIDES
Entred the orchard of Th'esperides, — Hero and Leander 2.298

THESSALE
She magick arts and Thessale charmes doth know, — Ovid's Elegies 1.8.5
No faithlesse witch in Thessale waters bath'd thee. — Ovid's Elegies 1.14.40

THESSALIAN (See also THESALIAN)
to their soules I think/As are Thessalian drugs or Mithradate. — 1Tamb 5.1.133 Tamb
Wars worse then civill on Thessalian playnes, — Lucan, First Booke 1

THESSALY
This was the wealthie King of Thessaly, — Dido 3.1.161 Dido

TH'ETERNALL
And race th'eternall Register of time: — Dido 3.2.7 Juno
Insooth th'eternall powers graunt maides society/Falsely to — Ovid's Elegies 3.3.11

THETHER
And see at home much, that thou nere broughtst thether. — Ovid's Elegies 3.4.48
Hearing her to be sicke, I thether ranne, — Ovid's Elegies 3.10.25
Though thether leades a rough steepe hilly way. — Ovid's Elegies 3.12.6

THETIS
And call both Thetis and [Cimothoe] <Cimodoae> <Cymodoce>,/To — Dido 1.1.132 Venus
Then Thetis hangs about Apolloes necke, — Dido 3.1.132 Dido
Shall hide his head in Thetis watery lap, — 2Tamb 1.3.169 Tamb
Like lovely Thetis in a Christall robe: — 2Tamb 3.4.51 Therid
If watry Thetis had her childe fordone? — Ovid's Elegies 2.14.14
Who doubts, with Pelius, Thetis did consort, — Ovid's Elegies 2.17.17
If Thetis, and the morne their sonnes did waile, — Ovid's Elegies 3.8.1
That now should shine on Thetis glassie bower, — Hero and Leander 2.203

TH'ETRURIAN
(as their old custome was)/They call th'Etrurian Augures, — Lucan, First Booke 584

TH'EVERLASTING
his promise, did despise/The love of th'everlasting Destinies. — Hero and Leander 1.462

THEY'
held up, all joyntly cryde/They'ill follow where he please: — Lucan, First Booke 389

THEY (See also TH, TH'AD, THAILE, THEILE)
When as they would have hal'd thee from my sight: — Dido 1.1.27 Jupitr
That they may trip more lightly ore the lawndes, — Dido 1.1.207 Venus
And they so wrackt and weltred by the waves, — Dido 1.1.223 Aeneas
In multitudes they swarme unto the shoare, — Dido 1.2.36 Serg
My selfe will see they shall not trouble ye, — Dido 1.2.38 Iarbus
Leave to lament lest they laugh at our feares. — Dido 2.1.38 Achat

THEY (cont.)

Where when they came, Ulysses on the sand/Assayd with honey	Dido	2.1.136		Aeneas
Where meeting with the rest, kill kill they cryed.	Dido	2.1.190		Aeneas
Father of fiftie sonnes, but they are slaine,	Dido	2.1.234		Aeneas
We heare they led her captive into Greece.	Dido	2.1.295		Achat
I was as farre from love, as they from hate.	Dido	3.1.167		Dido
Why should not they then joyne in marriage,	Dido	3.2.74		Juno
This day they both a hunting forth will ride/Into these woods,	Dido	3.2.87		Juno
Whil'st they were sporting in this darksome Cave?	Dido	4.1.24		Iarbus
They say Aeneas men are going abourd,	Dido	4.4.2		Dido
Unworthie are they of a Queenes reward:	Dido	4.4.12		Dido
See where they come, how might I doe to chide?	Dido	4.4.13		Dido
The ayre wherein they breathe, the water, fire,	Dido	4.4.75		Dido
All that they have, their lands, their goods, their lives,	Dido	4.4.76		Dido
Why burst you not, and they fell in the seas?	Dido	4.4.154		Dido
And they shall have what thing so ere thou needst.	Dido	5.1.74		Iarbus
or to what end/Launcht from the haven, lye they in the Rhode?	Dido	5.1.89		Dido
Then gan they drive into the Ocean,	Dido	5.1.231		Anna
They gan to move him to redresse my ruth,	Dido	5.1.238		Anna
That they may melt and I fall in his armes:	Dido	5.1.245		Dido
They may be still tormented with unrest,	Dido	5.1.305		Dido
Unlesse they have a wiser king than you.	1Tamb	1.1.92		Cosroe
Unlesse they have a wiser king than you?	1Tamb	1.1.93		Mycet
Or if they would, there are in readines/Ten thousand horse to	1Tamb	1.1.184		Ortyg
For they are friends that help to weane my state,	1Tamb	1.2.29		Tamb
As princely Lions when they rouse themselves,	1Tamb	1.2.52		Techel
But since they measure our deserts so meane,	1Tamb	1.2.63		Tamb
They shall be kept our forced followers,	1Tamb	1.2.66		Tamb
Till with their eies [they] <thee> view us Emperours.	1Tamb	1.2.67		Tamb
But are they rich? And is their armour good?	1Tamb	1.2.123		Tamb
And looke we friendly on them when they come:	1Tamb	1.2.141		Tamb
But if they offer word or violence,	1Tamb	1.2.142		Tamb
When with their fearfull tongues they shall confesse/Theise are	1Tamb	1.2.222		Usumc
And they will never leave thee till the death.	1Tamb	1.2.248		Tamb
They gather strength by power of fresh supplies.	1Tamb	2.2.21		Meandr
Suppose they be in number infinit,	1Tamb	2.2.43		Meandr
They knew not, ah, they knew not simple men,	1Tamb	2.4.2		Mycet
They cannot take away my crowne from me.	1Tamb	2.4.14		Mycet
I thinke the pleasure they enjoy in heaven/Can not compare with	1Tamb	2.5.58		Therid
I know they would with our perswasions.	1Tamb	2.5.80		Therid
Then thou for Parthia, they for Scythia and Medea.	1Tamb	2.5.83		Tamb
They say he is the King of Persea.	1Tamb	3.1.45		Argier
Which dies my lookes so livelesse as they are.	1Tamb	3.2.15		Zenoc
They sung for honor gainst Pierides,	1Tamb	3.2.51		Zenoc
are ful of brags/And menace more than they can wel performe:	1Tamb	3.3.4		Tamb
and my souldiers looke/As if they meant to conquer Affrica.	1Tamb	3.3.10		Tamb
For when they perish by our warlike hands,	1Tamb	3.3.24		Techel
Europe, and pursue/His scattered armie til they yeeld or die.	1Tamb	3.3.39		Therid
And when they chance to breath and rest a space,	1Tamb	3.3.51		Tamb
That they lie panting on the Gallies side,	1Tamb	3.3.53		Tamb
And strive for life at every stroke they give.	1Tamb	3.3.54		Tamb
Who, when they come unto their fathers age,	1Tamb	3.3.110		Bajzth
If they should yeeld their necks unto the sword,	1Tamb	3.3.142		Bajzth
For we will scorne they should come nere our selves.	1Tamb	3.3.186		Zenoc
Where they shall meete, and joine their force in one,	1Tamb	3.3.257		Tamb
If they would lay their crownes before my feet,	1Tamb	4.2.93		Tamb
And when they see me march in black aray.	1Tamb	4.2.119		Tamb
While they walke quivering on their citie walles,	1Tamb	4.4.3		Tamb
Halfe dead for feare before they feele my wrath:	1Tamb	4.4.4		Tamb
If with their lives they will be pleasde to yeeld,	1Tamb	4.4.89		Tamb
Casane, here are the cates you desire to finger, are they not?	1Tamb	4.4.108	P	Tamb
Nor shall they long be thine, I warrant them.	1Tamb	4.4.119		Bajzth
And they are worthy she investeth kings.	1Tamb	4.4.129		Tamb
Had never bene erected as they bee,	1Tamb	5.1.32		1Virgn
They know my custome:	1Tamb	5.1.67		Tamb
could they not as well/Have sent ye out, when first my	1Tamb	5.1.67		Tamb
They have refusde the offer of their lives,	1Tamb	5.1.126		Tamb
They have my Lord, and on Damascus wals/Have hoisted up their	1Tamb	5.1.130		Techel
If all the heavenly Quintessence they still/From their	1Tamb	5.1.165		Tamb
See, se Anippe if they breathe or no.	1Tamb	5.1.343		Zenoc
And they will (trembling) sound a quicke retreat,	2Tamb	1.1.150		Orcan
Bewraies they are too dainty for the wars.	2Tamb	1.3.28		Tamb
But that I know they issued from thy wombe,	2Tamb	1.3.33		Tamb
My gratious Lord, they have their mothers looks,	2Tamb	1.3.35		Zenoc
But when they list, their conquering fathers hart:	2Tamb	1.3.36		Zenoc
And shine in compleat vertue more than they,	2Tamb	1.3.51		Tamb
They are enough to conquer all the world/And you have won	2Tamb	1.3.67		Calyph
Dismaies their mindes before they come to proove/The wounding	2Tamb	1.3.86		Zenoc
The trumpets sound, Zenocrate, they come.	2Tamb	1.3.111		Tamb
Yet never did they recreate themselves,	2Tamb	1.3.182		Usumc
They shal Casane, and tis time yfaith.	2Tamb	1.3.185		Tamb
They have not long since massacred our Camp.	2Tamb	2.1.10		Fredrk
But as the faith which they prophanely plight/Is not by	2Tamb	2.1.37		Baldwn
Though I confesse the othes they undertake,	2Tamb	2.1.42		Sgsmnd
The houses burnt, wil looke as if they mourn'd,	2Tamb	2.4.139		Tamb
It may be they will yeeld it quietly,	2Tamb	3.3.12		Therid
Nor [any] issue foorth, but they shall die:	2Tamb	3.3.33		Techel
Sitting as if they were a telling ridles.	2Tamb	3.5.59		Tamb
Poore soules they looke as if their deaths were neere.	2Tamb	3.5.61		Usumc
The bullets fly at random where they list.	2Tamb	4.1.52		Calyph
They say I am a coward, (Perdicas) and I feare as litle their	2Tamb	4.1.67	P	Calyph
What a coyle they keepe, I beleeve there will be some hurt done	2Tamb	4.1.74	P	Calyph
That they may say, it is not chance doth this,	2Tamb	4.1.84		Amyras

THEY (cont.)

As if they were the teares of Mahomet/For hot consumption of	2Tamb	4.1.196	Tamb
And made so wanton that they knew their strengths,	2Tamb	4.3.14	Tamb
They shall to morrow draw my chariot,	2Tamb	4.3.30	Tamb
them for the funerall/They have bestowed on my abortive sonne.	2Tamb	4.3.66	Tamb
It seemes they meant to conquer us my Lord,	2Tamb	4.3.88	Therid
They will talk still my Lord, if you doe not bridle them.	2Tamb	5.1.146	P Amyras
Whom I have thought a God? they shal be burnt.	2Tamb	5.1.176	Tamb
Here they are my Lord.	2Tamb	5.1.177	Usumc
As when they swallow Assafitida,	2Tamb	5.1.208	Techel
And though they think their painfull date is out,	2Tamb	5.3.34	Usumc
Is greater far, than they can thus subdue.	2Tamb	5.3.39	Usumc
Yet will they reade me, and thereby attaine/To Peters Chayre:	Jew	Prol.11	Machvl
And when they cast me off,/Are poyson'd by my climing	Jew	Prol.12	Machvl
sure/When like the [Dracos] <Drancus> they were writ in blood.	Jew	Prol.21	Machvl
so richly pay/The things they traffique for with wedge of gold,	Jew	1.1.9	Barab
They are.	Jew	1.1.55	1Merch
They wondred how you durst with so much wealth/Trust such a	Jew	1.1.79	1Merch
Tush, they are wise; I know her and her strength:	Jew	1.1.81	Barab
Belike they coasted round by Candie shoare/About their Oyles,	Jew	1.1.91	Barab
Oh they were going up to Sicily:	Jew	1.1.98	Barab
They say we are a scatter'd Nation:	Jew	1.1.121	Barab
And they this day sit in the Counsell-house/To entertaine them	Jew	1.1.148	1Jew
Why let 'em come, so they come not to warre;	Jew	1.1.150	Barab
So they spare me, my daughter, and my wealth.	Jew	1.1.153	Barab
They would not come in warlike manner thus.	Jew	1.1.155	1Jew
What need they treat of peace that are in league?	Jew	1.1.158	Barab
Why, Barabas, they come for peace or warre.	Jew	1.1.161	1Jew
With whom they have attempted many times,	Jew	1.1.164	Barab
Were they not summon'd to appeare to day?	Jew	1.2.35	Govnr
They were, my Lord, and here they come.	Jew	1.2.36	Offcrs
And not simplicity, as they suggest.	Jew	1.2.161	Barab
Thou seest they have taken halfe our goods.	Jew	1.2.176	1Jew
And of me onely have they taken all.	Jew	1.2.179	Barab
Had they beene valued at indifferent rate,	Jew	1.2.186	Barab
Till they reduce the wrongs done to my father.	Jew	1.2.235	Abigal
Then shall they ne're be seene of Barrabas:	Jew	1.2.250	Abigal
For they have seiz'd upon thy house and wares.	Jew	1.2.251	Abigal
But they will give me leave once more, I trow,	Jew	1.2.252	Barab
That may they not:	Jew	1.2.253	Abigal
Displacing me; and of thy house they meane/To make a Nunnery,	Jew	1.2.255	Abigal
thus; thou toldst me they have turn'd my house/Into a Nunnery,	Jew	1.2.277	Barab
I, but father they will suspect me there.	Jew	1.2.283	Abigal
but be thou so precise/As they may thinke it done of Holinesse.	Jew	1.2.285	Barab
But here they come; be cunning Abigall.	Jew	1.2.299	Barab
Which they have now turn'd to a Nunnery.	Jew	1.2.320	Abigal
They fought it out, and not a man surviv'd/To bring the	Jew	2.2.50	Bosco
And so much must they yeeld or not be sold.	Jew	2.3.4	2Offcr
They hop'd my daughter would ha bin a Nun;	Jew	2.3.12	Barab
Heave up my shoulders when they call me dogge,	Jew	2.3.24	Barab
And seeing they are not idle, but still doing,	Jew	2.3.83	Barab
'Tis likely they in time may reape some fruit,	Jew	2.3.84	Barab
For though they doe a while increase and multiply,	Jew	2.3.89	Barab
Away, for here they come.	Jew	2.3.275	Barab
For they themselves hold it a principle,	Jew	2.3.310	Barab
As meet they will, and fighting dye; brave sport.	Jew	3.1.30	Ithimr
Oh bravely fought, and yet they thrust not home.	Jew	3.2.5	Barab
So, now they have shew'd themselves to be tall fellowes.	Jew	3.2.7	Barab
I, part 'em now they are dead: Farewell, farewell.	Jew	3.2.9	Barab
Till they [reveal] the causers of our smarts,	Jew	3.2.34	Govnr
And then they met, [and] as the story sayes,	Jew	3.3.20	Ithimr
In dolefull wise they ended both their dayes.	Jew	3.3.21	Ithimr
That by my favour they should both be slaine?	Jew	3.3.39	Abigal
This Even they use in Malta here ('tis call'd/Saint Jaques	Jew	3.4.75	Barab
Saint Jaques Even) and then I say they use/To send their Almes	Jew	3.4.76	Barab
There's a darke entry where they take it in,	Jew	3.4.79	Barab
Where they must neither see the messenger,	Jew	3.4.80	Barab
And Physicke will not helpe them; they must dye.	Jew	3.6.2	1Fryar
For every yeare they swell, and yet they live;	Jew	4.1.6	Barab
I smelt 'em e're they came.	Jew	4.1.22	Barab
I feare they know we sent the poyson'd broth.	Jew	4.1.26	Barab
I will not say that by a forged challenge they met.	Jew	4.1.45	P 2Fryar
I know they are, and I will be with you.	Jew	4.1.83	Barab
They weare no shirts, and they goe bare-foot too.	Jew	4.1.84	1Fryar
Which if they were reveal'd, would doe him harme.	Jew	4.2.65	Pilia
Sir, here they are.	Jew	4.3.50	Barab
Foh, me thinkes they stinke like a Holly-Hoke.	Jew	4.4.41	Pilia
Dead, my Lord, and here they bring his body.	Jew	5.1.53	1Offcr
Since they are dead, let them be buried.	Jew	5.1.57	Govnr
And since that time they have hir'd a slave my man/To accuse me	Jew	5.1.75	Barab
And being asleepe, belike they thought me dead,	Jew	5.1.81	Barab
I know; and they shall witnesse with their lives.	Jew	5.2.123	Barab
First, for his Army, they are sent before,	Jew	5.5.25	Barab
Stand close, for here they come:	Jew	5.5.46	Barab
As sooner shall they drinke the Ocean dry,	Jew	5.5.121	Govnr
How they did storme at these your nuptiall rites,	P 49	1.49	Admral
See where they be my good Lord, and he that smelles but to	P 73	2.16	P Pothec
they may become/As men that stand and gase against the Sunne.	P 162	2.105	Guise
They justly challenge their protection:	P 210	4.8	Charls
They that shalbe actors in this Massacre,	P 231	4.29	Guise
At which they all shall issue out and set the streetes.	P 237	4.35	Guise
Which when they heare, they shall begin to kill:	P 239	4.37	Guise
And under your direction see they keep/All trecherous violence	P 267	4.65	Charls

THEY (cont.)

That they which have already set the street/May know their	P 328	5.55	Guise
Harke, harke they come, Ile leap out at the window.	P 369	7.9	Taleus
How may we doe? I feare me they will live.	P 420	7.60	Guise
With bowes and dartes to shoot at them they see,	P 422	7.62	Dumain
And sinke them in the river as they swim.	P 423	7.63	Dumain
My Lord, they say/That all the protestants are massacred.	P 431	7.71	Navrre
I, so they are, but yet what remedy:	P 433	7.73	Anjoy
For Ile rule France, but they shall weare the crowne:	P 525	9.44	QnMoth
And if they storme, I then may pull them downe.	P 526	9.45	QnMoth
And so they shall, if fortune speed my will,	P 601	12.14	King
think they Henries heart/Will not both harbour love and	P 603	12.16	King
Put of that feare, they are already joynde,	P 605	12.18	King
Which they will put us to with sword and fire:	P 706	14.9	Navrre
Then in this bloudy brunt they may beholde,	P 713	14.16	Bartus
Not yet my Lord, for thereon doe they stay:	P 732	14.35	1Msngr
They should know how I scornde them and their mockes.	P 762	15.20	Guise
I, those are they that feed him with their golde,	P 845	17.40	King
Nay, they fear'd not to speak in the streetes,	P 876	17.71	Eprnon
Did they of Paris entertaine him so?	P 879	17.74	King
My head shall be my counsell, they are false:	P 884	17.79	King
They be my good Lord.	P 948	19.18	Capt
But are they resolute and armde to kill,	P 949	19.19	King
They were to blame that said I was displeasde,	P 969	19.39	King
Tut they are pesants, I am Duke of Guise:	P 998	19.68	Guise
How they beare armes against their soveraigne.	P1187	22.49	King
What? will they tyrannize upon the Church?	Edw	1.2.3	Lncstr
Then laide they violent hands upon him, next/Himselfe	Edw	1.2.36	ArchBp
How fast they run to banish him I love,	Edw	1.4.94	Edward
They would not stir, were it to do me good:	Edw	1.4.95	Edward
If all things sort out, as I hope they will,	Edw	2.1.79	Neece
Sweete husband be content, they all love you.	Edw	2.2.36	Queene
They love me not that hate my Gaveston.	Edw	2.2.37	Edward
They rate his ransome at five thousand pound.	Edw	2.2.117	Mortmr
the Mortimers/Are not so poore, but would they sell their land,	Edw	2.2.151	Mortmr
Do what they can, weele live in Tinmoth here,	Edw	2.2.221	Edward
O stay my lord, they will not injure you.	Edw	2.4.7	Gavstn
No doubt, such lessons they will teach the rest,	Edw	3.1.21	Spencr
As by their preachments they will profit much,	Edw	3.1.22	Spencr
And if they send me not my Gaveston,	Edw	3.1.26	Edward
Ah traitors, have they put my friend to death?	Edw	3.1.91	Edward
and when they flatly had denyed,/Refusing to receive me pledge	Edw	3.1.106	Arundl
So wish not they Iwis that sent thee hither,	Edw	3.1.152	Edward
Say they, and lovinglie advise your grace,	Edw	3.1.166	Herald
This graunted, they, their honors, and their lives,	Edw	3.1.170	Herald
A traitors, will they still display their pride?	Edw	3.1.172	Spencr
Rebels, will they appoint their soveraigne/His sports, his	Edw	3.1.174	Edward
For theile betray thee, traitors as they are.	Edw	3.1.203	Lncstr
Did they remoove that flatterer from thy throne.	Edw	3.1.231	Kent
What they intend, the hangman frustrates cleane.	Edw	3.1.275	Baldck
man, they say there is great execution/Done through the realme,	Edw	4.3.6	Edward
Why so, they barkt a pace a month agoe,	Edw	4.3.12	Edward
they intend to give king Edward battell in England, sooner then	Edw	4.3.34	P Spencr
diest, for Mortimer/And Isabell doe kisse while they conspire,	Edw	4.6.13	Kent
Yea madam, and they scape not easilie,	Edw	4.6.41	Mortmr
They shalbe started thence I doubt it not.	Edw	4.6.60	Mortmr
So fought not they that fought in Edwards right.	Edw	4.6.72	SpncrP
Your lives and my dishonor they pursue,	Edw	4.7.23	Edward
They stay your answer, will you yeeld your crowne?	Edw	5.1.50	Leistr
They passe not for thy frownes as late they did,	Edw	5.1.77	Edward
For if they goe, the prince shall lose his right.	Edw	5.1.92	Leistr
Farewell, I know the next newes that they bring,	Edw	5.1.125	Edward
Ah they do dissemble.	Edw	5.2.86	Kent
It is the chiefest marke they levell at.	Edw	5.3.12	Edward
The Spencers ghostes, where ever they remaine,	Edw	5.3.44	Edward
They thrust upon me the Protectorship,	Edw	5.4.56	Mortmr
Suscepi that provinciam as they terme it,	Edw	5.4.63	Mortmr
This dungeon where they keepe me, is the sincke,	Edw	5.5.56	Edward
They give me bread and water being a king,	Edw	5.5.62	Edward
Nor shall they now be tainted with a kings.	Edw	5.5.82	Ltborn
Now as I speake they fall, and yet with feare/Open againe.	Edw	5.5.95	Edward
Aye me, see where he comes, and they with him,	Edw	5.6.22	Queene
a point, to which when men aspire,/They tumble hedlong downe:	Edw	5.6.61	Mortmr
[Nor can they raise the winde, or rend the cloudes]:	F 86	1.1.58A	Faust
I'le leavy souldiers with the coyne they bring,	F 119	1.1.91	Faust
Like Lyons shall they guard us when we please,	F 151	1.1.123	Valdes
From <For> Venice shall they drag <dregge> huge Argosies,/And	F 157	1.1.129	Valdes
The spirits tell me they can dry the sea,	F 171	1.1.143	Cornel
damned Art/For which they two are infamous through the world.	F 222	1.2.29	1Schol
for they are as familiar with me, as if they payd for their	F 364	1.4.22	P Robin
me, as if they payd for their meate and drinke, I can tell you.	F 365	1.4.23	P Robin
O they are meanes to bring thee unto heaven.	F 406	2.1.18	GdAngl
[Here they are in this booke].	F 551.3	2.1.166A	P Mephst
[Heere they are too].	F 551.7	2.1.170A	P Mephst
[Here they be].	F 551.11	2.1.174A	P Mephst
But <tell me> have they all/One motion, both situ et tempore?	F 595	2.2.44	Faust
No Faustus they be but Fables.	F 613	2.2.62	P Mephst
Repent and they shall never raise thy skin.	F 633	2.2.82	GdAngl
O Faustus they are come to fetch <away> thy soule.	F 641	2.2.90	Faust
and the devill a peny they have left me, but a [bare] <small>	F 694	2.2.143	P Glutny
matters in hand, let the horses walk themselves and they will.	F 727	2.3.6	P Robin
into matters, as other men, if they were disposed to talke.	F 741	2.3.20	P Robin
And view their triumphs, as they passe this way.	F 857	3.1.79	Mephst

THEY (cont.)

And I'le performe it Faustus: heark they come:	F 866	3.1.88	Mephst
Long ere with Iron hands they punish men,	F 878	3.1.100	Pope
And as they turne their superstitious Bookes,	F 893	3.1.115	Faust
But whilst they sleepe within the Consistory,	F 943	3.1.165	Faust
So, they are safe:	F1035	3.2.55	Faust
Constantinople have they brought me now <am I hither brought>,	F1118	3.3.31	Mephst
[They put forth questions of Astrologie],	F1146	3.3.59A	3Chor
[As they admirde and wondred at his wit].	F1148	3.3.61A	3Chor
for they say, if a man be drunke over night, the Divell cannot	F1200	4.1.46	P Benvol
and they shall serve for buttons to his lips, to keepe his	F1387	4.2.63	P Benvol
they should be good, for they come from a farre Country I can	F1576	4.6.19	P Faust
be good, for they come from a farre Country I can tell you.	F1576	4.6.19	P Faust
that lye farre East, where they have fruit twice a yeare.	F1584	4.6.27	P Faust
And trust me, they are the sweetest grapes that e're I tasted.	F1587	4.6.30	P Lady
And then demand of them, what they would have.	F1590	4.6.33	Duke
What would they have?	F1599	4.6.42	Duke
They all cry out to speake with Doctor Faustus.	F1600	4.6.43	Servnt
They are good subject for a merriment.	F1606	4.6.49	Faust
Then I assure thee certainelie they are.	F1650	4.6.93	Faust
and see where they come, belike the feast is done.	F1680	5.1.7	P Wagner
See where they come.	F1815	5.2.19	Mephst
up my hands, but see they hold 'em <them>, they hold 'em <them>.	F1853	5.2.57	P Faust
my hands, but see they hold 'em <them>, they hold 'em <them>.	F1853	5.2.57	P Faust
All beasts are happy, for when they die,	F1969	5.2.173	Faust
about thee into familiars, and they shal teare thee in peeces.	F App	p.229 26	P Wagner
they are too familiar with me already, swowns they are as bolde	F App	p.229 27	P Clown
swowns they are as bolde with my flesh, as if they had payd for	F App	p.230 28	P Clown
with my flesh, as if they had payd for my meate and drinke.	F App	p.230 29	P Clown
Gridyrons, what be they?	F App	p.230 31	P Clown
they were never so knocht since they were divels, say I should	F App	p.230 46	P Clown
what, are they gone?	F App	p.230 51	P Clown
they have vilde long nailes, there was a hee divell and a shee	F App	p.230 51	P Clown
they say thou hast a familiar spirit, by whome thou canst	F App	p.236 4	P Emper
how they had wonne by prowesse such exploits, gote such riches,	F App	p.236 19	P Emper
or they that shal hereafter possesse our throne, shal (I feare	F App	p.236 21	P Emper
and attire/They usde to weare during their time of life,	F App	p.237 34	Emper
in that manner that they best liv'd in, in their most	F App	p.237 48	P Faust
heere they are my gratious Lord.	F App	p.238 59	P Faust
Where be they?	F App	p.241 160	P Mephst
here they be madam, wilt please you taste on them.	F App	p.242 15	P Faust
hither, as ye see, how do you like them Madame, be they good?	F App	p.242 24	P Faust
they be the best grapes that ere I tasted in my life before.	F App	p.242 25	P Duchss
I am glad they content you so Madam.	F App	p.242 27	P Faust
See where they come: belike the feast is ended.	F App	p.243 8	Wagner
Might they have won whom civil broiles have slaine,	Lucan, First Booke	14	
And they of Nilus mouth (if there live any).	Lucan, First Booke	20	
but being worne away/They both burst out, and each incounter	Lucan, First Booke	103	
They shooke for feare, and cold benumm'd their lims,	Lucan, First Booke	248	
Thus sighing whispered they, and none durst speake/And shew	Lucan, First Booke	259	
See how they quit our [bloud shed] <bloudshed> in the North;	Lucan, First Booke	302	
whilst with their dams/They kennel'd in Hircania, evermore/Wil	Lucan, First Booke	329	
And so they triumph, be't with whom ye wil.	Lucan, First Booke	342	
they had houses:	Lucan, First Booke	347	
force, they that now thwart right/In wars wil yeeld to wrong:	Lucan, First Booke	349	
They by Lemannus nooke forsooke their tents;	Lucan, First Booke	397	
They whom the Lingones foild with painted speares,	Lucan, First Booke	398	
They came that dwell/By Nemes fields, and bankes of Satirus,	Lucan, First Booke	420	
And they of Rhene and Leuca, cunning darters,	Lucan, First Booke	425	
where swift Rhodanus/Drives Araris to sea; They neere the hils,	Lucan, First Booke	435	
and fell Mercury <(Jove)>/They offer humane flesh, and where	Lucan, First Booke	441	
They stai'd not either to pray or sacrifice,	Lucan, First Booke	504	
As loath to leave Roome whom they held so deere,	Lucan, First Booke	506	
With slender trench they escape night stratagems,	Lucan, First Booke	514	
And they whom fierce Bellonaes fury moves/To wound their armes,	Lucan, First Booke	563	
(as their old custome was)/They call th'Etrurian Augures,	Lucan, First Booke	584	
then, they that keepe, and read/Sybillas secret works, and	Lucan, First Booke	598	
Say they are mine, and hands on thee impose.	Ovid's Elegies	1.4.40	
Where they may sport, and seeme to be unknowne.	Ovid's Elegies	1.5.8	
And guides my feete least stumbling falles they catch.	Ovid's Elegies	1.6.8	
Binde fast my hands, they have deserved chaines,	Ovid's Elegies	1.7.1	
Least they should fly, being tane, the tirant play.	Ovid's Elegies	1.8.70	
Who slumbring, they rise up in swelling armes.	Ovid's Elegies	1.9.26	
All for their Mistrisse, what they have, prepare.	Ovid's Elegies	1.10.58	
More fitly had [they] <thy> wrangling bondes contained/From	Ovid's Elegies	1.12.23	
Among day bookes and billes they had laine better/In which the	Ovid's Elegies	1.12.25	
Hold in thy rosie horses that they move not.	Ovid's Elegies	1.13.10	
But when thou comest they of their courses faile.	Ovid's Elegies	1.13.12	
But what had beene more faire had they beene kept?	Ovid's Elegies	1.14.3	
Not black, nor golden were they to our viewe,	Ovid's Elegies	1.14.9	
Ad <And> they were apt to curle an hundred waies,	Ovid's Elegies	1.14.13	
When they were slender, and like downy mosse,	Ovid's Elegies	1.14.23	
[Thy] <They> troubled haires, alas, endur'd great losse.	Ovid's Elegies	1.14.24	
How patiently hot irons they did take/In crooked [tramells]	Ovid's Elegies	1.14.25	
They well become thee, then to spare them turne.	Ovid's Elegies	1.14.28	
Such were they as [Dione] <Diana> painted stands/All naked	Ovid's Elegies	1.14.33	
Because [thy] <they> care too much thy Mistresse troubled.	Ovid's Elegies	2.2.8	
such faults are sad/Nor make they any man that heare them glad.	Ovid's Elegies	2.2.52	
Even kembed as they were, her lockes to rend,	Ovid's Elegies	2.5.45	
Also much better were they then I tell,	Ovid's Elegies	2.5.55	
Tis ill they pleas'd so much, for in my lips,	Ovid's Elegies	2.5.57	
No where can they be taught but in the bed,	Ovid's Elegies	2.5.61	
They that deserve paine, beare't with patience.	Ovid's Elegies	2.7.12	

THIEVISH (See THEEVISH)
THIGH
hellish fiend/Which made the sterne Lycurgus wound his thigh, Lucan, First Booke 573
How large a legge, and what a lustie thigh? Ovid's Elegies 1.5.22
The fathers thigh should unborne Bacchus lacke. Ovid's Elegies 3.3.40
And under mine her wanton thigh she flong, Ovid's Elegies 3.6.10
THIGHES
That loade their thighes with Hyblas honeys spoyles, Dido 5.1.13 Aeneas
Mingle not thighes, nor to his legge joyne thine, Ovid's Elegies 1.4.43
THIGHS
And mingle thighs, yours ever mine to beare. Ovid's Elegies 3.13.22
and there prie/Upon his brest, his thighs, and everie lim, Hero and Leander 2.189
TH'IMMORTALL
As Centinels to warne th'immortall soules, 2Tamb 2.4.16 Tamb
TH'IMPARTIALL
And with my prayers pierce [th']impartiall heavens, Jew 3.2.33 Govnr
TH'IMPERIALL
And here Queene Dido weares th'imperiall Crowne, Dido 2.1.63 Illion
Up to the pallace of th'imperiall heaven: 2Tamb 2.4.35 Tamb
And were the sinowes of th'imperiall seat/So knit and 2Tamb 3.1.10 Callap
THIN (See also THINNE)
And feeding them with thin and slender fare, 1Tamb 3.3.49 Tamb
A small thin skinne contain'd the vital parts, Lucan, First Booke 622
being thin, the harme was small,/Yet strivde she to be covered Ovid's Elegies 1.5.13
balde scalpes [thin] <thine> hoary flieces/And riveld cheekes I Ovid's Elegies 1.8.111
TH'INCHAUNTED
And stole away th'inchaunted gazers mind, Hero and Leander 1.104
TH'INCHAUNTING
O th'inchaunting words of that base slave, Dido 2.1.161 Aeneas
THINE (See also THYNE)
Sweet Jupiter, if ere I pleasde thine eye, Dido 1.1.19 Ganimd
Then dye Aeneas in thine innocence, Dido 1.1.80 Venus
The while thine eyes attract their sought for joyes: Dido 1.1.136 Venus
Feare not Iarbus, Dido may be thine. Dido 3.1.19 Dido
Should ere defile so faire a mouth as thine: Dido 3.2.27 Juno
Love my Aeneas, and desire is thine, Dido 3.2.60 Venus
The day, the night, my Swannes, my sweetes are thine. Dido 3.2.61 Venus
Why, man of Troy, doe I offend thine eyes? Dido 3.3.17 Iarbus
Speake of no other land, this land is thine, Dido 4.4.83 Dido
Dido is thine, henceforth Ile call thee Lord: Dido 4.4.84 Dido
To too forgetfull of thine owne affayres, Dido 5.1.30 Hermes
To sound this angrie message in thine eares. Dido 5.1.33 Hermes
been/When Didos beautie [chaind] <chaungd> thine eyes to her: Dido 5.1.114 Dido
dye to expiate/The griefe that tires upon thine inward soule. Dido 5.1.317 Iarbus
And mixe her bloud with thine, this shall I doe, Dido 5.1.326 Anna
Thus shall my heart be still combinde with thine, 1Tamb 1.2.235 Tamb
To dy by this resolved hand of thine, 1Tamb 3.2.98 Agidas
Thou wilt repent these lavish words of thine, 1Tamb 3.3.172 Zenoc
Nay, thine owne is easier to come by, plucke out that, and twil 1Tamb 4.4.13 P Tamb
Citties and townes/After my name and thine Zenocrate: 1Tamb 4.4.80 Tamb
Nor shall they long be thine, I warrant them. 1Tamb 4.4.119 Bajzth
I may poure foorth my soule into thine armes, 1Tamb 5.1.279 Bajzth
to Zenocrate/Than her owne life, or ought save thine owne love. 1Tamb 5.1.338 Zenoc
Blush, blush faire citie, at thine honors foile, 2Tamb 4.1.107 Tamb
Whose cruelties are not so harsh as thine, 2Tamb 4.1.169 Jrslem
Thine Argosie from Alexandria, Jew 1.1.85 2Merch
Thine and the rest. Jew 1.2.55 Govnr
we take particularly thine/To save the ruine of a multitude: Jew 1.2.96 Govnr
And wilt not see thine owne afflictions, Jew 1.2.353 1Fryar
That I intend my daughter shall be thine. Jew 2.3.254 Barab
My sonne lov'd thine. Jew 3.2.22 Mater
All that I have is thine when I am dead, Jew 3.4.44 Barab
My purse, my Coffer, and my selfe is thine. Jew 3.4.93 Barab
Nay [to] thine owne cost, villaine, if thou com'st. Jew 4.3.59 Barab
Slip not thine opportunity, for feare too late/Thou seek'st for Jew 5.2.45 Barab
No villain, that toung of thine, P 530 10.3 Guise
Nay for the Popes sake, and thine owne benefite. P 827 17.22 Eprnon
So thou wouldst smile and take me in thy <thine> armes. Edw 1.1.9 Gavstn
Here take my picture, and let me weare thine, Edw 1.4.127 Edward
My life for thine she will have Gaveston. Edw 2.1.28 Spencr
Tell me, where wast thou borne? What is thine armes? Edw 2.2.242 Edward
blood,/Of thine own people patron shouldst thou be/But thou-- Edw 4.4.13 Queene
Our lots are cast, I feare me so is thine. Edw 4.7.79 Baldck
These lookes of thine can harbor nought but death. Edw 5.5.73 Edward
Faustus, begin thine Incantations, F 233 1.3.5 Faust
The god thou serv'st is thine owne appetite, F 399 2.1.11 Faust
And wright a Deed of Gift with thine owne bloud; F 424 2.1.36 Mephst
Then Faustus stab thy <thine> Arme couragiously, F 438 2.1.50 Mephst
Why shouldst thou not? is not thy soule thine owne? F 457 2.1.69 Faust
She whom thine eye shall like, thy heart shall have, F 539 2.1.151 Mephst
'Twas thine own seeking Faustus, thanke thy selfe. F 555 2.2.4 Mephst
containes <containeth> for to delight thine eyes <thee with>, F 810 3.1.32 Mephst
By [cunning] <comming> in <of> thine Art to crosse the Pope,/Or F 859 3.1.81 Mephst
This deed of thine, in setting Bruno free/From his and our F1206 4.1.52 Emper
Shall adde more excellence unto thine Art, F1208 4.1.54 Emper
thee not to sleepe much, having such a head of thine owne. F1285 4.1.131 P Emper
Saies Faustus come, thine houre is almost come, F1727 5.1.54 Faust
the Scriptures, then I turn'd the leaves/And led thine eye. F1889 5.2.93 Mephst
Now Faustus let thine eyes with horror stare/Into that vaste F1909 5.2.113 BdAngl
If therefore thou, by cunning of thine Art, F App p.237 29 Emper
Caesar is thine, so please it thee, thy soldier; Lucan, First Booke 204
We are the Muses prophets, none of thine. Ovid's Elegies 1.1.10
Are all things thine? the Muses Tempe <Temple> thine? Ovid's Elegies 1.1.19

THINE (cont.)

Take these away, where is thy <thine> honor then?	Ovid's Elegies	1.2.38	
In spite of thee, forth will thy <thine> arrowes flie,	Ovid's Elegies	1.2.45	
If loftie titles cannot make me thine,	Ovid's Elegies	1.3.7	
And with my name shall thine be alwaies sung.	Ovid's Elegies	1.3.26	
Mingle not thighes, nor to his legge joyne thine,	Ovid's Elegies	1.4.43	
Giving the windes my words running in thine eare?	Ovid's Elegies	1.6.42	
Such is his forme as may with thine compare,	Ovid's Elegies	1.8.33	
When on thy lappe thine eyes thou dost deject,	Ovid's Elegies	1.8.37	
And let thine eyes constrained learne to weepe,	Ovid's Elegies	1.8.83	
balde scalpes [thin] <thine> hoary flieces/And riveld cheekes I	Ovid's Elegies	1.8.111	
But [heldst] <hadst> thou in thine armes some Caephalus,	Ovid's Elegies	1.13.39	
By thine owne hand and fault thy hurt doth growe,	Ovid's Elegies	1.14.43	
Knowing her scapes thine honour shall encrease,	Ovid's Elegies	2.2.27	
Thy mistrisse enseignes must be likewise thine.	Ovid's Elegies	2.3.10	
Not silent were thine eyes, the boord with wine/Was scribled,	Ovid's Elegies	2.5.17	
Forbid thine anger to procure my griefe.	Ovid's Elegies	2.7.14	
We people wholy given thee, feele thine armes,	Ovid's Elegies	2.9.11	
In white, with incense Ile thine Altars greete,	Ovid's Elegies	2.13.23	
And to thine owne losse was thy wit swift running.	Ovid's Elegies	3.7.46	
With thine, nor this last fire their presence misses.	Ovid's Elegies	3.8.54	
And by thine eyes whose radiance burnes out mine.	Ovid's Elegies	3.10.48	
Though thou be faire, yet be not thine owne thrall.	Hero and Leander	1.90	
Then shouldst thou bee his prisoner who is thine.	Hero and Leander	1.202	

TH'INFERNALL

And we discend into th'infernall vaults,	2Tamb	2.4.98	Tamb
as th'infernall spirits/On sweet Musaeus when he came to hell,	F 142	1.1.114	Faust
the brest of this slaine Bull are crept,/Th'infernall powers.	Lucan, First Booke	633	

THING

The thing that I will dye before I aske,	Dido	3.4.9	Dido
And they shall have what thing so ere thou needst.	Dido	5.1.74	Iarbus
As any thing of price with thy conceit?	2Tamb	5.1.14	Govnr
Makes walles a fresh with every thing that falles/Into the	2Tamb	5.1.18	Govnr
If any thing shall there concerne our state/Assure your selves	Jew	1.1.172	Barab
into the sea; why I'le doe any thing for your sweet sake.	Jew	3.4.40	P Ithimr
A thing that makes me tremble to unfold.	Jew	3.6.48	2Fryar
No, but a worse thing:	Jew	3.6.50	2Fryar
'Tis a strange thing of that Jew, he lives upon pickled	Jew	4.4.61	P Ithimr
Thou shalt not live in doubt of any thing.	Jew	5.5.45	Barab
within thy hands/To shuffle or cut, take this as surest thing:	P 147	2.90	Guise
Anjoy hath well advisde/Your highnes to consider of the thing,	P 220	4.18	Guise
And yet didst never sound any thing to the depth.	P 386	7.26	Guise
To work the way to bring this thing to passe:	P 649	12.62	QnMoth
Some thing he whispers in his childish eares.	Edw	5.2.76	Queene
Neede you any thing besides?	Edw	5.5.32	Gurney
to a Dog, or a Cat, or a Mouse, or a Rat, or any thing.	F 383	1.4.41	P Wagner
<why Faustus> think'st thou heaven is such a glorious thing?	F 556	2.2.5	Mephst
Villaine, have I not bound thee to tell me any thing?	F 622	2.2.71	P Faust
I pray you tell me, what is the thing you most desire to have?	F1567	4.6.10	P Faust
'Tis not so much worth; I pray you tel me one thing.	F1643	4.6.86	P Carter
One thing good servant let me crave of thee,	F1759	5.1.86	Faust
to a dogge, or a catte, or a mouse, or a ratte, or any thing.	F App	p.231 59	P Wagner
if you turne me into any thing, let it be in the likenesse of a	F App	p.231 61	P Clown
but I must tel you one thing before you have him, ride him not	F App	p.239 108	P Faust
I wil not hide from you the thing my heart desires, and were it	F App	p.242 9	P Duchss
were it a greater thing then this, so it would content you, you	F App	p.242 13	P Faust
The thing and place shall counsell us the rest.	Ovid's Elegies	1.4.54	
Her name comes from the thing:	Ovid's Elegies	1.8.3	
(Trust me) to give, it is a witty thing.	Ovid's Elegies	1.8.62	
What can be easier then the thing we pray?	Ovid's Elegies	2.2.66	
Well maiest thou one thing for thy Mistresse use.	Ovid's Elegies	2.8.24	
But seeing thee, I thinke my thing will swell,	Ovid's Elegies	2.15.25	
Not stronger am I, then the thing I move.	Ovid's Elegies	3.1.42	
Breathlesse spoke some thing, and sigh'd out the rest;	Hero and Leander	2.280	

THINGS

But what are you that aske of me these things?	Dido	1.1.214	Venus
And order all things at your high dispose,	Dido	5.1.303	Dido
Meet heaven and earth, and here let al things end,	2Tamb	5.3.249	Amyras
so richly pay/The things they traffique for with wedge of gold,	Jew	1.1.9	Barab
things past recovery/Are hardly cur'd with exclamations.	Jew	1.2.236	Barab
Has made me see the difference of things.	Jew	3.3.62	Abigal
This, Barabas; since things are in thy power,	Jew	5.2.57	Govnr
That at one instant all things may be done,	Jew	5.2.120	Barab
Then now are all things as my wish wud have 'em,	Jew	5.5.17	Barab
To meddle or attempt such dangerous things.	P 38	1.38	Admral
The plot is laide, and things shall come to passe,	P 164	2.107	Guise
In that I know the things that I have wrote,	P 403	7.43	Ramus
And all things that a King may wish besides:	P 595	12.8	QnMoth
Such things as these best please his majestie,	Edw	1.1.71	Gavstn
If all things sort out, as I hope they will,	Edw	2.1.79	Neece
Commit not to my youth things of more waight/Then fits a prince	Edw	3.1.74	Prince
All things that move betweene the quiet Poles/Shall be at my	F 83	1.1.55	Faust
Sweet Faustus think of heaven, and heavenly things.	F 409	2.1.21	GdAngl
I Faustus, and do greater things then these.	F 476	2.1.88	Mephst
I, so are all things else; but whereabouts <where about>?	F 507	2.1.119	Faust
let me be cloyd/With all things that delight the heart of man.	F 838	3.1.60	Faust
And see that all things be in readinesse,	F1011	3.2.31	Pope
Faustus had with pleasure tane the view]/[Of rarest things,	F1139	3.3.52A	3Chor
great bellyed women, do long for things, are rare and dainty.	F1569	4.6.12	P Faust
may exhort the wise/Onely to wonder at unlawfull things,	F2007	5.3.25	4Chor
his horse, and he would have his things rubd and made cleane:	F App	p.233 7	P Rafe
I can do al these things easily with it:	F App	p.234 22	P Robin
Time ends and to old Chaos all things turne;	Lucan, First Booke	74	

THINGS (cont.)			
All great things crush themselves, such end the gods/Allot the	Lucan, First Booke	81	
Curling their bloudy lockes, howle dreadfull things,	Lucan, First Booke	565	
to scarre/The quivering Romans, but worse things affright them.	Lucan, First Booke	673	
Are all things thine? the Muses Tempe <Temple> thine?	Ovid's Elegies	1.1.19	
That I may write things worthy thy faire lookes:	Ovid's Elegies	1.3.20	
Thankes worthely are due for things unbought,	Ovid's Elegies	1.10.43	
By speechlesse lookes we guesse at things succeeding.	Ovid's Elegies	1.11.18	
Your name approves you made for such like things,	Ovid's Elegies	1.12.27	
Let base conceited wits admire vilde things,	Ovid's Elegies	1.15.35	
The greedy spirits take the best things first,	Ovid's Elegies	2.6.39	
There good birds rest (if we beleeve things hidden)/Whence	Ovid's Elegies	2.6.51	
And then things found do ever further pace.	Ovid's Elegies	2.9.10	
There wine being fild, thou many things shalt tell,	Ovid's Elegies	2.11.49	
Fruites ripe will fall, let springing things increase,	Ovid's Elegies	2.14.25	
Vaine things why wish I?	Ovid's Elegies	2.15.27	
Not though thy face in all things make thee raigne,	Ovid's Elegies	2.17.11	
Small things with greater may be copulate.	Ovid's Elegies	2.17.14	
And tender love hath great things hatefull made.	Ovid's Elegies	2.18.4	
Wee skorne things lawfull, stolne sweetes we affect,	Ovid's Elegies	2.19.3	
Who covets lawfull things takes leaves from woods,	Ovid's Elegies	2.19.31	
Tis time to move grave things in lofty stile,	Ovid's Elegies	3.1.23	
And all things too much in their sole power drenches.	Ovid's Elegies	3.3.26	
Or Thamiras in curious painted things?	Ovid's Elegies	3.6.62	
But better things it gave, corne without ploughes,	Ovid's Elegies	3.7.39	
One [her] <she> commands, who many things can give.	Ovid's Elegies	3.7.62	
Outrageous death profanes all holy things/And on all creatures	Ovid's Elegies	3.8.19	
Be witnesse Crete (nor Crete doth all things feigne)/Crete	Ovid's Elegies	3.9.19	
Some other seeke, who will these things endure.	Ovid's Elegies	3.10.28	
As heaven preserves all things, so save thou one.	Hero and Leander	1.224	
Thinke water farre excels all earthly things:	Hero and Leander	1.260	
Things that are not at all, are never lost.	Hero and Leander	1.276	
And if these pleasures may thee <things thy minde may> move,	Passionate Shepherd	19	
TH'INHABITANTES			
the Gulfe, call'd by the name/Mare magiore, of th'inhabitantes:	2Tamb	1.3.215	Therid
TH'INHABITANTS			
Death and destruction to th'inhabitants.	2Tamb	3.2.5	Tamb
THINK			
If he think good, can from his garrisons,	1Tamb	3.3.21	Bassoe
To make me think of nought but blood and war.	1Tamb	4.2.55	Tamb
Doost thou think that Mahomet wil suffer this?	1Tamb	4.4.52	P Therid
Wel, lovely Virgins, think our countries care,	1Tamb	5.1.34	Govnr
A sight as banefull to their soules I think/As are Thessalian	1Tamb	5.1.132	Tamb
How canst thou think of this and offer war?	2Tamb	1.1.102	Orcan
Though she be dead, yet let me think she lives,	2Tamb	2.4.127	Tamb
Now my boyes, what think you of a wound?	2Tamb	3.2.129	Tamb
I know not what I should think of it.	2Tamb	3.2.130	P Calyph
For think ye I can live, and see him dead?	2Tamb	3.4.27	Sonne
I smile to think, how when this field is fought,	2Tamb	3.5.165	Techel
To think our helps will doe him any good.	2Tamb	4.1.21	Calyph
I think I make your courage something quaile.	2Tamb	5.1.126	Tamb
And though they think their painfull date is out,	2Tamb	5.3.34	Usumc
Tel me, what think you of my sicknes now?	2Tamb	5.3.81	Tamb
That's brave, master, but think you it wil not be known?	Jew	4.1.8	P Ithimr
I think so, and yet I cannot tell, for at the reading of the	Jew	4.2.6	P Pilia
Their deaths were like their lives, then think not of 'em;	Jew	5.1.56	Govnr
We think it good to goe and consumate/The rest, with hearing of	P 19	1.19	Charls
Sister, I think your selfe will beare us company.	P 21	1.21	Charls
For this, I wake, when others think I sleepe,	P 105	2.48	Guise
To think a word of such a simple sound,	P 125	2.68	Guise
think they Henries heart/Will not both harbour love and	P 603	12.16	King
I think for safety of your royall person,	P 887	17.82	Eprnon
Think you that we can brooke this upstart pride?	Edw	1.4.41	Warwck
Sweet Faustus think of heaven, and heavenly things.	F 409	2.1.21	GdAngl
Why, dost thou think <think'st thou then> that Faustus shall be	F 518	2.1.130	Faust
Thou art damn'd, think thou of hell>.	F 624	2.2.73	P Mephst
I think my Maister means to die shortly, he has made his will,	F1674	5.1.1	P Wagner
THINKE			
Made him to thinke Epeus pine-tree Horse/A sacrifize t'appease	Dido	2.1.162	Aeneas
Come let us thinke upon some pleasing sport,	Dido	2.1.302	Dido
Dido, that till now/Didst never thinke Aeneas beautifull:	Dido	3.1.83	Dido
Aeneas, thinke not Dido is in love:	Dido	3.1.136	Dido
And cannot talke nor thinke of ought but him:	Dido	3.2.73	Juno
Aeneas, thinke not but I honor thee,	Dido	3.3.1	Dido
I thinke some fell Inchantresse dwelleth here,	Dido	4.1.3	Iarbus
I thinke it was the divels revelling night,	Dido	4.1.9	Achat
Blush blush for shame, why shouldst thou thinke of love?	Dido	4.5.29	Nurse
Why doe I thinke of love now I should dye?	Dido	4.5.34	Nurse
Yet thinke upon Ascanius prophesie,	Dido	5.1.38	Hermes
I thinke some Fairies have beguiled me.	Dido	5.1.215	Nurse
And thorough your Planets I perceive you thinke,	1Tamb	1.1.19	Mycet
And thinke we prattle with distempered spirits:	1Tamb	1.2.62	Tamb
Thinke you I way this treasure more than you?	1Tamb	1.2.84	Tamb
We thinke it losse to make exchange for that/We are assured of	1Tamb	1.2.216	Techel
I thinke it would:	1Tamb	2.2.9	Mycet
Therefore in pollicie I thinke it good/To hide it close:	1Tamb	2.4.10	Mycet
Thinke thee invested now as royally,	1Tamb	2.5.2	Tamb
I thinke the pleasure they enjoy in heaven/Can not compare with	1Tamb	2.5.58	Therid
Who thinke you now is king of Persea?	1Tamb	2.7.56	Tamb
thou maist thinke thy selfe happie to be fed from my trencher.	1Tamb	4.4.92	P Tamb
To thinke thy puisant never staied arme/Will part their bodies,	1Tamb	5.1.88	1Virgn
Would make me thinke them Bastards, not my sons,	2Tamb	1.3.32	Tamb
Thinke them in number yet sufficient,	2Tamb	3.1.41	Orcan

THINKE (cont.)

I thinke it requisite and honorable,	2Tamb	3.1.70	Callap
To you? Why, do you thinke me weary of it?	2Tamb	3.3.17	Capt
Thinke of thy end, this sword shall lance thy throat.	2Tamb	3.5.78	Orcan
Why Madam, thinke ye to mocke me thus palpably?	2Tamb	4.2.67	Therid
Albeit the world thinke Machevill is dead,	Jew	Prol.1	Machvl
Why weepe you not to thinke upon my wrongs?	Jew	1.2.172	Barab
Thinke me to be a senselesse lumpe of clay/That will with every	Jew	1.2.216	Barab
thinke me not all so fond/As negligently to forgoe so much	Jew	1.2.241	Barab
in distresse/Thinke me so mad as I will hang my selfe,	Jew	1.2.263	Barab
but be thou so precise/As they may thinke it done of Holinesse.	Jew	1.2.285	Barab
And thinke upon the Jewels and the gold,	Jew	1.2.349	Barab
Thinke of me as thy father; Sonne farewell.	Jew	2.3.149	Barab
But goe you in, I'le thinke upon the account:	Jew	2.3.241	Barab
stands in feare/Of that which you, I thinke, ne're dreame upon,	Jew	2.3.283	Barab
Faith Master, I thinke by this/You purchase both their lives; is	Jew	2.3.365	Ithimr
That he shall verily thinke it comes from him.	Jew	2.3.376	Ithimr
I cannot thinke but that thou hat'st my life.	Jew	3.4.38	Barab
But doe you thinke that I beleeve his words?	Jew	4.1.105	Barab
Who would not thinke but that this Fryar liv'd?	Jew	4.1.156	Barab
And now I thinke on't, going to the execution, a fellow met me	Jew	4.2.27	P Ithimr
Malta's ruine, thinke you not/'Twere slender policy for Barabas	Jew	5.2.64	Barab
Thinke not but I am tragicall within:	P 894	17.89	King
Which whiles I have, I thinke my selfe as great,	Edw	1.1.172	Gavstn
Thinke me as base a groome as Gaveston.	Edw	1.4.291	Mortmr
And thinke I gaind, having bought so deare a friend.	Edw	1.4.310	Edward
And as she red, she smild, which makes me thinke,	Edw	2.1.21	Spencr
You have matters of more waight to thinke upon,	Edw	2.2.8	Mortmr
That thinke with high lookes thus to tread me down.	Edw	2.2.97	Edward
And Gaveston, thinke that I love thee well,	Edw	2.2.257	Edward
But thinke of Mortimer as he deserves.	Edw	2.4.58	Mortmr
To thinke that we can yet be tun'd together,	Edw	4.2.9	Queene
How say yong Prince, what thinke you of the match?	Edw	4.2.67	SrJohn
I thinke king Edward will out-run us all.	Edw	4.2.68	Prince
Edward will thinke we come to flatter him.	Edw	4.4.29	SrJohn
thinke not a thought so villanous/Can harbor in a man of noble	Edw	5.1.131	Bartly
Thinke therefore madam that imports [us] <as> much,	Edw	5.2.10	Mortmr
He is a traitor, thinke not on him, come.	Edw	5.4.115	Queene
Thinke not that I am frighted with thy words,	Edw	5.6.27	King
Because I thinke scorne to be accusde,	Edw	5.6.39	Mortmr
I doe not thinke her so unnaturall.	Edw	5.6.76	King
Thinke not to finde me slack or pitifull.	Edw	5.6.82	King
What bootes it then to thinke on <of> God or Heaven?	F 391	2.1.3	Faust
No Faustus, thinke of honour and of wealth.	F 410	2.1.22	BdAngl
<Come>, I thinke Hel's a fable.	F 516	2.1.128	Faust
I, thinke so still, till experience change thy mind.	F 517	2.1.129	Mephst
And if thou lovest me thinke no more of it.	F 536	2.1.148	Mephst
<Thinke thou on hell Faustus, for thou art damnd>.	F 624	(HC262)A	Mephst
Thinke Faustus upon God, that made the world.	F 625	2.2.74	P Faust
Thou should'st not thinke on <of> God.	F 644	2.2.93	Belzeb
Thinke [of] <on> the devill.	F 645	2.2.94	Lucifr
<Farewel Faustus, and thinke on the divel>.	F 720	(HC264)A	Lucifr
I thinke it be some Ghost crept out of Purgatory, and now is	F1059	3.2.79	P Archbp
to thinke I have beene such an Asse all this while, to stand	F1243	4.1.89	P Benvol
zounds hee'l raise up a kennell of Divels I thinke anon:	F1306	4.1.152	P Benvol
I do thinke my selfe my good Lord, highly recompenced, in that	F1563	4.6.6	P Faust
grace to thinke but well of that which Faustus hath performed.	F1564	4.6.7	P Faust
you thinke to carry it away with your Hey-passe, and Re-passe:	F1664	4.6.107	P Robin
Majesty, we should thinke our selves much beholding unto you.	F1686	5.1.13	P 1Schol
Therefore despaire, thinke onely upon hell;	F1881	5.2.85	Mephst
end be such/As every Christian heart laments to thinke on:	F1996	5.3.14	2Schol
I thinke I have met with you for it.	F App	p.238 78	P Faust
what, doost thinke I am a horse-doctor?	F App	p.240 120	P Faust
I thinke my maister meanes to die shortly,	F App	p.243 1	Wagner
Aske thou the boy, what thou enough doest thinke.	Ovid's Elegies		1.4.30
Least I should thinke thee guilty of offence.	Ovid's Elegies		1.4.50
Yet thinke no scorne to aske a wealthy churle,	Ovid's Elegies		1.10.53
Which I thinke gather'd from cold hemlocks flower/Wherein bad	Ovid's Elegies		1.12.9
fire/And [thinke] <thinkes> her chast whom many doe desire.	Ovid's Elegies		2.2.14
Thinke when she reades, her mother letters sent her,	Ovid's Elegies		2.2.19
to thinke the time more short/Lay downe thy forehead in thy lap	Ovid's Elegies		2.2.23
I thinke sheele doe, but deepely can dissemble.	Ovid's Elegies		2.4.16
[I thinke what one undeckt would be, being drest];	Ovid's Elegies		2.4.37
[Amber] <Yellow> trest is shee, then on the morne thinke I,/My	Ovid's Elegies		2.4.43
[wretch] <wench> I sawe when thou didst thinke I slumbred,	Ovid's Elegies		2.5.13
Ile thinke all true, though it be feigned matter.	Ovid's Elegies		2.11.53
But seeing thee, I thinke my thing will swell,	Ovid's Elegies		2.15.25
To serve a wench if any thinke it shame,	Ovid's Elegies		2.17.1
And one, I thinke, was longer, of her feete.	Ovid's Elegies		3.1.8
How to attaine, what is denyed, we thinke,	Ovid's Elegies		3.4.17
I know not, what men thinke should thee so move.	Ovid's Elegies		3.4.28
I thinke the great Gods greeved they had bestowde/This <The>	Ovid's Elegies		3.6.45
Or thinke soft verse in any stead to stand?	Ovid's Elegies		3.7.2
And some there be that thinke we have a deity.	Ovid's Elegies		3.8.18
By secreat thoughts to thinke there is a god.	Ovid's Elegies		3.8.36
Ceres, I thinke, no knowne fault will deny.	Ovid's Elegies		3.9.24
But victory, I thinke, will hap to love.	Ovid's Elegies		3.10.34
Or is I thinke my wish against the [starres] <starre>?	Ovid's Elegies		3.11.3
And I shall thinke you chaste, do what you can.	Ovid's Elegies		3.13.14
Deceive all, let me erre, and thinke I am right,	Ovid's Elegies		3.13.29
And like a wittall thinke thee voyde of slight.	Ovid's Elegies		3.13.30
My soule fleetes when I thinke what you have done,	Ovid's Elegies		3.13.37
being justified by two words, thinke/The cause acquits you not,	Ovid's Elegies		3.13.49

THINKE (cont.)			
Thinke water farre excels all earthly things:	Hero and Leander	1.260	
As Greece will thinke, if thus you live alone,	Hero and Leander	1.289	
And sigh'd to thinke upon th'approching sunne,	Hero and Leander	2.302	
THINKES			
Me thinkes that towne there should be Troy, yon Idas hill,	Dido	2.1.7	Aeneas
Yet thinkes my minde that this is Priamus:	Dido	2.1.25	Aeneas
Thinkes Dido I will goe and leave him here?	Dido	4.4.30	Aeneas
And thus me thinkes should men of judgement frame/This is the	Jew	1.1.34	Barab
Which me thinkes fits not their profession.	Jew	1.1.118	Barab
And now by that advantage thinkes, belike,	Jew	1.1.184	Barab
And now me thinkes that I am one of those:	Jew	2.1.28	Barab
Foh, me thinkes they stinke like a Holly-Hoke.	Jew	4.4.41	Pilia
Me thinkes he fingers very well.	Jew	4.4.49	Pilia
Me thinkes the gloves have a very strong perfume,	P 170	3.5	OldQn
Me thinkes my Lord, Anjoy hath well advisde/Your highnes to	P 219	4.17	Guise
me thinkes you hang the heads,/But weele advance them traitors,	Edw	3.1.223	Edward
Me thinkes I should revenge me of the wronges,	Edw	5.1.24	Edward
And thinkes your grace that Bartley will bee cruell?	Edw	5.1.151	Bartly
Nor I, and yet me thinkes I should commaund,	Edw	5.4.97	King
When as my sonne thinkes to abridge my daies.	Edw	5.6.84	Queene
doubt of that, for me thinkes you make no hast to wipe it out.	F1516	4.5.12	P Hostss
me thinkes you should have a wooden bedfellow of one of 'em.	F1653	4.6.96	P Carter
And yet me thinkes, if that death were neere,	F App	p.243 3	Wagner
fire/And [thinke] <thinkes> her chast whom many doe desire.	Ovid's Elegies	2.2.14	
Me thinkes she should <would> be nimble when shees downe.	Ovid's Elegies	2.4.14	
lies quiet/And slumbring, thinkes himselfe much blessed by it.	Ovid's Elegies	2.9.40	
Who thinkes her to be glad at lovers smart,	Ovid's Elegies	3.9.15	
THINKEST			
Then thinkest thou thy loose life is not showne?	Ovid's Elegies	1.13.34	
If I looke well, thou thinkest thou doest not move,	Ovid's Elegies	2.7.9	
THINKING			
Thinking the sea had swallowed up thy ships,	Dido	2.1.68	Illion
And thinking to goe downe, came Hectors ghost/With ashie	Dido	2.1.201	Aeneas
Thinking to beare her on my backe abourd,	Dido	2.1.284	Aeneas
And dart her plumes, thinking to pierce my brest,	Edw	1.1.41	Gavstn
Their lord rode home, thinking his prisoner safe,	Edw	3.1.117	Arundl
thinking some hidden mystery had beene in the horse, I had	F1485	4.4.29	P HrsCsr
I thinking that a little would serve his turne, bad him take as	F1528	4.5.24	P Carter
thinking the horse had had some [rare] quality that he would	F1542	4.5.38	P HrsCsr
thinking my horse had had some rare qualitie that he would not	F App	p.240 131	P HrsCsr
As nature wept, thinking she was undone;	Hero and Leander	1.46	
Pyn'd as they went, and thinking on her died.	Hero and Leander	1.130	
Thinking to traine Leander therewithall.	Hero and Leander	2.12	
Thinking to quench the sparckles new begonne.	Hero and Leander	2.138	
THINKS			
Me thinks I see kings kneeling at his feet,	1Tamb	1.2.55	Techel
Me thinks we should not, I am strongly moov'd,	1Tamb	2.5.75	Tamb
And thinks to rouse us from our dreadful siege/Of the famous	1Tamb	3.1.5	Bajzth
What thinks your greatnes best to be atchiev'd/In pursuit of	1Tamb	3.1.56	Fesse
Madame, she thinks perhaps she is too fine.	1Tamb	3.3.179	Ebea
Me thinks we martch as Meliager did,	1Tamb	4.3.1	Souldn
Me thinks, tis a great deale better than a consort of musicke.	1Tamb	4.4.60	P Therid
But yet me thinks their looks are amorous,	2Tamb	1.3.21	Tamb
Me thinks I see how glad the christian King/Is made, for joy of	2Tamb	2.2.20	Uribas
Me thinks tis a pitifull sight.	2Tamb	3.2.130	P Calyph
Me thinks the slave should make a lusty theefe.	2Tamb	3.5.96	Jrslem
Me thinks I could sustaine a thousand deaths,	2Tamb	5.2.22	Callap
Now worthy Faustus: me thinks your looks are chang'd.	F1821	5.2.25	1Schol
THINK'ST			
thou think'st I see thee not;/Away, I'de wish thee, and let me	Jew	4.1.169	1Fryar
And what think'st thou, will he come?	Jew	4.2.5	P Curtzn
Think'st thou that I [who] saw the face of God,	F 305	1.3.77	Mephst
Why, dost thou think <think'st thou then> that Faustus shall be	F 518	2.1.130	Faust
Think'st thou that Faustus, is so fond to imagine,	F 522	2.1.134	Faust
<why Faustus> think'st thou heaven is such a glorious thing?	F 556	2.2.5	Mephst
rise/And who thou never think'st should fall downe lies.	Ovid's Elegies	1.9.30	
THINKST			
What thinkst thou man, shal come of our attemptes?	1Tamb	2.3.3	Cosroe
What, thinkst thou Tamburlain esteems thy gold?	1Tamb	3.3.262	Tamb
What thinkst thou shall become of it and thee?	Jew	5.2.56	Barab
and when thow thinkst I have foregotten this	Paris	ms20,p391	Guise
THINNE			
did looke/Dead, and discoulour'd; th'other leane and thinne.	Lucan, First Booke	628	
being fine and thinne/Like to the silke the curious Seres	Ovid's Elegies	1.14.5	
A decent forme, thinne robe, a lovers looke,	Ovid's Elegies	3.1.9	
Which lie hid under her thinne veile suppresst.	Ovid's Elegies	3.2.36	
THIRD			
As durst resist us till our third daies siege:	2Tamb	5.1.59	Techel
And of the third part of the Persian ships,	Jew	1.1.2	Barab
And what art thou the third?	F 678	2.2.127	P Faust
the second time, aware the third, I give you faire warning.	F App	p.232 20	P Faust
like a Beare, the third an Asse, for doing this enterprise.	F App	p.235 33	P Mephst
In this sweete good, why hath a third to do?	Ovid's Elegies	2.5.32	
Sulmo, Pelignies third part me containes,	Ovid's Elegies	2.16.1	
Why seek'st not heav'n the third realme to frequent?	Ovid's Elegies	3.7.50	
THIRDLY			
Thirdly, that Mephostophilis shall doe for him, and bring him	F 488	2.1.100	P Faust
THIRLING			
(When yawning dragons draw her thirling carre,	Hero and Leander	1.108	
TH'IRREVOCABLE			
Th'irrevocable people flie in troupes.	Lucan, First Booke	507	
THIRST (See also ATHIRST)			
The thirst of raigne and sweetnes of a crown,	1Tamb	2.7.12	Tamb

THIRST (cont.)			
glut our swords/That thirst to drinke the feble Perseans blood.	1Tamb	3.3.165	Bajzth
Hunger and [thirst] <cold>, right adjuncts of the war.	2Tamb	3.2.58	Tamb
Nor care for blood when wine wil quench my thirst.	2Tamb	4.1.30	Calyph
And yet gapes stil for more to quench his thirst,	2Tamb	5.2.14	Amasia
That thirst so much for Principality.	Jew	1.1.135	Barab
For this, my quenchles thirst whereon I builde,	P 107	2.50	Guise
O water gentle friends to coole my thirst,	Edw	5.3.25	Edward
And none of both [them] <then> thirst for Edmunds bloud.	Edw	5.4.107	Kent
Perpetuall thirst, and winters lasting rage.	Ovid's Elegies		1.8.114
Pure waters moisture thirst away did keepe.	Ovid's Elegies		2.6.32
THIRSTER			
That fiery thirster after Soveraigntie:	1Tamb	2.6.31	Cosroe
THIRSTIE			
What thirstie traveller ever drunke of thee?	Ovid's Elegies		3.5.97
THIRSTING			
And either lanch his greedy thirsting throat,	1Tamb	1.2.146	Tamb
Thirsting with soverainty, with love of armes:	1Tamb	2.1.20	Menaph
Or thirsting after immortalitie,	Hero and Leander		1.427
THIRSTY (See also THYRSTY)			
Or Scythia; or hot Libiaes thirsty sands.	Lucan, First Booke		369
THIRTIE			
'Tis thirtie winters long since some of us/Did stray so farre	Jew	1.2.308	Abbass
Wherein are thirtie thousand able men,	P 139	2.82	Guise
THIRTY			
and thirty Kingdomes late contributory to his mighty father.	2Tamb	3.1.5	P Orcan
Ten thousand horse, and thirty thousand foot,	2Tamb	3.5.48	Soria
Goe send 'um threescore Camels, thirty Mules,	Jew	1.1.59	Barab
<as> Saturne in thirty yeares, Jupiter in twelve, Mars in four,	F 604	2.2.53	P Faust
and that buyes me <is> thirty meales a day, and ten Beavers:	F 695	2.2.144	P Glutny
remember that I have beene a student here these thirty yeares,	F1841	5.2.45	P Faust
THIS (See also O'THIS)			
By Saturnes soule, and this earth threatning [haire] <aire>,	Dido	1.1.10	Jupitr
Grace my immortall beautie with this boone,	Dido	1.1.21	Ganimd
But as this one Ile teare them all from him,	Dido	1.1.40	Jupitr
I, this is it, you can sit toying there,	Dido	1.1.50	Venus
Come Ganimed, we must about this geare.	Dido	1.1.121	Jupitr
To succour him in this extremitie.	Dido	1.1.133	Venus
For this so friendly ayde in time of neede.	Dido	1.1.138	Venus
Here in this bush disguised will I stand,	Dido	1.1.139	Venus
And rost our new found victuals on this shoare.	Dido	1.1.168	Aeneas
Hold, take this candle and goe light a fire,	Dido	1.1.171	Aeneas
And shrowdes thy beautie in this borrowd shape:	Dido	1.1.192	Aeneas
And lighten our extreames with this one boone,	Dido	1.1.196	Aeneas
good heaven/We breathe as now, and what this world is calde,	Dido	1.1.198	Aeneas
And this right hand shall make thy Altars crack/With mountaine	Dido	1.1.201	Aeneas
maides to weare/Their bowe and quiver in this modest sort,	Dido	1.1.205	Venus
In sending thee unto this curteous Coast:	Dido	1.1.232	Venus
Follow ye Troians, follow this brave Lord,	Dido	1.2.1	Illion
And in this humor is Achates to,	Dido	2.1.10	Achat
but saving ayre/Is nothing here, and what is this but stone?	Dido	2.1.14	Achat
O yet this stone doth make Aeneas weepe,	Dido	2.1.15	Aeneas
O Priamus is left and this is he,	Dido	2.1.21	Aeneas
Achates though mine eyes say this is stone,	Dido	2.1.24	Aeneas
Yet thinkes my minde that this is Priamus:	Dido	2.1.25	Aeneas
Sweete father leave to weepe, this is not he:	Dido	2.1.35	Ascan
Lords of this towne, or whatsoever stile/Belongs unto your	Dido	2.1.39	Aeneas
vouchsafe of ruth/To tell us who inhabits this faire towne,	Dido	2.1.41	Aeneas
For we are strangers driven on this shore,	Dido	2.1.43	Aeneas
Like Illioneus speakes this Noble man,	Dido	2.1.47	Achat
Sit in this chaire and banquet with a Queene,	Dido	2.1.83	Dido
This is no seate for one thats comfortles,	Dido	2.1.86	Aeneas
And if this be thy sonne as I suppose,	Dido	2.1.92	Dido
This place beseemes me not, O pardon me.	Dido	2.1.94	Aeneas
But all in this that Troy is overcome,	Dido	2.1.112	Dido
Beates forth my senses from this troubled soule,	Dido	2.1.116	Aeneas
And so came in this fatall instrument:	Dido	2.1.176	Aeneas
By this the Campe was come unto the walles,	Dido	2.1.188	Aeneas
Frighted with this confused noyse, I rose,	Dido	2.1.191	Aeneas
and with this sword/Sent many of their savadge ghosts to hell.	Dido	2.1.211	Aeneas
All which hemd me about, crying, this is he.	Dido	2.1.219	Aeneas
King of this Citie, but my Troy is fired,	Dido	2.1.236	Aeneas
This butcher whil'st his hands were yet held up,	Dido	2.1.241	Aeneas
As lothing Pirrhus for this wicked act:	Dido	2.1.258	Aeneas
By this I got my father on my backe,	Dido	2.1.265	Aeneas
This young boy in mine armes, and by the hand/Led faire Creusa	Dido	2.1.266	Aeneas
and had not we/Fought manfully, I had not told this tale:	Dido	2.1.271	Aeneas
But how scapt Helen, she that causde this warre?	Dido	2.1.292	Dido
And this yong Prince shall be thy playfellow.	Dido	2.1.307	Venus
I, and my mother gave me this fine bow.	Dido	2.1.309	Cupid
and in this grove/Amongst greene brakes Ile lay Ascanius,	Dido	2.1.316	Venus
Then touch her white breast with this arrow head,	Dido	2.1.326	Venus
Convey this golden arrowe in thy sleeve,	Dido	3.1.3	Cupid
And tell me where [learndst] <learnst> thou this pretie song?	Dido	3.1.27	Dido
What will you give me now? Ile have this Fanne.	Dido	3.1.32	Cupid
Ungentle Queene, is this thy love to me?	Dido	3.1.36	Iarbus
Full soone wouldst thou abjure this single life.	Dido	3.1.60	Dido
But now for quittance of this oversight,	Dido	3.1.84	Dido
I saw this man at Troy ere Troy was sackt.	Dido	3.1.141	Achat
I this in Greece when Paris stole faire Helen.	Dido	3.1.142	Aeneas
This man and I were at Olympus games.	Dido	3.1.143	Illion
I know this face, he is a Persian borne,	Dido	3.1.144	Serg
And I in Athens with this gentleman,	Dido	3.1.146	Cloan

THIS (cont.)

This was an Orator, and thought by words/To compasse me, but	Dido	3.1.155	Dido
And this a Spartan Courtier vaine and wilde,	Dido	3.1.157	Dido
This was Alcion, a Musition,	Dido	3.1.159	Dido
This was the wealthie King of Thessaly,	Dido	3.1.161	Dido
This Meleagers sonne, a warlike Prince,	Dido	3.1.163	Dido
What should this meane?	Dido	3.2.21	Venus
Is this then all the thankes that I shall have,	Dido	3.2.37	Juno
How highly I doe prize this amitie,	Dido	3.2.67	Juno
Well could I like this reconcilements meanes,	Dido	3.2.81	Venus
This day they both a hunting forth will ride/Into these woods,	Dido	3.2.87	Juno
Be it as you will have [it] for this once,	Dido	3.2.97	Venus
Stoute friend Achates, doest thou know this wood?	Dido	3.3.50	Aeneas
I, this it is which wounds me to the death,	Dido	3.3.63	Iarbus
This Troians end will be thy envies aime,	Dido	3.3.73	Iarbus
Tell me deare love, how found you out this Cave?	Dido	3.4.3	Dido
What meanes faire Dido by this doubtfull speech?	Dido	3.4.31	Aeneas
With this my hand I give to you my heart,	Dido	3.4.43	Aeneas
And by this Sword that saved me from the Greekes,	Dido	3.4.48	Aeneas
These golden bracelets, and this wedding ring,	Dido	3.4.62	Dido
In all this coyle, where have ye left the Queene?	Dido	4.1.14	Iarbus
Come forth the Cave: can heaven endure this sight?	Dido	4.1.17	Iarbus
Whil'st they were sporting in this darksome Cave?	Dido	4.1.24	Iarbus
But where were you Iarbus all this while?	Dido	4.1.31	Dido
partake with me the cause/Of this devotion that detaineth you,	Dido	4.2.28	Anna
Anna, against this Troian doe I pray,	Dido	4.2.30	Iarbus
In this delight of dying pensivenes:	Dido	4.2.44	Anna
Hermes this night descending in a dreame,	Dido	4.3.3	Aeneas
This is no life for men at armes to live,	Dido	4.3.33	Achat
I may not dure this female drudgerie,	Dido	4.3.55	Aeneas
Is this thy love to me?	Dido	4.4.16	Dido
me, for I forgot/That yong Ascanius lay with me this night:	Dido	4.4.32	Dido
And punish me Aeneas for this crime.	Dido	4.4.36	Dido
This kisse shall be faire Didos punishment.	Dido	4.4.37	Aeneas
How vaine am I to weare this Diadem,	Dido	4.4.40	Aeneas
And beare this golden Scepter in my hand?	Dido	4.4.41	Aeneas
This is the harbour that Aeneas seekes,	Dido	4.4.59	Aeneas
Speake of no other land, this land is thine,	Dido	4.4.83	Dido
Armies of foes resolv'd to winne this towne,	Dido	4.4.113	Dido
Is this the wood that grew in Carthage plaines,	Dido	4.4.136	Dido
Theres not so much as this base tackling too,	Dido	4.4.151	Dido
For this will Dido tye ye full of knots,	Dido	4.4.155	Dido
That I might live to see this boy a man,	Dido	4.5.18	Nurse
What length or bredth shal this brave towne containe?	Dido	5.1.16	Achat
And beautifying the Empire of this Queene,	Dido	5.1.28	Hermes
To sound this angrie message in thine eares.	Dido	5.1.33	Hermes
This was my mother that beguild the Queene,	Dido	5.1.42	Aeneas
Welcome sweet child, where hast thou been this long?	Dido	5.1.46	Aeneas
Spendst thou thy time about this little boy,	Dido	5.1.51	Hermes
Whil'st I rest thankfull for this curtesie.	Dido	5.1.77	Aeneas
this day swift Mercury/When I was laying a platforme for these	Dido	5.1.93	Aeneas
To leave this towne and passe to Italy,	Dido	5.1.100	Aeneas
Farewell: is this the mends for Didos love?	Dido	5.1.105	Dido
By this right hand, and by our spousall rites,	Dido	5.1.134	Dido
Ah foolish Dido to forbeare this long!	Dido	5.1.160	Dido
Wast thou not wrackt upon this Libian shoare,	Dido	5.1.161	Dido
By this is he got to the water side,	Dido	5.1.188	Dido
I crave but this, he stay a tide or two,	Dido	5.1.207	Dido
fleete, what shall I doe/But dye in furie of this oversight?	Dido	5.1.269	Dido
That shall consume all that this stranger left,	Dido	5.1.285	Dido
I, I, Iarbus, after this is done,	Dido	5.1.289	Dido
So, leave me now, let none approach this place.	Dido	5.1.291	Dido
Shall burne to cinders in this pretious flame.	Dido	5.1.301	Dido
That may revenge this treason to a Queene,	Dido	5.1.307	Dido
Betwixt this land and that be never league,	Dido	5.1.309	Dido
And mixe her bloud with thine, this shall I doe,	Dido	5.1.326	Anna
That Gods and men may pitie this my death,	Dido	5.1.327	Anna
View but his picture in this tragicke glasse,	1Tamb	Prol.7	Prolog
I might command you to be slaine for this,	1Tamb	1.1.23	Mycet
How like you this, my honorable Lords?	1Tamb	1.1.54	Mycet
Thou shalt be leader of this thousand horse,	1Tamb	1.1.62	Mycet
And ad this to them, that all Asia/Lament to see the follie of	1Tamb	1.1.95	Cosroe
Well here I sweare by this my royal seat--	1Tamb	1.1.97	Mycet
But this it is that doth excruciate/The verie substance of my	1Tamb	1.1.113	Cosroe
This should intreat your highnesse to rejoice,	1Tamb	1.1.123	Menaph
By curing of this maimed Emperie.	1Tamb	1.1.126	Menaph
But Menaphon, what means this trumpets sound?	1Tamb	1.1.133	Cosroe
And commons of this mightie Monarchie,	1Tamb	1.1.138	Ortyg
Come lady, let not this appal your thoughts.	1Tamb	1.2.1	Tamb
But Lady, this faire face and heavenly hew,	1Tamb	1.2.36	Tamb
This compleat armor, and this curtle-axe/Are adjuncts more	1Tamb	1.2.42	Tamb
and this curtle-axe/Are adjuncts more beseeming Tamburlaine.	1Tamb	1.2.42	Tamb
whatsoever you esteeme/Of this successe, and losse unvallued,	1Tamb	1.2.45	Tamb
Thinke you I way this treasure more than you?	1Tamb	1.2.84	Tamb
But this is she with whom I am in love.	1Tamb	1.2.108	Tamb
How say you Lordings, Is not this your hope?	1Tamb	1.2.116	Tamb
Where is this Scythian Tamburlaine?	1Tamb	1.2.152	Therid
Noble and milde this Persean seemes to be,	1Tamb	1.2.162	Tamb
He sends this Souldans daughter rich and brave,	1Tamb	1.2.186	Tamb
Besides thy share of this Egyptian prise,	1Tamb	1.2.190	Tamb
Joine with me now in this my meane estate,	1Tamb	1.2.202	Tamb
Come my Meander, let us to this geere,	1Tamb	2.2.1	Mycet
On this same theevish villaine Tamburlaine.	1Tamb	2.2.3	Mycet

THIS (cont.)

This countrie swarmes with vile outragious men,	1Tamb	2.2.22	Meandr
Here will I hide it in this simple hole.	1Tamb	2.4.15	Mycet
Is this your Crowne?	1Tamb	2.4.27	Tamb
O Gods, is this Tamburlaine the thiefe,	1Tamb	2.4.41	Mycet
Then shall we send to this triumphing King,	1Tamb	2.5.87	Techel
What means this divelish shepheard to aspire/With such a	1Tamb	2.6.1	Cosroe
So will I send this monstrous slave to hell,	1Tamb	2.6.7	Cosroe
Shall make me leave so rich a prize as this:	1Tamb	2.7.54	Tamb
To dispossesse me of this Diadem:	1Tamb	2.7.60	Tamb
As great commander of this Easterne world,	1Tamb	2.7.62	Tamb
All this is true as holy Mahomet,	1Tamb	3.1.54	Bajzth
destruction/Redeeme you from this deadly servitude.	1Tamb	3.2.34	Agidas
To dy by this resolved hand of thine,	1Tamb	3.2.98	Agidas
And with this stab slumber eternally.	1Tamb	3.2.106	Agidas
Bassoe, by this thy Lord and maister knowes,	1Tamb	3.3.1	Tamb
And for the expedition of this war,	1Tamb	3.3.20	Bassoe
This hand shal set them on your conquering heads:	1Tamb	3.3.31	Tamb
Note the presumption of this Scythian slave:	1Tamb	3.3.68	Bajzth
By this my sword that conquer'd Persea,	1Tamb	3.3.82	Tamb
Sit here upon this royal chaire of state,	1Tamb	3.3.112	Bajzth
Untill I bring this sturdy Tamburlain,	1Tamb	3.3.114	Bajzth
By this the Turks lie weltring in their blood/And Tamburlaine	1Tamb	3.3.201	Zenoc
Thou, by the fortune of this damned [foile] <soile>.	1Tamb	3.3.213	Bajzth
For though the glorie of this day be lost,	1Tamb	3.3.241	Bajzth
And by this meanes Ile win the world at last.	1Tamb	3.3.260	Tamb
Come bring them in, and for this happy conquest/Triumph, and	1Tamb	3.3.272	Tamb
This arme should send him downe to Erebus,	1Tamb	4.1.45	Souldn
faire Arabian king/That hath bene disapointed by this slave,	1Tamb	4.1.69	Souldn
And poure it in this glorious Tyrants throat.	1Tamb	4.2.7	Bajzth
But Villaine, thou that wishest this to me,	1Tamb	4.2.12	Tamb
With Eban Scepter strike this hatefull earth,	1Tamb	4.2.28	Bajzth
Even in Bythinia, when I took this Turke:	1Tamb	4.2.42	Tamb
Is this a place for mighty Bajazeth?	1Tamb	4.2.83	Bajzth
For he that gives him other food than this:	1Tamb	4.2.89	Tamb
This is my minde, and I will have it so.	1Tamb	4.2.91	Tamb
Even from this day to Platoes wondrous yeare,	1Tamb	4.2.96	Tamb
To tame the pride of this presumptuous Beast,	1Tamb	4.3.15	Souldn
And leave your venoms in this Tyrants dish.	1Tamb	4.4.22	Bajzth
And may this banquet proove as omenous,	1Tamb	4.4.23	Zabina
them leave Madam, this speech is a goodly refreshing to them.	1Tamb	4.4.32	P Techel
Doost thou think that Mahomet wil suffer this?	1Tamb	4.4.52	P Therid
And with this pen reduce them to a Map,	1Tamb	4.4.78	Tamb
say you to this (Turke) these are not your contributorie kings.	1Tamb	4.4.118	P Tamb
Stil dooth this man or rather God of war,	1Tamb	5.1.1	Govnr
That this devise may proove propitious,	1Tamb	5.1.52	2Virgn
(sacred Emperour)/The prostrate service of this wretched towne.	1Tamb	5.1.100	1Virgn
And take in signe thereof this gilded wreath,	1Tamb	5.1.101	1Virgn
And then shall we in this detested guyse,	1Tamb	5.1.235	Bajzth
By living long in this oppression,	1Tamb	5.1.251	Zabina
In this obscure infernall servitude?	1Tamb	5.1.254	Zabina
That in this terrour Tamburlaine may live.	1Tamb	5.1.299	Bajzth
wert thou the cause of this/That tearm'st Zenocrate thy dearest	1Tamb	5.1.335	Zenoc
Ah Madam, this their slavery hath Enforc'd,	1Tamb	5.1.345	Anippe
In this great Turk and haplesse Emperesse.	1Tamb	5.1.368	Zenoc
Of this infamous Tyrants souldiers,	1Tamb	5.1.404	Arabia
accidents/Have chanc'd thy merits in this worthles bondage.	1Tamb	5.1.425	Arabia
Which had ere this bin bathde in streames of blood,	1Tamb	5.1.438	Tamb
And I am pleasde with this my overthrow,	1Tamb	5.1.482	Souldn
Even by this hand that shall establish them,	1Tamb	5.1.492	Tamb
With this great Turke and his faire Emperesse:	1Tamb	5.1.532	Tamb
And make this champion mead a bloody Fen.	2Tamb	1.1.32	Orcan
Shall by this battell be the bloody Sea.	2Tamb	1.1.38	Orcan
Wilt thou have war, then shake this blade at me,	2Tamb	1.1.83	Sgsmnd
How canst thou think of this and offer war?	2Tamb	1.1.102	Orcan
And vow to keepe this peace inviolable.	2Tamb	1.1.136	Sgsmnd
I sweare to keepe this truce inviolable:	2Tamb	1.1.142	Orcan
of Natolia/Confirm'd this league beyond Danubius streame,	2Tamb	1.1.149	Orcan
Forbids you further liberty than this.	2Tamb	1.2.8	Almeda
Wel sir, what of this?	2Tamb	1.2.18	Almeda
And more than this, for all I cannot tell.	2Tamb	1.2.53	Callap
sent a thousand armed men/To intercept this haughty enterprize,	2Tamb	1.2.71	Almeda
This lovely boy the yongest of the three,	2Tamb	1.3.37	Zenoc
Larissa plaines/With hostes apeece against this Turkish crue,	2Tamb	1.3.108	Tamb
of Fesse have brought/To aide thee in this Turkish expedition,	2Tamb	1.3.131	Usumc
Whose lookes make this inferiour world to quake,	2Tamb	1.3.139	Techel
Meaning to aid [thee] <them> in this <these> Turkish armes,	2Tamb	1.3.144	Techel
For halfe the world shall perish in this fight:	2Tamb	1.3.171	Tamb
This should be treacherie and violence,	2Tamb	2.1.31	Sgsmnd
If we neglect this offered victory.	2Tamb	2.1.59	Fredrk
power and puritie/Behold and venge this Traitors perjury.	2Tamb	2.2.54	Orcan
Be now reveng'd upon this Traitors soule,	2Tamb	2.2.58	Orcan
In this my mortall well deserved wound,	2Tamb	2.3.6	Sgsmnd
And let this death wherein to sinne I die,	2Tamb	2.3.8	Sgsmnd
Whose power had share in this our victory:	2Tamb	2.3.35	Orcan
And since this miscreant hath disgrac'd his faith,	2Tamb	2.3.36	Orcan
ceaslesse lamps/That gently look'd upon this loathsome earth,	2Tamb	2.4.19	Tamb
And in this sweet and currious harmony,	2Tamb	2.4.30	Tamb
The God that tunes this musicke to our soules,	2Tamb	2.4.31	Tamb
That this my life may be as short to me/As are the daies of	2Tamb	2.4.36	Tamb
And if she passe this fit, the worst is past.	2Tamb	2.4.40	1Phstn
That when this fraile and transitory flesh/Hath suckt the	2Tamb	2.4.43	Zenoc
Than this base earth should shroud your majesty:	2Tamb	2.4.60	Zenoc

THIS (cont.)

To martch with me under this bloody flag:	2Tamb	2.4.116	Tamb
And all this raging cannot make her live,	2Tamb	2.4.120	Therid
This cursed towne will I consume with fire,	2Tamb	2.4.137	Tamb
Because this place bereft me of my Love:	2Tamb	2.4.138	Tamb
Then should you see this Thiefe of Scythia,	2Tamb	3.1.14	Callap
This proud usurping king of Persea,	2Tamb	3.1.15	Callap
not but your royall cares/Hath so provided for this cursed foe,	2Tamb	3.1.21	Callap
to as high a pitch/In this our strong and fortunate encounter.	2Tamb	3.1.31	Callap
By this my friendly keepers happy meanes,	2Tamb	3.1.34	Callap
All which will joine against this Tamburlain,	2Tamb	3.1.61	Soria
The poisoned braines of this proud Scythian.	2Tamb	3.1.67	Orcan
Wel then my noble Lords, for this my friend,	2Tamb	3.1.68	Callap
So, burne the turrets of this cursed towne,	2Tamb	3.2.1	Tamb
Threatning a death <dearth> and famine to this land,	2Tamb	3.2.9	Tamb
This Piller plac'd in memorie of her,	2Tamb	3.2.15	Calyph
Greek, is writ/This towne being burnt by Tamburlaine the great,	2Tamb	3.2.17	Calyph
And here this mournful streamer shal be plac'd/Wrought with the	2Tamb	3.2.19	Amyras
And here this table as a Register/Of all her vertues and	2Tamb	3.2.23	Celeb
Boyes leave to mourne, this towne shall ever mourne,	2Tamb	3.2.45	Tamb
And after this, to scale a castle wal,	2Tamb	3.2.59	Tamb
When this is learn'd for service on the land,	2Tamb	3.2.83	Tamb
When this is done, then are ye souldiers,	2Tamb	3.2.91	Tamb
My Lord, but this is dangerous to be done,	2Tamb	3.2.93	Calyph
a souldier, and this wound/As great a grace and majesty to me,	2Tamb	3.2.117	Tamb
My speech of war, and this my wound you see,	2Tamb	3.2.142	Tamb
And this is Balsera their chiefest hold,	2Tamb	3.3.3	Therid
No hope is left to save this conquered hold.	2Tamb	3.4.3	Olymp
Wel, this must be the messenger for thee.	2Tamb	3.4.15	Olymp
Ah sacred Mahomet, if this be sin,	2Tamb	3.4.31	Olymp
Then scortch a face so beautiful as this,	2Tamb	3.4.74	Techel
And let the end of this my fatall journey,	2Tamb	3.4.81	Olymp
Who by this time is at Natolia,	2Tamb	3.4.86	Therid
Rifling this Fort, devide in equall shares:	2Tamb	3.4.89	Therid
This Lady shall have twice so much againe,	2Tamb	3.4.90	Therid
with an hoste of men/Lies Tamburlaine, this king of Persea:	2Tamb	3.5.4	2Msngr
The field wherin this battaile shall be fought,	2Tamb	3.5.18	Callap
In memorie of this our victory.	2Tamb	3.5.20	Callap
Thinke of thy end, this sword shall lance thy throat.	2Tamb	3.5.78	Orcan
Come Almeda, receive this crowne of me,	2Tamb	3.5.129	Callap
See ye this rout, and know ye this same king?	2Tamb	3.5.151	Tamb
The glorie of this happy day is yours:	2Tamb	3.5.161	Tamb
I smile to think, how when this field is fought,	2Tamb	3.5.165	Techel
That they may say, it is not chance doth this,	2Tamb	4.1.84	Amyras
But wher's this coward, villaine, not my sonne,	2Tamb	4.1.89	Tamb
And joy'd the fire of this martiall flesh,	2Tamb	4.1.106	Tamb
For earth and al this aery region/Cannot containe the state of	2Tamb	4.1.119	Tamb
twixt our selves and thee/In this thy barbarous damned tyranny.	2Tamb	4.1.139	Orcan
Making them burie this effeminate brat,	2Tamb	4.1.162	Tamb
And since this earth, dew'd with thy brinish teares,	2Tamb	4.2.8	Olymp
Nor yet this aier, beat often with thy sighes,	2Tamb	4.2.10	Olymp
Let this invention be the instrument.	2Tamb	4.2.13	Olymp
Which beates against this prison to get out,	2Tamb	4.2.35	Olymp
Leave this my Love, and listen more to me.	2Tamb	4.2.38	Therid
will keep it for/The richest present of this Easterne world.	2Tamb	4.2.78	Therid
Cut off this arme that murthered my Love:	2Tamb	4.2.83	Therid
In whom the learned Rabies of this age,	2Tamb	4.2.84	Therid
To entertaine this Queene of chastitie,	2Tamb	4.2.96	Therid
Than you by this unconquered arme of mine.	2Tamb	4.3.16	Tamb
and to subdew/This proud contemner of thy dreadfull power,	2Tamb	4.3.40	Orcan
I Turke, I tel thee, this same Boy is he,	2Tamb	4.3.57	Tamb
That must (advaunst in higher pompe than this)/Rifle the	2Tamb	4.3.58	Tamb
And tremble when ye heare this Scourge wil come,	2Tamb	4.3.99	Tamb
Until my soule dissevered from this flesh,	2Tamb	4.3.131	Tamb
When this our famous lake of Limnasphaltis/Makes walles a fresh	2Tamb	5.1.17	Govnr
Though this be held his last daies dreadfull siege,	2Tamb	5.1.29	1Citzn
And this eternisde citie Babylon,	2Tamb	5.1.35	Govnr
Upon the ruines of this conquered towne.	2Tamb	5.1.85	Tamb
When this is done, we'll martch from Babylon,	2Tamb	5.1.127	Tamb
That I may sheath it in this breast of mine,	2Tamb	5.1.143	Jrslem
our hearts/More than the thought of this dooth vexe our soules.	2Tamb	5.1.145	Jrslem
and let this wound appease/The mortall furie of great	2Tamb	5.1.153	Govnr
And let this Captaine be remoov'd the walles,	2Tamb	5.1.215	Therid
To joine with you against this Tamburlaine.	2Tamb	5.2.35	Amasia
This is the time that must eternize me,	2Tamb	5.2.54	Callap
And guide this massy substance of the earthe,	2Tamb	5.3.18	Techel
Why, shal I sit and languish in this paine?	2Tamb	5.3.56	Tamb
No, strike the drums, and in revenge of this,	2Tamb	5.3.57	Tamb
Sit stil my gratious Lord, this griefe wil cease,	2Tamb	5.3.64	Techel
Pleaseth your Majesty to drink this potion,	2Tamb	5.3.78	Phsitn
Besides my Lord, this day is Criticall,	2Tamb	5.3.91	Phsitn
Yet if your majesty may escape this day,	2Tamb	5.3.98	Phsitn
As much too high for this disdainfull earth.	2Tamb	5.3.122	Tamb
Unto the rising of this earthly globe,	2Tamb	5.3.147	Tamb
And shall I die, and this unconquered?	2Tamb	5.3.150	Tamb
And shal I die, and this unconquered?	2Tamb	5.3.158	Tamb
But sons, this subject not of force enough,	2Tamb	5.3.168	Tamb
with what a broken hart/And damned spirit I ascend this seat,	2Tamb	5.3.207	Amyras
Let it be plac'd by this my fatall chaire,	2Tamb	5.3.211	Tamb
is come from France/To view this Land, and frolicke with his	Jew	Prol.4	Machvl
I crave but this, Grace him as he deserves,	Jew	Prol.33	Machvl
Fye; what a trouble tis to count this trash.	Jew	1.1.7	Barab
And of a Carrect of this quantity,	Jew	1.1.30	Barab

THIS (cont.)

of judgement frame/This is the ware wherein consists my wealth:	Jew	1.1.33	Barab
But this we heard some of our sea-men say,	Jew	1.1.78	1Merch
And yet I wonder at this Argosie.	Jew	1.1.84	Barab
And they this day sit in the Counsell-house/To entertaine them	Jew	1.1.148	1Jew
And Barabas now search this secret out.	Jew	1.1.177	Barab
To what this ten yeares tribute will amount/That we have cast,	Jew	1.2.46	Govnr
Lastly, he that denies this, shall absolutely lose al he has.	Jew	1.2.76	P Reader
Why know you what you did by this device?	Jew	1.2.84	Barab
gather of these goods/The mony for this tribute of the Turke.	Jew	1.2.156	Govnr
Oh silly brethren, borne to see this day!	Jew	1.2.170	Barab
Why pine not I, and dye in this distresse?	Jew	1.2.173	Barab
hardly can we brooke/The cruell handling of our selves in this:	Jew	1.2.175	1Jew
I, let me sorrow for this sudden chance,	Jew	1.2.206	Barab
Fearing the worst of this before it fell,	Jew	1.2.246	Barab
You partiall heavens, have I deserv'd this plague?	Jew	1.2.259	Barab
No, I will live; nor loath I this my life:	Jew	1.2.266	Barab
This shall follow then;/There have I hid close underneath the	Jew	1.2.295	Barab
No, Abigall, in this/It is not necessary I be seene.	Jew	1.2.301	Barab
Be close, my girle, for this must fetch my gold.	Jew	1.2.304	Barab
But, Madam, this house/And waters of this new made Nunnery	Jew	1.2.310	1Fryar
And waters of this new made Nunnery/Will much delight you.	Jew	1.2.311	1Fryar
No doubt, brother, but this proceedeth of the spirit.	Jew	1.2.327	1Fryar
Whose this?	Jew	1.2.366	Mthias
sudden fall/Has humbled her and brought her downe to this:	Jew	1.2.368	Mthias
and direct the hand/Of Abigall this night; or let the day/Turne	Jew	2.1.15	Barab
night; or let the day/Turne to eternall darkenesse after this:	Jew	2.1.16	Barab
fortune were so good/As but to be about this happy place;	Jew	2.1.32	Abigal
And 'bout this time the Nuns begin to wake;	Jew	2.1.56	Abigal
This truce we have is but in hope of gold,	Jew	2.2.26	1Knght
My Lord and King hath title to this Isle,	Jew	2.2.37	Bosco
On this condition shall thy Turkes be sold.	Jew	2.2.42	Govnr
This is the Market-place, here let 'em stand:	Jew	2.3.1	1Offcr
I heare the wealthy Jew walked this way;	Jew	2.3.32	Lodowk
marketplace; whats the price of this slave, two hundred Crowns?	Jew	2.3.98	P Barab
Ratest thou this Moore but at two hundred plats?	Jew	2.3.107	Lodowk
Why should this Turke be dearer then that Moore?	Jew	2.3.109	Barab
I, marke him, you were best, for this is he	Jew	2.3.132	Barab
This Moore is comeliest, is he not? speake son.	Jew	2.3.144	Mater
No, this is the better, mother, view this well.	Jew	2.3.145	Mthias
Oh brave, master, I worship your nose for this.	Jew	2.3.173	Ithimr
Why this is something:	Jew	2.3.213	Barab
For now by this has he kist Abigall;	Jew	2.3.246	Barab
What, hand in hand, I cannot suffer this.	Jew	2.3.276	Mthias
This is thy Diamond, tell me, shall I have it?	Jew	2.3.292	Lodowk
yet let me talke to her;/This off-spring of Cain, this Jebusite	Jew	2.3.301	Barab
This gentle Magot, Lodowicke I meane,	Jew	2.3.305	Barab
This followes well, and therefore daughter feare not.	Jew	2.3.313	Barab
For this I'le have his heart.	Jew	2.3.344	Mthias
Now tell me, Ithimore, how lik'st thou this?	Jew	2.3.364	Barab
Faith Master, I thinke by this/You purchase both their lives; is	Jew	2.3.365	Ithimr
Oh, master, that I might have a hand in this.	Jew	2.3.368	Ithimr
Take this and beare it to Mathias streight,	Jew	2.3.370	Barab
As I behave my selfe in this, imploy me hereafter.	Jew	2.3.379	Ithimr
Since this Towne was besieg'd, my gaine growes cold:	Jew	3.1.1	Curtzn
Tell me, how cam'st thou by this?	Jew	3.1.16	Curtzn
rumbling in the house; so I tooke onely this, and runne my way:	Jew	3.1.21	P Pilia
This is the place, now Abigall shall see/Whether Mathias holds	Jew	3.2.1	Mthias
What sight is this? my [Lodovico] <Lodowicke> slaine!	Jew	3.2.10	Govnr
Who is this? my sonne Mathias slaine!	Jew	3.2.12	Mater
Well, Ithimore, let me request thee this,	Jew	3.3.26	Abigal
Go to, sirra sauce, is this your question?	Jew	3.3.34	P Abigal
Was this the pursuit of thy policie?	Jew	3.3.37	Abigal
Who taught thee this?	Jew	3.3.66	1Fryar
Repentance? Spurca: what pretendeth this?	Jew	3.4.6	Barab
And [less] <least> thou yeeld to this that I intreat,	Jew	3.4.37	Barab
Onely know this, that thus thou art to doe:	Jew	3.4.48	Barab
I but Ithimore seest thou this?	Jew	3.4.67	Barab
This Even they use in Malta here ('tis call'd/Saint Jaques	Jew	3.4.75	Barab
Among the rest beare this, and set it there;	Jew	3.4.78	Barab
There Ithimore must thou goe place this [pot] <plot>:	Jew	3.4.84	Barab
Breake from the fiery kingdome; and in this/Vomit your venome,	Jew	3.4.103	Barab
For by this Answer, broken is the league,	Jew	3.5.34	Govnr
That in this house I liv'd religiously,	Jew	3.6.13	Abigal
To worke my peace, this I confesse to thee;	Jew	3.6.31	Abigal
First helpe to bury this, then goe with me/And helpe me to	Jew	3.6.45	2Fryar
What needs all this? I know I am a Jew.	Jew	4.1.33	Barab
Would pennance serve for this my sinne,	Jew	4.1.58	Barab
But yesterday two ships went from this Towne,	Jew	4.1.69	Barab
All this I'le give to some religious house/So I may be baptiz'd	Jew	4.1.75	Barab
Come to my house at one a clocke this night.	Jew	4.1.91	Barab
This is meere frailty, brethren, be content.	Jew	4.1.98	Barab
Who would not thinke but that this Fryar liv'd?	Jew	4.1.156	Barab
This is the houre/Wherein I shall proceed; Oh happy houre,	Jew	4.1.160	1Fryar
But soft, is not this Bernardine?	Jew	4.1.164	1Fryar
And understanding I should come this way,	Jew	4.1.165	1Fryar
That being importun'd by this Bernardine/To be a Christian, I	Jew	4.1.187	Barab
No, for this example I'le remaine a Jew:	Jew	4.1.195	Barab
I never knew a man take his death so patiently as this Fryar;	Jew	4.2.21	P Ithimr
This is the Gentleman you writ to.	Jew	4.2.37	P Pilia
I did Sir, and from this Gentlewoman, who as my selfe, and the	Jew	4.2.43	P Pilia
What shall we doe with this base villaine then?	Jew	4.2.62	Curtzn
I charge thee send me three hundred by this bearer, and this	Jew	4.2.75	P Ithimr

THIS (cont.)

by this bearer, and this shall be your warrant; if you doe not,	Jew		4.2.76	P Ithimr
Content, but we will leave this paltry land,	Jew		4.2.88	Ithimr
I must make this villaine away:	Jew		4.3.29	P Barab
this angers me,/That he who knowes I love him as my selfe	Jew		4.3.41	Barab
I love him as my selfe/Should write in this imperious vaine!	Jew		4.3.43	Barab
This shall with me unto the Governor.	Jew		4.4.25	Pilia
here's to thee with a--pox on this drunken hick-up.	Jew		4.4.33	P Ithimr
What a slave's this?	Jew		4.4.63	P Barab
Had we but proofe of this--	Jew		5.1.15	Govnr
For none of this can prejudice my life.	Jew		5.1.39	Barab
This sudden death of his is very strange.	Jew		5.1.54	Bosco
I'le be reveng'd on this accursed Towne;	Jew		5.1.62	Barab
And by this meanes the City is your owne.	Jew		5.1.94	Barab
If this be true, I'le make thee Governor.	Jew		5.1.95	Calym
No, Barabas, this must be look'd into;	Jew		5.2.34	Barab
This is the reason that I sent for thee;	Jew		5.2.51	Barab
This, Barabas; since things are in thy power,	Jew		5.2.57	Govnr
as once you said, within this Ile/In Malta here, that I have got	Jew		5.2.67	Barab
And in this City still have had successe,	Jew		5.2.69	Barab
What will you give him that procureth this?	Jew		5.2.83	Barab
Doe but bring this to passe which thou pretendest,	Jew		5.2.84	Govnr
Nay more, doe this, and live thou Governor still.	Jew		5.2.89	Govnr
Nay, doe thou this, Ferneze, and be free;	Jew		5.2.90	Barab
Then will I, Barabas, about this coyne,	Jew		5.2.107	Govnr
This is the life we Jewes are us'd to lead;	Jew		5.2.115	Barab
Well, now about effecting this device:	Jew		5.2.117	Barab
And how secure this conquer'd Iland stands/Inviron'd with the	Jew		5.3.6	Calym
Wee'll in this Summer Evening feast with him.	Jew		5.3.41	Calym
In this, my Countrimen, be rul'd by me,	Jew		5.4.1	Govnr
Or you released of this servitude.	Jew		5.4.7	Govnr
The floore whereof, this Cable being cut,	Jew		5.5.34	Barab
And fire the house; say, will not this be brave?	Jew		5.5.41	Barab
Why, is not this/A kingly kinde of trade	Jew		5.5.46	Barab
How now, what means this?	Jew		5.5.64	Calym
See Calymath, this was devis'd for thee.	Jew		5.5.66	Govnr
And had I but escap'd this stratagem,	Jew		5.5.84	Barab
Tell me, you Christians, what doth this portend?	Jew		5.5.90	Calym
This traine he laid to have intrap'd thy life;	Jew		5.5.91	Govnr
Was this the banquet he prepar'd for us?	Jew		5.5.95	Calym
And doe attend my comming there by this.	Jew		5.5.104	Calym
I wishe this union and religious league,	P	3	1.3	Charls
That kindled first this motion in our hearts,	P	7	1.7	Charls
From time to time, but specially in this,	P	10	1.10	Navrre
Let us goe to honor this solemnitie.	P	25	1.25	Charls
And make his Gospel flourish in this land.	P	57	1.57	Navrre
This day, this houre, this fatall night,	P	64	2.7	Guise
For this, I wake, when others think I sleepe,	P	105	2.48	Guise
For this, I waite, that scornes attendance else:	P	106	2.49	Guise
For this, my quenchles thirst whereon I builde,	P	107	2.50	Guise
For this, this head, this heart, this hand and sworde,	P	109	2.52	Guise
For this, hath heaven engendred me of earth,	P	113	2.56	Guise
For this, this earth sustaines my bodies [waight],	P	114	2.57	Guise
And with this wait Ile counterpoise a Crowne,	P	115	2.58	Guise
For this, from Spaine the stately Catholickes/Sends Indian	P	117	2.60	Guise
For this have I a largesse from the Pope,	P	119	2.62	Guise
All this and more, if more may be comprisde,	P	143	2.86	Guise
within thy hands/To shuffle or cut, take this as surest thing:	P	147	2.90	Guise
Maddame, I beseech your grace to except this simple gift.	P	166	3.1	P Pothec
Thanks my good freend, holde, take thou this reward.	P	168	3.3	OldQn
Let not this heavy chaunce my dearest Lord,	P	191	3.26	QnMarg
betraide, come my Lords, and let us goe tell the King of this.	P	200	3.35	P Navrre
Oh fatall was this mariage to us all.	P	202	3.37	Admral
They that shalbe actors in this Massacre,	P	231	4.29	Guise
I sweare by this to be unmercifull.	P	277	5.4	Dumain
Shall in the entrance of this Massacre,	P	286	5.13	Guise
In lucky time, come let us keep this lane,	P	298	5.25	Anjoy
Then pray unto our Ladye, kisse this crosse.	P	302	5.29	Gonzag
And when this just revenge is finished,	P	318	5.45	Anjoy
I sweare by this crosse, wee'l not be partiall,	P	325	5.52	Anjoy
I, I, for this Seroune, and thou shalt [ha't] <hate>.	P	351	6.6	Mntsrl
Then take this with you.	P	360	6.15	Mntsrl
And ipse dixi with this quidditie,	P	394	7.34	Guise
Not for my life doe I desire this pause,	P	401	7.41	Ramus
And this for Aristotle will I say,	P	408	7.48	Ramus
I have done what I could to stay this broile.	P	434	7.74	Anjoy
That you were one that made this Massacre.	P	436	7.76	Navrre
And now sirs for this night let our fury stay.	P	443	7.83	Guise
If your commission serve to warrant this,	P	475	8.25	Anjoy
All this and more your highnes shall commaund,	P	479	8.29	Lord
all doubts, be rulde by me, lets hang him heere upon this tree.	P	492	9.11	P 2Atndt
As I could long ere this have wisht him there.	P	496	9.15	QnMoth
And dayly meet about this time of day,	P	503	9.22	Guise
All this and more hath Henry with his crowne.	P	596	12.9	QnMoth
And long may Henry enjoy all this and more.	P	597	12.10	Cardnl
To punish those that doe prophane this holy feast.	P	617	12.30	Mugern
Hands of good fellow, I will be his baile/For this offence:	P	623	12.36	King
Till this our Coronation day be past:	P	624	12.37	King
To work the way to bring this thing to passe:	P	649	12.62	QnMoth
And then determine of this enterprise.	P	656	12.69	QnMoth
O would to God this quill that heere doth write,	P	667	13.11	Duchss
This wrathfull hand should strike thee to the hart.	P	690	13.34	Guise
And rent our true religion from this land:	P	703	14.6	Navrre

THIS (cont.)

Then in this bloudy brunt they may beholde,	P 713	14.16	Bartus
This is the Guise that hath incenst the King,	P 729	14.32	Navrre
How now my Lord, faith this is more then need,	P 757	15.15	Guise
That villain for whom I beare this deep disgrace,	P 766	15.24	Guise
Beleeve me this jest bites sore.	P 771	15.29	King
I like not this, come Epernoune/Lets goe seek the Duke and make	P 785	15.43	King
The terrour of this happy victory,	P 791	16.5	Bartus
Come my Lords, now that this storme is overpast,	P 804	16.18	Navrre
yet I meane to keepe you out, which I will if this geare holde:	P 815	17.10	P Souldr
Holde thee tall Souldier, take thee this and flye.	P 817	17.12	Guise
First let us set our hand and seale to this,	P 890	17.85	King
So, convey this to the counsell presently.	P 892	17.87	King
Then sirs take your standings within this Chamber,	P 940	19.10	Capt
How fares it this morning with your excellence?	P 966	19.36	King
Why this tis to have an army in the fielde.	P 980	19.50	Guise
So will I triumph over this wanton King,	P 983	19.53	Guise
To dye by Pesantes, what a greefe is this?	P1009	19.79	Guise
Ah this sweet sight is phisick to my soule,	P1020	19.90	King
I nere was King of France untill this houre:	P1027	19.97	King
This is the traitor that hath spent my golde,	P1028	19.98	King
Let Christian princes that shall heare of this,	P1041	19.111	King
our Guise is dead)/Rest satisfied with this that heer I sweare,	P1043	19.113	King
My father slaine, who hath done this deed?	P1047	19.117	YngGse
Art thou King, and hast done this bloudy deed?	P1050	19.120	YngGse
But what availeth that this traitors dead,	P1054	19.124	King
Mother, how like you this device of mine?	P1065	19.135	King
Pray God thou be a King now this is done.	P1068	19.138	QnMoth
Tis warre that must asswage this tyrantes pride.	P1128	21.22	Dumain
We will goe talke more of this within.	P1138	21.32	Dumain
Girting this strumpet Cittie with our siege,	P1152	22.14	King
I like not this Friers look.	P1159	22.21	Eprnon
Ile send my sister England newes of this,	P1189	22.51	King
What this detested Jacobin hath done.	P1195	22.57	King
Tell her for all this that I hope to live,	P1196	22.58	King
To see your highnes in this vertuous minde.	P1210	22.72	Navrre
Fight in the quarrell of this valiant Prince,	P1229	22.91	King
Ah Epernoune, is this thy love to me?	P1235	22.97	King
this is againste the lawe ser:	Paris	ms14,p390	P Souldr
Hold thee tale soldier take the this and flye	Paris	ms18,p390	Guise
and when thow thinkst I have foregotten this	Paris	ms20,p391	Guise
Will you not graunt me this?--	Edw	1.1.77	Edward
Mine unckle heere, this Earle, and I my selfe,	Edw	1.1.82	Mortmr
This sword of mine that should offend your foes,	Edw	1.1.86	Mortmr
Thou shouldst not plod one foote beyond this place.	Edw	1.1.181	Gavstn
For this offence be thou accurst of God.	Edw	1.1.199	BshpCv
Whose there? conveie this priest to the tower.	Edw	1.1.200	Edward
This ground which is corrupted with their steps,	Edw	1.2.5	Lncstr
We may not, nor we will not suffer this.	Edw	1.2.15	MortSr
This certifie the Pope, away, take horsse.	Edw	1.2.38	ArchBp
My lords, to eaze all this, but heare me speake.	Edw	1.2.68	ArchBp
But say my lord, where shall this meeting bee?	Edw	1.2.74	Warwck
What man of noble birth can brooke this sight?	Edw	1.4.12	MortSr
Is this the dutie that you owe your king?	Edw	1.4.22	Kent
Think you that we can brooke this upstart pride?	Edw	1.4.41	Warwck
Meete you for this, proud overdaring peeres?	Edw	1.4.47	Edward
This Ile shall fleete upon the Ocean,	Edw	1.4.49	Edward
if this content you not,/Make severall kingdomes of this	Edw	1.4.69	Edward
Make severall kingdomes of this monarchie,	Edw	1.4.70	Edward
This will be good newes to the common sort.	Edw	1.4.92	Penbrk
Is all my hope turnd to this hell of greefe.	Edw	1.4.116	Gavstn
Thou from this land, I from my selfe am banisht.	Edw	1.4.118	Edward
And onely this torments my wretched soule,	Edw	1.4.123	Edward
O might I keepe thee heere, as I doe this,	Edw	1.4.128	Edward
In saying this, thou wrongst me Gaveston,	Edw	1.4.149	Queene
Witnesse this hart, that sighing for thee breakes,	Edw	1.4.165	Queene
This wils my lord, and this must I performe,	Edw	1.4.202	Queene
Can this be true twas good to banish him,	Edw	1.4.245	Lncstr
And is this true to call him home againe?	Edw	1.4.246	Lncstr
This which I urge, is of a burning zeale,	Edw	1.4.256	Mortmr
I, but how chance this was not done before?	Edw	1.4.272	Lncstr
My lords, if to performe this I be slack,	Edw	1.4.290	Mortmr
In this I count me highly gratified,	Edw	1.4.295	Mortmr
And when this favour Isabell forgets,	Edw	1.4.297	Queene
Is new returnd, this newes will glad him much,	Edw	1.4.301	Queene
Then I may fetch from this ritch treasurie:	Edw	1.4.332	Queene
Once more receive my hand, and let this be,	Edw	1.4.334	Edward
This salutation overjoyes my heart.	Edw	1.4.344	Lncstr
And with this sword, Penbrooke wil fight for you.	Edw	1.4.352	Penbrk
In this your grace hath highly honoured me,	Edw	1.4.364	MortSr
In this, or ought, your highnes shall commaund us.	Edw	1.4.384	Warwck
But this I scorne, that one so baselie borne,	Edw	1.4.403	Mortmr
Unckle, tis this that makes me impatient.	Edw	1.4.419	Mortmr
learne this of me, a factious lord/Shall hardly do himselfe	Edw	2.1.6	Spencr
Leave of this jesting, here my lady comes.	Edw	2.1.56	Baldck
This letter came from my sweete Gaveston,	Edw	2.1.59	Neece
This argues the entire love of my Lord.	Edw	2.1.63	Neece
this fish my lord I beare,/The motto this:	Edw	2.2.27	Lncstr
The motto this: Undique mors est.	Edw	2.2.28	Lncstr
Is this the love you beare your soveraigne?	Edw	2.2.30	Edward
Is this the fruite your reconcilement beares?	Edw	2.2.31	Edward
What call you this but private libelling,	Edw	2.2.34	Edward
Yet I disdaine not to doe this for you.	Edw	2.2.79	Lncstr

THIS (cont.)

The life of thee shall salve this foule disgrace.	Edw	2.2.83	Gavstn
Deare shall you both abie this riotous deede:	Edw	2.2.88	Edward
I marry, such a garde as this dooth well.	Edw	2.2.131	Mortmr
How now, what noise is this?	Edw	2.2.139	Edward
Your minion Gaveston hath taught you this.	Edw	2.2.149	Lncstr
To Englands high disgrace, have made this Jig,	Edw	2.2.189	Lncstr
Cosin, this day shalbe your mariage feast,	Edw	2.2.256	Edward
My lords, of love to this our native land,	Edw	2.3.1	Kent
now my lords know this,/That Gaveston is secretlie arrivde,	Edw	2.3.15	Lncstr
This tottered ensigne of my auncesters,	Edw	2.3.21	Mortmr
Will I advaunce upon this castell walles,	Edw	2.3.24	Mortmr
O that mine armes could close this Ile about,	Edw	2.4.17	Queene
Whose this, the Queene?	Edw	2.4.22	Mortmr
That this your armie going severall waies,	Edw	2.4.42	Queene
Madam, stay you within this castell here.	Edw	2.4.50	Mortmr
And Gaveston this blessed day be slaine.	Edw	2.4.69	Queene
gratifie the king/In other matters, he must pardon us in this,	Edw	2.5.44	Warwck
I know it lords, it is this life you aime at,	Edw	2.5.48	Gavstn
it is this life you aime at,/Yet graunt king Edward this.	Edw	2.5.49	Gavstn
It is honourable in thee to offer this,	Edw	2.5.67	Mortmr
Touching the sending of this Gaveston,	Edw	2.5.76	Penbrk
Provided this, that you my lord of Arundell/Will joyne with me.	Edw	2.5.81	Penbrk
My lord of Lancaster, what say you in this?	Edw	2.5.89	Arundl
I do commit this Gaveston to thee,	Edw	2.5.107	Penbrk
Be thou this night his keeper, in the morning/We will discharge	Edw	2.5.108	Penbrk
O must this day be period of my life,	Edw	2.6.4	Gavstn
this rage, and suffer uncontrowld/These Barons thus to beard me	Edw	3.1.13	Spencr
This haught resolve becomes your majestie,	Edw	3.1.28	Baldck
Spencer, this love, this kindnes to thy King,	Edw	3.1.47	Edward
These be the letters, this the messenger.	Edw	3.1.65	Queene
Sib, if this be all/Valoys and I will soone be friends againe.	Edw	3.1.66	Edward
Madam in this matter/We will employ you and your little sonne,	Edw	3.1.69	Edward
this towardnes makes thy mother feare/Thou art not markt to	Edw	3.1.79	Queene
And this our sonne, [Levune] <Lewne> shall follow you,	Edw	3.1.82	Edward
I will this undertake, to have him hence,	Edw	3.1.111	Arundl
By this right hand, and by my fathers sword,	Edw	3.1.130	Edward
And in this place of honor and of trust,	Edw	3.1.143	Edward
You will this greefe have ease and remedie,	Edw	3.1.160	Herald
That from your princely person you remoove/This Spencer, as a	Edw	3.1.162	Herald
This graunted, they, their honors, and their lives,	Edw	3.1.170	Herald
This day I shall powre vengeance with my sword/On those proud	Edw	3.1.186	Edward
And this retire refresheth horse and man.	Edw	3.1.193	SpncrP
Grone for this greefe, behold how thou art maimed.	Edw	3.1.251	Mortmr
Edward this day hath crownd him king a new.	Edw	3.1.261	Edward
Nature, yeeld to my countries cause in this.	Edw	4.1.3	Kent
A boye, thou art deceivde at least in this,	Edw	4.2.8	Queene
To this distressed Queene his sister heere,	Edw	4.2.63	SrJohn
This noble gentleman, forward in armes,	Edw	4.2.76	Mortmr
this is all the newes of import.	Edw	4.3.36	P Spencr
Misgoverned kings are cause of all this wrack,	Edw	4.4.9	Queene
Arrivde and armed in this princes right,	Edw	4.4.18	Mortmr
And in this bed of [honor] <honors> die with fame.	Edw	4.5.7	Edward
O no my lord, this princely resolution/Fits not the time, away,	Edw	4.5.8	Baldck
This way he fled, but I am come too late.	Edw	4.6.1	Kent
to whom in justice it belongs/To punish this unnaturall revolt:	Edw	4.6.9	Kent
Edward, this Mortimer aimes at thy life:	Edw	4.6.10	Kent
O fly him then, but Edmund calme this rage,	Edw	4.6.11	Kent
Deale you my lords in this, my loving lords,	Edw	4.6.28	Queene
I like not this relenting moode in Edmund,	Edw	4.6.38	Mortmr
This, Edward, is the ruine of the realme.	Edw	4.6.45	Kent
In signe of love and dutie to this presence,	Edw	4.6.48	Rice
Present by me this traitor to the state,	Edw	4.6.49	Rice
Your loving care in this,/Deserveth princelie favors and	Edw	4.6.53	Mortmr
Care of my countrie cald me to this warre.	Edw	4.6.65	Queene
Meane while, have hence this rebell to the blocke,	Edw	4.6.69	Mortmr
As daunger of this stormie time requires.	Edw	4.7.7	Abbot
Father, this life contemplative is heaven,	Edw	4.7.20	Edward
O that I might this life in quiet lead,	Edw	4.7.21	Edward
good father on thy lap/Lay I this head, laden with mickle care,	Edw	4.7.40	Edward
Never againe lift up this drooping head,	Edw	4.7.42	Edward
O never more lift up this dying hart!	Edw	4.7.43	Edward
Baldock, this drowsines/Betides no good, here even we are	Edw	4.7.44	Spencr
Here man, rip up this panting brest of mine,	Edw	4.7.66	Edward
My heart with pittie earnes to see this sight,	Edw	4.7.70	Abbot
The gentle heavens have not to do in this.	Edw	4.7.76	Edward
Reduce we all our lessons unto this,	Edw	4.7.110	Baldck
Whilst I am lodgd within this cave of care,	Edw	5.1.32	Edward
That bleedes within me for this strange exchange.	Edw	5.1.35	Edward
But if proud Mortimer do weare this crowne,	Edw	5.1.43	Edward
That I may gaze upon this glittering crowne,	Edw	5.1.60	Edward
Let never silent night possesse this clime,	Edw	5.1.65	Edward
And in this torment, comfort finde I none,	Edw	5.1.81	Edward
This answer weele returne, and so farewell.	Edw	5.1.90	BshpWn
Make me despise this transitorie pompe,	Edw	5.1.108	Edward
is there in a Tigers jawes,/[Then] <This> his imbrasements:	Edw	5.1.117	Edward
beare this to the queene,/Wet with my teares, and dried againe	Edw	5.1.117	Edward
This poore revenge hath something easd my minde,	Edw	5.1.141	Edward
So may his limmes be torne, as is this paper,	Edw	5.1.142	Edward
I know not, but of this am I assured,	Edw	5.1.152	Edward
Further, or this letter was sealed, Lord Bartley came,	Edw	5.2.30	BshpWn
And this above the rest, because we heare/That Edmund casts to	Edw	5.2.57	Mortmr
Whither goes this letter, to my lord the king?	Edw	5.2.68	Queene

THIS (cont.)

And beare him this, as witnesse of my love.	Edw		5.2.72		Queene
Come sonne, and go with this gentle Lorde and me.	Edw		5.2.109		Queene
If mine will serve, unbowell straight this brest,	Edw		5.3.10		Edward
Not so my liege, the Queene hath given this charge,	Edw		5.3.13		Gurney
This usage makes my miserie increase.	Edw		5.3.16		Edward
Lay hands upon the earle for this assault.	Edw		5.3.54		Gurney
This letter written by a friend of ours,	Edw		5.4.6		Mortmr
Within this roome is lockt the messenger,	Edw		5.4.17		Mortmr
Deliver this to Gurney and Matrevis,	Edw		5.4.41		Mortmr
Take this, away, and never see me more.	Edw		5.4.43		Mortmr
And that this be the coronation day,	Edw		5.4.70		Mortmr
And thou compelst this prince to weare the crowne.	Edw		5.4.88		Kent
But stay, whose this?	Edw		5.5.14		Matrvs
Know you this token? I must have the king.	Edw		5.5.19		Ltborn
This villain's sent to make away the king.	Edw		5.5.21		Matrvs
Heere is the keyes, this is the lake,/Doe as you are commaunded	Edw		5.5.25		Matrvs
So,/Now must I about this geare, nere was there any/So finely	Edw		5.5.39		Ltborn
nere was there any/So finely handled as this king shalbe.	Edw		5.5.40		Ltborn
For she relents at this your miserie.	Edw		5.5.49		Ltborn
To see a king in this most pittious state?	Edw		5.5.51		Ltborn
This dungeon where they keepe me, is the sincke,	Edw		5.5.56		Edward
This ten dayes space, and least that I should sleepe,	Edw		5.5.60		Edward
As doth this water from my tattered robes:	Edw		5.5.67		Edward
O speake no more my lorde, this breakes my heart.	Edw		5.5.71		Ltborn
Lie on this bed, and rest your selfe a while.	Edw		5.5.72		Ltborn
One jewell have I left, receive thou this.	Edw		5.5.84		Edward
Let this gift change thy minde, and save thy soule,	Edw		5.5.88		Edward
This feare is that which makes me tremble thus,	Edw		5.5.105		Edward
I feare mee that this crie will raise the towne,	Edw		5.5.114		Matrvs
Excellent well, take this for thy rewarde.	Edw		5.5.117		Gurney
Whether thou wilt be secret in this,	Edw		5.6.5		Mortmr
But hath your grace no other proofe then this?	Edw		5.6.43		Mortmr
Yes, if this be the hand of Mortimer.	Edw		5.6.44		King
Tis my hand, what gather you by this.	Edw		5.6.47		Mortmr
This argues, that you spilt my fathers bloud,	Edw		5.6.70		King
Is this report raisde on poore Isabell.	Edw		5.6.75		Queene
Then come sweete death, and rid me of this greefe.	Edw		5.6.92		Queene
Thou hadst not hatcht this monstrous treacherie!	Edw		5.6.97		King
I offer up this wicked traitors head,	Edw		5.6.100		King
<daunt> his heavenly verse;/Onely this, Gentles <Gentlemen>:	F	7	Prol.7		1Chor
And this the man that in his study sits.	F	28	Prol.28		1Chor
Affoords this Art no greater miracle?	F	37	1.1.9		Faust
Then this profession were to be esteem'd.	F	54	1.1.26		Faust
This <His> study fits a Mercenarie drudge,	F	61	1.1.33		Faust
What doctrine call you this? Che sera, sera:	F	74	1.1.46		Faust
But his dominion that exceeds <excells> in this,	F	87	1.1.59		Faust
How am I glutted with conceipt of this?	F	105	1.1.77		Faust
Then gentle friends aid me in this attempt,	F	138	1.1.110		Faust
Valdes, as resolute am I in this,	F	161	1.1.133		Faust
And more frequented for this mysterie,	F	169	1.1.141		Cornel
Nothing Cornelius; O this cheeres my soule:	F	176	1.1.148		Faust
This night I'le conjure tho I die therefore.	F	193	1.1.165		Faust
with Valdes and Cornelius, as this wine, if it could speake,	F	216	1.2.23	P	Wagner
Within this circle is Jehova's Name,	F	236	1.3.8		Faust
Who would not be proficient in this Art?	F	256	1.3.28		Faust
How pliant is this Mephostophilis?	F	257	1.3.29		Faust
hath <I have> already done, and holds <hold> this principle,	F	283	1.3.55		Faust
This word Damnation, terrifies not me <him>,	F	286	1.3.58		Faust
Why this is hell: nor am I out of it.	F	304	1.3.76		Mephst
I'le live in speculation of this Art/Till Mephostophilis	F	341	1.3.113		Faust
you Maister, will you teach me this conjuring Occupation?	F	380	1.4.38	P	Robin
Abjure this Magicke, turne to God againe.	F	396	2.1.8		Faust
Veiw here this <the> bloud that trickles from mine arme,	F	446	2.1.58		Faust
Is it unwilling I should write this byll?	F	454	2.1.66		Faust
this byll is ended,/And Faustus hath bequeath'd his soule to	F	463	2.1.75		Faust
But what is this Inscription on mine Arme?	F	465	2.1.77		Faust
I see it plaine, even heere <in this place> is writ/Homo fuge:	F	469	2.1.81		Faust
What meanes this shew? speake Mephostophilis.	F	472	2.1.84		Faust
Then Mephostophilis receive this scrole,	F	477	2.1.89		Faust
<Here Mephastophilis> receive this scrole,	F	477	(HC260)A		Faust
Speake Faustus, do you deliver this as your Deed?	F	501	2.1.113		Mephst
That after this life there is any paine?	F	523	2.1.135		Faust
Nay, and this be hell, I'le willingly be damn'd <damned here>.	F	527	2.1.139		Faust
But leaving <off> this, let me have a wife, the fairest Maid in	F	529	2.1.141	P	Faust
What sight is this?	F	532	2.1.144		Faust
<Here>, take this booke, <and> peruse it [thoroughly] <well>:	F	543	2.1.155		Mephst
The framing of this circle on the ground/Brings Thunder,	F	545	2.1.157		Mephst
Pronounce this thrice devoutly to thy selfe,	F	547	2.1.159		Mephst
Thankes Mephostophilis for this sweete booke.	F	550	2.1.162		Faust
This will I keepe, as chary as my life.	F	551	2.1.163		Faust
[Here they are in this booke].	F	551.3	2.1.166A	P	Mephst
I will renounce this Magicke and repent.	F	562	2.2.11		Faust
And long e're this, I should have done the deed <slaine	F	575	2.2.24		Faust
As is the substance of this centricke earth?	F	588	2.2.37		Faust
<Well>, Resclve me then in this one question:	F	614	2.2.63	P	Faust
I, that is not against our kingdome: <but> this is.	F	623	2.2.72	P	Mephst
Remember this.--	F	626	2.2.75	P	Mephst
And this is my companion Prince in hell.	F	640	2.2.89		Lucifr
pardon [me] <him> for <in> this,/And Faustus vowes never to	F	647	2.2.96		Faust
not of Paradice or <nor> Creation, but marke the <this> shew.	F	659	2.2.108	P	Lucifr
<I would desire, that this house,	F	675	(HC263)A	P	Covet
and might I now obtaine <have> my wish, this house, you and all,	F	675	2.2.124	P	Covet

THIS (cont.)

run up and downe the world with these <this> case of Rapiers,	F 688	2.2.137	P	Wrath
<Now Faustus, how dost thou like this>?	F 711	(HC264)A		Lucifr
O how this sight doth delight <this feedes> my soule.	F 712	2.2.164		Faust
Meane while peruse this booke, and view it throughly,	F 717	2.2.169		Lucifr
<in mean time take this booke, peruse it throwly>,	F 717	(HC264)A		Lucifr
[This will I keepe as chary as my life].	F 719.1	2.2.172		Faust
And whirling round with this circumference,	F 764	2.3.43		2Chor
The which <That to> this day is highly solemnized.	F 778	2.3.57		2Chor
But tell me now, what resting place is this?	F 800	3.1.22		Faust
This is the goodly Palace of the Pope:	F 804	3.1.26		Mephst
Know that this City stands upon seven hils,	F 811	3.1.33		Mephst
The which this day with high solemnity,	F 833	3.1.55		Mephst
This day is held through Rome and Italy,	F 834	3.1.56		Mephst
That Faustus name, whilst this bright frame doth stand,	F 841	3.1.63		Faust
Then in this shew let me an Actor be,	F 854	3.1.76		Faust
be,/That this proud Pope may Faustus [cunning] <comming> see.	F 855	3.1.77		Faust
And view their triumphs, as they passe this way.	F 857	3.1.79		Mephst
Or dash the pride of this solemnity;	F 860	3.1.82		Mephst
This day shall make thee be admir'd in Rome.	F 867	3.1.89		Mephst
Thy selfe and I, may parly with this Pope:	F 896	3.1.118		Faust
This proud confronter of the Emperour,	F 897	3.1.119		Faust
despite of all his Holinesse/Restore this Bruno to his liberty,	F 899	3.1.121		Faust
Adding this golden sentence to our praise;	F 917	3.1.139		Pope
Behold this Silver Belt whereto is fixt/Seven golden [keys]	F 932	3.1.154		Pope
The Cardinals will be plagu'd for this anon.	F 976	3.1.198		Faust
And charme thee with this Magicke wand,	F 996	3.2.16		Mephst
First weare this girdle, then appeare/Invisible to all are	F 997	3.2.17		Mephst
As best beseemes this solemne festivall.	F1012	3.2.32		Pope
What needs this question?	F1016	3.2.36		Pope
False Prelates, for this hatefull treachery,	F1033	3.2.53		Pope
To the Bishop of Millaine, for this so rare a present.	F1042	3.2.62		Pope
yee Lubbers look about/And find the man that doth this villany,	F1056	3.2.76		Pope
I pray my Lords have patience at this troublesome banquet.	F1058	3.2.78		Pope
To lay the fury of this same troublesome ghost.	F1064	3.2.84		Pope
Damb'd be this soule for ever, for this deed.	F1070	3.2.90		Pope
that your devill can answere the stealing of this same cup,	F1089	3.3.2	P	Dick
To purge the rashnesse of this cursed deed,	F1125	3.3.38		Mephst
First, be thou turned to this ugly shape,	F1126	3.3.39		Mephst
That all this day the sluggard keepes his bed.	F1176	4.1.22		Mrtino
What of this?	F1184	4.1.30	P	Benvol
and thou shalt see/This Conjurer performe such rare exploits,	F1186	4.1.32		Mrtino
Speake, wilt thou come and see this sport?	F1193	4.1.39		Fredrk
I am content for this once to thrust my head out at a window:	F1200	4.1.46	P	Benvol
This deed of thine, in setting Bruno free/From his and our	F1206	4.1.52		Emper
And if this Bruno thou hast late redeem'd,	F1212	4.1.58		Emper
Present before this royall Emperour,	F1238	4.1.84		Faust
to thinke I have beene such an Asse all this while, to stand	F1243	4.1.89	P	Benvol
thoughts are ravished so/With sight of this renowned Emperour,	F1261	4.1.107		Emper
To satisfie my longing thoughts at full,/Let me this tell thee:	F1265	4.1.111		Emper
That this faire Lady, whilest she liv'd on earth,	F1266	4.1.112		Emper
And in this sight thou better pleasest me,	F1271	4.1.117		Emper
This sport is excellent: wee'l call and wake him.	F1281	4.1.127		Emper
this [is] most horrible:	F1291	4.1.137	P	Faust
Zounds Doctor, is this your villany?	F1293	4.1.139	P	Benvol
Or bring before this royall Emperour/The mightie Monarch,	F1296	4.1.142		Faust
hath Faustus justly requited this injurious knight, which being	F1313	4.1.159	P	Faust
to clap hornes of honest mens heades o'this order,	F1317	4.1.163	P	Benvol
But an I be not reveng'd for this, would I might be turn'd to a	F1319	4.1.165	P	Benvol
In recompence of this thy high desert,	F1322	4.1.168		Emper
us sway thy thoughts/From this attempt against the Conjurer.	F1326	4.2.2		Mrtino
If you will aid me in this enterprise,	F1334	4.2.10		Benvol
And kill that Doctor if he come this way.	F1339	4.2.15		Fredrk
By this (I know) the Conjurer is neere,	F1343	4.2.19		Benvol
this blow ends all,/Hell take his soule, his body thus must	F1362	4.2.38		Benvol
Was this that sterne aspect, that awfull frowne,	F1370	4.2.46		Fredrk
Was this that damned head, whose heart <art> conspir'd	F1373	4.2.49		Mrtino
I, [all] <I call> your hearts to recompence this deed.	F1394	4.2.70		Faust
Or hew'd this flesh and bones as small as sand,	F1398	4.2.74		Faust
Go Belimothe, and take this caitife hence,	F1408	4.2.84		Faust
Take thou this other, dragge him through the woods,	F1410	4.2.86		Faust
This Traytor flies unto some steepie rocke,	F1413	4.2.89		Faust
Yet to encounter this your weake attempt,	F1429	4.2.105		Faust
What devill attends this damn'd Magician,	F1445	4.3.15		Benvol
Till time shall alter this our brutish shapes:	F1454	4.3.24		Benvol
I beseech you sir accept of this; I am a very poore man, and	F1463	4.4.7	P	HrsCsr
late by horse flesh, and this bargaine will set me up againe.	F1464	4.4.8	P	HrsCsr
O what a cosening Doctor was this?	F1484	4.4.28	P	HrsCsr
I'le out-run him, and cast this leg into some ditch or other.	F1495	4.4.39	P	HrsCsr
Who's this, that stands so solemnly by himselfe:	F1513	4.5.9	P	Hostss
This is but a small matter:	F1574	4.6.17	P	Faust
Madam, I will do more then this for your content.	F1575	4.6.18	P	Faust
This makes me wonder more then all the rest, that at this time	F1578	4.6.21	P	Duke
that at this time of the yeare, when every Tree is barren of	F1578	4.6.21	P	Duke
We are much beholding to this learned man.	F1670	4.6.113		Lady
<Was this faire Hellen, whose admired worth>/<Made Greece with	F1696	(HC269)B		2Schol
and for this blessed sight <glorious deed>/Happy and blest be	F1704	5.1.31		1Schol
<Wee'l take our leaves>, and for this blessed sight	F1704	(HC269)B		1Schol
O gentle Faustus leave this damned Art,	F1707	5.1.34		OldMan
This Magicke, that will charme thy soule to hell,	F1708	5.1.35		OldMan
It may be this my exhortation/Seemes harsh, and all unpleasant;	F1717	5.1.44		OldMan
And so have hope, that this my kinde rebuke,	F1722	5.1.49		OldMan
<Faustus> This, or what else my Faustus shall <thou shalt>	F1766	5.1.93		Mephst

THIS (cont.)

Was this the face that Launcht a thousand ships,	F1768	5.1.95		Faust
[As in this furnace God shal try my faith],	F1792	5.1.119A		OldMan
And this gloomy night,/Here in this roome will wretched Faustus	F1803	5.2.7		Mephst
Here in this roome will wretched Faustus be.	F1804	5.2.8		Mephst
O my deere Faustus what imports this feare?	F1827	5.2.31		1Schol
this is the time <the time wil come>, and he will fetch mee.	F1861	5.2.65	P	Faust
Why did not Faustus tell us of this before, that Divines might	F1862	5.2.66	P	1Schol
this ever-burning chaire,/Is for ore-tortur'd soules to rest	F1914	5.2.118		BdAngl
or let this houre be but/A yeare, a month, a weeke, a naturall	F1932	5.2.136		Faust
Or why is this immortall that thou hast?	F1965	5.2.169		Faust
This soule should flie from me, and I be chang'd/[Unto] <Into>	F1967	5.2.171		Faust
That sometime grew within this learned man:	F2004	5.3.22		4Chor
My Lord, this dish was sent me from the Cardinall of Florence.	F App	p.231 9	P	Pope
Friers prepare a dirge to lay the fury of this ghost, once	F App	p.232 16	P	Pope
O this is admirable!	F App	p.233 1	P	Robin
tell thee, we were for ever made by this doctor Faustus booke?	F App	p.234 2	P	Robin
our horses shal eate no hay as long as this lasts.	F App	p.234 3	P	Robin
Wel, tone of you hath this goblet about you.	F App	p.235 16	P	Vintnr
like a Beare, the third an Asse, for doing this enterprise.	F App	p.235 33	P	Mephst
this therefore is my request, that thou let me see some proofe	F App	p.236 5	P	Emper
Canst raise this man from hollow vaults below,	F App	p.237 30		Emper
where lies intombde this famous Conquerour,	F App	p.237 31		Emper
this Lady while she liv'd had a wart or moale in her necke,	F App	p.238 60	P	Emper
hath Faustus worthily requited this injurious knight, which	F App	p.238 83	P	Faust
til I am past this faire and pleasant greene, ile walke on	F App	p.239 96	P	Faust
I have beene al this day seeking one maister Fustian:	F App	p.239 98	P	HrsCsr
I tell thee he has not slept this eight nights.	F App	p.240 144	P	Mephst
And he have not slept this eight weekes Ile speake with him.	F App	p.240 145	P	HrsCsr
I, this is he, God save ye maister doctor, maister doctor,	F App	p.241 148	P	HrsCsr
his labour; wel, this tricke shal cost him fortie dollers more.	F App	p.241 166	P	Faust
Beleeve me maister Doctor, this merriment hath much pleased me.	F App	p.242 1	P	Duke
you take no delight in this, I have heard that great bellied	F App	p.242 4	P	Faust
were it a greater thing then this, so it would content you, you	F App	p.242 13	P	Faust
this makes me wonder above the rest, that being in the dead	F App	p.242 16	P	Duke
this learned man for the great kindnes he hath shewd to you.	F App	p.243 29	P	Duke
my Lord, and whilst I live, Rest beholding for this curtesie.	F App	p.243 31	P	Duchss
Thou Caesar at this instant art my God,	Lucan, First Booke	63		
Thy power inspires the Muze that sings this war.	Lucan, First Booke	66		
So when this worlds compounded union breakes,	Lucan, First Booke	73		
This need no forraine proofe, nor far fet story:	Lucan, First Booke	94		
Such humors stirde them up; but this warrs seed,	Lucan, First Booke	159		
Againe, this people could not brooke calme peace,	Lucan, First Booke	172		
this spectacle/Stroake Caesars hart with feare, his hayre	Lucan, First Booke	194		
This said, he laying aside all lets of war,	Lucan, First Booke	206		
This said, the restles generall through the darke/(Swifter then	Lucan, First Booke	230		
Wagons or tents, then in this frontire towne.	Lucan, First Booke	255		
But gods and fortune prickt him to this war,	Lucan, First Booke	265		
Speake, when shall this thy long usurpt power end?	Lucan, First Booke	333		
This spoke none answer'd, but a murmuring buz/Th'unstable	Lucan, First Booke	353		
We grieve at this thy patience and delay:	Lucan, First Booke	362		
This [band] <hand> that all behind us might be quail'd,	Lucan, First Booke	370		
This hand (albeit unwilling) should performe it;	Lucan, First Booke	379		
what ere thou be whom God assignes/This great effect, art hid.	Lucan, First Booke	420		
this makes them/Run on the swords point and desire to die,	Lucan, First Booke	456		
were the Commons only strooke to heart/With this vaine terror;	Lucan, First Booke	484		
And in the brest of this slaine Bull are crept,	Lucan, First Booke	632		
skill in stars, and tune-full planeting,/In this sort spake.	Lucan, First Booke	641		
Disclosing Phoebus furie in this sort:	Lucan, First Booke	676		
under Hemus mount/Philippi plaines; Phoebus what radge is this?	Lucan, First Booke	680		
This headlesse trunke that lies on Nylus sande/I know:	Lucan, First Booke	684		
This said, being tir'd with fury she sunke downe.	Lucan, First Booke	694		
Then scarse can Phoebus say, this harpe is mine.	Ovid's Elegies	1.1.20		
When in this [workes] <worke> first verse I trod aloft,	Ovid's Elegies	1.1.21		
Thy mother shall from heaven applaud this show,	Ovid's Elegies	1.2.39		
Yet this Ile see, but if thy gowne ought cover,	Ovid's Elegies	1.4.41		
But though this night thy fortune be to trie it,	Ovid's Elegies	1.4.69		
Jove send me more such afternoones as this.	Ovid's Elegies	1.5.26		
Why enviest me, this hostile [denne] <dende> unbarre,	Ovid's Elegies	1.6.17		
On this hard threshold till the morning lay.	Ovid's Elegies	1.6.68		
Io, a strong man conquerd this Wench, hollow.	Ovid's Elegies	1.7.38		
red shame becomes white cheekes, but this/If feigned, doth well;	Ovid's Elegies	1.8.35		
That this, or that man may thy cheekes moist keepe.	Ovid's Elegies	1.8.84		
If this thou doest, to me by long use knowne,	Ovid's Elegies	1.8.105		
His Mistris dores this; that his Captaines keepes.	Ovid's Elegies	1.9.8		
He Citties greate, this thresholds lies before:	Ovid's Elegies	1.9.19		
This breakes Towne gates, but he his Mistris dore.	Ovid's Elegies	1.9.20		
A faire maides care expeld this sluggishnesse,	Ovid's Elegies	1.9.43		
No more this beauty mine eyes captivates.	Ovid's Elegies	1.10.10		
This cause hath thee from pleasing me debard.	Ovid's Elegies	1.10.12		
Let this word, come, alone the tables fill.	Ovid's Elegies	1.11.24		
This day denyall hath my sport adjourned.	Ovid's Elegies	1.12.2		
[All] <This> could I beare, but that the wench should rise,/Who	Ovid's Elegies	1.13.25		
That Nature shall dissolve this earthly bowre.	Ovid's Elegies	1.15.24		
what meanes learnd/Hath this same Poet my sad chaunce discernd?	Ovid's Elegies	2.1.10		
And asking why, this answeare she redoubled,	Ovid's Elegies	2.2.7		
Do this and soone thou shalt thy freedome reape.	Ovid's Elegies	2.2.40		
he will lament/And say this blabbe shall suffer punnishment.	Ovid's Elegies	2.2.60		
This for her looks, that for her woman-hood:	Ovid's Elegies	2.4.46		
In this sweete good, why hath a third to do?	Ovid's Elegies	2.5.32		
This, and what grife inforc'd me say I say'd,	Ovid's Elegies	2.5.33		
This grieves me not, no joyned kisses spent,	Ovid's Elegies	2.5.59		
Thy tunes let this rare birdes sad funerall borrowe,	Ovid's Elegies	2.6.9		

THIS (cont.)

Line	Work	Reference	Speaker
But what availde this faith? her rarest hue?	Ovid's Elegies	2.6.17	
This tombe approoves, I pleasde my mistresse well,	Ovid's Elegies	2.6.61	
The Gods from this sinne rid me of suspition,	Ovid's Elegies	2.7.19	
My selfe unguilty of this crime I know.	Ovid's Elegies	2.7.28	
This seemes the fairest, so doth that to mee,	Ovid's Elegies	2.10.7	
[And] this doth please me most, and so doth she.	Ovid's Elegies	2.10.8	
So with this love and that, wavers my minde.	Ovid's Elegies	2.10.10	
Yet this is better farre then lie alone,	Ovid's Elegies	2.10.15	
Let others tell this, and what each one speakes/Beleeve, no	Ovid's Elegies	2.11.21	
Let Nereus bend the waves unto this shore,	Ovid's Elegies	2.11.39	
Let the bright day-starre cause in heaven this day be,	Ovid's Elegies	2.11.55	
Do but deserve gifts with this title grav'd.	Ovid's Elegies	2.13.26	
To have this skirmish fought, let it suffice thee.	Ovid's Elegies	2.13.28	
Had ancient Mothers this vile custome cherisht,	Ovid's Elegies	2.14.9	
Againe by some in this unpeopled world.	Ovid's Elegies	2.14.12	
Forgive her gratious Gods this one delict,	Ovid's Elegies	2.14.43	
This kinde of verse is not alike, yet fit,	Ovid's Elegies	2.17.21	
Wily Corinna sawe this blemish in me,	Ovid's Elegies	2.19.9	
This doth delight me, this my courage cheares.	Ovid's Elegies	2.19.24	
Let this care some-times bite thee to the quick,	Ovid's Elegies	2.19.43	
And this is he whom fierce love burnes, they cry.	Ovid's Elegies	3.1.20	
This thou wilt say to be a worthy ground.	Ovid's Elegies	3.1.26	
This saied, she mov'd her buskins gaily varnisht,	Ovid's Elegies	3.1.31	
This goddesse company doth to me befall.	Ovid's Elegies	3.1.44	
The places lawes this benefit allowe.	Ovid's Elegies	3.2.20	
And this townes well knowne customes not beleeves,	Ovid's Elegies	3.4.38	
This said he: shee her modest eyes held downe,	Ovid's Elegies	3.5.67	
This said: her coate hood-winckt her fearefull eyes,	Ovid's Elegies	3.5.79	
To this I fondly loves of flouds told plainly:	Ovid's Elegies	3.5.101	
To this ad shame, shame to performe it quaild mee,	Ovid's Elegies	3.6.37	
the great Gods greeved they had bestowde/This <The> benefite,	Ovid's Elegies	3.6.46	
And least her maide should know of this disgrace,	Ovid's Elegies	3.6.83	
Knowest not this head a helme was wont to beare,	Ovid's Elegies	3.7.13	
This side that serves thee, a sharpe sword did weare.	Ovid's Elegies	3.7.14	
Confessing this, why doest thou touch him than?	Ovid's Elegies	3.7.22	
Homer without this shall be nothing worth.	Ovid's Elegies	3.7.28	
With thine, nor this last fire their presence misses.	Ovid's Elegies	3.8.54	
This was [their] <there> meate, the soft grasse was their bed.	Ovid's Elegies	3.9.10	
good growes by this griefe,/Oft bitter juice brings to the	Ovid's Elegies	3.10.7	
Yet this is lesse, then if he had seene me,	Ovid's Elegies	3.10.15	
choose this course,/Wilt have me willing, or to love by force?	Ovid's Elegies	3.10.49	
This bed, and that by tumbling made uneven,	Ovid's Elegies	3.13.32	
Graunt this, that what you do I may not see,	Ovid's Elegies	3.13.35	
This last end to my Elegies is set,	Ovid's Elegies	3.14.2	
But this is true, so like was one the other,	Hero and Leander	1.39	
Came lovers home, from this great festivall.	Hero and Leander	1.96	
On this feast day, O cursed day and hower,	Hero and Leander	1.131	
So faire a church as this, had Venus none,	Hero and Leander	1.135	
For know, that underneath this radiant floure,	Hero and Leander	1.145	
This sacrifice (whose sweet perfume descending,	Hero and Leander	1.209	
But this faire jem, sweet in the losse alone,	Hero and Leander	1.247	
All heaven would come to claime this legacie,	Hero and Leander	1.250	
This idoll which you terme Virginitie,	Hero and Leander	1.269	
Such sacrifice as this, Venus demands.	Hero and Leander	1.310	
Come thither; As she spake this, her toong tript,	Hero and Leander	1.357	
On her, this god/Enamoured was, and with his snakie rod,	Hero and Leander	1.397	
But long this blessed time continued not;	Hero and Leander	1.459	
Yet as a punishment they added this,	Hero and Leander	1.469	
And to this day is everie scholler poore,	Hero and Leander	1.471	
By this, sad Hero, with love unacquainted,	Hero and Leander	2.1	
Yet she this rashnesse sodainly repented,	Hero and Leander	2.33	
To see how he this captive Nymph beguil'd.	Hero and Leander	2.40	
Like Aesops cocke, this jewell he enjoyed,	Hero and Leander	2.51	
Than Hero this inestimable gemme.	Hero and Leander	2.78	
Jewels being lost are found againe, this never,	Hero and Leander	2.85	
Ere halfe this tale was done,/Aye me, Leander cryde,	Hero and Leander	2.201	
When this fresh bleeding wound Leander viewd,	Hero and Leander	2.213	
By this Leander being nere the land,	Hero and Leander	2.227	
Such sights as this, to tender maids are rare.	Hero and Leander	2.238	
This head was beat with manie a churlish billow,	Hero and Leander	2.251	
Much like a globe, (a globe may I tearme this,	Hero and Leander	2.275	
this strife of hers (like that/Which made the world) another	Hero and Leander	2.291	
And now she wisht this night were never done,	Hero and Leander	2.301	
Should know the pleasure of this blessed night,	Hero and Leander	2.304	
And round about the chamber this false morne,	Hero and Leander	2.321	
By this Apollos golden harpe began,	Hero and Leander	2.327	

THISTLE

Line	Work	Reference	Speaker
And leaves it off to snap on Thistle tops:	Jew	5.2.42	Barab

THITHER (See also THETHER)

Line	Work	Reference	Speaker
Thither made we,	Dido	1.2.25	Cloan
But hereby child, we shall get thither straight.	Dido	4.5.14	Nurse
Being caried thither by the cannons force,	2Tamb	5.1.66	Tamb
Go thither some of you and take his gold,	2Tamb	5.1.123	Tamb
Gonzago conduct them thither, and then/Beset his house that not	P 288	5.15	Guise
And thither will I to put them to the sword.	P 504	9.23	Guise
So now away, post thither wards amaine.	Edw	5.2.67	Mortmr
Thither shall your honour go, and so farewell.	Edw	5.3.62	Matrvs
That thither thou didst send a murtherer.	Edw	5.6.48	King
be carried thither againe by Gluttony and Letchery <Leachery>],	F 705.2	2.2.156A	P Sloth
And thither wee'le repaire and live obscure,	F1453	4.3.23	Benvol
Thither resorted many a wandring guest,	Hero and Leander	1.94	
Come thither; As she spake this, her toong tript,	Hero and Leander	1.357	

THITHER (cont.)			
For unawares (Come thither) from her slipt, . . .	Hero and Leander		1.358
THITHER WARDS			
So now away, post thither wards amaine.	Edw	5.2.67	Mortmr
THO			
Tho countermin'd <countermur'd> with walls of brasse, to love,	Jew	1.2.386	Mthias
This night I'le conjure tho I die therefore. . . .	F 193	1.1.165	Faust
to the devill, for a shoulder of Mutton, tho it were bloud raw.	F 350	1.4.8	P Wagner
And therefore tho we would we cannot erre. . . .	F 931	3.1.153	Pope
[No marvel tho the angry Greekes pursu'd]/[With tenne yeares	F1699	5.1.26A	3Schol
tho Faustus end be such/As every Christian heart laments to	F1995	5.3.13	2Schol
Although the nights be long, I sleepe not tho, . . .	Ovid's Elegies		1.2.3
THOGH			
And love to Room (thogh slaughter steeld their harts/And minds	Lucan, First Booke		355
THOMBE			
Thy Rosie cheekes be to thy thombe inclinde. . . .	Ovid's Elegies		1.4.22
TH'ONE			
Vanish vilaines, th'one like an Ape, an other like a Beare, the	F App	p.235 32	P Mephst
With scepters, and high buskins th'one would dresse me, .	Ovid's Elegies		3.1.63
THONGS			
Thongs at his heeles, by which Achilles horse/Drew him in	Dido	2.1.205	Aeneas
TH'OPPOSED			
Th'opposed starre of Mars hath done thee harme, . .	Ovid's Elegies		1.8.29
THORBONEST			
And thats because the blockish [Sorbonests] <thorbonest> .	P 411	7.51	Ramus
TH'ORIZON			
And now the sunne that through th'orizon peepes, . .	Hero and Leander		2.99
THORNES			
Amongst the pricking thornes, and sharpest briers, . .	F1411	4.2.87	Faust
THORNS			
And choakt with thorns, that greedy earth wants hinds, .	Lucan, First Booke		29
THORNY			
Standard round, that stood/As bristle-pointed as a thorny wood.	1Tamb	4.1.27	2Msngr
THOROUGH			
And thorough your Planets I perceive you thinke, . .	1Tamb	1.1.19	Mycet
And make a bridge, thorough the moving Aire, . . .	F 333	1.3.105	Faust
Thorough a rocke of stone in one nights space: . . .	F 793	3.1.15	Faust
but as the fields/When birds are silent thorough winters rage;	Lucan, First Booke		261
inconsiderate multitude/Thorough the Citty hurried headlong on,	Lucan, First Booke		493
And thorough everie vaine doth cold bloud runne, . .	Ovid's Elegies		3.13.38
THOROUGHLY (See also THROUGHLY, THROWLY)			
<Here>, take this booke, <and> peruse it [thoroughly] <well>:	F 543	2.1.155	Mephst
THOROUGHOUT			
To gather for him thoroughout the realme.	Edw	2.2.148	Edward
THOROW			
To safe conduct us thorow Affrica.	1Tamb	1.2.16	Zenoc
That ere made passage thorow Persean Armes. . . .	1Tamb	2.3.56	Tamb
Shall lead thee Captive thorow Affrica.	1Tamb	3.3.73	Tamb
Thorow the streets with troops of conquered kings, . .	2Tamb	4.3.114	Tamb
At every little breath that thorow heaven is blowen: .	2Tamb	4.3.124	Tamb
Went Hero thorow Sestos, from her tower/To Venus temple, .	Hero and Leander		1.132
THOROWE			
March in your armour thorowe watery Fens, ...	2Tamb	3.2.56	Tamb
THOSE			
In those faire walles I promist him of yore: . . .	Dido	1.1.85	Jupitr
In mannaging those fierce barbarian mindes: . . .	Dido	1.1.92	Jupitr
Shall build his throne amidst those starrie towers, . .	Dido	1.1.98	Jupitr
And chaunging heavens may those good daies returne, . .	Dido	1.1.150	Aeneas
And quell those hopes that thus employ your [cares] <eares>.	Dido	4.1.35	Dido
Those that dislike what Dido gives in charge, . . .	Dido	4.4.71	Dido
And see if those will serve in steed of sailes: . .	Dido	4.4.160	Dido
Let some of those thy followers goe with me, . . .	Dido	5.1.73	Iarbus
The Gods, what Gods be those that seeke my death? . .	Dido	5.1.128	Dido
Those thousand horse shall sweat with martiall spoile/Of .	1Tamb	1.2.191	Tamb
And by those steps that he hath scal'd the heavens, . .	1Tamb	1.2.200	Tamb
And rid the world of those detested troopes? . . .	1Tamb	2.2.19	Meandr
Shall massacre those greedy minded slaves. . . .	1Tamb	2.2.67	Meandr
How those were hit by pelting Cannon shot, . . .	1Tamb	2.4.3	Mycet
Then will we march to all those Indian Mines, . . .	1Tamb	2.5.41	Cosroe
Now in his majesty he leaves those lookes, . . .	1Tamb	3.2.61	Agidas
Those words of favour, and those comfortings, . . .	1Tamb	3.2.62	Agidas
And rifle all those stately Janisars.	1Tamb	3.3.26	Techel
But wil those Kings accompany your Lord?	1Tamb	3.3.27	Tamb
and then inlarge/Those Christian Captives, which you keep as	1Tamb	3.3.47	Tamb
those that lead my horse/Have to their names tytles of dignity,	1Tamb	3.3.69	Bajzth
And know thou Turke, that those which lead my horse, .	1Tamb	3.3.72	Tamb
I long to see those crownes won by our swords, . . .	1Tamb	3.3.98	Therid
The pillers that have bolstered up those tearmes, . .	1Tamb	3.3.229	Tamb
But ere I die those foule Idolaters/Shall make me bonfires with	1Tamb	3.3.239	Bajzth
Those walled garrisons wil I subdue, ...	1Tamb	3.3.244	Tamb
The Galles and those pilling Briggandines, . . .	1Tamb	3.3.248	Tamb
He dies, and those that kept us out so long. . . .	1Tamb	4.2.118	Tamb
I will confute those blind Geographers/That make a triple	1Tamb	4.4.75	Tamb
Those that are proud of fickle Empery, ...	1Tamb	5.1.352	Zenoc
Shall meet those Christians fleeting with the tyde, . .	2Tamb	1.1.40	Orcan
Desart of Arabia/To those that stand on Badgeths lofty Tower,	2Tamb	1.1.109	Sgsmnd
We are not bound to those accomplishments, . . .	2Tamb	2.1.35	Baldwn
Yet those infirmities that thus defame/Their faiths, their	2Tamb	2.1.44	Sgsmnd
and confound/The trustlesse force of those false Christians.	2Tamb	2.2.62	Orcan
Now are those Spheares where Cupid usde to sit, . .	2Tamb	2.4.81	Tamb
Or had those wanton Poets, for whose byrth/Olde Rome was proud,	2Tamb	2.4.91	Tamb
[Those] <Whose> looks will shed such influence in my campe,/As	2Tamb	3.2.39	Tamb
Intrench with those dimensions I prescribed: . . .	2Tamb	3.3.42	Therid

THOSE (cont.)

And join'd those stars that shall be opposite,	2Tamb	3.5.81	Tamb
I must apply my selfe to fit those tearmes,	2Tamb	4.1.155	Tamb
Then bring those Turkish harlots to my tent,	2Tamb	4.1.165	Tamb
Dangerous tc those, whose Chrisis is as yours:	2Tamb	5.3.92	Phsitn
that the soule/Wanting those Organnons by which it mooves,	2Tamb	5.3.96	Phsitn
In vaine I strive and raile against those powers,	2Tamb	5.3.120	Tamb
Sit up my boy, and with those silken raines,	2Tamb	5.3.202	Tamb
Bridle the steeled stomackes of those Jades.	2Tamb	5.3.203	Tamb
So, raigne my sonne, scourge and controlle those slaves,	2Tamb	5.3.228	Tamb
Admir'd I am of those that hate me most:	Jew	Prol.9	Machvl
As for those [Samnites] <Samintes>, and the men of Uzz,/That	Jew	1.1.4	Barab
How chance you came not with those other ships/That sail'd by	Jew	1.1.89	Barab
scambled up/More wealth by farre then those that brag of faith.	Jew	1.1.123	Barab
The Turkes and those of Malta are in league.	Jew	1.1.159	Barab
and those other Iles/That lye betwixt the Mediterranean seas.	Jew	1.2.3	Basso
What's Cyprus, Candy, and those other Iles/To us, or Malta?	Jew	1.2.5	Govnr
Goe one and call those Jewes of Malta hither:	Jew	1.2.34	Govnr
but for every one of those,/Had they beene valued at	Jew	1.2.185	Barab
Now I remember those old womens words,	Jew	2.1.24	Barab
And now me thinkes that I am one of those:	Jew	2.1.28	Barab
So shall you imitate those you succeed:	Jew	2.2.47	Bosco
And yet I know the prayers of those Nuns/And holy Fryers,	Jew	2.3.80	Barab
Thou in those Groves, by Dis above,	Jew	4.2.97	Ithimr
Where are those perfumed gloves which I sent/To be poysoned,	P 70	2.13	Guise
Guise, begins those deepe ingendred thoughts/To burst abroad,	P 91	2.34	Guise
ingendred thoughts/To burst abroad, those never dying flames,	P 92	2.35	Guise
Him will we--but first lets follow those in France,	P 153	2.96	Guise
Those that hate me, will I learn to loath.	P 156	2.99	Guise
That those which doe beholde, they may become/As men that stand	P 162	2.105	Guise
To get those pedantes from the King Navarre,	P 426	7.66	Guise
Murder the Hugonets, take those pedantes hence.	P 438	7.78	Guise
To punish those that doe prophane this holy feast.	P 617	12.30	Mugern
And keep those relicks from our countries coastes.	P 803	16.17	Navrre
I, those are they that feed him with their golde,	P 845	17.40	King
To overthrow those [sectious] <sexious> <factious> Puritans:	P 850	17.45	Guise
And in remembrance of those bloudy broyles,	P1024	19.94	King
And all those traitors to the Church of Rome,	P1120	21.14	Dumain
As Rome and all those popish Prelates there,	P1248	22.110	Navrre
To hide those parts which men delight to see,	Edw	1.1.65	Gavstn
He nods, and scornes, and smiles at those that passe.	Edw	1.2.24	Warwck
Or with those armes that twind about my neck,	Edw	1.4.175	Queene
But one of those that saith quandoquidem,	Edw	2.1.54	Spencr
Thy court is naked, being bereft of those,	Edw	2.2.174	Mortmr
with my sword/On those proud rebels that are up in armes,	Edw	3.1.187	Edward
Your selfe, and those your chosen companie,	Edw	4.7.6	Abbot
Upon my life, those be the men ye seeke.	Edw	4.7.46	Mower
I would those wordes proceeded from your heart.	Edw	5.2.100	Kent
I these are those that Faustus most desires.	F 79	1.1.51	Faust
And scorne those Joyes thou never shalt possesse.	F 314	1.3.86	Faust
Go beare these <those> tydings to great Lucifer,	F 315	1.3.87	Faust
Because thou hast depriv'd me of those Joyes.	F 554	2.2.3	Faust
that you have taken no pleasure in those sights; therefor I	F1566	4.6.9	P Faust
deny/The just [requests] <request> of those that wish him well,	F1691	5.1.18	Faust
Those <These> thoughts that do disswade me from my vow,	F1764	5.1.91	Faust
Those soules which sinne seales the blacke sonnes of hell,	F1799	5.2.3	Lucifr
hadst set/In yonder throne, like those bright shining Saints,	F1905	5.2.109	GdAngl
those two deceased princes which long since are consumed to	F App	p.237 42	P Faust
but the true substantiall bodies of those two deceased princes.	F App	p.238 65	P Emper
Those of Bituriges and light Axon pikes;	Lucan, First Booke		424
And Vangions who like those of Sarmata,	Lucan, First Booke		431
trumpets clang incites, and those that dwel/By Cyngas streame,	Lucan, First Booke		433
Those that inhabited the suburbe fieldes/Fled, fowle Erinnis	Lucan, First Booke		569
Those in their lovers, pretty maydes desire.	Ovid's Elegies		1.9.6
Men handle those, all manly hopes resigne,	Ovid's Elegies		2.3.9
Who would nct love those hands for their swift running?	Ovid's Elegies		2.4.28
And by those numbers is thy first youth spent.	Ovid's Elegies		3.1.28
And feare those, that to feare them least intend.	Ovid's Elegies		3.3.32
Now wish I those wings noble Perseus had,	Ovid's Elegies		3.5.13
for they tooke delite/To play upon those hands, they were so	Hero and Leander		1.30
Those with sweet water oft her handmaid fils,	Hero and Leander		1.35
Those orient cheekes and lippes, exceeding his/That leapt into	Hero and Leander		1.73
Than she the hearts of those that neere her stood.	Hero and Leander		1.112
And as shee spake those words, came somewhat nere him.	Hero and Leander		1.180
Foorth from those two tralucent cesternes brake,	Hero and Leander		1.296
And to those sterne nymphs humblie made request,	Hero and Leander		1.379
in being bold/To eie those parts, which no eie should behold.	Hero and Leander		1.408
And those on whom heaven, earth, and hell relies,	Hero and Leander		1.443
Love alwaies makes those eloquent that have it.	Hero and Leander		2.72
By those white limmes, which sparckled through the lawne.	Hero and Leander		2.242
Yet ever as he greedily assayd/To touch those dainties, she the	Hero and Leander		2.270

TH'OTHER

did looke/Dead, and discoulour'd; th'other leane and thinne.	Lucan, First Booke		628
The one his first love, th'other his new care.	Ovid's Elegies		3.8.32

THOU'

Hast thou't?	Jew	2.1.45	Barab
Here, Hast thou't?	Jew	2.1.46	P Abigal

THOU (See also TH, TH'ART, THOW)

And my nine Daughters sing when thou art sad,	Dido	1.1.33	Jupitr
Doe thou but say their colour pleaseth me.	Dido	1.1.41	Jupitr
Put thou about thy necke my owne sweet heart,	Dido	1.1.44	Jupitr
And shall have Ganimed, if thou wilt be my love.	Dido	1.1.49	Jupitr
False Jupiter, rewardst thou vertue so?	Dido	1.1.78	Venus

THOU (cont.)

Venus, how art thou compast with content,	Dido	1.1.135	Venus
Great Jupiter, still honourd maist thou be,	Dido	1.1.137	Venus
Brave Prince of Troy, thou onely art our God,	Dido	1.1.152	Achat
Doe thou but smile, and clowdie heaven will cleare,	Dido	1.1.155	Achat
Alas sweet boy, thou must be still a while,	Dido	1.1.164	Aeneas
How neere my sweet Aeneas art thou driven?	Dido	1.1.170	Venus
Thou art a Goddesse that delud'st our eyes,	Dido	1.1.191	Aeneas
But whether thou the Sunnes bright Sister be,	Dido	1.1.193	Aeneas
But for the land whereof thou doest enquire,	Dido	1.1.209	Venus
Fortune hath favord thee what ere thou be,	Dido	1.1.231	Venus
And for thy ships which thou supposest lost,	Dido	1.1.235	Venus
Too cruell, why wilt thou forsake me thus?	Dido	1.1.243	Aeneas
But thou art gone and leav'st me here alone,	Dido	1.1.247	Aeneas
O were I not at all so thou mightst be.	Dido	2.1.28	Aeneas
O Illioneus, art thou yet alive?	Dido	2.1.55	Achat
What stranger art thou that doest eye me thus?	Dido	2.1.74	Dido
Remember who thou art, speake like thy selfe,	Dido	2.1.100	Dido
Then be assured thou art not miserable.	Dido	2.1.104	Dido
When thou Achates with thy sword mad'st way,	Dido	2.1.268	Aeneas
ships, thou knowest/We sawe Cassandra sprauling in the streetes,	Dido	2.1.273	Aeneas
Faire child stay thou with Didos waiting maide,	Dido	2.1.304	Venus
Lest she imagine thou art Venus sonne:	Dido	3.1.4	Cupid
Tis not enough that thou doest graunt me love,	Dido	3.1.8	Iarbus
know that thou of all my wooers/(And yet have I had many	Dido	3.1.11	Dido
Weepe not sweet boy, thou shalt be Didos sonne,	Dido	3.1.24	Dido
And tell me where [learndst] <learnst> thou this pretie song?	Dido	3.1.27	Dido
Goe thou away, Ascanius shall stay.	Dido	3.1.35	Dido
Why staiest thou here? thou art no love of mine.	Dido	3.1.39	Dido
No, live Iarbus, what hast thou deserv'd,	Dido	3.1.41	Dido
That I should say thou art no love of mine?	Dido	3.1.42	Dido
Something thou hast deserv'd.--	Dido	3.1.43	Dido
What telst thou me of rich Getulia?	Dido	3.1.48	Dido
O Anna, didst thou know how sweet love were,	Dido	3.1.59	Dido
Full soone wouldst thou abjure this single life.	Dido	3.1.60	Dido
And thou Aeneas, Didos treasurie,	Dido	3.1.91	Dido
Aeneas, art thou there?	Dido	3.1.99	Dido
but now thou art here, tell me in sooth/In what might Dido	Dido	3.1.101	Dido
Conditionally that thou wilt stay with me,	Dido	3.1.114	Dido
Which if thou lose shall shine above the waves:	Dido	3.1.121	Dido
Achates, thou shalt be so [manly] <meanly> clad,	Dido	3.1.128	Dido
Then never say that thou art miserable,	Dido	3.1.169	Dido
Because it may be thou shalt be my love:	Dido	3.1.170	Dido
But not so much for thee, thou art but one,	Dido	3.1.175	Dido
Out hatefull hag, thou wouldst have slaine my sonne,	Dido	3.2.32	Venus
If thou but lay thy fingers on my boy.	Dido	3.2.36	Venus
But that thou maist more easilie perceive,	Dido	3.2.66	Juno
Thy sonne thou knowest with Dido now remaines,	Dido	3.2.70	Juno
My princely robes thou seest are layd aside,	Dido	3.3.3	Dido
Or art thou grievde thy betters presse so nye?	Dido	3.3.18	Iarbus
What, darest thou looke a Lyon in the face?	Dido	3.3.39	Dido
Stoute friend Achates, doest thou know this wood?	Dido	3.3.50	Aeneas
You to the vallies, thou unto the house.	Dido	3.3.62	Dido
Aeneas, thou art he, what did I say?	Dido	3.4.29	Dido
Sicheus, not Aeneas be thou calde:	Dido	3.4.59	Dido
And be thou king of Libia, by my guift.	Dido	3.4.64	Dido
The woman that thou wild us entertaine,	Dido	4.2.11	Iarbus
Now if thou beest a pitying God of power,	Dido	4.2.19	Iarbus
Thou and Achates ment to saile away.	Dido	4.4.28	Dido
Sway thou the Punike Scepter in my steede,	Dido	4.4.35	Dido
O that the Clowdes were here wherein thou [fledst] <fleest>,	Dido	4.4.50	Dido
That thou and I unseene might sport our selves:	Dido	4.4.51	Dido
And thou and I Achates, for revenge,	Dido	4.4.88	Aeneas
O cursed tree, hadst thou but wit or sense,	Dido	4.4.139	Dido
Thou wouldst have leapt from out the Sailers hands,	Dido	4.4.141	Dido
And yet I blame thee not, thou art but wood.	Dido	4.4.143	Dido
No, thou shalt goe with me unto my house,	Dido	4.5.3	Nurse
Where thou shalt see the red gild fishes leape,	Dido	4.5.10	Nurse
Blush blush for shame, why shouldst thou thinke of love?	Dido	4.5.29	Nurse
Why wilt thou so betray thy sonnes good hap?	Dido	5.1.31	Hermes
Vaine man, what Monarky expectst thou here?	Dido	5.1.34	Hermes
Or with what thought sleepst thou in Libia shoare?	Dido	5.1.35	Hermes
And thou despise the praise of such attempts:	Dido	5.1.37	Hermes
No marvell Dido though thou be in love,	Dido	5.1.44	Aeneas
Welcome sweet child, where hast thou been this long?	Dido	5.1.46	Aeneas
Spendst thou thy time about this little boy,	Dido	5.1.51	Hermes
I tell thee thou must straight to Italy,	Dido	5.1.53	Hermes
And they shall have what thing so ere thou needst.	Dido	5.1.74	Iarbus
Why look'st thou toward the sea?	Dido	5.1.113	Dido
Am I lesse faire then when thou sawest me first?	Dido	5.1.115	Dido
Say thou wilt stay in Carthage with [thy] <my> Queene,	Dido	5.1.117	Dido
Aeneas, say, how canst thou take thy leave?	Dido	5.1.119	Dido
Wilt thou kisse Dido?	Dido	5.1.120	Dido
canst thou take her hand?	Dido	5.1.121	Dido
Therefore unkind Aeneas, must thou say,	Dido	5.1.123	Dido
O Queene of Carthage, wert thou ugly blacke,	Dido	5.1.125	Aeneas
Hast thou forgot how many neighbour kings/Were up in armes, for	Dido	5.1.141	Dido
So thou wouldst prove as true as Paris did,	Dido	5.1.146	Dido
Now if thou goest, what canst thou leave behind,	Dido	5.1.151	Dido
In vaine my love thou spendst thy fainting breath,	Dido	5.1.153	Aeneas
And wilt thou not be mov'd with Didos words?	Dido	5.1.155	Dido
But thou art sprung from Scythian Caucasus,	Dido	5.1.158	Dido
Wast thou not wrackt upon this Libian shoare,	Dido	5.1.161	Dido

THOU (cont.)

Wilt thou now slay me with thy venomed sting,	Dido	5.1.167		Dido
And thou shalt perish in the billowes waies,	Dido	5.1.172		Dido
Where thou and false Achates first set foote:	Dido	5.1.175		Dido
Though thou nor he will pitie me a whit.	Dido	5.1.178		Dido
Why star'st thou in my face?	Dido	5.1.179		Dido
if thou wilt stay,/Leape in mine armes, mine armes are open	Dido	5.1.179		Dido
For though thou hast the heart to say farewell,	Dido	5.1.182		Dido
Once didst thou goe, and he came backe againe,	Dido	5.1.196		Dido
Now bring him backe, and thou shalt be a Queene,	Dido	5.1.197		Dido
Thou for some pettie guift hast let him goe,	Dido	5.1.218		Dido
None in the world shall have my love but thou:	Dido	5.1.290		Dido
Thou shalt burne first, thy crime is worse then his:	Dido	5.1.297		Dido
When first he came on shoare, perish thou to:	Dido	5.1.299		Dido
Meander, thou my faithfull Counsellor,	1Tamb	1.1.28		Mycet
Ful true thou speakst, and like thy selfe my lord,	1Tamb	1.1.49		Mycet
Thou shalt be leader of this thousand horse,	1Tamb	1.1.62		Mycet
Go frowning foorth, but come thou smyling home,	1Tamb	1.1.65		Mycet
And with thy lookes thou conquerest all thy foes:	1Tamb	1.1.75		Mycet
Ah, Menaphon, why staiest thou thus behind,	1Tamb	1.1.83		Mycet
(If as thou seem'st, thou art so meane a man)/And seeke not to	1Tamb	1.2.8		Zenoc
thou art so meane a man)/And seeke not to inrich thy followers,	1Tamb	1.2.8		Zenoc
Even as thou hop'st to be eternized,	1Tamb	1.2.72		Zenoc
Thou shalt be drawen amidst the frosen Pooles,	1Tamb	1.2.99		Tamb
Whom seekst thou Persean? I am Tamburlain.	1Tamb	1.2.153		Tamb
In thee (thou valiant man of Persea)	1Tamb	1.2.166		Tamb
Art thou but Captaine of a thousand horse,	1Tamb	1.2.168		Tamb
Draw foorth thy sword, thou mighty man at Armes,	1Tamb	1.2.178		Tamb
If thou wilt stay with me, renowmed man,	1Tamb	1.2.188		Tamb
Then shalt thou be Competitor with me,	1Tamb	1.2.208		Tamb
Then thou shalt find my vaunts substantiall.	1Tamb	1.2.213		Tamb
Wel hast thou pourtraid in thy tearms of life,	1Tamb	2.1.31		Cosroe
Wel, wel (Meander) thou art deeply read:	1Tamb	2.2.55		Mycet
What thinkst thou man, shal come of our attemptes?	1Tamb	2.3.3		Cosroe
Thou liest.	1Tamb	2.4.18		Mycet
Base villaine, darst thou give the lie?	1Tamb	2.4.19		Tamb
Thou breakst the law of Armes unlesse thou kneele,	1Tamb	2.4.21		Mycet
I, Didst thou ever see a fairer?	1Tamb	2.4.28		Mycet
Then shalt thou see me pull it from thy head:	1Tamb	2.4.39		Tamb
Thou art no match for mightie Tamburlaine.	1Tamb	2.4.40		Tamb
And till thou overtake me Tamburlaine,	1Tamb	2.5.44		Cosroe
Why say Theridamas, wilt thou be a king?	1Tamb	2.5.65		Tamb
Then thou for Parthia, they for Scythia and Medea.	1Tamb	2.5.83		Tamb
Then shalt thou see the Scythian Tamburlaine,	1Tamb	2.5.97		Tamb
Then stay thou with him, say I bid thee so.	1Tamb	3.1.35		Bajzth
have measured heaven/With triple circuit thou regreet us not,	1Tamb	3.1.37		Bajzth
It saies, Agydas, thou shalt surely die,	1Tamb	3.2.95		Agidas
And dar'st thou bluntly call me Bajazeth?	1Tamb	3.3.71		Bajzth
And know thou Turke, that those which lead my horse,	1Tamb	3.3.72		Tamb
And dar'st thou bluntly call me Tamburlaine?	1Tamb	3.3.74		Tamb
As if thou wert the Empresse of the world.	1Tamb	3.3.125		Tamb
Stir not Zenocrate untill thou see/Me martch victoriously with	1Tamb	3.3.126		Tamb
Til then take thou my crowne, vaunt of my worth,	1Tamb	3.3.130		Tamb
Now shalt thou feel the force of Turkish arms,	1Tamb	3.3.134		Bajzth
Thou knowest not (foolish hardy Tamburlaine)/What tis to meet	1Tamb	3.3.145		Bajzth
must thou be plac'd by me/That am the Empresse of the mighty	1Tamb	3.3.166		Zabina
Cal'st thou me Concubine that am betroath'd/Unto the great and	1Tamb	3.3.169		Zenoc
Thou wilt repent these lavish words of thine,	1Tamb	3.3.172		Zenoc
Thou shalt be Landresse to my waiting maid.	1Tamb	3.3.177		Zabina
How lik'st thou her Ebea, will she serve?	1Tamb	3.3.178		Zabina
Hearst thou Anippe, how thy drudge doth talk,	1Tamb	3.3.182		Zenoc
Thou art deceiv'd, I heard the Trumpets sound,	1Tamb	3.3.203		Zabina
Thou, by the fortune of this damned [foile] <soile>.	1Tamb	3.3.213		Bajzth
No Tamburlain, though now thou gat the best,	1Tamb	3.3.222		Zabina
Thou shalt not yet be Lord of Affrica.	1Tamb	3.3.223		Zabina
What, thinkst thou Tamburlain esteems thy gold?	1Tamb	3.3.262		Tamb
But Villaine, thou that wishest this to me,	1Tamb	4.2.12		Tamb
First shalt thou rip my bowels with thy sword,	1Tamb	4.2.16		Bajzth
Feends looke on me, and thou dread God of hell,	1Tamb	4.2.27		Bajzth
Dar'st thou that never saw an Emperour,	1Tamb	4.2.58		Zabina
Before thou met my husband in the field,	1Tamb	4.2.59		Zabina
And thou his wife shalt feed him with the scraps/My servitures	1Tamb	4.2.87		Tamb
Capolin, hast thou survaid our powers?	1Tamb	4.3.50		Souldn
And now Bajazeth, hast thou any stomacke?	1Tamb	4.4.10		Tamb
Villain, knowest thou to whom thou speakest?	1Tamb	4.4.39	P	Usumc
Doost thou think that Mahomet wil suffer this?	1Tamb	4.4.52	P	Therid
pray thee tel, why art thou so sad?	1Tamb	4.4.63	P	Tamb
If thou wilt have a song, the Turke shall straine his voice:	1Tamb	4.4.63	P	Tamb
And wouldst thou have me buy thy Fathers love/With such a	1Tamb	4.4.83		Tamb
thou maist thinke thy selfe happie to be fed from my trencher.	1Tamb	4.4.92	P	Tamb
Here Turk, wilt thou have a cleane trencher?	1Tamb	4.4.101	P	Tamb
wert thou the cause of this/That tearm'st Zenocrate thy dearest	1Tamb	5.1.335		Zenoc
Thou that in conduct of thy happy stars,	1Tamb	5.1.358		Zenoc
eies beholde/That as for her thou bearst these wretched armes,	1Tamb	5.1.409		Arabia
Even so for her thou diest in these armes:	1Tamb	5.1.410		Arabia
Thou hast with honor usde Zenocrate.	1Tamb	5.1.484		Souldn
Then sit thou downe divine Zenocrate,	1Tamb	5.1.506		Tamb
Viceroy of Byron, wisely hast thou said:	2Tamb	1.1.54		Orcan
Take which thou wilt, for as the Romans usde/I here present	2Tamb	1.1.81		Sgsmnd
Wilt thou have war, then shake this blade at me,	2Tamb	1.1.83		Sgsmnd
forgetst thou I am he/That with the Cannon shooke Vienna	2Tamb	1.1.86		Orcan
Forgetst thou that I sent a shower of dartes/Mingled with	2Tamb	1.1.91		Orcan
That thou thy self, then County-Pallatine,	2Tamb	1.1.94		Orcan

THOU (cont.)

Forgetst thou, that to have me raise my siege,	2Tamb	1.1.98	Orcan
How canst thou think of this and offer war?	2Tamb	1.1.102	Orcan
I know thou wouldst depart from hence with me.	2Tamb	1.2.11	Callap
Then shalt thou see a hundred kings and more/Upon their knees,	2Tamb	1.2.28	Callap
Choose which thou wilt, all are at thy command.	2Tamb	1.2.31	Callap
And as thou rid'st in triumph through the streets,	2Tamb	1.2.41	Callap
And when thou goest, a golden Canapie/Enchac'd with pretious	2Tamb	1.2.48	Callap
Thou shalt be crown'd a king and be my mate.	2Tamb	1.2.66	Callap
when wilt thou leave these armes/And save thy sacred person	2Tamb	1.3.9	Zenoc
Wel done my boy, thou shalt have shield and lance,	2Tamb	1.3.43	Tamb
If thou wilt love the warres and follow me,	2Tamb	1.3.47	Tamb
Thou shalt be made a King and raigne with me,	2Tamb	1.3.48	Tamb
If thou exceed thy elder Brothers worth,	2Tamb	1.3.50	Tamb
Thou shalt be king before them, and thy seed/Shall issue	2Tamb	1.3.52	Tamb
These words assure me boy, thou art my sonne,	2Tamb	1.3.58	Tamb
Be thou the scourge and terrour of the world.	2Tamb	1.3.60	Tamb
Of all the provinces I have subdued/Thou shalt not have a foot,	2Tamb	1.3.72	Tamb
a foot, unlesse thou beare/A mind corragious and invincible:	2Tamb	1.3.72	Tamb
Open thou shining vaile of Cynthia/And make a passage from the	2Tamb	2.2.47	Orcan
Thou Christ that art esteem'd omnipotent,	2Tamb	2.2.55	Orcan
If thou wilt proove thy selfe a perfect God,	2Tamb	2.2.56	Orcan
What saiest thou yet Gazellus to his foile:	2Tamb	2.3.27	Orcan
And if thou pitiest Tamburlain the great,	2Tamb	2.4.117	Tamb
her soule be, thou shalt stay with me/Embalm'd with Cassia,	2Tamb	2.4.129	Tamb
And till I die thou shalt not be interr'd.	2Tamb	2.4.132	Tamb
Thou shalt not beautifie Larissa plaines,	2Tamb	3.2.34	Tamb
Thou shalt be set upon my royall tent.	2Tamb	3.2.37	Tamb
Villain, art thou the sonne of Tamburlaine,	2Tamb	3.2.95	Tamb
Hast thou beheld a peale of ordinance strike/A ring of pikes,	2Tamb	3.2.98	Tamb
And canst thou Coward stand in feare of death?	2Tamb	3.2.102	Tamb
Hast thou not seene my horsmen charge the foe,	2Tamb	3.2.103	Tamb
And wilt thou shun the field for feare of woundes?	2Tamb	3.2.109	Tamb
It shall suffice thou darst abide a wound.	2Tamb	3.2.136	Tamb
My boy, Thou shalt not loose a drop of blood,	2Tamb	3.2.137	Tamb
Captaine, that thou yeeld up thy hold to us.	2Tamb	3.3.16	Therid
Nay Captain, thou art weary of thy life,	2Tamb	3.3.18	Techel
If thou withstand the friends of Tamburlain.	2Tamb	3.3.19	Techel
Death, whether art thou gone that both we live?	2Tamb	3.4.11	Olymp
death, why comm'st thou not?	2Tamb	3.4.14	Olymp
Tell me sweet boie, art thou content to die?	2Tamb	3.4.18	Olymp
Thou shalt with us to Tamburlaine the great,	2Tamb	3.4.39	Techel
Who when he heares how resolute thou wert,	2Tamb	3.4.40	Techel
And thou shalt see a man greater than Mahomet,	2Tamb	3.4.46	Therid
Now thou art fearfull of thy armies strength,	2Tamb	3.5.75	Orcan
Thou wouldst with overmatch of person fight,	2Tamb	3.5.76	Orcan
first thou shalt kneele to us/And humbly crave a pardon for thy	2Tamb	3.5.108	Orcan
Seest thou not death within my wrathfull looks?	2Tamb	3.5.119	Tamb
For if thou livest, not any Element/Shal shrowde thee from the	2Tamb	3.5.126	Tamb
Doost thou aske him leave?	2Tamb	3.5.134	P Callap
What, dar'st thou then be absent from the fight,	2Tamb	4.1.22	Amyras
Thou doost dishonor manhood, and thy house.	2Tamb	4.1.32	Celeb
Come, thou and I wil goe to cardes to drive away the time.	2Tamb	4.1.61	P Calyph
Thou hast procur'd a greater enemie,	2Tamb	4.1.127	Tamb
Whereat thou trembling hid'st thee in the aire,	2Tamb	4.1.130	Tamb
Thou shewest the difference twixt our selves and thee/In this	2Tamb	4.1.138	Orcan
Which with thy beauty thou wast woont to light,	2Tamb	4.2.16	Therid
Tell me Olympia, wilt thou graunt my suit?	2Tamb	4.2.21	Therid
And eb againe, as thou departst from me.	2Tamb	4.2.32	Therid
Thou shalt be stately Queene of faire Argier,	2Tamb	4.2.39	Therid
O thou that swaiest the region under earth,	2Tamb	4.3.32	Orcan
Come as thou didst in fruitfull Scicilie,	2Tamb	4.3.34	Orcan
And as thou took'st the faire Proserpina,	2Tamb	4.3.36	Orcan
wilt thou so defame/The hatefull fortunes of thy victory,	2Tamb	4.3.77	Orcan
Villaine, respects thou more thy slavish life,	2Tamb	5.1.10	Govnr
Thou desperate Governour of Babylon,	2Tamb	5.1.49	Therid
Or els be sure thou shalt be forc'd with paines,	2Tamb	5.1.52	Therid
Thou seest us prest to give the last assault,	2Tamb	5.1.60	Techel
Shouldst thou have entred, cruel Tamburlaine:	2Tamb	5.1.102	Govnr
Yet shouldst thou die, shoot at him all at once.	2Tamb	5.1.157	Tamb
Now Mahomet, if thou have any power,	2Tamb	5.1.187	Tamb
Thou art not woorthy to be worshipped,	2Tamb	5.1.189	Tamb
Why send'st thou not a furious whyrlwind downe,	2Tamb	5.1.192	Tamb
Where men report, thou sitt'st by God himselfe,	2Tamb	5.1.194	Tamb
thou that hast seene/Millions of Turkes perish by Tamburlaine,	2Tamb	5.2.24	Callap
let me see how well/Thou wilt become thy fathers majestie.	2Tamb	5.3.184	Tamb
As precious is the charge thou undertak'st/As that which	2Tamb	5.3.230	Tamb
The ships are safe thou saist, and richly fraught.	Jew	1.1.54	Barab
But art thou master in a ship of mine,	Jew	1.1.61	Barab
Sirra, which of my ships art thou Master of?	Jew	1.1.70	Barab
And saw'st thou not/Mine Argosie at Alexandria?	Jew	1.1.71	Barab
Thou couldst not come from Egypt, or by Caire/But at the entry	Jew	1.1.73	Barab
Thou needs must saile by Alexandria.	Jew	1.1.76	Barab
[But] <by> goe, goe thou thy wayes, discharge thy Ship,	Jew	1.1.82	Barab
Tut, Jew, we know thou art no souldier;	Jew	1.2.52	1Knght
Thou art a Merchant, and a monied man,	Jew	1.2.53	1Knght
Why Barabas wilt thou be christened?	Jew	1.2.81	Govnr
No, Jew, thou hast denied the Articles,	Jew	1.2.92	Govnr
But here in Malta, where thou gotst thy wealth,	Jew	1.2.101	Govnr
Live still; and if thou canst, get more.	Jew	1.2.102	Govnr
From nought at first thou camst to little welth,	Jew	1.2.105	1Knght
Sham'st thou not thus to justifie thy selfe,	Jew	1.2.119	Govnr
If thou rely upon thy righteousnesse,	Jew	1.2.121	Govnr

THOU (cont.)

Content thee, Barabas, thou hast nought but right.	Jew	1.2.152		Govnr
and all mens hatred/Inflict upon them, thou great Primus Motor.	Jew	1.2.164		Barab
Thou seest they have taken halfe our goods.	Jew	1.2.176		1Jew
thou perceiv'st the plight/Wherein these Christians have	Jew	1.2.270		Barab
thus; thou toldst me they have turn'd my house/Into a Nunnery,	Jew	1.2.277		Barab
but be thou so precise/As they may thinke it done of Holinesse.	Jew	1.2.284		Barab
Till thou hast gotten to be entertain'd.	Jew	1.2.288		Barab
As good dissemble that thou never mean'st/As first meane truth,	Jew	1.2.290		Barab
What art thou, daughter?	Jew	1.2.316		Abbass
now Abigall, what mak'st thou/Amongst these hateful Christians?	Jew	1.2.338		Barab
Hinder her not, thou man of little faith,	Jew	1.2.340		1Fryar
What wilt thou doe among these hatefull fiends?	Jew	1.2.345		Barab
I charge thee on my blessing that thou leave/These divels, and	Jew	1.2.346		Barab
Barabas, although thou art in mis-beleefe,	Jew	1.2.352		1Fryar
Wilt thou forsake mee too in my distresse,	Jew	1.2.358		Barab
No come not at me, if thou wilt be damn'd,	Jew	1.2.362		Barab
Out, out thou wretch.	Jew	1.2.365		Barab
Oh thou that with a fiery piller led'st/The sonnes of Israel	Jew	2.1.12		Barab
Now Captaine tell us whither thou art bound?	Jew	2.2.1		Govnr
And why thou cam'st ashore without our leave?	Jew	2.2.3		Govnr
Delbosco, as thou lovest and honour'st us,	Jew	2.2.24		1Knght
Bosco, thou shalt be Malta's Generall;	Jew	2.2.44		Govnr
Claime tribute where thou wilt, we are resolv'd,	Jew	2.2.55		Govnr
Barabas, thou know'st I am the Governors sonne.	Jew	2.3.40		Lodowk
Whither walk'st thou, Barabas?	Jew	2.3.43		Lodowk
Ratest thou this Moore but at two hundred plats?	Jew	2.3.107		Lodowk
and thou hast, breake my head with it, I'le forgive thee.	Jew	2.3.111	P	Barab
Tell me, hast thou thy health well?	Jew	2.3.121	P	Barab
Where was thou borne?	Jew	2.3.127	P	Barab
So much the better, thou art for my turne.	Jew	2.3.129		Barab
Thou hast thy Crownes, fellow, come let's away.	Jew	2.3.158		Mater
Hast thou no Trade?	Jew	2.3.167		Barab
First be thou voyd of these affections,	Jew	2.3.169		Barab
Be mov'd at nothing, see thou pitty none,	Jew	2.3.171		Barab
But tell me now, How hast thou spent thy time?	Jew	2.3.201		Barab
Be true and secret, thou shalt want no gold.	Jew	2.3.216		Barab
Thou know'st, and heaven can witnesse it is true,	Jew	2.3.253		Barab
I, Barabas, or else thou wrong'st me much.	Jew	2.3.255		Mthias
Mathias, as thou lov'st me, not a word.	Jew	2.3.277		Barab
Barabas, thou know'st I have lov'd thy daughter long.	Jew	2.3.288		Lodowk
Oh wretched Abigal, what hast [thou] <thee> done?	Jew	2.3.320		Abigal
Shee is thy wife, and thou shalt be mine heire.	Jew	2.3.328		Barab
But thou must dote upon a Christian?	Jew	2.3.360		Barab
Now tell me, Ithimore, how lik'st thou this?	Jew	2.3.364		Barab
I, so thou shalt, 'tis thou must doe the deed:	Jew	2.3.369		Barab
Tell me, how cam'st thou by this?	Jew	3.1.16		Curtzn
Zoon's what a looking thou keep'st, thou'lt betraye's anon.	Jew	3.1.25		Pilia
I did it, and revenge it if thou dar'st.	Jew	3.2.4		Mthias
hadst thou perish'd by the Turke,/Wretched Ferneze might have	Jew	3.2.13		Govnr
Why, how now Ithimore, why laugh'st thou so?	Jew	3.3.4		Abigal
Why, what ayl'st thou?	Jew	3.3.6		Abigal
Admit thou lov'dst not Lodowicke for his [sire] <sinne>,	Jew	3.3.40		Abigal
But thou wert set upon extreme revenge,	Jew	3.3.42		Abigal
And then thou didst not like that holy life.	Jew	3.3.58		1Fryar
Abigal I will, but see thou change no more,	Jew	3.3.70		1Fryar
Though thou deservest hardly at my hands,	Jew	3.3.74		Abigal
False, and unkinde; what, hast thou lost thy father?	Jew	3.4.2		Barab
Art thou againe got to the Nunnery?	Jew	3.4.4		Barab
When saw'st thou Abigall?	Jew	3.4.18		Barab
And [less] <least> thou yeeld to this that I intreat,	Jew	3.4.37		Barab
I cannot thinke but that thou hat'st my life.	Jew	3.4.38		Barab
Goe buy thee garments: but thou shalt not want:	Jew	3.4.47		Barab
Onely know this, that thus thou art to doe:	Jew	3.4.48		Barab
What, hast thou brought the Ladle with thee too?	Jew	3.4.57		Barab
Now shalt thou see the death of Abigall,	Jew	3.4.62		Barab
That thou mayst freely live to be my heire.	Jew	3.4.63		Barab
I but Ithimore seest thou this?	Jew	3.4.67		Barab
There Ithimore must thou goe place this [pot] <plot>:	Jew	3.4.84		Barab
Prethe doe: what saist thou now?	Jew	3.4.88		Barab
Assure thy selfe thou shalt have broth by the eye.	Jew	3.4.92		Barab
go set it downe/And come againe so soone as thou hast done,	Jew	3.4.109		Barab
since thou hast broke the league/By flat denyall of the	Jew	3.5.19		Basso
Thou know'st 'tis death and if it be reveal'd.	Jew	3.6.51		2Fryar
Thou shalt not need, for now the Nuns are dead,	Jew	4.1.15		Barab
Thou hast offended, therefore must be damn'd.	Jew	4.1.25		1Fryar
Barabas, thou hast--	Jew	4.1.28		2Fryar
I, that thou hast--	Jew	4.1.29		1Fryar
Thou art a--	Jew	4.1.31		2Fryar
I, that thou art a--	Jew	4.1.32		1Fryar
Thou hast committed--	Jew	4.1.40		2Fryar
Bernardine--/Wilt thou not speake?	Jew	4.1.169		1Fryar
thou think'st I see thee not;/Away, I'de wish thee, and let me	Jew	4.1.169		1Fryar
No, wilt thou not?	Jew	4.1.171		1Fryar
As thou lik'st that, stop me another time.	Jew	4.1.173		1Fryar
Why, how now Jacomo, what hast thou done?	Jew	4.1.174		Barab
Pilia-borza, didst thou meet with Ithimore?	Jew	4.2.1	P	Curtzn
And didst thou deliver my letter?	Jew	4.2.3	P	Curtzn
And what think'st thou, will he come?	Jew	4.2.5	P	Curtzn
Canst thou be so unkind to leave me thus?	Jew	4.2.52		Curtzn
I'le be thy Jason, thou my golden Fleece;	Jew	4.2.90		Ithimr
I'le be Adonis, thou shalt be Loves Queene.	Jew	4.2.94		Ithimr
Thou in those Groves, by Dis above,	Jew	4.2.97		Ithimr

THOU (cont.)

hast thou the gold?	Jew	4.2.100	P Ithimr
Take thou the mony, spend it for my sake.	Jew	4.2.123	Ithimr
Why, wantst thou any of thy tale?	Jew	4.3.19	P Barab
Nay [to] thine owne cost, villaine, if thou com'st.	Jew	4.3.59	Barab
Saist thou me so?	Jew	4.4.2	P Ithimr
There, if thou lov'st me doe not leave a drop.	Jew	4.4.6	P Ithimr
What wudst thou doe if he should send thee none?	Jew	4.4.13	Pilia
Thou and thy Turk; 'twas you that slew my son.	Jew	5.1.27	Govnr
Art thou that Jew whose goods we heard were sold/For	Jew	5.1.73	Calym
Canst thou, as thou reportest, make Malta ours?	Jew	5.1.85	Calym
Thus hast thou gotten, by thy policie,	Jew	5.2.27	Barab
And since by wrong thou got'st Authority,	Jew	5.2.35	Barab
for feare too late/Thou seek'st for much, but canst not	Jew	5.2.46	Barab
Thou seest thy life, and Malta's happinesse,	Jew	5.2.52	Barab
What thinkst thou shall become of it and thee?	Jew	5.2.56	Barab
What wilt thou give me, Governor, to procure/A dissolution of	Jew	5.2.76	Barab
Doe but bring this to passe which thou pretendest,	Jew	5.2.84	Govnr
Deale truly with us as thou intimatest,	Jew	5.2.85	Govnr
Nay more, doe this, and live thou Governor still.	Jew	5.2.89	Govnr
Nay, doe thou this, Ferneze, and be free;	Jew	5.2.90	Barab
And let me see what mony thou canst make;	Jew	5.2.94	Barab
Where be thou present onely to performe/One stratagem that I'le	Jew	5.2.98	Barab
I will be there, and doe as thou desirest;	Jew	5.2.103	Govnr
And banquet with him e're thou leav'st the Ile.	Jew	5.3.19	Msngr
returne me word/That thou wilt come, and I am satisfied.	Jew	5.5.12	Barab
That thou maist feast them in thy Citadell.	Jew	5.5.16	Msngr
Pounds saist thou, Governor, wel since it is no more/I'le	Jew	5.5.21	Barab
Here, hold that knife, and when thou seest he comes,	Jew	5.5.37	Barab
Thou shalt not live in doubt of any thing.	Jew	5.5.45	Barab
See his end first, and flye then if thou canst.	Jew	5.5.69	Govnr
But wish thou hadst behav'd thee otherwise.	Jew	5.5.75	Govnr
For with thy Gallyes couldst thou not get hence,	Jew	5.5.100	Govnr
Tush, Governor, take thou no care for that,	Jew	5.5.102	Calym
Why, hardst thou not the trumpet sound a charge?	Jew	5.5.105	Govnr
The ruines done to Malta and to us,/Thou canst not part:	Jew	5.5.113	Govnr
Content thee, Calymath, here thou must stay,	Jew	5.5.118	Govnr
The love thou bear'st unto the house of Guise:	P 69	2.12	Guise
gloves which I sent/To be poysoned, hast thou done them?	P 71	2.14	Guise
Then thou remainest resolute.	P 75	2.18	Guise
Now come thou forth and play thy tragick part,	P 85	2.28	Guise
And when thou seest the Admirall ride by,	P 87	2.30	Guise
Since thou hast all the Cardes within thy hands/To shuffle or	P 146	2.89	Guise
That right or wrong, thou deale thy selfe a King.	P 148	2.91	Guise
Thanks my good freend, holde, take thou this reward.	P 168	3.3	OldQn
And thou a traitor to thy soule and him.	P 342	5.69	Lorein
I, I, for this Seroune, and thou shalt [ha't] <hate>.	P 351	6.6	Mntsrl
Why, darst thou presume to call on Christ,	P 356	6.11	Mntsrl
Flye Ramus flye, if thou wilt save thy life.	P 365	7.5	Taleus
What art thou?	P 373	7.13	Gonzag
Come Ramus, more golde, or thou shalt have the stabbe.	P 376	7.16	Gonzag
Was it not thou that scoftes the Organon,	P 387	7.27	Guise
Thou traitor Guise, lay of thy bloudy hands.	P 439	7.79	Navrre
O say not so, thou kill'st thy mothers heart.	P 539	11.4	QnMoth
What art thou dead, sweet sonne speak to thy Mother.	P 551	11.16	QnMoth
Heere hast thou a country voide of feares,	P 591	12.4	QnMoth
How meanst thou that?	P 618	12.31	King
I prethee say to whome thou writes?	P 671	13.15	Guise
Thou trothles and unjust, what lines are these?	P 680	13.24	Guise
And fly my presence if thou looke to live.	P 692	13.36	Guise
But canst thou tell who is their generall?	P 731	14.34	Navrre
At thy request I am content thou goe,	P 746	15.4	King
How now Mugeroun, metst thou not the Guise at the doore?	P 774	15.32	King
Marry if thou hadst, thou mightst have had the stab,	P 776	15.34	King
Revenge it Henry as thou list or dare,	P 819	17.14	Guise
What Peere in France but thou (aspiring Guise)/Durst be in	P 828	17.23	Eprnon
Thou shouldst perceive the Duke of Guise is mov'd.	P 832	17.27	Guise
Least thou perceive the King of France be mov'd.	P 834	17.29	King
Thou able to maintaine an hoast in pay,	P 841	17.36	Eprnon
Else all France knowes how poor a Duke thou art.	P 844	17.39	Eprnon
Guise, weare our crowne, and be thou King of France,	P 859	17.54	King
Be thou proclaimde a traitor throughout France.	P 864	17.59	King
Then farwell Guise, the King and thou are freends.	P 870	17.65	King
And perish in the pit thou mad'st for me.	P 963	19.33	King
Villaine, why dost thou look so gastly? speake.	P 989	19.59	Guise
Pardon thee, why what hast thou done?	P 991	19.61	Guise
To which thou didst alure me being alive:	P1025	19.95	King
him, and will slay/Thee too, and thou prove such a traitor.	P1049	19.119	King
Art thou King, and hast done this bloudy deed?	P1050	19.120	YngGse
King, why so thou wert before.	P1067	19.137	QnMoth
Pray God thou be a King now this is done.	P1068	19.138	QnMoth
I cannot speak for greefe: when thou wast borne,	P1072	19.142	QnMoth
My sonne: thou art a changeling, not my sonne.	P1074	19.144	QnMoth
Sweet Guise, would he had died so thou wert heere:	P1082	19.152	QnMoth
Wert thou the Pope thou mightst not scape from us.	P1092	20.2	1Mur
Now thou art dead, heere is no stay for us:	P1111	21.5	Dumain
But how wilt thou get opportunitye?	P1135	21.29	Dumain
Frier, thou dost acknowledge me thy King?	P1164	22.26	King
Then come thou neer, and tell what newes thou bringst.	P1166	22.28	King
Search Surgeon and resolve me what thou seest.	P1193	22.55	King
Surgeon, why saist thou so? the King may live.	P1224	22.86	Navrre
Oh no Navarre, thou must be King of France.	P1225	22.87	King
So thou wouldst smile and take me in thy <thine> armes.	Edw	1.1.9	Gavstn

THOU (cont.)

What canst thou doe?	Edw	1.1.26	Gavstn
But I have no horses. What art thou?	Edw	1.1.28	Gavstn
Let me see, thou wouldst do well/To waite at my trencher, and	Edw	1.1.30	Gavstn
And what art thou?	Edw	1.1.33	Gavstn
Frownst thou thereat, aspiring Lancaster,	Edw	1.1.93	Edward
Why shouldst thou kneele, knowest thou not who I am?	Edw	1.1.142	Edward
Then thou hast beene of me since thy exile.	Edw	1.1.145	Edward
If for these dignities thou be envied,	Edw	1.1.163	Edward
Fearst thou thy person? thou shalt have a guard:	Edw	1.1.166	Edward
Wants thou gold? go to my treasurie:	Edw	1.1.167	Edward
Wouldst thou be lovde and fearde?	Edw	1.1.168	Edward
Thou shouldst not plod one foote beyond this place.	Edw	1.1.181	Gavstn
And Gaveston unlesse thou be reclaimd,	Edw	1.1.183	BshpCv
So will I now, and thou shalt back to France.	Edw	1.1.185	BshpCv
Be thou lord bishop, and receive his rents,	Edw	1.1.194	Edward
I give him thee, here use him as thou wilt.	Edw	1.1.196	Edward
I, to the tower, the fleete, or where thou wilt.	Edw	1.1.198	Edward
For this offence be thou accurst of God.	Edw	1.1.199	BshpCv
Come follow me, and thou shalt have my guarde,	Edw	1.1.204	Edward
Go whether thou wilt seeing I have Gaveston.	Edw	1.2.54	Queene
Thou villaine, wherfore talkes thou of a king,	Edw	1.4.28	Mortmr
Here Mortimer, sit thou in Edwards throne,	Edw	1.4.36	Edward
Thou Lancaster, high admirall of our fleete,	Edw	1.4.66	Edward
you lord Warwick, president of the North,/And thou of Wales:	Edw	1.4.69	Edward
And thou must hence, or I shall be deposd,	Edw	1.4.110	Edward
Live where thou wilt, ile send thee gould enough,	Edw	1.4.113	Edward
And long thou shalt not stay, or if thou doost,	Edw	1.4.114	Edward
Thou from this land, I from my selfe am banisht.	Edw	1.4.118	Edward
That whether I will or no thou must depart:	Edw	1.4.124	Edward
Thou shalt not hence, ile hide thee Gaveston.	Edw	1.4.131	Edward
The time is little that thou hast to stay,	Edw	1.4.138	Edward
In saying this, thou wrongst me Gaveston,	Edw	1.4.149	Queene
Ist not enough, that thou corrupts my lord,	Edw	1.4.150	Queene
But thou must call mine honor thus in question?	Edw	1.4.152	Queene
Thou art too familiar with that Mortimer,	Edw	1.4.154	Edward
Or thou shalt nere be reconcild to me.	Edw	1.4.157	Edward
Villaine, tis thou that robst me of my lord.	Edw	1.4.160	Queene
And witnesse heaven how deere thou art to me.	Edw	1.4.167	Edward
Assure thy selfe thou comst not in my sight.	Edw	1.4.169	Edward
And therefore as thou lovest and tendrest me,	Edw	1.4.211	Queene
Be thou my advocate unto these peeres.	Edw	1.4.212	Queene
As thou wilt soone subscribe to his repeale.	Edw	1.4.227	Queene
For thee faire Queene, if thou lovest Gaveston,	Edw	1.4.327	Edward
Seeing thou hast pleaded with so good successe.	Edw	1.4.329	Edward
Live thou with me as my companion.	Edw	1.4.343	Edward
Be thou commaunder of our royall fleete,	Edw	1.4.354	Edward
Nephue, I must to Scotland, thou staiest here.	Edw	1.4.386	MortSr
Thou seest by nature he is milde and calme,	Edw	1.4.388	MortSr
Which of the nobles dost thou meane to serve?	Edw	2.1.3	Baldck
Spencer, thou knowest I hate such formall toies,	Edw	2.1.44	Baldck
What needst thou, love, thus to excuse thy selfe?	Edw	2.1.60	Neece
I know thou couldst not come and visit me.	Edw	2.1.61	Neece
Though thou comparst him to a flying Fish,	Edw	2.2.43	Edward
Ah furious Mortimer what hast thou done?	Edw	2.2.85	Queene
Yes more then thou canst answer though he live,	Edw	2.2.87	Edward
Complaines, that thou hast left her all forlorne.	Edw	2.2.173	Lncstr
I meane the peeres, whom thou shouldst dearly love:	Edw	2.2.176	Mortmr
When wert thou in the field with banner spred?	Edw	2.2.182	Mortmr
Art thou an enemie to my Gaveston?	Edw	2.2.212	Edward
Traitor be gone, whine thou with Mortimer.	Edw	2.2.214	Edward
No marvell though thou scorne thy noble peeres,	Edw	2.2.217	Kent
Tell me, where wast thou borne? What is thine armes?	Edw	2.2.242	Edward
The fitter art thou Baldock for my turne,	Edw	2.2.245	Edward
Waite on me, and ile see thou shalt not want.	Edw	2.2.246	Edward
Knowest thou him Gaveston?	Edw	2.2.248	Edward
So well hast thou deserv'de sweete Mortimer.	Edw	2.4.59	Queene
Thou proud disturber of thy countries peace,	Edw	2.5.9	Mortmr
Upon my weapons point here shouldst thou fall,	Edw	2.5.13	Mortmr
Lancaster, why talkst thou to the slave?	Edw	2.5.19	Warwck
But for thou wert the favorit of a King,	Edw	2.5.27	Warwck
Thou shalt have so much honor at our hands.	Edw	2.5.28	Warwck
Shalt thou appoint/What we shall graunt?	Edw	2.5.49	Mortmr
But for we know thou art a noble gentleman,	Edw	2.5.68	Mortmr
How meanst thou Mortimer? that is over base.	Edw	2.5.71	Gavstn
Penbrooke, what wilt thou do?	Edw	2.5.82	Warwck
Be thou this night his keeper, in the morning/We will discharge	Edw	2.5.108	Penbrk
Unhappie-Gaveston, whether goest thou now.	Edw	2.5.110	Gavstn
Welcome old man, comst thou in Edwards aide?	Edw	3.1.34	Edward
Then tell thy prince, of whence, and what thou art.	Edw	3.1.35	Edward
Thou shalt have crownes of us, t'out bid the Barons,	Edw	3.1.55	Edward
thy mother feare/Thou art not markt to many daies on earth.	Edw	3.1.80	Queene
What lord [Arundell] <Matre>, dost thou come alone?	Edw	3.1.89	Edward
Tell me [Arundell] <Matre>, died he ere thou camst,	Edw	3.1.92	Edward
Or didst thou see my friend to take his death?	Edw	3.1.93	Edward
Thou comst from Mortimer and his complices,	Edw	3.1.153	Edward
Yet ere thou go, see how I do devorce	Edw	3.1.176	Edward
Away base upstart, brav'st thou nobles thus?	Edw	3.1.205	Penbrk
Then Edward, thou wilt fight it to the last,	Edw	3.1.211	Mortmr
That thou proud Warwicke watcht the prisoner,	Edw	3.1.237	Edward
As much as thou in rage out wentst the rest.	Edw	3.1.240	Edward
Tis but temporall that thou canst inflict.	Edw	3.1.242	Warwck
Grone for this greefe, behold how thou art maimed.	Edw	3.1.251	Mortmr

THOU (cont.)

Yea, but [Levune] <Lewne> thou seest,/These Barons lay their	Edw	3.1.273	Baldck
Proud Edward, doost thou banish me thy presence?	Edw	4.1.5	Kent
A boye, thou art deceivde at least in this,	Edw	4.2.8	Queene
Whether, O whether doost thou bend thy steps?	Edw	4.2.12	Queene
If, doost thou say?	Edw	4.3.21	Edward
And Edward thou art one among them all,	Edw	4.4.10	Queene
blood,/Of thine own people patron shouldst thou be/But thou--	Edw	4.4.13	Queene
Of thine own people patron shouldst thou be/But thou--	Edw	4.4.14	Queene
Proud traytor Mortimer why doost thou chase/Thy lawfull king	Edw	4.6.3	Kent
Vilde wretch, and why hast thou of all unkinde,	Edw	4.6.5	Kent
Raigne showers of vengeance on my cursed head/Thou God, to whom	Edw	4.6.8	Kent
Dissemble or thou diest, for Mortimer/And Isabell doe kisse	Edw	4.6.12	Kent
O hadst thou ever beene a king, thy hart/Pierced deeply with	Edw	4.7.9	Edward
That in our famous nurseries of artes/Thou suckedst from Plato,	Edw	4.7.19	Edward
A litter hast thou, lay me in a hearse,	Edw	4.7.87	Edward
Leister, thou staist for me,/And go I must, life farewell with	Edw	4.7.98	Edward
For kinde and loving hast thou alwaies beene:	Edw	5.1.7	Edward
Continue ever thou celestiall sunne,	Edw	5.1.64	Edward
But haplesse Edward, thou art fondly led,	Edw	5.1.76	Edward
Call thou them back, I have no power to speake.	Edw	5.1.93	Edward
Be thou perswaded, that I love thee well,	Edw	5.2.16	Queene
Conclude against his father what thou wilt,	Edw	5.2.19	Queene
As thou intendest to rise by Mortimer,	Edw	5.2.52	Mortmr
Seeke all the meanes thou canst to make him droope,	Edw	5.2.54	Mortmr
Thou being his unckle, and the next of bloud,	Edw	5.2.88	Mortmr
Inconstant Edmund, doost thou favor him,	Edw	5.2.101	Mortmr
Why yongling, s'dainst thou so of Mortimer.	Edw	5.2.111	Mortmr
For me, both thou, and both the Spencers died,	Edw	5.3.42	Edward
Edmund, yeeld thou thy self, or thou shalt die.	Edw	5.3.56	Matrvs
Come forth. Art thou as resolute as thou wast?	Edw	5.4.22	Mortmr
And hast thou cast how to accomplish it?	Edw	5.4.24	Mortmr
But at his lookes Lightborne thou wilt relent.	Edw	5.4.26	Mortmr
At every ten miles end thou hast a horse.	Edw	5.4.42	Mortmr
Unlesse thou bring me newes of Edwards death.	Edw	5.4.46	Mortmr
And thou compelst this prince to weare the crowne.	Edw	5.4.88	Kent
Art thou king, must I die at thy commaund?	Edw	5.4.103	Kent
I, stay a while, thou shalt have answer straight.	Edw	5.5.20	Matrvs
Whose there, what light is that, wherefore comes thou?	Edw	5.5.42	Edward
Villaine, I know thou comst to murther me.	Edw	5.5.45	Edward
Weepst thou already?	Edw	5.5.52	Edward
What meanes thou to dissemble with me thus?	Edw	5.5.80	Edward
One jewell have I left, receive thou this.	Edw	5.5.84	Edward
O if thou harborst murther in thy hart,	Edw	5.5.87	Edward
O wherefore sits thou heare?	Edw	5.5.96	Edward
No, no, for if thou meanst to murther me,	Edw	5.5.98	Edward
Thou wilt returne againe, and therefore stay.	Edw	5.5.99	Edward
And therefore tell me, wherefore art thou come?	Edw	5.5.106	Edward
if thou now growest penitent/Ile be thy ghostly father,	Edw	5.6.3	Mortmr
Whether thou wilt be secret in this,	Edw	5.6.5	Mortmr
And thou shalt die, and on his mournefull hearse,	Edw	5.6.29	King
And plainely saith, twas thou that murdredst him.	Edw	5.6.42	King
That thither thou didst send a murtherer.	Edw	5.6.48	King
A Mortimer, thou knowest that he is slaine,	Edw	5.6.50	King
And so shalt thou be too: why staies he heere?	Edw	5.6.51	King
As thou receivedst thy life from me,	Edw	5.6.68	Queene
Thou hadst not hatcht this monstrous treacherie!	Edw	5.6.97	King
and begin/To sound the depth of that thou wilt professe,	F 30	1.1.2	Faust
Sweet Analitikes <Anulatikes>, tis thou hast ravisht me,	F 34	1.1.6	Faust
Then read no more, thou hast attain'd that <the> end;	F 38	1.1.10	Faust
Why Faustus, hast thou not attain'd that end?	F 46	1.1.18	Faust
Yet art thou still but Faustus, and a man.	F 51	1.1.23	Faust
Couldst <Wouldst> thou make men <man> to live eternally,	F 52	1.1.24	Faust
Be thou on earth as Jove is in the skye,	F 103	1.1.75	BdAngl
As thou to live, therefore object it not.	F 162	1.1.134	Faust
And then wilt thou be perfecter then I.	F 189	1.1.161	Valdes
Why, dost not thou know then?	F 199	1.2.6	P 2Schol
<Why, didst thou not say thou knewst>?	F 204	(HC258)A	P 2Schol
That thou art <he is> falne into that damned Art/For which they	F 221	1.2.28	1Schol
Seeing thou hast pray'd and sacrific'd to them.	F 235	1.3.7	Faust
Thou art too ugly to attend on me:	F 252	1.3.24	Faust
thou art Conjurer laureate]/[That canst commaund great	F 260	1.3.32A	Faust
Now Faustus what wouldst thou have me do?	F 263	1.3.35	Mephst
How comes it then that thou art out of hell?	F 303	1.3.75	Faust
Think'st thou that I [who] saw the face of God,	F 305	1.3.77	Mephst
Learne thou of Faustus manly fortitude,	F 313	1.3.85	Faust
And scorne those Joyes thou never shalt possesse.	F 314	1.3.86	Faust
Sirra, hast thou no commings in?	F 346	1.4.4	P Wagner
Sirra, wilt thou be my man and waite on me?	F 354	1.4.12	P Wagner
Why so thou shalt be, whether thou dost it or no:	F 360	1.4.18	P Wagner
thou dost not presently bind thy selfe to me for seven yeares,	F 361	1.4.19	P Wagner
So, now thou art to bee at an howres warning, whensoever, and	F 369	1.4.27	P Wagner
Not I, thou art Prest, prepare thy selfe, for I will presently	F 372	1.4.30	P Wagner
left heele, that thou maist, Quasi vestigiis nostris insistere.	F 387	1.4.45	P Wagner
Now Faustus, must thou needs be damn'd,	F 389	2.1.1	Faust
[And] canst <thou> not [now] be sav'd.	F 390	2.1.2	Faust
Why waverst thou?	F 395	2.1.7	Faust
The god thou serv'st is thine owne appetite,	F 399	2.1.11	Faust
Faustus thou art safe.	F 414	2.1.26	Faust
But now <Faustus> thou must bequeath it solemnly,	F 423	2.1.35	Mephst
If thou deny it I must <wil> backe to hell.	F 426	2.1.38	Mephst
And give thee more then thou hast wit to aske.	F 436	2.1.48	Mephst
And then be thou as great as Lucifer.	F 441	2.1.53	Mephst

THOU (cont.)

But Faustus/<thou must> Write it in manner of a Deed of Gift.	F 449	2.1.61		Mephst
Why shouldst thou not? is not thy soule thine owne?	F 457	2.1.69		Faust
But yet conditionally, that thou performe/All Covenants, and	F 479	2.1.91		Faust
So, now Faustus aske me what thou wilt.	F 503	2.1.115		Mephst
Why, dost thou think <think'st thou then> that Faustus shall be	F 518	2.1.130		Faust
In which <Wherein> thou hast given thy soule to Lucifer.	F 520	2.1.132		Mephst
Think'st thou that Faustus, is so fond to imagine,	F 522	2.1.134		Faust
<Well thou wilt have one, sit there till I come,	F 531	(HC261)A	P	Mephst
Well Faustus, thou shalt have a wife.	F 531	2.1.143		Mephst
Now Faustus wilt thou have a wife?	F 533	2.1.145		Mephst
<Tel Faustus, how dost thou like thy wife>?	F 533	(HC261)A	P	Mephst
And if thou lovest me thinke no more of it.	F 536	2.1.148		Mephst
Ready to execute what thou commandst <desirst>.	F 549	2.1.161		Mephst
[O thou art deceived].	F 551.12	2.1.175A	P	Faust
Because thou hast depriv'd me of those Joyes.	F 554	2.2.3		Faust
<why Faustus> think'st thou heaven is such a glorious thing?	F 556	2.2.5		Mephst
I tell thee Faustus it is <tis> not halfe so faire/As thou, or	F 558	2.2.7		Mephst
How prov'st thou that?	F 559	2.2.8		Faust
Thou art a spirit, God cannot pity thee.	F 564	2.2.13		BdAngl
[Faustus, thou art damn'd, then swords <guns> and knives],	F 572	2.2.21A		Faust
Thou art damn'd, think thou of hell>.	F 624	2.2.73	P	Mephst
<Thinke thou on hell Faustus, for thou art damnd>.	F 624	(HC262)A		Mephst
Thou art damn'd, think thou of hell>.	F 624	2.2.73	P	Mephst
<Thinke thou on hell Faustus, for thou art damnd>.	F 624	(HC262)A		Mephst
'Tis thou hast damn'd distressed Faustus soule.	F 628	2.2.77		Faust
If thou repent, devils will <shall> teare thee in peeces.	F 632	2.2.81		BdAngl
O what art thou that look'st so [terrible] <terribly>.	F 638	2.2.87		Faust
We are come to tell thee thou dost injure us.	F 642	2.2.91		Belzeb
Thou calst on <talkst of> Christ contrary to thy promise.	F 643	2.2.92		Lucifr
Thou should'st not thinke on <of> God.	F 644	2.2.93		Belzeb
So shalt thou shew thy selfe an obedient servant <Do so>,/And	F 652	2.2.101		Lucifr
thou shalt behold <see al> the seven deadly sinnes appeare to	F 655	2.2.104	P	Belzeb
That shall I soone: What art thou the first?	F 663	2.2.112		Faust
Thou art a proud knave indeed:	F 672	2.2.121	P	Faust
What art thou the second?	F 672	2.2.121	P	Faust
And what art thou the third?	F 678	2.2.127	P	Faust
live along, then thou should'st see how fat I'de <I would> be.	F 683	2.2.132	P	Envy
but must thou sit, and I stand?	F 683	2.2.132	P	Envy
But what art thou the fourth?	F 685	2.2.134		Faust
And what are thou the fift?	F 692	2.2.141		Faust
Now Faustus thou hast heard all my progeny, wilt thou bid me to	F 700	2.2.149	P	Glutny
thou hast heard all my progeny, wilt thou bid me to supper?	F 701	2.2.150	P	Glutny
<No, Ile see thee hanged, thou wilt eate up all my victualls>.	F 702	(HC264)A	P	Faust
Choke thy selfe Glutton: What are thou the sixt?	F 704	2.2.153		Faust
<Now Faustus, how dost thou like this>?	F 711	(HC264)A		Lucifr
Faustus, thou shalt, at midnight I will send for thee;	F 716	2.2.168		Lucifr
And thou shalt turne thy selfe into what shape thou wilt.	F 718	2.2.170		Lucifr
keepe further from me O thou illiterate, and unlearned Hostler.	F 729	2.3.8	P	Robin
'Snayles, what hast thou got there, a book?	F 730	2.3.9	P	Dick
why thou canst not tell ne're a word on't.	F 730	2.3.9	P	Dick
That thou shalt see presently:	F 732	2.3.11	P	Robin
a paire of hornes on's head as e're thou sawest in thy life.	F 737	2.3.16	P	Robin
Thou needst not do that, for my Mistresse hath done it.	F 739	2.3.18	P	Dick
Hast thou, as earst I did command,	F 801	3.1.23		Faust
But <And> now my Faustus, that thou maist perceive,	F 809	3.1.31		Mephst
Where thou shalt see such store of Ordinance,	F 819	3.1.41		Mephst
<Where thou shalt see a troupe of bald-pate Friers>,	F 833	(HC265)A		Mephst
Sweete Mephostophilis, thou pleasest me:	F 836	3.1.58		Faust
come then stand by me/And thou shalt see them come immediately.	F 844	3.1.66		Mephst
Thou know'st within the compasse of eight daies,	F 847	3.1.69		Faust
Or any villany thou canst devise,	F 865	3.1.87		Mephst
To me and Peter, shalt thou groveling lie,	F 873	3.1.95		Pope
Both he and thou shalt stand excommunicate,	F 908	3.1.130		Pope
Then he and thou, and all the world shall stoope,	F 937	3.1.159		Pope
Faustus thou shalt, then kneele downe presently,	F 994	3.2.14		Mephst
Do what thou wilt, thou shalt not be discern'd.	F1005	3.2.25		Mephst
First, be thou turned to this ugly shape,	F1126	3.3.39		Mephst
And so thou shalt:	F1130	3.3.43		Mephst
be thou transformed to/A dog, and carry him upon thy backe;	F1130	3.3.43		Mephst
and thou shalt see/This Conjurer performe such rare exploits,	F1185	4.1.31		Mrtino
Speake, wilt thou come and see this sport?	F1193	4.1.39		Fredrk
Wilt thou stand in thy Window, and see it then?	F1195	4.1.41		Mrtino
Thou couldst command the worlds obedience:	F1210	4.1.56		Emper
And if this Bruno thou hast late redeem'd,	F1212	4.1.58		Emper
Thou shalt be famous through all Italy,	F1215	4.1.61		Emper
Then Faustus as thou late didst promise us,	F1230	4.1.76		Emper
and thou bring Alexander and his Paramour before the Emperour,	F1254	4.1.100	P	Benvol
And in this sight thou better pleasest me,	F1271	4.1.117		Emper
Thou shalt command the state of Germany,	F1323	4.1.169		Emper
Thou soone shouldst see me quit my foule disgrace.	F1356	4.2.32		Benvol
Take thou this other, dragge him through the woods,	F1410	4.2.86		Faust
thou canst not buy so good a horse, for so small a price:	F1459	4.4.3	P	Faust
sell him, but if thou likest him for ten Dollors more, take him,	F1460	4.4.4	P	Faust
more, take him, because I see thou hast a good minde to him.	F1461	4.4.5	P	Faust
hedge and ditch, or where thou wilt, but not into the water:	F1473	4.4.17	P	Faust
What art thou Faustus but a man condemn'd to die?	F1478	4.4.22		Faust
Sirra Dick, dost thou know why I stand so mute?	F1509	4.5.5	P	Robin
Do as thou wilt Faustus, I give thee leave.	F1607	4.6.50		Duke
My woodden leg? what dost thou meane by that?	F1628	4.6.71		Faust
Wouldst thou make a Colossus of me, that thou askest me such	F1646	4.6.89	P	Faust
thou make a Colossus of me, that thou askest me such questions?	F1646	4.6.89	P	Faust
But wherefore dost thou aske?	F1652	4.6.95		Faust

THOU (cont.)

Though thou hast now offended like a man,	F1710	5.1.37	OldMan
Yet, yet, thou hast an amiable soule,	F1712	5.1.39	OldMan
Then thou art banisht from the sight of heaven;	F1715	5.1.42	OldMan
Where art thou Faustus? wretch, what hast thou done?	F1724	5.1.51	Faust
[Damned art thou Faustus, damned, despaire and die],	F1725	5.1.52A	Faust
Accursed Faustus, <wretch what hast thou done>?	F1739	(HC270)B	Faust
Thou traytor Faustus, I arrest thy soule,	F1743	5.1.70	Mephst
This, or what else my Faustus shall <thou shalt> desire,	F1766	5.1.93	Mephst
O thou art fairer then the evenings <evening> aire,	F1781	5.1.108	Faust
Brighter art thou then flaming Jupiter,	F1783	5.1.110	Faust
And none but thou shalt be my Paramour.	F1787	5.1.114	Faust
Say Wagner, thou hast perus'd my will,	F1816	5.2.20	Faust
Say Wagner, thou hast perus'd my will,/How dost thou like it?	F1817	5.2.21	Faust
Pray thou, and we will pray, that God may have mercie upon	F1875	5.2.79	P 2Schol
I, Faustus, now thou hast no hope of heaven,	F1880	5.2.84	Mephst
O thou bewitching fiend, 'twas thy temptation,	F1883	5.2.87	Faust
'Twas I, that when thou wer't i'the way to heaven,	F1886	5.2.90	Mephst
Damb'd up thy passage; when thou took'st the booke,	F1887	5.2.91	Mephst
What, weep'st thou?	F1890	5.2.94	Mephst
Oh <Ah> Faustus, if thou hadst given eare to me,	F1892	5.2.96	GdAngl
But thou didst love the world.	F1894	5.2.98	GdAngl
O thou hast lost celestiall happinesse,	F1899	5.2.103	GdAngl
Hadst thou affected sweet divinitie,	F1901	5.2.105	GdAngl
Hadst thou kept on that way, Faustus behold,	F1903	5.2.107	GdAngl
In what resplendant glory thou hadst set/In yonder throne, like	F1904	5.2.108	GdAngl
that hast thou lost,/And now poore soule must thy good Angell	F1906	5.2.110	GdAngl
thou shalt see/Ten thousand tortures that more horrid be.	F1919	5.2.123	BdAngl
Nay, thou must feele them, taste the smart of all:	F1922	5.2.126	BdAngl
Then wilt thou tumble in confusion.	F1925	5.2.129	BdAngl
Now hast thou but one bare houre to live,	F1927	5.2.131	Faust
And then thou must be damn'd perpetually.	F1928	5.2.132	Faust
[O God, if thou wilt not have mercy on my soule],	F1958	5.2.162A	Faust
Why wert thou not a creature wanting soule?	F1964	5.2.168	Faust
Or why is this immortall that thou hast?	F1965	5.2.169	Faust
Tel me sirra, hast thou any commings in?	F App	p.229 4	P Wagner
wilt thou serve me, and Ile make thee go like Qui mihi	F App	p.229 13	P Wagner
So thou shalt, whether thou beest with me, or no:	F App	p.229 22	P Wagner
thou art at an houres warning whensoever or wheresoever the	F App	p.230 36	P Wagner
what doest thou with that same booke thou canst not reade?	F App	p.233 13	P Rafe
Canst thou conjure with it?	F App	p.233 21	P Rafe
if thou hast any mind to Nan Spit our kitchin maide, then turn	F App	p.234 26	P Robin
hir to thy owne use, as often as thou wilt, and at midnight.	F App	p.234 28	P Robin
O nomine Domine, what meanst thou Robin?	F App	p.235 26	P Vintnr
thou hast no goblet.	F App	p.235 26	P Vintnr
they say thou hast a familiar spirit, by whome thou canst	F App	p.236 4	P Emper
by whome thou canst accomplish what thou list, this therefore	F App	p.236 4	P Emper
by whome thou canst accomplish what thou list, this therefore	F App	p.236 5	P Emper
that thou let me see some proofe of thy skil, that mine eies	F App	p.236 6	P Emper
that what ever thou doest, thou shalt be no wayes prejudiced or	F App	p.236 9	P Emper
thou doest, thou shalt be no wayes prejudiced or indamaged.	F App	p.236 9	P Emper
If therefore thou, by cunning of thine Art,	F App	p.237 29	Emper
Thou shalt both satisfie my just desire,	F App	p.237 35	Emper
why I has thought thou hadst beene a batcheler, but now I see	F App	p.238 69	P Emper
but now I see thou hast a wife, that not only gives thee	F App	p.238 70	P Emper
Thou damned wretch, and execrable dogge,	F App	p.238 72	Knight
How darst thou thus abuse a Gentleman?	F App	p.238 74	Knight
Vilaine I say, undo what thou hast done.	F App	p.238 75	Knight
if thou likst him for fifty, take him.	F App	p.239 103	P Faust
over hedge or ditch, or where thou wilt, but not into the water.	F App	p.239 112	P Faust
what art thou Faustus but a man condemnd to die?	F App	p.240 121	P Faust
Why, thou seest he heares thee not.	F App	p.241 151	P Mephst
By which sweete path thou maist attaine the gole/That shall	F App	p.243 36	OldMan
Roome, if thou take delight in impious warre,	Lucan, First Booke	21	
as yet thou wants not foes.	Lucan, First Booke	23	
Fierce Pirhus, neither thou nor Hanniball/Art cause, no forraine	Lucan, First Booke	30	
thee (seeing thou being old/Must shine a star) shal heaven	Lucan, First Booke	45	
being old/Must shine a star) shal heaven (whom thou lovest),	Lucan, First Booke	46	
Receive with shouts; where thou wilt raigne as King,	Lucan, First Booke	47	
Whence thou shouldst view thy Roome with squinting beams.	Lucan, First Booke	55	
If any one part of vast heaven thou swayest,	Lucan, First Booke	56	
[There] <Their> Caesar may'st thou shine and no cloud dim thee;	Lucan, First Booke	59	
Thou Caesar at this instant art my God,	Lucan, First Booke	63	
longer life/Thou hadst restrainde thy headstrong husbands rage,	Lucan, First Booke	116	
Thou feard'st (great Pompey) that late deeds would dim/Olde	Lucan, First Booke	121	
Would dash the wreath thou wearst for Pirats wracke.	Lucan, First Booke	123	
And staring, thus bespoke: what mean'st thou Caesar?	Lucan, First Booke	192	
Thou thunderer that guardst/Roomes mighty walles built on	Lucan, First Booke	197	
In ten yeares wonst thou France; Roome may be won/With farre	Lucan, First Booke	283	
Nor shalt thou triumph when thou comst to Roome;	Lucan, First Booke	287	
denies all, with thy bloud must thou/Abie thy conquest past:	Lucan, First Booke	289	
decrees/To expel the father; share the world thou canst not;	Lucan, First Booke	291	
share the world thou canst not;/Injoy it all thou maiest:	Lucan, First Booke	292	
so Pompey thou having lickt/Warme goare from Syllas sword art	Lucan, First Booke	330	
What doubtst thou us?	Lucan, First Booke	363	
mainly throw the dart; wilt thou indure/These purple groomes?	Lucan, First Booke	365	
shouldst thou bid me/Intombe my sword within my brothers	Lucan, First Booke	376	
What wals thou wilt be leaveld with the ground,	Lucan, First Booke	384	
Albeit the Citty thou wouldst have so ra'st/Be Roome it selfe.	Lucan, First Booke	386	
for unto me/Thou cause, what ere thou be whom God assignes/This	Lucan, First Booke	419	
cause, what ere thou be whom God assignes/This great effect,	Lucan, First Booke	419	
And Trevier; thou being glad that wars are past thee;	Lucan, First Booke	437	
Thou Roome at name of warre runst from thy selfe,	Lucan, First Booke	517	

THOU (cont.)

O Phoebus shouldst thou with thy rayes now sing/The fell Nemean	Lucan, First Booke	654
'tis thou enflam'st/The threatning Scorpion with the burning	Lucan, First Booke	657
Why art thou thus enrag'd?	Lucan, First Booke	659
thou lead'st me toward th'east,/Where Nile augmenteth the	Lucan, First Booke	682
If reading five thou plainst of tediousnesse,	Ovid's Elegies	1.1.3
Ambitious Imp, why seekst thou further charge?	Ovid's Elegies	1.1.18
What needes thou warre, I sue to thee for grace,	Ovid's Elegies	1.2.21
The people thee applauding thou shalte stand,	Ovid's Elegies	1.2.25
Yong men and women, shalt thou lead as thrall,	Ovid's Elegies	1.2.27
Thou with these souldiers conquerest gods and men,	Ovid's Elegies	1.2.37
Unlesse I erre, full many shalt thou burne,	Ovid's Elegies	1.2.43
live with thee, and die, or <ere> thou shalt <shall> grieve.	Ovid's Elegies	1.3.18
Be thou the happie subject of my Bookes,	Ovid's Elegies	1.3.19
But how thou shouldst behave thy selfe now know;	Ovid's Elegies	1.4.11
Lines thou shalt read in wine by my hand writ.	Ovid's Elegies	1.4.20
If ought of me thou speak'st in inward thought,	Ovid's Elegies	1.4.23
When thou doest wish thy husband at the devill.	Ovid's Elegies	1.4.28
Aske thou the boy, what thou enough doest thinke.	Ovid's Elegies	1.4.30
When thou hast tasted, I will take the cup,	Ovid's Elegies	1.4.31
And where thou drinkst, on that part I will sup.	Ovid's Elegies	1.4.32
If thou givest kisses, I shall all disclose,	Ovid's Elegies	1.4.39
Do not thou so, but throw thy mantle hence,	Ovid's Elegies	1.4.49
There touch what ever thou canst touch of mee.	Ovid's Elegies	1.4.58
his tender mother/And smiling sayed, be thou as bold as other.	Ovid's Elegies	1.6.12
When thou stood'st naked ready to be beate,	Ovid's Elegies	1.6.19
Gratis thou maiest be free, give like for like,	Ovid's Elegies	1.6.23
Nor servile water shalt thou drinke for ever.	Ovid's Elegies	1.6.26
O harder then the dores thou gardest I prove thee.	Ovid's Elegies	1.6.62
No pritty wenches keeper maist thou bee:	Ovid's Elegies	1.6.63
But thou my crowne, from sad haires tane away,	Ovid's Elegies	1.6.67
What ere thou art, farewell, be like me paind,	Ovid's Elegies	1.6.71
Go now thou Conqueror, glorious triumphs raise,	Ovid's Elegies	1.7.35
But doubt thou not (revenge doth griefe appease)/With thy	Ovid's Elegies	1.7.63
Mistris thou knowest, thou hast a blest youth pleas'd,	Ovid's Elegies	1.8.23
As thou art faire, would thou wert fortunate,	Ovid's Elegies	1.8.27
Wert thou rich, poore should not be my state.	Ovid's Elegies	1.8.28
Would he not buy thee thou for him shouldst care.	Ovid's Elegies	1.8.34
When on thy lappe thine eyes thou dost deject,	Ovid's Elegies	1.8.37
Nor, so thou maist obtaine a wealthy prize,	Ovid's Elegies	1.8.63
Make a small price, while thou thy nets doest lay,	Ovid's Elegies	1.8.69
Nor, if thou couzenst one, dread to for-sweare,	Ovid's Elegies	1.8.85
Servants fit for thy purpose thou must hire/To teach thy lover,	Ovid's Elegies	1.8.87
When thou hast so much as he gives no more,	Ovid's Elegies	1.8.101
Pray him to lend what thou maist nere restore.	Ovid's Elegies	1.8.102
If this thou doest, to me by long use knowne,	Ovid's Elegies	1.8.105
Oft thou wilt say, live well, thou wilt pray oft,	Ovid's Elegies	1.8.107
rise/And who thou never think'st should fall downe lies.	Ovid's Elegies	1.9.30
Since maist thou see me watch and night warres move:	Ovid's Elegies	1.9.45
Such wert thou, and I fear'd the Bull and Eagle/And what ere	Ovid's Elegies	1.10.7
Ask'st why I chaunge? because thou crav'st reward:	Ovid's Elegies	1.10.11
While thou wert plaine, I lov'd thy minde and face:	Ovid's Elegies	1.10.13
and thou gaine by the pleasure/Which man and woman reape in	Ovid's Elegies	1.10.35
wood be flying/And thou the waxe stuft full with notes denying,	Ovid's Elegies	1.12.8
Yet as if mixt with red leade thou wert ruddy,	Ovid's Elegies	1.12.11
Aurora whither slidest thou?	Ovid's Elegies	1.13.3
Whither runst thou, that men, and women, love not?	Ovid's Elegies	1.13.9
Ere thou rise starres teach seamen where to saile,	Ovid's Elegies	1.13.11
But when thou comest they of their courses faile.	Ovid's Elegies	1.13.12
Thou coosnest boyes of sleepe, and dost betray them/To Pedants,	Ovid's Elegies	1.13.17
Thou makste the suretie to the lawyer runne,	Ovid's Elegies	1.13.19
Both whom thou raisest up to toyle anew.	Ovid's Elegies	1.13.22
Thou setst their labouring hands to spin and card.	Ovid's Elegies	1.13.24
Whither gost thou hateful nimph?	Ovid's Elegies	1.13.31
Then thinkest thou thy loose life is not showne?	Ovid's Elegies	1.13.34
Thou leav'st his bed, because hees faint through age,	Ovid's Elegies	1.13.37
But [heldst] <hadst> thou in thine armes some Caephalus,	Ovid's Elegies	1.13.39
Then wouldst thou cry, stay night and runne not thus.	Ovid's Elegies	1.13.40
Thou art as faire as shee, then kisse and play.	Ovid's Elegies	1.13.44
Jove that thou shouldst not hast but wait his leasure,	Ovid's Elegies	1.13.45
Now hast thou left no haires at all to die.	Ovid's Elegies	1.14.2
Feardst thou to dresse them?	Ovid's Elegies	1.14.5
Thou mad'st thy head with compound poyson flow.	Ovid's Elegies	1.14.44
O thou oft wilt blush/And say he likes me for my borrowed bush,	Ovid's Elegies	1.14.47
Cheere up thy selfe, thy losse thou maiest repaire,	Ovid's Elegies	1.14.55
Envie, why carpest thou my time is spent so ill,	Ovid's Elegies	1.15.1
Keeper if thou be wise cease hate to cherish,	Ovid's Elegies	2.2.9
Wilt thou her fault learne, she may make thee tremble,	Ovid's Elegies	2.2.17
Feare to be guilty, then thou maiest desemble.	Ovid's Elegies	2.2.18
Object thou then what she may well excuse,	Ovid's Elegies	2.2.37
Do this and soone thou shalt thy freedome reape.	Ovid's Elegies	2.2.40
On tell-tales neckes thou seest the linke-knitt chaines,	Ovid's Elegies	2.2.41
If he loves not, deafe eares thou doest importune,	Ovid's Elegies	2.2.53
To kinde requests thou wouldst more gentle prove,	Ovid's Elegies	2.3.5
Thou wert not borne to ride, or armes to beare,	Ovid's Elegies	2.3.7
If she discardes thee, what use servest thou for?	Ovid's Elegies	2.3.12
Shee may deceive thee, though thou her protect,	Ovid's Elegies	2.3.15
While thou hast time yet to bestowe that gift.	Ovid's Elegies	2.3.18
[wretch] <wench> I sawe when thou didst thinke I slumbred,	Ovid's Elegies	2.5.13
What doest, I cryed, transportst thou my delight?	Ovid's Elegies	2.5.29
But most thou friendly turtle-dove, deplore.	Ovid's Elegies	2.6.12
What helpes it thou wert given to please my wench,	Ovid's Elegies	2.6.19
Thou with thy quilles mightst make greene Emeralds darke,	Ovid's Elegies	2.6.21

THOU (cont.)

Thou spokest thy words so well with stammering sound.	Ovid's Elegies	2.6.24
Envy hath rapt thee, no fierce warres thou movedst,	Ovid's Elegies	2.6.25
Vaine babling speech, and pleasant peace thou lovedst.	Ovid's Elegies	2.6.26
The seventh day came, none following mightst thou see,	Ovid's Elegies	2.6.45
Thou arguest she doth secret markes unfold.	Ovid's Elegies	2.7.6
If I praise any, thy poore haires thou tearest,	Ovid's Elegies	2.7.7
If blame, dissembling of my fault thou fearest.	Ovid's Elegies	2.7.8
If I looke well, thou thinkest thou doest not move,	Ovid's Elegies	2.7.9
If ill, thou saiest I die for others love.	Ovid's Elegies	2.7.10
Thou Goddesse doest command a warme South-blast,	Ovid's Elegies	2.8.19
Well maiest thou one thing for thy Mistresse use.	Ovid's Elegies	2.8.24
If thou deniest foole, Ile our deeds expresse,	Ovid's Elegies	2.8.25
Hence with great laude thou maiest a triumph move.	Ovid's Elegies	2.9.16
Heere thou hast strength, here thy right hand doth rest.	Ovid's Elegies	2.9.36
Long shalt thou rest when Fates expire thy breath.	Ovid's Elegies	2.9.42
Light art thou, and more windie then thy winges,	Ovid's Elegies	2.9.49
Joyes with uncertaine faith thou takest and brings.	Ovid's Elegies	2.9.50
Yet Love, if thou with thy faire mother heare,	Ovid's Elegies	2.9.51
So of both people shalt thou homage gaine.	Ovid's Elegies	2.9.54
Graecinus (well I wot) thou touldst me once,	Ovid's Elegies	2.10.1
Venus, why doublest thou my endlesse smart?	Ovid's Elegies	2.10.11
Why addst thou starres to heaven, leaves to greene woods	Ovid's Elegies	2.10.13
Thou shalt admire no woods or Citties there,	Ovid's Elegies	2.11.11
Then wilt thou Laedas noble twinne-starres pray,	Ovid's Elegies	2.11.29
Yet Galatea favour thou her ship.	Ovid's Elegies	2.11.34
There wine being fild, thou many things shalt tell,	Ovid's Elegies	2.11.49
Thou that frequents Canopus pleasant fields,	Ovid's Elegies	2.13.7
Thou givest my mistris life, she mine againe.	Ovid's Elegies	2.13.16
On labouring women thou doest pitty take,	Ovid's Elegies	2.13.19
Worthy she is, thou shouldst in mercy save her.	Ovid's Elegies	2.13.22
Wilt thou thy wombe-inclosed off-spring wracke?	Ovid's Elegies	2.14.8
Thou also, that wert borne faire, hadst decayed,	Ovid's Elegies	2.14.19
Thou ring that shalt my faire girles finger binde,	Ovid's Elegies	2.15.1
Blest ring thou in my mistris hand shalt lye,	Ovid's Elegies	2.15.7
Or [be] a loade thou shouldst refuse to beare.	Ovid's Elegies	2.15.22
Thou swearest, devision should not twixt us rise,	Ovid's Elegies	2.16.43
If any godly care of me thou hast,	Ovid's Elegies	2.16.47
to detaine)/Thou oughtst therefore to scorne me for thy mate,	Ovid's Elegies	2.17.13
And thou my light accept me how so ever,	Ovid's Elegies	2.17.23
Nor in my bookes shall one but thou be writ,	Ovid's Elegies	2.17.33
Thou doest alone give matter to my wit.	Ovid's Elegies	2.17.34
To tragick verse while thou Achilles trainst,	Ovid's Elegies	2.18.1
Unlesse I erre to these thou more incline,	Ovid's Elegies	2.18.39
Foole if to keepe thy wife thou hast no neede,	Ovid's Elegies	2.19.1
Thou also that late tookest mine eyes away,	Ovid's Elegies	2.19.19
But thou of thy faire damsell too secure,	Ovid's Elegies	2.19.37
Thou doest beginne, she shall be mine no longer.	Ovid's Elegies	2.19.48
Thou suffrest what no husband can endure,	Ovid's Elegies	2.19.51
By thy default thou doest our joyes defraude.	Ovid's Elegies	2.19.58
A laughing stocke thou art to all the citty,	Ovid's Elegies	3.1.21
While without shame thou singst thy lewdnesse ditty.	Ovid's Elegies	3.1.22
Long hast thou loyterd, greater workes compile.	Ovid's Elegies	3.1.24
This thou wilt say to be a worthy ground.	Ovid's Elegies	3.1.26
art thou aye gravely plaied?	Ovid's Elegies	3.1.36
Thou deignst unequall lines should thee rehearse,	Ovid's Elegies	3.1.37
Thou fightst against me using mine owne verse.	Ovid's Elegies	3.1.38
And I deserve more then thou canst in verity,	Ovid's Elegies	3.1.47
Thou hast my gift, which she would from thee sue.	Ovid's Elegies	3.1.60
Yet whom thou favourst, pray may conquerour be.	Ovid's Elegies	3.2.2
That thou maiest know with love thou mak'st me flame.	Ovid's Elegies	3.2.4
Thou viewst the course, I thee:	Ovid's Elegies	3.2.5
What horse-driver thou favourst most is best,	Ovid's Elegies	3.2.7
But spare my wench thou at her right hand seated,	Ovid's Elegies	3.2.21
And sit thou rounder, that behind us see,	Ovid's Elegies	3.2.23
The more thou look'st, the more the gowne envide.	Ovid's Elegies	3.2.28
Flames into flame, flouds thou powrest seas into.	Ovid's Elegies	3.2.34
What Venus promisd, promise thou we pray,	Ovid's Elegies	3.2.59
For evermore thou shalt my mistris be.	Ovid's Elegies	3.2.62
thou maiest, if that be best,/[A] <Or> while thy tiptoes on the	Ovid's Elegies	3.2.63
I see whom thou affectest:	Ovid's Elegies	3.2.67
Though thou her body guard, her minde is staind:	Ovid's Elegies	3.4.5
Although thou chafe, stolne pleasure is sweet play,	Ovid's Elegies	3.4.31
Kindly thy mistris use, if thou be wise.	Ovid's Elegies	3.4.43
So shalt thou go with youths to feasts together,	Ovid's Elegies	3.4.47
And see at home much, that thou nere broughtst thether.	Ovid's Elegies	3.4.48
Thou hast no bridge, nor boate with ropes to throw,	Ovid's Elegies	3.5.3
With snow thaw'd from the next hill now thou rushest,	Ovid's Elegies	3.5.7
And in thy foule deepe waters thicke thou [gushest] <rushest>.	Ovid's Elegies	3.5.8
Rather thou large banke over-flowing river,	Ovid's Elegies	3.5.19
Slide in thy bounds, so shalt thou runne for ever.	Ovid's Elegies	3.5.20
(Trust me) land-streame thou shalt no envie lack,	Ovid's Elegies	3.5.21
Thou saiest broke with Alcides angry hand.	Ovid's Elegies	3.5.36
To stay thy tresses white veyle hast thou none?	Ovid's Elegies	3.5.56
Thou ore a hundreth Nimphes, or more shalt raigne:	Ovid's Elegies	3.5.63
much (I crave)/Gifts then my promise greater thou shalt have.	Ovid's Elegies	3.5.66
And I beleeve some wench thou hast affected:	Ovid's Elegies	3.5.83
How wouldst thou flowe wert thou a noble floud,	Ovid's Elegies	3.5.89
Thou hast no name, but com'st from snowy mountaines;	Ovid's Elegies	3.5.91
No certaine house thou hast, nor any fountaines.	Ovid's Elegies	3.5.92
Harmefull to beasts, and to the fields thou proves:	Ovid's Elegies	3.5.99
Lie downe with shame, and see thou stirre no more,	Ovid's Elegies	3.6.69
Seeing now thou wouldst deceive me as before:	Ovid's Elegies	3.6.70

THOU (cont.)

Thou [cousenst] <cousendst> mee, by thee surprizde am I,	Ovid's Elegies	3.6.71	
Why mockst thou me she cried, or being ill,	Ovid's Elegies	3.6.77	
Or jaded camst thou from some others bed.	Ovid's Elegies	3.6.80	
Foole canst thou him in thy white armes embrace?	Ovid's Elegies	3.7.11	
Foole canst thou lie in his enfolding space?	Ovid's Elegies	3.7.12	
Confessing this, why doest thou touch him than?	Ovid's Elegies	3.7.22	
Against thy selfe, mans nature, thou wert cunning,	Ovid's Elegies	3.7.45	
With th'earth thou wert content,/Why seek'st not heav'n the	Ovid's Elegies	3.7.49	
Heaven thou affects, with Romulus, temples brave/Bacchus,	Ovid's Elegies	3.7.51	
Ah now a name too true thou hast, I finde.	Ovid's Elegies	3.8.4	
Live godly, thou shalt die, though honour heaven,	Ovid's Elegies	3.8.37	
Was I: thou liv'dst, while thou esteemdst my faith.	Ovid's Elegies	3.8.56	
And thou, if falsely charged to wrong thy friend,	Ovid's Elegies	3.8.63	
I know not whom thou lewdly didst imbrace,	Ovid's Elegies	3.10.11	
Or lesse faire, or lesse lewd would thou mightst bee,	Ovid's Elegies	3.10.41	
What ere thou art mine art thou:	Ovid's Elegies	3.10.49	
Seeing thou art faire, I barre not thy false playing,	Ovid's Elegies	3.13.1	
But that thou wouldst dissemble when tis paste.	Ovid's Elegies	3.13.4	
Say but thou wert injurously accusde.	Ovid's Elegies	3.13.42	
Leander, thou art made for amorous play:	Hero and Leander	1.88	
Why art thou not in love, and lov'd of all?	Hero and Leander	1.89	
Though thou be faire, yet be not thine owne thrall.	Hero and Leander	1.90	
Then shouldst thou bee his prisoner who is thine.	Hero and Leander	1.202	
As thou in beautie doest exceed Loves mother/Nor heaven, nor	Hero and Leander	1.222	
Loves mother/Nor heaven, nor thou, were made to gaze upon,	Hero and Leander	1.223	
As heaven preserves all things, so save thou one.	Hero and Leander	1.224	
Why vowest thou then to live in Sestos here,	Hero and Leander	1.227	
Wilt thou live single still?	Hero and Leander	1.257	
one shalt thou bee,/Though never-singling Hymen couple thee.	Hero and Leander	1.257	
Tell me, to whom mad'st thou that heedlesse oath?	Hero and Leander	1.294	
For thou in vowing chastitie, hast sworne/To rob her name and	Hero and Leander	1.304	
But heale the heart, that thou hast wounded thus,	Hero and Leander	1.324	

THOUGH (See also THO, THOGH)

Though we be now in extreame miserie,	Dido	1.1.157	Achat
Achates though mine eyes say this is stone,	Dido	2.1.24	Aeneas
For though my birth be great, my fortunes meane,	Dido	2.1.88	Aeneas
What though I was offended with thy sonne,	Dido	3.2.40	Juno
So doth he now, though not with equall gaine,	Dido	3.3.83	Iarbus
But though he goe, he stayes in Carthage still,	Dido	4.4.133	Dido
No marvell Dido though thou be in love,	Dido	5.1.44	Aeneas
Though she repairde my fleete and gave me ships,	Dido	5.1.59	Aeneas
Pardon me though I aske, love makes me aske.	Dido	5.1.90	Dido
Though thou nor he will pitie me a whit.	Dido	5.1.178	Dido
For though thou hast the heart to say farewell,	Dido	5.1.182	Dido
Which seene to all, though he beheld me not,	Dido	5.1.237	Anna
Graunt, though the traytors land in Italy,	Dido	5.1.304	Dido
Though straight the passage and the port be made,	1Tamb	2.1.42	Cosroe
Nay, though I praise it, I can live without it.	1Tamb	2.5.66	Therid
Though Mars himselfe the angrie God of armes,	1Tamb	2.7.58	Tamb
You see though first the King of Persea/(Being a Shepheard)	1Tamb	3.2.59	Agidas
No Tamburlain, though now thou gat the best,	1Tamb	3.3.222	Zabina
Though he be prisoner, he may be ransomed.	1Tamb	3.3.231	Zabina
For though the glorie of this day be lost,	1Tamb	3.3.241	Bajzth
Though my right hand have thus enthralled thee,	1Tamb	5.1.435	Tamb
Though with the losse of Egypt and my Crown.	1Tamb	5.1.444	Souldn
Though from the shortest Northren Paralell,	2Tamb	1.1.25	Orcan
That though the stones, as at Deucalions flood,	2Tamb	1.3.163	Tamb
Though I confesse the othes they undertake,	2Tamb	2.1.42	Sgsmnd
Though she be dead, yet let me think she lives,	2Tamb	2.4.127	Tamb
Though this be held his last daies dreadfull siege,	2Tamb	5.1.29	1Citzn
For though thy cannon shooke the citie walles,	2Tamb	5.1.105	Govnr
No, though Asphaltis lake were liquid gold,	2Tamb	5.1.155	Tamb
Though God himselfe and holy Mahomet,	2Tamb	5.2.37	Amasia
And though they think their painfull date is out,	2Tamb	5.3.34	Usumc
Shal still retaine my spirit, though I die,	2Tamb	5.3.173	Tamb
Though some speake openly against my bookes,	Jew	Prol.10	Machvl
Small though the number was that kept the Towne,	Jew	2.2.49	Bosco
For though they doe a while increase and multiply,	Jew	2.3.89	Barab
Pardon me though I weepe; the Governors sonne/Will, whether I	Jew	2.3.257	Barab
Though thou deservest hardly at my hands,	Jew	3.3.74	Abigal
Or though it wrought, it would have done no good,	Jew	4.1.5	Barab
True, I have mony, what though I have?	Jew	4.1.30	Barab
Though womans modesty should hale me backe,	Jew	4.2.45	Curtzn
Though gentle mindes should pittie others paines,	P 215	4.13	Anjoy
though I come not to take possession (as I would I might) yet I	P 813	17.8	P Souldr
And Epernoune though I seeme milde and calme,	P 893	17.88	King
And therefore though I pleade for his repeall,	Edw	1.4.241	Mortmr
Though inwardly licentious enough,	Edw	2.1.50	Baldck
I will not long be from thee though I die:	Edw	2.1.62	Neece
Though thou comparst him to a flying Fish,	Edw	2.2.43	Edward
Yes more then thou canst answer though he live,	Edw	2.2.87	Edward
No marvell though thou scorne thy noble peeres,	Edw	2.2.217	Kent
What care I though the Earles begirt us round?	Edw	2.2.223	Edward
And though devorsed from king Edwards eyes,	Edw	2.5.3	Gavstn
As though your highnes were a schoole boy still,	Edw	3.1.30	Baldck
Where weapons want, and though a many friends/Are made away, as	Edw	4.2.51	Mortmr
But Edwards name survives, though Edward dies.	Edw	5.1.48	Edward
And so must die, though pitied by many.	Edw	5.3.24	Edward
If you be guiltie, though I be your sonne,	Edw	5.6.81	King
Though thou hast now offended like a man,	F1710	5.1.37	OldMan
Though my heart pant <pants> and quiver <quivers> to remember	F1839	5.2.43	P Faust
the Divel for a shoulder of mutton, though it were blood rawe.	F App	p.229 9	P Wagner

THOUGH (cont.)

to the Divel for a shoulder of mutton though twere blood rawe? F App p.229 10 P Clown
though I must confesse my selfe farre inferior to the report F App p.236 12 P Faust
Undaunted though her former guide be chang'd. . . . Lucan, First Booke 50
Who though his root be weake, and his owne waight/Keepe him Lucan, First Booke 139
Though every blast it nod, and seeme to fal, . . . Lucan, First Booke 142
who though lockt and chaind in stalls,/Souse downe the wals, Lucan, First Booke 295
Marveile not though the faire Bride did incite/The drunken Ovid's Elegies 1.4.7
Before thy husband come, though I not see/What may be done, yet Ovid's Elegies 1.4.13
But though this night thy fortune be to trie it, . . Ovid's Elegies 1.4.69
Though it be so, shut me not out therefore, . . Ovid's Elegies 1.6.47
But though I like a swelling floud was driven, . . . Ovid's Elegies 1.7.43
(Anger will helpe thy hands though nere so weake). . . Ovid's Elegies 1.7.66
Poore travailers though tierd, rise at thy sight, . . Ovid's Elegies 1.13.13
Then though death rackes <rakes> my bones in funerall fier, Ovid's Elegies 1.15.41
Let him goe see her though she doe not languish/And then report Ovid's Elegies 2.2.21
Nor is it easily prov'd though manifest, ... Ovid's Elegies 2.2.55
Though himselfe see; heele credit her denyall, . . . Ovid's Elegies 2.2.57
Shee may deceive thee, though thou her protect, . . Ovid's Elegies 2.3.15
Though her sowre looks a Sabines browe resemble, . . Ovid's Elegies 2.4.15
Bewaile I onely, though I them lament. . . . . Ovid's Elegies 2.5.60
His sword layed by, safe, though rude places yeelds. . Ovid's Elegies 2.9.20
Though I am slender, I have store of pith, . . . Ovid's Elegies 2.10.23
Ile thinke all true, though it be feigned matter. . . Ovid's Elegies 2.11.53
But tender Damsels do it, though with paine, . . . Ovid's Elegies 2.14.37
I would get off though straight, and sticking fast, . . Ovid's Elegies 2.15.13
ground/Conteines me, though the streames in fields surround, Ovid's Elegies 2.16.34
Though Hindes in brookes the running waters bring, . . Ovid's Elegies 2.16.35
Not though thy face in all things make thee raigne, . . Ovid's Elegies 2.17.11
Venus with Vulcan, though smiths tooles laide by, . . Ovid's Elegies 2.17.19
But though I apt were for such high deseignes, . . . Ovid's Elegies 2.18.14
Though thou her body guard, her minde is staind: . . Ovid's Elegies 3.4.5
Came forth a mother, though a maide there put. . . . Ovid's Elegies 3.4.22
Penelope, though no watch look'd unto her, . . . Ovid's Elegies 3.4.23
Whom Ilia pleasd, though in her lookes griefe reveld, . Ovid's Elegies 3.5.47
Though both of us performd our true intent, . . . Ovid's Elegies 3.6.5
Now, Sabine-like, though chast she seemes to live, . . Ovid's Elegies 3.7.61
Live godly, thou shalt die, though honour heaven, . . Ovid's Elegies 3.8.37
Nor is she, though she loves the fertile fields, . . Ovid's Elegies 3.9.17
That I may love yet, though against my minde. . . . Ovid's Elegies 3.10.52
Though thether leades a rough steepe hilly way. . . Ovid's Elegies 3.12.6
Though while the deede be doing you be tooke, . . . Ovid's Elegies 3.13.43
Though thou be faire, yet be not thine owne thrall. . . Hero and Leander 1.90
Though never-singling Hymen couple thee. . . . Hero and Leander 1.258
Though neither gods nor men may thee deserve, . . . Hero and Leander 1.315
though Hero would not yeeld/So soone to part from that she Hero and Leander 2.83
Though it was morning, did he take his flight. . . . Hero and Leander 2.102
For though the rising yv'rie mount he scal'd, . . . Hero and Leander 2.273

THOUGHE

thoughe you take out none but your owne treasure . . Paris ms 3,p390 P Souldr
enter by defaulte | whatt thoughe you were once in possession Paris ms11,p390 P Souldr
And thoughe I come not to keep possessione as I wold I mighte Paris ms14,p390 P Souldr

THOUGHT

Albeit the Gods doe know no wanton thought/Had ever residence Dido 3.1.16 Dido
This was an Orator, and thought by words/To compasse me, but yet Dido 3.1.155 Dido
Or with what thought sleepst thou in Libia shoare? . . Dido 5.1.35 Hermes
That never nourisht thought against thy rule, . . . 1Tamb 5.1.98 1Virgn
One thought, one grace, one woonder at the least, . . 1Tamb 5.1.172 Tamb
but that you wil be thought/More childish valourous than manly 2Tamb 4.1.16 Calyph
Shrowd any thought may holde my striving hands/From martiall 2Tamb 4.1.95 Tamb
Forbids my mind to entertaine a thought/That tends to love, but 2Tamb 4.2.25 Olymp
our hearts/More than the thought of this dooth vexe our soules. 2Tamb 5.1.145 Jrslem
Whom I have thought a God? they shal be burnt. . . . 2Tamb 5.1.176 Tamb
Retaine a thought of joy, or sparke of life? . . . 2Tamb 5.3.163 Amyras
A reaching thought will search his deepest wits, . . Jew 1.2.221 Barab
were ne're thought upon/Till Titus and Vespasian conquer'd us) Jew 2.3.9 Barab
Oh heaven forbid I should have such a thought. . . . Jew 2.3.256 Barab
I had not thought he had been so brave a man. . . . Jew 4.4.16 Curtzn
And being asleepe, belike they thought me dead, . . Jew 5.1.81 Barab
Is in your judgment thought a learned man. . . . P 391 7.31 Guise
And by his graces councell it is thought, ... P 465 8.15 Anjoy
Because my lords, it was not thought upon: . . . Edw 1.4.273 Mortmr
But I had thought the match had beene broke off, . . Edw 2.1.25 Baldck
Thy service Spencer shalbe thought upon. . . . . Edw 2.1.80 Neece
My lord, tis thought, the Earles are up in armes. . . Edw 2.2.225 Queene
I, and tis likewise thought you favour him <them> <'em> <hem>. Edw 2.2.226 Edward
Farre be it from the thought of Lancaster, . . . Edw 2.4.33 Lncstr
thinke not a thought so villanous/Can harbor in a man of noble Edw 5.1.131 Bartly
I thought as much. . . . . Edw 5.5.22 Gurney
Forgive my thought, for having such a thought, . . . Edw 5.5.83 Edward
thought you did not sneake up and downe after her for nothing. F 742 2.3.21 P Dick
And on a proud pac'd Steed, as swift as thought, . . F 984 3.2.4 Mephst
plague take you, I thought 'twas your knavery to take it away: F1110 3.3.23 P Vintnr
Oft have I thought to have done so: . . . . . F1864 5.2.68 P Faust
one, me thought/I heard him shreeke and call aloud for helpe: F1991 5.3.9 3Schol
I, I thought that was al the land his father left him: . F App p.229 17 P Clown
why I has thought thou hadst beene a batcheler, but now I see F App p.238 69 P Emper
And thought his name sufficient to uphold him, . . . Lucan, First Booke 136
You would have thought their houses had bin fierd/Or . Lucan, First Booke 490
If ought of me thou speak'st in inward thought, . . Ovid's Elegies 1.4.23
Dissemble so, as lov'd he may be thought, ... Ovid's Elegies 1.8.71
Phoebus gave not Diana such tis thought, ... Ovid's Elegies 2.5.27
And my presages of no weight be thought. . . . . Ovid's Elegies 2.14.42

THOUGHT (cont.)
Is by Evadne thought to take such flame, ... Ovid's Elegies 3.5.41
What sweete thought is there but I had the same? . . Ovid's Elegies 3.6.63
And would be thought to graunt against her will. . . Hero and Leander 1.336
And ever as he thought himselfe most nigh it, . . . Hero and Leander 2.74
And in her owne mind thought her selfe secure, . . . Hero and Leander 2.265
Treason was in her thought,/And cunningly to yeeld her selfe Hero and Leander 2.293
THOUGHTES
but most astonied/To see his choller shut in secrete thoughtes, 1Tamb 3.2.70 Agidas
late felt frownes/That sent a tempest to my daunted thoughtes, 1Tamb 3.2.86 Agidas
armours fight/A doubtfull battell with my tempted thoughtes, 1Tamb 5.1.152 Tamb
with horror aie/Griping our bowels with retorqued thoughtes, 1Tamb 5.1.237 Bajzth
As your supreame estates instruct our thoughtes, . . 2Tamb 5.3.20 Techel
For if thy body thrive not full of thoughtes/As pure and fiery 2Tamb 5.3.236 Tamb
THOUGHTLES
And I will either move the thoughtles flint, . . . Dido 4.2.40 Iarbus
THOUGHTS
What? dares she strike the darling of my thoughts? . . Dido 1.1.9 Jupitr
Such force is farre from our unweaponed thoughts, . . Dido 1.2.14 Illion
To rid me from these melancholly thoughts. . . . Dido 2.1.303 Dido
And in my thoughts is shrin'd another [love] <Iove>: . . Dido 3.1.58 Dido
Lest with these sweete thoughts I melt cleane away. . . Dido 3.1.76 Dido
give Dido leave/To be more modest then her thoughts admit, Dido 3.1.95 Dido
And finde the way to wearie such fond thoughts: . . Dido 3.2.86 Juno
And interchangeably discourse their thoughts, . . . Dido 3.2.93 Juno
And overjoy my thoughts with their escape: . . . . Dido 3.3.57 Aeneas
Aeneas thoughts dare not ascend so high/As Didos heart, which Dido 3.4.33 Aeneas
Father of gladnesse, and all frollicke thoughts, . . Dido 4.2.5 Iarbus
O leave me, leave me to my silent thoughts, . . . Dido 4.2.38 Iarbus
O what meane I to have such foolish thoughts! . . . Dido 4.5.25 Nurse
have I found a meane/To rid me from these thoughts of Lunacie: Dido 5.1.273 Dido
Come lady, let not this appal your thoughts. . . . 1Tamb 1.2.1 Tamb
Affecting thoughts coequall with the cloudes, . . . 1Tamb 1.2.65 Tamb
And stuft with treasure for his highest thoughts? . . 1Tamb 2.1.59 Ceneus
Yet since a farther passion feeds my thoughts, . . . 1Tamb 3.2.13 Zenoc
Had fed the feeling of their maisters thoughts, . . 1Tamb 5.1.162 Tamb
To harbour thoughts effeminate and faint? . . . . 1Tamb 5.1.177 Tamb
O life more loathsome to my vexed thoughts, . . . 1Tamb 5.1.255 Bajzth
From whence the issues of my thoughts doe breake: . . 1Tamb 5.1.274 Bajzth
May styl excruciat his tormented thoughts. . . . 1Tamb 5.1.301 Bajzth
What motion is it that inflames your thoughts, . . . 2Tamb 2.1.2 Sgsmnd
Yet in my thoughts shall Christ be honoured, . . . 2Tamb 2.3.33 Orcan
Then let some holy trance convay my thoughts, . . . 2Tamb 2.4.34 Tamb
That flies with fury swifter than our thoughts, . . . 2Tamb 4.1.5 Amyras
A woful change my Lord, that daunts our thoughts, . . 2Tamb 5.3.181 Therid
Nor quiet enter my distemper'd thoughts, ... Jew 2.1.18 Barab
Then were my thoughts so fraile and unconfirm'd, . . Jew 3.3.59 Abigal
Guise, begins those deepe ingendred thoughts/To burst abroad, P 91 2.34 Guise
And yeeld your thoughts to height of my desertes. . . P 602 12.15 King
We know that noble mindes change not their thoughts/For wearing P 610 12.23 Mugern
For his aspiring thoughts aime at the crowne, . . . P 923 18.24 Navrre
Surchargde with surfet of ambitious thoughts: . . . P 953 19.23 King
Whose murderous thoughts will be his overthrow. . . P1116 21.10 Dumain
These words revive my thoughts and comforts me, . . P1209 22.71 Navrre
Whose mounting thoughts did never creepe so low, . . Edw 2.2.77 Gavstn
Which fils my mind with strange despairing thoughts, . Edw 5.1.79 Edward
Which thoughts are martyred with endles torments. . . Edw 5.1.80 Edward
By desperate thoughts against Joves Deity: . . . F 317 1.3.89 Faust
my thoughts are ravished so/With sight of this renowned . F1260 4.1.106 Emper
To satisfie my longing thoughts at full, ... F1264 4.1.110 Emper
let us sway thy thoughts/From this attempt against the . F1325 4.2.1 Mrtino
Despaire doth drive distrust into my thoughts. . . . F1480 4.4.24 Faust
His Artfull sport, drives all sad thoughts away. . . F1673 4.6.116 Duke
Those <These> thoughts that do disswade me from my vow, . F1764 5.1.91 Faust
sundry thoughts arose, about the honour of mine auncestors, F App p.236 18 P Emper
Dispaire doth drive distrust unto my thoughts, . . . F App p.240 123 Faust
use stirde, and thoughts that alwaies scorn'd/A second place; Lucan, First Booke 124
My thoughts sole goddes, aide mine enterprise, . . . Lucan, First Booke 202
thou must hire/To teach thy lover, what thy thoughts desire. Ovid's Elegies 1.8.88
My idle thoughts delighted her no more, ... Ovid's Elegies 3.6.39
By secreat thoughts to thinke there is a god. . . . Ovid's Elegies 3.8.36
To lead thy thoughts, as thy faire lookes doe mine, . . Hero and Leander 1.201
Fearing her owne thoughts made her to be hated. . . Hero and Leander 2.44
Relenting thoughts, remorse and pittie rests. . . . Hero and Leander 2.216
and higher set/The drooping thoughts of base declining soules, Hero and Leander 2.257
THOU'LT (See also THOU'T)
be under colour of shaving, thou'lt cut my throat for my goods. Jew 2.3.120 P Barab
Zoon's what a looking thou keep'st, thou'lt betraye's anon. Jew 3.1.25 Pilia
THOUSAND
And guarded with a thousand grislie ghosts, ... Dido 1.1.59 Venus
That doe complaine the wounds of thousand waves, . . . Dido 1.2.8 Illion
Which thousand battering Rams could never pierce, . . . Dido 2.1.175 Aeneas
And after him a thousand Grecians more, ... Dido 2.1.185 Aeneas
Threatning a thousand deaths at every glaunce. . . . Dido 2.1.231 Aeneas
Yet not from Carthage for a thousand worlds. . . . Dido 3.1.51 Iarbus
Then twentie thousand Indiaes can affoord: . . . . Dido 3.1.93 Dido
And with one shaft provoke ten thousand darts: . . . Dido 3.3.72 Iarbus
Ten thousand Cupids hover in the ayre, ... Dido 4.4.48 Dido
Our kinsmens [lives] <loves>, and thousand guiltles soules, Dido 4.4.90 Aeneas
Musk-roses, and a thousand sort of flowers, ... Dido 4.5.8 Nurse
Not past foure thousand paces at the most. . . . . Dido 5.1.17 Aeneas
And yong Iulus more then thousand yeares, ... Dido 5.1.39 Hermes
Nor sent a thousand ships unto the walles, ... Dido 5.1.204 Dido

THOUSAND (cont.)

Chardg'd with a thousand horse, to apprehend/And bring him	1Tamb	1.1.47	Meandr
To send my thousand horse incontinent, ...	1Tamb	1.1.52	Mycet
Thou shalt be leader of this thousand horse, ...	1Tamb	1.1.62	Mycet
Theridamas, farewel ten thousand times.	1Tamb	1.1.82	Mycet
are in readines/Ten thousand horse to carie you from hence,	1Tamb	1.1.185	Ortyg
A thousand Persean horsmen are at hand, ...	1Tamb	1.2.111	Souldr
Such hope, such fortune have the thousand horse. . . .	1Tamb	1.2.118	Tamb
A thousand horsmen? We five hundred foote?	1Tamb	1.2.121	Tamb
Art thou but Captaine of a thousand horse, ...	1Tamb	1.2.168	Tamb
And lead thy thousand horse with my conduct, ...	1Tamb	1.2.189	Tamb
Those thousand horse shall sweat with martiall spoile/Of .	1Tamb	1.2.191	Tamb
A thousand thankes worthy Theridamas:	1Tamb	1.2.252	Tamb
A thousand sworne and overmatching foes:	1Tamb	2.1.39	Cosroe
Our army will be forty thousand strong, ...	1Tamb	2.1.61	Cosroe
And have a thousand horsmen tane away?	1Tamb	2.2.6	Mycet
giftes and promises/Inveigle him that lead a thousand horse,	1Tamb	2.2.26	Meandr
With twenty thousand expert souldiers.	1Tamb	2.5.25	Cosroe
A jest to chardge on twenty thousand men?	1Tamb	2.5.91	Therid
Techelles, take a thousand horse with thee, ...	1Tamb	2.5.99	Tamb
Two thousand horse shall forrage up and downe, ...	1Tamb	3.1.61	Bajzth
Will tell how many thousand men he slew.	1Tamb	3.2.43	Agidas
Hath now in armes ten thousand Janisaries, ...	1Tamb	3.3.15	Bassoe
Two hundred thousand footmen that have serv'd/In two set .	1Tamb	3.3.18	Bassoe
Three hundred thousand men in armour clad, ...	1Tamb	4.1.21	2Msngr
Five hundred thousand footmen threatning shot, ...	1Tamb	4.1.24	2Msngr
A monster of five hundred thousand heades, ...	1Tamb	4.3.7	Souldn
A hundred and fifty thousand horse, ...	1Tamb	4.3.53	Capol
Two hundred thousand foot, brave men at armes, ...	1Tamb	4.3.54	Capol
and feare presents/A thousand sorrowes to my martyred soule:	1Tamb	5.1.384	Zenoc
will send/A hundred thousand horse train'd to the war, .	2Tamb	1.1.154	Sgsmnd
A thousand Gallies mann'd with Christian slaves/I freely give	2Tamb	1.2.32	Callap
Although he sent a thousand armed men/To intercept this haughty	2Tamb	1.2.70	Almeda
Under my collors march ten thousand Greeks, ...	2Tamb	1.3.118	Therid
frontier townes/Twise twenty thousand valiant men at armes,	2Tamb	1.3.120	Therid
A hundred thousand expert souldiers:	2Tamb	1.3.132	Usumc
drops that fall/When Boreas rents a thousand swelling cloudes,	2Tamb	1.3.160	Tamb
And drew a thousand ships to Tenedos, ...	2Tamb	2.4.88	Tamb
I have a hundred thousand men in armes, ...	2Tamb	3.1.38	Orcan
From Soria with seventy thousand strong, ...	2Tamb	3.1.57	Soria
And roome within to lodge sixe thousand men.	2Tamb	3.2.72	Tamb
three score thousand fighting men/Are come since last we shewed	2Tamb	3.5.33	Jrslem
Came forty thousand warlike foot and horse, ...	2Tamb	3.5.38	Orcan
and stout Bythinians/Came to my bands full fifty thousand more,	2Tamb	3.5.42	Trebiz
Ten thousand horse, and thirty thousand foot, ...	2Tamb	3.5.48	Soria
royall is esteem'd/Six hundred thousand valiant fighting men.	2Tamb	3.5.51	Soria
And should I goe and kill a thousand men, ...	2Tamb	4.1.53	Calyph
A thousand deathes could not torment our hearts/More than the	2Tamb	5.1.144	Jrslem
Me thinks I could sustaine a thousand deaths, ...	2Tamb	5.2.22	Callap
to lode thy barke/With soules of thousand mangled carkasses.	2Tamb	5.3.74	Tamb
Backeward and forwards nere five thousand leagues. . .	2Tamb	5.3.144	Tamb
he had seven thousand sheepe,/Three thousand Camels, and two	Jew	1.2.182	Barab
Three thousand Camels, and two hundred yoake/Of labouring Oxen,	Jew	1.2.183	Barab
Ten thousand Portagues besides great Perles, ...	Jew	1.2.244	Barab
A hundred thousand Crownes.	Jew	2.2.36	Govnr
Their voyage will be worth ten thousand Crownes. . . .	Jew	4.1.70	Barab
Ten hundred thousand crownes,--Master Barabas. . . .	Jew	4.2.71	P Ithimr
Oh that ten thousand nights were put in one, ...	Jew	4.2.130	Ithimr
now; Bid him deliver thee a thousand Crownes, by the same token,	Jew	4.4.75	P Ithimr
have hir'd a slave my man/To accuse me of a thousand villanies:	Jew	5.1.76	Barab
With free consent a hundred thousand pounds.	Jew	5.5.20	Govnr
Wherein are thirtie thousand able men, ...	P 139	2.82	Guise
Besides a thousand sturdy student Catholicks, ...	P 140	2.83	Guise
Surchargde with guilt of thousand massacres, ...	P1022	19.92	King
O wordes of power to kill a thousand men.	P1126	21.20	Dumain
No, rather will I die a thousand deaths, ...	Edw	1.4.196	Queene
They rate his ransome at five thousand pound.	Edw	2.2.117	Mortmr
Welcome ten thousand times, old man againe.	Edw	3.1.46	Edward
A loves me better than a thousand Spencers.	Edw	4.2.7	Prince
And for your sakes, a thousand wronges ile take, . . .	Edw	5.3.43	Edward
And thousand desperate maladies beene cur'd <eas'd>? .	F 50	1.1.22	Faust
Am not tormented with ten thousand hels, ...	F 307	1.3.79	Mephst
<Then theres inough for a thousand soules>, ...	F 477	(HC260) A	Faust
And at his heeles a thousand furies waite, ...	F1182	4.1.28	Mrtino
of golden plate; besides two thousand duckets ready coin'd:	F1676	5.1.3	P Wagner
Was this the face that Launcht a thousand ships, . . .	F1768	5.1.95	Faust
Clad in the beauty of a thousand starres:	F1782	5.1.109	Faust
thou shalt see/Ten thousand tortures that more horrid be.	F1920	5.2.124	BdAngl
Let Faustus live in hell a thousand yeares, ...	F1961	5.2.165	Faust
A hundred thousand, and at last be sav'd.	F1962	5.2.166	Faust
Upon whose altars thousand soules do lie, ...	F App	p.235 36	Mephst
you that with me have borne/A thousand brunts, and tride me ful	Lucan, First Booke		301
Or Layis of a thousand [wooers] <lovers> [sped] <spread>.	Ovid's Elegies		1.5.12
And therof many thousand he rehearses.	Ovid's Elegies		1.8.58
Cypassis that a thousand wayes trimst haire, ...	Ovid's Elegies		2.8.1
And thousand kisses gives, that worke my harmes: . . .	Ovid's Elegies		2.18.10
We make Enceladus use a thousand armes, ...	Ovid's Elegies		3.11.27
Practise a thousand sports when there you come, . . .	Ovid's Elegies		3.13.24
Threatning a thousand deaths at everie glaunce, . . .	Hero and Leander		1.382
And a thousand fragrant [posies] <poesies>, ...	Passionate Shepherd		10

THOUSANDS

Our Crowne the pin that thousands seeke to cleave. . .	1Tamb	2.4.9	Mycet
Let thousands die, their slaughtered Carkasses/Shall serve for	1Tamb	3.3.138	Bajzth

THOUSANDS (cont.)
of that Spheare/Enchac'd with thousands ever shining lamps, — 1Tamb 4.2.9 Tamb
And hundred thousands subjects to each score: — 2Tamb 2.2.12 Gazell
Thousands of men drown'd in Asphaltis Lake, — 2Tamb 5.1.204 Techel

THOU'ST
Thou'st doom'd thy selfe, assault it presently. — Jew 5.1.97 Calym

THOU'T (Homograph)
Hast thou't? — Jew 2.1.45 Barab
Here, Hast thou't? — Jew 2.1.46 P Abigal
Do but speake what thou't have me to do, and I'le do't: — F 745 2.3.24 P Robin
If thou't dance naked, put off thy cloathes, and I'le conjure — F 746 2.3.25 P Robin
Or if thou't go but to the Taverne with me, I'le give thee — F 747 2.3.26 P Robin

THOW
Trayterouse guise ah thow hast murthered me — Paris ms17,p390 Minion
revenge it henry yf thow liste or darst — Paris ms23,p391 Guise
fondlie hast thow in censte the guises sowle — Paris ms25,p391 Guise
and when thow thinkst I have foregotten this — Paris ms20,p391 Guise
and that thow most reposest one my faythe — Paris ms31,p391 Guise

THRACE (See also TRACE)
The headstrong Jades of Thrace, Alcides tam'd, — 2Tamb 4.3.12 Tamb

THRACIA
Amasia, Thracia, Illyria, Carmonia and al the hundred and — 2Tamb 3.1.4 P Orcan

THRACIAN (See also THRATIAN)
As Prognes to th'adulterous Thracian King, — 1Tamb 4.4.24 Zabina
Beates Thracian Boreas; or when trees [bowe] <bowde> down, — Lucan, First Booke 391
So the fierce troupes of Thracian Rhesus fell/And Captive — Ovid's Elegies 1.9.23
Yet seemely like a Thracian Bacchinall/That tyr'd doth rashly — Ovid's Elegies 1.14.21
The Thracian Harpe with cunning to have strooke, — Ovid's Elegies 2.11.32
To Thracian Orpheus what did parents good? — Ovid's Elegies 3.8.21

THRACIANS
[Illirians] <Illicians>, Thracians, and Bythinians, — 2Tamb 1.1.64 Orcan

THRALDOM
Thrust under yoke and thraldom of a thiefe. — 1Tamb 5.1.261 Bajzth

THRALDOME
Hath shaken off the thraldome of the tower, — Edw 4.2.41 Mortmr

THRALDOMS
But Roome at thraldoms feet to rid from tyrants. — Lucan, First Booke 352

THRALL
Yong men and women, shalt thou lead as thrall, — Ovid's Elegies 1.2.27
Though thou be faire, yet be not thine owne thrall. — Hero and Leander 1.90

THRALLES
[A white wench thralles me, so doth golden yellowe], — Ovid's Elegies 2.4.39

THRALS
Rather then thus to live as Turkish thrals, — Jew 5.4.8 1Knght

THRASIMEN
Not marching <now> in the fields of Thrasimen, — F 1 Prol.1 1Chor

THRATIAN
The barbarous Thratian soldier moov'd with nought, — Hero and Leander 1.81

THREAD (See THRED)

THREADS
That sheares the slender threads of humane life, — Hero and Leander 1.448

THREAT
When as the waves doe threat our Chrystall world, — Dido 1.1.75 Venus
I but the barbarous sort doe threat our ships, — Dido 1.2.34 Serg
Shall threat the Gods more than Cyclopian warres, — 1Tamb 2.3.21 Tamb
Be patient Guise and threat not Epernoune, — P 833 17.28 King
It bootes me not to threat, I must speake faire, — Edw 1.4.63 Edward
what [rockes] <rocke> the feard Cerannia <Ceraunia> threat, — Ovid's Elegies 2.11.19

THREATEN
Blow windes, threaten ye Rockes and sandie shelfes, — Dido 4.4.58 Aeneas
mated and amaz'd/To heare the king thus threaten like himselfe? — 1Tamb 1.1.108 Menaph
Begin in troopes to threaten civill warre, — 1Tamb 1.1.148 Ceneus
Or els to threaten death and deadly armes, — 1Tamb 3.1.19 Fesse
Threaten our citie with a generall spoile: — 1Tamb 5.1.10 Govnr
And threaten conquest on our Soveraigne: — 2Tamb 5.3.14 Therid
And threaten him whose hand afflicts my soul, — 2Tamb 5.3.47 Tamb
To threaten England and to menace me? — P1034 19.104 King
And strike off his that makes you threaten us. — Edw 1.1.124 Mortmr
We are no traitors, therefore threaten not. — Edw 1.4.25 MortSr
No, threaten not my lord, but pay them home. — Edw 1.4.26 Gavstn
What Mortimer, you will not threaten him? — Edw 2.2.146 Kent
For now the wrathfull nobles threaten warres, — Edw 2.2.210 Kent
and every vaine/Did threaten horror from the host of Caesar; — Lucan, First Booke 621

THREATENEST
And threatenest death whether he rise or fall, — Edw 2.2.44 Edward

THREATENS
Nor blazing Commets threatens Didos death, — Dido 4.4.119 Dido
That to my face he threatens civill warres. — Edw 2.2.233 Edward

THREATES
Ah Menaphon, I passe not for his threates, — 1Tamb 1.1.109 Cosroe
That threates the starres with her aspiring top, — F 796 3.1.18 Faust

THREATINGS
Nor thunder in rough threatings haughty pride? — Ovid's Elegies 1.7.46

THREATNED
Threatned with frowning wrath and jealousie, — 1Tamb 3.2.67 Agidas
working tooles present/The naked action of my threatned end. — 1Tamb 3.2.94 Agidas
And make us desperate of our threatned lives: — 1Tamb 5.1.6 Govnr
Which threatned more than if the region/Next underneath the — 2Tamb 5.1.87 Tamb
but the Divel threatned to teare me in peeces if I nam'd God: — F1865 5.2.69 P Faust

THREATNING
By Saturnes soule, and this earth threatning [haire] <aire>, — Dido 1.1.10 Jupitr
Threatning a thousand deaths at every glaunce. — Dido 2.1.231 Aeneas
Threatning the world with high astounding tearms/And scourging — 1Tamb Prol.5 Prolog

THREATNING (cont.)				
Stretching their pawes, and threatning heardes of Beastes,	1Tamb	1.2.53		Techel
Five hundred thousand footmen threatning shot, ...	1Tamb	4.1.24		2Msngr
Threatning a death <dearth> and famine to this land, .	2Tamb	3.2.9		Tamb
And have no terrour but his threatning lookes?	2Tamb	5.1.23		Govnr
Write not so submissively, but threatning him.	Jew	4.2.72	P	Pilia
<a threatning Arme, an angry Brow>.	F1944	(HC271)B		Faust
Trumpets and drums, like deadly threatning other, . .	Lucan, First Booke	6		
the angry threatning gods/Fill'd both the earth and seas with	Lucan, First Booke	522		
The threatning Scorpion with the burning taile/And fier'st his	Lucan, First Booke	658		
And calves from whose feard front no threatning flyes, .	Ovid's Elegies	3.12.15		
Threatning a thousand deaths at everie glaunce, . . .	Hero and Leander	1.382		
THREATS				
But if these threats moove not submission, ...	1Tamb	4.1.58		2Msngr
Your threats, your larums, and your hote pursutes, . .	Edw	2.5.2		Gavstn
Tyrant, I scorne thy threats and menaces, ...	Edw	3.1.241		Warwck
Thus after many threats of wrathfull warre, ...	Edw	4.3.1		Edward
no threats or prayers move thee,/O harder then the dores thou	Ovid's Elegies	1.6.61		
THRED				
Controule proud Fate, and cut the thred of time. . .	Dido	1.1.29		Jupitr
Shortning my dayes and thred of vitall life, ...	F App	p.239 92		Faust
THREE				
Three winters shall he with the Rutiles warre, ...	Dido	1.1.89		Jupitr
And full three Sommers likewise shall he waste, . . .	Dido	1.1.91		Jupitr
Thus in stoute Hectors race three hundred yeares, . .	Dido	1.1.104		Jupitr
I would intreat you to speak but three wise wordes. . .	1Tamb	2.4.25		Tamb
Zabina, mother of three braver boies, ...	1Tamb	3.3.103		Bajzth
Three hundred thousand men in armour clad, ...	1Tamb	4.1.21		2Msngr
Now take these three crownes, and pledge me, my contributorie	1Tamb	4.4.115	P	Tamb
This lovely boy the yongest of the three, ...	2Tamb	1.3.37		Zenoc
three score thousand fighting men/Are come since last we shewed	2Tamb	3.5.33		Jrslem
To note me Emperour of the three fold world:	2Tamb	4.3.118		Tamb
Three thousand Camels, and two hundred yoake/Of labouring Oxen,	Jew	1.2.183		Barab
And if he has, he is worth three hundred plats. . . .	Jew	2.3.102		Barab
I charge thee send me three hundred by this bearer, and this	Jew	4.2.75	P	Ithimr
Barabas send me three hundred Crownes.	Jew	4.3.1		Barab
And I by him must send three hundred crownes. . . .	Jew	4.3.15		Barab
No; but three hundred will not serve his turne. . . .	Jew	4.3.20	P	Pilia
have a shag-rag knave to come [demand]/Three hundred Crownes,	Jew	4.3.62		Barab
Love thee, fill me three glasses.	Jew	4.4.7		Curtzn
Three and fifty dozen, I'le pledge thee.	Jew	4.4.8	P	Ithimr
Two, three, foure month Madam.	Jew	4.4.55	P	Barab
Anjoy, Gonzago, Retes, if that you three, ...	P 322	5.49		Guise
Because my places being but three, contains all his: .	P 405	7.45		Ramus
[Divinitie is basest of the three], ...	F 135	1.1.107A		Faust
Be alwaies serviceable to us three:	F 150	1.1.122		Valdes
Then tell me Faustus what shall we three want?	F 175	1.1.147		Cornel
bad him take as much as he would for three-farthings; so he	F1529	4.5.25	P	Carter
O horrible, had the Doctor three legs?	F1658	4.6.101	P	All
Thy selfe thus shivered out to three mens shares: . .	Lucan, First Booke	85		
Being three daies old inforst the floud to swell, . .	Lucan, First Booke	220		
We which were Ovids five books, now are three, . . .	Ovid's Elegies	1.1.1		
And gives the viper curled Dogge three heads. . . .	Ovid's Elegies	3.11.26		
THREE-FARTHINGS				
bad him take as much as he would for three-farthings; so he	F1529	4.5.25	P	Carter
THREE FOLD				
To note me Emperour of the three fold world:	2Tamb	4.3.118		Tamb
THREEFOLD				
Your threefold armie and my hugie hoste, ...	1Tamb	3.3.94		Bajzth
Above the threefold Astracisme of heaven, ...	2Tamb	4.3.62		Tamb
THREESCORE				
Goe send 'um threescore Camels, thirty Mules, ...	Jew	1.1.59		Barab
THRE-SHOLD				
when she departed/Nape by stumbling on the thre-shold started.	Ovid's Elegies	1.12.4		
And on thy thre-shold let me lie dispred, ...	Ovid's Elegies	2.19.21		
THRESHOLD				
On this hard threshold till the morning lay.	Ovid's Elegies	1.6.68		
THRESHOLDS				
And farewell cruell posts, rough thresholds block, . .	Ovid's Elegies	1.6.73		
He Citties greate, this thresholds lies before: . . .	Ovid's Elegies	1.9.19		
THREW				
flags/Through which sweet mercie threw her gentle beams, .	1Tamb	5.1.69		Tamb
of the war/Threw naked swords and sulphur bals of fire, .	2Tamb	3.2.41		Tamb
You run swifter when you threw my gold out of my Window. .	Jew	4.4.52	P	Barab
belike they thought me dead,/And threw me o're the wals: .	Jew	5.1.82		Barab
For which God threw him from the face of heaven. . .	F 296	1.3.68		Mephst
About her naked necke his bare armes threw.	Hero and Leander	1.42		
And [throw] <threw> him gawdie toies to please his eie, .	Hero and Leander	2.187		
THRICE				
Nor thee, nor them, thrice noble Tamburlain, ...	1Tamb	1.2.249		Therid
So do I thrice renowmed man at armes, ...	1Tamb	2.5.6		Cosroe
O sight thrice welcome to my joiful soule, ...	1Tamb	5.1.440		Zenoc
Thrice worthy kings of Natolia, and the rest, ...	2Tamb	3.1.7		Callap
And winds it twice or thrice about his eare;	Jew	4.3.8		Barab
Souldiers a largis, and thrice welcome all.	Edw	3.1.57		Edward
Pronounce this thrice devoutly to thy selfe, ...	F 547	2.1.159		Mephst
Thrice learned Faustus, welcome to our Court. . . .	F1205	4.1.51		Emper
Before her feete thrice prostrate downe I fell, . . .	Ovid's Elegies	1.7.61		
My feared hands thrice back she did repell.	Ovid's Elegies	1.7.62		
Thrice she prepar'd to flie, thrice she did stay, . . .	Ovid's Elegies	3.5.69		
THRIDS				
with thrids on wrong wheeles spun/And what with Mares ranck	Ovid's Elegies	1.8.7		
Or thrids which spiders slender foote drawes out/Fastning her	Ovid's Elegies	1.14.7		

THRISE			
That shaken thrise, makes Natures buildings quake,	Dido	1.1.11	Jupitr
And Libas, and the white cheek'de Pitho thrise,	Ovid's Elegies		3.6.24
THRIV'D			
Had forraine wars ill thriv'd; or wrathful France/Pursu'd us	Lucan, First Booke		308
THRIVE			
For if thy body thrive not full of thoughtes/As pure and fiery	2Tamb	5.3.236	Tamb
THRIVES			
So in a spring thrives he that told so much,	Ovid's Elegies		3.6.51
THROAND			
Titan himselfe throand in the midst of heaven,	Lucan, First Booke		538
THROANE			
That meane t'invest me in a higher throane,	2Tamb	5.3.121	Tamb
learne with awfull eie/To sway a throane as dangerous as his:	2Tamb	5.3.235	Tamb
THROANES			
To see the devils mount in Angels throanes,	2Tamb	5.3.32	Usumc
THROAT (See also THROTE)			
Then from the navell to the throat at once,	Dido	2.1.255	Aeneas
And either lanch his greedy thirsting throat,	1Tamb	1.2.146	Tamb
And poure it in this glorious Tyrants throat.	1Tamb	4.2.7	Bajzth
Who gently now wil lance thy Ivory throat,	2Tamb	3.4.24	Olymp
Thinke of thy end, this sword shall lance thy throat.	2Tamb	3.5.78	Orcan
To proove it, I wil noint my naked throat,	2Tamb	4.2.68	Olymp
Tyrant, I turne the traitor in thy throat,	2Tamb	5.1.54	Govnr
be under colour of shaving, thou'lt cut my throat for my goods.	Jew	2.3.120 P	Barab
I'de cut thy throat if I did.	Jew	4.1.11	Barab
Cry out, exclaime, houle till thy throat be hoarce,	P1077	19.147	King
THROATE			
Or fathers throate; or womens groning wombe;	Lucan, First Booke		378
THROATS			
Their carelesse swords shal lanch their fellowes throats/And	1Tamb	2.2.49	Meandr
Our Turky blades shal glide through al their throats,	2Tamb	1.1.31	Orcan
Downe to the channels of your hatefull throats,	2Tamb	4.1.183	Tamb
I steale/To travellers Chambers, and there cut their throats:	Jew	2.3.207	Ithimr
THROES			
And like light Salmacis, her body throes/Upon his bosome, where	Hero and Leander		2.46
THRONE (See also THROANE)			
Shall build his throne amidst those starrie towers,	Dido	1.1.98	Jupitr
Or els in Carthage make his kingly throne.	Dido	2.1.331	Venus
Shall chaine felicitie unto their throne.	Dido	3.2.80	Juno
to apprehend/And bring him Captive to your Highnesse throne.	1Tamb	1.1.48	Meandr
their Spheares/That guides his steps and actions to the throne,	1Tamb	2.1.17	Menaph
I long to sit upon my brothers throne.	1Tamb	2.5.47	Cosroe
Scarce being seated in my royall throne,	1Tamb	2.7.5	Cosroe
That I may rise into my royall throne.	1Tamb	4.2.15	Tamb
And on whose throne the holy Graces sit.	1Tamb	5.1.77	1Virgn
Fearing my power should pull him from his throne.	1Tamb	5.1.453	Tamb
as when Bajazeth/My royall Lord and father fild the throne,	2Tamb	3.1.12	Callap
Ready to levie power against thy throne,	2Tamb	4.1.117	Tamb
To blow thy Alcaron up to thy throne,	2Tamb	5.1.193	Tamb
Your sacred vertues pour'd upon his throne,	2Tamb	5.3.11	Therid
Or looke to see the throne where you should sit,	Edw	1.1.131	Lncstr
Here Mortimer, sit thou in Edwards throne,	Edw	1.4.36	Edward
Did they remoove that flatterer from thy throne.	Edw	3.1.231	Kent
And hart and hand to heavens immortall throne,	Edw	4.7.108	Baldck
[And fliest the throne of his tribunall seate],	F1790	5.1.117A	OldMan
seate of God, the Throne of the Blessed, the Kingdome of Joy,	F1845	5.2.49 P	Faust
In what resplendant glory thou hadst set/In yonder throne, like	F1905	5.2.109	GdAngl
or they that shal hereafter possesse our throne, shal (I feare	F App	p.236 22 P	Emper
And offred as a dower his burning throne,	Hero and Leander		1.7
THRONES			
And both our soules aspire celestiall thrones.	1Tamb	1.2.237	Tamb
(and gods not sleightly/Purchase immortal thrones; nor Jove	Lucan, First Booke		35
THRONG			
And lofty Caesar in the thickest throng,	Lucan, First Booke		247
Have care to walke in middle of the throng.	Ovid's Elegies		1.4.56
THRONGS			
Ran in the thickest throngs, and with this sword/Sent many of	Dido	2.1.211	Aeneas
But then run desperate through the thickest throngs,	2Tamb	3.2.139	Tamb
THROTE			
To strangle with a lawne thrust through the throte,	Edw	5.4.32	Ltborn
THROTES			
Returne it to their throtes, ile be thy warrant.	Edw	2.2.73	Edward
THROUGH (See also THOROUGH, THOROW, THOROWE)			
Drawne through the heavens by Steedes of Boreas brood,	Dido	1.1.55	Venus
See where her servitors passe through the hall/Bearing a	Dido	2.1.70	Serg
Through which it could not enter twas so huge.	Dido	2.1.171	Aeneas
And through the breach did march into the streetes,	Dido	2.1.189	Aeneas
Old men with swords thrust through their aged sides,	Dido	2.1.197	Aeneas
Achilles horse/Drew him in triumph through the Greekish Campe,	Dido	2.1.206	Aeneas
Through which he could not passe for slaughtred men:	Dido	2.1.262	Aeneas
Through which the water shall delight to play:	Dido	3.1.119	Dido
And cut a passage through his toples hilles:	Dido	4.3.12	Aeneas
And follow them as footemen through the deepe:	Dido	4.3.24	Aeneas
let him ride/As Didos husband through the Punicke streetes,	Dido	4.4.67	Dido
And make Aeneas famous through the world,	Dido	5.1.293	Dido
And through my provinces you must expect/Letters of conduct	1Tamb	1.2.23	Tamb
And ride in triumph through Persepolis.	1Tamb	2.5.49	Menaph
And ride in triumph through Persepolis?	1Tamb	2.5.50	Tamb
And ride in triumph through Persepolis?	1Tamb	2.5.54	Tamb
And with my blood my life slides through my wound,	1Tamb	2.7.43	Cosroe
As looks the sun through Nilus flowing stream,	1Tamb	3.2.47	Zenoc
Fearing his love through my unworthynesse.	1Tamb	3.2.65	Zenoc

THROUGH (cont.)
Thy fall shall make me famous through the world: 1Tamb 3.3.83 Tamb
Which glided through the bowels of the Greekes. 1Tamb 3.3.92 Argier
In sounding through the world his partiall praise. 1Tamb 4.3.49 Arabia
And through the eies and eares of Tamburlaine, 1Tamb 5.1.53 2Virgn
flags/Through which sweet mercie threw her gentle beams, 1Tamb 5.1.69 Tamb
Volleyes of shot pierce through thy charmed Skin, 1Tamb 5.1.221 Bajzth
Pierce through the center of my withered heart, 1Tamb 5.1.303 Bajzth
And makes my deeds infamous through the world. 1Tamb 5.1.391 Zenoc
To spread my fame through hell and up to heaven: 1Tamb 5.1.467 Tamb
Our Turky blades shal glide through al their throats, 2Tamb 1.1.31 Orcan
And as thou rid'st in triumph through the streets, 2Tamb 1.2.41 Callap
And I would strive to swim through pooles of blood, 2Tamb 1.3.92 Amyras
How through the midst of Verna and Bulgaria/And almost to the 2Tamb 2.1.8 Fredrk
shall breath/Through shady leaves of every sencelesse tree, 2Tamb 2.3.16 Orcan
Shall lead his soule through Orcus burning gulfe: 2Tamb 2.3.25 Orcan
Like tried silver runs through Paradice/To entertaine divine 2Tamb 2.4.24 Tamb
Whose hornes shall sprinkle through the tainted aire, 2Tamb 3.1.66 Orcan
That you may dryfoot martch through lakes and pooles, 2Tamb 3.2.86 Tamb
Shot through the armes, cut overthwart the hands, 2Tamb 3.2.104 Tamb
But then run desperate through the thickest throngs, 2Tamb 3.2.139 Tamb
A deadly bullet gliding through my side, 2Tamb 3.4.4 Capt
as the battaile is done, Ile ride in triumph through the Camp. 2Tamb 3.5.146 P Tamb
Breake through the hedges of their hateful mouthes, 2Tamb 4.3.46 Therid
Be famous through the furthest continents, 2Tamb 4.3.110 Tamb
And drawen with princely Eagles through the path, 2Tamb 4.3.127 Tamb
So will I ride through Samarcanda streets, 2Tamb 4.3.130 Tamb
Pierce through the coffin and the sheet of gold, 2Tamb 5.3.226 Tamb
Through rocks more steepe and sharp than Caspian cliftes. 2Tamb 5.3.241 Tamb
downe by Candie shoare/To Malta, through our Mediterranean sea. Jew 1.1.47 Barab
For through our sufferance of your hatefull lives, Jew 1.2.63 Govnr
piller led'st/The sonnes of Israel through the dismall shades, Jew 2.1.13 Barab
No, but I doe it through a burning zeale, Jew 2.3.87 Barab
Yet through the key-hole will he talke to her, Jew 2.3.263 Barab
through the Gardens I chanc'd to cast mine eye up to the Jewes Jew 3.1.17 P Pilia
I'le lead five hundred souldiers through the Vault, Jew 5.1.91 Barab
all his men/To come ashore, and march through Malta streets, Jew 5.5.15 Msngr
I my good Lord, shot through the arme. P 198 3.33 Admral
Madam, it wilbe noted through the world, P 207 4.5 Charls
See where my Souldier shot him through the arm. P 310 5.37 Guise
One like Actaeon peeping through the grove, Edw 1.1.67 Gavstn
they say there is great execution/Done through the realme, my Edw 4.3.7 Edward
Gallop a pace bright Phoebus through the skie, Edw 4.3.43 Edward
To strangle with a lawne thrust through the throte, Edw 5.4.32 Ltborn
My father's murdered through thy treacherie, Edw 5.6.28 King
damned Art/For which they two are infamous through the world. F 222 1.2.29 1Schol
O that there would come a famine over <through> all the world, F 682 2.2.131 P Envy
Just through the midst runnes flowing Tybers streame, F 813 3.1.35 Mephst
This day is held through Rome and Italy, F 834 3.1.56 Mephst
May be admired through the furthest Land. F 842 3.1.64 Faust
[Touching his journey through the world and ayre], F1145 3.3.58A 3Chor
Thou shalt be famous through all Italy, F1215 4.1.61 Emper
that shall pierce through/The Ebon gates of ever-burning hell, F1223 4.1.69 Faust
Take thou this other, dragge him through the woods, F1410 4.2.86 Faust
Through which the Furies drag'd me by the heeles. F1435 4.3.5 Mrtino
Now Babilon, (proud through our spoile) should stoop, Lucan, First Booke 10
Peace through the world from Janus Phane shal flie, Lucan, First Booke 61
the restles generall through the darke/(Swifter then bullets Lucan, First Booke 230
Through which the wood peer'd, headles darts, olde swords/With Lucan, First Booke 244
warre, wherein through use he's known/To exceed his maister, Lucan, First Booke 325
Which wont to run their course through empty night/At noone day Lucan, First Booke 534
did Thiestes towne/(Mycenae), Phoebus flying through the East: Lucan, First Booke 542
a dead blacknesse/Ranne through the bloud, that turn'd it all Lucan, First Booke 618
liver/Squis'd matter; through the cal, the intralls pearde, Lucan, First Booke 624
So runnes a Matron through th'amazed streetes, Lucan, First Booke 675
New factions rise; now through the world againe/I goe; o Phoebus Lucan, First Booke 691
So likewise we will through the world be rung, Ovid's Elegies 1.3.25
Such as Amimone through the drie fields strayed/When on her Ovid's Elegies 1.10.5
Thou leav'st his bed, because hees faint through age, Ovid's Elegies 1.13.37
Wee seeke that through thee safely love we may, Ovid's Elegies 2.2.65
And through the gemme let thy lost waters pash. Ovid's Elegies 2.15.24
With her I durst the Lybian Syrtes breake through, Ovid's Elegies 2.16.21
So through the world shold bright renown expresse me. Ovid's Elegies 3.1.64
Strayd bare-foote through sole places on a time. Ovid's Elegies 3.5.50
What, wast my limbs through some Thesalian charms, Ovid's Elegies 3.6.27
Now is the goat brought through the boyes with darts, Ovid's Elegies 3.12.21
And having wandred now through sea and land, Ovid's Elegies 3.12.33
Which as shee went would cherupe through the bils. Hero and Leander 1.36
Through regular and formall puritie. Hero and Leander 1.308
And here and there her eies through anger rang'd. Hero and Leander 1.360
And now the sunne that through th'orizon peepes, Hero and Leander 2.99
Which made his love through Sestos to bee knowne, Hero and Leander 2.111
By those white limmes, which sparckled through the lawne. Hero and Leander 2.242
Through numming cold, all feeble, faint and wan: Hero and Leander 2.246
A kind of twilight breake, which through the heare, Hero and Leander 2.319

THROUGHLY
Meane while peruse this booke, and view it throughly, F 717 2.2.169 Lucifr

THROUGHOUT
And disperse themselves throughout the Realme of France, P 507 9.26 QnMoth
Be thou proclaimde a traitor throughout France. P 864 17.59 King
now throughout the aire I flie,/To doubtfull Sirtes and drie Lucan, First Booke 685

THROW (See also THROES)
And throw them in the triple mote of Hell, 2Tamb 2.4.100 Tamb

THROW (cont.)
run to some rocke and throw my selfe headlong into the sea; Jew 3.4.39 P Ithimr
For the Jewes body, throw that o're the wals, Jew 5.1.58 Govnr
Then throw him down. P 306 5.33 Guise
Come dragge him away and throw him in a ditch. P 345 5.72 Guise
Lets throw him into the river. P 487 9.6 P 1Atndt
Then throw him into the ditch. P 490 9.9 P 1Atndt
Sirs, take him away and throw him in some ditch. P 499 9.18 Guise
Make for a new life man, throw up thy eyes, Edw 4.7.107 Baldck
yesternight/I opened but the doore to throw him meate,/And I Edw 5.5.8 Gurney
And melting, heavens conspir'd his over-throw: F 22 Prol.22 1Chor
If unto [God] <heaven>, hee'le throw me <thee> downe to hell. F 467 2.1.79 Faust
and strong armes/Can mainly throw the dart; wilt thou indure Lucan, First Booke 365
Do not thou so, but throw thy mantle hence, Ovid's Elegies 1.4.49
Thou hast no bridge, nor boate with ropes to throw, Ovid's Elegies 3.5.3
She on my necke her Ivorie armes did throw, Ovid's Elegies 3.6.7
And [throw] <threw> him gawdie toies to please his eie, Hero and Leander 2.187

THROWE
Throwe of his golden miter, rend his stole, Edw 1.1.187 Edward
My lordly hands ile throwe upon my right. Ovid's Elegies 2.5.30
At me Joves right-hand lightning hath to throwe. Ovid's Elegies 3.3.30

THROWEN
Now throwen to roomes of blacke abjection, 1Tamb 5.1.267 Bajzth

THROWES
And murdrous Fates throwes al his triumphs down. 2Tamb Prol.5 Prolog
Filling the world, leapes out and throwes forth fire, Lucan, First Booke 154
Jove throwes downe woods, and Castles with his fire: Ovid's Elegies 3.3.35
All headlong throwes her selfe the clouds among/And now Leander Hero and Leander 2.90

THROWLY
<in mean time take this booke, peruse it throwly>, F 717 (HC264)A Lucifr

THROWN
Yea and thy father to, and swords thrown down, Lucan, First Booke 117

THROWNE
The glozing head of thy base minion throwne. Edw 1.1.133 Lncstr
the darke/(Swifter then bullets throwne from Spanish slinges, Lucan, First Booke 231
As evill wood throwne in the high-waies lie, Ovid's Elegies 1.12.13
First to be throwne upon the untill'd ground. Ovid's Elegies 3.5.16

THRUST
Old men with swords thrust through their aged sides, Dido 2.1.197 Aeneas
Would make one thrust and strive to be retain'd/In such a great 1Tamb 2.3.31 Therid
But as he thrust them underneath the hils, 1Tamb 2.6.5 Cosroe
To thrust his doting father from his chaire, 1Tamb 2.7.14 Tamb
For as when Jove did thrust old Saturn down, 1Tamb 2.7.36 Usumc
take it from my swords point, or Ile thrust it to thy heart. 1Tamb 4.4.41 P Tamb
Thrust under yoke and thraldom of a thiefe. 1Tamb 5.1.261 Bajzth
Seiz'd all I had, and thrust me out a doores, Jew 2.3.76 Barab
Oh bravely fought, and yet they thrust not home. Jew 3.2.5 Barab
Keepe them a sunder, thrust in the king. Edw 5.3.52 Matrvs
To strangle with a lawne thrust through the throte, Edw 5.4.32 Ltborn
They thrust upon me the Protectorship, Edw 5.4.56 Mortmr
I am content for this once to thrust my head out at a window: F1200 4.1.46 P Benvol
These hands shall thrust the ram, and make them flie, Lucan, First Booke 385
I have sustainde so oft thrust from the dore, Ovid's Elegies 3.10.9
But like exiled aire thrust from his sphere, Hero and Leander 2.118

THRUSTES
Or as a sodaine gale thrustes into sea, Ovid's Elegies 2.9.31

THRUSTS
beast is yon, that thrusts his head out at [the] window. F1274 4.1.120 P Faust
And with the waters sees death neere him thrusts, Ovid's Elegies 2.11.26
fire filcht by Prometheus;/And thrusts him down from heaven: Hero and Leander 1.439

TH'THEATER'S
Isis may be done/Nor feare least she to th'theater's runne. Ovid's Elegies 2.2.26

THUMBE (See also THOMBE)
Yet rending with enraged thumbe her tresses, Ovid's Elegies 3.5.71

THUNDER
And with the thunder of his martial tooles/Makes Earthquakes in 2Tamb 2.2.7 Orcan
Betwixt which, shall our ordinance thunder foorth, 2Tamb 3.3.58 Therid
And ratling cannons thunder in our eares/Our proper ruine, 2Tamb 4.1.13 Amyras
From whom the thunder and the lightning breaks, 2Tamb 5.1.184 Tamb
Ile thunder such a peale into his eares, Edw 2.2.128 Mortmr
The framing of this circle on the ground/Brings Thunder, F 546 2.1.158 Mephst
[But feareful ecchoes thunder <thunders> in mine eares], F 571 2.2.20A Faust
So thunder which the wind teares from the cloudes, Lucan, First Booke 152
The thunder hov'd horse in a crooked line, Lucan, First Booke 222
Nor thunder in rough threatings haughty pride? Ovid's Elegies 1.7.46
as might make/Wrath-kindled Jove away his thunder shake. Ovid's Elegies 2.5.52

THUNDERBOLTS
And bullets like Joves dreadfull Thunderbolts, 1Tamb 2.3.19 Tamb
that in her wings/Caries the fearfull thunderbolts of Jove. 2Tamb 1.1.101 Orcan
Which if a shower of wounding thunderbolts/Should breake out 2Tamb 2.2.13 Gazell
Jove and Joves thunderbolts I had in hand/Which for his heaven Ovid's Elegies 2.1.15

THUNDERCLAPS
With shivering speares enforcing thunderclaps, 1Tamb 3.2.80 Agidas
nostrels breathe/Rebellious winds and dreadfull thunderclaps: 1Tamb 5.1.298 Bajzth
Flieng Dragons, lightning, fearfull thunderclaps, 2Tamb 3.2.10 Tamb

THUNDERED
And God hath thundered vengeance from on high, 2Tamb 2.3.2 Sgsmnd

THUNDERER
Thou thunderer that guardst/Roomes mighty walles built on Lucan, First Booke 197

THUNDERS
[But feareful ecchoes thunder <thunders> in mine eares], F 571 2.2.20A Faust

THUNDRING
For it requires a great and thundring speech: 1Tamb 1.1.3 Mycet

Line	Work	Ref	Speaker
THUNDRING (cont.)			
And calme the rage of thundring Jupiter:	1Tamb	3.3.123	Tamb
While thundring Cannons rattle on their Skins.	1Tamb	4.1.11	Souldn
Strooke with the voice of thundring Jupiter.	1Tamb	4.2.25	Tamb
Stead/That stampt on others with their thundring hooves,	1Tamb	5.1.331	Zenoc
Affrica, and Greece/Follow my Standard and my thundring Drums:	2Tamb	1.1.159	Orcan
TH'UNSTABLE			
none answer'd, but a murmuring buz/Th'unstable people made:	Lucan, First Booke		354
THUS			
Thus in stoute Hectors race three hundred yeares,	Dido	1.1.104	Jupitr
That durst thus proudly wrong our kinsmans peace.	Dido	1.1.119	Jupitr
Too cruell, why wilt thou forsake me thus?	Dido	1.1.243	Aeneas
Why stands my sweete Aeneas thus amazde?	Dido	2.1.2	Achat
What stranger art thou that doest eye me thus?	Dido	2.1.74	Dido
To whom the aged King thus trembling spoke:	Dido	2.1.232	Aeneas
That thus in person goe with thee to hunt:	Dido	3.3.2	Dido
What shall I doe thus wronged with disdaine?	Dido	3.3.69	Iarbus
And quell those hopes that thus employ your [cares] <eares>.	Dido	4.1.35	Dido
Doe Troians use to quit their Lovers thus?	Dido	5.1.106	Dido
What meanes my sister thus to rave and crye?	Dido	5.1.193	Anna
If he depart thus suddenly, I dye:	Dido	5.1.209	Dido
And I am thus deluded of my boy:	Dido	5.1.219	Dido
And must I rave thus for a runnagate?	Dido	5.1.265	Dido
What fatall destinie envies me thus,	Dido	5.1.323	Anna
Ah, Menaphon, why staiest thou thus behind,	1Tamb	1.1.83	Mycet
mated and amaz'd/To heare the king thus threaten like himselfe?	1Tamb	1.1.108	Menaph
And cause the souldiers that thus honour me,	1Tamb	1.1.172	Cosroe
That thus oppresse poore friendles passengers.	1Tamb	1.2.70	Zenoc
Thus shall my heart be still combinde with thine,	1Tamb	1.2.235	Tamb
Thus farre are we towards Theridamas,	1Tamb	2.1.1	Cosroe
That thus opposeth him against the Gods,	1Tamb	2.6.39	Cosroe
Thus to deprive me of my crowne and life.	1Tamb	2.7.2	Cosroe
And thus the Grecians shall be conquered.	1Tamb	3.1.67	Bajzth
And all his Captaines that thus stoutly stand,	1Tamb	3.3.79	Bajzth
Why stay we thus prolonging all their lives?	1Tamb	3.3.97	Techel
How dare you thus abuse my Majesty?	1Tamb	3.3.226	Zabina
O cursed Mahomet that makest us thus/The slaves to Scythians	1Tamb	3.3.270	Zabina
Being thy Captive, thus abuse his state,	1Tamb	4.2.60	Zabina
Confusion light on him that helps thee thus.	1Tamb	4.2.84	Bajzth
And where I goe be thus in triumph drawne:	1Tamb	4.2.86	Tamb
ruthlesse Governour/Have thus refusde the mercie of thy hand,	1Tamb	5.1.93	1Virgn
I thus conceiving and subduing both:	1Tamb	5.1.183	Tamb
When my poore pleasures are devided thus,	1Tamb	5.1.386	Zenoc
Though my right hand have thus enthralled thee,	1Tamb	5.1.435	Tamb
Yet those infirmities that thus defame/Their faiths, their	2Tamb	2.1.44	Sgsmnd
Thus have wee martcht Northwarde from Tamburlaine,	2Tamb	3.3.1	Therid
againe, you shall not trouble me thus to come and fetch you.	2Tamb	3.5.101 P	Tamb
How may my hart, thus fired with mine eies,	2Tamb	4.1.93	Tamb
Why Madam, thinke ye to mocke me thus palpably?	2Tamb	4.2.67	Therid
To Byron here where thus I honor you?	2Tamb	4.3.6	Tamb
Thus am I right the Scourge of highest Jove,	2Tamb	4.3.24	Tamb
And thus be drawen with these two idle kings.	2Tamb	4.3.28	Amyras
When we are thus defenc'd against our Foe,	2Tamb	5.1.22	Govnr
That thus intreat their shame and servitude?	2Tamb	5.1.37	Govnr
Is greater far, than they can thus subdue.	2Tamb	5.3.39	Usumc
What daring God torments my body thus,	2Tamb	5.3.42	Tamb
That thus invie the health of Tamburlaine.	2Tamb	5.3.53	Tamb
Thus are the villaines, cowards fled for feare,	2Tamb	5.3.115	Tamb
So that of thus much that returne was made:	Jew	1.1.1	Barab
Would make a miracle of thus much coyne:	Jew	1.1.13	Barab
And thus me thinkes should men of judgement frame/This is the	Jew	1.1.34	Barab
Thus trowles our fortune in by land and Sea,	Jew	1.1.103	Barab
And thus are wee on every side inrich'd:	Jew	1.1.104	Barab
for earthly man/Then thus to powre out plenty in their laps,	Jew	1.1.108	Barab
Rather had I a Jew be hated thus,	Jew	1.1.114	Barab
Why flocke you thus to me in multitudes?	Jew	1.1.144	Barab
They would not come in warlike manner thus.	Jew	1.1.155	1Jew
Thus: Since your hard conditions are such	Jew	1.2.18	Govnr
And therefore thus we are determined;	Jew	1.2.66	Govnr
And will you basely thus submit your selves/To leave your goods	Jew	1.2.79	Barab
Sham'st thou not thus to justifie thy selfe,	Jew	1.2.119	Govnr
For that is theft; and if you rob me thus,	Jew	1.2.126	Barab
That thus have dealt with me in my distresse.	Jew	1.2.168	Barab
Why stand you thus unmov'd with my laments?	Jew	1.2.171	Barab
I wot his wealth/Was written thus:	Jew	1.2.182	Barab
What, will you thus oppose me, lucklesse Starres,	Jew	1.2.260	Barab
And since you leave me in the Ocean thus/To sinke or swim, and	Jew	1.2.267	Barab
Then thus; thou toldst me they have turn'd my house/Into a	Jew	1.2.277	Barab
Thus father shall I much dissemble.	Jew	1.2.289	Abigal
The boord is marked thus that covers it,	Jew	1.2.350	Barab
The boord is marked thus	Jew	1.2.356	Barab
For I had rather dye, then see her thus.	Jew	1.2.357	Barab
Thus like the sad presaging Raven that tolls/The sicke mans	Jew	2.1.1	Barab
As good goe on, as sit so sadly thus.	Jew	2.1.40	Barab
I weigh it thus much; I have wealth enough.	Jew	2.3.245	Barab
Father, why have you thus incenst them both?	Jew	2.3.356	Abigal
Say, knave, why rail'st upon my father thus?	Jew	3.3.11	Abigal
Onely know this, that thus thou art to doe:	Jew	3.4.48	Barab
Thus every villaine ambles after wealth/Although he ne're be	Jew	3.4.52	Barab
Thus Ithimore:	Jew	3.4.74	Barab
and invenome her/That like a fiend hath left her father thus.	Jew	3.4.105	Barab
fares Callymath, What wind drives you thus into Malta rhode?	Jew	3.5.2 P	Govnr
To you of Malta thus saith Calymath:	Jew	3.5.7	Basso

THUS (cont.)

You loyter, master, wherefore stay [we] <me> thus?	Jew	4.1.139	Ithimr
Was up thus early; with intent to goe/Unto your Friery, because	Jew	4.1.191	Barab
Canst thou be so unkind to leave me thus?	Jew	4.2.52	Curtzn
and look'd upon him thus; told him he were best to send it;	Jew	4.2.105	P Pilia
The more villaine he to keep me thus:	Jew	4.2.111	Ithimr
Thus Bellamira esteemes of gold;	Jew	4.2.125	Curtzn
But thus of thee.--	Jew	4.2.126	Curtzn
I'le goe alone, dogs, do not hale me thus.	Jew	5.1.19	Barab
much better/To [have] kept thy promise then be thus surpriz'd?	Jew	5.2.5	Calym
Thus hast thou gotten, by thy policie,	Jew	5.2.27	Barab
I, Lord, thus slaves will learne.	Jew	5.2.49	Barab
And thus we cast it:	Jew	5.2.96	Barab
And thus farre roundly goes the businesse:	Jew	5.2.110	Barab
Thus loving neither, will I live with both,	Jew	5.2.111	Barab
Thus have we view'd the City, seene the sacke,	Jew	5.3.1	Calym
I wonder how it could be conquer'd thus?	Jew	5.3.12	Calym
Selim, for that, thus saith the Governor,	Jew	5.3.26	Msngr
discharg'd/By him that beares the Linstocke, kindled thus;	Jew	5.4.4	Govnr
Rather then thus to live as Turkish thrals,	Jew	5.4.8	1Knght
No, thus I'le see thy treachery repaid,	Jew	5.5.74	Govnr
Thus he determin'd to have handled thee,	Jew	5.5.93	Govnr
Knit in these hands, thus joyn'd in nuptiall rites,	P 4	1.4	Charls
Thus Madame.	P 230	4.28	Guise
Thus in despite of thy Religion,	P 314	5.41	Guise
Dearely beloved brother, thus tis written.	P 343	5.70	Guise
With Poland therfore must I covenant thus,	P 471	8.21	Anjoy
And whilste he sleepes securely thus in ease,	P 635	12.48	QnMoth
Am I thus to be jested at and scornde?	P 758	15.16	Guise
Thus God we see doth ever guide the right,	P 789	16.3	Navrre
My Lord, to speak more plainely, thus it is:	P 847	17.42	Guise
Thus Caesar did goe foorth, and thus he dyed.	P1015	19.85	Guise
thus fall Imperfett exhalatione/which our great sonn of fraunce	Paris	ms19,p390	Guise
That crosse me thus, shall know I am displeasd.	Edw	1.1.79	Edward
My lord, why do you thus incense your peeres,	Edw	1.1.99	Lncstr
Thus arme in arme, the king and he dooth marche:	Edw	1.2.20	Lncstr
Thus leaning on the shoulder of the king,	Edw	1.2.23	Warwck
Is it not straunge, that he is thus bewitcht?	Edw	1.2.55	MortSr
We will not thus be facst and overpeerd.	Edw	1.4.19	Mortmr
My lord, you may not thus disparage us,	Edw	1.4.32	Lncstr
Was ever king thus over rulde as I?	Edw	1.4.38	Edward
As for the peeres that backe the cleargie thus,	Edw	1.4.104	Edward
Stay Gaveston, I cannot leave thee thus.	Edw	1.4.135	Edward
But thou must call mine honor thus in question?	Edw	1.4.152	Queene
The king my lord thus to abandon me:	Edw	1.4.177	Queene
Then thus, but none shal heare it but our selves.	Edw	1.4.229	Queene
Hees gone, and for his absence thus I moorne,	Edw	1.4.305	Edward
What needst thou, love, thus to excuse thy selfe?	Edw	2.1.60	Neece
Seeing that he talkes thus of my mariage day?	Edw	2.1.69	Neece
But seeing you are so desirous, thus it is:	Edw	2.2.15	Mortmr
If in his absence thus he favors him,	Edw	2.2.47	Mortmr
Stil wil these Earles and Barrons use me thus?	Edw	2.2.70	Edward
Looke to your owne crowne, if you back him thus.	Edw	2.2.93	Warwck
Nay all of them conspire to crosse me thus,	Edw	2.2.95	Edward
That thinke with high lookes thus to tread me down.	Edw	2.2.97	Edward
Shall I still be haunted thus?	Edw	2.2.154	Edward
When I thy brother am rejected thus.	Edw	2.2.218	Kent
Thus do you still suspect me without cause.	Edw	2.2.227	Queene
From my imbracements thus he breakes away,	Edw	2.4.16	Queene
That muster rebels thus against your king)/To see his royall	Edw	2.5.6	Gavstn
Thus weele gratifie the king,	Edw	2.5.51	Mortmr
O treacherous Warwicke thus to wrong thy friend!	Edw	2.6.1	Gavstn
suffer uncontrowld/These Barons thus to beard me in my land,	Edw	3.1.14	Spencr
You would not suffer thus your majestie/Be counterbuft of your	Edw	3.1.17	Spencr
The earle of Penbrooke mildlie thus bespake,	Edw	3.1.108	Arundl
Away base upstart, brav'st thou nobles thus?	Edw	3.1.205	Penbrk
I traitors all, rather then thus be bravde,	Edw	3.1.214	Edward
Thus after many threats of wrathfull warre,	Edw	4.3.1	Edward
Is thus misled to countenance their ils.	Edw	4.3.49	Edward
My lord, why droope you thus?	Edw	4.7.60	Leistr
A sweet Spencer, thus then must we part.	Edw	4.7.73	Edward
That thus hath pent and mu'd me in a prison,	Edw	5.1.18	Edward
My lord, why waste you thus the time away,	Edw	5.1.49	Leistr
And thus, most humbly do we take our leave.	Edw	5.1.124	Trussl
Thus lives old Edward not reliev'd by any,	Edw	5.3.23	Edward
Why strive you thus? your labour is in vaine.	Edw	5.3.33	Matrvs
Base villaines, wherefore doe you gripe mee thus?	Edw	5.3.57	Kent
But read it thus, and thats an other sence:	Edw	5.4.10	Mortmr
Unpointed as it is, thus shall it goe,	Edw	5.4.13	Mortmr
If that my Unckle shall be murthered thus?	Edw	5.4.110	King
Tell Isabell the Queene, I lookt not thus,	Edw	5.5.68	Edward
What meanes your highnesse to mistrust me thus?	Edw	5.5.79	Ltborn
What meanes thou to dissemble with me thus?	Edw	5.5.80	Edward
This feare is that which makes me tremble thus,	Edw	5.5.105	Edward
You could not beare his death thus patiently,	Edw	5.6.36	King
Thus madam, tis the kings will you shall hence.	Edw	5.6.89	2Lord
Thus having triumpht over you, I will set my countenance like a	F 213	1.2.20	P Wagner
set my countenance like a Precisian, and begin to speake thus:	F 214	1.2.21	P Wagner
Is that the reason why he tempts us thus?	F 430	2.1.42	Faust
The second thus:	F 604	2.2.53	P Faust
Thus hitherto hath Faustus spent his time.	F 799	3.1.21	Faust
But thus I fall to Peter, not to thee.	F 872	3.1.94	Bruno
Sound Trumpets then, for thus Saint Peters Heire,	F 875	3.1.97	Pope

THUS (cont.)

Thus, as the Gods creepe on with feete of wool,	F 877	3.1.99	Pope
<holy> Synod/Of Priests and Prelates, it is thus decreed:	F 953	3.1.175	Faust
The Statutes Decretall have thus decreed,	F 961	3.1.183	Faust
So, so, was never Divell thus blest before.	F 974	3.1.196	Mephst
Away, you love me not, to urge me thus,	F1327	4.2.3	Benvol
Hell take his soule, his body thus must fall.	F1363	4.2.39	Benvol
Thus will I end his griefes immediatly.	F1367	4.2.43	Benvol
My friends transformed thus:	F1441	4.3.11	Benvol
Sith blacke disgrace hath thus eclipst our fame,	F1455	4.3.25	Benvol
what he meanes, if death were nie, he would not frolick thus:	F1678	5.1.5	P Wagner
Thus from infernall Dis do we ascend/To view the subjects of	F1797	5.2.1	Lucifr
The devils whom Faustus serv'd have torne him thus:	F1990	5.3.8	3Schol
How darst thou thus abuse a Gentleman?	F App	p.238 74	Knight
Thy selfe thus shivered out to three mens shares:	Lucan, First Booke		85
And staring, thus bespoke: what mean'st thou Caesar?	Lucan, First Booke		192
He thus cride out:	Lucan, First Booke		197
And muttering much, thus to themselves complain'd:	Lucan, First Booke		249
Thus sighing whispered they, and none durst speake/And shew	Lucan, First Booke		259
thus Curio spake,/And therewith Caesar prone ennough to warre,	Lucan, First Booke		292
And thus he spake:	Lucan, First Booke		300
were we bestead/When comming conqueror, Roome afflicts me thus?	Lucan, First Booke		310
Thus in his fright did each man strengthen Fame,	Lucan, First Booke		481
While these thus in and out had circled Roome,	Lucan, First Booke		604
Thus in ambiguous tearmes,/Involving all, did Aruns darkly	Lucan, First Booke		636
Why art thou thus enrag'd?	Lucan, First Booke		659
where shall I fall,/Thus borne aloft?	Lucan, First Booke		678
Thus I complaind, but Love unlockt his quiver,	Ovid's Elegies		1.1.25
And striving thus as one that would be cast,	Ovid's Elegies		1.5.15
As thus she spake, my shadow me betraide,	Ovid's Elegies		1.8.109
Then wouldst thou cry, stay night and runne not thus.	Ovid's Elegies		1.13.40
While thus I speake, blacke dust her white robes ray:	Ovid's Elegies		3.2.41
While thus I speake, the waters more abounded:	Ovid's Elegies		3.5.85
And thus Leander was enamoured.	Hero and Leander		1.162
Chast Hero to her selfe thus softly said:	Hero and Leander		1.178
Thus while dum signs their yeelding harts entangled,	Hero and Leander		1.187
With cheerefull hope thus he accosted her.	Hero and Leander		1.198
As Greece will thinke, if thus you live alone,	Hero and Leander		1.289
Hee thus replide:	Hero and Leander		1.299
And her in humble manner thus beseech.	Hero and Leander		1.314
But heale the heart, that thou hast wounded thus,	Hero and Leander		1.324
Thus having swallow'd Cupids golden hooke,	Hero and Leander		1.333
his spreading armes away she cast her,/And thus bespake him:	Hero and Leander		1.343
Likewise the angrie sisters thus deluded,	Hero and Leander		1.473
O Hero, Hero, thus he cry'de full oft,	Hero and Leander		2.147
Whereon Leander sitting, thus began,	Hero and Leander		2.245
Thus neere the bed she blushing stood upright,	Hero and Leander		2.317
THUSCAN			
If to incampe on Thuscan Tybers streames,	Lucan, First Booke		382
THWART			
force, they that now thwart right/In wars wil yeeld to wrong:	Lucan, First Booke		349
THY (See also TH, TH'ART, THIE)			
And I will spend my time in thy bright armes.	Dido	1.1.22	Ganimd
What ist sweet wagge I should deny thy youth?	Dido	1.1.23	Jupitr
As I exhal'd with thy fire darting beames,	Dido	1.1.25	Jupitr
Sit on my knee, and call for thy content,	Dido	1.1.28	Jupitr
Why, are not all the Gods at thy commaund,	Dido	1.1.30	Jupitr
And heaven and earth the bounds of thy delight?	Dido	1.1.31	Jupitr
To make thee fannes wherewith to coole thy face,	Dido	1.1.35	Jupitr
To sweeten out the slumbers of thy bed:	Dido	1.1.37	Jupitr
If that thy fancie in his feathers dwell,	Dido	1.1.39	Jupitr
Put thou about thy necke my owne sweet heart,	Dido	1.1.44	Jupitr
And tricke thy armes and shoulders with my theft.	Dido	1.1.45	Jupitr
Content thee Cytherea in thy care,	Dido	1.1.82	Jupitr
Since thy Aeneas wandring fate is firme,	Dido	1.1.83	Jupitr
How may I credite these thy flattering termes,	Dido	1.1.109	Venus
Venus farewell, thy sonne shall be our care:	Dido	1.1.120	Jupitr
That erst-while issued from thy watrie loynes,	Dido	1.1.128	Venus
And had my being from thy bubling froth:	Dido	1.1.129	Venus
That by thy vertues freest us from annoy,	Dido	1.1.153	Achat
Whose night and day descendeth from thy browes:	Dido	1.1.156	Achat
Ascanius, goe and drie thy drenched lims,	Dido	1.1.174	Aeneas
Nor speech bewraies ought humaine in thy birth,	Dido	1.1.190	Aeneas
And shrowdes thy beautie in this borrowd shape:	Dido	1.1.192	Aeneas
And this right hand shall make thy Altars crack/With mountaine	Dido	1.1.201	Aeneas
And for thy ships which thou supposest lost,	Dido	1.1.235	Venus
And so I leave thee to thy fortunes lot,	Dido	1.1.238	Venus
Wishing good lucke unto thy wandring steps.	Dido	1.1.239	Venus
Stay gentle Venus, flye not from thy sonne,	Dido	1.1.242	Aeneas
Thy mind Aeneas that would have it so/Deludes thy eye sight,	Dido	2.1.31	Achat
Thy mind Aeneas that would have it so/Deludes thy eye sight,	Dido	2.1.32	Achat
Thinking the sea had swallowed up thy ships,	Dido	2.1.68	Illion
Thy fortune may be greater then thy birth,	Dido	2.1.90	Dido
And if this be thy sonne as I suppose,	Dido	2.1.92	Dido
Heres to thy better fortune and good starres.	Dido	2.1.98	Dido
Remember who thou art, speake like thy selfe,	Dido	2.1.100	Dido
O Hector who weepes not to heare thy name?	Dido	2.1.209	Dido
When thou Achates with thy sword mad'st way,	Dido	2.1.268	Aeneas
Troian, thy ruthfull tale hath made me sad:	Dido	2.1.301	Dido
And this yong Prince shall be thy playfellow.	Dido	2.1.307	Venus
And sticke these spangled feathers in thy hat,	Dido	2.1.314	Venus
And nothing interrupt thy quiet sleepe,	Dido	2.1.338	Venus
To be inamourd of thy brothers lookes,	Dido	3.1.2	Cupid

THY (cont.)

Convey this golden arrowe in thy sleeve, ...	Dido	3.1.3	Cupid
Take it Ascanius, for thy fathers sake.	Dido	3.1.33	Dido
Ungentle Queene, is this thy love to me?	Dido	3.1.36	Iarbus
No, for thy sake Ile love thy father well.	Dido	3.1.81	Dido
Aeneas, Ile repaire thy Troian ships, ...	Dido	3.1.113	Dido
Thy Anchors shall be hewed from Christall Rockes, . .	Dido	3.1.120	Dido
The Masts whereon thy swelling sailes shall hang, . .	Dido	3.1.122	Dido
As Seaborne Nymphes shall swarme about thy ships, . .	Dido	3.1.129	Dido
Had not my Doves discov'rd thy entent:	Dido	3.2.33	Venus
But I will teare thy eyes fro forth thy head, ...	Dido	3.2.34	Venus
If thou but lay thy fingers on my boy.	Dido	3.2.36	Venus
What though I was offended with thy sonne, ...	Dido	3.2.40	Juno
Sister of Jove, if that thy love be such, ...	Dido	3.2.53	Venus
As these thy protestations doe paint forth, ...	Dido	3.2.54	Venus
Cupid shall lay his arrowes in thy lap, ...	Dido	3.2.56	Venus
And thy faire peacockes by my pigeons pearch: . . .	Dido	3.2.59	Venus
how may I deserve/Such amourous favours at thy beautious hand?	Dido	3.2.65	Juno
Which I will make in quittance of thy love:	Dido	3.2.69	Juno
Thy sonne thou knowest with Dido now remaines, . . .	Dido	3.2.70	Juno
Or art thou grievde thy betters presse so nye? . . .	Dido	3.3.18	Iarbus
Pesant, goe seeke companions like thy selfe, ...	Dido	3.3.21	Dido
This Troians end will be thy envies aime, ...	Dido	3.3.73	Iarbus
And make love drunken with thy sweete desire: . . .	Dido	3.3.75	Iarbus
That resteth in the rivall of thy paine, ...	Dido	3.3.84	Iarbus
That should detaine thy eye in his defects?	Dido	3.4.17	Aeneas
Stoute love in mine armes make thy Italy, ...	Dido	3.4.57	Dido
Whose Crowne and kingdome rests at thy commande: . . .	Dido	3.4.58	Dido
Hold, take these Jewels at thy Lovers hand, ...	Dido	3.4.61	Dido
That with thy gloomie hand corrects the heaven, . . .	Dido	4.2.6	Iarbus
Who seekes to rob me of thy Sisters love, ...	Dido	4.2.31	Iarbus
For her that so delighteth in thy paine:	Dido	4.2.34	Anna
Away with Dido, Anna be thy song, ...	Dido	4.2.45	Anna
And strewe thy walkes with my discheveld haire. . .	Dido	4.2.56	Anna
Since destinie doth call me from [thy] <the> shoare: . .	Dido	4.3.2	Aeneas
And let me linke [thy] <my> bodie to my <thy> lips, . . .	Dido	4.3.28	Aeneas
Is this thy love to me?	Dido	4.4.16	Dido
A grave, and not a lover fits thy age:--	Dido	4.5.30	Nurse
While Italy is cleane out of thy minde?	Dido	5.1.29	Hermes
Why wilt thou so betray thy sonnes good hap?	Dido	5.1.31	Hermes
That daylie dandlest Cupid in thy armes:	Dido	5.1.45	Aeneas
Spendst thou thy time about this little boy, ...	Dido	5.1.51	Hermes
If that be all, then cheare thy drooping lookes, . . .	Dido	5.1.71	Iarbus
Let some of those thy followers goe with me, ...	Dido	5.1.73	Iarbus
Thankes good Iarbus for thy friendly ayde, ...	Dido	5.1.75	Aeneas
But here he is, now Dido trie thy wit.	Dido	5.1.86	Dido
Aeneas, wherefore goe thy men abourd?	Dido	5.1.87	Dido
Why are thy ships new rigd?	Dido	5.1.88	Dido
Say thou wilt stay in Carthage with [thy] <my> Queene, . .	Dido	5.1.117	Dido
Aeneas, say, how canst thou take thy leave?	Dido	5.1.119	Dido
O thy lips have sworne/To stay with Dido:	Dido	5.1.120	Dido
Thy hand and mine have plighted mutuall faith, . . .	Dido	5.1.122	Dido
In vaine my love thou spendst thy fainting breath, . .	Dido	5.1.153	Aeneas
Thy mother was no Goddesse perjurd man, ...	Dido	5.1.156	Dido
Nor Dardanus the author of thy stocke:	Dido	5.1.157	Dido
Repairde not I thy ships, made thee a King, ...	Dido	5.1.163	Dido
And all thy needie followers Noblemen?	Dido	5.1.164	Dido
Wilt thou now slay me with thy venomed sting, . . .	Dido	5.1.167	Dido
That slayest me with thy harsh and hellish tale, . . .	Dido	5.1.217	Dido
And he hath all [my] <thy> fleete, what shall I doe/But dye in	Dido	5.1.268	Dido
Lay to thy hands and helpe me make a fire, ...	Dido	5.1.284	Dido
Now Dido, with these reliques burne thy selfe, . . .	Dido	5.1.292	Dido
Thou shalt burne first, thy crime is worse then his: .	Dido	5.1.297	Dido
Meaning to mangle all thy Provinces.	1Tamb	1.1.17	Cosroe
Ful true thou speakst, and like thy selfe my lord, . .	1Tamb	1.1.49	Mycet
Whom I may tearme a Damon for thy love.	1Tamb	1.1.50	Mycet
Then heare thy charge, valiant Theridamas, ...	1Tamb	1.1.57	Mycet
Go, stout Theridamas, thy words are swords, ...	1Tamb	1.1.74	Mycet
And with thy lookes thou conquerest all thy foes: . .	1Tamb	1.1.75	Mycet
Monster of Nature, shame unto thy stocke, ...	1Tamb	1.1.104	Mycet
That dar'st presume thy Soveraigne for to mocke. . . .	1Tamb	1.1.105	Mycet
thou art so meane a man)/And seeke not to inrich thy followers,	1Tamb	1.2.9	Zenoc
Thy person is more woorth to Tamburlaine, ...	1Tamb	1.2.90	Tamb
Thy Garments shall be made of Medean silke, ...	1Tamb	1.2.95	Tamb
Which with thy beautie will be soone resolv'd. . . .	1Tamb	1.2.101	Tamb
I see the folly of thy Emperour:	1Tamb	1.2.167	Tamb
That by Characters graven in thy browes, ...	1Tamb	1.2.169	Tamb
And by thy martiall face and stout aspect, ...	1Tamb	1.2.170	Tamb
Forsake thy king and do but joine with me/And we will triumph	1Tamb	1.2.172	Tamb
Draw foorth thy sword, thou mighty man at Armes, . . .	1Tamb	1.2.178	Tamb
And lead thy thousand horse with my conduct, ...	1Tamb	1.2.189	Tamb
Besides thy share of this Egyptian prise, ...	1Tamb	1.2.190	Tamb
Won with thy words, and conquered with thy looks, . . .	1Tamb	1.2.228	Therid
To be partaker of thy good or ill, ...	1Tamb	1.2.230	Therid
Thy selfe and them shall never part from me, ...	1Tamb	1.2.245	Tamb
Wel hast thou pourtraid in thy tearms of life, . . .	1Tamb	2.1.31	Cosroe
Thy wit will make us Conquerors to day.	1Tamb	2.2.58	Mycet
In thy approoved Fortunes all my hope, ...	1Tamb	2.3.2	Cosroe
I take thy doome for satisfaction.	1Tamb	2.3.5	Cosroe
now whet thy winged sword/And lift thy lofty arme into the	1Tamb	2.3.51	Cosroe
whet thy winged sword/And lift thy lofty arme into the cloudes,	1Tamb	2.3.52	Cosroe
Thy words assure me of kind successe:	1Tamb	2.3.60	Cosroe
Then shalt thou see me pull it from thy head:	1Tamb	2.4.39	Tamb

THY (cont.)

Now send Ambassage to thy neighbor Kings,	1Tamb	2.5.20		Cosroe
Judge by thy selfe Theridamas, not me,	1Tamb	2.5.93		Tamb
Who entring at the breach thy sword hath made,	1Tamb	2.7.9		Cosroe
Moov'd me to manage armes against thy state.	1Tamb	2.7.16		Tamb
Tell him thy Lord the Turkish Emperour,	1Tamb	3.1.22		Bajzth
Which thy prolonged Fates may draw on thee:	1Tamb	3.2.101		Agidas
Wherewith he may excruciate thy soule.	1Tamb	3.2.104		Agidas
Bassoe, by this thy Lord and maister knowes,	1Tamb	3.3.1		Tamb
Thy fall shall make me famous through the world:	1Tamb	3.3.83		Tamb
souldier of my Camp/Shall smile to see thy miserable state.	1Tamb	3.3.86		Tamb
And on thy head weare my Emperiall crowne,	1Tamb	3.3.113		Bajzth
That with thy lookes canst cleare the darkened Sky:	1Tamb	3.3.122		Tamb
Which I will bring as Vassals to thy feete.	1Tamb	3.3.129		Tamb
Thy souldiers armes could not endure to strike/So many blowes	1Tamb	3.3.143		Bajzth
When thy great Bassoe-maister and thy selfe,	1Tamb	3.3.173		Zenoc
Hearst thou Anippe, how thy drudge doth talk,	1Tamb	3.3.182		Zenoc
That offered jewels to thy sacred shrine,	1Tamb	3.3.199		Zabina
Straight will I use thee as thy pride deserves:	1Tamb	3.3.206		Zabina
Prepare thy selfe to live and die my slave.	1Tamb	3.3.207		Zabina
What, thinkst thou Tamburlain esteems thy gold?	1Tamb	3.3.262		Tamb
First shalt thou rip my bowels with thy sword,	1Tamb	4.2.16		Bajzth
Unworthy king, that by thy crueltie,	1Tamb	4.2.56		Zabina
Being thy Captive, thus abuse his state,	1Tamb	4.2.60		Zabina
And treading him beneath thy loathsome feet,	1Tamb	4.2.64		Zabina
Thy names and tytles, and thy dignities,	1Tamb	4.2.79		Tamb
my spirit doth foresee/The utter ruine of thy men and thee.	1Tamb	4.3.60		Arabia
To dim thy basenesse and obscurity,	1Tamb	4.3.65		Souldn
To race and scatter thy inglorious crue,	1Tamb	4.3.67		Souldn
Tamburlane) as I could willingly feed upon thy blood-raw hart.	1Tamb	4.4.12	P	Bajzth
to come by, plucke out that, and twil serve thee and thy wife:	1Tamb	4.4.14	P	Tamb
take it from my swords point, or Ile thrust it to thy heart.	1Tamb	4.4.41	P	Tamb
will make thee slice the brawnes of thy armes into carbonadoes,	1Tamb	4.4.44	P	Tamb
And wouldst thou have me buy thy Fathers love/With such a	1Tamb	4.4.83		Tamb
Content thy selfe, his person shall be safe,	1Tamb	4.4.87		Tamb
thou maist thinke thy selfe happie to be fed from my trencher.	1Tamb	4.4.92	P	Tamb
To thinke thy puisant never staied arme/Will part their bodies,	1Tamb	5.1.88		1Virgn
ruthlesse Governour/Have thus refusde the mercie of thy hand,	1Tamb	5.1.93		1Virgn
That never nourisht thought against thy rule,	1Tamb	5.1.98		1Virgn
To be investers of thy royall browes,	1Tamb	5.1.104		1Virgn
That in thy passion for thy countries love,	1Tamb	5.1.137		Tamb
And feare to see thy kingly Fathers harme,	1Tamb	5.1.138		Tamb
With haire discheweld wip'st thy watery cheeks:	1Tamb	5.1.139		Tamb
And sprinklest Saphyrs on thy shining face,	1Tamb	5.1.143		Tamb
Taking instructions from thy flowing eies:	1Tamb	5.1.146		Tamb
In silence of thy solemn Evenings walk,	1Tamb	5.1.148		Tamb
And gore thy body with as many wounds.	1Tamb	5.1.216		Bajzth
Sharpe forked arrowes light upon thy horse:	1Tamb	5.1.217		Bajzth
Volleyes of shot pierce through thy charmed Skin,	1Tamb	5.1.221		Bajzth
Or roaring Cannons sever all thy joints,	1Tamb	5.1.223		Bajzth
Sweet Bajazeth, I will prolong thy life,	1Tamb	5.1.283		Zabina
Now Bajazeth, abridge thy banefull daies,	1Tamb	5.1.286		Bajzth
And beat thy braines out of thy conquer'd head:	1Tamb	5.1.287		Bajzth
Hide now thy stained face in endles night,	1Tamb	5.1.292		Bajzth
Thy Fathers subjects and thy countrimen.	1Tamb	5.1.321		Zenoc
Thy streetes strowed with dissevered jointes of men,	1Tamb	5.1.322		Zenoc
the cause of this/That tearm'st Zenocrate thy dearest love?	1Tamb	5.1.336		Zenoc
Earth cast up fountaines from thy entralles,	1Tamb	5.1.347		Zenoc
And wet thy cheeks for their untimely deathes:	1Tamb	5.1.348		Zenoc
Thou that in conduct of thy happy stars,	1Tamb	5.1.358		Zenoc
Sleep'st every night with conquest on thy browes,	1Tamb	5.1.359		Zenoc
Leaving thy blood for witnesse of thy love.	1Tamb	5.1.411		Arabia
As much as thy faire body is for me.	1Tamb	5.1.416		Zenoc
accidents/Have chanc'd thy merits in this worthles bondage.	1Tamb	5.1.425		Arabia
Of thy deserv'd contentment and thy love:	1Tamb	5.1.427		Arabia
But making now a vertue of thy sight,	1Tamb	5.1.428		Arabia
Since thy desired hand shall close mine eies.	1Tamb	5.1.432		Arabia
A title higher than thy Souldans name:	1Tamb	5.1.434		Tamb
Thy princely daughter here shall set thee free.	1Tamb	5.1.436		Tamb
Mighty hath God and Mahomet made thy hand/(Renowmed Tamburlain)	1Tamb	5.1.479		Souldn
If as beseemes a person of thy state,	1Tamb	5.1.483		Souldn
Shall pay a yearly tribute to thy Syre.	1Tamb	5.1.519		Tamb
Thy first betrothed Love, Arabia,	1Tamb	5.1.530		Tamb
That thou thy self, then County-Pallatine,	2Tamb	1.1.94		Orcan
it out, or manage armes/Against thy selfe or thy confederates:	2Tamb	1.1.129		Sgsmnd
And sweare in sight of heaven and by thy Christ.	2Tamb	1.1.132		Orcan
if any Christian King/Encroche upon the confines of thy realme,	2Tamb	1.1.147		Orcan
Choose which thou wilt, all are at thy command.	2Tamb	1.2.31		Callap
With naked Negros shall thy coach be drawen,	2Tamb	1.2.40		Callap
The pavement underneath thy chariot wheels/With Turky Carpets	2Tamb	1.2.42		Callap
Fit objects for thy princely eie to pierce.	2Tamb	1.2.45		Callap
Betweene thy sons that shall be Emperours,	2Tamb	1.3.7		Tamb
leave these armes/And save thy sacred person free from scathe:	2Tamb	1.3.10		Zenoc
But that I know they issued from thy wombe,	2Tamb	1.3.33		Tamb
And I will teach thee how to charge thy foe,	2Tamb	1.3.45		Tamb
If thou exceed thy elder Brothers worth,	2Tamb	1.3.50		Tamb
them, and thy seed/Shall issue crowned from their mothers wombe.	2Tamb	1.3.52		Tamb
And cleave his Pericranion with thy sword.	2Tamb	1.3.101		Tamb
In all affection at thy kingly feet.	2Tamb	1.3.116		Therid
Wel said Argier, receive thy crowne againe.	2Tamb	1.3.127		Tamb
Is Barbary unpeopled for thy sake,	2Tamb	1.3.134		Usumc
All Barbary is unpeopled for thy sake.	2Tamb	1.3.149		Techel
Thanks king of Fesse, take here thy crowne again.	2Tamb	1.3.150		Tamb

THY (cont.)

papers as our sacrifice/And witnesse of thy servants perjury.	2Tamb	2.2.46	Orcan
If thou wilt proove thy selfe a perfect God,	2Tamb	2.2.56	Orcan
Techelles, draw thy sword,/And wound the earth, that it may	2Tamb	2.4.96	Tamb
For she is dead? thy words doo pierce my soule.	2Tamb	2.4.125	Tamb
or with a Curtle-axe/To hew thy flesh and make a gaping wound?	2Tamb	3.2.97	Tamb
View me thy father that hath conquered kings,	2Tamb	3.2.110	Tamb
Captaine, that thou yeeld up thy hold to us.	2Tamb	3.3.16	Therid
Nay Captain, thou art weary of thy life,	2Tamb	3.3.18	Techel
shall raise a hill/Of earth and fagots higher than thy Fort,	2Tamb	3.3.22	Therid
And over thy Argins and covered waies/Shal play upon the	2Tamb	3.3.23	Therid
Shal play upon the bulwarks of thy hold/Volleies of ordinance	2Tamb	3.3.24	Therid
not heaven it selfe/Shall ransome thee, thy wife and family.	2Tamb	3.3.28	Therid
That bring fresh water to thy men and thee:	2Tamb	3.3.30	Techel
And lie in trench before thy castle walles,	2Tamb	3.3.31	Techel
Now ugly death stretch out thy Sable wings,	2Tamb	3.4.16	Olymp
Therefore die by thy loving mothers hand,	2Tamb	3.4.23	Olymp
Who gently now wil lance thy Ivory throat,	2Tamb	3.4.24	Olymp
And him faire Lady shall thy eies behold.	2Tamb	3.4.67	Therid
Then welcome Tamburlaine unto thy death.	2Tamb	3.5.52	Callap
Now thou art fearfull of thy armies strength,	2Tamb	3.5.75	Orcan
Thinke of thy end, this sword shall lance thy throat.	2Tamb	3.5.78	Orcan
thou shalt kneele to us/And humbly crave a pardon for thy life.	2Tamb	3.5.109	Orcan
And all have jointly sworne thy cruell death,	2Tamb	3.5.112	Soria
Or rip thy bowels, and rend out thy heart,	2Tamb	3.5.121	Tamb
Searing thy hatefull flesh with burning yrons,	2Tamb	3.5.123	Tamb
while all thy joints/Be rackt and beat asunder with the wheele,	2Tamb	3.5.124	Tamb
So he shal, and weare thy head in his Scutchion.	2Tamb	3.5.138	P Orcan
Knowing my father hates thy cowardise,	2Tamb	4.1.23	Amyras
Thou doost dishonor manhood, and thy house.	2Tamb	4.1.32	Celeb
Cherish thy valour stil with fresh supplies:	2Tamb	4.1.87	Tamb
my striving hands/From martiall justice on thy wretched soule.	2Tamb	4.1.96	Tamb
Can never wash from thy distained browes.	2Tamb	4.1.110	Tamb
Made of the mould whereof thy selfe consists,	2Tamb	4.1.115	Tamb
Ready to levie power against thy throne,	2Tamb	4.1.117	Tamb
By Mahomet, thy mighty friend I sweare,	2Tamb	4.1.121	Tamb
Than he that darted mountaines at thy head,	2Tamb	4.1.128	Tamb
twixt our selves and thee/In this thy barbarous damned tyranny.	2Tamb	4.1.139	Orcan
Thy victories are growne so violent,	2Tamb	4.1.140	Jrslem
with the meteors/Of blood and fire thy tyrannies have made,	2Tamb	4.1.142	Jrslem
Will poure down blood and fire on thy head:	2Tamb	4.1.143	Jrslem
Whose scalding drops wil pierce thy seething braines,	2Tamb	4.1.144	Jrslem
whose weeping eies/Since thy arrivall here beheld no Sun,	2Tamb	4.2.2	Olymp
Hath stain'd thy cheekes, and made thee look like death,	2Tamb	4.2.4	Olymp
Devise some meanes to rid thee of thy life,	2Tamb	4.2.5	Olymp
And since this earth, dew'd with thy brinish teares,	2Tamb	4.2.8	Olymp
Nor yet this aier, beat often with thy sighes,	2Tamb	4.2.10	Olymp
Nor thy close Cave a sword to murther thee,	2Tamb	4.2.12	Olymp
Which with thy beauty thou wast woont to light,	2Tamb	4.2.16	Therid
him, in whom thy looks/Have greater operation and more force	2Tamb	4.2.28	Therid
For with thy view my joyes are at the full,	2Tamb	4.2.31	Therid
Nothing, but stil thy husband and thy sonne?	2Tamb	4.2.37	Therid
Commanding all thy princely eie desires,	2Tamb	4.2.43	Therid
What, have I slaine her? Villaine, stab thy selfe:	2Tamb	4.2.82	Therid
Thy youth forbids such ease my kingly boy,	2Tamb	4.3.29	Tamb
and to subdew/This proud contemner of thy dreadfull power,	2Tamb	4.3.40	Orcan
wilt thou so defame/The hatefull fortunes of thy victory,	2Tamb	4.3.78	Orcan
The violence of thy common Souldiours lust?	2Tamb	4.3.80	Orcan
Villaine, respects thou more thy slavish life,	2Tamb	5.1.10	Govnr
Than honor of thy countrie or thy name?	2Tamb	5.1.11	Govnr
As any thing of price with thy conceit?	2Tamb	5.1.14	Govnr
To save thy life, and us a litle labour,	2Tamb	5.1.50	Therid
Tyrant, I turne the traitor in thy throat,	2Tamb	5.1.54	Govnr
Tis not thy bloody tents can make me yeeld,	2Tamb	5.1.103	Govnr
Nor yet thy selfe, the anger of the highest,	2Tamb	5.1.104	Govnr
For though thy cannon shooke the citie walles,	2Tamb	5.1.105	Govnr
Do all thy wurst, nor death, nor Tamburlaine,	2Tamb	5.1.112	Govnr
First let thy Scythyan horse teare both our limmes/Rather then	2Tamb	5.1.138	Orcan
teare both our limmes/Rather then we should draw thy chariot,	2Tamb	5.1.139	Orcan
Rather lend me thy weapon Tamburlain,	2Tamb	5.1.142	Jrslem
And offer'd me as ransome for thy life,	2Tamb	5.1.156	Tamb
Come downe thy selfe and worke a myracle,	2Tamb	5.1.188	Tamb
fire to burne the writ/Wherein the sum of thy religion rests.	2Tamb	5.1.191	Tamb
To blow thy Alcaron up to thy throne,	2Tamb	5.1.193	Tamb
That shakes his sword against thy majesty,	2Tamb	5.1.196	Tamb
And spurns the Abstracts of thy foolish lawes.	2Tamb	5.1.197	Tamb
Aid thy obedient servant Callapine,	2Tamb	5.2.28	Callap
Blush heaven to loose the honor of thy name,	2Tamb	5.3.28	Usumc
To see thy foot-stoole set upon thy head,	2Tamb	5.3.29	Usumc
And let no basenesse in thy haughty breast,	2Tamb	5.3.30	Usumc
Which makes them manage armes against thy state,	2Tamb	5.3.36	Usumc
Thy instrument and note of Majesty,	2Tamb	5.3.38	Usumc
For if he die, thy glorie is disgrac'd,	2Tamb	5.3.40	Usumc
I and myne armie come to lode thy barke/With soules of thousand	2Tamb	5.3.73	Tamb
let me see how well/Thou wilt become thy fathers majestie.	2Tamb	5.3.184	Tamb
Let not thy love exceed thyne honor sonne,	2Tamb	5.3.199	Tamb
Nor bar thy mind that magnanimitie,	2Tamb	5.3.200	Tamb
Guiding thy chariot with thy Fathers hand.	2Tamb	5.3.229	Tamb
For if thy body thrive not full of thoughtes/As pure and fiery	2Tamb	5.3.236	Tamb
The nature of thy chariot wil not beare/A guide of baser temper	2Tamb	5.3.242	Tamb
Thy ships are safe, riding in Malta Rhode:	Jew	1.1.50	1Merch
And is thy credit not enough for that?	Jew	1.1.62	Barab
[But] <by> goe, goe thou thy wayes, discharge thy Ship,	Jew	1.1.82	Barab

THY (cont.)

Summon thy sences, call thy wits together:	Jew	1.1.178		Barab
And 'tis thy mony, Barabas, we seeke.	Jew	1.2.54		1Knght
Then pay thy halfe.	Jew	1.2.83		Govnr
But here in Malta, where thou gotst thy wealth,	Jew	1.2.101		Govnr
If your first curse fall heavy on thy head,	Jew	1.2.107		1Knght
'Tis not our fault, but thy inherent sinne.	Jew	1.2.109		1Knght
Sham'st thou not thus to justifie thy selfe,	Jew	1.2.119		Govnr
As if we knew not thy profession?	Jew	1.2.120		Govnr
If thou rely upon thy righteousnesse,	Jew	1.2.121		Govnr
Be patient and thy riches will increase.	Jew	1.2.122		Govnr
Thy fatall birth-day, forlorne Barabas;	Jew	1.2.192		Barab
Thy father has enough in store for thee.	Jew	1.2.227		Barab
to forgoe so much/Without provision for thy selfe and me.	Jew	1.2.243		Barab
For they have seiz'd upon thy house and wares.	Jew	1.2.251		Abigal
Displacing me; and of thy house they meane/To make a Nunnery,	Jew	1.2.255		Abigal
And seeme to them as if thy sinnes were great,	Jew	1.2.287		Barab
Well, daughter, say, what is thy suit with us?	Jew	1.2.321		Abbass
Child of perdition, and thy fathers shame,	Jew	1.2.344		Barab
Away accursed from thy fathers sight.	Jew	1.2.351		Barab
Yet let thy daughter be no longer blinde.	Jew	1.2.354		1Fryar
Blind, Fryer, I wrecke not thy perswasions.	Jew	1.2.355		Barab
Then father here receive thy happinesse.	Jew	2.1.44		Abigal
But I will practise thy enlargement thence:	Jew	2.1.53		Barab
Whence is thy ship that anchors in our Rhoad?	Jew	2.2.2		Govnr
But to admit a sale of these thy Turkes/We may not, nay we dare	Jew	2.2.21		Govnr
On this condition shall thy Turkes be sold.	Jew	2.2.42		Govnr
Tell me, hast thou thy health well?	Jew	2.3.121	P	Barab
Thinke of me as thy father; Sonne farewell.	Jew	2.3.149		Barab
Thou hast thy Crownes, fellow, come let's away.	Jew	2.3.158		Mater
Now let me know thy name, and therewithall/Thy birth,	Jew	2.3.163		Barab
Now let me know thy name, and therewithall/Thy birth, condition,	Jew	2.3.164		Barab
But to thy selfe smile when the Christians moane.	Jew	2.3.172		Barab
But tell me now, How hast thou spent thy time?	Jew	2.3.201		Barab
make account of me/As of thy fellow; we are villaines both:	Jew	2.3.214		Barab
Barabas, thou know'st I have lov'd thy daughter long.	Jew	2.3.288		Lodowk
This is thy Diamond, tell me, shall I have it?	Jew	2.3.292		Lodowk
'Tis not thy wealth, but her that I esteeme,	Jew	2.3.298		Lodowk
Yet crave I thy consent.	Jew	2.3.299		Lodowk
let him have thy hand,/But keepe thy heart till Don Mathias	Jew	2.3.306		Barab
But keepe thy heart till Don Mathias comes.	Jew	2.3.307		Barab
Then gentle Abigal plight thy faith to me.	Jew	2.3.315		Lodowk
Shee is thy wife, and thou shalt be mine heire.	Jew	2.3.328		Barab
I cannot choose but like thy readinesse:	Jew	2.3.377		Barab
These armes of mine shall be thy Sepulchre.	Jew	3.2.11		Govnr
Wretched Ferneze might have veng'd thy death.	Jew	3.2.14		Govnr
Thy sonne slew mine, and I'le revenge his death.	Jew	3.2.15		Mater
Looke, Katherin, looke, thy sonne gave mine these wounds.	Jew	3.2.16		Govnr
Was this the pursuit of thy policie?	Jew	3.3.37		Abigal
Abigal it is not yet long since/That I did labour thy admition,	Jew	3.3.57		1Fryar
For that will be most heavy to thy soule.	Jew	3.3.71		1Fryar
Thy father's, how?	Jew	3.3.72		1Fryar
Yet never shall these lips bewray thy life.	Jew	3.3.75		Abigal
False, and unkinde; what, hast thou lost thy father?	Jew	3.4.2		Barab
Come neere, my love, come neere, thy masters life,	Jew	3.4.14		Barab
And for thy sake, whom I so dearely love,	Jew	3.4.61		Barab
Assure thy selfe thou shalt have broth by the eye.	Jew	3.4.92		Barab
I'de cut thy throat if I did.	Jew	4.1.11		Barab
Thy daughter--	Jew	4.1.34		2Fryar
I, thy daughter--	Jew	4.1.35		1Fryar
Why does he goe to thy house? let him begone.	Jew	4.1.101		1Fryar
Sweet Bellamira, would I had my Masters wealth for thy sake.	Jew	4.2.55	P	Ithimr
I'le be thy Jason, thou my golden Fleece;	Jew	4.2.90		Ithimr
'Tis not thy mony, but thy selfe I weigh:	Jew	4.2.124		Curtzn
Why, wantst thou any of thy tale?	Jew	4.3.19	P	Barab
Whilst I in thy incony lap doe tumble.	Jew	4.4.29		Ithimr
Like thy breath, sweet-hart, no violet like 'em.	Jew	4.4.40		Ithimr
I bring thee newes by whom thy sonne was slaine:	Jew	5.1.10		Curtzn
Thou and thy Turk; 'twas you that slew my son.	Jew	5.1.27		Govnr
Ferneze, 'twas thy sonne that murder'd him.	Jew	5.1.45		Mater
Thou'st doom'd thy selfe, assault it presently.	Jew	5.1.97		Calym
much better/To [have] kept thy promise then be thus surpriz'd?	Jew	5.2.5		Calym
For thy desert we make thee Governor,	Jew	5.2.10		Calym
thy desert we make thee Governor,/Use them at thy discretion.	Jew	5.2.11		Calym
and Barabas we give/To guard thy person, these our Janizaries:	Jew	5.2.16		Calym
Thus hast thou gotten, by thy policie,	Jew	5.2.27		Barab
When as thy life shall be at their command?	Jew	5.2.33		Barab
Thou seest thy life, and Malta's happinesse,	Jew	5.2.52		Barab
This, Barabas; since things are in thy power,	Jew	5.2.57		Govnr
'Tis not thy life which can availe me ought,	Jew	5.2.62		Barab
privately procure/Great summes of mony for thy recompence:	Jew	5.2.88		Govnr
Goe walke about the City, see thy friends:	Jew	5.2.92		Barab
Tush, send not letters to 'em, goe thy selfe,	Jew	5.2.93		Barab
Wherein no danger shall betide thy life,	Jew	5.2.100		Barab
With all thy Bashawes and brave followers.	Jew	5.3.39		Msngr
That thou maist feast them in thy Citadell.	Jew	5.5.16		Msngr
I trust thy word, take what I promis'd thee.	Jew	5.5.43		Govnr
Should I in pitty of thy plaints or thee,	Jew	5.5.72		Govnr
No, thus I'le see thy treachery repaid,	Jew	5.5.74		Govnr
Then Barabas breath forth thy latest fate,	Jew	5.5.78		Barab
And in the fury of thy torments, strive/To end thy life with	Jew	5.5.79		Barab
fury of thy torments, strive/To end thy life with resolution:	Jew	5.5.80		Barab
Know, Governor, 'twas I that slew thy sonne;	Jew	5.5.81		Barab

THY (cont.)

Know, Calymath, I aym'd thy overthrow,	Jew	5.5.83	Barab
Dye life, flye soule, tongue curse thy fill and dye.	Jew	5.5.89	Barab
This traine he laid to have intrap'd thy life;	Jew	5.5.91	Govnr
But I have rather chose to save thy life.	Jew	5.5.94	Govnr
For with thy Gallyes couldst thou not get hence,	Jew	5.5.100	Govnr
Blowne up, and all thy souldiers massacred.	Jew	5.5.107	Govnr
till thy father hath made good/The ruines done to Malta and to	Jew	5.5.111	Govnr
Thankes my good freend, I will requite thy love.	P 78	2.21	Guise
Now come thou forth and play thy tragick part,	P 85	2.28	Guise
Discharge thy musket and perfourme his death:	P 88	2.31	Guise
Since thou hast all the Cardes within thy hands/To shuffle or	P 146	2.89	Guise
That right or wrong, thou deale thy selfe a King.	P 148	2.91	Guise
is massacred)/Infect thy gracious brest with fresh supply,	P 193	3.28	QnMarg
Thus in despite of thy Religion,	P 314	5.41	Guise
The Duke of Guise stampes on thy liveles bulke.	P 315	5.42	Guise
And thou a traitor to thy soule and him.	P 342	5.69	Lorein
Flye Ramus flye, if thou wilt save thy life.	P 365	7.5	Taleus
The Guisians are hard at thy doore,	P 367	7.7	Taleus
Thou traitor Guise, lay of thy bloudy hands.	P 439	7.79	Navrre
O say not so, thou kill'st thy mothers heart.	P 539	11.4	QnMoth
What art thou dead, sweet sonne speak to thy Mother.	P 551	11.16	QnMoth
Welcome to France thy fathers royall seate,	P 590	12.3	QnMoth
A warlike people to maintaine thy right,	P 592	12.5	QnMoth
A loving mother to preserve thy state,	P 594	12.7	QnMoth
Thy brother Guise and we may now provide,	P 636	12.49	QnMoth
Am I growne olde, or is thy lust growne yong,	P 681	13.25	Guise
In sight and judgement of thy lustfull eye?	P 687	13.31	Guise
Mor du, wert <were> not the fruit within thy wombe,	P 688	13.32	Guise
Hence strumpet, hide thy head for shame,	P 691	13.35	Guise
At thy request I am content thou goe,	P 746	15.4	King
Regarding still the danger of thy life.	P 748	15.6	King
For he hath solemnely sworne thy death.	P 777	15.35	King
The Pope and King of Spaine are thy good frends,	P 843	17.38	Eprnon
I cannot brook thy hauty insolence,	P 862	17.57	King
Dismisse thy campe or else by our Edict,	P 863	17.58	King
Then come proud Guise and heere disgordge thy brest,	P 952	19.22	King
And end thy endles treasons with thy death.	P 955	19.25	King
Come Guise and see thy traiterous guile outreacht,	P 962	19.32	King
Cry out, exclaime, houle till thy throat be hoarce,	P1077	19.147	King
Oh what may I doe, for to revenge thy death?	P1108	21.2	Dumain
I am thy brother, and ile revenge thy death,	P1112	21.6	Dumain
Frier, thou dost acknowledge me thy King?	P1164	22.26	King
Agent for England, send thy mistres word,	P1194	22.56	King
Navarre, give me thy hand, I heere do sweare,	P1203	22.65	King
Sweet Epernoune thy King must dye.	P1228	22.90	King
Ah Epernoune, is this thy love to me?	P1235	22.97	King
Henry thy King wipes of these childish teares,	P1236	22.98	King
And bids thee whet thy sword on Sextus bones,	P1237	22.99	King
enoughe to worke/thy Just degestione with extreamest shame	Paris	ms27,p391	Guise
And share the kingdom with thy deerest friend.	Edw	1.1.2	Gavstn
Sweete prince I come, these these thy amorous lines,	Edw	1.1.6	Gavstn
So thou wouldst smile and take me in thy <thine> armes.	Edw	1.1.9	Gavstn
Shall sleepe within the scabberd at thy neede,	Edw	1.1.87	Mortmr
And underneath thy banners march who will,	Edw	1.1.88	Mortmr
Beseemes it thee to contradict thy king?	Edw	1.1.92	Edward
The sworde shall plane the furrowes of thy browes,	Edw	1.1.94	Edward
Bridle thy anger gentle Mortimer.	Edw	1.1.121	Warwck
To floate in bloud, and at thy wanton head,	Edw	1.1.132	Lncstr
The glozing head of thy base minion throwne.	Edw	1.1.133	Lncstr
Thy friend, thy selfe, another Gaveston.	Edw	1.1.143	Edward
Then thou hast beene of me since thy exile.	Edw	1.1.145	Edward
I have my wish, in that I joy thy sight,	Edw	1.1.151	Edward
Thy woorth sweet friend is far above my guifts,	Edw	1.1.161	Edward
Fearst thou thy person? thou shalt have a guard:	Edw	1.1.166	Edward
What so thy minde affectes or fancie likes.	Edw	1.1.170	Edward
And make him serve thee as thy chaplaine,	Edw	1.1.195	Edward
For these thy superstitious taperlights,	Edw	1.4.98	Edward
Wherewith thy antichristian churches blaze,	Edw	1.4.99	Edward
Ile fire thy crased buildings, and enforce/The papall towers,	Edw	1.4.100	Edward
Rend not my hart with thy too piercing words,	Edw	1.4.117	Edward
But come sweete friend, ile beare thee on thy way.	Edw	1.4.140	Edward
And by thy meanes is Gaveston exilde.	Edw	1.4.155	Edward
Assure thy selfe thou comst not in my sight.	Edw	1.4.169	Edward
Fie Mortimer, dishonor not thy selfe,	Edw	1.4.244	Lncstr
Ile hang a golden tongue about thy neck,	Edw	1.4.328	Edward
A second mariage twixt thy selfe and me.	Edw	1.4.335	Edward
Couragious Lancaster, imbrace thy king,	Edw	1.4.340	Edward
Even so let hatred with thy [soveraignes] <soveraigne> smile.	Edw	1.4.342	Edward
Leave now to oppose thy selfe against the king,	Edw	1.4.387	MortSr
What needst thou, love, thus to excuse thy selfe?	Edw	2.1.60	Neece
Thy service Spencer shalbe thought upon.	Edw	2.1.80	Neece
But tell me Mortimer, whats thy devise,	Edw	2.2.11	Edward
Welcome to Tinmouth, welcome to thy friend,	Edw	2.2.51	Edward
Thy absence made me droope, and pine away,	Edw	2.2.52	Edward
and now thy sight/Is sweeter farre, then was thy parting hence	Edw	2.2.56	Edward
then was thy parting hence/Bitter and irkesome to my sobbing	Edw	2.2.57	Edward
Returne it to their throtes, ile be thy warrant.	Edw	2.2.73	Edward
Villaine thy life, unlesse I misse mine aime.	Edw	2.2.84	Mortmr
Warwicke, these words do ill beseeme thy years.	Edw	2.2.94	Kent
Have drawne thy treasure drie, and made thee weake,	Edw	2.2.159	Mortmr
Thy garrisons are beaten out of Fraunce,	Edw	2.2.162	Lncstr
While in the harbor ride thy ships unrigd.	Edw	2.2.169	Mortmr

THY (cont.)

Thy gentle Queene, sole sister to Valoys,	Edw		2.2.172	Lncstr
Thy court is naked, being bereft of those,	Edw		2.2.174	Mortmr
Ballads and rimes, made of thy overthrow.	Edw		2.2.178	Mortmr
But once, and then thy souldiers marcht like players,	Edw		2.2.183	Mortmr
not armor, and thy selfe/Bedaubd with golde, rode laughing at	Edw		2.2.184	Mortmr
Nodding and shaking of thy spangled crest,	Edw		2.2.186	Mortmr
Edward, unfolde thy pawes,/And let their lives bloud slake thy	Edw		2.2.204	Edward
And let their lives bloud slake thy furies hunger:	Edw		2.2.205	Edward
No marvell though thou scorne thy noble peeres,	Edw		2.2.217	Kent
When I thy brother am rejected thus.	Edw		2.2.218	Kent
No farewell, to poore Isabell, thy Queene?	Edw		2.4.13	Queene
Thou proud disturber of thy countries peace,	Edw		2.5.9	Mortmr
Corrupter of thy king, cause of these broiles,	Edw		2.5.10	Mortmr
weapons point here shouldst thou fall,/And welter in thy goare.	Edw		2.5.14	Mortmr
Gaveston, short warning/Shall serve thy turne:	Edw		2.5.22	Warwck
That here severelie we will execute/Upon thy person:	Edw		2.5.24	Warwck
Renowmed Edward, how thy name/Revives poore Gaveston.	Edw		2.5.41	Gavstn
Question with thy companions and thy mates.	Edw		2.5.73	Mortmr
in the morning/We will discharge thee of thy charge, be gon.	Edw		2.5.109	Penbrk
O treacherous Warwicke thus to wrong thy friend!	Edw		2.6.1	Gavstn
Come, let thy shadow parley with king Edward.	Edw		2.6.14	Warwck
Then tell thy prince, of whence, and what thou art.	Edw		3.1.35	Edward
Thy father Spencer?	Edw		3.1.43	Edward
Spencer, this love, this kindnes to thy King,	Edw		3.1.47	Edward
Argues thy noble minde and disposition:	Edw		3.1.48	Edward
this towardnes makes thy mother feare/Thou art not markt to	Edw		3.1.79	Queene
Well, say thy message.	Edw		3.1.155	Edward
now get thee to thy lords,/And tell them I will come to	Edw		3.1.177	Edward
Edward with fire and sword, followes at thy heeles.	Edw		3.1.180	Edward
No Edward, no, thy flatterers faint and flie.	Edw		3.1.201	Mortmr
Traitor on thy face, rebellious Lancaster.	Edw		3.1.204	Spencr
And rather bathe thy sword in subjects bloud,	Edw		3.1.212	Mortmr
Brother, in regard of thee and of thy land,	Edw		3.1.230	Kent
Did they remoove that flatterer from thy throne.	Edw		3.1.231	Kent
For which thy head shall over looke the rest,	Edw		3.1.239	Edward
Tyrant, I scorne thy threats and menaces,	Edw		3.1.241	Warwck
England, unkinde to thy nobilitie,	Edw		3.1.250	Mortmr
ragged stonie walles/Immure thy vertue that aspires to heaven?	Edw		3.1.257	Mortmr
A brother, no, a butcher of thy friends,	Edw		4.1.4	Kent
Proud Edward, doost thou banish me thy presence?	Edw		4.1.5	Kent
Mortimer I stay thy sweet escape,	Edw		4.1.10	Kent
But hath thy potion wrought so happilie?	Edw		4.1.14	Kent
Whether, O whether doost thou bend thy steps?	Edw		4.2.12	Queene
Oh my sweet hart, how do I mone thy wrongs,	Edw		4.2.27	Queene
Sir John of Henolt, be it thy renowne,	Edw		4.2.78	Mortmr
Whose loosnes hath betrayed thy land to spoyle,	Edw		4.4.11	Queene
thou chase/Thy lawfull king thy soveraigne with thy sword?	Edw		4.6.4	Kent
Borne armes against thy brother and thy king?	Edw		4.6.6	Kent
Edward, this Mortimer aimes at thy life:	Edw		4.6.10	Kent
Proud Mortimer pries neare into thy walkes.	Edw		4.6.18	Kent
Father, thy face should harbor no deceit,	Edw		4.7.8	Edward
a king, thy hart/Pierced deeply with sence of my distresse,	Edw		4.7.9	Edward
good father on thy lap/Lay I this head, laden with mickle care,	Edw		4.7.39	Edward
Rent sphere of heaven, and fier forsake thy orbe,	Edw		4.7.102	Spencr
Make for a new life man, throw up thy eyes,	Edw		4.7.107	Baldck
Thy speeches long agoe had easde my sorrowes,	Edw		5.1.6	Edward
They passe not for thy frownes as late they did,	Edw		5.1.77	Edward
Come death, and with thy fingers close my eyes,	Edw		5.1.110	Edward
And tell thy message to my naked brest.	Edw		5.1.130	Edward
Edmund, yeeld thou thy self, or thou shalt die.	Edw		5.3.56	Matrvs
Art thou king, must I die at thy commaund?	Edw		5.4.103	Kent
Feare not sweete boye, ile garde thee from thy foes,	Edw		5.4.111	Queene
Had Edmund liv'de, he would have sought thy death.	Edw		5.4.112	Queene
Small comfort findes poore Edward in thy lookes,	Edw		5.5.44	Edward
And then thy heart, were it as Gurneys is,	Edw		5.5.53	Edward
I see my tragedie written in thy browes,	Edw		5.5.74	Edward
Yet stay a while, forbeare thy bloudie hande,	Edw		5.5.75	Edward
O if thou harborst murther in thy hart,	Edw		5.5.87	Edward
Let this gift change thy minde, and save thy soule,	Edw		5.5.88	Edward
To rid thee of thy life. Matrevis come.	Edw		5.5.107	Ltborn
Excellent well, take this for thy rewarde.	Edw		5.5.117	Gurney
if thou now growest penitent/Ile be thy ghostly father,	Edw		5.6.4	Mortmr
Thinke not that I am frighted with thy words,	Edw		5.6.27	King
My father's murdered through thy treacherie,	Edw		5.6.28	King
Thy hatefull and accursed head shall lie,	Edw		5.6.30	King
To witnesse to the world, that by thy meanes,	Edw		5.6.31	King
now I see, that in thy wheele/There is a point, to which when	Edw		5.6.59	Mortmr
As thou receivedst thy life from me,	Edw		5.6.68	Queene
Sweete father heere, unto thy murdered ghost,	Edw		5.6.99	King
Settle thy studies Faustus, and begin/To sound the depth of	F	29	1.1.1	Faust
[Is not thy common talke sound Aphorismes]?	F	47	1.1.19A	Faust
Are not thy bils hung up as monuments,	F	48	1.1.20	Faust
god>,/Here <Faustus> tire my <trie thy> braines to get a Deity.	F	90	1.1.62	Faust
And gaze not on it least it tempt thy soule,	F	98	1.1.70	GdAngl
And heape Gods heavy wrath upon thy head.	F	99	1.1.71	GdAngl
Faustus, these bookes, thy wit, and our experience,	F	146	1.1.118	Valdes
How now sirra, where's thy Maister?	F	197	1.2.4	P 1Schol
And try if devils will obey thy Hest,	F	234	1.3.6	Faust
I charge thee to returne, and change thy shape,	F	251	1.3.23	Faust
Tell me, what is that Lucifer, thy Lord?	F	290	1.3.62	Faust
And then resolve me of thy Maisters mind.	F	328	1.3.100	Faust
thou dost not presently bind thy selfe to me for seven yeares,	F	361	1.4.19	P Wagner

THY (cont.)

prepare thy selfe, for I will presently raise up two devils to	F 372	1.4.30	P	Wagner
I sirra, I'le teach thee to turne thy selfe to a Dog, or a Cat,	F 382	1.4.40	P	Wagner
Now tell me what saith <sayes> Lucifer thy Lord.	F 419	2.1.31		Faust
And tell me, what good will my soule do thy Lord?	F 428	2.1.40		Faust
But tell me Faustus, shall I have thy soule?	F 434	2.1.46		Mephst
And I will be thy slave and waite on thee,	F 435	2.1.47		Mephst
Then Faustus stab thy <thine> Arme couragiously,	F 438	2.1.50		Mephst
And bind thy soule, that at some certaine day/Great Lucifer may	F 439	2.1.51		Mephst
Why shouldst thou not? is not thy soule thine owne?	F 457	2.1.69		Faust
Nothing Faustus but to delight thy mind <withall>,/And let thee	F 473	2.1.85		Mephst
I, thinke so still, till experience change thy mind.	F 517	2.1.129		Mephst
In which <Wherein> thou hast given thy soule to Lucifer.	F 520	2.1.132		Mephst
<Tel Faustus, how dost thou like thy wife>?	F 533	(HC261)A	P	Mephst
And bring them every morning to thy bed:	F 538	2.1.150		Mephst
She whom thine eye shall like, thy heart shall have,	F 539	2.1.151		Mephst
Pronounce this thrice devoutly to thy selfe,	F 547	2.1.159		Mephst
'Twas thine own seeking Faustus, thanke thy selfe.	F 555	2.2.4		Mephst
Repent and they shall never raise thy skin.	F 633	2.2.82		GdAngl
Christ cannot save thy soule, for he is just,	F 636	2.2.85		Lucifr
O Faustus they are come to fetch <away> thy soule.	F 641	2.2.90		Faust
Thou calst on <talkst of> Christ contrary to thy promise.	F 643	2.2.92		Lucifr
So shalt thou shew thy selfe an obedient servant <Do so>,/And	F 652	2.2.101		Lucifr
Choke thy selfe Glutton: What are thou the sixt?	F 704	2.2.153		Faust
And thou shalt turne thy selfe into what shape thou wilt.	F 718	2.2.170		Lucifr
a paire of hornes on's head as e're thou sawest in thy life.	F 738	2.3.17	P	Robin
put off thy cloathes, and I'le conjure thee about presently:	F 746	2.3.25	P	Robin
And then devise what best contents thy minde,	F 858	3.1.80		Mephst
Whilst on thy backe his hollinesse ascends/Saint Peters Chaire	F 869	3.1.91		Raymnd
And smite with death thy hated enterprise.	F 880	3.1.102		Pope
Thy selfe and I, may parly with this Pope:	F 896	3.1.118		Faust
Now Faustus, come prepare thy selfe for mirth,	F 981	3.2.1		Mephst
Whilst on thy head I lay my hand,	F 995	3.2.15		Mephst
That no eye may thy body see.	F1003	3.2.23		Mephst
Now Robin, now or never shew thy cunning.	F1095	3.3.8	P	Dick
and stir not for thy life, Vintner you shall have your cup	F1113	3.3.26	P	Robin
be thou transformed to/A dog, and carry him upon thy backe;	F1131	3.3.44		Mephst
Come leave thy chamber first, and thou shalt see/This Conjurer	F1185	4.1.31		Mrtino
Wilt thou stand in thy Window, and see it then?	F1195	4.1.41		Mrtino
Nay, and thy hornes hold, tis no matter for thy head, for that's	F1288	4.1.134	P	Emper
hold, tis no matter for thy head, for that's arm'd sufficiently.	F1288	4.1.134	P	Emper
In recompence of this thy high desert,	F1322	4.1.168		Emper
let us sway thy thoughts/From this attempt against the	F1325	4.2.1		Mrtino
Then Faustus try thy skill:	F1425	4.2.101		Faust
Thy fatall time drawes to a finall end;	F1479	4.4.23		Faust
With all my heart kind Doctor, please thy selfe,	F1623	4.6.66		Duke
Our servants, and our Courts at thy command.	F1624	4.6.67		Duke
'faith Ile drinke a health to thy woodden leg for that word.	F1627	4.6.70	P	HrsCsr
This Magicke, that will charme thy soule to hell,	F1708	5.1.35		OldMan
And pitty of thy future miserie.	F1721	5.1.48		OldMan
Checking thy body, may amend thy soule.	F1723	5.1.50		OldMan
[Ah] <O> stay good Faustus, stay thy desperate steps.	F1729	5.1.56		OldMan
I see an Angell hover <hovers> ore thy head,	F1730	5.1.57		OldMan
Offers to poure the same into thy soule,	F1732	5.1.59		OldMan
I feele thy words to comfort my distressed soule,	F1735	5.1.62		Faust
Fearing the enemy <ruine> of thy haplesse <hopelesse> soule.	F1738	5.1.65		OldMan
Thou traytor Faustus, I arrest thy soule,	F1743	5.1.70		Mephst
Revolt, or I'le in peece-meale teare thy flesh.	F1745	5.1.72		Mephst
intreat thy Lord/To pardon my unjust presumption,	F1747	5.1.74		Faust
Lest greater dangers <danger> do attend thy drift.	F1752	5.1.79		Mephst
That durst disswade me from thy Lucifer,	F1754	5.1.81		Faust
And weare thy colours on my plumed crest.	F1778	5.1.105		Faust
[That from thy soule exclud'st the grace of heaven],	F1789	5.1.116A		OldMan
To wait upon thy soule; the time is come/Which makes it	F1802	5.2.6		Lucifr
For that must be thy mansion, there to dwell.	F1882	5.2.86		Mephst
O thou bewitching fiend, 'twas thy temptation,	F1883	5.2.87		Faust
Damb'd up thy passage; when thou took'st the booke,	F1887	5.2.91		Mephst
O what will all thy riches, pleasures, pompes,	F1896	5.2.100		GdAngl
And now poore soule must thy good Angell leave thee,	F1907	5.2.111		GdAngl
No Faustus, curse thy selfe, curse Lucifer,	F1973	5.2.177		Faust
I will teach thee to turne thy selfe to anything, to a dogge,	F App	p.231 58	P	Wagner
and let thy left eye be diametarily fixt upon my right heele,	F App	p.231 69	P	Wagner
then turn her and wind hir to thy owne use, as often as thou	F App	p.234 27	P	Robin
Ile feede thy divel with horse-bread as long as he lives,	F App	p.234 30	P	Rafe
Peccatum peccatorum, heeres thy goblet, good Vintner.	F App	p.235 28	P	Rafe
good divel forgive me now, and Ile never rob thy Library more.	F App	p.235 31	P	Robin
Ifaith thy head will never be out of the potage pot.	F App	p.236 48	P	Robin
have heard strange report of thy knowledge in the blacke Arte,	F App	p.236 2	P	Emper
that thou let me see some proofe of thy skil, that mine eies	F App	p.236 6	P	Emper
thee hornes, but makes thee weare them, feele on thy head.	F App	p.238 71	P	Emper
Thy fatall time doth drawe to finall ende,	F App	p.240 122		Faust
To guide thy steps unto the way of life,	F App	p.243 35		OldMan
heavinesse/Of thy most vilde and loathsome filthinesse,	F App	p.243 40		OldMan
But mercie Faustus of thy Saviour sweete,	F App	p.243 44		OldMan
Whose bloud alone must wash away thy guilt.	F App	p.243 45		OldMan
conquer all the earth, then turne thy force/Against thy selfe:	Lucan, First Booke			22
conquer all the earth, then turne thy force/Against thy selfe:	Lucan, First Booke			23
But neither chuse the north t'erect thy seat;	Lucan, First Booke			53
Whence thou shouldst view thy Roome with squinting beams.	Lucan, First Booke			55
The burdened axes with thy force will bend;	Lucan, First Booke			57
Thy power inspires the Muze that sings this war.	Lucan, First Booke			66
O Roome thy selfe art cause of all these evils,	Lucan, First Booke			84
Thy selfe thus shivered out to three mens shares:	Lucan, First Booke			85

THY (cont.)

longer life/Thou hadst restrainde thy headstrong husbands rage,	Lucan, First Booke	116
Yea and thy father to, and swords thrown down,	Lucan, First Booke	117
Thy death broake amity and trainde to war,	Lucan, First Booke	119
Caesar is thine, so please it thee, thy soldier;	Lucan, First Booke	204
Five yeeres I lengthned thy commaund in France:	Lucan, First Booke	277
let thy sword bring us home.	Lucan, First Booke	280
denies all, with thy bloud must thou/Abie thy conquest past:	Lucan, First Booke	289
denies all, with thy bloud must thou/Abie thy conquest past:	Lucan, First Booke	290
Speake, when shall this thy long usurpt power end?	Lucan, First Booke	333
At last learne wretch to leave thy monarchy;	Lucan, First Booke	335
We grieve at this thy patience and delay:	Lucan, First Booke	362
Caesar; he whom I heare thy trumpets charge/I hould no Romaine;	Lucan, First Booke	374
by these ten blest ensignes/And all thy several triumphs,	Lucan, First Booke	376
Thou Roome at name of warre runst from thy selfe,	Lucan, First Booke	517
And wilt not trust thy Citty walls one night:	Lucan, First Booke	518
Or if Fate rule them, Rome thy Cittizens/Are neere some plague:	Lucan, First Booke	643
O Phoebus shouldst thou with thy rayes now sing/The fell Nemean	Lucan, First Booke	654
And heaven tormented with thy chafing heate,	Lucan, First Booke	656
But thy fiers hurt not; Mars, 'tis thou enflam'st/The	Lucan, First Booke	657
Two tane away, thy labor will be lesse:	Ovid's Elegies	1.1.4
[What] <That> if thy Mother take Dianas bowe,	Ovid's Elegies	1.1.11
Great are thy kingdomes, over strong and large,	Ovid's Elegies	1.1.17
Loe I confesse, I am thy captive I,	Ovid's Elegies	1.2.19
Yoke Venus Doves, put Mirtle on thy haire,	Ovid's Elegies	1.2.23
Guiding the harmelesse Pigeons with thy hand.	Ovid's Elegies	1.2.26
So will thy [triumph] <triumphs> seeme magnificall.	Ovid's Elegies	1.2.28
Io, triumphing shall thy people sing.	Ovid's Elegies	1.2.34
Take these away, where is thy <thine> honor then?	Ovid's Elegies	1.2.38
Thy mother shall from heaven applaud this show,	Ovid's Elegies	1.2.39
With beautie of thy wings, thy faire haire guilded,	Ovid's Elegies	1.2.41
In spite of thee, forth will thy <thine> arrowes flie,	Ovid's Elegies	1.2.45
Then seeing I grace thy show in following thee,	Ovid's Elegies	1.2.49
Forbeare to hurt thy selfe in spoyling mee.	Ovid's Elegies	1.2.50
Beholde thy kinsmans Caesars prosperous bandes,	Ovid's Elegies	1.2.51
And Cupide who hath markt me for thy pray,	Ovid's Elegies	1.3.12
That I may write things worthy thy faire lookes:	Ovid's Elegies	1.3.20
Thy husband to a banquet goes with me,	Ovid's Elegies	1.4.1
About thy neck shall he at pleasure skippe?	Ovid's Elegies	1.4.6
But how thou shouldst behave thy selfe now know;	Ovid's Elegies	1.4.11
Before thy husband come, though I not see/What may be done, yet	Ovid's Elegies	1.4.13
When our lascivious toyes come in thy minde,	Ovid's Elegies	1.4.21
Thy Rosie cheekes be to thy thombe inclinde.	Ovid's Elegies	1.4.22
Let thy soft finger to thy eare be brought.	Ovid's Elegies	1.4.24
Turne round thy gold-ring, as it were to ease thee.	Ovid's Elegies	1.4.26
When thou doest wish thy husband at the devill.	Ovid's Elegies	1.4.28
Let not thy necke by his vile armes be prest,	Ovid's Elegies	1.4.35
Nor [leane] <leave> thy soft head on his boistrous brest.	Ovid's Elegies	1.4.36
Thy bosomes Roseat buds let him not finger,	Ovid's Elegies	1.4.37
Chiefely on thy lips let not his lips linger.	Ovid's Elegies	1.4.38
Yet this Ile see, but if thy gowne ought cover,	Ovid's Elegies	1.4.41
Nor thy soft foote with his hard foote combine.	Ovid's Elegies	1.4.44
Do not thou so, but throw thy mantle hence,	Ovid's Elegies	1.4.49
Entreat thy husband drinke, but do not kisse,	Ovid's Elegies	1.4.51
At night thy husband clippes thee, I will weepe/And to the	Ovid's Elegies	1.4.61
I will weepe/And to the dores sight of thy selfe [will] keepe:	Ovid's Elegies	1.4.62
Constrain'd against thy will give it the pezant,	Ovid's Elegies	1.4.65
But though this night thy fortune be to trie it,	Ovid's Elegies	1.4.69
Thy lightning can my life in pieces batter.	Ovid's Elegies	1.6.16
For thee I did thy mistris faire entreate.	Ovid's Elegies	1.6.20
But now perchaunce thy wench with thee doth rest,	Ovid's Elegies	1.6.45
Ah howe thy lot is above my lot blest:	Ovid's Elegies	1.6.46
Come breake these deafe dores with thy boysterous wind.	Ovid's Elegies	1.6.54
Deflowr'd except, within thy Temple wall.	Ovid's Elegies	1.7.18
Pay vowes to Jove, engirt thy hayres with baies,	Ovid's Elegies	1.7.36
And let the troupes which shall thy Chariot follow,	Ovid's Elegies	1.7.37
griefe appease)/With thy sharpe nayles upon my face to seaze.	Ovid's Elegies	1.7.64
(Anger will helpe thy hands though nere so weake).	Ovid's Elegies	1.7.66
Put in their place thy keembed haires againe.	Ovid's Elegies	1.7.68
He staide, and on thy lookes his gazes seaz'd.	Ovid's Elegies	1.8.24
none thy face exceedes,/Aye me, thy body hath no worthy weedes.	Ovid's Elegies	1.8.25
Aye me, thy body hath no worthy weedes.	Ovid's Elegies	1.8.26
Venus thy side doth warme,/And brings good fortune, a rich	Ovid's Elegies	1.8.30
a rich lover plants/His love on thee, and can supply thy wants.	Ovid's Elegies	1.8.32
When on thy lappe thine eyes thou dost deject,	Ovid's Elegies	1.8.37
Shake off these wrinckles that thy front assault,	Ovid's Elegies	1.8.45
Poore lover with thy gransires I exile thee.	Ovid's Elegies	1.8.66
Make a small price, while thou thy nets doest lay,	Ovid's Elegies	1.8.69
Deny him oft, feigne now thy head doth ake:	Ovid's Elegies	1.8.73
To beggers shut, to bringers ope thy gate,	Ovid's Elegies	1.8.77
Thy fault with his fault so repuls'd will vanish.	Ovid's Elegies	1.8.80
That this, or that man may thy cheekes moist keepe.	Ovid's Elegies	1.8.84
Servants fit for thy purpose thou must hire/To teach thy lover,	Ovid's Elegies	1.8.87
Servants fit for thy purpose thou must hire/To teach thy lover,	Ovid's Elegies	1.8.88
thou must hire/To teach thy lover, what thy thoughts desire.	Ovid's Elegies	1.8.88
By keeping of thy birth make but a shift.	Ovid's Elegies	1.8.94
let him viewe/And thy neck with lascivious markes made blew.	Ovid's Elegies	1.8.98
Let thy tongue flatter, while thy minde harme-workes:	Ovid's Elegies	1.8.103
While thou wert plaine, I lov'd thy minde and face:	Ovid's Elegies	1.10.13
Now inward faults thy outward forme disgrace.	Ovid's Elegies	1.10.14
Or prostitute thy beauty for bad prize.	Ovid's Elegies	1.10.42
He wants no gifts into thy lap to hurle.	Ovid's Elegies	1.10.54
Thy service for nights scapes is knowne commodious/And to give	Ovid's Elegies	1.11.3

THY (cont.)

Corinna clips me oft by thy perswasion,	Ovid's Elegies	1.11.5
Never to harme me made thy faith evasion.	Ovid's Elegies	1.11.6
are in thy soft brest/But pure simplicity in thee doth rest.	Ovid's Elegies	1.11.9
Defend the ensignes of thy warre in mee.	Ovid's Elegies	1.11.12
dore more wisely/And som-what higher beare thy foote precisely.	Ovid's Elegies	1.12.6
More fitly had [they] <thy> wrangling bondes contained/From	Ovid's Elegies	1.12.23
Hold in thy rosie horses that they move not.	Ovid's Elegies	1.13.10
Poore travailers though tierd, rise at thy sight,	Ovid's Elegies	1.13.13
The lawier and the client <both do> hate thy view,	Ovid's Elegies	1.13.21
By thy meanes women of their rest are bard,	Ovid's Elegies	1.13.23
Nor morning starres shunne thy uprising face.	Ovid's Elegies	1.13.28
How oft, that either wind would breake thy coche,	Ovid's Elegies	1.13.29
Memnon the elfe/Received his cole-blacke colour from thy selfe.	Ovid's Elegies	1.13.32
Say that thy love with Caephalus were not knowne,	Ovid's Elegies	1.13.33
Then thinkest thou thy loose life is not showne?	Ovid's Elegies	1.13.34
And early mountest thy hatefull carriage:	Ovid's Elegies	1.13.38
Leave colouring thy tresses I did cry,	Ovid's Elegies	1.14.1
Beyond thy robes thy dangling [lockes] <lackes> had sweept.	Ovid's Elegies	1.14.4
[Thy] <They> troubled haires, alas, endur'd great losse.	Ovid's Elegies	1.14.24
Thy very haires will the hot bodkin teach.	Ovid's Elegies	1.14.30
Why doest thy ill kembd tresses losse lament?	Ovid's Elegies	1.14.35
Why in thy glasse doest looke being discontent?	Ovid's Elegies	1.14.36
To please thy selfe, thy selfe put out of minde.	Ovid's Elegies	1.14.38
No envious tongue wrought thy thicke lockes decay.	Ovid's Elegies	1.14.42
By thine owne hand and fault thy hurt doth growe,	Ovid's Elegies	1.14.43
Thou mad'st thy head with compound poyson flow.	Ovid's Elegies	1.14.44
Cheere up thy selfe, thy losse thou maiest repaire,	Ovid's Elegies	1.14.55
Thy scope is mortall, mine eternall fame,	Ovid's Elegies	1.15.7
Thy verses sweet Tibullus shall be spoken.	Ovid's Elegies	1.15.28
I Ovid Poet of [my] <thy> wantonnesse,	Ovid's Elegies	2.1.1
Pardon me Jove, thy weapons ayde me nought,	Ovid's Elegies	2.1.19
Bagous whose care doth thy Mistrisse bridle,	Ovid's Elegies	2.2.1
Because [thy] <they> care too much thy Mistresse troubled.	Ovid's Elegies	2.2.8
the time more short/Lay downe thy forehead in thy lap to snort.	Ovid's Elegies	2.2.24
And what lesse labour then to hold thy peace?	Ovid's Elegies	2.2.28
Of wealth and honour so shall grow thy heape,	Ovid's Elegies	2.2.39
Do this and soone thou shalt thy freedome reape.	Ovid's Elegies	2.2.40
Or if he loves, thy tale breedes his misfortune.	Ovid's Elegies	2.2.54
If ever wench had made luke-warme thy love:	Ovid's Elegies	2.3.6
Thy hands agree not with the warlike speare.	Ovid's Elegies	2.3.8
Thy mistrisse enseignes must be likewise thine.	Ovid's Elegies	2.3.10
Minding thy fault, with death I wish to revill,	Ovid's Elegies	2.5.3
No intercepted lines thy deedes display,	Ovid's Elegies	2.5.5
No gifts given secretly thy crime bewray.	Ovid's Elegies	2.5.6
the boord with wine/Was scribled, and thy fingers writ a line.	Ovid's Elegies	2.5.18
Thy tunes let this rare birdes sad funerall borrowe,	Ovid's Elegies	2.6.9
Birdes haples glory, death thy life doth quench.	Ovid's Elegies	2.6.20
Thou with thy quilles mightst make greene Emeralds darke,	Ovid's Elegies	2.6.21
Thou spokest thy words so well with stammering sound.	Ovid's Elegies	2.6.24
Thy mouth to taste of many meates did balke.	Ovid's Elegies	2.6.30
Nuts were thy food, and Poppie causde thee sleepe,	Ovid's Elegies	2.6.31
Yet words in thy benummed palate rung,	Ovid's Elegies	2.6.47
Farewell Corinna cryed thy dying tongue.	Ovid's Elegies	2.6.48
If I praise any, thy poore haires thou tearest,	Ovid's Elegies	2.7.7
Now rash accusing, and thy vaine beliefe,	Ovid's Elegies	2.7.13
Behold Cypassis wont to dresse thy head,	Ovid's Elegies	2.7.17
Adde she was diligent thy locks to braide,	Ovid's Elegies	2.7.23
Apt to thy mistrisse, but more apt to me.	Ovid's Elegies	2.8.4
In both [thy] <my> cheekes she did perceive thee blush,	Ovid's Elegies	2.8.16
Well maiest thou one thing for thy Mistresse use.	Ovid's Elegies	2.8.24
Telling thy mistresse, where I was with thee,	Ovid's Elegies	2.8.27
Why me that alwayes was thy souldiour found,	Ovid's Elegies	2.9.3
Doest harme, and in thy tents why doest me wound?	Ovid's Elegies	2.9.4
Why burnes thy brand, why strikes thy bow thy friends?	Ovid's Elegies	2.9.5
More glory by thy vanquisht foes assends.	Ovid's Elegies	2.9.6
Thy dull hand stayes thy striving enemies harmes.	Ovid's Elegies	2.9.12
Doest joy to have thy hooked Arrowes shaked,	Ovid's Elegies	2.9.13
Heere thou hast strength, here thy right hand doth rest.	Ovid's Elegies	2.9.36
Here of themselves thy shafts come, as if shot,	Ovid's Elegies	2.9.37
Long shalt thou rest when Fates expire thy breath.	Ovid's Elegies	2.9.42
And thy step-father fights by thy example.	Ovid's Elegies	2.9.48
Light art thou, and more windie then thy winges,	Ovid's Elegies	2.9.49
Yet Love, if thou with thy faire mother heare,	Ovid's Elegies	2.9.51
Subdue the wandring wenches to thy raigne,	Ovid's Elegies	2.9.53
In all thy face will be no crimsen bloud.	Ovid's Elegies	2.11.28
Request milde Zephires helpe for thy availe,	Ovid's Elegies	2.11.41
And with thy hand assist [the] <thy> swelling saile.	Ovid's Elegies	2.11.42
I from the shore thy knowne ship first will see,	Ovid's Elegies	2.11.43
For thy returne shall fall the vowd oblation,	Ovid's Elegies	2.11.46
How almost wrackt thy ship in maine seas fell.	Ovid's Elegies	2.11.50
new to enter/Warres, just Latinus, in thy kingdomes center:	Ovid's Elegies	2.12.22
So in thy Temples shall Osiris stay,	Ovid's Elegies	2.13.12
And the dull snake about thy offrings creepe,	Ovid's Elegies	2.13.13
And in thy pompe hornd Apis with thee keepe,	Ovid's Elegies	2.13.14
Turne thy lookes hether, and in one spare twaine,	Ovid's Elegies	2.13.15
My selfe will bring vowed gifts before thy feete,	Ovid's Elegies	2.13.24
Because thy belly should rough wrinckles lacke,	Ovid's Elegies	2.14.7
Wilt thou thy wombe-inclosed off-spring wracke?	Ovid's Elegies	2.14.8
If such a worke thy mother had assayed.	Ovid's Elegies	2.14.20
And hide thy left hand underneath her lappe.	Ovid's Elegies	2.15.12
Weare me, when warmest showers thy members wash,	Ovid's Elegies	2.15.23
And through the gemme let thy lost waters pash.	Ovid's Elegies	2.15.24

THY (cont.)

Nor thy gulfes crooked Malea, would I feare.	Ovid's Elegies	2.16.24
With thy white armes upon my shoulders seaze,	Ovid's Elegies	2.16.29
By me, and by my starres, thy radiant eyes.	Ovid's Elegies	2.16.44
Adde deeds unto thy promises at last.	Ovid's Elegies	2.16.48
And with swift Naggs drawing thy little Coach,	Ovid's Elegies	2.16.49
Not though thy face in all things make thee raigne,	Ovid's Elegies	2.17.11
to detaine)/Thou oughtst therefore to scorne me for thy mate,	Ovid's Elegies	2.17.13
Then warres, and from thy tents wilt come to mine.	Ovid's Elegies	2.18.40
Foole if to keepe thy wife thou hast no neede,	Ovid's Elegies	2.19.1
And on thy thre-shold let me lie dispred,	Ovid's Elegies	2.19.21
But thou of thy faire damsell too secure,	Ovid's Elegies	2.19.37
Beginne to shut thy house at evening sure.	Ovid's Elegies	2.19.38
Wilt nothing do, why I should wish thy death?	Ovid's Elegies	2.19.56
By thy default thou doest our joyes defraude.	Ovid's Elegies	2.19.58
And first [she] <he> sayd, when will thy love be spent,	Ovid's Elegies	3.1.15
O Poet carelesse of thy argument?	Ovid's Elegies	3.1.16
Wine-bibbing banquets tell thy naughtinesse,	Ovid's Elegies	3.1.17
While without shame thou singst thy lewdnesse ditty.	Ovid's Elegies	3.1.22
The subject hides thy wit, mens acts resound,	Ovid's Elegies	3.1.25
Thy muse hath played what may milde girles content,	Ovid's Elegies	3.1.27
And by those numbers is thy first youth spent.	Ovid's Elegies	3.1.28
To fill my lawes thy wanton spirit frame.	Ovid's Elegies	3.1.30
Thy lofty stile with mine I not compare,	Ovid's Elegies	3.1.39
What gate thy stately words cannot unlocke,	Ovid's Elegies	3.1.45
By suffring much not borne by thy severity.	Ovid's Elegies	3.1.48
First of thy minde the happy seedes I knewe,	Ovid's Elegies	3.1.59
Graunt Tragedie thy Poet times least tittle,	Ovid's Elegies	3.1.67
Thy labour ever lasts, she askes but little.	Ovid's Elegies	3.1.68
Because on him thy care doth hap to rest.	Ovid's Elegies	3.2.8
By thy sides touching ill she is entreated.	Ovid's Elegies	3.2.22
For shame presse not her backe with thy hard knee.	Ovid's Elegies	3.2.24
But on the ground thy cloathes too loosely lie,	Ovid's Elegies	3.2.25
That from thy fanne, mov'd by my hand may blow?	Ovid's Elegies	3.2.38
Souldiour applaud thy Mars:	Ovid's Elegies	3.2.49
Thy legges hang-downe:	Ovid's Elegies	3.2.63
[A] <Or> while thy tiptoes on the foote-stoole rest.	Ovid's Elegies	3.2.64
The horses seeme, as [thy] <they> desire they knewe.	Ovid's Elegies	3.2.68
What doest? thy wagon in lesse compasse bring.	Ovid's Elegies	3.2.70
least their gownes tosse thy haire,/To hide thee in my bosome	Ovid's Elegies	3.2.75
Rude man, 'tis vaine, thy damsell to commend/To keepers trust:	Ovid's Elegies	3.4.1
Sooner shall kindnesse gaine thy wills fruition.	Ovid's Elegies	3.4.12
Thy feare is, then her body, valued more.	Ovid's Elegies	3.4.30
She must be honest to thy servants credit.	Ovid's Elegies	3.4.36
Kindly thy mistris use, if thou be wise.	Ovid's Elegies	3.4.43
Honour what friends thy wife gives, sheele give many:	Ovid's Elegies	3.4.45
<redde-growne> slime bankes, till I be past/Thy waters stay:	Ovid's Elegies	3.5.2
Thee I have pass'd, and knew thy streame none such,	Ovid's Elegies	3.5.5
When thy waves brim did scarse my anckles touch.	Ovid's Elegies	3.5.6
And in thy foule deepe waters thicke thou [gushest] <rushest>.	Ovid's Elegies	3.5.8
Slide in thy bounds, so shalt thou runne for ever.	Ovid's Elegies	3.5.20
When nimph-Neaera rapt thy lookes Scamander.	Ovid's Elegies	3.5.28
If Achelous, I aske where thy hornes stand,	Ovid's Elegies	3.5.35
Where's thy attire? why wand'rest heere alone?	Ovid's Elegies	3.5.55
To stay thy tresses white veyle hast thou none?	Ovid's Elegies	3.5.56
Why weepst? and spoilst with teares thy watry eyes?	Ovid's Elegies	3.5.57
And fiercely knockst thy brest that open lyes?	Ovid's Elegies	3.5.58
That seeing thy teares can any joy then feele.	Ovid's Elegies	3.5.60
If thy great fame in every region stood?	Ovid's Elegies	3.5.90
Thy springs are nought but raine and melted snowe:	Ovid's Elegies	3.5.93
But for thy merits I wish thee, white streame,	Ovid's Elegies	3.5.105
Who bad thee lie downe here against thy will?	Ovid's Elegies	3.6.78
Foole canst thou him in thy white armes embrace?	Ovid's Elegies	3.7.11
Ah whether is [thy] <they> brests soft nature [fled] <sled>?	Ovid's Elegies	3.7.18
At thy deafe dores in verse sing my abuses.	Ovid's Elegies	3.7.24
Against thy selfe, mans nature, thou wert cunning,	Ovid's Elegies	3.7.45
And to thine owne losse was thy wit swift running.	Ovid's Elegies	3.7.46
Why gird'st thy citties with a towred wall?	Ovid's Elegies	3.7.47
Sad Elegia thy wofull haires unbinde:	Ovid's Elegies	3.8.3
Tibullus, thy workes Poet, and thy fame,	Ovid's Elegies	3.8.5
Faire-fac'd Iulus, he went forth thy court.	Ovid's Elegies	3.8.14
Yet shall thy life be forcibly bereaven.	Ovid's Elegies	3.8.38
Nor feared they thy body to annoy?	Ovid's Elegies	3.8.42
Thy dying eyes here did thy mother close,	Ovid's Elegies	3.8.49
Nor did thy ashes her last offrings lose.	Ovid's Elegies	3.8.50
Part of her sorrowe heere thy sister bearing,	Ovid's Elegies	3.8.51
Nemesis and thy first wench joyne their kisses,	Ovid's Elegies	3.8.53
And thou, if falsely charged to wrong thy friend,	Ovid's Elegies	3.8.63
With these thy soule walkes, soules if death release,	Ovid's Elegies	3.8.65
Thy bones I pray may in the urne safe rest,	Ovid's Elegies	3.8.67
And may th'earths weight thy ashes nought molest.	Ovid's Elegies	3.8.68
Why are our pleasures by thy meanes forborne?	Ovid's Elegies	3.9.4
As in thy sacrifize we them forbeare?	Ovid's Elegies	3.9.44
Long have I borne much, mad thy faults me make:	Ovid's Elegies	3.10.1
When have not I fixt to thy side close layed?	Ovid's Elegies	3.10.17
I have thy husband, guard, and fellow plaied.	Ovid's Elegies	3.10.18
Leave thy once powerfull words, and flatteries,	Ovid's Elegies	3.10.31
And by thy face to me a powre divine,	Ovid's Elegies	3.10.47
Seeing thou art faire, I barre not thy false playing,	Ovid's Elegies	3.13.1
But let not mee poore soule know of thy straying.	Ovid's Elegies	3.13.2
To lead thy thoughts, as thy faire lookes doe mine,	Hero and Leander	1.201
Dutifull service may thy love procure,	Hero and Leander	1.220
Ah simple Hero, learne thy selfe to cherish,	Hero and Leander	1.241

THY (cont.)				
Perhaps, thy sacred Priesthood makes thee loath,	Hero and Leander			1.293
Nor staine thy youthfull years with avarice,	Hero and Leander			1.325
Me in thy bed and maiden bosome take,	Hero and Leander			2.248
And therefore let it rest upon thy pillow.	Hero and Leander			2.252
And if these pleasures may thee <things thy minde may> move,	Passionate Shepherd			19
For thy delight each May-morning.	Passionate Shepherd			22
If these delights thy minde may move;	Passionate Shepherd			23
THYESTES (See THIESTES)				
THYNE				
Let not thy love exceed thyne honor sonne,	2Tamb	5.3.199		Tamb
Her shut gates greater lightning then thyne brought.	Ovid's Elegies			2.1.20
THYRSTY				
That his teare-thyrsty and unquenched hate,	2Tamb	5.3.222		Techel
THYSELF (See THIE SELFE)				
THY SELF				
That thou thy self, then County-Pallatine,	2Tamb	1.1.94		Orcan
Edmund, yeeld thou thy self, or thou shalt die.	Edw	5.3.56		Matrvs
THY SELFE				
Remember who thou art, speake like thy selfe,	Dido	2.1.100		Dido
Pesant, goe seeke companions like thy selfe,	Dido	3.3.21		Dido
Now Dido, with these reliques burne thy selfe,	Dido	5.1.292		Dido
Ful true thou speakst, and like thy selfe my lord,	1Tamb	1.1.49		Mycet
Thy selfe and them shall never part from me,	1Tamb	1.2.245		Tamb
Judge by thy selfe Theridamas, not me,	1Tamb	2.5.93		Tamb
When thy great Bassoe-maister and thy selfe,	1Tamb	3.3.173		Zenoc
Prepare thy selfe to live and die my slave.	1Tamb	3.3.207		Zabina
Content thy selfe, his person shall be safe,	1Tamb	4.4.87		Tamb
thou maist thinke thy selfe happie to be fed from my trencher.	1Tamb	4.4.92	P	Tamb
it out, or manage armes/Against thy selfe or thy confederates:	2Tamb	1.1.129		Sgsmnd
If thou wilt proove thy selfe a perfect God,	2Tamb	2.2.56		Orcan
Made of the mould whereof thy selfe consists,	2Tamb	4.1.115		Tamb
What, have I slaine her? Villaine, stab thy selfe:	2Tamb	4.2.82		Therid
Nor yet thy selfe, the anger of the highest,	2Tamb	5.1.104		Govnr
Come downe thy selfe and worke a myracle,	2Tamb	5.1.188		Tamb
Sham'st thou not thus to justifie thy selfe,	Jew	1.2.119		Govnr
to forgoe so much/Without provision for thy selfe and me.	Jew	1.2.243		Barab
But to thy selfe smile when the Christians moane.	Jew	2.3.172		Barab
Assure thy selfe thou shalt have broth by the eye.	Jew	3.4.92		Barab
'Tis not thy mony, but thy selfe I weigh:	Jew	4.2.124		Curtzn
Thou'st doom'd thy selfe, assault it presently.	Jew	5.1.97		Calym
Tush, send not letters to 'em, goe thy selfe,	Jew	5.2.93		Barab
That right or wrong, thou deale thy selfe a King.	P 148	2.91		Guise
Thy friend, thy selfe, another Gaveston.	Edw	1.1.143		Edward
Assure thy selfe thou comst not in my sight.	Edw	1.4.169		Edward
Fie Mortimer, dishonor not thy selfe,	Edw	1.4.244		Lncstr
A second mariage twixt thy selfe and me.	Edw	1.4.335		Edward
Leave now to oppose thy selfe against the king,	Edw	1.4.387		MortSr
What needst thou, love, thus to excuse thy selfe?	Edw	2.1.60		Neece
not armor, and thy selfe/Bedaubd with golde, rode laughing at	Edw	2.2.184		Mortmr
thou dost not presently bind thy selfe to me for seven yeares,	F 361	1.4.19	P	Wagner
prepare thy selfe, for I will presently raise up two devils to	F 372	1.4.30	P	Wagner
I sirra, I'le teach thee to turne thy selfe to a Dog, or a Cat,	F 382	1.4.40	P	Wagner
Pronounce this thrice devoutly to thy selfe,	F 547	2.1.159		Mephst
'Twas thine own seeking Faustus, thanke thy selfe.	F 555	2.2.4		Mephst
So shalt thou shew thy selfe an obedient servant <Do so>,/And	F 652	2.2.101		Lucifr
Choke thy selfe Glutton: What are thou the sixt?	F 704	2.2.153		Faust
And thou shalt turne thy selfe into what shape thou wilt.	F 718	2.2.170		Lucifr
Thy selfe and I, may parly with this Pope:	F 896	3.1.118		Faust
Now Faustus, come prepare thy selfe for mirth,	F 981	3.2.1		Mephst
With all my heart kind Doctor, please thy selfe,	F1623	4.6.66		Duke
No Faustus, curse thy selfe, curse Lucifer,	F1973	5.2.177		Faust
I will teach thee to turne thy selfe to anything, to a dogge,	F App	p.231 58	P	Wagner
conquer all the earth, then turne thy force/Against thy selfe:	Lucan, First Booke			23
O Roome thy selfe art cause of all these evils,	Lucan, First Booke			84
Thy selfe thus shivered out to three mens shares:	Lucan, First Booke			85
Thou Roome at name of warre runst from thy selfe,	Lucan, First Booke			517
Forbeare to hurt thy selfe in spoyling mee.	Ovid's Elegies			1.2.50
But how thou shouldst behave thy selfe now know;	Ovid's Elegies			1.4.11
I will weepe/And to the dores sight of thy selfe [will] keepe:	Ovid's Elegies			1.4.62
Memnon the elfe/Received his cole-blacke colour from thy selfe.	Ovid's Elegies			1.13.32
To please thy selfe, thy selfe put out of minde.	Ovid's Elegies			1.14.38
Cheere up thy selfe, thy losse thou maiest repaire,	Ovid's Elegies			1.14.55
Against thy selfe, mans nature, thou wert cunning,	Ovid's Elegies			3.7.45
Ah simple Hero, learne thy selfe to cherish,	Hero and Leander			1.241
TIBER (See also TYBERS)				
bands were spread/Along Nar floud that into Tiber fals,	Lucan, First Booke			472
TIBERS				
With slaughtered priests [make] <may> Tibers channell swell,	Edw	1.4.102		Edward
TIBI				
Si bene quid de te merui, fuit aut tibi quidquam/Dulce meum,	Dido	5.1.136		Dido
I saluted with an old hempen proverb, Hodie tibi, cras mihi,	Jew	4.2.19	P	Pilia
TIBULLUS				
Thy verses sweet Tibullus shall be spoken.	Ovid's Elegies			1.15.28
Tibullus, thy workes Poet, and thy fame,	Ovid's Elegies			3.8.5
And Venus grieves, Tibullus life being spent,	Ovid's Elegies			3.8.15
Trust in good verse, Tibullus feeles deaths paines,	Ovid's Elegies			3.8.39
Tibullus doth Elysiums joy inherit.	Ovid's Elegies			3.8.60
The godly, sweete Tibullus doth increase.	Ovid's Elegies			3.8.66
TIBURS				
In Tiburs field with watry fome art rumbling,	Ovid's Elegies			3.5.46
TICE				
That I may tice a Dolphin to the shoare,	Dido	5.1.249		Dido

TICE (cont.)
What stronge enchantments tice my yeelding soule? . . 1Tamb 1.2.224 Therid
TICING
Whose ticing tongue was made of Hermes pipe, . . . Dido 2.1.145 Aeneas
O had that ticing strumpet nere been borne: . . . Dido 2.1.300 Dido
Banish that ticing dame from forth your mouth, . . . Dido 4.3.31 Achat
Who wild me sacrifize his ticing relliques: . . . Dido 5.1.277 Dido
TICKLE
And tickle not your Spirits with desire/Stil to be train'd in 2Tamb 4.1.80 Tamb
tickle the pretie wenches plackets Ile be amongst them ifaith. F App p.231 63 P Clown
nay Ile tickle you Vintner, looke to the goblet Rafe, . F App p.235 23 P Robin
TIDE (See also TYDE)
As every tide tilts twixt their oken sides: . . . . Dido 1.1.224 Aeneas
Before my sorrowes tide have any stint. . . . . Dido 4.2.42 Iarbus
I crave but this, he stay a tide or two, ... Dido 5.1.207 Dido
Hether the windes blowe, here the spring-tide rore. . . Ovid's Elegies 2.11.40
Either th'art muddy in mid winter tide: . . . . Ovid's Elegies 3.5.95
TIDINGS (See also TYDINGS)
Will dye with very tidings of his death: . . . . Dido 3.3.77 Iarbus
that the Souldan is/No more dismaide with tidings of his fall, 1Tamb 4.3.31 Souldn
Letters my lord, and tidings foorth of Fraunce, . . Edw 4.3.25 Post
TIE (See also TYE)
And hold my conquered hands for thee to tie. . . . Ovid's Elegies 1.2.20
TIED
By Mahomet he shal be tied in chaines, ... 2Tamb 3.5.92 Jrslem
Not to be tied to their affection, ... Edw 3.1.29 Baldck
loves wrack/Shall follow thee, their hands tied at their backe. Ovid's Elegies 1.2.32
TIERD
Poore travailers though tierd, rise at thy sight, . . Ovid's Elegies 1.13.13
TIGERS (See also TYGERS)
Inhumaine creatures, nurst with Tigers milke, . . . Edw 5.1.71 Edward
More safetie is there in a Tigers jawes, ... Edw 5.1.116 Edward
TIGRIS
Of Euphrates and Tigris swiftly runs, ... 2Tamb 5.2.3 Callap
TIL
Europe, and pursue/His scattered armie til they yeeld or die. 1Tamb 3.3.39 Therid
Til then take thou my crowne, vaunt of my worth, . . 1Tamb 3.3.130 Tamb
Will never be dispenc'd with til our deaths. . . . 1Tamb 5.1.17 Govnr
Til fire and sword have found them at a bay. . . . 2Tamb 3.2.151 Tamb
of thy hold/Volleies of ordinance til the breach be made, 2Tamb 3.3.25 Therid
Which til it may defend you, labour low: . . . . 2Tamb 3.3.44 Therid
And til by vision, or by speach I heare/Immortall Jove say, 2Tamb 4.1.198 Tamb
So honour heaven til heaven dissolved be, ... 2Tamb 5.3.26 Techel
til I am past this faire and pleasant greene, ile walke on F App p.239 96 P Faust
TILL (Homograph; See also TYLL, UNTIL)
Till that a Princesse priest conceav'd by Mars, . . Dido 1.1.106 Jupitr
Till we have fire to dresse the meate we kild: . . . Dido 1.1.165 Aeneas
We banquetted till overcome with wine, ... Dido 2.1.178 Aeneas
Till I returne and take thee hence againe. . . . Dido 2.1.339 Venus
Dido, that till now/Didst never thinke Aeneas beautifull: Dido 3.1.82 Dido
Who nere will cease to soare till he be slaine. . . Dido 3.3.85 Iarbus
Till he hath furrowed Neptunes glassie fieldes, . . . Dido 4.3.11 Aeneas
Till men and kingdomes help to strengthen it: . . . 1Tamb 1.2.30 Tamb
Till with their eies [they] <thee> view us Emperours. . 1Tamb 1.2.67 Tamb
his chaine shall serve/For Manackles, till he be ransom'd home. 1Tamb 1.2.148 Tamb
And they will never leave thee till the death. . . . 1Tamb 1.2.248 Tamb
Till I may see thee hem'd with armed men. . . . 1Tamb 2.4.38 Tamb
And till thou overtake me Tamburlaine, ... 1Tamb 2.5.44 Cosroe
Till we have made us ready for the field. . . . . 1Tamb 5.1.212 Tamb
And till I die thou shalt not be interr'd. . . . 2Tamb 2.4.132 Tamb
That may endure till heaven be dissolv'd, ... 2Tamb 3.2.7 Tamb
Even till the dissolution of the world, ... 2Tamb 3.5.82 Tamb
Till we prepare our martch to Babylon, ... 2Tamb 4.3.93 Tamb
As durst resist us till our third daies siege: . . . 2Tamb 5.1.59 Techel
Yet could not enter till the breach was made. . . . 2Tamb 5.1.100 Tamb
by a Spanish Fleet/That never left us till within a league, Jew 1.1.96 2Merch
Till they reduce the wrongs done to my father. . . . Jew 1.2.235 Abigal
Till thou hast gotten to be entertain'd. . . . . Jew 1.2.288 Barab
Till I have answer of my Abigall. . . . . . . Jew 2.1.19 Barab
Till Titus and Vespasian conquer'd us)/Am I become as wealthy Jew 2.3.10 Barab
But keepe thy heart till Don Mathias comes. . . . Jew 2.3.307 Barab
Nay, if you will, stay till she comes her selfe. . . Jew 2.3.352 Barab
Till I have set 'em both at enmitie. . . . . . Jew 2.3.383 Barab
Till they [reveal] the causers of our smarts, . . . Jew 3.2.34 Govnr
In prison till the Law has past on him. . . . . Jew 5.1.49 Govnr
shut/His souldiers, till I have consum'd 'em all with fire? Jew 5.2.82 Barab
intreat your Highnesse/Not to depart till he has feasted you. Jew 5.3.33 Msngr
Till you shall heare a Culverin discharg'd/By him that beares Jew 5.4.3 Govnr
till thy father hath made good/The ruines done to Malta and to Jew 5.5.111 Govnr
May not desolve, till death desolve our lives, . . . P 5 1.5 Charls
I am my Lord, in what your grace commaundes till death. . P 76 2.19 P Pothec
Till this our Coronation day be past: . . . . . P 624 12.37 King
I may be stabd, and live till he be dead, ... P 778 15.36 Mugern
Cry out, exclaime, houle till thy throat be hoarce, . . P1077 19.147 King
Whose service he may still commaund till death. . . P1149 22.11 Navrre
Till surfeiting with our afflicting armes, ... P1153 22.15 King
And there abide till fortune call thee home. . . . Edw 1.4.126 Edward
There weepe, for till my Gaveston be repeald, . . . Edw 1.4.168 Edward
I Mortimer, for till he be restorde, ... Edw 1.4.209 Queene
Come lead the way, I long till I am there. . . . Edw 2.1.82 Neece
Farewell sweete unckle till we meete againe. . . . Edw 2.4.11 Neece
Till hee pay deerely for their companie. . . . . Edw 3.1.198 Lncstr
Till Edmund be arrivde for Englands good, ... Edw 4.1.2 Kent

TILL (cont.)				
Till I be strong enough to breake a staffe, . . .	Edw	4.2.24		Prince
keepe these preachments till you come to the place appointed.	Edw	4.7.113	P	Rice
But stay a while, let me be king till night, . . .	Edw	5.1.59		Edward
[Till] <And> at the last, he come to Killingworth, . .	Edw	5.2.60		Mortmr
Till being interrupted by my friends, ...	Edw	5.4.62		Mortmr
Till further triall may be made thereof.	Edw	5.6.80		King
Till swolne with cunning of a selfe conceit, ...	F 20	Prol.20		1Chor
in speculation of this Art/Till Mephostophilis returne againe.	F 342	1.3.114		Faust
I, thinke so still, till experience change thy mind. .	F 517	2.1.129		Mephst
<Well thou wilt have one, sit there till I come, . .	F 531	(HC261)A	P	Mephst
What Dick, looke to the horses there till I come againe. .	F 722	2.3.1	P	Robin
Till with my sword I have that Conjurer slaine. . .	F1333	4.2.9		Benvol
Till time shall alter this our brutish shapes: . . .	F1454	4.3.24		Benvol
Come sirs, what shall we do now till mine Hostesse comes?	F1520	4.5.16	P	Dick
he never left eating, till he had eate up all my loade of hay.	F1531	4.5.27	P	Carter
till I had pul'd me his leg quite off, and now 'tis at home in	F1551	4.5.47	P	HrsCsr
if I live till morning, Il'e visit you:	F1877	5.2.81	P	Faust
And so I leave thee Faustus till anon, ...	F1924	5.2.128		BdAngl
Who seeing hunters pauseth till fell wrath/And kingly rage	Lucan, First Booke			209
what store of ground/For servitors to till?	Lucan, First Booke			345
Both verses were alike till Love (men say)/Began to smile and	Ovid's Elegies			1.1.7
And quiver bearing Dian till the plaine:	Ovid's Elegies			1.1.14
Watching till after mid-night did not tire thee. . . .	Ovid's Elegies			1.6.44
On this hard threshold till the morning lay. . . .	Ovid's Elegies			1.6.68
Sooth Lovers watch till sleepe the hus-band charmes, .	Ovid's Elegies			1.9.25
Till Cupids bow, and fierie shafts be broken, . . .	Ovid's Elegies			1.15.27
But till the [keeper] <keepes> went forth, I forget not, .	Ovid's Elegies			3.1.55
On swift steedes mounted till the race were done. . .	Ovid's Elegies			3.2.10
<redde-growne> slime bankes, till I be past/Thy waters stay:	Ovid's Elegies			3.5.1
Till then, rough was her father, she severe, . . .	Ovid's Elegies			3.7.31
A greater ground with great horse is to till. . . .	Ovid's Elegies			3.14.18
Till with the fire that from his count'nance blazed, .	Hero and Leander			1.164
Till in his twining armes he lockt her fast, . . .	Hero and Leander			1.403
Till to the solitarie tower he got.	Hero and Leander			2.230
Till gentle parlie did the truce obtaine.	Hero and Leander			2.278
Till she o'recome with anguish, shame, and rage, . .	Hero and Leander			2.333
TILL'D (See also UNTILD, UNTILL'D)				
The ground which Curius and Camillus till'd, . . .	Lucan, First Booke			170
TILT (Homograph; See also TYLTE)				
Fighting for passage, tilt within the earth. . . .	1Tamb	1.2.51		Tamb
with winged Steads/All sweating, tilt about the watery heavens,	1Tamb	3.2.79		Agidas
Weele have a generall tilt and turnament, ...	Edw	1.4.376		Edward
When for her sake I ran at tilt in Fraunce, . . .	Edw	5.5.69		Edward
TILTING				
Trotting the ring, and tilting at a glove:	2Tamb	1.3.39		Zenoc
Run tilting round about the firmament, ...	2Tamb	4.1.203		Tamb
TILTS				
As every tide tilts twixt their oken sides: . . .	Dido	1.1.224		Aeneas
TIMBRELL				
joies/Then nymphs and sheapheards, when the timbrell rings,	Hero and Leander			2.233
TIME (See also MIDTIME)				
And I will spend my time in thy bright armes. . . .	Dido	1.1.22		Ganimd
Controule proud Fate, and cut the thred of time. . .	Dido	1.1.29		Jupitr
For this so friendly ayde in time of neede. . . .	Dido	1.1.138		Venus
Now is the time for me to play my part:	Dido	1.1.182		Venus
That in such peace long time did rule the same: . .	Dido	1.2.24		Cloan
Blest be the time I see Achates face.	Dido	2.1.56		Illion
And race th'eternall Register of time:	Dido	3.2.7		Juno
O no God wot, I cannot watch my time, ...	Dido	3.2.14		Juno
Wherefore I [chaungd] <chaunge> my counsell with the time,	Dido	3.2.51		Juno
She likewise in admyring spends her time, ...	Dido	3.2.72		Juno
Meane time, Ascanius shall be my charge, ...	Dido	3.2.98		Venus
Meane time these wanton weapons serve my warre, . .	Dido	3.3.37		Cupid
But time will discontinue her content, ...	Dido	3.3.78		Iarbus
But may be slackt untill another time:	Dido	4.2.26		Anna
Twas time to runne, Aeneas had been gone, ...	Dido	4.4.14		Anna
Spendst thou thy time about this little boy, . . .	Dido	5.1.51		Hermes
the time hath been/When Didos beautie [chaind] <chaungd> thine	Dido	5.1.113		Dido
That like a Foxe in midst of harvest time, ...	1Tamb	1.1.31		Mycet
Returne with speed, time passeth swift away, . . .	1Tamb	1.1.67		Mycet
So I can when I see my time.	1Tamb	2.4.26		Mycet
Your Highnesse needs not doubt but in short time, . .	1Tamb	3.2.32		Agidas
But as I live that towne shall curse the time/That Tamburlaine	1Tamb	3.3.59		Tamb
Not now Theridamas, her time is past:	1Tamb	3.3.228		Tamb
So might your highnesse, had you time to sort/Your fighting men,	1Tamb	4.1.36		Capol
But when Aurora mounts the second time, ...	1Tamb	4.1.54		2Msngr
Then let me find no further time to grace/Her princely Temples	1Tamb	5.1.488		Tamb
For now her mariage time shall worke us rest. . . .	1Tamb	5.1.504		Techel
Least time be past, and lingring let us both. . . .	2Tamb	1.2.75		Callap
How have ye spent your absent time from me?	2Tamb	1.3.173		Tamb
They shal Casane, and tis time yfaith.	2Tamb	1.3.185		Tamb
then that your Majesty/Take all advantages of time and power,	2Tamb	2.1.12		Fredrk
Your Majesty may choose some pointed time, ...	2Tamb	3.1.75		Jrslem
Who by this time is at Natolia, ...	2Tamb	3.4.86		Therid
Come, thou and I wil goe to cardes to drive away the time.	2Tamb	4.1.62	P	Calyph
twere but time indeed,/Lost long before you knew what honour	2Tamb	4.3.86		Tamb
This is the time that must eternize me, ...	2Tamb	5.2.54		Callap
And all his life time hath bin tired, ...	Jew	1.1.15		Barab
And seeke in time to intercept the worst, ...	Jew	1.1.187		Barab
We may have time to make collection/Amongst the Inhabitants of	Jew	1.2.20		Govnr
Let's know their time, perhaps it is not long; . . .	Jew	1.2.24		Calym
toyl'd to inherit here/The months of vanity and losse of time,	Jew	1.2.197		Barab

TIME (cont.)

That measure nought but by the present time.	Jew	1.2.220	Barab
And cast with cunning for the time to come:	Jew	1.2.222	Barab
And time may yeeld us an occasion/Which on the sudden cannot	Jew	1.2.239	Barab
'Twere time well spent to goe and visit her:	Jew	1.2.389	Lodowk
The incertaine pleasures of swift-footed time/Have tane their	Jew	2.1.7	Barab
Now have I happily espy'd a time/To search the plancke my	Jew	2.1.20	Abigal
And 'bout this time the Nuns begin to wake;	Jew	2.1.56	Abigal
'Tis likely they in time may reape some fruit,	Jew	2.3.84	Barab
might be got/To keepe him for his life time from the gallowes.	Jew	2.3.104	Barab
But tell me now, How hast thou spent thy time?	Jew	2.3.201	Barab
One time I was an Hostler in an Inne,	Jew	2.3.205	Ithimr
And in the night time secretly would I steale/To travellers	Jew	2.3.206	Ithimr
In good time, father, here are letters come/From Ormus, and the	Jew	2.3.222	Abigal
Well, let it passe, another time shall serve.	Jew	2.3.278	Mthias
The time has bin, that but for one bare night/A hundred Duckets	Jew	3.1.2	Curtzn
If so, 'tis time that it be seene into:	Jew	3.4.9	Barab
The time you tooke for respite, is at hand,	Jew	3.5.8	Basso
What time a night is't now, sweet Ithimore?	Jew	4.1.157	Barab
As thou lik'st that, stop me another time.	Jew	4.1.173	1Fryar
And since that time they have hir'd a slave my man/To accuse me	Jew	5.1.75	Barab
I will be there, and doe as thou desirest;/When is the time?	Jew	5.2.104	Govnr
From time to time, but specially in this,	P 10	1.10	Navrre
In lucky time, come let us keep this lane,	P 298	5.25	Anjoy
And in the mean time my Lord, could we devise,	P 425	7.65	Guise
And dayly meet about this time of day,	P 503	9.22	Guise
Doe so sweet Guise, let us delay no time,	P 505	9.24	QnMoth
Be gone, delay no time sweet Guise.	P 509	9.28	QnMoth
Come Pleshe, lets away whilste time doth serve.	P 587	11.52	Navrre
No person, place, or time, or circumstance,	P 606	12.19	King
If that be all, the next time that I meet her,	P 781	15.39	Mugern
Be gone I say, tis time that we were there.	P 919	18.20	Navrre
And all my former time was spent in vaine:	P 986	19.56	Guise
As pale as ashes, nay then tis time to look about.	P1001	19.71	Guise
Shall curse the time that ere Navarre was King,	P1249	22.111	Navrre
well/To waite at my trencher, and tell me lies at dinner time,	Edw	1.1.31	Gavstn
But in the meane time Gaveston away,	Edw	1.1.202	Edward
And in the meane time ile intreat you all,	Edw	1.2.77	ArchBp
The time is little that thou hast to stay,	Edw	1.4.138	Edward
But see in happie time, my lord the king,	Edw	1.4.299	Queene
Meane time my lord of Penbrooke and my selfe,	Edw	2.2.122	Warwck
Forslowe no time, sweet Lancaster lets march.	Edw	2.4.40	Warwck
traitors, now tis time/To be avengd on you for all your braves,	Edw	3.1.224	Edward
Betweene you both, shorten the time I pray,	Edw	4.3.45	Edward
O no my lord, this princely resolution/Fits not the time, away,	Edw	4.5.9	Baldck
As daunger of this stormie time requires.	Edw	4.7.7	Abbot
My lord, why waste you thus the time away,	Edw	5.1.49	Leistr
Tis not the first time I have killed a man.	Edw	5.4.30	Ltborn
Eclipses, all at one time, but in some years we have more, in	F 616	2.2.65	P Faust
<in mean time take this booke, peruse it throwly>,	F 717	(HC264) A	Lucifr
Thus hitherto hath Faustus spent his time.	F 799	3.1.21	Faust
I, and I fall not asleepe i'th meane time.	F1196	4.1.42	Benvol
Till time shall alter this our brutish shapes:	F1454	4.3.24	Benvol
Thy fatall time drawes to a finall end;	F1479	4.4.23	Faust
bad me ride him night and day, and spare him no time; but,	F1541	4.5.37	P HrsCsr
a dead time of the Winter, I would request no better meate,	F1572	4.6.15	P Lady
that at this time of the yeare, when every Tree is barren of	F1579	4.6.22	P Duke
To wait upon thy soule; the time is come/Which makes it forfeit.	F1802	5.2.6	Lucifr
this is the time <the time wil come>, and he will fetch mee.	F1861	5.2.65	P Faust
That time may cease, and midnight never come.	F1930	5.2.134	Faust
The Stars move still, Time runs, the Clocke will strike,	F1936	5.2.140	Faust
At which selfe time the house seem'd all on fire,	F1993	5.3.11	3Schol
Well, theres the second time, aware the third, I give you faire	F App	p.232 20	P Faust
and attire/They usde to weare during their time of life,	F App	p.237 34	Emper
course that time doth runne with calme and silent foote,	F App	p.239 90	P Faust
Thy fatall time doth drawe to finall ende,	F App	p.240 122	Faust
Why hee's fast asleepe, come some other time.	F App	p.240 141	P Mephst
and the dead time of the winter, I would desire no better meate	F App	p.242 10	P Duchss
that being in the dead time of winter, and in the month of	F App	p.242 17	P Duke
Time ends and to old Chaos all things turne;	Lucan, First Booke	74	
In summer time the purple Rubicon,	Lucan, First Booke	215	
And shal he triumph long before his time,	Lucan, First Booke	316	
She may perceive how we the time did wast:	Ovid's Elegies	1.6.70	
Time flying slides hence closely, and deceaves us,	Ovid's Elegies	1.8.49	
But never give a spatious time to ire,	Ovid's Elegies	1.8.81	
he doth not chide/Nor to hoist saile attends fit time and tyde.	Ovid's Elegies	1.9.14	
Time passeth while I speake, give her my writ/But see that	Ovid's Elegies	1.11.15	
Envie, why carpest thou my time is spent so ill,	Ovid's Elegies	1.15.1	
to thinke the time more short/Lay downe thy forehead in thy lap	Ovid's Elegies	2.2.23	
While thou hast time yet to bestowe that gift.	Ovid's Elegies	2.3.18	
And time it was for me to live in quiet,	Ovid's Elegies	2.9.23	
To bring that happy time so soone as may be.	Ovid's Elegies	2.11.56	
I borne much, hoping time would beate thee/To guard her well,	Ovid's Elegies	2.19.49	
Tis time to move grave things in lofty stile,	Ovid's Elegies	3.1.23	
And seaven [times] <time> shooke her head with thicke locks	Ovid's Elegies	3.1.32	
She gave me leave, soft loves in time make hast,	Ovid's Elegies	3.1.69	
Yet in the meane time wilt small windes bestowe,	Ovid's Elegies	3.2.37	
Strayd bare-foote through sole places on a time.	Ovid's Elegies	3.5.50	
Both loves to whom my heart long time did yeeld,	Ovid's Elegies	3.14.15	
Since Heroes time, hath halfe the world beene blacke.	Hero and Leander	1.50	
Which long time lie untoucht, will harshly jarre.	Hero and Leander	1.230	
In time it will returne us two for one.	Hero and Leander	1.236	
But long this blessed time continued not;	Hero and Leander	1.459	

TIME (cont.)
And she her selfe before the pointed time, . . . Hero and Leander 2.20
TIMELES
And brought by murder to their timeles ends. . . . P 46 1.46 Navrre
Shall be their timeles sepulcher, or mine. . . . Edw 1.2.6 Lncstr
TIMELESSE
Let earth and heaven his timelesse death deplore, . . 2Tamb 5.3.252 Amyras
Him timelesse death tooke, she was deifide. . . . Ovid's Elegies 2.2.46
TIMERE
Edwardum occidere nolite timere bonum est. . . . Edw 5.4.8 Mortmr
Edwardum occidere nolite timere bonum est. . . . Edw 5.4.11 Mortmr
Edwardum occidere nolite timere, ... Edw 5.5.17 Matrvs
TIMES
And then Ile hugge with you an hundred times. . . . Dido 1.1.48 Ganimd
Theridamas, farewel ten thousand times. . . . . 1Tamb 1.1.82 Mycet
Twere requisite he should be ten times more, . . . 1Tamb 3.1.47 Argier
With whom they have attempted many times, . . . Jew 1.1.164 Barab
the Nuns are dead/That sound at other times like Tinkers pans? Jew 4.1.3 Barab
Considering of these dangerous times. . . . . P 175 3.10 Admral
O gracious God, what times are these? . . . . P 188 3.23 Navrre
Welcome ten thousand times, old man againe. . . . Edw 3.1.46 Edward
Despite of times, despite of enemies. . . . . Edw 3.1.147 Edward
And there stay times advantage with your sonne? . . Edw 4.2.18 SrJohn
All times and seasons rest you at a stay, ... Edw 5.1.67 Edward
at all times, in what shape [or] <and> forme soever he please. F 492 2.1.104 P Faust
At al times charging home, and making havock; . . . Lucan, First Booke 148
Which is nor sea, nor land, but oft times both, . . . Lucan, First Booke 411
But in times past I fear'd vaine shades, and night, . . Ovid's Elegies 1.6.9
But what entreates for thee some-times tooke place, . . Ovid's Elegies 1.6.21
And as first wrongd the wronged some-times banish, . . Ovid's Elegies 1.8.79
Nothing I love, that at all times availes me. . . . Ovid's Elegies 2.19.8
Let this care some-times bite thee to the quick, . . Ovid's Elegies 2.19.43
And seaven [times] <time> shooke her head with thicke locks Ovid's Elegies 3.1.32
Graunt Tragedie thy Poet times least tittle, . . . Ovid's Elegies 3.1.67
Wit was some-times more pretious then gold, . . . Ovid's Elegies 3.7.3
Come were the times of Ceres sacrifize, ... Ovid's Elegies 3.9.1
For whom succeeding times make greater mone. . . . Hero and Leander 1.54
Receives no blemish, but oft-times more grace, . . . Hero and Leander 1.217
T'INCOUNTER
T'incounter with the strength of Tamburlaine. . . . 1Tamb 3.3.7 Tamb
I meane t'incounter with that Bajazeth. . . . . 1Tamb 3.3.65 Tamb
T'incounter with the cruell Tamburlain, ... 2Tamb 2.2.5 Orcan
TINCTURE
And silver tincture of her cheekes, that drew/The love of Hero and Leander 1.396
TINDER
Gentle Achates, reach the Tinder boxe, ... Dido 1.1.166 Aeneas
TINKERS
the Nuns are dead/That sound at other times like Tinkers pans? Jew 4.1.3 Barab
TINMOTH
Do what they can, weele live in Tinmoth here, . . . Edw 2.2.221 Edward
And here in Tinmoth frollicks with the king. . . . Edw 2.3.17 Lncstr
TINMOUTH
Welcome to Tinmouth, welcome to thy friend, . . . Edw 2.2.51 Edward
T'INVEST
That meane t'invest me in a higher throane, . . . 2Tamb 5.3.121 Tamb
TIPHEUS
Whose flintie darts slept in Tipheus den, ... Dido 4.1.19 Iarbus
TIPPET
and when the Hangman had put on his hempen Tippet, he made such Jew 4.2.23 P Ithimr
TIPTOES
[A] <Or> while thy tiptoes on the foote-stoole rest. . Ovid's Elegies 3.2.64
TIRANNICALL
An action bloudy and tirannicall: . . . . . . P 208 4.6 Charls
TIRANNIE
As made Love sigh, to see his tirannie. . . . . Hero and Leander 1.374
TIRANNOUS
Love Hero then, and be not tirannous, ... Hero and Leander 1.323
TIRANNY
In murder, mischeefe, or in tiranny. . . . . . P 41 1.41 Condy
TIRANT
Least they should fly, being tane, the tirant play. . . Ovid's Elegies 1.8.70
TIR'D
These hands are tir'd, with haling of my lord/From Gaveston, Edw 2.4.26 Queene
This said, being tir'd with fury she sunke downe. . . Lucan, First Booke 694
Being wrackt, carowse the sea tir'd by their ships: . . Ovid's Elegies 2.10.34
TIRE (Homograph; See also ATTIRE, TIERD, TYRE)
god>,/Here <Faustus> tire my <trie thy> braines to get a Deity. F 90 1.1.62 Faust
Watching till after mid-night did not tire thee. . . Ovid's Elegies 1.6.44
TIRED
The Grecian souldiers tired with ten yeares warre, . . Dido 2.1.126 Aeneas
Achates speake, sorrow hath tired me quite. . . . Dido 2.1.293 Aeneas
And all his life time hath bin tired, ... Jew 1.1.15 Barab
fitter for a tale of love/Then to be tired out with Orizons: Jew 1.2.370 Mthias
TIRES
dye to expiate/The griefe that tires upon thine inward soule. Dido 5.1.317 Iarbus
And like a Harpyr <Harpye> tires on my life. . . . 1Tamb 2.7.50 Cosroe
TIRIEN
It is the use for [Tirien] <Turen> maides to weare/Their bowe Dido 1.1.204 Venus
'TIS
'twere in my power/To favour you, but 'tis my fathers cause, Jew 1.2.11 Calym
And 'tis more Kingly to obtaine by peace/Then to enforce . Jew 1.2.25 Calym
And 'tis thy mony, Barabas, we seeke. . . . . Jew 1.2.54 1Knght
'Tis not our fault, but thy inherent sinne. . . . Jew 1.2.109 1Knght

'TIS (cont.)

And covetousnesse, oh 'tis a monstrous sinne.	Jew	1.2.124		Govnr
'Tis necessary that be look'd unto:	Jew	1.2.157		1Knght
'Tis in the trouble of my spirit I speake;	Jew	1.2.207		Barab
but trust me 'tis a misery/To see a man in such affliction:	Jew	1.2.211		2Jew
'Tis thirtie winters long since some of us/Did stray so farre	Jew	1.2.308		Abbass
As but to be about this happy place;/'Tis not so happy:	Jew	2.1.33		Abigal
Peace, Abigal, 'tis I.	Jew	2.1.43		Barab
'Tis true, my Lord, therefore intreat him well.	Jew	2.2.8		1Knght
'tis a custome held with us,/That when we speake with Gentiles	Jew	2.3.44		Barab
'Tis likely they in time may reape some fruit,	Jew	2.3.84		Barab
'tis not a stone of beef a day will maintaine you in these	Jew	2.3.124	P	Barab
I feare me 'tis about faire Abigall.	Jew	2.3.139		Mthias
on the Machabees/I have it, Sir, and 'tis at your command.	Jew	2.3.154		Barab
'Tis not thy wealth, but her that I esteeme,	Jew	2.3.298		Lodowk
Oh muse not at it, 'tis the Hebrewes guize,	Jew	2.3.325		Barab
I, so thou shalt, 'tis thou must doe the deed:	Jew	2.3.369		Barab
'Tis poyson'd, is it not?	Jew	2.3.372		Ithimr
'Tis silver, I disdaine it.	Jew	3.1.13		Curtzn
I feare she knowes ('tis so) of my device/In Don Mathias and	Jew	3.4.7		Barab
If so, 'tis time that it be seene into:	Jew	3.4.9		Barab
Here 'tis, Master.	Jew	3.4.55	P	Ithimr
This Even they use in Malta here ('tis call'd/Saint Jaques	Jew	3.4.75		Barab
Peace, Ithimore, 'tis better so then spar'd.	Jew	3.4.91		Barab
Thou know'st 'tis death and if it be reveal'd.	Jew	3.6.51		2Fryar
Then 'tis not for me; and I am resolv'd/You shall confesse me,	Jew	4.1.85		Barab
Therefore 'tis not requisite he should live.	Jew	4.1.121		Barab
No, 'tis an order which the Fryars use:	Jew	4.1.134		Barab
'Tis neatly done, Sir, here's no print at all.	Jew	4.1.151		Ithimr
'Tis not thy mony, but thy selfe I weigh:	Jew	4.2.124		Curtzn
'Tis not five hundred Crownes that I esteeme,	Jew	4.3.40		Barab
'Tis a strange thing of that Jew, he lives upon pickled	Jew	4.4.61	P	Ithimr
'Tis our command:	Jew	5.2.15		Calym
'Tis not thy life which can availe me ought,	Jew	5.2.62		Barab
'Tis magick, magick, that hath ravisht me.	F 137	1.1.109		Faust
'Tis thou hast damn'd distressed Faustus soule.	F 628	2.2.77		Faust
'Tis well said Faustus, come then stand by me/And thou shalt	F 843	3.1.65		Mephst
'Tis no matter, let him come; an he follow us, I'le so conjure	F1091	3.3.4	P	Robin
Here 'tis:	F1094	3.3.7	P	Dick
Nay there you lie, 'tis beyond us both.	F1109	3.3.22	P	Robin
me his leg quite off, and now 'tis at home in mine Hostry.	F1551	4.5.47	P	HrsCsr
'Tis not so much worth; I pray you tel me one thing.	F1643	4.6.86	P	Carter
and now ['tis] <'ts> too late.	F1866	5.2.70	P	Faust
'tis too late, despaire, farewell,/Fooles that will laugh on	F1890	5.2.94		Mephst
Where is it now? 'tis gone.	F1943	5.2.147		Faust
'tis thou enflam'st/The threatning Scorpion with the burning	Lucan, First Booke			657
So farre 'tis safe, but to go farther dread.	Ovid's Elegies			2.11.16
Rude man, 'tis vaine, thy damsell to commend/To keepers trust:	Ovid's Elegies			3.4.1
A free-borne wench, no right 'tis up to locke:	Ovid's Elegies			3.4.33
In mid Bithynia 'tis said Inachus,	Ovid's Elegies			3.5.25
'Tis so: by my witte her abuse is growne.	Ovid's Elegies			3.11.8
'Tis doubtfull whether verse availe, or harme,	Ovid's Elegies			3.11.13
'Tis wisedome to give much, a gift prevailes,	Hero and Leander			2.225

T'IS

T'is lost but once, and once lost, lost for ever.	Hero and Leander			2.86
So beautie, sweetly quickens when t'is ny,	Hero and Leander			2.126

TIS

Achates, tis my mother that is fled,	Dido	1.1.240		Aeneas
Renowmed Dido, tis our Generall:	Dido	2.1.77		Illion
Tis not enough that thou doest graunt me love,	Dido	3.1.8		Iarbus
If there be any heaven in earth, tis love:	Dido	4.5.27		Nurse
O then Aeneas, tis for griefe of thee:	Dido	5.1.116		Dido
Therefore tis good and meete for to be wise.	1Tamb	1.1.34		Mycet
Therefore tis best, if so it lik you all,	1Tamb	1.1.51		Mycet
And tis a prety toy to be a Poet.	1Tamb	2.2.54		Mycet
Then tis mine.	1Tamb	2.4.34		Tamb
O my Lord, tis sweet and full of pompe.	1Tamb	2.5.55		Techel
Tis more then pitty such a heavenly face/Should by hearts	1Tamb	3.2.4		Agidas
hardy Tamburlaine)/What tis to meet me in the open field,	1Tamb	3.3.146		Bajzth
Tis like he wil, when he cannot let it.	1Tamb	4.4.53	P	Techel
Me thinks, tis a great deale better than a consort of musicke.	1Tamb	4.4.60	P	Therid
Tis enough for us to see them, and for Tamburlaine onely to	1Tamb	4.4.111	P	Techel
Tis requisit to parle for a peace/With Sigismond the king of	2Tamb	1.1.50		Gazell
They shal Casane, and tis time yfaith.	2Tamb	1.3.185		Tamb
Assure your Grace tis superstition/To stand so strictly on	2Tamb	2.1.49		Fredrk
Tis but the fortune of the wars my Lord,	2Tamb	2.3.31		Gazell
Tis nought for your majesty to give a kingdome.	2Tamb	3.1.77		Jrslem
Me thinks tis a pitifull sight.	2Tamb	3.2.130	P	Calyph
Tis nothing: give me a wound father.	2Tamb	3.2.132	P	Celeb
Tis not thy bloody tents can make me yeeld,	2Tamb	5.1.103		Govnr
Tis brave indeed my boy, wel done,	2Tamb	5.1.150		Tamb
Fye; what a trouble tis to count this trash.	Jew	1.1.7		Barab
Tis but a nook of France,/Sufficient yet for such a pettie	P 149	2.92		Guise
Cosin tis he, I know him by his look.	P 309	5.36		Guise
Dearely beloved brother, thus tis written.	P 343	5.70		Guise
Tis Taleus, Ramus bedfellow.	P 372	7.12		Retes
Tis Ramus, the Kings professor of Logick.	P 381	7.21		Retes
Tis well advisde Dumain, goe see it strait be done.	P 424	7.64		Guise
But tis the house of Burbon that he meanes.	P 644	12.57		Cardnl
And tell him that tis for his Countries good,	P 646	12.59		Cardnl
Sweet Mugeroune, tis he that hath my heart,	P 660	13.4		Duchss
Tis more then kingly or Emperious.	P 759	15.17		Guise
What I have done tis for the Gospell sake.	P 826	17.21		Guise

TIS (cont.)

Tis for your safetie and your enemies wrack.	P 858	17.53	Guise
Be gone I say, tis time that we were there.	P 919	18.20	Navrre
Why this tis to have an army in the fielde.	P 980	19.50	Guise
As pale as ashes, nay then tis time to look about.	P1001	19.71	Guise
Tis warre that must asswage this tyrantes pride.	P1128	21.22	Dumain
What danger tis to stand against your king.	Edw	1.1.97	Edward
Tis true, and but for reverence of these robes,	Edw	1.1.180	Gavstn
Tis true, the Bishop is in the tower,	Edw	1.2.1	Warwck
Tis done, and now accursed hand fall off.	Edw	1.4.88	Edward
Tis true sweete Gaveston, oh were it false.	Edw	1.4.108	Edward
Tis something to be pitied of a king.	Edw	1.4.130	Gavstn
Villaine, tis thou that robst me of my lord.	Edw	1.4.160	Queene
Madam, tis you that rob me of my lord.	Edw	1.4.161	Gavstn
I know tis long of Gaveston she weepes.	Edw	1.4.191	Mortmr
For tis against my will he should returne.	Edw	1.4.217	Queene
Tis for my selfe I speake, and not for him.	Edw	1.4.219	Queene
Tis not for his sake, but for our availe:	Edw	1.4.242	Mortmr
Tis hard for us to worke his overthrow.	Edw	1.4.262	Mortmr
Tis treason to be up against the king.	Edw	1.4.281	Mortmr
Tis not the king can buckler Gaveston,	Edw	1.4.288	Mortmr
Unckle, tis this that makes me impatient.	Edw	1.4.419	Mortmr
Tis like enough, for since he was exild,	Edw	2.1.23	Baldck
Tis not a black coate and a little band,	Edw	2.1.33	Spencr
Tis not the hugest monster of the sea,	Edw	2.2.45	Edward
Tis warre that must abate these Barons pride.	Edw	2.2.99	Edward
And when tis gone, our swordes shall purchase more.	Edw	2.2.197	Lncstr
My lord, tis thought, the Earles are up in armes.	Edw	2.2.225	Queene
I, and tis likewise thought you favour him <them> <'em> <hem>.	Edw	2.2.226	Edward
Come, come aboord, tis but an houres sailing.	Edw	2.4.49	Lncstr
Tis verie kindlie spoke my lord of Penbrooke,	Edw	2.5.104	Arundl
Tis not amisse my liege for eyther part,	Edw	3.1.190	SpncrP
traitors, now tis time/To be avengd on you for all your braves,	Edw	3.1.224	Edward
Tis but temporall that thou canst inflict.	Edw	3.1.242	Warwck
Mortimer tis I,	Edw	4.1.13	Kent
Tis not in her controulment, nor in ours,	Edw	4.6.35	Mortmr
Madam, tis good to looke to him betimes.	Edw	4.6.39	Mortmr
Tis in the name of Isabell the Queene:	Edw	4.7.59	Leistr
Must! tis somwhat hard, when kings must go.	Edw	4.7.83	Edward
No, tis for Mortimer, not Edwards head,	Edw	5.1.40	Edward
I, my most gratious lord, so tis decreed.	Edw	5.1.138	Bartly
And when tis done, we will subscribe our name.	Edw	5.2.50	Mortmr
I tell thee tis not meet, that one so false/Should come about	Edw	5.2.104	Mortmr
Feare not to kill the king tis good he die.	Edw	5.4.9	Mortmr
Kill not the king tis good to feare the worst.	Edw	5.4.12	Mortmr
Tis not the first time I have killed a man.	Edw	5.4.30	Ltborn
Tis for your highnesse good, and for the realmes.	Edw	5.4.101	Mortmr
Tis my hand, what gather you by this.	Edw	5.6.47	Mortmr
Thus madam, tis the kings will you shall hence.	Edw	5.6.89	2Lord
Sweet Analitikes <Anulatikes>, tis thou hast ravisht me,	F 34	1.1.6	Faust
I tell thee Faustus it is <tis> not halfe so faire/As thou, or	F 557	2.2.6	Mephst
<Tut, tis no matter man>, wee'l be bold with his <good cheare>.	F 808	(HC265) A P	Mephst
Looke up Benvolio, tis the Emperour calls.	F1286	4.1.132	Saxony
hold, tis no matter for thy head, for that's arm'd sufficiently.	F1288	4.1.134 P	Emper
<to cure him, tis but a surffet, never feare man>.	F1831	(HC270) A P	2Schol
Tis but a surfet sir, feare nothing.	F1832	5.2.36	3Schol
You lie Drawer, tis afore me:	F App	p.235 17 P	Robin
which of both/Had justest cause unlawful tis to judge:	Lucan, First Booke		127
Tis cruell love turmoyles my captive hart.	Ovid's Elegies		1.2.8
Tis shame for eld in warre or love to be.	Ovid's Elegies		1.9.4
Oft to invade the sleeping foe tis good/And arm'd to shed	Ovid's Elegies		1.9.21
Tis shame their wits should be more excelent.	Ovid's Elegies		1.10.26
Tis shame sould tongues the guilty should defend/Or great	Ovid's Elegies		1.10.39
Tis shame to grow rich by bed merchandize,	Ovid's Elegies		1.10.41
In verse to praise kinde Wenches tis my part,	Ovid's Elegies		1.10.59
And tis suppos'd Loves bowe hath wounded thee,	Ovid's Elegies		1.11.11
I cryed, tis sinne, tis sinne, these haires to burne,	Ovid's Elegies		1.14.27
Phoebus gave not Diana such tis thought,	Ovid's Elegies		2.5.27
Tis ill they pleas'd so much, for in my lips,	Ovid's Elegies		2.5.57
Tis credible some [god-head] <good head> haunts the place.	Ovid's Elegies		3.1.2
Tis time to move grave things in lofty stile,	Ovid's Elegies		3.1.23
Tis not enough, she shakes your record off,	Ovid's Elegies		3.3.19
Tis said the slippery streame held up her brest,	Ovid's Elegies		3.5.81
Tis well, if some wench for the poore remaine.	Ovid's Elegies		3.7.60
But that thou wouldst dissemble when tis paste.	Ovid's Elegies		3.13.4
Slippe still, onely denie it when tis done,	Ovid's Elegies		3.13.15

TISIPHON

Or like the snakie wreathe of Tisiphon,	Edw	5.1.45	Edward

TITAN

As far as Titan springs where night dims heaven,	Lucan, First Booke		15
While Titan strives against the worlds swift course;	Lucan, First Booke		90
Or flaming Titan (feeding on the deepe)/Puls them aloft, and	Lucan, First Booke		416
Titan himselfe throand in the midst of heaven,	Lucan, First Booke		538

TITERUS

*Aeneas warre, and Titerus shall be read,	Ovid's Elegies		1.15.25

TITHON

Would Tithon might but talke of thee a while,	Ovid's Elegies		1.13.35
And Tithon livelier then his yeeres require.	Ovid's Elegies		3.6.42

TITLE (See also TYTLE)

A title higher than thy Souldans name:	1Tamb	5.1.434	Tamb
Many will talke of Title to a Crowne:	Jew	Prol.18	Machvl
My Lord and King hath title to this Isle,	Jew	2.2.37	Bosco
Do but deserve gifts with this title grav'd.	Ovid's Elegies		2.13.26

TITLES			
My lord, these titles far exceed my worth.	Edw	1.1.157	Gavstn
No greater titles happen unto me,	Edw	2.2.254	Spencr
Stand not on titles, but obay th'arrest,	Edw	4.7.58	Leistr
If loftie titles cannot make me thine,	Ovid's Elegies		1.3.7
TITTLE			
Within a while great heapes grow of a tittle.	Ovid's Elegies		1.8.90
Graunt Tragedie thy Poet times least tittle,	Ovid's Elegies		3.1.67
TITUS			
Till Titus and Vespasian conquer'd us)/Am I become as wealthy	Jew	2.3.10	Barab
TITYRUS (See TITERUS)			
TITYUS			
Our verse great Tityus a huge space out-spreads,	Ovid's Elegies		3.11.25
'TMAY			
Nay stay, my Lord, 'tmay be he will confesse.	Jew	5.1.25	1Knght
'TMUST			
For to be short, amongst you 'tmust be had.	Jew	1.2.56	Govnr
TO AND FRO			
Whence the wind blowes stil forced to and fro;	Lucan, First Booke		414
My sides are sore with tumbling to and fro.	Ovid's Elegies		1.2.4
TO DAY			
To day when as I fild into your cups,	Dido	1.1.5	Ganimd
Our life is fraile, and we may die to day.	1Tamb	1.1.68	Mycet
Thy wit will make us Conquerors to day.	1Tamb	2.2.58	Mycet
belike he hath not bene watered to day, give him some drinke.	1Tamb	4.4.55	P Tamb
Hath Bajazeth bene fed to day?	1Tamb	5.1.192	Tamb
Were they not summon'd to appeare to day?	Jew	1.2.35	Govnr
To day.	Jew	3.4.19	P Ithimr
The Pope will curse them for their sloth to day,	F 987	3.2.7	Faust
Benvolio's head was grac't with hornes to day?	F1331	4.2.7	Benvol
Let me lie with thee browne Cypasse to day.	Ovid's Elegies		2.8.22
TODOS			
Bien para todos mi ganado no es:	Jew	2.1.39	Barab
TOGETHER			
Why talke we not together hand in hand?	Dido	1.1.245	Aeneas
That tyed together by the striving tongues,	Dido	4.3.29	Aeneas
The Souldan and the Arabian king together/Martch on us with	1Tamb	5.1.199	Techel
Summon thy sences, call thy wits together:	Jew	1.1.178	Barab
Come my deare love, let's in and sleepe together.	Jew	4.2.129	Curtzn
That wee might sleepe seven yeeres together afore we wake.	Jew	4.2.131	Ithimr
These Barons lay their heads on blocks together,	Edw	3.1.274	Baldck
To thinke that we can yet be tun'd together,	Edw	4.2.9	Queene
Be both your legs bedfellowes every night together?	F1645	4.6.88	P Carter
The world (were it together) is by cowards/Left as a pray now	Lucan, First Booke		511
And loving Doves kisse eagerly together.	Ovid's Elegies		2.6.56
So shalt thou go with youths to feasts together,	Ovid's Elegies		3.4.47
TOGITHER			
Good forme there is, yeares apt to play togither,	Ovid's Elegies		2.3.13
TOIES			
Spencer, thou knowest I hate such formall toies,	Edw	2.1.44	Baldck
And [throw] <threw> him gawdie toies to please his eie,	Hero and Leander		2.187
TOILE (See also TOYLE)			
But as the Gods to end the Troyans toile,	1Tamb	5.1.392	Zenoc
Roome may be won/With farre lesse toile, and yet the honors	Lucan, First Booke		284
TOKEN			
a thousand Crownes, by the same token, that the Nuns lov'd Rice,	Jew	4.4.75	P Ithimr
My Lord, in token of my true humilitie,	P 866	17.61	Guise
And by a secret token that he beares,	Edw	5.4.19	Mortmr
Know you this token? I must have the king.	Edw	5.5.19	Ltborn
In token of our seven-fold power from heaven,	F 934	3.1.156	Pope
Yet when a token of great worth we send,	Hero and Leander		2.80
TOLD			
And when we told her she would weepe for griefe,	Dido	2.1.67	Illion
and had not we/Fought manfully, I had not told this tale:	Dido	2.1.271	Aeneas
Nor quit good turnes with double fee downe told:	Dido	3.2.15	Juno
And told me that Aeneas ment to goe:	Dido	4.4.142	Dido
As for the Diamond, Sir, I told you of,	Jew	2.3.91	Barab
Where is the Diamond you told me of?	Jew	2.3.219	Lodowk
'twas told me in shrift,/Thou know'st 'tis death and if it be	Jew	3.6.50	2Fryar
told him he were best to send it; then he hug'd and imbrac'd	Jew	4.2.106	P Pilia
and told me he lov'd me for your sake, and said what a	Jew	4.2.108	P Pilia
A friend of mine told me in secrecie,	Edw	2.1.17	Spencr
To this I fondly loves of flouds told plainly:	Ovid's Elegies		3.5.101
So in a spring thrives he that told so much,	Ovid's Elegies		3.6.51
Thereat smilde Neptune, and then told a tale,	Hero and Leander		2.193
TOLDE			
Madam, as in secrecy I was tolde,	P 641	12.54	Cardnl
What age of Varroes name shall not be tolde,	Ovid's Elegies		1.15.21
TOLDST			
thus; thou toldst me they have turn'd my house/Into a Nunnery,	Jew	1.2.277	Barab
TOLE			
set the street/May know their watchword, then tole the bell,	P 329	5.56	Guise
TOLLS			
Thus like the sad presaging Raven that tolls/The sicke mans	Jew	2.1.1	Barab
TOMB'D			
Whose body shall be tomb'd with all the pompe/The treasure of	2Tamb	4.2.97	Therid
TOMBE			
Then would I wish me with Anchises Tombe,	Dido	3.3.44	Aeneas
Then in as rich a tombe as Mausolus,	2Tamb	2.4.133	Tamb
There saw we learned Maroes golden tombe:	F 791	3.1.13	Faust
This tombe approoves, I pleasde my mistresse well,	Ovid's Elegies		2.6.61
O would in my fore-fathers tombe deepe layde,	Ovid's Elegies		3.5.73
TO MORROW			
They shall to morrow draw my chariot,	2Tamb	4.3.30	Tamb

TO MORROW (cont.)			
To morrow early I'le be at the doore.	Jew	1.2.361	Barab
Farewell, Remember to morrow morning.	Jew	1.2.364	Barab
To morrow is the Sessions; you shall to it.	Jew	4.1.199	Barab
To morrow, sitting in our Consistory,	F 967	3.1.189	Pope
To morrow we would sit i'th Consistory,	F1017	3.2.37	Pope
To me to morrow constantly deny it.	Ovid's Elegies	1.4.70	
TON (See TUN)			
TONE			
Wel, tone of you hath this goblet about you.	F App	p.235 16	P Vintnr
TONGUE (See also TOONG, TOUNG)			
Then speake Aeneas with Achilles tongue,	Dido	2.1.121	Aeneas
Whose ticing tongue was made of Hermes pipe,	Dido	2.1.145	Aeneas
and she shal looke/That these abuses flow not from her tongue:	1Tamb	4.2.70	Zenoc
Would lend an howers license to my tongue:	1Tamb	5.1.423	Arabia
Dye life, flye soule, tongue curse thy fill and dye.	Jew	5.5.89	Barab
Ile hang a golden tongue about thy neck,	Edw	1.4.328	Edward
buttons to his lips, to keepe his tongue from catching cold.	F1388	4.2.64	P Benvol
oh hee stayes my tongue:	F1852	5.2.56	P Faust
and whose tongue/Could tune the people to the Nobles mind:	Lucan, First Booke	272	
She nothing said, pale feare her tongue had tyed.	Ovid's Elegies	1.7.20	
Nor doth her tongue want harmefull eloquence.	Ovid's Elegies	1.8.20	
Let thy tongue flatter, while thy minde harme-workes:	Ovid's Elegies	1.8.103	
No envious tongue wrought thy thicke lockes decay.	Ovid's Elegies	1.14.42	
(Such with my tongue it likes me to purloyne).	Ovid's Elegies	2.5.24	
Lay her whole tongue hid, mine in hers she dips.	Ovid's Elegies	2.5.58	
Farewell Corinna cryed thy dying tongue.	Ovid's Elegies	2.6.48	
And eagerlie she kist me with her tongue,	Ovid's Elegies	3.6.9	
There in your rosie lippes my tongue intombe,	Ovid's Elegies	3.13.23	
Teach but your tongue to say, I did it not,	Ovid's Elegies	3.13.48	
TONGUES			
That tyed together by the striving tongues,	Dido	4.3.29	Aeneas
When with their fearfull tongues they shall confesse/Theise are	1Tamb	1.2.222	Usumc
To make these captives reine their lavish tongues.	1Tamb	4.2.67	Techel
Ile bridle al your tongues/And bind them close with bits of	2Tamb	4.1.181	Tamb
To bridle their contemptuous cursing tongues,	2Tamb	4.3.44	Therid
to restraine/These coltish coach-horse tongues from blasphemy.	2Tamb	4.3.52	Usumc
But such as love me, gard me from their tongues,	Jew	Prol.6	Machvl
Preach upon poles for trespasse of their tongues.	Edw	1.1.118	Kent
Inricht with tongues, well seene in Minerals,	F 166	1.1.138	Cornel
Tis shame sould tongues the guilty should defend/Or great	Ovid's Elegies	1.10.39	
flying touch/Tantalus seekes, his long tongues gaine is such.	Ovid's Elegies	2.2.44	
What should I tell her vaine tongues filthy lyes,	Ovid's Elegies	3.10.21	
TO NIGHT			
I'le be with you to night.	Jew	4.1.90	2Fryar
TOO (Homograph)			
Too cruell, why wilt thou forsake me thus?	Dido	1.1.243	Aeneas
Too meane to be companion to a Queene.	Dido	2.1.89	Aeneas
Lest you be mov'd too much with my sad tale.	Dido	2.1.125	Aeneas
In being too familiar with Iarbus:	Dido	3.1.15	Dido
Poore soule I know too well the sower of love,	Dido	3.1.61	Anna
Theres not so much as this base tackling too,	Dido	4.4.151	Dido
To too forgetfull of thine owne affayres,	Dido	5.1.30	Hermes
He loves me to too well to serve me so:	Dido	5.1.185	Dido
Traytoresse too [keene] <keend> <kind> and cursed Sorceresse.	Dido	5.1.221	Dido
The [Lords] <Lord> would not be too exasperate,	1Tamb	1.1.182	Ortyg
An ods too great, for us to stand against:	1Tamb	1.2.122	Tamb
To bid him battaile ere he passe too farre,	1Tamb	2.5.95	Tamb
Too harsh a subject for your dainty eares.	1Tamb	3.2.46	Agidas
Madame, she thinks perhaps she is too fine.	1Tamb	3.3.179	Ebea
For Fame I feare hath bene too prodigall,	1Tamb	4.3.48	Arabia
Sirra, why fall you not too, are you so daintily brought up, you	1Tamb	4.4.36	P Tamb
sir, you must be dieted, too much eating will make you surfeit.	1Tamb	4.4.103	P Tamb
Would not with too much cowardize or feare,	1Tamb	5.1.37	Govnr
And tels for trueth, submissions comes too late.	1Tamb	5.1.73	Tamb
Faire is too foule an Epithite for thee,	1Tamb	5.1.136	Tamb
Too deare a witnesse for such love my Lord.	1Tamb	5.1.412	Zenoc
With them Arabia too hath left his life,	1Tamb	5.1.473	Tamb
Bewraies they are too dainty for the wars.	2Tamb	1.3.28	Tamb
Hold him, and cleave him too, or Ile cleave thee,	2Tamb	1.3.104	Tamb
(Too litle to defend our guiltlesse lives)/Sufficient to	2Tamb	2.2.60	Orcan
Go too sirha, take your crown, and make up the halfe dozen.	2Tamb	3.5.135	P Tamb
If Jove esteeming me too good for earth,	2Tamb	4.3.60	Tamb
kings Concubines)/Take them, devide them and their jewels too,	2Tamb	4.3.72	Tamb
As much too high for this disdainfull earth.	2Tamb	5.3.122	Tamb
I, and of a moving spirit too, brother; but come,	Jew	1.2.328	2Fryar
Wilt thou forsake mee too in my distresse,	Jew	1.2.358	Barab
And so will I too, or it shall goe hard.--	Jew	1.2.392	Lodowk
Oh Abigal, Abigal, that I had thee here too,	Jew	2.1.51	Barab
And buy it basely too for summes of gold?	Jew	2.2.29	Bosco
I, and his sonnes too, or it shall goe hard.	Jew	2.3.17	Barab
I wud you were his father too, Sir, that's al the harm I wish	Jew	2.3.41	P Barab
So doe I too.	Jew	2.3.61	Barab
alas, hath pac'd too long/The fatall Labyrinth of misbeleefe,	Jew	3.3.63	Abigal
What, hast thou brought the Ladle with thee too?	Jew	3.4.57	Barab
And I shall dye too, for I feele death comming.	Jew	3.6.8	Abigal
I, and a Virgin too, that grieves me most:	Jew	3.6.41	2Fryar
And reason too;	Jew	4.1.12	Ithimr
Is't not too late now to turne Christian?	Jew	4.1.50	Barab
They weare no shirts, and they goe bare-foot too.	Jew	4.1.84	1Fryar
I, and our lives too, therfore pull amaine.	Jew	4.1.150	Ithimr
Take in the staffe too, for that must be showne:	Jew	4.1.204	Barab
I'le make him send me half he has, and glad he scapes so too.	Jew	4.2.67	P Ithimr

TOO (cont.)

And bid the Jeweller come hither too.	Jew	4.2.86		Ithimr
I, and the rest too, or else--	Jew	4.3.28	P	Pilia
the Nuns, and he and I, snicle hand too fast, strangled a Fryar.	Jew	4.4.21	P	Ithimr
Take my goods too, and seize upon my lands:	Jew	5.1.66		Barab
not thine opportunity, for feare too late/Thou seek'st for much,	Jew	5.2.45		Barab
Now tell me, Governor, and plainely too,	Jew	5.2.55		Barab
And reason too, for Christians doe the like:	Jew	5.2.116		Barab
Will be too costly and too troublesome:	Jew	5.3.23		Calym
A pension and a dispensation too:	P 120	2.63		Guise
Too late it is my Lord if that be true/To blame her highnes,	P 181	3.16		QnMarg
What, all alone my love, and writing too:	P 670	13.14		Guise
If it be not too free there's the question:	P 813	17.8	P	Souldr
slew him, and will slay/Thee too, and thou prove such a traitor.	P1049	19.119		King
He died a death too good, the devill of hell/Torture his wicked	P1218	22.80		Bartus
Rend not my hart with thy too piercing words,	Edw	1.4.117		Edward
Thou art too familiar with that Mortimer,	Edw	1.4.154		Edward
Repeald, the newes is too sweet to be true.	Edw	1.4.323		Edward
I am that Cedar, shake me not too much,	Edw	2.2.38		Edward
Now let them thanke themselves, and rue too late.	Edw	2.2.207		Edward
Yea gentle Spencer, we have beene too milde,	Edw	3.1.24		Edward
Too kinde to them, but now have drawne our sword,	Edw	3.1.25		Edward
that we can yet be tun'd together,/No, no, we jarre too farre.	Edw	4.2.10		Queene
This way he fled, but I am come too late.	Edw	4.6.1		Kent
Too true it is, quem dies vidit veniens superbum,	Edw	4.7.53		Leistr
Here, take my crowne, the life of Edward too,	Edw	5.1.57		Edward
Unlesse it be with too much clemencie?	Edw	5.1.123		Edward
Heare me immortall Jove, and graunt it too.	Edw	5.1.143		Edward
Let him be king, I am too yong to raigne.	Edw	5.2.93		Prince
I am too weake and feeble to resist,	Edw	5.5.108		Edward
But not too hard, least that you bruse his body.	Edw	5.5.113		Ltborn
His kingly body was too soone interrde.	Edw	5.6.32		King
And so shalt thou be too: why staies he heere?	Edw	5.6.51		King
My lord, I feare me it will proove too true.	Edw	5.6.77		2Lord
Nay, to my death, for too long have I lived,	Edw	5.6.83		Queene
Too servile <The devill> and illiberall for mee.	F 63	1.1.35		Faust
Thou art too ugly to attend on me:	F 252	1.3.24		Faust
Yes, and goings out too, you may see sir.	F 347	1.4.5	P	Robin
I, and body too, but what of that:	F 521	2.1.133		Faust
[Heere they are too].	F 551.7	2.1.170A	P	Mephst
Ist not too late?	F 629	2.2.78		Faust
Too late.	F 630	2.2.79		BdAngl
Never too late, if Faustus will <can> repent.	F 631	2.2.80		GdAngl
Lord Raymond pray fall too, I am beholding/To the Bishop of	F1041	3.2.61		Pope
I'le have that too.	F1048	3.2.68		Faust
My wine gone too?	F1055	3.2.75		Pope
I, I, and I am content too:	F1254	4.1.100	P	Benvol
some on's have cause to know him; did he conjure thee too?	F1524	4.5.20	P	HrsCsr
'Faith you are too outragious, but come neere,	F1609	4.6.52		Faust
Too simple is my wit to tell her worth <praise>,/Whom all the	F1697	5.1.24		2Schol
Then Faustus, will repentance come too late,	F1714	5.1.41		OldMan
and now ['tis] <'ts> too late.	F1866	5.2.70	P	Faust
'tis too late, despaire, farewell,/Fooles that will laugh on	F1890	5.2.94		Mephst
I, and goings out too, you may see else.	F App	p.229 5	P	Clown
they are too familiar with me already, swowns they are as bolde	F App	p.229 27	P	Clown
Fall too, and the divel choake you and you spare.	F App	p.231 2	P	Faust
to lay the fury of this ghost, once again my Lord fall too.	F App	p.232 17	P	Pope
and ware robes/Too light for women; Poverty (who hatcht/Roomes	Lucan, First Booke			166
O wals unfortunate too neere to France,	Lucan, First Booke			250
And with them Curio, sometime Tribune too,	Lucan, First Booke			271
Th'Averni too, which bouldly faine themselves/The Romanes	Lucan, First Booke			428
Sword-girt Orions side glisters too bright.	Lucan, First Booke			664
I aske too much, would she but let me love hir,	Ovid's Elegies			1.3.3
Thee feare I too much:	Ovid's Elegies			1.6.15
The Sabine gauntlets were too dearely wunne/That unto death did	Ovid's Elegies			1.10.49
Because [thy] <they> care too much thy Mistresse troubled.	Ovid's Elegies			2.2.8
While Junos watch-man Io too much eyde,	Ovid's Elegies			2.2.45
and too much his griefe doth favour/That seekes the conquest by	Ovid's Elegies			2.5.11
Too late you looke back, when with anchors weighd,	Ovid's Elegies			2.11.23
Fat love, and too much fulsome me annoyes,	Ovid's Elegies			2.19.25
But thou of thy faire damsell too secure,	Ovid's Elegies			2.19.37
But on the ground thy cloathes too loosely lie,	Ovid's Elegies			3.2.25
Alas he runnes too farre about the ring,	Ovid's Elegies			3.2.69
And all things too much in their sole power drenches.	Ovid's Elegies			3.3.26
He is too clownish, whom a lewd wife grieves,	Ovid's Elegies			3.4.37
Ah now a name too true thou hast, I finde.	Ovid's Elegies			3.8.4
Before the roome be cleere, and doore put too.	Ovid's Elegies			3.13.10
passions to asswage)/Compile sharpe satyrs, but alas too late,	Hero and Leander			1.127
Beautie alone is lost, too warily kept.	Hero and Leander			1.328
And too too well the faire vermilion knew,	Hero and Leander			1.395
(Love is too full of faith, too credulous,	Hero and Leander			2.221

TOOK

Even in Bythinia, when I took this Turke:	1Tamb	4.2.42		Tamb
I took the king, and lead him bound in chaines/Unto Damasco,	2Tamb	1.3.204		Techel
He took his rouse with stopes of Rhennish wine,	F1174	4.1.20		Mrtino

TOOKE

Yet he undaunted tooke his fathers flagge,	Dido	2.1.259		Aeneas
Whom I tooke up to beare unto our ships:	Dido	2.1.277		Aeneas
No, I tooke it prisoner.	1Tamb	2.4.32		Tamb
Therfore I tooke my course to Manico:	2Tamb	1.3.198		Techel
where I tooke/The Turke and his great Empresse prisoners,	2Tamb	5.3.128		Tamb
then we [luft] <left>, and [tackt] <tooke>, and fought at ease:	Jew	2.2.14		Bosco
rumbling in the house; so I tooke onely this, and runne my way:	Jew	3.1.21	P	Pilia

TOOKE (cont.)			
The time you tooke for respite, is at hand,	Jew	3.5.8	Basso
I tooke him by the [beard] <sterd>, and look'd upon him thus;	Jew	4.2.105	P Pilia
be he that strucke <tooke> fryer Sandelo a blow on the pate.	F1081	3.2.101	P 1Frier
Cursed be he that tooke away his holinesse wine.	F1085	3.2.105	1Frier
I seeing that, tooke him by the leg, and never rested pulling,	F1550	4.5.46	P HrsCsr
Cursed be he that tooke Frier Sandelo a blow on the pate.	F App	p.232 35	Frier
Cursed be he that tooke away his holinesse wine.	F App	p.233 39	Frier
Men tooke delight in Jewels, houses, plate,	Lucan, First Booke		164
(men say)/Began to smile and [tooke] <take> one foote away.	Ovid's Elegies		1.1.8
Tooke out the shaft, ordaind my hart to shiver:	Ovid's Elegies		1.1.26
But what entreates for thee some-times tooke place,	Ovid's Elegies		1.6.21
Toyes, and light Elegies my darts I tooke,	Ovid's Elegies		2.1.21
Him timelesse death tooke, she was deifide.	Ovid's Elegies		2.2.46
<blushe>, and by that blushfull [glance] <glasse> am tooke:	Ovid's Elegies		2.4.12
One among many is to grieve thee tooke.	Ovid's Elegies		2.7.4
Nor can an other say his helpe I tooke.	Ovid's Elegies		2.12.12
By her footes blemish greater grace she tooke.	Ovid's Elegies		3.1.10
How long her lockes were, ere her oath she tooke:	Ovid's Elegies		3.3.3
She sawe, and as her marrowe tooke the flame,	Ovid's Elegies		3.9.27
By whom disclosd, she in the high woods tooke,	Ovid's Elegies		3.12.19
Though while the deede be doing you be tooke,	Ovid's Elegies		3.13.43
for they tooke delite/To play upon those hands, they were so	Hero and Leander		1.29
And with still panting rockt, there tooke his rest.	Hero and Leander		1.44
Because she tooke more from her than she left,	Hero and Leander		1.47
Imbrast her sodainly, tooke leave, and kist,	Hero and Leander		2.92
their loves/On heapes of heavie gold, and tooke great pleasure,	Hero and Leander		2.163
Or speake to him who in a moment tooke,	Hero and Leander		2.308
Whence his admiring eyes more pleasure tooke,	Hero and Leander		2.325
TOOKEN			
So at her presence all surpris'd and tooken,	Hero and Leander		1.122
TOOKEST			
Thou also that late tookest mine eyes away,	Ovid's Elegies		2.19.19
TOOK'ST			
And as thou took'st the faire Proserpina,	2Tamb	4.3.36	Orcan
Damb'd up thy passage; when thou took'st the booke,	F1887	5.2.91	Mephst
TOOLES			
For words are vaine where working tooles present/The naked	1Tamb	3.2.93	Agidas
And with the thunder of his martial tooles/Makes Earthquakes in	2Tamb	2.2.7	Orcan
Venus with Vulcan, though smiths tooles laide by,	Ovid's Elegies		2.17.19
TOONG			
Come thither; As she spake this, her toong tript,	Hero and Leander		1.357
Her mind pure, and her toong untaught to glose.	Hero and Leander		1.392
TOONGD			
Is with that smoothe toongd scholler Baldock gone,	Edw	4.6.57	Rice
TOONGS			
So she be faire, but some vile toongs will blot?	Hero and Leander		1.286
TOO'T			
Soft Barabas, there's more longs too't than so.	Jew	1.2.45	Govnr
TOOTH			
And with a wantons tooth, your necke new raste?	Ovid's Elegies		3.13.34
TOP			
But when you see his actions [top] <stop> his speech,	1Tamb	2.3.26	Therid
Or mount the top with my aspiring winges,	P 103	2.46	Guise
On whose top-branches Kinglie Eagles pearch,	Edw	2.2.17	Mortmr
Did mount him up <himselfe> to scale Olimpus top.	F 757	2.3.36	2Chor
That threates the starres with her aspiring top,	F 796	3.1.18	Faust
TOPAS			
Jacints, hard Topas, grasse-greene Emeraulds,	Jew	1.1.26	Barab
TOP-BRANCHES			
On whose top-branches Kinglie Eagles pearch,	Edw	2.2.17	Mortmr
TOPFLAG			
Twill make him vaile the topflag of his pride,	Edw	1.4.276	Mortmr
TOPLES			
And cut a passage through his toples hilles:	Dido	4.3.12	Aeneas
TOPLESSE			
And burnt the toplesse Towers of Ilium?	F1769	5.1.96	Faust
TOPPE			
Shaking her snakie haire and crooked pine/With flaming toppe,	Lucan, First Booke		572
With hoarie toppe, and under Hemus mount/Philippi plaines;	Lucan, First Booke		679
With earthes revenge and how Olimpus toppe/High Ossa bore,	Ovid's Elegies		2.1.13
TOPS			
And scale the ysie mountaines lofty tops:	1Tamb	1.2.100	Tamb
Whose tops are covered with Tartarian thieves,	1Tamb	2.2.16	Meandr
And leaves it off to snap on Thistle tops:	Jew	5.2.42	Barab
Weele steele it on their crest, and powle their tops.	Edw	3.1.27	Edward
Environed round with airy mountaine tops,	F 781	3.1.3	Faust
Or waters tops with the warme south-winde taken.	Ovid's Elegies		1.7.56
TORCH			
Now spearlike, long; now like a spreading torch:	Lucan, First Booke		530
TORCHES			
Come, come, away, now put the torches out,	Edw	5.3.47	Matrvs
TORMENT			
I must conceale/The torment, that it bootes me not reveale,/And	Dido	3.4.26	Dido
You must devise some torment worsse, my Lord,	1Tamb	4.2.66	Techel
That dares torment the body of my Love,	2Tamb	2.4.79	Tamb
Shall so torment thee and that Callapine,	2Tamb	3.5.85	Tamb
Save griefe and sorrow which torment my heart,	2Tamb	4.2.24	Olymp
A thousand deathes could not torment our hearts/More than the	2Tamb	5.1.144	Jrslem
no soule in hell/Hath felt more torment then poore Gaveston.	Edw	1.1.147	Gavstn
And in this torment, comfort finde I none,	Edw	5.1.81	Edward
Torment sweet friend, that base and [crooked age] <aged man>,	F1753	5.1.80	Faust
With greatest [torments] <torment> that our hell affoords.	F1755	5.1.82	Faust

TORMENT (cont.)			
Unwilling Lovers, love doth more torment,	Ovid's Elegies	1.2.17	
Her owne request to her owne torment turnd.	Ovid's Elegies	3.3.38	
TORMENTED			
They may be still tormented with unrest,	Dido	5.1.305	Dido
May styl excruciat his tormented thoughts.	1Tamb	5.1.301	Bajzth
Vex'd and tormented runnes poore Barabas/With fatall curses	Jew	2.1.5	Barab
breast a long great Scrowle/How I with interest tormented him.	Jew	2.3.198	Barab
Was ever Jew tormented as I am?	Jew	4.3.60	Barab
Am not tormented with ten thousand hels,	F 307	1.3.79	Mephst
And heaven tormented with thy chafing heate,	Lucan, First Booke	656	
Deserv'd thereby with death to be tormented.	Ovid's Elegies	2.14.6	
TORMENTING			
And millions of his strong tormenting spirits:	2Tamb	1.3.147	Techel
That legions of tormenting spirits may vex/Your slavish bosomes	2Tamb	5.1.45	Govnr
TORMENTS			
An uncouth paine torments my grieved soule,	1Tamb	2.7.7	Cosroe
Than stay the torments he and heaven have sworne.	1Tamb	3.2.99	Agidas
Remooved from the Torments and the hell:	1Tamb	3.2.103	Agidas
sparke of breath/Can quench or coole the torments of my griefe.	1Tamb	5.1.285	Zabina
Or bind thee in eternall torments wrath.	2Tamb	3.5.113	Soria
earth may eccho foorth/The far resounding torments ye sustaine,	2Tamb	4.1.186	Tamb
What daring God torments my body thus,	2Tamb	5.3.42	Tamb
And eielesse Monster that torments my soule,	2Tamb	5.3.217	Tamb
And one offence torments me more then all.	Jew	3.6.19	Abigal
And in the fury of thy torments, strive/To end thy life with	Jew	5.5.79	Barab
With death delay'd and torments never usde,	P 257	4.55	Charls
Just torments for his trechery.	P1175	22.37	King
And onely this torments my wretched soule,	Edw	1.4.123	Edward
Which thoughts are martyred with endles torments.	Edw	5.1.80	Edward
'sbloud I am never able to endure these torments.	F1307	4.1.153	P Benvol
With greatest [torments] <torment> that our hell affoords.	F1755	5.1.82	Faust
TORNE			
His armes torne from his shoulders, and his breast/Furrowd with	Dido	2.1.203	Aeneas
That may command thee peecemeale to be torne,	1Tamb	4.2.23	Tamb
Mangled and torne, and all my entrals bath'd/In blood that	2Tamb	3.4.8	Capt
First were his sacred garments rent and torne,	Edw	1.2.35	ArchBp
So may his limmes be torne, as is this paper,	Edw	5.1.142	Edward
All torne asunder by the hand of death.	F1989	5.3.7	2Schol
The devils whom Faustus serv'd have torne him thus:	F1990	5.3.8	3Schol
Mourning appear'd, whose hoary hayres were torne,	Lucan, First Booke	189	
And rough jades mouths with stubburn bits are torne,	Ovid's Elegies	1.2.15	
For wofull haires let piece-torne plumes abound,	Ovid's Elegies	2.6.5	
Why with hid irons are your bowels torne?	Ovid's Elegies	2.14.27	
TORPEDO			
I meane that vile Torpedo, Gaveston,	Edw	1.4.223	Mortmr
TORRID			
And thence by land unto the Torrid Zone,	1Tamb	4.4.124	Tamb
I to the Torrid Zone where midday burnes,	Lucan, First Booke	16	
TORTUR'D			
And sink not quite into my tortur'd soule.	1Tamb	5.1.263	Bajzth
Where we are tortur'd, and remaine for ever.	F 509	2.1.121	Mephst
Is for ore-tortur'd soules to rest them in.	F1915	5.2.119	BdAngl
TORTURE			
Or els invent some torture worse than that.	2Tamb	3.4.22	Olymp
T'appease my wrath, or els Ile torture thee,	2Tamb	3.5.122	Tamb
Torture or paine can daunt my dreadlesse minde.	2Tamb	5.1.113	Govnr
That we might torture him with some new found death.	P1217	22.79	Eprnon
a death too good, the devill of hell/Torture his wicked soule.	P1219	22.81	Bartus
Why, have you any paine that torture other <tortures others>?	F 432	2.1.44	Faust
with horror stare/Into that vaste perpetuall torture-house,	F1910	5.2.114	BdAngl
O, I have seene enough to torture me.	F1921	5.2.125	Faust
TORTURE-HOUSE			
with horror stare/Into that vaste perpetuall torture-house,	F1910	5.2.114	BdAngl
TORTURES			
to everlasting paines/And extreme tortures of the fiery deepe,	Jew	1.2.167	Barab
Why, have you any paine that torture other <tortures others>?	F 432	2.1.44	Faust
thou shalt see/Ten thousand tortures that more horrid be.	F1920	5.2.124	BdAngl
TOSS'D			
When well-toss'd mattocks did the ground prepare,	Ovid's Elegies	3.9.31	
TOSSE			
But if that Triton tosse the troubled floud,	Ovid's Elegies	2.11.27	
least their gownes tosse thy haire,/To hide thee in my bosome	Ovid's Elegies	3.2.75	
TOSSING			
There are the Furies tossing damned soules,	F1911	5.2.115	BdAngl
TOST			
Whose shattered lims, being tost as high as heaven,	2Tamb	3.2.100	Tamb
Even as a boate, tost by contrarie winde,	Ovid's Elegies	2.10.9	
Like one start up your haire tost and displast,	Ovid's Elegies	3.13.33	
TOSTU			
Belseborams framanto pacostiphos tostu Mephastophilis,	F App	p.235 25	P Robin
T'OTHER			
As I was going to Wittenberge t'other day, with a loade of Hay,	F1526	4.5.22	P Carter
TOTTER			
That now the walles of houses halfe [rear'd] <reaer'd> totter,	Lucan, First Booke	24	
TOTTER'D			
He sent a shaggy totter'd staring slave,	Jew	4.3.6	Barab
TOTTERED			
This tottered ensigne of my auncesters,	Edw	2.3.21	Mortmr
TOUCH			
Then touch her white breast with this arrow head,	Dido	2.1.326	Venus
As every touch shall wound Queene Didos heart.	Dido	2.1.333	Cupid
Then shall I touch her breast and conquer her.	Dido	3.1.6	Cupid

TOUCH (cont.)			
Why did it suffer thee to touch her breast,	Dido	4.4.145	Dido
Away, I am the King: go, touch me not.	1Tamb	2.4.20	Mycet
Ah villaines, dare ye touch my sacred armes?	1Tamb	3.3.268	Bajzth
Unworthy to imbrace or touch the ground,	1Tamb	4.2.20	Tamb
my souldiers march/Shal rise aloft and touch the horned Moon,	2Tamb	1.3.14	Tamb
That touch the end of famous Euphrates.	2Tamb	3.1.53	Trebiz
Should I but touch the rusty gates of hell,	2Tamb	5.1.96	Tamb
Villaines, I am a sacred person, touch me not.	Jew	4.1.201	1Fryar
The Law shall touch you, we'll but lead you, we:	Jew	4.1.202	Barab
Away then, touch me not, come Gaveston.	Edw	1.4.159	Edward
His faith is great, I cannot touch his soule;	F1756	5.1.83	Mephst
While others touch the damsell I love best?	Ovid's Elegies		1.4.4
There touch what ever thou canst touch of mee.	Ovid's Elegies		1.4.58
What armes and shoulders did I touch and see,	Ovid's Elegies		1.5.19
Water in waters, and fruite flying touch/Tantalus seekes, his	Ovid's Elegies		2.2.43
Or if one touch the lute with art and cunning,	Ovid's Elegies		2.4.27
Then would I wish thee touch my mistris pappe,	Ovid's Elegies		2.15.11
Would first my beautious wenches moist lips touch,	Ovid's Elegies		2.15.17
When thy waves brim did scarse my ankles touch.	Ovid's Elegies		3.5.6
Yet might her touch make youthfull Pilius fire,	Ovid's Elegies		3.6.41
And lookes uppon the fruits he cannot touch.	Ovid's Elegies		3.6.52
Canst touch that hand wherewith some one lie dead?	Ovid's Elegies		3.7.17
Confessing this, why doest thou touch him than?	Ovid's Elegies		3.7.22
These lovers parled by the touch of hands,	Hero and Leander		1.185
youth forbeare/To touch the sacred garments which I weare.	Hero and Leander		1.344
As might have made heaven stoope to have a touch,	Hero and Leander		1.366
Yet ever as he greedily assayd/To touch those dainties, she the	Hero and Leander		2.270
TOUCH'D			
son; he and I kild 'em both, and yet never touch'd 'em.	Jew	4.4.18	P Ithimr
TOUCHE			
None be so hardie as to touche the King,	Edw	2.3.27	Lncstr
TOUCHES			
But when he touches it, it will be foild:	Jew	2.3.57	Barab
TOUCHING			
that with touching of a string/May draw the pliant king which	Edw	1.1.52	Gavstn
Touching the sending of this Gaveston,	Edw	2.5.76	Penbrk
I long to heare an answer from the Barons/Touching my friend,	Edw	3.1.2	Edward
[Touching his journey through the world and ayre],	F1145	3.3.58A	3Chor
The [haven] <heaven> touching barcke now nere the lea,	Ovid's Elegies		2.9.32
By thy sides touching ill she is entreated.	Ovid's Elegies		3.2.22
So was his necke in touching, and surpast/The white of Pelops	Hero and Leander		1.64
He toucht her hand, in touching it she trembled,	Hero and Leander		1.183
TOUCHT			
With whose instinct the soule of man is toucht,	1Tamb	5.1.179	Tamb
And rude boyes toucht with unknowne love me reade,	Ovid's Elegies		2.1.6
And sweet toucht harpe that to move stones was able?	Ovid's Elegies		3.11.40
We toucht the walles, Camillus wonne by thee.	Ovid's Elegies		3.12.2
He toucht her hand, in touching it she trembled,	Hero and Leander		1.183
TOUCHTE			
that point I touchte,/And seeing there was no place to mount up	Edw	5.6.61	Mortmr
TOULD			
Tould us at our arrivall all the newes,	Edw	4.2.48	Mortmr
TOULDST			
Graecinus (well I wot) thou touldst me once,	Ovid's Elegies		2.10.1
TOUNG			
No villain, that toung of thine,	P 530	10.3	Guise
TOURNAMENT (See TURNAMENT)			
TOURNY			
And spend some daies in barriers, tourny, tylte,	P 628	12.41	King
T'OUT BID			
Thou shalt have crownes of us, t'out bid the Barons,	Edw	3.1.55	Edward
TOWARD			
Why look'st thou toward the sea?	Dido	5.1.113	Dido
And take my other toward brother here,	2Tamb	4.1.34	Calyph
Will take his leave and saile toward Ottoman.	Jew	5.2.106	Barab
And toward Calabria, back'd by Sicily,	Jew	5.3.9	Calym
thou lead'st me toward th'east,/Where Nile augmenteth the	Lucan, First Booke		682
TOWARDNES			
this towardnes makes thy mother feare/Thou art not markt to	Edw	3.1.79	Queene
TOWARDS			
Thus farre are we towards Theridamas,	1Tamb	2.1.1	Cosroe
now come let us martch/Towards Techelles and Theridamas,	2Tamb	3.2.146	Tamb
Cast up the earth towards the castle wall,	2Tamb	3.3.43	Therid
Here I began to martch towards Persea,	2Tamb	5.3.126	Tamb
but to passe along/Towards Venice by the Adriatick Sea;	Jew	1.1.163	Barab
poore Barabas/With fatall curses towards these Christians.	Jew	2.1.6	Barab
Father, it draweth towards midnight now,	Jew	2.1.55	Abigal
Looke not towards him, let's away:	Jew	3.1.24	Pilia
The other Chambers open towards the street.	Jew	4.1.138	Barab
Towards one.	Jew	4.1.158	P Ithimr
Are gone towards Lambeth, there let them remaine.	Edw	1.3.5	Gavstn
March towards Roome; and you fierce men of Rhene/Leaving your	Lucan, First Booke		460
Then towards the pallace of the Destinies,	Hero and Leander		1.377
TOWER			
Desart of Arabia/To those that stand on Badgeths lofty Tower,	2Tamb	1.1.109	Sgsmnd
And cast the fame of Ilions Tower to hell.	2Tamb	4.3.113	Tamb
A warning-peece shall be shot off from the Tower,	Jew	5.5.39	Barab
Then Ile have a peale of ordinance shot from the tower,	P 236	4.34	Guise
I, to the tower, the fleete, or where thou wilt.	Edw	1.1.198	Edward
Whose there? conveie this priest to the tower.	Edw	1.1.200	Edward
Tis true, the Bishop is in the tower,	Edw	1.2.1	Warwck
When she was lockt up in a brasen tower,	Edw	2.2.54	Edward

TOWER (cont.)
Why do you not commit him to the tower? | Edw 2.2.234 | Gavstn
Go take that haughtie Mortimer to the tower, | Edw 3.1.252 | Edward
Hath shaken off the thraldome of the tower, | Edw 4.2.41 | Mortmr
From the lieutenant of the tower my lord. | Edw 4.3.9 | Arundl
And therefore we commit you to the Tower, | Edw 5.6.79 | King
And in the strongest Tower inclose him fast. | F 966 3.1.188 | Pope
In brazen tower had not Danae dwelt, | Ovid's Elegies | 2.19.27
Went Hero thorow Sestos, from her tower/To Venus temple, [where] | Hero and Leander | 1.132
Was Danaes statue in a brazen tower, | Hero and Leander | 1.146
And therefore to her tower he got by stealth. | Hero and Leander | 2.18
Where having spy'de her tower, long star'd he on't, | Hero and Leander | 2.149
Descends upon my radiant Heroes tower. | Hero and Leander | 2.204
Till to the solitarie tower he got. | Hero and Leander | 2.230

TOWERS
Shall build his throne amidst those starrie towers, | Dido 1.1.98 | Jupitr
Whose wealthie streames may waite upon her towers, | Dido 5.1.9 | Aeneas
Now may we see Damascus lofty towers, | 1Tamb 4.2.102 | Tamb
The towers and cities of these hatefull Turks, | 2Tamb 3.2.148 | Tamb
like armed men/Are seene to march upon the towers of heaven, | 2Tamb 4.1.202 | Tamb
And with brasse-bullets batter downe your Towers, | Jew 3.5.24 | Basso
<incense>/The papall towers to kisse the [lowly] <holy> earth. | P1202 22.64 | King
and enforce/The papall towers, to kisse the lowlie ground, | Edw 1.4.101 | Edward
As I have manors, castels, townes, and towers: | Edw 3.1.133 | Edward
And burnt the toplesse Towers of Ilium? | F1769 5.1.96 | Faust
There, he who rules the worlds starre-spangled towers, | Ovid's Elegies | 3.9.21

TOWN
The town is ours my Lord, and fresh supply/Of conquest, and of | 1Tamb 5.1.196 | Techel

TOWNE
Before he be the Lord of Turnus towne, | Dido 1.1.87 | Jupitr
Adjoyning on Agenors stately towne, | Dido 1.1.211 | Venus
Me thinkes that towne there should be Troy, yon Idas hill, | Dido 2.1.7 | Aeneas
Lords of this towne, or whatsoever stile/Belongs unto your | Dido 2.1.39 | Aeneas
vouchsafe of ruth/To tell us who inhabits this faire towne, | Dido 2.1.41 | Aeneas
Some say Antenor did betray the towne, | Dido 2.1.110 | Dido
Ulysses sent to our unhappie towne: | Dido 2.1.149 | Aeneas
Troy is a fire, the Grecians have the towne. | Dido 2.1.208 | Aeneas
That onely Juno rules in Rhamnuse towne. | Dido 3.2.20 | Juno
And bring forth mightie Kings to Carthage towne, | Dido 3.2.75 | Juno
Whiles Dido lives and rules in Junos towne, | Dido 3.4.50 | Aeneas
Come Dido, let us hasten to the towne, | Dido 4.1.26 | Aeneas
She crav'd a hide of ground to build a towne, | Dido 4.2.13 | Iarbus
And build the towne againe the Greekes did burne? | Dido 4.3.40 | Illion
Armies of foes resolv'd to winne this towne, | Dido 4.4.113 | Dido
What length or bredth shal this brave towne containe? | Dido 5.1.16 | Achat
Welcome to Carthage new erected towne. | Dido 5.1.26 | Aeneas
To leave this towne and passe to Italy, | Dido 5.1.100 | Aeneas
But as I live that towne shall curse the time/That Tamburlaine | 1Tamb 3.3.59 | Tamb
The men, the treasure, and the towne is ours. | 1Tamb 4.2.110 | Tamb
My lord, to see my fathers towne besieg'd, | 1Tamb 4.4.65 | Zenoc
(sacred Emperour)/The prostrate service of this wretched towne. | 1Tamb 5.1.100 | 1Virgn
Bring him forth, and let us know if the towne be ransackt. | 1Tamb 5.1.194 | P Tamb
This cursed towne will I consume with fire, | 2Tamb 2.4.137 | Tamb
So, burne the turrets of this cursed towne, | 2Tamb 3.2.1 | Tamb
Greek, is writ/This towne being burnt by Tamburlaine the great, | 2Tamb 3.2.17 | Calyph
At every towne and castle I besiege, | 2Tamb 3.2.36 | Tamb
Boyes leave to mourne, this towne shall ever mourne, | 2Tamb 3.2.45 | Tamb
As is that towne, so is my heart consum'd, | 2Tamb 3.2.49 | Amyras
Besiege a fort, to undermine a towne, | 2Tamb 3.2.60 | Tamb
Fire the towne and overrun the land. | 2Tamb 3.5.9 | 2Msngr
Yeeld up the towne, save our wives and children: | 2Tamb 5.1.39 | 2Citzn
nor the towne will never yeeld/As long as any life is in my | 2Tamb 5.1.47 | Govnr
That made us all the labour for the towne, | 2Tamb 5.1.82 | Therid
Upon the ruines of this conquered towne. | 2Tamb 5.1.85 | Tamb
Leave not a Babylonian in the towne. | 2Tamb 5.1.171 | Tamb
comes to more/Then many Merchants of the Towne are worth, | Jew 1.1.64 | 1Merch
To seize upon the Towne: I, that he seekes. | Jew 1.1.185 | Barab
Why let 'em enter, let 'em take the Towne. | Jew 1.1.190 | Barab
Small though the number was that kept the Towne, | Jew 2.2.49 | Bosco
the Towne-seale might be got/To keepe him for his life time | Jew 2.3.103 | Barab
I have as much coyne as will buy the Towne. | Jew 2.3.200 | Barab
Since this Towne was besieg'd, my gaine growes cold: | Jew 3.1.1 | Curtzn
But yesterday two ships went from this Towne, | Jew 4.1.69 | Barab
Will winne the Towne, or dye before the wals. | Jew 5.1.5 | Govnr
So, now away and fortifie the Towne. | Jew 5.1.60 | Govnr
I'le be reveng'd on this accursed Towne; | Jew 5.1.62 | Barab
can spy a place/Where you may enter, and surprize the Towne: | Jew 5.1.71 | Barab
And rise with them i'th middle of the Towne, | Jew 5.1.92 | Barab
wee'll walke about/The ruin'd Towne, and see the wracke we | Jew 5.2.19 | Calym
For Callymath, when he hath view'd the Towne, | Jew 5.2.105 | Barab
Two lofty Turrets that command the Towne. | Jew 5.3.11 | Calym
to feast my traine/Within a Towne of warre so lately pillag'd, | Jew 5.3.22 | Calym
is a monastery/Which standeth as an out-house to the Towne; | Jew 5.3.37 | Msngr
Follow me to the towne. | Edw 4.7.119 | Rice
I feare mee that this crie will raise the towne, | Edw 5.5.114 | Matrvs
In Germany, within a Towne cal'd [Rhode] <Rhodes>: | F 12 Prol.12 | 1Chor
in every good towne and Citie>, | F 699 (HC264)A | P Glutny
Past with delight the stately Towne of Trier: | F 780 3.1.2 | Faust
[Quarter <Quarters> the towne in foure equivolence]. | F 790 3.1.12A | Faust
A towne with one poore church set them at oddes. | Lucan, First Booke | 97
And deem'd renowne to spoile their native towne, | Lucan, First Booke | 176
Wagons or tents, then in this frontire towne. | Lucan, First Booke | 255
making men/Dispaire of day; as did Thiestes towne/(Mycenae), | Lucan, First Booke | 541

TOWNE (cont.)
And went the round, in, and without the towne. — Lucan, First Booke 594
This breakes Towne gates, but he his Mistris dore. — Ovid's Elegies 1.9.20
They say Peneus neere Phthias towne did hide. — Ovid's Elegies 3.5.32
The towne of Sestos cal'd it Venus glasse. — Hero and Leander 1.142
Far from the towne (where all is whist and still, — Hero and Leander 1.346

TOWNES
Now living idle in the walled townes, — 1Tamb 1.1.146 Ceneus
The townes-men maske in silke and cloath of gold, — 1Tamb 4.2.108 Tamb
Provinces, Citties and townes/After my name and thine Zenocrate: — 1Tamb 4.4.79 Tamb
To Alexandria, and the frontier townes, — 2Tamb 1.1.48 Gazell
And of Argier and Affriks frontier townes/Twise twenty thousand — 2Tamb 1.3.119 Therid
Riso, Sancina, and the bordering townes, — 2Tamb 3.1.52 Trebiz
The cursed Scythian sets on all their townes, — 2Tamb 3.1.55 Trebiz
That we have sent before to fire the townes, — 2Tamb 3.2.147 Tamb
A kingly kinde of trade to purchase Townes/By treachery, and — Jew 5.5.47 Barab
As I have manors, castels, townes, and towers: — Edw 3.1.133 Edward
Make Englands civill townes huge heapes of stones, — Edw 3.1.215 Edward
rid him intc the deepe pond at the townes ende, I was no sooner — F App p.240 133 P HrsCsr
huge heapes of stone/Lye in our townes, that houses are — Lucan, First Booke 26
To mannage greater deeds; the bordering townes/He garrison'd; — Lucan, First Booke 463
Shall townes be swallowed? — Lucan, First Booke 645
No little ditched townes, no lowlie walles, — Ovid's Elegies 2.12.7
And this townes well knowne customes not beleeves, — Ovid's Elegies 3.4.38
Love kindling fire, to burne such townes as Troy, — Hero and Leander 1.153

TOWNE-SEALE
the Towne-seale might be got/To keepe him for his life time — Jew 2.3.103 Barab

TOWNES-MEN
The townes-men maske in silke and cloath of gold, — 1Tamb 4.2.108 Tamb

TOW'RED
(for loftie pride that dwels/In tow'red courts, is oft in — Hero and Leander 1.394

TOWRED
Why gird'st thy citties with a towred wall? — Ovid's Elegies 3.7.47
Built walles high towred with a prosperous hand. — Ovid's Elegies 3.12.34

TOY (See also TOIES)
Foolish is love, a toy.-- — Dido 4.5.26 Nurse
And tis a prety toy to be a Poet. — 1Tamb 2.2.54 Mycet
I count Religion but a childish Toy, — Jew Prol.14 Machvl
<Tut Faustus>, Marriage is but a ceremoniall toy, — F 535 2.1.147 Mephst
But be surpris'd with every garish toy. — Hero and Leander 1.480

TOYED
And as a brother with his sister toyed, — Hero and Leander 2.52

TOYES
For riper yeares will weane him from such toyes. — Edw 1.4.401 MortSr
When our lascivious toyes come in thy minde, — Ovid's Elegies 1.4.21
Toyes, and light Elegies my darts I tooke, — Ovid's Elegies 2.1.21
(Nor am I by such wanton toyes defamde)/Heire of an antient — Ovid's Elegies 3.14.4

TOYING
I, this is it, you can sit toying there, — Dido 1.1.50 Venus

TOYINGS
The bed is for lascivious toyings meete, — Ovid's Elegies 3.13.17

TOYL'D
For onely I have toyl'd to inherit here/The months of vanity — Jew 1.2.196 Barab

TOYLD
Yet there with Sysiphus he toyld in vaine, — Hero and Leander 2.277

TOYLE
And therefore will take pitie on his toyle, — Dido 1.1.131 Venus
Who would not undergoe all kind of toyle, — Dido 3.3.58 Aeneas
Which he hath pitcht within his deadly toyle. — P 54 1.54 Navrre
Within the compasse of a deadly toyle, — P 205 4.3 QnMoth
To rest his bones after his weary toyle, — F 769 2.3.48 2Chor
Both whom thou raisest up to toyle anew. — Ovid's Elegies 1.13.22

TOYLES
Huntsmen, why pitch you not your toyles apace, — Dido 3.3.30 Dido
The Mutin toyles; the fleet at Leuca suncke; — Lucan, First Booke 42

TOYLING
And would be toyling in the watrie billowes, — Dido 4.4.137 Dido
But sorrow seaze upon my toyling soule, — P1089 19.159 QnMoth
And pray'd the narrow toyling Hellespont, — Hero and Leander 2.150

TRACE (Homograph)
Doe trace these Libian deserts all despisde, — Dido 1.1.228 Aeneas
Excluding Regions which I meane to trace, — 1Tamb 4.4.77 Tamb
In Trace; brought up in Arabia. — Jew 2.3.128 P Ithimr
paths, wherein the gods might trace/To Joves high court. — Hero and Leander 1.298

TRADE
And turne him to his ancient trade againe. — 2Tamb 3.5.95 Jrslem
That trade in mettall of the purest mould; — Jew 1.1.20 Barab
Their meanes of traffique from the vulgar trade, — Jew 1.1.35 Barab
Hast thou no Trade? — Jew 2.3.167 Barab
A kingly kinde of trade to purchase Townes/By treachery, and — Jew 5.5.47 Barab

TRADES
Pillage and murder are his usuall trades. — 1Tamb 4.1.66 Souldn

TRADING
[Trading] <Treading> by land unto the Westerne Isles, — 1Tamb 1.1.38 Meandr

TRAFFIQUE
so richly pay/The things they traffique for with wedge of gold, — Jew 1.1.9 Barab
Their meanes of traffique from the vulgar trade, — Jew 1.1.35 Barab

TRAGEDIE
Valoyses lyne ends in my tragedie. — P1231 22.93 King
I see my tragedie written in thy browes, — Edw 5.5.74 Edward
Now Mortimer begins our tragedie. — Edw 5.6.23 Queene
Then with huge steps came violent Tragedie, — Ovid's Elegies 3.1.11
Now give the Roman Tragedie a name, — Ovid's Elegies 3.1.29

TRAGEDIE (cont.)			
With lofty wordes stout Tragedie (she sayd)/Why treadst me	Ovid's Elegies		3.1.35
Graunt Tragedie thy Poet times least tittle,	Ovid's Elegies		3.1.67
(Whose tragedie divine Musaeus soong)/Dwelt at Abidus; since	Hero and Leander		1.52
TRAGEDIES			
Yet tragedies, and scepters fild my lines,	Ovid's Elegies		2.18.13
TRAGEDY			
But to present the Tragedy of a Jew,	Jew	Prol.30	Machvl
TRAGICALL			
Thinke not but I am tragicall within:	P 894	17.89	King
TRAGICK			
Now come thou forth and play thy tragick part,	P 85	2.28	Guise
To tragick verse while thou Achilles trainst,	Ovid's Elegies		2.18.1
TRAGICKE			
View but his picture in this tragicke glasse,	1Tamb	Prol.7	Prolog
TRAILE			
lakes of gore/Your headles trunkes, your bodies will I traile,	Edw	3.1.136	Edward
TRAIN'D			
will send/A hundred thousand horse train'd to the war,	2Tamb	1.1.154	Sgsmnd
Spirits with desire/Stil to be train'd in armes and chivalry?	2Tamb	4.1.81	Tamb
TRAIND			
That like the Greekish strumpet traind to armes/And bloudie	Edw	2.5.15	Lncstr
TRAINDE			
And with an hoste of Moores trainde to the war,	2Tamb	1.3.141	Techel
Thy death broake amity and trainde to war,	Lucan, First Booke		119
TRAINE (Homograph)			
And charg'd him drowne my sonne with all his traine.	Dido	1.1.61	Venus
And in your confines with his lawlesse traine,	1Tamb	1.1.39	Meandr
Shall buy the meanest souldier in my traine.	1Tamb	1.2.86	Tamb
Beside the spoile of him and all his traine:	1Tamb	2.2.34	Meandr
That damned traine, the scum of Affrica,	1Tamb	3.3.56	Tamb
Or els discended to his winding traine:	2Tamb	2.4.54	Tamb
to feast my traine/Within a Towne of warre so lately pillag'd,	Jew	5.3.21	Calym
This traine he laid to have intrap'd thy life;	Jew	5.5.91	Govnr
That in the Court I bare so great a traine.	P 968	19.38	Guise
And floute our traine, and jest at our attire:	Edw	1.4.418	Mortmr
The king hath left him, and his traine is small.	Edw	2.4.39	Queene
Stately and proud, in riches and in traine,	Edw	4.7.12	Edward
Thinking to traine Leander therewithall.	Hero and Leander		2.12
Where kingly Neptune and his traine abode.	Hero and Leander		2.166
TRAINES			
Whose flaming traines should reach down to the earth/Could not	2Tamb	5.1.90	Tamb
TRAINS			
Th'ad best betimes forsake [them] <thee> and their trains,	Edw	3.1.202	Lncstr
TRAINST			
To tragick verse while thou Achilles trainst,	Ovid's Elegies		2.18.1
TRAITEROUS			
And of that false Cosroe, my traiterous brother.	1Tamb	2.2.4	Mycet
Come Guise and see thy traiterous guile outreacht,	P 962	19.32	King
Tretcherous Warwicke, traiterous Mortimer,	Edw	3.1.134	Edward
On your accursed traiterous progenie,	Edw	3.1.141	Edward
TRAITEROUSLY			
Riding the streetes was traiterously shot,	P 244	4.42	Man
TRAITOR (See also TRAYTOR)			
But shall I proove a Traitor to my King?	1Tamb	1.2.226	Therid
See here the perjur'd traitor Hungary,	2Tamb	2.3.12	Gazell
And died a traitor both to heaven and earth,	2Tamb	2.3.37	Orcan
With that accursed traitor Almeda,	2Tamb	3.2.150	Tamb
That curst and damned Traitor Almeda.	2Tamb	3.2.154	Usumc
Villaine, traitor, damned fugitive,	2Tamb	3.5.117	Tamb
But traitor to my name and majesty.	2Tamb	4.1.90	Tamb
More exquisite than ever Traitor felt.	2Tamb	5.1.53	Therid
Tyrant, I turne the traitor in thy throat,	2Tamb	5.1.54	Govnr
to fall into the hands/Of such a Traitor and unhallowed Jew!	Jew	5.2.13	Govnr
And thou a traitor to thy soule and him.	P 342	5.69	Lorein
Thou traitor Guise, lay of thy bloudy hands.	P 439	7.79	Navrre
Why I am no traitor to the crowne of France.	P 825	17.20	Guise
Be thou proclaimde a traitor throughout France.	P 864	17.59	King
This is the traitor that hath spent my golde,	P1028	19.98	King
him, and will slay/Thee too, and thou prove such a traitor.	P1049	19.119	King
Traitor to God, and to the realme of France.	P1076	19.146	QnMoth
Lay hands on that traitor Mortimer.	Edw	1.4.20	Edward
Lay hands on that traitor Gaveston.	Edw	1.4.21	MortSr
Treason, treason: whers the traitor?	Edw	2.2.80	Edward
Traitor be gone, whine thou with Mortimer.	Edw	2.2.214	Edward
Traitor on thy face, rebellious Lancaster.	Edw	3.1.204	Spencr
Present by me this traitor to the state,	Edw	4.6.49	Rice
What traitor have wee there with blades and billes?	Edw	5.4.82	Mortmr
Strike of my head? base traitor I defie thee.	Edw	5.4.90	Kent
He is a traitor, thinke not on him, come.	Edw	5.4.115	Queene
Traitor, in me my loving father speakes,	Edw	5.6.41	King
Hence with the traitor, with the murderer.	Edw	5.6.58	King
What, suffer you the traitor to delay?	Edw	5.6.67	King
use he's known/To exceed his maister, that arch-traitor Sylla.	Lucan, First Booke		326
TRAITORS			
Or impious traitors vowde to have my life,	Dido	4.4.114	Dido
Who brings that Traitors head Theridamas,	1Tamb	2.2.32	Meandr
Traitors, villaines, damned Christians.	2Tamb	2.2.29	Orcan
power and puritie/Behold and venge this Traitors perjury.	2Tamb	2.2.54	Orcan
Be now reveng'd upon this Traitors soule,	2Tamb	2.2.58	Orcan
Villaines, cowards, Traitors to our state,	2Tamb	5.1.43	Govnr
But what availeth that this traitors dead,	P1054	19.124	King
And all those traitors to the Church of Rome,	P1120	21.14	Dumain

TRAITORS (cont.)			
We are no traitors, therefore threaten not.	Edw	1.4.25	MortSr
Ah traitors, have they put my friend to death?	Edw	3.1.91	Edward
Yea Spencer, traitors all.	Edw	3.1.102	Edward
A traitors, will they still display their pride?	Edw	3.1.172	Spencr
For theile betray thee, traitors as they are.	Edw	3.1.203	Lncstr
I traitors all, rather then thus be bravde,	Edw	3.1.214	Edward
But weele advance them traitors, now tis time/To be avengd on	Edw	3.1.224	Edward
When we may meet these traitors in the field.	Edw	4.3.47	Edward
Traitors be gon, and joine you with Mortimer,	Edw	5.1.87	Edward
Traitors away, what will you murther me,	Edw	5.3.29	Edward
Lay downe your weapons, traitors, yeeld the king.	Edw	5.3.55	Kent
I offer up this wicked traitors head,	Edw	5.6.100	King
TRAITOUR			
And as a traitour mine owne fault confesse.	Ovid's Elegies		2.8.26
TRALUCENT			
Foorth from those two tralucent cesternes brake,	Hero and Leander		1.296
TRAMELLS			
take/In crooked [tramells] <trannels> crispy curles to make.	Ovid's Elegies		1.14.26
TRAMPLE			
Cupid by thee, Mars in great doubt doth trample,	Ovid's Elegies		2.9.47
TRAMPLING			
Trampling their bowels with our horses hooffes:	1Tamb	3.3.150	Tamb
Steeds, disdainfully/With wanton paces trampling on the ground.	1Tamb	4.1.23	2Msngr
TRANCE			
Then let some holy trance convay my thoughts,	2Tamb	2.4.34	Tamb
TRANNELS			
take/In crocked [tramells] <trannels> crispy curles to make.	Ovid's Elegies		1.14.26
TRANSCENDS			
My feare transcends my words,/Yet more will happen then I can	Lucan, First Booke		633
TRANSFORMD			
Epeus horse, to Aetnas hill transformd,	Dido	1.1.66	Venus
TRANSFORMDE			
Shall by the angrie goddesse be transformde,	Edw	1.1.68	Gavstn
TRANSFORME			
Mephostophilis, transforme him; and hereafter sir, looke you	F1314	4.1.160	P Faust
presumption, I transforme thee into an Ape, and thee into a Dog,	F App	p.235 43	P Mephst
Mephastophilis, transforme him strait.	F App	p.238 85	P Faust
TRANSFORMED			
For Apish deeds transformed to an Ape.	F1127	3.3.40	Mephst
be thou transformed to/A dog, and carry him upon thy backe;	F1130	3.3.43	Mephst
My friends transformed thus:	F1441	4.3.11	Benvol
TRANSFOURME			
May never such a change transfourme my love/In whose sweet	2Tamb	2.4.47	Tamb
TRANSFUSE			
Or in mine eyes good wench no paine transfuse.	Ovid's Elegies		3.3.48
TRANSGRESSE			
Were to transgresse against all lawes of love:	Dido	4.3.48	Aeneas
TRANSGRESSION			
Shall I be tryed by their transgression?	Jew	1.2.115	Barab
TRANSGREST			
and bid him rule/Better then I, yet how have I transgrest,	Edw	5.1.122	Edward
TRANSITORIE			
Make me despise this transitorie pompe,	Edw	5.1.108	Edward
TRANSITORY			
That when this fraile and transitory flesh/Hath suckt the	2Tamb	2.4.43	Zenoc
TRANSPORT			
Then beare the ship that shall transport thee hence:	Edw	1.1.153	Edward
That may transport me without oares to rowe.	Ovid's Elegies		3.5.4
TRANSPORTST			
What doest, I cryed, transportst thou my delight?	Ovid's Elegies		2.5.29
TRAP			
And beates his braines to catch us in his trap,	P 53	1.53	Navrre
TRAPT			
Trapt with the wealth and riches of the world,	2Tamb	1.1.43	Orcan
TRASH			
Fye; what a trouble tis to count this trash.	Jew	1.1.7	Barab
Who aimes at nothing but externall trash,	F 62	1.1.34	Faust
TRASIMEN (See THRASIMEN)			
TRAVAILE			
Souldiers must travaile farre:	Ovid's Elegies		1.9.9
That meane to travaile some long irkesome way.	Ovid's Elegies		2.16.16
What day and night to travaile in her quest?	Ovid's Elegies		3.5.10
TRAVAILERS			
Poore travailers though tierd, rise at thy sight,	Ovid's Elegies		1.13.13
TRAVAILES			
gods/Sweate teares to shew the travailes of their citty.	Lucan, First Booke		555
Or when the Moone travailes with charmed steedes.	Ovid's Elegies		2.5.38
TRAVEILE			
That we may traveile into Siria,	1Tamb	1.2.77	Agidas
We meane to traveile to th'Antartique Pole,	1Tamb	4.4.136	Tamb
As Pilgrimes traveile to our Hemi-spheare,	2Tamb	3.2.32	Tamb
And traveile hedlong to the lake of hell:	2Tamb	3.5.24	Orcan
TRAVEILER			
Or as the Ocean to the Traveiler/That restes upon the snowy	2Tamb	1.1.110	Sgsmnd
TRAVEILING			
Who traveiling with these Medean Lords/To Memphis, from my	1Tamb	1.2.11	Zenoc
TRAVELD			
I traveld with him to Aetolia.	Dido	3.1.145	Serg
TRAVELLER			
A traveller.	Edw	1.1.29	2PrMan
That scornes the world, and as a traveller,	Edw	5.6.65	Mortmr
What thirstie traveller ever drunke of thee?	Ovid's Elegies		3.5.97

TRAVELLERS			
the night time secretly would I steale/To travellers Chambers,	Jew	2.3.207	Ithimr
TRAVELS			
Triumph, my mates, our travels are at end, ...	Dido	5.1.1	Aeneas
TRAYTEROUSE			
Trayterouse guise ah thow hast murthered me	Paris	ms17,p390	Minion
TRAYTOR			
I traytor, and the waves shall cast thee up, ...	Dido	5.1.174	Dido
Proud traytor Mortimer why doost thou chase/Thy lawfull king	Edw	4.6.3	Kent
This Traytor flies unto some steepie rocke, ...	F1413	4.2.89	Faust
Thou traytor Faustus, I arrest thy soule, ...	F1743	5.1.70	Mephst
TRAYTORESSE			
Traytoresse too [keene] <keend> <kind> and cursed Sorceresse.	Dido	5.1.221	Dido
TRAYTORS			
Graunt, though the traytors land in Italy, ...	Dido	5.1.304	Dido
Knew you not Traytors, I was limitted/For foure and twenty	F1395	4.2.71	Faust
Go horse these traytors on your fiery backes, ...	F1403	4.2.79	Faust
TREACHERIE			
This should be treacherie and violence, ...	2Tamb	2.1.31	Sgsmnd
My father's murdered through thy treacherie, ...	Edw	5.6.28	King
Thou hadst not hatcht this monstrous treacherie! . .	Edw	5.6.97	King
And hell shall after plague their treacherie.	F1407	4.2.83	Faust
TREACHERIES			
Their bloud and yours shall seale these treacheries. .	Edw	5.1.89	Edward
TREACHEROUS			
Treacherous and false Theridamas, ...	1Tamb	2.7.3	Cosroe
The treacherous army of the Christians, ...	2Tamb	2.2.25	1Msngr
Oh treacherous Lodowicke!	Jew	2.3.266	Mthias
Now let the treacherous Mortimers conspire, ...	Edw	1.1.149	Edward
O treacherous Warwicke thus to wrong thy friend! . .	Edw	2.6.1	Gavstn
Treacherous earle, shall I not see the king? . . .	Edw	2.6.15	Gavstn
TREACHERY (See also TRETCHEROUS)			
A kingly kinde of trade to purchase Townes/By treachery, and	Jew	5.5.48	Barab
No, thus I'le see thy treachery repaid, ...	Jew	5.5.74	Govnr
False Prelates, for this hatefull treachery, ...	F1033	3.2.53	Pope
To sheild me from your hated treachery:	F1428	4.2.104	Faust
TREAD			
That we may tread upon his captive necke, ...	2Tamb	3.2.157	Tamb
Who set themselves to tread us under foot, ...	P 702	14.5	Navrre
But if I live, ile tread upon their heads, ...	Edw	2.2.96	Edward
That thinke with high lookes thus to tread me down. . .	Edw	2.2.97	Edward
That Peters heires should tread on Emperours, ...	F 918	3.1.140	Pope
his limbes he spread/Upon the bed, but on my foote first tread.	Ovid's Elegies		1.4.16
Maides on the shore, with marble white feete tread, . .	Ovid's Elegies		2.11.15
Then on the rough Alpes should I tread aloft, . . .	Ovid's Elegies		2.16.19
We vanquish, and tread tam'd love under feete, . . .	Ovid's Elegies		3.10.5
There use all tricks, and tread shame under feete. . .	Ovid's Elegies		3.13.18
TREADE			
heaven beholde/Their Scourge and Terrour treade on Emperours.	1Tamb	4.2.32	Tamb
TREADES			
And treades the deserts snowy heapes [do] <to> cover. .	Ovid's Elegies		1.9.12
TREADETH			
That treadeth Fortune underneath his feete, ...	2Tamb	3.4.52	Therid
TREADING			
Treading upon his breast, strooke off his hands. . .	Dido	2.1.242	Aeneas
[Trading] <Treading> by land unto the Westerne Isles, .	1Tamb	1.1.38	Meandr
And treading him beneath thy loathsome feet, ...	1Tamb	4.2.64	Zabina
For treading on the back of Bajazeth, ...	1Tamb	4.2.77	Bajzth
Treading the Lyon, and the Dragon downe, ...	F 920	3.1.142	Pope
TREADST			
lofty wordes stout Tragedie (she sayd)/Why treadst me downe?	Ovid's Elegies		3.1.36
Saying, why sadly treadst my banckes upon, ...	Ovid's Elegies		3.5.53
TREASON			
I know not what you meane by treason, I, ...	Dido	5.1.222	Nurse
That may revenge this treason to a Queene, ...	Dido	5.1.307	Dido
That with such treason seek our overthrow, ...	2Tamb	2.2.34	Gazell
Or treason in the fleshly heart of man, ...	2Tamb	2.2.37	Orcan
Treason, treason! Bashawes, flye.	Jew	5.5.67	Calym
Oh monstrous treason!	Jew	5.5.108	Calym
For he that did by treason worke our fall, ...	Jew	5.5.109	Govnr
By treason hath delivered thee to us:	Jew	5.5.110	Govnr
That Guise hath slaine by treason of his heart, . . .	P 45	1.45	Navrre
I challenge thee for treason in the cause.	P 830	17.25	Eprnon
Then meanes he present treason to our state. . . .	P 880	17.75	King
To hatch forth treason gainst their naturall Queene? .	P1032	19.102	King
Tis treason to be up against the king.	Edw	1.4.281	Mortmr
Treason, treason: whers the traitor?	Edw	2.2.80	Edward
Some treason, or some villanie was cause.	Edw	3.1.114	Spencr
I arrest you of high treason here, ...	Edw	4.7.57	Leistr
Treason was in her thought,/And cunningly to yeeld her selfe	Hero and Leander		2.293
TREASONS			
And end thy endles treasons with thy death.	P 955	19.25	King
TREASURE			
The jewels and the treasure we have tane/Shall be reserv'd, and	1Tamb	1.2.2	Tamb
If you intend to keep your treasure safe.	1Tamb	1.2.25	Tamb
I hope our Ladies treasure and our owne, ...	1Tamb	1.2.74	Agidas
Thinke you I way this treasure more than you? . . .	1Tamb	1.2.84	Tamb
Open the Males, yet guard the treasure sure, ...	1Tamb	1.2.138	Tamb
And stuft with treasure for his highest thoughts? . . .	1Tamb	2.1.59	Ceneus
And dig for treasure to appease my wrath:	1Tamb	3.3.265	Tamb
The men, the treasure, and the towne is ours. . . .	1Tamb	4.2.110	Tamb
Wherein is all the treasure of the land.	2Tamb	3.3.4	Therid
shall sweat/With carrieng pearle and treasure on their backes.	2Tamb	3.5.167	Techel

TREASURE (cont.)			
with all the pompe/The treasure of my kingdome may affoord.	2Tamb	4.2.98	Therid
Adding their wealth and treasure to my store.	2Tamb	4.3.101	Tamb
glide by night/About the place where Treasure hath bin hid:	Jew	2.1.27	Barab
Come and receive the Treasure I have found.	Jew	2.1.38	Abigal
To spend the treasure that should strength my land,	P1037	19.107	King
For all the wealth and treasure of the world.	P1163	22.25	King
thoughe you take out none but your owne treasure	Paris	ms 3,p390 P	Souldr
And riote it with the treasure of the realme,	Edw	1.4.405	Mortmr
Have drawne thy treasure drie, and made thee weake,	Edw	2.2.159	Mortmr
Bestowe that treasure on the lords of Fraunce,	Edw	3.1.265	Spencr
Yet gentle monkes, for treasure, golde nor fee,	Edw	4.7.24	Edward
Art/Wherein all natures [treasury] <treasure> is contain'd:	F 102	1.1.74	BdAngl
And fetch the treasure of all forraine wrackes:	F 172	1.1.144	Cornel
Therefore in signe her treasure suffred wracke,	Hero and Leander		1.49
Then treasure is abus'de,/When misers keepe it; being put to	Hero and Leander		1.234
To spurne in carelesse sort, the shipwracke treasure.	Hero and Leander		2.164
TREASURIE			
And thou Aeneas, Didos treasurie,	Dido	3.1.91	Dido
For ballace, emptie Didos treasurie,	Dido	3.1.126	Dido
And dive into blacke tempests treasurie,	Dido	4.1.5	Iarbus
Deliver them into my treasurie.	1Tamb	3.3.217	Tamb
And every house is as a treasurie.	1Tamb	4.2.109	Tamb
Out of the coffers of our treasurie.	2Tamb	3.4.91	Therid
Opening the doores of his rich treasurie,	2Tamb	4.2.95	Therid
Rifling the bowels of her treasurie,	P 135	2.78	Guise
Wants thou gold? go to my treasurie:	Edw	1.1.167	Edward
Then I may fetch from this ritch treasurie:	Edw	1.4.332	Queene
That havocks Englands wealth and treasurie.	Edw	4.4.27	Mortmr
Reveld in Englands wealth and treasurie.	Edw	4.6.52	Rice
TREASURY			
And bring his gold into our treasury.	Jew	4.1.163	1Fryar
Art/Wherein all natures [treasury] <treasure> is contain'd:	F 102	1.1.74	BdAngl
That yearely [stuffes] <stuff'd> old Phillips treasury,	F 159	1.1.131	Valdes
And leave it in the Churches treasury.	F 971	3.1.193	Pope
And put into the Churches treasury.	F1028	3.2.48	Raymnd
TREAT			
To breake his sword, and mildly treat of love,	1Tamb	5.1.327	Zenoc
King of Natolia, let us treat of peace,	2Tamb	1.1.13	Gazell
crost Danubius stream/To treat of friendly peace or deadly war:	2Tamb	1.1.80	Sgsmnd
Or treat of peace with the Natolian king?	2Tamb	1.1.113	Sgsmnd
What need they treat of peace that are in league?	Jew	1.1.158	Barab
TREBIZON			
Danubius stream that runs to Trebizon,	2Tamb	1.1.33	Orcan
chiefe of my army hence/To faire Natolia, and to Trebizon,	2Tamb	1.1.162	Orcan
Of Soria, Trebizon and Amasia,	2Tamb	2.3.44	Orcan
Emperour of Natolia, Jerusalem, Trebizon, Soria, Amasia,	2Tamb	3.1.4	P Orcan
And I as many bring from Trebizon,	2Tamb	3.1.49	Trebiz
From Trebizon in Asia the lesse,	2Tamb	3.5.40	Trebiz
TREBLE			
And treble all his fathers slaveries.	2Tamb	3.2.158	Tamb
would he lov'd me/But halfe so much, then were I treble blest.	Edw	1.4.304	Queene
TRECHERIE			
Murder, rape, warre, lust and trecherie,	Hero and Leander		1.457
TRECHEROUS			
I deepely sorrow for your trecherous wrong:	P 263	4.61	Charls
see they keep/All trecherous violence from our noble freend,	P 268	4.66	Charls
And give her warning of her trecherous foes.	P1190	22.52	King
Fire Paris where these trecherous rebels lurke.	P1241	22.103	King
TRECHERY			
Just torments for his trechery.	P1175	22.37	King
TRED			
She hath not trode <tred> awrie that doth denie it,	Ovid's Elegies		3.13.5
TREE			
Made him to thinke Epeus pine-tree Horse/A sacrifize t'appease	Dido	2.1.162	Aeneas
O cursed tree, hadst thou but wit or sense,	Dido	4.4.139	Dido
shall breath/Through shady leaves of every sencelesse tree,	2Tamb	2.3.16	Orcan
And feeds upon the banefull tree of hell,	2Tamb	2.3.19	Orcan
Like to an almond tree ymounted high,	2Tamb	4.3.119	Tamb
all doubts, be rulde by me, lets hang him heere upon this tree.	P 492	9.11	P 2Atndt
And in his sportfull hands an Olive tree,	Edw	1.1.64	Gavstn
A loftie Cedar tree faire flourishing,	Edw	2.2.16	Mortmr
As for my selfe, I stand as Joves huge tree,	Edw	5.6.11	Mortmr
And <Faustus all> jointly move upon one Axle-tree,	F 592	2.2.41	Mephst
Pluto's blew fire, and Hecat's tree,	F1001	3.2.21	Mephst
when every Tree is barren of his fruite, from whence you had	F1579	4.6.22	P Duke
Poore wretches on the tree themselves did strangle,	Ovid's Elegies		1.12.17
for the lovely boy/That now is turn'd into a Cypres tree,	Hero and Leander		1.155
Like to the tree of Tantalus she fled,	Hero and Leander		2.75
describe, but hee/That puls or shakes it from the golden tree:	Hero and Leander		2.300
TREES			
Wound on the barkes of odoriferous trees,	Dido	3.1.117	Dido
And all the trees are blasted with our breathes.	1Tamb	3.1.55	Bajzth
Or scattered like the lofty Cedar trees,	1Tamb	4.2.24	Tamb
see al plants, hearbes and trees that grow upon the earth].	F 551.9	2.1.172A	P Faust
and our followers/Close in an ambush there behinde the trees,	F1342	4.2.18	Benvol
For loe these Trees remove at my command,	F1426	4.2.102	Faust
Beates Thracian Boreas; or when trees [bowe] <bowde> down,/And	Lucan, First Booke		391
Elisium hath a wood of holme trees black,	Ovid's Elegies		2.6.49
Memphis, and Pharos that sweete date trees yeelds,	Ovid's Elegies		2.13.8
Why takest increasing grapes from Vine-trees full?	Ovid's Elegies		2.14.23
And coole gales shake the tall trees leavy spring,	Ovid's Elegies		2.16.36
And fruit from trees, when ther's no wind at al.	Ovid's Elegies		3.6.34

TREES (cont.)				
There stands an old wood with thick trees darke clouded,	Ovid's Elegies	3.12.7		
TREMBLE				
were woont to quake/And tremble at the Persean Monarkes name,	1Tamb	1.1.116		Cosroe
True (Argier) and tremble at my lookes.	1Tamb	3.1.49		Bajzth
As all the world shall tremble at their view.	2Tamb	1.3.57		Celeb
And tremble when ye heare this Scourge wil come,	2Tamb	4.3.99		Tamb
Whose tender blossoms tremble every one,	2Tamb	4.3.123		Tamb
A thing that makes me tremble to unfold.	Jew	3.6.48		2Fryar
This feare is that which makes me tremble thus,	Edw	5.5.105		Edward
All tremble at my name, and I feare none,	Edw	5.6.13		Mortmr
Tremble and quake at his commanding charmes?	F1372	4.2.48		Fredrk
heare [me] with patience, and tremble not at my speeches.	F1839	5.2.43	P	Faust
I tremble to unfould/What you intend, great Jove is now	Lucan, First Booke	630		
Wilt thou her fault learne, she may make thee tremble,	Ovid's Elegies	2.2.17		
TREMBLED				
Before whose bow th'Arcadian wild beasts trembled.	Ovid's Elegies	1.7.14		
He toucht her hand, in touching it she trembled,	Hero and Leander	1.183		
TREMBLING				
To whom the aged King thus trembling spoke:	Dido	2.1.232		Aeneas
And they will (trembling) sound a quicke retreat,	2Tamb	1.1.150		Orcan
Whereat thou trembling hid'st thee in the aire,	2Tamb	4.1.130		Tamb
the Alpes/Shooke the old snow from off their trembling laps.	Lucan, First Booke	552		
Then, that the trembling Citizens should walke/About the City;	Lucan, First Booke	591		
Her halfe dead joynts, and trembling limmes I sawe,	Ovid's Elegies	1.7.53		
Her trembling hand writ back she might not doo.	Ovid's Elegies	2.2.6		
Her trembling mouth these unmeete sounds expresses.	Ovid's Elegies	3.5.72		
But follow trembling campes, and battailes sterne,	Ovid's Elegies	3.7.26		
She trembling strove, this strife of hers (like that/Which made	Hero and Leander	2.291		
TRENCH				
Then shall our footmen lie within the trench,	1Tamb	3.1.64		Bajzth
Minions, Fauknets, and Sakars to the trench,	2Tamb	3.3.6		Techel
That with his ruine fils up all the trench.	2Tamb	3.3.26		Therid
And lie in trench before thy castle walles,	2Tamb	3.3.31		Techel
measure the height/And distance of the castle from the trench,	2Tamb	3.3.51		Techel
bringing of our ordinance/Along the trench into the battery,	2Tamb	3.3.55		Therid
With slender trench they escape night stratagems,	Lucan, First Booke	514		
TRENCHE				
And bare him to his death, and in a trenche/Strake off his head,	Edw	3.1.119		Arundl
TRENCHER				
thou maist thinke thy selfe happie to be fed from my trencher.	1Tamb	4.4.93	P	Tamb
Here Turk, wilt thou have a cleane trencher?	1Tamb	4.4.101	P	Tamb
thou wouldst do well/To waite at my trencher, and tell me lies	Edw	1.1.31		Gavstn
TRENT				
What by the holy Councell held at Trent,	F 884	3.1.106		Pope
TRESPASSE				
Preach upon poles for trespasse of their tongues.	Edw	1.1.118		Kent
TRESSES				
pooles, refraines/To taint his tresses in the Tyrrhen maine?	Dido	1.1.112		Venus
Shaking her silver tresses in the aire,	1Tamb	5.1.141		Tamb
Her white necke hid with tresses hanging downe,	Ovid's Elegies	1.5.10		
Could I therefore her comely tresses teare?	Ovid's Elegies	1.7.11		
But cruelly her tresses having rent,	Ovid's Elegies	1.7.49		
Leave colouring thy tresses I did cry,	Ovid's Elegies	1.14.1		
Why doest thy ill kembd tresses losse lament?	Ovid's Elegies	1.14.35		
To stay thy tresses white veyle hast thou none?	Ovid's Elegies	3.5.56		
Yet rending with enraged thumbe her tresses,	Ovid's Elegies	3.5.71		
Jewels, and gold their Virgin tresses crowne,	Ovid's Elegies	3.12.25		
His dangling tresses that were never shorne,	Hero and Leander	1.55		
He clapt his plumpe cheekes, with his tresses playd,	Hero and Leander	2.181		
TREST				
On Priams loose-trest daughter when he gazed.	Ovid's Elegies	1.9.38		
[Amber] <Yellow> trest is shee, then on the morne thinke I,/My	Ovid's Elegies	2.4.43		
TRESTE				
Who'le set the faire treste [sunne] <sonne> in battell ray,	Ovid's Elegies	1.1.15		
TRETCHEROUS				
Tretcherous Warwicke, traiterous Mortimer,	Edw	3.1.134		Edward
TREVIER				
And Trevier; thou being glad that wars are past thee;	Lucan, First Booke	437		
TRIALL (See also TRYALL)				
Make triall now of that philosophie,	Edw	4.7.17		Edward
Till further triall may be made thereof.	Edw	5.6.80		King
[What there he did in triall of his art],	F1153	3.3.66A		3Chor
TRIBE				
But say the Tribe that I descended of/Were all in generall cast	Jew	1.2.113		Barab
I am not of the Tribe of Levy, I,	Jew	2.3.18		Barab
TRIBUNALL				
[And fliest the throne of his tribunall seate],	F1790	5.1.117A		OldMan
TRIBUNE				
And with them Curio, sometime Tribune too,	Lucan, First Booke	271		
TRIBUNES				
That lawes were broake, Tribunes with Consuls strove,	Lucan, First Booke	179		
From doubtfull Roome wrongly expel'd the Tribunes,	Lucan, First Booke	269		
TRIBUTARY				
nay we dare not give consent/By reason of a Tributary league.	Jew	2.2.23		Govnr
TRIBUTE				
Shall pay a yearly tribute to thy Syre.	1Tamb	5.1.519		Tamb
Shall pay me tribute for, in Babylon.	2Tamb	5.1.167		Tamb
Where Nilus payes his tribute to the maine,	Jew	1.1.75		Barab
Which Tribute all in policie, I feare,	Jew	1.1.181		Barab
The ten yeares tribute that remaines unpaid.	Jew	1.2.7		Calym
are such/That you will needs have ten yeares tribute past,	Jew	1.2.19		Govnr
To levie of us ten yeares tribute past,	Jew	1.2.41		Govnr

TRIBUTE (cont.)

To what this ten yeares tribute will amount/That we have cast,	Jew	1.2.46	Govnr
Are strangers with your tribute to be tax'd?	Jew	1.2.59	Barab
tribute mony of the Turkes shall all be levyed amongst the	Jew	1.2.68	P Reader
gather of these goods/The mony for this tribute of the Turke.	Jew	1.2.156	Govnr
Claime tribute where thou wilt, we are resolv'd,	Jew	2.2.55	Govnr
And for the Tribute-mony I am sent.	Jew	3.5.10	Basso
Bashaw, in briefe, shalt have no tribute here,	Jew	3.5.11	Govnr
hast broke the league/By flat denyall of the promis'd Tribute,	Jew	3.5.20	Basso
thou that Jew whose goods we heard were sold/For Tribute-mony?	Jew	5.1.74	Calym

TRIBUTE-MONY

And for the Tribute-mony I am sent.	Jew	3.5.10	Basso
thou that Jew whose goods we heard were sold/For Tribute-mony?	Jew	5.1.74	Calym

TRICE

Even he that in a trice vanquisht two kings,	1Tamb	3.3.36	Therid
O spare me, or dispatche me in a trice.	Edw	5.5.111	Edward

TRICK

Some wicked trick or other.	Jew	2.3.119	P Barab

TRICKE

And tricke thy armes and shoulders with my theft.	Dido	1.1.45	Jupitr
Belike he has some new tricke for a purse;	Jew	2.3.101	Barab
Well use that tricke no more, I would advise you.	F App	p.232 19	Faust
his labour; wel, this tricke shal cost him fortie dollers more.	F App	p.241 166	P Faust

TRICKES

Nay, you shall pardon me, none shall knowe my trickes.	Edw	5.4.39	Ltborn
let me have the carrying of him about to shew some trickes.	F1129	3.3.42	P Robin

TRICKLES

Veiw here this <the> bloud that trickles from mine arme,	F 446	2.1.58	Faust

TRICKLING

And downe her cheekes, the trickling teares did flow,	Ovid's Elegies		1.7.57

TRICKS

And tricks belonging unto Brokery,	Jew	2.3.192	Barab
There use all tricks, and tread shame under feete.	Ovid's Elegies		3.13.18

TRIDE

me have borne/A thousand brunts, and tride me ful ten yeeres,	Lucan, First Booke		301
Judge you the rest, being tyrde <tride> she bad me kisse.	Ovid's Elegies		1.5.25
Penelope in bowes her youths strength tride,	Ovid's Elegies		1.8.47

TRIE

But here he is, now Dido trie thy wit.	Dido	5.1.86	Dido
be put in the front of such a battaile once, to trie my valour.	2Tamb	4.1.73	P Calyph
That I dissemble not, trie it on me.	2Tamb	4.2.76	Olymp
god>,/Here <Faustus> tire my <trie thy> braines to get a Deity.	F 90	1.1.62	Faust
Yet let us see <trie> what we can do.	F 228	1.2.35	2Schol
Warre and the destinies shall trie my cause.	Lucan, First Booke		229
But though this night thy fortune be to trie it,	Ovid's Elegies		1.4.69

TRIED

Like tried silver runs through Paradice/To entertaine divine	2Tamb	2.4.24	Tamb
Lets use our tried force, they that now thwart right/In wars	Lucan, First Booke		349
Compar'd with marriage, had you tried them both,	Hero and Leander		1.263

TRIER

Past with delight the stately Towne of Trier:	F 780	3.1.2	Faust

TRIES

Let him surcease: love tries wit best of all.	Ovid's Elegies		1.9.32

TRIFLE

A trifle, weele expell him when we please:	Edw	2.2.10	Edward
a small trifle to suffice nature.	F 695	2.2.144	P Glutny

TRIFLES

But leaving these vaine trifles of mens soules,	F 289	1.3.61	Faust
[Tush] <No>, these are trifles, and meere old wives Tales.	F 524	2.1.136	Faust
<Tush>, These slender questions <trifles> Wagner can decide:	F 600	2.2.49	Faust

TRIM'D

Nor she her selfe but first trim'd up discernes.	Ovid's Elegies		2.17.10

TRIMST

Cypassis that a thousand wayes trimst haire,	Ovid's Elegies		2.8.1

TRINITY

conjuring/Is stoutly to abjure [the Trinity] <all godlinesse>,	F 281	1.3.53	Mephst

TRIP

That they may trip more lightly ore the lawndes,	Dido	1.1.207	Venus

TRIPLE (See also TREBLE)

And triple wise intrench her round about:	Dido	5.1.10	Aeneas
[and] <To> pull the triple headed dog from hell.	1Tamb	1.2.161	Therid
have measured heaven/With triple circuit thou regreet us not,	1Tamb	3.1.37	Bajzth
And crave his triple worthy buriall.	1Tamb	3.2.112	Usumc
Now cleare the triple region of the aire,	1Tamb	4.2.30	Tamb
those blind Geographers/That make a triple region in the world,	1Tamb	4.4.76	Tamb
Whose triple Myter I did take by force,	2Tamb	1.3.189	Techel
And throw them in the triple mote of Hell,	2Tamb	2.4.100	Tamb
Before I conquere all the triple world.	2Tamb	4.3.63	Tamb
And in my helme a triple plume shal spring,	2Tamb	4.3.116	Tamb
The triple headed Cerberus would howle,	2Tamb	5.1.97	Tamb
And know my Lord, the Pope will sell his triple crowne,	P 851	17.46	Guise
These bloudy hands shall teare his triple Crowne,	P1199	22.61	King
And point like Antiques at his triple Crowne:	F 862	3.1.84	Mephst
Did seeke to weare the triple Dyadem,	F 959	3.1.181	Faust
Here, take his triple Crowne along with you,	F 970	3.1.192	Pope
With his rich triple crowne to be reserv'd,	F1027	3.2.47	Raymnd
In peace possesse the triple Diadem,	F1213	4.1.59	Emper
Beat downe the bold waves with his triple mace,	Hero and Leander		2.172

TRIPLEX

Dei Acherontis propitii, valeat numen triplex Jehovae, Ignei,	F 244	1.3.16	P Faust

TRIPOLY

Brought to the war by men of Tripoly:	1Tamb	3.3.17	Bassoe
That lanching from Argier to Tripoly,	2Tamb	1.3.124	Therid

TRIPOLY (cont.)			
Tane from Aleppo, Soldino, Tripoly,	2Tamb	3.1.58	Soria
TRIPS			
Trips she, it likes me well, plods she, what than?	Ovid's Elegies		2.4.23
Wherewith as one displeas'd, away she trips.	Hero and Leander		2.4
TRIPT			
Come thither; As she spake this, her toong tript,	Hero and Leander		1.357
TRITON			
Triton I know hath fild his trumpe with Troy,	Dido	1.1.130	Venus
But if that Triton tosse the troubled floud,	Ovid's Elegies		2.11.27
And made his capring Triton sound alowd,	Hero and Leander		2.156
TRITONS			
That I may swim to him like Tritons neece:	Dido	5.1.247	Dido
TRIUMPH			
Achilles horse/Drew him in triumph through the Greekish Campe,	Dido	2.1.206	Aeneas
And then in triumph ran into the streetes,	Dido	2.1.261	Aeneas
Nor Venus triumph in his tender youth:	Dido	3.2.9	Juno
Triumph, my mates, our travels are at end,	Dido	5.1.1	Aeneas
To triumph over many Provinces.	1Tamb	1.1.173	Cosroe
do but joine with me/And we will triumph over all the world.	1Tamb	1.2.173	Tamb
their fellowes throats/And make us triumph in their overthrow.	1Tamb	2.2.50	Meandr
May triumph in our long expected Fate.	1Tamb	2.3.44	Tamb
And ride in triumph through Persepolis.	1Tamb	2.5.49	Menaph
And ride in triumph through Persepolis?	1Tamb	2.5.50	Tamb
And ride in triumph through Persepolis?	1Tamb	2.5.54	Tamb
Whose smiling stars gives him assured hope/Of martiall triumph,	1Tamb	3.3.43	Tamb
and for this happy conquest/Triumph, and solemnize a martiall	1Tamb	3.3.273	Tamb
And where I goe be thus in triumph drawne:	1Tamb	4.2.86	Tamb
And as thou rid'st in triumph through the streets,	2Tamb	1.2.41	Callap
Then wil we triumph, banquet and carouse,	2Tamb	1.3.218	Tamb
as the battaile is done, Ile ride in triumph through the Camp.	2Tamb	3.5.145	P Tamb
Ninus and great Alexander/Have rode in triumph, triumphs	2Tamb	5.1.70	Tamb
To triumph after all our victories.	2Tamb	5.1.213	Tamb
To triumph over cursed Tamburlaine.	2Tamb	5.2.30	Callap
Let us away with triumph to our tents.	P 805	16.19	Navrre
So will I triumph over this wanton King,	P 983	19.53	Guise
Against the stately triumph we decreed?	Edw	2.2.12	Edward
And triumph Edward with his friends uncontrould.	Edw	4.3.3	Edward
[My faith, vile hel, shall triumph over thee],	F1793	5.1.120A	OldMan
Will ye wadge war, for which you shall not triumph?	Lucan, First Booke		12
Nor shalt thou triumph when thou comst to Roome;	Lucan, First Booke		287
And shal he triumph long before his time,	Lucan, First Booke		316
And so they triumph, be't with whom ye wil.	Lucan, First Booke		342
So will thy [triumph] <triumphs> seeme magnificall.	Ovid's Elegies		1.2.28
Hence with great laude thou maiest a triumph move.	Ovid's Elegies		2.9.16
That victory doth chiefely triumph merit,	Ovid's Elegies		2.12.5
O care-got triumph hetherwards advance.	Ovid's Elegies		2.12.16
TRIUMPHANT			
Since I arriv'd with my triumphant hoste,	1Tamb	5.1.458	Tamb
With captive kings at his triumphant Carre.	Edw	1.1.174	Gavstn
In peace triumphant, fortunate in warres.	Edw	3.1.33	SpncrP
In honour of the Popes triumphant victory.	F 835	3.1.57	Mephst
Then with triumphant laurell will I grace them/And in the midst	Ovid's Elegies		1.11.25
About my temples go triumphant bayes,	Ovid's Elegies		2.12.1
TRIUMPHE			
Who in the triumphe will be challenger,	Edw	1.4.382	Edward
Yet triumphe in the hope of thee my joye?	Edw	4.2.28	Queene
TRIUMPHES			
The former triumphes of our mightines,	1Tamb	5.1.253	Zabina
in her browes/Triumphes and Trophees for my victories:	1Tamb	5.1.513	Tamb
In sollemne triumphes, and in publike showes,	Edw	1.4.350	Edward
The idle triumphes, maskes, lascivious showes/And prodigall	Edw	2.2.157	Mortmr
TRIUMPHETH			
Triumpheth Englands Edward with his friends,	Edw	4.3.2	Edward
And Love triumpheth ore his buskind Poet.	Ovid's Elegies		2.18.18
TRIUMPHING			
Then shall we send to this triumphing King,	1Tamb	2.5.87	Techel
Triumphing over him and these his kings,	1Tamb	3.3.128	Tamb
Triumphing in his fall whom you advaunst,	2Tamb	5.3.23	Techel
Io, triumphing shall thy people sing.	Ovid's Elegies		1.2.34
TRIUMPHS			
And murdrous Fates throwes al his triumphs down.	2Tamb	Prol.5	Prolog
and great Alexander/Have rode in triumph, triumphs Tamburlaine,	2Tamb	5.1.70	Tamb
And view their triumphs, as they passe this way.	F 857	3.1.79	Mephst
(great Pompey) that late deeds would dim/Olde triumphs,	Lucan, First Booke		122
by these ten blest ensignes/And all thy several triumphs,	Lucan, First Booke		376
So will thy [triumph] <triumphs> seeme magnificall.	Ovid's Elegies		1.2.28
Go now thou Conqueror, glorious triumphs raise,	Ovid's Elegies		1.7.35
TRIUMPHT			
Have triumpht over Affrike, and the bounds/Of Europe wher the	1Tamb	1.1.9	Cosroe
And I that triumpht so be overcome.	1Tamb	1.2.115	Tamb
Thus having triumpht over you, I will set my countenance like a	F 213	1.2.20	P Wagner
like those bright shining Saints,/And triumpht over hell:	F1906	5.2.110	GdAngl
TROD			
When in this [workes] <worke> first verse I trod aloft,	Ovid's Elegies		1.1.21
TRODE			
Hath trode the Meisures, do my souldiers martch,	2Tamb	5.1.75	Tamb
Trode on the neck of Germane Fredericke,	F 916	3.1.138	Pope
She hath not trode <tred> awrie that doth denie it,	Ovid's Elegies		3.13.5
TROIAN (See also TROYANE)			
And every Troian be as welcome here,	Dido	1.2.40	Iarbus
Sometime I was a Troian, mightie Queene:	Dido	2.1.75	Aeneas
Troian, thy ruthfull tale hath made me sad:	Dido	2.1.301	Dido

TROIAN (cont.)			
Aeneas, Ile repaire thy Troian ships,	Dido	3.1.113	Dido
when for the hate of Troian Ganimed,	Dido	3.2.42	Juno
Faire Troian, hold my golden bowe awhile,	Dido	3.3.7	Dido
Anna, against this Troian doe I pray,	Dido	4.2.30	Iarbus
To rob their mistresse of her Troian guest?	Dido	4.4.138	Dido
Led by Achates to the Troian fleete:	Dido	5.1.84	Dido
TROIANE			
Whom Troiane ships fecht from Europa farre.	Ovid's Elegies		1.10.2
TROIANES			
Troianes destroy the Greeke wealth, while you may.	Ovid's Elegies		1.9.34
TROIANS			
Follow ye Troians, follow this brave Lord,	Dido	1.2.1	Illion
But tell me Troians, Troians if you be,	Dido	1.2.17	Iarbus
Who looking on the scarres we Troians gave,	Dido	2.1.131	Aeneas
This Troians end will be thy envies aime,	Dido	3.3.73	Iarbus
Troians abourd, and I will follow you,	Dido	4.3.45	Aeneas
O foolish Troians that would steale from hence,	Dido	4.4.5	Dido
Doe Troians use to quit their Lovers thus?	Dido	5.1.106	Dido
TROLL (See TROWLES)			
TROOPE (See also TROUPE)			
Leading a troope of Gentlemen and Lords,	1Tamb	2.1.58	Ceneus
And with a troope of theeves and vagabondes,	1Tamb	4.1.6	Souldn
to see the Sun-bright troope/Of heavenly vyrgins and unspotted	1Tamb	5.1.324	Zenoc
We may discourage all the pagan troope,	2Tamb	2.1.25	Fredrk
TROOPES			
And so in troopes all marcht to Tenedos:	Dido	2.1.135	Aeneas
Have swarm'd in troopes into the Easterne India:	1Tamb	1.1.120	Cosroe
Begin in troopes to threaten civill warre,	1Tamb	1.1.148	Ceneus
And rid the world of those detested troopes?	1Tamb	2.2.19	Meandr
That live confounded in disordered troopes,	1Tamb	2.2.60	Meandr
(Staying to order all the scattered troopes)/Farewell Lord	1Tamb	2.5.45	Cosroe
Environed with troopes of noble men,	1Tamb	5.1.526	Tamb
When he himselfe amidst the thickest troopes/Beats downe our	2Tamb	4.1.25	Amyras
meet not me/With troopes of harlots at your slothful heeles.	2Tamb	4.3.82	Tamb
Be you the generall of the levied troopes,	Edw	1.4.362	Edward
Which troopes hath alwayes bin on Cupids side:	Ovid's Elegies		1.2.36
TROOPS			
Thorow the streets with troops of conquered kings,	2Tamb	4.3.114	Tamb
TROPHEES			
in her browes/Triumphes and Trophees for my victories:	1Tamb	5.1.513	Tamb
TROPICK			
Even from the midst of fiery Cancers Tropick,	2Tamb	1.1.73	Orcan
The [Tropicks] <Tropick>, Zones, and quarters of the skye,	F 761	2.3.40	2Chor
TROPICKE			
Cutting the Tropicke line of Capricorne,	2Tamb	5.3.138	Tamb
TROPICKS			
The [Tropicks] <Tropick>, Zones, and quarters of the skye,	F 761	2.3.40	2Chor
TROT			
a bawde aright/Give eare, there is an old trot Dipsas hight.	Ovid's Elegies		1.8.2
TROTH			
Troth master, I'm loth such a pot of pottage should be spoyld.	Jew	3.4.89	P Ithimr
to speake <say> troth,/Both short and long please me, for I	Ovid's Elegies		2.4.35
TROTHLES			
Thou trothles and unjust, what lines are these?	P 680	13.24	Guise
TROTTING			
Trotting the ring, and tilting at a glove:	2Tamb	1.3.39	Zenoc
Or Lapland Giants trotting by our sides:	F 153	1.1.125	Valdes
TROUBLE			
My selfe will see they shall not trouble ye,	Dido	1.2.38	Iarbus
Avaunt old witch and trouble not my wits.	Dido	3.2.25	Venus
That worke such trouble to your woonted rest:	1Tamb	3.2.3	Agidas
againe, you shall not trouble me thus to come and fetch you.	2Tamb	3.5.101	P Tamb
Fye; what a trouble tis to count this trash.	Jew	1.1.7	Barab
'Tis in the trouble of my spirit I speake;	Jew	1.2.207	Barab
Trouble her not, sweet Lodowicke depart:	Jew	2.3.327	Barab
You shall not need trouble your selves so farre,	Jew	3.5.22	Basso
Away, no more, let him not trouble me.	Jew	5.2.26	Barab
Trouble me not, I neare offended him,	P1005	19.75	Guise
Out of my sight, and trouble me no more.	Edw	2.2.216	Edward
And trouble not the Duke.	F1598	4.6.41	Servnt
TROUBLED			
Beates forth my senses from this troubled soule,	Dido	2.1.116	Aeneas
nor the Turk/Troubled my sences with conceit of foile,	1Tamb	5.1.158	Tamb
Making a passage for my troubled soule,	2Tamb	4.2.34	Olymp
Was ever troubled with injurious warres:	P1142	22.4	King
His mind was troubled, and he aim'd at war,	Lucan, First Booke		186
[Thy] <They> troubled haires, alas, endur'd great losse.	Ovid's Elegies		1.14.24
Because [thy] <they> care too much thy Mistresse troubled.	Ovid's Elegies		2.2.8
But if that Triton tosse the troubled floud,	Ovid's Elegies		2.11.27
Nor hanging oares the troubled seas did sweepe,	Ovid's Elegies		3.7.43
TROUBLES			
they come to proove/The wounding troubles angry war affoords.	2Tamb	1.3.87	Zenoc
TROUBLESOME			
Will be too costly and too troublesome:	Jew	5.3.23	Calym
I pray my Lords have patience at this troublesome banquet.	F1058	3.2.78	Pope
To lay the fury of this same troublesome ghost.	F1064	3.2.84	Pope
TROUBLETH			
Blindes Europs eyes and troubleth our estate:	P 152	2.95	Guise
TROUBLOUS			
Fill all the aire with troublous bellowing:	2Tamb	4.1.190	Tamb
TROUNCE			
But secretlie her lookes with checks did trounce mee,	Ovid's Elegies		1.7.21

TROUPE (See also TROOPE)			
<Where thou shalt see a troupe of bald-pate Friers>, .	F 833	(HC265)A	Mephst
Twas his troupe hem'd in Milo being accusde; . . .	Lucan, First Booke		323
Next, an inferiour troupe, in tuckt up vestures, . .	Lucan, First Booke		595
TROUPES			
Give me my horse and lets r'enforce our troupes: . .	Edw	4.5.6	Edward
Raw soldiours lately prest; and troupes of gownes; . .	Lucan, First Booke		312
These troupes should soone pull down the church of Jove. .	Lucan, First Booke		381
delay/Might crosse him, he withdrew his troupes from France,	Lucan, First Booke		395
One sweares his troupes of daring horsemen fought/Upon Mevanias	Lucan, First Booke		469
heady rout/That in chain'd troupes breake forth at every port;	Lucan, First Booke		489
Th'irrevocable people flie in troupes.	Lucan, First Booke		507
And let the troupes which shall thy Chariot follow, . .	Ovid's Elegies		1.7.37
So the fierce troupes of Thracian Rhesus fell/And Captive	Ovid's Elegies		1.9.23
Nor being arm'd fierce troupes to follow farre? . .	Ovid's Elegies		2.14.2
And forth the gay troupes on swift horses flie. . .	Ovid's Elegies		3.2.78
TROW			
But they will give me leave once more, I trow, . . .	Jew	1.2.252	Barab
No my lord Mortimer, not I, I trow.	Edw	4.2.44	Prince
TROWE			
Is it not, trowe ye, to assemble aide, ...	Edw	3.1.207	SpncrP
I trowe/The lords of Fraunce love Englands gold so well, .	Edw	4.3.14	Edward
TROWLES			
Thus trowles our fortune in by land and Sea, . . .	Jew	1.1.103	Barab
TROY			
Poore Troy must now be sackt upon the Sea, . . .	Dido	1.1.64	Venus
Which once performd, poore Troy so long supprest, . .	Dido	1.1.93	Jupitr
Who will eternish Troy in their attempts.	Dido	1.1.108	Jupitr
Triton I know hath fild his trumpe with Troy, . . .	Dido	1.1.130	Venus
Brave Prince of Troy, thou onely art our God, . . .	Dido	1.1.152	Achat
Of Troy am I, Aeneas is my name, ...	Dido	1.1.216	Aeneas
Wretches of Troy, envied of the windes, ...	Dido	1.2.4	Illion
Me thinkes that towne there should be Troy, yon Idas hill,	Dido	2.1.7	Aeneas
that under his conduct/We might saile backe to Troy, and be	Dido	2.1.18	Aeneas
He is alive, Troy is not overcome.	Dido	2.1.30	Aeneas
But Troy is not, what shall I say I am?	Dido	2.1.76	Aeneas
O Priamus, O Troy, oh Hecuba!	Dido	2.1.105	Aeneas
And truely to, how Troy was overcome:	Dido	2.1.107	Dido
But all in this that Troy is overcome, ...	Dido	2.1.112	Dido
What, faints Aeneas to remember Troy?	Dido	2.1.118	Dido
Troy is invincible, why stay we here?	Dido	2.1.128	Aeneas
And prophecied Troy should be overcome:	Dido	2.1.142	Aeneas
we were commanded straight/With reverence to draw it into Troy.	Dido	2.1.168	Aeneas
O had it never entred, Troy had stood.	Dido	2.1.172	Aeneas
Troy is a fire, the Grecians have the towne. . . .	Dido	2.1.208	Aeneas
Which made the funerall flame that burnt faire Troy: .	Dido	2.1.218	Aeneas
King of this Citie, but my Troy is fired, ...	Dido	2.1.236	Aeneas
My cosin Helen taught it me in Troy.	Dido	3.1.28	Cupid
where shall be wrought/The warres of Troy, but not Troyes	Dido	3.1.125	Dido
I saw this man at Troy ere Troy was sackt. . . .	Dido	3.1.141	Achat
Troy shall no more call him her second hope, . . .	Dido	3.2.8	Juno
Why, man of Troy, doe I offend thine eyes? . . .	Dido	3.3.17	Iarbus
For Troy, for Priam, for his fiftie sonnes, . . .	Dido	4.4.89	Aeneas
Here will Aeneas build a statelier Troy, ...	Dido	5.1.2	Aeneas
But what shall it be calde, Troy as before? . . .	Dido	5.1.18	Illion
And raise a new foundation to old Troy, ...	Dido	5.1.79	Aeneas
Would, as faire Troy was, Carthage might be sackt, . .	Dido	5.1.147	Dido
I never vow'd at Aulis gulfe/The desolation of his native Troy,	Dido	5.1.203	Dido
And had she liv'd before the siege of Troy, . . .	2Tamb	2.4.86	Tamb
worth>/<Made Greece with ten yeares warres afflict poore Troy>?	F1696	(HC269)B	2Schol
In stead of Troy shall Wittenberg <Wertenberge> be sack't,/And	F1776	5.1.103	Faust
When Troy by ten yeares battle tumbled downe, . . .	Ovid's Elegies		2.12.9
Troy had not yet beene ten yeares siege out-stander, .	Ovid's Elegies		3.5.27
When Thebes, when Troy, when Caesar should be writ, . .	Ovid's Elegies		3.11.15
Love kindling fire, to burne such townes as Troy, . .	Hero and Leander		1.153
TROYANE			
Had Venus spoilde her bellies Troyane fruite, . . .	Ovid's Elegies		2.14.17
TROYANES			
A woman forc'd the Troyanes new to enter/Warres, just Latinus,	Ovid's Elegies		2.12.21
TROYANS			
But as the Gods to end the Troyans toile, ...	1Tamb	5.1.392	Zenoc
TROYES			
Who for Troyes sake hath entertaind us all, . . .	Dido	2.1.64	Illion
shall be wrought/The warres of Troy, but not Troyes overthrow:	Dido	3.1.125	Dido
The worke of Poets lasts Troyes labours fame, . . .	Ovid's Elegies		3.8.29
TRUCE			
Tell him, I am content to take a truce, ...	1Tamb	3.1.31	Bajzth
And with my father take a frindly truce.	1Tamb	4.4.72	Zenoc
For Tamburlaine takes truce with al the world. . . .	1Tamb	5.1.529	Tamb
the king of Hungary/Should meet our person to conclude a truce.	2Tamb	1.1.10	Orcan
basely on their knees/In all your names desirde a truce of me?	2Tamb	1.1.97	Orcan
But whilst I live will be at truce with thee. . . .	2Tamb	1.1.130	Sgsmnd
I sweare to keepe this truce inviolable:	2Tamb	1.1.142	Orcan
the christian King/Is made, for joy of your admitted truce:	2Tamb	2.2.21	Uribas
Then hang out flagges (my Lord) of humble truce, . .	2Tamb	5.1.6	Maxim
Offer submission, hang up flags of truce, ...	2Tamb	5.1.26	1Citzn
This truce we have is but in hope of gold, ...	Jew	2.2.26	1Knght
Feare not, my Lord, for here, against the [sluice] <Truce>,/The	Jew	5.1.86	Barab
Till gentle parlie did the truce obtaine.	Hero and Leander		2.278
So that the truce was broke, and she alas, . . .	Hero and Leander		2.285
TRUE			
So thou wouldst prove as true as Paris did, . . .	Dido	5.1.146	Dido
I am as true as any one of yours.	Dido	5.1.223	Nurse

TRUE (cont.)			
in the darksome Cave/He drew, and swore by to be true to me,	Dido	5.1.296	Dido
Ful true thou speakst, and like thy selfe my lord,	1Tamb	1.1.49	Mycet
Nor are Apollos Oracles more true,	1Tamb	1.2.212	Tamb
I tel you true my heart is swolne with wrath,	1Tamb	2.2.2	Mycet
He tells you true, my maisters, so he does.	1Tamb	2.2.74	Mycet
True (Argier) and tremble at my lookes.	1Tamb	3.1.49	Bajzth
All this is true as holy Mahomet,	1Tamb	3.1.54	Bajzth
Even with the true Egyptian Diadem.	1Tamb	5.1.105	1Virgn
And fashions men with true nobility.	1Tamb	5.1.190	Tamb
In whom no faith nor true religion rests,	2Tamb	2.1.34	Baldwn
With love and patience let your true love die,	2Tamb	2.4.67	Zenoc
And of my Lords whose true nobilitie/Have merited my latest	2Tamb	2.4.73	Zenoc
for his vertues)/Revives the spirits of true Turkish heartes,	2Tamb	3.1.24	Callap
You say true.	2Tamb	4.1.41	Calyph
'Tis true, my Lord, therefore intreat him well.	Jew	2.2.8	1Knght
Be true and secret, thou shalt want no gold.	Jew	2.3.216	Barab
Thou know'st, and heaven can witnesse it is true,	Jew	2.3.253	Barab
True; and it shall be cunningly perform'd.	Jew	2.3.367	Barab
Then of true griefe let us take equall share.	Jew	3.2.37	Govnr
True, I have mony, what though I have?	Jew	4.1.30	Barab
Why true, therefore did I place him there:	Jew	4.1.137	Barab
If this be true, I'le make thee Governor.	Jew	5.1.95	Calym
And if it be not true, then let me dye.	Jew	5.1.96	Barab
I now am Governour of Malta; true,	Jew	5.2.29	Barab
Too late it is my Lord if that be true/To blame her highnes,	P 181	3.16	QnMarg
The vertues of our true Religion,	P 577	11.42	Pleshe
And true profession of his holy word:	P 586	11.51	Navrre
And rent our true religion from this land:	P 703	14.6	Navrre
To plant the true succession of the faith,	P 715	14.18	Bartus
My Lord, in token of my true humilitie,	P 866	17.61	Guise
Tis true, and but for reverence of these robes,	Edw	1.1.180	Gavstn
True, true.	Edw	1.1.201	BshpCv
Tis true, the Bishop is in the tower,	Edw	1.2.1	Warwck
Tis true sweete Gaveston, oh were it false.	Edw	1.4.108	Edward
Can this be true twas good to banish him,	Edw	1.4.245	Lncstr
And is this true to call him home againe?	Edw	1.4.246	Lncstr
In no respect can contraries be true.	Edw	1.4.249	Lncstr
He saith true.	Edw	1.4.271	Penbrk
Repeald, the newes is too sweet to be true.	Edw	1.4.323	Edward
To make away a true man for a theefe.	Edw	2.5.70	Mortmr
True, and it like your grace,/That powres in lieu of all your	Edw	3.1.43	Spencr
Spencer, as true as death,/He is in Englands ground, our	Edw	4.3.21	Edward
Too true it is, quem dies vidit veniens superbum,	Edw	4.7.53	Leistr
Dares but affirme, that Edwards not true king,	Edw	5.4.76	Champn
My lord, I feare me it will proove too true.	Edw	5.6.77	2Lord
Without election, and a true consent:	F 887	3.1.109	Pope
if that bee true, I have a charme in my head, shall controule	F1202	4.1.48	P Benvol
In their true shapes, and state Majesticall,	F1233	4.1.79	Emper
How may I prove that saying to be true?	F1268	4.1.114	Emper
True Maister Doctor, and since I finde you so kind I will make	F1570	4.6.13	P Lady
<Oh> Pythagoras Metemsycosis <metem su cossis>; were that true,	F1966	5.2.170	Faust
You say true, Ile hate.	F App	p.231 11	P Faust
True Rafe, and more Rafe, if thou hast any mind to Nan Spit our	F App	p.234 26	P Robin
true substantiall bodies of those two deceased princes which	F App	p.237 42	P Faust
Ifaith thats as true as Diana turned me to a stag.	F App	p.237 54	P Knight
but the true substantiall bodies of those two deceased princes.	F App	p.238 64	P Emper
Romans if ye be,/And beare true harts, stay heare:	Lucan, First Booke		194
Vaine fame increast true feare, and did invade/The peoples	Lucan, First Booke		465
but this/If feigned, doth well; if true it doth amisse.	Ovid's Elegies		1.8.36
Vaine causes faine of him the true to hide,	Ovid's Elegies		2.2.31
Ile thinke all true, though it be feigned matter.	Ovid's Elegies		2.11.53
My selfe would sweare, the wenches true did sweare,	Ovid's Elegies		3.3.45
Though both of us performd our true intent,	Ovid's Elegies		3.6.5
Ah now a name too true thou hast, I finde.	Ovid's Elegies		3.8.4
Nor have their words true histories pretence,	Ovid's Elegies		3.11.42
On Hellespont guiltie of True-loves blood,	Hero and Leander		1.1
But this is true, so like was one the other,	Hero and Leander		1.39
True love is mute, and oft amazed stands.	Hero and Leander		1.186
TRUELIE			
No truelie sir, I would make nothing of you, but I would faine	F1648	4.6.91	P Carter
TRUE-LOVES			
On Hellespont guiltie of True-loves blood,	Hero and Leander		1.1
TRUELY			
And truely to, how Troy was overcome:	Dido	2.1.107	Dido
Truely my deere brethren, my Maister is within at dinner, with	F 214	1.2.21	P Wagner
TRUEST			
And reape no guerdon for my truest love?	Dido	5.1.282	Iarbus
Live false Aeneas, truest Dido dyes,	Dido	5.1.312	Dido
Lady, the last was truest of the twaine,	Edw	4.2.39	Mortmr
TRUETH			
And tels for trueth, submissions comes too late.	1Tamb	5.1.73	Tamb
a signe of grace in you, when you will confesse the trueth.	F App	p.237 45	P Knight
TRUETHS			
And calling Christ for record of our trueths?	2Tamb	2.1.30	Sgsmnd
TRULIE			
And saying, trulie ant may please your honor,	Edw	2.1.40	Spencr
TRULLES			
And make us jeasting Pageants for their Trulles.	2Tamb	4.3.89	Therid
TRULS			
And common souldiers jest with all their Truls.	2Tamb	4.3.91	Tamb
TRULY			
Deale truly with us as thou intimatest,	Jew	5.2.85	Govnr

TRULY (cont.)			
Truly Ile none of them.	F App	p.230 39	P Wagner
Truly but you shall.	F App	p.230 40	P Clown
TRUMPE			
Triton I know hath fild his trumpe with Troy,	Dido	1.1.130	Venus
Fame hovereth, sounding of her golden Trumpe:	2Tamb	3.4.63	Therid
TRUMPET			
Why, hardst thou not the trumpet sound a charge?	Jew	5.5.105	Govnr
TRUMPETS			
But Menaphon, what means this trumpets sound?	1Tamb	1.1.133	Cosroe
Sound up the trumpets then, God save the King.	1Tamb	1.1.188	Ortyg
Thou art deceiv'd, I heard the Trumpets sound,	1Tamb	3.3.203	Zabina
heare the clange/Of Scythian trumpets, heare the Basiliskes,	1Tamb	4.1.2	Souldn
The trumpets sound, Zenocrate, they come.	2Tamb	1.3.111	Tamb
Trumpets and drums, alarum presently,	2Tamb	3.3.62	Techel
Sound drums and trumpets, marche with me my friends,	Edw	3.1.260	Edward
Sound trumpets my lord and forward let us martch,	Edw	4.4.28	SrJohn
The trumpets sound, I must go take my place.	Edw	5.4.72	Mortmr
None comes, sound trumpets.	Edw	5.4.79	Mortmr
Sound Trumpets then, for thus Saint Peters Heire,	F 875	3.1.97	Pope
And with a solemne noyse of trumpets sound,	F1237	4.1.83	Faust
Trumpets and drums, like deadly threatning other,	Lucan, First Booke		6
colours, with confused noise/Of trumpets clange, shril cornets,	Lucan, First Booke		240
Caesar; he whom I heare thy trumpets charge/I hould no Romaine;	Lucan, First Booke		374
Whome trumpets clang incites, and those that dwel/By Cyngas	Lucan, First Booke		433
Trumpets were heard to sound; and with what noise/An armed	Lucan, First Booke		577
For long shrild trumpets let your notes resound.	Ovid's Elegies		2.6.6
TRUNCK			
that is all he gets/Of Gaveston, or else his sencelesse trunck.	Edw	2.5.54	Mortmr
TRUNKE			
We wil both watch and ward shall keepe his trunke/Amidst these	2Tamb	2.3.38	Orcan
This headlesse trunke that lies on Nylus sande/I know:	Lucan, First Booke		684
TRUNKES			
in lakes of gore/Your headles trunkes, your bodies will I	Edw	3.1.136	Edward
TRUST (See also TROWE)			
how you durst with so much wealth/Trust such a crazed Vessell,	Jew	1.1.80	1Merch
but trust me 'tis a misery/To see a man in such affliction:	Jew	1.2.211	2Jew
For if I keepe not promise, trust not me.	Jew	5.5.23	Barab
I trust thy word, take what I promis'd thee.	Jew	5.5.43	Govnr
But trust him not my Lord,	P 871	17.66	Eprnon
was Plantagenet/False of his word, and therefore trust we thee.	Edw	2.3.12	Mortmr
I will not trust them, Gaveston away.	Edw	2.4.8	Edward
Then if you will not trust his grace in keepe,	Edw	2.5.65	Arundl
But if you dare trust Penbrooke with the prisoner,	Edw	2.5.87	Penbrk
Our friend [Levune] <Lewne>, faithfull and full of trust,	Edw	3.1.60	Queene
Then shall your charge committed to my trust.	Edw	3.1.78	Prince
And in this place of honor and of trust,	Edw	3.1.143	Edward
[Levune] <Lewne>, the trust that we repose in thee,/Begets the	Edw	3.1.262	Spencr
Your worship I trust will remember me?	Edw	4.7.117	Mower
And therefore trust him not.	Edw	5.2.107	Mortmr
Despair in GOD, and trust in Belzebub:	F 393	2.1.5	Faust
[makes men] <make them> foolish that do use <trust> them most.	F 408	2.1.20	BdAngl
order, Il'e nere trust smooth faces, and small ruffes more.	F1318	4.1.164	P Benvol
And trust me, they are the sweetest grapes that e're I tasted.	F1587	4.6.30	P Lady
And wilt not trust thy Citty walls one night:	Lucan, First Booke		518
(Trust me) to give, it is a witty thing.	Ovid's Elegies		1.8.62
Trust me all husbands for such faults are sad/Nor make they any	Ovid's Elegies		2.2.51
Applaud you Neptune, that dare trust his wave,	Ovid's Elegies		3.2.47
Rude man, 'tis vaine, thy damsell to commend/To keepers trust:	Ovid's Elegies		3.4.2
(Trust me) land-streame thou shalt no envie lack,	Ovid's Elegies		3.5.21
Trust in good verse, Tibullus feeles deaths paines,	Ovid's Elegies		3.8.39
And I will trust your words more then mine eies.	Ovid's Elegies		3.13.46
TRUSTIE			
Why turnes Aeneas from his trustie friends?	Dido	2.1.57	Cloan
No, but the trustie friend of Tamburlaine.	1Tamb	1.2.227	Tamb
Ortigius and Menaphon, my trustie friendes,	1Tamb	2.5.29	Cosroe
But what the secret trustie night conceal'd,	Hero and Leander		2.103
TRUSTING			
Urging his fortune, trusting in the gods,	Lucan, First Booke		149
TRUSTLESSE			
and confound/The trustlesse force of those false Christians.	2Tamb	2.2.62	Orcan
TRUSTY			
My trusty servant, nay, my second [selfe] <life>;	Jew	3.4.15	Barab
Oh trusty Ithimore; no servant, but my friend;	Jew	3.4.42	Barab
And after that, I and my trusty Turke--	Jew	4.1.127	Barab
TRUTH (See also TROTH, TRUETH)			
As good dissemble that thou never mean'st/As first meane truth,	Jew	1.2.291	Barab
Truth Pleshe, and God so prosper me in all,	P 584	11.49	Navrre
As I entend to labour for the truth,	P 585	11.50	Navrre
That lift themselves against the perfect truth,	P 799	16.13	Navrre
Mine honor shalbe hostage of my truth,	Edw	2.3.9	Kent
we deceive our selves, and there is <theres> no truth in us.	F 70	1.1.42	P Faust
you may be ashamed to burden honest men with a matter of truth.	F App	p.234 15	P Rafe
So be I may be bold to speake a truth,	Lucan, First Booke		361
so (if truth you sing)/Death brings long life.	Lucan, First Booke		453
Accept him that will love with spotlesse truth:	Ovid's Elegies		1.3.6
To staine all faith in truth, by false crimes use.	Ovid's Elegies		2.2.38
Full of simplicitie and naked truth.	Hero and Leander		1.208
TRUTHLESS (See TROTHLES)			
TRUTHS			
With privy signes, and talke dissembling truths?	Ovid's Elegies		3.10.24
TRY (See also TRIE)			
Faustus may try his cunning by himselfe.	F 187	1.1.159	Cornel

TRY (cont.)
For e're I sleep, I'le try what I can do: F 192 1.1.164 Faust
And try if devils will obey thy Hest, F 234 1.3.6 Faust
resolute/And try the utmost <uttermost> Magicke can performe. F 243 1.3.15 Faust
Then Faustus try thy skill: F1425 4.2.101 Faust
[As in this furnace God shal try my faith], F1792 5.1.119A OldMan
The sport being such, as both alike sweete try it, Ovid's Elegies 1.10.33
What neede she [tyre] <try> her hand to hold the quill, Ovid's Elegies 1.11.23

TRYALL
Condemne his eyes, and say there is no tryall. Ovid's Elegies 2.2.58

TRYED
Shall I be tryed by their transgression? Jew 1.2.115 Barab

'TS
and now ['tis] <'ts> too late. F1866 5.2.70 P Faust

TU
[Quid tu moraris] <quod tumeraris>; per Jehovam, Gehennam, et F 248 1.3.20 P Faust

TUCKT
Next, an inferiour troupe, in tuckt up vestures, Lucan, First Booke 595
Coate-tuckt Dianas legges are painted like them, Ovid's Elegies 3.2.31

TUE
Tue, tue, tue,/Let none escape, P 336 5.63 Guise
Tue, tue, tue, let none escape: P 534 10.7 Guise

TUIS
Desine meque tuis incendere teque querelis, Dido 5.1.139 Aeneas

TULLIE
The Romaine Tullie loved Octavius, Edw 1.4.396 MortSr

TUMBLE
Whilst I in thy incony lap doe tumble. Jew 4.4.29 Ithimr
a point, to which when men aspire,/They tumble hedlong downe: Edw 5.6.61 Mortmr
Then wilt thou tumble in confusion. F1925 5.2.129 BdAngl

TUMBLED
When Troy by ten yeares battle tumbled downe, Ovid's Elegies 2.12.9

TUMBLING
My sides are sore with tumbling to and fro. Ovid's Elegies 1.2.4
On all the [bed mens] <beds men> tumbling let him viewe/And thy Ovid's Elegies 1.8.97
Nor passe I thee, who hollow rocks downe tumbling, Ovid's Elegies 3.5.45
This bed, and that by tumbling made uneven, Ovid's Elegies 3.13.32
And tumbling with the Rainbow in a cloud: Hero and Leander 1.150
And tumbling in the grasse, he often strayd/Beyond the bounds Hero and Leander 1.406

TUMERARIS
[Quid tu moraris] <quod tumeraris>; per Jehovam, Gehennam, et F 248 1.3.20 P Faust

TUMULT
his grave looke appeasd/The wrastling tumult, and right hand Lucan, First Booke 299

TUMULTES
Day rose and viewde these tumultes of the war; Lucan, First Booke 235

TUN
word a Merchant's fled/That owes me for a hundred Tun of Wine: Jew 2.3.244 Barab

TUNA
Must tuna my Lute for sound, twang twang first. Jew 4.4.31 Barab

TUN'D
To thinke that we can yet be tun'd together, Edw 4.2.9 Queene
Of his gilt Harpe the well tun'd strings doth hold. Ovid's Elegies 1.8.60

TUNE (See also TUNA)
Pardona moy, be no in tune yet; so, now, now all be in. Jew 4.4.45 P Barab
and whose tongue/Could tune the people to the Nobles mind: Lucan, First Booke 273
Memphis never had/For skill in stars, and tune-full planeting, Lucan, First Booke 640

TUNE-FULL
Memphis never had/For skill in stars, and tune-full planeting, Lucan, First Booke 640

TUNES
The God that tunes this musicke to our soules, 2Tamb 2.4.31 Tamb
Thy tunes let this rare birdes sad funerall borrowe, Ovid's Elegies 2.6.9
Here when the Pipe with solemne tunes doth sound, Ovid's Elegies 3.12.11

TUNYS
From Azamor to Tunys neare the sea, 2Tamb 1.3.133 Usumc

TUREN
It is the use for [Tirien] <Turen> maides to weare/Their bowe Dido 1.1.204 Venus

TURFE
And suddaine rampire raisde of turfe snatcht up/Would make them Lucan, First Booke 515

TURFFE
A grassie turffe the moistened earth doth hide. Ovid's Elegies 2.16.10

TURK
As fits the Legate of the stately Turk. 1Tamb 3.1.44 Bassoe
The field is ours, the Turk, his wife and all. 1Tamb 3.3.163 Tamb
Here Turk, wilt thou have a cleane trencher? 1Tamb 4.4.101 P Tamb
nor the Turk/Troubled my sences with conceit of foile, 1Tamb 5.1.157 Tamb
O Bajazeth, O Turk, O Emperor. 1Tamb 5.1.309 Zabina
Behold the Turk and his great Emperesse. 1Tamb 5.1.357 Zenoc
In this great Turk and haplesse Emperesse. 1Tamb 5.1.368 Zenoc
The Turk and his great Emperesse as it seems, 1Tamb 5.1.470 Tamb
Thou and thy Turk; 'twas you that slew my son. Jew 5.1.27 Govnr

TURKE
Have past the armie of the mightie Turke: 1Tamb 1.2.14 Zenoc
As if the Turke, the Pope, Affrike and Greece, 1Tamb 2.5.85 Tamb
Alas (poore Turke) his fortune is to weake, 1Tamb 3.3.6 Tamb
Wil first subdue the Turke, and then inlarge/Those Christian 1Tamb 3.3.46 Tamb
And know thou Turke, that those which lead my horse, 1Tamb 3.3.72 Tamb
thou be plac'd by me/That am the Empresse of the mighty Turke? 1Tamb 3.3.167 Zabina
Come bind them both and one lead in the Turke. 1Tamb 3.3.266 Tamb
Even in Bythinia, when I took this Turke: 1Tamb 4.2.42 Tamb
Come bring in the Turke. 1Tamb 4.2.126 Tamb
he persecutes/The noble Turke and his great Emperesse? 1Tamb 4.3.27 Arabia
not the Turke and his wife make a goodly showe at a banquet? 1Tamb 4.4.57 P Tamb
If thou wilt have a song, the Turke shall straine his voice: 1Tamb 4.4.64 P Tamb

TURKE (cont.)			
say you to this (Turke) these are not your contributorie kings.	1Tamb	4.4.118	P Tamb
Behold the Turke and his great Emperesse.	1Tamb	5.1.354	Zenoc
Behold the Turke and his great Emperesse.	1Tamb	5.1.362	Zenoc
With this great Turke and his faire Emperesse:	1Tamb	5.1.532	Tamb
Before we meet the armie of the Turke.	2Tamb	3.2.138	Tamb
Ready to charge the army of the Turke.	2Tamb	3.4.87	Therid
I Turke, I tel thee, this same Boy is he,	2Tamb	4.3.57	Tamb
where I tooke/The Turke and his great Empresse prisoners,	2Tamb	5.3.129	Tamb
That had the Gallies of the Turke in chase.	Jew	1.1.97	2Merch
Long to the Turke did Malta contribute;	Jew	1.1.180	Barab
gather of these goods/The mony for this tribute of the Turke.	Jew	1.2.156	Govnr
Perswade our Governor against the Turke;	Jew	2.2.25	1Knght
Do the [Turkes] <Turke> weigh so much?	Jew	2.3.98	P Barab
Why should this Turke be dearer then that Moore?	Jew	2.3.109	Barab
hadst thou perish'd by the Turke,/Wretched Ferneze might have	Jew	3.2.13	Govnr
Marry the Turke shall be one of my godfathers,	Jew	4.1.111	Barab
And after that, I and my trusty Turke--	Jew	4.1.127	Barab
Why, a Turke could ha done no more.	Jew	4.1.198	P Ithimr
he flouts me, what gentry can be in a poore Turke of ten pence?	Jew	4.2.39	P Ithimr
So is the Turke, and Barabas the Jew.	Jew	5.1.51	1Offcr
slavish Bands/Wherein the Turke hath yoak'd your land and you?	Jew	5.2.78	Barab
And on the other side against the Turke,	P 462	8.12	Anjoy
If any Christian, Heathen, Turke, or Jew,	Edw	5.4.75	Champn
TURKES			
Now Turkes and Tartars shake their swords at thee,	1Tamb	1.1.16	Cosroe
As many circumcised Turkes we have,	1Tamb	3.1.8	Bajzth
Turkes are ful of brags/And menace more than they can wel	1Tamb	3.3.3	Tamb
I have of Turkes, Arabians, Moores and Jewes/Enough to cover	1Tamb	3.3.136	Bajzth
Who shal kisse the fairest of the Turkes Concubines first, when	2Tamb	4.1.64	P Calyph
thou that hast seene/Millions of Turkes perish by Tamburlaine,	2Tamb	5.2.25	Callap
The Turkes and those of Malta are in league.	Jew	1.1.159	Barab
The Turkes have let increase to such a summe,	Jew	1.1.182	Barab
mony of the Turkes shall all be levyed amongst the Jewes,	Jew	1.2.68	P Reader
But to admit a sale of these thy Turkes/We may not, nay we dare	Jew	2.2.21	Govnr
Will Knights of Malta be in league with Turkes,	Jew	2.2.28	Bosco
and you were stated here/To be at deadly enmity with Turkes.	Jew	2.2.33	Bosco
On this condition shall thy Turkes be sold.	Jew	2.2.42	Govnr
will follow thee/Against these barbarous mis-beleeving Turkes.	Jew	2.2.46	Govnr
Do the [Turkes] <Turke> weigh so much?	Jew	2.3.98	P Barab
Pitty in Jewes, nor piety in Turkes.	Jew	3.3.48	Abigal
flie amaine/Unto my Faustus to the great Turkes Court.	F1137	3.3.50	Mephst
TURKESSE			
Disdainful Turkesse and unreverend Bosse,	1Tamb	3.3.168	Zenoc
Give her the Crowne Turkesse, you wer best.	1Tamb	3.3.224	Therid
The Turkesse let my Loves maid lead away.	1Tamb	3.3.267	Tamb
TURKEY			
Are come from Turkey, and lye in our Rhode:	Jew	1.1.147	1Jew
From the Emperour of Turkey is arriv'd/Great Selim-Calymath,	Jew	1.2.39	Govnr
To saile to Turkey, to great Ottoman,	Jew	5.3.16	Msngr
Nay rather, Christians, let me goe to Turkey,	Jew	5.5.115	Calym
TURKIE			
of our Empery/Once lost, All Turkie would be overthrowne:	2Tamb	1.1.56	Orcan
All Turkie is in armes with Callapine.	2Tamb	5.2.51	Callap
TURKISH			
Tell him thy Lord the Turkish Emperour,	1Tamb	3.1.22	Bajzth
More mighty than the Turkish Emperour:	1Tamb	3.3.37	Therid
What meanes the mighty Turkish Emperor/To talk with one so base	1Tamb	3.3.87	Fesse
Now shalt thou feel the force of Turkish arms,	1Tamb	3.3.134	Bajzth
Now strengthen him against the Turkish Bajazeth,	1Tamb	3.3.191	Zenoc
Nay take the Turkish Crown from her, Zenocrate,	1Tamb	3.3.220	Tamb
And never had the Turkish Emperour/So great a foile by any	1Tamb	3.3.234	Bajzth
wherin at anchor lies/A Turkish Gally of my royall fleet,	2Tamb	1.2.21	Callap
We quickly may in Turkish seas arrive.	2Tamb	1.2.27	Callap
Where Egypt and the Turkish Empire parts,	2Tamb	1.3.6	Tamb
When we shall meet the Turkish Deputie/And all his Viceroies,	2Tamb	1.3.99	Tamb
Larissa plaines/With hostes apeece against this Turkish crue,	2Tamb	1.3.108	Tamb
of Fesse have brought/To aide thee in this Turkish expedition,	2Tamb	1.3.131	Usumc
Meaning to aid [thee] <them> in this <these> Turkish armes,	2Tamb	1.3.144	Techel
Such lavish will I make of Turkish blood,	2Tamb	1.3.165	Tamb
That strikes a terrour to all Turkish hearts,	2Tamb	2.1.15	Fredrk
for his vertues)/Revives the spirits of true Turkish heartes,	2Tamb	3.1.24	Callap
suborn'd/That villaine there, that slave, that Turkish dog,	2Tamb	3.5.87	Tamb
Then bring those Turkish harlots to my tent,	2Tamb	4.1.165	Tamb
Now fetch me out the Turkish Concubines,	2Tamb	4.3.64	Tamb
Now Casane, wher's the Turkish Alcaron,	2Tamb	5.1.173	Tamb
Our Turkish swords shal headlong send to hell,	2Tamb	5.2.15	Amasia
Because we vail'd not to the [Turkish] <Spanish> Fleet,/Their	Jew	2.2.11	Bosco
and under Turkish yokes/Shall groning beare the burthen of our	Jew	5.2.7	Calym
Rather then thus to live as Turkish thrals,	Jew	5.4.8	1Knght
Damn'd Christians, dogges, and Turkish Infidels;	Jew	5.5.86	Barab
TURKS			
By this the Turks lie weltring in their blood/And Tamburlaine	1Tamb	3.3.201	Zenoc
Cicilians, Jewes, Arabians, Turks, and Moors,	2Tamb	1.1.62	Orcan
Whose arches should be fram'd with bones of Turks,	2Tamb	1.3.94	Amyras
These heathnish Turks and Pagans lately made,	2Tamb	2.1.6	Fredrk
The towers and cities of these hatefull Turks,	2Tamb	3.2.148	Tamb
Naturalized Turks and stout Bythinians/Came to my bands full	2Tamb	3.5.41	Trebiz
Come fight ye Turks, or yeeld us victory.	2Tamb	3.5.169	Tamb
in their glories shine the golden crownes/Of these proud Turks,	2Tamb	4.1.2	Amyras
Ransacke the tents and the pavilions/Of these proud Turks, and	2Tamb	4.1.161	Tamb
My sword hath sent millions of Turks to hell,	2Tamb	5.1.180	Tamb
Our fraught is Grecians, Turks, and Africk Moores.	Jew	2.2.9	Bosco

TURKY
And means to fire Turky as he goes: 2Tamb 1.1.18 Gazell
Our Turky blades shal glide through al their throats, 2Tamb 1.1.31 Orcan
We came from Turky to confirme a league, 2Tamb 1.1.115 Gazell
thy chariot wheels/With Turky Carpets shall be covered: 2Tamb 1.2.43 Callap
And after martch to Turky with our Campe, 2Tamb 1.3.158 Tamb
Long live Callepinus, Emperour of Turky. 2Tamb 3.1.6 P Orcan
Viceroies and Peeres of Turky play the men, 2Tamb 3.5.14 Callap

TURKYE
Ye petty kings of Turkye I am come, 2Tamb 3.5.64 Tamb

TURMOILES
Turmoiles the coast, and enterance forbids; Lucan, First Booke 409

TURMOYLES
Tis cruell love turmoyles my captive hart. Ovid's Elegies 1.2.8

TURN
then turn her and wind hir to thy owne use, as often as thou F App p.234 27 P Robin

TURNAMENT
Weele have a generall tilt and turnament, Edw 1.4.376 Edward

TURN'D
Turn'd to dispaire, would break my wretched breast, 2Tamb 2.4.64 Zenoc
Turn'd into pearle and proffered for my stay, 2Tamb 4.1.44 Amyras
thus; thou toldst me they have turn'd my house/Into a Nunnery, Jew 1.2.277 Barab
Which they have now turn'd to a Nunnery. Jew 1.2.320 Abigal
One turn'd my daughter, therefore he shall dye; Jew 4.1.119 Barab
of love/In Courts of Kings, where state is over-turn'd, F 4 Prol.4 1Chor
would I might be turn'd to a gaping Oyster, and drinke nothing F1319 4.1.165 P Benvol
one of his devils turn'd me into the likenesse of an Apes face. F1554 4.5.50 P Dick
Is all our pleasure turn'd to melancholy? F1828 5.2.32 2Schol
view the Scriptures, then I turn'd the leaves/And led thine eye. F1888 5.2.92 Mephst
Woods turn'd to ships; both land and sea against us: Lucan, First Booke 307
Ranne through the bloud, that turn'd it all to gelly, Lucan, First Booke 618
Shall water be conjeal'd and turn'd to ice? Lucan, First Booke 647
for the lovely boy/That now is turn'd into a Cypres tree, Hero and Leander 1.155
And yet at everie word shee turn'd aside, Hero and Leander 1.195
And as she wept, her teares to pearle he turn'd, Hero and Leander 1.375
And would have turn'd againe, but was afrayd, Hero and Leander 2.8
And turn'd aside, and to her selfe lamented. Hero and Leander 2.34

TURND
And drie with griefe was turnd into a stone, Dido 2.1.5 Aeneas
and both his eyes/Turnd up to heaven as one resolv'd to dye, Dido 2.1.152 Aeneas
Lord of my fortune, but my fortunes turnd, Dido 2.1.235 Aeneas
reading of the letter, he star'd and stamp'd, and turnd aside. Jew 4.2.105 P Pilia
Is all my hope turnd to this hell of greefe. Edw 1.4.116 Gavstn
And Isabell, whose eyes [being] <beene> turnd to steele, Edw 5.1.104 Edward
and all the people in it were turnd> to Gold, F 676 (HC263)A P Covet
Her owne request to her owne torment turnd. Ovid's Elegies 3.3.38
Eryx bright Empresse turnd her lookes aside, Ovid's Elegies 3.8.45
The Sunne turnd backe from Atreus cursed table? Ovid's Elegies 3.11.39
Then standing at the doore, she turnd about, Hero and Leander 2.97
And as he turnd, cast many a lustfull glaunce, Hero and Leander 2.186

TURNDE
Were turnde to men, he should be overcome: 2Tamb 1.3.164 Tamb
If ever day were turnde to ugly night, P 62 2.5 Guise

TURNE
Charge him from me to turne his stormie powers, Dido 1.1.117 Jupitr
on the sand/Assayd with honey words to turne them backe: Dido 2.1.137 Aeneas
Now Cupid turne thee to Ascanius shape, Dido 2.1.323 Venus
turne the hand of fate/Unto that happie day of my delight, Dido 3.3.80 Iarbus
If not, turne from me, and Ile turne from thee: Dido 5.1.181 Dido
And with my hand turne Fortunes wheel about, 1Tamb 1.2.175 Tamb
Untill our bodies turne to Elements: 1Tamb 1.2.236 Tamb
And bid him turne [him] <his> back to war with us, 1Tamb 2.5.100 Tamb
But I shall turne her into other weedes, 1Tamb 3.3.180 Ebea
To turne them al upon their proper heades. 1Tamb 4.4.31 Tamb
That she shall stay and turne her wheele no more, 1Tamb 5.1.374 Anippe
And turne him to his ancient trade againe. 2Tamb 3.5.95 Jrslem
Tyrant, I turne the traitor in thy throat, 2Tamb 5.1.54 Govnr
us an occasion/Which on the sudden cannot serve the turne. Jew 1.2.240 Barab
night; or let the day/Turne to eternall darkenesse after this: Jew 2.1.16 Barab
We turne into the Ayre to purge our selves: Jew 2.3.46 Barab
Yet I have one left that will serve your turne: Jew 2.3.50 Barab
So much the better, thou art for my turne. Jew 2.3.129 Barab
Oh that my sighs could turne to lively breath; Jew 3.2.18 Govnr
And turne proud Malta to a wildernesse/For these intolerable Jew 3.5.25 Basso
Is't not too late now to turne Christian? Jew 4.1.50 Barab
will you turne Christian, when holy Friars turne devils and Jew 4.1.193 P Ithimr
when holy Friars turne devils and murder one another. Jew 4.1.194 P Ithimr
No; but three hundred will not serve his turne. Jew 4.3.20 P Pilia
Not serve his turne, Sir? Jew 4.3.21 P Barab
My sinnewes shrinke, my braines turne upside downe, P 549 11.14 Charls
The fitter art thou Baldock for my turne, Edw 2.2.245 Edward
Gaveston, short warning/Shall serve thy turne: Edw 2.5.22 Warwck
Heavens turne it to a blaze of quenchelesse fier, Edw 5.1.44 Edward
Who now makes Fortunes wheele turne as he please, Edw 5.2.53 Mortmr
I'le turne all the lice about thee into Familiars, and make F 362 1.4.20 P Wagner
I sirra, I'le teach thee to turne thy selfe to a Dog, or a Cat, F 382 1.4.40 P Wagner
Abjure this Magicke, turne to God againe. F 396 2.1.8 Faust
[I and Faustus will turne to God againe]. F 397 2.1.9A Faust
should turne to Gold, that I might locke you safe into <uppe F 676 2.2.125 P Covet
And thou shalt turne thy selfe into what shape thou wilt. F 718 2.2.170 Lucifr
And as they turne their superstitious Bookes, F 893 3.1.115 Faust
the Emperour, Il'e be Acteon, and turne my selfe to a Stagge. F1255 4.1.101 P Benvol
In bold Acteons shape to turne a Stagge. F1299 4.1.145 Faust

TURNE (cont.)
I thinking that a little would serve his turne, bad him take as F1528 4.5.24 P Carter
<O> It strikes, it strikes; now body turne to aire, F1975 5.2.179 Faust
or Ile turne al the lice about thee into familiars, and they F App p.229 25 P Wagner
I will teach thee to turne thy selfe to anything, to a dogge, F App p.231 58 P Wagner
if you turne me into any thing, let it be in the likenesse of a F App p.231 61 P Clown
conquer all the earth, then turne thy force/Against thy selfe: Lucan, First Booke 22
Time ends and to old Chaos all things turne; Lucan, First Booke 74
Turne all to good, be Augury vaine, and Tages/Th'arts master Lucan, First Booke 635
Whither turne I now? Lucan, First Booke 682
And give woundes infinite at everie turne. Ovid's Elegies 1.2.44
Turne round thy gold-ring, as it were to ease thee. Ovid's Elegies 1.4.26
Or I more sterne then fire or sword will turne, Ovid's Elegies 1.6.57
They well become thee, then to spare them turne. Ovid's Elegies 1.14.28
Or such, as least long yeares should turne the die, Ovid's Elegies 2.5.39
For which good turne my sweete reward repay, Ovid's Elegies 2.8.21
Turne thy lookes hether, and in one spare twaine, Ovid's Elegies 2.13.15
(Alas my precepts turne my selfe to smart)/We write, or what Ovid's Elegies 2.18.20
With wheeles bent inward now the ring-turne ride. Ovid's Elegies 3.2.12
To thee Minerva turne the craftes-mens hands. Ovid's Elegies 3.2.52
For faithfull love will never turne to hate. Hero and Leander 1.128

TURNED
Or Monster turned to a manly shape, 1Tamb 2.6.16 Ortyg
First, be thou turned to this ugly shape, F1126 3.3.39 Mephst
for your horse is turned to a bottle of Hay,--Maister Doctor. F1490 4.4.34 P HrsCsr
Ifaith thats as true as Diana turned me to a stag. F App p.237 54 P Knight
or do the turned hinges sound,/And opening dores with creaking Ovid's Elegies 1.6.49
And turned streames run back-ward to their fountaines. Ovid's Elegies 2.1.26

TURNES
Then would we hope to quite such friendly turnes, Dido 1.2.46 Serg
Why turnes Aeneas from his trustie friends? Dido 2.1.57 Cloan
Nor quit good turnes with double fee downe told: Dido 3.2.15 Juno
And yet wouldst shun the wavering turnes of war, 1Tamb 5.1.360 Zenoc
That being concocted, turnes to crimson blood, 2Tamb 3.2.108 Tamb
And let them equally serve all your turnes. 2Tamb 4.3.73 Tamb
And with the noise turnes up my giddie braine, Edw 1.4.314 Edward
He turnes away, and smiles upon his minion. Edw 2.4.29 Queene
Turnes all the goodly <godly> birdes to what she please. Ovid's Elegies 2.6.58
Jove turnes himselfe into a Swanne, or gold, Ovid's Elegies 3.11.33

TURNING
and excusde/For turning my poore charge to his direction. 1Tamb 2.3.29 Therid
Will send up fire to your turning Spheares, 1Tamb 4.2.39 Tamb
That I might moove the turning Spheares of heaven, 2Tamb 4.1.118 Tamb
And then turning my selfe to a wrought Smocke do what I list. F 668 2.2.117 P Pride

TURNUS
Before he be the Lord of Turnus towne, Dido 1.1.87 Jupitr
Comes now as Turnus gainst Eneas did, 1Tamb 5.1.380 Philem
Prevented Turnus of Lavinia, 1Tamb 5.1.393 Zenoc

TURRET
And looking from a turret, might behold/Young infants swimming Dido 2.1.192 Aeneas
And from a turret Ile behold my love. Dido 4.4.86 Dido
And on her Turret-bearing head disperst, Lucan, First Booke 190
My turret stands, and there God knowes I play/With Venus Hero and Leander 1.351
That he would leave her turret and depart. Hero and Leander 2.38

TURRET-BEARING
And on her Turret-bearing head disperst, Lucan, First Booke 190

TURRETS
Will batter Turrets with their manly fists. 1Tamb 3.3.111 Bajzth
That roaring, shake Damascus turrets downe. 1Tamb 4.1.3 Souldn
Batter our walles, and beat our Turrets downe. 1Tamb 5.1.2 Govnr
So, burne the turrets of this cursed towne, 2Tamb 3.2.1 Tamb
Upon the marble turrets of my Court/Sit like to Venus in her 2Tamb 4.2.41 Therid
Whose shyning Turrets shal dismay the heavens, 2Tamb 4.3.112 Tamb
Two lofty Turrets that command the Towne. Jew 5.3.11 Calym

TURTLE
But most thou friendly turtle-dove, deplore. Ovid's Elegies 2.6.12
Such to the parrat was the turtle dove. Ovid's Elegies 2.6.16

TURTLE-DOVE
But most thou friendly turtle-dove, deplore. Ovid's Elegies 2.6.12

TURTLE DOVE
Such to the parrat was the turtle dove. Ovid's Elegies 2.6.16

TURTLES
What, are the Turtles fraide out of their neastes? 1Tamb 5.1.64 Tamb
There Hero sacrificing turtles blood, Hero and Leander 1.158

TUSCANE (See also THUSCAN, TUSKAN)
Which with the grasse of Tuscane fields are fed. Ovid's Elegies 3.12.14

TUSCIA
When fruite fild Tuscia should a wife give me, Ovid's Elegies 3.12.1

TUSH
Tush. Turkes are ful of brags/And menace more 1Tamb 3.3.3 Tamb
Tush, who amongst 'em knowes not Barrabas? Jew 1.1.67 Barab
Tush, they are wise; I know her and her strength: Jew 1.1.81 Barab
Tush, tell not me 'twas done of policie. Jew 1.1.140 1Jew
tush, take not from me then,/For that is theft; and if you rob Jew 1.2.125 Barab
Tush,/As good dissemble that thou never mean'st Jew 1.2.289 Barab
Tush man, we talk'd of Diamonds, not of Abigal. Jew 2.3.151 Barab
Tush, send not letters to 'em, goe thy selfe, Jew 5.2.93 Barab
Tush, Governor, take thou no care for that, Jew 5.5.102 Calym
Tush man, let me alone with him, P 648 12.61 QnMoth
Tush, all shall dye unles I have my will: P 653 12.66 QnMoth
tush, were he heere, we would kill him presently. P 934 19.4 P 1Mur
Tush, to be short, he meant to make me Munke, P1039 19.109 King
Tush my Lord, let me alone for that. P1136 21.30 P Frier

TUSH (cont.)			
tush Sib, if this be all/Valoys and I will soone be friends	Edw	3.1.66	Edward
Wish well to mine, then tush, for them ile die.	Edw	5.3.45	Edward
[Tush] <No>, these are trifles, and meere old wives Tales.	F 524	2.1.136	Faust
<Tush>, These slender questions <trifles> Wagner can decide:	F 600	2.2.49	Faust
[Tush], these are fresh mens [suppositions] <questions>:	F 606	2.2.55	P Faust
Tush, Christ did call the Theefe upon the Crosse,	F1482	4.4.26	Faust
Tush, Christ did call the thiefe upon the Crosse,	F App	p.240 125	Faust
TUSKAN			
and in his tuskan cap/A jewell of more value then the crowne.	Edw	1.4.414	Mortmr
TUSKED			
And overtake the tusked Bore in chase.	Dido	1.1.208	Venus
TUT			
Tut, I am simple, without [minde] <made> to hurt,	Dido	3.2.16	Juno
Tut, tut, there is some other matter in't.	Jew	1.1.160	Barab
Tut, Jew, we know thou art no souldier;	Jew	1.2.52	1Knght
Tut, she were fitter for a tale of love/Then to be tired out	Jew	1.2.369	Mthias
Tut they are pesants, I am Duke of Guise:	P 998	19.68	Guise
<Tut Faustus>, Marriage is but a ceremoniall toy,	F 535	2.1.147	Mephst
[Tut I warrant thee].	F 551.13	2.1.176A	P Mephst
[Tut] <But> Faustus, in hell is all manner of delight.	F 713	2.2.165	Lucifr
<Tut, tis no matter man>, wee'l be bold with his <good cheare>.	F 808	(HC265)A	P Mephst
Tut, men should not their courage so consume.	Ovid's Elegies		3.3.34
TUTORS			
That are tutors to him and the prince of Condy--	P 427	7.67	Guise
TWAIN			
His Skul al rivin in twain, his braines dasht out?	1Tamb	5.1.306	Zabina
TWAINE			
And wound the earth, that it may cleave in twaine,	2Tamb	2.4.97	Tamb
Lady, the last was truest of the twaine,	Edw	4.2.39	Mortmr
Parted in twaine, and with a double point/Rose like the Theban	Lucan, First Booke		549
Turne thy lookes hether, and in one spare twaine,	Ovid's Elegies		2.13.15
To part in twaine, that hee might come and go,	Hero and Leander		2.151
TWANG			
Must tuna my Lute for sound, twang twang first.	Jew	4.4.31	Barab
'TWAS			
But 'twas ill done of you to come so farre/Without the ayd or	Jew	1.1.93	Barab
Tush, tell not me 'twas done of policie.	Jew	1.1.140	1Jew
'twas told me in shrift,/Thou know'st 'tis death and if it be	Jew	3.6.50	2Fryar
We two, and 'twas never knowne, nor never shall be for me.	Jew	4.4.23	P Ithimr
'Twas sent me for a present from the great Cham.	Jew	4.4.68	Barab
Thou and thy Turk; 'twas you that slew my son.	Jew	5.1.27	Govnr
Ferneze, 'twas thy sonne that murder'd him.	Jew	5.1.45	Mater
'Twas bravely done:	Jew	5.1.84	Calym
Know, Governor, 'twas I that slew thy sonne;	Jew	5.5.81	Barab
'Twas thine own seeking Faustus, thanke thy selfe.	F 555	2.2.4	Mephst
'Twas <It was> made for man; then he's <therefore is man> more	F 560	2.2.9	Mephst
If Heaven was <it were> made for man, 'twas made for me:	F 561	2.2.10	Faust
plague take you, I thought 'twas your knavery to take it away:	F1110	3.3.23	P Vintnr
O thou bewitching fiend, 'twas thy temptation,	F1883	5.2.87	Faust
'Twas I, that when thou wer't i'the way to heaven,	F1886	5.2.90	Mephst
T'WAS			
T'was peace against their wils; betwixt them both/Stept Crassus	Lucan, First Booke		99
stil poore/Did vild deeds, then t'was worth the price of bloud,	Lucan, First Booke		175
T'was so, he stroke me with a slender dart,	Ovid's Elegies		1.2.7
When t'was the odour which her breath foorth cast.	Hero and Leander		1.22
TWAS			
Others report twas Sinons perjurie:	Dido	2.1.111	Dido
Through which it could not enter twas so huge.	Dido	2.1.171	Aeneas
Twas time to runne, Aeneas had been gone,	Dido	4.4.14	Anna
But when you were abourd twas calme enough,	Dido	4.4.27	Dido
Twas I my lord that gat the victory,	1Tamb	5.1.445	Tamb
Twas bravely done, and like a souldiers wife.	2Tamb	3.4.38	Techel
Sirra twas I that slew him, and will slay/Thee too, and thou	P1048	19.118	King
Can this be true twas good to banish him,	Edw	1.4.245	Lncstr
Twas in your wars, you should ransome him.	Edw	2.2.144	Lncstr
And plainely saith, twas thou that murdredst him.	Edw	5.6.42	King
Twas his troupe hem'd in Milo being accusde;	Lucan, First Booke		323
TWELVE			
With twise twelve Phrigian ships I plowed the deepe,	Dido	1.1.220	Aeneas
<as> Saturne in thirty yeares, Jupiter in twelve, Mars in four,	F 604	2.2.53	P Faust
For twixt the houres of twelve and one, me thought/I heard him	F1991	5.3.9	3Schol
TWENTIE			
Then twentie thousand Indiaes can affoord:	Dido	3.1.93	Dido
grant unto them that foure and twentie yeares being expired,	F 496	2.1.108	P Faust
TWENTY			
With twenty thousand expert souldiers.	1Tamb	2.5.25	Cosroe
A jest to chardge on twenty thousand men?	1Tamb	2.5.91	Therid
frontier townes/Twise twenty thousand valiant men at armes,	2Tamb	1.3.120	Therid
What, can ye draw but twenty miles a day,	2Tamb	4.3.2	Tamb
chiefe selected men/Of twenty severall kingdomes at the least:	2Tamb	5.2.49	Callap
And twenty Waggons to bring up the ware.	Jew	1.1.60	Barab
[Cossin] <Cosin> <Cousin>, take twenty of our strongest guarde,	P 266	4.64	Charls
So he will spare him foure and twenty yeares,	F 319	1.3.91	Faust
West, in foure and twenty houres, upon the poles of the world,	F 597	2.2.46	P Mephst
Venus, and Mercury in a yeare; the Moone in twenty eight daies.	F 606	2.2.55	P Faust
My foure and twenty yeares of liberty/I'le spend in pleasure	F 839	3.1.61	Faust
I was limitted/For foure and twenty yeares, to breathe on	F1396	4.2.72	Faust
and twenty yeares hath Faustus lost eternall joy and felicitie.	F1859	5.2.63	P Faust
Or he who war'd and wand'red twenty yeare?	Ovid's Elegies		2.1.31
'TWERE			
grave [Governour], 'twere in my power/To favour you, but 'tis my	Jew	1.2.10	Calym
'Twere time well spent to goe and visit her:	Jew	1.2.389	Lodowk

'TWERE (cont.)			
If 'twere above ground I could, and would have it; but hee	Jew	4.2.57	P Ithimr
'Twere slender policy for Barabas/To dispossesse himselfe of	Jew	5.2.65	Barab
TWERE			
Twere requisite he should be ten times more,	1Tamb	3.1.47	Argier
twere better he kild his wife, and then she shall be sure not	1Tamb	4.4.45	P Usumc
twere but time indeed,/Lost long before you knew what honour	2Tamb	4.3.86	Tamb
My Lord, twere good to make them frends,	P 772	15.30	Eprnon
Twere hard with me if I should doubt my kinne,	P 971	19.41	King
Twere not amisse my Lord, if he were searcht.	P1160	22.22	Eprnon
to the Divel for a shoulder of mutton though twere blood rawe?	F App	p.229 11	P Clown
TWICE (See also TWISE)			
This Lady shall have twice so much againe,	2Tamb	3.4.90	Therid
And winds it twice or thrice about his eare;	Jew	4.3.8	Barab
Oh raskall! I change my selfe twice a day.	Jew	4.4.65	Barab
that lye farre East, where they have fruit twice a yeare.	F1584	4.6.27	P Faust
TWIGGER			
Youle be a twigger when you come to age.	Dido	4.5.20	Nurse
TWIL			
Twil proove a pretie jest (in faith) my friends.	1Tamb	2.5.90	Tamb
to come by, plucke out that, and twil serve thee and thy wife:	1Tamb	4.4.14	P Tamb
I shal be found, and then twil greeve me more.	Edw	1.4.132	Gavstn
TWILIGHT			
Like twilight glimps at setting of the sunne,	Ovid's Elegies		1.5.5
A kind of twilight breake, which through the heare,	Hero and Leander		2.319
'TWILL			
I'le gage my credit, 'twill content your grace.	F1622	4.6.65	Faust
'twill all be past anone:	F1957	5.2.161	Faust
TWILL			
Twill please my mind as wel to heare both you/Have won a heape	2Tamb	4.1.36	Calyph
Oh twill corrupt the water, and the water the fish, and by the	P 488	9.7	P 2Atndt
Twill make him vaile the topflag of his pride,	Edw	1.4.276	Mortmr
Nay, do your pleasures, I know how twill proove.	Edw	2.5.93	Warwck
TWINCKLE			
Vanish and returne in a twinckle.	Jew	4.2.79	P Ithimr
TWINCKLES			
It twinckles like a Starre.	Jew	4.2.128	P Ithimr
TWINCLES			
Which gave such light, as twincles in a wood,	Ovid's Elegies		1.5.4
TWIND			
Or with those armes that twind about my neck,	Edw	1.4.175	Queene
TWINING			
Till in his twining armes he lockt her fast,	Hero and Leander		1.403
TWINKLING			
Shall be perform'd in twinkling of an eye.	F1767	5.1.94	Mephst
TWINNE			
Then wilt thou Laedas noble twinne-starres pray,	Ovid's Elegies		2.11.29
Remus and Romulus, Ilias twinne-borne seed.	Ovid's Elegies		3.4.40
TWINNE-BORNE			
Remus and Romulus, Ilias twinne-borne seed.	Ovid's Elegies		3.4.40
TWINNES			
In swelling wombe her twinnes had Ilia kilde?	Ovid's Elegies		2.14.15
TWINNE-STARRES			
Then wilt thou Laedas noble twinne-starres pray,	Ovid's Elegies		2.11.29
TWISE			
With twise twelve Phrigian ships I plowed the deepe,	Dido	1.1.220	Aeneas
frontier townes/Twise twenty thousand valiant men at armes,	2Tamb	1.3.120	Therid
Yet boorded I the golden Chie twise,	Ovid's Elegies		3.6.23
'TWIXT			
And in the warres 'twixt France and Germanie,	Jew	2.3.187	Barab
TWIXT			
To hang her meteor like twixt heaven and earth,	Dido	1.1.13	Jupitr
As every tide tilts twixt their oken sides:	Dido	1.1.224	Aeneas
Twixt his manly pitch,/A pearle more worth, then all the world	1Tamb	2.1.11	Menaph
Where twixt the Isles of Cyprus and of Creete,	2Tamb	1.2.26	Callap
Approove the difference twixt himself and you.	2Tamb	4.1.137	Tamb
Thou shewest the difference twixt our selves and thee/In this	2Tamb	4.1.138	Orcan
A second mariage twixt thy selfe and me.	Edw	1.4.335	Edward
Twixt theirs and yours, shall be no enmitie.	Edw	5.3.46	Matrvs
And stand as Bulwarkes twixt your selves and me,	F1427	4.2.103	Faust
For twixt the houres of twelve and one, me thought/I heard him	F1991	5.3.9	3Schol
Borne twixt the Alpes and Rhene, which he hath brought/From out	Lucan, First Booke		478
Which rashly twixt the sharpe rocks in the deepe,	Ovid's Elegies		2.11.3
Thou swearest, devision should not twixt us rise,	Ovid's Elegies		2.16.43
TWO (See also TWAIN)			
Was with two winged Serpents stung to death.	Dido	2.1.166	Aeneas
We two will goe a hunting in the woods,	Dido	3.1.174	Dido
And banquet as two Sisters with the Gods?	Dido	3.2.29	Juno
We two as friends one fortune will devide:	Dido	3.2.55	Venus
let there be a match confirmd/Betwixt these two, whose loves	Dido	3.2.78	Juno
Lords goe before, we two must talke alone.	Dido	3.3.9	Dido
We two will talke alone, what words be these?	Dido	3.3.12	Iarbus
I crave but this, he stay a tide or two,	Dido	5.1.207	Dido
And these his two renowmed friends my Lord,	1Tamb	2.3.30	Therid
Holde thee Cosroe, weare two imperiall Crownes.	1Tamb	2.5.1	Tamb
Two thousand horse shall forrage up and downe,	1Tamb	3.1.61	Bajzth
Two hundred thousand footmen that have serv'd/In two set	1Tamb	3.3.18	Bassoe
footmen that have serv'd/In two set battels fought in Grecia:	1Tamb	3.3.19	Bassoe
Even he that in a trice vanquisht two kings,	1Tamb	3.3.36	Therid
Two hundred thousand foot, brave men at armes,	1Tamb	4.3.54	Capol
Now have we martcht from faire Natolia/Two hundred leagues, and	2Tamb	1.1.7	Orcan
Knowing two kings, the [friends] <friend> to Tamburlain,	2Tamb	3.3.13	Therid
And thus be drawen with these two idle kings.	2Tamb	4.3.28	Amyras

TWO (cont.)			
Three thousand Camels, and two hundred yoake/Of labouring Oxen,	Jew	1.2.183	Barab
marketplace; whats the price of this slave, two hundred Crowns?	Jew	2.3.98	P Barab
Ratest thou this Moore but at two hundred plats? . .	Jew	2.3.107	Lodowk
talke with him was [but]/About the borrowing of a booke or two.	Jew	2.3.156	Mthias
How can it if we two be secret.	Jew	4.1.9	Barab
Look, look, master, here come two religious Caterpillers.	Jew	4.1.21	P Ithimr
But yesterday two ships went from this Towne, . . .	Jew	4.1.69	Barab
I have don't, but no body knowes it but you two, I may escape.	Jew	4.1.181	P 1Fryar
Put in two hundred at least.	Jew	4.2.74	P Pilia
You two alone?	Jew	4.4.22	Curtzn
We two, and 'twas never knowne, nor never shall be for me.	Jew	4.4.23	P Ithimr
There's two crownes for thee, play.	Jew	4.4.47	Pilia
Two, three, foure month Madam.	Jew	4.4.55	P Barab
Two lofty Turrets that command the Towne.	Jew	5.3.11	Calym
These two will make one entire Duke of Guise, . . .	P1060	19.130	King
Ile have my will, and these two Mortimers, . . .	Edw	1.1.78	Edward
And both the Mortimers, two goodly men, ...	Edw	1.3.3	Gavstn
Two of my fathers servants whilst he liv'de, . . .	Edw	2.2.240	Neece
Two kings in England cannot raigne at once: . . .	Edw	5.1.58	Edward
damned Art/For which they two are infamous through the world.	F 222	1.2.29	1Schol
for I will presently raise up two devils to carry thee away:	F 373	1.4.31	P Wagner
With winding bankes that cut it in two parts; . . .	F 814	3.1.36	Mephst
Over the which [foure] <two> stately Bridges leane, . .	F 815	3.1.37	Mephst
Mephostophilis, and two such Cardinals/Ne're serv'd a holy Pope,	F 941	3.1.163	Faust
me for the matter, for sure the cup is betweene you two. .	F1108	3.3.21	P Vintnr
What a devill ayle you two?	F1179	4.1.25	P Benvol
Two spreading hornes most strangely fastened/Upon the head of	F1277	4.1.123	Emper
the yeare is divided into two circles over the whole world, so	F1581	4.6.24	P Faust
of golden plate; besides two thousand duckets ready coin'd:	F1676	5.1.3	P Wagner
two divels presently to fetch thee away Baliol and Belcher.	F App	p.230 43	P Wagner
two deceased princes which long since are consumed to dust.	F App	p.237 42	P Faust
but the true substantiall bodies of those two deceased princes.	F App	p.238 65	P Emper
earth, the sea, the world it selfe,/Would not admit two Lords:	Lucan, First Booke		111
Two tane away, thy labor will be lesse:	Ovid's Elegies		1.1.4
Thee Pompous birds and him two tygres drew. . . .	Ovid's Elegies		1.2.48
and in her eyes/Two eye-balles shine, and double light thence	Ovid's Elegies		1.8.16
words she sayd/While closely hid betwixt two dores I layed.	Ovid's Elegies		1.8.22
Nor one or two men are sufficient.	Ovid's Elegies		1.8.54
Such as the cause was of two husbands warre, . . .	Ovid's Elegies		1.10.1
The number two no good divining bringes.	Ovid's Elegies		1.12.28
Made two nights one to finish up his pleasure. . . .	Ovid's Elegies		1.13.46
What two determine never wants effect.	Ovid's Elegies		2.3.16
Such blisse is onely common to us two, ...	Ovid's Elegies		2.5.31
For now I love two women equallie:	Ovid's Elegies		2.10.4
If one can doote, if not, two everie night, . . .	Ovid's Elegies		2.10.22
And I see when you ope the two leavde booke: . . .	Ovid's Elegies		3.13.44
And being justified by two words, thinke/The cause acquits you	Ovid's Elegies		3.13.49
In view and opposit two citties stood, ...	Hero and Leander		1.2
When two are stript, long ere the course begin, . .	Hero and Leander		1.169
Of two gold Ingots like in each respect.	Hero and Leander		1.172
In time it will returne us two for one.	Hero and Leander		1.236
Foorth from those two tralucent cesternes brake, . .	Hero and Leander		1.296
TWO LEAVDE			
And I see when you ope the two leavde booke: . . .	Ovid's Elegies		3.13.44
TWOO			
the yeere is divided into twoo circles over the whole worlde,	F App	p.242 19	P Faust
I could not be in love with twoo at once, ...	Ovid's Elegies		2.10.2
'TWOULD			
As had you seene her 'twould have mov'd your heart, . .	Jew	1.2.385	Mthias
TYBERS			
Just through the midst runnes flowing Tybers streame, .	F 813	3.1.35	Mephst
If to incampe on Thuscan Tybers streames, ...	Lucan, First Booke		382
TYDE			
Shall meet those Christians fleeting with the tyde, . .	2Tamb	1.1.40	Orcan
he doth not chide/Nor to hoist saile attends fit time and tyde.	Ovid's Elegies		1.9.14
TYDIDES			
Tydides left worst signes of villanie, ...	Ovid's Elegies		1.7.31
TYDINGS			
Go beare these <those> tydings to great Lucifer, . .	F 315	1.3.87	Faust
Mephostophilis come/And bring glad tydings from great Lucifer.	F 416	2.1.28	Faust
TYE			
For this will Dido tye ye full of knots, ...	Dido	4.4.155	Dido
And tye white linnen scarfes about their armes. . .	P 233	4.31	Guise
TYED			
That tyed together by the striving tongues, . . .	Dido	4.3.29	Aeneas
She nothing said, pale feare her tongue had tyed. . .	Ovid's Elegies		1.7.20
TYERS			
Now Germany shall captive haire-tyers send thee, . .	Ovid's Elegies		1.14.45
TYGARS			
[As] <A> brood of barbarous Tygars having lapt/The bloud of	Lucan, First Booke		327
TYGERS			
And Tygers of Hircania gave thee sucke:	Dido	5.1.159	Dido
Armenian Tygers never did so ill, ...	Ovid's Elegies		2.14.35
TYGRES			
Thee Pompous birds and him two tygres drew. . . .	Ovid's Elegies		1.2.48
TYLL			
and tyll the ground that he himself should occupy, which is his	P 811	17.6	P Souldr
TYLTE			
And spend some daies in barriers, tourny, tylte, . .	P 628	12.41	King
TYNEMOUTH (See TINMOTH)			
TYPHOEUS (See TIPHEUS)			
TYPHONS			
of a bigger size/Than all the brats ysprong from Typhons loins:	1Tamb	3.3.109	Bajza

E			
st in disdaine of wrong and tyrannie,	1Tamb	2.1.55	Ceneus
NNIES			
know not how to take their tyrannies.	1Tamb	2.7.41	Cosroe
with the meteors/Of blood and fire thy tyrannies have made,	2Tamb	4.1.142	Jrslem
these terrours and these tyrannies/(If tyrannies wars justice	2Tamb	4.1.146	Tamb
tyrannies/(If tyrannies wars justice ye repute)/I execute,	2Tamb	4.1.147	Tamb
To practize tauntes and bitter tyrannies?	2Tamb	4.3.56	Jrslem
TYRANNISE			
The Scythians shall not tyrannise on me.	2Tamb	3.4.29	Sonne
And sent from hell to tyrannise on earth,	2Tamb	5.1.111	Govnr
TYRANNISING			
Letting out death and tyrannising war,	2Tamb	2.4.115	Tamb
TYRANNIZE			
What? will they tyrannize upon the Church?	Edw	1.2.3	Lncstr
TYRANNOUS (See also TIRANNOUS)			
If I be cruell, and growe tyrannous,	Edw	2.2.206	Edward
TYRANNY (See also TIRANNIE)			
twixt our selves and thee/In this thy barbarous damned tyranny.	2Tamb	4.1.139	Orcan
Against the wrath and tyranny of death,	2Tamb	5.3.221	Techel
that Senates tyranny?	Lucan, First Booke		366
TYRANT (See also TIRANT)			
I Tyrant, and more meat.	1Tamb	4.4.102	P Bajzth
Injurious tyrant, wilt thou so defame/The hatefull fortunes of	2Tamb	4.3.77	Orcan
Tyrant, I turne the traitor in thy throat,	2Tamb	5.1.54	Govnr
Vild Tyrant, barbarous bloody Tamburlain.	2Tamb	5.1.133	Trebiz
never sepulchre/Shall grace that base-borne Tyrant Tamburlaine.	2Tamb	5.2.18	Amasia
For conquering the Tyrant of the world.	2Tamb	5.2.55	Callap
Tyrant, I scorne thy threats and menaces,	Edw	3.1.241	Warwck
TYRANTES			
Tis warre that must asswage this tyrantes pride.	P1128	21.22	Dumain
TYRANTS			
Go wander free from feare of Tyrants rage,	1Tamb	3.2.102	Agidas
And poure it in this glorious Tyrants throat.	1Tamb	4.2.7	Bajzth
And leave your venoms in this Tyrants dish.	1Tamb	4.4.22	Bajzth
Of this infamous Tyrants souldiers,	1Tamb	5.1.404	Arabia
Ah cruel Brat, sprung from a tyrants loines,	2Tamb	4.3.54	Jrslem
And these must die under a tyrants sword.	Edw	4.7.92	Edward
To seeke for mercie at a tyrants hand.	Edw	5.3.36	Edward
But Roome at thraldoms feet to rid from tyrants.	Lucan, First Booke		352
TYR'D			
These Jades are broken winded, and halfe tyr'd,	2Tamb	5.1.129	Tamb
Bacchinall/That tyr'd doth rashly on the greene grasse fall.	Ovid's Elegies		1.14.22
TYRDE			
Judge you the rest, being tyrde <tride> she bad me kisse.	Ovid's Elegies		1.5.26
TYRE			
run over hedge and ditch, and never tyre, I gave him his money;	F1539	4.5.35	P HrsCsr
What neede she [tyre] <try> her hand to hold the quill,	Ovid's Elegies		1.11.23
TYRED			
I saw when forth a tyred lover went,	Ovid's Elegies		3.10.13
TYRIAN (See TIRIEN)			
TYRO			
Drye Enipeus, Tyro to embrace,	Ovid's Elegies		3.5.43
TYROS			
Where by the river Tyros I subdew'd/Stoka, Padalia, and	2Tamb	1.3.209	Therid
TYRRHEN			
pooles, refraines/To taint his tresses in the Tyrrhen maine?	Dido	1.1.112	Venus
Or that the Tyrrhen sea were in mine armes,	Dido	4.4.101	Dido
TYTLE			
To gaine the tytle of a Conquerour,	1Tamb	1.1.125	Menaph
To injure or suppresse your woorthy tytle.	1Tamb	1.1.183	Ortyg
(For that's the style and tytle I have yet)/Although he sent a	2Tamb	1.2.69	Almeda
Ere I would loose the tytle of a king.	2Tamb	1.3.91	Celeb
Ere I would loose the tytle of a king.	2Tamb	1.3.95	Amyras
me, that I may resigne/My place and proper tytle to my sonne:	2Tamb	5.3.176	Tamb
TYTLES			
those that lead my horse/Have to their names tytles of dignity,	1Tamb	3.3.70	Bajzth
Thy names and tytles, and thy dignities,	1Tamb	4.2.79	Tamb
Deserve these tytles I endow you with,	1Tamb	4.4.125	Tamb
UBI			
[Seeing ubi desinit philosophus, ibi incipit medicus].	F 41	1.1.13A	Faust
UGLIE			
where my slave, the uglie monster death/Shaking and quivering,	2Tamb	5.3.67	Tamb
UGLY (See also OUGLY)			
That ugly impe that shall outweare my wrath,	Dido	3.2.4	Juno
Not with Aeneas in the ugly Cave.	Dido	4.1.32	Iarbus
O Queene of Carthage, wert thou ugly blacke,	Dido	5.1.125	Aeneas
Upon his browes was pourtraid ugly death,	1Tamb	3.2.72	Agidas
Hover about the ugly Ferriman,	1Tamb	5.1.246	Zabina
Let ugly darknesse with her rusty coach/Engyrt with tempests	1Tamb	5.1.294	Bajzth
With ugly Furies bearing fiery flags,	2Tamb	1.3.146	Techel
Now ugly death stretch out thy Sable wings,	2Tamb	3.4.16	Olymp
By whose proud side the ugly furies run,	2Tamb	3.4.59	Therid
If ever day were turnde to ugly night,	P 62	2.5	Guise
Thou art too ugly to attend on me:	F 252	1.3.24	Faust
I, go accursed spirit to ugly hell:	F 627	2.2.76	Faust
First, be thou turned to this ugly shape,	F1126	3.3.39	Mephst
Ugly hell gape not; come not Lucifer,	F1981	5.2.185	Faust
olde swords/With ugly teeth of blacke rust fouly scarr'd:	Lucan, First Booke		245
Prodigious birthes with more and ugly jointes/Then nature	Lucan, First Booke		560
ULISSES			
White-cheekt Penelope knewe Ulisses signe,	Ovid's Elegies		2.18.29
The East winds in Ulisses baggs we shut,	Ovid's Elegies		3.11.29

ULYSSES			
See how the night Ulysses-like comes forth,	Dido	1.1.70	Venus
Ulysses on the sand/Assayd with honey words to turne them	Dido	2.1.136	Aeneas
Ulysses sent to our unhappie towne:	Dido	2.1.149	Aeneas
my selfe to smart)/We write, or what Penelope sends Ulysses,	Ovid's Elegies		2.18.21
ULYSSES-LIKE			
See how the night Ulysses-like comes forth,	Dido	1.1.70	Venus
'UM (See also 'EM)			
Goe send 'um threescore Camels, thirty Mules,	Jew	1.1.59	Barab
Speake, shall I have 'um, Sir?	Jew	4.3.49	Pilia
UMBRAS			
Sic sic juvat ire sub umbras.	Dido	5.1.313	Dido
UMH (See also HUM)			
Umh; All the Jewes in Malta must be there?	Jew	1.1.169	Barab
UN			
defence/When [un-protected] <un-protested> ther is no expence?	Ovid's Elegies		2.2.12
UNA			
Si una eademque res legatur duobus, alter rem, alter valorem	F 56	1.1.28	P Faust
UNABLE			
The Sun unable to sustaine the sight,	2Tamb	1.3.168	Tamb
UNACQUAINTED			
With unacquainted power of our hoste.	2Tamb	2.2.23	Uribas
By this, sad Hero, with love unacquainted,	Hero and Leander		2.1
UNAFFRIGHTED			
As Crocodiles that unaffrighted rest,	1Tamb	4.1.10	Souldn
UNAPT			
You are unapt my looser lines to heare.	Ovid's Elegies		2.1.4
UNARMED			
sleeping foe tis good/And arm'd to shed unarmed peoples bloud.	Ovid's Elegies		1.9.22
UNAWARES			
yett comminge upon you once unawares he frayde you out againe.	Paris	ms12,p390	P Souldr
And sodenly surprize them unawares.	Edw	2.3.19	Lncstr
For unawares (Come thither) from her slipt,	Hero and Leander		1.358
UNBARD			
To get the dore with little noise unbard.	Ovid's Elegies		3.1.50
UNBARRE			
Why enviest me, this hostile [denne] <dende> unbarre,	Ovid's Elegies		1.6.17
UNBARRED			
Fierce Mulciber unbarred Aetna's gate,	Lucan, First Booke		543
UNBINDE			
Sad Elegia thy wofull haires unbinde:	Ovid's Elegies		3.8.3
UNBORNE			
But if for Nero (then unborne) the fates/Would find no other	Lucan, First Booke		33
Who unborne infants first to slay invented,	Ovid's Elegies		2.14.5
And why dire poison give you babes unborne?	Ovid's Elegies		2.14.28
The fathers thigh should unborne Bacchus lacke.	Ovid's Elegies		3.3.40
UNBOUGHT			
Thankes worthely are due for things unbought,	Ovid's Elegies		1.10.43
UNBOWELL			
If mine will serve, unbowell straight this brest,	Edw	5.3.10	Edward
UNBURDEN			
Shall here unburden their exhaled sweetes,	Dido	5.1.14	Aeneas
UNBURDENED			
And all of them unburdened of their loade,	Dido	1.1.225	Aeneas
UNCERTAINE (See also INCERTAINE)			
And others came from that uncertaine shore,	Lucan, First Booke		410
Joyes with uncertaine faith thou takest and brings.	Ovid's Elegies		2.9.50
UNCHOSEN			
(Unchosen Nation, never circumciz'd;	Jew	2.3.8	Barab
UNCIVIL (See INCIVILL)			
UNCKLE			
Mine unckle heere, this Earle, and I my selfe,	Edw	1.1.82	Mortmr
Come unckle, let us leave the brainsick king,	Edw	1.1.125	Mortmr
Yong Mortimer and his unckle shalbe earles,	Edw	1.4.67	Edward
Unckle, his wanton humor greeves not me,	Edw	1.4.402	Mortmr
Unckle, tis this that makes me impatient.	Edw	1.4.419	Mortmr
You know my minde, come unckle lets away.	Edw	1.4.424	Mortmr
Wigmore shall flie, to set my unckle free.	Edw	2.2.196	Mortmr
Sweet unckle speake more kindly to the queene.	Edw	2.2.228	Neece
Farewell sweete unckle till we meete againe.	Edw	2.4.11	Neece
Tell me good unckle, what Edward doe you meane?	Edw	4.6.32	Prince
Thou being his unckle, and the next of bloud,	Edw	5.2.88	Mortmr
Helpe unckle Kent, Mortimer will wrong me.	Edw	5.2.113	Prince
My lord, he is my unckle, and shall live.	Edw	5.4.91	King
My lord, if you will let my unckle live,	Edw	5.4.99	King
If that my Unckle shall be murthered thus?	Edw	5.4.110	King
And shall my Unckle Edmund ride with us?	Edw	5.4.114	King
UNCKLES			
My unckles taken prisoner by the Scots.	Edw	2.2.115	Mortmr
Mine unckles taken prisoner by the Scots.	Edw	2.2.142	Mortmr
and then a Fig/For all my unckles frienship here in Fraunce.	Edw	4.2.5	Prince
UNCLEANE			
things hidden)/Whence uncleane fowles are said to be forbidden.	Ovid's Elegies		2.6.52
UNCLES			
these Medean Lords/To Memphis, from my uncles country of Medea,	1Tamb	1.2.12	Zenoc
She wailing Mars sinne, and her uncles crime,	Ovid's Elegies		3.5.49
UNCONFIRM'D			
Then were my thoughts so fraile and unconfirm'd,	Jew	3.3.59	Abigal
UNCONQUERD			
Pallas launce strikes me with unconquerd arme.	Ovid's Elegies		3.3.28
UNCONQUERED			
Than you by this unconquered arme of mine.	2Tamb	4.3.16	Tamb
And shall I die, and this unconquered?	2Tamb	5.3.150	Tamb

UNCONQUERED (cont.)
And shal I die, and this unconquered? 2Tamb 5.3.158 Tamb
UNCONSTANT
By Mortimer, and my unconstant Queene, Edw 5.1.30 Edward
UNCONSTRAIN'D
And all unknowne, and unconstrain'd of me, Jew 3.4.3 Barab
UNCONTROLDE
The gentle King whose pleasure uncontrolde, P 127 2.70 Guise
UNCONTROULD
And triumph Edward with his friends uncontrould. Edw 4.3.3 Edward
UNCONTROULDE
Lives uncontroulde within the English pale, Edw 2.2.165 Lncstr
UNCONTROWLD
and suffer uncontrowld/These Barons thus to beard me in my Edw 3.1.13 Spencr
UNCOUTH
An uncouth paine torments my grieved soule, 1Tamb 2.7.7 Cosroe
UNCUT
An old wood, stands uncut of long yeares space, Ovid's Elegies 3.1.1
UNDAS
league,/Littora littoribus contraria, fluctibus undas/Imprecor: Dido 5.1.310 Dido
UNDAUNTED
Yet he undaunted tooke his fathers flagge, Dido 2.1.259 Aeneas
The undaunted spirit of Percie was appeasd, Edw 1.1.114 Kent
Undaunted though her former guide be chang'd. Lucan, First Booke 50
UNDECKT
[I thinke what one undeckt would be, being drest]; Ovid's Elegies 2.4.37
UNDER
As to instruct us under what good heaven/We breathe as now, and Dido 1.1.197 Aeneas
it life, that under his conduct/We might saile backe to Troy, Dido 2.1.17 Aeneas
Oft hath she askt us under whom we serv'd, Dido 2.1.66 Illion
But he clapt under hatches saild away. Dido 5.1.240 Anna
And [pitcht] <pitch> our tents under the Georgean hilles, 1Tamb 2.2.15 Meandr
and the Easterne theeves/Under the conduct of one Tamburlaine, 1Tamb 3.1.3 Bajzth
He stamps it under his feet my Lord. 1Tamb 4.4.42 P Therid
Thrust under yoke and thraldom of a thiefe. 1Tamb 5.1.261 Bajzth
To Amazonia under Capricorne, 2Tamb 1.1.74 Orcan
Your Keeper under Tamburlaine the great, 2Tamb 1.2.68 Almeda
Have under me as many kings as you, 2Tamb 1.3.55 Celeb
Under my collors march ten thousand Greeks, 2Tamb 1.3.118 Therid
Five hundred Briggandines are under saile, 2Tamb 1.3.122 Therid
And all the men in armour under me, 2Tamb 1.3.135 Usumc
To martch with me under this bloody flag: 2Tamb 2.4.116 Tamb
pearle of welthie India/Were mounted here under a Canapie: 2Tamb 3.2.122 Tamb
O thou that swaiest the region under earth, 2Tamb 4.3.32 Orcan
Under a hollow bank, right opposite/Against the Westerne gate 2Tamb 5.1.121 Govnr
My Viceroies bondage under Tamburlaine, 2Tamb 5.2.21 Callap
Loaden with Spice and Silkes, now under saile, Jew 1.1.45 Barab
And send to keepe our Gallies under-saile, Jew 1.2.15 Calym
It may be under colour of shaving, thou'lt cut my throat for my Jew 2.3.119 P Barab
abroad a nights/And kill sicke people groaning under walls: Jew 2.3.175 Barab
Under pretence of helping Charles the fifth, Jew 2.3.188 Barab
buries it up as Partridges doe their egges, under the earth. Jew 4.2.58 P Ithimr
tell him, I scorne to write a line under a hundred crownes. Jew 4.2.121 P Ithimr
he weares, Judas left under the Elder when he hang'd himselfe. Jew 4.4.66 P Ithimr
and under Turkish yokes/Shall groning beare the burthen of our Jew 5.2.7 Calym
Cheefely since under safetie of our word, P 209 4.7 Charls
And under your direction see they keep/All trecherous violence P 267 4.65 Charls
Who set themselves to tread us under foot, P 702 14.5 Navrre
Sweet Epernoune all Rebels under heaven, P1185 22.47 King
Then live in infamie under such a king. Edw 3.1.244 Lncstr
And these must die under a tyrants sword. Edw 4.7.92 Edward
the greater sway/When as a kings name shall be under writ. Edw 5.2.14 Mortmr
Under the heavens. F 506 2.1.118 Mephst
I had nothing under me but a little straw, and had much ado to F1486 4.4.30 P HrsCsr
and he would by no meanes sell him under forty Dollors; so sir, F1537 4.5.33 P HrsCsr
I marry can I, we are under heaven. F1615 4.6.58 P Carter
under whose blacke survey/Great Potentates do kneele with awful F App p.235 34 Mephst
Under great burdens fals are ever greevous; Lucan, First Booke 71
Under the frosty beare, or parching East, Lucan, First Booke 254
our wintering/Under the Alpes; Roome rageth now in armes/As if Lucan, First Booke 304
Under the rockes by crooked Vogesus; Lucan, First Booke 399
Under whose hoary rocks Gebenna hangs; Lucan, First Booke 436
With hoarie toppe, and under Hemus mount/Philippi plaines; Lucan, First Booke 679
Wilt lying under him his bosome clippe? Ovid's Elegies 1.4.5
I and my wench oft under clothes did lurke, Ovid's Elegies 1.4.47
How smoothe a bellie, under her waste sawe I, Ovid's Elegies 1.5.21
Under sweete hony deadly poison lurkes. Ovid's Elegies 1.8.104
Which lie hid under her thinne veile supprest. Ovid's Elegies 3.2.36
And under mine her wanton thigh she flong, Ovid's Elegies 3.6.10
And Juno like with Dis raignes under ground? Ovid's Elegies 3.9.46
We vanquish, and tread tam'd love under feete, Ovid's Elegies 3.10.5
There use all tricks, and tread shame under feete. Ovid's Elegies 3.13.18
Under whose shade the Wood-gods love to bee. Hero and Leander 1.156
For under water he was almost dead, Hero and Leander 2.170
UNDERGOE
Who would not undergoe all kind of toyle, Dido 3.3.58 Aeneas
UNDER GROUND
And Juno like with Dis raignes under ground? Ovid's Elegies 3.9.46
UNDERMINE
Besiege a fort, to undermine a towne, 2Tamb 3.2.60 Tamb
Raise mounts, batter, intrench, and undermine, 2Tamb 3.3.38 Capt
To undermine us with a showe of love. Edw 2.3.6 Lncstr
UNDERNEATH
But as he thrust them underneath the hils, 1Tamb 2.6.5 Cosroe

UNDERNEATH (cont.)			
Conquering the pecple underneath our feet, ...	1Tamb	4.4.137	Tamb
The pavement underneath thy chariot wheels/With Turky Carpets	2Tamb	1.2.42	Callap
That treadeth Fortune underneath his feete, ...	2Tamb	3.4.52	Therid
more than if the regicn/Next underneath the Element of fire,	2Tamb	5.1.88	Tamb
There have I hid close underneath the plancke/That runs along	Jew	1.2.296	Barab
But perish underneath my bitter curse/Like Cain by Adam, for	Jew	3.4.32	Barab
and underneath/In severall places are field-pieces pitch'd,	Jew	5.5.26	Barab
Now tell me, worldlings, underneath the [sunne] <summe>, .	Jew	5.5.49	Barab
Navarre that cloakes them underneath his wings, . .	P 855	17.50	Guise
And underneath thy banners march who will, ...	Edw	1.1.88	Mortmr
And hide thy left hand underneath her lappe. . . .	Ovid's Elegies		2.15.12
For know, that underneath this radiant floure, . . .	Hero and Leander		1.145
Upon a rocke, and underneath a hill, ...	Hero and Leander		1.345
UNDERPROP			
That underprop <underprops> the ground-worke of the same:	F 812	3.1.34	Mephst
UNDERPROPS			
That earth-borne Atlas groning underprops:	Dido	1.1.99	Jupitr
That underprop <underprops> the ground-worke of the same:	F 812	3.1.34	Mephst
UNDER-SAILE			
And send to keepe our Gallies under-saile, ...	Jew	1.2.15	Calym
UNDERSTAND			
I understand your highnesse sent for me.	Dido	3.1.100	Aeneas
And not let Dido understand their drift:	Dido	4.4.6	Dido
Pleaseth your mightinesse to understand, ...	1Tamb	4.1.47	2Msngr
And now Madam as I understand, ...	P 500	9.19	Guise
of Guise, we understand that you/Have gathered a power of men.	P 821	17.16	King
Let her my faith with thee given understand. . . .	Ovid's Elegies		2.15.28
UNDERSTANDE			
My Lord, as by our scoutes we understande, ...	P 724	14.27	1Msngr
UNDERSTANDING			
And understanding I should come this way, ...	Jew	4.1.165	1Fryar
UNDERSTOODE			
Yet understcode by ncne.	P 112	2.55	Guise
UNDERTAKE			
Though I confesse the othes they undertake, ...	2Tamb	2.1.42	Sgsmnd
That if I undertake to weare the crowne/Of Poland, it may	P 466	8.16	Anjoy
I thankfully shall undertake the charge/Of you and yours, and	P 476	8.26	Anjoy
We undertake to mannage these our warres/Against the proud	P 699	14.2	Navrre
I will upon mine honor undertake/To carrie him, and bring him	Edw	2.5.79	Penbrk
That I would undertake to carrie him/Unto your highnes, and to	Edw	3.1.99	Arundl
I will this undertake, to have him hence, ...	Edw	3.1.111	Arundl
To be reveng'd on Jove, did undertake, ...	Hero and Leander		1.442
UNDERTAK'ST			
As precious is the charge thou undertak'st/As that which .	2Tamb	5.3.230	Tamb
UNDERTOOKE			
And Penbrooke undertooke for his returne, ...	Edw	3.1.236	Edward
UNDETECTED			
But woods and groves keepe your faults undetected. . .	Ovid's Elegies		3.5.84
UNDIQUE			
The motto this: Undique mors est.	Edw	2.2.28	Lncstr
UNDO			
Vilaine I say, undo what thou hast done.	F App	p.238 75	Knight
UNDOE			
To undoe a Jew is charity, and not sinne.	Jew	4.4.81	Ithimr
UNDONE			
She has confest, and we are both undone, ...	Jew	4.1.46	Barab
I my good Lord, I would it were undone.	Edw	5.6.2	Matrvs
Alas I am undone, what shall I do?	F1492	4.4.36	P HrsCsr
Alas, I am undone, what shall I do:	F App	p.241 154	P HrsCsr
That with one worde hath nigh himselfe undone, . . .	Ovid's Elegies		1.13.20
As nature wept, thinking she was undone;	Hero and Leander		1.46
UNEQUALD			
father Phoebus layed/To sing with his unequald harpe is sayed.	Ovid's Elegies		3.8.24
UNEQUALL			
Thou deignst unequall lines should thee rehearse, . .	Ovid's Elegies		3.1.37
UNEVEN			
This bed, and that by tumbling made uneven, ...	Ovid's Elegies		3.13.32
UNFAIN'D			
For that I know your friendship is unfain'd, . . .	F1689	5.1.16	Faust
UNFAINED			
Hence fained weeds, unfained are my woes, ...	Edw	4.7.97	Edward
Do it then Faustus <quickly>, with unfained heart, . .	F1751	5.1.78	Mephst
UNFELD			
In unféld wcods, and sacred groves you dwell, . . .	Lucan, First Booke		448
UNFITTING			
Small doores unfitting for large houses are. . . .	Ovid's Elegies		3.1.40
UNFOLD			
Himselfe in presence shal unfold at large. . . .	2Tamb	Prol.9	Prolog
A thing that makes me tremble to unfold.	Jew	3.6.48	2Fryar
Yet more will happen then I can unfold;	Lucan, First Booke		634
Thou arguest she doth secret markes unfold. . . .	Ovid's Elegies		2.7.6
UNFOLDE			
Edward, unfolde thy pawes,/And let their lives bloud slake thy	Edw	2.2.204	Edward
UNFORTUNATE (See alsc INFORTUNATE)			
O wals unfortunate too neere to France, ...	Lucan, First Booke		250
UNFOULD			
A wofull tale bids Dido to unfould, ...	Dido	2.1.114	Aeneas
The causes first I purpose to unfould/Of these garboiles,	Lucan, First Booke		67
I tremble to unfould/What you intend, great Jove is now .	Lucan, First Booke		630
UNFOYL'D			
Win it, and weare it, it is yet [unfoyl'd] <unsoyl'd>. .	Jew	2.3.293	Barab
UNFRAME			
And that slowe webbe nights fals-hood did unframe. . .	Ovid's Elegies		3.8.30

UNFREQUENTED			
And wander to the unfrequented Inde.	Edw	1.4.50	Edward
UNGENTLE			
Ungentle Queene, is this thy love to me?	Dido	3.1.36	Iarbus
Ungentle, can she wrong Iarbus so?	Dido	3.3.10	Iarbus
On Mortimer, with whom ungentle Queene--	Edw	1.4.147	Gavstn
Proud Mortimer, ungentle Lancaster,	Edw	2.2.29	Edward
sith the ungentle king/Of Fraunce refuseth to give aide of	Edw	4.2.61	SrJohn
UNGRATE			
Ungrate why feignest new feares?	Ovid's Elegies		2.8.23
UNGUARDED			
Few love, what others have unguarded left.	Ovid's Elegies		3.4.26
UNGUILTY			
My selfe unguilty of this crime I know.	Ovid's Elegies		2.7.28
UNHALLOWED			
to fall into the hands/Of such a Traitor and unhallowed Jew!	Jew	5.2.13	Govnr
Now Selim note the unhallowed deeds of Jewes:	Jew	5.5.92	Govnr
UNHAPPIE			
Ulysses sent to our unhappie towne:	Dido	2.1.149	Aeneas
In which unhappie worke was I employd,	Dido	2.1.169	Aeneas
Dido in these flames/Hath burnt her selfe, aye me, unhappie me!	Dido	5.1.315	Anna
Unhappie Persea, that in former age/Hast bene the seat of	1Tamb	1.1.6	Cosroe
Unhappie Gaveston, whether goest thou now.	Edw	2.5.110	Gavstn
Unhappie Isabell, when Fraunce rejects,	Edw	4.2.11	Queene
[Unhappie] <Unhappies> <Unhappy is> Edward, chaste from	Edw	4.6.62	Kent
Friends, whither must unhappie Edward go,	Edw	5.3.4	Edward
UNHAPPIES			
[Unhappie] <Unhappies> <Unhappy is> Edward, chaste from	Edw	4.6.62	Kent
UNHAPPILYE			
from her tower/To Venus temple, [where] <were> unhappilye,	Hero and Leander		1.133
UNHAPPY			
Oh unhappy day,	Jew	3.4.26	Barab
[Unhappie] <Unhappies> <Unhappy is> Edward, chaste from	Edw	4.6.62	Kent
Unhappy spirits that [fell] <live> with Lucifer,	F 298	1.3.70	Mephst
What doest, unhappy?	Ovid's Elegies		3.2.71
UNHARNESSE			
Unharnesse them, and let me have fresh horse:	2Tamb	5.1.130	Tamb
UNHEARD			
He shewes me how unheard to passe the watch,	Ovid's Elegies		1.6.7
To move her feete unheard in [setting] <sitting> downe.	Ovid's Elegies		3.1.52
UNHORSTE			
And there unhorste the duke of Cleremont.	Edw	5.5.70	Edward
UNION			
I wishe this union and religious league,	P 3	1.3	Charls
So when this worlds compounded union breakes,	Lucan, First Booke		73
UNITE			
Or els unite you to his life and soule,	1Tamb	3.2.23	Zenoc
Let us unite our royall bandes in one,	1Tamb	4.3.17	Souldn
UNITED			
The number of your hostes united is,	1Tamb	4.3.52	Capol
Which forc'd their hands divide united hearts:	Jew	3.2.35	Govnr
Looke how their hands, so were their hearts united,	Hero and Leander		2.27
UNIVERSALL			
And universall body of the law <Church>.	F 60	1.1.32	Faust
UNJUST			
Thou trothles and unjust, what lines are these?	P 680	13.24	Guise
O wicked sexe, perjured and unjust,	P 693	13.37	Guise
intreat thy Lord/To pardon my unjust presumption,	F1748	5.1.75	Faust
The unjust Judge for bribes becomes a stale.	Ovid's Elegies		1.10.38
The unjust seas all blewish do appeare.	Ovid's Elegies		2.11.12
UNJUSTLY			
That him from her unjustly did detaine.	Hero and Leander		2.122
UNKEEMBD			
Comes forth her [unkeembd] <unkeembe> locks a sunder tearing.	Ovid's Elegies		3.8.52
UNKEEMBE			
Comes forth her [unkeembd] <unkeembe> locks a sunder tearing.	Ovid's Elegies		3.8.52
UNKIND			
Therefore unkind Aeneas, must thou say,	Dido	5.1.123	Dido
To cure my minde that melts for unkind love.	Dido	5.1.287	Dido
Hard-hearted Father, unkind Barabas,	Jew	3.3.36	Abigal
Canst thou be so unkind to leave me thus?	Jew	4.2.52	Curtzn
Be not unkind and faire, mishapen stuffe/Are of behaviour	Hero and Leander		1.203
UNKINDE			
False, and unkinde; what, hast thou lost thy father?	Jew	3.4.2	Barab
England, unkinde to thy nobilitie,	Edw	3.1.250	Mortmr
The lords are cruell, and the king unkinde,	Edw	4.2.2	Queene
Unkinde Valoys,/Unhappie Isabell, when Fraunce rejects,	Edw	4.2.10	Queene
How hard the nobles, how unkinde the king/Hath shewed himself:	Edw	4.2.49	Mortmr
Vilde wretch, and why hast thou of all unkinde,	Edw	4.6.5	Kent
Both unkinde parents, but for causes sad,	Ovid's Elegies		2.14.31
UNKINDENES			
I heare sweete lady of the kings unkindenes,	Edw	4.2.15	SrJohn
UNKINDLY			
Why do you lowre unkindly on a king?	Edw	4.7.63	Edward
UNKNOWN			
Great store of strange and unknown stars were seene/Wandering	Lucan, First Booke		524
UNKNOWNE			
But haples I, God wot, poore and unknowne,	Dido	1.1.227	Aeneas
And all unknowne, and unconstrain'd of me,	Jew	3.4.3	Barab
And unto your good mistris as unknowne.	Jew	4.3.48	Barab
Goes to discover countries yet unknowne.	Edw	5.6.66	Mortmr
Was stretcht unto the fields of hinds unknowne;	Lucan, First Booke		171
Where they may sport, and seeme to be unknowne.	Ovid's Elegies		1.5.8

UNKNOWNE (cont.)
Praysing for me some unknowne Guelder dame, Ovid's Elegies 1.14.49
And rude boyes toucht with unknowne love me reade, Ovid's Elegies 2.1.6
Let him goe forth knowne, that unknowne did enter, Ovid's Elegies 2.2.20
And wish hereby them all unknowne to leave. Ovid's Elegies 2.5.54
if Corcyras Ile/Had thee unknowne interr'd in ground most vile. Ovid's Elegies 3.8.48
Which made the world) another world begat,/Of unknowne joy. Hero and Leander 2.293

UNLAWFUL
which of both/Had justest cause unlawful tis to judge: Lucan, First Booke 127

UNLAWFULL
may exhort the wise/Onely to wonder at unlawfull things, F2007 5.3.25 4Chor
I sawe you then unlawfull kisses joyne, Ovid's Elegies 2.5.23
Deflowr'd and stained in unlawfull bed? Ovid's Elegies 3.5.76

UNLAWFULLY
Unlawfully usurpest the Persean seat: 1Tamb 4.2.57 Zabina

UNLEARNED
keepe further from me O thou illiterate, and unlearned Hostler. F 729 2.3.8 P Robin

UNLES
Tush, all shall dye unles I have my will: P 653 12.66 QnMoth
Unles he meane to be betraide and dye: P 898 17.93 King

UNLESSE
Unlesse I be deceiv'd disputed once. Dido 3.1.147 Cloan
I, and unlesse the destinies be false, Dido 4.4.81 Aeneas
Dido I am, unlesse I be deceiv'd, Dido 5.1.264 Dido
Unlesse they have a wiser king than you. 1Tamb 1.1.92 Cosroe
Unlesse they have a wiser king than you? 1Tamb 1.1.93 Mycet
Thou breakst the law of Armes unlesse thou kneele, 1Tamb 2.4.21 Mycet
My jointes benumb'd, unlesse I eat, I die. 1Tamb 4.4.98 Bajzth
a foot, unlesse thou beare/A mind corragious and invincible: 2Tamb 1.3.72 Tamb
Unlesse your unrelenting flinty hearts/Suppresse all pitty in Jew 1.2.141 Barab
And Gaveston unlesse thou be reclaimd, Edw 1.1.183 BshpCv
Unlesse his brest be sword proofe he shall die. Edw 1.2.8 Mortmr
Unlesse he be declinde from that base pesant. Edw 1.4.7 Mortmr
Unlesse the sea cast up his shipwrack body. Edw 1.4.205 Lncstr
Villaine thy life, unlesse I misse mine aime. Edw 2.2.84 Mortmr
Unlesse it be with too much clemencie? Edw 5.1.123 Edward
Unlesse thou bring me newes of Edwards death. Edw 5.4.46 Mortmr
Nor will we come unlesse he use such meanes, F 278 1.3.50 Mephst
unlesse <except> the ground be <were> perfum'd, and cover'd F 670 2.2.119 P Pride
Unlesse you bring them forth immediatly: F1031 3.2.51 Pope
Unlesse I erre, full many shalt thou burne, Ovid's Elegies 1.2.43
Unlesse I erre to these thou more incline, Ovid's Elegies 2.18.39
Now I forewarne, unlesse to keepe her stronger, Ovid's Elegies 2.19.47

UNLIKE
And not unlike a bashfull puretaine, Edw 5.4.59 Mortmr
Or that unlike the line from whence I [sprong] <come>, Ovid's Elegies 1.15.3

UNLOCKE
What gate thy stately words cannot unlocke, Ovid's Elegies 3.1.45

UNLOCKT
Then he unlockt the Horse, and suddenly/From out his entrailes, Dido 2.1.182 Aeneas
Thus I complaind, but Love unlockt his quiver, Ovid's Elegies 1.1.25

UNLOOKT
Thankes gentle Lord for such unlookt for grace. Dido 1.2.44 Serg

UNLOOSDE
Kist him, imbrast him, and unloosde his bands, Dido 2.1.158 Aeneas

UNMEETE
Unmeete is beauty without use to wither. Ovid's Elegies 2.3.14
Her trembling mouth these unmeete sounds expresses. Ovid's Elegies 3.5.72

UNMERCIFULL
I sweare by this to be unmercifull. P 277 5.4 Dumain

UNMOV'D
Why stand you thus unmov'd with my laments? Jew 1.2.171 Barab

UNNATURAL
Unnatural wars, where subjects brave their king, Edw 3.1.86 Queene

UNNATURALL
A desperate and unnaturall resolution, Edw 3.1.217 Warwck
Unnaturall king, to slaughter noble men/And cherish flatterers: Edw 4.1.8 Kent
to whom in justice it belongs/To punish this unnaturall revolt: Edw 4.6.9 Kent
And that unnaturall Queene false Isabell, Edw 5.1.17 Edward
I doe not thinke her so unnaturall. Edw 5.6.76 King

UNPAID
The ten yeares tribute that remaines unpaid. Jew 1.2.7 Calym

UNPEOPLED
Is Barbary unpeopled for thy sake, 2Tamb 1.3.134 Usumc
All Barbary is unpeopled for thy sake. 2Tamb 1.3.149 Techel
Againe by some in this unpeopled world. Ovid's Elegies 2.14.12

UNPEOPLING
Unpeopling Westerne Affrica and Greece: 1Tamb 3.3.34 Usumc

UNPLEASANT
[Unpleasant, harsh, contemptible and vilde]: F 136 1.1.108A Faust
my exhortation/Seemes harsh, and all unpleasant; let it not, F1718 5.1.45 OldMan
Forbeare sweet wordes, and be your sport unpleasant. Ovid's Elegies 1.4.66

UNPLEASING
And plead in vaine, unpleasing soverainty. 2Tamb 5.3.198 Amyras

UNPOINTED
Unpointed as it is, thus shall it goe, Edw 5.4.13 Mortmr
Gurney, it was left unpointed for the nonce, Edw 5.5.16 Matrvs

UNPROFITABLY
At least unprofitably lose it not: Jew 5.2.37 Barab

UN-PROTECTED
defence/When [un-protected] <un-protested> ther is no expence? Ovid's Elegies 2.2.12

UN-PROTESTED
defence/When [un-protected] <un-protested> ther is no expence? Ovid's Elegies 2.2.12

UNPROVIDED			
<Faustus I have, and because we wil not be unprovided, .	F 805	(HC265)A	P Mephst
UNPUNISHT			
if she unpunisht you deceive,/For others faults, why do I losse	Ovid's Elegies		3.3.15
UNQUENCHED			
That his teare-thyrsty and unquenched hate, . . .	2Tamb	5.3.222	Techel
UNQUIET			
may I presume/To know the cause of these unquiet fits: .	1Tamb	3.2.2	Agidas
UNREADINESSE			
by expedition/Advantage takes of your unreadinesse. . .	1Tamb	4.1.39	Capol
UNRELENTING			
if the unrelenting eares/Of death and hell be shut against my	2Tamb	5.3.191	Amyras
Unlesse your unrelenting flinty hearts/Suppresse all pitty in	Jew	1.2.141	Barab
Then send for unrelenting Mortimer/And Isabell, whose eyes	Edw	5.1.103	Edward
UNRENOWMED			
Commaunds me leave these unrenowmed [reames] <beames>, .	Dido	4.3.18	Aeneas
UNRESISTED			
That hath so many unresisted friends:	Dido	3.2.50	Juno
Where unresisted I remoov'd my campe.	2Tamb	1.3.199	Techel
And unresisted, drave away riche spoiles.	Edw	2.2.167	Lncstr
UNREST			
And heaven and earth with his unrest acquaints. . .	Dido	1.1.141	Venus
They may be still tormented with unrest, ...	Dido	5.1.305	Dido
UNREVENG'D			
While slaughtred Crassus ghost walks unreveng'd, . .	Lucan, First Booke		11
UNREVENGD			
Let them not unrevengd murther your friends, . . .	Edw	3.1.125	Spencr
And unrevengd mockt Gods with me doth scoffe. . . .	Ovid's Elegies		3.3.20
UNREVENGING			
Iarbus, curse that unrevenging Jove, ...	Dido	4.1.18	Iarbus
UNREVEREND			
Disdainful Turkesse and unreverend Bosse, ...	1Tamb	3.3.168	Zenoc
UNRIGD			
Yet Queene of Affricke, are my ships unrigd, . . .	Dido	3.1.105	Aeneas
While in the harbor ride thy ships unrigd. . . .	Edw	2.2.169	Mortmr
UNRIVAL'D			
Beware least he unrival'd loves secure, ...	Ovid's Elegies		1.8.95
UNRULY			
That like unruly never broken Jades, ...	2Tamb	4.3.45	Therid
My horsmen brandish their unruly blades.	2Tamb	5.1.79	Tamb
UNSACKT			
pompe than this)/Rifle the kingdomes I shall leave unsackt,	2Tamb	4.3.59	Tamb
UNSEEMLY			
But how unseemly is it for my Sex, ...	1Tamb	5.1.174	Tamb
UNSEENE			
That thou and I unseene might sport our selves: . .	Dido	4.4.51	Dido
A counterfet profession is better/Then unseene hypocrisie.	Jew	1.2.293	Barab
And here behold (unseene) where I have found/The gold, the	Jew	2.1.22	Abigal
Alas, see where he sits, and hopes unseene, ...	Edw	4.7.51	Leistr
And doe what ere I please, unseene of any. . . .	F 993	3.2.13	Faust
<to do what I please unseene of any whilst I stay in Rome>.	F 993	(HC266)A	P Faust
UNSETLED			
And Caesars mind unsetled musing stood;	Lucan, First Booke		264
UNSHEATH'D			
My hands an unsheath'd shyning weapon have not. . .	Ovid's Elegies		2.2.64
UNSOLD			
At Alexandria, Merchandize unsold:	Jew	4.1.68	Barab
UNSOYL'D			
Win it, and weare it, it is yet [unfoyl'd] <unsoyl'd>. .	Jew	2.3.293	Barab
UNSPEAKEABLE			
Pleasures unspeakeable, blisse without end.	F1900	5.2.104	GdAngl
UNSPOTTED			
Let us have hope that their unspotted praiers, ...	1Tamb	5.1.20	Govnr
the Sun-bright troope/Of heavenly vyrgins and unspotted maides,	1Tamb	5.1.325	Zenoc
UNSTABLE			
To gaine the light unstable commons love, ...	Lucan, First Booke		133
none answer'd, but a murmuring buz/Th'unstable people made:	Lucan, First Booke		354
UNSURPRIZD			
Yet liveth Pierce of Gaveston unsurprizd, ...	Edw	2.5.4	Gavstn
UNTAUGHT			
Her mind pure, and her toong untaught to glose. . .	Hero and Leander		1.392
UNTIL (See also TIL, TILL)			
But if he stay until the bloody flag/Be once advanc'd on my	1Tamb	4.2.116	Tamb
Until with greater honors I be grac'd.	1Tamb	4.4.140	Tamb
Until my soule dissevered from this flesh, ...	2Tamb	4.3.131	Tamb
UNTIL'D			
Italy many yeares hath lyen until'd, ...	Lucan, First Booke		28
UNTILD (See also TILT)			
And untild ground with crooked plough-shares broake. .	Ovid's Elegies		3.9.14
UNTILL			
Untill I gird my quiver to my side:	Dido	3.3.8	Dido
But may be slackt untill another time:	Dido	4.2.26	Anna
Untill our bodies turne to Elements:	1Tamb	1.2.236	Tamb
Untill we reach the ripest fruit of all, ...	1Tamb	2.7.27	Tamb
Untill I bring this sturdy Tamburlain, ...	1Tamb	3.3.114	Bajzth
Stir not Zenocrate untill thou see/Me martch victoriously with	1Tamb	3.3.126	Tamb
Untill the Persean Fleete and men of war, ...	1Tamb	3.3.252	Tamb
make no period/Untill Natolia kneele before your feet. .	2Tamb	1.3.217	Therid
And not depart untill I see you free.	Jew	2.2.41	Bosco
And never cease untill that bell shall cease, . . .	P 240	4.38	Guise
I nere was King of France untill this houre: . . .	P1027	19.97	King
And pants untill I see that Conjurer dead. . . .	F1352	4.2.28	Benvol
Untill the cruel Giants war was done)/We plaine not heavens,	Lucan, First Booke		36

UNTILL (cont.)			
Untill some honourable deed be done.	Hero and Leander	1.282	
UNTILL'D (See also TILT)			
First to be throwne upon the untill'd ground.	Ovid's Elegies	3.5.16	
UNTIMELY			
To worke my downfall and untimely end.	1Tamb	2.7.6	Cosroe
And wet thy cheeks for their untimely deathes:	1Tamb	5.1.348	Zenoc
UNTO			
To make us live unto our former heate,	Dido	1.1.160	Achat
In sending thee unto this curteous Coast:	Dido	1.1.232	Venus
Wishing good lucke unto thy wandring steps.	Dido	1.1.239	Venus
Unto what fruitfull quarters were ye bound,	Dido	1.2.18	Iarbus
In multitudes they swarme unto the shoare,	Dido	1.2.36	Serg
or whatsoever stile/Belongs unto your name, vouchsafe of ruth	Dido	2.1.40	Aeneas
Began to crye, let us unto our ships,	Dido	2.1.127	Aeneas
And brought unto the Court of Priamus:	Dido	2.1.154	Aeneas
By this the Campe was come unto the walles,	Dido	2.1.188	Aeneas
And as we went unto our ships, thou knowest/We sawe Cassandra	Dido	2.1.273	Aeneas
Whom I tooke up to beare unto our ships:	Dido	2.1.277	Aeneas
And yet God knowes intangled unto one.--	Dido	3.1.154	Dido
I mustred all the windes unto his wracke,	Dido	3.2.45	Juno
Shall chaine felicitie unto their throne.	Dido	3.2.80	Juno
Unto the purpose which we now propound.	Dido	3.2.95	Juno
And better able unto other armes.	Dido	3.3.36	Cupid
Some to the mountaines, some unto the soyle,	Dido	3.3.61	Dido
You to the vallies, thou unto the house.	Dido	3.3.62	Dido
And mould her minde unto newe fancies shapes:	Dido	3.3.79	Iarbus
turne the hand of fate/Unto that happie day of my delight,	Dido	3.3.81	Iarbus
To move unto the measures of delight:	Dido	3.4.54	Dido
I might have stakte them both unto the earth,	Dido	4.1.23	Iarbus
O Anna, runne unto the water side,	Dido	4.4.1	Dido
No, thou shalt goe with me unto my house,	Dido	4.5.3	Nurse
And bore yong Cupid unto Cypresse Ile.	Dido	5.1.41	Hermes
Sergestus, beare him hence unto our ships,	Dido	5.1.49	Aeneas
And givest not eare unto the charge I bring?	Dido	5.1.52	Hermes
Now will I haste unto Lavinian shoare,	Dido	5.1.78	Aeneas
Nor sent a thousand ships unto the walles,	Dido	5.1.204	Dido
And ore his ships will soare unto the Sunne,	Dido	5.1.244	Dido
Or els Ile make a prayer unto the waves,	Dido	5.1.246	Dido
And ride upon his backe unto my love:	Dido	5.1.250	Dido
Daughter unto the Nimphs Hesperides,	Dido	5.1.276	Dido
Good brother tell the cause unto my Lords,	1Tamb	1.1.4	Mycet
[Trading] <Treading> by land unto the Westerne Isles,	1Tamb	1.1.38	Meandr
Monster of Nature, shame unto thy stocke,	1Tamb	1.1.104	Mycet
Where kings shall crouch unto our conquering swords,	1Tamb	1.2.220	Usumc
We yeeld unto thee happie Tamburlaine.	1Tamb	1.2.257	Agidas
And make him false his faith unto his King,	1Tamb	2.2.27	Meandr
To swarme unto the Ensigne I support.	1Tamb	2.3.14	Tamb
Who, when they come unto their fathers age,	1Tamb	3.3.110	Bajzth
If they should yeeld their necks unto the sword,	1Tamb	3.3.142	Bajzth
that am betroath'd/Unto the great and mighty Tamburlaine?	1Tamb	3.3.170	Zenoc
So from the East unto the furthest West,	1Tamb	3.3.246	Tamb
And thence unto the straightes of Jubalter:	1Tamb	3.3.256	Tamb
Unto the hallowed person of a prince,	1Tamb	4.3.40	Souldn
banquet and carouse/Full bowles of wine unto the God of war,	1Tamb	4.4.6	Tamb
Or if my love unto your majesty/May merit favour at your	1Tamb	4.4.69	Zenoc
Unto the watry mornings ruddy [bower] <hower>,	1Tamb	4.4.123	Tamb
And thence by land unto the Torrid Zone,	1Tamb	4.4.124	Tamb
Whose sorrowes lay more siege unto my soule,	1Tamb	5.1.155	Tamb
That will we chiefly see unto, Theridamas,	1Tamb	5.1.206	Tamb
From Barbary unto the Westerne Inde,	1Tamb	5.1.518	Tamb
From strong Tesella unto Biledull,	2Tamb	1.3.148	Techel
And all the land unto the coast of Spaine.	2Tamb	1.3.179	Usumc
From thence unto Cazates did I martch,	2Tamb	1.3.191	Techel
and lead him bound in chaines/Unto Damasco, where I staid	2Tamb	1.3.205	Techel
And so unto my citie of Damasco,	2Tamb	3.1.59	Soria
And wife unto the Monarke of the East.	2Tamb	3.2.22	Amyras
Whom I brought bound unto Damascus walles.	2Tamb	3.2.125	Tamb
Unto the frontier point of Soria:	2Tamb	3.3.2	Therid
if our artillery/Will carie full point blancke unto their wals.	2Tamb	3.3.53	Techel
My Lord deceast, was dearer unto me,	2Tamb	3.4.42	Olymp
Unto the shining bower where Cynthia sits,	2Tamb	3.4.50	Therid
Then welcome Tamburlaine unto thy death.	2Tamb	3.5.52	Callap
our mighty hoste/Shal bring thee bound unto the Generals tent.	2Tamb	3.5.111	Trebiz
And make a bridge unto the battered walles.	2Tamb	5.1.68	Tamb
And thence unto Bythinia, where I tooke/The Turke and his great	2Tamb	5.3.128	Tamb
Unto the rising of this earthly globe,	2Tamb	5.3.147	Tamb
our state/Assure your selves I'le looke--unto my selfe.	Jew	1.1.173	Barab
From little unto more, from more to most:	Jew	1.2.106	1Knght
'Tis necessary that be look'd unto:	Jew	1.2.157	1Knght
Vizadmirall unto the Catholike King.	Jew	2.2.7	Bosco
I'le write unto his Majesty for ayd,	Jew	2.2.40	Bosco
For unto us the Promise doth belong.	Jew	2.3.47	Barab
And tricks belonging unto Brokery,	Jew	2.3.192	Barab
What, is he gone unto my mother?	Jew	2.3.351	Mthias
and then I say they use/To send their Almes unto the Nunneries:	Jew	3.4.77	Barab
early; with intent to goe/Unto your Friery, because you staid.	Jew	4.1.192	Barab
I'le write unto him, we'le have mony strait.	Jew	4.2.69	P Ithimr
no childe, and unto whom/Should I leave all but unto Ithimore?	Jew	4.3.44	Barab
no childe, and unto whom/Should I leave all but unto Ithimore?	Jew	4.3.45	Barab
And unto your good mistris as unknowne.	Jew	4.3.48	Barab
This shall with me unto the Governor.	Jew	4.4.25	Pilia
your sonne and Mathias were both contracted unto Abigall; [he]	Jew	5.1.29	P Ithimr

UNTO (cont.)

Now whilst you give assault unto the wals,	Jew	5.1.90	Barab
Malta's Governor, I bring/A message unto mighty Calymath;	Jew	5.3.14	Msngr
The love thou bear'st unto the house of Guise:	P 69	2.12	Guise
Then pray unto our Ladye, kisse this crosse.	P 302	5.29	Gonzag
Unto mount Faucon will we dragge his coarse:	P 319	5.46	Anjoy
O let me pray unto my God.	P 359	6.14	Seroun
[Sorbonests] <thorbonest>/Attribute as much unto their workes,	P 412	7.52	Ramus
Mountsorrell unto Roan, and spare not one/That you suspect of	P 446	7.86	Guise
That I may write unto my dearest Lord.	P 659	13.3	Duchss
the Duke of Joyeux/Hath made great sute unto the King therfore.	P 734	14.37	1Msngr
Ile secretly convay me unto Bloyse,	P 895	17.90	King
To shew your love unto the King of France:	P 904	18.5	Bartus
grace the Duke of Guise doth crave/Accesse unto your highnes.	P 960	19.30	Eprnon
of Loraine by the Kings consent is lately strangled unto death.	P1124	21.18	P Frier
the President of Paris, that craves accesse unto your grace.	P1157	22.19	P 1Msngr
Yet dare you brave the king unto his face.	Edw	1.1.116	Kent
For heele complaine unto the sea of Rome.	Edw	1.1.190	Kent
Let him complaine unto the sea of hell,	Edw	1.1.191	Gavstn
Unto the forrest gentle Mortimer,	Edw	1.2.47	Queene
Madam, returne unto the court againe:	Edw	1.2.56	Mortmr
Aspir'st unto the guidance of the sunne.	Edw	1.4.17	Warwck
Speake not unto her, let her droope and pine.	Edw	1.4.162	Edward
To sue unto you all for his repeale:	Edw	1.4.201	Queene
Be thou my advocate unto these peeres.	Edw	1.4.212	Queene
My heart is as an anvill unto sorrow,	Edw	1.4.312	Edward
Unto our cosin, the earle of Glosters heire.	Edw	1.4.379	Edward
Having read unto her since she was a childe.	Edw	2.1.30	Baldck
He wils me to repaire unto the court,	Edw	2.1.67	Neece
And gets unto the highest bough of all,	Edw	2.2.19	Mortmr
Unto the proudest peere of Britanie:	Edw	2.2.42	Edward
Weele haile him by the eares unto the block.	Edw	2.2.91	Lncstr
As never subject did unto his King.	Edw	2.2.129	Mortmr
Unto the walles of Yorke the Scots made rode,	Edw	2.2.166	Lncstr
No greater titles happen unto me,	Edw	2.2.254	Spencr
neece, the onely heire/Unto the Earle of Gloster late deceased.	Edw	2.2.259	Edward
Hees gone by water unto Scarborough,	Edw	2.4.37	Queene
For favors done in him, unto us all.	Edw	3.1.42	SpncrP
That I would undertake to carrie him/Unto your highnes, and to	Edw	3.1.100	Arundl
For being delivered unto Penbrookes men,	Edw	3.1.116	Arundl
in a trenche/Strake off his head, and marcht unto the campe.	Edw	3.1.120	Arundl
Desires accesse unto your majestie.	Edw	3.1.149	Spencr
But hath your grace got shipping unto Fraunce?	Edw	4.1.17	Mortmr
Of love and care unto his royall person,	Edw	4.6.25	Queene
Reduce we all our lessons unto this,	Edw	4.7.110	Baldck
a letter presently/Unto the Lord of Bartley from our selfe,	Edw	5.2.48	Mortmr
If he have such accesse unto the prince,	Edw	5.2.77	Mortmr
Why speake you not unto my lord the king?	Edw	5.6.38	1Lord
Bring him unto a hurdle, drag him foorth,	Edw	5.6.52	King
Then sue for life unto a paltrie boye.	Edw	5.6.57	Mortmr
Sweete father heere, unto thy murdered ghost,	Edw	5.6.99	King
Leapes from th'Antarticke world unto the skie,	F 231	1.3.3	Faust
O they are meanes to bring thee unto heaven.	F 406	2.1.18	GdAngl
If unto [God] <heaven>, hee'le throw me <thee> downe to hell.	F 467	2.1.79	Faust
grant unto them that foure and twentie yeares being expired,	F 495	2.1.107	P Faust
Even from the Moone unto the Emperiall Orbe,	F 590	2.2.39	Mephst
That sight will be as pleasant to <pleasing unto> me, as	F 657	2.2.106	P Faust
Lord Raymond, I drink unto your grace.	F1053	3.2.73	Pope
Purgatory, and now is come unto your holinesse for his pardon.	F1060	3.2.80	P Archbp
flie amaine/Unto my Faustus to the great Turkes Court.	F1137	3.3.50	Mephst
Shall adde more excellence unto thine Art,	F1208	4.1.54	Emper
Come souldiers, follow me unto the grove,	F1348	4.2.24	Fredrk
This Traytor flies unto some steepie rocke,	F1413	4.2.89	Faust
Go bid the Hostler deliver him unto you, and remember what I	F1474	4.4.18	P Faust
kind I will make knowne unto you what my heart desires to have,	F1571	4.6.14	P Lady
Majesty, we should thinke our selves much beholding unto you.	F1687	5.1.14	P 1Schol
That I may <might> have unto my paramour,	F1761	5.1.88	Faust
[Hence hel, for hence I flie unto my God].	F1796	5.1.123A	OldMan
you <yee> heare, come not unto me, for nothing can rescue me.	F1874	5.2.78	P Faust
from me, and I be chang'd/[Unto] <Into> some brutish beast.	F1968	5.2.172	Faust
and binde your selfe presently unto me for seaven yeeres, or	F App	p.229 24	P Wagner
Dispaire doth drive distrust unto my thoughts,	F App	p.240 123	Faust
To guide thy steps unto the way of life,	F App	p.243 35	OldMan
Was stretcht unto the fields of hinds unknowne;	Lucan, First Booke		171
As soone as Caesar got unto the banke/And bounds of Italy;	Lucan, First Booke		225
Straight summon'd he his severall companies/Unto the standard:	Lucan, First Booke		298
Philosophers looke you, for unto me/Thou cause, what ere thou be	Lucan, First Booke		418
And as a pray unto blinde anger given,	Ovid's Elegies		1.7.44
too dearely wunne/That unto death did presse the holy Nunne.	Ovid's Elegies		1.10.50
lookes to my verse/Which golden love doth unto me rehearse.	Ovid's Elegies		2.1.38
Which do perchance old age unto them give.	Ovid's Elegies		2.6.28
Let Nereus bend the waves unto this shore,	Ovid's Elegies		2.11.39
Adde deeds unto thy promises at last.	Ovid's Elegies		2.16.48
Penelope, though no watch look'd unto her,	Ovid's Elegies		3.4.23
And Crusa unto Zanthus first affide,	Ovid's Elegies		3.5.31
Had they beene cut, and unto Colchos borne,	Hero and Leander		1.56
He kneel'd, but unto her devoutly praid;	Hero and Leander		1.177
And Jupiter unto his place restor'd.	Hero and Leander		1.464
Therefore unto him hastily she goes,	Hero and Leander		2.45
Mov'd by Loves force, unto ech other lep?	Hero and Leander		2.58
Therefore unto his bodie, hirs he clung,	Hero and Leander		2.65
And thence unto Abydus sooner blowne,	Hero and Leander		2.112
Unto her was he led, or rather drawne,	Hero and Leander		2.241

UNTO (cont.)			
That Meremaid-like unto the floore she slid,	Hero and Leander		2.315
UNTOLD			
[I leave untold, your eyes shall see performd].	F1154	3.3.67A	3Chor
UNTOUCHT			
And yet I live untoucht by Mahomet:	2Tamb	5.1.182	Tamb
Which long time lie untoucht, will harshly jarre.	Hero and Leander		1.230
UNTROD			
of armes was heard, in untrod woods/Shrill voices schright,	Lucan, First Booke		567
UNTRUE			
That rumor is untrue, for loving thee,	Edw	5.6.74	Queene
UNTUN'D			
Like untun'd golden strings all women are,	Hero and Leander		1.229
UNVALLUED			
whatsoever you esteeme/Of this successe, and losse unvallued,	1Tamb	1.2.45	Tamb
UNWEAPONED			
Such force is farre from our unweaponed thoughts,	Dido	1.2.14	Illion
UNWEDDED			
Sometimes like women or unwedded Maides,	F 154	1.1.126	Valdes
UNWILLING			
And with unwilling souldiers faintly arm'd,	1Tamb	2.1.66	Cosroe
Is it unwilling I should write this byll?	F 454	2.1.66	Faust
This hand (albeit unwilling) should performe it;	Lucan, First Booke		379
Unwilling Lovers, love doth more torment,	Ovid's Elegies		1.2.17
UNWISE			
O how unwise was I to say him nay!	Dido	4.5.37	Nurse
I am not as I was before, unwise.	Ovid's Elegies		3.10.32
UNWORTHIE			
Unworthie are they of a Queenes reward:	Dido	4.4.12	Dido
UNWORTHY			
Unworthy to imbrace or touch the ground,	1Tamb	4.2.20	Tamb
Unworthy king, that by thy crueltie,	1Tamb	4.2.56	Zabina
Stand up, ye base unworthy souldiers,	2Tamb	4.1.99	Tamb
Although unworthy of that Sister-hood.	Jew	3.3.69	Abigal
Unworthy porter, bound in chaines full sore,	Ovid's Elegies		1.6.1
Aye me rare gifts unworthy such a happe.	Ovid's Elegies		1.14.54
UNWORTHYNESSE			
Fearing his love through my unworthynesse.	1Tamb	3.2.65	Zenoc
UP (See also UPPE)			
And all Aeolia to be up in armes:	Dido	1.1.63	Venus
Pluck up your hearts, since fate still rests our friend,	Dido	1.1.149	Aeneas
Thinking the sea had swallowed up thy ships,	Dido	2.1.68	Illion
Looke up and speake.	Dido	2.1.120	Dido
Gave up their voyces to dislodge the Campe,	Dido	2.1.134	Aeneas
and both his eyes/Turnd up to heaven as one resolv'd to dye,	Dido	2.1.152	Aeneas
Headles carkasses piled up in heapes,	Dido	2.1.194	Aeneas
He with his faulchions poynt raisde up at once,	Dido	2.1.229	Aeneas
This butcher whil'st his hands were yet held up,	Dido	2.1.241	Aeneas
Whereat he lifted up his bedred lims,	Dido	2.1.250	Aeneas
Whom I tooke up to beare unto our ships:	Dido	2.1.277	Aeneas
altar, where Ile offer up/As many kisses as the Sea hath sands,	Dido	3.1.87	Dido
Whose short conclusion will seale up their hearts,	Dido	3.2.94	Juno
And dead to honour that hath brought me up.	Dido	3.3.45	Aeneas
Where straying in our borders up and downe,	Dido	4.2.12	Iarbus
Yeelds up her beautie to a strangers bed,	Dido	4.2.17	Iarbus
The sailes were hoysing up, and he abourd.	Dido	4.4.15	Anna
As oft as he attempts to hoyst up saile:	Dido	4.4.103	Dido
But dares to heape up sorrowe to my heart:	Dido	4.4.152	Dido
Was it not you that hoysed up these sailes?	Dido	4.4.153	Dido
Flote up and downe where ere the billowes drive?	Dido	5.1.58	Aeneas
Hast thou forgot how many neighbour kings/Were up in armes, for	Dido	5.1.142	Dido
I traytor, and the waves shall cast thee up,	Dido	5.1.174	Dido
And spying me, hoyst up the sailes amaine:	Dido	5.1.227	Anna
Then gan he wagge his hand, which yet held up,	Dido	5.1.229	Anna
See see, the billowes heave him up to heaven,	Dido	5.1.252	Dido
By plowing up his Countries with the Sword:	Dido	5.1.308	Dido
That holds us up, and foiles our neighbour foes.	1Tamb	1.1.61	Mycet
Sound up the trumpets then, God save the King.	1Tamb	1.1.188	Ortyg
with Russian stems/Plow up huge furrowes in the Caspian sea,	1Tamb	1.2.195	Tamb
Therefore cheere up your mindes, prepare to fight,	1Tamb	2.2.29	Meandr
And while the base borne Tartars take it up,	1Tamb	2.2.65	Meandr
Strike up the Drum and martch corragiously,	1Tamb	2.2.72	Meandr
To cast up hils against the face of heaven:	1Tamb	2.6.3	Cosroe
Then strike up Drum, and all the Starres that make/The	1Tamb	2.6.36	Cosroe
Two thousand horse shall forrage up and downe,	1Tamb	3.1.61	Bajzth
Shall swallow up these base borne Perseans.	1Tamb	3.3.95	Bajzth
The pillers that have bolstered up those tearmes,	1Tamb	3.3.229	Tamb
every fixed starre/To sucke up poison from the moorish Fens,	1Tamb	4.2.6	Bajzth
Will send up fire to your turning Spheares,	1Tamb	4.2.39	Tamb
And in your hands bring hellish poison up,	1Tamb	4.4.19	Bajzth
are you so daintily brought up, you cannot eat your owne flesh?	1Tamb	4.4.37	P Tamb
Take it up Villaine, and eat it, or I will make thee slice the	1Tamb	4.4.43	P Tamb
Yet musicke woulde doe well to cheare up Zenocrate:	1Tamb	4.4.62	P Tamb
on Damascus wals/Have hoisted up their slaughtered carcases.	1Tamb	5.1.131	Techel
Breake up the earth, and with their firebrands,	1Tamb	5.1.219	Bajzth
Why live we Bajazeth, and build up neasts,	1Tamb	5.1.249	Zabina
Brought up and propped by the hand of fame,	1Tamb	5.1.265	Bajzth
On horsmens Lances to be hoisted up,	1Tamb	5.1.328	Zenoc
Earth cast up fountaines from thy entralles,	1Tamb	5.1.347	Zenoc
To spread my fame through hell and up to heaven:	1Tamb	5.1.467	Tamb
Mount up your royall places of estate,	1Tamb	5.1.525	Tamb
Hang up your weapons on Alcides poste,	1Tamb	5.1.528	Tamb
Closde in a coffyn mounted up the aire,	2Tamb	1.1.140	Orcan

UP (cont.)

Which when I come aboord will hoist up saile,	2Tamb	1.2.24	Callap
The sailes wrapt up, the mast and tacklings downe,	2Tamb	1.2.59	Callap
Sit up and rest thee like a lovely Queene.	2Tamb	1.3.16	Tamb
place himselfe therin/Must armed wade up to the chin in blood.	2Tamb	1.3.84	Tamb
And sent them marching up to Belgasar,	2Tamb	2.1.19	Fredrk
Up to the pallace of th'imperiall heaven:	2Tamb	2.4.35	Tamb
And here will I set up her stature <statue>/And martch about it	2Tamb	2.4.140	Tamb
sir, for being a king, for Tamburlain came up of nothing.	2Tamb	3.1.74	P Almeda
Forbids the world to build it up againe.	2Tamb	3.2.18	Calyph
Captaine, that thou yeeld up thy hold to us.	2Tamb	3.3.16	Therid
That with his ruine fils up all the trench.	2Tamb	3.3.26	Therid
Cast up the earth towards the castle wall,	2Tamb	3.3.43	Therid
Go too sirha, take your crown, and make up the halfe dozen.	2Tamb	3.5.135	P Tamb
Stand up, ye base unworthy souldiers,	2Tamb	4.1.99	Tamb
Stand up my boyes, and I wil teach ye arms,	2Tamb	4.1.103	Tamb
(wanting moisture and remorsefull blood)/Drie up with anger,	2Tamb	4.1.180	Soria
Offer submission, hang up flags of truce,	2Tamb	5.1.26	1Citzn
Yeeld up the towne, save our wives and children:	2Tamb	5.1.39	2Citzn
Call up the souldiers to defend these wals.	2Tamb	5.1.56	Govnr
Wel, now Ile make it quake, go draw him up,	2Tamb	5.1.107	Tamb
Hang him up in chaines upon the citie walles,	2Tamb	5.1.108	Tamb
Up with him then, his body shalbe scard.	2Tamb	5.1.114	Tamb
Take them, and hang them both up presently.	2Tamb	5.1.132	Tamb
To blow thy Alcaron up to thy throne,	2Tamb	5.1.193	Tamb
Amasde, swim up and downe upon the waves,	2Tamb	5.1.207	Techel
Sit up my sonne, let me see how well/Thou wilt become thy	2Tamb	5.3.183	Tamb
Sit up my boy, and with those silken raines,	2Tamb	5.3.202	Tamb
the Easterne rockes/Without controule can picke his riches up,	Jew	1.1.22	Barab
and the bordering Iles/Are gotten up by Nilus winding bankes:	Jew	1.1.43	Barab
And twenty Waggons to bring up the ware.	Jew	1.1.60	Barab
Oh they were going up to Sicily:	Jew	1.1.98	Barab
but we have scambled up/More wealth by farre then those that	Jew	1.1.122	Barab
Heave up my shoulders when they call me dogge,	Jew	2.3.24	Barab
In Trace; brought up in Arabia.	Jew	2.3.128	P Ithimr
And when he comes, she lockes her selfe up fast;	Jew	2.3.262	Barab
up to the Jewes counting-house where I saw some bags of mony,	Jew	3.1.18	P Pilia
and in the night I clamber'd up with my hooks, and as I was	Jew	3.1.19	P Pilia
Then take them up, and let them be interr'd/Within one sacred	Jew	3.2.29	Govnr
Upon which Altar I will offer up/My daily sacrifice of sighes	Jew	3.2.31	Govnr
And as you profitably take up Armes,	Jew	3.5.32	Govnr
Then is it as it should be, take him up.	Jew	4.1.152	Barab
Was up thus early; with intent to goe/Unto your Friery, because	Jew	4.1.191	Barab
but hee hides and buries it up as Partridges doe their egges,	Jew	4.2.58	P Ithimr
Or climbe up to my Counting-house window:	Jew	4.3.34	P Barab
Of that condition I wil drink it up; here's to thee.	Jew	4.4.4	P Ithimr
here's to thee with a--pox on this drunken hick-up.	Jew	4.4.33	P Ithimr
I'le reare up Malta now remedilesse.	Jew	5.2.73	Barab
Blowne up, and all thy souldiers massacred.	Jew	5.5.107	Govnr
O holde me up, my sight begins to faile,	P 548	11.13	Charls
Ile muster up an army secretly,	P 572	11.37	Navrre
his market, and set up your standing where you should not:	P 809	17.4	P Souldr
Pleshe, goe muster up our men with speed,	P 916	18.17	Navrre
That hatcheth up such bloudy practises.	P1205	22.67	King
Come Lords, take up the body of the King,	P1245	22.107	Navrre
displeases him | And fill up his rome that he shold occupie.	Paris	ms 4,p390	P Souldr
Rakt up in embers of their povertie,	Edw	1.1.21	Gavstn
For Mortimer will hang his armor up.	Edw	1.1.89	Mortmr
And at the court gate hang the pessant up,	Edw	1.2.30	Mortmr
What neede I, God himselfe is up in armes,	Edw	1.2.40	ArchBp
Unlesse the sea cast up his shipwrack body.	Edw	1.4.205	Lncstr
Tis treason to be up against the king.	Edw	1.4.281	Mortmr
And with the noise turnes up my giddie braine,	Edw	1.4.314	Edward
And by the barke a canker creepes me up,	Edw	2.2.18	Mortmr
No sooner is it up, but thers a foule,	Edw	2.2.26	Lncstr
When she was lockt up in a brasen tower,	Edw	2.2.54	Edward
Their wives and children slaine, run up and downe,	Edw	2.2.180	Lncstr
My lord, tis thought, the Earles are up in armes.	Edw	2.2.225	Queene
Upon these Barons, harten up your men,	Edw	3.1.124	Spencr
The Barons up in armes, by me salute/Your highnes, with long	Edw	3.1.156	Herald
with my sword/On those proud rebels that are up in armes,	Edw	3.1.187	Edward
in England/Would cast up cappes, and clap their hands for joy,	Edw	4.2.55	Mortmr
And all the land I know is up in armes,	Edw	4.7.31	Spencr
Never againe lift up this drooping head,	Edw	4.7.42	Edward
O never more lift up this dying hart!	Edw	4.7.43	Edward
Looke up my lord.	Edw	4.7.44	Spencr
Here man, rip up this panting brest of mine,	Edw	4.7.66	Edward
Make for a new life man, throw up thy eyes,	Edw	4.7.107	Baldck
being strucke/Runnes to an herbe that closeth up the wounds,	Edw	5.1.10	Edward
lowly earth/Should drinke his bloud, mounts up into the ayre:	Edw	5.1.14	Edward
Full often am I sowring up to heaven,	Edw	5.1.21	Edward
And joyntly both yeeld up their wished right.	Edw	5.1.63	Edward
Being in a vault up to the knees in water,	Edw	5.5.2	Matrvs
Much more a king brought up so tenderlie.	Edw	5.5.6	Matrvs
Hang him I say, and set his quarters up,	Edw	5.6.53	King
And seeing there was no place to mount up higher,	Edw	5.6.62	Mortmr
I offer up this wicked traitors head,	Edw	5.6.100	King
Whereas his kinsmen chiefly brought him up;	F 14	Prol.14	1Chor
Be a Phisitian Faustus, heape up gold,	F 42	1.1.14	Faust
Are not thy bils hung up as monuments,	F 48	1.1.20	Faust
Say he surrenders up to him his soule,	F 318	1.3.90	Faust
for I will presently raise up two devils to carry thee away:	F 373	1.4.31	P Wagner
But may I raise such <up> spirits when I please?	F 475	2.1.87	Faust

UP (cont.)
and incantations, that I might raise up spirits when I please]. F 551.2 2.1.165A P Faust
run up and downe the world with these <this> case of Rapiers, F 688 2.2.137 P Wrath
<No, Ile see thee hanged, thou wilt eate up all my victualls>. F 702 (HC264)A P Faust
thought you did not sneake up and downe after her for nothing. F 742 2.3.21 P Dick
Did mount him up <himselfe> to scale Olimpus top. F 757 2.3.36 2Chor
Then up to Naples rich Campania, F 787 3.1.9 Faust
I have taken up his holinesse privy chamber for our use>. F 806 (HC265)A P Mephst
Looke up Benvolio, tis the Emperour calls. F1286 4.1.132 Saxony
zounds hee'l raise up a kennell of Divels I thinke anon: F1305 4.1.151 P Benvol
late by horse flesh, and this bargaine will set me up againe. F1465 4.4.9 P HrsCsr
looke up into th'hall there ho. F1519 4.5.15 P Hostss
he never left eating, till he had eate up all my loade of hay. F1531 4.5.27 P Carter
Do you remember sir, how you cosened me and eat up my load of-- F1659 4.6.102 P Carter
Yet Faustus looke up to heaven, and remember [Gods] mercy is F1835 5.2.39 P 2Schol
I would lift up my hands, but see they hold 'em <them>, they F1852 5.2.56 P Faust
Damb'd up thy passage; when thou took'st the booke, F1887 5.2.91 Mephst
O I'le leape up to [my God] <heaven>: who puls me downe? F1938 5.2.142 Faust
Now draw up Faustus like a foggy mist, F1952 5.2.156 Faust
serve you, would you teach me to raise up Banios and Belcheos? F App p.230 57 P Clown
keep out, or else you are blowne up, you are dismembred Rafe, F App p.233 10 P Robin
When all the woods about stand bolt up-right, Lucan, First Booke 143
Such humors stirde them up; but this warrs seed, Lucan, First Booke 159
spectacle/Stroake Caesars hart with feare, his hayre stoode up, Lucan, First Booke 195
having whiskt/His taile athwart his backe, and crest heav'd up, Lucan, First Booke 211
And snatcht armes neer their houshold gods hung up/Such as Lucan, First Booke 242
me,/Because at his commaund I wound not up/My conquering Eagles? Lucan, First Booke 339
And with their hands held up, all joyntly cryde/They'll follow Lucan, First Booke 388
And rustling swing up as the wind fets breath. Lucan, First Booke 392
And suddaine rampire raisde of turfe snatcht up/Would make them Lucan, First Booke 515
Next, an inferiour troupe, in tuckt up vestures, Lucan, First Booke 595
Who slumbring, they rise up in swelling armes. Ovid's Elegies 1.9.26
Both whom thou raisest up to toyle anew. Ovid's Elegies 1.13.22
Made two nights one to finish up his pleasure. Ovid's Elegies 1.13.46
Cheere up thy selfe, thy losse thou maiest repaire, Ovid's Elegies 1.14.55
how Olimpus toppe/High Ossa bore, mount Pelion up to proppe. Ovid's Elegies 2.1.14
Foldes up her armes, and makes low curtesie. Ovid's Elegies 2.4.30
But may soft love rowse up my drowsie eies, Ovid's Elegies 2.10.19
Nor she her selfe but first trim'd up discernes. Ovid's Elegies 2.17.10
Gather them up, or lift them loe will I. Ovid's Elegies 3.2.26
And each give signes by casting up his cloake. Ovid's Elegies 3.2.74
A free-borne wench, no right 'tis up to locke: Ovid's Elegies 3.4.33
Tis said the slippery streame held up her brest, Ovid's Elegies 3.5.81
Yea, and she soothde me up, and calde me sir <sire>, Ovid's Elegies 3.6.11
Rather Ile hoist up saile, and use the winde, Ovid's Elegies 3.10.51
When you are up and drest, be sage and grave, Ovid's Elegies 3.13.19
Like one start up your haire tost and displast, Ovid's Elegies 3.13.33
From Latmus mount up to the glomie skie, Hero and Leander 1.109
He started up, she blusht as one asham'd; Hero and Leander 1.181
Heav'd up her head, and halfe the world upon, Hero and Leander 1.190
Who builds a pallace and rams up the gate, Hero and Leander 1.239
In heaping up a masse of drossie pelfe, Hero and Leander 1.244
Which th'earth from ougly Chaos den up-wayd: Hero and Leander 1.450
She offers up her selfe a sacrifice, Hero and Leander 2.48
He heav'd him up, and looking on his face, Hero and Leander 2.171
Which mounted up, intending to have kist him, Hero and Leander 2.173
Leander being up, began to swim, Hero and Leander 2.175
And up againe, and close beside him swim, Hero and Leander 2.190
Gote-footed Satyrs, and up-staring <upstarting> Fawnes, Hero and Leander 2.200

UPE
the markett and sett upe your standinge where you shold not: Paris ms 6,p390 P Souldr

UPHEAV'D
And from the mid foord his hoarse voice upheav'd, Ovid's Elegies 3.5.52

UPHOLD
And thought his name sufficient to uphold him, Lucan, First Booke 136
Did she uphold to Venus, and againe, Hero and Leander 1.367

UPLANDISH
That in the vast uplandish countrie dwelt, Hero and Leander 1.80

UPON (See also UPPON)
My Juno ware upon her marriage day, Dido 1.1.43 Jupitr
Poore Troy must now be sackt upon the Sea, Dido 1.1.64 Venus
And will not let us lodge upon the sands: Dido 1.2.35 Serg
I cannot choose but fall upon my knees, Dido 2.1.11 Achat
And scarcely doe agree upon one poynt: Dido 2.1.109 Dido
With sacrificing wreathes upon his head, Dido 2.1.148 Aeneas
for that one Laocoon/Breaking a speare upon his hollow breast, Dido 2.1.165 Aeneas
Neoptolemus/Setting his speare upon the ground, leapt forth, Dido 2.1.184 Aeneas
Treading upon his breast, strooke off his hands. Dido 2.1.242 Aeneas
Come let us thinke upon some pleasing sport, Dido 2.1.302 Dido
That she may dote upon Aeneas love: Dido 2.1.327 Venus
When first you set your foote upon the shoare, Dido 3.3.53 Achat
To waite upon him as their soveraigne Lord. Dido 4.4.69 Dido
And let rich Carthage fleete upon the seas, Dido 4.4.134 Dido
Which I bestowd upon his followers: Dido 4.4.162 Dido
Whose wealthie streames may waite upon her towers, Dido 5.1.9 Aeneas
Yet thinke upon Ascanius prophesie, Dido 5.1.38 Hermes
Wast thou not wrackt upon this Libian shoare, Dido 5.1.161 Dido
And weepe upon your liveles carcases, Dido 5.1.177 Dido
And looke upon him with a Mermaides eye, Dido 5.1.201 Dido
And ride upon his backe unto my love: Dido 5.1.250 Dido
dye to expiate/The griefe that tires upon thine inward soule. Dido 5.1.317 Iarbus
And shining stones upon their loftie Crestes: 1Tamb 1.1.145 Ceneus
With milke-white Hartes upon an Ivorie sled, 1Tamb 1.2.98 Tamb

UPON (cont.)

His fierie eies are fixt upon the earth,	1Tamb	1.2.158	Therid
Both we wil walke upon the lofty clifts,	1Tamb	1.2.193	Tamb
In happy hower we have set the Crowne/Upon your kingly head,	1Tamb	2.1.51	Ortyg
of my company/Scowting abroad upon these champion plaines,	1Tamb	2.2.40	Spy
Fortune her selfe dooth sit upon our Crests.	1Tamb	2.2.73	Meandr
I long to sit upon my brothers throne.	1Tamb	2.5.47	Cosroe
We will not steale upon him cowardly,	1Tamb	2.5.102	Tamb
Where flames shall ever feed upon his soule.	1Tamb	2.6.8	Cosroe
And fearefull vengeance light upon you both.	1Tamb	2.7.52	Cosroe
For neither rain can fall upon the earth,	1Tamb	3.1.51	Moroc
Upon his browes was pourtraid ugly death,	1Tamb	3.2.72	Agidas
Attend upon the person of your Lord,	1Tamb	3.3.62	Bajzth
Sit here upon this royal chaire of state,	1Tamb	3.3.112	Bajzth
That leave no ground for thee to martch upon.	1Tamb	3.3.147	Bajzth
marshal us the way/We use to march upon the slaughtered foe:	1Tamb	3.3.149	Tamb
Resting her selfe upon my milk-white Tent:	1Tamb	3.3.161	Tamb
Upon their pransing Steeds, disdainfully/With wanton paces	1Tamb	4.1.22	2Msngr
feathered bird/That spreads her wings upon the citie wals,	1Tamb	4.2.106	Tamb
I long to breake my speare upon his crest,	1Tamb	4.3.46	Arabia
Reflexing hewes of blood upon their heads,	1Tamb	4.4.2	Tamb
Tamburlane) as I could willingly feed upon thy blood-raw hart.	1Tamb	4.4.12	P Bajzth
That fed upon the substance of his child.	1Tamb	4.4.25	Zabina
To turne them al upon their proper heades.	1Tamb	4.4.31	Tamb
Whiles only danger beat upon our walles,	1Tamb	5.1.30	1Virgn
Sharpe forked arrowes light upon thy horse:	1Tamb	5.1.217	Bajzth
Enforce thee run upon the banefull pikes.	1Tamb	5.1.220	Bajzth
Sharp hunger bites upon and gripes the root,	1Tamb	5.1.273	Bajzth
in peeces, give me the sworde with a ball of wildefire upon it.	1Tamb	5.1.312	P Zabina
Gazing upon the beautie of their lookes:	1Tamb	5.1.334	Zenoc
Then let us set the crowne upon her head,	1Tamb	5.1.501	Therid
When he arrived last upon our stage,	2Tamb	Prol.2	Prolog
And made it dance upon the Continent:	2Tamb	1.1.88	Orcan
fethered steele/So thick upon the blink-ei'd Burghers heads,	2Tamb	1.1.93	Orcan
Ocean to the Traveiler/That restes upon the snowy Appenines:	2Tamb	1.1.111	Sgsmnd
if Sigismond/Speake as a friend, and stand not upon tearmes,	2Tamb	1.1.123	Orcan
if any Christian King/Encroche upon the confines of thy realme,	2Tamb	1.1.147	Orcan
Then shalt thou see a hundred kings and more/Upon their knees,	2Tamb	1.2.29	Callap
And worke revenge upon these Infidels:	2Tamb	2.1.13	Fredrk
And issue sodainly upon the rest:	2Tamb	2.1.23	Fredrk
of the clowdes/And fall as thick as haile upon our heads,	2Tamb	2.2.15	Gazell
Hel and confusion light upon their heads,	2Tamb	2.2.33	Gazell
Be now reveng'd upon this Traitors soule,	2Tamb	2.2.58	Orcan
And feeds upon the banefull tree of hell,	2Tamb	2.3.19	Orcan
keepe his trunke/Amidst these plaines, for Foules to pray upon.	2Tamb	2.3.39	Orcan
ceaslesse lamps/That gently look'd upon this loathsome earth,	2Tamb	2.4.19	Tamb
Onely to gaze upon Zenocrate.	2Tamb	3.2.33	Tamb
Thou shalt be set upon my royall tent.	2Tamb	3.2.37	Tamb
Upon the heads of all our enemies.	2Tamb	3.2.42	Tamb
Ile have you learne to sleepe upon the ground,	2Tamb	3.2.55	Tamb
That we may tread upon his captive necke,	2Tamb	3.2.157	Tamb
And enter in, to seaze upon the gold:	2Tamb	3.3.8	Techel
Shal play upon the bulwarks of thy hold/Volleies of ordinance	2Tamb	3.3.24	Therid
That humbly craves upon her knees to stay,	2Tamb	3.4.70	Olymp
That feeds upon her sonnes and husbands flesh.	2Tamb	3.4.72	Olymp
And in a stable lie upon the planks.	2Tamb	3.5.107	Tamb
See father, how Almeda the Jaylor lookes upon us.	2Tamb	3.5.116	Celeb
like armed men/Are seene to march upon the towers of heaven,	2Tamb	4.1.202	Tamb
Upon the marble turrets of my Court/Sit like to Venus in her	2Tamb	4.2.41	Therid
souldiers now that fought/So Lion-like upon Asphaltis plaines?	2Tamb	4.3.68	Tamb
To exercise upon such guiltlesse Dames,	2Tamb	4.3.79	Orcan
Upon the lofty and celestiall mount,	2Tamb	4.3.120	Tamb
Upon the ruines of this conquered towne.	2Tamb	5.1.85	Tamb
Hang him up in chaines upon the citie walles,	2Tamb	5.1.108	Tamb
Amasde, swim up and downe upon the waves,	2Tamb	5.1.207	Techel
And pull proud Tamburlaine upon his knees,	2Tamb	5.2.40	Amasia
Your sacred vertues pour'd upon his throne,	2Tamb	5.3.11	Therid
To see thy foot-stoole set upon thy head,	2Tamb	5.3.29	Usumc
your absence in the field, offers to set upon us presently.	2Tamb	5.3.104	P 3Msngr
May be upon himselfe reverberate.	2Tamb	5.3.223	Techel
To seize upon the Towne: I, that he seekes.	Jew	1.1.185	Barab
If thou rely upon thy righteousnesse,	Jew	1.2.121	Govnr
my Lord, we have seiz'd upon the goods/And wares of Barabas,	Jew	1.2.132	Offcrs
and all mens hatred/Inflict upon them, thou great Primus Motor.	Jew	1.2.164	Barab
And here upon my knees, striking the earth,	Jew	1.2.165	Barab
Why weepe you not to thinke upon my wrongs?	Jew	1.2.172	Barab
And yet have kept enough to live upon;	Jew	1.2.190	Barab
For they have seiz'd upon thy house and wares.	Jew	1.2.251	Abigal
And thinke upon the Jewels and the gold,	Jew	1.2.349	Barab
For late upon the coast of Corsica,	Jew	2.2.10	Bosco
were ne're thought upon/Till Titus and Vespasian conquer'd us)	Jew	2.3.9	Barab
Hoping to see them starve upon a stall,	Jew	2.3.26	Barab
And be reveng'd upon the--Governor.	Jew	2.3.143	Barab
studied Physicke, and began/To practise first upon the Italian;	Jew	2.3.182	Barab
Pinning upon his breast a long great Scrowle/How I with	Jew	2.3.197	Barab
But goe you in, I'le thinke upon the account:	Jew	2.3.241	Barab
stands in feare/Of that which you, I thinke, ne're dreame upon,	Jew	2.3.283	Barab
But thou must dote upon a Christian?	Jew	2.3.360	Barab
That we may venge their blood upon their heads.	Jew	3.2.28	Mater
Upon which Altar I will offer up/My daily sacrifice of sighes	Jew	3.2.31	Govnr
Say, knave, why rail'st upon my father thus?	Jew	3.3.11	Abigal
But thou wert set upon extreme revenge,	Jew	3.3.42	Abigal
And couldst not venge it, but upon his sonne,	Jew	3.3.44	Abigal

UPON (cont.)

me in the pot of Rice/That for our supper stands upon the fire.	Jew	3.4.50	Barab
Nor shall the Heathens live upon our spoyle:	Jew	3.5.12	Govnr
so, let him leane upon his staffe; excellent, he stands as if he	Jew	4.1.154	P Ithimr
Fie upon 'em, master, will you turne Christian, when holy	Jew	4.1.193	P Ithimr
Upon mine owne free-hold within fortie foot of the gallowes,	Jew	4.2.16	P Pilia
and now would I were gone, I am not worthy to looke upon her.	Jew	4.2.36	P Ithimr
and look'd upon him thus; told him he were best to send it;	Jew	4.2.105	P Pilia
So, now I am reveng'd upon 'em all.	Jew	4.4.42	Barab
Jew, he lives upon pickled Grashoppers, and sauc'd Mushrumbs.	Jew	4.4.61	P Ithimr
Take my goods too, and seize upon my lands:	Jew	5.1.66	Barab
And by that priviledge to worke upon,	P 121	2.64	Guise
Upon the cursed breakers of our peace.	P 270	4.68	Charls
Goe place some men upon the bridge,	P 421	7.61	Dumain
all doubts, be rulde by me, lets hang him heere upon this tree.	P 492	9.11	P 2Atndt
For to revenge their deaths upon us all.	P 518	9.37	Cardnl
A griping paine hath ceasde upon my heart:	P 537	11.2	Charls
Upon the hauty mountains of my brest:	P 718	14.21	Navrre
To make his glory great upon the earth.	P 790	16.4	Navrre
you will take upon you to be his, and tyll the ground that he	P 811	17.6	P Souldr
What should I doe but stand upon my guarde?	P 839	17.34	Guise
Ah Sextus, be reveng'd upon the King,	P1010	19.80	Guise
But sorrow seaze upon my toyling soule,	P1089	19.159	QnMoth
To revenge our deaths upon that cursed King,	P1100	20.10	Cardnl
Upon whose heart may all the furies gripe,	P1101	20.11	Cardnl
Sweet Duke of Guise our prop to leane upon,	P1110	21.4	Dumain
Sancte [Jacobe] <Jacobus>, now have mercye upon me.	P1172	22.34	Frier
ser where he is your landlorde you take upon you to be his |	Paris	ms10,p390	P Souldr
yett comminge upon you once unawares he frayde you out againe.	Paris	ms12,p390	P Souldr
And like Leander gaspt upon the sande,	Edw	1.1.8	Gavstn
The king, upon whose bosome let me die,	Edw	1.1.14	Gavstn
Preach upon poles for trespasse of their tongues.	Edw	1.1.118	Kent
No, spare his life, but seaze upon his goods,	Edw	1.1.193	Edward
What? will they tyrannize upon the Church?	Edw	1.2.3	Lncstr
Nay more, the guarde upon his lordship waites:	Edw	1.2.21	Lncstr
Then laide they violent hands upon him, next/Himselfe	Edw	1.2.36	ArchBp
But dotes upon the love of Gaveston.	Edw	1.2.50	Queene
Nay, then lay violent hands upon your king,	Edw	1.4.35	Edward
This Ile shall fleete upon the Ocean,	Edw	1.4.49	Edward
Because my lords, it was not thought upon:	Edw	1.4.273	Mortmr
Harke how he harpes upon his minion.	Edw	1.4.311	Queene
Which beates upon it like the Cyclops hammers,	Edw	1.4.313	Edward
Thy service Spencer shalbe thought upon.	Edw	2.1.80	Neece
I feare me he is wrackt upon the sea.	Edw	2.2.2	Edward
You have matters of more waight to thinke upon,	Edw	2.2.8	Mortmr
But if I live, ile tread upon their heads,	Edw	2.2.96	Edward
For my sake let him waite upon your grace,	Edw	2.2.250	Gavstn
Then Spencer waite upon me, for his sake/Ile grace thee with a	Edw	2.2.252	Edward
Will I advaunce upon this castell walles,	Edw	2.3.24	Mortmr
He turnes away, and smiles upon his minion.	Edw	2.4.29	Queene
Upon him souldiers, take away his weapons.	Edw	2.5.8	Warwck
Upon my weapons point here shouldst thou fall,	Edw	2.5.13	Mortmr
That here severelie we will execute/Upon thy person:	Edw	2.5.24	Warwck
I will upon mine honor undertake/To carrie him, and bring him	Edw	2.5.79	Penbrk
Upon mine oath I will returne him back.	Edw	2.5.88	Penbrk
And said, upon the honour of my name,	Edw	3.1.98	Arundl
Upon these Barons, harten up your men,	Edw	3.1.124	Spencr
upon them lords,/This day I shall powre vengeance with my sword	Edw	3.1.185	Edward
Upon my life, those be the men ye seeke.	Edw	4.7.46	Mower
That I may gaze upon this glittering crowne,	Edw	5.1.60	Edward
But that I feele the crowne upon my head,	Edw	5.1.82	Edward
That if he slip will seaze upon us both,	Edw	5.2.8	Mortmr
That waites upon my poore distressed soule,	Edw	5.3.38	Edward
O levell all your lookes upon these daring men,	Edw	5.3.39	Edward
Lay hands upon the earle for this assault.	Edw	5.3.54	Gurney
They thrust upon me the Protectorship,	Edw	5.4.56	Mortmr
One plaies continually upon a Drum,	Edw	5.5.61	Edward
And vowes to be revengd upon us both,	Edw	5.6.19	Queene
He surfets upon cursed Necromancie:	F 25	Prol.25	1Chor
And heape Gods heavy wrath upon thy head.	F 99	1.1.71	GdAngl
should stand upon; therefore acknowledge your errour,	F 203	1.2.10	P Wagner
I charge thee waite upon me whilst I live/To do what ever	F 264	1.3.36	Faust
your right eye be alwaies Diametrally fixt upon my left heele,	F 386	1.4.44	P Wagner
see al plants, hearbes and trees that grow upon the earth].	F 551.9	2.1.172A	P Faust
And <Faustus all> jointly move upon one Axle-tree,	F 592	2.2.41	Mephst
upon the poles of the world, but differ in their motions	F 598	2.2.47	P Mephst
in their motions <motion> upon the poles of the Zodiacke.	F 599	2.2.48	P Mephst
Thinke Faustus upon God, that made the world.	F 625	2.2.74	P Faust
Sometimes, like a Perriwig, I sit upon her Brow:	F 666	2.2.115	P Pride
And mounted then upon a Dragons backe,	F 771	2.3.50	2Chor
Know that this City stands upon seven hils,	F 811	3.1.33	Mephst
Upon the Bridge, call'd Ponte Angelo,	F 817	3.1.39	Mephst
Or clap huge hornes, upon the Cardinals heads:	F 864	3.1.86	Mephst
And walke upon the dreadfull Adders backe,	F 919	3.1.141	Pope
be thou transformed to/A dog, and carry him upon thy backe;	F1131	3.3.44	Mephst
He was upon the devils backe late enough; and if he be so farre	F1190	4.1.36	P Benvol
hornes most strangely fastened/Upon the head of yong Benvolio.	F1278	4.1.124	Emper
A plague upon you, let me sleepe a while.	F1283	4.1.129	Benvol
Tush, Christ did call the Theefe upon the Crosse,	F1482	4.4.26	Faust
horse vanisht away, and I sate straddling upon a bottle of Hay.	F1545	4.5.41	P HrsCsr
I, I, he does not stand much upon that.	F1630	4.6.73	P HrsCsr
No faith, not much upon a woodden leg.	F1631	4.6.74	Faust
To wait upon thy soule; the time is come/Which makes it	F1802	5.2.6	Lucifr

UPON (cont.)
thou, and we will pray, that God may have mercie upon thee. F1876 5.2.80 P 2Schol
Therefore despaire, thinke onely upon hell; F1881 5.2.85 Mephst
Shall waite upon his heavy funerall. F2001 5.3.19 2Schol
and let thy left eye be diametarily fixt upon my right heele, F App p.231 70 P Wagner
goe and make cleane our bootes which lie foule upon our handes, F App p.234 33 P Robin
Upon whose altars thousand soules do lie, F App p.235 36 Mephst
Tush, Christ did call the thiefe upon the Crosse, F App p.240 125 Faust
and I sat upon a bottle of hey, never so neare drowning in my F App p.240 135 P HrsCsr
Or Cynthia nights Queene waights upon the day; Lucan, First Booke 91
or his speare/Sticks in his side) yet runs upon the hunter. Lucan, First Booke 214
his troupes of daring horsemen fought/Upon Mevanias plaine, Lucan, First Booke 470
And bent his sinewy bow upon his knee, Ovid's Elegies 1.1.27
when his limbes he spread/Upon the bed, but on my foote first Ovid's Elegies 1.4.16
griefe appease)/With thy sharpe nayles upon my face to seaze. Ovid's Elegies 1.7.64
love please/[Am] <And> driven like a ship upon rough seas, Ovid's Elegies 2.4.8
My lordly hands ile throwe upon my right. Ovid's Elegies 2.5.30
Shee oft hath serv'd thee upon certaine dayes, Ovid's Elegies 2.13.17
Upon the cold earth pensive let them lay, Ovid's Elegies 2.16.15
With thy white armes upon my shoulders seaze, Ovid's Elegies 2.16.29
My foote upon the further banke to set. Ovid's Elegies 3.5.12
First to be throwne upon the untill'd ground. Ovid's Elegies 3.5.16
Saying, why sadly treadst my banckes upon, Ovid's Elegies 3.5.53
She prais'd me, yet the gate shutt fast upon her, Ovid's Elegies 3.7.7
Upon their heads the holy mysteries had. Ovid's Elegies 3.12.28
Where she should sit for men to gaze upon. Hero and Leander 1.8
Upon her head she ware a myrtle wreath, Hero and Leander 1.17
for they tooke delite/To play upon those hands, they were so Hero and Leander 1.30
And laid his childish head upon her brest, Hero and Leander 1.43
So ran the people foorth to gaze upon her, Hero and Leander 1.117
Heav'd up her head, and halfe the world upon, Hero and Leander 1.190
Loves mother/Nor heaven, nor thou, were made to gaze upon, Hero and Leander 1.223
Upon a rocke, and underneath a hill, Hero and Leander 1.345
The while upon a hillocke downe he lay, Hero and Leander 1.400
Impos'd upon her lover such a taske, Hero and Leander 1.429
To dote upon deceitfull Mercurie. Hero and Leander 1.446
her body throes/Upon his bosome, where with yeelding eyes, Hero and Leander 2.47
dive into the water, and there prie/Upon his brest, his thighs, Hero and Leander 2.189
Descends upon my radiant Heroes tower. Hero and Leander 2.204
And as he spake, upon the waves he springs. Hero and Leander 2.206
And therefore let it rest upon thy pillow. Hero and Leander 2.252
His hands he cast upon her like a snare, Hero and Leander 2.259
And sigh'd to thinke upon th'approching sunne, Hero and Leander 2.302
And wee will sit upon the Rocks, Passionate Shepherd 5
UPPE
that I might locke you safe into <uppe in> my <goode> Chest: F 676 2.2.125 P Covet
UPPER
the plancke/That runs along the upper chamber floore, Jew 1.2.297 Barab
UPPON
Dooth pray uppon my flockes of Passengers, 1Tamb 1.1.32 Mycet
To rest my limbes, uppon a bedde I lay, Ovid's Elegies 1.5.2
And therefore filles the bed she lies uppon: Ovid's Elegies 2.4.34
And lookes uppon the fruits he cannot touch. Ovid's Elegies 3.6.52
UPREARD
Muse upreard <prepar'd> I [meant] <meane> to sing of armes, Ovid's Elegies 1.1.5
Seeing her face, mine upreard armes discended, Ovid's Elegies 2.5.47
UPREARED
Never to leave these newe upreared walles, Dido 3.4.49 Aeneas
UP-RIGHT
When all the woods about stand bolt up-right, Lucan, First Booke 143
UPRIGHT
here are Bugges/Wil make the haire stand upright on your heads, 2Tamb 3.5.148 Tamb
Now when he should not jette, he boults upright, Ovid's Elegies 3.6.67
Thus neere the bed she blushing stood upright, Hero and Leander 2.317
UPRISE
Shall make the morning hast her gray uprise, Dido 1.1.102 Jupitr
UPRISING
Nor morning starres shunne thy uprising face. Ovid's Elegies 1.13.28
UPROARES
We first sustain'd the uproares of the Gaules, Lucan, First Booke 256
UPROOTED
Armies alied, the kingdoms league uprooted, Lucan, First Booke 4
UPSIDE
My sinnewes shrinke, my braines turne upside downe, P 549 11.14 Charls
UPSIDE DOWNE
My sinnewes shrinke, my braines turne upside downe, P 549 11.14 Charls
UP-STARING
Gote-footed Satyrs, and up-staring <upstarting> Fawnes, Hero and Leander 2.200
UPSTART
That makes these upstart heresies in Fraunce: P 81 2.24 Guise
Then pittie or releeve these upstart hereticks. P 222 4.20 Guise
Think you that we can brooke this upstart pride? Edw 1.4.41 Warwck
I will not yeeld to any such upstart. Edw 1.4.423 Mortmr
Away base upstart, brav'st thou nobles thus? Edw 3.1.205 Penbrk
UPSTARTING
Gote-footed Satyrs, and up-staring <upstarting> Fawnes, Hero and Leander 2.200
UPSTARTS
Whose brightnes such pernitious upstarts dim, Edw 3.1.165 Herald
UPWARDS
Like his desire, lift upwards and divine, 1Tamb 2.1.8 Menaph
That mooves not upwards, nor by princely deeds/Doth meane to 1Tamb 2.7.32 Therid
UP-WAYD
Which th'earth from ougly Chaos den up-wayd: Hero and Leander 1.450

URE			
And alwayes kept the Sexton's armes in ure/With digging graves	Jew	2.3.184	Barab
URG'D			
And urg'd each Element to his annoy:	Dido	3.2.46	Juno
And Crownes come either by succession/Or urg'd by force; and	Jew	1.1.132	Barab
And urg'd thereto with my afflictions,	Jew	1.2.231	Abigal
That might be urg'd to witnesse our false playing.	Ovid's Elegies		2.8.8
URGD			
The Queenes commission, urgd by Mortimer,	Edw	4.7.49	Leistr
URGE			
Let me alone to urge it now I know the meaning.	Jew	4.4.79	Pilia
Urge him, my lord.	Edw	1.4.83	MortSr
This which I urge, is of a burning zeale,	Edw	1.4.256	Mortmr
Away, you love me not, to urge me thus,	F1327	4.2.3	Benvol
Some greater worke will urge me on at last.	Ovid's Elegies		3.1.70
URGENT			
Have been most urgent suiters for my love,	Dido	3.1.151	Dido
URGING			
Urging his fortune, trusting in the gods,	Lucan, First Booke		149
The angry Senate urging Grachus deeds,	Lucan, First Booke		268
URIBASSA			
Gazellus, Uribassa, and the rest,	2Tamb	2.2.1	Orcan
Go Uribassa, give it straight in charge.	2Tamb	2.3.40	Orcan
URINE			
I view'd your urine, and the [Hipostasis] <Hipostates>/Thick	2Tamb	5.3.82	Phsitn
URNE			
Scarse rests of all what a small urne conteines.	Ovid's Elegies		3.8.40
Thy bones I pray may in the urne safe rest,	Ovid's Elegies		3.8.67
US (See also LET'S, LETS, LETTS)			
Priams misfortune followes us by sea,	Dido	1.1.143	Aeneas
That by thy vertues freest us from annoy,	Dido	1.1.153	Achat
To make us live unto our former heate,	Dido	1.1.160	Achat
That we may make a fire to warme us with,	Dido	1.1.167	Aeneas
To know what coast the winde hath driven us on,	Dido	1.1.176	Aeneas
As to instruct us under what good heaven/We breathe as now, and	Dido	1.1.197	Aeneas
Tell us, O tell us that are ignorant,	Dido	1.1.200	Aeneas
There is a place Hesperia term'd by us,	Dido	1.2.20	Cloan
From thence a fewe of us escapt to land,	Dido	1.2.30	Cloan
And will not let us lodge upon the sands:	Dido	1.2.35	Serg
vouchsafe of ruth/To tell us who inhabits this faire towne,	Dido	2.1.41	Aeneas
He [names] <meanes> Aeneas, let us kisse his feete.	Dido	2.1.51	Illion
Who for Troyes sake hath entertaind us all,	Dido	2.1.64	Illion
And clad us in these wealthie robes we weare.	Dido	2.1.65	Illion
Oft hath she askt us under whom we serv'd,	Dido	2.1.66	Illion
Began to crye, let us unto our ships,	Dido	2.1.127	Aeneas
But suddenly the Grecians followed us,	Dido	2.1.278	Aeneas
Come let us thinke upon some pleasing sport,	Dido	2.1.302	Dido
Come Dido, leave Ascanius, let us walke.	Dido	3.1.34	Iarbus
To challenge us with your comparisons?	Dido	3.3.20	Dido
Come Dido, let us hasten to the towne,	Dido	4.1.26	Aeneas
The woman that thou wild us entertaine,	Dido	4.2.11	Iarbus
Why, let us build a Citie of our owne,	Dido	4.3.37	Illion
Then let Aeneas goe abourd with us.	Dido	4.4.23	Achat
That holds us up, and foiles our neighbour foes.	1Tamb	1.1.61	Mycet
To safe conduct us thorow Affrica.	1Tamb	1.2.16	Zenoc
Till with their eies [they] <thee> view us Emperours.	1Tamb	1.2.67	Tamb
Therefore at least admit us libertie,	1Tamb	1.2.71	Zenoc
Sent from the King to overcome us all.	1Tamb	1.2.112	Souldr
An ods too great, for us to stand against:	1Tamb	1.2.122	Tamb
Our swordes shall play the Orators for us.	1Tamb	1.2.132	Techel
Come let us meet them at the mountain foot,	1Tamb	1.2.133	Usumc
Come let us martch.	1Tamb	1.2.136	Techel
Shall vaile to us, as Lords of all the Lake.	1Tamb	1.2.196	Tamb
And hostes of souldiers stand amaz'd at us,	1Tamb	1.2.221	Usumc
Welcome renowmed Persean to us all.	1Tamb	1.2.239	Techel
Long may Theridamas remaine with us.	1Tamb	1.2.240	Usumc
and brave Theridamas/Have met us by the river Araris:	1Tamb	2.1.63	Cosroe
Come my Meander, let us to this geere,	1Tamb	2.2.1	Mycet
their fellowes throats/And make us triumph in their overthrow.	1Tamb	2.2.50	Meandr
Thy wit will make us Conquerors to day.	1Tamb	2.2.58	Mycet
Came creeping to us with their crownes apace.	1Tamb	2.5.86	Tamb
And bid him turne [him] <his> back to war with us,	1Tamb	2.5.100	Tamb
That onely made him King to make us sport.	1Tamb	2.5.101	Tamb
Let us put on our meet incountring mindes,	1Tamb	2.6.19	Ortyg
Nature that fram'd us of foure Elements,	1Tamb	2.7.18	Tamb
Doth teach us all to have aspyring minds:	1Tamb	2.7.20	Tamb
Wils us to weare our selves and never rest,	1Tamb	2.7.26	Tamb
And that made us, the friends of Tamburlaine,	1Tamb	2.7.34	Techel
And thinks to rouse us from our dreadful siege/Of the famous	1Tamb	3.1.5	Bajzth
have measured heaven/With triple circuit thou regreet us not,	1Tamb	3.1.37	Bajzth
Let us afford him now the bearing hence.	1Tamb	3.2.111	Usumc
Yet we assure us of the victorie.	1Tamb	3.3.35	Usumc
Our conquering swords shall marshal us the way/We use to march	1Tamb	3.3.148	Tamb
But come my Lords, to weapons let us fall.	1Tamb	3.3.162	Tamb
let us glut our swords/That thirst to drinke the feble Perseans	1Tamb	3.3.164	Bajzth
O cursed Mahomet that makest us thus/The slaves to Scythians	1Tamb	3.3.270	Zabina
Whom he detaineth in despight of us,	1Tamb	4.1.44	Souldn
May have fresh warning to go war with us,	1Tamb	4.1.71	Souldn
And make it swallow both of us at once.	1Tamb	4.2.29	Bajzth
Shall lead him with us wheresoere we goe.	1Tamb	4.2.100	Tamb
He dies, and those that kept us out so long.	1Tamb	4.2.118	Tamb
Raves in Egyptia, and annoyeth us.	1Tamb	4.3.10	Souldn
That dares controll us in our Territories.	1Tamb	4.3.14	Souldn

US (cont.)

Let us unite our royall bandes in one,	1Tamb	4.3.17	Souldn
Then let us freely banquet and carouse/Full bowles of wine unto	1Tamb	4.4.5	Tamb
Let us live in spite of them, looking some happie power will	1Tamb	4.4.99	P Zabina
of them, looking some happie power will pitie and inlarge us.	1Tamb	4.4.100	P Zabina
Tis enough for us to see them, and for Tamburlaine onely to	1Tamb	4.4.111	P Techel
Take them away againe and make us slaves.	1Tamb	4.4.133	Therid
And make us desperate of our threatned lives:	1Tamb	5.1.6	Govnr
Let us have hope that their unspotted praiers,	1Tamb	5.1.20	Govnr
And use us like a loving Conquerour.	1Tamb	5.1.23	Govnr
Submit your selves and us to servitude.	1Tamb	5.1.39	Govnr
And bring us pardon in your chearfull lookes.	1Tamb	5.1.47	Govnr
Leave us my Lord, and loving countrimen,	1Tamb	5.1.60	2Virgn
For us, for infants, and for all our bloods,	1Tamb	5.1.97	1Virgn
O pitie us.	1Tamb	5.1.119	Omnes
Bring him forth, and let us know if the towne be ransackt.	1Tamb	5.1.194	P Tamb
and fresh supply/Of conquest, and of spoile is offered us.	1Tamb	5.1.197	Techel
Arabian king together/Martch on us with such eager violence,	1Tamb	5.1.200	Techel
As if there were no way but one with us.	1Tamb	5.1.201	Techel
But let us save the reverend Souldans life,	1Tamb	5.1.204	Therid
Till we have made us ready for the field.	1Tamb	5.1.212	Tamb
Pray for us Bajazeth, we are going.	1Tamb	5.1.213	Tamb
not but faire Zenocrate/Will soone consent to satisfy us both.	1Tamb	5.1.499	Tamb
Then let us set the crowne upon her head,	1Tamb	5.1.501	Therid
For now her mariage time shall worke us rest.	1Tamb	5.1.504	Techel
King of Natolia, let us treat of peace,	2Tamb	1.1.13	Gazell
Whose holy Alcaron remaines with us,	2Tamb	1.1.138	Orcan
Come let us goe and banquet in our tents:	2Tamb	1.1.160	Orcan
Come banquet and carouse with us a while,	2Tamb	1.1.165	Orcan
Thanks gentle Almeda, then let us haste,	2Tamb	1.2.74	Callap
Least time be past, and lingring let us both.	2Tamb	1.2.75	Callap
No Madam, these are speeches fit for us,	2Tamb	1.3.88	Celeb
And made Canarea cal us kings and Lords,	2Tamb	1.3.181	Usumc
Cookes shall have pensions to provide us cates,	2Tamb	1.3.219	Tamb
And glut us with the dainties of the world,	2Tamb	1.3.220	Tamb
Come let us banquet and carrouse the whiles.	2Tamb	1.3.225	Tamb
Should not give us presumption to the like.	2Tamb	2.1.46	Sgsmnd
Comes marching on us, and determines straight,	2Tamb	2.2.27	1Msngr
To bid us battaile for our dearest lives.	2Tamb	2.2.28	1Msngr
To armes my Lords, on Christ still let us crie,	2Tamb	2.2.63	Orcan
let us haste and meete/Our Army and our brother of Jerusalem,	2Tamb	2.3.42	Orcan
Of Greekish wine now let us celebrate/Our happy conquest,	2Tamb	2.3.46	Orcan
Do us such honor and supremacie,	2Tamb	3.1.16	Callap
Usumcasane now come let us martch/Towards Techelles and	2Tamb	3.2.145	Tamb
Then let us see if coward Calapine/Dare levie armes against our	2Tamb	3.2.155	Tamb
Then let us bring our light Artilery,	2Tamb	3.3.5	Techel
Captaine, that thou yeeld up thy hold to us.	2Tamb	3.3.16	Therid
and let us haste from hence/Along the cave that leads beyond	2Tamb	3.4.1	Olymp
Come back again (sweet death) and strike us both:	2Tamb	3.4.12	Olymp
Will hew us peecemeale, put us to the wheele,	2Tamb	3.4.21	Olymp
Thou shalt with us to Tamburlaine the great,	2Tamb	3.4.39	Techel
But Lady goe with us to Tamburlaine,	2Tamb	3.4.45	Therid
Madam, sooner shall fire consume us both,	2Tamb	3.4.73	Techel
That you must goe with us, no remedy.	2Tamb	3.4.79	Therid
Souldiers now let us meet the Generall,	2Tamb	3.4.85	Therid
Come puissant Viceroies, let us to the field,	2Tamb	3.5.53	Callap
first thou shalt kneele to us/And humbly crave a pardon for thy	2Tamb	3.5.108	Orcan
See father, how Almeda the Jaylor lookes upon us.	2Tamb	3.5.116	Celeb
Away, let us to the field, that the villaine may be slaine.	2Tamb	3.5.143	P Trebiz
Loden with Lawrell wreathes to crowne us all.	2Tamb	3.5.164	Tamb
Come fight ye Turks, or yeeld us victory.	2Tamb	3.5.169	Tamb
Goe, goe tall stripling, fight you for us both,	2Tamb	4.1.33	Calyph
sonnes have had no shares/In all the honors he proposde for us.	2Tamb	4.1.48	Amyras
Let al of us intreat your highnesse pardon.	2Tamb	4.1.98	Tec&Us
O pity us my Lord, and save our honours.	2Tamb	4.3.83	Ladies
It seemes they meant to conquer us my Lord,	2Tamb	4.3.88	Therid
And make us jeasting Pageants for their Trulles.	2Tamb	4.3.89	Therid
Let us not be idle then my Lord,	2Tamb	4.3.95	Techel
with the martiall spoiles/We will convay with us to Persea.	2Tamb	4.3.106	Tamb
And use us like a loving Conquerour.	2Tamb	5.1.28	1Citzn
To save thy life, and us a litle labour,	2Tamb	5.1.50	Therid
As durst resist us till our third daies siege:	2Tamb	5.1.59	Techel
Thou seest us prest to give the last assault,	2Tamb	5.1.60	Techel
That made us all the labour for the towne,	2Tamb	5.1.82	Therid
I, good my Lord, let us in hast to Persea,	2Tamb	5.1.214	Therid
let us lie in wait for him/And if we find him absent from his	2Tamb	5.2.56	Callap
Come let us march against the powers of heaven,	2Tamb	5.3.48	Tamb
Come let us chardge our speares and pierce his breast,	2Tamb	5.3.58	Tamb
Techelles let us march,/And weary Death with bearing soules to	2Tamb	5.3.76	Tamb
your absence in the field, offers to set upon us presently.	2Tamb	5.3.104	P 3Msngr
by a Spanish Fleet/That never left us till within a league,	Jew	1.1.96	2Merch
Give us a peacefull rule, make Christians Kings,	Jew	1.1.134	Barab
Come therefore let us goe to Barrabas;	Jew	1.1.141	2Jew
I feare their comming will afflict us all.	Jew	1.1.156	2Jew
I know you will; well brethren let us goe.	Jew	1.1.174	1Jew
What's Cyprus, Candy, and those other Iles/To us, or Malta?	Jew	1.2.6	Govnr
I hope your Highnesse will consider us.	Jew	1.2.9	Govnr
Then give us leave, great Selim-Calymath.	Jew	1.2.13	Govnr
To levie of us ten yeares tribute past,	Jew	1.2.41	Govnr
Now then here know that it concerneth us--	Jew	1.2.42	Govnr
Alas, my Lord, the most of us are poore!	Jew	1.2.57	1Jew
Have strangers leave with us to get their wealth?	Jew	1.2.60	2Knght
Then let them with us contribute.	Jew	1.2.61	2Knght

US (cont.)

our hands with blood/Is farre from us and our profession.	Jew	1.2.145		Govnr
let us in, and gather of these goods/The mony for this tribute	Jew	1.2.155		Govnr
Come, let us leave him in his irefull mood,	Jew	1.2.209		1Jew
And time may yeeld us an occasion/Which on the sudden cannot	Jew	1.2.239		Barab
it be to injure them/That have so manifestly wronged us,	Jew	1.2.275		Abigal
'Tis thirtie winters long since some of us/Did stray so farre	Jew	1.2.308		Abbass
Well, daughter, say, what is thy suit with us?	Jew	1.2.321		Abbass
Proceed from sinne, or want of faith in us,	Jew	1.2.323		Abigal
Let us intreat she may be entertain'd.	Jew	1.2.329		2Fryar
Come daughter, follow us.	Jew	1.2.337		Abbass
To shun suspition, therefore, let us part.	Jew	2.1.57		Abigal
Now Captaine tell us whither thou art bound?	Jew	2.2.1		Govnr
Their creeping Gallyes had us in the chase:	Jew	2.2.12		Bosco
Welcome to Malta, and to all of us;	Jew	2.2.20		Govnr
Delbosco, as thou lovest and honour'st us,	Jew	2.2.24		1Knght
He'de give us present mony for them all.	Jew	2.3.6		1Offcr
Till Titus and Vespasian conquer'd us)/Am I become as wealthy	Jew	2.3.10		Barab
'tis a custome held with us,/That when we speake with Gentiles	Jew	2.3.44		Barab
For unto us the Promise doth belong.	Jew	2.3.47		Barab
Come home and there's no price shall make us part,	Jew	2.3.92		Barab
Yonder comes Don Mathias, let us stay;	Jew	2.3.140		Barab
Then of true griefe let us take equall share.	Jew	3.2.37		Govnr
And nought to us more welcome is then wars.	Jew	3.5.36		Govnr
Blame not us but the proverb, Confes and be hang'd.	Jew	4.1.146	P	Barab
No, let us beare him to the Magistrates.	Jew	4.1.183		Ithimr
Oh bring us to the Governor.	Jew	5.1.7		Curtzn
Deale truly with us as thou intimatest,	Jew	5.2.85		Govnr
For well has Barabas deserv'd of us.	Jew	5.3.25		Calym
And now, bold Bashawes, let us to our Tents,	Jew	5.3.43		Calym
And meditate how we may grace us best/To solemnize our	Jew	5.3.44		Calym
busie Barrabas is there above/To entertaine us in his Gallery;	Jew	5.5.53		Calym
Let us salute him. Save thee, Barabas.	Jew	5.5.54		Calym
Was this the banquet he prepar'd for us?	Jew	5.5.95		Calym
By treason hath delivered thee to us:	Jew	5.5.110		Govnr
thy father hath made good/The ruines done to Malta and to us,	Jew	5.5.112		Govnr
[all] <call> the world/To rescue thee, so will we guard us now,	Jew	5.5.120		Govnr
Then conquer Malta, or endanger us.	Jew	5.5.122		Govnr
Sister, I think your selfe will beare us company.	P 21	1.21		Charls
Let us goe to honor this solemnitie.	P 25	1.25		Charls
Now Guise may storme but doe us little hurt:	P 28	1.28		Navrre
And thats the cause that Guise so frowns at us,	P 52	1.52		Navrre
And beates his braines to catch us in his trap,	P 53	1.53		Navrre
Come my Lords let us beare her body hence,	P 195	3.30		Admral
betraide, come my Lords, and let us goe tell the King of this.	P 199	3.34	P	Navrre
Oh fatall was this mariage to us all.	P 202	3.37		Admral
In lucky time, come let us keep this lane,	P 298	5.25		Anjoy
And now my Lords let us closely to our busines.	P 332	5.59		Guise
And meane to murder us:	P 368	7.8		Taleus
Come let us goe tell the King.	P 440	7.80		Condy
Why let us burne him for an heretick.	P 483	9.2	P	2Atndt
Doe so sweet Guise, let us delay no time,	P 505	9.24		QnMoth
It will be hard for us to worke their deaths.	P 508	9.27		QnMoth
For to revenge their deaths upon us all.	P 518	9.37		Cardnl
Come my Lord [let] <lets> us goe.	P 527	9.46		QnMoth
And he nor heares, nor sees us what we doe:	P 553	11.18		QnMoth
And bid him come without delay to us.	P 559	11.24		QnMoth
Come let us take his body hence.	P 564	11.29		QnMoth
Will shew his mercy and preserve us still.	P 576	11.41		Navrre
Lets goe my Lords, our dinner staies for us.	P 630	12.43		King
Come my [Lord] <Lords>, let us goe seek the Guise,	P 655	12.68		QnMoth
Who set themselves to tread us under foot,	P 702	14.5		Navrre
Which they will put us to with sword and fire:	P 706	14.9		Navrre
To send his power to meet us in the field.	P 712	14.15		Navrre
But come my Lords, let us away with speed,	P 741	14.44		Navrre
Let us away with triumph to our tents.	P 805	16.19		Navrre
First let us set our hand and seale to this,	P 890	17.85		King
And send us safely to arrive in France:	P 928	18.29		Navrre
Let us alone, I warrant you.	P 939	19.9	P	1Mur
You will give us our money?	P 942	19.12	P	AllMur
Wert thou the Pope thou mightst not scape from us.	P1092	20.2		1Mur
Now thou art dead, heere is no stay for us:	P1111	21.5		Dumain
Come let us away and leavy men,	P1127	21.21		Dumain
If you love us my lord, hate Gaveston.	Edw	1.1.80		MortSr
And strike off his that makes you threaten us.	Edw	1.1.124		Mortmr
Come unckle, let us leave the brainsick king,	Edw	1.1.125		Mortmr
Will be the ruine of the realme and us.	Edw	1.2.32		Mortmr
Then wil you joine with us that be his peeres/To banish or	Edw	1.2.42		Mortmr
My lord, you may not thus disparage us,	Edw	1.4.32		Lncstr
Learne then to rule us better and the realme.	Edw	1.4.39		Lncstr
My lords, now let us all be resolute,	Edw	1.4.45		Mortmr
Nothing shall alter us, wee are resolv'd.	Edw	1.4.74		ArchBp
Therefore with dum imbracement let us part.	Edw	1.4.134		Edward
But madam, would you have us cal him home?	Edw	1.4.208		Mortmr
As he will front the mightiest of us all,	Edw	1.4.260		Mortmr
Tis hard for us to worke his overthrow.	Edw	1.4.262		Mortmr
Nay more, when he shall know it lies in us,	Edw	1.4.274		Mortmr
Should beare us downe of the nobilitie,	Edw	1.4.286		Mortmr
Now let us in, and feast it roiallie:	Edw	1.4.374		Edward
In this, or ought, your highnes shall commaund us.	Edw	1.4.384		Warwck
a factious lord/Shall hardly do himselfe good, much lesse us,	Edw	2.1.7		Spencr
May with one word, advaunce us while we live:	Edw	2.1.9		Spencr
He meanes to make us stoope by force of armes,	Edw	2.2.103		Lncstr

US (cont.)

And therefore let us jointlie here protest, ...	Edw	2.2.104		Lncstr
Looke next to see us with our ensignes spred.	Edw	2.2.199		Lncstr
What care I though the Earles begirt us round? . . .	Edw	2.2.223		Edward
To undermine us with a showe of love.	Edw	2.3.6		Lncstr
Let us with these our followers scale the walles, . .	Edw	2.3.18		Lncstr
Cease to lament, and tell us wheres the king? . . .	Edw	2.4.30		Mortmr
Tell us where he remaines, and he shall die. . . .	Edw	2.4.36		Lncstr
Nay, rather saile with us to Scarborough.	Edw	2.4.52		Mortmr
gratifie the king/In other matters, he must pardon us in this,	Edw	2.5.44		Warwck
Come fellowes, it booted not for us to strive, ...	Edw	2.6.18		James
For favors done in him, unto us all.	Edw	3.1.42		SpncrP
Thou shalt have crownes of us, t'out bid the Barons, .	Edw	3.1.55		Edward
Informeth us, by letters and by words, ...	Edw	3.1.61		Queene
And go in peace, leave us in warres at home. . . .	Edw	3.1.85		Edward
By earth, the common mother of us all, ...	Edw	3.1.128		Edward
Accursed wretches, wast in regard of us, ...	Edw	3.1.233		Edward
to request/He might be spared to come to speake with us, .	Edw	3.1.235		Edward
A boye, our friends do faile us all in Fraunce, . .	Edw	4.2.1		Queene
Tould us at our arrivall all the newes, ...	Edw	4.2.48		Mortmr
To see us there appointed for our foes.	Edw	4.2.56		Mortmr
I thinke king Edward will out-run us all.	Edw	4.2.68		Prince
Sir John of Henolt, pardon us I pray, ...	Edw	4.2.71		Kent
Binde us in kindenes all at your commaund. . . .	Edw	4.2.73		Kent
I pray let us see it, what have we there?	Edw	4.3.10		Edward
Come friends to Bristow, there to make us strong, . .	Edw	4.3.50		Edward
And for the open wronges and injuries/Edward hath done to us,	Edw	4.4.22		Mortmr
Sound trumpets my lord and forward let us martch, . .	Edw	4.4.28		SrJohn
To keepe your royall person safe with us, ...	Edw	4.7.3		Abbot
Do you betray us and our companie.	Edw	4.7.25		Edward
A gave a long looke after us my lord, ...	Edw	4.7.30		Spencr
To let us take our farewell of his grace.	Edw	4.7.69		Spencr
And Leister say, what shall become of us?	Edw	4.7.81		Edward
Parted from hence, never to see us more!	Edw	4.7.101		Spencr
That if he slip will seaze upon us both, ...	Edw	5.2.8		Mortmr
Thinke therefore madam that imports [us] <as> much, . .	Edw	5.2.10		Mortmr
as long as he survives/What safetie rests for us, or for my	Edw	5.2.43		Queene
and Mortimer/Shall rule the realme, the king, and none rule us,	Edw	5.4.66		Mortmr
And shall my Unckle Edmund ride with us?	Edw	5.4.114		King
Let us assaile his minde another while.	Edw	5.5.12		Matrvs
And therefore let us take horse and away.	Edw	5.5.115		Matrvs
Come let us cast the body in the mote, ...	Edw	5.5.118		Gurney
Betray us both, therefore let me flie.	Edw	5.6.8		Matrvs
And vowes to be revengd upon us both, ...	Edw	5.6.19		Queene
we deceive our selves, and there is <theres> no truth in us.	F 70	1.1.42	P	Faust
Shall make all Nations to Canonize us:	F 147	1.1.119		Valdes
Be alwaies serviceable to us three:	F 150	1.1.122		Valdes
Like Lyons shall they guard us when we please, . . .	F 151	1.1.123		Valdes
Go to sirra, leave your jesting, and tell us where he is.	F 201	1.2.8	P	1Schol
Then <Well> you will not tell us?	F 205	1.2.12	P	2Schol
But come, let us go, and informe the Rector: . . .	F 225	1.2.32		2Schol
Yet let us see <trie> what we can do.	F 228	1.2.35		2Schol
Is that the reason why he tempts us thus?	F 430	2.1.42		Faust
thou performe/All Covenants, and Articles, betweene us both.	F 480	2.1.92		Faust
All <articles prescrib'd> <covenant-articles> betweene us both.	F 480	(HC260)		Faust
To effect all promises betweene us [made] <both>. . .	F 482	2.1.94		Mephst
Come Mephostophilis let us dispute againe, ...	F 584	2.2.33		Faust
We are come to tell thee thou dost injure us. . . .	F 642	2.2.91		Belzeb
I, there be of us here, that have waded as deepe into matters,	F 740	2.3.19	P	Robin
I hope his Holinesse will bid us welcome.	F 807	3.1.29		Faust
Away and bring us word <again> with speed. . . .	F 888	3.1.110		Pope
Is not all power on earth bestowed on us?	F 930	3.1.152		Pope
Resigne, or seale, or what so pleaseth us.	F 936	3.1.158		Pope
Let us salute his reverend Father-hood.	F 944	3.1.166		Faust
And by their folly make some <us> merriment, . . .	F 990	3.2.10		Faust
You brought us word even now, it was decreed, . . .	F1019	3.2.39		Pope
Your Grace mistakes, you gave us no such charge. . .	F1024	3.2.44		1Card
Lord Archbishop of Reames, sit downe with us. . . .	F1037	3.2.57		Pope
same cup, for the Vintners boy followes us at the hard heeles.	F1090	3.3.3	P	Dick
let him come; an he follow us, I'le so conjure him, as he was	F1091	3.3.4	P	Robin
Nay there you lie, 'tis beyond us both.	F1109	3.3.22	P	Robin
Then Faustus as thou late didst promise us, ...	F1230	4.1.76		Emper
let us sway thy thoughts/From this attempt against the .	F1325	4.2.1		Mrtino
Take you the wealth, leave us the victorie.	F1347	4.2.23		Benvol
Pitie us gentle Faustus, save our lives.	F1417	4.2.93		Fredrk
And make us laughing stockes to all the world. . . .	F1450	4.3.20		Benvol
Why Hostesse, I say, fetch us some Beere.	F1518	4.5.14	P	Dick
so that when it is Winter with us, in the contrary circle it is	F1582	4.6.25	P	Faust
Commit with us, he were as good commit with his father, as	F1603	4.6.46	P	Dick
us, he were as good commit with his father, as commit with us.	F1604	4.6.47	P	Dick
Zons fill us some Beere, or we'll breake all the barrels in the	F1618	4.6.61	P	HrsCsr
if you will doe us so much <that> favour, as to let us see that	F1685	5.1.12	P	1Schol
as to let us see that peerelesse dame of Greece, whom all the	F1685	5.1.12	P	1Schol
[Let us depart], and for this blessed sight <glorious deed>	F1704	5.1.31		1Schol
Bringing with us lasting damnation, ...	F1801	5.2.5		Lucifr
Why did not Faustus tell us of this before, that Divines might	F1862	5.2.66	P	1Schol
but let us into the next roome, and [there] pray for him.	F1871	5.2.75	P	1Schol
Come Gentlemen, let us go visit Faustus, ...	F1983	5.3.1		1Schol
O help us heaven, see, here are Faustus limbs, . . .	F1988	5.3.6		2Schol
Therefore sweet Mephastophilis, let us make haste to Wertenberge	F App	p.239 94		Faust
that when it is heere winter with us, in the contrary circle it	F App	p.242 20	P	Faust
let us in, where you must wel reward this learned man for the	F App	p.243 28	P	Duke
Come, maister Doctor follow us, and receive your reward. .	F App	p.243 33	P	Duke

US (cont.)			
nor Hanniball/Art cause, no forraine foe could so afflict us,	Lucan, First Booke	31	
Parthians y'afflict us more then ye suppose,	Lucan, First Booke	107	
When fortune made us lords of all, wealth flowed,	Lucan, First Booke	161	
let thy sword bring us home.	Lucan, First Booke	280	
Woods turn'd to ships; both land and sea against us:	Lucan, First Booke	307	
or wrathful France/Pursu'd us hither, how were we bestead/When	Lucan, First Booke	309	
the gods are with us,/Neither spoile, nor kingdom seeke we by	Lucan, First Booke	350	
What doubtst thou us?	Lucan, First Booke	363	
Well, leade us then to Syrtes desart shoare;	Lucan, First Booke	368	
This [band] <hand> that all behind us might be quail'd,	Lucan, First Booke	370	
War onely gives us peace, o Rome continue/The course of	Lucan, First Booke	669	
When pleasure mov'd us to our sweetest worke.	Ovid's Elegies	1.4.48	
The thing and place shall counsell us the rest.	Ovid's Elegies	1.4.54	
Time flying slides hence closely, and deceaves us,	Ovid's Elegies	1.8.49	
And with swift horses the swift yeare soone leaves us.	Ovid's Elegies	1.8.50	
Such blisse is onely common to us two,	Ovid's Elegies	2.5.31	
Thou swearest, devision should not twixt us rise,	Ovid's Elegies	2.16.43	
Let us both lovers hope, and feare a like,	Ovid's Elegies	2.19.5	
Let us all conquer by our mistris favour.	Ovid's Elegies	3.2.18	
In vaine why flyest backe? force conjoynes us now:	Ovid's Elegies	3.2.19	
And sit thou rounder, that behind us see,	Ovid's Elegies	3.2.23	
Though both of us performd our true intent,	Ovid's Elegies	3.6.5	
What profit to us hath our pure life bred?	Ovid's Elegies	3.8.33	
If ought remaines of us but name, and spirit,	Ovid's Elegies	3.8.59	
Scylla by us her fathers rich haire steales,	Ovid's Elegies	3.11.21	
For will in us is over-rul'd by fate.	Hero and Leander	1.168	
In time it will returne us two for one.	Hero and Leander	1.236	
What vertue is it that is borne with us?	Hero and Leander	1.278	
In silence of the night to viste us),	Hero and Leander	1.350	
With follie and false hope deluding us).	Hero and Leander	2.222	
USAGE			
This usage makes my miserie increase.	Edw	5.3.16	Edward
US'D			
Let me be us'd but as my brethren are.	Jew	1.2.91	Barab
This is the life we Jewes are us'd to lead;	Jew	5.2.115	Barab
After went Mercurie, who us'd such cunning,	Hero and Leander	1.417	
USD			
Let him please, haunt the house, be kindly usd,	Ovid's Elegies	2.2.29	
US'DE			
for both not us'de,/Are of like worth.	Hero and Leander	1.233	
These arguments he us'de, and many more,	Hero and Leander	1.329	
USDE			
Thou hast with honor usde Zenocrate.	1Tamb	5.1.484	Souldn
for as the Romans usde/I here present thee with a naked sword.	2Tamb	1.1.81	Sgsmnd
Now are those Spheares where Cupid usde to sit,	2Tamb	2.4.81	Tamb
And usde such slender reckning of [your] <you> majesty.	2Tamb	5.1.83	Therid
With death delay'd and torments never usde,	P 257	4.55	Charls
and attire/They usde to weare during their time of life,	F App	p.237 34	Emper
Yet blusht I not, nor usde I any saying,	Ovid's Elegies	2.8.7	
I shame so great names to have usde so vainly:	Ovid's Elegies	3.5.102	
And usde all speech that might provoke and stirre.	Ovid's Elegies	3.6.12	
Nor usde the slight nor <and> cunning which she could,	Ovid's Elegies	3.6.56	
USE			
It is the use for [Tirien] <Turen> maides to weare/Their bowe	Dido	1.1.204	Venus
But if I use such ceremonious thankes,	Dido	4.3.49	Aeneas
In steed of oares, let him use his hands,	Dido	4.4.163	Dido
Doe Troians use to quit their Lovers thus?	Dido	5.1.106	Dido
Could use perswasions more patheticall.	1Tamb	1.2.211	Therid
marshal us the way/We use to march upon the slaughtered foe:	1Tamb	3.3.149	Tamb
Straight will I use thee as thy pride deserves:	1Tamb	3.3.206	Zabina
And use us like a loving Conquerour.	1Tamb	5.1.23	Govnr
Wherin the change I use condemns my faith,	1Tamb	5.1.390	Zenoc
Use all their voices and their instruments/To entertaine divine	2Tamb	2.4.28	Tamb
According to our ancient use, shall beare/The figure of the	2Tamb	3.1.64	Orcan
Ile use some other means to make you yeeld,	2Tamb	4.2.51	Therid
And use us like a loving Conquerour.	2Tamb	5.1.28	1Citzn
Use him as if he were a--Philistine.	Jew	2.3.228	Barab
And whilst I live use halfe; spend as my selfe;	Jew	3.4.45	Barab
This Even they use in Malta here ('tis call'd/Saint Jaques	Jew	3.4.75	Barab
Saint Jaques Even) and then I say they use/To send their Almes	Jew	3.4.76	Barab
No, 'tis an order which the Fryars use:	Jew	4.1.134	Barab
Yes, 'cause you use to confesse.	Jew	4.1.145	Ithimr
Let me alone, I'le use him in his kinde.	Jew	4.2.80	Pilia
thy desert we make thee Governor,/Use them at thy discretion.	Jew	5.2.11	Calym
and use a counterfeite key to his privie Chamber doore:	P 807	17.2	P Souldr
duke a cuckolde and use a counterfeyt key to his privy chamber	Paris	ms 2,p390	P Souldr
I give him thee, here use him as thou wilt.	Edw	1.1.196	Edward
And use them but of meere hypocrisie.	Edw	2.1.45	Baldck
Stil wil these Earles and Barrons use me thus?	Edw	2.2.70	Edward
We never beg, but use such praiers as these.	Edw	2.2.153	Mortmr
Even so betide my soule as I use him.	Edw	5.1.148	Bartly
Use Edmund friendly, as if all were well.	Edw	5.2.79	Queene
Relent, ha, ha, I use much to relent.	Edw	5.4.27	Ltborn
Nor will we come unlesse he use such meanes,	F 278	1.3.50	Mephst
[makes men] <make them> foolish that do use <trust> them most.	F 408	2.1.20	BdAngl
I chuse his privy chamber for our use.	F 806	3.1.28	Mephst
I have taken up his holinesse privy chamber for our use>.	F 806	(HC265)A	P Mephst
What use shall we put his beard to?	F1383	4.2.59	P Mrtino
Well use that tricke no more, I would advise you.	F App	p.232 19	Faust
and ifaith I meane to search some circles for my owne use:	F App	p.233 3	P Robin
then turn her and wind hir to thy owne use, as often as thou	F App	p.234 28	P Robin
O brave Robin, shal I have Nan Spit, and to mine owne use?	F App	p.234 30	P Rafe

USE (cont.)			
Thee wars use stirde, and thoughts that alwaies scorn'd/A	Lucan, First Booke	124	
warre, wherein through use he's known/To exceed his maister,	Lucan, First Booke	325	
Lets use our tried force, they that now thwart right/In wars	Lucan, First Booke	349	
Long Love my body to such use [makes] <make> slender/And to get	Ovid's Elegies	1.6.5	
Excludst a lover, how wouldst use a foe?	Ovid's Elegies	1.6.31	
Brasse shines with use; good garments would be worne,	Ovid's Elegies	1.8.51	
Receive him soone, least patient use he gaine,	Ovid's Elegies	1.8.75	
If this thou doest, to me by long use knowne,	Ovid's Elegies	1.8.105	
To staine all faith in truth, by false crimes use.	Ovid's Elegies	2.2.38	
If she discardes thee, what use servest thou for?	Ovid's Elegies	2.3.12	
Unmeete is beauty without use to wither.	Ovid's Elegies	2.3.14	
Well maiest thou one thing for thy Mistresse use.	Ovid's Elegies	2.8.24	
The sea I use not: me my earth must have.	Ovid's Elegies	3.2.48	
But yet their gift more moderately use,	Ovid's Elegies	3.3.47	
So use we women of strange nations stocke.	Ovid's Elegies	3.4.34	
Kindly thy mistris use, if thou be wise.	Ovid's Elegies	3.4.43	
Chuf-like had I not gold, and could not use it?	Ovid's Elegies	3.6.50	
Rather Ile hoist up saile, and use the winde,	Ovid's Elegies	3.10.51	
Nor, as use will not Poets record heare,	Ovid's Elegies	3.11.19	
We make Enceladus use a thousand armes,	Ovid's Elegies	3.11.27	
As is the use, the Nunnes in white veyles clad,	Ovid's Elegies	3.12.27	
There use all tricks, and tread shame under feete.	Ovid's Elegies	3.13.18	
difference betwixt the richest mine/And basest mold, but use?	Hero and Leander	1.233	
she wanting no excuse/To feed him with delaies, as women use:	Hero and Leander	1.426	
And kist againe, as lovers use to do.	Hero and Leander	2.94	
In such warres women use but halfe their strength.	Hero and Leander	2.296	
USED			
To whom he used action so pitifull,	Dido	2.1.155	Aeneas
Intreat them well, as we have used thee.	Jew	5.2.17	Calym
The Queene sent me, to see how you were used,	Edw	5.5.48	Ltborn
Buskins of shels all silvered, used she,	Hero and Leander	1.31	
USES			
And him that hew'd you out for needfull uses/Ile prove had	Ovid's Elegies	1.12.15	
USING			
Thou fightst against me using mine owne verse.	Ovid's Elegies	3.1.38	
USUALL			
Pillage and murder are his usuall trades.	1Tamb	4.1.66	Souldn
USUMCASANE (See also CASANE)			
Usumcasane and Techelles both,	1Tamb	2.3.36	Cosroe
Usumcasane and Techelles come,	1Tamb	2.3.63	Tamb
Usumcasane and Theridamas,	1Tamb	2.5.52	Tamb
Usumcasane, see how right the man/Hath hit the meaning of my	1Tamb	3.2.107	Techel
Techelles King of Fesse, and Usumcasane King of Morocus.	1Tamb	4.4.117	P Tamb
Usumcasane now come let us martch/Towards Techelles and	2Tamb	3.2.145	Tamb
USURER			
Then after that was I an Usurer,	Jew	2.3.190	Barab
I must needs say that I have beene a great usurer.	Jew	4.1.39	Barab
USURIE			
And ransome them with fame and usurie.	1Tamb	2.5.43	Cosroe
USURPER			
That Jove, usurper of his fathers seat,	Hero and Leander	1.452	
USURPES			
And Guise usurpes it, cause I am his wife:	P 661	13.5	Duchss
USURPEST			
Unlawfully usurpest the Persean seat:	1Tamb	4.2.57	Zabina
USURPING			
That such a base usurping vagabond/Should brave a king, or	1Tamb	4.3.21	Souldn
This proud usurping king of Persea,	2Tamb	3.1.15	Callap
To make usurping Mortimer a king?	Edw	5.1.37	Edward
USURPS			
The slave usurps the glorious name of war.	1Tamb	4.1.67	Souldn
USURPT			
Speake, when shall this thy long usurpt power end?	Lucan, First Booke	333	
USURY			
Hence interest and devouring usury sprang,	Lucan, First Booke	183	
UT			
propitiamus vos, ut appareat, et surgat Mephostophilis.	F 247	1.3.19	P Faust
UTMOST			
with amitie we yeeld/Our utmost service to the faire Cosroe.	1Tamb	2.3.34	Techel
With utmost vertue of my faith and dutie.	1Tamb	2.5.17	Meandr
Ah sweete sir John, even to the utmost verge/Of Europe, or the	Edw	4.2.29	Queene
resolute/And try the utmost <uttermost> Magicke can performe.	F 243	1.3.15	Faust
Shall make poore Faustus to his utmost power,	F1218	4.1.64	Faust
UTTER			
my spirit doth foresee/The utter ruine of thy men and thee.	1Tamb	4.3.60	Arabia
UTTERED			
(Uttered with teares of wretchednesse and blood,	1Tamb	5.1.25	1Virgn
UTTERLY			
sacke, and utterly consume/Your cities and your golden pallaces,	2Tamb	4.1.192	Tamb
UTTERMOST			
resolute/And try the utmost <uttermost> Magicke can performe.	F 243	1.3.15	Faust
UZZ			
As for those [Samnites] <Samintes>, and the men of Uzz,/That	Jew	1.1.4	Barab
VAGABOND			
That such a base usurping vagabond/Should brave a king, or	1Tamb	4.3.21	Souldn
VAGABONDES			
And with a troope of theeves and vagabondes,	1Tamb	4.1.6	Souldn
VAGRANT			
in Asia, or display/His vagrant Ensigne in the Persean fields,	1Tamb	1.1.45	Meandr
VAIL			
shine as bright/As that faire vail that covers all the world:	2Tamb	1.2.50	Callap
VAIL'D			
Because we vail'd not to the [Turkish] <Spanish> Fleet,/Their	Jew	2.2.11	Bosco

VAILD (Homograph)			
Vaild his resplendant glorie from your view.	Dido	1.1.126	Venus
But justice of the quarrell and the cause,/Vaild is your pride:	Edw	3.1.223	Edward
then the Nunnes/And their vaild Matron, who alone might view	Lucan, First Booke		597
Vaild to the ground, vailing her eie-lids close,	Hero and Leander		1.159
VAILE (Homograph)			
Shall vaile to us, as Lords of all the Lake.	1Tamb	1.2.196	Tamb
Even from the fiery spangled vaile of heaven,	1Tamb	5.1.185	Tamb
Open thou shining vaile of Cynthia/And make a passage from the	2Tamb	2.2.47	Orcan
Now vaile your pride you captive Christians,	Jew	5.2.1	Calym
Twill make him vaile the topflag of his pride,	Edw	1.4.276	Mortmr
From whence her vaile reacht to the ground beneath.	Hero and Leander		1.18
Her vaile was artificiall flowers and leaves,	Hero and Leander		1.19
VAILES			
And Flamins last, with networke wollen vailes.	Lucan, First Booke		603
VAILING			
whom he vouchsafes/For vailing of his bonnet one good looke.	Edw	1.2.19	Lncstr
Vaild to the ground, vailing her eie-lids close,	Hero and Leander		1.159
VAINE (Homograph)			
And this a Spartan Courtier vaine and wilde,	Dido	3.1.157	Dido
Alas poore King that labours so in vaine,	Dido	4.2.33	Anna
How vaine am I to weare this Diadem,	Dido	4.4.40	Aeneas
Vaine man, what Monarky expectst thou here?	Dido	5.1.34	Hermes
In vaine my love thou spendst thy fainting breath,	Dido	5.1.153	Aeneas
Sackes every vaine and artier of my heart.	1Tamb	2.7.10	Cosroe
For words are vaine where working tooles present/The naked	1Tamb	3.2.93	Agidas
in vaine ye labour to prevent/That which mine honor sweares	1Tamb	5.1.106	Tamb
vaine or Artier feed/The cursed substance of that cruel heart,	2Tamb	4.1.177	Soria
In vaine I see men worship Mahomet,	2Tamb	5.1.179	Tamb
In vaine I strive and raile against those powers,	2Tamb	5.3.120	Tamb
And plead in vaine, unpleasing soverainty.	2Tamb	5.3.198	Amyras
Compassion, love, vaine hope, and hartlesse feare,	Jew	2.3.170	Barab
I love him as my selfe/Should write in this imperious vaine!	Jew	4.3.43	Barab
For his othes are seldome spent in vaine.	P 773	15.31	Eprnon
And all my former time was spent in vaine:	P 986	19.56	Guise
And yet I love in vaine, heele nere love me.	Edw	1.4.197	Queene
Freely enjoy that vaine light-headed earle,	Edw	1.4.400	MortSr
And all in vaine, for when I speake him faire,	Edw	2.4.28	Queene
In vaine I looke for love at Edwards hand,	Edw	2.4.61	Queene
And shall or Warwicks sword shal smite in vaine.	Edw	3.1.199	Warwck
Farewell vaine worlde.	Edw	3.1.249	Warwck
That Isabell shall make her plaints in vaine,	Edw	3.1.278	Levune
My lord, it is in vaine to greeve or storme,	Edw	4.7.77	Baldck
And tell him, that I labour all in vaine,	Edw	5.2.70	Queene
Why strive you thus? your labour is in vaine.	Edw	5.3.33	Matrvs
But all in vaine, so vainely do I strive,	Edw	5.3.35	Edward
O would my bloud dropt out from every vaine,	Edw	5.5.66	Edward
But leaving these vaine trifles of mens soules,	F 289	1.3.61	Faust
Away with such vaine fancies, and despaire,	F 392	2.1.4	Faust
To over-reach the Divell, but all in vaine;	F1811	5.2.15	Mephst
vaine pleasure of foure and twenty yeares hath Faustus lost	F1859	5.2.63	P Faust
Vaine fame increast true feare, and did invade/The peoples	Lucan, First Booke		465
were the Commons only strooke to heart/With this vaine terror;	Lucan, First Booke		484
No vaine sprung out but from the yawning gash,	Lucan, First Booke		613
and every vaine/Did threaten horror from the host of Caesar;	Lucan, First Booke		620
all to good, be Augury vaine, and Tages/Th'arts master falce.	Lucan, First Booke		635
But in times past I fear'd vaine shades, and night,	Ovid's Elegies		1.6.9
The vaine name of inferiour slaves despize.	Ovid's Elegies		1.8.64
Presages are not vaine, when she departed/Nape by stumbling on	Ovid's Elegies		1.12.3
For ever lasts high Sophocles proud vaine,	Ovid's Elegies		1.15.15
Vaine causes faine of him the true to hide,	Ovid's Elegies		2.2.31
O would my proofes as vaine might be withstood,	Ovid's Elegies		2.5.7
Vaine babling speech, and pleasant peace thou lovedst.	Ovid's Elegies		2.6.26
Now rash accusing, and thy vaine beliefe,	Ovid's Elegies		2.7.13
Vaine things why wish I?	Ovid's Elegies		2.15.27
Maides words more vaine and light then falling leaves,	Ovid's Elegies		2.16.45
In vaine why flyest backe? force conjoynes us now:	Ovid's Elegies		3.2.19
God is a name, no substance, feard in vaine,	Ovid's Elegies		3.3.23
Rude man, 'tis vaine, thy damsell to commend/To keepers trust:	Ovid's Elegies		3.4.1
Even her I had, and she had me in vaine,	Ovid's Elegies		3.6.43
What should I tell her vaine tongues filthy lyes,	Ovid's Elegies		3.10.21
And thorough everie vaine doth cold bloud runne,	Ovid's Elegies		3.13.38
Then thee whom I must love I hate in vaine,	Ovid's Elegies		3.13.39
And there for honie, bees have sought in vaine,	Hero and Leander		1.23
the night (that might be better spent)/In vaine discourse,	Hero and Leander		1.356
Vow'd spotlesse chastitie, but all in vaine.	Hero and Leander		1.368
Having striv'ne in vaine, was now about to crie,	Hero and Leander		1.413
Yet there with Sysiphus he toyld in vaine,	Hero and Leander		2.277
VAINELY			
But all in vaine, so vainely do I strive,	Edw	5.3.35	Edward
His rider vainely striving him to stay,	Ovid's Elegies		2.9.30
VAINES			
• My vaines are withered, and my sinewes drie,	Dido	4.5.33	Nurse
From jygging vaines of riming mother wits,	1Tamb	Prol.1	Prolog
My vaines are pale, my sinowes hard and drie,	1Tamb	4.4.97	Bajzth
Filling their empty vaines with aiery wine,	2Tamb	3.2.107	Tamb
I feele my liver pierc'd and all my vaines,	2Tamb	3.4.6	Capt
Your vaines are full of accidentall heat,	2Tamb	5.3.84	Phsitn
Your Artiers which alongst the vaines convey/The lively spirits	2Tamb	5.3.93	Phsitn
VAINLY			
the Planets/Alter their course; and vainly dim their vertue?	Lucan, First Booke		663
I shame so great names to have usde so vainly:	Ovid's Elegies		3.5.102
VALDES			
The Germane Valdes and Cornelius,	F 88	1.1.64	Faust

VALDES (cont.)			
Come Germane Valdes and Cornelius,	F 125	1.1.97	Faust
Valdes, sweete Valdes, and Cornelius,	F 127	1.1.99	Faust
Valdes, as resolute am I in this,	F 161	1.1.133	Faust
Valdes, first let him know the words of Art,	F 185	1.1.157	Cornel
is within at dinner, with Valdes and Cornelius, as this wine,	F 215	1.2.22	P Wagner
VALE			
How that a sheapheard sitting in a vale,	Hero and Leander		2.194
VALEAT			
Dei Acherontis propitii, valeat numen triplex Jehovae, Ignei,	F 244	1.3.16	P Faust
VALES			
And creepes along the vales, deviding just/The bounds of Italy,	Lucan, First Booke		217
VALIANT			
Then heare thy charge, valiant Theridamas,	1Tamb	1.1.57	Mycet
In thee (thou valiant man of Persea)	1Tamb	1.2.166	Tamb
And valiant Tamburlaine, the man of fame,	1Tamb	2.1.2	Cosroe
Go valiant Souldier, go before and charge/The fainting army of	1Tamb	2.3.61	Cosroe
Because I heare he beares a valiant mind.	1Tamb	3.1.32	Bajzth
Your men are valiant but their number few,	1Tamb	3.3.11	Bassoe
Ye Moores and valiant men of Barbary,	1Tamb	3.3.89	Moroc
frontier townes/Twise twenty thousand valiant men at armes,	2Tamb	1.3.120	Therid
royall is esteem'd/Six hundred thousand valiant fighting men.	2Tamb	3.5.51	Soria
Which makes me valiant, proud, ambitious,	2Tamb	4.1.116	Tamb
Fight in the quarrell of this valiant Prince,	P1229	22.91	King
traind to armes/And bloudie warres, so many valiant knights,	Edw	2.5.16	Lncstr
immortal pens/Renowne the valiant soules slaine in your wars,	Lucan, First Booke		444
Her valiant lover followes without end.	Ovid's Elegies		1.9.10
VALIANTLY			
In whose defence he fought so valiantly:	Dido	2.1.119	Dido
VALLEIES			
Covers the hils, the valleies and the plaines.	2Tamb	3.5.13	Callap
VALLIES			
You to the vallies, thou unto the house.	Dido	3.3.62	Dido
And falling vallies be the smooth-wayes crowne.	Ovid's Elegies		2.16.52
That Vallies, groves, hills and fieldes,	Passionate Shepherd		3
VALLOURS			
Then shall your meeds and vallours be advaunst/To roomes of	1Tamb	2.3.40	Cosroe
VALOIS (See also VALOYS)			
The wicked branch of curst Valois his line.	P1013	19.83	Guise
VALOREM			
eademque res legatur duobus, alter rem, alter valorem rei, &c.	F 56	1.1.28	P Faust
VALOUR (See also VALURE)			
Betokening valour and excesse of strength:	1Tamb	2.1.28	Menaph
With reasons of his valour and his life,	1Tamb	2.1.38	Cosroe
And let my Fortunes and my valour sway,	1Tamb	2.3.11	Tamb
that is rapt with love/Of fame, of valour, and of victory,	1Tamb	5.1.181	Tamb
be put in the front of such a battaile once, to trie my valour.	2Tamb	4.1.73	P Calyph
Cherish thy valour stil with fresh supplies:	2Tamb	4.1.87	Tamb
Were not subdew'd with valour more divine,	2Tamb	4.3.15	Tamb
Then for all your valour, you would save your life.	2Tamb	5.1.119	Tamb
VALOUROUS			
you wil be thought/More childish valourous than manly wise:	2Tamb	4.1.17	Calyph
VALOYES			
That lord Valoyes our brother, king of Fraunce,	Edw	3.1.62	Queene
VALOYS			
And roote Valoys his line from forth of France,	P1113	21.7	Dumain
Thy gentle Queene, sole sister to Valoys,	Edw	2.2.172	Lncstr
Sib, if this be all/Valoys and I will soone be friends againe.	Edw	3.1.67	Edward
Unkinde Valoys,/Unhappie Isabell, when Fraunce rejects,	Edw	4.2.10	Queene
VALOYSES			
I am a Prince of the Valoyses line,/Therfore an enemy to the	P 835	17.30	Guise
Valoyses lyne ends in my tragedie.	P1231	22.93	King
VALUE			
By [valure] <value and by magnanimity.	1Tamb	4.4.126	Tamb
and in his tuskan cap/A jewell of more value then the crowne.	Edw	1.4.415	Mortmr
VALUED			
which being valued/Amount to more then all the wealth in Malta.	Jew	1.2.133	Offcrs
Had they beene valued at indifferent rate,	Jew	1.2.186	Barab
As be it valued but indifferently,	Jew	5.3.29	Msngr
Thy feare is, then her body, valued more.	Ovid's Elegies		3.4.30
VALURE			
By [valure] <value and by magnanimity.	1Tamb	4.4.126	Tamb
VALURES			
And stirs your valures to such soddaine armes?	2Tamb	2.1.3	Sgsmnd
VALUROUS			
More rich and valurous than Zenocrates.	1Tamb	1.2.97	Tamb
VANES			
Ha, to the East? yes: See how stands the Vanes?	Jew	1.1.40	Barab
VANGIONS			
And Vangions who like those of Sarmata,	Lucan, First Booke		431
VANHOLT			
the Duke of Vanholt doth earnestly entreate your company, and	F1500	4.4.44	P Wagner
Sir, the Duke of Vanholt doth earnestly entreate your company.	F App	p.241 168	P Wagner
The Duke of Vanholt!	F App	p.241 170	P Faust
VANHOLT'S			
The Duke of Vanholt's an honourable Gentleman, and one to whom	F1503	4.4.47	P Faust
VANISH			
Weepe heavens, and vanish into liquid teares,	2Tamb	5.3.1	Therid
That I may vanish ore the earth in ayre,	Jew	1.2.264	Barab
Vanish and returne in a twinckle.	Jew	4.2.79	P Ithimr
But dayes bright beames dooth vanish fast away,	Edw	5.1.69	Edward
Vanish vilaines, th'one like an Ape, an other like a Beare, the	F App	p.235 32	P Mephst
Thy fault with his fault so repuls'd will vanish.	Ovid's Elegies		1.8.80

VANISHT			
Like Summers vapours, vanisht by the Sun.	2Tamb	5.3.116	Tamb
and when I came just in the midst my horse vanisht away, and I	F1544	4.5.40 P	HrsCsr
pond, but my horse vanisht away, and I sat upon a bottle of hey,	F App	p.240 134 P	HrsCsr
VANITIES			
And said it was a heape of vanities?	P 388	7.28	Guise
VANITY			
toyl'd to inherit here/The months of vanity and losse of time,	Jew	1.2.197	Barab
I'le buy you, and marry you to Lady vanity, if you doe well.	Jew	2.3.116 P	Barab
VANQUISH			
We vanquish, and tread tam'd love under feete, ...	Ovid's Elegies		3.10.5
VANQUISHT			
Even he that in a trice vanquisht two kings, ...	1Tamb	3.3.36	Therid
the vanquisht rise/And who thou never think'st should fall	Ovid's Elegies		1.9.29
And vanquisht people curious dressings lend thee, . .	Ovid's Elegies		1.14.46
More glory by thy vanquisht foes assends.	Ovid's Elegies		2.9.6
VANTAGE			
And takes his vantage on Religion, ...	P 924	18.25	Navrre
VAPORS			
Contagious smels, and vapors to infect thee, ...	2Tamb	4.2.11	Olymp
VAPOURS			
Like Summers vapours, vanisht by the Sun.	2Tamb	5.3.116	Tamb
And as grosse vapours perish by the sunne, . . .	Edw	1.4.341	Edward
VARIES			
For she that varies from me in beleefe/Gives great presumption	Jew	3.4.10	Barab
VARLETS			
Why saucy varlets, dare you be so bold.	F1594	4.6.37	Servnt
VARNA (See VERNA)			
VARNISHT			
This saied, she mov'd her buskins gaily varnisht, . .	Ovid's Elegies		3.1.31
VARROES			
What age of Varroes name shall not be tolde, ...	Ovid's Elegies		1.15.21
VARUS			
And frontier Varus that the campe is farre, ...	Lucan, First Booke		405
VASSAILE			
Ignoble vassaile that like Phaeton, ...	Edw	1.4.16	Warwck
VASSALL			
Base villain, vassall, slave to Tamburlaine:	1Tamb	4.2.19	Tamb
VASSALS			
Which I will bring as Vassals to thy feete.	1Tamb	3.3.129	Tamb
But foorth ye vassals, what so ere it be, ...	2Tamb	5.1.221	Tamb
And far more barbarous then the French (his vassals)/And that	Lucan, First Booke		476
VAST			
Chiefe Lord of all the wide vast Euxine sea, ...	1Tamb	1.1.167	Ortyg
As vast and deep as Euphrates or Nile.	1Tamb	5.1.439	Tamb
Vast Gruntland compast with the frozen sea, ...	2Tamb	1.1.26	Orcan
That hides these plaines, and seems as vast and wide, .	2Tamb	1.1.107	Sgsmnd
Of Joves vast pallace the imperiall Orbe, ...	2Tamb	3.4.49	Therid
If any one part of vast heaven thou swayest, ...	Lucan, First Booke		56
And to the vast deep sea fresh water flouds?	Ovid's Elegies		2.10.14
Rich Nile by seaven mouthes to the vast sea flowing, .	Ovid's Elegies		3.5.39
That in the vast uplandish countrie dwelt, ...	Hero and Leander		1.80
VASTE			
with horror stare/Into that vaste perpetuall torture-house,	F1910	5.2.114	BdAngl
VAULT			
I'le lead five hundred souldiers through the Vault, . .	Jew	5.1.91	Barab
Being in a vault up to the knees in water, ...	Edw	5.5.2	Matrvs
VAULTS			
Or meant to pierce Avernus darksome vaults, ...	1Tamb	1.2.160	Therid
And we discend into th'infernall vaults, ...	2Tamb	2.4.98	Tamb
Canst raise this man from hollow vaults below, . . .	F App	p.237 30	Emper
VAUNT			
Which Pergama did vaunt in all her pride.	Dido	1.1.151	Aeneas
Carthage shall vaunt her pettie walles no more, . . .	Dido	5.1.4	Aeneas
Til then take thou my crowne, vaunt of my worth, . .	1Tamb	3.3.130	Tamb
When I shall vaunt as victor in revenge.	P 722	14.25	Navrre
Intends our Muse to vaunt <daunt> his heavenly verse; .	F 6	Prol.6	1Chor
VAUNTS			
Then thou shalt find my vaunts substantiall. . . .	1Tamb	1.2.213	Tamb
VAUSIS			
As Jupiter to sillie [Baucis] <Vausis> house: . . .	Dido	1.2.41	Iarbus
VEILE (See also VAILD, VEYLE)			
<superfluities>/Is covered with a liquid purple veile, .	2Tamb	1.3.80	Tamb
Which lie hid under her thinne veile suppresst. . . .	Ovid's Elegies		3.2.36
VEINES (See also VAINE, VEYNES)			
Suspitious feare in all my veines will hover, . . .	Ovid's Elegies		1.4.42
VEIW			
Veiw here this <the> bloud that trickles from mine arme, .	F 446	2.1.58	Faust
VEIW'D			
We veiw'd the face of heaven, of earth and hell. . . .	F 848	3.1.70	Faust
VELVET			
A Velvet cap'de cloake, fac'st before with Serge, . .	Edw	2.1.34	Spencr
VENEMOUS			
In steed of red bloud wallowed venemous gore. . . .	Lucan, First Booke		614
VENETIAN			
That yeerely saile to the Venetian gulfe, ...	1Tamb	3.3.249	Tamb
VENG'D			
Wretched Ferneze might have veng'd thy death. . . .	Jew	3.2.14	Govnr
And he who on his mother veng'd his sire, ...	Ovid's Elegies		1.7.9
Their wedlocks pledges veng'd their husbands bad. . .	Ovid's Elegies		2.14.32
As meaning to be veng'd for darting it.	Hero and Leander		2.212
VENGE			
That God hath given to venge our Christians death/And scourge	2Tamb	2.1.52	Fredrk

VENGE (cont.)

power and puritie/Behold and venge this Traitors perjury. 2Tamb 2.2.54 Orcan
That we may venge their blood upon their heads. . . Jew 3.2.28 Mater
And couldst not venge it, but upon his sonne, . . . Jew 3.3.44 Abigal
To venge themselves on Hermes, have concluded/That Midas brood Hero and Leander 1.474

VENGEANCE

Say vengeance, now shall her Ascanius dye? . . . Dido 3.2.13 Juno
And fearefull vengeance light upon you both. . . . 1Tamb 2.7.52 Cosroe
So surely will the vengeance of the highest/And jealous anger 2Tamb 2.1.56 Fredrk
And God hath thundered vengeance from on high, . . . 2Tamb 2.3.2 Sgsmnd
Bearing the vengeance of our fathers wrongs, . . . 2Tamb 3.1.17 Callap
Or vengeance on the head of Tamburlain, ... 2Tamb 5.1.195 Tamb
With a vengeance. . . . . Jew 2.3.67 Barab
Ile pay thee with a vengeance Ithamore. . . . . Jew 3.4.116 Barab
The power of vengeance now incampes it selfe, . . . P 717 14.20 Navrre
My lord, referre your vengeance to the sword, . . . Edw 3.1.123 Spencr
This day I shall powre vengeance with my sword/On those proud Edw 3.1.186 Edward
Raigne showers of vengeance on my cursed head/Thou God, to whom Edw 4.6.7 Kent
come downe with a vengeance. . . . . . . F 684 2.2.133 P Envy
I say, least I send you into the Ostry with a vengeance. . F 733 2.3.12 P Robin
So shall our sleeping vengeance now arise, . . . F 879 3.1.101 Pope
a vengeance on them, they have vilde long nailes, there was a F App p.230 51 P Clown
fury moves/To wound their armes, sing vengeance, Sibils priests, Lucan, First Booke 564

VENGER

If of scornd lovers god be venger just, ... Ovid's Elegies 3.7.65

VENI

Veni veni Mephostophile. . . . . F 418 2.1.30 Faust

VENICE

but to passe along/Towards Venice by the Adriatick Sea; . Jew 1.1.163 Barab
From Venice Merchants, and from Padua/Were wont to come . Jew 3.1.6 Curtzn
In Florence, Venice, Antwerpe, London, Civill, . . . Jew 4.1.71 Barab
From <For> Venice shall they drag <dregge> huge Argosies,/And F 157 1.1.129 Valdes
From thence to Venice, Padua, and the [rest] <East>, . F 794 3.1.16 Faust

VENIENS

Too true it is, quem dies vidit veniens superbum, . . Edw 4.7.53 Leistr

VENISON

All's one, for wee'l be bold with his Venison. . . . F 808 3.1.30 Mephst

VENOME

and in this/Vomit your venome, and invenome her/That like a Jew 3.4.104 Barab
Who swolne with venome of ambitious pride, . . . Edw 1.2.31 Mortmr

VENOMED

Wilt thou now slay me with thy venomed sting, . . . Dido 5.1.167 Dido

VENOMOUS

Sprong of the teeth of Dragons venomous, ... 1Tamb 2.2.48 Meandr
That sprong of teeth of Dragons venomous? . . . . 1Tamb 2.2.52 Mycet
that in his infancie/Did pash the jawes of Serpents venomous: 1Tamb 3.3.105 Bajzth

VENOMS

And leave your venoms in this Tyrants dish. . . . 1Tamb 4.4.22 Bajzth

VENT'ROUS

Would have allur'd the vent'rous youth of Greece, . . Hero and Leander 1.57

VENTROUS

I like a ventrous youth, rid him into the deepe pond at the F App p.240 133 P HrsCsr

VENTURE

Yet would I venture to conduct your Grace, . . . 2Tamb 1.2.72 Almeda
There was the venture summ'd and satisfied. . . . Jew 1.1.3 Barab

VENUS

And Venus Swannes shall shed their silver downe, . . . Dido 1.1.36 Jupitr
Venus farewell, thy sonne shall be our care: . . . Dido 1.1.120 Jupitr
Venus, how art thou compast with content, ... Dido 1.1.135 Venus
And made that way my mother Venus led: . . . . Dido 1.1.221 Aeneas
Stay gentle Venus, flye not from thy sonne, . . . Dido 1.1.242 Aeneas
My mother Venus jealous of my health, ... Dido 2.1.221 Aeneas
Lest she imagine thou art Venus sonne: . . . . Dido 3.1.4 Cupid
Nor Venus triumph in his tender youth: . . . . Dido 3.2.9 Juno
Say Paris, now shall Venus have the ball? . . . . Dido 3.2.12 Juno
Fie Venus, that such causeles words of wrath, . . . Dido 3.2.26 Juno
Venus, sweete Venus, how may I deserve/Such amourous favours at Dido 3.2.64 Juno
sweete Venus, how may I deserve/Such amourous favours at thy Dido 3.2.64 Juno
And Venus, let there be a match confirmd/Betwixt these two, Dido 3.2.77 Juno
And here we met faire Venus virgine like, ... Dido 3.3.54 Achat
By chance sweete Queene, as Mars and Venus met. . . Dido 3.4.4 Aeneas
Or for the love of Venus, would she leave/The angrie God of 1Tamb 5.1.124 Tamb
turrets of my Court/Sit like to Venus in her chaire of state, 2Tamb 4.2.42 Therid
the Sun, Venus, and Mercury in a yeare; the Moone in twenty F 605 2.2.54 P Faust
Venus is faint; swift Hermes retrograde; . . . . Lucan, First Booke 661
Yoke Venus Doves, put Mirtle on thy haire, . . . Ovid's Elegies 1.2.23
Venus thy side doth warme,/And brings good fortune, a rich Ovid's Elegies 1.8.30
And Venus rules in her Aeneas Citty. . . . . . Ovid's Elegies 1.8.42
Venus to mockt men lendes a sencelesse eare. . . . Ovid's Elegies 1.8.86
What age fits Mars, with Venus doth agree, . . . Ovid's Elegies 1.9.3
will I grace them/And in the midst of Venus temple place them. Ovid's Elegies 1.11.26
That cannot Venus mutuall pleasure taste. . . . . Ovid's Elegies 2.3.2
But Venus often to her Mars such brought. . . . . Ovid's Elegies 2.5.28
With Venus game who will a servant grace? . . . . Ovid's Elegies 2.7.21
I sweare by Venus, and the wingd boyes bowe, . . . Ovid's Elegies 2.7.27
By Venus Deity how did I protest. . . . . . Ovid's Elegies 2.8.18
Venus, why doublest thou my endlesse smart? . . . Ovid's Elegies 2.10.11
Had Venus spoilde her bellies Troyane fruite, . . . Ovid's Elegies 2.14.17
Venus with Vulcan, though smiths tooles laide by, . . . Ovid's Elegies 2.17.19
Wee Macer sit in Venus slothfull shade, ... Ovid's Elegies 2.18.3
Venus without me should be rusticall, ... Ovid's Elegies 3.1.43
Thee gentle Venus, and the boy that flies, . . . Ovid's Elegies 3.2.55
What Venus promisd, promise thou we pray, ... Ovid's Elegies 3.2.59

VENUS	(cont.)			
And Venus grieves, Tibullus life being spent,	• • •	Ovid's Elegies	3.8.15	
Festivall dayes aske Venus, songs, and wine,	• • •	Ovid's Elegies	3.9.47	
Where Venus in her naked glory strove,	• • •	Hero and Leander	1.12	
So lovely faire was Hero, Venus Nun,	• • •	Hero and Leander	1.45	
from her tower/To Venus temple, [where] <were> unhappilye,		Hero and Leander	1.133	
So faire a church as this, had Venus none,	•	Hero and Leander	1.135	
The towne of Sestos cal'd it Venus glasse.	•	Hero and Leander	1.142	
From Venus altar to your footsteps bending)/Doth testifie that		Hero and Leander	1.210	
To Venus, answered shee, and as shee spake,	• • •	Hero and Leander	1.295	
Such sacrifice as this, Venus demands.	• • •	Hero and Leander	1.310	
Then shall you most resemble Venus Nun,	• • •	Hero and Leander	1.319	
When Venus sweet rites are perform'd and done.	• • •	Hero and Leander	1.320	
God knowes I play/With Venus swannes and sparrowes all the day.		Hero and Leander	1.352	
Did she uphold to Venus, and againe,	• • •	Hero and Leander	1.367	

VERBE				
And hath a speciall gift to forme a verbe.	• • •	Edw	2.1.55	Spencr

VERGE				
Ah sweete sir John, even to the utmost verge/Of Europe, or the		Edw	4.2.29	Queene

VERIE				
of Persea, and the verie legges/Whereon our state doth leane,		1Tamb	1.1.59	Mycet
is that doth excruciate/The verie substance of my vexed soule:		1Tamb	1.1.114	Cosroe
How can it but afflict my verie soule?	• • •	1Tamb	4.4.67	Zenoc
Tis verie kindlie spoke my lord of Penbrooke,	• •	Edw	2.5.104	Arundl
Yes, I do verie well remember that.	• • •	F1638	4.6.81	P Faust

VERILY				
That he shall verily thinke it comes from him.	• • •	Jew	2.3.376	Ithimr

VERITAS				
Si peccasse negamus, fallimur, et nulla est in nobis veritas:		F 68	1.1.40	P Faust

VERITY				
And I deserve more then thou canst in verity,	• •	Ovid's Elegies	3.1.47	

VERLETE				
Holla verlete, hey: Epernoune, where is the King?	• •	P 956	19.26	Guise

VERMILION				
until the bloody flag/Be once advanc'd on my vermilion Tent,		1Tamb	4.2.117	Tamb
And too too well the faire vermilion knew,	• • •	Hero and Leander	1.395	

VERMILLION				
Sirha, the view of our vermillion tents,	• • •	2Tamb	5.1.86	Tamb

VERMINE				
that's good to kill Vermine:	• • • •	F 358	1.4.16	P Robin
then belike, if I were your man, I should be ful of vermine.		F App	p.229 22	P Clown

VERNA				
How through the midst of Verna and Bulgaria/And almost to the		2Tamb	2.1.8	Fredrk

VERONE				
in Catul Verone,/Of me Pelignis nation boasts alone,	•	Ovid's Elegies	3.14.7	

VERSE				
conning his neck-verse I take it, looking of a Fryars		Jew	4.2.17	P Pilia
Intends our Muse to vaunt <daunt> his heavenly verse;	•	F 6	Prol.6	1Chor
What, in Verse?	• • • • • •	F 356	1.4.14	P Robin
How, in verse?	• • • • • •	F App	p.229 15	P Clown
When in this [workes] <worke> first verse I trod aloft,	•	Ovid's Elegies	1.1.21	
Let my first verse be sixe, my last five feete,	•	Ovid's Elegies	1.1.31	
In verse to praise kinde Wenches tis my part,	•	Ovid's Elegies	1.10.59	
The fame that verse gives doth for ever last.	•	Ovid's Elegies	1.10.62	
Verse is immortall, and shall nere decay.	• •	Ovid's Elegies	1.15.32	
Let Kings give place to verse, and kingly showes,		Ovid's Elegies	1.15.33	
Snakes leape by verse from caves of broken mountaines/And		Ovid's Elegies	2.1.25	
Wenches apply your faire lookes to my verse/Which golden love		Ovid's Elegies	2.1.37	
This kinde of verse is not alike, yet fit,	• •	Ovid's Elegies	2.17.21	
To tragick verse while thou Achilles trainst,	•	Ovid's Elegies	2.18.1	
Thou fightst against me using mine owne verse.	•	Ovid's Elegies	3.1.38	
Come therefore, and to long verse shorter frame.	•	Ovid's Elegies	3.1.66	
Nere was, nor shall be, what my verse mentions.	•	Ovid's Elegies	3.5.18	
Or thinke soft verse in any stead to stand?	• •	Ovid's Elegies	3.7.2	
At thy deafe dores in verse sing my abuses.	• •	Ovid's Elegies	3.7.24	
And for a good verse drawe the first dart forth,	•	Ovid's Elegies	3.7.27	
Trust in good verse, Tibullus feeles deaths paines,	•	Ovid's Elegies	3.8.39	
'Tis doubtfull whether verse availe, or harme,	•	Ovid's Elegies	3.11.13	
Our verse great Tityus a huge space out-spreads,	•	Ovid's Elegies	3.11.25	

VERSES				
Both verses were alike till Love (men say) /Began to smile and		Ovid's Elegies	1.1.7	
By verses horned Io got hir name,	• • •	Ovid's Elegies	1.3.21	
Behold what gives the Poet but new verses?	•	Ovid's Elegies	1.8.57	
Let her make verses, and some blotted letter/On the last edge		Ovid's Elegies	1.11.21	
Thy verses sweet Tibullus shall be spoken.	• • •	Ovid's Elegies	1.15.28	
Verses [deduce] <reduce> the horned bloudy moone/And call the		Ovid's Elegies	2.1.23	
Verses ope dores, and lockes put in the poast/Although of oake,		Ovid's Elegies	2.1.27	
put in the poast/Although of oake, to yeeld to verses boast.		Ovid's Elegies	2.1.28	
The little stones these little verses have.	•	Ovid's Elegies	2.6.60	
For great revenews I good verses have,	• •	Ovid's Elegies	2.17.27	
Verses alone are with continuance crown'd.	• •	Ovid's Elegies	3.8.28	

VERTUE				
False Jupiter, rewardst thou vertue so?	• • •	Dido	1.1.78	Venus
With utmost vertue of my faith and dutie.	• •	1Tamb	2.5.17	Meandr
For vertue is the fount whence honor springs.	•	1Tamb	4.4.128	Tamb
Which into words no vertue can digest:	• •	1Tamb	5.1.173	Tamb
That Vertue solely is the sum of glorie,	• •	1Tamb	5.1.189	Tamb
With vertue of a gentle victorie,	• • •	1Tamb	5.1.398	Zenoc
But making now a vertue of thy sight,	• •	1Tamb	5.1.428	Arabia
And shine in compleat vertue more than they,	•	2Tamb	1.3.51	Tamb
May never day give vertue to his eies,	• •	2Tamb	4.1.174	Trebiz
And when my soule hath vertue of your sight,	•	2Tamb	5.3.225	Tamb
To cherish vertue and nobilitie,	• • •	Edw	3.1.167	Herald

VERTUE (cont.)

ragged stonie walles/Immure thy vertue that aspires to heaven? Edw 3.1.257 Mortmr
I see there's vertue in my heavenly words. F 255 1.3.27 Faust
the Planets/Alter their course; and vainly dim their vertue? Lucan, First Booke 663
Let all Lawes yeeld, sinne beare the name of vertue, Lucan, First Booke 666
Such force and vertue hath an amorous looke. Hero and Leander 1.166
What vertue is it that is borne with us? Hero and Leander 1.278

VERTUES

That by thy vertues freest us from annoy, Dido 1.1.153 Achat
Whose vertues carie with it life and death, 1Tamb 2.5.61 Therid
(An Emperour so honoured for his vertues)/Revives the spirits 2Tamb 3.1.23 Callap
this table as a Register/Of all her vertues and perfections. 2Tamb 3.2.24 Celeb
Your sacred vertues pour'd upon his throne, 2Tamb 5.3.11 Therid
The vertues of our true Religion, P 577 11.42 Pleshe

VERTUOUS

Nor Sun reflexe his vertuous beames thereon, 1Tamb 3.1.52 Moroc
To see your highnes in this vertuous minde. P1210 22.72 Navrre
Men foolishly doe call it vertuous, Hero and Leander 1.277
And few great lords in vertuous deeds shall joy, Hero and Leander 1.479

VERY (See also VERIE)

Will dye with very tidings of his death: Dido 3.3.77 Iarbus
of Verna and Bulgaria/And almost to the very walles of Rome, 2Tamb 2.1.9 Fredrk
The very Custome barely comes to more/Then many Merchants of Jew 1.1.63 1Merch
And very wisely sayd, it may be so. Jew 1.1.166 3Jew
Alas, Sir, I am a very youth. Jew 2.3.115 P Slave
And he is very seldome from my house; Jew 3.1.10 Curtzn
A very feeling one; have not the Nuns fine sport with the Jew 3.3.32 P Ithimr
Very well, Ithimore, then now be secret; Jew 3.4.60 Barab
Me thinkes he fingers very well. Jew 4.4.49 Pilia
Very mush, Mounsier, you no be his man? Jew 4.4.57 P Barab
This sudden death of his is very strange. Jew 5.1.54 Bosco
The very same, my Lord: Jew 5.1.74 Barab
Me thinkes the gloves have a very strong perfume, P 170 3.5 OldQn
But come lets walke aside, th'airs not very sweet. P 497 9.16 QnMoth
Now doe I see that from the very first, P 694 13.38 Guise
My swelling hart for very anger breakes, Edw 2.2.200 Edward
That you were dead, or very neare your death. Edw 4.2.38 Queene
Very well. Edw 5.5.31 Matrvs
I am a very poore man, and have lost very much of late by horse F1463 4.4.7 P HrsCsr
and have lost very much of late by horse flesh, and this F1464 4.4.8 P HrsCsr
The very cullor scard him; a dead blacknesse/Ranne through the Lucan, First Booke 617
Thy very haires will the hot bodkin teach. Ovid's Elegies 1.14.30

VESPASIAN

Till Titus and Vespasian conquer'd us)/Am I become as wealthy Jew 2.3.10 Barab

VESSELL

how you durst with so much wealth/Trust such a crazed Vessell, Jew 1.1.80 1Merch

VESSELS

Servants, come fetch these emptie vessels here, Dido 4.2.49 Iarbus
Vessels of Brasse oft handled, brightly shine, Hero and Leander 1.231

VESTALL

rites and Latian Jove advanc'd/On Alba hill o Vestall flames, Lucan, First Booke 201
Fierce Mastives hould; the vestall fires went out, Lucan, First Booke 547
Why being a vestall am I wooed to wed, Ovid's Elegies 3.5.75
And she her vestall virgin Priests doth follow. Ovid's Elegies 3.12.30

VESTIGIAS

upon my right heele, with quasi vestigias nostras insistere. F App p.231 70 P Wagner

VESTIGIIS

left heele, that thou maist, Quasi vestigiis nostris insistere. F 387 1.4.45 P Wagner

VESTURES

Next, an inferiour troupe, in tuckt up vestures, Lucan, First Booke 595

VEX

That most may vex his body and his soule. 2Tamb 3.5.99 Callap
That legions of tormenting spirits may vex/Your slavish bosomes 2Tamb 5.1.45 Govnr

VEX'D

Vex'd and tormented runnes poore Barabas/With fatall curses Jew 2.1.5 Barab

VEXE

our hearts/More than the thought of this dooth vexe our soules. 2Tamb 5.1.145 Jrslem
Nothing but vexe thee more,/To want in hell, that had on earth F1897 5.2.101 BdAngl

VEXED

is that doth excruciate/The verie substance of my vexed soule: 1Tamb 1.1.114 Cosroe
O life more loathsome to my vexed thoughts, 1Tamb 5.1.255 Bajzth
Must I be vexed like the nightly birde, Edw 5.3.6 Edward
How am I vexed by these villaines Charmes? F1117 3.3.30 Mephst
How am I vexed with these vilaines charmes? F App p.235 37 Mephst

VEXT

And with mistrust of the like measure vext. Ovid's Elegies 1.4.46
So having vext she nourisht my warme fire, Ovid's Elegies 2.19.15

VEYLE

To stay thy tresses white veyle hast thou none? Ovid's Elegies 3.5.56

VEYLES

As is the use, the Nunnes in white veyles clad, Ovid's Elegies 3.12.27

VEYNES

A small, but wholesome soyle with watrie veynes. Ovid's Elegies 2.16.2

VIAL (See VYOLL)

VICE

Forbeare to kindle vice by prohibition, Ovid's Elegies 3.4.11

VICE-ADMIRAL (See VIZADMIRALL)

VICEROIES

Therefore Viceroies the Christians must have peace. 2Tamb 1.1.77 Orcan
When we shall meet the Turkish Deputie/And all his Viceroies, 2Tamb 1.3.100 Tamb
With all his viceroies shall be so affraide, 2Tamb 1.3.162 Tamb
Viceroies and Peeres of Turky play the men, 2Tamb 3.5.14 Callap
Tell me Viceroies the number of your men, 2Tamb 3.5.30 Callap

VICEROIES (cont.)
Come puissant Viceroies, let us to the field, 2Tamb 3.5.53 Callap
Come Asian Viceroies, to your taskes a while/And take such 2Tamb 5.1.136 Tamb
My Viceroies bondage under Tamburlaine, 2Tamb 5.2.21 Callap

VICEROY
Viceroy of Byron, wisely hast thou said: 2Tamb 1.1.54 Orcan
Wil match thee with a viceroy or a king. 2Tamb 3.4.41 Techel
Than any Viceroy, King or Emperour. 2Tamb 3.4.43 Olymp
But as for you (Viceroy) you shal have bits, 2Tamb 3.5.103 Tamb

VICEROYES
Egregious Viceroyes of these Eastern parts/Plac'd by the issue 2Tamb 1.1.1 Orcan

VICES
Or justifie my vices being many, Ovid's Elegies 2.4.2
Ah, she doth more worth then her vices prove. Ovid's Elegies 3.10.44

VICIOUS
But vicious, harebraind, and illit'rat hinds? Hero and Leander 2.218

VICTOR
When made a victor in these hautie arms, 2Tamb 4.1.46 Amyras
When I shall vaunt as victor in revenge. P 722 14.25 Navrre

VICTORIE
Whose fading weale of victorie forsooke, Dido 1.2.15 Illion
Yet we assure us of the victorie. 1Tamb 3.3.35 Usumc
Returne with victorie, and free from wound. 1Tamb 3.3.133 Zenoc
That never fought but had the victorie: 1Tamb 3.3.153 Tamb
Then Victorie begins to take her flight, 1Tamb 3.3.160 Tamb
Graunt that these signes of victorie we yeeld/May bind the 1Tamb 5.1.55 2Virgn
We know the victorie is ours my Lord, 1Tamb 5.1.203 Therid
Go, never to returne with victorie: 1Tamb 5.1.214 Bajzth
With vertue of a gentle victorie, 1Tamb 5.1.398 Zenoc
And take the victorie our God hath given. 2Tamb 2.1.63 Sgsmnd
If there be Christ, we shall have victorie. 2Tamb 2.2.64 Orcan
Assaile it and be sure of victorie. 2Tamb 5.2.59 Callap
Take you the wealth, leave us the victorie. F1347 4.2.23 Benvol

VICTORIES
in her browes/Triumphes and Trophees for my victories: 1Tamb 5.1.513 Tamb
Thy victories are growne so violent, 2Tamb 4.1.140 Jrslem
For honor of my woondrous victories. 2Tamb 4.1.205 Tamb
To triumph after all our victories. 2Tamb 5.1.213 Tamb
and the victories/Wherewith he hath so sore dismaide the world, 2Tamb 5.2.43 Callap
Proclaime king Edwards warres and victories. Edw 3.1.281 Spencr

VICTORIOUS
And set it safe on my victorious head. 1Tamb 2.3.54 Cosroe
And proove the waight of his victorious arme: 1Tamb 4.3.47 Arabia
Victorious wreathes at length my Temples greete. Ovid's Elegies 3.10.6
Victorious Perseus a wingd steedes back takes. Ovid's Elegies 3.11.24

VICTORIOUSLY
untill thou see/Me martch victoriously with all my men, 1Tamb 3.3.127 Tamb

VICTORY
And more regarding gaine than victory: 1Tamb 2.2.46 Meandr
that is rapt with love/Of fame, of valour, and of victory, 1Tamb 5.1.181 Tamb
Whom should I wish the fatall victory, 1Tamb 5.1.385 Zenoc
Nor fortune keep them selves from victory. 1Tamb 5.1.406 Arabia
Twas I my lord that gat the victory, 1Tamb 5.1.445 Tamb
Al sights of power to grace my victory: 1Tamb 5.1.474 Tamb
to them should not infringe/Our liberty of armes and victory. 2Tamb 2.1.41 Baldwn
If we neglect this offered victory. 2Tamb 2.1.59 Fredrk
Whose power had share in this our victory: 2Tamb 2.3.35 Orcan
In memorie of this our victory. 2Tamb 3.5.20 Callap
Nor ere returne but with the victory, 2Tamb 3.5.44 Trebiz
My sterne aspect shall make faire Victory, 2Tamb 3.5.162 Tamb
Come fight ye Turks, or yeeld us victory. 2Tamb 3.5.169 Tamb
wilt thou so defame/The hatefull fortunes of thy victory, 2Tamb 4.3.78 Orcan
Where resolution strives for victory. P 165 2.108 Guise
And we are grac'd with wreathes of victory: P 788 16.2 Navrre
The terrour of this happy victory, P 791 16.5 Bartus
In honour of the Popes triumphant victory. F 835 3.1.57 Mephst
Drinke to our late and happy victory. F 980 3.1.202 Pope
That victory doth chiefely triumph merit, Ovid's Elegies 2.12.5
First Victory is brought with large spred wing, Ovid's Elegies 3.2.45
But victory, I thinke, will hap to love. Ovid's Elegies 3.10.34

VICTUALL
Victuall his Souldiers, give him wealthie gifts, Dido 2.1.329 Venus
starv'd, and he be provided for a moneths victuall before hand. 1Tamb 4.4.47 P Usumc
That no supply of victuall shall come in, 2Tamb 3.3.32 Techel

VICTUALLS
<No, Ile see thee hanged, thou wilt eate up all my victualls>. F 702 (HC264)A P Faust

VICTUALS
And rost our new found victuals on this shoare. Dido 1.1.168 Aeneas
Wel Zenocrate, Techelles, and the rest, fall to your victuals. 1Tamb 4.4.15 P Tamb

VIDIT
Too true it is, quem dies vidit veniens superbum, Edw 4.7.53 Leistr
Hunc dies vidit fugiens jacentem. Edw 4.7.54 Leistr

VIENNA
thou I am he/That with the Cannon shooke Vienna walles, 2Tamb 1.1.87 Orcan
Vienna was besieg'd, and I was there, 2Tamb 1.1.103 Sgsmnd

VIEW (See also VEIW)
Vaild his resplendant glorie from your view. Dido 1.1.126 Venus
Whose lookes set forth no mortall forme to view, Dido 1.1.189 Aeneas
Looke where she comes: Aeneas [view] <viewd> her well. Dido 2.1.72 Illion
Well may I view her, but she sees not me. Dido 2.1.73 Aeneas
View but his picture in this tragicke glasse, 1Tamb Prol.7 Prolog
That I may view these milk-white steeds of mine, 1Tamb 1.1.77 Mycet
Till with their eies [they] <thee> view us Emperours. 1Tamb 1.2.67 Tamb

VIEW (cont.)			
Lay out our golden wedges to the view,	1Tamb	1.2.139	Tamb
View well my Camp, and speake indifferently,	1Tamb	3.3.8	Tamb
and let the Feends infernall view/As are the blasted banks of	1Tamb	5.1.242	Zabina
But now Orcanes, view my royall hoste,	2Tamb	1.1.106	Sgsmnd
As all the world shall tremble at their view.	2Tamb	1.3.57	Celeb
View me thy father that hath conquered kings,	2Tamb	3.2.110	Tamb
And set his warlike person to the view/Of fierce Achilles,	2Tamb	3.5.67	Tamb
For with thy view my joyes are at the full,	2Tamb	4.2.31	Therid
Sirha, the view of our vermillion tents,	2Tamb	5.1.86	Tamb
is come from France/To view this Land, and frolicke with his	Jew	Prol.4	Machvl
No, this is the better, mother, view this well.	Jew	2.3.145	Mthias
Now cosin view him well,	P 307	5.34	Anjoy
I view the prince with Aristarchus eyes,	Edw	5.4.54	Mortmr
Jeromes Bible Faustus, view it well:	F 65	1.1.37	Faust
Longing to view Orions drisling looke <looks>,	F 230	1.3.2	Faust
Meane while peruse this booke, and view it throughly,	F 717	2.2.169	Lucifr
There did we view the Kingdomes of the world,	F 852	3.1.74	Faust
And view their triumphs, as they passe this way.	F 857	3.1.79	Mephst
To view the sentence of the reverend Synod,	F1014	3.2.34	1Card
Then wherefore would you have me view that booke?	F1023	3.2.43	Pope
[When Faustus had with pleasure tane the view]/[Of rarest	F1138	3.3.51A	3Chor
Dis do we ascend/To view the subjects of our Monarchy,	F1798	5.2.2	Lucifr
To view the Scriptures, then I turn'd the leaves/And led thine	F1888	5.2.92	Mephst
Whence thou shouldst view thy Roome with squinting beams.	Lucan, First Booke		55
And their vaild Matron, who alone might view/Minervas statue;	Lucan, First Booke		597
View me, my becks, and speaking countenance:	Ovid's Elegies		1.4.17
The lawier and the client <both do> hate thy view,	Ovid's Elegies		1.13.21
In view and opposit two citties stood,	Hero and Leander		1.2
VIEW'D			
Have view'd the army of the Scythians,	1Tamb	2.2.41	Spy
The Westerne part of Affrike, where I view'd/The Ethiopian sea,	2Tamb	1.3.195	Techel
I view'd your urine, and the [Hipostasis] <Hipostates>/Thick	2Tamb	5.3.82	Phsitn
For Callymath, when he hath view'd the Towne,	Jew	5.2.105	Barab
Thus have we view'd the City, seene the sacke,	Jew	5.3.1	Calym
And all that view'd her, were enamour'd on her.	Hero and Leander		1.118
VIEWD			
Looke where she comes: Aeneas [view] <viewd> her well.	Dido	2.1.72	Illion
Which when I viewd, I cride, Aeneas stay,	Dido	5.1.232	Anna
And yet I have not viewd my Lord the king,	Edw	1.1.45	Gavstn
When this fresh bleeding wound Leander viewd,	Hero and Leander		2.213
VIEWDE			
Day rose and viewde these tumultes of the war;	Lucan, First Booke		235
VIEWE			
On all the [bed mens] <beds men> tumbling let him viewe/And thy	Ovid's Elegies		1.8.97
Not black, nor golden were they to our viewe,	Ovid's Elegies		1.14.9
She viewed the earth: the earth to viewe, beseem'd her.	Ovid's Elegies		2.5.43
VIEWED			
Whose lovely faces never any viewed,	2Tamb	3.2.30	Tamb
She viewed the earth: the earth to viewe, beseem'd her.	Ovid's Elegies		2.5.43
VIEWES			
the Pilot stands/And viewes a strangers ship rent in the winds,	1Tamb	4.3.33	Souldn
He viewes the cloudes, the Planets, and the Starres,	F 760	2.3.39	2Chor
She holds, and viewes her old lockes in her lappe,	Ovid's Elegies		1.14.53
VIEWING			
Which Sinon viewing, causde the Greekish spyes/To hast to	Dido	2.1.180	Aeneas
Viewing the fire wherewith rich Ilion burnt.	Dido	2.1.264	Aeneas
Jove viewing me in armes, lookes pale and wan,	1Tamb	5.1.452	Tamb
And some guest viewing watry Sulmoes walles,	Ovid's Elegies		3.14.11
Viewing Leanders face, fell downe and fainted.	Hero and Leander		2.2
VIEWST			
Thou viewst the course, I thee:	Ovid's Elegies		3.2.5
VIGOR			
With strange infusion of his sacred vigor,	2Tamb	2.2.52	Orcan
And was the second cause why vigor failde mee:	Ovid's Elegies		3.6.38
VILAINE			
in his nakednesse, the vilaine is bare, and out of service,	F App	p.229 7	P Wagner
Vilaine, call me Maister Wagner, and let thy left eye be	F App	p.231 69	P Wagner
Vilaine I say, undo what thou hast done.	F App	p.238 75	Knight
VILAINES			
Vanish vilaines, th'one like an Ape, an other like a Beare, the	F App	p.235 32	P Mephst
How am I vexed with these vilaines charmes?	F App	p.235 37	Mephst
VILD			
Vild Tyrant, barbarous bloody Tamburlain.	2Tamb	5.1.133	Trebiz
greedy desire stil poore/Did vild deeds, then t'was worth the	Lucan, First Booke		175
each mans mony/And seekes vild wealth by selling of her Cony,	Ovid's Elegies		1.10.22
VILDE			
Vilde wretch, and why hast thou of all unkinde,	Edw	4.6.5	Kent
[Unpleasant, harsh, contemptible and vilde]:	F 136	1.1.108A	Faust
they have vilde long nailes, there was a hee divell and a shee	F App	p.230 52	P Clown
heavinesse/Of thy most vilde and loathsome filthinesse,	F App	p.243 40	OldMan
Let base conceited wits admire vilde things,	Ovid's Elegies		1.15.35
To meete for poyson or vilde facts we crave not,	Ovid's Elegies		2.2.63
VILE			
This countrie swarmes with vile outragious men,	1Tamb	2.2.22	Meandr
Let not a man so vile and barbarous,	1Tamb	3.2.26	Agidas
I shall now revenge/My fathers vile abuses and mine owne.	2Tamb	3.5.91	Callap
Vile monster, borne of some infernal hag,	2Tamb	5.1.110	Govnr
abject our princely mindes/To vile and ignominious servitude.	2Tamb	5.1.141	Orcan
And that vile Carkasse drawne by warlike kings,	2Tamb	5.2.16	Amasia
I meane that vile Torpedo, Gaveston,	Edw	1.4.223	Mortmr
[My faith, vile hel, shall triumph over thee],	F1793	5.1.120A	OldMan
Let not thy necke by his vile armes be prest,	Ovid's Elegies		1.4.35

VILE (cont.)				
to her I consecrate/My faithfull tables being vile maple late.	Ovid's Elegies	1.11.28		
Not one in heaven should be more base and vile.	Ovid's Elegies	1.13.36		
Had ancient Mothers this vile custome cherisht,	Ovid's Elegies	2.14.9		
if Corcyras Ile/Had thee unknowne interr'd in ground most vile.	Ovid's Elegies	3.8.48		
So she be faire, but some vile toongs will blot?	Hero and Leander	1.286		
VILLAGES				
In setting Christian villages on fire,	Jew	2.3.203		Ithimr
VILLAIN (See also VILAINES)				
Villain, I tell thee, were that Tamburlaine/As monsterous as	1Tamb	4.1.17		Souldn
Base villain, vassall, slave to Tamburlaine:	1Tamb	4.2.19		Tamb
Villain, knowest thou to whom thou speakest?	1Tamb	4.4.39	P	Usumc
Villain, art thou the sonne of Tamburlaine,	2Tamb	3.2.95		Tamb
Villain, the shepheards issue, at whose byrth/Heaven did	2Tamb	3.5.79		Tamb
What, dares the villain write in such base terms?	Jew	3.2.3		Lodowk
How liberally the villain gives me mine own gold.	Jew	4.4.48	P	Barab
No villain, that toung of thine,	P 530	10.3		Guise
That villain for whom I beare this deep disgrace,	P 766	15.24		Guise
VILLAINE				
On this same theevish villaine Tamburlaine.	1Tamb	2.2.3		Mycet
Base villaine, darst thou give the lie?	1Tamb	2.4.19		Tamb
I tell thee villaine, those that lead my horse/Have to their	1Tamb	3.3.69		Bajzth
Mercilesse villaine, Pesant ignorant,	1Tamb	4.1.64		Souldn
But Villaine, thou that wishest this to me,	1Tamb	4.2.12		Tamb
Stoop villaine, stoope, stoope for so he bids,	1Tamb	4.2.22		Tamb
Take it up Villaine, and eat it, or I will make thee slice the	1Tamb	4.4.43	P	Tamb
a roguish runnaway, suborn'd/That villaine there, that slave,	2Tamb	3.5.87		Tamb
Villaine, traitor, damned fugitive,	2Tamb	3.5.117		Tamb
Goe villaine, cast thee headlong from a rock,	2Tamb	3.5.120		Tamb
Away, let us to the field, that the villaine may be slaine.	2Tamb	3.5.143	P	Trebiz
But wher's this coward, villaine, not my sonne,	2Tamb	4.1.89		Tamb
What, have I slaine her? Villaine, stab thy selfe:	2Tamb	4.2.82		Therid
Villaine, respects thou more thy slavish life,	2Tamb	5.1.10		Govnr
Go bind the villaine, he shall hang in chaines,	2Tamb	5.1.84		Tamb
villaine I say,/Should I but touch the rusty gates of hell,	2Tamb	5.1.95		Tamb
Villaine away, and hie thee to the field,	2Tamb	5.3.72		Tamb
There comes the villaine, now I'le be reveng'd.	Jew	2.3.333		Lodowk
A Fryar? false villaine, he hath done the deed.	Jew	3.4.22		Barab
Thus every villaine ambles after wealth/Although he ne're be	Jew	3.4.52		Barab
What shall we doe with this base villaine then?	Jew	4.2.62		Curtzn
The more villaine he to keep me thus:	Jew	4.2.111		Ithimr
I must make this villaine away:	Jew	4.3.29	P	Barab
Nay [to] thine owne cost, villaine, if thou com'st.	Jew	4.3.59		Barab
And how the villaine revels with my gold.	Jew	4.3.68		Barab
Oh villaine, Heaven will be reveng'd on thee.	Jew	5.2.25		Govnr
No, villaine, no.	Jew	5.5.76		Govnr
Christ, villaine?	P 355	6.10		Mntsrl
But villaine he to whom these lines should goe,	P 696	13.40		Guise
Villaine, why dost thou look so gastly? speake.	P 989	19.59		Guise
To murder me, villaine?	P 993	19.63		Guise
No, let the villaine dye, and feele in hell,	P1174	22.36		King
Take hence that damned villaine from my sight.	P1182	22.44		King
O that that damned villaine were alive againe,	P1216	22.78		Eprnon
That villaine Mortimer, ile be his death.	Edw	1.1.81		Gavstn
That villaine Gaveston is made an Earle.	Edw	1.2.11		Lncstr
Thou villaine, wherfore talkes thou of a king,	Edw	1.4.28		Mortmr
Villaine, tis thou that robst me of my lord.	Edw	1.4.160		Queene
Villaine thy life, unlesse I misse mine aime.	Edw	2.2.84		Mortmr
By heaven, the abject villaine shall not live.	Edw	2.2.106		Mortmr
Goe, take the villaine, soldiers come away,	Edw	2.6.11		Warwck
Villaine, I know thou comst to murther me.	Edw	5.5.45		Edward
Villaine.	Edw	5.6.25		King
Villaine, call me Maister Wagner, and see that you walke	F 385	1.4.43	P	Wagner
Villaine, have I not bound thee to tell me any thing?	F 622	2.2.71	P	Faust
O help, help, the villaine hath murder'd me.	F1493	4.4.37	P	Faust
Away you villaine:	F App	p.240 120	P	Faust
Come villaine to the Constable.	F App	p.241 157	P	Mephst
VILLAINES				
Injurious villaines, thieves, runnagates,	1Tamb	3.3.225		Zabina
Ah villaines, dare ye touch my sacred armes?	1Tamb	3.3.268		Bajzth
Traitors, villaines, damned Christians.	2Tamb	2.2.29		Orcan
And vow to burne the villaines cruell heart.	2Tamb	3.1.56		Trebiz
Villaines, these terrours and these tyrannies/(If tyrannies	2Tamb	4.1.146		Tamb
Are ye not gone ye villaines with your spoiles?	2Tamb	4.3.84		Tamb
Villaines, cowards, Traitors to our state,	2Tamb	5.1.43		Govnr
There should not one of all the villaines power/Live to give	2Tamb	5.3.108		Tamb
Thus are the villaines, cowards fled for feare,	2Tamb	5.3.115		Tamb
Oh earth-mettall'd villaines, and no Hebrews born!	Jew	1.2.78		Barab
Who for the villaines have no wit themselves,	Jew	1.2.215		Barab
poore villaines, were ne're thought upon/Till Titus and	Jew	2.3.9		Barab
make account of me/As of thy fellow; we are villaines both:	Jew	2.3.214		Barab
Villaines, I am a sacred person, touch me not.	Jew	4.1.201		1Fryar
And villaines, know you cannot helpe me now.	Jew	5.5.77		Barab
Hath he been hurt with villaines in the street?	P 254	4.52		Charls
You villaines that have slaine my Gaveston:	Edw	3.1.142		Edward
A villaines, hath that Mortimer escapt?	Edw	4.3.38		Edward
Base villaines, wherefore doe you gripe mee thus?	Edw	5.3.57		Kent
Staie villaines.	Edw	5.4.93		Kent
O villaines!	Edw	5.5.58		Ltborn
nakednesse, I know the Villaines out of service, and so hungry,	F 349	1.4.7	P	Wagner
Villaines why speake you not?	F1045	3.2.65		Pope
How am I vexed by these villaines Charmes?	F1117	3.3.30		Mephst
That rowling downe, may breake the villaines bones,	F1414	4.2.90		Faust

VILLAINES (cont.)			
wel villaines, for your presumption, I transforme thee into an	F App	p.235 43	P Mephst
VILLAIN'S			
This villain's sent to make away the king.	Edw	5.5.21	Matrvs
VILLAINS			
I, villains, you must yeeld, and under Turkish yokes/Shall	Jew	5.2.7	Calym
VILLANESSE			
And Villanesse to shame, disdaine, and misery:	1Tamb	5.1.269	Bajzth
VILLANIE			
Is far from villanie or servitude.	1Tamb	3.2.38	Zenoc
To be reveng'd of all his Villanie.	2Tamb	5.2.23	Callap
That by my helpe shall doe much villanie.	Jew	2.3.133	Barab
And apt for any kinde of villanie.	Edw	2.1.51	Baldck
Some treason, or some villanie was cause.	Edw	3.1.114	Spencr
Tydides left worst signes of villanie,	Ovid's Elegies	1.7.31	
VILLANIES			
have hir'd a slave my man/To accuse me of a thousand villanies:	Jew	5.1.76	Barab
Justly rewarded for his villanies.	F1376	4.2.52	Benvol
VILLANOUS			
thinke not a thought so villanous/Can harbor in a man of noble	Edw	5.1.131	Bartly
VILLANOUSLY			
Now sirs, you shall heare how villanously he serv'd mee:	F1535	4.5.31	P HrsCsr
VILLANY			
Bloody and breathlesse for his villany.	2Tamb	2.3.13	Gazell
Why, was there ever seene such villany,	Jew	3.3.1	Ithimr
Oh monstrous villany.	Jew	3.6.30	2Fryar
for in his villany/He will tell all he knowes and I shall dye	Jew	4.3.64	Barab
Or any villany thou canst devise,	F 865	3.1.87	Mephst
yee Lubbers look about/And find the man that doth this villany,	F1056	3.2.76	Pope
Zounds Doctor, is this your villany?	F1293	4.1.139	P Benvol
VINE			
That deads the royall vine, whose golden leaves/Empale your	Edw	3.1.163	Herald
So shall not Englands [Vine] <Vines> be perished,	Edw	5.1.47	Edward
Take clustred grapes from an ore-laden vine,	Ovid's Elegies	1.10.55	
Why takest increasing grapes from Vine-trees full?	Ovid's Elegies	2.14.23	
But without thee, although vine-planted ground/Conteines me,	Ovid's Elegies	2.16.33	
A livelie vine of greene sea agget spread;	Hero and Leander	1.138	
VINE-PLANTED			
But without thee, although vine-planted ground/Conteines me,	Ovid's Elegies	2.16.33	
VINES			
So shall not Englands [Vine] <Vines> be perished,	Edw	5.1.47	Edward
Whose bankes are set with Groves of fruitfull Vines.	F 786	3.1.8	Faust
With corne the earth abounds, with vines much more,	Ovid's Elegies	2.16.7	
Elmes love the Vines, the Vines with Elmes abide,	Ovid's Elegies	2.16.41	
By charmes maste drops from okes, from vines grapes fall,	Ovid's Elegies	3.6.33	
VINE-TREES			
Why takest increasing grapes from Vine-trees full?	Ovid's Elegies	2.14.23	
VINEYARDS			
And Bacchus vineyards [over-spread] <ore-spread> the world:	Jew	4.2.92	Ithimr
VINTNER			
life, Vintner you shall have your cup anon, say nothing Dick:	F1113	3.3.26	P Robin
But Robin, here comes the vintner.	F App	p.234 4	P Rafe
nay Ile tickle you Vintner, looke to the goblet Rafe,	F App	p.235 23	P Robin
Peccatum peccatorum, heeres thy goblet, good Vintner.	F App	p.235 29	P Rafe
VINTNERS			
same cup, for the Vintners boy followes us at the hard heeles.	F1089	3.3.2	P Dick
VIOLATE			
Violate any promise to possesse him.	Edw	2.5.64	Warwck
Is charg'd to violate her mistresse bed.	Ovid's Elegies	2.7.18	
VIOLATED			
Nor ever violated faith to him:	Dido	5.1.205	Dido
VIOLENCE			
But if they offer word or violence,	1Tamb	1.2.142	Tamb
Arabian king together/Martch on us with such eager violence,	1Tamb	5.1.200	Techel
This should be treacherie and violence,	2Tamb	2.1.31	Sgsmnd
The violence of thy common Souldiours lust?	2Tamb	4.3.80	Orcan
Or die some death of quickest violence,	2Tamb	5.1.41	2Citzn
see they keep/All trecherous violence from our noble freend,	P 268	4.66	Charls
He is hard hearted, therfore pull with violence.	P1105	20.15	1Mur
And will not offer violence to their King,	P1162	22.24	King
When violence is offered to the church.	Edw	1.2.41	ArchBp
To offer violence to his soveraigne,	Edw	2.4.34	Lncstr
To scape the violence of the streame first waded,	Lucan, First Booke	223	
Alcides like, by mightie violence,	Hero and Leander	2.120	
VIOLENT			
The motion was so over violent.	Dido	4.1.13	Achat
Thy victories are growne so violent,	2Tamb	4.1.140	Jrslem
And cannot last, it is so violent.	2Tamb	5.3.65	Techel
either by succession/Or urg'd by force; and nothing violent,	Jew	1.1.132	Barab
Ah brother, lay not violent hands on him,	Edw	1.1.189	Kent
Then laide they violent hands upon him, next/Himselfe	Edw	1.2.36	ArchBp
Nay, then lay violent hands upon your king,	Edw	1.4.35	Edward
Nor violent South-windes did thee ought affright.	Ovid's Elegies	2.11.52	
Then with huge steps came violent Tragedie,	Ovid's Elegies	3.1.11	
And some (their violent passions to asswage)/Compile sharpe	Hero and Leander	1.126	
VIOLET			
Like thy breath, sweet-hart, no violet like 'em.	Jew	4.4.40	Ithimr
VIOLETS			
And strewe him with sweete smelling Violets,	Dido	2.1.318	Venus
VIPER			
And gives the viper curled Dogge three heads.	Ovid's Elegies	3.11.26	
VIRGIL			
In Virgil Mantua joyes:	Ovid's Elegies	3.14.7	

VIRGIN (See also VYRGINS)			
But what may I faire Virgin call your name?	Dido	1.1.188	Aeneas
I, and a Virgin too, that grieves me most:	Jew	3.6.41	2Fryar
Griping his false hornes with hir virgin hand:	Ovid's Elegies	1.3.24	
With virgin waxe hath some imbast my joynts,	Ovid's Elegies	3.6.29	
Jewels, and gold their Virgin tresses crowne,	Ovid's Elegies	3.12.25	
And she her vestall virgin Priests doth follow.	Ovid's Elegies	3.12.30	
VIRGINE			
And here we met faire Venus virgine like,	Dido	3.3.54	Achat
VIRGINES			
Therefore, for these our harmlesse virgines sakes,	1Tamb	5.1.18	Govnr
VIRGINITIE			
Virginitie, albeit some highly prise it,	Hero and Leander	1.262	
This idoll which you terme Virginitie,	Hero and Leander	1.269	
Abandon fruitlesse cold Virginitie,	Hero and Leander	1.317	
VIRGINS			
Virgins halfe dead dragged by their golden haire,	Dido	2.1.195	Aeneas
Wel, lovely Virgins, think our countries care,	1Tamb	5.1.34	Govnr
What simple Virgins may perswade, we will.	1Tamb	5.1.61	2Virgn
Farewell (sweet Virgins) on whose safe return/Depends our	1Tamb	5.1.62	Govnr
Virgins, in vaine ye labour to prevent/That which mine honor	1Tamb	5.1.106	Tamb
What, have your horsmen shewen the virgins Death?	1Tamb	5.1.129	Tamb
The Grecian virgins shall attend on thee,	2Tamb	1.2.36	Callap
Grave Abbasse, and you happy Virgins guide,	Jew	1.2.314	Abigal
Th'Arcadian Virgins constant love hath wunne?	Ovid's Elegies	3.5.30	
VIRGO			
Virgo, salve.	Jew	3.3.50	1Fryar
VIRTUE (See VERTUE)			
VISAG'D			
Whereat the saphir visag'd god grew prowd,	Hero and Leander	2.155	
VISAGE			
came Hectors ghost/With ashie visage, blewish sulphure eyes,	Dido	2.1.202	Aeneas
The purple moone with sanguine visage stood.	Ovid's Elegies	1.8.12	
By fear'd Anubis visage I thee pray,	Ovid's Elegies	2.13.11	
VISAGES			
With furious words and frowning visages,	2Tamb	5.1.78	Tamb
VISION			
And til by vision, or by speach I heare/Immortall Jove say,	2Tamb	4.1.198	Tamb
At night in dreadful vision fearefull Roome,	Lucan, First Booke	188	
VISIT			
'Twere time well spent to goe and visit her:	Jew	1.2.389	Lodowk
Yet would I gladly visit Barabas,	Jew	5.3.24	Calym
I know thou couldst not come and visit me.	Edw	2.1.61	Neece
And I will visit him, why stay you me?	Edw	5.3.60	Kent
Request them earnestly to visit me.	F 93	1.1.65	Faust
if I live till morning, Il'e visit you:	F1877	5.2.81	P Faust
Come Gentlemen, let us go visit Faustus,	F1983	5.3.1	1Schol
VISITE			
<humble> intreates your Majestie/To visite him sick in his bed.	P 246	4.44	Man
Your Majesty were best goe visite him,	P 249	4.47	QnMoth
Content, I will goe visite the Admirall.	P 251	4.49	Charls
And every hower I will visite you.	P 272	4.70	Charls
And tell him ere it be long, Ile visite him.	P 912	18.13	Navrre
VISTE			
In silence of the night to viste us),	Hero and Leander	1.350	
O let mee viste Hero ere I die.	Hero and Leander	2.178	
VITAL			
Then will I comfort all my vital parts,	2Tamb	5.3.100	Tamb
A small thin skinne contain'd the vital parts,	Lucan, First Booke	622	
VITALL			
Hath suckt the measure of that vitall aire/That feeds the body	2Tamb	2.4.44	Zenoc
Shortning my dayes and thred of vitall life,	F App	p.239 92	Faust
VITTLES			
I must have one that's sickly, and be but for sparing vittles:	Jew	2.3.124	P Barab
VIVE			
Vive [le] <la> Roy, vive [le] <la> Roy.	P 588	12.1	All
Vive [le] <la> Roy, vive [le] <la> Roy.	P 598	12.11	All
Vive la messe, perish Hugonets,	P1014	19.84	Guise
VIZADMIRALL			
Vizadmirall unto the Catholike King.	Jew	2.2.7	Bosco
VOGESUS			
Under the rockes by crooked Vogesus;	Lucan, First Booke	399	
VOICE (See also VOYCE)			
And death arrests the organe of my voice,	1Tamb	2.7.8	Cosroe
Strooke with the voice of thundring Jupiter.	1Tamb	4.2.25	Tamb
If thou wilt have a song, the Turke shall straine his voice:	1Tamb	4.4.64	P Tamb
If woords might serve, our voice hath rent the aire,	2Tamb	2.4.121	Therid
He cannot heare the voice of Tamburlain,	2Tamb	5.1.199	Tamb
Stand close, he is comming, I know him by his voice.	P1000	19.70	P 1Mur
Even from your cheekes parte of a voice did breake.	Ovid's Elegies	2.5.16	
Or voice that howe to change the wilde notes knew?	Ovid's Elegies	2.6.18	
No such voice-feigning bird was on the ground,	Ovid's Elegies	2.6.23	
Dead is that speaking image of mans voice,	Ovid's Elegies	2.6.37	
And from the mid foord his hoarse voice upheav'd,	Ovid's Elegies	3.5.52	
VOICE-FEIGNING			
No such voice-feigning bird was on the ground,	Ovid's Elegies	2.6.23	
VOICES			
Use all their voices and their instruments/To entertaine divine	2Tamb	2.4.28	Tamb
of offices, and peoples voices/Bought by themselves and solde,	Lucan, First Booke	180	
in untrod woods/Shrill voices schright, and ghoasts incounter	Lucan, First Booke	568	
VOID (See also VOYD)			
Yet being void of Martiall discipline,	1Tamb	2.2.44	Meandr
which the heart ingenders/Are partcht and void of spirit,	2Tamb	5.3.95	Phsitn

VOIDE			
Quite voide of skars, and cleare from any wound,	2Tamb	3.2.112	Tamb
Heere hast thou a country voide of feares,	P 591	12.4	QnMoth
Supplying their voide places with the worst.	Ovid's Elegies		2.6.40
VOLGA (See also VUOLGAS)			
The rogue of Volga holds Zenocrate,	1Tamb	4.1.4	Souldn
VOLLEIES			
of thy hold/Volleies of ordinance til the breach be made,	2Tamb	3.3.25	Therid
But I have sent volleies of shot to you,	2Tamb	5.1.99	Tamb
VOLLEYES			
Volleyes of shot pierce through thy charmed Skin,	1Tamb	5.1.221	Bajzth
VOLLUMES			
And comments vollumes with her Yvory pen,	1Tamb	5.1.145	Tamb
VOLUPTUOUSNESSE			
Letting him live in all voluptuousnesse,	F 320	1.3.92	Faust
VOMIT			
and in this/Vomit your venome, and invenome her/That like a	Jew	3.4.104	Barab
VOMITE			
That when you vomite forth into the aire,	F1954	5.2.158	Faust
VOS			
et Demogorgon, propitiamus vos, ut appareat, et surgat	F 246	1.3.18	P Faust
VOTA			
nunc facio; et per vota nostra ipse nunc surgat nobis dicatus	F 249	1.3.21	P Faust
VOUCHSAFE			
vouchsafe of ruth/To tell us who inhabits this faire towne,	Dido	2.1.40	Aeneas
answered Love, nor would vouchsafe so much/As one poore word,	Hero and Leander		1.383
At least vouchsafe these armes some little roome,	Hero and Leander		2.249
VOUCHSAFES			
whom he vouchsafes/For vailing of his bonnet one good looke.	Edw	1.2.18	Lncstr
VOUCHSAFT			
And since your highnesse hath so well vouchsaft,	1Tamb	4.4.130	Therid
With whom (being women) I vouchsaft a league,	2Tamb	1.3.193	Techel
VOUCHSAFTE			
That ever I vouchsafte my dearest freends.	P1146	22.8	King
VOUSTRE			
A voustre commandemente Madam.	Jew	4.4.38	Barab
VOW			
I vow, if she but once frowne on thee more,	Dido	1.1.12	Jupitr
And vow by all the Gods of Hospitalitie,	Dido	3.4.44	Aeneas
And vow to weare it for my countries good:	1Tamb	1.1.158	Cosroe
And call'd the Gods to witnesse of my vow,	1Tamb	1.2.234	Tamb
Emperour in humblest tearms/I vow my service to your Majestie,	1Tamb	2.5.16	Meandr
A sacred vow to heaven and him I make,	1Tamb	4.3.36	Souldn
And vow to keepe this peace inviolable.	2Tamb	1.1.136	Sgsmnd
So what we vow to them should not infringe/Our liberty of armes	2Tamb	2.1.40	Baldwn
And vow to burne the villaines cruell heart.	2Tamb	3.1.56	Trebiz
Dissemble, sweare, protest, vow to love him,	Jew	2.3.229	Barab
I vow and sweare as I am King of France,	P 255	4.53	Charls
Madam, I have heard him solemnly vow,	P 516	9.35	Cardnl
I vow as I am lawfull King of France,	P1143	22.5	King
And then I vow for to revenge his death,	P1247	22.109	Navrre
Will make thee vow to study nothing else.	F 164	1.1.136	Cornel
againe I will confirme/The <My> former vow I made to Lucifer.	F1750	5.1.77	Faust
Those <These> thoughts that do disswade me from my vow,	F1764	5.1.91	Faust
And keepe [mine oath] <my vow> I made to Lucifer.	F1765	5.1.92	Faust
VOW'D			
I never vow'd at Aulis gulfe/The desolation of his native Troy,	Dido	5.1.202	Dido
Yet for her sake whom you have vow'd to serve,	Hero and Leander		1.316
Vow'd spotlesse chastitie, but all in vaine.	Hero and Leander		1.368
When first religious chastitie she vow'd:	Hero and Leander		2.110
VOWD			
Are to your highnesse vowd and consecrate.	Edw	3.1.171	Herald
For thy returne shall fall the vowd oblation,	Ovid's Elegies		2.11.46
Still vowd he love, she wanting no excuse/To feed him with	Hero and Leander		1.425
VOWDE			
Or impious traitors vowde to have my life,	Dido	4.4.114	Dido
VOWED			
My selfe will bring vowed gifts before thy feete,	Ovid's Elegies		2.13.24
Sappho her vowed harpe laies at Phoebus feete.	Ovid's Elegies		2.18.34
VOWES			
Lookes so remorcefull, vowes so forcible,	Dido	2.1.156	Aeneas
And she vowes love to him, and hee to her.	Jew	2.3.247	Barab
And vowes to be revengd upon us both,	Edw	5.6.19	Queene
And Faustus vowes never to looke to heaven,	F 648	2.2.97	Faust
when she bewayles/Her perjur'd Theseus flying vowes and sayles,	Ovid's Elegies		1.7.16
Pay vowes to Jove, engirt thy hayres with baies,	Ovid's Elegies		1.7.36
My wenches vowes for thee what should I show,	Ovid's Elegies		2.6.43
Her vowes above the emptie aire he flings:	Hero and Leander		1.370
Saying, let your vowes and promises be kept.	Hero and Leander		2.96
VOWEST			
Why vowest thou then to live in Sestos here,	Hero and Leander		1.227
VOWING			
Vowing our loves to equall death and life.	1Tamb	2.6.28	Cosroe
For thou in vowing chastitie, hast sworne/To rob her name and	Hero and Leander		1.304
VOYAGE			
and the bounds of Affrike/And made a voyage into Europe,	2Tamb	1.3.208	Therid
Their voyage will be worth ten thousand Crownes.	Jew	4.1.70	Barab
VOYCE			
I heare Aeneas voyce, but see him not,	Dido	2.1.45	Illion
Moved with her voyce, I lept into the sea,	Dido	2.1.283	Aeneas
Hell claimes his <calls for> right, and with a roaring voyce,	F1726	5.1.53	Faust
Words without voyce shall on my eye browes sit,	Ovid's Elegies		1.4.19
Nor set my voyce to sale in everie cause?	Ovid's Elegies		1.15.6

VOYCE (cont.)
Who sayd with gratefull voyce perpetuall bee? . . . . Ovid's Elegies 3.5.98
VOYCES
Gave up their voyces to dislodge the Campe, . . . Dido 2.1.134 Aeneas
VOYD
First be thou voyd of these affections, ... Jew 2.3.169 Barab
VOYDE
And like a wittall thinke thee voyde of slight. . . Ovid's Elegies 3.13.30
VOYDED
Good Fredericke see the roomes be voyded straight, . . F1157 4.1.3 Mrtino
VULCAN
Vulcan shall daunce to make thee laughing sport, . . Dido 1.1.32 Jupitr
Vulcan will give thee Chariots rich and faire. . . . Ovid's Elegies 1.2.24
Venus with Vulcan, though smiths tooles laide by, . . Ovid's Elegies 2.17.19
Which limping Vulcan and his Cyclops set: . . . . . Hero and Leander 1.152
VULCANS
And fetter them in Vulcans sturdie brasse, . . . Dido 1.1.118 Jupitr
VULGAR
Shall vulgar pesants storme at what I doe? . . . Dido 4.4.73 Dido
Their meanes of traffique from the vulgar trade, . . Jew 1.1.35 Barab
VULTURE
The ravenous vulture lives, the Puttock hovers/Around the aire, Ovid's Elegies 2.6.33
VULTURES
To be a prey for Vultures and wild beasts. . . . Jew 5.1.59 Govnr
Vultures and furies nestled in the boughes. . . . Ovid's Elegies 1.12.20
VUOLGAS
Wun on the fiftie headed Vuolgas waves, ... 1Tamb 1.2.103 Tamb
VYOLL
And with a vyoll full of pretious grace, ... F1731 5.1.58 OldMan
VYRGINS
the Sun-bright troope/Of heavenly vyrgins and unspotted maides, 1Tamb 5.1.325 Zenoc
WADE
place himselfe therin/Must armed wade up to the chin in blood. 2Tamb 1.3.84 Tamb
WADED
of us here, that have waded as deepe into matters, as other men, F 740 2.3.19 P Robin
To scape the violence of the streame first waded, . . Lucan, First Booke 223
WADGE
Will ye wadge war, for which you shall not triumph? . . Lucan, First Booke 12
WAFTED
we were wafted by a Spanish Fleet/That never left us till Jew 1.1.95 2Merch
WAG
Come Amorous wag, first banquet and then sleep. . . Jew 4.2.132 Curtzn
WAGE (See also WADGE)
And with that summe he craves might we wage warre. . . Jew 2.2.27 1Knght
Let others tell how winds fierce battailes wage, . . Ovid's Elegies 2.11.17
WAGES
Pay me my wages for my worke is done. . . . . . Jew 3.4.115 Ithimr
WAGGE (Homograph)
What ist sweet wagge I should deny thy youth? . . . Dido 1.1.23 Jupitr
I wagge, and give thee leave to kisse her to. . . . Dido 3.1.31 Dido
How pretilie he laughs, goe ye wagge, ... Dido 4.5.19 Nurse
Then gan he wagge his hand, which yet held up, . . . Dido 5.1.229 Anna
WAGGONS
And twenty Waggons to bring up the ware. . . . . Jew 1.1.60 Barab
WAGNER
Wagner, commend me to me deerest friends, ... F 91 1.1.63 Faust
I good Wagner, take away the devill then. . . . . F 377 1.4.35 P Robin
O brave Wagner. . . . . F 384 1.4.42 P Robin
call me Maister Wagner, and see that you walke attentively, F 385 1.4.43 P Wagner
<Tush>, These slender questions <trifles> Wagner can decide: F 600 2.2.49 Faust
How now Wagner what newes with thee? . . . . . . F1499 4.4.43 P Faust
such belly-cheere, as Wagner in his life nere saw the like: F1679 5.1.6 P Wagner
He and his servant Wagner are at hand, ... F1813 5.2.17 Mephst
Say Wagner, thou hast perus'd my will, ... F1816 5.2.20 Faust
Gramercies Wagner. Welcome gentlemen. . . . . . F1820 5.2.24 Faust
But doe you heare Wagner? . . . . F App p.231 66 P Clown
call me Maister Wagner, and let thy left eye be diametarily F App p.231 69 P Wagner
How now Wagner, what's the newes with thee? . . . . F App p.241 167 P Faust
As Wagner nere beheld in all his life. . . . . . F App p.243 7 Wagner
WAGON
What doest? thy wagon in lesse compasse bring. . . . Ovid's Elegies 3.2.70
WAGONS
Wagons of gold were set before my tent: . . . . . 2Tamb 1.1.99 Orcan
Wagons or tents, then in this frontire towne. . . . Lucan, First Booke 255
WAGS (See also WAGGE)
Achates, see King Priam wags his hand, ... Dido 2.1.29 Aeneas
WAIES
And thou shalt perish in the billowes waies, ... Dido 5.1.172 Dido
It must have high Argins and covered waies/To keep the bulwark 2Tamb 3.2.75 Tamb
And over thy Argins and covered waies/Shal play upon the . 2Tamb 3.3.23 Therid
That this your armie going severall waies, ... Edw 2.4.42 Queene
As evill wood throwne in the high-waies lie, ... Ovid's Elegies 1.12.13
Ad <And> they were apt to curle an hundred waies, . . . Ovid's Elegies 1.14.13
raught/Ill waies by rough seas wondring waves first taught, Ovid's Elegies 2.11.2
Each crosse waies corner doth as much expresse. . . Ovid's Elegies 3.1.18
Was divers waies distract with love, and shame. . . Ovid's Elegies 3.9.28
And like a planet, mooving severall waies, ... Hero and Leander 1.361
WAIGHT (Homograph)
On whom the nimble windes may all day waight, ... Dido 4.3.23 Aeneas
As with their waight shall make the mountains quake, . 1Tamb 1.2.49 Tamb
That beares the honor of my royall waight. . . . . 1Tamb 4.2.21 Tamb
And proove the waight of his victorious arme: . . . . 1Tamb 4.3.47 Arabia
Honor still waight on happy Tamburlaine: . . . . . 1Tamb 4.4.85 Zenoc

WAIGHT (cont.)			
Shake with their waight in signe of feare and griefe: .	1Tamb	5.1.349	Zenoc
For this, this earth sustaines my bodies [waight], . .	P 114	2.57	Guise
You have matters of more waight to thinke upon, . .	Edw	2.2.8	Mortmr
Commit not to my youth things of more waight/Then fits a prince	Edw	3.1.74	Prince
root be weake, and his owne waight/Keepe him within the ground,	Lucan, First Booke		139
Whose waight consists in nothing but her name, ...	Hero and Leander		2.114
WAIGHTE			
And I will tell thee reasons of such waighte, ...	Edw	1.4.226	Queene
WAIGHTIE			
Nay, no such waightie busines of import, ...	Dido	4.2.25	Anna
WAIGHTS			
Or Cynthia nights Queene waights upon the day;	Lucan, First Booke		91
WAILE (See also WAYLES)			
If Thetis, and the morne their sonnes did waile, . .	Ovid's Elegies		3.8.1
WAILING			
She wailing Mars sinne, and her uncles crime, ...	Ovid's Elegies		3.5.49
WAINE (Homograph)			
and Phoebe's waine/Chace Phoebus and inrag'd affect his place,	Lucan, First Booke		77
And now least age might waine his state, he casts/For civill	Lucan, First Booke		324
Or least his love oft beaten backe should waine. . .	Ovid's Elegies		1.8.76
[Doest] punish <ye >me, because yeares make him waine? .	Ovid's Elegies		1.13.41
WAINES			
She waines againe, and so shall his I hope, ...	2Tamb	5.2.47	Callap
WAIST (See WASTE)			
WAIT (Homograph; See also WAIGHT)			
And such shall wait on worthy Tamburlaine.	1Tamb	2.1.60	Cosroe
But here these kings that on my fortunes wait, . . .	1Tamb	5.1.490	Tamb
let us lie in wait for him/And if we find him absent from his	2Tamb	5.2.56	Callap
And all good fortune wait on Calymath.	Jew	1.2.33	Govnr
Now Governor--stand by there, wait within.--	Jew	5.2.50	Barab
And with this wait Ile counterpoise a Crowne, . . .	P 115	2.58	Guise
We will wait heere about the court.	Edw	1.1.49	Omnes
To wait upon thy soule; the time is come/Which makes it .	F1802	5.2.6	Lucifr
Jove that thou shouldst not hast but wait his leasure, .	Ovid's Elegies		1.13.45
WAITE			
May it please your grace to let Aeneas waite:	Dido	2.1.87	Aeneas
To waite upon him as their soveraigne Lord. . . .	Dido	4.4.69	Dido
Whose wealthie streames may waite upon her towers, . .	Dido	5.1.9	Aeneas
Achates and the rest shall waite on thee, ...	Dido	5.1.76	Aeneas
On whom death and the fatall sisters waite, ...	2Tamb	3.4.54	Therid
For this, I waite, that scornes attendance else: . .	P 106	2.49	Guise
thou wouldst do well/To waite at my trencher, and tell me lies	Edw	1.1.31	Gavstn
That waite attendance for a gratious looke, ...	Edw	1.4.338	Queene
Waite on me, and ile see thou shalt not want. . . .	Edw	2.2.246	Edward
For my sake let him waite upon your grace, ...	Edw	2.2.250	Gavstn
Then Spencer waite upon me, for his sake/Ile grace thee with a	Edw	2.2.252	Edward
I charge thee waite upon me whilst I live/To do what ever	F 264	1.3.36	Faust
Sirra, wilt thou be my man and waite on me?	F 354	1.4.12	P Wagner
That I shall waite on Faustus whilst he lives, ...	F 420	2.1.32	Mephst
And I will be thy slave and waite on thee, ...	F 435	2.1.47	Mephst
And at his heeles a thousand furies waite, ...	F1182	4.1.28	Mrtino
Shall waite upon his heavy funerall.	F2001	5.3.19	2Schol
WAITES			
On whom ruth and compassion ever waites, ...	Dido	4.2.20	Iarbus
Nay more, the guarde upon his lordship waites:	Edw	1.2.21	Lncstr
That waites your pleasure, and the day growes old. . .	Edw	4.7.85	Leistr
That waites upon my poore distressed soule, ...	Edw	5.3.38	Edward
WAITING			
Faire child stay thou with Didos waiting maide, . . .	Dido	2.1.304	Venus
That lie in ambush, waiting for a pray:	1Tamb	2.2.17	Meandr
Thou shalt be Landresse to my waiting maid.	1Tamb	3.3.177	Zabina
Waiting the back returne of Charons boat, ...	1Tamb	5.1.464	Tamb
Waiting my comming to the river side, ...	2Tamb	1.2.22	Callap
WAITING MAID			
Thou shalt be Landresse to my waiting maid. . . .	1Tamb	3.3.177	Zabina
WAITS			
My duty waits on you.	Jew	3.3.76	Abigal
WAKE			
And wake blacke Jove to crouch and kneele to me, . .	2Tamb	5.1.98	Tamb
may dreame/A golden dreame, and of the sudden [wake] <walke>,	Jew	2.1.37	Abigal
And 'bout this time the Nuns begin to wake;	Jew	2.1.56	Abigal
And for the Raven wake the morning Larke, ...	Jew	2.1.61	Barab
That wee might sleepe seven yeeres together afore we wake.	Jew	4.2.131	Ithimr
For this, I wake, when others think I sleepe, ...	P 105	2.48	Guise
then will I wake thee from thie folishe dreame/and lett thee	Paris	ms32,p391	Guise
And tels me, if I sleepe I never wake, ...	Edw	5.5.104	Edward
This sport is excellent: wee'l call and wake him. . .	F1281	4.1.127	Emper
and whooping in his eares, but all could not wake him: .	F1549	4.5.45	P HrsCsr
No, will you not wake?	F App	p.241 153	P HrsCsr
Ile make you wake ere I goe.	F App	p.241 153	P HrsCsr
WAKING			
But that greefe keepes me waking, I shoulde sleepe, . .	Edw	5.5.93	Edward
WAL			
And after this, to scale a castle wal, ...	2Tamb	3.2.59	Tamb
WALDE			
Or seemed faire walde in with Egles wings, ...	Dido	1.1.20	Ganimd
WALES			
you lord Warwick, president of the North,/And thou of Wales:	Edw	1.4.69	Edward
WALK			
In silence of thy solemn Evenings walk, ...	1Tamb	5.1.148	Tamb
Now walk the angels on the walles of heaven, ...	2Tamb	2.4.15	Tamb
Ile goe [take] <make> a walk/On purpose from the Court to meet	P 783	15.41	Mugern

WALK (cont.)				
What Robin, you must come away and walk the horses.	F 725	2.3.4	P	Dick
matters in hand, let the horses walk themselves and they will.	F 727	2.3.6	P	Robin
WALKE				
Come Dido, leave Ascanius, let us walke.	Dido	3.1.34		Iarbus
Both we wil walke upon the lofty clifts,	1Tamb	1.2.193		Tamb
While they walke quivering on their citie walles,	1Tamb	4.4.3		Tamb
lord, specially having so smal a walke, and so litle exercise.	1Tamb	4.4.106	P	Therid
And when I dye, here shall my spirit walke.	Jew	2.1.30		Barab
may dreame/A golden dreame, and of the sudden [wake] <walke>,	Jew	2.1.37		Abigal
I walke abroad a nights/And kill sicke people groaning under	Jew	2.3.174		Barab
I have it for you, Sir; please you walke in with me:	Jew	2.3.220		Barab
come, wee'll walke about/The ruin'd Towne, and see the wracke we	Jew	5.2.18		Calym
Goe walke about the City, see thy friends:	Jew	5.2.92		Barab
Pale death may walke in furrowes of my face:	P 158	2.101		Guise
But come lets walke aside, th'airs not very sweet.	P 497	9.16		QnMoth
And in the day when he shall walke abroad,	Edw	1.1.57		Gavstn
Whiles other walke below, the king and he/From out a window,	Edw	1.4.416		Mortmr
And so I walke with him about the walles,	Edw	2.2.222		Edward
and see that you walke attentively, and let your right eye be	F 385	1.4.43	P	Wagner
I walke the horses, I scorn't 'faith, I have other matters in	F 726	2.3.5	P	Robin
And walke upon the dreadfull Adders backe,	F 919	3.1.141		Pope
That I may walke invisible to all,	F 992	3.2.12		Faust
I am past this faire and pleasant greene, ile walke on foote.	F App	p.239 96	P	Faust
Sylla's ghost/Was seene to walke, singing sad Oracles,/And	Lucan, First Booke			580
Then, that the trembling Citizens should walke/About the City;	Lucan, First Booke			591
Have care to walke in middle of the throng.	Ovid's Elegies			1.4.56
Heere while I walke hid close in shadie grove,	Ovid's Elegies			3.1.5
Be more advisde, walke as a puritane,	Ovid's Elegies			3.13.13
WALKED				
I heare the wealthy Jew walked this way;	Jew	2.3.32		Lodowk
Wondring if any walked without light.	Ovid's Elegies			1.6.10
WALKES				
And strewe thy walkes with my discheveld haire.	Dido	4.2.56		Anna
But wherefore walkes yong Mortimer aside?	Edw	1.4.353		Edward
She neither walkes abroad, nor comes in sight:	Edw	2.1.24		Baldck
Proud Mortimer pries neare into thy walkes.	Edw	4.6.18		Kent
With these thy soule walkes, soules if death release,	Ovid's Elegies			3.8.65
WALKETH				
Holla, who walketh there, ist you my lord?	Edw	4.1.12		Mortmr
WALKING				
That I may, walking in my Gallery,	Jew	2.3.179		Barab
walking the backe lanes through the Gardens I chanc'd to cast	Jew	3.1.17	P	Pilia
That charming Circes walking on the waves,	Edw	1.4.172		Queene
What, sleeping, eating, walking and disputing?	F 528	2.1.140		Faust
And all alone, comes walking in his gowne;	F1358	4.2.34		Fredrk
I saw the damsell walking yesterday/There where the porch doth	Ovid's Elegies			2.2.3
WALKS				
Yond walks the Jew, now for faire Abigall.	Jew	2.3.38		Lodowk
Madam, whether walks your majestie so fast?	Edw	1.2.46		Mortmr
While slaughtred Crassus ghost walks unreveng'd,	Lucan, First Booke			11
WALK'ST				
Whither walk'st thou, Barabas?	Jew	2.3.43		Lodowk
WALL (See also WAL, WALDE)				
Inforst a wide breach in that rampierd wall,	Dido	2.1.174		Aeneas
Cast up the earth towards the castle wall,	2Tamb	3.3.43		Therid
As there be breaches in her battered wall.	2Tamb	5.1.160		Tamb
I'le have them wall all Germany with Brasse,	F 115	1.1.87		Faust
Deflowr'd except, within thy Temple wall.	Ovid's Elegies			1.7.18
Why gird'st thy citties with a towred wall?	Ovid's Elegies			3.7.47
WALLED				
Now living idle in the walled townes,	1Tamb	1.1.146		Ceneus
Those walled garrisons wil I subdue,	1Tamb	3.3.244		Tamb
WALLES				
Prepared stands to wracke their woodden walles,	Dido	1.1.67		Venus
In those faire walles I promist him of yore:	Dido	1.1.85		Jupitr
Where am I now? these should be Carthage walles.	Dido	2.1.1		Aeneas
Lovely Aeneas, these are Carthage walles,	Dido	2.1.62		Illion
By this the Campe was come unto the walles,	Dido	2.1.188		Aeneas
forth will ride/Into these woods, adjoyning to these walles,	Dido	3.2.88		Juno
Never to leave these newe upreared walles,	Dido	3.4.49		Aeneas
Carthage shall vaunt her pettie walles no more,	Dido	5.1.4		Aeneas
swift Mercury/When I was laying a platforme for these walles,	Dido	5.1.94		Aeneas
Nor sent a thousand ships unto the walles,	Dido	5.1.204		Dido
Or breathles lie before the citie walles.	1Tamb	3.1.15		Bajzth
with their Cannons mouth'd like Orcus gulfe/Batter the walles,	1Tamb	3.1.66		Bajzth
Carkasses/Shall serve for walles and bulwarkes to the rest:	1Tamb	3.3.139		Bajzth
your sounding Drummes/Direct our Souldiers to Damascus walles.	1Tamb	4.3.62		Souldn
While they walke quivering on their citie walles,	1Tamb	4.4.3		Tamb
Then raise your seige from faire Damascus walles,	1Tamb	4.4.71		Zenoc
Batter our walles, and beat our Turrets downe.	1Tamb	5.1.2		Govnr
Whiles only danger beat upon our walles,	1Tamb	5.1.30		1Virgn
Than all my Army to Damascus walles.	1Tamb	5.1.156		Tamb
Damascus walles di'd with Egyptian blood:	1Tamb	5.1.320		Zenoc
thou I am he/That with the Cannon shooke Vienna walles,	2Tamb	1.1.87		Orcan
And cloath of Arras hung about the walles,	2Tamb	1.2.44		Callap
of Verna and Bulgaria/And almost to the very walles of Rome,	2Tamb	2.1.9		Fredrk
Now walk the angels on the walles of heaven,	2Tamb	2.4.15		Tamb
Murther the Foe and save [the] <their> walles from breach.	2Tamb	3.2.82		Tamb
Whom I brought bound unto Damascus walles.	2Tamb	3.2.125		Tamb
Filling the ditches with the walles wide breach,	2Tamb	3.3.7		Techel
Stand at the walles, with such a mighty power.	2Tamb	3.3.14		Therid
And lie in trench before thy castle walles,	2Tamb	3.3.31		Techel

WALLES (cont.)
Who meanes to gyrt Natolias walles with siege, 2Tamb 3.5.8 2Msngr
Have we not hope, for all our battered walles, 2Tamb 5.1.15 Govnr
Makes walles a fresh with every thing that falles/Into the 2Tamb 5.1.18 Govnr
For I wil cast my selfe from off these walles, 2Tamb 5.1.40 2Citzn
And make a bridge unto the battered walles. 2Tamb 5.1.68 Tamb
For though thy cannon shooke the citie walles, 2Tamb 5.1.105 Govnr
Hang him up in chaines upon the citie walles, 2Tamb 5.1.108 Tamb
And let this Captaine be remoov'd the walles, 2Tamb 5.1.215 Therid
Then heere wee'l lye before [Lutetia] <Lucrecia> walles, P1151 22.13 King
Unto the walles of Yorke the Scots made rode, Edw 2.2.166 Lncstr
And so I walke with him about the walles, Edw 2.2.222 Edward
Let us with these our followers scale the walles, Edw 2.3.18 Lncstr
Will I advaunce upon this castell walles, Edw 2.3.24 Mortmr
can ragged stonie walles/Immure thy vertue that aspires to Edw 3.1.256 Mortmr
And hath not he that built the walles of Thebes/With ravishing F 579 2.2.28 Faust
Conducted me within the walles of Rome? F 802 3.1.24 Faust
<Within whose walles such store of ordnance are>, F 819 (HC265)A Mephst
That now the walles of houses halfe [rear'd] <reaer'd> totter, Lucan, First Booke 24
Roomes infant walles were steept in brothers bloud; Lucan, First Booke 95
that guardst/Roomes mighty walles built on Tarpeian rocke, Lucan, First Booke 198
No little ditched townes, no lowlie walles, Ovid's Elegies 2.12.7
In stone, and Yron walles Danae shut, Ovid's Elegies 3.4.21
The posts of brasse, the walles of iron were. Ovid's Elegies 3.7.32
We toucht the walles, Camillus wonne by thee. Ovid's Elegies 3.12.2
Built walles high towred with a prosperous hand. Ovid's Elegies 3.12.34
And some guest viewing watry Sulmoes walles, Ovid's Elegies 3.14.11

WALLOWED
In steed of red bloud wallowed venemous gore. Lucan, First Booke 614

WALLS
Tho countermin'd <countermur'd> with walls of brasse, to love, Jew 1.2.386 Mthias
abroad a nights/And kill sicke people groaning under walls: Jew 2.3.175 Barab
And wilt not trust thy Citty walls one night: Lucan, First Booke 518

WALS
feathered bird/That spreads her wings upon the citie wals, 1Tamb 4.2.106 Tamb
and on Damascus wals/Have hoisted up their slaughtered 1Tamb 5.1.130 Techel
Counterscarps/Narrow and steepe, the wals made high and broad, 2Tamb 3.2.69 Tamb
And let the burning of Larissa wals, 2Tamb 3.2.141 Tamb
if our artillery/Will carie full point blancke unto their wals. 2Tamb 3.3.53 Techel
Call up the souldiers to defend these wals. 2Tamb 5.1.56 Govnr
First will we race the City wals our selves, Jew 3.5.13 Govnr
Talke not of racing downe your City wals, Jew 3.5.21 Basso
Will winne the Towne, or dye before the wals. Jew 5.1.5 Govnr
For the Jewes body, throw that o're the wals, Jew 5.1.58 Govnr
belike they thought me dead,/And threw me o're the wals: Jew 5.1.82 Barab
Now whilst you give assault unto the wals, Jew 5.1.90 Barab
I cannot feast my men in Malta wals, Jew 5.3.34 Calym
With wals of Flint, and deepe intrenched Lakes, F 782 3.1.4 Faust
Had fild Assirian Carras wals with bloud, Lucan, First Booke 105
O wals unfortunate too neere to France, Lucan, First Booke 250
Souse downe the wals, and make a passage forth: Lucan, First Booke 296
What wals thou wilt be leaveld with the ground, Lucan, First Booke 384
the suburbe fieldes/Fled, fowle Erinnis stalkt about the wals, Lucan, First Booke 570
the sacred priests/That with divine lustration purg'd the wals, Lucan, First Booke 593
The wals were of discoloured Jasper stone, Hero and Leander 1.136

WAN
a heavenly face/Should by hearts sorrow wax so wan and pale, 1Tamb 3.2.5 Agidas
Jove viewing me in armes, lookes pale and wan, 1Tamb 5.1.452 Tamb
My Lord, your presence makes them pale and wan. 2Tamb 3.5.60 Usumc
monster death/Shaking and quivering, pale and wan for feare, 2Tamb 5.3.68 Tamb
Through numming cold, all feeble, faint and wan: Hero and Leander 2.246

WAND
And charme thee with this Magicke wand, F 996 3.2.16 Mephst
His bodie was as straight as Circes wand, Hero and Leander 1.61

WANDER
Go wander free from feare of Tyrants rage, 1Tamb 3.2.102 Agidas
And wander to the unfrequented Inde. Edw 1.4.50 Edward

WANDERING
strange and unknown stars were seene/Wandering about the North, Lucan, First Booke 525

WANDERS
Whiles my Aeneas wanders on the Seas, Dido 1.1.52 Venus
Wanders about the black circumference, 2Tamb 4.2.90 Therid

WAND'RED
Or he who war'd and wand'red twenty yeare? Ovid's Elegies 2.1.31

WANDRED
And having wandred now through sea and land, Ovid's Elegies 3.12.33

WAND'REST
Where's thy attire? why wand'rest heere alone? Ovid's Elegies 3.5.55

WANDRING
Since thy Aeneas wandring fate is firme, Dido 1.1.83 Jupitr
men, saw you as you came/Any of all my Sisters wandring here? Dido 1.1.184 Venus
Wishing good lucke unto thy wandring steps. Dido 1.1.239 Venus
And measure every wandring plannets course: 1Tamb 2.7.23 Tamb
The wandring Sailers of proud Italy, 2Tamb 1.1.39 Orcan
When wandring Phoebes Ivory cheeks were scortcht/And all the 2Tamb 5.3.232 Tamb
Or that the wandring maine follow the moone; Lucan, First Booke 415
that knew/The hearts of beasts, and flight of wandring foules; Lucan, First Booke 587
Subdue the wandring wenches to thy raigne, Ovid's Elegies 2.9.53
Thither resorted many a wandring guest, Hero and Leander 1.94
Nor that night-wandring pale and watrie starre, Hero and Leander 1.107
he wandring here,/In mournfull tearmes, with sad and heavie Hero and Leander 1.439

WANE (See WAINE)

WANES
Wanes with enforst and necessary change. 2Tamb 2.4.46 Zenoc

WANT					
	Forgetting both his want of strength and hands,	Dido	2.1.252		Aeneas
	When as I want both rigging for my fleete,	Dido	5.1.69		Aeneas
	Shal want my heart to be with gladnes pierc'd/To do you honor	1Tamb	1.2.250		Therid
	For want of nourishment to feed them both,	1Tamb	2.7.47		Cosroe
	Argue their want of courage and of wit:	2Tamb	1.3.24		Tamb
	And feed my mind that dies for want of her:	2Tamb	2.4.128		Tamb
	And better one want for a common good,	Jew	1.2.98		Govnr
	You that/Were ne're possest of wealth, are pleas'd with want.	Jew	1.2.201		Barab
	Proceed from sinne, or want of faith in us,	Jew	1.2.323		Abigal
	Be true and secret, thou shalt want no gold.	Jew	2.3.216		Barab
	Goe buy thee garments: but thou shalt not want:	Jew	3.4.47		Barab
	Ere I shall want, will cause his Indians,	P 853	17.48		Guise
	As dooth the want of my sweete Gaveston,	Edw	1.4.307		Edward
	While souldiers mutinie for want of paie.	Edw	1.4.406		Mortmr
	Waite on me, and ile see thou shalt not want.	Edw	2.2.246		Edward
	Where weapons want, and though a many friends/Are made away, as	Edw	4.2.51		Mortmr
	Where I am sterv'd for want of sustenance,	Edw	5.3.20		Edward
	So that for want of sleepe and sustenance,	Edw	5.5.63		Edward
	Then tell me Faustus what shall we three want?	F 175	1.1.147		Cornel
	To want in hell, that had on earth such store.	F1898	5.2.102		BdAngl
	Nor doth her tongue want harmefull eloquence.	Ovid's Elegies	1.8.20		
	Nor want I strength, but weight to presse her with:	Ovid's Elegies	2.10.24		
	Who, because meanes want, doeth not, she doth.	Ovid's Elegies	3.4.4		
WANTED					
	Better I could part of my selfe have wanted.	Ovid's Elegies	1.7.24		
WANTES					
	That these my boies may finish all my wantes.	2Tamb	5.3.125		Tamb
	He that wantes these, and is suspected of heresie,	P 234	4.32		Guise
WANTETH					
	There wanteth nothing but the Governors pelfe,	Jew	5.5.18		Barab
WANTING					
	Wanting both pay and martiall discipline,	1Tamb	1.1.147		Ceneus
	But (wanting moisture and remorsefull blood)/Drie up with	2Tamb	4.1.179		Soria
	that the soule/Wanting those Organnons by which it mooves,	2Tamb	5.3.96		Phsitn
	Why wert thou not a creature wanting soule?	F1964	5.2.168		Faust
	vowd he love, she wanting no excuse/To feed him with delaies,	Hero and Leander	1.425		
	But know you not that creatures wanting sence,	Hero and Leander	2.55		
	And wanting organs to advaunce a step,	Hero and Leander	2.57		
WANTON					
	And playing with that female wanton boy,	Dido	1.1.51		Venus
	Albeit the Gods doe know no wanton thought/Had ever residence	Dido	3.1.16		Dido
	And wanton Mermaides court thee with sweete songs,	Dido	3.1.130		Dido
	Meane time these wanton weapons serve my warre,	Dido	3.3.37		Cupid
	And wanton motions of alluring eyes,	Dido	4.3.35		Achat
	Making it daunce with wanton majestie:	1Tamb	2.1.26		Menaph
	Steeds, disdainfully/With wanton paces trampling on the ground.	1Tamb	4.1.23		2Msngr
	Or had those wanton Poets, for whose byrth/Olde Rome was proud,	2Tamb	2.4.91		Tamb
	And made so wanton that they knew their strengths,	2Tamb	4.3.14		Tamb
	So will I triumph over this wanton King,	P 983	19.53		Guise
	I must have wanton Poets, pleasant wits,	Edw	1.1.51		Gavstn
	To floate in bloud, and at thy wanton head,	Edw	1.1.132		Lncstr
	His wanton humor will be quicklie left.	Edw	1.4.199		Lncstr
	Unckle, his wanton humor greeves not me,	Edw	1.4.402		Mortmr
	Spencer, the father to that wanton Spencer,	Edw	4.6.50		Rice
	for I am wanton and lascivious, and cannot live without a wife.	F 530	2.1.142	P	Faust
	In wanton Arethusa's [azur'd] <azure> armes,	F1786	5.1.113		Faust
	Being fittest matter for a wanton wit,	Ovid's Elegies	1.1.24		
	I have beene wanton, therefore am perplext,	Ovid's Elegies	1.4.45		
	To serve for pay beseemes not wanton gods.	Ovid's Elegies	1.10.20		
	To fill my lawes thy wanton spirit frame.	Ovid's Elegies	3.1.30		
	The other smilde, (I wot) with wanton eyes,	Ovid's Elegies	3.1.33		
	And under mine her wanton thigh she flong,	Ovid's Elegies	3.6.10		
	Alone Corinna moves my wanton wit.	Ovid's Elegies	3.11.16		
	Forbare no wanton words you there would speake,	Ovid's Elegies	3.13.25		
	(Nor am I by such wanton toyes defamde)/Heire of an antient	Ovid's Elegies	3.14.4		
WANTONLY					
	And smiling wantonly, his love bewrayd.	Hero and Leander	2.182		
WANTONNESSE					
	I Ovid Poet of [my] <thy> wantonnesse,	Ovid's Elegies	2.1.1		
	Oft have I spent the night in wantonnesse,	Ovid's Elegies	2.10.27		
WANTONS					
	with kissing/And on her necke a wantons marke not missing.	Ovid's Elegies	1.7.42		
	And with a wantons tooth, your necke new raste?	Ovid's Elegies	3.13.34		
WANTS					
	Which piteous wants if Dido will supplie,	Dido	3.1.111		Aeneas
	Her state and person wants no pomp you see,	1Tamb	5.1.485		Tamb
	Now wants the fewell that enflamde his beames:	2Tamb	2.4.4		Tamb
	To supply my wants and necessitie.	P 136	2.79		Guise
	Wants thou gold? go to my treasurie:	Edw	1.1.167		Edward
	as yet thou wants not foes.	Lucan, First Booke	23		
	And choakt with thorns, that greedy earth wants hinds,	Lucan, First Booke	29		
	a rich lover plants/His love on thee, and can supply thy wants.	Ovid's Elegies	1.8.32		
	He wants no gifts into thy lap to hurle.	Ovid's Elegies	1.10.54		
	What two determine never wants effect.	Ovid's Elegies	2.3.16		
WANTST					
	Why, wantst thou any of thy tale?	Jew	4.3.19	P	Barab
WAR (See also WARRE, WARRS)					
	Weele leade you to the stately tent of War:	1Tamb	Prol.3		Prolog
	Accurst be he that first invented war,	1Tamb	2.4.1		Mycet
	Since he is yeelded to the stroke of War,	1Tamb	2.5.12		Cosroe
	And bid him turne [him] <his> back to war with us,	1Tamb	2.5.100		Tamb
	Will rattle foorth his facts of war and blood.	1Tamb	3.2.45		Agidas

WAR (cont.)
Brought to the war by men of Tripoly: 1Tamb 3.3.17 Bassoe
And for the expedition of this war, 1Tamb 3.3.20 Bassoe
Nor in Pharsalia was there such hot war, 1Tamb 3.3.154 Tamb
Untill the Persean Fleete and men of war, 1Tamb 3.3.252 Tamb
The slave usurps the glorious name of war. 1Tamb 4.1.67 Souldn
May have fresh warning to go war with us, 1Tamb 4.1.71 Souldn
To make me think of nought but blood and war. 1Tamb 4.2.55 Tamb
banquet and carouse/Full bowles of wine unto the God of war, 1Tamb 4.4.6 Tamb
Stil dooth this man or rather God of war, 1Tamb 5.1.1 Govnr
And yet wouldst shun the wavering turnes of war, 1Tamb 5.1.360 Zenoc
The God of war resignes his roume to me, 1Tamb 5.1.450 Tamb
crost Danubius stream/To treat of friendly peace or deadly war: 2Tamb 1.1.80 Sgsmnd
Wilt thou have war, then shake this blade at me, 2Tamb 1.1.83 Sgsmnd
How canst thou think of this and offer war? 2Tamb 1.1.102 Orcan
will send/A hundred thousand horse train'd to the war, 2Tamb 1.1.154 Sgsmnd
I thank thee Sigismond, but when I war/All Asia Minor, Affrica, 2Tamb 1.1.157 Orcan
And dangerous chances of the wrathfull war? 2Tamb 1.3.11 Zenoc
Harbors revenge, war, death and cruelty: 2Tamb 1.3.78 Tamb
they come to proove/The wounding troubles angry war affoords. 2Tamb 1.3.87 Zenoc
And with an hoste of Moores trainde to the war, 2Tamb 1.3.141 Techel
Or cease one day from war and hot alarms, 2Tamb 1.3.183 Usumc
That dare attempt to war with Christians. 2Tamb 2.1.26 Fredrk
Letting out death and tyrannising war, 2Tamb 2.4.115 Tamb
Goddesse of the war/Threw naked swords and sulphur bals of 2Tamb 3.2.40 Tamb
That meane to teach you rudiments of war: 2Tamb 3.2.54 Tamb
Hunger and [thirst] <cold>, right adjuncts of the war. 2Tamb 3.2.58 Tamb
My speech of war, and this my wound you see, 2Tamb 3.2.142 Tamb
In war, in blood, in death, in crueltie, 2Tamb 4.1.156 Tamb
Come carie me to war against the Gods, 2Tamb 5.3.52 Tamb
And war must be the meanes, or heele stay stil. Edw 1.2.63 Warwck
Will ye wadge war, for which you shall not triumph? Lucan, First Booke 12
Untill the cruel Giants war was done)/We plaine not heavens, Lucan, First Booke 36
Then men from war shal bide in league, and ease, Lucan, First Booke 60
Thy power inspires the Muze that sings this war. Lucan, First Booke 66
Being conquered, we are plaugde with civil war. Lucan, First Booke 108
Thy death broake amity and trainde to war, Lucan, First Booke 119
Caesars renowne for war was lesse, he restles, Lucan, First Booke 145
Them freedome without war might not suffice, Lucan, First Booke 173
Faiths breach, and hence came war to most men welcom. Lucan, First Booke 184
His mind was troubled, and he aim'd at war, Lucan, First Booke 186
This said, he laying aside all lets of war, Lucan, First Booke 206
Day rose and viewde these tumultes of the war; Lucan, First Booke 235
But gods and fortune prickt him to this war, Lucan, First Booke 265
Is conquest got by civill war so hainous? Lucan, First Booke 367
When Caesar saw his army proane to war, Lucan, First Booke 393
and swiftly bringing newes/Of present war, made many lies and Lucan, First Booke 468
War onely gives us peace, o Rome continue/The course of Lucan, First Booke 669
Why grapples Rome, and makes war, having no foes? Lucan, First Booke 681

WARBLEST
Elegian Muse, that warblest amorous laies, Ovid's Elegies 1.1.33

WAR'D
When first he war'd against the Christians. 1Tamb 3.3.200 Zabina
Or he who war'd and wand'red twenty yeare? Ovid's Elegies 2.1.31

WARD (Homograph)
To ward the blow, and shield me safe from harme. 1Tamb 1.2.181 Tamb
We wil both watch and ward shall keepe his trunke/Amidst these 2Tamb 2.3.38 Orcan
And turned streames run back-ward to their fountaines. Ovid's Elegies 2.1.26

WARDEN
Lord warden of the realme, and sith the fates/Have made his Edw 4.6.26 Queene

WARDERS
It hath my lord, the warders all a sleepe, Edw 4.1.15 Mortmr

WARDS
So now away, post thither wards amaine. Edw 5.2.67 Mortmr

WARE (Homograph)
My Juno ware upon her marriage day, Dido 1.1.43 Jupitr
Goe fetch the garment which Sicheus ware: Dido 2.1.80 Dido
is Aeneas, were he clad/In weedes as bad as ever Irus ware. Dido 2.1.85 Dido
of judgement frame/This is the ware wherein consists my wealth: Jew 1.1.33 Barab
And twenty Waggons to bring up the ware. Jew 1.1.60 Barab
Ware-houses stuft with spices and with drugs, Jew 4.1.64 Barab
scorn'd old sparing diet, and ware robes/Too light for women; Lucan, First Booke 165
Upon her head she ware a myrtle wreath, Hero and Leander 1.17
She ware no gloves for neither sunne nor wind/Would burne or Hero and Leander 1.27

WARE-HOUSES
Ware-houses stuft with spices and with drugs, Jew 4.1.64 Barab

WARES
we have seiz'd upon the goods/And wares of Barabas, which being Jew 1.2.133 Offcrs
For they have seiz'd upon thy house and wares. Jew 1.2.251 Abigal

WARILY
Warily garding that which I ha got. Jew 1.1.188 Barab
Beautie alone is lost, too warily kept. Hero and Leander 1.328

WARLICKE
Where Mars did mate the warlicke Carthagens <Carthaginians>, F 2 Prol.2 1Chor
this royall Emperour/The mightie Monarch, warlicke Alexander. F1297 4.1.143 Faust

WARLIKE
Warlike Aeneas. Dido 2.1.78 Illion
Warlike Aeneas, and in these base robes? Dido 2.1.79 Dido
This Meleagers sonne, a warlike Prince, Dido 3.1.163 Dido
Nay, where is my warlike father, can you tell? Dido 4.1.15 Cupid
Shall either perish by our warlike hands, 1Tamb 1.1.72 Therid
The warlike Souldiers, and the Gentlemen, 1Tamb 1.1.140 Ceneus
And warlike bands of Christians renied, 1Tamb 3.1.9 Bajzth

WARLIKE (cont.)			
For when they perish by our warlike hands, . . .	1Tamb	3.3.24	Techel
Whose hands are made to gripe a warlike Lance, . . .	1Tamb	3.3.106	Bajzth
Their warlike Engins and munition/Exceed the forces of their	1Tamb	4.1.28	2Msngr
Our warlike hoste in compleat armour rest, . . .	2Tamb	1.1.8	Orcan
Shal end the warlike progresse he intends, . . .	2Tamb	3.5.23	Orcan
Came forty thousand warlike foot and horse, . . .	2Tamb	3.5.38	Orcan
And set his warlike person to the view/Of fierce Achilles, .	2Tamb	3.5.67	Tamb
And that vile Carkasse drawne by warlike kings, . .	2Tamb	5.2.16	Amasia
A Fleet of warlike Gallyes, Barabas, ...	Jew	1.1.146	1Jew
They would not come in warlike manner thus. . . .	Jew	1.1.155	1Jew
We and our warlike Knights will follow thee/Against these	Jew	2.2.45	Govnr
A warlike people to maintaine thy right, ...	P 592	12.5	QnMoth
The royall shapes and warlike semblances/Of Alexander and his	F1170	4.1.16	Mrtino
Thy hands agree not with the warlike speare. . . .	Ovid's Elegies		2.3.8
WARME			
That we may make a fire to warme us with, ...	Dido	1.1.167	Aeneas
And offer luke-warme bloud, of new borne babes. . .	F 402	2.1.14	Faust
having lickt/Warme goare from Syllas sword art yet athirst,	Lucan, First Booke		331
Or waters tops with the warme south-winde taken. . .	Ovid's Elegies		1.7.56
Venus thy side doth warme,/And brings good fortune, a rich	Ovid's Elegies		1.8.30
If ever wench had made luke-warme thy love: . . .	Ovid's Elegies		2.3.6
Thou Goddesse doest command a warme South-blast, .	Ovid's Elegies		2.8.19
So having vext she nourisht my warme fire, . . .	Ovid's Elegies		2.19.15
Her wofull bosome a warme shower did drowne. . . .	Ovid's Elegies		3.5.68
A clowne, nor no love from her warme brest yeelds. . .	Ovid's Elegies		3.9.18
or parch her hands, but to her mind,/Or warme or coole them:	Hero and Leander		1.29
And in her luke-warme place Leander lay.	Hero and Leander		2.254
WARMEST			
Weare-me, when warmest showers thy members wash, . .	Ovid's Elegies		2.15.23
WARMING			
and a Dagger with a hilt like a warming-pan, and he gave me a	Jew	4.2.29	P Ithimr
WARMING-PAN			
and a Dagger with a hilt like a warming-pan, and he gave me a	Jew	4.2.29	P Ithimr
WARMTH			
To feele the lovely warmth of shepheards flames, . .	1Tamb	5.1.186	Tamb
WARN'D			
And oft hath warn'd thee to be stil in field, . . .	2Tamb	4.1.24	Amyras
Be warn'd by him then, learne with awfull eie/To sway a throane	2Tamb	5.3.234	Tamb
WARNE			
Who warne me of such daunger prest at hand, . . .	Dido	3.2.22	Venus
and warne him to his ships/That now afflicts me with his .	Dido	4.2.21	Iarbus
As Centinels to warne th'immortall soules, . . .	2Tamb	2.4.16	Tamb
Brawle not (I warne you) for your lechery, . . .	2Tamb	4.3.75	Tamb
Aye me I warne what profits some few howers, . . .	Ovid's Elegies		1.4.59
WARNING			
But give him warning and more warriours.	1Tamb	2.5.103	Tamb
May have fresh warning to go war with us, ...	1Tamb	4.1.71	Souldn
I'le give him such a warning e're he goes/As he shall have	Jew	2.3.273	Barab
A warning-peece shall be shot off from the Tower, . .	Jew	5.5.39	Barab
And give her warning of her trecherous foes. . . .	P1190	22.52	King
Gaveston, short warning/Shall serve thy turne: . . .	Edw	2.5.21	Warwck
So, now thou art to bee at an howres warning, whensoever, and	F 369	1.4.27	P Wagner
warning whensoever or wheresoever the divell shall fetch thee.	F App	p.230 36	P Wagner
the second time, aware the third, I give you faire warning.	F App	p.232 21	P Faust
WARNING-PEECE			
A warning-peece shall be shot off from the Tower, . .	Jew	5.5.39	Barab
WARNINGS			
Let these be warnings for you then my slave, . . .	1Tamb	4.2.72	Anippe
Nor let the windes away my warnings blowe. . . .	Ovid's Elegies		1.4.12
Aye me, let not my warnings cause my paine. . . .	Ovid's Elegies		2.19.34
WARRANT			
Nor shall they long be thine, I warrant them. . . .	1Tamb	4.4.119	Bajzth
No more there is not I warrant thee Techelles. . . .	1Tamb	5.1.202	Tamb
hee shall not be put to that exigent, I warrant thee. .	2Tamb	3.5.157	P Soria
I warrant thee, Barabas.	Jew	4.1.113	1Fryar
by this bearer, and this shall be your warrant; if you doe not,	Jew	4.2.76	P Ithimr
I warrant your worship shall hav't.	Jew	4.2.119	P Pilia
And I will warrant Malta free for ever.	Jew	5.2.101	Barab
If your commission serve to warrant this, ...	P 475	8.25	Anjoy
Let us alone, I warrant you.	P 939	19.9	P 1Mur
I warrant ye my Lord.	P 951	19.21	Capt
The wound I warrant ye is deepe my Lord, ...	P1192	22.54	King
Clarke of the crowne, direct our warrant forth, . . .	Edw	1.4.369	Edward
Returne it to their throtes, ile be thy warrant. . .	Edw	2.2.73	Edward
I warrant you.	Edw	2.2.126	Warwck
I warrant you, ile winne his highnes quicklie, . . .	Edw	4.2.6	Prince
I warrant you my lord.	Edw	5.2.56	Gurney
Well sir, I warrant you.	F 388	1.4.46	P Robin
[Tut I warrant thee].	F 551.13	2.1.176A	P Mephst
him, as he was never conjur'd in his life, I warrant him:	F1092	3.3.5	P Robin
Fast a sleepe I warrant you, ...	F1173	4.1.19	Mrtino
shall controule him as well as the Conjurer, I warrant you.	F1203	4.1.49	P Benvol
it will weare out ten birchin broomes I warrant you. .	F1385	4.2.61	P Benvol
I warrant you sir; O joyfull day:	F1476	4.4.20	P HrsCsr
WARRANTS			
These more than dangerous warrants of our death, . .	1Tamb	5.1.31	1Virgn
A faire commission warrants what we do.	Edw	4.7.48	Rice
WARRE			
And Neptunes waves be envious men of warre, . . .	Dido	1.1.65	Venus
Three winters shall he with the Rutiles warre, . . .	Dido	1.1.89	Jupitr
Who driven by warre from forth my native world, . .	Dido	1.1.217	Aeneas
The Grecian souldiers tired with ten yeares warre, . .	Dido	2.1.126	Aeneas

WARRE (cont.)			
But how scapt Helen, she that causde this warre?	Dido	2.1.292	Dido
To warre against my bordering enemies:	Dido	3.1.135	Dido
Bootles I sawe it was to warre with fate,	Dido	3.2.49	Juno
Meane time these wanton weapons serve my warre,	Dido	3.3.37	Cupid
fond man, that were to warre gainst heaven,/And with one shaft	Dido	3.3.71	Iarbus
When ayrie creatures warre amongst themselves:	Dido	4.2.7	Iarbus
Effeminate our mindes inur'd to warre.	Dido	4.3.36	Achat
Begin in troopes to threaten civill warre,	1Tamb	1.1.148	Ceneus
Why let 'em come, so they come not to warre;	Jew	1.1.150	Barab
Or let 'em warre, so we be conquerors:	Jew	1.1.151	Barab
Why, Barabas, they come for peace or warre.	Jew	1.1.161	1Jew
And with that summe he craves might we wage warre.	Jew	2.2.27	1Knght
to feast my traine/Within a Towne of warre so lately pillag'd,	Jew	5.3.22	Calym
Spaine is the place where he makes peace and warre,	P 710	14.13	Navrre
And as Dictator make or warre or peace,	P 860	17.55	King
Tis warre that must asswage this tyrantes pride.	P1128	21.22	Dumain
I have no warre, and therefore sir be gone.	Edw	1.1.36	Gavstn
Whose great atchivements in our forrain warre,	Edw	1.4.360	Edward
For with my nature warre doth best agree.	Edw	1.4.365	MortSr
Tis warre that must abate these Barons pride.	Edw	2.2.99	Edward
Now lustie lords, now not by chance of warre,	Edw	3.1.221	Edward
Thus after many threats of wrathfull warre,	Edw	4.3.1	Edward
Care of my countrie cald me to this warre.	Edw	4.6.65	Queene
Yea stranger engines for the brunt of warre,	F 122	1.1.94	Faust
pursu'd]/[With tenne yeares warre the rape of such a queene],	F1700	5.1.27A	3Schol
what huge lust of warre/Hath made Barbarians drunke with Latin	Lucan, First Booke		8
Roome, if thou take delight in impious warre,	Lucan, First Booke		21
Warre and the destinies shall trie my cause.	Lucan, First Booke		229
And therewith Caesar prone ennough to warre,	Lucan, First Booke		293
Who sees not warre sit by the quivering Judge;	Lucan, First Booke		320
he casts/For civill warre, wherein through use he's known/To	Lucan, First Booke		325
and flying/Left hateful warre decreed to both the Consuls.	Lucan, First Booke		486
Thou Roome at name of warre runst from thy selfe,	Lucan, First Booke		517
Se impious warre defiles the Senat house,	Lucan, First Booke		690
Fare well sterne warre, for blunter Poets meete.	Ovid's Elegies		1.1.32
What needes thou warre, I sue to thee for grace,	Ovid's Elegies		1.2.21
All Lovers warre, and Cupid hath his tent,	Ovid's Elegies		1.9.1
Atticke, all lovers are to warre farre sent.	Ovid's Elegies		1.9.2
Tis shame for eld in warre or love to be.	Ovid's Elegies		1.9.4
Doubtfull is warre and love, the vanquisht rise/And who thou	Ovid's Elegies		1.9.29
Such as the cause was of two husbands warre,	Ovid's Elegies		1.10.1
Defend the ensignes of thy warre in mee.	Ovid's Elegies		1.11.12
Aeneas warre, and Titerus shall be read,	Ovid's Elegies		1.15.25
What helpes it Woman to be free from warre?	Ovid's Elegies		2.14.1
Heroes lookes yeelded, but her words made warre,	Hero and Leander		1.331
Murder, rape, warre, lust and trecherie,	Hero and Leander		1.457
WARRES			
where shall be wrought/The warres of Troy, but not Troyes	Dido	3.1.125	Dido
Shall threat the Gods more than Cyclopian warres,	1Tamb	2.3.21	Tamb
The wrath of Tamburlain, and power of warres.	1Tamb	5.1.44	Govnr
If thou wilt love the warres and follow me,	2Tamb	1.3.47	Tamb
That by the warres lost not a dram of blood,	2Tamb	3.2.113	Tamb
and tel me if the warres/Be not a life that may illustrate	2Tamb	4.1.78	Tamb
And what the jealousie of warres must doe.	2Tamb	4.1.104	Tamb
but cannot compasse it/By reason of the warres, that robb'd our	Jew	1.2.48	Govnr
And in the warres 'twixt France and Germanie,	Jew	2.3.187	Barab
And nought is to be look'd for now but warres,	Jew	3.5.35	Govnr
To please himselfe with mannage of the warres,	P 459	8.9	Anjoy
The greatest warres within our Christian bounds,	P 460	8.10	Anjoy
I meane our warres against the Muscovites:	P 461	8.11	Anjoy
We undertake to mannage these our warres/Against the proud	P 699	14.2	Navrre
In making forraine warres and civile broiles.	P1029	19.99	King
Was ever troubled with injurious warres:	P1142	22.4	King
Seeing he is taken prisoner in his warres?	Edw	2.2.119	Mortmr
For now the wrathfull nobles threaten warres,	Edw	2.2.210	Kent
That to my face he threatens civill warres.	Edw	2.2.233	Edward
like the Greekish strumpet traind to armes/And bloudie warres,	Edw	2.5.16	Lncstr
In peace triumphant, fortunate in warres.	Edw	3.1.33	SpncrP
And go in peace, leave us in warres at home.	Edw	3.1.85	Edward
Proclaime king Edwards warres and victories.	Edw	3.1.281	Spencr
worth>/<Made Greece with ten yeares warres afflict poore Troy>?	F1696	(HC269)B	2Schol
Since maist thou see me watch and night warres move:	Ovid's Elegies		1.9.45
Envy hath rapt thee, no fierce warres thou movedst,	Ovid's Elegies		2.6.25
Nor is my warres cause new, but for a Queene/Europe, and Asia	Ovid's Elegies		2.12.17
A woman forc'd the Troyanes new to enter/Warres, just Latinus,	Ovid's Elegies		2.12.22
Rome did send/The Sabine Fathers, who sharpe warres intend.	Ovid's Elegies		2.12.24
Domesticke acts, and mine owne warres to sing.	Ovid's Elegies		2.18.12
Then warres, and from thy tents wilt come to mine.	Ovid's Elegies		2.18.40
no warres we move,/Peace pleaseth me, and in mid peace is love.	Ovid's Elegies		3.2.49
What ere he hath his body gaind in warres.	Ovid's Elegies		3.7.20
they manadge peace, and rawe warres bloudy jawes,	Ovid's Elegies		3.7.58
Or shall I plaine some God against me warres?	Ovid's Elegies		3.11.4
Not onely by warres rage made Gentleman.	Ovid's Elegies		3.14.6
In such warres women use but halfe their strength.	Hero and Leander		2.296
WARRIAR			
Nay madam, if you be a warriar,	Edw	4.4.15	Mortmr
WARRING			
Whereas the Wind-god warring now with Fate,	Dido	1.1.115	Jupitr
a greater [task]/Fits Menaphon, than warring with a Thiefe:	1Tamb	1.1.88	Cosroe
Warring within our breasts for regiment,	1Tamb	2.7.19	Tamb
WARRIOUR			
And every warriour that is rapt with love/Of fame, of valour,	1Tamb	5.1.180	Tamb

WARRIOURS			
But give him warning and more warriours.	1Tamb	2.5.103	Tamb
WARRS			
Such humors stirde them up; but this warrs seed,	Lucan, First Booke		159
WARS			
Bewraies they are too dainty for the wars.	2Tamb	1.3.28	Tamb
Tis but the fortune of the wars my Lord,	2Tamb	2.3.31	Gazell
Blood is the God of Wars rich livery.	2Tamb	3.2.116	Tamb
tyrannies/(If tyrannies wars justice ye repute)/I execute,	2Tamb	4.1.147	Tamb
And nought to us more welcome is then wars.	Jew	3.5.36	Govnr
Twas in your wars, you should ransome him.	Edw	2.2.144	Lncstr
Unnatural wars, where subjects brave their king,	Edw	3.1.86	Queene
Wars worse then civill on Thessalian playnes,	Lucan, First Booke		1
Thee wars use stirde, and thoughts that alwaies scorn'd/A	Lucan, First Booke		124
all lands else/Have stable peace, here wars rage first begins,	Lucan, First Booke		252
But law being put to silence by the wars,	Lucan, First Booke		278
Had forraine wars ill thriv'd; or wrathful France/Pursu'd us	Lucan, First Booke		308
force, they that now thwart right/In wars wil yeeld to wrong:	Lucan, First Booke		350
prone) restrain'd them; but wars love/And Caesars awe dasht all:	Lucan, First Booke		356
And Trevier; thou being glad that wars are past thee;	Lucan, First Booke		437
immortal pens/Renowne the valiant soules slaine in your wars,	Lucan, First Booke		444
Wars radge draws neare; and to the swords strong hand,	Lucan, First Booke		665
Wars dustie <rustie> honors are refused being yong,	Ovid's Elegies		1.15.4
WART			
Had on her necke a little wart, or mole;	F1267	4.1.113	Emper
this Lady while she liv'd had a wart or moale in her necke,	F App	p.238 61 P	Emper
WARWICK			
With Guie of Warwick that redoubted knight,	Edw	1.3.4	Gavstn
And you lord Warwick, president of the North,	Edw	1.4.68	Edward
Warwick shalbe my chiefest counseller:	Edw	1.4.345	Edward
Chide me sweete Warwick, if I go astray.	Edw	1.4.348	Edward
Thankes gentle Warwick, come lets in and revell.	Edw	1.4.385	Edward
How say you my lord of Warwick?	Edw	2.5.92	Mortmr
Warwick I know is roughe, and Lancaster/Inexorable, and I shall	Edw	3.1.6	Edward
The earle of Warwick would not bide the hearing,	Edw	3.1.104	Arundl
The earle of Warwick seazde him on his way,	Edw	3.1.115	Arundl
But ere he came, Warwick in ambush laie,	Edw	3.1.118	Arundl
and though a many friends/Are made away, as Warwick, Lancaster,	Edw	4.2.52	Mortmr
WARWICKE			
Wherfore is Guy of Warwicke discontent?	Edw	1.2.10	Mortmr
Warwicke and Lancaster, weare you my crowne,	Edw	1.4.37	Edward
Warwicke, these words do ill beseeme thy years.	Edw	2.2.94	Kent
Why my Lord of Warwicke,	Edw	2.5.46	Gavstn
O treacherous Warwicke thus to wrong thy friend!	Edw	2.6.1	Gavstn
Tretcherous Warwicke, traiterous Mortimer,	Edw	3.1.134	Edward
That thou proud Warwicke watcht the prisoner,	Edw	3.1.237	Edward
These lustie leaders Warwicke and Lancaster,	Edw	3.1.246	Edward
WARWICKES			
If Warwickes wit and policie prevaile.	Edw	2.5.96	Warwck
WARWICKS			
And shall or Warwicks sword shal smite in vaine.	Edw	3.1.199	Warwck
WARWICKSHIRE			
All Warwickshire will love him for my sake.	Edw	1.1.128	Warwck
WAS (See also 'TWAS, TWAS, WAST)			
And flourish once againe that erst was dead:	Dido	1.1.95	Jupitr
And drie with griefe was turnd into a stone,	Dido	2.1.5	Aeneas
Here she was wont to sit, but saving ayre/Is nothing here, and	Dido	2.1.13	Achat
Sometime I was a Troian, mightie Queene:	Dido	2.1.75	Aeneas
And truely to, how Troy was overcome:	Dido	2.1.107	Dido
And heaven was darkned with tempestuous clowdes:	Dido	2.1.140	Aeneas
Whose ticing tongue was made of Hermes pipe,	Dido	2.1.145	Aeneas
Was with two winged Serpents stung to death.	Dido	2.1.166	Aeneas
In which unhappie worke was I employd,	Dido	2.1.169	Aeneas
By this the Campe was come unto the walles,	Dido	2.1.188	Aeneas
Achilles sonne, remember what I was,	Dido	2.1.233	Aeneas
And I alas, was forst to let her lye.	Dido	2.1.279	Aeneas
Was by the cruell Mirmidons surprizd,	Dido	2.1.287	Aeneas
And so was reconcil'd to Menelaus.	Dido	2.1.299	Achat
I saw this man at Troy ere Troy was sackt.	Dido	3.1.141	Achat
This was an Orator, and thought by words/To compasse me, but	Dido	3.1.155	Dido
and thought by words/To compasse me, but yet he was deceiv'd:	Dido	3.1.156	Dido
This was Alcion, a Musition,	Dido	3.1.159	Dido
This was the wealthie King of Thessaly,	Dido	3.1.161	Dido
I was as farre from love, as they from hate.	Dido	3.1.167	Dido
What though I was offended with thy sonne,	Dido	3.2.40	Juno
That was advanced by my Hebes shame,	Dido	3.2.43	Juno
Bootles I sawe it was to warre with fate,	Dido	3.2.49	Juno
Why, that was in a net, where we are loose,	Dido	3.4.5	Dido
Something it was that now I have forgot.	Dido	3.4.30	Dido
It was because I sawe no King like thee,	Dido	3.4.35	Dido
I thinke it was the divels revelling night,	Dido	4.1.9	Achat
There was such hurly burly in the heavens:	Dido	4.1.10	Achat
The motion was so over violent.	Dido	4.1.13	Achat
And shrunke not backe, knowing my love was there?	Dido	4.4.146	Dido
Was it not you that hoysed up these sailes?	Dido	4.4.153	Dido
O how unwise was I to say him nay!	Dido	4.5.37	Nurse
This was my mother that beguild the Queene,	Dido	5.1.42	Aeneas
swift Mercury/When I was laying a platforme for these walles,	Dido	5.1.94	Aeneas
Would, as faire Troy was, Carthage might be sackt,	Dido	5.1.147	Dido
Thy mother was no Goddesse perjurd man,	Dido	5.1.156	Dido
And in the morning he was stolne from me,	Dido	5.1.214	Nurse
Before I came, Aeneas was abourd,	Dido	5.1.226	Anna
Wrapped in curles, as fierce Achilles was,	1Tamb	2.1.24	Menaph

WAS (cont.)

Was there such brethren, sweet Meander, say,	1Tamb	2.2.51	Mycet
Was but a handful to that we will have.	1Tamb	2.3.17	Tamb
For he was never sprong of humaine race,	1Tamb	2.6.11	Meandr
Upon his browes was pourtraid ugly death,	1Tamb	3.2.72	Agidas
Faith, and Techelles, it was manly done:	1Tamb	3.2.109	Usumc
And since he was so wise and honorable,	1Tamb	3.2.110	Usumc
Nor in Pharsalia was there such hot war,	1Tamb	3.3.154	Tamb
As was the fame of [Clymens] <Clymeus> brain-sicke sonne,/That	1Tamb	4.2.49	Tamb
As was to Jason Colchos golden fleece.	1Tamb	4.4.9	Tamb
The countrie wasted where my selfe was borne,	1Tamb	4.4.66	Zenoc
The Sun was downe.	1Tamb	5.1.314	P Zabina
And pardon me that was not moov'd with ruthe,	1Tamb	5.1.369	Zenoc
Vienna was besieg'd, and I was there,	2Tamb	1.1.103	Sgsmnd
And what we did, was in extremity:	2Tamb	1.1.105	Sgsmnd
As faire as was Pigmalions Ivory gyrle,	2Tamb	1.2.38	Callap
for whose byrth/Olde Rome was proud, but gasde a while on her,	2Tamb	2.4.92	Tamb
To signifie she was a princesse borne,	2Tamb	3.2.21	Amyras
And Moores, in whom was never pitie found,	2Tamb	3.4.20	Olymp
My Lord deceast, was dearer unto me,	2Tamb	3.4.42	Olymp
to put him in remembrance he was a Jailor, that when I take	2Tamb	3.5.140	P Tamb
I, my Lord, he was Calapines keeper.	2Tamb	3.5.152	P Therid
Wherein was neither corrage, strength or wit,	2Tamb	4.1.125	Tamb
My purpose was (my Lord) to spend it so,	2Tamb	4.2.73	Olymp
But was prevented by his sodaine end.	2Tamb	4.2.74	Olymp
Yet could not enter till the breach was made.	2Tamb	5.1.100	Tamb
Which when the citie was besieg'd I hid,	2Tamb	5.1.117	Govnr
Eastward behold/As much more land, which never was descried,	2Tamb	5.3.155	Tamb
Yet was his soule but flowne beyond the Alpes,	Jew	Prol.2	Machvl
Which mony was not got without my meanes.	Jew	Prol.32	Machvl
So that of thus much that returne was made:	Jew	1.1.1	Barab
There was the venture summ'd and satisfied.	Jew	1.1.3	Barab
And herein was old Abrams happinesse:	Jew	1.1.106	Barab
Governour, it was not got so easily;	Jew	1.2.86	Barab
I wot his wealth/Was written thus:	Jew	1.2.182	Barab
And leave no memory that e're I was.	Jew	1.2.265	Barab
And let me lodge where I was wont to lye.	Jew	1.2.333	Abigal
But say, What was she?	Jew	1.2.382	Lodowk
Was lately lost, and you were stated here/To be at deadly	Jew	2.2.32	Bosco
Small though the number was that kept the Towne,	Jew	2.2.49	Bosco
and Vespasian conquer'd us)/Am I become as wealthy as I was:	Jew	2.3.11	Barab
The Diamond that I talke of, ne'r was foild:	Jew	2.3.56	Barab
Where was thou borne?	Jew	2.3.127	P Barab
and my talke with him was [but]/About the borrowing of a booke	Jew	2.3.155	Mthias
And after that I was an Engineere,	Jew	2.3.186	Barab
Then after that was I an Usurer,	Jew	2.3.190	Barab
One time I was an Hostler in an Inne,	Jew	2.3.205	Ithimr
His father was my chiefest enemie.	Jew	2.3.250	Barab
Since this Towne was besieg'd, my gaine growes cold:	Jew	3.1.1	Curtzn
and as I was taking my choyce, I heard a rumbling in the house;	Jew	3.1.20	P Pilia
Nay Madam stay, that weapon was my son's,	Jew	3.2.25	Govnr
Why, was there ever seene such villany,	Jew	3.3.1	Ithimr
No, what was it?	Jew	3.3.17	Abigal
And was my father furtherer of their deaths?	Jew	3.3.22	Abigal
Was this the pursuit of thy policie?	Jew	3.3.37	Abigal
And I was chain'd to follies of the world:	Jew	3.3.60	Abigal
That was my father's fault.	Jew	3.3.72	Abigal
Whereof his sire, the Pope, was poysoned.	Jew	3.4.99	Barab
was ever pot of rice porredge so sauc't?	Jew	3.4.106	P Ithimr
Mathias was the man that I held deare,	Jew	3.6.24	Abigal
So, say how was their end?	Jew	3.6.26	2Fryar
I was afraid the poyson had not wrought;	Jew	4.1.4	Barab
Fornication? but that was in another Country:	Jew	4.1.41	Barab
Was up thus early; with intent to goe/Unto your Friery, because	Jew	4.1.191	Barab
he was ready to leape off e're the halter was about his necke;	Jew	4.2.22	P Ithimr
with his lips; the effect was, that I should come to her house.	Jew	4.2.31	P Ithimr
He was not wont to call me Barabas.	Jew	4.3.3	Barab
Was ever Jew tormented as I am?	Jew	4.3.60	Barab
The scent thereof was death, I poyson'd it.	Jew	4.4.43	Barab
He never put on cleane shirt since he was circumcis'd.	Jew	4.4.64	P Ithimr
I bring thee newes by whom thy sonne was slaine:	Jew	5.1.10	Curtzn
Mathias did it not, it was the Jew.	Jew	5.1.11	Curtzn
his man's now at my lodging/That was his Agent, he'll confesse	Jew	5.1.17	Curtzn
What a damn'd slave was I?	Jew	5.1.23	Barab
Was my Mathias murder'd by the Jew?	Jew	5.1.44	Mater
Be patient, gentle Madam, it was he,	Jew	5.1.46	Govnr
I was imprison'd, but escap'd their hands.	Jew	5.1.77	Barab
Hearing his Soveraigne was bound for Sea,	Jew	5.3.15	Msngr
See Calymath, this was devis'd for thee.	Jew	5.5.66	Govnr
Was this the banquet he prepar'd for us?	Jew	5.5.95	Calym
Why, then the house was fir'd,/Blowne up, and all thy souldiers	Jew	5.5.106	Govnr
Your grace was ill advisde to take them then,	P 174	3.9	Admral
Oh fatall was this mariage to us all.	P 202	3.37	Admral
Riding the streetes was traiterously shot,	P 244	4.42	Man
[Sanctus] <Sancta> Jacobus hee was my Saint, pray to him.	P 358	6.13	Mntsrl
Was it not thou that scoftes the Organon,	P 387	7.27	Guise
And said it was a heape of vanities?	P 388	7.28	Guise
Nere was there Colliars sonne so full of pride.	P 416	7.56	Anjoy
Madam, as in secrecy I was tolde,	P 641	12.54	Cardnl
Whose light was deadly to the Protestants:	P 945	19.15	Capt
Breath out that life wherein my death was hid,	P 954	19.24	King
I heard your Majestie was scarsely pleasde,	P 967	19.37	Guise
They were to blame that said I was displeasde,	P 969	19.39	King

WAS (cont.)

And all my former time was spent in vaine:	P 986	19.56		Guise
I nere was King of France untill this houre:	P1027	19.97		King
Nere was there King of France so yoakt as I.	P1044	19.114		King
Nay he was King and countermanded me,	P1069	19.139		King
That ever I was prov'd your enemy,	P1140	22.2		King
Was ever troubled with injurious warres:	P1142	22.4		King
Shall curse the time that ere Navarre was King,	P1249	22.111		Navrre
that of it self was hote enoughe to worke/thy Just degestione	Paris	ms26,p391		Guise
The undaunted spirit of Percie was appeasd,	Edw	1.1.114		Kent
Not Hilas was more mourned of Hercules,	Edw	1.1.144		Edward
I did no more then I was bound to do,	Edw	1.1.182		BshpCv
Was ever king thus over rulde as I?	Edw	1.4.38		Edward
Remember how the Bishop was abusde,	Edw	1.4.59		ArchBp
Either banish him that was the cause thereof,	Edw	1.4.60		ArchBp
Would when I left sweet France and was imbarkt,	Edw	1.4.171		Queene
I, but how chance this was not done before?	Edw	1.4.272		Lncstr
Because my lords, it was not thought upon:	Edw	1.4.273		Mortmr
When I was forst to leave my Gaveston.	Edw	1.4.318		Edward
I Isabell, nere was my heart so light.	Edw	1.4.368		Edward
Tis like enough, for since he was exild,	Edw	2.1.23		Baldck
Having read unto her since she was a childe.	Edw	2.1.30		Baldck
Mine old lord whiles he livde, was so precise,	Edw	2.1.46		Baldck
The greefe for his exile was not so much,	Edw	2.1.57		Neece
When she was lockt up in a brasen tower,	Edw	2.2.54		Edward
then was thy parting hence/Bitter and irkesome to my sobbing	Edw	2.2.57		Edward
Stay Edmund, never was Plantagenet/False of his word, and	Edw	2.3.11		Mortmr
Neither my lord, for as he was surprizd,	Edw	3.1.94		Arundl
Some treason, or some villanie was cause.	Edw	3.1.114		Spencr
A ranker route of rebels never was:	Edw	3.1.154		Edward
To whome right well you knew our soule was knit,	Edw	3.1.227		Edward
the newes was heere my lord,/That you were dead, or very neare	Edw	4.2.37		Queene
Lady, the last was truest of the twaine,	Edw	4.2.39		Mortmr
Was borne I see to be our anchor hold.	Edw	4.2.77		Mortmr
What, was I borne to flye and runne away,	Edw	4.5.4		Edward
Whilom I was, powerfull and full of pompe,	Edw	4.7.13		Edward
Further, or this letter was sealed, Lord Bartley came,	Edw	5.2.30		BshpWn
And I was almost stifeled with the savor.	Edw	5.5.9		Gurney
Gurney, it was left unpointed for the nonce,	Edw	5.5.16		Matrvs
geare, nere was there any/So finely handled as this king shalbe.	Edw	5.5.39		Ltborn
Tell me sirs, was it not bravelie done?	Edw	5.5.116		Ltborn
His kingly body was too soone interrde.	Edw	5.6.32		King
Forbid not me to weepe, he was my father,	Edw	5.6.34		King
And seeing there was no place to mount up higher,	Edw	5.6.62		Mortmr
That shortly he was grac'd with Doctors name,	F 17	Prol.17		1Chor
was the fiery keele at [Antwerpe] <Anwerpe> <Antwarpes>	F 123	1.1.95		Faust
Will be as cunning as Agrippa was,	F 144	1.1.116		Faust
become of Faustus that/Was wont to make our schooles ring,	F 195	1.2.2		1Schol
That was the cause, but yet per accidens:	F 274	1.3.46		Mephst
Was not that Lucifer an Angell once?	F 292	1.3.64		Faust
Were <Be> she as chaste as was Penelope,	F 540	2.1.152		Mephst
Saba, or as beautifull/As was bright Lucifer before his fall.	F 542	2.1.154		Mephst
'Twas <It was> made for man; then he's <therefore is man> more	F 560	2.2.9		Mephst
If Heaven was <it were> made for man, 'twas made for me:	F 561	2.2.10		Faust
me, as Paradise was to Adam the first day of his creation.	F 657	2.2.106	P	Faust
out of a Lyons mouth when I was scarce <half> an houre old,	F 687	2.2.136	P	Wrath
I was borne in hell, and look to it, for some of you shall be	F 690	2.2.139	P	Wrath
my father <grandfather> was a Gammon of Bacon, and my mother	F 696	2.2.145	P	Glutny
and my mother <grandmother> was a Hogshead of Claret Wine.	F 697	2.2.146	P	Glutny
O she was an ancient Gentlewoman, her name was <mistress>	F 699	2.2.148	P	Glutny
Gentlewoman, her name was <mistress> Margery March-beere:	F 700	2.2.149	P	Glutny
I was begotten on a sunny bank:	F 705	2.2.154	P	Sloth
I was elected by the Emperour.	F 905	3.1.127		Bruno
So, so, was never Divell thus blest before.	F 974	3.1.196		Mephst
You brought us word even now, it was decreed,	F1019	3.2.39		Pope
we all are witnesses/That Bruno here was late delivered you,	F1026	3.2.46		Raymnd
Was sent me from a Cardinall in France.	F1047	3.2.67		Pope
him, as he was never conjur'd in his life, I warrant him:	F1092	3.3.5	P	Robin
As never yet was seene in Germany.	F1188	4.1.34		Mrtino
He was upon the devils backe late enough; and if he be so farre	F1189	4.1.35	P	Benvol
Benvolio's head was grac't with hornes to day?	F1331	4.2.7		Benvol
My head is lighter then it was by th'hornes,	F1350	4.2.26		Benvol
Was this that sterne aspect, that awfull frowne,	F1370	4.2.46		Fredrk
Was this that damned head, whose heart <art> conspir'd	F1373	4.2.49		Mrtino
you not Traytors, I was limitted/For foure and twenty yeares,	F1395	4.2.71		Faust
O what a cosening Doctor was this?	F1484	4.4.28	P	HrsCsr
As I was going to Wittenberge t'other day, with a loade of Hay,	F1525	4.5.21	P	Carter
which was the beautifullest in all the world, we have	F1682	5.1.9	P	1Schol
that Hellen of Greece was the admirablest Lady that ever liv'd:	F1683	5.1.10	P	1Schol
<Was this faire Hellen, whose admired worth>/<Made Greece with	F1696	(HC269) B		2Schol
Was this the face that Launcht a thousand ships,	F1768	5.1.95		Faust
For such a dreadfull night, was never seene,	F1984	5.3.2		1Schol
Yet for he was a Scholler, once admired/For wondrous knowledge	F1997	5.3.15		2Schol
I, I thought that was al the land his father left him:	F App	p.229 17	P	Clown
there was a hee divell and a shee divell, Ile tell you how you	F App	p.230 52	P	Clown
here is a daintie dish was sent me from the Bishop of Millaine.	F App	p.231 5	P	Pope
My Lord, this dish was sent me from the Cardinall of Florence.	F App	p.231 9	P	Pope
for conjuring that ere was invented by any brimstone divel.	F App	p.233 20	P	Robin
I shall say, As I was sometime solitary set, within my Closet,	F App	p.236 17	P	Emper
send for the knight that was so pleasent with me here of late?	F App	p.238 67	P	Faust
mas Doctor Lopus was never such a Doctor, has given me a	F App	p.240 128	P	HrsCsr
but yet like an asse as I was, I would not be ruled by him, for	F App	p.240 130	P	HrsCsr
I was no sooner in the middle of the pond, but my horse vanisht	F App	p.240 134	P	HrsCsr

WAS (cont.)

Untill the cruel Giants war was done)/We plaine not heavens,	Lucan, First Booke	36
Roome was so great it could not beare it selfe:	Lucan, First Booke	72
Nor then was land, or sea, to breed such hate,	Lucan, First Booke	96
T'was peace against their wils; betwixt them both/Stept Crassus	Lucan, First Booke	99
Both differ'd much, Pompey was strooke in yeares,	Lucan, First Booke	130
Caesars renowne for war was lesse, he restles,	Lucan, First Booke	145
Was even the same that wrack's all great [dominions]	Lucan, First Booke	160
Poverty (who hatcht/Roomes greatest wittes) was loath'd, and al	Lucan, First Booke	167
Was stretcht unto the fields of hinds unknowne;	Lucan, First Booke	171
stil poore/Did vild deeds, then t'was worth the price of bloud,	Lucan, First Booke	175
His mind was troubled, and he aim'd at war,	Lucan, First Booke	186
As oft as Roome was sackt, here gan the spoile:	Lucan, First Booke	258
One that was feed for Caesar, and whose tongue/Could tune the	Lucan, First Booke	272
to warre,/Was so incenst as are Eleius steedes/With clamors:	Lucan, First Booke	294
Clashing of armes was heard, in untrod woods/Shrill voices	Lucan, First Booke	567
Sylla's ghost/Was seene to walke, singing sad Oracles,/And	Lucan, First Booke	580
To these ostents (as their old custome was)/They call	Lucan, First Booke	583
T'was so, he stroke me with a slender dart,	Ovid's Elegies	1.2.7
So having conquerd Inde, was Bacchus hew,	Ovid's Elegies	1.2.47
being thin, the harme was small,/Yet strivde she to be covered	Ovid's Elegies	1.5.13
Yet was she graced with her ruffled hayre.	Ovid's Elegies	1.7.12
So fayre she was, Atalanta she resembled,	Ovid's Elegies	1.7.13
Such Ariadne was, when she bewayles/Her perjur'd Theseus flying	Ovid's Elegies	1.7.15
That I was mad, and barbarous all men cried,	Ovid's Elegies	1.7.19
But though I like a swelling floud was driven,	Ovid's Elegies	1.7.43
Of horne the bowe was that approv'd their side.	Ovid's Elegies	1.8.48
to passe/The souldiours, and poore lovers worke ere was.	Ovid's Elegies	1.9.28
Great Agamemnon was, men say, amazed,	Ovid's Elegies	1.9.37
In heaven was never more notorious fable.	Ovid's Elegies	1.9.40
My selfe was dull, and faint, to sloth inclinde,	Ovid's Elegies	1.9.41
Such as the cause was of two husbands warre,	Ovid's Elegies	1.10.1
Such as was Leda, whom the God deluded/In snowe-white plumes of	Ovid's Elegies	1.10.3
Oft was she drest before mine eyes, yet never,	Ovid's Elegies	1.14.17
But I remember when it was my fame.	Ovid's Elegies	1.14.50
[His Arte excelld, although his witte was weake].	Ovid's Elegies	1.15.14
Even Jove himselfe out off my wit was reft.	Ovid's Elegies	2.1.18
Him timelesse death tooke, she was deifide.	Ovid's Elegies	2.2.46
The man did grieve, the woman was defam'd.	Ovid's Elegies	2.2.50
Why so was Ledas, yet was Leda faire.	Ovid's Elegies	2.4.42
the boord with wine/Was scribled, and thy fingers writ a line.	Ovid's Elegies	2.5.18
To these, or some of these like was her colour,	Ovid's Elegies	2.5.41
With her owne armor was my wench defended.	Ovid's Elegies	2.5.48
I that ere-while was fierce, now humbly sue,	Ovid's Elegies	2.5.49
Full concord all your lives was you betwixt,	Ovid's Elegies	2.6.13
Such to the parrat was the turtle dove.	Ovid's Elegies	2.6.16
No such voice-feigning bird was on the ground,	Ovid's Elegies	2.6.23
Adde she was diligent thy locks to braide,	Ovid's Elegies	2.7.23
Telling thy mistresse, where I was with thee,	Ovid's Elegies	2.8.27
Why me that alwayes was thy souldiour found,	Ovid's Elegies	2.9.3
And time it was for me to live in quiet,	Ovid's Elegies	2.9.23
Was not one wench inough to greeve my heart?	Ovid's Elegies	2.10.12
I was both horse-man, foote-man, standard bearer.	Ovid's Elegies	2.12.14
Angry I was, but feare my wrath exempted.	Ovid's Elegies	2.13.4
Had then swum over, but the way was blinde.	Ovid's Elegies	2.16.32
And was againe most apt to my desire.	Ovid's Elegies	2.19.16
And one, I thinke, was longer, of her feete.	Ovid's Elegies	3.1.8
Sterne was her front, her [cloake] <looke> on ground did lie.	Ovid's Elegies	3.1.12
What gift with me was on her birth day sent,	Ovid's Elegies	3.1.57
But cruelly by her was drown'd and rent.	Ovid's Elegies	3.1.58
Ah Pelops from his coach was almost feld,	Ovid's Elegies	3.2.15
Faire white with rose red was before commixt:	Ovid's Elegies	3.3.5
Her foote was small: her footes forme is most fit:	Ovid's Elegies	3.3.7
Comely tall was she, comely tall shee's yet.	Ovid's Elegies	3.3.8
Was not defilde by any gallant wooer.	Ovid's Elegies	3.4.24
Nere was, nor shall be, what my verse mentions.	Ovid's Elegies	3.5.18
One Deianira was more worth then these.	Ovid's Elegies	3.5.38
My bones had beene, while yet I was a maide.	Ovid's Elegies	3.5.74
Either she was foule, or her attire was bad,	Ovid's Elegies	3.6.1
Or she was not the wench I wisht t'have had.	Ovid's Elegies	3.6.2
Or shade, or body was [I] <Io>, who can say?	Ovid's Elegies	3.6.16
And was the second cause why vigor failde mee:	Ovid's Elegies	3.6.38
Why was I blest?	Ovid's Elegies	3.6.49
Worthy she was to move both Gods and men,	Ovid's Elegies	3.6.59
But neither was I man, nor lived then.	Ovid's Elegies	3.6.60
Wit was some-times more pretious then gold,	Ovid's Elegies	3.7.3
Knowest not this head a helme was wont to beare,	Ovid's Elegies	3.7.13
A target bore: bloud sprinckled was his right.	Ovid's Elegies	3.7.16
Till then, rough was her father, she severe,	Ovid's Elegies	3.7.31
In hell were harbourd, here was found no masse.	Ovid's Elegies	3.7.38
And to thine owne losse was thy wit swift running.	Ovid's Elegies	3.7.46
Was I: thou liv'dst, while thou esteemdst my faith.	Ovid's Elegies	3.8.56
Nor on the earth was knowne the name of floore.	Ovid's Elegies	3.9.8
This was [their] <there> meate, the soft grasse was their bed.	Ovid's Elegies	3.9.10
Was divers waies distract with love, and shame.	Ovid's Elegies	3.9.28
Onely was Crete fruitfull that plenteous yeare,	Ovid's Elegies	3.9.37
Where Ceres went each place was harvest there.	Ovid's Elegies	3.9.38
Which by the wild boare in the woods was shorne.	Ovid's Elegies	3.9.40
My love was cause that more mens love she seazd.	Ovid's Elegies	3.10.20
But with my rivall sicke she was not than.	Ovid's Elegies	3.10.26
I am not as I was before, unwise.	Ovid's Elegies	3.10.32
What day was that, which all sad haps to bring,	Ovid's Elegies	3.11.1
Who mine was cald, whom I lov'd more then any,	Ovid's Elegies	3.11.5

WAS (cont.)

And sweet toucht harpe that to move stones was able?	Ovid's Elegies	3.11.40	
Such was the Greeke pompe, Agamemnon dead,	Ovid's Elegies	3.12.31	
Sweare I was blinde, yeeld not <deny>, if you be wise,	Ovid's Elegies	3.13.45	
Her kirtle blew, whereon was many a staine,	Hero and Leander	1.15	
Her vaile was artificiall flowers and leaves,	Hero and Leander	1.19	
And looking in her face, was strooken blind.	Hero and Leander	1.38	
But this is true, so like was one the other,	Hero and Leander	1.39	
As he imagyn'd Hero was his mother.	Hero and Leander	1.40	
So lovely faire was Hero, Venus Nun,	Hero and Leander	1.45	
As nature wept, thinking she was undone;	Hero and Leander	1.46	
His bodie was as straight as Circes wand,	Hero and Leander	1.61	
So was his necke in touching, and surpast/The white of Pelops	Hero and Leander	1.64	
How smooth his brest was, and how white his bellie,	Hero and Leander	1.66	
Was moov'd with him, and for his favour sought.	Hero and Leander	1.82	
Some swore he was a maid in mans attire,	Hero and Leander	1.83	
And such as knew he was a man would say,	Hero and Leander	1.87	
So was her beautie to the standers by.	Hero and Leander	1.106	
Wherein was Proteus carved, and o'rehead,	Hero and Leander	1.137	
Of Christall shining faire, the pavement was,	Hero and Leander	1.141	
Was Danaes statue in a brazen tower,	Hero and Leander	1.146	
And thus Leander was enamoured.	Hero and Leander	1.162	
Relenting Heroes gentle heart was strooke,	Hero and Leander	1.165	
Wherewith Leander much more was inflam'd.	Hero and Leander	1.182	
The aire with sparkes of living fire was spangled,	Hero and Leander	1.188	
Wherewith she yeelded, that was woon before.	Hero and Leander	1.330	
The more she striv'd, the deeper was she strooke.	Hero and Leander	1.334	
so much/As one poore word, their hate to him was such.	Hero and Leander	1.384	
Yet prowd she was, (for loftie pride that dwels/In tow'red	Hero and Leander	1.393	
On her, this god/Enamoured was, and with his snakie rod,/Did	Hero and Leander	1.398	
Whose only dower was her chastitie,	Hero and Leander	1.412	
Having striv'ne in vaine, was now about to crie,	Hero and Leander	1.413	
courted her, was glad/That she such lovelinesse and beautie had	Hero and Leander	1.421	
and beautie had/As could provoke his liking, yet was mute,	Hero and Leander	1.423	
And would have turn'd againe, but was afrayd,	Hero and Leander	2.8	
He askt, she gave, and nothing was denied,	Hero and Leander	2.25	
Supposing nothing else was to be done,	Hero and Leander	2.53	
Long was he taking leave, and loath to go,	Hero and Leander	2.93	
Though it was morning, did he take his flight.	Hero and Leander	2.102	
With Cupids myrtle was his bonet crownd,	Hero and Leander	2.105	
but he must weare/The sacred ring wherewith she was endow'd,	Hero and Leander	2.109	
So to his mind was yoong Leanders looke.	Hero and Leander	2.130	
His secret flame apparantly was seene,	Hero and Leander	2.135	
where the ground/Was strewd with pearle, and in low corrall	Hero and Leander	2.161	
But when he knew it was not Ganimed,	Hero and Leander	2.169	
For under water he was almost dead,	Hero and Leander	2.170	
Ere halfe this tale was done,/Aye me, Leander cryde,	Hero and Leander	2.201	
Neptune was angrie that hee gave no eare,	Hero and Leander	2.207	
Thereon concluded that he was beloved.	Hero and Leander	2.220	
Unto her was he led, or rather drawne,	Hero and Leander	2.241	
This head was beat with manie a churlish billow,	Hero and Leander	2.251	
And everie kisse to her was as a charme,	Hero and Leander	2.283	
So that the truce was broke, and she alas,	Hero and Leander	2.285	
(Poore sillie maiden) at his mercie was.	Hero and Leander	2.286	
Treason was in her thought,/And cunningly to yeeld her selfe	Hero and Leander	2.293	
Seeming not woon, yet woon she was at length,	Hero and Leander	2.295	
One halfe appear'd, the other halfe was hid.	Hero and Leander	2.316	
Brought foorth the day before the day was borne.	Hero and Leander	2.322	

WASH

And in my blood wash all your hands at once,	2Tamb	3.2.127	Tamb
Can never wash from thy distained browes.	2Tamb	4.1.110	Tamb
lumpe of clay/That will with every water wash to dirt:	Jew	1.2.217	Barab
No, but wash your face, and shave away your beard,	Edw	5.3.31	Gurney
Whose bloud alone must wash away thy guilt.	F App	p.243 45	OldMan
secret works, and [wash] <washt> their saint/In Almo's floud:	Lucan, First Booke	599	
Weare me, when warmest showers thy members wash,	Ovid's Elegies	2.15.23	

WASHETH

Phrigia to the sea/Which washeth Cyprus with his brinish waves,	2Tamb	3.5.12	Callap

WASHT

secret works, and [wash] <washt> their saint/In Almo's floud:	Lucan, First Booke	599	

WA'ST

Wa'st not enough the fearefull Wench to chide?	Ovid's Elegies	1.7.45	

WAST (Homograph)

Wast thou not wrackt upon this Libian shoare,	Dido	5.1.161	Dido
Which with thy beauty thou wast woont to light,	2Tamb	4.2.16	Therid
What wast I prethe?	Jew	1.2.377	Lodowk
I cannot speak for greefe: when thou wast borne,	P1072	19.142	QnMoth
Tell me, where wast thou borne? What is thine armes?	Edw	2.2.242	Edward
Accursed wretches, wast in regard of us,	Edw	3.1.233	Edward
That wast a cause of his imprisonment?	Edw	5.2.102	Mortmr
Come forth. Art thou as resolute as thou wast?	Edw	5.4.22	Mortmr
She may perceive how we the time did wast:	Ovid's Elegies	1.6.70	
Which to her wast her girdle still kept downe.	Ovid's Elegies	1.7.48	
Garments do weare, jewells and gold do wast,	Ovid's Elegies	1.10.61	
What, wast my limbs through some Thesalian charms,	Ovid's Elegies	3.6.27	

WASTE (Homograph; See also WAST)

And full three Sommers likewise shall he waste,	Dido	1.1.91	Jupitr
their neckes/Hangs massie chaines of golde downe to the waste,	1Tamb	1.2.126	Souldr
To waste and spoile the sweet Aonian fieldes.	1Tamb	4.3.6	Souldn
Kingdomes made waste, brave cities sackt and burnt,	2Tamb	5.2.26	Callap
Lay waste the Iland, hew the Temples downe,	Jew	3.5.14	Govnr
Weakneth his body, and will waste his Realme,	P 128	2.71	Guise
My lord, why waste you thus the time away,	Edw	5.1.49	Leistr

WASTE (cont.)			
How smoothe a bellie, under her waste sawe I,	Ovid's Elegies		1.5.21
WASTED			
The countrie wasted where my selfe was borne,	1Tamb	4.4.66	Zenoc
And body with continuall moorning wasted:	Edw	2.4.25	Queene
WASTFULL			
Open an entrance for the wastfull sea,	Jew	3.5.16	Govnr
WASTING			
All wasting years have that complaint [out] <not> worne.	Ovid's Elegies		2.6.8
WATCH			
O no God wot, I cannot watch my time,	Dido	3.2.14	Juno
We wil both watch and ward shall keepe his trunke/Amidst these	2Tamb	2.3.38	Orcan
Do [match] <watch> the number of the daies contain'd,	F 821	3.1.43	Mephst
He shewes me how unheard to passe the watch,	Ovid's Elegies		1.6.7
Both of them watch: each on the hard earth sleepes:	Ovid's Elegies		1.9.7
Sooth Lovers watch till sleepe the hus-band charmes,	Ovid's Elegies		1.9.25
Since maist thou see me watch and night warres move:	Ovid's Elegies		1.9.45
While Junos watch-man Io too much eyde,	Ovid's Elegies		2.2.45
Penelope, though no watch look'd unto her,	Ovid's Elegies		3.4.23
When I to watch supplyed a servants place.	Ovid's Elegies		3.10.12
WATCHES			
Stand still you watches of the element,	Edw	5.1.66	Edward
WATCHFULL			
To force an hundred watchfull eyes to sleepe:	Dido	2.1.146	Aeneas
No sleepe can fasten on my watchfull eyes,	Jew	2.1.17	Barab
A watchfull Senate for ordaining lawes,	P 593	12.6	QnMoth
Which watchfull Hesperus no sooner heard,	Hero and Leander		2.329
WATCHING			
Watching till after mid-night did not tire thee.	Ovid's Elegies		1.6.44
Nor canst by watching keepe her minde from sinne.	Ovid's Elegies		3.4.7
WATCH-MAN			
While Junos watch-man Io too much eyde,	Ovid's Elegies		2.2.45
WATCHT			
to your maister/My friend, and tell him that I watcht it well.	Edw	2.6.13	Warwck
That thou proud Warwicke watcht the prisoner,	Edw	3.1.237	Edward
He watcht his armes, and as they opend wide,	Hero and Leander		2.183
WATCHWORD			
And then the watchword being given, a bell shall ring,	P 238	4.36	Guise
which have already set the street/May know their watchword,	P 329	5.56	Guise
WATER			
Through which the water shall delight to play:	Dido	3.1.119	Dido
O Anna, runne unto the water side,	Dido	4.4.1	Dido
As in the Sea are little water drops:	Dido	4.4.63	Dido
The ayre wherein they breathe, the water, fire,	Dido	4.4.75	Dido
The water which our Poets terme a Nimph,	Dido	4.4.144	Dido
The water is an Element, no Nimph,	Dido	4.4.147	Dido
White Swannes, and many lovely water fowles:	Dido	4.5.11	Nurse
By this is he got to the water side,	Dido	5.1.188	Dido
As hath the Ocean or the Terrene sea/Small drops of water, when	1Tamb	3.1.11	Bajzth
Cut of the water, that by leaden pipes/Runs to the citie from	1Tamb	3.1.59	Bajzth
Fetch me some water for my burning breast,	1Tamb	5.1.276	Bajzth
Water and ayre being simbolisde in one,	2Tamb	1.3.23	Tamb
Ile teach you how to make the water mount,	2Tamb	3.2.85	Tamb
That bring fresh water to thy men and thee:	2Tamb	3.3.30	Techel
Cut off the water, all convoies that can,	2Tamb	3.3.39	Capt
Have made the water swell above the bankes,	2Tamb	5.1.205	Techel
lumpe of clay/That will with every water wash to dirt:	Jew	1.2.217	Barab
Oh twill corrupt the water, and the water the fish, and by the	P 488	9.7	P 2Atndt
and the water the fish, and by the fish our selves when we eate	P 488	9.7	P 2Atndt
With haire that gilds the water as it glides,	Edw	1.1.62	Gavstn
Hees gone by water unto Scarborough,	Edw	2.4.37	Queene
O water gentle friends to coole my thirst,	Edw	5.3.25	Edward
Heeres channell water, as our charge is given.	Edw	5.3.27	Matrvs
Or choake your soveraigne with puddle water?	Edw	5.3.30	Edward
Being in a vault up to the knees in water,	Edw	5.5.2	Matrvs
They give me bread and water being a king,	Edw	5.5.62	Edward
As doth this water from my tattered robes:	Edw	5.5.67	Edward
turn'd to a gaping Oyster, and drinke nothing but salt water.	F1320	4.1.166	P Benvol
in any case, ride him not into the water.	F1469	4.4.13	P Faust
How sir, not into the water?	F1470	4.4.14	P HrsCsr
waters, but ride him not into the water; o're hedge and ditch,	F1473	4.4.17	P Faust
hedge and ditch, or where thou wilt, but not into the water:	F1474	4.4.18	P Faust
I riding my horse into the water, thinking some hidden mystery	F1485	4.4.29	P HrsCsr
time; but, quoth he, in any case ride him not into the water.	F1541	4.5.37	P HrsCsr
you remember you bid he should not ride [him] into the water?	F1637	4.6.80	P Carter
O soule be chang'd into <to> [little] <small> water drops,	F1977	5.2.181	Faust
before you have him, ride him not into the water at any hand.	F App	p.239 109	P Faust
but ride him not into the water, ride him over hedge or ditch,	F App	p.239 112	P Faust
hedge or ditch, or where thou wilt, but not into the water.	F App	p.239 113	P Faust
at ease, if I bring his water to you, youle tel me what it is?	F App	p.240 118	P HrsCsr
by him, for he bade me I should ride him into no water; now,	F App	p.240 131	P HrsCsr
Shall water be conjeal'd and turn'd to ice?	Lucan, First Booke		647
Nor servile water shalt thou drinke for ever.	Ovid's Elegies		1.6.26
Like water gushing from consuming snowe.	Ovid's Elegies		1.7.58
the drie fields strayed/When on her head a water pitcher laied.	Ovid's Elegies		1.10.6
Water in waters, and fruite flying touch/Tantalus seekes, his	Ovid's Elegies		2.2.43
And to the vast deep sea fresh water flouds?	Ovid's Elegies		2.10.14
And into water desperately she flies.	Ovid's Elegies		3.5.80
To cover it, spilt water in <on> the place.	Ovid's Elegies		3.6.84
Those with sweet water oft her handmaid fils,	Hero and Leander		1.35
his/That leapt into the water for a kis/Of his owne shadow,	Hero and Leander		1.74
Thinke water farre excels all earthly things:	Hero and Leander		1.260
Differs as much, as wine and water doth.	Hero and Leander		1.264

WATER (cont.)				
Are reeking water, and dull earthlie fumes.	Hero and Leander	2.116		
For under water he was almost dead,	Hero and Leander	2.170		
And dive into the water, and there prie/Upon his brest, his	Hero and Leander	2.188		
Least water-nymphs should pull him from the brinke.	Hero and Leander	2.198		
WATERED				
belike he hath not bene watered to day, give him some drinke.	1Tamb	4.4.55	P	Tamb
If teares, our eies have watered all the earth:	2Tamb	2.4.122		Therid
WATER FOWLES				
White Swannes, and many lovely water fowles:	Dido	4.5.11		Nurse
WATER-NYMPHS				
Least water-nymphs should pull him from the brinke.	Hero and Leander	2.198		
WATERS				
And waters of this new made Nunnery/Will much delight you.	Jew	1.2.311		1Fryar
why will he not drink of all waters?	F1471	4.4.15	P	HrsCsr
he will drinke of all waters, but ride him not into the water;	F1472	4.4.16	P	Faust
why sir, wil he not drinke of all waters?	F App	p.239 110	P	HrsCsr
he wil drinke of al waters, but ride him not into the water,	F App	p.239 111	P	Faust
Or waters tops with the warme south-winde taken.	Ovid's Elegies	1.7.56		
No faithlesse witch in Thessale waters bath'd thee.	Ovid's Elegies	1.14.40		
Water in waters, and fruite flying touch/Tantalus seekes, his	Ovid's Elegies	2.2.43		
Pure waters moisture thirst away did keepe.	Ovid's Elegies	2.6.32		
The Argos wrackt had deadly waters drunke.	Ovid's Elegies	2.11.6		
How Scyllaes and Caribdis waters rage.	Ovid's Elegies	2.11.18		
And with the waters sees death neere him thrusts,	Ovid's Elegies	2.11.26		
And through the gemme let thy lost waters pash.	Ovid's Elegies	2.15.24		
And waters force, force helping Gods to faile,	Ovid's Elegies	2.16.28		
Though Hindes in brookes the running waters bring,	Ovid's Elegies	2.16.35		
And drinkes stolne waters in surrownding floudes.	Ovid's Elegies	2.19.32		
<redder-growne> slime bankes, till I be past/Thy waters stay:	Ovid's Elegies	3.5.2		
And in thy foule deepe waters thicke thou [gushest] <rushest>.	Ovid's Elegies	3.5.8		
Who so well keepes his waters head from knowing,	Ovid's Elegies	3.5.40		
While thus I speake, the waters more abounded:	Ovid's Elegies	3.5.85		
With joy heares Neptunes swelling waters sound.	Ovid's Elegies	3.10.30		
And blabbing Tantalus in mid-waters put.	Ovid's Elegies	3.11.30		
WATER SIDE				
O Anna, runne unto the water side,	Dido	4.4.1		Dido
By this is he got to the water side,	Dido	5.1.188		Dido
WATERY				
with winged Steads/All sweating, tilt about the watery heavens,	1Tamb	3.2.79		Agidas
With haire discheweld wip'st thy watery cheeks:	1Tamb	5.1.139		Tamb
Shall hide his head in Thetis watery lap,	2Tamb	1.3.169		Tamb
March in your armour thorowe watery Fens,	2Tamb	3.2.56		Tamb
operation and more force/Than Cynthias in the watery wildernes,	2Tamb	4.2.30		Therid
WAT'RED				
See how the gates with my teares wat'red are.	Ovid's Elegies	1.6.18		
WATRIE				
That erst-while issued from thy watrie loynes,	Dido	1.1.128		Venus
Are ballassed with billowes watrie weight.	Dido	1.1.226		Aeneas
Ile make the Clowdes dissolve their watrie workes,	Dido	3.2.90		Juno
And would be toyling in the watrie billowes,	Dido	4.4.137		Dido
A small, but wholesome soyle with watrie veynes.	Ovid's Elegies	2.16.2		
Nor that night-wandring pale and watrie starre,	Hero and Leander	1.107		
WAT'RY				
But now the winters wrath and wat'ry moone,	Lucan, First Booke	219		
WATRY				
Unto the watry mornings ruddy [bower] <hower>,	1Tamb	4.4.123		Tamb
Such as in hilly Idas watry plaines,	Ovid's Elegies	1.14.11		
If watry Thetis had her childe fordone?	Ovid's Elegies	2.14.14		
In Tiburs field with watry fome art rumbling,	Ovid's Elegies	3.5.46		
Why weepst? and spoilst with teares thy watry eyes?	Ovid's Elegies	3.5.57		
And some guest viewing watry Sulmoes walles,	Ovid's Elegies	3.14.11		
WAVE				
from the breach/Of Libian Syrtes roules a monstrous wave,	Lucan, First Booke	497		
painted stands/All naked holding in her wave-moist hands.	Ovid's Elegies	1.14.34		
Applaud you Neptune, that dare trust his wave,	Ovid's Elegies	3.2.47		
WAVE-MOIST				
painted stands/All naked holding in her wave-moist hands.	Ovid's Elegies	1.14.34		
WAVERING				
And yet wouldst shun the wavering turnes of war,	1Tamb	5.1.360		Zenoc
Our Ladies first love is not wavering,	Edw	2.1.27		Spencr
So wavering Cupid bringes me backe amaine,	Ovid's Elegies	2.9.33		
WAVERS				
So with this love and that, wavers my minde.	Ovid's Elegies	2.10.10		
WAVERST				
Why waverst thou?	F 395	2.1.7		Faust
WAVES				
And Neptunes waves be envious men of warre,	Dido	1.1.65		Venus
When as the waves doe threat our Chrystall world,	Dido	1.1.75		Venus
And they so wrackt and weltred by the waves,	Dido	1.1.223		Aeneas
That doe complaine the wounds of thousand waves,	Dido	1.2.8		Illion
Which if thou lose shall shine above the waves:	Dido	3.1.121		Dido
I traytor, and the waves shall cast thee up,	Dido	5.1.174		Dido
Or els Ile make a prayer unto the waves,	Dido	5.1.246		Dido
Wun on the fiftie headed Vuolgas waves,	1Tamb	1.2.103		Tamb
Against the terrour of the winds and waves.	1Tamb	3.2.84		Agidas
For all the wealth of Gehons golden waves.	1Tamb	5.1.123		Tamb
Shall carie wrapt within his scarlet waves,	2Tamb	1.1.34		Orcan
That danc'd with glorie on the silver waves,	2Tamb	2.4.3		Tamb
And make a Fortresse in the raging waves,	2Tamb	3.2.88		Tamb
Phrigia to the sea/Which washeth Cyprus with his brinish waves,	2Tamb	3.5.12		Callap
city Samarcanda/And christall waves of fresh Jaertis streame,	2Tamb	4.3.108		Tamb
Amasde, swim up and downe upon the waves,	2Tamb	5.1.207		Techel

WAVES (cont.)

That charming Circes walking on the waves, ... Edw 1.4.172 Queene
raught/Ill waies by rough seas wondring waves first taught, Ovid's Elegies 2.11.2
Let Nereus bend the waves unto this shore, . . . Ovid's Elegies 2.11.39
No flowing waves with drowned ships forth poured, . . Ovid's Elegies 2.16.25
When thy waves brim did scarse my anckles touch. . . Ovid's Elegies 3.5.6
Her, from his swift waves, the bold floud perceav'd, . Ovid's Elegies 3.5.51
Leander striv'd, the waves about him wound, . . . Hero and Leander 2.159
Beat downe the bold waves with his triple mace, . . Hero and Leander 2.172
And as he spake, upon the waves he springs. . . . Hero and Leander 2.206

WAX

a heavenly face/Should by hearts sorrow wax so wan and pale, 1Tamb 3.2.5 Agidas

WAXE (Homograph)

Ile frame me wings of waxe like Icarus, ... Dido 5.1.243 Dido
Then when the Sky shal waxe as red as blood, . . . 1Tamb 4.2.53 Tamb
Now waxe all pale and withered to the death, . . . 1Tamb 5.1.91 1Virgn
wood be flying/And thou the waxe stuft full with notes denying, Ovid's Elegies 1.12.8
age you wrackes/And sluttish white-mould overgrowe the waxe. Ovid's Elegies 1.12.30
Least to the waxe the hold-fast drye gemme cleaves, . . Ovid's Elegies 2.15.16
With virgin waxe hath some imbast my joynts, . . . Ovid's Elegies 3.6.29

WAXED

Strooke with th'earths suddaine shadow waxed pale, . . Lucan, First Booke 537

WAXEN (Homograph)

Heavens envious of our joyes is waxen pale, ... Dido 4.4.52 Dido
His waxen wings did mount above his reach, ... F 21 Prol.21 1Chor

WAXETH

My bloodlesse body waxeth chill and colde, ... 1Tamb 2.7.42 Cosroe

WAXT

Desirde her more, and waxt outragious, ... Edw 2.2.55 Edward
He inly storm'd, and waxt more furious, ... Hero and Leander 1.437
Now waxt she jealous, least his love abated, . . . Hero and Leander 2.43

WAY (Homograph; See also WAIES)

And made that way my mother Venus led: . . . . . Dido 1.1.221 Aeneas
When thou Achates with thy sword mad'st way, . . . Dido 2.1.268 Aeneas
And finde the way to wearie such fond thoughts: . . . Dido 3.2.86 Juno
Who having wrought her shame, is straight way fled: . . Dido 4.2.18 Iarbus
Doe as I bid thee sister, leade the way, ... Dido 4.4.85 Dido
Thinke you I way this treasure more than you? . . . 1Tamb 1.2.84 Tamb
Our conquering swords shall marshal us the way/We use to march 1Tamb 3.3.148 Tamb
As if there were no way but one with us. . . . . 1Tamb 5.1.201 Techel
Then next, the way to fortifie your men, ... 2Tamb 3.2.62 Tamb
And strowes the way with braines of slaughtered men: . 2Tamb 3.4.58 Therid
Shall mount the milk-white way and meet him there. . . 2Tamb 4.3.132 Tamb
I heare the wealthy Jew walked this way; . . . . . Jew 2.3.32 Lodowk
No, no, and yet it might be done that way: . . . . Jew 2.3.373 Barab
rumbling in the house; so I tooke onely this, and runne my way: Jew 3.1.21 P Pilia
And understanding I should come this way, ... Jew 4.1.165 1Fryar
nay then I'le force my way;/And see, a staffe stands ready for Jew 4.1.171 1Fryar
Now am I cleane, or rather fouly out of the way. . . Jew 4.2.47 P Ithimr
That perill is the cheefest way to happines, ... P 95 2.38 Guise
To work the way to bring this thing to passe: . . . P 649 12.62 QnMoth
But which way is he gone? . . . . P 783 15.41 Mugern
of a string/May draw the pliant king which way I please: . Edw 1.1.53 Gavstn
But come sweete friend, ile beare thee on thy way. . . Edw 1.4.140 Edward
Having brought the Earle of Cornewall on his way, . . . Edw 1.4.300 Queene
Come lead the way, I long till I am there. . . . . Edw 2.1.82 Neece
Lead on the way. . . . . Edw 2.2.132 Lncstr
My house is not farre hence, out of the way/A little, but our Edw 2.5.100 Penbrk
The earle of Warwick seazde him on his way, ... Edw 3.1.115 Arundl
This way he fled, but I am come too late. . . . . Edw 4.6.1 Kent
way how hardly I can brooke/To loose my crowne and kingdome, Edw 5.1.51 Edward
And by the way to make him fret the more, ... Edw 5.2.62 Mortmr
I, I, and none shall know which way he died. . . . Edw 5.4.25 Ltborn
But yet I have a braver way then these. . . . . . Edw 5.4.37 Ltborn
The way he cut, an English mile in length, ... F 792 3.1.14 Faust
And view their triumphs, as they passe this way. . . F 857 3.1.79 Mephst
And kill that Doctor if he come this way. . . . . F1339 4.2.15 Fredrk
'Twas I, that when thou wer't i'the way to heaven, . . F1886 5.2.90 Mephst
Hadst thou kept on that way, Faustus behold, . . . F1903 5.2.107 GdAngl
To guide thy steps unto the way of life, ... F App p.243 35 OldMan
His losse made way for Roman outrages. . . . . . Lucan, First Booke 106
And glad when bloud, and ruine made him way: . . . . Lucan, First Booke 151
No sicknesse harm'd thee, farre be that a way, . . . Ovid's Elegies 1.14.41
That meane to travaile some long irkesome way. . . . Ovid's Elegies 2.16.16
My hard way with my mistrisse would seeme soft. . . . Ovid's Elegies 2.16.20
Had then swum over, but the way was blinde. . . . . Ovid's Elegies 2.16.32
Argus had either way an hundred eyes, ... Ovid's Elegies 3.4.19
Now love, and hate my light brest each way move; . . . Ovid's Elegies 3.10.33
Though thether leades a rough steepe hilly way. . . . Ovid's Elegies 3.12.6
Women receave perfection everie way. . . . . . . Hero and Leander 1.268
his parentage, would needs discover/The way to new Elisium: Hero and Leander 1.411
To linger by the way, and once she stayd, ... Hero and Leander 2.7

WAYD

Which th'earth from ougly Chaos den up-wayd: . . . . Hero and Leander 1.450

WAYE

Not yet my lorde, ile beare you on your waye. . . . . Edw 5.1.155 Leistr

WAYES

[But] <by> goe, goe thou thy wayes, discharge thy Ship, . Jew 1.1.82 Barab
thou doest, thou shalt be no wayes prejudiced or indamaged. F App p.236 9 P Emper
Cypassis that a thousand wayes trimst haire, ... Ovid's Elegies 2.8.1
Corinna meanes, and dangerous wayes to take. . . . Ovid's Elegies 2.11.8
And falling vallies be the smooth-wayes crowne. . . . Ovid's Elegies 2.16.52
Shew large wayes with their garments there displayed. . Ovid's Elegies 3.12.24

WAYLES			
better/In which the Merchant wayles his banquerout debter.	Ovid's Elegies	1.12.26	
WAYWARD			
Swell raging seas, frowne wayward destinies,	Dido	4.4.57	Aeneas
WE (See also WE'L, WE'LE, WEE, WEE'LL, WEELE)			
Come Ganimed, we must about this geare.	Dido	1.1.121	Jupitr
How many dangers have we over past?	Dido	1.1.145	Aeneas
Though we be now in extreame miserie,	Dido	1.1.157	Achat
Till we have fire to dresse the meate we kild:	Dido	1.1.165	Aeneas
That we may make a fire to warme us with,	Dido	1.1.167	Aeneas
As to instruct us under what good heaven/We breathe as now, and	Dido	1.1.198	Aeneas
On which by tempests furie we are cast.	Dido	1.1.199	Aeneas
Why talke we not together hand in hand?	Dido	1.1.245	Aeneas
We come not we to wrong your Libian Gods,	Dido	1.2.10	Illion
Which now we call Italia of his name,	Dido	1.2.23	Cloan
Thither made we,	Dido	1.2.25	Cloan
The rest we feare are foulded in the flouds.	Dido	1.2.31	Cloan
Might we but once more see Aeneas face,	Dido	1.2.45	Serg
Then would we hope to quite such friendly turnes,	Dido	1.2.46	Serg
that under his conduct/We might saile backe to Troy, and be	Dido	2.1.18	Aeneas
For we are strangers driven on this shore,	Dido	2.1.43	Aeneas
And scarcely know within what Clime we are.	Dido	2.1.44	Aeneas
And clad us in these wealthie robes we weare.	Dido	2.1.65	Illion
Oft hath she askt us under whom we serv'd,	Dido	2.1.66	Illion
And when we told her she would weepe for griefe,	Dido	2.1.67	Illion
And Priam dead, yet how we heare no newes.	Dido	2.1.113	Dido
Troy is invincible, why stay we here?	Dido	2.1.128	Aeneas
Who looking on the scarres we Troians gave,	Dido	2.1.131	Aeneas
we were commanded straight/With reverence to draw it into Troy.	Dido	2.1.167	Aeneas
We banquetted till overcome with wine,	Dido	2.1.178	Aeneas
And we were round inviron'd with the Greekes:	Dido	2.1.269	Aeneas
and had not we/Fought manfully, I had not told this tale:	Dido	2.1.270	Aeneas
Yet manhood would not serve, of force we fled,	Dido	2.1.272	Aeneas
And as we went unto our ships, thou knowest/We sawe Cassandra	Dido	2.1.273	Aeneas
thou knowest/We sawe Cassandra sprauling in the streetes,	Dido	2.1.274	Aeneas
Then got we to our ships, and being abourd,	Dido	2.1.280	Aeneas
What happened to the Queene we cannot shewe,	Dido	2.1.294	Achat
We heare they led her captive into Greece.	Dido	2.1.295	Achat
We will account her author of our lives.	Dido	3.1.112	Aeneas
We two will goe a hunting in the woods,	Dido	3.1.174	Dido
Are not we both sprong of celestiall rase,	Dido	3.2.28	Juno
We two as friends one fortune will devide:	Dido	3.2.55	Venus
Unto the purpose which we now propound.	Dido	3.2.95	Juno
The woods are wide, and we have store of game:	Dido	3.3.6	Dido
Lords goe before, we two must talke alone.	Dido	3.3.9	Dido
We two will talke alone, what words be these?	Dido	3.3.12	Iarbus
We could have gone without your companie.	Dido	3.3.14	Dido
And here we met faire Venus virgine like,	Dido	3.3.54	Achat
Why, that was in a net, where we are loose,	Dido	3.4.5	Dido
With whom we did devide both lawes and land,	Dido	4.2.14	Iarbus
We may as one saile into Italy.	Dido	4.3.30	Aeneas
No no, she cares not how we sinke or swimme,	Dido	4.3.41	Illion
We will not stay a minute longer here.	Dido	4.3.44	Cloan
And when we whisper, then the starres fall downe,	Dido	4.4.53	Dido
But hereby child, we shall get thither straight.	Dido	4.5.14	Nurse
Our life is fraile, and we may die to day.	1Tamb	1.1.68	Mycet
We in the name of other Persean states,	1Tamb	1.1.137	Ortyg
We will invest your Highnesse Emperour:	1Tamb	1.1.151	Ceneus
We here doo crowne thee Monarch of the East,	1Tamb	1.1.161	Ortyg
Whether we presently will flie (my Lords)/To rest secure	1Tamb	1.1.177	Cosroe
We knew my Lord, before we brought the crowne,	1Tamb	1.1.179	Ortyg
The jewels and the treasure we have tane/Shall be reserv'd, and	1Tamb	1.2.2	Tamb
And since we have arriv'd in Scythia,	1Tamb	1.2.17	Magnet
We have his highnesse letters to command/Aide and assistance if	1Tamb	1.2.19	Magnet
letters to command/Aide and assistance if we stand in need.	1Tamb	1.2.20	Magnet
And thinke we prattle with distempered spirits:	1Tamb	1.2.62	Tamb
That we may traveile into Siria,	1Tamb	1.2.77	Agidas
And wheresoever we repose our selves,	1Tamb	1.2.80	Magnet
We will report but well of Tamburlaine.	1Tamb	1.2.81	Magnet
Shall all we offer to Zenocrate,	1Tamb	1.2.104	Tamb
We hope your selfe wil willingly restore them.	1Tamb	1.2.117	Agidas
A thousand horsmen? We five hundred foote?	1Tamb	1.2.121	Tamb
Then shall we fight couragiously with them.	1Tamb	1.2.128	Tamb
And looke we friendly on them when they come:	1Tamb	1.2.141	Tamb
Before we part with our possession.	1Tamb	1.2.144	Tamb
And gainst the Generall we will lift our swords,	1Tamb	1.2.145	Tamb
I heare them come, shal we encounter them?	1Tamb	1.2.149	Techel
do but joine with me/And we will triumph over all the world.	1Tamb	1.2.173	Tamb
Both we wil walke upon the lofty clifts,	1Tamb	1.2.193	Tamb
Both we will raigne as Consuls of the earth,	1Tamb	1.2.197	Tamb
May we become immortall like the Gods.	1Tamb	1.2.201	Tamb
We are his friends, and if the Persean king/Should offer	1Tamb	1.2.214	Techel
We thinke it losse to make exchange for that/We are assured of	1Tamb	1.2.216	Techel
exchange for that/We are assured of by our friends successe.	1Tamb	1.2.217	Techel
And kingdomes at the least we all expect,	1Tamb	1.2.218	Usumc
Whose [statues] <statutes> we adore in Scythia,	1Tamb	1.2.244	Tamb
We yeeld unto thee happie Tamburlaine.	1Tamb	1.2.257	Agidas
Thus farre are we towards Theridamas,	1Tamb	2.1.1	Cosroe
Proud is his fortune if we pierce it not.	1Tamb	2.1.44	Cosroe
In happy hower we have set the Crowne/Upon your kingly head,	1Tamb	2.1.50	Ortyg
What should we doe but bid them battaile straight,	1Tamb	2.2.18	Meandr
Least if we let them lynger here a while,	1Tamb	2.2.20	Meandr
And as we know) remaines with Tamburlaine,	1Tamb	2.2.36	Meandr

WE (cont.)

We have our Cammels laden all with gold:	1Tamb	2.2.62	Meandr
Was but a handful to that we will have.	1Tamb	2.3.17	Tamb
and with our Sun-bright armour as we march,	1Tamb	2.3.221	Tamb
With dutie [and] <not> with amitie we yeeld/Our utmost service	1Tamb	2.3.33	Techel
we have discovered the enemie/Ready to chardge you with a	1Tamb	2.3.49	1Msngr
We are enough to scarre the enemy,	1Tamb	2.3.64	Tamb
On your submission we with thanks excuse,	1Tamb	2.5.13	Cosroe
And now we will to faire Persepolis,	1Tamb	2.5.24	Cosroe
And as we ever [aim'd] <and> at your behoofe,	1Tamb	2.5.32	Ortyg
So will we with our powers and our lives,	1Tamb	2.5.34	Ortyg
Then will we march to all those Indian Mines,	1Tamb	2.5.41	Cosroe
shall we wish for ought/The world affoords in greatest	1Tamb	2.5.72	Tamb
Me thinks we should not, I am strongly moov'd,	1Tamb	2.5.75	Tamb
If we should aime at such a dignitie?	1Tamb	2.5.79	Tamb
Then shall we send to this triumphing King,	1Tamb	2.5.87	Techel
We will not steale upon him cowardly,	1Tamb	2.5.102	Tamb
Haste thee Techelles, we will follow thee.	1Tamb	2.5.104	Tamb
And since we all have suckt one wholsome aire,	1Tamb	2.6.25	Cosroe
same proportion of Elements/Resolve, I hope we are resembled,	1Tamb	2.6.27	Cosroe
Untill we reach the ripest fruit of all,	1Tamb	2.7.27	Tamb
So do we hope to raign in Asia,	1Tamb	2.7.38	Usumc
We heare, the Tartars and the Easterne theeves/Under the	1Tamb	3.1.2	Bajzth
As many circumcised Turkes we have,	1Tamb	3.1.8	Bajzth
Yet would we not be brav'd with forrain power,	1Tamb	3.1.13	Bajzth
We meane to take his mornings next arise/For messenger, he will	1Tamb	3.1.38	Bajzth
like Orcus gulfe/Batter the walles, and we will enter in:	1Tamb	3.1.66	Bajzth
The entertainment we have had of him,	1Tamb	3.2.37	Zenoc
Agreed Casane, we wil honor him.	1Tamb	3.2.113	Techel
We meane to seate our footmen on their Steeds,	1Tamb	3.3.25	Techel
Yet we assure us of the victorie.	1Tamb	3.3.35	Usumc
Why stay we thus prolonging all their lives?	1Tamb	3.3.97	Techel
That we may raigne as kings of Affrica.	1Tamb	3.3.99	Therid
And manage words with her as we will armes.	1Tamb	3.3.131	Tamb
marshal us the way/We use to march upon the slaughtered foe:	1Tamb	3.3.149	Tamb
For we will scorne they should come nere our selves.	1Tamb	3.3.186	Zenoc
We have their crownes, their bodies strowe the fielde.	1Tamb	3.3.215	Techel
Ah faire Zabina, we have lost the field.	1Tamb	3.3.233	Bajzth
To faire Damascus, where we now remaine,	1Tamb	4.2.99	Tamb
Shall lead him with us wheresoere we goe.	1Tamb	4.2.100	Tamb
Now may we see Damascus lofty towers,	1Tamb	4.2.102	Tamb
Me thinks we martch as Meliager did,	1Tamb	4.3.1	Souldn
offences feele/Such plagues as heaven and we can poure on him.	1Tamb	4.3.45	Arabia
If we deserve them not with higher meeds/Then erst our states	1Tamb	4.4.131	Therid
We meane to traveile to th'Antartique Pole,	1Tamb	4.4.136	Tamb
We see his tents have now bene altered,	1Tamb	5.1.7	Govnr
And if we should with common rites of Armes,	1Tamb	5.1.11	Govnr
Nor you depend on such weake helps as we.	1Tamb	5.1.33	1Virgn
Endure as we the malice of our stars,	1Tamb	5.1.43	Govnr
With knees and hearts submissive we intreate/Grace to our words	1Tamb	5.1.50	2Virgn
Graunt that these signes of victorie we yeeld/May bind the	1Tamb	5.1.55	2Virgn
What simple Virgins may perswade, we will.	1Tamb	5.1.61	2Virgn
O then for these, and such as we our selves,	1Tamb	5.1.96	1Virgn
Wherein as in a myrrour we perceive/The highest reaches of a	1Tamb	5.1.167	Tamb
We know the victorie is ours my Lord,	1Tamb	5.1.203	Therid
That will we chiefly see unto, Theridamas,	1Tamb	5.1.206	Tamb
Till we have made us ready for the field.	1Tamb	5.1.212	Tamb
Pray for us Bajazeth, we are going.	1Tamb	5.1.213	Tamb
Ah faire Zabina, we may curse his power,	1Tamb	5.1.230	Bajzth
And then shall we in this detested guyse,	1Tamb	5.1.235	Bajzth
Why should we live, O wretches, beggars, slaves,	1Tamb	5.1.248	Zabina
Why live we Bajazeth, and build up neasts,	1Tamb	5.1.249	Zabina
Left to themselves while we were at the fight,	1Tamb	5.1.471	Tamb
And here we crowne thee Queene of Persea,	1Tamb	5.1.507	Tamb
Shall we with honor (as beseemes) entombe,	1Tamb	5.1.531	Tamb
We wil our celebrated rites of mariage solemnize.	1Tamb	5.1.534	Tamb
Now have we martcht from faire Natolia/Two hundred leagues, and	2Tamb	1.1.6	Orcan
Shall we parle with the Christian,/Or crosse the streame, and	2Tamb	1.1.11	Orcan
We all are glutted with the Christians blood,	2Tamb	1.1.14	Gazell
Will hazard that we might with surety hold.	2Tamb	1.1.24	Uribas
We have revolted Grecians, Albanees,	2Tamb	1.1.61	Orcan
And what we did, was in extremity:	2Tamb	1.1.105	Sgsmnd
We came from Turky to confirme a league,	2Tamb	1.1.115	Gazell
And we from Europe to the same intent,	2Tamb	1.1.118	Fredrk
So prest are we, but yet if Sigismond/Speake as a friend, and	2Tamb	1.1.122	Orcan
And then depart we to our territories.	2Tamb	1.1.166	Orcan
We quickly may in Turkish seas arrive.	2Tamb	1.2.27	Callap
But need we not be spied going aboord?	2Tamb	1.2.56	Almeda
When we shall meet the Turkish Deputie/And all his Viceroies,	2Tamb	1.3.99	Tamb
For we will martch against them presently.	2Tamb	1.3.105	Tamb
Now will we banquet on these plaines a while,	2Tamb	1.3.157	Tamb
For since we left you at the Souldans court,	2Tamb	1.3.177	Usumc
We have subdude the Southerne Guallatia,	2Tamb	1.3.178	Usumc
We kept the narrow straight of Gibralter,	2Tamb	1.3.180	Usumc
Then wil we triumph, banquet and carouse,	2Tamb	1.3.218	Tamb
I, liquid golde when we have conquer'd him,	2Tamb	1.3.223	Tamb
We may discourage all the pagan troope,	2Tamb	2.1.25	Fredrk
Grace to memorie/The league we lately made with king Orcanes,	2Tamb	2.1.28	Sgsmnd
We are not bound to those accomplishments,	2Tamb	2.1.35	Baldwn
So what we vow to them should not infringe/Our liberty of armes	2Tamb	2.1.40	Baldwn
And should we lose the opportunity/That God hath given to venge	2Tamb	2.1.51	Fredrk
If we neglect this offered victory.	2Tamb	2.1.59	Fredrk
Now will we march from proud Orminius mount/To faire Natolia,	2Tamb	2.2.2	Orcan

WE (cont.)

And now come we to make his sinowes shake,	2Tamb	2.2.9	Gazell
And solemne covenants we have both confirm'd,	2Tamb	2.2.31	Orcan
If there be Christ, we shall have victorie.	2Tamb	2.2.64	Orcan
Which we referd to justice of his Christ,	2Tamb	2.3.28	Orcan
We wil both watch and ward shall keepe his trunke/Amidst these	2Tamb	2.3.38	Orcan
And we discend into th'infernall vaults,	2Tamb	2.4.98	Tamb
We both will rest and have one Epitaph/Writ in as many severall	2Tamb	2.4.134	Tamb
We shall not need to nourish any doubt,	2Tamb	3.1.26	Callap
We may be slaine or wounded ere we learne.	2Tamb	3.2.94	Calyph
Before we meet the armie of the Turke.	2Tamb	3.2.138	Tamb
That we have sent before to fire the townes,	2Tamb	3.2.147	Tamb
That we may tread upon his captive necke,	2Tamb	3.2.157	Tamb
How say ye Souldiers, Shal we not?	2Tamb	3.3.9	Techel
And when we enter in, not heaven it selfe/Shall ransome thee,	2Tamb	3.3.27	Therid
We will my Lord.	2Tamb	3.3.46	Pionrs
Both we (Theridamas) wil intrench our men,	2Tamb	3.3.49	Techel
That we may know if our artillery/Will carie full point blancke	2Tamb	3.3.52	Techel
Where we will have [Gabions] <Galions> of sixe foot broad,/To	2Tamb	3.3.56	Therid
Death, whether art thou gone that both we live?	2Tamb	3.4.11	Olymp
fighting men/Are come since last we shewed your majesty.	2Tamb	3.5.34	Jrslem
Since last we numbred to your Majesty.	2Tamb	3.5.39	Orcan
Since last we numbred to your majesty.	2Tamb	3.5.45	Trebiz
Since last we numbred to your majestie:	2Tamb	3.5.49	Soria
Nay, when the battaile ends, al we wil meet,	2Tamb	3.5.97	Callap
when we are fighting, least hee hide his crowne as the foolish	2Tamb	3.5.154	P Tamb
No, we wil meet thee slavish Tamburlain.	2Tamb	3.5.170	Orcan
Now brother, follow we our fathers sword,	2Tamb	4.1.4	Amyras
Content my Lord, but what shal we play for?	2Tamb	4.1.63	P Perdic
Shal we let goe these kings again my Lord/To gather greater	2Tamb	4.1.82	Amyras
And we wil force him to the field hereafter.	2Tamb	4.1.102	Amyras
We will my Lord.	2Tamb	4.1.167	Soldrs
we wil break the hedges of their mouths/And pul their kicking	2Tamb	4.3.48	Techel
We thank your majesty.	2Tamb	4.3.74	Soldrs
Till we prepare our martch to Babylon,	2Tamb	4.3.93	Tamb
Whether we next make expedition.	2Tamb	4.3.94	Tamb
We wil Techelles, forward then ye Jades:	2Tamb	4.3.97	Tamb
with the martiall spoiles/We will convay with us to Persea.	2Tamb	4.3.106	Tamb
Have we not hope, for all our battered walles,	2Tamb	5.1.15	Govnr
When we are thus defenc'd against our Foe,	2Tamb	5.1.22	Govnr
we offer more/Than ever yet we did to such proud slaves,	2Tamb	5.1.57	Techel
we offer more/Than ever yet we did to such proud slaves,	2Tamb	5.1.58	Techel
Assault and spare not, we wil never yeeld.	2Tamb	5.1.62	Govnr
teare both our limmes/Rather then we should draw thy chariot,	2Tamb	5.1.139	Orcan
But that we leave sufficient garrison/And presently depart to	2Tamb	5.1.211	Tamb
And here may we behold great Babylon,	2Tamb	5.2.4	Callap
Doubt not my lord, but we shal conquer him.	2Tamb	5.2.12	Amasia
For we have here the chiefe selected men/Of twenty severall	2Tamb	5.2.48	Callap
And never wil we sunder camps and armes,	2Tamb	5.2.52	Callap
lie in wait for him/And if we find him absent from his campe,	2Tamb	5.2.57	Callap
For by your life we entertaine our lives.	2Tamb	5.3.167	Celeb
But this we heard some of our sea-men say,	Jew	1.1.78	1Merch
Sir we saw 'em not.	Jew	1.1.90	2Merch
we were wafted by a Spanish Fleet/That never left us till	Jew	1.1.95	2Merch
They say we are a scatter'd Nation:	Jew	1.1.121	Barab
but we have scambled up/More wealth by farre then those that	Jew	1.1.122	Barab
I must confesse we come not to be Kings:	Jew	1.1.129	Barab
Or let 'em warre, so we be conquerors:	Jew	1.1.151	Barab
Know Knights of Malta, that we came from Rhodes,	Jew	1.2.2	Basso
For happily we shall not tarry here:	Jew	1.2.16	Calym
We may have time to make collection/Amongst the Inhabitants of	Jew	1.2.20	Govnr
We grant a month, but see you keep your promise.	Jew	1.2.28	Calym
To what this ten yeares tribute will amount/That we have cast,	Jew	1.2.47	Govnr
And therefore are we to request your ayd.	Jew	1.2.49	Govnr
Alas, my Lord, we are no souldiers:	Jew	1.2.50	Barab
Tut, Jew, we know thou art no souldier;	Jew	1.2.52	1Knght
And 'tis thy mony, Barabas, we seeke.	Jew	1.2.54	1Knght
And therefore thus we are determined;	Jew	1.2.66	Govnr
Oh my Lord we will give halfe.	Jew	1.2.77	3Jews
Either pay that, or we will seize on all.	Jew	1.2.89	Govnr
we take particularly thine/To save the ruine of a multitude:	Jew	1.2.96	Govnr
Yet Barrabas we will not banish thee,	Jew	1.2.100	Govnr
As if we knew not thy profession?	Jew	1.2.120	Govnr
my Lord, we have seiz'd upon the goods/And wares of Barabas,	Jew	1.2.132	Offcrs
And of the other we have seized halfe.	Jew	1.2.135	Offcrs
For if we breake our day, we breake the league,	Jew	1.2.158	1Knght
as hardly can we brooke/The cruell handling of our selves in	Jew	1.2.174	1Jew
by me, for in extremitie/We ought to make barre of no policie.	Jew	1.2.273	Barab
We now are almost at the new made Nunnery.	Jew	1.2.306	1Fryar
The better; for we love not to be seene:	Jew	1.2.307	Abbass
Well, daughter, we admit you for a Nun.	Jew	1.2.330	Abbass
How say you, shall we?	Jew	1.2.390	Lodowk
yet when we parted last,/He said he wud attend me in the morne.	Jew	2.1.33	Abigal
Because we vail'd not to the [Turkish] <Spanish> Fleet,/Their	Jew	2.2.11	Bosco
And then we [luft] <left>, and [tackt] <tooke>, and fought at	Jew	2.2.14	Bosco
Some have we fir'd, and many have we sunke;	Jew	2.2.15	Bosco
Of whom we would make sale in Malta here.	Jew	2.2.18	Bosco
But to admit a sale of these thy Turkes/We may not, nay we dare	Jew	2.2.22	Govnr
nay we dare not give consent/By reason of a Tributary league.	Jew	2.2.22	Govnr
This truce we have is but in hope of gold,	Jew	2.2.26	1Knght
And with that summe he craves might we wage warre.	Jew	2.2.27	1Knght
Captaine we know it, but our force is small.	Jew	2.2.34	Govnr
We and our warlike Knights will follow thee/Against these	Jew	2.2.45	Govnr

WE (cont.)

So will we fight it out; come, let's away:	Jew	2.2.52	Govnr
Claime tribute where thou wilt, we are resolv'd,	Jew	2.2.55	Govnr
We Jewes can fawne like Spaniels when we please;	Jew	2.3.20	Barab
And when we grin we bite, yet are our lookes/As innocent and	Jew	2.3.21	Barab
That when we speake with Gentiles like to you,	Jew	2.3.45	Barab
We turne into the Ayre to purge our selves:	Jew	2.3.46	Barab
Oh my Lord we will not jarre about the price;	Jew	2.3.65	Barab
Tush man, we talk'd of Diamonds, not of Abigal.	Jew	2.3.151	Barab
make account of me/As of thy fellow; we are villaines both:	Jew	2.3.214	Barab
Both circumcized, we hate Christians both:	Jew	2.3.215	Barab
That we may venge their blood upon their heads.	Jew	3.2.28	Mater
Come, shall we goe?	Jew	3.3.76	1Fryar
First will we race the City wals our selves,	Jew	3.5.13	Govnr
How can it if we two be secret.	Jew	4.1.9	Barab
I feare they know we sent the poyson'd broth.	Jew	4.1.26	Barab
She has confest, and we are both undone,	Jew	4.1.46	Barab
I feare me he mistrusts what we intend.	Jew	4.1.133	Ithimr
You loyter, master, wherefore stay [we] <me> thus?	Jew	4.1.139	Ithimr
The Law shall touch you, we'll but lead you, we:	Jew	4.1.202	Barab
What shall we doe with this base villaine then?	Jew	4.2.62	Curtzn
Content, but we will leave this paltry land,	Jew	4.2.88	Ithimr
That wee might sleepe seven yeeres together afore we wake.	Jew	4.2.131	Ithimr
We two, and 'twas never knowne, nor never shall be for me.	Jew	4.4.23	P Ithimr
Pardona moy, Mounsier, [me] <we> be no well.	Jew	4.4.71	Barab
And dye he shall, for we will never yeeld.	Jew	5.1.6	1Knght
Had we but proofe of this--	Jew	5.1.15	Govnr
Whom have we there, a spy?	Jew	5.1.69	Calym
Art thou that Jew whose goods we heard were sold/For	Jew	5.1.73	Calym
What should I say? we are captives and must yeeld.	Jew	5.2.6	Govnr
And Barabas, as erst we promis'd thee,	Jew	5.2.9	Calym
For thy desert we make thee Governor,	Jew	5.2.10	Calym
and Barabas we give/To guard thy person, these our Janizaries:	Jew	5.2.15	Calym
Intreat them well, as we have used thee.	Jew	5.2.17	Calym
walke about/The ruin'd Towne, and see the wracke we made:	Jew	5.2.19	Calym
And thus we cast it:	Jew	5.2.96	Barab
This is the life we Jewes are us'd to lead;	Jew	5.2.115	Barab
Thus have we view'd the City, seene the sacke,	Jew	5.3.1	Calym
We rent in sunder at our entry:	Jew	5.3.4	Calym
Well, tell the Governor we grant his suit,	Jew	5.3.40	Calym
And meditate how we may grace us best/To solemnize our	Jew	5.3.44	Calym
What will we not adventure?	Jew	5.4.9	1Knght
We shall, my Lord, and thanke you.	Jew	5.5.8	Crpntr
Nay, Selim, stay, for since we have thee here,	Jew	5.5.97	Govnr
We will not let thee part so suddenly:	Jew	5.5.98	Govnr
Besides, if we should let thee goe, all's one,	Jew	5.5.99	Govnr
[all] <call> the world/To rescue thee, so will we guard us now,	Jew	5.5.120	Govnr
Thanks sonne Navarre, you see we love you well,	P 13	1.13	QnMoth
We think it good to goe and consumate/The rest, with hearing of	P 19	1.19	Charls
Him will we--but first lets follow those in France,	P 153	2.96	Guise
We are betraide, come my Lords, and let us goe tell the King of	P 199	3.34	P Navrre
Now have we got the fatall stragling deere,	P 204	4.2	QnMoth
And as we late decreed we may perfourme.	P 206	4.4	QnMoth
What shall we doe now with the Admirall?	P 248	4.46	Charls
He mist him neer, but we have strook him now.	P 311	5.38	Guise
Unto mount Faucon will we dragge his coarse:	P 319	5.46	Anjoy
But slay as many as we can come neer.	P 326	5.53	Anjoy
Which we have chaste into the river [Sene] <Rene>,	P 418	7.58	Guise
How may we doe? I feare me they will live.	P 420	7.60	Guise
And in the mean time my Lord, could we devise,	P 425	7.65	Guise
Yet will we not that the Massacre shall end:	P 444	7.84	Guise
Now sirra, what shall we doe with the Admirall?	P 482	9.1	P 1Atndt
and the fire the aire, and so we shall be poysoned with him.	P 485	9.4	P 1Atndt
What shall we doe then?	P 486	9.5	P 2Atndt
water the fish, and by the fish our selves when we eate them.	P 489	9.8	P 2Atndt
And he nor heares, nor sees us what we doe:	P 553	11.18	QnMoth
But that we presently despatch Embassadours/To Poland, to call	P 555	11.20	QnMoth
We will with all the speed we can, provide/For Henries	P 562	11.27	QnMoth
We know that noble mindes change not their thoughts/For wearing	P 610	12.23	Mugern
I tell thee Mugeroun we will be freends,	P 614	12.27	King
Thy brother Guise and we may now provide,	P 636	12.49	QnMoth
Where we may one injoy the others sight.	P 665	13.9	Duchss
We undertake to mannage these our warres/Against the proud	P 699	14.2	Navrre
We must with resolute mindes resolve to fight,	P 707	14.10	Navrre
My Lord, as by our scoutes we understande,	P 724	14.27	1Msngr
And we are grac'd with wreathes of victory:	P 788	16.2	Navrre
Thus God we see doth ever guide the right,	P 789	16.3	Navrre
But God we know will alwaies put them downe,	P 798	16.12	Navrre
of Guise, we understand that you/Have gathered a power of men.	P 821	17.16	King
What your intent is yet we cannot learn,	P 823	17.18	King
But we presume it is not for our good.	P 824	17.19	King
Assure him all the aide we can provide,	P 909	18.10	Navrre
For we must aide the King against the Guise.	P 918	18.19	Navrre
Be gone I say, tis time that we were there.	P 919	18.20	Navrre
tush, were he heere, we would kill him presently.	P 934	19.4	P 1Mur
But when will he come that we may murther him?	P 937	19.7	P 3Mur
O Lord no: for we entend to strangle you.	P1095	20.5	2Mur
We will goe talke more of this within.	P1138	21.32	Dumain
We might have punisht him to his deserts.	P1184	22.46	Eprnon
That we might torture him with some new found death.	P1217	22.79	Eprnon
That we may see it honourably interde:	P1246	22.108	Navrre
We thanke your worship.	Edw	1.1.47	Omnes
We will wait heere about the court.	Edw	1.1.49	Omnes

WE (cont.)

We may not, nor we will not suffer this.	Edw	1.2.15	MortSr
Why post we not from hence to levie men?	Edw	1.2.16	Mortmr
The king shall lose his crowne, for we have power,	Edw	1.2.59	Mortmr
We and the rest that are his counsellers,	Edw	1.2.69	ArchBp
What we confirme the king will frustrate.	Edw	1.2.72	Lncstr
Then may we lawfully revolt from him.	Edw	1.2.73	Mortmr
It is our pleasure, we will have it so.	Edw	1.4.9	Edward
We will not thus be facst and overpeerd.	Edw	1.4.19	Mortmr
We know our duties, let him know his peeres.	Edw	1.4.23	Warwck
We are no traitors, therefore threaten not.	Edw	1.4.25	MortSr
What we have done, our hart bloud shall maintaine.	Edw	1.4.40	Mortmr
Think you that we can brooke this upstart pride?	Edw	1.4.41	Warwck
And see what we your councellers have done.	Edw	1.4.44	ArchBp
Subscribe as we have done to his exile.	Edw	1.4.53	ArchBp
he refuse, and then may we/Depose him and elect an other king.	Edw	1.4.54	Mortmr
O that we might as well returne as goe.	Edw	1.4.143	Edward
All that he speakes, is nothing, we are resolv'd.	Edw	1.4.251	Warwck
Then may we with some colour rise in armes,	Edw	1.4.279	Mortmr
For howsoever we have borne it out,	Edw	1.4.280	Mortmr
So shall we have the people of our side,	Edw	1.4.282	Mortmr
Lord Mortimer, we leave you to your charge:	Edw	1.4.373	Edward
Such newes we heare my lord.	Edw	1.4.380	Lncstr
Spare for no cost, we will requite your love.	Edw	1.4.383	Edward
And promiseth as much as we can wish,	Edw	1.4.399	MortSr
below, the king and he/From out a window, laugh at such as we,	Edw	1.4.417	Mortmr
May with one word, advaunce us while we live:	Edw	2.1.9	Spencr
And will be at the court as soone as we.	Edw	2.1.77	Neece
A trifle, weele expell him when we please:	Edw	2.2.10	Edward
Against the stately triumph we decreed?	Edw	2.2.12	Edward
About it then, and we will follow you.	Edw	2.2.124	Mortmr
Why, so he may, but we will speake to him.	Edw	2.2.136	Lncstr
May we not?	Edw	2.2.138	Mortmr
Who have we there, ist you?	Edw	2.2.140	Edward
We never beg, but use such praiers as these.	Edw	2.2.153	Mortmr
He is your brother, therefore have we cause/To cast the worst,	Edw	2.3.7	Warwck
was Plantagenet/False of his word, and therefore trust we thee.	Edw	2.3.12	Mortmr
Whereof we got the name of Mortimer,	Edw	2.3.23	Mortmr
Farewell sweete unckle till we meete againe.	Edw	2.4.11	Neece
That when I had him we might never part.	Edw	2.4.21	Queene
We would but rid the realme of Gaveston,	Edw	2.4.35	Lncstr
cause,/That here severelie we will execute/Upon thy person:	Edw	2.5.23	Warwck
Arundell, we will gratifie the king/In other matters, he must	Edw	2.5.43	Warwck
Shalt thou appoint/What we shall graunt?	Edw	2.5.50	Mortmr
We wot, he that the care of realme remits,	Edw	2.5.61	Warwck
But for we know thou art a noble gentleman,	Edw	2.5.68	Mortmr
We will not wrong thee so,	Edw	2.5.69	Mortmr
is it not enough/That we have taken him, but must we now/Leave	Edw	2.5.84	Warwck
That we have taken him, but must we now/Leave him on had-I-wist,	Edw	2.5.84	Warwck
My lord of Penbrooke, we deliver him you,	Edw	2.5.97	Mortmr
We that have prettie wenches to our wives,	Edw	2.5.102	Penbrk
in the morning/We will discharge thee of thy charge, be gon.	Edw	2.5.109	Penbrk
We will in hast go certifie our Lord.	Edw	2.6.19	James
Yea gentle Spencer, we have beene too milde,	Edw	3.1.24	Edward
Because we heare Lord Bruse dooth sell his land,	Edw	3.1.53	Edward
Madam in this matter/We will employ you and your little sonne,	Edw	3.1.70	Edward
Madam, we will that you with speed be shipt,	Edw	3.1.81	Edward
With all the hast we can dispatch him hence.	Edw	3.1.83	Edward
And meerely of our love we do create thee/Earle of Gloster, and	Edw	3.1.145	Edward
For now, even now, we marche to make them stoope,	Edw	3.1.183	Edward
Why do we sound retreat?	Edw	3.1.185	Edward
When we had sent our messenger to request/He might be spared to	Edw	3.1.234	Edward
[Levune] <Lewne>, the trust that we repose in thee,/Begets the	Edw	3.1.262	Spencr
The lords are cruell, and the king unkinde,/What shall we doe?	Edw	4.2.3	Queene
To thinke that we can yet be tun'd together,	Edw	4.2.9	Queene
that we can yet be tun'd together,/No, no, we jarre too farre.	Edw	4.2.10	Queene
Will we with thee to Henolt, so we will.	Edw	4.2.31	Queene
But gentle lords, friendles we are in Fraunce.	Edw	4.2.46	Queene
Yet have we friends, assure your grace, in England/Would cast	Edw	4.2.54	Mortmr
We will finde comfort, money, men, and friends/Ere long, to bid	Edw	4.2.65	SrJohn
I pray let us see it, what have we there?	Edw	4.3.10	Edward
My lord, we have, and if he be in England,	Edw	4.3.19	Spencr
When we may meet these traitors in the field.	Edw	4.3.47	Edward
Our kindest friends in Belgia have we left,	Edw	4.4.3	Queene
Lords, sith that we are by sufferance of heaven,	Edw	4.4.17	Mortmr
Heere for our countries cause sweare we to him/All homage,	Edw	4.4.19	Mortmr
We come in armes to wrecke it with the [sword] <swords>:	Edw	4.4.23	Mortmr
and withall/We may remoove these flatterers from the king,	Edw	4.4.26	Mortmr
Edward will thinke we come to flatter him.	Edw	4.4.29	SrJohn
Shape we our course to Ireland there to breath.	Edw	4.5.3	Spencr
princely resolution/Fits not the time, away, we are pursu'd.	Edw	4.5.9	Baldck
Since then succesfully we have prevayled,	Edw	4.6.21	Queene
Ere farther we proceede my noble lordes,	Edw	4.6.23	Queene
We heere create our welbeloved sonne,	Edw	4.6.24	Queene
We thanke you all.	Edw	4.6.53	Queene
And we must seeke to right it as we may,	Edw	4.6.68	Mortmr
We in meane while madam, must take advise,	Edw	4.6.77	Mortmr
As silent and as carefull will we be,	Edw	4.7.2	Abbot
But we alas are chaste, and you my friends,	Edw	4.7.22	Edward
We were imbarkt for Ireland, wretched we,	Edw	4.7.33	Baldck
this drowsines/Betides no good, here even we are betraied.	Edw	4.7.45	Spencr
A faire commission warrants what we do.	Edw	4.7.48	Rice
A sweet Spencer, thus then must we part.	Edw	4.7.73	Edward

WE (cont.)

We must my lord, so will the angry heavens.	Edw		4.7.74		Spencr
Here humblie of your grace we take our leaves, ...	Edw		4.7.78		Baldck
For we shall see them shorter by the heads.	Edw		4.7.94		Rice
part we must,/Sweete Spencer, gentle Baldocke, part we must.	Edw		4.7.95		Edward
Sweete Spencer, gentle Baldocke, part we must.	Edw		4.7.96		Edward
We are deprivde the sun-shine of our life, ...	Edw		4.7.106		Baldck
Reduce we all our lessons unto this, ...	Edw		4.7.110		Baldck
And princely Edwards right we crave the crowne. . .	Edw		5.1.39		BshpWn
And thus, most humbly do we take our leave.	Edw		5.1.124		Trussl
Faire Isabell, now have we our desire, ...	Edw		5.2.1		Mortmr
Be rulde by me, and we will rule the realme, ...	Edw		5.2.5		Mortmr
For now we hould an old Wolfe by the eares, ...	Edw		5.2.7		Mortmr
To erect your sonne with all the speed we may, ...	Edw		5.2.11		Mortmr
And we have heard that Edmund laid a plot, ...	Edw		5.2.32		BshpWn
And none but we shall know where he lieth.	Edw		5.2.41		Mortmr
And when tis done, we will subscribe our name. . . .	Edw		5.2.50		Mortmr
rest, because we heare/That Edmund casts to worke his libertie,	Edw		5.2.57		Mortmr
Brother Edmund, strive not, we are his friends, . . .	Edw		5.2.114		Queene
My lord, be not pensive, we are your friends.	Edw		5.3.1		Matrvs
Wherefore stay we? on sirs to the court.	Edw		5.3.65		Souldr
And we be quit that causde it to be done:	Edw		5.4.16		Mortmr
As we were bringing him to Killingworth.	Edw		5.4.85		Souldr
More then we can enflict, and therefore now, ...	Edw		5.5.11		Matrvs
His fathers dead, and we have murdered him.	Edw		5.6.16		Queene
And therefore we commit you to the Tower, ...	Edw		5.6.79		King
we must now performe/The forme of Faustus fortunes, good or	F	7	Prol.7		1Chor
And now <so> to patient judgements we appeale <our plaude>,	F	9	Prol.9		1Chor
If we say that we have no sinne we deceive our selves, and	F	69	1.1.41	P	Faust
Why then belike/We must sinne, and so consequently die,/I, we	F	72	1.1.44		Faust
I, we must die, an everlasting death.	F	73	1.1.45		Faust
Like Lyons shall they guard us when we please, ...	F	151	1.1.123		Valdes
Then tell me Faustus what shall we three want?	F	175	1.1.147		Cornel
We will informe thee e're our conference cease. . . .	F	184	1.1.156		Valdes
That shall we presently know, <for see> here comes his boy.	F	196	1.2.3		2Schol
Yet let us see <trie> what we can do.	F	228	1.2.35		2Schol
No more then he commands, must we performe.	F	270	1.3.42		Mephst
For when we heare one racke the name of God, ...	F	275	1.3.47		Mephst
We flye in hope to get his glorious soule:	F	277	1.3.49		Mephst
Nor will we come unlesse he use such meanes, ...	F	278	1.3.50		Mephst
Where we are tortur'd, and remaine for ever.	F	509	2.1.121		Mephst
but <for> where we are is hell,/And where hell is there must we	F	511	2.1.123		Mephst
And where hell is there must we ever be.	F	512	2.1.124		Mephst
all at one time, but in some years we have more, in some lesse?	F	616	2.2.65	P	Faust
We are come to tell thee thou dost injure us.	F	642	2.2.91		Belzeb
And we will highly gratify thee for it.	F	653	2.2.102		Lucifr
we are come from hell in person to shew thee some pastime:	F	654	2.2.103	P	Belzeb
We saw the River Maine, fall into Rhine <Rhines>, . . .	F	785	3.1.7		Faust
There saw we learned Maroes golden tombe:	F	791	3.1.13		Faust
And cause we are no common guests, ...	F	805	3.1.27		Mephst
<Faustus I have, and because we wil not be unprovided, .	F	805	(HC265) A	P	Mephst
We veiw'd the face of heaven, of earth and hell. . . .	F	848	3.1.70		Faust
There did we view the Kingdomes of the world, ...	F	852	3.1.74		Faust
We go my Lord.	F	889	3.1.111		1Card
We will depose the Emperour for that deed, ...	F	906	3.1.128		Pope
So will we quell that haughty Schismatique;	F	922	3.1.144		Pope
And therefore tho we would we cannot erre.	F	931	3.1.153		Pope
Now tell me Faustus, are we not fitted well?	F	940	3.1.162		Mephst
two such Cardinals/Ne're serv'd a holy Pope, as we shall do.	F	942	3.1.164		Faust
We will determine of his life or death.	F	969	3.1.191		Pope
That we may solemnize Saint Peters feast, ...	F	978	3.1.200		Pope
To morrow we would sit i'th Consistory, ...	F	1017	3.2.37		Pope
we all are witnesses/That Bruno here was late delivered you,	F	1025	3.2.45		Raymnd
By holy Paul we saw them not.	F	1029	3.2.49		BthCrd
That we receive such great indignity?	F	1050	3.2.70		Pope
we were best looke that your devill can answere the stealing of	F	1088	3.3.1	P	Dick
we steale a cup?	F	1099	3.3.12	P	Robin
what you say, we looke not like cup-stealers I can tell you.	F	1099	3.3.12	P	Robin
your searching; we scorne to steale your cups I can tell you.	F	1106	3.3.19	P	Dick
We would behold that famous Conquerour, ...	F	1231	4.1.77		Emper
That we may wonder at their excellence.	F	1234	4.1.80		Emper
Be it as Faustus please, we are content.	F	1253	4.1.99		Emper
Nay, we will stay with thee, betide what may, ...	F	1338	4.2.14		Fredrk
Where shall we place our selves Benvolio?	F	1353	4.2.29		Mrtino
Here will we stay to bide the first assault, ...	F	1354	4.2.30		Benvol
let's devise how we may adde more shame/To the blacke scandall	F	1377	4.2.53		Fredrk
What use shall we put his beard to?	F	1383	4.2.59	P	Mrtino
Nay feare not man, we have no power to kill.	F	1440	4.3.10		Mrtino
Nay chafe not man, we all are sped.	F	1444	4.3.14		Mrtino
What may we do, that we may hide our shames?	F	1447	4.3.17		Fredrk
If we should follow him to worke revenge, ...	F	1448	4.3.18		Benvol
What shall we then do deere Benvolio?	F	1451	4.3.21		Mrtino
Come sirs, what shall we do now till mine Hostesse comes?	F	1520	4.5.16	P	Dick
What rude disturbers have we at the gate?	F	1588	4.6.31		Duke
We have no reason for it, therefore a fig for him. . . .	F	1593	4.6.36	P	Dick
I hope sir, we have wit enough to be more bold then welcome.	F	1595	4.6.38	P	HrsCsr
I, and we will speake with him.	F	1601	4.6.44		Carter
we will be wellcome for our mony, and we will pay for what we	F	1611	4.6.54	P	Robin
be wellcome for our mony, and we will pay for what we take:	F	1611	4.6.54	P	Robin
be wellcome for our mony, and we will pay for what we take:	F	1612	4.6.55	P	Robin
I marry can I, we are under heaven.	F	1615	4.6.58	P	Carter
We are much beholding to this learned man.	F	1670	4.6.113		Lady
So are we Madam, which we will recompence/With all the love and	F	1671	4.6.114		Duke

WE (cont.)

which we will recompence/With all the love and kindnesse that	F1671	4.6.114	Duke
we will recompence/With all the love and kindnesse that we may.	F1672	4.6.115	Duke
we have determin'd with our selves, that Hellen of Greece was	F1682	5.1.9	P 1Schol
Majesty, we should thinke our selves much beholding unto you.	F1686	5.1.13	P 1Schol
Now <Since> we have seene the pride of Natures worke <workes>,	F1702	5.1.29	1Schol
Thus from infernall Dis do we ascend/To view the subjects of	F1797	5.2.1	Lucifr
'Mong which as chiefe, Faustus we come to thee,	F1800	5.2.4	Lucifr
O what may <shal> we do to save Faustus?	F1868	5.2.72	P 2Schol
Pray thou, and we will pray, that God may have mercie upon thee.	F1875	5.2.79	P 2Schol
Come on Mephastophilis, what shall we do?	F App	p.232 22	P Faust
Nay I know not, we shalbe curst with bell, booke, and candle.	F App	p.232 23	P Mephst
tell thee, we were for ever made by this doctor Faustus booke?	F App	p.234 1	P Robin
as we that do succeede, or they that shal hereafter possesse	F App	p.236 21	P Emper
We sing, whose conquering swords their own breasts launcht,	Lucan, First Booke	3	
Untill the cruel Giants war was done)/We plaine not heavens,	Lucan, First Booke	37	
Being conquered, we are plaugde with civil war.	Lucan, First Booke	108	
And then we grew licencious and rude,	Lucan, First Booke	162	
We bide the first brunt, safer might we dwel,	Lucan, First Booke	253	
We first sustain'd the uproares of the Gaules,	Lucan, First Booke	256	
wars,/We from our houses driven, most willingly/Suffered exile:	Lucan, First Booke	279	
Pursu'd us hither, how were we bestead/When comming conqueror,	Lucan, First Booke	309	
Neither spoile, nor kingdom seeke we by these armes,	Lucan, First Booke	351	
We grieve at this thy patience and delay:	Lucan, First Booke	362	
Why should we wish the gods should ever end them?	Lucan, First Booke	668	
We which were Ovids five books, now are three,	Ovid's Elegies	1.1.1	
We are the Muses prophets, none of thine.	Ovid's Elegies	1.1.10	
Yeelding or striving <strugling> doe we give him might,	Ovid's Elegies	1.2.9	
So likewise we will through the world be rung,	Ovid's Elegies	1.3.25	
When to go homewards we rise all along,	Ovid's Elegies	1.4.55	
But we must part, when heav'n with black night lowers.	Ovid's Elegies	1.4.60	
Erre we? or do the turned hinges sound,	Ovid's Elegies	1.6.49	
We erre: a strong blast seem'd the gates to ope:	Ovid's Elegies	1.6.51	
She may perceive how we the time did wast:	Ovid's Elegies	1.6.70	
For beds ill hyr'd we are indebted nought.	Ovid's Elegies	1.10.44	
By speechlesse lookes we guesse at things succeeding.	Ovid's Elegies	1.11.18	
Beleeve me, whom we feare, we wish to perish.	Ovid's Elegies	2.2.10	
To meete for poyson or vilde facts we crave not,	Ovid's Elegies	2.2.63	
Wee seeke that through thee safely love we may,	Ovid's Elegies	2.2.65	
What can be easier then the thing we pray?	Ovid's Elegies	2.2.66	
Oh how the burthen irkes, that we should shun.	Ovid's Elegies	2.4.6	
Seeing she likes my bookes, why should we jarre?	Ovid's Elegies	2.4.20	
There good birds rest (if we beleeve things hidden)/Whence	Ovid's Elegies	2.6.51	
How oft, and by what meanes we did agree.	Ovid's Elegies	2.8.28	
We people wholy given thee, feele thine armes,	Ovid's Elegies	2.9.11	
Nor of our love to be asham'd we need,	Ovid's Elegies	2.17.26	
What lawfull is, or we professe Loves art,	Ovid's Elegies	2.18.19	
(Alas my precepts turne my selfe to smart)/We write, or what	Ovid's Elegies	2.18.21	
Wee skorne things lawfull, stolne sweetes we affect,	Ovid's Elegies	2.19.3	
no warres we move,/Peace pleaseth me, and in mid peace is love.	Ovid's Elegies	3.2.49	
We praise: great goddesse ayde my enterprize.	Ovid's Elegies	3.2.56	
What Venus promisd, promise thou we pray,	Ovid's Elegies	3.2.59	
One slowe we favour, Romans him revoke:	Ovid's Elegies	3.2.73	
How to attaine, what is denyed, we thinke,	Ovid's Elegies	3.4.17	
What's kept, we covet more: the care makes theft:	Ovid's Elegies	3.4.25	
So use we women of strange nations stocke.	Ovid's Elegies	3.4.34	
And nine sweete bouts had we before day light.	Ovid's Elegies	3.6.26	
Now poverty great barbarisme we hold.	Ovid's Elegies	3.7.4	
Not what we slouthfull [knowe] <knewe>, let wise men learne,	Ovid's Elegies	3.7.25	
Gold from the earth in steade of fruits we pluck,	Ovid's Elegies	3.7.53	
The gods care we are cald, and men of piety,	Ovid's Elegies	3.8.17	
And some there be that thinke we have a deity.	Ovid's Elegies	3.8.18	
As in thy sacrifize we them forbeare?	Ovid's Elegies	3.9.44	
We vanquish, and tread tam'd love under feete,	Ovid's Elegies	3.10.5	
We make Enceladus use a thousand armes,	Ovid's Elegies	3.11.27	
The East winds in Ulisses baggs we shut,	Ovid's Elegies	3.11.29	
Niobe flint, Callist we make a Beare,	Ovid's Elegies	3.11.31	
We toucht the walles, Camillus wonne by thee.	Ovid's Elegies	3.12.2	
We wish that one should loose, the other win.	Hero and Leander	1.170	
And one especiallie doe we affect,	Hero and Leander	1.171	
What we behold is censur'd by our eies.	Hero and Leander	1.174	
We humane creatures should enjoy that blisse.	Hero and Leander	1.254	
Base boullion for the stampes sake we allow,	Hero and Leander	1.265	
Even so for mens impression do we you.	Hero and Leander	1.266	
Above our life we love a stedfast friend,	Hero and Leander	2.79	
Yet when a token of great worth we send,	Hero and Leander	2.80	
We often kisse it, often looke thereon,	Hero and Leander	2.81	
Even as a bird, which in our hands we wring,	Hero and Leander	2.289	
And we will all the pleasures prove,	Passionate Shepherd	2	
Which from our pretty Lambes we pull,	Passionate Shepherd	14	

WEAKE

And the remainder weake and out of heart,	Dido	2.1.133	Aeneas
Alas (poore Turke) his fortune is to weake,	1Tamb	3.3.6	Tamb
Nor you depend on such weake helps as we.	1Tamb	5.1.33	1Virgn
Have drawne thy treasure drie, and made thee weake,	Edw	2.2.159	Mortmr
I am too weake and feeble to resist,	Edw	5.5.108	Edward
Yet to encounter this your weake attempt,	F1429	4.2.105	Faust
And I will combat with weake Menelaus,	F1777	5.1.104	Faust
Who though his root be weake, and his owne waight/Keepe him	Lucan, First Booke	139	
Now while their part is weake, and feares, march hence,	Lucan, First Booke	281	
(Anger will helpe thy hands though nere so weake).	Ovid's Elegies	1.7.66	
[His Arte excelld, although his witte was weake].	Ovid's Elegies	1.15.14	
Weake Elegies, delightfull Muse farewell;	Ovid's Elegies	3.14.19	

WEAKNETH			
Weakneth his body, and will waste his Realme,	P 128	2.71	Guise
WEALE			
Whose fading weale of victorie forsooke,	Dido	1.2.15	Illion
The citie and my native countries weale,	2Tamb	5.1.13	Govnr
WEALTH (See also WEALE, WELTH)			
And fertile in faire Ceres furrowed wealth,	Dido	1.2.22	Cloan
In whose faire bosome I will locke more wealth,	Dido	3.1.92	Dido
If wealth or riches may prevaile with them,	1Tamb	2.2.61	Meandr
For all the wealth of Gehons golden waves.	1Tamb	5.1.123	Tamb
Trapt with the wealth and riches of the world,	2Tamb	1.1.43	Orcan
Adding their wealth and treasure to my store.	2Tamb	4.3.101	Tamb
of judgement frame/This is the ware wherein consists my wealth:	Jew	1.1.33	Barab
And as their wealth increaseth, so inclose/Infinite riches in a	Jew	1.1.36	Barab
They wondred how you durst with so much wealth/Trust such a	Jew	1.1.79	1Merch
Or who is honour'd now but for his wealth?	Jew	1.1.113	Barab
scambled up/More wealth by farre then those that brag of faith.	Jew	1.1.123	Barab
So they spare me, my daughter, and my wealth.	Jew	1.1.153	Barab
As all the wealth of Malta cannot pay;	Jew	1.1.183	Barab
Have strangers leave with us to get their wealth?	Jew	1.2.60	2Knght
Halfe of my substance is a Cities wealth.	Jew	1.2.85	Barab
But here in Malta, where thou gotst thy wealth,	Jew	1.2.101	Govnr
Excesse of wealth is cause of covetousnesse:	Jew	1.2.123	Govnr
which being valued/Amount to more then all the wealth in Malta.	Jew	1.2.134	Offcrs
You have my goods, my mony, and my wealth,	Jew	1.2.138	Barab
You have my wealth, the labour of my life,	Jew	1.2.149	Barab
I wot his wealth/Was written thus:	Jew	1.2.181	Barab
You that/Were ne're possest of wealth, are pleas'd with want.	Jew	1.2.201	Barab
My gold, my gold, and all my wealth is gone.	Jew	1.2.258	Barab
Who in my wealth wud tell me winters tales,	Jew	2.1.25	Barab
I weigh it thus much; I have wealth enough.	Jew	2.3.245	Barab
'Tis not thy wealth, but her that I esteeme,	Jew	2.3.298	Lodowk
Thus every villaine ambles after wealth/Although he ne're be	Jew	3.4.52	Barab
And now for store of wealth may I compare/With all the Jewes in	Jew	4.1.55	Barab
may I compare/With all the Jewes in Malta; but what is wealth?	Jew	4.1.56	Barab
You shall convert me, you shall have all my wealth.	Jew	4.1.81	Barab
Sweet Bellamira, would I had my Masters wealth for thy sake.	Jew	4.2.55	P Ithimr
maintaine/The wealth and safety of your kingdomes right.	P 478	8.28	Anjoy
For all the wealth and treasure of the world.	P1163	22.25	King
about my neck/Then these my lord, nor let me have more wealth,	Edw	1.4.331	Queene
That havocks Englands wealth and treasurie.	Edw	4.4.27	Mortmr
Reveld in Englands wealth and treasurie.	Edw	4.6.52	Rice
Yea <I> all the wealth that our fore-fathers hid,	F 173	1.1.145	Cornel
No Faustus, thinke of honour and of wealth.	F 410	2.1.22	BdAngl
<Of> Wealth?	F 411	2.1.23	Faust
Take you the wealth, leave us the victorie.	F1347	4.2.23	Benvol
he has made his will, and given me his wealth, his house, his	F1675	5.1.2	P Wagner
When fortune made us lords of all, wealth flowed,	Lucan, First Booke		161
By many hands great wealth is quickly got.	Ovid's Elegies		1.8.92
Troianes destroy the Greeke wealth, while you may.	Ovid's Elegies		1.9.34
each mans mony/And seekes vild wealth by selling of her Cony,	Ovid's Elegies		1.10.22
should defend/Or great wealth from a judgement seate ascend.	Ovid's Elegies		1.10.40
Of wealth and honour so shall grow thy heape,	Ovid's Elegies		2.2.39
Let marchants seeke wealth, [and] with perjured lips,	Ovid's Elegies		2.10.33
Which wealth, cold winter doth on thee bestowe.	Ovid's Elegies		3.5.94
See a rich chuffe whose wounds great wealth inferr'd,	Ovid's Elegies		3.7.9
Courts shut the poore out; wealth gives estimation,	Ovid's Elegies		3.7.55
Which fact, and country wealth Halesus fled.	Ovid's Elegies		3.12.32
Wherein the liberall graces lock'd their wealth,	Hero and Leander		2.17
WEALTHIE			
And clad us in these wealthie robes we weare.	Dido	2.1.65	Illion
Victuall his Souldiers, give him wealthie gifts,	Dido	2.1.329	Venus
This was the wealthie King of Thessaly,	Dido	3.1.161	Dido
Whose wealthie streames may waite upon her towers,	Dido	5.1.9	Aeneas
The men of wealthie Sestos, everie yeare,	Hero and Leander		1.91
WEALTHIER			
I, wealthier farre then any Christian.	Jew	1.1.128	Barab
WEALTHY (See also WELTHY)			
at the spoile/Of great Darius and his wealthy hoast.	1Tamb	1.1.154	Ceneus
But ere I martch to wealthy Persea,	1Tamb	4.2.47	Tamb
in mine eies/Than all the wealthy kingdomes I subdewed:	2Tamb	1.3.19	Tamb
The wealthy Moore, that in the Easterne rockes/Without	Jew	1.1.21	Barab
Many in France, and wealthy every one:	Jew	1.1.127	Barab
and Vespasian conquer'd us)/Am I become as wealthy as I was:	Jew	2.3.11	Barab
I heare the wealthy Jew walked this way;	Jew	2.3.32	Lodowk
Nor, so thou maist obtaine a wealthy prize,	Ovid's Elegies		1.8.63
Yet thinke no scorne to aske a wealthy churle,	Ovid's Elegies		1.10.53
Who should have Priams wealthy substance wonne,	Ovid's Elegies		2.14.13
WEANE			
For they are friends that help to weane my state,	1Tamb	1.2.29	Tamb
For riper yeares will weane him from such toyes.	Edw	1.4.401	MortSr
WEAPON			
Direct my weapon to his barbarous heart,	1Tamb	2.6.38	Cosroe
Rather lend me thy weapon Tamburlain,	2Tamb	5.1.142	Jrslem
Lend me that weapon that did kill my sonne,	Jew	3.2.23	Mater
Nay Madam stay, that weapon was my son's,	Jew	3.2.25	Govnr
My hands an unsheath'd shyning weapon have not.	Ovid's Elegies		2.2.64
WEAPON'D			
And their owne privie weapon'd hands destroy them.	Ovid's Elegies		2.14.4
WEAPONLES			
Weaponles must I fall and die in bands,	Edw	2.6.3	Gavstn
WEAPONS			
But weapons gree not with my tender yeares:	Dido	3.1.164	Dido

WEAPONS (cont.)
Meane time these wanton weapons serve my warre, — Dido 3.3.37 Cupid
Direct our Bullets and our weapons pointes/And make our <your> — 1Tamb 3.3.157 Tamb
But come my Lords, to weapons let us fall. — 1Tamb 3.3.162 Tamb
Hang up your weapons on Alcides poste, — 1Tamb 5.1.528 Tamb
Which when you stab, looke on your weapons point, — 2Tamb 4.2.69 Olymp
and mark your weapons point/That wil be blunted if the blow be — 2Tamb 4.2.79 Olymp
Upon him souldiers, take away his weapons. — Edw 2.5.8 Warwck
Upon my weapons point here shouldst thou fall, — Edw 2.5.13 Mortmr
Begirt with weapons, and with enemies round, — Edw 3.1.95 Arundl
Where weapons want, and though a many friends/Are made away, as — Edw 4.2.51 Mortmr
in others and their sides/With their owne weapons gorde, — Edw 4.4.8 Queene
Lay downe your weapons, traitors, yeeld the king. — Edw 5.3.55 Kent
Then draw your weapons, and be resolute: — F1335 4.2.11 Benvol
Pardon me Jove, thy weapons ayde me nought, — Ovid's Elegies 2.1.19

WEAR (See WARE)

WEARE
It is the use for [Tirien] <Turen> maides to weare/Their bowe — Dido 1.1.204 Venus
And clad us in these wealthie robes we weare. — Dido 2.1.65 Illion
Weare the emperiall Crowne of Libia, — Dido 4.4.34 Dido
How vaine am I to weare this Diadem, — Dido 4.4.40 Aeneas
And vow to weare it for my countries good: — 1Tamb 1.1.158 Cosroe
Lie here ye weedes that I disdaine to weare, — 1Tamb 1.2.41 Tamb
Holde thee Cosroe, weare two imperiall Crownes. — 1Tamb 2.5.1 Tamb
To weare a Crowne enchac'd with pearle and golde, — 1Tamb 2.5.60 Therid
Wils us to weare our selves and never rest, — 1Tamb 2.7.26 Tamb
Yet will I weare it in despight of them, — 1Tamb 2.7.61 Tamb
And on thy head weare my Emperiall crowne, — 1Tamb 3.3.113 Bajzth
vagabond/Should brave a king, or weare a princely crowne. — 1Tamb 4.3.22 Souldn
Alight and weare a woful mourning weed. — 2Tamb 1.1.44 Orcan
For he shall weare the crowne of Persea, — 2Tamb 1.3.74 Tamb
And sirha, if you meane to weare a crowne, — 2Tamb 1.3.98 Tamb
So he shal, and weare thy head in his Scutchion. — 2Tamb 3.5.138 P Orcan
Win it, and weare it, it is yet [unfoyl'd] <unsoyl'd>. — Jew 2.3.293 Barab
To fast, to pray, and weare a shirt of haire, — Jew 4.1.61 Barab
They weare no shirts, and they goe bare-foot too. — Jew 4.1.84 1Fryar
Shall weare white crosses on their Burgonets, — P 232 4.30 Guise
That if I undertake to weare the crowne/Of Poland, it may — P 466 8.16 Anjoy
And Henry then shall weare the diadem. — P 522 9.41 QnMoth
For Ile rule France, but they shall weare the crowne: — P 525 9.44 QnMoth
To weare his brothers crowne and dignity. — P 557 11.22 QnMoth
And then shall Mounser weare the diadem. — P 652 12.65 QnMoth
Guise, weare our crowne, and be thou King of France, — P 859 17.54 King
Now let the house of Bourbon weare the crowne, — P1232 22.94 King
Warwicke and Lancaster, weare you my crowne, — Edw 1.4.37 Edward
Here take my picture, and let me weare thine, — Edw 1.4.127 Edward
I weare the crowne, but am contrould by them, — Edw 5.1.29 Edward
But if proud Mortimer do weare this crowne, — Edw 5.1.43 Edward
See monsters see, ile weare my crowne againe, — Edw 5.1.74 Edward
And therefore let me weare it yet a while. — Edw 5.1.83 Edward
Mother, perswade me not to weare the crowne, — Edw 5.2.92 Prince
And thou compelst this prince to weare the crowne. — Edw 5.4.88 Kent
Did seeke to weare the triple Dyadem, — F 959 3.1.181 Faust
First weare this girdle, then appeare/Invisible to all are — F 997 3.2.17 Mephst
it will weare out ten birchin broomes I warrant you. — F1384 4.2.60 P Benvol
Do you remember how you made me weare an Apes-- — F1661 4.6.104 P Dick
And weare thy colours on my plumed crest. — F1778 5.1.105 Faust
and attire/They usde to weare during their time of life, — F App p.237 34 Emper
gives thee hornes, but makes thee weare them, feele on thy head. — F App p.238 71 P Emper
Garments do weare, jewells and gold do wast, — Ovid's Elegies 1.10.61
Therefore when flint and yron weare away, — Ovid's Elegies 1.15.31
I guide and souldiour wunne the field and weare her, — Ovid's Elegies 2.12.13
Weare me, when warmest showers thy members wash, — Ovid's Elegies 2.15.23
This side that serves thee, a sharpe sword did weare. — Ovid's Elegies 3.7.14
youth forbeare/To touch the sacred garments which I weare. — Hero and Leander 1.344
but he must weare/The sacred ring wherewith she was endow'd, — Hero and Leander 2.108

WEARES
And here Queene Dido weares th'imperiall Crowne, — Dido 2.1.63 Illion
The Hat he weares, Judas left under the Elder when he hang'd — Jew 4.4.66 P Ithimr
He weares a lords revenewe on his back, — Edw 1.4.407 Mortmr
He weares a short Italian hooded cloake, — Edw 1.4.413 Mortmr

WEARIE
Whose wearie lims shall shortly make repose, — Dido 1.1.84 Jupitr
And finde the way to wearie such fond thoughts: — Dido 3.2.86 Juno
Nurse I am wearie, will you carrie me? — Dido 4.5.15 Cupid
Shall overway his wearie witlesse head, — 1Tamb 2.1.46 Cosroe
Wearie Corinna hath her life in doubt. — Ovid's Elegies 2.13.2
Cast downe his wearie feet, and felt the sand. — Hero and Leander 2.228

WEARIED
Dishonest love my wearied brest forsake, — Ovid's Elegies 3.10.2

WEARING
noble mindes change not their thoughts/For wearing of a crowne: — P 611 12.24 Mugern

WEARST
Would dash the wreath thou wearst for Pirats wracke. — Lucan, First Booke 123

WEARY
To you? Why, do you thinke me weary of it? — 2Tamb 3.3.17 Capt
Nay Captain, thou art weary of thy life, — 2Tamb 3.3.18 Techel
Which being faint and weary with the siege, — 2Tamb 5.2.7 Callap
And weary Death with bearing soules to hell. — 2Tamb 5.3.77 Tamb
Or with seditions weary all the worlde: — P 116 2.59 Guise
To rest his bones after his weary toyle, — F 769 2.3.48 2Chor
The weary souldiour hath the conquerd fields, — Ovid's Elegies 2.9.19

WEARYING
Wearying his fingers ends with telling it, — Jew 1.1.16 Barab

WEATHER
That shew faire weather to the neighbor morne. . . . . 2Tamb 3.1.48 Jrslem
WEATHERBEATEN
And rest the map of weatherbeaten woe: . . . . Dido 1.1.158 Achat
WEB
foote drawes out/Fastning her light web some old beame about. Ovid's Elegies 1.14.8
WEBBE
And that slowe webbe nights fals-hood did unframe. . . Ovid's Elegies 3.8.30
WED
To wed thee to our neece, the onely heire/Unto the Earle of Edw 2.2.258 Edward
I did not bid thee wed an aged swaine. . . . . Ovid's Elegies 1.13.42
Why being a vestall am I wooed to wed, ... Ovid's Elegies 3.5.75
WEDDED
I had been wedded ere Aeneas came: . . . . . . Dido 3.1.138 Dido
WEDDING
These golden bracelets, and this wedding ring, . . . Dido 3.4.62 Dido
WEDGE
so richly pay/The things they traffique for with wedge of gold, Jew 1.1.9 Barab
WEDGES
Lay out our golden wedges to the view, ... 1Tamb 1.2.139 Tamb
The skipping Salii with shields like wedges; . . . Lucan, First Booke 602
WEDLOCKS
Their wedlocks pledges veng'd their husbands bad. . . Ovid's Elegies 2.14.32
WEE
Wee with our Peeres have crost Danubius stream/To treat of 2Tamb 1.1.79 Sgsmnd
Thus have wee martcht Northwarde from Tamburlaine, . . 2Tamb 3.3.1 Therid
Wee may lie ready to encounter him, ... 2Tamb 5.2.8 Callap
And thus are wee on every side inrich'd: . . . . Jew 1.1.104 Barab
That wee might sleepe seven yeeres together afore we wake. Jew 4.2.131 Ithimr
Nothing shall alter us, wee are resolv'd. . . . . Edw 1.4.74 ArchBp
That shall wee see, looke where his lordship comes. . . Edw 2.2.49 Lncstr
grace may sit secure, if none but wee/Doe wot of your abode. Edw 4.7.26 Monk
In heaven wee may, in earth never shall wee meete, . . Edw 4.7.80 Edward
To die sweet Spencer, therefore live wee all, . . . Edw 4.7.111 Baldck
What traitor have wee there with blades and billes? . . Edw 5.4.82 Mortmr
Why are <have wee> not Conjunctions, Oppositions, Aspects, F 615 2.2.64 P Faust
you heartily sir; for wee cal'd you but in jeast I promise you. F1123 3.3.36 P Dick
Wee seeke that through thee safely love we may, . . Ovid's Elegies 2.2.65
Wee Macer sit in Venus slothfull shade, ... Ovid's Elegies 2.18.3
Wee skorne things lawfull, stolne sweetes we affect, . Ovid's Elegies 2.19.3
Wee cause feete flie, wee mingle haires with snakes, . Ovid's Elegies 3.11.23
Honour is purchac'd by the deedes wee do. . . . . Hero and Leander 1.280
And wee will sit upon the Rocks, ... Passionate Shepherd 5
WEED
Jove sometime masked in a Shepheards weed, . . . 1Tamb 1.2.199 Tamb
Alight and weare a woful mourning weed. . . . . 2Tamb 1.1.44 Orcan
WEEDES
is Aeneas, were he clad/In weedes as bad as ever Irus ware. Dido 2.1.85 Dido
Lie here ye weedes that I disdaine to weare, . . . 1Tamb 1.2.41 Tamb
But I shall turne her into other weedes, ... 1Tamb 3.3.180 Ebea
Aye me, thy body hath no worthy weedes. . . . . Ovid's Elegies 1.8.26
WEEDS
And martch in cottages of strowed weeds: . . . . . 1Tamb 5.1.187 Tamb
Hence fained weeds, unfained are my woes, ... Edw 4.7.97 Edward
Whereat she starts, puts on her purple weeds, . . . Hero and Leander 2.88
WEEKE
let this houre be but/A yeare, a month, a weeke, a naturall day, F1933 5.2.137 Faust
WEEKES
And he have not slept this eight weekes Ile speake with him. F App p.240 145 P HrsCsr
WEE'L
I sweare by this crosse, wee'l not be partiall, . . P 325 5.52 Anjoy
Wee'l beat him back, and drive him to his death, . . P 929 18.30 Navrre
Then heere wee'l lye before [Lutetia] <Lucrecia> walles, . P1151 22.13 King
All's one, for wee'l be bold with his Venison. . . . F 808 3.1.30 Mephst
<Tut, tis no matter man>, wee'l be bold with his <good cheare>. F 808 (HC265)A P Mephst
This sport is excellent: wee'l call and wake him. . . F1281 4.1.127 Emper
Wee'l sell it to a Chimny-sweeper: . . . . . . F1384 4.2.60 P Benvol
Wee'l put out his eyes, and they shall serve for buttons to his F1387 4.2.63 P Benvol
<Wee'l take our leaves>, and for this blessed sight . . F1704 (HC269)B 1Schol
And here wee'l stay, ... F1805 5.2.9 Belzeb
If it be so, wee'l have Physitians, ... F1830 5.2.34 2Schol
WEEL
Weel chase the Stars from heaven, and dim their eies/That stand 1Tamb 2.3.23 Tamb
Weel have him ransomd man, be of good cheere. . . . Edw 2.2.116 Lncstr
Weel make quick worke, commend me to your maister/My friend, Edw 2.6.12 Warwck
WEE'LE
hold belly hold, and wee'le not pay one peny for it. . F 749 2.3.28 P Robin
But wee'le pul downe his haughty insolence: . . . F 914 3.1.136 Pope
And thither wee'le repaire and live obscure, . . . F1453 4.3.23 Benvol
WEELE
Weele leade you to the stately tent of War: . . . 1Tamb Prol.3 Prolog
Weele fight five hundred men at armes to one, . . . 1Tamb 1.2.143 Tamb
Weele hale him from the bosome of the king, . . . Edw 1.2.29 Mortmr
That slie inveigling Frenchman weele exile, ... Edw 1.2.57 Mortmr
No, but weele lift Gaveston from hence. . . . . . Edw 1.2.62 Lncstr
Weele pull him from the strongest hould he hath. . . . Edw 1.4.289 Mortmr
Weele have a generall tilt and turnament, ... Edw 1.4.376 Edward
A trifle, weele expell him when we please: . . . . Edw 2.2.10 Edward
Weele haile him by the eares unto the block. . . . Edw 2.2.91 Lncstr
Do what they can, weele live in Tinmoth here, . . . Edw 2.2.221 Edward
Why then weele have him privilie made away. . . . Edw 2.2.236 Gavstn
Thus weele gratifie the king, ... Edw 2.5.51 Mortmr
Weele send his head by thee, let him bestow/His teares on that, Edw 2.5.52 Mortmr

WEELE (cont.)
My lord, weele quicklie be at Cobham. Edw 2.5.111 HrsBoy
Weele steele it on their crest, and powle their tops. Edw 3.1.27 Edward
But weele advance them traitors, now tis time/To be avengd on Edw 3.1.224 Edward
This answer weele returne, and so farewell. Edw 5.1.90 BshpWn
Feare not my Lord, weele do as you commaund. Edw 5.2.66 Matrvs
Sit downe, for weele be Barbars to your grace. Edw 5.3.28 Matrvs
Weele enter in by darkenes to Killingworth. Edw 5.3.48 Matrvs
Come sonne, weele ride a hunting in the parke. Edw 5.4.113 Queene
And in the forme of beds weele strowe soft sand, Ovid's Elegies 2.11.47

WEE'LL
Where wee'll attend the respit you have tane, Jew 1.2.30 Calym
Then wee'll take order for the residue. Jew 1.2.136 Govnr
Wee'll send [thee] <the> bullets wrapt in smoake and fire: Jew 2.2.54 Govnr
come, wee'll walke about/The ruin'd Towne, and see the wracke we Jew 5.2.18 Calym
Wee'll in this Summer Evening feast with him. Jew 5.3.41 Calym

WEENETH
What weeneth the king of England, Edw 2.2.193 Lncstr

WEEP
Weep not sweet Navarre, but revenge my death. P1234 22.96 King

WEEPE
O yet this stone doth make Aeneas weepe, Dido 2.1.15 Aeneas
Sweete father leave to weepe, this is not he: Dido 2.1.35 Ascan
And when we told her she would weepe for griefe, Dido 2.1.67 Illion
his breast/Furrowd with wounds, and that which made me weepe, Dido 2.1.204 Aeneas
Weepe not sweet boy, thou shalt be Didos sonne, Dido 3.1.24 Dido
And weepe upon your liveles carcases, Dido 5.1.177 Dido
Weepe heavens, and vanish into liquid teares, 2Tamb 5.3.1 Therid
my soule dooth weepe to see/Your sweet desires depriv'd my 2Tamb 5.3.246 Tamb
Why weepe you not to thinke upon my wrongs? Jew 1.2.172 Barab
Pardon me though I weepe; the Governors sonne/Will, whether I Jew 2.3.257 Barab
That maidens new betroth'd should weepe a while: Jew 2.3.326 Barab
'Las I could weepe at your calamity. Jew 4.1.203 Barab
There weepe, for till my Gaveston be repeald, Edw 1.4.168 Edward
and in any case/Let no man comfort him, if he chaunce to weepe, Edw 5.2.64 Mortmr
Weepe not sweete sonne. Edw 5.6.33 Queene
Forbid not me to weepe, he was my father, Edw 5.6.34 King
Farewell faire Queene, weepe not for Mortimer, Edw 5.6.64 Mortmr
<O> my God, I would weepe, but the Divell drawes in my teares. F1850 5.2.54 P Faust
Fooles that will laugh on earth, [must] <most> weepe in hell. F1891 5.2.95 Mephst
I will weepe/And to the dores sight of thy selfe [will] keepe: Ovid's Elegies 1.4.61
And let thine eyes constrained learne to weepe, Ovid's Elegies 1.8.83

WEEPES
O Hector who weepes not to heare thy name? Dido 2.1.209 Dido
I know tis long of Gaveston she weepes. Edw 1.4.191 Mortmr
My Mistresse weepes whom my mad hand did harme. Ovid's Elegies 1.7.4
Alas she almost weepes, and her white cheekes, Ovid's Elegies 1.14.51

WEEPING (See also WEPING)
whose weeping eies/Since thy arrivall here beheld no Sun, 2Tamb 4.2.1 Olymp
That at my funeralles some may weeping crie, Ovid's Elegies 2.10.37
Sylvanus weeping for the lovely boy/That now is turn'd into a Hero and Leander 1.154

WEEP'ST
What, weep'st thou? F1890 5.2.94 Mephst

WEEPST
Weepst thou already? Edw 5.5.52 Edward
Why weepst? and spoilst with teares thy watry eyes? Ovid's Elegies 3.5.57

WEIGH (See also OUTWAIES, UP-WAYD, WAY, WEY)
And weigh not men, and therefore not mens words. Jew Prol.8 Machvl
Do the [Turkes] <Turke> weigh so much? Jew 2.3.98 P Barab
I weigh it thus much; I have wealth enough. Jew 2.3.245 Barab
'Tis not thy mony, but thy selfe I weigh: Jew 4.2.124 Curtzn

WEIGH'D
liberties and lives were weigh'd/In equall care and ballance 1Tamb 5.1.41 Govnr

WEIGHD
Too late you looke back, when with anchors weighd, Ovid's Elegies 2.11.23

WEIGHT (See also WAIGHT, WAIT)
Are ballassed with billowes watrie weight. Dido 1.1.226 Aeneas
Receive them free, and sell them by the weight; Jew 1.1.24 Barab
Besides I know not how much weight in Pearle/Orient and round, Jew 4.1.66 Barab
Nor want I strength, but weight to presse her with: Ovid's Elegies 2.10.24
And my presages of no weight be thought. Ovid's Elegies 2.14.42
Gold, silver, irons heavy weight, and brasse, Ovid's Elegies 3.7.37
And may th'earths weight thy ashes nought molest. Ovid's Elegies 3.8.68

WE'L
See, see his window's ope, we'l call to him. F1177 4.1.23 Fredrk

WEL
Wel, since I see the state of Persea droope, 1Tamb 1.1.155 Cosroe
I know it wel my Lord, and thanke you all. 1Tamb 1.1.187 Cosroe
Wel hast thou pourtraid in thy tearms of life, 1Tamb 2.1.31 Cosroe
wel then, by heavens I sweare,/Aurora shall not peepe out of 1Tamb 2.2.9 Mycet
Wel, wel (Meander) thou art deeply read: 1Tamb 2.2.55 Mycet
Wel, I meane you shall have it againe. 1Tamb 2.4.36 Tamb
Why, that's wel said Techelles, so would I, 1Tamb 2.5.69 Tamb
are ful of brags/And menace more than they can wel performe: 1Tamb 3.3.4 Tamb
Wel said Theridamas, speake in that mood, 1Tamb 3.3.40 Tamb
Wel said my stout contributory kings, 1Tamb 3.3.93 Bajzth
Wel Zenocrate, Techelles, and the rest, fall to your victuals. 1Tamb 4.4.14 P Tamb
Wel, here is now to the Souldane of Egypt, the King of Arabia, 1Tamb 4.4.113 P Tamb
Wel said Theridamas, when holy Fates/Shall stablish me in 1Tamb 4.4.134 Tamb
Wel, lovely Virgins, think our countries care, 1Tamb 5.1.34 Govnr
Thats wel Techelles, what's the newes? 1Tamb 5.1.198 Tamb
Wel met my only deare Zenocrate, 1Tamb 5.1.443 Souldn
Wel sir, what of this? 2Tamb 1.2.18 Almeda

WEL (cont.)

Wel done my boy, thou shalt have shield and lance,	2Tamb	1.3.43		Tamb
Why may not I my Lord, as wel as he,	2Tamb	1.3.61		Amyras
Wel lovely boies, you shal be Emperours both,	2Tamb	1.3.96		Tamb
Wel said Argier, receive thy crowne againe.	2Tamb	1.3.127		Tamb
Wel then my noble Lords, for this my friend,	2Tamb	3.1.68		Callap
Wel, this must be the messenger for thee.	2Tamb	3.4.15		Olymp
Wel sirs, diet your selves, you knowe I shall have occasion	2Tamb	3.5.114	P	Tamb
Wel, in despight of thee he shall be king:	2Tamb	3.5.128		Callap
Wel, now you see hee is a king, looke to him Theridamas, when	2Tamb	3.5.153	P	Tamb
Twill please my mind as wel to heare both you/Have won a heape	2Tamb	4.1.36		Calyph
Wel, bark ye dogs.	2Tamb	4.1.181		Tamb
Wel met Olympia, I sought thee in my tent,	2Tamb	4.2.14		Therid
Wel, now Ile make it quake, go draw him up,	2Tamb	5.1.107		Tamb
Tis brave indeed my boy, wel done,	2Tamb	5.1.150		Tamb
Wel said, let there be a fire presently.	2Tamb	5.1.178		Tamb
Wel souldiers, Mahomet remaines in hell,	2Tamb	5.1.198		Tamb
Wel then my friendly Lordes, what now remaines/But that we	2Tamb	5.1.210		Tamb
wel since it is no more/I'le satisfie my selfe with that;	Jew	5.5.21		Barab
Not wel, but do remember such a man.	P 173	3.8		OldQn
Graunt that our deeds may wel deserve your loves:	P 600	12.13		King
Wel, let that peevish Frenchman guard him sure,	Edw	1.2.7		Mortmr
Your grace doth wel to place him by your side,	Edw	1.4.10		Lncstr
burladie I had neede have it wel roasted, and good sawce to it,	F App	p.229 12	P	Clown
wel, wilt thou serve me, and Ile make thee go like Qui mihi	F App	p.229 13	P	Wagner
wel, do you heare sirra?	F App	p.230 30	P	Wagner
Wel sirra, come.	F App	p.231 65	P	Wagner
Wel, tone of you hath this goblet about you.	F App	p.235 16	P	Vintnr
wel villaines, for your presumption, I transforme thee into an	F App	p.235 43	P	Mephst
What horse-courser, you are wel met.	F App	p.239 100	P	Faust
Wel, come give me your money, my boy wil deliver him to you:	F App	p.239 107	P	Faust
Wel sir, Now am I made man for ever, Ile not leave my horse for	F App	p.239 114	P	HrsCsr
slicke as an Ele; wel god buy sir, your boy wil deliver him me:	F App	p.240 117	P	HrsCsr
his labour; wel, this tricke shal cost him fortie dollers more.	F App	p.241 165	P	Faust
My gratious Lord, I am glad it contents you so wel:	F App	p.242 3	P	Faust
wel reward this learned man for the great kindnes he hath shewd	F App	p.243 28	P	Duke
But seeing white Eagles, and Roomes flags wel known,	Lucan, First Booke			246
Wel might these feare, when Pompey fear'd and fled.	Lucan, First Booke			519
Both are wel favoured, both rich in array,	Ovid's Elegies			2.10.5

WELBELOVED

We heere create our welbeloved sonne,	Edw	4.6.24		Queene
<a jolly gentlewoman, and welbeloved	F 699	(HC264)A	P	Glutny

WELCOM

Faiths breach, and hence came war to most men welcom.	Lucan, First Booke			184

WELCOME (See also WELLCOME)

And every Troian be as welcome here,	Dido	1.2.40		Iarbus
Brave Prince, welcome to Carthage and to me,	Dido	2.1.81		Dido
Welcome to Carthage new erected towne.	Dido	5.1.26		Aeneas
Welcome sweet child, where hast thou been this long?	Dido	5.1.46		Aeneas
Returnes amaine: welcome, welcome my love:	Dido	5.1.191		Dido
See where he comes, welcome, welcome my love.	Dido	5.1.261		Dido
Techelles, and Casane, welcome him.	1Tamb	1.2.238		Tamb
Welcome renowmed Persean to us all.	1Tamb	1.2.239		Techel
Faste and welcome sir, while hunger make you eat.	1Tamb	4.4.56	P	Tamb
O sight thrice welcome to my joiful soule,	1Tamb	5.1.440		Zenoc
kings and more/Upon their knees, all bid me welcome home.	2Tamb	1.2.29		Callap
Welcome Theridamas, king of Argier.	2Tamb	1.3.112		Tamb
Kings of Morocus and of Fesse, welcome.	2Tamb	1.3.128		Tamb
Then welcome Tamburlaine unto thy death.	2Tamb	3.5.52		Callap
Welcome Theridamas and Techelles both,	2Tamb	3.5.150		Tamb
Welcome the first beginner of my blisse:	Jew	2.1.50		Barab
Welcome to Malta, and to all of us;	Jew	2.2.20		Govnr
Abigall, bid him welcome for my sake.	Jew	2.3.232		Barab
For your sake and his own he's welcome hither.	Jew	2.3.233		Abigal
Welcome grave Fryar; Ithamore begon,	Jew	3.3.52		Abigal
Welcome, great [Bashaw] <Bashaws>, how fares/Callymath,	Jew	3.5.1		Govnr
And let's provide to welcome Calymath:	Jew	3.5.30		Govnr
And nought to us more welcome is then wars.	Jew	3.5.36		Govnr
I can with-hold no longer; welcome sweet love.	Jew	4.2.46		Curtzn
Welcome great Calymath.	Jew	5.5.55		Barab
Welcome from Poland Henry once agayne,	P 589	12.2		QnMoth
Welcome to France thy fathers royall seate,	P 590	12.3		QnMoth
What Gaveston, welcome:	Edw	1.1.140		Edward
I know it, brother welcome home my friend.	Edw	1.1.148		Edward
Welcome to Tinmouth, welcome to thy friend,	Edw	2.2.51		Edward
Salute him? yes: welcome Lord Chamberlaine.	Edw	2.2.65		Lncstr
Welcome is the good Earle of Cornewall.	Edw	2.2.66		Mortmr
Welcome Lord governour of the Ile of Man.	Edw	2.2.67		Warwck
Welcome maister secretarie.	Edw	2.2.68		Penbrk
Welcome old man, comst thou in Edwards aide?	Edw	3.1.34		Edward
Welcome ten thousand times, old man againe.	Edw	3.1.46		Edward
Souldiers a largis, and thrice welcome all.	Edw	3.1.57		Edward
Welcome [Levune] <Lewne>, tush Sib, if this be all/Valoys and I	Edw	3.1.66		Edward
His grace I dare presume will welcome me,	Edw	4.2.33		Queene
Welcome to Fraunce:	Edw	4.2.37		Queene
That Englands peeres may Henolts welcome see.	Edw	4.2.82		SrJohn
Welcome a Gods name Madam and your sonne,	Edw	4.3.41		Edward
England shall welcome you, and all your route.	Edw	4.3.42		Edward
Welcome to England all with prosperous windes,	Edw	4.4.2		Queene
Will be my death, and welcome shall it be,	Edw	5.1.126		Edward
I hope his Holinesse will bid us welcome.	F 807	3.1.29		Faust
Welcome grave Fathers, answere presently,	F 946	3.1.168		Pope
Welcome Lord Cardinals: come sit downe.	F1009	3.2.29		Pope

WELCOME (cont.)

Thrice learned Faustus, welcome to our Court.	F1205	4.1.51	Emper
welcome.	F1508	4.5.4	P Hostss
I hope sir, we have wit enough to be more bold then welcome.	F1596	4.6.39	P HrsCsr
I have procur'd your pardons: welcome all.	F1610	4.6.53	Faust
Gramercies Wagner. Welcome gentlemen.	F1820	5.2.24	Faust
Be welcome to her, gladly let her take thee,	Ovid's Elegies		2.15.3

WELCOMES

The generall welcomes Tamburlain receiv'd,	2Tamb	Prol.1	Prolog

WE'LE

I'le write unto him, we'le have mony strait.	Jew	4.2.69	P Ithimr
with me, and after meate/We'le canvase every quidditie thereof:	F 191	1.1.163	Faust
conjuring bookes, and now we'le have such knavery, as't passes.	F 724	2.3.3	P Robin
We'le rather die with griefe, then live with shame.	F1456	4.3.26	Benvol
we'le into another roome and drinke a while, and then we'le go	F1556	4.5.52	P Robin
and drinke a while, and then we'le go seeke out the Doctor.	F1557	4.5.53	P Robin

WELFARE

Then to misdoe the welfare of their King:	P 546	11.11	Charls

WEL FAVOURED

Both are wel favoured, both rich in array,	Ovid's Elegies		2.10.5

WELKIN

Whose hideous ecchoes make the welkin howle,	Dido	4.2.9	Iarbus
Fighting for passage, [makes] <make> the Welkin cracke,	1Tamb	4.2.45	Tamb
And dyms the Welkin, with her pitchy breathe:	F 232	1.3.4	Faust

WEL KNOWN

But seeing white Eagles, and Roomes flags wel known,	Lucan, First Booke		246

WE'LL

When this is done, we'll martch from Babylon,	2Tamb	5.1.127	Tamb
The Law shall touch you, we'll but lead you, we:	Jew	4.1.202	Barab
Give me a Reame of paper, we'll have a kingdome of gold for't.	Jew	4.2.115	P Ithimr
or we'll breake all the barrels in the house, and dash out all	F1618	4.6.61	P HrsCsr
We'll give his mangled limbs due buryall:	F1999	5.3.17	2Schol

WELL

I love thee well, say Juno what she will.	Dido	1.1.2	Jupitr
Whose beautious burden well might make you proude,	Dido	1.1.124	Venus
Looke where she comes: Aeneas [view] <viewd> her well.	Dido	2.1.72	Illion
Well may I view her, but she sees not me.	Dido	2.1.73	Aeneas
Poore soule I know too well the sower of love,	Dido	3.1.61	Anna
Aeneas well deserves to be your love,	Dido	3.1.70	Anna
No, for thy sake Ile love thy father well.	Dido	3.1.81	Dido
The rest are such as all the world well knowes,	Dido	3.1.165	Dido
Well could I like this reconcilements meanes,	Dido	3.2.81	Venus
To be well stor'd with such a winters tale?	Dido	3.3.59	Aeneas
Achates and Ascanius, well met.	Dido	4.1.28	Dido
Well, if he come a wooing he shall speede,	Dido	4.5.36	Nurse
Fare well may Dido, so Aeneas stay,	Dido	5.1.107	Dido
He loves me to too well to serve me so:	Dido	5.1.185	Dido
Brother, I see your meaning well enough.	1Tamb	1.1.18	Mycet
Well here I sweare by this my royal seat--	1Tamb	1.1.97	Mycet
You may doe well to kisse it then.	1Tamb	1.1.98	Cosroe
We will report but well of Tamburlaine.	1Tamb	1.2.81	Magnet
And well his merits show him to be made/His Fortunes maister,	1Tamb	2.1.35	Cosroe
And might content the Queene of heaven as well,	1Tamb	3.2.11	Zenoc
View well my Camp, and speake indifferently,	1Tamb	3.3.8	Tamb
Yet musicke woulde doe well to cheare up Zenocrate:	1Tamb	4.4.62	P Tamb
And since your highnesse hath so well vouchsaft,	1Tamb	4.4.130	Therid
could they not as well/Have sent ye out, when first my	1Tamb	5.1.67	Tamb
As well for griefe our ruthlesse Governour/Have thus refusde	1Tamb	5.1.92	1Virgn
I like that well:	2Tamb	1.2.61	P Almeda
Well done Techelles: what saith Theridamas?	2Tamb	1.3.206	Tamb
In this my mortall well deserved wound,	2Tamb	2.3.6	Sgsmnd
That can endure so well your royall presence,	2Tamb	5.3.111	Usumc
let me see how well/Thou wilt become thy fathers majestie.	2Tamb	5.3.183	Tamb
Well fare the Arabians, who so richly pay/The things they	Jew	1.1.8	Barab
the Custome-house/Will serve as well as I were present there.	Jew	1.1.58	Barab
Well, goe/And bid the Merchants and my men dispatch	Jew	1.1.99	Barab
I know you will; well brethren let us goe.	Jew	1.1.174	1Jew
Your Lordship shall doe well to let them have it.	Jew	1.2.44	Barab
Well then my Lord, say, are you satisfied?	Jew	1.2.137	Barab
I, fare you well.	Jew	1.2.213	Barab
Well father, say I be entertain'd,	Jew	1.2.294	Abigal
Well, daughter, say, what is thy suit with us?	Jew	1.2.321	Abbass
Well, daughter, we admit you for a Nun.	Jew	1.2.330	Abbass
'Twere time well spent to goe and visit her:	Jew	1.2.389	Lodowk
'Tis true, my Lord, therefore intreat him well.	Jew	2.2.8	1Knght
Well, Barabas, canst helpe me to a Diamond?	Jew	2.3.48	Lodowk
I'le buy you, and marry you to Lady vanity, if you doe well.	Jew	2.3.117	P Barab
Tell me, hast thou thy health well?	Jew	2.3.121	P Barab
I, passing well.	Jew	2.3.122	P Slave
No, this is the better, mother, view this well.	Jew	2.3.145	Mthias
Oh Barabas well met;	Jew	2.3.218	Lodowk
Well, let it passe, another time shall serve.	Jew	2.3.278	Mthias
This followes well, and therefore daughter feare not.	Jew	2.3.313	Barab
Well, let him goe.	Jew	2.3.336	Lodowk
Well, but for me, as you went in at dores/You had bin stab'd,	Jew	2.3.337	Barab
Well, I have deliver'd the challenge in such sort,	Jew	3.1.29	Ithimr
So neatly plotted, and so well perform'd?	Jew	3.3.2	Ithimr
Well, Ithimore, let me request thee this,	Jew	3.3.26	Abigal
Well, sirra, what is't?	Jew	3.3.31	Abigal
Well said, Ithimore;	Jew	3.4.56	Barab
Very well, Ithimore, then now be secret;	Jew	3.4.60	Barab
Well, master, I goe.	Jew	3.4.94	P Ithimr
Well, Governor, since thou hast broke the league/By flat	Jew	3.5.19	Basso

WELL (cont.)

To fast and be well whipt; I'le none of that.	Jew	4.1.124	Barab
hee had had another Cure to serve; well, goe whither he will,	Jew	4.2.25	P Ithimr
Well, my hope is, he will not stay there still;	Jew	4.3.16	Barab
Might he not as well come as send; pray bid him come and fetch	Jew	4.3.26	P Barab
Fare you well.	Jew	4.3.58	Pilia
Well, I must seeke a meanes to rid 'em all,	Jew	4.3.63	Barab
Me thinkes he fingers very well.	Jew	4.4.49	Pilia
Pardona moy, Mounsier, [me] <we> be no well.	Jew	4.4.71	Barab
And see that Malta be well fortifi'd;	Jew	5.1.2	Govnr
What, all alone? well fare sleepy drinke.	Jew	5.1.61	Barab
Intreat them well, as we have used thee.	Jew	5.2.17	Calym
Well, now about effecting this device:	Jew	5.2.117	Barab
For well has Barabas deserv'd of us.	Jew	5.3.25	Calym
Well, tell the Governor we grant his suit,	Jew	5.3.40	Calym
Thanks sonne Navarre, you see we love you well,	P 13	1.13	QnMoth
Well Madam, let that rest:	P 17	1.17	Charls
Might well have moved your highnes to beware/How you did meddle	P 179	3.14	Navrre
Anjoy hath well advisde/Your highnes to consider of the thing,	P 219	4.17	Guise
Well Madam, I referre it to your Majestie,	P 225	4.23	Charls
And make a shew as if all were well.	P 250	4.48	QnMoth
Now cosin view him well,	P 307	5.34	Anjoy
Well, say on.	P 400	7.40	Anjoy
Tis well advisde Dumain, goe see it strait be done.	P 424	7.64	Guise
Beleeve me Guise he becomes the place so well,	P 495	9.14	QnMoth
Well, let me alone, whose within there?	P 881	17.76	King
Well then, I see you are resolute.	P 938	19.8	Capt
Let me see, thou wouldst do well/To waite at my trencher, and	Edw	1.1.30	Gavstn
If I speed well, ile entertaine you all.	Edw	1.1.46	Gavstn
Well Mortimer, ile make thee rue these words,	Edw	1.1.91	Edward
Well doone, Ned.	Edw	1.1.98	Gavstn
For which, had not his highnes lov'd him well,	Edw	1.1.112	Kent
the least of these may well suffice/For one of greater birth	Edw	1.1.158	Kent
O that we might as well returne as goe.	Edw	1.4.143	Edward
Well of necessitie it must be so.	Edw	1.4.238	Mortmr
No, his companion, for he loves me well,	Edw	2.1.13	Spencr
I marry, such a garde as this dooth well.	Edw	2.2.131	Mortmr
I dare not, for the people love him well.	Edw	2.2.235	Edward
His name is Spencer, he is well alied,	Edw	2.2.249	Gavstn
And Gaveston, thinke that I love thee well,	Edw	2.2.257	Edward
So well hast thou deserv'de sweete Mortimer.	Edw	2.4.59	Queene
to your maister/My friend, and tell him that I watcht it well.	Edw	2.6.13	Warwck
Well, and how fortunes that he came not?	Edw	3.1.113	Edward
Well, say thy message.	Edw	3.1.155	Edward
our men with sweat and dust/All chockt well neare, begin to	Edw	3.1.192	SpncrP
To whome right well you knew our soule was knit,	Edw	3.1.227	Edward
And please my father well, and then a Fig/For all my unckles	Edw	4.2.4	Prince
Well said my lord.	Edw	4.2.26	SrJohn
Would all were well, and Edward well reclaimd,	Edw	4.2.57	Kent
I trowe/The lords of Fraunce love Englands gold so well,	Edw	4.3.15	Edward
Well, that shalbe, shalbe:	Edw	4.7.95	Edward
Well may I rent his name, that rends my hart.	Edw	5.1.140	Edward
Be thou perswaded, that I love thee well,	Edw	5.2.16	Queene
Use Edmund friendly, as if all were well.	Edw	5.2.79	Queene
Well, if my Lorde your brother were enlargde.	Edw	5.2.82	Queene
Wish well to mine, then tush, for them ile die.	Edw	5.3.45	Edward
Well, do it bravely, and be secret.	Edw	5.4.28	Mortmr
Very well.	Edw	5.5.31	Matrvs
Excellent well, take this for thy rewarde.	Edw	5.5.117	Gurney
And had you lov'de him halfe so well as I,	Edw	5.6.35	King
Is to dispute well Logickes chiefest end?	F 36	1.1.8	Faust
Jeromes Bible Faustus, view it well:	F 65	1.1.37	Faust
Inricht with tongues, well seene in Minerals,	F 166	1.1.138	Cornel
Then <Well> you will not tell us?	F 205	1.2.12	P 2Schol
I had need to have it well rosted, and good sauce to it,	F 352	1.4.10	P Robin
Well sirra, leave your jesting, and take these Guilders.	F 367	1.4.25	P Wagner
Well sir, I warrant you.	F 388	1.4.46	P Robin
Well Faustus, thou shalt have a wife.	F 531	2.1.143	Mephst
<Well thou wilt have one, sit there till I come,	F 531	(HC261)A	P Mephst
<Here>, take this booke, <and> peruse it [thoroughly] <well>:	F 543	2.1.155	Mephst
<Well>, Resolve me then in this one question:	F 614	2.2.63	P Faust
Well, I am answer'd:	F 618	2.2.67	P Faust
'Tis well said Faustus, come then stand by me/And thou shalt	F 843	3.1.65	Mephst
Now tell me Faustus, are we not fitted well?	F 940	3.1.162	Mephst
<Well, I am content, to compasse then some sport>,	F 989	(HC266)A	Faust
let the Maids looke well to their porridge-pots, for I'le into	F1133	3.3.46	P Robin
Well, go you attend the Emperour:	F1199	4.1.45	P Benvol
shall controule him as well as the Conjurer, I warrant you.	F1203	4.1.49	P Benvol
Well Master Doctor, an your Divels come not away quickly, you	F1241	4.1.87	P Benvol
him; and hereafter sir, looke you speake well of Schollers.	F1315	4.1.161	P Faust
Speake well of yee?	F1316	4.1.162	P Benvol
Well, I will not stand with thee, give me the money:	F1466	4.4.10	P Faust
Well I'le go rouse him, and make him give me my forty Dollors	F1487	4.4.31	P HrsCsr
grace to thinke but well of that which Faustus hath performed.	F1564	4.6.7	P Faust
Yes, I do verie well remember that.	F1638	4.6.81	P Faust
deny/The just [requests] <request> of those that wish him well,	F1691	5.1.18	Faust
Sir, so wondrous well,/As in all humble dutie, I do yeeld	F1817	5.2.21	Wagner
He is not well with being over solitarie.	F1829	5.2.33	3Schol
Well Gentlemen, tho Faustus end be such/As every Christian	F1995	5.3.13	2Schol
Well, I will cause two divels presently to fetch thee away	F App	p.230 43	P Wagner
Well sirra follow me.	F App	p.230 55	P Wagner
Well, Ile folow him, Ile serve him, thats flat.	F App	p.231 72	P Clown
Well use that tricke no more, I would advise you.	F App	p.232 19	Faust

WELL (cont.)
Well, theres the second time, aware the third, I give you faire   F App p.232 20 P Faust
and sir knight, hereafter speake well of Scholers: . .   F App p.238 85 P Faust
Well, leade us then to Syrtes desart shoare; . . . .   Lucan, First Booke 368
And Sequana that well could manage steeds; . . . .   Lucan, First Booke 426
Well skild in Pyromancy; one that knew/The hearts of beasts,   Lucan, First Booke 586
Fare well sterne warre, for blunter Poets meete. . . .   Ovid's Elegies 1.1.32
Yet scarse my hands from thee containe I well. . . .   Ovid's Elegies 1.4.10
To leave the rest, all likt me passing well, . . .   Ovid's Elegies 1.5.23
Well I remember when I first did hire thee, . . .   Ovid's Elegies 1.6.43
cheekes, but this/If feigned, doth well; if true it doth amisse.   Ovid's Elegies 1.8.36
Of his gilt Harpe the well tun'd strings doth hold. . .   Ovid's Elegies 1.8.60
Take strife away, love doth not well endure. . . .   Ovid's Elegies 1.8.96
Oft thou wilt say, live well, thou wilt pray oft, . .   Ovid's Elegies 1.8.107
Rhesus fell/And Captive horses bad their Lord fare-well. .   Ovid's Elegies 1.9.24
If ever, now well lies she by my side. . . . .   Ovid's Elegies 1.13.6
They well become thee, then to spare them turne. . .   Ovid's Elegies 1.14.28
Hundred-hand Gyges, and had done it well, ...   Ovid's Elegies 2.1.12
Object thou then what she may well excuse, . . .   Ovid's Elegies 2.2.37
Trips she, it likes me well, plods she, what than? . .   Ovid's Elegies 2.4.23
Thou spokest thy words so well with stammering sound. .   Ovid's Elegies 2.6.24
This tombe approoves, I pleasde my mistresse well, . .   Ovid's Elegies 2.6.61
If I looke well, thou thinkest thou doest not move, . .   Ovid's Elegies 2.7.9
Well maiest thou one thing for thy Mistresse use. . .   Ovid's Elegies 2.8.24
Graecinus (well I wot) thou touldst me once, . . .   Ovid's Elegies 2.10.1
Fit her so well, as she is fit for me: . . . . .   Ovid's Elegies 2.15.5
And even the ring performe a mans part well. . . .   Ovid's Elegies 2.15.26
Aye me why is it knowne to her so well? . . . .   Ovid's Elegies 2.17.8
hoping time would beate thee/To guard her well, that well I   Ovid's Elegies 2.19.50
beate thee/To guard her well, that well I might entreate thee.   Ovid's Elegies 2.19.50
The Gods have eyes, and brests as well as men. . . .   Ovid's Elegies 3.3.42
And this townes well knowne customes not beleeves, . .   Ovid's Elegies 3.4.38
Who so well keepes his waters head from knowing, . .   Ovid's Elegies 3.5.40
Well, I beleeve she kist not as she should, . . .   Ovid's Elegies 3.6.55
Tis well, if some wench for the poore remaine. . .   Ovid's Elegies 3.7.60
When well-toss'd mattocks did the ground prepare, . .   Ovid's Elegies 3.9.31
To know their rites, well recompenc'd my stay, . . .   Ovid's Elegies 3.12.5
A stately builded ship, well rig'd and tall, . . .   Hero and Leander 1.225
Well therefore by the gods decreed it is, ...   Hero and Leander 1.253
And too too well the faire vermilion knew, . . .   Hero and Leander 1.395

WELLCOME
yow are wellcome ser have at you . . . . . .   Paris ms16,p390 P Souldr
we will be wellcome for our mony, and we will pay for what we   F1611 4.6.54 P Robin

WELL-KNOWNE (See WEL KNOWN)

WELL KNOWNE
And this townes well knowne customes not beleeves, . .   Ovid's Elegies 3.4.38

WELLS
Sometimes I goe about and poyson wells; . . . . .   Jew 2.3.176 Barab

WELL-TOSS'D
When well-toss'd mattocks did the ground prepare, . .   Ovid's Elegies 3.9.31

WELTER
weapons point here shouldst thou fall,/And welter in thy goare.   Edw 2.5.14 Mortmr

WELTH
From nought at first thou camst to little welth, . . .   Jew 1.2.105 1Knght

WELTHIE
And fairest pearle of welthie India/Were mounted here under a   2Tamb 3.2.121 Tamb

WELTHY
Not all the Gold in Indias welthy armes, ...   1Tamb 1.2.85 Tamb

WELTRED
And they so wrackt and weltred by the waves, . . .   Dido 1.1.223 Aeneas

WELTRING
By this the Turks lie weltring in their blood/And Tamburlaine   1Tamb 3.3.201 Zenoc

WEN
Not one wen in her bodie could I spie, ...   Ovid's Elegies 1.5.18

WENCH
Hold thee, wench, there's something for thee to spend. .   Jew 3.1.12 Pilia
And besides, the Wench is dead. . . . .   Jew 4.1.42 Barab
like to Ovids Flea, I can creepe into every corner of a Wench: F 665 2.2.114 P Pride
I and my wench oft under clothes did lurke, . . .   Ovid's Elegies 1.4.47
But now perchaunce thy wench with thee doth rest, . .   Ovid's Elegies 1.6.45
For rage against my wench mov'd my rash arme, . . .   Ovid's Elegies 1.7.3
Io, a strong man conquerd this Wench, hollow. . . .   Ovid's Elegies 1.7.38
Wa'st not enough the fearefull Wench to chide? . . .   Ovid's Elegies 1.7.45
the wench forth send,/Her valiant lover followes without end.   Ovid's Elegies 1.9.9
[All] <This> could I beare, but that the wench should rise,/Who   Ovid's Elegies 1.13.25
Snatching the combe, to beate the wench out drive <drave> her.   Ovid's Elegies 1.14.18
My wench her dore shut, Joves affares I left, . . .   Ovid's Elegies 2.1.17
Enjoy the wench, let all else be refusd. . . . .   Ovid's Elegies 2.2.30
His fauning wench with her desire he crownes. . . .   Ovid's Elegies 2.2.34
If ever wench had made luke-warme thy love: . . .   Ovid's Elegies 2.3.6
[A white wench thralles me, so doth golden yellowe], .   Ovid's Elegies 2.4.39
A yong wench pleaseth, and an old is good, . . .   Ovid's Elegies 2.4.45
Alas a wench is a perpetuall evill. . . . . . .   Ovid's Elegies 2.5.4
To whom his wench can say, I never did it. . . .   Ovid's Elegies 2.5.10
[wretch] <wench> I sawe when thou didst thinke I slumbred,   Ovid's Elegies 2.5.13
With her owne armor was my wench defended. . . .   Ovid's Elegies 2.5.48
What helpes it thou wert given to please my wench, . .   Ovid's Elegies 2.6.19
If some faire wench me secretly behold, ...   Ovid's Elegies 2.7.5
To like a base wench of despisd condition. . . .   Ovid's Elegies 2.7.20
Was not one wench inough to greeve my heart? . . .   Ovid's Elegies 2.10.12
Let one wench cloy me with sweete loves delight, . .   Ovid's Elegies 2.10.21
The losse of such a wench much blame will gather, . .   Ovid's Elegies 2.11.35
My wench, Lucina, I intreat thee favour, ...   Ovid's Elegies 2.13.21

WENCH (cont.)			
To serve a wench if any thinke it shame,	Ovid's Elegies	2.17.1	
I know a wench reports her selfe Corinne,	Ovid's Elegies	2.17.29	
Often at length, my wench depart, I bid,	Ovid's Elegies	2.18.5	
But spare my wench thou at her right hand seated,	Ovid's Elegies	3.2.21	
Or in mine eyes good wench no paine transfuse.	Ovid's Elegies	3.3.48	
A free-borne wench, no right 'tis up to locke:	Ovid's Elegies	3.4.33	
And I beleeve some wench thou hast affected:	Ovid's Elegies	3.5.83	
Or she was not the wench I wisht t'have had.	Ovid's Elegies	3.6.2	
Nay more, the wench did not disdaine a whit,	Ovid's Elegies	3.6.73	
Tis well, if some wench for the poore remaine.	Ovid's Elegies	3.7.60	
Nemesis and thy first wench joyne their kisses,	Ovid's Elegies	3.8.53	
The wench by my fault is set forth to sell.	Ovid's Elegies	3.11.10	
And my wench ought to have seem'd falsely praisd,	Ovid's Elegies	3.11.43	
WENCHES			
We that have prettie wenches to our wives,	Edw	2.5.102	Penbrk
tickle the pretie wenches plackets Ile be amongst them ifaith.	F App	p.231 63	P Clown
No pritty wenches keeper maist thou bee:	Ovid's Elegies	1.6.63	
In verse to praise kinde Wenches tis my part,	Ovid's Elegies	1.10.59	
But when I praise a pretty wenches face/Shee in requitall doth	Ovid's Elegies	2.1.33	
Wenches apply your faire lookes to my verse/Which golden love	Ovid's Elegies	2.1.37	
But such kinde wenches let their lovers have.	Ovid's Elegies	2.5.26	
My wenches vowes for thee what should I show,	Ovid's Elegies	2.6.43	
That have so oft serv'd pretty wenches dyet.	Ovid's Elegies	2.9.24	
Subdue the wandring wenches to thy raigne,	Ovid's Elegies	2.9.53	
Would first my beautious wenches moist lips touch,	Ovid's Elegies	2.15.17	
Or if there be a God, he loves fine wenches,	Ovid's Elegies	3.3.25	
My selfe would sweare, the wenches true did sweare,	Ovid's Elegies	3.3.45	
WEND			
If he gives nothing, let him from thee wend.	Ovid's Elegies	1.8.100	
WENDS			
But whither wends my beauteous Abigall?	Jew	1.2.224	Barab
WENT			
And as we went unto our ships, thou knowest/We sawe Cassandra	Dido	2.1.273	Aeneas
I went to take my farewell of Achates.	Dido	4.4.18	Aeneas
but for me, as you went in at dores/You had bin stab'd, but not	Jew	2.3.337	Barab
But yesterday two ships went from this Towne,	Jew	4.1.69	Barab
And since I went from hence, no soule in hell/Hath felt more	Edw	1.1.146	Gavstn
At <of> riper yeares to Wittenberg <Wertenberg> he went,	F 13	Prol.13	1Chor
I went to him yesterday to buy a horse of him, and he would by	F1536	4.5.32	P HrsCsr
it; I went me home to his house, and there I found him asleepe;	F1548	4.5.44	P HrsCsr
Fierce Mastives hould; the vestall fires went out,	Lucan, First Booke	547	
The earth went off hir hinges; And the Alpes/Shooke the old	Lucan, First Booke	551	
And went the round, in, and without the towne.	Lucan, First Booke	594	
Hector to armes went from his wives embraces,	Ovid's Elegies	1.9.35	
The sonne slew her, that forth to meete him went,	Ovid's Elegies	1.10.51	
But till the [keeper] <keepes> went forth, I forget not,	Ovid's Elegies	3.1.55	
I might not go, whether my papers went.	Ovid's Elegies	3.7.6	
Faire-fac'd Iulus, he went forth thy court.	Ovid's Elegies	3.8.14	
Where Ceres went each place was harvest there.	Ovid's Elegies	3.9.38	
I saw when forth a tyred lover went,	Ovid's Elegies	3.10.13	
Which as shee went would cherupe through the bils.	Hero and Leander	1.36	
Firmament/Glistered with breathing stars, who where they went,	Hero and Leander	1.98	
Pyn'd as they went, and thinking on her died.	Hero and Leander	1.130	
Went Hero thorow Sestos, from her tower/To Venus temple,	Hero and Leander	1.132	
And shot a shaft that burning from him went,	Hero and Leander	1.372	
After went Mercurie, who us'd such cunning,	Hero and Leander	1.417	
Yet as she went, full often look'd behind,	Hero and Leander	2.5	
He flung at him his mace, but as it went,	Hero and Leander	2.209	
His colour went and came, as if he rewd/The greefe which	Hero and Leander	2.214	
And as her silver body downeward went,	Hero and Leander	2.263	
WENTST			
As much as thou in rage out wentst the rest.	Edw	3.1.240	Edward
WEPING			
halfe to weping framed,/Aye me she cries, to love, why art	Ovid's Elegies	2.18.7	
WEPT			
Who for her sonnes death wept out life and breath,	Dido	2.1.4	Aeneas
If I had wept a sea of teares for her,	2Tamb	3.2.47	Calyph
The conquering [Hercules] <Hector> for Hilas wept,	Edw	1.4.393	MortSr
As nature wept, thinking she was undone;	Hero and Leander	1.46	
And as she wept, her teares to pearle he turn'd,	Hero and Leander	1.375	
Sad Hero wroong him by the hand, and wept,	Hero and Leander	2.95	
WER			
Give her the Crowne Turkesse, you wer best.	1Tamb	3.3.224	Therid
WERE (See also TWERE, 'TWERE)			
Unto what fruitfull quarters were ye bound,	Dido	1.2.18	Iarbus
O were I not at all so thou mightst be.	Dido	2.1.28	Aeneas
For were it Priam he would smile on me.	Dido	2.1.36	Ascan
is Aeneas, were he clad/In weedes as bad as ever Irus ware.	Dido	2.1.84	Dido
we were commanded straight/With reverence to draw it into Troy.	Dido	2.1.167	Aeneas
This butcher whil'st his hands were yet held up,	Dido	2.1.241	Aeneas
And we were round environ'd with the Greekes:	Dido	2.1.269	Aeneas
For all our ships were launcht into the deepe:	Dido	2.1.285	Aeneas
O Anna, didst thou know how sweet love were,	Dido	3.1.59	Dido
O sister, were you Empresse of the world,	Dido	3.1.69	Anna
This man and I were at Olympus games.	Dido	3.1.143	Illion
fond man, that were to warre gainst heaven,/And with one shaft	Dido	3.3.71	Iarbus
And yet I am not free, oh would I were.	Dido	3.4.6	Dido
Whil'st they were sporting in this darksome Cave?	Dido	4.1.24	Iarbus
But where were you Iarbus all this while?	Dido	4.1.31	Dido
Were to transgresse against all lawes of love:	Dido	4.3.48	Aeneas
The sailes were hoysing up, and he abourd.	Dido	4.4.15	Anna
But when you were abourd twas calme enough,	Dido	4.4.27	Dido

WERE (cont.)

O that the Clowdes were here wherein thou [fledst] <fleest>,	Dido	4.4.50	Dido
Or that the Tyrrhen sea were in mine armes,	Dido	4.4.101	Dido
These were the instruments that launcht him forth,	Dido	4.4.150	Dido
Hast thou forgot how many neighbour kings/Were up in armes, for	Dido	5.1.142	Dido
Had I a sonne by thee, the griefe were lesse,	Dido	5.1.149	Dido
If words might move me I were overcome.	Dido	5.1.154	Aeneas
To see our neighbours that were woont to quake/And tremble at	1Tamb	1.1.115	Cosroe
Than if you were arriv'd in Siria,	1Tamb	1.2.4	Tamb
How those were hit by pelting Cannon shot,	1Tamb	2.4.3	Mycet
In what a lamentable case were I,	1Tamb	2.4.6	Mycet
Meander, you that were our brothers Guide,	1Tamb	2.5.10	Cosroe
If I were matcht with mightie Tamburlaine.	1Tamb	3.2.55	Zenoc
I tell thee, were that Tamburlaine/As monsterous as Gorgon,	1Tamb	4.1.17	Souldn
Were in that citie all the world contain'd,	1Tamb	4.2.121	Tamb
Zenocrate, were Egypt Joves owne land,	1Tamb	4.4.73	Tamb
And be renowm'd, as never Emperours were.	1Tamb	4.4.138	Tamb
Were but to bring our wilfull overthrow,	1Tamb	5.1.5	Govnr
Before all hope of rescue were denied,	1Tamb	5.1.38	Govnr
liberties and lives were weigh'd/In equall care and ballance	1Tamb	5.1.41	Govnr
As if there were no way but one with us.	1Tamb	5.1.201	Techel
Whose lives were dearer to Zenocrate/Than her owne life, or	1Tamb	5.1.337	Zenoc
Left to themselves while we were at the fight,	1Tamb	5.1.471	Tamb
As Juno, when the Giants were supprest,	1Tamb	5.1.510	Tamb
Wagons of gold were set before my tent:	2Tamb	1.1.99	Orcan
Ah were I now but halfe so eloquent/To paint in woords, what	2Tamb	1.2.9	Callap
For if his chaire were in a sea of blood,	2Tamb	1.3.89	Celeb
all the christall gates of Joves high court/Were opened wide,	2Tamb	1.3.154	Tamb
Were turnde to men, he should be overcome:	2Tamb	1.3.164	Tamb
And were the sinowes of th'imperiall seat/So knit and	2Tamb	3.1.10	Callap
pearle of welthie India/Were mounted here under a Canapie:	2Tamb	3.2.122	Tamb
Were you that are the friends of Tamburlain,	2Tamb	3.3.35	Capt
Sitting as if they were a telling ridles.	2Tamb	3.5.59	Tamb
Poore soules they looke as if their deaths were neere.	2Tamb	3.5.61	Usumc
My father were enough to scar the foe:	2Tamb	4.1.19	Calyph
Were all the lofty mounts of Zona mundi,	2Tamb	4.1.42	Amyras
I were as soone rewarded with a shot,	2Tamb	4.1.54	Calyph
As if they were the teares of Mahomet/For hot consumption of	2Tamb	4.1.196	Tamb
Were not subdew'd with valour more divine,	2Tamb	4.3.15	Tamb
(I meane such Queens as were kings Concubines)/Take them,	2Tamb	4.3.71	Tamb
Were woont to guide the seaman in the deepe,	2Tamb	5.1.65	Tamb
Were full of Commets and of blazing stars,	2Tamb	5.1.89	Tamb
not perswade you to submission,/But stil the ports were shut:	2Tamb	5.1.95	Tamb
No, though Asphaltis lake were liquid gold,	2Tamb	5.1.155	Tamb
health and majesty/Were strangely blest and governed by heaven,	2Tamb	5.3.25	Techel
When wandring Phoebes Ivory cheeks were scortcht/And all the	2Tamb	5.3.232	Tamb
and Lawes were then most sure/When like the [Dracos] <Drancus>	Jew	Prol.20	Machvl
sure/When like the [Dracos] <Drancus> they were writ in blood.	Jew	Prol.21	Machvl
the Custome-house/Will serve as well as I were present there.	Jew	1.1.58	Barab
we were wafted by a Spanish Fleet/That never left us till	Jew	1.1.95	2Merch
Oh they were going up to Sicily:	Jew	1.1.98	Barab
Were it for confirmation of a League,	Jew	1.1.154	1Jew
Were they not summon'd to appeare to day?	Jew	1.2.35	Govnr
They were, my Lord, and here they come.	Jew	1.2.36	Offcrs
that I descended of/Were all in generall cast away for sinne,	Jew	1.2.114	Barab
You were a multitude, and I but one,	Jew	1.2.178	Barab
You that/Were ne're possest of wealth, are pleas'd with want.	Jew	1.2.201	Barab
And seeme to them as if thy sinnes were great,	Jew	1.2.287	Barab
she were fitter for a tale of love/Then to be tired out with	Jew	1.2.369	Mthias
What, Barabas, whose goods were lately seiz'd?	Jew	1.2.383	Lodowk
Now that my fathers fortune were so good/As but to be about	Jew	2.1.31	Abigal
Then my desires were fully satisfied,	Jew	2.1.52	Barab
and you were stated here/To be at deadly enmity with Turkes.	Jew	2.2.32	Bosco
were ne're thought upon/Till Titus and Vespasian conquer'd us)	Jew	2.3.9	Barab
I wud you were his father too, Sir, that's al the harm I wish	Jew	2.3.41	P Barab
And as it were in Catechising sort,	Jew	2.3.73	Barab
I, marke him, you were best, for this is he	Jew	2.3.132	Barab
Use him as if he were a--Philistine.	Jew	2.3.228	Barab
and from Padua/Were wont to come rare witted Gentlemen,	Jew	3.1.7	Curtzn
Then were my thoughts so fraile and unconfirm'd,	Jew	3.3.59	Abigal
is there/Set downe at large, the Gallants were both slaine.	Jew	3.6.29	Abigal
staffe; excellent, he stands as if he were begging of Bacon.	Jew	4.1.154	P Ithimr
and now would I were gone, I am not worthy to looke upon her.	Jew	4.2.36	P Ithimr
Which if they were reveal'd, would doe him harme.	Jew	4.2.65	Pilia
told him he were best to send it; then he hug'd and imbrac'd	Jew	4.2.106	P Pilia
Oh that ten thousand nights were put in one,	Jew	4.2.130	Ithimr
And when he comes: Oh that he were but here!	Jew	4.3.17	Barab
words, Sir, and send it you, were best see; there's his letter.	Jew	4.3.24	P Pilia
Ha, to the Jew, and send me mony you were best.	Jew	4.4.12	P Ithimr
your sonne and Mathias were both contracted unto Abigall; [he]	Jew	5.1.29	P Ithimr
Their deaths were like their lives, then think not of 'em;	Jew	5.1.56	Govnr
Art thou that Jew whose goods we heard were sold/For	Jew	5.1.73	Calym
If ever day were turnde to ugly night,	P 62	2.5	Guise
Your Majesty were best goe visite him,	P 249	4.47	QnMoth
And make a shew as if all were well.	P 250	4.48	QnMoth
That you were one that made this Massacre.	P 436	7.76	Navrre
diadem, before/You were invested in the crowne of France.	P 613	12.26	Mugern
Mor du, wert <were> not the fruit within thy wombe,	P 688	13.32	Guise
Ah base Epernoune, were not his highnes heere,	P 831	17.26	Guise
It would be good the Guise were made away,	P 888	17.83	Eprnon
Be gone I say, tis time that we were there.	P 919	18.20	Navrre
tush, were he heere, we would kill him presently.	P 934	19.4	P 1Mur
O that his heart were leaping in my hand.	P 936	19.6	P 2Mur

WERE (cont.)

They were to blame that said I was displeasde,	P 969	19.39	King
Twere not amisse my Lord, if he were searcht.	P1160	22.22	Eprnon
O that that damned villaine were alive againe,	P1216	22.78	Eprnon
enter by defaulte | whatt thoughe you were once in possession	Paris	ms11,p390 P	Souldr
Were sworne to your father at his death,	Edw	1.1.83	Mortmr
And Mowberie and he were reconcild:	Edw	1.1.115	Kent
Were all the Earles and Barons of my minde,	Edw	1.2.28	Mortmr
First were his sacred garments rent and torne,	Edw	1.2.35	ArchBp
Were I a king--	Edw	1.4.27	Gavstn
Were he a peasant, being my minion,	Edw	1.4.30	Edward
They would not stir, were it to do me good:	Edw	1.4.95	Edward
Tis true sweete Gaveston, oh were it false.	Edw	1.4.108	Edward
Happie were I, but now most miserable.	Edw	1.4.129	Edward
Do you not wish that Gaveston were dead?	Edw	1.4.252	Mortmr
I would he were.	Edw	1.4.253	Penbrk
But were he here, detested as he is,	Edw	1.4.264	Mortmr
would he lov'd me/But halfe so much, then were I treble blest.	Edw	1.4.304	Queene
No more then I would answere were he slaine.	Edw	2.2.86	Mortmr
Base flatterer, yeeld, and were it not for shame,	Edw	2.5.11	Mortmr
Were I king Edward, Englands soveraigne,	Edw	3.1.10	Spencr
As though your highnes were a schoole boy still,	Edw	3.1.30	Baldck
That you were dead, or very neare your death.	Edw	4.2.38	Queene
I would it were no worse,/But gentle lords, friendles we are in	Edw	4.2.45	Queene
Would all were well, and Edward well reclaimd,	Edw	4.2.57	Kent
As you injurious were to beare them foorth.	Edw	4.3.52	Edward
We were imbarkt for Ireland, wretched we,	Edw	4.7.33	Baldck
Imagine Killingworth castell were your court,	Edw	5.1.2	Leistr
First would I heare newes that hee were deposde,	Edw	5.2.21	Mortmr
I would hee were, so it were not by my meanes.	Edw	5.2.45	Queene
Use Edmund friendly, as if all were well.	Edw	5.2.79	Queene
Well, if my Lorde your brother were enlargde.	Edw	5.2.82	Queene
Whose lookes were as a breeching to a boye.	Edw	5.4.55	Mortmr
As we were bringing him to Killingworth.	Edw	5.4.85	Souldr
That were enough to poison any man,	Edw	5.5.5	Matrvs
The Queene sent me, to see how you were used,	Edw	5.5.48	Ltborn
And then thy heart, were it as Gurneys is,	Edw	5.5.53	Edward
These handes were never stainde with innocent bloud,	Edw	5.5.81	Ltborn
I my good Lord, I would it were undone.	Edw	5.6.2	Matrvs
Then this profession were to be esteem'd.	F 54	1.1.26	Faust
yet if you were not dunces, you would never aske me such a	F 206	1.2.13	P Wagner
were not for you to come within fortie foot of the place of	F 210	1.2.17	P Wagner
Were he a stranger, <and> not allyed to me,	F 223	1.2.30	2Schol
to the devill, for a shoulder of Mutton, tho it were bloud raw.	F 350	1.4.8	P Wagner
Were <Be> she as chaste as was Penelope,	F 540	2.1.152	Mephst
If Heaven was <it were> made for man, 'twas made for me:	F 561	2.2.10	Faust
unlesse <except> the ground be <were> perfum'd, and cover'd	F 670	2.2.119	P Pride
and all the people in it were turnd> to Gold,	F 676	(HC263)A	P Covet
cannot read, and therefore wish all books burn'd <were burnt>.	F 680	2.2.129	P Envy
My godfathers were these:	F 698	2.2.147	P Glutny
I see hell, and returne againe safe, how happy were I then.	F 715	2.2.167	P Faust
into matters, as other men, if they were disposed to talke.	F 741	2.3.20	P Robin
Were by the holy Councell both condemn'd/For lothed Lollords,	F1021	3.2.41	Pope
were best looke that your devill can answere the stealing of	F1088	3.3.1	P Dick
O were that damned Hell-hound but in place,	F1355	4.2.31	Benvol
heart desires to have, and were it now Summer, as it is January,	F1571	4.6.14	P Lady
us, he were as good commit with his father, as commit with us.	F1603	4.6.46	P Dick
sir, did not I pull off one of your legs when you were asleepe?	F1656	4.6.99	P HrsCsr
what he meanes, if death were nie, he would not frolick thus:	F1677	5.1.4	P Wagner
Were gluttons, and lov'd only delicates,	F1917	5.2.121	BdAngl
<Oh> Pythagoras Metemsycosis <metem su cossis>; were that true,	F1966	5.2.170	Faust
Such fearefull shrikes, and cries, were never heard,	F1986	5.3.4	1Schol
the Divel for a shoulder of mutton, though it were blood rawe.	F App	p.229 9	P Wagner
why then belike, if I were your man, I should be ful of vermine.	F App	p.229 21	P Clown
crownes a man were as good have as many english counters,	F App	p.230 33	P Clown
they were never so knocht since they were divels, say I should	F App	p.230 46	P Clown
tell thee, we were for ever made by this doctor Faustus booke?	F App	p.234 1	P Robin
my heart desires, and were it nowe summer, as it is January,	F App	p.242 9	P Duchss
were it a greater thing then this, so it would content you, you	F App	p.242 13	P Faust
And yet me thinkes, if that death were neere,	F App	p.243 3	Wagner
Roomes infant walles were steept in brothers bloud;	Lucan, First Booke		95
Quarrels were rife, greedy desire stil poore/Did vild deeds,	Lucan, First Booke		174
Hence came it that th'edicts were overrul'd,	Lucan, First Booke		178
That lawes were broake, Tribunes with Consuls strove,	Lucan, First Booke		179
Mourning appear'd, whose hoary hayres were torne,	Lucan, First Booke		189
Whether the gods, or blustring south were cause/I know not, but	Lucan, First Booke		236
Or sea far from the land, so all were whist.	Lucan, First Booke		262
rageth now in armes/As if the Carthage Hannibal were neere;	Lucan, First Booke		305
Pursu'd us hither, how were we bestead/When comming conqueror,	Lucan, First Booke		309
steeld their harts/And minds were prone) restrain'd them;	Lucan, First Booke		356
And Vangions who like those of Sarmata,/Were open slops:	Lucan, First Booke		432
who were wont/In large spread heire to exceed the rest of	Lucan, First Booke		438
Other that Caesars barbarous bands were spread/Along Nar floud	Lucan, First Booke		471
Nor were the Commons only strooke to heart/With this vaine	Lucan, First Booke		483
(that did remaine/To their afflictions) were t'abandon Roome.	Lucan, First Booke		495
The world (were it together) is by cowards/Left as a pray now	Lucan, First Booke		511
Great store of strange and unknown stars were seene/Wandering	Lucan, First Booke		524
birds/Defil'd the day, and <at night> wilde beastes were seene,	Lucan, First Booke		557
Cattell were seene that muttered humane speech:	Lucan, First Booke		559
And dismall Prophesies were spread abroad:	Lucan, First Booke		562
Trumpets were heard to sound; and with what noise/An armed	Lucan, First Booke		577
If cold noysome Saturne/Were now exalted, and with blew beames	Lucan, First Booke		651
These sad presages were enough to scarre/The quivering Romans,	Lucan, First Booke		672

WERE (cont.)
We which were Ovids five books, now are three, ... Ovid's Elegies 1.1.1
Both verses were alike till Love (men say)/Began to smile and Ovid's Elegies 1.1.7
Were Love the cause, it's like I shoulde descry him, . Ovid's Elegies 1.2.5
Turne round thy gold-ring, as it were to ease thee. . . Ovid's Elegies 1.4.26
How apt her breasts were to be prest by me, . . . Ovid's Elegies 1.5.20
I am alone, were furious Love discarded. . . . . Ovid's Elegies 1.6.34
Meeter it were her lips were blewe with kissing/And on her Ovid's Elegies 1.7.41
My bloud, the teares were that from her descended. . . Ovid's Elegies 1.7.60
The Sabine gauntlets were too dearely wunne/That unto death did Ovid's Elegies 1.10.49
Say that thy love with Caephalus were not knowne, . . Ovid's Elegies 1.13.33
Not black, nor golden were they to our viewe, . . . Ovid's Elegies 1.14.9
Ad <And> they were apt to curle an hundred waies, . . Ovid's Elegies 1.14.13
When they were slender, and like downy mosse, . . . Ovid's Elegies 1.14.23
from their crowne/Phoebus and Bacchus wisht were hanging downe. Ovid's Elegies 1.14.32
Such were they as [Dione] <Diana> painted stands/All naked Ovid's Elegies 1.14.33
Not silent were thine eyes, the boord with wine/Was scribled, Ovid's Elegies 2.5.17
Now many guests were gone, the feast being done, . . Ovid's Elegies 2.5.21
Even kembed as they were, her lockes to rend, . . . Ovid's Elegies 2.5.45
Also much better were they then I tell, ... Ovid's Elegies 2.5.55
Nuts were thy food, and Poppie causde thee sleepe, . . Ovid's Elegies 2.6.31
Would I were culpable of some offence, ... Ovid's Elegies 2.7.11
Who that our bodies were comprest bewrayde? . . . Ovid's Elegies 2.8.5
But though I apt were for such high deseignes, . . . Ovid's Elegies 2.18.14
On swift steedes mounted till the race were done. . . Ovid's Elegies 3.2.10
Ere these were seene, I burnt: what will these do? . . Ovid's Elegies 3.2.33
How long her lockes were, ere her oath she tooke: . . Ovid's Elegies 3.3.3
And by mine eyes, and mine were pained sore. . . . Ovid's Elegies 3.3.14
Were I a God, I should give women leave, ... Ovid's Elegies 3.3.43
wish the chariot, whence corne [seedes] <fields> were found, Ovid's Elegies 3.5.15
Her cheekes were scratcht, her goodly haires discheveld. . Ovid's Elegies 3.5.48
That were as white as is <Her armes farre whiter, then> the Ovid's Elegies 3.6.8
The posts of brasse, the walles of iron were. . . . Ovid's Elegies 3.7.32
In hell were harbourd, here was found no masse. . . Ovid's Elegies 3.7.38
Come were the times of Ceres sacrifize, ... Ovid's Elegies 3.9.1
Love conquer'd shame, the furrowes dry were burnd, . . Ovid's Elegies 3.9.29
And seedes were equally in large fields cast, . . . Ovid's Elegies 3.9.33
The plough-mans hopes were frustrate at the last. . . Ovid's Elegies 3.9.34
Ceres what sports to thee so grievous were, . . . Ovid's Elegies 3.9.43
Against my good they were an envious charme. . . . Ovid's Elegies 3.11.14
And blush, and seeme as you were full of grace. . . Ovid's Elegies 3.13.28
The outside of her garments were of lawne, . . . Hero and Leander 1.9
they tooke delite/To play upon those hands, they were so white. Hero and Leander 1.30
His dangling tresses that were never shorne, . . . Hero and Leander 1.55
For in his lookes were all that men desire, . . . Hero and Leander 1.84
And all that view'd her, were enamour'd on her. . . Hero and Leander 1.118
And many seeing great princes were denied, . . . Hero and Leander 1.129
from her tower/To Venus temple, [where] <were> unhappilye, Hero and Leander 1.133
The wals were of discoloured Jasper-stone, . . . Hero and Leander 1.136
Were I the saint hee worships, I would heare him, . . Hero and Leander 1.179
Loves mother/Nor heaven, nor thou, were made to gaze upon, Hero and Leander 1.223
And crave the helpe of sheap-heards that were nie. . . Hero and Leander 1.414
Were with Jove clos'd in Stigian Emperie. . . . . Hero and Leander 1.458
Seeing in their loves, the Fates were injured. . . . Hero and Leander 1.484
Both to each other quickly were affied. . . . . Hero and Leander 2.26
Looke how their hands, so were their hearts united, . . Hero and Leander 2.27
To slake his anger, if he were displeas'd, . . . Hero and Leander 2.49
yet he suspected/Some amorous rites or other were neglected. Hero and Leander 2.64
O that these tardie armes of mine were wings, . . . Hero and Leander 2.205
Breathlesse albeit he were, he rested not, . . . Hero and Leander 2.229
And now she wisht this night were never done, . . . Hero and Leander 2.301
But as her naked feet were whipping out, ... Hero and Leander 2.313

WER'T
'Twas I, that when thou wer't i'the way to heaven, . . F1886 5.2.90 Mephst

WERT
O Queene of Carthage, wert thou ugly blacke, . . . Dido 5.1.125 Aeneas
As if thou wert the Empresse of the world. . . . 1Tamb 3.3.125 Tamb
wert thou the cause of this/That tearm'st Zenocrate thy dearest 1Tamb 5.1.335 Zenoc
Who when he heares how resolute thou wert, . . . 2Tamb 3.4.40 Techel
But thou wert set upon extreme revenge, ... Jew 3.3.42 Abigal
Mor du, wert <were> not the fruit within thy wombe, . . P 688 13.32 Guise
King, why so thou wert before. . . . . P1067 19.137 QnMoth
Sweet Guise, would he had died so thou wert heere: . . P1082 19.152 QnMoth
Wert thou the Pope thou mightst not scape from us. . . P1092 20.2 1Mur
That wert the onely cause of his exile. . . . . Edw 1.1.179 Edward
When wert thou in the field with banner spred? . . . Edw 2.2.182 Mortmr
But for thou wert the favorit of a King, ... Edw 2.5.27 Warwck
Why wert thou not a creature wanting soule? . . . F1964 5.2.168 Faust
As thou art faire, would thou wert fortunate, . . . Ovid's Elegies 1.8.27
Wert thou rich, poore should not be my state. . . . Ovid's Elegies 1.8.28
Such wert thou, and I fear'd the Bull and Eagle/And what ere Ovid's Elegies 1.10.7
While thou wert plaine, I lov'd thy minde and face: . . Ovid's Elegies 1.10.13
Yet as if mixt with red leade thou wert ruddy, . . . Ovid's Elegies 1.12.11
Thou wert not borne to ride, or armes to beare, . . . Ovid's Elegies 2.3.7
What helpes it thou wert given to please my wench, . . Ovid's Elegies 2.6.19
Thou also, that wert borne faire, hadst decayed, . . . Ovid's Elegies 2.14.19
How wouldst thou flowe wert thou a noble floud, . . . Ovid's Elegies 3.5.89
Against thy selfe, mans nature, thou wert cunning, . . Ovid's Elegies 3.7.45
with th'earth thou wert content,/Why seek'st not heav'n the Ovid's Elegies 3.7.49
Say but thou wert injurously accusde. . . . . Ovid's Elegies 3.13.42

WERTENBERG
At <of> riper yeares to Wittenberg <Wertenberg> he went, . F 13 Prol.13 1Chor

WERTENBERGE

And made the flowring pride of Wittenberg <Wertenberge>	F 141	1.1.113	Faust
I John Faustus of Wittenberg <Wertenberge>, Doctor, by these	F 493	2.1.105	P Faust
In stead of Troy shall Wittenberg <Wertenberge> be sack't,/And	F1776	5.1.103	Faust
O would I had never seene Wittenberg <Wertenberge>, never read	F1841	5.2.45	P Faust
Therefore sweet Mephastophilis, let us make haste to Wertenberge	F App	p.239 94	Faust

WEST

Measuring the limits of his Emperie/By East and west, as	1Tamb	1.2.40	Tamb
So from the East unto the furthest West,	1Tamb	3.3.246	Tamb
Stretching your conquering armes from east to west:	2Tamb	1.3.97	Tamb
The Terrene west, the Caspian north north-east,	2Tamb	4.3.103	Tamb
All <joyntly> move from East to West, in foure and twenty	F 597	2.2.46	P Mephst
From East to West his Dragons swiftly glide,	F 766	2.3.45	2Chor
rocks, and where the north-west wind/Nor Zephir rules not,	Lucan, First Booke		407
And Gallus shall be knowne from East to West,	Ovid's Elegies		1.15.29
For thee the East and West winds make me pale,	Ovid's Elegies		2.11.9

WESTERN

Born to be Monarch of the Western world:	2Tamb	1.2.3	Callap

WESTERNE

[Trading] <Treading> by land unto the Westerne Isles,	1Tamb	1.1.38	Meandr
Unpeopling Westerne Affrica and Greece:	1Tamb	3.3.34	Usumc
From Barbary unto the Westerne Inde,	1Tamb	5.1.518	Tamb
The Westerne part of Affrike, where I view'd/The Ethiopian sea,	2Tamb	1.3.195	Techel
bank, right opposite/Against the Westerne gate of Babylon.	2Tamb	5.1.122	Govnr
That's to be gotten in the Westerne Inde:	Jew	3.5.5	Govnr

WESTWARD

Lies westward from the midst of Cancers line,	2Tamb	5.3.146	Tamb

WET

And wet thy cheeks for their untimely deathes:	1Tamb	5.1.348	Zenoc
Wet with my teares, and dried againe with sighes,	Edw	5.1.118	Edward

WEY

O no, the Gods wey not what Lovers doe,	Dido	5.1.131	Dido
If you wey not ill speeches, yet wey mee:	Ovid's Elegies		3.13.36

WHAT (See also WHATT)

I love thee well, say Juno what she will.	Dido	1.1.2	Jupitr
What? dares she strike the darling of my thoughts?	Dido	1.1.9	Jupitr
What ist sweet wagge I should deny thy youth?	Dido	1.1.23	Jupitr
What shall I doe to save thee my sweet boy?	Dido	1.1.74	Venus
What? is not pietie exempt from woe?	Dido	1.1.79	Venus
What? doe I see my sonne now come on shoare:	Dido	1.1.134	Venus
See what strange arts necessitie findes out,	Dido	1.1.169	Venus
To know what coast the winde hath driven us on,	Dido	1.1.176	Aeneas
But what may I faire Virgin call your name?	Dido	1.1.188	Aeneas
As to instruct us under what good heaven/We breathe as now, and	Dido	1.1.197	Aeneas
good heaven/We breathe as now, and what this world is calde,	Dido	1.1.198	Aeneas
But what are you that aske of me these things?	Dido	1.1.214	Venus
Fortune hath favord thee what ere thou be,	Dido	1.1.231	Venus
Why, what are you, or wherefore doe you sewe?	Dido	1.2.3	Iarbus
Unto what fruitfull quarters were ye bound,	Dido	1.2.18	Iarbus
but saving ayre/Is nothing here, and what is this but stone?	Dido	2.1.14	Achat
What meanes Aeneas?	Dido	2.1.23	Achat
What kind of people, and who governes them:	Dido	2.1.42	Aeneas
And scarcely know within what Clime we are.	Dido	2.1.44	Aeneas
O what destinies/Have brought my sweete companions in such	Dido	2.1.59	Aeneas
What stranger art thou that doest eye me thus?	Dido	2.1.74	Dido
But Troy is not, what shall I say I am?	Dido	2.1.76	Aeneas
What, faints Aeneas to remember Troy?	Dido	2.1.118	Dido
Achilles sonne, remember what I was,	Dido	2.1.233	Aeneas
O what became of aged Hecuba?	Dido	2.1.290	Anna
What happened to the Queene we cannot shewe,	Dido	2.1.294	Achat
But that I may enjoy what I desire:	Dido	3.1.9	Iarbus
What will you give me now? Ile have this Fanne.	Dido	3.1.32	Cupid
No, live Iarbus, what hast thou deserv'd,	Dido	3.1.41	Dido
What telst thou me of rich Getulia?	Dido	3.1.48	Dido
here, tell me in sooth/In what might Dido highly pleasure thee.	Dido	3.1.102	Dido
Take what ye will, but leave Aeneas here.	Dido	3.1.127	Dido
What should this meane?	Dido	3.2.21	Venus
Juno, my mortall foe, what make you here?	Dido	3.2.24	Venus
What though I was offended with thy sonne,	Dido	3.2.40	Juno
We two will talke alone, what words be these?	Dido	3.3.12	Iarbus
What makes Iarbus here of all the rest?	Dido	3.3.13	Dido
Aeneas, be not movde at what he sayes,	Dido	3.3.23	Dido
What, darest thou looke a Lyon in the face?	Dido	3.3.39	Dido
I, and outface him to, doe what he can.	Dido	3.3.40	Cupid
What shall I doe thus wronged with disdaine?	Dido	3.3.69	Iarbus
And then, what then? Iarbus shall but love:	Dido	3.3.82	Iarbus
Why, what is it that Dido may desire/And not obtaine, be it in	Dido	3.4.7	Aeneas
What, hath Iarbus angred her in ought?	Dido	3.4.13	Aeneas
What ailes my Queene, is she falne sicke of late?	Dido	3.4.24	Aeneas
Aeneas, thou art he, what did I say?	Dido	3.4.29	Dido
What meanes faire Dido by this doubtfull speech?	Dido	3.4.31	Aeneas
But now that I have found what to effect,	Dido	3.4.37	Dido
What more then Delian musicke doe I heare,	Dido	3.4.52	Dido
What willes our Lord, or wherefore did he call?	Dido	4.3.15	Achat
And Mercury to flye for what he calles?	Dido	4.4.47	Dido
Lets see what tempests can anoy me now.	Dido	4.4.60	Aeneas
What if the Citizens repine thereat?	Dido	4.4.70	Anna
Those that dislike what Dido gives in charge,	Dido	4.4.71	Dido
Shall vulgar pesants storme at what I doe?	Dido	4.4.73	Dido
What if I sinke his ships? O heele frowne:	Dido	4.4.110	Dido
Say Dido what she will I am not old,	Dido	4.5.21	Nurse
O what meane I to have such foolish thoughts!	Dido	4.5.25	Nurse
What length or bredth shal this brave towne containe?	Dido	5.1.16	Achat

WHAT (cont.)

But what shall it be calde, Troy as before?	Dido	5.1.18		Illion
Vaine man, what Monarky expectst thou here?	Dido	5.1.34		Hermes
Or with what thought sleepst thou in Libia shoare?	Dido	5.1.35		Hermes
What, would the Gods have me, Deucalion like,	Dido	5.1.57		Aeneas
How now Aeneas, sad, what meanes these dumpes?	Dido	5.1.62		Iarbus
Nor I devise by what meanes to contrive.	Dido	5.1.66		Aeneas
And they shall have what thing so ere thou needst.	Dido	5.1.74		Iarbus
or to what end/Launcht from the haven, lye they in the Rhode?	Dido	5.1.88		Dido
The Gods, what Gods be those that seeke my death?	Dido	5.1.128		Dido
O no, the Gods wey not what Lovers doe,	Dido	5.1.131		Dido
Now if thou goest, what canst thou leave behind,	Dido	5.1.151		Dido
What meanes my sister thus to rave and crye?	Dido	5.1.193		Anna
I know not what you meane by treason, I,	Dido	5.1.222		Nurse
And stay a while to heare what I could say,	Dido	5.1.239		Anna
fleete, what shall I doe/But dye in furie of this oversight?	Dido	5.1.268		Dido
What can my teares or cryes prevaile me now?	Dido	5.1.319		Anna
What fatall destinie envies me thus,	Dido	5.1.323		Anna
What, shall I call thee brother?	1Tamb	1.1.103		Mycet
what, mated and amaz'd/To heare the king thus threaten like	1Tamb	1.1.107		Menaph
But Menaphon, what means this trumpets sound?	1Tamb	1.1.133		Cosroe
What now? In love?	1Tamb	1.2.106		Techel
With what a majesty he rears his looks:--	1Tamb	1.2.165		Tamb
What stronge enchantments tice my yeelding soule?	1Tamb	1.2.224		Therid
What stature wields he, and what personage?	1Tamb	2.1.6		Cosroe
What will he doe supported by a king?	1Tamb	2.1.57		Ceneus
What should we doe but bid them battaile straight,	1Tamb	2.2.18		Meandr
What thinkst thou man, shal come of our attemptes?	1Tamb	2.3.3		Cosroe
You see my Lord, what woorking woordes he hath.	1Tamb	2.3.25		Therid
In what a lamentable case were I,	1Tamb	2.4.6		Mycet
What, fearful coward, stragling from the camp/When Kings	1Tamb	2.4.16		Tamb
From one that knew not what a King should do,	1Tamb	2.5.22		Cosroe
To one that can commaund what longs thereto:	1Tamb	2.5.23		Cosroe
What saies my other friends, wil you be kings?	1Tamb	2.5.67		Tamb
What then my Lord?	1Tamb	2.5.71		Usumc
What saith Theridamas?	1Tamb	2.5.105		Tamb
What means this divelish shepheard to aspire/With such a	1Tamb	2.6.1		Cosroe
What God or Feend, or spirit of the earth,	1Tamb	2.6.15		Ortyg
Or of what mould or mettel he be made,	1Tamb	2.6.17		Ortyg
What star or state soever governe him,	1Tamb	2.6.18		Ortyg
What better president than mightie Jove?	1Tamb	2.7.17		Tamb
What if you sent the Bassoes of your guard,	1Tamb	3.1.17		Fesse
What thinks your greatnes best to be atchiev'd/In pursuit of	1Tamb	3.1.56		Fesse
He bids you prophesie what it imports.	1Tamb	3.2.89		Techel
What meanes the mighty Turkish Emperor/To talk with one so base	1Tamb	3.3.87		Fesse
What Coward wold not fight for such a prize?	1Tamb	3.3.100		Usumc
hardy Tamburlaine)/What tis to meet me in the open field,	1Tamb	3.3.146		Bajzth
What, thinkst thou Tamburlain esteems thy gold?	1Tamb	3.3.262		Tamb
But speake, what power hath he?	1Tamb	4.1.20		Souldn
what, not a bit?	1Tamb	4.4.54	P	Tamb
What simple Virgins may perswade, we will.	1Tamb	5.1.61		2Virgn
What, are the Turtles fraide out of their neastes?	1Tamb	5.1.64		Tamb
Behold my sword, what see you at the point?	1Tamb	5.1.108		Tamb
What, have your horsmen shewen the virgins Death?	1Tamb	5.1.129		Tamb
What is beauty, saith my sufferings then?	1Tamb	5.1.160		Tamb
What do mine eies behold, my husband dead?	1Tamb	5.1.305		Zabina
Ah what may chance to thee Zenocrate?	1Tamb	5.1.371		Zenoc
What other heavie news now brings Philemus?	1Tamb	5.1.377		Zenoc
What cursed power guides the murthering hands,	1Tamb	5.1.403		Arabia
What saith the noble Souldane and Zenocrate?	1Tamb	5.1.495		Tamb
But what became of faire Zenocrate,	2Tamb	Prol.6		Prolog
What? Shall we parle with the Christian,	2Tamb	1.1.11		Orcan
And what we did, was in extremity:	2Tamb	1.1.105		Sgsmnd
so eloquent/To paint in woords, what Ile perfourme in deeds,	2Tamb	1.2.10		Callap
Wel sir, what of this?	2Tamb	1.2.18		Almeda
Well done Techelles: what saith Theridamas?	2Tamb	1.3.206		Tamb
What motion is it that inflames your thoughts,	2Tamb	2.1.2		Sgsmnd
I am sure/What cruell slaughter of our Christian bloods,	2Tamb	2.1.5		Fredrk
So what we vow to them should not infringe/Our liberty of armes	2Tamb	2.1.40		Baldwn
What saiest thou yet Gazellus to his foile:	2Tamb	2.3.27		Orcan
What, is she dead?	2Tamb	2.4.96		Tamb
What God so ever holds thee in his armes,	2Tamb	2.4.109		Tamb
In champion grounds, what figure serves you best,	2Tamb	3.2.63		Tamb
Now my boyes, what think you of a wound?	2Tamb	3.2.129		Tamb
I know not what I should think of it.	2Tamb	3.2.130	P	Calyph
What requier you my maisters?	2Tamb	3.3.15		Capt
the plaines/To spie what force comes to relieve the holde.	2Tamb	3.3.48		Techel
How now Madam, what are you doing?	2Tamb	3.4.34		Therid
And what our Army royall is esteem'd.	2Tamb	3.5.31		Callap
That fighting, knowes not what retreat doth meane,	2Tamb	3.5.43		Trebiz
What, take it man.	2Tamb	3.5.132	P	Orcan
ho, what, given so much to sleep/You cannot leave it, when our	2Tamb	4.1.11		Amyras
What, dar'st thou then be absent from the fight,	2Tamb	4.1.22		Amyras
I know sir, what it is to kil a man,	2Tamb	4.1.27		Calyph
Content my Lord, but what shal we play for?	2Tamb	4.1.63	P	Perdic
What a coyle they keepe, I beleeve there will be some hurt done	2Tamb	4.1.74	P	Calyph
And what the jealousie of warres must doe.	2Tamb	4.1.104		Tamb
What is it?	2Tamb	4.2.58		Therid
What, have I slaine her? Villaine, stab thy selfe:	2Tamb	4.2.82		Therid
What, can ye draw but twenty miles a day,	2Tamb	4.3.2		Tamb
Lost long before you knew what honour meant.	2Tamb	4.3.87		Tamb
What saith Maximus?	2Tamb	5.1.1		Govnr
What faintnesse should dismay our courages,	2Tamb	5.1.21		Govnr

WHAT (cont.)

What shal be done with their wives and children my Lord.	2Tamb	5.1.168	P	Techel
Lordes, what now remaines/But that we leave sufficient garrison	2Tamb	5.1.210		Tamb
What is it dares distemper Tamburlain?	2Tamb	5.1.219		Techel
Something Techelles, but I know not what,	2Tamb	5.1.220		Tamb
But foorth ye vassals, what so ere it be,	2Tamb	5.1.221		Tamb
What daring God torments my body thus,	2Tamb	5.3.42		Tamb
Ah friends, what shal I doe, I cannot stand,	2Tamb	5.3.51		Tamb
Tel me, what think you of my sicknes now?	2Tamb	5.3.81		Tamb
Looke here my boies, see what a world of ground,	2Tamb	5.3.145		Tamb
Here lovely boies, what death forbids my life,	2Tamb	5.3.159		Tamb
With what a flinty bosome should I joy,	2Tamb	5.3.185		Amyras
with what a broken hart/And damned spirit I ascend this seat,	2Tamb	5.3.206		Amyras
What right had Caesar to the [Empery] <Empire>?	Jew	Prol.19		Machvl
Fye; what a trouble tis to count this trash.	Jew	1.1.7		Barab
Into what corner peeres my Halcions bill?	Jew	1.1.39		Barab
What more may Heaven doe for earthly man/Then thus to powre out	Jew	1.1.107		Barab
What accident's betided to the Jewes?	Jew	1.1.145		Barab
Fond men, what dreame you of their multitudes?	Jew	1.1.157		Barab
What need they treat of peace that are in league?	Jew	1.1.158		Barab
Now Bassoes, what demand you at our hands?	Jew	1.2.1		Govnr
What at our hands demand ye?	Jew	1.2.6		Govnr
What Callapine, a little curtesie.	Jew	1.2.23		Calym
What respit aske you [Governour]?	Jew	1.2.27		Calym
Have you determin'd what to say to them?	Jew	1.2.37		1Knght
To what this ten yeares tribute will amount/That we have cast,	Jew	1.2.46		Govnr
Why know you what you did by this device?	Jew	1.2.84		Barab
Christians; what, or how can I multiply?	Jew	1.2.103		Barab
What? bring you Scripture to confirm your wrongs?	Jew	1.2.110		Barab
What tell you me of Job?	Jew	1.2.181		Barab
Oh what has made my lovely daughter sad?	Jew	1.2.225		Barab
What, woman, moane not for a little losse:	Jew	1.2.226		Barab
What, will you thus oppose me, lucklesse Starres,	Jew	1.2.260		Barab
what e're it be to injure them/That have so manifestly wronged	Jew	1.2.274		Abigal
have so manifestly wronged us,/What will not Abigall attempt?	Jew	1.2.276		Abigal
Well father, say I be entertain'd,/What then shall follow?	Jew	1.2.295		Abigal
What art thou, daughter?	Jew	1.2.316		Abbass
Well, daughter, say, what is thy suit with us?	Jew	1.2.321		Abbass
now Abigall, what mak'st thou/Amongst these hateful Christians?	Jew	1.2.338		Barab
What wilt thou doe among these hatefull fiends?	Jew	1.2.345		Barab
What wast I prethe?	Jew	1.2.377		Lodowk
But say, What was she?	Jew	1.2.382		Lodowk
What, Barabas, whose goods were lately seiz'd?	Jew	1.2.383		Lodowk
But stay, what starre shines yonder in the East?	Jew	2.1.41		Barab
What is the summe that Calymath requires?	Jew	2.2.35		Bosco
What sparkle does it give without a foile?	Jew	2.3.55		Lodowk
What, can he steale that you demand so much?	Jew	2.3.100		Barab
What, hast the Philosophers stone?	Jew	2.3.111	P	Barab
What makes the Jew and Lodowicke so private?	Jew	2.3.138		Mthias
My profession what you please.	Jew	2.3.166		Ithimr
What, ho, Abigall; open the doore I say.	Jew	2.3.221		Barab
What, hand in hand, I cannot suffer this.	Jew	2.3.276		Mthias
My death? what, is the base borne peasant mad?	Jew	2.3.281		Lodowk
What, shall I be betroth'd to Lodowicke?	Jew	2.3.308		Abigal
Oh wretched Abigal, what hast [thou] <thee> done?	Jew	2.3.320		Abigal
What greater gift can poore Mathias have?	Jew	2.3.346		Mthias
What, is he gone unto my mother?	Jew	2.3.351		Mthias
Zoon's what a looking thou keep'st, thou'lt betraye's anon.	Jew	3.1.25		Pilia
What, dares the villain write in such base terms?	Jew	3.2.3		Lodowk
What sight is this? my [Lodovico] <Lodowicke> slaine!	Jew	3.2.10		Govnr
Why, what ayl'st thou?	Jew	3.3.6		Abigal
No, what was it?	Jew	3.3.17		Abigal
Well, sirra, what is't?	Jew	3.3.31		Abigal
What, Abigall become a Nunne againe?	Jew	3.4.1		Barab
False, and unkinde; what, hast thou lost thy father?	Jew	3.4.2		Barab
Repentance? Spurca: what pretendeth this?	Jew	3.4.6		Barab
What, hast thou brought the Ladle with thee too?	Jew	3.4.57		Barab
Prethe doe: what saist thou now?	Jew	3.4.88		Barab
What a blessing has he given't?	Jew	3.4.106	P	Ithimr
what shall I doe with it?	Jew	3.4.107	P	Ithimr
fares Callymath, What wind drives you thus into Malta rhode?	Jew	3.5.2	P	Govnr
Oh what a sad confession will there be?	Jew	3.6.4		2Fryar
What, all dead save onely Abigall?	Jew	3.6.7		2Fryar
What then?	Jew	3.6.16		2Fryar
Yes, what of them?	Jew	3.6.21		2Fryar
Why? what has he done?	Jew	3.6.47		1Fryar
What, has he crucified a child?	Jew	3.6.49		1Fryar
True, I have mony, what though I have?	Jew	4.1.30		Barab
What needs all this? I know I am a Jew.	Jew	4.1.33		Barab
Why, what of them?	Jew	4.1.44	P	Barab
may I compare/With all the Jewes in Malta; but what is wealth?	Jew	4.1.56		Barab
What if I murder'd him e're Jacomo comes?	Jew	4.1.116		Barab
Yes; and I know not what the reason is:	Jew	4.1.130		Ithimr
Doe what I can he will not strip himselfe,	Jew	4.1.131		Ithimr
I feare me he mistrusts what we intend.	Jew	4.1.133		Ithimr
What, doe you meane to strangle me?	Jew	4.1.144		2Fryar
What, will you [have] <save> my life?	Jew	4.1.148		2Fryar
What time a night is't now, sweet Ithimore?	Jew	4.1.157		Barab
Why, how now Jacomo, what hast thou done?	Jew	4.1.174		Barab
Heaven blesse me; what, a Fryar a murderer?	Jew	4.1.196		Barab
And what think'st thou, will he come?	Jew	4.2.5	P	Curtzn
And what said he?	Jew	4.2.11	P	Curtzn
I wonder what the reason is.	Jew	4.2.32	P	Ithimr

WHAT (cont.)

he flouts me, what gentry can be in a poore Turke of ten pence?	Jew	4.2.38	P	Ithimr
What shall we doe with this base villaine then?	Jew	4.2.62		Curtzn
for your sake, and said what a faithfull servant you had bin.	Jew	4.2.109	P	Pilia
What an eye she casts on me?	Jew	4.2.127	P	Ithimr
what hee writes for you, ye shall have streight.	Jew	4.3.27	P	Barab
What wudst thou doe if he should send thee none?	Jew	4.4.13		Pilia
nothing; but I know what I know.	Jew	4.4.14	P	Ithimr
What a slave's this?	Jew	4.4.63	P	Barab
What e're I am, yet Governor heare me speake;	Jew	5.1.9		Curtzn
Nuns, strangled a Fryar, and I know not what mischiefe beside.	Jew	5.1.14	P	Pilia
What a damn'd slave was I?	Jew	5.1.23		Barab
Confesse; what meane you, Lords, who should confesse?	Jew	5.1.26		Barab
For what?	Jew	5.1.36		Barab
What, all alone? well fare sleepy drinke.	Jew	5.1.61		Barab
What should I say? we are captives and must yeeld.	Jew	5.2.6		Govnr
What greater misery could heaven inflict?	Jew	5.2.14		Govnr
me/My life's in danger, and what boots it thee/Poore Barabas,	Jew	5.2.31		Barab
What thinkst thou shall become of it and thee?	Jew	5.2.56		Barab
What wilt thou give me, Governor, to procure/A dissolution of	Jew	5.2.76		Barab
What will you give me if I render you/The life of Calymath,	Jew	5.2.79		Barab
What will you give him that procureth this?	Jew	5.2.83		Barab
And let me see what mony thou canst make;	Jew	5.2.94		Barab
To what event my secret purpose drives,	Jew	5.2.122		Barab
What will we not adventure?	Jew	5.4.9		1Knght
Now sirra, what, will he come?	Jew	5.5.13		Barab
I trust thy word, take what I promis'd thee.	Jew	5.5.43		Govnr
How now, what means this?	Jew	5.5.64		Calym
Tell me, you Christians, what doth this portend?	Jew	5.5.90		Calym
Yes, what of that?	Jew	5.5.106		Calym
In what Queen Mother or your grace commands.	P 12	1.12		Navrre
For what he doth the Pope will ratifie:	P 40	1.40		Condy
I am my Lord, in what your grace commaundes till death.	P 76	2.19	P	Pothec
What glory is there in a common good,	P 97	2.40		Guise
If I repaire not what he ruinates:	P 129	2.72		Guise
An eare, to heare what my detractors say,	P 160	2.103		Guise
O gracious God, what times are these?	P 188	3.23		Navrre
What are you hurt my Lord high Admiral?	P 197	3.32		Condy
What you determine, I will ratifie.	P 227	4.25		Charls
What order wil you set downe for the Massacre?	P 229	4.27		QnMoth
How now fellow, what newes?	P 242	4.40		Charls
What shall we doe now with the Admirall?	P 248	4.46		Charls
Gonzago, what, is he dead?	P 304	5.31		Guise
What fearfull cries comes from the river [Sene] <Rene>,/That	P 361	7.1		Ramus
What art thou?	P 373	7.13		Gonzag
I, so they are, but yet what remedy:	P 433	7.73		Anjoy
I have done what I could to stay this broile.	P 434	7.74		Anjoy
Now sirra, what shall we doe with the Admirall?	P 482	9.1	P	1Atndt
What shall we doe then?	P 486	9.5	P	2Atndt
What art thou dead, sweet sonne speak to thy Mother.	P 551	11.16		QnMoth
And he nor heares, nor sees us what we doe:	P 553	11.18		QnMoth
My Lords, what resteth there now for to be done?	P 554	11.19		QnMoth
What saies our Minions, think they Henries heart/Will not both	P 603	12.16		King
And fellowes to, what ever stormes arise.	P 615	12.28		King
What now remaines, but for a while to feast,	P 627	12.40		King
And if he doe deny what I doe say,	P 650	12.63		QnMoth
What, all alone my love, and writing too:	P 670	13.14		Guise
Thou trothles and unjust, what lines are these?	P 680	13.24		Guise
How now sirra, what newes?	P 723	14.26		Navrre
So he be safe he cares not what becomes,	P 739	14.42		Navrre
Not I my Lord, what if I had?	P 775	15.33		Mugern
what are ye come so soone?	P 815	17.10	P	Souldr
What your intent is yet we cannot learn,	P 823	17.18		King
What I have done tis for the Gospell sake.	P 826	17.21		Guise
What Peere in France but thou (aspiring Guise)/Durst be in	P 828	17.23		Eprnon
What should I doe but stand upon my guarde?	P 839	17.34		Guise
For had your highnesse seene with what a pompe/He entred Paris,	P 872	17.67		Eprnon
And then Ile tell thee what I meane to doe.	P 891	17.86		King
Come on sirs, what, are you resolutely bent,	P 931	19.1		Capt
What, will you not feare when you see him come?	P 933	19.3		Capt
Pardon thee, why what hast thou done?	P 991	19.61		Guise
To dye by Pesantes, what a greefe is this?	P1009	19.79		Guise
What, have you done?	P1016	19.86		Capt
But what availeth that this traitors dead,	P1054	19.124		King
And all for thee my Guise: what may I doe?	P1088	19.158		QnMoth
What, will you fyle your handes with Churchmens bloud?	P1093	20.3		Cardnl
Oh what may I doe, for to revenge thy death?	P1108	21.2		Dumain
But what doth move thee above the rest to doe the deed?	P1132	21.26	P	Dumain
Then come thou neer, and tell what newes thou bringst.	P1166	22.28		King
What, is your highnes hurt?	P1176	22.38		Navrre
What irreligeous Pagans partes be these,	P1180	22.42		King
Search Surgeon and resolve me what thou seest.	P1193	22.55		King
What this detested Jacobin hath done.	P1195	22.57		King
what, shall the French king dye,/Wounded and poysoned, both at	P1214	22.76		King
What greater blisse can hap to Gaveston,	Edw	1.1.4		Gavstn
What neede the artick people love star-light,	Edw	1.1.16		Gavstn
But how now, what are these?	Edw	1.1.24		Gavstn
What canst thou doe?	Edw	1.1.26		Gavstn
But I have no horses. What art thou?	Edw	1.1.28		Gavstn
And what art thou?	Edw	1.1.33		Gavstn
What danger tis to stand against your king.	Edw	1.1.97		Edward
What Gaveston, welcome:	Edw	1.1.140		Edward
What so thy minde affectes or fancie likes.	Edw	1.1.170		Edward

WHAT (cont.)

What should a priest do with so faire a house?	Edw	1.1.206	Gavstn
What? will they tyrannize upon the Church?	Edw	1.2.3	Lncstr
What neede I, God himselfe is up in armes,	Edw	1.2.40	ArchBp
What els my lords, for it concernes me neere,	Edw	1.2.44	ArchBp
What we confirme the king will frustrate.	Edw	1.2.72	Lncstr
What? are you mov'd that Gaveston sits heere?	Edw	1.4.8	Edward
What man of noble birth can brooke this sight?	Edw	1.4.12	MortSr
See what a scornfull looke the pesant casts.	Edw	1.4.14	MortSr
What we have done, our hart bloud shall maintaine.	Edw	1.4.40	Mortmr
And see what we your councellers have done.	Edw	1.4.44	ArchBp
What, would ye have me plead for Gaveston?	Edw	1.4.213	Mortmr
Yet good my lord, heare what he can alledge.	Edw	1.4.250	Queene
Diablo, what passions call you these?	Edw	1.4.319	Lncstr
If it be so, what will not Edward do?	Edw	1.4.325	Edward
What, meane you then to be his follower?	Edw	2.1.12	Baldck
What needst thou, love, thus to excuse thy selfe?	Edw	2.1.60	Neece
How now, what newes, is Gaveston arrivde?	Edw	2.2.6	Edward
Nothing but Gaveston, what means your grace?	Edw	2.2.7	Mortmr
And what is yours my lord of Lancaster?	Edw	2.2.21	Edward
What call you this but private libelling,	Edw	2.2.34	Edward
What will he do when as he shall be present?	Edw	2.2.48	Mortmr
Ah furious Mortimer what hast thou done?	Edw	2.2.85	Queene
How now, what noise is this?	Edw	2.2.139	Edward
What Mortimer, you will not threaten him?	Edw	2.2.146	Kent
What forraine prince sends thee embassadors?	Edw	2.2.170	Lncstr
What weeneth the king of England,	Edw	2.2.193	Lncstr
Do what they can, weele live in Tinmoth here,	Edw	2.2.221	Edward
What care I though the Earles begirt us round?	Edw	2.2.223	Edward
But let them go, and tell me what are these.	Edw	2.2.239	Edward
Tell me, where wast thou borne? What is thine armes?	Edw	2.2.242	Edward
What would you with the king, ist him you seek?	Edw	2.4.31	Queene
Shalt thou appoint/What we shall graunt?	Edw	2.5.50	Mortmr
Penbrooke, what wilt thou do?	Edw	2.5.82	Warwck
My lord of Lancaster, what say you in this?	Edw	2.5.89	Arundl
Then tell thy prince, of whence, and what thou art.	Edw	3.1.35	Edward
Madam, what newes?	Edw	3.1.58	Edward
What lord [Arundell] <Matre>, dost thou come alone?	Edw	3.1.89	Edward
What rebels, do you shrinke, and sound retreat?	Edw	3.1.200	Edward
What Mortimer?	Edw	3.1.256	Mortmr
What they intend, the hangman frustrates cleane.	Edw	3.1.275	Baldck
And certifie what Edwards loosenes is.	Edw	4.1.7	Kent
The lords are cruell, and the king unkinde,/What shall we doe?	Edw	4.2.3	Queene
Madam, what cheere?	Edw	4.2.13	SrJohn
How say yong Prince, what thinke you of the match?	Edw	4.2.67	SrJohn
What newes my lord?	Edw	4.3.5	Spencr
I pray let us see it, what have we there?	Edw	4.3.10	Edward
What now remaines, have you proclaimed, my lord,	Edw	4.3.17	Edward
How now, what newes with thee, from whence come these?	Edw	4.3.24	Edward
What, was I borne to flye and runne away,	Edw	4.5.4	Edward
Tell me good unckle, what Edward doe you meane?	Edw	4.6.32	Prince
My lord of Kent, what needes these questions?	Edw	4.6.34	Mortmr
Madam, what resteth, why stand ye in a muse?	Edw	4.6.63	SrJohn
But what is he, whome rule and emperie/Have not in life or	Edw	4.7.14	Edward
A faire commission warrants what we do.	Edw	4.7.48	Rice
What cannot gallant Mortimer with the Queene?	Edw	4.7.50	Leistr
And Leister say, what shall become of us?	Edw	4.7.81	Edward
Remember thee fellow? what else?	Edw	4.7.118	Rice
But what are kings, when regiment is gone,	Edw	5.1.26	Edward
But what the heavens appoint, I must obaye,	Edw	5.1.56	Edward
What, feare you not the furie of your king?	Edw	5.1.75	Edward
Elect, conspire, install, do what you will,	Edw	5.1.88	Edward
Take it: what are you moovde, pitie you me?	Edw	5.1.102	Edward
An other poast, what newes bringes he?	Edw	5.1.128	Leistr
Conclude against his father what thou wilt,	Edw	5.2.19	Queene
as long as he survives/What safetie rests for us, or for my	Edw	5.2.43	Queene
Traitors away, what will you murther me,	Edw	5.3.29	Edward
What else my lord? and farre more resolute.	Edw	5.4.23	Ltborn
I seale, I cancell, I do what I will,	Edw	5.4.51	Mortmr
And what I list commaund, who dare controwle?	Edw	5.4.68	Mortmr
What traitor have wee there with blades and billes?	Edw	5.4.82	Mortmr
What hath he done?	Edw	5.4.83	King
What safetie may I looke for at his hands,	Edw	5.4.109	King
let him have the king,/What else?	Edw	5.5.25	Matrvs
I know what I must do, get you away,	Edw	5.5.27	Ltborn
What else, a table and a fetherbed.	Edw	5.5.33	Ltborn
Whose there, what light is that, wherefore comes thou?	Edw	5.5.42	Edward
And what eyes can refraine from shedding teares,	Edw	5.5.50	Ltborn
What meanes your highnesse to mistrust me thus?	Edw	5.5.79	Ltborn
What meanes thou to dissemble with me thus?	Edw	5.5.80	Edward
What if he have? the king is yet a childe.	Edw	5.6.17	Mortmr
Tis my hand, what gather you by this.	Edw	5.6.47	Mortmr
What murtherer? bring foorth the man I sent.	Edw	5.6.49	Mortmr
What, suffer you the traitor to delay?	Edw	5.6.67	King
What doctrine call you this? Che sera, sera:	F 74	1.1.46	Faust
What will be, shall be; Divinitie adeiw.	F 75	1.1.47	Faust
O what a world of profite and delight,	F 80	1.1.52	Faust
Shall I make spirits fetch me what I please?	F 106	1.1.78	Faust
Performe what desperate enterprise I will?	F 108	1.1.80	Faust
Then tell me Faustus what shall we three want?	F 175	1.1.147	Cornel
For e're I sleep, I'le try what I can do:	F 192	1.1.164	Faust
Yet let us see <trie> what we can do.	F 228	1.2.35	2Schol
Now Faustus what wouldst thou have me do?	F 263	1.3.35	Mephst

WHAT (cont.)

upon me whilst I live/To do what ever Faustus shall command:	F 265	1.3.37		Faust
Tell me, what is that Lucifer, thy Lord?	F 290	1.3.62		Faust
And what are you that live with Lucifer?	F 297	1.3.69		Faust
What, is great Mephostophilis so passionate/For being deprived	F 311	1.3.83		Faust
Now that I have obtain'd what I desir'd <desire>/I'le live in	F 340	1.3.112		Faust
What, in Verse?	F 356	1.4.14	P	Robin
What bootes it then to thinke on <of> God or Heaven?	F 391	2.1.3		Faust
what of these <them>?	F 405	2.1.17		Faust
shall stand by me,/What [god] <power> can hurt me <thee>?	F 414	2.1.26		Faust
Now tell me what saith <sayes> Lucifer thy Lord.	F 419	2.1.31		Faust
And tell me, what good will my soule do thy Lord?	F 428	2.1.40		Faust
What might the staying of my bloud portend?	F 453	2.1.65		Faust
What will nct I do to obtaine his soule?	F 462	2.1.74		Mephst
But what is this Inscription on mine Arme?	F 465	2.1.77		Faust
What meanes this shew? speake Mephostophilis.	F 472	2.1.84		Faust
And let thee see <shewe thee> what Magicke can performe.	F 474	2.1.86		Mephst
at all times, in what shape [or] <and> forme soever he please.	F 492	2.1.104	P	Faust
So, now Faustus aske me what thou wilt.	F 503	2.1.115		Mephst
I, and body too, but what of that:	F 521	2.1.133		Faust
What, sleeping, eating, walking and disputing?	F 528	2.1.140		Faust
What sight is this?	F 532	2.1.144		Faust
Ready to execute what thou commandst <desirst>.	F 549	2.1.161		Mephst
O what art thou that look'st so [terrible] <terribly>.	F 638	2.2.87		Faust
That shall I soone: What art thou the first?	F 663	2.2.112		Faust
<indeede I doe, what doe I not>?	F 668	(HC263) A	P	Pride
And then turning my selfe to a wrought Smocke do what I list.	F 668	2.2.117	P	Pride
But fye, what a smell <scent> is heere?	F 669	2.2.118	P	Pride
What art thou the second?	F 672	2.2.121	P	Faust
And what art thou the third?	F 678	2.2.127	P	Faust
But what art thou the fourth?	F 685	2.2.134		Faust
And what are thou the fift?	F 692	2.2.141		Faust
Choke thy selfe Glutton: What are thou the sixt?	F 704	2.2.153		Faust
And what are you Mistris Minkes, the seventh and last?	F 707	2.2.159		Faust
And thou shalt turne thy selfe into what shape thou wilt.	F 718	2.2.170		Lucifr
What Dick, looke to the horses there till I come againe.	F 722	2.3.1	P	Robin
What Robin, you must come away and walk the horses.	F 725	2.3.4	P	Dick
'Snayles, what hast thou got there, a book?	F 730	2.3.9	P	Dick
I'le tell thee what, an my Maister come here, I'le clap as	F 736	2.3.15	P	Robin
Do but speake what thou't have me to do, and I'le do't:	F 745	2.3.24	P	Robin
But tell me now, what resting place is this?	F 800	3.1.22		Faust
What Rome containes <containeth> for to delight thine eyes	F 810	3.1.32		Mephst
And what might please mine eye, I there beheld.	F 853	3.1.75		Faust
And then devise what best contents thy minde,	F 858	3.1.80		Mephst
What by the holy Councell held at Trent,	F 884	3.1.106		Pope
Resigne, or seale, or what so pleaseth us.	F 936	3.1.158		Pope
What have our holy Councell there decreed,	F 947	3.1.169		Pope
<to do what I please unseene of any whilst I stay in Rome>.	F 993	(HC266) A	P	Faust
And doe what ere I please, unseene of any.	F 993	3.2.13		Faust
Do what thou wilt, thou shalt not be discern'd.	F1005	3.2.25		Mephst
What needs this question?	F1016	3.2.36		Pope
What Lollards do attend our Hollinesse,	F1049	3.2.69		Pope
Now Faustus, what will you do now?	F1071	3.2.91	P	Mephst
take heed what you say, we looke not like cup-stealers I can	F1099	3.3.12	P	Robin
[And in their conference of what befell],	F1144	3.3.57A		3Chor
[What there he did in triall of his art],	F1153	3.3.66A		3Chor
What ho, Officers, Gentlemen,	F1155	4.1.1		Mrtino
What hoe, Benvolio.	F1178	4.1.24		Mrtino
What a devill ayle you two?	F1179	4.1.25	P	Benvol
To accomplish what soever the Doctor please.	F1183	4.1.29		Mrtino
What of this?	F1184	4.1.30	P	Benvol
who comes to see/What wonders by blacke spels may compast be.	F1198	4.1.44		Mrtino
what strange beast is yon, that thrusts his head out at [the]	F1274	4.1.120	P	Faust
What, is he asleepe, or dead?	F1279	4.1.125		Saxony
What ho, Benvolio.	F1282	4.1.128		Emper
Why how now sir Knight, what, hang'd by the hornes?	F1290	4.1.136	P	Faust
Nay, we will stay with thee, betide what may,	F1338	4.2.14		Fredrk
What use shall we put his beard to?	F1383	4.2.59	P	Mrtino
What shall [his] eyes doe?	F1386	4.2.62	P	Fredrk
and now sirs, having divided him, what shall the body doe?	F1390	4.2.66	P	Mrtino
What ho, Benvolio.	F1431	4.3.1		Mrtino
Here, what Frederick, ho.	F1431	4.3.1		Benvol
What devill attends this damn'd Magician,	F1445	4.3.15		Benvol
What may we do, that we may hide our shames?	F1447	4.3.17		Fredrk
What shall we then do deere Benvolio?	F1451	4.3.21		Mrtino
bid the Hostler deliver him unto you, and remember what I say.	F1475	4.4.19	P	Faust
What art thou Faustus but a man condemn'd to die?	F1478	4.4.22		Faust
O what a cosening Doctor was this?	F1484	4.4.28	P	HrsCsr
Alas I am undone, what shall I do?	F1492	4.4.36	P	HrsCsr
How now Wagner what newes with thee?	F1499	4.4.43	P	Faust
I'le bring you to the best beere in Europe, what ho, Hostis;	F1506	4.5.2	P	Carter
How now, what lacke you?	F1507	4.5.3	P	Hostss
What my old Guesse?	F1507	4.5.3	P	Hostss
what my old Guest?	F1513	4.5.9	P	Hostss
Come sirs, what shall we do now till mine Hostesse comes?	F1520	4.5.16	P	Dick
me what he should give me for as much Hay as he could eate;	F1527	4.5.23	P	Carter
what did I but rid him into a great river, and when I came just	F1543	4.5.39	P	HrsCsr
I pray you tell me, what is the thing you most desire to have?	F1567	4.6.10	P	Faust
kind I will make knowne unto you what my heart desires to have,	F1571	4.6.14	P	Lady
What rude disturbers have we at the gate?	F1588	4.6.31		Duke
And then demand of them, what they would have.	F1590	4.6.33		Duke
Why how now Maisters, what a coyle is there?	F1591	4.6.34		Servnt
What is the reason you disturbe the Duke?	F1592	4.6.35		Servnt

WHAT (cont.)

What would they have?	F1599	4.6.42		Duke
be wellcome for our mony, and we will pay for what we take:	F1612	4.6.55	P	Robin
What ho, give's halfe a dosen of Beere here, and be hang'd.	F1612	4.6.55	P	Robin
I but sir sauce box, know you in what place?	F1616	4.6.59		Servnt
My woodden leg? what dost thou meane by that?	F1628	4.6.71		Faust
I wonder what he meanes, if death were nie, he would not	F1677	5.1.4	P	Wagner
Where art thou Faustus? wretch, what hast thou done?	F1724	5.1.51		Faust
Accursed Faustus, <wretch what hast thou done>?	F1739	(HC270)B		Faust
What shall I doe to shun the snares of death?	F1742	5.1.69		Faust
But what I may afflict his body with,	F1757	5.1.84		Mephst
This, or what else my Faustus shall <thou shalt> desire,	F1766	5.1.93		Mephst
What ailes Faustus?	F1823	5.2.27		2Schol
<what meanes Faustus>?	F1827	(HC270)A	P	2Schol
O my deere Faustus what imports this feare?	F1827	5.2.31		1Schol
and what wonders I have done, all Germany can witnesse, yea all	F1842	5.2.46	P	Faust
friends, what shall become of Faustus being in hell for ever?	F1846	5.2.50	P	Faust
O what may <shal> we do to save Faustus?	F1868	5.2.72	P	2Schol
and what noyse soever you <yee> heare, come not unto me, for	F1873	5.2.77	P	Faust
What, weep'st thou?	F1890	5.2.94		Mephst
O what will all thy riches, pleasures, pompes,	F1896	5.2.100		GdAngl
In what resplendant glory thou hadst set/In yonder throne, like	F1904	5.2.108		GdAngl
Gridyrons, what be they?	F App	p.230 31	P	Clown
have as many english counters, and what should I do with these?	F App	p.230 34	P	Clown
divels, say I should kill one of them, what would folkes say?	F App	p.230 47	P	Clown
what, are they gone?	F App	p.230 51	P	Clown
What againe?	F App	p.231 12	P	Pope
What, are you crossing of your selfe?	F App	p.232 18		Faust
Come on Mephastophilis, what shall we do?	F App	p.232 22	P	Faust
what doest thou with that same booke thou canst not reade?	F App	p.233 13	P	Rafe
Why Robin what booke is that?	F App	p.233 18	P	Rafe
What booke?	F App	p.233 19	P	Robin
what meane you sirra?	F App	p.235 21	P	Vintnr
Ile tel you what I meane.	F App	p.235 22	P	Robin
O nomine Domine, what meanst thou Robin?	F App	p.235 26	P	Vintnr
Misericordia pro nobis, what shal I doe?	F App	p.235 30	P	Robin
by whome thou canst accomplish what thou list, this therefore	F App	p.236 5	P	Emper
be witnesses to confirme what mine eares have heard reported,	F App	p.236 7	P	Emper
that what ever thou doest, thou shalt be no wayes prejudiced or	F App	p.236 9	P	Emper
Faustus, marke what I shall say, As I was sometime solitary set,	F App	p.236 17	P	Emper
Vilaine I say, undo what thou hast done.	F App	p.238 75		Knight
what, wil you goe on horse backe, or on foote?	F App	p.239 95	P	Mephst
What horse-courser, you are wel met.	F App	p.239 100	P	Faust
at ease, if I bring his water to you, youle tel me what it is?	F App	p.240 119	P	HrsCsr
what, doost thinke I am a horse-doctor?	F App	p.240 120	P	Faust
what art thou Faustus but a man condemnd to die?	F App	p.240 121	P	Faust
why sir, what would you?	F App	p.240 139	P	Mephst
Alas, I am undone, what shall I do:	F App	p.241 154	P	HrsCsr
What is he gone?	F App	p.241 164	P	Faust
women do long for some dainties or other, what is it Madame?	F App	p.242 5	P	Faust
what madnes, what huge lust of warre/Hath made Barbarians	Lucan, First Booke	8		
what huge lust of warre/Hath made Barbarians drunke with Latin	Lucan, First Booke	8		
Ay me, O what a world of land and sea,	Lucan, First Booke	13		
What God it please thee be, or where to sway:	Lucan, First Booke	52		
And what made madding people shake off peace.	Lucan, First Booke	69		
Destroying what withstood his proud desires,	Lucan, First Booke	150		
And staring, thus bespoke: what mean'st thou Caesar?	Lucan, First Booke	192		
What should I talke of mens corne reapt by force,	Lucan, First Booke	318		
What end of mischiefe?	Lucan, First Booke	334		
What, now Scicillian Pirats are suppresт,	Lucan, First Booke	336		
What seates for their deserts?	Lucan, First Booke	344		
what store of ground/For servitors to till?	Lucan, First Booke	344		
what Colonies/To rest their bones?	Lucan, First Booke	345		
What doubtst thou us?	Lucan, First Booke	363		
What wals thou wilt be leaveld with the ground,	Lucan, First Booke	384		
cause, what ere thou be whom God assignes/This great effect,	Lucan, First Booke	419		
And without ground, fear'd, what themselves had faind:	Lucan, First Booke	482		
heard to sound; and with what noise/An armed battaile joines,	Lucan, First Booke	577		
Looke what the lightning blasted, Aruns takes/And it inters	Lucan, First Booke	605		
By these he seeing what myschiefes must ensue,	Lucan, First Booke	629		
I tremble to unfould/What you intend, great Jove is now	Lucan, First Booke	631		
what mischiefe shall insue?	Lucan, First Booke	644		
O Gods what death prepare ye?	Lucan, First Booke	648		
with what plague/Meane ye to radge?	Lucan, First Booke	648		
under Hemus mount/Philippi plaines; Phoebus what radge is this?	Lucan, First Booke	680		
[What] <That> if thy Mother take Dianas bowe,	Ovid's Elegies	1.1.11		
What makes my bed seem hard seeing it is soft?	Ovid's Elegies	1.2.1		
What needes thou warre, I sue to thee for grace,	Ovid's Elegies	1.2.21		
though I not see/What may be done, yet there before him bee.	Ovid's Elegies	1.4.14		
What wine he fills thee, wisely will him drinke,	Ovid's Elegies	1.4.29		
Aske thou the boy, what thou enough doest thinke.	Ovid's Elegies	1.4.30		
If hee gives thee what first himselfe did tast,	Ovid's Elegies	1.4.33		
There touch what ever thou canst touch of mee.	Ovid's Elegies	1.4.58		
Aye me I warne what profits some few howers,	Ovid's Elegies	1.4.59		
What armes and shoulders did I touch and see,	Ovid's Elegies	1.5.19		
How large a legge, and what a lustie thigh?	Ovid's Elegies	1.5.22		
But what entreates for thee some-times tooke place,	Ovid's Elegies	1.6.21		
What ere thou art, farewell, be like me paind,	Ovid's Elegies	1.6.71		
wheeles spun/And what with Mares ranck humour may be done.	Ovid's Elegies	1.8.8		
Behold what gives the Poet but new verses?	Ovid's Elegies	1.8.57		
What he will give, with greater instance crave.	Ovid's Elegies	1.8.68		
And Isis now will shew what scuse to make.	Ovid's Elegies	1.8.74		
thou must hire/To teach thy lover, what thy thoughts desire.	Ovid's Elegies	1.8.88		

WHAT (cont.)

Let them aske some-what, many asking little,	Ovid's Elegies	1.8.89
Pray him to lend what thou maist nere restore.	Ovid's Elegies	1.8.102
What age fits Mars, with Venus doth agree,	Ovid's Elegies	1.9.3
What yeares in souldiours Captaines do require,	Ovid's Elegies	1.9.5
Bull and Eagle/And what ere love made Jove should thee invegle.	Ovid's Elegies	1.10.8
And doth constraind, what you do of good will.	Ovid's Elegies	1.10.24
Farmes out her-self on nights for what she can.	Ovid's Elegies	1.10.30
And lets what both delight, what both desire,	Ovid's Elegies	1.10.31
All for their Mistrisse, what they have, prepare.	Ovid's Elegies	1.10.58
Leave asking, and Ile give what I refraine.	Ovid's Elegies	1.10.64
If, what I do, she askes, say hope for night,	Ovid's Elegies	1.11.13
What neede she [tyre] <try> her hand to hold the quill,	Ovid's Elegies	1.11.23
dore more wisely/And som-what higher beare thy foote precisely.	Ovid's Elegies	1.12.6
But what had beene more faire had they beene kept?	Ovid's Elegies	1.14.3
What age of Varroes name shall not be tolde,	Ovid's Elegies	1.15.21
And long admiring say by what meanes learnd/Hath this same Poet	Ovid's Elegies	2.1.9
What helpes it me of fierce Achill to sing?	Ovid's Elegies	2.1.29
What good to me wil either Ajax bring?	Ovid's Elegies	2.1.30
what needes defence/When [un-protected] <un-protested> ther is	Ovid's Elegies	2.2.11
Enquire not what with Isis may be done/Nor feare least she to	Ovid's Elegies	2.2.25
And what lesse labour then to hold thy peace?	Ovid's Elegies	2.2.28
And what she likes, let both hold ratifide.	Ovid's Elegies	2.2.32
Object thou then what she may well excuse,	Ovid's Elegies	2.2.37
What can be easier then the thing we pray?	Ovid's Elegies	2.2.66
If she discardes thee, what use servest thou for?	Ovid's Elegies	2.3.12
What two determine never wants effect.	Ovid's Elegies	2.3.16
Trips she, it likes me well, plods she, what than?	Ovid's Elegies	2.4.23
[I thinke what one undeckt would be, being drest];	Ovid's Elegies	2.4.37
Nay what is she that any Romane loves,	Ovid's Elegies	2.4.47
I knew your speech (what do not lovers see)?	Ovid's Elegies	2.5.19
What doest, I cryed, transportst thou my delight?	Ovid's Elegies	2.5.29
This, and what grife inforc'd me say I say'd,	Ovid's Elegies	2.5.33
What Pylades did to Orestes prove,	Ovid's Elegies	2.6.15
But what availde this faith? her rarest hue?	Ovid's Elegies	2.6.17
What helpes it thou wert given to please my wench,	Ovid's Elegies	2.6.19
My wenches vowes for thee what should I show,	Ovid's Elegies	2.6.43
Turnes all the goodly <godly> birdes to what she please.	Ovid's Elegies	2.6.58
What if a man with bond-women offend,	Ovid's Elegies	2.8.9
What graced Kings, in me no shame I deeme.	Ovid's Elegies	2.8.14
How oft, and by what meanes we did agree.	Ovid's Elegies	2.8.28
Foole, what is sleepe but image of cold death,	Ovid's Elegies	2.9.41
what [rockes] <rocke> the feard Cerannia <Ceraunia> threat,	Ovid's Elegies	2.11.19
In what gulfe either Syrtes have their seate.	Ovid's Elegies	2.11.20
Let others tell this, and what each one speakes/Beleeve, no	Ovid's Elegies	2.11.21
me, or I am sure/I oft have done, what might as much procure.	Ovid's Elegies	2.13.6
What helpes it Woman to be free from warre?	Ovid's Elegies	2.14.1
What Tereus, what Jason you provokes,	Ovid's Elegies	2.14.33
My heate is heere, what moves my heate is gone.	Ovid's Elegies	2.16.12
What would not she give that faire name to winne?	Ovid's Elegies	2.17.30
What lawfull is, or we professe Loves art,	Ovid's Elegies	2.18.19
my selfe to smart)/We write, or what Penelope sends Ulysses,	Ovid's Elegies	2.18.21
What thanklesse Jason, Macareus, and Paris,	Ovid's Elegies	2.18.23
And what poore Dido with her drawne sword sharpe,	Ovid's Elegies	2.18.25
What should I do with fortune that nere failes me?	Ovid's Elegies	2.19.7
And craftily knowes by what meanes to winne me.	Ovid's Elegies	2.19.10
To please me, what faire termes and sweet words ha's shee,	Ovid's Elegies	2.19.17
Great gods what kisses, and how many gave she?	Ovid's Elegies	2.19.18
What ever haps, by suffrance harme is done,	Ovid's Elegies	2.19.35
What flies, I followe, what followes me I shunne.	Ovid's Elegies	2.19.36
Thou suffrest what no husband can endure,	Ovid's Elegies	2.19.51
To finde, what worke my muse might move, I strove.	Ovid's Elegies	3.1.6
Thy muse hath played what may milde girles content,	Ovid's Elegies	3.1.27
What gate thy stately words cannot unlocke,	Ovid's Elegies	3.1.45
What gift with me was on her birth day sent,	Ovid's Elegies	3.1.57
let either heed/What please them, and their eyes let either	Ovid's Elegies	3.2.6
What horse-driver thou favourst most is best,	Ovid's Elegies	3.2.7
Ere these were seene, I burnt: what will these do?	Ovid's Elegies	3.2.33
What Venus promisd, promise thou we pray,	Ovid's Elegies	3.2.59
What doest? thy wagon in lesse compasse bring.	Ovid's Elegies	3.2.70
What doest, unhappy?	Ovid's Elegies	3.2.71
What, are there Gods?	Ovid's Elegies	3.3.1
How to attaine, what is denyed, we thinke,	Ovid's Elegies	3.4.17
Few love, what others have unguarded left.	Ovid's Elegies	3.4.26
I know not, what men thinke should thee so move.	Ovid's Elegies	3.4.28
Honour what friends thy wife gives, sheele give many:	Ovid's Elegies	3.4.45
What helpes my hast: what to have tane small rest?	Ovid's Elegies	3.5.9
What day and night to travaile in her quest?	Ovid's Elegies	3.5.10
Nere was, nor shall be, what my verse mentions.	Ovid's Elegies	3.5.18
What? not Alpheus in strange lands to runne,	Ovid's Elegies	3.5.29
What should I name Aesope, that Thebe lov'd,	Ovid's Elegies	3.5.33
And kindly gave her, what she liked best.	Ovid's Elegies	3.5.82
What thirstie traveller ever drunke of thee?	Ovid's Elegies	3.5.97
I know not what expecting, I ere while/Nam'd Achelaus, Inachus,	Ovid's Elegies	3.5.103
What will my age do, age I cannot shunne,	Ovid's Elegies	3.6.17
What, wast my limbs through some Thesalian charms,	Ovid's Elegies	3.6.27
What might I crave more if I aske againe?	Ovid's Elegies	3.6.44
What sweete thought is there but I had the same?	Ovid's Elegies	3.6.63
What man will now take liberall arts in hand,	Ovid's Elegies	3.7.1
What ere he hath his body gaind in warres.	Ovid's Elegies	3.7.20
Not what we slouthfull [knowe] <knewe>, let wise men learne,	Ovid's Elegies	3.7.25
What doest with seas?	Ovid's Elegies	3.7.49
To Thracian Orpheus what did parents good?	Ovid's Elegies	3.8.21

WHAT (cont.)
What profit to us hath our pure life bred? . . . Ovid's Elegies 3.8.33
What to have laine alone in empty bed? . . . . Ovid's Elegies 3.8.34
Scarse rests of all what a small urne conteines. . . Ovid's Elegies 3.8.40
Ceres what sports to thee so grievous were, . . . Ovid's Elegies 3.9.43
And what I have borne, shame to beare againe. . . Ovid's Elegies 3.10.4
What should I tell her vaine tongues filthy lyes, . . Ovid's Elegies 3.10.21
What secret becks in banquets with her youths, . . . Ovid's Elegies 3.10.23
These hardned me, with what I keepe obscure, . . . Ovid's Elegies 3.10.27
Bulles hate the yoake, yet what they hate have still. . Ovid's Elegies 3.10.36
What ere thou art mine art thou: . . . . . . Ovid's Elegies 3.10.49
What day was that, which all sad haps to bring, . . Ovid's Elegies 3.11.1
Proteus what should I name? teeth, Thebes first seed? . Ovid's Elegies 3.11.35
What madnesse ist to tell night <nights> prankes by day, . Ovid's Elegies 3.13.7
And I shall thinke you chaste, do what you can. . . Ovid's Elegies 3.13.14
Graunt this, that what you do I may not see, . . . Ovid's Elegies 3.13.35
My soule fleetes when I thinke what you have done, . . Ovid's Elegies 3.13.37
What we behold is censur'd by our eies. . . . . Hero and Leander 1.174
What difference betwixt the richest mine/And basest mold, but Hero and Leander 1.232
What vertue is it that is borne with us? . . . . Hero and Leander 1.278
He readie to accomplish what she wil'd, ... Hero and Leander 1.433
Which being knowne (as what is hid from Jove)? . . . Hero and Leander 1.436
They granted what he crav'd, and once againe, . . . Hero and Leander 1.455
He being a novice, knew not what she meant, . . . Hero and Leander 2.13
And what he did, she willingly requited. . . . . Hero and Leander 2.28
O what god would not therewith be appeas'd? . . . Hero and Leander 2.50
But what the secret trustie night conceal'd, . . . Hero and Leander 2.103
What is it now, but mad Leander dares? . . . . Hero and Leander 2.146
WHAT ERE
Fortune hath favord thee what ere thou be, . . . Dido 1.1.231 Venus
And doe what ere I please, unseene of any. . . . F 993 3.2.13 Faust
cause, what ere thou be whom God assignes/This great effect, Lucan, First Booke 419
What ere thou art, farewell, be like me paind, . . . Ovid's Elegies 1.6.71
Bull and Eagle/And what ere love made Jove should thee invegle. Ovid's Elegies 1.10.8
What ere he hath his body gaind in warres. . . . Ovid's Elegies 3.7.20
What ere thou art mine art thou: . . . . . . Ovid's Elegies 3.10.49
WHAT E'RE
what e're it be to injure them/That have so manifestly wronged Jew 1.2.274 Abigal
What e're I am, yet Governor heare me speake; . . . Jew 5.1.9 Curtzn
WHAT EVER
And fellowes to, what ever stormes arise. . . . . P 615 12.28 King
upon me whilst I live/To do what ever Faustus shall command: F 265 1.3.37 Faust
that what ever thou doest, thou shalt be no wayes prejudiced or F App p.236 9 P Emper
There touch what ever thou canst touch of mee. . . . Ovid's Elegies 1.4.58
What ever haps, by suffrance harme is done, . . . Ovid's Elegies 2.19.35
WHAT'S
How now, what's the matter? . . . . 1Tamb 1.2.110 Tamb
Thats wel Techelles, what's the newes? . . . . . 1Tamb 5.1.198 Tamb
What's Cyprus, Candy, and those other Iles/To us, or Malta? Jew 1.2.5 Govnr
And what's our aid against so great a Prince? . . . Jew 1.2.51 Barab
How, a Christian? Hum, what's here to doe? . . . Jew 1.2.75 Barab
And what's the price? . . . . Jew 2.3.64 Lodowk
What's that to thee? . . . . Jew 2.3.357 Barab
I wonder what's become of Faustus that/Was wont to make our F 194 1.2.1 1Schol
What's here? an ambush to betray my life: . . . . F1424 4.2.100 Faust
What's that? . . . . F1644 4.6.87 P Faust
How now Wagner, what's the newes with thee? . . . F App p.241 167 P Faust
What's kept, we covet more: the care makes theft: . . Ovid's Elegies 3.4.25
Nemesis answeares, what's my losse to thee? . . . Ovid's Elegies 3.8.57
WHATS
marketplace; whats the price of this slave, two hundred Crowns? Jew 2.3.97 P Barab
But tell me Mortimer, whats thy devise, ... Edw 2.2.11 Edward
But whats the reason you should leave him now? . . . Edw 2.3.13 Penbrk
their sides/With their owne weapons gorde, but whats the helpe? Edw 4.4.8 Queene
Whats that? . . . . Edw 5.4.38 Mortmr
Whats heere? I know not how to conster it. . . . Edw 5.5.15 Gurney
Still feare I, and I know not whats the cause, . . . Edw 5.5.85 Edward
WHAT SO ERE
But foorth ye vassals, what so ere it be, ... 2Tamb 5.1.221 Tamb
WHATSOERE
To compasse whatsoere your grace commands. . . . F1226 4.1.72 Faust
WHAT SOEVER
To accomplish what soever the Doctor please. . . . F1183 4.1.29 Mrtino
WHATSOEVER
Lords of this towne, or whatsoever stile/Belongs unto your name, Dido 2.1.39 Aeneas
And Maddam, whatsoever you esteeme/Of this successe, and losse 1Tamb 1.2.44 Tamb
Whatsoever any whisper in mine eares, ... P 974 19.44 King
And whatsoever else is requisite, ... F 183 1.1.155 Valdes
To give me whatsoever I shall aske; . . . . . . F 322 1.3.94 Faust
To tell me whatsoever I demand: . . . . F 323 1.3.95 Faust
Mephostophilis shall doe for him, and bring him whatsoever. F 489 2.1.101 P Faust
I am content to do whatsoever your majesty shall command me. F App p.236 15 P Faust
WHATT
enter by defaulte | whatt thoughe you were once in possession Paris ms11,p390 P Souldr
WHEAT
Cellers of Wine, and Sollers full of Wheat, . . . Jew 4.1.63 Barab
WHEEL
And with my hand turne Fortunes wheel about, . . . 1Tamb 1.2.175 Tamb
WHEELE
That she shall stay and turne her wheele no more, . . 1Tamb 5.1.374 Anippe
Will hew us peecemeale, put us to the wheele, . . . 2Tamb 3.4.21 Olymp
while all thy joints/Be rackt and beat asunder with the wheele, 2Tamb 3.5.125 Tamb
Who now makes Fortunes wheele turne as he please, . . Edw 5.2.53 Mortmr

WHEELE (cont.)
now I see, that in thy wheele/There is a point, to which when   Edw   5.6.59   Mortmr
WHEELES
Made Hebe to direct her ayrie wheeles/Into the windie countrie   Dido   1.1.56   Venus
Whose chariot wheeles have burst th'Assirians bones,   2Tamb   5.1.71   Tamb
And he shall follow my proud Chariots wheeles.   P 984   19.54   Guise
with thrids on wrong wheeles spun/And what with Mares ranck   Ovid's Elegies   1.8.7
Be broake with wheeles of chariots passing by.   Ovid's Elegies   1.12.14
With wheeles bent inward now the ring-turne ride.   Ovid's Elegies   3.2.12
WHEELS
The pavement underneath thy chariot wheels/With Turky Carpets   2Tamb   1.2.42   Callap
WHELM'D
And whelm'd the world in darknesse, making men/Dispaire of day;   Lucan, First Booke   540
WHELPES
Nor dares the Lyonesse her young whelpes kill.   Ovid's Elegies   2.14.36
WHEN
To day when as I fild into your cups,   Dido   1.1.5   Ganimd
When as they would have hal'd thee from my sight: Dido   1.1.27   Jupitr
And my nine Daughters sing when thou art sad,   Dido   1.1.33   Jupitr
When as the waves doe threat our Chrystall world,   Dido   1.1.75   Venus
When yet both sea and sands beset their ships,   Dido   1.1.110   Venus
When suddenly gloomie Orion rose,   Dido   1.2.26   Cloan
And when I know it is not, then I dye.   Dido   2.1.9   Aeneas
And when my grieved heart sighes and sayes no,   Dido   2.1.26   Aeneas
And when we told her she would weepe for griefe,   Dido   2.1.67   Illion
Where when they came, Ulysses on the sand/Assayd with honey   Dido   2.1.136   Aeneas
When thou Achates with thy sword mad'st way,   Dido   2.1.268   Aeneas
And when she strokes thee softly on the head,   Dido   3.1.5   Cupid
How lovely is Ascanius when he smiles?   Dido   3.1.29   Dido
You shall not hurt my father when he comes.   Dido   3.1.80   Cupid
I this in Greece when Paris stole faire Helen.   Dido   3.1.142   Aeneas
When for the hate of Troian Ganimed,   Dido   3.2.42   Juno
When in the midst of all their gamesome sports,   Dido   3.2.89   Juno
When first you set your foote upon the shoare,   Dido   3.3.53   Achat
When as he buts his beames on Floras bed,   Dido   3.4.20   Dido
That can call them forth when as she please,   Dido   4.1.4   Iarbus
When as she meanes to maske the world with clowdes.   Dido   4.1.6   Iarbus
When ayrie creatures warre amongst themselves: Dido   4.2.7   Iarbus
When sleepe but newly had imbrast the night,   Dido   4.3.17   Aeneas
Which Circes sent Sicheus when he lived: Dido   4.4.11   Dido
But when you were abourd twas calme enough,   Dido   4.4.27   Dido
And when we whisper, then the starres fall downe,   Dido   4.4.53   Dido
When I leave thee, death be my punishment,   Dido   4.4.56   Aeneas
Youle be a twigger when you come to age.   Dido   4.5.20   Nurse
When as I want both rigging for my fleete,   Dido   5.1.69   Aeneas
swift Mercury/When I was laying a platforme for these walles,   Dido   5.1.94   Aeneas
been/When Didos beautie [chaind] <chaungd> thine eyes to her: Dido   5.1.114   Dido
Am I lesse faire then when thou sawest me first?   Dido   5.1.115   Dido
Which when I viewd, I cride, Aeneas stay,   Dido   5.1.232   Anna
How can ye goe when he hath all your fleete?   Dido   5.1.242   Anna
When first he came on shoare, perish thou to: Dido   5.1.299   Dido
When other men prease forward for renowne: 1Tamb   1.1.84   Mycet
Even as when windy exhalations,   1Tamb   1.2.50   Tamb
As princely Lions when they rouse themselves,   1Tamb   1.2.52   Techel
Looke for orations when the foe is neere.   1Tamb   1.2.131   Techel
And looke we friendly on them when they come: 1Tamb   1.2.141   Tamb
admyre me not)/And when my name and honor shall be spread,   1Tamb   1.2.205   Tamb
When with their fearfull tongues they shall confesse/Theise are   1Tamb   1.2.222   Usumc
Then when our powers in points of swords are join'd,   1Tamb   2.1.40   Cosroe
And when the princely Persean Diadem,   1Tamb   2.1.45   Cosroe
When Tamburlain and brave Theridamas/Have met us by the river   1Tamb   2.1.62   Cosroe
And when their scattered armie is subdu'd,   1Tamb   2.2.68   Meandr
Drums, why sound ye not when Meander speaks.   1Tamb   2.2.75   Mycet
But when you see his actions [top] <stop> his speech,   1Tamb   2.3.26   Therid
When she that rules in Rhamnis golden gates,   1Tamb   2.3.37   Cosroe
from the camp/When Kings themselves are present in the field?   1Tamb   2.4.17   Tamb
So I can when I see my time.   1Tamb   2.4.26   Mycet
When looks breed love, with lookes to gaine the prize.   1Tamb   2.5.63   Therid
For as when Jove did thrust old Saturn down,   1Tamb   2.7.36   Usumc
when the Moon begins/To joine in one her semi-circled hornes: 1Tamb   3.1.11   Bajzth
When your offensive rape by Tamburlaine,   1Tamb   3.2.6   Agidas
Who when he shall embrace you in his armes,   1Tamb   3.2.42   Agidas
And when you looke for amorous discourse,   1Tamb   3.2.44   Agidas
Or when the morning holds him in her armes: 1Tamb   3.2.48   Zenoc
Or when Minerva did with Neptune strive.   1Tamb   3.2.52   Zenoc
As when the Sea-man sees the Hyades/Gather an armye of Cemerian   1Tamb   3.2.76   Agidas
For when they perish by our warlike hands,   1Tamb   3.3.24   Techel
And when they chance to breath and rest a space,   1Tamb   3.3.51   Tamb
Who, when they come unto their fathers age,   1Tamb   3.3.110   Bajzth
And when she sees our bloody Collours spread,   1Tamb   3.3.159   Tamb
When thy great Bassoe-maister and thy selfe,   1Tamb   3.3.173   Zenoc
When first he war'd against the Christians.   1Tamb   3.3.200   Zabina
As when my Emperour overthrew the Greeks: 1Tamb   3.3.204   Zabina
The first day when he pitcheth downe his tentes,   1Tamb   4.1.49   2Msngr
But when Aurora mounts the second time,   1Tamb   4.1.54   2Msngr
Even in Bythinia, when I took this Turke: 1Tamb   4.2.42   Tamb
As when a fiery exhalation/Wrapt in the bowels of a freezing   1Tamb   4.2.43   Tamb
Then when the Sky shal waxe as red as blood,   1Tamb   4.2.53   Tamb
And when they see me march in black aray.   1Tamb   4.2.119   Tamb
Than in the haven when the Pilot stands/And viewes a strangers   1Tamb   4.3.32   Souldn
Tis like he wil, when he cannot let it.   1Tamb   4.4.53   P Techel
Theridamas, when holy Fates/Shall stablish me in strong Egyptia,   1Tamb   4.4.134   Tamb
when first my milkwhite flags/Through which sweet mercie threw   1Tamb   5.1.68   Tamb

WHEN (cont.)

As now when furie and incensed hate/Flings slaughtering terrour	1Tamb	5.1.71		Tamb
Eies when that Ebena steps to heaven,	1Tamb	5.1.147		Tamb
When al their riders chardg'd their quivering speares/Began to	1Tamb	5.1.332		Zenoc
When my poore pleasures are devided thus,	1Tamb	5.1.386		Zenoc
When men presume to manage armes with him.	1Tamb	5.1.478		Tamb
As Juno, when the Giants were supprest,	1Tamb	5.1.510		Tamb
When he arrived last upon our stage,	2Tamb	Prol.2		Prolog
As when the massy substance of the earth,	2Tamb	1.1.89		Orcan
Whose glorious body when he left the world,	2Tamb	1.1.139		Orcan
I thank thee Sigismond, but when I war/All Asia Minor, Affrica,	2Tamb	1.1.157		Orcan
Which when I come aboord will hoist up saile,	2Tamb	1.2.24		Callap
And when thou goest, a golden Canapie/Enchac'd with pretious	2Tamb	1.2.48		Callap
When Phoebus leaping from his Hemi-Spheare,	2Tamb	1.2.51		Callap
When you will my Lord, I am ready.	2Tamb	1.2.76		Almeda
when wilt thou leave these armes/And save thy sacred person	2Tamb	1.3.9		Zenoc
When heaven shal cease to moove on both the poles/And when the	2Tamb	1.3.12		Tamb
And when the ground wheron my souldiers march/Shal rise aloft	2Tamb	1.3.13		Tamb
When these my sonnes, more precious in mine eies/Than all the	2Tamb	1.3.18		Tamb
But when they list, their conquering fathers hart:	2Tamb	1.3.36		Zenoc
Which when he tainted with his slender rod,	2Tamb	1.3.40		Zenoc
When I am old and cannot mannage armes,	2Tamb	1.3.59		Tamb
When we shall meet the Turkish Deputie/And all his Viceroies,	2Tamb	1.3.99		Tamb
drops that fall/When Boreas rents a thousand swelling cloudes,	2Tamb	1.3.160		Tamb
I, liquid golde when we have conquer'd him,	2Tamb	1.3.223		Tamb
That when this fraile and transitory flesh/Hath suckt the	2Tamb	2.4.43		Zenoc
the sun and Moone as darke/As when opposde in one Diamiter,	2Tamb	2.4.52		Tamb
as when Bajazeth/My royall Lord and father fild the throne,	2Tamb	3.1.11		Callap
And when I meet an armie in the field,	2Tamb	3.2.38		Tamb
When this is learn'd for service on the land,	2Tamb	3.2.83		Tamb
When this is done, then are ye souldiers,	2Tamb	3.2.91		Tamb
And when we enter in, not heaven it selfe/Shall ransome thee,	2Tamb	3.3.27		Therid
Who when he heares how resolute thou wert,	2Tamb	3.4.40		Techel
Harkening when he shall bid them plague the world.	2Tamb	3.4.60		Therid
Than when she gave eternall Chaos forme,	2Tamb	3.4.76		Techel
Nay, when the battaile ends, al we wil meet,	2Tamb	3.5.97		Callap
And when ye stay, be lasht with whips of wier:	2Tamb	3.5.105		Tamb
that when I take him, I may knocke out his braines with them,	2Tamb	3.5.140	P	Tamb
in the stable, when you shall come sweating from my chariot.	2Tamb	3.5.142	P	Tamb
when we are fighting, least hee hide his crowne as the foolish	2Tamb	3.5.154	P	Tamb
I smile to think, how when this field is fought,	2Tamb	3.5.165		Techel
when our enemies drums/And ratling cannons thunder in our eares	2Tamb	4.1.12		Amyras
When he himselfe amidst the thickest troopes/Beats downe our	2Tamb	4.1.25		Amyras
Nor care for blood when wine wil quench my thirst.	2Tamb	4.1.30		Calyph
When made a victor in these hautie arms,	2Tamb	4.1.46		Amyras
Turkes Concubines first, when my father hath conquered them.	2Tamb	4.1.65	P	Calyph
As when an heard of lusty Cymbrian Buls,	2Tamb	4.1.187		Tamb
But when I saw the place obscure and darke,	2Tamb	4.2.15		Therid
Which when you stab, looke on your weapons point,	2Tamb	4.2.69		Olymp
And tremble when ye heare this Scourge wil come,	2Tamb	4.3.99		Tamb
When all the Gods stand gazing at his pomp:	2Tamb	4.3.129		Tamb
When this our famous lake of Limnasphaltis/Makes walles a fresh	2Tamb	5.1.17		Govnr
When we are thus defenc'd against our Foe,	2Tamb	5.1.22		Govnr
Which when the citie was besieg'd I hid,	2Tamb	5.1.117		Govnr
When this is done, we'll martch from Babylon,	2Tamb	5.1.127		Tamb
As when they swallow Assafitida,	2Tamb	5.1.208		Techel
When I record my Parents slavish life,	2Tamb	5.2.19		Callap
Yet when the pride of Cynthia is at full,	2Tamb	5.2.46		Callap
And when I look away, comes stealing on:	2Tamb	5.3.71		Tamb
And when my soule hath vertue of your sight,	2Tamb	5.3.225		Tamb
When wandring Phoebes Ivory cheeks were scortcht/And all the	2Tamb	5.3.232		Tamb
And when they cast me off,/Are poyson'd by my climing	Jew	Prol.12		Machvl
sure/When like the [Dracos] <Drancus> they were writ in blood.	Jew	Prol.21		Machvl
And when I dye, here shall my spirit walke.	Jew	2.1.30		Barab
yet when we parted last,/He said he wud attend me in the morne.	Jew	2.1.33		Abigal
For when their hideous force inviron'd Rhodes,	Jew	2.2.48		Bosco
We Jewes can fawne like Spaniels when we please;	Jew	2.3.20		Barab
And when we grin we bite, yet are our lookes/As innocent and	Jew	2.3.21		Barab
Heave up my shoulders when they call me dogge,	Jew	2.3.24		Barab
That when the offering-Bason comes to me,	Jew	2.3.28		Barab
That when we speake with Gentiles like to you,	Jew	2.3.45		Barab
But when he touches it, it will be foild:	Jew	2.3.57		Barab
When you have brought her home, come to my house;	Jew	2.3.148		Barab
But to thy selfe smile when the Christians moane.	Jew	2.3.172		Barab
And when he comes, she lockes her selfe up fast;	Jew	2.3.262		Barab
looking out/When you should come and hale him from the doore.	Jew	2.3.265		Barab
Revenge it on him when you meet him next.	Jew	2.3.343		Barab
When, ducke you?	Jew	3.3.51	P	Ithimr
When saw'st thou Abigall?	Jew	3.4.18		Barab
All that I have is thine when I am dead,	Jew	3.4.44		Barab
when holy Friars turne devils and murder one another.	Jew	4.1.193	P	Ithimr
When shall you see a Jew commit the like?	Jew	4.1.197		Barab
and when the Hangman had put on his hempen Tippet, he made such	Jew	4.2.23	P	Ithimr
That when he speakes, drawes out his grisly beard,	Jew	4.3.7		Barab
Who when he speakes, grunts like a hog, and looks/Like one that	Jew	4.3.11		Barab
And when he comes: Oh that he were but here!	Jew	4.3.17		Barab
Pray when, Sir, shall I see you at my house?	Jew	4.3.56		Barab
So did you when you stole my gold.	Jew	4.4.50		Barab
You run swifter when you threw my gold out of my Window.	Jew	4.4.52	P	Barab
he weares, Judas left under the Elder when he hang'd himselfe.	Jew	4.4.66	P	Ithimr
When as thy life shall be at their command?	Jew	5.2.33		Barab
I will be there, and doe as thou desirest;/When is the time?	Jew	5.2.104		Govnr
For Callymath, when he hath view'd the Towne,	Jew	5.2.105		Barab

WHEN (cont.)

[Where] <When> Siracusian Dionisius reign'd,	Jew	5.3.10		Calym
Here, hold that knife, and when thou seest he comes,	Jew	5.5.37		Barab
To give thee knowledge when to cut the cord,	Jew	5.5.40		Barab
And when thou seest the Admirall ride by,	P 87	2.30		Guise
For this, I wake, when others think I sleepe,	P 105	2.48		Guise
Give me a look, that when I bend the browes,	P 157	2.100		Guise
Which when they heare, they shall begin to kill:	P 239	4.37		Guise
And when this just revenge is finished,	P 318	5.45		Anjoy
And when you see me in, then follow hard.	P 429	7.69		Anjoy
water the fish, and by the fish our selves when we eate them.	P 489	9.8	P	2Atndt
To such a one my Lord, as when she reads my lines,	P 672	13.16		Duchss
That change their coulour when the winter comes,	P 721	14.24		Navrre
When I shall vaunt as victor in revenge.	P 722	14.25		Navrre
What, will you not feare when you see him come?	P 933	19.3		Capt
But when will he come that we may murther him?	P 937	19.7	P	3Mur
And all his Minions stoup when I commaund:	P 979	19.49		Guise
When Duke Dumaine his brother is alive,	P1055	19.125		King
I cannot speak for greefe: when thou wast borne,	P1072	19.142		QnMoth
and when thow thinkst I have foregotten this	Paris	ms20,p391		Guise
And in the day when he shall walke abroad,	Edw	1.1.57		Gavstn
When violence is offered to the church.	Edw	1.2.41		ArchBp
And when I come, he frownes, as who should say,	Edw	1.2.53		Queene
Would when I left sweet France and was imbarkt,	Edw	1.4.171		Queene
Nay more, when he shall know it lies in us,	Edw	1.4.274		Mortmr
And when the commons and the nobles joyne,	Edw	1.4.287		Mortmr
And when this favour Isabell forgets,	Edw	1.4.297		Queene
When I was forst to leave my Gaveston.	Edw	1.4.318		Edward
Slay me my lord, when I offend your grace.	Edw	1.4.349		Warwck
When I forsake thee, death seaze on my heart,	Edw	2.1.64		Neece
A trifle, weele expell him when we please:	Edw	2.2.10		Edward
What will he do when as he shall be present?	Edw	2.2.48		Mortmr
When she was lockt up in a brasen tower,	Edw	2.2.54		Edward
Aye me poore soule when these begin to jarre.	Edw	2.2.72		Queene
When wert thou in the field with banner spred?	Edw	2.2.182		Mortmr
And when tis gone, our swordes shall purchase more.	Edw	2.2.197		Lncstr
When I thy brother am rejected thus.	Edw	2.2.218		Kent
Come lets away, and when the mariage ends,	Edw	2.2.264		Edward
That when I had him we might never part.	Edw	2.4.21		Queene
And all in vaine, for when I speake him faire,	Edw	2.4.28		Queene
When, can you tell?	Edw	2.5.60		Warwck
and when they flatly had denyed,/Refusing to receive me pledge	Edw	3.1.106		Arundl
When we had sent our messenger to request/He might be spared to	Edw	3.1.234		Edward
Unhappie Isabell, when Fraunce rejects,	Edw	4.2.11		Queene
When we may meet these traitors in the field.	Edw	4.3.47		Edward
When force to force is knit, and sword and gleave/In civill	Edw	4.4.5		Queene
Must! tis somwhat hard, when kings must go.	Edw	4.7.83		Edward
But when the imperiall Lions flesh is gorde,	Edw	5.1.11		Edward
But when I call to minde I am a king,	Edw	5.1.23		Edward
But what are kings, when regiment is gone,	Edw	5.1.26		Edward
the greater sway/When as a kings name shall be under writ.	Edw	5.2.14		Mortmr
And when tis done, we will subscribe our name.	Edw	5.2.50		Mortmr
When will the furie of his minde asswage?	Edw	5.3.8		Edward
When will his hart be satisfied with bloud?	Edw	5.3.9		Edward
When all my sences are anoyde with stenche?	Edw	5.3.18		Edward
Is sure to pay for it when his sonne is of age,	Edw	5.4.4		Mortmr
Shall he be murdered when the deed is done.	Edw	5.4.20		Mortmr
And when I frowne, make all the court looke pale,	Edw	5.4.53		Mortmr
I will requite it when I come to age.	Edw	5.4.100		King
And when the murders done,/See how he must be handled for his	Edw	5.5.22		Matrvs
I, I, so: when I call you, bring it in.	Edw	5.5.35		Ltborn
When for her sake I ran at tilt in Fraunce,	Edw	5.5.69		Edward
That <and> even then when I shall lose my life,	Edw	5.5.77		Edward
that in thy wheele/There is a point, to which when men aspire,	Edw	5.6.60		Mortmr
When as my sonne thinkes to abridge my daies.	Edw	5.6.84		Queene
When all is done, Divinitie is best:	F 64	1.1.36		Faust
as th'infernall spirits/On sweet Musaeus when he came to hell,	F 143	1.1.115		Faust
Like Lyons shall they guard us when we please,	F 151	1.1.123		Valdes
For when we heare one racke the name of God,	F 275	1.3.47		Mephst
When Mephostophilis shall stand by me,	F 413	2.1.25		Faust
But may I raise such <up> spirits when I please?	F 475	2.1.87		Faust
And to be short <conclude>, when all the world dissolves,	F 513	2.1.125		Mephst
and incantations, that I might raise up spirits when I please].	F 551.2	2.1.165A	P	Faust
When I behold the heavens then I repent/And curse thee wicked	F 552	2.2.1		Faust
out of a Lyons mouth when I was scarce <half> an houre old,	F 687	2.2.136	P	Wrath
my selfe when I could get none <had no body> to fight withall:	F 689	2.2.138	P	Wrath
when, can you tell?	F1112	3.3.25	P	Robin
[When Faustus had with pleasure tane the view]/[Of rarest	F1138	3.3.51A		3Chor
That when my Spirits present the royall shapes/Of Alexander and	F1249	4.1.95		Faust
When every servile groome jeasts at my wrongs,	F1329	4.2.5		Benvol
so when I had my horse, Doctor Fauster bad me ride him night	F1539	4.5.35	P	HrsCsr
and when I came just in the midst my horse vanisht away, and I	F1544	4.5.40	P	HrsCsr
when every Tree is barren of his fruite, from whence you had	F1579	4.6.22	P	Duke
so that when it is Winter with us, in the contrary circle it is	F1582	4.6.25	P	Faust
sir, did not I pull off one of your legs when you were asleepe?	F1656	4.6.99	P	HrsCsr
Then when sir Paris crost the seas with <for> her,	F1694	5.1.21		Faust
When he appear'd to haplesse Semele:	F1784	5.1.111		Faust
'Twas I, that when thou wer't i'the way to heaven,	F1886	5.2.90		Mephst
Damb'd up thy passage; when thou took'st the booke,	F1887	5.2.91		Mephst
That when you vomite forth into the aire,	F1954	5.2.158		Faust
All beasts are happy, for when they die,	F1969	5.2.173		Faust
As when I heare but motion made of him,	F App	p.237 27		Emper
a signe of grace in you, when you will confesse the trueth.	F App	p.237 45	P	Knight

WHEN (cont.)

No sir, but when Acteon died, he left the hornes for you:	F App	p.237 55 P Faust
that when it is heere winter with us, in the contrary circle it	F App	p.242 20 P Faust
So when this worlds compounded union breakes,	Lucan, First Booke	73
So when as Crassus wretched death who stayd them,	Lucan, First Booke	104
When all the woods about stand bolt up-right,	Lucan, First Booke	143
When yre, or hope provokt, heady, and bould,	Lucan, First Booke	147
And glad when bloud, and ruine made him way:	Lucan, First Booke	151
When fortune made us lords of all, wealth flowed,	Lucan, First Booke	161
shoot) marcht on/And then (when Lucifer did shine alone,	Lucan, First Booke	233
but as the fields/When birds are silent thorough winters rage;	Lucan, First Booke	261
Nor shalt thou triumph when thou comst to Roome;	Lucan, First Booke	287
how were we bestead/When comming conqueror, Roome afflicts me	Lucan, First Booke	310
Speake, when shall this thy long usurpt power end?	Lucan, First Booke	333
even nowe when youthfull bloud/Pricks forth our lively bodies,	Lucan, First Booke	363
As when against pine bearing Ossa's rocks,	Lucan, First Booke	390
Beates Thracian Boreas; or when trees [bowe] <bowde> down,/And	Lucan, First Booke	391
When Caesar saw his army proane to war,	Lucan, First Booke	393
Looke how when stormy Auster from the breach/Of Libian Syrtes	Lucan, First Booke	496
When Romans are besieg'd by forraine foes,	Lucan, First Booke	513
Wel might these feare, when Pompey fear'd and fled.	Lucan, First Booke	519
when by Junoes taske/He had before lookt Pluto in the face.	Lucan, First Booke	575
Shall Dian fanne when love begins to glowe?	Ovid's Elegies	1.1.12
When in this [workes] <worke> first verse I trod aloft,	Ovid's Elegies	1.1.21
Lie with him gently, when his limbes he spread/Upon the bed, but	Ovid's Elegies	1.4.15
When our lascivious toyes come in thy minde,	Ovid's Elegies	1.4.21
When I (my light) do or say ought that please thee,	Ovid's Elegies	1.4.25
When thou doest wish thy husband at the devill.	Ovid's Elegies	1.4.28
When thou hast tasted, I will take the cup,	Ovid's Elegies	1.4.31
When pleasure mov'd us to our sweetest worke.	Ovid's Elegies	1.4.48
When to go homewards we rise all along,	Ovid's Elegies	1.4.55
But we must part, when heav'n with black night lowers.	Ovid's Elegies	1.4.60
When thou stood'st naked ready to be beate,	Ovid's Elegies	1.6.19
Well I remember when I first did hire thee,	Ovid's Elegies	1.6.43
That when my mistresse there beholds thee cast,	Ovid's Elegies	1.6.69
when she bewayles/Her perjur'd Theseus flying vowes and sayles,	Ovid's Elegies	1.7.15
When she will, cloudes the darckned heav'n obscure,	Ovid's Elegies	1.8.9
When she will, day shines every where most pure.	Ovid's Elegies	1.8.10
When on thy lappe thine eyes thou dost deject,	Ovid's Elegies	1.8.37
Perhaps the Sabines rude, when Tatius raignde,	Ovid's Elegies	1.8.39
When causes fale thee to require a gift,	Ovid's Elegies	1.8.93
When thou hast so much as he gives no more,	Ovid's Elegies	1.8.101
On Priams loose-trest daughter when he gazed.	Ovid's Elegies	1.9.38
the drie fields strayed/When on her head a water pitcher laied.	Ovid's Elegies	1.10.6
when she departed/Nape by stumbling on the thre-shold started.	Ovid's Elegies	1.12.3
But when thou comest they of their courses faile.	Ovid's Elegies	1.13.12
When they were slender, and like downy mosse,	Ovid's Elegies	1.14.23
But I remember when it was my fame.	Ovid's Elegies	1.14.50
Therefore when flint and yron weare away,	Ovid's Elegies	1.15.31
But when I praise a pretty wenches face/Shee in requitall doth	Ovid's Elegies	2.1.33
defence/When [un-protected] <un-protested> ther is no expence?	Ovid's Elegies	2.2.12
Thinke when she reades, her mother letters sent her,	Ovid's Elegies	2.2.19
When most her husband bends the browes and frownes,	Ovid's Elegies	2.2.33
Me thinkes she should <would> be nimble when shees downe.	Ovid's Elegies	2.4.14
And when one sweetely sings, then straight I long,	Ovid's Elegies	2.4.25
[wretch] <wench> I sawe when thou didst thinke I slumbred,	Ovid's Elegies	2.5.13
Or when the Moone travailes with charmed steedes.	Ovid's Elegies	2.5.38
But when on thee her angry eyes did rush,	Ovid's Elegies	2.8.15
For when my loathing it of heate deprives me,	Ovid's Elegies	2.9.27
Long shalt thou rest when Fates expire thy breath.	Ovid's Elegies	2.9.42
But when I die, would I might droope with doing,	Ovid's Elegies	2.10.35
Too late you looke back, when with anchors weighd,	Ovid's Elegies	2.11.23
When Troy by ten yeares battle tumbled downe,	Ovid's Elegies	2.12.9
Weare me, when warmest showers thy members wash,	Ovid's Elegies	2.15.23
But when she comes, [you] <your> swelling mounts sinck downe,	Ovid's Elegies	2.16.51
While Juno Io keepes when hornes she wore,	Ovid's Elegies	2.19.29
And first [she] <he> sayd, when will thy love be spent,	Ovid's Elegies	3.1.15
When strong wilde beasts, she stronger hunts to strike them.	Ovid's Elegies	3.2.32
But when her lover came, had she drawne backe,	Ovid's Elegies	3.3.39
When he perceivd the reines let slacke, he stayde,	Ovid's Elegies	3.4.15
When thy waves brim did scarse my anckles touch.	Ovid's Elegies	3.5.6
When nimph-Neaera rapt thy lookes Scamander.	Ovid's Elegies	3.5.28
Seeing <When> in my prime my force is spent and done?	Ovid's Elegies	3.6.18
And fruit from trees, when ther's no wind at al.	Ovid's Elegies	3.6.34
Can deafe [eares] <yeares> take delight when Phemius sings,/Or	Ovid's Elegies	3.6.61
Now when he should not jette, he boults upright,	Ovid's Elegies	3.6.67
But when she saw it would by no meanes stand,	Ovid's Elegies	3.6.75
When our bookes did my mistris faire content,	Ovid's Elegies	3.7.5
But when in gifts the wise adulterer came,	Ovid's Elegies	3.7.33
Yet when old Saturne heavens rule possest,	Ovid's Elegies	3.7.35
As when the wilde boare Adons groine had rent.	Ovid's Elegies	3.8.16
When bad fates take good men, I am forbod,	Ovid's Elegies	3.8.35
When well-toss'd mattocks did the ground prepare,	Ovid's Elegies	3.9.31
Why am I sad, when Proserpine is found,	Ovid's Elegies	3.9.45
When I to watch supplyed a servants place.	Ovid's Elegies	3.10.12
I saw when forth a tyred lover went,	Ovid's Elegies	3.10.13
When have not I fixt to thy side close layed?	Ovid's Elegies	3.10.17
When Thebes, when Troy, when Caesar should be writ,	Ovid's Elegies	3.11.15
When fruite fild Tuscia should a wife give me,	Ovid's Elegies	3.12.1
Here when the Pipe with solemne tunes doth sound,	Ovid's Elegies	3.12.11
When the chiefe pompe comes, lowd the people hollow,	Ovid's Elegies	3.12.29
But that thou wouldst dissemble when tis paste.	Ovid's Elegies	3.13.4
Slippe still, onely denie it when tis done,	Ovid's Elegies	3.13.15

WHEN (cont.)			
When you are up and drest, be sage and grave,	Ovid's Elegies	3.13.19	
Practise a thousand sports when there you come,	Ovid's Elegies	3.13.24	
My soule fleetes when I thinke what you have done,	Ovid's Elegies	3.13.37	
And I see when you ope the two leavde booke:	Ovid's Elegies	3.13.44	
When carefull Rome in doubt their prowesse held.	Ovid's Elegies	3.14.10	
When t'was the odour which her breath foorth cast.	Hero and Leander	1.22	
(When yawning dragons draw her thirling carre,	Hero and Leander	1.108	
Even as, when gawdie Nymphs pursue the chace,	Hero and Leander	1.113	
When two are stript, long ere the course begin,	Hero and Leander	1.169	
When misers keepe it; being put to lone,	Hero and Leander	1.235	
When you fleet hence, can be bequeath'd to none.	Hero and Leander	1.248	
When Venus sweet rites are perform'd and done.	Hero and Leander	1.320	
Women are woon when they begin to jarre.	Hero and Leander	1.332	
When like desires and affections meet,	Hero and Leander	2.30	
Yet when a token of great worth we send,	Hero and Leander	2.80	
When first religious chastitie she vow'd:	Hero and Leander	2.110	
Home when he came, he seem'd not to be there,	Hero and Leander	2.117	
So beautie, sweetly quickens when t'is ny,	Hero and Leander	2.126	
But when he knew it was not Ganimed,	Hero and Leander	2.169	
And when hee sported in the fragrant lawnes,	Hero and Leander	2.199	
When this fresh bleeding wound Leander viewd,	Hero and Leander	2.213	
When deepe perswading Oratorie failes.	Hero and Leander	2.226	
joies/Then nymphs and sheapheards, when the timbrell rings,	Hero and Leander	2.233	
Or crooked Dolphin when the sailer sings;	Hero and Leander	2.234	
Like chast Diana, when Acteon spyde her,	Hero and Leander	2.261	
WHENCE			
Whence may you come, or whither will you goe?	Dido	1.1.215	Venus
From whence my radiant mother did descend,	Dido	3.4.47	Aeneas
For vertue is the fount whence honor springs.	1Tamb	4.4.128	Tamb
From whence the issues of my thoughts doe breake:	1Tamb	5.1.274	Bajzth
From whence the starres doo borrow all their light,	2Tamb	4.2.89	Therid
Whence is thy ship that anchors in our Rhoad?	Jew	2.2.2	Govnr
The Christian Ile of Rhodes, from whence you came,	Jew	2.2.31	Bosco
Whence none can possibly escape alive:	Jew	5.5.31	Barab
Letters, from whence?	Edw	2.2.112	Mortmr
Then tell thy prince, of whence, and what thou art.	Edw	3.1.35	Edward
How now, what newes with thee, from whence come these?	Edw	4.3.24	Edward
Letters, from whence?	Edw	5.2.23	Mortmr
From whence a dampe continually ariseth,	Edw	5.5.4	Matrvs
is barren of his fruite, from whence you had these ripe grapes.	F1580	4.6.23 P	Duke
From whence, by meanes of a swift spirit that I have, I had	F1585	4.6.28 P	Faust
Whence thou shouldst view thy Roome with squinting beams.	Lucan, First Booke	55	
Of these garboiles, whence springs [a long] <along> discourse,	Lucan, First Booke	68	
Whence the wind blowes stil forced to and fro;	Lucan, First Booke	414	
Or that unlike the line from whence I [sprong] <come>,	Ovid's Elegies	1.15.3	
things hidden)/Whence uncleane fowles are said to be forbidden.	Ovid's Elegies	2.6.52	
Whence knowes Corinna that with thee I playde?	Ovid's Elegies	2.8.6	
wish the chariot, whence corne [seedes] <fields> were found,	Ovid's Elegies	3.5.15	
From whence her vaile reacht to the ground beneath.	Hero and Leander	1.18	
Whence his admiring eyes more pleasure tooke,	Hero and Leander	2.325	
WHENSOEVER			
whensoever, and wheresoever the devill shall fetch thee.	F 369	1.4.27 P	Wagner
warning whensoever or wheresoever the divell shall fetch thee.	F App	p.230 36 P	Wagner
WHER			
and the bounds/Of Europe wher the Sun dares scarce appeare,	1Tamb	1.1.10	Cosroe
Wher Beauty, mother to the Muses sits,	1Tamb	5.1.144	Tamb
Wher death cuts off the progres of his pomp,	2Tamb	Prol.4	Prolog
wher raging Lantchidol/Beates on the regions with his	2Tamb	1.1.69	Orcan
Wher Amazonians met me in the field:	2Tamb	1.3.192	Techel
WHERBY			
Wherby whole Cities have escap't the plague,	F 49	1.1.21	Faust
WHERE			
Where finding Aeolus intrencht with stormes,	Dido	1.1.58	Venus
Where Dido will receive ye with her smiles:	Dido	1.1.234	Venus
Where am I now? these should be Carthage walles.	Dido	2.1.1	Aeneas
And kisse his hand: O where is Hecuba?	Dido	2.1.12	Achat
See where her servitors passe through the hall/Bearing a	Dido	2.1.70	Serg
Looke where she comes: Aeneas [view] <viewd> her well.	Dido	2.1.72	Illion
Where when they came, Ulysses on the sand/Assayd with honey	Dido	2.1.136	Aeneas
Where meeting with the rest, kill kill they cryed.	Dido	2.1.190	Aeneas
And tell me where [learndst] <learnst> thou this pretie song?	Dido	3.1.27	Dido
So lovely is he that where ere he goes,	Dido	3.1.71	Anna
altar, where Ile offer up/As many kisses as the Sea hath sands,	Dido	3.1.87	Dido
of foulded Lawne, where shall be wrought/The warres of Troy,	Dido	3.1.124	Dido
See where the pictures of my suiters hang,	Dido	3.1.139	Dido
And planted love where envie erst had sprong.	Dido	3.2.52	Juno
Why, that was in a net, where we are loose,	Dido	3.4.5	Dido
The man that I doe eye where ere I am,	Dido	3.4.18	Dido
In all this coyle, where have ye left the Queene?	Dido	4.1.14	Iarbus
Nay, where is my warlike father, can you tell?	Dido	4.1.15	Cupid
Behold where both of them come forth the Cave.	Dido	4.1.16	Anna
But where were you Iarbus all this while?	Dido	4.1.31	Dido
Where straying in our borders up and downe,	Dido	4.2.12	Iarbus
Mine eye is fixt where fancie cannot start,	Dido	4.2.37	Iarbus
That doe pursue my peace where ere it goes.	Dido	4.2.51	Iarbus
Where daliance doth consume a Souldiers strength,	Dido	4.3.34	Achat
See where they come, how might I doe to chide?	Dido	4.4.13	Dido
O where is Ganimed to hold his cup,	Dido	4.4.46	Dido
Ile hang ye in the chamber where I lye,	Dido	4.4.128	Dido
A garden where are Bee hives full of honey,	Dido	4.5.7	Nurse
Where thou shalt see the red gild fishes leape,	Dido	4.5.10	Nurse
Whom I have brought from Ida where he slept,	Dido	5.1.40	Hermes

WHERE (cont.)

Welcome sweet child, where hast thou been this long?	Dido	5.1.46		Aeneas
Flote up and downe where ere the billowes drive?	Dido	5.1.58		Aeneas
Where thou and false Achates first set foote:	Dido	5.1.175		Dido
See where he comes, welcome, welcome my love.	Dido	5.1.261		Dido
Where you shall heare the Scythian Tamburlaine,	1Tamb	Prol.4		Prolog
O where is dutie and allegeance now?	1Tamb	1.1.101		Mycet
Where all my youth I have bene governed,	1Tamb	1.2.13		Zenoc
Where her betrothed Lord Alcidamus,	1Tamb	1.2.78		Agidas
Where is this Scythian Tamburlaine?	1Tamb	1.2.152		Therid
Where kings shall crouch unto our conquering swords,	1Tamb	1.2.220		Usumc
Where honor sits invested royally:	1Tamb	2.1.18		Menaph
See where it is, the keenest Cutle-axe <curtle-axe>,/That ere	1Tamb	2.3.55		Tamb
Where flames shall ever feed upon his soule.	1Tamb	2.6.8		Cosroe
For words are vaine where working tooles present/The naked	1Tamb	3.2.93		Agidas
Where are your stout contributorie kings?	1Tamb	3.3.214		Tamb
Where they shall meete, and joine their force in one,	1Tamb	3.3.257		Tamb
And where I goe be thus in triumph drawne:	1Tamb	4.2.86		Tamb
To faire Damascus, where we now remaine,	1Tamb	4.2.99		Tamb
The countrie wasted where my selfe was borne,	1Tamb	4.4.66		Zenoc
His cole-blacke collours every where advaunst,	1Tamb	5.1.9		Govnr
bed, where many a Lord/In prime and glorie of his loving joy,	1Tamb	5.1.83		1Virgn
Where shaking ghosts with ever howling grones,	1Tamb	5.1.245		Zabina
Where ere I come the fatall sisters sweat,	1Tamb	5.1.454		Tamb
And here in Affrick where it seldom raines,	1Tamb	5.1.457		Tamb
Where Sigismond the king of Hungary/Should meet our person to	2Tamb	1.1.9		Orcan
Where twixt the Isles of Cyprus and of Creete,	2Tamb	1.2.26		Callap
Where Egypt and the Turkish Empire parts,	2Tamb	1.3.6		Tamb
Machda, where the mighty Christian Priest/Cal'd John the great,	2Tamb	1.3.187		Techel
The Westerne part of Affrike, where I view'd/The Ethiopian sea,	2Tamb	1.3.195		Techel
Where unresisted I remoov'd my campe.	2Tamb	1.3.199		Techel
I came to Cubar, where the Negros dwell,	2Tamb	1.3.201		Techel
lead him bound in chaines/Unto Damasco, where I staid before.	2Tamb	1.3.205		Techel
Where by the river Tyros I subdew'd/Stoka, Padalia, and	2Tamb	1.3.209		Therid
And Nigra Silva, where the Devils dance,	2Tamb	1.3.212		Therid
where our neighbour kings/Expect our power and our royall	2Tamb	2.2.3		Orcan
But every where fils every Continent,	2Tamb	2.2.51		Orcan
Now are those Spheares where Cupid usde to sit,	2Tamb	2.4.81		Tamb
Where ere her soule be, thou shalt stay with me/Embalm'd with	2Tamb	2.4.129		Tamb
them seeme as black/As is the Island where the Furies maske,	2Tamb	3.2.12		Tamb
Where in Arabian, Hebrew, Greek, is writ/This towne being burnt	2Tamb	3.2.16		Calyph
And sharpest where th'assault is desperate.	2Tamb	3.2.67		Tamb
Pioners away, and where I stuck the stake,	2Tamb	3.3.41		Therid
Where we will have [Gabions] <Galions> of sixe foot broad,/To	2Tamb	3.3.56		Therid
And carie both our soules, where his remaines.	2Tamb	3.4.17		Olymp
Unto the shining bower where Cynthia sits,	2Tamb	3.4.50		Therid
Then carie me I care not where you will,	2Tamb	3.4.80		Olymp
quyvering leaves/Of Idas forrest, where your highnesse hounds,	2Tamb	3.5.6		2Msngr
Where legions of devils (knowing he must die/Here in Natolia,	2Tamb	3.5.25		Orcan
The bullets fly at random where they list.	2Tamb	4.1.52		Calyph
O Samarcanda, where I breathed first,	2Tamb	4.1.105		Tamb
But that where every period ends with death,	2Tamb	4.2.47		Olymp
But from Asphaltis, where I conquer'd you,	2Tamb	4.3.5		Tamb
To Byron here where thus I honor you?	2Tamb	4.3.6		Tamb
Where are my common souldiers now that fought/So Lion-like upon	2Tamb	4.3.67		Tamb
Where Belus, Ninus and great Alexander/Have rode in triumph,	2Tamb	5.1.69		Tamb
Now in the place where faire Semiramis,	2Tamb	5.1.73		Tamb
where brave Assirian Dames/Have rid in pompe like rich	2Tamb	5.1.76		Tamb
Where about lies it?	2Tamb	5.1.120		Tamb
Where men report, thou sitt'st by God himselfe,	2Tamb	5.1.194		Tamb
Marcheth in Asia major, where the streames,	2Tamb	5.2.2		Callap
Where Tamburlaine with all his armie lies,	2Tamb	5.2.6		Callap
See where my slave, the uglie monster death/Shaking and	2Tamb	5.3.67		Tamb
Looke where he goes, but see, he comes againe/Because I stay:	2Tamb	5.3.75		Tamb
where I tooke/The Turke and his great Empresse prisoners,	2Tamb	5.3.128		Tamb
Graecia, and from thence/To Asia, where I stay against my will,	2Tamb	5.3.142		Tamb
Which is from Scythia, where I first began,	2Tamb	5.3.143		Tamb
Where Nilus payes his tribute to the maine,	Jew	1.1.75		Barab
Where wee'll attend the respit you have tane,	Jew	1.2.30		Calym
But here in Malta, where thou gotst thy wealth,	Jew	1.2.101		Govnr
Where father?	Jew	1.2.248		Abigal
To make a Nunnery, where none but their owne sect/Must enter in;	Jew	1.2.256		Abigal
And let me lodge where I was wont to lye.	Jew	1.2.333		Abigal
And here behold (unseene) where I have found/The gold, the	Jew	2.1.22		Abigal
glide by night/About the place where Treasure hath bin hid:	Jew	2.1.27		Barab
Then, gentle sleepe, where e're his bodie rests,	Jew	2.1.35		Abigal
Claime tribute where thou wilt, we are resolv'd,	Jew	2.2.55		Govnr
Where was thou borne?	Jew	2.3.127	P	Barab
Once at Jerusalem, where the pilgrims kneel'd,	Jew	2.3.208		Ithimr
Where is the Diamond you told me of?	Jew	2.3.219		Lodowk
up to the Jewes counting-house where I saw some bags of mony,	Jew	3.1.18	P	Pilia
There's a darke entry where they take it in,	Jew	3.4.79		Barab
Where they must neither see the messenger,	Jew	3.4.80		Barab
Where is the Fryar that converst with me?	Jew	3.6.9		Abigal
Frankeford, Lubecke, Mosco, and where not,	Jew	4.1.72		Barab
And where didst meet him?	Jew	4.2.15	P	Curtzn
but the Exercise being done, see where he comes.	Jew	4.2.20	P	Pilia
Where are my Maids?	Jew	4.2.83		Curtzn
Where painted Carpets o're the meads are hurl'd,	Jew	4.2.91		Ithimr
Where Woods and Forrests goe in goodly greene,	Jew	4.2.93		Ithimr
Where is the Jew, where is that murderer?	Jew	5.1.48		Mater
one that can spy a place/Where you may enter, and surprize the	Jew	5.1.71		Barab
Where be thou present onely to performe/One stratagem that I'le	Jew	5.2.98		Barab

WHERE (cont.)

[Where] <When> Siracusian Dionisius reign'd,	Jew	5.3.10		Calym
Where are those perfumed gloves which I sent/To be poysoned,	P 70	2.13		Guise
See where they be my good Lord, and he that smelles but to	P 73	2.16	P	Pothec
Where resolution strives for victory.	P 165	2.108		Guise
Where is the Admirall?	P 300	5.27		Gonzag
See where my Souldier shot him through the arm.	P 310	5.37		Guise
Where we may one injoy the others sight.	P 665	13.9		Duchss
Spaine is the place where he makes peace and warre,	P 710	14.13		Navrre
his market, and set up your standing where you should not:	P 810	17.5	P	Souldr
Holla verlete, hey: Epernoune, where is the King?	P 956	19.26		Guise
But see where he comes.	P1018	19.88		Capt
My Lord, see where the Guise is slaine.	P1019	19.89		Capt
Boy, look where your father lyes.	P1046	19.116		King
see where she comes, as if she droupt/To heare these newes.	P1062	19.132		Eprnon
Fire Paris where these trecherous rebels lurke.	P1241	22.103		King
the markett and sett upe your standinge where you shold not:	Paris	ms 6,p390	P	Souldr
ser where he is your landlorde you take upon you to be his |	Paris	ms 9,p390	P	Souldr
Or looke to see the throne where you should sit,	Edw	1.1.131		Lncstr
I, to the tower, the fleete, or where thou wilt.	Edw	1.1.198		Edward
But say my lord, where shall this meeting bee?	Edw	1.2.74		Warwck
For no where else the new earle is so safe.	Edw	1.4.11		Lncstr
My lord I heare it whispered every where,	Edw	1.4.106		Gavstn
Live where thou wilt, ile send thee gould enough,	Edw	1.4.113		Edward
For no where else seekes he felicitie.	Edw	1.4.122		Gavstn
Looke where the sister of the king of Fraunce,	Edw	1.4.187		Lncstr
But rest thee here where Gaveston shall sleepe.	Edw	2.1.65		Neece
That shall wee see, looke where his lordship comes.	Edw	2.2.49		Lncstr
Where womens favors hung like labels downe.	Edw	2.2.187		Mortmr
Tell me, where wast thou borne? What is thine armes?	Edw	2.2.242		Edward
O tell me Spencer, where is Gaveston?	Edw	2.4.1		Edward
That I might pull him to me where I would,	Edw	2.4.18		Queene
Tell us where he remaines, and he shall die.	Edw	2.4.36		Lncstr
Unnatural wars, where subjects brave their king,	Edw	3.1.86		Queene
Where weapons want, and though a many friends/Are made away, as	Edw	4.2.51		Mortmr
Alas, see where he sits, and hopes unseene,	Edw	4.7.51		Leistr
Where sorrow at my elbow still attends,	Edw	5.1.33		Edward
And none but we shall know where he lieth.	Edw	5.2.41		Mortmr
Where I am sterv'd for want of sustenance,	Edw	5.3.20		Edward
The Spencers ghostes, where ever they remaine,	Edw	5.3.44		Edward
Where is the court but heere, heere is the king,	Edw	5.3.59		Kent
The court is where lord Mortimer remaines,	Edw	5.3.61		Matrvs
Where lords keepe courts, and kings are lockt in prison!	Edw	5.3.64		Kent
This dungeon where they keepe me, is the sincke,	Edw	5.5.56		Edward
I feele a hell of greefe: where is my crowne?	Edw	5.5.90		Edward
Aye me, see where he comes, and they with him,	Edw	5.6.22		Queene
Goe fetche my fathers hearse, where it shall lie,	Edw	5.6.94		King
Where Mars did mate the warlicke Carthagens <Carthaginians>,	F 2	Prol.2		1Chor
of love/In Courts of Kings, where state is over-turn'd,	F 4	Prol.4		1Chor
Physicke farewell: where is Justinian?	F 55	1.1.27		Faust
Go to sirra, leave your jesting, and tell us where he is.	F 201	1.2.8	P	1Schol
Where are you damn'd?	F 301	1.3.73		Faust
Tell me, where is the place that men call Hell?	F 505	2.1.117		Faust
I, so are all things else; but whereabouts <where about>?	F 507	2.1.119		Faust
Where we are tortur'd, and remaine for ever.	F 509	2.1.121		Mephst
but <for> where we are is hell,/And where hell is there must we	F 511	2.1.123		Mephst
And where hell is there must we ever be.	F 512	2.1.124		Mephst
where I might see al characters of <and> planets of the	F 551.4	2.1.167A	P	Faust
[where I have laine ever since, and you have done me great	F 705.1	2.2.155A	P	Sloth
Where sitting <Being seated> in a Chariot burning bright,	F 758	2.3.37		2Chor
Where thou shalt see such store of Ordinance,	F 819	3.1.41		Mephst
<Where thou shalt see a troupe of bald-pate Friers>,	F 833	(HC265)A		Mephst
Faustus no more: see where the Cardinals come.	F1008	3.2.28		Mephst
[Where such as beare <bare> his absence but with griefe],	F1141	3.3.54A		3Chor
But where is Bruno our elected Pope,	F1160	4.1.6		Fredrk
Where is Benvolio?	F1172	4.1.18		Fredrk
The Emperour? where? O zounds my head.	F1287	4.1.133		Benvol
Where shall we place our selves Benvolio?	F1353	4.2.29		Mrtino
and let them hang/Within the window where he yoak'd me first,	F1381	4.2.57		Benvol
See where he comes, dispatch, and kill the slave.	F1423	4.2.99		2Soldr
O help me gentle friend; where is Martino?	F1432	4.3.2		Fredrk
hedge and ditch, or where thou wilt, but not into the water:	F1473	4.4.17	P	Faust
best beere in Europe, what ho, Hostis; where be these Whores?	F1506	4.5.2	P	Carter
that lye farre East, where they have fruit twice a yeare.	F1584	4.6.27	P	Faust
It appeares so, pray be bold else-where,	F1597	4.6.40		Servnt
Nay, hearke you, can you tell me where you are?	F1614	4.6.57		Faust
where ther's such belly-cheere, as Wagner in his life nere saw	F1678	5.1.5	P	Wagner
and see where they come, belike the feast is done.	F1679	5.1.6	P	Wagner
Where art thou Faustus? wretch, what hast thou done?	F1724	5.1.51		Faust
Accursed Faustus, [where is mercy now]?	F1739	5.1.66		Faust
Her lips sucke <suckes> forth my soule, see where it flies.	F1771	5.1.98		Faust
See where they come.	F1815	5.2.19		Mephst
[See see where Christs bloud streames in the firmament],	F1939	5.2.143A		Faust
Where is it now?	F1943	5.2.147		Faust
And see [where God]/[Stretcheth out his Arme, and bends his	F1943	5.2.147		Faust
that I may be here and there and every where, O Ile tickle the	F App	p.231 63	P	Clown
where lies intombde this famous Conquerour,	F App	p.237 31		Emper
masse see where he is, God save you maister doctor.	F App	p.239 99	P	HrsCsr
over hedge or ditch, or where thou wilt, but not into the water.	F App	p.239 112	P	Faust
See where he is fast asleepe.	F App	p.241 147	P	Mephst
Where be they?	F App	p.241 160	P	Mephst
where you must wel reward this learned man for the great	F App	p.243 28	P	Duke
See where they come: belike the feast is ended.	F App	p.243 8		Wagner

WHERE (cont.)			
As far as Titan springs where night dims heaven,	Lucan, First Booke	15	
I to the Torrid Zone where midday burnes,	Lucan, First Booke	16	
And where stiffe winter whom no spring resolves,	Lucan, First Booke	17	
Receive with shouts; where thou wilt raigne as King,	Lucan, First Booke	47	
What God it please thee be, or where to sway:	Lucan, First Booke	52	
Shaming to strive but where he did subdue,	Lucan, First Booke	146	
resisting it/Falls, and returnes, and shivers where it lights.	Lucan, First Booke	158	
Where men are ready, lingering ever hurts:	Lucan, First Booke	282	
held up, all joyntly cryde/They'ill follow where he please:	Lucan, First Booke	389	
rocks, and where the north-west wind/Nor Zephir rules not,	Lucan, First Booke	407	
Where Tarbels winding shoares imbrace the sea,	Lucan, First Booke	422	
Cyngas streame, and where swift Rhodanus/Drives Araris to sea;	Lucan, First Booke	434	
And where to Hesus, and fell Mercury <(Jove)>/They offer humane	Lucan, First Booke	440	
humane flesh, and where [Jove] <it> seemes/Bloudy like Dian,	Lucan, First Booke	441	
Or Plutoes bloodles kingdom, but else where/Resume a body:	Lucan, First Booke	452	
horsemen fought/Upon Mevanias plaine, where Buls are graz'd;	Lucan, First Booke	470	
At that bunch where the liver is, appear'd/A knob of flesh,	Lucan, First Booke	626	
where shall I fall,/Thus borne aloft?	Lucan, First Booke	677	
Where Nile augmenteth the Pelusian sea:	Lucan, First Booke	683	
and drie Affricke, where/A fury leades the Emathian bandes,	Lucan, First Booke	686	
Or lies he close, and shoots where none can spie him?	Ovid's Elegies	1.2.6	
Take these away, where is thy <thine> honor then?	Ovid's Elegies	1.2.38	
And where thou drinkst, on that part I will sup.	Ovid's Elegies	1.4.32	
Where they may sport, and seeme to be unknowne.	Ovid's Elegies	1.5.8	
When she will, day shines every where most pure.	Ovid's Elegies	1.8.10	
He hath no bosome, where to hide base pelfe.	Ovid's Elegies	1.10.18	
Ere thou rise starres teach seamen where to saile,	Ovid's Elegies	1.13.11	
yesterday/There where the porch doth Danaus fact display.	Ovid's Elegies	2.2.4	
but where love please/[Am] <And> driven like a ship upon rough	Ovid's Elegies	2.4.7	
No where can they be taught but in the bed,	Ovid's Elegies	2.5.61	
Telling thy mistresse, where I was with thee,	Ovid's Elegies	2.8.27	
And where swift Nile in his large channell slipping <skipping>,	Ovid's Elegies	2.13.9	
Where the French rout engirt themselves with Bayes.	Ovid's Elegies	2.13.18	
And by the rising herbes, where cleare springs slide,	Ovid's Elegies	2.16.9	
Where round about small birdes most sweetely sing.	Ovid's Elegies	3.1.4	
Where Mars his sonnes not without fault did breed,	Ovid's Elegies	3.4.39	
If Achelous, I aske where thy hornes stand,	Ovid's Elegies	3.5.35	
Yet could I not cast ancor where I meant,	Ovid's Elegies	3.6.6	
Where Linus by his father Phoebus layed/To sing with his	Ovid's Elegies	3.8.23	
Where Ceres went each place was harvest there.	Ovid's Elegies	3.9.38	
Where Juno comes, each youth, and pretty maide,	Ovid's Elegies	3.12.23	
Where little ground to be inclosd befalles,	Ovid's Elegies	3.14.12	
Where she should sit for men to gaze upon.	Hero and Leander	1.8	
Where Venus in her naked glory strove,	Hero and Leander	1.12	
Where sparrowes pearcht, of hollow pearle and gold,	Hero and Leander	1.33	
Firmament/Glistered with breathing stars, who where they went,	Hero and Leander	1.98	
Where crown'd with blazing light and majestie,	Hero and Leander	1.110	
from her tower/To Venus temple, [where] <were> unhappilye,	Hero and Leander	1.133	
Where by one hand, light headed Bacchus hoong,	Hero and Leander	1.139	
Where both deliberat, the love is slight,	Hero and Leander	1.175	
Far from the towne (where all is whist and still,	Hero and Leander	1.346	
That hops about the chamber where I lie,	Hero and Leander	1.354	
Where fancie is in equall ballance pais'd).	Hero and Leander	2.32	
her body throes/Upon his bosome, where with yeelding eyes,	Hero and Leander	2.47	
Burnes where it cherisht, murders where it loved.	Hero and Leander	2.128	
Leanders Father knew where hee had beene,	Hero and Leander	2.136	
Where having spy'de her tower, long star'd he on't,	Hero and Leander	2.149	
him to the bottome, where the ground/Was strewd with pearle,	Hero and Leander	2.160	
Where kingly Neptune and his traine abode.	Hero and Leander	2.166	
Where seeing a naked man, she scriecht for feare,	Hero and Leander	2.237	
(as men say)/But deaffe and cruell, where he meanes to pray.	Hero and Leander	2.288	
WHERE ABOUT			
I, so are all things else; but whereabouts <where about>?	F 507	2.1.119	Faust
WHEREABOUTS			
I, so are all things else; but whereabouts <where about>?	F 507	2.1.119	Faust
WHEREAS			
Whereas the Wind-god warring now with Fate,	Dido	1.1.115	Jupitr
Whereas Sidonian Dido rules as Queene.	Dido	1.1.213	Venus
Whereas the Southerne winde with brackish breath,	Dido	1.2.28	Cloan
Whereas Nobilitie abhors to stay,	Dido	4.3.19	Aeneas
Whereas the Fort may fittest be assailde,	2Tamb	3.2.66	Tamb
Whereas the Terren and the red sea meet,	2Tamb	5.3.132	Tamb
Whereas the Sun declining from our sight,	2Tamb	5.3.148	Tamb
and whereas hee is your Landlord, you will take upon you to be	P 810	17.5	P Souldr
And whereas he shall live and be belovde,	Edw	1.4.261	Mortmr
Whereas his kinsmen chiefly brought him up;	F 14	Prol.14	1Chor
WHEREAT			
Whereat agast, we were commanded straight/With reverence to	Dido	2.1.167	Aeneas
Whereat he lifted up his bedred lims,	Dido	2.1.250	Aeneas
Whereat the Souldiers will conceive more joy,	1Tamb	1.1.152	Ceneus
Whereat thou trembling hid'st thee in the aire,	2Tamb	4.1.130	Tamb
Whereat she starts, puts on her purple weeds,	Hero and Leander	2.88	
Whereat the saphir visag'd god grew prowd,	Hero and Leander	2.155	
Whereat agast, the poore soule gan to crie,	Hero and Leander	2.177	
WHERE BY			
Where by one hand, light headed Bacchus hoong,	Hero and Leander	1.139	
WHEREBY			
Whereby the moisture of your blood is dried,	2Tamb	5.3.85	Phsitn
Whereby he is in danger to be damn'd:	F 279	1.3.51	Mephst
WHERE ERE			
So lovely is he that where ere he goes,	Dido	3.1.71	Anna
The man that I doe eye where ere I am,	Dido	3.4.18	Dido

WHERE ERE (cont.)			
That doe pursue my peace where ere it goes.	Dido	4.2.51	Iarbus
Flote up and downe where ere the billowes drive?	Dido	5.1.58	Aeneas
Where ere I come the fatall sisters sweat,	1Tamb	5.1.454	Tamb
Where ere her soule be, thou shalt stay with me/Embalm'd with	2Tamb	2.4.129	Tamb
WHERE E'RE			
Then, gentle sleepe, where e're his bodie rests,	Jew	2.1.35	Abigal
WHERE EVER			
The Spencers ghostes, where ever they remaine,	Edw	5.3.44	Edward
WHEREFORE			
Why, what are you, or wherefore doe you sewe?	Dido	1.2.3	Iarbus
Wherefore doth Dido bid Iarbus goe?	Dido	3.1.56	Anna
Wherefore would Dido have Aeneas stay?	Dido	3.1.134	Aeneas
Wherefore I [chaungd] <chaunge> my counsell with the time,	Dido	3.2.51	Juno
What willes our Lord, or wherefore did he call?	Dido	4.3.15	Achat
Aeneas, wherefore goe thy men abourd?	Dido	5.1.87	Dido
But wherefore talk'd Don Lodowick with you?	Jew	2.3.150	Mthias
You loyter, master, wherefore stay [we] <me> thus?	Jew	4.1.139	Ithimr
But wherefore walkes yong Mortimer aside?	Edw	1.4.353	Edward
Base villaines, wherefore doe you gripe mee thus?	Edw	5.3.57	Kent
Wherefore stay we? on sirs to the court.	Edw	5.3.65	Souldr
Whose there, what light is that, wherefore comes thou?	Edw	5.5.42	Edward
O wherefore sits thou heare?	Edw	5.5.96	Edward
And therefore tell me, wherefore art thou come?	Edw	5.5.106	Edward
Then wherefore should you aske me such a question?	F 208	1.2.15	P Wagner
Then wherefore would you have me view that booke?	F1023	3.2.43	Pope
But wherefore doe I dally my revenge?	F1401	4.2.77	Faust
But wherefore dost thou aske?	F1652	4.6.95	Faust
Wherefore Leanders fancie to surprize,	Hero and Leander		2.223
WHEREIN			
The boy wherein false destinie delights,	Dido	3.2.2	Juno
O that the Clowdes were here wherein thou [fledst] <fleest>,	Dido	4.4.50	Dido
The ayre wherein they breathe, the water, fire,	Dido	4.4.75	Dido
Wherein the day may evermore delight:	Dido	5.1.7	Aeneas
Wherein have I offended Jupiter,	Dido	5.1.129	Dido
Wherein by curious soveraintie of Art,	1Tamb	2.1.13	Menaph
Wherein he wrought such ignominious wrong,	1Tamb	4.3.39	Souldn
Wherein as in a myrrour we perceive/The highest reaches of a	1Tamb	5.1.167	Tamb
Wherein as in a mirrour may be seene,	1Tamb	5.1.476	Tamb
And let this death wherein to sinne I die,	2Tamb	2.3.8	Sgsmnd
Wherein is all the treasure of the land.	2Tamb	3.3.4	Therid
Wherein an incorporeall spirit mooves,	2Tamb	4.1.114	Tamb
Wherein was neither corrage, strength or wit,	2Tamb	4.1.125	Tamb
Wherein he spareth neither man nor child,	2Tamb	5.1.30	1Citzn
fire to burne the writ/Wherein the sum of thy religion rests.	2Tamb	5.1.191	Tamb
Wherein are rockes of Pearle, that shine as bright/As all the	2Tamb	5.3.156	Tamb
of judgement frame/This is the ware wherein consists my wealth:	Jew	1.1.33	Barab
Wherein I may not, nay I dare not dally.	Jew	1.2.12	Calym
the plight/Wherein these Christians have oppressed me:	Jew	1.2.271	Barab
Wherein?	Jew	3.3.13	Abigal
Wherein?	Jew	3.3.54	1Fryar
This is the houre/Wherein I shall proceed; Oh happy houre,	Jew	4.1.161	1Fryar
Wherein I shall convert an Infidell,	Jew	4.1.162	1Fryar
slavish Bands/Wherein the Turke hath yoak'd your land and you?	Jew	5.2.78	Barab
Wherein no danger shall betide thy life,	Jew	5.2.100	Barab
Wherein are thirtie thousand able men,	P 139	2.82	Guise
Wherein hath Ramus been so offencious?	P 384	7.24	Ramus
Breath out that life wherein my death was hid,	P 954	19.24	King
Wherein my lord, have I deservd these words?	Edw	1.4.163	Queene
Wherein the filthe of all the castell falles.	Edw	5.5.57	Edward
Art/Wherein all natures [treasury] <treasure> is contain'd:	F 102	1.1.74	BdAngl
Wherein is fixt the love of Belzebub,	F 400	2.1.12	Faust
In which <Wherein> thou hast given thy soule to Lucifer.	F 520	2.1.132	Mephst
have a booke wherein I might beholde al spels and incantations,	F 551.1	2.1.164A	P Faust
wherein I might see al plants, hearbes and trees that grow upon	F 551.9	2.1.172A	P Faust
warre, wherein through use he's known/To exceed his maister,	Lucan, First Booke		325
cold hemlocks flower/Wherein bad hony Corsicke Bees did power.	Ovid's Elegies		1.12.10
Wherein is seene the givers loving minde:	Ovid's Elegies		2.15.2
Wherein was Proteus carved, and o'rehead,	Hero and Leander		1.137
Wherein the liberall graces lock'd their wealth,	Hero and Leander		2.17
Wherein Leander on her quivering brest,	Hero and Leander		2.279
WHEREOF			
But for the land whereof thou doest enquire,	Dido	1.1.209	Venus
Made of the mould whereof thy selfe consists,	2Tamb	4.1.115	Tamb
Whereof a man may easily in a day/Tell that which may maintaine	Jew	1.1.10	Barab
Whereof his sire, the Pope, was poysoned.	Jew	3.4.99	Barab
The floore whereof, this Cable being cut,	Jew	5.5.34	Barab
The sent whereof doth make my head to ake.	P 171	3.6	OldQn
Whereof we got the name of Mortimer,	Edw	2.3.23	Mortmr
For proofe whereof, if so your Grace be pleas'd,	F1221	4.1.67	Faust
the sight whereof so delighted me, as nothing in the world	F1560	4.6.3	P Duke
The stench whereof corrupts the inward soule/With such	F App	p.243 41	OldMan
appear'd/A knob of flesh, whereof one halfe did looke/Dead, and	Lucan, First Booke		627
WHEREON			
The Masts whereon thy swelling sailes shall hang,	Dido	3.1.122	Dido
and the verie legges/Whereon our state doth leane, as on a	1Tamb	1.1.60	Mycet
For this, my quenchles thirst whereon I builde,	P 107	2.50	Guise
His left hand whereon gold doth ill alight,	Ovid's Elegies		3.7.15
Her kirtle blew, whereon was many a staine,	Hero and Leander		1.15
Whereon Leander sitting, thus began,	Hero and Leander		2.245
WHERE'S			
Now where's the hope you had of haughty Spaine?	Jew	5.2.3	Calym
How now sirra, where's thy Maister?	F 197	1.2.4	P 1Schol

WHERE'S (cont.)

pray where's the cup you stole from the Taverne? F1097 3.3.10 P Vintnr
you, hey, passe, where's your maister? F App p.240 138 P HrsCsr
Where's thy attire? why wand'rest heere alone? Ovid's Elegies 3.5.55

WHERES

But wheres Aeneas? ah hees gone hees gone! Dido 5.1.192 Dido
Cease to lament, and tell us wheres the king? Edw 2.4.30 Mortmr
But wheres the king and the other Spencer fled? Edw 4.6.55 Mortmr

WHERESOERE

Shall lead him with us wheresoere we goe. 1Tamb 4.2.100 Tamb

WHERESOEVER

And wheresoever we repose our selves, 1Tamb 1.2.80 Magnet
whensoever, and wheresoever the devill shall fetch thee. F 370 1.4.28 P Wagner
[and] bloud, <or goods> into their habitation wheresoever. F 499 2.1.111 P Faust
warning whensoever or wheresoever the divell shall fetch thee. F App p.230 37 P Wagner

WHERETO

Whereto ech man of rule hath given his hand, 1Tamb 5.1.102 1Virgn
Behold this Silver Belt whereto is fixt/Seven golden [keys] F 932 3.1.154 Pope

WHEREWITH

To make thee fannes wherewith to coole thy face, Dido 1.1.35 Jupitr
Viewing the fire wherewith rich Ilion burnt. Dido 2.1.264 Aeneas
Wherewith my husband woo'd me yet a maide, Dido 3.4.63 Dido
Wherewith his burning beames like labouring Bees, Dido 5.1.12 Aeneas
Wherewith he may excruciate thy soule. 1Tamb 3.2.104 Agidas
The slaverie wherewith he persecutes/The noble Turke and his 1Tamb 4.3.26 Arabia
Expell the hate wherewith he paines our soules. 2Tamb 4.1.173 Orcan
and the victories/Wherewith he hath so sore dismaide the world, 2Tamb 5.2.44 Callap
Wherewith thy antichristian churches blaze, Edw 1.4.99 Edward
Wherewith the Students shall be bravely clad. F 118 1.1.90 Faust
Canst touch that hand wherewith some one lie dead? Ovid's Elegies 3.7.17
Wherewith Leander much more was inflam'd. Hero and Leander 1.182
Wherewith she yeelded, that was woon before. Hero and Leander 1.330
Wherewith she strooken, look'd so dolefully, Hero and Leander 1.373
Wherewith the king of Gods and men is feasted. Hero and Leander 1.432
Wherewith as one displeas'd, away she trips. Hero and Leander 2.4
Wherewith she wreath'd her largely spreading heare, Hero and Leander 2.107
but he must weare/The sacred ring wherewith she was endow'd, Hero and Leander 2.109

WHERFORE

Tell me Taleus, wherfore should I flye? P 366 7.6 Ramus
But wherfore beares he me such deadly hate? P 779 15.37 Mugern
Wherfore is Guy of Warwicke discontent? Edw 1.2.10 Mortmr
Thou villaine, wherfore talkes thou of a king, Edw 1.4.28 Mortmr

WHERIN

Wherin the change I use condemns my faith, 1Tamb 5.1.390 Zenoc
The Terrene main wherin Danubius fals, 2Tamb 1.1.37 Orcan
wherin at anchor lies/A Turkish Gally of my royall fleet, 2Tamb 1.2.20 Callap
The field wherin this battaile shall be fought, 2Tamb 3.5.18 Callap

WHERON

And when the ground wheron my souldiers march/Shal rise aloft 2Tamb 1.3.13 Tamb
paths, wheron the gods might trace/To Joves high court. Hero and Leander 1.298

WHER'S

But wher's this coward, villaine, not my sonne, 2Tamb 4.1.89 Tamb
Now Casane, wher's the Turkish Alcaron, 2Tamb 5.1.173 Tamb

WHERS

Treason, treason: whers the traitor? Edw 2.2.80 Edward

WHET

now whet thy winged sword/And lift thy lofty arme into the 1Tamb 2.3.51 Cosroe
Whet all your swords to mangle Tamburlain, 2Tamb 3.5.15 Callap
And bids thee whet thy sword on Sextus bones, P1237 22.99 King

WHETHER (Homograph)

Or whether men or beasts inhabite it. Dido 1.1.177 Aeneas
But whether thou the Sunnes bright Sister be, Dido 1.1.193 Aeneas
Whether we presently will flie (my Lords)/To rest secure 1Tamb 1.1.177 Cosroe
Whether from earth, or hell, or heaven he grow. 1Tamb 2.6.23 Ortyg
And tell me whether I should stoope so low, 2Tamb 1.1.112 Sgsmnd
Death, whether art thou gone that both we live? 2Tamb 3.4.11 Olymp
Whether we next make expedition. 2Tamb 4.3.94 Tamb
sent me to know/Whether your selfe will come and custome them. Jew 1.1.53 1Merch
Against my will, and whether I would or no, Jew 2.3.75 Barab
the Governors sonne/Will, whether I will or no, have Abigall: Jew 2.3.258 Barab
now Abigall shall see/Whether Mathias holds her deare or no. Jew 3.2.2 Mthias
Whether now, Fidler? Jew 4.4.70 Pilia
Whether he have dishonoured me or no. P 769 15.27 Guise
Whether goes my Lord of Coventrie so fast? Edw 1.1.175 Edward
Madam, whether walks your majestie so fast? Edw 1.2.46 Mortmr
Go whether thou wilt seeing I have Gaveston. Edw 1.2.54 Queene
Whether will you beare him, stay or ye shall die. Edw 1.4.24 Edward
That whether I will or no thou must depart: Edw 1.4.124 Edward
Whether goes my lord? Edw 1.4.144 Queene
And threatenest death whether he rise or fall, Edw 2.2.44 Edward
Unhappie Gaveston, whether goest thou now. Edw 2.5.110 Gavstn
Whether, O whether doost thou bend thy steps? Edw 4.2.12 Queene
Whether you will, all places are alike, Edw 5.1.145 Edward
I, lead me whether you will, even to my death, Edw 5.3.66 Kent
And therefore soldiers whether will you hale me? Edw 5.4.108 Kent
And whether I have limmes or no, I know not. Edw 5.5.65 Edward
Whether thou wilt be secret in this, Edw 5.6.5 Mortmr
Why so thou shalt be, whether thou dost it or no: F 360 1.4.18 P Wagner
Homo fuge: whether should I flye? F 466 2.1.78 Faust
So thou shalt, whether thou beest with me, or no: F App p.229 22 P Wagner
or moale in her necke, how shal I know whether it be so or no? F App p.238 61 P Emper
Whether goes my standarde? Lucan, First Booke 193
Whether the gods, or blustring south were cause/I know not, but Lucan, First Booke 236

WHETHER (cont.)			
Whether now shal these olde bloudles soules repaire?	Lucan, First Booke	343	
Whether the sea roul'd alwaies from that point,	Lucan, First Booke	413	
I know not whether my mindes whirle-wind drives me.	Ovid's Elegies	2.9.28	
Whether the subtile maide lines bringes and carries,	Ovid's Elegies	2.19.41	
I might not go, whether my papers went.	Ovid's Elegies	3.7.6	
Ah whether is [thy] <they> brests soft nature [fled] <sled>?	Ovid's Elegies	3.7.18	
'Tis doubtfull whether verse availe, or harme,	Ovid's Elegies	3.11.13	
WHICH			
Which once performd, poore Troy so long suppressed,	Dido	1.1.93	Jupitr
Which Pergama did vaunt in all her pride.	Dido	1.1.151	Aeneas
On which by tempests furie we are cast.	Dido	1.1.199	Aeneas
And for thy ships which thou supposest lost,	Dido	1.1.235	Venus
Which now we call Italia of his name,	Dido	1.2.23	Cloan
Grecians, which rejoyce/That nothing now is left of Priamus:	Dido	2.1.19	Aeneas
Goe fetch the garment which Sicheus ware:	Dido	2.1.80	Dido
In which unhappie worke was I employd,	Dido	2.1.169	Aeneas
Through which it could not enter twas so huge.	Dido	2.1.171	Aeneas
Which thousand battering Rams could never pierce,	Dido	2.1.175	Aeneas
Which Sinon viewing, causde the Greekish spyes/To hast to	Dido	2.1.180	Aeneas
his breast/Furrowd with wounds, and that which made me weepe,	Dido	2.1.204	Aeneas
by which Achilles horse/Drew him in triumph through the	Dido	2.1.205	Aeneas
Which made the funerall flame that burnt faire Troy:	Dido	2.1.218	Aeneas
All which hemd me about, crying, this is he.	Dido	2.1.219	Aeneas
At which the franticke Queene leapt on his face,	Dido	2.1.244	Aeneas
Which sent an eccho to the wounded King:	Dido	2.1.249	Aeneas
Which he disdaining whiskt his sword about,	Dido	2.1.253	Aeneas
Through which he could not passe for slaughtred men:	Dido	2.1.262	Aeneas
That love is childish which consists in words.	Dido	3.1.10	Iarbus
Which piteous wants if Dido will supplie,	Dido	3.1.111	Aeneas
Through which the water shall delight to play:	Dido	3.1.119	Dido
Which if thou lose shall shine above the waves:	Dido	3.1.121	Dido
All these and others which I never sawe,	Dido	3.1.150	Dido
Which I will make in quittance of thy love:	Dido	3.2.69	Juno
Unto the purpose which we now propound.	Dido	3.2.95	Juno
Which I will breake betwixt a Lyons jawes.	Dido	3.3.38	Cupid
I, this it is which wounds me to the death,	Dido	3.3.63	Iarbus
ascend so high/As Didos heart, which Monarkes might not scale.	Dido	3.4.34	Aeneas
Which Circes sent Sicheus when he lived:	Dido	4.4.11	Dido
onely Aeneas frowne/Is that which terrifies poore Didos heart:	Dido	4.4.116	Dido
The water which our Poets terme a Nimph,	Dido	4.4.144	Dido
Which I bestowd upon his followers:	Dido	4.4.162	Dido
Then that which grim Atrides overthrew:	Dido	5.1.3	Aeneas
Which neither art nor reason may atchieve,	Dido	5.1.65	Aeneas
I hope that that which love forbids me doe,	Dido	5.1.170	Dido
Which if it chaunce, Ile give ye buriall,	Dido	5.1.176	Dido
Then gan he wagge his hand, which yet held up,	Dido	5.1.229	Anna
Which when I viewd, I cride, Aeneas stay,	Dido	5.1.232	Anna
Which seene to all, though he beheld me not,	Dido	5.1.237	Anna
Here lye the garment which I cloath'd him in,	Dido	5.1.298	Dido
Which is (God knowes) about that Tamburlaine,	1Tamb	1.1.30	Mycet
Which will revolt from Persean government,	1Tamb	1.1.91	Cosroe
And that which might resolve me into teares,	1Tamb	1.1.118	Cosroe
Which gratious starres have promist at my birth.	1Tamb	1.2.92	Tamb
Which with thy beautie will be soone resolv'd.	1Tamb	1.2.101	Tamb
Which is as much as if I swore by heaven,	1Tamb	1.2.233	Tamb
On which the breath of heaven delights to play,	1Tamb	2.1.25	Menaph
And which is worst to have his Diadem/Sought for by such scalde	1Tamb	2.2.7	Mycet
Which make reports it far exceeds the Kings.	1Tamb	2.2.42	Spy
Which you that be but common souldiers,	1Tamb	2.2.63	Meandr
which by fame is said/To drinke the mightie Parthian Araris,	1Tamb	2.3.15	Tamb
Which I esteeme as portion of my crown.	1Tamb	2.3.35	Cosroe
The heat and moisture which did feed each other,	1Tamb	2.7.46	Cosroe
Not all the curses which the furies breathe,	1Tamb	2.7.53	Tamb
(Which of your whole displeasures should be most)/Hath seem'd	1Tamb	3.2.7	Agidas
Which dies my lookes so livelesse as they are.	1Tamb	3.2.15	Zenoc
Which thy prolonged Fates may draw on thee:	1Tamb	3.2.101	Agidas
inlarge/Those Christian Captives, which you keep as slaves,	1Tamb	3.3.47	Tamb
And know thou Turke, that those which lead my horse,	1Tamb	3.3.72	Tamb
Which glided through the bowels of the Greekes.	1Tamb	3.3.92	Argier
Which I will bring as Vassals to thy feete.	1Tamb	3.3.129	Tamb
Which lately made all Europe quake for feare:	1Tamb	3.3.135	Bajzth
Excluding Regions which I meane to trace,	1Tamb	4.4.77	Tamb
Which he observes as parcell of his fame,	1Tamb	5.1.14	Govnr
flags/Through which sweet mercie threw her gentle beams,	1Tamb	5.1.69	Tamb
to prevent/That which mine honor sweares shal be perform'd:	1Tamb	5.1.107	Tamb
Which into words no vertue can digest:	1Tamb	5.1.173	Tamb
That which hath [stoopt] <stopt> the tempest of the Gods,	1Tamb	5.1.184	Tamb
Which fils the nookes of Hell with standing aire,	1Tamb	5.1.257	Bajzth
Which had ere this bin bathde in streames of blood,	1Tamb	5.1.438	Tamb
Which kept his father in an yron cage:	2Tamb	1.1.5	Orcan
Take which thou wilt, for as the Romans usde/I here present	2Tamb	1.1.81	Sgsmnd
which basely on their knees/In all your names desirde a truce	2Tamb	1.1.96	Orcan
Which if your General refuse or scorne,	2Tamb	1.1.119	Fredrk
Which when I come aboord will hoist up saile,	2Tamb	1.2.24	Callap
Choose which thou wilt, all are at thy command.	2Tamb	1.2.31	Callap
slaves/I freely give thee, which shall cut the straights,	2Tamb	1.2.33	Callap
which shine as bright/As that faire vail that covers all the	2Tamb	1.2.49	Callap
Which should be like the quilles of Porcupines,	2Tamb	1.3.26	Tamb
Which when he tainted with his slender rod,	2Tamb	1.3.40	Zenoc
Which being wroth, sends lightning from his eies,	2Tamb	1.3.76	Tamb
All which have sworne to sacke Natolia:	2Tamb	1.3.121	Therid
Which with my crowne I gladly offer thee.	2Tamb	1.3.136	Usumc

WHICH (cont.)

Which in despight of them I set on fire:	2Tamb	1.3.213	Therid
But as the faith which they prophanely plight/Is not by	2Tamb	2.1.37	Baldwn
Which if a shower of wounding thunderbolts/Should breake out	2Tamb	2.2.13	Gazell
Which we referd to justice of his Christ,	2Tamb	2.3.28	Orcan
which here appeares as full/As raies of Cynthia to the clearest	2Tamb	2.3.29	Orcan
with which I burst/The rusty beames of Janus Temple doores,	2Tamb	2.4.113	Tamb
All which will joine against this Tamburlain,	2Tamb	3.1.61	Soria
To shew her beautie, which the world admyr'd,	2Tamb	3.2.26	Tamb
For [which] <with> the quinque-angle fourme is meet:	2Tamb	3.2.64	Tamb
Which til it may defend you, labour low:	2Tamb	3.3.44	Therid
Betwixt which, shall our ordinance thunder foorth,	2Tamb	3.3.58	Therid
Which measureth the glorious frame of heaven,	2Tamb	3.4.65	Therid
In frame of which, Nature hath shewed more skill,	2Tamb	3.4.75	Techel
Phrigia to the sea/Which washeth Cyprus with his brinish waves,	2Tamb	3.5.12	Callap
which all the good I have/Join'd with my fathers crowne would	2Tamb	4.1.57	Calyph
And shame of nature [which] <with> Jaertis streame,	2Tamb	4.1.108	Tamb
Which makes me valiant, proud, ambitious,	2Tamb	4.1.116	Tamb
Which with thy beauty thou wast woont to light,	2Tamb	4.2.16	Therid
Save griefe and sorrow which torment my heart,	2Tamb	4.2.24	Olymp
Which beates against this prison to get out,	2Tamb	4.2.35	Olymp
An ointment which a cunning Alcumist/Distilled from the purest	2Tamb	4.2.59	Olymp
In which the essentiall fourme of Marble stone,	2Tamb	4.2.62	Olymp
With which if you but noint your tender Skin,	2Tamb	4.2.65	Olymp
Which when you stab, looke on your weapons point,	2Tamb	4.2.69	Olymp
By which I hold my name and majesty.	2Tamb	4.3.26	Tamb
Which threatned more than if the region/Next underneath the	2Tamb	5.1.87	Tamb
Which when the citie was besieg'd I hid,	2Tamb	5.1.117	Govnr
<Affrica>/Which hath bene subject to the Persean king,	2Tamb	5.1.166	Tamb
Which makes them fleet aloft and gaspe for aire.	2Tamb	5.1.209	Techel
Which being faint and weary with the siege,	2Tamb	5.2.7	Callap
Which makes them manage armes against thy state,	2Tamb	5.3.36	Usumc
Which ad much danger to your malladie.	2Tamb	5.3.55	Therid
Which wil abate the furie of your fit,	2Tamb	5.3.79	Phsitn
and Calor, which some holde/Is not a parcell of the Elements,	2Tamb	5.3.86	Phsitn
Which being the cause of life, imports your death.	2Tamb	5.3.90	Phsitn
Your Artiers which alongst the vaines convey/The lively spirits	2Tamb	5.3.93	Phsitn
The lively spirits which the heart ingenders/Are partcht and	2Tamb	5.3.94	Phsitn
that the soule/Wanting those Organnons by which it mooves,	2Tamb	5.3.96	Phsitn
Which onely will dismay the enemy.	2Tamb	5.3.112	Usumc
Which is from Scythia, where I first began,	2Tamb	5.3.143	Tamb
Eastward behold/As much more land, which never was descried,	2Tamb	5.3.155	Tamb
As that which [Clymens] <Clymeus> brainsicke sonne did guide,	2Tamb	5.3.231	Tamb
Which maxime had Phaleris observ'd,	Jew	Prol.24	Machvl
Which mony was not got without my meanes.	Jew	Prol.32	Machvl
easily in a day/Tell that which may maintaine him all his life.	Jew	1.1.11	Barab
Sirra, which of my ships art thou Master of?	Jew	1.1.70	Barab
Which me thinkes fits not their profession.	Jew	1.1.118	Barab
Which Tribute all in policie, I feare,	Jew	1.1.181	Barab.
Warily garding that which I ha got.	Jew	1.1.188	Barab
And which of you can charge me otherwise?	Jew	1.2.117	Barab
which being valued/Amount to more then all the wealth in Malta.	Jew	1.2.133	Offcrs
us an occasion/Which on the sudden cannot serve the turne.	Jew	1.2.240	Barab
The gold and Jewels which I kept for thee.	Jew	1.2.298	Barab
Which they have now turn'd to a Nunnery.	Jew	1.2.320	Abigal
Fearing the afflictions which my father feeles,	Jew	1.2.322	Abigal
I have found/The gold, the perles, and Jewels which he hid.	Jew	2.1.23	Abigal
no, but happily he stands in feare/Of that which you, I thinke,	Jew	2.3.283	Barab
Now have I that for which my soule hath long'd.	Jew	2.3.318	Lodowk
Upon which Altar I will offer up/My daily sacrifice of sighes	Jew	3.2.31	Govnr
Which forc'd their hands divide united hearts:	Jew	3.2.35	Govnr
be it to her as the draught/Of which great Alexander drunke,	Jew	3.4.97	Barab
And by my father's practice, which is there/Set downe at large,	Jew	3.6.28	Abigal
No, 'tis an order which the Fryars use:	Jew	4.1.134	Barab
Which if they were reveal'd, would doe him harme.	Jew	4.2.65	Pilia
'Tis not thy life which can availe me ought,	Jew	5.2.62	Barab
Doe but bring this to passe which thou pretendest,	Jew	5.2.84	Govnr
Which with our Bombards shot and Basiliske,	Jew	5.3.3	Calym
is a monastery/Which standeth as an out-house to the Towne;	Jew	5.3.37	Msngr
The many favours which your grace hath showne,	P 9	1.9	Navrre
Which Ile desolve with bloud and crueltie.	P 26	1.26	QnMoth
Which he hath pitcht within his deadly toyle.	P 54	1.54	Navrre
Where are those perfumed gloves which I sent/To be poysoned,	P 70	2.13	Guise
Which cannot be extinguisht but by bloud.	P 93	2.36	Guise
That those which doe beholde, they may become/As men that stand	P 162	2.105	Guise
At which they all shall issue out and set the streetes.	P 237	4.35	Guise
Which when they heare, they shall begin to kill:	P 239	4.37	Guise
That they which have already set the street/May know their	P 328	5.55	Guise
Who is that which knocks there?	P 346	6.1	P SrnsWf
Which is no sooner receiv'd but it is spent.	P 379	7.19	Ramus
To contradict which, I say Ramus shall dye:	P 396	7.36	Guise
Which as I heare one [Shekius] <Shekins> takes it ill,	P 404	7.44	Ramus
Which we have chaste into the river [Sene] <Rene>,	P 418	7.58	Guise
Which in the woods doe holde their synagogue:	P 502	9.21	Guise
For the late nights worke which my Lord of Guise/Did make in	P 514	9.33	QnMoth
Which [are] <as> he saith, to kill the Puritans,	P 643	12.56	Cardnl
Is all my love forgot which helde thee deare?	P 684	13.28	Guise
Which they will put us to with sword and fire:	P 706	14.9	Navrre
Which are already mustered in the land,	P 726	14.29	1Msngr
Which your wife writ to my deare Minion,	P 755	15.13	King
But which way is he gone?	P 783	15.41	Mugern
Which Ile maintaine so long as life doth last:	P 800	16.14	Navrre
yet you put in that which displeaseth him, and so forestall his	P 809	17.4	P Souldr

WHICH (cont.)

that he himself should occupy, which is his own free land.	P 812	17.7	P Souldr
yet I meane to keepe you out, which I will if this geare holde:	P 815	17.10	P Souldr
Which cannot but be thankfully receiv'd.	P 906	18.7	Bartus
To which thou didst alure me being alive:	P1025	19.95	King
Which if I doe, the Papall Monarck goes/To wrack, and [his]	P1197	22.59	King
exhalatione/which our great sonn of fraunce cold not effecte	Paris	ms20,p390	Guise
of a string/May draw the pliant king which way I please:	Edw	1.1.53	Gavstn
To hide those parts which men delight to see,	Edw	1.1.65	Gavstn
For which, had not his highnes lov'd him well,	Edw	1.1.112	Kent
Which whiles I have, I thinke my selfe as great,	Edw	1.1.172	Gavstn
This ground which is corrupted with their steps,	Edw	1.2.5	Lncstr
Which being caught, strikes him that takes it dead,	Edw	1.4.222	Mortmr
This which I urge, is of a burning zeale,	Edw	1.4.256	Mortmr
Which may in Ireland purchase him such friends,	Edw	1.4.259	Mortmr
Which for his fathers sake leane to the king,	Edw	1.4.283	Mortmr
Which beates upon it like the Cyclops hammers,	Edw	1.4.313	Edward
Which of the nobles dost thou meane to serve?	Edw	2.1.3	Baldck
And as she red, she smild, which makes me thinke,	Edw	2.1.21	Spencr
Which made me curate-like in mine attire,	Edw	2.1.49	Baldck
Which all the other fishes deadly hate,	Edw	2.2.24	Lncstr
Which swept the desart shore of that dead sea,	Edw	2.3.22	Mortmr
For which ere long, their heads shall satisfie,	Edw	3.1.209	Edward
For which thy head shall over looke the rest,	Edw	3.1.239	Edward
Which in a moment will abridge his life:	Edw	5.1.42	Edward
In which extreame my minde here murthered is:	Edw	5.1.55	Edward
Which fils my mind with strange despairing thoughts,	Edw	5.1.79	Edward
Which thoughts are martyred with endles torments.	Edw	5.1.80	Edward
I, I, and none shall know which way he died.	Edw	5.4.25	Ltborn
To which the channels of the castell runne,	Edw	5.5.3	Matrvs
This feare is that which makes me tremble thus,	Edw	5.5.105	Edward
that in thy wheele/There is a point, to which when men aspire,	Edw	5.6.60	Mortmr
Which he preferres before his chiefest blisse;	F 27	Prol.27	1Chor
of argument, which <that> you, being Licentiats <licentiate>,	F 202	1.2.9	P Wagner
Then I feare that which I have long suspected:	F 220	1.2.27	1Schol
damned Art/For which they two are infamous through the world.	F 222	1.2.29	1Schol
By which the spirits are inforc'd to rise:	F 241	1.3.13	Faust
For which God threw him from the face of heaven.	F 296	1.3.68	Mephst
Which [strike] <strikes> a terror to my fainting soule.	F 310	1.3.82	Mephst
In which <Wherein> thou hast given thy soule to Lucifer.	F 520	2.1.132	Mephst
The which <That to> this day is highly solemnized.	F 778	2.3.57	2Chor
In [midst] <one> of which a sumptuous Temple stands,	F 795	3.1.17	Faust
Over the which [foure] <two> stately Bridges leane,	F 815	3.1.37	Mephst
That <which> Julius caesar brought from Affrica.	F 824	3.1.46	Mephst
The which this day with high solemnity,	F 833	3.1.55	Mephst
[Which Faustus answered with such learned skill],	F1147	3.3.60A	3Chor
which being all I desire, I am content to remove his hornes.	F1313	4.1.159	P Faust
Through which the Furies drag'd me by the heeles.	F1435	4.3.5	Mrtino
grace to thinke but well of that which Faustus hath performed.	F1564	4.6.7	P Faust
which we will recompence/With all the love and kindnesse that	F1671	4.6.114	Duke
which was the beautifullest in all the world, we have	F1682	5.1.9	P 1Schol
I will attempt, which is but little worth.	F1758	5.1.85	Mephst
That heavenly Hellen, which I saw of late,	F1762	5.1.89	Faust
Those soules which sinne seales the blacke sonnes of hell,	F1799	5.2.3	Lucifr
'Mong which as chiefe, Faustus we come to thee,	F1800	5.2.4	Lucifr
wait upon thy soule; the time is come/Which makes it forfeit.	F1803	5.2.7	Lucifr
for which Faustus hath lost both Germany and the world, yea	F1843	5.2.47	P Faust
At which selfe time the house seem'd all on fire,	F1993	5.3.11	3Schol
How now, whose that which spake?	F App	p.231 3	P Pope
How now, whose that which snatcht the meate from me?	F App	p.231 8	P Pope
goe and make cleane our bootes which lie foule upon our handes,	F App	p.234 33	P Robin
amongest which kings is Alexander the great, chiefe spectacle	F App	p.237 23	P Emper
two deceased princes which long since are consumed to dust.	F App	p.237 43	P Faust
which I doubt not shal sufficiently content your Imperiall	F App	p.237 48	P Faust
which being all I desire, I am content to release him of his	F App	p.238 83	P Faust
By which sweete path thou maist attaine the gole/That shall	F App	p.243 36	OldMan
Will ye wadge war, for which you shall not triumph?	Lucan, First Booke		12
Which made thee Emperor; thee (seeing thou being old/Must shine	Lucan, First Booke		45
superior, which of both/Had justest cause unlawful tis to judge:	Lucan, First Booke		126
So thunder which the wind teares from the cloudes,	Lucan, First Booke		152
al the world/Ransackt for golde, which breeds the world decay;	Lucan, First Booke		168
The ground which Curius and Camillus till'd,	Lucan, First Booke		170
Which issues from a small spring, is but shallow,	Lucan, First Booke		216
Which being broke the foot had easie passage.	Lucan, First Booke		224
Or darts which Parthians backward shoot) marcht on/And then	Lucan, First Booke		232
Through which the wood peer'd, headles darts, olde swords/With	Lucan, First Booke		244
That crost them; both which now approacht the camp,	Lucan, First Booke		270
Which is nor sea, nor land, but oft times both,	Lucan, First Booke		411
too, which bouldly faine themselves/The Romanes brethren,	Lucan, First Booke		428
And shame to spare life which being lost is wonne.	Lucan, First Booke		458
and Rhene, which he hath brought/From out their Northren parts,	Lucan, First Booke		478
Which makes the maine saile fal with hideous sound;	Lucan, First Booke		498
Which wont to run their course through empty night/At noone day	Lucan, First Booke		534
Which flamed not on high; but headlong pitcht/Her burning head	Lucan, First Booke		544
hellish fiend/Which made the sterne Lycurgus wound his thigh,	Lucan, First Booke		573
And which (aie me) ever pretendeth ill,	Lucan, First Booke		625
We which were Ovids five books, now are three,	Ovid's Elegies		1.1.1
Which being not shakt <slackt>, I saw it die at length.	Ovid's Elegies		1.2.12
Then oxen which have drawne the plow before.	Ovid's Elegies		1.2.14
Which troopes hath alwayes bin on Cupids side:	Ovid's Elegies		1.2.36
My spotlesse life, which but to Gods [gives] <give> place,	Ovid's Elegies		1.3.13
Which gave such light, as twincles in a wood,	Ovid's Elegies		1.5.4
And let the troupes which shall thy Chariot follow,	Ovid's Elegies		1.7.37

WHICH (cont.)

Which to her wast her girdle still kept downe.	Ovid's Elegies	1.7.48
Chiefely shew him the gifts, which others send:	Ovid's Elegies	1.8.99
by the pleasure/Which man and woman reape in equall measure?	Ovid's Elegies	1.10.36
Which I thinke gather'd from cold hemlocks flower/Wherein bad	Ovid's Elegies	1.12.9
better/In which the Merchant wayles his banquerout debter.	Ovid's Elegies	1.12.26
Or thrids which spiders slender foote drawes out/Fastning her	Ovid's Elegies	1.14.7
which from their crowne/Phoebus and Bacchus wisht were hanging	Ovid's Elegies	1.14.31
Which some admiring, O thou oft wilt blush/And say he likes me	Ovid's Elegies	1.14.47
[And] <The> banks ore which gold bearing Tagus flowes.	Ovid's Elegies	1.15.34
I had in hand/Which for his heaven fell on the Gyants band.	Ovid's Elegies	2.1.16
lookes to my verse/Which golden love doth unto me rehearse.	Ovid's Elegies	2.1.38
Which giving her, she may give thee againe.	Ovid's Elegies	2.2.16
Which do perchance old age unto them give.	Ovid's Elegies	2.6.28
Which stormie South-windes into sea did blowe?	Ovid's Elegies	2.6.44
For which good turne my sweete reward repay,	Ovid's Elegies	2.8.21
Which is the loveliest it is hard to say:	Ovid's Elegies	2.10.6
Which rashly twixt the sharpe rocks in the deepe,	Ovid's Elegies	2.11.3
Which without bloud-shed doth the pray inherit.	Ovid's Elegies	2.12.6
Pelignian fields [with] <which> liqued rivers flowe,	Ovid's Elegies	2.16.5
Which as it seemes, hence winde and sea bereaves.	Ovid's Elegies	2.16.46
Thou hast my gift, which she would from thee sue.	Ovid's Elegies	3.1.60
Which lie hid under her thinne veile suppreast.	Ovid's Elegies	3.2.36
By which she perjurd oft hath lyed [to] <by> me.	Ovid's Elegies	3.3.10
Which wealth, cold winter doth on thee bestowe.	Ovid's Elegies	3.5.94
Then did the robe or garment which she wore <more>,	Ovid's Elegies	3.6.40
they had bestowde/This <The> benefite, which lewdly I forslowd:	Ovid's Elegies	3.6.46
Nor usde the slight nor <and> cunning which she could,	Ovid's Elegies	3.6.56
Which by the wild boare in the woods was shorne.	Ovid's Elegies	3.9.40
And doubt to which desire the palme to give.	Ovid's Elegies	3.10.40
What day was that, which all sad haps to bring,	Ovid's Elegies	3.11.1
Which with the grasse of Tuscane fields are fed.	Ovid's Elegies	3.12.14
Which fact, and country wealth Halesus fled.	Ovid's Elegies	3.12.32
Which I Pelignis foster-child have framde,	Ovid's Elegies	3.14.3
When t'was the odour which her breath foorth cast.	Hero and Leander	1.22
Which lightned by her necke, like Diamonds shone.	Hero and Leander	1.26
Which as shee went would cherupe through the bils.	Hero and Leander	1.36
Frighted the melancholie earth, which deem'd,	Hero and Leander	1.99
Which limping Vulcan and his Cyclops set:	Hero and Leander	1.152
Which like sweet musicke entred Heroes eares,	Hero and Leander	1.194
Which makes me hope, although I am but base,	Hero and Leander	1.218
Which long time lie untoucht, will harshly jarre.	Hero and Leander	1.230
Which after his disceasse, some other gains.	Hero and Leander	1.246
By which alone, our reverend fathers say,	Hero and Leander	1.267
This idoll which you terme Virginitie,	Hero and Leander	1.269
Of that which hath no being, doe not boast,	Hero and Leander	1.275
of liquid pearle, which downe her face/Made milk-white paths,	Hero and Leander	1.297
The rites/In which Loves beauteous Empresse most delites,/Are	Hero and Leander	1.300
To expiat which sinne, kisse and shake hands,	Hero and Leander	1.309
Which makes him quickly re-enforce his speech,	Hero and Leander	1.313
youth forbeare/To touch the sacred garments which I weare.	Hero and Leander	1.344
in being bold/To eie those parts, which no eie should behold.	Hero and Leander	1.408
Which being knowne (as what is hid from Jove)?	Hero and Leander	1.436
Which th'earth from ougly Chaos den up-wayd:	Hero and Leander	1.450
To which the Muses sonnes are only heire:	Hero and Leander	1.476
Which joyfull Hero answered in such sort,	Hero and Leander	2.15
Which taught him all that elder lovers know,	Hero and Leander	2.69
Which made his love through Sestos to bee knowne,	Hero and Leander	2.111
Which mounted up, intending to have kist him,	Hero and Leander	2.173
went and came, as if he rewd/The greefe which Neptune felt.	Hero and Leander	2.215
And knockt and cald, at which celestiall noise,	Hero and Leander	2.231
By those white limmes, which sparckled through the lawne.	Hero and Leander	2.242
Which is with azure circling lines empal'd,	Hero and Leander	2.274
By which love sailes to regions full of blis),	Hero and Leander	2.276
Which so prevail'd, as he with small ado,	Hero and Leander	2.281
Even as a bird, which in our hands we wring,	Hero and Leander	2.289
of hers (like that/Which made the world) another world begat,	Hero and Leander	2.292
That which so long so charily she kept,	Hero and Leander	2.309
A kind of twilight breake, which through the heare,	Hero and Leander	2.319
Which watchfull Hesperus no sooner heard,	Hero and Leander	2.329
Which from our pretty Lambes we pull,	Passionate Shepherd	14

WHILE

That erst-while issued from thy watrie loynes,	Dido	1.1.128		Venus
The while thine eyes attract their sought for joyes:	Dido	1.1.136		Venus
Alas sweet boy, thou must be still a while,	Dido	1.1.164		Aeneas
A little while prolong'd her husbands life:	Dido	2.1.246		Aeneas
No more my child, now talke another while,	Dido	3.1.26		Dido
Iarbus pardon me, and stay a while.	Dido	3.1.46		Dido
But where were you Iarbus all this while?	Dido	4.1.31		Dido
While Italy is cleane out of thy minde?	Dido	5.1.29		Hermes
And stay a while to heare what I could say,	Dido	5.1.239		Anna
Least if we let them lynger here a while,	1Tamb	2.2.20		Meandr
And while the base borne Tartars take it up,	1Tamb	2.2.65		Meandr
Here take it for a while, I lend it thee,	1Tamb	2.4.37		Tamb
While you faint-hearted base Egyptians,	1Tamb	4.1.8		Souldn
While thundring Cannons rattle on their Skins.	1Tamb	4.1.11		Souldn
While they walke quivering on their citie walles,	1Tamb	4.4.3		Tamb
dispatch her while she is fat, for if she live but a while	1Tamb	4.4.48	P	Tamb
for if she live but a while longer, shee will fall into a	1Tamb	4.4.49	P	Tamb
Faste and welcome sir, while hunger make you eat.	1Tamb	4.4.56	P	Tamb
Left to themselves while we were at the fight,	1Tamb	5.1.471		Tamb
Come banquet and carouse with us a while,	2Tamb	1.1.165		Orcan
But while my brothers follow armes my lord,	2Tamb	1.3.65		Calyph

WHILE (cont.)

Now will we banquet on these plaines a while,	2Tamb	1.3.157	Tamb
And therefore let them rest a while my Lord.	2Tamb	1.3.184	Usumc
But since my life is lengthened yet a while,	2Tamb	2.4.71	Zenoc
for whose byrth/Olde Rome was proud, but gasde a while on her,	2Tamb	2.4.92	Tamb
While I sit smiling to behold the sight.	2Tamb	3.2.128	Tamb
But stay a while, summon a parle, Drum,	2Tamb	3.3.11	Therid
while all thy joints/Be rackt and beat asunder with the wheele,	2Tamb	3.5.124	Tamb
Ile dispose them as it likes me best,/Meane while take him in.	2Tamb	4.1.167	Tamb
While these their fellow kings may be refresht.	2Tamb	4.3.31	Tamb
to your taskes a while/And take such fortune as your fellowes	2Tamb	5.1.136	Tamb
And could I but a while pursue the field,	2Tamb	5.3.117	Tamb
For though they doe a while increase and multiply,	Jew	2.3.89	Barab
Whither goes Don Mathias? stay a while.	Jew	2.3.251	Barab
While she runs to the window looking out/When you should come	Jew	2.3.264	Barab
That maidens new betroth'd should weepe a while:	Jew	2.3.326	Barab
Then breath a while.	P 241	4.39	Guise
O let me stay and rest me heer a while,	P 536	11.1	Charls
what now remaines, but for a while to feast,	P 627	12.40	King
For while she lives Katherine will be Queene.	P 654	12.67	QnMoth
Then stay a while and Ile goe call the King,	P1017	19.87	Capt
O my Lord, let him live a while.	P1173	22.35	Eprnon
Sweete Mortimer, sit downe by me a while,	Edw	1.4.225	Queene
While souldiers mutinie for want of paie.	Edw	1.4.406	Mortmr
May with one word, advaunce us while we live:	Edw	2.1.9	Spencr
I for a while, but Baldock marke the end,	Edw	2.1.16	Spencr
While in the harbor ride thy ships unrigd.	Edw	2.2.169	Mortmr
To breathe a while, our men with sweat and dust/All chockt well	Edw	3.1.191	SpncrP
diest, for Mortimer/And Isabell doe kisse while they conspire,	Edw	4.6.13	Kent
Meane while, have hence this rebell to the blocke,	Edw	4.6.69	Mortmr
We in meane while madam, must take advise,	Edw	4.6.77	Mortmr
But stay a while, let me be king till night,	Edw	5.1.59	Edward
And therefore let me weare it yet a while.	Edw	5.1.83	Edward
While at the councell table, grave enough,	Edw	5.4.58	Mortmr
Let us assaile his minde another while.	Edw	5.5.12	Matrvs
I, stay a while, thou shalt have answer straight.	Edw	5.5.20	Matrvs
list a while to me,/And then thy heart, were it as Gurneys is,	Edw	5.5.52	Edward
Lie on this bed, and rest your selfe a while.	Edw	5.5.72	Ltborn
Yet stay a while, forbeare thy bloudie hande,	Edw	5.5.75	Edward
O let me not die yet, stay, O stay a while.	Edw	5.5.101	Edward
Meane while peruse this booke, and view it throughly,	F 717	2.2.169	Lucifr
to thinke I have beene such an Asse all this while, to stand	F1244	4.1.90	P Benvol
A plague upon you, let me sleepe a while.	F1283	4.1.129	Benvol
Come Faustus while the Emperour lives.	F1321	4.1.167	Emper
we'le into another roome and drinke a while, and then we'le go	F1556	4.5.52	P Robin
My Lord, beseech you give me leave a while,	F1621	4.6.64	Faust
Leave me a while, to ponder on my sinnes.	F1736	5.1.63	Faust
Adders and serpents, let me breathe a while:	F1980	5.2.184	Faust
this Lady while she liv'd had a wart or moale in her necke,	F App	p.238 60	P Emper
While slaughtred Crassus ghost walks unreveng'd,	Lucan, First Booke	11	
While th'earth the sea, and ayre the earth sustaines;	Lucan, First Booke	89	
While Titan strives against the worlds swift course;	Lucan, First Booke	90	
Caesar (said he) while eloquence prevail'd,	Lucan, First Booke	274	
Now while their part is weake, and feares, march hence,	Lucan, First Booke	281	
While these thus in and out had circled Roome,	Lucan, First Booke	604	
While Mars doth take the Aonian harpe to play?	Ovid's Elegies	1.1.16	
While others touch the damsell I love best?	Ovid's Elegies	1.4.4	
And while he drinkes, to adde more do not misse,	Ovid's Elegies	1.4.52	
While rage is absent, take some friend the paynes.	Ovid's Elegies	1.7.2	
words she sayd/While closely hid betwixt two dores I layed.	Ovid's Elegies	1.8.22	
Make a small price, while thou thy nets doest lay,	Ovid's Elegies	1.8.69	
Within a while great heapes grow of a tittle.	Ovid's Elegies	1.8.90	
Let thy tongue flatter, while thy minde harme-workes:	Ovid's Elegies	1.8.103	
Troianes destroy the Greeke wealth, while you may.	Ovid's Elegies	1.9.34	
While thou wert plaine, I lov'd thy minde and face:	Ovid's Elegies	1.10.13	
Time passeth while I speake, give her my writ/But see that	Ovid's Elegies	1.11.15	
Would Tithon might but talke of thee a while,	Ovid's Elegies	1.13.35	
Homer shall live while Tenedos stands and Ide,	Ovid's Elegies	1.15.9	
Ascreus lives, while grapes with new wine swell,	Ovid's Elegies	1.15.11	
While bond-men cheat, fathers [be hard] <hoord>, bawds hoorish,	Ovid's Elegies	1.15.17	
While Rome of all the [conquered] <conquering> world is head.	Ovid's Elegies	1.15.26	
While I speake some fewe, yet fit words be idle.	Ovid's Elegies	2.2.2	
While Junos watch-man Io too much eyde,	Ovid's Elegies	2.2.45	
While thou hast time yet to bestowe that gift.	Ovid's Elegies	2.3.18	
I that ere-while was fierce, now humbly sue,	Ovid's Elegies	2.5.49	
While rashly her wombes burthen she casts out,	Ovid's Elegies	2.13.1	
Let me be slandered, while my fire she hides,	Ovid's Elegies	2.17.3	
To tragick verse while thou Achilles trainst,	Ovid's Elegies	2.18.1	
While Juno Io keepes when hornes she wore,	Ovid's Elegies	2.19.29	
Heere while I walke hid close in shadie grove,	Ovid's Elegies	3.1.5	
While without shame thou singst thy lewdnesse ditty.	Ovid's Elegies	3.1.22	
Hippodameias lookes while he beheld.	Ovid's Elegies	3.2.16	
While thus I speake, blacke dust her white robes ray:	Ovid's Elegies	3.2.41	
[A] <Or> while thy tiptoes on the foote-stoole rest.	Ovid's Elegies	3.2.64	
My bones had beene, while yet I was a maide.	Ovid's Elegies	3.5.74	
While thus I speake, the waters more abounded:	Ovid's Elegies	3.5.85	
I know not what expecting, I ere while/Nam'd Achelaus, Inachus,	Ovid's Elegies	3.5.103	
Was I: thou liv'dst, while thou esteemdst my faith.	Ovid's Elegies	3.8.56	
Though while the deede be doing you be tooke,	Ovid's Elegies	3.13.43	
Thus while dum signs their yeelding harts entangled,	Hero and Leander	1.187	
So having paus'd a while, at last shee said:	Hero and Leander	1.337	
Harken a while, and I will tell you why:	Hero and Leander	1.385	
The while upon a hillocke downe he lay,	Hero and Leander	1.400	

WHILES
And held the cloath of pleasance whiles you dranke, Dido 1.1.6 Ganimd
Whiles my Aeneas wanders on the Seas, Dido 1.1.52 Venus
Whiles my Aeneas spends himselfe in plaints, Dido 1.1.140 Venus
Whiles I with my Achates roave abroad, Dido 1.1.175 Aeneas
Whiles Dido lives and rules in Junos towne, Dido 3.4.50 Aeneas
Whiles these adulterors surfetted with sinne: Dido 4.1.20 Iarbus
There whiles he lives, shal Bajazeth be kept, 1Tamb 4.2.85 Tamb
Whiles only danger beat upon our walles, 1Tamb 5.1.30 1Virgn
Come let us banquet and carrouse the whiles. 2Tamb 1.3.225 Tamb
Which whiles I have, I thinke my selfe as great, Edw 1.1.172 Gavstn
Whiles other walke below, the king and he/From out a window, Edw 1.4.416 Mortmr
But whiles I have a sword, a hand, a hart, Edw 1.4.422 Mortmr
Mine old lord whiles he livde, was so precise, Edw 2.1.46 Baldck
WHILEST
That this faire Lady, whilest she liv'd on earth, F1266 4.1.112 Emper
WHILOM
Whilom I was, powerfull and full of pompe, Edw 4.7.13 Edward
WHIL'ST
This butcher whil'st his hands were yet held up, Dido 2.1.241 Aeneas
Whil'st they were sporting in this darksome Cave? Dido 4.1.24 Iarbus
Whil'st I rest thankfull for this curtesie. Dido 5.1.77 Aeneas
WHILST
But whilst I live will be at truce with thee. 2Tamb 1.1.130 Sgsmnd
For whilst I live, here lives my soules sole hope, Jew 2.1.29 Barab
And whilst I live use halfe; spend as my selfe; Jew 3.4.45 Barab
Whilst I in thy incony lap doe tumble. Jew 4.4.29 Ithimr
Now whilst you give assault unto the wals, Jew 5.1.90 Barab
Two of my fathers servants whilst he liv'de, Edw 2.2.240 Neece
Whilst I am lodgd within this cave of care, Edw 5.1.32 Edward
Ile not resigne, but whilst I live, [be king]. Edw 5.1.86 Edward
Or whilst one is a sleepe, to take a quill/And blowe a little Edw 5.4.34 Ltborn
I charge thee waite upon me whilst I live/To do what ever F 264 1.3.36 Faust
That I shall waite on Faustus whilst he lives, F 420 2.1.32 Mephst
Whilst I am here on earth let me be cloyd/With all things that F 837 3.1.59 Faust
That Faustus name, whilst this bright frame doth stand, F 841 3.1.63 Faust
Whilst on thy backe his hollinesse ascends/Saint Peters Chaire F 869 3.1.91 Raymnd
But whilst they sleepe within the Consistory, F 943 3.1.165 Faust
<to do what I please unseene of any whilst I stay in Rome>. F 993 (HC266)A P Faust
Whilst on thy head I lay my hand, F 995 3.2.15 Mephst
Whilst with my gentle Mephostophilis, F1412 4.2.88 Faust
And give me cause to praise thee whilst I live. F App p.237 36 Emper
my Lord, and whilst I live, Rest beholding for this curtesie. F App p.243 30 P Duchss
many a heard, whilst with their dams/They kennel'd in Hircania, Lucan, First Booke 328
WHILSTE
And now Navarre whilste that these broiles doe last, P 565 11.30 Navrre
Come Pleshe, lets away whilste time doth serve. P 587 11.52 Navrre
And whilste he sleepes securely thus in ease, P 635 12.48 QnMoth
Whilste I cry placet like a Senator. P 861 17.56 King
WHINE
Traitor be gone, whine thou with Mortimer. Edw 2.2.214 Edward
WHIP
I could afford to whip my selfe to death. Jew 4.1.59 Barab
Then be themselves base subjects to the whip. P 218 4.16 Anjoy
Come sirs, Ile whip you to death with my punniards point. P 441 7.81 Guise
WHIPPINCRUST
Muskadine, Malmesey and Whippincrust, hold belly hold, and F 749 2.3.28 P Robin
WHIPPING
But as her naked feet were whipping out, Hero and Leander 2.313
WHIPS
And when ye stay, be lasht with whips of wier: 2Tamb 3.5.105 Tamb
Sirha, prepare whips, and bring my chariot to my Tent: 2Tamb 3.5.144 P Tamb
That whips downe cities, and controwleth crownes, 2Tamb 4.3.100 Tamb
WHIPT
Or els I sweare to have you whipt stark nak'd. 1Tamb 4.2.74 Anippe
To fast and be well whipt; I'le none of that. Jew 4.1.124 Barab
And, rowing in a Gally, whipt to death. Jew 5.1.68 Barab
WHIRL
I goe as whirl-windes rage before a storme. P 511 9.30 Guise
WHIRL'D
Cole-blacke Charibdis whirl'd a sea of bloud; Lucan, First Booke 546
WHIRLE
Some whirle winde fetche them backe, or sincke them all:-- Edw 4.6.59 Mortmr
Brings Thunder, Whirle-winds, Storme <tempests> and Lightning: F 546 2.1.158 Mephst
I know not whether my mindes whirle-wind drives me. Ovid's Elegies 2.9.28
As his deepe whirle-pooles could not quench the same. Ovid's Elegies 3.5.42
WHIRLE-POOLES
As his deepe whirle-pooles could not quench the same. Ovid's Elegies 3.5.42
WHIRLE-WIND (See also WHYRLWIND)
I know not whether my mindes whirle-wind drives me. Ovid's Elegies 2.9.28
WHIRLE WINDE
Some whirle winde fetche them backe, or sincke them all:-- Edw 4.6.59 Mortmr
WHIRLE-WINDS
Brings Thunder, Whirle-winds, Storme <tempests> and Lightning: F 546 2.1.158 Mephst
WHIRLING
And whirling round with this circumference, F 764 2.3.43 2Chor
WHIRL-WINDES
I goe as whirl-windes rage before a storme. P 511 9.30 Guise
WHISKING
Or whisking of these leaves, all shall be still, Dido 2.1.337 Venus
WHISKT
Which he disdaining whiskt his sword about, Dido 2.1.253 Aeneas
rage increase, then having whiskt/His taile athwart his backe, Lucan, First Booke 210

WHISPER			
And when we whisper, then the starres fall downe,	Dido	4.4.53	Dido
Whatsoever any whisper in mine eares,	P 974	19.44	King
And now she lets him whisper in her eare,	Hero and Leander		2.267
WHISPERED			
My lord I heare it whispered every where,	Edw	1.4.106	Gavstn
Thus sighing whispered they, and none durst speake/And shew	Lucan, First Booke		259
WHISPERS			
Smiles in his face, and whispers in his eares,	Edw	1.2.52	Queene
Some thing he whispers in his childish eares.	Edw	5.2.76	Queene
WHIST			
The ayre is cleere, and Southerne windes are whist,	Dido	4.1.25	Aeneas
Or sea far from the land, so all were whist.	Lucan, First Booke		262
Far from the towne (where all is whist and still,	Hero and Leander		1.346
WHISTLES			
And silver whistles to controule the windes,	Dido	4.4.10	Dido
WHISTLING			
noise/Of trumpets clange, shril cornets, whistling fifes;	Lucan, First Booke		240
WHIT			
Though thou nor he will pitie me a whit.	Dido	5.1.178	Dido
My teares nor plaints could mollifie a whit:	Dido	5.1.235	Anna
And so mistake you not a whit my Lord.	1Tamb	2.3.6	Tamb
No whit my Lord:	2Tamb	2.1.33	Baldwn
Nay more, the wench did not disdaine a whit,	Ovid's Elegies		3.6.73
WHITE			
Altars crack/With mountaine heapes of milke white Sacrifize.	Dido	1.1.202	Aeneas
These milke white Doves shall be his Centronels:	Dido	2.1.320	Venus
Then touch her white breast with this arrow head,	Dido	2.1.326	Venus
White Swannes, and many lovely water fowles:	Dido	4.5.11	Nurse
That I may view these milk-white steeds of mine,	1Tamb	1.1.77	Mycet
With milke-white Hartes upon an Ivorie sled,	1Tamb	1.2.98	Tamb
Brave horses, bred on the white Tartarian hils:	1Tamb	3.3.151	Tamb
Resting her selfe upon my milk-white Tent:	1Tamb	3.3.161	Tamb
White is their hew, and on his silver crest/A snowy Feather	1Tamb	4.1.50	2Msngr
on his silver crest/A snowy Feather spangled white he beares,	1Tamb	4.1.51	2Msngr
Your tentes of white now pitch'd before the gates/And gentle	1Tamb	4.2.111	Therid
Streamers white, Red, Blacke.	1Tamb	5.1.315	P Zabina
Their haire as white as milke and soft as Downe,	2Tamb	1.3.25	Tamb
Priest/Cal'd John the great, sits in a milk-white robe,	2Tamb	1.3.188	Techel
queintly dect/With bloomes more white than Hericinas browes,	2Tamb	4.3.122	Tamb
Shall mount the milk-white way and meet him there.	2Tamb	4.3.132	Tamb
And the white leprosie.	Jew	2.3.54	Barab
Shall weare white crosses on their Burgonets,	P 232	4.30	Guise
And tye white linnen scarfes about their armes.	P 233	4.31	Guise
Such reasons make white blacke, and darke night day.	Edw	1.4.247	Lncstr
Then has <in> the white breasts of the Queene of love.	F 156	1.1.128	Valdes
but to the Taverne with me, I'le give thee white wine, red wine,	F 748	2.3.27	P Robin
But seeing white Eagles, and Roomes flags wel known,	Lucan, First Booke		246
Her white necke hid with tresses hanging downe,	Ovid's Elegies		1.5.10
lockes spred/On her white necke but for hurt cheekes be led.	Ovid's Elegies		1.7.40
her bloodlesse white lookes shewed/Like marble from the Parian	Ovid's Elegies		1.7.51
red shame becomes white cheekes, but this/If feigned, doth	Ovid's Elegies		1.8.35
God deluded/In snowe-white plumes of a false swanne included.	Ovid's Elegies		1.10.4
age you wrackes/And sluttish white-mould overgrowe the waxe.	Ovid's Elegies		1.12.30
Alas she almost weepes, and her white cheekes,	Ovid's Elegies		1.14.51
And call the sunnes white horses [backe] <blacke> at noone.	Ovid's Elegies		2.1.24
[A white wench thralles me, so doth golden yellowe],	Ovid's Elegies		2.4.39
If her white necke be shadowde with blacke haire,	Ovid's Elegies		2.4.41
Maides on the shore, with marble white feete tread,	Ovid's Elegies		2.11.15
I saw how Bulls for a white Heifer strive,	Ovid's Elegies		2.12.25
In white, with incense Ile thine Altars greete,	Ovid's Elegies		2.13.23
With thy white armes upon my shoulders seaze,	Ovid's Elegies		2.16.29
White-cheekt Penelope knewe Ulisses signe,	Ovid's Elegies		2.18.29
While thus I speake, blacke dust her white robes ray:	Ovid's Elegies		3.2.41
Faire white with rose red was before commixt:	Ovid's Elegies		3.3.5
Now shine her lookes pure white and red betwixt.	Ovid's Elegies		3.3.6
To stay thy tresses white veyle hast thou none?	Ovid's Elegies		3.5.56
But for thy merits I wish thee, white streame,	Ovid's Elegies		3.5.105
That were as white as is <Her armes farre whiter, then> the	Ovid's Elegies		3.6.8
And Libas, and the white cheek'de Pitho thrise,	Ovid's Elegies		3.6.24
Foole canst thou him in thy white armes embrace?	Ovid's Elegies		3.7.11
White birdes to lovers did not alwayes sing.	Ovid's Elegies		3.11.2
White Heifers by glad people forth are led,	Ovid's Elegies		3.12.13
As is the use, the Nunnes in white veyles clad,	Ovid's Elegies		3.12.27
they tooke delite/To play upon those hands, they were so white.	Hero and Leander		1.30
necke in touching, and surpast/The white of Pelops shoulder.	Hero and Leander		1.65
How smooth his brest was, and how white his bellie,	Hero and Leander		1.66
which downe her face/Made milk-white paths, wheron the gods	Hero and Leander		1.298
By those white limmes, which sparckled through the lawne.	Hero and Leander		2.242
WHITE-CHEEKT			
White-cheekt Penelope knewe Ulisses signe,	Ovid's Elegies		2.18.29
WHITE-MOULD			
age you wrackes/And sluttish white-mould overgrowe the waxe.	Ovid's Elegies		1.12.30
WHITER			
That were as white as is <Her armes farre whiter, then> the	Ovid's Elegies		3.6.8
WHITEST			
Fairer than whitest snow on Scythian hils,	1Tamb	1.2.89	Tamb
WHITHER (See also WHETHER)			
Whence may you come, or whither will you goe?	Dido	1.1.215	Venus
Whither must I goe? Ile stay with my mother.	Dido	4.5.2	Cupid
But whither am I bound, I come not, I,	Jew	Prol.28	Machvl
But whither wends my beauteous Abigall?	Jew	1.2.224	Barab
Now Captaine tell us whither thou art bound?	Jew	2.2.1	Govnr

WHITHER (cont.)

Whither walk'st thou, Barabas?	Jew	2.3.43	Lodowk
Whither goes Don Mathias? stay a while.	Jew	2.3.251	Barab
Whither but to my faire love Abigall?	Jew	2.3.252	Mthias
goe whither he will, I'le be none of his followers in haste:	Jew	4.2.25	P Ithimr
Whither so soone?	Jew	4.2.48	Curtzn
Whither will I not goe with gentle Ithimore?	Jew	4.2.99	Curtzn
Whither will your lordships?	Edw	2.2.133	Guard
Whither else but to the King.	Edw	2.2.134	Mortmr
is gone, whither if you aske, with sir John of Henolt, brother	Edw	4.3.31	P Spencr
Whither goes this letter, to my lord the king?	Edw	5.2.68	Queene
Friends, whither must unhappie Edward go,	Edw	5.3.4	Edward
Pean whither am I halde?	Lucan, First Booke		677
Whither turne I now?	Lucan, First Booke		682
Aurora whither slidest thou?	Ovid's Elegies		1.13.3
Whither runst thou, that men, and women, love not?	Ovid's Elegies		1.13.9
Whither gost thou hateful nimph?	Ovid's Elegies		1.13.31

WHO

Who with the Sunne devides one radiant shape,	Dido	1.1.97	Jupitr
Who will eternish Troy in their attempts.	Dido	1.1.108	Jupitr
Who driven by warre from forth my native world,	Dido	1.1.217	Aeneas
Who shall confirme my words with further deedes.	Dido	1.2.43	Iarbus
Who for her sonnes death wept out life and breath,	Dido	2.1.4	Aeneas
vouchsafe of ruth/To tell us who inhabits this faire towne,	Dido	2.1.41	Aeneas
What kind of people, and who governes them:	Dido	2.1.42	Aeneas
Who for Troyes sake hath entertaind us all,	Dido	2.1.64	Illion
Remember who thou art, speake like thy selfe,	Dido	2.1.100	Dido
And who so miserable as Aeneas is?	Dido	2.1.102	Aeneas
Who looking on the scarres we Troians gave,	Dido	2.1.131	Aeneas
Who groveling in the mire of Zanthus bankes,	Dido	2.1.150	Aeneas
Who with steele Pol-axes dasht out their braines.	Dido	2.1.199	Aeneas
O Hector who weepes not to heare thy name?	Dido	2.1.209	Dido
Who then ran to the pallace of the King,	Dido	2.1.224	Aeneas
Yet who so wretched but desires to live?	Dido	2.1.238	Aeneas
Who if that any seeke to doe him hurt,	Dido	2.1.321	Venus
who in stead of him/Will set thee on her lap and play with	Dido	2.1.324	Venus
Who warne me of such daunger prest at hand,	Dido	3.2.22	Venus
Who would not undergoe all kind of toyle,	Dido	3.3.58	Aeneas
Who nere will cease to soare till he be slaine.	Dido	3.3.85	Iarbus
Who then of all so cruell may he be,	Dido	3.4.16	Aeneas
Who having wrought her shame, is straight way fled:	Dido	4.2.18	Iarbus
Who seekes to rob me of thy Sisters love,	Dido	4.2.31	Iarbus
Who ever since hath luld me in her armes.	Dido	5.1.48	Ascan
Who have no sailes nor tackling for my ships?	Dido	5.1.56	Aeneas
Sweet sister cease, remember who you are.	Dido	5.1.263	Anna
Who wild me sacrifize his ticing relliques:	Dido	5.1.277	Dido
Who traveiling with these Medean Lords/To Memphis, from my	1Tamb	1.2.11	Zenoc
Who brings that Traitors head Theridamas,	1Tamb	2.2.32	Meandr
Who entring at the breach thy sword hath made,	1Tamb	2.7.9	Cosroe
Who thinke you now is king of Persea?	1Tamb	2.7.56	Tamb
Who when he shall embrace you in his armes,	1Tamb	3.2.42	Agidas
Who, when they come unto their fathers age,	1Tamb	3.3.110	Bajzth
Now king of Bassoes, who is Conqueror?	1Tamb	3.3.212	Tamb
Who lives in Egypt, prisoner to that slave,	2Tamb	1.1.4	Orcan
who hath followed long/The martiall sword of mighty	2Tamb	3.1.27	Callap
Who gently now wil lance thy Ivory throat,	2Tamb	3.4.24	Olymp
Who when he heares how resolute thou wert,	2Tamb	3.4.40	Techel
Who by this time is at Natolia,	2Tamb	3.4.86	Therid
Who meanes to gyrt Natolias walles with siege,	2Tamb	3.5.8	2Msngr
Who now with Jove opens the firmament,	2Tamb	3.5.56	Callap
Who shal kisse the fairest of the Turkes Concubines first, when	2Tamb	4.1.64	P Calyph
Who have ye there my Lordes?	2Tamb	5.1.80	Tamb
Who flies away at every glance I give,	2Tamb	5.3.70	Tamb
Who smiles to see how full his bags are cramb'd,	Jew	Prol.31	Machvl
who so richly pay/The things they traffique for with wedge of	Jew	1.1.8	Barab
But who comes heare? How now.	Jew	1.1.48	Barab
Tush, who amongst 'em knowes not Barrabas?	Jew	1.1.67	Barab
Who hateth me but for my happinesse?	Jew	1.1.112	Barab
Or who is honour'd now but for his wealth?	Jew	1.1.113	Barab
And all I have is hers. But who comes here?	Jew	1.1.139	Barab
Who stand accursed in the sight of heaven,	Jew	1.2.64	Govnr
Who for the villaines have no wit themselves,	Jew	1.2.215	Barab
It may be so: but who comes here?	Jew	1.2.313	Abbass
Who in my wealth wud tell me winters tales,	Jew	2.1.25	Barab
Who of meere charity and Christian ruth,	Jew	2.3.71	Barab
Who is this? my sonne Mathias slaine!	Jew	3.2.12	Mater
Who made them enemies?	Jew	3.2.20	Mater
Who taught thee this?	Jew	3.3.66	1Fryar
But who comes here?	Jew	3.4.13	Barab
Who I, master?	Jew	3.4.39	P Ithimr
Nor make enquiry who hath sent it them.	Jew	3.4.81	Barab
But Barabas, who shall be your godfathers,	Jew	4.1.109	1Fryar
Who would not thinke but that this Fryar liv'd?	Jew	4.1.156	Barab
Who is it?	Jew	4.1.176	Barab
only gave me a nod, as who shold say, Is it even so; and so I	Jew	4.2.12	P Pilia
me ever since she saw me, and who would not requite such love?	Jew	4.2.34	P Ithimr
this Gentlewoman, who as my selfe, and the rest of the family,	Jew	4.2.43	P Pilia
Who when he speakes, grunts like a hog, and looks/Like one that	Jew	4.3.11	Barab
That he who knowes I love him as my selfe/Should write in this	Jew	4.3.42	Barab
Who, besides the slaughter of these Gentlemen, poyson'd his	Jew	5.1.12	P Pilia
Confesse; what meane you, Lords, who should confesse?	Jew	5.1.26	Barab
Who carried that challenge?	Jew	5.1.31	Barab
I carried it, I confesse, but who writ it?	Jew	5.1.32	P Ithimr

WHO (cont.)

I am disguisde and none knows who I am,	P 278	5.5	Anjoy
Who is that which knocks there?	P 346	6.1	P SrnsWf
Who goes there?	P 371	7.11	Gonzag
Who have you there?	P 380	7.20	Anjoy
Who I? you are deceived, I rose but now.	P 437	7.77	Anjoy
Who set themselves to tread us under foot,	P 702	14.5	Navrre
But canst thou tell who is their generall?	P 731	14.34	Navrre
My father slaine, who hath done this deed?	P1047	19.117	YngGse
Or who will helpe to builde Religion?	P1084	19.154	QnMoth
And underneath thy banners march who will,	Edw	1.1.88	Mortmr
Why shouldst thou kneele, knowest thou not who I am?	Edw	1.1.142	Edward
Who swolne with venome of ambitious pride,	Edw	1.2.31	Mortmr
And when I come, he frownes, as who should say,	Edw	1.2.53	Queene
Who in the triumphe will be challenger,	Edw	1.4.382	Edward
Who should defray the money, but the King,	Edw	2.2.118	Mortmr
Who have we there, ist you?	Edw	2.2.140	Edward
Who loves thee? but a sort of flatterers.	Edw	2.2.171	Mortmr
Holla, who walketh there, ist you my lord?	Edw	4.1.12	Mortmr
His grace I dare presume will welcome me,/But who are these?	Edw	4.2.34	Queene
Mortimer, who talkes of Mortimer,	Edw	4.7.37	Edward
Who wounds me with the name of Mortimer/That bloudy man?	Edw	4.7.38	Edward
Who spots my nuptiall bed with infamie,	Edw	5.1.31	Edward
And who must keepe mee now, must you my lorde?	Edw	5.1.137	Edward
Who now makes Fortunes wheele turne as he please,	Edw	5.2.53	Mortmr
who should protect the sonne,/But she that gave him life, I	Edw	5.2.90	Kent
How now, who comes there?	Edw	5.3.49	Gurney
And what I list commaund, who dare controwle?	Edw	5.4.68	Mortmr
Lets see who dare impeache me for his death?	Edw	5.6.14	Mortmr
Who is the man dare say I murdered him?	Edw	5.6.40	Mortmr
Who aimes at nothing but externall trash,	F 62	1.1.34	Faust
Who would not be proficient in this Art?	F 256	1.3.28	Faust
Think'st thou that I [who] saw the face of God,	F 305	1.3.77	Mephst
Who buzzeth in mine eares I am a spirit?	F 565	2.2.14	Faust
Who knowes not the double motion of the Planets?	F 602	2.2.51	Faust
now tell me who made the world?	F 618	2.2.67	P Faust
I <who I sir, I> am Gluttony; my parents are all dead, and the	F 693	2.2.142	P Glutny
Who I <I I> sir?	F 708	2.2.160	P Ltchry
How now? who snatch't the meat from me!	F1044	3.2.64	Pope
who comes to see/What wonders by blacke spels may compast be.	F1197	4.1.43	Mrtino
Who kils him shall have gold, and endlesse love.	F1349	4.2.25	Fredrk
Who payes for the Ale?	F1666	4.6.109	P Hostss
have sent away my guesse, I pray who shall pay me for my A--	F1667	4.6.110	P Hostss
Who, Faustus?	F1854	5.2.58	P AllSch
O I'le leape up to [my God] <heaven>: who puls me downe?	F1938	5.2.142	Faust
who are at supper with such belly-cheere,	F App	p.243 6	Wagner
So when as Crassus wretched death who stayd them,	Lucan, First Booke	104	
Who though his root be weake, and his owne waight/Keepe him	Lucan, First Booke	139	
women; Poverty (who hatcht/Roomes greatest wittes) was loath'd,	Lucan, First Booke	166	
And armes all naked, who with broken sighes,	Lucan, First Booke	191	
Who seeing hunters pauseth till fell wrath/And kingly rage	Lucan, First Booke	209	
who though lockt and chaind in stalls,/Souse downe the wals,	Lucan, First Booke	295	
Who sees not warre sit by the quivering Judge;	Lucan, First Booke	320	
Who running long, fals in a greater floud,	Lucan, First Booke	401	
And Vangions who like those of Sarmata,	Lucan, First Booke	431	
who were wont/In large spread heire to exceed the rest of	Lucan, First Booke	438	
And their vaild Matron, who alone might view/Minervas statue;	Lucan, First Booke	597	
Rash boy, who gave thee power to change a line?	Ovid's Elegies	1.1.9	
Who gardes [the] <thee> conquered with his conquering hands.	Ovid's Elegies	1.2.52	
And Cupide who hath markt me for thy pray,	Ovid's Elegies	1.3.12	
Who feares these armes? who wil not go to meete them?	Ovid's Elegies	1.6.39	
And he who on his mother veng'd his sire,	Ovid's Elegies	1.7.9	
There is, who ere will knowe a bawde aright/Give eare, there is	Ovid's Elegies	1.8.1	
Who seekes, for being faire, a night to have,	Ovid's Elegies	1.8.67	
Who but a souldiour or a lover is bould/To suffer storme mixt	Ovid's Elegies	1.9.15	
Who slumbring, they rise up in swelling armes.	Ovid's Elegies	1.9.26	
rise/And who thou never think'st should fall downe lies.	Ovid's Elegies	1.9.30	
Therefore who ere love sloathfulnesse doth call,	Ovid's Elegies	1.9.31	
Who can indure, save him with whom none lies?	Ovid's Elegies	1.13.26	
Or he who war'd and wand'red twenty yeare?	Ovid's Elegies	2.1.31	
Who first depriv'd yong boyes of their best part,	Ovid's Elegies	2.3.3	
Who would not love those hands for their swift running?	Ovid's Elegies	2.4.28	
With Venus game who will a servant grace?	Ovid's Elegies	2.7.21	
Who that our bodies were comprest bewrayde?	Ovid's Elegies	2.8.5	
Hees happie who loves mutuall skirmish slayes <layes>,	Ovid's Elegies	2.10.29	
Rome did send/The Sabine Fathers, who sharpe warres intend.	Ovid's Elegies	2.12.24	
Who unborne infants first to slay invented,	Ovid's Elegies	2.14.5	
Who should have Priams wealthy substance wonne,	Ovid's Elegies	2.14.13	
And who ere see her, worthily lament.	Ovid's Elegies	2.14.40	
Who doubts, with Pelius, Thetis did consort,	Ovid's Elegies	2.17.17	
Who covets lawfull things takes leaves from woods,	Ovid's Elegies	2.19.31	
Search at the dore who knocks oft in the darke,	Ovid's Elegies	2.19.39	
Who now will care the Altars to perfume?	Ovid's Elegies	3.3.33	
Who, without feare, is chaste, is chast in sooth:	Ovid's Elegies	3.4.3	
Who, because meanes want, doeth not, she doth.	Ovid's Elegies	3.4.4	
Who may offend, sinnes least; power to do ill,	Ovid's Elegies	3.4.9	
Thebe who Mother of five Daughters prov'd?	Ovid's Elegies	3.5.34	
Who so well keepes his waters head from knowing,	Ovid's Elegies	3.5.40	
Nor passe I thee, who hollow rocks downe tumbling,	Ovid's Elegies	3.5.45	
Who sayd with gratefull voyce perpetuall bee?	Ovid's Elegies	3.5.98	
Or shade, or body was [I] <Io>, who can say?	Ovid's Elegies	3.6.16	
Who bad thee lie downe here against thy will?	Ovid's Elegies	3.6.78	
One [her] <she> commands, who many things can give.	Ovid's Elegies	3.7.62	

WHO (cont.)			
Who thinkes her to be glad at lovers smart,	Ovid's Elegies		3.9.15
There, he who rules the worlds starre-spangled towers,	Ovid's Elegies		3.9.21
Some other seeke, who will these things endure.	Ovid's Elegies		3.10.28
fellow bed, by all/The Gods who by thee to be perjurde fall,	Ovid's Elegies		3.10.46
Who mine was cald, whom I lov'd more then any,	Ovid's Elegies		3.11.5
Who sees it, graunts some deity there is shrowded.	Ovid's Elegies		3.12.8
Firmament/Glistered with breathing stars, who where they went,	Hero and Leander		1.98
Who ever lov'd, that lov'd not at first sight?	Hero and Leander		1.176
Then shouldst thou bee his prisoner who is thine.	Hero and Leander		1.202
Who on Loves seas more glorious wouldst appeare?	Hero and Leander		1.228
Who builds a pallace and rams up the gate,	Hero and Leander		1.239
Who taught thee Rhethoricke to deceive a maid?	Hero and Leander		1.338
After went Mercurie, who us'd such cunning,	Hero and Leander		1.417
Who with incroching guile, keepes learning downe.	Hero and Leander		1.482
At last he came, O who can tell the greeting,	Hero and Leander		2.23
And who have hard hearts, and obdurat minds,	Hero and Leander		2.217
Who hoping to imbrace thee, cherely swome.	Hero and Leander		2.250
Or speake to him who in a moment tooke,	Hero and Leander		2.308
WHO ERE			
There is, who ere will knowe a bawde aright/Give eare, there is	Ovid's Elegies		1.8.1
Therefore who ere love sloathfulnesse doth call,	Ovid's Elegies		1.9.31
And who ere see her, worthily lament.	Ovid's Elegies		2.14.40
WHO EVER			
Who ever since hath luld me in her armes.	Dido	5.1.48	Ascan
Who ever lov'd, that lov'd not at first sight?	Hero and Leander		1.176
WHO'LE			
Who'le set the faire treste [sunne] <sonne> in battell ray,	Ovid's Elegies		1.1.15
WHOLE			
(Which of your whole displeasures should be most)/Hath seem'd	1Tamb	3.2.7	Agidas
And make whole cyties caper in the aire.	2Tamb	3.2.61	Tamb
Here's a drench to poyson a whole stable of Flanders mares:	Jew	3.4.111	P Ithimr
Whole Chests of Gold, in Bullion, and in Coyne,	Jew	4.1.65	Barab
Bombards, whole Barrels full of Gunpowder,	Jew	5.5.28	Barab
Wherby whole Cities have escap't the plague,	F 49	1.1.21	Faust
O monstrous, eate a whole load of Hay!	F1532	4.5.28	P All
the yeare is divided into two circles over the whole world, so	F1582	4.6.25	P Faust
nor in the whole world can compare with thee, for the rare	F App	p.236 3	P Emper
the yeere is divided into twoo circles over the whole worlde,	F App	p.242 20	P Faust
Lay her whole tongue hid, mine in hers she dips.	Ovid's Elegies		2.5.58
WHOLESOME			
A small, but wholesome soyle with watrie veynes.	Ovid's Elegies		2.16.2
WHOLSOME			
And since we all have suckt one wholsome aire,	1Tamb	2.6.25	Cosroe
WHOLY			
And binde it wholy to the Sea of Rome:	P 926	18.27	Navrre
We people wholy given thee, feele thine armes,	Ovid's Elegies		2.9.11
WHOM			
And spare our lives whom every spite pursues.	Dido	1.2.9	Illion
Oft hath she askt us under whom we serv'd,	Dido	2.1.66	Illion
To whom he used action so pitifull,	Dido	2.1.155	Aeneas
To whom the aged King thus trembling spoke:	Dido	2.1.232	Aeneas
Whom Ajax ravisht in Dianas [Fane] <Fawne>,	Dido	2.1.275	Aeneas
Whom I tooke up to beare unto our ships:	Dido	2.1.277	Aeneas
O happie shall he be whom Dido loves.	Dido	3.1.168	Aeneas
Whom kindred and acquaintance counites?	Dido	3.2.31	Juno
Whom casualtie of sea hath made such friends?	Dido	3.2.76	Juno
Whom I will beare to Ida in mine armes,	Dido	3.2.99	Venus
With whom we did devide both lawes and land,	Dido	4.2.14	Iarbus
On whom ruth and compassion ever waites,	Dido	4.2.20	Iarbus
I will not leave Iarbus whom I love,	Dido	4.2.43	Anna
On whom the nimble windes may all day waight,	Dido	4.3.23	Aeneas
Whom doe I see, Joves winged messenger?	Dido	5.1.25	Aeneas
Whom I have brought from Ida where he slept,	Dido	5.1.40	Hermes
To whom poore Dido doth bequeath revenge.	Dido	5.1.173	Dido
Whom I may tearme a Damon for thy love.	1Tamb	1.1.50	Mycet
But this is she with whom I am in love.	1Tamb	1.2.108	Tamb
Whom seekst thou Persean? I am Tamburlain.	1Tamb	1.2.153	Tamb
These are my friends in whom I more rejoice,	1Tamb	1.2.241	Tamb
To whom sweet Menaphon, direct me straight.	1Tamb	2.1.68	Cosroe
He cals me Bajazeth, whom you call Lord.	1Tamb	3.3.67	Bajzth
Whom I have brought to see their overthrow.	1Tamb	3.3.81	Bajzth
Whom he detaineth in despight of us,	1Tamb	4.1.44	Souldn
Villain, knowest thou to whom thou speakest?	1Tamb	4.4.39	P Usumc
Whom should I wish the fatall victory,	1Tamb	5.1.385	Zenoc
(Renowmed Tamburlain) to whom all kings/Of force must yeeld	1Tamb	5.1.480	Souldn
With whom (being women) I vouchsaft a league,	2Tamb	1.3.193	Techel
In whom no faith nor true religion rests,	2Tamb	2.1.34	Baldwn
Whom I brought bound unto Damascus walles.	2Tamb	3.2.125	Tamb
And Moores, in whom was never pitie found,	2Tamb	3.4.20	Olymp
On whom death and the fatall sisters waite,	2Tamb	3.4.54	Therid
Before whom (mounted on a Lions backe)/Rhamnusia beares a	2Tamb	3.4.56	Therid
With whom I buried al affections,	2Tamb	4.2.23	Olymp
him, in whom thy looks/Have greater operation and more force	2Tamb	4.2.28	Therid
In whom the learned Rabies of this age,	2Tamb	4.2.84	Therid
Whom I have thought a God? they shal be burnt.	2Tamb	5.1.176	Tamb
From whom the thunder and the lightning breaks,	2Tamb	5.1.184	Tamb
Triumphing in his fall whom you advaunst,	2Tamb	5.3.23	Techel
Daughter, whom I hold as deare/As Agamemnon did his Iphegen:	Jew	1.1.137	Barab
With whom they have attempted many times,	Jew	1.1.164	Barab
Of whom we would make sale in Malta here.	Jew	2.2.18	Bosco
With whom?	Jew	3.4.20	Barab
And for thy sake, whom I so dearely love,	Jew	3.4.61	Barab

WHOM (cont.)

whom I saluted with an old hempen proverb, Hodie tibi,	Jew	4.2.18	P Pilia
no childe, and unto whom/Should I leave all but unto Ithimore?	Jew	4.3.44	Barab
I bring thee newes by whom thy sonne was slaine:	Jew	5.1.10	Curtzn
Whom have we there, a spy?	Jew	5.1.69	Calym
And he from whom my most advantage comes,	Jew	5.2.113	Barab
And such a King whom practise long hath taught,	P 458	8.8	Anjoy
But villaine he to whom these lines should goe,	P 696	13.40	Guise
Whom I respect as leaves of boasting greene,	P 720	14.23	Navrre
That villain for whom I beare this deep disgrace,	P 766	15.24	Guise
To whom shall I bewray my secrets now,	P1083	19.153	QnMoth
Whom God hath blest for hating Papestry.	P1208	22.70	King
To whom the sunne shines both by day and night.	Edw	1.1.17	Gavstn
whom he vouchsafes/For vailing of his bonnet one good looke.	Edw	1.2.18	Lncstr
On whom but on my husband should I fawne?	Edw	1.4.146	Queene
On Mortimer, with whom ungentle Queene--	Edw	1.4.147	Gavstn
I meane the peeres, whom thou shouldst dearly love:	Edw	2.2.176	Mortmr
to whom in justice it belongs/To punish this unnaturall revolt:	Edw	4.6.8	Kent
To whom Faustus doth dedicate himselfe.	F 285	1.3.57	Faust
She whom thine eye shall like, thy heart shall have,	F 539	2.1.151	Mephst
and one to whom I must be no niggard of my cunning; Come,	F1504	4.4.48	P Faust
whom all the world admires for Majesty, we should thinke	F1686	5.1.13	P 1Schol
Whom all the world admires for majesty.	F1698	5.1.25	2Schol
On God, whom Faustus hath abjur'd?	F1849	5.2.53	P Faust
on God, whom Faustus hath blasphem'd?	F1849	5.2.53	P Faust
The devils whom Faustus serv'd have torne him thus:	F1990	5.3.8	3Schol
to whom I must be no niggard of my cunning, come	F App	p.241 170	P Faust
Might they have won whom civil broiles have slaine,	Lucan, First Booke		14
And where stiffe winter whom no spring resolves,	Lucan, First Booke		17
being old/Must shine a star) shal heaven (whom thou lovest),	Lucan, First Booke		46
Let come their [leader] <leaders whom long peace hath quail'd;	Lucan, First Booke		311
Brabbling Marcellus; Cato whom fooles reverence;	Lucan, First Booke		313
(Whom from his youth he bribde) needs make him king?	Lucan, First Booke		315
And so they triumph, be't with whom ye wil.	Lucan, First Booke		342
Caesar; he whom I heare thy trumpets charge/I hould no Romaine;	Lucan, First Booke		374
They whom the Lingones foild with painted speares,	Lucan, First Booke		398
cause, what ere thou be whom God assignes/This great effect,	Lucan, First Booke		419
[Jove] <it> seemes/Bloudy like Dian, whom the Scythians serve;	Lucan, First Booke		442
men/Whom death the greatest of all feares affright not,	Lucan, First Booke		455
As loath to leave Roome whom they held so deere,	Lucan, First Booke		506
And they whom fierce Bellonaes fury moves/To wound their armes,	Lucan, First Booke		563
was)/They call th'Etrurian Augures, amongst whom/The gravest,	Lucan, First Booke		584
And she to whom in shape of [Swanne] <Bull> Jove came.	Ovid's Elegies		1.3.22
My Mistresse weepes whom my mad hand did harme.	Ovid's Elegies		1.7.4
Yet he harm'd lesse, whom I profess'd to love,	Ovid's Elegies		1.7.33
Faire women play, shee's chast whom none will have,	Ovid's Elegies		1.8.43
Whom Troiane ships fecht from Europa farre.	Ovid's Elegies		1.10.2
whom the God deluded/In snowe-white plumes of a false swanne	Ovid's Elegies		1.10.3
And whom I like eternize by mine art.	Ovid's Elegies		1.10.60
Both whom thou raisest up to toyle anew.	Ovid's Elegies		1.13.22
Who can indure, save him with whom none lies?	Ovid's Elegies		1.13.26
So shall Licoris whom he loved best:	Ovid's Elegies		1.15.30
Let Maydes whom hot desire to husbands leade,	Ovid's Elegies		2.1.5
Or wofull Hector whom wilde jades did teare?	Ovid's Elegies		2.1.32
Beleeve me, whom we feare, we wish to perish.	Ovid's Elegies		2.2.10
fire/And [thinke] <thinkes> her chast whom many doe desire.	Ovid's Elegies		2.2.14
By whom the husband his wives incest knewe.	Ovid's Elegies		2.2.48
To whom his wench can say, I never did it.	Ovid's Elegies		2.5.10
Did not Pelides whom his Speare did grieve,	Ovid's Elegies		2.9.7
And he is happy whom the earth holds, say.	Ovid's Elegies		2.11.30
She whom her husband, guard, and gate as foes,	Ovid's Elegies		2.12.3
Cruell is he, that loves whom none protect.	Ovid's Elegies		2.19.4
And this is he whom fierce love burnes, they cry.	Ovid's Elegies		3.1.20
Yet whom thou favourst, pray may conquerour be.	Ovid's Elegies		3.2.2
I see whom thou affectest:	Ovid's Elegies		3.2.67
He is too clownish, whom a lewd wife grieves,	Ovid's Elegies		3.4.37
Whom Ilia pleasd, though in her lookes griefe reveld,	Ovid's Elegies		3.5.47
I know not whom thou lewdly didst imbrace,	Ovid's Elegies		3.10.11
Who mine was cald, whom I lov'd more then any,	Ovid's Elegies		3.11.5
By whom disclosd, she in the high woods tooke,	Ovid's Elegies		3.12.19
Then thee whom I must love I hate in vaine,	Ovid's Elegies		3.13.39
Whom liberty to honest armes compeld,	Ovid's Elegies		3.14.9
Both loves to whom my heart long time did yeeld,	Ovid's Elegies		3.14.15
Whom young Apollo courted for her haire,	Hero and Leander		1.6
For whom succeeding times make greater mone.	Hero and Leander		1.54
(For his sake whom their goddesse held so deare,	Hero and Leander		1.92
He whom she favours lives, the other dies.	Hero and Leander		1.124
To whom you offer, and whose Nunne you are.	Hero and Leander		1.212
Tell me, to whom mad'st thou that heedlesse oath?	Hero and Leander		1.294
Yet for her sake whom you have vow'd to serve,	Hero and Leander		1.316
And those on whom heaven, earth, and hell relies,	Hero and Leander		1.443
By being possest of him for whom she long'd:	Hero and Leander		2.36

WHOME

For whome the Powers divine have made the world,	1Tamb	5.1.76	1Virgn
I prethee say to whome thou writes?	P 671	13.15	Guise
Why should you love him, whome the world hates so?	Edw	1.4.76	Mortmr
To whome right well you knew our soule was knit,	Edw	3.1.227	Edward
whome rule and emperie/Have not in life or death made	Edw	4.7.14	Edward
Whome I esteeme as deare as these mine eyes,	Edw	5.2.18	Queene
by whome thou canst accomplish what thou list, this therefore	F App	p.236 4	P Emper
Whome trumpets clang incites, and those that dwel/By Cyngas	Lucan, First Booke		433

WHOOPING

I kept a hallowing and whooping in his eares, but all could not	F1549	4.5.45	P HrsCsr

WHORE (See also HOORISH)
Here's a hot whore indeed; no, I'le no wife. F 534 2.1.146 Faust
<A plague on her for a hote whore>. F 534 (HC261)A P Faust
The whore stands to be bought for each mans mony/And seekes Ovid's Elegies 1.10.21
She is not chaste, that's kept, but a deare whore: Ovid's Elegies 3.4.29
men point at me for a whore,/Shame, that should make me blush, Ovid's Elegies 3.5.77
WHORES
crosbiting, such a Rogue/As is the husband to a hundred whores: Jew 4.3.14 Barab
best beere in Europe, what ho, Hostis; where be these Whores? F1506 4.5.2 P Carter
WHORESON
You whoreson conjuring scab, do you remember how you cosened me F1662 4.6.105 P HrsCsr
WHO'S (See also WHOSE)
Who's within there? 1Tamb 5.1.191 Tamb
Who's there? Jew 2.1.43 Barab
Who's that? Jew 2.1.43 Abigal
Who's that spoke? Friers looke about. F1040 3.2.60 Pope
Who's this, that stands so solemnly by himselfe: F1513 4.5.9 P Hostss
WHOSE (Homograph)
Whose face reflects such pleasure to mine eyes, Dido 1.1.24 Jupitr
Whose wearie lims shall shortly make repose, Dido 1.1.84 Jupitr
Whose azured gates enchased with his name, Dido 1.1.101 Jupitr
Whose beautious burden well might make you proude, Dido 1.1.124 Venus
Whose night and day descendeth from thy browes: Dido 1.1.156 Achat
Whose lookes set forth no mortall forme to view, Dido 1.1.189 Aeneas
Whose fading weale of victorie forsooke, Dido 1.2.15 Illion
Whose memorie like pale deaths stony mace, Dido 2.1.115 Aeneas
In whose defence he fought so valiantly: Dido 2.1.119 Dido
With whose outcryes Atrides being apal'd, Dido 2.1.129 Aeneas
Whose ticing tongue was made of Hermes pipe, Dido 2.1.145 Aeneas
At whose accursed feete as overjoyed, Dido 2.1.177 Aeneas
In whose sterne faces shin'd the quenchles fire, Dido 2.1.186 Aeneas
About whose withered necke hung Hecuba, Dido 2.1.226 Aeneas
at whose latter gaspe/Joves marble statue gan to bend the brow, Dido 2.1.256 Aeneas
In whose faire bosome I will locke more wealth, Dido 3.1.92 Dido
a match confirmd/Betwixt these two, whose loves are so alike, Dido 3.2.78 Juno
Whose armed soule alreadie on the sea, Dido 3.2.83 Venus
Whose short conclusion will seale up their hearts, Dido 3.2.94 Juno
Whose glittering pompe Dianas shrowdes supplies, Dido 3.3.4 Dido
Whose bloud will reconcile thee to content, Dido 3.3.74 Iarbus
Whose amorous face like Pean sparkles fire, Dido 3.4.19 Dido
Whose golden Crowne might ballance my content: Dido 3.4.36 Dido
Whose Crowne and kingdome rests at thy commande: Dido 3.4.58 Dido
Whose flintie darts slept in Tipheus den, Dido 4.1.19 Iarbus
Whose emptie Altars have enlarg'd our illes. Dido 4.2.3 Iarbus
Whose hideous ecchoes make the welkin howle, Dido 4.2.9 Iarbus
Whose yeelding heart may yeeld thee more reliefe. Dido 4.2.36 Anna
Whose golden fortunes clogd with courtly ease, Dido 4.3.8 Aeneas
Whose wealthie streames may waite upon her towers, Dido 5.1.9 Aeneas
Yet he whose [hearts] <heart> of adamant or flint, Dido 5.1.234 Anna
At whose byrth-day Cynthia with Saturne joinde, 1Tamb 1.1.13 Cosroe
Whose foming galle with rage and high disdaine, 1Tamb 1.1.63 Mycet
Whose ransome made them martch in coates of gold, 1Tamb 1.1.143 Ceneus
By whose desires of discipline in Armes, 1Tamb 1.1.174 Cosroe
Whose [statues] <statutes> we adore in Scythia, 1Tamb 1.2.244 Tamb
Whose fiery cyrcles beare encompassed/A heaven of heavenly 1Tamb 2.1.15 Menaph
Whose tops are covered with Tartarian thieves, 1Tamb 2.2.16 Meandr
Whose vertues carie with it life and death, 1Tamb 2.5.61 Therid
whose faculties can comprehend/The wondrous Architecture of the 1Tamb 2.7.21 Tamb
Whose smiling stars gives him assured hope/Of martiall triumph, 1Tamb 3.3.42 Tamb
Whose hands are made to gripe a warlike Lance, 1Tamb 3.3.106 Bajzth
Whose eies are brighter than the Lamps of heaven, 1Tamb 3.3.120 Tamb
Whose feet the kings of Affrica have kist. 1Tamb 4.2.65 Zabina
Whose honors and whose lives relie on him: 1Tamb 5.1.19 Govnr
Farewell (sweet Virgins) on whose safe return/Depends our 1Tamb 5.1.62 Govnr
And on whose throne the holy Graces sit. 1Tamb 5.1.77 1Virgn
In whose sweete person is compriz'd the Sum/Of natures Skill 1Tamb 5.1.78 1Virgn
within whose silver haires/Honor and reverence evermore have 1Tamb 5.1.81 1Virgn
Whose cheekes and hearts so punisht with conceit, 1Tamb 5.1.87 1Virgn
(Whose scepter Angels kisse, and Furies dread)/As for their 1Tamb 5.1.94 1Virgn
Whose sorrowes lay more siege unto my soule, 1Tamb 5.1.155 Tamb
With whose instinct the soule of man is toucht, 1Tamb 5.1.179 Tamb
whose worthinesse/Deserves a conquest over every hart: 1Tamb 5.1.207 Tamb
Accursed Bajazeth, whose words of ruth, 1Tamb 5.1.270 Bajzth
whose moaning entercourse/Hath hetherto bin staid, with wrath 1Tamb 5.1.280 Bajzth
Whose lookes might make the angry God of armes, 1Tamb 5.1.326 Zenoc
Whose lives were dearer to Zenocrate/Than her owne life, or 1Tamb 5.1.337 Zenoc
the cursed object/Whose Fortunes never mastered her griefs: 1Tamb 5.1.414 Zenoc
Whose sight with joy would take away my life, 1Tamb 5.1.419 Arabia
Whose holy Alcaron remaines with us, 2Tamb 1.1.138 Orcan
Whose glorious body when he left the world, 2Tamb 1.1.139 Orcan
Of whose conditions, and our solemne othes/Sign'd with our 2Tamb 1.1.143 Orcan
with my heart/Wish your release, but he whose wrath is death, 2Tamb 1.2.6 Almeda
Whose beames illuminate the lamps of heaven, 2Tamb 1.3.2 Tamb
Whose chearful looks do cleare the clowdy aire/And cloath it in 2Tamb 1.3.3 Tamb
Whose head hath deepest scarres, whose breast most woundes, 2Tamb 1.3.75 Tamb
For in a field whose [superficies] <superfluities>/Is covered 2Tamb 1.3.79 Tamb
Whose arches should be fram'd with bones of Turks, 2Tamb 1.3.94 Amyras
Whose lookes make this inferiour world to quake, 2Tamb 1.3.139 Techel
Whose coleblacke faces make their foes retire, 2Tamb 1.3.142 Techel
Whose triple Myter I did take by force, 2Tamb 1.3.189 Techel
Whose shape is figure of the highest God? 2Tamb 2.2.38 Orcan
From paine to paine, whose change shal never end: 2Tamb 2.3.26 Orcan
Whose power is often proov'd a myracle. 2Tamb 2.3.32 Gazell

WHOSE (cont.)

Whose power had share in this our victory:	2Tamb	2.3.35	Orcan
Whose eies shot fire from their Ivory bowers,	2Tamb	2.4.9	Tamb
Whose jealousie admits no second Mate,	2Tamb	2.4.12	Tamb
The christall springs whose taste illuminates/Refined eies with	2Tamb	2.4.22	Tamb
transfourme my love/In whose sweet being I repose my life,	2Tamb	2.4.48	Tamb
Whose heavenly presence beautified with health,	2Tamb	2.4.49	Tamb
Whose absence make the sun and Moone as darke/As when opposde	2Tamb	2.4.51	Tamb
And of my Lords whose true nobilitie/Have merited my latest	2Tamb	2.4.73	Zenoc
Whose darts do pierce the Center of my soule:	2Tamb	2.4.84	Tamb
Hellen, whose beauty sommond Greece to armes,	2Tamb	2.4.87	Tamb
Or had those wanton Poets, for whose byrth/Olde Rome was proud,	2Tamb	2.4.91	Tamb
Whose cursed fate hath so dismembred it,	2Tamb	3.1.13	Callap
Whose courages are kindled with the flames,	2Tamb	3.1.54	Trebiz
Whose hornes shall sprinkle through the tainted aire,	2Tamb	3.1.66	Orcan
Whose lovely faces never any viewed,	2Tamb	3.2.30	Tamb
[Those] <Whose> looks will shed such influence in my campe,/As	2Tamb	3.2.39	Tamb
Whose shattered lims, being tost as high as heaven,	2Tamb	3.2.100	Tamb
Whose body with his fathers I have burnt,	2Tamb	3.4.36	Olymp
In whose high lookes is much more majesty/Than from the Concave	2Tamb	3.4.47	Therid
By whose proud side the ugly furies run,	2Tamb	3.4.59	Therid
Over whose Zenith cloth'd in windy aire,	2Tamb	3.4.61	Therid
land, whose brave Metropolis/Reedified the faire Semyramis,	2Tamb	3.5.36	Orcan
issue, at whose byrth/Heaven did affoord a gratious aspect,	2Tamb	3.5.79	Tamb
Whose matter is the flesh of Tamburlain,	2Tamb	4.1.113	Tamb
Whose scalding drops wil pierce thy seething braines,	2Tamb	4.1.144	Jrslem
Whose cruelties are not so harsh as thine,	2Tamb	4.1.169	Jrslem
Whose sight composde of furie and of fire/Doth send such sterne	2Tamb	4.1.175	Trebiz
whose weeping eies/Since thy arrivall here beheld no Sun,	2Tamb	4.2.1	Olymp
Whose drift is onely to dishonor thee.	2Tamb	4.2.7	Olymp
Affoords no hearbs, whose taste may poison thee,	2Tamb	4.2.9	Olymp
Whose body shall be tomb'd with all the pompe/The treasure of	2Tamb	4.2.97	Therid
Whose shyning Turrets shal dismay the heavens,	2Tamb	4.3.112	Tamb
Whose tender blossoms tremble every one,	2Tamb	4.3.123	Tamb
Whose state he ever pitied and reliev'd,	2Tamb	5.1.32	1Citzn
Whose lofty Pillers, higher than the cloudes,	2Tamb	5.1.64	Tamb
Whose chariot wheeles have burst th'Assirians bones,	2Tamb	5.1.71	Tamb
Whose flaming traines should reach down to the earth/Could not	2Tamb	5.1.90	Tamb
Whose Scourge I am, and him will I obey.	2Tamb	5.1.185	Tamb
And threaten him whose hand afflicts my soul,	2Tamb	5.3.47	Tamb
Whose shoulders beare the Axis of the world,	2Tamb	5.3.59	Tamb
Dangerous to those, whose Chrisis is as yours:	2Tamb	5.3.92	Phsitn
Whose matter is incorporat in your flesh.	2Tamb	5.3.165	Amyras
But he whose steele-bard coffers are cramb'd full,	Jew	1.1.14	Barab
Whose this?	Jew	1.2.366	Mthias
What, Barabas, whose goods were lately seiz'd?	Jew	1.2.383	Lodowk
Having Fernezes hand, whose heart I'le have;	Jew	2.3.16	Barab
The Abbasse of the house/Whose zealous admonition I embrace:	Jew	3.3.67	Abigal
Whose operation is to binde, infect,	Jew	3.4.70	Barab
Whose billowes beating the resistlesse bankes,	Jew	3.5.17	Govnr
Whose face has bin a grind-stone for mens swords,	Jew	4.3.9	Barab
Art thou that Jew whose goods we heard were sold/For	Jew	5.1.73	Calym
The gentle King whose pleasure uncontrolde,	P 127	2.70	Guise
(For whose effects my soule is massacred)/Infect thy gracious	P 192	3.27	QnMarg
Whose army shall discomfort all your foes,	P 579	11.44	Pleshe
Of whose encrease I set some longing hope,	P 689	13.33	Guise
Well, let me alone, whose within there?	P 881	17.76	King
Now fals the star whose influence governes France,	P 944	19.14	Capt
Whose light was deadly to the Protestants:	P 945	19.15	Capt
Upon whose heart may all the furies gripe,	P1101	20.11	Cardnl
Whose murderous thoughts will be his overthrow.	P1116	21.10	Dumain
Whose service he may still commaund till death.	P1149	22.11	Navrre
The king, upon whose bosome let me die,	Edw	1.1.14	Gavstn
Whose there? conveie this priest to the tower.	Edw	1.1.200	Edward
in whose gratious lookes/The blessednes of Gaveston remaines,	Edw	1.4.120	Gavstn
Whose great atchivements in our forrain warre,	Edw	1.4.360	Edward
Then let his grace, whose youth is flexible,	Edw	1.4.398	MortSr
Whose proud fantastick liveries make such show,	Edw	1.4.410	Mortmr
On whose good fortune Spencers hope depends.	Edw	2.1.11	Spencr
Whose there, Balduck?	Edw	2.1.70	Neece
On whose top-branches Kinglie Eagles pearch,	Edw	2.2.17	Mortmr
Whose mounting thoughts did never creepe so low,	Edw	2.2.77	Gavstn
Content, ile beare my part, holla whose there?	Edw	2.2.130	Lncstr
Whose this, the Queene?	Edw	2.4.22	Mortmr
Whose pining heart, her inward sighes have blasted,	Edw	2.4.24	Queene
Whose eyes are fixt on none but Gaveston:	Edw	2.4.62	Queene
the royall vine, whose golden leaves/Empale your princelie head,	Edw	3.1.163	Herald
Whose brightnes such pernitious upstarts dim,	Edw	3.1.165	Herald
Whose loosnes hath betrayed thy land to spoyle,	Edw	4.4.11	Queene
whose dauntlesse minde/The ambitious Mortimer would seeke to	Edw	5.1.15	Edward
And Isabell, whose eyes [being] <beene> turnd to steele,	Edw	5.1.104	Edward
By Mortimer, whose name is written here,	Edw	5.1.139	Edward
Whose there? call hither Gurney and Matrevis.	Edw	5.2.38	Mortmr
Whose sight is loathsome to all winged fowles?	Edw	5.3.7	Edward
Whose lookes were as a breeching to a boye.	Edw	5.4.55	Mortmr
But stay, whose this?	Edw	5.5.14	Matrvs
Whose there, what light is that, wherefore comes thou?	Edw	5.5.42	Edward
[whose sweete delight's] dispute/In th'heavenly matters of	F 18	Prol.18	1Chor
Excelling all, <whose sweete delight disputes>	F 18	(HC256)A	1Chor
Whose [shadows] made all Europe honour him.	F 145	1.1.117	Faust
Whose termine <terminine>, is tearmed the worlds wide Pole	F 593	2.2.42	Mephst
Whose bankes are set with Groves of fruitfull Vines.	F 786	3.1.8	Faust
[The] <Whose> buildings faire, and gorgeous to the eye,	F 788	3.1.10	Faust

WHOSE (cont.)

[Whose] <The> streetes straight forth, and paved with finest	F 789	3.1.11	Faust
Whose frame is paved with sundry coloured stones,	F 797	3.1.19	Faust
<Within whose walles such store of ordnance are>,	F 819	(HC265)A	Mephst
<Whose summum bonum is in belly-cheare>.	F 834	(HC265)A	Mephst
at whose pallace now]/[Faustus is feasted mongst his noblemen].	F1151	3.3.64A	3Chor
whose heart <art> conspir'd/Benvolio's shame before the	F1373	4.2.49	Mrtino
whose admired worth>/<Made Greece with ten yeares warres	F1696	(HC269)B	2Schol
[Whose heavenly beauty passeth all compare].	F1701	5.1.28A	3Schol
Whose sweet embraces <imbracings> may extinguish cleare	F1763	5.1.90	Faust
Whose influence hath allotted death and hell;	F1951	5.2.155	Faust
[Yet for Christs sake, whose bloud hath ransom'd me],	F1959	5.2.163A	Faust
Whose fiendfull fortune may exhort the wise/Onely to wonder at	F2006	5.3.24	4Chor
Whose deepnesse doth intice such forward wits,	F2008	5.3.26	4Chor
How now, whose that which spake?	F App	p.231 3 P	Pope
How now, whose that which snatcht the meate from me?	F App	p.231 8 P	Pope
under whose blacke survey/Great Potentates do kneele with awful	F App	p.235 34	Mephst
Upon whose altars thousand soules do lie,	F App	p.235 36	Mephst
The bright shining of whose glorious actes/Lightens the world	F App	p.237 25	Emper
Whose bloud alone must wash away thy guilt.	F App	p.243 45	OldMan
We sing, whose conquering swords their own breasts launcht,	Lucan, First Booke		3
Mourning appear'd, whose hoary hayres were torne,	Lucan, First Booke		189
and whose tongue/Could tune the people to the Nobles mind:	Lucan, First Booke		272
so did Alcides port, whose seas/Eate hollow rocks, and where the	Lucan, First Booke		406
Under whose hoary rocks Gebenna hangs;	Lucan, First Booke		436
whose immortal pens/Renowne the valiant soules slaine in your	Lucan, First Booke		443
ugly jointes/Then nature gives, whose sight appauls the mother,	Lucan, First Booke		561
Whose like Aegiptian Memphis never had/For skill in stars, and	Lucan, First Booke		639
Before whose bow th'Arcadian wild beasts trembled.	Ovid's Elegies		1.7.14
Nape free-borne, whose cunning hath no border,	Ovid's Elegies		1.11.2
Bagous whose care doth thy Mistrisse bridle,	Ovid's Elegies		2.2.1
All you whose pineons in the cleare aire sore,	Ovid's Elegies		2.6.11
Whose life nine ages scarce bring out of date.	Ovid's Elegies		2.6.36
Whose earth doth not perpetuall greene-grasse lacke,	Ovid's Elegies		2.6.50
Whose blast may hether strongly be inclinde,	Ovid's Elegies		2.11.38
Whose bodies with their heavy burthens ake.	Ovid's Elegies		2.13.20
Wild me, whose slowe feete sought delay, be flying.	Ovid's Elegies		2.19.12
See a rich chuffe whose wounds great wealth inferr'd,	Ovid's Elegies		3.7.9
See Homer from whose fountaine ever fild,	Ovid's Elegies		3.8.25
And by thine eyes whose radiance burnes out mine.	Ovid's Elegies		3.10.48
Oxen in whose mouthes burning flames did breede?	Ovid's Elegies		3.11.36
The ships, whose God-head in the sea now glisters?	Ovid's Elegies		3.11.38
And calves from whose feard front no threatning flyes,	Ovid's Elegies		3.12.15
Whose workmanship both man and beast deceaves.	Hero and Leander		1.20
(Whose tragedie divine Musaeus soong)/Dwelt at Abidus; since	Hero and Leander		1.52
And whose immortall fingars did imprint,	Hero and Leander		1.67
Under whose shade the Wood-gods love to bee.	Hero and Leander		1.156
This sacrifice (whose sweet perfume descending,	Hero and Leander		1.209
To whom you offer, and whose Nunne you are.	Hero and Leander		1.212
Whose name is it, if she be false or not,	Hero and Leander		1.285
Whose sound allures the golden Morpheus,	Hero and Leander		1.349
Whose carelesse haire, in stead of pearle t'adorne it,	Hero and Leander		1.389
Whose only dower was her chastitie,	Hero and Leander		1.412
Whose waight consists in nothing but her name,	Hero and Leander		2.114
Is swifter than the wind, whose tardie plumes,	Hero and Leander		2.115
Whose lively heat like fire from heaven fet,	Hero and Leander		2.255
Whose fruit none rightly can describe, but hee/That puls or	Hero and Leander		2.299
By shallow Rivers, to whose falls,	Passionate Shepherd		7

WHY

Why, are not all the Gods at thy commaund,	Dido	1.1.30	Jupitr
Too cruell, why wilt thou forsake me thus?	Dido	1.1.243	Aeneas
Why talke we not together hand in hand?	Dido	1.1.245	Aeneas
Why, what are you, or wherefore doe you sewe?	Dido	1.2.3	Iarbus
Why stands my sweete Aeneas thus amazde?	Dido	2.1.2	Achat
Why turnes Aeneas from his trustie friends?	Dido	2.1.57	Cloan
Troy is invincible, why stay we here?	Dido	2.1.128	Aeneas
Why staiest thou here? thou art no love of mine.	Dido	3.1.39	Dido
Why is it then displeasure should disjoyne,	Dido	3.2.30	Juno
Why should not they then joyne in marriage,	Dido	3.2.74	Juno
Why, man of Troy, doe I offend thine eyes?	Dido	3.3.17	Iarbus
Huntsmen, why pitch you not your toyles apace,	Dido	3.3.30	Dido
Why, that was in a net, where we are loose,	Dido	3.4.5	Dido
Why, what is it that Dido may desire/And not obtaine, be it in	Dido	3.4.7	Aeneas
Nature, why mad'st me not some poysonous beast,	Dido	4.1.21	Iarbus
Why, let us build a Citie of our owne,	Dido	4.3.37	Illion
Why did it suffer thee to touch her breast,	Dido	4.4.145	Dido
Why should I blame Aeneas for his flight?	Dido	4.4.148	Dido
Why burst you not, and they fell in the seas?	Dido	4.4.154	Dido
Blush blush for shame, why shouldst thou thinke of love?	Dido	4.5.29	Nurse
why, I may live a hundred yeares,/Fourescore is but a girles	Dido	4.5.31	Nurse
Why doe I thinke of love now I should dye?	Dido	4.5.34	Nurse
Why cosin, stand you building Cities here,	Dido	5.1.27	Hermes
Why wilt thou so betray thy sonnes good hap?	Dido	5.1.31	Hermes
Why are thy ships new rigd?	Dido	5.1.88	Dido
O pardon me, if I resolve thee why:	Dido	5.1.91	Aeneas
Why look'st thou toward the sea?	Dido	5.1.113	Dido
Why star'st thou in my face?	Dido	5.1.179	Dido
Ah, Menaphon, why staiest thou thus behind,	1Tamb	1.1.83	Mycet
Drums, why sound ye not when Meander speaks.	1Tamb	2.2.75	Mycet
Why say Theridamas, wilt thou be a king?	1Tamb	2.5.65	Tamb
Why, that's wel said Techelles, so would I,	1Tamb	2.5.69	Tamb
Why then Casane, shall we wish for ought/The world affoords in	1Tamb	2.5.72	Tamb
Why then Theridamas, Ile first assay,	1Tamb	2.5.81	Tamb

WHY (cont.)

Why stay we thus prolonging all their lives?	1Tamb	3.3.97		Techel
Each man a crown? why kingly fought ifaith.	1Tamb	3.3.216		Tamb
Sirra, why fall you not too, are you so daintily brought up, you	1Tamb	4.4.36	P	Tamb
pray thee tel, why art thou so sad?	1Tamb	4.4.63	P	Tamb
but why is it?	1Tamb	4.4.64	P	Tamb
Why should we live, O wretches, beggars, slaves,	1Tamb	5.1.248		Zabina
Why live we Bajazeth, and build up neasts,	1Tamb	5.1.249		Zabina
Why feed ye still on daies accursed beams,	1Tamb	5.1.262		Bajzth
Why may not I my Lord, as wel as he,	2Tamb	1.3.61		Amyras
Why, I thank your Majesty.	2Tamb	3.1.79	P	Almeda
To you? Why, do you thinke me weary of it?	2Tamb	3.3.17		Capt
death, why comm'st thou not?	2Tamb	3.4.14		Olymp
Why, so he is Casane, I am here,	2Tamb	3.5.62		Tamb
Why Madam, thinke ye to mocke me thus palpably?	2Tamb	4.2.67		Therid
Why gave you not your husband some of it,	2Tamb	4.2.71		Therid
How like you that sir king? why speak you not?	2Tamb	4.3.53		Celeb
Why send'st thou not a furious whyrlwind downe,	2Tamb	5.1.192		Tamb
Why, shal I sit and languish in this paine?	2Tamb	5.3.56		Tamb
why then I hope my ships/I sent for Egypt and the bordering	Jew	1.1.41		Barab
Why then goe bid them come ashore,/And bring with them their	Jew	1.1.55		Barab
Why, how now Countrymen?	Jew	1.1.143		Barab
Why flocke you thus to me in multitudes?	Jew	1.1.144		Barab
Why let 'em come, so they come not to warre;	Jew	1.1.150		Barab
Why, Barabas, they come for peace or warre.	Jew	1.1.161		1Jew
like enough, why then let every man/Provide him, and be there	Jew	1.1.170		Barab
Why let 'em enter, let 'em take the Towne.	Jew	1.1.190		Barab
Why Barabas wilt thou be christened?	Jew	1.2.81		Govnr
Why know you what you did by this device?	Jew	1.2.84		Barab
Why I esteeme the injury farre lesse,	Jew	1.2.146		Barab
Why stand you thus unmov'd with my laments?	Jew	1.2.171		Barab
Why weepe you not to thinke upon my wrongs?	Jew	1.2.172		Barab
Why pine not I, and dye in this distresse?	Jew	1.2.173		Barab
Why, Barabas, as hardly can we brooke/The cruell handling of	Jew	1.2.174		1Jew
Why did you yeeld to their extortion?	Jew	1.2.177		Barab
Why so,/Then thus; thou toldst me they have turn'd my house	Jew	1.2.276		Barab
Why how now Abigall, what mak'st thou/Amongst these hateful	Jew	1.2.338		Barab
Why how now Don Mathias, in a dump?	Jew	1.2.374		Lodowk
Why, the rich Jewes daughter.	Jew	1.2.382		Mthias
And why thou cam'st ashore without our leave?	Jew	2.2.3		Govnr
Why should this Turke be dearer then that Moore?	Jew	2.3.109		Barab
Why this is something:	Jew	2.3.213		Barab
Why, loves she Don Mathias?	Jew	2.3.285		Lodowk
Why on the sudden is your colour chang'd?	Jew	2.3.321		Lodowk
Father, why have you thus incenst them both?	Jew	2.3.356		Abigal
Why, was there ever seene such villany,	Jew	3.3.1		Ithimr
Why, how now Ithimore, why laugh'st thou so?	Jew	3.3.4		Abigal
Why, what ayl'st thou?	Jew	3.3.6		Abigal
Say, knave, why rail'st upon my father thus?	Jew	3.3.11		Abigal
Why, know you not?	Jew	3.3.14	P	Ithimr
Why, no.	Jew	3.3.15		Abigal
Why the devil invented a challenge, my master writ it, and I	Jew	3.3.18	P	Ithimr
Why Abigal it is not yet long since/That I did labour thy	Jew	3.3.56		1Fryar
Why, made mine Abigall a Nunne.	Jew	3.4.24		Barab
Why I'le run to some rocke and throw my selfe headlong into the	Jew	3.4.39	P	Ithimr
into the sea; why I'le doe any thing for your sweet sake.	Jew	3.4.40	P	Ithimr
Why, master, wil you poison her with a messe of rice	Jew	3.4.64	P	Ithimr
Why? what has he done?	Jew	3.6.47		1Fryar
Why, what of them?	Jew	4.1.44	P	Barab
Why goe, get you away.	Jew	4.1.93		2Fryar
Why does he goe to thy house? let him begone.	Jew	4.1.101		1Fryar
Why, Brother, you converted Abigall;	Jew	4.1.106		Barab
Why true, therefore did I place him there:	Jew	4.1.137		Barab
Why, how now Jacomo, what hast thou done?	Jew	4.1.174		Barab
Why, stricken him that would have stroke at me.	Jew	4.1.175		1Fryar
Why, a Turke could ha done no more.	Jew	4.1.198	P	Ithimr
Why so?	Jew	4.2.8	P	Curtzn
And if he aske why I demand so much, tell him, I scorne to	Jew	4.2.120	P	Ithimr
Why, wantst thou any of thy tale?	Jew	4.3.19	P	Barab
why Sir,/You know I have no childe, and unto whom	Jew	4.3.43		Barab
Why now I see that you have Art indeed.	Jew	5.5.4		Barab
Why, is not this/A kingly kinde of trade	Jew	5.5.46		Barab
Governour, why stand you all so pittilesse?	Jew	5.5.71		Barab
Why, hardst thou not the trumpet sound a charge?	Jew	5.5.105		Govnr
Why, then the house was fir'd,/Blowne up, and all thy souldiers	Jew	5.5.106		Govnr
Why, darst thou presume to call on Christ,	P 356	6.11		Mntsrl
Why suffer you that peasant to declaime?	P 414	7.54		Guise
Why let us burne him for an heretick.	P 483	9.2	P	2Atndt
Why I am no traitor to the crowne of France.	P 825	17.20		Guise
Why? I am a Prince of the Valoyses line,	P 835	17.30		Guise
Why this tis to have an army in the fielde.	P 980	19.50		Guise
Villaine, why dost thou look so gastly? speake.	P 989	19.59		Guise
Pardon thee, why what hast thou done?	P 991	19.61		Guise
King, why so thou wert before.	P1067	19.137		QnMoth
Surgeon, why saist thou so? the King may live.	P1224	22.86		Navrre
Why there are hospitals for such as you,	Edw	1.1.35		Gavstn
My lord, why do you thus incense your peeres,	Edw	1.1.99		Lncstr
Why shouldst thou kneele, knowest thou not who I am?	Edw	1.1.142		Edward
How now, why droops the earle of Lancaster?	Edw	1.2.9		MortSr
Why post we not from hence to levie men?	Edw	1.2.16		Mortmr
Why are you moov'd, be patient my lord,	Edw	1.4.43		ArchBp
Why should you love him, whome the world hates so?	Edw	1.4.76		Mortmr
Why should a king be subject to a priest?	Edw	1.4.96		Edward

WHY (cont.)

Why?	Edw	1.4.192	MortSr
Why then my lord, give me but leave to speak.	Edw	1.4.254	Mortmr
why do I stay,/Seeing that he talkes thus of my mariage day?	Edw	2.1.68	Neece
The winde is good, I wonder why he stayes,	Edw	2.2.1	Edward
Why how now cosin, how fares all our friends?	Edw	2.2.114	Lncstr
Why, so he may, but we will speake to him.	Edw	2.2.136	Lncstr
Why do you not commit him to the tower?	Edw	2.2.234	Gavstn
Why then weele have him privilie made away.	Edw	2.2.236	Gavstn
Lancaster, why talkst thou to the slave?	Edw	2.5.19	Warwck
by me, yet but he may/See him before he dies, for why he saies,	Edw	2.5.37	Arundl
Why my Lord of Warwicke,	Edw	2.5.46	Gavstn
Why I say, let him go on Penbrookes word.	Edw	2.5.90	Lncstr
Why do we sound retreat?	Edw	3.1.185	Edward
Not sonne, why not?	Edw	4.2.45	Queene
Why man, they say there is great execution/Done through the	Edw	4.3.6	Edward
Why so, they barkt a pace a month agoe,	Edw	4.3.12	Edward
Proud traytor Mortimer why doost thou chase/Thy lawfull king	Edw	4.6.3	Kent
Vilde wretch, and why hast thou of all unkinde,	Edw	4.6.5	Kent
Madam, what resteth, why stand ye in a muse?	Edw	4.6.63	SrJohn
My lord, why droope you thus?	Edw	4.7.60	Leistr
Why do you lowre unkindly on a king?	Edw	4.7.63	Edward
My lord, why waste you thus the time away,	Edw	5.1.49	Leistr
Why gape you for your soveraignes overthrow?	Edw	5.1.72	Edward
Why, is he dead?	Edw	5.2.98	Prince
Why yongling, s'dainst thou so of Mortimer.	Edw	5.2.111	Mortmr
Why strive you thus? your labour is in vaine.	Edw	5.3.33	Matrvs
And I will visit him, why stay you me?	Edw	5.3.60	Kent
Why speake you not unto my lord the king?	Edw	5.6.38	1Lord
And so shalt thou be too: why staies he heere?	Edw	5.6.51	King
Why should I greeve at my declining fall?	Edw	5.6.63	Mortmr
Why Faustus, hast thou not attain'd that end?	F 46	1.1.18	Faust
Why then belike/We must sinne, and so consequently die,	F 71	1.1.43	Faust
Why, dost not thou know then?	F 199	1.2.6	P 2Schol
<Why, didst thou not say thou knewst>?	F 204	(HC258) A	P 2Schol
Why this is hell: nor am I out of it.	F 304	1.3.76	Mephst
Why so thou shalt be, whether thou dost it or no:	F 360	1.4.18	P Wagner
Why waverst thou?	F 395	2.1.7	Faust
[To God]? <Why> he loves thee not:	F 398	2.1.10	Faust
Why, the Signory of Embden shall be mine:	F 412	2.1.24	Faust
Is that the reason why he tempts us thus?	F 430	2.1.42	Faust
Why, have you any paine that torture other <tortures others>?	F 432	2.1.44	Faust
Why streames it not, that I may write a fresh?	F 455	2.1.67	Faust
Why shouldst thou not? is not thy soule thine owne?	F 457	2.1.69	Faust
Why, dost thou think <think'st thou then> that Faustus shall be	F 518	2.1.130	Faust
<why Faustus> think'st thou heaven is such a glorious thing?	F 556	2.2.5	Mephst
Why should I die then, or basely despaire?	F 582	2.2.31	Faust
Why are <have wee> not Conjunctions, Oppositions, Aspects,	F 615	2.2.64	P Faust
why thou canst not tell ne're a word on't.	F 730	2.3.9	P Dick
Villaines why speake you not?	F1045	3.2.65	Pope
Why how now sir Knight, what, hang'd by the hornes?	F1290	4.1.136	P Faust
why will he not drink of all waters?	F1470	4.4.14	P HrsCsr
Sirra Dick, dost thou know why I stand so mute?	F1509	4.5.5	P Robin
No Robin, why is't?	F1510	4.5.6	P Dick
Why Hostesse, I say, fetch us some Beere.	F1518	4.5.14	P Dick
Why how now Maisters, what a coyle is there?	F1591	4.6.34	Servnt
Why saucy varlets, dare you be so bold.	F1594	4.6.37	Servnt
Why, how now my [good] <goods> friends?	F1608	4.6.51	Faust
Why, do you heare sir, did not I pull off one of your legs when	F1655	4.6.98	P HrsCsr
Why, Lucifer and Mephostophilis:	F1855	5.2.59	Faust
Why did not Faustus tell us of this before, that Divines might	F1862	5.2.66	P 1Schol
Why wert thou not a creature wanting soule?	F1964	5.2.168	Faust
Or why is this immortall that thou hast?	F1965	5.2.169	Faust
staves acre, why then belike, if I were your man, I should be	F App	p.229 21	P Clown
Why french crownes.	F App	p.230 32	P Wagner
Why now sirra thou art at an houres warning whensoever or	F App	p.230 36	P Wagner
Why Robin what booke is that?	F App	p.233 18	P Rafe
why the most intollerable booke for conjuring that ere was	F App	p.233 19	P Robin
why I has thought thou hadst beene a batcheler, but now I see	F App	p.238 69	P Emper
why sir, wil he not drinke of all waters?	F App	p.239 110	P HrsCsr
why sir, what would you?	F App	p.240 139	P Mephst
Why hee's fast asleepe, come some other time.	F App	p.240 141	P Mephst
Why, thou seest he heares thee not.	F App	p.241 151	P Mephst
Why joine you force to share the world betwixt you?	Lucan, First Booke		88
Why art thou thus enrag'd?	Lucan, First Booke		659
why doe the Planets/Alter their course; and vainly dim their	Lucan, First Booke		662
Why should we wish the gods should ever end them?	Lucan, First Booke		668
Why grapples Rome, and makes war, having no foes?	Lucan, First Booke		681
Ambitious Imp, why seekst thou further charge?	Ovid's Elegies		1.1.18
Or why slips downe the Coverlet so oft?	Ovid's Elegies		1.2.2
Why enviest me, this hostile [denne] <dende> unbarre,	Ovid's Elegies		1.6.17
In midst of peace why art of armes afraide?	Ovid's Elegies		1.6.30
Why? Ajax, maister of the seven-foulds shield,	Ovid's Elegies		1.7.7
And why shouldst not please?	Ovid's Elegies		1.8.25
Ask'st why I chaunge? because thou crav'st reward:	Ovid's Elegies		1.10.11
Why should one sell it, and the other buy it?	Ovid's Elegies		1.10.34
Why should I loose, and thou gaine by the pleasure/Which man	Ovid's Elegies		1.10.35
Why doest thy ill kembd tresses losse lament?	Ovid's Elegies		1.14.35
Why in thy glasse doest looke being discontent?	Ovid's Elegies		1.14.36
Envie, why carpest thou my time is spent so ill,	Ovid's Elegies		1.15.1
And asking why, this answeare she redoubled,	Ovid's Elegies		2.2.7
Why fightst gainst oddes?	Ovid's Elegies		2.2.61
Seeing she likes my bookes, why should we jarre?	Ovid's Elegies		2.4.20

WHY (cont.)
Why so was Ledas, yet was Leda faire. Ovid's Elegies 2.4.42
Aye me poore soule, why is my cause so good. Ovid's Elegies 2.5.8
In this sweete good, why hath a third to do? Ovid's Elegies 2.5.32
Why Philomele doest Tereus leudnesse mourne? Ovid's Elegies 2.6.7
Ungrate why feignest new feares? Ovid's Elegies 2.8.23
Why me that alwayes was thy souldiour found, Ovid's Elegies 2.9.3
Doest harme, and in thy tents why doest me wound? Ovid's Elegies 2.9.4
Why burnes thy brand, why strikes thy bow thy friends? Ovid's Elegies 2.9.5
Venus, why doublest thou my endlesse smart? Ovid's Elegies 2.10.11
Why addst thou starres to heaven, leaves to greene woods Ovid's Elegies 2.10.13
Mine owne desires why should my selfe not flatter? Ovid's Elegies 2.11.54
Why takest increasing grapes from Vine-trees full? Ovid's Elegies 2.14.23
With cruell hand why doest greene Apples pull? Ovid's Elegies 2.14.24
Why with hid irons are your bowels torne? Ovid's Elegies 2.14.27
And why dire poison give you babes unborne? Ovid's Elegies 2.14.28
Vaine things why wish I? Ovid's Elegies 2.15.27
Why doth my mistresse from me oft devide? Ovid's Elegies 2.16.42
Aye me why is it knowne to her so well? Ovid's Elegies 2.17.8
Aye me she cries, to love, why art a shamed? Ovid's Elegies 2.18.8
In nights deepe silence why the ban-dogges barke. Ovid's Elegies 2.19.40
Why she alone in empty bed oft tarries. Ovid's Elegies 2.19.42
Wilt nothing do, why I should wish thy death? Ovid's Elegies 2.19.56
lofty wordes stout Tragedie (she sayd)/Why treadst me downe? Ovid's Elegies 3.1.36
In vaine why flyest backe? force conjoynes us now: Ovid's Elegies 3.2.19
For others faults, why do I losse receive? Ovid's Elegies 3.3.16
Why grieve I? and of heaven reproches pen? Ovid's Elegies 3.3.41
Saying, why sadly treadst my banckes upon, Ovid's Elegies 3.5.53
Where's thy attire? why wand'rest heere alone? Ovid's Elegies 3.5.55
Why weepst? and spoilst with teares thy watry eyes? Ovid's Elegies 3.5.57
Why being a vestall am I wooed to wed, Ovid's Elegies 3.5.75
Why stay I? Ovid's Elegies 3.5.77
Mad streame, why doest our mutuall joyes deferre? Ovid's Elegies 3.5.87
Clowne, from my journey why doest me deterre? Ovid's Elegies 3.5.88
Why might not then my sinews be inchanted, Ovid's Elegies 3.6.35
And was the second cause why vigor failde mee: Ovid's Elegies 3.6.38
Why was I blest? Ovid's Elegies 3.6.49
why made king [to refuse] <and refusde> it? Ovid's Elegies 3.6.49
Why mockst thou me she cried, or being ill, Ovid's Elegies 3.6.77
Confessing this, why doest thou touch him than? Ovid's Elegies 3.7.22
Why gird'st thy citties with a towred wall? Ovid's Elegies 3.7.47
Why letst discordant hands to armour fall? Ovid's Elegies 3.7.48
Why seek'st not heav'n the third realme to frequent? Ovid's Elegies 3.7.50
Why are our pleasures by thy meanes forborne? Ovid's Elegies 3.9.4
Why am I sad, when Proserpine is found, Ovid's Elegies 3.9.45
And justly: for her praise why did I tell? Ovid's Elegies 3.11.9
Why see I lines so oft receivde and given, Ovid's Elegies 3.13.31
Why art thou not in love, and lov'd of all? Hero and Leander 1.89
Why should you worship her? Hero and Leander 1.213
Why vowest thou then to live in Sestos here, Hero and Leander 1.227
Harken a while, and I will tell you why: Hero and Leander 1.385

WHYRLWIND
Why send'st thou not a furious whyrlwind downe, 2Tamb 5.1.192 Tamb

WICKED
As lothing Pirrhus for this wicked act: Dido 2.1.258 Aeneas
Wicked Aeneas. Dido 5.1.199 Anna
Call him not wicked, sister, speake him faire, Dido 5.1.200 Dido
Have sworne the death of wicked Tamburlaine. 1Tamb 1.1.64 Mycet
Fit Souldiers for the wicked Tamburlaine. 1Tamb 2.2.24 Meandr
Some Jewes are wicked, as all Christians are: Jew 1.2.112 Barab
Some wicked trick or other. Jew 2.3.119 P Barab
Stay wicked Jew, repent, I say, and stay. Jew 4.1.24 2Fryar
Plaine Barabas: oh that wicked Curtezane! Jew 4.3.2 Barab
O wicked sexe, perjured and unjust, P 693 13.37 Guise
That wicked Guise I feare me much will be, P 921 18.22 Navrre
The wicked branch of curst Valois his line. P1013 19.83 Guise
Wicked Navarre will get the crowne of France, P1086 19.156 QnMoth
To ruinate that wicked Church of Rome, P1204 22.66 King
a death too good, the devill of hell/Torture his wicked soule. P1219 22.81 Bartus
But is that wicked Gaveston returnd? Edw 1.1.177 BshpCv
Ah wicked king, accurssed Gaveston, Edw 1.2.4 Lncstr
with haling of my lord/From Gaveston, from wicked Gaveston, Edw 2.4.27 Queene
I offer up this wicked traitors head, Edw 5.6.100 King
the heavens then I repent/And curse thee wicked Mephostophilis, F 553 2.2.2 Faust

WICKEDNESSE
That durst to so great wickednesse aspire. Ovid's Elegies 3.8.44

WIDE
Exild forth Europe and wide Asia both, Dido 1.1.229 Aeneas
Inforst a wide breach in that rampierd wall, Dido 2.1.174 Aeneas
The woods are wide, and we have store of game: Dido 3.3.6 Dido
Leape in mine armes, mine armes are open wide: Dido 5.1.180 Dido
Chiefe Lord of all the wide vast Euxine sea, 1Tamb 1.1.167 Ortyg
Have swelling cloudes drawen from wide gasping woundes, 1Tamb 5.1.459 Tamb
That hides these plaines, and seems as vast and wide, 2Tamb 1.1.107 Sgsmnd
all the christall gates of Joves high court/Were opened wide, 2Tamb 1.3.154 Tamb
Filling the ditches with the walles wide breach, 2Tamb 3.3.7 Techel
Whose termine <terminine>, is tearmed the worlds wide Pole. F 593 2.2.42 Mephst
With jawes wide open ghastly roaring out; Lucan, First Booke 212
Quickly soft words hard dores wide open strooke. Ovid's Elegies 2.1.22
My flatt'ring speeches soone wide open knocke. Ovid's Elegies 3.1.46
to thee our Court stands open wide,/There shalt be lov'd: Ovid's Elegies 3.5.61
Her gate by my hands is set open wide. Ovid's Elegies 3.11.12
Her wide sleeves greene, and bordered with a grove, Hero and Leander 1.11

WIDE (cont.)
Wide open stood the doore, hee need not clime, Hero and Leander 2.19
He watcht his armes, and as they opend wide, Hero and Leander 2.183
WIDOWE
Ile be no more a widowe, I am young, Dido 4.5.22 Nurse
WIDOWES
Barabas, is not that the widowes sonne? Jew 2.3.279 Lodowk
WIELDS
What stature wields he, and what personage? 1Tamb 2.1.6 Cosroe
WIER
And when ye stay, be lasht with whips of wier: 2Tamb 3.5.105 Tamb
WIFE (See also SIB)
mine armes, and by the hand/Led faire Creusa my beloved wife, Dido 2.1.267 Aeneas
O there I lost my wife: Dido 2.1.270 Aeneas
The field is ours, the Turk, his wife and all. 1Tamb 3.3.163 Tamb
And thou his wife shalt feed him with the scraps/My servitures 1Tamb 4.2.87 Tamb
to come by, plucke out that, and twil serve thee and thy wife: 1Tamb 4.4.14 P Tamb
twere better he kild his wife, and then she shall be sure not 1Tamb 4.4.45 P Usumc
not the Turke and his wife make a goodly showe at a banquet? 1Tamb 4.4.57 P Tamb
The jealous bodie of his fearfull wife, 1Tamb 5.1.86 1Virgn
You see my wife, my Queene and Emperesse, 1Tamb 5.1.264 Bajzth
And wife unto the Monarke of the East. 2Tamb 3.2.22 Amyras
not heaven it selfe/Shall ransome thee, thy wife and family. 2Tamb 3.3.28 Therid
Farewell sweet wife, sweet son farewell, I die. 2Tamb 3.4.10 Capt
Twas bravely done, and like a souldiers wife. 2Tamb 3.4.38 Techel
Shee is thy wife, and thou shalt be mine heire. Jew 2.3.328 Barab
And Guise usurpes it, cause I am his wife: P 661 13.5 Duchss
So kindely Cosin of Guise you and your wife/Doe both salute our P 752 15.10 King
Which your wife writ to my deare Minion, P 755 15.13 King
Because his wife beares thee such kindely love. P 780 15.38 King
<off> this, let me have a wife, the fairest Maid in Germany, F 529 2.1.141 P Faust
<How, a wife? I prithee Faustus talke not of a wife>. F 530 (HC261)A P Mephst
for I am wanton and lascivious, and cannot live without a wife. F 530 2.1.142 P Faust
Ile fetch thee a wife in the divels name>. F 531 (HC261)A P Mephst
Well Faustus, thou shalt have a wife. F 531 2.1.143 Mephst
Now Faustus wilt thou have a wife? F 533 2.1.145 Mephst
<Tel Faustus, how dost thou like thy wife>? F 533 (HC261)A P Mephst
Here's a hot whore indeed; no, I'le no wife. F 534 2.1.146 Faust
I am Envy, begotten of a Chimney-sweeper, and an Oyster-wife: F 680 2.2.129 P Envy
but now I see thou hast a wife, that not only gives thee F App p.238 70 P Emper
felow, and he has a great charge, neither wife nor childe. F App p.239 106 P Mephst
Foole if to keepe thy wife thou hast no neede, Ovid's Elegies 2.19.1
That can effect <affect> a foolish wittalls wife. Ovid's Elegies 2.19.46
He is too clownish, whom a lewd wife grieves, Ovid's Elegies 3.4.37
Honour what friends thy wife gives, sheele give many: Ovid's Elegies 3.4.45
When fruite fild Tuscia should a wife give me, Ovid's Elegies 3.12.1
WIGHT (See WITES)
WIGMORE
Wigmore shall flie, to set my unckle free. Edw 2.2.196 Mortmr
WIL (Homograph)
We hope your selfe wil willingly restore them. 1Tamb 1.2.117 Agidas
Both we wil walke upon the lofty clifts, 1Tamb 1.2.193 Tamb
You will not sell it, wil ye? 1Tamb 2.4.29 Tamb
What saies my other friends, wil you be kings? 1Tamb 2.5.67 Tamb
I wil the captive Pioners of Argier, 1Tamb 3.1.58 Bajzth
Agreed Casane, we wil honor him. 1Tamb 3.2.113 Techel
But wil those Kings accompany your Lord? 1Tamb 3.3.27 Tamb
For Wil and Shall best fitteth Tamburlain, 1Tamb 3.3.41 Tamb
Wil first subdue the Turke, and then inlarge/Those Christian 1Tamb 3.3.46 Tamb
Those walled garrisons wil I subdue, 1Tamb 3.3.244 Tamb
Doost thou think that Mahomet wil suffer this? 1Tamb 4.4.52 P Therid
Tis like he wil, when he cannot let it. 1Tamb 4.4.53 P Techel
We wil our celebrated rites of mariage solemnize. 1Tamb 5.1.534 Tamb
And I wil sheath it to confirme the same. 2Tamb 1.1.85 Sgsmnd
Then wil we triumph, banquet and carouse, 2Tamb 1.3.218 Tamb
An hundred kings by scores wil bid him armes, 2Tamb 2.2.11 Gazell
We wil both watch and ward shall keepe his trunke/Amidst these 2Tamb 2.3.38 Orcan
Phisitions, wil no phisicke do her good? 2Tamb 2.4.38 Tamb
Some musicke, and my fit wil cease my Lord. 2Tamb 2.4.77 Zenoc
The houses burnt, wil looke as if they mourn'd, 2Tamb 2.4.139 Tamb
Then wil I shortly keep my promise Almeda. 2Tamb 3.1.78 P Callap
That hanging here, wil draw the Gods from heaven: 2Tamb 3.2.28 Tamb
Both we (Theridamas) wil intrench our men, 2Tamb 3.3.49 Techel
Who gently now wil lance thy Ivory throat, 2Tamb 3.4.24 Olymp
Wil match thee with a viceroy or a king. 2Tamb 3.4.41 Techel
Nay, when the battaile ends, al we wil meet, 2Tamb 3.5.97 Callap
here are Bugges/Wil make the haire stand upright on your heads, 2Tamb 3.5.148 Tamb
No, we wil meet thee slavish Tamburlain. 2Tamb 3.5.170 Orcan
Wil send a deadly lightening to his heart. 2Tamb 4.1.10 Celeb
but that you wil be thought/More childish valourous than manly 2Tamb 4.1.16 Calyph
Nor care for blood when wine wil quench my thirst. 2Tamb 4.1.30 Calyph
You wil not goe then? 2Tamb 4.1.40 Amyras
Come, thou and I wil goe to cardes to drive away the time. 2Tamb 4.1.61 P Calyph
And we wil force him to the field hereafter. 2Tamb 4.1.102 Amyras
Stand up my boyes, and I wil teach ye arms, 2Tamb 4.1.103 Tamb
Whose scalding drops wil pierce thy seething braines, 2Tamb 4.1.144 Jrslem
Nay Lady, then if nothing wil prevaile, 2Tamb 4.2.50 Therid
I must and wil be pleasde, and you shall yeeld: 2Tamb 4.2.53 Therid
Stay good my Lord, and wil you save my honor, 2Tamb 4.2.55 Olymp
To proove it, I wil noint my naked throat, 2Tamb 4.2.68 Olymp
I wil Olympia, and will keep it for/The richest present of this 2Tamb 4.2.77 Therid
your weapons point/That wil be blunted if the blow be great. 2Tamb 4.2.80 Olymp
we wil break the hedges of their mouths/And pul their kicking 2Tamb 4.3.48 Techel

WIL (cont.)
We wil Techelles, forward then ye Jades: 2Tamb 4.3.97 Tamb
And tremble when ye heare this Scourge wil come, 2Tamb 4.3.99 Tamb
Wil get his pardon if your grace would send. 2Tamb 5.1.33 1Citzn
My Lord, if ever you wil win our hearts, 2Tamb 5.1.38 2Citzn
For I wil cast my selfe from off these walles, 2Tamb 5.1.40 2Citzn
And wil defend it in despight of thee. 2Tamb 5.1.55 Govnr
Assault and spare not, we wil never yeeld. 2Tamb 5.1.62 Govnr
Save but my life and I wil give it thee. 2Tamb 5.1.118 Govnr
I have fulfil'd your highnes wil, my Lord, 2Tamb 5.1.203 Techel
And never wil we sunder camps and armes, 2Tamb 5.2.52 Callap
Sit stil my gratious Lord, this griefe wil cease, 2Tamb 5.3.64 Techel
Which wil abate the furie of your fit, 2Tamb 5.3.79 Phsitn
I know it wil Casane: 2Tamb 5.3.113 Tamb
rebelling Jades/Wil take occasion by the slenderest haire, 2Tamb 5.3.239 Tamb
The nature of thy chariot wil not beare/A guide of baser temper 2Tamb 5.3.242 Tamb
For both their woorths wil equall him no more. 2Tamb 5.3.253 Amyras
I pray, mistris, wil you answer me to one question? Jew 3.3.30 P Ithimr
master, wil you poison her with a messe of rice [porredge]? Jew 3.4.64 P Ithimr
that wil preserve life, make her round and plump, and batten Jew 3.4.65 P Ithimr
That's brave, master, but think you it wil not be known? Jew 4.1.8 P Ithimr
Of that condition I wil drink it up; here's to thee. Jew 4.4.4 P Ithimr
What order wil you set downe for the Massacre? P 229 4.27 QnMoth
Then wil you joine with us that be his peeres/To banish or Edw 1.2.42 Mortmr
I wil endure a melancholie life, Edw 1.2.66 Queene
And with this sword, Penbrooke wil fight for you. Edw 1.4.352 Penbrk
Stil wil these Earles and Barrons use me thus? Edw 2.2.70 Edward
The wind that bears him hence, wil fil our sailes, Edw 2.4.48 Lncstr
If thou deny it I must <wil> backe to hell. F 426 2.1.38 Mephst
<Faustus I have, and because we wil not be unprovided, F 805 (HC265) A P Mephst
this is the time <the time wil come>, and he will fetch mee. F1861 5.2.65 P Faust
wil I make al the maidens in our parish dance at my pleasure F App p.233 3 P Robin
wil you take sixe pence in your purse to pay for your supper, F App p.235 41 P Robin
what, wil you goe on horse backe, or on foote? F App p.239 95 P Mephst
Wel, come give me your money, my boy wil deliver him to you: F App p.239 107 P Faust
why sir, wil he not drinke of all waters? F App p.239 110 P HrsCsr
he wil drinke of al waters, but ride him not into the water, F App p.239 111 P Faust
slicke as an Ele; wel god buy sir, your boy wil deliver him me: F App p.240 117 P HrsCsr
But I wil speake with him. F App p.240 140 P HrsCsr
I wil not hide from you the thing my heart desires, and were it F App p.242 8 P Duchss
And so I wil my Lord, and whilst I live, Rest beholding for F App p.243 30 P Duchss
They kennel'd in Hircania, evermore/Wil rage and pray: Lucan, First Booke 330
And so they triumph, be't with whom ye wil. Lucan, First Booke 342
force, they that now thwart right/In wars wil yeeld to wrong: Lucan, First Booke 350
Who feares these armes? who wil not go to meete them? Ovid's Elegies 1.6.39
What good to me wil either Ajax bring? Ovid's Elegies 2.1.30

WILBE
Madam, it wilbe noted through the world, P 207 4.5 Charls

WIL'D
He readie to accomplish what she wil'd, Hero and Leander 1.433

WILD
The woman that thou wild us entertaine, Dido 4.2.11 Iarbus
Who wild me sacrifize his ticing relliques: Dido 5.1.277 Dido
To be a prey for Vultures and wild beasts. Jew 5.1.59 Govnr
Hee wild the Governour of Orleance in his name, P1117 21.11 Dumain
And that he's much chang'd, looking wild and big, Lucan, First Booke 475
Before whose bow th'Arcadian wild beasts trembled. Ovid's Elegies 1.7.14
And to her tentes wild me my selfe addresse. Ovid's Elegies 1.9.44
Wild me, whose slowe feete sought delay, be flying. Ovid's Elegies 2.19.12
With strong hand striking wild-beasts brist'led hyde. Ovid's Elegies 3.9.26
Which by the wild boare in the woods was shorne. Ovid's Elegies 3.9.40
Wild savages, that drinke of running springs, Hero and Leander 1.259

WILD-BEASTS
With strong hand striking wild-beasts brist'led hyde. Ovid's Elegies 3.9.26

WILDE
With balles of wilde fire in their murdering pawes, Dido 2.1.217 Aeneas
And this a Spartan Courtier vaine and wilde, Dido 3.1.157 Dido
Grave Socrates, wilde Alcibiades: Edw 1.4.397 MortSr
The wilde Oneyle, with swarmes of Irish Kernes, Edw 2.2.164 Lncstr
Scythia and wilde Armenia had bin yoakt, Lucan, First Booke 19
birds/Defil'd the day, and <at night> wilde beastes were seene, Lucan, First Booke 557
Or wofull Hector whom wilde jades did teare? Ovid's Elegies 2.1.32
Or voice that howe to change the wilde notes knew? Ovid's Elegies 2.6.18
When strong wilde beasts, she stronger hunts to strike them. Ovid's Elegies 3.2.32
As when the wilde boare Adons groine had rent. Ovid's Elegies 3.8.16
Or songs amazing wilde beasts of the wood? Ovid's Elegies 3.8.22
Had wilde Hippolitus, Leander seene, Hero and Leander 1.77

WILDEFIRE
in peeces, give me the sworde with a ball of wildefire upon it. 1Tamb 5.1.312 P Zabina

WILDERNES
operation and more force/Than Cynthias in the watery wildernes, 2Tamb 4.2.30 Therid

WILDERNESSE
And turne proud Malta to a wildernesse/For these intolerable Jew 3.5.25 Basso

WILES
Sister, I see you savour of my wiles, Dido 3.2.96 Venus

WILFULL
Were but to bring our wilfull overthrow, 1Tamb 5.1.5 Govnr

WILL (Homograph)
I love thee well, say Juno what she will. Dido 1.1.2 Jupitr
That will not shield me from her shrewish blowes: Dido 1.1.4 Ganimd
And I will spend my time in thy bright armes. Dido 1.1.22 Ganimd
Who will eternish Troy in their attempts. Dido 1.1.108 Jupitr
I will take order for that presently: Dido 1.1.113 Jupitr

WILL (cont.)

And therefore will take pitie on his toyle,	Dido	1.1.131	Venus
Here in this bush disguised will I stand,	Dido	1.1.139	Venus
Doe thou but smile, and clowdie heaven will cleare,	Dido	1.1.155	Achat
Whence may you come, or whither will you goe?	Dido	1.1.215	Venus
Where Dido will receive ye with her smiles:	Dido	1.1.234	Venus
And will not let us lodge upon the sands:	Dido	1.2.35	Serg
My selfe will see they shall not trouble ye,	Dido	1.2.38	Iarbus
And now she sees thee how will she rejoyce?	Dido	2.1.69	Illion
And so I will sweete child:	Dido	2.1.97	Dido
Will Dido give to sweete Ascanius:	Dido	2.1.312	Venus
Eate Comfites in mine armes, and I will sing.	Dido	2.1.315	Venus
Will quickly flye to [Cithereas] <Citheidas> fist.	Dido	2.1.322	Venus
in stead of him/Will set thee on her lap and play with thee:	Dido	2.1.325	Venus
I will faire mother, and so play my part,	Dido	2.1.332	Cupid
No Dido will not take me in her armes,	Dido	3.1.22	Cupid
Will Dido let me hang about her necke?	Dido	3.1.30	Cupid
What will you give me now? Ile have this Fanne.	Dido	3.1.32	Cupid
In stead of musicke I will heare him speake,	Dido	3.1.89	Dido
In whose faire bosome I will locke more wealth,	Dido	3.1.92	Dido
That will Aeneas shewe your majestie.	Dido	3.1.98	Achat
Which piteous wants if Dido will supplie,	Dido	3.1.111	Aeneas
We will account her author of our lives.	Dido	3.1.112	Aeneas
Take what ye will, but leave Aeneas here.	Dido	3.1.127	Dido
We two will goe a hunting in the woods,	Dido	3.1.174	Dido
But I will take another order now,	Dido	3.2.6	Juno
But I will teare thy eyes fro forth thy head,	Dido	3.2.34	Venus
We two as friends one fortune will devide:	Dido	3.2.55	Venus
Which I will make in quittance of thy love:	Dido	3.2.69	Juno
But much I feare my sonne will nere consent,	Dido	3.2.82	Venus
Faire Queene of love, I will devorce these doubts,	Dido	3.2.85	Juno
This day they both a hunting forth will ride/Into these woods,	Dido	3.2.87	Juno
Whose short conclusion will seale up their hearts,	Dido	3.2.94	Juno
Be it as you will have [it] for this once,	Dido	3.2.97	Venus
Whom I will beare to Ida in mine armes,	Dido	3.2.99	Venus
We two will talke alone, what words be these?	Dido	3.3.12	Iarbus
For otherwhile he will be out of joynt.	Dido	3.3.24	Dido
Which I will breake betwixt a Lyons jawes.	Dido	3.3.38	Cupid
This Troians end will be thy envies aime,	Dido	3.3.73	Iarbus
Whose bloud will reconcile thee to content,	Dido	3.3.74	Iarbus
Will dye with very tidings of his death:	Dido	3.3.77	Iarbus
But time will discontinue her content,	Dido	3.3.78	Iarbus
Who nere will cease to soare till he be slaine.	Dido	3.3.85	Iarbus
The thing that I will dye before I aske,	Dido	3.4.9	Dido
And will she be avenged on his life?	Dido	3.4.14	Aeneas
Doe shame her worst, I will disclose my griefe:--	Dido	3.4.28	Dido
But I will soone put by that stumbling blocke,	Dido	4.1.34	Dido
And I will either move the thoughtles flint,	Dido	4.2.40	Iarbus
I will not leave Iarbus whom I love,	Dido	4.2.43	Anna
I may nor will list to such loathsome chaunge,	Dido	4.2.47	Iarbus
For I will flye from these alluring eyes,	Dido	4.2.50	Iarbus
And none but base Aeneas will abide:	Dido	4.3.20	Aeneas
Will Dido raise old Priam forth his grave,	Dido	4.3.39	Illion
We will not stay a minute longer here.	Dido	4.3.44	Cloan
Troians abourd, and I will follow you,	Dido	4.3.45	Aeneas
Her silver armes will coll me round about,	Dido	4.3.51	Aeneas
Each word she sayes will then containe a Crowne,	Dido	4.3.53	Aeneas
It may be he will steale away with them:	Dido	4.4.3	Dido
Thinkes Dido I will goe and leave him here?	Dido	4.4.30	Aeneas
And will my guard with Mauritanian darts,	Dido	4.4.68	Dido
Will leade an hoste against the hatefull Greekes,	Dido	4.4.91	Aeneas
I, but it may be he will leave my love,	Dido	4.4.97	Dido
I must prevent him, wishing will not serve:	Dido	4.4.104	Dido
Aeneas will not goe without his sonne:	Dido	4.4.107	Dido
For this will Dido tye ye full of knots,	Dido	4.4.155	Dido
And see if those will serve in steed of sailes:	Dido	4.4.160	Dido
Now speake Ascanius, will ye goe or no?	Dido	4.5.12	Nurse
Nurse I am wearie, will you carrie me?	Dido	4.5.15	Cupid
Say Dido what she will I am not old,	Dido	4.5.21	Nurse
Here will Aeneas build a statelier Troy,	Dido	5.1.2	Aeneas
For I will grace them with a fairer frame,	Dido	5.1.5	Aeneas
From golden India Ganges will I fetch,	Dido	5.1.8	Aeneas
Nay, I will have it calde Anchisaeon,	Dido	5.1.22	Aeneas
For I will furnish thee with such supplies:	Dido	5.1.72	Iarbus
Now will I haste unto Lavinian shoare,	Dido	5.1.78	Aeneas
Aeneas will not faine with his deare love,	Dido	5.1.92	Aeneas
But yet Aeneas will not leave his love?	Dido	5.1.98	Dido
And Didos beautie will returne againe:	Dido	5.1.118	Dido
But rather will augment then ease my woe?	Dido	5.1.152	Dido
The Rockes and Sea-gulfes will performe at large,	Dido	5.1.171	Dido
Though thou nor he will pitie me a whit.	Dido	5.1.178	Dido
Will, being absent, be obdurate still.	Dido	5.1.187	Dido
And leaving me will saile to Italy.	Dido	5.1.195	Dido
And I will live a private life with him.	Dido	5.1.198	Dido
O Anna, Anna, I will follow him.	Dido	5.1.241	Dido
And ore his ships will soare unto the Sunne,	Dido	5.1.244	Dido
No but I am not, yet I will be straight.	Dido	5.1.271	Dido
How long will Dido mourne a strangers flight,	Dido	5.1.279	Iarbus
But afterwards will Dido graunt me love?	Dido	5.1.288	Iarbus
Which will revolt from Persean government,	1Tamb	1.1.91	Cosroe
We will invest your Highnesse Emperour:	1Tamb	1.1.151	Ceneus
Whereat the Souldiers will conceive more joy,	1Tamb	1.1.152	Ceneus
Whether we presently will flie (my Lords)/To rest secure	1Tamb	1.1.177	Cosroe

WILL (cont.)

That even to death will follow Tamburlaine.	1Tamb	1.2.59		Usumc
Will never prosper your intended driftes,	1Tamb	1.2.69		Zenoc
We will report but well of Tamburlaine.	1Tamb	1.2.81		Magnet
Which with thy beautie will be soone resolv'd.	1Tamb	1.2.101		Tamb
And gainst the Generall we will lift our swords,	1Tamb	1.2.145		Tamb
My selfe will bide the danger of the brunt.	1Tamb	1.2.151		Tamb
do but joine with me/And we will triumph over all the world.	1Tamb	1.2.173		Tamb
And Jove himselfe will stretch his hand from heaven,	1Tamb	1.2.180		Tamb
Both we will raigne as Consuls of the earth,	1Tamb	1.2.197		Tamb
And they will never leave thee till the death.	1Tamb	1.2.248		Tamb
If you will willingly remaine with me,	1Tamb	1.2.254		Tamb
What will he doe supported by a king?	1Tamb	2.1.57		Ceneus
Our army will be forty thousand strong,	1Tamb	2.1.61		Cosroe
I will my Lord.	1Tamb	2.1.69		Menaph
But I will have Cosroe by the head,	1Tamb	2.2.11		Mycet
Will quickly win such as are like himselfe.	1Tamb	2.2.28		Meandr
Thy wit will make us Conquerors to day.	1Tamb	2.2.58		Mycet
The world will strive with hostes of men at armes,	1Tamb	2.3.13		Tamb
Was but a handful to that we will have.	1Tamb	2.3.17		Tamb
Your speech will stay, or so extol his worth,	1Tamb	2.3.27		Therid
Here will I hide it in this simple hole.	1Tamb	2.4.15		Mycet
You will not sell it, wil ye?	1Tamb	2.4.29		Tamb
Such another word, and I will have thee executed.	1Tamb	2.4.30		Mycet
And now we will to faire Persepolis,	1Tamb	2.5.24		Cosroe
Now will i gratify your former good,	1Tamb	2.5.30		Cosroe
So will we with our powers and our lives,	1Tamb	2.5.34		Ortyg
I will not thank thee (sweet Ortigius)/Better replies shall	1Tamb	2.5.36		Cosroe
Then will we march to all those Indian Mines,	1Tamb	2.5.41		Cosroe
And lose more labor than the gaine will quight.	1Tamb	2.5.96		Tamb
We will not steale upon him cowardly,	1Tamb	2.5.102		Tamb
Haste thee Techelles, we will follow thee.	1Tamb	2.5.104		Tamb
So will I send this monstrous slave to hell,	1Tamb	2.6.7		Cosroe
Yet will I weare it in despight of them,	1Tamb	2.7.61		Tamb
mornings next arise/For messenger, he will not be reclaim'd,	1Tamb	3.1.39		Bajzth
Your Bassoe will accomplish your behest:	1Tamb	3.1.42		Bassoe
like Orcus gulfe/Batter the walles, and we will enter in:	1Tamb	3.1.66		Bajzth
He will with Tamburlaines destruction/Redeeme you from this	1Tamb	3.2.33		Agidas
Will tell how many thousand men he slew.	1Tamb	3.2.43		Agidas
Will rattle foorth his facts of war and blood.	1Tamb	3.2.45		Agidas
I will not tell thee how Ile handle thee,	1Tamb	3.3.84		Tamb
Will batter Turrets with their manly fists.	1Tamb	3.3.111		Bajzth
Which I will bring as Vassals to thy feete.	1Tamb	3.3.129		Tamb
And manage words with her as we will armes.	1Tamb	3.3.131		Tamb
How lik'st thou her Ebea, will she serve?	1Tamb	3.3.178		Zabina
For we will scorne they should come nere our selves.	1Tamb	3.3.186		Zenoc
Straight will I use thee as thy pride deserves:	1Tamb	3.3.206		Zabina
But that he lives and will be Conquerour.	1Tamb	3.3.211		Zenoc
Now will the Christian miscreants be glad,	1Tamb	3.3.236		Bajzth
Will sooner burne the glorious frame of Heaven,	1Tamb	4.2.10		Tamb
Will send up fire to your turning Spheares,	1Tamb	4.2.39		Tamb
That will maintaine it against a world of Kings.	1Tamb	4.2.81		Tamb
This is my minde, and I will have it so.	1Tamb	4.2.91		Tamb
I doubt not but the Governour will yeeld,	1Tamb	4.2.113		Therid
will make thee slice the brawnes of thy armes into carbonadoes,	1Tamb	4.4.43	P	Tamb
shee will fall into a consumption with freatting, and then she	1Tamb	4.4.49	P	Tamb
with freatting, and then she will not bee woorth the eating.	1Tamb	4.4.50	P	Tamb
I will confute those blind Geographers/That make a triple	1Tamb	4.4.75		Tamb
Here at Damascus will I make the Point/That shall begin the	1Tamb	4.4.81		Tamb
If with their lives they will be pleasde to yeeld,	1Tamb	4.4.89		Tamb
of them, locking some happie power will pitie and inlarge us.	1Tamb	4.4.100	P	Zabina
sir, you must be dieted, too much eating will make you surfeit.	1Tamb	4.4.103	P	Tamb
Zenocrate, I will not crowne thee yet,	1Tamb	4.4.139		Tamb
Will never be dispenc'd with til our deaths.	1Tamb	5.1.17		Govnr
and hartie humble mones/Will melt his furie into some remorse:	1Tamb	5.1.22		Govnr
What simple Virgins may perswade, we will.	1Tamb	5.1.61		2Virgn
To thinke thy puisant never staied arme/Will part their bodies,	1Tamb	5.1.89		1Virgn
I will not spare these proud Egyptians,	1Tamb	5.1.121		Tamb
That will we chiefly see unto, Theridamas,	1Tamb	5.1.206		Tamb
That all the world will see and laugh to scorne,	1Tamb	5.1.252		Zabina
Sweet Bajazeth, I will prolong thy life,	1Tamb	5.1.283		Zabina
not but faire Zenocrate/Will soone consent to satisfy us both.	1Tamb	5.1.499		Tamb
Will hazard that we might with surety hold.	2Tamb	1.1.24		Uribas
But whilst I live will be at truce with thee.	2Tamb	1.1.130		Sgsmnd
And they will (trembling) sound a quicke retreat,	2Tamb	1.1.150		Orcan
Sigismond will send/A hundred thousand horse train'd to the	2Tamb	1.1.153		Sgsmnd
I will dispatch chiefe of my army hence/To faire Natolia, and	2Tamb	1.1.161		Orcan
Which when I come aboord will hoist up saile,	2Tamb	1.2.24		Callap
When you will my Lord, I am ready.	2Tamb	1.2.76		Almeda
And I will teach thee how to charge thy foe,	2Tamb	1.3.45		Tamb
If any man will hold him, I will strike,	2Tamb	1.3.102		Calyph
For we will martch against them presently.	2Tamb	1.3.105		Tamb
Will quickly ride before Natolia:	2Tamb	1.3.125		Therid
Now will we banquet on these plaines a while,	2Tamb	1.3.157		Tamb
Such lavish will I make of Turkish blood,	2Tamb	1.3.165		Tamb
So surely will the vengeance of the highest/And jealous anger	2Tamb	2.1.56		Fredrk
Now will we march from proud Orminius mount/To faire Natolia,	2Tamb	2.2.2		Orcan
I will my Lord.	2Tamb	2.3.41		Uribas
We both will rest and have one Epitaph/Writ in as many severall	2Tamb	2.4.134		Tamb
This cursed towne will I consume with fire,	2Tamb	2.4.137		Tamb
And here will I set up her stature <statue>/And martch about it	2Tamb	2.4.140		Tamb
I will requite your royall gratitudes/With all the benefits my	2Tamb	3.1.8		Callap
Will now retaine her olde inconstancie,	2Tamb	3.1.29		Callap

WILL (cont.)

Will poure it downe in showers on our heads:	2Tamb	3.1.36	Callap
All which will joine against this Tamburlain, ...	2Tamb	3.1.61	Soria
[Those] <Whose> looks will shed such influence in my campe,/As	2Tamb	3.2.39	Tamb
It may be they will yeeld it quietly, ...	2Tamb	3.3.12	Therid
We will my Lord.	2Tamb	3.3.46	Pionrs
if our artillery/Will carie full point blancke unto their wals.	2Tamb	3.3.53	Techel
Where we will have [Gabions] <Galions> of sixe foot broad,/To	2Tamb	3.3.56	Therid
Will hew us peecemeale, put us to the wheele, ...	2Tamb	3.4.21	Olymp
And for his sake here will I end my daies.	2Tamb	3.4.44	Olymp
Then carie me I care not where you will, ...	2Tamb	3.4.80	Olymp
To think our helps will doe him any good.	2Tamb	4.1.21	Calyph
Take you the honor, I will take my ease, ...	2Tamb	4.1.49	Calyph
I beleeve there will be some hurt done anon amongst them.	2Tamb	4.1.74	P Calyph
That will not see the strength of Tamburlaine, ...	2Tamb	4.1.133	Tamb
Will poure down blood and fire on thy head:	2Tamb	4.1.143	Jrslem
We will my Lord.	2Tamb	4.1.167	Soldrs
I will with Engines, never exercisde, ...	2Tamb	4.1.191	Tamb
I will persist a terrour to the world, ...	2Tamb	4.1.200	Tamb
And I will cast off armes and sit with thee, ...	2Tamb	4.2.44	Therid
and will keep it for/The richest present of this Easterne	2Tamb	4.2.77	Therid
I will prefer them for the funerall/They have bestowed on my	2Tamb	4.3.65	Tamb
with the martiall spoiles/We will convay with us to Persea.	2Tamb	4.3.106	Tamb
So will I ride through Samarcanda streets, ...	2Tamb	4.3.130	Tamb
And now will work a refuge to our lives, ...	2Tamb	5.1.25	1Citzn
nor the towne will never yeeld/As long as any life is in my	2Tamb	5.1.47	Govnr
I will my Lord.	2Tamb	5.1.135	Therid
They will talk still my Lord, if you doe not bridle them.	2Tamb	5.1.146	P Amyras
And to command the citie, I will build/A Cytadell, that all	2Tamb	5.1.164	Tamb
I will about it straight, come Souldiers.	2Tamb	5.1.172	Techel
Whose Scourge I am, and him will I obey.	2Tamb	5.1.185	Tamb
Will him to send Apollo hether straight, ...	2Tamb	5.3.62	Tamb
Then will I comfort all my vital parts, ...	2Tamb	5.3.100	Tamb
Which onely will dismay the enemy.	2Tamb	5.3.112	Usumc
In spight of death I will goe show my face.	2Tamb	5.3.114	Tamb
Graecia, and from thence/To Asia, where I stay against my will,	2Tamb	5.3.142	Tamb
Yet will they reade me, and thereby attaine/To Peters Chayre:	Jew	Prol.11	Machvl
Birds of the Aire will tell of murders past;	Jew	Prol.16	Machvl
Many will talke of Title to a Crowne:	Jew	Prol.18	Machvl
sent me to know/Whether your selfe will come and custome them.	Jew	1.1.53	1Merch
the Custome-house/Will serve as well as I were present there.	Jew	1.1.58	Barab
I feare their comming will afflict us all.	Jew	1.1.156	2Jew
I know you will; well brethren let us goe.	Jew	1.1.174	1Jew
I hope your Highnesse will consider us.	Jew	1.2.9	Govnr
are such/That you will needs have ten yeares tribute past,	Jew	1.2.19	Govnr
To what this ten yeares tribute will amount/That we have cast,	Jew	1.2.46	Govnr
Oh my Lord we will give halfe.	Jew	1.2.77	3Jews
And will you basely thus submit your selves/To leave your goods	Jew	1.2.79	Barab
No, Governour, I will be no convertite.	Jew	1.2.82	Barab
Nor will I part so slightly therewithall.	Jew	1.2.87	Barab
Either pay that, or we will seize on all.	Jew	1.2.89	Govnr
Will you then steale my goods?	Jew	1.2.94	Barab
Yet Barrabas we will not banish thee, ...	Jew	1.2.100	Govnr
Be patient and thy riches will increase.	Jew	1.2.122	Govnr
His house will harbour many holy Nuns.	Jew	1.2.130	1Knght
And that will prove but simple policie.	Jew	1.2.159	1Knght
Our words will but increase his extasie.	Jew	1.2.210	1Jew
lumpe of clay/That will with every water wash to dirt:	Jew	1.2.217	Barab
A reaching thought will search his deepest wits, . . .	Jew	1.2.221	Barab
But I will learne to leave these fruitlesse teares, . . .	Jew	1.2.230	Abigal
But they will give me leave once more, I trow, . . .	Jew	1.2.252	Barab
What, will you thus oppose me, lucklesse Starres, . . .	Jew	1.2.260	Barab
in distresse/Thinke me so mad as I will hang my selfe,	Jew	1.2.263	Barab
No, I will live; nor loath I this my life:	Jew	1.2.266	Barab
have so manifestly wronged us,/What will not Abigall attempt?	Jew	1.2.276	Abigal
I, but father they will suspect me there.	Jew	1.2.283	Abigal
For I will seeme offended with thee for't.	Jew	1.2.303	Barab
And waters of this new made Nunnery/Will much delight you.	Jew	1.2.312	1Fryar
I must and will, Sir, there's no remedy.	Jew	1.2.391	Mthias
And so will I too, or it shall goe hard.--	Jew	1.2.392	Lodowk
But I will practise thy enlargement thence:	Jew	2.1.53	Barab
Will Knights of Malta be in league with Turkes, . . .	Jew	2.2.28	Bosco
We and our warlike Knights will follow thee/Against these	Jew	2.2.45	Govnr
So will we fight it out; come, let's away:	Jew	2.2.52	Govnr
And there in spite of Malta will I dwell:	Jew	2.3.15	Barab
will I shew my selfe to have more of the Serpent then the Dove;	Jew	2.3.36	P Barab
Yet I have one left that will serve your turne: . . .	Jew	2.3.50	Barab
But when he touches it, it will be foild:	Jew	2.3.57	Barab
Oh my Lord we will not jarre about the price; . . .	Jew	2.3.65	Barab
Come to my house and I will giv't your honour-- . . .	Jew	2.3.66	Barab
No, Barabas, I will deserve it first.	Jew	2.3.68	Lodowk
Against my will, and whether I would or no, ...	Jew	2.3.75	Barab
It shall goe hard but I will see your death.	Jew	2.3.94	Barab
I will serve you, Sir.	Jew	2.3.118	P Slave
not a stone of beef a day will maintaine you in these chops;	Jew	2.3.124	P Barab
Marry will I, Sir.	Jew	2.3.160	Barab
And I will teach [thee] that shall sticke by thee: . . .	Jew	2.3.168	Barab
I have as much coyne as will buy the Towne.	Jew	2.3.200	Barab
though I weepe; the Governors sonne/Will, whether I will or no,	Jew	2.3.258	Barab
the Governors sonne/Will, whether I will or no, have Abigall:	Jew	2.3.258	Barab
Yet through the key-hole will he talke to her, ...	Jew	2.3.263	Barab
He has my heart, I smile against my will.	Jew	2.3.287	Abigal
I have intreated her, and she will grant.	Jew	2.3.314	Barab

WILL (cont.)

Nay, if you will, stay till she comes her selfe.	Jew	2.3.352	Barab
I will have Don Mathias, he is my love.	Jew	2.3.361	Abigal
So, now will I goe in to Lodowicke,	Jew	2.3.381	Barab
But now against my will I must be chast.	Jew	3.1.4	Curtzn
And I will have it or it shall goe hard.	Jew	3.1.15	Pilia
As meet they will, and fighting dye; brave sport.	Jew	3.1.30	Ithimr
Upon which Altar I will offer up/My daily sacrifice of sighes	Jew	3.2.31	Govnr
I will forsooth, Mistris.	Jew	3.3.35	P Ithimr
Abigal I will, but see thou change no more,	Jew	3.3.70	1Fryar
For that will be most heavy to thy soule.	Jew	3.3.71	1Fryar
First will we race the City wals our selves,	Jew	3.5.13	Govnr
And Physicke will not helpe them; they must dye.	Jew	3.6.2	1Fryar
Oh what a sad confession will there be?	Jew	3.6.4	2Fryar
I will not say that by a forged challenge they met.	Jew	4.1.45	P 2Fryar
And so could I; but pennance will not serve.	Jew	4.1.60	Ithimr
Their voyage will be worth ten thousand Crownes.	Jew	4.1.70	Barab
I know they are, and I will be with you.	Jew	4.1.83	Barab
I will not goe for thee.	Jew	4.1.94	1Fryar
And so I will, oh Jacomo, faile not but come.	Jew	4.1.108	Barab
not both these wise men to suppose/That I will leave my house,	Jew	4.1.123	Barab
Doe what I can he will not strip himselfe,	Jew	4.1.131	Ithimr
What, will you [have] <save> my life?	Jew	4.1.148	2Fryar
Then will not Jacomo be long from hence.	Jew	4.1.159	Barab
will you turne Christian, when holy Friars turne devils and	Jew	4.1.193	P Ithimr
And what think'st thou, will he come?	Jew	4.2.5	P Curtzn
goe whither he will, I'le be none of his followers in haste:	Jew	4.2.25	P Ithimr
Tell him you will confesse.	Jew	4.2.77	P Pilia
Content, but we will leave this paltry land,	Jew	4.2.88	Ithimr
Whither will I not goe with gentle Ithimore?	Jew	4.2.99	Curtzn
Or else I will confesse: I, there it goes:	Jew	4.3.4	Barab
Well, my hope is, he will not stay there still;	Jew	4.3.16	Barab
No; but three hundred will not serve his turne.	Jew	4.3.20	P Pilia
Here take 'em, fellow, with as good a will--	Jew	4.3.52	Barab
his villany/He will tell all he knowes and I shall dye for't.	Jew	4.3.65	Barab
I will in some disguize goe see the slave,	Jew	4.3.67	Barab
Any of 'em will doe it.	Jew	4.4.78	P Ithimr
Will winne the Towne, or dye before the wals.	Jew	5.1.5	Govnr
And dye he shall, for we will never yeeld.	Jew	5.1.6	1Knght
Nay stay, my Lord, 'tmay be he will confesse.	Jew	5.1.25	1Knght
I hope the poyson'd flowers will worke anon.	Jew	5.1.43	Barab
Oh villaine, Heaven will be reveng'd on thee.	Jew	5.2.25	Govnr
But Barabas will be more circumspect.	Jew	5.2.43	Barab
I, Lord, thus slaves will learne.	Jew	5.2.49	Barab
Nor feare I death, nor will I flatter thee.	Jew	5.2.60	Govnr
Will Barabas recover Malta's losse?	Jew	5.2.74	Govnr
Will Barabas be good to Christians?	Jew	5.2.75	Govnr
What will you give me if I render you/The life of Calymath,	Jew	5.2.79	Barab
What will you give him that procureth this?	Jew	5.2.83	Barab
And I will send amongst the Citizens/And by my letters	Jew	5.2.86	Govnr
To a solemne feast/I will invite young Selim-Calymath,/Where be	Jew	5.2.97	Barab
And I will warrant Malta free for ever.	Jew	5.2.101	Barab
I will be there, and doe as thou desirest;	Jew	5.2.103	Govnr
Will take his leave and saile toward Ottoman.	Jew	5.2.106	Barab
Then will I, Barabas, about this coyne,	Jew	5.2.107	Govnr
Thus loving neither, will I live with both,	Jew	5.2.111	Barab
Will be too costly and too troublesome:	Jew	5.3.23	Calym
The price thereof will serve to entertaine/Selim and all his	Jew	5.3.30	Msngr
There will he banquet them, but thee at home,	Jew	5.3.38	Msngr
What will we not adventure?	Jew	5.4.9	1Knght
Now sirra, what, will he come?	Jew	5.5.13	Barab
He will; and has commanded all his men/To come ashore, and	Jew	5.5.14	Msngr
And fire the house; say, will not this be brave?	Jew	5.5.41	Barab
For I will shew thee greater curtesie/Then Barabas would have	Jew	5.5.61	Govnr
You will not helpe me then?	Jew	5.5.76	Barab
We will not let thee part so suddenly:	Jew	5.5.98	Govnr
To keepe me here will nought advantage you.	Jew	5.5.117	Calym
[all] <call> the world/To rescue thee, so will we guard us now,	Jew	5.5.120	Govnr
Shall binde me ever to your highnes will,	P 11	1.11	Navrre
Sister, I think your selfe will beare us company.	P 21	1.21	Charls
I will my good Lord.	P 22	1.22	QnMarg
The rest that will not goe (my Lords) may stay:	P 23	1.23	Charls
For what he doth the Pope will ratifie:	P 40	1.40	Condy
And will revenge the bloud of innocents,	P 44	1.44	Navrre
Will every savour breed a pangue of death?	P 72	2.15	Guise
Thankes my good freend, I will requite thy love.	P 78	2.21	Guise
I will my Lord.	P 90	2.33	P Souldr
Weakneth his body, and will waste his Realme,	P 128	2.71	Guise
To bring the will of our desires to end.	P 144	2.87	Guise
Him will we--but first lets follow those in France,	P 153	2.96	Guise
Those that hate me, will I learn to loath.	P 156	2.99	Guise
Yet will the wisest note their proper greefes:	P 216	4.14	Anjoy
What you determine, I will ratifie.	P 227	4.25	Charls
Messenger, tell him I will see him straite.	P 247	4.45	Charls
Content, I will goe visite the Admirall.	P 251	4.49	Charls
And I will goe take order for his death.	P 252	4.50	Guise
And every hower I will visite you.	P 272	4.70	Charls
And so will I.	P 280	5.7	Gonzag
Plac'd by my brother, will betray his Lord:	P 294	5.21	Anjoy
Unto mount Faucon will we dragge his coarse:	P 319	5.46	Anjoy
Will be as resolute as I and Dumaine:	P 323	5.50	Guise
I will my Lord.	P 331	5.58	Mntsrl
Anjoy will follow thee.	P 333	5.60	Anjoy

WILL (cont.)

And so will Dumaine.	P 334	5.61	Dumain
He that will be a flat decotamest,	P 389	7.29	Guise
And this for Aristotle will I say,	P 408	7.48	Ramus
How may we doe? I feare me they will live.	P 420	7.60	Guise
Yet will we not that the Massacre shall end:	P 444	7.84	Guise
O no, his bodye will infect the fire, and the fire the aire, and	P 484	9.3	P 1Atndt
And thither will I to put them to the sword.	P 504	9.23	Guise
It will be hard for us to worke their deaths.	P 508	9.27	QnMoth
For Katherine must have her will in France:	P 520	9.39	QnMoth
And if he grudge or crosse his Mothers will,	P 523	9.42	QnMoth
But God will sure restore you to your health.	P 542	11.7	Navrre
Madam, I will.	P 560	11.25	Eprnon
We will with all the speed we can, provide/For Henries	P 562	11.27	QnMoth
Will shew his mercy and preserve us still.	P 576	11.41	Navrre
And so they shall, if fortune speed my will,	P 601	12.14	King
they Henries heart/Will not both harbour love and Majestie?	P 604	12.17	King
I tell thee Mugeroun we will be freends,	P 614	12.27	King
Hands of good fellow, I will be his baile/For this offence:	P 622	12.35	King
Tush, all shall dye unles I have my will:	P 653	12.66	QnMoth
For while she lives Katherine will be Queene.	P 654	12.67	QnMoth
I will Madam.	P 658	13.2	Maid
Will laugh I feare me at their good aray.	P 673	13.17	Duchss
Which they will put us to with sword and fire:	P 706	14.9	Navrre
It will not countervaile his paines I hope,	P 735	14.38	Navrre
I hope will make the King surcease his hate:	P 792	16.6	Bartus
But God we know will alwaies put them downe,	P 798	16.12	Navrre
you will take upon you to be his, and tyll the ground that he	P 811	17.6	P Souldr
yet I meane to keepe you out, which I will if this geare holde:	P 815	17.10	P Souldr
To countermaund our will and check our freends.	P 846	17.41	King
And know my Lord, the Pope will sell his triple crowne,	P 851	17.46	Guise
Ere I shall want, will cause his Indians,	P 853	17.48	Guise
For not effecting of his holines will.	P 878	17.73	Eprnon
And Epernoune I will be rulde by thee.	P 885	17.80	King
I will my Lord.	P 913	18.14	Bartus
That wicked Guise I feare me much will be,	P 921	18.22	Navrre
What, will you not feare when you see him come?	P 933	19.3	Capt
But when will he come that we may murther him?	P 937	19.7	P 3Mur
For anon the Guise will come.	P 941	19.11	Capt
You will give us our money?	P 942	19.12	P AllMur
So will I triumph over this wanton King,	P 983	19.53	Guise
Nor will I aske forgivenes of the King.	P1006	19.76	Guise
Sirra twas I that slew him, and will slay/Thee too, and thou	P1048	19.118	King
And will him in my name to kill the Duke.	P1058	19.128	King
These two will make one entire Duke of Guise,	P1060	19.130	King
But now I will be King and rule my selfe,	P1070	19.140	King
And now will I to armes, come Epernoune:	P1079	19.149	King
And let her greeve her heart out if she will.	P1080	19.150	King
Or who will helpe to builde Religion?	P1084	19.154	QnMoth
The Protestants will glory and insulte,	P1085	19.155	QnMoth
Wicked Navarre will get the crowne of France,	P1086	19.156	QnMoth
For since the Guise is dead, I will not live.	P1090	19.160	QnMoth
What, will you fyle your handes with Churchmens bloud?	P1093	20.3	Cardnl
Whose murderous thoughts will be his overthrow.	P1116	21.10	Dumain
the Jacobyns, that for my conscience sake will kill the King.	P1131	21.25	P Frier
We will goe talke more of this within.	P1138	21.32	Dumain
And will not offer violence to their King,	P1162	22.24	King
I my good Lord, and will dye therein.	P1165	22.27	Frier
But you will saye you leave him rome enoughe besides:	Paris	ms 6,p390	P Souldr
and will needs enter by defaulte | whatt thoughe you were once	Paris	ms10,p390	P Souldr
then will I wake thee from thie folishe dreame/and lett thee	Paris	ms32,p391	Guise
We will wait heere about the court.	Edw	1.1.49	Omnes
Will you not graunt me this?--	Edw	1.1.77	Edward
Ile have my will, and these two Mortimers,	Edw	1.1.78	Edward
And know my lord, ere I will breake my oath,	Edw	1.1.85	Mortmr
And underneath thy banners march who will,	Edw	1.1.88	Mortmr
For Mortimer will hang his armor up.	Edw	1.1.89	Mortmr
I will have Gaveston, and you shall know,	Edw	1.1.96	Edward
These will I sell to give my souldiers paye,	Edw	1.1.104	Lncstr
I cannot, nor I will not, I must speake.	Edw	1.1.122	Mortmr
All Warwickshire will love him for my sake.	Edw	1.1.128	Warwck
So will I now, and thou shalt back to France.	Edw	1.1.185	BshpCv
What? will they tyrannize upon the Church?	Edw	1.2.3	Lncstr
We may not, nor we will not suffer this.	Edw	1.2.15	MortSr
Will be the ruine of the realme and us.	Edw	1.2.32	Mortmr
My lord, will you take armes against the king?	Edw	1.2.39	Lncstr
Will meete, and with a generall consent,	Edw	1.2.70	ArchBp
What we confirme the king will frustrate.	Edw	1.2.72	Lncstr
I, if words will serve, if not, I must.	Edw	1.2.83	Mortmr
It is our pleasure, we will have it so.	Edw	1.4.9	Edward
We will not thus be facst and overpeerd.	Edw	1.4.19	Mortmr
Whether will you beare him, stay or ye shall die.	Edw	1.4.24	Edward
I there it goes, but yet I will not yeeld,	Edw	1.4.56	Edward
Or I will presentlie discharge these lords,	Edw	1.4.61	ArchBp
The Legate of the Pope will be obayd:	Edw	1.4.64	Edward
This will be good newes to the common sort.	Edw	1.4.92	Penbrk
The Legate of the Pope will have it so,	Edw	1.4.109	Edward
But I will raigne to be reveng'd of them,	Edw	1.4.111	Edward
That whether I will or no thou must depart:	Edw	1.4.124	Edward
The peeres will frowne.	Edw	1.4.141	Gavstn
Like frantick Juno will I fill the earth,	Edw	1.4.178	Queene
But that will more exasperate his wrath,	Edw	1.4.182	Queene
No, rather will I die a thousand deaths,	Edw	1.4.196	Queene

WILL (cont.)

His wanton humor will be quicklie left.	Edw	1.4.199	Lncstr
Plead for him he that will, I am resolvde.	Edw	1.4.214	MortSr
For tis against my will he should returne.	Edw	1.4.217	Queene
No speaking will prevaile, and therefore cease.	Edw	1.4.220	Penbrk
And I will tell thee reasons of such waighte,	Edw	1.4.226	Queene
Will you be resolute and hold with me?	Edw	1.4.231	Lncstr
As he will front the mightiest of us all,	Edw	1.4.260	Mortmr
On that condition Lancaster will graunt.	Edw	1.4.292	Lncstr
And so will Penbrooke and I.	Edw	1.4.293	Warwck
And Mortimer will rest at your commaund.	Edw	1.4.296	Mortmr
Is new returnd, this newes will glad him much,	Edw	1.4.301	Queene
But will you love me, if you finde it so?	Edw	1.4.324	Queene
If it be so, what will not Edward do?	Edw	1.4.325	Edward
These silver haires will more adorne my court,	Edw	1.4.346	Edward
Who in the triumphe will be challenger,	Edw	1.4.382	Edward
Spare for no cost, we will requite your love.	Edw	1.4.383	Edward
Let him without controulement have his will.	Edw	1.4.390	MortSr
For riper yeares will weane him from such toyes.	Edw	1.4.401	MortSr
I will not yeeld to any such upstart.	Edw	1.4.423	Mortmr
My life for thine she will have Gaveston.	Edw	2.1.28	Spencr
I will not long be from thee though I die:	Edw	2.1.62	Neece
And will be at the court as soone as we.	Edw	2.1.77	Neece
If all things sort out, as I hope they will,	Edw	2.1.79	Neece
I have the [gesses] <gresses> that will pull you downe,	Edw	2.2.40	Edward
What will he do when as he shall be present?	Edw	2.2.48	Mortmr
Will none of you salute my Gaveston?	Edw	2.2.64	Edward
Will to Newcastell heere, and gather head.	Edw	2.2.123	Warwck
About it then, and we will follow you.	Edw	2.2.124	Mortmr
Cosin, and if he will not ransome him,	Edw	2.2.127	Mortmr
Whither will your lordships?	Edw	2.2.133	Guard
Why, so he may, but we will speake to him.	Edw	2.2.136	Lncstr
What Mortimer, you will not threaten him?	Edw	2.2.146	Kent
And so will I, and then my lord farewell.	Edw	2.2.156	Lncstr
Will be the ruine of the realme and you,	Edw	2.2.209	Kent
So will I, rather then with Gaveston.	Edw	2.2.215	Kent
I know my lord, many will stomack me,	Edw	2.2.260	Gavstn
Will be the first that shall adventure life.	Edw	2.3.4	Kent
If that will not suffice, farwell my lords.	Edw	2.3.10	Kent
Will I advaunce upon this castell walles,	Edw	2.3.24	Mortmr
Spencer and I will post away by land.	Edw	2.4.6	Edward
O stay my lord, they will not injure you.	Edw	2.4.7	Gavstn
I will not trust them, Gaveston away.	Edw	2.4.8	Edward
Mine honour will be cald in question,	Edw	2.4.55	Queene
My sonne and I will over into France,	Edw	2.4.65	Queene
But yet I hope my sorrowes will have end,	Edw	2.4.68	Queene
cause,/That here severelie we will execute/Upon thy person:	Edw	2.5.23	Warwck
He will be mindfull of the curtesie.	Edw	2.5.40	Arundl
Arundell, we will gratifie the king/In other matters, he must	Edw	2.5.43	Warwck
Will not these delaies beget my hopes?	Edw	2.5.47	Gavstn
He will but talke with him and send him backe.	Edw	2.5.59	Arundl
For Gaveston, will if he [seaze] <zease> <sees> him once,	Edw	2.5.63	Warwck
Then if you will not trust his grace in keepe,	Edw	2.5.65	Arundl
My lords, I will be pledge for his returne.	Edw	2.5.66	Arundl
We will not wrong thee so,	Edw	2.5.69	Mortmr
I will upon mine honor undertake/To carrie him, and bring him	Edw	2.5.79	Penbrk
Provided this, that you my lord of Arundell/Will joyne with me.	Edw	2.5.82	Penbrk
My lords, I will not over wooe your honors,	Edw	2.5.86	Penbrk
Upon mine oath I will returne him back.	Edw	2.5.88	Penbrk
in the morning/We will discharge thee of thy charge, be gon.	Edw	2.5.109	Penbrk
Strive you no longer, I will have that Gaveston.	Edw	2.6.7	Warwck
We will in hast go certifie our Lord.	Edw	2.6.19	James
No doubt, such lessons they will teach the rest,	Edw	3.1.21	Spencr
As by their preachments they will profit much,	Edw	3.1.22	Spencr
And daily will enrich thee with our favour,	Edw	3.1.50	Edward
Sib, if this be all/Valoys and I will soone be friends againe.	Edw	3.1.67	Edward
Madam in this matter/We will employ you and your little sonne,	Edw	3.1.70	Edward
Madam, we will that you with speed be shipt,	Edw	3.1.81	Edward
I will this undertake, to have him hence,	Edw	3.1.111	Arundl
I will have heads, and lives, for him as many,	Edw	3.1.132	Edward
lakes of gore/Your headles trunkes, your bodies will I traile,	Edw	3.1.136	Edward
You will this greefe have ease and remedie,	Edw	3.1.160	Herald
A traitors, will they still display their pride?	Edw	3.1.172	Spencr
Rebels, will they appoint their soveraigne/His sports, his	Edw	3.1.174	Edward
And tell them I will come to chastise them,	Edw	3.1.178	Edward
I doubt it not my lord, right will prevaile.	Edw	3.1.189	Spencr
will your grace with me to Henolt,/And there stay times	Edw	4.2.17	SrJohn
How say you my Lord, will you go with your friends,	Edw	4.2.19	SrJohn
Will we with thee to Henolt, so we will.	Edw	4.2.31	Queene
His grace I dare presume will welcome me,	Edw	4.2.33	Queene
The king will nere forsake his flatterers.	Edw	4.2.60	Mortmr
We will finde comfort, money, men, and friends/Ere long, to bid	Edw	4.2.65	SrJohn
I thinke king Edward will out-run us all.	Edw	4.2.68	Prince
A will be had ere long I doubt it not.	Edw	4.3.20	Spencr
And will sir John of Henolt lead the round?	Edw	4.3.40	Edward
Edward will thinke we come to flatter him.	Edw	4.4.29	SrJohn
How will you deale with Edward in his fall?	Edw	4.6.31	Kent
As silent and as carefull will we be,	Edw	4.7.2	Abbot
We must my lord, so will the angry heavens.	Edw	4.7.74	Spencr
Nay so will hell, and cruell Mortimer,	Edw	4.7.75	Edward
Will your Lordships away?	Edw	4.7.116	Rice
Your worship I trust will remember me?	Edw	4.7.117	Mower
Which in a moment will abridge his life:	Edw	5.1.42	Edward

WILL (cont.)

They stay your answer, will you yeeld your crowne?	Edw	5.1.50	Leistr
And therefore say, will you resigne or no.	Edw	5.1.85	Trussl
Elect, conspire, install, do what you will,	Edw	5.1.88	Edward
And will be called the murtherer of a king,	Edw	5.1.101	Edward
Will sooner sparkle fire then shed a teare:	Edw	5.1.105	Edward
Yet stay, for rather then I will looke on them,	Edw	5.1.106	Edward
Will be my death, and welcome shall it be,	Edw	5.1.126	Edward
Whether you will, all places are alike,	Edw	5.1.145	Edward
And thinkes your grace that Bartley will bee cruell?	Edw	5.1.151	Bartly
Be rulde by me, and we will rule the realme,	Edw	5.2.5	Mortmr
That if he slip will seaze upon us both,	Edw	5.2.8	Mortmr
For our behoofe will beare the greater sway/When as a kings	Edw	5.2.13	Mortmr
And I my selfe will willinglie subscribe.	Edw	5.2.20	Queene
And when tis done, we will subscribe our name.	Edw	5.2.50	Mortmr
I will madam.	Edw	5.2.73	Matrvs
Our plots and stratagems will soone be dasht.	Edw	5.2.78	Mortmr
Let me but see him first, and then I will.	Edw	5.2.95	Prince
With you I will, but not with Mortimer.	Edw	5.2.110	Prince
Then I will carrie thee by force away.	Edw	5.2.112	Mortmr
Helpe unckle Kent, Mortimer will wrong me.	Edw	5.2.113	Prince
Edward is my sonne, and I will keepe him.	Edw	5.2.117	Queene
Hence will I haste to Killingworth castle,	Edw	5.2.119	Kent
Will hatefull Mortimer appoint no rest?	Edw	5.3.5	Edward
When will the furie of his minde asswage?	Edw	5.3.8	Edward
When will his hart be satisfied with bloud?	Edw	5.3.9	Edward
If mine will serve, unbowell straight this brest,	Edw	5.3.10	Edward
Traitors away, what will you murther me,	Edw	5.3.29	Edward
And I will visit him, why stay you me?	Edw	5.3.60	Kent
I, lead me whether you will, even to my death,	Edw	5.3.66	Kent
And therefore will I do it cunninglie.	Edw	5.4.5	Mortmr
That will I quicklie do, farewell my lord.	Edw	5.4.47	Ltborn
I seale, I cancell, I do what I will,	Edw	5.4.51	Mortmr
Mine enemies will I plague, my friends advance,	Edw	5.4.67	Mortmr
And will avcuche his saying with the sworde,	Edw	5.4.77	Champn
I am the Champion that will combate him!	Edw	5.4.78	Champn
My lord, if you will let my unckle live,	Edw	5.4.99	King
I will requite it when I come to age.	Edw	5.4.100	King
Let me but stay and speake, I will not go,	Edw	5.4.105	Kent
And therefore soldiers whether will you hale me?	Edw	5.4.108	Kent
Send for him out thence, and I will anger him.	Edw	5.5.13	Gurney
Yet will it melt, ere I have done my tale.	Edw	5.5.55	Edward
I feare mee that this crie will raise the towne,	Edw	5.5.114	Matrvs
Gurney, my lord, is fled, and will I feare,	Edw	5.6.7	Matrvs
Madam, intreat not, I will rather die,	Edw	5.6.56	Mortmr
My lord, I feare me it will proove too true.	Edw	5.6.77	2Lord
Thus madam, tis the kings will you shall hence.	Edw	5.6.89	2Lord
What will be, shall be; Divinitie adeiw.	F 75	1.1.47	Faust
I will sir.	F 94	1.1.66	Wagner
Their conference will be a greater helpe to me,	F 95	1.1.67	Faust
Performe what desperate enterprise I will?	F 108	1.1.80	Faust
[That will receive no object, for my head]/[But ruminates on	F 131	1.1.103A	Faust
Will be as cunning as Agrippa was,	F 144	1.1.116	Faust
If learned Faustus will be resolute.	F 160	1.1.132	Valdes
The miracles that magick will performe,	F 163	1.1.135	Cornel
Will make thee vow to study nothing else.	F 164	1.1.136	Cornel
We will informe thee e're our conference cease.	F 184	1.1.156	Valdes
Then <Well> you will not tell us?	F 205	1.2.12	P 2Schol
You are deceiv'd, for <Yes sir>, I will tell you:	F 206	1.2.13	P Wagner
I will set my countenance like a Precisian, and begin to speake	F 213	1.2.20	P Wagner
<O but> I feare me, nothing will <can> reclaime him now.	F 227	1.2.34	1Schol
And try if devils will obey thy Hest,	F 234	1.3.6	Faust
Nor will we come unlesse he use such meanes,	F 278	1.3.50	Mephst
So he will spare him foure and twenty yeares,	F 319	1.3.91	Faust
And alwaies be obedient to my will.	F 325	1.3.97	Faust
I will Faustus.	F 329	1.3.101	Mephst
and I will make thee go, like Qui mihi discipulus.	F 354	1.4.12	P Wagner
for I will presently raise up two devils to carry thee away:	F 372	1.4.30	P Wagner
How now sir, will you serve me now?	F 376	1.4.34	P Wagner
I will sir; but hearke you Maister, will you teach me this	F 380	1.4.38	P Robin
you Maister, will you teach me this conjuring Occupation?	F 380	1.4.38	P Robin
[I and Faustus will turne to God againe].	F 397	2.1.9A	Faust
So he will buy my service with his soule.	F 421	2.1.33	Mephst
And tell me, what good will my soule do thy Lord?	F 428	2.1.40	Faust
And I will be thy slave and waite on thee,	F 435	2.1.47	Mephst
I so I do <will>; but Mephostophilis,	F 450	2.1.62	Faust
Now will I make an end immediately.	F 461	2.1.73	Faust
What will not I do to obtaine his soule?	F 462	2.1.74	Mephst
First, I will question [with] thee about hell:	F 504	2.1.116	Faust
<Nay sweete Mephastophilis fetch me one, for I will have one>.	F 530	(HC261)A	P Faust
This will I keepe, as chary as my life.	F 551	2.1.163	Faust
I will renounce this Magicke and repent.	F 562	2.2.11	Faust
Faustus repent, yet God will pitty thee.	F 563	2.2.12	GdAngl
Yea <I>, God will pitty me if I repent.	F 567	2.2.16	Faust
I will not.	F 619	2.2.68	P Mephst
Move me not Faustus <for I will not tell thee>.	F 621	2.2.70	P Mephst
Never too late, if Faustus will <can> repent.	F 631	2.2.80	GdAngl
If thou repent, devils will <shall> teare thee in peeces.	F 632	2.2.81	BdAngl
Nor will [I] <Faustus> henceforth:	F 647	2.2.96	Faust
And we will highly gratify thee for it.	F 653	2.2.102	Lucifr
That sight will be as pleasant to <pleasing unto> me, as	F 657	2.2.106	P Faust
Faustus, thou shalt, at midnight I will send for thee;	F 716	2.2.168	Lucifr
[This will I keepe as chary as my life].	F 719.1	2.2.172	Faust

WILL (cont.)

matters in hand, let the horses walk themselves and they will.	F 727	2.3.6	P	Robin
And as I guesse will first arrive at Rome,	F 775	2.3.54		2Chor
I hope his Holinesse will bid us welcome.	F 807	3.1.29		Faust
We will depose the Emperour for that deed,	F 906	3.1.128		Pope
So will we quell that haughty Schismatique;	F 922	3.1.144		Pope
We will determine of his life or death.	F 969	3.1.191		Pope
The Cardinals will be plagu'd for this anon.	F 976	3.1.198		Faust
The Pope will curse them for their sloth to day,	F 987	3.2.7		Faust
Now Faustus, what will you do now?	F1071	3.2.91	P	Mephst
will it please you to take a shoulder of Mutton to supper, and	F1120	3.3.33	P	Robin
Will not his grace consort the Emperour?	F1162	4.1.8		Fredrk
Faustus I will.	F1240	4.1.86		Mephst
If you will aid me in this enterprise,	F1334	4.2.10		Benvol
here will Benvolio die,/But Faustus death shall quit my	F1336	4.2.12		Benvol
Nay, we will stay with thee, betide what may,	F1338	4.2.14		Fredrk
Here will we stay to bide the first assault,	F1354	4.2.30		Benvol
Thus will I end his griefes immediatly.	F1367	4.2.43		Benvol
it will weare out ten birchin broomes I warrant you.	F1384	4.2.60	P	Benvol
Faustus will have heads and hands,/I, [all] <I call> your	F1393	4.2.69		Faust
late by horse flesh, and this bargaine will set me up againe.	F1465	4.4.9	P	HrsCsr
Well, I will not stand with thee, give me the money:	F1466	4.4.10	P	Faust
why will he not drink of all waters?	F1470	4.4.14	P	HrsCsr
he will drinke of all waters, but ride him not into the water;	F1472	4.4.16	P	Faust
kind I will make knowne unto you what my heart desires to have,	F1570	4.6.13	P	Lady
Madam, I will do more then this for your content.	F1575	4.6.18	P	Faust
I, and we will speake with him.	F1601	4.6.44		Carter
Will you sir? Commit the Rascals.	F1602	4.6.45		Duke
we will be wellcome for our mony, and we will pay for what we	F1611	4.6.54	P	Robin
be wellcome for our mony, and we will pay for what we take:	F1611	4.6.54	P	Robin
which we will recompence/With all the love and kindnesse that	F1671	4.6.114		Duke
to die shortly, he has made his will, and given me his wealth,	F1675	5.1.2	P	Wagner
if you will doe us so much <that> favour, as to let us see that	F1684	5.1.11	P	1Schol
This Magicke, that will charme thy soule to hell,	F1708	5.1.35		OldMan
Then Faustus, will repentance come too late,	F1714	5.1.41		OldMan
And Faustus now will come to do thee right.	F1728	5.1.55		Faust
And with my bloud againe I will confirme/The <My> former vow I	F1749	5.1.76		Faust
I will attempt, which is but little worth.	F1758	5.1.85		Mephst
Here will I dwell, for heaven is <be> in these lippes,	F1773	5.1.100		Faust
I will be Paris <Pacis>, and for love of thee,	F1775	5.1.102		Faust
And I will combat with weake Menelaus,	F1777	5.1.104		Faust
Yea, I will wound Achilles in the heele,	F1779	5.1.106		Faust
Here in this roome will wretched Faustus be.	F1804	5.2.8		Mephst
Both come from drawing Faustus latest will.	F1814	5.2.18		Mephst
Say Wagner, thou hast perus'd my will,	F1816	5.2.20		Faust
this is the time <the time wil come>, and he will fetch mee.	F1861	5.2.65	P	Faust
God will strengthen me, I will stay with Faustus.	F1870	5.2.74	P	3Schol
Pray thou, and we will pray, that God may have mercie upon thee.	F1875	5.2.79	P	2Schol
Fooles that will laugh on earth, [must] <most> weepe in hell.	F1891	5.2.95		Mephst
O what will all thy riches, pleasures, pompes,	F1896	5.2.100		GdAngl
The Stars move still, Time runs, the Clocke will strike,	F1936	5.2.140		Faust
The devill will come, and Faustus must be damn'd.	F1937	5.2.141		Faust
One drop <of bloud will save me; oh> my Christ.	F1940	(HC271) B		Faust
Yet will I call on him: O spare me Lucifer.	F1942	5.2.146		Faust
Then will I headlong run into the earth:	F1948	5.2.152		Faust
Gape earth; O no, it will not harbour me.	F1949	5.2.153		Faust
Or Lucifer will beare thee quicke to hell.	F1976	5.2.180		Faust
will cause two divels presently to fetch thee away Baliol and	F App	p.230 43	P	Wagner
I will teach thee to turne thy selfe to anything, to a dogge,	F App	p.231 58	P	Wagner
will no man looke?	F App	p.231 9	P	Pope
Ifaith thy head will never be out of the potage pot.	F App	p.236 48	P	Robin
a signe of grace in you, when you will confesse the trueth.	F App	p.237 45	P	Knight
No, will you not wake?	F App	p.241 153	P	HrsCsr
Will ye wadge war, for which you shall not triumph?	Lucan, First Booke	12		
The burdened axes with thy force will bend;	Lucan, First Booke	57		
draw the Commons minds/To favour thee, against the Senats will,	Lucan, First Booke	276		
Love over-rules my will, I must obay thee,	Lucan, First Booke	373		
Yet more will happen then I can unfold;	Lucan, First Booke	634		
Two tane away, thy labor will be lesse:	Ovid's Elegies	1.1.4		
Vulcan will give thee Chariots rich and faire.	Ovid's Elegies	1.2.24		
So will thy [triumph] <triumphs> seeme magnificall.	Ovid's Elegies	1.2.28		
I lately cought, will have a new made wound,	Ovid's Elegies	1.2.29		
In spite of thee, forth will thy <thine> arrowes flie,	Ovid's Elegies	1.2.45		
Accept him that will serve thee all his youth,	Ovid's Elegies	1.3.5		
Accept him that will love with spotlesse truth:	Ovid's Elegies	1.3.6		
So likewise we will through the world be rung,	Ovid's Elegies	1.3.25		
What wine he fills thee, wisely will him drinke,	Ovid's Elegies	1.4.29		
When thou hast tasted, I will take the cup,	Ovid's Elegies	1.4.31		
And where thou drinkst, on that part I will sup.	Ovid's Elegies	1.4.32		
Suspitious feare in all my veines will hover,	Ovid's Elegies	1.4.42		
There will I finde thee, or be found by thee,	Ovid's Elegies	1.4.57		
I will weepe/And to the dores sight of thy selfe [will] keepe:	Ovid's Elegies	1.4.61		
I will weepe/And to the dores sight of thy selfe [will] keepe:	Ovid's Elegies	1.4.62		
Then will he kisse thee, and not onely kisse/But force thee	Ovid's Elegies	1.4.63		
Constrain'd against thy will give it the pezant,	Ovid's Elegies	1.4.65		
The gate halfe ope my bent side in will take.	Ovid's Elegies	1.6.4		
Or I more sterne then fire or sword will turne,	Ovid's Elegies	1.6.57		
(Anger will helpe thy hands though nere so weake).	Ovid's Elegies	1.7.66		
There is, who ere will knowe a bawde aright/Give eare, there is	Ovid's Elegies	1.8.1		
When she will, cloudes the darckned heav'n obscure,	Ovid's Elegies	1.8.9		
When she will, day shines every where most pure.	Ovid's Elegies	1.8.10		
Faire women play, shee's chast whom none will have,	Ovid's Elegies	1.8.43		
What he will give, with greater instance crave.	Ovid's Elegies	1.8.68		

WILL (cont.)
And Isis now will shew what scuse to make. Ovid's Elegies 1.8.74
Thy fault with his fault so repuls'd will vanish. Ovid's Elegies 1.8.80
He that will not growe slothfull let him love. Ovid's Elegies 1.9.46
Will you for gaine have Cupid sell himselfe? Ovid's Elegies 1.10.17
And doth constraind, what you do of good will. Ovid's Elegies 1.10.24
Ill gotten goods good end will never have. Ovid's Elegies 1.10.48
Straight being read, will her to write much backe, Ovid's Elegies 1.11.19
Then with triumphant laurell will I grace them/And in the midst Ovid's Elegies 1.11.25
Thy very haires will the hot bodkin teach. Ovid's Elegies 1.14.30
he will lament/And say this blabbe shall suffer punnishment. Ovid's Elegies 2.2.59
With Venus game who will a servant grace? Ovid's Elegies 2.7.21
In all thy face will be no crimsen bloud. Ovid's Elegies 2.11.28
The losse of such a wench much blame will gather, Ovid's Elegies 2.11.35
I from the shore thy knowne ship first will see, Ovid's Elegies 2.11.43
My selfe will bring vowed gifts before thy feete, Ovid's Elegies 2.13.24
Fruites ripe will fall, let springing things increase, Ovid's Elegies 2.14.25
My life, that I will shame thee never feare, Ovid's Elegies 2.15.21
But seeing thee, I thinke my thing will swell, Ovid's Elegies 2.15.25
Or els will maidens, yong-mens mates, to go/If they determine Ovid's Elegies 2.16.17
So sweete a burthen I will beare with eaze. Ovid's Elegies 2.16.30
Her lover let her mocke, that long will raigne, Ovid's Elegies 2.19.33
But of my love it will an end procure. Ovid's Elegies 2.19.52
And first [she] <he> sayd, when will thy love be spent, Ovid's Elegies 3.1.15
Some greater worke will urge me on at last. Ovid's Elegies 3.1.70
And from my hands the reines will slip away. Ovid's Elegies 3.2.14
Gather them up, or lift them loe will I. Ovid's Elegies 3.2.26
Ere these were seene, I burnt: what will these do? Ovid's Elegies 3.2.33
Who now will care the Altars to perfume? Ovid's Elegies 3.3.33
Nor, least she will, can any be restrainde. Ovid's Elegies 3.4.6
What will my age do, age I cannot shunne, Ovid's Elegies 3.6.17
Who bad thee lie downe here against thy will? Ovid's Elegies 3.6.78
What man will now take liberall arts in hand, Ovid's Elegies 3.7.1
Ceres, I thinke, no knowne fault will deny. Ovid's Elegies 3.9.24
Some other seeke, who will these things endure. Ovid's Elegies 3.10.28
But victory, I thinke, will hap to love. Ovid's Elegies 3.10.34
Ile hate, if I can; if not, love gainst my will: Ovid's Elegies 3.10.35
Nor, as use will not Poets record heare, Ovid's Elegies 3.11.19
The strumpet with the stranger will not do, Ovid's Elegies 3.13.9
Will you make shipwracke of your honest name, Ovid's Elegies 3.13.11
And I will trust your words more then mine eies. Ovid's Elegies 3.13.46
For faithfull love will never turne to hate. Hero and Leander 1.128
For will in us is over-rul'd by fate. Hero and Leander 1.168
And I in dutie will excell all other, Hero and Leander 1.221
Which long time lie untoucht, will harshly jarre. Hero and Leander 1.230
In time it will returne us two for one. Hero and Leander 1.236
So she be faire, but some vile toongs will blot? Hero and Leander 1.286
As Greece will thinke, if thus you live alone, Hero and Leander 1.289
And would be thought to graunt against her will. Hero and Leander 1.336
Harken a while, and I will tell you why: Hero and Leander 1.385
Will mount aloft, and enter heaven gate, Hero and Leander 1.466
Now he her favour and good will had wone. Hero and Leander 2.54
And we will all the pleasures prove, Passionate Shepherd 2
And wee will sit upon the Rocks, Passionate Shepherd 5
And I will make thee beds of Roses, Passionate Shepherd 9

WILLES
What willes our Lord, or wherefore did he call? Dido 4.3.15 Achat

WILLING
My lord, the king is willing to resigne. Edw 5.1.94 Leistr
Strike with a willing hand, his head is off. F1368 4.2.44 Mrtino
Wilt have me willing, or to love by force? Ovid's Elegies 3.10.50

WILLINGLIE
Come willinglie, therfore. 2Tamb 3.4.84 Techel
And I my selfe will willinglie subscribe. Edw 5.2.20 Queene

WILLINGLY
I willingly receive th'emperiall crowne, 1Tamb 1.1.157 Cosroe
We hope your selfe wil willingly restore them. 1Tamb 1.2.117 Agidas
If you will willingly remaine with me, 1Tamb 1.2.254 Tamb
As these my followers willingly would have: 1Tamb 3.3.155 Tamb
Tamburlane) as I could willingly feed upon thy blood-raw hart. 1Tamb 4.4.12 P Bajzth
The king hath willingly resignde his crowne. Edw 5.2.28 BshpWn
Nay, and this be hell, I'le willingly be damn'd <damned here>. F 527 2.1.139 Faust
wars,/We from our houses driven, most willingly/Suffered exile: Lucan, First Booke 279
And what he did, she willingly requited. Hero and Leander 2.28

WILLS (Homograph)
So Cupid wills, farre hence be the severe, Ovid's Elegies 2.1.3
Sooner shall kindnesse gaine thy wills fruition. Ovid's Elegies 3.4.12

WILL'T
Will't please thee, mighty Selim-Calymath, Jew 5.5.57 Barab

WILS
Jove wils it so, my mother wils it so: Dido 4.3.5 Aeneas
Dido, faire Dido wils Aeneas stay: Dido 5.1.233 Anna
But see, Achates wils him put to sea, Dido 5.1.258 Dido
Yet live, yea, live, Mycetes wils it so: 1Tamb 1.1.27 Mycet
Wils us to weare our selves and never rest, 1Tamb 2.7.26 Tamb
Wils and commands (for say not I intreat)/Not once to set his 1Tamb 3.1.27 Bajzth
Now here she writes, and wils me to repent. Jew 3.4.5 Barab
Law wils that each particular be knowne. Jew 4.1.205 Barab
And either have our wils, or lose our lives. Edw 1.4.46 Mortmr
This wils my lord, and this must I performe, Edw 1.4.202 Queene
He wils me to repaire unto the court, Edw 2.1.67 Neece
T'was peace against their wils; betwixt them both/Stept Crassus Lucan, First Booke 99

WILSHIRE
Wilshire hath men enough to save our heads. Edw 1.1.127 Mortmr

WILSHIRE (cont.)			
Spencer, I heere create thee earle of Wilshire,	Edw	3.1.49	Edward
WILT (See also THOU'LT, THOU'T)			
And shall have Ganimed, if thou wilt be my love.	Dido	1.1.49	Jupitr
Too cruell, why wilt thou forsake me thus?	Dido	1.1.243	Aeneas
Conditionally that thou wilt stay with me,	Dido	3.1.114	Dido
Hard hearted, wilt not deigne to heare me speake?	Dido	4.2.54	Anna
Why wilt thou so betray thy sonnes good hap?	Dido	5.1.31	Hermes
Say thou wilt stay in Carthage with [thy] <my> Queene,	Dido	5.1.117	Dido
Wilt thou kisse Dido?	Dido	5.1.120	Dido
And wilt thou not be mov'd with Didos words?	Dido	5.1.155	Dido
Wilt thou now slay me with thy venomed sting,	Dido	5.1.167	Dido
if thou wilt stay,/Leape in mine armes, mine armes are open	Dido	5.1.179	Dido
If thou wilt stay with me, renowmed man,	1Tamb	1.2.188	Tamb
Why say Theridamas, wilt thou be a king?	1Tamb	2.5.65	Tamb
Thou wilt repent these lavish words of thine,	1Tamb	3.3.172	Zenoc
If thou wilt have a song, the Turke sh·ll straine his voice:	1Tamb	4.4.63	P Tamb
Here Turk, wilt thou have a cleane tre..cher?	1Tamb	4.4.101	P Tamb
Take which thou wilt, for as the Romans usde/I here present	2Tamb	1.1.81	Sgsmnd
Wilt thou have war, then shake this blade at me,	2Tamb	1.1.83	Sgsmnd
Choose which thou wilt, all are at thy command.	2Tamb	1.2.31	Callap
when wilt thou leave these armes/And save thy sacred person	2Tamb	1.3.9	Zenoc
If thou wilt love the warres and follow me,	2Tamb	1.3.47	Tamb
If thou wilt proove thy selfe a perfect God,	2Tamb	2.2.56	Orcan
And wilt thou shun the field for feare of woundes?	2Tamb	3.2.109	Tamb
Tell me Olympia, wilt thou graunt my suit?	2Tamb	4.2.21	Therid
wilt thou so defame/The hatefull fortunes of thy victory,	2Tamb	4.3.77	Orcan
let me see how well/Thou wilt become thy fathers majestie.	2Tamb	5.3.184	Tamb
Why Barabas wilt thou be christened?	Jew	1.2.81	Govnr
What wilt thou doe among these hatefull fiends?	Jew	1.2.345	Barab
And wilt not see thine owne afflictions,	Jew	1.2.353	1Fryar
Wilt thou forsake mee too in my distresse,	Jew	1.2.358	Barab
No come not at me, if thou wilt be damn'd,	Jew	1.2.362	Barab
Claime tribute where thou wilt, we are resolv'd,	Jew	2.2.55	Govnr
Bernardine--/Wilt thou not speake?	Jew	4.1.169	1Fryar
No, wilt thou not?	Jew	4.1.171	1Fryar
Wilt drinke French-man, here's to thee with a--pox on this	Jew	4.4.32	P Ithimr
What wilt thou give me, Governor, to procure/A dissolution of	Jew	5.2.76	Barab
returne me word/That thou wilt come, and I am satisfied.	Jew	5.5.12	Barab
Flye Ramus flye, if thou wilt save thy life.	P 365	7.5	Taleus
But how wilt thou get opportunitye?	P1135	21.29	Dumain
I give him thee, here use him as thou wilt.	Edw	1.1.196	Edward
I, to the tower, the fleete, or where thou wilt.	Edw	1.1.198	Edward
Go whether thou wilt seeing I have Gaveston.	Edw	1.2.54	Queene
Live where thou wilt, ile send thee gould enough,	Edw	1.4.113	Edward
As thou wilt soone subscribe to his repeale.	Edw	1.4.227	Queene
Penbrooke, what wilt thou do?	Edw	2.5.82	Warwck
Then Edward, thou wilt fight it to the last,	Edw	3.1.211	Mortmr
Conclude against his father what thou wilt,	Edw	5.2.19	Queene
But at his lookes Lightborne thou wilt relent.	Edw	5.4.26	Mortmr
Thou wilt returne againe, and therefore stay.	Edw	5.5.99	Edward
Whether thou wilt be secret in this,	Edw	5.6.5	Mortmr
and begin/To sound the depth of that thou wilt professe,	F 30	1.1.2	Faust
And then wilt thou be perfecter then I.	F 189	1.1.161	Valdes
Sirra, wilt thou be my man and waite on me?	F 354	1.4.12	P Wagner
So, now Faustus aske me what thou wilt.	F 503	2.1.115	Mephst
<Well thou wilt have one, sit there till I come,	F 531	(HC261)A	P Mephst
Now Faustus wilt thou have a wife?	F 533	2.1.145	Mephst
thou hast heard all my progeny, wilt thou bid me to supper?	F 701	2.2.150	P Glutny
<No, Ile see thee hanged, thou wilt eate up all my victualls>.	F 702	(HC264)A	P Faust
And thou shalt turne thy selfe into what shape thou wilt.	F 718	2.2.170	Lucifr
Do what thou wilt, thou shalt not be discern'd.	F1005	3.2.25	Mephst
Speake, wilt thou come and see this sport?	F1193	4.1.39	Fredrk
Wilt thou stand in thy Window, and see it then?	F1195	4.1.41	Mrtino
hedge and ditch, or where thou wilt, but not into the water:	F1473	4.4.17	P Faust
Do as thou wilt Faustus, I give thee leave.	F1607	4.6.50	Duke
Then wilt thou tumble in confusion.	F1925	5.2.129	BdAngl
[O God, if thou wilt not have mercy on my soule],	F1958	5.2.162A	Faust
wilt thou serve me, and Ile make thee go like Qui mihi	F App	p.229 13	P Wagner
My Lord of Lorraine, wilt please you draw neare.	F App	p.231 1	P Pope
hir to thy owne use, as often as thou wilt, and at midnight.	F App	p.234 28	P Robin
wilt please your highnes now to send for the knight that was so	F App	p.238 66	P Faust
over hedge or ditch, or where thou wilt, but not into the water.	F App	p.239 112	P Faust
here they be madam, wilt please you taste on them.	F App	p.242 15	P Faust
Receive with shouts; where thou wilt raigne as King,	Lucan, First Booke		47
mainly throw the dart; wilt thou indure/These purple groomes?	Lucan, First Booke		365
What wals thou wilt be leaveld with the ground,	Lucan, First Booke		384
And wilt not trust thy Citty walls one night:	Lucan, First Booke		518
Wilt lying under him his bosome clippe?	Ovid's Elegies		1.4.5
Hard-Hearted Porter doest and wilt not heare?	Ovid's Elegies		1.6.27
Oft thou wilt say, live well, thou wilt pray oft,	Ovid's Elegies		1.8.107
O thou oft wilt blush/And say he likes me for my borrowed bush,	Ovid's Elegies		1.14.47
Wilt thou her fault learne, she may make thee tremble,	Ovid's Elegies		2.2.17
Then wilt thou Laedas noble twinne-starres pray,	Ovid's Elegies		2.11.29
Wilt thou thy wombe-inclosed off-spring wracke?	Ovid's Elegies		2.14.8
Then warres, and from thy tents wilt come to mine.	Ovid's Elegies		2.18.40
Wilt nothing do, why I should wish thy death?	Ovid's Elegies		2.19.56
This thou wilt say to be a worthy ground.	Ovid's Elegies		3.1.26
Yet in the meane time wilt small windes bestowe,	Ovid's Elegies		3.2.37
Wilt have me willing, or to love by force?	Ovid's Elegies		3.10.50
Wilt thou live single still?	Hero and Leander		1.257
WILTSHIRE (See WILSHIRE)			
WILY			
Wily Corinna sawe this blemish in me,	Ovid's Elegies		2.19.9

WIN (See also WINNE, WOONE, WUN)			
That he may win the Babylonians hearts,	1Tamb	1.1.90	Cosroe
Will quickly win such as are like himselfe.	1Tamb	2.2.28	Meandr
Make but a jest to win the Persean crowne.	1Tamb	2.5.98	Tamb
And by this meanes Ile win the world at last.	1Tamb	3.3.260	Tamb
And for their power, ynow to win the world.	2Tamb	3.1.43	Orcan
My Lord, if ever you wil win our hearts,	2Tamb	5.1.38	2Citzn
Win it, and weare it, it is yet [unfoyl'd] <unsoyl'd>.	Jew	2.3.293	Barab
We wish that one should loose, the other win.	Hero and Leander		1.170
WINCHESTER			
my lord of Winchester,/These lustie leaders Warwicke and	Edw	3.1.245	Edward
Thankes gentle Winchester: sirra, be gon.	Edw	5.2.27	Queene
WINCKT			
her coate hood-winckt her fearefull eyes,/And into water	Ovid's Elegies		3.5.79
WIND (Homograph)			
Whereas the Wind-god warring now with Fate,	Dido	1.1.115	Jupitr
And with the [wind] <wound> thereof the King fell downe:	Dido	2.1.254	Aeneas
But now how stands the wind?	Jew	1.1.38	Barab
But suddenly the wind began to rise,	Jew	2.2.13	Bosco
fares Callymath, What wind drives you thus into Malta rhode?	Jew	3.5.2	P Govnr
The wind that bloweth all the world besides,	Jew	3.5.3	Basso
The wind that bears him hence, wil fil our sailes,	Edw	2.4.48	Lncstr
To pierce the wind-pipe with a needles point,	Edw	5.4.33	Ltborn
then turn her and wind hir to thy owne use, as often as thou	F App	p.234 27	P Robin
So thunder which the wind teares from the cloudes,	Lucan, First Booke		152
And rustling swing up as the wind fets breath.	Lucan, First Booke		392
rocks, and where the north-west wind/Nor Zephir rules not,	Lucan, First Booke		407
Whence the wind blowes stil forced to and fro;	Lucan, First Booke		414
Come breake these deafe dores with thy boysterous wind.	Ovid's Elegies		1.6.54
How oft, that either wind would breake thy coche,	Ovid's Elegies		1.13.29
I know not whether my mindes whirle-wind drives me.	Ovid's Elegies		2.9.28
And fruit from trees, when ther's no wind at al.	Ovid's Elegies		3.6.34
She ware no gloves for neither sunne nor wind/Would burne or	Hero and Leander		1.27
Is swifter than the wind, whose tardie plumes,	Hero and Leander		2.115
WINDE			
To know what coast the winde hath driven us on,	Dido	1.1.176	Aeneas
Whereas the Southerne winde with brackish breath,	Dido	1.2.28	Cloan
My Sailes all rent in sunder with the winde,	Dido	3.1.106	Aeneas
Ile [fawne] <fanne> first on the winde,/That glaunceth at my	Edw	1.1.22	Gavstn
The winde is good, I wonder why he stayes,	Edw	2.2.1	Edward
Faire blowes the winde for Fraunce, blowe gentle gale,	Edw	4.1.1	Kent
Some whirle winde fetche them backe, or sincke them all:--	Edw	4.6.59	Mortmr
[Nor can they raise the winde, or rend the cloudes]:	F 86	1.1.58A	Faust
Or waters tops with the warme south-winde taken.	Ovid's Elegies		1.7.56
Even as a boate, tost by contrarie winde,	Ovid's Elegies		2.10.9
Go, minding to returne with prosperous winde,	Ovid's Elegies		2.11.37
Which as it seemes, hence winde and sea bereaves.	Ovid's Elegies		2.16.46
Rather Ile hoist up saile, and use the winde,	Ovid's Elegies		3.10.51
WINDED			
These Jades are broken winded, and halfe tyr'd,	2Tamb	5.1.129	Tamb
WINDES			
Then gan the windes breake ope their brazen doores,	Dido	1.1.62	Venus
Wretches of Troy, envied of the windes,	Dido	1.2.4	Illion
his entent/The windes did drive huge billowes to the shoare,	Dido	2.1.139	Aeneas
The crye of beasts, the ratling of the windes,	Dido	2.1.336	Venus
Our Masts the furious windes strooke over bourd:	Dido	3.1.110	Aeneas
I mustred all the windes unto his wracke,	Dido	3.2.45	Juno
The ayre is cleere, and Southerne windes are whist,	Dido	4.1.25	Aeneas
On whom the nimble windes may all day waight,	Dido	4.3.23	Aeneas
And silver whistles to controule the windes,	Dido	4.4.10	Dido
The sea is rough, the windes blow to the shoare.	Dido	4.4.25	Aeneas
Blow windes, threaten ye Rockes and sandie shelfes,	Dido	4.4.58	Aeneas
O that I had a charme to keepe the windes/Within the closure of	Dido	4.4.99	Dido
Packt with the windes to beare Aeneas hence?	Dido	4.4.127	Dido
Ile set the casement open that the windes/May enter in, and	Dido	4.4.130	Dido
I goe as whirl-windes rage before a storme.	P 511	9.30	Guise
And windes as equall be to bring them in,	Edw	4.3.51	Edward
Welcome to England all with prosperous windes,	Edw	4.4.2	Queene
With awkward windes, and sore tempests driven/To fall on	Edw	4.7.34	Baldck
Nor let the windes away my warnings blowe.	Ovid's Elegies		1.4.12
Giving the windes my words running in thine eare?	Ovid's Elegies		1.6.42
Nor let my words be with the windes hence blowne,	Ovid's Elegies		1.8.106
East windes he doth not chide/Nor to hoist saile attends fit	Ovid's Elegies		1.9.13
Which stormie South-windes into sea did blowe?	Ovid's Elegies		2.6.44
Hether the windes blowe, here the spring-tide rore.	Ovid's Elegies		2.11.40
Nor violent South-windes did thee ought affright.	Ovid's Elegies		2.11.52
Yet in the meane time wilt small windes bestowe,	Ovid's Elegies		3.2.37
WINDFALL			
You shall have leaves and windfall bowes enow/Neere to these	Dido	1.1.172	Aeneas
WIND-GOD			
Whereas the Wind-god warring now with Fate,	Dido	1.1.115	Jupitr
WINDIE			
her ayrie wheeles/Into the windie countrie of the clowdes,	Dido	1.1.57	Venus
Light art thou, and more windie then thy winges,	Ovid's Elegies		2.9.49
But if sterne Neptunes windie powre prevaile,	Ovid's Elegies		2.16.27
WINDING			
Or els discended to his winding traine:	2Tamb	2.4.54	Tamb
and the bordering Iles/Are gotten up by Nilus winding bankes:	Jew	1.1.43	Barab
With winding bankes that cut it in two parts;	F 814	3.1.36	Mephst
Where Tarbels winding shoares imbrace the sea,	Lucan, First Booke		422
Then wreathes about my necke her winding armes,	Ovid's Elegies		2.18.9
WINDOW			
While she runs to the window looking out/When you should come	Jew	2.3.264	Barab

WINDOW (cont.)				
Or climbe up to my Counting-house window:	Jew	4.3.34	P	Barab
You run swifter when you threw my gold out of my Window.	Jew	4.4.53	P	Barab
Stand in some window opening neere the street,	P 86	2.29		Guise
Harke, harke they come, Ile leap out at the window.	P 369	7.9		Taleus
below, the king and he/From out a window, laugh at such as we,	Edw	1.4.417		Mortmr
wilt thou stand in thy Window, and see it then?	F1195	4.1.41		Mrtino
I am content for this once to thrust my head out at a window:	F1200	4.1.46	P	Benvol
beast is yon, that thrusts his head out at [the] window.	F1275	4.1.121	P	Faust
and let them hang/Within the window where he yoak'd me first,	F1381	4.2.57		Benvol
One window shut, the other open stood,	Ovid's Elegies			1.5.3
WINDOWES				
And shut the windowes of the lightsome heavens.	1Tamb	5.1.293		Bajzth
him now, or Ile breake his glasse-windowes about his eares.	F App	p.240 142	P	HrsCsr
WINDOW'S				
See, see his window's ope, we'l call to him.	F1177	4.1.23		Fredrk
WIND-PIPE				
To pierce the wind-pipe with a needles point,	Edw	5.4.33		Ltborn
WINDS (Homograph)				
Against the terrour of the winds and waves.	1Tamb	3.2.84		Agidas
the Pilot stands/And viewes a strangers ship rent in the winds,	1Tamb	4.3.33		Souldn
nostrels breathe/Rebellious winds and dreadfull thunderclaps:	1Tamb	5.1.298		Bajzth
and al the winds shall breath/Through shady leaves of every	2Tamb	2.3.15		Orcan
and the winds/To drive their substance with successefull	Jew	1.1.110		Barab
And winds it twice or thrice about his eare;	Jew	4.3.8		Barab
Brings Thunder, Whirle-winds, Storme <tempests> and Lightning:	F 546	2.1.158		Mephst
And frozen Alpes thaw'd with resolving winds.	Lucan, First Booke			221
For thee the East and West winds make me pale,	Ovid's Elegies			2.11.9
Let others tell how winds fierce battailes wage,	Ovid's Elegies			2.11.17
And raging Seas in boistrous South-winds plough.	Ovid's Elegies			2.16.22
The East winds in Ulisses baggs we shut,	Ovid's Elegies			3.11.29
WINDY (See also WINDIE)				
Even as when windy exhalations,	1Tamb	1.2.50		Tamb
Over whose Zenith cloth'd in windy aire,	2Tamb	3.4.61		Therid
WINE				
We banquetted till overcome with wine,	Dido	2.1.178		Aeneas
banquet and carouse/Full bowles of wine unto the God of war,	1Tamb	4.4.6		Tamb
Of Greekish wine now let us celebrate/Our happy conquest,	2Tamb	2.3.46		Orcan
Filling their empty vaines with aiery wine,	2Tamb	3.2.107		Tamb
Nor care for blood when wine wil quench my thirst.	2Tamb	4.1.30		Calyph
word a Merchant's fled/That owes me for a hundred Tun of Wine:	Jew	2.3.244		Barab
And with her let it worke like Borgias wine,	Jew	3.4.98		Barab
Cellers of Wine, and Sollers full of Wheat,	Jew	4.1.63		Barab
Give him a crowne, and fill me out more wine.	Jew	4.4.46		Ithimr
That labours with a load of bread and wine,	Jew	5.2.41		Barab
with Valdes and Cornelius, as this wine, if it could speake,	F 216	1.2.23	P	Wagner
and my mother <grandmother> was a Hogshead of Claret Wine.	F 697	2.2.146	P	Glutny
but to the Taverne with me, I'le give thee white wine, red wine,	F 748	2.3.27	P	Robin
with me, I'le give thee white wine, red wine, claret wine, Sacke	F 748	2.3.27	P	Robin
give thee white wine, red wine, claret wine, Sacke, Muskadine,	F 748	2.3.27	P	Robin
Fetch me some wine.	F1051	3.2.71		Pope
My wine gone too?	F1055	3.2.75		Pope
Cursed be he that tooke away his holinesse wine.	F1085	3.2.105		1Frier
He took his rouse with stopes of Rhennish wine,	F1174	4.1.20		Mrtino
Cursed be he that tooke away his holinesse wine.	F App	p.233 39		Frier
the Altar/He laies a ne're-yoakt Bull, and powers downe wine,	Lucan, First Booke			608
As [Maenas] <Maenus> full of wine on Pindus raves,	Lucan, First Booke			674
Lines thou shalt read in wine by my hand writ.	Ovid's Elegies			1.4.20
What wine he fills thee, wisely will him drinke,	Ovid's Elegies			1.4.29
If hee lyes downe with Wine and sleepe opprest,	Ovid's Elegies			1.4.53
See Love with me, wine moderate in my braine,	Ovid's Elegies			1.6.37
Night, Love, and wine to all extreames perswade:	Ovid's Elegies			1.6.59
Night shamelesse, wine and Love are fearelesse made.	Ovid's Elegies			1.6.60
Ascreus lives, while grapes with new wine swell,	Ovid's Elegies			1.15.11
Not drunke, your faults [in] <on> the spilt wine I numbred.	Ovid's Elegies			2.5.14
Not silent were thine eyes, the boord with wine/Was scribled,	Ovid's Elegies			2.5.17
There wine being fild, thou many things shalt tell,	Ovid's Elegies			2.11.49
Wine-bibbing banquets tell thy naughtinesse,	Ovid's Elegies			3.1.17
Festivall dayes aske Venus, songs, and wine,	Ovid's Elegies			3.9.47
And with the other, wine from grapes out wroong.	Hero and Leander			1.140
But they that dayly tast neat wine, despise it.	Hero and Leander			1.261
Differs as much, as wine and water doth.	Hero and Leander			1.264
WINE-BIBBING				
Wine-bibbing banquets tell thy naughtinesse,	Ovid's Elegies			3.1.17
WINES				
Lachrima Christi and Calabrian wines/Shall common Souldiers	2Tamb	1.3.221		Tamb
That bought my Spanish Oyles, and Wines of Greece,	Jew	1.1.5		Barab
Downe to the Celler, taste of all my wines.	Jew	5.5.7		Barab
WING				
a fellow met me with a muschatoes like a Ravens wing, and a	Jew	4.2.28	P	Ithimr
Had late been pluckt from out faire Cupids wing:	P 668	13.12		Duchss
I'le wing my selfe and forth-with flie amaine/Unto my Faustus	F1136	3.3.49		Mephst
First Victory is brought with large spred wing,	Ovid's Elegies			3.2.45
Foorth plungeth, and oft flutters with her wing,	Hero and Leander			2.290
WINGD				
I sweare by Venus, and the wingd boyes bowe,	Ovid's Elegies			2.7.27
Victorious Perseus a wingd steedes back takes.	Ovid's Elegies			3.11.24
WINGED				
Was with two winged Serpents stung to death.	Dido	2.1.166		Aeneas
Whom doe I see, Joves winged messenger?	Dido	5.1.25		Aeneas
now whet thy winged sword/And lift thy lofty arme into the	1Tamb	2.3.51		Cosroe
(Auster and Aquilon with winged Steads/All sweating, tilt about	1Tamb	3.2.78		Agidas
Or winged snakes of Lerna cast your stings,	1Tamb	4.4.21		Bajzth

WINGED (cont.)
That Jove shall send his winged Messenger/To bid me sheath my — 2Tamb 1.3.166 Tamb
The winged Hermes, to convay thee hence: — 2Tamb 4.2.19 Therid
Whose sight is loathsome to all winged fowles? — Edw 5.3.7 Edward
But if my words with winged stormes hence slip, — Ovid's Elegies 2.11.33
Heavens winged herrald, Jove-borne Mercury, — Hero and Leander 1.386
WINGES
Or mount the top with my aspiring winges, — P 103 2.46 Guise
with him, Ile clippe his winges/Or ere he passe my handes, — P1052 19.122 King
Light art thou, and more windie then thy winges, — Ovid's Elegies 2.9.49
WINGS
Or seemed faire walde in with Egles wings, — Dido 1.1.20 Ganimd
Hermes no more shall shew the world his wings, — Dido 1.1.38 Jupitr
Ile frame me wings of waxe like Icarus, — Dido 5.1.243 Dido
As far as Boreas claps his brazen wings, — 1Tamb 1.2.206 Tamb
These are the wings shall make it flie as swift, — 1Tamb 2.3.57 Tamb
feathered bird/That spreads her wings upon the citie wals, — 1Tamb 4.2.106 Tamb
Stampt with the princely Foule that in her wings/Caries the — 2Tamb 1.1.100 Orcan
Now ugly death stretch out thy Sable wings, — 2Tamb 3.4.16 Olymp
And Eagles wings join'd to her feathered breast, — 2Tamb 3.4.62 Therid
And cuts down armies with his [conquering] <conquerings> wings. — 2Tamb 4.1.6 Amyras
of the silent night/Doth shake contagion from her sable wings; — Jew 2.1.4 Barab
Navarre that cloakes them underneath his wings, — P 855 17.50 Guise
As with the wings of rancor and disdaine, — Edw 5.1.20 Edward
His waxen wings did mount above his reach, — F 21 Prol.21 1Chor
That with his wings did part the subtle aire, — F 772 2.3.51 2Chor
With beautie of thy wings, thy faire haire guilded, — Ovid's Elegies 1.2.41
Now wish I those wings noble Perseus had, — Ovid's Elegies 3.5.13
How piteously with drouping wings he stands, — Ovid's Elegies 3.8.9
Cupid beats downe her praiers with his wings, — Hero and Leander 1.369
O that these tardie armes of mine were wings, — Hero and Leander 2.205
WINKE
two words, thinke/The cause acquits you not, but I that winke. — Ovid's Elegies 3.13.50
WINNE
Armies of foes resolv'd to winne this towne, — Dido 4.4.113 Dido
Will winne the Towne, or dye before the wals. — Jew 5.1.5 Govnr
Him as a childe I dayly winne with words, — P 130 2.73 Guise
My Lords, albeit the Queen winne Mortimer, — Edw 1.4.230 Lncstr
I warrant you, ile winne his highnes quicklie, — Edw 4.2.6 Prince
Least Arte should winne her, firmely did inclose. — Ovid's Elegies 2.12.4
What would not she give that faire name to winne? — Ovid's Elegies 2.17.30
And craftily knowes by what meanes to winne me. — Ovid's Elegies 2.19.10
Least labour so shall winne great grace of any. — Ovid's Elegies 3.4.46
To winne the maide came in a golden shewer. — Ovid's Elegies 3.7.30
WINTER
That change their coulour when the winter comes, — P 721 14.24 Navrre
a dead time of the Winter, I would request no better meate, — F1572 4.6.15 P Lady
so that when it is Winter with us, in the contrary circle it is — F1582 4.6.25 P Faust
and the dead time of the winter, I would desire no better meate — F App p.242 10 P Duchss
that being in the dead time of winter, and in the month of — F App p.242 17 P Duke
that when it is heere winter with us, in the contrary circle it — F App p.242 20 P Faust
And where stiffe winter whom no spring resolves, — Lucan, First Booke 17
Which wealth, cold winter doth on thee bestowe. — Ovid's Elegies 3.5.94
Either th'art muddy in mid winter tide: — Ovid's Elegies 3.5.95
WINTERING
and our wounds; our wintering/Under the Alpes; Roome rageth now — Lucan, First Booke 303
WINTERS
Three winters shall he with the Rutiles warre, — Dido 1.1.89 Jupitr
To be well stor'd with such a winters tale? — Dido 3.3.59 Aeneas
'Tis thirtie winters long since some of us/Did stray so farre — Jew 1.2.308 Abbass
Who in my wealth wud tell me winters tales, — Jew 2.1.25 Barab
The sheepeherd nipt with biting winters rage, — Edw 2.2.61 Gavstn
But now the winters wrath and wat'ry moone, — Lucan, First Booke 219
but as the fields/When birds are silent thorough winters rage; — Lucan, First Booke 261
Perpetuall thirst, and winters lasting rage. — Ovid's Elegies 1.8.114
Drye winters aye, and sunnes in heate extreame. — Ovid's Elegies 3.5.106
WIPE
doubt of that, for me thinkes you make no hast to wipe it out. — F1517 4.5.13 P Hostss
WIPES
Henry thy King wipes of these childish teares, — P1236 22.98 King
WIP'ST
with haire discheweld wip'st thy watery cheeks: — 1Tamb 5.1.139 Tamb
WIRE (See WIER)
WISDOMES
As to your wisdomes fittest seemes in all. — Edw 4.6.29 Queene
WISE
And triple wise intrench her round about: — Dido 5.1.10 Aeneas
I am not wise enough to be a kinge, — 1Tamb 1.1.20 Mycet
Therefore tis good and meete for to be wise. — 1Tamb 1.1.34 Mycet
I would intreat you to speak but three wise wordes. — 1Tamb 2.4.25 Tamb
And since he was so wise and honorable, — 1Tamb 3.2.110 Usumc
you wil be thought/More childish valourous than manly wise: — 2Tamb 4.1.17 Calyph
Tush, they are wise; I know her and her strength: — Jew 1.1.81 Barab
In dolefull wise they ended both their dayes. — Jew 3.3.21 Ithimr
But are not both these wise men to suppose/That I will leave my — Jew 4.1.122 Barab
Not a wise word, only gave me a nod, as who shold say, Is it — Jew 4.2.12 P Pilia
You, and such as you are, have made wise worke in England. — Edw 4.7.114 P Rice
And beare wise Bacons, and [Abanus] <Albanus> <Albertus> — F 181 1.1.153 Valdes
As wise as Saba, or as beautifull/As was bright Lucifer before — F 541 2.1.153 Mephst
Whose fiendfull fortune may exhort the wise/Onely to wonder at — F2006 5.3.24 4Chor
she being wise,/Sees not the morne on rosie horses rise. — Ovid's Elegies 1.8.3
Keeper if thou be wise cease hate to cherish, — Ovid's Elegies 2.2.9
Nor is her husband wise, what needes defence/When — Ovid's Elegies 2.2.11

WISE (cont.)
Kindly thy mistris use, if thou be wise. — Ovid's Elegies 3.4.43
Not what we slouthfull [knowe] <knewe>, let wise men learne, — Ovid's Elegies 3.7.25
But when in gifts the wise adulterer came, — Ovid's Elegies 3.7.33
Sweare I was blinde, yeeld not <deny>, if you be wise, — Ovid's Elegies 3.13.45

WISEDOME
My wisedome shall excuse my cowardise: — 2Tamb 4.1.50 Calyph
'Tis wisedome to give much, a gift prevailes, — Hero and Leander 2.225

WISEDOMES
If Nature had not given me wisedomes lore? — 1Tamb 2.4.7 Mycet

WISELY
Viceroy of Byron, wisely hast thou said: — 2Tamb 1.1.54 Orcan
And very wisely sayd, it may be so. — Jew 1.1.166 3Jew
What wine he fills thee, wisely will him drinke, — Ovid's Elegies 1.4.29
Going out againe passe forth the dore more wisely/And som-what — Ovid's Elegies 1.12.5

WISER
Unlesse they have a wiser king than you. — 1Tamb 1.1.92 Cosroe
Unlesse they have a wiser king than you? — 1Tamb 1.1.93 Mycet

WISEST
Yet will the wisest note their proper greefes: — P 216 4.14 Anjoy
And not kings onelie, but the wisest men, — Edw 1.4.395 MortSr

WISH
And wish that I had never wrongd him so: — Dido 3.2.48 Juno
Then would I wish me with Anchises Tombe, — Dido 3.3.44 Aeneas
Then would I wish me in faire Didos armes, — Dido 3.3.48 Iarbus
Your Majestie shall shortly have your wish, — 1Tamb 2.5.48 Menaph
shall we wish for ought/The world affoords in greatest — 1Tamb 2.5.72 Tamb
Whom should I wish the fatall victory, — 1Tamb 5.1.385 Zenoc
and with my heart/Wish your release, but he whose wrath is — 2Tamb 1.2.6 Almeda
Ile make thee wish the earth had swallowed thee: — 2Tamb 3.5.118 Tamb
I wish, grave [Governour], 'twere in my power/To favour you, — Jew 1.2.10 Calym
And henceforth wish for an eternall night, — Jew 1.2.193 Barab
you were his father too, Sir, that's al the harm I wish you: — Jew 2.3.42 P Barab
Away, I'de wish thee, and let me goe by: — Jew 4.1.170 1Fryar
Then now are all things as my wish wud have 'em, — Jew 5.5.17 Barab
But wish thou hadst behav'd thee otherwise. — Jew 5.5.75 Govnr
And all things that a King may wish besides: — P 595 12.8 QnMoth
I yours, and therefore I would wish you graunt. — Edw 1.1.120 Edward
I have my wish, in that I joy thy sight, — Edw 1.1.151 Edward
But I would wish thee reconcile the lords, — Edw 1.4.156 Edward
Do you not wish that Gaveston were dead? — Edw 1.4.252 Mortmr
And promiseth as much as we can wish, — Edw 1.4.399 MortSr
So wish not they Iwis that sent thee hither, — Edw 3.1.152 Edward
Wish well to mine, then tush, for them ile die. — Edw 5.3.45 Edward
And let it be propitious for my wish. — F 447 2.1.59 Faust
bag; and might I now obtaine <have> my wish, this house, — F 675 2.2.124 P Covet
cannot read, and therefore wish all books burn'd <were burnt>. — F 680 2.2.129 P Envy
deny/The just [requests] <request> of those that wish him well, — F1691 5.1.18 Faust
Gentlemen farewell: the same wish I to you. — F1706 5.1.33 Faust
Why should we wish the gods should ever end them? — Lucan, First Booke 668
When thou doest wish thy husband at the devill. — Ovid's Elegies 1.4.28
Beleeve me, whom we feare, we wish to perish. — Ovid's Elegies 2.2.10
Cupid flie)/That my chiefe wish should be so oft to die. — Ovid's Elegies 2.5.2
Minding thy fault, with death I wish to revill, — Ovid's Elegies 2.5.3
And wish hereby them all unknowne to leave. — Ovid's Elegies 2.5.54
Then would I wish thee touch my mistris pappe, — Ovid's Elegies 2.15.11
Vaine things why wish I? — Ovid's Elegies 2.15.27
Wilt nothing do, why I should wish thy death? — Ovid's Elegies 2.19.56
Wish in his hands graspt did Hippomenes. — Ovid's Elegies 3.2.30
My mistris wish confirme with my request. — Ovid's Elegies 3.2.80
My mistris hath her wish, my wish remaine: — Ovid's Elegies 3.2.81
Now wish I those wings noble Perseus had, — Ovid's Elegies 3.5.13
Now wish the chariot, whence corne [seedes] <fields> were — Ovid's Elegies 3.5.15
But for thy merits I wish thee, white streame, — Ovid's Elegies 3.5.105
Or is I thinke my wish against the [starres] <starre>? — Ovid's Elegies 3.11.3
We wish that one should loose, the other win. — Hero and Leander 1.170

WISHE
I wishe this union and religious league, — P 3 1.3 Charls

WISHED
And joyntly both yeeld up their wished right. — Edw 5.1.63 Edward
And needes I must resigne my wished crowne. — Edw 5.1.70 Edward
Now my ship in the wished haven crownd, — Ovid's Elegies 3.10.29
As soone as he his wished purpose got, — Hero and Leander 1.460

WISHES
And may repulse place for our wishes strike. — Ovid's Elegies 2.19.6
her good wishes fade,/Let with strong hand the reine to bend be — Ovid's Elegies 3.2.71

WISHEST
But Villaine, thou that wishest this to me, — 1Tamb 4.2.12 Tamb

WISHING
Wishing good lucke unto thy wandring steps. — Dido 1.1.239 Venus
I must prevent him, wishing will not serve: — Dido 4.4.104 Dido

WISHT
And wisht as worthy subjects happy meanes, — 1Tamb 5.1.103 1Virgn
As I could long ere this have wisht him there. — P 496 9.15 QnMoth
How oft wisht I night would not give thee place, — Ovid's Elegies 1.13.27
from their crowne/Phoebus and Bacchus wisht were hanging downe. — Ovid's Elegies 1.14.32
Or she was not the wench I wisht t'have had. — Ovid's Elegies 3.6.2
I wisht to be received in, <and> in I [get] <got> me, — Ovid's Elegies 3.6.47
And wisht the goddesse long might feele loves fire. — Ovid's Elegies 3.9.42
Faire Cinthia wisht, his armes might be her spheare, — Hero and Leander 1.59
I, and shee wisht, albeit not from her hart, — Hero and Leander 2.37
And now she wisht this night were never done, — Hero and Leander 2.301

WIST
him, but must we now/Leave him on had-I-wist, and let him go? — Edw 2.5.84 Warwck

WIT (See also WITTE)

O cursed tree, hadst thou but wit or sense,	Dido	4.4.139	Dido
But here he is, now Dido trie thy wit.	Dido	5.1.86	Dido
I know you have a better wit than I.	1Tamb	1.1.5	Mycet
That knowe my wit, and can be witnesses:	1Tamb	1.1.22	Mycet
Thy wit will make us Conquerors to day.	1Tamb	2.2.58	Mycet
in a myrrour we perceive/The highest reaches of a humaine wit:	1Tamb	5.1.168	Tamb
Argue their want of courage and of wit:	2Tamb	1.3.24	Tamb
Wherein was neither corrage, strength or wit,	2Tamb	4.1.125	Tamb
Who for the villaines have no wit themselves,	Jew	1.2.215	Barab
If Warwickes wit and policie prevaile.	Edw	2.5.96	Warwck
A greater subject fitteth Faustus wit:	F 39	1.1.11	Faust
Faustus, these bookes, thy wit, and our experience,	F 146	1.1.118	Valdes
And give thee more then thou hast wit to aske.	F 436	2.1.48	Mephst
[As they admirde and wondred at his wit].	F1148	3.3.61A	3Chor
I hope sir, we have wit enough to be more bold then welcome.	F1595	4.6.38	P HrsCsr
Too simple is my wit to tell her worth <praise>,/Whom all the	F1697	5.1.24	2Schol
Being fittest matter for a wanton wit,	Ovid's Elegies		1.1.24
Let him surcease: love tries wit best of all.	Ovid's Elegies		1.9.32
commodious/And to give signes dull wit to thee is odious.	Ovid's Elegies		1.11.4
Rude Ennius, and Plautus full of wit,	Ovid's Elegies		1.15.19
Even Jove himselfe out off my wit was reft.	Ovid's Elegies		2.1.18
Thou doest alone give matter to my wit.	Ovid's Elegies		2.17.34
I yeeld, and back my wit from battells bring,	Ovid's Elegies		2.18.11
The subject hides thy wit, mens acts resound,	Ovid's Elegies		3.1.25
Wit was some-times more pretious then gold,	Ovid's Elegies		3.7.3
And to thine owne losse was thy wit swift running.	Ovid's Elegies		3.7.46
Alone Corinna moves my wanton wit.	Ovid's Elegies		3.11.16

WITCH

Avaunt old witch and trouble not my wits.	Dido	3.2.25	Venus
No faithlesse witch in Thessale waters bath'd thee.	Ovid's Elegies		1.14.40

WITCHT

Either th'art witcht with blood <bould> of frogs new dead,	Ovid's Elegies		3.6.79

WITES

in a brasen Bull/Of great ones envy; o'th poore petty wites,	Jew	Prol.26	Machvl

WITH

Come gentle Ganimed and play with me,	Dido	1.1.1	Jupitr
And bind her hand and foote with golden cordes,	Dido	1.1.14	Jupitr
O how would I with Helens brother laugh,	Dido	1.1.17	Ganimd
Or seemed faire walde in with Egles wings,	Dido	1.1.20	Ganimd
Grace my immortall beautie with this boone,	Dido	1.1.21	Ganimd
As I exhal'd with thy fire darting beames,	Dido	1.1.25	Jupitr
And tricke thy armes and shoulders with my theft.	Dido	1.1.45	Jupitr
And then Ile hugge with you an hundred times.	Dido	1.1.48	Ganimd
And playing with that female wanton boy,	Dido	1.1.51	Venus
Where finding Aeolus intrencht with stormes,	Dido	1.1.58	Venus
And guarded with a thousand grislie ghosts,	Dido	1.1.59	Venus
And charg'd him drowne my sonne with all his traine.	Dido	1.1.61	Venus
Three winters shall he with the Rutiles warre,	Dido	1.1.89	Jupitr
And in the end subdue them with his sword,	Dido	1.1.90	Jupitr
Who with the Sunne devides one radiant shape,	Dido	1.1.97	Jupitr
Whose azured gates enchased with his name,	Dido	1.1.101	Jupitr
To feede her eyes with his engraven fame.	Dido	1.1.103	Jupitr
Whereas the Wind-god warring now with Fate,	Dido	1.1.115	Jupitr
And court Aeneas with your calmie cheere,	Dido	1.1.123	Venus
Had not the heavens conceav'd with hel-borne clowdes,	Dido	1.1.125	Venus
Triton I know hath fild his trumpe with Troy,	Dido	1.1.130	Venus
Venus, how art thou compast with content,	Dido	1.1.135	Venus
And heaven and earth with his unrest acquaints.	Dido	1.1.141	Venus
That we may make a fire to warme us with,	Dido	1.1.167	Aeneas
Whiles I with my Achates roave abroad,	Dido	1.1.175	Aeneas
And lighten our extreames with this one boone,	Dido	1.1.196	Aeneas
Altars crack/With mountaine heapes of milke white Sacrifize.	Dido	1.1.202	Aeneas
With twise twelve Phrigian ships I plowed the deepe,	Dido	1.1.220	Aeneas
Are ballassed with billowes watrie weight.	Dido	1.1.226	Aeneas
Where Dido will receive ye with her smiles:	Dido	1.1.234	Venus
To dull the ayre with my discoursive moane.	Dido	1.1.248	Aeneas
Before that Boreas buckled with your sailes?	Dido	1.2.19	Iarbus
Whereas the Southerne winde with brackish breath,	Dido	1.2.28	Cloan
Come in with me, Ile bring you to my Queene,	Dido	1.2.42	Iarbus
Who shall confirme my words with further deedes.	Dido	1.2.43	Iarbus
And drie with griefe was turnd into a stone,	Dido	2.1.5	Aeneas
Sit in this chaire and banquet with a Queene,	Dido	2.1.83	Dido
Then speake Aeneas with Achilles tongue,	Dido	2.1.121	Aeneas
Peeres/Heare me, but yet with Mirmidons harsh eares,	Dido	2.1.123	Aeneas
Lest you be mov'd too much with my sad tale.	Dido	2.1.125	Aeneas
The Grecian souldiers tired with ten yeares warre,	Dido	2.1.126	Aeneas
With whose outcryes Atrides being apal'd,	Dido	2.1.129	Aeneas
on the sand/Assayd with honey words to turne them backe:	Dido	2.1.137	Aeneas
And heaven was darkned with tempestuous clowdes:	Dido	2.1.140	Aeneas
With sacrificing wreathes upon his head,	Dido	2.1.148	Aeneas
Was with two winged Serpents stung to death.	Dido	2.1.166	Aeneas
we were commanded straight/With reverence to draw it into Troy.	Dido	2.1.168	Aeneas
We banquetted till overcome with wine,	Dido	2.1.178	Aeneas
Where meeting with the rest, kill kill they cryed.	Dido	2.1.190	Aeneas
Frighted with this confused noyse, I rose,	Dido	2.1.191	Aeneas
And with maine force flung on a ring of pikes,	Dido	2.1.196	Aeneas
Old men with swords thrust through their aged sides,	Dido	2.1.197	Aeneas
Who with steele Pol-axes dasht out their braines.	Dido	2.1.199	Aeneas
came Hectors ghost/With ashie visage, blewish sulphure eyes,	Dido	2.1.202	Aeneas
and his breast/Furrowd with wounds, and that which made me	Dido	2.1.204	Aeneas
and with this sword/Sent many of their savadge ghosts to hell.	Dido	2.1.211	Aeneas
With balles of wilde fire in their murdering pawes,	Dido	2.1.217	Aeneas

WITH (cont.)

He with his faulchions poynt raisde up at once,	Dido	2.1.229	Aeneas
And with Megeras eyes stared in their face,	Dido	2.1.230	Aeneas
And would have grappeld with Achilles sonne,	Dido	2.1.251	Aeneas
And with the [wind] <wound> thereof the King fell downe:	Dido	2.1.254	Aeneas
When thou Achates with thy sword mad'st way,	Dido	2.1.268	Aeneas
And we were round inviron'd with the Greekes:	Dido	2.1.269	Aeneas
Her cheekes swolne with sighes, her haire all rent,	Dido	2.1.276	Aeneas
Moved with her voyce, I lept into the sea,	Dido	2.1.283	Aeneas
I dye with melting ruth, Aeneas leave.	Dido	2.1.289	Dido
Faire child stay thou with Didos waiting maide,	Dido	2.1.304	Venus
And strewe him with sweete smelling Violets,	Dido	2.1.318	Venus
in stead of him/Will set thee on her lap and play with thee:	Dido	2.1.325	Venus
Then touch her white breast with this arrow head,	Dido	2.1.326	Venus
In being too familiar with Iarbus:	Dido	3.1.15	Dido
little sonne/Playes with your garments and imbraceth you.	Dido	3.1.21	Anna
O stay Iarbus, and Ile goe with thee.	Dido	3.1.37	Dido
Lest with these sweete thoughts I melt cleane away.	Dido	3.1.76	Dido
My Sailes all rent in sunder with the winde,	Dido	3.1.106	Aeneas
Yea all my Navie split with Rockes and Shelfes:	Dido	3.1.108	Aeneas
Conditionally that thou wilt stay with me,	Dido	3.1.114	Dido
And wanton Mermaides court thee with sweete songs,	Dido	3.1.130	Dido
So that Aeneas may but stay with me.	Dido	3.1.133	Dido
I traveld with him to Aetolia.	Dido	3.1.145	Serg
And I in Athens with this gentleman,	Dido	3.1.146	Cloan
But weapons gree not with my tender yeares:	Dido	3.1.164	Dido
And wrong my deitie with high disgrace:	Dido	3.2.5	Juno
And feede infection with his [let] <left> out life:	Dido	3.2.11	Juno
Nor quit good turnes with double fee downe told:	Dido	3.2.15	Juno
And banquet as two Sisters with the Gods?	Dido	3.2.29	Juno
And feast the birds with their bloud-shotten balles,	Dido	3.2.35	Venus
What though I was offended with thy sonne,	Dido	3.2.40	Juno
Bootles I sawe it was to warre with fate,	Dido	3.2.49	Juno
Wherefore I [chaungd] <chaunge> my counsell with the time,	Dido	3.2.51	Juno
That overcloy my soule with their content:	Dido	3.2.63	Juno
Thy sonne thou knowest with Dido now remaines,	Dido	3.2.70	Juno
And feedes his eyes with favours of her Court,	Dido	3.2.71	Juno
And drench Silvanus dwellings with their shewers,	Dido	3.2.91	Juno
That thus in person goe with thee to hunt:	Dido	3.3.2	Dido
To challenge us with your comparisons?	Dido	3.3.20	Dido
And meddle not with any that I love:	Dido	3.3.22	Dido
And loade his speare with Grecian Princes heads,	Dido	3.3.43	Aeneas
Then would I wish me with Anchises Tombe,	Dido	3.3.44	Aeneas
And overjoy my thoughts with their escape:	Dido	3.3.57	Aeneas
To be well stor'd with such a winters tale?	Dido	3.3.59	Aeneas
What shall I doe thus wronged with disdaine?	Dido	3.3.69	Iarbus
And with one shaft provoke ten thousand darts:	Dido	3.3.72	Iarbus
And make love drunken with thy sweete desire:	Dido	3.3.75	Iarbus
Will dye with very tidings of his death:	Dido	3.3.77	Iarbus
So doth he now, though not with equall gaine,	Dido	3.3.83	Iarbus
With this my hand I give to you my heart,	Dido	3.4.43	Aeneas
When as she meanes to maske the world with clowdes.	Dido	4.1.6	Iarbus
Whiles these adulterors surfetted with sinne:	Dido	4.1.20	Iarbus
That with the sharpnes of my edged sting,	Dido	4.1.22	Iarbus
Not with Aeneas in the ugly Cave.	Dido	4.1.32	Iarbus
That with thy gloomie hand corrects the heaven,	Dido	4.2.6	Iarbus
With whom we did devide both lawes and land,	Dido	4.2.14	Iarbus
him to his ships/That now afflicts me with his flattering eyes.	Dido	4.2.22	Iarbus
I Anna, is there ought you would with me?	Dido	4.2.24	Iarbus
Yet if you would partake with me the cause/Of this devotion	Dido	4.2.27	Anna
Away with Dido, Anna be thy song,	Dido	4.2.45	Anna
For I have honey to present thee with:	Dido	4.2.53	Anna
Ile follow thee with outcryes nere the lesse,	Dido	4.2.55	Anna
And strewe thy walkes with my discheveld haire.	Dido	4.2.56	Anna
Whose golden fortunes clogd with courtly ease,	Dido	4.3.8	Aeneas
And slice the Sea with sable coloured ships,	Dido	4.3.22	Aeneas
And every speech be ended with a kisse:	Dido	4.3.54	Aeneas
It may be he will steale away with them:	Dido	4.4.3	Dido
Then let Aeneas goe abourd with us.	Dido	4.4.23	Achat
me, for I forgot/That yong Ascanius lay with me this night:	Dido	4.4.32	Dido
And will my guard with Mauritanian darts,	Dido	4.4.68	Dido
And heele make me immortall with a kisse.	Dido	4.4.123	Dido
Your Nurse is gone with yong Ascanius,	Dido	4.4.124	Lord
Packt with the windes to beare Aeneas hence?	Dido	4.4.127	Dido
And sheere ye all asunder with her hands:	Dido	4.4.156	Dido
My Lord Ascanius, ye must goe with me.	Dido	4.5.1	Nurse
Whither must I goe? Ile stay with my mother.	Dido	4.5.2	Cupid
No, thou shalt goe with me unto my house,	Dido	4.5.3	Nurse
I, so youle dwell with me and call me mother.	Dido	4.5.16	Nurse
For I will grace them with a fairer frame,	Dido	5.1.5	Aeneas
That loade their thighes with Hyblas honeys spoyles,	Dido	5.1.13	Aeneas
And plant our pleasant suburbes with her fumes.	Dido	5.1.15	Aeneas
That have I not determinde with my selfe.	Dido	5.1.19	Aeneas
Or with what thought sleepst thou in Libia shoare?	Dido	5.1.35	Hermes
Eating sweet Comfites with Queene Didos maide,	Dido	5.1.47	Ascan
With speede he bids me saile to Italy,	Dido	5.1.68	Aeneas
For I will furnish thee with such supplies:	Dido	5.1.72	Iarbus
Let some of those thy followers goe with me,	Dido	5.1.73	Iarbus
Aeneas will not faine with his deare love,	Dido	5.1.92	Aeneas
Say thou wilt stay in Carthage with [thy] <my> Queene,	Dido	5.1.117	Dido
O thy lips have sworne/To stay with Dido:	Dido	5.1.121	Dido
Desires Aeneas to remaine with her:	Dido	5.1.135	Dido
And wilt thou not be mov'd with Didos words?	Dido	5.1.155	Dido

WITH (cont.)

Wilt thou now slay me with thy venomed sting,	Dido	5.1.167	Dido
And I will live a private life with him.	Dido	5.1.198	Dido
And looke upon him with a Mermaides eye,	Dido	5.1.201	Dido
he lay with me last night,/And in the morning he was stolne	Dido	5.1.213	Nurse
That slayest me with thy harsh and hellish tale,	Dido	5.1.217	Dido
Away with her to prison presently,	Dido	5.1.220	Dido
Away with her, suffer her not to speake.	Dido	5.1.224	Dido
How long shall I with griefe consume my daies,	Dido	5.1.281	Iarbus
Now Dido, with these reliques burne thy selfe,	Dido	5.1.292	Dido
They may be still tormented with unrest,	Dido	5.1.305	Dido
By plowing up his Countries with the Sword:	Dido	5.1.308	Dido
And mixe her bloud with thine, this shall I doe,	Dido	5.1.326	Anna
Threatning the world with high astounding tearms/And scourging	1Tamb	Prol.5	Prolog
tearms/And scourging kingdoms with his conquering sword.	1Tamb	Prol.6	Prolog
At whose byrth-day Cynthia with Saturne joinde,	1Tamb	1.1.13	Cosroe
And in your confines with his lawlesse traine,	1Tamb	1.1.39	Meandr
prophesies)/To raigne in Asia, and with barbarous Armes,	1Tamb	1.1.42	Meandr
Chardg'd with a thousand horse, to apprehend/And bring him	1Tamb	1.1.47	Meandr
Whose foming galle with rage and high disdaine,	1Tamb	1.1.63	Mycet
As did Sir Paris with the Grecian Dame:	1Tamb	1.1.66	Mycet
Returne with speed, time passeth swift away,	1Tamb	1.1.67	Mycet
And with thy lookes thou conquerest all thy foes:	1Tamb	1.1.75	Mycet
All loden with the heads of killed men.	1Tamb	1.1.78	Mycet
Besmer'd with blood, that makes a dainty show.	1Tamb	1.1.80	Mycet
a greater [task]/Fits Menaphon, than warring with a Thiefe:	1Tamb	1.1.88	Cosroe
Embost with silke as best beseemes my state,	1Tamb	1.1.99	Mycet
Lading their shippes with golde and pretious stones:	1Tamb	1.1.121	Cosroe
How easely may you with a mightie hoste,	1Tamb	1.1.129	Menaph
Present thee with th'Emperiall Diadem.	1Tamb	1.1.139	Ortyg
That heretofore have fild Persepolis/With Affrike Captaines,	1Tamb	1.1.142	Ceneus
With costlie jewels hanging at their eares,	1Tamb	1.1.144	Ceneus
And with the Armie of Theridamas,	1Tamb	1.1.176	Cosroe
Who traveiling with these Medean Lords/To Memphis, from my	1Tamb	1.2.11	Zenoc
As with their waight shall make the mountains quake,	1Tamb	1.2.49	Tamb
And he with frowning browes and fiery lookes,	1Tamb	1.2.56	Techel
And thinke we prattle with distempered spirits:	1Tamb	1.2.62	Tamb
Affecting thoughts coequall with the cloudes,	1Tamb	1.2.65	Tamb
Till with their eies [they] <thee> view us Emperours.	1Tamb	1.2.67	Tamb
Disdaines Zenocrate to live with me?	1Tamb	1.2.82	Tamb
Enchast with precious juelles of mine owne:	1Tamb	1.2.96	Tamb
With milke-white Hartes upon an Ivorie sled,	1Tamb	1.2.98	Tamb
Which with thy beautie will be soone resolv'd.	1Tamb	1.2.101	Tamb
My martiall prises with five hundred men,	1Tamb	1.2.102	Tamb
But this is she with whom I am in love.	1Tamb	1.2.108	Tamb
Their plumed helmes are wrought with beaten golde.	1Tamb	1.2.124	Souldr
Then shall we fight couragiously with them.	1Tamb	1.2.128	Tamb
And with a sodaine and an hot alarme/Drive all their horses	1Tamb	1.2.134	Usumc
Before we part with our possession.	1Tamb	1.2.144	Tamb
so imbellished/With Natures pride, and richest furniture?	1Tamb	1.2.156	Therid
With what a majesty he rears his looks:--	1Tamb	1.2.165	Tamb
Forsake thy king and do but joine with me/And we will triumph	1Tamb	1.2.172	Tamb
And with my hand turne Fortunes wheel about,	1Tamb	1.2.175	Tamb
If thou wilt stay with me, renowmed man,	1Tamb	1.2.188	Tamb
And lead thy thousand horse with my conduct,	1Tamb	1.2.189	Tamb
Those thousand horse shall sweat with martiall spoile/Of	1Tamb	1.2.191	Tamb
And Christian Merchants that with Russian stems/Plow up huge	1Tamb	1.2.194	Tamb
Joine with me now in this my meane estate,	1Tamb	1.2.202	Tamb
Then shalt thou be Competitor with me,	1Tamb	1.2.208	Tamb
And sit with Tamburlaine in all his majestie.	1Tamb	1.2.209	Tamb
When with their fearfull tongues they shall confesse/Theise are	1Tamb	1.2.222	Usumc
Won with thy words, and conquered with thy looks,	1Tamb	1.2.228	Therid
Thus shall my heart be still combinde with thine.	1Tamb	1.2.235	Tamb
Long may Theridamas remaine with us.	1Tamb	1.2.240	Usumc
Shal want my heart to be with gladnes pierc'd/To do you honor	1Tamb	1.2.250	Therid
If you will willingly remaine with me,	1Tamb	1.2.254	Tamb
Or els you shall be forc'd with slaverie.	1Tamb	1.2.256	Tamb
wrought in him with passion,/Thirsting with soverainty, with	1Tamb	2.1.19	Menaph
Thirsting with soverainty, with love of armes:	1Tamb	2.1.20	Menaph
Making it daunce with wanton majestie:	1Tamb	2.1.26	Menaph
Nature doth strive with Fortune and his stars,	1Tamb	2.1.33	Cosroe
With reasons of his valour and his life,	1Tamb	2.1.38	Cosroe
And fall like mellowed fruit, with shakes of death,	1Tamb	2.1.47	Cosroe
In joyning with the man, ordain'd by heaven/To further every	1Tamb	2.1.52	Ortyg
He that with Shepheards and a litle spoile,	1Tamb	2.1.54	Ceneus
And stuft with treasure for his highest thoughts?	1Tamb	2.1.59	Ceneus
And with unwilling souldiers faintly arm'd,	1Tamb	2.1.66	Cosroe
I tel you true my heart is swolne with wrath,	1Tamb	2.2.2	Mycet
And kill proud Tamburlaine with point of sword.	1Tamb	2.2.12	Mycet
Whose tops are covered with Tartarian thieves,	1Tamb	2.2.16	Meandr
This countrie swarmes with vile outragious men,	1Tamb	2.2.22	Meandr
And he that could with giftes and promises/Inveigle him that	1Tamb	2.2.25	Meandr
And as we know) remaines with Tamburlaine,	1Tamb	2.2.36	Meandr
And be reclaim'd with princely lenitie.	1Tamb	2.2.38	Meandr
If wealth or riches may prevaile with them,	1Tamb	2.2.61	Meandr
We have our Cammels laden all with gold:	1Tamb	2.2.62	Meandr
The world will strive with hostes of men at armes,	1Tamb	2.3.13	Tamb
and with our Sun-bright armour as we march,	1Tamb	2.3.221	Tamb
With dutie [and] <not> with amitie we yeeld/Our utmost service	1Tamb	2.3.33	Techel
That I with these my friends and all my men,	1Tamb	2.3.43	Tamb
Meete with the foole, and rid your royall shoulders/Of such a	1Tamb	2.3.46	Tamb
discovered the enemie/Ready to chardge you with a mighty armie.	1Tamb	2.3.50	1Msngr
Till I may see thee hem'd with armed men.	1Tamb	2.4.38	Tamb

WITH (cont.)

With greatest pompe had crown'd thee Emperour.	1Tamb	2.5.5	Tamb
On your submission we with thanks excuse,	1Tamb	2.5.13	Cosroe
With utmost vertue of my faith and dutie.	1Tamb	2.5.17	Meandr
With twenty thousand expert souldiers.	1Tamb	2.5.25	Cosroe
With litle slaughter take Meanders course,	1Tamb	2.5.27	Cosroe
And grace your calling with a greater sway.	1Tamb	2.5.31	Cosroe
So will we with our powers and our lives,	1Tamb	2.5.34	Ortyg
And ransome them with fame and usurie.	1Tamb	2.5.43	Cosroe
enjoy in heaven/Can not compare with kingly joyes in earth.	1Tamb	2.5.59	Therid
To weare a Crowne enchac'd with pearle and golde,	1Tamb	2.5.60	Therid
Whose vertues carie with it life and death,	1Tamb	2.5.61	Therid
When looks breed love, with lookes to gaine the prize.	1Tamb	2.5.63	Therid
I, if I could with all my heart my Lord.	1Tamb	2.5.68	Techel
I could attaine it with a woondrous ease,	1Tamb	2.5.77	Tamb
I know they would with our perswasions.	1Tamb	2.5.80	Therid
Came creeping to us with their crownes apace.	1Tamb	2.5.86	Tamb
Techelles, take a thousand horse with thee,	1Tamb	2.5.99	Tamb
And bid him turne [him] <his> back to war with us,	1Tamb	2.5.100	Tamb
divelish shepheard to aspire/With such a Giantly presumption,	1Tamb	2.6.2	Cosroe
Since with the spirit of his fearefull pride,	1Tamb	2.6.12	Meandr
And with the same proportion of Elements/Resolve, I hope we are	1Tamb	2.6.26	Cosroe
And that made me to joine with Tamburlain,	1Tamb	2.7.30	Therid
And with my blood my life slides through my wound,	1Tamb	2.7.43	Cosroe
dooth gastly death/With greedy tallents gripe my bleeding hart,	1Tamb	2.7.49	Cosroe
Presume a bickering with your Emperour:	1Tamb	3.1.4	Bajzth
Yet would we not be brav'd with forrain power,	1Tamb	3.1.13	Bajzth
He be so mad to manage Armes with me,	1Tamb	3.1.34	Bajzth
Then stay thou with him, say I bid thee so.	1Tamb	3.1.35	Bajzth
have measured heaven/With triple circuit thou regreet us not,	1Tamb	3.1.37	Bajzth
The ground is mantled with such multitudes.	1Tamb	3.1.53	Moroc
And all the trees are blasted with our breathes.	1Tamb	3.1.55	Bajzth
And with their Cannons mouth'd like Orcus gulfe/Batter the	1Tamb	3.1.65	Bajzth
With ceaselesse and disconsolate conceits,	1Tamb	3.2.14	Zenoc
That I may live and die with Tamburlaine.	1Tamb	3.2.24	Zenoc
With Tamburlaine?	1Tamb	3.2.25	Agidas
Be honored with your love, but for necessity.	1Tamb	3.2.30	Agidas
He will with Tamburlaines destruction/Redeeme you from this	1Tamb	3.2.33	Agidas
[Agidas], leave to wound me with these words:	1Tamb	3.2.35	Zenoc
Or when Minerva did with Neptune strive.	1Tamb	3.2.52	Zenoc
If I were matcht with mightie Tamburlaine.	1Tamb	3.2.55	Zenoc
Threatned with frowning wrath and jealousie,	1Tamb	3.2.67	Agidas
Surpriz'd with feare of hideous revenge,	1Tamb	3.2.68	Agidas
(Auster and Aquilon with winged Steads/All sweating, tilt about	1Tamb	3.2.78	Agidas
With shivering speares enforcing thunderclaps,	1Tamb	3.2.80	Agidas
He needed not with words confirme my feare,	1Tamb	3.2.92	Agidas
And with this stab slumber eternally.	1Tamb	3.2.106	Agidas
T'incounter with the strength of Tamburlaine.	1Tamb	3.3.7	Tamb
Burdening their bodies with your heavie chaines,	1Tamb	3.3.48	Tamb
And feeding them with thin and slender fare,	1Tamb	3.3.49	Tamb
Are punisht with Bastones so grievously,	1Tamb	3.3.52	Tamb
Inhabited with stragling Runnagates,	1Tamb	3.3.57	Tamb
I meane t'incounter with that Bajazeth.	1Tamb	3.3.65	Tamb
mighty Turkish Emperor/To talk with one so base as Tamburlaine?	1Tamb	3.3.88	Fesse
Will batter Turrets with their manly fists.	1Tamb	3.3.111	Bajzth
That with thy lookes canst cleare the darkened Sky:	1Tamb	3.3.122	Tamb
adorned with my Crowne,/As if thou wert the Empresse of the	1Tamb	3.3.124	Tamb
untill thou see/Me martch victoriously with all my men,	1Tamb	3.3.127	Tamb
And manage words with her as we will armes.	1Tamb	3.3.131	Tamb
Returne with victorie, and free from wound.	1Tamb	3.3.133	Zenoc
Trampling their bowels with our horses hooffes:	1Tamb	3.3.150	Tamb
That dare to manage armes with him,	1Tamb	3.3.198	Zabina
Ringing with joy their superstitious belles:	1Tamb	3.3.237	Bajzth
foule Idolaters/Shall make me bonfires with their filthy bones,	1Tamb	3.3.240	Bajzth
And with a troope of theeves and vagabondes,	1Tamb	4.1.6	Souldn
That with his terrour and imperious eies,	1Tamb	4.1.14	2Msngr
Steeds, disdainfully/With wanton paces trampling on the ground.	1Tamb	4.1.23	2Msngr
That satiate with spoile refuseth blood.	1Tamb	4.1.53	2Msngr
Then must his kindled wrath bee quencht with blood:	1Tamb	4.1.56	2Msngr
He raceth all his foes with fire and sword.	1Tamb	4.1.63	2Msngr
May have fresh warning to go war with us,	1Tamb	4.1.71	Souldn
Staining his Altars with your purple blood:	1Tamb	4.2.4	Bajzth
of that Spheare/Enchac'd with thousands ever shining lamps,	1Tamb	4.2.9	Tamb
First shalt thou rip my bowels with thy sword,	1Tamb	4.2.16	Bajzth
Strooke with the voice of thundring Jupiter.	1Tamb	4.2.25	Tamb
With Eban Scepter strike this hatefull earth,	1Tamb	4.2.28	Bajzth
First rising in the East with milde aspect,	1Tamb	4.2.37	Tamb
Fill all the aire with fiery meteors.	1Tamb	4.2.52	Tamb
Are fled from Bajazeth, and remaine with me,	1Tamb	4.2.80	Tamb
And thou his wife shalt feed him with the scraps/My servitures	1Tamb	4.2.87	Tamb
Shall lead him with us wheresoere we goe.	1Tamb	4.2.100	Tamb
That with their beauties grac'd the Memphion fields:	1Tamb	4.2.104	Tamb
With mournfull streamers hanging down their heads,	1Tamb	4.2.120	Tamb
Environed with brave Argolian knightes,	1Tamb	4.3.2	Souldn
Or Cephalus with lustie Thebane youths,	1Tamb	4.3.4	Souldn
Joine your Arabians with the Souldans power:	1Tamb	4.3.16	Souldn
that the Souldan is/No more dismaide with tidings of his fall,	1Tamb	4.3.31	Souldn
Confirming it with Ibis holy name,	1Tamb	4.3.37	Souldn
And leads with him the great Arabian King,	1Tamb	4.3.64	Souldn
shee will fall into a consumption with freatting, and then she	1Tamb	4.4.50	P Tamb
And with my father take a frindly truce.	1Tamb	4.4.72	Zenoc
Yet would I with my sword make Jove to stoope.	1Tamb	4.4.74	Tamb
And with this pen reduce them to a Map,	1Tamb	4.4.78	Tamb

WITH (cont.)

wouldst thou have me buy thy Fathers love/With such a losse?	1Tamb	4.4.84	Tamb
If with their lives they will be pleasde to yeeld, . .	1Tamb	4.4.89	Tamb
I (my Lord) but none save kinges must feede with these. .	1Tamb	4.4.109	P Therid
You that have martcht with happy Tamburlaine, ...	1Tamb	4.4.121	Tamb
Deserve these tytles I endow you with, ...	1Tamb	4.4.125	Tamb
If we deserve them not with higher meeds/Then erst our states	1Tamb	4.4.131	Therid
Until with greater honors I be grac'd.	1Tamb	4.4.140	Tamb
And to resist with longer stubbornesse, ...	1Tamb	5.1.3	Govnr
With terrours to the last and cruelst hew:	1Tamb	5.1.8	Govnr
Threaten our citie with a generall spoile:	1Tamb	5.1.10	Govnr
And if we should with common rites of Armes, ...	1Tamb	5.1.11	Govnr
Will never be dispenc'd with til our deaths.	1Tamb	5.1.17	Govnr
(Uttered with teares of wretchednesse and blood, . . .	1Tamb	5.1.25	1Virgn
Would not with too much cowardize or feare, ...	1Tamb	5.1.37	Govnr
lives were weigh'd/In equall care and ballance with our owne,	1Tamb	5.1.42	Govnr
With knees and hearts submissive we intreate/Grace to our words	1Tamb	5.1.50	2Virgn
With happy looks of ruthe and lenity.	1Tamb	5.1.59	2Virgn
Embraceth now with teares of ruth and blood, ...	1Tamb	5.1.85	1Virgn
Whose cheekes and hearts so punisht with conceit, . . .	1Tamb	5.1.87	1Virgn
Even with the true Egyptian Diadem.	1Tamb	5.1.105	1Virgn
Away with them I say and shew them death.	1Tamb	5.1.120	Tamb
would she leave/The angrie God of Armes, and lie with me.	1Tamb	5.1.125	Tamb
With haire discheweld wip'st thy watery cheeks: . . .	1Tamb	5.1.139	Tamb
And comments vollumes with her Yvory pen, ...	1Tamb	5.1.145	Tamb
armours fight/A doubtfull battell with my tempted thoughtes,	1Tamb	5.1.152	Tamb
nor the Turk/Troubled my sences with conceit of foile, .	1Tamb	5.1.158	Tamb
With whose instinct the soule of man is toucht, . . .	1Tamb	5.1.179	Tamb
And every warriour that is rapt with love/Of fame, of valour,	1Tamb	5.1.180	Tamb
And fashions men with true nobility.	1Tamb	5.1.190	Tamb
Arabian king together/Martch on us with such eager violence,	1Tamb	5.1.200	Techel
As if there were no way but one with us.	1Tamb	5.1.201	Techel
Go, never to returne with victorie:	1Tamb	5.1.214	Bajzth
And gore thy body with as many wounds.	1Tamb	5.1.216	Bajzth
Breake up the earth, and with their firebrands, . . .	1Tamb	5.1.219	Bajzth
With shame, with hungar, and with horror aie/Griping our bowels	1Tamb	5.1.236	Bajzth
with hungar, and with horror aie/Griping our bowels with .	1Tamb	5.1.236	Bajzth
and with horror aie/Griping our bowels with retorqued .	1Tamb	5.1.236	Bajzth
with horror aie/Griping our bowels with retorqued thoughtes,	1Tamb	5.1.237	Bajzth
Where shaking ghosts with ever howling grones, ...	1Tamb	5.1.245	Zabina
Which fils the nookes of Hell with standing aire, . . .	1Tamb	5.1.257	Bajzth
Infecting all the Ghosts with curelesse griefs: . . .	1Tamb	5.1.258	Bajzth
Smear'd with blots of basest drudgery:	1Tamb	5.1.268	Bajzth
That would with pity chear Zabinas heart, ...	1Tamb	5.1.271	Bajzth
To coole and comfort me with longer date, ...	1Tamb	5.1.277	Bajzth
may poure foorth my soule into thine armes,/With words of love:	1Tamb	5.1.280	Bajzth
staid, with wrath and hate/Of our expreslesse band inflictions.	1Tamb	5.1.281	Bajzth
Accursed day infected with my griefs, ...	1Tamb	5.1.291	Bajzth
Let ugly darknesse with her rusty coach/Engyrt with tempests	1Tamb	5.1.294	Bajzth
her rusty coach/Engyrt with tempests wrapt in pitchy clouds,	1Tamb	5.1.295	Bajzth
Smother the earth with never fading mistes:	1Tamb	5.1.296	Bajzth
in peeces, give me the sworde with a ball of wildefire upon it.	1Tamb	5.1.311	P Zabina
Downe with him, downe with him.	1Tamb	5.1.312	P Zabina
Damascus walles di'd with Egyptian blood:	1Tamb	5.1.320	Zenoc
Thy streetes strowed with dissevered jointes of men, .	1Tamb	5.1.322	Zenoc
Stead/That stampt on others with their thundring hooves, .	1Tamb	5.1.331	Zenoc
How are ye glutted with these grievous objects, . . .	1Tamb	5.1.341	Zenoc
Shake with their waight in signe of feare and griefe: .	1Tamb	5.1.349	Zenoc
Sleep'st every night with conquest on thy browes, . .	1Tamb	5.1.359	Zenoc
And pardon me that was not moov'd with ruthe, . . .	1Tamb	5.1.369	Zenoc
Armed with lance into the Egyptian fields, ...	1Tamb	5.1.381	Philem
With vertue of a gentle victorie, ...	1Tamb	5.1.398	Zenoc
With happy safty of my fathers life, ...	1Tamb	5.1.401	Zenoc
Then shal I die with full contented heart, ...	1Tamb	5.1.417	Arabia
Whose sight with joy would take away my life, . . .	1Tamb	5.1.419	Arabia
Depriv'd of care, my heart with comfort dies, . . .	1Tamb	5.1.431	Arabia
Though with the losse of Egypt and my Crown. . . .	1Tamb	5.1.444	Souldn
Since I arriv'd with my triumphant hoste, ...	1Tamb	5.1.458	Tamb
Hell and Elisian swarme with ghosts of men, ...	1Tamb	5.1.465	Tamb
With them Arabia too hath left his life, ...	1Tamb	5.1.473	Tamb
When men presume to manage armes with him.	1Tamb	5.1.478	Tamb
And I am pleasde with this my overthrow, ...	1Tamb	5.1.482	Souldn
Thou hast with honor usde Zenocrate.	1Tamb	5.1.484	Souldn
time to grace/Her princely Temples with the Persean crowne:	1Tamb	5.1.489	Tamb
Shal now, adjoining al their hands with mine, ...	1Tamb	5.1.493	Tamb
I yeeld with thanks and protestations/Of endlesse honor to thee	1Tamb	5.1.496	Souldn
Environed with troopes of noble men, ...	1Tamb	5.1.526	Tamb
For Tamburlaine takes truce with al the world. . . .	1Tamb	5.1.529	Tamb
Shall we with honor (as beseemes) entombe, ...	1Tamb	5.1.531	Tamb
With this great Turke and his faire Emperesse: . . .	1Tamb	5.1.532	Tamb
And with how manie cities sacrifice/He celebrated her [sad]	2Tamb	Prol.7	Prolog
Shall we parle with the Christian,/Or crosse the streame, and	2Tamb	1.1.11	Orcan
We all are glutted with the Christians blood, ...	2Tamb	1.1.14	Gazell
Muffes, and Danes/That with the Holbard, Lance, and murthering	2Tamb	1.1.23	Uribas
Will hazard that we might with surety hold.	2Tamb	1.1.24	Uribas
Vast Gruntland compast with the frozen sea, ...	2Tamb	1.1.26	Orcan
Inhabited with tall and sturdy men, ...	2Tamb	1.1.27	Orcan
Shall meet those Christians fleeting with the tyde, . .	2Tamb	1.1.40	Orcan
Trapt with the wealth and riches of the world, . . .	2Tamb	1.1.43	Orcan
Marching from Cairon northward with his camp, . . .	2Tamb	1.1.47	Gazell
to parle for a peace/With Sigismond the king of Hungary: .	2Tamb	1.1.51	Gazell
Lantchidol/Beates on the regions with his boysterous blowes,	2Tamb	1.1.70	Orcan
All Asia is in Armes with Tamburlaine.	2Tamb	1.1.72	Orcan

WITH (cont.)

All Affrike is in Armes with Tamburlaine.	2Tamb	1.1.76	Orcan
Wee with our Peeres have crost Danubius stream/To treat of	2Tamb	1.1.79	Sgsmnd
for as the Romans usde/I here present thee with a naked sword.	2Tamb	1.1.82	Sgsmnd
thou I am he/That with the Cannon shooke Vienna walles,	2Tamb	1.1.87	Orcan
Mingled with powdered shot and fethered steele/So thick upon	2Tamb	1.1.92	Orcan
Stampt with the princely Foule that in her wings/Caries the	2Tamb	1.1.100	Orcan
Or treat of peace with the Natolian king?	2Tamb	1.1.113	Sgsmnd
Drawen with advise of our Ambassadors.	2Tamb	1.1.126	Orcan
But whilst I live will be at truce with thee.	2Tamb	1.1.130	Sgsmnd
But (Sigismond) confirme it with an oath,	2Tamb	1.1.131	Orcan
Whose holy Alcaron remaines with us,	2Tamb	1.1.138	Orcan
and our solemne othes/Sign'd with our handes, each shal retaine	2Tamb	1.1.144	Orcan
Come banquet and carouse with us a while,	2Tamb	1.1.165	Orcan
My Lord I pitie it, and with my heart/Wish your release, but he	2Tamb	1.2.5	Almeda
I know thou wouldst depart from hence with me.	2Tamb	1.2.11	Callap
A thousand Gallies mann'd with Christian slaves/I freely give	2Tamb	1.2.32	Callap
Fraughted with golde of rich America:	2Tamb	1.2.35	Callap
With naked Negros shall thy coach be drawen,	2Tamb	1.2.40	Callap
thy chariot wheels/With Turky Carpets shall be covered:	2Tamb	1.2.43	Callap
a golden Canapie/Enchac'd with pretious stones, which shine as	2Tamb	1.2.49	Callap
Which when he tainted with his slender rod,	2Tamb	1.3.40	Zenoc
Thou shalt be made a King and raigne with me,	2Tamb	1.3.48	Tamb
And martch with such a multitude of men,	2Tamb	1.3.56	Celeb
<superfluities>/Is covered with a liquid purple veile,	2Tamb	1.3.80	Tamb
And sprinkled with the braines of slaughtered men,	2Tamb	1.3.81	Tamb
Whose arches should be fram'd with bones of Turks,	2Tamb	1.3.94	Amyras
And cleave his Pericranion with thy sword.	2Tamb	1.3.101	Tamb
And cleave him to the channell with my sword.	2Tamb	1.3.103	Calyph
Larissa plaines/With hostes apeece against this Turkish crue,	2Tamb	1.3.108	Tamb
Which with my crowne I gladly offer thee.	2Tamb	1.3.136	Usumc
I here present thee with the crowne of Fesse,	2Tamb	1.3.140	Techel
And with an hoste of Moores trainde to the war,	2Tamb	1.3.141	Techel
With ugly Furies bearing fiery flags,	2Tamb	1.3.146	Techel
And after martch to Turky with our Campe,	2Tamb	1.3.158	Tamb
With all his viceroies shall be so affraide,	2Tamb	1.3.162	Tamb
have martcht/Foure hundred miles with armour on their backes,	2Tamb	1.3.175	Usumc
With whom (being women) I vouchsaft a league,	2Tamb	1.3.193	Techel
And with my power did march to Zansibar,	2Tamb	1.3.194	Techel
And glut us with the dainties of the world,	2Tamb	1.3.220	Tamb
Mingled with corrall and with [orient] <orientall> pearle:	2Tamb	1.3.224	Tamb
That dare attempt to war with Christians.	2Tamb	2.1.26	Fredrk
Grace to memorie/The league we lately made with king Orcanes,	2Tamb	2.1.28	Sgsmnd
for with such Infidels,/In whom no faith nor true religion	2Tamb	2.1.33	Baldwn
his fearefull arme/Be pour'd with rigour on our sinfull heads,	2Tamb	2.1.58	Fredrk
With expedition to assaile the Pagan,	2Tamb	2.1.62	Sgsmnd
T'incounter with the cruell Tamburlain,	2Tamb	2.2.5	Orcan
And with the thunder of his martial tooles/Makes Earthquakes in	2Tamb	2.2.7	Orcan
With greater power than erst his pride hath felt,	2Tamb	2.2.10	Gazell
With unacquainted power of our hoste.	2Tamb	2.2.23	Uribas
That with such treason seek our overthrow,	2Tamb	2.2.34	Gazell
With strange infusion of his sacred vigor,	2Tamb	2.2.52	Orcan
With apples like the heads of damned Feends.	2Tamb	2.3.23	Orcan
And happily with full Natolian bowles/Of Greekish wine now let	2Tamb	2.3.45	Orcan
That danc'd with glorie on the silver waves,	2Tamb	2.4.3	Tamb
And all with faintnesse and for foule disgrace,	2Tamb	2.4.5	Tamb
He bindes his temples with a frowning cloude,	2Tamb	2.4.6	Tamb
Ready to darken earth with endlesse night:	2Tamb	2.4.7	Tamb
And tempered every soule with lively heat,	2Tamb	2.4.10	Tamb
her latest breath/All dasled with the hellish mists of death.	2Tamb	2.4.14	Tamb
whose taste illuminates/Refined eies with an eternall sight,	2Tamb	2.4.23	Tamb
of that vitall aire/That feeds the body with his dated health,	2Tamb	2.4.45	Zenoc
Wanes with enforst and necessary change.	2Tamb	2.4.46	Zenoc
Whose heavenly presence beautified with health,	2Tamb	2.4.49	Tamb
With love and patience let your true love die,	2Tamb	2.4.67	Zenoc
And let me die with kissing of my Lord.	2Tamb	2.4.70	Zenoc
Wounding the world with woonder and with love,	2Tamb	2.4.82	Tamb
Sadly supplied with pale and ghastly death,	2Tamb	2.4.83	Tamb
And with the cannon breake the frame of heaven,	2Tamb	2.4.104	Tamb
with which I burst/The rusty beames of Janus Temple doores,	2Tamb	2.4.113	Tamb
To martch with me under this bloody flag:	2Tamb	2.4.116	Tamb
Come downe from heaven and live with me againe.	2Tamb	2.4.118	Tamb
her soule be, thou shalt stay with me/Embalm'd with Cassia,	2Tamb	2.4.129	Tamb
thou shalt stay with me/Embalm'd with Cassia, Amber Greece and	2Tamb	2.4.130	Tamb
As I have conquered kingdomes with my sword.	2Tamb	2.4.136	Tamb
This cursed towne will I consume with fire,	2Tamb	2.4.137	Tamb
stature <statue>/And martch about it with my mourning campe,	2Tamb	2.4.141	Tamb
your royall gratitudes/With all the benefits my Empire yeelds:	2Tamb	3.1.9	Callap
That Jove surchardg'd with pity of our wrongs,	2Tamb	3.1.35	Callap
That on mount Sinay with their ensignes spread,	2Tamb	3.1.46	Jrslem
Whose courages are kindled with the flames,	2Tamb	3.1.54	Trebiz
From Soria with seventy thousand strong,	2Tamb	3.1.57	Soria
Fed with the fresh supply of earthly dregs,	2Tamb	3.2.8	Tamb
Compast with Lethe, Styx, and Phlegeton,	2Tamb	3.2.13	Tamb
shal be plac'd/Wrought with the Persean and Egyptian armes,	2Tamb	3.2.20	Amyras
With griefe and sorrow for my mothers death.	2Tamb	3.2.50	Amyras
For [which] <with> the quinque-angle fourme is meet:	2Tamb	3.2.64	Tamb
With Cavalieros and thicke counterforts,	2Tamb	3.2.71	Tamb
Fenc'd with the concave of a monstrous rocke,	2Tamb	3.2.89	Tamb
or with a Curtle-axe/To hew thy flesh and make a gaping wound?	2Tamb	3.2.96	Tamb
ordinance strike/A ring of pikes, mingled with shot and horse,	2Tamb	3.2.99	Tamb
Dieng their lances with their streaming blood,	2Tamb	3.2.105	Tamb
Filling their empty vaines with aiery wine,	2Tamb	3.2.107	Tamb

WITH (cont.)

And with his hoste [martcht] <martch> round about the earth,	2Tamb	3.2.111	Tamb
Enchac'd with Diamondes, Saphyres, Rubies/And fairest pearle of	2Tamb	3.2.120	Tamb
And I sat downe, cloth'd with the massie robe,	2Tamb	3.2.123	Tamb
Come boyes and with your fingers search my wound,	2Tamb	3.2.126	Tamb
With that accursed traitor Almeda,	2Tamb	3.2.150	Tamb
I long to pierce his bowels with my sword,	2Tamb	3.2.152	Usumc
Filling the ditches with the walles wide breach,	2Tamb	3.3.7	Techel
Stand at the walles, with such a mighty power.	2Tamb	3.3.14	Therid
That with his ruine fils up all the trench.	2Tamb	3.3.26	Therid
Intrench with those dimensions I prescribed:	2Tamb	3.3.42	Therid
And with the Jacobs staffe measure the height/And distance of	2Tamb	3.3.50	Techel
And with the breaches fall, smoake, fire, and dust,	2Tamb	3.3.59	Therid
Whose body with his fathers I have burnt,	2Tamb	3.4.36	Olymp
Thou shalt with us to Tamburlaine the great,	2Tamb	3.4.39	Techel
Wil match thee with a viceroy or a king.	2Tamb	3.4.41	Techel
But Lady goe with us to Tamburlaine,	2Tamb	3.4.45	Therid
With naked swords and scarlet liveries:	2Tamb	3.4.55	Therid
And strowes the way with braines of slaughtered men:	2Tamb	3.4.58	Therid
Madam, I am so far in love with you,	2Tamb	3.4.78	Therid
That you must goe with us, no remedy.	2Tamb	3.4.79	Therid
Here at Alepo with an hoste of men/Lies Tamburlaine, this king	2Tamb	3.5.3	2Msngr
With open crie pursues the wounded Stag:	2Tamb	3.5.7	2Msngr
Who meanes to gyrt Natolias walles with siege,	2Tamb	3.5.8	2Msngr
Phrigia to the sea/Which washeth Cyprus with his brinish waves,	2Tamb	3.5.12	Callap
Streching their monstrous pawes, grin with their teeth,	2Tamb	3.5.28	Orcan
Nor ere returne but with the victory,	2Tamb	3.5.44	Trebiz
Who now with Jove opens the firmament,	2Tamb	3.5.56	Callap
Thou wouldst with overmatch of person fight,	2Tamb	3.5.76	Orcan
Rowing with Christians in a Brigandine,	2Tamb	3.5.93	Jrslem
And when ye stay, be lasht with whips of wier:	2Tamb	3.5.105	Tamb
Searing thy hatefull flesh with burning yrons,	2Tamb	3.5.123	Tamb
while all thy joints/Be rackt and beat asunder with the wheele,	2Tamb	3.5.125	Tamb
I may knocke out his braines with them, and lock you in the	2Tamb	3.5.141	P Tamb
Loden with Lawrell wreathes to crowne us all.	2Tamb	3.5.164	Tamb
shall sweat/With carrieng pearle and treasure on their backes.	2Tamb	3.5.167	Techel
That flies with fury swifter than our thoughts,	2Tamb	4.1.5	Amyras
And cuts down armies with his [conquering] <conquerings> wings.	2Tamb	4.1.6	Amyras
If halfe our campe should sit and sleepe with me,	2Tamb	4.1.18	Calyph
As if I lay with you for company.	2Tamb	4.1.39	Calyph
I were as soone rewarded with a shot,	2Tamb	4.1.54	Calyph
the good I have/Join'd with my fathers crowne would never cure.	2Tamb	4.1.58	Calyph
I should be affraid, would put it off and come to bed with me.	2Tamb	4.1.70	P Calyph
And tickle not your Spirits with desire/Stil to be train'd in	2Tamb	4.1.80	Tamb
Cherish thy valour stil with fresh supplies:	2Tamb	4.1.87	Tamb
And glut it not with stale and daunted foes.	2Tamb	4.1.88	Tamb
How may my hart, thus fired with mine eies,	2Tamb	4.1.93	Tamb
Wounded with shame, and kill'd with discontent,	2Tamb	4.1.94	Tamb
And shame of nature [which] <with> Jaertis streame,	2Tamb	4.1.108	Tamb
Embracing thee with deepest of his love,	2Tamb	4.1.109	Tamb
Cloth'd with a pitchy cloud for being seene.	2Tamb	4.1.131	Tamb
fild with the meteors/Of blood and fire thy tyrannies have	2Tamb	4.1.141	Jrslem
And with our bloods, revenge our bloods on thee.	2Tamb	4.1.145	Jrslem
Souldier shall defile/His manly fingers with so faint a boy.	2Tamb	4.1.164	Tamb
Nor yet imposd, with such a bitter hate.	2Tamb	4.1.170	Jrslem
(wanting moisture and remorsefull blood)/Drie up with anger,	2Tamb	4.1.180	Soria
remorsefull blood)/Drie up with anger, and consume with heat.	2Tamb	4.1.180	Soria
your tongues/And bind them close with bits of burnisht steele,	2Tamb	4.1.182	Tamb
And with the paines my rigour shall inflict,	2Tamb	4.1.184	Tamb
And stung with furie of their following,	2Tamb	4.1.189	Tamb
Fill all the aire with troublous bellowing:	2Tamb	4.1.190	Tamb
I will with Engines, never exercisde,	2Tamb	4.1.191	Tamb
And with the flames that beat against the clowdes/Incense the	2Tamb	4.1.194	Tamb
And since this earth, dew'd with thy brinish teares,	2Tamb	4.2.8	Olymp
Nor yet this aier, beat often with thy sighes,	2Tamb	4.2.10	Olymp
Which with thy beauty thou wast woont to light,	2Tamb	4.2.16	Therid
My Lord and husbandes death, with my sweete sons,	2Tamb	4.2.22	Olymp
With whom I buried al affections,	2Tamb	4.2.23	Olymp
For with thy view my joyes are at the full,	2Tamb	4.2.31	Therid
And I will cast off armes and sit with thee,	2Tamb	4.2.44	Therid
But that where every period ends with death,	2Tamb	4.2.47	Olymp
And every line begins with death againe:	2Tamb	4.2.48	Olymp
With which if you but noint your tender Skin,	2Tamb	4.2.65	Olymp
And you shall se't rebated with the blow.	2Tamb	4.2.70	Olymp
Whose body shall be tomb'd with all the pompe/The treasure of	2Tamb	4.2.97	Therid
That King Egeus fed with humaine flesh,	2Tamb	4.3.13	Tamb
Were not subdew'd with valour more divine,	2Tamb	4.3.15	Tamb
You shal be fed with flesh as raw as blood,	2Tamb	4.3.18	Tamb
If you can live with it, then live, and draw/My chariot swifter	2Tamb	4.3.20	Tamb
And thus be drawen with these two idle kings.	2Tamb	4.3.28	Amyras
meet not me/With troopes of harlots at your slothful heeles.	2Tamb	4.3.82	Tamb
Are ye not gone ye villaines with your spoiles?	2Tamb	4.3.84	Tamb
And common souldiers jest with all their Truls.	2Tamb	4.3.91	Tamb
Shal al be loden with the martiall spoiles/We will convay with	2Tamb	4.3.105	Tamb
with the martiall spoiles/We will convay with us to Persea.	2Tamb	4.3.106	Tamb
Thorow the streets with troops of conquered kings,	2Tamb	4.3.114	Tamb
Spangled with Diamonds dancing in the aire,	2Tamb	4.3.117	Tamb
queintly dect/With bloomes more white than Hericinas browes,	2Tamb	4.3.122	Tamb
Mounted his shining [chariot] <chariots>, gilt with fire,	2Tamb	4.3.126	Tamb
And drawen with princely Eagles through the path,	2Tamb	4.3.127	Tamb
Pav'd with bright Christall, and enchac'd with starres,	2Tamb	4.3.128	Tamb
As any thing of price with thy conceit?	2Tamb	5.1.14	Govnr
Makes walles a fresh with every thing that falles/Into the	2Tamb	5.1.18	Govnr

WITH (cont.)

Fill'd with a packe of faintheart Fugitives,	2Tamb	5.1.36	Govnr
spirits may vex/Your slavish bosomes with continuall paines,	2Tamb	5.1.46	Govnr
Or els be sure thou shalt be forc'd with paines,	2Tamb	5.1.52	Therid
Drawen with these kings on heaps of carkasses.	2Tamb	5.1.72	Tamb
With furious words and frowning visages,	2Tamb	5.1.78	Tamb
That with his sword hath quail'd all earthly kings,	2Tamb	5.1.93	Tamb
Up with him then, his body shalbe scard.	2Tamb	5.1.114	Tamb
The rest forward with execution,	2Tamb	5.1.124	Tamb
Away with him hence, let him speake no more:	2Tamb	5.1.125	Tamb
What shal be done with their wives and children my Lord.	2Tamb	5.1.168	P Techel
Circled about with Limnasphaltis Lake,	2Tamb	5.2.5	Callap
Where Tamburlaine with all his armie lies,	2Tamb	5.2.6	Callap
Which being faint and weary with the siege,	2Tamb	5.2.7	Callap
Marching about the ayer with armed men,	2Tamb	5.2.34	Amasia
To joine with you against this Tamburlaine.	2Tamb	5.2.35	Amasia
All Turkie is in armes with Callapine.	2Tamb	5.2.51	Callap
Muffle your beauties with eternall clowdes,	2Tamb	5.3.6	Therid
And Death with armies of Cymerian spirits/Gives battile gainst	2Tamb	5.3.8	Therid
Stands aiming at me with his murthering dart,	2Tamb	5.3.69	Tamb
to lode thy barke/With soules of thousand mangled carkasses.	2Tamb	5.3.74	Tamb
And weary Death with bearing soules to hell.	2Tamb	5.3.77	Tamb
Begins the day with our Antypodes:	2Tamb	5.3.149	Tamb
bleeding harts/Wounded and broken with your Highnesse griefe,	2Tamb	5.3.162	Amyras
With what a flinty bosome should I joy,	2Tamb	5.3.185	Amyras
Pierc'd with the joy of any dignity?	2Tamb	5.3.190	Amyras
Sit up my boy, and with those silken raines,	2Tamb	5.3.202	Tamb
with what a broken hart/And damned spirit I ascend this seat,	2Tamb	5.3.206	Amyras
And glut your longings with a heaven of joy.	2Tamb	5.3.227	Tamb
Guiding thy chariot with thy Fathers hand.	2Tamb	5.3.229	Tamb
learne with awfull eie/To sway a throane as dangerous as his:	2Tamb	5.3.234	Tamb
from France/To view this Land, and frolicke with his friends.	Jew	Prol.4	Machvl
so richly pay/The things they traffique for with wedge of gold,	Jew	1.1.9	Barab
Wearying his fingers ends with telling it,	Jew	1.1.16	Barab
Loaden with Spice and Silkes, now under saile,	Jew	1.1.45	Barab
And all the Merchants with other Merchandize/Are safe arriv'd,	Jew	1.1.51	1Merch
And bring with them their bils of entry:	Jew	1.1.56	Barab
They wondred how you durst with so much wealth/Trust such a	Jew	1.1.79	1Merch
Laden with riches, and exceeding store/Of Persian silkes, of	Jew	1.1.87	2Merch
How chance you came not with those other ships/That sail'd by	Jew	1.1.89	Barab
the winds/To drive their substance with successefull blasts?	Jew	1.1.111	Barab
With whom they have attempted many times,	Jew	1.1.164	Barab
Are strangers with your tribute to be tax'd?	Jew	1.2.59	Barab
Have strangers leave with us to get their wealth?	Jew	1.2.60	2Knght
Then let them with us contribute.	Jew	1.2.61	2Knght
to staine our hands with blood/Is farre from us and our	Jew	1.2.144	Govnr
That thus have dealt with me in my distresse.	Jew	1.2.168	Barab
Why stand you thus unmov'd with my laments?	Jew	1.2.171	Barab
You that/Were ne're possest of wealth, are pleas'd with want.	Jew	1.2.201	Barab
lumpe of clay/That will with every water wash to dirt:	Jew	1.2.217	Barab
And cast with cunning for the time to come:	Jew	1.2.222	Barab
And urg'd thereto with my afflictions,	Jew	1.2.231	Abigal
With fierce exclaimes run to the Senate-house,	Jew	1.2.232	Abigal
And rent their hearts with tearing of my haire,	Jew	1.2.234	Abigal
things past recovery/Are hardly cur'd with exclamations.	Jew	1.2.237	Barab
Then father, goe with me.	Jew	1.2.300	Abigal
For I will seeme offended with thee for't.	Jew	1.2.303	Barab
Well, daughter, say, what is thy suit with us?	Jew	1.2.321	Abbass
fitter for a tale of love/Then to be tired out with Orizons:	Jew	1.2.370	Mthias
Tho countermin'd <countermur'd> with walls of brasse, to love,	Jew	1.2.386	Mthias
poore Barabas/With fatall curses towards these Christians.	Jew	2.1.6	Barab
Oh thou that with a fiery piller led'st/The sonnes of Israel	Jew	2.1.12	Barab
That I may hover with her in the Ayre,	Jew	2.1.62	Barab
And with that summe he craves might we wage warre.	Jew	2.2.27	1Knght
Will Knights of Malta be in league with Turkes,	Jew	2.2.28	Bosco
and you were stated here/To be at deadly enmity with Turkes.	Jew	2.2.33	Bosco
Honor is bought with bloud and not with gold.	Jew	2.2.56	Govnr
'tis a custome held with us,/That when we speake with Gentiles	Jew	2.3.44	Barab
That when we speake with Gentiles like to you,	Jew	2.3.45	Barab
With a vengeance.	Jew	2.3.67	Barab
and thou hast, breake my head with it, I'le forgive thee.	Jew	2.3.112	P Barab
But wherefore talk'd Don Lodowick with you?	Jew	2.3.150	Mthias
and my talke with him was [but]/About the borrowing of a booke	Jew	2.3.155	Mthias
Converse not with him, he is cast off from heaven.	Jew	2.3.157	Mater
There I enrich'd the Priests with burials,	Jew	2.3.183	Barab
armes in ure/With digging graves and ringing dead mens knels:	Jew	2.3.185	Barab
Slew friend and enemy with my stratagems.	Jew	2.3.189	Barab
And with extorting, cozening, forfeiting,	Jew	2.3.191	Barab
I fill'd the Jailes with Bankrouts in a yeare,	Jew	2.3.193	Barab
And with young Orphans planted Hospitals,	Jew	2.3.194	Barab
breast a long great Scrowle/How I with interest tormented him.	Jew	2.3.198	Barab
I have it for you, Sir; please you walke in with me:	Jew	2.3.220	Barab
the Governors sonne/With all the curtesie you can affoord;	Jew	2.3.226	Barab
And I am sure he is with Abigall.	Jew	2.3.268	Barab
Doth she not with her smiling answer you?	Jew	2.3.286	Barab
your Lordship wud disdaine/To marry with the daughter of a Jew:	Jew	2.3.295	Barab
a golden crosse/With Christiān posies round about the ring.	Jew	2.3.297	Barab
Faith is not to be held with Heretickes;	Jew	2.3.311	Barab
And Natures beauty choake with stifeling clouds,	Jew	2.3.331	Lodowk
Hee's with your mother, therefore after him.	Jew	2.3.350	Barab
Shee'll dye with griefe.	Jew	2.3.354	Mthias
and in the night I clamber'd up with my hooks, and as I was	Jew	3.1.19	P Pilia
And with my prayers pierce [th']impartiall heavens,	Jew	3.2.33	Govnr

WITH (cont.)

And say, I pray them come and speake with me.	Jew	3.3.29	Abigal
one; have not the Nuns fine sport with the Fryars now and then?	Jew	3.3.32	P Ithimr
But here comes cursed Ithimore with the Fryar.	Jew	3.3.49	Abigal
But now experience, purchased with griefe,	Jew	3.3.61	Abigal
With whom?	Jew	3.4.20	Barab
from hence/Ne're shall she grieve me more with her disgrace;	Jew	3.4.29	Barab
What, hast thou brought the Ladle with thee too?	Jew	3.4.57	Barab
saies, he that eats with the devil had need of a long spoone.	Jew	3.4.58	P Ithimr
master, wil you poison her with a messe of rice [porredge]?	Jew	3.4.64	P Ithimr
And with her let it worke like Borgias wine,	Jew	3.4.98	Barab
what shall I doe with it?	Jew	3.4.107	P Ithimr
I'le carry't to the Nuns with a powder.	Jew	3.4.112	P Ithimr
Ile pay thee with a vengeance Ithamore.	Jew	3.4.116	Barab
Shall overflow it with their refluence.	Jew	3.5.18	Govnr
And with brasse-bullets batter downe your Towers,	Jew	3.5.24	Basso
Where is the Fryar that converst with me?	Jew	3.6.9	Abigal
this, then goe with me/And helpe me to exclaime against the Jew.	Jew	3.6.45	2Fryar
They'll dye with griefe.	Jew	4.1.16	Barab
Oh speake not of her, then I dye with griefe.	Jew	4.1.36	Barab
for store of wealth may I compare/With all the Jewes in Malta;	Jew	4.1.56	Barab
Ware-houses stuft with spices and with drugs,	Jew	4.1.64	Barab
I know they are, and I will be with you.	Jew	4.1.83	Barab
Rid him away, and goe you home with me.	Jew	4.1.89	Barab
I'le be with you to night.	Jew	4.1.90	2Fryar
Fryar Barnardine goe you with Ithimore.	Jew	4.1.99	Barab
You know my mind, let me alone with him.	Jew	4.1.100	Barab
Off with your girdle, make a hansom noose;	Jew	4.1.142	Barab
So might my man and I hang with you for company.	Jew	4.1.182	Barab
Was up thus early; with intent to goe/Unto your Friery, because	Jew	4.1.191	Barab
Pilia-borza, didst thou meet with Ithimore?	Jew	4.2.1	P Curtzn
whom I saluted with an old hempen proverb, Hodie tibi,	Jew	4.2.18	P Pilia
a fellow met me with a muschatoes like a Ravens wing, and a	Jew	4.2.28	P Ithimr
and a Dagger with a hilt like a warming-pan, and he gave me a	Jew	4.2.28	P Ithimr
sort as if he had meant to make cleane my Boots with his lips;	Jew	4.2.31	P Ithimr
I can with-hold no longer; welcome sweet love.	Jew	4.2.46	Curtzn
What shall we doe with this base villaine then?	Jew	4.2.62	Curtzn
Shalt live with me and be my love.	Jew	4.2.98	Ithimr
Whither will I not goe with gentle Ithimore?	Jew	4.2.99	Curtzn
please you dine with me, Sir, and you shal be most hartily	Jew	4.3.29	P Barab
Oh that I should part with so much gold!	Jew	4.3.51	Barab
Here take 'em, fellow, with as good a will--	Jew	4.3.52	Barab
And how the villaine revels with my gold.	Jew	4.3.68	Barab
This shall with me unto the Governor.	Jew	4.4.25	Pilia
French-man, here's to thee with a--pox on this drunken hick-up.	Jew	4.4.32	P Ithimr
Away with her, she is a Curtezane.	Jew	5.1.8	Govnr
Away with him, his sight is death to me.	Jew	5.1.35	Govnr
Once more away with him; you shall have law.	Jew	5.1.40	Govnr
And rise with them i'th middle of the Towne,	Jew	5.1.92	Barab
To prison with the Governour and these/Captaines, his consorts	Jew	5.2.23	Barab
That labours with a load of bread and wine,	Jew	5.2.41	Barab
shut/His souldiers, till I have consum'd 'em all with fire?	Jew	5.2.82	Barab
Deale truly with us as thou intimatest,	Jew	5.2.85	Govnr
Governor, I enlarge thee, live with me,	Jew	5.2.91	Barab
And bring it with me to thee in the evening.	Jew	5.2.108	Govnr
Thus loving neither, will I live with both,	Jew	5.2.111	Barab
I know; and they shall witnesse with their lives.	Jew	5.2.123	Barab
Which with our Bombards shot and Basiliske,	Jew	5.3.3	Calym
conquer'd Iland stands/Inviron'd with the mediterranean Sea,	Jew	5.3.7	Calym
Strong contermin'd <countermur'd> with other petty Iles;	Jew	5.3.8	Calym
And banquet with him e're thou leav'st the Ile.	Jew	5.3.19	Msngr
To banquet with him in his Citadell?	Jew	5.3.20	Calym
With all thy Bashawes and brave followers.	Jew	5.3.39	Msngr
Wee'll in this Summer Evening feast with him.	Jew	5.3.41	Calym
With free consent a hundred thousand pounds.	Jew	5.5.20	Govnr
wel since it is no more/I'le satisfie my selfe with that; nay,	Jew	5.5.22	Barab
And with his Bashawes shall be blithely set,	Jew	5.5.38	Barab
fury of thy torments, strive/To end thy life with resolution:	Jew	5.5.80	Barab
the extremity of heat/To pinch me with intolerable pangs:	Jew	5.5.88	Barab
For with thy Gallyes couldst thou not get hence,	Jew	5.5.100	Govnr
That linke you in mariage with our daughter heer:	P 14	1.14	QnMoth
to goe and consumate/The rest, with hearing of a holy Masse:	P 20	1.20	Charls
Which Ile desolve with bloud and crueltie.	P 26	1.26	QnMoth
And had his alters deckt with duskie lightes:	P 59	2.2	Guise
If ever sunne stainde heaven with bloudy clowdes,	P 60	2.3	Guise
And made it look with terrour on the worlde:	P 61	2.4	Guise
And then Ile guerdon thee with store of crownes.	P 89	2.32	Guise
Ile either rend it with my nayles to naught,	P 102	2.45	Guise
Or mount the top with my aspiring winges,	P 103	2.46	Guise
And with this wait Ile counterpoise a Crowne,	P 115	2.58	Guise
Or with seditions weary all the worlde:	P 116	2.59	Guise
Him as a childe I dayly winne with words,	P 130	2.73	Guise
That with a rablement of his hereticks,	P 151	2.94	Guise
A hand, that with a graspe may gripe the world,	P 159	2.102	Guise
to beware/How you did meddle with such dangerous giftes.	P 180	3.15	Navrre
O graunt sweet God my daies may end with hers,	P 189	3.24	Navrre
That I with her may dye and live againe.	P 190	3.25	Navrre
is massacred)/Infect thy gracious brest with fresh supply,	P 193	3.28	QnMarg
And see it honoured with just solemnitie.	P 196	3.31	Admral
What shall we doe now with the Admirall?	P 248	4.46	Charls
How fares it with my Lord high Admiral,	P 253	4.51	Charls
Hath he been hurt with villaines in the street?	P 254	4.52	Charls
To finde and to repay the man with death:	P 256	4.54	Charls

WITH (cont.)

With death delay'd and torments never usde,	P 257	4.55	Charls
Repaying all attempts with present death,	P 269	4.67	Charls
Away with him, cut of his head and handes,	P 316	5.43	Anjoy
down, heer's one would speak with you from the Duke of Guise.	P 348	6.3	P SrnsWf
To speek with me from such a man as he?	P 350	6.5	Seroun
Then take this with you.	P 360	6.15	Mntsrl
And ipse dixi with this quidditie,	P 394	7.34	Guise
With bowes and dartes to shoot at them they see,	P 422	7.62	Dumain
Come sirs, Ile whip you to death with my punniards point.	P 441	7.81	Guise
Away with them both.	P 442	7.82	Anjoy
To please himselfe with mannage of the warres,	P 459	8.9	Anjoy
With Poland therfore must I covenant thus,	P 471	8.21	Anjoy
on me, then with your leaves/I may retire me to my native home.	P 473	8.23	Anjoy
Now sirra, what shall we doe with the Admirall?	P 482	9.1	P 1Atndt
and the fire the aire, and so we shall be poysoned with him.	P 485	9.4	P 1Atndt
With the rebellious King of Navarre,	P 517	9.36	Cardnl
Downe with the Hugonites, murder them.	P 528	10.1	Guise
We will with all the speed we can, provide/For Henries	P 562	11.27	QnMoth
For feare that Guise joyn'd with the King of Spaine,	P 573	11.38	Navrre
Cannot but march with many graces more:	P 578	11.43	Pleshe
All this and more hath Henry with his crowne.	P 596	12.9	QnMoth
To plant our selves with such authoritie,	P 637	12.50	QnMoth
Now Madam must you insinuate with the King,	P 645	12.58	Cardnl
Tush man, let me alone with him,	P 648	12.61	QnMoth
Ile dispatch him with his brother presently,	P 651	12.64	QnMoth
Faine would I finde some means to speak with him/But cannot,	P 662	13.6	Duchss
Shall buy her love even with his dearest bloud.	P 697	13.41	Guise
Which they will put us to with sword and fire:	P 706	14.9	Navrre
We must with resolute mindes resolve to fight,	P 707	14.10	Navrre
Plaies with her goary coulours of revenge,	P 719	14.22	Navrre
A mighty army comes from France with speed:	P 725	14.28	1Msngr
But come my Lords, let us away with speed,	P 741	14.44	Navrre
Shall buy that strumpets favour with his blood,	P 768	15.26	Guise
Ile make her shake off love with her heeles.	P 782	15.40	Mugern
<make> a walk/On purpose from the Court to meet with him.	P 784	15.42	Mugern
And we are grac'd with wreathes of victory:	P 788	16.2	Navrre
And with the Queene of England joyne my force,	P 801	16.15	Navrre
Let us away with triumph to our tents.	P 805	16.19	Navrre
I, those are they that feed him with their golde,	P 845	17.40	King
Intending to dislodge my campe with speed.	P 869	17.64	Guise
For had your highnesse seene with what a pompe/He entred Paris,	P 872	17.67	Eprnon
With gifts and shewes did entertaine him/And promised to be at	P 874	17.69	Eprnon
Pleshe, goe muster up our men with speed,	P 916	18.17	Navrre
Surchargde with surfet of ambitious thoughts:	P 953	19.23	King
And end thy endles treasons with thy death.	P 955	19.25	King
How fares it this morning with your excellence?	P 966	19.36	King
Twere hard with me if I should doubt my kinne,	P 971	19.41	King
And princes with their lookes ingender feare.	P 999	19.69	Guise
Downe with him, downe with him.	P1002	19.72	P AllMur
Surchargde with guilt of thousand massacres,	P1022	19.92	King
our Guise is dead)/Rest satisfied with this that heer I sweare,	P1043	19.113	King
Away to prison with him, Ile clippe his winges/Or ere he passe	P1052	19.122	King
Ile clippe his winges/Or ere he passe my handes, away with him.	P1053	19.123	King
Especially with our olde mothers helpe.	P1061	19.131	King
What, will you fyle your handes with Churchmens bloud?	P1093	20.3	Cardnl
And with their pawes drench his black soule in hell.	P1102	20.12	Cardnl
He is hard hearted, therfore pull with violence.	P1105	20.15	1Mur
That basely seekes to joyne with such a King,	P1115	21.9	Dumain
That I with speed should have beene put to death.	P1118	21.12	Dumain
Frier come with me,	P1137	21.31	Dumain
Was ever troubled with injurious warres:	P1142	22.4	King
With all the honors and affections,	P1145	22.7	King
Girting this strumpet Cittie with our siege,	P1152	22.14	King
Till surfeiting with our afflicting armes,	P1153	22.15	King
For you are stricken with a poysoned knife.	P1213	22.75	Srgeon
That we might torture him with some new found death.	P1217	22.79	Eprnon
enoughe to worke/thy Just degestione with extreamest shame	Paris	ms27,p391	Guise
And share the kingdom with thy deerest friend.	Edw	1.1.2	Gavstn
Ah words that make me surfet with delight:	Edw	1.1.3	Gavstn
And with the world be still at enmitie:	Edw	1.1.15	Gavstn
That wouldst reward them with an hospitall.	Edw	1.1.38	3PrMan
that with touching of a string/May draw the pliant king which	Edw	1.1.52	Gavstn
Shall with their Goate feete daunce an antick hay.	Edw	1.1.60	Gavstn
With haire that gilds the water as it glides,	Edw	1.1.62	Gavstn
He should have lost his head, but with his looke,	Edw	1.1.113	Kent
And henceforth parle with our naked swords.	Edw	1.1.126	Mortmr
Ile bandie with the Barons and the Earles,	Edw	1.1.137	Edward
And eyther die, or live with Gaveston.	Edw	1.1.138	Edward
Is Edward pleazd with kinglie regiment.	Edw	1.1.165	Edward
With captive kings at his triumphant Carre.	Edw	1.1.174	Gavstn
What should a priest do with so faire a house?	Edw	1.1.206	Gavstn
This ground which is corrupted with their steps,	Edw	1.2.5	Lncstr
Who swolne with venome of ambitious pride,	Edw	1.2.31	Mortmr
Then wil you joine with us that be his peeres/To banish or	Edw	1.2.42	Mortmr
And let him frollick with his minion.	Edw	1.2.67	Queene
Will meete, and with a generall consent,	Edw	1.2.70	ArchBp
Confirme his banishment with our handes and seales.	Edw	1.2.71	ArchBp
To crosse to Lambeth, and there stay with me.	Edw	1.2.78	ArchBp
With Guie of Warwick that redoubted knight,	Edw	1.3.4	Gavstn
Away I say with hatefull Gaveston.	Edw	1.4.33	Lncstr
And with the earle of Kent that favors him.	Edw	1.4.34	MortSr
To frolike with my deerest Gaveston.	Edw	1.4.73	Edward

WITH (cont.)

In steede of inke, ile write it with my teares.	Edw	1.4.86	Edward
With slaughtered priests [make] <may> Tibers channell swell,	Edw	1.4.102	Edward
And bankes raisd higher with their sepulchers:	Edw	1.4.103	Edward
Rend not my hart with thy too piercing words,	Edw	1.4.117	Edward
Therefore with dum imbracement let us part.	Edw	1.4.134	Edward
On Mortimer, with whom ungentle Queene--	Edw	1.4.147	Gavstn
Thou art too familiar with that Mortimer,	Edw	1.4.154	Edward
Or with those armes that twind about my neck,	Edw	1.4.175	Queene
With gastlie murmure of my sighes and cries,	Edw	1.4.179	Queene
Will you be resolute and hold with me?	Edw	1.4.231	Lncstr
To greet his lordship with a poniard,	Edw	1.4.266	Mortmr
Then may we with some colour rise in armes,	Edw	1.4.279	Mortmr
And with the noise turnes up my giddie braine,	Edw	1.4.314	Edward
And with my kinglie scepter stroke me dead,	Edw	1.4.317	Edward
That you have parled with your Mortimer?	Edw	1.4.321	Edward
Seeing thou hast pleaded with so good successe.	Edw	1.4.329	Edward
Even so let hatred with thy [soveraignes] <soveraigne> smile.	Edw	1.4.342	Edward
Live thou with me as my companion.	Edw	1.4.343	Edward
And with this sword, Penbrooke wil fight for you.	Edw	1.4.352	Penbrk
For with my nature warre doth best agree.	Edw	1.4.365	MortSr
And riote it with the treasure of the realme,	Edw	1.4.405	Mortmr
With base outlandish cullions at his heeles,	Edw	1.4.409	Mortmr
Larded with pearle, and in his tuskan cap/A jewell of more	Edw	1.4.414	Mortmr
May with one word, advaunce us while we live:	Edw	2.1.9	Spencr
With letters to our ladie from the King,	Edw	2.1.20	Spencr
A Velvet cap'de cloake, fac'st before with Serge,	Edw	2.1.34	Spencr
Or looking downeward, with your eye lids close,	Edw	2.1.39	Spencr
Can get you any favour with great men.	Edw	2.1.41	Spencr
Desirde her more, and waxt outragious,/So did it sure with me:	Edw	2.2.56	Edward
The sheepeherd nipt with biting winters rage,	Edw	2.2.61	Gavstn
That thinke with high lookes thus to tread me down.	Edw	2.2.97	Edward
Cosin it is no dealing with him now,	Edw	2.2.102	Lncstr
The wilde Oneyle, with swarmes of Irish Kernes,	Edw	2.2.164	Lncstr
When wert thou in the field with banner spred?	Edw	2.2.182	Mortmr
With garish robes, not armor, and thy selfe/Bedaubd with golde,	Edw	2.2.184	Mortmr
and thy selfe/Bedaubd with golde, rode laughing at the rest,	Edw	2.2.185	Mortmr
With a heave and a ho,	Edw	2.2.192	Lncstr
With a rombelow.	Edw	2.2.195	Lncstr
Looke next to see us with our ensignes spred.	Edw	2.2.199	Lncstr
Traitor be gone, whine thou with Mortimer.	Edw	2.2.214	Edward
So will I, rather then with Gaveston.	Edw	2.2.215	Kent
And so I walke with him about the walles,	Edw	2.2.222	Edward
My lord, dissemble with her, speake her faire.	Edw	2.2.229	Gavstn
me, for his sake/Ile grace thee with a higher stile ere long.	Edw	2.2.253	Edward
I come to joine with you, and leave the king,	Edw	2.3.2	Kent
To undermine us with a showe of love.	Edw	2.3.6	Lncstr
And here in Tinmoth frollicks with the king.	Edw	2.3.17	Lncstr
Let us with these our followers scale the walles,	Edw	2.3.18	Lncstr
And body with continuall moorning wasted:	Edw	2.4.25	Queene
These hands are tir'd, with haling of my lord/From Gaveston,	Edw	2.4.26	Queene
What would you with the king, ist him you seek?	Edw	2.4.31	Queene
force, and with the power/That he intendeth presentlie to raise,	Edw	2.4.43	Queene
Nay, rather saile with us to Scarborough.	Edw	2.4.52	Mortmr
As if he heare I have but talkt with you,	Edw	2.4.54	Queene
As Isabell could live with thee for ever.	Edw	2.4.60	Queene
Yet once more ile importune him with praiers,	Edw	2.4.63	Queene
Souldiers away with him.	Edw	2.5.45	Warwck
Souldiers away with him:	Edw	2.5.50	Mortmr
He will but talke with him and send him backe.	Edw	2.5.59	Arundl
Question with thy companions and thy mates.	Edw	2.5.73	Mortmr
Provided this, that you my lord of Arundell/Will joyne with me.	Edw	2.5.82	Penbrk
But if you dare trust Penbrooke with the prisoner,	Edw	2.5.87	Penbrk
My Lord, you shall go with me,	Edw	2.5.99	Penbrk
Come, let thy shadow parley with king Edward.	Edw	2.6.14	Warwck
The Barons overbeare me with their pride.	Edw	3.1.9	Edward
Loe, with a band of bowmen and of pikes,	Edw	3.1.36	SpncrP
And daily will enrich thee with our favour,	Edw	3.1.50	Edward
You shall go parley with the king of Fraunce.	Edw	3.1.71	Edward
And do your message with a majestie.	Edw	3.1.73	Edward
Madam, we will that you with speed be shipt,	Edw	3.1.81	Edward
With all the hast we can dispatch him hence.	Edw	3.1.83	Edward
Begirt with weapons, and with enemies round,	Edw	3.1.95	Arundl
And staine my roiall standard with the same,	Edw	3.1.138	Edward
armes, by me salute/Your highnes, with long life and happines,	Edw	3.1.157	Herald
Edward with fire and sword, followes at thy heeles.	Edw	3.1.180	Edward
This day I shall powre vengeance with my sword/On those proud	Edw	3.1.186	Edward
a while, our men with sweat and dust/All chockt well neare,	Edw	3.1.191	SpncrP
to request/He might be spared to come to speake with us,	Edw	3.1.235	Edward
Away with them:	Edw	3.1.245	Edward
I charge you roundly off with both their heads,	Edw	3.1.247	Edward
Sound drums and trumpets, marche with me my friends,	Edw	3.1.260	Edward
Therefore be gon in hast, and with advice,	Edw	3.1.264	Spencr
France/Makes friends, to crosse the seas with her yong sonne,	Edw	3.1.270	Spencr
Among the lords of France with Englands golde,	Edw	3.1.277	Levune
And Fraunce shall be obdurat with her teares.	Edw	3.1.279	Levune
will your grace with me to Henolt,/And there stay times	Edw	4.2.17	SrJohn
And there stay times advantage with your sonne?	Edw	4.2.18	SrJohn
How say you my Lord, will you go with your friends,	Edw	4.2.19	SrJohn
Will we with thee to Henolt, so we will.	Edw	4.2.31	Queene
distressed Queene his sister heere,/Go you with her to Henolt:	Edw	4.2.64	SrJohn
Madam along, and you my lord, with me,	Edw	4.2.81	SrJohn
Triumpheth Englands Edward with his friends,	Edw	4.3.2	Edward

WITH (cont.)

And triumph Edward with his friends uncontrould.	Edw		4.3.3	Edward
How now, what newes with thee, from whence come these?	Edw		4.3.24	Edward
behalfe, dealt with the king of Fraunce his lords, and effected,	Edw		4.3.29	P Spencr
if you aske, with sir John of Henolt, brother to the Marquesse,	Edw		4.3.31	P Spencr
with them are gone lord Edmund, and the lord Mortimer, having	Edw		4.3.32	P Spencr
With him is Edmund gone associate?	Edw		4.3.39	Edward
Welcome to England all with prosperous windes,	Edw		4.4.2	Queene
friends in Belgia have we left,/To cope with friends at home:	Edw		4.4.4	Queene
in others and their sides/With their owne weapons gorde,	Edw		4.4.8	Queene
And made the channels overflow with blood,	Edw		4.4.12	Queene
We come in armes to wrecke it with the [sword] <swords>:	Edw		4.4.23	Mortmr
And in this bed of [honor] <honors> die with fame.	Edw		4.5.7	Edward
thou chase/Thy lawfull king thy soveraigne with thy sword?	Edw		4.6.4	Kent
How will you deale with Edward in his fall?	Edw		4.6.31	Kent
Baldock is with the king,/A goodly chauncelor, is he not my	Edw		4.6.42	Queene
Is with that smoothe toongd scholler Baldock gone,	Edw		4.6.57	Rice
And shipt but late for Ireland with the king.	Edw		4.6.58	Rice
Madam, have done with care and sad complaint,	Edw		4.6.66	Mortmr
To keepe your royall person safe with us,	Edw		4.7.3	Abbot
a king, thy hart/Pierced deeply with sence of my distresse,	Edw		4.7.10	Edward
Armes that pursue our lives with deadly hate.	Edw		4.7.32	Spencr
With awkward windes, and sore tempests driven/To fall on	Edw		4.7.34	Baldck
Who wounds me with the name of Mortimer/That bloudy man?	Edw		4.7.38	Edward
good father on thy lap/Lay I this head, laden with mickle care,	Edw		4.7.40	Edward
What cannot gallant Mortimer with the Queene?	Edw		4.7.50	Leistr
Away with them.	Edw		4.7.68	Rice
My heart with pittie earnes to see this sight,	Edw		4.7.70	Abbot
And go I must, life farewell with my friends.	Edw		4.7.99	Edward
Pay natures debt with cheerefull countenance,	Edw		4.7.109	Baldck
He rends and teares it with his wrathfull pawe,	Edw		5.1.12	Edward
And so it fares with me, whose dauntlesse minde/The ambitious	Edw		5.1.15	Edward
As with the wings of rancor and disdaine,	Edw		5.1.20	Edward
Who spots my nuptiall bed with infamie,	Edw		5.1.31	Edward
To companie my hart with sad laments,	Edw		5.1.34	Edward
Inhumaine creatures, nurst with Tigers milke,	Edw		5.1.71	Edward
Which fils my mind with strange despairing thoughts,	Edw		5.1.79	Edward
Which thoughts are martyred with endles torments.	Edw		5.1.80	Edward
Traitors be gon, and joine you with Mortimer,	Edw		5.1.87	Edward
Come death, and with thy fingers close my eyes,	Edw		5.1.110	Edward
Wet with my teares, and dried againe with sighes,	Edw		5.1.118	Edward
If with the sight thereof she be not mooved,	Edw		5.1.119	Edward
Unlesse it be with too much clemencie?	Edw		5.1.123	Edward
Your grace must hence with mee to Bartley straight.	Edw		5.1.144	Bartly
To erect your sonne with all the speed we may,	Edw		5.2.11	Mortmr
But amplifie his greefe with bitter words.	Edw		5.2.65	Mortmr
Heere comes the yong prince, with the Earle of Kent.	Edw		5.2.75	Mortmr
Sweete sonne come hither, I must talke with thee.	Edw		5.2.87	Queene
Come sonne, and go with this gentle Lorde and me.	Edw		5.2.109	Queene
With you I will, but not with Mortimer.	Edw		5.2.110	Prince
When will his hart be satisfied with bloud?	Edw		5.3.9	Edward
When all my sences are anoyde with stenche?	Edw		5.3.18	Edward
Or choake your soveraigne with puddle water?	Edw		5.3.30	Edward
To strangle with a lawne thrust through the throte,	Edw		5.4.32	Ltborn
To pierce the wind-pipe with a needles point,	Edw		5.4.33	Ltborn
And with a lowly conge to the ground,	Edw		5.4.49	Mortmr
I view the prince with Aristarchus eyes,	Edw		5.4.54	Mortmr
And will avouche his saying with the sworde,	Edw		5.4.77	Champn
What traitor have wee there with blades and billes?	Edw		5.4.82	Mortmr
At our command, once more away with him.	Edw		5.4.104	Mortmr
And shall my Unckle Edmund ride with us?	Edw		5.4.114	King
And I was almost stifeled with the savor.	Edw		5.5.9	Gurney
Foh, heeres a place in deed with all my hart.	Edw		5.5.41	Ltborn
What meanes thou to dissemble with me thus?	Edw		5.5.80	Edward
These handes were never stainde with innocent bloud,	Edw		5.5.81	Ltborn
Nor shall they now be tainted with a kings.	Edw		5.5.82	Ltborn
Now as I speake they fall, and yet with feare/Open againe.	Edw		5.5.95	Edward
Aye me, see where he comes, and they with him,	Edw		5.6.22	Queene
Thinke not that I am frighted with thy words,	Edw		5.6.27	King
But you I feare, conspirde with Mortimer.	Edw		5.6.37	King
Hence with the traitor, with the murderer.	Edw		5.6.58	King
Awaye with her, her wordes inforce these teares,	Edw		5.6.85	King
And with the rest accompanie him to his grave?	Edw		5.6.88	Queene
That shortly he was grac'd with Doctors name,	F	17	Prol.17	1Chor
Till swolne with cunning of a selfe conceit,	F	20	Prol.20	1Chor
And glutted now <more> with learnings golden gifts,	F	24	Prol.24	1Chor
How am I glutted with conceipt of this?	F	105	1.1.77	Faust
I'le have them wall all Germany with Brasse,	F	115	1.1.87	Faust
I'le have them fill the publique Schooles with [silke] <skill>,	F	117	1.1.89	Faust
I'le leavy souldiers with the coyne they bring,	F	119	1.1.91	Faust
And make me blest with your sage conference.	F	126	1.1.98	Faust
have with [concise] <subtle> Sillogismes <Consissylogismes>	F	139	1.1.111	Faust
Like Almaine Rutters with their horsemens staves,	F	152	1.1.124	Valdes
Inricht with tongues, well seene in Minerals,	F	166	1.1.138	Cornel
Then come and dine with me, and after meate/We'le canvase every	F	190	1.1.162	Faust
that/Was wont to make our schooles ring, with sic probo.	F	195	1.2.2	1Schol
is within at dinner, with Valdes and Cornelius, as this wine,	F	215	1.2.22	P Wagner
And dyms the Welkin, with her pitchy breathe:	F	232	1.3.4	Faust
My <His> Ghost be with the old Phylosophers.	F	288	1.3.60	Faust
And what are you that live with Lucifer?	F	297	1.3.69	Faust
Unhappy spirits that [fell] <live> with Lucifer,	F	298	1.3.70	Mephst
Conspir'd against our God with Lucifer,	F	299	1.3.71	Mephst
And are for ever damn'd with Lucifer.	F	300	1.3.72	Mephst

WITH (cont.)

Am not tormented with ten thousand hels,	F 307	1.3.79		Mephst
To passe the Ocean with a band of men,	F 334	1.3.106		Faust
seene many boyes with [such pickadevaunts] <beards> I am sure.	F 345	1.4.3	P	Robin
for they are as familiar with me, as if they payd for their	F 365	1.4.23	P	Robin
Away with such vaine fancies, and despaire,	F 392	2.1.4		Faust
So he will buy my service with his soule.	F 421	2.1.33		Mephst
And wright a Deed of Gift with thine owne bloud;	F 424	2.1.36		Mephst
and with his <my> proper bloud/Assures his <assure my> soule to	F 443	2.1.55		Faust
First, I will question [with] thee about hell:	F 504	2.1.116		Faust
walles of Thebes/With ravishing sound of his melodious Harpe,	F 580	2.2.29		Faust
Made musicke with my Mephostophilis?	F 581	2.2.30		Faust
the ground be <were> perfum'd, and cover'd with cloth of Arras.	F 670	2.2.119	P	Pride
I am leane with seeing others eate:	F 681	2.2.130	P	Envy
come downe with a vengeance.	F 684	2.2.133	P	Envy
run up and downe the world with these <this> case of Rapiers,	F 688	2.2.137	P	Wrath
the first letter of my name begins with Letchery <leachery>.	F 710	2.2.162	P	Ltchry
I say, least I send you into the Ostry with a vengeance.	F 733	2.3.12	P	Robin
Or if thou't go but to the Taverne with me, I'le give thee	F 747	2.3.26	P	Robin
And whirling round with this circumference,	F 764	2.3.43		2Chor
That with his wings did part the subtle aire,	F 772	2.3.51		2Chor
Past with delight the stately Towne of Trier:	F 780	3.1.2		Faust
Invironed round with airy mountaine tops,	F 781	3.1.3		Faust
With wals of Flint, and deepe intrenched Lakes,	F 782	3.1.4		Faust
Whose bankes are set with Groves of fruitfull Vines.	F 786	3.1.8		Faust
<The> streetes straight forth, and paved with finest bricke,	F 789	3.1.11		Faust
That threates the starres with her aspiring top,	F 796	3.1.18		Faust
Whose frame is paved with sundry coloured stones,	F 797	3.1.19		Faust
And roof't aloft with curious worke in gold.	F 798	3.1.20		Faust
All's one, for wee'l be bold with his Venison.	F 808	3.1.30		Mephst
<Tut, tis no matter man>, wee'l be bold with his <good cheare>.	F 808	(HC265)A	P	Mephst
containes <containeth> for to delight thine eyes <thee with>,	F 810	3.1.32		Mephst
With winding bankes that cut it in two parts;	F 814	3.1.36		Mephst
The which this day with high solemnity,	F 833	3.1.55		Mephst
let me be cloyd/With all things that delight the heart of man.	F 838	3.1.60		Faust
Thus, as the Gods creepe on with feete of wool,	F 877	3.1.99		Pope
Long ere with Iron hands they punish men,	F 878	3.1.100		Pope
And smite with death thy hated enterprise.	F 880	3.1.102		Pope
Go forth-with to our holy Consistory,	F 882	3.1.104		Pope
Away and bring us word <again> with speed.	F 888	3.1.110		Pope
Strike them with sloth, and drowsy idlenesse;	F 894	3.1.116		Faust
Thy selfe and I, may parly with this Pope:	F 896	3.1.118		Faust
Seven golden [keys] <seales> fast sealed with seven seales,	F 933	3.1.155		Pope
With all our College of grave Cardinals,	F 968	3.1.190		Pope
Here, take his triple Crowne along with you,	F 970	3.1.192		Pope
And with Lord Raymond, King of Hungary,	F 979	3.1.201		Pope
And charme thee with this Magicke wand,	F 996	3.2.16		Mephst
With Magicke spels so compasse thee,	F1002	3.2.22		Mephst
With his rich triple crowne to be reserv'd,	F1027	3.2.47		Raymnd
Hale them to prison, lade their limbes with gyves:	F1032	3.2.52		Pope
Lord Archbishop of Reames, sit downe with us.	F1037	3.2.57		Pope
Must every bit be spiced with a Crosse?	F1066	3.2.86		Faust
for I can tell you, you'le be curst with Bell, Booke, and	F1072	3.2.92	P	Mephst
Come brethren, let's about our businesse with good devotion.	F1076	3.2.96	P	1Frier
Now with the flames of ever-burning fire,	F1135	3.3.48		Mephst
I'le wing my selfe and forth-with flie amaine/Unto my Faustus	F1136	3.3.49		Mephst
[When Faustus had with pleasure tane the view]/[Of rarest	F1138	3.3.51A		3Chor
[Where such as beare <bare> his absence but with griefe],	F1141	3.3.54A		3Chor
[Did gratulate his safetie with kinde words],	F1143	3.3.56A		3Chor
[Which Faustus answered with such learned skill],	F1147	3.3.60A		3Chor
And with him comes the Germane Conjurer,	F1164	4.1.10		Mrtino
He took his rouse with stopes of Rhennish wine,	F1174	4.1.20		Mrtino
and if he be so farre in love with him, I would he would post	F1191	4.1.37	P	Benvol
love with him, I would he would post with him to Rome againe.	F1191	4.1.37	P	Benvol
And with a solemne noyse of trumpets sound,	F1237	4.1.83		Faust
thoughts are ravished so/With sight of this renowned Emperour,	F1261	4.1.107		Emper
as to delight your Majesty with some mirth, hath Faustus justly	F1312	4.1.158	P	Faust
Benvolio's head was grac't with hornes to day?	F1331	4.2.7		Benvol
Till with my sword I have that Conjurer slaine.	F1333	4.2.9		Benvol
Nay, we will stay with thee, betide what may,	F1338	4.2.14		Fredrk
And take his leave, laden with rich rewards.	F1345	4.2.21		Benvol
Breake may his heart with grones: deere Frederik see,	F1366	4.2.42		Benvol
Strike with a willing hand, his head is off.	F1368	4.2.44		Mrtino
And had you cut my body with your swords,	F1397	4.2.73		Faust
And mount aloft with them as high as heaven,	F1404	4.2.80		Faust
Whilst with my gentle Mephostophilis,	F1412	4.2.88		Faust
I heard them parly with the Conjurer.	F1422	4.2.98		1Soldr
O hellish spite,/Your heads are all set with hornes.	F1442	4.3.12		Benvol
We'le rather die with griefe, then live with shame.	F1456	4.3.26		Benvol
Well, I will not stand with thee, give me the money:	F1466	4.4.10	P	Faust
Confound these passions with a quiet sleepe:	F1481	4.4.25		Faust
How now Wagner what newes with thee?	F1499	4.4.43	P	Faust
of his men to attend you with provision fit for your journey.	F1502	4.4.46	P	Wagner
to Wittenberge t'other day, with a loade of Hay, he met me,	F1526	4.5.22	P	Carter
so that when it is Winter with us, in the contrary circle it is	F1582	4.6.25	P	Faust
in the contrary circle it is likewise Summer with them, as in	F1583	4.6.26	P	Faust
They all cry out to speake with Doctor Faustus.	F1600	4.6.43		Servnt
I, and we will speake with him.	F1601	4.6.44		Carter
Commit with us, he were as good commit with his father, as	F1603	4.6.46	P	Dick
us, he were as good commit with his father, as commit with us.	F1603	4.6.46	P	Dick
us, he were as good commit with his father, as commit with us.	F1604	4.6.47	P	Dick
in the house, and dash out all your braines with your Bottles.	F1619	4.6.62	P	HrsCsr
With all my heart kind Doctor, please thy selfe,	F1623	4.6.66		Duke

WITH (cont.)

that flesh and bloud should be so fraile with your Worship:	F1632	4.6.75	P	Carter
scab, do you remember how you cosened me with <of> a ho--	F1663	4.6.106	P	HrsCsr
you thinke to carry it away with your Hey-passe, and Re-passe:	F1664	4.6.107	P	Robin
we will recompence/With all the love and kindnesse that we may.	F1672	4.6.115		Duke
hee's now at supper with the schollers, where ther's such	F1678	5.1.5	P	Wagner
we have determin'd with our selves, that Hellen of Greece was	F1683	5.1.10	P	1Schol
Then when sir Paris crost the seas with <for> her,	F1694	5.1.21		Faust
worth>/<Made Greece with ten yeares warres afflict poore Troy>?	F1696	(HC269) B		2Schol
pursu'd]/[With tenne yeares warre the rape of such a queene],	F1700	5.1.27A		3Schol
Hell claimes his <calls for> right, and with a roaring voyce,	F1726	5.1.53		Faust
And with a vyoll full of pretious grace,	F1731	5.1.58		OldMan
Faustus I leave thee, but with griefe of heart,	F1737	5.1.64		OldMan
<I goe sweete Faustus, but with heavy cheare>,	F1737	(HC269) A		OldMan
Hell strives with grace for conquest in my breast:	F1741	5.1.68		Faust
And with my bloud againe I will confirme/The <My> former vow I	F1749	5.1.76		Faust
Do it then Faustus <quickly>, with unfained heart,	F1751	5.1.78		Mephst
With greatest [torments] <torment> that our hell affoords.	F1755	5.1.82		Faust
But what I may afflict his body with,	F1757	5.1.84		Mephst
Sweet Hellen make me immortall with a kisse:	F1770	5.1.97		Faust
And I will combat with weake Menelaus,	F1777	5.1.104		Faust
[Sathan begins to sift me with his pride]:	F1791	5.1.118A		OldMan
Bringing with us lasting damnation,	F1801	5.2.5		Lucifr
How should he, but in <with> desperate lunacie.	F1807	5.2.11		Mephst
Fond worldling, now his heart bloud dries with griefe;	F1808	5.2.12		Mephst
His store of pleasures must be sauc'd with paine.	F1812	5.2.16		Mephst
chamber-fellow, had I liv'd with thee, then had I lived still,	F1824	5.2.28	P	Faust
He is not well with being over solitarie.	F1829	5.2.33		3Schol
heare [me] with patience, and tremble not at my speeches.	F1839	5.2.43	P	Faust
I writ them a bill with mine owne bloud, the date is expired:	F1860	5.2.64	P	Faust
Gentlemen away, least you perish with me.	F1867	5.2.71	P	Faust
God will strengthen me, I will stay with Faustus.	F1870	5.2.74	P	3Schol
Now Faustus let thine eyes with horror stare/Into that vaste	F1909	5.2.113		BdAngl
These, that are fed with soppes of flaming fire,	F1916	5.2.120		BdAngl
With dreadfull horror of these damned fiends.	F1994	5.3.12		3Schol
you have seene many boyes with such pickadevaunts as I have.	F App	p.229 3	P	Clown
So thou shalt, whether thou beest with me, or no:	F App	p.229 22	P	Wagner
they are too familiar with me already, swowns they are as bolde	F App	p.230 28	P	Clown
swowns they are as bolde with my flesh, as if they had payd for	F App	p.230 28	P	Clown
have as many english counters, and what should I do with these?	F App	p.230 34	P	Clown
upon my right heele, with quasi vestigias nostras insistere.	F App	p.231 70	P	Wagner
Nay I know not, we shalbe curst with bell, booke, and candle.	F App	p.232 23	P	Mephst
Come brethren, lets about our businesse with good devotion.	F App	p.232 29	P	Frier
he keepes such a chafing with my mistris about it, and she has	F App	p.233 8	P	Rafe
what doest thou with that same booke thou canst not reade?	F App	p.233 13	P	Rafe
study, shee's borne to beare with me, or else my Art failes.	F App	p.233 17	P	Robin
Canst thou conjure with it?	F App	p.233 21	P	Rafe
I can do al these things easily with it:	F App	p.234 22	P	Robin
druncke with ipocrase at any taberne in Europe for nothing,	F App	p.234 23	P	Robin
Ile feede thy divel with horse-bread as long as he lives,	F App	p.234 30	P	Rafe
Drawer, I hope al is payd, God be with you, come Rafe.	F App	p.234 6	P	Robin
a word with you, I must yet have a goblet payde from you ere	F App	p.234 7	P	Vintnr
I meane so sir with your favor.	F App	p.234 11	P	Vintnr
you may be ashamed to burden honest men with a matter of truth.	F App	p.234 15	P	Rafe
blacke survey/Great Potentates do kneele with awful feare,	F App	p.235 35		Mephst
How am I vexed with these vilaines charmes?	F App	p.235 37		Mephst
Ile have fine sport with the boyes, Ile get nuts and apples	F App	p.236 45	P	Robin
nor in the whole world can compare with thee, for the rare	F App	p.236 3	P	Emper
glorious actes/Lightens the world with his reflecting beames,	F App	p.237 26		Emper
And bring with him his beauteous Paramour,	F App	p.237 32		Emper
Ile meete with you anone for interrupting me so:	F App	p.238 58	P	Faust
send for the knight that was so pleasent with me here of late?	F App	p.238 67	P	Faust
how you crossed me in my conference with the emperour?	F App	p.238 77	P	Faust
I thinke I have met with you for it.	F App	p.238 78	P	Faust
as to delight you with some mirth, hath Faustus worthily	F App	p.238 82	P	Faust
course that time doth runne with calme and silent foote,	F App	p.239 91	P	Faust
Confound these passions with a quiet sleepe:	F App	p.240 124		Faust
you cannot speake with him.	F App	p.240 139	P	Mephst
But I wil speake with him.	F App	p.240 140	P	HrsCsr
Ile speake with him now, or Ile breake his glasse-windowes	F App	p.240 142	P	HrsCsr
And he have not slept this eight weekes Ile speake with him.	F App	p.240 146	P	HrsCsr
How now Wagner, what's the newes with thee?	F App	p.241 167	P	Faust
that when it is heere winter with us, in the contrary circle it	F App	p.242 20	P	Faust
us, in the contrary circle it is summer with them, as in India,	F App	p.242 21	P	Faust
who are at supper with such belly-cheere,	F App	p.243 6		Wagner
Breake heart, drop bloud, and mingle it with teares,	F App	p.243 38		OldMan
the inward soule/With such flagitious crimes of hainous sinnes,	F App	p.243 42		OldMan
lust of warre/Hath made Barbarians drunke with Latin bloud?	Lucan, First Booke	9		
Fetters the Euxin sea, with chaines of yce:	Lucan, First Booke	18		
And choakt with thorns, that greedy earth wants hinds,	Lucan, First Booke	29		
Pharsalia grone with slaughter;/And Carthage soules be glutted	Lucan, First Booke	38		
And Carthage soules be glutted with our blouds;	Lucan, First Booke	39		
Receive with shouts; where thou wilt raigne as King,	Lucan, First Booke	47		
And with bright restles fire compasse the earth,	Lucan, First Booke	49		
Whence thou shouldst view thy Roome with squinting beams.	Lucan, First Booke	55		
The burdened axes with thy force will bend;	Lucan, First Booke	57		
And boult the brazen gates with barres of Iron.	Lucan, First Booke	62		
O faintly joyn'd friends with ambition blind,	Lucan, First Booke	87		
A towne with one poore church set them at oddes.	Lucan, First Booke	97		
Had fild Assirian Carras wals with bloud,	Lucan, First Booke	105		
Being conquered, we are plaugde with civil war.	Lucan, First Booke	108		
for Julia/Snatcht hence by cruel fates with ominous howles,	Lucan, First Booke	112		
With cracke of riven ayre and hideous sound,	Lucan, First Booke	153		

WITH (cont.)

and blasts their eyes/With overthwarting flames, and raging	Lucan, First Booke	156
That lawes were broake, Tribunes with Consuls strove,	Lucan, First Booke	179
And armes all naked, who with broken sighes,	Lucan, First Booke	191
this spectacle/Stroake Caesars hart with feare, his hayre	Lucan, First Booke	195
Approcht the swelling streame with drum and ensigne,	Lucan, First Booke	207
With jawes wide open ghastly roaring out;	Lucan, First Booke	212
And frozen Alpes thaw'd with resolving winds.	Lucan, First Booke	221
There spred the colours, with confused noise/Of trumpets clange,	Lucan, First Booke	239
olde swords/With ugly teeth of blacke rust fouly scarr'd:	Lucan, First Booke	245
And with them Curio, sometime Tribune too,	Lucan, First Booke	271
Roome may be won/With farre lesse toile, and yet the honors	Lucan, First Booke	284
Few battailes fought with prosperous successe/May bring her	Lucan, First Booke	285
successe/May bring her downe, and with her all the world;	Lucan, First Booke	286
Nor capitall be adorn'd with sacred bayes:	Lucan, First Booke	288
denies all, with thy bloud must thou/Abie thy conquest past:	Lucan, First Booke	289
Was so incenst as are Eleius steedes/With clamors:	Lucan, First Booke	295
you that with me have borne/A thousand brunts, and tride me ful	Lucan, First Booke	300
Must Pompeis followers with strangers ayde,	Lucan, First Booke	314
many a heard, whilst with their dams/They kennel'd in Hircania,	Lucan, First Booke	328
Jawes flesht with bloud continue murderous.	Lucan, First Booke	332
And so they triumph, be't with whom ye wil.	Lucan, First Booke	342
the gods are with us,/Neither spoile, nor kingdom seeke we by	Lucan, First Booke	350
then Laelius/The chiefe Centurion crown'd with Oaken leaves,	Lucan, First Booke	358
Hath with thee past the swelling Ocean;	Lucan, First Booke	371
What wals thou wilt be leaveld with the ground,	Lucan, First Booke	384
And with their hands held up, all joyntly cryde/They'ill follow	Lucan, First Booke	388
They whom the Lingones foild with painted speares,	Lucan, First Booke	398
The stubborne Nervians staind with Cottas bloud;	Lucan, First Booke	430
townes/He garrison'd; and Italy he fild with soldiours.	Lucan, First Booke	464
(his vassals)/And that he lags behind with them of purpose,	Lucan, First Booke	477
were the Commons only strooke to heart/With this vaine terror;	Lucan, First Booke	484
Then with their feare, and danger al distract,	Lucan, First Booke	487
had bin fierd/Or dropping-ripe, ready to fall with Ruine,	Lucan, First Booke	491
Which makes the maine saile fal with hideous sound;	Lucan, First Booke	498
Roome that flowes/With Citizens and [Captives] <Captaines>, and	Lucan, First Booke	510
With slender trench they escape night stratagems,	Lucan, First Booke	514
threatning gods/Fill'd both the earth and seas with prodegies;	Lucan, First Booke	523
Strooke with th'earths suddaine shadow waxed pale,	Lucan, First Booke	537
and with a double point/Rose like the Theban brothers funerall	Lucan, First Booke	549
Prodigious birthes with more and ugly jointes/Then nature	Lucan, First Booke	560
Shaking her snakie haire and crooked pine/With flaming toppe,	Lucan, First Booke	572
heard to sound; and with what noise/An armed battaile joines,	Lucan, First Booke	577
the sacred priests/That with divine lustration purg'd the wals,	Lucan, First Booke	593
The skipping Salii with shields like wedges;	Lucan, First Booke	602
And Flamins last, with networke wollen vailes.	Lucan, First Booke	603
blasted, Aruns takes/And it inters with murmurs dolorous,	Lucan, First Booke	606
And stain'd the bowels with darke lothsome spots:	Lucan, First Booke	619
The liver swell'd with filth, and every vaine/Did threaten	Lucan, First Booke	620
with what plague/Meane ye to radge?	Lucan, First Booke	648
noysome Saturne/Were now exalted, and with blew beames shinde,	Lucan, First Booke	651
O Phoebus shouldst thou with thy rayes now sing/The fell Nemean	Lucan, First Booke	654
And heaven tormented with thy chafing heate,	Lucan, First Booke	656
The threatning Scorpion with the burning taile/And fier'st his	Lucan, First Booke	658
With hoarie toppe, and under Hemus mount/Philippi plaines;	Lucan, First Booke	679
This said, being tir'd with fury she sunke downe.	Lucan, First Booke	694
With Muse upreard <prepar'd> I [meant] <meane> to sing of	Ovid's Elegies	1.1.5
Girt my shine browe with sea banke mirtle praise <sprays>.	Ovid's Elegies	1.1.34
My sides are sore with tumbling to and fro.	Ovid's Elegies	1.2.4
T'was so, he stroke me with a slender dart,	Ovid's Elegies	1.2.7
And rough jades mouths with stubburn bits are torne,	Ovid's Elegies	1.2.15
With armes to conquer armlesse men is base,	Ovid's Elegies	1.2.22
Guiding the harmelesse Pigeons with thy hand.	Ovid's Elegies	1.2.26
Thou with these souldiers conquerest gods and men,	Ovid's Elegies	1.2.37
With beautie of thy wings, thy faire haire guilded,	Ovid's Elegies	1.2.41
Who gardes [the] <thee> conquered with his conquering hands.	Ovid's Elegies	1.2.52
Love <Jove> knowes with such like praiers, I dayly move hir:	Ovid's Elegies	1.3.4
Accept him that will love with spotlesse truth:	Ovid's Elegies	1.3.6
If men have Faith, Ile live with thee for ever.	Ovid's Elegies	1.3.16
Ile live with thee, and die, or <ere> thou shalt <shall>	Ovid's Elegies	1.3.18
Griping his false hornes with hir virgin hand:	Ovid's Elegies	1.3.24
And with my name shall thine be alwaies sung.	Ovid's Elegies	1.3.26
Thy husband to a banquet goes with me,	Ovid's Elegies	1.4.1
Lie with him gently, when his limbes he spread/Upon the bed,	Ovid's Elegies	1.4.15
Nor thy soft foote with his hard foote combine.	Ovid's Elegies	1.4.44
And with mistrust of the like measure vext.	Ovid's Elegies	1.4.46
If hee lyes downe with Wine and sleepe opprest,	Ovid's Elegies	1.4.53
But we must part, when heav'n with black night lowers.	Ovid's Elegies	1.4.60
Her white necke hid with tresses hanging downe,	Ovid's Elegies	1.5.10
Love hearing it laugh'd with his tender mother/And smiling	Ovid's Elegies	1.6.11
Forth-with Love came, no darke night-flying spright/Nor hands	Ovid's Elegies	1.6.13
See how the gates with my teares wat'red are.	Ovid's Elegies	1.6.18
With stiffe oake propt the gate doth still appeare.	Ovid's Elegies	1.6.28
With armes or armed men I come not guarded,	Ovid's Elegies	1.6.33
See Love with me, wine moderate in my braine,	Ovid's Elegies	1.6.37
Night runnes away; with open entrance greete them.	Ovid's Elegies	1.6.40
But now perchaunce thy wench with thee doth rest,	Ovid's Elegies	1.6.45
And opening dores with creaking noyse abound?	Ovid's Elegies	1.6.50
Come breake these deafe dores with thy boysterous wind.	Ovid's Elegies	1.6.54
And with my brand these gorgeous houses burne.	Ovid's Elegies	1.6.58
Carelesse, farewell, with my falt not distaind.	Ovid's Elegies	1.6.72
And dores conjoynd with an hard iron lock.	Ovid's Elegies	1.6.74
Or holy gods with cruell strokes abus'd.	Ovid's Elegies	1.7.6

WITH (cont.)

Yet was she graced with her ruffled hayre.	Ovid's Elegies	1.7.12
But secretlie her lookes with checks did trounce mee,	Ovid's Elegies	1.7.21
Pay vowes to Jove, engirt thy hayres with baies,	Ovid's Elegies	1.7.36
Let the sad captive formost with lockes spred/On her white	Ovid's Elegies	1.7.39
Meeter it were her lips were blewe with kissing/And on her	Ovid's Elegies	1.7.41
Like Popler leaves blowne with a stormy flawe,	Ovid's Elegies	1.7.54
Or slender eares, with gentle Zephire shaken,	Ovid's Elegies	1.7.55
Or waters tops with the warme south-winde taken.	Ovid's Elegies	1.7.56
griefe appease)/With thy sharpe nayles upon my face to seaze.	Ovid's Elegies	1.7.64
She knows with gras, with thrids on wrong wheeles spun/And what	Ovid's Elegies	1.8.7
with thrids on wrong wheeles spun/And what with Mares ranck	Ovid's Elegies	1.8.7
wheeles spun/And what with Mares ranck humour may be done.	Ovid's Elegies	1.8.8
The purple moone with sanguine visage stood.	Ovid's Elegies	1.8.12
she chides/And with long charmes the solide earth divides.	Ovid's Elegies	1.8.18
Such is his forme as may with thine compare,	Ovid's Elegies	1.8.33
And with swift horses the swift yeare soone leaves us.	Ovid's Elegies	1.8.50
Brasse shines with use; good garments would be worne,	Ovid's Elegies	1.8.51
Houses not dwelt in, are with filth forlorne.	Ovid's Elegies	1.8.52
Beauty not exercisde with age is spent,	Ovid's Elegies	1.8.53
Poore lover with thy gransires I exile thee.	Ovid's Elegies	1.8.66
What he will give, with greater instance crave.	Ovid's Elegies	1.8.68
Thy fault with his fault so repuls'd will vanish.	Ovid's Elegies	1.8.80
let him viewe/And thy neck with lascivious markes made blew.	Ovid's Elegies	1.8.98
Nor let my words be with the windes hence blowne,	Ovid's Elegies	1.8.106
With much a do my hands I scarsely staide.	Ovid's Elegies	1.8.110
What age fits Mars, with Venus doth agree,	Ovid's Elegies	1.9.3
is bould/To suffer storme mixt snowes with nights sharpe cold?	Ovid's Elegies	1.9.16
Now all feare with my mindes hot love abates,	Ovid's Elegies	1.10.9
Love and Loves sonne are with fierce armes to oddes;	Ovid's Elegies	1.10.19
give her my writ/But see that forth-with shee peruseth it.	Ovid's Elegies	1.11.16
Then with triumphant laurell will I grace them/And in the midst	Ovid's Elegies	1.11.25
wood be flying/And thou the waxe stuft full with notes denying,	Ovid's Elegies	1.12.8
Yet as if mixt with red leade thou wert ruddy,	Ovid's Elegies	1.12.11
Be broake with wheeles of chariots passing by.	Ovid's Elegies	1.12.14
for needfull uses/Ile prove had hands impure with all abuses.	Ovid's Elegies	1.12.16
committed/And then with sweete words to my Mistrisse fitted.	Ovid's Elegies	1.12.22
dost betray them/To Pedants, that with cruell lashes pay them.	Ovid's Elegies	1.13.18
That with one worde hath nigh himselfe undone,	Ovid's Elegies	1.13.20
Who can indure, save him with whom none lies?	Ovid's Elegies	1.13.26
Or steeds might fal forcd with thick clouds approch.	Ovid's Elegies	1.13.30
Say that thy love with Caephalus were not knowne,	Ovid's Elegies	1.13.33
The Moone sleepes with Endemion everie day,	Ovid's Elegies	1.13.43
Bee not to see with wonted eyes inclinde,	Ovid's Elegies	1.14.37
Thou mad'st thy head with compound poyson flow.	Ovid's Elegies	1.14.44
Died red with shame, to hide from shame she seekes.	Ovid's Elegies	1.14.52
And be heereafter seene with native haire.	Ovid's Elegies	1.14.56
Ascreus lives, while grapes with new wine swell,	Ovid's Elegies	1.15.11
Or men with crooked sickles corne downe fell.	Ovid's Elegies	1.15.12
With sunne and moone Aratus shall remaine.	Ovid's Elegies	1.15.16
And rude boyes toucht with unknowne love me reade,	Ovid's Elegies	2.1.6
That some youth hurt as I am with loves bowe/His owne flames	Ovid's Elegies	2.1.7
With earthes revenge and how Olimpus toppe/High Ossa bore,	Ovid's Elegies	2.1.13
Enquire not what with Isis may be done/Nor feare least she to	Ovid's Elegies	2.2.25
His fauning wench with her desire he crownes.	Ovid's Elegies	2.2.34
I sawe ones legges with fetters blacke and blewe,	Ovid's Elegies	2.2.47
With selfe same woundes he gave, he ought to smart.	Ovid's Elegies	2.3.4
Thy hands agree not with the warlike speare.	Ovid's Elegies	2.3.8
If any eie mee with a modest looke,	Ovid's Elegies	2.4.11
Yet would I lie with her if that I might.	Ovid's Elegies	2.4.22
She would be nimbler, lying with a man.	Ovid's Elegies	2.4.24
Or if one touch the lute with art and cunning,	Ovid's Elegies	2.4.27
And she <her> I like that with a majestie,	Ovid's Elegies	2.4.29
To leave my selfe, that am in love [with all] <withall>,	Ovid's Elegies	2.4.31
If her white necke be shadowde with blacke haire,	Ovid's Elegies	2.4.41
Minding thy fault, with death I wish to revill,	Ovid's Elegies	2.5.3
Not silent were thine eyes, the boord with wine/Was scribled,	Ovid's Elegies	2.5.17
(Such with my tongue it likes me to purloyne).	Ovid's Elegies	2.5.24
Such as a rose mixt with a lilly breedes,	Ovid's Elegies	2.5.37
Or when the Moone travailes with charmed steedes.	Ovid's Elegies	2.5.38
With her owne armor was my wench defended.	Ovid's Elegies	2.5.48
Least with worse kisses she should me indue.	Ovid's Elegies	2.5.50
And with rough clawes your tender cheekes assaile.	Ovid's Elegies	2.6.4
Thou with thy quilles mightst make greene Emeralds darke,	Ovid's Elegies	2.6.21
Thou spokest thy words so well with stammering sound.	Ovid's Elegies	2.6.24
Supplying their voide places with the worst.	Ovid's Elegies	2.6.40
The Parrat into wood receiv'd with these,	Ovid's Elegies	2.6.57
They that deserve paine, beare't with patience.	Ovid's Elegies	2.7.12
Duld with much beating slowly forth doth passe.	Ovid's Elegies	2.7.16
With Venus game who will a servant grace?	Ovid's Elegies	2.7.21
Or any back made rough with stripes imbrace?	Ovid's Elegies	2.7.22
Whence knowes Corinna that with thee I playde?	Ovid's Elegies	2.8.6
What if a man with bond-women offend,	Ovid's Elegies	2.8.9
Achilles burnt with face of captive Briseis,	Ovid's Elegies	2.8.11
Let me lie with thee browne Cypasse to day.	Ovid's Elegies	2.8.22
Telling thy mistresse, where I was with thee,	Ovid's Elegies	2.8.27
Being requirde, with speedy helpe relieve?	Ovid's Elegies	2.9.8
Hence with great laude thou maiest a triumph move.	Ovid's Elegies	2.9.16
With strawie cabins now her courts should build.	Ovid's Elegies	2.9.18
Joyes with uncertaine faith thou takest and brings.	Ovid's Elegies	2.9.50
Yet Love, if thou with thy faire mother heare,	Ovid's Elegies	2.9.51
I could not be in love with twoo at once,	Ovid's Elegies	2.10.2
So with this love and that, wavers my minde.	Ovid's Elegies	2.10.10

WITH (cont.)

Let one wench cloy me with sweete loves delight,	Ovid's Elegies	2.10.21
Nor want I strength, but weight to presse her with:	Ovid's Elegies	2.10.24
I pay them home with that they most desire:	Ovid's Elegies	2.10.26
And with his <their> bloud eternall honour gaine,	Ovid's Elegies	2.10.32
Let marchants seeke wealth, [and] with perjured lips,	Ovid's Elegies	2.10.33
But when I die, would I might droope with doing,	Ovid's Elegies	2.10.35
With Icy Boreas, and the Southerne gale:	Ovid's Elegies	2.11.10
The sucking shore with their aboundance swels.	Ovid's Elegies	2.11.14
Maides on the shore, with marble white feete tread,	Ovid's Elegies	2.11.15
with what [rockes] <rocke> the feard Cerannia <Ceraunia>	Ovid's Elegies	2.11.19
Too late you looke back, when with anchors weighd,	Ovid's Elegies	2.11.23
And with the waters sees death neere him thrusts,	Ovid's Elegies	2.11.26
The Thracian Harpe with cunning to have strooke,	Ovid's Elegies	2.11.32
But if my words with winged stormes hence slip,	Ovid's Elegies	2.11.33
Go, minding to returne with prosperous winde,	Ovid's Elegies	2.11.37
And with thy hand assist [the] <thy> swelling saile.	Ovid's Elegies	2.11.42
Ile clip and kisse thee with all contentation,	Ovid's Elegies	2.11.45
With the Atrides many gainde renowne.	Ovid's Elegies	2.12.10
And me with many, but yet me without murther,	Ovid's Elegies	2.12.27
She secretly with me such harme attempted,	Ovid's Elegies	2.13.3
And in thy pompe hornd Apis with thee keepe,	Ovid's Elegies	2.13.14
Where the French rout engirt themselves with Bayes.	Ovid's Elegies	2.13.18
Whose bodies with their heavy burthens ake.	Ovid's Elegies	2.13.20
In white, with incense Ile thine Altars greete,	Ovid's Elegies	2.13.23
Subscribing, Naso with Corinna sav'd:	Ovid's Elegies	2.13.25
Do but deserve gifts with this title grav'd.	Ovid's Elegies	2.13.26
Deserv'd thereby with death to be tormented.	Ovid's Elegies	2.14.6
My selfe that better dye with loving may/Had seene, my mother	Ovid's Elegies	2.14.21
With cruell hand why doest greene Apples pull?	Ovid's Elegies	2.14.24
Why with hid irons are your bowels torne?	Ovid's Elegies	2.14.27
At Colchis stain'd with childrens bloud men raile,	Ovid's Elegies	2.14.29
To plague your bodies with such harmefull strokes?	Ovid's Elegies	2.14.34
But tender Damsels do it, though with paine,	Ovid's Elegies	2.14.37
Shee dyes, and with loose haires to grave is sent,	Ovid's Elegies	2.14.39
Let her my faith with thee given understand.	Ovid's Elegies	2.15.28
A small, but wholesome soyle with watrie veynes.	Ovid's Elegies	2.16.2
Pelignian fields [with] <which> liqued rivers flowe,	Ovid's Elegies	2.16.5
With corne the earth abounds, with vines much more,	Ovid's Elegies	2.16.7
My hard way with my mistrisse would seeme soft.	Ovid's Elegies	2.16.20
With her I durst the Lybian Syrtes breake through,	Ovid's Elegies	2.16.21
No flowing waves with drowned ships forth poured,	Ovid's Elegies	2.16.25
With thy white armes upon my shoulders seaze,	Ovid's Elegies	2.16.29
So sweete a burthen I will beare with eaze.	Ovid's Elegies	2.16.30
And rockes dyed crimson with Prometheus bloud.	Ovid's Elegies	2.16.40
Elmes love the Vines, the Vines with Elmes abide,	Ovid's Elegies	2.16.41
And with swift Naggs drawing thy little Coach,	Ovid's Elegies	2.16.49
Small things with greater may be copulate.	Ovid's Elegies	2.17.14
Who doubts, with Pelius, Thetis did consort,	Ovid's Elegies	2.17.17
Egeria with just Numa had good sport,	Ovid's Elegies	2.17.18
Venus with Vulcan, though smiths tooles laide by,	Ovid's Elegies	2.17.19
With his stumpe-foote he halts ill-favouredly.	Ovid's Elegies	2.17.20
With shorter numbers the heroicke sit.	Ovid's Elegies	2.17.22
And rule so soone with private hands acquainted.	Ovid's Elegies	2.18.16
And what poore Dido with her drawne sword sharpe,	Ovid's Elegies	2.18.25
Doth say, with her that lov'd the Aonian harpe.	Ovid's Elegies	2.18.26
With Laodameia mate to her dead Lord.	Ovid's Elegies	2.18.38
What should I do with fortune that nere failes me?	Ovid's Elegies	2.19.7
Nor never with nights sharpe revenge afflicted?	Ovid's Elegies	2.19.54
Some other seeke that may in patience strive with thee,	Ovid's Elegies	2.19.59
To pleasure me, for-bid me to corive with thee.	Ovid's Elegies	2.19.60
Elegia came with haires perfumed sweete,	Ovid's Elegies	3.1.7
Then with huge steps came violent Tragedie,	Ovid's Elegies	3.1.11
And seaven [times] <time> shooke her head with thicke locks	Ovid's Elegies	3.1.32
The other smilde, (I wot) with wanton eyes,	Ovid's Elegies	3.1.33
With lofty wordes stout Tragedie (she sayd)/Why treadst me	Ovid's Elegies	3.1.35
Thy lofty stile with mine I not compare,	Ovid's Elegies	3.1.39
Light am I, and with me, my care, light love,	Ovid's Elegies	3.1.41
To get the dore with little noise unbard.	Ovid's Elegies	3.1.50
What gift with me was on her birth day sent,	Ovid's Elegies	3.1.57
With scepters, and high buskins th'one would dresse me,	Ovid's Elegies	3.1.63
To sit, and talke with thee I hether came,	Ovid's Elegies	3.2.3
That thou maiest know with love thou mak'st me flame.	Ovid's Elegies	3.2.4
With wheeles bent inward now the ring-turne ride.	Ovid's Elegies	3.2.12
For shame presse not her backe with thy hard knee.	Ovid's Elegies	3.2.24
First Victory is brought with large spred wing,	Ovid's Elegies	3.2.45
With Augures Phoebus, Phoebe with hunters standes,	Ovid's Elegies	3.2.51
The Gods, and their rich pompe witnesse with me,	Ovid's Elegies	3.2.61
Let with strong hand the reine to bend be made.	Ovid's Elegies	3.2.72
My mistris wish confirme with my request.	Ovid's Elegies	3.2.80
She smilde, and with quicke eyes behight some grace:	Ovid's Elegies	3.2.83
Faire white with rose red was before commixt:	Ovid's Elegies	3.3.5
And unrevengd mockt Gods with me doth scoffe.	Ovid's Elegies	3.3.20
Pallas launce strikes me with unconquerd arme.	Ovid's Elegies	3.3.28
Jove throwes downe woods, and Castles with his fire:	Ovid's Elegies	3.3.35
With lying lips my God-head to deceave,	Ovid's Elegies	3.3.44
So shalt thou go with youths to feasts together,	Ovid's Elegies	3.4.47
Floud with [reede-growne] <redde-growne> slime bankes, till I	Ovid's Elegies	3.5.1
Thou hast no bridge, nor boate with ropes to throw,	Ovid's Elegies	3.5.3
With snow thaw'd from the next hill now thou rushest,	Ovid's Elegies	3.5.7
Bearing the head with dreadfull [Adders] <Arrowes> clad,	Ovid's Elegies	3.5.14
Thou saiest broke with Alcides angry hand.	Ovid's Elegies	3.5.36
In Tiburs field with watry fome art rumbling,	Ovid's Elegies	3.5.46

WITH (cont.)

Why weepst? and spoilst with teares thy watry eyes?	Ovid's Elegies	3.5.57
Yet rending with enraged thumbe her tresses,	Ovid's Elegies	3.5.71
Who sayd with gratefull voyce perpetuall bee?	Ovid's Elegies	3.5.98
Idly I lay with her, as if I lovde <her> not,	Ovid's Elegies	3.6.3
And eagerlie she kist me with her tongue,	Ovid's Elegies	3.6.9
Or one that with her tender brother lies,	Ovid's Elegies	3.6.22
With virgin waxe hath some imbast my joynts,	Ovid's Elegies	3.6.29
And pierst my liver with sharpe needle poynts <needles>?	Ovid's Elegies	3.6.30
And I grow faint, as with some spirit haunted?	Ovid's Elegies	3.6.36
To kisse, I kisse, to lie with her shee let me.	Ovid's Elegies	3.6.48
And with sweete words cause deafe rockes to have loved <moned>,	Ovid's Elegies	3.6.58
Lie downe with shame, and see thou stirre no more,	Ovid's Elegies	3.6.69
And bide sore losse, with endlesse infamie.	Ovid's Elegies	3.6.72
To take it in her hand and play with it.	Ovid's Elegies	3.6.74
Either th'art witcht with blood <bould> of frogs new dead,	Ovid's Elegies	3.6.79
With that her loose gowne on, from me she cast her,	Ovid's Elegies	3.6.81
I heere and there go witty with dishonour.	Ovid's Elegies	3.7.8
With strong plough shares no man the earth did cleave,	Ovid's Elegies	3.7.41
Why gird'st thy citties with a towred wall?	Ovid's Elegies	3.7.47
What doest with seas?	Ovid's Elegies	3.7.49
with th'earth thou wert content,/Why seek'st not heav'n the	Ovid's Elegies	3.7.49
Heaven thou affects, with Romulus, temples brave/Bacchus,	Ovid's Elegies	3.7.51
How piteously with drouping wings he stands,	Ovid's Elegies	3.8.9
And knocks his bare brest with selfe-angry hands.	Ovid's Elegies	3.8.10
father Phoebus layed/To sing with his unequald harpe is sayed.	Ovid's Elegies	3.8.24
Verses alone are with continuance crown'd.	Ovid's Elegies	3.8.28
With thine, nor this last fire their presence misses.	Ovid's Elegies	3.8.54
Their <Your> youthfull browes with Ivie girt to meete him,/With	Ovid's Elegies	3.8.61
With Calvus learnd Catullus comes <come> and greete him.	Ovid's Elegies	3.8.62
With these thy soule walkes, soules if death release,	Ovid's Elegies	3.8.65
Golden-hair'd Ceres crownd with eares of corne,	Ovid's Elegies	3.9.3
And ripe-earde corne with sharpe-edg'd sithes to fell.	Ovid's Elegies	3.9.12
And untild ground with crooked plough-shares broake.	Ovid's Elegies	3.9.14
With strong hand striking wild-beasts brist'led hyde.	Ovid's Elegies	3.9.26
Was divers waies distract with love, and shame.	Ovid's Elegies	3.9.28
And corne with least part of it selfe returnd.	Ovid's Elegies	3.9.30
Being fit broken with the crooked share,	Ovid's Elegies	3.9.32
Ida the seate of groves did sing with corne,	Ovid's Elegies	3.9.39
And Juno like with Dis raignes under ground?	Ovid's Elegies	3.9.46
What secret becks in banquets with her youths,	Ovid's Elegies	3.10.23
With privy signes, and talke dissembling truths?	Ovid's Elegies	3.10.24
But with my rivall sicke she was not than.	Ovid's Elegies	3.10.26
These hardned me, with what I keepe obscure,	Ovid's Elegies	3.10.27
With joy heares Neptunes swelling waters sound.	Ovid's Elegies	3.10.30
Nor with thee, nor without thee can I live,	Ovid's Elegies	3.10.39
Beauty with lewdnesse doth right ill agree.	Ovid's Elegies	3.10.42
I feare with me is common now to many.	Ovid's Elegies	3.11.6
With Muse oppos'd would I my lines had done,	Ovid's Elegies	3.11.17
Wee cause feete flie, wee mingle haires with snakes,	Ovid's Elegies	3.11.23
With famous pageants, and their home-bred beasts.	Ovid's Elegies	3.12.4
There stands an old wood with thick trees darke clouded,	Ovid's Elegies	3.12.7
Here when the Pipe with solemne tunes doth sound,	Ovid's Elegies	3.12.11
Which with the grasse of Tuscane fields are fed.	Ovid's Elegies	3.12.14
And Rams with hornes their hard heads wreathed back.	Ovid's Elegies	3.12.17
Now is the goat brought through the boyes with darts,	Ovid's Elegies	3.12.21
Shew large wayes with their garments there displayed.	Ovid's Elegies	3.12.24
Built walles high towred with a prosperous hand.	Ovid's Elegies	3.12.34
The strumpet with the stranger will not do,	Ovid's Elegies	3.13.9
And with your pastime let the bedsted creake,	Ovid's Elegies	3.13.26
But with your robes, put on an honest face,	Ovid's Elegies	3.13.27
And with a wantons tooth, your necke new raste?	Ovid's Elegies	3.13.34
And would be dead, but dying <dead> with thee remaine.	Ovid's Elegies	3.13.40
A greater ground with great horse is to till.	Ovid's Elegies	3.14.18
The lining, purple silke, with guilt starres drawne,	Hero and Leander	1.10
Her wide sleeves greene, and bordered with a grove,	Hero and Leander	1.11
Made with the blood of wretched Lovers slaine.	Hero and Leander	1.16
And branch't with blushing corall to the knee;	Hero and Leander	1.32
Those with sweet water oft her handmaid fils,	Hero and Leander	1.35
And with still panting rockt, there tooke his rest.	Hero and Leander	1.44
That heavenly path, with many a curious dint,	Hero and Leander	1.68
The barbarous Thratian soldier moov'd with nought,	Hero and Leander	1.81
Was moov'd with him, and for his favour sought.	Hero and Leander	1.82
street like to a Firmament/Glistered with breathing stars,	Hero and Leander	1.98
Where crown'd with blazing light and majestie,	Hero and Leander	1.110
Incenst with savage heat, gallop amaine,	Hero and Leander	1.115
Poore soldiers stand with fear of death dead strooken,	Hero and Leander	1.121
And with the other, wine from grapes out wroong.	Hero and Leander	1.140
To dallie with Idalian Ganimed:	Hero and Leander	1.148
And tumbling with the Rainbow in a cloud:	Hero and Leander	1.150
Thence flew Loves arrow with the golden head,	Hero and Leander	1.161
Till with the fire that from his count'nance blazed,	Hero and Leander	1.164
The aire with sparkes of living fire was spangled,	Hero and Leander	1.188
to display/Loves holy fire, with words, with sighs and teares,	Hero and Leander	1.193
With chearefull hope thus he accosted her.	Hero and Leander	1.198
And with intestine broiles the world destroy,	Hero and Leander	1.251
Compar'd with marriage, had you tried them both,	Hero and Leander	1.263
What vertue is it that is borne with us?	Hero and Leander	1.278
Nor staine thy youthfull years with avarice,	Hero and Leander	1.325
With that Leander stoopt, to have imbrac'd her,	Hero and Leander	1.341
God knowes I play/With Venus swannes and sparrowes all the day.	Hero and Leander	1.352
Cupid beats downe her praiers with his wings,	Hero and Leander	1.369
Laden with languishment and griefe he flies.	Hero and Leander	1.378

WITH (cont.)

But with a ghastly dreadfull countenaunce,	Hero and Leander	1.381	
Glist'red with deaw, as one that seem'd to skorne it:	Hero and Leander	1.390	
On her, this god/Enamoured was, and with his snakie rod,/Did	Hero and Leander	1.398	
And with smooth speech, her fancie to assay,	Hero and Leander	1.402	
And then he woo'd with kisses, and at last,	Hero and Leander	1.404	
she wanting no excuse/To feed him with delaies, as women use:	Hero and Leander	1.426	
tearmes, with sad and heavie cheare/Complaind to Cupid;	Hero and Leander	1.440	
He wounds with love, and forst them equallie,	Hero and Leander	1.445	
Were with Jove clos'd in Stigian Emperie.	Hero and Leander	1.458	
Hermes had slept in hell with ignoraunce.	Hero and Leander	1.468	
But be surpris'd with every garish toy.	Hero and Leander	1.480	
Who with incroching guile, keepes learning downe.	Hero and Leander	1.482	
By this, sad Hero, with love unacquainted,	Hero and Leander	2.1	
Had spread the boord, with roses strowed the roome,	Hero and Leander	2.21	
her body throes/Upon his bosome, where with yeelding eyes,	Hero and Leander	2.47	
And as a brother with his sister toyed,	Hero and Leander	2.52	
Long dallying with Hero, nothing saw/That might delight him	Hero and Leander	2.62	
on the rushes to be flung,/Striv'd with redoubled strength:	Hero and Leander	2.67	
Shee, with a kind of graunting, put him by it,	Hero and Leander	2.73	
With Cupids myrtle was his bonet crownd,	Hero and Leander	2.105	
Spits foorth the ringled bit, and with his hoves,	Hero and Leander	2.143	
With that hee stript him to the yv'rie skin,	Hero and Leander	2.153	
where the ground/Was strewd with pearle, and in low corrall	Hero and Leander	2.161	
Meremaids, sported with their loves/On heapes of heavie gold,	Hero and Leander	2.162	
Beat downe the bold waves with his triple mace,	Hero and Leander	2.172	
He clapt his plumpe cheekes, with his tresses playd,	Hero and Leander	2.181	
Playd with a boy so faire and [so] kind,	Hero and Leander	2.195	
The god seeing him with pittie to be moved,	Hero and Leander	2.219	
With follie and false hope deluding us).	Hero and Leander	2.222	
And drunke with gladnesse, to the dore she goes.	Hero and Leander	2.236	
This head was beat with manie a churlish billow,	Hero and Leander	2.251	
She overcome with shame and sallow feare,	Hero and Leander	2.260	
With both her hands she made the bed a tent,	Hero and Leander	2.264	
O'recast with dim and darksome coverture.	Hero and Leander	2.266	
Which is with azure circling lines empal'd,	Hero and Leander	2.274	
Yet there with Sysiphus he toyld in vaine,	Hero and Leander	2.277	
Which so prevail'd, as he with small ado,	Hero and Leander	2.281	
Foorth plungeth, and oft flutters with her wing,	Hero and Leander	2.290	
And with his flaring beames mockt ougly night,	Hero and Leander	2.332	
Till she o'recome with anguish, shame, and rage,	Hero and Leander	2.333	
Come live with mee, and be my love,	Passionate Shepherd	1	
Imbroydred all with leaves of Mirtle.	Passionate Shepherd	12	
With buckles of the purest gold.	Passionate Shepherd	16	
With Corall clasps and Amber studs,	Passionate Shepherd	18	
Come <Then> live with mee, and be my love.	Passionate Shepherd	20	
Then live with mee, and be my love.	Passionate Shepherd	24	

WITHALL

bowes enow/Neere to these woods, to rost your meate withall:	Dido	1.1.173	Aeneas
Then have at him to begin withall.	2Tamb	5.1.152	Therid
So precious, and withall so orient,	Jew	5.3.28	Msngr
And that the Mortimers are in hand withall,	Edw	3.1.54	Edward
and withall/We may remoove these flatterers from the king,	Edw	4.4.25	Mortmr
Nothing Faustus but to delight thy mind <withall>,/And let thee	F 473	2.1.85	Mephst
my selfe when I could get none <had no body> to fight withall:	F 689	2.2.138	P Wrath
To leave my selfe, that am in love [with all] <withall>,	Ovid's Elegies	2.4.31	

WITHDRAW

And cause them to withdraw their forces home,	1Tamb	1.1.131	Menaph
Withdraw as many more to follow him.	1Tamb	3.3.22	Bassoe

WITHDREW

delay/Might crosse him, he withdrew his troupes from France,	Lucan, First Booke	395

WITHER

Unmeete is beauty without use to wither.	Ovid's Elegies	2.3.14

WITHERED

About whose withered necke hung Hecuba,	Dido	2.1.226	Aeneas
My vaines are withered, and my sinewes drie,	Dido	4.5.33	Nurse
Or withered leaves that Autume shaketh downe:	1Tamb	4.1.32	Souldn
Now waxe all pale and withered to the death,	1Tamb	5.1.91	1Virgn
Pierce through the center of my withered heart,	1Tamb	5.1.303	Bajzth

WITH-HOLD

I can with-hold no longer; welcome sweet love.	Jew	4.2.46	Curtzn

WITHIN

And scarcely know within what Clime we are.	Dido	2.1.44	Aeneas
Our Phrigian [shepherds] <shepherd> haled within the gates,/And	Dido	2.1.153	Aeneas
charme to keepe the windes/Within the closure of a golden ball,	Dido	4.4.100	Dido
Fighting for passage, tilt within the earth.	1Tamb	1.2.51	Tamb
Warring within our breasts for regiment,	1Tamb	2.7.19	Tamb
Then shall our footmen lie within the trench,	1Tamb	3.1.64	Bajzth
within whose silver haires/Honor and reverence evermore have	1Tamb	5.1.81	1Virgn
Who's within there?	1Tamb	5.1.191	Tamb
So high within the region of the aire,	1Tamb	5.1.250	Zabina
Shall carie wrapt within his scarlet waves,	2Tamb	1.1.34	Orcan
But keep within the circle of mine armes.	2Tamb	3.2.35	Tamb
And roome within to lodge sixe thousand men.	2Tamb	3.2.72	Tamb
And yet at night carrouse within my tent,	2Tamb	3.2.106	Tamb
Seest thou not death within my wrathfull looks?	2Tamb	3.5.119	Tamb
But closde within the compasse of a tent,	2Tamb	4.2.3	Olymp
by a Spanish Fleet/That never left us till within a league,	Jew	1.1.96	2Merch
are letters come/From Ormus, and the Post stayes here within.	Jew	2.3.223	Abigal
and let them be interr'd/Within one sacred monument of stone;	Jew	3.2.30	Govnr
Be blest of me, nor come within my gates,	Jew	3.4.31	Barab
much weight in Pearle/Orient and round, have I within my house;	Jew	4.1.67	Barab
For he that shriv'd her is within my house.	Jew	4.1.115	Barab

WITHIN (cont.)

Upon mine owne free-hold within fortie foot of the gallowes,	Jew	4.2.16	P	Pilia
Within [there] <here>.	Jew	5.2.47		Barab
Now Governor--stand by there, wait within.--	Jew	5.2.50		Barab
as once you said, within this Ile/In Malta here, that I have got	Jew	5.2.67		Barab
to feast my traine/Within a Towne of warre so lately pillag'd,	Jew	5.3.22		Calym
Which he hath pitcht within his deadly toyle.	P 54	1.54		Navrre
Since thou hast all the Cardes within thy hands/To shuffle or	P 146	2.89		Guise
the fatall poyson/Workes within my head, my brain pan breakes,	P 185	3.20		OldQn
Within the compasse of a deadly toyle,	P 205	4.3		QnMoth
The greatest warres within our Christian bounds,	P 460	8.10		Anjoy
That it might print these lines within his heart.	P 669	13.13		Duchss
Mor du, wert <were> not the fruit within thy wombe,	P 688	13.32		Guise
But he doth lurke within his drousie couch,	P 737	14.40		Navrre
Well, let me alone, whose within there?	P 881	17.76		King
Thinke not but I am tragicall within:	P 894	17.89		King
Then sirs take your standings within this Chamber,	P 940	19.10		Capt
We will goe talke more of this within.	P1138	21.32		Dumain
O the fatall poyson workes within my brest,	P1221	22.83		King
Shall sleepe within the scabberd at thy neede,	Edw	1.1.87		Mortmr
Ere Gaveston shall stay within the realme.	Edw	1.1.105		Lncstr
Lives uncontroulde within the English pale,	Edw	2.2.165		Lncstr
Madam, stay you within this castell here.	Edw	2.4.50		Mortmr
Whilst I am lodgd within this cave of care,	Edw	5.1.32		Edward
That bleedes within me for this strange exchange.	Edw	5.1.35		Edward
Within a dungeon Englands king is kept,	Edw	5.3.19		Edward
Within this roome is lockt the messenger,	Edw	5.4.17		Mortmr
In Germany, within a Towne cal'd [Rhode] <Rhodes>:	F 12	Prol.12		1Chor
Within the massy entrailes of the earth:	F 174	1.1.146		Cornel
for you to come within fortie foot of the place of execution,	F 211	1.2.18	P	Wagner
my Maister is within at dinner, with Valdes and Cornelius,	F 215	1.2.22	P	Wagner
Within this circle is Jehova's Name,	F 236	1.3.8		Faust
Within the bowels of these Elements,	F 508	2.1.120		Mephst
Within the concave compasse of the Pole,	F 765	2.3.44		2Chor
Not long he stayed within his quiet house,	F 768	2.3.47		2Chor
Conducted me within the walles of Rome?	F 802	3.1.24		Faust
<Within whose walles such store of ordnance are>,	F 819	(HC265)A		Mephst
<As match the dayes within one compleate yeare>,	F 821	(HC265)A		Mephst
Within the compasse of one compleat yeare:	F 822	3.1.44		Mephst
Thou know'st within the compasse of eight daies,	F 847	3.1.69		Faust
But whilst they sleepe within the Consistory,	F 943	3.1.165		Faust
and let them hang/Within the window where he yoak'd me first,	F1381	4.2.57		Benvol
That sometime grew within this learned man:	F2004	5.3.22		4Chor
sometime solitary set, within my Closet, sundry thoughts arose,	F App	p.236 18	P	Emper
and his owne waight/Keepe him within the ground, his armes al	Lucan, First Booke			140
thou bid me/Intombe my sword within my brothers bowels;	Lucan, First Booke			377
Deflowr'd except, within thy Temple wall.	Ovid's Elegies			1.7.18
Let him within heare bard out lovers prate.	Ovid's Elegies			1.8.78
Within a while great heapes grow of a tittle.	Ovid's Elegies			1.8.90
Within my brest no desert empire beare.	Ovid's Elegies			2.9.52
All being shut out, th'adulterer is within.	Ovid's Elegies			3.4.8

WITHOUT

As without blushing I can aske no more:	Dido	3.1.104		Aeneas
Tut, I am simple, without [minde] <made> to hurt,	Dido	3.2.16		Juno
We could have gone without your companie.	Dido	3.3.14		Dido
Aeneas will not goe without his sonne:	Dido	4.4.107		Dido
Now is he come on shoare safe without hurt:	Dido	5.1.257		Dido
Nay, though I praise it, I can live without it.	1Tamb	2.5.66		Therid
Without respect of Sex, degree or age,	1Tamb	4.1.62		2Msngr
Which mony was not got without my meanes.	Jew	Prol.32		Machvl
the Easterne rockes/Without controule can picke his riches up,	Jew	1.1.22		Barab
you to come so farre/Without the ayd or conduct of their ships.	Jew	1.1.94		Barab
to forgoe so much/Without provision for thy selfe and me.	Jew	1.2.243		Barab
And why thou cam'st ashore without our leave?	Jew	2.2.3		Govnr
What sparkle does it give without a foile?	Jew	2.3.55		Lodowk
Without fresh men to rigge and furnish them.	Jew	5.5.101		Govnr
Guise/Dares once adventure without the Kings consent,	P 37	1.37		Admral
Without the intercession of some Saint?	P 357	6.12		Mntsrl
And bid him come without delay to us.	P 559	11.24		QnMoth
As not a man may live without our leaves.	P 638	12.51		QnMoth
(aspiring Guise)/Durst be in armes without the Kings consent?	P 829	17.24		Eprnon
Let him without controulement have his will.	Edw	1.4.390		MortSr
That cannot speake without propterea quod.	Edw	2.1.53		Baldck
Thus do you still suspect me without cause.	Edw	2.2.227		Queene
That if without effusion of bloud,	Edw	3.1.159		Herald
Madam, without offence if I may aske,	Edw	4.6.30		Kent
I can brooke/To loose my crowne and kingdome, without cause,	Edw	5.1.52		Edward
And may not follow thee without his leave;	F 269	1.3.41		Mephst
for I am wanton and lascivious, and cannot live without a wife.	F 530	2.1.142	P	Faust
Without election, and a true consent:	F 887	3.1.109		Pope
Without inforcement of the German Peeres,	F 958	3.1.180		Faust
Pleasures unspeakeable, blisse without end.	F1900	5.2.104		GdAngl
Them freedome without war might not suffice,	Lucan, First Booke			173
And without ground, fear'd, what themselves had faind:	Lucan, First Booke			482
Lightning in silence, stole forth without clouds,	Lucan, First Booke			531
And went the round, in, and without the towne.	Lucan, First Booke			594
Words without voyce shall on my eye browes sit,	Ovid's Elegies			1.4.19
Wondring if any walked without light.	Ovid's Elegies			1.6.10
Now Mars doth rage abroad without all pitty,	Ovid's Elegies			1.8.41
Her valiant lover followes without end.	Ovid's Elegies			1.9.10
Unmeete is beauty without use to wither.	Ovid's Elegies			2.3.14
So many men and maidens without love,	Ovid's Elegies			2.9.15
Live without love, so sweete ill is a maide.	Ovid's Elegies			2.9.26

WITHOUT (cont.)
Which without bloud-shed doth the pray inherit. . . Ovid's Elegies 2.12.6
And me with many, but yet me without murther, . . . Ovid's Elegies 2.12.27
If without battell selfe-wrought wounds annoy them, . . Ovid's Elegies 2.14.3
In heaven without thee would I not be fixt. . . . Ovid's Elegies 2.16.14
But without thee, although vine-planted ground/Conteines me, Ovid's Elegies 2.16.33
While without shame thou singst thy lewdnesse ditty. . Ovid's Elegies 3.1.22
Venus without me should be rusticall, ... Ovid's Elegies 3.1.43
Who, without feare, is chaste, is chast in sooth: . . . Ovid's Elegies 3.4.3
Where Mars his sonnes not without fault did breed, . . Ovid's Elegies 3.4.39
That may transport me without oares to rowe. . . . Ovid's Elegies 3.5.4
Homer without this shall be nothing worth. . . . Ovid's Elegies 3.7.28
But better things it gave, corne without ploughes, . . Ovid's Elegies 3.7.39
His broken bowe, his fire-brand without light. . . . Ovid's Elegies 3.8.8
Nor with thee, nor without thee can I live, ... Ovid's Elegies 3.10.39
Faire creature, let me speake without offence, . . . Hero and Leander 1.199
Without the sweet societie of men. . . . . . Hero and Leander 1.256
WITHSTAND
Be able to withstand and conquer him. . . . . 2Tamb 2.2.19 Gazell
If thou withstand the friends of Tamburlain. . . . 2Tamb 3.3.19 Techel
WITHSTOOD
Destroying what withstood his proud desires, . . . Lucan, First Booke 150
O would my proofes as vaine might be withstood, . . Ovid's Elegies 2.5.7
WITLESSE
Shall overway his wearie witlesse head, ... 1Tamb 2.1.46 Cosroe
And all conjoin'd to meet the witlesse King, . . . 1Tamb 2.1.64 Cosroe
My witlesse brother to the Christians lost: . . . 1Tamb 2.5.42 Cosroe
WITNES
Witnes the Gods, and witnes heaven and earth, . . . Dido 5.1.80 Aeneas
Heavens witnes me, with what a broken hart/And damned spirit I 2Tamb 5.3.206 Amyras
WITNESSE
And call'd the Gods to witnesse of my vow, . . . 1Tamb 1.2.234 Tamb
Leaving thy blood for witnesse of thy love. . . . 1Tamb 5.1.411 Arabia
Too deare a witnesse for such love my Lord. . . . 1Tamb 5.1.412 Zenoc
As memorable witnesse of our league. . . . . . . 2Tamb 1.1.145 Orcan
papers as our sacrifice/And witnesse of thy servants perjury. 2Tamb 2.2.46 Orcan
Thou know'st, and heaven can witnesse it is true, . . Jew 2.3.253 Barab
And witnesse that I dye a Christian. . . . . . Jew 3.6.40 Abigal
I know; and they shall witnesse with their lives. . . Jew 5.2.123 Barab
Witnesse the teares that Isabella sheds, ... Edw 1.4.164 Queene
Witnesse this hart, that sighing for thee breakes, . . Edw 1.4.165 Queene
And witnesse heaven how deere thou art to me. . . . Edw 1.4.167 Edward
Heavens can witnesse, I love none but you. . . . Edw 2.4.15 Queene
And beare him this, as witnesse of my love. . . . Edw 5.2.72 Queene
To witnesse to the world, that by thy meanes, . . . Edw 5.6.31 King
Be witnesse of my greefe and innocencie. . . . . Edw 5.6.102 King
<Have you any witnesse on't>? . . . . F 204 (HC258)A P Wagner
I have done, all Germany can witnesse, yea all the world: F1843 5.2.47 P Faust
Beare witnesse I gave them him. . . . . F App p.230 41 P Wagner
Beare witnesse I give them you againe. . . . . . F App p.230 42 P Clown
That might be urg'd to witnesse our false playing. . . Ovid's Elegies 2.8.8
The Gods, and their rich pompe witnesse with me, . . Ovid's Elegies 3.2.61
Be witnesse Crete (nor Crete doth all things feigne)/Crete Ovid's Elegies 3.9.19
Faith to the witnesse Joves praise doth apply, . . . Ovid's Elegies 3.9.23
And let the world be witnesse of the same? . . . Ovid's Elegies 3.13.12
WITNESSES
That knowe my wit, and can be witnesses: . . . . . 1Tamb 1.1.22 Mycet
we all are witnesses/That Bruno here was late delivered you, F1025 3.2.45 Raymnd
be witnesses to confirme what mine eares have heard reported, F App p.236 7 P Emper
WITS
Avaunt old witch and trouble not my wits. . . . . Dido 3.2.25 Venus
From jygging vaines of riming mother wits, . . . 1Tamb Prol.1 Prolog
Summon thy sences, call thy wits together: . . . Jew 1.1.178 Barab
A reaching thought will search his deepest wits, . . Jew 1.2.221 Barab
I must have wanton Poets, pleasant wits, ... Edw 1.1.51 Gavstn
Both Law and Physicke are for petty wits: . . . . F 134 1.1.106 Faust
Whose deepnesse doth intice such forward wits, . . . F2008 5.3.26 4Chor
Tis shame their wits should be more excelent. . . . Ovid's Elegies 1.10.26
Let base conceited wits admire vilde things, . . . Ovid's Elegies 1.15.35
their wits should them defend. . . . . Ovid's Elegies 3.4.2
And fruitfull wits that in aspiring <inaspiring> are, . Hero and Leander 1.477
WITTALL
And like a wittall thinke thee voyde of slight. . . Ovid's Elegies 3.13.30
WITTALLS
That can effect <affect> a foolish wittalls wife. . . Ovid's Elegies 2.19.46
WITTE
[His Arte excelld, although his witte was weake]. . . Ovid's Elegies 1.15.14
'Tis so: by my witte her abuse is growne. . . . . Ovid's Elegies 3.11.8
WITTED
and from Padua/Were wont to come rare witted Gentlemen, . Jew 3.1.7 Curtzn
WITTENBERG (See also WERTENBERG)
At <of> riper yeares to Wittenberg <Wertenberg> he went, . F 13 Prol.13 1Chor
And made the flowring pride of Wittenberg <Wertenberge> . F 141 1.1.113 Faust
I John Faustus of Wittenberg <Wertenberge>, Doctor, by these F 493 2.1.105 P Faust
In stead of Troy shall Wittenberg <Wertenberge> be sack't,/And F1776 5.1.103 Faust
O would I had never seene Wittenberg <Wertenberge>, never read F1841 5.2.45 P Faust
WITTENBERGE
And make swift Rhine, circle faire Wittenberge <Wertenberge>: F 116 1.1.88 Faust
The learned Faustus, fame of Wittenberge, ... F1165 4.1.11 Mrtino
As I was going to Wittenberge t'other day, with a loade of Hay, F1525 4.5.21 P Carter
WITTES
Poverty (who hatcht/Roomes greatest wittes) was loath'd, and al Lucan, First Booke 167
WITTOL (See WITTALL)

WITTY			
Are you the witty King of Persea?	1Tamb	2.4.23	Tamb
(Trust me) to give, it is a witty thing.	Ovid's Elegies	1.8.62	
I heere and there go witty with dishonour. . . .	Ovid's Elegies	3.7.8	
WIVES			
Some made your wives, and some your children)/Might have .	1Tamb	5.1.27	1Virgn
Yeeld up the towne, save our wives and children: . .	2Tamb	5.1.39	2Citzn
What shal be done with their wives and children my Lord. .	2Tamb	5.1.168	P Techel
I'le helpe to slay their children and their wives, . .	Jew	5.1.64	Barab
Their wives and children slaine, run up and downe, . .	Edw	2.2.180	Lncstr
We that have prettie wenches to our wives, . . .	Edw	2.5.102	Penbrk
[Tush] <No>, these are trifles, and meere old wives Tales.	F 524	2.1.136	Faust
Hector to armes went from his wives embraces, . . .	Ovid's Elegies	1.9.35	
By whom the husband his wives incest knewe. . . .	Ovid's Elegies	2.2.48	
WOE			
What? is not pietie exempt from woe?	Dido	1.1.79	Venus
And rest the map of weatherbeaten woe:	Dido	1.1.158	Achat
And wrought him mickle woe on sea and land, . . .	Dido	3.2.41	Juno
But rather will augment then ease my woe?	Dido	5.1.152	Dido
Oh woe is me, he never shootes but hits, ...	Ovid's Elegies	1.1.29	
WOES			
Hence fained weeds, unfained are my woes, ...	Edw	4.7.97	Edward
WOFUL			
Alight and weare a woful mourning weed.	2Tamb	1.1.44	Orcan
A woful change my Lord, that daunts our thoughts, . .	2Tamb	5.3.181	Therid
WOFULL			
A wofull tale bids Dido to unfould, ...	Dido	2.1.114	Aeneas
And wofull Dido by these blubbred cheekes, . . .	Dido	5.1.133	Dido
These comforts that you give our wofull queene, . .	Edw	4.2.72	Kent
There to salute the wofull Emperour.	F 986	3.2.6	Mephst
Or wofull Hector whom wilde jades did teare? . . .	Ovid's Elegies	2.1.32	
For wofull haires let piece-torne plumes abound, . .	Ovid's Elegies	2.6.5	
Her wofull bosome a warme shower did drowne. . . .	Ovid's Elegies	3.5.68	
Sad Elegia thy wofull haires unbinde:	Ovid's Elegies	3.8.3	
WOLD			
What Coward wold not fight for such a prize? . . .	1Tamb	3.3.100	Usumc
And thoughe I come not to keep possessione as I wold I mighte	Paris	ms15,p390	P Souldr
WOLFE (See also WOOLFE)			
For now we hould an old Wolfe by the eares, . . .	Edw	5.2.7	Mortmr
WOLLEN			
And Flamins last, with networke wollen vailes. . . .	Lucan, First Booke		603
WOLVES (See WOOLVES)			
WOMAN			
The woman that thou wild us entertaine, ...	Dido	4.2.11	Iarbus
Not farre from hence/There is a woman famoused for arts, .	Dido	5.1.275	Dido
Techelles, Drowne them all, man, woman, and child, . .	2Tamb	5.1.170	Tamb
What, woman, moane not for a little losse: . . .	Jew	1.2.226	Barab
O no my Lord, a woman only must/Partake the secrets of my heart.	P 675	13.19	Duchss
Only a Woman gets spoiles from a Man, ...	Ovid's Elegies	1.10.29	
by the pleasure/Which man and woman reape in equall measure?	Ovid's Elegies	1.10.36	
The man did grieve, the woman was defam'd. . . .	Ovid's Elegies	2.2.50	
This for her looks, that for her woman-hood: . . .	Ovid's Elegies	2.4.46	
The Laphithes, and the Centaures for a woman, . . .	Ovid's Elegies	2.12.19	
A woman forc'd the Troyanes new to enter/Warres, just Latinus,	Ovid's Elegies	2.12.21	
A woman against late-built Rome did send/The Sabine Fathers,	Ovid's Elegies	2.12.23	
What helpes it Woman to be free from warre? . . .	Ovid's Elegies	2.14.1	
You are deceav'd, I am no woman I.	Hero and Leander		2.192
WOMAN-HOOD			
This for her looks, that for her woman-hood: . . .	Ovid's Elegies	2.4.46	
WOMANS			
Though womans modesty should hale me backe, . . .	Jew	4.2.45	Curtzn
WOMBE			
But that I know they issued from thy wombe, . . .	2Tamb	1.3.33	Tamb
and thy seed/Shall issue crowned from their mothers wombe.	2Tamb	1.3.53	Tamb
Mor du, wert <were> not the fruit within thy wombe, . .	P 688	13.32	Guise
Or fathers throate; or womens groning wombe; . . .	Lucan, First Booke		378
Wilt thou thy wombe-inclosed off-spring wracke? . .	Ovid's Elegies	2.14.8	
In swelling wombe her twinnes had Ilia kilde? . . .	Ovid's Elegies	2.14.15	
And Scyllaes wombe mad raging dogs conceales. . . .	Ovid's Elegies	3.11.22	
WOMBE-INCLOSED			
Wilt thou thy wombe-inclosed off-spring wracke? . .	Ovid's Elegies	2.14.8	
WOMBES			
While rashly her wombes burthen she casts out, . . .	Ovid's Elegies	2.13.1	
WOMEN			
Women may wrong by priviledge of love:	Dido	3.3.25	Iarbus
Especially in women of [our] <your> yeares.-- . . .	Dido	4.5.28	Nurse
Techelles, women must be flatered.	1Tamb	1.2.107	Tamb
With whom (being women) I vouchsaft a league, . . .	2Tamb	1.3.193	Techel
Sometimes like women or unwedded Maides, ...	F 154	1.1.126	Valdes
I have heard that great bellyed women, do long for things, are	F1568	4.6.11	P Faust
that great bellied women do long for some dainties or other,	F App	p.242 5	P Faust
and ware robes/Too light for women; Poverty (who hatcht/Roomes	Lucan, First Booke		166
Yong men and women, shalt thou lead as thrall, . . .	Ovid's Elegies	1.2.27	
She drawes chast women to incontinence, ...	Ovid's Elegies	1.8.19	
Faire women play, shee's chast whom none will have, . .	Ovid's Elegies	1.8.43	
Whither runst thou, that men, and women, love not? . .	Ovid's Elegies	1.13.9	
By thy meanes women of their rest are bard, . . .	Ovid's Elegies	1.13.23	
What if a man with bond-women offend, ...	Ovid's Elegies	2.8.9	
For now I love two women equallie:	Ovid's Elegies	2.10.4	
On labouring women thou doest pitty take, ...	Ovid's Elegies	2.13.19	
Were I a God, I should give women leave, ...	Ovid's Elegies	3.3.43	
So use we women of strange nations stocke. . . .	Ovid's Elegies	3.4.34	
Like untun'd golden strings all women are, . . .	Hero and Leander		1.229

WOMEN (cont.)			
Lone women like to emptie houses perish.	Hero and Leander		1.242
Women receave perfection everie way.	Hero and Leander		1.268
Women are woon when they begin to jarre.	Hero and Leander		1.332
she wanting no excuse/To feed him with delaies, as women use:	Hero and Leander		1.426
All women are ambitious naturallie:	Hero and Leander		1.428
In such warres women use but halfe their strength.	Hero and Leander		2.296
WOMENS			
O love, O hate, O cruell womens hearts,	Dido	3.3.66	Iarbus
Now I remember those old womens words,	Jew	2.1.24	Barab
Where womens favors hung like labels downe.	Edw	2.2.187	Mortmr
Or fathers throate; or womens groning wombe;	Lucan, First Booke		378
parents/Keep back their sons, or womens teares their husbands;	Lucan, First Booke		503
Ist womens love my captive brest doth frie?	Ovid's Elegies		3.2.40
WON (See also WONE, WONST, WOON, WOONE, WUN)			
Won with thy words, and conquered with thy looks,	1Tamb	1.2.228	Therid
I long to see those crownes won by our swords,	1Tamb	3.3.98	Therid
His royall Crowne againe, so highly won.	1Tamb	3.3.219	Zenoc
conquer all the world/And you have won enough for me to keep.	2Tamb	1.3.68	Calyph
wel to heare both you/Have won a heape of honor in the field,	2Tamb	4.1.37	Calyph
Know that your words have won me at the last,	F 128	1.1.100	Faust
Might they have won whom civil broiles have slaine,	Lucan, First Booke		14
The soldiours having won the market place,	Lucan, First Booke		238
wonst thou France; Roome may be won/With farre lesse toile,	Lucan, First Booke		283
WONDER (See also WOONDER)			
And bring the Gods to wonder at the game:	Dido	1.1.18	Ganimd
As shall surpasse the wonder of our speech.	Dido	1.2.47	Serg
Lest I be made a wonder to the world.	Dido	3.1.96	Dido
And yet I wonder at this Argosie.	Jew	1.1.84	Barab
I wonder what the reason is.	Jew	4.2.32	P Ithimr
Wonder not at it, Sir, the heavens are just:	Jew	5.1.55	Govnr
I wonder how it could be conquer'd thus?	Jew	5.3.12	Calym
The winde is good, I wonder why he stayes,	Edw	2.2.1	Edward
I wonder how he scapt.	Edw	2.4.22	Lncstr
Gurney, I wonder the king dies not,	Edw	5.5.1	Matrvs
I wonder what's become of Faustus that/Was wont to make our	F 194	1.2.1	1Schol
The wonder of the world for Magick Art;	F1166	4.1.12	Mrtino
Wonder of men, renown'd Magitian,	F1204	4.1.50	Emper
That we may wonder at their excellence.	F1234	4.1.80	Emper
in your head for shame, let not all the world wonder at you.	F1292	4.1.138	P Faust
This makes me wonder more then all the rest, that at this time	F1578	4.6.21	P Duke
I wonder what he meanes, if death were nie, he would not	F1677	5.1.4	P Wagner
may exhort the wise/Onely to wonder at unlawfull things,	F2007	5.3.25	4Chor
this makes me wonder above the rest, that being in the dead	F App	p.242 16	P Duke
WONDERFULL			
I speake old Poets wonderfull inventions,	Ovid's Elegies		3.5.17
WONDERS			
The Mother Queene workes wonders for my sake,	P 133	2.76	Guise
who comes to see/What wonders by blacke spels may compast be.	F1198	4.1.44	Mrtino
and what wonders I have done, all Germany can witnesse, yea all	F1842	5.2.46	P Faust
WONDRED			
They wondred how you durst with so much wealth/Trust such a	Jew	1.1.79	1Merch
[As they admirde and wondred at his wit].	F1148	3.3.61A	3Chor
WONDRING			
Wondring if any walked without light.	Ovid's Elegies		1.6.10
raught/Ill waies by rough seas wondring waves first taught,	Ovid's Elegies		2.11.2
WONDROUS (See also WOONDROUS)			
can comprehend/The wondrous Architecture of the world:	1Tamb	2.7.22	Tamb
Even from this day to Platoes wondrous yeare,	1Tamb	4.2.96	Tamb
Are wondrous; and indeed doe no man good:	Jew	2.3.82	Barab
And be eterniz'd for some wondrous cure:	F 43	1.1.15	Faust
O wondrous sight:	F1276	4.1.122	Emper
Sir, so wondrous well,/As in all humble dutie, I do yeeld	F1817	5.2.21	Wagner
once admired/For wondrous knowledge in our Germane schooles,	F1998	5.3.16	2Schol
And of such wondrous beautie her bereft:	Hero and Leander		1.48
But you are faire (aye me) so wondrous faire,	Hero and Leander		1.287
WONE			
Beleeve me Hero, honour is not wone,	Hero and Leander		1.281
Now he her favour and good will had wone.	Hero and Leander		2.54
WONNE			
Not to be wonne by any conquering Prince:	F 783	3.1.5	Faust
how they had wonne by prowesse such exploits, gote such riches,	F App	p.236 19	P Emper
And shame to spare life which being lost is wonne.	Lucan, First Booke		458
Who should have Priams wealthy substance wonne,	Ovid's Elegies		2.14.13
We toucht the walles, Camillus wonne by thee.	Ovid's Elegies		3.12.2
WONST			
In ten yeares wonst thou France; Roome may be won/With farre	Lucan, First Booke		283
WONT (See also WOONT)			
Here she was wont to sit, but saving ayre/Is nothing here, and	Dido	2.1.13	Achat
And let me lodge where I was wont to lye.	Jew	1.2.333	Abigal
and from Padua/Were wont to come rare witted Gentlemen,	Jew	3.1.7	Curtzn
He was not wont to call me Barabas.	Jew	4.3.3	Barab
become of Faustus that/Was wont to make our schooles ring,	F 195	1.2.2	1Schol
who were wont/In large spread heire to exceed the rest of	Lucan, First Booke		438
Which wont to run their course through empty night/At noone day	Lucan, First Booke		534
Behold Cypassis wont to dresse thy head,	Ovid's Elegies		2.7.17
Knowest not this head a helme was wont to beare,	Ovid's Elegies		3.7.13
WONTED			
Bee not to see with wonted eyes inclinde,	Ovid's Elegies		1.14.37
WOO (See also WOOE)			
Shee pleas'd me, soone I sent, and did her woo,	Ovid's Elegies		2.2.5
WOO'D			
Wherewith my husband woo'd me yet a maide,	Dido	3.4.63	Dido

WOO'D (cont.)			
And then he woo'd with kisses, and at last,	Hero and Leander	1.404	
WOOD			
Stoute friend Achates, doest thou know this wood?	Dido	3.3.50	Aeneas
As others did, by running to the wood.	Dido	4.1.30	Anna
Is this the wood that grew in Carthage plaines,	Dido	4.4.136	Dido
And yet I blame thee not, thou art but wood.	Dido	4.4.143	Dido
Standard round, that stood/As bristle-pointed as a thorny wood.	1Tamb	4.1.27	2Msngr
I'le sacrifice her on a pile of wood.	Jew	2.3.52	Barab
Through which the wood peer'd, headles darts, olde swords/With	Lucan, First Booke	244	
Which gave such light, as twincles in a wood,	Ovid's Elegies	1.5.4	
funerall wood be flying/And thou the waxe stuft full with notes	Ovid's Elegies	1.12.7	
As evill wood throwne in the high-waies lie,	Ovid's Elegies	1.12.13	
Elisium hath a wood of holme trees black,	Ovid's Elegies	2.6.49	
The Parrat into wood receiv'd with these,	Ovid's Elegies	2.6.57	
addst thou starres to heaven, leaves to greene woods <wood>,	Ovid's Elegies	2.10.13	
An old wood, stands uncut of long yeares space,	Ovid's Elegies	3.1.1	
Or songs amazing wilde beasts of the wood?	Ovid's Elegies	3.8.22	
There stands an old wood with thick trees darke clouded,	Ovid's Elegies	3.12.7	
Under whose shade the Wood-gods love to bee.	Hero and Leander	1.156	
WOODDEN			
Prepared stands to wracke their woodden walles,	Dido	1.1.67	Venus
'faith Ile drinke a health to thy woodden leg for that word.	F1627	4.6.70	P HrsCsr
My woodden leg? what dost thou meane by that?	F1628	4.6.71	Faust
No faith, not much upon a woodden leg.	F1631	4.6.74	Faust
WOODDIE			
In wooddie groves ist meete that Ceres Raigne,	Ovid's Elegies	1.1.13	
WOODEN			
me thinkes you should have a wooden bedfellow of one of 'em.	F1654	4.6.97	P Carter
WOOD-GODS			
Under whose shade the Wood-gods love to bee.	Hero and Leander	1.156	
WOODS			
shall have leaves and windfall bowes enow/Neere to these woods,	Dido	1.1.173	Aeneas
We two will goe a hunting in the woods,	Dido	3.1.174	Dido
This day they both a hunting forth will ride/Into these woods,	Dido	3.2.88	Juno
The woods are wide, and we have store of game:	Dido	3.3.6	Dido
And all the woods Eliza to resound:	Dido	4.2.10	Iarbus
hunters in the chace/Of savage beastes amid the desart woods.	1Tamb	4.3.57	Capol
Where Woods and Forrests goe in goodly greene,	Jew	4.2.93	Ithimr
Which in the woods doe holde their synagogue:	P 502	9.21	Guise
Take thou this other, dragge him through the woods,	F1410	4.2.86	Faust
I have a Castle joyning neere these woods,	F1452	4.3.22	Benvol
When all the woods about stand bolt up-right,	Lucan, First Booke	143	
Woods turn'd to ships; both land and sea against us:	Lucan, First Booke	307	
In unfeld woods, and sacred groves you dwell,	Lucan, First Booke	448	
Leaving the woods, lodge in the streetes of Rome.	Lucan, First Booke	558	
of armes was heard, in untrod woods/Shrill voices schright,	Lucan, First Booke	567	
I am no halfe horse, nor in woods I dwell,	Ovid's Elegies	1.4.9	
Horse freed from service range abroad the woods.	Ovid's Elegies	2.9.22	
addst thou starres to heaven, leaves to greene woods <wood>,	Ovid's Elegies	2.10.13	
Thou shalt admire no woods or Citties there,	Ovid's Elegies	2.11.11	
Who covets lawfull things takes leaves from woods,	Ovid's Elegies	2.19.31	
Jove throwes downe woods, and Castles with his fire:	Ovid's Elegies	3.3.35	
But woods and groves keepe your faults undetected.	Ovid's Elegies	3.5.84	
The graine-rich goddesse in high woods did stray,	Ovid's Elegies	3.9.35	
Which by the wild boare in the woods was shorne.	Ovid's Elegies	3.9.40	
By whom disclosd, she in the high woods tooke,	Ovid's Elegies	3.12.19	
Woods, or steepie mountaine yeeldes.	Passionate Shepherd	4	
WOOE			
My lords, I will not over wooe your honors,	Edw	2.5.86	Penbrk
WOOED			
Oft couzen me, oft being wooed say nay.	Ovid's Elegies	2.19.20	
Why being a vestall am I wooed to wed,	Ovid's Elegies	3.5.75	
WOOER			
Was not defilde by any gallant wooer.	Ovid's Elegies	3.4.24	
WOOERS			
know that thou of all my wooers/(And yet have I had many	Dido	3.1.11	Dido
Or Layis of a thousand [wooers] <lovers> [sped] <spread>.	Ovid's Elegies	1.5.12	
WOOING			
Well, if he come a wooing he shall speede,	Dido	4.5.36	Nurse
WOOL (See also WOLLEN)			
Thus, as the Gods creepe on with feete of wool,	F 877	3.1.99	Pope
WOOLFE			
Against the Woolfe that angrie Themis sent,	1Tamb	4.3.5	Souldn
WOOLL			
A gowne made of the finest wooll,	Passionate Shepherd	13	
WOOLVES			
For hees a lambe, encompassed by Woolves,	Edw	5.1.41	Edward
From dog-kept flocks come preys to woolves most gratefull.	Ovid's Elegies	1.8.56	
WOON			
Wherewith she yeelded, that was woon before.	Hero and Leander	1.330	
Women are woon when they begin to jarre.	Hero and Leander	1.332	
Maids are not woon by brutish force and might,	Hero and Leander	1.419	
Seeming not woon, yet woon she was at length,	Hero and Leander	2.295	
WOONDER			
One thought, one grace, one woonder at the least,	1Tamb	5.1.172	Tamb
Wounding the world with woonder and with love,	2Tamb	2.4.82	Tamb
Such as the world would woonder to behold:	Hero and Leander	1.34	
WOONDROUS			
The face and personage of a woondrous man:	1Tamb	2.1.32	Cosroe
I could attaine it with a woondrous ease,	1Tamb	2.5.77	Tamb
For honor of my woondrous victories.	2Tamb	4.1.205	Tamb
Might find as many woondrous myracles,	2Tamb	4.2.85	Therid

WOONE			
So soone to have woone Scotland,	Edw	2.2.194	Lncstr
WOONT			
To see our neighbours that were woont to quake/And tremble at	1Tamb	1.1.11	Cosroe
Which with thy beauty thou wast woont to light,	2Tamb	4.2.16	Therid
Were woont to guide the seaman in the deepe,	2Tamb	5.1.65	Tamb
WOONTED			
That worke such trouble to your woonted rest:	1Tamb	3.2.3	Agidas
Now in defiance of that woonted love,	2Tamb	5.3.10	Therid
WOORD			
Send woord, Orcanes of Natolia/Confirm'd this league beyond	2Tamb	1.1.148	Orcan
WOORDES			
You see my Lord, what woorking woordes he hath.	1Tamb	2.3.25	Therid
WOORDS			
Ah were I now but halfe so eloquent/To paint in woords, what	2Tamb	1.2.10	Callap
If woords might serve, our voice hath rent the aire,	2Tamb	2.4.121	Therid
WOORKE			
And make her daintie fingers fall to woorke.	1Tamb	3.3.181	Ebea
WOORKING			
You see my Lord, what woorking woordes he hath.	1Tamb	2.3.25	Therid
WOORSE			
The more he is restrain'd, the woorse he fares,	Hero and Leander		2.145
WOORTH			
Thy person is more woorth to Tamburlaine,	1Tamb	1.2.90	Tamb
To make him famous in accomplisht woorth:	1Tamb	2.1.34	Cosroe
with freatting, and then she will not bee woorth the eating.	1Tamb	4.4.50	P Tamb
Thy woorth sweet friend is far above my guifts,	Edw	1.1.161	Edward
WOORTHS			
For both their woorths wil equall him no more.	2Tamb	5.3.253	Amyras
WOORTHY			
To injure or suppresse your woorthy tytle.	1Tamb	1.1.183	Ortyg
Thou art not woorthy to be worshipped,	2Tamb	5.1.189	Tamb
WORD (See also WOORD)			
Each word she sayes will then containe a Crowne,	Dido	4.3.53	Aeneas
But if they offer word or violence,	1Tamb	1.2.142	Tamb
Such another word, and I will have thee executed.	1Tamb	2.4.30	Mycet
my Lord, if I should goe, would you bee as good as your word?	2Tamb	1.2.62	P Almeda
Daughter, a word more; kisse him, speake him faire,	Jew	2.3.234	Barab
My Factor sends me word a Merchant's fled/That owes me for a	Jew	2.3.243	Barab
Mathias, as thou lov'st me, not a word.	Jew	2.3.277	Barab
Stay her,--but let her not speake one word more.	Jew	2.3.323	Barab
went in at dores/You had bin stab'd, but not a word on't now;	Jew	2.3.338	Barab
But not a word to any of your Covent.	Jew	4.1.112	Barab
now I to keepe my word,/And give my goods and substance to your	Jew	4.1.189	Barab
Not a wise word, only gave me a nod, as who shold say, Is it	Jew	4.2.12	P Pilia
I'le send by word of mouth now; Bid him deliver thee a thousand	Jew	4.4.74	P Ithimr
Now Selim-Calymath, returne me word/That thou wilt come, and I	Jew	5.5.11	Barab
I trust thy word, take what I promis'd thee.	Jew	5.5.43	Govnr
To think a word of such a simple sound,	P 125	2.68	Guise
Cheefely since under safetie of our word,	P 209	4.7	Charls
I am a preacher of the word of God,	P 341	5.68	Lorein
O good my Lord, let me but speak a word.	P 399	7.39	Ramus
And true profession of his holy word:	P 586	11.51	Navrre
Agent for England, send thy mistres word,	P1194	22.56	King
All stomack him, but none dare speake a word.	Edw	1.2.26	Lncstr
May with one word, advaunce us while we live:	Edw	2.1.9	Spencr
never was Plantagenet/False of his word, and therefore trust we	Edw	2.3.12	Mortmr
And sends you word, he knowes that die he shall,	Edw	2.5.38	Arundl
Why I say, let him go on Penbrookes word.	Edw	2.5.90	Lncstr
And neither give him kinde word, nor good looke.	Edw	5.2.55	Mortmr
This word Damnation, terrifies not me <him>,	F 286	1.3.58	Faust
not speake a word more for a Kings ransome <an other worde>,	F 669	2.2.118	P Pride
I'le not speake <an other word for a King's raunsome>.	F 706	(HC264)A	P Sloth
I'le not speake <a word more for a kings ransome>.	F 706	(HC264)B	P Sloth
I'le not speake [an other] word.	F 706	2.2.158	P Sloth
why thou canst not tell ne're a word on't.	F 731	2.3.10	P Dick
Away and bring us word <again> with speed.	F 888	3.1.110	Pope
You brought us word even now, it was decreed,	F1019	3.2.39	Pope
'faith Ile drinke a health to thy woodden leg for that word.	F1627	4.6.70	P HrsCsr
a word with you, I must yet have a goblet payde from you ere	F App	p.234 7	P Vintnr
Let this word, come, alone the tables fill.	Ovid's Elegies		1.11.24
And yet at everie word shee turn'd aside,	Hero and Leander		1.195
nor would vouchsafe so much/As one poore word, their hate to	Hero and Leander		1.384
WORDE			
My lord of Cornewall now, at every worde,	Edw	1.2.17	Lncstr
Souldiers, let me but talke to him one worde.	Edw	5.3.53	Kent
Sonne, be content, I dare not speake a worde.	Edw	5.4.96	Queene
not speake a word more for a Kings ransome <an other worde>,	F 670	2.2.119	P Pride
That with one worde hath nigh himselfe undone,	Ovid's Elegies		1.13.20
WORDES			
I would intreat you to speak but three wise wordes.	1Tamb	2.4.25	Tamb
O wordes of power to kill a thousand men.	P1126	21.20	Dumain
I, I, these wordes of his move me as much,	Edw	1.1.39	Gavstn
Kinde wordes, and mutuall talke, makes our greefe greater,	Edw	1.4.133	Edward
If he be straunge and not regarde my wordes,	Edw	2.4.64	Queene
I would those wordes proceeded from your heart.	Edw	5.2.100	Kent
Awaye with her, her wordes inforce these teares,	Edw	5.6.85	King
Forbeare sweet wordes, and be your sport unpleasant.	Ovid's Elegies		1.4.66
With lofty wordes stout Tragedie (she sayd)/Why treadst me	Ovid's Elegies		3.1.35
WORDS			
Who shall confirme my words with further deedes.	Dido	1.2.43	Iarbus
on the sand/Assayd with honey words to turne them backe:	Dido	2.1.137	Aeneas
O th'inchaunting words of that base slave,	Dido	2.1.161	Aeneas

WORDS (cont.)

That love is childish which consists in words.	Dido	3.1.10	Iarbus
This was an Orator, and thought by words/To compasse me, but yet	Dido	3.1.155	Dido
Fie Venus, that such causeles words of wrath,	Dido	3.2.26	Juno
More then melodious are these words to me,	Dido	3.2.62	Juno
We two will talke alone, what words be these?	Dido	3.3.12	Iarbus
These words proceed not from Aeneas heart.	Dido	5.1.102	Dido
These words are poyson to poore Didos soule,	Dido	5.1.111	Dido
If words might move me I were overcome.	Dido	5.1.154	Aeneas
And wilt thou not be mov'd with Didos words?	Dido	5.1.155	Dido
Go, stout Theridamas, thy words are swords,	1Tamb	1.1.74	Mycet
These are his words, Meander set them downe.	1Tamb	1.1.94	Mycet
To be reveng'd for these contemptuous words.	1Tamb	1.1.100	Mycet
Won with thy words, and conquered with thy looks,	1Tamb	1.2.228	Therid
Thy words assure me of kind successe:	1Tamb	2.3.60	Cosroe
[Agidas], leave to wound me with these words:	1Tamb	3.2.35	Zenoc
Those words of favour, and those comfortings,	1Tamb	3.2.62	Agidas
He needed not with words confirme my feare,	1Tamb	3.2.92	Agidas
For words are vaine where working tooles present/The naked	1Tamb	3.2.93	Agidas
Leave words and let them feele your lances pointes,	1Tamb	3.3.91	Argier
I speake it, and my words are oracles.	1Tamb	3.3.102	Tamb
And manage words with her as we will armes.	1Tamb	3.3.131	Tamb
Thou wilt repent these lavish words of thine,	1Tamb	3.3.172	Zenoc
we intreate/Grace to our words and pitie to our lookes,	1Tamb	5.1.51	2Virgn
Which into words no vertue can digest:	1Tamb	5.1.173	Tamb
Accursed Bajazeth, whose words of ruth,	1Tamb	5.1.270	Bajzth
may poure foorth my soule into thine armes,/With words of love:	1Tamb	5.1.280	Bajzth
These words assure me boy, thou art my sonne,	2Tamb	1.3.58	Tamb
For she is dead? thy words doo pierce my soule.	2Tamb	2.4.125	Tamb
With furious words and frowning visages,	2Tamb	5.1.78	Tamb
Ah good my Lord, leave these impatient words,	2Tamb	5.3.54	Therid
And weigh not men, and therefore not mens words.	Jew	Prol.8	Machvl
Our words will but increase his extasie.	Jew	1.2.210	1Jew
Now I remember those old womens words,	Jew	2.1.24	Barab
then listen to my words,/And I will teach [thee] that shall	Jew	2.3.167	Barab
But doe you thinke that I beleeve his words?	Jew	4.1.105	Barab
I'le feast you, lodge you, give you faire words,	Jew	4.1.126	Barab
Oh good words, Sir, and send it you, were best see; there's his	Jew	4.3.24	P Pilia
Here's many words but no crownes; the crownes.	Jew	4.3.46	P Pilia
Governor, good words, be not so furious;	Jew	5.2.61	Barab
Him as a childe I dayly winne with words,	P 130	2.73	Guise
Even for your words that have incenst me so,	P 767	15.25	Guise
These words revive my thoughts and comforts me,	P1209	22.71	Navrre
Ah words that make me surfet with delight:	Edw	1.1.3	Gavstn
Well Mortimer, ile make thee rue these words,	Edw	1.1.91	Edward
Cease brother, for I cannot brooke these words:	Edw	1.1.160	Edward
I, if words will serve, if not, I must.	Edw	1.2.83	Mortmr
Rend not my hart with thy too piercing words,	Edw	1.4.117	Edward
Wherein my lord, have I deservd these words?	Edw	1.4.163	Queene
Feare not, the queens words cannot alter him.	Edw	1.4.233	Penbrk
Can you in words make showe of amitie,	Edw	2.2.32	Edward
Yet have I words left to expresse my joy:	Edw	2.2.60	Gavstn
Warwicke, these words do ill beseeme thy years.	Edw	2.2.94	Kent
Informeth us, by letters and by words,	Edw	3.1.61	Queene
A king to beare these words and proud commaunds.	Edw	4.7.71	Abbot
Leister, if gentle words might comfort me,	Edw	5.1.5	Edward
But amplifie his greefe with bitter words.	Edw	5.2.65	Mortmr
Thinke not that I am frighted with thy words,	Edw	5.6.27	King
Know that your words have won me at the last,	F 128	1.1.100	Faust
[Yet not your words onely, but mine owne fantasie],	F 130	1.1.102A	Faust
Valdes, first let him know the words of Art,	F 185	1.1.157	Cornel
I see there's vertue in my heavenly words.	F 255	1.3.27	Faust
[Did gratulate his safetie with kinde words],	F1143	3.3.56A	3Chor
These gracious words, most royall Carolus,	F1217	4.1.63	Faust
No words:	F1362	4.2.38	Benvol
Be silent then, for danger is in words.	F1696	5.1.23	Faust
I feele thy words to comfort my distressed soule,	F1735	5.1.62	Faust
My feare transcends my words,/Yet more will happen then I can	Lucan, First Booke		633
Words without voyce shall on my eye browes sit,	Ovid's Elegies		1.4.19
Giving the windes my words running in thine eare?	Ovid's Elegies		1.6.42
these words she sayd/While closely hid betwixt two dores I	Ovid's Elegies		1.8.21
Nor let my words be with the windes hence blowne,	Ovid's Elegies		1.8.106
committed/And then with sweete words to my Mistrisse fitted.	Ovid's Elegies		1.12.22
Quickly soft words hard dores wide open strooke.	Ovid's Elegies		2.1.22
While I speake some fewe, yet fit words be idle.	Ovid's Elegies		2.2.2
And words that seem'd for certaine markes to be.	Ovid's Elegies		2.5.20
Thou spokest thy words so well with stammering sound.	Ovid's Elegies		2.6.24
The Parrat given me, the farre [worlds] <words> best choice.	Ovid's Elegies		2.6.38
Yet words in thy benummed palate rung,	Ovid's Elegies		2.6.47
But me let crafty damsells words deceive,	Ovid's Elegies		2.9.43
But if my words with winged stormes hence slip,	Ovid's Elegies		2.11.33
But in the ayre let these words come to nought,	Ovid's Elegies		2.14.41
Maides words more vaine and light then falling leaves,	Ovid's Elegies		2.16.45
To please me, what faire termes and sweet words ha's shee,	Ovid's Elegies		2.19.17
What gate thy stately words cannot unlocke,	Ovid's Elegies		3.1.45
And with sweete words cause deafe rockes to have loved <moned>,	Ovid's Elegies		3.6.58
Leave thy once powerfull words, and flatteries,	Ovid's Elegies		3.10.31
Would I my words would any credit beare.	Ovid's Elegies		3.11.20
Nor have their words true histories pretence,	Ovid's Elegies		3.11.42
Forbare no wanton words you there would speake,	Ovid's Elegies		3.13.25
And I will trust your words more then mine eies.	Ovid's Elegies		3.13.46
And being justified by two words, thinke/The cause acquits you	Ovid's Elegies		3.13.49
And as shee spake those words, came somewhat nere him.	Hero and Leander		1.180

WORDS (cont.)			
to display/Loves holy fire, with words, with sighs and teares,	Hero and Leander		1.193
I would my rude words had the influence,	Hero and Leander		1.200
My words shall be as spotlesse as my youth,	Hero and Leander		1.207
Heroes lookes yeelded, but her words made warre,	Hero and Leander		1.331
Aye me, such words as these should I abhor,	Hero and Leander		1.339
WORE			
While Juno Io keepes when hornes she wore,	Ovid's Elegies		2.19.29
Then did the robe or garment which she wore <more>,	Ovid's Elegies		3.6.40
WORK (See also WOORKE)			
send for them/To do the work my chamber maid disdaines.	1Tamb	3.3.188	Anippe
And now will work a refuge to our lives,	2Tamb	5.1.25	1Citzn
To work the way to bring this thing to passe:	P 649	12.62	QnMoth
WORKE			
But bright Ascanius, beauties better worke,	Dido	1.1.96	Jupitr
In which unhappie worke was I employd,	Dido	2.1.169	Aeneas
To worke my downfall and untimely end.	1Tamb	2.7.6	Cosroe
That worke such trouble to your woonted rest:	1Tamb	3.2.3	Agidas
For now her mariage time shall worke us rest.	1Tamb	5.1.504	Techel
And worke revenge upon these Infidels:	2Tamb	2.1.13	Fredrk
Come downe thy selfe and worke a myracle,	2Tamb	5.1.188	Tamb
And with her let it worke like Borgias wine,	Jew	3.4.98	Barab
Pay me my wages for my worke is done.	Jew	3.4.115	Ithimr
To worke my peace, this I confesse to thee;	Jew	3.6.31	Abigal
I hope the poyson'd flowers will worke anon.	Jew	5.1.43	Barab
For he that did by treason worke our fall,	Jew	5.5.109	Govnr
And by that priviledge to worke upon,	P 121	2.64	Guise
It will be hard for us to worke their deaths.	P 508	9.27	QnMoth
For the late nights worke which my Lord of Guise/Did make in	P 514	9.33	QnMoth
goe sirra, worke no more,/Till this our Coronation day be past:	P 623	12.36	King
that of it self was hote enoughe to worke/thy Just degestione	Paris	ms26,p391	Guise
Tis hard for us to worke his overthrow.	Edw	1.4.262	Mortmr
Weel make quick worke, commend me to your maister/My friend,	Edw	2.6.12	Warwck
You, and such as you are, have made wise worke in England.	Edw	4.7.114	P Rice
rest, because we heare/That Edmund casts to worke his libertie,	Edw	5.2.58	Mortmr
To ease his greefe, and worke his libertie:	Edw	5.2.71	Queene
And roof't aloft with curious worke in gold.	F 798	3.1.20	Faust
That underprop <underprops> the ground-worke of the same:	F 812	3.1.34	Mephst
If we should follow him to worke revenge,	F1448	4.3.18	Benvol
Now <Since> we have seene the pride of Natures worke <workes>,	F1702	5.1.29	1Schol
Rafe, keepe out, for I am about a roaring peece of worke.	F App	p.233 12	P Robin
When in this [workes] <worke> first verse I trod aloft,	Ovid's Elegies		1.1.21
Saying, Poet heers a worke beseeming thee.	Ovid's Elegies		1.1.28
When pleasure mov'd us to our sweetest worke.	Ovid's Elegies		1.4.48
And crowing Cocks poore soules to worke awake.	Ovid's Elegies		1.6.66
to passe/The souldiours, and poore lovers worke ere was.	Ovid's Elegies		1.9.28
But being present, might that worke the best,	Ovid's Elegies		2.8.17
If such a worke thy mother had assayed.	Ovid's Elegies		2.14.20
And thousand kisses gives, that worke my harmes:	Ovid's Elegies		2.18.10
To finde, what worke my muse might move, I strove.	Ovid's Elegies		3.1.6
Some greater worke will urge me on at last.	Ovid's Elegies		3.1.70
The worke of Poets lasts Troyes labours fame,	Ovid's Elegies		3.8.29
And Phoebus had forsooke my worke begun.	Ovid's Elegies		3.11.18
A worke, that after my death, heere shall dwell	Ovid's Elegies		3.14.20
WORKES			
Ile make the Clowdes dissolve their watrie workes,	Dido	3.2.90	Juno
The Mother Queene workes wonders for my sake,	P 133	2.76	Guise
the fatall poyson/Workes within my head, my brain pan breakes,	P 185	3.20	OldQn
[Sorbonests] <thorbonest>/Attribute as much unto their workes,	P 412	7.52	Ramus
O the fatall poyson workes within my brest,	P1221	22.83	King
And live and die in Aristotles workes.	F 33	1.1.5	Faust
beare wise Bacons, and [Abanus] <Albanus> <Albertus> workes,	F 181	1.1.153	Valdes
Now <Since> we have seene the pride of Natures worke <workes>,	F1702	5.1.29	1Schol
in Europe for nothing, thats one of my conjuring workes.	F App	p.234 24	P Robin
When in this [workes] <worke> first verse I trod aloft,	Ovid's Elegies		1.1.21
Let thy tongue flatter, while thy minde harme-workes:	Ovid's Elegies		1.8.103
Long hast thou loyterd, greater workes compile.	Ovid's Elegies		3.1.24
Tibullus, thy workes Poet, and thy fame,	Ovid's Elegies		3.8.5
WORKING			
For words are vaine where working tooles present/The naked	1Tamb	3.2.93	Agidas
WORKMANSHIP			
Whose workmanship both man and beast deceaves.	Hero and Leander		1.20
WORKS			
It works remorse of conscience in me,	2Tamb	4.1.28	Calyph
and read/Sybillas secret works, and [wash] <washt> their saint	Lucan, First Booke		599
And tearmes <termst> [my] <our> works fruits of an idle quill?	Ovid's Elegies		1.15.2
WORLD			
Hermes no more shall shew the world his wings,	Dido	1.1.38	Jupitr
When as the waves doe threat our Chrystall world,	Dido	1.1.75	Venus
good heaven/We breathe as now, and what this world is calde,	Dido	1.1.198	Aeneas
Who driven by warre from forth my native world,	Dido	1.1.217	Aeneas
O sister, were you Empresse of the world,	Dido	3.1.69	Anna
Lest I be made a wonder to the world.	Dido	3.1.96	Dido
The rest are such as all the world well knowes,	Dido	3.1.165	Dido
When as she meanes to maske the world with clowdes.	Dido	4.1.6	Iarbus
Not all the world can take thee from mine armes,	Dido	4.4.61	Dido
And all the world calles me a second Helen,	Dido	5.1.144	Dido
None in the world shall have my love but thou:	Dido	5.1.290	Dido
And make Aeneas famous through the world,	Dido	5.1.293	Dido
Threatning the world with high astounding tearms/And scourging	1Tamb	Prol.5	Prolog
And meanes to be a terrour to the world,	1Tamb	1.2.38	Tamb
do but joine with me/And we will triumph over all the world.	1Tamb	1.2.173	Tamb
shall confesse/Theise are the men that all the world admires.	1Tamb	1.2.223	Usumc

WORLD (cont.)

A pearle more worth, then all the world is plaste:	1Tamb	2.1.12	Menaph
Should make the world subdued to Tamburlaine.	1Tamb	2.1.30	Menaph
And rid the world of those detested troopes?	1Tamb	2.2.19	Meandr
The world will strive with hostes of men at armes,	1Tamb	2.3.13	Tamb
we wish for ought/The world affoords in greatest noveltie,	1Tamb	2.5.73	Tamb
can comprehend/The wondrous Architecture of the world:	1Tamb	2.7.22	Tamb
As great commander of this Easterne world,	1Tamb	2.7.62	Tamb
The high and highest Monarke of the world,	1Tamb	3.1.26	Bajzth
The onely feare and terrour of the world,	1Tamb	3.3.45	Tamb
Thy fall shall make me famous through the world:	1Tamb	3.3.83	Tamb
As if thou wert the Empresse of the world.	1Tamb	3.3.125	Tamb
Not all the world shall ransom Bajazeth.	1Tamb	3.3.232	Tamb
And by this meanes Ile win the world at last.	1Tamb	3.3.260	Tamb
That will maintaine it against a world of Kings.	1Tamb	4.2.81	Tamb
Were in that citie all the world contain'd,	1Tamb	4.2.121	Tamb
Not for the world Zenocrate, if I have sworn:	1Tamb	4.2.125	Tamb
In sounding through the world his partiall praise.	1Tamb	4.3.49	Arabia
those blind Geographers/That make a triple region in the world,	1Tamb	4.4.76	Tamb
Intending so to terrifie the world:	1Tamb	5.1.15	Govnr
For whome the Powers divine have made the world,	1Tamb	5.1.76	1Virgn
Shal give the world to note, for all my byrth,	1Tamb	5.1.188	Tamb
That all the world will see and laugh to scorne,	1Tamb	5.1.252	Zabina
And makes my deeds infamous through the world.	1Tamb	5.1.391	Zenoc
Meaning to make me Generall of the world,	1Tamb	5.1.451	Tamb
For Tamburlaine takes truce with al the world.	1Tamb	5.1.529	Tamb
Trapt with the wealth and riches of the world,	2Tamb	1.1.43	Orcan
Yet stout Orcanes, Prorex of the world,	2Tamb	1.1.45	Gazell
He brings a world of people to the field,	2Tamb	1.1.67	Orcan
By him that made the world and sav'd my soule,	2Tamb	1.1.133	Sgsmnd
Whose glorious body when he left the world,	2Tamb	1.1.139	Orcan
Born to be Monarch of the Western world:	2Tamb	1.2.3	Callap
shine as bright/As that faire vail that covers all the world:	2Tamb	1.2.50	Callap
And every one Commander of a world.	2Tamb	1.3.8	Tamb
As all the world shall tremble at their view.	2Tamb	1.3.57	Celeb
Be thou the scourge and terrour of the world.	2Tamb	1.3.60	Tamb
Be tearm'd the scourge and terrour of the world?	2Tamb	1.3.62	Amyras
Be al a scourge and terror to the world,	2Tamb	1.3.63	Tamb
They are enough to conquer all the world/And you have won	2Tamb	1.3.67	Calyph
Arch-Monarke of the world, I offer here,	2Tamb	1.3.114	Therid
Whose lookes make this inferiour world to quake,	2Tamb	1.3.139	Techel
For halfe the world shall perish in this fight:	2Tamb	1.3.171	Tamb
And glut us with the dainties of the world,	2Tamb	1.3.220	Tamb
Wounding the world with woonder and with love,	2Tamb	2.4.82	Tamb
As all the world should blot our dignities/Out of the booke of	2Tamb	3.1.18	Callap
And for their power, ynow to win the world.	2Tamb	3.1.43	Orcan
Forbids the world to build it up againe.	2Tamb	3.2.18	Calyph
To shew her beautie, which the world admyr'd,	2Tamb	3.2.26	Tamb
Harkening when he shall bid them plague the world.	2Tamb	3.4.60	Therid
Gods great lieftenant over all the world:	2Tamb	3.5.2	2Msngr
The Emperour of the world, and earthly God,	2Tamb	3.5.22	Orcan
Even till the dissolution of the world,	2Tamb	3.5.82	Tamb
Nor am I made Arch-monark of the world,	2Tamb	4.1.150	Tamb
The Scourge of God and terrour of the world,	2Tamb	4.1.154	Tamb
I will persist a terrour to the world,	2Tamb	4.1.200	Tamb
As all the world cannot affoord the like.	2Tamb	4.2.57	Olymp
will keep it for/The richest present of this Easterne world.	2Tamb	4.2.78	Therid
As in the Theoria of the world.	2Tamb	4.2.86	Therid
Before I conquere all the triple world.	2Tamb	4.3.63	Tamb
To note me Emperour of the three fold world:	2Tamb	4.3.118	Tamb
and the victories/Wherewith he hath so sore dismaide the world,	2Tamb	5.2.44	Callap
For conquering the Tyrant of the world.	2Tamb	5.2.55	Callap
That have bene tearm'd the terrour of the world?	2Tamb	5.3.45	Tamb
Whose shoulders beare the Axis of the world,	2Tamb	5.3.59	Tamb
let me see how much/Is left for me to conquer all the world,	2Tamb	5.3.124	Tamb
Looke here my boies, see what a world of ground,	2Tamb	5.3.145	Tamb
More worth than Asia, and the world beside,	2Tamb	5.3.153	Tamb
Albeit the world thinke Machevill is dead,	Jew	Prol.1	Machvl
How ere the world goe, I'le make sure for one,	Jew	1.1.186	Barab
And make thee poore and scorn'd of all the world,	Jew	1.2.108	1Knght
And I was chain'd to follies of the world:	Jew	3.3.60	Abigal
The wind that bloweth all the world besides,	Jew	3.5.3	Basso
reading of the letter, he look'd like a man of another world.	Jew	4.2.7	P Pilia
And Bacchus vineyards [over-spread] <ore-spread> the world:	Jew	4.2.92	Ithimr
For so I live, perish may all the world.	Jew	5.5.10	Barab
Malta prisoner; for come [all] <call> the world/To rescue thee,	Jew	5.5.119	Govnr
A hand, that with a graspe may gripe the world,	P 159	2.102	Guise
Madam, it wilbe noted through the world,	P 207	4.5	Charls
(As all the world shall know our Guise is dead)/Rest satisfied	P1042	19.112	King
For all the wealth and treasure of the world.	P1163	22.25	King
And with the world be still at enmitie:	Edw	1.1.15	Gavstn
Why should you love him, whome the world hates so?	Edw	1.4.76	Mortmr
Because he loves me more then all the world:	Edw	1.4.77	Edward
That makes a king seeme glorious to the world,	Edw	2.2.175	Mortmr
To witnesse to the world, that by thy meanes,	Edw	5.6.31	King
That scornes the world, and as a traveller,	Edw	5.6.65	Mortmr
O what a world of profite and delight,	F 80	1.1.52	Faust
And search all corners of the new-found-world/For pleasant	F 111	1.1.83	Faust
damned Art/For which they two are infamous through the world.	F 222	1.2.29	1Schol
Leapes from th'Antarticke world unto the skie,	F 231	1.3.3	Faust
Or the Ocean to overwhelme the world.	F 267	1.3.39	Faust
By him, I'le be great Emperour of the world,	F 332	1.3.104	Faust
And to be short <conclude>, when all the world dissolves,	F 513	2.1.125	Mephst

WORLD (cont.)				
upon the poles of the world, but differ in their motions	F 598	2.2.47	P	Mepnst
now tell me who made the world?	F 618	2.2.67	P	Faust
Thinke Faustus upon God, that made the world.	F 625	2.2.74	P	Faust
O that there would come a famine over <through> all the world,	F 682	2.2.131	P	Envy
run up and downe the world with these <this> case of Rapiers,	F 688	2.2.137	P	Wrath
There did we view the Kingdomes of the world,	F 852	3.1.74		Faust
Then he and thou, and all the world shall stoope,	F 937	3.1.159		Pope
[Touching his journey through the world and ayre],	F1145	3.3.58A		3Chor
The wonder of the world for Magick Art;	F1166	4.1.12		Mrtino
in your head for shame, let not all the world wonder at you.	F1292	4.1.138	P	Faust
That all the world may see my just revenge.	F1382	4.2.58		Benvol
Yet stay, the world shall see their miserie,	F1406	4.2.82		Faust
And make us laughing stockes to all the world.	F1450	4.3.20		Benvol
so delighted me, as nothing in the world could please me more.	F1561	4.6.4	P	Duke
be it in the world, it shall be yours:	F1567	4.6.10	P	Faust
the yeare is divided into two circles over the whole world, so	F1582	4.6.25	P	Faust
which was the beautifullest in all the world, we have	F1682	5.1.9	P	1Schol
whom all the world admires for Majesty, we should thinke	F1686	5.1.13	P	1Schol
Whom all the world admires for majesty.	F1698	5.1.25		2Schol
Begets a world of idle fantasies,	F1810	5.2.14		Mephst
I have done, all Germany can witnesse, yea all the world:	F1843	5.2.47	P	Faust
for which Faustus hath lost both Germany and the world, yea	F1844	5.2.48	P	Faust
But thou didst love the world.	F1894	5.2.98		GdAngl
nor in the whole world can compare with thee, for the rare	F App	p.236 3	P	Emper
glorious actes/Lightens the world with his reflecting beames,	F App	p.237 26		Emper
Ay me, O what a world of land and sea,	Lucan, First Booke			13
Peace through the world from Janus Phane shal flie,	Lucan, First Booke			61
day, and ful of strife/Disolve the engins of the broken world.	Lucan, First Booke			80
Why joine you force to share the world betwixt you?	Lucan, First Booke			88
that made Roome/Governe the earth, the sea, the world it selfe,	Lucan, First Booke			110
Filling the world, leapes out and throwes forth fire,	Lucan, First Booke			154
wittes) was loath'd, and al the world/Ransackt for golde,	Lucan, First Booke			167
al the world/Ransackt for golde, which breeds the world decay;	Lucan, First Booke			168
successe/May bring her downe, and with her all the world;	Lucan, First Booke			286
decrees/To expel the father; share the world thou canst not;	Lucan, First Booke			291
The world (were it together) is by cowards/Left as a pray now	Lucan, First Booke			511
And whelm'd the world in darknesse, making men/Dispaire of day;	Lucan, First Booke			540
New factions rise; now through the world againe/I goe; o Phoebus	Lucan, First Booke			691
So likewise we will through the world be rung,	Ovid's Elegies			1.3.25
That all the world [may] <might> ever chaunt my name.	Ovid's Elegies			1.15.8
[The world shall of Callimachus ever speake],	Ovid's Elegies			1.15.13
While Rome of all the [conquered] <conquering> world is head.	Ovid's Elegies			1.15.26
Rome if her strength the huge world had not fild,	Ovid's Elegies			2.9.17
Againe by some in this unpeopled world.	Ovid's Elegies			2.14.12
So through the world shold bright renown expresse me.	Ovid's Elegies			3.1.64
And doth the world in fond beliefe deteine.	Ovid's Elegies			3.3.24
And let the world be witnesse of the same?	Ovid's Elegies			3.13.12
Such as the world would woonder to behold:	Hero and Leander			1.34
Since Heroes time, hath halfe the world beene blacke.	Hero and Leander			1.50
Heav'd up her head, and halfe the world upon,	Hero and Leander			1.190
And with intestine broiles the world destroy,	Hero and Leander			1.251
of hers (like that/Which made the world) another world begat,	Hero and Leander			2.292
WORLDE				
My Lord, the great Commander of the worlde,	1Tamb	3.3.13		Bassoe
And made it look with terrour on the worlde:	P 61	2.4		Guise
Or with seditions weary all the worlde:	P 116	2.59		Guise
Farewell vaine worlde.	Edw	3.1.249		Warwck
the yeere is divided into twoo circles over the whole worlde,	F App	p.242 20	P	Faust
WORLDES				
chiefe spectacle of the worldes preheminence, The bright	F App	p.237 24	P	Emper
WORLDLING				
Fond worldling, now his heart bloud dries with griefe;	F1808	5.2.12		Mephst
WORLDLINGS				
Now tell me, worldlings, underneath the [sunne] <summe>,	Jew	5.5.49		Barab
WORLDS				
Yet not from Carthage for a thousand worlds.	Dido	3.1.51		Iarbus
Now bright Zenocrate, the worlds faire eie,	2Tamb	1.3.1		Tamb
Whose termine <terminine>, is tearmed the worlds wide Pole.	F 593	2.2.42		Mephst
Thou couldst command the worlds obedience:	F1210	4.1.56		Emper
Since first the worlds creation did begin.	F1985	5.3.3		1Schol
Th'affrighted worlds force bent on publique spoile,	Lucan, First Booke			5
So when this worlds compounded union breakes,	Lucan, First Booke			73
While Titan strives against the worlds swift course;	Lucan, First Booke			90
The worlds swift course is lawlesse/And casuall; all the	Lucan, First Booke			641
The Parrat given me, the farre [worlds] <words> best choice.	Ovid's Elegies			2.6.38
There, he who rules the worlds starre-spangled towers,	Ovid's Elegies			3.9.21
WORMEATEN				
gods hung up/Such as peace yeelds; wormeaten leatherne targets,	Lucan, First Booke			243
WORNE				
Hath worne the Poland diadem, before/You were invested in the	P 612	12.25		Mugern
each from other, but being worne away/They both burst out,	Lucan, First Booke			102
Brasse shines with use; good garments would be worne,	Ovid's Elegies			1.8.51
All wasting years have that complaint [out] <not> worne.	Ovid's Elegies			2.6.8
Neither themselves nor others, if not worne.	Hero and Leander			1.238
WORSE (See also WOORSE, WORSSE)				
Thou shalt burne first, thy crime is worse then his:	Dido	5.1.297		Dido
Or els invent some torture worse than that.	2Tamb	3.4.22		Olymp
And let him not be entertain'd the worse/Because he favours me.	Jew	Prol.34		Machvl
I, but theft is worse:	Jew	1.2.125		Barab
So much the worse; I must have one that's sickly, and be but	Jew	2.3.123	P	Barab
No, but a worse thing:	Jew	3.6.50		2Fryar
God graunt my neerest freends may prove no worse.	P 547	11.12		Charls

WORSE (cont.)
I would it were no worse,/But gentle lords, friendles we are in — Edw 4.2.45 Queene
Wars worse then civill on Thessalian playnes, — Lucan, First Booke 1
say Pompey, are these worse/Then Pirats of Sycillia? — Lucan, First Booke 346
to scarre/The quivering Romans, but worse things affright them. — Lucan, First Booke 673
Least with worse kisses she should me indue. — Ovid's Elegies 2.5.50
honour, and thereby/Commit'st a sinne far worse than perjurie. — Hero and Leander 1.306

WORSHIP
Worthy the worship of all faithfull hearts, — 2Tamb 2.2.57 Orcan
In vaine I see men worship Mahomet, — 2Tamb 5.1.179 Tamb
Oh brave, master, I worship your nose for this. — Jew 2.3.173 Ithimr
I warrant your worship shall hav't. — Jew 4.2.119 P Pilia
We thanke your worship. — Edw 1.1.47 Omnes
Your worship I trust will remember me? — Edw 4.7.117 Mower
I beseech your Worship accept of these forty Dollors. — F1457 4.4.1 P HrsCsr
that flesh and bloud should be so fraile with your Worship: — F1633 4.6.76 P Carter
Thee all shall feare and worship as a King, — Ovid's Elegies 1.2.33
Why should you worship her? — Hero and Leander 1.213

WORSHIPPED
Thou art not woorthy to be worshipped, — 2Tamb 5.1.189 Tamb

WORSHIPS
Such as desire your worships service. — Edw 1.1.25 Poorem
wine, if it could speake, <it> would informe your Worships: — F 216 1.2.23 P Wagner
Were I the saint hee worships, I would heare him, — Hero and Leander 1.179

WORSHIPT
And worshipt by their paine, and lying apart? — Ovid's Elegies 3.9.16

WORSSE
You must devise some torment worsse, my Lord, — 1Tamb 4.2.66 Techel

WORST (See also WURST)
Doe shame her worst, I will disclose my griefe:-- — Dido 3.4.28 Dido
And which is worst to have his Diadem/Sought for by such scalde — 1Tamb 2.2.7 Mycet
And if she passe this fit, the worst is past. — 2Tamb 2.4.40 1Phstn
I would not yeeld it: therefore doo your worst. — 2Tamb 3.3.37 Capt
And seeke in time to intercept the worst, — Jew 1.1.187 Barab
Fearing the worst of this before it fell, — Jew 1.2.246 Barab
Devils doe your worst, [I'le] <I> live in spite of you. — Jew 5.1.41 Barab
Curse me, depose me, doe the worst you can. — Edw 1.4.57 Edward
therefore have we cause/To cast the worst, and doubt of your — Edw 2.3.8 Warwck
The worst is death, and better die to live, — Edw 3.1.243 Lncstr
Kill not the king tis good to feare the worst. — Edw 5.4.12 Mortmr
Tydides left worst signes of villanie, — Ovid's Elegies 1.7.31
Supplying their voide places with the worst. — Ovid's Elegies 2.6.40

WORTH (See also WOORTH)
Flinging in favours of more soveraigne worth, — Dido 3.1.131 Dido
A pearle more worth, then all the world is plaste: — 1Tamb 2.1.12 Menaph
Your speech will stay, or so extol his worth, — 1Tamb 2.3.27 Therid
Til then take thou my crowne, vaunt of my worth, — 1Tamb 3.3.130 Tamb
If thou exceed thy elder Brothers worth, — 2Tamb 1.3.50 Tamb
There lies more gold than Babylon is worth, — 2Tamb 5.1.116 Govnr
More worth than Asia, and the world beside, — 2Tamb 5.3.153 Tamb
comes to more/Then many Merchants of the Towne are worth, — Jew 1.1.64 1Merch
As much I hope as all I hid is worth. — Jew 1.2.336 Barab
And if he has, he is worth three hundred plats. — Jew 2.3.102 Barab
Their voyage will be worth ten thousand Crownes. — Jew 4.1.70 Barab
I'le not leave him worth a gray groat. — Jew 4.2.114 P Ithimr
My lord, these titles far exceed my worth. — Edw 1.1.157 Gavstn
A homely one my lord, not worth the telling. — Edw 2.2.13 Mortmr
'Tis not so much worth; I pray you tel me one thing. — F1643 4.6.86 P Carter
whose admired worth>/<Made Greece with ten yeares warres — F1696 (HC269)B 2Schol
Too simple is my wit to tell her worth <praise>,/Whom all the — F1697 5.1.24 2Schol
I will attempt, which is but little worth. — F1758 5.1.85 Mephst
stil poore/Did vild deeds, then t'was worth the price of bloud, — Lucan, First Booke 175
Healthfull Peligny I esteeme nought worth, — Ovid's Elegies 2.16.37
One Deianira was more worth then these. — Ovid's Elegies 3.5.38
Homer without this shall be nothing worth. — Ovid's Elegies 3.7.28
Ah, she doth more worth then her vices prove. — Ovid's Elegies 3.10.44
A Diamond set in lead his worth retaines, — Hero and Leander 1.215
for both not us'de,/Are of like worth. — Hero and Leander 1.234
Yet when a token of great worth we send, — Hero and Leander 2.80

WORTHELY
Thankes worthely are due for things unbought, — Ovid's Elegies 1.10.43

WORTHIE
Is not Aeneas worthie Didos love? — Dido 3.1.68 Dido

WORTHIEST
(The worthiest knight that ever brandisht sword)/Challenge in — 2Tamb 3.5.71 Tamb

WORTHILY
hath Faustus worthily requited this injurious knight, which — F App p.238 83 P Faust
And who ere see her, worthily lament. — Ovid's Elegies 2.14.40

WORTHINESSE
made one Poems period/And all combin'd in Beauties worthinesse, — 1Tamb 5.1.170 Tamb
whose worthinesse/Deserves a conquest over every hart: — 1Tamb 5.1.207 Tamb

WORTHLES
I am much better for your worthles love, — Dido 1.1.3 Ganimd
accidents/Have chanc'd thy merits in this worthles bondage. — 1Tamb 5.1.425 Arabia

WORTHLESSE
Being supposde his worthlesse Concubine, — 1Tamb 3.2.29 Agidas

WORTHS
As my despised worths, that shun all praise, — Dido 3.4.42 Aeneas

WORTHY
A thousand thankes worthy Theridamas: — 1Tamb 1.2.252 Tamb
And such shall wait on worthy Tamburlaine. — 1Tamb 2.1.60 Cosroe
Now worthy Tamburlaine, have I reposde, — 1Tamb 2.3.1 Cosroe
And crave his triple worthy buriall. — 1Tamb 3.2.112 Usumc

WORTHY (cont.)			
And made my lordly Love her worthy King:	1Tamb	3.3.190	Zenoc
And they are worthy she investeth kings.	1Tamb	4.4.129	Tamb
And wisht as worthy subjects happy meanes,	1Tamb	5.1.103	1Virgn
Worthy the worship of all faithfull hearts,	2Tamb	2.2.57	Orcan
Thrice worthy kings of Natolia, and the rest,	2Tamb	3.1.7	Callap
And worthy sonnes of Tamburlain the great.	2Tamb	3.2.92	Tamb
and now would I were gone, I am not worthy to looke upon her.	Jew	4.2.36	P Ithimr
A martiall people, worthy such a King,	P 455	8.5	Anjoy
Now worthy Faustus: me thinks your looks are chang'd.	F1821	5.2.25	1Schol
That I may write things worthy thy faire lookes:	Ovid's Elegies		1.3.20
Aye me, thy body hath no worthy weedes.	Ovid's Elegies		1.8.26
Worthy to keembe none but a Goddesse faire,	Ovid's Elegies		2.8.2
Worthy she is, thou shouldst in mercy save her.	Ovid's Elegies		2.13.22
This thou wilt say to be a worthy ground.	Ovid's Elegies		3.1.26
Worthy she was to move both Gods and men,	Ovid's Elegies		3.6.59
WORTHYNESSE			
And have bene crown'd for prooved worthynesse:	1Tamb	5.1.491	Tamb
WOT			
But haples I, God wot, poore and unknowne,	Dido	1.1.227	Aeneas
O no God wot, I cannot watch my time,	Dido	3.2.14	Juno
I wot his wealth/Was written thus:	Jew	1.2.181	Barab
For wot you not that I have made him sure,	Edw	1.4.378	Edward
We wot, he that the care of realme remits,	Edw	2.5.61	Warwck
grace may sit secure, if none but wee/Doe wot of your abode.	Edw	4.7.27	Monk
Graecinus (well I wot) thou touldst me once,	Ovid's Elegies		2.10.1
The other smilde, (I wot) with wanton eyes,	Ovid's Elegies		3.1.33
WOULD (See also WOLD, WUD)			
O how would I with Helens brother laugh,	Dido	1.1.17	Ganimd
When as they would have hal'd thee from my sight:	Dido	1.1.27	Jupitr
I would have a jewell for mine eare,	Dido	1.1.46	Ganimd
Then would we hope to quite such friendly turnes,	Dido	1.2.46	Serg
And would my prayers (as Pigmalions did)/Could give it life,	Dido	2.1.16	Aeneas
Then would it leape out to give Priam life:	Dido	2.1.27	Aeneas
Thy mind Aeneas that would have it so/Deludes thy eye sight,	Dido	2.1.31	Achat
For were it Priam he would smile on me.	Dido	2.1.36	Ascan
And when we told her she would weepe for griefe,	Dido	2.1.67	Illion
Then he alleag'd the Gods would have them stay,	Dido	2.1.141	Aeneas
And would have grappeld with Achilles sonne,	Dido	2.1.251	Aeneas
Yet manhood would not serve, of force we fled,	Dido	2.1.272	Aeneas
Wherefore would Dido have Aeneas stay?	Dido	3.1.134	Aeneas
That would have kild him sleeping as he lay?	Dido	3.2.39	Juno
I would have either drunke his dying bloud,	Dido	3.3.28	Iarbus
Or els I would have given my life in gage.	Dido	3.3.29	Iarbus
Then would I wish me with Anchises Tombe,	Dido	3.3.44	Aeneas
Then would I wish me in faire Didos armes,	Dido	3.3.48	Iarbus
Who would not undergoe all kind of toyle,	Dido	3.3.58	Aeneas
And yet I am not free, oh would I were.	Dido	3.4.6	Dido
I Anna, is there ought you would with me?	Dido	4.2.24	Iarbus
Yet if you would partake with me the cause/Of this devotion	Dido	4.2.27	Anna
I would be thankfull for such curtesie.	Dido	4.2.29	Anna
I faine would goe, yet beautie calles me backe:	Dido	4.3.46	Aeneas
O foolish Troians that would steale from hence,	Dido	4.4.5	Dido
I would have given Achates store of gold,	Dido	4.4.7	Dido
Because I feard your grace would keepe me here.	Dido	4.4.20	Achat
And would be toyling in the watrie billowes,	Dido	4.4.137	Dido
What, would the Gods have me, Deucalion like,	Dido	5.1.57	Aeneas
Would, as faire Troy was, Carthage might be sackt,	Dido	5.1.147	Dido
Yet he that in my sight would not relent,	Dido	5.1.186	Dido
Made me suppose he would have heard me speake:	Dido	5.1.230	Anna
The [Lords] <Lord> would not be too exasperate,	1Tamb	1.1.182	Ortyg
Or if they would, there are in readines/Ten thousand horse to	1Tamb	1.1.184	Ortyg
Would it not grieve a King to be so abusde,	1Tamb	2.2.5	Mycet
I thinke it would:	1Tamb	2.2.9	Mycet
Would make one thrust and strive to be retain'd/In such a great	1Tamb	2.3.31	Therid
I would intreat you to speak but three wise wordes.	1Tamb	2.4.25	Tamb
Why, that's wel said Techelles, so would I,	1Tamb	2.5.69	Tamb
And so would you my maisters, would you not?	1Tamb	2.5.70	Tamb
And would not all our souldiers soone consent,	1Tamb	2.5.78	Tamb
I know they would with our perswasions.	1Tamb	2.5.80	Therid
Yet would we not be brav'd with forrain power,	1Tamb	3.1.13	Bajzth
And higher would I reare my estimate,	1Tamb	3.2.53	Zenoc
As these my followers willingly would have:	1Tamb	3.3.155	Tamb
The Souldane would not start a foot from him.	1Tamb	4.1.19	Souldn
Yet would the Souldane by his conquering power,	1Tamb	4.1.33	Souldn
If they would lay their crownes before my feet,	1Tamb	4.2.93	Tamb
Yet would you have some pitie for my sake,	1Tamb	4.2.123	Zenoc
But if his highnesse would let them be fed, it would doe them	1Tamb	4.4.34	P Therid
highnesse would let them be fed, it would doe them more good.	1Tamb	4.4.34	P Therid
Yet would I with my sword make Jove to stoope.	1Tamb	4.4.74	Tamb
So it would my lord, specially having so smal a walke, and so	1Tamb	4.4.105	P Therid
Would not with too much cowardize or feare,	1Tamb	5.1.37	Govnr
for the love of Venus, would she leave/The angrie God of Armes,	1Tamb	5.1.124	Tamb
That would with pity chear Zabinas heart,	1Tamb	5.1.271	Bajzth
Whose sight with joy would take away my life,	1Tamb	5.1.419	Arabia
Would lend an howers license to my tongue:	1Tamb	5.1.423	Arabia
of our Empery/Once lost, All Turkie would be overthrowne:	2Tamb	1.1.56	Orcan
my Lord, if I should goe, would you bee as good as your word?	2Tamb	1.2.62	P Almeda
Yet would I venture to conduct your Grace,	2Tamb	1.2.72	Almeda
Would make me thinke them Bastards, not my sons,	2Tamb	1.3.32	Tamb
I would prepare a ship and saile to it,	2Tamb	1.3.90	Celeb
Ere I would loose the tytle of a king.	2Tamb	1.3.91	Celeb
And I would strive to swim through pooles of blood,	2Tamb	1.3.92	Amyras

WOULD (cont.)

Ere I would loose the tytle of a king.	2Tamb	1.3.95	Amyras
That would not kill and curse at Gods command,	2Tamb	2.1.55	Fredrk
Turn'd to dispaire, would break my wretched breast,	2Tamb	2.4.64	Zenoc
And furie would confound my present rest.	2Tamb	2.4.65	Zenoc
It would not ease the sorrow I sustaine.	2Tamb	3.2.48	Calyph
I would not yeeld it: therefore doo your worst.	2Tamb	3.3.37	Capt
I see how fearfully ye would refuse,	2Tamb	3.5.73	Tamb
I would not bide the furie of my father:	2Tamb	4.1.45	Amyras
the good I have/Join'd with my fathers crowne would never cure.	2Tamb	4.1.58	Calyph
I should be affraid, would put it off and come to bed with me.	2Tamb	4.1.70	P Calyph
Such a feare (my Lord) would never make yee retire.	2Tamb	4.1.71	P Perdic
would my father would let me be put in the front of such a	2Tamb	4.1.72	P Calyph
would let me be put in the front of such a battaile once,	2Tamb	4.1.72	P Calyph
Wil get his pardon if your grace would send.	2Tamb	5.1.33	1Citzn
The triple headed Cerberus would howle,	2Tamb	5.1.97	Tamb
Then for all your valour, you would save your life.	2Tamb	5.1.119	Tamb
Would make a miracle of thus much coyne:	Jew	1.1.13	Barab
Would in his age be loath to labour so,	Jew	1.1.17	Barab
They would not come in warlike manner thus.	Jew	1.1.155	1Jew
As much as would have bought his beasts and him,	Jew	1.2.189	Barab
And better would she farre become a bed/Embraced in a friendly	Jew	1.2.371	Mthias
Of whom we would make sale in Malta here.	Jew	2.2.18	Bosco
They hop'd my daughter would ha bin a Nun;	Jew	2.3.12	Barab
Against my will, and whether I would or no,	Jew	2.3.75	Barab
And in the night time secretly would I steale/To travellers	Jew	2.3.206	Ithimr
And therewithall their knees would rankle, so/That I have	Jew	2.3.210	Ithimr
would I give a hundred of the Jewes Crownes that I had such a	Jew	3.1.27	P Ithimr
Or though it wrought, it would have done no good,	Jew	4.1.5	Barab
An Hebrew borne, and would become a Christian?	Jew	4.1.19	Barab
That would for Lucars sake have sold my soule.	Jew	4.1.53	Barab
Would pennance serve for this my sinne,	Jew	4.1.58	Barab
Pull hard, I say, you would have had my goods.	Jew	4.1.149	Barab
Who would not thinke but that this Fryar liv'd?	Jew	4.1.156	Barab
Why, stricken him that would have stroke at me.	Jew	4.1.175	1Fryar
me ever since she saw me, and who would not requite such love?	Jew	4.2.34	P Ithimr
and now would I were gone, I am not worthy to looke upon her.	Jew	4.2.36	P Ithimr
Sweet Bellamira, would I had my Masters wealth for thy sake.	Jew	4.2.55	P Ithimr
and would have it; but hee hides and buries it up as Partridges	Jew	4.2.57	P Ithimr
Which if they were reveal'd, would doe him harme.	Jew	4.2.65	Pilia
He humbly would intreat your Majesty/To come and see his homely	Jew	5.3.17	Msngr
Yet would I gladly visit Barabas,	Jew	5.3.24	Calym
Therefore he humbly would intreat your Highnesse/Not to depart	Jew	5.3.32	Msngr
thee greater curtesie/Then Barabas would have affoorded thee.	Jew	5.5.62	Govnr
I would have brought confusion on you all,	Jew	5.5.85	Barab
down, heer's one would speak with you from the Duke of Guise.	P 348	6.3	P SrnsWf
Faine would I finde some means to speak with him/But cannot,	P 662	13.6	Duchss
O would to God this quill that heere doth write,	P 667	13.11	Duchss
I would the Guise in his steed might have come,	P 736	14.39	Navrre
possession (as I would I might) yet I meane to keepe you out,	P 814	17.9	P Souldr
It would be good the Guise were made away,	P 888	17.83	Eprnon
tush, were he heere, we would kill him presently.	P 934	19.4	P 1Mur
I slew the Guise, because I would be King.	P1066	19.136	King
I would that I had murdered thee my sonne.	P1073	19.143	QnMoth
Sweet Guise, would he had died so thou wert heere:	P1082	19.152	QnMoth
That naturally would love and honour you,	Edw	1.1.100	Lncstr
I yours, and therefore I would wish you graunt.	Edw	1.1.120	Edward
Would seeke the ruine of my Gaveston,	Edw	1.4.79	Edward
They would not stir, were it to do me good:	Edw	1.4.95	Edward
But I would wish thee reconcile the lords,	Edw	1.4.156	Edward
Would when I left sweet France and was imbarkt,	Edw	1.4.171	Queene
Theres none here, but would run his horse to death.	Edw	1.4.207	Warwck
But madam, would you have us cal him home?	Edw	1.4.208	Mortmr
What, would ye have me plead for Gaveston?	Edw	1.4.213	Mortmr
I would he were.	Edw	1.4.253	Penbrk
more/Then he can Gaveston, would he lov'd me/But halfe so much,	Edw	1.4.303	Queene
I would freelie give it to his enemies,	Edw	1.4.309	Edward
And would have once preferd me to the king.	Edw	2.1.14	Spencr
That he would take exceptions at my buttons,	Edw	2.1.47	Baldck
I knew the King would have him home againe.	Edw	2.1.78	Spencr
No more then I would answere were he slaine.	Edw	2.2.86	Mortmr
the Mortimers/Are not so poore, but would they sell their land,	Edw	2.2.151	Mortmr
Would levie men enough to anger you.	Edw	2.2.152	Mortmr
Would Lancaster and he had both carroust,	Edw	2.2.237	Edward
That I might pull him to me where I would,	Edw	2.4.18	Queene
What would you with the king, ist him you seek?	Edw	2.4.31	Queene
We would but rid the realme of Gaveston,	Edw	2.4.35	Lncstr
would I beare/These braves, this rage, and suffer uncontrowld	Edw	3.1.12	Spencr
You would not suffer thus your majestie/Be counterbuft of your	Edw	3.1.17	Spencr
That I would undertake to carrie him/Unto your highnes, and to	Edw	3.1.99	Arundl
And tell me, would the rebels denie me that?	Edw	3.1.101	Edward
The earle of Warwick would not bide the hearing,	Edw	3.1.104	Arundl
I would it were no worse,/But gentle lords, friendles we are in	Edw	4.2.45	Queene
in England/Would cast up cappes, and clap their hands for joy,	Edw	4.2.55	Mortmr
Would all were well, and Edward well reclaimd,	Edw	4.2.57	Kent
I would he never had bin flattered more.	Edw	4.4.30	Kent
dauntlesse minde/The ambitious Mortimer would seeke to curbe,	Edw	5.1.16	Edward
O would I might, but heavens and earth conspire/To make me	Edw	5.1.96	Edward
And save you from your foes, Bartley would die.	Edw	5.1.134	Bartly
First would I heare newes that hee were deposde,	Edw	5.2.21	Mortmr
Alas poore soule, would I could ease his greefe.	Edw	5.2.26	Queene
I would hee were, so it were not by my meanes.	Edw	5.2.45	Queene
I would those wordes proceeded from your heart.	Edw	5.2.100	Kent

WOULD (cont.)

A would have taken the king away perforce,	Edw	5.4.84	Souldr
Had Edmund liv'de, he would have sought thy death.	Edw	5.4.112	Queene
O would my bloud dropt out from every vaine,	Edw	5.5.66	Edward
I my good Lord, I would it were undone.	Edw	5.6.2	Matrvs
Els would you not intreate for Mortimer.	Edw	5.6.71	King
you were not dunces, you would never aske me such a question:	F 207	1.2.14	P Wagner
would say) it were not for you to come within fortie foot of	F 210	1.2.17	P Wagner
wine, if it could speake, <it> would informe your Worships:	F 216	1.2.23	P Wagner
The danger of his soule would make me mourne:	F 224	1.2.31	2Schol
Who would not be proficient in this Art?	F 256	1.3.28	Faust
that <I know> he would give his soule to the devill, for a	F 349	1.4.7	P Wagner
would I have a booke wherein I might beholde al spels and	F 551.1	2.1.164A	P Faust
would I have a booke where I might see al characters of <and>	F 551.4	2.1.167A	P Faust
<I would desire, that this house,	F 675	(HC263)A	P Covet
O that there would come a famine over <through> all the world,	F 681	2.2.130	P Envy
live along, then thou should'st see how fat I'de <I would> be.	F 683	2.2.132	P Envy
And therefore tho we would we cannot erre.	F 931	3.1.153	Pope
To morrow we would sit i'th Consistory,	F1017	3.2.37	Pope
Then wherefore would you have me view that booke?	F1023	3.2.43	Pope
love with him, I would he would post with him to Rome againe.	F1191	4.1.37	P Benvol
We would behold that famous Conquerour,	F1231	4.1.77	Emper
That in mine armes I would have compast him.	F1262	4.1.108	Emper
would I might be turn'd to a gaping Oyster, and drinke nothing	F1319	4.1.165	P Benvol
I thinking that a little would serve his turne, bad him take as	F1528	4.5.24	P Carter
bad him take as much as he would for three-farthings; so he	F1529	4.5.25	P Carter
and he would by no meanes sell him under forty Dollors; so sir,	F1536	4.5.32	P HrsCsr
such a horse, as would run over hedge and ditch, and never tyre,	F1538	4.5.34	P HrsCsr
had had some [rare] quality that he would not have me know of,	F1542	4.5.38	P HrsCsr
I would request no better meate, then a dish of ripe grapes.	F1573	4.6.16	P Lady
And then demand of them, what they would have.	F1590	4.6.33	Duke
What would they have?	F1599	4.6.42	Duke
sir, I would make nothing of you, but I would faine know that.	F1648	4.6.91	P Carter
what he meanes, if death were nie, he would not frolick thus:	F1677	5.1.4	P Wagner
O would I had never seene Wittenberg <Wertenberge>, never read	F1841	5.2.45	P Faust
<O> my God, I would weepe, but the Divell drawes in my teares.	F1850	5.2.54	P Faust
I would lift up my hands, but see they hold 'em <them>, they	F1852	5.2.56	P Faust
One drop [would save my soule, halfe a drop, ah] my Christ.	F1940	5.2.144	Faust
he would give his soule to the Divel for a shoulder of mutton,	F App	p.229 8	P Wagner
Doe yee heare, I would be sorie to robbe you of your living.	F App	p.229 18	P Clown
divels, say I should kill one of them, what would folkes say?	F App	p.230 47	P Clown
serve you, would you teach me to raise up Banios and Belcheos?	F App	p.230 56	P Clown
Well use that tricke no more, I would advise you.	F App	p.232 19	Faust
his horse, and he would have his things rubd and made cleane:	F App	p.233 7	P Rafe
I would not be ruled by him, for he bade me I should ride him	F App	p.240 130	P HrsCsr
had some rare qualitie that he would not have had me knowne of,	F App	p.240 132	P HrsCsr
why sir, what would you?	F App	p.240 139	P Mephst
I would desire no better meate then a dish of ripe grapes.	F App	p.242 10	P Duchss
thing then this, so it would content you, you should have it	F App	p.242 14	P Faust
He would not banquet, and carowse, and swill/Amongst the	F App	p.243 4	Wagner
for Nero (then unborne) the fates/Would find no other meanes,	Lucan, First Booke		34
earth, the sea, the world it selfe,/Would not admit two Lords:	Lucan, First Booke		111
Thou feard'st (great Pompey) that late deeds would dim/Olde	Lucan, First Booke		121
Would dash the wreath thou wearst for Pirats wracke.	Lucan, First Booke		123
You would have thought their houses had bin fierd/Or	Lucan, First Booke		490
and would hould/The world (were it together) is by cowards	Lucan, First Booke		510
snatcht up/Would make them sleepe securely in their tents.	Lucan, First Booke		516
Then Gaynimede would renew Deucalions flood,	Lucan, First Booke		652
rayes now sing/The fell Nemean beast, th'earth would be fired,	Lucan, First Booke		655
I aske too much, would she but let me love hir,	Ovid's Elegies		1.3.3
And striving thus as one that would be cast,	Ovid's Elegies		1.5.15
Although I would, I cannot him cashiere/Before I be divided	Ovid's Elegies		1.6.35
Would of mine armes, my shoulders had beene scanted,	Ovid's Elegies		1.7.23
As thou art faire, would thou wert fortunate,	Ovid's Elegies		1.8.27
Would he not buy thee thou for him shouldst care.	Ovid's Elegies		1.8.34
Or, but for bashfulnesse her selfe would crave.	Ovid's Elegies		1.8.44
Brasse shines with use; good garments would be worne,	Ovid's Elegies		1.8.51
hoary flieces/And riveld cheekes I would have puld a pieces.	Ovid's Elegies		1.8.112
How oft wisht I night would not give thee place,	Ovid's Elegies		1.13.27
How oft, that either wind would breake thy coche,	Ovid's Elegies		1.13.29
Would Tithon might but talke of thee a while,	Ovid's Elegies		1.13.35
Me thinkes she should <would> be nimble when shees downe.	Ovid's Elegies		2.4.14
If not, because shees simple I would have her.	Ovid's Elegies		2.4.18
Yet would I lie with her if that I might.	Ovid's Elegies		2.4.22
She would be nimbler, lying with a man.	Ovid's Elegies		2.4.24
Who would not love those hands for their swift running?	Ovid's Elegies		2.4.28
[I thinke what one undeckt would be, being drest];	Ovid's Elegies		2.4.37
O would my proofes as vaine might be withstood,	Ovid's Elegies		2.5.7
Would I were culpable of some offence,	Ovid's Elegies		2.7.11
But when I die, would I might droope with doing,	Ovid's Elegies		2.10.35
O would that no Oares might in seas have suncke,	Ovid's Elegies		2.11.5
O would that sodainly into my gift,	Ovid's Elegies		2.15.9
Then would I wish thee touch my mistris pappe,	Ovid's Elegies		2.15.11
I would get off though straight, and sticking fast,	Ovid's Elegies		2.15.13
Would first my beautious wenches moist lips touch,	Ovid's Elegies		2.15.17
I would not out, might I in one place hit,	Ovid's Elegies		2.15.19
In heaven without thee would I not be fixt.	Ovid's Elegies		2.16.14
My hard way with my mistrisse would seeme soft.	Ovid's Elegies		2.16.20
Nor thy gulfes crooked Malea, would I feare.	Ovid's Elegies		2.16.24
Would I had beene my mistresse gentle prey,	Ovid's Elegies		2.17.5
What would not she give that faire name to winne?	Ovid's Elegies		2.17.30
I borne much, hoping time would beate thee/To guard her well,	Ovid's Elegies		2.19.49
Thou hast my gift, which she would from thee sue.	Ovid's Elegies		3.1.60

WOULD (cont.)

With scepters, and high buskins th'one would dresse me,	Ovid's Elegies 3.1.63
I would bravely runne,/On swift steedes mounted till the race	Ovid's Elegies 3.2.9
Now would I slacke the reines, now lash their hide,	Ovid's Elegies 3.2.11
My selfe would sweare, the wenches true did sweare,	Ovid's Elegies 3.3.45
And I would be none of the Gods severe.	Ovid's Elegies 3.3.46
O would in my fore-fathers tombe deepe layde,	Ovid's Elegies 3.5.73
But when she saw it would by no meanes stand,	Ovid's Elegies 3.6.75
If I should give, both would the house forbeare.	Ovid's Elegies 3.7.64
Or lesse faire, or lesse lewd would thou mightst bee,	Ovid's Elegies 3.10.41
With Muse oppos'd would I my lines had done,	Ovid's Elegies 3.11.17
Would I my words would any credit beare.	Ovid's Elegies 3.11.20
Forbare no wanton words you there would speake,	Ovid's Elegies 3.13.25
And would be dead, but dying <dead> with thee remaine.	Ovid's Elegies 3.13.40
Many would praise the sweet smell as she past,	Hero and Leander 1.21
for neither sunne nor wind/Would burne or parch her hands,	Hero and Leander 1.28
Such as the world would woonder to behold:	Hero and Leander 1.34
Which as shee went would cherupe through the bils.	Hero and Leander 1.36
Would have allur'd the vent'rous youth of Greece,	Hero and Leander 1.57
And such as knew he was a man would say,	Hero and Leander 1.87
Were I the saint hee worships, I would heare him,	Hero and Leander 1.179
I would my rude words had the influence,	Hero and Leander 1.200
All heaven would come to claime this legacie,	Hero and Leander 1.250
And would be thought to graunt against her will.	Hero and Leander 1.336
answered Love, nor would vouchsafe so much/As one poore word,	Hero and Leander 1.383
his parentage, would needs discover/The way to new Elisium:	Hero and Leander 1.410
And neither would denie, nor graunt his sute.	Hero and Leander 1.424
And would have turn'd againe, but was afrayd,	Hero and Leander 2.8
That he would leave her turret and depart.	Hero and Leander 2.38
O what god would not therewith be appeas'd?	Hero and Leander 2.50
And stay the messenger that would be gon:	Hero and Leander 2.82
though Hero would not yeeld/So soone to part from that she	Hero and Leander 2.83
He would have chac'd away the swelling maine,	Hero and Leander 2.121
At every stroke, betwixt them would he slide,	Hero and Leander 2.184
and up-staring <upstarting> Fawnes,/Would steale him thence.	Hero and Leander 2.201
Would animate grosse clay, and higher set/The drooping thoughts	Hero and Leander 2.256
And faine by stealth away she would have crept,	Hero and Leander 2.310

WOULDE

Yet musicke woulde doe well to cheare up Zenocrate:	1Tamb	4.4.62	P	Tamb

WOULDST

Full soone wouldst thou abjure this single life.	Dido	3.1.60	Dido
Out hatefull hag, thou wouldst have slaine my sonne,	Dido	3.2.32	Venus
Thou wouldst have leapt from out the Sailers hands,	Dido	4.4.141	Dido
So thou wouldst prove as true as Paris did,	Dido	5.1.146	Dido
And wouldst thou have me buy thy Fathers love/With such a	1Tamb	4.4.83	Tamb
And yet wouldst shun the wavering turnes of war,	1Tamb	5.1.360	Zenoc
I know thou wouldst depart from hence with me.	2Tamb	1.2.11	Callap
Thou wouldst with overmatch of person fight,	2Tamb	3.5.76	Orcan
So thou wouldst smile and take me in thy <thine> armes.	Edw	1.1.9	Gavstn
Let me see, thou wouldst do well/To waite at my trencher, and	Edw	1.1.30	Gavstn
That wouldst reward them with an hospitall.	Edw	1.1.38	3PrMan
Wouldst thou be lovde and fearde?	Edw	1.1.168	Edward
Couldst <Wouldst> thou make men <man> to live eternally,	F 52	1.1.24	Faust
Now Faustus what wouldst thou have me do?	F 263	1.3.35	Mephst
Wouldst thou make a Colossus of me, that thou askest me such	F1646	4.6.89	P Faust
Albeit the Citty thou wouldst have so ra'st/Be Roome it selfe.	Lucan, First Booke	386	
Excludst a lover, how wouldst use a foe?	Ovid's Elegies	1.6.31	
Then wouldst thou cry, stay night and runne not thus.	Ovid's Elegies	1.13.40	
To kinde requests thou wouldst more gentle prove,	Ovid's Elegies	2.3.5	
How wouldst thou flowe wert thou a noble floud,	Ovid's Elegies	3.5.89	
Seeing now thou wouldst deceive me as before:	Ovid's Elegies	3.6.70	
But that thou wouldst dissemble when tis paste.	Ovid's Elegies	3.13.4	
Who on Loves seas more glorious wouldst appeare?	Hero and Leander	1.228	

WOUND (Homograph)

And with the [wind] <wound> thereof the King fell downe:	Dido	2.1.254	Aeneas
As every touch shall wound Queene Didos heart.	Dido	2.1.333	Cupid
Wound on the barkes of odoriferous trees,	Dido	3.1.117	Dido
And with my blood my life slides through my wound,	1Tamb	2.7.43	Cosroe
[Agidas], leave to wound me with these words:	1Tamb	3.2.35	Zenoc
Returne with victorie, and free from wound.	1Tamb	3.3.133	Zenoc
make our <your> strokes to wound the sencelesse [aire] <lure>.	1Tamb	3.3.158	Tamb
As now it bringeth sweetnesse to my wound,	1Tamb	5.1.420	Arabia
In this my mortall well deserved wound,	2Tamb	2.3.6	Sgsmnd
And wound the earth, that it may cleave in twaine,	2Tamb	2.4.97	Tamb
or with a Curtle-axe/To hew thy flesh and make a gaping wound?	2Tamb	3.2.97	Tamb
Quite voide of skars, and cleare from any wound,	2Tamb	3.2.112	Tamb
A wound is nothing be it nere so deepe,	2Tamb	3.2.115	Tamb
a souldier, and this wound/As great a grace and majesty to me,	2Tamb	3.2.117	Tamb
Come boyes and with your fingers search my wound,	2Tamb	3.2.126	Tamb
Now my boyes, what think you of a wound?	2Tamb	3.2.129	Tamb
give me a wound father.	2Tamb	3.2.132	P Celeb
It shall suffice thou darst abide a wound.	2Tamb	3.2.136	Tamb
My speech of war, and this my wound you see,	2Tamb	3.2.142	Tamb
and let this wound appease/The mortall furie of great	2Tamb	5.1.153	Govnr
Oh I have my deaths wound, give me leave to speak.	P1003	19.73	Guise
Pleaseth your grace to let the Surgeon search your wound.	P1191	22.53	Navrre
The wound I warrant ye is deepe my Lord,	P1192	22.54	King
Alas my Lord, the wound is dangerous,	P1212	22.74	Srgeon
Yea, I will wound Achilles in the heele,	F1779	5.1.106	Faust
me,/Because at his commaund I wound not up/My conquering Eagles?	Lucan, First Booke	339	
And they whom fierce Bellonaes fury moves/To wound their armes,	Lucan, First Booke	564	
hellish fiend/Which made the sterne Lycurgus wound his thigh,	Lucan, First Booke	573	
I lately cought, will have a new made wound,	Ovid's Elegies	1.2.29	

WOUND (cont.)
About my head be quivering Mirtle wound, Ovid's Elegies 1.15.37
Doest harme, and in thy tents why doest me wound? Ovid's Elegies 2.9.4
And give to him that the first wound imparts. Ovid's Elegies 3.12.22
And wound them on his arme, and for her mourn'd. Hero and Leander 1.376
About his armes the purple riband wound, Hero and Leander 2.106
Leander striv'd, the waves about him wound, Hero and Leander 2.159
When this fresh bleeding wound Leander viewd, Hero and Leander 2.213
WOUNDED
Which sent an eccho to the wounded King: Dido 2.1.249 Aeneas
And wounded bodies gasping yet for life. 1Tamb 5.1.323 Zenoc
Lye down Arabia, wounded to the death, 1Tamb 5.1.407 Arabia
Behold her wounded in conceit for thee, 1Tamb 5.1.415 Zenoc
If I had not bin wounded as I am. 1Tamb 5.1.421 Arabia
We may be slaine or wounded ere we learne. 2Tamb 3.2.94 Calyph
With open crie pursues the wounded Stag: 2Tamb 3.5.7 2Msngr
Wounded with shame, and kill'd with discontent, 2Tamb 4.1.94 Tamb
bleeding harts/Wounded and broken with your Highnesse griefe, 2Tamb 5.3.162 Amyras
Wounded and poysoned, both at once? P1215 22.77 King
And tis suppos'd Loves bowe hath wounded thee, Ovid's Elegies 1.11.11
But heale the heart, that thou hast wounded thus, Hero and Leander 1.324
WOUNDES
Have swelling cloudes drawen from wide gasping woundes, 1Tamb 5.1.459 Tamb
Whose head hath deepest scarres, whose breast most woundes, 2Tamb 1.3.75 Tamb
And wilt thou shun the field for feare of woundes? 2Tamb 3.2.109 Tamb
And give woundes infinite at everie turne. Ovid's Elegies 1.2.44
With selfe same woundes he gave, he ought to smart. Ovid's Elegies 2.3.4
WOUNDING
they come to proove/The wounding troubles angry war affoords. 2Tamb 1.3.87 Zenoc
Which if a shower of wounding thunderbolts/Should breake out 2Tamb 2.2.13 Gazell
Wounding the world with woonder and with love, 2Tamb 2.4.82 Tamb
wounding my selfe when I could get none <had no body> to fight F 689 2.2.138 P Wrath
WOUNDS (See also ZOUNDS)
That doe complaine the wounds of thousand waves, Dido 1.2.8 Illion
and his breast/Furrowd with wounds, and that which made me Dido 2.1.204 Aeneas
I, this it is which wounds me to the death, Dido 3.3.63 Iarbus
And gore thy body with as many wounds. 1Tamb 5.1.216 Bajzth
Dreadlesse of blowes, of bloody wounds and death: 2Tamb 3.2.140 Tamb
Looke, Katherin, looke, thy sonne gave mine these wounds. Jew 3.2.16 Govnr
Who wounds me with the name of Mortimer/That bloudy man? Edw 4.7.38 Edward
being strucke/Runnes to an herbe that closeth up the wounds, Edw 5.1.10 Edward
friends death; and our wounds; our wintering/Under the Alpes; Lucan, First Booke 303
If without battell selfe-wrought wounds annoy them, Ovid's Elegies 2.14.3
See a rich chuffe whose wounds great wealth inferr'd, Ovid's Elegies 3.7.9
He wounds with love, and forst them equallie, Hero and Leander 1.445
WRACK
Tis for your safetie and your enemies wrack. P 858 17.53 Guise
The Popedome cannot stand, all goes to wrack, P1087 19.157 QnMoth
the Papall Monarck goes/To wrack, and [his] antechristian P1198 22.60 King
Misgoverned kings are cause of all this wrack, Edw 4.4.9 Queene
shame, and such as seeke loves wrack/Shall follow thee, their Ovid's Elegies 1.2.31
WRACKE
Prepared stands to wracke their woodden walles, Dido 1.1.67 Venus
I mustred all the windes unto his wracke, Dido 3.2.45 Juno
And hover in the straightes for Christians wracke, 1Tamb 3.3.250 Tamb
walke about/The ruin'd Towne, and see the wracke we made: Jew 5.2.19 Calym
I see no reason but of Malta's wracke, Jew 5.2.58 Govnr
Would dash the wreath thou wearst for Pirats wracke. Lucan, First Booke 123
Wilt thou thy wombe-inclosed off-spring wracke? Ovid's Elegies 2.14.8
Therefore in signe her treasure suffred wracke, Hero and Leander 1.49
WRACKES
And fetch the treasure of all forraine wrackes: F 172 1.1.144 Cornel
I pray that rotten age you wrackes/And sluttish white-mould Ovid's Elegies 1.12.29
WRACKFULL
Disperst them all amongst the wrackfull Rockes: Dido 1.2.29 Cloan
WRACK'S
even the same that wrack's all great [dominions] <dominion>. Lucan, First Booke 160
WRACKT
And they so wrackt and weltred by the waves, Dido 1.1.223 Aeneas
Wast thou not wrackt upon this Libian shoare, Dido 5.1.161 Dido
I feare me he is wrackt upon the sea. Edw 2.2.2 Edward
Being wrackt, carowse the sea tir'd by their ships: Ovid's Elegies 2.10.34
The Argos wrackt had deadly waters drunke. Ovid's Elegies 2.11.6
How almost wrackt thy ship in maine seas fell. Ovid's Elegies 2.11.50
WRANGLING
More fitly had [they] <thy> wrangling bondes contained/From Ovid's Elegies 1.12.23
WRAPPED
Wrapped in curles, as fierce Achilles was, 1Tamb 2.1.24 Menaph
WRAPT
And wrapt in silence of his angry soule. 1Tamb 3.2.71 Agidas
a fiery exhalation/Wrapt in the bowels of a freezing cloude, 1Tamb 4.2.44 Tamb
her rusty coach/Engyrt with tempests wrapt in pitchy clouds, 1Tamb 5.1.295 Bajzth
Shall carie wrapt within his scarlet waves, 2Tamb 1.1.34 Orcan
The sailes wrapt up, the mast and tacklings downe, 2Tamb 1.2.59 Callap
Wee'll send [thee] <the> bullets wrapt in smoake and fire: Jew 2.2.54 Govnr
Oft dyes she that her paunch-wrapt child hath slaine. Ovid's Elegies 2.14.38
WRASTLING
his grave looke appeasd/The wrastling tumult, and right hand Lucan, First Booke 299
WRATH (See also WROTH)
Epeus pine-tree Horse/A sacrifize t'appease Minervas wrath: Dido 2.1.163 Aeneas
So I escapt the furious Pirrhus wrath: Dido 2.1.223 Aeneas
That ugly impe that shall outweare my wrath, Dido 3.2.4 Juno
Fie Venus, that such causeles words of wrath, Dido 3.2.26 Juno

WRATH (cont.)			
Or els abide the wrath of frowning Jove.	Dido	5.1.54	Hermes
I tel you true my heart is swolne with wrath, ...	1Tamb	2.2.2	Mycet
Least he incurre the furie of my wrath.	1Tamb	3.1.30	Bajzth
Threatned with frowning wrath and jealousie, ...	1Tamb	3.2.67	Agidas
I that am tearm'd the Scourge and Wrath of God, . . .	1Tamb	3.3.44	Tamb
And dig for treasure to appease my wrath:	1Tamb	3.3.265	Tamb
Then must his kindled wrath bee quencht with blood: . .	1Tamb	4.1.56	2Msngr
Halfe dead for feare before they feele my wrath: . .	1Tamb	4.4.4	Tamb
The wrath of Tamburlain, and power of warres. . . .	1Tamb	5.1.44	Govnr
staid, with wrath and hate/Of our expreslesse band inflictions.	1Tamb	5.1.281	Bajzth
with my heart/Wish your release, but he whose wrath is death,	2Tamb	1.2.6	Almeda
Or bind thee in eternall torments wrath.	2Tamb	3.5.113	Soria
T'appease my wrath, or els Ile torture thee, ...	2Tamb	3.5.122	Tamb
any Element/Shal shrowde thee from the wrath of Tamburlaine.	2Tamb	3.5.127	Tamb
Wrath kindled in the furnace of his breast, . . .	2Tamb	4.1.9	Celeb
That Tamburlains intollorable wrath/May be suppresst by our	2Tamb	5.1.8	Maxim
Before I bide the wrath of Tamburlaine.	2Tamb	5.1.42	2Citzn
There is a God full of revenging wrath, ...	2Tamb	5.1.183	Tamb
Against the wrath and tyranny of death, ...	2Tamb	5.3.221	Techel
But that will more exasperate his wrath, ...	Edw	1.4.182	Queene
Moov'd may he be, and perish in his wrath.	Edw	2.2.101	Mortmr
T'appeaze the wrath of their offended king.	Edw	3.1.210	Edward
To them that fight in right and feare his wrath: . . .	Edw	4.6.20	Queene
And heape Gods heavy wrath upon thy head.	F 99	1.1.71	GdAngl
slow to wrath, and prone to letcherie (to love I would say) it	F 210	1.2.17	P Wagner
I am Wrath:	F 686	2.2.135	P Wrath
For gentle sonne, I speake it not in wrath, ...	F1719	5.1.46	OldMan
And hide me from the heavy wrath of [God] <heaven>. . .	F1946	5.2.150	Faust
Who seeing hunters pauseth till fell wrath/And kingly rage	Lucan, First Booke		209
But now the winters wrath and wat'ry moone, ...	Lucan, First Booke		219
as might make/Wrath-kindled Jove away his thunder shake. .	Ovid's Elegies		2.5.52
Angry I was, but feare my wrath exempted.	Ovid's Elegies		2.13.4
WRATHFUL			
forraine wars ill thriv'd; or wrathful France/Pursu'd us hither,	Lucan, First Booke		308
WRATHFULL			
And know my customes are as peremptory/As wrathfull Planets,	1Tamb	5.1.128	Tamb
And dangerous chances of the wrathfull war?	2Tamb	1.3.11	Zenoc
Seest thou not death within my wrathfull looks? . . .	2Tamb	3.5.119	Tamb
The wrathfull messenger of mighty Jove, ...	2Tamb	5.1.92	Tamb
This wrathfull hand should strike thee to the hart. . .	P 690	13.34	Guise
Anger and wrathfull furie stops my speech.	Edw	1.4.42	Edward
For now the wrathfull nobles threaten warres, ...	Edw	2.2.210	Kent
Thus after many threats of wrathfull warre, ...	Edw	4.3.1	Edward
He rends and teares it with his wrathfull pawe, . . .	Edw	5.1.12	Edward
WRATH-KINDLED			
as might make/Wrath-kindled Jove away his thunder shake. .	Ovid's Elegies		2.5.52
WREAKE			
These plagues arise from wreake of civill power. . . .	Lucan, First Booke		32
WREAKES			
what each one speakes/Beleeve, no tempest the beleever wreakes.	Ovid's Elegies		2.11.22
WREATH			
And take in signe thereof this gilded wreath, ...	1Tamb	5.1.101	1Virgn
Would dash the wreath thou wearst for Pirats wracke. .	Lucan, First Booke		123
Upon her head she ware a myrtle wreath, ...	Hero and Leander		1.17
WREATH'D			
Wherewith she wreath'd her largely spreading heare, . . .	Hero and Leander		2.107
WREATHE			
Or like the snakie wreathe of Tisiphon, ...	Edw	5.1.45	Edward
WREATHED			
And Rams with hornes their hard heads wreathed back. .	Ovid's Elegies		3.12.17
WREATHES			
With sacrificing wreathes upon his head, ...	Dido	2.1.148	Aeneas
Loden with Lawrell wreathes to crowne us all.	2Tamb	3.5.164	Tamb
And we are grac'd with wreathes of victory:	P 788	16.2	Navrre
Then wreathes about my necke her winding armes, . . .	Ovid's Elegies		2.18.9
Victorious wreathes at length my Temples greete. . .	Ovid's Elegies		3.10.6
WRECKE (See also WRACKE)			
Blind, Fryer, I wrecke not thy perswasions.	Jew	1.2.355	Barab
We come in armes to wrecke it with the [sword] <swords>: .	Edw	4.4.23	Mortmr
WRENNE			
The Wrenne may strive against the Lions strength, . . .	Edw	5.3.34	Edward
WRESTLING (See WRASTLING)			
WRETCH			
O cursed hagge and false dissembling wretch!	Dido	5.1.216	Dido
Out, out thou wretch.	Jew	1.2.365	Barab
Hard harted to the poore, a covetous wretch, ...	Jew	4.1.52	Barab
Looke for no other fortune wretch then death, ...	Edw	2.5.17	Lncstr
Vilde wretch, and why hast thou of all unkinde, . . .	Edw	4.6.5	Kent
Out envious wretch <Away envious rascall>:	F 685	2.2.134	Faust
Where art thou Faustus? wretch, what hast thou done? .	F1724	5.1.51	Faust
Accursed Faustus, <wretch what hast thou done>? . . .	F1739	(HC270)B	Faust
Thou damned wretch, and execrable dogge, ...	F App	p.238 72	Knight
At last learne wretch to leave thy monarchy;	Lucan, First Booke		335
[wretch] <wench> I sawe when thou didst thinke I slumbred,	Ovid's Elegies		2.5.13
My selfe poore wretch mine owne gifts now envie. . .	Ovid's Elegies		2.15.8
WRETCHED			
Yet who so wretched but desires to live?	Dido	2.1.238	Aeneas
I must be pleasde perforce, wretched Zenocrate. . . .	1Tamb	1.2.259	Zenoc
Yet in compassion of his wretched state, ...	1Tamb	4.3.35	Souldn
(sacred Emperour)/The prostrate service of this wretched towne.	1Tamb	5.1.100	1Virgn
Wretched Zenocrate, that livest to see, ...	1Tamb	5.1.319	Zenoc
Ah wretched eies, the enemies of my hart, ...	1Tamb	5.1.340	Zenoc

WRETCHED (cont.)
eies beholde/That as for her thou bearst these wretched armes, 1Tamb 5.1.409 Arabia
Turn'd to dispaire, would break my wretched breast, 2Tamb 2.4.64 Zenoc
my striving hands/From martiall justice on thy wretched soule. 2Tamb 4.1.96 Tamb
Your soul gives essence to our wretched subjects, 2Tamb 5.3.164 Amyras
Out wretched Barabas, Jew 1.2.118 Govnr
The Jew of Malta, wretched Barabas; Jew 1.2.318 Abigal
Oh wretched Abigal, what hast [thou] <thee> done? Jew 2.3.320 Abigal
Wretched Ferneze might have veng'd thy death. Jew 3.2.14 Govnr
And onely this torments my wretched soule, Edw 1.4.123 Edward
We were imbarkt for Ireland, wretched we, Edw 4.7.33 Baldck
To wretched men death is felicitie. Edw 5.1.127 Edward
Here in this roome will wretched Faustus be. F1804 5.2.8 Mephst
So when as Crassus wretched death who stayd them, Lucan, First Booke 104
Made with the blood of wretched Lovers slaine. Hero and Leander 1.16
Wretched Ixions shaggie footed race, Hero and Leander 1.114
WRETCHEDNESSE
(Uttered with teares of wretchednesse and blood, 1Tamb 5.1.25 1Virgn
WRETCHES
Wretches of Troy, envied of the windes, Dido 1.2.4 Illion
Why should we live, O wretches, beggars, slaves, 1Tamb 5.1.248 Zabina
Accursed wretches, wast in regard of us, Edw 3.1.233 Edward
Poore wretches on the tree themselves did strangle, Ovid's Elegies 1.12.17
WRIGHT
And wright a Deed of Gift with thine owne bloud; F 424 2.1.36 Mephst
WRINCKLES
Shake off these wrinckles that thy front assault, Ovid's Elegies 1.8.45
Wrinckles in beauty is a grievous fault. Ovid's Elegies 1.8.46
Because thy belly should rough wrinckles lacke, Ovid's Elegies 2.14.7
WRING (See also WROONG)
Even as a bird, which in our hands we wring, Hero and Leander 2.289
WRINGING
Sits wringing of her hands, and beats her brest. Edw 1.4.188 Lncstr
WRINGS
I, I, but he teares his haire, and wrings his handes, Edw 5.6.18 Queene
WRIT
rest and have one Epitaph/Writ in as many severall languages, 2Tamb 2.4.135 Tamb
Greek, is writ/This towne being burnt by Tamburlaine the great, 2Tamb 3.2.16 Calyph
That suffers flames of fire to burne the writ/Wherein the sum 2Tamb 5.1.190 Tamb
sure/When like the [Dracos] <Drancus> they were writ in blood. Jew Prol.21 Machvl
devil invented a challenge, my master writ it, and I carried it, Jew 3.3.18 P Ithimr
This is the Gentleman you writ to. Jew 4.2.37 P Pilia
I carried it, I confesse, but who writ it? Jew 5.1.32 P Ithimr
Which your wife writ to my deare Minion, P 755 15.13 King
the greater sway/When as a kings name shall be under writ. Edw 5.2.14 Mortmr
My sences are deceiv'd, here's nothing writ: F 468 2.1.80 Faust
I see it plaine, even heere <in this place> is writ/Homo fuge: F 469 2.1.81 Faust
I writ them a bill with mine owne bloud, the date is expired: F1860 5.2.64 P Faust
Lines thou shalt read in wine by my hand writ. Ovid's Elegies 1.4.20
give her my writ/But see that forth-with shee peruseth it. Ovid's Elegies 1.11.15
Are both in Fames eternall legend writ. Ovid's Elegies 1.15.20
Her trembling hand writ back she might not doo. Ovid's Elegies 2.2.6
the boord with wine/Was scribled, and thy fingers writ a line. Ovid's Elegies 2.5.18
Nor in my bookes shall one but thou be writ, Ovid's Elegies 2.17.33
When Thebes, when Troy, when Caesar should be writ, Ovid's Elegies 3.11.15
WRITE (See also WRIGHT)
And write my selfe great Lord of Affrica: 1Tamb 3.3.245 Tamb
I'le write unto his Majesty for ayd, Jew 2.2.40 Bosco
What, dares the villain write in such base terms? Jew 3.2.3 Lodowk
So sure did your father write, and I cary the chalenge. Jew 3.3.25 P Ithimr
I'le write unto him, we'le have mony strait. Jew 4.2.69 P Ithimr
Write not so submissively, but threatning him. Jew 4.2.72 P Pilia
Write for five hundred Crownes. Jew 4.2.116 P Pilia
tell him, I scorne to write a line under a hundred crownes. Jew 4.2.121 P Ithimr
I love him as my selfe/Should write in this imperious vaine! Jew 4.3.43 Barab
Prethe sweet love, one more, and write it sharp. Jew 4.4.73 Curtzn
That I may write unto my dearest Lord. P 659 13.3 Duchss
to speak with him/But cannot, and therfore am enforst to write, P 663 13.7 Duchss
O would to God this quill that heere doth write, P 667 13.11 Duchss
Quick quick my lorde, I long to write my name. Edw 1.4.4 Lncstr
In steede of inke, ile write it with my teares. Edw 1.4.86 Edward
write a letter presently/Unto the Lord of Bartley from Edw 5.2.47 Mortmr
But Faustus/<thou must> Write it in manner of a Deed of Gift. F 449 2.1.61 Mephst
My bloud congeales, and I can write no more. F 451 2.1.63 Faust
Is it unwilling I should write this byll? F 454 2.1.66 Faust
Why streames it not, that I may write a fresh? F 455 2.1.67 Faust
Then write againe: Faustus gives to thee his soule. F 458 2.1.70 Faust
That I may write things worthy thy faire lookes: Ovid's Elegies 1.3.20
The rest my hand doth in my letters write. Ovid's Elegies 1.11.14
Straight being read, will her to write much backe, Ovid's Elegies 1.11.19
Borne at Peligny, to write more addresse. Ovid's Elegies 2.1.2
Another railes at me, and that I write, Ovid's Elegies 2.4.21
(Alas my precepts turne my selfe to smart)/We write, or what Ovid's Elegies 2.18.21
WRITES
Now here she writes, and wils me to repent. Jew 3.4.5 Barab
for she writes further, that she loves me ever since she saw Jew 4.2.33 P Ithimr
what hee writes for you, ye shall have streight. Jew 4.3.27 P Barab
I prethee say to whome thou writes? P 671 13.15 Guise
WRITING
What, all alone my love, and writing too: P 670 13.14 Guise
WRITINGS
And writings did from diverse places frame, Ovid's Elegies 2.18.28
WRITTE
I hate faire paper should writte matter lacke. Ovid's Elegies 1.11.20

WRITTEN
Shall finde it written on confusions front, Dido 3.2.19 Juno
I wot his wealth/Was written thus: Jew 1.2.182 Barab
Every ones price is written on his backe, Jew 2.3.3 2Offcr
Dearely beloved brother, thus tis written. P 343 5.70 Guise
By Mortimer, whose name is written here, Edw 5.1.139 Edward
This letter written by a friend of ours, Edw 5.4.6 Mortmr
I see my tragedie written in thy browes, Edw 5.5.74 Edward
above written being inviolate, full power to fetch or carry the F 497 2.1.109 P Faust

WRONG
That durst thus proudly wrong our kinsmans peace. Dido 1.1.119 Jupitr
We come not we to wrong your Libian Gods, Dido 1.2.10 Illion
And wrong my deitie with high disgrace: Dido 3.2.5 Juno
Ungentle, can she wrong Iarbus so? Dido 3.3.10 Iarbus
Women may wrong by priviledge of love: Dido 3.3.25 Iarbus
Durst in disdaine of wrong and tyrannie, 1Tamb 2.1.55 Ceneus
Wherein he wrought such ignominious wrong, 1Tamb 4.3.39 Souldn
And therefore ne're distinguish of the wrong. Jew 1.2.151 Barab
Your extreme right does me exceeding wrong: Jew 1.2.153 Barab
Stands here a purpose, meaning me some wrong, Jew 4.1.166 1Fryar
And since by wrong thou got'st Authority, Jew 5.2.35 Barab
That right or wrong, thou deale thy selfe a King. P 148 2.91 Guise
I deepely sorrow for your trecherous wrong: P 263 4.61 Charls
We will not wrong thee so, Edw 2.5.69 Mortmr
O treacherous Warwicke thus to wrong thy friend! Edw 2.6.1 Gavstn
And wrong our lord, your honorable friend. Edw 2.6.9 James
Helpe unckle Kent, Mortimer will wrong me. Edw 5.2.113 Prince
force, they that now thwart right/In wars wil yeeld to wrong: Lucan, First Booke 350
with thrids on wrong wheeles spun/And what with Mares ranck Ovid's Elegies 1.8.7
And doing wrong made shew of innocence. Ovid's Elegies 2.19.14
And thou, if falsely charged to wrong thy friend, Ovid's Elegies 3.8.63

WRONG'D
And know that some have wrong'd Dianas name? Hero and Leander 1.284
As if her name and honour had beene wrong'd, Hero and Leander 2.35

WRONGD
And wish that I had never wrongd him so: Dido 3.2.48 Juno
Your king hath wrongd your countrie and himselfe, Edw 4.6.67 Mortmr
O Gaveston, it is for thee that I am wrongd, Edw 5.3.41 Edward
And as first wrongd the wronged some-times banish, Ovid's Elegies 1.8.79

WRONGDE
Mortimer shall know that he hath wrongde mee. Edw 5.2.118 Kent

WRONGED
What shall I doe thus wronged with disdaine? Dido 3.3.69 Iarbus
it be to injure them/That have so manifestly wronged us, Jew 1.2.275 Abigal
But ile to Fraunce, and cheere the wronged Queene, Edw 4.1.6 Kent
And as first wrongd the wronged some-times banish, Ovid's Elegies 1.8.79
The wronged Gods dread faire ones to offend, Ovid's Elegies 3.3.31

WRONGES
And for the open wronges and injuries/Edward hath done to us, Edw 4.4.21 Mortmr
Me thinkes I should revenge me of the wronges, Edw 5.1.24 Edward
That wronges their liege and soveraigne, Englands king. Edw 5.3.40 Edward
And for your sakes, a thousand wronges ile take, Edw 5.3.43 Edward

WRONGFULLY
That holdes it from your highnesse wrongfully: P 582 11.47 Pleshe

WRONGING
And to my losse God-wronging perjuries? Ovid's Elegies 3.10.22

WRONGLY
From doubtfull Roome wrongly expel'd the Tribunes, Lucan, First Booke 269

WRONGS
Redresse these wrongs, and warne him to his ships/That now Dido 4.2.21 Iarbus
Bearing the vengeance of our fathers wrongs, 2Tamb 3.1.17 Callap
That Jove surchardg'd with pity of our wrongs, 2Tamb 3.1.35 Callap
What? bring you Scripture to confirm your wrongs? Jew 1.2.110 Barab
Why weepe you not to thinke upon my wrongs? Jew 1.2.172 Barab
Till they reduce the wrongs done to my father. Jew 1.2.235 Abigal
Malta to a wildernesse/For these intolerable wrongs of yours; Jew 3.5.26 Basso
Oh my sweet hart, how do I mone thy wrongs, Edw 4.2.27 Queene
When every servile groome jeasts at my wrongs, F1329 4.2.5 Benvol
First, on his head, in quittance of my wrongs, F1379 4.2.55 Benvol
That spite of spite, our wrongs are doubled? F1446 4.3.16 Benvol

WRONG'ST
I, Barabas, or else thou wrong'st me much. Jew 2.3.255 Mthias

WRONGST
In saying this, thou wrongst me Gaveston, Edw 1.4.149 Queene

WROONG
And with the other, wine from grapes out wroong. Hero and Leander 1.140
Sad Hero wroong him by the hand, and wept, Hero and Leander 2.95

WROTE
Her name had bene in every line he wrote: 2Tamb 2.4.90 Tamb
In that I know the things that I have wrote, P 403 7.43 Ramus

WROTH
Which being wroth, sends lightning from his eies, 2Tamb 1.3.76 Tamb

WROUGHT
of foulded Lawne, where shall be wrought/The warres of Troy, Dido 3.1.124 Dido
And wrought him mickle woe on sea and land, Dido 3.2.41 Juno
Who having wrought her shame, is straight way fled: Dido 4.2.18 Iarbus
Their plumed helmes are wrought with beaten golde. 1Tamb 1.2.124 Souldr
wrought in him with passion,/Thirsting with soverainty, with 1Tamb 2.1.19 Menaph
Wherein he wrought such ignominious wrong, 1Tamb 4.3.39 Souldn
shal be plac'd/Wrought with the Persean and Egyptian armes, 2Tamb 3.2.20 Amyras
I was afraid the poyson had not wrought; Jew 4.1.4 Barab
Or though it wrought, it would have done no good, Jew 4.1.5 Barab
But hath thy potion wrought so happilie? Edw 4.1.14 Kent

WROUGHT (cont.)			
And then turning my selfe to a wrought Smocke do what I list.	F 668	2.2.117	P Pride
No envious tongue wrought thy thicke lockes decay. . .	Ovid's Elegies		1.14.42
If without battell selfe-wrought wounds annoy them, . .	Ovid's Elegies		2.14.3
Her long haires eare-wrought garland fell away. . .	Ovid's Elegies		3.9.36
WUD			
Who in my wealth wud tell me winters tales, ...	Jew	2.1.25	Barab
He said he wud attend me in the morne.	Jew	2.1.34	Abigal
I wud you were his father too, Sir, that's al the harm I wish	Jew	2.3.41	P Barab
Oh but I know your Lordship wud disdaine/To marry with the	Jew	2.3.294	Barab
As I wud see thee hang'd; oh, love stops my breath: . .	Jew	4.3.53	Barab
Then now are all things as my wish wud have 'em, . .	Jew	5.5.17	Barab
WUDST			
What wudst thou doe if he should send thee none? . .	Jew	4.4.13	Pilia
WUN			
Wun on the fiftie headed Vuolgas waves, ...	1Tamb	1.2.103	Tamb
WUNNE			
The Sabine gauntlets were too dearely wunne/That unto death did	Ovid's Elegies		1.10.49
I guide and souldiour wunne the field and weare her, .	Ovid's Elegies		2.12.13
Th'Arcadian Virgins constant love hath wunne?	Ovid's Elegies		3.5.30
WURST			
Do all thy wurst, nor death, nor Tamburlaine, ...	2Tamb	5.1.112	Govnr
XANTHUS (See ZANTHUS)			
XERXES			
The host of Xerxes, which by fame is said/To drinke the mightie	1Tamb	2.3.15	Tamb
Y'			
Parthians y'afflict us more then ye suppose, ...	Lucan, First Booke		107
Y'AFFLICT			
Parthians y'afflict us more then ye suppose, ...	Lucan, First Booke		107
YAWNING			
No vaine sprung out but from the yawning gash, . . .	Lucan, First Booke		613
(When yawning dragons draw her thirling carre, . . .	Hero and Leander		1.108
YCE			
Fetters the Euxin sea, with chaines of yce:	Lucan, First Booke		18
YE (See also Y', YEE)			
And Helens rape doth haunt [ye] <thee> at the heeles. .	Dido	1.1.144	Aeneas
Where Dido will receive ye with her smiles:	Dido	1.1.234	Venus
Follow ye Troians, follow this brave Lord, ...	Dido	1.2.1	Illion
Unto what fruitfull quarters were ye bound, ...	Dido	1.2.18	Iarbus
My selfe will see they shall not trouble ye, ...	Dido	1.2.38	Iarbus
Take what ye will, but leave Aeneas here.	Dido	3.1.127	Dido
How now Getulian, are ye growne so brave, ...	Dido	3.3.19	Dido
In all this coyle, where have ye left the Queene? . . .	Dido	4.1.14	Iarbus
Blow windes, threaten ye Rockes and sandie shelfes, . . .	Dido	4.4.58	Aeneas
Ile hang ye in the chamber where I lye, ...	Dido	4.4.128	Dido
For this will Dido tye ye full of knots, ...	Dido	4.4.155	Dido
And sheere ye all asunder with her hands:	Dido	4.4.156	Dido
Ye shall no more offend the Carthage Queene.	Dido	4.4.158	Dido
My Lord Ascanius, ye must goe with me.	Dido	4.5.1	Nurse
Now speake Ascanius, will ye goe or no?	Dido	4.5.12	Nurse
How pretilie he laughs, goe ye wagge, ...	Dido	4.5.19	Nurse
Which if it chaunce, Ile give ye buriall, ...	Dido	5.1.176	Dido
How can ye goe when he hath all your fleete?	Dido	5.1.242	Anna
And now ye gods that guide the starrie frame, ...	Dido	5.1.302	Dido
Lie here ye weedes that I disdaine to weare, ...	1Tamb	1.2.41	Tamb
Soft ye my Lords and sweet Zenocrate.	1Tamb	1.2.119	Tamb
Drums, why sound ye not when Meander speaks.	1Tamb	2.2.75	Mycet
You will not sell it, wil ye?	1Tamb	2.4.29	Tamb
Ye Moores and valiant men of Barbary, ...	1Tamb	3.3.89	Moroc
How can ye suffer these indignities?	1Tamb	3.3.90	Moroc
Ye Gods and powers that governe Persea, ...	1Tamb	3.3.189	Zenoc
Ah villaines, dare ye touch my sacred armes?	1Tamb	3.3.268	Bajzth
Awake ye men of Memphis, heare the clange/Of Scythian trumpets,	1Tamb	4.1.1	Souldn
Ye holy Priests of heavenly Mahomet, ...	1Tamb	4.2.2	Bajzth
have ye lately heard/The overthrow of mightie Bajazeth, .	1Tamb	4.3.23	Arabia
Ye Furies that can maske invisible, ...	1Tamb	4.4.17	Bajzth
could they not as well/Have sent ye out, when first my .	1Tamb	5.1.68	Tamb
in vaine ye labour to prevent/That which mine honor sweares	1Tamb	5.1.106	Tamb
Why feed ye still on daies accursed beams, ...	1Tamb	5.1.262	Bajzth
How are ye glutted with these grievous objects, . . .	1Tamb	5.1.341	Zenoc
A friendly parle might become ye both.	2Tamb	1.1.117	Gazell
But now my friends, let me examine ye, ...	2Tamb	1.3.172	Tamb
How have ye spent your absent time from me?	2Tamb	1.3.173	Tamb
When this is done, then are ye souldiers, ...	2Tamb	3.2.91	Tamb
How say ye Souldiers, Shal we not?	2Tamb	3.3.9	Techel
For think ye I can live, and see him dead?	2Tamb	3.4.27	Sonne
The gold, the silver, and the pearle ye got, ...	2Tamb	3.4.88	Therid
Ye petty kings of Turkye I am come, ...	2Tamb	3.5.64	Tamb
I see how fearfully ye would refuse, ...	2Tamb	3.5.73	Tamb
As ye shal curse the byrth of Tamburlaine.	2Tamb	3.5.89	Tamb
And when ye stay, be lasht with whips of wier:	2Tamb	3.5.105	Tamb
How now ye pety kings, loe, here are Bugges/Wil make the haire	2Tamb	3.5.147	Tamb
See ye this rout, and know ye this same king?	2Tamb	3.5.151	Tamb
Come fight ye Turks, or yeeld us victory.	2Tamb	3.5.169	Tamb
Away ye fools, my father needs not me, ...	2Tamb	4.1.15	Calyph
See now ye slaves, my children stoops your pride/And leads your	2Tamb	4.1.76	Tamb
Stand up, ye base unworthy souldiers, ...	2Tamb	4.1.99	Tamb
Know ye not yet the argument of Armes?	2Tamb	4.1.100	Tamb
Stand up my boyes, and I wil teach ye arms, ...	2Tamb	4.1.103	Tamb
And now ye cankred curres of Asia, ...	2Tamb	4.1.132	Tamb
tyrannies/(If tyrannies wars justice ye repute)/I execute, .	2Tamb	4.1.147	Tamb
Wel, bark ye dogs.	2Tamb	4.1.181	Tamb
Ile make ye roare, that earth may eccho foorth/The far .	2Tamb	4.1.185	Tamb

YE (cont.)			
earth may eccho foorth/The far resounding torments ye sustaine,	2Tamb	4.1.186	Tamb
Why Madam, thinke ye to mocke me thus palpably?	2Tamb	4.2.67	Therid
Holla, ye pampered Jades of Asia:	2Tamb	4.3.1	Tamb
What, can ye draw but twenty miles a day,	2Tamb	4.3.2	Tamb
As you (ye slaves) in mighty Tamburlain.	2Tamb	4.3.11	Tamb
Hold ye tal souldiers, take ye Queens apeece/(I meane such	2Tamb	4.3.70	Tamb
take ye Queens apeece/(I meane such Queens as were kings	2Tamb	4.3.70	Tamb
Live [continent] <content> then (ye slaves) and meet not me	2Tamb	4.3.81	Tamb
Are ye not gone ye villaines with your spoiles?	2Tamb	4.3.84	Tamb
We wil Techelles, forward then ye Jades:	2Tamb	4.3.97	Tamb
Now crowch ye kings of greatest Asia,	2Tamb	4.3.98	Tamb
And tremble when ye heare this Scourge wil come,	2Tamb	4.3.99	Tamb
Who have ye there my Lordes?	2Tamb	5.1.80	Tamb
But foorth ye vassals, what so ere it be,	2Tamb	5.1.221	Tamb
O then ye Powers that sway eternal seates,	2Tamb	5.3.17	Techel
Cannot behold the teares ye shed for me,	2Tamb	5.3.218	Tamb
What at our hands demand ye?	Jew	1.2.6	Govnr
That ye be both made sure e're you come out.	Jew	2.3.236	Barab
get ye gon.	Jew	3.3.34	P Abigal
And ye did but know how she loves you, Sir.	Jew	4.2.53	Pilia
what hee writes for you, ye shall have streight.	Jew	4.3.27	P Barab
what are ye come so soone?	P 815	17.10	P Souldr
have at ye sir.	P 816	17.11	P Souldr
I warrant ye my Lord.	P 951	19.21	Capt
The wound I warrant ye is deepe my Lord,	P1192	22.54	King
Whether will you beare him, stay or ye shall die.	Edw	1.4.24	Edward
Feare ye not Madam, now his minions gone,	Edw	1.4.198	Lncstr
What, would ye have me plead for Gaveston?	Edw	1.4.213	Mortmr
And you the Eagles, sore ye nere so high,	Edw	2.2.39	Edward
If ye be moov'de, revenge it as you can,	Edw	2.2.198	Lncstr
Is it not, trowe ye, to assemble aide,	Edw	3.1.207	SpncrP
Ye must not grow so passionate in speeches:	Edw	4.4.16	Mortmr
Madam, what resteth, why stand ye in a muse?	Edw	4.6.63	SrJohn
Upon my life, those be the men ye seeke.	Edw	4.7.46	Mower
do ye see yonder tall fellow in the round slop, hee has kild	F App	p.230 47	P Clown
sirra you, Ile teach ye to impeach honest men:	F App	p.235 17	P Robin
but hark ye sir, if my horse be sick, or ill at ease, if I	F App	p.240 118	P HrsCsr
this is he, God save ye maister doctor, maister doctor, maister	F App	p.241 148	P HrsCsr
had them brought hither, as ye see, how do you like them Madame,	F App	p.242 23	P Faust
Will ye wadge war, for which you shall not triumph?	Lucan, First Booke	12	
Parthians y'afflict us more then ye suppose,	Lucan, First Booke	107	
Romans if ye be,/And beare true harts, stay heare:	Lucan, First Booke	193	
Ye gods of Phrigia and Iulus line,	Lucan, First Booke	199	
And so they triumph, be't with whom ye wil.	Lucan, First Booke	342	
O Gods what death prepare ye?	Lucan, First Booke	648	
with what plague/Meane ye to radge?	Lucan, First Booke	649	
[Doest] punish <ye >me, because yeares make him waine?	Ovid's Elegies	1.13.41	
I could tell ye,/How smooth his brest was, and how white his	Hero and Leander	1.65	
And from her countenance behold ye might,	Hero and Leander	2.318	
YEA			
Yea all my Navie split with Rockes and Shelfes:	Dido	3.1.108	Aeneas
Yea little sonne, are you so forward now?	Dido	3.3.34	Dido
Yet live, yea, live, Mycetes wils it so:	1Tamb	1.1.27	Mycet
Yea gentle Spencer, we have beene too milde,	Edw	3.1.24	Edward
Yea my good lord, for Gaveston is dead.	Edw	3.1.90	Arundl
Yea Spencer, traitors all.	Edw	3.1.102	Edward
Yea, but [Levune] <Lewne> thou seest,/These Barons lay their	Edw	3.1.273	Baldck
Yea gentle brother, and the God of heaven,	Edw	4.2.74	Queene
Yea madam, and they scape not easilie,	Edw	4.6.41	Mortmr
Yea stranger engines for the brunt of warre,	F 122	1.1.94	Faust
Yea <I> all the wealth that our fore-fathers hid,	F 173	1.1.145	Cornel
Yea <I>, God will pitty me if I repent.	F 567	2.2.16	Faust
Yea, I will wound Achilles in the heele,	F1779	5.1.106	Faust
I have done, all Germany can witnesse, yea all the world:	F1843	5.2.47	P Faust
hath lost both Germany and the world, yea heaven it selfe:	F1844	5.2.48	P Faust
Gush forth bloud in stead of teares, yea life and soule:	F1852	5.2.56	P Faust
Yea and thy father to, and swords thrown down,	Lucan, First Booke	117	
Yea, let my foes sleepe in an emptie bed,	Ovid's Elegies	2.10.17	
Yea, and she soothde me up, and calde me sir <sire>,	Ovid's Elegies	3.6.11	
YEARE (See also YEERE)			
Even from this day to Platoes wondrous yeare,	1Tamb	4.2.96	Tamb
I fill'd the Jailes with Bankrouts in a yeare,	Jew	2.3.193	Barab
For every yeare they swell, and yet they live;	Jew	4.1.6	Barab
Venus, and Mercury in a yeare; the Moone in twenty eight daies.	F 605	2.2.54	P Faust
<As match the dayes within one compleate yeare>,	F 821	(HC265) A	Mephst
Within the compasse of one compleat yeare:	F 822	3.1.44	Mephst
that at this time of the yeare, when every Tree is barren of	F1579	4.6.22	P Duke
the yeare is divided into two circles over the whole world, so	F1581	4.6.24	P Faust
that lye farre East, where they have fruit twice a yeare.	F1585	4.6.28	P Faust
or let this houre be but/A yeare, a month, a weeke, a naturall	F1933	5.2.137	Faust
and every yeare/Frauds and corruption in the field of Mars;	Lucan, First Booke	181	
Many a yeare these [furious] <firious> broiles let last,	Lucan, First Booke	667	
And with swift horses the swift yeare soone leaves us.	Ovid's Elegies	1.8.50	
Or he who war'd and wand'red twenty yeare?	Ovid's Elegies	2.1.31	
Onely was Crete fruitfull that plenteous yeare,	Ovid's Elegies	3.9.37	
The men of wealthie Sestos, everie yeare,	Hero and Leander	1.91	
YEARELY			
That yearely [stuffes] <stuff'd> old Phillips treasury,	F 159	1.1.131	Valdes
YEARES (Homograph)			
Thus in stoute Hectors race three hundred yeares,	Dido	1.1.104	Jupitr
The Grecian souldiers tired with ten yeares warre,	Dido	2.1.126	Aeneas
But weapons gree not with my tender yeares:	Dido	3.1.164	Dido

Line	Work	Reference	Speaker
YEARES (cont.)			
Especially in women of [our] <your> yeares.--	Dido	4.5.28	Nurse
why, I may live a hundred yeares,/Fourescore is but a girles	Dido	4.5.31	Nurse
And yong Iulus more then thousand yeares,	Dido	5.1.39	Hermes
The ten yeares tribute that remaines unpaid.	Jew	1.2.7	Calym
are such/That you will needs have ten yeares tribute past,	Jew	1.2.19	Govnr
To levie of us ten yeares tribute past,	Jew	1.2.41	Govnr
To what this ten yeares tribute will amount/That we have cast,	Jew	1.2.46	Govnr
A faire young maid scarce fourteene yeares of age,	Jew	1.2.378	Mthias
For riper yeares will weane him from such toyes.	Edw	1.4.401	MortSr
At <of> riper yeares to Wittenberg <Wertenberg> he went,	F 13	Prol.13	1Chor
So he will spare him foure and twenty yeares,	F 319	1.3.91	Faust
thou dost not presently bind thy selfe to me for seven yeares,	F 362	1.4.20	P Wagner
grant unto them that foure and twentie yeares being expired,	F 496	2.1.108	P Faust
<as> Saturne in thirty yeares, Jupiter in twelve, Mars in four,	F 604	2.2.53	P Faust
My foure and twenty yeares of liberty/I'le spend in pleasure	F 839	3.1.61	Faust
I was limitted/For foure and twenty yeares, to breathe on	F1396	4.2.72	Faust
worth>/<Made Greece with ten yeares warres afflict poore Troy>?	F1696	(HC269)B	2Schol
pursu'd]/[With tenne yeares warre the rape of such a queene],	F1700	5.1.27A	3Schol
remember that I have beene a student here these thirty yeares,	F1841	5.2.45	P Faust
and twenty yeares hath Faustus lost eternall joy and felicitie.	F1859	5.2.63	P Faust
Let Faustus live in hell a thousand yeares,	F1961	5.2.165	Faust
Calls for the payment of my latest yeares,	F App	p.239 93	Faust
Italy many yeares hath lyen until'd,	Lucan, First Booke		28
Both differ'd much, Pompey was strooke in yeares,	Lucan, First Booke		130
In ten yeares wonst thou France; Roome may be won/With farre	Lucan, First Booke		283
The yeares that fatall destenie shall give,	Ovid's Elegies		1.3.17
What yeares in souldiours Captaines do require,	Ovid's Elegies		1.9.5
Love is a naked boy, his yeares saunce staine,	Ovid's Elegies		1.10.15
[Doest] punish <ye >me, because yeares make him waine?	Ovid's Elegies		1.13.41
Good forme there is, yeares apt to play togither,	Ovid's Elegies		2.3.13
Or such, as least long yeares should turne the die,	Ovid's Elegies		2.5.39
When Troy by ten yeares battle tumbled downe,	Ovid's Elegies		2.12.9
So shall my love continue many yeares,	Ovid's Elegies		2.19.23
An old wood, stands uncut of long yeares space,	Ovid's Elegies		3.1.1
Troy had not yet beene ten yeares siege out-stander,	Ovid's Elegies		3.5.27
Can deafe [eares] <yeares> take delight when Phemius sings,/Or	Ovid's Elegies		3.6.61
Law-giving Minos did such yeares desire;	Ovid's Elegies		3.9.41
YEARLY			
Shall pay a yearly tribute to thy Syre.	1Tamb	5.1.519	Tamb
And birds for <from> Memnon yearly shall be slaine.	Ovid's Elegies		1.13.4
YEARS			
Warwicke, these words do ill beseeme thy years.	Edw	2.2.94	Kent
all at one time, but in some years we have more, in some lesse?	F 616	2.2.65	P Faust
spread these flags that ten years space have conquer'd,	Lucan, First Booke		348
All wasting years have that complaint [out] <not> worne.	Ovid's Elegies		2.6.8
Nor staine thy youthfull years with avarice,	Hero and Leander		1.325
YEE			
Such a feare (my Lord) would never make yee retire.	2Tamb	4.1.71	P Perdic
And yee be men,/Speede to the king.	Edw	2.6.5	Gavstn
doubt yee not,/We will finde comfort, money, men, and friends	Edw	4.2.64	SrJohn
yee Lubbers look about/And find the man that doth this villany,	F1055	3.2.75	Pope
Speake well of yee?	F1316	4.1.162	P Benvol
Here, now taste yee these, they should be good, for they come	F1576	4.6.19	P Faust
and what noyse soever you <yee> heare, come not unto me, for	F1873	5.2.77	P Faust
Doe yee heare, I would be sorie to robbe you of your living.	F App	p.229 18	P Clown
YEELD			
Shall yeeld to dignitie a dubble birth,	Dido	1.1.107	Jupitr
Whose yeelding heart may yeeld thee more reliefe.	Dido	4.2.36	Anna
I yeeld my selfe, my men and horse to thee:	1Tamb	1.2.229	Therid
We yeeld unto thee happie Tamburlaine.	1Tamb	1.2.257	Agidas
With dutie [and] <not> with amitie we yeeld/Our utmost service	1Tamb	2.3.33	Techel
And gladly yeeld them to my gracious rule:	1Tamb	2.5.28	Cosroe
Nor raise our siege before the Gretians yeeld,	1Tamb	3.1.14	Bajzth
Europe, and pursue/His scattered armie til they yeeld or die.	1Tamb	3.3.39	Therid
If they should yeeld their necks unto the sword,	1Tamb	3.3.142	Bajzth
Before I yeeld to such a slavery.	1Tamb	4.2.18	Bajzth
I doubt not but the Governour will yeeld,	1Tamb	4.2.113	Therid
If with their lives they will be pleasde to yeeld,	1Tamb	4.4.89	Tamb
Graunt that these signes of victorie we yeeld/May bind the	1Tamb	5.1.55	2Virgn
whom all kings/Of force must yeeld their crownes and Emperies:	1Tamb	5.1.481	Souldn
I yeeld with thanks and protestations/Of endlesse honor to thee	1Tamb	5.1.496	Souldn
It may be they will yeeld it quietly,	2Tamb	3.3.12	Therid
Captaine, that thou yeeld up thy hold to us.	2Tamb	3.3.16	Therid
And therefore Captaine, yeeld it quietly.	2Tamb	3.3.34	Techel
I would not yeeld it: therefore doo your worst.	2Tamb	3.3.37	Capt
Come fight ye Turks, or yeeld us victory.	2Tamb	3.5.169	Tamb
Rather than yeeld to his detested suit,	2Tamb	4.2.6	Olymp
Ile use some other means to make you yeeld,	2Tamb	4.2.51	Therid
I must and wil be pleasde, and you shall yeeld:	2Tamb	4.2.53	Therid
Yeeld up the towne, save our wives and children:	2Tamb	5.1.39	2Citzn
nor the towne will never yeeld/As long as any life is in my	2Tamb	5.1.47	Govnr
Yeeld speedily the citie to our hands,	2Tamb	5.1.51	Therid
Yeeld foolish Governour, we offer more/Than ever yet we did to	2Tamb	5.1.57	Techel
Assault and spare not, we wil never yeeld.	2Tamb	5.1.62	Govnr
Tis not thy bloody tents can make me yeeld,	2Tamb	5.1.103	Govnr
Why did you yeeld to their extortion?	Jew	1.2.177	Barab
And time may yeeld us an occasion/Which on the sudden cannot	Jew	1.2.239	Barab
And so much must they yeeld or not be sold.	Jew	2.3.4	2Offcr
And [less] <least> thou yeeld to this that I intreat,	Jew	3.4.37	Barab
And dye he shall, for we will never yeeld.	Jew	5.1.6	1Knght
What should I say? we are captives and must yeeld.	Jew	5.2.6	Govnr
you must yeeld, and under Turkish yokes/Shall groning beare the	Jew	5.2.7	Calym

YEELD (cont.)				
And yeeld your thoughts to height of my desertes.	P 602	12.15		King
I there it goes, but yet I will not yeeld,	Edw	1.4.56		Edward
I will not yeeld to any such upstart.	Edw	1.4.423		Mortmr
Base flatterer, yeeld, and were it not for shame,	Edw	2.5.11		Mortmr
Nature, yeeld to my countries cause in this.	Edw	4.1.3		Kent
They stay your answer, will you yeeld your crowne?	Edw	5.1.50		Leistr
And joyntly both yeeld up their wished right.	Edw	5.1.63		Edward
Lay downe your weapons, traitors, yeeld the king.	Edw	5.3.55		Kent
Edmund, yeeld thou thy self, or thou shalt die.	Edw	5.3.56		Matrvs
dutie, I do yeeld/My life and lasting service for your love.	F1818	5.2.22		Wagner
force, they that now thwart right/In wars wil yeeld to wrong:	Lucan, First Booke	350		
Let all Lawes yeeld, sinne beare the name of vertue,	Lucan, First Booke	666		
Lets yeeld, a burden easly borne is light.	Ovid's Elegies	1.2.10		
To yeeld their love to more then one disdainde.	Ovid's Elegies	1.8.40		
Let Homer yeeld to such as presents bring,	Ovid's Elegies	1.8.61		
put in the poast/Although of oake, to yeeld to verses boast.	Ovid's Elegies	2.1.28		
I yeeld, and back my wit from battells bring,	Ovid's Elegies	2.18.11		
Sweare I was blinde, yeeld not <deny>, if you be wise,	Ovid's Elegies	3.13.45		
Both loves to whom my heart long time did yeeld,	Ovid's Elegies	3.14.15		
though Hero would not yeeld/So soone to part from that she	Hero and Leander	2.83		
And cunningly to yeeld her selfe she sought.	Hero and Leander	2.294		
YEELDED				
Since he is yeelded to the stroke of War,	1Tamb	2.5.12		Cosroe
Betrayde her selfe, and yeelded at the last.	Ovid's Elegies	1.5.16		
Wherewith she yeelded, that was woon before.	Hero and Leander	1.330		
Heroes lookes yeelded, but her words made warre,	Hero and Leander	1.331		
YEELDES				
Woods, or steepie mountaine yeeldes.	Passionate Shepherd	4		
YEELDING				
Whose yeelding heart may yeeld thee more reliefe.	Dido	4.2.36		Anna
What stronge enchantments tice my yeelding soule?	1Tamb	1.2.224		Therid
Yeelding or striving <strugling> doe we give him might,	Ovid's Elegies	1.2.9		
Thus while dum signs their yeelding harts entangled,	Hero and Leander	1.187		
her body throes/Upon his bosome, where with yeelding eyes,	Hero and Leander	2.47		
YEELDS				
Yeelds up her beautie to a strangers bed,	Dido	4.2.17		Iarbus
your royall gratitudes/With all the benefits my Empire yeelds:	2Tamb	3.1.9		Callap
armes neer their houshold gods hung up/Such as peace yeelds;	Lucan, First Booke	243		
His sword layed by, safe, though rude places yeelds.	Ovid's Elegies	2.9.20		
Memphis, and Pharos that sweete date trees yeelds,	Ovid's Elegies	2.13.8		
A clowne, nor no love from her warme brest yeelds.	Ovid's Elegies	3.9.18		
From him that yeelds the garland <palme> is quickly got,	Ovid's Elegies	3.13.47		
YEERE				
the yeere is divided into twoo circles over the whole worlde,	F App	p.242 19	P	Faust
YEERELY				
That yeerely saile to the Venetian gulfe,	1Tamb	3.3.249		Tamb
YEERES				
That wee might sleepe seven yeeres together afore we wake.	Jew	4.2.131		Ithimr
and binde your selfe presently unto me for seaven yeeres, or	F App	p.229 25	P	Wagner
Five yeeres I lengthned thy command in France:	Lucan, First Booke	277		
me have borne/A thousand brunts, and tride me ful ten yeeres,	Lucan, First Booke	301		
And Tithon livelier then his yeeres require.	Ovid's Elegies	3.6.42		
YELLOW				
Dewberries, Apples, yellow Orenges,	Dido	4.5.6		Nurse
The yellow Ruthens left their garrisons;	Lucan, First Booke	403		
[Amber] <Yellow> trest is shee, then on the morne thinke I,/My	Ovid's Elegies	2.4.43		
Save that the sea playing on yellow sand,	Hero and Leander	1.347		
YELLOWE				
[A white wench thralles me, so doth golden yellowe],	Ovid's Elegies	2.4.39		
YELPING				
By yelping hounds puld downe, and seeme to die.	Edw	1.1.70		Gavstn
YES (See also YEA)				
Yes, and Iarbus foule and favourles.	Dido	3.1.64		Anna
Yes, and Iarbus rude and rusticall.	Dido	3.1.66		Anna
Yes, my Lord.	1Tamb	4.4.59	P	Zenoc
Yes father, you shal see me if I live,	2Tamb	1.3.54		Celeb
Yes, my Lord, yes, come lets about it.	2Tamb	3.3.10		Soldrs
Ha, to the East? yes: See how stands the Vanes?	Jew	1.1.40		Barab
Yes, give me leave, and Hebrews now come neare.	Jew	1.2.38		Govnr
Yes, Madam, and my talke with him was [but]/About the borrowing	Jew	2.3.155		Mthias
Yes, you shall have him: Goe put her in.	Jew	2.3.362		Barab
Yes.	Jew	3.3.24		Abigal
Yes, Sir, the proverb saies, he that eats with the devil had	Jew	3.4.58	P	Ithimr
Yes, what of them?	Jew	3.6.21		2Fryar
Yes; and I know not what the reason is:	Jew	4.1.130		Ithimr
Yes, 'cause you use to confesse.	Jew	4.1.145		Ithimr
Yes.	Jew	4.2.101	P	Pilia
Yes, my good Lord, one that can spy a place/Where you may	Jew	5.1.70		Barab
Yes, what of that?	Jew	5.5.106		Calym
Yes Navarre, but not to death I hope.	P1177	22.39		King
Salute him? yes: welcome Lord Chamberlaine.	Edw	2.2.65		Lncstr
Yes more then thou canst answer though he live,	Edw	2.2.87		Edward
Yes, yes, for Mortimer your lovers sake.	Edw	2.4.14		Edward
Yes, if this be the hand of Mortimer.	Edw	5.6.44		King
Yes, I know, but that followes not.	F 200	1.2.7	P	Wagner
<Yes sirre, I heard you>.	F 204	(HC258) A	P	1Schol
You are deceiv'd, for <Yes sir>, I will tell you:	F 206	1.2.13	P	Wagner
Yes Faustus, and most deerely lov'd of God.	F 293	1.3.65		Mephst
Yes, and goings out too, you may see sir.	F 347	1.4.5	P	Robin
Yes marry sir, and I thanke you to.	F 368	1.4.26	P	Robin
O yes, I see it plaine, even heere <in this place> is writ/Homo	F 469	2.1.81		Faust
Yes Mephostophilis, and two such Cardinals/Ne're serv'd a holy	F 941	3.1.163		Faust

YES (cont.)				
O yes,/And with him comes the Germane Conjurer,	F1163	4.1.9		Mrtino
Yes, he will drinke of all waters, but ride him not into the	F1472	4.4.16	P	Faust
Yes, yes, that may be; for I have heard of one, that ha's eate	F1533	4.5.29	P	Robin
Yes, I remember I sold one a horse.	F1635	4.6.78		Faust
Yes, I do verie well remember that.	F1638	4.6.81	P	Faust
Yes, my maister and mistris shal finde that I can reade, he for	F App	p.233 15	P	Robin
O yes, he wil drinke of al waters, but ride him not into the	F App	p.239 111	P	Faust
YESTERDAY				
But yesterday two ships went from this Towne,	Jew	4.1.69		Barab
I went to him yesterday to buy a horse of him, and he would by	F1536	4.5.32	P	HrsCsr
I sawe the damsell walking yesterday/There where the porch doth	Ovid's Elegies			2.2.3
Drouping more then a Rose puld yesterday:	Ovid's Elegies			3.6.66
YESTERNIGHT				
yesternight/I opened but the doore to throw him meate,	Edw	5.5.7		Gurney
So kindly yesternight to Bruno's health,	F1175	4.1.21		Mrtino
YET				
When yet both sea and sands beset their ships,	Dido	1.1.110		Venus
grim Ceranias seate/Have you oregone, and yet remaine alive?	Dido	1.1.148		Aeneas
Yet shall the aged Sunne shed forth his [haire] <aire>,	Dido	1.1.159		Achat
Yet much I marvell that I cannot finde,	Dido	1.1.180		Achat
O yet this stone doth make Aeneas weepe,	Dido	2.1.15		Aeneas
Yet thinkes my minde that this is Priamus:	Dido	2.1.25		Aeneas
O Illioneus, art thou yet alive?	Dido	2.1.55		Achat
And Priam dead, yet how we heare no newes.	Dido	2.1.113		Dido
Peeres/Heare me, but yet with Mirmidons harsh eares,	Dido	2.1.123		Aeneas
Yet flung I forth, and desperate of my life,	Dido	2.1.210		Aeneas
Yet who so wretched but desires to live?	Dido	2.1.238		Aeneas
This butcher whil'st his hands were yet held up,	Dido	2.1.241		Aeneas
Yet he undaunted tooke his fathers flagge,	Dido	2.1.259		Aeneas
Yet manhood would not serve, of force we fled,	Dido	2.1.272		Aeneas
(And yet have I had many mightier Kings)/Hast had the greatest	Dido	3.1.12		Dido
Yet not from Carthage for a thousand worlds.	Dido	3.1.51		Iarbus
Yet must I heare that lothsome name againe?	Dido	3.1.78		Dido
Yet Queene of Affricke, are my ships unrigd,	Dido	3.1.105		Aeneas
Yet none obtaind me, I am free from all.--	Dido	3.1.153		Dido
And yet God knowes intangled unto one.--	Dido	3.1.154		Dido
and thought by words/To compasse me, but yet he was deceiv'd:	Dido	3.1.156		Dido
Yet how <here> <now> I sweare by heaven and him I love,	Dido	3.1.166		Dido
Yet boast not of it, for I love thee not,	Dido	3.1.171		Dido
not of it, for I love thee not,/And yet I hate thee not:--	Dido	3.1.172		Dido
Yet now I doe repent me of his ruth,	Dido	3.2.47		Juno
And yet I am not free, oh would I were.	Dido	3.4.6		Dido
And yet desire to have before I dye.	Dido	3.4.10		Dido
And yet Ile speake, and yet Ile hold my peace,	Dido	3.4.27		Dido
Wherewith my husband woo'd me yet a maide,	Dido	3.4.63		Dido
Yet if you would partake with me the cause/Of this devotion	Dido	4.2.27		Anna
Yet Dido casts her eyes like anchors out,	Dido	4.3.25		Aeneas
I faine would goe, yet beautie calles me backe:	Dido	4.3.46		Aeneas
Yet lest he should, for I am full of feare,	Dido	4.4.108		Dido
And yet I blame thee not, thou art but wood.	Dido	4.4.143		Dido
Yet thinke upon Ascanius prophesie,	Dido	5.1.38		Hermes
Yet hath she tane away my oares and masts,	Dido	5.1.60		Aeneas
But yet Aeneas will not leave his love?	Dido	5.1.98		Dido
And yet I may not stay, Dido farewell.	Dido	5.1.104		Aeneas
Yet must he not gainsay the Gods behest.	Dido	5.1.127		Aeneas
Yet he that in my sight would not relent,	Dido	5.1.186		Dido
Then gan he wagge his hand, which yet held up,	Dido	5.1.229		Anna
Yet he whose [hearts] <heart> of adamant or flint,	Dido	5.1.234		Anna
No but I am not, yet I will be straight.	Dido	5.1.271		Dido
Yet insufficient to expresse the same:	1Tamb	1.1.2		Mycet
I meane it not, but yet I know I might,	1Tamb	1.1.26		Mycet
Yet live, yea, live, Mycetes wils it so:	1Tamb	1.1.27		Mycet
And yet a shepheard by my Parentage:	1Tamb	1.2.35		Tamb
Open the Males, yet guard the treasure sure,	1Tamb	1.2.138		Tamb
(I cal it meane, because being yet obscure,	1Tamb	1.2.203		Tamb
Yet being void of Martiall discipline,	1Tamb	2.2.44		Meandr
Yet will I weare it in despight of them,	1Tamb	2.7.61		Tamb
Yet would we not be brav'd with forrain power,	1Tamb	3.1.13		Bajzth
Yet since a farther passion feeds my thoughts,	1Tamb	3.2.13		Zenoc
Yet be not so inconstant in your love,	1Tamb	3.2.56		Agidas
Yet we assure us of the victorie.	1Tamb	3.3.35		Usumc
Yet somtimes let your highnesse send for them/To do the work my	1Tamb	3.3.187		Anippe
Yet should he not perswade me otherwise,	1Tamb	3.3.210		Zenoc
Thou shalt not yet be Lord of Affrica.	1Tamb	3.3.223		Zabina
Yet set a ransome on me Tamburlaine.	1Tamb	3.3.261		Bajzth
Yet would the Souldane by his conquering power,	1Tamb	4.1.33		Souldn
Yet in revenge of faire Zenocrate,	1Tamb	4.1.43		Souldn
Yet would you have some pitie for my sake,	1Tamb	4.2.123		Zenoc
Yet in compassion of his wretched state,	1Tamb	4.3.35		Souldn
Yet musicke woulde doe well to cheare up Zenocrate:	1Tamb	4.4.62		Tamb
Yet would I with my sword make Jove to stoope.	1Tamb	4.4.74		Tamb
Yet give me leave to plead for him my Lord.	1Tamb	4.4.86		Zenoc
Zenocrate, I will not crowne thee yet,	1Tamb	4.4.139		Tamb
soules/From heavens of comfort, yet their age might beare,	1Tamb	5.1.90		1Virgn
Yet should ther hover in their restlesse heads,	1Tamb	5.1.171		Tamb
And wounded bodies gasping yet for life.	1Tamb	5.1.323		Zenoc
And yet wouldst shun the wavering turnes of war,	1Tamb	5.1.360		Zenoc
to your dominions/Than ever yet confirm'd th'Egyptian Crown.	1Tamb	5.1.449		Tamb
Yet stout Orcanes, Prorex of the world,	2Tamb	1.1.45		Gazell
Yet scarse enough t'encounter Tamburlaine.	2Tamb	1.1.66		Orcan
That never sea-man yet discovered:	2Tamb	1.1.71		Orcan
So prest are we, but yet if Sigismond/Speake as a friend, and	2Tamb	1.1.122		Orcan

YET (cont.)

Yet here detain'd by cruell Tamburlaine.	2Tamb	1.2.4	Callap
Yet heare me speake my gentle Almeda.	2Tamb	1.2.13	Callap
(For that's the style and tytle I have yet)/Although he sent a	2Tamb	1.2.69	Almeda
Yet would I venture to conduct your Grace, . . .	2Tamb	1.2.72	Almeda
But yet me thinks their looks are amorous, ...	2Tamb	1.3.21	Tamb
Yet never did they recreate themselves, ...	2Tamb	1.3.182	Usumc
Yet shall my souldiers make no period/Untill Natolia kneele	2Tamb	1.3.216	Therid
Yet those infirmities that thus defame/Their faiths, their	2Tamb	2.1.44	Sgsmnd
Yet should our courages and steeled crestes, . . .	2Tamb	2.2.17	Gazell
Yet flourisheth as Flora in her pride, ...	2Tamb	2.3.22	Orcan
What saiest thou yet Gazellus to his foile: . . .	2Tamb	2.3.27	Orcan
Yet in my thoughts shall Christ be honoured, . . .	2Tamb	2.3.33	Orcan
But let me die my Love, yet let me die, ...	2Tamb	2.4.66	Zenoc
Yet let me kisse my Lord before I die, ...	2Tamb	2.4.69	Zenoc
But since my life is lengthened yet a while, . . .	2Tamb	2.4.71	Zenoc
Though she be dead, yet let me think she lives, . . .	2Tamb	2.4.127	Tamb
Thinke them in number yet sufficient, ...	2Tamb	3.1.41	Orcan
And yet at night carrouse within my tent, ...	2Tamb	3.2.106	Tamb
Yet I am resolute, and so farewell.	2Tamb	3.3.40	Capt
But yet Ile save their lives and make them slaves. . .	2Tamb	3.5.63	Tamb
Yet pardon him I pray your Majesty.	2Tamb	4.1.97	Therid
Know ye not yet the argument of Armes?	2Tamb	4.1.100	Tamb
Nor yet imposd, with such a bitter hate.	2Tamb	4.1.170	Jrslem
Nor yet this aier, beat often with thy sighes, . . .	2Tamb	4.2.10	Olymp
Yet are there Christians of Georgia here, ...	2Tamb	5.1.31	1Citzn
we offer more/Than ever yet we did to such proud slaves, .	2Tamb	5.1.58	Techel
Yet could not enter till the breach was made. . . .	2Tamb	5.1.100	Tamb
Nor yet thy selfe, the anger of the highest, . . .	2Tamb	5.1.104	Govnr
Yet save my life, and let this wound appease/The mortall furie	2Tamb	5.1.153	Govnr
Yet shouldst thou die, shoot at him all at once. . .	2Tamb	5.1.157	Tamb
And yet I live untoucht by Mahomet:	2Tamb	5.1.182	Tamb
And yet gapes stil for more to quench his thirst, . .	2Tamb	5.2.14	Amasia
Yet might your mighty hoste incounter all, ...	2Tamb	5.2.39	Amasia
Yet when the pride of Cynthia is at full, ...	2Tamb	5.2.46	Callap
Yet make them feele the strength of Tamburlain, . . .	2Tamb	5.3.37	Usumc
Yet if your majesty may escape this day, ...	2Tamb	5.3.98	Phsitn
Yet was his soule but flowne beyond the Alpes, . . .	Jew	Prol.2	Machvl
Yet will they reade me, and thereby attaine/To Peters Chayre:	Jew	Prol.11	Machvl
And yet I wonder at this Argosie.	Jew	1.1.84	Barab
Yet Barrabas we will not banish thee, ...	Jew	1.2.100	Govnr
Oh yet be patient, gentle Barabas.	Jew	1.2.169	1Jew
Yet brother Barabas remember Job.	Jew	1.2.180	1Jew
And yet have kept enough to live upon;	Jew	1.2.190	Barab
Yet let thy daughter be no longer blinde.	Jew	1.2.354	1Fryar
yet when we parted last,/He said he wud attend me in the morne.	Jew	2.1.33	Abigal
bite, yet are our lookes/As innocent and harmelesse as a Lambes.	Jew	2.3.21	Barab
Yet I have one left that will serve your turne: . .	Jew	2.3.50	Barab
And yet I know the prayers of those Nuns/And holy Fryers,	Jew	2.3.80	Barab
yet I say make love to him;/Doe, it is requisite it should be	Jew	2.3.238	Barab
Yet through the key-hole will he talke to her, . . .	Jew	2.3.263	Barab
Win it, and weare it, it is yet [unfoyl'd] <unsoyl'd>. .	Jew	2.3.293	Barab
And yet I'le give her many a golden crosse/With Christian	Jew	2.3.296	Barab
Yet crave I thy consent.	Jew	2.3.299	Lodowk
And mine you have, yet let me talke to her; . . .	Jew	2.3.300	Barab
Nor our Messias that is yet to come, ...	Jew	2.3.304	Barab
So have not I, but yet I hope I shall.	Jew	2.3.319	Barab
No, no, and yet it might be done that way: . . .	Jew	2.3.373	Barab
And yet I know my beauty doth not faile.	Jew	3.1.5	Curtzn
Oh bravely fought, and yet they thrust not home. . .	Jew	3.2.5	Barab
Yet Don Mathias ne're offended thee:	Jew	3.3.41	Abigal
Why Abigal it is not yet long since/That I did labour thy	Jew	3.3.56	1Fryar
Yet never shall these lips bewray thy life. . . .	Jew	3.3.75	Abigal
yet not appeare/In forty houres after it is tane. . .	Jew	3.4.71	Barab
For every yeare they swell, and yet they live; . . .	Jew	4.1.6	Barab
You see I answer him, and yet he stayes;	Jew	4.1.88	Barab
Yet if he knew our meanings, could he scape? . . .	Jew	4.1.135	Barab
so, and yet I cannot tell, for at the reading of the letter,	Jew	4.2.6	P Pilia
son; he and I kild 'em both, and yet never touch'd 'em. .	Jew	4.4.18	P Ithimr
Pardona moy, be no in tune yet; so, now, now all be in. .	Jew	4.4.45	P Barab
What e're I am, yet Governor heare me speake; . . .	Jew	5.1.9	Curtzn
Yet you doe live, and live for me you shall: . . .	Jew	5.2.63	Barab
Yet would I gladly visit Barabas, ...	Jew	5.3.24	Calym
Yet understoode by none.	P 112	2.55	Guise
Sufficient yet for such a pettie King:	P 150	2.93	Guise
Yet will the wisest note their proper greefes: . . .	P 216	4.14	Anjoy
And yet didst never sound any thing to the depth. . .	P 386	7.26	Guise
I, so they are, but yet what remedy:	P 433	7.73	Anjoy
But yet my Lord the report doth run, ...	P 435	7.75	Navrre
Yet will we not that the Massacre shall end: . . .	P 444	7.84	Guise
Yet by my brother Charles our King of France, . . .	P 464	8.14	Anjoy
Yet is [their] <there> pacience of another sort, . . .	P 545	11.10	Charls
Not yet my Lord, for thereon doe they stay:	P 732	14.35	1Msngr
yet you put in that which displeaseth him, and so forestall his	P 808	17.3	P Souldr
possession (as I would I might) yet I meane to keepe you out,	P 814	17.9	P Souldr
What your intent is yet we cannot learn, ...	P 823	17.18	King
Yet Caesar shall goe forth.	P 996	19.66	Guise
Yet lives/My brother Duke Dumaine, and many moe: . . .	P1098	20.8	Cardnl
yet I come to keepe you out ser.	Paris	ms15,p390	P Souldr
But yet it is no paine to speake men faire, ...	Edw	1.1.42	Gavstn
And yet I have not viewd my Lord the king, ...	Edw	1.1.45	Gavstn
Yet dare you brave the king unto his face.	Edw	1.1.116	Kent
and yet ere that day come,/The king shall lose his crowne, for	Edw	1.2.58	Mortmr

YET (cont.)

But yet lift not your swords against the king.	Edw	1.2.61	ArchBp
I there it goes, but yet I will not yeeld,	Edw	1.4.56	Edward
And yet heele ever dote on Gaveston,	Edw	1.4.185	Queene
And yet I love in vaine, heele nere love me.	Edw	1.4.197	Queene
Yet good my lord, heare what he can alledge.	Edw	1.4.250	Queene
returnd, this newes will glad him much,/Yet not so much as me.	Edw	1.4.302	Queene
That day, if not for him, yet for my sake,	Edw	1.4.381	Edward
Yet have I words left to expresse my joy:	Edw	2.2.60	Gavstn
Yet I disdaine not to doe this for you.	Edw	2.2.79	Lncstr
Yet, shall the crowing of these cockerels,	Edw	2.2.203	Edward
Yet once more ile importune him with praiers,	Edw	2.4.63	Queene
But yet I hope my sorrowes will have end,	Edw	2.4.68	Queene
Yet lustie lords I have escapt your handes,	Edw	2.5.1	Gavstn
Yet liveth Pierce of Gaveston unsurprizd,	Edw	2.5.4	Gavstn
Intreateth you by me, yet but he may/See him before he dies, for	Edw	2.5.36	Arundl
it is this life you aime at,/Yet graunt king Edward this.	Edw	2.5.49	Gavstn
Cause yet more bloudshed:	Edw	2.5.83	Warwck
Sweete soveraigne, yet I come/To see thee ere I die.	Edw	2.5.94	Gavstn
Yet not perhaps,	Edw	2.5.95	Warwck
Yet ere thou go, see how I do devorce	Edw	3.1.176	Edward
To thinke that we can yet be tun'd together,	Edw	4.2.9	Queene
Yet triumphe in the hope of thee my joye?	Edw	4.2.28	Queene
Yet have we friends, assure your grace, in England/Would cast	Edw	4.2.54	Mortmr
And yet she beares a face of love forsooth:	Edw	4.6.14	Kent
Shall I not see the king my father yet?	Edw	4.6.61	Prince
Yet gentle monkes, for treasure, golde nor fee,	Edw	4.7.24	Edward
It may become thee yet,/To let us take our farewell of his	Edw	4.7.68	Spencr
And therefore let me weare it yet a while.	Edw	5.1.83	Edward
Yet stay, for rather then I will looke on them,	Edw	5.1.106	Edward
and bid him rule/Better then I, yet how have I transgrest,	Edw	5.1.122	Edward
Not yet my lorde, ile beare you on your waye.	Edw	5.1.155	Leistr
Yet he that is the cause of Edwards death,	Edw	5.4.3	Mortmr
Containes his death, yet bids them save his life.	Edw	5.4.7	Mortmr
But yet I have a braver way then these.	Edw	5.4.37	Ltborn
Nor I, and yet me thinkes I should commaund,	Edw	5.4.97	King
Yet be not farre off, I shall need your helpe,	Edw	5.5.28	Ltborn
Yet will it melt, ere I have done my tale.	Edw	5.5.55	Edward
Yet stay a while, forbeare thy bloudie hande,	Edw	5.5.75	Edward
Now as I speake they fall, and yet with feare/Open againe.	Edw	5.5.95	Edward
O let me not die yet, stay, O stay a while.	Edw	5.5.101	Edward
What if he have? the king is yet a childe.	Edw	5.6.17	Mortmr
Goes to discover countries yet unknowne.	Edw	5.6.66	Mortmr
Yet levell at the end of every Art,	F 32	1.1.4	Faust
Yet art thou still but Faustus, and a man.	F 51	1.1.23	Faust
[Yet not your words onely, but mine owne fantasie],	F 130	1.1.102A	Faust
yet if you were not dunces, you would never aske me such a	F 206	1.2.13	P Wagner
<yet should I grieve for him>:	F 224	(HC258)A	2Schol
Yet let us see <trie> what we can do.	F 228	1.2.35	2Schol
That was the cause, but yet per accidens:	F 274	1.3.46	Mephst
yet shall not Faustus flye.	F 470	2.1.82	Faust
But yet conditionally, that thou performe/All Covenants, and	F 479	2.1.91	Faust
[Yet faine would I have a booke wherein I might beholde al	F 551.1	2.1.164A	P Faust
Faustus repent, yet God will pitty thee.	F 563	2.2.12	GdAngl
Be I a devill yet God may pitty me,	F 566	2.2.15	Faust
As never yet was seene in Germany.	F1188	4.1.34	Mrtino
Has not the Pope enough of conjuring yet?	F1189	4.1.35	P Benvol
But yet my [heart's] <heart> more ponderous then my head,	F1351	4.2.27	Benvol
Yet in a minute had my spirit return'd,	F1399	4.2.75	Faust
Yet stay, the world shall see their miserie,	F1406	4.2.82	Faust
Yet to encounter this your weake attempt,	F1429	4.2.105	Faust
Yet, yet, thou hast an amiable soule,	F1712	5.1.39	OldMan
I do repent, and yet I doe despaire,	F1740	5.1.67	Faust
Yet Faustus looke up to heaven, and remember [Gods] mercy is	F1835	5.2.39	P 2Schol
Yet Faustus call on God.	F1848	5.2.52	P 2Schol
But yet all these are nothing, thou shalt see/Ten thousand	F1919	5.2.123	BdAngl
Yet will I call on him: O spare me Lucifer.	F1942	5.2.146	Faust
[Yet for Christs sake, whose bloud hath ransom'd me],	F1959	5.2.163A	Faust
Yet for he was a Scholler, once admired/For wondrous knowledge	F1997	5.3.15	2Schol
so by that meanes I shal see more then ere I felt, or saw yet.	F App	p.233 5	P Robin
with you, I must yet have a goblet payde from you ere you goe.	F App	p.234 7	P Vintnr
yet for that love and duety bindes me thereunto, I am content	F App	p.236 14	P Faust
Doctor, yet ere you goe, expect from me a bounteous reward.	F App	p.239 88	P Emper
but yet like an asse as I was, I would not be ruled by him, for	F App	p.240 129	P HrsCsr
And yet me thinkes, if that death were neere,	F App	p.243 3	Wagner
as yet thou wants not foes.	Lucan, First Booke		23
Yet Room is much bound to these civil armes,	Lucan, First Booke		44
Nor yet the adverse reking southerne pole,	Lucan, First Booke		54
Yet he alone is held in reverence.	Lucan, First Booke		144
or his speare/Sticks in his side) yet runs upon the hunter.	Lucan, First Booke		214
may be won/With farre lesse toile, and yet the honors more;	Lucan, First Booke		284
having lickt/Warme goare from Syllas sword art yet athirst,	Lucan, First Booke		331
Yet for long service done, reward these men,	Lucan, First Booke		341
and the rest/Marcht not intirely, and yet hide the ground,	Lucan, First Booke		474
Yet more will happen then I can unfold;	Lucan, First Booke		634
Yet scarse my hands from thee containe I well.	Ovid's Elegies		1.4.10
though I not see/What may be done, yet there before him bee.	Ovid's Elegies		1.4.14
Yet this Ile see, but if thy gowne ought cover,	Ovid's Elegies		1.4.41
Or night being past, and yet not day begunne.	Ovid's Elegies		1.5.6
Yet strivde she to be covered therewithall,	Ovid's Elegies		1.5.14
Yet was she graced with her ruffled hayre.	Ovid's Elegies		1.7.12
Yet he harm'd lesse, whom I profess'd to love,	Ovid's Elegies		1.7.33
Yet greedy Bauds command she curseth still,	Ovid's Elegies		1.10.23

YET (cont.)			
Yet thinke no scorne to aske a wealthy churle,	Ovid's Elegies	1.10.53	
Yet as if mixt with red leade thou wert ruddy,	Ovid's Elegies	1.12.11	
Yet lingered not the day, but morning scard me.	Ovid's Elegies	1.13.48	
Yet although [neither] <either>, mixt of eithers hue,	Ovid's Elegies	1.14.10	
Oft was she drest before mine eyes, yet never,	Ovid's Elegies	1.14.17	
Oft in the morne her haires not yet digested,	Ovid's Elegies	1.14.19	
Yet seemely like a Thracian Bacchinall/That tyr'd doth rashly	Ovid's Elegies	1.14.21	
While I speake some fewe, yet fit words be idle.	Ovid's Elegies	2.2.2	
But yet sometimes to chide thee let her fall/Counterfet teares:	Ovid's Elegies	2.2.35	
While thou hast time yet to bestowe that gift.	Ovid's Elegies	2.3.18	
I loathe, yet after that I loathe, I runne:	Ovid's Elegies	2.4.5	
Yet would I lie with her if that I might.	Ovid's Elegies	2.4.22	
Why so was Ledas, yet was Leda faire.	Ovid's Elegies	2.4.42	
And Hector dyed his brothers yet alive.	Ovid's Elegies	2.6.42	
Yet words in thy benummed palate rung,	Ovid's Elegies	2.6.47	
Yet blusht I not, nor usde I any saying,	Ovid's Elegies	2.8.7	
Yet should I curse a God, if he but said,	Ovid's Elegies	2.9.25	
Yet Love, if thou with thy faire mother heare,	Ovid's Elegies	2.9.51	
Yet this is better farre then lie alone,	Ovid's Elegies	2.10.15	
Yet Galatea favour thou her ship.	Ovid's Elegies	2.11.34	
And me with many, but yet me without murther,	Ovid's Elegies	2.12.27	
This kinde of verse is not alike, yet fit,	Ovid's Elegies	2.17.21	
Yet tragedies, and scepters fild my lines,	Ovid's Elegies	2.18.13	
Yet whom thou favourst, pray may conquerour be.	Ovid's Elegies	3.2.2	
Yet he attain'd by her support to have her,	Ovid's Elegies	3.2.17	
Yet in the meane time wilt small windes bestowe,	Ovid's Elegies	3.2.37	
He holdes the palme: my palme is yet to gaine.	Ovid's Elegies	3.2.82	
And yet remaines the face she had before.	Ovid's Elegies	3.3.2	
Comely tall was she, comely tall shee's yet.	Ovid's Elegies	3.3.8	
But yet their gift more moderately use,	Ovid's Elegies	3.3.47	
Yet by deceit Love did them all surprize.	Ovid's Elegies	3.4.20	
Troy had not yet beene ten yeares siege out-stander,	Ovid's Elegies	3.5.27	
Yet rending with enraged thumbe her tresses,	Ovid's Elegies	3.5.71	
My bones had beene, while yet I was a maide.	Ovid's Elegies	3.5.74	
Yet could I not cast ancor where I meant,	Ovid's Elegies	3.6.6	
Yet like as if cold hemlocke I had drunke,	Ovid's Elegies	3.6.13	
Yet boorded I the golden Chie twise,	Ovid's Elegies	3.6.23	
Yet might her touch make youthfull Pilius fire,	Ovid's Elegies	3.6.41	
Yet notwithstanding, like one dead it lay,	Ovid's Elegies	3.6.65	
She prais'd me, yet the gate shutt fast upon her,	Ovid's Elegies	3.7.7	
Yet when old Saturne heavens rule possest,	Ovid's Elegies	3.7.35	
Yet shall thy life be forcibly bereaven.	Ovid's Elegies	3.8.38	
Yet better ist, then if Corcyras Ile/Had thee unknowne interr'd	Ovid's Elegies	3.8.47	
Yet this is lesse, then if he had seene me,	Ovid's Elegies	3.10.15	
Bulles hate the yoake, yet what they hate have still.	Ovid's Elegies	3.10.36	
That I may love yet, though against my minde.	Ovid's Elegies	3.10.52	
If you wey not ill speeches, yet wey mee:	Ovid's Elegies	3.13.36	
Though thou be faire, yet be not thine owne thrall.	Hero and Leander	1.90	
And yet at everie word shee turn'd aside,	Hero and Leander	1.195	
As put thereby, yet might he hope for mo.	Hero and Leander	1.312	
Yet for her sake whom you have vow'd to serve,	Hero and Leander	1.316	
Yet evilly faining anger, strove she still,	Hero and Leander	1.335	
And yet I like them for the Orator.	Hero and Leander	1.340	
Yet prowd she was, (for loftie pride that dwels/In tow'red	Hero and Leander	1.393	
and beautie had/As could provoke his liking, yet was mute,	Hero and Leander	1.423	
As he ought not performe, nor yet she aske.	Hero and Leander	1.430	
Yet as a punishment they added this,	Hero and Leander	1.469	
Yet as she went, full often look'd behind,	Hero and Leander	2.5	
Yet she this rashnesse sodainly repented,	Hero and Leander	2.33	
yet he suspected/Some amorous rites or other were neglected.	Hero and Leander	2.63	
As in plaine termes (yet cunningly) he crav'd it,	Hero and Leander	2.71	
Yet when a token of great worth we send,	Hero and Leander	2.80	
If not for love, yet love for pittie sake,	Hero and Leander	2.247	
Yet ever as he greedily assayd/To touch those dainties, she the	Hero and Leander	2.269	
Yet there with Sysiphus he toyld in vaine,	Hero and Leander	2.277	
Seeming not woon, yet woon she was at length,	Hero and Leander	2.295	
YETT			
yett you putt in that displeases him | And fill up his rome	Paris	ms 4,p390	P Souldr
yett comminge upon you once unawares he frayde you out againe.	Paris	ms12,p390	P Souldr
YF			
yf it be not to free theres the questione | now ser where he is	Paris	ms 8,p390	P Souldr
revenge it henry yf thow liste or darst	Paris	ms23,p391	Guise
YFAITH			
They shal Casane, and tis time yfaith.	2Tamb	1.3.185	Tamb
Agreed yfaith.	2Tamb	4.1.66	P Perdic
YIELD (See YEELD)			
YMOUNTED			
Like to an almond tree ymounted high,	2Tamb	4.3.119	Tamb
YNOW			
And for their power, ynow to win the world.	2Tamb	3.1.43	Orcan
YOAK'D			
slavish Bands/Wherein the Turke hath yoak'd your land and you?	Jew	5.2.78	Barab
and let them hang/Within the window where he yoak'd me first,	F1381	4.2.57	Benvol
YOAKE			
Three thousand Camels, and two hundred yoake/Of labouring Oxen,	Jew	1.2.183	Barab
Slow oxen early in the yoake are pent.	Ovid's Elegies	1.13.16	
She first constraind bulles necks to beare the yoake,	Ovid's Elegies	3.9.13	
Bulles hate the yoake, yet what they hate have still.	Ovid's Elegies	3.10.36	
YOAKT			
Nere was there King of France so yoakt as I.	P1044	19.114	King
Scythia and wilde Armenia had bin yoakt,	Lucan, First Booke	19	
on the Altar/He laies a ne're-yoakt Bull, and powers downe	Lucan, First Booke	608	

YOKE			
Thrust under yoke and thraldom of a thiefe. . . .	1Tamb	5.1.261	Bajzth
Yoke Venus Doves, put Mirtle on thy haire, . . .	Ovid's Elegies		1.2.23
YOKED			
Drawne by the strength of yoked <yoky> Dragons neckes; .	F 759	2.3.38	2Chor
YOKES			
to be enthral'd/To forraine powers, and rough imperious yokes:	1Tamb	5.1.36	Govnr
and under Turkish yokes/Shall groning beare the burthen of our	Jew	5.2.7	Calym
YOKT			
Yong oxen newly yokt are beaten more, ...	Ovid's Elegies		1.2.13
YOKY			
Drawne by the strength of yoked <yoky> Dragons neckes; .	F 759	2.3.38	2Chor
YON			
Me thinkes that towne there should be Troy, yon Idas hill,	Dido	2.1.7	Aeneas
what strange beast is yon, that thrusts his head out at [the]	F1274	4.1.120	P Faust
Into the entrals of yon labouring cloud, ...	F1953	5.2.157	Faust
YOND			
Yond walks the Jew, now for faire Abigall. . . .	Jew	2.3.38	Lodowk
YONDER			
But stay, what starre shines yonder in the East? . .	Jew	2.1.41	Barab
Yonder comes Don Mathias, let us stay;	Jew	2.3.140	Barab
Yonder is Edward among his flatterers.	Edw	3.1.196	Mortmr
Yonder he comes:	F1094	3.3.7	P Dick
In what resplendant glory thou hadst set/In yonder throne, like	F1905	5.2.109	GdAngl
do ye see yonder tall fellow in the round slop, hee has kild	F App	p.230 47	P Clown
O yonder is his snipper snapper, do you heare?	F App	p.240 137	P HrsCsr
YONG			
Hoe yong men, saw you as you came/Any of all my Sisters .	Dido	1.1.183	Venus
And this yong Prince shall be thy playfellow.	Dido	2.1.307	Venus
me, for I forgot/That yong Ascanius lay with me this night:	Dido	4.4.32	Dido
Goe, bid my Nurse take yong Ascanius, ...	Dido	4.4.105	Dido
Your Nurse is gone with yong Ascanius, ...	Dido	4.4.124	Lord
And yong Iulus more then thousand yeares, ...	Dido	5.1.39	Hermes
And bore yong Cupid unto Cypresse Ile.	Dido	5.1.41	Hermes
But let the yong Arabian live in hope, ...	1Tamb	3.2.57	Agidas
yong Callapine that lately fled from your majesty, hath nowe	2Tamb	5.3.102	P 3Msngr
Am I growne olde, or is thy lust growne yong, ...	P 681	13.25	Guise
Yong Mortimer and his unckle shalbe earles, ...	Edw	1.4.67	Edward
But wherefore walkes yong Mortimer aside?	Edw	1.4.353	Edward
things of more waight/Then fits a prince so yong as I to beare,	Edw	3.1.75	Prince
France/Makes friends, to crosse the seas with her yong sonne,	Edw	3.1.270	Spencr
How say yong Prince, what thinke you of the match? . .	Edw	4.2.67	SrJohn
Heere comes the yong prince, with the Earle of Kent. .	Edw	5.2.75	Mortmr
Let him be king, I am too yong to raigne.	Edw	5.2.93	Prince
hornes most strangely fastened/Upon the head of yong Benvolio.	F1278	4.1.124	Emper
Yong oxen newly yokt are beaten more, ...	Ovid's Elegies		1.2.13
Yong men and women, shalt thou lead as thrall, . . .	Ovid's Elegies		1.2.27
Wars dustie <rustie> honors are refused being yong, . .	Ovid's Elegies		1.15.4
Who first depriv'd yong boyes of their best part, . .	Ovid's Elegies		2.3.3
A yong wench pleaseth, and an old is good, ...	Ovid's Elegies		2.4.45
yong-mens mates, to go/If they determine to persever so. .	Ovid's Elegies		2.16.17
Hath any rose so from a fresh yong maide, ...	Ovid's Elegies		3.6.53
YONGER			
The yonger Mortimer is growne so brave, ...	Edw	2.2.232	Edward
I know the malice of the yonger Mortimer, ...	Edw	3.1.5	Edward
YONGEST			
and on his speare/The mangled head of Priams yongest sonne,	Dido	2.1.215	Aeneas
This lovely boy the yongest of the three, ...	2Tamb	1.3.37	Zenoc
YONGLING			
Why yongling, s'dainst thou so of Mortimer.	Edw	5.2.111	Mortmr
YONG-MENS			
yong-mens mates, to go/If they determine to persever so. .	Ovid's Elegies		2.16.17
YOONG			
Amorous Leander, beautifull and yoong, ...	Hero and Leander		1.51
So yoong, so gentle, and so debonaire, ...	Hero and Leander		1.288
So to his mind was yoong Leanders looke.	Hero and Leander		2.130
YORE			
In those faire walles I promist him of yore: . . .	Dido	1.1.85	Jupitr
YORKE			
Unto the walles of Yorke the Scots made rode, . . .	Edw	2.2.166	Lncstr
YOU (See also Y', YE, YEE, YOW)			
And held the cloath of pleasance whiles you dranke, . .	Dido	1.1.6	Ganimd
And then Ile hugge with you an hundred times. . . .	Dido	1.1.48	Ganimd
I, this is it, you can sit toying there, ...	Dido	1.1.50	Venus
Whose beautious burden well might make you proude, . .	Dido	1.1.124	Venus
You sonnes of care, companions of my course, . . .	Dido	1.1.142	Aeneas
and grim Ceranias seate/Have you oregone, and yet remaine	Dido	1.1.148	Aeneas
You shall have leaves and windfall bowes enow/Neere to these	Dido	1.1.172	Aeneas
men, saw you as you came/Any of all my Sisters wandring here?	Dido	1.1.183	Venus
But what are you that aske of me these things? . . .	Dido	1.1.214	Venus
Whence may you come, or whither will you goe? . . .	Dido	1.1.215	Venus
Why, what are you, or wherefore doe you sewe? . . .	Dido	1.2.3	Iarbus
But tell me Troians, Troians if you be, ...	Dido	1.2.17	Iarbus
Your men and you shall banquet in our Court, . . .	Dido	1.2.39	Iarbus
Come in with me, Ile bring you to my Queene, . . .	Dido	1.2.42	Iarbus
You are Achates, or I [am] deciv'd.	Dido	2.1.49	Serg
Madame, you shall be my mother.	Dido	2.1.96	Ascan
And Dido and you Carthaginian Peeres/Heare me, but yet with	Dido	2.1.122	Aeneas
Lest you be mov'd too much with my sad tale. . . .	Dido	2.1.125	Aeneas
Are you Queene Didos sonne?	Dido	2.1.308	Ascan
little sonne/Playes with your garments and imbraceth you.	Dido	3.1.21	Anna
What will you give me now? Ile have this Fanne. . .	Dido	3.1.32	Cupid
O sister, were you Empresse of the world, ...	Dido	3.1.69	Anna

YOU (cont.)

You shall not hurt my father when he comes.	Dido	3.1.80	Cupid
But speake Aeneas, know you none of these?	Dido	3.1.148	Dido
Juno, my mortall foe, what make you here?	Dido	3.2.24	Venus
Sister, I see you savour of my wiles,	Dido	3.2.96	Venus
Be it as you will have [it] for this once,	Dido	3.2.97	Venus
Huntsmen, why pitch you not your toyles apace,	Dido	3.3.30	Dido
Yea little sonne, are you so forward now?	Dido	3.3.34	Dido
As I remember, here you shot the Deere,	Dido	3.3.51	Achat
When first you set your foote upon the shoare,	Dido	3.3.53	Achat
You to the vallies, thou unto the house.	Dido	3.3.62	Dido
Tell me deare love, how found you out this Cave?	Dido	3.4.3	Dido
With this my hand I give to you my heart,	Dido	3.4.43	Aeneas
Nay, where is my warlike father, can you tell?	Dido	4.1.15	Cupid
Faire Anna, how escapt you from the shower?	Dido	4.1.29	Aeneas
But where were you Iarbus all this while?	Dido	4.1.31	Dido
I Anna, is there ought you would with me?	Dido	4.2.24	Iarbus
Yet if you would partake with me the cause/Of this devotion	Dido	4.2.27	Anna
partake with me the cause/Of this devotion that detaineth you,	Dido	4.2.28	Anna
Troians abourd, and I will follow you,	Dido	4.3.45	Aeneas
Get you abourd, Aeneas meanes to stay.	Dido	4.4.24	Dido
But when you were abourd twas calme enough,	Dido	4.4.27	Dido
Henceforth you shall be our Carthage Gods:	Dido	4.4.96	Dido
Drive if you can my house to Italy:	Dido	4.4.129	Dido
Was it not you that hoysed up these sailes?	Dido	4.4.153	Dido
Why burst you not, and they fell in the seas?	Dido	4.4.154	Dido
Nurse I am wearie, will you carrie me?	Dido	4.5.15	Cupid
Youle be a twigger when you come to age.	Dido	4.5.20	Nurse
Why cosin, stand you building Cities here,	Dido	5.1.27	Hermes
As how I pray, may I entreate you tell.	Dido	5.1.67	Iarbus
I know not what you meane by treason, I,	Dido	5.1.222	Nurse
Sweet sister cease, remember who you are.	Dido	5.1.263	Anna
Weele leade you to the stately tent of War:	1Tamb	Prol.3	Prolog
Where you shall heare the Scythian Tamburlaine,	1Tamb	Prol.4	Prolog
And then applaud his fortunes if you please.	1Tamb	Prol.8	Prolog
I know you have a better wit than I.	1Tamb	1.1.5	Mycet
And thorough your Planets I perceive you thinke,	1Tamb	1.1.19	Mycet
I might command you to be slaine for this,	1Tamb	1.1.23	Mycet
Therefore tis best, if so it lik you all,	1Tamb	1.1.51	Mycet
How like you this, my honorable Lords?	1Tamb	1.1.54	Mycet
It cannot choose, because it comes from you.	1Tamb	1.1.56	Cosroe
Nay, pray you let him stay, a greater [task]/Fits Menaphon, than	1Tamb	1.1.87	Cosroe
Unlesse they have a wiser king than you.	1Tamb	1.1.92	Cosroe
Unlesse they have a wiser king than you?	1Tamb	1.1.93	Mycet
You may doe well to kisse it then.	1Tamb	1.1.98	Cosroe
Since Fortune gives you opportunity,	1Tamb	1.1.124	Menaph
How easely may you with a mightie hoste,	1Tamb	1.1.129	Menaph
Least you subdue the pride of Christendome?	1Tamb	1.1.132	Menaph
Bringing the Crowne to make you Emperour.	1Tamb	1.1.135	Menaph
are in readines/Ten thousand horse to carie you from hence,	1Tamb	1.1.185	Ortyg
I know it wel my Lord, and thanke you all.	1Tamb	1.1.187	Cosroe
we have tane/Shall be reserv'd, and you in better state,	1Tamb	1.2.3	Tamb
Than if you were arriv'd in Siria,	1Tamb	1.2.4	Tamb
But now you see these letters and commandes,	1Tamb	1.2.21	Tamb
And through my provinces you must expect/Letters of conduct	1Tamb	1.2.23	Tamb
If you intend to keep your treasure safe.	1Tamb	1.2.25	Tamb
As easely may you get the Souldans crowne,	1Tamb	1.2.27	Tamb
I am (my Lord), for so you do import.	1Tamb	1.2.33	Zenoc
And Maddam, whatsoever you esteeme/Of this successe, and losse	1Tamb	1.2.44	Tamb
Both may invest you Empresse of the East:	1Tamb	1.2.46	Tamb
Or you my Lordes to be my followers?	1Tamb	1.2.83	Tamb
Thinke you I way this treasure more than you?	1Tamb	1.2.84	Tamb
How say you Lordings, Is not this your hope?	1Tamb	1.2.116	Tamb
You must be forced from me ere you goe:	1Tamb	1.2.120	Tamb
Or looke you, I should play the Orator?	1Tamb	1.2.129	Tamb
Before I crowne you kings in Asia.	1Tamb	1.2.246	Tamb
heart to be with gladnes pierc'd/To do you honor and securitie.	1Tamb	1.2.251	Therid
If you will willingly remaine with me,	1Tamb	1.2.254	Tamb
You shall have honors, as your merits be:	1Tamb	1.2.255	Tamb
Or els you shall be forc'd with slaverie.	1Tamb	1.2.256	Tamb
For you then Maddam, I am out of doubt.	1Tamb	1.2.258	Tamb
I tel you true my heart is swolne with wrath,	1Tamb	2.2.2	Mycet
Tell you the rest (Meander) I have said.	1Tamb	2.2.13	Mycet
Which you that be but common souldiers,	1Tamb	2.2.63	Meandr
You fighting more for honor than for gold,	1Tamb	2.2.66	Meandr
And you march on their slaughtered carkasses:	1Tamb	2.2.69	Meandr
He tells you true, my maisters, so he does.	1Tamb	2.2.74	Mycet
And so mistake you not a whit my Lord.	1Tamb	2.3.6	Tamb
And doubt you not, but if you favour me,	1Tamb	2.3.10	Tamb
You see my Lord, what woorking woordes he hath.	1Tamb	2.3.25	Therid
But when you see his actions [top] <stop> his speech,	1Tamb	2.3.26	Therid
discovered the enemie/Ready to chardge you with a mighty armie.	1Tamb	2.3.50	1Msngr
Are you the witty King of Persea?	1Tamb	2.4.23	Tamb
I marie am I: have you any suite to me?	1Tamb	2.4.24	Mycet
I would intreat you to speak but three wise wordes.	1Tamb	2.4.25	Tamb
You will not sell it, wil ye?	1Tamb	2.4.29	Tamb
You lie, I gave it you.	1Tamb	2.4.33	Mycet
No, I meane, I let you keep it.	1Tamb	2.4.35	Mycet
Wel, I meane you shall have it againe.	1Tamb	2.4.36	Tamb
Meander, you that were our brothers Guide,	1Tamb	2.5.10	Cosroe
And give you equall place in our affaires.	1Tamb	2.5.14	Cosroe
What saies my other friends, wil you be kings?	1Tamb	2.5.67	Tamb
And so would you my maisters, would you not?	1Tamb	2.5.70	Tamb

YOU (cont.)

And fearefull vengeance light upon you both.	1Tamb	2.7.52		Cosroe
Who thinke you now is King of Persea?	1Tamb	2.7.56		Tamb
If you but say that Tamburlaine shall raigne.	1Tamb	2.7.63		Tamb
You know our Armie is invincible:	1Tamb	3.1.7		Bajzth
What if you sent the Bassoes of your guard,	1Tamb	3.1.17		Fesse
Or els unite you to his life and soule,	1Tamb	3.2.23		Zenoc
That holds you from your father in despight,	1Tamb	3.2.27		Agidas
And keeps you from the honors of a Queene,	1Tamb	3.2.28		Agidas
So now the mighty Souldan heares of you,	1Tamb	3.2.31		Agidas
destruction/Redeeme you from this deadly servitude.	1Tamb	3.2.34		Agidas
How can you fancie one that lookes so fierce,	1Tamb	3.2.40		Agidas
Who when he shall embrace you in his armes,	1Tamb	3.2.42		Agidas
And when you looke for amorous discourse,	1Tamb	3.2.44		Agidas
You see though first the King of Persea/(Being a Shepheard)	1Tamb	3.2.59		Agidas
the King of Persea/(Being a Shepheard) seem'd to love you much,	1Tamb	3.2.60		Agidas
See you Agidas how the King salutes you.	1Tamb	3.2.88		Techel
He bids you prophesie what it imports.	1Tamb	3.2.89		Techel
inlarge/Those Christian Captives, which you keep as slaves,	1Tamb	3.3.47		Tamb
He cals me Bajazeth, whom you call Lord.	1Tamb	3.3.67		Bajzth
Fight all couragiously and be you kings.	1Tamb	3.3.101		Tamb
Give her the Crowne Turkesse, you wer best.	1Tamb	3.3.224		Therid
How dare you thus abuse my Majesty?	1Tamb	3.3.226		Zabina
Here Madam, you are Empresse, she is none.	1Tamb	3.3.227		Therid
While you faint-hearted base Egyptians,	1Tamb	4.1.8		Souldn
So might your highnesse, had you time to sort/Your fighting men,	1Tamb	4.1.36		Capol
And cause the Sun to borrowe light of you.	1Tamb	4.2.40		Tamb
You must devise some torment worsse, my Lord,	1Tamb	4.2.66		Techel
Let these be warnings for you then my slave,	1Tamb	4.2.72		Anippe
How you abuse the person of the king:	1Tamb	4.2.73		Anippe
Or els I sweare to have you whipt stark nak'd.	1Tamb	4.2.74		Anippe
Yet would you have some pitie for my sake,	1Tamb	4.2.123		Zenoc
And make Damascus spoiles as rich to you,	1Tamb	4.4.8		Tamb
you suffer these outragious curses by these slaves of yours?	1Tamb	4.4.26	P	Zenoc
I pray you give them leave Madam, this speech is a goodly	1Tamb	4.4.32	P	Techel
Sirra, why fall you not too, are you so daintily brought up, you	1Tamb	4.4.36	P	Tamb
are you so daintily brought up, you cannot eat your owne flesh?	1Tamb	4.4.36	P	Tamb
are you so daintily brought up, you cannot eat your owne flesh?	1Tamb	4.4.37	P	Tamb
Faste and welcome sir, while hunger make you eat.	1Tamb	4.4.56	P	Tamb
If any love remaine in you my Lord,	1Tamb	4.4.68		Zenoc
Feede you slave, thou maist thinke thy selfe happie to be fed	1Tamb	4.4.92	P	Tamb
sir, you must be dieted, too much eating will make you surfeit.	1Tamb	4.4.103	P	Tamb
sir, you must be dieted, too much eating will make you surfeit.	1Tamb	4.4.104	P	Tamb
Casane, here are the cates you desire to finger, are they not?	1Tamb	4.4.108	P	Tamb
I crowne you here (Theridamas) King of Argier:	1Tamb	4.4.116	P	Tamb
say you to this (Turke) these are not your contributorie kings.	1Tamb	4.4.117	P	Tamb
You that have martcht with happy Tamburlaine,	1Tamb	4.4.121		Tamb
Deserve these tytles I endow you with,	1Tamb	4.4.125		Tamb
Nor you depend on such weake helps as we.	1Tamb	5.1.33		1Virgn
must you be first shal feele/The sworne destruction of	1Tamb	5.1.65		Tamb
Behold my sword, what see you at the point?	1Tamb	5.1.108		Tamb
But I am pleasde you shall not see him there:	1Tamb	5.1.113		Tamb
You hope of libertie and restitution:	1Tamb	5.1.210		Tamb
You see my wife, my Queene and Emperesse,	1Tamb	5.1.264		Bajzth
Her state and person wants no pomp you see,	1Tamb	5.1.485		Tamb
Gainst him my Lord must you addresse your power.	2Tamb	1.1.19		Gazell
Ready to charge you ere you stir your feet.	2Tamb	1.1.121		Fredrk
Forbids you further liberty than this.	2Tamb	1.2.8		Almeda
No talke of running, I tell you sir.	2Tamb	1.2.16		Almeda
How far hence lies the Galley, say you?	2Tamb	1.2.54		Almeda
but tel me my Lord, if I should let you goe,	2Tamb	1.2.61	P	Callap
my Lord, if I should goe, would you bee as good as your word?	2Tamb	1.2.62	P	Almeda
And die before I brought you backe again.	2Tamb	1.2.73		Almeda
When you will my Lord, I am ready.	2Tamb	1.2.76		Almeda
Yes father, you shal see me if I live,	2Tamb	1.3.54		Celeb
Have under me as many kings as you,	2Tamb	1.3.55		Celeb
Or els you are not sons of Tamburlaine.	2Tamb	1.3.64		Tamb
conquer all the world/And you have won enough for me to keep.	2Tamb	1.3.68		Calyph
Wel lovely boies, you shal be Emperours both,	2Tamb	1.3.96		Tamb
And sirha, if you meane to weare a crowne,	2Tamb	1.3.98		Tamb
For since we left you at the Souldans court,	2Tamb	1.3.177		Usumc
Then should you see this Thiefe of Scythia,	2Tamb	3.1.14		Callap
That meane to teach you rudiments of war:	2Tamb	3.2.54		Tamb
Ile have you learne to sleepe upon the ground,	2Tamb	3.2.55		Tamb
In champion grounds, what figure serves you best,	2Tamb	3.2.63		Tamb
Ile teach you how to make the water mount,	2Tamb	3.2.85		Tamb
That you may dryfoot martch through lakes and pooles,	2Tamb	3.2.86		Tamb
And see him lance his flesh to teach you all.	2Tamb	3.2.114		Tamb
Now my boyes, what think you of a wound?	2Tamb	3.2.129		Tamb
Here father, cut it bravely as you did your own.	2Tamb	3.2.135	P	Celeb
My speech of war, and this my wound you see,	2Tamb	3.2.142		Tamb
Teach you my boyes to beare couragious minds,	2Tamb	3.2.143		Tamb
What requier you my maisters?	2Tamb	3.3.15		Capt
To you? Why, do you thinke me weary of it?	2Tamb	3.3.17		Capt
Were you that are the friends of Tamburlain,	2Tamb	3.3.35		Capt
Which til it may defend you, labour low:	2Tamb	3.3.44		Therid
How now Madam, what are you doing?	2Tamb	3.4.34		Therid
Madam, I am so far in love with you,	2Tamb	3.4.78		Therid
That you must goe with us, no remedy.	2Tamb	3.4.79		Therid
Then carie me I care not where you will,	2Tamb	3.4.80		Olymp
I doe you honor in the simile,	2Tamb	3.5.69		Tamb
that ever brandisht sword)/Challenge in combat any of you all,	2Tamb	3.5.72		Tamb
againe, you shall not trouble me thus to come and fetch you.	2Tamb	3.5.101	P	Tamb

YOU (cont.)

againe, you shall not trouble me thus to come and fetch you.	2Tamb	3.5.102	P	Tamb
But as for you (Viceroy) you shal have bits, ...	2Tamb	3.5.103		Tamb
Ile have you learne to feed on provander, ...	2Tamb	3.5.106		Tamb
you knowe I shall have occasion shortly to journey you. .	2Tamb	3.5.114	P	Tamb
you knowe I shall have occasion shortly to journey you. .	2Tamb	3.5.115	P	Tamb
So sirha, now you are a king you must give armes. . .	2Tamb	3.5.137	P	Tamb
and lock you in the stable, when you shall come sweating from	2Tamb	3.5.141	P	Tamb
in the stable, when you shall come sweating from my chariot.	2Tamb	3.5.142	P	Tamb
Wel, now you see hee is a king, looke to him Theridamas, when we	2Tamb	3.5.153	P	Tamb
You knowe not sir:	2Tamb	3.5.158		Tamb
Fight as you ever did, like Conquerours, ...	2Tamb	3.5.160		Tamb
You shall be princes all immediatly:	2Tamb	3.5.168		Tamb
given so much to sleep/You cannot leave it, when our enemies	2Tamb	4.1.12		Amyras
Nor you in faith, but that you wil be thought/More childish	2Tamb	4.1.16		Calyph
but that you wil be thought/More childish valourous than manly	2Tamb	4.1.16		Calyph
You doo dishonor to his majesty, ...	2Tamb	4.1.20		Calyph
Goe, goe tall stripling, fight you for us both, . . .	2Tamb	4.1.33		Calyph
Twill please my mind as wel to heare both you/Have won a heape	2Tamb	4.1.36		Calyph
As if I lay with you for company.	2Tamb	4.1.39		Calyph
You wil not goe then?	2Tamb	4.1.40		Amyras
You say true.	2Tamb	4.1.41		Calyph
Take you the honor, I will take my ease, ...	2Tamb	4.1.49		Calyph
Now you shal feele the strength of Tamburlain, ...	2Tamb	4.1.135		Tamb
Approove the difference twixt himself and you. . . .	2Tamb	4.1.137		Tamb
Ile use some other means to make you yeeld, ...	2Tamb	4.2.51		Therid
I must and wil be pleasde, and you shall yeeld: . . .	2Tamb	4.2.53		Therid
Stay good my Lord, and wil you save my honor, ...	2Tamb	4.2.55		Olymp
With which if you but noint your tender Skin, ...	2Tamb	4.2.65		Olymp
Which when you stab, looke on your weapons point, . . .	2Tamb	4.2.69		Olymp
And you shall se't rebated with the blow.	2Tamb	4.2.70		Olymp
Why gave you not your husband some of it, ...	2Tamb	4.2.71		Therid
If you loved him, and it so precious?	2Tamb	4.2.72		Therid
But from Asphaltis, where I conquer'd you, ...	2Tamb	4.3.5		Tamb
To Byron here where thus I honor you?	2Tamb	4.3.6		Tamb
As you (ye slaves) in mighty Tamburlain.	2Tamb	4.3.11		Tamb
Than you by this unconquered arme of mine.	2Tamb	4.3.16		Tamb
To make you fierce, and fit my appetite, ...	2Tamb	4.3.17		Tamb
You shal be fed with flesh as raw as blood, ...	2Tamb	4.3.18		Tamb
If you can live with it, then live, and draw/My chariot swifter	2Tamb	4.3.20		Tamb
How like you that sir king? why speak you not? . . .	2Tamb	4.3.53		Celeb
Brawle not (I warne you) for your lechery, ...	2Tamb	4.3.75		Tamb
Lost long before you knew what honour meant. . . .	2Tamb	4.3.87		Tamb
My Lord, if ever you did deed of ruth, ...	2Tamb	5.1.24		1Citzn
My Lord, if ever you wil win our hearts, ...	2Tamb	5.1.38		2Citzn
And usde such slender reckning of [your] <you> majesty. .	2Tamb	5.1.83		Therid
traines should reach down to the earth/Could not affright you,	2Tamb	5.1.91		Tamb
Could not perswade you to submission, ...	2Tamb	5.1.94		Tamb
But I have sent volleies of shot to you, ...	2Tamb	5.1.99		Tamb
Then for all your valour, you would save your life. . .	2Tamb	5.1.119		Tamb
Go thither some of you and take his gold, ...	2Tamb	5.1.123		Tamb
They will talk still my Lord, if you doe not bridle them.	2Tamb	5.1.146	P	Amyras
To joine with you against this Tamburlaine.	2Tamb	5.2.35		Amasia
If you retaine desert of holinesse, ...	2Tamb	5.3.19		Techel
Triumphing in his fall whom you advaunst, ...	2Tamb	5.3.23		Techel
And cause some milder spirits governe you.	2Tamb	5.3.80		Phsitn
Tel me, what think you of my sicknes now?	2Tamb	5.3.81		Tamb
No doubt, but you shal soone recover all.	2Tamb	5.3.99		Phsitn
draw you slaves,/In spight of death I will goe show my face.	2Tamb	5.3.113		Tamb
My Lord, you must obey his majesty, ...	2Tamb	5.3.204		Therid
They wondred how you durst with so much wealth/Trust such a	Jew	1.1.79		1Merch
How chance you came not with those other ships/That sail'd by	Jew	1.1.89		Barab
But 'twas ill done of you to come so farre/Without the ayd or	Jew	1.1.93		Barab
Why flocke you thus to me in multitudes?	Jew	1.1.144		Barab
Fond men, what dreame you of their multitudes?	Jew	1.1.157		Barab
I know you will; well brethren let us goe.	Jew	1.1.174		1Jew
Now Bassoes, what demand you at our hands?	Jew	1.2.1		Govnr
'twere in my power/To favour you, but 'tis my fathers cause,	Jew	1.2.11		Calym
Now [Governour], how are you resolv'd?	Jew	1.2.17		Calym
are such/That you will needs have ten yeares tribute past,	Jew	1.2.19		Govnr
What respit aske you [Governour]?	Jew	1.2.27		Calym
We grant a month, but see you keep your promise. . . .	Jew	1.2.28		Calym
Where wee'll attend the respit you have tane, ...	Jew	1.2.30		Calym
Have you determin'd what to say to them?	Jew	1.2.37		1Knght
For to be short, amongst you 'tmust be had.	Jew	1.2.56		Govnr
And will you basely thus submit your selves/To leave your goods	Jew	1.2.79		Barab
Why know you what you did by this device?	Jew	1.2.84		Barab
Corpo di dio stay, you shall have halfe, ...	Jew	1.2.90		Barab
Will you then steale my goods?	Jew	1.2.94		Barab
What? bring you Scripture to confirm your wrongs? . . .	Jew	1.2.110		Barab
And which of you can charge me otherwise?	Jew	1.2.117		Barab
For that is theft; and if you rob me thus, ...	Jew	1.2.126		Barab
It shall be so: now Officers have you done?	Jew	1.2.131		Govnr
Well then my Lord, say, are you satisfied?	Jew	1.2.137		Barab
You have my goods, my mony, and my wealth, ...	Jew	1.2.138		Barab
And having all, you can request no more;	Jew	1.2.140		Barab
And now shall move you to bereave my life.	Jew	1.2.143		Barab
You have my wealth, the labour of my life, ...	Jew	1.2.149		Barab
But take it to you i'th devils name.	Jew	1.2.154		Barab
Why stand you thus unmov'd with my laments?	Jew	1.2.171		Barab
Why weepe you not to thinke upon my wrongs?	Jew	1.2.172		Barab
Why did you yeeld to their extortion?	Jew	1.2.177		Barab
You were a multitude, and I but one, ...	Jew	1.2.178		Barab

YOU (cont.)

What tell you me of Job?	Jew	1.2.181		Barab
You that/Were ne're possest of wealth, are pleas'd with want.	Jew	1.2.200		Barab
I, fare you well.	Jew	1.2.213		Barab
You partiall heavens, have I deserv'd this plague?	Jew	1.2.259		Barab
What, will you thus oppose me, lucklesse Starres,	Jew	1.2.260		Barab
And since you leave me in the Ocean thus/To sinke or swim, and	Jew	1.2.267		Barab
And waters of this new made Nunnery/Will much delight you.	Jew	1.2.312		1Fryar
Grave Abbasse, and you happy Virgins guide,	Jew	1.2.314		Abigal
Well, daughter, we admit you for a Nun.	Jew	1.2.330		Abbass
As had you seene her 'twould have mov'd your heart,	Jew	1.2.385		Mthias
And if she be so faire as you report,	Jew	1.2.388		Lodowk
How say you, shall we?	Jew	1.2.390		Lodowk
The Christian Ile of Rhodes, from whence you came,	Jew	2.2.31		Bosco
and you were stated here/To be at deadly enmity with Turkes.	Jew	2.2.32		Bosco
And he meanes quickly to expell you hence;	Jew	2.2.38		Bosco
And not depart untill I see you free.	Jew	2.2.41		Bosco
So shall you imitate those you succeed:	Jew	2.2.47		Bosco
I wud you were his father too, Sir, that's al the harm I wish	Jew	2.3.41	P	Barab
you were his father too, Sir, that's al the harm I wish you:	Jew	2.3.42	P	Barab
That when we speake with Gentiles like to you,	Jew	2.3.45		Barab
Pointed it is, good Sir,--but not for you.	Jew	2.3.60		Barab
Your life and if you have it.--	Jew	2.3.64		Barab
As for the Diamond, Sir, I told you of,	Jew	2.3.91		Barab
What, can he steale that you demand so much?	Jew	2.3.100		Barab
Let me see, sirra, are you not an old shaver?	Jew	2.3.114	P	Barab
I'le buy you, and marry you to Lady vanity, if you doe well.	Jew	2.3.116	P	Barab
I'le buy you, and marry you to Lady vanity, if you doe well.	Jew	2.3.117	P	Barab
I will serve you, Sir.	Jew	2.3.118	P	Slave
not a stone of beef a day will maintaine you in these chops;	Jew	2.3.125	P	Barab
Here's a leaner, how like you him?	Jew	2.3.126	P	1Offcr
I, marke him, you were best, for this is he	Jew	2.3.132		Barab
My Lord farewell: Come Sirra you are mine.	Jew	2.3.134		Barab
When you have brought her home, come to my house;	Jew	2.3.148		Barab
But wherefore talk'd Don Lodowick with you?	Jew	2.3.150		Mthias
My profession what you please.	Jew	2.3.166		Ithimr
Where is the Diamond you told me of?	Jew	2.3.219		Lodowk
I have it for you, Sir; please you walke in with me:	Jew	2.3.220		Barab
Give me the letters, daughter, doe you heare?	Jew	2.3.224		Barab
the Governors sonne/With all the curtesie you can affoord;	Jew	2.3.226		Barab
Provided, that you keepe your Maiden-head.	Jew	2.3.227		Barab
That ye be both made sure e're you come out.	Jew	2.3.236		Barab
But goe you in, I'le thinke upon the account:	Jew	2.3.241		Barab
looking out/When you should come and hale him from the doore.	Jew	2.3.265		Barab
If you love me, no quarrels in my house;	Jew	2.3.271		Barab
But steale you in, and seeme to see him not;	Jew	2.3.272		Barab
no, but happily he stands in feare/Of that which you, I thinke,	Jew	2.3.283		Barab
Doth she not with her smiling answer you?	Jew	2.3.286		Barab
And so has she done you, even from a child.	Jew	2.3.289		Barab
Nor I the affection that I beare to you.	Jew	2.3.291		Barab
And mine you have, yet let me talke to her;	Jew	2.3.300		Barab
but for me, as you went in at dores/You had bin stab'd, but not	Jew	2.3.337		Barab
as you went in at dores/You had bin stab'd, but not a word on't	Jew	2.3.338		Barab
Revenge it on him when you meet him next.	Jew	2.3.343		Barab
Nay, if you will, stay till she comes her selfe.	Jew	2.3.352		Barab
Father, why have you thus incenst them both?	Jew	2.3.356		Abigal
Yes, you shall have him: Goe put her in.	Jew	2.3.362		Barab
I thinke by this/You purchase both their lives; is it not so?	Jew	2.3.366		Ithimr
Why, know you not?	Jew	3.3.14	P	Ithimr
Know you not of Mathias and Don Lodowickes disaster?	Jew	3.3.16	P	Ithimr
I pray, mistris, wil you answer me to one question?	Jew	3.3.30	P	Ithimr
When, ducke you?	Jew	3.3.51	P	Ithimr
Nay, you shall pardon me:	Jew	3.3.73		Abigal
My duty waits on you.	Jew	3.3.76		Abigal
I have brought you a Ladle.	Jew	3.4.59	P	Ithimr
master, wil you poison her with a messe of rice [porredge]?	Jew	3.4.64	P	Ithimr
make her round and plump, and batten more then you are aware.	Jew	3.4.66	P	Ithimr
Pray doe, and let me help you, master.	Jew	3.4.86	P	Ithimr
fares Callymath, What wind drives you thus into Malta rhode?	Jew	3.5.2	P	Govnr
To you of Malta thus saith Calymath:	Jew	3.5.7		Basso
The time you tooke for respite, is at hand,	Jew	3.5.8		Basso
You shall not need trouble your selves so farre,	Jew	3.5.22		Basso
And now you men of Malta looke about,	Jew	3.5.29		Govnr
And as you profitably take up Armes,	Jew	3.5.32		Govnr
sent for him, but seeing you are come/Be you my ghostly father;	Jew	3.6.11		Abigal
but seeing you are come/Be you my ghostly father; and first	Jew	3.6.12		Abigal
You knew Mathias and Don Lodowicke?	Jew	3.6.20		Abigal
That's brave, master, but think you it wil not be known?	Jew	4.1.8	P	Ithimr
For my part feare you not.	Jew	4.1.10		Ithimr
Doe you not sorrow for your daughters death?	Jew	4.1.17		Ithimr
of my sinnes/Lye heavy on my soule; then pray you tell me,	Jew	4.1.49		Barab
And Barabas, you know--	Jew	4.1.79		2Fryar
You shall convert me, you shall have all my wealth.	Jew	4.1.81		Barab
I know they are, and I will be with you.	Jew	4.1.83		Barab
and I am resolv'd/You shall confesse me, and have all my goods.	Jew	4.1.86		Barab
You see I answer him, and yet he stayes;	Jew	4.1.88		Barab
Rid him away, and goe you home with me.	Jew	4.1.89		Barab
I'le be with you to night.	Jew	4.1.90		2Fryar
You heare your answer, and you may be gone.	Jew	4.1.92		1Fryar
Why goe, get you away.	Jew	4.1.93		2Fryar
Fryar Barnardine goe you with Ithimore.	Jew	4.1.99		Barab
You know my mind, let me alone with him.	Jew	4.1.100		Barab
But doe you thinke that I beleeve his words?	Jew	4.1.105		Barab

YOU (cont.)

Why, Brother, you converted Abigall;	Jew	4.1.106		Barab
For presently you shall be shriv'd.	Jew	4.1.110		1Fryar
Now Fryar Bernardine I come to you,	Jew	4.1.125		Barab
I'le feast you, lodge you, give you faire words,	Jew	4.1.126		Barab
You loyter, master, wherefore stay [we] <me> thus?	Jew	4.1.139		Ithimr
What, doe you meane to strangle me?	Jew	4.1.144		2Fryar
Yes, 'cause you use to confesse.	Jew	4.1.145		Ithimr
What, will you [have] <save> my life?	Jew	4.1.148		2Fryar
Pull hard, I say, you would have had my goods.	Jew	4.1.149		Barab
I have don't, but no body knowes it but you two, I may escape.	Jew	4.1.180	P	1Fryar
So might my man and I hang with you for company.	Jew	4.1.182		Barab
early; with intent to goe/Unto your Friery, because you staid.	Jew	4.1.192		Barab
will you turne Christian, when holy Friars turne devils and	Jew	4.1.193	P	Ithimr
When shall you see a Jew commit the like?	Jew	4.1.197		Barab
To morrow is the Sessions; you shall to it.	Jew	4.1.199		Barab
The Law shall touch you, we'll but lead you, we:	Jew	4.1.202		Barab
by such a tall man as I am, from such a beautifull dame as you.	Jew	4.2.10	P	Pilia
This is the Gentleman you writ to.	Jew	4.2.37	P	Pilia
sweet youth; did not you, Sir, bring the sweet youth a letter?	Jew	4.2.41	P	Ithimr
And ye did but know how she loves you, Sir.	Jew	4.2.53		Pilia
And you can have it, Sir, and if you please.	Jew	4.2.56		Pilia
Let me alone, doe but you speake him faire:	Jew	4.2.63		Pilia
But you know some secrets of the Jew,	Jew	4.2.64		Pilia
and this shall be your warrant; if you doe not, no more but so.	Jew	4.2.76	P	Ithimr
Tell him you will confesse.	Jew	4.2.77	P	Pilia
for your sake, and said what a faithfull servant you had bin.	Jew	4.2.109	P	Pilia
as you love your life send me five hundred crowns, and give the	Jew	4.2.117	P	Ithimr
words, Sir, and send it you, were best see; there's his letter.	Jew	4.3.24	P	Pilia
what hee writes for you, ye shall have streight.	Jew	4.3.27	P	Barab
please you dine with me, Sir, and you shal be most hartily	Jew	4.3.29	P	Barab
you dine with me, Sir, and you shal be most hartily poyson'd.	Jew	4.3.30	P	Barab
you know my meaning.	Jew	4.3.34	P	Barab
You know I have no childe, and unto whom/Should I leave all but	Jew	4.3.44		Barab
Pray when, Sir, shall I see you at my house?	Jew	4.3.56		Barab
Fare you well.	Jew	4.3.58		Pilia
have at it; and doe you heare?	Jew	4.4.2	P	Ithimr
Ha, to the Jew, and send me mony you were best.	Jew	4.4.12	P	Ithimr
You knew Mathias and the Governors son; he and I kild 'em both,	Jew	4.4.17	P	Ithimr
You two alone?	Jew	4.4.22		Curtzn
Sirra, you must give my mistris your posey.	Jew	4.4.37		Pilia
So did you when you stole my gold.	Jew	4.4.50		Barab
You run swifter when you threw my gold out of my Window.	Jew	4.4.52	P	Barab
Very mush, Mounsier, you no be his man?	Jew	4.4.57	P	Barab
Now, Gentlemen, betake you to your Armes,	Jew	5.1.1		Govnr
And it behoves you to be resolute;	Jew	5.1.3		Govnr
Nor me neither, I cannot out-run you Constable, oh my belly.	Jew	5.1.20	P	Ithimr
Confesse; what meane you, Lords, who should confesse?	Jew	5.1.26		Barab
Thou and thy Turk; 'twas you that slew my son.	Jew	5.1.27		Govnr
you men of Malta, heare me speake;/Shee is a Curtezane and he a	Jew	5.1.36		Barab
Once more away with him; you shall have law.	Jew	5.1.40		Govnr
Devils doe your worst, [I'le] <I> live in spite of you.	Jew	5.1.41		Barab
one that can spy a place/Where you may enter, and surprize the	Jew	5.1.71		Barab
Now whilst you give assault unto the wals,	Jew	5.1.90		Barab
Open the gates for you to enter in,	Jew	5.1.93		Barab
Now vaile your pride you captive Christians,	Jew	5.2.1		Calym
Now where's the hope you had of haughty Spaine?	Jew	5.2.3		Calym
you must yeeld, and under Turkish yokes/Shall groning beare the	Jew	5.2.7		Calym
Yet you doe live, and live for me you shall:	Jew	5.2.63		Barab
Malta's ruine, thinke you not/'Twere slender policy for Barabas	Jew	5.2.64		Barab
For sith, as once you said, within this Ile/In Malta here, that	Jew	5.2.67		Barab
slavish Bands/Wherein the Turke hath yoak'd your land and you?	Jew	5.2.78		Barab
What will you give me if I render you/The life of Calymath,	Jew	5.2.79		Barab
What will you give him that procureth this?	Jew	5.2.83		Barab
intreat your Highnesse/Not to depart till he has feasted you.	Jew	5.3.33		Msngr
Till you shall heare a Culverin discharg'd/By him that beares	Jew	5.4.3		Govnr
Or you released of this servitude.	Jew	5.4.7		Govnr
Why now I see that you have Art indeed.	Jew	5.5.4		Barab
There, Carpenters, divide that gold amongst you:	Jew	5.5.5		Barab
We shall, my Lord, and thanke you.	Jew	5.5.8		Crpntr
And if you like them, drinke your fill and dye:	Jew	5.5.9		Barab
Governour, why stand you all so pittilesse?	Jew	5.5.71		Barab
You will not helpe me then?	Jew	5.5.76		Barab
And villaines, know you cannot helpe me now.	Jew	5.5.77		Barab
I would have brought confusion on you all,	Jew	5.5.85		Barab
Tell me, you Christians, what doth this portend?	Jew	5.5.90		Calym
To keepe me here will nought advantage you.	Jew	5.5.117		Calym
Thanks sonne Navarre, you see we love you well,	P 13	1.13		QnMoth
That linke you in mariage with our daughter heer:	P 14	1.14		QnMoth
And as you know, our difference in Religion/Might be a meanes	P 15	1.15		QnMoth
in Religion/Might be a meanes to crosse you in your love.	P 16	1.16		QnMoth
Have you not heard of late how he decreed,	P 32	1.32		Navrre
My Lord you need not mervaile at the Guise,	P 39	1.39		Condy
My Lord, but did you mark the Cardinall/The Guises brother, and	P 47	1.47		Admral
Doth not your grace know the man that gave them you?	P 172	3.7		Navrre
to beware/How you did meddle with such dangerous giftes.	P 180	3.15		Navrre
What are you hurt my Lord high Admiral?	P 197	3.32		Condy
What you determine, I will ratifie.	P 227	4.25		Charls
What order wil you set downe for the Massacre?	P 229	4.27		QnMoth
Then I am carefull you should be preserved.	P 265	4.63		Charls
And every hower I will visite you.	P 272	4.70		Charls
To kill all that you suspect of heresie.	P 276	5.3		Guise
Swizers keepe you the streetes,/And at ech corner shall the	P 290	5.17		Anjoy

YOU (cont.)

Anjoy, Gonzago, Retes, if that you three,	P 322	5.49	Guise
Are you a preacher of these heresies?	P 340	5.67	Guise
down, heer's one would speak with you from the Duke of Guise.	P 349	6.4	P SrnsWf
Then take this with you.	P 360	6.15	Mntsrl
Who have you there?	P 380	7.20	Anjoy
How answere you that?	P 397	7.37	Guise
Why suffer you that peasant to declaime?	P 414	7.54	Guise
For that let me alone, Cousin stay you heer,	P 428	7.68	Anjoy
And when you see me in, then follow hard.	P 429	7.69	Anjoy
How now my Lords, how fare you?	P 430	7.70	Anjoy
That you were one that made this Massacre.	P 436	7.76	Navrre
Who I? you are deceived, I rose but now.	P 437	7.77	Anjoy
Come sirs, Ile whip you to death with my punniards point.	P 441	7.81	Guise
Gonzago poste you to Orleance, Retes to Deep,	P 445	7.85	Guise
unto Roan, and spare not one/That you suspect of heresy.	P 447	7.87	Guise
I thankfully shall undertake the charge/Of you and yours, and	P 477	8.27	Anjoy
Now Madame, how like you our lusty Admirall?	P 494	9.13	Guise
My Lord of Loraine have you markt of late,/How Charles our	P 512	9.31	QnMoth
But God will sure restore you to your health.	P 542	11.7	Navrre
Thanks to you al.	P 599	12.12	King
As now you are, so shall you still persist,	P 608	12.21	King
diadem, before/You were invested in the crowne of France.	P 613	12.26	Mugern
His minde you see runnes on his minions,	P 633	12.46	QnMoth
Now Madam must you insinuate with the King,	P 645	12.58	Cardnl
But for you know our quarrell is no more,	P 704	14.7	Navrre
So kindely Cosin of Guise you and your wife/Doe both salute our	P 752	15.10	King
Remember you the letter gentle sir,	P 754	15.12	King
Sir, to you sir, that dares make the Duke a cuckolde, and use a	P 806	17.1	P Souldr
And although you take out nothing but your owne, yet you put in	P 808	17.3	P Souldr
yet you put in that which displeaseth him, and so forestall his	P 808	17.3	P Souldr
his market, and set up your standing where you should not:	P 810	17.5	P Souldr
you will take upon you to be his, and tyll the ground that he	P 811	17.6	P Souldr
possession (as I would I might) yet I meane to keepe you out,	P 814	17.9	P Souldr
of Guise, we understand that you/Have gathered a power of men.	P 821	17.16	King
Come on sirs, what, are you resolutely bent,	P 931	19.1	Capt
What, will you not feare when you see him come?	P 933	19.3	Capt
Feare him said you?	P 934	19.4	P 1Mur
Well then, I see you are resolute.	P 938	19.8	Capt
Let us alone, I warrant you.	P 939	19.9	P 1Mur
You will give us our money?	P 942	19.12	P AllMur
And you good Cosin to imagine it.	P 970	19.40	King
Cousin, assure you I am resolute,	P 973	19.43	King
O my Lord, I am one of them that is set to murder you.	P 992	19.62	P 3Mur
Philip and Parma, I am slaine for you:	P1011	19.81	Guise
What, have you done?	P1016	19.86	Capt
And heere in presence of you all I sweare,	P1026	19.96	King
Get you away and strangle the Cardinall.	P1059	19.129	King
Mother, how like you this device of mine?	P1065	19.135	King
What, will you fyle your handes with Churchmens bloud?	P1093	20.3	Cardnl
O Lord no: for we entend to strangle you.	P1095	20.5	2Mur
Yours my Lord Cardinall, you should have saide.	P1103	20.13	1Mur
I come to bring you newes, that your brother the Cardinall of	P1122	21.16	P Frier
And that the sweet and princely minde you beare,	P1141	22.3	King
For you are stricken with a poysoned knife.	P1213	22.75	Srgeon
Long may you live, and still be King of France.	P1226	22.88	Navrre
you that dares make a duke a cuckolde and use a counterfeyt key	Paris	ms 1,p390	P Souldr
thoughe you take out none but your owne treasure	Paris	ms 3,p390	P Souldr
yett you putt in that displeases him | And fill up his rome	Paris	ms 4,p390	P Souldr
you forestalle the markett and sett upe your standinge where	Paris	ms 5,p390	P Souldr
the markett and sett upe your standinge where you shold not:	Paris	ms 6,p390	P Souldr
But you will saye you leave him rome enoughe besides:	Paris	ms 6,p390	P Souldr
But you will saye you leave him rome enoughe besides:	Paris	ms 7,p390	P Souldr
ser where he is your landlorde you take upon you to be his |	Paris	ms10,p390	P Souldr
enter by defaulte | whatt thoughe you were once in possession	Paris	ms11,p390	P Souldr
yett comminge upon you once unawares he frayde you out againe.	Paris	ms12,p390	P Souldr
yet I come to keepe you out ser.	Paris	ms16,p390	P Souldr
yow are wellcome ser have at you	Paris	ms16,p390	P Souldr
And as I like your discoursing, ile have you.	Edw	1.1.32	Gavstn
Why there are hospitals for such as you,	Edw	1.1.35	Gavstn
You know that I came lately out of France,	Edw	1.1.44	Gavstn
If I speed well, ile entertaine you all.	Edw	1.1.46	Gavstn
Will you not graunt me this?--	Edw	1.1.77	Edward
If you love us my lord, hate Gaveston.	Edw	1.1.80	MortSr
I will have Gaveston, and you shall know,	Edw	1.1.96	Edward
My lord, why do you thus incense your peeres,	Edw	1.1.99	Lncstr
That naturally would love and honour you,	Edw	1.1.100	Lncstr
Yet dare you brave the king unto his face.	Edw	1.1.116	Kent
I yours, and therefore I would wish you graunt.	Edw	1.1.120	Edward
And strike off his that makes you threaten us.	Edw	1.1.124	Mortmr
Or looke to see the throne where you should sit,	Edw	1.1.131	Lncstr
Saving your reverence, you must pardon me.	Edw	1.1.186	Gavstn
My lord, will you take armes against the king?	Edw	1.2.39	Lncstr
Then wil you joine with us that be his peeres/To banish or	Edw	1.2.42	Mortmr
And in the meane time ile intreat you all,	Edw	1.2.77	ArchBp
What? are you mov'd that Gaveston sits heere?	Edw	1.4.8	Edward
Is this the dutie that you owe your king?	Edw	1.4.22	Kent
Whether will you beare him, stay or ye shall die.	Edw	1.4.24	Edward
Ile make the prowdest of you stoope to him.	Edw	1.4.31	Edward
My lord, you may not thus disparage us,	Edw	1.4.32	Lncstr
Warwicke and Lancaster, weare you my crowne,	Edw	1.4.37	Edward
Think you that we can brooke this upstart pride?	Edw	1.4.41	Warwck
Why are you moov'd, be patient my lord,	Edw	1.4.43	ArchBp

YOU (cont.)

Meete you for this, proud overdaring peeres?	Edw	1.4.47	Edward
You know that I am legate to the Pope,	Edw	1.4.51	ArchBp
Curse me, depose me, doe the worst you can.	Edw	1.4.57	Edward
My lord, you shalbe Chauncellor of the realme,	Edw	1.4.65	Edward
And you lord Warwick, president of the North,	Edw	1.4.68	Edward
if this content you not,/Make severall kingdomes of this	Edw	1.4.69	Edward
And share it equally amongst you all,	Edw	1.4.71	Edward
Why should you love him, whome the world hates so?	Edw	1.4.76	Mortmr
You that be noble borne should pitie him.	Edw	1.4.80	Edward
You that are princely borne should shake him off,	Edw	1.4.81	Warwck
Are you content to banish him the realme?	Edw	1.4.84	ArchBp
But to forsake you, in whose gratious lookes/The blessednes of	Edw	1.4.120	Gavstn
I say no more, judge you the rest my lord.	Edw	1.4.148	Gavstn
Madam, tis you that rob me of my lord.	Edw	1.4.161	Gavstn
To sue unto you all for his repeale:	Edw	1.4.201	Queene
But madam, would you have us cal him home?	Edw	1.4.208	Mortmr
will you be resolute and hold with me?	Edw	1.4.231	Lncstr
Do you not wish that Gaveston were dead?	Edw	1.4.252	Mortmr
Know you not Gaveston hath store of golde,	Edw	1.4.258	Mortmr
Marke you but that my lord of Lancaster.	Edw	1.4.263	Warwck
Diablo, what passions call you these?	Edw	1.4.319	Lncstr
My gratious lord, I come to bring you newes.	Edw	1.4.320	Queene
That you have parled with your Mortimer?	Edw	1.4.321	Edward
But will you love me, if you finde it so?	Edw	1.4.324	Queene
And with this sword, Penbrooke wil fight for you.	Edw	1.4.352	Penbrk
As England shall be quiet, and you safe.	Edw	1.4.358	Mortmr
And as for you, lord Mortimer of Chirke,	Edw	1.4.359	Edward
Be you the generall of the levied troopes,	Edw	1.4.362	Edward
Lord Mortimer, we leave you to your charge:	Edw	1.4.373	Edward
For wot you not that I have made him sure,	Edw	1.4.378	Edward
But nephew, now you see the king is changd.	Edw	1.4.420	MortSr
You know my minde, come unckle lets away.	Edw	1.4.424	Mortmr
What, meane you then to be his follower?	Edw	2.1.12	Baldck
Then Balduck, you must cast the scholler off,	Edw	2.1.31	Spencr
Can get you any favour with great men.	Edw	2.1.41	Spencr
You must be proud, bold, pleasant, resolute,	Edw	2.1.42	Spencr
Spencer, stay you and beare me companie,	Edw	2.1.74	Neece
You have matters of more waight to thinke upon,	Edw	2.2.8	Mortmr
But seeing you are so desirous, thus it is:	Edw	2.2.15	Mortmr
Is this the love you beare your soveraigne?	Edw	2.2.30	Edward
Can you in words make showe of amitie,	Edw	2.2.32	Edward
What call you this but private libelling,	Edw	2.2.34	Edward
Sweete husband be content, they all love you.	Edw	2.2.36	Queene
And you the Eagles, sore ye nere so high,	Edw	2.2.39	Edward
I have the [gesses] <gresses> that will pull you downe,	Edw	2.2.40	Edward
Will none of you salute my Gaveston?	Edw	2.2.64	Edward
Brother, doe you heare them?	Edw	2.2.69	Kent
As to bestow a looke on such as you.	Edw	2.2.78	Gavstn
Yet I disdaine not to doe this for you.	Edw	2.2.79	Lncstr
Deare shall you both abie this riotous deede:	Edw	2.2.88	Edward
Looke to your owne crowne, if you back him thus.	Edw	2.2.93	Warwck
About it then, and we will follow you.	Edw	2.2.124	Mortmr
I warrant you.	Edw	2.2.126	Warwck
You may not in, my lord.	Edw	2.2.137	Guard
Who have we there, ist you?	Edw	2.2.140	Edward
Nay, stay my lord, I come to bring you newes,	Edw	2.2.141	Mortmr
Twas in your wars, you should ransome him.	Edw	2.2.144	Lncstr
And you shall ransome him, or else--	Edw	2.2.145	Mortmr
What Mortimer, you will not threaten him?	Edw	2.2.146	Kent
Quiet your self, you shall have the broad seale,	Edw	2.2.147	Edward
Your minion Gaveston hath taught you this.	Edw	2.2.149	Lncstr
Would levie men enough to anger you.	Edw	2.2.152	Mortmr
Nay, now you are heere alone, ile speake my minde.	Edw	2.2.155	Mortmr
Maids of England, sore may you moorne,	Edw	2.2.190	Lncstr
For your lemmons you have lost, at Bannocks borne,	Edw	2.2.191	Lncstr
If ye be moov'de, revenge it as you can,	Edw	2.2.198	Lncstr
Will be the ruine of the realme and you,	Edw	2.2.209	Kent
I, and tis likewise thought you favour him <them> <'em> <hem>.	Edw	2.2.226	Edward
Thus do you still suspect me without cause.	Edw	2.2.227	Queene
Why do you not commit him to the tower?	Edw	2.2.234	Gavstn
Scarce shall you finde a man of more desart.	Edw	2.2.251	Gavstn
I come to joine with you, and leave the king,	Edw	2.3.2	Kent
I feare me you are sent of pollicie,	Edw	2.3.5	Lncstr
But whats the reason you should leave him now?	Edw	2.3.13	Penbrk
But neither spare you Gaveston, nor his friends.	Edw	2.3.28	Lncstr
O stay my lord, they will not injure you.	Edw	2.4.7	Gavstn
Heavens can witnesse, I love none but you.	Edw	2.4.15	Queene
What would you with the king, ist him you seek?	Edw	2.4.31	Queene
Madam, stay you within this castell here.	Edw	2.4.50	Mortmr
You know the king is so suspitious,	Edw	2.4.53	Queene
As if he heare I have but talkt with you,	Edw	2.4.54	Queene
Madam, I cannot stay to answer you,	Edw	2.4.57	Mortmr
I thanke you all my lords, then I perceive,	Edw	2.5.29	Gavstn
My lords, king Edward greetes you all by me.	Edw	2.5.33	Arundl
Hearing that you had taken Gaveston,	Edw	2.5.35	Arundl
Intreateth you by me, yet but he may/See him before he dies,	Edw	2.5.36	Arundl
And sends you word, he knowes that die he shall,	Edw	2.5.38	Arundl
And if you gratifie his grace so farre,	Edw	2.5.39	Arundl
I know it lords, it is this life you aime at,	Edw	2.5.48	Gavstn
When, can you tell?	Edw	2.5.60	Warwck
Then if you will not trust his grace in keepe,	Edw	2.5.65	Arundl
My lord Mortimer, and you my lords each one,	Edw	2.5.74	Penbrk

YOU (cont.)

Provided this, that you my lord of Arundell/Will joyne with me.	Edw	2.5.81	Penbrk
But if you dare trust Penbrooke with the prisoner,	Edw	2.5.87	Penbrk
My lord of Lancaster, what say you in this?	Edw	2.5.89	Arundl
And you lord Mortimer?	Edw	2.5.91	Penbrk
How say you my lord of Warwick?	Edw	2.5.92	Mortmr
My lord of Penbrooke, we deliver him you,	Edw	2.5.97	Mortmr
My Lord, you shall go with me,	Edw	2.5.99	Penbrk
Strive you no longer, I will have that Gaveston.	Edw	2.6.7	Warwck
Did you retaine your fathers magnanimitie,	Edw	3.1.16	Spencr
You would not suffer thus your majestie/Be counterbuft of your	Edw	3.1.17	Spencr
Madam in this matter/We will employ you and your little sonne,	Edw	3.1.70	Edward
You shall go parley with the king of Fraunce.	Edw	3.1.71	Edward
Boye, see you beare you bravelie to the king,	Edw	3.1.72	Edward
Madam, we will that you with speed be shipt,	Edw	3.1.81	Edward
And this our sonne, [Levune] <Lewne> shall follow you,	Edw	3.1.82	Edward
Choose of our lords to beare you companie,	Edw	3.1.84	Edward
That you may drinke your fill, and quaffe in bloud,	Edw	3.1.137	Edward
You villaines that have slaine my Gaveston:	Edw	3.1.142	Edward
You will this greefe have ease and remedie,	Edw	3.1.160	Herald
That from your princely person you remoove/This Spencer, as a	Edw	3.1.161	Herald
My [lords] <lord>, perceive you how these rebels swell:	Edw	3.1.181	Edward
What rebels, do you shrinke, and sound retreat?	Edw	3.1.200	Edward
me thinkes you hang the heads,/But weele advance them traitors,	Edw	3.1.223	Edward
traitors, now tis time/To be avengd on you for all your braves,	Edw	3.1.225	Edward
To whome right well you knew our soule was knit,	Edw	3.1.227	Edward
A rebels, recreants, you made him away.	Edw	3.1.229	Edward
So sir, you have spoke, away, avoid our presence.	Edw	3.1.232	Edward
I charge you roundly off with both their heads,	Edw	3.1.247	Edward
Have you no doubts my lords, ile [clap so] <claps> close,/Among	Edw	3.1.276	Levune
Holla, who walketh there, ist you my lord?	Edw	4.1.12	Mortmr
I warrant you, ile winne his highnes quicklie,	Edw	4.2.6	Prince
How say you my Lord, will you go with your friends,	Edw	4.2.19	SrJohn
Madam, long may you live,	Edw	4.2.34	Kent
That you were dead, or very neare your death.	Edw	4.2.38	Queene
How meane you, and the king my father lives?	Edw	4.2.43	Prince
distressed Queene his sister heere,/Go you with her to Henolt:	Edw	4.2.64	SrJohn
How say yong Prince, what thinke you of the match?	Edw	4.2.67	SrJohn
and you must not discourage/Your friends that are so forward in	Edw	4.2.69	Queene
These comforts that you give our wofull queene,	Edw	4.2.72	Kent
Madam along, and you my lord, with me,	Edw	4.2.81	SrJohn
My lord of Gloster, do you heare the newes?	Edw	4.3.4	Edward
the realme, my lord of Arundell/You have the note, have you not?	Edw	4.3.8	Edward
realme, my lord of Arundell/You have the note, have you not?	Edw	4.3.8	Edward
What now remaines, have you proclaimed, my lord,	Edw	4.3.17	Edward
To you my lord of Gloster from [Levune] <Lewne>.	Edw	4.3.26	Post
is gone, whither if you aske, with sir John of Henolt, brother	Edw	4.3.31	P Spencr
England shall welcome you, and all your route.	Edw	4.3.42	Edward
Betweene you both, shorten the time I pray,	Edw	4.3.45	Edward
As you injurious were to beare them foorth.	Edw	4.3.52	Edward
Nay madam, if you be a warriar,	Edw	4.4.15	Mortmr
Thankes be heavens great architect and you.	Edw	4.6.22	Queene
Deale you my lords in this, my loving lords,	Edw	4.6.28	Queene
How will you deale with Edward in his fall?	Edw	4.6.31	Kent
Tell me good unckle, what Edward doe you meane?	Edw	4.6.32	Prince
We thanke you all.	Edw	4.6.53	Queene
Take him away, he prates. You Rice ap Howell,	Edw	4.6.73	Mortmr
Have you no doubt my Lorde, have you no feare,	Edw	4.7.1	Abbot
But we alas are chaste, and you my friends,	Edw	4.7.22	Edward
Do you betray us and our companie.	Edw	4.7.25	Edward
I arrest you of high treason here,	Edw	4.7.57	Leistr
My lord, why droope you thus?	Edw	4.7.60	Leistr
Why do you lowre unkindly on a king?	Edw	4.7.63	Edward
keepe these preachments till you come to the place appointed.	Edw	4.7.113	P Rice
You, and such as you are, have made wise worke in England.	Edw	4.7.114	P Rice
And that you lay for pleasure here a space,	Edw	5.1.3	Leistr
My lord, why waste you thus the time away,	Edw	5.1.49	Leistr
They stay your answer, will you yeeld your crowne?	Edw	5.1.50	Leistr
Stand still you watches of the element,	Edw	5.1.66	Edward
All times and seasons rest you at a stay,	Edw	5.1.67	Edward
Why gape you for your soveraignes overthrow?	Edw	5.1.72	Edward
What, feare you not the furie of your king?	Edw	5.1.75	Edward
And therefore say, will you resigne or no.	Edw	5.1.85	Trussl
Traitors be gon, and joine you with Mortimer,	Edw	5.1.87	Edward
Elect, conspire, install, do what you will,	Edw	5.1.88	Edward
He of you all that most desires my bloud,	Edw	5.1.100	Edward
Take it: what are you moovde, pitie you me?	Edw	5.1.102	Edward
And save you from your foes, Bartley would die.	Edw	5.1.134	Bartly
And who must keepe mee now, must you my lorde?	Edw	5.1.137	Edward
Whether you will, all places are alike,	Edw	5.1.145	Edward
Favor him my lord, as much as lieth in you.	Edw	5.1.147	Leistr
Not yet my lorde, ile beare you on your waye.	Edw	5.1.155	Leistr
I warrant you my lord.	Edw	5.2.56	Gurney
Feare not my Lord, weele do as you commaund.	Edw	5.2.66	Matrvs
Brother, you know it is impossible.	Edw	5.2.97	Queene
With you I will, but not with Mortimer.	Edw	5.2.110	Prince
Traitors away, what will you murther me,	Edw	5.3.29	Edward
Least you be knowne, and so be rescued.	Edw	5.3.32	Gurney
Why strive you thus? your labour is in vaine.	Edw	5.3.33	Matrvs
Base villaines, wherefore doe you gripe mee thus?	Edw	5.3.57	Kent
And I will visit him, why stay you me?	Edw	5.3.60	Kent
I, lead me whether you will, even to my death,	Edw	5.3.66	Kent
You shall not need to give instructions,	Edw	5.4.29	Ltborn

YOU (cont.)

Nay, you shall pardon me, none shall knowe my trickes.	Edw	5.4.39	Ltborn
Did you attempt his rescue, Edmund speake?	Edw	5.4.86	Mortmr
My lord, if you will let my unckle live,	Edw	5.4.99	King
How often shall I bid you beare him hence?	Edw	5.4.102	Mortmr
And therefore soldiers whether will you hale me?	Edw	5.4.108	Kent
My lord protector greetes you.	Edw	5.5.14	Ltborn
Know you this token? I must have the king.	Edw	5.5.19	Ltborn
Doe as you are commaunded by my lord.	Edw	5.5.26	Matrvs
I know what I must do, get you away,	Edw	5.5.27	Ltborn
Neede you any thing besides?	Edw	5.5.32	Gurney
I, I, so: when I call you, bring it in.	Edw	5.5.35	Ltborn
Feare not you that.	Edw	5.5.36	Matrvs
To comfort you, and bring you joyfull newes.	Edw	5.5.43	Ltborn
To murther you my most gratious lorde?	Edw	5.5.46	Ltborn
Farre is it from my hart to do you harme,	Edw	5.5.47	Ltborn
The Queene sent me, to see how you were used,	Edw	5.5.48	Ltborn
If you mistrust me, ile be gon my lord.	Edw	5.5.97	Ltborn
But not too hard, least that you bruse his body.	Edw	5.5.113	Ltborn
Feare not my lord, know that you are a king.	Edw	5.6.24	1Lord
And had you lov'de him halfe so well as I,	Edw	5.6.35	King
You could not beare his death thus patiently,	Edw	5.6.36	King
But you I feare, conspirde with Mortimer.	Edw	5.6.37	King
Why speake you not unto my lord the king?	Edw	5.6.38	1Lord
Tis my hand, what gather you by this.	Edw	5.6.47	Mortmr
What, suffer you the traitor to delay?	Edw	5.6.67	King
This argues, that you spilt my fathers bloud,	Edw	5.6.70	King
Els would you not intreate for Mortimer.	Edw	5.6.71	King
I, madam, you, for so the rumor runnes.	Edw	5.6.73	King
Mother, you are suspected for his death,	Edw	5.6.78	King
And therefore we commit you to the Tower,	Edw	5.6.79	King
If you be guiltie, though I be your sonne,	Edw	5.6.81	King
Thus madam, tis the kings will you shall hence.	Edw	5.6.89	2Lord
What doctrine call you this? Che sera, sera:	F 74	1.1.46	Faust
of argument, which <that> you, being Licentiats <licentiate>,	F 202	1.2.9	P Wagner
<Have you any witnesse on't>?	F 204	(HC258)A	P Wagner
<Yes sirre, I heard you>.	F 204	(HC258)A	P 1Schol
Then <Well> you will not tell us?	F 205	1.2.12	P 2Schol
You are deceiv'd, for <Yes sir>, I will tell you:	F 206	1.2.13	P Wagner
yet if you were not dunces, you would never aske me such a	F 206	1.2.13	P Wagner
you were not dunces, you would never aske me such a question:	F 207	1.2.14	P Wagner
Then wherefore should you aske me such a question?	F 209	1.2.16	P Wagner
for you to come within fortie foot of the place of execution,	F 211	1.2.18	P Wagner
I do not doubt but to see you both hang'd the next Sessions.	F 212	1.2.19	P Wagner
Thus having triumpht over you, I will set my countenance like a	F 213	1.2.20	P Wagner
and so the Lord blesse you, preserve you, and keepe you, my	F 217	1.2.24	P Wagner
you, and keepe you, my deere brethren <my deare brethren>.	F 217	1.2.24	P Wagner
And what are you that live with Lucifer?	F 297	1.3.69	Faust
Where are you damn'd?	F 301	1.3.73	Faust
you have seene many boyes with [such pickadevaunts] <beards> I	F 345	1.4.3	P Robin
Yes, and goings out too, you may see sir.	F 347	1.4.5	P Robin
and good sauce to it, if I pay so deere, I can tell you.	F 353	1.4.11	P Robin
then belike if I serve you, I shall be lousy.	F 359	1.4.17	P Robin
you may save your selfe a labour, for they are as familiar with	F 364	1.4.22	P Robin
me, as if they payd for their meate and drinke, I can tell you.	F 366	1.4.24	P Robin
Yes marry sir, and I thanke you to.	F 368	1.4.26	P Robin
How now sir, will you serve me now?	F 376	1.4.34	P Wagner
but hearke you Maister, will you teach me this conjuring	F 380	1.4.38	P Robin
you Maister, will you teach me this conjuring Occupation?	F 380	1.4.38	P Robin
and see that you walke attentively, and let your right eye be	F 385	1.4.43	P Wagner
Well sir, I warrant you.	F 388	1.4.46	P Robin
Why, have you any paine that torture other <tortures others>?	F 432	2.1.44	Faust
Speake Faustus, do you deliver this as your Deed?	F 501	2.1.113	Mephst
this house, you and all, should turne to Gold, that I might	F 675	2.2.124	P Covet
that I might locke you safe into <uppe in> my <goode> Chest:	F 676	2.2.125	P Covet
in hell, and look to it, for some of you shall be my father.	F 690	2.2.139	P Wrath
and you have done me great injury to bring me from thence, let	F 705.1	2.2.155A	P Sloth
And what are you Mistris Minkes, the seventh and last?	F 707	2.2.159	Faust
What Robin, you must come away and walk the horses.	F 725	2.3.4	P Dick
I say, least I send you into the Ostry with a vengeance.	F 733	2.3.12	P Robin
you had best leave your foolery, for an my Maister come, he'le	F 734	2.3.13	P Dick
your foolery, for an my Maister come, he'le conjure you 'faith.	F 735	2.3.14	P Dick
A plague take you, I thought you did not sneake up and downe	F 742	2.3.21	P Dick
thought you did not sneake up and downe after her for nothing.	F 742	2.3.21	P Dick
Here, take his triple Crowne along with you,	F 970	3.1.192	Pope
Did I not tell you,/To morrow we would sit i'th Consistory,	F1016	3.2.36	Pope
You brought us word even now, it was decreed,	F1019	3.2.39	Pope
Then wherefore would you have me view that booke?	F1023	3.2.43	Pope
Your Grace mistakes, you gave us no such charge.	F1024	3.2.44	1Card
we all are witnesses/That Bruno here was late delivered you,	F1026	3.2.46	Raymnd
By Peter you shall dye,	F1030	3.2.50	Pope
Unlesse you bring them forth immediatly:	F1031	3.2.51	Pope
Fall to, the Divell choke you an you spare.	F1039	3.2.59	Faust
I thanke you sir.	F1043	3.2.63	Faust
Villaines why speake you not?	F1045	3.2.65	Pope
Or by our sanctitude you all shall die.	F1057	3.2.77	Pope
Now Faustus, what will you do now?	F1071	3.2.91	P Mephst
for I can tell you, you'le be curst with Bell, Booke, and	F1072	3.2.92	P Mephst
O, are you here?	F1096	3.3.9	P Vintnr
I am glad I have found you, you are a couple of fine	F1096	3.3.9	P Vintnr
am glad I have found you, you are a couple of fine companions:	F1096	3.3.9	P Vintnr
pray where's the cup you stole from the Taverne?	F1097	3.3.10	P Vintnr
take heed what you say, we looke not like cup-stealers I can	F1099	3.3.12	P Robin

YOU (cont.)

what you say, we looke not like cup-stealers I can tell you.	F1100	3.3.13	P	Robin
Never deny't, for I know you have it, and I'le search you.	F1101	3.3.14	P	Vintnr
Come on sirra, let me search you now.	F1104	3.3.17	P	Vintnr
your searching; we scorne to steale your cups I can tell you.	F1106	3.3.19	P	Dick
me for the matter, for sure the cup is betweene you two.	F1108	3.3.21	P	Vintnr
Nay there you lie, 'tis beyond us both.	F1109	3.3.22	P	Robin
A plague take you, I thought 'twas your knavery to take it	F1110	3.3.23	P	Vintnr
when, can you tell?	F1112	3.3.25	P	Robin
life, Vintner you shall have your cup anon, say nothing Dick:	F1113	3.3.26	P	Robin
You Princely Legions of infernall Rule,	F1116	3.3.29		Mephst
you have had a shroud journey of it, will it please you to take	F1120	3.3.33	P	Robin
will it please you to take a shoulder of Mutton to supper, and	F1121	3.3.34	P	Robin
I pray you heartily sir; for wee cal'd you but in jeast I	F1123	3.3.36	P	Dick
you heartily sir; for wee cal'd you but in jeast I promise you.	F1123	3.3.36	P	Dick
you heartily sir; for wee cal'd you but in jeast I promise you.	F1124	3.3.37	P	Dick
Fast a sleepe I warrant you,	F1173	4.1.19		Mrtino
What a devill ayle you two?	F1179	4.1.25	P	Benvol
Speak softly sir, least the devil heare you:	F1180	4.1.26		Mrtino
Well, go you attend the Emperour:	F1199	4.1.45	P	Benvol
shall controule him as well as the Conjurer, I warrant you.	F1203	4.1.49	P	Benvol
come not away quickly, you shall have me asleepe presently:	F1242	4.1.88	P	Benvol
Il'e make you feele something anon, if my Art faile me not.	F1246	4.1.92	P	Faust
And Il'e play Diana, and send you the hornes presently.	F1257	4.1.103	P	Faust
My gracious Lord, you doe forget your selfe,	F1258	4.1.104		Faust
A plague upon you, let me sleepe a while.	F1283	4.1.129		Benvol
in your head for shame, let not all the world wonder at you.	F1292	4.1.138	P	Faust
If Faustus do it, you are streight resolv'd,	F1298	4.1.144		Faust
Let me intreate you to remove his hornes,	F1309	4.1.155		Emper
him; and hereafter sir, looke you speake well of Schollers.	F1315	4.1.161	P	Faust
Away, you love me not, to urge me thus,	F1327	4.2.3		Benvol
If you will aid me in this enterprise,	F1334	4.2.10		Benvol
Take you the wealth, leave us the victorie.	F1347	4.2.23		Benvol
Grone you Master Doctor?	F1365	4.2.41		Fredrk
it will weare out ten birchin broomes I warrant you.	F1385	4.2.61	P	Benvol
Knew you not Traytors, I was limitted/For foure and twenty	F1395	4.2.71		Faust
And had you cut my body with your swords,	F1397	4.2.73		Faust
You hit it right,/It is your owne you meane, feele on your	F1442	4.3.12		Fredrk
It is your owne you meane, feele on your head.	F1443	4.3.13		Fredrk
I beseech you sir accept of this; I am a very poore man, and	F1463	4.4.7	P	HrsCsr
now sirra I must tell you, that you may ride him o're hedge and	F1467	4.4.11	P	Faust
that you may ride him o're hedge and ditch, and spare him not;	F1467	4.4.11	P	Faust
him o're hedge and ditch, and spare him not; but do you heare?	F1468	4.4.12	P	Faust
Go bid the Hostler deliver him unto you, and remember what I	F1474	4.4.18	P	Faust
I warrant you sir; O joyfull day:	F1476	4.4.20	P	HrsCsr
Ho sirra Doctor, you cosoning scab; Maister Doctor awake, and	F1488	4.4.32	P	HrsCsr
If it please you, the Duke of Vanholt doth earnestly entreate	F1500	4.4.44	P	Wagner
of his men to attend you with provision fit for your journey.	F1502	4.4.46	P	Wagner
Maisters, I'le bring you to the best beere in Europe, what ho,	F1505	4.5.1	P	Carter
How now, what lacke you?	F1507	4.5.3	P	Hostss
O Hostisse how do you?	F1515	4.5.11	P	Robin
doubt of that, for me thinkes you make no hast to wipe it out.	F1516	4.5.12	P	Hostss
You shall presently:	F1519	4.5.15	P	Hostss
I'le tell you the bravest tale how a Conjurer serv'd me; you	F1521	4.5.17	P	Carter
bravest tale how a Conjurer serv'd me; you know Doctor Fauster?	F1522	4.5.18	P	Carter
I'le tell you how he serv'd me:	F1525	4.5.21	P	Carter
Now sirs, you shall heare how villanously he serv'd mee:	F1535	4.5.31	P	HrsCsr
But you shall heare how bravely I serv'd him for it; I went me	F1547	4.5.43	P	HrsCsr
Hearke you, we'le into another roome and drinke a while, and	F1556	4.5.52	P	Robin
that you have taken no pleasure in those sights; therefor I	F1565	4.6.8	P	Faust
therefor I pray you tell me, what is the thing you most desire	F1566	4.6.9	P	Faust
I pray you tell me, what is the thing you most desire to have?	F1567	4.6.10	P	Faust
you so kind I will make knowne unto you what my heart desires	F1570	4.6.13	P	Lady
kind I will make knowne unto you what my heart desires to have,	F1571	4.6.14	P	Lady
be good, for they come from a farre Country I can tell you.	F1577	4.6.20	P	Faust
is barren of his fruite, from whence you had these ripe grapes.	F1580	4.6.23	P	Duke
spirit that I have, I had these grapes brought as you see.	F1586	4.6.29	P	Faust
What is the reason you disturbe the Duke?	F1592	4.6.35		Servnt
Why saucy varlets, dare you be so bold.	F1594	4.6.37		Servnt
Will you sir? Commit the Rascals.	F1602	4.6.45		Duke
'Faith you are too outragious, but come neere,	F1609	4.6.52		Faust
Nay, hearke you, can you tell me where you are?	F1614	4.6.57		Faust
I but sir sauce box, know you in what place?	F1616	4.6.59		Servnt
Be not so furious: come you shall have Beere.	F1620	4.6.63		Faust
My Lord, beseech you give me leave a while,	F1621	4.6.64		Faust
do not you remember a Horse-courser you sold a horse to?	F1633	4.6.76	P	Carter
you remember you bid he should not ride [him] into the water?	F1636	4.6.79	P	Carter
And do you remember nothing of your leg?	F1639	4.6.82	P	Carter
I thank you sir.	F1642	4.6.85	P	Faust
'Tis not so much worth; I pray you tel me one thing.	F1643	4.6.86	P	Carter
sir, I would make nothing of you, but I would faine know that.	F1648	4.6.91	P	Carter
I thanke you, I am fully satisfied.	F1651	4.6.94	P	Carter
me thinkes you should have a wooden bedfellow of one of 'em.	F1653	4.6.96	P	Carter
do you heare sir, did not I pull off one of your legs when you	F1655	4.6.98	P	HrsCsr
sir, did not I pull off one of your legs when you were asleepe?	F1656	4.6.99	P	HrsCsr
looke you heere sir.	F1657	4.6.100	P	Faust
Do you remember sir, how you cosened me and eat up my load of--	F1659	4.6.102	P	Carter
Do you remember how you made me weare an Apes--	F1661	4.6.104	P	Dick
You whoreson conjuring scab, do you remember how you cosened me	F1662	4.6.105	P	HrsCsr
scab, do you remember how you cosened me with <of> a ho--	F1662	4.6.105	P	HrsCsr
scab, do you remember how you cosened me with <of> a ho--	F1663	4.6.106	P	HrsCsr
Ha' you forgotten me?	F1664	4.6.107	P	Robin
you thinke to carry it away with your Hey-passe, and Re-passe:	F1664	4.6.107	P	Robin

YOU (cont.)

do you remember the dogs fa--	F1665	4.6.108	P	Robin
heare you Maister Doctor, now you have sent away my guesse, I	F1666	4.6.109	P	Hostss
now you have sent away my guesse, I pray who shall pay me for	F1667	4.6.110	P	Hostss
if you will doe us so much <that> favour, as to let us see that	F1684	5.1.11	P	1Schol
Majesty, we should thinke our selves much beholding unto you.	F1687	5.1.14	P	1Schol
You shall behold that peerelesse dame of Greece,	F1692	5.1.19		Faust
Gentlemen farewell: the same wish I to you.	F1706	5.1.33		Faust
Gentlemen away, least you perish with me.	F1867	5.2.71	P	Faust
and what noyse soever you <yee> heare, come not unto me, for	F1873	5.2.77	P	Faust
if I live till morning, Il'e visit you:	F1877	5.2.81	P	Faust
Stand still you ever moving Spheares of heaven,	F1929	5.2.133		Faust
You Starres that raign'd at my nativity,	F1950	5.2.154		Faust
That when you vomite forth into the aire,	F1954	5.2.158		Faust
you have seene many boyes with such pickadevaunts as I have.	F App	p.229 2	P	Clown
I, and goings out too, you may see else.	F App	p.229 5	P	Clown
Doe yee heare, I would be sorie to robbe you of your living.	F App	p.229 18	P	Clown
Doe you heare sir?	F App	p.229 27	P	Clown
you may save that labour, they are too familiar with me	F App	p.229 27	P	Clown
wel, do you heare sirra?	F App	p.230 30	P	Wagner
Truly but you shall.	F App	p.230 40	P	Clown
Beare witnesse I give them you againe.	F App	p.230 42	P	Clown
Ile tell you how you shall know them, all hee divels has	F App	p.230 52	P	Clown
Ile tell you how you shall know them, all hee divels has	F App	p.230 53	P	Clown
But do you hear?	F App	p.230 56	P	Clown
if I should serve you, would you teach me to raise up Banios	F App	p.230 56	P	Clown
serve you, would you teach me to raise up Banios and Belcheos?	F App	p.230 56	P	Clown
if you turne me into any thing, let it be in the likenesse of a	F App	p.231 61	P	Clown
But doe you heare Wagner?	F App	p.231 66	P	Clown
My Lord of Lorraine, wilt please you draw neare.	F App	p.231 1	P	Pope
Fall too, and the divel choake you and you spare.	F App	p.231 2	P	Faust
I thanke you sir.	F App	p.231 7	P	Faust
You say true, Ile hate.	F App	p.231 11	P	Faust
What, are you crossing of your selfe?	F App	p.232 18		Faust
Well use that tricke no more, I would advise you.	F App	p.232 19		Faust
the second time, aware the third, I give you faire warning.	F App	p.232 20	P	Faust
Anon you shal heare a hogge grunt, a calfe bleate, and an asse	F App	p.232 27	P	Faust
keep out, or else you are blowne up, you are dismembred Rafe,	F App	p.233 10	P	Robin
or else you are blowne up, you are dismembred Rafe, keepe out,	F App	p.233 10	P	Robin
Drawer, I hope al is payd, God be with you, come Rafe.	F App	p.234 6	P	Robin
a word with you, I must yet have a goblet payde from you ere	F App	p.234 7	P	Vintnr
with you, I must yet have a goblet payde from you ere you goe.	F App	p.234 8	P	Vintnr
I scorne you:	F App	p.234 9	P	Robin
and you are but a &c.	F App	p.234 9	P	Robin
How say you now?	F App	p.234 12	P	Robin
I must say somewhat to your felow, you sir.	F App	p.234 13	P	Vintnr
you may be ashamed to burden honest men with a matter of truth.	F App	p.234 14	P	Rafe
Wel, tone of you hath this goblet about you.	F App	p.235 16	P	Vintnr
You lie Drawer, tis afore me:	F App	p.235 17	P	Robin
sirra you, Ile teach ye to impeach honest men:	F App	p.235 17	P	Robin
stand by, Ile scowre you for a goblet, stand aside you had best,	F App	p.235 18	P	Robin
stand aside you had best, I charge you in the name of Belzabub:	F App	p.235 19	P	Robin
what meane you sirra?	F App	p.235 21	P	Vintnr
Ile tel you what I meane.	F App	p.235 22	P	Robin
nay Ile tickle you Vintner, looke to the goblet Rafe,	F App	p.235 23	P	Robin
you have had a great journey, wil you take sixe pence in your	F App	p.235 40	P	Robin
wil you take sixe pence in your purse to pay for your supper,	F App	p.235 41	P	Robin
now theres a signe of grace in you, when you will confesse the	F App	p.237 45	P	Knight
a signe of grace in you, when you will confesse the trueth.	F App	p.237 45	P	Knight
Do you heare maister Doctor?	F App	p.237 51	P	Knight
you bring Alexander and his paramour before the emperor?	F App	p.237 51	P	Knight
No sir, but when Acteon died, he left the hornes for you:	F App	p.237 55	P	Faust
Nay, and you go to conjuring, Ile be gone.	F App	p.237 57	P	Knight
Ile meete with you anone for interrupting me so:	F App	p.238 58	P	Faust
One of you call him foorth.	F App	p.238 68	P	Emper
you remembred how you crossed me in my conference with the	F App	p.238 76	P	Faust
how you crossed me in my conference with the emperour?	F App	p.238 77	P	Faust
I thinke I have met with you for it.	F App	p.238 78	P	Faust
as to delight you with some mirth, hath Faustus worthily	F App	p.238 82	P	Faust
Doctor, yet ere you goe, expect from me a bounteous reward.	F App	p.239 88	P	Emper
what, wil you goe on horse backe, or on foote?	F App	p.239 95	P	Mephst
masse see where he is, God save you maister doctor.	F App	p.239 99	P	HrsCsr
What horse-courser, you are wel met.	F App	p.239 100	P	Faust
Do you heare sir?	F App	p.239 101	P	HrsCsr
I have brought you forty dollers for your horse.	F App	p.239 101	P	HrsCsr
Alas sir, I have no more, I pray you speake for me.	F App	p.239 104	P	HrsCsr
I pray you let him have him, he is an honest felow, and he has	F App	p.239 105	P	Mephst
Wel, come give me your money, my boy wil deliver him to you:	F App	p.239 108	P	Faust
but I must tel you one thing before you have him, ride him not	F App	p.239 108	P	Faust
at ease, if I bring his water to you, youle tel me what it is?	F App	p.240 119	P	HrsCsr
Away you villaine:	F App	p.240 120	P	Faust
O yonder is his snipper snapper, do you heare?	F App	p.240 138	P	HrsCsr
you, hey, passe, where's your maister?	F App	p.240 138	P	HrsCsr
why sir, what would you?	F App	p.240 139	P	Mephst
you cannot speake with him.	F App	p.240 139	P	Mephst
No, will you not wake?	F App	p.241 153	P	HrsCsr
Ile make you wake ere I goe.	F App	p.241 153	P	HrsCsr
O Lord sir, let me goe, and Ile give you fortie dollers more.	F App	p.241 158	P	HrsCsr
have none about me, come to my Oastrie, and Ile give them you.	F App	p.241 162	P	HrsCsr
My gratious Lord, I am glad it contents you so wel:	F App	p.242 3	P	Faust
you take no delight in this, I have heard that great bellied	F App	p.242 4	P	Faust
tell me, and you shal have it.	F App	p.242 6	P	Faust
I wil not hide from you the thing my heart desires, and were it	F App	p.242 9	P	Duchss

YOU (cont.)

Line	Source	Reference		Speaker
thing then this, so it would content you, you should have it	F App	p.242 14	P	Faust
here they be madam, wilt please you taste on them.	F App	p.242 15	P	Faust
in the month of January, how you shuld come by these grapes.	F App	p.242 18	P	Duke
hither, as ye see, how do you like them Madame, be they good?	F App	p.242 23	P	Faust
I am glad they content you so Madam.	F App	p.242 27	P	Faust
you must wel reward this learned man for the great kindnes he	F App	p.243 28	P	Duke
this learned man for the great kindnes he hath shewd to you.	F App	p.243 29	P	Duke
Will ye wadge war, for which you shall not triumph?	Lucan, First Booke	12		
Why joine you force to share the world betwixt you?	Lucan, First Booke	88		
you that with me have borne/A thousand brunts, and tride me ful	Lucan, First Booke	300		
Philosophers looke you, for unto me/Thou cause, what ere thou	Lucan, First Booke	418		
And you late shorne Ligurians, who were wont/In large spread	Lucan, First Booke	438		
And you French Bardi, whose immortal pens/Renowne the valiant	Lucan, First Booke	443		
And Druides you now in peace renew/Your barbarous customes, and	Lucan, First Booke	446		
In unfeld woods, and sacred groves you dwell,	Lucan, First Booke	448		
And only gods and heavenly powers you know,	Lucan, First Booke	449		
gods and heavenly powers you know,/Or only know you nothing.	Lucan, First Booke	450		
For you hold/That soules passe not to silent Erebus	Lucan, First Booke	450		
so (if truth you sing)/Death brings long life.	Lucan, First Booke	453		
You likewise that repulst the Caicke foe,	Lucan, First Booke	459		
and you fierce men of Rhene/Leaving your countrey open to the	Lucan, First Booke	460		
You would have thought their houses had bin fierd/Or	Lucan, First Booke	490		
I tremble to unfould/What you intend, great Jove is now	Lucan, First Booke	631		
Soone may you plow the little lands <land> I have,	Ovid's Elegies	1.3.9		
Judge you the rest, being tyrde <tride> she bad me kisse.	Ovid's Elegies	1.5.25		
Troianes destroy the Greeke wealth, while you may.	Ovid's Elegies	1.9.34		
Will you for gaine have Cupid sell himselfe?	Ovid's Elegies	1.10.17		
And doth constraind, what you do of good will.	Ovid's Elegies	1.10.24		
And him that hew'd you out for needfull uses/Ile prove had	Ovid's Elegies	1.12.15		
Your name approves you made for such like things,	Ovid's Elegies	1.12.27		
I pray that rotten age you wrackes/And sluttish white-mould	Ovid's Elegies	1.12.29		
You are unapt my looser lines to heare.	Ovid's Elegies	2.1.4		
I sawe you then unlawfull kisses joyne,	Ovid's Elegies	2.5.23		
All you whose pineons in the cleare aire sore,	Ovid's Elegies	2.6.11		
Full concord all your lives was you betwixt,	Ovid's Elegies	2.6.13		
Too late you looke back, when with anchors weighd,	Ovid's Elegies	2.11.23		
And why dire poison give you babes unborne?	Ovid's Elegies	2.14.28		
What Tereus, what Jason you provokes,	Ovid's Elegies	2.14.33		
But when she comes, [you] <your> swelling mounts sinck downe,	Ovid's Elegies	2.16.51		
She left; I say'd, you both I must beseech,	Ovid's Elegies	3.1.61		
Applaud you Neptune, that dare trust his wave,	Ovid's Elegies	3.2.47		
if she unpunisht you deceive,/For others faults, why do I losse	Ovid's Elegies	3.3.15		
But did you not so envy Cepheus Daughter,	Ovid's Elegies	3.3.17		
Will you make shipwracke of your honest name,	Ovid's Elegies	3.13.11		
And I shall thinke you chaste, do what you can.	Ovid's Elegies	3.13.14		
When you are up and drest, be sage and grave,	Ovid's Elegies	3.13.19		
And in the bed hide all the faults you have,	Ovid's Elegies	3.13.20		
Be not ashamed to strippe you being there,	Ovid's Elegies	3.13.21		
Practise a thousand sports when there you come,	Ovid's Elegies	3.13.24		
Forbare no wanton words you there would speake,	Ovid's Elegies	3.13.25		
And blush, and seeme as you were full of grace.	Ovid's Elegies	3.13.28		
Graunt this, that what you do I may not see,	Ovid's Elegies	3.13.35		
If you wey not ill speeches, yet wey mee:	Ovid's Elegies	3.13.36		
My soule fleetes when I thinke what you have done,	Ovid's Elegies	3.13.37		
Though while the deede be doing you be tooke,	Ovid's Elegies	3.13.43		
And I see when you ope the two leavde booke:	Ovid's Elegies	3.13.44		
Sweare I was blinde, yeeld not <deny>, if you be wise,	Ovid's Elegies	3.13.45		
two words, thinke/The cause acquits you not, but I that winke.	Ovid's Elegies	3.13.50		
How such a Poet could you bring forth, sayes,	Ovid's Elegies	3.14.13		
How small so ere, Ile you for greatest praise.	Ovid's Elegies	3.14.14		
There might you see one sigh, another rage,	Hero and Leander	1.125		
There might you see the gods in sundrie shapes,	Hero and Leander	1.143		
O shun me nct, but heare me ere you goe,	Hero and Leander	1.205		
God knowes I cannot force love, as you doe.	Hero and Leander	1.206		
footsteps bending)/Doth testifie that you exceed her farre,	Hero and Leander	1.211		
To whom you offer, and whose Nunne you are.	Hero and Leander	1.212		
Why should you worship her?	Hero and Leander	1.213		
her you surpasse,/As much as sparkling Diamonds flaring glasse.	Hero and Leander	1.213		
In heaping up a masse of drossie pelfe,/Than such as you:	Hero and Leander	1.245		
When you fleet hence, can be bequeath'd to none.	Hero and Leander	1.248		
Compar'd with marriage, had you tried them both,	Hero and Leander	1.263		
Even so for mens impression do we you.	Hero and Leander	1.266		
This idoll which you terme Virginitie,	Hero and Leander	1.269		
Seeke you for chastitie, immortall fame,	Hero and Leander	1.283		
But you are faire (aye me) so wondrous faire,	Hero and Leander	1.287		
As Greece will thinke, if thus you live alone,	Hero and Leander	1.289		
Some one or other keepes you as his owne.	Hero and Leander	1.290		
Yet for her sake whom you have vow'd to serve,	Hero and Leander	1.316		
Then shall you most resemble Venus Nun,	Hero and Leander	1.319		
Harken a while, and I will tell you why:	Hero and Leander	1.385		
But know you not that creatures wanting sence,	Hero and Leander	2.55		
You are deceav'd, I am no woman I.	Hero and Leander	2.192		

YOU'D

Line	Source	Reference		Speaker
You'd make a rich Poet, Sir.	Jew	4.2.122	P	Pilia
I know you'd <faine> see the Pope/And take some part of holy	F 831	3.1.53		Mephst

YOU'LE

Line	Source	Reference		Speaker
You'le like it better farre a nights than dayes.	Jew	2.3.63		Barab
for I can tell you, you'le be curst with Bell, Booke, and	F1072	3.2.92	P	Mephst

YOULE

Line	Source	Reference		Speaker
Then sister youle abjure Iarbus love?	Dido	3.1.77		Anna
I, so youle dwell with me and call me mother.	Dido	4.5.16		Nurse
So youle love me, I care not if I doe.	Dido	4.5.17		Cupid

YOULE (cont.)			
Youle be a twigger when you come to age.	Dido	4.5.20	Nurse
at ease, if I bring his water to you, youle tel me what it is?	F App	p.240 119 P	HrsCsr
YOU'LL			
You'll make 'em friends?	Jew	2.3.358	Barab
YOUNG (See also YONG, YOONG)			
Bequeath her young ones to our scanted foode.	Dido	1.1.162	Achat
might behold/Young infants swimming in their parents bloud,	Dido	2.1.193	Aeneas
This young boy in mine armes, and by the hand/Led faire Creusa	Dido	2.1.266	Aeneas
Ile be no more a widowe, I am young,	Dido	4.5.22	Nurse
A faire young maid scarce fourteene yeares of age,	Jew	1.2.378	Mthias
Singing ore these, as she does ore her young.	Jew	2.1.63	Barab
Because he is young and has more qualities.	Jew	2.3.110	1Offcr
Being young I studied Physicke, and began/To practise first	Jew	2.3.181	Barab
And with young Orphans planted Hospitals,	Jew	2.3.194	Barab
To a solemne feast/I will invite young Selim-Calymath,/Where be	Jew	5.2.97	Barab
And that young Cardinall that is growne so proud?	P1056	19.126	King
The people started; young men left their beds,	Lucan, First Booke		241
Nor dares the Lyonesse her young whelpes kill.	Ovid's Elegies		2.14.36
Great flouds ought to assist young men in love,	Ovid's Elegies		3.5.23
Whom young Apollo courted for her haire,	Hero and Leander		1.6
YOUR (See also BURLADIE)			
I am much better for your worthles love,	Dido	1.1.3	Ganimd
To day when as I fild into your cups,	Dido	1.1.5	Ganimd
Disquiet Seas lay downe your swelling lookes,	Dido	1.1.122	Venus
And court Aeneas with your calmie cheere,	Dido	1.1.123	Venus
Vaild his resplendant glorie from your view.	Dido	1.1.126	Venus
Pluck up your hearts, since fate still rests our friend,	Dido	1.1.149	Aeneas
bowes enow/Neere to these woods, to rost your meate withall:	Dido	1.1.173	Aeneas
But what may I faire Virgin call your name?	Dido	1.1.188	Aeneas
And plaine to him the summe of your distresse.	Dido	1.2.2	Illion
That crave such favour at your honors feete,	Dido	1.2.5	Illion
We come not we to wrong your Libian Gods,	Dido	1.2.10	Illion
Or steale your houshold lares from their shrines:	Dido	1.2.11	Illion
Before that Boreas buckled with your sailes?	Dido	1.2.19	Iarbus
Your men and you shall banquet in our Court,	Dido	1.2.39	Iarbus
or whatsoever stile/Belongs unto your name, vouchsafe of ruth	Dido	2.1.40	Aeneas
Your sight amazde me, O what destinies/Have brought my sweete	Dido	2.1.59	Aeneas
May it please your grace to let Aeneas waite:	Dido	2.1.87	Aeneas
In all humilitie I thanke your grace.	Dido	2.1.99	Aeneas
little sonne/Playes with your garments and imbraceth you.	Dido	3.1.21	Anna
Aeneas well deserves to be your love,	Dido	3.1.70	Anna
Achates, how doth Carthage please your Lord?	Dido	3.1.97	Dido
That will Aeneas shewe your majestie.	Dido	3.1.98	Achat
I understand your highnesse sent for me.	Dido	3.1.100	Aeneas
We could have gone without your companie.	Dido	3.3.14	Dido
To presse beyond acceptance to your sight.	Dido	3.3.16	Aeneas
To challenge us with your comparisons?	Dido	3.3.20	Dido
Huntsmen, why pitch you not your toyles apace,	Dido	3.3.30	Dido
That sav'd your famisht souldiers lives from death,	Dido	3.3.52	Achat
When first you set your foote upon the shoare,	Dido	3.3.53	Achat
If that your majestie can looke so lowe,	Dido	3.4.41	Aeneas
I see Aeneas sticketh in your minde,	Dido	4.1.33	Dido
And quell those hopes that thus employ your [cares] <eares>.	Dido	4.1.35	Dido
How now Iarbus, at your prayers so hard?	Dido	4.2.23	Anna
Banish that ticing dame from forth your mouth,	Dido	4.3.31	Achat
And follow your foreseeing starres in all;	Dido	4.3.32	Achat
Because I feard your grace would keepe me here.	Dido	4.4.20	Achat
Your Nurse is gone with yong Ascanius,	Dido	4.4.124	Lord
Come come, Ile goe, how farre hence is your house?	Dido	4.5.13	Cupid
Especially in women of [our] <your> yeares.--	Dido	4.5.28	Nurse
Let it be term'd Aenea by your name.	Dido	5.1.20	Cloan
Rather Ascania by your little sonne.	Dido	5.1.21	Serg
And weepe upon your liveles carcases,	Dido	5.1.177	Dido
O Dido, your little sonne Ascanius/Is gone!	Dido	5.1.212	Nurse
How can ye goe when he hath all your fleete?	Dido	5.1.242	Anna
And order all things at your high dispose,	Dido	5.1.303	Dido
Brother, I see your meaning well enough.	1Tamb	1.1.18	Mycet
And thorough your Planets I perceive you thinke,	1Tamb	1.1.19	Mycet
Oft have I heard your Majestie complain,	1Tamb	1.1.35	Meandr
That robs your merchants of Persepolis,	1Tamb	1.1.37	Meandr
And in your confines with his lawlesse traine,	1Tamb	1.1.39	Meandr
Your Grace hath taken order by Theridamas,	1Tamb	1.1.46	Meandr
to apprehend/And bring him Captive to your Highnesse throne.	1Tamb	1.1.48	Meandr
Or plead for mercie at your highnesse feet.	1Tamb	1.1.73	Therid
This should intreat your highnesse to rejoice,	1Tamb	1.1.123	Menaph
Affrike and Europe bordering on your land,	1Tamb	1.1.127	Menaph
And continent to your Dominions:	1Tamb	1.1.128	Menaph
We will invest your Highnesse Emperour:	1Tamb	1.1.151	Ceneus
Then I may seeke to gratifie your love,	1Tamb	1.1.171	Cosroe
Intending your investion so neere/The residence of your	1Tamb	1.1.180	Ortyg
your investion so neere/The residence of your dispised brother,	1Tamb	1.1.181	Ortyg
To injure or suppresse your woorthy tytle.	1Tamb	1.1.183	Ortyg
Come lady, let not this appal your thoughts.	1Tamb	1.2.1	Tamb
Even in the circle of your Fathers armes:	1Tamb	1.2.5	Tamb
If you intend to keep your treasure safe.	1Tamb	1.2.25	Tamb
But tell me Maddam, is your grace betroth'd?	1Tamb	1.2.32	Tamb
Will never prosper your intended driftes,	1Tamb	1.2.69	Zenoc
Now must your jewels be restor'd againe:	1Tamb	1.2.114	Tamb
How say you Lordings, Is not this your hope?	1Tamb	1.2.116	Tamb
We hope your selfe wil willingly restore them.	1Tamb	1.2.117	Agidas
Keep all your standings, and not stir a foote,	1Tamb	1.2.150	Tamb
You shall have honors, as your merits be:	1Tamb	1.2.255	Tamb

YOUR (cont.)

In happy hower we have set the Crowne/Upon your kingly head,	1Tamb	2.1.51		Ortyg
Therefore cheere up your mindes, prepare to fight,	1Tamb	2.2.29		Meandr
Go on my Lord, and give your charge I say,	1Tamb	2.2.57		Mycet
To some direction in your martiall deeds,	1Tamb	2.3.12		Tamb
Your speech will stay, or so extol his worth,	1Tamb	2.3.27		Therid
Then shall your meeds and vallours be advaunst/To roomes of	1Tamb	2.3.40		Cosroe
The King your Brother is now hard at hand,	1Tamb	2.3.45		Tamb
with the foole, and rid your royall shoulders/Of such a burthen,	1Tamb	2.3.46		Tamb
Is this your Crowne?	1Tamb	2.4.27		Tamb
On your submission we with thanks excuse,	1Tamb	2.5.13		Cosroe
Emperour in humblest tearms/I vow my service to your Majestie,	1Tamb	2.5.16		Meandr
Now will i gratify your former good,	1Tamb	2.5.30		Cosroe
And grace your calling with a greater sway.	1Tamb	2.5.31		Cosroe
And as we ever [aim'd] <and> at your behoofe,	1Tamb	2.5.32		Ortyg
And sought your state all honor it deserv'd,	1Tamb	2.5.33		Ortyg
Your Majestie shall shortly have your wish,	1Tamb	2.5.48		Menaph
To save your King and country from decay:	1Tamb	2.6.35		Cosroe
Presume a bickering with your Emperour:	1Tamb	3.1.4		Bajzth
What if you sent the Bassoes of your guard,	1Tamb	3.1.17		Fesse
Your Bassoe will accomplish your behest:	1Tamb	3.1.42		Bassoe
And show your pleasure to the Persean,	1Tamb	3.1.43		Bassoe
But if he dare attempt to stir your siege,	1Tamb	3.1.46		Argier
For all flesh quakes at your magnificence.	1Tamb	3.1.48		Argier
The spring is hindred by your smoothering host,	1Tamb	3.1.50		Moroc
What thinks your greatnes best to be atchiev'd/In pursuit of	1Tamb	3.1.56		Fesse
That worke such trouble to your woonted rest:	1Tamb	3.2.3		Agidas
When your offensive rape by Tamburlaine,	1Tamb	3.2.6		Agidas
(Which of your whole displeasures should be most)/Hath seem'd	1Tamb	3.2.7		Agidas
That holds you from your father in despight,	1Tamb	3.2.27		Agidas
Be honored with your love, but for necessity.	1Tamb	3.2.30		Agidas
Your Highnesse needs not doubt but in short time,	1Tamb	3.2.32		Agidas
Too harsh a subject for your dainty eares.	1Tamb	3.2.46		Agidas
Yet be not so inconstant in your love,	1Tamb	3.2.56		Agidas
After your rescue to enjoy his choise.	1Tamb	3.2.58		Agidas
Your men are valiant but their number few,	1Tamb	3.3.11		Bassoe
But wil those Kings accompany your Lord?	1Tamb	3.3.27		Tamb
This hand shal set them on your conquering heads:	1Tamb	3.3.31		Tamb
Burdening their bodies with your heavie chaines,	1Tamb	3.3.48		Tamb
Attend upon the person of your Lord,	1Tamb	3.3.62		Bajzth
Techelles, and the rest prepare your swordes,	1Tamb	3.3.64		Tamb
Leave words and let them feele your lances pointes,	1Tamb	3.3.91		Argier
Your threefold armie and my hugie hoste,	1Tamb	3.3.94		Bajzth
make our <your> strokes to wound the sencelesse [aire] <lure>.	1Tamb	3.3.158		Tamb
And sue to me to be your Advocates.	1Tamb	3.3.175		Zenoc
Yet somtimes let your highnesse send for them/To do the work my	1Tamb	3.3.187		Anippe
Where are your stout contributorie kings?	1Tamb	3.3.214		Tamb
Nay (mightie Souldan) did your greatnes see/The frowning lookes	1Tamb	4.1.12		2Msngr
It might amaze your royall majesty.	1Tamb	4.1.16		2Msngr
So might your highnesse, had you time to sort/Your fighting	1Tamb	4.1.36		Capol
had you time to sort/Your fighting men, and raise your royall	1Tamb	4.1.37		Capol
time to sort/Your fighting men, and raise your royall hoste.	1Tamb	4.1.37		Capol
by expedition/Advantage takes of your unreadinesse.	1Tamb	4.1.39		Capol
Pleaseth your mightinesse to understand,	1Tamb	4.1.47		2Msngr
That sacrificing slice and cut your flesh,	1Tamb	4.2.3		Bajzth
Staining his Altars with your purple blood:	1Tamb	4.2.4		Bajzth
Will send up fire to your turning Spheares,	1Tamb	4.2.39		Tamb
Zenocrate, looke better to your slave.	1Tamb	4.2.68		Tamb
Your tentes of white now pitch'd before the gates/And gentle	1Tamb	4.2.111		Therid
Offering Damascus to your Majesty.	1Tamb	4.2.114		Therid
Joine your Arabians with the Souldans power:	1Tamb	4.3.16		Souldn
The number of your hostes united is,	1Tamb	4.3.52		Capol
Then reare your standardes, let your sounding Drummes/Direct	1Tamb	4.3.61		Souldn
let your sounding Drummes/Direct our Souldiers to Damascus	1Tamb	4.3.61		Souldn
That meanes to fill your helmets full of golde:	1Tamb	4.4.7		Tamb
Wel Zenocrate, Techelles, and the rest, fall to your victuals.	1Tamb	4.4.15	P	Tamb
Fall to, and never may your meat digest.	1Tamb	4.4.16		Bajzth
And in your hands bring hellish poison up,	1Tamb	4.4.19		Bajzth
Or winged snakes of Lerna cast your stings,	1Tamb	4.4.21		Bajzth
And leave your venoms in this Tyrants dish.	1Tamb	4.4.22		Bajzth
are you so daintily brought up, you cannot eat your owne flesh?	1Tamb	4.4.37	P	Tamb
Go to, fal to your meat:	1Tamb	4.4.54	P	Tamb
Or if my love unto your majesty/May merit favour at your	1Tamb	4.4.69		Zenoc
unto your majesty/May merit favour at your highnesse handes,	1Tamb	4.4.70		Zenoc
Then raise your seige from faire Damascus walles,	1Tamb	4.4.71		Zenoc
say you to this (Turke) these are not your contributorie kings.	1Tamb	4.4.118	P	Tamb
Your byrthes shall be no blemish to your fame,	1Tamb	4.4.127		Tamb
And since your highnesse hath so well vouchsaft,	1Tamb	4.4.130		Therid
Some made your wives, and some your children)/Might have	1Tamb	5.1.27		1Virgn
and some your children)/Might have intreated your obdurate	1Tamb	5.1.27		1Virgn
some your children)/Might have intreated your obdurate breasts,	1Tamb	5.1.28		1Virgn
Submit your selves and us to servitude.	1Tamb	5.1.39		Govnr
Therefore in that your safeties and our owne,	1Tamb	5.1.40		Govnr
Your honors, liberties and lives were weigh'd/In equall care	1Tamb	5.1.41		Govnr
And bring us pardon in your chearfull lookes.	1Tamb	5.1.47		Govnr
Reflexing them on your disdainfull eies:	1Tamb	5.1.70		Tamb
Your fearfull minds are thicke and mistie then,	1Tamb	5.1.110		Tamb
What, have your horsmen shewen the virgins Death?	1Tamb	5.1.129		Tamb
Madam content your self and be resolv'd,	1Tamb	5.1.372		Anippe
Your love hath fortune so at his command,	1Tamb	5.1.373		Anippe
That fights for honor to adorne your head.	1Tamb	5.1.376		Anippe
Madam, your father and th'Arabian king,	1Tamb	5.1.378		Philem
The first affecter of your excellence,	1Tamb	5.1.379		Philem

YOUR (cont.)

And therfore grieve not at your overthrow,	1Tamb	5.1.446	Tamb
Since I shall render all into your hands.	1Tamb	5.1.447	Tamb
And ad more strength to your dominions/Than ever yet confirm'd	1Tamb	5.1.448	Tamb
That purchac'd kingdomes by your martiall deeds,	1Tamb	5.1.523	Tamb
Cast off your armor, put on scarlet roabes.	1Tamb	5.1.524	Tamb
Mount up your royall places of estate,	1Tamb	5.1.525	Tamb
And there make lawes to rule your provinces:	1Tamb	5.1.527	Tamb
Hang up your weapons on Alcides poste,	1Tamb	5.1.528	Tamb
Gainst him my Lord must you addresse your power.	2Tamb	1.1.19	Gazell
basely on their knees/In all your names desirde a truce of me?	2Tamb	1.1.97	Orcan
Which if your General refuse or scorne,	2Tamb	1.1.119	Fredrk
Ready to charge you ere you stir your feet.	2Tamb	1.1.121	Fredrk
and with my heart/Wish your release, but he whose wrath is	2Tamb	1.2.6	Almeda
No speach to that end, by your favour sir.	2Tamb	1.2.14	Almeda
my Lord, if I should goe, would you bee as good as your word?	2Tamb	1.2.62	P Almeda
Your Keeper under Tamburlaine the great,	2Tamb	1.2.68	Almeda
Yet would I venture to conduct your Grace,	2Tamb	1.2.72	Almeda
Stretching your conquering armes from east to west:	2Tamb	1.3.97	Tamb
Meet for your service on the sea, my Lord,	2Tamb	1.3.123	Therid
Thanks king of Morocus, take your crown again.	2Tamb	1.3.137	Tamb
Your presence (loving friends and fellow kings)/Makes me to	2Tamb	1.3.151	Tamb
It could not more delight me than your sight.	2Tamb	1.3.156	Tamb
How have ye spent your absent time from me?	2Tamb	1.3.173	Tamb
make no period/Untill Natolia kneele before your feet.	2Tamb	1.3.217	Therid
What motion is it that inflames your thoughts,	2Tamb	2.1.2	Sgsmnd
And stirs your valures to such soddaine armes?	2Tamb	2.1.3	Sgsmnd
Your Majesty remembers I am sure/What cruell slaughter of our	2Tamb	2.1.4	Fredrk
It resteth now then that your Majesty/Take all advantages of	2Tamb	2.1.11	Fredrk
Your Highnesse knowes for Tamburlaines repaire,	2Tamb	2.1.14	Fredrk
But cals not then your Grace to memorie/The league we lately	2Tamb	2.1.27	Sgsmnd
Assure your Grace tis superstition/To stand so strictly on	2Tamb	2.1.49	Fredrk
the christian King/Is made, for joy of your admitted truce:	2Tamb	2.2.21	Uribas
Taking advantage of your slender power,	2Tamb	2.2.26	1Msngr
My Lord, your Majesty shall soone perceive:	2Tamb	2.4.39	1Phstn
the fiery Element/Dissolve, and make your kingdome in the Sky,	2Tamb	2.4.59	Zenoc
Than this base earth should shroud your majesty:	2Tamb	2.4.60	Zenoc
For should I but suspect your death by mine,	2Tamb	2.4.61	Zenoc
happinesse/And hope to meet your highnesse in the heavens,	2Tamb	2.4.63	Zenoc
With love and patience let your true love die,	2Tamb	2.4.67	Zenoc
Your griefe and furie hurtes my second life:	2Tamb	2.4.68	Zenoc
And in your lives your fathers excellency.	2Tamb	2.4.76	Zenoc
I will requite your royall gratitudes/With all the benefits my	2Tamb	3.1.8	Callap
And now I doubt not but your royall cares/Hath so provided for	2Tamb	3.1.20	Callap
And bring him captive to your highnesse feet.	2Tamb	3.1.62	Soria
Your Majesty may choose some pointed time,	2Tamb	3.1.75	Jrslem
Perfourming all your promise to the full:	2Tamb	3.1.76	Jrslem
Tis nought for your majesty to give a kingdome.	2Tamb	3.1.77	Jrslem
Why, I thank your Majesty.	2Tamb	3.1.79	P Almeda
And now my Lords, advance your speares againe,	2Tamb	3.2.43	Tamb
Being burnt to cynders for your mothers death.	2Tamb	3.2.46	Tamb
March in your armour thorowe watery Fens,	2Tamb	3.2.56	Tamb
Then next, the way to fortifie your men,	2Tamb	3.2.62	Tamb
Come boyes and with your fingers search my wound,	2Tamb	3.2.126	Tamb
And in my blood wash all your hands at once,	2Tamb	3.2.127	Tamb
Come sirra, give me your arme.	2Tamb	3.2.134	P Tamb
Here father, cut it bravely as you did your own.	2Tamb	3.2.135	P Celeb
I would not yeeld it: therefore doo your worst.	2Tamb	3.3.37	Capt
Give me your knife (good mother) or strike home:	2Tamb	3.4.28	Sonne
No Madam, but the beginning of your joy,	2Tamb	3.4.83	Techel
quyvering leaves/Of Idas forrest, where your highnesse hounds,	2Tamb	3.5.6	2Msngr
Whet all your swords to mangle Tamburlain,	2Tamb	3.5.15	Callap
by your highnesse hands)/All brandishing their brands of	2Tamb	3.5.26	Orcan
Tell me Viceroies the number of your men,	2Tamb	3.5.30	Callap
fighting men/Are come since last we shewed your majesty.	2Tamb	3.5.34	Jrslem
Since last we numbred to your Majesty.	2Tamb	3.5.39	Orcan
Since last we numbred to your majesty.	2Tamb	3.5.45	Trebiz
Halla is repair'd/And neighbor cities of your highnesse land,	2Tamb	3.5.47	Soria
Since last we numbred to your majestie:	2Tamb	3.5.49	Soria
My Lord, your presence makes them pale and wan.	2Tamb	3.5.60	Usumc
Ile hang a clogge about your necke for running away againe, you	2Tamb	3.5.100	P Tamb
diet your selves, you knowe I shall have occasion shortly to	2Tamb	3.5.114	P Tamb
Go too sirha, take your crown, and make up the halfe dozen.	2Tamb	3.5.135	P Tamb
here are Bugges/Wil make the haire stand upright on your heads,	2Tamb	3.5.148	Tamb
And cast your crownes in slavery at their feet.	2Tamb	3.5.149	Tamb
And left your slender carkasses behind,	2Tamb	4.1.38	Calyph
my children stoops your pride/And leads your glories <bodies>	2Tamb	4.1.76	Tamb
pride/And leads your glories <bodies> sheep-like to the sword.	2Tamb	4.1.77	Tamb
And tickle not your Spirits with desire/Stil to be train'd in	2Tamb	4.1.80	Tamb
Yet pardon him I pray your Majesty.	2Tamb	4.1.97	Therid
Let al of us intreat your highnesse pardon.	2Tamb	4.1.98	Tec&Us
And let your hates extended in his paines,	2Tamb	4.1.172	Orcan
Ile bridle al your tongues/And bind them close with bits of	2Tamb	4.1.181	Tamb
Downe to the channels of your hatefull throats,	2Tamb	4.1.183	Tamb
and utterly consume/Your cities and your golden pallaces,	2Tamb	4.1.193	Tamb
Ah, pity me my Lord, and draw your sword,	2Tamb	4.2.33	Olymp
Ile give your Grace a present of such price,	2Tamb	4.2.56	Olymp
With which if you but noint your tender Skin,	2Tamb	4.2.65	Olymp
Nor Pistol, Sword, nor Lance can pierce your flesh.	2Tamb	4.2.66	Olymp
Which when you stab, looke on your weapons point,	2Tamb	4.2.69	Olymp
Why gave you not your husband some of it,	2Tamb	4.2.71	Therid
and mark your weapons point/That wil be blunted if the blow be	2Tamb	4.2.79	Olymp
And have so proud a chariot at your heeles,	2Tamb	4.3.3	Tamb

YOUR (cont.)

Your Majesty must get some byts for these,	2Tamb	4.3.43	Therid
Your Majesty already hath devisde/A meane, as fit as may be to	2Tamb	4.3.50	Usumc
And let them equally serve all your turnes.	2Tamb	4.3.73	Tamb
We thank your majesty.	2Tamb	4.3.74	Soldrs
Brawle not (I warne you) for your lechery,	2Tamb	4.3.75	Tamb
meet not me/With troopes of harlots at your sloothful heeles.	2Tamb	4.3.82	Tamb
Are ye not gone ye villaines with your spoiles?	2Tamb	4.3.84	Tamb
Save your honours?	2Tamb	4.3.86	Tamb
Wil get his pardon if your grace would send.	2Tamb	5.1.33	1Citzn
spirits may vex/Your slavish bosomes with continuall paines,	2Tamb	5.1.46	Govnr
And usde such slender reckning of [your] <you> majesty.	2Tamb	5.1.83	Therid
Then for all your valour, you would save your life.	2Tamb	5.1.119	Tamb
I think I make your courage something quaile.	2Tamb	5.1.126	Tamb
to your taskes a while/And take such fortune as your fellowes	2Tamb	5.1.136	Tamb
taskes a while/And take such fortune as your fellowes felt.	2Tamb	5.1.137	Tamb
I have fulfil'd your highnes wil, my Lord,	2Tamb	5.1.203	Techel
Should come in person to resist your power,	2Tamb	5.2.38	Amasia
Yet might your mighty hoste incounter all,	2Tamb	5.2.39	Amasia
To sue for mercie at your highnesse feete.	2Tamb	5.2.41	Amasia
Muffle your beauties with eternall clowdes,	2Tamb	5.3.6	Therid
Your sacred vertues pour'd upon his throne,	2Tamb	5.3.11	Therid
But if he die, your glories are disgrac'd,	2Tamb	5.3.15	Therid
As your supreame estates instruct our thoughtes,	2Tamb	5.3.20	Techel
Be not inconstant, carelesse of your fame,	2Tamb	5.3.21	Techel
Beare not the burthen of your enemies joyes,	2Tamb	5.3.22	Techel
Techelles and the rest, come take your swords,	2Tamb	5.3.46	Tamb
Which ad much danger to your malladie.	2Tamb	5.3.55	Therid
Pleaseth your Majesty to drink this potion,	2Tamb	5.3.78	Phsitn
Which wil abate the furie of your fit,	2Tamb	5.3.79	Phsitn
I view'd your urine, and the [Hipostasis] <Hipostates>/Thick	2Tamb	5.3.82	Phsitn
<Hipostates>/Thick and obscure doth make your danger great,	2Tamb	5.3.83	Phsitn
Your vaines are full of accidentall heat,	2Tamb	5.3.84	Phsitn
Whereby the moisture of your blood is dried,	2Tamb	5.3.85	Phsitn
Which being the cause of life, imports your death.	2Tamb	5.3.90	Phsitn
Your Artiers which alongst the vaines convey/The lively spirits	2Tamb	5.3.93	Phsitn
Yet if your majesty may escape this day,	2Tamb	5.3.98	Phsitn
yong Callapine that lately fled from your majesty, hath nowe	2Tamb	5.3.102	P 3Msngr
and hearing your absence in the field, offers to set upon us	2Tamb	5.3.103	P 3Msngr
I joy my Lord, your highnesse is so strong,	2Tamb	5.3.110	Usumc
That can endure so well your royall presence,	2Tamb	5.3.111	Usumc
That let your lives command in spight of death.	2Tamb	5.3.160	Tamb
bleeding harts/Wounded and broken with your Highnesse griefe,	2Tamb	5.3.162	Amyras
Your soul gives essence to our wretched subjects,	2Tamb	5.3.164	Amyras
Whose matter is incorporat in your flesh.	2Tamb	5.3.165	Amyras
Your paines do pierce our soules, no hope survives,	2Tamb	5.3.166	Celeb
For by your life we entertaine our lives.	2Tamb	5.3.167	Celeb
By equall portions into both your breasts:	2Tamb	5.3.171	Tamb
My flesh devided in your precious shapes,	2Tamb	5.3.172	Tamb
And live in all your seedes immortally:	2Tamb	5.3.174	Tamb
Then feeles your majesty no sovereraigne ease,	2Tamb	5.3.213	Usumc
Joy any hope of your recovery?	2Tamb	5.3.215	Usumc
Now eies, injoy your latest benefite,	2Tamb	5.3.224	Tamb
And when my soule hath vertue of your sight,	2Tamb	5.3.225	Tamb
And glut your longings with a heaven of joy.	2Tamb	5.3.227	Tamb
dooth weepe to see/Your sweet desires depriv'd my company,	2Tamb	5.3.247	Tamb
sent me to know/Whether your selfe will come and custome them.	Jew	1.1.53	1Merch
shall there concerne our state/Assure your selves I'le looke--	Jew	1.1.173	Barab
I hope your Highnesse will consider us.	Jew	1.2.9	Govnr
Since your hard conditions are such/That you will needs have	Jew	1.2.18	Govnr
We grant a month, but see you keep your promise.	Jew	1.2.28	Calym
Then good my Lord, to keepe your quiet still,	Jew	1.2.43	Barab
Your Lordship shall doe well to let them have it.	Jew	1.2.44	Barab
And therefore are we to request your ayd.	Jew	1.2.49	Govnr
Then let the rich increase your portions.	Jew	1.2.58	Govnr
Are strangers with your tribute to be tax'd?	Jew	1.2.59	Barab
For through our sufferance of your hatefull lives,	Jew	1.2.63	Govnr
And will you basely thus submit your selves/To leave your goods	Jew	1.2.79	Barab
submit your selves/To leave your goods to their arbitrament?	Jew	1.2.80	Barab
Is theft the ground of your Religion?	Jew	1.2.95	Barab
If your first curse fall heavy on thy head,	Jew	1.2.107	1Knght
What? bring you Scripture to confirm your wrongs?	Jew	1.2.110	Barab
Unlesse your unrelenting flinty hearts/Suppresse all pitty in	Jew	1.2.141	Barab
flinty hearts/Suppresse all pitty in your stony breasts,	Jew	1.2.142	Barab
Your extreme right does me exceeding wrong:	Jew	1.2.153	Barab
And be a Novice in your Nunnery,	Jew	1.2.325	Abigal
Novice learne to frame/My solitary life to your streight lawes,	Jew	1.2.332	Abigal
I doe not doubt by your divine precepts/And mine owne industry,	Jew	1.2.334	Abigal
As had you seene her 'twould have mov'd your heart,	Jew	1.2.385	Mthias
I, I, no doubt but shee's at your command.	Jew	2.3.39	Barab
Oh, Sir, your father had my Diamonds.	Jew	2.3.49	Barab
Yet I have one left that will serve your turne:	Jew	2.3.50	Barab
Your life and if you have it.--	Jew	2.3.64	Barab
Come to my house and I will giv't your honour--	Jew	2.3.66	Barab
Your father has deserv'd it at my hands,	Jew	2.3.70	Barab
No doubt your soule shall reape the fruit of it.	Jew	2.3.78	Lodowk
Even for your Honourable fathers sake.	Jew	2.3.93	Barab
It shall goe hard but I will see your death.	Jew	2.3.94	Barab
All that I have shall be at your command.	Jew	2.3.137	Barab
Seeme not to know me here before your mother/Lest she mistrust	Jew	2.3.146	Barab
on the Machabees/I have it, Sir, and 'tis at your command.	Jew	2.3.154	Barab
Oh brave, master, I worship your nose for this.	Jew	2.3.173	Ithimr
Provided, that you keepe your Maiden-head.	Jew	2.3.227	Barab

YOUR (cont.)

For your sake and his own he's welcome hither.	Jew	2.3.233	Abigal
Not for all Malta, therefore sheath your sword;	Jew	2.3.270	Barab
I, and take heed, for he hath sworne your death.	Jew	2.3.280	Barab
Oh but I know your Lordship wud disdaine/To marry with the	Jew	2.3.294	Barab
Why on the sudden is your colour chang'd?	Jew	2.3.321	Lodowk
Be made an accessary of your deeds;	Jew	2.3.342	Barab
My heart misgives me, that to crosse your love,	Jew	2.3.349	Barab
Hee's with your mother, therefore after him.	Jew	2.3.350	Barab
So sure did your father write, and I cary the chalenge.	Jew	3.3.25	P Ithimr
Go to, sirra sauce, is this your question?	Jew	3.3.34	P Abigal
into the sea; why I'le doe any thing for your sweet sake.	Jew	3.4.40	P Ithimr
and in this/Vomit your venome, and invenome her/That like a	Jew	3.4.104	Barab
For the performance of your promise past;	Jew	3.5.9	Basso
Talke not of racing downe your City wals,	Jew	3.5.21	Basso
You shall not need trouble your selves so farre,	Jew	3.5.22	Basso
And with brasse-bullets batter downe your Towers,	Jew	3.5.24	Basso
Close your Port-cullise, charge your Basiliskes,	Jew	3.5.31	Govnr
Doe you not sorrow for your daughters death?	Jew	4.1.17	Ithimr
You heare your answer, and you may be gone.	Jew	4.1.92	1Fryar
But Barabas, who shall be your godfathers,	Jew	4.1.109	1Fryar
But not a word to any of your Covent.	Jew	4.1.112	Barab
Off with your girdle, make a hansom noose;	Jew	4.1.142	Barab
And give my goods and substance to your house,	Jew	4.1.190	Barab
early; with intent to goe/Unto your Friery, because you staid.	Jew	4.1.192	Barab
'Las I could weepe at your calamity.	Jew	4.1.203	Barab
and the rest of the family, stand or fall at your service.	Jew	4.2.44	P Pilia
by this bearer, and this shall be your warrant; if you doe not,	Jew	4.2.76	P Ithimr
and told me he lov'd me for your sake, and said what a	Jew	4.2.109	P Pilia
as you love your life send me five hundred crowns, and give the	Jew	4.2.117	P Ithimr
I warrant your worship shall hav't.	Jew	4.2.119	P Pilia
Oh, if that be all, I can picke ope your locks.	Jew	4.3.33	Pilia
enough, and therfore talke not to me of your Counting-house:	Jew	4.3.36	P Pilia
And unto your good mistris as unknowne.	Jew	4.3.48	Barab
Soone enough to your cost, Sir:	Jew	4.3.57	Pilia
A French Musician, come let's heare your skill?	Jew	4.4.30	Curtzn
Sirra, you must give my mistris your posey.	Jew	4.4.37	Pilia
Play, Fidler, or I'le cut your cats guts into chitterlins.	Jew	4.4.44	P Ithimr
Now, Gentlemen, betake you to your Armes,	Jew	5.1.1	Govnr
your sonne and Mathias were both contracted unto Abigall; [he]	Jew	5.1.28	P Ithimr
Devils doe your worst, [I'le] <I> live in spite of you.	Jew	5.1.41	Barab
The Jew is here, and rests at your command.	Jew	5.1.83	Barab
And by this meanes the City is your owne.	Jew	5.1.94	Barab
Now vaile your pride you captive Christians,	Jew	5.2.1	Calym
And kneele for mercy to your conquering foe:	Jew	5.2.2	Calym
And now at length am growne your Governor,	Jew	5.2.70	Barab
Your selves shall see it shall not be forgot:	Jew	5.2.71	Barab
slavish Bands/Wherein the Turke hath yoak'd your land and you?	Jew	5.2.78	Barab
He humbly would intreat your Majesty/To come and see his homely	Jew	5.3.17	Msngr
Therefore he humbly would intreat your Highnesse/Not to depart	Jew	5.3.32	Msngr
And if you like them, drinke your fill and dye:	Jew	5.5.9	Barab
In person there to [mediate] <meditate> your peace;	Jew	5.5.116	Calym
The many favours which your grace hath showne,	P 9	1.9	Navrre
Shall binde me ever to your highnes will,	P 11	1.11	Navrre
In what Queen Mother or your grace commands.	P 12	1.12	Navrre
in Religion/Might be a meanes to crosse you in your love.	P 16	1.16	QnMoth
Sister, I think your selfe will beare us company.	P 21	1.21	Charls
How they did storme at these your nuptiall rites,	P 49	1.49	Admral
And joynes your linnage to the crowne of France?	P 51	1.51	Admral
I am my Lord, in what your grace commaundes till death.	P 76	2.19	P Pothec
Maddame, I beseech your grace to except this simple gift.	P 166	3.1	P Pothec
I humbly thank your Majestie.	P 169	3.4	P Pothec
Doth not your grace know the man that gave them you?	P 172	3.7	Navrre
Your grace was ill advisde to take them then,	P 174	3.9	Admral
The heavens forbid your highnes such mishap.	P 177	3.12	QnMarg
Might well have moved your highnes to beware/How you did meddle	P 179	3.14	Navrre
Anjoy hath well advisde/Your highnes to consider of the thing,	P 220	4.18	Guise
And rather chuse to seek your countries good,	P 221	4.19	Guise
Well Madam, I referre it to your Majestie,	P 225	4.23	Charls
And it please your grace the Lord high Admirall,	P 243	4.41	Man
And most [humbly] <humble> intreates your Majestie/To visite	P 245	4.43	Man
Your Majesty were best goe visite him,	P 249	4.47	QnMoth
Assure your selfe my good Lord Admirall,	P 262	4.60	Charls
I deepely sorrow for your trecherous wrong:	P 263	4.61	Charls
And under your direction see they keep/All trecherous violence	P 267	4.65	Charls
I humbly thank your royall Majestie.	P 273	4.71	Admral
Gonzago, Retes, sweare by/The argent crosses in your burgonets,	P 275	5.2	Guise
Is in your judgment thought a learned man.	P 391	7.31	Guise
your nego argumentum/Cannot serve, sirra:	P 397	7.37	Guise
The offer of your Prince Electors, farre/Beyond the reach of my	P 452	8.2	Anjoy
on me, then with your leaves/I may retire me to my native home.	P 473	8.23	Anjoy
If your commission serve to warrant this,	P 475	8.25	Anjoy
maintaine/The wealth and safety of your kingdomes right.	P 478	8.28	Anjoy
All this and more your highnes shall commaund,	P 479	8.29	Lord
Comfort your selfe my Lord and have no doubt,	P 541	11.6	Navrre
But God will sure restore you to your health.	P 542	11.7	Navrre
Whose army shall discomfort all your foes,	P 579	11.44	Pleshe
That holdes it from your highnesse wrongfully:	P 582	11.47	Pleshe
Your Majestie her rightfull Lord and Soveraigne.	P 583	11.48	Pleshe
Graunt that our deeds may wel deserve your loves:	P 600	12.13	King
And yeeld your thoughts to height of my desertes.	P 602	12.15	King
Remooveles from the favours of your King.	P 609	12.22	King
in that your grace,/Hath worne the Poland diadem, before	P 611	12.24	Mugern

YOUR (cont.)

Then may it please your Majestie to give me leave,	P 616	12.29	Mugern
Come sir, give me my buttons and heers your eare.	P 620	12.33	Mugern
How likes your grace my sonnes pleasantnes?	P 632	12.45	QnMoth
Are these your secrets that no man must know?	P 678	13.22	Guise
The sole endevour of your princely care,	P 714	14.17	Guise
And meanes to meet your highnes in the field.	P 727	14.30	Bartus
Thanks to your Majestie, and so I take my leave.	P 749	15.7	1Msngr
So kindely Cosin of Guise you and your wife/Doe both salute our	P 752	15.10	Joyeux
Which your wife writ to my deare Minion,	P 755	15.13	King
I love your Minions?	P 763	15.21	King
dote on them your selfe,/I know none els but holdes them in	P 763	15.21	Guise
Even for your words that have incenst me so,	P 767	15.25	Guise
And although you take out nothing but your owne, yet you put in	P 808	17.3	P Souldr
his market, and set up your standing where you should not:	P 810	17.5	P Souldr
and whereas hee is your Landlord, you will take upon you to be	P 810	17.5	P Souldr
What your intent is yet we cannot learn,	P 823	17.18	King
Your highnes needs not feare mine armies force,	P 857	17.52	Guise
Tis for your safetie and your enemies wrack.	P 858	17.53	Guise
And simple meaning to your Majestie,	P 867	17.62	Guise
I kisse your graces hand, and take my leave,	P 868	17.63	Guise
For had your highnesse seene with what a pompe/He entred Paris,	P 872	17.67	Eprnon
I think for safety of your royall person,	P 887	17.82	Eprnon
And so to quite your grace of all suspect.	P 889	17.84	Eprnon
Then hath your grace fit oportunitie,	P 903	18.4	Bartus
To shew your love unto the King of France:	P 904	18.5	Bartus
Then sirs take your standings within this Chamber,	P 940	19.10	Capt
And please your grace the Duke of Guise doth crave/Accesse unto	P 959	19.29	Eprnon
grace the Duke of Guise doth crave/Accesse unto your highnes.	P 960	19.30	Eprnon
Good morrow to your Majestie.	P 964	19.34	Guise
How fares it this morning with your excellence?	P 966	19.36	King
I heard your Majestie was scarsely pleasde,	P 967	19.37	Guise
Boy, look where your father lyes.	P1046	19.116	King
What, will you fyle your handes with Churchmens bloud?	P1093	20.3	Cardnl
Shed your bloud?	P1094	20.4	2Mur
No remedye, therefore prepare your selfe.	P1097	20.7	1Mur
your brother the Cardinall of Loraine by the Kings consent is	P1122	21.16	P Frier
That ever I was prov'd your enemy,	P1140	22.2	King
To recompence your reconciled love,	P1144	22.6	King
your Majestie heere is a Frier of the order of the Jacobins,	P1155	22.17	P 1Msngr
the President of Paris, that craves accesse unto your grace.	P1157	22.19	P 1Msngr
The President of Paris greetes your grace,	P1168	22.30	Frier
Humblye craving your gracious reply.	P1170	22.32	Frier
What, is your highnes hurt?	P1176	22.38	Navrre
God shield your grace from such a sodaine death:	P1178	22.40	Navrre
Ah, had your highnes let him live,	P1183	22.45	Eprnon
Pleaseth your grace to let the Surgeon search your wound.	P1191	22.53	Navrre
To see your highnes in this vertuous minde.	P1210	22.72	Navrre
Alas my Lord, your highnes cannot live.	P1223	22.85	Srgeon
For he is your lawfull King and my next heire:	P1230	22.92	King
thoughe you take out none but your owne treasure	Paris	ms 3,p390	P Souldr
the markett and sett upe your standinge where you shold not:	Paris	ms 6,p390	P Souldr
ser where he is your landlorde you take upon you to be his |	Paris	ms10,p390	P Souldr
therefore your entrye is mere Intrusione	Paris	ms13,p390	P Souldr
Such as desire your worships service.	Edw	1.1.25	Poorem
And as I like your discoursing, ile have you.	Edw	1.1.32	Gavstn
We thanke your worship.	Edw	1.1.47	Omnes
Were sworne to your father at his death,	Edw	1.1.83	Mortmr
This sword of mine that should offend your foes,	Edw	1.1.86	Mortmr
What danger tis to stand against your king.	Edw	1.1.97	Edward
My lord, why do you thus incense your peeres,	Edw	1.1.99	Lncstr
Barons and Earls, your pride hath made me mute,	Edw	1.1.107	Kent
Adew my Lord, and either change your minde,	Edw	1.1.130	Lncstr
It shall suffice me to enjoy your love,	Edw	1.1.171	Gavstn
To celebrate your fathers exequies,	Edw	1.1.176	BshpCv
Saving your reverence, you must pardon me.	Edw	1.1.186	Gavstn
Madam, whether walks your majestie so fast?	Edw	1.2.46	Mortmr
But yet lift not your swords against the king.	Edw	1.2.61	ArchBp
May it please your lordship to subscribe your name.	Edw	1.4.2	Lncstr
Your grace doth wel to place him by your side,	Edw	1.4.10	Lncstr
Is this the dutie that you owe your king?	Edw	1.4.22	Kent
Nay, then lay violent hands upon your king,	Edw	1.4.35	Edward
And see what we your councellers have done.	Edw	1.4.44	ArchBp
On your allegeance to the sea of Rome,	Edw	1.4.52	ArchBp
I meane not so, your grace must pardon me.	Edw	1.4.153	Gavstn
Your highnes knowes, it lies not in my power.	Edw	1.4.158	Queene
Madam, how fares your grace?	Edw	1.4.192	Mortmr
It is impossible, but speake your minde.	Edw	1.4.228	Mortmr
I hope your honors make no question,	Edw	1.4.240	Mortmr
And Mortimer will rest at your command.	Edw	1.4.296	Mortmr
That you have parled with your Mortimer?	Edw	1.4.321	Edward
And on their knees salute your majestie.	Edw	1.4.339	Queene
Slay me my lord, when I offend your grace.	Edw	1.4.349	Warwck
My lord, ile marshall so your enemies,	Edw	1.4.357	Mortmr
In this your grace hath highly honoured me,	Edw	1.4.364	MortSr
Lord Mortimer, we leave you to your charge:	Edw	1.4.373	Edward
Spare for no cost, we will requite your love.	Edw	1.4.383	Edward
In this, or ought, your highnes shall commaund us.	Edw	1.4.384	Warwck
Or holding of a napkin in your hand,	Edw	2.1.36	Spencr
Or looking downeward, with your eye lids close,	Edw	2.1.39	Spencr
And saying, trulie ant may please your honor,	Edw	2.1.40	Spencr
I humbly thanke your Ladieship.	Edw	2.1.81	Spencr
Nothing but Gaveston, what means your grace?	Edw	2.2.7	Mortmr

YOUR (cont.)

Is this the love you beare your soveraigne?	Edw	2.2.30	Edward
Is this the fruite your reconcilement beares?	Edw	2.2.31	Edward
And in your shields display your rancorous minds?	Edw	2.2.33	Edward
Sweet Lord and King, your speech preventeth mine,	Edw	2.2.59	Gavstn
Then I doe to behold your Majestie.	Edw	2.2.63	Gavstn
Base leaden Earles that glorie in your birth,	Edw	2.2.74	Gavstn
Goe sit at home and eate your tenants beefe:	Edw	2.2.75	Gavstn
Looke to your owne heads, his is sure enough.	Edw	2.2.92	Edward
Looke to your owne crowne, if you back him thus.	Edw	2.2.93	Warwck
Whither will your lordships?	Edw	2.2.133	Guard
Twas in your wars, you should ransome him.	Edw	2.2.144	Lncstr
Quiet your self, you shall have the broad seale,	Edw	2.2.147	Edward
Your minion Gaveston hath taught you this.	Edw	2.2.149	Lncstr
For your lemmons you have lost, at Bannocks borne,	Edw	2.2.191	Lncstr
My lord, I see your love to Gaveston,	Edw	2.2.208	Kent
Your pardon is quicklie got of Isabell.	Edw	2.2.231	Queene
Mait please your grace to entertaine them now.	Edw	2.2.241	Neece
I humblie thanke your majestie.	Edw	2.2.247	Baldck
For my sake let him waite upon your grace,	Edw	2.2.250	Gavstn
Then to be favoured of your majestie.	Edw	2.2.255	Spencr
Cosin, this day shalbe your mariage feast,	Edw	2.2.256	Edward
And in your quarrell and the realmes behoofe,	Edw	2.3.3	Kent
He is your brother, therefore have we cause/To cast the worst,	Edw	2.3.7	Warwck
have we cause/To cast the worst, and doubt of your revolt.	Edw	2.3.8	Warwck
Yes, yes, for Mortimer your lovers sake.	Edw	2.4.14	Edward
That this your armie going severall waies,	Edw	2.4.42	Queene
Yet lustie lords I have escapt your handes,	Edw	2.5.1	Gavstn
Your threats, your larums, and your hote pursutes,	Edw	2.5.2	Gavstn
Breathing, in hope (malgrado all your beards,	Edw	2.5.5	Gavstn
That muster rebels thus against your king)/To see his royall	Edw	2.5.6	Gavstn
Arundell, say your message.	Edw	2.5.34	Warwck
My lords, I will not over wooe your honors,	Edw	2.5.86	Penbrk
Nay, do your pleasures, I know how twill proove.	Edw	2.5.93	Warwck
Returne him on your honor. Sound, away.	Edw	2.5.98	Mortmr
Your honor hath an adamant, of power/To drawe a prince.	Edw	2.5.105	Arundl
I see it is your life these armes pursue.	Edw	2.6.2	James
Your lordship doth dishonor to your selfe,	Edw	2.6.8	James
And wrong our lord, your honorable friend.	Edw	2.6.9	James
Weel make quick worke, commend me to your maister/My friend, and	Edw	2.6.12	Warwck
Did you retaine your fathers magnanimitie,	Edw	3.1.16	Spencr
You would not suffer thus your majestie/Be counterbuft of your	Edw	3.1.17	Spencr
not suffer thus your majestie/Be counterbuft of your nobilitie.	Edw	3.1.19	Spencr
This haught resolve becomes your majestie,	Edw	3.1.28	Baldck
As though your highnes were a schoole boy still,	Edw	3.1.30	Baldck
I come in person to your majestie,	Edw	3.1.39	SpncrP
Bound to your highnes everlastinglie,	Edw	3.1.41	SpncrP
True, and it like your grace,/That powres in lieu of all your	Edw	3.1.43	Spencr
That powres in lieu of all your goodnes showne,	Edw	3.1.44	Spencr
His life, my lord, before your princely feete.	Edw	3.1.45	Spencr
Because your highnesse hath beene slack in homage,	Edw	3.1.63	Queene
Madam in this matter/We will employ you and your little sonne,	Edw	3.1.70	Edward
And do your message with a majestie.	Edw	3.1.73	Edward
Then shall your charge committed to my trust.	Edw	3.1.78	Prince
I did your highnes message to them all,	Edw	3.1.96	Arundl
That I would undertake to carrie him/Unto your highnes, and to	Edw	3.1.100	Arundl
And see him redelivered to your hands.	Edw	3.1.112	Arundl
My lord, referre your vengeance to the sword,	Edw	3.1.123	Spencr
Upon these Barons, harten up your men,	Edw	3.1.124	Spencr
Let them not unrevengd murther your friends,	Edw	3.1.125	Spencr
Advaunce your standard Edward in the field,	Edw	3.1.126	Spencr
in lakes of gore/Your headles trunkes, your bodies will I	Edw	3.1.136	Edward
lakes of gore/Your headles trunkes, your bodies will I traile,	Edw	3.1.136	Edward
That you may drinke your fill, and quaffe in bloud,	Edw	3.1.137	Edward
On your accursed traiterous progenie,	Edw	3.1.141	Edward
Desires accesse unto your majestie.	Edw	3.1.149	Spencr
armes, by me salute/Your highnes, with long life and happines,	Edw	3.1.157	Herald
And bid me say as plainer to your grace,	Edw	3.1.158	Herald
That from your princely person you remoove/This Spencer, as a	Edw	3.1.161	Herald
whose golden leaves/Empale your princelie head, your diadem,	Edw	3.1.164	Herald
Say they, and lovinglie advise your grace,	Edw	3.1.166	Herald
Are to your highnesse vowd and consecrate.	Edw	3.1.171	Herald
Souldiers, good harts, defend your soveraignes right,	Edw	3.1.182	Edward
And levie armes against your lawfull king?	Edw	3.1.208	SpncrP
But justice of the quarrell and the cause,/Vaild is your pride:	Edw	3.1.223	Edward
traitors, now tis time/To be avengd on you for all your braves,	Edw	3.1.225	Edward
But hath your grace got shipping unto Fraunce?	Edw	4.1.17	Mortmr
will your grace with me to Henolt,/And there stay times	Edw	4.2.17	SrJohn
And there stay times advantage with your sonne?	Edw	4.2.18	SrJohn
How say you my Lord, will you go with your friends,	Edw	4.2.19	SrJohn
Much happier then your friends in England do.	Edw	4.2.35	Kent
That you were dead, or very neare your death.	Edw	4.2.38	Queene
And lives t'advance your standard good my lord.	Edw	4.2.42	Mortmr
we friends, assure your grace, in England/Would cast up cappes,	Edw	4.2.54	Mortmr
not discourage/Your friends that are so forward in your aide.	Edw	4.2.70	Queene
Binde us in kindenes all at your commaund.	Edw	4.2.73	Kent
Prosper your happie motion good sir John.	Edw	4.2.75	Queene
My dutie to your honor [premised] <promised>, &c. I have	Edw	4.3.28	P Spencr
having in their company divers of your nation, and others,	Edw	4.3.33	P Spencr
Your honors in all service, [Levune] <Lewne>.	Edw	4.3.37	P Spencr
Welcome à Gods name Madam and your sonne,	Edw	4.3.41	Edward
England shall welcome you, and all your route.	Edw	4.3.42	Edward
As to your wisdomes fittest seemes in all.	Edw	4.6.29	Queene

YOUR (cont.)

Nephew, your father, I dare not call him king.	Edw	4.6.33	Kent
So shall your brother be disposed of.	Edw	4.6.37	Mortmr
Your loving care in this,/Deserveth princelie favors and	Edw	4.6.53	Mortmr
Your king hath wrongd your countrie and himselfe,	Edw	4.6.67	Mortmr
Your lordship cannot priviledge your head.	Edw	4.6.70	Mortmr
Being of countenance in your countrey here,	Edw	4.6.75	Mortmr
To keepe your royall person safe with us,	Edw	4.7.3	Abbot
and fell invasion/Of such as have your majestie in chase,	Edw	4.7.5	Abbot
Your selfe, and those your chosen companie,	Edw	4.7.6	Abbot
Your lives and my dishonor they pursue,	Edw	4.7.23	Edward
Your grace may sit secure, if none but wee/Doe wot of your	Edw	4.7.26	Monk
grace may sit secure, if none but wee/Doe wot of your abode.	Edw	4.7.27	Monk
Here humblie of your grace we take our leaves,	Edw	4.7.78	Baldck
Your majestie must go to Killingworth.	Edw	4.7.82	Leistr
Here is a Litter readie for your grace,	Edw	4.7.84	Leistr
That waites your pleasure, and the day growes old.	Edw	4.7.85	Leistr
Will your Lordships away?	Edw	4.7.116	Rice
Your worship I trust will remember me?	Edw	4.7.117	Mower
Imagine Killingworth castell were your court,	Edw	5.1.2	Leistr
Your grace mistakes, it is for Englands good,	Edw	5.1.38	BshpWn
They stay your answer, will you yeeld your crowne?	Edw	5.1.50	Leistr
Why gape you for your soveraignes overthrow?	Edw	5.1.72	Edward
What, feare you not the furie of your king?	Edw	5.1.75	Edward
To do your highnes service and devoire,	Edw	5.1.133	Bartly
And save you from your foes, Bartley would die.	Edw	5.1.134	Bartly
Your grace must hence with mee to Bartley straight.	Edw	5.1.144	Bartly
And thinkes your grace that Bartley will bee cruell?	Edw	5.1.151	Bartly
Not yet my lorde, ile beare you on your waye.	Edw	5.1.155	Leistr
To erect your sonne with all the speed we may,	Edw	5.2.11	Mortmr
In health sweete Mortimer, how fares your grace?	Edw	5.2.81	Kent
Well, if my Lorde your brother were enlargde.	Edw	5.2.82	Queene
I would those wordes proceeded from your heart.	Edw	5.2.100	Kent
My lord, be not pensive, we are your friends.	Edw	5.3.1	Matrvs
To keepe your grace in safetie,	Edw	5.3.14	Gurney
Your passions make your dolours to increase.	Edw	5.3.15	Gurney
Sit downe, for weele be Barbars to your grace.	Edw	5.3.28	Matrvs
Or choake your soveraigne with puddle water?	Edw	5.3.30	Edward
No, but wash your face, and shave away your beard,	Edw	5.3.31	Gurney
Why strive you thus? your labour is in vaine.	Edw	5.3.33	Matrvs
O levell all your lookes upon these daring men,	Edw	5.3.39	Edward
And for your sakes, a thousand wronges ile take,	Edw	5.3.43	Edward
Lay downe your weapons, traitors, yeeld the king.	Edw	5.3.55	Kent
Thither shall your honour go, and so farewell.	Edw	5.3.62	Matrvs
Lord Mortimer, now take him to your charge.	Edw	5.4.81	Queene
My lord, he is your enemie, and shall die.	Edw	5.4.92	Mortmr
Tis for your highnesse good, and for the realmes.	Edw	5.4.101	Mortmr
Yet be not farre off, I shall need your helpe,	Edw	5.5.28	Ltborn
For she relents at this your miserie.	Edw	5.5.49	Ltborn
Lie on this bed, and rest your selfe a while.	Edw	5.5.72	Ltborn
What meanes your highnesse to mistrust me thus?	Edw	5.5.79	Ltborn
Your overwatchde my lord, lie downe and rest.	Edw	5.5.92	Ltborn
I humblie thanke your honour.	Edw	5.6.10	Matrvs
But hath your grace no other proofe then this?	Edw	5.6.43	Mortmr
If you be guiltie, though I be your sonne,	Edw	5.6.81	King
And make me blest with your sage conference.	F 126	1.1.98	Faust
Know that your words have won me at the last,	F 128	1.1.100	Faust
[Yet not your words onely, but mine owne fantasie],	F 130	1.1.102A	Faust
Go to sirra, leave your jesting, and tell us where he is.	F 201	1.2.8	P 1Schol
stand upon: therefore acknowledge your errour, and be attentive.	F 203	1.2.10	P Wagner
wine, if it could speake, <it> would informe your Worships:	F 216	1.2.23	P Wagner
boy in your face, you have seene many boyes with [such	F 344	1.4.2	P Robin
you may save your selfe a labour, for they are as familiar with	F 364	1.4.22	P Robin
Well sirra, leave your jesting, and take these Guilders.	F 367	1.4.25	P Wagner
Here, take your Guilders [againe], I'le none of 'em.	F 371	1.4.29	P Robin
your right eye be alwaies Diametrally fixt upon my left heele,	F 386	1.4.44	P Wagner
Speake Faustus, do you deliver this as your Deed?	F 501	2.1.113	Mephst
you had best leave your foolery, for an my Maister come, he'le	F 734	2.3.13	P Dick
And by your death to clime Saint Peters Chaire,	F 960	3.1.182	Faust
here, take him to your charge,/And beare him streight to Ponte	F 964	3.1.186	Pope
Lest Faustus make your shaven crownes to bleed.	F1007	3.2.27	Faust
Lord Raymond, take your seate, Friers attend,	F1010	3.2.30	Pope
First, may it please your sacred Holinesse,	F1013	3.2.33	1Card
Your Grace mistakes, you gave us no such charge.	F1024	3.2.44	1Card
Curst be your soules to hellish misery.	F1034	3.2.54	Pope
I thanke your Holinesse.	F1038	3.2.58	Archbp
Lord Raymond, I drink unto your grace.	F1053	3.2.73	Pope
I pledge your grace.	F1054	3.2.74	Faust
Please it your holinesse, I thinke it be some Ghost crept out	F1059	3.2.79	P Archbp
Purgatory, and now is come unto your holinesse for his pardon.	F1060	3.2.80	P Archbp
that your devill can answere the stealing of this same cup,	F1088	3.3.1	P Dick
I feare not your searching; we scorne to steale your cups I can	F1105	3.3.18	P Dick
your searching; we scorne to steale your cups I can tell you.	F1106	3.3.19	P Dick
plague take you, I thought 'twas your knavery to take it away:	F1110	3.3.23	P Vintnr
life, Vintner you shall have your cup anon, say nothing Dick:	F1114	3.3.27	P Robin
to supper, and a Tester in your purse, and go backe againe.	F1122	3.3.35	P Robin
[I leave untold, your eyes shall see performd].	F1154	3.3.67A	3Chor
For proofe whereof, if so your Grace be pleas'd,	F1221	4.1.67	Faust
To compasse whatsoere your grace commands.	F1226	4.1.72	Faust
Your Majesty shall see them presently.	F1235	4.1.81	Faust
an your Divels come not away quickly, you shall have me asleepe	F1241	4.1.87	P Benvol
My Lord, I must forewarne your Majesty,	F1248	4.1.94	Faust
Your grace demand no questions of the King,	F1251	4.1.97	Faust

YOUR (cont.)

My gracious Lord, you doe forget your selfe,	F1258	4.1.104		Faust
Your Majesty may boldly goe and see.	F1269	4.1.115		Faust
pull in your head for shame, let not all the world wonder at	F1291	4.1.137	P	Faust
Zounds Doctor, is this your villany?	F1293	4.1.139	P	Benvol
And therefore my Lord, so please your Majesty,	F1300	4.1.146		Faust
as to delight your Majesty with some mirth, hath Faustus justly	F1312	4.1.158	P	Faust
Then draw your weapons, and be resolute:	F1335	4.2.11		Benvol
I, [all] <I call> your hearts to recompence this deed.	F1394	4.2.70		Faust
And had you cut my body with your swords,	F1397	4.2.73		Faust
Go horse these traytors on your fiery backes,	F1403	4.2.79		Faust
Come sirs, prepare your selves in readinesse,	F1420	4.2.96		1Soldr
And stand as Bulwarkes twixt your selves and me,	F1427	4.2.103		Faust
To sheild me from your hated treachery:	F1428	4.2.104		Faust
Yet to encounter this your weake attempt,	F1429	4.2.105		Faust
O hellish spite,/Your heads are all set with hornes.	F1442	4.3.12		Benvol
It is your owne you meane, feele on your head.	F1443	4.3.13		Fredrk
I beseech your Worship accept of these forty Dollors.	F1457	4.4.1	P	HrsCsr
for your horse is turned to a bottle of Hay,--Maister Doctor.	F1490	4.4.34	P	HrsCsr
the Duke of Vanholt doth earnestly entreate your company, and	F1501	4.4.45	P	Wagner
of his men to attend you with provision fit for your journey.	F1502	4.4.46	P	Wagner
your great deserts in erecting that inchanted Castle in the	F1559	4.6.2	P	Duke
your grace to thinke but well of that which Faustus hath	F1564	4.6.7	P	Faust
Madam, I will do more then this for your content.	F1575	4.6.18	P	Faust
Please it your grace, the yeare is divided into two circles	F1581	4.6.24	P	Faust
I do beseech your grace let them come in,	F1605	4.6.48		Faust
I thanke your grace.	F1608	4.6.51		Faust
I have procur'd your pardons: welcome all.	F1610	4.6.53		Faust
in the house, and dash out all your braines with your Bottles.	F1619	4.6.62	P	HrsCsr
I'le gage my credit, 'twill content your grace.	F1622	4.6.65		Faust
I humbly thanke your grace: then fetch some Beere.	F1625	4.6.68		Faust
that flesh and bloud should be so fraile with your Worship:	F1633	4.6.76	P	Carter
And do you remember nothing of your leg?	F1639	4.6.82	P	Carter
Then I pray remember your curtesie.	F1641	4.6.84	P	Carter
Be both your legs bedfellowes every night together?	F1645	4.6.88	P	Carter
sir, did not I pull off one of your legs when you were asleepe?	F1656	4.6.99	P	HrsCsr
you thinke to carry it away with your Hey-passe, and Re-passe:	F1665	4.6.108	P	Robin
For that I know your friendship is unfain'd,	F1689	5.1.16		Faust
see how the heavens smiles]/[At your repulse, and laughs your	F1795	5.1.122A		OldMan
smiles]/[At your repulse, and laughs your state to scorne],	F1795	5.1.122A		OldMan
dutie, I do yeeld/My life and lasting service for your love.	F1819	5.2.23		Wagner
Now worthy Faustus: me thinks your looks are chang'd.	F1821	5.2.25		1Schol
Talke not of me, but save your selves and depart.	F1869	5.2.73	P	Faust
My limbes may issue from your smoky mouthes,	F1955	5.2.159		Faust
Doe yee heare, I would be sorie to robbe you of your living.	F App	p.229 19	P	Clown
why then belike, if I were your man, I should be ful of vermine.	F App	p.229 21	P	Clown
leave your jesting, and binde your selfe presently unto me for	F App	p.229 24	P	Wagner
and binde your selfe presently unto me for seaven yeeres, or	F App	p.229 24	P	Wagner
No, no, here take your gridirons againe.	F App	p.230 38	P	Clown
Let your Balio and your Belcher come here, and Ile knocke them,	F App	p.230 45	P	Clown
Heere's no body, if it like your Holynesse.	F App	p.231 4	P	Frier
my Lord Ile drinke to your grace	F App	p.231 12	P	Pope
Ile pledge your grace.	F App	p.232 13	P	Faust
out of Purgatory come to begge a pardon of your holinesse.	F App	p.232 15	P	Lorein
What, are you crossing of your selfe?	F App	p.232 18		Faust
I meane so sir with your favor.	F App	p.234 11	P	Vintnr
I must say somewhat to your felow, you sir.	F App	p.234 13	P	Vintnr
me sir, me sir, search your fill:	F App	p.234 14	P	Rafe
wil you take sixe pence in your purse to pay for your supper,	F App	p.235 41	P	Robin
villaines, for your presumption, I transforme thee into an Ape,	F App	p.235 43	P	Mephst
and nothing answerable to the honor of your Imperial majesty,	F App	p.236 14	P	Faust
I am content to do whatsoever your majesty shall command me.	F App	p.236 16	P	Faust
I am ready to accomplish your request, so farre forth as by art	F App	p.237 37	P	Faust
But if it like your Grace, it is not in my abilitie to present	F App	p.237 41	P	Faust
it is not in my abilitie to present before your eyes, the true	F App	p.237 42	P	Faust
shal appeare before your Grace, in that manner that they best	F App	p.237 47	P	Faust
I doubt not shal sufficiently content your Imperiall majesty.	F App	p.237 49	P	Faust
Your highnes may boldly go and see.	F App	p.238 63	P	Faust
your highnes now to send for the knight that was so pleasent	F App	p.238 66	P	Faust
so much for the injury hee offred me heere in your presence,	F App	p.238 82	P	Faust
I have brought you forty dollers for your horse.	F App	p.239 102	P	HrsCsr
Wel, come give me your money, my boy wil deliver him to you:	F App	p.239 107	P	Faust
slicke as an Ele; wel god buy sir, your boy wil deliver him me:	F App	p.240 117	P	HrsCsr
you, hey, passe, where's your maister?	F App	p.240 138	P	HrsCsr
Sir, the Duke of Vanholt doth earnestly entreate your company.	F App	p.241 168	P	Wagner
And for I see your curteous intent to pleasure me, I wil not	F App	p.242 8	P	Duchss
If it like your grace, the yeere is divided into twoo circles	F App	p.242 19	P	Faust
I humbly thanke your Grace.	F App	p.243 32	P	Faust
Come, maister Doctor follow us, and receive your reward.	F App	p.243 33	P	Duke
immortal pens/Renowne the valiant soules slaine in your wars,	Lucan, First Booke	444		
And Druides you now in peace renew/Your barbarous customes, and	Lucan, First Booke	447		
fierce men of Rhene/Leaving your countrey open to the spoile.	Lucan, First Booke	461		
Forbeare, sweet wordes, and be your sport unpleasant.	Ovid's Elegies	1.4.66		
Your name approves you made for such like things,	Ovid's Elegies	1.12.27		
famous names/Farewel, your favour nought my minde inflames.	Ovid's Elegies	2.1.36		
Wenches apply your faire lookes to my verse/Which golden love	Ovid's Elegies	2.1.37		
Not drunke, your faults [in] <on> the spilt wine I numbred.	Ovid's Elegies	2.5.14		
I saw your nodding eye-browes much to speake,	Ovid's Elegies	2.5.15		
Even from your cheekes parte of a voice did breake.	Ovid's Elegies	2.5.16		
I knew your speech (what do not lovers see)?	Ovid's Elegies	2.5.19		
Go goodly <godly> birdes, striking your breasts bewaile,	Ovid's Elegies	2.6.3		
And with rough clawes your tender cheekes assaile.	Ovid's Elegies	2.6.4		
For long shrild trumpets let your notes resound.	Ovid's Elegies	2.6.6		

YOUR (cont.)

Full concord all your lives was you betwixt,	Ovid's Elegies	2.6.13	
And to the end your constant faith stood fixt.	Ovid's Elegies	2.6.14	
Why with hid irons are your bowels torne?	Ovid's Elegies	2.14.27	
To plague your bodies with such harmefull strokes?	Ovid's Elegies	2.14.34	
But when she comes, [you] <your> swelling mounts sinck downe,	Ovid's Elegies	2.16.51	
Tis not enough, she shakes your record off,	Ovid's Elegies	3.3.19	
But woods and groves keepe your faults undetected.	Ovid's Elegies	3.5.84	
Their <Your> youthfull browes with Ivie girt to meete him,/With	Ovid's Elegies	3.8.61	
Now your credulity harme to me hath raisd.	Ovid's Elegies	3.11.44	
Will you make shipwracke of your honest name,	Ovid's Elegies	3.13.11	
There in your rosie lippes my tongue intombe,	Ovid's Elegies	3.13.23	
And with your pastime let the bedsted creake,	Ovid's Elegies	3.13.26	
But with your robes, put on an honest face,	Ovid's Elegies	3.13.27	
Like one start up your haire tost and displast,	Ovid's Elegies	3.13.33	
And with a wantons tooth, your necke new raste?	Ovid's Elegies	3.13.34	
And I will trust your words more then mine eies.	Ovid's Elegies	3.13.46	
Teach but your tongue to say, I did it not,	Ovid's Elegies	3.13.48	
Your golden ensignes [plucke] <pluckt> out of my field,	Ovid's Elegies	3.14.16	
From Venus altar to your footsteps bending)/Doth testifie that	Hero and Leander	1.210	
But Pallas and your mistresse are at strife.	Hero and Leander	1.322	
Saying, let your vowes and promises be kept.	Hero and Leander	2.96	

YOURS

I am as true as any one of yours.	Dido	5.1.223	Nurse
Then fight couragiously, their crowns are yours.	1Tamb	3.3.30	Tamb
you suffer these outragious curses by these slaves of yours?	1Tamb	4.4.27	P Zenoc
And souldiers play the men, the [hold] <holds> is yours.	2Tamb	3.3.63	Techel
The glorie of this happy day is yours:	2Tamb	3.5.161	Tamb
Dangerous tc those, whose Chrisis is as yours:	2Tamb	5.3.92	Phsitn
As for the Diamond it shall be yours;	Jew	2.3.135	Barab
Malta to a wildernesse/For these intolerable wrongs of yours;	Jew	3.5.26	Basso
I thankfully shall undertake the charge/Of you and yours, and	P 477	8.27	Anjoy
Yours my Lord Cardinall, you should have saide.	P1103	20.13	1Mur
I yours, and therefore I would wish you graunt.	Edw	1.1.120	Edward
And what is yours my lord of Lancaster?	Edw	2.2.21	Edward
Mounsier le Grand, a noble friend of yours,	Edw	4.2.47	Mortmr
Her friends doe multiply and yours doe fayle,	Edw	4.5.2	Spencr
Their bloud and yours shall seale these treacheries.	Edw	5.1.89	Edward
Twixt theirs and yours, shall be no enmitie.	Edw	5.3.46	Matrvs
be it in the world, it shall be yours:	F1568	4.6.11	P Faust
And mingle thighs, yours ever mine to beare.	Ovid's Elegies	3.13.22	

YOUR SELF

Madam content your self and be resolv'd,	1Tamb	5.1.372	Anippe
Quiet your self, you shall have the broad seale,	Edw	2.2.147	Edward

YOUR SELFE

We hope your selfe wil willingly restore them.	1Tamb	1.2.117	Agidas
sent me to know/Whether your selfe will come and custome them.	Jew	1.1.53	1Merch
Sister, I think your selfe will beare us company.	P 21	1.21	Charls
Assure your selfe my good Lord Admirall,	P 262	4.60	Charls
Comfort your selfe my Lord and have no doubt,	P 541	11.6	Navrre
dote on them your selfe,/I know none els but holdes them in	P 763	15.21	Guise
No remedye, therefore prepare your selfe.	P1097	20.7	1Mur
Your lordship doth dishonor to your selfe,	Edw	2.6.8	James
Your selfe, and those your chosen companie,	Edw	4.7.6	Abbot
Lie on this bed, and rest your selfe a while.	Edw	5.5.72	Ltborn
you may save your selfe a labour, for they are as familiar with	F 364	1.4.22	P Robin
My gracious Lord, you doe forget your selfe,	F1258	4.1.104	Faust
and binde your selfe presently unto me for seaven yeeres, or	F App	p.229 24	P Wagner
What, are you crossing of your selfe?	F App	p.232 18	Faust

YOUR SELVES

Submit your selves and us to servitude.	1Tamb	5.1.39	Govnr
diet your selves, you knowe I shall have occasion shortly to	2Tamb	3.5.114	P Tamb
shall there concerne our state/Assure your selves I'le looke--	Jew	1.1.173	Barab
And will you basely thus submit your selves/To leave your goods	Jew	1.2.79	Barab
You shall not need trouble your selves so farre,	Jew	3.5.22	Basso
Your selves shall see it shall not be forgot:	Jew	5.2.71	Barab
Come sirs, prepare your selves in readinesse,	F1420	4.2.96	1Soldr
And stand as Bulwarkes twixt your selves and me,	F1427	4.2.103	Faust
Talke not of me, but save your selves and depart.	F1869	5.2.73	P Faust

YOUTH

What ist sweet wagge I should deny thy youth?	Dido	1.1.23	Jupitr
Nor Venus triumph in his tender youth:	Dido	3.2.9	Juno
Where all my youth I have bene governed,	1Tamb	1.2.13	Zenoc
Thy youth forbids such ease my kingly boy,	2Tamb	4.3.29	Tamb
Alas, Sir, I am a very youth.	Jew	2.3.115	P Slave
A youth?	Jew	2.3.116	P Barab
Is't not a sweet fac'd youth, Pilia?	Jew	4.2.40	P Curtzn
Agen, sweet youth; did not you, Sir, bring the sweet youth a	Jew	4.2.41	P Ithimr
sweet youth; did not you, Sir, bring the sweet youth a letter?	Jew	4.2.42	P Ithimr
Then let his grace, whose youth is flexible,	Edw	1.4.398	MortSr
Commit not to my youth things of more waight/Then fits a prince	Edw	3.1.74	Prince
I like a ventrous youth, rid him into the deepe pond at the	F App	p.240 133	P HrsCsr
(Whom from his youth he bribde) needs make him king?	Lucan, First Booke	315	
Accept him that will serve thee all his youth,	Ovid's Elegies	1.3.5	
Mistris thou knowest, thou hast a blest youth pleas'd,	Ovid's Elegies	1.8.23	
That some youth hurt as I am with loves bowe/His owne flames	Ovid's Elegies	2.1.7	
The youth oft swimming to his Hero kinde,	Ovid's Elegies	2.16.31	
And by those numbers is thy first youth spent.	Ovid's Elegies	3.1.28	
I prove neither youth nor man, but old and rustie.	Ovid's Elegies	3.6.20	
Where Juno comes, each youth, and pretty maide,	Ovid's Elegies	3.12.23	
Would have allur'd the vent'rous youth of Greece,	Hero and Leander	1.57	
My words shall be as spotlesse as my youth,	Hero and Leander	1.207	
Gentle youth forbeare/To touch the sacred garments which I	Hero and Leander	1.343	

YOUTH (cont.)			
Nor could the youth abstaine, but he must weare/The sacred ring	Hero and Leander	2.108	
YOUTHFULL			
even nowe when youthfull bloud/Pricks forth our lively bodies,	Lucan, First Booke	363	
The youthfull sort to divers pastimes runne.	Ovid's Elegies	2.5.22	
I blush, [that] <and> being youthfull, hot, and lustie,	Ovid's Elegies	3.6.19	
Yet might her touch make youthfull Pilius fire,	Ovid's Elegies	3.6.41	
Their <Your> youthfull browes with Ivie girt to meete him,/With	Ovid's Elegies	3.8.61	
Nor staine thy youthfull years with avarice,	Hero and Leander	1.325	
YOUTHS			
Or Cephalus with lustie Thebane youths,	1Tamb	4.3.4	Souldn
Penelope in bowes her youths strength tride,	Ovid's Elegies	1.8.47	
So shalt thou go with youths to feasts together,	Ovid's Elegies	3.4.47	
What secret becks in banquets with her youths,	Ovid's Elegies	3.10.23	
YOW			
yow are wellcome ser have at you	Paris	ms16,p390 P	Souldr
YRE			
When yre, or hope provokt, heady, and bould,	Lucan, First Booke	147	
YRON			
I hold the Fates bound fast in yron chaines,	1Tamb	1.2.174	Tamb
Shaking their swords, their speares and yron bils,	1Tamb	4.1.25	2Msngr
Which kept his father in an yron cage:	2Tamb	1.1.5	Orcan
Keeping in yron cages Emperours.	2Tamb	1.3.49	Tamb
Therefore when flint and yron weare away,	Ovid's Elegies	1.15.31	
In stone, and Yron walles Danae shut,	Ovid's Elegies	3.4.21	
Blood-quaffing Mars, heaving the yron net,	Hero and Leander	1.151	
YRONS			
Searing thy hatefull flesh with burning yrons,	2Tamb	3.5.123	Tamb
YSIE			
And scale the ysie mountaines lofty tops:	1Tamb	1.2.100	Tamb
YSPRONG			
of a bigger size/Than all the brats ysprong from Typhons loins:	1Tamb	3.3.109	Bajzth
YVORY			
And comments vollumes with her Yvory pen,	1Tamb	5.1.145	Tamb
YV'RIE			
With that hee stript him to the yv'rie skin,	Hero and Leander	2.153	
For though the rising yv'rie mount he scal'd,	Hero and Leander	2.273	
ZAARETH			
Doe so; Farewell Zaareth, farewell Temainte.	Jew	1.1.176	Barab
ZABINA			
Zabina, mother of three braver boies,	1Tamb	3.3.103	Bajzth
Ah faire Zabina, we have lost the field.	1Tamb	3.3.233	Bajzth
Ah faire Zabina, we may curse his power,	1Tamb	5.1.230	Bajzth
O poore Zabina, O my Queen, my Queen,	1Tamb	5.1.275	Bajzth
ZABINAS			
That would with pity chear Zabinas heart,	1Tamb	5.1.271	Bajzth
ZANSIBAR			
And with my power did march to Zansibar,	2Tamb	1.3.194	Techel
I conquered all as far as Zansibar.	2Tamb	5.3.139	Tamb
ZANTE (See ASANT)			
ZANTHUS			
There Zanthus streame, because here's Priamus,	Dido	2.1.8	Aeneas
Who groveling in the mire of Zanthus bankes,	Dido	2.1.150	Aeneas
And Crusa unto Zanthus first affide,	Ovid's Elegies	3.5.31	
ZEALE			
No, but I doe it through a burning zeale,	Jew	2.3.87	Barab
Being animated by Religious zeale,	P 848	17.43	Guise
This which I urge, is of a burning zeale,	Edw	1.4.256	Mortmr
ZEALOUS			
The Abbasse of the house/Whose zealous admonition I embrace:	Jew	3.3.67	Abigal
I have beene zealous in the Jewish faith,	Jew	4.1.51	Barab
ZEASE			
For Gaveston, will if he [seaze] <zease> <sees> him once,	Edw	2.5.63	Warwck
ZENITH			
Over my Zenith hang a blazing star,	2Tamb	3.2.6	Tamb
Over whose Zenith cloth'd in windy aire,	2Tamb	3.4.61	Therid
ZENOCRATE			
Disdaines Zenocrate to live with me?	1Tamb	1.2.82	Tamb
Zenocrate, lovelier than the Love of Jove,	1Tamb	1.2.87	Tamb
Shall all we offer to Zenocrate,	1Tamb	1.2.104	Tamb
And then my selfe to faire Zenocrate.	1Tamb	1.2.105	Tamb
How now my Lords of Egypt and Zenocrate?	1Tamb	1.2.113	Tamb
Soft ye my Lords and sweet Zenocrate.	1Tamb	1.2.119	Tamb
I must be pleasde perforce, wretched Zenocrate.	1Tamb	1.2.259	Zenoc
Madame Zenocrate, may I presume/To know the cause of these	1Tamb	3.2.1	Agidas
Before such hap fall to Zenocrate.	1Tamb	3.2.20	Agidas
Ah faire Zenocrate,/Let not a man so vile and barbarous,	1Tamb	3.2.25	Agidas
Zenocrate, the loveliest Maide alive,	1Tamb	3.3.117	Tamb
Stir not Zenocrate untill thou see/Me martch victoriously with	1Tamb	3.3.126	Tamb
Nay take the Turkish Crown from her, Zenocrate,	1Tamb	3.3.220	Tamb
The rogue of Volga holds Zenocrate,	1Tamb	4.1.4	Souldn
Yet in revenge of faire Zenocrate,	1Tamb	4.1.43	Souldn
Zenocrate, looke better to your slave.	1Tamb	4.2.68	Tamb
Not for the world Zenocrate, if I have sworn:	1Tamb	4.2.125	Tamb
Or kept the faire Zenocrate so long,	1Tamb	4.3.41	Souldn
Wel Zenocrate, Techelles, and the rest, fall to your victuals.	1Tamb	4.4.14 P	Tamb
To let them see (divine Zenocrate)/I glorie in the curses of my	1Tamb	4.4.28	Tamb
How now Zenocrate, dooth not the Turke and his wife make a	1Tamb	4.4.57 P	Tamb
Yet musicke woulde doe well to cheare up Zenocrate:	1Tamb	4.4.62 P	Tamb
Zenocrate, were Egypt Joves owne land,	1Tamb	4.4.73	Tamb
Citties and townes/After my name and thine Zenocrate:	1Tamb	4.4.80	Tamb
Tell me Zenocrate?	1Tamb	4.4.84	Tamb
And all the friendes of faire Zenocrate,	1Tamb	4.4.88	Tamb

ZENOCRATE (cont.)			
Zenocrate, I will not crowne thee yet, ...	1Tamb	4.4.139	Tamb
Ah faire Zenocrate, divine Zenocrate, ...	1Tamb	5.1.135	Tamb
His life that so consumes Zenocrate, ...	1Tamb	5.1.154	Tamb
So much by much, as dooth Zenocrate.	1Tamb	5.1.159	Tamb
For faire Zenocrate, that so laments his state. . .	1Tamb	5.1.205	Therid
For sweet Zenocrate, whose worthinesse/Deserves a conquest over	1Tamb	5.1.207	Tamb
Wretched Zenocrate, that livest to see, ...	1Tamb	5.1.319	Zenoc
the cause of this/That tearm'st Zenocrate thy dearest love?	1Tamb	5.1.336	Zenoc
Whose lives were dearer to Zenocrate/Than her owne life, or	1Tamb	5.1.337	Zenoc
Ah what may chance to thee Zenocrate?	1Tamb	5.1.371	Zenoc
Behold Zenocrate, the cursed object/Whose Fortunes never .	1Tamb	5.1.413	Zenoc
Having beheld devine Zenocrate, ...	1Tamb	5.1.418	Arabia
Come happy Father of Zenocrate, ...	1Tamb	5.1.433	Tamb
Wel met my only deare Zenocrate, ...	1Tamb	5.1.443	Souldn
Thou hast with honor usde Zenocrate.	1Tamb	5.1.484	Souldn
What saith the noble Souldane and Zenocrate? . . .	1Tamb	5.1.495	Tamb
Then doubt I not but faire Zenocrate/Will soone consent to	1Tamb	5.1.498	Tamb
Then sit thou downe divine Zenocrate, ...	1Tamb	5.1.506	Tamb
To gratify the <thee> sweet Zenocrate, ...	1Tamb	5.1.516	Tamb
But what became of faire Zenocrate, ...	2Tamb	Prol.6	Prolog
Now bright Zenocrate, the worlds faire eie, ...	2Tamb	1.3.1	Tamb
And not before, my sweet Zenocrate:	2Tamb	1.3.15	Tamb
The trumpets sound, Zenocrate, they come.	2Tamb	1.3.111	Tamb
Zenocrate that gave him light and life, ...	2Tamb	2.4.8	Tamb
To entertaine devine Zenocrate.	2Tamb	2.4.17	Tamb
no more, but deck the heavens/To entertaine divine Zenocrate.	2Tamb	2.4.21	Tamb
silver runs through Paradice/To entertaine divine Zenocrate.	2Tamb	2.4.25	Tamb
voices and their instruments/To entertaine divine Zenocrate.	2Tamb	2.4.29	Tamb
out his hand in highest majesty/To entertaine divine Zenocrate.	2Tamb	2.4.33	Tamb
life may be as short to me/As are the daies of sweet Zenocrate:	2Tamb	2.4.37	Tamb
Tell me, how fares my faire Zenocrate?	2Tamb	2.4.41	Tamb
Zenocrate had bene the argument/Of every Epigram or Eligie.	2Tamb	2.4.94	Tamb
For taking hence my faire Zenocrate.	2Tamb	2.4.101	Tamb
Behold me here divine Zenocrate, ...	2Tamb	2.4.111	Tamb
Drooping and pining for Zenocrate.	2Tamb	2.4.142	Tamb
Because my deare Zenocrate is dead.	2Tamb	3.2.14	Tamb
And here the picture of Zenocrate, ...	2Tamb	3.2.25	Tamb
Sweet picture of divine Zenocrate, ...	2Tamb	3.2.27	Tamb
Onely to gaze upon Zenocrate.	2Tamb	3.2.33	Tamb
Now fetch the hearse of faire Zenocrate, ...	2Tamb	5.3.210	Tamb
ZENOCRATES			
More rich and valurous than Zenocrates.	1Tamb	1.2.97	Tamb
And let Zenccrates faire eies beholde/That as for her thou	1Tamb	5.1.408	Arabia
ZEPHIR			
and where the north-west wind/Nor Zephir rules not, but the	Lucan, First Booke		408
ZEPHIRE			
Or slender eares, with gentle Zephire shaken, ...	Ovid's Elegies		1.7.55
ZEPHIRES			
Request milde Zephires helpe for thy availe, ...	Ovid's Elegies		2.11.41
ZOACUM			
That Zoacum, that fruit of bytternesse, ...	2Tamb	2.3.20	Orcan
ZODIACKE			
in their motions <motion> upon the poles of the Zodiacke.	F 599	2.2.48	P Mephst
ZONA			
Were all the lofty mounts of Zona mundi, ...	2Tamb	4.1.42	Amyras
ZONE			
And thence by land unto the Torrid Zone, ...	1Tamb	4.4.124	Tamb
I to the Torrid Zone where midday burnes, ...	Lucan, First Booke		16
ZONES			
The [Tropicks] <Tropick>, Zones, and quarters of the skye,/From	F 761	2.3.40	2Chor
'ZONS			
'Zons, hornes againe.	F1444	4.3.14	Benvol
ZONS			
Zons fill us some Beere, or we'll breake all the barrels in the	F1617	4.6.60	P HrsCsr
ZOON'S			
Zoon's what a looking thou keep'st, thou'lt betraye's anon.	Jew	3.1.25	Pilia
ZOUNDS (See also SWOWNS)			
Zounds, boy in your face, you have seene many boyes with [such	F 344	1.4.2	P Robin
zounds I could eate my selfe for anger, to thinke I have beene	F1242	4.1.88	P Benvol
The Emperour? where? O zounds my head.	F1287	4.1.133	Benvol
Zounds Doctor, is this your villany?	F1293	4.1.139	P Benvol
zounds hee'l raise up a kennell of Divels I thinke anon: .	F1305	4.1.151	P Benvol
Zounds the Divel's alive agen.	F1391	4.2.67	P Benvol
ZULA			
Betwixt the citie Zula and Danubius, ...	2Tamb	2.1.7	Fredrk

Concordance to the Stage Directions

ABBASSE			
<three> Fryars and [three] <two> Nuns [, one the Abbasse].	Jew of Malta		1.2.304.2
ABBOT			
Enter the Abbot, Monkes, Edward, Spencer, and Baldocke .	Edward II		4.7.0.1
ABIGALL			
Enter Abigall the Jewes daughter.	Jew of Malta		1.2.223.1
Enter Abigall above.	Jew of Malta		2.1.19.1
Enter Abigall.	Jew of Malta		2.3.221.1
[Exeunt Lodowicke and Abigall].	Jew of Malta		2.3.241.1
Enter Lodowicke, Abigall.	Jew of Malta		2.3.275.1
[Exit Abigall].	Jew of Malta		2.3.363.1
Enter Abigall.	Jew of Malta		3.3.3.1
Enter [the] two Fryars <and Abigall>.	Jew of Malta		3.6.0.1
Enter Abigall.	Jew of Malta		3.6.6.2
ABOUT			
three Phisitians about her bed, tempering potions. . .	2Tamburlaine		2.4.0.2
King, Baldock, and Spencer the sonne, flying about the stage.	Edward II		4.5.0.2
they runne about.	Faustus App.		p235 25.2
ABOVE			
[Enter above] Captaine with his wife [Olympia] and sonne.	2Tamburlaine		3.3.14.2
Enter Abigall above.	Jew of Malta		2.1.19.1
Enter Barabas above.	Jew of Malta		3.2.4.1
Enter [Barabas] with a Hammar above, very busie. . .	Jew of Malta		5.5.0.1
[enter] the Souldier [above, who] dischargeth his Musket at the	Paris	196.1	3.31.1
Enter [above Gonzago and others] into the Admirals house, and	Paris	297.1	5.24.1
Exeunt Gonzago and rest above].	Paris	306.1	5.33.1
Enter Lucifer and foure devils [above], Faustus to them with	Faustus	229.1	1.3.0.1
Exeunt [Faustus; Lucifer and devils above].	Faustus	342.1	1.3.114.1
Enter Benvolio above at a window, in his nightcap: . .	Faustus	1178.1	4.1.24.1
Enter [above] Lucifer, Belzebub, and Mephostophilis. .	Faustus	1797.1	5.2.0.1
[Exeunt Lucifer and devils above].	Faustus	1982.2	5.2.186.2
ACHATES			
Enter Aeneas with Ascanius [and Achates], with one or two more.	Dido		1.1.133.1
Enter Aeneas, Achates, and Ascanius [attended].	Dido		2.1.0.1
[Enter Aeneas, Achates, Sergestus, Illioneus, and Cloanthus].	Dido		3.1.96.1
Anna, Iarbus, Achates, [Cupid for Ascanius], and followers.	Dido		3.3.0.1
Enter Achates, [Cupid for] Ascanius, Iarbus, and Anna. .	Dido		4.1.0.1
Enter Achates, Cloanthus, Sergestus, and Illioneus. . .	Dido		4.3.14.1
Enter Anna, with Aeneas, Achates, Illioneus, and Sergestus.	Dido		4.4.13.1
the platforme of the citie, with him Achates, [Sergestus],	Dido		5.1.0.2
ADMIRALL			
the Lord high Admirall, and [Margaret] the Queene of Navarre,	Paris	0.2	1.0.2
manet Navar, the Prince of Condy, and the Lord high Admirall.	Paris	26.4	1.26.4
of Condy, the Admirall, and the Pothecary with the gloves,	Paris	166.2	3.0.2
who] dischargeth his Musket at the Lord Admirall [and exit].	Paris	196.2	3.31.2
Enter the Admirall in his bed.	Paris	252.2	4.50.2
ADMIRALS			
Enter the Admirals man.	Paris	241.1	4.39.1
Enter [above Gonzago and others] into the Admirals house, and	Paris	297.1	5.24.1
Enter two with the Admirals body.	Paris	482.1	9.0.1
AENEAS			
Enter Aeneas with Ascanius [and Achates], with one or two more.	Dido		1.1.133.1
Enter Aeneas, Achates, and Ascanius [attended]. . .	Dido		2.1.0.1
[Enter servant with robe and Aeneas puts it on]. . .	Dido		2.1.95.1
[Enter Aeneas, Achates, Sergestus, Illioneus, and Cloanthus].	Dido		3.1.96.1
Enter Dido, Aeneas, Anna, Iarbus, Achates, [Cupid for .	Dido		3.3.0.1
Enter Aeneas and Dido in the Cave at severall times. .	Dido		3.4.0.1
[Enter Aeneas and Dido].	Dido		4.1.24.1
Enter Aeneas alone.	Dido		4.3.0.1
[Exeunt omnes, manet Aeneas].	Dido		4.3.45.1
Enter Anna, with Aeneas, Achates, Illioneus, and Sergestus.	Dido		4.4.13.1
Enter Aeneas with a paper in his hand, drawing the platforme of	Dido		5.1.0.1
Exit Iarbus and Aeneas traine.	Dido		5.1.77.1
Enter Dido [attended] [to] <and> Aeneas.	Dido		5.1.82.1
[Exit Aeneas].	Dido		5.1.183.1
AFTER			
to the Battell, and after the battell, enter Cosroe wounded,	1Tamburlaine		2.7.0.1
Tamburlaine enjoyes the victory, after Arabia enters wounded.	1Tamburlaine		5.1.402.2
After Calapine, and after him other Lordes [and Almeda]: .	2Tamburlaine		3.1.0.3
devill playing on a Drum, after him another bearing an Ensigne:	Faustus	1430.1	4.2.106.1
AGAINE			
To the battell againe.	1Tamburlaine		3.3.200.1
Tamburlaine goes in, and comes out againe with al the rest.	2Tamburlaine		5.3.114.1
The Guise enters againe, with all the rest, with their Swords	Paris	335.2	5.62.2
They knocke againe, and call out to talke with Faustus. .	Faustus	1590.1	4.6.33.1
Enter Hellen againe, passing over betweene two Cupids. .	Faustus	1767.1	5.1.94.1
Crosse againe.	Faustus App.		p232 19.1
Crosse againe, and Faustus hits him a boxe of the eare, and	Faustus App.		p232 21.1
AGAINST			
He brains himself against the cage.	1Tamburlaine		5.1.304.1
She runs against the Cage and braines her selfe. . .	1Tamburlaine		5.1.318.1
AGEN			
Enter Mephostophilis agen with the grapes. . . .	Faustus	1575.1	4.6.18.1
AGENT			
Enter the English Agent.	Paris	1193.2	22.55.2
AGIDAS			
Lords [,Magnetes, Agidas], and Souldiers loden with treasure.	1Tamburlaine		1.2.0.2
[Enter] Agidas, Zenocrate, Anippe, with others. . .	1Tamburlaine		3.2.0.1
by the hand, looking wrathfully on Agidas, and sayes nothing.	1Tamburlaine		3.2.65.2
[Exeunt. Manet Agidas].	1Tamburlaine		3.2.65.3
AL			
Banquet, and to it commeth Tamburlain al in scarlet, Theridamas,	1Tamburlaine		4.4.0.1
Tamburlaine goes in, and comes out againe with al the rest.	2Tamburlaine		5.3.114.1

ALARME		
Alarme:	2Tamburlaine	4.1.0.1
Alarme, and Amyras and Celebinus run in.	2Tamburlaine	4.1.51.1
Alarme.	2Tamburlaine	4.1.73.1
Alarme, and they scale the walles.	2Tamburlaine	5.1.62.1
Alarme within.	2Tamburlaine	5.3.101.1
Alarme, Tamburlaine goes in, and comes out againe with al the	2Tamburlaine	5.3.114.1
ALARMES		
Alarmes.	Jew of Malta	5.2.0.1
ALARUMS		
Alarums within.	Paris 787.1	16.0.1
[Alarums].	Edward II	2.4.0.1
Enter the Barons, alarums.	Edward II	2.4.21.1
Alarums, excursions, a great fight, and a retreate.	Edward II	3.1.184.2
Alarums].	Edward II	3.1.220.1
ALEX		
exit Alex:	Faustus App.	p238 63.1
ALEXANDER		
Enter at one [dore] the Emperour Alexander, at the other	Faustus 1257.2	4.1.103.2
is throwne downe, Alexander kils him; takes off his Crowne,	Faustus 1257.3	4.1.103.3
with Alexander and his paramour.	Faustus App.	p238 59.1
ALGIERS (See ARGIER)		
ALL (See also AL)		
Tamburlaine all in blacke, and verie melancholy.	1Tamburlaine	5.1.63.3
Enter Theridamas, Techelles and all their traine.	2Tamburlaine	3.4.33.2
enters againe, with all the rest, with their Swords drawne,	Paris 335.2	5.62.2
All goe out, but Navarre and Pleshe.	Paris 564.1	11.29.1
and then all crye vive [le] <la> Roy two or three times.	Paris 588.1	12.0.1
Goe out all, but the Queene [Mother] and the Cardinall.	Paris 630.1	12.43.1
Enter Pope and all the Lords.	Faustus 1008.1	3.2.28.1
besmear'd with mud and durt; all having hornes on their heads.	Faustus 1431.3	4.3.0.3
Faustus hits him a boxe of the eare, and they all runne away.	Faustus App.	p232 21.2
Enter all the Friers to sing the Dirge.	Faustus App.	p232 28.1
Enter Horsecourser all wet, crying.	Faustus App.	p240 26.2
ALMEDA		
[Enter] Callapine with Almeda, his keeper.	2Tamburlaine	1.2.0.1
After Calapine, and after him other Lordes [and Almeda]:	2Tamburlaine	3.1.0.3
Orcanes, Jerusalem, Trebizon, Soria, Almeda, with their traine.	2Tamburlaine	3.5.0.1
ALONE		
Enter Aeneas alone.	Dido	4.3.0.1
and Mycetes comes out alone with his Crowne in his hand,	1Tamburlaine	2.4.0.1
[Enter] Olympia alone.	2Tamburlaine	4.2.0.1
[Enter] Edmund [earle of Kent] alone with a sword and target.	Edward II	4.6.0.1
Enter Mortimer alone.	Edward II	5.4.0.1
ALOOF		
[Governor stands aloof].	Jew of Malta	5.5.46.1
[Enter Old Man] [aloof].	Faustus 1774.1A	5.1.101.1
ALOOFE		
Enter [aloofe] Tamburlaine with Techelles and others.	1Tamburlaine	3.2.24.1
ALSO		
Enter also the Guise [and others].	Paris 528.2	10.0.2
AMASIA		
Enter Callapine, Amasia, [Captaine, Souldiers], with drums and	2Tamburlaine	5.2.0.1
AMBO		
Exeunt ambo [Penbrooke and Arundell, attended].	Edward II	2.5.111.1
AMBUSHT		
Enter the ambusht Souldiers.	Faustus 1419.2	4.2.95.2
AMONG		
Beate the Friers, fling fire workes among them, and Exeunt.	Faustus 1087.1	3.2.107.1
the Friers, and fling fier-workes among them, and so Exeunt.	Faustus App.	p233 41.1
AMYRAS		
Calyphas, Amyras, and Celebinus, with drummes and trumpets.	2Tamburlaine	1.3.0.2
[Calyphas], [Amyras, and Celebinus], foure bearing the hearse	2Tamburlaine	3.2.0.2
Amyras and Celebinus, issues from the tent where Caliphas sits	2Tamburlaine	4.1.0.1
Alarme, and Amyras and Celebinus run in.	2Tamburlaine	4.1.51.1
Usumcasane, Amyras, Celebinus, leading the Turkish kings.	2Tamburlaine	4.1.75.3
them, Techelles, Theridamas, Usumcasane, Amyras, Celebinus:	2Tamburlaine	4.3.0.4
and Soria], with Usumcasane, Amyras, and Celebinus, with others,	2Tamburlaine	5.1.62.3
drawn by the captive kings; Amyras, Celebinus, Physitians].	2Tamburlaine	5.3.41.1
[To Amyras].	2Tamburlaine	5.3.177.1
AN		
Enter Hugh Spencer an old man, father to the yong Spencer, with	Edward II	3.1.31.1
devill playing on a Drum, after him another bearing an Ensigne:	Faustus 1430.2	4.2.106.2
Enter an Old Man.	Faustus 1706.1	5.1.33.1
Enter an old man.	Faustus App.	p243 33.1
AND		
dandling Ganimed upon his knee, and Mercury lying asleepe.	Dido	1.1.0.2
Enter Aeneas with Ascanius [and Achates], with one or two more.	Dido	1.1.133.1
Enter [Iarbus, with] Illioneus, and Cloanthus [and Sergestus].	Dido	1.2.0.1
Enter [Iarbus, with] Illioneus, and Cloanthus [and Sergestus].	Dido	1.2.0.2
Enter Aeneas, Achates, and Ascanius [attended].	Dido	2.1.0.1
Enter Cloanthus, Sergestus, Illioneus [and others].	Dido	2.1.38.1
Enter Dido [with Anna and Iarbus] and her traine.	Dido	2.1.73.1
[Enter servant with robe and Aeneas puts it on].	Dido	2.1.95.1
doore, and takes Ascanius by the sleeve [as he is going off].	Dido	2.1.303.2
Enter Iarbus, Anna, and Dido.	Dido	3.1.6.1
[Enter Aeneas, Achates, Sergestus, Illioneus, and Cloanthus].	Dido	3.1.96.1
Anna, Iarbus, Achates, [Cupid for Ascanius], and followers.	Dido	3.3.0.2
Enter Aeneas and Dido in the Cave at severall times.	Dido	3.4.0.1
Enter Achates, [Cupid for] Ascanius, Iarbus, and Anna.	Dido	4.1.0.1
[Enter Aeneas and Dido].	Dido	4.1.24.1
Enter Achates, Cloanthus, Sergestus, and Illioneus.	Dido	4.3.14.1
Enter Dido and Anna [with traine].	Dido	4.4.0.1

AND (cont.)

Enter Anna, with Aeneas, Achates, Illioneus, and Sergestus.	Dido	4.4.13.1
[Gives him crowne and scepter].	Dido	4.4.36.1
citie, with him Achates, [Sergestus], Cloanthus, and Illioneus.	Dido	5.1.0.2
Exit Iarbus and Aeneas traine.	Dido	5.1.77.1
Enter Dido [attended] [to] <and> Aeneas.	Dido	5.1.82.1
Exeunt the Nurse [and Attendants].	Dido	5.1.224.1
[Enter Attendants with wood and fire].	Dido	5.1.282.1
Manent Cosroe and Menaphon.	1Tamburlaine	1.1.106.2
Enter Ortigius and [Ceneus] <Conerus> bearing a Crowne, with	1Tamburlaine	1.1.135.1
Lords [,Magnetes, Agidas], and Souldiers loden with treasure.	1Tamburlaine	1.2.0.2
[Enter] Mycetes, Meander, with other Lords and Souldiers.	1Tamburlaine	2.2.0.1
and Mycetes comes out alone with his Crowne in his hand,	1Tamburlaine	2.4.0.1
Sound trumpets to the battell, and he runs in.	1Tamburlaine	2.4.42.1
to the Battell, and after the battell, enter Cosroe wounded,	1Tamburlaine	2.7.0.1
He takes the Crowne and puts it on.	1Tamburlaine	2.7.52.2
kings of Fesse, Moroco, and Argier, with others, in great pompe.	1Tamburlaine	3.1.0.1
Enter [aloofe] Tamburlaine with Techelles and others.	1Tamburlaine	3.2.24.1
and takes her away lovingly by the hand, looking wrathfully on	1Tamburlaine	3.2.65.1
by the hand, looking wrathfully on Agidas, and sayes nothing.	1Tamburlaine	3.2.65.2
[Enter Techelles and Usumcasane].	1Tamburlaine	3.2.106.2
his Bassoes and contributorie Kinges [and Zabina and Ebea].	1Tamburlaine	3.3.60.1
his Bassoes and contributorie Kinges [and Zabina and Ebea].	1Tamburlaine	3.3.60.2
They sound [to] the battell within, and stay.	1Tamburlaine	3.3.188.1
Bajazeth flies [over the stage], and he pursues him.	1Tamburlaine	3.3.211.1
The battell short, and they enter, Bajazeth is overcome.	1Tamburlaine	3.3.211.2
He takes it from her, and gives it Zenocrate.	1Tamburlaine	3.3.224.1
of Egipt with three or four Lords, Capolin [, and a Messenger].	1Tamburlaine	4.1.0.2
drawing Bajazeth in his cage, and his wife following him.	1Tamburlaine	4.2.0.2
Capoline, with [streaming] <steaming> collors and Souldiers.	1Tamburlaine	4.3.0.1
Banquet, and to it commeth Tamburlain al in scarlet, Theridamas,	1Tamburlaine	4.4.0.1
He takes it and stamps upon it.	1Tamburlaine	4.4.41.1
They give him water to drinke, and he flings it on the ground.	1Tamburlaine	4.4.55.1
and foure Virgins, with branches of Laurell in their hands.	1Tamburlaine	5.1.0.2
Tamburlaine all in blacke, and verie melancholy.	1Tamburlaine	5.1.63.3
They [Techelles and soldiers] take them away.	1Tamburlaine	5.1.120.1
Enter Techelles, Theridamas, Usumcasane, and others.	1Tamburlaine	5.1.195.2
They bring in the Turke [in his cage, and Zabina].	1Tamburlaine	5.1.202.1
Exeunt. [Manent Bajazeth and Zabina].	1Tamburlaine	5.1.213.1
She runs against the Cage and braines her selfe.	1Tamburlaine	5.1.318.1
And Tamburlaine enjoyes the victory, after Arabia enters	1Tamburlaine	5.1.402.1
<Upibassa>, and their traine, with drums and trumpets.	2Tamburlaine	1.1.0.2
Fredericke, Baldwine, and their traine with drums and trumpets.	2Tamburlaine	1.1.77.1
Fredericke, Baldwine, and their traine with drums and trumpets.	2Tamburlaine	1.1.77.2
Tamburlaine with Zenocrate, and his three sonnes, Calyphas,	2Tamburlaine	1.3.0.1
Calyphas, Amyras, and Celebinus, with drummes and trumpets.	2Tamburlaine	1.3.0.2
Enter Theridamas, and his traine with Drums and Trumpets.	2Tamburlaine	1.3.111.1
Enter Theridamas, and his traine with Drums and Trumpets.	2Tamburlaine	1.3.111.2
Enter Techelles and Usumcasane together.	2Tamburlaine	1.3.127.1
Sound to the battell, and Sigismond comes out wounded.	2Tamburlaine	2.3.0.1
Exit Uribassa [and soldiers with body].	2Tamburlaine	2.3.41.1
The Arras is drawen and Zenocrate lies in her bed of state,	2Tamburlaine	2.4.0.1
Theridamas, Techelles, Usumcasane, and the three sonnes.	2Tamburlaine	2.4.0.3
The musicke sounds, and she dies.	2Tamburlaine	2.4.95.1
Enter the kings of Trebisond and Soria, one bringing a sword,	2Tamburlaine	3.1.0.1
and Soria, one bringing a sword, and another a scepter:	2Tamburlaine	3.1.0.1
Next Natolia and Jerusalem with the Emperiall crowne:	2Tamburlaine	3.1.0.2
After Calapine, and after him other Lordes [and Almeda]:	2Tamburlaine	3.1.0.3
Orcanes and Jerusalem crowne him, and the other give him the	2Tamburlaine	3.1.0.4
and Jerusalem crowne him, and the other give him the scepter.	2Tamburlaine	3.1.0.4
Tamburlaine with Usumcasane, and his three sons, [Calyphas],	2Tamburlaine	3.2.0.1
[Amyras, and Celebinus], foure bearing the hearse of Zenocrate,	2Tamburlaine	3.2.0.2
and the drums sounding a doleful martch, the Towne burning.	2Tamburlaine	3.2.0.2
[Enter] Techelles, Theridamas and their traine.	2Tamburlaine	3.3.0.1
[Enter above] Captaine with his wife [Olympia] and sonne.	2Tamburlaine	3.3.14.2
Enter [below] the Captaine with [Olympia] his wife and sonne.	2Tamburlaine	3.4.0.2
Enter Theridamas, Techelles and all their traine.	2Tamburlaine	3.4.33.2
Enter Theridamas, Techelles, and their traine.	2Tamburlaine	3.5.146.1
Amyras and Celebinus, issues from the tent where Caliphas sits	2Tamburlaine	4.1.0.1
Alarme, and Amyras and Celebinus run in.	2Tamburlaine	4.1.51.1
He goes in and brings him out.	2Tamburlaine	4.1.90.1
his chariot by Trebizon and Soria with bittes in their mouthes,	2Tamburlaine	4.3.0.1
and Jerusalem led by with five or six common souldiers.	2Tamburlaine	4.3.0.4
Governour of Babylon upon the walles with [Maximus and] others.	2Tamburlaine	5.1.0.2
Enter Theridamas and Techelles, with other souldiers.	2Tamburlaine	5.1.48.1
Alarme, and they scale the walles.	2Tamburlaine	5.1.62.1
[drawn in his chariot by the kings of Trebizon and Soria], with	2Tamburlaine	5.1.62.3
Amyras, and Celebinus, with others, the two spare kings	2Tamburlaine	5.1.62.3
King of Natolia, and King of Jerusalem, led by souldiers].	2Tamburlaine	5.1.62.4
Theridamas and Techelles bringing the Governor of Babylon.	2Tamburlaine	5.1.79.1
[Exit with the Kings of Trebizon and Soria].	2Tamburlaine	5.1.135.1
Amasia, [Captaine, Souldiers], with drums and trumpets.	2Tamburlaine	5.2.0.2
Tamburlaine goes in, and comes out againe with al the rest.	2Tamburlaine	5.3.114.1
Knights [and Officers], met by [Callapine and other] Bassoes of	Jew of Malta	1.2.0.1
met by [Callapine and other] Bassoes of the Turke; Calymath.	Jew of Malta	1.2.0.2
Enter Barabas, and three Jewes.	Jew of Malta	1.2.36.1
Exeunt. [Manent Barabas and the three Jewes].	Jew of Malta	1.2.159.1
<three> Fryars and [three] <two> Nuns [, one the Abbasse].	Jew of Malta	1.2.304.1
Enter Governor, Martin del Bosco, the Knights [and Officers].	Jew of Malta	2.2.0.1
Exeunt [Mater and slave].	Jew of Malta	2.3.158.1
[Exeunt Lodowicke and Abigall].	Jew of Malta	2.3.241.1
Enter [the] two Fryars <and Abigall>.	Jew of Malta	3.6.0.1
Exit [Ithimore and 2. Fryar].	Jew of Malta	4.1.101.1

AND (cont.)

Enter [come forward] Barabas [and Ithimore].	Jew of Malta		4.1.173.1
Enter Curtezane, and Pilia-borza.	Jew of Malta		4.2.0.1
Enter Turkes, Barabas, Governour, and Knights prisoners. .	Jew of Malta		5.2.0.1
Enter Calymath and Bashawes.	Jew of Malta		5.5.50.1
Enter del Bosco and Knights].	Jew of Malta		5.5.63.3
Admirall, and [Margaret] the Queene of Navarre, with others.	Paris	0.3	1.0.3
and [Margaret] the Queene of Navar [with others], and manet	Paris	26.2	1.26.2
of Navar [with others], and manet Navar, the Prince of Condy,	Paris	26.3	1.26.3
manet Navar, the Prince of Condy, and the Lord high Admirall.	Paris	26.4	1.26.4
Enter the King of Navar and Queen [Margaret], and his [olde]	Paris	166.1	3.0.1
and his [olde] Mother Queen [of Navarre], the Prince of Condy,	Paris	166.1	3.0.1
and the Pothecary with the gloves, and gives them to the olde	Paris	166.2	3.0.2
Pothecary with the gloves, and gives them to the olde Queene.	Paris	166.3	3.0.3
who] dischargeth his Musket at the Lord Admirall [and exit].	Paris	196.2	3.31.2
They beare away the [olde] Queene [of Navarre] and goe out.	Paris	202.1	3.37.1
Anjoy, Duke Demayne [and Cossin, Captain of the Kings Guard].	Paris	203.2	4.0.2
Gonzago, Retes, Montsorrell, and Souldiers to the massacre.	Paris	274.1	5.0.1
Exit Gonzago and others with him.	Paris	292.1	5.19.1
Enter [above Gonzago and others] into the Admirals house, and	Paris	297.1	5.24.1
Gonzago and others] into the Admirals house, and he in his bed.	Paris	297.1	5.24.1
Exeunt Gonzago and rest above].	Paris	306.1	5.33.1
Enter Loreine running, the Guise and the rest pursuing him.	Paris	338.2	5.65.2
Enter Mountsorrell and knocks at Serouns doore. . .	Paris	346.1	6.0.1
Stab him [and he falls within and dies].	Paris	360.1	6.15.1
Enter Gonzago and Retes.	Paris	370.1	7.10.1
Enter the Guise and Anjoy [, Dumaine, Mountsorrell, with .	Paris	379.1	7.19.1
and enter the King of Navarre and Prince of Condy, with their	Paris	429.1	7.69.1
Exeunt [Condy and Navarre].	Paris	440.1	7.80.1
Exit Anjoy [and soldiers with bodies].	Paris	442.1	7.82.1
of Guise, and Queene Mother, and the Cardinall [of Loraine].	Paris	493.2	9.12.2
five or sixe Protestants with bookes, and kneele together.	Paris	528.1	10.0.1
Enter also the Guise [and others].	Paris	528.2	10.0.2
[Charles] the King of France, Navar and Epernoune staying him:	Paris	536.1	11.0.1
enter Queene Mother, and the Cardinall [of Loraine, and Pleshe].	Paris	536.2	11.0.2
Queene Mother, and the Cardinall [of Loraine, and Pleshe].	Paris	536.2	11.0.2
All goe out, but Navarre and Pleshe.	Paris	564.1	11.29.1
and then all crye vive [le] <la> Roy two or three times. .	Paris	588.1	12.0.1
[Mugeroun], the kings Minions, with others, and the Cutpurse.	Paris	588.5	12.0.5
Goe out all, but the Queene [Mother] and the Cardinall.	Paris	630.1	12.43.1
Enter the Duchesse of Guise, and her Maide.	Paris	657.1	13.0.1
Enter the Maid with Inke and Paper.	Paris	665.1	13.9.1
Enter the King of Navarre, Pleshe and Bartus, and their train,	Paris	698.1	14.0.1
Pleshe and Bartus, and their train, with drums and trumpets.	Paris	698.1	14.0.1
Pleshe and Bartus, and their train, with drums and trumpets.	Paris	698.2	14.0.2
the King of France, Duke of Guise, Epernoune, and Duke Joyeux.	Paris	743.2	15.0.2
Enter the King of Navarre [, Bartus], and his traine. .	Paris	787.2	16.0.2
He shootes at him and killes him.	Paris	816.2	17.11.2
Enter the King and Epernoune.	Paris	820.2	17.15.2
Enter one with a pen and inke.	Paris	881.1	17.76.1
Enter the King of Navarre reading of a letter, and Bartus.	Paris	900.1	18.0.1
Enter the Captaine of the guarde, and three murtherers. .	Paris	931.1	19.0.1
Enter the King and Epernoune.	Paris	946.1	19.16.1
Enter the Guise [within] and knocketh.	Paris	955.1	19.25.1
Exit King [and Epernoune].	Paris	976.1	19.46.1
[Enter King and Epernoune attended].	Paris	1017.1	19.87.1
Exit the King and Epernoune.	Paris	1080.1	19.150.1
Sound Drumme and Trumpets, and enter the King of France, and	Paris	1139.1	22.0.1
Drumme and Trumpets, and enter the King of France, and Navarre,	Paris	1139.1	22.0.1
and enter the King of France, and Navarre, Epernoune, Bartus,	Paris	1139.1	22.0.1
France, and Navarre, Epernoune, Bartus, Pleshe and Souldiers.	Paris	1139.2	22.0.2
the letter, and then the King getteth the knife and killes him.	Paris	1172.2	22.34.2
Enter both the Mortimers, Warwicke, and Lancaster. . .	Edward II		1.2.0.1
Enter the [Archbishop] of Canterburie [and attendant]. .	Edward II		1.2.32.1
Enter Gaveston and the earle of Kent.	Edward II		1.3.0.1
Enter the King and Gaveston [and Kent].	Edward II		1.4.7.1
[Exeunt Kent and Gaveston guarded].	Edward II		1.4.34.1
Exeunt Edward and Gaveston.	Edward II		1.4.169.1
[Exeunt Clarke and Beamont].	Edward II		1.4.372.1
Enter Spencer and Balduck.	Edward II		2.1.0.1
Exit the King [, Queene, and Kent].	Edward II		2.2.99.1
[Enter the King and Kent].	Edward II		2.2.138.1
of these Neece to the King, Gaveston], Baldock, and Spencer.	Edward II		2.2.224.2
Enter [at several doors] the King and Spencer, to them .	Edward II		2.4.0.1
and Penbrookes men, foure souldiers [, one of them James].	Edward II		2.5.98.2
Exeunt ambo [Penbrooke and Arundell, attended]. . .	Edward II		2.5.111.1
and the earle of Penbrookes men [, James and three souldiers].	Edward II		2.6.0.1
and the earle of Penbrookes men [, James and three souldiers].	Edward II		2.6.0.2
Enter Warwicke and his companie.	Edward II		2.6.6.1
Exeunt Warwicke and his men, with Gaveston. . . .	Edward II		2.6.17.1
Enter king Edward and Spencer, [Baldock], with Drummes and	Edward II		3.1.0.1
king Edward and Spencer, [Baldock], with Drummes and Fifes.	Edward II		3.1.0.2
father to the yong Spencer, with his trunchion, and soldiers.	Edward II		3.1.31.2
Enter the Queene and her sonne, and [Levune] <Lewne> a .	Edward II		3.1.58.1
the Queene and her sonne, and [Levune] <Lewne> a Frenchman.	Edward II		3.1.58.1
Edward kneels, and saith.	Edward II		3.1.127.1
Alarums, excursions, a great fight, and a retreate. . .	Edward II		3.1.184.2
father, Spencer the sonne, and the noblemen of the kings side.	Edward II		3.1.184.4
Enter Edward, with the Barons [and Kent] captives. . .	Edward II		3.1.220.2
Manent Spencer filius, [Levune] <Lewne> and Baldock. .	Edward II		3.1.261.2
Enter the Queene and her sonne.	Edward II		4.2.0.1
Enter Edmund [earle of Kent] and Mortimer.	Edward II		4.2.34.1
her sonne, Edmund [earle of Kent], Mortimer, and sir John.	Edward II		4.4.0.2

AND (cont.)

King, Baldock, and Spencer the sonne, flying about the stage.	Edward II		4.5.0.1
[Enter] Edmund [earle of Kent] alone with a sword and target.	Edward II		4.6.0.1
the Queene, Mortimer, the young Prince and Sir John of Henolt.	Edward II		4.6.18.1
and the Maior of Bristow, with Spencer the father.	Edward II		4.6.45.2
Monkes, Edward, Spencer, and Baldocke [disguised as monks].	Edward II		4.7.0.1
hookes, Rice ap Howell, a Mower, and the Earle of Leicester.	Edward II		4.7.45.2
Exeunt Edward and Leicester.	Edward II		4.7.99.1
with a Bishop [of Winchester] for the crowne [and Trussell].	Edward II		5.1.0.2
[Exeunt Bishop of Winchester and Trussell].	Edward II		5.1.124.1
Enter Mortimer, and Queene Isabell.	Edward II		5.2.0.1
Enter Messenger [and then Bishop of Winchester with the crown].	Edward II		5.2.22.1
Enter Matrevis and Gurney.	Edward II		5.2.45.1
Exeunt Matrevis and Gurney.	Edward II		5.2.73.1
Manent Isabell and Mortimer.	Edward II		5.2.73.1
Enter the yong Prince, and the Earle of Kent talking with him.	Edward II		5.2.73.2
Enter Matrevis and Gurney with the King [and souldiers].	Edward II		5.3.0.1
They wash him with puddle water, and shave his beard away.	Edward II		5.3.36.1
Exeunt Matrevis and Gurney, with the king.	Edward II		5.3.62.1
Manent Edmund and the souldiers.	Edward II		5.3.62.2
They hale Edmund away, and carie him to be beheaded.	Edward II		5.4.108.1
Enter Matrevis and Gurney.	Edward II		5.5.0.1
[Exeunt Matrevis and Gurney].	Edward II		5.5.37.1
[Enter Matrevis, Gurney, and exeunt.	Edward II		5.5.109.1
Enter Mortimer and Matrevis [at different doors].	Edward II		5.6.0.1
[Exit Queene and 2. Lord].	Edward II		5.6.92.1
Enter the <good> Angell and Spirit <the evill Angell>.	Faustus	96.1	1.1.68.1
Enter Valdes and Cornelius.	Faustus	126.1	1.1.98.1
Enter Lucifer and foure devils [above], Faustus to them with	Faustus	229.1	1.3.0.1
Exeunt [Faustus; Lucifer and devils above].	Faustus	342.1	1.3.114.1
Enter Wagner and [Robin] the Clowne.	Faustus	343.1	1.4.0.1
Enter the two Angels <Enter good Angell, and Evill>.	Faustus	402.1	2.1.14.1
<with> Devils, giving Crownes and rich apparell to Faustus:	Faustus	471.2	2.1.83.2
they <and> dance, and then depart.	Faustus	471.3	2.1.83.3
Enter Faustus in his Study, and Mephostophilis.	Faustus	552.1	2.2.0.1
Enter the two Angels <good Angel, and evill Angell>.	Faustus	562.1	2.2.11.1
Enter Lucifer, Belzebub, and Mephostophilis.	Faustus	635.1	2.2.84.1
Enter Faustus and Mephostophilis.	Faustus	779.1	3.1.0.1
Enter the Cardinals and Bishops, some bearing Crosiers, some	Faustus	867.1	3.1.89.1
some the Pillars, Monkes and Friers, singing their Procession:	Faustus	867.2	3.1.89.2
Pope, and Raymond King of Hungary, with Bruno led in chaines.	Faustus	867.3	3.1.89.3
Exeunt Faustus and Mephostophilis.	Faustus	903.1	3.1.125.1
Enter Faustus and Mephostophilis like the Cardinals.	Faustus	939.1	3.1.161.1
Exeunt Faustus and Mephostophilis [with Bruno].	Faustus	976.1	3.1.198.1
and then Enter Faustus and Mephostophilis in their owne shapes.	Faustus	981.1	3.2.0.1
and then Enter Faustus and Mephostophilis in their owne shapes.	Faustus	981.2	3.2.0.2
Enter Pope and all the Lords.	Faustus	1008.1	3.2.28.1
Exeunt the Pope and his traine.	Faustus	1070.1	3.2.90.1
Enter the Friers with Bell, Booke, and Candle, for the Dirge.	Faustus	1075.1	3.2.95.1
Beate the Friers, fling fire workes among them, and Exeunt.	Faustus	1087.2	3.2.107.2
Enter [Robin the] Clowne and Dicke, with a Cup.	Faustus	1088.1	3.3.0.1
Enter Martino, and Frederick at severall dores.	Faustus	1155.1	4.1.0.1
Exeunt [Martino and Fredericke].	Faustus	1203.1	4.1.49.1
Faustus, Mephostophilis, Fredericke, Martino, and Attendants.	Faustus	1203.3	4.1.49.3
his Crowne, and offering to goe out, his Paramour meetes him,	Faustus	1257.4	4.1.103.4
her, and sets Darius Crowne upon her head; and comming backe,	Faustus	1257.5	4.1.103.5
upon her head; and comming backe, both salute the Emperour,	Faustus	1257.5	4.1.103.5
Then trumpets cease, and Musicke sounds.	Faustus	1257.8	4.1.103.8
Enter Benvolio, Martino, Fredericke, and Souldiers.	Faustus	1325.1	4.2.0.1
Enter Mephostophilis and other Divels.	Faustus	1402.1	4.2.78.1
and enter a devill playing on a Drum, after him another bearing	Faustus	1430.1	4.2.106.1
and divers with weapons, Mephostophilis with fire-workes; they	Faustus	1430.2	4.2.106.2
fire-workes; they set upon the Souldiers and drive them out.	Faustus	1430.3	4.2.106.3
Fredericke, and Martino, their heads and faces bloudy, and	Faustus	1431.1	4.3.0.1
their heads and faces bloudy, and besmear'd with mud and durt;	Faustus	1431.2	4.3.0.2
and besmear'd with mud and durt; all having hornes on their	Faustus	1431.2	4.3.0.2
and besmear'd with mud and durt; all having hornes on their	Faustus	1431.3	4.3.0.3
Enter Faustus, and the Horse-courser <and Mephistophilis>.	Faustus	1457.1	4.4.0.1
Enter [Robin the] Clowne, Dick, Horse-courser, and a Carter.	Faustus	1505.1	4.5.0.1
the Duke of Vanholt; his Dutches, Faustus, and Mephostophilis.	Faustus	1558.2	4.6.0.2
They knocke againe, and call out to talke with Faustus.	Faustus	1590.1	4.6.33.1
Enter [Robin] the Clowne, Dick, Carter, and Horse-courser.	Faustus	1608.1	4.6.51.1
Thunder and lightning:	Faustus	1674.1	5.1.0.1
Enter Faustus, Mephostophilis, and two or three Schollers.	Faustus	1680.2	5.1.7.2
brings in Hellen, she <and Helen> passeth over the stage.	Faustus	1696.2	5.1.23.2
Enter [above] Lucifer, Belzebub, and Mephostophilis.	Faustus	1797.1	5.2.0.1
Enter Faustus and Wagner.	Faustus	1815.1	5.2.19.1
Enter the Good Angell, and the Bad Angell at severall doores.	Faustus	1891.2	5.2.95.2
<Thunder and lightning>.	Faustus	1976.1A	HC p271
Thunder, and enter the devils.	Faustus	1978.1	5.2.182.1
[Exeunt Lucifer and devils above].	Faustus	1982.2	5.2.186.2
Enter Wagner and the Clowne.	Faustus App.		p229 0.1
Enter two divells, and the clowne runnes up and downe crying.	Faustus App.		p230 49.1
Enter two divells, and the clowne runnes up and downe crying.	Faustus App.		p230 49.2
enter the Pope and the Cardinall of Lorraine to the banket,	Faustus App.		p231 0.1
and Faustus hits him a boxe of the eare, and they all runne	Faustus App.		p232 21.1
Faustus hits him a boxe of the eare, and they all runne away.	Faustus App.		p232 21.2
the Friers, and fling fier-workes among them, and so Exeunt.	Faustus App.		p233 41.1
the Friers, and fling fier-workes among them, and so Exeunt.	Faustus App.		p233 41.2
Enter Robin and Rafe with a silver Goblet.	Faustus App.		p234 0.1
Enter Emperour, Faustus, and a Knight, with Attendants.	Faustus App.		p236 0.1
with Alexander and his paramour.	Faustus App.		p238 59.1
Pull him by the legge, and pull it away.	Faustus App.		p241 53.1

AND (cont.)			
Enter to them the Duke, and the Dutches, the Duke speakes.	Faustus App.	p242	0.1
ANGEL			
Enter the two Angels <good Angel, and evill Angell>.	Faustus	562.1	2.2.11.1
ANGELL			
Enter the <good> Angell and Spirit <the evill Angell>.	Faustus	96.1	1.1.68.1
Enter the two Angels <Enter good Angell, and Evill>.	Faustus	402.1	2.1.14.1
Enter the two Angels <good Angel, and evill Angell>.	Faustus	562.1	2.2.11.1
Enter the Good Angell, and the Bad Angell at severall doores.	Faustus	1891.2	5.2.95.2
ANGELS			
Exeunt Angels.	Faustus	104.1	1.1.76.1
Enter the two Angels <Enter good Angell, and Evill>.	Faustus	402.1	2.1.14.1
Exeunt Angels.	Faustus	410.1	2.1.22.1
Enter the two Angels <good Angel, and evill Angell>.	Faustus	562.1	2.2.11.1
Exeunt Angels.	Faustus	568.1	2.2.17.1
Enter the two Angels.	Faustus	629.1	2.2.78.1
Exeunt Angels.	Faustus	633.1	2.2.82.1
ANHOLT (See VANHOLT)			
ANIPPE			
[Enter] Agidas, Zenocrate, Anippe, with others.	1Tamburlaine		3.2.0.1
Theridamas, Bassoe, Zenocrate, [Anippe], with others.	1Tamburlaine		3.3.0.2
Zenocrate, Anippe, two Moores drawing Bajazeth in his cage, and	1Tamburlaine		4.2.0.2
Enter Zenocrate wyth Anippe.	1Tamburlaine		5.1.318.2
ANJOY			
Duke of Guise, Duke Anjoy, Duke Demayne [and Cossin, Captain o	Paris	203.2	4.0.2
Enter Guise, Anjoy, Dumaine, Gonzago, Retes, Montsorrell, and	Paris	274.1	5.0.1
Enter the Guise and Anjoy [, Dumaine, Mountsorrell, with	Paris	379.1	7.19.1
Exit Anjoy [and soldiers with bodies].	Paris	442.1	7.82.1
Enter Anjoy, with two Lords of Poland.	Paris	451.1	8.0.1
ANNA			
Enter Dido [with Anna and Iarbus] and her traine.	Dido		2.1.73.1
Enter Iarbus, Anna, and Dido.	Dido		3.1.6.1
Exit Anna.	Dido		3.1.79.1
Enter Dido, Aeneas, Anna, Iarbus, Achates, [Cupid for	Dido		3.3.0.1
Enter Achates, [Cupid for] Ascanius, Iarbus, and Anna.	Dido		4.1.0.1
Enter Anna.	Dido		4.2.22.1
Enter Dido and Anna [with traine].	Dido		4.4.0.1
[Exit Anna].	Dido		4.4.4.1
Enter Anna, with Aeneas, Achates, Illioneus, and Sergestus.	Dido		4.4.13.1
[Enter Anna].	Dido		5.1.192.1
Exit Anna.	Dido		5.1.211.1
Enter Anna.	Dido		5.1.225.1
Exit Anna.	Dido		5.1.278.1
Enter Anna.	Dido		5.1.313.2
ANOINT (See NOINTS)			
ANOTHER			
Enter Venus [with Cupid] at another doore, and takes Ascanius	Dido		2.1.303.2
and Soria, one bringing a sword, and another a scepter:	2Tamburlaine		3.1.0.2.
Enter another [1. Citizen], kneeling to the Governour.	2Tamburlaine		5.1.23.1
devill playing on a Drum, after him another bearing an Ensigne:	Faustus	1430.2	4.2.106.2
AP			
Enter Rice ap Howell, and the Maior of Bristow, with Spencer	Edward II		4.6.45.2
Enter with Welch hookes, Rice ap Howell, a Mower, and the Earle	Edward II		4.7.45.1
APART			
[They talk apart].	Faustus	890.1	3.1.112.1
APOTHECARY (See POTHECAIER)			
APPARELL			
<with> Devils, giving Crownes and rich apparell to Faustus:	Faustus	471.2	2.1.83.2
ARABIA			
[Enter] Souldane, Arabia, Capoline, with [streaming] <steaming>	1Tamburlaine		4.3.0.1
Tamburlaine enjoyes the victory, after Arabia enters wounded.	1Tamburlaine		5.1.402.2
ARCHBISHOP			
Enter the [Archbishop] of Canterburie [and attendant].	Edward II		1.2.32.1
Mortimer junior, the Archbishop of Canterburie, attended].	Edward II		1.4.0.2
Enter the yong King, [Archbishop] [of Canterbury], Champion,	Edward II		5.4.72.1
ARE			
The Concubines are brought in.	2Tamburlaine		4.3.66.1
[As they are leaving] Enter Mathias.	Jew of Malta		1.2.365.1
As they are going, [enter] the Souldier [above, who]	Paris	196.1	3.31.1
ARGIER			
kings of Fesse, Moroco, and Argier, with others, in great pompe.	1Tamburlaine		3.1.0.1
ARME			
He cuts his arme.	2Tamburlaine		3.2.114.1
ARMES			
Enter the Herald from the Barons, with his coate of armes.	Edward II		3.1.150.2
ARRAS			
The Arras is drawen and Zenocrate lies in her bed of state,	2Tamburlaine		2.4.0.1
The Arras is drawen.	2Tamburlaine		2.4.142.1
ARUNDELL			
Enter earle of Arundell.	Edward II		2.5.31.1
Manent Penbrooke, [Arundell] <Mat.>, Gaveston, and Penbrookes	Edward II		2.5.98.2
Exeunt ambo [Penbrooke and Arundell, attended].	Edward II		2.5.111.1
Enter lord [Arundell].	Edward II		3.1.88.1
Enter the King, [Arundell] <Matr.>, the two Spencers, with	Edward II		4.3.0.1
AS			
doore, and takes Ascanius by the sleeve [as he is going off].	Dido		2.1.303.3
[Enter] Machevil [as Prologue].	Jew of Malta		Prol.0.1
[As they are leaving] Enter Mathias.	Jew of Malta		1.2.365.1
[Enter Officers carrying Barabas, as dead].	Jew of Malta		5.1.53.1
As they are going, [enter] the Souldier [above, who]	Paris	196.1	3.31.1
[The murtherers go aside as if in the next room].	Paris	943.1	19.13.1
He stabs the King with a knife as he readeth the letter, and	Paris	1172.1	22.34.1
Monkes, Edward, Spencer, and Baldocke [disguised as monks].	Edward II		4.7.0.2

ASCANIUS			
Enter Aeneas with Ascanius [and Achates], with one or two more.	Dido		1.1.133.1
[Exit Ascanius with cthers].	Dido		1.1.177.1
Enter Aeneas, Achates, and Ascanius [attended].	Dido		2.1.0.1
dcore, and takes Ascanius by the sleeve [as he is going off].	Dido		2.1.303.3
Enter Cupid solus [for Ascanius].	Dido		3.1.0.1
Enter Juno to Ascanius asleepe.	Dido		3.2.0.1
Anna, Iarbus, Achates, [Cupid for Ascanius], and followers.	Dido		3.3.0.2
Enter Achates, [Cupid for] Ascanius, Iarbus, and Anna.	Dido		4.1.0.1
Enter the Nurse with Cupid for Ascanius.	Dido		4.5.0.1
Enter Hermes with Ascanius.	Dido		5.1.23.1
[Exit Sergestus with Ascanius].	Dido		5.1.50.1
ASCENDS			
A Flourish while he ascends.	Faustus	876.1	3.1.98.1
Exit. [Throne ascends].	Faustus	1908.1	5.2.112.1
ASIDE			
[Aside].	Dido		1.1.169.1
[Aside].	Dido		3.1.61.1
[Aside].	Dido		3.1.154.1
[Aside].	Dido		3.3.46.1
[Aside].	1Tamburlaine		1.2.106.1
[Aside].	1Tamburlaine		1.2.107.1
[Aside].	1Tamburlaine		1.2.154.1
Aside.	Jew of Malta		1.1.152.1
Aside.	Jew of Malta		1.1.173.1
[Aside].	Jew of Malta		1.2.71.1
[Aside].	Jew of Malta		1.2.75.1
Aside.	Jew of Malta		1.2.336.1
[Aside to her].	Jew of Malta		1.2.356.1
Aside to her.	Jew of Malta		1.2.359.1
Aside to her.	Jew of Malta		1.2.361.1
Aside.	Jew of Malta		1.2.364.1
[Aside].	Jew of Malta		1.2.392.1
[Aside].	Jew of Malta		2.3.42.1
Aside.	Jew of Malta		2.3.51.1
[Aside].	Jew of Malta		2.3.57.1
Aside.	Jew of Malta		2.3.60.1
Aside.	Jew of Malta		2.3.63.1
[Aside].	Jew of Malta		2.3.64.1
Aside.	Jew of Malta		2.3.67.1
Aside.	Jew of Malta		2.3.82.1
Aside.	Jew of Malta		2.3.88.1
Aside.	Jew of Malta		2.3.94.1
[Aside].	Jew of Malta		2.3.132.1
[Aside].	Jew of Malta		2.3.139.1
[Aside].	Jew of Malta		2.3.143.1
Aside.	Jew of Malta		2.3.228.1
[Aside].	Jew of Malta		2.3.234.1
[Aside].	Jew of Malta		2.3.287.1
Aside.	Jew of Malta		2.3.301.1
[Aside].	Jew of Malta		2.3.316.1
[Aside].	Jew of Malta		2.3.319.1
[Aside].	Jew of Malta		2.3.323.1
[Aside].	Jew of Malta		3.3.73.1
Aside.	Jew of Malta		4.1.47.1
[Aside to 2. Fryar].	Jew of Malta		4.1.81.1
[Aside to 2. Fryar].	Jew of Malta		4.1.83.1
[Aside to 1. Fryar].	Jew of Malta		4.1.86.1
[Aside to 1. Fryar].	Jew of Malta		4.1.89.1
[Aside to 2. Fryar].	Jew of Malta		4.1.91.1
[Aside to 2. Fryar].	Jew of Malta		4.1.100.1
[They go aside].	Jew of Malta		4.1.159.1
[Aside].	Jew of Malta		4.2.39.1
[Aside].	Jew of Malta		4.2.47.1
[Aside].	Jew of Malta		4.2.50.1
[Aside to Pilia-borza].	Jew of Malta		4.2.62.1
[Throw it aside].	Jew of Malta		4.2.125.1
Aside.	Jew of Malta		4.3.30.1
[Aside].	Jew of Malta		4.3.39.1
[Aside].	Jew of Malta		4.3.51.1
[Aside to Bellamira].	Jew of Malta		4.4.25.1
[Aside to Pilia-borza].	Jew of Malta		4.4.26.1
[Aside].	Jew of Malta		4.4.42.1
Aside.	Jew of Malta		4.4.48.1
Aside.	Jew of Malta		4.4.50.1
Aside.	Jew of Malta		4.4.53.1
[Aside].	Jew of Malta		4.4.60.1
Aside.	Jew of Malta		4.4.63.1
Aside.	Jew of Malta		4.4.65.1
Aside.	Jew of Malta		4.4.68.1
[Aside].	Jew of Malta		5.1.22.1
[They take body aside].	Jew of Malta		5.1.59.1
[Aside].	Paris	26.1	1.26.1
[Aside].	Paris	865.1	17.60.1
[The murtherers go aside as if in the next room].	Paris	943.1	19.13.1
[Aside].	Edward II		1.1.77.1
[Aside].	Edward II		2.5.95.1
[Aside].	Edward II		4.6.45.1
[Aside].	Edward II		4.6.59.1
[Aside].	Edward II		4.6.62.1
[Aside].	Edward II		4.7.49.1
[Aside].	Edward II		5.2.86.1
[aside].	Faustus	462.1	2.1.74.1

ASIDE (cont.)			
aside.	Faustus App.		p236 11.1
aside.	Faustus App.		p237 40.1
aside.	Faustus App.		p237 45.1
A SLEEPE			
Celebinus, issues from the tent where Caliphas sits a sleepe.	2Tamburlaine		4.1.0.2
ASLEEPE			
Ganimed upon his knee, and Mercury lying asleepe.	Dido		1.1.0.3
Enter Juno to Ascanius asleepe.	Dido		3.2.0.1
AT			
Enter Venus [with Cupid] at another doore, and takes Ascanius	Dido		2.1.303.2
Enter Aeneas and Dido in the Cave at severall times.	Dido		3.4.0.2
who] dischargeth his Musket at the Lord Admirall [and exit].	Paris	196.2	3.31.2
Enter Mountsorrell and knocks at Serouns doore.	Paris	346.1	6.0.1
He makes hornes at the Guise.	Paris	753.1	15.11.1
He shootes at him and killes him.	Paris	816.2	17.11.2
Enter [at several doors] the King and Spencer, to them	Edward II		2.4.0.1
Enter Mortimer and Matrevis [at different doors].	Edward II		5.6.0.1
Enter Martino, and Frederick at severall dores.	Faustus	1155.1	4.1.0.1
Enter Benvolio above at a window, in his nightcap:	Faustus	1178.1	4.1.24.1
Enter at one [dore] the Emperour Alexander, at the other	Faustus	1257.2	4.1.103.2
[dore] the Emperour Alexander, at the other Darius; they meete,	Faustus	1257.2	4.1.103.2
Enter at severall dores, Benvolio, Fredericke, and Martino,	Faustus	1431.1	4.3.0.1
The [Clownes] <Clowne> bounce at the gate, within.	Faustus	1587.1	4.6.30.1
Enter the Good Angell, and the Bad Angell at severall doores.	Faustus	1891.3	5.2.95.3
sets squibs at their backes:	Faustus App.		p235 25.1
ATTENDANT			
[Exit attendant].	Paris	1021.1	19.91.1
[Exit attendant].	Paris	1179.1	22.41.1
Enter the [Archbishop] of Canterburie [and attendant].	Edward II		1.2.32.1
[Exit attendant].	Edward II		1.2.38.1
ATTENDANTS			
Exeunt the Nurse [and Attendants].	Dido		5.1.224.1
[Enter Attendants with wood and fire].	Dido		5.1.282.1
[Exeunt attendants].	1Tamburlaine		5.1.195.1
Exit [the attendants taking up body of the Guise].	Paris	1090.1	19.160.1
[Exeunt attendants with body].	Paris	1182.1	22.44.1
Mortimer [junior], Warwicke, Penbrooke, Kent, attendants.	Edward II		2.2.0.2
Faustus, Mephostophilis, Fredericke, Martino, and Attendants.	Faustus	1203.4	4.1.49.4
Enter Emperour, Faustus, and a Knight, with Attendants.	Faustus App.		p236 0.2
ATTENDED			
Enter Aeneas, Achates, and Ascanius [attended].	Dido		2.1.0.1
Exeunt [attended].	Dido		4.4.165.1
Enter Dido [attended] [to] <and> Aeneas.	Dido		5.1.82.1
Exeunt [attended].	1Tamburlaine		1.1.188.1
Enter Governor, Mater [attended].	Jew of Malta		3.2.9.2
Enter the Guise [attended].	Paris	816.3	17.11.3
[Enter King and Epernoune attended].	Paris	1017.1	19.87.1
Enter Queene Mother [attended].	Paris	1063.1	19.133.1
Mortimer junior, the Archbishop of Canterburie, attended].	Edward II		1.4.0.2
Enter king Edward moorning [attended].	Edward II		1.4.304.1
[Exit Gaveston, attended].	Edward II		2.2.86.1
Exeunt ambo [Penbrooke and Arundell, attended].	Edward II		2.5.111.1
Exit [attended].	Edward II		3.1.261.1
[Exit Mortimer with 1. Lord attended].	Edward II		5.6.67.1
[Exeunt Cardinals attended].	Faustus	1034.1	3.2.54.1
ATTENDING			
the Cardinall of Lorraine to the banket, with Friers attending.	Faustus App.		p231 0.2
AWAY			
and takes her away lovingly by the hand, looking wrathfully on	1Tamburlaine		3.2.65.1
They [Techelles and soldiers] take them away.	1Tamburlaine		5.1.120.1
Exit, taking her away.	2Tamburlaine		4.2.98.1
They run away with the Ladies.	2Tamburlaine		4.3.84.1
They beare away the [olde] Queene [of Navarre] and goe out.	Paris	202.1	3.37.1
Carry away the dead body.	Paris	499.1	9.18.1
Take him away.	Paris	820.1	17.15.1
They wash him with puddle water, and shave his beard away.	Edward II		5.3.36.1
They hale Edmund away, and carie him to be beheaded.	Edward II		5.4.108.1
Faustus hits him a boxe of the eare, and they all runne away.	Faustus App.		p232 21.2
Pull him by the legge, and pull it away.	Faustus App.		p241 53.1
Horsecourser runnes away.	Faustus App.		p241 63.1
BABYLON			
Governour of Babylon upon the walles with [Maximus and] others.	2Tamburlaine		5.1.0.1
Theridamas and Techelles bringing the Governor of Babylon.	2Tamburlaine		5.1.79.2
hang the Governour of Babylon in chaines on the walles].	2Tamburlaine		5.1.148.2
BACK			
[Offers to go back].	Edward II		2.2.140.1
BACKE			
upon her head; and comming backe, both salute the Emperour,	Faustus	1257.6	4.1.103.6
BACKES			
sets squibs at their backes:	Faustus App.		p235 25.1
BAD			
Enter the Good Angell, and the Bad Angell at severall doores.	Faustus	1891.2	5.2.95.2
BAG			
[Gives him bag].	Jew of Malta		4.2.101.1
BAGS			
Throwes downe bags.	Jew of Malta		2.1.46.1
Hugs his bags.	Jew of Malta		2.1.54.1
BAJAZETH			
[Enter] Bajazeth, the kings of Fesse, Moroco, and Argier, with	1Tamburlaine		3.1.0.1
Bajazeth with his Bassoes and contributorie Kinges [and Zabina	1Tamburlaine		3.3.60.1
Bajazeth flies [over the stage], and he pursues him.	1Tamburlaine		3.3.211.1
The battell short, and they enter, Bajazeth is overcome.	1Tamburlaine		3.3.211.2

BAJAZETH (cont.)		
two Moores drawing Bajazeth in his cage, and his wife following	1Tamburlaine	4.2.0.2
Exeunt. [Manent Bajazeth and Zabina].	1Tamburlaine	5.1.213.1
BALDOCK		
Exit [Baldock].	Edward II	2.1.74.1
of these Neece to the king, Gaveston], Baldock, and Spencer.	Edward II	2.2.224.2
king Edward and Spencer, [Baldock], with Drummes and Fifes.	Edward II	3.1.0.1
Manent Spencer filius, [Levune] <Lewne> and Baldock.	Edward II	3.1.261.2
Enter the King, Baldock, and Spencer the sonne, flying about	Edward II	4.5.0.1
BALDOCKE		
Monkes, Edward, Spencer, and Baldocke [disguised as monks].	Edward II	4.7.0.1
BALDUCK		
Enter Spencer and Balduck.	Edward II	2.1.0.1
BALDWINE		
Fredericke, Baldwine, and their traine with drums and trumpets.	2Tamburlaine	1.1.77.1
[Enter] Sigismond, Fredericke, Baldwine, with their traine.	2Tamburlaine	2.1.0.1
BANKET		
enter the Pope and the Cardinall of Lorraine to the banket,	Faustus App.	p231 0.2
BANQUET		
The Banquet, and to it commeth Tamburlain al in scarlet,	1Tamburlaine	4.4.0.1
A Senit while the Banquet is brought in; and then Enter Faustus	Faustus 981.1	3.2.0.1
BARABAS		
Enter Barabas in his Counting-house, with heapes of gold before	Jew of Malta	1.1.0.1
Enter Barabas, and three Jewes.	Jew of Malta	1.2.36.1
Exeunt. [Manent Barabas and the three Jewes].	Jew of Malta	1.2.159.1
Enter Barabas with a light.	Jew of Malta	2.1.0.1
Enter Barabas.	Jew of Malta	2.3.4.1
Enter Barabas above.	Jew of Malta	3.2.4.1
Enter Barabas reading a letter.	Jew of Malta	3.4.0.1
Enter Barabas, Ithamore.	Jew of Malta	4.1.0.1
Enter [come forward] Barabas [and Ithimore].	Jew of Malta	4.1.173.1
Enter Barabas, reading a letter.	Jew of Malta	4.3.0.1
Enter Barabas with a Lute, disguis'd.	Jew of Malta	4.4.29.1
Exit [Barabas, Curtezane, Pilia-borza, with Officers].	Jew of Malta	5.1.43.1
[Enter Officers carrying Barabas, as dead].	Jew of Malta	5.1.53.1
Exeunt. [Manet Barabas].	Jew of Malta	5.1.60.1
Enter Turkes, Barabas, Governour, and Knights prisoners.	Jew of Malta	5.2.0.1
Exeunt. [Manet Barabas].	Jew of Malta	5.2.25.1
Enter [Barabas] with a Hammar above, very busie.	Jew of Malta	5.5.0.1
[Barabas falls into it.	Jew of Malta	5.5.63.3
BARONS		
Enter the Barons, alarums.	Edward II	2.4.21.1
[Exeunt Barons].	Edward II	2.4.58.1
Enter the Herald from the Barons, with his coate of armes.	Edward II	3.1.150.1
Enter the Barons, Mortimer, Lancaster, Warwick, Penbrooke, cum	Edward II	3.1.194.1
Enter Edward, with the Barons [and Kent] captives.	Edward II	3.1.220.2
[Barons led off by Spencer pater].	Edward II	3.1.249.1
BARTLEY		
<Enter Bartley>.	Edward II	5.1.111.1
[Enter Bartley to Leister with letter].	Edward II	5.1.127.1
BARTUS		
Enter the King of Navarre, Pleshe and Bartus, and their train,	Paris 698.1	14.0.1
Enter the King of Navarre [, Bartus], and his traine.	Paris 787.2	16.0.2
Enter the King of Navarre reading of a letter, and Bartus.	Paris 900.1	18.0.1
France, and Navarre, Epernoune, Bartus, Pleshe and Souldiers.	Paris 1139.2	22.0.2
BASHAW		
Enter Governor, Bosco, Knights, [Callapine, the] Bashaw.	Jew of Malta	3.5.0.1
BASHAWES		
Enter Calymath, Bashawes, Turkes.	Jew of Malta	5.1.68.1
Enter Calymath, Bashawes.	Jew of Malta	5.3.0.1
Enter Calymath and Bashawes.	Jew of Malta	5.5.50.1
BASSOE		
Exit Bassoe.	1Tamburlaine	3.1.44.1
Usumcasane, Theridamas, Bassoe, Zenocrate, [Anippe], with	1Tamburlaine	3.3.0.2
BASSOES		
his Bassoes and contributorie Kinges [and Zabina and Ebea].	1Tamburlaine	3.3.60.1
met by [Callapine and other] Bassoes of the Turke; Calymath.	Jew of Malta	1.2.0.2
BATTAILE		
[Exeunt] To the Battaile, and Mycetes comes out alone with his	1Tamburlaine	2.4.0.1
They sound to the battaile.	1Tamburlaine	5.1.402.1
BATTELL		
Sound trumpets to the battell, and he runs in.	1Tamburlaine	2.4.42.1
[Exeunt] <Enter> to the Battell, and after the battell, enter	1Tamburlaine	2.7.0.1
to the Battell, and after the battell, enter Cosroe wounded,	1Tamburlaine	2.7.0.1
They sound [to] the battell within, and stay.	1Tamburlaine	3.3.188.1
To the battell againe.	1Tamburlaine	3.3.200.1
The battell short, and they enter, Bajazeth is overcome.	1Tamburlaine	3.3.211.2
Sound to the battell, and Sigismond comes out wounded.	2Tamburlaine	2.3.0.1
Summon the battell.	2Tamburlaine	3.3.14.1
BE		
They hale Edmund away, and carie him to be beheaded.	Edward II	5.4.108.1
BEAMONT		
[Exeunt Clarke and Beamont].	Edward II	1.4.372.1
BEARD		
They wash him with puddle water, and shave his beard away.	Edward II	5.3.36.1
BEARE		
They beare away the [olde] Queene [of Navarre] and goe out.	Paris 202.1	3.37.1
BEARING		
Enter Ortigius and [Ceneus] <Conerus> bearing a Crowne, with	1Tamburlaine	1.1.135.1
foure bearing the hearse of Zenocrate, and the drums sounding a	2Tamburlaine	3.2.0.2
Cardinals and Bishops, some bearing Crosiers, some the Pillars,	Faustus 867.1	3.1.89.1
devill playing on a Drum, after him another bearing an Ensigne:	Faustus 1430.2	4.2.106.2
BEATE		
Beate the Friers, fling fire workes among them, and Exeunt.	Faustus 1083.1	3.2.107.1

BEATE (cont.)		
Beate the Friers, and fling fier-workes among them, and so	Faustus App.	p233 41.1
BEAUMONT (See BEAMONT)		
BED		
The Arras is drawen and Zenocrate lies in her bed of state,	2Tamburlaine	2.4.0.1
three Phisitians about her bed, tempering potions. . . .	2Tamburlaine	2.4.0.2
Enter the Admirall in his bed.	Paris 252.2	4.50.2
Gonzago and others] into the Admirals house, and he in his bed.	Paris 297.2	5.24.2
BEFORE		
Barabas in his Counting-house, with heapes of gold before him.	Jew of Malta	1.1.0.2
BEHEADED		
They hale Edmund away, and carie him to be beheaded. .	Edward II	5.4.108.1
BEING		
The ordinance being shot of, the bell tolles. . . .	Paris 334.1	5.61.1
BELL		
The ordinance being shot of, the bell tolles. . . .	Paris 334.1	5.61.1
Enter the Friers with Bell, Booke, and Candle, for the Dirge.	Faustus 1075.1	3.2.95.1
BELLAMIRA		
[Aside to Bellamira].	Jew of Malta	4.4.25.1
BELLS		
Bells within.	Jew of Malta	4.1.0.1
BELOW		
Enter [below] the Captaine with [Olympia] his wife and sonne.	2Tamburlaine	3.4.0.1
[below] Theridamas and Techelles bringing the Governor of	2Tamburlaine	5.1.79.1
[Enter Theridamas below].	2Tamburlaine	5.1.148.3
[Enter Mephostophilis below].	Faustus 1879.2	5.2.83.2
BELZEBUB		
Enter Lucifer, Belzebub, and Mephostophilis. . . .	Faustus 635.1	2.2.84.1
Enter [above] Lucifer, Belzebub, and Mephostophilis. .	Faustus 1797.1	5.2.0.1
BENVOLIO		
Enter Benvolio above at a window, in his nightcap: . .	Faustus 1178.1	4.1.24.1
Enter Benvolio, Martino, Fredericke, and Souldiers. . .	Faustus 1325.1	4.2.0.1
Enter at severall dores, Benvolio, Fredericke, and Martino,	Faustus 1431.1	4.3.0.1
BERKELEY (See BARTLEY)		
BESMEAR'D		
and besmear'd with mud and durt; all having hornes on their	Faustus 1431.2	4.3.0.2
BETWEENE		
Enter Hellen againe, passing over betweene two Cupids. .	Faustus 1767.1	5.1.94.1
BIND		
They bind them.	1Tamburlaine	3.3.267.1
BISHOP		
Enter the Bishop of Coventrie.	Edward II	1.1.174.1
with a Bishop [of Winchester] for the crowne [and Trussell].	Edward II	5.1.0.1
[Exeunt Bishop of Winchester and Trussell]. . . .	Edward II	5.1.124.1
Enter Messenger [and then Bishop of Winchester with the crown].	Edward II	5.2.22.1
BISHOPS		
Enter the Cardinals and Bishops, some bearing Crosiers, some	Faustus 867.1	3.1.89.1
BITTES		
his chariot by Trebizon and Soria with bittes in their mouthes,	2Tamburlaine	4.3.0.2
BLACKE		
Tamburlaine all in blacke, and verie melancholy. . .	1Tamburlaine	5.1.63.3
BLOUDY		
their heads and faces bloudy, and besmear'd with mud and durt;	Faustus 1431.2	4.3.0.2
BODIES		
[Burns the bodies].	2Tamburlaine	3.4.33.1
Exeunt [with bodies].	Jew of Malta	3.2.37.1
Exit Anjoy [and soldiers with bodies].	Paris 442.1	7.82.1
BODY		
[Exeunt with body].	1Tamburlaine	3.2.113.1
Exit Uribassa [and soldiers with body].	2Tamburlaine	2.3.41.1
[Exeunt with the body of Calyphas].	2Tamburlaine	4.1.167.1
[They take body aside].	Jew of Malta	5.1.59.1
[The body is thrown down.	Paris 306.1	5.33.1
Enter two with the Admirals body.	Paris 482.1	9.0.1
Carry away the dead body.	Paris 499.1	9.18.1
Exit [the attendants taking up body of the Guise]. . .	Paris 1090.1	19.160.1
[Exeunt attendants with body].	Paris 1182.1	22.44.1
They march out with the body of the King, lying on foure mens	Paris 1250.1	22.112.1
BOOKE		
Enter the Cardinals with a Booke.	Faustus 1008.2	3.2.28.2
Enter the Friers with Bell, Booke, and Candle, for the Dirge.	Faustus 1075.1	3.2.95.1
Enter Robin the Ostler with a booke in his hand . .	Faustus App.	p233 0.1
BOOKES		
Enter five or sixe Protestants with bookes, and kneele .	Paris 528.1	10.0.1
BOSCO		
Enter Governor, Martin del Bosco, the Knights [and Officers].	Jew of Malta	2.2.0.1
Enter Governor, Bosco, Knights, [Callapine, the] Bashaw. .	Jew of Malta	3.5.0.1
Enter Governor, Knights, Martin Del-Bosco.	Jew of Malta	5.1.0.1
Enter Governor, Knights, Del-bosco.	Jew of Malta	5.4.0.1
Enter del Bosco and Knights].	Jew of Malta	5.5.63.3
BOTH		
Enter both the Mortimers, Warwicke, and Lancaster. . .	Edward II	1.2.0.1
comming backe, both salute the Emperour, who leaving his State,	Faustus 1257.6	4.1.103.6
BOUNCE		
The [Clownes] <Clowne> bounce at the gate, within. . .	Faustus 1587.1	4.6.30.1
BOXE		
[Faustus hits him a boxe of the eare].	Faustus 1067.1A	3.2.87.1
and Faustus hits him a boxe of the eare, and they all runne	Faustus App.	p232 21.1
BOY		
Exit Boy.	Paris 1053.1	19.123.1
BRAINES		
She runs against the Cage and braines her selfe. . .	1Tamburlaine	5.1.318.1
BRAINS		
He brains himself against the cage.	1Tamburlaine	5.1.304.1

BRANCHES
and foure Virgins, with branches of Laurell in their hands. 1Tamburlaine 5.1.0.2
BRIDLE
They bridle them. 2Tamburlaine 5.1.148.1
BRING
They bring in the Turke [in his cage, and Zabina]. . . 1Tamburlaine 5.1.202.1
They bring in the hearse. 2Tamburlaine 5.3.223.1
BRINGING
and Soria, one bringing a sword, and another a scepter: . 2Tamburlaine 3.1.0.1
Theridamas and Techelles bringing the Governor of Babylon. 2Tamburlaine 5.1.79.1
BRINGS
He goes in and brings him out. 2Tamburlaine 4.1.90.1
One brings a Map. 2Tamburlaine 5.3.125.1
Mephostophilis brings in Hellen, she <and Helen> passeth over Faustus 1696.1 5.1.23.1
BRISTOW
and the Maior of Bristow, with Spencer the father. . . Edward II 4.6.45.2
BROUGHT
The Concubines are brought in. 2Tamburlaine 4.3.66.1
reading on a letter that was brought him from the king. . Edward II 1.1.0.2
A Senit while the Banquet is brought in; and then Enter Faustus Faustus 981.1 3.2.0.1
Enter Hostesse [brought hither by magic] with drinke. . Faustus 1649.1 4.6.92.1
BRUNO
Pope, and Raymond King of Hungary, with Bruno led in chaines. Faustus 867.4 3.1.89.4
Exeunt Faustus and Mephostophilis [with Bruno]. . . Faustus 976.1 3.1.198.1
[Enter] Charles the Germane Emperour, Bruno, [Duke of] Saxony, Faustus 1203.2 4.1.49.2
BURNING
and the drums sounding a dolefull martch, the Towne burning. 2Tamburlaine 3.2.0.3
BURNS
[Burns the bodies]. 2Tamburlaine 3.4.33.1
BUSIE
Enter [Barabas] with a Hammar above, very busie. . . Jew of Malta 5.5.0.1
BUT
All goe out, but Navarre and Pleshe. . . . . . Paris 564.1 11.29.1
Goe out all, but the Queene [Mother] and the Cardinall. . Paris 630.1 12.43.1
BUTTONING
buttoning. . . . . Faustus 1178.2 4.1.24.2
BUTTONS
Cutpurse eare, for cutting of the golde buttons off his cloake. Paris 617.2 12.30.2
BY
doore, and takes Ascanius by the sleeve [as he is going off]. Dido 2.1.303.3
and takes her away lovingly by the hand, looking wrathfully on 1Tamburlaine 3.2.65.1
Zenocrate lies in her bed of state, Tamburlaine sitting by her: 2Tamburlaine 2.4.0.2
his chariot by Trebizon and Soria with bittes in their mouthes, 2Tamburlaine 4.3.0.1
and Jerusalem led by with five or six common souldiers. . 2Tamburlaine 4.3.0.5
[drawn in his chariot by the kings of Trebizon and Soria], with 2Tamburlaine 5.1.62.2
King of Natolia, and King of Jerusalem, led by souldiers]. 2Tamburlaine 5.1.62.5
[Enter Tamburlaine, drawn by the captive kings; Amyras, . 2Tamburlaine 5.3.41.1
met by [Callapine and other] Bassoes of the Turke; Calymath. Jew of Malta 1.2.0.1
[Barons led off by Spencer pater]. . . . . . . Edward II 3.1.249.1
Enter the Seven Deadly Sinnes [led by a Piper]. . . Faustus 660.1 2.2.109.1
Enter Hostesse [brought hither by magic] with drinke. . Faustus 1649.1 4.6.92.1
Pull him by the legge, and pull it away. . . . . Faustus App. p241 53.1
BYRON
Gazellus, vice-roy of Byron, [Uribassa] <Upibassa>, and their 2Tamburlaine 1.1.0.1
CABLE
A charge, the cable cut, a Caldron discovered. . . . Jew of Malta 5.5.63.2
CAETERIS
Manet James cum caeteris. . . . . Edward II 2.6.17.2
Barons, Mortimer, Lancaster, Warwick, Penbrooke, cum caeteris. Edward II 3.1.194.2
CAGE
They take him out of the cage. 1Tamburlaine 4.2.1.1
two Moores drawing Bajazeth in his cage, and his wife following 1Tamburlaine 4.2.0.2
[They put him into the cage]. 1Tamburlaine 4.2.82.1
They bring in the Turke [in his cage, and Zabina]. . . 1Tamburlaine 5.1.202.1
He brains himself against the cage. 1Tamburlaine 5.1.304.1
She runs against the Cage and braines her selfe. . . 1Tamburlaine 5.1.318.1
CALAPINE
After Calapine, and after him other Lordes [and Almeda]: . 2Tamburlaine 3.1.0.3
CALDRON
A charge, the cable cut, a Caldron discovered. . . . Jew of Malta 5.5.63.2
CALIPHAS
Celebinus, issues from the tent where Caliphas sits a sleepe. 2Tamburlaine 4.1.0.2
CALL
They call musicke. 2Tamburlaine 2.4.77.1
They knocke againe, and call out to talke with Faustus. . Faustus 1590.1 4.6.33.1
CALLAPINE
[Enter] Callapine with Almeda, his keeper. 2Tamburlaine 1.2.0.1
Enter Callapine, Amasia, [Captaine, Souldiers], with drums and 2Tamburlaine 5.2.0.1
met by [Callapine and other] Bassoes of the Turke; Calymath. Jew of Malta 1.2.0.2
Enter Governor, Bosco, Knights, [Callapine, the] Bashaw. . Jew of Malta 3.5.0.1
CALLEPINE
[Enter] Callepine, Orcanes, Jerusalem, Trebizon, Soria, Almeda, 2Tamburlaine 3.5.0.1
CALLING
Enter Rafe calling Robin. . . . . Faustus App. p233 5.1
CALLS
[Calls]. . . . . Faustus 373.1 1.4.31.1
CALYMATH
met by [Callapine and other] Bassoes of the Turke; Calymath. Jew of Malta 1.2.0.2
Enter Calymath, Bashawes, Turkes. . . . . . . Jew of Malta 5.1.68.1
Enter Calymath, Bashawes. . . . . Jew of Malta 5.3.0.1
Enter Calymath and Bashawes. . . . . Jew of Malta 5.5.50.1
CALYPHAS
and his three sonnes, Calyphas, Amyras, and Celebinus, . 2Tamburlaine 1.3.0.1

CALYPHAS (cont.)
and his three sons, [Calyphas], [Amyras, and Celebinus], . 2Tamburlaine 3.2.0.1
[Stabs Calyphas]. 2Tamburlaine 4.1.120.1
[Exeunt with the body of Calyphas]. 2Tamburlaine 4.1.167.1

CANDLE
Enter the Friers with Bell, Booke, and Candle, for the Dirge. Faustus 1075.1 3.2.95.1

CANTERBURIE
Enter the [Archbishop] of Canterburie [and attendant]. . Edward II 1.2.32.1
Mortimer junior, the Archbishop of Canterburie, attended]. Edward II 1.4.0.2

CANTERBURY
Enter the yong King, [Archbishop] [of Canterbury], Champion, Edward II 5.4.72.1

CAPOLIN
of Egipt with three or four Lords, Capolin [, and a Messenger]. 1Tamburlaine 4.1.0.2

CAPOLINE
Capoline, with [streaming] <steaming> collors and Souldiers. 1Tamburlaine 4.3.0.1

CAPTAIN
Anjoy, Duke Demayne [and Cossin, Captain of the Kings Guard]. Paris 203.2 4.0.2

CAPTAINE
[Enter above] Captaine with his wife [Olympia] and sonne. 2Tamburlaine 3.3.14.2
Enter [below] the Captaine with [Olympia] his wife and sonne. 2Tamburlaine 3.4.0.1
Amasia, [Captaine, Souldiers], with drums and trumpets. . 2Tamburlaine 5.2.0.1
Enter the Captaine of the guarde, and three murtherers. . Paris 931.1 19.0.1
Enter Captaine of the Guarde. . . . . Paris 1015.2 19.85.2
[Exit Captaine of the Guarde]. . . . . Paris 1058.1 19.128.1

CAPTIVE
[Enter Tamburlaine, drawn by the captive kings; Amyras, . 2Tamburlaine 5.3.41.1

CAPTIVES
Enter Edward, with the Barons [and Kent] captives. . . Edward II 3.1.220.2

CARDENALL
Enter two [Murtherers] dragging in the Cardenall [of Loraine]. Paris 1091.1 20.0.1

CARDINALL
of Guise, and Queene Mother, and the Cardinall [of Loraine]. Paris 493.3 9.12.3
enter Queene Mother, and the Cardinall [of Loraine, and Pleshe]. Paris 536.2 11.0.2
Queene [Mother], Cardinall [of Loraine], Duke of Guise, . Paris 588.3 12.0.3
Goe out all, but the Queene [Mother] and the Cardinall. . Paris 630.1 12.43.1
enter the Pope and the Cardinall of Lorraine to the banket, Faustus App. p231 0.1

CARDINALS
Enter the Cardinals and Bishops, some bearing Crosiers, some Faustus 867.1 3.1.89.1
Exeunt Cardinals. . . . . Faustus 889.1 3.1.111.1
Enter Faustus and Mephostophilis like the Cardinals. . Faustus 939.1 3.1.161.1
Enter the Cardinals with a Booke. . . . . . . Faustus 1008.1 3.2.28.1
[Exeunt Cardinals attended]. . . . . Faustus 1034.1 3.2.54.1

CARIE
They hale Edmund away, and carie him to be beheaded. . Edward II 5.4.108.1

CARRY
Carry away the dead body. . . . . Paris 499.1 9.18.1

CARRYING
[Enter Officers carrying Barabas, as dead]. . . . . Jew of Malta 5.1.53.1

CARTER
Enter [Robin the] Clowne, Dick, Horse-courser, and a Carter. Faustus 1505.1 4.5.0.1
Enter [Robin] the Clowne, Dick, Carter, and Horse-courser. Faustus 1608.1 4.6.51.1

CATHERINE
French King, [Catherine] the Queene Mother, the King of Navarre Paris 0.1 1.0.1
the King, [Catherine the] Queene Mother, Duke of Guise, . Paris 203.1 4.0.1

CAVE
Enter Aeneas and Dido in the Cave at severall times. . Dido 3.4.0.1
Exeunt to the Cave. . . . . Dido 3.4.64.1

CEASE
Then trumpets cease, and Musicke sounds. . . . . . Faustus 1257.8 4.1.103.8

CELEBINUS
Calyphas, Amyras, and Celebinus, with drummes and trumpets. 2Tamburlaine 1.3.0.2
[Amyras, and Celebinus], foure bearing the hearse of Zenocrate, 2Tamburlaine 3.2.0.2
Amyras and Celebinus, issues from the tent where Caliphas sits 2Tamburlaine 4.1.0.1
Alarme, and Amyras and Celebinus run in. 2Tamburlaine 4.1.51.1
Usumcasane, Amyras, Celebinus, leading the Turkish kings. 2Tamburlaine 4.1.75.3
them, Techelles, Theridamas, Usumcasane, Amyras, Celebinus: 2Tamburlaine 4.3.0.4
Amyras, and Celebinus, with others, the two spare kings . 2Tamburlaine 5.1.62.3
drawn by the captive kings; Amyras, Celebinus, Physitians]. 2Tamburlaine 5.3.41.2

CENEUS
Meander, Theridamas, Ortygius, Ceneus, [Menaphon], with others. 1Tamburlaine 1.1.0.1
Enter Ortigius and [Ceneus] <Conerus> bearing a Crowne, with 1Tamburlaine 1.1.135.1
Cosroe, Menaphon, Ortygius, Ceneus, with other Souldiers. 1Tamburlaine 2.1.0.1

CHAFER
Enter Mephostophilis with the <a> Chafer of Fire <coles>. Faustus 458.1 2.1.70.1

CHAINES
hang the Governour of Babylon in chaines on the walles]. . 2Tamburlaine 5.1.148.2
Pope, and Raymond King of Hungary, with Bruno led in chaines. Faustus 867.4 3.1.89.4

CHAIRE
He gets up upon him to his chaire. 1Tamburlaine 4.2.29.1
Sleepe in his chaire. . . . . Faustus App. p240 26.1

CHAMPION
King, [Archbishop] [of Canterbury], Champion, Nobles, Queene. Edward II 5.4.72.1

CHARGE
A charge, the cable cut, a Caldron discovered. . . . Jew of Malta 5.5.63.2

CHARIOT
his chariot by Trebizon and Soria with bittes in their mouthes, 2Tamburlaine 4.3.0.1
[drawn in his chariot by the kings of Trebizon and Soria], with 2Tamburlaine 5.1.62.2

CHARLES
Enter Charles the French King, [Catherine] the Queene Mother, Paris 0.1 1.0.1
Exit [Charles] the King, Queene Mother, and [Margaret] the Paris 26.2 1.26.2
Enter [Charles] the King, [Catherine the] Queene Mother, Duke Paris 203.1 4.0.1
Enter [Charles] the King of France, Navar and Epernoune staying Paris 536.1 11.0.1
[Enter] Charles the Germane Emperour, Bruno, [Duke of] Saxony, Faustus 1203.2 4.1.49.2

CHARMES			
Faustus charmes him dumb.	Faustus	1660.1	4.6.103.1
[Faustus charmes him dumb].	Faustus	1661.1	4.6.104.1
[Faustus charmes him dumb].	Faustus	1663.1	4.6.106.1
[Faustus charmes him dumb].	Faustus	1665.1	4.6.108.1
[Faustus charmes her dumb].	Faustus	1668.1	4.6.111.1
CHASING			
the rest, with their Swords drawne, chasing the Protestants.	Paris	335.3	5.62.3
CHORUS			
Enter Chorus.	Faustus	0.1	Prol.0.1
Enter the Chorus <Wagner solus>.	Faustus	753.2	2.3.32.2
Enter Chorus.	Faustus	1137.2A	3.3.50.2
Enter Chorus.	Faustus	2001.2	5.3.19.2
CITIE			
his hand, drawing the platforme of the citie, with him Achates,	Dido		5.1.0.2
CITIZEN			
Enter another [1. Citizen], kneeling to the Governour.	2Tamburlaine		5.1.23.1
[enter 2. Citizen].	2Tamburlaine		5.1.37.1
CITIZENS			
of Damasco, with three or foure Citizens, and foure Virgins,	1Tamburlaine		5.1.0.1
CLARKE			
[Exeunt Clarke and Beamont].	Edward II		1.4.372.1
CLOAK			
[Takes off shepheards cloak].	1Tamburlaine		1.2.41.1
CLOAKE			
Cutpurse eare, for cutting of the golde buttons off his cloake.	Paris	617.2	12.30.2
CLOANTHUS			
Enter [Iarbus, with] Illioneus, and Cloanthus [and Sergestus].	Dido		1.2.0.1
Enter Cloanthus, Sergestus, Illioneus [and others].	Dido		2.1.38.1
[Enter Aeneas, Achates, Sergestus, Illioneus, and Cloanthus].	Dido		3.1.96.1
Enter Achates, Cloanthus, Sergestus, and Illioneus.	Dido		4.3.14.1
citie, with him Achates, [Sergestus], Cloanthus, and Illioneus.	Dido		5.1.0.2
CLOCK			
The Clock strikes eleven.	Faustus	1925.2	5.2.129.2
CLOCKE			
The clocke striketh twelve.	Faustus	1974.1	5.2.178.1
CLOSE			
[Close the studie].	Paris	416.1	7.56.1
CLOSES			
Exit. [Hell closes].	Faustus	1925.1	5.2.129.1
CLOWNE			
Enter Wagner and [Robin] the Clowne.	Faustus	343.1	1.4.0.1
Enter [Robin] the Clowne.	Faustus	722.1	2.3.0.1
Enter [Robin the] Clowne and Dicke, with a Cup.	Faustus	1088.1	3.3.0.1
Enter [Robin the] Clowne, Dick, Horse-courser, and a Carter.	Faustus	1505.1	4.5.0.1
The [Clownes] <Clowne> bounce at the gate, within.	Faustus	1587.1	4.6.30.1
Enter [Robin] the Clowne, Dick, Carter, and Horse-courser.	Faustus	1608.1	4.6.51.1
Enter Wagner and the Clowne.	Faustus App.	p229	0.1
Enter two divells, and the clowne runnes up and downe crying.	Faustus App.	p230	49.1
CLOWNES			
Exeunt the two Clownes.	Faustus	1134.1	3.3.47.1
The [Clownes] <Clowne> bounce at the gate, within.	Faustus	1587.1	4.6.30.1
Exeunt Clownes.	Faustus	1665.1	4.6.108.1
COATE			
Enter the Herald from the Barons, with his coate of armes.	Edward II		3.1.150.1
COLES			
Enter Mephostophilis with the <a> Chafer of Fire <coles>.	Faustus	458.1	2.1.70.1
COLLORS			
Capoline, with [streaming] <steaming> collors and Souldiers.	1Tamburlaine		4.3.0.1
COME			
Enter [come forward] Barabas [and Ithimore].	Jew of Malta		4.1.173.1
COMES			
and Mycetes comes out alone with his Crowne in his hand,	1Tamburlaine		2.4.0.1
Sound to the battell, and Sigismond comes out wounded.	2Tamburlaine		2.3.0.1
Tamburlaine goes in, and comes out againe with al the rest.	2Tamburlaine		5.3.114.1
[Comes forward].	Jew of Malta		5.5.60.1
The Guise comes to the King.	Paris	963.1	19.33.1
[Edward comes up or is discovered].	Edward II		5.5.41.1
COMMETH			
Banquet, and to it commeth Tamburlain al in scarlet, Theridamas,	1Tamburlaine		4.4.0.1
COMMING			
upon her head; and comming backe, both salute the Emperour,	Faustus	1257.6	4.1.103.6
COMMON			
and Jerusalem led by with five or six common souldiers.	2Tamburlaine		4.3.0.5
COMPANIE			
Enter Warwicke and his companie.	Edward II		2.6.6.1
CONCUBINES			
The Concubines are brought in.	2Tamburlaine		4.3.66.1
CONDY			
manet Navar, the Prince of Condy, and the Lord high Admirall.	Paris	26.3	1.26.3
Mother Queen [of Navarre], the Prince of Condy, the Admirall,	Paris	166.2	3.0.2
and enter the King of Navarre and Prince of Condy, with their	Paris	429.2	7.69.2
Exeunt [Condy and Navarre].	Paris	440.1	7.80.1
CONDYE			
King of Navarre, the Prince of Condye, the Lord high Admirall,	Paris	0.2	1.0.2
CONERUS			
Enter Ortigius and [Ceneus] <Conerus> bearing a Crowne, with	1Tamburlaine		1.1.135.1
CONJURE			
<Enter Faustus to conjure>.	Faustus	228.1A	HC p258
CONTRIBUTORIE			
his Bassoes and contributorie Kinges [and Zabina and Ebea].	1Tamburlaine		3.3.60.1
CORNELIUS			
Enter Valdes and Cornelius.	Faustus	126.1	1.1.98.1

COSROE
[Enter] Mycetes, Cosroe, Meander, Theridamas, Ortygius, Ceneus, 1Tamburlaine 1.1.0.1
Manent Cosroe and Menaphon. 1Tamburlaine 1.1.106.2
[Enter] Cosroe, Menaphon, Ortygius, Ceneus, with other 1Tamburlaine 2.1.0.1
[Enter] Cosroe, Tamburlaine, Theridamas, Techelles, Usumcasane, 1Tamburlaine 2.3.0.1
[Enter] Cosroe, Tamburlaine, Theridamas, Menaphon, Meander, 1Tamburlaine 2.5.0.1
[Enter] Cosroe, Meander, Ortygius, Menaphon, with other 1Tamburlaine 2.6.0.1
and after the battell, enter Cosroe wounded, Theridamas, 1Tamburlaine 2.7.0.1
COSSIN
Anjoy, Duke Demayne [and Cossin, Captain of the Kings Guard]. Paris 203.2 4.0.2
COUNTING
Enter Barabas in his Counting-house, with heapes of gold before Jew of Malta 1.1.0.1
COUNTING-HOUSE
Enter Barabas in his Counting-house, with heapes of gold before Jew of Malta 1.1.0.1
COURSE
Enter a second course of Crownes. 1Tamburlaine 4.4.106.1
COURSER
Enter Faustus, and the Horse-courser <and Mephistophilis>. Faustus 1457.1 4.4.0.1
Enter the Horse-courser wet. Faustus 1483.2 4.4.27.2
Enter [Robin the] Clowne, Dick, Horse-courser, and a Carter. Faustus 1505.1 4.5.0.1
Enter [Robin] the Clowne, Dick, Carter, and Horse-courser. Faustus 1608.1 4.6.51.1
enter a Horse-courser Faustus App. p239 97.1
COURTESAN (See CURTEZANE)
COVENTRIE
Enter the Bishop of Coventrie. Edward II 1.1.174.1
COVER'D
Enter devils with cover'd dishes; Mephostophilis leades them Faustus 1674.1 5.1.0.1
CROSIERS
Cardinals and Bishops, some bearing Crosiers, some the Pillars, Faustus 867.1 3.1.89.1
CROSSE
Crosse againe. Faustus App. p232 19.1
Crosse againe, and Faustus hits him a boxe of the eare, and Faustus App. p232 21.1
CROSSETH
[The Pope crosseth himselfe]. Faustus 1064.1A 3.2.84.1
The Pope crosseth himselfe. Faustus App. p232 17.1
CROWN
Enter Messenger [and then Bishop of Winchester with the crown]. Edward II 5.2.22.1
CROWND
Enter Henry crownd: Paris 588.3 12.0.3
CROWNE
[Gives him crowne and scepter]. Dido 4.4.36.1
Enter Ortigius and [Ceneus] <Conerus> bearing a Crowne, with 1Tamburlaine 1.1.135.1
and Mycetes comes out alone with his Crowne in his hand, 1Tamburlaine 2.4.0.2
He takes the Crowne and puts it on. 1Tamburlaine 2.7.52.2
Next Natolia and Jerusalem with the Emperiall crowne: 2Tamburlaine 3.1.0.3
Orcanes and Jerusalem crowne him, and the other give him the 2Tamburlaine 3.1.0.4
They crowne him. 2Tamburlaine 5.3.184.1
with a Bishop [of Winchester] for the crowne [and Trussell]. Edward II 5.1.0.2
kils him; takes off his Crowne, and offering to goe out, Faustus 1257.4 4.1.103.4
her, and sets Darius Crowne upon her head; and comming backe, Faustus 1257.5 4.1.103.5
CROWNES
Enter a second course of Crownes. 1Tamburlaine 4.4.106.1
<with> Devils, giving Crownes and rich apparell to Faustus: Faustus 471.2 2.1.83.2
CRYE
and then all crye vive [le] <la> Roy two or three times. Paris 588.1 12.0.1
CRYING
Enter two divells, and the clowne runnes up and downe crying. Faustus App. p230 49.2
Enter Horsecourser all wet, crying. Faustus App. p240 26.2
CUM
Exeunt Jupiter cum Ganimed. Dido 1.1.121.1
Exit [Gaveston] cum servis Penbrookis. Edward II 2.5.110.1
Manet James cum caeteris. Edward II 2.6.17.2
Barons, Mortimer, Lancaster, Warwick, Penbrooke, cum caeteris. Edward II 3.1.194.2
CUP
Enter [Robin the] Clowne and Dicke, with a Cup. Faustus 1088.1 3.3.0.1
CUPID
Enter Venus [with Cupid] at another doore, and takes Ascanius Dido 2.1.303.2
Enter Cupid solus [for Ascanius]. Dido 3.1.0.1
[Cupid sings]. Dido 3.1.25.1
Anna, Iarbus, Achates, [Cupid for Ascanius], and followers. Dido 3.3.0.1
Enter Achates, [Cupid for] Ascanius, Iarbus, and Anna. Dido 4.1.0.1
Enter the Nurse with Cupid for Ascanius. Dido 4.5.0.1
CUPIDS
Enter Hellen againe, passing over betweene two Cupids. Faustus 1767.1 5.1.94.1
CURTAINES
Here the Curtaines draw, there is discovered Jupiter dandling Dido 1.1.0.1
CURTEZANE
Enter a Curtezane. Jew of Malta 3.1.0.1
Enter Curtezane, and Pilia-borza. Jew of Malta 4.2.0.1
Enter Curtezane, Ithimore, Pilia-borza. Jew of Malta 4.4.0.1
Enter Curtezane, Pilia-borza. Jew of Malta 5.1.6.1
Exit [Barabas, Curtezane, Pilia-borza, with Officers]. Jew of Malta 5.1.43.1
CUT
A charge, the cable cut, a Caldron discovered. Jew of Malta 5.5.63.2
CUTPURSE
[Mugeroun], the kings Minions, with others, and the Cutpurse. Paris 588.5 12.0.5
He cuts of the Cutpurse eare, for cutting of the golde buttons Paris 617.1 12.30.1
CUTS
He cuts his arme. 2Tamburlaine 3.2.114.1
He cuts of the Cutpurse eare, for cutting of the golde buttons Paris 617.1 12.30.1
CUTTING
Cutpurse eare, for cutting of the golde buttons off his cloake. Paris 617.1 12.30.1
DAGGER
Enter Techelles with a naked dagger. 1Tamburlaine 3.2.87.1

DAGGER (cont.)

[Dagger].	2Tamburlaine		3.4.15.1
Shewing his dagger.	Paris	351.1	6.6.1
He offereth tc throwe his dagger.	Paris	1051.1	19.121.1
Mephostophilis gives him a dagger.	Faustus	1725.1	5.1.52.1
DAMASCO			
[Enter] The Governcur of Damasco, with three or foure Citizens,	1Tamburlaine		5.1.0.1
DANCE			
they <and> dance, and then depart.	Faustus	471.3	2.1.83.3
DANDLING			
there is discovered Jupiter dandling Ganimed upon his knee, and	Dido		1.1.0.1
DARIUS			
[dore] the Emperour Alexander, at the other Darius; they meete,	Faustus	1257.3	4.1.103.3
they meete, Darius is throwne downe, Alexander kils him; takes	Faustus	1257.3	4.1.103.3
her, and sets Darius Crowne upon her head; and comming backe,	Faustus	1257.5	4.1.103.5
DAUGHTER			
Enter Abigall the Jewes daughter.	Jew of Malta		1.2.223.1
DEAD			
[Enter Officers carrying Barabas, as dead].	Jew of Malta		5.1.53.1
Carry away the dead body.	Paris	499.1	9.18.1
lying on foure mens shoulders with a dead march, drawing	Paris	1250.3	22.112.3
DEADLY			
Enter the Seven Deadly Sinnes [led by a Piper].	Faustus	660.1	2.2.109.1
DEL-BOSCO			
Enter Governor, Knights, Martin Del-Bosco.	Jew of Malta		5.1.0.1
Enter Governor, Knights, Del-bosco.	Jew of Malta		5.4.0.1
DEL BOSCO			
Enter del Bosco and Knights].	Jew of Malta		5.5.63.3
DEMAYNE			
Anjoy, Duke Demayne [and Cossin, Captain of the Kings Guard].	Paris	203.2	4.0.2
DEPART			
they <and> dance, and then depart.	Faustus	471.3	2.1.83.3
DESCENDS			
Musicke while the Throne descends.	Faustus	1898.1	5.2.102.1
DEVILL (See also DIVELL)			
Enter a Devill.	Faustus	250.1	1.3.22.1
Exit Devill.	Faustus	254.1	1.3.26.1
He fetches in a woman devill.	Faustus	531.1	2.1.143.1
and enter a devill playing on a Drum, after him another bearing	Faustus	1430.1	4.2.106.1
DEVILS			
Enter Lucifer and foure devils [above], Faustus to them with	Faustus	229.1	1.3.0.1
Exeunt [Faustus; Lucifer and devils above].	Faustus	342.1	1.3.114.1
Enter two devils.	Faustus	375.1	1.4.33.1
Enter <with> Devils, giving Crownes and rich apparell to	Faustus	471.2	2.1.83.2
Enter devils with cover'd dishes; Mephostophilis leades them	Faustus	1674.1	5.1.0.1
Thunder, and enter the devils.	Faustus	1978.1	5.2.182.1
[Exeunt Lucifer and devils above].	Faustus	1982.2	5.2.186.2
DICK			
Enter Dick.	Faustus	724.1	2.3.3.1
Enter [Robin the] Clowne, Dick, Horse-courser, and a Carter.	Faustus	1505.1	4.5.0.1
Enter [Robin] the Clowne, Dick, Carter, and Horse-courser.	Faustus	1608.1	4.6.51.1
DICKE			
Enter [Robin the] Clowne and Dicke, with a Cup.	Faustus	1088.1	3.3.0.1
DIDO			
Enter Dido [with Anna and Iarbus] and her traine.	Dido		2.1.73.1
Enter Iarbus, Anna, and Dido.	Dido		3.1.6.1
Enter Dido, Aeneas, Anna, Iarbus, Achates, [Cupid for	Dido		3.3.0.1
Enter Aeneas and Dido in the Cave at severall times.	Dido		3.4.0.1
[Enter Aeneas and Dido].	Dido		4.1.24.1
Enter Dido and Anna [with traine].	Dido		4.4.0.1
Enter Dido [attended] [to] <and> Aeneas.	Dido		5.1.82.1
DIES (See also DYES)			
[Dies].	1Tamburlaine		2.7.52.1
[Dies].	1Tamburlaine		3.2.106.1
[Dies].	1Tamburlaine		5.1.432.1
[Dies].	2Tamburlaine		2.3.9.1
The musicke sounds, and she dies.	2Tamburlaine		2.4.95.1
[Dies].	2Tamburlaine		3.4.10.1
[Dies].	2Tamburlaine		5.3.248.1
[Dies].	Jew of Malta		3.6.40.1
[Dies].	Jew of Malta		4.1.150.1
Stab him [and he falls within and dies].	Paris	360.1	6.15.1
He dies.	Paris	550.1	11.15.1
[King dies].	Edward II		5.5.113.1
DIFFERENT			
Enter Mortimer and Matrevis [at different doors].	Edward II		5.6.0.1
DIRGE			
Enter the Friers with Bell, Booke, and Candle, for the Dirge.	Faustus	1075.2	3.2.95.2
Enter all the Friers to sing the Dirge.	Faustus	App.	p232 28.1
DIRT (See DURT)			
DISCHARGETH			
who] dischargeth his Musket at the Lord Admirall [and exit].	Paris	196.1	3.31.1
DISCOVERED			
there is discovered Jupiter dandling Ganimed upon his knee, and	Dido		1.1.0.1
A charge, the cable cut, a Caldron discovered.	Jew of Malta		5.5.63.2
[Edward comes up or is discovered].	Edward II		5.5.41.1
Hell is discovered.	Faustus	1908.2	5.2.112.2
DISGUIS'D			
Enter Barabas with a Lute, disguis'd.	Jew of Malta		4.4.29.1
DISGUISED			
Enter Mortimer disguised.	Edward II		4.1.11.1
Monkes, Edward, Spencer, and Baldocke [disguised as monks].	Edward II		4.7.0.2
DISHES			
Enter devils with cover'd dishes; Mephostophilis leades them	Faustus	1670.1	5.1.0.1

DIVELL			
<Enter with a divell drest like a woman, with fier workes>.	Faustus	531.1A	HC p261
DIVELLES			
[Enter the Divelles].	Faustus	1790.1A	5.1.117.1
DIVELLS			
Enter two divells, and the clowne runnes up and downe crying.	Faustus	App.	p230 49.1
DIVELS			
Enter Mephostophilis and other Divels.	Faustus	1402.1	4.2.78.1
DIVERS			
and divers with weapons, Mephostophilis with fire-workes; they	Faustus	1430.2	4.2.106.2
DOLEFULL			
and the drums sounding a dolefull martch, the Towne burning.	2Tamburlaine		3.2.0.3
DOORE			
Enter Venus [with Cupid] at another doore, and takes Ascanius	Dido		2.1.303.2
Enter Mountsorrell and knocks at Serouns doore.	Paris	346.1	6.0.1
DOORES			
Enter the Good Angell, and the Bad Angell at severall doores.	Faustus	1891.3	5.2.95.3
DOORS			
Enter [at several doors] the King and Spencer, to them	Edward II		2.4.0.1
Enter Mortimer and Matrevis [at different doors].	Edward II		5.6.0.1
DORE			
Enter at one [dore] the Emperour Alexander, at the other	Faustus	1257.2	4.1.103.2
Faustus strikes the dore, and enter a devill playing on a Drum,	Faustus	1430.1	4.2.106.1
DORES			
Enter Martino, and Frederick at severall dores.	Faustus	1155.1	4.1.0.1
Enter at severall dores, Benvolio, Fredericke, and Martino,	Faustus	1431.1	4.3.0.1
DOWN			
[The body is thrown down.	Paris	306.1	5.33.1
DOWNE			
Throwes downe bags.	Jew of Malta		2.1.46.1
they meete, Darius is throwne downe, Alexander kils him; takes	Faustus	1257.3	4.1.103.3
Enter two divells, and the clowne runnes up and downe crying.	Faustus	App.	p230 49.2
DRAGGING			
Enter two [Murtherers] dragging in the Cardenall [of Loraine].	Paris	1091.1	20.0.1
DRAGON			
[Dragon].	Faustus	247.1	1.3.19.1
DRAW			
Here the Curtaines draw, there is discovered Jupiter dandling	Dido		1.1.0.1
DRAWEN			
The Arras is drawen and Zenocrate lies in her bed of state,	2Tamburlaine		2.4.0.1
The Arras is drawen.	2Tamburlaine		2.4.142.1
drawen in his chariot by Trebizon and Soria with bittes in	2Tamburlaine		4.3.0.1
DRAWING			
his hand, drawing the platforme of the citie, with him Achates,	Dido		5.1.0.1
two Moores drawing Bajazeth in his cage, and his wife following	1Tamburlaine		4.2.0.2
shoulders with a dead march, drawing weapons on the ground.	Paris	1250.4	22.112.4
DRAWN			
[drawn in his chariot by the kings of Trebizon and Soria], with	2Tamburlaine		5.1.62.2
[Enter Tamburlaine, drawn by the captive kings; Amyras,	2Tamburlaine		5.3.41.1
DRAWNE			
all the rest, with their Swords drawne, chasing the Protestants.	Paris	335.3	5.62.3
DRAWS			
[Draws sword].	Edward II		2.2.79.1
DREST			
<Enter with a divell drest like a woman, with fier workes>.	Faustus	531.1A	HC p261
DRINKE			
They give him water to drinke, and he flings it on the ground.	1Tamburlaine		4.4.55.1
Enter Hostesse [brought hither by magic] with drinke.	Faustus	1649.1	4.6.92.1
DRINKS			
[Drinks].	Dido		2.1.98.1
[Drinks].	Edward II		5.4.80.1
DRIVE			
fire-workes; they set upon the Souldiers and drive them out.	Faustus	1430.3	4.2.106.3
DRUM			
and enter a devill playing on a Drum, after him another bearing	Faustus	1430.1	4.2.106.1
DRUMME			
Sound Drumme and Trumpets, and enter the King of France, and	Paris	1139.1	22.0.1
DRUMMES			
Calyphas, Amyras, and Celebinus, with drummes and trumpets.	2Tamburlaine		1.3.0.2
king Edward and Spencer, [Baldock], with Drummes and Fifes.	Edward II		3.1.0.2
DRUMS			
<Upibassa>, and their traine, with drums and trumpets.	2Tamburlaine		1.1.0.2
Fredericke, Baldwine, and their traine with drums and trumpets.	2Tamburlaine		1.1.77.2
Enter Theridamas, and his traine with Drums and Trumpets.	2Tamburlaine		1.3.111.1
and the drums sounding a dolefull martch, the Towne burning.	2Tamburlaine		3.2.0.3
Amasia, [Captaine, Souldiers], with drums and trumpets.	2Tamburlaine		5.2.0.1
Pleshe and Bartus, and their train, with drums and trumpets.	Paris	698.2	14.0.2
DUCHESSE (See also DUTCHES)			
Enter the Duchesse of Guise, and her Maide.	Paris	657.1	13.0.1
Exit [Duchesse].	Paris	692.1	13.36.1
DUKE			
Enter the Duke of Guise.	Paris	58.1	2.0.1
[Catherine the] Queene Mother, Duke of Guise, Duke Anjoy, Duke	Paris	203.1	4.0.1
Duke of Guise, Duke Anjoy, Duke Demayne [and Cossin, Captain o	Paris	203.2	4.0.2
Anjoy, Duke Demayne [and Cossin, Captaine of the Kings Guard].	Paris	203.2	4.0.2
Enter the Duke of Guise, and Queene Mother, and the Cardinall	Paris	493.2	9.12.2
Cardinall [of Loraine], Duke of Guise, Epernoone, [Mugeroun],	Paris	588.4	12.0.4
Enter [Henry] the King of France, Duke of Guise, Epernoune, and	Paris	743.1	15.0.1
the King of France, Duke of Guise, Epernoune, and Duke Joyeux.	Paris	743.2	15.0.2
The Duke Joyeux slaine.	Paris	787.1	16.0.1
Enter Duke Dumayn reading of a letter, with others.	Paris	1107.1	21.0.1
Emperour, Bruno, [Duke of] Saxony, Faustus, Mephostophilis,	Faustus	1203.2	4.1.49.2
Enter the Duke of Vanholt; his Dutches, Faustus, and	Faustus	1558.1	4.6.0.1

DUKE (cont.)			
Enter to them the Duke, and the Dutches, the Duke speakes.	Faustus App.		p242 0.1
Enter to them the Duke, and the Dutches, the Duke speakes.	Faustus App.		p242 0.2
DUMAINE (See also DEMAYNE)			
Enter Guise, Anjoy, Dumaine, Gonzago, Retes, Montsorreil, and	Paris	274.1	5.0.1
Enter the Guise and Anjoy [, Dumaine, Mountsorrell, with	Paris	379.1	7.19.1
[Exit Dumaine].	Paris	424.1	7.64.1
DUMAYN			
Enter Duke Dumayn reading of a letter, with others.	Paris	1107.1	21.0.1
DUMB			
Faustus charmes him dumb.	Faustus	1660.1	4.6.103.1
[Faustus charmes him dumb].	Faustus	1661.1	4.6.104.1
[Faustus charmes him dumb].	Faustus	1663.1	4.6.106.1
[Faustus charmes him dumb].	Faustus	1665.1	4.6.108.1
[Faustus charmes her dumb].	Faustus	1668.1	4.6.111.1
DURT			
and besmear'd with mud and durt; all having hornes on their	Faustus	1431.3	4.3.0.3
DUTCHES			
Enter the Duke of Vanholt; his Dutches, Faustus, and	Faustus	1558.1	4.6.0.1
Enter to them the Duke, and the Dutches, the Duke speakes.	Faustus App.		p242 0.1
DYES			
[Dyes].	Jew of Malta		5.5.89.1
She dyes.	Paris	186.1	3.21.1
He dyes.	Paris	1015.1	19.85.1
He dyes.	Paris	1244.1	22.106.1
EACH			
[Kill each other].	Jew of Malta		3.2.6.1
EARE			
He cuts of the Cutpurse eare, for cutting of the golde buttons	Paris	617.1	12.30.1
[Faustus hits him a boxe of the eare].	Faustus	1067.1A	3.2.87.1
and Faustus hits him a boxe of the eare, and they all runne	Faustus App.		p232 21.1
Hallow in his eare.	Faustus App.		p241 52.1
EARLE			
Mortimer junior, Edmund Earle of Kent, Guie Earle of Warwicke,	Edward II		1.1.73.2
junior, Edmund Earle of Kent, Guie Earle of Warwicke, &c.	Edward II		1.1.73.2
Enter Gaveston and the earle of Kent.	Edward II		1.3.0.1
Enter earle of Arundell.	Edward II		2.5.31.1
and the earle of Penbrookes men [, James and three souldiers].	Edward II		2.6.0.1
Enter Edmund [earle of Kent].	Edward II		4.1.0.1
Enter Edmund [earle of Kent] and Mortimer.	Edward II		4.2.34.1
her sonne, Edmund [earle of Kent], Mortimer, and sir John.	Edward II		4.4.0.1
[Enter] Edmund [earle of Kent] alone with a sword and target.	Edward II		4.6.0.1
hookes, Rice ap Howell, a Mower, and the Earle of Leicester.	Edward II		4.7.45.2
Enter the yong Prince, and the Earle of Kent talking with him.	Edward II		5.2.73.2
Enter Edmund [earle of Kent].	Edward II		5.3.48.1
Enter Souldiers with the Earle of Kent prisoner.	Edward II		5.4.81.1
EBEA			
his Bassoes and contributorie Kinges [and Zabina and Ebea].	1Tamburlaine		3.3.60.2
EDMUND			
Mortimer junior, Edmund Earle of Kent, Guie Earle of Warwicke,	Edward II		1.1.73.2
Enter Edmund [earle of Kent].	Edward II		4.1.0.1
Enter Edmund [earle of Kent] and Mortimer.	Edward II		4.2.34.1
her sonne, Edmund [earle of Kent], Mortimer, and sir John.	Edward II		4.4.0.1
[Enter] Edmund [earle of Kent] alone with a sword and target.	Edward II		4.6.0.1
Enter Edmund [earle of Kent].	Edward II		5.3.48.1
Manent Edmund and the souldiers.	Edward II		5.3.62.2
They hale Edmund away, and carie him to be beheaded.	Edward II		5.4.108.1
EDWARD			
Exeunt Edward and Gaveston.	Edward II		1.4.169.1
Enter king Edward moorning [attended].	Edward II		1.4.304.1
Enter Edward, the Queene, Lancaster, Mortimer [junior],	Edward II		2.2.0.1
Enter king Edward and Spencer, [Baldock], with Drummes and	Edward II		3.1.0.1
Edward kneels, and saith.	Edward II		3.1.127.1
Enter Edward, with the Barons [and Kent] captives.	Edward II		3.1.220.2
Monkes, Edward, Spencer, and Baldocke [disguised as monks].	Edward II		4.7.0.1
Exeunt Edward and Leicester.	Edward II		4.7.99.1
[Edward comes up or is discovered].	Edward II		5.5.41.1
EGIPT			
[Enter] Souldan of Egipt with three or four Lords, Capolin	1Tamburlaine		4.1.0.1
ELEVEN			
The Clock strikes eleven.	Faustus	1925.2	5.2.129.2
EMBRACE			
Embrace Spencer.	Edward II		3.1.176.1
leaving his State, offers to embrace them, which Faustus seeing,	Faustus	1257.7	4.1.103.7
EMBRACETH			
him, he embraceth her, and sets Darius Crowne upon her head;	Faustus	1257.5	4.1.103.5
EMPERIALL			
Next Natolia and Jerusalem with the Emperiall crowne:	2Tamburlaine		3.1.0.2
EMPEROUR			
[Enter] Charles the Germane Emperour, Bruno, [Duke of] Saxony,	Faustus	1203.2	4.1.49.2
Enter at one [dore] the Emperour Alexander, at the other	Faustus	1257.2	4.1.103.2
comming backe, both salute the Emperour, who leaving his State,	Faustus	1257.6	4.1.103.6
Enter Emperour, Faustus, and a Knight, with Attendants.	Faustus App.		p236 0.1
exit Emperour.	Faustus App.		p239 89.1
ENGLISH			
Enter the English Agent.	Paris	1193.2	22.55.2
ENJOYES			
And Tamburlaine enjoyes the victory, after Arabia enters	1Tamburlaine		5.1.402.1
ENSIGNE			
devill playing on a Drum, after him another bearing an Ensigne:	Faustus	1430.2	4.2.106.2
ENTER			
Enter Chorus.	Dido		Prol.0.1
Enter Venus.	Dido		1.1.49.1
Enter Aeneas with Ascanius [and Achates], with one or two more.	Dido		1.1.133.1

ENTER (cont.)

Enter [Iarbus, with] Illioneus, and Cloanthus [and Sergestus].	Dido	1.2.0.1
Enter Aeneas, Achates, and Ascanius [attended].	Dido	2.1.0.1
Enter Cloanthus, Sergestus, Illioneus [and others].	Dido	2.1.38.1
Enter Dido [with Anna and Iarbus] and her traine.	Dido	2.1.73.1
[Enter servant with robe and Aeneas puts it on].	Dido	2.1.95.1
Enter Venus [with Cupid] at another doore, and takes Ascanius	Dido	2.1.303.2
Enter Cupid solus [for Ascanius].	Dido	3.1.0.1
Enter Iarbus, Anna, and Dido.	Dido	3.1.6.1
[Enter Aeneas, Achates, Sergestus, Illioneus, and Cloanthus].	Dido	3.1.96.1
Enter Juno to Ascanius asleepe.	Dido	3.2.0.1
Enter Venus.	Dido	3.2.20.1
Enter Dido, Aeneas, Anna, Iarbus, Achates, [Cupid for	Dido	3.3.0.1
Enter Aeneas and Dido in the Cave at severall times.	Dido	3.4.0.1
Enter Achates, [Cupid for] Ascanius, Iarbus, and Anna.	Dido	4.1.0.1
[Enter Aeneas and Dido].	Dido	4.1.24.1
Enter Anna.	Dido	4.2.22.1
Enter Aeneas alone.	Dido	4.3.0.1
Enter Achates, Cloanthus, Sergestus, and Illioneus.	Dido	4.3.14.1
Enter Dido and Anna [with traine].	Dido	4.4.0.1
Enter Anna, with Aeneas, Achates, Illioneus, and Sergestus.	Dido	4.4.13.1
Enter a Lord.	Dido	4.4.123.1
Enter the Nurse with Cupid for Ascanius.	Dido	4.5.0.1
Enter Aeneas with a paper in his hand, drawing the platforme of	Dido	5.1.0.1
Enter Hermes with Ascanius.	Dido	5.1.23.1
Enter to them Iarbus.	Dido	5.1.61.1
Enter Dido [attended] [to] <and> Aeneas.	Dido	5.1.82.1
[Enter Anna].	Dido	5.1.192.1
Enter the Nurse.	Dido	5.1.211.2
Enter Anna.	Dido	5.1.225.1
Enter Iarbus.	Dido	5.1.278.2
[Enter Attendants with wood and fire].	Dido	5.1.282.1
Enter Anna.	Dido	5.1.313.2
Enter Iarbus running.	Dido	5.1.315.1
[Enter] Mycetes, Cosroe, Meander, Theridamas, Ortygius, Ceneus,	1Tamburlaine	1.1.0.1
Enter Ortigius and [Ceneus] <Conerus> bearing a Crowne, with	1Tamburlaine	1.1.135.1
[Enter] Tamburlaine leading Zenocrate:	1Tamburlaine	1.2.0.1
Enter a Souldier.	1Tamburlaine	1.2.108.1
The Souldiers enter.	1Tamburlaine	1.2.137.1
Enter Theridamas with others.	1Tamburlaine	1.2.151.1
[Enter] Cosroe, Menaphon, Ortygius, Ceneus, with other	1Tamburlaine	2.1.0.1
[Enter] Mycetes, Meander, with other Lords and Souldiers.	1Tamburlaine	2.2.0.1
[Enter a Spy].	1Tamburlaine	2.2.38.1
[Enter] Cosroe, Tamburlaine, Theridamas, Techelles, Usumcasane,	1Tamburlaine	2.3.0.1
[Enter a Messenger].	1Tamburlaine	2.3.48.1
Enter Tamburlain.	1Tamburlaine	2.4.15.1
[Enter] Cosroe, Tamburlaine, Theridamas, Menaphon, Meander,	1Tamburlaine	2.5.0.1
[Enter] Cosroe, Meander, Ortygius, Menaphon, with other	1Tamburlaine	2.6.0.1
[Exeunt] <Enter> to the Battell, and after the battell, enter	1Tamburlaine	2.7.0.1
and after the battell, enter Cosroe wounded, Theridamas,	1Tamburlaine	2.7.0.1
[Enter] Bajazeth, the kings of Fesse, Moroco, and Argier, with	1Tamburlaine	3.1.0.1
[Enter] Agidas, Zenocrate, Anippe, with others.	1Tamburlaine	3.2.0.1
Enter [aloofe] Tamburlaine with Techelles and others.	1Tamburlaine	3.2.24.1
Enter Techelles with a naked dagger.	1Tamburlaine	3.2.87.1
[Enter Techelles and Usumcasane].	1Tamburlaine	3.2.106.2
[Enter] Tamburlain, Techelles, Usumcasane, Theridamas, Bassoe,	1Tamburlaine	3.3.0.1
Enter Bajazeth with his Bassoes and contributorie Kinges [and	1Tamburlaine	3.3.60.1
The battell short, and they enter, Bajazeth is overcome.	1Tamburlaine	3.3.211.2
Enter Techelles, Theridamas, Usumcasane.	1Tamburlaine	3.3.214.1
[Enter] Souldan of Egipt with three or four Lords, Capolin	1Tamburlaine	4.1.0.1
[Enter] Tamburlain, Techelles, Theridamas, Usumcasane,	1Tamburlaine	4.2.0.1
[Enter] Souldane, Arabia, Capoline, with [streaming] <steaming>	1Tamburlaine	4.3.0.1
Enter a second course of Crownes.	1Tamburlaine	4.4.106.1
[Enter] The Governour of Damasco, with three or foure Citizens,	1Tamburlaine	5.1.0.1
[Enter] Tamburlaine, Techelles, Theridamas, Usumcasane, with	1Tamburlaine	5.1.63.2
Enter Techelles.	1Tamburlaine	5.1.128.1
Enter two or three.	1Tamburlaine	5.1.191.1
Enter Techelles, Theridamas, Usumcasane, and others.	1Tamburlaine	5.1.195.2
Enter Zabina.	1Tamburlaine	5.1.304.2
Enter Zenocrate wyth Anippe.	1Tamburlaine	5.1.318.2
Enter [Philemus], a Messenger.	1Tamburlaine	5.1.376.1
Enter Tamburlain leading the Souldane, Techelles, Theridamas,	1Tamburlaine	5.1.432.2
[Enter] Orcanes, king of Natolia, Gazellus, vice-roy of Byron,	2Tamburlaine	1.1.0.1
[Enter] Sigismond, Fredericke, Baldwine, and their traine with	2Tamburlaine	1.1.77.1
[Enter] Callapine with Almeda, his keeper.	2Tamburlaine	1.2.0.1
[Enter] Tamburlaine with Zenocrate, and his three sonnes,	2Tamburlaine	1.3.0.1
Enter Theridamas, and his traine with Drums and Trumpets.	2Tamburlaine	1.3.111.1
Enter Techelles and Usumcasane together.	2Tamburlaine	1.3.127.1
[Enter] Sigismond, Fredericke, Baldwine, with their traine.	2Tamburlaine	2.1.0.1
[Enter] Orcanes, Gazellus, Uribassa with their traine.	2Tamburlaine	2.2.0.1
Enter a Messenger.	2Tamburlaine	2.2.23.1
Enter Orcanes, Gazellus, Uribassa, with others.	2Tamburlaine	2.3.9.2
Enter the kings of Trebisond and Soria, one bringing a sword,	2Tamburlaine	3.1.0.1
[Enter] Tamburlaine with Usumcasane, and his three sons,	2Tamburlaine	3.2.0.1
[Enter] Techelles, Theridamas and their traine.	2Tamburlaine	3.3.0.1
[Enter above] Captaine with his wife [Olympia] and sonne.	2Tamburlaine	3.3.14.2
Enter [below] the Captaine with [Olympia] his wife and sonne.	2Tamburlaine	3.4.0.1
Enter Theridamas, Techelles and all their traine.	2Tamburlaine	3.4.33.2
[Enter] Callepine, Orcanes, Jerusalem, Trebizon, Soria, Almeda,	2Tamburlaine	3.5.0.1
[Enter] Tamburlaine with his three sonnes, Usumcasane with	2Tamburlaine	3.5.57.1
Enter Theridamas, Techelles, and their traine.	2Tamburlaine	3.5.146.1
[Enter Perdicas].	2Tamburlaine	4.1.59.1
Enter [with Souldiers] Tamburlain, Theridamas, Techelles,	2Tamburlaine	4.1.75.2

ENTER (cont.)

[Enter] Olympia alone.	2Tamburlaine		4.2.0.1
Enter Theridamas.	2Tamburlaine		4.2.13.1
[Enter] Tamburlaine drawen in his chariot by Trebizon and Soria	2Tamburlaine		4.3.0.1
Enter the Governour of Babylon upon the walles with [Maximus	2Tamburlaine		5.1.0.1
Enter another [1. Citizen], kneeling to the Governour.	2Tamburlaine		5.1.23.1
[enter 2. Citizen].	2Tamburlaine		5.1.37.1
Enter Theridamas and Techelles, with other souldiers.	2Tamburlaine		5.1.48.1
Enter Tamburlain, [drawn in his chariot by the kings of	2Tamburlaine		5.1.62.2
Enter [below] Theridamas and Techelles bringing the Governor of	2Tamburlaine		5.1.79.1
[Enter Theridamas below].	2Tamburlaine		5.1.148.3
[Enter Techelles].	2Tamburlaine		5.1.202.1
Enter Callapine, Amasia, [Captaine, Souldiers], with drums and	2Tamburlaine		5.2.0.1
[Enter] Theridamas, Techelles, Usumcasane.	2Tamburlaine		5.3.0.1
[Enter Tamburlaine, drawn by the captive kings; Amyras,	2Tamburlaine		5.3.41.1
[Enter a Messenger].	2Tamburlaine		5.3.101.2
[Enter] Machevil [as Prologue].	Jew of Malta		Prol.0.1
Enter Barabas in his Counting-house, with heapes of gold before	Jew of Malta		1.1.0.1
Enter a Merchant.	Jew of Malta		1.1.48.1
Enter a second Merchant.	Jew of Malta		1.1.84.1
Enter three Jewes.	Jew of Malta		1.1.139.1
Enter [Ferneze] [Governor] of Malta, Knights [and Officers],	Jew of Malta		1.2.0.1
Enter Barabas, and three Jewes.	Jew of Malta		1.2.36.1
Enter Officers.	Jew of Malta		1.2.130.1
Enter Abigall the Jewes daughter.	Jew of Malta		1.2.223.1
Enter [two] <three> Fryars and [three] <two> Nuns [, one the	Jew of Malta		1.2.304.1
[As they are leaving] Enter Mathias.	Jew of Malta		1.2.365.1
Enter Lodowicke.	Jew of Malta		1.2.373.1
Enter Barabas with a light.	Jew of Malta		2.1.0.1
Enter Abigall above.	Jew of Malta		2.1.19.1
Enter Governor, Martin del Bosco, the Knights [and Officers].	Jew of Malta		2.2.0.1
Enter Officers with slaves.	Jew of Malta		2.3.0.1
Enter Barabas.	Jew of Malta		2.3.4.1
Enter Lodowicke.	Jew of Malta		2.3.31.1
Enter Mathias, Mater.	Jew of Malta		2.3.137.1
Enter Lodowicke.	Jew of Malta		2.3.217.1
Enter Abigall.	Jew of Malta		2.3.221.1
Enter Mathias.	Jew of Malta		2.3.250.1
Enter Lodowicke, Abigall.	Jew of Malta		2.3.275.1
Enter Mathias.	Jew of Malta		2.3.333.1
Enter a Curtezane.	Jew of Malta		3.1.0.1
Enter Pilia-borza.	Jew of Malta		3.1.11.1
Enter Ithimore.	Jew of Malta		3.1.22.1
Enter Mathias.	Jew of Malta		3.2.0.1
Enter Lodowicke reading.	Jew of Malta		3.2.2.1
Enter Barabas above.	Jew of Malta		3.2.4.1
Enter Governor, Mater [attended].	Jew of Malta		3.2.9.2
Enter Ithimore.	Jew of Malta		3.3.0.1
Enter Abigall.	Jew of Malta		3.3.3.1
Enter Ithimore, 1. Fryar.	Jew of Malta		3.3.49.1
Enter Barabas reading a letter.	Jew of Malta		3.4.0.1
[Enter Ithimore].	Jew of Malta		3.4.12.1
Enter Ithimore with the pot.	Jew of Malta		3.4.54.1
Enter Governor, Bosco, Knights, [Callapine, the] Bashaw.	Jew of Malta		3.5.0.1
Enter [the] two Fryars <and Abigall>.	Jew of Malta		3.6.0.1
Enter Abigall.	Jew of Malta		3.6.6.2
Enter 1. Fryar.	Jew of Malta		3.6.43.1
Enter Barabas, Ithamore.	Jew of Malta		4.1.0.1
Enter the two Fryars.	Jew of Malta		4.1.20.1
Enter [1. Fryar] Jacomo.	Jew of Malta		4.1.159.2
Enter [come forward] Barabas [and Ithimore].	Jew of Malta		4.1.173.1
Enter Curtezane, and Pilia-borza.	Jew of Malta		4.2.0.1
Enter Ithimore.	Jew of Malta		4.2.20.1
Enter [Pilia-borza].	Jew of Malta		4.2.99.1
Enter Barabas, reading a letter.	Jew of Malta		4.3.0.1
Enter Pilia-borza.	Jew of Malta		4.3.17.1
Enter Curtezane, Ithimore, Pilia-borza.	Jew of Malta		4.4.0.1
Enter Barabas with a Lute, disguis'd.	Jew of Malta		4.4.29.1
Enter Governor, Knights, Martin Del-Bosco.	Jew of Malta		5.1.0.1
Enter Curtezane, Pilia-borza.	Jew of Malta		5.1.6.1
Enter Jew, Ithimore [with Officers].	Jew of Malta		5.1.18.2
Enter Mater.	Jew of Malta		5.1.43.2
Enter 1. Officer.	Jew of Malta		5.1.49.1
[Enter Officers carrying Barabas, as dead].	Jew of Malta		5.1.53.1
Enter Calymath, Bashawes, Turkes.	Jew of Malta		5.1.68.1
Enter Turkes, Barabas, Governour, and Knights prisoners.	Jew of Malta		5.2.0.1
Enter Governor with a guard.	Jew of Malta		5.2.47.1
Enter Calymath, Bashawes.	Jew of Malta		5.3.0.1
Enter a Messenger.	Jew of Malta		5.3.12.1
Enter Governor, Knights, Del-bosco.	Jew of Malta		5.4.0.1
Enter [Barabas] with a Hammar above, very busie.	Jew of Malta		5.5.0.1
Enter Messenger.	Jew of Malta		5.5.13.1
Enter Governour.	Jew of Malta		5.5.19.1
Enter Calymath and Bashawes.	Jew of Malta		5.5.50.1
Enter del Bosco and Knights].	Jew of Malta		5.5.63.3
Enter Charles the French King, [Catherine] the Queene Mother,	Paris	0.1	1.0.1
Enter the Duke of Guise.	Paris	58.1	2.0.1
Enter the Pothecarie.	Paris	66.1	2.9.1
Enter a Souldier.	Paris	83.2	2.26.2
Enter the King of Navar and Queen [Margaret], and his [olde]	Paris	166.1	3.0.1
[enter] the Souldier [above, who] dischargeth his Musket at the	Paris	196.1	3.31.1
Enter [Charles] the King, [Catherine the] Queene Mother, Duke	Paris	203.1	4.0.1
Enter the Admirals man.	Paris	241.1	4.39.1

ENTER (cont.)

Enter the Admirall in his bed.	Paris	252.2	4.50.2
Enter Guise, Anjoy, Dumaine, Gonzago, Retes, Montsorrell, and	Paris	274.1	5.0.1
Enter [above Gonzago and others] into the Admirals house, and	Paris	297.1	5.24.1
Enter Loreine running, the Guise and the rest pursuing him.	Paris	338.2	5.65.2
Enter Mountsorrell and knocks at Serouns doore.	Paris	346.1	6.0.1
Enter Seroune.	Paris	349.1	6.4.1
Enter Ramus in his studie.	Paris	361.1	7.0.1
Enter Taleus.	Paris	364.1	7.4.1
Enter Gonzago and Retes.	Paris	370.1	7.10.1
Enter Ramus [out of his studie].	Paris	375.2	7.15.2
Enter the Guise and Anjoy [, Dumaine, Mountsorrell, with	Paris	379.1	7.19.1
and enter the King of Navarre and Prince of Condy, with their	Paris	429.1	7.69.1
Enter [to them] Guise.	Paris	437.1	7.77.1
Enter Anjoy, with two Lords of Poland.	Paris	451.1	8.0.1
Enter two with the Admirals body.	Paris	482.1	9.0.1
Enter the Duke of Guise, and Queene Mother, and the Cardinall	Paris	493.2	9.12.2
Enter five or sixe Protestants with bookes, and kneele	Paris	528.1	10.0.1
Enter also the Guise [and others].	Paris	528.2	10.0.2
Enter [Charles] the King of France, Navar and Epernoune staying	Paris	536.1	11.0.1
enter Queene Mother, and the Cardinall [of Loraine, and	Paris	536.2	11.0.2
Enter Henry crownd:	Paris	588.3	12.0.3
Enter the Duchesse of Guise, and her Maide.	Paris	657.1	13.0.1
Enter the Maid with Inke and Paper.	Paris	665.1	13.9.1
Enter the Guise.	Paris	669.1	13.13.1
Enter the King of Navarre, Pleshe and Bartus, and their train,	Paris	698.1	14.0.1
Enter a Messenger.	Paris	722.1	14.25.1
Enter [Henry] the King of France, Duke of Guise, Epernoune, and	Paris	743.1	15.0.1
Enter Mugercun.	Paris	773.1	15.31.1
Enter the King of Navarre [, Bartus], and his traine.	Paris	787.2	16.0.2
Enter a Souldier.	Paris	806.1	17.0.1
Enter Mugercun.	Paris	816.1	17.11.1
Enter the Guise [attended].	Paris	816.3	17.11.3
Enter the King and Epernoune.	Paris	820.2	17.15.2
Enter one with a pen and inke.	Paris	881.1	17.76.1
Enter the King of Navarre reading of a letter, and Bartus.	Paris	900.1	18.0.1
Enter Pleshe.	Paris	914.1	18.15.1
Enter the Captaine of the guarde, and three murtherers.	Paris	931.1	19.0.1
Enter the King and Epernoune.	Paris	946.1	19.16.1
Enter the Guise [within] and knocketh.	Paris	955.1	19.25.1
Enter one of the Murtherers.	Paris	988.1	19.58.1
Enter Captaine of the Guarde.	Paris	1015.2	19.85.2
[Enter King and Epernoune attended].	Paris	1017.1	19.87.1
Enter the Guises sonne.	Paris	1045.1	19.115.1
Enter Queene Mother [attended].	Paris	1063.1	19.133.1
Enter two [Murtherers] dragging in the Cardenall [of Loraine].	Paris	1091.1	20.0.1
Enter Duke Dumayn reading of a letter, with others.	Paris	1107.1	21.0.1
Enter the Frier.	Paris	1121.1	21.15.1
Drumme and Trumpets, and enter the King of France, and Navarre,	Paris	1139.1	22.0.1
Enter a Messenger.	Paris	1154.1	22.16.1
Enter Frier with a Letter.	Paris	1158.1	22.20.1
[Enter Surgeon].	Paris	1190.1	22.52.1
Enter the English Agent.	Paris	1193.2	22.55.2
Enter A souldier with a muskett	Paris ms		p390 0.1
Enter minion He kills him	Paris ms		p390 16.1
Enter guise	Paris ms		p390 17.1
Enter Gaveston reading on a letter that was brought him from	Edward II		1.1.0.1
Enter three poore men.	Edward II		1.1.23.1
Enter the King, Lancaster, Mortimer senior, Mortimer junior,	Edward II		1.1.73.1
Enter the Bishop of Coventrie.	Edward II		1.1.174.1
Enter both the Mortimers, Warwicke, and Lancaster.	Edward II		1.2.0.1
Enter the [Archbishop] of Canterburie [and attendant].	Edward II		1.2.32.1
Enter the Queene.	Edward II		1.2.45.1
Enter Gaveston and the earle of Kent.	Edward II		1.3.0.1
Enter Nobiles [: Lancaster, Warwicke, Penbrooke, Mortimer	Edward II		1.4.0.1
Enter the King and Gaveston [and Kent].	Edward II		1.4.7.1
Enter Gaveston.	Edward II		1.4.105.1
Enter Queen Isabell.	Edward II		1.4.143.1
Enter the Nobles to the Queene.	Edward II		1.4.186.1
Enter king Edward moorning [attended].	Edward II		1.4.304.1
Enter Spencer and Balduck.	Edward II		2.1.0.1
Enter the Ladie [Neece to the king].	Edward II		2.1.56.1
Enter Edward, the Queene, Lancaster, Mortimer [junior],	Edward II		2.2.0.1
Enter Gaveston.	Edward II		2.2.49.1
Enter a Poast.	Edward II		2.2.111.1
[Enter a Guard].	Edward II		2.2.130.1
[Enter the King and Kent].	Edward II		2.2.138.1
Enter the Queene, three Ladies [, one of these Neece to the	Edward II		2.2.224.1
Enter Lancaster, Mortimer [junior], Warwick, Penbrooke, Kent.	Edward II		2.3.0.1
Enter [at several doors] the King and Spencer, to them	Edward II		2.4.0.1
Enter the Barons, alarums.	Edward II		2.4.21.1
Enter Gaveston pursued.	Edward II		2.5.0.1
Enter the Nobles.	Edward II		2.5.7.1
Enter earle of Arundell.	Edward II		2.5.31.1
Enter Gaveston moorning, and the earle of Penbrookes men	Edward II		2.6.0.1
Enter Warwicke and his companie.	Edward II		2.6.6.1
Enter King Edward and Spencer, [Baldock], with Drummes and	Edward II		3.1.0.1
Enter Hugh Spencer an old man, father to the yong Spencer, with	Edward II		3.1.31.1
Enter the Queene and her sonne, and [Levune] <Lewne> a	Edward II		3.1.58.1
Enter lord [Arundell].	Edward II		3.1.88.1
Enter the Herald from the Barons, with his coate of armes.	Edward II		3.1.150.1
Enter the King, Spencer the father, Spencer the sonne, and the	Edward II		3.1.184.3
Enter the Barons, Mortimer, Lancaster, Warwick, Penbrooke, cum	Edward II		3.1.194.1

ENTER (cont.)

Enter Edward, with the Barons [and Kent] captives.	Edward II		3.1.220.2
Enter Edmund [earle of Kent].	Edward II		4.1.0.1
Enter Mortimer disguised.	Edward II		4.1.11.1
Enter the Queene and her sonne.	Edward II		4.2.0.1
Enter sir John of Henolt.	Edward II		4.2.12.1
Enter Edmund [earle of Kent] and Mortimer.	Edward II		4.2.34.1
Enter the King, [Arundell] <Matr.>, the two Spencers, with	Edward II		4.3.0.1
Enter a Poaste.	Edward II		4.3.23.1
Enter the Queene, her sonne, Edmund [earle of Kent], Mortimer,	Edward II		4.4.0.1
Enter the King, Baldock, and Spencer the sonne, flying about	Edward II		4.5.0.1
[Enter] Edmund [earle of Kent] alone with a sword and target.	Edward II		4.6.0.1
Enter the Queene, Mortimer, the young Prince and Sir John of	Edward II		4.6.18.1
Enter Rice ap Howell, and the Maior of Bristow, with Spencer	Edward II		4.6.45.2
Enter the Abbot, Monkes, Edward, Spencer, and Baldocke	Edward II		4.7.0.1
Enter with Welch hookes, Rice ap Howell, a Mower, and the Earle	Edward II		4.7.45.1
Enter the King, Leicester, with a Bishop [of Winchester] for	Edward II		5.1.0.1
<Enter Bartley>.	Edward II		5.1.111.1
[Enter Bartley to Leister with letter].	Edward II		5.1.127.1
Enter Mortimer, and Queene Isabell.	Edward II		5.2.0.1
Enter Messenger [and then Bishop of Winchester with the crown].	Edward II		5.2.22.1
Enter Matrevis and Gurney.	Edward II		5.2.45.1
Enter the yong Prince, and the Earle of Kent talking with him.	Edward II		5.2.73.2
Enter Matrevis and Gurney with the King [and souldiers].	Edward II		5.3.0.1
Enter Edmund [earle of Kent].	Edward II		5.3.48.1
Enter Mortimer alone.	Edward II		5.4.0.1
[Enter Lightborn].	Edward II		5.4.22.1
Enter the yong King, [Archbishop] [of Canterbury], Champion,	Edward II		5.4.72.1
Enter Souldiers with the Earle of Kent prisoner.	Edward II		5.4.81.1
Enter Matrevis and Gurney.	Edward II		5.5.0.1
Enter Lightborne.	Edward II		5.5.14.1
[Enter Matrevis, Gurney, and exeunt.	Edward II		5.5.109.1
Enter Mortimer and Matrevis [at different doors].	Edward II		5.6.0.1
Enter the Queene.	Edward II		5.6.14.1
Enter the King, with the lords.	Edward II		5.6.23.1
[Enter 1. Lord].	Edward II		5.6.92.2
[Enter some with hearse].	Edward II		5.6.97.1
Enter Chorus.	Faustus	0.1	Prol.0.1
[Enter Faustus in his study].	Faustus	29.1	1.1.0.1
Enter Wagner.	Faustus	90.1	1.1.62.1
Enter the <good> Angell and Spirit <the evill Angell>.	Faustus	96.1	1.1.68.1
Enter Valdes and Cornelius.	Faustus	126.1	1.1.98.1
Enter two Schollers.	Faustus	194.1	1.2.0.1
Enter Wagner.	Faustus	195.1	1.2.2.1
<Enter Faustus to conjure>.	Faustus	228.1A	HC p258
Enter Lucifer and foure devils [above], Faustus to them with	Faustus	229.1	1.3.0.1
Enter a Devill.	Faustus	250.1	1.3.22.1
Enter Mephostophilis.	Faustus	262.1	1.3.34.1
Enter Wagner and [Robin] the Clowne.	Faustus	343.1	1.4.0.1
Enter two devils.	Faustus	375.1	1.4.33.1
Enter Faustus in his Study.	Faustus	389.1	2.1.0.1
Enter the two Angels <Enter good Angell, and Evill>.	Faustus	402.1	2.1.14.1
Enter Mephostophilis.	Faustus	418.1	2.1.30.1
Enter Mephostophilis with the <a> Chafer of Fire <coles>.	Faustus	458.1	2.1.70.1
Enter <with> Devils, giving Crownes and rich apparell to	Faustus	471.2	2.1.83.2
Enter Mephostophilis.	Faustus	471.4	2.1.83.4
<Enter with a divell drest like a woman, with fier workes>.	Faustus	531.1A	HC p261
Enter Faustus in his Study, and Mephostophilis.	Faustus	552.1	2.2.0.1
Enter the two Angels <good Angel, and evill Angell>.	Faustus	562.1	2.2.11.1
Enter the two Angels.	Faustus	629.1	2.2.78.1
Enter Lucifer, Belzebub, and Mephostophilis.	Faustus	635.1	2.2.84.1
Enter the Seven Deadly Sinnes [led by a Piper].	Faustus	660.1	2.2.109.1
Enter [Robin] the Clowne.	Faustus	722.1	2.3.0.1
Enter Dick.	Faustus	724.1	2.3.3.1
Enter the Chorus <Wagner solus>.	Faustus	753.2	2.3.32.2
Enter Faustus and Mephostophilis.	Faustus	779.1	3.1.0.1
Enter the Cardinals and Bishops, some bearing Crosiers, some	Faustus	867.1	3.1.89.1
Enter Faustus and Mephostophilis like the Cardinals.	Faustus	939.1	3.1.161.1
and then Enter Faustus and Mephostophilis in their owne shapes.	Faustus	981.1	3.2.0.1
Enter Pope and all the Lords.	Faustus	1008.1	3.2.28.1
Enter the Cardinals with a Booke.	Faustus	1008.1	3.2.28.1
Enter the Friers with Bell, Booke, and Candle, for the Dirge.	Faustus	1075.1	3.2.95.1
Enter [Robin the] Clowne and Dicke, with a Cup.	Faustus	1088.1	3.3.0.1
Enter Vintner.	Faustus	1093.1	3.3.6.1
Enter Mephostophilis.	Faustus	1115.1	3.3.28.1
Enter Chorus.	Faustus	1137.2A	3.3.50.2
Enter Martino, and Frederick at severall dores.	Faustus	1155.1	4.1.0.1
Enter Benvolio above at a window, in his nightcap:	Faustus	1178.1	4.1.24.1
[Enter] Charles the Germane Emperour, Bruno, [Duke of] Saxony,	Faustus	1203.2	4.1.49.2
[Enter Mephostophilis].	Faustus	1257.1	4.1.103.1
Enter at one [dore] the Emperour Alexander, at the other	Faustus	1257.2	4.1.103.2
Enter Benvolio, Martino, Fredericke, and Souldiers.	Faustus	1325.1	4.2.0.1
Enter Fredericke.	Faustus	1356.1	4.2.32.1
Enter Faustus with the false head.	Faustus	1361.1	4.2.37.1
Enter Mephostophilis and other Divels.	Faustus	1402.1	4.2.78.1
Enter the ambusht Souldiers.	Faustus	1419.2	4.2.95.2
and enter a devill playing on a Drum, after him another bearing	Faustus	1430.1	4.2.106.1
Enter at severall dores, Benvolio, Fredericke, and Martino,	Faustus	1431.1	4.3.0.1
Enter Faustus, and the Horse-courser <and Mephistophilis>.	Faustus	1457.1	4.4.0.1
Enter the Horse-courser wet.	Faustus	1483.2	4.4.27.2
Enter Wagner.	Faustus	1498.1	4.4.42.1
Enter [Robin the] Clowne, Dick, Horse-courser, and a Carter.	Faustus	1505.1	4.5.0.1
Enter Hostis.	Faustus	1506.1	4.5.2.1

ENTER (cont.)			
Enter the Duke of Vanholt; his Dutches, Faustus, and	Faustus	1558.1	4.6.0.1
Enter Mephostophilis agen with the grapes.	Faustus	1575.1	4.6.18.1
Enter [Robin] the Clowne, Dick, Carter, and Horse-courser.	Faustus	1608.1	4.6.51.1
Enter Hostesse [brought hither by magic] with drinke.	Faustus	1649.1	4.6.92.1
Enter devils with cover'd dishes; Mephostophilis leades them	Faustus	1674.1	5.1.0.1
Then enter Wagner.	Faustus	1674.3	5.1.0.3
Enter Faustus, Mephostophilis, and two or three Schollers.	Faustus	1680.2	5.1.7.2
Enter an Old Man.	Faustus	1706.1	5.1.33.1
Enter Helien againe, passing over betweene two Cupids.	Faustus	1767.1	5.1.94.1
[Enter Old Man] [aloof].	Faustus	1774.1A	5.1.101.1
[Enter the Divelles].	Faustus	1790.1A	5.1.117.1
Enter [above] Lucifer, Belzebub, and Mephostophilis.	Faustus	1797.1	5.2.0.1
Enter Faustus and Wagner.	Faustus	1815.1	5.2.19.1
Enter <Faustus with> the Scholers <Schollers>.	Faustus	1819.1	5.2.23.1
[Enter Mephostophilis below].	Faustus	1879.2	5.2.83.2
Enter the Good Angell, and the Bad Angell at severall doores.	Faustus	1891.2	5.2.95.2
Thunder, and enter the devils.	Faustus	1978.1	5.2.182.1
Enter the Schollers.	Faustus	1983.1	5.3.0.1
Enter Chorus.	Faustus	2001.2	5.3.19.2
Enter Wagner and the Clowne.	Faustus App.	p229	0.1
Enter two divells, and the clowne runnes up and downe crying.	Faustus App.	p230	49.1
enter the Pope and the Cardinall of Lorraine to the banket,	Faustus App.	p231	0.1
Enter all the Friers to sing the Dirge.	Faustus App.	p232	28.1
Enter Robin the Ostler with a booke in his hand	Faustus App.	p233	0.1
Enter Rafe calling Robin.	Faustus App.	p233	5.1
Enter Robin and Rafe with a silver Goblet.	Faustus App.	p234	0.1
enter the Vintner.	Faustus App.	p234	3.1
Enter Mephostophilis:	Faustus App.	p235	25.1
Enter to them Meph.	Faustus App.	p235	31.1
Enter Emperour, Faustus, and a Knight, with Attendants.	Faustus App.	p236	0.1
Enter Meph:	Faustus App.	p238	59.1
Enter the Knight with a paire of hornes on his head.	Faustus App.	p238	68.1
enter a Horse-courser	Faustus App.	p239	97.1
Enter Horsecourser all wet, crying.	Faustus App.	p240	26.2
Enter Wagner.	Faustus App.	p241	66.1
Enter to them the Duke, and the Dutches, the Duke speakes.	Faustus App.	p242	0.1
enter Mephasto:	Faustus App.	p242	14.1
enter Wagner solus.	Faustus App.	p243	0.1
Enter an old man.	Faustus App.	p243	33.1
ENTERS			
Enters Iarbus to Sacrifize.	Dido		4.2.0.1
Tamburlaine enjoyes the victory, after Arabia enters wounded.	1Tamburlaine		5.1.402.2
The Guise enters againe, with all the rest, with their Swords	Paris	335.2	5.62.2
EPERNOONE			
Duke of Guise, Epernoone, [Mugeroun], the kings Minions,	Paris	588.4	12.0.4
EPERNOUNE			
[Charles] the King of France, Navar and Epernoune staying him:	Paris	536.1	11.0.1
Exit Epernoune.	Paris	560.1	11.25.1
the King of France, Duke of Guise, Epernoune, and Duke Joyeux.	Paris	743.1	15.0.1
Enter the King and Epernoune.	Paris	820.2	17.15.2
Enter the King and Epernoune.	Paris	946.1	19.16.1
Exit King [and Epernoune].	Paris	976.1	19.46.1
[Enter King and Epernoune attended].	Paris	1017.1	19.87.1
Exit the King and Epernoune.	Paris	1080.1	19.150.1
of France, and Navarre, Epernoune, Bartus, Pleshe and Souldiers.	Paris	1139.2	22.0.2
&C.			
junior, Edmund Earle of Kent, Guie Earle of Warwicke, &c.	Edward II		1.1.73.2
and Spencer, to them Gaveston, &c. [the Queene, Neece, lords].	Edward II		2.4.0.2
EVILL			
Enter the <good> Angell and Spirit <the evill Angell>.	Faustus	96.1	1.1.68.1
Enter the two Angels <Enter good Angell, and Evill>.	Faustus	402.1	2.1.14.1
Enter the two Angels <good Angel, and evill Angell>.	Faustus	562.1	2.2.11.1
EXCURSIONS			
Alarums, excursions, a great fight, and a retreate.	Edward II		3.1.184.2
EXEUNT			
Exeunt Jupiter cum Ganimed.	Dido		1.1.121.1
Exeunt omnes.	Dido		2.1.303.1
Exeunt omnes:	Dido		3.3.62.2
Exeunt to the Cave.	Dido		3.4.64.1
[Exeunt omnes, manet Aeneas].	Dido		4.3.45.1
Exeunt [attended].	Dido		4.4.165.1
Exeunt the Nurse [and Attendants].	Dido		5.1.224.1
Exeunt [attended].	1Tamburlaine		1.1.188.1
[Exeunt] To the Battaile, and Mycetes comes out alone with his	1Tamburlaine		2.4.0.1
[Exeunt] <Enter> to the Battell, and after the battell, enter	1Tamburlaine		2.7.0.1
[Exeunt. Manet Agidas].	1Tamburlaine		3.2.65.3
[Exeunt with body].	1Tamburlaine		3.2.113.1
Exeunt. [Manent Virgins].	1Tamburlaine		5.1.63.1
Exeunt. [Manet Tamburlaine].	1Tamburlaine		5.1.134.1
[Exeunt attendants].	1Tamburlaine		5.1.195.1
Exeunt. [Manent Bajazeth and Zabina].	1Tamburlaine		5.1.213.1
[Exeunt with the body of Calyphas].	2Tamburlaine		4.1.167.1
[Exeunt souldiers several ways, some with Governour].	2Tamburlaine		5.1.126.1
[Exeunt three Jewes].	Jew of Malta		1.1.176.1
Exeunt [Turkes].	Jew of Malta		1.2.32.1
[Exeunt Officers].	Jew of Malta		1.2.93.1
Exeunt. [Manent Barabas and the three Jewes].	Jew of Malta		1.2.159.1
[Exeunt Officers].	Jew of Malta		2.2.43.1
Exeunt [Mater and slave].	Jew of Malta		2.3.158.1
[Exeunt Officers with slaves].	Jew of Malta		2.3.162.1
[Exeunt Lodowicke and Abigall].	Jew of Malta		2.3.241.1
Exeunt [with bodies].	Jew of Malta		3.2.37.1

EXEUNT (cont.)			
Exeunt. [Manet Barabas].	Jew of Malta		5.1.60.1
Exeunt. [Manet Barabas].	Jew of Malta		5.2.25.1
[Exeunt guard].	Jew of Malta		5.2.50.1
[Exeunt severally].	Jew of Malta		5.4.10.1
Exeunt omnes.	Paris	273.1	4.71.1
Exeunt Gonzago and rest above].	Paris	306.1	5.33.1
Exeunt [omnes].	Paris	345.1	5.72.1
Exeunt [Condy and Navarre].	Paris	440.1	7.80.1
[Exeunt attendants with body].	Paris	1182.1	22.44.1
Exeunt Nobiles.	Edward II		1.1.133.1
[Exeunt Kent and Gaveston guarded].	Edward II		1.4.34.1
Exeunt Nobiles.	Edward II		1.4.93.1
Exeunt Edward and Gaveston.	Edward II		1.4.169.1
[Exeunt Clarke and Beamont].	Edward II		1.4.372.1
Exeunt. Manent Mortimers.	Edward II		1.4.385.1
Exeunt Nobiles.	Edward II		2.2.199.1
Exeunt omnes.	Edward II		2.2.265.1
Exeunt omnes, manet Isabella.	Edward II		2.4.14.1
[Exeunt Barons].	Edward II		2.4.58.1
Exeunt ambo [Penbrooke and Arundell, attended].	Edward II		2.5.111.1
Exeunt Warwicke and his men, with Gaveston.	Edward II		2.6.17.1
[Exeunt severally.	Edward II		3.1.220.1
Exeunt omnes.	Edward II		3.1.281.1
Exeunt omnes.	Edward II		4.6.79.1
Exeunt Edward and Leicester.	Edward II		4.7.99.1
[Exeunt Bishop of Winchester and Trussell].	Edward II		5.1.124.1
Exeunt omnes.	Edward II		5.1.155.1
Exeunt Matrevis and Gurney.	Edward II		5.2.73.1
Exeunt omnes [severally].	Edward II		5.2.121.1
Exeunt Matrevis and Gurney, with the king.	Edward II		5.3.62.1
Exeunt omnes.	Edward II		5.3.67.1
Exeunt omnes.	Edward II		5.4.115.1
[Exeunt Matrevis and Gurney].	Edward II		5.5.37.1
[Enter Matrevis, Gurney, and exeunt.	Edward II		5.5.109.1
Exeunt omnes.	Edward II		5.5.120.1
Exeunt Angels.	Faustus	104.1	1.1.76.1
Exeunt omnes.	Faustus	193.1	1.1.165.1
Exeunt [Faustus; Lucifer and devils above].	Faustus	342.1	1.3.114.1
Exeunt Angels.	Faustus	410.1	2.1.22.1
Exeunt Angels.	Faustus	568.1	2.2.17.1
Exeunt Angels.	Faustus	633.1	2.2.82.1
Exeunt the Seven Sinnes.	Faustus	711.1	2.2.163.1
Exeunt omnes, severall waies.	Faustus	721.1	2.2.173.1
Exeunt Cardinals.	Faustus	889.1	3.1.111.1
Exeunt Faustus and Mephostophilis.	Faustus	903.1	3.1.125.1
Exeunt Faustus and Mephostophilis [with Bruno].	Faustus	976.1	3.1.198.1
[Exeunt Cardinals attended].	Faustus	1034.1	3.2.54.1
Exeunt the Pope and his traine.	Faustus	1070.1	3.2.90.1
Beate the Friers, fling fire workes among them, and Exeunt.	Faustus	1087.2	3.2.107.2
Exeunt the two Clownes.	Faustus	1134.1	3.3.47.1
Exeunt [Martino and Fredericke].	Faustus	1203.1	4.1.49.1
Exeunt omnes.	Faustus	1324.1	4.1.170.1
Exeunt Spirits with the knights.	Faustus	1419.1	4.2.95.1
[Exeunt omnes].	Faustus	1430.4	4.2.106.4
Exeunt omnes.	Faustus	1456.1	4.3.26.1
Exeunt omnes.	Faustus	1557.1	4.5.53.1
Exeunt Clownes.	Faustus	1665.1	4.6.108.1
Exeunt Schollers.	Faustus	1705.1	5.1.32.1
Exeunt Schollers.	Faustus	1879.1	5.2.83.1
Exeunt [with him].	Faustus	1982.1	5.2.186.1
[Exeunt Lucifer and devils above].	Faustus	1982.2	5.2.186.2
the Friers, and fling fier-workes among them, and so Exeunt.	Faustus	App.	p233 41.2
EXIT			
[Exit Mercury].	Dido		1.1.119.1
[Exit Ascanius with others].	Dido		1.1.177.1
[Exit servant].	Dido		2.1.80.1
Exit Iarbus.	Dido		3.1.55.1
Exit Anna.	Dido		3.1.79.1
[Exit Anna].	Dido		4.4.4.1
Exit [with Troians].	Dido		4.4.92.1
[Exit a Lord].	Dido		4.4.109.1
[Exit Sergestus with Ascanius].	Dido		5.1.50.1
Exit Iarbus and Aeneas traine.	Dido		5.1.77.1
[Exit Aeneas].	Dido		5.1.183.1
Exit Anna.	Dido		5.1.211.1
Exit Anna.	Dido		5.1.278.1
Exit Iarbus.	Dido		5.1.291.1
Exit Bassoe.	1Tamburlaine		3.1.44.1
Exit, with his followers.	1Tamburlaine		3.3.163.1
Exit, with his followers.	1Tamburlaine		3.3.165.1
Exit Uribassa [and soldiers with body].	2Tamburlaine		2.3.41.1
Exit, taking her away.	2Tamburlaine		4.2.98.1
[Exit with the Kings of Trebizon and Soria].	2Tamburlaine		5.1.135.1
[Exit 1. Merchant].	Jew of Malta		1.1.83.1
[Exit Lodowicke].	Jew of Malta		2.3.143.2
[Exit Mathias].	Jew of Malta		2.3.160.1
[Exit Abigall].	Jew of Malta		2.3.363.1
Exit [Ithimore].	Jew of Malta		3.3.52.1
Exit [Ithimore and 2. Fryar].	Jew of Malta		4.1.101.1
[Exit Officers].	Jew of Malta		5.1.18.1
Exit [Barabas, Curtezane, Pilia-borza, with Officers].	Jew of Malta		5.1.43.1
[Exit Governor].	Jew of Malta		5.2.109.1

EXIT (cont.)

Exit [Charles] the King, Queene Mother, and [Margaret] the	Paris	26.2	1.26.2
Exit Pothecaier.	Paris	83.1	2.26.1
Exit Souldier.	Paris	90.1	2.33.1
Exit Pothecary.	Paris	169.1	3.4.1
who] dischargeth his Musket at the Lord Admirall [and exit].	Paris	196.2	3.31.2
Exit Messenger.	Paris	247.1	4.45.1
Exit Guise.	Paris	252.1	4.50.1
Exit Gonzago and others with him.	Paris	292.1	5.19.1
Exit Mountsorrell.	Paris	331.1	5.58.1
Exit Taleus.	Paris	375.1	7.15.1
[Exit Dumaine].	Paris	424.1	7.64.1
Exit Anjoy [and soldiers with bodies].	Paris	442.1	7.82.1
Exit Guise	Paris	511.1	9.30.1
Exit Epernoune.	Paris	560.1	11.25.1
Exit Maid.	Paris	658.1	13.2.1
Exit [Duchesse].	Paris	692.1	13.36.1
Exit Joyeux.	Paris	751.1	15.9.1
Exit Souldier.	Paris	817.1	17.12.1
Exit Guise.	Paris	870.1	17.65.1
Exit one.	Paris	892.1	17.87.1
Exit King [and Epernoune].	Paris	976.1	19.46.1
[Exit attendant].	Paris	1021.1	19.91.1
Exit Boy.	Paris	1053.1	19.123.1
[Exit Captaine of the Guarde].	Paris	1058.1	19.128.1
[Exit Murtherers].	Paris	1059.1	19.129.1
Exit the King and Epernoune.	Paris	1080.1	19.150.1
Exit [the attendants taking up body of the Guise].	Paris	1090.1	19.160.1
[Exit attendant].	Paris	1179.1	22.41.1
[Exit guarded].	Edward II		1.1.201.1
[Exit attendant].	Edward II		1.2.38.1
Exit [Baldock].	Edward II		2.1.74.1
[Exit Gaveston, attended].	Edward II		2.2.86.1
Exit the King [, Queene, and Kent].	Edward II		2.2.99.1
Exit [Gaveston] cum servis Penbrookis.	Edward II		2.5.110.1
[Exit Herald].	Edward II		3.1.180.1
[Exit Kent].	Edward II		3.1.232.1
[Exit guarded].	Edward II		3.1.259.1
Exit [attended].	Edward II		3.1.261.1
[Exit Messenger].	Edward II		5.2.27.1
[Exit Winchester].	Edward II		5.2.36.1
[Exit Mortimer with 1. Lord attended].	Edward II		5.6.67.1
[Exit Queene and 2. Lord].	Edward II		5.6.92.1
Exit Devill.	Faustus	254.1	1.3.26.1
Exit <Wagner>.	Faustus	778.1	2.3.57.1
[Exit Vintner running].	Faustus	1115.1	3.3.28.1
Exit Show.	Faustus	1273.1	4.1.119.1
Exit Frederick with the Souldiers.	Faustus	1349.1	4.2.25.1
Exit Mephostophilis.	Faustus	1574.1	4.6.17.1
Exit Hostesse.	Faustus	1668.1	4.6.111.1
[Exit Wagner].	Faustus	1820.1	5.2.24.1
Exit. [Throne ascends].	Faustus	1908.1	5.2.112.1
Exit. [Hell closes].	Faustus	1925.1	5.2.129.1
exit Meph.	Faustus App.		p237 56.1
exit Kn:	Faustus App.		p237 57.1
exit Alex:	Faustus App.		p238 63.1
exit Emperour.	Faustus App.		p239 89.1
Exit Horsecourser.	Faustus App.		p240 19.1
exit Meph.	Faustus App.		p242 13.1

FACES

their heads and faces bloudy, and besmear'd with mud and durt;	Faustus	1431.2	4.3.0.2

FALLS

[Barabas falls into it.	Jew of Malta		5.5.63.3
Stab him [and he falls within and dies].	Paris	360.1	6.15.1

FALS

Strike him, he fals.	Jew of Malta		4.1.173.1

FALSE

Enter Faustus with the false head.	Faustus	1361.1	4.2.37.1

FATHER

an old man, father to the yong Spencer, with his trunchion,	Edward II		3.1.31.1
Enter the King, Spencer the father, Spencer the sonne, and the	Edward II		3.1.184.3
and the Maior of Bristow, with Spencer the father.	Edward II		4.6.45.3

FAUSTUS

[Enter Faustus in his study].	Faustus	29.1	1.1.0.1
<Enter Faustus to conjure>.	Faustus	228.1A	HC p258
and foure devils [above], Faustus to them with this speech.	Faustus	229.2	1.3.0.2
Exeunt [Faustus; Lucifer and devils above].	Faustus	342.1	1.3.114.1
Enter Faustus in his Study.	Faustus	389.1	2.1.0.1
<with> Devils, giving Crownes and rich apparell to Faustus:	Faustus	471.3	2.1.83.3
Enter Faustus in his Study, and Mephostophilis.	Faustus	552.1	2.2.0.1
Enter Faustus and Mephostophilis.	Faustus	779.1	3.1.0.1
Exeunt Faustus and Mephostophilis.	Faustus	903.1	3.1.125.1
Enter Faustus and Mephostophilis like the Cardinals.	Faustus	939.1	3.1.161.1
Exeunt Faustus and Mephostophilis [with Bruno].	Faustus	976.1	3.1.198.1
and then Enter Faustus and Mephostophilis in their owne shapes.	Faustus	981.2	3.2.0.2
[Faustus hits him a boxe of the eare].	Faustus	1067.1A	3.2.87.1
[Faustus strikes a friar].	Faustus	1080.1	3.2.100.1
Bruno, [Duke of] Saxony, Faustus, Mephostophilis, Fredericke,	Faustus	1203.3	4.1.49.3
to embrace them, which Faustus seeing, suddenly staies him.	Faustus	1257.7	4.1.103.7
Enter Faustus with the false head.	Faustus	1361.1	4.2.37.1
[Faustus rises].	Faustus	1390.1	4.2.66.1
Faustus strikes the dore, and enter a devill playing on a Drum,	Faustus	1430.1	4.2.106.1
Enter Faustus, and the Horse-courser <and Mephistophilis>.	Faustus	1457.1	4.4.0.1

FAUSTUS (cont.)		
the Duke of Vanholt; his Dutches, Faustus, and Mephostophilis.	Faustus 1558.2	4.6.0.2
They knocke againe, and call out to talke with Faustus.	Faustus 1590.1	4.6.33.1
Faustus charmes him dumb.	Faustus 1660.1	4.6.103.1
[Faustus charmes him dumb].	Faustus 1661.1	4.6.104.1
[Faustus charmes him dumb].	Faustus 1663.1	4.6.106.1
[Faustus charmes him dumb].	Faustus 1665.1	4.6.108.1
[Faustus charmes her dumb].	Faustus 1668.1	4.6.111.1
cover'd dishes; Mephostophilis leades them into Faustus Study:	Faustus 1674.2	5.1.0.2
Enter Faustus, Mephostophilis, and two or three Schollers.	Faustus 1680.2	5.1.7.2
Enter Faustus and Wagner.	Faustus 1815.1	5.2.19.1
Enter <Faustus with> the Scholers <Schollers>.	Faustus 1819.1	5.2.23.1
and Faustus hits him a boxe of the eare, and they all runne	Faustus App.	p232 21.1
Enter Emperour, Faustus, and a Knight, with Attendants.	Faustus App.	p236 0.1
FEATHER		
[Plucks a feather from Mercuries wings].	Dido	1.1.40.1
FERNEZE		
Enter [Ferneze] [Governor] of Malta, Knights [and Officers],	Jew of Malta	1.2.0.1
FESSE		
[Enter] Bajazeth, the kings of Fesse, Moroco, and Argier, with	1Tamburlaine	3.1.0.1
FETCHES		
He fetches in a woman devill.	Faustus 531.1	2.1.143.1
FIER		
<Enter with a divell drest like a woman, with fier workes>.	Faustus 531.1A	HC p261
the Friers, and fling fier-workes among them, and so Exeunt.	Faustus App.	p233 41.1
FIER-WORKES		
the Friers, and fling fier-workes among them, and so Exeunt.	Faustus App.	p233 41.1
FIER WORKES		
<Enter with a divell drest like a woman, with fier workes>.	Faustus 531.1A	HC p261
FIFES		
king Edward and Spencer, [Baldock], with Drummes and Fifes.	Edward II	3.1.0.2
FIGHT		
Fight:	Jew of Malta	3.2.4.1
Fight.	Jew of Malta	4.1.96.1
Alarums, excursions, a great fight, and a retreate.	Edward II	3.1.184.2
FILIUS		
Manent Spencer filius, [Levune] <Lewne> and Baldock.	Edward II	3.1.261.2
FIRE		
[Enter Attendants with wood and fire].	Dido	5.1.282.1
Enter Mephostophilis with the <a> Chafer of Fire <coles>.	Faustus 458.1	2.1.70.1
Beate the Friers, fling fire workes among them, and Exeunt.	Faustus 1087.1	3.2.107.1
Mephostophilis with fire-workes; they set upon the Souldiers	Faustus 1430.3	4.2.106.3
FIRE-WORKES		
Mephostophilis with fire-workes; they set upon the Souldiers	Faustus 1430.3	4.2.106.3
FIRE WORKES		
Beate the Friers, fling fire workes among them, and Exeunt.	Faustus 1087.1	3.2.107.1
FIVE		
and Jerusalem led by with five or six common souldiers.	2Tamburlaine	4.3.0.5
Enter five or sixe Protestants with bookes, and kneele	Paris 528.1	10.0.1
FLAMES		
[Throws herself into the flames].	Dido	5.1.313.1
FLIES		
Bajazeth flies [over the stage], and he pursues him.	1Tamburlaine	3.3.211.1
FLING		
Beate the Friers, fling fire workes among them, and Exeunt.	Faustus 1087.1	3.2.107.1
the Friers, and fling fier-workes among them, and so Exeunt.	Faustus App.	p233 41.1
FLINGS		
They give him water to drinke, and he flings it on the ground.	1Tamburlaine	4.4.55.1
FLOURISH		
A Flourish while he ascends.	Faustus 876.1	3.1.98.1
FLYING		
King, Baldock, and Spencer the sonne, flying about the stage.	Edward II	4.5.0.2
FOLLOWERS		
Anna, Iarbus, Achates, [Cupid for Ascanius], and followers.	Dido	3.3.0.2
Exit, with his followers.	1Tamburlaine	3.3.163.1
Exit, with his followers.	1Tamburlaine	3.3.165.1
FOLLOWING		
drawing Bajazeth in his cage, and his wife following him.	1Tamburlaine	4.2.0.3
FOR		
Enter Cupid solus [for Ascanius].	Dido	3.1.0.1
Anna, Iarbus, Achates, [Cupid for Ascanius], and followers.	Dido	3.3.0.2
Enter Achates, [Cupid for] Ascanius, Iarbus, and Anna.	Dido	4.1.0.1
Enter the Nurse with Cupid for Ascanius.	Dido	4.5.0.1
Cutpurse eare, for cutting of the golde buttons off his cloake.	Paris 617.1	12.30.1
with a Bishop [of Winchester] for the crowne [and Trussell].	Edward II	5.1.0.1
Enter the Friers with Bell, Booke, and Candle, for the Dirge.	Faustus 1075.2	3.2.95.2
FORWARD		
Enter [come forward] Barabas [and Ithimore].	Jew of Malta	4.1.173.1
[Comes forward].	Jew of Malta	5.5.60.1
FOUR		
[Enter] Souldan of Egipt with three or four Lords, Capolin	1Tamburlaine	4.1.0.1
FOURE		
of Damasco, with three or foure Citizens, and foure Virgins,	1Tamburlaine	5.1.0.1
and foure Virgins, with branches of Laurell in their hands.	1Tamburlaine	5.1.0.2
foure bearing the hearse of Zenocrate, and the drums sounding a	2Tamburlaine	3.2.0.2
lying on foure mens shoulders with a dead march, drawing	Paris 1250.3	22.112.3
and Penbrookes men, foure souldiers [, one of them James].	Edward II	2.5.98.2
Enter Lucifer and foure devils [above], Faustus to them with	Faustus 229.1	1.3.0.1
FRANCE		
Enter [Charles] the King of France, Navar and Epernoune staying	Paris 536.1	11.0.1
Enter [Henry] the King of France, Duke of Guise, Epernoune, and	Paris 743.1	15.0.1
Drumme and Trumpets, and enter the King of France, and Navarre,	Paris 1139.1	22.0.1
FREDERICK		
Enter Martino, and Frederick at severall dores.	Faustus 1151.1	4.1.0.1

FREDERICK (cont.)			
Exit Frederick with the Souldiers.	Faustus	1349.1	4.2.25.1
FREDERICKE			
[Enter] Sigismond, Fredericke, Baldwine, and their traine with	2Tamburlaine		1.1.77.1
[Enter] Sigismond, Fredericke, Baldwine, with their traine.	2Tamburlaine		2.1.0.1
Exeunt [Martino and Fredericke].	Faustus	1203.1	4.1.49.1
Faustus, Mephostophilis, Fredericke, Martino, and Attendants.	Faustus	1203.3	4.1.49.3
Enter Benvolio, Martino, Fredericke, and Souldiers.	Faustus	1325.1	4.2.0.1
Enter Fredericke.	Faustus	1356.1	4.2.32.1
Benvolio, Fredericke, and Martino, their heads and faces	Faustus	1431.1	4.3.0.1
FRENCH			
Enter Charles the French King, [Catherine] the Queene Mother,	Paris	0.1	1.0.1
FRENCHMAN			
the Queene and her sonne, and [Levune] <Lewne> a Frenchman.	Edward II		3.1.58.2
FRIAR (See also FRYAR)			
[Faustus strikes a friar].	Faustus	1080.1	3.2.100.1
FRIER			
Enter the Frier.	Paris	1121.1	21.15.1
Enter Frier with a Letter.	Paris	1158.1	22.20.1
FRIERS			
some the Pillars, Monkes and Friers, singing their Procession:	Faustus	867.2	3.1.89.2
Enter the Friers with Bell, Booke, and Candle, for the Dirge.	Faustus	1075.1	3.2.95.1
Beate the Friers, fling fire workes among them, and Exeunt.	Faustus	1087.1	3.2.107.1
the Cardinall of Lorraine to the banket, with Friers attending.	Faustus	App.	p231 0.2
Enter all the Friers to sing the Dirge.	Faustus	App.	p232 28.1
Beate the Friers, and fling fier-workes among them, and so	Faustus	App.	p233 41.1
FROM			
[Plucks a feather from Mercuries wings].	Dido		1.1.40.1
He takes it from her, and gives it Zenocrate.	1Tamburlaine		3.3.224.1
Celebinus, issues from the tent where Caliphas sits a sleepe.	2Tamburlaine		4.1.0.1
[Runs out from studie].	Paris	369.1	7.9.1
reading on a letter that was brought him from the king.	Edward II		1.1.0.2
Enter the Herald from the Barons, with his coate of armes.	Edward II		3.1.150.1
FRYAR			
Enter Ithimore, 1. Fryar.	Jew of Malta		3.3.49.1
Enter 1. Fryar.	Jew of Malta		3.6.43.1
[Aside to 2. Fryar].	Jew of Malta		4.1.81.1
[Aside to 2. Fryar].	Jew of Malta		4.1.83.1
[Aside to 1. Fryar].	Jew of Malta		4.1.86.1
[Aside to 1. Fryar].	Jew of Malta		4.1.89.1
[Aside to 2. Fryar].	Jew of Malta		4.1.91.1
[Aside to 2. Fryar].	Jew of Malta		4.1.100.1
Exit [Ithimore and 2. Fryar].	Jew of Malta		4.1.101.1
Enter [1. Fryar] Jacomo.	Jew of Malta		4.1.159.2
FRYARS			
<three> Fryars and [three] <two> Nuns [, one the Abbasse].	Jew of Malta		1.2.304.1
Enter [the] two Fryars <and Abigall>.	Jew of Malta		3.6.0.1
Enter the two Fryars.	Jew of Malta		4.1.20.1
GANIMED			
there is discovered Jupiter dandling Ganimed upon his knee, and	Dido		1.1.0.2
Exeunt Jupiter cum Ganimed.	Dido		1.1.121.1
GATE			
The [Clownes] <Clowne> bounce at the gate, within.	Faustus	1587.1	4.6.30.1
GAVESTON			
Gaveston reading on a letter that was brought him from the	Edward II		1.1.0.1
Enter Gaveston and the earle of Kent.	Edward II		1.3.0.1
Enter the King and Gaveston [and Kent].	Edward II		1.4.7.1
[Exeunt Kent and Gaveston guarded].	Edward II		1.4.34.1
Enter Gaveston.	Edward II		1.4.105.1
Exeunt Edward and Gaveston.	Edward II		1.4.169.1
Enter Gaveston.	Edward II		2.2.49.1
[Wounds Gaveston].	Edward II		2.2.84.1
[Exit Gaveston, attended].	Edward II		2.2.86.1
Ladies [, one of these Neece to the king, Gaveston], Baldock,	Edward II		2.2.224.2
doors] the King and Spencer, to them Gaveston, &c. [the Queene,	Edward II		2.4.0.2
Enter Gaveston pursued.	Edward II		2.5.0.1
[Arundell] <Mat.>, Gaveston, and Penbrookes men, foure	Edward II		2.5.98.2
Exit [Gaveston] cum servis Penbrookis.	Edward II		2.5.110.1
Enter Gaveston moorning, and the earle of Penbrookes men	Edward II		2.6.0.1
Exeunt Warwicke and his men, with Gaveston.	Edward II		2.6.17.1
GAZELLUS			
king of Natolia, Gazellus, vice-roy of Byron, [Uribassa]	2Tamburlaine		1.1.0.1
[Enter] Orcanes, Gazellus, Uribassa with their traine.	2Tamburlaine		2.2.0.1
Enter Orcanes, Gazellus, Uribassa, with others.	2Tamburlaine		2.3.9.2
GERMANE			
[Enter] Charles the Germane Emperour, Bruno, [Duke of] Saxony,	Faustus	1203.2	4.1.49.2
GETS			
He gets up upon him to his chaire.	1Tamburlaine		4.2.29.1
GETTETH			
the letter, and then the King getteth the knife and killes him.	Paris	1172.2	22.34.2
GIVE			
They give him water to drinke, and he flings it on the ground.	1Tamburlaine		4.4.55.1
and Jerusalem crowne him, and the other give him the scepter.	2Tamburlaine		3.1.0.4
GIVES			
[Gives jewells].	Dido		1.1.42.1
[Gives him crowne and scepter].	Dido		4.4.36.1
He takes it from her, and gives it Zenocrate.	1Tamburlaine		3.3.224.1
[Gives paper].	Jew of Malta		3.6.29.1
[Gives him bag].	Jew of Malta		4.2.101.1
Pothecary with the gloves, and gives them to the olde Queene.	Paris	166.3	3.0.3
Mephostophilis gives him a dagger.	Faustus	1725.1	5.1.52.1
GIVING			
<with> Devils, giving Crownes and rich apparell to Faustus:	Faustus	471.2	2.1.83.2

GLOVES			
and the Pothecary with the gloves, and gives them to the olde	Paris	166.3	3.0.3
GO			
[They go in the tent].	2Tamburlaine		4.1.75.1
[They go aside].	Jew of Malta		4.1.159.1
[The murtherers go aside as if in the next room].	Paris	943.1	19.13.1
[Offer to go].	Edward II		1.1.38.1
[Offers to go back].	Edward II		2.2.140.1
GOBLET			
Enter Robin and Rafe with a silver Goblet.	Faustus App.	p234	0.1
GOE			
They beare away the [olde] Queene [of Navarre] and goe out.	Paris	202.2	3.37.2
All goe out, but Navarre and Pleshe.	Paris	564.1	11.29.1
Goe out all, but the Queene [Mother] and the Cardinall.	Paris	630.1	12.43.1
his Crowne, and offering to goe out, his Paramour meetes him,	Faustus	1257.4	4.1.103.4
GOES			
Tamburlaine goes to her, and takes her away lovingly by the	1Tamburlaine		3.2.65.1
She goes out.	1Tamburlaine		5.1.285.1
He goes in and brings him out.	2Tamburlaine		4.1.90.1
Tamburlaine goes in, and comes out againe with al the rest.	2Tamburlaine		5.3.114.1
GOING			
doore, and takes Ascanius by the sleeve [as he is going off].	Dido		2.1.303.3
As they are going, [enter] the Souldier [above, who]	Paris	196.1	3.31.1
[Is going off].	Edward II		5.2.117.1
GOLD			
Barabas in his Counting-house, with heapes of gold before him.	Jew of Malta		1.1.0.2
GOLDE			
Cutpurse eare, for cutting of the golde buttons off his cloake.	Paris	617.1	12.30.1
GONZAGO			
Anjoy, Dumaine, Gonzago, Retes, Montsorrell, and Souldiers to	Paris	274.1	5.0.1
Exit Gonzago and others with him.	Paris	292.1	5.19.1
Enter [above Gonzago and others] into the Admirals house, and	Paris	297.1	5.24.1
Exeunt Gonzago and rest above].	Paris	306.1	5.33.1
Enter Gonzago and Retes.	Paris	370.1	7.10.1
GOOD			
Enter the <good> Angell and Spirit <the evill Angell>.	Faustus	96.1	1.1.68.1
Enter the two Angels <Enter good Angell, and Evill>.	Faustus	402.1	2.1.14.1
Enter the two Angels <good Angel, and evill Angell>.	Faustus	562.1	2.2.11.1
Enter the Good Angell, and the Bad Angell at severall doores.	Faustus	1891.2	5.2.95.2
GOVERNOR			
Theridamas and Techelles bringing the Governor of Babylon.	2Tamburlaine		5.1.79.1
Enter [Ferneze] [Governor] of Malta, Knights [and Officers],	Jew of Malta		1.2.0.1
Enter Governor, Martin del Bosco, the Knights [and Officers].	Jew of Malta		2.2.0.1
Enter Governor, Mater [attended].	Jew of Malta		3.2.9.2
Enter Governor, Bosco, Knights, [Callapine, the] Bashaw.	Jew of Malta		3.5.0.1
Enter Governor, Knights, Martin Del-Bosco.	Jew of Malta		5.1.0.1
Enter Governor with a guard.	Jew of Malta		5.2.47.1
[Exit Governor].	Jew of Malta		5.2.109.1
Enter Governor, Knights, Del-bosco.	Jew of Malta		5.4.0.1
[Governor stands aloof].	Jew of Malta		5.5.46.1
GOVERNOUR			
[Enter] The Governour of Damasco, with three or foure Citizens,	1Tamburlaine		5.1.0.1
Governour of Babylon upon the walles with [Maximus and] others.	2Tamburlaine		5.1.0.1
Enter another [1. Citizen], kneeling to the Governour.	2Tamburlaine		5.1.23.1
[Exeunt souldiers several ways, some with Governour].	2Tamburlaine		5.1.126.1
hang the Governour of Babylon in chaines on the walles].	2Tamburlaine		5.1.148.2
Enter Turkes, Barabas, Governour, and Knights prisoners.	Jew of Malta		5.2.0.1
Enter Governour.	Jew of Malta		5.5.19.1
GRAPES			
Enter Mephostophilis agen with the grapes.	Faustus	1575.1	4.6.18.1
with the grapes.	Faustus App.	p242	14.2
GREAT			
of Fesse, Moroco, and Argier, with others, in great pompe.	1Tamburlaine		3.1.0.2
Alarums, excursions, a great fight, and a retreate.	Edward II		3.1.184.2
GROUND			
They give him water to drinke, and he flings it on the ground.	1Tamburlaine		4.4.55.1
march, drawing weapons on the ground.	Paris	1250.5	22.112.5
GUARD			
Enter Governor with a guard.	Jew of Malta		5.2.47.1
[Exeunt guard].	Jew of Malta		5.2.50.1
Anjoy, Duke Demayne [and Cossin, Captain of the Kings Guard].	Paris	203.3	4.0.3
[Enter a Guard].	Edward II		2.2.130.1
GUARDE			
Enter the Captaine of the guarde, and three murtherers.	Paris	931.1	19.0.1
Enter Captaine of the Guarde.	Paris	1015.2	19.85.2
[Exit Captaine of the Guarde].	Paris	1058.1	19.128.1
GUARDED			
[Exit guarded].	Edward II		1.1.201.1
[Exeunt Kent and Gaveston guarded].	Edward II		1.4.34.1
[Exit guarded].	Edward II		3.1.259.1
GUIE			
junior, Edmund Earle of Kent, Guie Earle of Warwicke, &c.	Edward II		1.1.73.2
GUISE			
Enter the Duke of Guise.	Paris	58.1	2.0.1
[Catherine the] Queene Mother, Duke of Guise, Duke Anjoy, Duke	Paris	203.2	4.0.2
Exit Guise.	Paris	252.1	4.50.1
Enter Guise, Anjoy, Dumaine, Gonzago, Retes, Montsorrell, and	Paris	274.1	5.0.1
The Guise enters againe, with all the rest, with their Swords	Paris	335.2	5.62.2
Enter Loreine running, the Guise and the rest pursuing him.	Paris	338.2	5.65.2
Enter the Guise and Anjoy [, Dumaine, Mountsorrell, with	Paris	379.1	7.19.1
Enter [to them] Guise.	Paris	437.1	7.77.1
Enter the Duke of Guise, and Queene Mother, and the Cardinall	Paris	493.2	9.12.2
Exit Guise	Paris	511.1	9.30.1

GUISE (cont.)			
Enter also the Guise [and others].	Paris	528.2	10.0.2
Cardinall [cf Loraine], Duke of Guise, Epernoone, [Mugeroun],	Paris	588.4	12.0.4
Enter the Duchesse of Guise, and her Maide.	Paris	657.1	13.0.1
Enter the Guise.	Paris	669.1	13.13.1
Enter [Henry] the King of France, Duke of Guise, Epernoune, and	Paris	743.1	15.0.1
He makes hornes at the Guise.	Paris	753.1	15.11.1
Enter the Guise [attended].	Paris	816.3	17.11.3
Exit Guise.	Paris	870.1	17.65.1
Enter the Guise [within] and knocketh.	Paris	955.1	19.25.1
The Guise ccmes to the King.	Paris	963.1	19.33.1
Exit [the attendants taking up body of the Guise].	Paris	1090.1	19.160.1
Enter guise	Paris ms		p390 17.1
GUISES			
Enter the Guises sonne.	Paris	1045.1	19.115.1
GURNEY			
Enter Matrevis and Gurney.	Edward II		5.2.45.1
Exeunt Matrevis and Gurney.	Edward II		5.2.73.1
Enter Matrevis and Gurney with the King [and souldiers].	Edward II		5.3.0.1
Exeunt Matrevis and Gurney, with the king.	Edward II		5.3.62.1
Enter Matrevis and Gurney.	Edward II		5.5.0.1
[Exeunt Matrevis and Gurney].	Edward II		5.5.37.1
[Enter Matrevis, Gurney, and exeunt.	Edward II		5.5.109.1
Then Gurney stabs Lightborne.	Edward II		5.5.117.1
GUY (See GUIE)			
HAINAULT (See HENOLT)			
HALE			
They hale Edmund away, and carie him to be beheaded.	Edward II		5.4.108.1
HALLOW			
Hallow in his eare.	Faustus App.		p241 52.1
HAMMAR			
Enter [Barabas] with a Hammar above, very busie.	Jew of Malta		5.5.0.1
HAND			
Enter Aeneas with a paper in his hand, drawing the platforme of	Dido		5.1.0.1
and Mycetes comes out alone with his Crowne in his hand,	1Tamburlaine		2.4.0.2
and takes her away lovingly by the hand, looking wrathfully on	1Tamburlaine		3.2.65.1
mouthes, reines in his left hand, in his right hand a whip,	2Tamburlaine		4.3.0.2
hand, in his right hand a whip, with which he scourgeth them,	2Tamburlaine		4.3.0.2
[Lays hand on sword].	Edward II		2.2.153.1
Enter Robin the Ostler with a booke in his hand	Faustus App.		p233 0.1
HANDS			
and foure Virgins, with branches of Laurell in their hands.	1Tamburlaine		5.1.0.2
HANG			
hang the Governour of Babylon in chaines on the walles].	2Tamburlaine		5.1.148.2
They hang him.	Paris	493.1	9.12.1
HAUL (See HALE)			
HAVING			
besmear'd with mud and durt; all having hornes on their heads.	Faustus	1431.3	4.3.0.3
HE			
doore, and takes Ascanius by the sleeve [as he is going off].	Dido		2.1.303.3
Sound trumpets to the battell, and he runs in.	1Tamburlaine		2.4.42.1
He takes the Crowne and puts it on.	1Tamburlaine		2.7.52.2
Bajazeth flies [over the stage], and he pursues him.	1Tamburlaine		3.3.211.1
He takes it from her, and gives it Zenocrate.	1Tamburlaine		3.3.224.1
He gets up upon him to his chaire.	1Tamburlaine		4.2.29.1
He takes it and stamps upon it.	1Tamburlaine		4.4.41.1
They give him water to drinke, and he flings it on the ground.	1Tamburlaine		4.4.55.1
He brains himself against the cage.	1Tamburlaine		5.1.304.1
[He kisses her].	2Tamburlaine		2.4.70.1
He cuts his arme.	2Tamburlaine		3.2.114.1
He goes in and brings him out.	2Tamburlaine		4.1.90.1
his right hand a whip, with which he scourgeth them, Techelles,	2Tamburlaine		4.3.0.3
Strike him, he fals.	Jew of Malta		4.1.173.1
He writes.	Jew of Malta		4.2.71.1
Gonzago and others] into the Admirals house, and he in his bed.	Paris	297.1	5.24.1
He stabs him.	Paris	343.1	5.70.1
Stab him [and he falls within and dies].	Paris	360.1	6.15.1
He knocketh, and enter the King of Navarre and Prince of Condy,	Paris	429.1	7.69.1
He kils them.	Paris	441.1	7.81.1
He dies.	Paris	550.1	11.15.1
He cuts of the Cutpurse eare, for cutting of the golde buttons	Paris	617.1	12.30.1
He takes it.	Paris	677.1	13.21.1
He makes hornes at the Guise.	Paris	753.1	15.11.1
He shootes at him and killes him.	Paris	816.2	17.11.2
He writes.	Paris	891.1	17.86.1
He dyes.	Paris	1015.1	19.85.1
He offereth to throwe his dagger.	Paris	1051.1	19.121.1
He stabs the King with a knife as he readeth the letter, and	Paris	1172.1	22.34.1
He dyes.	Paris	1244.1	22.106.1
Enter minion He kills him	Paris ms		p390 16.1
He fetches in a woman devill.	Faustus	531.1	2.1.143.1
A Flourish while he ascends.	Faustus	876.1	3.1.98.1
him, he embraceth her, and sets Darius Crowne upon her head;	Faustus	1257.5	4.1.103.5
He sits to sleepe.	Faustus	1483.1	4.4.27.1
He puls off his leg.	Faustus	1491.1	4.4.35.1
He reades.	Faustus App.		p235 22.1
HEAD			
her, and sets Darius Crowne upon her head; and comming backe,	Faustus	1257.5	4.1.103.5
Enter Faustus with the false head.	Faustus	1361.1	4.2.37.1
Enter the Knight with a paire of hornes on his head.	Faustus App.		p238 68.1
HEADS			
their heads and faces bloudy, and besmear'd with mud and durt;	Faustus	1431.2	4.3.0.2
besmear'd with mud and durt; all having hornes on their heads.	Faustus	1431.3	4.3.0.3

HEAPES			
Barabas in his Counting-house, with heapes of gold before him.	Jew of Malta		1.1.0.1
HEARSE			
foure bearing the hearse of Zenocrate, and the drums sounding a	2Tamburlaine		3.2.0.2
They bring in the hearse.	2Tamburlaine		5.3.223.1
[Enter some with hearse].	Edward II		5.6.97.1
HELEN			
brings in Hellen, she <and Helen> passeth over the stage.	Faustus	1696.2	5.1.23.2
HELL			
Hell is discovered.	Faustus	1908.2	5.2.112.2
Exit. [Hell closes].	Faustus	1925.1	5.2.129.1
HELLEN			
Mephostophilis brings in Hellen, she <and Helen> passeth over	Faustus	1696.1	5.1.23.1
Enter Hellen againe, passing over betweene two Cupids.	Faustus	1767.1	5.1.94.1
HENOLT			
Enter sir John of Henolt.	Edward II		4.2.12.1
the Queene, Mortimer, the young Prince and Sir John of Henolt.	Edward II		4.6.18.2
HENRY			
Enter Henry crownd:	Paris	588.3	12.0.3
Enter [Henry] the King of France, Duke of Guise, Epernoune, and	Paris	743.1	15.0.1
HER			
Enter Dido [with Anna and Iarbus] and her traine.	Dido		2.1.73.1
Tamburlaine goes to her, and takes her away lovingly by the	1Tamburlaine		3.2.65.1
and takes her away lovingly by the hand, looking wrathfully on	1Tamburlaine		3.2.65.1
He takes it from her, and gives it Zenocrate.	1Tamburlaine		3.3.224.1
She runs against the Cage and braines her selfe.	1Tamburlaine		5.1.318.1
The Arras is drawen and Zenocrate lies in her bed of state,	2Tamburlaine		2.4.0.1
Zenocrate lies in her bed of state, Tamburlaine sitting by her:	2Tamburlaine		2.4.0.2
three Phisitians about her bed, tempering potions.	2Tamburlaine		2.4.0.2
[He kisses her].	2Tamburlaine		2.4.70.1
She noints her throat.	2Tamburlaine		4.2.78.1
[Stabs her].	2Tamburlaine		4.2.81.1
Exit, taking her away.	2Tamburlaine		4.2.98.1
Whispers to her.	Jew of Malta		1.2.348.1
[Aside to her].	Jew of Malta		1.2.356.1
Aside to her.	Jew of Malta		1.2.359.1
Aside to her.	Jew of Malta		1.2.361.1
[Whispers her].	Jew of Malta		4.4.2.1
Enter the Duchesse of Guise, and her Maide.	Paris	657.1	13.0.1
Enter the Queene and her sonne, and [Levune] <Lewne> a	Edward II		3.1.58.1
Enter the Queene and her sonne.	Edward II		4.2.0.1
Enter the Queene, her sonne, Edmund [earle of Kent], Mortimer,	Edward II		4.4.0.1
him, he embraceth her, and sets Darius Crowne upon her head;	Faustus	1257.5	4.1.103.5
her, and sets Darius Crowne upon her head; and comming backe,	Faustus	1257.5	4.1.103.5
[Faustus charmes her dumb].	Faustus	1668.1	4.6.111.1
HERALD			
Enter the Herald from the Barons, with his coate of armes.	Edward II		3.1.150.1
[Exit Herald].	Edward II		3.1.180.1
HERE			
Here the Curtaines draw, there is discovered Jupiter dandling	Dido		1.1.0.1
HERMES			
Enter Hermes with Ascanius.	Dido		5.1.23.1
HERSELF			
[Throws herself into the flames].	Dido		5.1.313.1
[Kills herself].	Dido		5.1.329.1
HER SELFE			
She runs against the Cage and braines her selfe.	1Tamburlaine		5.1.318.1
HIDE			
out alone with his Crowne in his hand, offering to hide it.	1Tamburlaine		2.4.0.2
HIGH			
the Lord high Admirall, and [Margaret] the Queene of Navarre,	Paris	0.2	1.0.2
manet Navar, the Prince of Condy, and the Lord high Admirall.	Paris	26.4	1.26.4
HIM			
[Gives him crowne and scepter].	Dido		4.4.36.1
the platforme of the citie, with him Achates, [Sergestus],	Dido		5.1.0.2
Bajazeth flies [over the stage], and he pursues him.	1Tamburlaine		3.3.211.1
They take him out of the cage.	1Tamburlaine		4.2.1.1
drawing Bajazeth in his cage, and his wife following him.	1Tamburlaine		4.2.0.3
He gets up upon him to his chaire.	1Tamburlaine		4.2.29.1
[They put him into the cage].	1Tamburlaine		4.2.82.1
They give him water to drinke, and he flings it on the ground.	1Tamburlaine		4.4.55.1
After Calapine, and after him other Lordes [and Almeda]:	2Tamburlaine		3.1.0.3
Orcanes and Jerusalem crowne him, and the other give him the	2Tamburlaine		3.1.0.4
and Jerusalem crowne him, and the other give him the scepter.	2Tamburlaine		3.1.0.4
She stabs him.	2Tamburlaine		3.4.30.1
He goes in and brings him out.	2Tamburlaine		4.1.90.1
They crowne him.	2Tamburlaine		5.3.184.1
Barabas in his Counting-house, with heapes of gold before him.	Jew of Malta		1.1.0.2
Strike him, he fals.	Jew of Malta		4.1.173.1
[Kisse him].	Jew of Malta		4.2.46.1
[Gives him bag].	Jew of Malta		4.2.101.1
Kisse him.	Jew of Malta		4.2.126.1
[His men work with him].	Jew of Malta		5.5.0.2
Exit Gonzago and others with him.	Paris	292.1	5.19.1
Stab him.	Paris	302.1	5.29.1
Enter Loreine running, the Guise and the rest pursuing him.	Paris	338.2	5.65.2
He stabs him.	Paris	343.1	5.70.1
Stab him [and he falls within and dies].	Paris	360.1	6.15.1
Kill him.	Paris	416.1	7.56.1
They hang him.	Paris	493.1	9.12.1
[Charles] the King of France, Navar and Epernoune staying him:	Paris	536.2	11.0.2
He shootes at him and killes him.	Paris	816.2	17.11.2
Take him away.	Paris	820.1	17.15.1

HIM (cont.)

They stabbe him.	Paris	1002.1	19.72.1
Now they strangle him.	Paris	1103.1	20.13.1
the letter, and then the King getteth the knife and killes him.	Paris	1172.2	22.34.2
Enter minion He kills him	Paris ms		p390 16.1
reading on a letter that was brought him from the king.	Edward II		1.1.0.2
[Lays hold on him].	Edward II		1.1.186.1
[Seize him].	Edward II		1.4.21.1
Enter the yong Prince, and the Earle of Kent talking with him.	Edward II		5.2.73.3
They wash him with puddle water, and shave his beard away.	Edward II		5.3.36.1
They hale Edmund away, and carie him to be beheaded.	Edward II		5.4.108.1
[Faustus hits him a boxe of the eare].	Faustus	1067.1A	3.2.87.1
is throwne downe, Alexander kils him; takes off his Crowne,	Faustus	1257.3	4.1.103.3
offering to goe out, his Paramour meetes him, he embraceth her,	Faustus	1257.5	4.1.103.5
to embrace them, which Faustus seeing, suddenly staies him.	Faustus	1257.7	4.1.103.7
devill playing on a Drum, after him another bearing an Ensigne:	Faustus	1430.2	4.2.106.2
Faustus charmes him dumb.	Faustus	1660.1	4.6.103.1
[Faustus charmes him dumb].	Faustus	1661.1	4.6.104.1
[Faustus charmes him dumb].	Faustus	1663.1	4.6.106.1
[Faustus charmes him dumb].	Faustus	1665.1	4.6.108.1
Mephostophilis gives him a dagger.	Faustus	1725.1	5.1.52.1
Exeunt [with him].	Faustus	1982.1	5.2.186.1
and Faustus hits him a boxe of the eare, and they all runne	Faustus App.		p232 21.1
Pull him by the legge, and pull it away.	Faustus App.		p241 53.1

HIMSELF

[Kills himself].	Dido		5.1.318.1
He brains himself against the cage.	1Tamburlaine		5.1.304.1
[Offers to stab himself].	Faustus	1728.1	5.1.55.1

HIMSELFE

[The Pope crosseth himselfe].	Faustus	1064.1A	3.2.84.1
The Pope crosseth himselfe.	Faustus App.		p232 17.1

HIS

there is discovered Jupiter dandling Ganimed upon his knee, and	Dido		1.1.0.2
Enter Aeneas with a paper in his hand, drawing the platforme of	Dido		5.1.0.1
and Mycetes comes out alone with his Crowne in his hand,	1Tamburlaine		2.4.0.2
his Bassoes and contributorie Kinges [and Zabina and Ebea].	1Tamburlaine		3.3.60.1
Exit, with his followers.	1Tamburlaine		3.3.163.1
Exit, with his followers.	1Tamburlaine		3.3.165.1
two Moores drawing Bajazeth in his cage, and his wife following	1Tamburlaine		4.2.0.2
drawing Bajazeth in his cage, and his wife following him.	1Tamburlaine		4.2.0.2
He gets up upon him to his chaire.	1Tamburlaine		4.2.29.1
They bring in the Turke [in his cage, and Zabina].	1Tamburlaine		5.1.202.1
[Enter] Callapine with Almeda, his keeper.	2Tamburlaine		1.2.0.1
Tamburlaine with Zenocrate, and his three sonnes, Calyphas,	2Tamburlaine		1.3.0.1
Enter Theridamas, and his traine with Drums and Trumpets.	2Tamburlaine		1.3.111.1
Tamburlaine with Usumcasane, and his three sons, [Calyphas],	2Tamburlaine		3.2.0.1
He cuts his arme.	2Tamburlaine		3.2.114.1
[Enter above] Captaine with his wife [Olympia] and sonne.	2Tamburlaine		3.3.14.2
Enter [below] the Captaine with [Olympia] his wife and sonne.	2Tamburlaine		3.4.0.1
[Enter] Tamburlaine with his three sonnes, Usumcasane with	2Tamburlaine		3.5.57.1
his chariot by Trebizon and Soria with bittes in their mouthes,	2Tamburlaine		4.3.0.1
mouthes, reines in his left hand, in his right hand a whip,	2Tamburlaine		4.3.0.2
hand, in his right hand a whip, with which he scourgeth them,	2Tamburlaine		4.3.0.2
[drawn in his chariot by the kings of Trebizon and Soria], with	2Tamburlaine		5.1.62.2
Enter Barabas in his Counting-house, with heapes of gold before	Jew of Malta		1.1.0.1
Hugs his bags.	Jew of Malta		2.1.54.1
[His men work with him].	Jew of Malta		5.5.0.2
Pointing to his Sworde.	Paris	153.1	2.96.1
and his [olde] Mother Queen [of Navarre], the Prince of Condy,	Paris	166.1	3.0.1
who] dischargeth his Musket at the Lord Admirall [and exit].	Paris	196.1	3.31.1
Enter the Admirall in his bed.	Paris	252.2	4.50.2
Gonzago and others] into the Admirals house, and he in his bed.	Paris	297.2	5.24.2
Shewing his dagger.	Paris	351.1	6.6.1
Enter Ramus in his studie.	Paris	361.1	7.0.1
Enter Ramus [out of his studie].	Paris	375.2	7.15.2
Cutpurse eare, for cutting of the golde buttons off his cloake.	Paris	617.2	12.30.2
Enter the King of Navarre [, Bartus], and his traine.	Paris	787.2	16.0.2
He offereth to throwe his dagger.	Paris	1051.1	19.121.1
Enter Warwicke and his companie.	Edward II		2.6.6.1
Exeunt Warwicke and his men, with Gaveston.	Edward II		2.6.17.1
father to the yong Spencer, with his trunchion, and soldiers.	Edward II		3.1.31.2
Enter the Herald from the Barons, with his coate of armes.	Edward II		3.1.150.1
They wash him with puddle water, and shave his beard away.	Edward II		5.3.36.1
[Enter Faustus in his study].	Faustus	29.1	1.1.0.1
Enter Faustus in his Study.	Faustus	389.1	2.1.0.1
Enter Faustus in his Study, and Mephostophilis.	Faustus	552.1	2.2.0.1
Exeunt the Pope and his traine.	Faustus	1070.1	3.2.90.1
Enter Benvolio above at a window, in his nightcap:	Faustus	1178.2	4.1.24.2
kils him; takes off his Crowne, and offering to goe out,	Faustus	1257.4	4.1.103.4
offering to goe out, his Paramour meetes him, he embraceth her,	Faustus	1257.4	4.1.103.4
the Emperour, who leaving his State, offers to embrace them,	Faustus	1257.6	4.1.103.6
He puls off his leg.	Faustus	1491.1	4.4.35.1
Enter the Duke of Vanholt; his Dutches, Faustus, and	Faustus	1558.1	4.6.0.1
Enter Robin the Ostler with a booke in his hand	Faustus App.		p233 0.1
with Alexander and his paramour.	Faustus App.		p238 59.1
Enter the Knight with a paire of hornes on his head.	Faustus App.		p238 68.1
Sleepe in his chaire.	Faustus App.		p240 26.1
Hallow in his eare.	Faustus App.		p241 52.1

HITHER

Enter Hostesse [brought hither by magic] with drinke.	Faustus	1649.1	4.6.92.1

HITS

[Faustus hits him a boxe of the eare].	Faustus	1067.1A	3.2.87.1
and Faustus hits him a boxe of the eare, and they all runne	Faustus App.		p232 21.1

HOLD			
[Lays hold on him].	Edward II		1.1.186.1
HOLLER (See HALLOW)			
HOOKES			
Enter with Welch hookes, Rice ap Howell, a Mower, and the Earle	Edward II		4.7.45.1
HORNES			
He makes hornes at the Guise.	Paris	753.1	15.11.1
besmear'd with mud and durt; all having hornes on their heads.	Faustus	1431.3	4.3.0.3
Enter the Knight with a paire of hornes on his head.	Faustus App.		p238 68.1
HORSE			
Enter Faustus, and the Horse-courser <and Mephistophilis>.	Faustus	1457.1	4.4.0.1
Enter the Horse-courser wet.	Faustus	1483.2	4.4.27.2
Enter [Robin the] Clowne, Dick, Horse-courser, and a Carter.	Faustus	1505.1	4.5.0.1
Enter [Robin] the Clowne, Dick, Carter, and Horse-courser.	Faustus	1608.1	4.6.51.1
enter a Horse-courser	Faustus App.		p239 97.1
HORSE-COURSER			
Enter Faustus, and the Horse-courser <and Mephistophilis>.	Faustus	1457.1	4.4.0.1
Enter the Horse-courser wet.	Faustus	1483.2	4.4.27.2
Enter [Robin the] Clowne, Dick, Horse-courser, and a Carter.	Faustus	1505.1	4.5.0.1
Enter [Robin] the Clowne, Dick, Carter, and Horse-courser.	Faustus	1608.1	4.6.51.1
enter a Horse-courser	Faustus App.		p239 97.1
HORSECOURSER			
Exit Horsecourser.	Faustus App.		p240 19.1
Enter Horsecourser all wet, crying.	Faustus App.		p240 26.2
Horsecourser runnes away.	Faustus App.		p241 63.1
HOSTESSE			
Enter Hostesse [brought hither by magic] with drinke.	Faustus	1649.1	4.6.92.1
Exit Hostesse.	Faustus	1668.1	4.6.111.1
HOSTIS			
Enter Hostis.	Faustus	1506.1	4.5.2.1
HOUSE			
Enter Barabas in his Counting-house, with heapes of gold before	Jew of Malta		1.1.0.1
Enter [above Gonzago and others] into the Admirals house, and	Paris	297.1	5.24.1
HOWELL			
Enter Rice ap Howell, and the Maior of Bristow, with Spencer	Edward II		4.6.45.2
Enter with Welch hookes, Rice ap Howell, a Mower, and the Earle	Edward II		4.7.45.1
HUGH			
Enter Hugh Spencer an old man, father to the yong Spencer, with	Edward II		3.1.31.1
HUGS			
Hugs his bags.	Jew of Malta		2.1.54.1
HUNGARY			
Pope, and Raymond King of Hungary, with Bruno led in chaines.	Faustus	867.3	3.1.89.3
IARBUS			
Enter [Iarbus, with] Illioneus, and Cloanthus [and Sergestus].	Dido		1.2.0.1
Enter Dido [with Anna and Iarbus] and her traine.	Dido		2.1.73.1
Enter Iarbus, Anna, and Dido.	Dido		3.1.6.1
Exit Iarbus.	Dido		3.1.55.1
Aeneas, Anna, Iarbus, Achates, [Cupid for Ascanius], and	Dido		3.3.0.1
[To Iarbus].	Dido		3.3.62.1
manet [Iarbus].	Dido		3.3.62.2
Enter Achates, [Cupid for] Ascanius, Iarbus, and Anna.	Dido		4.1.0.1
Enters Iarbus to Sacrifize.	Dido		4.2.0.1
Enter to them Iarbus.	Dido		5.1.61.1
Exit Iarbus and Aeneas traine.	Dido		5.1.77.1
Enter Iarbus.	Dido		5.1.278.2
Exit Iarbus.	Dido		5.1.291.1
Enter Iarbus running.	Dido		5.1.315.1
IF			
[The murtherers go aside as if in the next room].	Paris	943.1	19.13.1
ILLIONEUS			
Enter [Iarbus, with] Illioneus, and Cloanthus [and Sergestus].	Dido		1.2.0.1
Enter Cloanthus, Sergestus, Illioneus [and others].	Dido		2.1.38.1
[Enter Aeneas, Achates, Sergestus, Illioneus, and Cloanthus].	Dido		3.1.96.1
Enter Achates, Cloanthus, Sergestus, and Illioneus.	Dido		4.3.14.1
Enter Anna, with Aeneas, Achates, Illioneus, and Sergestus.	Dido		4.4.13.1
citie, with him Achates, [Sergestus], Cloanthus, and Illioneus.	Dido		5.1.0.2
IMPERIAL (See EMPERIALL)			
IN			
Enter Aeneas and Dido in the Cave at severall times.	Dido		3.4.0.1
Enter Aeneas with a paper in his hand, drawing the platforme of	Dido		5.1.0.1
and Mycetes comes out alone with his Crowne in his hand,	1Tamburlaine		2.4.0.2
Sound trumpets to the battell, and he runs in.	1Tamburlaine		2.4.42.1
of Fesse, Moroco, and Argier, with others, in great pompe.	1Tamburlaine		3.1.0.2
two Moores drawing Bajazeth in his cage, and his wife following	1Tamburlaine		4.2.0.2
Banquet, and to it commeth Tamburlain al in scarlet, Theridamas,	1Tamburlaine		4.4.0.1
and foure Virgins, with branches of Laurell in their hands.	1Tamburlaine		5.1.0.2
Tamburlaine all in blacke, and verie melancholy.	1Tamburlaine		5.1.63.3
They bring in the Turke [in his cage, and Zabina].	1Tamburlaine		5.1.202.1
The Arras is drawen and Zenocrate lies in her bed of state,	2Tamburlaine		2.4.0.1
Alarme, and Amyras and Celebinus run in.	2Tamburlaine		4.1.51.1
[They go in the tent].	2Tamburlaine		4.1.75.1
He goes in and brings him out.	2Tamburlaine		4.1.90.1
in his chariot by Trebizon and Soria with bittes in their	2Tamburlaine		4.3.0.1
his chariot by Trebizon and Soria with bittes in their mouthes,	2Tamburlaine		4.3.0.2
mouthes, reines in his left hand, in his right hand a whip,	2Tamburlaine		4.3.0.2
hand, in his right hand a whip, with which he scourgeth them,	2Tamburlaine		4.3.0.2
The Concubines are brought in.	2Tamburlaine		4.3.66.1
[drawn in his chariot by the kings of Trebizon and Soria], with	2Tamburlaine		5.1.62.2
hang the Governour of Babylon in chaines on the walles].	2Tamburlaine		5.1.148.2
Tamburlaine goes in, and comes out againe with al the rest.	2Tamburlaine		5.3.114.1
They bring in the hearse.	2Tamburlaine		5.3.223.1
Enter Barabas in his Counting-house, with heapes of gold before	Jew of Malta		1.1.0.1
Enter the Admirall in his bed.	Paris	252.2	4.50.2

IN (cont.)			
Gonzago and cthers] into the Admirals house, and he in his bed.	Paris	297.1	5.24.1
Enter Ramus in his studie.	Paris	361.1	7.0.1
[The murtherers gc aside as if in the next room].	Paris	943.1	19.13.1
Enter two [Murtherers] dragging in the Cardenall [of Loraine].	Paris	1091.1	20.0.1
[Enter Faustus in his study].	Faustus	29.1	1.1.0.1
Enter Faustus in his Study.	Faustus	389.1	2.1.0.1
He fetches in a wcman devill.	Faustus	531.1	2.1.143.1
Enter Faustus in his Study, and Mephostophilis.	Faustus	552.1	2.2.0.1
Pope, and Raymond King of Hungary, with Bruno led in chaines.	Faustus	867.4	3.1.89.4
A Senit while the Banquet is brought in; and then Enter Faustus	Faustus	981.1	3.2.0.1
and then Enter Faustus and Mephostophilis in their owne shapes.	Faustus	981.2	3.2.0.2
Enter Benvolio above at a window, in his nightcap:	Faustus	1178.2	4.1.24.2
Mephostophilis brings in Hellen, she <and Helen> passeth over	Faustus	1696.1	5.1.23.1
Enter Robin the Ostler with a booke in his hand	Faustus	App.	p233 0.1
Sleepe in his chaire.	Faustus	App.	p240 26.1
Hallow in his eare.	Faustus	App.	p241 52.1
INKE			
Enter the Maid with Inke and Paper.	Paris	665.1	13.9.1
Enter one with a pen and inke.	Paris	881.1	17.76.1
INTO			
[Throws herself into the flames].	Dido		5.1.313.1
[They put him intc the cage].	1Tamburlaine		4.2.82.1
[Barabas falls into it.	Jew of Malta		5.5.63.3
Enter [above Gonzago and others] into the Admirals house, and	Paris	297.1	5.24.1
cover'd dishes; Mephostophilis leades them into Faustus Study:	Faustus	1674.2	5.1.0.2
IS			
there is discovered Jupiter dandling Ganimed upon his knee, and	Dido		1.1.0.1
doore, and takes Ascanius by the sleeve [as he is going off].	Dido		2.1.303.3
The battell short, and they enter, Bajazeth is overcome.	1Tamburlaine		3.3.211.2
The Arras is drawen and Zenocrate lies in her bed of state,	2Tamburlaine		2.4.0.1
The Arras is drawen.	2Tamburlaine		2.4.142.1
[The body is thrown dcwn.	Paris	306.1	5.33.1
[Is going off].	Edward II		5.2.117.1
[Edward comes up or is discovered].	Edward II		5.5.41.1
A Senit while the Banquet is brought in; and then Enter Faustus	Faustus	981.1	3.2.0.1
they meete, Darius is throwne downe, Alexander kils him; takes	Faustus	1257.3	4.1.103.3
Hell is disccvered.	Faustus	1908.2	5.2.112.2
ISABELL			
Enter Queen Isabell.	Edward II		1.4.143.1
Enter Mortimer, and Queene Isabell.	Edward II		5.2.0.1
Manent Isabell and Mcrtimer.	Edward II		5.2.73.1
ISABELLA			
Exeunt omnes, manet Isabella.	Edward II		2.4.14.1
ISSUES			
Celebinus, issues frcm the tent where Caliphas sits a sleepe.	2Tamburlaine		4.1.0.1
IT			
[Enter servant with robe and Aeneas puts it on].	Dido		2.1.95.1
out alone with his Crowne in his hand, offering to hide it.	1Tamburlaine		2.4.0.2
He takes the Crowne and puts it on.	1Tamburlaine		2.7.52.2
He takes it from her, and gives it Zenocrate.	1Tamburlaine		3.3.224.1
Banquet, and to it ccmmeth Tamburlain al in scarlet, Theridamas,	1Tamburlaine		4.4.0.1
He takes it and stamps upon it.	1Tamburlaine		4.4.41.1
They give him water to drinke, and he flings it on the ground.	1Tamburlaine		4.4.55.1
[Throw it aside].	Jew of Malta		4.2.125.1
[Barabas falls into it.	Jew of Malta		5.5.63.3
He takes it.	Paris	677.1	13.21.1
[Snatch it].	Faustus	1043.1A	3.2.63.1
[Snatch it].	Faustus	1048.1	3.2.68.1
[Snatch it].	Faustus	1054.1	3.2.74.1
Snatch it.	Faustus	App.	p231 7.1
Pull him by the legge, and pull it away.	Faustus	App.	p241 53.1
ITHAMORE			
Enter Barabas, Ithamore.	Jew of Malta		4.1.0.1
ITHIMORE			
Enter Ithimcre.	Jew of Malta		3.1.22.1
Enter Ithimcre.	Jew of Malta		3.3.0.1
Enter Ithimcre, 1. Fryar.	Jew of Malta		3.3.49.1
Exit [Ithimcre].	Jew of Malta		3.3.52.1
[Enter Ithimore].	Jew of Malta		3.4.12.1
Enter Ithimcre with the pot.	Jew of Malta		3.4.54.1
Exit [Ithimcre and 2. Fryar].	Jew of Malta		4.1.101.1
Enter [come forward] Barabas [and Ithimore].	Jew of Malta		4.1.173.1
Enter Ithimcre.	Jew of Malta		4.2.20.1
Enter Curtezane, Ithimore, Pilia-borza.	Jew of Malta		4.4.0.1
Enter Jew, Ithimore [with Officers].	Jew of Malta		5.1.18.2
JACOMO			
Enter [1. Fryar] Jacomo.	Jew of Malta		4.1.159.2
JAMES			
and Penbrookes men, foure souldiers [, one of them James].	Edward II		2.5.98.3
and the earle of Penbrookes men [, James and three souldiers].	Edward II		2.6.0.2
Manet James cum caeteris.	Edward II		2.6.17.2
JERUSALEM			
Next Natolia and Jerusalem with the Emperiall crowne:	2Tamburlaine		3.1.0.2
Orcanes and Jerusalem crowne him, and the other give him the	2Tamburlaine		3.1.0.4
[Enter] Callepine, Orcanes, Jerusalem, Trebizon, Soria, Almeda,	2Tamburlaine		3.5.0.1
and Jerusalem led by with five or six common souldiers.	2Tamburlaine		4.3.0.5
King of Natclia, and King of Jerusalem, led by souldiers].	2Tamburlaine		5.1.62.4
JEW			
Enter Jew, Ithimore [with Officers].	Jew of Malta		5.1.18.2
JEWELLS			
[Gives jewells].	Dido		1.1.42.1
JEWES			
Enter three Jewes.	Jew of Malta		1.1.139.1

JEWES (cont.)			
[Exeunt three Jewes].	Jew of Malta		1.1.176.1
Enter Barabas, and three Jewes.	Jew of Malta		1.2.36.1
Exeunt. [Manent Barabas and the three Jewes].	Jew of Malta		1.2.159.1
Enter Abigall the Jewes daughter.	Jew of Malta		1.2.223.1
JOHN			
Enter sir John of Henolt.	Edward II		4.2.12.1
her sonne, Edmund [earle of Kent], Mortimer, and sir John.	Edward II		4.4.0.2
the Queene, Mortimer, the young Prince and Sir John of Henolt.	Edward II		4.6.18.2
JOYEUX			
the King of France, Duke of Guise, Epernoune, and Duke Joyeux.	Paris	743.2	15.0.2
Exit Joyeux.	Paris	751.1	15.9.1
The Duke Joyeux slaine.	Paris	787.1	16.0.1
JUNIOR			
Mortimer senior, Mortimer junior, Edmund Earle of Kent, Guie	Edward II		1.1.73.1
senior, Mortimer junior, the Archbishop of Canterburie,	Edward II		1.4.0.2
the Queene, Lancaster, Mortimer [junior], Warwicke, Penbrooke,	Edward II		2.2.0.1
Enter Lancaster, Mortimer [junior], Warwick, Penbrooke, Kent.	Edward II		2.3.0.1
JUNO			
Enter Juno to Ascanius asleepe.	Dido		3.2.0.1
JUPITER			
there is discovered Jupiter dandling Ganimed upon his knee, and	Dido		1.1.0.1
Exeunt Jupiter cum Ganimed.	Dido		1.1.121.1
KEEPER			
[Enter] Callapine with Almeda, his keeper.	2Tamburlaine		1.2.0.1
KENT			
Mortimer junior, Edmund Earle of Kent, Guie Earle of Warwicke,	Edward II		1.1.73.2
Enter Gaveston and the earle of Kent.	Edward II		1.3.0.1
Enter the King and Gaveston [and Kent].	Edward II		1.4.7.1
[Exeunt Kent and Gaveston guarded].	Edward II		1.4.34.1
Mortimer [junior], Warwicke, Penbrooke, Kent, attendants.	Edward II		2.2.0.2
Exit the King [, Queene, and Kent].	Edward II		2.2.99.1
[Enter the King and Kent].	Edward II		2.2.138.1
Enter Lancaster, Mortimer [junior], Warwick, Penbrooke, Kent.	Edward II		2.3.0.1
Enter Edward, with the Barons [and Kent] captives.	Edward II		3.1.220.2
[Exit Kent].	Edward II		3.1.232.1
Enter Edmund [earle of Kent].	Edward II		4.1.0.1
Enter Edmund [earle of Kent] and Mortimer.	Edward II		4.2.34.1
her sonne, Edmund [earle of Kent], Mortimer, and sir John.	Edward II		4.4.0.1
[Enter] Edmund [earle of Kent] alone with a sword and target.	Edward II		4.6.0.1
Enter the yong Prince, and the Earle of Kent talking with him.	Edward II		5.2.73.2
Enter Edmund [earle of Kent].	Edward II		5.3.48.1
Enter Souldiers with the Earle of Kent prisoner.	Edward II		5.4.81.1
KILL			
[Kill each other].	Jew of Malta		3.2.6.1
Kill him.	Paris	416.1	7.56.1
Kill them.	Paris	534.1	10.7.1
KILLES			
He shootes at him and killes him.	Paris	816.2	17.11.2
the letter, and then the King getteth the knife and killes him.	Paris	1172.2	22.34.2
KILLS			
[Kills himself].	Dido		5.1.318.1
[Kills herself].	Dido		5.1.329.1
Enter minion He kills him	Paris ms		p390 16.1
KILS			
He kils them.	Paris	441.1	7.81.1
is throwne downe, Alexander kils him; takes off his Crowne,	Faustus	1257.3	4.1.103.3
KING			
[Enter] Orcanes, king of Natolia, Gazellus, vice-roy of Byron,	2Tamburlaine		1.1.0.1
[Orcanes king of] Natolia, and Jerusalem led by with five or	2Tamburlaine		4.3.0.4
spare kings [Orcanes, King of Natolia, and King of Jerusalem,	2Tamburlaine		5.1.62.4
King of Natolia, and King of Jerusalem, led by souldiers].	2Tamburlaine		5.1.62.4
Enter Charles the French King, [Catherine] the Queene Mother,	Paris	0.1	1.0.1
the Queene Mother, the King of Navarre, the Prince of Condye,	Paris	0.2	1.0.2
Exit [Charles] the King, Queene Mother, and [Margaret] the	Paris	26.2	1.26.2
Enter the King of Navar and Queen [Margaret], and his [olde]	Paris	166.1	3.0.1
Enter [Charles] the King, [Catherine the] Queene Mother, Duke	Paris	203.1	4.0.1
and enter the King of Navarre and Prince of Condy, with their	Paris	429.1	7.69.1
Enter [Charles] the King of France, Navar and Epernoune staying	Paris	536.1	11.0.1
Enter the King of Navarre, Pleshe and Bartus, and their train,	Paris	698.1	14.0.1
Enter [Henry] the King of France, Duke of Guise, Epernoune, and	Paris	743.1	15.0.1
Enter the King of Navarre [, Bartus], and his traine.	Paris	787.2	16.0.2
Enter the King and Epernoune.	Paris	820.2	17.15.2
Enter the King of Navarre reading of a letter, and Bartus.	Paris	900.1	18.0.1
Enter the King and Epernoune.	Paris	946.1	19.16.1
The Guise comes to the King.	Paris	963.1	19.33.1
Exit King [and Epernoune].	Paris	976.1	19.46.1
[Enter King and Epernoune attended].	Paris	1017.1	19.87.1
Exit the King and Epernoune.	Paris	1080.1	19.150.1
Drumme and Trumpets, and enter the King of France, and Navarre,	Paris	1139.1	22.0.1
He stabs the King with a knife as he readeth the letter, and	Paris	1172.1	22.34.1
the letter, and then the King getteth the knife and killes him.	Paris	1172.2	22.34.2
They march out with the body of the King, lying on foure mens	Paris	1250.1	22.112.1
reading on a letter that was brought him from the king.	Edward II		1.1.0.2
Enter the King, Lancaster, Mortimer senior, Mortimer junior,	Edward II		1.1.73.1
Enter the King and Gaveston [and Kent].	Edward II		1.4.7.1
Enter king Edward moorning [attended].	Edward II		1.4.304.1
Enter the Ladie [Neece to the king].	Edward II		2.1.56.1
Exit the King [, Queene, and Kent].	Edward II		2.2.99.1
[Enter the King and Kent].	Edward II		2.2.138.1
three Ladies [, one of these Neece to the king, Gaveston],	Edward II		2.2.224.1
Enter [at several doors] the King and Spencer, to them	Edward II		2.4.0.1
Enter king Edward and Spencer, [Baldock], with Drummes and	Edward II		3.1.0.1

KING (cont.)
Enter the King, Spencer the father, Spencer the sonne, and the Edward II 3.1.184.3
Enter the King, [Arundell] <Matr.>, the two Spencers, with Edward II 4.3.0.1
Enter the King, Baldock, and Spencer the sonne, flying about Edward II 4.5.0.1
Enter the King, Leicester, with a Bishop [of Winchester] for Edward II 5.1.0.1
The king rageth. . . . . Edward II 5.1.85.1
Enter Matrevis and Gurney with the King [and souldiers]. . Edward II 5.3.0.1
Exeunt Matrevis and Gurney, with the king. . . . . Edward II 5.3.62.1
Enter the yong King, [Archbishop] [of Canterbury], Champion, Edward II 5.4.72.1
[King dies]. . . . . Edward II 5.5.113.1
Enter the King, with the lords. . . . . Edward II 5.6.23.1
Pope, and Raymond King of Hungary, with Bruno led in chaines. Faustus 867.3 3.1.89.3
KINGES
his Bassoes and contributorie Kinges [and Zabina and Ebea]. 1Tamburlaine 3.3.60.2
KINGS
[Enter] Bajazeth, the kings of Fesse, Moroco, and Argier, with 1Tamburlaine 3.1.0.1
Enter the kings of Trebisond and Soria, one bringing a sword, 2Tamburlaine 3.1.0.1
Usumcasane, Amyras, Celebinus, leading the Turkish kings. 2Tamburlaine 4.1.75.3
[drawn in his chariot by the kings of Trebizon and Soria], with 2Tamburlaine 5.1.62.2
with others, the two spare kings [Orcanes, King of Natolia, and 2Tamburlaine 5.1.62.4
[Exit with the Kings of Trebizon and Soria]. 2Tamburlaine 5.1.135.1
[Enter Tamburlaine, drawn by the captive kings; Amyras, 2Tamburlaine 5.3.41.1
Anjoy, Duke Demayne [and Cossin, Captain of the Kings Guard]. Paris 203.3 4.0.3
[Mugeroun], the kings Minions, with others, and the Cutpurse. Paris 588.4 12.0.4
father, Spencer the sonne, and the noblemen of the kings side. Edward II 3.1.184.4
KISSE
[Kisse him]. . . . . Jew of Malta 4.2.46.1
Kisse him. . . . . Jew of Malta 4.2.126.1
KISSES
[He kisses her]. 2Tamburlaine 2.4.70.1
KN
exit Kn: . . . . Faustus App. p237 57.1
KNEE
there is discovered Jupiter dandling Ganimed upon his knee, and Dido 1.1.0.2
KNEELE
five or sixe Protestants with bookes, and kneele together. Paris 528.1 10.0.1
KNEELING
Enter another [1. Citizen], kneeling to the Governour. . 2Tamburlaine 5.1.23.1
KNEELS
Edward kneels, and saith. . . . . Edward II 3.1.127.1
KNIFE
He stabs the King with a knife as he readeth the letter, and Paris 1172.1 22.34.1
the letter, and then the King getteth the knife and killes him. Paris 1172.2 22.34.2
KNIGHT
Enter Emperour, Faustus, and a Knight, with Attendants. . Faustus App. p236 0.1
Enter the Knight with a paire of hornes on his head. . Faustus App. p238 68.1
KNIGHTS
Knights [and Officers], met by [Callapine and other] Bassoes of Jew of Malta 1.2.0.1
Enter Governor, Martin del Bosco, the Knights [and Officers]. Jew of Malta 2.2.0.1
Enter Governor, Bosco, Knights, [Callapine, the] Bashaw. . Jew of Malta 3.5.0.1
Enter Governor, Knights, Martin Del-Bosco. . . . . Jew of Malta 5.1.0.1
Enter Turkes, Barabas, Governour, and Knights prisoners. . Jew of Malta 5.2.0.2
Enter Governor, Knights, Del-bosco. . . . . . . Jew of Malta 5.4.0.1
Enter del Bosco and Knights]. . . . . Jew of Malta 5.5.63.3
Exeunt Spirits with the knights. . . . . . . Faustus 1419.1 4.2.95.1
KNOCKE
They knocke againe, and call out to talke with Faustus. . Faustus 1590.1 4.6.33.1
KNOCKETH
He knocketh, and enter the King of Navarre and Prince of Condy, Paris 429.1 7.69.1
Enter the Guise [within] and knocketh. . . . . Paris 955.1 19.25.1
KNOCKS
Enter Mountsorrell and knocks at Serouns doore. . . Paris 346.1 6.0.1
LA
and then all crye vive [le] <la> Roy two or three times. . Paris 588.1 12.0.1
LADEN (See LODEN)
LADIE
Enter the Ladie [Neece to the king]. . . . . . . Edward II 2.1.56.1
LADIES
They run away with the Ladies. 2Tamburlaine 4.3.84.1
three Ladies [, one of these Neece to the king, Gaveston], Edward II 2.2.224.1
LANCASTER
Enter the King, Lancaster, Mortimer senior, Mortimer junior, Edward II 1.1.73.1
Enter both the Mortimers, Warwicke, and Lancaster. . . Edward II 1.2.0.1
Enter Nobiles [: Lancaster, Warwicke, Penbrooke, Mortimer Edward II 1.4.0.1
Edward, the Queene, Lancaster, Mortimer [junior], Warwicke, Edward II 2.2.0.1
Enter Lancaster, Mortimer [junior], Warwick, Penbrooke, Kent. Edward II 2.3.0.1
Enter the Barons, Mortimer, Lancaster, Warwick, Penbrooke, cum Edward II 3.1.194.1
LAURELL
and foure Virgins, with branches of Laurell in their hands. 1Tamburlaine 5.1.0.2
LAYS
[Lays hold on him]. . . . . Edward II 1.1.186.1
[Lays hand on sword]. . . . . Edward II 2.2.153.1
LE
and then all crye vive [le] <la> Roy two or three times. . Paris 588.1 12.0.1
LEADES
cover'd dishes; Mephostophilis leades them into Faustus Study: Faustus 1674.2 5.1.0.2
LEADING
[Enter] Tamburlaine leading Zenocrate: 1Tamburlaine 1.2.0.1
Enter Tamburlain leading the Souldane, Techelles, Theridamas, 1Tamburlaine 5.1.432.2
Usumcasane, Amyras, Celebinus, leading the Turkish kings. 2Tamburlaine 4.1.75.3
LEAVING
[As they are leaving] Enter Mathias. . . . . . . Jew of Malta 1.2.365.1
the Emperour, who leaving his State, offers to embrace them, Faustus 1257.6 4.1.103.6

LED		
and Jerusalem led by with five or six common souldiers.	2Tamburlaine	4.3.0.5
King of Natclia, and King of Jerusalem, led by souldiers].	2Tamburlaine	5.1.62.5
[Barons led cff by Spencer pater].	Edward II	3.1.249.1
[Spencer led cff].	Edward II	4.6.73.1
Enter the Seven Deadly Sinnes [led by a Piper].	Faustus 660.1	2.2.109.1
Pope, and Raymond King of Hungary, with Bruno led in chaines.	Faustus 867.4	3.1.89.4
LEFT		
mouthes, reines in his left hand, in his right hand a whip,	2Tamburlaine	4.3.0.2
LEG		
He puls off his leg.	Faustus 1491.1	4.4.35.1
LEGGE		
Pull him by the legge, and pull it away.	Faustus App.	p241 53.1
LEICESTER		
hookes, Rice ap Howell, a Mower, and the Earle of Leicester.	Edward II	4.7.45.2
Exeunt Edward and Leicester.	Edward II	4.7.99.1
Leicester, with a Bishop [of Winchester] for the crowne [and	Edward II	5.1.0.1
LEISTER		
[Enter Bartley to Leister with letter].	Edward II	5.1.127.1
LETTER		
Enter Barabas reading a letter.	Jew of Malta	3.4.0.1
Enter Barabas, reading a letter.	Jew of Malta	4.3.0.1
Enter the King of Navarre reading of a letter, and Bartus.	Paris 900.1	18.0.1
Enter Duke Dumayn reading of a letter, with others.	Paris 1107.1	21.0.1
Enter Frier with a Letter.	Paris 1158.1	22.20.1
He stabs the King with a knife as he readeth the letter, and	Paris 1172.1	22.34.1
reading on a letter that was brought him from the king.	Edward II	1.1.0.1
Spencer reades the letter.	Edward II	4.3.27.1
[Enter Bartley to Leister with letter].	Edward II	5.1.127.1
LEVUNE		
the Queene and her sonne, and [Levune] <Lewne> a Frenchman.	Edward II	3.1.58.1
Manent Spencer filius, [Levune] <Lewne> and Baldock.	Edward II	3.1.261.2
LEWNE		
the Queene and her sonne, and [Levune] <Lewne> a Frenchman.	Edward II	3.1.58.1
Manent Spencer filius, [Levune] <Lewne> and Baldock.	Edward II	3.1.261.2
LIES		
The Arras is drawen and Zenocrate lies in her bed of state,	2Tamburlaine	2.4.0.1
LIGHT		
Enter Barabas with a light.	Jew of Malta	2.1.0.1
LIGHTBORN		
[Enter Lightbcrn].	Edward II	5.4.22.1
LIGHTBORNE		
Enter Lightborne.	Edward II	5.5.14.1
Then Gurney stabs Lightborne.	Edward II	5.5.117.1
LIGHTNING		
Thunder and lightning:	Faustus 1674.1	5.1.0.1
<Thunder and lightning>.	Faustus 1976.1A	HC p271
LIKE		
<Enter with a divell drest like a woman, with fier workes>.	Faustus 531.1A	HC p261
Enter Faustus and Mephostophilis like the Cardinals.	Faustus 939.1	3.1.161.1
LODEN		
Lords [,Magnetes, Agidas], and Souldiers loden with treasure.	1Tamburlaine	1.2.0.2
LODOWICKE		
Enter Lodowicke.	Jew of Malta	1.2.373.1
Enter Lodowicke.	Jew of Malta	2.3.31.1
[Exit Lodowicke].	Jew of Malta	2.3.143.2
Enter Lodowicke.	Jew of Malta	2.3.217.1
[Exeunt Lodowicke and Abigall].	Jew of Malta	2.3.241.1
Enter Lodowicke, Abigall.	Jew of Malta	2.3.275.1
Enter Lodowicke reading.	Jew of Malta	3.2.2.1
LOOKING		
by the hand, looking wrathfully on Agidas, and sayes nothing.	1Tamburlaine	3.2.65.2
LORAINE		
of Guise, and Queene Mother, and the Cardinall [of Loraine].	Paris 493.3	9.12.3
enter Queene Mother, and the Cardinall [of Loraine, and Pleshe].	Paris 536.2	11.0.2
Queene [Mother], Cardinall [of Loraine], Duke of Guise,	Paris 588.3	12.0.3
Enter two [Murtherers] dragging in the Cardenall [of Loraine].	Paris 1091.1	20.0.1
LORD		
[Exit a Lord].	Dido	4.4.109.1
Enter a Lord.	Dido	4.4.123.1
the Lord high Admirall, and [Margaret] the Queene of Navarre,	Paris 0.2	1.0.2
manet Navar, the Prince of Condy, and the Lord high Admirall.	Paris 26.4	1.26.4
who] dischargeth his Musket at the Lord Admirall [and exit].	Paris 196.2	3.31.2
Enter lord [Arundell].	Edward II	3.1.88.1
[Exit Mortimer with 1. Lord attended].	Edward II	5.6.67.1
[Exit Queene and 2. Lord].	Edward II	5.6.92.1
[Enter 1. Lord].	Edward II	5.6.92.2
LORDES		
After Calapine, and after him other Lordes [and Almeda]:	2Tamburlaine	3.1.0.3
LORDS		
Usumcasane, other Lords [,Magnetes, Agidas], and Souldiers loden	1Tamburlaine	1.2.0.2
[Enter] Mycetes, Meander, with other Lords and Souldiers.	1Tamburlaine	2.2.0.1
[Enter] Souldan of Egipt with three or four Lords, Capolin	1Tamburlaine	4.1.0.1
Enter Anjoy, with two Lords of Poland.	Paris 451.1	8.0.1
and Spencer, to them Gaveston, &c. [the Queene, Neece, lords].	Edward II	2.4.0.2
Enter the King, with the lords.	Edward II	5.6.23.1
Enter Pope and all the Lords.	Faustus 1008.1	3.2.28.1
LOREINE		
Enter Loreine running, the Guise and the rest pursuing him.	Paris 338.2	5.65.2
LORRAINE		
enter the Pope and the Cardinall of Lorraine to the banket,	Faustus App.	p231 0.1
LOVINGLY		
and takes her away lovingly by the hand, looking wrathfully on	1Tamburlaine	3.2.65.1

Entry	Play	TLN	Reference
LUCIFER			
Enter Lucifer and foure devils [above], Faustus to them with	Faustus	229.1	1.3.0.1
Exeunt [Faustus; Lucifer and devils above].	Faustus	342.1	1.3.114.1
Enter Lucifer, Belzebub, and Mephostophilis.	Faustus	635.1	2.2.84.1
Enter [above] Lucifer, Belzebub, and Mephostophilis.	Faustus	1797.1	5.2.0.1
[Exeunt Lucifer and devils above].	Faustus	1982.2	5.2.186.2
LUTE			
Enter Barabas with a Lute, disguis'd.	Jew of Malta		4.4.29.1
LYING			
Ganimed upon his knee, and Mercury lying asleepe.	Dido		1.1.0.3
the body of the King, lying on foure mens shoulders with a dead	Paris	1250.1	22.112.1
MACHEVIL			
[Enter] Machevil [as Prologue].	Jew of Malta		Prol.0.1
MAGIC			
Enter Hostesse [brought hither by magic] with drinke.	Faustus	1649.1	4.6.92.1
MAGNETES			
Usumcasane, other Lords [,Magnetes, Agidas], and Souldiers loden	1Tamburlaine		1.2.0.2
MAID			
Exit Maid.	Paris	658.1	13.2.1
Enter the Maid with Inke and Paper.	Paris	665.1	13.9.1
MAIDE			
Enter the Duchesse of Guise, and her Maide.	Paris	657.1	13.0.1
MAIOR			
and the Maior of Bristow, with Spencer the father.	Edward II		4.6.45.2
MAKES			
He makes hornes at the Guise.	Paris	753.1	15.11.1
MALTA			
Enter [Perneze] [Governor] of Malta, Knights [and Officers],	Jew of Malta		1.2.0.1
MAN			
Enter the Admirals man.	Paris	241.1	4.39.1
Enter Hugh Spencer an old man, father to the yong Spencer, with	Edward II		3.1.31.1
Enter an Old Man.	Faustus	1706.1	5.1.33.1
[Enter Old Man] [aloof].	Faustus	1774.1A	5.1.101.1
Enter an old man.	Faustus App.		p243 33.1
MANENT			
Manent Cosrce and Menaphon.	1Tamburlaine		1.1.106.2
Manent Tamburlaine, Techelles, Theridamas, Usumcasane.	1Tamburlaine		2.5.49.2
Exeunt. [Manent Virgins].	1Tamburlaine		5.1.63.1
Exeunt. [Manent Bajazeth and Zabina].	1Tamburlaine		5.1.213.1
Exeunt. [Manent Barabas and the three Jewes].	Jew of Malta		1.2.159.1
Exeunt. Manent Mortimers.	Edward II		1.4.385.1
Manent Penbrocke, [Arundell] <Mat.>, Gaveston, and Penbrookes	Edward II		2.5.98.2
Manent Spencer filius, [Levune] <Lewne> and Baldock.	Edward II		3.1.261.2
Manent Isabell and Mortimer.	Edward II		5.2.73.1
Manent Edmund and the souldiers.	Edward II		5.3.62.2
MANET			
manet [Iarbus].	Dido		3.3.62.2
[Exeunt omnes, manet Aeneas].	Dido		4.3.45.1
[Exeunt. Manet Agidas].	1Tamburlaine		3.2.65.3
Exeunt. [Manet Tamburlaine].	1Tamburlaine		5.1.134.1
Exeunt. [Manet Barabas].	Jew of Malta		5.1.60.1
Exeunt. [Manet Barabas].	Jew of Malta		5.2.25.1
of Navar [with others], and manet Navar, the Prince of Condy,	Paris	26.3	1.26.3
Exeunt omnes, manet Isabella.	Edward II		2.4.14.1
Manet James cum caeteris.	Edward II		2.6.17.2
MAP			
One brings a Map.	2Tamburlaine		5.3.125.1
MARCH (See also MARTCH)			
They march out with the body of the King, lying on foure mens	Paris	1250.1	22.112.1
on foure mens shoulders with a dead march, drawing weapons on	Paris	1250.4	22.112.4
MARGARET			
Admirall, and [Margaret] the Queene of Navarre, with others.	Paris	0.3	1.0.3
and [Margaret] the Queene of Navar [with others], and manet	Paris	26.2	1.26.2
Enter the King of Navar and Queen [Margaret], and his [olde]	Paris	166.1	3.0.1
MARTCH			
and the drums sounding a dolefull martch, the Towne burning.	2Tamburlaine		3.2.0.3
MARTIN			
Enter Governor, Martin del Bosco, the Knights [and Officers].	Jew of Malta		2.2.0.1
Enter Governor, Knights, Martin Del-Bosco.	Jew of Malta		5.1.0.1
MARTINO			
Enter Martino, and Frederick at severall dores.	Faustus	1155.1	4.1.0.1
Exeunt [Martino and Fredericke].	Faustus	1203.1	4.1.49.1
Faustus, Mephostophilis, Fredericke, Martino, and Attendants.	Faustus	1203.3	4.1.49.3
Enter Benvolio, Martino, Fredericke, and Souldiers.	Faustus	1325.1	4.2.0.1
Fredericke, and Martino, their heads and faces bloudy, and	Faustus	1431.1	4.3.0.1
MASSACRE			
Gonzago, Retes, Montsorrell, and Souldiers to the massacre.	Paris	274.2	5.0.2
MAT.			
Manent Penbrooke, [Arundell] <Mat.>, gaveston, and Penbrookes	Edward II		2.5.98.2
MATER			
Enter Mathias, Mater.	Jew of Malta		2.3.137.1
Exeunt [Mater and slave].	Jew of Malta		2.3.158.1
Enter Governor, Mater [attended].	Jew of Malta		3.2.9.2
Enter Mater.	Jew of Malta		5.1.43.2
MATHIAS			
[As they are leaving] Enter Mathias.	Jew of Malta		1.2.365.1
Enter Mathias, Mater.	Jew of Malta		2.3.137.1
[Exit Mathias].	Jew of Malta		2.3.160.1
Enter Mathias.	Jew of Malta		2.3.250.1
Enter Mathias.	Jew of Malta		2.3.333.1
Enter Mathias.	Jew of Malta		3.2.0.1
MATR.			
Enter the King, [Arundell] <Matr.>, the two Spencers, with	Edward II		4.3.0.1

MATREVIS		
Enter Matrevis and Gurney.	Edward II	5.2.45.1
Exeunt Matrevis and Gurney.	Edward II	5.2.73.1
Enter Matrevis and Gurney with the King [and souldiers].	Edward II	5.3.0.1
Exeunt Matrevis and Gurney, with the king.	Edward II	5.3.62.1
Enter Matrevis and Gurney.	Edward II	5.5.0.1
[Exeunt Matrevis and Gurney].	Edward II	5.5.37.1
[Enter Matrevis, Gurney, and exeunt.	Edward II	5.5.109.1
Enter Mortimer and Matrevis [at different doors].	Edward II	5.6.0.1
MAXIMUS		
Governour of Babylon upon the walles with [Maximus and] others.	2Tamburlaine	5.1.0.2
MAYOR (See MAIOR)		
MEANDER		
[Enter] Mycetes, Cosroe, Meander, Theridamas, Ortygius, Ceneus,	1Tamburlaine	1.1.0.1
[Enter] Mycetes, Meander, with other Lords and Souldiers.	1Tamburlaine	2.2.0.1
Theridamas, Menaphon, Meander, Ortygius, Techelles, Usumcasane,	1Tamburlaine	2.5.0.1
[Enter] Cosroe, Meander, Ortygius, Menaphon, with other	1Tamburlaine	2.6.0.1
MEETE		
at the other Darius; they meete, Darius is throwne downe,	Faustus 1257.3	4.1.103.3
MEETES		
offering to goe out, his Paramour meetes him, he embraceth her,	Faustus 1257.4	4.1.103.4
MELANCHOLY		
Tamburlaine all in blacke, and verie melancholy.	1Tamburlaine	5.1.63.3
MEN		
[His men work with him].	Jew of Malta	5.5.0.2
Enter three poore men.	Edward II	1.1.23.1
and Penbrookes men, foure souldiers [, one of them James].	Edward II	2.5.98.2
and the earle of Penbrookes men [, James and three souldiers].	Edward II	2.6.0.2
Exeunt Warwicke and his men, with Gaveston.	Edward II	2.6.17.1
MENAPHON		
Meander, Theridamas, Ortygius, Ceneus, [Menaphon], with others.	1Tamburlaine	1.1.0.2
Manent Cosroe and Menaphon.	1Tamburlaine	1.1.106.2
[Enter] Cosroe, Menaphon, Ortygius, Ceneus, with other	1Tamburlaine	2.1.0.1
Tamburlaine, Theridamas, Menaphon, Meander, Ortygius,	1Tamburlaine	2.5.0.1
Cosroe, Meander, Ortygius, Menaphon, with other Souldiers.	1Tamburlaine	2.6.0.1
MENS		
lying on foure mens shoulders with a dead march, drawing	Paris 1250.3	22.112.3
MEPH		
Enter to them Meph.	Faustus App.	p235 31.1
exit Meph.	Faustus App.	p237 56.1
Enter Meph:	Faustus App.	p238 59.1
exit Meph.	Faustus App.	p242 13.1
MEPHASTO		
enter Mephasto:	Faustus App.	p242 14.1
MEPHISTOPHILIS		
Enter Faustus, and the Horse-courser <and Mephistophilis>.	Faustus 1457.1	4.4.0.1
MEPHOSTOPHILIS		
Enter Mephostophilis.	Faustus 262.1	1.3.34.1
Enter Mephostophilis.	Faustus 418.1	2.1.30.1
Enter Mephostophilis with the <a> Chafer of Fire <coles>.	Faustus 458.1	2.1.70.1
Enter Mephostophilis.	Faustus 471.4	2.1.83.4
Enter Faustus in his Study, and Mephostophilis.	Faustus 552.1	2.2.0.1
Enter Lucifer, Belzebub, and Mephostophilis.	Faustus 635.1	2.2.84.1
Enter Faustus and Mephostophilis.	Faustus 779.1	3.1.0.1
Exeunt Faustus and Mephostophilis.	Faustus 903.1	3.1.125.1
Enter Faustus and Mephostophilis like the Cardinals.	Faustus 939.1	3.1.161.1
Exeunt Faustus and Mephostophilis [with Bruno].	Faustus 976.1	3.1.198.1
and then Enter Faustus and Mephostophilis in their owne shapes.	Faustus 981.2	3.2.0.2
Enter Mephostophilis.	Faustus 1115.1	3.3.28.1
[Duke of] Saxony, Faustus, Mephostophilis, Fredericke, Martino,	Faustus 1203.3	4.1.49.3
[Enter Mephostophilis].	Faustus 1257.1	4.1.103.1
Enter Mephostophilis and other Divels.	Faustus 1402.1	4.2.78.1
Mephostophilis with fire-workes; they set upon the Souldiers	Faustus 1430.2	4.2.106.2
the Duke of Vanholt; his Dutches, Faustus, and Mephostophilis.	Faustus 1558.2	4.6.0.2
Exit Mephostophilis.	Faustus 1574.1	4.6.17.1
Enter Mephostophilis agen with the grapes.	Faustus 1575.1	4.6.18.1
cover'd dishes; Mephostophilis leades them into Faustus Study:	Faustus 1674.2	5.1.0.2
Enter Faustus, Mephostophilis, and two or three Schollers.	Faustus 1680.2	5.1.7.2
Mephostophilis brings in Hellen, she <and Helen> passeth over	Faustus 1696.1	5.1.23.1
Mephostophilis gives him a dagger.	Faustus 1725.1	5.1.52.1
Enter [above] Lucifer, Belzebub, and Mephostophilis.	Faustus 1797.1	5.2.0.1
[Enter Mephostophilis below].	Faustus 1879.2	5.2.83.2
Enter Mephostophilis:	Faustus App.	p235 25.1
MERCHANT		
Enter a Merchant.	Jew of Malta	1.1.48.1
[Exit 1. Merchant].	Jew of Malta	1.1.83.1
Enter a second Merchant.	Jew of Malta	1.1.84.1
MERCURIES		
[Plucks a feather from Mercuries wings].	Dido	1.1.40.1
MERCURY		
dandling Ganimed upon his knee, and Mercury lying asleepe.	Dido	1.1.0.2
[Exit Mercury].	Dido	1.1.119.1
MESSENGER		
[Enter a Messenger].	1Tamburlaine	2.3.48.1
of Egipt with three or four Lords, Capolin [, and a Messenger].	1Tamburlaine	4.1.0.2
Enter [Philemus], a Messenger.	1Tamburlaine	5.1.376.1
Enter a Messenger.	2Tamburlaine	2.2.23.1
[To them the Messenger].	2Tamburlaine	3.5.0.2
[Enter a Messenger].	2Tamburlaine	5.3.101.2
Enter a Messenger.	Jew of Malta	5.3.12.1
Enter Messenger.	Jew of Malta	5.5.13.1
Exit Messenger.	Paris 247.1	4.45.1
Enter a Messenger.	Paris 722.1	14.25.1

MESSENGER (cont.)

Enter a Messenger.	Paris	1154.1	22.16.1
Enter Messenger [and then Bishop of Winchester with the crown].	Edward II		5.2.22.1
[Exit Messenger].	Edward II		5.2.27.1
MET			
met by [Callapine and other] Bassoes of the Turke; Calymath.	Jew of Malta		1.2.0.1
MINION			
Enter minion He kills him	Paris ms		p390 16.1
MINIONS			
[Mugeroun], the kings Minions, with others, and the Cutpurse.	Paris	588.4	12.0.4
MONKES			
Enter the Abbot, Monkes, Edward, Spencer, and Baldocke	Edward II		4.7.0.1
some the Pillars, Monkes and Friers, singing their Procession:	Faustus	867.2	3.1.89.2
MONKS			
Monkes, Edward, Spencer, and Baldocke [disguised as monks].	Edward II		4.7.0.2
MONTSORRELL (See also MOUNTSORRELL)			
Gonzago, Retes, Montsorrell, and Souldiers to the massacre.	Paris	274.1	5.0.1
MOORES			
two Moores drawing Bajazeth in his cage, and his wife following	1Tamburlaine		4.2.0.2
MOORNING			
Enter king Edward moorning [attended].	Edward II		1.4.304.1
Enter Gaveston moorning, and the earle of Penbrookes men	Edward II		2.6.0.1
MORE			
Enter Aeneas with Ascanius [and Achates], with one or two more.	Dido		1.1.133.1
MOROCO			
Bajazeth, the kings of Fesse, Moroco, and Argier, with others,	1Tamburlaine		3.1.0.1
MORTIMER			
Lancaster, Mortimer senior, Mortimer junior, Edmund Earle of	Edward II		1.1.73.1
Mortimer senior, Mortimer junior, Edmund Earle of Kent, Guie	Edward II		1.1.73.1
Penbrooke, Mortimer senior, Mortimer junior, the Archbishop of	Edward II		1.4.0.1
senior, Mortimer junior, the Archbishop of Canterburie,	Edward II		1.4.0.2
the Queene, Lancaster, Mortimer [junior], Warwicke, Penbrooke,	Edward II		2.2.0.1
Enter Lancaster, Mortimer [junior], Warwick, Penbrooke, Kent.	Edward II		2.3.0.1
Enter the Barons, Mortimer, Lancaster, Warwick, Penbrooke, cum	Edward II		3.1.194.1
Enter Mortimer disguised.	Edward II		4.1.11.1
Enter Edmund [earle of Kent] and Mortimer.	Edward II		4.2.34.1
her sonne, Edmund [earle of Kent], Mortimer, and sir John.	Edward II		4.4.0.2
the Queene, Mortimer, the young Prince and Sir John of Henolt.	Edward II		4.6.18.1
Enter Mortimer, and Queene Isabell.	Edward II		5.2.0.1
Manent Isabell and Mortimer.	Edward II		5.2.73.1
Enter Mortimer alone.	Edward II		5.4.0.1
Enter Mortimer and Matrevis [at different doors].	Edward II		5.6.0.1
[Exit Mortimer with 1. Lord attended].	Edward II		5.6.67.1
MORTIMER JUNIOR			
senior, Mortimer junior, the Archbishop of Canterburie,	Edward II		1.4.0.2
MORTIMERS			
Enter both the Mortimers, Warwicke, and Lancaster.	Edward II		1.2.0.1
Exeunt. Manent Mortimers.	Edward II		1.4.385.1
MOTHER			
French King, [Catherine] the Queene Mother, the King of Navarre	Paris	0.1	1.0.1
Queene Mother, and [Margaret] the Queene of Navar [with	Paris	26.2	1.26.2
and his [olde] Mother Queen [of Navarre], the Prince of Condy,	Paris	166.1	3.0.1
the King, [Catherine the] Queene Mother, Duke of Guise,	Paris	203.1	4.0.1
of Guise, and Queene Mother, and the Cardinall [of Loraine].	Paris	493.2	9.12.2
enter Queene Mother, and the Cardinall [of Loraine, and	Paris	536.2	11.0.2
Queene [Mother], Cardinall [of Loraine], Duke of Guise,	Paris	588.3	12.0.3
Goe out all, but the Queene [Mother] and the Cardinall.	Paris	630.1	12.43.1
Enter Queene Mother [attended].	Paris	1063.1	19.133.1
MOUNTSORRELL			
Exit Mountsorrell.	Paris	331.1	5.58.1
Enter Mountsorrell and knocks at Serouns doore.	Paris	346.1	6.0.1
the Guise and Anjoy [, Dumaine, Mountsorrell, with soldiers].	Paris	379.1	7.19.1
MOUTHES			
his chariot by Trebizon and Soria with bittes in their mouthes,	2Tamburlaine		4.3.0.2
MOWER			
hookes, Rice ap Howell, a Mower, and the Earle of Leicester.	Edward II		4.7.45.1
MUD			
and besmear'd with mud and durt; all having hornes on their	Faustus	1431.3	4.3.0.3
MUGEROUN			
Guise, Epernoone, [Mugeroun], the kings Minions, with others,	Paris	588.4	12.0.4
Enter Mugeroun.	Paris	773.1	15.31.1
Enter Mugeroun.	Paris	816.1	17.11.1
MURTHERERS			
Enter the Captaine of the guarde, and three murtherers.	Paris	931.1	19.0.1
[The murtherers go aside as if in the next room].	Paris	943.1	19.13.1
Enter one of the Murtherers.	Paris	988.1	19.58.1
[Exit Murtherers].	Paris	1059.1	19.129.1
Enter two [Murtherers] dragging in the Cardenall [of Loraine].	Paris	1091.1	20.0.1
MUSICKE			
They call musicke.	2Tamburlaine		2.4.77.1
The musicke sounds, and she dies.	2Tamburlaine		2.4.95.1
Then trumpets cease, and Musicke sounds.	Faustus	1257.8	4.1.103.8
Musicke sound, Mephostophilis brings in Hellen, she <and Helen>	Faustus	1696.1	5.1.23.1
Musicke while the Throne descends.	Faustus	1898.1	5.2.102.1
MUSKET			
who] dischargeth his Musket at the Lord Admirall [and exit].	Paris	196.2	3.31.2
MUSKETT			
Enter A souldier with a muskett	Paris ms		p390 0.1
MYCETES			
[Enter] Mycetes, Cosroe, Meander, Theridamas, Ortygius, Ceneus,	1Tamburlaine		1.1.0.1
[Enter] Mycetes, Meander, with other Lords and Souldiers.	1Tamburlaine		2.2.0.1
and Mycetes comes out alone with his Crowne in his hand,	1Tamburlaine		2.4.0.1
NAKED			
Enter Techelles with a naked dagger.	1Tamburlaine		3.2.87.1

NAMES
Spencer reads their names. — Edward II 4.3.11.1

NATOLIA
[Enter] Orcanes, king of Natolia, Gazellus, vice-roy of Byron, — 2Tamburlaine 1.1.0.1
Next Natolia and Jerusalem with the Emperiall crowne: — 2Tamburlaine 3.1.0.2
[Orcanes king of] Natolia, and Jerusalem led by with five or — 2Tamburlaine 4.3.0.4
spare kings [Orcanes, King of Natolia, and King of Jerusalem, — 2Tamburlaine 5.1.62.4

NAVAR
and [Margaret] the Queene of Navar [with others], and manet — Paris 26.3 1.26.3
of Navar [with others], and manet Navar, the Prince of Condy, — Paris 26.3 1.26.3
Enter the King of Navar and Queen [Margaret], and his [olde] — Paris 166.1 3.0.1
[Charles] the King of France, Navar and Epernoune staying him: — Paris 536.1 11.0.1

NAVARRE
the Queene Mother, the King of Navarre, the Prince of Condye, — Paris 0.2 1.0.2
Admirall, and [Margaret] the Queene of Navarre, with others. — Paris 0.3 1.0.3
and his [olde] Mother Queen [of Navarre], the Prince of Condy, — Paris 166.2 3.0.2
They beare away the [olde] Queene [of Navarre] and goe out. — Paris 202.1 3.37.1
and enter the King of Navarre and Prince of Condy, with their — Paris 429.1 7.69.1
Exeunt [Condy and Navarre]. — Paris 440.1 7.80.1
All goe out, but Navarre and Pleshe. — Paris 564.1 11.29.1
Enter the King of Navarre, Pleshe and Bartus, and their train, — Paris 698.1 14.0.1
Enter the King of Navarre [, Bartus], and his traine. — Paris 787.2 16.0.2
Enter the King of Navarre reading of a letter, and Bartus. — Paris 900.1 18.0.1
and enter the King of France, and Navarre, Epernoune, Bartus, — Paris 1139.2 22.0.2

NEECE
Enter the Ladie [Neece to the king]. — Edward II 2.1.56.1
three Ladies [, one of these Neece to the king, Gaveston], — Edward II 2.2.224.1
and Spencer, to them Gaveston, &c. [the Queene, Neece, lords]. — Edward II 2.4.0.2

NEXT
Next Natolia and Jerusalem with the Emperiall crowne: — 2Tamburlaine 3.1.0.2
[The murtherers go aside as if in the next room]. — Paris 943.1 19.13.1

NIGHTCAP
Enter Benvolio above at a window, in his nightcap: — Faustus 1178.2 4.1.24.2

NOBILES
Exeunt Nobiles. — Edward II 1.1.133.1
Enter Nobiles [: Lancaster, Warwicke, Penbrooke, Mortimer — Edward II 1.4.0.1
Exeunt Nobiles. — Edward II 1.4.93.1
Exeunt Nobiles. — Edward II 2.2.199.1

NOBLEMEN
father, Spencer the sonne, and the noblemen of the kings side. — Edward II 3.1.184.4

NOBLES
Enter the Nobles to the Queene. — Edward II 1.4.186.1
Enter the Nobles. — Edward II 2.5.7.1
King, [Archbishop] [of Canterbury], Champion, Nobles, Queene. — Edward II 5.4.72.2

NOINTS
She noints her throat. — 2Tamburlaine 4.2.78.1

NOTHING
by the hand, looking wrathfully on Agidas, and sayes nothing. — 1Tamburlaine 3.2.65.2

NOW
Now they strangle him. — Paris 1103.1 20.13.1

NUNS
<three> Fryars and [three] <two> Nuns [, one the Abbasse]. — Jew of Malta 1.2.304.1

NURSE
Enter the Nurse with Cupid for Ascanius. — Dido 4.5.0.1
Enter the Nurse. — Dido 5.1.211.2
Exeunt the Nurse [and Attendants]. — Dido 5.1.224.1

OF (Homograph)
his hand, drawing the platforme of the citie, with him Achates, — Dido 5.1.0.1
[Enter] Bajazeth, the kings of Fesse, Moroco, and Argier, with — 1Tamburlaine 3.1.0.1
[Enter] Souldan of Egipt with three or four Lords, Capolin — 1Tamburlaine 4.1.0.1
They take him out of the cage. — 1Tamburlaine 4.2.1.1
Enter a second course of Crownes. — 1Tamburlaine 4.4.106.1
[Enter] The Governour of Damasco, with three or foure Citizens, — 1Tamburlaine 5.1.0.1
and foure Virgins, with branches of Laurell in their hands. — 1Tamburlaine 5.1.0.2
[Enter] Orcanes, king of Natolia, Gazellus, vice-roy of Byron, — 2Tamburlaine 1.1.0.1
Gazellus, vice-roy of Byron, [Uribassa] <Upibassa>, and their — 2Tamburlaine 1.1.0.1
The Arras is drawen and Zenocrate lies in her bed of state, — 2Tamburlaine 2.4.0.1
Enter the kings of Trebisond and Soria, one bringing a sword, — 2Tamburlaine 3.1.0.1
foure bearing the hearse of Zenocrate, and the drums sounding a — 2Tamburlaine 3.2.0.2
[Exeunt with the body of Calyphas]. — 2Tamburlaine 4.1.167.1
[Orcanes king of] Natolia, and Jerusalem led by with five or — 2Tamburlaine 4.3.0.4
Governour of Babylon upon the walles with [Maximus and] others. — 2Tamburlaine 5.1.0.1
[drawn in his chariot by the kings of Trebizon and Soria], with — 2Tamburlaine 5.1.62.2
spare kings [Orcanes, King of Natolia, and King of Jerusalem, — 2Tamburlaine 5.1.62.4
King of Natolia, and King of Jerusalem, led by souldiers]. — 2Tamburlaine 5.1.62.4
Theridamas and Techelles bringing the Governor of Babylon. — 2Tamburlaine 5.1.79.1
[Exit with the Kings of Trebizon and Soria]. — 2Tamburlaine 5.1.135.1
hang the Governour of Babylon in chaines on the walles]. — 2Tamburlaine 5.1.148.2
Barabas in his Counting-house, with heapes of gold before him. — Jew of Malta 1.1.0.2
Enter [Ferneze] [Governor] of Malta, Knights [and Officers], — Jew of Malta 1.2.0.1
met by [Callapine and other] Bassoes of the Turke; Calymath. — Jew of Malta 1.2.0.2
the Queene Mother, the King of Navarre, the Prince of Condye, — Paris 0.2 1.0.2
King of Navarre, the Prince of Condye, the Lord high Admirall, — Paris 0.2 1.0.2
Admirall, and [Margaret] the Queene of Navarre, with others. — Paris 0.3 1.0.3
and [Margaret] the Queene of Navar [with others], and manet — Paris 26.3 1.26.3
manet Navar, the Prince of Condy, and the Lord high Admirall. — Paris 26.3 1.26.3
Enter the Duke of Guise. — Paris 58.1 2.0.1
Enter the King of Navar and Queen [Margaret], and his [olde] — Paris 166.1 3.0.1
and his [olde] Mother Queen [of Navarre], the Prince of Condy, — Paris 166.2 3.0.2
Mother Queen [of Navarre], the Prince of Condy, the Admirall, — Paris 166.2 3.0.2
They beare away the [olde] Queene [of Navarre] and goe out. — Paris 202.1 3.37.1
[Catherine the] Queene Mother, Duke of Guise, Duke Anjoy, Duke — Paris 203.1 4.0.1
Anjoy, Duke Demayne [and Cossin, Captain of the Kings Guard]. — Paris 203.2 4.0.2

OF (cont.)
The ordinance being shot of, the bell tolles. Paris 334.1 5.61.1
Enter Ramus [out of his studie]. Paris 375.2 7.15.2
and enter the King of Navarre and Prince of Condy, with their Paris 429.1 7.69.1
and enter the King of Navarre and Prince of Condy, with their Paris 429.2 7.69.2
Enter Anjoy, with two Lords of Poland. Paris 451.1 8.0.1
Enter the Duke of Guise, and Queene Mother, and the Cardinall Paris 493.2 9.12.2
of Guise, and Queene Mother, and the Cardinall [of Loraine]. Paris 493.3 9.12.3
Enter [Charles] the King of France, Navar and Epernoune staying Paris 536.1 11.0.1
enter Queene Mother, and the Cardinall [of Loraine, and Pleshe]. Paris 536.2 11.0.2
Queene [Mother], Cardinall [of Loraine], Duke of Guise, Paris 588.3 12.0.3
Cardinall [of Loraine], Duke of Guise, Epernoone, [Mugeroun], Paris 588.4 12.0.4
He cuts of the Cutpurse eare, for cutting of the golde buttons Paris 617.1 12.30.1
Cutpurse eare, for cutting of the golde buttons off his cloake. Paris 617.1 12.30.1
Enter the Duchesse of Guise, and her Maide. Paris 657.1 13.0.1
Enter the King of Navarre, Pleshe and Bartus, and their train, Paris 698.1 14.0.1
Enter [Henry] the King of France, Duke of Guise, Epernoune, and Paris 743.1 15.0.1
Enter the King of Navarre [, Bartus], and his traine. Paris 787.2 16.0.2
Enter the King of Navarre reading of a letter, and Bartus. Paris 900.1 18.0.1
Enter the Captaine of the guarde, and three murtherers. Paris 931.1 19.0.1
Enter one of the Murtherers. Paris 988.1 19.58.1
Enter Captaine of the Guarde. Paris 1015.2 19.85.2
[Exit Captaine of the Guarde]. Paris 1058.1 19.128.1
Exit [the attendants taking up body of the Guise]. Paris 1090.1 19.160.1
Enter two [Murtherers] dragging in the Cardenall [of Loraine]. Paris 1091.1 20.0.1
Enter Duke Dumayn reading of a letter, with others. Paris 1107.1 21.0.1
Drumme and Trumpets, and enter the King of France, and Navarre, Paris 1139.1 22.0.1
They march out with the body of the King, lying on foure mens Paris 1250.1 22.112.1
Mortimer junior, Edmund Earle of Kent, Guie Earle of Warwicke, Edward II 1.1.73.2
junior, Edmund Earle of Kent, Guie Earle of Warwicke, &c. Edward II 1.1.73.2
Enter the Bishop of Coventrie. Edward II 1.1.174.1
Enter the [Archbishop] of Canterburie [and attendant]. Edward II 1.2.32.1
Enter Gaveston and the earle of Kent. Edward II 1.3.0.1
Mortimer junior, the Archbishop of Canterburie, attended]. Edward II 1.4.0.2
three Ladies [, one of these Neece to the king, Gaveston], Edward II 2.2.224.1
Enter earle of Arundell. Edward II 2.5.31.1
and Penbrookes men, foure souldiers [, one of them James]. Edward II 2.5.98.3
and the earle of Penbrookes men [, James and three souldiers]. Edward II 2.6.0.1
Enter the Herald from the Barons, with his coate of armes. Edward II 3.1.150.1
father, Spencer the sonne, and the noblemen of the kings side. Edward II 3.1.184.4
Enter Edmund [earle of Kent]. Edward II 4.1.0.1
Enter sir John of Henolt. Edward II 4.2.12.1
Enter Edmund [earle of Kent] and Mortimer. Edward II 4.2.34.1
her sonne, Edmund [earle of Kent], Mortimer, and sir John. Edward II 4.4.0.1
[Enter] Edmund [earle of Kent] alone with a sword and target. Edward II 4.6.0.1
the Queene, Mortimer, the young Prince and Sir John of Henolt. Edward II 4.6.18.2
and the Maior of Bristow, with Spencer the father. Edward II 4.6.45.2
hookes, Rice ap Howell, a Mower, and the Earle of Leicester. Edward II 4.7.45.2
with a Bishop [of Winchester] for the crowne [and Trussell]. Edward II 5.1.0.1
[Exeunt Bishop of Winchester and Trussell]. Edward II 5.1.124.1
Enter Messenger [and then Bishop of Winchester with the crown]. Edward II 5.2.22.1
Enter the yong Prince, and the Earle of Kent talking with him. Edward II 5.2.73.2
Enter Edmund [earle of Kent]. Edward II 5.3.48.1
Enter the yong King, [Archbishop] [of Canterbury], Champion, Edward II 5.4.72.1
Enter Souldiers with the Earle of Kent prisoner. Edward II 5.4.81.1
Enter Mephostophilis with the <a> Chafer of Fire <coles>. Faustus 458.1 2.1.70.1
Pope, and Raymond King of Hungary, with Bruno led in chaines. Faustus 867.3 3.1.89.3
[Faustus hits him a boxe of the eare]. Faustus 1067.1A 3.2.87.1
Emperour, Bruno, [Duke of] Saxony, Faustus, Mephostophilis, Faustus 1203.2 4.1.49.2
Enter the Duke of Vanholt; his Dutches, Faustus, and Faustus 1558.1 4.6.0.1
enter the Pope and the Cardinall of Lorraine to the banket, Faustus App. p231 0.1
and Faustus hits him a boxe of the eare, and they all runne Faustus App. p232 21.1
Enter the Knight with a paire of hornes on his head. Faustus App. p238 68.1

OFF (See also OF)
doore, and takes Ascanius by the sleeve [as he is going off]. Dido 2.1.303.3
[Takes off shepheards cloak]. 1Tamburlaine 1.2.41.1
Cutpurse eare, for cutting of the golde buttons off his cloake. Paris 617.2 12.30.2
[Barons led off by Spencer pater]. Edward II 3.1.249.1
[Spencer led off]. Edward II 4.6.73.1
[Is going off]. Edward II 5.2.117.1
kils him; takes off his Crowne, and offering to goe out, Faustus 1257.4 4.1.103.4
He puls off his leg. Faustus 1491.1 4.4.35.1

OFFER
[Offer to go]. Edward II 1.1.38.1

OFFERETH
He offereth to throwe his dagger. Paris 1051.1 19.121.1

OFFERING
out alone with his Crowne in his hand, offering to hide it. 1Tamburlaine 2.4.0.2
his Crowne, and offering to goe out, his Paramour meetes him, Faustus 1257.4 4.1.103.4

OFFERS
[Offers to go back]. Edward II 2.2.140.1
leaving his State, offers to embrace them, which Faustus seeing, Faustus 1257.6 4.1.103.6
[Offers to stab himself]. Faustus 1728.1 5.1.55.1

OFFICER
Enter 1. Officer. Jew of Malta 5.1.49.1

OFFICERS
Knights [and Officers], met by [Callapine and other] Bassoes of Jew of Malta 1.2.0.1
[Exeunt Officers]. Jew of Malta 1.2.93.1
Enter Officers. Jew of Malta 1.2.130.1
Enter Governor, Martin del Bosco, the Knights [and Officers]. Jew of Malta 2.2.0.1
[Exeunt Officers]. Jew of Malta 2.2.43.1
Enter Officers with slaves. Jew of Malta 2.3.0.1
[Exeunt Officers with slaves]. Jew of Malta 2.3.162.1

OFFICERS (cont.)

[Exit Officers].	Jew of Malta		5.1.18.1
Enter Jew, Ithimore [with Officers].	Jew of Malta		5.1.18.2
Exit [Barabas, Curtezane, Pilia-borza, with Officers].	Jew of Malta		5.1.43.1
[Enter Officers carrying Barabas, as dead].	Jew of Malta		5.1.53.1

OLD

Enter Hugh Spencer an old man, father to the yong Spencer, with	Edward II		3.1.31.1
Enter an Old Man.	Faustus	1706.1	5.1.33.1
[Enter Old Man] [aloof].	Faustus	1774.1A	5.1.101.1
Enter an old man.	Faustus App.	p243	33.1

OLDE

and his [olde] Mother Queen [of Navarre], the Prince of Condy,	Paris	166.1	3.0.1
Pothecary with the gloves, and gives them to the olde Queene.	Paris	166.3	3.0.3
They beare away the [olde] Queene [of Navarre] and goe out.	Paris	202.1	3.37.1

OLYMPIA

[Enter above] Captaine with his wife [Olympia] and sonne.	2Tamburlaine		3.3.14.2
Enter [below] the Captaine with [Olympia] his wife and sonne.	2Tamburlaine		3.4.0.1
[Enter] Olympia alone.	2Tamburlaine		4.2.0.1

OMNES

Exeunt omnes.	Dido		2.1.303.1
Exeunt omnes:	Dido		3.3.62.2
[Exeunt omnes, manet Aeneas].	Dido		4.3.45.1
Exeunt omnes.	Paris	273.1	4.71.1
Exeunt [omnes].	Paris	345.1	5.72.1
Exeunt omnes.	Edward II		2.2.265.1
Exeunt omnes, manet Isabella.	Edward II		2.4.14.1
Exeunt omnes.	Edward II		3.1.281.1
Exeunt omnes.	Edward II		4.6.79.1
Exeunt omnes.	Edward II		5.1.155.1
Exeunt omnes [severally].	Edward II		5.2.121.1
Exeunt omnes.	Edward II		5.3.67.1
Exeunt omnes.	Edward II		5.4.115.1
Exeunt omnes.	Edward II		5.5.120.1
Exeunt omnes.	Faustus	193.1	1.1.165.1
Exeunt omnes, severall waies.	Faustus	721.1	2.2.173.1
Exeunt omnes.	Faustus	1324.1	4.1.170.1
[Exeunt omnes].	Faustus	1430.4	4.2.106.4
Exeunt omnes.	Faustus	1456.1	4.3.26.1
Exeunt omnes.	Faustus	1557.1	4.5.53.1

ON

[Enter servant with robe and Aeneas puts it on].	Dido		2.1.95.1
He takes the Crowne and puts it on.	1Tamburlaine		2.7.52.2
by the hand, looking wrathfully on Agidas, and sayes nothing.	1Tamburlaine		3.2.65.2
They give him water to drinke, and he flings it on the ground.	1Tamburlaine		4.4.55.1
hang the Governour of Babylon in chaines on the walles].	2Tamburlaine		5.1.148.2
lying on foure mens shoulders with a dead march, drawing	Paris	1250.3	22.112.3
march, drawing weapons on the ground.	Paris	1250.5	22.112.5
reading on a letter that was brought him from the king.	Edward II		1.1.0.1
[Lays hold on him].	Edward II		1.1.186.1
[Lays hand on sword].	Edward II		2.2.153.1
and enter a devill playing on a Drum, after him another bearing	Faustus	1430.1	4.2.106.1
besmear'd with mud and durt; all having hornes on their heads.	Faustus	1431.3	4.3.0.3
Enter the Knight with a paire of hornes on his head.	Faustus App.		p238 68.1

ONE

Enter Aeneas with Ascanius [and Achates], with one or two more.	Dido		1.1.133.1
and Soria, one bringing a sword, and another a scepter:	2Tamburlaine		3.1.0.1
One brings a Map.	2Tamburlaine		5.3.125.1
<three> Fryars and [three] <two> Nuns [, one the Abbasse].	Jew of Malta		1.2.304.2
Enter one with a pen and inke.	Paris	881.1	17.76.1
Exit one.	Paris	892.1	17.87.1
Enter one of the Murtherers.	Paris	988.1	19.58.1
three Ladies [, one of these Neece to the king, Gaveston],	Edward II		2.2.224.1
and Penbrookes men, foure souldiers [, one of them James].	Edward II		2.5.98.3
Enter at one [dore] the Emperour Alexander, at the other	Faustus	1257.2	4.1.103.2

OR

Enter Aeneas with Ascanius [and Achates], with one or two more.	Dido		1.1.133.1
[Enter] Souldan of Egipt with three or four Lords, Capolin	1Tamburlaine		4.1.0.1
of Damasco, with three or foure Citizens, and foure Virgins,	1Tamburlaine		5.1.0.1
Enter two or three.	1Tamburlaine		5.1.191.1
and Jerusalem led by with five or six common souldiers.	2Tamburlaine		4.3.0.5
Enter five or sixe Protestants with bookes, and kneele	Paris	528.1	10.0.1
and then all crye vive [le] <la> Roy two or three times.	Paris	588.2	12.0.2
[Edward comes up or is discovered].	Edward II		5.5.41.1
Enter Faustus, Mephostophilis, and two or three Schollers.	Faustus	1680.2	5.1.7.2

ORCANES

[Enter] Orcanes, king of Natolia, Gazellus, vice-roy of Byron,	2Tamburlaine		1.1.0.1
[Enter] Orcanes, Gazellus, Uribassa with their traine.	2Tamburlaine		2.2.0.1
Enter Orcanes, Gazellus, Uribassa, with others.	2Tamburlaine		2.3.9.2
Orcanes and Jerusalem crowne him, and the other give him the	2Tamburlaine		3.1.0.4
[Enter] Callepine, Orcanes, Jerusalem, Trebizon, Soria, Almeda,	2Tamburlaine		3.5.0.1
[Orcanes king of] Natolia, and Jerusalem led by with five or	2Tamburlaine		4.3.0.4
with others, the two spare kings [Orcanes, King of Natolia, and	2Tamburlaine		5.1.62.4

ORDINANCE

The ordinance being shot of, the bell tolles.	Paris	334.1	5.61.1

ORTIGIUS

Enter Ortigius and [Ceneus] <Conerus> bearing a Crowne, with	1Tamburlaine		1.1.135.1

ORTYGIUS

Meander, Theridamas, Ortygius, Ceneus, [Menaphon], with others.	1Tamburlaine		1.1.0.1
Cosroe, Menaphon, Ortygius, Ceneus, with other Souldiers.	1Tamburlaine		2.1.0.1
Theridamas, Techelles, Usumcasane, Ortygius, with others.	1Tamburlaine		2.3.0.2
Menaphon, Meander, Ortygius, Techelles, Usumcasane, with	1Tamburlaine		2.5.0.2
Cosroe, Meander, Ortygius, Menaphon, with other Souldiers.	1Tamburlaine		2.6.0.1

OSTLER

Enter Robin the Ostler with a booke in his hand	Faustus App.		p233 0.1

OTHER			
Usumcasane, other Lords [,Magnetes, Agidas], and Souldiers loden	1Tamburlaine		1.2.0.2
Cosroe, Menaphon, Ortygius, Ceneus, with other Souldiers.	1Tamburlaine		2.1.0.1
[Enter] Mycetes, Meander, with other Lords and Souldiers.	1Tamburlaine		2.2.0.1
Cosroe, Meander, Ortygius, Menaphon, with other Souldiers.	1Tamburlaine		2.6.0.1
After Calapine, and after him other Lordes [and Almeda]:	2Tamburlaine		3.1.0.3
and Jerusalem crowne him, and the other give him the scepter.	2Tamburlaine		3.1.0.4
Tamburlaine with his three sonnes, Usumcasane with other.	2Tamburlaine		3.5.57.2
Enter Theridamas and Techelles, with other souldiers.	2Tamburlaine		5.1.48.1
met by [Callapine and other] Bassoes of the Turke; Calymath.	Jew of Malta		1.2.0.2
[Kill each other].	Jew of Malta		3.2.6.1
[dore] the Emperour Alexander, at the other Darius; they meete,	Faustus	1257.2	4.1.103.2
Enter Mephostophilis and other Divels.	Faustus	1402.1	4.2.78.1
OTHERS			
[Exit Ascanius with others].	Dido		1.1.177.1
Enter Cloanthus, Sergestus, Illioneus [and others].	Dido		2.1.38.1
Meander, Theridamas, Ortygius, Ceneus, [Menaphon], with others.	1Tamburlaine		1.1.0.2
with others.	1Tamburlaine		1.1.135.1
Enter Theridamas with others.	1Tamburlaine		1.2.151.1
Theridamas, Techelles, Usumcasane, Ortygius, with others.	1Tamburlaine		2.3.0.2
Meander, Ortygius, Techelles, Usumcasane, with others.	1Tamburlaine		2.5.0.2
Theridamas, Tamburlaine, Techelles, Usumcasane, with others.	1Tamburlaine		2.7.0.3
kings of Fesse, Moroco, and Argier, with others, in great pompe.	1Tamburlaine		3.1.0.2
[Enter] Agidas, Zenocrate, Anippe, with others.	1Tamburlaine		3.2.0.1
Enter [aloofe] Tamburlaine with Techelles and others.	1Tamburlaine		3.2.24.1
Theridamas, Bassoe, Zenocrate, [Anippe], with others.	1Tamburlaine		3.3.0.2
Theridamas, Techelles, Usumcasane, the Turke, with others.	1Tamburlaine		4.4.0.2
Tamburlaine, Techelles, Theridamas, Usumcasane, with others:	1Tamburlaine		5.1.63.3
Enter Techelles, Theridamas, Usumcasane, and others.	1Tamburlaine		5.1.195.2
the Souldane, Techelles, Theridamas, Usumcasane, with others.	1Tamburlaine		5.1.432.3
Enter Orcanes, Gazellus, Uribassa, with others.	2Tamburlaine		2.3.9.2
Governour of Babylon upon the walles with [Maximus and] others.	2Tamburlaine		5.1.0.2
and Celebinus, with others, the two spare kings [Orcanes, King	2Tamburlaine		5.1.62.3
Admirall, and [Margaret] the Queene of Navarre, with others.	Paris	0.3	1.0.3
and [Margaret] the Queene of Navar [with others], and manet	Paris	26.3	1.26.3
Exit Gonzago and others with him.	Paris	292.1	5.19.1
Enter [above Gonzago and others] into the Admirals house, and	Paris	297.1	5.24.1
Enter also the Guise [and others].	Paris	528.2	10.0.2
[Mugeroun], the kings Minions, with others, and the Cutpurse.	Paris	588.5	12.0.5
Enter Duke Dumayn reading of a letter, with others.	Paris	1107.1	21.0.1
the King, [Arundell] <Matr.>, the two Spencers, with others.	Edward II		4.3.0.2
OUT			
and Mycetes comes out alone with his Crowne in his hand,	1Tamburlaine		2.4.0.1
They take him out of the cage.	1Tamburlaine		4.2.1.1
She goes out.	1Tamburlaine		5.1.285.1
Sound to the battell, and Sigismond comes out wounded.	2Tamburlaine		2.3.0.1
He goes in and brings him out.	2Tamburlaine		4.1.90.1
Tamburlaine goes in, and comes out againe with al the rest.	2Tamburlaine		5.3.114.1
They beare away the [olde] Queene [of Navarre] and goe out.	Paris	202.2	3.37.2
[Runs out from studie].	Paris	369.1	7.9.1
Enter Ramus [out of his studie].	Paris	375.2	7.15.2
All goe out, but Navarre and Pleshe.	Paris	564.1	11.29.1
Goe out all, but the Queene [Mother] and the Cardinall.	Paris	630.1	12.43.1
They march out with the body of the King, lying on foure mens	Paris	1250.1	22.112.1
his Crowne, and offering to goe out, his Paramour meetes him,	Faustus	1257.4	4.1.103.4
fire-workes; they set upon the Souldiers and drive them out.	Faustus	1430.4	4.2.106.4
They knocke againe, and call out to talke with Faustus.	Faustus	1590.1	4.6.33.1
OVER			
Bajazeth flies [over the stage], and he pursues him.	1Tamburlaine		3.3.211.1
brings in Hellen, she <and Helen> passeth over the stage.	Faustus	1696.2	5.1.23.2
Enter Hellen againe, passing over betweene two Cupids.	Faustus	1767.1	5.1.94.1
OVERCOME			
The battell short, and they enter, Bajazeth is overcome.	1Tamburlaine		3.3.211.2
OWNE			
and then Enter Faustus and Mephostophilis in their owne shapes.	Faustus	981.2	3.2.0.2
PAIRE			
Enter the Knight with a paire of hornes on his head.	Faustus	App.	p238 68.1
PAPER			
Enter Aeneas with a paper in his hand, drawing the platforme of	Dido		5.1.0.1
[Gives paper].	Jew of Malta		3.6.29.1
Enter the Maid with Inke and Paper.	Paris	665.1	13.9.1
PARAMOUR			
offering to goe out, his Paramour meetes him, he embraceth her,	Faustus	1257.4	4.1.103.4
with Alexander and his paramour.	Faustus	App.	p238 59.1
PASSETH			
brings in Hellen, she <and Helen> passeth over the stage.	Faustus	1696.2	5.1.23.2
PASSING			
Enter Hellen againe, passing over betweene two Cupids.	Faustus	1767.1	5.1.94.1
PATER			
[Barons led off by Spencer pater].	Edward II		3.1.249.1
PEN			
Enter one with a pen and inke.	Paris	881.1	17.76.1
PENBROOKE			
Warwicke, Penbrooke, Mortimer senior, Mortimer junior,	Edward II		1.4.0.1
Mortimer [junior], Warwicke, Penbrooke, Kent, attendants.	Edward II		2.2.0.2
Enter Lancaster, Mortimer [junior], Warwick, Penbrooke, Kent.	Edward II		2.3.0.1
Manent Penbrooke, [Arundell] <Mat.>, Gaveston, and Penbrookes	Edward II		2.5.98.2
Exeunt ambo [Penbrooke and Arundell, attended].	Edward II		2.5.111.1
Barons, Mortimer, Lancaster, Warwick, Penbrooke, cum caeteris.	Edward II		3.1.194.2
PENBROOKES			
and Penbrookes men, foure souldiers [, one of them James].	Edward II		2.5.98.2
and the earle of Penbrookes men [, James and three souldiers].	Edward II		2.6.0.1
PENBROOKIS			
Exit [Gaveston] cum servis Penbrookis.	Edward II		2.5.109.1

PERDICAS			
[Enter Perdicas].	2Tamburlaine		4.1.59.1
PHILEMUS			
Enter [Philemus], a Messenger.	1Tamburlaine		5.1.376.1
PHISITIANS			
three Phisitians about her bed, tempering potions.	2Tamburlaine		2.4.0.2
PHYSITIANS			
drawn by the captive kings; Amyras, Celebinus, Physitians].	2Tamburlaine		5.3.41.2
PILIA-BORZA			
Enter Pilia-borza.	Jew of Malta		3.1.11.1
Enter Curtezane, and Pilia-borza.	Jew of Malta		4.2.0.1
[Aside to Pilia-borza].	Jew of Malta		4.2.62.1
Enter [Pilia-borza].	Jew of Malta		4.2.99.1
Enter Pilia-borza.	Jew of Malta		4.3.17.1
Enter Curtezane, Ithimore, Pilia-borza.	Jew of Malta		4.4.0.1
[Aside to Pilia-borza].	Jew of Malta		4.4.26.1
Enter Curtezane, Pilia-borza.	Jew of Malta		5.1.6.1
Exit [Barabas, Curtezane, Pilia-borza, with Officers].	Jew of Malta		5.1.43.1
PILLARS			
some bearing Crosiers, some the Pillars, Monkes and Friers,	Faustus	867.2	3.1.89.2
PIPER			
Enter the Seven Deadly Sinnes [led by a Piper].	Faustus	660.1	2.2.109.1
PLATFORME			
his hand, drawing the platforme of the citie, with him Achates,	Dido		5.1.0.1
PLAY			
They play.	2Tamburlaine		4.1.66.1
PLAYING			
and enter a devill playing on a Drum, after him another bearing	Faustus	1430.1	4.2.106.1
PLESHE			
Queene Mother, and the Cardinall [of Loraine, and Pleshe].	Paris	536.3	11.0.3
All goe out, but Navarre and Pleshe.	Paris	564.1	11.29.1
Enter the King of Navarre, Pleshe and Bartus, and their train,	Paris	698.1	14.0.1
Enter Pleshe.	Paris	914.1	18.15.1
France, and Navarre, Epernoune, Bartus, Pleshe and Souldiers.	Paris	1139.2	22.0.2
PLUCKS			
[Plucks a feather from Mercuries wings].	Dido		1.1.40.1
POAST			
Enter a Poast.	Edward II		2.2.111.1
POASTE			
Enter a Poaste.	Edward II		4.3.23.1
POINTING			
Pointing to his Sworde.	Paris	153.1	2.96.1
POLAND			
Enter Anjoy, with two Lords of Poland.	Paris	451.1	8.0.1
POMPE			
of Fesse, Moroco, and Argier, with others, in great pompe.	1Tamburlaine		3.1.0.2
POORE			
Enter three poore men.	Edward II		1.1.23.1
POPE			
Then the Pope, and Raymond King of Hungary, with Bruno led in	Faustus	867.3	3.1.89.3
Enter Pope and all the Lords.	Faustus	1008.1	3.2.28.1
[The Pope crosseth himselfe].	Faustus	1064.1A	3.2.84.1
Exeunt the Pope and his traine.	Faustus	1070.1	3.2.90.1
enter the Pope and the Cardinall of Lorraine to the banket,	Faustus App.	p231	0.1
The Pope crosseth himselfe.	Faustus App.	p232	17.1
POST (See POAST)			
POT			
Enter Ithimore with the pot.	Jew of Malta		3.4.54.1
POTHECAIER			
Exit Pothecaier.	Paris	83.1	2.26.1
POTHECARIE			
Enter the Pothecarie.	Paris	66.1	2.9.1
POTHECARY			
and the Pothecary with the gloves, and gives them to the olde	Paris	166.3	3.0.3
Exit Pothecary.	Paris	169.1	3.4.1
POTIONS			
three Phisitians about her bed, tempering potions.	2Tamburlaine		2.4.0.2
PRIAMS			
[Sees Priams statue].	Dido		2.1.6.1
PRINCE			
King of Navarre, the Prince of Condye, the Lord high Admirall,	Paris	0.2	1.0.2
manet Navar, the Prince of Condy, and the Lord high Admirall.	Paris	26.3	1.26.3
Mother Queen [of Navarre], the Prince of Condy, the Admirall,	Paris	166.2	3.0.2
and enter the King of Navarre and Prince of Condy, with their	Paris	429.2	7.69.2
the Queene, Mortimer, the young Prince and Sir John of Henolt.	Edward II		4.6.18.1
Enter the yong Prince, and the Earle of Kent talking with him.	Edward II		5.2.73.2
PRISONER			
Enter Souldiers with the Earle of Kent prisoner.	Edward II		5.4.81.1
PRISONERS			
Enter Turkes, Barabas, Governour, and Knights prisoners.	Jew of Malta		5.2.0.2
PROCESSION			
some the Pillars, Monkes and Friers, singing their Procession:	Faustus	867.2	3.1.89.2
PROLOGUE			
[Enter] Machevil [as Prologue].	Jew of Malta		Prol.0.1
PROTESTANTS			
the rest, with their Swords drawne, chasing the Protestants.	Paris	335.3	5.62.3
Enter five or sixe Protestants with bookes, and kneele	Paris	528.1	10.0.1
PUDDLE			
They wash him with puddle water, and shave his beard away.	Edward II		5.3.36.1
PULL			
Pull him by the legge, and pull it away.	Faustus App.	p241	53.1
PULS			
He puls off his leg.	Faustus	1491.1	4.4.35.1

PURSUED
Enter Gaveston pursued. Edward II 2.5.0.1
PURSUES
Bajazeth flies [over the stage], and he pursues him. 1Tamburlaine 3.3.211.1
PURSUING
Enter Loreine running, the Guise and the rest pursuing him. Paris 338.2 5.65.2
PUT
[They put him into the cage]. 1Tamburlaine 4.2.82.1
PUTS
[Enter servant with robe and Aeneas puts it on]. Dido 2.1.95.1
He takes the Crowne and puts it on. 1Tamburlaine 2.7.52.2
QUEEN
Enter the King of Navar and Queen [Margaret], and his [olde] Paris 166.1 3.0.1
and his [olde] Mother Queen [of Navarre], the Prince of Condy, Paris 166.2 3.0.2
Enter Queen Isabell. Edward II 1.4.143.1
QUEENE
French King, [Catherine] the Queene Mother, the King of Navarre Paris 0.1 1.0.1
Admirall, and [Margaret] the Queene of Navarre, with others. Paris 0.3 1.0.3
Queene Mother, and [Margaret] the Queene of Navar [with Paris 26.2 1.26.2
and [Margaret] the Queene of Navar [with others], and manet Paris 26.2 1.26.2
Pothecary with the gloves, and gives them to the olde Queene. Paris 166.3 3.0.3
They beare away the [olde] Queene [of Navarre] and goe out. Paris 202.1 3.37.1
the King, [Catherine the] Queene Mother, Duke of Guise, Paris 203.1 4.0.1
of Guise, and Queene Mother, and the Cardinall [of Loraine]. Paris 493.2 9.12.2
enter Queene Mother, and the Cardinall [of Loraine, and Paris 536.2 11.0.2
Queene [Mother], Cardinall [of Loraine], Duke of Guise, Paris 588.3 12.0.3
Goe out all, but the Queene [Mother] and the Cardinall. Paris 630.1 12.43.1
Enter Queene Mother [attended]. Paris 1063.1 19.133.1
Enter the Queene. Edward II 1.2.45.1
Enter the Nobles to the Queene. Edward II 1.4.186.1
Enter Edward, the Queene, Lancaster, Mortimer [junior], Edward II 2.2.0.1
Exit the King [, Queene, and Kent]. Edward II 2.2.99.1
Enter the Queene, three Ladies [, one of these Neece to the Edward II 2.2.224.1
and Spencer, to them Gaveston, &c. [the Queene, Neece, lords]. Edward II 2.4.0.2
Enter the Queene and her sonne, and [Levune] <Lewne> a Edward II 3.1.58.1
Enter the Queene and her sonne. Edward II 4.2.0.1
Enter the Queene, her sonne, Edmund [earle of Kent], Mortimer, Edward II 4.4.0.1
Enter the Queene, Mortimer, the young Prince and Sir John of Edward II 4.6.18.1
[To Queene]. Edward II 4.6.38.1
Enter Mortimer, and Queene Isabell. Edward II 5.2.0.1
King, [Archbishop] [of Canterbury], Champion, Nobles, Queene. Edward II 5.4.72.2
Enter the Queene. Edward II 5.6.14.1
[Exit Queene and 2. Lord]. Edward II 5.6.92.1
RAFE
Enter Rafe calling Robin. Faustus App. p233 5.1
Enter Robin and Rafe with a silver Goblet. Faustus App. p234 0.1
RAGETH
The king rageth. Edward II 5.1.85.1
RAMUS
Enter Ramus in his studie. Paris 361.1 7.0.1
Enter Ramus [out of his studie]. Paris 375.2 7.15.2
RAYMOND
Pope, and Raymond King of Hungary, with Bruno led in chaines. Faustus 867.3 3.1.89.3
READES
Spencer reades the letter. Edward II 4.3.27.1
He reades. Faustus App. p235 22.1
READETH
He stabs the King with a knife as he readeth the letter, and Paris 1172.1 22.34.1
READING
Enter Lodowicke reading. Jew of Malta 3.2.2.1
Enter Barabas reading a letter. Jew of Malta 3.4.0.1
Enter Barabas, reading a letter. Jew of Malta 4.3.0.1
Enter the King of Navarre reading of a letter, and Bartus. Paris 900.1 18.0.1
Enter Duke Dumayn reading of a letter, with others. Paris 1107.1 21.0.1
reading on a letter that was brought him from the king. Edward II 1.1.0.1
READS
Spencer reads their names. Edward II 4.3.11.1
REINES
mouthes, reines in his left hand, in his right hand a whip, 2Tamburlaine 4.3.0.2
REST
Tamburlaine goes in, and comes out againe with al the rest. 2Tamburlaine 5.3.114.1
Exeunt Gonzago and rest above]. Paris 306.1 5.33.1
enters againe, with all the rest, with their Swords drawne, Paris 335.2 5.62.2
Enter Loreine running, the Guise and the rest pursuing him. Paris 338.2 5.65.2
RETES
Gonzago, Retes, Montsorrell, and Souldiers to the massacre. Paris 274.1 5.0.1
Enter Gonzago and Retes. Paris 370.1 7.10.1
RETREATE
Alarums, excursions, a great fight, and a retreate. Edward II 3.1.184.2
RETURN
Return with table]. Edward II 5.5.109.1
RICE
Enter Rice ap Howell, and the Maior of Bristow, with Spencer Edward II 4.6.45.2
Enter with Welch hookes, Rice ap Howell, a Mower, and the Earle Edward II 4.7.45.1
RICE AP HOWELL
Enter Rice ap Howell, and the Maior of Bristow, with Spencer Edward II 4.6.45.2
Enter with Welch hookes, Rice ap Howell, a Mower, and the Earle Edward II 4.7.45.1
RICH
<with> Devils, giving Crownes and rich apparell to Faustus: Faustus 471.2 2.1.83.2
RIGHT
hand, in his right hand a whip, with which he scourgeth them, 2Tamburlaine 4.3.0.2
RING
[A ring]. Edward II 5.2.72.1

RISES			
[Rises].	Edward II		3.1.143.1
[Faustus rises].	Faustus	1390.1	4.2.66.1
ROBE			
[Enter servant with robe and Aeneas puts it on].	Dido		2.1.95.1
ROBIN			
Enter Wagner and [Robin] the Clowne.	Faustus	343.1	1.4.0.1
Enter [Robin] the Clowne.	Faustus	722.1	2.3.0.1
Enter [Robin the] Clowne and Dicke, with a Cup.	Faustus	1088.1	3.3.0.1
Enter [Robin the] Clowne, Dick, Horse-courser, and a Carter.	Faustus	1505.1	4.5.0.1
Enter [Robin] the Clowne, Dick, Carter, and Horse-courser.	Faustus	1608.1	4.6.51.1
Enter Robin the Ostler with a booke in his hand	Faustus App.		p233 0.1
Enter Rafe calling Robin.	Faustus App.		p233 5.1
Enter Robin and Rafe with a silver Goblet.	Faustus App.		p234 0.1
ROOM			
[The murtherers go aside as if in the next room].	Paris	943.1	19.13.1
ROY			
Gazellus, vice-roy of Byron, [Uribassa] <Upibassa>, and their	2Tamburlaine		1.1.0.1
and then all crye vive [le] <la> Roy two or three times.	Paris	588.1	12.0.1
RUN			
Alarme, and Amyras and Celebinus run in.	2Tamburlaine		4.1.51.1
They run away with the Ladies.	2Tamburlaine		4.3.84.1
RUNNE			
Faustus hits him a boxe of the eare, and they all runne away.	Faustus App.		p232 21.2
they runne about.	Faustus App.		p235 25.2
RUNNES			
Enter two divells, and the clowne runnes up and downe crying.	Faustus App.		p230 49.1
Horsecourser runnes away.	Faustus App.		p241 63.1
RUNNING			
Enter Iarbus running.	Dido		5.1.315.1
Enter Loreine running, the Guise and the rest pursuing him.	Paris	338.2	5.65.2
[Exit Vintner running].	Faustus	1115.1	3.3.28.1
RUNS			
Sound trumpets to the battell, and he runs in.	1Tamburlaine		2.4.42.1
She runs against the Cage and braines her selfe.	1Tamburlaine		5.1.318.1
[Runs out from studie].	Paris	369.1	7.9.1
SACRIFIZE			
Enters Iarbus to Sacrifize.	Dido		4.2.0.1
SAITH			
Edward kneels, and saith.	Edward II		3.1.127.1
SALUTE			
comming backe, both salute the Emperour, who leaving his State,	Faustus	1257.6	4.1.103.6
SAXONY			
Emperour, Bruno, [Duke of] Saxony, Faustus, Mephostophilis,	Faustus	1203.3	4.1.49.3
SAYES			
by the hand, looking wrathfully on Agidas, and sayes nothing.	1Tamburlaine		3.2.65.2
SCALE			
Alarme, and they scale the walles.	2Tamburlaine		5.1.62.1
SCARLET			
Banquet, and to it commeth Tamburlain al in scarlet, Theridamas,	1Tamburlaine		4.4.0.1
SCEPTER			
[Gives him crowne and scepter].	Dido		4.4.36.1
and Soria, one bringing a sword, and another a scepter:	2Tamburlaine		3.1.0.2
and Jerusalem crowne him, and the other give him the scepter.	2Tamburlaine		3.1.0.4
SCHOLERS			
Enter <Faustus with> the Scholers <Schollers>.	Faustus	1819.1	5.2.23.1
SCHOLLERS			
Enter two Schollers.	Faustus	194.1	1.2.0.1
Enter Faustus, Mephostophilis, and two or three Schollers.	Faustus	1680.3	5.1.7.3
Exeunt Schollers.	Faustus	1705.1	5.1.32.1
Enter <Faustus with> the Scholers <Schollers>.	Faustus	1819.1	5.2.23.1
Exeunt Schollers.	Faustus	1879.1	5.2.83.1
Enter the Schollers.	Faustus	1983.1	5.3.0.1
SCHOLMAISTERS			
King of Navarre and Prince of Condy, with their scholmaisters.	Paris	429.2	7.69.2
SCOURGETH			
his right hand a whip, with which he scourgeth them, Techelles,	2Tamburlaine		4.3.0.3
SEARCHETH			
The Surgeon searcheth.	Paris	1193.1	22.55.1
SECOND			
Enter a second course of Crownes.	1Tamburlaine		4.4.106.1
Enter a second Merchant.	Jew of Malta		1.1.84.1
SEEING			
to embrace them, which Faustus seeing, suddenly staies him.	Faustus	1257.7	4.1.103.7
SEES			
[Sees Priams statue].	Dido		2.1.6.1
SEIZE			
[Seize him].	Edward II		1.4.21.1
SELFE			
She runs against the Cage and braines her selfe.	1Tamburlaine		5.1.318.1
SENIOR			
Lancaster, Mortimer senior, Mortimer junior, Edmund Earle of	Edward II		1.1.73.1
Penbrooke, Mortimer senior, Mortimer junior, the Archbishop of	Edward II		1.4.0.1
SENIT (See also SONNET)			
A Senit while the Banquet is brought in; and then Enter Faustus	Faustus	981.1	3.2.0.1
A Senit.	Faustus	1203.2	4.1.49.2
Senit.	Faustus	1257.2	4.1.103.2
SERGESTUS			
Enter [Iarbus, with] Illioneus, and Cloanthus [and Sergestus].	Dido		1.2.0.2
Enter Cloanthus, Sergestus, Illioneus [and others].	Dido		2.1.38.1
[Enter Aeneas, Achates, Sergestus, Illioneus, and Cloanthus].	Dido		3.1.96.1
Enter Achates, Cloanthus, Sergestus, and Illioneus.	Dido		4.3.14.1
Enter Anna, with Aeneas, Achates, Illioneus, and Sergestus.	Dido		4.4.13.2

SERGESTUS (cont.)			
citie, with him Achates, [Sergestus], Cloanthus, and Illioneus.	Dido		5.1.0.2
[Exit Sergestus with Ascanius].	Dido		5.1.50.1
SEROUNE			
Enter Seroune.	Paris	349.1	6.4.1
SEROUNS			
Enter Mountsorrell and knocks at Serouns doore.	Paris	346.1	6.0.1
SERVANT			
[Exit servant].	Dido		2.1.80.1
[Enter servant with robe and Aeneas puts it on].	Dido		2.1.95.1
SERVIS			
Exit [Gaveston] cum servis Penbrookis.	Edward II		2.5.110.1
SET			
fire-workes; they set upon the Souldiers and drive them out.	Faustus	1430.3	4.2.106.3
SETS			
her, and sets Darius Crowne upon her head; and comming backe,	Faustus	1257.5	4.1.103.5
sets squibs at their backes:	Faustus App.		p235 25.1
SEVEN			
Enter the Seven Deadly Sinnes [led by a Piper].	Faustus	660.1	2.2.109.1
Exeunt the Seven Sinnes.	Faustus	711.1	2.2.163.1
SEVERAL			
[Exeunt souldiers several ways, some with Governour].	2Tamburlaine		5.1.126.1
Enter [at several doors] the King and Spencer, to them	Edward II		2.4.0.1
SEVERALL			
Enter Aeneas and Dido in the Cave at severall times.	Dido		3.4.0.2
Exeunt omnes, severall waies.	Faustus	721.1	2.2.173.1
Enter Martino, and Frederick at severall dores.	Faustus	1155.1	4.1.0.1
Enter at severall dores, Benvolio, Fredericke, and Martino,	Faustus	1431.1	4.3.0.1
Enter the Good Angell, and the Bad Angell at severall doores.	Faustus	1891.3	5.2.95.3
SEVERALLY			
[Exeunt severally].	Jew of Malta		5.4.10.1
[Exeunt severally.	Edward II		3.1.220.1
Exeunt omnes [severally].	Edward II		5.2.121.1
SHAPES			
and then Enter Faustus and Mephostophilis in their owne shapes.	Faustus	981.2	3.2.0.2
SHAVE			
They wash him with puddle water, and shave his beard away.	Edward II		5.3.36.1
SHE			
She goes out.	1Tamburlaine		5.1.285.1
She runs against the Cage and braines her selfe.	1Tamburlaine		5.1.318.1
The musicke sounds, and she dies.	2Tamburlaine		2.4.95.1
She stabs him.	2Tamburlaine		3.4.30.1
She noints her throat.	2Tamburlaine		4.2.78.1
She dyes.	Paris	186.1	3.21.1
She writes.	Paris	667.1	13.11.1
brings in Hellen, she <and Helen> passeth over the stage.	Faustus	1696.2	5.1.23.2
SHEPHEARDS			
[Takes off shepheards cloak].	1Tamburlaine		1.2.41.1
SHEWING			
Shewing his dagger.	Paris	351.1	6.6.1
SHOOTE			
They shoote.	2Tamburlaine		5.1.157.1
SHOOTES			
Theridamas shootes.	2Tamburlaine		5.1.152.1
He shootes at him and killes him.	Paris	816.2	17.11.2
SHORT			
The battell short, and they enter, Bajazeth is overcome.	1Tamburlaine		3.3.211.2
SHOT			
The ordinance being shot of, the bell tolles.	Paris	334.1	5.61.1
SHOULDERS			
lying on foure mens shoulders with a dead march, drawing	Paris	1250.3	22.112.3
SHOW			
Exit Show.	Faustus	1273.1	4.1.119.1
SIDE			
father, Spencer the sonne, and the noblemen of the kings side.	Edward II		3.1.184.4
SIGISMOND			
[Enter] Sigismond, Fredericke, Baldwine, and their traine with	2Tamburlaine		1.1.77.1
[Enter] Sigismond, Fredericke, Baldwine, with their traine.	2Tamburlaine		2.1.0.1
Sound to the battell, and Sigismond comes out wounded.	2Tamburlaine		2.3.0.1
SILVER			
Enter Robin and Rafe with a silver Goblet.	Faustus App.		p234 0.1
SING			
Enter all the Friers to sing the Dirge.	Faustus App.		p232 28.1
Sing this.	Faustus App.		p232 30.1
SINGING			
some the Pillars, Monkes and Friers, singing their Procession:	Faustus	867.2	3.1.89.2
SINGS			
[Cupid sings].	Dido		3.1.25.1
SINNES			
Enter the Seven Deadly Sinnes [led by a Piper].	Faustus	660.1	2.2.109.1
Exeunt the Seven Sinnes.	Faustus	711.1	2.2.163.1
SIR			
Enter sir John of Henolt.	Edward II		4.2.12.1
her sonne, Edmund [earle of Kent], Mortimer, and sir John.	Edward II		4.4.0.2
the Queene, Mortimer, the young Prince and Sir John of Henolt.	Edward II		4.6.18.2
SITS			
Celebinus, issues from the tent where Caliphas sits a sleepe.	2Tamburlaine		4.1.0.2
He sits to sleepe.	Faustus	1483.1	4.4.27.1
SITTING			
Zenocrate lies in her bed of state, Tamburlaine sitting by her:	2Tamburlaine		2.4.0.2
SIX			
and Jerusalem led by with five or six common souldiers.	2Tamburlaine		4.3.0.5
SIXE			
Enter five or sixe Protestants with bookes, and kneele	Paris	528.1	10.0.1

SLAINE		
The Duke Joyeux slaine.	Paris 787.1	16.0.1
SLAVE		
Exeunt [Mater and slave].	Jew of Malta	2.3.158.1
SLAVES		
Enter Officers with slaves.	Jew of Malta	2.3.0.1
[Exeunt Officers with slaves].	Jew of Malta	2.3.162.1
SLEEPE		
Celebinus, issues from the tent where Caliphas sits a sleepe.	2Tamburlaine	4.1.0.2
He sits to sleepe.	Faustus 1483.1	4.4.27.1
Sleepe in his chaire.	Faustus App.	p240 26.1
SLEEVE		
doore, and takes Ascanius by the sleeve [as he is going off].	Dido	2.1.303.3
SNATCH		
[Snatch it].	Faustus 1043.1A	3.2.63.1
[Snatch it].	Faustus 1048.1	3.2.68.1
[Snatch it].	Faustus 1054.1	3.2.74.1
Snatch it.	Faustus App.	p231 7.1
SO		
the Friers, and fling fier-workes among them, and so Exeunt.	Faustus App.	p233 41.2
SOLDIERS (See also SOULDIERS)		
They [Techelles and soldiers] take them away.	1Tamburlaine	5.1.120.1
Exit Uribassa [and soldiers with body].	2Tamburlaine	2.3.41.1
the Guise and Anjoy [, Dumaine, Mountsorrell, with soldiers].	Paris 379.1	7.19.1
Exit Anjoy [and soldiers with bodies].	Paris 442.1	7.82.1
father to the yong Spencer, with his trunchion, and soldiers.	Edward II	3.1.31.2
SOLUS		
Enter Cupid solus [for Ascanius].	Dido	3.1.0.1
Enter the Chorus <Wagner solus>.	Faustus 753.2	2.3.32.2
enter Wagner solus.	Faustus App.	p243 0.1
SOME		
[Exeunt souldiers several ways, some with Governour].	2Tamburlaine	5.1.126.1
[Enter some with hearse].	Edward II	5.6.97.1
Cardinals and Bishops, some bearing Crosiers, some the Pillars,	Faustus 867.1	3.1.89.1
some bearing Crosiers, some the Pillars, Monkes and Friers,	Faustus 867.1	3.1.89.1
SONG		
[Song].	Dido	2.1.315.1
SONNE		
[Enter above] Captaine with his wife [Olympia] and sonne.	2Tamburlaine	3.3.14.2
Enter [below] the Captaine with [Olympia] his wife and sonne.	2Tamburlaine	3.4.0.2
Enter the Guises sonne.	Paris 1045.1	19.115.1
Enter the Queene and her sonne, and [Levune] <Lewne> a	Edward II	3.1.58.1
father, Spencer the sonne, and the noblemen of the kings side.	Edward II	3.1.184.3
Enter the Queene and her sonne.	Edward II	4.2.0.1
Enter the Queene, her sonne, Edmund [earle of Kent], Mortimer,	Edward II	4.4.0.1
King, Baldock, and Spencer the sonne, flying about the stage.	Edward II	4.5.0.1
SONNES		
Tamburlaine with Zenocrate, and his three sonnes, Calyphas,	2Tamburlaine	1.3.0.1
Theridamas, Techelles, Usumcasane, and the three sonnes.	2Tamburlaine	2.4.0.3
[Enter] Tamburlaine with his three sonnes, Usumcasane with	2Tamburlaine	3.5.57.1
SONNET		
exit Sound a Sonnet, enter the Pope and the Cardinall of	Faustus App.	p231 0.1
SONS		
Tamburlaine with Usumcasane, and his three sons, [Calyphas],	2Tamburlaine	3.2.0.1
SORIA		
Enter the kings of Trebisond and Soria, one bringing a sword,	2Tamburlaine	3.1.0.1
Orcanes, Jerusalem, Trebizon, Soria, Almeda, with their traine.	2Tamburlaine	3.5.0.1
his chariot by Trebizon and Soria with bittes in their mouthes,	2Tamburlaine	4.3.0.1
[drawn in his chariot by the kings of Trebizon and Soria], with	2Tamburlaine	5.1.62.3
[Exit with the Kings of Trebizon and Soria].	2Tamburlaine	5.1.135.1
SOULDAN		
[Enter] Souldan of Egipt with three or four Lords, Capolin	1Tamburlaine	4.1.0.1
SOULDANE		
[Enter] Souldane, Arabia, Capoline, with [streaming] <steaming>	1Tamburlaine	4.3.0.1
Enter Tamburlain leading the Souldane, Techelles, Theridamas,	1Tamburlaine	5.1.432.2
SOULDIER		
Enter a Souldier.	1Tamburlaine	1.2.108.1
Enter a Souldier.	Paris 83.2	2.26.2
Exit Souldier.	Paris 90.1	2.33.1
[enter] the Souldier [above, who] dischargeth his Musket at the	Paris 196.1	3.31.1
Enter a Souldier.	Paris 806.1	17.0.1
Exit Souldier.	Paris 817.1	17.12.1
Enter A souldier with a muskett	Paris ms	p390 0.1
SOULDIERS		
Lords [,Magnetes, Agidas], and Souldiers loden with treasure.	1Tamburlaine	1.2.0.2
The Souldiers enter.	1Tamburlaine	1.2.137.1
Cosroe, Menaphon, Ortygius, Ceneus, with other Souldiers.	1Tamburlaine	2.1.0.1
[Enter] Mycetes, Meander, with other Lords and Souldiers.	1Tamburlaine	2.2.0.1
Cosroe, Meander, Ortygius, Menaphon, with other Souldiers.	1Tamburlaine	2.6.0.2
Capoline, with [streaming] <steaming> collors and Souldiers.	1Tamburlaine	4.3.0.2
Enter [with Souldiers] Tamburlain, Theridamas, Techelles,	2Tamburlaine	4.1.75.2
and Jerusalem led by with five or six common souldiers.	2Tamburlaine	4.3.0.5
Enter Theridamas and Techelles, with other souldiers.	2Tamburlaine	5.1.48.1
King of Natolia, and King of Jerusalem, led by souldiers].	2Tamburlaine	5.1.62.5
[Exeunt souldiers several ways, some with Governour].	2Tamburlaine	5.1.126.1
[Souldiers hang the Governour of Babylon in chaines on the	2Tamburlaine	5.1.148.2
Amasia, [Captaine, Souldiers], with drums and trumpets.	2Tamburlaine	5.2.0.1
Gonzago, Retes, Montsorrell, and Souldiers to the massacre.	Paris 274.2	5.0.2
France, and Navarre, Epernoune, Bartus, Pleshe and Souldiers.	Paris 1139.2	22.0.2
and Penbrookes men, foure souldiers [, one of them James].	Edward II	2.5.98.3
and the earle of Penbrookes men [, James and three souldiers].	Edward II	2.6.0.2
Enter Matrevis and Gurney with the King [and souldiers].	Edward II	5.3.0.1
Manent Edmund and the souldiers.	Edward II	5.3.62.2

SOULDIERS (cont.)		
Enter Souldiers with the Earle of Kent prisoner.	Edward II	5.4.81.1
[To Souldiers].	Edward II	5.4.102.1
Enter Benvolio, Martino, Fredericke, and Souldiers.	Faustus 1325.1	4.2.0.1
Exit Frederick with the Souldiers.	Faustus 1349.1	4.2.25.1
Enter the ambusht Souldiers.	Faustus 1419.2	4.2.95.2
fire-workes; they set upon the Souldiers and drive them out.	Faustus 1430.3	4.2.106.3
SOUND		
Sound trumpets to the battell, and he runs in.	1Tamburlaine	2.4.42.1
They sound [to] the battell within, and stay.	1Tamburlaine	3.3.188.1
They sound to the battaile.	1Tamburlaine	5.1.402.1
Sound to the battell, and Sigismond comes out wounded.	2Tamburlaine	2.3.0.1
Sound Trumpets within, and then all crye vive [le] <la> Roy two	Paris 588.1	12.0.1
Sound Trumpets.	Paris 588.1	12.1.1
Sound trumpets.	Paris 598.1	12.11.1
Sound Drumme and Trumpets, and enter the King of France, and	Paris 1139.1	22.0.1
Musicke sound, Mephostophilis brings in Hellen, she <and Helen>	Faustus 1696.1	5.1.23.1
exit Sound a Sonnet, enter the Pope and the Cardinall of	Faustus App.	p231 0.1
SOUNDING		
and the drums sounding a dolefull martch, the Towne burning.	2Tamburlaine	3.2.0.3
SOUNDS		
The musicke sounds, and she dies.	2Tamburlaine	2.4.95.1
Then trumpets cease, and Musicke sounds.	Faustus 1257.8	4.1.103.8
SPARE		
with others, the two spare kings [Orcanes, King of Natolia, and	2Tamburlaine	5.1.62.4
SPEAKES		
Enter to them the Duke, and the Dutches, the Duke speakes.	Faustus App.	p242 0.2
SPEECH		
and foure devils [above], Faustus to them with this speech.	Faustus 229.2	1.3.0.2
SPENCER		
Enter Spencer and Balduck.	Edward II	2.1.0.1
of these Neece to the king, Gaveston], Baldock, and Spencer.	Edward II	2.2.224.2
Enter [at several doors] the King and Spencer, to them	Edward II	2.4.0.1
Enter king Edward and Spencer, [Baldock], with Drummes and	Edward II	3.1.0.1
Enter Hugh Spencer an old man, father to the yong Spencer, with	Edward II	3.1.31.1
an old man, father to the yong Spencer, with his trunchion,	Edward II	3.1.31.1
Embrace Spencer.	Edward II	3.1.176.1
Enter the King, Spencer the father, Spencer the sonne, and the	Edward II	3.1.184.3
father, Spencer the sonne, and the noblemen of the kings side.	Edward II	3.1.184.3
[Barons led off by Spencer pater].	Edward II	3.1.249.1
Manent Spencer filius, [Levune] <Lewne> and Baldock.	Edward II	3.1.261.2
Spencer reads their names.	Edward II	4.3.11.1
Spencer reades the letter.	Edward II	4.3.27.1
King, Baldock, and Spencer the sonne, flying about the stage.	Edward II	4.5.0.1
and the Maior of Bristow, with Spencer the father.	Edward II	4.6.45.3
[Spencer led off].	Edward II	4.6.73.1
Monkes, Edward, Spencer, and Baldocke [disguised as monks].	Edward II	4.7.0.1
SPENCER FILIUS		
Manent Spencer filius, [Levune] <Lewne> and Baldock.	Edward II	3.1.261.2
SPENCER PATER		
[Barons led off by Spencer pater].	Edward II	3.1.249.1
SPENCERS		
the King, [Arundell] <Matr.>, the two Spencers, with others.	Edward II	4.3.0.1
SPIRIT		
Enter the <good> Angell and Spirit <the evill Angell>.	Faustus 96.1	1.1.68.1
SPIRITS		
Exeunt Spirits with the Knights.	Faustus 1419.1	4.2.95.1
SPY		
[Enter a Spy].	1Tamburlaine	2.2.38.1
SQUIBS		
sets squibs at their backes:	Faustus App.	p235 25.1
STAB		
Stab him.	Paris 302.1	5.29.1
Stab him [and he falls within and dies].	Paris 360.1	6.15.1
[Offers to stab himself].	Faustus 1728.1	5.1.55.1
STABBE		
They stabbe him.	Paris 1002.1	19.72.1
STABS		
She stabs him.	2Tamburlaine	3.4.30.1
[Stabs Calyphas].	2Tamburlaine	4.1.120.1
[Stabs her].	2Tamburlaine	4.2.81.1
He stabs him.	Paris 343.1	5.70.1
He stabs the King with a knife as he readeth the letter, and	Paris 1172.1	22.34.1
Then Gurney stabs Lightborne.	Edward II	5.5.117.1
STAGE		
Bajazeth flies [over the stage], and he pursues him.	1Tamburlaine	3.3.211.1
King, Baldock, and Spencer the sonne, flying about the stage.	Edward II	4.5.0.2
brings in Hellen, she <and Helen> passeth over the stage.	Faustus 1696.2	5.1.23.2
STAIES		
to embrace them, which Faustus seeing, suddenly staies him.	Faustus 1257.7	4.1.103.7
STAMPS		
He takes it and stamps upon it.	1Tamburlaine	4.4.41.1
STANDS		
[Governor stands aloof].	Jew of Malta	5.5.46.1
STATE		
The Arras is drawen and Zenocrate lies in her bed of state,	2Tamburlaine	2.4.0.1
the Emperour, who leaving his State, offers to embrace them,	Faustus 1257.6	4.1.103.6
STATUE		
[Sees Priams statue].	Dido	2.1.6.1
STAY (See also STAIES)		
They sound [to] the battell within, and stay.	1Tamburlaine	3.3.188.1
STAYING		
[Charles] the King of France, Navar and Epernoune staying him:	Paris 536.1	11.0.1

STEAMING			
Capoline, with [streaming] <steaming> collors and Souldiers.	1Tamburlaine		4.3.0.1
STORME			
The storme.	Dido		3.4.0.1
STRANGLE			
Now they strangle him.	Paris	1103.1	20.13.1
STREAMING			
Capoline, with [streaming] <steaming> collors and Souldiers.	1Tamburlaine		4.3.0.1
STRIKE			
Strike him, he fals.	Jew of Malta		4.1.173.1
STRIKES			
[Faustus strikes a friar].	Faustus	1080.1	3.2.100.1
Faustus strikes the dore, and enter a devill playing on a Drum,	Faustus	1430.1	4.2.106.1
The Clock strikes eleven.	Faustus	1925.2	5.2.129.2
The Watch strikes.	Faustus	1956.1	5.2.160.1
STRIKETH			
The clocke striketh twelve.	Faustus	1974.1	5.2.178.1
STUDIE			
Enter Ramus in his studie.	Paris	361.1	7.0.1
[Runs out from studie].	Paris	369.1	7.9.1
Enter Ramus [out of his studie].	Paris	375.2	7.15.2
[Close the studie].	Paris	416.1	7.56.1
STUDY			
[Enter Faustus in his study].	Faustus	29.1	1.1.0.1
Enter Faustus in his Study.	Faustus	389.1	2.1.0.1
Enter Faustus in his Study, and Mephostophilis.	Faustus	552.1	2.2.0.1
cover'd dishes; Mephostophilis leades them into Faustus Study:	Faustus	1674.2	5.1.0.2
SUDDENLY			
to embrace them, which Faustus seeing, suddenly staies him.	Faustus	1257.7	4.1.103.7
SULTAN (See SOULDANE)			
SUMMON			
Summon the battell.	2Tamburlaine		3.3.14.1
SURGEON			
[Enter Surgeon].	Paris	1190.1	22.52.1
The Surgeon searcheth.	Paris	1193.1	22.55.1
SWORD			
and Soria, one bringing a sword, and another a scepter:	2Tamburlaine		3.1.0.1
[Draws sword].	Edward II		2.2.79.1
[Lays hand on sword].	Edward II		2.2.153.1
[Enter] Edmund [earle of Kent] alone with a sword and target.	Edward II		4.6.0.1
SWORDE			
Pointing to his Sworde.	Paris	153.1	2.96.1
SWORDS			
all the rest, with their Swords drawne, chasing the Protestants.	Paris	335.3	5.62.3
TABLE			
Return with table].	Edward II		5.5.109.1
TAKE			
They take him out of the cage.	1Tamburlaine		4.2.1.1
They [Techelles and soldiers] take them away.	1Tamburlaine		5.1.120.1
[They take body aside].	Jew of Malta		5.1.59.1
Take him away.	Paris	820.1	17.15.1
TAKES			
doore, and takes Ascanius by the sleeve [as he is going off].	Dido		2.1.303.2
[Takes off shepheards cloak].	1Tamburlaine		1.2.41.1
He takes the Crowne and puts it on.	1Tamburlaine		2.7.52.2
and takes her away lovingly by the hand, looking wrathfully on	1Tamburlaine		3.2.65.1
He takes it from her, and gives it Zenocrate.	1Tamburlaine		3.3.224.1
He takes it and stamps upon it.	1Tamburlaine		4.4.41.1
He takes it.	Paris	677.1	13.21.1
kils him; takes off his Crowne, and offering to goe out,	Faustus	1257.4	4.1.103.4
TAKING			
Exit, taking her away.	2Tamburlaine		4.2.98.1
Exit [the attendants taking up body of the Guise].	Paris	1090.1	19.160.1
TALEUS			
Enter Taleus.	Paris	364.1	7.4.1
Exit Taleus.	Paris	375.1	7.15.1
TALK			
[They talk apart].	Faustus	890.1	3.1.112.1
TALKE			
They knocke againe, and call out to talke with Faustus.	Faustus	1590.1	4.6.33.1
TALKING			
Enter the yong Prince, and the Earle of Kent talking with him.	Edward II		5.2.73.2
TAMBURLAIN			
Enter Tamburlain.	1Tamburlaine		2.4.15.1
[Enter] Tamburlain, Techelles, Usumcasane, Theridamas, Bassoe,	1Tamburlaine		3.3.0.1
[Enter] Tamburlain, Techelles, Theridamas, Usumcasane,	1Tamburlaine		4.2.0.1
Banquet, and to it commeth Tamburlain al in scarlet, Theridamas,	1Tamburlaine		4.4.0.1
Enter Tamburlain leading the Souldane, Techelles, Theridamas,	1Tamburlaine		5.1.432.2
Enter [with Souldiers] Tamburlain, Theridamas, Techelles,	2Tamburlaine		4.1.75.2
Enter Tamburlain, [drawn in his chariot by the kings of	2Tamburlaine		5.1.62.2
TAMBURLAINE			
[Enter] Tamburlaine leading Zenocrate:	1Tamburlaine		1.2.0.1
[Enter] Cosroe, Tamburlaine, Theridamas, Techelles, Usumcasane,	1Tamburlaine		2.3.0.1
[Enter] Cosroe, Tamburlaine, Theridamas, Menaphon, Meander,	1Tamburlaine		2.5.0.1
Manent Tamburlaine, Techelles, Theridamas, Usumcasane.	1Tamburlaine		2.5.49.2
Cosroe wounded, Theridamas, Tamburlaine, Techelles, Usumcasane,	1Tamburlaine		2.7.0.2
Enter [aloofe] Tamburlaine with Techelles and others.	1Tamburlaine		3.2.24.1
Tamburlaine goes to her, and takes her away lovingly by the	1Tamburlaine		3.2.65.1
[Enter] Tamburlaine, Techelles, Theridamas, Usumcasane, with	1Tamburlaine		5.1.63.2
Tamburlaine all in blacke, and verie melancholy.	1Tamburlaine		5.1.63.3
Exeunt. [Manet Tamburlaine].	1Tamburlaine		5.1.134.1
And Tamburlaine enjoyes the victory, after Arabia enters	1Tamburlaine		5.1.402.1
[Enter] Tamburlaine with Zenocrate, and his three sonnes,	2Tamburlaine		1.3.0.1

TAMBURLAINE (cont.)		
Zenocrate lies in her bed of state, Tamburlaine sitting by her:	2Tamburlaine	2.4.0.1
[Enter] Tamburlaine with Usumcasane, and his three sons,	2Tamburlaine	3.2.0.1
[Enter] Tamburlaine with his three sonnes, Usumcasane with	2Tamburlaine	3.5.57.1
Tamburlaine drawen in his chariot by Trebizon and Soria with	2Tamburlaine	4.3.0.1
[Enter Tamburlaine, drawn by the captive kings; Amyras,	2Tamburlaine	5.3.41.1
Tamburlaine goes in, and comes out againe with al the rest.	2Tamburlaine	5.3.114.1
TARGET		
[Enter] Edmund [earle of Kent] alone with a sword and target.	Edward II	4.6.0.1
TECHELLES		
Techelles, Usumcasane, other Lords [,Magnetes, Agidas], and	1Tamburlaine	1.2.0.1
[To Techelles].	1Tamburlaine	1.2.162.1
Tamburlaine, Theridamas, Techelles, Usumcasane, Ortygius, with	1Tamburlaine	2.3.0.1
Meander, Ortygius, Techelles, Usumcasane, with others.	1Tamburlaine	2.5.0.2
Manent Tamburlaine, Techelles, Theridamas, Usumcasane.	1Tamburlaine	2.5.49.2
Theridamas, Tamburlaine, Techelles, Usumcasane, with others.	1Tamburlaine	2.7.0.2
Enter [aloofe] Tamburlaine with Techelles and others.	1Tamburlaine	3.2.24.1
Enter Techelles with a naked dagger.	1Tamburlaine	3.2.87.1
[Enter Techelles and Usumcasane].	1Tamburlaine	3.2.106.2
[Enter] Tamburlain, Techelles, Usumcasane, Theridamas, Bassoe,	1Tamburlaine	3.3.0.1
Enter Techelles, Theridamas, Usumcasane.	1Tamburlaine	3.3.214.1
[Enter] Tamburlain, Techelles, Theridamas, Usumcasane,	1Tamburlaine	4.2.0.1
al in scarlet, Theridamas, Techelles, Usumcasane, the Turke,	1Tamburlaine	4.4.0.2
[Enter] Tamburlaine, Techelles, Theridamas, Usumcasane, with	1Tamburlaine	5.1.63.2
They [Techelles and soldiers] take them away.	1Tamburlaine	5.1.120.1
Enter Techelles.	1Tamburlaine	5.1.128.1
Enter Techelles, Theridamas, Usumcasane, and others.	1Tamburlaine	5.1.195.2
Enter Tamburlain leading the Souldane, Techelles, Theridamas,	1Tamburlaine	5.1.432.2
Enter Techelles and Usumcasane together.	2Tamburlaine	1.3.127.1
Theridamas, Techelles, Usumcasane, and the three sonnes.	2Tamburlaine	2.4.0.3
[Enter] Techelles, Theridamas and their traine.	2Tamburlaine	3.3.0.1
Enter Theridamas, Techelles and all their traine.	2Tamburlaine	3.4.33.2
Enter Theridamas, Techelles, and their traine.	2Tamburlaine	3.5.146.1
Tamburlain, Theridamas, Techelles, Usumcasane, Amyras,	2Tamburlaine	4.1.75.2
with which he scourgeth them, Techelles, Theridamas,	2Tamburlaine	4.3.0.3
Enter Theridamas and Techelles, with other souldiers.	2Tamburlaine	5.1.48.1
Theridamas and Techelles bringing the Governor of Babylon.	2Tamburlaine	5.1.79.1
[Enter Techelles].	2Tamburlaine	5.1.202.1
[Enter] Theridamas, Techelles, Usumcasane.	2Tamburlaine	5.3.0.1
TEMPERING		
three Phisitians about her bed, tempering potions.	2Tamburlaine	2.4.0.2
TENT		
Celebinus, issues from the tent where Caliphas sits a sleepe.	2Tamburlaine	4.1.0.1
[They go in the tent].	2Tamburlaine	4.1.75.1
THAT		
reading on a letter that was brought him from the king.	Edward II	1.1.0.1
THEIR		
and foure Virgins, with branches of Laurell in their hands.	1Tamburlaine	5.1.0.2
<Upibassa>, and their traine, with drums and trumpets.	2Tamburlaine	1.1.0.2
Fredericke, Baldwine, and their traine with drums and trumpets.	2Tamburlaine	1.1.77.1
[Enter] Sigismond, Fredericke, Baldwine, with their traine.	2Tamburlaine	2.1.0.1
[Enter] Orcanes, Gazellus, Uribassa with their traine.	2Tamburlaine	2.2.0.1
[Enter] Techelles, Theridamas and their traine.	2Tamburlaine	3.3.0.1
Enter Theridamas, Techelles and all their traine.	2Tamburlaine	3.4.33.2
Orcanes, Jerusalem, Trebizon, Soria, Almeda, with their traine.	2Tamburlaine	3.5.0.2
Enter Theridamas, Techelles, and their traine.	2Tamburlaine	3.5.146.1
his chariot by Trebizon and Soria with bittes in their mouthes,	2Tamburlaine	4.3.0.2
all the rest, with their Swords drawne, chasing the Protestants.	Paris 335.2	5.62.2
King of Navarre and Prince of Condy, with their scholmaisters.	Paris 429.2	7.69.2
Pleshe and Bartus, and their train, with drums and trumpets.	Paris 698.2	14.0.2
Spencer reads their names.	Edward II	4.3.11.1
some the Pillars, Monkes and Friers, singing their Procession:	Faustus 867.2	3.1.89.2
and then Enter Faustus and Mephostophilis in their owne shapes.	Faustus 981.2	3.2.0.2
their heads and faces bloudy, and besmear'd with mud and durt;	Faustus 1431.2	4.3.0.2
besmear'd with mud and durt; all having hornes on their heads.	Faustus 1431.3	4.3.0.3
sets squibs at their backes:	Faustus App.	p235 25.1
THEM		
Enter to them Iarbus.	Dido	5.1.61.1
They bind them.	1Tamburlaine	3.3.267.1
They [Techelles and soldiers] take them away.	1Tamburlaine	5.1.120.1
[To them the Messenger].	2Tamburlaine	3.5.0.2
his right hand a whip, with which he scourgeth them, Techelles,	2Tamburlaine	4.3.0.3
They bridle them.	2Tamburlaine	5.1.148.1
Pothecary with the gloves, and gives them to the olde Queene.	Paris 166.3	3.0.3
Enter [to them] Guise.	Paris 437.1	7.77.1
He kils them.	Paris 441.1	7.81.1
Kill them.	Paris 534.1	10.7.1
doors] the King and Spencer, to them Gaveston, &c. [the Queene,	Edward II	2.4.0.1
and Penbrookes men, foure souldiers [, one of them James].	Edward II	2.5.98.3
and foure devils [above], Faustus to them with this speech.	Faustus 229.2	1.3.0.2
[There turne to them].	Faustus 551.3.A	2.1.166.1
[Turne to them].	Faustus 551.7.A	2.1.170.1
[Turne to them].	Faustus 551.13.A	2.1.176.1
Beate the Friers, fling fire workes among them, and Exeunt.	Faustus 1087.1	3.2.107.1
leaving his State, offers to embrace them, which Faustus seeing,	Faustus 1257.7	4.1.103.7
fire-workes; they set upon the Souldiers and drive them out.	Faustus 1430.3	4.2.106.3
cover'd dishes; Mephostophilis leades them into Faustus Study:	Faustus 1674.2	5.1.0.2
the Friers, and fling fier-workes among them, and so Exeunt.	Faustus App.	p233 41.1
Enter to them Meph.	Faustus App.	p235 31.1
Enter to them the Duke, and the Dutches, the Duke speakes.	Faustus App.	p242 0.1
THEN		
and then all crye vive [le] <la> Roy two or three times.	Paris 588.1	12.0.1
the letter, and then the King getteth the knife and killes him.	Paris 1172.2	22.34.2

THEN (cont.)		
Enter Messenger [and then Bishop of Winchester with the crown].	Edward II	5.2.22.1
Then Gurney stabs Lightborne.	Edward II	5.5.117.1
they <and> dance, and then depart.	Faustus 471.3	2.1.83.3
Then the Pope, and Raymond King of Hungary, with Bruno led in	Faustus 867.3	3.1.89.3
and then Enter Faustus and Mephostophilis in their owne shapes.	Faustus 981.1	3.2.0.1
Then trumpets cease, and Musicke sounds.	Faustus 1257.7	4.1.103.7
Then enter Wagner.	Faustus 1674.3	5.1.0.3
THERE		
there is discovered Jupiter dandling Ganimed upon his knee, and	Dido	1.1.0.1
[There turne to them].	Faustus 551.3.A	2.1.166.1
THERIDAMAS		
Cosroe, Meander, Theridamas, Ortygius, Ceneus, [Menaphon],	1Tamburlaine	1.1.0.1
Enter Theridamas with others.	1Tamburlaine	1.2.151.1
[To Theridamas].	1Tamburlaine	1.2.166.1
[Enter] Cosroe, Tamburlaine, Theridamas, Techelles, Usumcasane,	1Tamburlaine	2.3.0.1
[Enter] Cosroe, Tamburlaine, Theridamas, Menaphon, Meander,	1Tamburlaine	2.5.0.1
Manent Tamburlaine, Techelles, Theridamas, Usumcasane.	1Tamburlaine	2.5.49.2
enter Cosroe wounded, Theridamas, Tamburlaine, Techelles,	1Tamburlaine	2.7.0.2
Techelles, Usumcasane, Theridamas, Bassoe, Zenocrate, [Anippe],	1Tamburlaine	3.3.0.1
Enter Techelles, Theridamas, Usumcasane.	1Tamburlaine	3.3.214.1
Tamburlain, Techelles, Theridamas, Usumcasane, Zenocrate,	1Tamburlaine	4.2.0.1
to it commeth Tamburlain al in scarlet, Theridamas, Techelles,	1Tamburlaine	4.4.0.2
Tamburlaine, Techelles, Theridamas, Usumcasane, with others:	1Tamburlaine	5.1.63.2
Enter Techelles, Theridamas, Usumcasane, and others.	1Tamburlaine	5.1.195.2
the Souldane, Techelles, Theridamas, Usumcasane, with others.	1Tamburlaine	5.1.432.3
Enter Theridamas, and his traine with Drums and Trumpets.	2Tamburlaine	1.3.111.1
Theridamas, Techelles, Usumcasane, and the three sonnes.	2Tamburlaine	2.4.0.3
[Enter] Techelles, Theridamas and their traine.	2Tamburlaine	3.3.0.1
Enter Theridamas, Techelles and all their traine.	2Tamburlaine	3.4.33.2
Enter Theridamas, Techelles, and their traine.	2Tamburlaine	3.5.146.1
Enter [with Souldiers] Tamburlain, Theridamas, Techelles,	2Tamburlaine	4.1.75.2
Enter Theridamas.	2Tamburlaine	4.2.13.1
he scourgeth them, Techelles, Theridamas, Usumcasane, Amyras,	2Tamburlaine	4.3.0.3
Enter Theridamas and Techelles, with other souldiers.	2Tamburlaine	5.1.48.1
Theridamas and Techelles bringing the Governor of Babylon.	2Tamburlaine	5.1.79.1
[Enter Theridamas below].	2Tamburlaine	5.1.148.3
Theridamas shootes.	2Tamburlaine	5.1.152.1
[Enter] Theridamas, Techelles, Usumcasane.	2Tamburlaine	5.3.0.1
THESE		
three Ladies [, one of these Neece to the king, Gaveston],	Edward II	2.2.224.1
THEY		
They sound [to] the battell within, and stay.	1Tamburlaine	3.3.188.1
The battell short, and they enter, Bajazeth is overcome.	1Tamburlaine	3.3.211.2
They bind them.	1Tamburlaine	3.3.267.1
They take him out of the cage.	1Tamburlaine	4.2.1.1
[They put him into the cage].	1Tamburlaine	4.2.82.1
They give him water to drinke, and he flings it on the ground.	1Tamburlaine	4.4.55.1
They [Techelles and soldiers] take them away.	1Tamburlaine	5.1.120.1
They bring in the Turke [in his cage, and Zabina].	1Tamburlaine	5.1.202.1
They sound to the battaile.	1Tamburlaine	5.1.402.1
They call musicke.	2Tamburlaine	2.4.77.1
They play.	2Tamburlaine	4.1.66.1
[They go in the tent].	2Tamburlaine	4.1.75.1
They run away with the Ladies.	2Tamburlaine	4.3.84.1
Alarme, and they scale the walles.	2Tamburlaine	5.1.62.1
They bridle them.	2Tamburlaine	5.1.148.1
They shoote.	2Tamburlaine	5.1.157.1
They crowne him.	2Tamburlaine	5.3.184.1
They bring in the hearse.	2Tamburlaine	5.3.223.1
[As they are leaving] Enter Mathias.	Jew of Malta	1.2.365.1
[They go aside].	Jew of Malta	4.1.159.1
[They take body aside].	Jew of Malta	5.1.59.1
As they are going, [enter] the Souldier [above, who]	Paris 196.1	3.31.1
They beare away the [olde] Queene [of Navarre] and goe out.	Paris 202.1	3.37.1
They hang him.	Paris 493.1	9.12.1
They stabbe him.	Paris 1002.1	19.72.1
Now they strangle him.	Paris 1103.1	20.13.1
They march out with the body of the King, lying on foure mens	Paris 1250.1	22.112.1
They wash him with puddle water, and shave his beard away.	Edward II	5.3.36.1
They hale Edmund away, and carie him to be beheaded.	Edward II	5.4.108.1
they <and> dance, and then depart.	Faustus 471.3	2.1.83.3
[They talk apart].	Faustus 890.1	3.1.112.1
at the other Darius; they meete, Darius is throwne downe,	Faustus 1257.3	4.1.103.3
fire-workes; they set upon the Souldiers and drive them out.	Faustus 1430.3	4.2.106.3
They knocke againe, and call out to talke with Faustus.	Faustus 1590.1	4.6.33.1
Faustus hits him a boxe of the eare, and they all runne away.	Faustus App.	p232 21.2
they runne about.	Faustus App.	p235 25.2
THIS		
and foure devils [above], Faustus to them with this speech.	Faustus 229.2	1.3.0.2
Sing this.	Faustus App.	p232 30.1
THREE		
[Enter] Souldan of Egipt with three or four Lords, Capolin	1Tamburlaine	4.1.0.1
of Damasco, with three or foure Citizens, and foure Virgins,	1Tamburlaine	5.1.0.1
Enter two or three.	1Tamburlaine	5.1.191.1
Tamburlaine with Zenocrate, and his three sonnes, Calyphas,	2Tamburlaine	1.3.0.1
three Phisitians about her bed, tempering potions.	2Tamburlaine	2.4.0.2
Theridamas, Techelles, Usumcasane, and the three sonnes.	2Tamburlaine	2.4.0.3
Tamburlaine with Usumcasane, and his three sons, [Calyphas],	2Tamburlaine	3.2.0.1
[Enter] Tamburlaine with his three sonnes, Usumcasane with	2Tamburlaine	3.5.57.1
Enter three Jewes.	Jew of Malta	1.1.139.1
[Exeunt three Jewes].	Jew of Malta	1.1.176.1
Enter Barabas, and three Jewes.	Jew of Malta	1.2.36.1

THREE (cont.)			
Exeunt. [Manent Barabas and the three Jewes].	Jew of Malta		1.2.159.1
<three> Fryars and [three] <two> Nuns [, one the Abbasse].	Jew of Malta		1.2.304.1
and then all crye vive [le] <la> Roy two or three times.	Paris	588.2	12.0.2
Enter the Captaine of the guarde, and three murtherers.	Paris	931.1	19.0.1
Enter three poore men.	Edward II		1.1.23.1
three Ladies [, one of these Neece to the king, Gaveston],	Edward II		2.2.224.1
and the earle of Penbrookes men [, James and three souldiers].	Edward II		2.6.0.2
Enter Faustus, Mephostophilis, and two or three Schollers.	Faustus	1680.2	5.1.7.2
THROAT			
She noints her throat.	2Tamburlaine		4.2.78.1
THRONE			
Musicke while the Throne descends.	Faustus	1898.1	5.2.102.1
Exit. [Throne ascends].	Faustus	1908.1	5.2.112.1
THROW			
[Throw it aside].	Jew of Malta		4.2.125.1
THROWE			
He offereth to throwe his dagger.	Paris	1051.1	19.121.1
THROWES			
Throwes downe bags.	Jew of Malta		2.1.46.1
THROWN			
[The body is thrown down.	Paris	306.1	5.33.1
THROWNE			
they meete, Darius is throwne downe, Alexander kils him; takes	Faustus	1257.3	4.1.103.3
THROWS			
[Throws herself into the flames].	Dido		5.1.313.1
THUNDER			
Thunder.	Faustus	229.1	1.3.0.1
[Thunder].	Faustus	243.1	1.3.15.1
Thunder and lightning:	Faustus	1674.1	5.1.0.1
Thunder.	Faustus	1797.1	5.2.0.1
<Thunder and lightning>.	Faustus	1976.1A	HC p271
Thunder, and enter the devils.	Faustus	1978.1	5.2.182.1
TIMES			
Enter Aeneas and Dido in the Cave at severall times.	Dido		3.4.0.2
and then all crye vive [le] <la> Roy two or three times.	Paris	588.2	12.0.2
TO			
Enter Juno to Ascanius asleepe.	Dido		3.2.0.1
[To Iarbus].	Dido		3.3.62.1
Exeunt to the Cave.	Dido		3.4.64.1
Enters Iarbus to Sacrifize.	Dido		4.2.0.1
Enter to them Iarbus.	Dido		5.1.61.1
Enter Dido [attended] [to] <and> Aeneas.	Dido		5.1.82.1
[To Techelles].	1Tamburlaine		1.2.162.1
[To Theridamas].	1Tamburlaine		1.2.166.1
[Exeunt] To the Battaile, and Mycetes comes out alone with his	1Tamburlaine		2.4.0.1
out alone with his Crowne in his hand, offering to hide it.	1Tamburlaine		2.4.0.2
Sound trumpets to the battell, and he runs in.	1Tamburlaine		2.4.42.1
[Exeunt] <Enter> to the Battell, and after the battell, enter	1Tamburlaine		2.7.0.1
Tamburlaine goes to her, and takes her away lovingly by the	1Tamburlaine		3.2.65.1
They sound [to] the battell within, and stay.	1Tamburlaine		3.3.188.1
To the battell againe.	1Tamburlaine		3.3.200.1
He gets up upon him to his chaire.	1Tamburlaine		4.2.29.1
Banquet, and to it commeth Tamburlain al in scarlet, Theridamas,	1Tamburlaine		4.4.0.1
They give him water to drinke, and he flings it on the ground.	1Tamburlaine		4.4.55.1
They sound to the battaile.	1Tamburlaine		5.1.402.1
Sound to the battell, and Sigismond comes out wounded.	2Tamburlaine		2.3.0.1
[To them the Messenger].	2Tamburlaine		3.5.0.2
Enter another [1. Citizen], kneeling to the Governour.	2Tamburlaine		5.1.23.1
[To Amyras].	2Tamburlaine		5.3.177.1
Whispers to her.	Jew of Malta		1.2.348.1
[Aside to her].	Jew of Malta		1.2.356.1
Aside to her.	Jew of Malta		1.2.359.1
Aside to her.	Jew of Malta		1.2.361.1
[Aside to 2. Fryar].	Jew of Malta		4.1.81.1
[Aside to 2. Fryar].	Jew of Malta		4.1.83.1
[Aside to 1. Fryar].	Jew of Malta		4.1.86.1
[Aside to 1. Fryar].	Jew of Malta		4.1.89.1
[Aside to 2. Fryar].	Jew of Malta		4.1.91.1
[Aside to 2. Fryar].	Jew of Malta		4.1.100.1
[Aside to Pilia-borza].	Jew of Malta		4.2.62.1
[Aside to Bellamira].	Jew of Malta		4.4.25.1
[Aside to Pilia-borza].	Jew of Malta		4.4.26.1
Pointing to his Sworde.	Paris	153.1	2.96.1
Pothecary with the gloves, and gives them to the olde Queene.	Paris	166.3	3.0.3
Gonzago, Retes, Montsorrell, and Souldiers to the massacre.	Paris	274.2	5.0.2
Enter [to them] Guise.	Paris	437.1	7.77.1
The Guise comes to the King.	Paris	963.1	19.33.1
He offereth to throwe his dagger.	Paris	1051.1	19.121.1
[Offer to go].	Edward II		1.1.38.1
Enter the Nobles to the Queene.	Edward II		1.4.186.1
Enter the Ladie [Neece to the king].	Edward II		2.1.56.1
[Offers to go back].	Edward II		2.2.140.1
three Ladies [, one of these Neece to the king, Gaveston],	Edward II		2.2.224.1
doors] the King and Spencer, to them Gaveston, &c. [the Queene,	Edward II		2.4.0.1
an old man, father to the yong Spencer, with his trunchion,	Edward II		3.1.31.1
[To Queene].	Edward II		4.6.38.1
[Enter Bartley to Leister with letter].	Edward II		5.1.127.1
[To Souldiers].	Edward II		5.4.102.1
They hale Edmund away, and carie him to be beheaded.	Edward II		5.4.108.1
<Enter Faustus to conjure>.	Faustus	228.1A	HC p258
and foure devils [above], Faustus to them with this speech.	Faustus	229.2	1.3.0.2
<with> Devils, giving Crownes and rich apparell to Faustus:	Faustus	471.2	2.1.83.2

TO (cont.)
[There turne to them]. Faustus 551.3.A 2.1.166.1
[Turne to them]. Faustus 551.7.A 2.1.170.1
[Turne to them]. Faustus551.13.A 2.1.176.1
his Crowne, and offering to goe out, his Paramour meetes him, Faustus 1257.4 4.1.103.4
leaving his State, offers to embrace them, which Faustus seeing, Faustus 1257.7 4.1.103.7
He sits to sleepe. Faustus 1483.1 4.4.27.1
They knocke againe, and call out to talke with Faustus. Faustus 1590.1 4.6.33.1
[Offers to stab himself]. Faustus 1728.1 5.1.55.1
enter the Pope and the Cardinall of Lorraine to the banket, Faustus App. p231 0.2
Enter all the Friers to sing the Dirge. Faustus App. p232 28.1
Enter to them Meph. Faustus App. p235 31.1
Enter to them the Duke, and the Dutches, the Duke speakes. Faustus App. p242 0.1

TOGETHER
Enter Techelles and Usumcasane together. 2Tamburlaine 1.3.127.1
five or sixe Protestants with bookes, and kneele together. Paris 528.1 10.0.1

TOLLES
The ordinance being shot of, the bell tolles. Paris 334.1 5.61.1

TOWNE
and the drums sounding a dolefull martch, the Towne burning. 2Tamburlaine 3.2.0.3

TRAIN
Pleshe and Bartus, and their train, with drums and trumpets. Paris 698.2 14.0.2

TRAINE
Enter Dido [with Anna and Iarbus] and her traine. Dido 2.1.73.1
Enter Dido and Anna [with traine]. Dido 4.4.0.1
Exit Iarbus and Aeneas traine. Dido 5.1.77.1
<Upibassa>, and their traine, with drums and trumpets. 2Tamburlaine 1.1.0.2
Fredericke, Baldwine, and their traine with drums and trumpets. 2Tamburlaine 1.1.77.1
Enter Theridamas, and his traine with Drums and Trumpets. 2Tamburlaine 1.3.111.1
[Enter] Sigismond, Fredericke, Baldwine, with their traine. 2Tamburlaine 2.1.0.1
[Enter] Orcanes, Gazellus, Uribassa with their traine. 2Tamburlaine 2.2.0.1
[Enter] Techelles, Theridamas and their traine. 2Tamburlaine 3.3.0.1
Enter Theridamas, Techelles and all their traine. 2Tamburlaine 3.4.33.2
Orcanes, Jerusalem, Trebizon, Soria, Almeda, with their traine. 2Tamburlaine 3.5.0.2
Enter Theridamas, Techelles, and their traine. 2Tamburlaine 3.5.146.1
Enter the King of Navarre [, Bartus], and his traine. Paris 787.2 16.0.2
Exeunt the Pope and his traine. Faustus 1070.1 3.2.90.1

TREASURE
Lords [,Magnetes, Agidas], and Souldiers loden with treasure. 1Tamburlaine 1.2.0.2

TREBISOND
Enter the kings of Trebisond and Soria, one bringing a sword, 2Tamburlaine 3.1.0.1

TREBIZON
Orcanes, Jerusalem, Trebizon, Soria, Almeda, with their traine. 2Tamburlaine 3.5.0.1
his chariot by Trebizon and Soria with bittes in their mouthes, 2Tamburlaine 4.3.0.1
[drawn in his chariot by the kings of Trebizon and Soria], with 2Tamburlaine 5.1.62.2
[Exit with the Kings of Trebizon and Soria]. 2Tamburlaine 5.1.135.1

TROIANS
Exit [with Troians]. Dido 4.4.92.1

TRUMPETS
Sound trumpets to the battell, and he runs in. 1Tamburlaine 2.4.42.1
<Upibassa>, and their traine, with drums and trumpets. 2Tamburlaine 1.1.0.2
Fredericke, Baldwine, and their traine with drums and trumpets. 2Tamburlaine 1.1.77.2
Calyphas, Amyras, and Celebinus, with drummes and trumpets. 2Tamburlaine 1.3.0.2
Enter Theridamas, and his traine with Drums and Trumpets. 2Tamburlaine 1.3.111.2
Amasia, [Captaine, Souldiers], with drums and trumpets. 2Tamburlaine 5.2.0.2
Sound Trumpets. Paris 588.1 12.1.1
Sound Trumpets within, and then all crye vive [le] <la> Roy two Paris 588.1 12.0.1
Sound trumpets. Paris 598.1 12.11.1
Pleshe and Bartus, and their train, with drums and trumpets. Paris 698.2 14.0.2
Sound Drumme and Trumpets, and enter the King of France, and Paris 1139.1 22.0.1
Then trumpets cease, and Musicke sounds. Faustus 1257.8 4.1.103.8

TRUNCHION
father to the yong Spencer, with his trunchion, and soldiers. Edward II 3.1.31.2

TRUSSELL
with a Bishop [of Winchester] for the crowne [and Trussell]. Edward II 5.1.0.2
[Exeunt Bishop of Winchester and Trussell]. Edward II 5.1.124.1

TURKE
Theridamas, Techelles, Usumcasane, the Turke, with others. 1Tamburlaine 4.4.0.2
They bring in the Turke [in his cage, and Zabina]. 1Tamburlaine 5.1.202.1
met by [Callapine and other] Bassoes of the Turke; Calymath. Jew of Malta 1.2.0.2

TURKES
Exeunt [Turkes]. Jew of Malta 1.2.32.1
Enter Calymath, Bashawes, Turkes. Jew of Malta 5.1.68.1
Enter Tûrkes, Barabas, Governour, and Knights prisoners. Jew of Malta 5.2.0.1

TURKISH
Usumcasane, Amyras, Celebinus, leading the Turkish kings. 2Tamburlaine 4.1.75.3

TURNE
[There turne to them]. Faustus 551.3.A 2.1.166.1
[Turne to them]. Faustus 551.7.A 2.1.170.1
[Turne to them]. Faustus551.13.A 2.1.176.1

TWELVE
The clocke striketh twelve. Faustus 1974.1 5.2.178.1

TWO
Enter Aeneas with Ascanius [and Achates], with one or two more. Dido 1.1.133.1
two Moores drawing Bajazeth in his cage, and his wife following 1Tamburlaine 4.2.0.2
Enter two or three. 1Tamburlaine 5.1.191.1
with others, the two spare kings [Orcanes, King of Natolia, and 2Tamburlaine 5.1.62.4
[two] <three> Fryars and [three] <two> Nuns [, one the Jew of Malta 1.2.304.1
<three> Fryars and [three] <two> Nuns [, one the Abbasse]. Jew of Malta 1.2.304.1
Enter [the] two Fryars <and Abigall>. Jew of Malta 3.6.0.1
Enter the two Fryars. Jew of Malta 4.1.20.1
Enter Anjoy, with two Lords of Poland. Paris 451.1 8.0.1
Enter two with the Admirals body. Paris 482.1 9.0.1

TWO (cont.)

and then all crye vive [le] <la> Roy two or three times.	Paris	588.2	12.0.2
Enter two [Murtherers] dragging in the Cardenall [of Loraine].	Paris	1091.1	20.0.1
the King, [Arundell] <Matr.>, the two Spencers, with others.	Edward II		4.3.0.1
Enter two Schollers.	Faustus	194.1	1.2.0.1
Enter two devils.	Faustus	375.1	1.4.33.1
Enter the two Angels <Enter good Angell, and Evill>.	Faustus	402.1	2.1.14.1
Enter the two Angels <good Angel, and evill Angell>.	Faustus	562.1	2.2.11.1
Enter the two Angels.	Faustus	629.1	2.2.78.1
Exeunt the two Clownes.	Faustus	1134.1	3.3.47.1
Enter Faustus, Mephostophilis, and two or three Schollers.	Faustus	1680.2	5.1.7.2
Enter Hellen againe, passing over betweene two Cupids.	Faustus	1767.1	5.1.94.1
Enter two divells, and the clowne runnes up and downe crying.	Faustus App.		p230 49.1

UP

He gets up upon him to his chaire.	1Tamburlaine		4.2.29.1
Exit [the attendants taking up body of the Guise].	Paris	1090.1	19.160.1
[Edward comes up or is discovered].	Edward II		5.5.41.1
Enter two divells, and the clowne runnes up and downe crying.	Faustus App.		p230 49.1

UPIBASSA

vice-roy of Byron, [Uribassa] <Upibassa>, and their traine, with	2Tamburlaine		1.1.0.2

UPON

there is discovered Jupiter dandling Ganimed upon his knee, and	Dido		1.1.0.2
He gets up upon him to his chaire.	1Tamburlaine		4.2.29.1
He takes it and stamps upon it.	1Tamburlaine		4.4.41.1
Governour of Babylon upon the walles with [Maximus and] others.	2Tamburlaine		5.1.0.1
her, and sets Darius Crowne upon her head; and comming backe,	Faustus	1257.5	4.1.103.5
fire-workes; they set upon the Souldiers and drive them out.	Faustus	1430.3	4.2.106.3

URIBASSA

vice-roy of Byron,/[Uribassa] <Upibassa>, and their traine, with	2Tamburlaine		1.1.0.2
[Enter] Orcanes, Gazellus, Uribassa with their traine.	2Tamburlaine		2.2.0.1
Enter Orcanes, Gazellus, Uribassa, with others.	2Tamburlaine		2.3.9.2
Exit Uribassa [and soldiers with body].	2Tamburlaine		2.3.41.1

USUMCASANE

Techelles, Usumcasane, other Lords [,Magnetes, Agidas], and	1Tamburlaine		1.2.0.1
Theridamas, Techelles, Usumcasane, Ortygius, with others.	1Tamburlaine		2.3.0.1
Meander, Ortygius, Techelles, Usumcasane, with others.	1Tamburlaine		2.5.0.2
Manent Tamburlaine, Techelles, Theridamas, Usumcasane.	1Tamburlaine		2.5.49.2
Theridamas, Tamburlaine, Techelles, Usumcasane, with others.	1Tamburlaine		2.7.0.3
[Enter Techelles and Usumcasane].	1Tamburlaine		3.2.106.2
[Enter] Tamburlain, Techelles, Usumcasane, Theridamas, Bassoe,	1Tamburlaine		3.3.0.1
Enter Techelles, Theridamas, Usumcasane.	1Tamburlaine		3.3.214.1
Techelles, Theridamas, Usumcasane, Zenocrate, Anippe, two	1Tamburlaine		4.2.0.1
Theridamas, Techelles, Usumcasane, the Turke, with others.	1Tamburlaine		4.4.0.2
Tamburlaine, Techelles, Theridamas, Usumcasane, with others:	1Tamburlaine		5.1.63.2
Enter Techelles, Theridamas, Usumcasane, and others.	1Tamburlaine		5.1.195.2
the Souldane, Techelles, Theridamas, Usumcasane, with others.	1Tamburlaine		5.1.432.3
Enter Techelles and Usumcasane together.	2Tamburlaine		1.3.127.1
Theridamas, Techelles, Usumcasane, and the three sonnes.	2Tamburlaine		2.4.0.3
[Enter] Tamburlaine with Usumcasane, and his three sons,	2Tamburlaine		3.2.0.1
Tamburlaine with his three sonnes, Usumcasane with other.	2Tamburlaine		3.5.57.1
Theridamas, Techelles, Usumcasane, Amyras, Celebinus, leading	2Tamburlaine		4.1.75.3
them, Techelles, Theridamas, Usumcasane, Amyras, Celebinus:	2Tamburlaine		4.3.0.3
by the kings of Trebizon and Soria], with Usumcasane, Amyras,	2Tamburlaine		5.1.62.3
[Enter] Theridamas, Techelles, Usumcasane.	2Tamburlaine		5.3.0.1

VALDES

Enter Valdes and Cornelius.	Faustus	126.1	1.1.98.1

VANHOLT

Enter the Duke of Vanholt; his Dutches, Faustus, and	Faustus	1558.1	4.6.0.1

VENUS

Enter Venus.	Dido		1.1.49.1
Enter Venus [with Cupid] at another doore, and takes Ascanius	Dido		2.1.303.2
Enter Venus.	Dido		3.2.20.1

VERIE

Tamburlaine all in blacke, and verie melancholy.	1Tamburlaine		5.1.63.3

VERY

Enter [Barabas] with a Hammar above, very busie.	Jew of Malta		5.5.0.1

VICE

Gazellus, vice-roy of Byron, [Uribassa] <Upibassa>, and their	2Tamburlaine		1.1.0.1

VICE-ROY

Gazellus, vice-roy of Byron, [Uribassa] <Upibassa>, and their	2Tamburlaine		1.1.0.1

VICTORY

And Tamburlaine enjoyes the victory, after Arabia enters	1Tamburlaine		5.1.402.2

VINTNER

Enter Vintner.	Faustus	1093.1	3.3.6.1
[Exit Vintner running].	Faustus	1115.1	3.3.28.1
enter the Vintner.	Faustus App.		p234 3.1

VIRGINS

and foure Virgins, with branches of Laurell in their hands.	1Tamburlaine		5.1.0.2
Exeunt. [Manent Virgins].	1Tamburlaine		5.1.63.1

VIVE

and then all crye vive [le] <la> Roy two or three times.	Paris	588.1	12.0.1

WAGNER

Enter Wagner.	Faustus	90.1	1.1.62.1
Enter Wagner.	Faustus	195.1	1.2.2.1
Enter Wagner and [Robin] the Clowne.	Faustus	343.1	1.4.0.1
Enter the Chorus <Wagner solus>.	Faustus	753.2	2.3.32.2
Exit <Wagner>.	Faustus	778.1	2.3.57.1
Enter Wagner.	Faustus	1498.1	4.4.42.1
Then enter Wagner.	Faustus	1674.3	5.1.0.3
Enter Faustus and Wagner.	Faustus	1815.1	5.2.19.1
[Exit Wagner].	Faustus	1820.1	5.2.24.1
Enter Wagner and the Clowne.	Faustus App.		p229 0.1
Enter Wagner.	Faustus App.		p241 66.1

WAGNER (cont.)		
enter Wagner solus.	Faustus App.	p243 0.1
WAIES		
Exeunt omnes, severall waies.	Faustus 721.1	2.2.173.1
WALLES		
Governour of Babylon upon the walles with [Maximus and] others.	2Tamburlaine	5.1.0.1
Alarme, and they scale the walles.	2Tamburlaine	5.1.62.1
hang the Governour of Babylon in chaines on the walles]. .	2Tamburlaine	5.1.148.2
WARWICK		
Enter Lancaster, Mortimer [junior], Warwick, Penbrooke, Kent.	Edward II	2.3.0.1
Barons, Mortimer, Lancaster, Warwick, Penbrooke, cum caeteris.	Edward II	3.1.194.1
WARWICKE		
junior, Edmund Earle of Kent, Guie Earle of Warwicke, &c.	Edward II	1.1.73.2
Enter both the Mortimers, Warwicke, and Lancaster. . .	Edward II	1.2.0.1
Enter Nobiles [: Lancaster, Warwicke, Penbrooke, Mortimer	Edward II	1.4.0.1
Lancaster, Mortimer [junior], Warwicke, Penbrooke, Kent, .	Edward II	2.2.0.2
Enter Warwicke and his companie.	Edward II	2.6.6.1
Exeunt Warwicke and his men, with Gaveston. . . .	Edward II	2.6.17.1
WAS		
reading on a letter that was brought him from the king. .	Edward II	1.1.0.1
WASH		
They wash him with puddle water, and shave his beard away.	Edward II	5.3.36.1
WATCH		
The Watch strikes.	Faustus 1956.1	5.2.160.1
WATER		
They give him water to drinke, and he flings it on the ground.	1Tamburlaine	4.4.55.1
They wash him with puddle water, and shave his beard away.	Edward II	5.3.36.1
WAYS (See also WAIES)		
[Exeunt souldiers several ways, some with Governour]. .	2Tamburlaine	5.1.126.1
WEAPONS		
shoulders with a dead march, drawing weapons on the ground.	Paris 1250.4	22.112.4
and divers with weapons, Mephostophilis with fire-workes; they	Faustus 1430.2	4.2.106.2
WELCH		
Enter with Welch hookes, Rice ap Howell, a Mower, and the Earle	Edward II	4.7.45.1
WET		
Enter the Horse-courser wet.	Faustus 1483.2	4.4.27.2
Enter Horsecourser all wet, crying.	Faustus App.	p240 26.2
WHERE		
Celebinus, issues from the tent where Caliphas sits a sleepe.	2Tamburlaine	4.1.0.2
WHICH		
his right hand a whip, with which he scourgeth them, Techelles,	2Tamburlaine	4.3.0.3
to embrace them, which Faustus seeing, suddenly staies him.	Faustus 1257.7	4.1.103.7
WHILE		
A Flourish while he ascends.	Faustus 876.1	3.1.98.1
A Senit while the Banquet is brought in; and then Enter Faustus	Faustus 981.1	3.2.0.1
Musicke while the Throne descends.	Faustus 1898.1	5.2.102.1
WHIP		
hand, in his right hand a whip, with which he scourgeth them,	2Tamburlaine	4.3.0.3
WHISPERS		
Whispers to her.	Jew of Malta	1.2.348.1
[Whispers her].	Jew of Malta	4.4.2.1
WHO		
who] dischargeth his Musket at the Lord Admirall [and exit].	Paris 196.1	3.31.1
the Emperour, who leaving his State, offers to embrace them,	Faustus 1257.6	4.1.103.6
WIFE		
drawing Bajazeth in his cage, and his wife following him.	1Tamburlaine	4.2.0.2
[Enter above] Captaine with his wife [Olympia] and sonne.	2Tamburlaine	3.3.14.2
Enter [below] the Captaine with [Olympia] his wife and sonne.	2Tamburlaine	3.4.0.1
WINCHESTER		
with a Bishop [of Winchester] for the crowne [and Trussell].	Edward II	5.1.0.1
[Exeunt Bishop of Winchester and Trussell]. . . .	Edward II	5.1.124.1
Enter Messenger [and then Bishop of Winchester with the crown].	Edward II	5.2.22.1
[Exit Winchester].	Edward II	5.2.36.1
WINDOW		
Enter Benvolio above at a window, in his nightcap: . .	Faustus 1178.1	4.1.24.1
WINGS		
[Plucks a feather from Mercuries wings].	Dido	1.1.40.1
WITH (See also WYTH)		
Enter Aeneas with Ascanius [and Achates], with one or two more.	Dido	1.1.133.1
[Exit Ascanius with others].	Dido	1.1.177.1
Enter [Iarbus, with] Illioneus, and Cloanthus [and Sergestus].	Dido	1.2.0.1
Enter Dido [with Anna and Iarbus] and her traine. . .	Dido	2.1.73.1
[Enter servant with robe and Aeneas puts it on]. . .	Dido	2.1.95.1
Enter Venus [with Cupid] at another doore, and takes Ascanius	Dido	2.1.303.2
Enter Dido and Anna [with traine].	Dido	4.4.0.1
Enter Anna, with Aeneas, Achates, Illioneus, and Sergestus.	Dido	4.4.13.1
Exit [with Troians].	Dido	4.4.92.1
Enter the Nurse with Cupid for Ascanius.	Dido	4.5.0.1
Enter Aeneas with a paper in his hand, drawing the platforme of	Dido	5.1.0.1
the platforme of the citie, with him Achates, [Sergestus],	Dido	5.1.0.2
Enter Hermes with Ascanius.	Dido	5.1.23.1
[Exit Sergestus with Ascanius].	Dido	5.1.50.1
[Enter Attendants with wood and fire].	Dido	5.1.282.1
Meander, Theridamas, Ortygius, Ceneus, [Menaphon], with others.	1Tamburlaine	1.1.0.2
Ortigius and [Ceneus] <Conerus> bearing a Crowne, with others.	1Tamburlaine	1.1.135.2
Lords [:Magnetes, Agidas], and Souldiers loden with treasure.	1Tamburlaine	1.2.0.2
Enter Theridamas with others.	1Tamburlaine	1.2.151.1
Cosroe, Menaphon, Ortygius, Ceneus, with other Souldiers.	1Tamburlaine	2.1.0.1
[Enter] Mycetes, Meander, with other Lords and Souldiers.	1Tamburlaine	2.2.0.1
Theridamas, Techelles, Usumcasane, Ortygius, with others.	1Tamburlaine	2.3.0.2
and Mycetes comes out alone with his Crowne in his hand, .	1Tamburlaine	2.4.0.1
Meander, Ortygius, Techelles, Usumcasane, with others. .	1Tamburlaine	2.5.0.2
Cosroe, Meander, Ortygius, Menaphon, with other Souldiers.	1Tamburlaine	2.6.0.1

WITH (cont.)

Theridamas, Tamburlaine, Techelles, Usumcasane, with others.	1Tamburlaine		2.7.0.3
kings of Fesse, Moroco, and Argier, with others, in great pompe.	1Tamburlaine		3.1.0.1
[Enter] Agidas, Zenocrate, Anippe, with others.	1Tamburlaine		3.2.0.1
Enter [aloofe] Tamburlaine with Techelles and others.	1Tamburlaine		3.2.24.1
Enter Techelles with a naked dagger.	1Tamburlaine		3.2.87.1
[Exeunt with body].	1Tamburlaine		3.2.113.1
Theridamas, Bassoe, Zenocrate, [Anippe], with others.	1Tamburlaine		3.3.0.2
with his Bassoes and contributorie Kinges [and Zabina and	1Tamburlaine		3.3.60.1
Exit, with his followers.	1Tamburlaine		3.3.163.1
Exit, with his followers.	1Tamburlaine		3.3.165.1
[Enter] Souldan of Egipt with three or four Lords, Capolin	1Tamburlaine		4.1.0.1
Capoline, with [streaming] <steaming> collors and Souldiers.	1Tamburlaine		4.3.0.1
Theridamas, Techelles, Usumcasane, the Turke, with others.	1Tamburlaine		4.4.0.2
of Damasco, with three or foure Citizens, and foure Virgins,	1Tamburlaine		5.1.0.1
and foure Virgins, with branches of Laurell in their hands.	1Tamburlaine		5.1.0.2
Tamburlaine, Techelles, Theridamas, Usumcasane, with others:	1Tamburlaine		5.1.63.2
the Souldane, Techelles, Theridamas, Usumcasane, with others.	1Tamburlaine		5.1.432.3
<Upibassa>, and their traine, with drums and trumpets.	2Tamburlaine		1.1.0.2
Fredericke, Baldwine, and their traine with drums and trumpets.	2Tamburlaine		1.1.77.1
[Enter] Callapine with Almeda, his keeper.	2Tamburlaine		1.2.0.1
[Enter] Tamburlaine with Zenocrate, and his three sonnes,	2Tamburlaine		1.3.0.1
Calyphas, Amyras, and Celebinus, with drummes and trumpets.	2Tamburlaine		1.3.0.2
Enter Theridamas, and his traine with Drums and Trumpets.	2Tamburlaine		1.3.111.1
[Enter] Sigismond, Fredericke, Baldwine, with their traine.	2Tamburlaine		2.1.0.1
[Enter] Orcanes, Gazellus, Uribassa with their traine.	2Tamburlaine		2.2.0.1
Enter Orcanes, Gazellus, Uribassa, with others.	2Tamburlaine		2.3.9.2
Exit Uribassa [and soldiers with body].	2Tamburlaine		2.3.41.1
Next Natolia and Jerusalem with the Emperiall crowne:	2Tamburlaine		3.1.0.2
[Enter] Tamburlaine with Usumcasane, and his three sons,	2Tamburlaine		3.2.0.1
[Enter above] Captaine with his wife [Olympia] and sonne.	2Tamburlaine		3.3.14.2
Enter [below] the Captaine with [Olympia] his wife and sonne.	2Tamburlaine		3.4.0.1
Orcanes, Jerusalem, Trebizon, Soria, Almeda, with their traine.	2Tamburlaine		3.5.0.2
[Enter] Tamburlaine with his three sonnes, Usumcasane with	2Tamburlaine		3.5.57.1
Tamburlaine with his three sonnes, Usumcasane with other.	2Tamburlaine		3.5.57.2
Enter [with Souldiers] Tamburlain, Theridamas, Techelles,	2Tamburlaine		4.1.75.2
[Exeunt with the body of Calyphas].	2Tamburlaine		4.1.167.1
his chariot by Trebizon and Soria with bittes in their mouthes,	2Tamburlaine		4.3.0.2
his right hand a whip, with which he scourgeth them, Techelles,	2Tamburlaine		4.3.0.3
and Jerusalem led by with five or six common souldiers.	2Tamburlaine		4.3.0.5
They run away with the Ladies.	2Tamburlaine		4.3.84.1
Governour of Babylon upon the walles with [Maximus and] others.	2Tamburlaine		5.1.0.1
Enter Theridamas and Techelles, with other souldiers.	2Tamburlaine		5.1.48.1
by the kings of Trebizon and Soria], with Usumcasane, Amyras,	2Tamburlaine		5.1.62.3
and Celebinus, with others, the two spare kings [Orcanes, King	2Tamburlaine		5.1.62.3
[Exeunt souldiers several ways, some with Governour].	2Tamburlaine		5.1.126.1
[Exit with the Kings of Trebizon and Soria].	2Tamburlaine		5.1.135.1
Amasia, [Captaine, Souldiers], with drums and trumpets.	2Tamburlaine		5.2.0.1
Tamburlaine goes in, and comes out againe with al the rest.	2Tamburlaine		5.3.114.1
Barabas in his Counting-house, with heapes of gold before him.	Jew of Malta		1.1.0.1
Enter Barabas with a light.	Jew of Malta		2.1.0.1
Enter Officers with slaves.	Jew of Malta		2.3.0.1
[Exeunt Officers with slaves].	Jew of Malta		2.3.162.1
Exeunt [with bodies].	Jew of Malta		3.2.37.1
Enter Ithimore with the pot.	Jew of Malta		3.4.54.1
Enter Barabas with a Lute, disguis'd.	Jew of Malta		4.4.29.1
Enter Jew, Ithimore [with Officers].	Jew of Malta		5.1.18.2
Exit [Barabas, Curtezane, Pilia-borza, with Officers].	Jew of Malta		5.1.43.1
Enter Governor with a guard.	Jew of Malta		5.2.47.1
Enter [Barabas] with a Hammar above, very busie.	Jew of Malta		5.5.0.1
[His men work with him].	Jew of Malta		5.5.0.2
Admirall, and [Margaret] the Queene of Navarre, with others.	Paris	0.3	1.0.3
and [Margaret] the Queene of Navar [with others], and manet	Paris	26.3	1.26.3
and the Pothecary with the gloves, and gives them to the olde	Paris	166.3	3.0.3
Exit Gonzago and others with him.	Paris	292.1	5.19.1
enters againe, with all the rest, with their Swords drawne,	Paris	335.2	5.62.2
all the rest, with their Swords drawne, chasing the Protestants.	Paris	335.2	5.62.2
the Guise and Anjoy [, Dumaine, Mountsorrell, with soldiers].	Paris	379.1	7.19.1
King of Navarre and Prince of Condy, with their scholmaisters.	Paris	429.2	7.69.2
Exit Anjoy [and soldiers with bodies].	Paris	442.1	7.82.1
Enter Anjoy, with two Lords of Poland.	Paris	451.1	8.0.1
Enter two with the Admirals body.	Paris	482.1	9.0.1
Enter five or sixe Protestants with bookes, and kneele	Paris	528.1	10.0.1
[Mugeroun], the kings Minions, with others, and the Cutpurse.	Paris	588.5	12.0.5
Enter the Maid with Inke and Paper.	Paris	665.1	13.9.1
Pleshe and Bartus, and their train, with drums and trumpets.	Paris	698.2	14.0.2
Enter one with a pen and inke.	Paris	881.1	17.76.1
Enter Duke Dumayn reading of a letter, with others.	Paris	1107.1	21.0.1
Enter Frier with a Letter.	Paris	1158.1	22.20.1
He stabs the King with a knife as he readeth the letter, and	Paris	1172.1	22.34.1
[Exeunt attendants with body].	Paris	1182.1	22.44.1
They march cut with the body of the King, lying on foure mens	Paris	1250.1	22.112.1
lying on foure mens shoulders with a dead march, drawing	Paris	1250.3	22.112.3
Enter A souldier with a muskett	Paris ms		p390 0.1
Exeunt Warwicke and his men, with Gaveston.	Edward II		2.6.17.1
King Edward and Spencer, [Baldock], with Drummes and Fifes.	Edward II		3.1.0.1
father to the yong Spencer, with his trunchion, and soldiers.	Edward II		3.1.31.2
Enter the Herald from the Barons, with his coate of armes.	Edward II		3.1.150.1
Enter Edward, with the Barons [and Kent] captives.	Edward II		3.1.220.2
the King, [Arundell] <Matr.>, the two Spencers, with others.	Edward II		4.3.0.2
[Enter] Edmund [earle of Kent] alone with a sword and target.	Edward II		4.6.0.1
and the Maior of Bristow, with Spencer the father.	Edward II		4.6.45.2
Enter with Welch hookes, Rice ap Howell, a Mower, and the Earle	Edward II		4.7.45.1

WITH (cont.)			
with a Bishcp [of Winchester] for the crowne [and Trussell].	Edward II		5.1.0.1
[Enter Bartley to Leister with letter].	Edward II		5.1.127.1
Enter Messenger [and then Bishop of Winchester with the crown].	Edward II		5.2.22.1
Enter the ycng Prince, and the Earle of Kent talking with him.	Edward II		5.2.73.3
Enter Matrevis and Gurney with the King [and souldiers].	Edward II		5.3.0.1
They wash him with puddle water, and shave his beard away.	Edward II		5.3.36.1
Exeunt Matrevis and Gurney, with the king.	Edward II		5.3.62.1
Enter Souldiers with the Earle of Kent prisoner.	Edward II		5.4.81.1
Return with table].	Edward II		5.5.109.1
Enter the King, with the lords.	Edward II		5.6.23.1
[Exit Mortimer with 1. Lord attended].	Edward II		5.6.67.1
[Enter some with hearse].	Edward II		5.6.97.1
and foure devils [abcve], Faustus to them with this speech.	Faustus	229.2	1.3.0.2
Enter Mephostophilis with the <a> Chafer of Fire <coles>.	Faustus	458.1	2.1.70.1
Enter <with> Devils, giving Crownes and rich apparell to	Faustus	471.2	2.1.83.2
<Enter with a divell drest like a woman, with fier workes>.	Faustus	531.1A	HC p261
Pope, and Raymond King of Hungary, with Bruno led in chaines.	Faustus	867.4	3.1.89.4
Exeunt Faustus and Mephostophilis [with Bruno].	Faustus	976.1	3.1.198.1
Enter the Cardinals with a Booke.	Faustus	1008.2	3.2.28.2
Enter the Friers with Bell, Booke, and Candle, for the Dirge.	Faustus	1075.1	3.2.95.1
Enter [Robin the] Clowne and Dicke, with a Cup.	Faustus	1088.1	3.3.0.1
Exit Frederick with the Souldiers.	Faustus	1349.1	4.2.25.1
Enter Faustus with the false head.	Faustus	1361.1	4.2.37.1
Exeunt Spirits with the knights.	Faustus	1419.1	4.2.95.1
and divers with weapons, Mephostophilis with fire-workes; they	Faustus	1430.2	4.2.106.2
Mephostophilis with fire-workes; they set upon the Souldiers	Faustus	1430.3	4.2.106.3
and besmear'd with mud and durt; all having hornes on their	Faustus	1431.2	4.3.0.2
Enter Mephostophilis agen with the grapes.	Faustus	1575.1	4.6.18.1
They knocke againe, and call out to talke with Faustus.	Faustus	1590.1	4.6.33.1
Enter Hostesse [brought hither by magic] with drinke.	Faustus	1649.1	4.6.92.1
Enter devils with cover'd dishes; Mephostophilis leades them	Faustus	1674.1	5.1.0.1
Enter <Faustus with> the Scholers <Schollers>.	Faustus	1819.1	5.2.23.1
Exeunt [with him].	Faustus	1982.1	5.2.186.1
the Cardinall of Lorraine to the banket, with Friers attending.	Faustus App.		p231 0.2
Enter Robin the Ostler with a booke in his hand	Faustus App.		p233 0.1
Enter Robin and Rafe with a silver Goblet.	Faustus App.		p234 0.1
Enter Emperour, Faustus, and a Knight, with Attendants.	Faustus App.		p236 0.2
with Alexander and his paramour.	Faustus App.		p238 59.1
Enter the Knight with a paire of hornes on his head.	Faustus App.		p238 68.1
with the grapes.	Faustus App.		p242 14.2
WITHIN			
They sound [to] the battell within, and stay.	1Tamburlaine		3.3.188.1
Alarme within.	2Tamburlaine		5.3.101.1
Bells within.	Jew of Malta		4.1.0.1
[Within].	Jew of Malta		5.5.63.1
[Within].	Paris	346.1	6.1.1
Stab him [and he falls within and dies].	Paris	360.1	6.15.1
Sound Trumpets within, and then all crye vive [le] <la> Roy two	Paris	588.1	12.0.1
Alarums within.	Paris	787.1	16.0.1
Enter the Guise [within] and knocketh.	Paris	955.1	19.25.1
The [Clownes] <Clcwne> bounce at the gate, within.	Faustus	1587.1	4.6.30.1
WOMAN			
He fetches in a woman devill.	Faustus	531.1	2.1.143.1
<Enter with a divell drest like a woman, with fier workes>.	Faustus	531.1A	HC p261
WOOD			
[Enter Attendants with wood and fire].	Dido		5.1.282.1
WORK			
[His men work with him].	Jew of Malta		5.5.0.2
WORKES			
<Enter with a divell drest like a woman, with fier workes>.	Faustus	531.1A	HC p261
Beate the Friers, fling fire workes among them, and Exeunt.	Faustus	1087.1	3.2.107.1
Mephostophilis with fire-workes; they set upon the Souldiers	Faustus	1430.3	4.2.106.3
the Friers, and fling fier-workes among them, and so Exeunt.	Faustus App.		p233 41.1
WOUNDED			
and after the battell, enter Cosroe wounded, Theridamas,	1Tamburlaine		2.7.0.2
Tamburlaine enjoyes the victory, after Arabia enters wounded.	1Tamburlaine		5.1.402.2
Sound to the battell, and Sigismond comes out wounded.	2Tamburlaine		2.3.0.1
WOUNDS			
[Wounds Gaveston].	Edward II		2.2.84.1
WRATHFULLY			
by the hand, looking wrathfully on Agidas, and sayes nothing.	1Tamburlaine		3.2.65.2
WRITES			
He writes.	Jew of Malta		4.2.71.1
She writes.	Paris	667.1	13.11.1
He writes.	Paris	891.1	17.86.1
WYTH			
Enter Zenocrate wyth Anippe.	1Tamburlaine		5.1.318.2
YONG			
an old man, father to the yong Spencer, with his trunchion,	Edward II		3.1.31.1
Enter the yong Prince, and the Earle of Kent talking with him.	Edward II		5.2.73.2
Enter the yong King, [Archbishop] [of Canterbury], Champion,	Edward II		5.4.72.1
YOUNG			
the Queene, Mortimer, the young Prince and Sir John of Henolt.	Edward II		4.6.18.1
ZABINA			
his Bassoes and contributorie Kinges [and Zabina and Ebea].	1Tamburlaine		3.3.60.2
They bring in the Turke [in his cage, and Zabina].	1Tamburlaine		5.1.202.1
Exeunt. [Manent Bajazeth and Zabina].	1Tamburlaine		5.1.213.1
Enter Zabina.	1Tamburlaine		5.1.304.2
ZENOCRATE			
[Enter] Tamburlaine leading Zenocrate:	1Tamburlaine		1.2.0.1
[Enter] Agidas, Zenocrate, Anippe, with others.	1Tamburlaine		3.2.0.1
Theridamas, Bassoe, Zenocrate, [Anippe], with others.	1Tamburlaine		3.3.0.2

ZENOCRATE (ccnt.)

He takes it from her, and gives it Zenocrate.	1Tamburlaine	3.3.224.1
Usumcasane, Zenocrate, Anippe, two Moores drawing Bajazeth in	1Tamburlaine	4.2.0.1
Enter Zenocrate wyth Anippe.	1Tamburlaine	5.1.318.2
[Enter] Tamburlaine with Zenocrate, and his three sonnes,	2Tamburlaine	1.3.0.1
The Arras is drawen and Zenocrate lies in her bed of state,	2Tamburlaine	2.4.0.1
foure bearing the hearse of Zenocrate, and the drums sounding a	2Tamburlaine	3.2.0.2

APPENDIXES

-
ANDON'D
ANDOND
ANDONS
ANUS
ATED
ATES
BOTS
BYES
ETTED
HOR
HOR'D
IDUS
IGAIL
IGAILE
ILITIE
JECTION
JUR'D
ORTIVE
OUNDANCE
OUNDED
OUNDS
RAHAM
RAHAMS
RAMS
REVIATED
SOLUTE
SOLUTELY
STAINE
STRACTS
US'DE
YDOS
YDUS
ANTHA
CEPTANCE
CESSARY
CIDENS
CIDENTALL
CIDENT'S
CIDENTS
COMPANIE
COMPLISHMENTS
COMPLISHT
CORD
COSTED
COUNTED
CURSSED
CUSE
CUSING
CUSTOME
HELAUS
HELOUS
HERONTIS
HILL
HILLIS
CLOCKE
COMMING
QUAINTANCE
QUAINTS
QUITS
TAEON
TEONS
TES
TOR
TORS
AMANTES
AMANTINE
DED
DES
DST
EIW
EW
CHUC
JOINING
JOURNED
JUNCT
MIRABLE
MIRABLEST
MIRDE
MITION
MITS
MONISHT
MONITION
MYR'D
MYRE
MYRING
DO
CONS
CORNED
ORIAN
CRIATICK
DRY

ADUE
ADULTERORS
ADVANCED
ADVERTISED
ADVICE
ADVIZE
ADVOCATE
ADVOCATES
AEGEAN
AEGIPTIAN
AENEA
AEOLIA
AERII
AERY
AESOPS
AETNA'S
AETNAS
A FARRE
AFFARES
AFFAYRES
AFFECTER
AFFECTES
AFFECTEST
AFFECTING
AFFECTS
AFFIDE
AFFIED
AFFIRME
AFFLICTED
AFFLICTING
AFFLICTION
AFFOORDED
AFFORDING
AFFRAID
AFFRAIDE
AFFRIGHTED
AFFRIGHTS
AFFRIK
AFFRIKS
A FOOTE
AFRAIDE
AFRAYD
AFRICK
AFRIGHTED
AFTERNOONES
AFTERWARDS
AGAINSTE
AGAVE
AGAYNE
AGENORS
AGGET
AGONY
AGOOD
AGRAMITHIST
AGRAVATE
AGREEDE
AGREEV'D
AGRIPPA
AGROUND
AIER
AIERY
AIMED
AIMING
AIRIE
AIRS
AIRY
AKED
ALARMS
ALBANEES
ALBANUS
ALBERTUS
ALCIBIADES
ALCIDAMUS
ALCINOUS
ALCION
ALCUMIST
ALDEBORAN
ALE
ALEPO
ALEPPO
ALEXANDERS
AL-FOWLES
ALIANCE
ALIFE
A LIKE
ALLAYDE
ALLEAG'D
ALLEDGE
ALLOT
ALLOTTED
ALLOW
ALLOWE
ALLOWES

ALLUDES
ALLUR'D
ALLURES
ALLYED
ALMAINE
ALMES
ALMIGHTY
ALMOND
ALMO'S
ALOUD
ALOUDE
ALOWD
ALPHEUS
ALREADIE
ALTERED
ALTERS
ALURE
AMASDE
AMATISTS
AMAZING
AMAZON
AMAZONIA
AMAZONIANS
AMBASSADORS
AMBASSAGE
AMBER GREECE
AMBIGUITIES
AMBIGUOUS
AMBITION
AMBLES
AMBROSIA
AMEND
AMIABLE
AMID
AMIMONE
AMITY
AMONGEST
AMOUROUS
AMPLIFIE
AMYRAS
ANAGRAMATIS'D
ANALITIKES
ANCHISAEON
ANCKLES
ANCONA
ANCOR
ANDROMACHE
ANEW
ANGERS
ANGRING
A NIGHT
A NIGHTS
ANIMATE
ANIMATED
ANNAS
ANNOYES
ANNOYETH
ANNUALL
ANOY
ANOYDE
ANSWEARE
ANSWEARES
ANSWERABLE
ANSWERING
ANT
ANTARTICKE
ANTECHRISTIAN
ANTENOR
ANTICHRISTIAN
ANTICK
ANTIOCH
ANTIPODES
ANTIQUES
ANTS
ANTWARPES
ANTWERPES
ANTYPODES
ANUBIS
ANULATIKES
ANVILL
ANWERPE
ANYTHING
AP
APAL'D
APART
APHORISMES
A PIECES
APIS
APOLLO'S
APÓTHEÇARIE
APPAL
APPARANT
APPARANTLY

APPAREAT
APPAULS
APPEALE
APPEARD
APPEARDE
APPEARING
APPEAZE
APPENINES
APPETENCE
APPLAUDED
APPLAUDING
APPLE
APPROACHT
APPROCH
APPROCHING
APPROCHT
APPROOVE
APPROOVED
APPROV'D
APPROVE
APPROVES
APRILL
AQUAM
AQUATANI
AQUATICI
AQUILON
ARABICUS
ARACHNE
ARATUS
ARCHES
ARCHIPELLAGO
ARCHITECT
ARCHITECTURE
ARCH-MONARK
ARCH-MONARKE
ARCH-REGENT
ARCH-TRAITOR
ARDENTIS
ARETHUSA'Ŝ
ARGEIRE
ARGENT
ARGIRON
ARGOLIAN
ARGOSES
ARGOSIES
ARGUEST
ARGUMENTS
ARIADAN
ARIADNE
ARIGHT
ARIONS
ARISETH
ARISTARCHUS
ARISTOTLES
ARIVED
ARKE
ARM
ARMA
ARMADOS
ARMDE
ARMES-BEARING
ARMIS
ARMLESSE
ARMOURS
AROUND
ARRESTS
ARRIMINUM
ARRIVED
ARROWE
ARTES
ARTFULL
ARTICKS
ARTIERS
ARTIFICIALL
ARTILERY
ARTIZAN
ASANT
ASCANIA
ASCEASD
ASCREUŞ
ASCRIB'D
ASHAMDE
A SHAMED
ASHIE
ASIAN
ASIAS
ASKED
ASKEST
ASK'ST
ASK'T
ASPECTS
ASPEN
ASPIRES

ASPIR'ST
ASPYRING
ASSAFITIDA
ASSAIES
ASSAULTS
ASSAYED
ASSEMBLE
ASSENDS
ASSENT
ASSIGNES
ASSIRIANS
ASSISTANCE
ASSOCIATE
ASSOCIATES
ASSUME
ASSURES
ASSYRIAN
AS'T
ASTONIED
ASTOUNDING
ASTRACISME
ASTRAEUS
ASTRAY
ASTROLOGIE
ASTRONOMY
ATALANTA
ATALANTAS
ATAX
ATCHIEV'D
ATCHIVE
ATCHIVEMENTS
ATHENS
ATHIRST
ATHWART
ATREUS
ATTEMPLESSE
ATTENTIVE
ATTENTIVELY
ATTICKE
ATTIRED
ATTONEMENT
ATTRACT
ATTRACTIVE
ATTRIBUTE
ATTURNEY
AUDACIOUS
AUGMENT
AUGMENTETH
AUGMENTS
AUGURY
AUKWARD
AULIS
AUNCESTERS
AUNCESTORS
AUNTIENT
AUSTRICH
AUT
AUTUME
AVAILDE
AVAILES
AVAILETH
AVARICE
AVAUNT
AVENGD
AVENGED
AVERNE
AVERNI
AVOID
AVOUCHE
AVOYD
AW
AWAIT
A WAY
AWAYE
AWDE
AWE
AWFUL
AWHILE
AWKWARD
A WOOING
AWRIE
AXIOMS
AXIS
AXLE
AXLE-TREE
AXLETREE
AXON
AYER
AYLE
AYL'ST
AYM'D
AYME
AZAMOR

-1- (CONT.)

AZUR'D
AZURED
BABILON
BABLING
BABYLONIANS
BACCHINALL
BACK'D
BACKT
BACK-WARD
BACONS
BADE
BADGETHS
BAG
BAGDETS
BAGGE
BAGGS
BAGOUS
BAIES
BAILE
BAIRSETH
BAITED
BAK'D
BALAAM
BALDE
BALD-PATE
BALEFULL
BALIO
BALIOL
BALLACE
BALLADS
BALLASSED
BALLE
BALS
BALSAMUM
BALSERA
BAN
BANCHO
BANCKES
BANDIE
BAN-DOGGES
BANIOS
BANISHD
BANISHED
BANKROUTS
BANNE
BANNER
BANNERS
BANNOCKS
BANNOCKS BORNE
BANQUEROUT
BANQUETTED
BAPTIZ'D
BAR
BARBARIANS
BARBARISME
BARBARS
BARCKE
BARDE
BARDI
BARE-FOOTE
BARGAINE
BARK
BARKES
BARKT
BARNARDINE
BARQUE
BARRAINE
BARR'D
BARRENNESSE
BARRES
BARRONS
BASE-BORNE
BASE-BRED
BASELIE
BASENES
BASHAWS
BASHFULNESSE
BASON
BASSOE-MAISTER
BASTARDLY
BASTARDS
BASTONES
BATAVIANS
BATCHELER
BATHDE
BATHING
BATTEL
BATTELS
BATTEN
BATTILE
BATTLE
BAUCIS
BAUDE
BAUDS
BAWD
BAWDS
BEADES
BEAKE
BEAME
BEAMONT
BEAR
BEARDED
BEARE'
BEARE'T
BEARS
BEAR'ST
BEARST
BEAUTIFIED
BEAUTIFUL
BEAUTIFULLEST
BEAUTIFYING
BEAVERS
BECKT
BEDAUBD
BEDDE
BEDFELLOWES
BEDRED
BED-RID
BEDSTED
BEEF
BEE HIVES
BEELZEBUB
BEFALL
BEFALLES
BEFAL'NE
BEFORE HAND
BE-FRIENDED
BEG
BEGAT
BEGET
BEGGARS
BEGGE
BEGGERS
BEGGERY
BEGGING
BEGINNER
BEGINNES
BEGINNING
BEGON
BEGONNE
BEGUILD
BEGUILE
BEGUILED
BEGUN
BEGUNNE
BEHALFE
BEHAV'D
BEHEAD
BEHIGHT
BEHINDE
BEHOLDS
BEHOULD
BEHOVES
BEL
BELCH
BELCHEOS
BELDAME
BELEEVER
BELEEVES
BELEEVING
BELGASAR
BELGIA
BELGIANS
BELIMOTHE
BELLES
BELLIED
BELLIES
BELLONA
BELLONAES
BELLOWED
BELLY-CHEARE
BELLYED
BELONG
BELONGING
BELOVDE
BELOWE
BELSEBORAMS
BELUS
BELZABUB
BENEFIT
BENEFITS
BENIGHTED
BENUMB'D
BENUMM'D
BENUMMED
BEREAVEN
BEREAVES
BESCRATCH
BESEEM'D
BESEIGED
BESMER'D
BESPEAKE
BESPOKE
BESTEAD
BESTOWD
BESTOWDE
BESTRID
BE'T
BETAKE
BETIDED
BETIDES
BETOKENING
BETRAID
BETRAIES
BETRAYD
BETRAYDE
BETRAYED
BETRAYE'S
BETROATH'D
BETTERS
BETWEEN
BEWAILD
BEWAYLES
BEWITCHING
BEWITCHT
BEWRAYD
BEWRAYDE
BIBBING
BIBLE
BICKERING
BIDENTALL
BIEN
BIGNESSE
BILEDULL
BILLOW
BINDING
BIRCHIN
BIRD-CHANGED
BIRDE
BIRTH-DAY
BIRTH DAY
BIRTHES
BISHOPRICK
BITING
BITTE
BITTERLY
BITURIGES
BLABBE
BLABBING
BLACKNESSE
BLACK-SMITHES
BLADE
BLANCKE
BLASPHEM'D
BLASPHEMDE
BLASPHEMOUS
BLASTING
BLAZ'D
BLAZON
BLEARE
BLEATE
BLEED
BLEEDES
BLESSEDNES
BLESSINGS
BLINDES
BLINK
BLINK-EI'D
BLIS
BLITHELY
BLOATS
BLOCKISH
BLOCKS
BLOODLES
BLOOD-QUAFFING
BLOOD-RAW
BLOOMES
BLOSSOMS
BLOTS
BLOTTED
BLOUDLES
BLOUDLESSE
BLOUDS
BLOUD-SHED
BLOUD-SHOTTEN
BLOWEN
BLOWETH
BLOYSE
BLUBBERED
BLUBBRED
BLUNTED
BLUNTER
BLUSHE
BLUSHFULL
BLUSTRING
BOASTS
BOAT
BOATS
BODKIN
BODYE
BOETES
BOHEME
BOHEMIA
BOIE
BOISTEROUS
BOLDE
BOLSTERED
BOLT
BONDES
BONDMAN
BOND-MEN
BOND-WOMEN
BONET
BONNET
BOORDED
BOORE
BOORES
BOOT
BOOTED
BOOTLES
BOOTLESSE
BORDER
BORDERED
BORDERERS
BORDERS
BORDRING
BORGIAS
BORROWD
BORROWING
BOSSE
BOTTLE-NOS'D
BOTTLES
BOUGHS
BOULLION
BOULT
BOUNDLESSE
BOUNTIFULL
BOUNTY
BOURBON
BOURD
'BOUT
BOUTS
BOWDE
BOWERS
BOWLE
BOWMEN
BOWRE
BOX
BOXE
BOYLE
BRABBLING
BRACELET
BRACKISH
BRAG
BRAGS
BRAIDE
BRAINDE
BRAINS
BRAINSICK
BRAIN-SICKE
BRAINSICKE
BRAKE
BRAKES
BRANCHE
BRANCHES
BRANCHT
BRANDISH
BRANDISHING
BRANDS
BRASSE-BULLETS
BRATS
BRAVDE
BRAV'ST
BRAWLE
BRAWLING
BRAWNES
BRAYE
BREADTH
BREAKERS
BREAKST
BREATHED
BREATHLES
BREDTH
BREECHING
BRENT
BRESTED
BREVIATED
BRIBDE
BRIBES
BRICKE
BRIDE
BRIDGES
BRIEFE
BRIERS
BRIGANDINE
BRIGHT-BEAR
BRIGHTEST
BRIGHTNES
BRIGHTNESSE
BRIGHTSOME
BRIM
BRIMSTONE
BRINCKE
BRINGERS
BRINGETH
BRINGST
BRINKE
BRISKE
BRISTLE
BRIST'LED
BRISTLE-POI
BRITAINE
BRITISH
BRITTAINE
BRITTISH
BROILE
BROKEN WINDE
BROKERY
BROOK
BROOKES
BROOMES
BROTHER'S
BROUCH
BROUGHTST
BROYLE
BROYLING
BRUNTS
BUBLING
BUCKLES
BUD
BUDA
BUGGES
BUILDING
BUILDS
BULGARIA
BULKE
BULLION
BULLS
BULWARK
BUNDLE
BURBONITES
BURDENED
BURDENING
BURDENS
BURIALS
BURIE
BURIES
BURLADIE
BURLY
BURNED
BURTHENS
BURYALL
BURYING
BUSHY
BUSINESSES
BUSKIN
BUSKIND
BUSKINES
BUSSETH
BUTCHERD
BUTS
BUTTING
BUTTOCKE
BUYES
BUZ
BUZZETH
BYATHER
BYRDS
BYRTH-DAY
BYRTHES
BY-SOUTH
BYTS
BYTTERNESSE
CABINS

(CONT.)
E
NET
SSE
ARIA
S
KE
E
ON
IFE
BRIA
BRIAN
PINES
ONIAN
PINUS
E
DONIAN
ED
EPINE
EPINUS
IST
DE
IE
R
E
ST
T
ES
US
DON
PSO
ELS
ANIA
ES
S
AN
REA
ELL
YAN
S
RED
ONIERS
N
NIZE
NS
PUS
ERBURIES
ASE
BLE
DE
TALL
TOLL
ES
ING
AIN'S
AINS
IVATES
IVITIE
S
ONADOES
INALLS
DST
FULLY
-GOT
LES
LESLY
BDIS
ES
ONIA
ON
WSING
ATHIAN
ENTERS
EST
AS
ECT
IENG
OUST
YING
Y'T
S
T
HAGENS
HAGINIANS
Y
EMATES
EMENT
IERE
EA
EAN
SIA

CASTILIANO
CASTING
CASUALL
CASUALTIE
CATCHING
CATECHISING
CATERPILLERS
CATHOLICKES
CATHOLIKE
CATHOLIQUES
CATILINE
CATS
CATTELL
CATUL
CATULLUS
CATZERIE
CAUGHT
'CAUSE
CAUSELES
CAZATES
CAZZO
CEASDE
CEAŞELESSE
CEASLES
CEASLESSE
CEASSLES
CELESTIAL
CELLER
CELLERS
CELS
CEMERIAN
CENSTE
CENSUR'D
CENSURE
CENTERS
CENTINELS
CENTRICKE
CENTRONELS
CENTURION
CEPHALUS
CEPHEUS
CERANIAS
CERANNIA
CERAUNIA
CERBERUS
CEREMONIALL
CEREMONIES
CEREMONIOUS
CEREMONY
CERTAINELIE
CESTERNES
CHAC'D
CHAINING
CHALENGE
CHALLENGER
CHAMBER-FELLOW
CHAMBER MAID
CHAMPIONS
CHANCES
CHANGED
CHANGELING
CHANGETH
CHAPLAINE
CHAPLET
CHARGED
CHARGING
CHARILY
CHARIOT-HORSES
CHARITIE
CHARMING
CHARMS
CHARRIOT
CHASTEST
CHASTISE
CHASTIZE
CHAUNC'D
CHAUNCELLOR
CHAUNCELOR
CHAUNGING
CHAYRE
CHE
CHEAR
CHEAREFULL
CHEARES
CHEARFUL
CHEARFULL
CHEAT
CHECK
CHECKE
CHECKES
CHECKING
CHECKS
CHECKT

CHEEF
CHEEFELY
CHEEFEST
CHEEK
CHEEK'DE
CHEERELES
CHEERES
CHERUBINS
CHERUPE
CHEST
CHESTS
CHID
CHIDES
CHIE
CHIMNEY
CHIMNEY-SWEEPER
CHIMNY
CHIMNY-SWEEPER
CHIN
CHIO
CHIRKE
CHITTERLINS
CHIVALRIE
CHIVALRY
CHOAKT
CHOCKT
CHOICE
CHOISE
CHOISEST
CHOLLER
CHOOSING
CHOPS
CHOSE
CHOYSE
CHRISEIS
CHRISIS
CHRISTAL
CHRISTALINUM
CHRISTEN
CHRISTENED
CHRISTI
CHRONICLE
CHUF
CHUFFE
CHUF-LIKE
CHURCHMENS
CHURLES
CICILIANS
CILICIA
CIMODOAE
CIMOTHOE
CINDERS
CINTHIA
CINTHIA'S
CIPHER
CIRCLING
CIRCUMCIS'D
CIRCUMCISED
CIRCUMCIZ'D
CIRCUMCIZED
CIRCUMSCRIB'D
CIRCUMSCRIPTIBLE
CIRCUMSPECT
CIRCUMSTANCE
CISALPIN
CITHEIDAS
CITHERA
CITHEREA'S
CITHEREAS
CITIZEN
CITTIZENS
CITTYES
CIVILE
CLAIMES
CLAMBER'D
CLAMORS
CLANG
CLARKE
CLASHING
CLASPS
CLAWES
CLEAREST
CLEARGIE
CLEAVES
CLEREMONT
CLEYES
CLIENT
CLIFTES
CLIMAT
CLIMBE
CLING'D
CLINGED
CLIP

CLIPPES
CLIPS
CLOAK
CLOAKES
CLOANTHUS
CLOATHED
CLOGD
CLOGGE
CLOS'D
CLOSD
CLOSETH
CLOSURE
CLOTH
CLOUDED
CLOUDIE
CLOUDY
CLOUTS
CLOVEN
CLOWDIE
CLOWNAGE
CLOWNISH
CLOY
CLOYD
CLOYE
CLOYED
CLOYES
CLOYSTER
CLUNG
CLUSTERS
CLUSTRED
COACHE
COACH-HORSE
COACHMAN
COARSE
COASTED
COASTES
COASTS
COAT
COATE-TUCKT
COBHAM
COCHE
COCKE
COCKERELS
COCKS
CODEMIA
COELUM
COEQUALL
COFFER
COFFIN
COFFYN
COIN'D
COLCHIS
COLDLY
COLEBLACK
COLEBLACKE
COLES
COLL
COLLECTION
COLLEDGE
COLLEDGES
COLLIARS
COLLORS
COLONIES
COLOSSUS
COLOURING
COLTISH
COLTS
COMBATE
COMBE
COMBES
COMBIN'D
COMBINDE
COMBINE
COMEDIES
COMELIEST
COMEST
COMETS
COMFORTED
COMFORTINGS
COMFORTLES
COMING
COMMANDE
COMMANDEMENT
COMMANDEMENTE
COMMANDST
COMMAUNDER
COMMAUNDES
COMMAUNDING
COMME
COMMENC'D
COMMENTS
COMMINGE
COMMINGS IN

COMMISERATION
COMMITS
COMMIT'ST
COMMITTING
COMMIXT
COMMODIOUS
COMMONWEALE
COMM'ST
COMPANIES
COMPANION-BASHAWES
COMPAR'D
COMPARD
COMPARISONS
COMPARST
COMPELD
COMPELST
COMPETITOR
COMPLAIN
COMPLAIN'D
COMPLAINES
COMPLEATE
COMPLET
COMPOSDE
COMPOUND
COMPOUNDED
COMPREHEND
COMPREST
COMPRISDE
COMPRIZ'D
COMPULSION
CONCEALE
CONCEALED
CONCEALES
CONCEIPT
CONCEIPTED
CONCEITED
CONCEITES
CONCEIVED
CONCEPTION
CONCERNE
CONCERNES
CONCERNETH
CONCISE
CONCLUSION
CONCOCTED
CONCORD
CONDEMND
CONDEMNS
CONDUCTED
CONFES
CONFESSETH
CONFESSING
CONFIRM
CONFIRMATION
CONFIRMD
CONFIRMING
CONFOUNDED
CONFOUNDS
CONFRONT
CONFRONTER
CONFUSDE
CONFUSIONS
CONFUTE
CONGE
CONGEALES
CONJEAL'D
CONJEALED
CONJOIN'D
CONJOYNES
CONJUNCTIONS
CONJUR'D
CONNING
CONQUERE
CONQUERERS
CONQUERINGS
CONQUERS
CONQUESTES
CONQUESTS
CONSAITS
CONSECRATAM
CONSEQUENTLY
CONSERVE
CONSERVES
CONSIDERING
CONSINUATE
CONSISSYLOGISMES
CONSPIRACIE
CONSPIRDE
CONSTANTLY
CONSTER
CONSTRAIN'D
CONSTRAINED
CONSTRAINT

-1- (CONT.)

- (CONT.)

LIGENT
MENSIONS
MS
NEROS
NT
O
OMEDES
ONE
ONISIUS
P
PS
PSAS
REFUL
RT
SAPOINTED
SARM'D
SASTER
SCARDED
SCARDES
SCEASSE
SCEND
SCENDETH
SCENT
SCERN'D
SCERND
SCERNES
SCHARGD
SCHEWELD
SCLOSD
SCLOSING
SCOLOURED
SCOMFITED
SCOMFORTED
SCONSOLATE
SCONTENTED
SCONTINUE
SCORDANT
SCOULOUR'D
SCOURSING
SCOURSIVE
SCOV'RD
SDAINDE
SDAINFUL
SDAINFULLY
SDAINING
SDAYNE
SGORDGE
SGUISDE
SGUISED
SGUIZE
ISHONEST
ISHONORD
ISHONOURED
ISINHERITE
SJOIN'D
SJOYNE
ISLOYALTYE
ISMAIES
ISMISSE
ISMIST
ISMOUNT
ISOBEDIENCE
ISOLVE
ISORDERED
ISPARADGEMENT
ISPARAGE
ISPATCH'D
ISPATCHE
ISPATCHED
ISPEARST
ISPENC'D
ISPENSATION
ISPENSIVE
ISPERSE
ISPIGHT
ISPISED
ISPLACING
ISPLAID
ISPLAIDE
ISPLAIE
ISPLAST
ISPLAYED
ISPLAYES
ISPLEASDE
ISPLEASED
ISPLEASES
ISPLEASETH
ISPLEASURES
ISPORTES
ISPOSITION
ISPOSSEST
ISPRED

DISPUTED
DISPUTES
DISPUTING
DISQUIET
DISSERERE
DISSEVER
DISSOLVED
DISSOLVES
DISTAFFE
DISTAIN
DISTAIND
DISTAINED
DISTANCE
DISTANT
DISTEMPER
DISTEMPER'D
DISTILD
DISTILL
DISTILLED
DISTINGUISH
DISTINIE
DISTURBE
DISTURBER
DITCHED
DITCHER
DITTY
DIVELLISH
DIVERSE
DIVIDES
DIVINES
DIVINING
DIVISION
DIXI
DOCKE
DOCTRINE
DOETH
DOG-KEPT
DOG-STARRE
DOLEFULL
DOLEFULLY
DOLON
DOLORIS
DOLOROUS
DOLOUR
DOLOURS
DOLPHIAN
DOMESTICKE
DOMINE
DOMOOPHON
DOMUS
DON'T
DOOING
DOOM'D
DOOME
DOONE
DOOTE
DORICK
DOSEN
DO'T
DOTED
DOTING
DOUBLEST
DOUBTLESLY
DOUBTST
DOWAY
DOWNWARD
DOWNWARDS
DOWNY
DRACOS
DRAG'D
DRAGGED
DRANCUS
DRAWETH
DRAWS
DREAMING
DREARY
DREGGE
DREGGES
DREGS
DRENCHED
DRENCHES
DRERIE
DRESSINGS
DREWE
DRIES
DRIFTES
DRIFTS
DRINKS
DRINKST
DRISSELL
DRIVER
DROOPS
DROOPT

DROPPING-RIPE
DROPT
DROSSE
DROSSIE
DROUGHS
DROUP
DROUSIE
DROWND
DROWNED
DROWSIE
DROWSINES
DROWSY
DRUDGERIE
DRUDGERY
DRUGGES
DRUIDES
DRUMMES
DRYFOOT
DUBBLE
DUETIE
DUGARD
DUKEDOMES
DULCE
DULD
DUMBE
DUMP
DUNCES
DUOBUS
DURE
DURING
DUSTIE
DUTCH
DUTIES
DUTIFULL
DWARFISH
DWELLETH
DWELLINGS
DWELS
DYADEM
DYAMETER
DYET
DYMS
DYV'D
DYVILS
E.
EACUS
EADEMQUE
EAGER
EAGERLIE
EAGERLY
EAGLE
EARDE
EARED
EARE-WROUGHT
EARLS
EARNED
EARNES
EARNESTLIE
EARTH-BORNE
EARTHE
EARTHES
EARTHLIE
EARTH-METTALL'D
EARTHQUAKES
EAS'D
EASD
EASDE
EASLY
EASTERN
EASTWARD
EAST WINDS
EATS
EB
EBAN
EBBES
EBEA
EBENA
EBON
ECCE
ECCHOE
ECLIPSES
ECLIPST
ECUES
EDG'D
EDGED
EDICT
EDICTS
EFFECTE
EFFECTED
EFFUSION
EGERIA
EGEUS
EGGES

EGLES
EGO
EGREGIOUS
EGYPTS
EI'D
EIELESSE
EIE-LIDS
EIGHTEENE
EITHERS
ELBOW
ELD
ELDEST
ELE
ELECTION
ELECTORS
ELECTRA
ELEGIAN
ELEIUS
ELENOR
ELFE
ELIGIE
ELISA
ELIZA
ELL
ELSE-WHERE
ELSE WHERE
ELYSIUMS
EMATHIAN
EMBALM'D
EMBASSADORS
EMBASSADOURS
EMBASSIE
EMBDEN
EMBERS
EMBOST
EMBRACED
EMBRACETH
EMBRACING
EMERALDS
EMERAULDS
EMPAL'D
EMPALE
EMPERESSES
EMPERIES
EMPERIOUS
EMPERORS
EMPIRES
EMPLOYD
EMPLOYED
EMULOUS
ENAMILED
ENAMOUR'D
ENCELADUS
ENCHANTMENTS
ENCHASED
ENCHAST
ENCROCHE
ENDANGER
ENDEMION
ENDEVOUR
ENDOW
ENDOW'D
ENDUR'D
ENFLAMDE
ENFLAM'ST
ENFLICT
ENFOLDING
ENFORC'D
ENFORCING
ENFORMD
ENFORMDE
ENGENDRED
ENGINEERE
ENGRASPED
ENGRAV'D
ENGRAVEN
ENGYRT
ENIMIE
ENIPEUS
ENJOIN'D
ENJOY'D
ENJOYED
ENLARG'D
ENLARGDE
ENLARGEMENT
ENMITY
ENNIUS
ENNOUGH
ENQUIRY
ENRAGED
ENRICH
ENRICH'D
ENRICHT

ENROLDE
ENROWLE
ENSEIGNES
ENSUE
ENTANGLED
ENTENDS
ENTERANCE
ENTERCOURSE
ENTERTAIND
ENTERTAINMENT
ENTHRAL'D
ENTHRALLED
ENTOMBE
ENTOMBES
ENTRALLES
ENTREATED
ENTREATES
ENTREATETH
ENTREATING
ENTRING
ENTRYE
ENVIDE
ENVIEST
ENVIRONING
ENVY'D
EPHESTION
EPIGRAM
EPITAPH
EPITHITE
EPITOMIES
EQUI
EQUINOCTIALL
EQUIVOLENCE
ERECTING
ERE-WHILE
ERICINE
ERINNIS
ERROR
ERROUR
ERST-WHILE
ERYX
ES
ESCAP'T
ESCAPTE
ESPECIALLIE
ESPERIDES
ESPY'D
ESPY'DE
ESSENTIALL
ESTABLISH
ESTEEMDST
ESTEEMED
ESTEEMES
ESTEEMING
ESTEEMS
ESTIMATE
ESTIMATES
ESTIMATION
& (ET)
ETERNISDE
ETERNISH
ETERNITIE
ETERNIZ'D
ETERNIZED
ETRURIAN
EUNUCH
EUNUCHES
EUNUKE
EUROPAS
EUROP'S
EUROPS
EUROTAS
EUXIN
EVADNE
EVASION
EVE
EVENT
EVERIE DAY
EVERLASTINGLIE
EVERY DAY
EVERY ONES
EVERY THING
EVIDENCE
EVILLY
EWE
EXALTED
EXCEDING
EXCEEDES
EXCEEDETH
EXCEEDINGLY
EXCELENT
EXCELLD
EXCELLENCY

-1- (CONT.)

EXCELLS
EXCELS
EXCEPTING
EXCESSIVE
EXCLAIMES
EXCLAMATIONS
EXCLAMES
EXCLUDING
EXCLUD'ST
EXCLUDST
EXCREMENTS
EXCRUCIAT
EXCUSES
EXECUTED
EXECUTES
EXEMPTED
EXHALATION
EXHALATIONE
EXHAL'D
EXHALED
EXHEREDITARE
EXHIBITION
EXHORT
EXHORTATION
EXIGENT
EXIGENTS
EXILDE
EXPECTED
EXPECTING
EXPECTS
EXPECTST
EXPEL'D
EXPELD
EXPENCE
EXPIAT
EXPIATE
EXPIRE
EXPRESLESSE
EXPRESSES
EXQUISITE
EXTASIE
EXTASIES
EXTENDED
EXTERIOR
EXTERNALL
EXTERPATIONE
EXTINGUISH
EXTINGUISHED
EXTINGUISHT
EXTOL
EXTORTING
EXTORTION
EXTRACTS
EXTREAMEST
EXTREAMS
EXTREMITIES
EXUE
EYDE
EYE-BALLES
EYE-BEAMES
EYE-BROWES
EYE BROWES
EYE LIDS
EYELIDS
EYE SIGHT
FA
FABLES
FACIO
FAC'ST
FACST
FACTION
FACTIONS
FACTORS
FACULTIES
FAILDE
FAIN'D
FAINED
FAINING
FAINTED
FAINT-HEARTED
FAINTHEARTED
FAINTNES
FAINTS
FAIR
FAIRE-FAC'D
FAIRIES
FALCE
FALE
FALLEN
FALLIMUR
FALS-HOOD
FALT
FAMASTBO
FAMILIE
FAMISHT
FANE
FANNES
FANTASIE
FARE-WELL
FARE WELL
FAR FET
FARMES
FARTHINGS
FARWEL
FASHIONED
FASHIONS
FASHION-SAKE
FASTE
FASTEN
FASTENED
FASTNING
FATALLY
FATHER-HOOD
FATTE
FAUCON
FAUKNETS
FAULCHIONS
FAUNING
FAVORD
FAVORET
FAVORITE
FAVOUREDLY
FAVOURLES
FAWNES
FAYLE
FAYTHE
FEALTIE
FEAR
FEARDE
FEARD'ST
FEARDST
FEAREFUL
FEAREST
FEARFUL
FEARFULLY
FEAR'ST
FEARST
FEASTING
FEATURE
FECHT
FEEL
FEELD
FEIGN'D
FEIGND
FEIGNEST
FEIGNING
FEIRSE
FELD
FELICITY
FELLOWE
FELON
FEMALS
FEN
FENC'D
FENCE
FERMAMENT
FERNEZES
FERRIMAN
FETCH'D
FETHERBED
FETHERED
FETIALES
FETS
FEWELD
FEWELL
FIELD-PIECES
FIENDFULL
FIERCELY
FIERD
FIER'ST
FIFES
FIFTH
FIGS
FIGULUS
FILCHT
FIL'D
FILIUM
FILLES
FILLS
FILTHE
FILTHINESSE
FINER
FINGARS
FINGRED
FINIS
FINISHED
FINISHT
FIRE-BRAND
FIREBRANDS
FIRIOUS
FIRMELY
FISHER
FIST
FISTS
FITLY
FIXING
FLAGGE
FLAGGES
FLAGITIOUS
FLAME BEARING
FLAMED
FLAMINS
FLANDERS
FLANKE
FLASH
FLATERED
FLATTERED
FLATTERIES
FLATT'RING
FLAUNDERS
FLAWE
FLEDST
FLEECED
FLEERING
FLEEST
FLEETED
FLEETES
FLEGMATIQUE
FLEIGHT
FLEMISH
FLESHLESSE
FLESHLY
FLESHT
FLEXIBLE
FLIECES
FLIENG
FLIEST
FLIETH
FLINGING
FLINT-BRESTED
FLINTIE
FLOATE
FLOCKE
FLONG
FLORAS
FLORISHING
FLOTE
FLOTES
FLOUD-BEATE
FLOUDES
FLOURE
FLOURISHETH
FLOURISHING
FLOUTE
FLOUTS
FLOWED
FLOWNE
FLOWRIE
FLOWRING
FLUCTIBUS
FLUTTERS
FLYEST
FOE-MAN
FOGGY
FOILES
FOLISHE
FOLKE
FOLKES
FOLLIES
FOLLOWER
FOLOW
FOME
FONDLIE
FOODE
FOOLERIES
FOOLERY
FOOLS
FOORDS
FOOTE-MAN
FOOTEMEN
FOOTE-STOOLE
FOOTMANSHIP
FOOTSTEPS
FORBADE
FORBARE
FOR-BEARE
FOR-BID
FORBOD
FORBORNE
FORCD
FORCELESSE
FORCETH
FORCIBLE
FORCIBLY
FORDONE
FOREGOTTEN
FORESEE
FORESEEING
FORESTALL
FORESTALLE
FORFEITING
FORGETFULL
FORGETS
FORGETTING
FORGIVEN
FORGOE
FORHEAD
FORKES
FORMOST
FORNICATION
FORRAGE
FORREINE
FORREN
FORRESTS
FORSLOWD
FORSLOWE
FOR-SWEARE
FORSWORE
FORTIFI'D
FORTITUDE
FORTRESSE
FORTUNA
FORWARDNES
FORWARDS
FOSTER
FOSTER-CHILD
FOUGHTEN
FOULD
FOULDING
FOUNDATION
FOUNT
FOUNTAINE
FOUR
FOURESCORE
FOURTEENE
FOURTH
FOURTHLY
FOWLE
FOWLEST
FOXE
FRAIDE
FRAILTY
FRAMANTO
FRAMED
FRAMING
FRANKEFORD
FRANTICKE
FRATRIS
FRAUDS
FRAUGHTED
FRAYDE
FREATTING
FREDERIK
FREEDOM
FREE-HOLD
FREELAND
FREELIE
FREEST
FRENCH-MAN
FREQUENTED
FREQUENTS
FRESH MENS
FRET
FRIARS
FRIE
FRIENDED
FRIENSHIP
FRIERY
FRIGHTES
FRINDLY
FRISKING
FRIVOLOUS
FROGS
FROLICK
FROLICKS
FROLLICK
FROLLICKE
FROLLICKS
FRONTIRE
FRONTS
FROSEN
FROST
FROTH
FROWARD
FROWN
FROWND
FROWNS
FROWNST
FRUITLES
FRUSTRATES
FRYDE
FUELL
FUGIENS
FUGITIVE
FUGITIVES
FUIT
FULFIL'D
FULLER
FULNESSE
FULSOME
FUNERALLES
FUNERALS
FURIOUSLY
FURROWD
FURTHERER
FURTHERMORE
FYERY
FYLE
GABINE
GABIONS
GAILY
GAINDE
GAINS
GAINSAY
GALATEA
GALEN
GALES
GALIONS
GALL
GALLANTS
GALLE
GALLES
GALLEY
GALLY-SLAVES
GAMBALS
GAMES
GAMESOME
GAMMON
GANADO
GAPES
GARBOILES
GARD
GARDENS
GARDES
GARDEST
GARDING
GARNISHT
GARRISON
GARRISON'D
GASDE
GASE
GASH
GASPT
GASTLIE
GATHERING
GAUDIE
GAULES
GAUNTLETS
GAVESTONS
GAY
GAYNIMEDE
GAZA
GAZERS
GAZES
GAZETH
GEBENNA
GEHENNAM
GEHONS
GELLY
GEMS
GENERAL
GENERALLY
GENERALS
GENNET
GENTILES
GENTLES
GENTRIE
GENTRY
GEOGRAPHERS
GEORGEAN
GEORGIA
GERMAN
GERMANIE

- (CONT.)

SSES
STURE
ULIAN
DASTS
DSTES
ANTLY
BRALTER
DIE
.D
.DED
.DERS
.DS
TY
D
DED
RD'ST
RTING
RTS
EN'T
ER
ERS
E'S
'T
ADNES
ASSES
ASSE-WINDOWES
AUNCETH
AVE
DED
DES
MPS
MPS'D
STERED
STERING
ST'RED
TER'D
MIE
SE
W
WE
ZING
TTON
TTONS
MSE
RY
T
BETS
LETS
BUY
DES
DESSES
HEAD
LINESSE
MOTHER
-WRONGING
TH
NGS OUT
DEN-FLEECED
DEN-HAIR'D
D-RING
E
DE
DES
DESSES
DNES
SE
GE
GIOUS
PEL
PELL
T
E-POOTED
'ST
ST
LD
ERN'D
ERND
ERNOR'S
CHUS
C'T
ECINUS
INE
INE-RICH
MERCIES
MERCY
NDFATHER
NDMOTHER
ND-SIRES
NSIRES
NTED
PPELD
PPLES

GRAS
GRASHOPPERS
GRASPE
GRASPT
GRASSE-GREENE
GRASSIE
GRATIFIED
GRATIS
GRATITUDES
GRATULATE
GRAUNTED
GRAUNTING
GRAUNTS
GRAV'D
GRAVEL'D
GRAVELY
GRAVER
GRAVISSIMUM
GRAZ'D
GRAZING
GREATE
GREATLY
GREE
GREEDIE
GREEDILY
GREEK
GREENE-GRASSE
GREET
GREETING
GREEV'D
GREEVDE
GREEVED
GREEVOUS
GRESSES
GRETIANS
GRIDIRONS
GRIDYRONS
GRIESLY
GRIEV'D
GRIEVDE
GRIFE
GRIND
GRIND-STONE
GRIPES
GRIPT
GRISLIE
GRISLY
GROANING
GROINE
GROUNDS
GROUND-WORKE
GROWEST
GRUNT
GRUNTLAND
GRUNTS
GUALLATIA
GUARDIAN
GUARDST
GUELDER
GUIDER
GUIE
GUIFTS
GUILDED
GUILTLESLY
GUL
GUM
GUNNES
GUNPOWDER
GUNS
GURNEYS
GUSH
GUSHEST
GUSHING
GUSTS
GUTS
GUY
GUYRONS
GUYSE
GYGES
GYRLE
GYRT
GYVES
H'
H.
HA'
HABITATION
HABUISSE
HACKT
HAD-I-WIST
HAEC
HAGGE
HAGS
HAILD

HAIR'D
HAIRE-TYERS
HALCIONS
HAL'D
HALDE
HALED
HALESUS
HALFE A DOSEN
HALFE DEAD
HALFE DOZEN
HALLA
HALLES
HALLOWED
HALLOWING
HALTER
HALTERS
HALTS
HAMMERS
HANDE
HANDFUL
HANDFULL
HANDLING
HANDMAID
HANDMAIDS
HANGD
HANG-DOWNE
HANGED
HANG-MAN
HANNIBAL
HANNIBALL
HANSOM
HANSOME
HAOLE
HAPPENED
HAPPILIE
HARBENGER
HARBORD
HARBORST
HARBOURD
HARBOURS
HARDEN
HARDER
HARDEST
HARD HARTED
HARDIE
HARDINESSE
HARDST
HARDY
HAREBRAIND
HARK
HARKEN
HARKENING
HARLOT
HARM
HARME-WORKES
HARMING
HARMLESSE
HARNEST
HARPES
HARPEY
HARPIE
HARPYE
HARPYR
HARSHLY
HART BLOUD
HARTEN
HARTES
HARTIE
HARTILY
HARTLESSE
HARTY
HASTILY
HA'T
HATCH
HATCHES
HATCHEST
HATÈTH
HAT'ST
HAUGHT
HAUGHTIE
HAUNTS
HAVENS
HAVOCKS
HAZARDED
HEADDIE
HEADING
HEADLESSE
HEALE
HEALTHFULL
HEAPING
HEAPT
HEAR
HEARBES

HEARBS
HEARDES
HEARK
HEARST
HEART BREAKING
HEARTES
HEARTILY
HEART'S
HEATETH
HEATHENS
HEATHNISH
HEAVIE HEADED
HEAVINESSE
HEAVING
HEBES
HEBON
HECAT'S
HE'D
HE'DE
HEEDLESSE
HEE'L
HE'ELE
HEE'LE
HEEREAFTER
HEERETOFORE
HEER'S
HEIFER
HEIFERS
HEIRES
HEL-BORNE
HELDE
HELDST
HE'LE
HE'LL
HELLES
HELL-HOUND
HELMES
HELMETS
HEL'S
HEM
HEMD
HEMLOCKE
HEMLOCKS
HEMUS
HENOLTS
HERALD
HERALDRIE
HERALDS
HERBE
HEREABOUTS
HERESY
HERETICK
HERETICKES
HERETOFORE
HERICINAS
HERMOSO
HEROICKE
HERRALD
HERRALDS
HER-SELF
HES
HESPERIA
HESPERIDES
HESPERUS
HESPERY
HEST
HESUS
HETHERWARDS
HETRURIANS
HEWES
HEWNE
HEY-PASSE
H'HAD
HICK
HICK-UP
HID'ST
HIER
HIGH MINDED
HIGH-WAIES
HILLOCKE
HILLS
HILT
HINDE
HINDES
HINDRED
HIPOLITE
HIPOSTASIS
HIPOSTATES
HIPPODAMEIAS
HIPPOLITUS
HIPPOMENES
HIPSIPILE
HIR'D

HIRER
HIRS
HISSE
HISSES
HISTORIE
HISTORIES
HITS
HIVES
HOARCE
HOARIE
HODIE
HOGGE
HOGS
HOGSHEAD
HOG-STIES
HOIE
HOKE
HOLBARD
HOLDETH
HOLD-FAST
HOLINES
HOLLY
HOLLY-HOKE
HOLME
HOLYNESSE
HOMAG
HOME-BRED
HOMERS
HOMEWARDS
HONEYS
HONIE
HONORED
HONOURABLY
HONOURD
HONOUR'ST
HOODED
HOOD-WINCKT
HOOFES
HOOFFES
HOOKE
HOOKED
HOOKES
HOOKS
HOONG
HOOPE
HOORD
HOORISH
HOOVES
HOP'D
HOPS
HOP'ST
HORND
HORNE
HORRID
HORSE BACKE
HORSE-BREAD
HORSECOURSER
HORSED
HORSE-DOCTOR
HORSE-DRIVER
HORSE-KEEPERS
HORSE-MAN
HORSEMENS
HORSSE
HOSPITALITIE
HOSPITALL
HOSTAGE
HOSTILE
HOSTIS
HOSTISSE
HOSTRY
HOULE
HOUND
HOUSHOULD
HOV'D
HOVER'D
HOVERETH
HOVERING
HOVES
HOWELL
HOW EVER
HOWLES
HOWRES
HOW SO EVER
HOWSOEVER
HOYSED
HOYSING
HUG'D
HUGEST
HUGGE
HUGH
HUGONET
HUM

-1- (CONT.)

HUMBLED
HUMBLEST
HUMBLYE
HUMIDUM
HUMILITY
HUMORS
HUNC
HUNDRED-HAND
HUNGAR
HUNGARIANS
HUNGARIE
HUNTER
HUNTS
HUNTSMEN
HUNTSPEARE
HURDLE
HURL'D
HURLD
HURLY
HURLY BURLY
HURRIED
HURTES
HURTS
HUS
HUS-BAND
HUSBANDES
HUSBAND-MEN
HUSH
HUSH'T
HYACINTHE
HYADES
HYBLAS
HYDE
HYR'D
HYS
IASION
IBI
IBIS
ICARIAN
ICARUS
ICE
ICY
IDAEAN
IDALIAN
IDIOT
IDLY
IDOLATERS
IDOLL
IGNEI
IGNEUM
IGNOBLE
IGNORANCE
IGNORAUNCE
IL
ILIADS
ILIAN
ILIAS
ILION
ILIONS
ILIUM
ILL-BEAUTIOUS
ILL-FAVOUREDLY
ILL GOTTEN
ILLIBERALL
ILLICIANS
ILLIRIANS
ILLITERATE
ILLIT'RAT
ILLUMINATE
ILLUMINATES
ILLUSIONS
ILLUSTRATE
ILLYRIA
ILS
I'M
IMAGINES
IMAGINING
IMAGYN'D
IMBAST
IMBECILITIE
IMBELLISHED
IMBRACEMENT
IMBRACETH
IMBRACINGS
IMBRASEMENTS
IMBRODERED
IMBROTHERIE
IMBROYDRED
IMMENSE
IMMODEST
IMMORTALLIE
IMMORTALLY
IMMURE
IMP
IMPART
IMPARTIALL
IMPARTING
IMPARTS
IMPE
IMPEACH
IMPEACHE
IMPERFETT
IMPLOY
IMPLOY'D
IMPORTANT
IMPORTE
IMPORTUN'D
IMPOS'D
IMPOSD
IMPRECATIONS
IMPRECOR
IMPRESSION
IMPRESSIONS
IMPRIMIS
IMPRINT
IMPRINTED
IMPRISON'D
IMPRISONED
IMPRISONMENT
IMPURE
INAMOURD
INARTIFICIALE
INASPIRING
INCAMPE
INCAMPES
INCENDERE
INCENSED
IN CENSTE
INCERTAINE
INCESSANT
INCH
INCHANTRESSE
INCHASTITY
INCHAUNTING
INCIPIT
INCIRCLING
INCITE
INCITES
INCIVILL
INCLOS'D
INCLOSD
INCLOSED
INCLUDED
INCONSIDERATE
INCONSTANCIE
INCONTINENCE
INCONY
INCORPORAT
INCORPOREAL
INCORPOREALL
INCOUNTRING
INCREASETH
INCREASING
INCREAST
INCROCHING
INCUR'D
INCURRE
INDAMAGED
INDEBTED
IN DEED
INDEEDE
INDEVOR
INDEX
INDIAES
INDIANS
INDIAS
INDIFFERENT
INDIGNITIES
INDIGNITY
INDUE
INDUSTRY
INEXCELLENCE
INFAMIES
INFECTED
INFECTING
INFECTION
INFERIOR
INFERNAL
INFERNI
INFERR'D
INFIDELL
INFIRMITIES
INFLAM'D
INFLICTIONS
INFORCE
INFORCEMENT
INFORMETH
INFORSE
INFORTUNATE
INFRINGE
INFRINGING
INFUSION
INGENDER
INGENDERS
INGLORIOUS
INGOTS
INGRAFT
INGRATITUDE
INHABIT
INHABITANTES
INHABITE
INHABITS
INHERENT
INHERITANCE
INHUMAINE
INJOINE
INJOYNDE
INJURED
INJURES
INJURIE
INJUROUSLY
INLARG'D
INMATE
INMATES
INNE
INNOCENCIE
INNOCENTS
INNOVATION
INNUMERABLE
INQUIR'D
INRAG'D
INRICH'D
INSATIATE
INSCRIPTION
INSOLENT
INSOOTH
INSPIR'D
INSPIRES
INSTALL
IN STEADE
IN STEEDE
INSTINCT
INSTITUTE
INSUE
INSUFFICIENT
INSULTE
INTELIGENTIJ
INTELLECT
INTELLIGENTIA
INTEMPERATE
INTENDEST
INTENDETH
INTERCEPTED
INTERCESSION
INTERCHANGEABLY
INTERDE
INTERDICTED
INTERRDE
INTERRUPT
INTERRUPTED
INTERRUPTING
INTERS
INTESTINE
INTHRALLD
INTHRONIZED
INTICE
INTIMATES
INTIMATEST
INTIRELY
IN TO
INTOLLERABLE
INTOMBDE
INTOO'T
INTRAILES
INTRALLS
INTRAP
INTRAP'D
INTREATES
INTREATETH
INTREATY
INTRENCHED
INTRENCHT
INTRUSIONE
INVASION
INVEGLE
INVEIGLE
INVENOMB'D
INVENOME
INVENTING
INVENTION
INVESTERS
INVESTETH
INVESTION
INVIE
INVIRONED
INVISIBLIE
INVITE
INVOCATE
INVOLVING
INWARDLY
IONIAN
IOVE
IPHEGEN
IPOCRASE
IPSIQUE
IRIS
IRKSOME
IRRATIONALL
IRRELIGEOUS
IRREVOCABLE
IRUS
ISABELLAS
ISARA
ISLAND
ISRAEL
ISSUINGS
ISTAM
ISTE
ISTHMOS
ITALIA
ITALIAM
ITERATING
I'THE
ITHIMOR
IT SELF
ITYS
IWIS
IXIONS
JACENTEM
JACINTS
JACK
JACOBE
JACOBIN
JACOBINES
JACOBINS
JACOBS
JACOBYNS
JAILES
JAILOR
JAIRIM
JANGLING
JANISARS
JANIZARIES
JARRES
JARRING
JASPER
JAVELIN
JAYLOR
JAYNES
JEAST
JEASTING
JEASTS
JEAT
JEBUSITE
JEER'D
JEERES
JEHOVAE
JEHOVAM
JEHOVA'S
JEM
JEROMES
JESTED
JESTETH
JESTS
JESUS
JETS
JETTE
JETTY
JEWELLER
JEWELLS
JEWISH
JEWS
JIG
JOIDE
JOIFUL
JOINDE
JOINES
JOINTE
JOINTLIE
JOLLY
JOUYCE
JOVE-BORNE
JOY'D
JOYE
JOYED
JOYING
JOYNDE
JOYNED
JOYNES
JUBALTER
JUDAEA
JUDAS
JUDGD
JUDGEMENTS
JUDGES
JUDGMENT
JUELLES
JUICE
JUROR
JUSTEST
JUSTIFIED
JUSTINIAN
JUVAT
JUYCE
JYGGING
KAI
KATHERIN
KATHERINA
KEELES
KEEMBE
KEEMBED
KEEND
KEENE
KEENEST
KEENLY
KEEP'ST
KEIES
KEMBED
KENNEL'D
KERNES
KEY-HOLE
KEYS
KICKING
KILDE
KILL'D
KILL DIVELL
KILL'ST
KIN
KINDENES
KINDEST
KINDLIE
KINDLING
KINGE
KING'S
KINNE
KINSMENS
KIRRIAH
KISSED
KNAVELY
KNELS
KNEWST
KNIGHTED
KNIGHTLY
KNITT
KNIVES
KNOB
KNOCHT
KNOCKST
KNOCKT
KNOTS
KNOWEN
KNUCKLES
LABELS
LABENTIS
LABORING
LABYRINTH
LACE
LACEDEMON
LACES
LACHRIMA
LACKES
LAD
LADE
LADIESHIP
LADING
LADYE
LAEDAS
LAELIUS
LAGS
LAIE
LAIED
LAIRE
LAISIE
LAMBE

L- (CONT.)

AME
AMENTABLE
AMENTED
AMENTETH
ANCERES
ANCHING
ANDLORD
ANDLORDE
ANDRESSE
AND-STREAME
ANE
ANGUAGES
ANGUISHMENT
ANTCHIDOL
AOCOON
AODAMEIA
AOMEDON
APHITHES
APLAND
ARDED
ARES
ARGESSE
ARGIS
ARKE
ARUMS
AS
ASH
ASHES
ASHT
ATE-BUILT
ATIAN
ATIN
ATINUS
ATITUDE
ATMUS
ATONAS
AT'RALLY
AUDE
AUGHED
AUGH'ST
AUNCE
AUREATE
AURELL
AVINIA
AVINIAN
AVINIAS
AWFUL
AWFULLY
AW GIVER
AW-GIVING
AWIER
AWNDES
AWYER
AYDE
AYIS
EA
EAD'ST
EAFE
EAGRE
EAP
EARNDE
EARNDST
EARNINGS
EARNST
EASURE
EATHER
EAVDE
EAVELD
ECHEROUS
ECHERY
ECTURE
EDAS
ED'ST
EEFEST
EGACIE
EGACIES
EGATES
EGATS
EGATUR
EGEND
EMANNUS
EMMONS
ENDES
ENGTHENED
ENGTHNED
ENITIE
ENITY
EOPARDS
EP
EPROSIE
EPT
ERNA
ERNA'S
LESBIA
LESS
LETCHERIE
LETHE
LETST
LETT
LETTS
LEUDNESSE
LEVIN
LEVY
LEVYED
LIBAS
LIBELLING
LIBELS
LIBERAL
LIBERALLY
LIBIAES
LIBRARIE
LIBRARY
LICENCIOUS
LICENSE
LICENTIATE
LICENTIATS
LICENTIOUS
LICKT
LICORIS
LIEST
LIEU
LIEUTENANT
LIFE'S
LIFE TIME
LIFTED
LIGHTBORN
LIGHTBORNE
LIGHT-BRAINDE
LIGHTED
LIGHTENS
LIGHTER
LIGHTES
LIGHT FOOTE
LIGHT-HEADED
LIGHT HEADED
LIGHTS
LIGHTSOME
LIGURIANS
LIK
LIKELY
LIKENES
LIKEST
LIKING
LIKST
LILLY
LIMIT
LIMITED
LIMITTED
LIMNASPHALTES
LINCOLNE
LINEAMENTS
LINED
LINGONES
LINGRED
LINING
LINKED
LINKE-KNITT
LINNAGE
LINNEN
LINSTOCKE
LINUS
LION-LIKE
LIQUED
LIQUOR
LISTE
LISTS
LITTORA
LITTORIBUS
LIVDE
LIV'DST
LIVELESSE
LIVELIE
LIVELIER
LIVERY
LOADEN
LOADING
LOADSTARRE
LOATH'D
LOATHING
LOCK'D
LOCUS
LODE
LODGD
LODOVICOES
LODOWICKES
LOGGES
LOGICES
LOGICKES
LOINES
LOLLARDS
LOME
LONGINGS
LOOKED
LOOKETH
LOOK'T
LOOSELY
LOOSENES
LOOSER
LOOSETH
LOOSE-TREST
LOOSING
LOOSNES
LOPUS
LORAYNE
LORDINGS
LORE
LORRAINE
LOS
LOSSES
LOTH'D
LOTHED
LOTHING
LOTS
LOUSY
LOV'DE
LOV'DST
LOVEDST
LOVELIER
LOVELINESSE
LOVE-SICK
LOVE-SNARDE
LOVETH
LOVINGLIE
LOWD
LOWERS
LOWNE
LOWR'D
LOWRE
LOYTER
LOYTERD
LUBBERS
LUBECKE
LUCARS
LUCIFERS
LUCINA
LUCK
LUCK-LESSE
LUCKLESSE
LUCKY
LUCRECIA
LUCRETIUS
LUFT
LULD
LUMPE
LUNA
LUNACY
LUNATICK
LURE
LURKES
LUSTRATION
LUTETIA
LYBIAN
LYCURGUS
LYDIAN
LYED
LYEN
LYEST
LYMNASPHALTIS
LYNE
LYNGER
LYONESSE
MACAREUS
MACEDONIANS
MACHABEES
MACHDA
MADDAME
MADDING
MADNES
MADRIGALLS
MAENAS
MAENUS
MAGICALL
MAGICIAN
MAGIORE
MAGISTRATES
MAGITIANS
MAGNIFICALL
MAGNIFICENCE
MAGOT
MAIDEN-HEAD
MAIME
MAIN
MAINELY
MAINE SAILE
MAINLY
MAIT
MAJESTIES
MAKERS
MAKEST
MAKETH
MAKSTE
MALADIES
MALEA
MALES
MALGRADO
MALIGN'D
MALLADIE
MALLICE
MALMESEY
MANACKLES
MANACLED
MANADGE
MANAGDE
MANDRAKE
MANE
MANER
MANFULLY
MANICO
MANIFESTLY
MANNA
MANNAGING
MANN'D
MANNERS
MANORS
MANTLED
MANTUA
MAPLE
MARCELLUS
MARCHANTS
MARCH-BEERE
MARCHETH
MARE-MAJOR
MARGARET
MARGERY
MARIA
MARIE
MARIUS
MARKET-PLACE
MARKETPLACE
MARKETT
MAROES
MARQUES
MARQUESSE
MARRINERS
MARROWE
MARSHAL
MARTCH'D
MARTLEMASSE
MARTLEMASSE-BEEFE
MARVEL
MASKED
MASTE
MASTER'S
MASTIVES
MASTY
MATCHT
MATED
MATTINS
MATTOCKS
MAUSOLUS
MAXIME
MAXIMUS
MAYDENHEAD
MAYDS
MAY-MORNING
MAY'ST
MAYST
MAYSTERS
MEAD
MEADE
MEALE
MEALES
MEANDERS
MEANINGS
MEANLY
MEASURED
MEASURETH
MEASURING
MEATES
MECA
MECAS
MEDIATE
MEDICINAE
MEDICINE
MEDICUS
MEERELY
MEETER
MEETES
MEGAERA
MEGERAS
MEISURES
MELANCHOLLY
MELANCHOLY
MELEAGERS
MELIAGER
MELLOWED
MELTED
MELTS
MEMORABLE
MEMORY
MEMPHION
MENACETH
MENACING
MENANDER
MEND
MENDS
MEN OF WAR
MEN OF WARRE
MENTEM
MENTIONS
MEPHOSTOPHILE
MEQUE
MERCENARIE
MERCHANT'S
MERCIES
MERCYE
MERE
MEREMAID
MEREMAID-LIKE
MEREMAIDS
MERIDIAN
MERITE
MERITED
MERITORIOUS
MERMAIDS
MERUI
MESOPOTAMIA
MESSIAS
METAMORPHIS'D
METAMORPHOSED
METAPHISICALL
METAPHISICKS
METEM SU COSSIS
METEMSYCOSIS
ME THOUGHT
METROPOLIS
METST
METTALL
METTALL'D
METTEL
MEUM
MEVANIAS
MEXICO
MI
MIDDAY
MID-NIGHT
MIDNIGHT-REVELL
MIDTIME
MID-WATERS
MID WINTER
MIGHTE
MIGHTIER
MIGHTINES
MIHIMET
MILD
MILDER
MILDLIE
MILDNESSE
MILE
MILKE-WHITE
MILKE WHITE
MILKWHITE
MILO
MINISTER
MINKES
MINOR
MINOS
MIRACLES
MIRROUR
MIRTHFULL
MIS-BELEEFE
MISBELEEFE
MIS-BELEEVING
MISCHEEFE
MISCHIEFES

-1- (CONT.)

MISCHIEFS
MISCREANTS
MISDOE
MISERERE
MISERICORDIA
MISERIS
MISERS
MISGIVES
MISGOVERNED
MISHAP
MISHAPEN
MISSING
MISTIE
MISTRES
MISTRESS
MISTRUSTS
MISTS
MISUS'D
MITER
MITHRADATE
MIXE
MO
MOALE
MOANING
MOCKED
MOCKES
MOCKST
MODERATE
MODERATELY
MODESTIE
MODESTLY
MODESTY
MOE
MOISTENED
MOLE
MOLEST
MOLLIFIDE
MONARCHA
MONARKY
MONASTRY
MONED
MONES
MONESTARIES
'MONG
MONGER
MONGST
MONIED
MONKS
MONSTEROUS
MONTHS
MONUMENT
MOODE
MOORISH
MOORNING
MOORS
MOOV'DE
MOOVER
MORA
MORARIS
MORES
MOROCCUS
MORT
MOSCO
MOSSE
MOTES
MOTHER-MURTHERD
MOTHER QUEENE
MOTHER WITS
MOTOR
MOUGHT
MOUNTEST
MOUNTING
MOURNED
MOURNEFULL
MOURNFUL
MOUTH'D
MOVDE
MOVEDST
MOVINGS
MU'D
MUDDY
MUFFLE
MUGEROUNE
MULCIBER
MUNDA
MUNDI
MUNITION
MUNKE
MURDREDST
MURDROUS
MURMURES
MURMURS
MURTHERD
MURTHERERS
MURTHEROUS
MUSCADELL
MUSCADINE
MUSCATTERS
MUSCHATOES
MUSCOVITES
MUS'D
MUSH
MUSHRUMBS
MUSHRUMP
MUSING
MUSITIANS
MUSITION
MUSK
MUSKADINE
MUSK-ROSES
MUSTERS
MUTIN
MUTINIE
MUTTERED
MUTTERING
MUTUALLY
MUZE
MYCENAE
MYGHTY
MYNE
MYNES
MYRACLES
MYRRE
MYRROUR
MYSCHIEFES
MY SELF
MYSTERIE
MYSTERY
MYSTIE
MYSTY
MYTER
NAGGS
NAILE
NAILES
NAK'D
NAME'S
NAMING
NAPKIN
NAR
NASO
NASTY
NATOLIANS
NATOLIAS
NATURALE
NATURALIZED
NATURALLIE
NATURALLY
NAUGHT
NAVELL
NAVIE
NEAERA
NEAREST
NEASTES
NEASTS
NEAT
NECKELACE
NECK-LACE
NECKT
NECK-VERSE
NECROMANCIE
NECROMANTICK
NED
NEEDED
NEEDETH
NEEDFULL
NEEDIE
NEEDLE POYNTS
NEEDY
NEEREST
NEGAMUS
NEGLECT
NEGLECTED
NEGLECTING
NEGLIGENTLY
NEGO
NEGROMANTICK
NEGROMANTIQUE
NEIGBOR
NEIGHBOURS
NEMEAN
NEMES
NEPHUE
NEPOTES
NE'R
NER'E
NERE THE LESSE
NERETHELESSE
NEREUS
NE'RE-YOAKT
NERO
NEROS
NERVIANS
NESTLED
NETWORKE
NEVER-SINGLING
NEW BORNE
NEWCASTELL
NEW COME
NEW FOUND
NEW-FOUND-WORLD
NICE
NIGHT-FLYING
NIGHT-GOWNE
NIGHTLY
NIGHT TIME
NIGHT-WANDRING
NIGRA
NIMBLER
NIMPH-NEAERA
NINUS
NIPT
NISI
NOCERE
NOCTIS
NODS
NOISOME
NOMINE
NONES
NONE SUCH
NON-PLUS
NOOK
NOOKES
NOONE DAY
NOOSE
NORTH-EAST
NORTHERNE
NORTHWARDE
NORTH-WEST
NOS'D
NOSEGAY
NOSTERILS
NOSTRA
NOSTRAS
NOSTRELS
NOSTRIS
NOTED
NOTORIOUS
NOTWITHSTANDING
NOURCERY
NOURISHMENT
NOVELL
NOVELTIE
NOYSOME
NULLA
NUMA
NUMBER'S
NUMDE
NUMEN
NUMM'D
NUMMING
NUNNERIES
NURSERIES
NURST
NUT
NUT-BROWNE
NY
NYE
NYLUS
NYMPH
NYMPHES
OAKEN
OASTRIE
OATHES
OBAYD
OBAYE
OBED
OBEIED
OBEY'D
OBLIA
OBLOQUIE
OBSCURDE
OBSCURITY
OBSERVATIONS
OBSERV'D
OBSERVES
OBTAIN'D
OBTAIND
OCCASION'S
OCCUPATION
OCCUPIE
OCCUPY
OCEANUS
OCTAVIUS
ODORIFEROUS
ODORS
ODOUR
ODS
OENONS
O'ER
OFFENCES
OFFENCIOUS
OFFENSIVE
OFFER'D
OFFERING-BASON
OFFICE
OFFICES
OFFRING
OFSPRING
OFTENTIMES
OFT-TIMES
OINTMENT
OKEN
OLIVE
OLIVES
OMENOUS
OMNIPOTENCE
OMNIPOTENT
ONCAYMAEON
ONEYLE
ON KAI ME ON
ONSET
ONUS
OPALS
OPEND
OPENLIE
OPENS
OPINION
OPORTUNITIE
OPPORTUNITYE
OPPOS'D
OPPOSDE
OPPOSED
OPPOSETH
OPPOSIT
OPPOSITIONS
OPPRESSE
OPPRESSED
OPPRESSION
OPPROBRIOUS
ORATIONS
ORATORIE
ORATORS
ORBES
ORCHARDS
ORDAIN'D
ORDAINING
ORDNANCE
O'RECAST
ORECAST
O'RECOME
OREGONE
O'REHEAD
ORE-LADEN
ORENGES
ORE-SPREAD
ORE-TORTUR'D
OREWHELME
ORGANE
ORGANNONS
ORGANS
ORGON
ORIENTIS
ORIFEX
ORIGINALL
ORION
ORITHYAS
ORIZON
ORIZONS
ORMUS
ORO
ORPHANS
ORPHEUS
ORTYGIUS
OSIRIS
OSSA
OSSA'S
OSTENTS
OSTRY
O'TH
OTH
OTHERWAIES
OTHERWHILE
O'THIS
OUGHTST
OUR SELFE
OUT A DOORES
OUT FACE
OUTFACE
OUTLANDISH
OUT OF DATE
OUTRAGE
OUTRAGEOUS
OUTREACHT
OUT-RUNNE
OUTSHINES
OUTSIDE
OUT-SPREADS
OUT-STANDER
OUTSTRETCHED
OUTWAIES
OUTWEARE
OVERBEARE
OVER BOURD
OVERCLOY
OVER-COME
OVERDARE
OVERDARING
OVER-FLOWING
OVERGREAT
OVERGROWE
OVERJOY
OVERJOYES
OVER LOOKE
OVERMATCH
OVERMATCHING
OVER NIGHT
OVER PAST
OVERPEERD
OVER-PEERES
OVER-REACH
OVER-RUL'D
OVERRUL'D
OVERRUN
OVER-SPREAD
OVERSTRETCHED
OVER-THROW
OVERTHROWES
OVERTHROWNE
OVERTHWART
OVERTHWARTING
OVER-TURN'D
OVERWATCHDE
OVERWAY
OVERWEIGHING
OVERWHELME
OVERWHELMES
OWE
OWES
OWING
OWLES
OWNER
OXFORD
OYSTER-WIFE
PACIENCE
PACIENT
PACIS
PACKE
PACKT
PACOSTIPHOS
PADALIA
PAGANISME
PAGEANT
PAGES
PAIE
PAILES
PAIND
PAINED
PAINEFULL
PAIRE
PAISANT
PAIS'D
PALACE
PALATE
PALESTINA
PALPABLY
PAMPELONIA
PAMPERED
PANG
PANGES
PANGEUS
PANGS
PANGUE
PANS
PANT

- (CONT.)

PESTRY
PPE
R
RA
RADISE
RALELL
RAPETS
RBREAK
RCEL
RCH
RCHING
RDONED
RDONS
RIAN
RLAMENT
RLEE
RLIAMENT
ARRELL
RSON
RTAKER
RTCHT
RTHIAN
RTI
RTI-COLOURED
RTICULAR
RTICULARLY
RTIE
RTNER
RTNERS
RTNERSHIP
RTRIDGES
SS'D
SSEOVER
SSEPORT
SSES
STE
STIMES
STORS
CER
CES
CHETICALL
CHS
CROCLUS
CRONES
CRONESSE
CRONS
JL
NCH
JNCH-WRAPT
JS'D
JSE
JSETH
VILIONS
YE
YDE
YE
YETH
YMENT
YNES
YNTED
ACEFULL
ACOCKES
ARCE
ARCHT
ARDE
BLE
BLE STONE
CCASSE
CCATI
CCATORUM
CATUM
DIGREE
ECE-MEALE
EPE
EPES
EPING
ER'D
ERING
ERLESSE
EVISH
GASUS
LIDES
LIGNIAN
LIGNIES
IUS
TING
USIAN
NALTY
NDANTS
NEUS
NITENCE
NITENT

PENSION
PENSIONS
PENTION
PERAMIDES
PERCEAV'D
PERCEIVD
PERCEIV'ST
PERCHAUNCE
PERCHES
PERDITION
PEREAT
PEREMPTORY
PERFECTER
PERFECTIONS
PERFORMANCE
PERFORMED
PERFOURM'D
PERFOURMING
PERFUM'D
PERGAMA
PERICRANION
PERIPHRASTICON
PERISH'D
PERISHED
PERJURDE
PERLE
PERMANENT
PERMITS
PERNICIOUS
PERNITIOUS
PERPENDICULAR
PERPLEXT
PERRIWIG
PERSEAS
PERSECUTES
PERSIANS
PERSWADING
PERSWASION
PERT
PERUS'D
PERUSETH
PERUSIAN
PESANTES
PESSANT
PESTILENCE
PETY
PEZANT
PHALERIS
PHANE
PHANGS
PHAROS
PHEDRA
PHEMIUS
PHENISSA
PHILEMUS
PHILISTINE
PHILLIPS
PHILOMELE
PHILOSOPHUS
PHISICK
PHISICKE
PHISITIAN
PHOEBE'S
PHOENIX
PHTHIAS
PHYLOSOPHERS
PHYSITIANS
PHYTEUS
PIBBLE
PIBBLE-STONES
PICKELD
PICKELD-HERRING
PICKLE
PICKLED
PICKLE-HERRING
PICTURES
PIECE
PIECE-TORNE
PIERCED
PIERCETH
PIERIAN
PIERIDES
PIERST
PIETIE
PIGGS
PILED
PILGRIMES
PILGRIMS
PILIUS
PILLAG'D
PILLAGE
PILLING
PILLOW

PIN
PIN'D
PINDUS
PINE-BEARING
PINEONS
PINE-TREE
PINION'D
PINNING
PINS
PIPER
PIRATES
PIRENE
PIRHUS
PISTOL
PITCHER
PITCHETH
PITEOUS
PITEOUSLY
PITH
PITHO
PITIEST
PITTILESSE
PITTIOUS
PITTYING
PITYING
PLACER
PLACET
PLACING
PLACKETS
PLAGUING
PLAINER
PLAINING
PLAINLY
PLAINST
PLAINTES
PLANE
PLANET
PLANETING
PLANKS
PLANNETS
PLANTAGENET
PLASTE
PLATFORME
PLATO
PLATOES
PLAUDE
PLAUGDE
PLAUTUS
PLAYDE
PLAYED
PLAYERS
PLAYES
PLAYFELLOW
PLAYNES
PLEACE
PLEADS
PLEASANCE
PLEASANTNES
PLEASED
PLEASENT
PLEAZD
PLEDGES
PLENTEOUS
PLENTIE
PLENTY
PLIGHTED
PLIGHTES
PLINIE
PLODS
PLOTS
PLOTTED
PLOUGHES
PLOUGH-MANS
PLOUGH-SHARES
PLOWED
PLOWES
PLOWING
PLOWMAN
PLUME BEARING
PLUMP
PLUMPE
PLUMS
PLUNG'D
PLUNGETH
PLUS
PLUTO
PLUTOES
PLUTO'S
PLUTOS
PO
POEMS
POESIE
POESIES

POESY
POETRIE
POL
POLANDS
POL-AXES
POLICYE
POLIXENA
POLLAND
POLLICIES
POLLUTED
POLLYCY
POLONIE
POLYPHEME
POLYPRAGMOS
POMPEIS
POMPES
POMPEYS
POMPOUS
PONDER
PONDEROUS
PONIARD
PONTIFICALL
PONTUS
POOR
POPEDOME
POPELINGS
POPLAR
POPLAR-BEARING
POPLER
POPPIE
POPPY
POPULAR
PORCH
PORCUPINES
PORE
PORPINTINE
PORRIDGE
PORRIDGE-POTS
PORTAGUES
PORT-CULLISE
PORTINGALE
PORTION
PORT-MAISTERS
PORTS
PORTUGALL
POSSESSIONE
POSSESSIONS
POSSIBLY
POSSIT
POSTED
POTAGE
POTEST
POTS
POTTAGE
POURED
POWDERED
POWLE
POWRES
POWREST
POX
POYNTS
POYSONOUS
POYSONS
PRACTICE
PRACTISES
PRACTIZE
PRAETOR
PRAID
PRAIDE
PRAIS'D
PRAISD
PRANKES
PRANSING
PRATE
PRATES
PRATTLE
PRAYD
PRAYES
PRAYSING
PREASE
PRECIBUS
PRECINCT
PRECISELY
PRECISIAN
PREDESTINATE
PREFER
PREFERR'D
PREFERRETH
PREHEMINENCE
PREJUDICED
PREMISED
PREORDAINDE
PREPARATION

PREPARED
PRESAGETH
PRESCRIB'D
PRESCRIBED
PRESERVED
PRESERVES
PRESERVETH
PRESUMING
PRESUMPTUOUS
PRETENDED
PRETENDEST
PRETILIE
PRETTIE
PRETY
PREVAYLED
PREVENTETH
PREVENTION
PREYS
PRICKE
PRICKING
PRICKS
PRICKT
PRIE
PRIES
PRIESTHOOD
PRIMROSE
PRIMUM
PRIMUS
PRINCEPS
PRINCESSE PRIE
PRINCIPALITY
PRINCIPLES
PRIORIES
PRISES
PRISONERS
PRITHEE
PRITTY
PRIVATELY
PRIVILIE
PRIZES
PRO
PROANE
PROBLEMES
PROBO
PROCEEDE
PROCEEDED
PROCEEDETH
PROCLAIMDE
PROCLAIME
PROCLAIMED
PROCURETH
PRODEGIES
PRODIGIOUS
PROFANES
PROFESS'D
PROFESSED
PROFESSOR
PROFFERED
PROFICIENT
PROFITABLY
PROFITE
PROGENIE
PROGENITORS
PROGENITOUR
PROGENY
PROGENYE
PROGNE
PROGNES
PROGRES
PROGRESSE
PROHIBITION
PROLOCUTOR
PROLONG
PROLONG'D
PROLONGED
PROLONGING
PROMISD
PRONOUNST
PROOFES
PROOV'D
PROOVED
PROP
PROPHANE
PROPHANELY
PROPHETS
PROPITIAMUS
PROPITII
PROPORTION
PROPORTIONED
PROPOSDE
PROPOUND
PROPPE
PROPPED

- 1- (CONT.)

- (CONT.)

CRAMENT
CRIFIC'D
CRIFIZDE
CRILEGE
DNESSE
FER
FFRONS
FTIE
FTY
IDE
IED
IL'D
ILD
ILDE
ILER
KARS
LII
LLOW
LLY
LMACIS
LSBURIE
LUTATION
LUTES
LUTING
LVETE
MINTES
MNITES
NCINA
NCTA
NCTE
NCTITUDE
NCTOBULORUM
NCTUS
NDIE
NGUINE
NITAS
NTONS
PHIR
PHIRES
PHYRES
PHYRS
PPHO
RELL
RMATA
THAN
TIATE
TIRUS
TISFACTION
TISFY
TURN
TURNIA
TYRES
UC'T
UCY
ULE
UNCE
USINESSE
VADGE
V'DE
VOR
WCE
XON
XONY
YE
YLES
CABBERD
CALDE
CALDES
CALONIANS
CALPES
CAMANDER
CAMBLED
CANDALL
CAR
CAR'D
CARFES
CARR'D
CATHE
CATTER'D
CEPTRED
CHISMATIQUE
CHOLERISME
CHOLERS
CHOOLE
CHOOLE BOY
CHRIGHT
CICILIE
CICILLIAN
CIENCE
CILLA
CITHEAN
CITUATION
SCLAVONIANS
SCOFTES
SCOPE
SCORCH
SCORCHING
SCORES
SCORND
SCORNEFULL
SCORNFULL
SCORN'T
SCORTCH
SCORTCHING
SCOT
SCOURE
SCOUT
SCOUTES
SCOWRE
SCOWTING
SCRAPS
SCRATCHT
SCRIBLED
SCRICH
SCRICH-OWLES
SCRIECHT
SCRIPTURE
SCUSE
SCUTCHION
SCYLLA
SCYTHYAN
S'DAINST
SE'
SEA BANKE
SEABORDERERS
SEABORDERS
SEABORNE
SEA-GULFES
SEAMAN
SEA-MEN
SEAMEN
SEA-NIMPHS
SEARCHT
SEARING
SEASETH
SEASONS
SEAZD
SEAZDE
SEAZED
SECREAT
SECRECY
SECRETARY
SECRETE
SECT
SECTIOUS
SECURITIES
SECURITY
SEDGE
SEDITIONS
SEDUCED
SEDULOUS
SEEDE
SEEM
SEEMELY
SEEM'ST
SEEN
SEETHING
SEIGE
SEILDSENE
SEIZED
SEIZETH
SEL
SELDOM
SELECTED
SELFE-ANGRY
SELFE CONCEIT
SELFE SAME
SELFE-WROUGHT
SELF-SAME
SELIMS
SELINUS
SELLING
SEMBLANCE
SEMBLANCES
SEMINARY
SEMPER
SEMYRAMIS
SENAT
SENATES
SENATOR
SENATORS
SENATS
SENCELES
SEND'ST
SENSE
SENSELESSE
SENUS
SEPARATED
SEPULCHERS
SEQUANA
SEQUEL
SEQUOR
SERAPHINS
SERES
SERGE
SEROUNE
SERVEST
SERVICEABLE
SERVISES
SERVITURES
SERV'ST
SE'T
SETST
SETT
SETTLE
SEVEN-FOLD
SEVEN-FOULD
SEVENTY
SEVER
SEVERALLY
SEVERELIE
SEVERITY
SEW
SEWE
SEXE
SEXIOUS
SEXTON'S
SHADIE
SHADOWDE
SHADOWS
SHADY
SHAG
SHAGGIE
SHAGGY
SHAG-RAG
SHAKED
SHAKETH
SHAKT
SHALTE
SHAMED
SHAMEFASTE
SHAMEFULLY
SHAMES
SHAMING
SHAM'ST
SHARPE-EDG'D
SHARPNES
SHATILLIAN
SHATTERED
SHAVEN
SHAVER
SHAVING
SHEAD
SHEADING
SHEAPHEARD
SHEARES
SHEDDING
SHEE'LL
SHEEP
SHEEPEHERD
SHEEP-LIKE
SHEERE
SHEILD
SHEKINS
SHEKIUS
SHELLES
SHELS
SHELVES
SHEPHERD
SHEPHERDS
SHE'S
SHEW'D
SHEWD
SHEWEN
SHEWER
SHEWERS
SHEWEST
SHIELDES
SHIFTS
SHINDE
SHINED
SHIPBOYES
SHIP-MAN
SHIPPES
SHIPWRACK
SHIRTS
SHIVERING
SHIVERS
SHOARES
SHONE
SHOOTE
SHOOTES
SHORTEN
SHORTNED
SHORTNING
SHOTTEN
SHOUT
SHOUTS
SHOWTS
SHREEKE
SHREWDLY
SHREWISH
SHRIFT
SHRIKES
SHRIL
SHRILD
SHRIN'D
SHRINE
SHRINES
SHROWD
SHROWDE
SHROWDED
SHRUBS
SHUFFLE
SHULD
SHUTT
SIB
SIBILS
SICKLES
SICKLY
SIDONIAN
SIGN'D
SIGNET
SIGNIFY
SIGNORY
SIGNS
SIGNUM
SIGNUMQUE
SILK
SILKEN
SILLOGISMES
SILVA
SILVANUS
SILVERBINGS
SILVERED
SILVERLINGS
SIMBOLISDE
SIMILE
SIMPLEST
SINAY
SINCK
SINDG'D
SINDGE
SINEWS
SINEWY
SINGLING
SINGST
SINISTER
SINK
SINN'D
SINNER
SINNEWES
SINOD
SINONS
SINOWIE
SINOWY
SINS
SINT
SIPT
SIRACUSIAN
SIRENS
SIRES
SIRRE
SIRTES
SITHES
SITTETH
SITT'ST
SITU
SITUATION
SIX
SIXT
SIZE
SKARRE
SKARRES
SKARS
SKATHD
SKIL
SKILD
SKILFUL
SKILFULD
SKILFULL
SKINNE
SKINS
SKIPPE
SKUL
SLAIN
SLANDERED
SLAUGHTERING
SLAVE'S
SLAVONIANS
SLAYES
SLAYEST
SLEEPIE
SLEEP'ST
SLEEPST
SLEEVE
SLEEVES
SLEIGHTLY
SLENDEREST
SLEWE
SLICING
SLICKE
SLID
SLIDEST
SLIE
SLIGHTLY
SLIME
SLINGES
SLIPPE
SLIPPERS
SLIPS
SLOATHFULNESSE
SLOOTHFUL
SLOP
SLOPS
SLOUTHFULL
SLOWLY
SLUGGARD
SLUGGISHNESSE
SLUICE
SLUMBER
SLUMBERING
SLUMBERS
SLUMBRED
SLUTTISH
SLYLIE
SMACK
SMAL
SMARTS
SMEAR'D
SMELLES
SMELS
SMELT
SMIL'D
SMITHES
SMITHS
SMOCKE
SMOKY
SMOLDERING
SMOOTHERING
SMOOTHE TOONGD
SMOOTHLY
SMOOTHNESSE
SMOOTH-WAYES
SMOTHER
SMOTHER'D
SMYLING
SNAKE
SNAP
SNAPPER
SNARDE
SNARE
SNARES
SNATCH
SNATCH'T
'SNAYLES
SNEAKE
SNICLE
SNIPPER
SNIPPER SNAPPER
SNORT
SNOWDE
SNOWES
SNOWE-WHITE
SOAR'D
SOBBES
SOBBING
SOBS
SOCIETIE
SOCIETIES
SOCIOS
SOCRATES
SODDAINE
SODENLY

-1- (CONT.)

SO EVER
SOILE
SOLAMEN
SOLDE
SOLDINO
SOLEMN
SOLEMNELY
SOLICIT
SOLIDE
SOLLEMNE
SOLLEMNLY
SOLLERS
SOLLICIT
SOLLICITE
SOM
SOME-WHAT
SOMMERS
SOMMON
SOMMOND
SOMMONS
SOMTIMES
SOM-WHAT
SOMWHAT
SONN
SON'S
SOON
SOONEST
SOONG
SOOTHDE
SOPHOCLES
SOPPES
SORBONESTS
SORCERESSE
SORER
SORIE
SORROWING
SORTE
SOULD
SOULDIORS
SOULDYER
SOUNDETH
SOUSE
SOUTH-BLAST
SOUTHERN
SOUTHSAYERS
SOUTH-WINDE
SOUTH-WINDS
SOVERAIGNTIE
SOVERAINTIE
SOVERERAIGNE
SOW'D
SOWER
SOWLE
SOWRE
SOWRING
SPAINES
SPANIELS
SPARCKLED
SPARCKLES
SPAR'D
SPARED
SPARETH
SPARGO
SPARTAN
SPEAD
SPEAKEST
SPEAKS
SPEAK'ST
SPEAKST
SPEARLIKE
SPECIFIED
SPECTACLES
SPECULATION
SPEECHE
SPEECHLESSE
SPEEDIE
SPEEDY
SPEEDYE
SPEEK
SPELLES
SPENDING
SPERANZA
SPIALS
SPICED
SPICES
SPIDERS
SPIGHTFULL
SPILDE
SPIN
SPINNE
SPIRITUS
SPITS
SPLENDENT
SPLIT
SPOILDE
SPOILST
SPOKEN
SPOKEST
SPONTE
SPOONE
SPORTE
SPORTFULL
SPOUSALL
SPOYLED
SPOYLING
SPRANG
SPRAULING
SPRAYS
SPRIGHT
SPRINCKLED
SPRINGE
SPRINGING
SPRING-TIDE
SPRINKLE
SPRINKLED
SPRINKLEST
SPUN
SPURCA
SPURNING
SPURNS
SPY'DE
SPYDE
SPYE
SPYES
SQUARE
SQUEASE
SQUINTING
SQUIS'D
STABBE
STAB'D
STABD
STABLISH
STAGE
STAGGERING
STAI'D
STAIE
STAIED
STAINING
STAIST
STAKE
STAKTE
STALKT
STALL
STALLS
STAMMERING
STAMP'D
STAMPE
STAMPS
STANDARDE
STANDARDES
STANDER
STANDERD
STANDERS BY
STANDES
STANDETH
STANDINGE
STARE
STARED
STARK
STAR-LIGHT
STARRE-SPANGLED
STARRY
STAR'ST
STARTING
STARTS
STARV'D
STARVES
STATED
STATELIER
STAYED
STAYNES
STAYRES
STEADE
STEADS
STEALERS
STEALES
STEEL
STEELD
STEELE-BARD
STEEPLE
STEEPT
STEMS
STENCH
STENCHE
STEPDAME
STEP-FATHER
STERD
STERN
STERV'D
STICK
STICKETH
STICKING
STICKS
STIES
STIFELED
STIFELING
STIFFE-NECKT
STIFLED
STIGIAN
STILTS
STINKE
STINT
STIPEND
STIRD
STIRS
STOCKFISH
STOKA
STOMACKES
STONE-PAV'D
STONE STILL
STOODE
STOOD'ST
STOOPING
STOOPS
STOPES
STOR'D
STORM'D
STRADDLING
STRAGLERS
STRAIGHTLY
STRAIGHTS
STRAIND
STRAINE
STRAINED
STRAINETH
STRAKE
STRANGLING
STRATAGEME
STRAWIE
STRAYED
STREAMER
STREAMING
STREAMS
STRECHING
STRENGTHNED
STRENGTHS
STRETCHT
STREWD
STRICT
STRICTLY
STRING
STRIP
STRIPLING
STRIPPE
STRIVDE
STRIVED
STRIV'NE
STROAKE
STRONGE
STROOK
STROW
STROWES
STRUGGLED
STUBBORNESSE
STUBBURN
STUCK
STUDIE
STUDIED
STUDIES
STUDIOUS
STUDS
STUFF'D
STUFFE
STUFFES
STUMPE
STUMPE-FOOTE
STYL
STYLE
SUB
SUBBORND
SUBDEW
SUBDU'D
SUBDUING
SUBMISSIONS
SUBMISSIVELY
SUBORN'D
SUBTIL
SUBTILL
SUBURBE
SUBURBES
SUCCEED
SUCCEEDE
SUCCESFULL
SUCCESFULLY
SUCCESSEFULL
SUCCESSIVE
SUCKEDST
SUCKES
SUCKING
SUDAINLY
SUES
SUFFERINGS
SUFFERS
SUFFER'T
SUFFICENTLY
SUFFICETH
SUFFRANCE
SUFFRED
SUFFREST
SUGAR-ALMONDS
SUITES
SULMO
SULMOES
SULPHUR
SULPHURE
SUMM'D
SUMMOND
SUMMONED
SUMPTUOUS
SUNDRIE
SUNS
SUP
SUPERBUM
SUPERFLUITIES
SUPERIOR
SUPERNATURALLY
SUPERSTICIOUS
SUPERSTITION
SUPPLIE
SUPPLIED
SUPPLYED
SUPPLYING
SUPPORTED
SUPPORTS
SUPPOS'D
SUPPOSEST
SUPPOSITIONS
SUPPRESST
SUPPRISDE
SUPREAME
SURCHARDG'D
SURER
SUREST
SURETIE
SURETY
SURFEIT
SURFEITING
SURFETS
SURFFET
SURGE
SURGES
SURMOUNTS
SURPAST
SURPRISDE
SURPRIZDE
SURRENDERS
SURROUND
SURROUNDED
SURROWNDING
SURVAID
SURVAIENG
SURVAY
SURVEY
SURVIV'D
SUSCEPI
SUSPICIOUS
SUSTAIN'D
SUSTAIND
SUSTAINDE
SWAIES
SWAIEST
SWALLOW'D
SWAMME
SWANS
SWARM'D
SWAYEST
SWEAREST
SWEATE
SWEEPE
SWEEPT
SWEETEN
SWEET-HART
SWEET HART
SWEET HEART
SWEETNESSE
SWELS
SWIFT-FOOTED
SWIMME
SWINE
SWINE-EATING
SWING
SWIZERS
SWOME
SWONG
SWORD-GIRT
SWORN
SYBILLAS
SYCILLIA
SYLLAES
SYLLA'S
SYLLAS
SYLVAN
SYLVANUS
SYLVIAN
SYMOIS
SYRE
SYSIPHUS
SYTHIA
T.
T'ABANDON
TABERNE
TACKLINGS
TACKT
T'ADORNE
T'ADVANCE
TAGES
TAGUS
TAINE
TAINTLESSE
TAL
TALKT
TALLENTS
TAMBURLAINS
TAMBURLANE
TAME
TANAISE
TANTARAS
TANTI
TAPERLIGHTS
T'APPEAZE
TARA
TARA TANTARAS
TARBELS
TARE
TARGET
TARGETIERS
TARGETS
TARPEIAN
TARRIE
TARTAR
TARTARY
TASK
TASKES
TATIUS
TATTERED
TAUNTED
TAUNTES
TAV'RON
TAX'D
TAXES
TE
TEACHING
TEAREST
TEARE-THYRSTY
TEARMED
TEARM'ST
TEARS
TEATE
TEATE-DISTILL
TEDIOUSNESSE
TELLS
TELL-TALES
TELST
TEMAINTE
TEMPE
TEMPER
TEMPESTUOUS
TEMPORALL
TEMPORE
TEMPTATION
TEMPTS
TENANTS
T'ENCOUNTER
TEND

- (CONT.)

NDERLIE
NDREST
NDS
NNE
QUE
'ERECT
RMINE
RMININE
RMS
RMST
RREFIE
RREN
RRENI
RRIFIE
RRIFIED
RRIFY
'ESCAPE
ESELLA
ESTAMENT
ESTER
ESTIFIE
ESTIMONII
ESTIMONIS
EXT
H'ABREVIATED
H'AD
H'ADULTERER
H'ADULTEROUS
H'ADVANTAGES
H'AFFRIGHTED
HAILE
H'AIRS
H'ALMIGHTY
H'AMAZED
HAMIRAS
HANKLESSE
H'ANTARTICKE
H'ANTIPODES
H'APPROCHING
H'ARABIAN
H'ARREST
H'ARRIVALL
H'ARTS
H'ASPIRING
H'ASSAULT
H'ASSIRIANS
'HAVE
H'AVERNI
HEAMES
H'EARLE
H'EAST
HEATER
HEATER'S
HEATERS
HEBANE
H'EDICTS
HEEVISH
HEIRS
HEISE
HEMIS
HEM SELVES
H'ENAMELD
TH'ENAMOURED
HEOLOGIE
HEORIA
HEREFOR
HEREUNTO
HEREWITH ALL
HERIN
HEROF
HERS
HERSITES
HESALIAN
HESEUS
TH'ESPERIDES
HESSALY
TH'ETRURIAN
TH'EVERLASTING
THEY'
THEY'ILL
THEYR
TH'HALL
TH'HEAVENLY
TH'HETRURIANS
TH'HORNES
THICKNED
THIE SELFE
THIESTES
TH'IMMORTALL
TH'IMPARTIALL
TH'INCHAUNTED
TH'INCHAUNTING

TH'INHABITANTES
TH'INHABITANTS
THIRDLY
THIRLING
TH'IRREVOCABLE
THIRSTER
THIRSTIE
THIRSTY
THISTLE
THITHER WARDS
THOGH
THOMBE
THONGS
TH'OPPOSED
THORBONEST
TH'ORIZON
THORNES
THORNS
THORNY
THOROUGHLY
THOROUGHOUT
THOROWE
THOUGHTLES
THOU'ST
THRACE
THRACIA
THRACIANS
THRALDOM
THRALDOME
THRALDOMS
THRALLES
THRALS
THRASIMEN
THRATIAN
THREADS
THREATENEST
THREATINGS
THREE-FARTHINGS
THREE FOLD
THREESCORE
THRESHOLD
THRIV'D
THRIVE
THRIVES
THROAND
THROANES
THROATE
THROES
THROTE
THROTES
THROUGHLY
THROWEN
THROWLY
THROWN
THRUSTES
TH'THEATER'S
THUMBE
THUNDERED
THUNDERER
THUNDERS
TH'UNSTABLE
THUSCAN
THWART
THYRSTY
TIBER
TIBERS
TIBURS
TIE
TIERD
TIGRIS
TILL'D
TILTS
TIMBRELL
TINCTURE
TINDER
TINKERS
TINMOUTH
T'INVEST
TIPHEUS
TIPPET
TIPTOES
TIRANNICALL
TIRANNIE
TIRANNOUS
TIRANNY
TIRANT
TIRIEN
TISIPHON
TITERUS
TITUS
TITYUS
'TMAY
'TMUST

TODOS
TOGITHER
TOLDST
TOLE
TOLLS
TOMB'D
TONE
TO NIGHT
TOOKEN
TOOKEST
TOONGD
TOONGS
TOO'T
TOOTH
TOPAS
TOP-BRANCHES
TOPFLAG
TOPLES
TOPLESSE
TORCH
TORCHES
TORPEDO
TORTURE-HOUSE
TOSS'D
TOSSING
TOSTU
T'OTHER
TOTTER
TOTTER'D
TOTTERED
TOUCH'D
TOUCHE
TOUCHES
TOUCHTE
TOULD
TOULDST
TOUNG
TOURNY
T'OUT BID
TOWARDNES
TOWN
TOWNE-SEALE
TOWNES-MEN
TOW'RED
TOYED
TOYING
TOYINGS
TOYL'D
TOYLD
TRADES
TRADING
TRAGEDIES
TRAGEDY
TRAGICALL
TRAGICKE
TRAILE
TRAIND
TRAINES
TRAINS
TRAINST
TRAITEROUSLY
TRAITOUR
TRALUCENT
TRAMELLS
TRAMPLE
TRANCE
TRANNELS
TRANSCENDS
TRANSFORMD
TRANSFORMDE
TRANSFOURME
TRANSFUSE
TRANSGRESSE
TRANSGRESSION
TRANSGREST
TRANSITORIE
TRANSITORY
TRANSPORTST
TRAP
TRAPT
TRAVAILERS
TRAVEILER
TRAVEILING
TRAVELD
TRAVELLERS
TRAVELS
TRAYTEROUSE
TRAYTORESSE
TREACHERIES
TREADE
TREADES
TREADETH
TREASONS

TRECHERIE
TRECHERY
TRED
TRENCHE
TRENT
TRESPASSE
TRESTE
TRETCHEROUS
TREVIER
TRIBUNALL
TRIBUNE
TRIBUTARY
TRICK
TRICKLES
TRICKLING
TRIER
TRIES
TRIM'D
TRIMST
TRINITY
TRIP
TRIPLEX
TRIPT
TRITONS
TROD
TROIANE
TROIANES
TROOPS
TROPHEES
TROPICKE
TROPICKS
TROT
TROTHLES
TROUBLES
TROUBLETH
TROUBLOUS
TROUNCE
TROWLES
TROYANE
TROYANES
TROYANS
TRUELIE
TRUE-LOVES
TRUETHS
TRULIE
TRULLES
TRULS
TRUMPET
TRUNCK
TRUNKES
TRUSTING
TRUSTLESSE
TRUTHS
TRYALL
TRYED
'TS
TU
TUIS
TULLIE
TUMBLED
TUMERARIS
TUMULT
TUMULTES
TUN
TUNA
TUNE-FULL
TUNYS
TUREN
TURFE
TURFFE
TURKYE
TURMOILES
TURMOYLES
TURN
TURNAMENT
TURRET-BEARING
TURTLE-DOVE
TURTLE DOVE
TUSCANE
TUSCIA
TUSKAN
TUSKED
TUTORS
TWAIN
TWIGGER
TWINCKLE
TWINCKLES
TWINCLES
TWIND
TWINING
TWINKLING
TWINNE-BORNE
TWINNES

TWINNE-STARRES
'TWIXT
TWO LEAVDE
'TWOULD
TYDIDES
TYERS
TYGARS
TYGRES
TYLL
TYLTE
TYPHONS
TYRANNIE
TYRANNISING
TYRANNIZE
TYRANNOUS
TYRANTES
TYRDE
TYRED
TYRO
TYROS
UBI
UGLIE
ULYSSES-LIKE
UMBRAS
UMH
UNA
UNABLE
UNAFFRIGHTED
UNAPT
UNARMED
UNBARD
UNBARRE
UNBARRED
UNBINDE
UNBOUGHT
UNBOWELL
UNBURDEN
UNBURDENED
UNCHOSEN
UNCLEANE
UNCONFIRM'D
UNCONQUERD
UNCONSTANT
UNCONSTRAIN'D
UNCONTROLDE
UNCONTROULD
UNCONTROULDE
UNCONTROWLD
UNCOUTH
UNCUT
UNDAS
UNDECKT
UNDERGOE
UNDER GROUND
UNDERPROP
UNDER-SAILE
UNDERSTANDE
UNDERSTANDING
UNDERSTOODE
UNDERTAK'ST
UNDERTOOKE
UNDETECTED
UNDIQUE
UNDO
UNDOE
UNEQUALD
UNEQUALL
UNEVEN
UNFAIN'D
UNFELD
UNFITTING
UNFOLDE
UNFORTUNATE
UNFOYL'D
UNFRAME
UNFREQUENTED
UNGRATE
UNGUARDED
UNGUILTY
UNHAPPIES
UNHAPPILYE
UNHARNESSE
UNHORSTE
UNIVERSALL
UNJUSTLY
UNKEEMBD
UNKEEMBE
UNKINDENES
UNKINDLY
UNKNOWN
UNLAWFUL
UNLAWFULLY
UNLEARNED

-1- (CONT.)

UNLOCKE
UNLOOKT
UNLOOSDE
UNMERCIFULL
UNMOV'D
UNNATURAL
UNPAID
UNPEOPLING
UNPLEASING
UNPROFITABLY
UN-PROTECTED
UN-PROTESTED
UNPROVIDED
UNPUNISHT
UNQUENCHED
UNQUIET
UNREADINESSE
UNRENOWMED
UNREVENG'D
UNREVENGING
UNREVEREND
UNRIVAL'D
UNSACKT
UNSEEMLY
UNSETLED
UNSHEATH'D
UNSOLD
UNSOYL'D
UNSPEAKEABLE
UNSURPRIZD
UNTAUGHT
UNTIL'D
UNTILD
UNTILL'D
UNTOLD
UNTROD
UNTRUE
UNTUN'D
UNVALLUED
UNWEAPONED
UNWEDDED
UNWORTHIE
UNWORTHYNESSE
UPE
UPHEAV'D
UPLANDISH
UPPE
UPPER
UPREARED
UP-RIGHT
UPRISE
UPRISING
UPROARES
UPROOTED
UPSIDE
UPSIDE DOWNE
UP-STARING
UPSTARTING
UPSTARTS
UP-WAYD
URE
URGD
URGENT
URINE
USAGE
USD
USES
USING
USUALL
USURIE
USURPER
USURPES
USURPEST
USURPS
USURPT
USURY
UT
UTTER
UTTERED
UTTERLY
UTTERMOST
UZZ
VAGABOND
VAGABONDES
VAGRANT
VAIL
VAIL'D
VAILES
VALE
VALEAT
VALES
VALIANTLY
VALLEIES
VALLOURS
VALOIS
VALOREM
VALOUROUS
VALOYES
VALURE
VALURES
VALUROUS
VANES
VANGIONS
VANHOLT'S
VANITIES
VANQUISH
VANTAGE
VAPORS
VARIES
VARLETS
VARNISHT
VARROES
VARUS
VASSAILE
VASSALL
VASTE
VAUNTS
VAUSIS
VEINES
VEIW
VEIW'D
VELVET
VENEMOUS
VENETIAN
VENGER
VENIENS
VENISON
VENOMED
VENOMS
VENT'ROUS
VENTROUS
VERBE
VERGE
VERILY
VERITAS
VERITY
VERLETE
VERMILLION
VERNA
VERONE
VESPASIAN
VESSELL
VESTIGIAS
VESTIGIIS
VESTURES
VEX'D
VEYLE
VEYLES
VEYNES
VICE
VICEROYES
VICIOUS
VICTORIOUSLY
VICTUALLS
VIEWDE
VIEWST
VILLAGES
VILLAIN'S
VILLAINS
VILLANESSE
VILLANOUS
VILLANOUSLY
VINE-PLANTED
VINE-TREES
VINEYARDS
VINTNERS
VIOLATED
VIOLET
VIOLETS
VIPER
VIRGIL
VIRGINE
VIRGINES
VIRGO
VISAG'D
VISAGES
VITTLES
VIZADMIRALL
VOGESUS
VOICE-FEIGNING
VOLGA
VOLLEYES
VOLLUMES
VOLUPTUOUSNESSE
VOMIT
VOMITE
VOS
VOTA
VOUCHSAFES
VOUCHSAFTE
VOUSTRE
VOWDE
VOWEST
VOYCES
VOYD
VOYDE
VOYDED
VULCANS
VULTURE
VUOLGAS
VYOLL
VYRGINS
WADE
WADGE
WAFTED
WAG
WAGES
WAGGONS
WAGON
WAGS
WAIGHTE
WAIGHTIE
WAIGHTS
WAILE
WAILING
WAINES
WAITING MAID
WAITS
WAKING
WAL
WALDE
WALES
WALKETH
WALK'ST
WALLOWED
WANDERING
WAND'RED
WANDRED
WAND'REST
WANES
WANTED
WANTETH
WANTONLY
WANTST
WARBLEST
WARDEN
WARDERS
WARDS
WARE-HOUSES
WARMEST
WARMING
WARMING-PAN
WARMTH
WARNING-PEECE
WARRIAR
WARRIOUR
WARRIOURS
WARRS
WARWICKES
WARWICKS
WARWICKSHIRE
WASHETH
WASHT
WA'ST
WASTFULL
WASTING
WATCHES
WATCH-MAN
WATER FOWLES
WATER-NYMPHS
WAT'RED
WAT'RY
WAVE-MOIST
WAVERS
WAVERST
WAX
WAXED
WAXETH
WAYD
WAYE
WAYLES
WAYWARD
WEAKNETH
WEALTHIER
WEAPON'D
WEAPONLES
WEARIED
WEARING
WEARST
WEARYING
WEATHER
WEATHERBEATEN
WEB
WEBBE
WEDDED
WEDDING
WEDGE
WEDLOCKS
WEEKE
WEEKES
WEENETH
WEEP
WEEP'ST
WEIGH'D
WEIGHD
WE'L
WELCOM
WELCOMES
WELFARE
WEL FAVOURED
WEL KNOWN
WELL KNOWNE
WELLS
WELL-TOSS'D
WELTER
WELTH
WELTHIE
WELTHY
WELTRED
WELTRING
WEN
WEND
WENDS
WENTST
WEPING
WER
WER'T
WERTENBERG
WESTERN
WESTWARD
WHAT SO ERE
WHATSOERE
WHAT SOEVER
WHATT
WHEAT
WHEEL
WHEELS
WHELM'D
WHELPES
WHERBY
WHERE ABOUT
WHEREABOUTS
WHERE BY
WHERE E'RE
WHERE EVER
WHERESOERE
WHERS
WHILEST
WHILOM
WHINE
WHIPPINCRUST
WHIPPING
WHIRL
WHIRL'D
WHIRLE-POOLES
WHIRLE-WIND
WHIRLE WINDE
WHIRLE-WINDS
WHIRLING
WHIRL-WINDES
WHISKING
WHISTLES
WHISTLING
WHITE-CHEEKT
WHITE-MOULD
WHITER
WHITEST
WHO'LE
WHOLESOME
WHOLSOME
WHOOPING
WHORESON
WHYRLWIND
WICKEDNESSE
WIDOWE
WIDOWES
WIELDS
WIER
WIGMORE
WILBE
WIL'D
WILD-BEAS
WILDEFIRE
WILDERNES
WILDERNES
WILES
WILFULL
WILLES
WILL'T
WILY
WINCKT
WINDED
WINDFALL
WIND-GOD
WINDOW'S
WIND-PIPE
WINE-BIBB
WINKE
WINTERING
WIPE
WIPES
WIP'ST
WISDOMES
WISEDOMES
WISHE
WISHEST
WIST
WITCHT
WITES
WITHDREW
WITHER
WITH-HOLD
WITTALL
WITTALLS
WITTED
WITTES
WOES
WOLFE
WOLLEN
WOMAN-HOOD
WOMANS
WOMBE-INCL
WOMBES
WONDERFULL
WONST
WONTED
WOO
WOODDIE
WOODEN
WOOD-GODS
WOOE
WOOER
WOOING
WOOL
WOOLFE
WOOLL
WOONE
WOORD
WOORDES
WOORKE
WOORKING
WOORSE
WOORTHS
WORKING
WORKMANSHI
WORLDES
WORLDLING
WORLDLINGS
WORMEATEN
WORSHIPPED
WORSHIPT
WORSSE
WORTHELY
WORTHIE
WORTHIEST
WORTHLESSE
WORTHS
WORTHYNESS
WOULDE
WRACKFULL
WRACK'S
WRANGLING
WRAPPED
WRASTLING
WRATHFUL
WRATH-KIND
WREAKE
WREAKES
WREATH'D
WREATHE
WREATHED
WRENNE
WRETCHEDNES
WRIGHT

-1- (CONT.)

WRING
WRINGING
WRINGS
WRITING
WRITINGS
WRITTE
WRONGDE
WRONGFULLY
WRONGING
WRONGLY
WRONG'ST
WRONGST
WROTH
WUDST
WUN
WURST
XERXES
Y'
Y'AFFLICT
YCE
YEARELY
YEELDES
YEERE
YEERELY
YELLOWE
YELPING
YMOUNTED
YNOW
YOKED
YOKT
YOKY
YOND
YONGLING
YONG-MENS
YORE
YORKE
YOU'LL
YOW
YRE
YRONS
YSIE
YSPRONG
YVORY
ZAARETH
ZABINAS
ZEASE
ZEPHIR
ZEPHIRE
ZEPHIRES
ZOACUM
ZODIACKE
ZONA
ZONES
'ZONS
ZONS
ZOON'S
ZULA

-2-

ABATE
ABHORS
ABIE
ABJECT
ABODE
ABOUND
ABUS'D
ABUSDE
ACCOMPANY
ACHERON
ACKNOWLEDGE
ACQUAINTED
ACT
ADAM
ADAMANT
ADJOYNING
ADJUNCTS
ADMIR'D
ADMYRED
ADO
ADOPT
ADORN'D
ADULTERER
ADULTEROUS
ADVANTAGES
AEQUE
AESOPE
AETNA
AETOLIA
AFFAIRES
AFFECTED
AFFORD
A FIRE
AFORE
AFRAID
A FRESH
AGES
AGREED
AILES
AIM'D
AIMES
AKER
ALARME
ALARMES
ALBA
ALBANIA
ALIED
ALIGHT
ALL'S
ALLURING
ALMAIN
ALMAINS
ALMONDS
ALONGST
AMAZDE
AMAZE
AMEN
AMENDS
AMOUNT
ANCHISES
A NEW
ANGELO
ANGRED
ANSWER'D
ANTARTIQUE
ANTWERPE
A PACE
APACE
APEECE
APISH
APOSTOLICALL
APPEARES
APPEAS'D
APPEASD
APPETITE
APPLAUSE
APPREHEND
APPROOVES
ARAY
ARAYED
ARBITRAMENT
ARCADIAN
ARCHBISHOP
ARGINS
ARGOS
ARGUE
ARGUMENTUM
ARGUS
ARISTOTLE
ARMENIAN
ARMYE
ARRAS
ARRAY
ARROW
ARTIER
ARTILLERY
ASCENDS
ASHAMED
ASKT
A SLEEPE
ASSAILDE
ASSAY
ASSAYD
ASSES
ASSIRIAN
ASTEROTH
ASTROLOGY
A SUNDER
ATCHIEVE
ATTEMPTES
ATTENDANCE
AUSTER
AUTHORITIE
AVERNUS
AWARE
AWFULL
AXES
AYRIE
BABES
BACKEWARD
BACON
BALD
BALDUCK
BALIOLL
BALKE
BANE
BANIO
BANISHMENT
BANK
BANKET
BARBARIAN
BARE-FOOT
BARELY
BARKING
BARRELS
BARREN
BARRIERS
BARTUS
BASENESSE
BASER
BASHAW
BASHFULL
BASILISKE
BASILISKES
BATH'D
BATHE
BATTERING
BATTERY
BAWDE
BEARDS
BEAUTIFIE
BECKS
BEDFELLOW
BEEFE
BEEST
BEFELL
BEGETS
BEGINNE
BEGIRT
BEGUIL'D
BEHAVE
BEHEST
BELEEFE
BELIEFE
BELIMOTH
BELLIE
BELLOWING
BELLY-CHEERE
BELS
BELT
BENEATH
BEQUEATH'D
BEREAVE
BESEEME
BESEEMING
BESPAKE
BEWARE
BIGGER
BILL
BILLES
BINDES
BITES
BITHYNIA
BLASPHEMY
BLAZE
BLESSE
BLEWE
BLEWISH
BLOCK
BLOODLESSE
BLUNTLY
BOATE
BOMBARDS
BOND
BONFIRES
BOONE
BOOTS
BORN
BORNO
BORROW
BORROWE
BORROWED
BOSCO
BOSOMES
BOTTOME
BOUGHES
BOULDLY
BOULES
BOULTS
BOUNDES
BOUNTEOUS
BOYSTEROUS
BRAIN
BRANCH
BRANDISHT
BRASEN
BRAV'D
BRAVELIE
BRAVER
BRAVES
BREACHES
BREAKS
BREATHES
BREEDES
BRIGGANDINES
BRIGHTLY
BRINISH
BRISEIS
BRITANIE
BROWE
BRUSE
BUCKLED
BUCKLER
BUDS
BUILDE
BUILDED
BULS
BULWARKES
BULWARKS
BUNCH
BURGHERS
BURGONET
BURGONETS
BURN'D
BURND
BURY
BUSH
BUSIE
BUTCHER
BYLL
BYRON
BYTHINIANS
CAEPHALUS
CAIN
CAIRO
CALAMITY
CALAPINE
CALLIMACHUS
CALLYMATH
CAMILLUS
CANAPIE
CANCERS
CANDIE
CANDY
CANKER
CAN NOT
CAP
CAPER
CAPOLIN
CAPRICORNE
CAPTAIN
CAPTIVITY
CARDENALL
CARIED
CARIO
CARKASSE
CAROWSE
CARPETS
CARRIAGE
CARRIES
CARROUSE
CARVED
CASSANDRA
CASTELS
CASTLES
CASTOR
CAT
CATCH
CATES
CATHOLICKS
CATO
CATTE
CAUCASUS
CAUS'D
CAVALIEROS
CAVES
CELEBRATE
CELEBRATED
CENTAURES
CHAFE
CHAFING
CHAIN'D
CHAM
CHAMBERS
CHANC'D
CHARDG'D
CHARG'D
CHARGD
CHARIBDIS
CHARONS
CHARY
CHAUNT
CHEEFE
CHEEKE
CHEEKT
CHEEREFULL
CHERISHT
CHIEFLY
CHILDRENS
CHILL
CHOSEN
CHOYCE
CHRISTS
CHRYSTALL
CHURLE
CHURLISH
CIRCUIT
CITTIE
CLANGE
CLAPT
CLARET
CLAY
CLEMENCIE
CLIFTS
CLIMING
CLIPPE
CLOATH'D
CLOCKE
CLOSET
CLOTHED
CLOUDE
CLOWDY
CLYMENS
CLYMEUS
COATES
COCH
COCITUS
COFFERS
COLCHOS
COMFITES
COMFORTS
COMMANDES
COMMANDING
COMMAUNDED
COMMENDED
COMMENT
COMMINGS
COMPACT
COMPILE
COMPLAIND
COMPLAINT
COMPLEXION
COM'ST
CONCEAL'D
CONCEAV'D
CONCEITS
CONCEIV'D
CONCEIVING
CONCERNING
CONCLUDED
CONDITIONALLY
CONFESSION
CONFEST
CONJOYND
CONQUEREST
CONQUEROURS
CONSIDER
CONSORTS
CONSTABLE
CONSTRAIND
CONSUMATE
CONSUMPTION
CONTEINES
CONTEMPTUOUS
CONTENTS
CONTINUALL
CONTINUALLY
CONTRADICT
CONTRIBUTE
CONVEIE
COOLING
CORALL
CORNERS
CORNETS
CORPS
CORRAGE
CORRALL
CORRUPTED
CORRUPTS
COSENED
COSSIN
COUCH

-2- (CONT.)

COUGHT
COUNTERFEIT
COUNTERFET
COUNTERMANDED
COUNTERMUR'D
COUNT'NANCE
COUNTY
COUNTY-PALLATINE
COUPLE
COVENANT
COVENTRIE
COVERTURE
COWARDISE
COWARDLY
CRAGGIE
CRAMB'D
CRASED
CREATED
CRESTES
CRITICALL
CROSSES
CROWING
CRUE
CRUELLY
CUCKOLDE
CUPS
CURIO
CURLED
CURLES
CURSING
CUTS
CYMERIAN
CYPASSIS
DAGGER
DALIANCE
DALLIANCE
DALLY
DAMASCO
DAMB'D
DAMNATION
DANES
DANGERS
DANGLING
DARKNES
DARTED
DARTING
DATED
DAUNGER
DAUNT
DAUNTED
DEALT
DEARTH
DEATHES
DEBARD
DECEAVES
DECIDE
DECRETALL
DEEDE
DEEM'D
DEFAME
DEFAULT
DEFIE
DEFILE
DEFLOWR'D
DEITIE
DELAIES
DELBOSCO
DELIA
DELICATES
DELIGHTED
DEMOGORGON
DEN
DENYED
DEPENDS
DEPLORE
DEPTH
DESCENDING
DESERTES
DESIR'D
DESIRDE
DESIRED
DESPATCH
DESTITUTE
DETAINETH
DEUCALIONS
DEVIDED
DEVIS'D
DEVORCE
DEVOUTLY
DIENG
DIEST
DIGEST
DINE
DIPT
DIRE
DISCENDED
DISCHEVELD
DISCIPULUS
DISCLOSE
DISCOMFORT
DISCOVER
DISCOVERS
DISCRETION
DISDAINEFULL
DISHONOUR
DISLIKE
DISLODGE
DISMAIDE
DISMEMBER
DISMEMBRED
DISPERST
DISPLEASD
DISPLEASURE
DISPOSDE
DISPOSITIONS
DISPOSSESSE
DISSEMBLED
DISSEVERED
DISSOLUTION
DISSWADE
DISTILLING
DISTRACT
DISTREST
DISTRUST
DISTURBETH
DISWADE
DIVELISH
DIVEL'S
DIVIDE
DOCTORS
DOGGES
DOLPHIN
DOTES
DOUBLED
DOUBTLES
DOWER
DOZEN
DRAG
DRAGON
DRAM
DRANKE
DRAUGHT
DRAVE
DRAWER
DREADFUL
DREADLESSE
DREAMES
DRENCHT
DRIED
DRINKES
DROOPES
DROUPING
DROUPT
DROWNING
DRUDGE
DRUNCKE
DU
DUCKE
DUCKETS
DUETY
DUM
DUMAIN
DUMPES
DURT
DUSKIE
DWEL
DY
EARLDOMES
EARST
EASELY
EASIER
EAZE
ECCHO
ECCHOES
EDGE
EDMUNDS
EFFECTING
EFFECTS
ELEGIA
ELISIUM
ELIZIUM
ELMES
ELOQUENCE
EMBRACES
ENAMELD
ENCHAUNTED
ENCOMPASSE
ENCOMPASSED
ENCREASE
ENDE
ENLARGE
ENOUGHE
ENQUIRE
ENTENT
ENTER'D
ENTERPRIZE
ENTIRE
ENTRAILES
ENTRALS
ENTREAT
ENVIES
ERECT
ERRING
ESCAP'D
ESPECIALLY
ESTATES
ETERNAL
ETERNIZE
ETHIOPIAN
EUROPA
EUXINE
EVENINGS
EVENTS
EVERLIVING
EXAMINE
EXASPERATE
EXCEPTIONS
EXCESSE
EXCHANGE
EXCOMMUNICATE
EXCRUCIATE
EXCUSDE
EXECRABLE
EXEMPT
EXERCISDE
EXHALATIONS
EXILD
EXILED
EXPEL
EXPERT
EXPIRED
EXTEND
EXTREMITIE
EXTREMITY
EYE-LIDS
EYTHER
FABLE
FAC'D
FACT
FACTIOUS
FACTOR
FACTS
FADE
FADING
FAGOTS
FAIND
FAINTHEART
FAINTLY
FAINTNESSE
FAITHLESSE
FALLS
FALSHOOD
FAMES
FAMILIARS
FAMILY
FAMOUSED
FAN
FANTASIES
FANTASTICK
FARTHEST
FASHION
FAUSTER
FAVOURST
FAYRE
FEARED
FEASTS
FEATHER
FEBLE
FEE
FEEDING
FEIGNED
FELOW
FEMALE
FENS
FETCHE
FETCHT
FETTER
FETTERS
FEWE
FICKLE
FIELDE
FIERIE
FIERS
FIFT
FIG
FIGHTST
FIGURES
FIL
FILTH
FINDING
FINELY
FINEST
FINISH
FIR'D
FITTED
FITTETH
FLAG
FLARING
FLATTERER
FLEA
FLEW
FLINGS
FLINTY
FLOCKES
FLORA
FLOWE
FLOWER
FLYES
FOH
FOLD
FOLDED
FOLLOWE
FOLLY
FOMING
FONDLY
FOOD
FOOLISHLY
FOORD
FOOTES
FOOTSTOOLE
FORE
FORE-FATHERS
FOREHEAD
FOREWARNE
FORFEIT
FORG'D
FORGED
FORGIVENES
FORMALL
FORRAIN
FORSAKEN
FORTIFIE
FOULDED
FOULY
FOURME
FOWER
FRAMDE
FRANCISCAN
FRANTICK
FREDERICK
FREE-BORNE
FRENCHMAN
FRENDS
FREQUENT
FRIENDES
FRIENDLES
FRIENDSHIP
FRIGHT
FROLICKE
FROLIKE
FROSTY
FRUITLESSE
FRYER
FRYERS
FUGE
FUMES
FURNACE
FURNISH
FURROWED
FUTURE
GAGE
GAIN'D
GAIND
GALLANT
GALLOP
GALLUS
GANGES
GARDEN
GARISH
GARLAND
GASPE
GASPING
GAT
GATHER'D
GAWDIE
GAZED
GEERE
GEORGE
GETULIA
GHOSTLY
GIFTES
GLADNESSE
GLASSIE
GLIDING
GLISTERS
GLITTERING
GLOSTERS
GLOVE
GLUTTONY
GOARE
GOATE
GOD-A-MERCY
GOINGS
GORDE
GORGEOUS
GORGON
GOTE
GOVERNES
GOWNES
GRACED
GRAND
GRAVEN
GRAVEST
GRAY
GREATNES
GREEFES
GREEKE
GREEKS
GRIEVED
GRIEVOUSLY
GRIN
GROAT
GRONES
GROVELING
GRUDGE
GUARDED
GUESTS
GUIDANCE
GUIDING
GUIFT
GUILDERS
GUILE
GUILTLES
GUIZE
GULFES
GYANTS
HABIT
HAG
HALF
HALING
HANGES
HAPPE
HAPPIER
HAPPINES
HARBORS
HARD-HEARTE
HARD HEARTE
HARDNED
HARLOTS
HARNESSE
HARTED
HA'S
HASTING
HATCHETH
HATRED
HAUNT
HAUTY
HAVOCK
HAV'T
HAYRE
HAYRES
HAZARD
HEAD-STRONG
HEADSTRONG
HEADY
HEARDS
HEATHEN
HEBREWES
HEBREWS
HECTORS
HEDGES
HEDLONG
HEERE'S
HELLESPONT

- (CONT.)

LMET
LPING
LS
M'D
MI
MI-SPHEARE
MPEN
RBES
REBY
REIN
REOF
REWITH
RRING
THERTO
W'D
WED
GHT
LAS
LLY
NDER
RCANIA
THERTO
ARSE
E
G
ISTED
LDING
LE
LES
LLINESSE
MO
NOUR'D
NOURS
PELESSE
RRIBLE
RSEMEN
RSMENS
SPITALS
VERS
WERS
WLING
GIE
GONITES
MOUR
MOURS
NDRETH
RLE
DRA
E
POCRISIE
PPOLITUS
LENESSE
NOMINIOUS
NORANT
AND
LES
BARKT
BRAC'D
BRACEMENTS
ITATE
MEDIATELY
MORTAL
MORTALITIE
PERIAL
PORTUNE
POSE
POSSIBLE
ACHUS
CANTATIONS
CEST
CHANTED
CHAUNTED
CLINE
CONTINENT
ESTIMABLE
EXORABLE
FANCIE
FANT
FINIT
FORC'D
FORST
GENDRED
HABITANTS
LARGE
LY
NOCENCE
QUIRE
RICH
RICHT
SINUATE
SISTERE
STANCE

INSTEAD
IN'T
INTANGLED
INTENDED
INTERCEPTS
INTERDICT
INTOLERABLE
INTOLLORABLE
INTOMBE
INUR'D
INVEIGLING
INVENTIONS
INVIOLABLE
INVIOLATE
IPSE
IREFULL
IRISH
IRKES
IRKESOME
ISABELLA
ISIS
ISLE
ISSUED
ISSUES
ITHAMORE
ITIS
IT'S
IVIE
JACOBUS
JADED
JAERTIS
JAMES
JANISARIES
JANUS
JAQUES
JASONS
JOB
JOINTLY
JOYNING
JOYNT
JULIA
JUSTIFIE
KATHERINE
KEELE
KEEPS
KEMBD
KENNELL
KIL
KILLED
KILS
KINDELY
KINDLE
KINDNES
KINDNESSE
KINDRED
KINSMEN
KIRTLE
KISSING
KITCHIN
KNAVERY
KNAVES
KNEEL'D
KNEELING
KNIGHTES
KNOT
LABOR
LACK
LADIE
LADLE
LAMBES
LAMBETH
LANES
LAPS
LAPT
LARGELY
LASTLY
LATTER
LAUGHT
LAWLES
LAWNES
LAWRELL
LAYES
LAYING
LEACHERY
LEADERS
LEADES
LEANER
LEANING
LEAPING
LEARN
LEARNES
LEARNING
LEATHERNE

LEDA
LENTE
LESSER
LESSONS
LETCHERY
LETTING
LEVIED
LEWDLY
LEWDNESSE
LICE
LIEFTENANT
LIETH
LIFTING
LIGHTEN
LIGHTLY
LIGHTNED
LIKED
LIKT
LIM
LIMNASPHALTIS
LIMPING
LINGERED
LINGRING
LION
LISTEN
LITTER
LIV'DE
LIVELES
LIVERIE
LIVERIES
LIVETH
LOATHE
LOATHED
LODGING
LODOVICO
LODOWICK
LOGICK
LOINS
LOLLORDS
LONDON
LONE
LONG'D
LONGS
LONGSHANKES
LOOKT
LORDSHIPS
LOUD
LOVELIE
LOV'ST
LOWEST
LOWLIE
LOYNES
LUCKE
LUNACIE
LUSTLESSE
LUTHERANES
MACER
MACHEVILL
MADNESSE
MAGITIAN
MAGNANIMITIE
MAGNANIMITY
MAGNIFICENT
MAINTAINES
MAIOR
MAJESTICALL
MAK'ST
MANGLE
MANHOOD
MANIE
MANIFEST
MAN'S
MANSION
MANTLE
MARES
MARK
MARKED
MARTIN
MARTINO
MARTYRED
MARVEILE
MARY
MAS
MASSACRES
MAST
MASTERED
MASTERS
MATCHLESSE
MATRE
MATRON
MAURITANIAN
MAYD
MAYDES

MEADS
MEANEST
MEAN'ST
MEAN TIME
MEASURES
MEEDS
MELANCHOLIE
MELTING
MEMNON
MENACES
MENELAUS
MENT
MERCILESSE
MERMAIDES
MERVAILE
MESSE
MICKLE
MIDAS
MIGHTIEST
MIGHTINESSE
MILDLY
MILLAINE
MINDFULL
MINDING
MINERVAS
MINISTERS
MIRACLE
MIRE
MIS
MISCREANT
MISLED
MISSES
MISTAKE
MISTAKES
MISTES
MOBILE
MOLLIFIE
MOMENT
MONARCHY
MONARCK
MONARK
MONARKES
MONASTERY
MONE
MONETHS
MONKES
MONSTERS
MOOD
MOON
MOOVDE
MORPHEUS
MORS
MOTE
MOTTC
MOUNTAIN
MOURN'D
MOURNFULL
MOUTHS
MOWBERIE
MOY
MUD
MUFFES
MUGEROUN
MURDERING
MURDEROUS
MURMURING
MUSAEUS
MUSICIAN
MUSKET
MUSTRED
MUTINIES
MYCETES
MYRTLE
MYSTERIES
NAKEDNESSE
NAN
NAPE
NAPLES
NATOLIAN
NAUGHTINESSE
NEATLY
NECKS
NEEDLE
NEEDLES
NEERER
NEGROS
NEOPTOLEMUS
NETS
NEWE
NEWS
NIE
NIGGARD
NIOBE

NOBILITY
NOBLEMEN
NOD
NODDING
NOINT
NONCE
NOOKE
NOONE
NORMANDIE
NORTHWARD
NOURISH
NOURISHT
NUBIA
NUTS
O'
OAKES
OBAY
OBDURAT
OBDURATE
OBLATION
OFFENDS
OFFRINGS
OHO
OKES
OLIMPUS
OLYMPUS
OMINOUS
OMNES
ONELIE
OPENLY
OPERATION
OPPOSITE
OPPREST
OPS
ORACLE
ORCHARD
ORCUS
ORDAIND
ORESTES
ORGANON
ORMINIUS
OUGLY
OUTCRYES
OUT-HOUSE
OUTRAGES
OVERFLOW
OVERJOYED
OVERPAST
OVER RULDE
OVER-RULES
OVERSIGHT
OVERTAKE
OVERTHREW
OVID
OVIDS
OYLES
OYSTER
PAC'D
PAGAN
PAGANS
PAGEANTS
PAINT
PALLACES
PALLATINE
PALTRIE
PAN
PANTS
PAPHOS
PARADICE
PARAGON
PARDONA
PARISH
PARKE
PARLED
PARLEY
PARLY
PARMA
PARTAKERS
PARTE
PARTES
PARTHIANS
PARTING
PASH
PASSENGERS
PASTIME
PASTURES
PATRON
PAV'D
PAVED
PAVEMENT
PAVILION
PAYES
PEAN

-2- (CONT.)

PEARCH
PEDANTES
PEDANTS
PEERE
PEERELESSE
PELIGNIS
PELIGNY
PELION
PELOPS
PENNANCE
PENS
PENSIVENES
PENT
PENY
PERCHANCE
PERCIE
PERDICAS
PERFECTION
PERFORCE
PERFUMED
PERILL
PERISHT
PERJURED
PERLES
PERPETUALLY
PERSEUS
PERSEVER
PERSIST
PERSONAGE
PERSWADED
PHARSALIA
PHILIPPI
PHILLIS
PHILOSOPHERS
PHILOSOPHIE
PHILOSOPHY
PHISITIONS
PHLEGETON
PHOEBE
PHOEBES
PHRIGIA
PICKADEVAUNTS
PICKE
PIERCING
PIETY
PIGEONS
PIGMALIONS
PILE
PILLER
PILLERS
PILOT
PINCH
PINING
PIPES
PITCH'D
PITTIED
PLAGE
PLAGU'D
PLAIED
PLANCKE
PLANTS
PLATS
PLEADED
PLEASD
PLEASEST
PLOD
PLUCKE
PLUCKT
PLUMED
POINTES
POLLICIE
POLLUX
POND
PONTE
POOLE
POPISH
PORREDGE
PORTEND
PORTER
PORTIONS
PORTLY
POSEY
POSIES
POSSIBLE
POSTE
POSTS
POTENTATES
POTION
POUND
POUNDS
POUR'D
POURTRAID
POVERTIE
POYNT
PRAY'D
PRAYER
PREACHER
PREACHMENTS
PRECEPTS
PRECISE
PREFERRES
PREJUDICE
PRESAGING
PRESERVING
PRETENCE
PRETENDETH
PREVAIL'D
PREVAILES
PREY
PRIESTES
PRIME
PRINCELIE
PRINCESSE
PRINCIPLE
PRINT
PRISE
PROCUR'D
PRODIGALL
PROFESSE
PROFITS
PROMISETH
PRONOUNCE
PROPHECIED
PROPHESIE
PROPHESIES
PROPITIOUS
PROREX
PROTESTATIONS
PROUDE
PUBLIQUE
PUBLISHED
PUDDLE
PUL
PUNNISHMENT
PURCHAC'D
PURGATORY
PURITANS
PURITIE
PURSUED
PURSUES
PURSUIT
PYRAMIDES
QUAFFING
QUALITIE
QUANTITY
QUARRELS
QUARTER
QUASI
QUAVER
QUEENES
QUELL
QUENCHLES
QUI
QUID
QUIDDITIE
QUIETLY
QUILLES
QUOTH
RACKE
RACKT
RAIGN
RAIN
RAISD
RAMPIERD
RAMPIERS
RANGE
RANNE
RANSACKE
RANSACKT
RANSOM'D
RAREST
RASE
RASHNESSE
RAT
RATE
RATIFIE
RATTE
RATTLE
RAVE
RAVEN
RAVENS
RAVES
RAY
RAYES
RE
REACHT
READINES
REALMES
REAMES
REAPT
RECEIVED
RECLAIM'D
RECLAIMD
RECLAIME
RECONCILD
RECONCILE
RECOVER
RECREANTS
REDEEME
REDOUBLED
REDRESSE
REFERRE
REFLEXING
REFRAINE
REFT
REFUGE
REFUSETH
REFUSING
REGALL
REHEARSE
REINE
REJOICE
RELEAST
RELENTS
RELIEV'D
RELIEVE
REMEDYE
REMEMBRING
REMOOVDE
RENDS
RENE
RENOWM'D
RENOWNED
REPAIR'D
REPAIRDE
REPAY
REPLIDE
REQUESTS
RESEMBLED
RESERV'D
RESISTING
RESISTLESSE
RESPIT
RESPLENDANT
RESTING
RESTLESSE
RESTOR'D
RESTRAIN'D
RESTRAINDE
RETAIN'D
RETAINES
RETURN'D
RETURNED
RETURNES
RETURNING
REVEALE
REVELD
REVELL
REVENGING
REVOLTED
REWARDED
REWARDS
RHESUS
RHINE
RICHE
RIFLE
RIFLING
RIGHTLY
RIGOUR
RINGING
RIPER
RIVELD
ROCK
ROD
ROMANES
ROMULUS
ROOM
ROOT
ROST
ROUND ABOUT
ROUNDER
ROUNDLY
ROUTE
ROWE
ROWING
ROWSE
ROYALLY
RUBICON
RUDDY
RUDIMENTS
RUFFLED
RUMBLING
RUMOR
RUNG
RUNST
RUSHEST
RUSTICALL
RUTHE
RUTHLESSE
SAFETIES
SAGE
SAILING
SAKES
SALT
SALUTED
SALVATION
SALVE
SANCTI
SANDE
SANDELO
SATE
SATURNES
SATYRS
SAUC'D
SAVAGES
SAVED
SAVOUR
SAWEST
SAW'ST
SAY'D
SAYED
'SBLOUD
SCAB
SCAL'D
SCALDING
SCANTED
SCAPT
SCARCELY
SCARRE
SCARRES
SCARSELY
SCATTER
SCENT
SCHISMATIQUES
SCOFFE
SCORNDE
SCORNING
SCORPION
SCORTCHT
SCOURGING
SCRATCH
SCROLE
SCYLLAES
SEALED
SEA-MAN
SEA-NIMPHES
SEARCHING
SEATES
SEAZ'D
SECONDLY
SECRECIE
SECRETARIE
SECRETLIE
SECURELY
SEEDS
SEEKS
SEEK'ST
SEEKST
SEEMED
SEEMING
SEEMS
SELDOME
SEMELE
SEMI
SEMI-CIRCLED
SEMIRAMIS
SENATE-HOUSE
SENE
SENSES
SERA
SETS
SEVENTH
SEVERAL
SEXTUS
SHADOWING
SHAMELESSE
SHARPEST
SHAVE
SHEAP
SHEAP-HEARDS
SHEAPHEARDS
SHEDS
SHEELE
SHEEPE
SHEEPHEARDS
SHEET
SHELFES
SHEWES
SHIELDS
SHIFT
SHIN'D
SHIRT
SHIVER
SHIVERED
SHORTEST
SHOULDE
SHOULD'ST
SHRILL
SHRINKE
SHRINKES
SHRIV'D
SHROWDES
SHRUNKE
SHYNING
SICKNES
SIFT
SIGHS
SIGNIFIE
SIMPLICITY
SINCKE
SINEWES
SINFULL
SINON
SIRIA
SISTER-HOOD
SKIES
SKIRMISH
SKYE
SLAKE
SLAUGHTRED
SLAVERIE
SLAVERIES
SLED
SLEEPS
SLEEPY
SLIDES
SLIPPERY
SLIPPING
SLOW
SLUMBRING
SMELLING
SMILD
SMITE
SMOAKE
SMOOTHE
SNATCHING
SOCIETY
SO ERE
SOLELY
SOLEMNITIE
SOLEMNITY
SOLEMNIZED
SOME ONE
SOME THING
SOPHISTER
SORIANS
SOUL
SOUNDLY
SOUTH-WINDES
SOVERAINTY
SPARKE
SPARKLE
SPARKLES
SPARKLING
SPARROWES
SPATIOUS
SPEACH
SPEAKETH
SPECIALL
SPEEDILY
SPENDST
SPIDE
SPIED
SPILL
SPORTED
SPORTING
SPOTS
SPOTTED
SPOYLD
SPOYLES
SPREADS
SPURNE
STAG
STAGGE

(CONT.)

DE
ND
NDE
NED
E
PES
PT
DERS
'D
KE
RIE
UES
ES-AKER
DE
LTH
FAST
DE
PIE
T
KE
G
GS
ENDIUM
DE

KES
IE
P
PT
T
MY
Y
P
TLY
IGHTES
NGEST
UNGE
W
Y
YD
YING
ETE
TCHETH
TCHING
WE
CKEN
NGS
PES
PT
WE
CKE
GLING
MPETS
BORNE
ENT
G
DIE

EW'D
EWED
UDE
ISSIVE
CRIBING
ILE
LE
T
ERED
ISE
RING
R
EST
E
ERS
ON'D
UM

E
Y
RFICIES
ORT
OSDE
OSING
RESSE
EMACIE
HARGDE
ETTED
AT
ASSE
RIS'D
RIZ'D
RIZD
MES

SWEATING
SWEEPER
SWEETER
SWEETNES
SWELL'D
SWEPT
SWILL
SWIMMING
SWOMME
SWOWNS
SWUM
SYLLA
SYNAGOGUE
SYNOD
TAILE
TAINT
TAKEST
TALK'D
TALKST
TAMBURLAINES
TAM'D
TANDEM
T'APPEASE
TARDIE
TARRIES
TARRY
TAVERNE
TEARING
TEARME
TEMPERED
TEMPTED
TEREUS
TERM'D
TERRIBLE
TERRIBLY
TERRIFIES
TERRITORIES
TERROURS
THANKFULL
THANKFULLY
TH'ANTARTIQUE
TH'ARCADIAN
THAW'D
TH'EARTHS
THEBE
TH'EGYPTIAN
TH'EMPERIALL
THER
THESSALE
THESSALIAN
TH'ETERNALL
THEY'LL
THIEVES
THIGHES
THIGHS
THINKEST
THIRTIE
TH'ONE
TH'OTHER
THOU'
THOU'LT
THRALL
THREATENS
THREATES
THRED
THREEFOLD
THRE-SHOLD
THRESHOLDS
THRIDS
THRISE
THROANE
THRONES
THRONG
THRONGS
THYNE
THY SELF
TIBI
TICE
TIGERS
TILTING
TIMELES
TIMELESSE
TINMOTH
TIRE
TIRES
T'IS
TITHON
TITTLE
TO AND FRO
TOIES
TOILE
TOLDE
TOOK'ST

TOONG
TORMENTING
TORRID
TOSSE
TOWRED
TOYLES
TRAFFIQUE
TRAGICK
TRAIN'D
TRAINDE
TRAMPLING
TRANSPORT
TRASH
TRAVAILES
TREADST
TREBLE
TREMBLED
TREST
TRIBE
TRIBUNES
TRIBUTE-MONY
TRICE
TRICKES
TRICKS
TRIFLE
TRIPS
TRIUMPHE
TRIUMPHETH
TROPICK
TROTH
TROTTING
TROW
TROWE
TRUELY
TRUETH
TRUMPE
TRUNKE
TUCKT
TUN'D
TURKIE
TURNDE
TURTLE
TURTLES
TWANG
TWENTIE
TWILIGHT
'TWILL
TWINNE
TWOO
TYBERS
TYDE
TYDINGS
TYE
TYED
TYGERS
TYRANNISE
TYR'D
TYRE
TYRRHEN
ULISSES
'UM
UN
UNACQUAINTED
UNCERTAINE
UNCLES
UNDERPROPS
UNFAINED
UNHALLOWED
UNHEARD
UNION
UNITE
UNLES
UNLIKE
UNLOCKT
UNMEETE
UNPOINTED
UNREST
UNREVENGD
UNRIGD
UNRULY
UNSPOTTED
UNSTABLE
UNTIMELY
UNTOUCHT
UNWISE
UPHOLD
UPREARD
UPWARDS
URGING
URIBASSA
URNE
US'DE
USURER

VAILING
VAINELY
VAINLY
VALOYSES
VALUE
VANITY
VAPOURS
VAULT
VEILE
VENI
VENOME
VENTURE
VERMILION
VERMINE
VESSELS
VEX
VEXE
VEXT
VICES
VICTOR
VICTUALS
VIDIT
VIENNA
VIEWED
VIGOR
VILAINES
VILLANIES
VIOLATE
VISION
VISTE
VITAL
VITALL
VOID
VOLLEIES
VOUCHSAFT
VOWED
VOWING
VOYAGE
VULGAR
VULTURES
WADED
WAGE
WAGONS
WALKED
WALLED
WAND
WANDER
WANDERS
WANTES
WANTONNESSE
WANTONS
WAR'D
WARES
WARILY
WARLICKE
WARN'D
WARRANTS
WART
WASTED
WATCHING
WATCHWORD
WATERED
WATER SIDE
WAXEN
WEALE
WEANE
WEDGES
WEED
WEEPST
WELBELOVED
WELLCOME
WET
WHAT E'RE
WHENSOEVER
WHEREBY
WHERETO
WHERON
WHER'S
WHISKT
WHISPERED
WHISPERS
WHO EVER
WHOLY
WHORES
WILLINGLIE
WILLS
WILSHIRE
WINCHESTER
WINDOWES
WINDY
WINGD
WISEDOME
WISER

WISEST
WISHES
WISHING
WITCH
WITHDRAW
WITHSTAND
WITHSTOOD
WITTE
WOFUL
WOLD
WONDRED
WONDRING
WONE
WOO'D
WOOED
WOOERS
WOOLVES
WOONTED
WOORDS
WOORTHY
WORE
WORTHILY
WORTHINESSE
WORTHLES
WRACKES
WRECKE
WRONG'D
WROONG
WROTE
YAWNING
YEARLY
YESTERNIGHT
YETT
YF
YFAITH
YOAK'D
YOKE
YOKES
YONGER
YONGEST
YOU'D
YOU'LE
YOUR SELF
YV'RIE
ZANSIBAR
ZEALOUS
ZENITH
ZENOCRATES
ZONE

-3-

ABHORRE
ABRIDGE
ACCUSDE
ACTEON
ACTIONS
ACTS
ADDERS
ADDING
ADDRESSE
ADMIRAL
ADMIRALS
ADMIRE
ADMIRED
ADMIRES
ADMIRING
ADMITTED
ADORE
ADVANC'D
ADVENTURE
ADVERSE
AEOLUS
AFFRICK
AFFRICKE
AGAST
AGEN
AGENT
AGYDAS
A HUNTING
AIE
AJAX
AKE
ALARUM
ALLEGEANCE
AMAZ'D
AMAZED
AMERICA
AMISSE
ANGELL
ANGLE

-3- (CONT.)

3- (CONT.)

NSTRUMENT
NTERCEPT
NTEREST
NTERR'D
NTREATED
NVADE
NVENT
NVIRON'D
ULUS
VORIE
ANUARY
OINTES
OINTS
OYEUX
OYN'D
OYNTS
UNOES
UNOS
EY
EYES
INGDOM
INGDOMS
INSMANS
IS
NELL
NOCKE
NOCKS
NOWS
AMP
ANCH
ANGUISH
ASTING
AUGH'D
AUGHS
AWE
EADEN
EADER
EAPES
EARN'D
EARND
EAV'ST
EICESTER
EUCA
EVELD
EVELL
IBERTIES
IEGE
IGHTENING
IKENESSE
IK'ST
IMBS
IMITS
INGERING
INKE
IVEST
OCK
OCKE
ODEN
OOK'ST
OREINE
OT
OTH
OTHSOME
OVDE
OVELIEST
OWE
OWLY
UKE
UKE-WARME
URKE
UTE
YON
YONS
ADDAM
AIMED
AJOR
ALE
AP
ARSHALL
ARTIAL
EDDLE
EDEAN
EDITERRANEAN
ELODIOUS
EMBERS
ERCHANDIZE
ERIT
ERRIE
ETEOR
IDDLE
ILES
INDED

MINERALS
MINERVA
MINUTE
MIRMIDONS
MIRTH
MISFORTUNE
MOANE
MOCKE
MOCKT
MOLD
MONUMENTS
MOOVED
MOOVING
MOR
MORNINGS
MOUNTAINS
MOUNTSORRELL
MOVES
MOVING
MULES
MULTIPLY
MURDERS
MURMURE
MUSTERED
MYRACLE
NATIVITY
NEECE
NEEDST
NEIGHBOUR
NEMESIS
NEWLY
NIMBLE
NIMPHS
NOBIS
NOBLY
NO BODY
NOLITE
NON
NOSE
NOVICE
NOWE
NO WHERE
NUNC
NUNNES
NUPTIALL
OAKE
OBEDIENT
OCCIDERE
ODDES
ODIOUS
OFFERING
OFFERS
OFFRED
OFF-SPRING
ON'S
OPENED
OPENING
OPPOSE
ORATOR
ORIENTALL
ORIONS
ORLEANCE
ORTIGIUS
OTHES
OTTOMAN
OUT-RUN
OUTWARD
PACE
PACES
PACIFIE
PADUA
PAINFULL
PANTING
PAPERS
PARCELL
PARLEMENT
PARLIE
PARTAKE
PARTHIA
PATE
PATH
PAYD
PEALE
PEECE
PEECEMEALE
PELFE
PENANCE
PENBROOKES
PENCE
PENSIVE
PERFORMD
PERFUME
PERJUR'D

PERJURIES
PERJURY
PERSIAN
PERSWASIONS
PERUSE
PETTIE
PHAETON
PHILIP
PHRIGIAN
PIECES
PIERC'D
PILIA-BORZA
PIONERS
PIRATS
PIT
PLAIES
PLAINELY
PLATE
PLEADE
PLIANT
PLOW
PLUME
POINTS
POISONED
POSSEST
PREFERD
PRELATES
PRESAGE
PRESAGES
PRESENTLIE
PREVENTED
PRIVY CHAMBER
PROCEED
PROMETHEUS
PROMISED
PRONE
PROPHET
PROSTRATE
PROUDLY
PROV'D
PROVERB
PROVISION
PROVOKE
PROWESSE
PUISSANT
PUREST
PURG'D
PURSU'D
PYN'D
QUAIL'D
QUICKE
QUOD
RAILE
RAISDE
RAMS
RAPT
RASH
RASHLY
RATLING
RAVISHT
RAWE
REARE
REBELL
RECOVERY
REFUSDE
REGARDING
REGISTER
RELENTING
RELIEFE
REMEDY
REMOOV'D
REMOOVED
REMOVE
RENDER
RENTS
REPEALE
REPENTANCE
REPORTS
REPULSE
REQUIRES
REQUITED
RESIDENCE
RESOUND
RESTED
RETES
REVENGD
REVIVES
RICHLY
ROMAN
ROMANE
RUINES
RUNNAGATES
RUSTIE

RUSTY
RUTHFULL
SABA
SABINE
SABINES
SACRIFICING
SADLY
SAFELY
SAFETY
SAIEST
SAMARCANDA
SAT
SAUCE
SCARBOROUGH
SCARD
SCEPTERS
SCHOOLES
SCORN'D
SCOTLAND
SCROWLE
SCUM
SEATS
SECURITIE
SEIZE
SENDING
SEPULCHER
SERPENT
SERVES
SERVITORS
SESSIONS
SEVERE
SEX
SHAFT
SHAKEN
SHARP
SHEES
SHEWE
SHIPPING
SHIPT
SHOOTS
SHORNE
SHORTER
SHOWE
SHROUD
SIC
SICHEUS
SICILY
SICK
SICKNESSE
SIGH
SIGH'D
SIGHING
SILLIE
SIMPLICITIE
SINOWES
SKORNE
SLACK
SLACKT
SLAVERY
SLEEP
SLIGHT
SLOTHFULL
SLOWE
SMELL
SMILDE
SNAKIE
SNOWE
SOFTLY
SOLDIERS
SOLEMNLY
SOLITARIE
SOLITARY
SONGS
SORROWE
SOUNDS
SOVERAIGN
SOYLE
SPARING
SPARKES
SPECIALLY
SPECTACLE
SPEEDE
SPENDS
SPHERE
SPICE
SPILT
SPIRITES
SPY
SPYING
STAIES
STAIEST
STAIN'D
STANDARD BEARER

STANDINGS
STARING
START
STARVE
STATES
STATUTES
STAVES ACRE
STAYING
STEALING
STEELED
STIRRE
STOMACK
STONY
STOPS
STORMES
STORMIE
STOUTE
STRAGLING
STRAITE
STREAM
STREAMERS
STRETCH
STRIKING
STRIV'D
STRONGER
STRONGLY
STROOKEN
STUDENTS
STUFT
STUMBLING
STYGIAN
SUBMIT
SUCCEEDING
SUCCESSION
SUCCOUR
SUCKE
SUDDAINE
SUFFERANCE
SUFFICIENTLY
SUMMERS
SUMMES
SUMMON
SUN-BRIGHT
SUNCKE
SUN-SHINE
SUPERSTITIOUS
SURCEASE
SURELY
SURVIVE
SUSPITIOUS
SUSTAINES
SUSTENANCE
SUTE
SWAINE
SWAINES
SWALLOWED
SWANNE
SWEARES
SWEETELY
SWEETES
TAINTED
TALEUS
TALKES
TANTALUS
TASKE
TAST
TEARM'D
TEARMS
TELS
TEMPEST
TEMPT
TERROR
TH'ART
THEBAN
THEILE
THEREIN
THEREWITH
THER'S
THETHER
THIE
TH'IMPERIALL
TH'INFERNALL
THIRSTING
THOUGHE
THROUGHOUT
THROWE
THRUSTS
THUNDERCLAPS
TICKLE
TIDINGS
TIED
TIMERE
T'INCOUNTER

-3- (CONT.)

TIR'D
TOOK
TOOLES
TOPPE
TORTUR'D
TORTURES
TOST
TOYLING
TRANSFORME
TRANSFORMED
TRAVAILE
TRAVELLER
TRAYTORS
TRENCHER
TRIALL
TRIDE
TRIED
TRIFLES
TRIPOLY
TRITON
TRODE
TROUBLESOME
TROUPE
TROYES
TRUEST
TRULY
TRUSTY
TUMBLE
TUNE
TUNES
TURKESSE
TURNUS
TWELVE
TWIL
TWISE
TYRANNY
TYTLES
UNAWARES
UNCKLES
UNCONQUERED
UNDAUNTED
UNDERMINE
UNFOULD
UNITED
UNLAWFULL
UNPEOPLED
UNPLEASANT
UNRELENTING
UNRESISTED
UNTIL
UPRIGHT
US'D
USURPING
VALLIES
VANHOLT
VANISHT
VASSALS
VAULTS
VENOMOUS
VICTUALL
VIEWE
VIEWES
VILAINE
VILD
VIRGINITIE
VISAGE
VOICES
VOIDE
VOUCHSAFE
VOWD
WALKS
WALLS
WARD
WARNINGS
WARRING
WATCHT
WAVE
WAVERING
WAXT
WED
WEEDS
WEEL
WEE'LE
WEEPING
WELKIN
WEY
WHERES
WHET
WHIL'ST
WHIP
WHIPS
WHIPT
WHISPER
WHIST
WHO ERE
WILLING
WINDIE
WINES
WINGES
WITLESSE
WITNES
WITNESSES
WITTENBERGE
WITTY
WONDERS
WOONDER
WOONT
WORK
WORKS
WORSHIPS
WREATH
WRINCKLES
WUNNE
YOAKT
YON
YOONG
ZANTHUS
ZEALE

-4-

ABANDON
ABBASSE
ABUSES
ACCESSE
ACCORDING
ACCOUNT
ACCURST
ACRE
ACTION
ADONIS
ADORNE
ADVAUNST
ADVISDE
ADVISE
AFFLICTS
AGIDAS
ALCARON
AMASIA
AMBER
AMBUSH
ANCHORS
ANNOY
ANTIENT
APOLLOS
APPLAUD
ARABIANS
ARCH
ARISE
ARRIVDE
ARTE
ARUNS
ASHORE
ASPHALTIS
ASPIRE
ASSIST
ASUNDER
AURORA
BAGS
BALDOCKE
BALL
BANEFULL
BANKS
BASSOE
BAY
BEATING
BEAUTIOUS
BEHOLDING
BEHOOFE
BELONGS
BESTOWE
BESTOWED
BETRAIED
BETROTHED
BEWAILE
BEWRAIES
BEWRAY
BITE
BLAST
BLAZING
BLEEDING
BLEW
BLINDE
BLUSHING
BLUSHT
BOLDLY
BONDAGE
BONUM
BOULD
BRAINE
BREAK
BRIGHTER
BRINGES
BRISTOW
BROAD
BROAKE
BROW
BROWNE
BRUNT
BURIALL
BUSINESSE
CAL
CALL'D
CALS
CAPTIVES
CARRIE
CAUSES
CEDAR
CERTAINE
CHACE
CHAMBERLAINE
CHANNELS
CHARACTERS
CHARDGE
CHARLES
CHARMED
CHUSE
CIRCLED
CIRCLES
CITADELL
CLEERE
CLIME
CLOAKE
COATE
COLDE
COLE
COLE-BLACKE
COLOURED
COMELY
COMMISSION
COMPASSION
COMPLEAT
COMPLICES
CONCAVE
CONDEMN'D
CONFINES
CONFIRM'D
CONFUSION
CONQUEROR
CONQUERORS
CONSTANTINOPLE
CONTAIN'D
CONTAINES
CONTRARY
CONTRIBUTORIE
CONTROULE
CONVERT
CORONATION
COSTLY
COUNTRIMEN
COURSER
COVER
CREATURE
CREEPING
CREPT
CRETE
CRIDE
CRIES
CROWND
CRUELTIE
CURSES
CURTLE
CURTLE-AXE
CYPRUS
DAMES
DANAE
DARKNESSE
DARKSOME
DASHT
DAYLY
DE
DEARER
DECEIT
DEEDES
DEEPEST
DELUDED
DENIES
DESERT
DESTINIE
DESTROY
DEVINE
DIGNITIE
DIGNITIES
DIGNITY
DING
DIRGE
DISCHARG'D
DISMAY
DISPLEAS'D
DISPUTE
DISSEMBLING
DISSOLV'D
DISSOLVE
DIVIDED
DOMINION
DOMINIONS
DOWNFALL
DRAGGE
DRAWE
DROOPING
DRUGS
DRUNKEN
DRYE
EARLY
EARNESTLY
EASIE
EASILIE
EASILY
EGYPTIA
EGYPTIANS
EMPEROR
EMPERY
ENAMOURED
ENFORCE
ENSIGNE
ENTRY
EUPHRATES
EVER-BURNING
EVERLASTING
EVILL
EXCEEDING
EXECUTE
EXPELL
EXPERIENCE
FALNE
FATHER'S
FEATHERS
FEELES
FEENDS
FIDLER
FIFTY
FINGER
FIRES
FIXED
FLAT
FLOW
FLUNG
FOLLOWED
FOLLOWING
FOOLES
FOOTMEN
FOOT-STOOLE
FORLORNE
FORREST
FOR'T
FORTH-WITH
FORTUNATE
FOULES
FOWLES
FRAILE
FREED
FRONTIER
FRUSTRATE
FULLY
FUSTIAN
GALE
GAPE
GAPING
GATHERED
GILT
GIRDLE
GLAUNCE
GLOBE
GLORIES
GREEVES
GRONING
GROOME
GUESSE
GUIDES
HALL
HANGMAN
HAPPEN
HARBOR
HARKE
HARMELESSE
HARMONY
HAT
HATEFUL
HATES
HATING
HAVEN
HEAPS
HEAV'N
HECUBA
HEDGE
HELEN
HELME
HELPES
HERESIE
HIE
HIMSELF
HIRE
HOARY
HOAST
HOLLA
HOMAGE
HORROR
HOSTES
HOUSHOLD
HOWE
HOWLE
HUGONETS
HUNGER
ILES
ILIA
IMBRAST
IMMEDIATLY
IMPERIOUS
IMPORTS
INCLINDE
INCLOSE
INCONSTANT
INDE
INFAMOUS
INFECT
INFIDELS
INHERIT
INSTRUMENTS
INTENDS
INTRENCH
INVENTED
INVESTED
INVINCIBLE
IRE
IRONS
ISLES
ITALIAN
I'TH
JASON
JEALOUSIE
JESTING
JOIES
JOIN'D
JOYFULL
JOYNTLY
JUDGEMENT
JULIUS
JUSTLY
KEEPERS
KINGES
KINGLIE
KNOWN
LAIES
LAINE
LAKES
LAMENTS
LAPPE
LASTS
LAUGHING
LAWLESSE
LAWNE
LAYED
LEADING
LEADS
LEAGUES
LEAVY
LEGATE
LEWD
LIBERALL
LIMBES
LINGER
LOAD

CONT.)

NE
S
Y
ULL
N
ED
E
S
T
LL
S
CRED
E
WHILE
T
ATE
IS
T ARMES
ANT
RIE
S
MENT
E
ED
UST
URE
CHIE
E
US
FIED
ER
IER
AINE
TUDES
R'D
R
W
N
ALL
S
SITIE
SITY
S
R
ED
S
ENCE
T
TS
ION
ERS
RTUNITY
RY
R
TAGE
AT
ED
CALL
ETH
ON
ES
ECT
OURME
URD
NTS
R
IUS

PITCHY
PITIED
PITIFULL
PLAGUES
PLAINTS
PLANT
PLANTED
PLAYD
PLAYING
PLESHE
PLOUGH
PLUCK
POLICY
POMP
POPES
POTENTATE
POWERFULL
PREACH
PRETHE
PREVENT
PRIVIE
PRIVILEDGE
PROMIS'D
PROMISES
PROMIST
PROTECT
PROUDEST
PROWD
PUISANT
PULS
PUNISHT
QUAM
QUEENS
QUILL
RADGE
RAIGN'D
RAINE
RAINES
RAPINE
READIE
READINESSE
REDUCE
REGARD
REINES
RELEASE
REMEMBRANCE
REMORSE
RENEW
REPEALD
REPOSE
RESEMBLE
RESOLVED
RESTETH
RESTLES
RETREAT
REVEAL'D
RHENE
RHODES
RIDING
RIP
RIVALL
RIVERS
RODE
ROGUE
ROSIE
ROUT
ROY
SABLE
SAILERS
SAINTS
SAVAGE
SAVING
SCATTERED
SCHOLLERS
SCORNES
SCRIPTURES
SEALES
SEAVEN
SEEKING
SENTENCE
SERGESTUS
SHADE
SHADES
SHADOWES
SHAFTS
SHALLOW
SHEE'S
SHEWED
SHIPWRACKE
SHOWER
SHUNNE
SI
SILKES

SINGING
SINGLE
SIXE
SKIPPING
SLACKE
SLICE
SLIPT
SNOW
SOARE
SOEVER
SOLDIER
SOLDIOURS
SOLEMNIZE
SOME-TIMES
SOOTH
SOUNDING
SOVERAIGNES
SPED
SPIE
SPIT
SPORTS
SPOTLESSE
SPOYLE
SPREADING
STAID
STARTED
STATUE
STATURE
STEEPE
STEP
STIFFE
STILE
STOMACKE
STRANGELY
STRANGLED
STRATAGEM
STRATAGEMS
STRENGTHEN
STRIFE
STRIVES
STROKES
STROWED
SUBDUED
SUBSTANTIALL
SUIT
SUPPLIES
SURVIVES
SUSPITION
SWANNES
SWEETLY
SWOLNE
SWORDES
SYRTES
T
TALK
TELLING
TENEDOS
TENTES
TERME
TH'EARTH
THEBES
THEEFE
THEREAT
THEREBY
THERETO
THICKEST
THIGH
THIN
THINKST
THINNE
THROATS
THROWES
THROWNE
THUNDERBOLTS
TICING
TILT
TIRED
TITAN
TITLE
TITLES
TOYES
TRACE
TRAITEROUS
TRAVEILE
TRAYTOR
TREACHERIE
TREACHERY
TRECHEROUS
TRICKE
TRIUMPHES
TRIUMPHING
TRIUMPHT
TROOPE

TRUSTIE
TURKEY
TURNING
T'WAS
'TWERE
TWICE
TWILL
ULYSSES
UNBORNE
UNFOLD
UNHAPPY
UNWILLING
UPPON
URG'D
USED
VAILD
VALOYS
VALUED
VANQUISHT
VENG'D
VERTUOUS
VESTALL
VICEROY
VICTORIOUS
VIEWD
VINTNER
VOW'D
VULCAN
WAGGE
WAINE
WAITES
WATCHFULL
WEARES
WEEDES
WEEPES
WEIGH
WHERESOEVER
WHERFORE
WHERIN
WHILSTE
WHIRLE
WISELY
WISHED
WOODDEN
WOONDROUS
WOORTH
WOUNDING
WRETCHES
WRITES
WRONGD
WRONGES
YEELDED
YELLOW
YESTERDAY
YOAKE
YOUTHS
ZABINA

-5-

ABIDE
ABJURE
ABOORD
ACCEPT
ADVAUNCE
AFFECT
AFFECTION
AFFLICTIONS
AFFOORD
AFFOORDS
AGAMEMNON
AGOE
ALSO
AMIDST
ANGELS
ANJOY
ANSWERED
APE
APOLLO
APPEASE
APPLES
APPOINT
ARGOSIE
ARMOR
ARROWES
ASHES
ATTAINE
ATTEMPTS
AUTHORITY
AVAILE
BACKWARD

BANKE
BARKE
BARRABAS
BARRE
BASE BORNE
BATTAILES
BEARD
BEARER
BEDS
BELOVED
BESIEG'D
BILS
BISHOP
BLASTED
BLIND
BLOODS
BLOUDIE
BLOWNE
BORE
BRAZEN
BREATHLESSE
BREED
BUILDINGS
BYTHINIA
CAL'D
CANNON
CAREFULL
CAROLUS
CARRIED
CARRY
CASPIAN
CASTELL
CAUSDE
CHAMPION
CHAUNGE
CHEEKS
CITTIES
CLAP
CLOATH
CLOSELY
CLOTH'D
CLOUD
CLOWNE
COMMANDER
COMPANION
COMPAST
COMST
CONCUBINES
CONDITIONS
CONSISTORY
CONTAINE
CONTINUE
CONVAY
CORNELIUS
COURAGIOUSLY
COUSIN
CRAVES
CREATE
CREATURES
CREEPE
CROST
CRYE
CRYED
CURTEZANE
DAILY
DAINTY
DAMSELL
DANCE
DARING
DARST
DASH
DAUNCE
DEALE
DECAY
DEFENCE
DEPOSE
DESPISE
DETESTED
DEVICE
DEVIDE
DIANA
DIFFERENCE
DISCHARGE
DISCIPLINE
DIVE
DOGS
DOLLORS
DOTE
DOVES
DRESSE
DRIFT
DRUM
DRY

-5- (CONT.)

DUMAINE
DYED
EASTERNE
ECH
EIGHT
EMBRACE
ENCHAC'D
ENDED
ENTERTAIN'D
ENTRANCE
ENTRED
ENVIE
EVERY WHERE
EXCELLENCE
EXCLAIME
EXPECT
EXPEDITION
EXTREME
'FAITH
FALLING
FARTHER
FARWELL
FAVORS
FEEDS
FELICITIE
FIELDES
FIER
FIGHTS
FIGURE
FLAMING
FLEECE
FLOORE
FORCES
FORSOOKE
FOUNTAINES
FRO
FROWNES
FRUITS
FRYARS
GENTLY
GIRLES
GIVING
GLUT
GODLY
GONZAGO
GOVERNMENT
GRATIFIE
GREEKISH
GREETE
GREEVE
GREW
GROSSE
GROWE
HANDLED
HEARES
HEARSE
HEARTED
HENCEFORTH
HERCULES
HEREAFTER
HERES
HERS
HIDDEN
HIT
HOMER
HONEY
HONORABLE
HONOURED
HORNED
HOST
HOTE
HOULD
HOURES
HOWER
HUMBLIE
HUNGARY
HUNTERS
I'
I'DE
IMAGE
IMAGINE
IMPATIENT
IMPORT
INFAMIE
INFLICT
INJURE
INNOCENT
IN STEAD
INTENDING
INTENT
INTREATE
INVEST
INVISIBLE
IVORY
JACOMO
JEWELL
KEEPING
KILD
KILLING
KNAVE
KNEE
KNEWE
KNOWLEDGE
KNOW'ST
LABOURS
LACKE
LAID
LAIDE
LARISSA
LASCIVIOUS
LAUNCHT
LAVISH
LAYD
LEGIONS
LEGS
LIBERTIE
LIDS
LIMMES
LIONS
LIPPES
LIVED
LIVER
LOCKS
LOCKT
LODGE
LOVED
LOVEST
MAD'ST
MAIDENS
MAIDS
MANNAGE
MARCHT
MASSE
MASSY
MATE
MATES
MEETING
MENACE
MERCURY
MILKE
MILK-WHITE
MIRTLE
MIST
MIXT
MONARKE
MOOVE
MOOVES
MOTIONS
MOULD
MOURNING
MOVED
MURDERER
MURTHERER
MURTHERING
MUTE
MUTTON
NATIONS
NECESSARY
NEEDES
NEER
NEIGHBOR
NIMPH
NORTHREN
NURSE
OBEY
OFFERED
ONES
ORACLES
O'RE
OUTRAGIOUS
OXEN
PALLAS
PARLE
PATIENTLY
PAWES
PENELOPE
PERFORM'D
PERIOD
PERJURIE
PESANT
PETTY
PHYSICKE
PICTURE
PLEAS'D
PLEASING
POAST
POINTED
POLE
PORT
POT
POWDER
POWRE
PRESENTS
PRESIDENT
PRESSE
PRETIE
PRIAMS
PROFIT
PROTECTOR
PROTEUS
PROVIDED
PUNISH
PURGE
PURSE
QUITTANCE
RAPE
RAYMOND
READING
REAPE
REASONS
REBELLIOUS
RECEIV'D
REGENT
REGIMENT
REGIONS
REJOYCE
REQUIRE
REQUISITE
RESTORE
RETURND
REVENGDE
REVEREND
REVOLT
RICE
RICHEST
RINGS
RISING
ROARING
ROBE
ROMAINE
ROSES
RUTTERS
SAIST
SALE
SAVIOUR
SCAPES
SCHOLLER
SCORE
SCOTS
SE
SEATED
SEED
SEEDES
SEIZ'D
SENCE
SENCES
SEPULCHRE
SERPENTS
SERVILE
SETTING
SHAKES
SHARES
SHEATH
SHEPHEARD
SHEPHEARDS
SHINES
SHOOKE
SHOOT
SHOWNE
SIGHTS
SIN
SIRE
SLEEPES
SLIDE
SLIP
SNAKES
SOMETIMES
SOMEWHAT
SONG
SORIA
SOULDAN
SPEAKING
SPRUNG
STABLE
STANDING
STOOLE
STRAIT
STRANGLE
STREET
STRONGEST
STUDY
STURDY
SUBMISSION
SUM
SUNDER
SUNDRY
SUNNES
SUPPOSE
SURFET
SUSPECTED
SWALLOW
SWEAT
SWEETEST
SWIFTLY
SWORDE
TABLES
TAKING
TARTARS
TASTED
TERMES
TH
THEEVES
THICK
THOUSANDS
THOU'T
THOW
THREATNED
THREATS
TIDE
TOMBE
TOP
TOUCHT
TOWARD
TOY
TRADE
TREADING
TREASURY
TREAT
TURRET
TWAINE
TYRANNIES
UNGENTLE
UNJUST
UNKIND
UNNATURALL
UPSTART
URGE
UTMOST
VAUNT
VENGE
VENICE
VERIE
VEXED
VIEWING
VISITE
VIVE
WAITING
WALK
WALKES
WAN
WARNE
WATERY
WEALTHIE
WEAPON
WEE'LL
WE'LL
WERTENBERGE
WHAT EVER
WHEELE
WHER
WHERE'S
WHIT
WHORE
WHO'S
WINDING
WING
WITHERED
WITTENBERG
WOE
WONNE
WOON
WORDE
WORLDE
WORNE
WOUNDES
WRACK
WREATHES
WRONGED
YEARS
YEELDING
YEERES
YOULE

-6-

ABSENCE
ABSENT
ABUSE
ACCOMPLISH
ADDE
ADVANCE
AFFLICT
AIME
ALTARS
ALTER
ALWAYES
AMITIE
ANCHOR
APPEAR'D
ARABIAN
ARGUMENT
ARM'D
ARRIV'D
ARTS
ASPECT
ATLAS
AXE
BANISHT
BARBARY
BASELY
BATTELL
BEATE
BEATEN
BEATES
BEAUTIES
BEAUTIFULL
BELLY
BEND
BESIDE
BETRAIDE
BITTER
BLEMISH
BLOWE
BLOWES
BOORD
BOOTES
BORDERING
BOTTLE
BRED
BRINGING
BROKE
BUILT
BURST
BYRTH
CALLES
CARES
CENTER
CHARIOTS
CHASTITIE
CHEARE
CHERISH
CHILDE
CHRISTENDOME
COAST
COLLOURS
COMPANIONS
COMPARE
COMPLAINE
CONCLUDE
CONCUBINE
CONDITION
CONFERENCE
CONFOUND
CONSCIENCE
CONSISTS
CONTINENT
COOLE
COST
COULDST
COWARDS
CREST
CRUELTY
CURE
CURIOUS
CURST
DANUBIUS
DAR'ST
DART
DATE
DEAFE
DECEIV'D
DEEP

-6- (CONT.)

DEEREST
DENIE
DENIED
DESERTS
DESPITE
DIAMONDS
DIANAS
DIS
DISCONTENT
DISH
DIVINITIE
DOGGE
DOUBLE
DOUBTFULL
DOUBTS
DREAME
DUE
EMPTY
ENCOUNTER
ENGLISH
ENVY
EQUALLY
ESCAPT
ESTEEM'D
EVENING
EXCEPT
EXCUSE
EXECUTION
EXERCISE
EXPRESSE
FACES
FAIRER
FAL
FALLES
FALS
FAMILIAR
FANNE
FAREWEL
FAWNE
FERNEZE
FILS
FISH
FLAGS
FLOURISH
FORBID
FORGIVE
FRAM'D
FRUITE
FURROWES
GALLIES
GARRISONS
GETS
GHOSTS
GLADLY
GLOOMIE
GLOSTER
GLUTTED
GOTTEN
GRAC'D
GRACES
GRANT
GRIEVES
GRIEVOUS
GRIPE
GROWES
GUILTY
GUISIANS
GULFE
ANG'D
ANGS
AP
ARBOUR
ARSH
AUGHTY
EAVIE
EED
EER
EERES
EIGHT
IDEOUS
IDES
OOD
OPING
UMANE
UMBLE
LLIONEUS
NCENSE
NDIAN
NFINITE
NJURY
ARRE
EST
JUSTICE
KINDLED
KINDLY
KNIFE
KNIT
LA
LADEN
LADIES
LE
LEANDERS
LEAPE
LEGGES
LEISTER
LEND
LIBIA
LIBIAN
LOADE
LONGING
LYING
MAGICK
MALICE
MALTA'S
MARCHING
MARRIAGE
MARTCHT
MATTERS
MEMORIE
MIGHTST
MISCHIEFE
MODEST
MONEY
MOURNE
MOUTHES
MULTITUDE
MUTUALL
NIMPHES
NOISE
NUNNE
OLYMPIA
ON'T
OTHERWISE
PASSING
PASSIONATE
PEASANT
PEECES
PER
PIKES
PITCH
PITCHT
PLEAD
PLIGHT
POOLES
POSSESSE
POURE
POVERTY
PRACTISE
PRESERVE
PRESUMPTION
PRETIOUS
PRETTY
PROSPER
PROTEST
PULD
PUNISHMENT
QUARRELL
QUARTERS
QUESTIONS
QUICKLIE
QUIT
RADIANT
RAW
RECORD
REFUSE
RELENT
REQUITE
RESIST
RETAINE
RETIRE
REVERENCE
RHODE
ROMANS
ROUSE
RUE
RUL'D
SACKE
SAND
SAYD
SCARSE
SEEK
SELIM-CALYMATH
SENCELESSE
SER
SHIELD
SHOLD
SHOWES
SILLY
SINGS
SIRHA
SKIN
SKY
SLEEPING
SMART
SMOOTH
SNATCHT
SNOWY
SOLD
SOMETIME
SOULDANE
SOULDIOUR
SOUTHERNE
SPANISH
SPELS
SPENCERS
SPHEARE
SPIGHT
SPRED
STAFFE
STAINE
STAR
STAVES
STAYD
STEED
STEEDES
STOCKE
STREETS
STRIVING
STROVE
STRUMPET
SUMMER
SUPPLY
SUPPREST
SURGEON
SURPRIZE
SUSTAINE
SWARME
SWIFTER
TALES
TARTARIAN
TEARMES
TERRENE
THEFT
THEREON
THICKE
THIRTY
THOROUGH
THOROW
THOUGHTES
THRACIAN
THREAT
THUNDRING
TIBULLUS
TOKEN
TOPS
TOYLE
TREACHEROUS
TREBIZON
TRIUMPHANT
TUE
TUMBLING
TURNED
TYTLE
UNDERSTAND
UNDONE
UNSEENE
UNWORTHY
USUMCASANE
VALDES
VANISH
VERTUES
VICTORIES
VIEW'D
VILDE
VILLANIE
VINE
VINES
VIRGIN
VOYCE
WALKING
WALL
WATRIE
WATRY
WAYES
WEARIE
WE'LE
WEPT
WESTERNE
WHEELES
WHERE ERE
WHEREON
WOMENS
WRACKT
WUD
YOUTHFULL
ZOUNDS

-7-

AD
ADVANTAGE
AFFECTIONS
AGREE
ALCIDES
ALIKE
ASSAILE
ASSE
ASSURED
ATTIRE
AWAKE
AYDE
BALDOCK
BASHAWES
BASSOES
BEAUTEOUS
BEERE
BEHOLDE
BERNARDINE
BESEEMES
BETWEENE
BIRD
BOIES
BULLETS
BURNES
CALME
CANDLE
CARIE
CARKASSES
CHANNELL
CHIDE
CHILDISH
CHILDREN
CITIZENS
CITTY
CLEAVE
COMMEND
CONVEY
CORNER
COUNCELL
COURTS
COVERED
COWARD
COYNE
DAME
DEITY
DEPRIV'D
DESART
DETERMINE
DIAMOND
DICK
DIRECT
DISPLAY
DOES
DOING
DOLLERS
DOORES
DRAWEN
DREAD
DREW
DRINK
DRIVES
DROOPE
DUST
DWELT
DYING
EATING
EGYPTIAN
ELEMENT
EMPERIE
ENDLESSE
ENEMIE
ENTERPRISE
ENTREATE
ERST
&C.
EVERMORE
FAINTING
FAIREST
FEARD
FEEDE
FELLOWES
FESSE
FIE
FLATTERERS
FLEET
FLOWING
FOILE
FOND
FORC'D
FORGET
FORT
FREELY
FREEND
FRIER
FRONT
GOVERNORS
GRECIAN
GRECIANS
GUEST
HAPLESSE
HAPPILY
HARTS
HEADED
HEAPE
HEARING
HECTOR
HELLEN
HELLISH
HEROES
HONOURABLE
HORSMEN
HUMAINE
IFAITH
IMBRACE
INCENST
INCOUNTER
INJURIOUS
IO
IRELAND
IRON
JEALOUS
JERUSALEM
JOURNEY
KNIGHTS
LABOURING
LANCES
LAUGH
LEAPT
LEAVING
LIMS
LIQUID
LUST
MANNER
MARBLE
MEANE TIME
MEAT
MELT
MERCHANTS
MESSAGE
METEORS
MILK
MILLIONS
MISERY
MONARCH
MONTH
MOOV'D
MOUNTS
MURTHERED
NOTE
NUMBERS
OATH
ORCANES
ORIENT
OWN
PAPALL
PASSIONS
PATIENCE
PEN
PERPETUALL
PERSEANS
PERSWADE
PITY
PLOT
POLAND
POLES
POMPEY
POSSESSION
POST
PRETHEE
PRIAM
PRIVY
PROCURE

-7- (CONT.)

PROSPEROUS
PROTESTANTS
PROVIDE
PURCHASE
QUEEN
QUENCH
QUICK
RECOMPENCE
RELIGIOUS
REMOOVE
RESOLUTION
RIPE
ROYAL
SACRIFIZE
SAFETIE
SANDS
SATISFIE
SATISFIED
SATURNE
SAV'D
SAYES
SCALE
SCARLET
SECRETLY
SECRETS
SENATE
SESTOS
SHADOW
SHUN
SIDES
SIGNE
SINKE
SITH
SLAVISH
SLOTH
SMILING
SODAINLY
SON
SORROWES
SOULDIOURS
SPANGLED
SPRONG
STAYES
STIR
STOLNE
STOP
STREIGHT
STRIKES
SUDDENLY
SUFFICE
SUMME
SUPPER
SWORE
TACKLING
TEETH
TEMPESTS
THANK
THEREWITHALL
THINK'ST
THO
THREW
TO MORROW
TRENCH
TRIE
TRIUMPHS
TURKY
TURRETS
TWERE
TYRANT
UNKINDE
VAILE
VAINES
VILLANY
VISIT
WANTING
WASH
WAXE
WEARY
WEIGHT
WHAT ERE
WHATS
WHEREAT
WOMBE
WRAPT
YEELDS
YONDER
YRON

-8-

ADMIT
AFFRIGHT
AGAIN
ALEXANDRIA
ALPES
ANCIENT
AN OTHER
ANY THING
ARMIES
ARTICLES
ARUNDELL
ASCEND
ASPIRING
ASSAULT
BANDS
BEAST
BECOMES
BE GON
BESEECH
BIRDES
BIRDS
BLESSED
BOREAS
BREAKES
BRIDGE
BRIDLE
BULL
CALD
CALDE
CAMP
CANNONS
CARDINALL
CARELESSE
CASE
CASTS
CHURCHES
CLOUDS
COMMONS
CONCEIT
CONJURE
CONSPIRE
COURAGE
CREDIT
CRIME
CROWN'D
CRUEL
CRY
CYNTHIA
DEAREST
DECEIVE
DELAY
DEMAND
DESERVES
DESTINIES
DISCOURSE
DISHONOR
DOMINUS
DRAGONS
DRAWES
DRUMS
DULL
DYES
EAGLES
EARLES
EAT
EFFECT
EMPERIALL
EMPIRE
EMPRESSE
ENEMY
ENSIGNES
ERRE
EST
EXCEED
EXCELLENT
FAILE
FAITHFULL
FAULTS
FEAR'D
FEARFULL
FINE
FIRMAMENT
FLINT
FLOWERS
FOLLOWES
FOOLE
FORTY
FREENDS
FROWNING
GAN
GIRLE
GLASSE
GOWNE
GRASSE
GREEDY
GREEKES
GROVE
GROVES
GUARDE
GUISES
GURNEY
HAPPINESSE
HATED
HEES
HENOLT
HE'S
HEW
HIR
HONEST
HOPES
HOVER
IL'E
INDEED
INWARD
IS'T
JAWES
KEEPER
KENT
KILLINGWORTH
KNOWE
KNOWING
LAMPS
LANDS
LEADE
LEANE
LEGGE
LENGTH
LEVIE
LEVUNE
LEWNE
LIBERTY
LIVELY
LOATHSOME
LORDSHIP
LOW
LUSTIE
LYES
MAID
MAIDES
MAIEST
MAISTERS
MALEDICAT
MEASURE
MENAPHON
MID
MIDNIGHT
MILDE
MINIONS
MISERIE
MORTALL
MORTIMERS
MURDERED
NEEDE
NEPHEW
NEPTUNES
NILE
NOBILITIE
NUN
OBTAINE
ORDINANCE
OURS
PAINTED
PARTS
PERSEPOLIS
PLUMES
POYSONED
PRAIERS
PRECIOUS
PREPAR'D
PRESUME
PRIVATE
PRIZE
RAMUS
REGION
REND
ROCKS
RULDE
SACKT
SAIES
SCAPE
SEAZE
SELF
SERVITUDE
SEVERALL
SIGHES
SILKE
SITTING
SKIE
SLAUGHTERED
SLEPT
SMILES
SONS
SOUTH
SPACE
STEAD
STRANGER
STRANGERS
SUBDUE
SUBSCRIBE
SUFFICIENT
TEMPLE
THETIS
THIRD
TORMENTED
TORTURE
TOUCHING
TRAGEDIE
TROIANS
TRY
TYRANTS
UNDERTAKE
UNHAPPIE
VALOUR
VICEROIES
WARWICKE
WASTE
WHATSOEVER
WHOME
WIN
WITHALL
WOFULL
WOT
WRACKE
WRITTEN
YEE

-9-

ABLE
ALREADY
ALTAR
ANSWERE
BAND
BARTLEY
BATTER
BEHELD
BELCHER
BELL
BETRAY
BIDS
BILLOWES
BOW
BOYE
BROILES
CASTLE
CHANG'D
CHARME
CHASE
CHAUNCE
CHRISTALL
COACH
COLOUR
COMMIT
CONSUME
CORNEWALL
COUNTENANCE
CRIE
CROWN
CUPIDS
DELIVER
DESERVE
DESPIGHT
DEVISE
DISTRESSED
DITCH
DIVEL
DOO
DORE
ELEMENTS
ESTATE
ESTEEME
EXILE
FAINE
FANCIE
FEARES
FELT
FIGHTING
FLY
FORGOT
FORTIE
FRIERS
GANIMED
GAZE
GERMANE
GOVERNE
GROW
HANGING
HAY
HEATE
HEL
HETHER
HUNG
INFLUENCE
INTEND
IT SELFE
JADES
KNEELE
LAMENT
LANCE
LATEST
LIKEWISE
LOATH
LOFTIE
MANLY
MANS
MASSACRE
MATREVIS
MINION
MISTRISSE
MORNE
MORROW
MOUNTAINES
MUSES
NATURES
NECK
NEPTUNE
PITTIE
PLEASDE
PLEDGE
POISON
POYSON'D
PRAYERS
PREST
PREVAILE
PRIAMUS
PROPER
QUIVERING
RAFE
RAGING
RAN
REACH
RENOWNE
REPAIRE
RESCUE
RESPECT
ROOMES
RUNNES
SCARCE
SCYTHIA
SCYTHIANS
SECURE
SEEM'D
SEEMES
SHAKING
SHORTLY
SHOULDER
SHOW
SHOWERS
SILENCE
SOULDANS
SOULDIER
SPEAKES
SPEARE
SPEND
SPOILES
SPOKE
STAB
STANDARD
STROKE
SUE
SWAY
SWELL
SWIM
TABLE
TAUGHT
TIL
TROIAN
TROUBLED

-9- (CONT.)

TURK
VAST
VILLAIN
VIRGINS
VOWES
WAIT
WARE
WARNING
WEST
WILLINGLY
WINTER
WINTERS
WIVES
WON
WONDROUS
WONT
WORDES
WRATHFULL
YOUR SELVES
HERMES
KISSES
KIST
KNIGHT
KNOWEST
LAWFULL
LIKES
LIV'D
LIVING
LOOK'D
MAINE
MANAGE
MATCH
ME THINKS
MONSTER
MOTION
NATIVE
NORTH
NUNNERY
OARES
OFFENCE
OFFEND
OFFENDED
OLDE
PARAMOUR
PATIENT
PERHAPS
PLANETS
PRIEST
PRINCES
PROVINCES
RACE
RARE
READE
ROB
SCEPTER
SHOULDERS
SINNES
SISTERS
SLEW
SOLEMNE
SORE
SPEARES
SPRINGS
STARRE
STEEDS
STOLE
SUBJECTS
SUDDEN
THERES
THIEFE
THROAT
TO DAY
TREAD
TREMBLING
TURNES
USDE
VIOLENT
WAIES
WANTS
WATCH
WEALTHY
WHEREAS
WINGED
WINNE
WISHT
WORSHIP

-10-

ABIGAL
AFFRIKE
AGED
AID
ANGRIE
BACCHUS
BATTAILE
BE GONE
BEHIND
BENT
BEYOND
BIND
BINDE
LAZED
BODIE
BRASSE
BREASTS
BREATHE
BROOKE
CALLAPINE
CARDINALS
CAVE
CELESTIALL
CERES
CHASTE
CHEERE
CHOOSE
CLAD
CLEARE
CONDUCT
CONFIRME
COSROE
COUNSELL
COUNTRIE
CURTESIE
DAYES
DIED
DISPATCH
DOG
DRIE
DRIVEN
DROPS
DRUNKE
EMPTIE
ENVIOUS
ET
FARE
FAVOURS
FEAREFULL
FEARING
FITS
FLOUD
FORBEARE
FORBIDS
FRENCH
FRUITFULL
FUL
GARMENTS
GATHER
GHOST
GLORIE
GOBLET
GON
GRACIOUS
HALE
HANDES
HEAPES
HENRY

-11-

ACHILLES
ALBEIT
ALMEDA
ALOFT
AMBITIOUS
ANON
APT
ARGIER
ASLEEPE
BANKES
BENVOLIO
BIDE
BOUGHT
BRAVELY
BREACH
BRETHREN
BUILD
BURTHEN
CHARMES
CHIEFE
CHIEFEST
CIRCLE
COMMANDS
COMPANY
CONQUER'D
CONQUEROUR
DANGEROUS
DECREED
DESPAIRE
DIES
DIM
DIVELS
DOORE
DOOST
DROP
DUTIE
DWELL
EMPERESSE
FLATTER
FORMER
FORSAKE
FRUIT
FUNERALL
GLORY
HARPE
HEAT
HEELE
HEY
HILL
HILS
HOURE
HUSBANDS
IMPERIALL
INCREASE
INDIA
JOYNE
LEG
LIGHTNING
LIST
LITLE
LOCKES
LOE
MADAME
MAINTAINE
MAIST
MEANS
MERCY
MINDS
MONSTROUS
MOORES
NAMES
NEARE
NOBLES
OBSCURE
PALLACE
PARENTS
PETERS
PINE
PLAC'D
PLACES
PLEASETH
PLEASURES
POLICIE
PRIESTS
PROFESSION
PURSUE
QUAKE
QUITE
RESIGNE
RICHES
ROBIN
ROCKE
SALUTE
SAYING
SEALE
SERV'D
SHAPES
SHED
SLAY
SMILE
SODAINE
SOUGHT
SPAKE
SPHEARES
STEELE
STEPS
STOOPE
SUCCESSE
TASTE
THANKS
THIRST
THUNDER
TORNE
TOWERS
TROOPES
TROUPES
TURKS
TUT
TWAS
VERSES
VOICE
WAIGHT
WARWICK
WEE'L
WHEREOF
WHOLE
WILD
WINDOW
WITS
WORLDS
WRONGS

-12-

ABROAD
AMAINE
ARABIA
ARMED
ATTEMPT
BANISH
BELIKE
BLACK
BLOW
BLUSH
CAESARS
CAPTAINE
CAPTAINES
CHALLENGE
CHANCE
CITY
COMMING
COMPANIE
CONJURING
CORINNA
CORNE
CUSTOME
DESERV'D
DISTRESSE
DORES
EARTHLY
ENDURE
ENJOY
ESCAPE
FARES
FED
FEW
FIND
FIXT
FLIES
FLIGHT
FLOUDS
FLYING
FOOLISH
FORRAINE
FURIOUS
GRAPES
HARDLY
HEAVY
HEELES
HOLDS
JOHN
JOINE
KEEPES
LATELY
LEST
LIFT
LOSE
MAD
MARIAGE
MARRY
MEANDER
MEANT
MEPHASTOPHILIS
MOUNTED
MURTHER
OVERCOME
PENBROOKE
POETS
PRISONER
PROOFE
PURPOSE
QUIVER
REBELS
REPORT
RESTS
RULES
RUTH
SERVANTS
SEVEN
SHARE
SHORT
SIGISMOND
SILENT
SKILL
SOLE
SPEED
SPITE
STOUT
STREAMES
STROOKE
TAKES
TEMPLES
THRICE
TOGETHER
TONGUES
TORMENT
TREASURIE
TREMBLE
TRESSES
TROUBLE
TRUTH
TURND
UNKNOWNE
VIOLENCE
WAKE
WANDRING
WARME
WAST
WEAKE
WILDE
WINDS
WOUNDED
WOUNDS
WRETCH

-13-

ADMIRALL
ALMOST
ALWAIES
AMONG
ANSWER
APPEARE
ASSURE
BABYLON
BAD
BEAT
BEGAN
BLISSE
BOOKES
BOWE
BROKEN
BRUNO
CIVILL
CLEANE
CONJURER
CONQUEST
CONSENT
COUNTRY
DARKE
DARTS
DENY
DISGRACE
DIVELL
EATE
ENDS
FINGERS
FRIENDLY
FURY
GAINST
GERMANY
GLORIOUS
GOODLY
GUIDE
HEADLONG
HELP
HIGHLY
HITHER
HOLDE
HOLLOW
IDLE
INFERNALL
IST
JUNO
LAP
LED

INDEX WORDS ORDERED BY FREQUENCY

LONGER
MERCIE
MINDES
MOTHERS
MUSE
NUMBER
OPE
PITTY
PLAINE
POYSON
PRISON
PURE
QUESTION
RENOWMED
RESOLVE
REWARD
SEAT
SEATE
SEES
SEEST
SELL
SHINING
SICKE
SIEGE
SIGNES
SOMETHING
SPEAK
SPRING
STIL
STORME
STREETES
SUSPECT
TEL
TENDER
THEREOF
THERFORE
THINKING
THINKS
TOLD
TOWARDS
TREES
TWIXT
VICTORIE
WENCHES
WHAT'S
WHILES
WILS
WINDE
WORKES
WORSE
WORST

-14-

ALEXANDER
ARMIE
ASIDE
BEEN
BLAME
BOUNDS
BOYES
BRAINES
BRINGS
CHAST
CITIES
CLOUDES
CLOWDES
CROOKED
CUP
DANGER
DEERE
DISDAINE
DISSEMBLE
DRAWNE
DRIVE
EIE
EMPEROURS
EPERNOUNE
EQUALL
FILD
FOURE
FROWNE
GATE
GOING
GREATEST
GREENE
HADST
HEIRE
HIGHER
HIGHEST
HOUSES
JUDGE
JUPITER
KIND
KNEES
LEARNED
MAGICKE
MARKE
MEATE
MISERABLE
MISTRESSE
MOUTH
MUSICKE
PLAINES
PLEASANT
POET
PRICE
REVENG'D
ROCKES
ROSE
RUNS
SACRIFICE
SAINT
SEEKES
SELIM
SERVANT
SHORE
SIMPLE
SPEECHES
STERNE
SUBJECT
SUBSTANCE
SWELLING
TALL
TANE
THITHER
THREATEN
THREATNING
TRAINE
TRUCE
TWENTY
UNDERNEATH
UNTILL
VALIANT
VILE
WAGNER
WOMAN
WROUGHT
YOUR SELFE

-15-

ARMOUR
ATTEND
BARONS
BEAMES
BLOUDY
BONES
BOWELS
BUY
CASANE
CHAIRE
CHAMBER
COSIN
DARES
DESPERATE
DEVILS
DIADEM
DREADFULL
DURST
EGYPT
EUROPE
FATE
FLAME
FORWARD
GENTLEMAN
GIFT
GRIEVE
GROWNE
HEALTH
HOT
KINDE
KINGDOME
LOOKING
MESSENGER
MET
ME THINKES
OFTEN
ORDER
PERCEIVE
PLAGUE
PREPARE
REASON
REMAINES
RIVER
ROUGH
RUDE
SAITH
SCYTHIAN
SHARPE
TAKEN
TALE
'TWAS
WEAPONS
YOUNG

-16-

AIDE
ALIVE
BARE
BEASTS
BELEEVE
BLOODY
BOLD
BURNT
CHURCH
COMFORT
CONQUERED
DEATHS
DESIRES
DOOTH
EDWARDS
FAINT
FAULT
FEED
FLEETE
FORME
FORTUNES
FRAME
GLAD
GUARD
HUMBLY
JOYES
LADY
LAKE
LAW
LOFTY
MEANING
MOV'D
NEEDS
PASSAGE
PROMISE
PROOVE
PURPLE
RANSOME
RENT
RITES
ROBES
SAWE
SEARCH
SECOND
SENDS
SHALBE
SHAPE
SHIP
SHUT
SIRS
SLAUGHTER
SLENDER
SOONER
SPAINE
STEALE
STONES
TEARE
TENT
THERE'S
THRUST
TORMENTS
TREE
TRIBUTE
UGLY
UNCKLE
YEARE

-17-

ABOURD
AMOROUS
ANGRY
COMPASSE
DEVILL
EARE
FATES
FINDE
FOUGHT
FOULE
FRYAR
FURIES
GODDESSE
HAPPIE
HERE'S
JEWELS
LOVER
MAIDE
MENS
NE'RE
NUNS
ORE
PAINES
QUIET
RED
RELIGION
RING
RUINE
SORT
STRANGE
SWORNE
TENTS
TERROUR
THROW
TURKES
VENGEANCE
VERTUE
WAITE
WOOD

-18-

ALONG
BEARES
BEAUTIE
BECOME
BEGIN
BEGINS
BETWIXT
BIN
BIRTH
BLEST
BOSOME
CAMPE
CEASE
CHAINES
CHILD
CONQUER
COURSE
DAMASCUS
DAMN'D
DEFEND
DEPART
DON
ENTER
E'RE
EVERIE
FILL
FLAMES
FRESH
GIFTS
GREECE
HOLINESSE
HURT
IMMORTALL
LABOUR
LAWES
LEARNE
LETTER
LOOK
LORDE
MAKING
MOONE
MORNING
NEED
ONLY
OUR SELVES
POINT
PRAISE
PROVE
REPENT
RESOLV'D
RID
RUNNING
SAILES
SECRET
SEEME
SHAKE
SORROW
STATELY
STONE
STRIVE
TEACH
THANKES
TOWNES
TRUMPETS
TURN'D
VOW
WARS
WHEREWITH
WIDE
YOURS

-19-

AYE
BARBAROUS
BENE
BROTHERS
CHARIOT
COUNTRIES
CROSSE
DIDST
EASE
FELLOW
FURTHER
GAINE
GREEFE
HAIRES
HASTE
HER SELFE
HID
HO
HUGE
ISSUE
KINGDOMES
LETTERS
LINE
LIPS
LOOKS
MATTER
MIDST
NATOLIA
READ
REQUEST
SITS
SPORT
STARS
STOOD
STREAME
T'
TONGUE
TREASON
TRIPLE
WHEREFORE
WIND
WONDER
WORTHY
WRIT
YEA

-20-

ACCURSED
ALTHOUGH
ANGER
ARMY
BOUND
BURNE
CHANGE
CRAVE
CUPID
DAIES
DOST
EDMUND
FAMOUS
FLED
FOLLOWERS
FOR EVER
GENERALL
GENTLEMEN
JOVES
KNOWNE
LARGE

INES
OSSE
ARTIALL
CEAN
UGHT
ARIS
RESENCE
UICKLY
ONNES
POILE
PREAD
UFFER
HANKE
RAITORS
ICKED
INGS

-21-

NNA
ROWES
EADLY
OWN
LS
NTERTAINE
OLDE
ARME
ORSES
NTREAT
YE
URDER
EXT
IGHTS
VERTHROW
ERFORME
HOEBUS
OWERS
ESOLUTE
COURGE
HINE
HOULDST
TORE
UNNE
HAT'S
HATS
OWER
USH
ALS
ARLIKE
EE
EEPE
HILST
HITHER
ISE
RETCHED
RONG

-22-

FFRICA
MONGST
ANQUET
EARING
EAUTY
BEAST
ALYMATH
EEDS
EET
IELDS
LYE
OOT
RATIOUS
A
ATEFULL
INGLY
CV'D
ALE
EARLE
EERES
OMPE
AIGNE
EADY
OUND
UNNE
CORNE
ILVER
ING
LAVES
PEECH

SPENT
UNLESSE
VERY
VICTORY
WATERS
WEELE

-23-

ASCANIUS
AYRE
BESIDES
CAPTIVE
CHEEKES
CITIE
DIVINE
DRAW
ENGLANDS
FIERCE
FIERY
FIVE
GATES
GRAVE
HEAVENLY
HONORS
KEEP
LEAGUE
LET'S
LOOSE
MARTCH
MEETE
NAVARRE
NOUGHT
PERISH
RAGE
SHOARE
SHOT
SOFT
SUN
THINKES
THRONE
VERSE
WANT
WARRANT
WOULDST

-24-

BODIES
CAESAR
CONFESSE
DEED
EITHER
ETERNALL
FEAST
FEELE
FELL
FOOTE
HELD
HOSTE
JEWES
JUST
LEAD
LEAVES
NECKE
OFFER
PIERCE
PULL
SINNE
WHENCE
WITNESSE
YOUTH

-25-

ABOVE
ANOTHER
BEE
BURNING
CHRIST
COLD
CUNNING
CURSE
ENGLAND
GOVERNOUR
GRAUNT
HERO

ISABELL
LEANDER
LESSE
LODOWICKE
LOVELY
MEE
MONY
PAINE
PERSEAN
PITIE
REMAINE
RULE
SEAS
SERVICE
SPARE
SWIFT
TIMES
WALKE
WAVES
WERT
WOMEN
YONG

-26-

AGE
COMMAND
COMMAUND
COMMON
DARE
DEARE
DIDOS
ENEMIES
FAR
FATALL
FOE
FOES
FURIE
GOES
MARS
MIGHTIE
MOUNT
NATURE
SIDE
SPIRIT
STANDS
TREASURE
TURKISH
VILLAINES
WANTON
WINDES
WOODS
WORTH

-27-

ARME
BREATH
BREST
CLOSE
CONQUERING
DEEPE
GOODS
MARCH
RAISE
RISE
SAW
SPIRITS
TRUST
WIT
WRITE

-28-

ACHATES
ASIA
EAST
FEETE
FLESH
FLIE
FOORTH
FOUND
FREE
HAPPY
HEARTS
HIGHNES
ITALY

KEPT
KNEW
KNOWES
LOVING
MISTRIS
RUN
SAILE
WENT

-29-

BAJAZETH
CARTHAGE
DRINKE
FAST
GIVEN
HAIRE
HUSBAND
ILL
ITHIMORE
MIND
NEERE
OPEN
SACRED
SAME
STARRES
THENCE
THINK

-30-

BRIGHT
CRUELL
DAMNED
EARLE
FAVOUR
FRAUNCE
GOVERNOR
LIES
PAY
PEOPLE
SELVES
SHEE
STRENGTH
TRAITOR

-31-

ASKE
BACK
BLACKE
BOOKE
BREAKE
CUT
FIT
GOT
HIDE
HORNES
KILL
LOST
MATHIAS
PAST
PERSON
PLAY
SOVERAIGNE
THEMSELVES
THREE
TOUCH

-32-

ABIGALL
DUKE
EYE
FAME
HONOUR
LANCASTER
MOVE
NAKED
SISTER

-33-

EARES
GIVES
JOY
LETS
LUCIFER
PERSEA
RECEIVE
RIDE
SHEW
STRIKE
STRONG
TECHELLES
TRIUMPH

-34-

EIES
FIGHT
LOVERS
NERE
OTHERS
PASSE
POPE
PRESENT
PRINCELY
REALME
SAD
SWEARE

-35-

CANST
CHRISTIAN
DOUBT
EACH
ELSE
FALSE
FETCH
HART
HEARD
HELPE
SAFE
TALKE
THING
TOOKE
TURKE
VIEW
WIFE

-36-

GET
RATHER
REMEMBER
SMALL
SPENCER
SURE
WOUND
WRATH

-37-

ALAS
CHRISTIANS
DOEST
GRIEFE
HANG
HIGHNESSE
IARBUS
MAHOMET
NEITHER
ROOME
SEEKE
TEN
WARRES
WINE

-38-

MASTER
PLEASURE

INDEX WORDS ORDERED BY FREQUENCY

SEENE
SLEEPE
SWORDS

-39-

DAUGHTER
HALFE
KISSE
PARDON
PRINCE
RETURNE
ROME
SAID
SLAVE
SOUND
STRAIGHT

-40-

A WHILE
BEENE
BEHOLD
BID
BROUGHT
GAVE
NEWES
WORD
WORKE
YEARES
YES

-41-

DELIGHT
DESIRE
HEE
MAISTER
NEW
TROY
WENCH
WHEREIN
WHETHER

-42-

BRAVE
CARE
COURT
CURSED
HEADS
SEEING
SLAINE
SOULES
THERIDAMAS

-43-

AFTER
AL
BOY
'EM
PRESENTLY
ROYALL
SAKE

-44-

MAJESTIE
MEET
ONELY
PRIDE
REVENGE
SOONE

-45-

CROWNES
FRIEND
GREATER
HAVING
HOME
LAY
WISH

-46-

BEST
LIE
MEPHOSTOPHILIS
SIRRA
STATE

-47-

BETTER
EDWARD
FAITH
TAMBURLAIN
THOUGHT

-48-

AIRE
CONTENT
HAS
HATE
LITTLE
MALTA
MIGHTY
NOBLE
SHIPS
VILLAINE

-49-

BED
ENOUGH
FIELD
GROUND
SERVE
WEARE

-50-

ALONE
BORNE
FORTUNE
HARD
LATE
OLD
RICH
WARRE
WAY

-51-

BECAUSE
CHARGE
VENUS

-52-

CAST
HEAVENS
HIMSELFE
LAST
MINDE
OVER

-53-

FATHERS
JEW
PEACE
WAR
WEALTH

-54-

DOCTOR
PUT
WHITE

-55-

FORCE
OFF
TEARES
WALLES

-56-

HOLY
PART
'TIS
WEL

-57-

HIGH
MAJESTY
SHAME
THY SELFE
UNDER
WATER
WELCOME
WITHOUT
YEELD

-58-

HOLD
RIGHT
SIT
THOUGHTS

-59-

BASE
FARRE
LEAST
LIGHT
VAINE

-60-

BACKE
DYE
FOLLOW
FRANCE
KEEPE
LEFT
OFT
THINGS
TURNE

-61-

BLOOD
EMPEROUR
END
GOLDEN
ONCE

-62-

MOTHER
SAVE

-63-

CAME
GENTLE
HONOR
MAKES
PROUD

-64-

BODY
FULL
MOST
SIGHT

-65-

CALL
HEERE
LOOKES
LOVES
MEANES
NOTHING
SENT
USE

-66-

LAND

-67-

ZENOCRATE

-68-

GUISE
OWNE

-69-

EVEN
FACE
PLEASE
TOWNE

-70-

DIDO
HUNDRED
SET
TWO

-71-

BROTHER
FALL
SEND
TH'
TRUE
WITHIN

-72-

CAUSE
LIVES
STILL

-73-

GONE
MADAM

-74-

FAREWELL
SINCE

-75-

SOULDIERS

-76-

FRIENDS
HORSE

-77-

MY SELFE
STAND

-78-

DEAD
MEANE

-79-

BARABAS
PLACE

-80-

EYES
JOVE

-81-

ERE
HOUSE
SWEETE
SWORD

-82-

POORE

-83-

BLOUD
NAY

-84-

FORTH
GOLD
NONE
PRAY
TILL

-85-

AH
COULD
HENCE

-86-

SHAL

INDEX WORDS ORDERED BY FREQUENCY

-87-

THINE

-88-

WIL

-89-

BEARE
POWER
WILT

-90-

HOPE

-91-

CANNOT
COMES
OH

-92-

QUEENE

-94-

MANY
NIGHT

-95-

EVERY

-96-

FIRE
GODS
OTHER

-97-

BRING

-99-

HEARE

-100-

LOOKE
LORDS
WORDS

-101-

HANDS

-102-

DIE

-103-

GO
MORTIMER
THROUGH

-104-

REST
THOUSAND

-105-

THAN

-106-

KINGS
NAME
THOUGH

-107-

EVER
SEA

-109-

FATHER
YE

-111-

SHALT

-112-

GRACE
HEART
HELL
TIS

-113-

CROWNE
GAVESTON
I'LE
WHILE

-115-

AGAINST
ANY
DONE
SONNE

-116-

SPEAKE

-117-

THEREFORE

-118-

ABOUT

-120-

THINKE
THOSE

-122-

AGAINE
DAY

-123-

BEFORE

-124-

HAST
HEAD

-126-

WHOM

-130-

DOWNE
TOO

-131-

FIRST

-133-

SWEET

-135-

SIR

-136-

BEING
HAND
TAMBURLAINE
TIME

-137-

LONG

-138-

FEARE

-141-

LEAVE
MUCH

-142-

EARTH

-143-

AENEAS

-145-

MIGHT

-147-

INTO

-152-

ART
SOULE
STAY

-157-

DOTH

-158-

SAY

-160-

BOTH

-161-

WORLD

-163-

AN
GOD

-164-

MINE

-166-

TELL

-169-

LIVE
NEVER

-170-

GIVE

-176-

DOE

-178-

MAN
UNTO

-181-

FAIRE
OUT

-185-

GREAT

-186-

WHO

-188-

KNOW

-189-

ARMES

-190-

SELFE

-192-

MADE
WELL

-194-

CAN

-196-

GOE

-197-

LIFE
SOME

-200-

DO

-202-

HEAVEN

-203-

GOOD

-204-

UP

-205-

ILE

INDEX WORDS ORDERED BY FREQUENCY

-207-
AWAY

-216-
DEATH

-219-
FAUSTUS

-223-
THUS

-224-
NOR

-225-
MEN

-226-
WHOSE

-229-
TAKE

-232-
ONE

-236-
THERE

-238-
MUST

-242-
HAD

-245-
DID

-248-
AM

-249-
SHOULD

-251-
UPON

-266-
WERE

-270-
WHY

-274-
LIKE

-277-
HATH
WHERE

-278-
HERE

-289-
WOULD

-293-
SUCH

-303-
O

-304-
MAKE

-328-
YET

-335-
MORE

-338-
WHICH

-348-
HOW

-372-
US

-373-
SEE

-377-
WAS

-380-
WHEN

-382-
THEM

-383-
KING

-388-
SHE

-403-
MAY

-409-
THESE

-417-
THEY

-421-
LOVE

-429-
AT

-434-
COME

-495-
ARE

-497-
LET

-502-
IF

-505-
ON

-510-
LORD

-523-
OR

-531-
NO

-568-
THEIR

-615-
FROM

-625-
BY

-638-
OUR

-647-
WE

-664-
THEN

-680-
NOW

-690-
THEE

-707-
HER

-722-
SHALL

-729-
ALL

-735-
WHAT

-770-
SO

-798-
WILL

-812-
HAVE

-825-
HIM

-855-
YOUR

-862-
IT

-937-
HE

-1017-
AS

-1018-
THY

-1063-
IS

-1071-
THIS

-1082-
THOU

-1105-
BUT

-1177-
YOU

-1205-

BE

-1223-

NOT

-1320-

HIS

-1335-

FOR

-1384-

ME

-1686-

WITH

-1791-

A

-1892-

THAT

-1908-

IN

-2506-

MY

-3011-

I

-3022-

OF

-3359-

TO

-5182-

THE

-5478-

AND

INDEX WORDS ORDERED ALPHABETICALLY

1791 A
4 ABANDON
4 ABBASSE
3 ABHORRE
5 ABIDE
10 ABIGAL
32 ABIGALL
5 ABJURE
9 ABLE
5 ABOORD
17 ABOURD
118 ABOUT
25 ABOVE
3 ABRIDGE
12 ABROAD
6 ABSENCE
6 ABSENT
6 ABUSE
4 ABUSES
5 ACCEPT
4 ACCESSE
6 ACCOMPLISH
4 ACCORDING
4 ACCOUNT
20 ACCURSED
4 ACCURST
3 ACCUSDE
28 ACHATES
11 ACHILLES
4 ACRE
3 ACTEON
4 ACTION
3 ACTIONS
3 ACTS
7 AD
6 ADDE
3 ADDERS
3 ADDING
3 ADDRESSE
3 ADMIRAL
13 ADMIRALL
3 ADMIRALS
3 ADMIRE
3 ADMIRED
3 ADMIRES
3 ADMIRING
8 ADMIT
3 ADMITTED
4 ADONIS
3 ADORE
4 ADORNE
3 ADVANC'D
6 ADVANCE
7 ADVANTAGE
5 ADVAUNCE
4 ADVAUNST
3 ADVENTURE
3 ADVERSE
4 ADVISDE
4 ADVISE
143 AENEAS
3 AEOLUS
5 AFFECT
5 AFFECTION
7 AFFECTIONS
6 AFFLICT
5 AFFLICTIONS
4 AFFLICTS
5 AFFOORD
5 AFFOORDS
22 AFFRICA
3 AFFRICK
3 AFFRICKE
8 AFFRIGHT
10 AFFRIKE
43 AFTER
8 AGAIN
122 AGAINE
115 AGAINST
5 AGAMEMNON
3 AGAST
26 AGE
10 AGED
3 AGEN
3 AGENT
4 AGIDAS
5 AGOE
7 AGREE
3 AGYDAS
85 AH
3 A HUNTING
10 AID
16 AIDE
3 AIE
6 AIME
48 AIRE
3 AJAX
3 AKE
43 AL
3 ALARUM
37 ALAS
11 ALBEIT
4 ALCARON
7 ALCIDES
14 ALEXANDER
8 ALEXANDRIA
7 ALIKE
16 ALIVE
729 ALL
3 ALLEGEANCE
11 ALMEDA
13 ALMOST
11 ALOFT
50 ALONE
18 ALONG
8 ALPES
9 ALREADY
5 ALSO
9 ALTAR
6 ALTARS
6 ALTER
20 ALTHOUGH
13 ALWAIES
6 ALWAYES
248 AM
12 AMAINE
4 AMASIA
3 AMAZ'D
3 AMAZED
4 AMBER
11 AMBITIOUS
4 AMBUSH
3 AMERICA
5 AMIDST
3 AMISSE
6 AMITIE
13 AMONG
22 AMONGST
17 AMOROUS
163 AN
6 ANCHOR
4 ANCHORS
8 ANCIENT
5478 AND
3 ANGELL
5 ANGELS
20 ANGER
3 ANGLE
10 ANGRIE
17 ANGRY
3 ANGUISH
3 ANIPPE
5 ANJOY
21 ANNA
4 ANNOY
11 ANON
3 ANONE
8 AN OTHER
25 ANOTHER
13 ANSWER
9 ANSWERE
5 ANSWERED
4 ANTIENT
115 ANY
8 ANY THING
3 AONIAN
5 APE
3 APES
5 APOLLO
3 APOLLOES
4 APOLLOS
6 APPEAR'D
13 APPEARE
5 APPEASE
4 APPLAUD
5 APPLES
3 APPLY
5 APPOINT
3 APPOINTED
3 APPROACH
11 APT
12 ARABIA
6 ARABIAN
4 ARABIANS
3 ARARIS
4 ARCH
495 ARE
11 ARGIER
5 ARGOSIE
3 ARGUES
6 ARGUMENT
4 ARISE
6 ARM'D
27 ARME
12 ARMED
3 ARMENIA
189 ARMES
14 ARMIE
8 ARMIES
5 ARMOR
15 ARMOUR
3 ARMS
20 ARMY
3 AROSE
3 ARREST
3 ARRIVALL
6 ARRIV'D
4 ARRIVDE
3 ARRIVE
5 ARROWES
152 ART
4 ARTE
3 ARTICK
8 ARTICLES
6 ARTS
8 ARUNDELL
4 ARUNS
1017 AS
23 ASCANIUS
8 ASCEND
3 ASHAM'D
5 ASHES
4 ASHORE
28 ASIA
14 ASIDE
31 ASKE
3 ASKES
3 ASKING
11 ASLEEPE
6 ASPECT
4 ASPHALTIS
4 ASPIRE
8 ASPIRING
7 ASSAILE
8 ASSAULT
7 ASSE
3 ASSIRIA
4 ASSIST
3 ASSURANCE
13 ASSURE
7 ASSURED
3 ASSWAGE
4 ASUNDER
429 AT
6 ATLAS
3 ATRIDES
3 ATTAIN'D
5 ATTAINE
12 ATTEMPT
3 ATTEMPTED
5 ATTEMPTS
15 ATTEND
3 ATTENDS
7 ATTIRE
3 AUGURES
4 AURORA
3 AUTHOR
5 AUTHORITY
5 AVAILE
7 AWAKE
207 AWAY
40 A WHILE
6 AXE
3 AXELTREE
3 AY
3 AYD
7 AYDE
19 AYE
23 AYRE
3 AZURE
13 BABYLON
10 BACCHUS
31 BACK
60 BACKE
3 BACKES
5 BACKWARD
13 BAD
4 BAGS
29 BAJAZETH
7 BALDOCK
4 BALDOCKE
4 BALL
3 BALLANCE
3 BALLES
9 BAND
3 BANDES
8 BANDS
4 BANEFULL
12 BANISH
6 BANISHT
5 BANKE
11 BANKES
4 BANKS
22 BANQUET
3 BANQUETS
79 BARABAS
19 BARBAROUS
6 BARBARY
3 BARD
16 BARE
5 BARKE
15 BARONS
5 BARRABAS
5 BARRE
9 BARTLEY
59 BASE
5 BASE BORNE
6 BASELY
3 BASEST
7 BASHAWES
4 BASSOE
7 BASSOES
10 BATTAILE
5 BATTAILES
6 BATTELL
3 BATTELLS
9 BATTER
3 BATTERED
4 BAY
3 BAYES
1205 BE
15 BEAMES
3 BEAMS
5 BEARD
89 BEARE
5 BEARER
18 BEARES
22 BEARING
8 BEAST
3 BEASTES
16 BEASTS
13 BEAT
6 BEATE
6 BEATEN
6 BEATES
4 BEATING
3 BEATS
7 BEAUTEOUS
18 BEAUTIE
6 BEAUTIES
6 BEAUTIFULL
4 BEAUTIOUS
22 BEAUTY
3 BECAME
51 BECAUSE
18 BECOME
8 BECOMES
49 BED
5 BEDS
25 BEE
14 BEEN
40 BEENE
7 BEERE
3 BEES
123 BEFORE
13 BEGAN
18 BEGIN
18 BEGINS
8 BE GON
10 BE GONE
3 BEGONE
3 BEGOTTEN
3 BEHAVIOUR
9 BEHELD
10 BEHIND
40 BEHOLD
7 BEHOLDE
4 BEHOLDING
4 BEHOOFE
136 BEING
9 BELCHER
16 BELEEVE

12 BELIKE
9 BELL
3 BELLAMIRA
6 BELLY
4 BELONGS
3 BELOV'D
5 BELOVED
3 BELOW
3 BELZEBUB
6 BEND
3 BENDING
3 BENDS
19 BENE
3 BENEFITE
10 BENT
11 BENVOLIO
3 BENVOLIO'S
3 BEQUEATH
3 BEREFT
7 BERNARDINE
8 BESEECH
7 BESEEMES
3 BESET
6 BESIDE
23 BESIDES
5 BESIEG'D
3 BESIEGE
46 BEST
3 BESTOW
4 BESTOWE
4 BESTOWED
3 BETIDE
3 BETIMES
6 BETRAIDE
4 BETRAIED
9 BETRAY
3 BETROTH'D
4 BETROTHED
47 BETTER
7 BETWEENE
18 BETWIXT
4 BEWAILE
4 BEWRAIES
4 BEWRAY
10 BEYOND
40 BID
11 BIDE
9 BIDS
3 BIG
9 BILLOWES
5 BILS
18 BIN
10 BIND
10 BINDE
7 BIRD
8 BIRDES
8 BIRDS
18 BIRTH
5 BISHOP
3 BIT
4 BITE
3 BITS
6 BITTER
12 BLACK
31 BLACKE
3 BLADES
14 BLAME
4 BLAST
5 BLASTED
3 BLASTS
10 LAZED
4 BLAZING
4 BLEEDING
6 BLEMISH
8 BLESSED
3 BLESSING
18 BLEST
4 BLEW
5 BLIND
4 BLINDE
13 BLISSE
3 BLOCKE
61 BLOOD
5 BLOODS
16 BLOODY
3 BLOT
83 BLOUD
5 BLOUDIE
3 BLOUDSHED
15 BLOUDY
12 BLOW
6 BLOWE
6 BLOWES
5 BLOWNE
12 BLUSH
4 BLUSHING
4 BLUSHT
3 BOARE
3 BOAST
3 BOASTING
10 BODIE
24 BODIES
64 BODY
7 BOIES
3 BOISTROUS
16 BOLD
4 BOLDLY
4 BONDAGE
15 BONES
4 BONUM
3 BOOK
31 BOOKE
13 BOOKES
3 BOOKS
6 BOORD
6 BOOTES
6 BORDERING
5 BORE
8 BOREAS
50 BORNE
18 BOSOME
160 BOTH
6 BOTTLE
3 BOUGH
11 BOUGHT
4 BOULD
20 BOUND
14 BOUNDS
9 BOW
13 BOWE
15 BOWELS
3 BOWER
3 BOWES
3 BOWLES
43 BOY
9 BOYE
14 BOYES
3 BRACELETS
4 BRAINE
14 BRAINES
3 BRAND
10 BRASSE
3 BRAT
42 BRAVE
11 BRAVELY
3 BRAVEST
5 BRAZEN
11 BREACH
3 BREAD
4 BREAK
31 BREAKE
8 BREAKES
3 BREAKING
22 BREAST
10 BREASTS
27 BREATH
3 BREATH'D
10 BREATHE
3 BREATHING
5 BREATHLESSE
6 BRED
5 BREED
3 BREEDE
3 BREEDS
27 BREST
3 BRESTS
11 BRETHREN
8 BRIDGE
8 BRIDLE
30 BRIGHT
4 BRIGHTER
97 BRING
4 BRINGES
6 BRINGING
14 BRINGS
4 BRISTOW
4 BROAD
4 BROAKE
9 BROILES
6 BROKE
13 BROKEN
3 BROOD
10 BROOKE
3 BROTH
71 BROTHER
19 BROTHERS
40 BROUGHT
4 BROW
21 BROWES
4 BROWNE
3 BROYLES
13 BRUNO
3 BRUNO'S
4 BRUNT
3 BRUTISH
11 BUILD
5 BUILDINGS
6 BUILT
8 BULL
3 BULLES
3 BULLET
7 BULLETS
3 BURBON
3 BURDEN
4 BURIALL
3 BURIED
20 BURNE
7 BURNES
25 BURNING
3 BURNISHT
16 BURNT
6 BURST
11 BURTHEN
3 BUSINES
4 BUSINESSE
3 BUSKINS
1105 BUT
3 BUTTONS
15 BUY
625 BY
6 BYRTH
5 BYTHINIA
24 CAESAR
12 CAESARS
3 CAGE
4 CAL
5 CAL'D
8 CALD
8 CALDE
65 CALL
10 CALLAPINE
4 CALL'D
6 CALLES
3 CALLING
3 CALLS
7 CALME
4 CALS
22 CALYMATH
63 CAME
3 CAMELS
8 CAMP
18 CAMPE
3 CAM'ST
3 CAMST
194 CAN
7 CANDLE
5 CANNON
8 CANNONS
91 CANNOT
35 CANST
12 CAPTAINE
12 CAPTAINES
23 CAPTIVE
4 CAPTIVES
3 CARCASES
3 CARDES
8 CARDINALL
10 CARDINALS
42 CARE
5 CAREFULL
8 CARELESSE
6 CARES
7 CARIE
7 CARKASSES
5 CAROLUS
3 CAROUSE
3 CARRE
4 CARRIE
5 CARRIED
5 CARRY
29 CARTHAGE
3 CARTHAGINIAN
15 CASANE
8 CASE
5 CASPIAN
52 CAST
5 CASTELL
9 CASTLE
8 CASTS
3 CATHOLICK
5 CAUSDE
72 CAUSE
3 CAUSERS
4 CAUSES
10 CAVE
18 CEASE
4 CEDAR
10 CELESTIALL
6 CENTER
10 CERES
4 CERTAINE
3 CERTIFIE
4 CHACE
3 CHAIND
3 CHAINE
18 CHAINES
15 CHAIRE
12 CHALLENGE
15 CHAMBER
4 CHAMBERLAINE
5 CHAMPION
12 CHANCE
9 CHANG'D
3 CHANGD
20 CHANGE
7 CHANNELL
4 CHANNELS
3 CHAOS
4 CHARACTERS
4 CHARDGE
51 CHARGE
19 CHARIOT
6 CHARIOTS
3 CHARITY
4 CHARLES
9 CHARME
4 CHARMED
11 CHARMES
9 CHASE
14 CHAST
10 CHASTE
6 CHASTITIE
9 CHAUNCE
3 CHAUNGD
5 CHAUNGE
6 CHEARE
23 CHEEKES
5 CHEEKS
10 CHEERE
6 CHERISH
7 CHIDE
11 CHIEFE
3 CHIEFELY
11 CHIEFEST
18 CHILD
6 CHILDE
7 CHILDISH
7 CHILDREN
3 CHOAKE
3 CHOKE
10 CHOOSE
25 CHRIST
9 CHRISTALL
6 CHRISTENDOME
35 CHRISTIAN
37 CHRISTIANS
16 CHURCH
8 CHURCHES
4 CHUSE
3 CIRCES
11 CIRCLE
4 CIRCLED
4 CIRCLES
3 CIRCUMFERENCE
4 CITADELL
23 CITIE
14 CITIES
7 CITIZENS
5 CITTIES
7 CITTY
12 CITY
3 CIVIL
13 CIVILL
10 CLAD
3 CLAIME
5 CLAP
3 CLAPS
13 CLEANE
10 CLEARE
7 CLEAVE
4 CLEERE
4 CLIME

4 DIRGE
6 DIS
4 DISCHARG'D
5 DISCHARGE
5 DISCIPLINE
6 DISCONTENT
3 DISCOURAGE
8 DISCOURSE
3 DISCOVERED
14 DISDAINE
3 DISDAINES
3 DISDAINFULL
3 DISGRAC'D
13 DISGRACE
6 DISH
8 DISHONOR
3 DISMALL
4 DISMAY
3 DISPAIRE
10 DISPATCH
3 DISPATCHT
7 DISPLAY
3 DISPLAYD
4 DISPLEAS'D
3 DISPOSE
3 DISPOSED
4 DISPUTE
14 DISSEMBLE
4 DISSEMBLING
4 DISSOLV'D
4 DISSOLVE
3 DISTEMPERED
12 DISTRESSE
9 DISTRESSED
3 DISTURBERS
9 DITCH
3 DITCHES
5 DIVE
9 DIVEL
13 DIVELL
11 DIVELS
3 DIVERS
4 DIVIDED
23 DIVINE
6 DIVINITIE
200 DO
54 DOCTOR
176 DOE
7 DOES
37 DOEST
10 DOG
6 DOGGE
5 DOGS
7 DOING
7 DOLLERS
5 DOLLORS
4 DOMINION
4 DOMINIONS
8 DOMINUS
18 DON
115 DONE
9 DOO
11 DOORE
7 DOORES
11 DOOST
16 DOOTH
9 DORE
12 DORES
20 DOST
5 DOTE
157 DOTH
6 DOUBLE
35 DOUBT
6 DOUBTFULL
6 DOUBTS
3 DOVE
5 DOVES
21 DOWN
130 DOWNE
3 DOWNEWARD
4 DOWNFALL
4 DRAGGE
8 DRAGONS
23 DRAW
4 DRAWE
7 DRAWEN
8 DRAWES
3 DRAWING
14 DRAWNE
7 DREAD
15 DREADFULL
6 DREAME
3 DRENCH
5 DRESSE
3 DREST
7 DREW
10 DRIE
5 DRIFT
7 DRINK
29 DRINKE
3 DRISLING
14 DRIVE
10 DRIVEN
7 DRIVES
7 DROOPE
4 DROOPING
11 DROP
3 DROPPING
10 DROPS
3 DROWN'D
3 DROWNE
4 DRUGS
5 DRUM
8 DRUMS
10 DRUNKE
4 DRUNKEN
5 DRY
4 DRYE
6 DUE
32 DUKE
8 DULL
5 DUMAINE
3 DUNGEON
15 DURST
7 DUST
11 DUTIE
3 DUTY
11 DWELL
7 DWELT
60 DYE
5 DYED
8 DYES
7 DYING
35 EACH
8 EAGLES
17 EARE
33 EARES
30 EARLE
8 EARLES
4 EARLY
4 EARNESTLY
142 EARTH
12 EARTHLY
3 EARTHS
19 EASE
4 EASIE
4 EASILIE
4 EASILY
28 EAST
5 EASTERNE
8 EAT
13 EATE
7 EATING
5 ECH
20 EDMUND
47 EDWARD
16 EDWARDS
3 EDWARDUM
8 EFFECT
3 EFFEMINATE
15 EGYPT
4 EGYPTIA
7 EGYPTIAN
4 EGYPTIANS
14 EIE
34 EIES
5 EIGHT
24 EITHER
3 ELDER
3 ELECT
3 ELECTED
3 ELEGIES
7 ELEMENT
9 ELEMENTS
3 ELISIAN
3 ELOQUENT
21 ELS
35 ELSE
43 'EM
5 EMBRACE
11 EMPERESSE
8 EMPERIALL
7 EMPERIE
4 EMPEROR
61 EMPEROUR
14 EMPEROURS
4 EMPERY
8 EMPIRE
3 EMPLOY
8 EMPRESSE
10 EMPTIE
6 EMPTY
4 ENAMOURED
5 ENCHAC'D
6 ENCOUNTER
61 END
5 ENDED
3 ENDLES
7 ENDLESSE
13 ENDS
12 ENDURE
3 ENEAS
7 ENEMIE
26 ENEMIES
8 ENEMY
4 ENFORCE
3 ENFORST
3 ENGINES
3 ENGINS
3 ENGIRT
25 ENGLAND
23 ENGLANDS
6 ENGLISH
12 ENJOY
3 ENMITIE
49 ENOUGH
3 ENOW
3 ENRAG'D
4 ENSIGNE
8 ENSIGNES
3 ENTEND
18 ENTER
7 ENTERPRISE
5 ENTERTAIN'D
21 ENTERTAINE
5 ENTRANCE
7 ENTREATE
5 ENTRED
4 ENTRY
5 ENVIE
3 ENVIED
10 ENVIOUS
3 ENVIRONED
6 ENVY
14 EPERNOUNE
3 EPEUS
14 EQUALL
3 EQUALLIE
6 EQUALLY
18 E'RE
81 ERE
3 EREBUS
3 ERECTED
8 ERRE
7 ERST
12 ESCAPE
6 ESCAPT
3 ESSENCE
8 EST
9 ESTATE
6 ESTEEM'D
9 ESTEEME
10 ET
7 &C.
24 ETERNALL
3 ETERNALLY
4 EUPHRATES
15 EUROPE
69 EVEN
6 EVENING
107 EVER
4 EVER-BURNING
18 EVERIE
4 EVERLASTING
7 EVERMORE
95 EVERY
5 EVERY WHERE
4 EVILL
3 EVILS
3 EXAMPLE
8 EXCEED
4 EXCEEDING
3 EXCEEDS
3 EXCELL
5 EXCELLENCE
8 EXCELLENT
3 EXCELLING
6 EXCEPT
5 EXCLAIME
6 EXCUSE
4 EXECUTE
6 EXECUTION
3 EXEQUIES
6 EXERCISE
9 EXILE
5 EXPECT
5 EXPEDITION
4 EXPELL
4 EXPERIENCE
3 EXPLOITS
6 EXPRESSE
3 EXTREAME
3 EXTREAMES
5 EXTREME
32 EYE
80 EYES
69 FACE
6 FACES
8 FAILE
3 FAILES
9 FAINE
16 FAINT
7 FAINTING
181 FAIRE
6 FAIRER
7 FAIREST
5 'FAITH
47 FAITH
8 FAITHFULL
3 FAITHS
6 FAL
71 FALL
6 FALLES
5 FALLING
4 FALNE
6 FALS
35 FALSE
3 FALSELY
32 FAME
6 FAMILIAR
3 FAMINE
20 FAMOUS
9 FANCIE
3 FANCIES
6 FANNE
26 FAR
10 FARE
12 FARES
6 FAREWEL
74 FAREWELL
59 FARRE
5 FARTHER
5 FARWELL
29 FAST
3 FAT
26 FATALL
15 FATE
17 FATES
109 FATHER
4 FATHER'S
53 FATHERS
16 FAULT
8 FAULTS
219 FAUSTUS
3 FAVOR
3 FAVORIT
5 FAVORS
30 FAVOUR
3 FAVOURED
10 FAVOURS
6 FAWNE
8 FEAR'D
7 FEARD
138 FEARE
10 FEAREFULL
3 FEARELESSE
9 FEARES
8 FEARFULL
10 FEARING
24 FEAST
3 FEASTED
3 FEATHERED
4 FEATHERS
12 FED
3 FEEBLE
16 FEED
7 FEEDE
3 FEEDES
5 FEEDS
24 FEELE
4 FEELES
3 FEELING

INDEX WORDS ORDERED ALPHABETICALLY

8 GUARDE
3 GUERDON
4 GUESSE
7 GUEST
13 GUIDE
4 GUIDES
3 GUILT
3 GUILTIE
3 GUILTLESSE
6 GUILTY
68 GUISE
8 GUISES
6 GUISIANS
6 GULFE
8 GURNEY
22 HA
242 HAD
14 HADST
3 HAILE
3 HAINOUS
29 HAIRE
19 HAIRES
10 HALE
39 HALFE
4 HALL
136 HAND
10 HANDES
3 HANDLE
5 HANDLED
101 HANDS
37 HANG
6 HANG'D
9 HANGING
4 HANGMAN
6 HANGS
6 HAP
3 HAPLES
7 HAPLESSE
4 HAPPEN
17 HAPPIE
7 HAPPILY
8 HAPPINESSE
28 HAPPY
3 HAPS
4 HARBOR
6 HARBOUR
50 HARD
12 HARDLY
4 HARKE
3 HARM'D
21 HARME
3 HARMEFULL
4 HARMELESSE
3 HARMES
4 HARMONY
11 HARPE
6 HARSH
35 HART
7 HARTS
3 HARVEST
48 HAS
124 HAST
19 HASTE
3 HASTEN
4 HAT
3 HATCHT
48 HATE
8 HATED
4 HATEFUL
22 HATEFULL
4 HATES
277 HATH
4 HATING
6 HAUGHTY
3 HAUNTED
3 HAUTIE
812 HAVE
4 HAVEN
45 HAVING
9 HAY
937 HE
124 HEAD
7 HEADED
3 HEADES
3 HEADLES
13 HEADLONG
42 HEADS
15 HEALTH
7 HEAPE
10 HEAPES
4 HEAPS
35 HEARD
99 HEARE
5 HEARES
7 HEARING
3 HEARKE
5 HEARSE
112 HEART
5 HEARTED
28 HEARTS
11 HEAT
9 HEATE
3 HEAV'D
3 HEAVE
202 HEAVEN
23 HEAVENLY
52 HEAVENS
6 HEAVIE
4 HEAV'N
12 HEAVY
3 HEBE
3 HEBREW
7 HECTOR
4 HECUBA
4 HEDGE
41 HEE
6 HEED
11 HEELE
12 HEELES
6 HEER
65 HEERE
6 HEERES
3 HEERS
3 HEE'S
8 HEES
6 HEIGHT
14 HEIRE
9 HEL
24 HELD
4 HELEN
3 HELENA
3 HELENS
112 HELL
7 HELLEN
7 HELLISH
4 HELME
13 HELP
35 HELPE
4 HELPES
3 HELPS
85 HENCE
5 HENCEFORTH
8 HENOLT
3 HENRIES
10 HENRY
707 HER
5 HERCULES
278 HERE
5 HEREAFTER
17 HERE'S
5 HERES
4 HERESIE
3 HERESIES
3 HERETICKS
10 HERMES
25 HERO
7 HEROES
5 HERS
19 HER SELFE
8 HE'S
9 HETHER
8 HEW
11 HEY
19 HID
5 HIDDEN
31 HIDE
6 HIDEOUS
6 HIDES
4 HIE
57 HIGH
14 HIGHER
14 HIGHEST
13 HIGHLY
28 HIGHNES
37 HIGHNESSE
11 HILL
3 HILLES
11 HILS
825 HIM
4 HIMSELF
52 HIMSELFE
3 HINDS
3 HINGES
8 HIR
4 HIRE
1320 HIS
5 HIT
13 HITHER
19 HO
4 HOARY
4 HOAST
3 HOIST
58 HOLD
13 HOLDE
3 HOLDES
12 HOLDS
18 HOLINESSE
4 HOLLA
13 HOLLOW
56 HOLY
4 HOMAGE
45 HOME
3 HOMELY
5 HOMER
8 HONEST
5 HONEY
63 HONOR
5 HONORABLE
23 HONORS
32 HONOUR
7 HONOURABLE
5 HONOURED
3 HONY
6 HOOD
90 HOPE
8 HOPES
6 HOPING
5 HORNED
31 HORNES
4 HORROR
76 HORSE
3 HORSE-COURSER
21 HORSES
7 HORSMEN
5 HOST
24 HOSTE
4 HOSTES
3 HOSTESSE
3 HOSTLER
15 HOT
5 HOTE
3 HOULD
3 HOUNDS
11 HOURE
5 HOURES
81 HOUSE
14 HOUSES
4 HOUSHOLD
8 HOVER
348 HOW
4 HOWE
5 HOWER
4 HOWLE
3 HOYST
3 HUE
19 HUGE
4 HUGONETS
7 HUMAINE
6 HUMANE
6 HUMBLE
5 HUMBLIE
16 HUMBLY
3 HUMILITIE
3 HUMOR
70 HUNDRED
9 HUNG
5 HUNGARY
4 HUNGER
3 HUNGRY
3 HUNT
5 HUNTERS
3 HUNTING
18 HURT
29 HUSBAND
11 HUSBANDS
3 HYMEN
5 I'
3011 I
37 IARBUS
3 IDA
3 IDAS
5 I'DE
3 IDE
13 IDLE
502 IF
7 IFAITH
113 I'LE
8 IL'E
205 ILE
4 ILES
4 ILIA
29 ILL
6 ILLIONEUS
5 IMAGE
5 IMAGINE
7 IMBRACE
4 IMBRAST
4 IMMEDIATLY
18 IMMORTALL
5 IMPATIENT
11 IMPERIALL
4 IMPERIOUS
3 IMPIOUS
5 IMPORT
4 IMPORTS
1908 IN
6 INCENSE
7 INCENST
4 INCLINDE
4 INCLOSE
4 INCONSTANT
7 INCOUNTER
11 INCREASE
4 INDE
8 INDEED
11 INDIA
6 INDIAN
3 INDIFFERENTLY
3 INDURE
5 INFAMIE
4 INFAMOUS
3 INFANTS
4 INFECT
3 INFERIOUR
13 INFERNALL
4 INFIDELS
6 INFINITE
3 INFLAMES
5 INFLICT
9 INFLUENCE
3 INFORME
3 INHABITED
4 INHERIT
3 INJOY
5 INJURE
3 INJURIES
7 INJURIOUS
6 INJURY
3 INKE
5 INNOCENT
3 INOUGH
3 INSOLENCE
3 INSTANT
5 IN STEAD
3 IN STEED
3 INSTRUCT
3 INSTRUCTIONS
3 INSTRUMENT
4 INSTRUMENTS
9 INTEND
5 INTENDING
4 INTENDS
5 INTENT
3 INTERCEPT
3 INTEREST
3 INTERR'D
147 INTO
21 INTREAT
5 INTREATE
3 INTREATED
4 INTRENCH
3 INVADE
3 INVENT
4 INVENTED
5 INVEST
4 INVESTED
4 INVINCIBLE
3 INVIRON'D
5 INVISIBLE
8 INWARD
7 IO
4 IRE
7 IRELAND
7 IRON
4 IRONS
1063 IS
25 ISABELL
4 ISLES
19 ISSUE
8 IS'T
13 IST
862 IT

INDEX WORDS ORDERED ALPHABETICALLY

4 ITALIAN
28 ITALY
4 I'TH
29 ITHIMORE
9 IT SELFE
3 IULUS
3 IVORIE
5 IVORY
5 JACOMO
9 JADES
3 JANUARY
6 JARRE
4 JASON
8 JAWES
7 JEALOUS
4 JEALOUSIE
7 JERUSALEM
6 JEST
4 JESTING
53 JEW
5 JEWELL
17 JEWELS
24 JEWES
12 JOHN
4 JOIES
4 JOIN'D
12 JOINE
3 JOINTES
3 JOINTS
7 JOURNEY
80 JOVE
20 JOVES
33 JOY
16 JOYES
3 JOYEUX
4 JOYFULL
3 JOYN'D
11 JOYNE
4 JOYNTLY
3 JOYNTS
14 JUDGE
4 JUDGEMENT
4 JULIUS
13 JUNO
3 JUNOES
3 JUNOS
14 JUPITER
24 JUST
6 JUSTICE
4 JUSTLY
23 KEEP
60 KEEPE
8 KEEPER
4 KEEPERS
12 KEEPES
5 KEEPING
8 KENT
28 KEPT
3 KEY
3 KEYES
5 KILD
31 KILL
5 KILLING
8 KILLINGWORTH
14 KIND
15 KINDE
6 KINDLED
6 KINDLY
383 KING
3 KINGDOM
15 KINGDOME
19 KINGDOMES
3 KINGDOMS
4 KINGES
4 KINGLIE
22 KINGLY
106 KINGS
3 KINSMANS
3 KIS
39 KISSE
10 KISSES
10 KIST
5 KNAVE
5 KNEE
9 KNEELE
14 KNEES
3 KNELL
28 KNEW
5 KNEWE
6 KNIFE
10 KNIGHT
7 KNIGHTS
6 KNIT
3 KNOCKE
3 KNOCKS
188 KNOW
8 KNOWE
28 KNOWES
10 KNOWEST
8 KNOWING
5 KNOWLEDGE
4 KNOWN
20 KNOWNE
3 KNOWS
5 KNOW'ST
6 LA
18 LABOUR
7 LABOURING
5 LABOURS
5 LACKE
6 LADEN
6 LADIES
16 LADY
5 LAID
5 LAIDE
4 LAIES
4 LAINE
16 LAKE
4 LAKES
9 LAMENT
4 LAMENTS
3 LAMP
8 LAMPS
32 LANCASTER
9 LANCE
7 LANCES
3 LANCH
66 LAND
8 LANDS
3 LANGUISH
13 LAP
4 LAPPE
20 LARGE
5 LARISSA
5 LASCIVIOUS
52 LAST
3 LASTING
4 LASTS
50 LATE
12 LATELY
9 LATEST
7 LAUGH
3 LAUGH'D
4 LAUGHING
3 LAUGHS
5 LAUNCHT
5 LAVISH
16 LAW
3 LAWE
18 LAWES
10 LAWFULL
4 LAWLESSE
4 LAWNE
45 LAY
5 LAYD
4 LAYED
6 LE
24 LEAD
8 LEADE
3 LEADEN
3 LEADER
4 LEADING
4 LEADS
23 LEAGUE
4 LEAGUES
25 LEANDER
6 LEANDERS
8 LEANE
6 LEAPE
3 LEAPES
7 LEAPT
3 LEARN'D
3 LEARND
18 LEARNE
14 LEARNED
59 LEAST
141 LEAVE
24 LEAVES
7 LEAVING
3 LEAV'ST
4 LEAVY
13 LED
60 LEFT
11 LEG
4 LEGATE
8 LEGGE
6 LEGGES
5 LEGIONS
5 LEGS
3 LEICESTER
6 LEISTER
6 LEND
8 LENGTH
25 LESSE
12 LEST
497 LET
23 LET'S
33 LETS
18 LETTER
19 LETTERS
3 LEUCA
3 LEVELD
3 LEVELL
8 LEVIE
8 LEVUNE
4 LEWD
8 LEWNE
4 LIBERALL
5 LIBERTIE
3 LIBERTIES
8 LIBERTY
6 LIBIA
6 LIBIAN
5 LIDS
46 LIE
3 LIEGE
30 LIES
197 LIFE
12 LIFT
59 LIGHT
3 LIGHTENING
11 LIGHTNING
274 LIKE
3 LIKENESSE
10 LIKES
9 LIKEWISE
3 LIK'ST
4 LIMBES
3 LIMBS
3 LIMITS
5 LIMMES
7 LIMS
19 LINE
20 LINES
4 LINGER
3 LINGERING
3 LINKE
5 LIONS
5 LIPPES
19 LIPS
7 LIQUID
11 LIST
11 LITLE
48 LITTLE
10 LIV'D
169 LIVE
5 LIVED
8 LIVELY
5 LIVER
72 LIVES
3 LIVEST
10 LIVING
4 LOAD
6 LOADE
9 LOATH
8 LOATHSOME
3 LOCK
3 LOCKE
11 LOCKES
5 LOCKS
5 LOCKT
3 LODEN
5 LODGE
25 LODOWICKE
11 LOE
9 LOFTIE
16 LOFTY
137 LONG
13 LONGER
6 LONGING
18 LOOK
10 LOOK'D
100 LOOKE
65 LOOKES
15 LOOKING
19 LOOKS
3 LOOK'ST
23 LOOSE
4 LORAINE
510 LORD
18 LORDE
4 LORDES
4 LORDLY
100 LORDS
8 LORDSHIP
3 LOREINE
12 LOSE
20 LOSSE
31 LOST
3 LOT
3 LOTH
3 LOTHSOME
22 LOV'D
3 LOVDE
421 LOVE
5 LOVED
3 LOVELIEST
25 LOVELY
17 LOVER
34 LOVERS
65 LOVES
5 LOVEST
28 LOVING
8 LOW
3 LOWE
3 LOWLY
33 LUCIFER
3 LUKE
3 LUKE-WARME
3 LURKE
7 LUST
4 LUSTFULL
8 LUSTIE
4 LUSTY
3 LUTE
21 LYE
8 LYES
6 LYING
3 LYON
3 LYONS
4 MACE
12 MAD
73 MADAM
11 MADAME
3 MADDAM
192 MADE
5 MAD'ST
6 MAGICK
14 MAGICKE
37 MAHOMET
8 MAID
17 MAIDE
4 MAIDEN
5 MAIDENS
8 MAIDES
5 MAIDS
8 MAIEST
3 MAIMED
10 MAINE
11 MAINTAINE
11 MAIST
41 MAISTER
8 MAISTERS
44 MAJESTIE
57 MAJESTY
3 MAJOR
304 MAKE
63 MAKES
18 MAKING
3 MALE
8 MALEDICAT
6 MALICE
48 MALTA
6 MALTA'S
178 MAN
10 MANAGE
4 MANGLED
9 MANLY
5 MANNAGE
7 MANNER
9 MANS
94 MANY
3 MAP
7 MARBLE
27 MARCH
4 MARCHE
6 MARCHING
5 MARCHT
4 MARE
12 MARIAGE
14 MARKE
4 MARKES

INDEX WORDS ORDERED ALPHABETICALLY

4 MARKET
4 MARKT
6 MARRIAGE
12 MARRY
26 MARS
3 MARSHALL
23 MARTCH
6 MARTCHT
3 MARTIAL
20 MARTIALL
4 MARVELL
4 MASKE
4 MASKES
9 MASSACRE
4 MASSACRED
5 MASSE
4 MASSIE
5 MASSY
38 MASTER
4 MASTS
10 MATCH
5 MATE
5 MATES
31 MATHIAS
9 MATREVIS
19 MATTER
6 MATTERS
403 MAY
1384 ME
4 MEAN
12 MEANDER
78 MEANE
65 MEANES
7 MEANE TIME
4 MEANE WHILE
16 MEANING
11 MEANS
4 MEANST
12 MEANT
8 MEASURE
7 MEAT
14 MEATE
3 MEDDLE
4 MEDEA
3 MEDEAN
4 MEDITATE
3 MEDITERRANEAN
25 MEE
4 MEERE
44 MEET
23 MEETE
5 MEETING
3 MELODIOUS
7 MELT
3 MEMBERS
6 MEMORIE
4 MEMPHIS
225 MEN
5 MENACE
8 MENAPHON
4 MEN AT ARMES
17 MENS
12 MEPHASTOPHILIS
46 MEPHOSTOPHILIS
3 MERCHANDIZE
4 MERCHANT
7 MERCHANTS
13 MERCIE
4 MERCURIE
5 MERCURY
11 MERCY
3 MERIT
4 MERITS
3 MERRIE
4 MERRIMENT
7 MESSAGE
15 MESSENGER
15 MET
3 METEOR
7 METEORS
15 ME THINKES
10 ME THINKS
8 MID
3 MIDDLE
8 MIDNIGHT
19 MIDST
145 MIGHT
26 MIGHTIE
6 MIGHTST
48 MIGHTY
4 MIHI
8 MILDE
3 MILES
7 MILK
5 MILKE
5 MILK-WHITE
7 MILLIONS
29 MIND
52 MINDE
3 MINDED
13 MINDES
11 MINDS
164 MINE
3 MINERALS
3 MINERVA
4 MINES
4 MINGLE
4 MINGLED
9 MINION
8 MINIONS
3 MINUTE
3 MIRMIDONS
3 MIRTH
5 MIRTLE
6 MISCHIEFE
14 MISERABLE
8 MISERIE
7 MISERY
3 MISFORTUNE
4 MISSE
5 MIST
14 MISTRESSE
28 MISTRIS
9 MISTRISSE
4 MISTRUST
5 MIXT
3 MOANE
3 MOCKE
3 MOCKT
6 MODEST
4 MOIST
4 MOISTURE
3 MOLD
7 MONARCH
4 MONARCHIE
5 MONARKE
6 MONEY
10 MONSTER
11 MONSTROUS
7 MONTH
3 MONUMENTS
25 MONY
18 MOONE
4 MOORE
11 MOORES
4 MOORNE
7 MOOV'D
5 MOOVE
3 MOOVED
5 MOOVES
3 MOOVING
3 MOR
335 MORE
9 MORNE
18 MORNING
3 MORNINGS
4 MOROCUS
9 MORROW
8 MORTALL
4 MORTIFIED
103 MORTIMER
8 MORTIMERS
64 MOST
62 MOTHER
13 MOTHERS
10 MOTION
5 MOTIONS
5 MOULD
4 MOUNSER
4 MOUNSIER
26 MOUNT
4 MOUNTAINE
9 MOUNTAINES
3 MOUNTAINS
12 MOUNTED
7 MOUNTS
3 MOUNTSORRELL
6 MOURNE
5 MOURNING
4 MOUSE
14 MOUTH
6 MOUTHES
16 MOV'D
32 MOVE
5 MOVED
3 MOVES
3 MOVING
141 MUCH
3 MULES
3 MULTIPLY
6 MULTITUDE
4 MULTITUDES
21 MURDER
4 MURDER'D
8 MURDERED
5 MURDERER
3 MURDERS
3 MURMURE
12 MURTHER
7 MURTHERED
5 MURTHERER
5 MURTHERING
13 MUSE
9 MUSES
14 MUSICKE
238 MUST
4 MUSTER
3 MUSTERED
5 MUTE
5 MUTTON
6 MUTUALL
2506 MY
3 MYRACLE
77 MY SELFE
32 NAKED
4 NAM'D
106 NAME
11 NAMES
4 NARROW
4 NATION
5 NATIONS
10 NATIVE
3 NATIVITY
19 NATOLIA
4 NATURALL
26 NATURE
9 NATURES
23 NAVARRE
83 NAY
4 NAYLES
11 NEARE
5 NECESSARY
4 NECESSITIE
4 NECESSITY
9 NECK
24 NECKE
4 NECKES
4 NECTAR
3 NEECE
18 NEED
8 NEEDE
5 NEEDES
16 NEEDS
3 NEEDST
5 NEER
29 NEERE
5 NEIGHBOR
3 NEIGHBOUR
37 NEITHER
3 NEMESIS
8 NEPHEW
9 NEPTUNE
8 NEPTUNES
17 NE'RE
34 NERE
4 NET
169 NEVER
41 NEW
40 NEWES
3 NEWLY
21 NEXT
4 NIGH
94 NIGHT
21 NIGHTS
8 NILE
4 NILUS
3 NIMBLE
5 NIMPH
6 NIMPHES
3 NIMPHS
4 NINE
531 NO
8 NOBILITIE
3 NOBIS
48 NOBLE
11 NOBLES
3 NOBLY
3 NO BODY
6 NOISE
3 NOLITE
3 NON
84 NONE
224 NOR
10 NORTH
5 NORTHREN
3 NOSE
1223 NOT
7 NOTE
4 NOTES
65 NOTHING
23 NOUGHT
3 NOVICE
680 NOW
3 NOWE
3 NO WHERE
4 NOYSE
13 NUMBER
7 NUMBERS
4 NUMBRED
8 NUN
3 NUNC
6 NUNNE
10 NUNNERY
3 NUNNES
17 NUNS
3 NUPTIALL
5 NURSE
4 NYMPHS
303 O
3 OAKE
10 OARES
7 OATH
4 OBEDIENCE
3 OBEDIENT
5 OBEY
4 OBJECT
4 OBJECTS
11 OBSCURE
8 OBTAINE
4 OCCASION
3 OCCIDERE
20 OCEAN
3 ODDES
3 ODIOUS
3022 OF
55 OFF
10 OFFENCE
10 OFFEND
10 OFFENDED
24 OFFER
5 OFFERED
3 OFFERING
3 OFFERS
4 OFFICERS
3 OFFRED
3 OFF-SPRING
60 OFT
15 OFTEN
91 OH
50 OLD
10 OLDE
6 OLYMPIA
505 ON
61 ONCE
232 ONE
44 ONELY
5 ONES
18 ONLY
3 ON'S
6 ON'T
13 OPE
29 OPEN
3 OPENED
3 OPENING
4 OPPORTUNITY
3 OPPOSE
523 OR
5 ORACLES
3 ORATOR
4 ORBE
7 ORCANES
15 ORDER
8 ORDINANCE
5 O'RE
17 ORE
7 ORIENT
3 ORIENTALL
3 ORIONS
3 ORLEANCE
3 ORTIGIUS
96 OTHER
34 OTHERS

6 OTHERWISE
3 OTHES
3 OTTOMAN
20 OUGHT
638 OUR
8 OURS
18 OUR SELVES
181 OUT
5 OUTRAGIOUS
3 OUT-RUN
3 OUTWARD
52 OVER
12 OVERCOME
21 OVERTHROW
7 OWN
68 OWNE
5 OXEN
3 PACE
3 PACES
3 PACIFIE
3 PADUA
25 PAINE
17 PAINES
3 PAINFULL
8 PAINTED
22 PALE
11 PALLACE
5 PALLAS
4 PALME
4 PALTRY
3 PANTING
7 PAPALL
4 PAPER
3 PAPERS
10 PARAMOUR
3 PARCELL
39 PARDON
4 PARENTAGE
11 PARENTS
20 PARIS
5 PARLE
3 PARLEMENT
3 PARLIE
4 PARRAT
56 PART
3 PARTAKE
4 PARTED
3 PARTHIA
4 PARTIALL
8 PARTS
16 PASSAGE
34 PASSE
4 PASSETH
6 PASSING
4 PASSION
6 PASSIONATE
7 PASSIONS
31 PAST
3 PATE
3 PATH
7 PATIENCE
10 PATIENT
5 PATIENTLY
5 PAWES
30 PAY
3 PAYD
53 PEACE
3 PEALE
22 PEARLE
6 PEASANT
3 PEECE
3 PEECEMEALE
6 PEECES
22 PEERES
3 PELFE
7 PEN
3 PENANCE
12 PENBROOKE
3 PENBROOKES
3 PENCE
5 PENELOPE
3 PENSIVE
30 PEOPLE
4 PEOPLES
6 PER
15 PERCEIVE
4 PERFECT
5 PERFORM'D
3 PERFORMD
21 PERFORME
4 PERFOURME
3 PERFUME
10 PERHAPS
5 PERIOD
23 PERISH
3 PERJUR'D
4 PERJURD
5 PERJURIE
3 PERJURIES
3 PERJURY
7 PERPETUALL
33 PERSEA
25 PERSEAN
7 PERSEANS
8 PERSEPOLIS
3 PERSIAN
31 PERSON
7 PERSWADE
3 PERSWASIONS
3 PERUSE
5 PESANT
4 PESANTS
4 PETER
11 PETERS
3 PETTIE
5 PETTY
3 PHAETON
3 PHILIP
21 PHOEBUS
3 PHRIGIAN
5 PHYSICKE
5 PICTURE
3 PIECES
3 PIERC'D
24 PIERCE
6 PIKES
3 PILIA-BORZA
11 PINE
3 PIONERS
4 PIPE
3 PIRATS
4 PIRRHUS
3 PIT
6 PITCH
6 PITCHT
4 PITCHY
25 PITIE
4 PITIED
4 PITIFULL
9 PITTIE
13 PITTY
7 PITY
11 PLAC'D
79 PLACE
11 PLACES
15 PLAGUE
4 PLAGUES
3 PLAIES
13 PLAINE
3 PLAINELY
14 PLAINES
4 PLAINTS
10 PLANETS
4 PLANT
4 PLANTED
3 PLATE
31 PLAY
4 PLAYD
4 PLAYING
6 PLEAD
3 PLEADE
14 PLEASANT
5 PLEAS'D
9 PLEASDE
69 PLEASE
11 PLEASETH
5 PLEASING
38 PLEASURE
11 PLEASURES
9 PLEDGE
4 PLESHE
3 PLIANT
6 PLIGHT
7 PLOT
4 PLOUGH
3 PLOW
4 PLUCK
3 PLUME
8 PLUMES
5 POAST
14 POET
12 POETS
18 POINT
5 POINTED
3 POINTS
9 POISON
3 POISONED
7 POLAND
5 POLE
7 POLES
11 POLICIE
4 POLICY
4 POMP
22 POMPE
7 POMPEY
6 POOLES
82 POORE
34 POPE
4 POPES
5 PORT
6 POSSESSE
7 POSSESSION
3 POSSEST
7 POST
5 POT
4 POTENTATE
6 POURE
6 POVERTY
5 POWDER
89 POWER
4 POWERFULL
21 POWERS
5 POWRE
13 POYSON
9 POYSON'D
8 POYSONED
6 PRACTISE
8 PRAIERS
18 PRAISE
84 PRAY
9 PRAYERS
4 PREACH
8 PRECIOUS
3 PREFERD
3 PRELATES
8 PREPAR'D
15 PREPARE
3 PRESAGE
3 PRESAGES
20 PRESENCE
34 PRESENT
3 PRESENTLIE
43 PRESENTLY
5 PRESENTS
6 PRESERVE
5 PRESIDENT
5 PRESSE
9 PREST
8 PRESUME
6 PRESUMPTION
4 PRETHE
7 PRETHEE
5 PRETIE
6 PRETIOUS
6 PRETTY
9 PREVAILE
4 PREVENT
3 PREVENTED
7 PRIAM
5 PRIAMS
9 PRIAMUS
14 PRICE
44 PRIDE
10 PRIEST
11 PRIESTS
39 PRINCE
34 PRINCELY
10 PRINCES
13 PRISON
12 PRISONER
8 PRIVATE
4 PRIVIE
4 PRIVILEDGE
7 PRIVY
3 PRIVY CHAMBER
8 PRIZE
3 PROCEED
7 PROCURE
11 PROFESSION
5 PROFIT
3 PROMETHEUS
4 PROMIS'D
16 PROMISE
3 PROMISED
4 PROMISES
4 PROMIST
3 PRONE
12 PROOFE
16 PROOVE
9 PROPER
3 PROPHET
6 PROSPER
7 PROSPEROUS
3 PROSTRATE
4 PROTECT
5 PROTECTOR
6 PROTEST
7 PROTESTANTS
5 PROTEUS
63 PROUD
4 PROUDEST
3 PROUDLY
3 PROV'D
18 PROVE
3 PROVERB
7 PROVIDE
5 PROVIDED
10 PROVINCES
3 PROVISION
3 PROVOKE
4 PROWD
3 PROWESSE
4 PUISANT
3 PUISSANT
6 PULD
24 PULL
4 PULS
5 PUNISH
6 PUNISHMENT
4 PUNISHT
7 PURCHASE
13 PURE
3 PUREST
3 PURG'D
5 PURGE
16 PURPLE
12 PURPOSE
5 PURSE
3 PURSU'D
11 PURSUE
54 PUT
3 PYN'D
3 QUAIL'D
11 QUAKE
4 QUAM
6 QUARRELL
6 QUARTERS
7 QUEEN
92 QUEENE
4 QUEENS
7 QUENCH
13 QUESTION
6 QUESTIONS
7 QUICK
3 QUICKE
6 QUICKLIE
20 QUICKLY
17 QUIET
4 QUILL
6 QUIT
11 QUITE
5 QUITTANCE
12 QUIVER
9 QUIVERING
3 QUOD
10 RACE
4 RADGE
6 RADIANT
9 RAFE
23 RAGE
9 RAGING
4 RAIGN'D
22 RAIGNE
3 RAILE
4 RAINE
4 RAINES
3 RAISDE
27 RAISE
3 RAMS
8 RAMUS
9 RAN
16 RANSOME
5 RAPE
4 RAPINE
3 RAPT
10 RARE
3 RASH
3 RASHLY
36 RATHER
3 RATLING
3 RAVISHT
6 RAW

INDEX WORDS ORDERED ALPHABETICALLY

3 RAWE
5 RAYMOND
9 REACH
19 READ
10 READE
4 READIE
4 READINESSE
5 READING
22 READY
34 REALME
5 REAPE
3 REARE
15 REASON
5 REASONS
3 REBELL
5 REBELLIOUS
12 REBELS
5 RECEIV'D
33 RECEIVE
7 RECOMPENCE
6 RECORD
3 RECOVERY
17 RED
4 REDUCE
3 REFUSDE
6 REFUSE
4 REGARD
3 REGARDING
5 REGENT
5 REGIMENT
8 REGION
5 REGIONS
3 REGISTER
4 REINES
5 REJOYCE
4 RELEASE
6 RELENT
3 RELENTING
3 RELIEFE
17 RELIGION
7 RELIGIOUS
25 REMAINE
15 REMAINES
3 REMEDY
36 REMEMBER
4 REMEMBRANCE
3 REMOOV'D
7 REMOOVE
3 REMOOVED
4 REMORSE
3 REMOVE
8 REND
3 RENDER
4 RENEW
13 RENOWMED
9 RENOWNE
16 RENT
3 RENTS
9 REPAIRE
4 REPEALD
3 REPEALE
18 REPENT
3 REPENTANCE
12 REPORT
3 REPORTS
4 REPOSE
3 REPULSE
19 REQUEST
5 REQUIRE
3 REQUIRES
5 REQUISITE
6 REQUITE
3 REQUITED
9 RESCUE
4 RESEMBLE
3 RESIDENCE
11 RESIGNE
6 RESIST
21 RESOLUTE
7 RESOLUTION
18 RESOLV'D
13 RESOLVE
4 RESOLVED
3 RESOUND
9 RESPECT
104 REST
3 RESTED
4 RESTETH
4 RESTLES
5 RESTORE
12 RESTS
6 RETAINE
3 RETES
6 RETIRE
4 RETREAT
5 RETURND
39 RETURNE
4 REVEAL'D
14 REVENG'D
3 REVENGD
5 REVENGDE
44 REVENGE
6 REVERENCE
5 REVEREND
3 REVIVES
5 REVOLT
13 REWARD
4 RHENE
6 RHODE
4 RHODES
5 RICE
50 RICH
11 RICHES
5 RICHEST
3 RICHLY
18 RID
33 RIDE
4 RIDING
58 RIGHT
17 RING
5 RINGS
4 RIP
7 RIPE
27 RISE
5 RISING
16 RITES
4 RIVALL
15 RIVER
4 RIVERS
5 ROARING
10 ROB
5 ROBE
16 ROBES
11 ROBIN
11 ROCKE
14 ROCKES
8 ROCKS
4 RODE
4 ROGUE
5 ROMAINE
3 ROMAN
3 ROMANE
6 ROMANS
39 ROME
37 ROOME
9 ROOMES
14 ROSE
5 ROSES
4 ROSIE
15 ROUGH
22 ROUND
6 ROUSE
4 ROUT
4 ROY
7 ROYAL
43 ROYALL
15 RUDE
6 RUE
17 RUINE
3 RUINES
6 RUL'D
8 RULDE
25 RULE
12 RULES
28 RUN
3 RUNNAGATES
22 RUNNE
9 RUNNES
18 RUNNING
14 RUNS
3 RUSTIE
3 RUSTY
12 RUTH
3 RUTHFULL
5 RUTTERS
3 SABA
3 SABINE
3 SABINES
4 SABLE
6 SACKE
8 SACKT
29 SACRED
14 SACRIFICE
3 SACRIFICING
7 SACRIFIZE
34 SAD
3 SADLY
35 SAFE
3 SAFELY
7 SAFETIE
3 SAFETY
39 SAID
8 SAIES
3 SAIEST
28 SAILE
4 SAILERS
18 SAILES
14 SAINT
4 SAINTS
5 SAIST
15 SAITH
43 SAKE
5 SALE
11 SALUTE
3 SAMARCANDA
29 SAME
6 SAND
7 SANDS
3 SAT
7 SATISFIE
7 SATISFIED
7 SATURNE
3 SAUCE
4 SAVAGE
7 SAV'D
62 SAVE
4 SAVING
5 SAVIOUR
27 SAW
16 SAWE
158 SAY
6 SAYD
7 SAYES
11 SAYING
7 SCALE
8 SCAPE
5 SCAPES
3 SCARBOROUGH
9 SCARCE
3 SCARD
7 SCARLET
6 SCARSE
4 SCATTERED
10 SCEPTER
3 SCEPTERS
5 SCHOLLER
4 SCHOLLERS
3 SCHOOLES
5 SCORE
3 SCORN'D
22 SCORNE
4 SCORNES
3 SCOTLAND
5 SCOTS
21 SCOURGE
4 SCRIPTURES
3 SCROWLE
3 SCUM
9 SCYTHIA
15 SCYTHIAN
9 SCYTHIANS
5 SE
107 SEA
11 SEALE
4 SEALES
16 SEARCH
25 SEAS
13 SEAT
13 SEATE
5 SEATED
3 SEATS
4 SEAVEN
8 SEAZE
16 SECOND
18 SECRET
7 SECRETLY
7 SECRETS
9 SECURE
3 SECURITIE
373 SEE
5 SEED
5 SEEDES
42 SEEING
6 SEEK
37 SEEKE
14 SEEKES
4 SEEKING
9 SEEM'D
18 SEEME
9 SEEMES
38 SEENE
13 SEES
13 SEEST
5 SEIZ'D
3 SEIZE
8 SELF
190 SELFE
14 SELIM
6 SELIM-CALYMATH
13 SELL
30 SELVES
7 SENATE
5 SENCE
6 SENCELESSE
5 SENCES
71 SEND
3 SENDING
16 SENDS
65 SENT
4 SENTENCE
3 SEPULCHER
5 SEPULCHRE
6 SER
4 SERGESTUS
3 SERPENT
5 SERPENTS
14 SERVANT
12 SERVANTS
11 SERV'D
49 SERVE
3 SERVES
25 SERVICE
5 SERVILE
3 SERVITORS
8 SERVITUDE
3 SESSIONS
7 SESTOS
70 SET
5 SETTING
12 SEVEN
8 SEVERALL
3 SEVERE
3 SEX
4 SHADE
4 SHADES
7 SHADOW
4 SHADOWES
3 SHAFT
4 SHAFTS
18 SHAKE
3 SHAKEN
5 SHAKES
9 SHAKING
86 SHAL
16 SHALBE
722 SHALL
4 SHALLOW
111 SHALT
57 SHAME
16 SHAPE
11 SHAPES
12 SHARE
5 SHARES
3 SHARP
15 SHARPE
388 SHE
5 SHEATH
11 SHED
30 SHEE
4 SHEE'S
3 SHEES
5 SHEPHEARD
5 SHEPHEARDS
33 SHEW
3 SHEWE
4 SHEWED
6 SHIELD
21 SHINE
5 SHINES
13 SHINING
16 SHIP
3 SHIPPING
48 SHIPS
3 SHIPT
4 SHIPWRACKE
23 SHOARE
6 SHOLD
5 SHOOKE
5 SHOOT
3 SHOOTS
14 SHORE
3 SHORNE

12 SHORT
3 SHORTER
9 SHORTLY
23 SHOT
249 SHOULD
9 SHOULDER
10 SHOULDERS
21 SHOULDST
9 SHOW
3 SHOWE
4 SHOWER
9 SHOWERS
6 SHOWES
5 SHOWNE
3 SHROUD
7 SHUN
4 SHUNNE
16 SHUT
4 SI
3 SIC
3 SICHEUS
3 SICILY
3 SICK
13 SICKE
3 SICKNESSE
26 SIDE
7 SIDES
13 SIEGE
3 SIGH
3 SIGH'D
8 SIGHES
3 SIGHING
64 SIGHT
5 SIGHTS
12 SIGISMOND
7 SIGNE
13 SIGNES
9 SILENCE
12 SILENT
8 SILKE
4 SILKES
3 SILLIE
6 SILLY
22 SILVER
14 SIMPLE
3 SIMPLICITIE
5 SIN
74 SINCE
22 SING
4 SINGING
4 SINGLE
6 SINGS
7 SINKE
24 SINNE
10 SINNES
3 SINOWES
135 SIR
5 SIRE
6 SIRHA
46 SIRRA
16 SIRS
32 SISTER
10 SISTERS
58 SIT
7 SITH
19 SITS
8 SITTING
4 SIXE
8 SKIE
12 SKILL
6 SKIN
4 SKIPPING
3 SKORNE
6 SKY
3 SLACK
4 SLACKE
3 SLACKT
42 SLAINE
16 SLAUGHTER
8 SLAUGHTERED
39 SLAVE
3 SLAVERY
22 SLAVES
7 SLAVISH
11 SLAY
3 SLEEP
38 SLEEPE
5 SLEEPES
6 SLEEPING
16 SLENDER
8 SLEPT
10 SLEW
4 SLICE
5 SLIDE
3 SLIGHT
5 SLIP
4 SLIPT
7 SLOTH
3 SLOTHFULL
3 SLOWE
36 SMALL
6 SMART
3 SMELL
3 SMILDE
11 SMILE
8 SMILES
7 SMILING
6 SMOOTH
5 SNAKES
3 SNAKIE
6 SNATCHT
4 SNOW
3 SNOWE
6 SNOWY
770 SO
4 SOARE
11 SODAINE
7 SODAINLY
4 SOEVER
23 SOFT
3 SOFTLY
6 SOLD
4 SOLDIER
3 SOLDIERS
4 SOLDIOURS
12 SOLE
10 SOLEMNE
4 SOLEMNIZE
3 SOLEMNLY
3 SOLITARIE
3 SOLITARY
197 SOME
13 SOMETHING
6 SOMETIME
4 SOME-TIMES
5 SOMETIMES
5 SOMEWHAT
7 SON
5 SONG
3 SONGS
115 SONNE
20 SONNES
8 SONS
44 SOONE
16 SOONER
4 SOOTH
10 SORE
5 SORIA
18 SORROW
3 SORROWE
7 SORROWES
17 SORT
11 SOUGHT
5 SOULDAN
6 SOULDANE
9 SOULDANS
9 SOULDIER
75 SOULDIERS
6 SOULDIOUR
7 SOULDIOURS
152 SOULE
42 SOULES
39 SOUND
4 SOUNDING
3 SOUNDS
8 SOUTH
6 SOUTHERNE
3 SOVERAIGN
31 SOVERAIGNE
4 SOVERAIGNES
3 SOYLE
8 SPACE
16 SPAINE
11 SPAKE
7 SPANGLED
6 SPANISH
25 SPARE
3 SPARING
3 SPARKES
13 SPEAK
116 SPEAKE
9 SPEAKES
5 SPEAKING
9 SPEARE
10 SPEARES
3 SPECIALLY
3 SPECTACLE
4 SPED
22 SPEECH
14 SPEECHES
12 SPEED
3 SPEEDE
6 SPELS
36 SPENCER
6 SPENCERS
9 SPEND
3 SPENDS
22 SPENT
6 SPHEARE
11 SPHEARES
3 SPHERE
3 SPICE
4 SPIE
6 SPIGHT
3 SPILT
26 SPIRIT
3 SPIRITES
27 SPIRITS
4 SPIT
12 SPITE
20 SPOILE
9 SPOILES
9 SPOKE
19 SPORT
4 SPORTS
4 SPOTLESSE
4 SPOYLE
20 SPREAD
4 SPREADING
6 SPRED
13 SPRING
10 SPRINGS
7 SPRONG
5 SPRUNG
3 SPY
3 SPYING
9 STAB
5 STABLE
6 STAFFE
4 STAID
3 STAIES
3 STAIEST
3 STAIN'D
6 STAINE
77 STAND
9 STANDARD
3 STANDARD BEARER
5 STANDING
3 STANDINGS
26 STANDS
6 STAR
3 STARING
10 STARRE
29 STARRES
19 STARS
3 START
4 STARTED
3 STARVE
46 STATE
18 STATELY
3 STATES
4 STATUE
4 STATURE
3 STATUTES
6 STAVES
3 STAVES ACRE
152 STAY
6 STAYD
7 STAYES
3 STAYING
8 STEAD
16 STEALE
3 STEALING
6 STEED
6 STEEDES
10 STEEDS
11 STEELE
3 STEELED
4 STEEPE
4 STEP
11 STEPS
14 STERNE
4 STIFFE
13 STIL
4 STILE
72 STILL
7 STIR
3 STIRRE
6 STOCKE
10 STOLE
7 STOLNE
3 STOMACK
4 STOMACKE
18 STONE
16 STONES
3 STONY
19 STOOD
5 STOOLE
11 STOOPE
7 STOP
3 STOPS
21 STORE
13 STORME
3 STORMES
3 STORMIE
12 STOUT
3 STOUTE
3 STRAGLING
39 STRAIGHT
5 STRAIT
3 STRAITE
17 STRANGE
4 STRANGELY
8 STRANGER
8 STRANGERS
5 STRANGLE
4 STRANGLED
4 STRATAGEM
4 STRATAGEMS
3 STREAM
19 STREAME
3 STREAMERS
12 STREAMES
5 STREET
13 STREETES
6 STREETS
7 STREIGHT
30 STRENGTH
4 STRENGTHEN
3 STRETCH
4 STRIFE
33 STRIKE
7 STRIKES
3 STRIKING
3 STRIV'D
18 STRIVE
4 STRIVES
6 STRIVING
9 STROKE
4 STROKES
33 STRONG
3 STRONGER
5 STRONGEST
3 STRONGLY
12 STROOKE
3 STROOKEN
6 STROVE
4 STROWED
6 STRUMPET
3 STUDENTS
5 STUDY
3 STUFT
3 STUMBLING
5 STURDY
3 STYGIAN
8 SUBDUE
4 SUBDUED
14 SUBJECT
10 SUBJECTS
5 SUBMISSION
3 SUBMIT
8 SUBSCRIBE
14 SUBSTANCE
4 SUBSTANTIALL
3 SUCCEEDING
11 SUCCESSE
3 SUCCESSION
3 SUCCOUR
293 SUCH
3 SUCKE
3 SUDDAINE
10 SUDDEN
7 SUDDENLY
9 SUE
20 SUFFER
3 SUFFERANCE
7 SUFFICE
8 SUFFICIENT
3 SUFFICIENTLY
4 SUIT
5 SUM
7 SUMME

6 SUMMER
3 SUMMERS
3 SUMMES
3 SUMMON
23 SUN
3 SUN-BRIGHT
3 SUNCKE
5 SUNDER
5 SUNDRY
21 SUNNE
5 SUNNES
3 SUN-SHINE
3 SUPERSTITIOUS
7 SUPPER
4 SUPPLIES
6 SUPPLY
5 SUPPOSE
6 SUPPREST
3 SURCEASE
36 SURE
3 SURELY
5 SURFET
6 SURGEON
6 SURPRIZE
3 SURVIVE
4 SURVIVES
13 SUSPECT
5 SUSPECTED
4 SUSPITION
3 SUSPITIOUS
6 SUSTAINE
3 SUSTAINES
3 SUSTENANCE
3 SUTE
3 SWAINE
3 SWAINES
5 SWALLOW
3 SWALLOWED
3 SWANNE
4 SWANNES
6 SWARME
9 SWAY
34 SWEARE
3 SWEARES
5 SWEAT
133 SWEET
81 SWEETE
3 SWEETELY
3 SWEETES
5 SWEETEST
4 SWEETLY
9 SWELL
14 SWELLING
25 SWIFT
6 SWIFTER
5 SWIFTLY
9 SWIM
4 SWOLNE
81 SWORD
5 SWORDE
4 SWORDES
38 SWORDS
7 SWORE
17 SWORNE
4 SYRTES
19 T'
4 T
9 TABLE
5 TABLES
7 TACKLING
3 TAINTED
229 TAKE
15 TAKEN
12 TAKES
5 TAKING
15 TALE
6 TALES
3 TALEUS
4 TALK
35 TALKE
3 TALKES
14 TALL
47 TAMBURLAIN
136 TAMBURLAINE
14 TANE
3 TANTALUS
6 TARTARIAN
5 TARTARS
3 TASKE
3 TAST
11 TASTE
5 TASTED
9 TAUGHT
18 TEACH
16 TEARE
55 TEARES
3 TEARM'D
6 TEARMES
3 TEARMS
33 TECHELLES
7 TEETH
13 TEL
166 TELL
4 TELLING
3 TELS
3 TEMPEST
7 TEMPESTS
8 TEMPLE
12 TEMPLES
3 TEMPT
37 TEN
13 TENDER
4 TENEDOS
16 TENT
4 TENTES
17 TENTS
4 TERME
5 TERMES
6 TERRENE
3 TERROR
17 TERROUR
71 TH'
5 TH
105 THAN
7 THANK
20 THANKE
18 THANKES
11 THANKS
3 TH'ART
1892 THAT
21 THAT'S
21 THATS
5182 THE
4 TH'EARTH
3 THEBAN
4 THEBES
690 THEE
4 THEEFE
5 THEEVES
6 THEFT
3 THEILE
568 THEIR
382 THEM
31 THEMSELVES
664 THEN
29 THENCE
236 THERE
4 THEREAT
4 THEREBY
117 THEREFORE
3 THEREIN
13 THEREOF
6 THEREON
16 THERE'S
10 THERES
4 THERETO
3 THEREWITH
7 THEREWITHALL
13 THERFORE
42 THERIDAMAS
3 THER'S
409 THESE
3 THETHER
8 THETIS
417 THEY
5 THICK
6 THICKE
4 THICKEST
3 THIE
10 THIEFE
4 THIGH
3 TH'IMPERIALL
4 THIN
87 THINE
3 TH'INFERNALL
35 THING
60 THINGS
29 THINK
120 THINKE
23 THINKES
13 THINKING
13 THINKS
7 THINK'ST
4 THINKST
4 THINNE
8 THIRD
11 THIRST
3 THIRSTING
6 THIRTY
1071 THIS
14 THITHER
7 THO
6 THOROUGH
6 THOROW
120 THOSE
1082 THOU
106 THOUGH
3 THOUGHE
47 THOUGHT
6 THOUGHTES
58 THOUGHTS
104 THOUSAND
5 THOUSANDS
5 THOU'T
5 THOW
6 THRACIAN
6 THREAT
14 THREATEN
5 THREATNED
14 THREATNING
5 THREATS
31 THREE
7 THREW
12 THRICE
10 THROAT
4 THROATS
23 THRONE
103 THROUGH
3 THROUGHOUT
17 THROW
3 THROWE
4 THROWES
4 THROWNE
16 THRUST
3 THRUSTS
11 THUNDER
4 THUNDERBOLTS
3 THUNDERCLAPS
6 THUNDRING
223 THUS
1018 THY
57 THY SELFE
6 TIBULLUS
4 TICING
3 TICKLE
5 TIDE
3 TIDINGS
3 TIED
9 TIL
84 TILL
4 TILT
136 TIME
3 TIMERE
25 TIMES
3 T'INCOUNTER
3 TIR'D
4 TIRED
56 'TIS
112 TIS
4 TITAN
4 TITLE
4 TITLES
3359 TO
10 TO DAY
12 TOGETHER
6 TOKEN
13 TOLD
5 TOMBE
7 TO MORROW
19 TONGUE
12 TONGUES
130 TOO
3 TOOK
35 TOOKE
3 TOOLES
5 TOP
3 TOPPE
6 TOPS
12 TORMENT
8 TORMENTED
16 TORMENTS
11 TORNE
3 TORTUR'D
8 TORTURE
3 TORTURES
3 TOST
31 TOUCH
8 TOUCHING
5 TOUCHT
5 TOWARD
13 TOWARDS
21 TOWER
11 TOWERS
69 TOWNE
18 TOWNES
5 TOY
4 TOYES
6 TOYLE
3 TOYLING
4 TRACE
5 TRADE
8 TRAGEDIE
14 TRAINE
4 TRAITEROUS
30 TRAITOR
20 TRAITORS
3 TRANSFORME
3 TRANSFORMED
3 TRAVAILE
4 TRAVEILE
3 TRAVELLER
4 TRAYTOR
3 TRAYTORS
4 TREACHERIE
6 TREACHEROUS
4 TREACHERY
10 TREAD
5 TREADING
19 TREASON
26 TREASURE
12 TREASURIE
5 TREASURY
5 TREAT
6 TREBIZON
4 TRECHEROUS
16 TREE
13 TREES
12 TREMBLE
10 TREMBLING
7 TRENCH
3 TRENCHER
12 TRESSES
3 TRIALL
16 TRIBUTE
4 TRICKE
3 TRIDE
7 TRIE
3 TRIED
3 TRIFLES
19 TRIPLE
3 TRIPOLY
3 TRITON
33 TRIUMPH
6 TRIUMPHANT
4 TRIUMPHES
4 TRIUMPHING
7 TRIUMPHS
4 TRIUMPHT
3 TRODE
9 TROIAN
8 TROIANS
4 TROOPE
11 TROOPES
12 TROUBLE
9 TROUBLED
3 TROUBLESOME
3 TROUPE
11 TROUPES
41 TROY
3 TROYES
14 TRUCE
71 TRUE
3 TRUEST
3 TRULY
18 TRUMPETS
27 TRUST
4 TRUSTIE
3 TRUSTY
12 TRUTH
8 TRY
6 TUE
3 TUMBLE
6 TUMBLING
3 TUNE
3 TUNES
9 TURK
35 TURKE
17 TURKES
3 TURKESSE
4 TURKEY
26 TURKISH
11 TURKS

7 TURKY
18 TURN'D
12 TURND
60 TURNE
6 TURNED
10 TURNES
4 TURNING
3 TURNUS
5 TURRET
7 TURRETS
21 TUSH
11 TUT
5 TWAINE
15 'TWAS
4 T'WAS
11 TWAS
3 TWELVE
14 TWENTY
4 'TWERE
7 TWERE
4 TWICE
3 TWIL
4 TWILL
3 TWISE
13 TWIXT
70 TWO
5 TYRANNIES
3 TYRANNY
7 TYRANT
8 TYRANTS
6 TYTLE
3 TYTLES
16 UGLY
4 ULYSSES
3 UNAWARES
4 UNBORNE
16 UNCKLE
3 UNCKLES
3 UNCONQUERED
3 UNDAUNTED
57 UNDER
3 UNDERMINE
14 UNDERNEATH
6 UNDERSTAND
8 UNDERTAKE
6 UNDONE
4 UNFOLD
3 UNFOULD
5 UNGENTLE
8 UNHAPPIE
4 UNHAPPY
3 UNITED
5 UNJUST
5 UNKIND
7 UNKINDE
12 UNKNOWNE
3 UNLAWFULL
22 UNLESSE
5 UNNATURALL
3 UNPEOPLED
3 UNPLEASANT
3 UNRELENTING
3 UNRESISTED
6 UNSEENE
3 UNTIL
14 UNTILL
178 UNTO
4 UNWILLING
6 UNWORTHY
204 UP
251 UPON
4 UPPON
3 UPRIGHT
5 UPSTART
4 URG'D
5 URGE
372 US
3 US'D
10 USDE
65 USE
4 USED
6 USUMCASANE
3 USURPING
5 UTMOST
4 VAILD
7 VAILE
59 VAINE
7 VAINES
6 VALDES
14 VALIANT
3 VALLIES
8 VALOUR
4 VALOYS
4 VALUED
3 VANHOLT
6 VANISH
3 VANISHT
4 VANQUISHT
3 VASSALS
9 VAST
3 VAULTS
5 VAUNT
4 VENG'D
5 VENGE
17 VENGEANCE
5 VENICE
3 VENOMOUS
51 VENUS
5 VERIE
23 VERSE
11 VERSES
17 VERTUE
6 VERTUES
4 VERTUOUS
22 VERY
4 VESTALL
5 VEXED
8 VICEROIES
4 VICEROY
13 VICTORIE
6 VICTORIES
4 VICTORIOUS
22 VICTORY
3 VICTUALL
35 VIEW
6 VIEW'D
4 VIEWD
3 VIEWE
3 VIEWES
5 VIEWING
3 VILAINE
3 VILD
6 VILDE
14 VILE
9 VILLAIN
48 VILLAINE
26 VILLAINES
6 VILLANIE
7 VILLANY
6 VINE
6 VINES
4 VINTNER
12 VIOLENCE
10 VIOLENT
6 VIRGIN
3 VIRGINITIE
9 VIRGINS
3 VISAGE
7 VISIT
5 VISITE
5 VIVE
11 VOICE
3 VOICES
3 VOIDE
3 VOUCHSAFE
18 VOW
4 VOW'D
3 VOWD
9 VOWES
6 VOYCE
4 VULCAN
4 WAGGE
14 WAGNER
10 WAIES
11 WAIGHT
4 WAINE
9 WAIT
17 WAITE
4 WAITES
5 WAITING
12 WAKE
5 WALK
25 WALKE
5 WALKES
6 WALKING
3 WALKS
6 WALL
55 WALLES
3 WALLS
21 WALS
5 WAN
12 WANDRING
23 WANT
7 WANTING
26 WANTON
10 WANTS
53 WAR
3 WARD
9 WARE
21 WARLIKE
12 WARME
5 WARNE
9 WARNING
3 WARNINGS
23 WARRANT
50 WARRE
37 WARRES
3 WARRING
18 WARS
11 WARWICK
8 WARWICKE
377 WAS
7 WASH
12 WAST
8 WASTE
10 WATCH
4 WATCHFULL
3 WATCHT
57 WATER
22 WATERS
5 WATERY
6 WATRIE
6 WATRY
3 WAVE
3 WAVERING
25 WAVES
7 WAXE
3 WAXT
50 WAY
6 WAYES
647 WE
12 WEAKE
53 WEALTH
5 WEALTHIE
10 WEALTHY
5 WEAPON
15 WEAPONS
49 WEARE
4 WEARES
6 WEARIE
7 WEARY
3 WED
21 WEE
4 WEEDES
3 WEEDS
11 WEE'L
3 WEEL
3 WEE'LE
22 WEELE
5 WEE'LL
21 WEEPE
4 WEEPES
3 WEEPING
4 WEIGH
7 WEIGHT
56 WEL
57 WELCOME
6 WE'LE
3 WELKIN
5 WE'LL
192 WELL
41 WENCH
13 WENCHES
28 WENT
6 WEPT
266 WERE
25 WERT
5 WERTENBERGE
9 WEST
6 WESTERNE
3 WEY
735 WHAT
7 WHAT ERE
5 WHAT EVER
13 WHAT'S
7 WHATS
8 WHATSOEVER
8 WHEELE
6 WHEELES
380 WHEN
24 WHENCE
5 WHER
277 WHERE
10 WHEREAS
7 WHEREAT
6 WHERE ERE
19 WHEREFORE
41 WHEREIN
11 WHEREOF
6 WHEREON
5 WHERE'S
3 WHERES
4 WHERESOEVER
18 WHEREWITH
4 WHERFORE
4 WHERIN
3 WHET
41 WHETHER
338 WHICH
113 WHILE
13 WHILES
3 WHIL'ST
21 WHILST
4 WHILSTE
3 WHIP
3 WHIPS
3 WHIPT
4 WHIRLE
3 WHISPER
3 WHIST
5 WHIT
54 WHITE
21 WHITHER
186 WHO
3 WHO ERE
11 WHOLE
126 WHOM
8 WHOME
5 WHORE
5 WHO'S
226 WHOSE
270 WHY
20 WICKED
18 WIDE
35 WIFE
88 WIL
11 WILD
12 WILDE
798 WILL
3 WILLING
9 WILLINGLY
13 WILS
89 WILT
8 WIN
19 WIND
13 WINDE
26 WINDES
3 WINDIE
5 WINDING
11 WINDOW
12 WINDS
37 WINE
3 WINES
5 WING
10 WINGED
3 WINGES
20 WINGS
10 WINNE
9 WINTER
9 WINTERS
21 WISE
4 WISELY
45 WISH
4 WISHED
10 WISHT
27 WIT
1686 WITH
8 WITHALL
5 WITHERED
71 WITHIN
57 WITHOUT
3 WITLESSE
3 WITNES
24 WITNESSE
3 WITNESSES
11 WITS
5 WITTENBERG
3 WITTENBERGE
3 WITTY
9 WIVES
5 WOE
8 WOFULL
14 WOMAN
7 WOMBE
25 WOMEN
6 WOMENS
9 WON
19 WONDER
3 WONDERS
9 WONDROUS
5 WONNE
9 WONT

A CLOCKE
A COMMING
A DO
A DRY
A FARRE
A FIRE
A FOOTE
A FRESH
A HUNTING
A LIKE
A NEW
A NIGHT
A NIGHTS
A PACE
A PIECES
A SHAMED
A SLEEPE
A SUNDER
A WAY
A WHILE
A WOOING
AL-FOWLES
AMBER GREECE
AN OTHER
ANY THING
ARCH-MONARK
ARCH-MONARKE
ARCH-REGENT
ARCH-TRAITOR
ARMES-BEARING
AXLE-TREE
BACK-WARD
BALD-PATE
BAN-DOGGES
BANNOCKS BORNE
BARE-FOOT
BARE-FOOTE
BASE-BORNE
BASE-BRED
BASE BORNE
BASSOE-MAISTER
BE-FRIENDED
BE GON
BE GONE
BED-RID
BEE HIVES
BEFORE HAND
BELLY-CHEARE
BELLY-CHEERE
BIRD-CHANGED
BIRTH-DAY
BIRTH DAY
BLACK-SMITHES
BLINK-EI'D
BLOOD-QUAFFING
BLOOD-RAW
BLOUD-SHED
BLOUD-SHOTTEN
BOND-MEN
BOND-WOMEN
BOTTLE-NOS'D
BRAIN-SICKE
BRASSE-BULLETS
BRIGHT-BEARING
BRISTLE-POINTED
BROKEN WINDED
BY-SOUTH
BYRTH-DAY
CAN NOT
CARE-GOT
CHAMBER-FELLOW
CHAMBER MAID
CHARIOT-HORSES
CHIMNEY-SWEEPER
CHIMNY-SWEEPER
CHUF-LIKE
COACH-HORSE
COATE-TUCKT
COLE-BLACKE
COMMINGS IN
COMPANION-BASHAWES
CORPS-DUGARD
COSTER-MONGER
COUNSELL-HOUSE
COUNTING-HOUSE
COUNTRY-MEN
COUNTY-PALLATINE
COVENANT-ARTICLES
CRAFTES-MENS
CUCKOLD-MAKERS
CUP-STEALERS
CURATE-LIKE
CURTLE-AXE
CUSTOME-HOUSE
CUTLE-AXE
DAY-LIGHT
DAY-STARRE
DAY LIGHT
DEL BOSCO
DEMI-GOD
DOG-KEPT
DOG-STARRE
DROPPING-RIPE
EARE-WROUGHT
EARTH-BORNE
EARTH-METTALL'D
EAST WINDS
EIE-LIDS
ELSE-WHERE
ELSE WHERE
ERE-WHILE
ERST-WHILE
EVER-BURNING
EVERIE DAY
EVERY DAY
EVERY ONES
EVERY THING
EVERY WHERE
EYE-BALLES
EYE-BEAMES
EYE-BROWES
EYE-LIDS
EYE BROWES
EYE LIDS
EYE SIGHT
FAINT-HEARTED
FAIRE-FAC'D
FALS-HOOD
FAR FET
FARE-WELL
FARE WELL
FASHION-SAKE
FATHER-HOOD
FIELD-PIECES
FIRE-BRAND
FLAME BEARING
FLINT-BRESTED
FLOUD-BEATE
FOE-MAN
FOOT-STOOLE
FOOTE-MAN
FOOTE-STOOLE
FOR-BEARE
FOR-BID
FOR-SWEARE
FOR EVER
FORE-FATHERS
FORTH-WITH
FOSTER-CHILD
FREE-BORNE
FREE-HOLD
FRENCH-MAN
FRESH MENS
GALLY-SLAVES
GLASSE-WINDOWES
GOD-A-MERCY
GOD-HEAD
GOD-WRONGING
GOD BUY
GOINGS OUT
GOLD-RING
GOLDEN-FLEECED
GOLDEN-HAIR'D
GOTE-FOOTED
GRAINE-RICH
GRAND-SIRES
GRASSE-GREENE
GREENE-GRASSE
GRIND-STONE
GROUND-WORKE
HAD-I-WIST
HAIRE-TYERS
HALFE A DOSEN
HALFE DEAD
HALFE DOZEN
HANG-DOWNE
HANG-MAN
HARD-HEARTED
HARD HARTED
HARD HEARTED
HARME-WORKES
HART BLOUD
HEAD-STRONG
HEART BREAKING
HEAVIE HEADED
HEL-BORNE
HELL-HOUND
HEMI-SPHEARE
HER-SELF
HER SELFE
HEY-PASSE
HICK-UP
HIGH-WAIES
HIGH MINDED
HOG-STIES
HOLD-FAST
HOLLY-HOKE
HOME-BRED
HOOD-WINCKT
HORSE-BREAD
HORSE-COURSER
HORSE-DOCTOR
HORSE-DRIVER
HORSE-KEEPERS
HORSE-MAN
HORSE BACKE
HOW EVER
HOW SO EVER
HUNDRED-HAND
HURLY BURLY
HUS-BAND
HUSBAND-MEN
ILL-BEAUTIOUS
ILL-FAVOUREDLY
ILL GOTTEN
IN CENSTE
IN DEED
IN STEAD
IN STEADE
IN STEED
IN STEEDE
IN TO
IT SELF
IT SELFE
JOVE-BORNE
KEY-HOLE
KILL DIVELL
LAND-STREAME
LATE-BUILT
LAW-GIVING
LAW GIVER
LIFE TIME
LIGHT-BRAINDE
LIGHT-HEADED
LIGHT FOOTE
LIGHT HEADED
LINKE-KNITT
LION-LIKE
LOOSE-TREST
LOVE-SICK
LOVE-SNARDE
LUCK-LESSE
LUKE-WARME
MAIDEN-HEAD
MAINE SAILE
MARCH-BEERE
MARE-MAJOR
MARKET-PLACE
MARTLEMASSE-BEEFE
MAY-MORNING
ME THINKES
ME THINKS
ME THOUGHT
MEAN TIME
MEANE TIME
MEANE WHILE
MEN AT ARMES
MEN OF WAR
MEN OF WARRE
MEREMAID-LIKE
METEM SU COSSIS
MID-NIGHT
MID-WATERS
MID WINTER
MIDNIGHT-REVELL
MILK-WHITE
MILKE-WHITE
MILKE WHITE
MIS-BELEEFE
MIS-BELEEVING
MOTHER-MURTHERD
MOTHER QUEENE
MOTHER WITS
MUSK-ROSES
MY SELF
MY SELFE
NECK-LACE
NECK-VERSE
NEEDLE POYNTS

NE'RE-YOAKT
NERE THE LESSE
NEVER-SINGLING
NEW-FOUND-WORLD
NEW BORNE
NEW COME
NEW FOUND
NIGHT-FLYING
NIGHT-GOWNE
NIGHT-WANDRING
NIGHT TIME
NIMPH-NEAERA
NO BODY
NO WHERE
NON-PLUS
NONE SUCH
NOONE DAY
NORTH-EAST
NORTH-WEST
NUT-BROWNE
OFF-SPRING
OFFERING-BASON
OFT-TIMES
ON KAI ME ON
ORE-LADEN
ORE-SPREAD
ORE-TORTUR'D
OUR SELFE
OUR SELVES
OUT-HOUSE
OUT-RUN
OUT-RUNNE
OUT-SPREADS
OUT-STANDER
OUT A DOORES
OUT FACE
OUT OF DATE
OVER-COME
OVER-FLOWING
OVER-PEERES
OVER-REACH
OVER-RUL'D
OVER-RULES
OVER-SPREAD
OVER-THROW
OVER-TURN'D
OVER BOURD
OVER LOOKE
OVER NIGHT
OVER PAST
OVER RULDE
OYSTER-WIFE
PARTI-COLOURED
PAUNCH-WRAPT
PEBLE STONE
PEECE-MEALE
PIBBLE-STONES
PICKELD-HERRING
PICKLE-HERRING
PIECE-TORNE
PILIA-BORZA
PINE-BEARING
PINE-TREE
PLOUGH-MANS
PLOUGH-SHARES
PLUME BEARING
POL-AXES
POPLAR-BEARING
PORRIDGE-POTS
PORT-CULLISE
PORT-MAISTERS
PRINCESSE PRIEST
PRIVY CHAMBER
PROUD-DARING
QUEEN MOTHER
QUEENE MOTHER
QUICK SILVER
QUINQUE-ANGLE
QUOTH A
RAINE-DOUBLED
RARE WITTED
RE-ENFORCE
RE-PASSE
REDDE-GROWNE
REEDE-GROWNE
RICE AP HOWELL
RIGHT-HAND
RING-TURNE
RIPE-EARDE
RIVER SIDE
ROSE-CHEEKT
ROUND ABOUT
SABINE-LIKE
SCHOOLE BOY
SCRICH-OWLES
SEA-GULFES
SEA-MAN
SEA-MEN
SEA-NIMPHES
SEA-NIMPHS
SEA BANKE
SELF-SAME
SELFE-ANGRY
SELFE-WROUGHT
SELFE CONCEIT
SELFE SAME
SELIM-CALYMATH
SEMI-CIRCLED
SENATE-HOUSE
SEVEN-FOLD
SEVEN-FOULD
SHAG-RAG
SHARPE-EDG'D
SHEAP-HEARDS
SHEEP-LIKE
SHIP-MAN
SISTER-HOOD
SMOOTH-WAYES
SMOOTHE TOONGD
SNIPPER SNAPPER
SNOWE-WHITE
SO ERE
SO EVER
SOM-WHAT
SOME-TIMES
SOME-WHAT
SOME ONE
SOME THING
SOUTH-BLAST
SOUTH-WINDE
SOUTH-WINDES
SOUTH-WINDS
SPRING-TIDE
STANDARD BEARER
STANDERS BY
STAR-LIGHT
STARRE-SPANGLED
STAVES-AKER
STAVES ACRE
STEELE-BARD
STEP-FATHER
STIFFE-NECKT
STONE-PAV'D
STONE STILL
STUMPE-FOOTE
SUGAR-ALMONDS
SUN-BRIGHT
SUN-SHINE
SWEET-HART
SWEET HART
SWEET HEART
SWIFT-FOOTED
SWINE-EATING
SWORD-GIRT
TARA TANTARAS
TEARE-THYRSTY
TEATE-DISTILLING
TELL-TALES
THEM SELVES
THEREWITH ALL
THIE SELFE
THITHER WARDS
THRE-SHOLD
THREE-FARTHINGS
THREE FOLD
THY SELF
THY SELFE
TO AND FRO
TO DAY
TO MORROW
TO NIGHT
TOP-BRANCHES
TORTURE-HOUSE
T'OUT BID
TOWNE-SEALE
TOWNES-MEN
TRIBUTE-MONY
TRUE-LOVES
TUNE-FULL
TURRET-BEARING
TURTLE-DOVE
TURTLE DOVE
TWINNE-BORNE
TWINNE-STARRES
TWO LEAVDE
ULYSSES-LIKE
UN-PROTECTED
UN-PROTESTED
UNDER-SAILE
UNDER GROUND
UP-RIGHT
UP-STARING
UP-WAYD
UPSIDE DOWNE
VINE-PLANTED
VINE-TREES
VOICE-FEIGNING
WAITING MAID
WARE-HOUSES
WARMING-PAN
WARNING-PEECE
WATCH-MAN
WATER-NYMPHS
WATER FOWLES
WATER SIDE
WAVE-MOIST
WEL FAVOURED
WEL KNOWN
WELL-TOSS'D
WELL KNOWNE
WHAT E'RE
WHAT ERE
WHAT EVER
WHAT SO ERE
WHAT SOEVER
WHERE ABOUT
WHERE BY
WHERE E'RE
WHERE ERE
WHERE EVER
WHIRL-WINDES
WHIRLE-POOLES
WHIRLE-WIND
WHIRLE-WINDS
WHIRLE WINDE
WHITE-CHEEKT
WHITE-MOULD
WHO ERE
WHO EVER
WILD-BEASTS
WIND-GOD
WIND-PIPE
WINE-BIBBING
WITH-HOLD
WOMAN-HOOD
WOMBE-INCLOSED
WOOD-GODS
WRATH-KINDLED
YONG-MENS
YOUR SELF
YOUR SELFE
YOUR SELVES

GOD-A-MERCY
HALFE A DOSEN
OUT A DOORES
QUOTH A
ROUND ABOUT
WHERE ABOUT
STAVES ACRE
STAVES-AKER
THEREWITH ALL
SUGAR-ALMONDS
TO AND FRO
QUINQUE-ANGLE
SELFE-ANGRY
RICE AP HOWELL
COVENANT-ARTICLES
MEN AT ARMES
CURTLE-AXE
CUTLE-AXE
POL-AXES
HORSE BACKE
EYE-BALLES
HUS-BAND
SEA BANKE
STEELE-BARD
COMPANION-BASHAWES
OFFERING-BASON
EYE-BEAMES
FOR-BEARE
STANDARD BEARER
ARMES-BEARING
BRIGHT-BEARING
FLAME BEARING
PINE-BEARING
PLUME BEARING
POPLAR-BEARING
TURRET-BEARING
WILD-BEASTS
FLOUD-BEATE
ILL-BEAUTIOUS
MARTLEMASSE-BEEFE
MARCH-BEERE
MIS-BELEEFE
MIS-BELEEVING
WINE-BIBBING
FOR-BID
T'OUT BID
COLE-BLACKE
SOUTH-BLAST
HART BLOUD
NO BODY
BANNOCKS BORNE
BASE-BORNE
BASE BORNE
EARTH-BORNE
FREE-BORNE
HEL-BORNE
JOVE-BORNE
NEW BORNE
TWINNE-BORNE
PILIA-BORZA
DEL BOSCO
OVER BOURD
SCHOOLE BOY
LIGHT-BRAINDE
TOP-BRANCHES
FIRE-BRAND
HORSE-BREAD
HEART BREAKING
BASE-BRED
HOME-BRED
FLINT-BRESTED
SUN-BRIGHT
EYE-BROWES
EYE BROWES
NUT-BROWNE
LATE-BUILT
BRASSE-BULLETS
HURLY BURLY
EVER-BURNING
GOD BUY
STANDERS BY
WHERE BY
SELIM-CALYMATH
IN CENSTE
PRIVY CHAMBER
BIRD-CHANGED
BELLY-CHEARE
ROSE-CHEEKT
WHITE-CHEEKT
BELLY-CHEERE
FOSTER-CHILD
SEMI-CIRCLED
A CLOCKE

PARTI-COLOURED
NEW COME
OVER-COME
A COMMING
SELFE CONCEIT
HORSE-COURSER
PORT-CULLISE
PROUD-DARING
BIRTH-DAY
BIRTH DAY
BYRTH-DAY
EVERIE DAY
EVERY DAY
NOONE DAY
TO DAY
HALFE DEAD
IN DEED
TEATE-DISTILLING
KILL DIVELL
A DO
HORSE-DOCTOR
BAN-DOGGES
RAINE-DOUBLED
TURTLE-DOVE
TURTLE DOVE
HANG-DOWNE
UPSIDE DOWNE
HALFE DOZEN
HORSE-DRIVER
A DRY
CORPS-DUGARD
RIPE-EARDE
NORTH-EAST
SWINE-EATING
SHARPE-EDG'D
BLINK-EI'D
RE-ENFORCE
SO ERE
WHAT E'RE
WHAT ERE
WHERE E'RE
WHERE ERE
WHO ERE
FOR EVER
HOW EVER
SO EVER
WHAT EVER
WHERE EVER
WHO EVER
FAIRE-FAC'D
OUT FACE
A FARRE
THREE-FARTHINGS
HOLD-FAST
STEP-FATHER
FORE-FATHERS
WEL FAVOURED
ILL-FAVOUREDLY
VOICE-FEIGNING
CHAMBER-FELLOW
FAR FET
A FIRE
GOLDEN-FLEECED
OVER-FLOWING
NIGHT-FLYING
SEVEN-FOLD
THREE FOLD
BARE-FOOT
A FOOTE
BARE-FOOTE
LIGHT FOOTE
STUMPE-FOOTE
GOTE-FOOTED
SWIFT-FOOTED
SEVEN-FOULD
NEW-FOUND-WORLD
NEW FOUND
AL-FOWLES
WATER FOWLES
A FRESH
BE-FRIENDED
TUNE-FULL
SWORD-GIRT
LAW GIVER
LAW-GIVING
DEMI-GOD
WIND-GOD
WOOD-GODS
BE GON
BE GONE
CARE-GOT
ILL GOTTEN
NIGHT-GOWNE

GREENE-GRASSE
AMBER GREECE
GRASSE-GREENE
UNDER GROUND
REDDE-GROWNE
REEDE-GROWNE
SEA-GULFES
GOLDEN-HAIR'D
BEFORE HAND
HUNDRED-HAND
RIGHT-HAND
SWEET-HART
SWEET HART
HARD HARTED
GOD-HEAD
MAIDEN-HEAD
HEAVIE HEADED
LIGHT-HEADED
LIGHT HEADED
SHEAP-HEARDS
SWEET HEART
FAINT-HEARTED
HARD-HEARTED
HARD HEARTED
PICKELD-HERRING
PICKLE-HERRING
BEE HIVES
HOLLY-HOKE
FREE-HOLD
WITH-HOLD
KEY-HOLE
FALS-HOOD
FATHER-HOOD
SISTER-HOOD
WOMAN-HOOD
COACH-HORSE
CHARIOT-HORSES
HELL-HOUND
COUNSELL-HOUSE
COUNTING-HOUSE
CUSTOME-HOUSE
OUT-HOUSE
SENATE-HOUSE
TORTURE-HOUSE
WARE-HOUSES
A HUNTING
HAD-I-WIST
COMMINGS IN
WOMBE-INCLOSED
ON KAI ME ON
HORSE-KEEPERS
DOG-KEPT
WRATH-KINDLED
LINKE-KNITT
WEL KNOWN
WELL KNOWNE
NECK-LACE
ORE-LADEN
TWO LEAVDE
LUCK-LESSE
EIE-LIDS
EYE-LIDS
EYE LIDS
DAY-LIGHT
DAY LIGHT
STAR-LIGHT
A LIKE
CHUF-LIKE
CURATE-LIKE
LION-LIKE
MEREMAID-LIKE
SABINE-LIKE
SHEEP-LIKE
ULYSSES-LIKE
OVER LOOKE
TRUE-LOVES
CHAMBER MAID
WAITING MAID
BASSOE-MAISTER
PORT-MAISTERS
MARE-MAJOR
CUCKOLD-MAKERS
FOE-MAN
FOOTE-MAN
FRENCH-MAN
HANG-MAN
HORSE-MAN
SEA-MAN
SHIP-MAN
WATCH-MAN
PLOUGH-MANS
PEECE-MEALE
BOND-MEN

COMPOUNDS ORDERED BY SECOND ELEMENT

COUNTRY-MEN
HUSBAND-MEN
SEA-MEN
TOWNES-MEN
CRAFTES-MENS
FRESH MENS
YONG-MENS
EARTH-METTALL'D
HIGH MINDED
WAVE-MOIST
ARCH-MONARK
ARCH-MONARKE
COSTER-MONGER
TRIBUTE-MONY
MAY-MORNING
TO MORROW
QUEEN MOTHER
QUEENE MOTHER
WHITE-MOULD
MOTHER-MURTHERD
NIMPH-NEAERA
STIFFE-NECKT
A NEW
A NIGHT
MID-NIGHT
OVER NIGHT
TO NIGHT
A NIGHTS
SEA-NIMPHES
SEA-NIMPHS
BOTTLE-NOS'D
CAN NOT
WATER-NYMPHS
MEN OF WAR
MEN OF WARRE
OUT OF DATE
SOME ONE
EVERY ONES
AN OTHER
GOINGS OUT
SCRICH-OWLES
A PACE
COUNTY-PALLATINE
WARMING-PAN
HEY-PASSE
RE-PASSE
OVER PAST
BALD-PATE
STONE-PAV'D
WARNING-PEECE
OVER-PEERES
A PIECES
FIELD-PIECES
WIND-PIPE
MARKET-PLACE
VINE-PLANTED
NON-PLUS
BRISTLE-POINTED
WHIRLE-POOLES
PORRIDGE-POTS
NEEDLE POYNTS
PRINCESSE PRIEST
UN-PROTECTED
UN-PROTESTED
BLOOD-QUAFFING
MOTHER QUEENE
SHAG-RAG
BLOOD-RAW
OVER-REACH
ARCH-REGENT
MIDNIGHT-REVELL
GRAINE-RICH
BED-RID
UP-RIGHT
GOLD-RING
DROPPING-RIPE
MUSK-ROSES
OVER-RUL'D
OVER RULDE
OVER-RULES
OUT-RUN
OUT-RUNNE
MAINE SAILE
UNDER-SAILE
FASHION-SAKE
SELF-SAME
SELFE SAME
TOWNE-SEALE
HER-SELF
IT SELF
MY SELF
THY SELF
YOUR SELF
HER SELFE
IT SELFE
MY SELFE
OUR SELFE
THIE SELFE
THY SELFE
YOUR SELFE
OUR SELVES
THEM SELVES
YOUR SELVES
A SHAMED
PLOUGH-SHARES
BLOUD-SHED
SUN-SHINE
THRE-SHOLD
BLOUD-SHOTTEN
LOVE-SICK
BRAIN-SICKE
RIVER SIDE
WATER SIDE
EYE SIGHT
QUICK SILVER
NEVER-SINGLING
GRAND-SIRES
GALLY-SLAVES
A SLEEPE
BLACK-SMITHES
SNIPPER SNAPPER
LOVE-SNARDE
HOW SO EVER
WHAT SO ERE
WHAT SOEVER
BY-SOUTH
STARRE-SPANGLED
HEMI-SPHEARE
ORE-SPREAD
OVER-SPREAD
OUT-SPREADS
OFF-SPRING
OUT-STANDER
UP-STARING
DAY-STARRE
DOG-STARRE
TWINNE-STARRES
IN STEAD
IN STEADE
CUP-STEALERS
IN STEED
IN STEEDE
HOG-STIES
STONE STILL
GRIND-STONE
PEBLE STONE
PIBBLE-STONES
FOOT-STOOLE
FOOTE-STOOLE
LAND-STREAME
HEAD-STRONG
METEM SU COSSIS
NONE SUCH
A SUNDER
FOR-SWEARE
CHIMNEY-SWEEPER
CHIMNY-SWEEPER
TELL-TALES
TARA TANTARAS
NERE THE LESSE
ANY THING
EVERY THING
SOME THING
ME THINKES
ME THINKS
ME THOUGHT
OVER-THROW
TEARE-THYRSTY
SPRING-TIDE
LIFE TIME
MEAN TIME
MEANE TIME
NIGHT TIME
OFT-TIMES
SOME-TIMES
IN TO
SMOOTHE TOONGD
PIECE-TORNE
ORE-TORTUR'D
WELL-TOSS'D
ARCH-TRAITOR
AXLE-TREE
PINE-TREE
VINE-TREES
LOOSE-TREST
COATE-TUCKT
OVER-TURN'D
RING-TURNE
HAIRE-TYERS
HICK-UP
NECK-VERSE
HIGH-WAIES
NIGHT-WANDRING
BACK-WARD
THITHER WARDS
LUKE-WARME
MID-WATERS
A WAY
UP-WAYD
SMOOTH-WAYES
FARE-WELL
FARE WELL
NORTH-WEST
SOM-WHAT
SOME-WHAT
ELSE-WHERE
ELSE WHERE
EVERY WHERE
NO WHERE
A WHILE
ERE-WHILE
ERST-WHILE
MEANE WHILE
MILK-WHITE
MILKE-WHITE
MILKE WHITE
SNOWE-WHITE
OYSTER-WIFE
HOOD-WINCKT
WHIRLE-WIND
SOUTH-WINDE
WHIRLE WINDE
BROKEN WINDED
SOUTH-WINDES
WHIRL-WINDES
GLASSE-WINDOWES
EAST WINDS
SOUTH-WINDS
WHIRLE-WINDS
MID WINTER
FORTH-WITH
MOTHER WITS
RARE WITTED
BOND-WOMEN
A WOOING
GROUND-WORKE
HARME-WORKES
PAUNCH-WRAPT
GOD-WRONGING
EARE-WROUGHT
SELFE-WROUGHT
NE'RE-YOAKT

COMPOUNDS ORDERED BY THIRD ELEMENT

MEN AT ARMES
METEM SU COSSIS
OUT OF DATE
OUT A DOORES
HALFE A DOSEN
WHAT SO ERE
HOW SO EVER
TO AND FRO
RICE AP HOWELL
NERE THE LESSE
ON KAI ME ON
GOD-A-MERCY
MEN OF WAR
MEN OF WARRE
HAD-I-WIST
NEW-FOUND-WORLD

WORDS CONTAINING APOSTROPHES

ABANDON'D
ABHOR'D
ABJUR'D
ABUS'D
ABUS'DE
ACCIDENT'S
ADMIR'D
ADMYR'D
ADORN'D
ADVANC'D
AETNA'S
AGREEV'D
AIM'D
ALL'S
ALLEAG'D
ALLUR'D
ALMO'S
AMAZ'D
ANAGRAMATIS'D
ANSWER'D
APAL'D
APOLLO'S
APPEAR'D
APPEAS'D
APPROV'D
ARETHUSA'S
ARM'D
ARRIV'D
AS'T
ASCRIB'D
ASHAM'D
ASK'ST
ASK'T
ASPIR'ST
ATCHIEV'D
ATTAIN'D
AYL'ST
AYM'D
AZUR'D
BACK'D
BAK'D
BAPTIZ'D
BARR'D
BATH'D
BE'T
BEAR'ST
BEARE'
BEARE'T
BEFAL'NE
BEGUIL'D
BEHAV'D
BELOV'D
BENUMB'D
BENUMM'D
BENVOLIO'S
BEQUEATH'D
BESEEM'D
BESIEG'D
BESMER'D
BETRAYE'S
BETROATH'D
BETROTH'D
BLASPHEM'D
BLAZ'D
BLINK-EI'D
BOTTLE-NOS'D
'BOUT
BRAV'D
BRAV'ST
BREATH'D
BRIST'LED
BROTHER'S
BRUNO'S
BURN'D
CAL'D
CAL'ST
CALL'D
CAM'ST
CAP'DE
CAPTAIN'S
CAR'DST
CARRY'T
CAUS'D
'CAUSE
CENSUR'D
CHAC'D
CHAIN'D
CHANC'D
CHANG'D
CHARDG'D
CHARG'D
CHAUNC'D
CHEEK'DE
CINTHIA'S
CIRCUMCIS'D
CIRCUMCIZ'D
CIRCUMSCRIB'D
CITHEREA'S
CLAMBER'D
CLING'D
CLOATH'D
CLOS'D
CLOTH'D
COIN'D
COM'ST
COMBIN'D
COMM'ST
COMMENC'D
COMMIT'ST
COMPAR'D
COMPLAIN'D
COMPRIZ'D
CONCEAL'D
CONCEAV'D
CONCEIV'D
CONDEMN'D
CONFIRM'D
CONJEAL'D
CONJOIN'D
CONJUR'D
CONQUER'D
CONSPIR'D
CONSTRAIN'D
CONSUM'D
CONTAIN'D
CONTERMIN'D
CONTROL'D
CONVINC'D
COUNT'NANCE
COUNTERMIN'D
COUNTERMUR'D
COVER'D
CRAMB'D
CRAV'D
CRAV'ST
CROWN'D
CRY'DE
CUR'D
DAMB'D
DAMN'D
DANC'D
DANG'D
DAR'ST
DECEAV'D
DECEIV'D
DECEIV'ST
DECIV'D
DECLIN'D
DEEM'D
DEFAM'D
DEFENC'D
DEFIL'D
DEFLOWR'D
DELAY'D
DELIGHT'S
DELIVER'D
DELUD'ST
DENI'D
DENY'T
DEPRIV'D
DESERV'D
DESERV'DE
DESERV'ST
DESIR'D
DETAIN'D
DETERMIN'D
DEVIS'D
DEW'D
DIFFER'D
DIGG'D
DISARM'D
DISCERN'D
DISCHARG'D
DISCOULOUR'D
DISCOV'RD
DISGRAC'D
DISJOIN'D
DISPATCH'D
DISPENC'D
DISPLEAS'D
DISSOLV'D
DISTEMPER'D
DIVEL'S
DO'T
DON'T
DOOM'D
DRAG'D
DROWN'D
DYV'D
E'RE
EARTH-METTALL'D
EAS'D
EDG'D
EI'D
'EM
EMBALM'D
EMPAL'D
ENAMOUR'D
ENCHAC'D
ENDOW'D
ENDUR'D
ENFLAM'ST
ENFORC'D
ENGRAV'D
ENJOIN'D
ENJOY'D
ENLARG'D
ENRAG'D
ENRICH'D
ENTER'D
ENTERTAIN'D
ENTHRAL'D
ENVY'D
ESCAP'D
ESCAP'T
ESPY'D
ESPY'DE
ESTEEM'D
ETERNIZ'D
EUROP'S
EXCLUD'ST
EXHAL'D
EXPEL'D
FAC'D
FAC'ST
FAIN'D
FAIRE-FAC'D
'FAITH
FATHER'S
FEAR'D
FEAR'ST
FEARD'ST
FEIGN'D
FENC'D
FETCH'D
FIER'ST
FIL'D
FILL'D
FIR'D
FLATT'RING
FOR'T
FORC'D
FORG'D
FORTIFI'D
FRAM'D
FULFIL'D
GAIN'D
GARRISON'D
GATHER'D
GIRD'ST
GIV'T
GIVE'S
GIVEN'T
GLIMPS'D
GLIST'RED
GLITER'D
GOLDEN-HAIR'D
GOT'ST
GOVERN'D
GOVERNOR'S
GRAC'D
GRAC'T
GRAV'D
GRAVEL'D
GRAZ'D
GREEV'D
GRIEV'D
H'
H'HAD
HA'
HA'S
HA'T
HAIR'D
HAL'D
HANG'D
HARM'D
HAT'ST
HAV'T
HE'D
HE'DE
HE'ELE
HE'LE
HE'LL
HE'S
HEART'S
HEAV'D
HEAV'N
HECAT'S
HEE'L
HEE'LE
HEE'S
HEER'S
HEERE'S
HEL'S
HEM'D
HERE'S
HEW'D
HID'ST
HIR'D
HONOUR'D
HONOUR'ST
HOP'D
HOP'ST
HOV'D
HOVER'D
HUG'D
HURL'D
HUSH'T
HYR'D
I'
I'DE
I'LE
I'M
I'TH
I'THE
IL'E
ILLIT'RAT
IMAGYN'D
IMBRAC'D
IMPLOY'D
IMPORTUN'D
IMPOS'D
IMPRISON'D
IN'T
INCLOS'D
INCUR'D
INFERR'D
INFLAM'D
INFORC'D
INLARG'D
INQUIR'D
INRAG'D
INRICH'D
INSPIR'D
INTERR'D
INTOO'T
INTRAP'D
INUR'D
INVENOMB'D
INVIRON'D
IS'T
IT'S
JEER'D
JEHOVA'S
JOIN'D
JOY'D
JOYN'D
KEEP'ST
KENNEL'D
KILL'D
KILL'ST
KING'S
KNEEL'D
KNOW'ST
'LAS
LAT'RALLY
LAUGH'D
LAUGH'ST
LEAD'ST
LEARN'D
LEAV'ST
LED'ST
LERNA'S
LET'S
LIFE'S
LIK'ST
LIV'D
LIV'DE
LIV'DST
LOATH'D
LOCK'D
LONG'D
LOOK'D
LOOK'ST
LOOK'T
LOTH'D
LOV'D
LOV'DE
LOV'DST
LOV'ST
LOWR'D
MAD'ST
MAK'ST
MALIGN'D
MALTA'S
MAN'S
MANN'D
MARTCH'D
MASTER'S
MAY'ST
MEAN'ST
MERCHANT'S
METAMORPHIS'
METTALL'D
MISUS'D
'MONG
MOOV'D
MOOV'DE
MOURN'D
MOUTH'D
MOV'D
MU'D
MURDER'D
MUS'D
NAK'D
NAM'D
NAME'S
NE'R
NE'RE
NE'RE-YOAKT
NER'E
NOS'D
NUMBER'S
NUMM'D
O'
O'ER
O'RE
O'RECAST
O'RECOME
O'REHEAD
O'TH
O'THIS
OBEY'D
OBSERV'D
OBTAIN'D
OCCASION'S
OFFER'D
ON'S
ON'T
OPPOS'D
ORDAIN'D
ORE-TORTUR'D
OSSA'S
OVER-RUL'D
OVERRUL'D
OVER-TURN'D
PAC'D
PAIS'D
'PARRELL
PASS'D
PAUS'D
PAV'D
PEER'D
PERCEAV'D
PERCEIV'ST
PERFORM'D
PERFOURM'D
PERFUM'D
PERISH'D
PERJUR'D
PERUS'D
PHOEBE'S
PIERC'D
PILLAG'D
PIN'D
PINION'D
PITCH'D
PLAC'D
PLAGU'D
PLEAS'D
PLUNG'D
PLUTO'S
POUR'D
POYSON'D
PRAIS'D

WORDS CONTAINING APOSTROPHES

PRAY'D
PREFERR'D
PREPAR'D
PRESCRIB'D
PREVAIL'D
PROCUR'D
PROFESS'D
PROLONG'D
PROMIS'D
PROOV'D
PROV'D
PROV'ST
PUL'D
PULL'D
PURCHAC'D
PURG'D
PURIFI'D
PURSU'D
PYN'D
QUAIL'D
R'ENFORCE
RA'ST
RAIGN'D
RAIL'ST
RAIN'D
RAIN'ST
RAIS'D
RANG'D
RANSOM'D
REAER'D
REAR'D
REBUK'T
RECALL'D
RECEIV'D
RECLAIM'D
RECOMPENC'D
RECONCIL'D
REDEEM'D
REDUC'D
REFRAIN'D
REIGN'D
REJOIN'D
RELIEV'D
REMOOV'D
RENOWM'D
RENOWN'D
REPAIR'D
REPULS'D
RESERV'D
RESOLV'D
RESTOR'D
RESTRAIN'D
RETAIN'D
RETURN'D
REVEAL'D
REVENG'D
RID'ST
RIG'D
ROB'D
ROBB'D
ROOF'T
ROUL'D
RUIN'D
RUL'D
S'DAINST
SACK'T
SACRIFIC'D
SAIL'D
SAUC'D
SAUC'T
SAV'D
SAV'DE
SAW'ST
SAY'D
'SBLOUD
SCAL'D
SCAR'D
SCARR'D
SCATTER'D
SCORN'D
SCORN'T
SE'
SE'T
SEAZ'D
SEEK'ST
SEEM'D
SEEM'ST
SEIZ'D
SEND'ST
SERV'D
SERV'ST
SEXTON'S
SHAM'ST
SHARPE-EDG'D
SHE'S
SHEE'LL
SHEE'S
SHEW'D
SHIN'D
SHOULD'ST
SHRIN'D
SHRIV'D
SIGH'D
SIGN'D
SINDG'D
SINN'D
SITT'ST
SLAVE'S
SLEEP'ST
SMEAR'D
SMIL'D
SMOTHER'D
SNATCH'T
'SNAYLES
SOAR'D
SON'S
SOW'D
SPAR'D
SPEAK'ST
SPY'DE
SQUIS'D
STAB'D
STAI'D
STAIN'D
STAMP'D
STAR'D
STAR'ST
STARV'D
STERV'D
STONE-PAV'D
STOOD'ST
STOR'D
STORM'D
STRIV'D
STRIV'NE
STUFF'D
SUBDEW'D
SUBDU'D
SUBORN'D
SUFFER'T
SUMM'D
SUMMON'D
SUPPOS'D
SURCHARDG'D
SURPRIS'D
SURPRIZ'D
SURVIV'D
SUSTAIN'D
SWALLOW'D
SWARM'D
SWELL'D
SYLLA'S
T'
T'ABANDON
T'ADORNE
T'ADVANCE
T'APPEASE
T'APPEAZE
T'ENCOUNTER
T'ERECT
T'ESCAPE
T'HAVE
T'INCOUNTER
T'INVEST
T'IS
T'OTHER
T'OUT BID
T'WAS
TALK'D
TAM'D
TAV'RON
TAX'D
TEARM'D
TEARM'ST
TERM'D
TH'
TH'ABREVIATED
TH'AD
TH'ADULTERER
TH'ADULTEROUS
TH'ADVANTAGES
TH'AFFRIGHTED
TH'AIRS
TH'ALMIGHTY
TH'AMAZED
TH'ANTARTICKE
TH'ANTARTIQUE
TH'ANTIPODES
TH'APPROCHING
TH'ARABIAN
TH'ARCADIAN
TH'ARREST
TH'ARRIVALL
TH'ART
TH'ARTS
TH'ASPIRING
TH'ASSAULT
TH'ASSIRIANS
TH'AVERNI
TH'EARLE
TH'EARTH
TH'EARTHS
TH'EAST
TH'EDICTS
TH'EGYPTIAN
TH'EMPERIALL
TH'ENAMELD
TH'ENAMOURED
TH'ESPERIDES
TH'ETERNALL
TH'ETRURIAN
TH'EVERLASTING
TH'HALL
TH'HEAVENLY
TH'HETRURIANS
TH'HORNES
TH'IMMORTALL
TH'IMPARTIALL
TH'IMPERIALL
TH'INCHAUNTED
TH'INCHAUNTING
TH'INFERNALL
TH'INHABITANTES
TH'INHABITANTS
TH'IRREVOCABLE
TH'ONE
TH'OPPOSED
TH'ORIZON
TH'OTHER
TH'THEATER'S
TH'UNSTABLE
THAT'S
THAW'D
THEATER'S
THER'S
THERE'S
THEY'
THEY'ILL
THEY'LL
THINK'ST
THOU'
THOU'LT
THOU'ST
THOU'T
THRIV'D
TILL'D
TIR'D
'TIS
'TMAY
'TMUST
TOMB'D
TOO'T
TOOK'ST
TORTUR'D
TOSS'D
TOTTER'D
TOUCH'D
TOW'RED
TOYL'D
TRAIN'D
TRIM'D
'TS
TUN'D
TURN'D
'TWAS
'TWERE
'TWILL
'TWIXT
'TWOULD
TYR'D
'UM
UNCONFIRM'D
UNCONSTRAIN'D
UNDERTAK'ST
UNFAIN'D
UNFOYL'D
UNMOV'D
UNREVENG'D
UNRIVAL'D
UNSHEATH'D
UNSOYL'D
UNTIL'D
UNTILL'D
UNTUN'D
UPHEAV'D
URG'D
US'D
US'DE
VAIL'D
VANHOLT'S
VEIW'D
VENG'D
VENT'ROUS
VEX'D
VIEW'D
VILLAIN'S
VISAG'D
VOW'D
WA'ST
WALK'ST
WAND'RED
WAND'REST
WAR'D
WARN'D
WAT'RED
WAT'RY
WE'L
WE'LE
WE'LL
WEAPON'D
WEE'L
WEE'LE
WEE'LL
WEEP'ST
WEIGH'D
WELL-TOSS'D
WER'T
WHAT'S
WHAT E'RE
WHELM'D.
WHER'S
WHERE'S
WHERE E'RE
WHIL'ST
WHIRL'D
WHO'LE
WHO'S
WIL'D
WILL'T
WINDOW'S
WIP'ST
WOO'D
WRACK'S
WREATH'D
WRONG'D
WRONG'ST
Y'
Y'AFFLICT
YOAK'D
YOU'D
YOU'LE
YOU'LL
YV'RIE
'ZONS
ZOON'S

WORDS CONTAINING APOSTROPHES--ORDERED BY SECOND ELEMENT

T'ABANDON
TH'ABREVIATED
TH'AD
T'ADORNE
TH'ADULTERER
TH'ADULTEROUS
T'ADVANCE
TH'ADVANTAGES
Y'AFFLICT
TH'AFFRIGHTED
TH'AIRS
TH'ALMIGHTY
TH'AMAZED
TH'ANTARTICKE
TH'ANTARTIQUE
TH'ANTIPODES
T'APPEASE
T'APPEAZE
TH'APPROCHING
TH'ARABIAN
TH'ARCADIAN
TH'ARREST
TH'ARRIVALL
TH'ART
TH'ARTS
TH'ASPIRING
TH'ASSAULT
TH'ASSIRIANS
TH'AVERNI
ABANDON'D
ABHOR'D
ABJUR'D
ABUS'D
ADMIR'D
ADMYR'D
ADORN'D
ADVANC'D
AGREEV'D
AIM'D
ALLEAG'D
ALLUR'D
AMAZ'D
ANAGRAMATIS'D
ANSWER'D
APAL'D
APPEAR'D
APPEAS'D
APPROV'D
ARM'D
ARRIV'D
ASCRIB'D
ASHAM'D
ATCHIEV'D
ATTAIN'D
AYM'D
AZUR'D
BACK'D
BAK'D
BAPTIZ'D
BARR'D
BATH'D
BEGUIL'D
BEHAV'D
BELOV'D
BENUMB'D
BENUMM'D
BEQUEATH'D
BESEEM'D
BESIEG'D
BESMER'D
BETROATH'D
BETROTH'D
BLASPHEM'D
BLAZ'D
BLINK-EI'D
BOTTLE-NOS'D
BRAV'D
BREATH'D
BURN'D
CAL'D
CALL'D
CAUS'D
CENSUR'D
CHAC'D
CHAIN'D
CHANC'D
CHANG'D
CHARDG'D
CHARG'D
CHAUNC'D
CIRCUMCIS'D
CIRCUMCIZ'D
CIRCUMSCRIB'D
CLAMBER'D
CLING'D
CLOATH'D
CLOS'D
CLOTH'D
COIN'D
COMBIN'D
COMMENC'D
COMPAR'D
COMPLAIN'D
COMPRIZ'D
CONCEAL'D
CONCEAV'D
CONCEIV'D
CONDEMN'D
CONFIRM'D
CONJEAL'D
CONJOIN'D
CONJUR'D
CONQUER'D
CONSPIR'D
CONSTRAIN'D
CONSUM'D
CONTAIN'D
CONTERMIN'D
CONTROL'D
CONVINC'D
COUNTERMIN'D
COUNTERMUR'D
COVER'D
CRAMB'D
CRAV'D
CROWN'D
CUR'D
DAMB'D
DAMN'D
DANC'D
DANG'D
DECEAV'D
DECEIV'D
DECIV'D
DECLIN'D
DEEM'D
DEFAM'D
DEFENC'D
DEFIL'D
DEFLOWR'D
DELAY'D
DELIVER'D
DENI'D
DEPRIV'D
DESERV'D
DESIR'D
DETAIN'D
DETERMIN'D
DEVIS'D
DEW'D
DIFFER'D
DIGG'D
DISARM'D
DISCERN'D
DISCHARG'D
DISCOULOUR'D
DISGRAC'D
DISJOIN'D
DISPATCH'D
DISPENC'D
DISPLEAS'D
DISSOLV'D
DISTEMPER'D
DOOM'D
DRAG'D
DROWN'D
DYV'D
EARTH-METTALL'D
EAS'D
EDG'D
EI'D
EMBALM'D
EMPAL'D
ENAMOUR'D
ENCHAC'D
ENDOW'D
ENDUR'D
ENFORC'D
ENGRAV'D
ENJOIN'D
ENJOY'D
ENLARG'D
ENRAG'D
ENRICH'D
ENTER'D
ENTERTAIN'D
ENTHRAL'D
ENVY'D
ESCAP'D
ESPY'D
ESTEEM'D
ETERNIZ'D
EXHAL'D
EXPEL'D
FAC'D
FAIN'D
FAIRE-FAC'D
FEAR'D
FEIGN'D
FENC'D
FETCH'D
FIL'D
FILL'D
FIR'D
FORC'D
FORG'D
FORTIFI'D
FRAM'D
FULFIL'D
GAIN'D
GARRISON'D
GATHER'D
GLIMPS'D
GLITER'D
GOLDEN-HAIR'D
GOVERN'D
GRAC'D
GRAV'D
GRAVEL'D
GRAZ'D
GREEV'D
GRIEV'D
HAIR'D
HAL'D
HANG'D
HARM'D
HE'D
HEAV'D
HEM'D
HEW'D
HIR'D
HONOUR'D
HOP'D
HOV'D
HOVER'D
HUG'D
HURL'D
HYR'D
IMAGYN'D
IMBRAC'D
IMPLOY'D
IMPORTUN'D
IMPOS'D
IMPRISON'D
INCLOS'D
INCUR'D
INFERR'D
INFLAM'D
INFORC'D
INLARG'D
INQUIR'D
INRAG'D
INRICH'D
INSPIR'D
INTERR'D
INTRAP'D
INUR'D
INVENOMB'D
INVIRON'D
JEER'D
JOIN'D
JOY'D
JOYN'D
KENNEL'D
KILL'D
KNEEL'D
LAUGH'D
LEARN'D
LIV'D
LOATH'D
LOCK'D
LONG'D
LOOK'D
LOTH'D
LOV'D
LOWR'D
MALIGN'D
MANN'D
MARTCH'D
METAMORPHIS'D
METTALL'D
MISUS'D
MOOV'D
MOURN'D
MOUTH'D
MOV'D
MU'D
MURDER'D
MUS'D
NAK'D
NAM'D
NOS'D
NUMM'D
OBEY'D
OBSERV'D
OBTAIN'D
OFFER'D
OPPOS'D
ORDAIN'D
ORE-TORTUR'D
OVER-RUL'D
OVER-TURN'D
OVERRUL'D
PAC'D
PAIS'D
PASS'D
PAUS'D
PAV'D
PEER'D
PERCEAV'D
PERFORM'D
PERFOURM'D
PERFUM'D
PERISH'D
PERJUR'D
PERUS'D
PIERC'D
PILLAG'D
PIN'D
PINION'D
PITCH'D
PLAC'D
PLAGU'D
PLEAS'D
PLUNG'D
POUR'D
POYSON'D
PRAIS'D
PRAY'D
PREFERR'D
PREPAR'D
PRESCRIB'D
PREVAIL'D
PROCUR'D
PROFESS'D
PROLONG'D
PROMIS'D
PROOV'D
PROV'D
PUL'D
PULL'D
PURCHAC'D
PURG'D
PURIFI'D
PURSU'D
PYN'D
QUAIL'D
RAIGN'D
RAIN'D
RAIS'D
RANG'D
RANSOM'D
REAER'D
REAR'D
RECALL'D
RECEIV'D
RECLAIM'D
RECOMPENC'D
RECONCIL'D
REDEEM'D
REDUC'D
REFRAIN'D
REIGN'D
REJOIN'D
RELIEV'D
REMOOV'D
RENOWM'D
RENOWN'D
REPAIR'D
REPULS'D
RESERV'D
RESOLV'D
RESTOR'D
RESTRAIN'D
RETAIN'D
RETURN'D
REVEAL'D
REVENG'D
RIG'D
ROB'D
ROBB'D
ROUL'D
RUIN'D
RUL'D
SACRIFIC'D
SAIL'D
SAUC'D
SAV'D
SAY'D
SCAL'D
SCAR'D
SCARR'D
SCATTER'D
SCORN'D
SEAZ'D
SEEM'D
SEIZ'D
SERV'D
SHARPE-EDG'D
SHEW'D
SHIN'D
SHRIN'D
SHRIV'D
SIGH'D
SIGN'D
SINDG'D
SINN'D
SMEAR'D
SMIL'D
SMOTHER'D
SOAR'D
SOW'D
SPAR'D
SQUIS'D
STAB'D
STAI'D
STAIN'D
STAMP'D
STAR'D
STARV'D
STERV'D
STONE-PAV'D
STOR'D
STORM'D
STRIV'D
STUFF'D
SUBDEW'D
SUBDU'D
SUBORN'D
SUMM'D
SUMMON'D
SUPPOS'D
SURCHARDG'D
SURPRIS'D
SURPRIZ'D
SURVIV'D
SUSTAIN'D
SWALLOW'D
SWARM'D
SWELL'D
TALK'D
TAM'D
TAX'D
TEARM'D
TERM'D
THAW'D
THRIV'D
TILL'D
TIR'D
TOMB'D
TORTUR'D
TOSS'D
TOTTER'D
TOUCH'D
TOYL'D
TRAIN'D
TRIM'D
TUN'D
TURN'D
TYR'D
UNCONFIRM'D
UNCONSTRAIN'D
UNFAIN'D
UNFOYL'D
UNMOV'D

UNREVENG'D
UNRIVAL'D
UNSHEATH'D
UNSOYL'D
UNTIL'D
UNTILL'D
UNTUN'D
UPHEAV'D
URG'D
US'D
VAIL'D
VEIW'D
VENG'D
VEX'D
VIEW'D
VISAG'D
VOW'D
WAR'D
WARN'D
WEAPON'D
WEIGH'D
WELL-TOSS'D
WHELM'D
WHIRL'D
WIL'D
WOO'D
WREATH'D
WRONG'D
YOAK'D
YOU'D
S'DAINST
ABUS'DE
CAP'DE
CHEEK'DE
CRY'DE
DESERV'DE
ESPY'DE
HE'DE
I'DE
LIV'DE
LOV'DE
MOOV'DE
SAV'DE
SPY'DE
US'DE
CAR'DST
LIV'DST
LOV'DST
IL'E
NER'E
TH'EARLE
TH'EARTH
TH'EARTHS
TH'EAST
TH'EDICTS
TH'EGYPTIAN
HE'ELE
TH'EMPERIALL
TH'ENAMELD
TH'ENAMOURED
T'ENCOUNTER
R'ENFORCE
O'ER
T'ERECT
T'ESCAPE
TH'ESPERIDES
TH'ETERNALL
TH'ETRURIAN
TH'EVERLASTING
H'HAD
TH'HALL
T'HAVE
TH'HEAVENLY
TH'HETRURIANS
TH'HORNES
THEY'ILL
TH'IMMORTALL
TH'IMPARTIALL
TH'IMPERIALL
TH'INCHAUNTED
TH'INCHAUNTING
T'INCOUNTER
TH'INFERNALL
TH'INHABITANTES
TH'INHABITANTS
T'INVEST
TH'IRREVOCABLE
T'IS
HEE'L
WE'L
WEE'L
HE'LE
HEE'LE
I'LE
WE'LE
WEE'LE
WHO'LE
YOU'LE
BRIST'LED
HE'LL
SHEE'LL
THEY'LL
WE'LL
WEE'LL
YOU'LL
THOU'LT
I'M
HEAV'N
COUNT'NANCE
BEFAL'NE
STRIV'NE
TH'ONE
TH'OPPOSED
TH'ORIZON
T'OTHER
TH'OTHER
T'OUT BID
NE'R
LAT'RALLY
ILLIT'RAT
DISCOV'RD
E'RE
NE'RE
O'RE
WHAT E'RE
WHERE E'RE
O'RECAST
O'RECOME
GLIST'RED
TOW'RED
WAND'RED
WAT'RED
O'REHEAD
WAND'REST
NE'RE-YOAKT
YV'RIE
FLATT'RING
TAV'RON
VENT'ROUS
WAT'RY
ACCIDENT'S
AETNA'S
ALL'S
ALMO'S
APOLLO'S
ARETHUSA'S
BENVOLIO'S
BETRAYE'S
BROTHER'S
BRUNO'S
CAPTAIN'S
CINTHIA'S
CITHEREA'S
DELIGHT'S
DIVEL'S
EUROP'S
FATHER'S
GIVE'S
GOVERNOR'S
HA'S
HE'S
HEART'S
HECAT'S
HEE'S
HEER'S
HEERE'S
HEL'S
HERE'S
IT'S
JEHOVA'S
KING'S
LERNA'S
LET'S
LIFE'S
MALTA'S
MAN'S
MASTER'S
MERCHANT'S
NAME'S
NUMBER'S
OCCASION'S
ON'S
OSSA'S
PHOEBE'S
PLUTO'S
SEXTON'S
SHE'S
SHEE'S
SLAVE'S
SON'S
SYLLA'S
THAT'S
THEATER'S
THER'S
THERE'S
VANHOLT'S
VILLAIN'S
WHAT'S
WHER'S
WHERE'S
WHO'S
WINDOW'S
WRACK'S
ZOON'S
ASK'ST
ASPIR'ST
AYL'ST
BEAR'ST
BRAV'ST
CAL'ST
CAM'ST
COM'ST
COMM'ST
COMMIT'ST
CRAV'ST
DAR'ST
DECEIV'ST
DELUD'ST
DESERV'ST
ENFLAM'ST
EXCLUD'ST
FAC'ST
FEAR'ST
FEARD'ST
FIER'ST
GIRD'ST
GOT'ST
HAT'ST
HID'ST
HONOUR'ST
HOP'ST
KEEP'ST
KILL'ST
KNOW'ST
LAUGH'ST
LEAD'ST
LEAV'ST
LED'ST
LIK'ST
LOOK'ST
LOV'ST
MAD'ST
MAK'ST
MAY'ST
MEAN'ST
PERCEIV'ST
PROV'ST
RA'ST
RAIL'ST
RAIN'ST
RID'ST
SAW'ST
SEEK'ST
SEEM'ST
SEND'ST
SERV'ST
SHAM'ST
SHOULD'ST
SITT'ST
SLEEP'ST
SPEAK'ST
STAR'ST
STOOD'ST
TEARM'ST
THINK'ST
THOU'ST
TOOK'ST
UNDERTAK'ST
WA'ST
WALK'ST
WEEP'ST
WHIL'ST
WIP'ST
WRONG'ST
AS'T
ASK'T
BE'T
BEARE'T
CARRY'T
DENY'T
DO'T
DON'T
ESCAP'T
FOR'T
GIV'T
GIVEN'T
GRAC'T
HA'T
HAV'T
HUSH'T
IN'T
INTOO'T
IS'T
LOOK'T
ON'T
REBUK'T
ROOF'T
SACK'T
SAUC'T
SCORN'T
SE'T
SNATCH'T
SUFFER'T
THOU'T
TOO'T
WER'T
WILL'T
I'TH
O'TH
I'THE
TH'THEATER'S
O'THIS
TH'UNSTABLE
T'WAS

FOREIGN WORDS

-LATIN-

ACCIDENS
ACHERONTIS
AD
ADHUC
AEQUE
AERII
ALTER
APPAREAT
AQUAM
AQUATANI
AQUATICI
ARDENTIS
ARGUMENTUM
ARMA
ARMIS
ARTE
AUT
BENE
BONUM
CALOR
CAROLUS
CHRISTALINUM
COELUM
CONSECRATAM
CONSUMMATUM
CONTRARIA
CONVENIUNT
CORPUS
CRAS
CRUCIS
CUI
CURRITE
DE
DEI
DESINE
DESINIT
DIABOLE
DICATUS
DIES
DISCIPULUS
DISSERERE
DIXI
DOLORIS
DOMINE
DOMINUS
DOMUS
DULCE
DUOBUS
EADEMQUE
ECCE
EDWARDUM
EGO
EQUI
EST
ET
& (ET)
&C.
EXHEREDITARE
EXUE
FACIO
FALLIMUR
FETIALES
FILIUM
FINIS
FLUCTIBUS
FORTUNA
FRATRIS
FUGE
FUGIENS
FUIT
GEHENNAM
GRATIS
GRAVISSIMUM
HABUISSE
HAEC
HODIE
HOMO
HUMIDUM
HUNC
IBI
IGNEI
IGNEUM
IMPRECOR
IMPRIMIS
IN
INARTIFICIALE
INCENDERE
INCIPIT
INFERNI
INSISTERE
INTELIGENTIJ
INTELLIGENTIA
IPSE
IPSIQUE
IRE
ISTAM
ISTE
ITALIAM
JACENTEM
JACOBE
JACOBUS
JEHOVAE
JEHOVAM
JUVAT
LABENTIS
LEGATUR
LENTE
LITTORA
LITTORIBUS
LOCUS
LOGICES
MAJOR
MALE
MALEDICAT
MARE
MEDICINAE
MEDICUS
MENTEM
MEPHOSTOPHILE
MEQUE
MERUI
MEUM
MIHI
MIHIMET
MISERERE
MISERICORDIA
MISERIS
MOBILE
MONARCHA
MORARIS
MORS
MOTOR
MUNDI
NATURALE
NEGAMUS
NEGO
NEPOTES
NISI
NOBIS
NOCERE
NOCTIS
NOLITE
NOMINE
NON
NOSTRA
NOSTRAS
NOSTRIS
NULLA
NUMEN
NUNC
OCCIDERE
OMNES
ONUS
ORIENTIS
ORO
PATER
PECCASSE
PECCATI
PECCATORUM
PECCATUM
PER
PEREAT
PHILOSOPHUS
POSSIT
POTEST
PRECIBUS
PRIMUM
PRIMUS
PRINCEPS
PRO
PROBO
PROPITIAMUS
PROPITII
PROPTEREA
PROVINCIAM
PROXIMUS
PUGNENT
QUAM
QUANDOQUIDEM
QUASI
QUEM
QUERELIS
QUI
QUID
QUIDQUAM
QUIN
QUIS
QUOD
REDIS
REGIS
REI
REM
RES
SALVE
SALVETE
SANCTA
SANCTE
SANCTI
SANCTUS
SANITAS
SE
SEMPER
SEQUOR
SI
SIC
SIGNUM
SIGNUMQUE
SINT
SITU
SOCIOS
SOLAMEN
SPARGO
SPIRITUS
SPONTE
STIPENDIUM
SUB
SUM
SUMMUM
SUPERBUM
SURGAT
SUSCEPI
TANDEM
TANTI
TE
TEMPORE
TEQUE
TERRENI
TESTIMONII
TESTIMONIS
THEORIA
TIBI
TIMERE
TRIPLEX
TU
TUIS
UBI
UMBRAS
UNA
UNDAS
UNDIQUE
UT
VALEAT
VALOREM
VENI
VENIENS
VERITAS
VESTIGIAS
VESTIGIIS
VIDIT
VIRGO
VOS
VOTA
ZONA

-ITALIAN-

ANGELO
BANCHO
CASTILIANO
CAZZO
CHE
CORPO
DI
DIABOLO
DIO
MAGIORE
MALGRADO
MARE
PONTE
RIVO
SERA
SPURCA

-SPANISH-

BIEN
DE
DIABLO
DINEROS
ES
GANADO
HERMOSO
LOS
MI
PARA
PLACER
TODOS

-FRENCH-

A
ADEIW
COMMANDEMENTE
CONGE
CORPS
CORPS-DUGARD
COUPE
DE
DEVOIRE
DIEU
DU
DUGARD
ECUES
GORGE
GRAMERCY
GRAND
IL
LA
LE
MESSE
MOR
MORA
MORT
MOUNSER
MOUNSIER
MOY
NON-PLUS
PAR
PARDONA
PLACET
ROY
SAUNCE
TUE
VERLETE
VIVE
VOUSTRE

-GREEK-

KAI
ME
METEM SU COSSIS
METEMSYCOSIS
ON

-PSEUDO-FOREIGN-

BELSEBORAMS
FRAMANTO
PACOSTIPHOS
PERIPHRASTICON
POLYPRAGMOS
SANCTOBULORUM
TOSTU
TUMERARIS

HOMOGRAPHS

A
AD
ALTER
AMBER
AN
AND
ANGLE
ARME
ARMES
ART
ARTE
AYE
BAD
BAND
BANDS
BARE
BARKE
BASE
BAY
BEARE
BEE
BENE
BILL
BILLES
BILS
BIT
BLOW
BLOWE
BLOWES
BOOTES
BOOTS
BORE
BORNE
BOTTLE
BOUND
BOUNDS
BOW
BOWE
BOWES
BRUSE
BUY
CAL
CASE
CHASTE
CLEAVE
CLIFTS
CLIME
CLIPPE
COLD
CONTENT
CORPS
COSIN
DAMB'D
DATE
DE
DEARE
DEERE
DESERT
DESERTS
DIE
DIED
DIENG
DIES
DOWNE
DYED
EARES
EFFECT
ELDER
'EM
ERE
EVEN
FAINE
FALS
FAST
FAWNE
FELL
FIT
FITS
FLEET
FLEETE
FLIE
FLIES
FLIGHT
FLY
FLYE
FLYES
FLYING
FOILD
FOILE
FOULE
GATE
GORGON
GOTE
GRAND
GRAVE
GREECE
GUILT
GUIZE
HA
HAILE
HART
HAST
HATE
HEELE
HEERE
HEIRE
HELME
HEROES
HEW
HEY
HIDE
HO
HOLLOW
HOOD
HOST
I
IDE
ILE
IN
IRE
LAIES
LAPT
LAST
LEAD
LEADE
LEAGUE
LEAGUES
LEANE
LEAVE
LEAVES
LEAVY
LEFT
LET
LETS
LEUCA
LIE
LIES
LIGHT
LIKE
LIST
LOCKES
LOCKS
LONE
LONG
LOOSE
LYE
LYES
LYING
MAINE
MAN
MARCH
MARE
MARKE
MARRY
MASSE
MAST
MAY
ME
MEAN
MEANE
MEANES
MEANS
MEET
MEETE
MESSE
MIGHT
MINE
MINES
MIST
MOLD
MOR
MOTION
MOULD
MOUNT
MOUNTS
MUSE
MUSES
NERE
NON
O
OF
OFF
ON
ONCAYMAEON
ONE
OUGHT
PALE
PARIS
PIERCE
PINE
PLAINE
PLIGHT
POAST
POLES
PORT
POST
POSTE
PRAY
PRESIDENT
PREST
QUIT
QUITE
RACE
RACKE
RAIN
RAINES
RAISE
RASE
REAMES
RED
RENT
RENTS
REPAIR'D
REPAIRE
REST
RESTETH
RESTS
REVELD
RHENE
RHODE
RICE
RID
RING
RINGS
RODE
ROME
ROOME
ROOMES
ROSE
ROUSE
ROUT
SACKE
SALVE
SAVE
SAVING
SCARD
SE
SEA
SENT
SHOLD
SIGHT
SING
SLIGHT
SONNE
SOUND
SPIT
STABLE
STALE
STATURE
STATUTES
STAVES
STEAD
STEED
STERNE
STOLE
STRAIGHT
STRAIT
STREIGHT
STROKE
STROKES
SUM
T'
TALE
TEARE
TEARES
TEMPLES
TH'
THAN
THE
THEN
THOU'T
TILL
TILT
TIRE
TO
TOO
TRACE
TRAINE
VAILD
VAILE
VAINE
WAGGE
WAIGHT
WAINE
WAIT
WARD
WARE
WAST
WASTE
WAXE
WAXEN
WAY
WHETHER
WHOSE
WIL
WILL
WIND
WINDS
WOUND
YEARES

Library of Congress Cataloging in Publication Data

Fehrenbach, Robert J., 1936–
A concordance to the plays, poems, and translations of Christopher Marlowe.

(The Cornell concordances)
"Based on the critical old-spelling edition of The complete works of Christopher Marlowe, Fredso
Bowers, editor, published by the Cambridge University Press, 2nd ed., 1981"—Pref.
1. Marlowe, Christoper, 1564–1593—Concordances.
I. Boone, Lea Ann. II. Di Cesare, Mario A. III. Marlowe, Christopher, 1564–1593. Works. 198
IV. Title. V. Series.
PR2672.F43 1982 822'.3 81-67175
ISBN 0-8014-1420-2

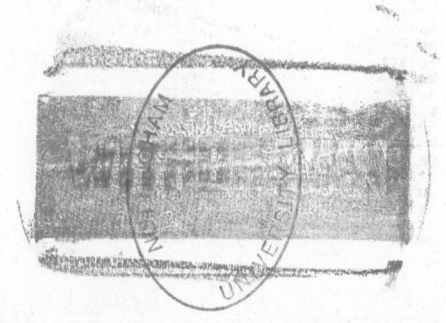